POCKET OXFORD CHINE

POCKET OXFORD CHINESE DICTIONARY

English • Chinese
Chinese • English
英汉·汉英

Monolingual English text edited by:
Martin H. Manser

English-Chinese Dictionary edited and translated by:
Zhu Yuan Wang Liangbi Ren Yongchang

Chinese-English Dictionary edited by:
Wu Jingrong Mei Ping Ren Xiaoping Shi Qinan

Fourth edition revised by:
Ren Xiaoping Liu Tong
The Dictionaries Department of Oxford University Press

OXFORD
UNIVERSITY PRESS

商務印書館
The Commercial Press

Oxford University Press is a department of the University of Oxford. It furthers the University's objective of excellence in research, scholarship, and education by publishing worldwide. Oxford is a registered trade mark of Oxford University Press in the UK and in certain other countries

Published in Hong Kong by
Oxford University Press (China) Limited
18th Floor, Warwick House East, Taikoo Place, 979 King's Road, Quarry Bay, Hong Kong

Pocket Oxford Chinese Dictionary English-Chinese Chinese-English

First published as the Concise English-Chinese Chinese-English Dictionary 1986
The revised and updated edition published as the Pocket Chinese Dictionary 1999
Third edition published as the Oxford Chinese Dictionary 2003
Fourth edition published as Oxford Chinese Desk Dictionary 2009

ISBN: 978-0-19-800594-0 (UK & US paperback)
ISBN: 978-0-19-800595-7 (UK paperback with CD-ROM)
ISBN: 978-0-19-800596-4 (US hardback with CD-ROM)

This impression (lowest digit)
10 9 8 7 6 5

7218416013997941

前　言

此第四版对原来的旧版进行了修订，增补了由于英汉两种语言的发展变化而产生的许多新词新义。这些新词语反映了科学和技术方面，特别是资讯科技和电信领域的日新月异，同时也体现出政治、经济、文化和社会生活等各个方面的各项变化。

汉英部份中收录的不少新词精选自商务印书馆出版的汉语词典，如《现代汉语词典》（第 5 版）等。这些新增的词条见证了工作环境的急促变化，中国新经济的蓬勃发展以及中国与英语世界日益频繁的接触。英汉部份的新词则精选自“牛津英语语料库”。这个规模庞大的英语语言资料库是所有牛津英语词典的主要信息来源。英汉部分的修订也得益于《牛津英语大词典》(*Oxford English Dictionary*) 最新网络版本的应用。

本词典简明易用、权威可靠、参考性强，能满足中级程度的学生、旅游爱好者和商界专业人士的不同需要，既可供汉语读者学习和使用英语时参考，也是操英语人士学习和使用汉语的必备工具书。

编　者

2009 年 4 月

Preface

This fourth edition has been updated to take account of new vocabulary and recent developments in Chinese and English. New words and phrases reflect scientific and technical innovations, particularly in the areas of business, information technology and telecommunications, as well as changes in politics, culture, and society.

Many of the new additions to the Chinese-English section have been selected from the Commercial Press's Chinese dictionaries, especially *A Dictionary of Current Chinese* (*5th edition*). The new entries bear testimony to the accelerating pace of change in the workplace and the rise of the New Economy in China as well as the ever-increasing contacts between China and the English-speaking world. Additions to the English-Chinese section have been selected using the Oxford English Corpus — the vast English-language databanks which form a major resource for all Oxford English Dictionaries — and with online access to the latest version of the text of the *Oxford English Dictionary*.

Designed to meet the needs of a wide range of users, from the student at intermediate level and above to the enthusiastic traveller and business professional, this dictionary is an essential, easy-to-use, and authoritative reference tool for all Chinese-speaking learners of English and English-speaking learners of Chinese.

The Editors
April 2009

目录 CONTENTS

英 汉 词 典

English-Chinese Dictionary

用法说明
GUIDE TO THE USE OF THE DICTIONARY

本词
HEADWORDS

本词排黑正体　Headwords appear in bold type:

dance

table

同形异义词作为不同词目出现时，在右上角用数码标出　Headwords spelt the same but with different meanings are entered separately with a raised number after each:

head^1

head^2

复合词和派生词
COMPOUNDS AND DERIVATIVES

复合词和派生词用黑正体排在词条的末尾部分　Compounds and derivatives appear under the headword which forms their first element:

huge /hjuːdʒ/ *adj* ... **hugely** *adv* ...

house^1/haʊs/ *n* [C] ... ˈ**housework** *n* [U] ...

习语和短语动词
IDIOMS AND PHRASAL VERBS

习语和短语动词排黑正体，用简明的释义和例证阐明其用法　Idioms and phrasal verbs appear in bold type, followed by concise explanations and examples to illustrate their usage:

hook /hʊk/ *n* [C] **1** 钩 gōu；挂〔掛〕钩 guàgōu. **2** (拳击)肘弯〔彎〕击〔擊〕zhǒuwānjī. **3** [习语] **off the** ˈ**hook** (**a**) (电话听筒)未挂上 wèi guàshàng. (**b**) [非正式用语]脱离〔離〕困境 tuōlí kùnjìng: *let/get sb off the* ～ 使某人脱离困境.

名 词
NOUNS

名词可用作单数(a dog)或复数(some dogs)的,用[C](countable, 可数的)表示 Countable senses of a noun are marked [C]:

label /ˈleɪbl/ *n* [C]

没有复数形式的名词(如 sugar、milk),标以[U](uncountable, 不可数的),这类名词与 some、much、a lot of、enough 等连用 Uncountable senses of a noun are marked [U]:

linen /ˈlɪnɪn/ *n* [U]

可用作可数名词也可用作不可数名词的,用[C, U]表示,如 **coffee** 这个词在 Two coffees, please. (要两杯咖啡。)这个句子里是可数名词,在 Have you got any coffee left? (你还有咖啡吗?)这个句子里是不可数名词。大多数名词的复数是有规则的,即加 s,如 dog — dogs,或名词末尾是 s、z、x、ch 或 sh 时加 es,如 church — churches. 如果是不规则变化则予以标出 Nouns with both countable and uncountable forms are marked [C, U]. Irregular plural forms of nouns are clearly shown within the entries:

man[1] /mæn/ *n* (*pl* **men** /men/)

lady /ˈleɪdɪ/ *n* [C] (*pl* **-ies**)

life /laɪf/ *n* (*pl* **lives** /laɪvz/)

形 容 词
ADJECTIVES

所有以辅音字母结尾的单音节形容词(如 kind、green)都以加-er 和-est 的方法来构成比较级和最高级。单音节或双音节形容词不以此种方法,而以加-r、-st、-ier、-iest 的方法来构成比较级和最高级的,本词典都予以标出 Irregular comparative and superlative forms of adjectives are given in square brackets after the part of speech:

free /friː/ *adj* [~**r** /-ə(r)/, ~**st**]

gentle /ˈdʒentl/ *adj* [~**r** /-lə(r)/, ~**st** /-lɪst/]

happy /ˈhæpɪ/ *adj* [**-ier**, **-iest**]

动　词
VERBS

动词过去时和过去分词的拼法和发音为不规则变化的，都在词条的开头予以标出　The past tense and past participle of irregular verbs are given at the beginning of the entry:

know /nəʊ/ *v* [*pt* **knew** /njuː; *US* nuː/, *pp* ~**n** /nəʊn/]

rise /raɪz/ *v* [*pt* **rose** /rəʊz/, *pp* ~**n** /ˈrɪzn/]

双写辅音字母　Doubling of Consonants　末尾为单个辅音字母的动词在构成过去时、过去分词及现在分词时，需将此辅音字母双写(如 stop — stopped — stopping)。某些形容词在构成比较级和最高级时，亦需双写此辅音字母(如 hot — hotter — hottest)。以上两种情况本词典都予以标出　The doubling of a final consonant before **-ed** or **-ing** is also shown:

rot /rɒt/ *v* [**-tt-**]

sad /sæd/ *adj* [~**der**, ~**dest**]

动词、形容词、名词同介词的搭配
PREPOSITIONS TO USE WITH VERBS, ADJECTIVES AND NOUNS

许多动词、形容词和名词通常都后接某一特定的介词。这类最常用的搭配，本词典以斜体字予以标出，加圆括号的是不固定搭配，不加圆括号的是固定搭配　The prepositions which typically follow verbs, adjectives or nouns are shown in italics in round brackets if optional and without brackets if fixed:

familiarize /fəˈmɪlɪəraɪz/ *v* [T] *with*

sensitive /ˈsensətɪv/ *adj* **1** (*to*)

释　义
MEANINGS

汉语释义中的简化汉字用六角括号注出繁体字(同一词条中再次出现时不重

复注，常用的简化偏旁不注）；汉语释义都加注汉语拼音，并加声调符号（ˉ阴平，ˊ阳平，ˇ上声，ˋ去声，不加调号者为轻声） In translations, orthodox Chinese characters are given in hexagonal brackets immediately following their simplified form (except those reappearing in the same entry or those simplified radicals that are easily recognized). All Chinese translations are followed by pinyin romanization and tones (ˉ first tone or *yinping*, ˊ second tone or *yangping*, ˇ third tone or *shangsheng*, ˋ fourth tone or *qusheng* and no mark for a light tone):

honourable (美语 **-nor-**) /ˈɒnərəbl/ *adj* **1** 光荣〔榮〕的 guāngróngde；荣誉〔譽〕的 róngyùde

若干符号用法
BRACKETS AND SYMBOLS

1. () 圆括号用于注出拼法、内容或意义的补充说明，以及代换部分、可省略部分。Round brackets () are used to show spelling variants, extra information, clarification of a meaning, words that can be substituted or omitted, etc.

2. [ ] 方括号用于注出语法、用法、文体、修辞色彩、学科等。Square brackets [ ] are used to show information about grammar, usage, forms, rhetorical devices, subject fields, etc.

3. 〔〕六角括号用于注出简体汉字的繁体字。Hexagonal brackets 〔〕 give the orthodox version of simplified Chinese characters.

4. ～ 代字号用于代表本词。A swung dash (～) represents the headword.

5. ⇨ 箭头号表示“参见”。An arrow (⇨) cross-refers the user to another entry.

6. / 斜线号用于英语中词语的代换。A forward slash (/) separates alternative structures.

7. ⚠ 提醒号表示“禁忌语”。(⚠) alerts the user to slang or informal language which should be used with care.

略 语 表

ABBREVIATIONS USED IN THE DICTIONARY

abbr = abbreviation 缩略语

adj = adjective 形容词

adv = adverb 副词

aux v = auxiliary verb 助动词

[C] = countable 可数的

conj = conjunction 连接词

fem = feminine 阴性

[I] = intransitive 不及物的

interj = interjection 感叹词

modal v = modal verb 情态动词

n = noun 名词

P = proprietary 专利

pl = plural 复数

pp = past participle 过去分词

prep = preposition 介词

pres part = present participle 现在分词

pron = pronoun 代词

pt = past tense 过去时

rel pron = relative pronoun 关系代词

sb = somebody 某人

sing = singular 单数

sth = something 某事物

[T] = transitive 及物的

[U] = uncountable 不可数的

US = American 美语

v = verb 动词

发音简表
GUIDE TO ENGLISH PRONUNCIATION

元音和双元音
VOWELS AND DIPHTHONGS

音标 Phonetic symbol	例词 Example	读音 Pronunciation
iː	see	/siː/
ɪ	sit	/sɪt/
e	ten	/ten/
æ	hat	/hæt/
ɑː	arm	/ɑːm/
ɒ	got	/gɒt/
ɔː	saw	/sɔː/
ʊ	put	/pʊt/
uː	too	/tuː/
ʌ	cup	/kʌp/
ɜː	fur	/fɜː(r)/
ə	ago	/əˈgəʊ/
eɪ	page	/peɪdʒ/
əʊ	home	/həʊm/
aɪ	five	/faɪv/
aʊ	now	/naʊ/
ɔɪ	join	/dʒɔɪn/
ɪə	near	/nɪə(r)/
eə	hair	/heə(r)/
ʊə	pure	/pjʊə(r)/

辅 音
CONSONANTS

音标 Phonetic symbol	例词 Example	读音 Pronunciation
p	pen	/pen/
b	bad	/bæd/
t	tea	/tiː/
d	did	/dɪd/
k	cat	/kæt/
g	got	/gɒt/
tʃ	chin	/tʃɪn/
dʒ	June	/dʒuːn/
f	fall	/fɔːl/
v	voice	/vɔɪs/
θ	thin	/θɪn/
ð	then	/ðen/
s	so	/səʊ/
z	zoo	/zuː/
ʃ	she	/ʃiː/
ʒ	vision	/ˈvɪʒn/
h	how	/haʊ/
m	man	/mæn/
n	no	/nəʊ/
ŋ	sing	/sɪŋ/
l	leg	/leg/
r	red	/red/
j	yes	/jes/
w	wet	/wet/

/ˈ/ 主重音符号 primary stress: **about** /əˈbaʊt/

/ˌ/ 次重音符号 secondary stress: **academic** /ˌækəˈdemɪk/

(r) 用于英国英语发音，表示如果后面紧接以元音开始的词，发 r 音，否则省略 is sounded in British pronunciation when the word immediately following begins with a vowel. Otherwise it is not pronounced.

/-/ 表示省略了的相同的音标 indicates the part of phonetic transcription being repeated.

拼 写 法
SPELLING

如果不了解一个词开头的音是怎么写的，有时在词典里是很难查到这个词的。以下所列是最常遇到的困难　If the exact spelling of the first syllable of a word is not known, it is sometimes difficult to look it up in the dictionary. Here are some common problems：

首字母不发音　First letter not sounded

wh- 有时读作 sometimes pronounced as /h-/：who, whole.

wr- 读作 pronounced as /r-/：write, wrist.

kn- 读作 pronounced as /n-/：knife, know.

ho- 有时读作 sometimes pronounced as /ɒ-/：honest, honour.

ps- 读作 pronounced as /s-/：psychology.

pn- 读作 pronounced as /n-/：pneumonia.

第二个字母不发音　Second letter not sounded

wh- 有时读作 sometimes pronounced as /w-/：which, whether.

gu- 有时读作 sometimes pronounced as /g-/：guest, guess.

gh- 读作 pronounced as /g-/：ghastly, ghost.

bu- 有时读作 sometimes pronounced as /b-/，如 build, buoy.

头两个字母发特殊的音　First two letters with special pronunciation

ph- 读作 pronounced as /f-/：photo.

qu- 通常读作 usually pronounced as /kw-/：quick.

ch- 有时读作 sometimes pronounced as /k-/：chorus.

请记住　Remember

c- 可读作 may be pronounced as /k-/：call, 或读作 or pronounced as /s-/：centre.

g- 可读作 may be pronounced as /g-/: good, 或读作 or pronounced as /dʒ-/: general.

如果在词典中查不到某个词，下表可用作查找的指南 If you have difficulty in looking up a word, the following table may help:

读音 Pronunciation	可能的拼法 Possible spelling
f-	**ph-** (如 e.g. *photo*)
g-	**gh-** (如 e.g. *ghost*) 或 or
	gu- (如 e.g. *guest*)
h-	**wh-** (如 e.g. *who, whole*)
k-	**ch-** (如 e.g. *character*)
kw-	**qu-** (如 e.g. *quick*)
n-	**kn-** (如 e.g. *knife*) 或 or
	pn- (如 e.g. *pneumonia*)
r-	**wr-** (如 e.g. *write*)
s-	**c-** (如 e.g. *centre*) 或 or
	ps- (如 e.g. *psychology*)
dʒ-	**j-** (如 e.g. *job*) 或 or
	g- (如 e.g. *general*)
ʃ-	**sh-** (如 e.g. *shop*) 或 or
	ch- (如 e.g. *chalet*)
iː	**ea-** (如 e.g. *each*)
ɪ	**e-** (如 e.g. *enjoy*)
e	**a-** (如 e.g. *any*)
ɑː	**au-** (如 e.g. *aunt*)
ɒ	**ho-** (如 e.g. *honest*)
ɔː	**au-** (如 e.g. *author*)或 or
	oa- (如 e.g. *oar*)
ə	**a-** (如 e.g. *awake*)或 or
	o- (如 e.g. *obey*)

ɜː	**ear-** (如 e.g. *early*)或 or
	ir- (如 e.g. *irk*)
eɪ	**ai-** (如 e.g. *aim*)或 or
	ei- (如 e.g. *eight*)
əʊ	**oa-** (如 e.g. *oath*)
aɪ	**ei-** (如 e.g. *either*)
juː	**eu-** (如 e.g. *Europe*)

A a

A, a[1] /eɪ/ [*pl* A's, a's /eɪz/] 英语的第一个〔個〕字母 yīngyǔde dìyīgè zìmǔ. **A level** *n* [C] [英国英语]中学〔學〕生高级考试 zhōngxuéshēng gāojí kǎoshì.

A[2] *abbr* ampere(s)

a /ə 强式:eɪ/ (亦作 an /ən 强式:æn/) *indefinite article* [*an* 用于以元音开头的词前] 1 一 yī;一个〔個〕yī gè: *a book* 一本书. *a teacher* 一位教师. *a million pounds* 一百万英镑. 2 (表示数量、群等): *a lot of money* 很多钱. 3 每 měi; 每一 měi yī: *70 miles an hour* 每小时70英里.

A2 level *n* [C] [英国英语]A2级别考试 jíbié kǎoshì.

aback /əˈbæk/ *adv* [短语动词] take sb aback ⇨ TAKE[1].

abacus /ˈæbəkəs/ *n* [C] 算盘〔盤〕suànpán.

abandon /əˈbændən/ *v* [T] 1 离〔離〕弃〔棄〕líqì;遗弃 yíqì. 2 放弃 fàngqì: ~ *an idea* 放弃一种想法. 3 [正式用语] ~ oneself to 陷于(某种感情) xiàn yú. **abandoned** *adj* 1 被遗弃的 bèi yíqì de. 2 (行为)放荡〔蕩〕的 fàngdàngde. **abandonment** *n* [U].

abashed /əˈbæʃt/ *adj* 窘迫的 jiǒngpòde; 羞愧的 xiūkuìde.

abate /əˈbeɪt/ *v* [I] [正式用语]减少 jiǎnshǎo;减轻〔輕〕jiǎnqīng. **abatement** *n* [U]: *noise ~ment* 减轻噪音.

abattoir /ˈæbətwɑː(r); *US* æbəˈtwɑːr/ *n* [C] 屠宰场〔場〕túzǎichǎng.

abbess /ˈæbes/ *n* [C] 女修道院院长〔長〕nǚxiūdàoyuàn yuànzhǎng.

abbey /ˈæbɪ/ *n* [C] 修道院 xiūdàoyuàn.

abbot /ˈæbət/ *n* [C] 修道院院长 xiūdàoyuàn yuànzhǎng;寺庙〔廟〕住持 sìmiào zhùchí.

abbreviate /əˈbriːvɪeɪt/ *v* [T] 简略 jiǎnlüè; 缩写〔寫〕suōxiě. **abbreviation** /əˌbriːvɪˈeɪʃn/ *n* [C] 缩略 suōlüè;缩略语 suōlüèyǔ.

abdicate /ˈæbdɪkeɪt/ *v* [I, T] 让〔讓〕(位) ràng;放弃〔棄〕(责任等) fàngqì. **abdication** /ˌæbdɪˈkeɪʃn/ *n* [U].

abdomen /ˈæbdəmən/ *n* [C] 腹 fù;腹部 fùbù. **abdominal** /æbˈdɒmɪnl/ *adj*.

abduct /əbˈdʌkt, æb-/ *v* [T] 绑架 bǎngjià. **abduction** /əbˈdʌkʃn, æb-/ *n* [U, C].

aberration /ˌæbəˈreɪʃn/ *n* [C, U] 越轨 yuèguǐ.

abet /əˈbet/ *v* [-tt-] [习语] aid and abet ⇨ AID.

abhor /əbˈhɔː(r)/ *v* [-rr-] [T] [正式用语]憎恨 zènghèn;厌〔厭〕恶〔惡〕yànwù. **abhorrence** /əbˈhɒrəns/ *n* [U]. **abhorrent** /-ənt/ *adj*.

abide /əˈbaɪd/ *v* 1 [T] 忍受 rěnshòu;容忍 róngrěn: *She can't ~ that man*. 她不能容忍那个男人. 2 [I] *by* 遵守 zūnshǒu;坚〔堅〕持 jiānchí. **abiding** *adj* 持久的 chíjiǔde.

ability /əˈbɪlətɪ/ *n* [C, U] [*pl* -ies] 才干〔幹〕cáigàn;能力 nénglì.

abject /ˈæbdʒekt/ *adj* [正式用语] 1 情况可怜〔憐〕的 qíngkuàng kělián de: ~ *poverty* 赤贫. 2 卑鄙的 bēibǐde. **abjectly** *adv*.

ablaze /əˈbleɪz/ *adj* 1 着火 zháo huǒ;燃烧 ránshāo. 2 [喻] 闪耀 shǎnyào.

able /ˈeɪbl/ *adj* [~r, ~st] 1 *to* 能够的 nénggòude;能 (有能力、有办法、有机会)做某事 néngzuò mǒushì: *Are you ~ to come with us?* 你能同我们一起走吗? 2 聪〔聰〕明的 cōngmíngde;能干〔幹〕的 nénggànde. ˌ**able-ˈbodied** *adj* 健壮〔壯〕的 jiànzhuàngde. **ably** *adv*.

abnormal /ˌæbˈnɔːml/ *adj* 变〔變〕态〔態〕的 biàntàide;反常的 fǎnchángde. **abnormality** /ˌæbnɔːˈmælətɪ/ *n* [C, U] [*pl* -ies]. **abnormally** *adv*.

aboard /əˈbɔːd/ *adv*, *prep* 在船上 zài chuán shang;在飞机〔機〕上 zài fēijī shang;在火车上 zài huǒchē shang;在公共汽车上 zài gōnggòngqìchē shang.

abode /əˈbəʊd/ *n* [sing] [正式用语] 1 住所 zhùsuǒ. 2 [习语] (of) ˌno fixed aˈbode 无〔無〕固定住所 wú gùdìng zhùsuǒ.

abolish /əˈbɒlɪʃ/ *v* [T] 废〔廢〕除 fèichú: ~ *taxes* 废除赋税. **abolition** /ˌæbəˈlɪʃən/ *n* [U].

abominable /əˈbɒmɪnəbl; *US* -mən-/ *adj* 1 [非正式用语] 讨厌〔厭〕的 tǎoyànde: ~ *weather* 讨厌的天气. 2 [正式用语]极〔極〕坏〔壞〕的 jíhuàide: ~ *behaviour* 恶〔惡〕劣的行为. **abominably** *adv*.

aboriginal /ˌæbəˈrɪdʒənl/ *adj* (人或动物)某地区〔區〕土生土长〔長〕的 mǒu dìqū tǔshēngtǔzhǎng de. **aboriginal** (亦作 **Aboriginal**) *n* [C] 澳大利亚〔亞〕土著人 Aodàlìyà tǔzhù rén.

Aborigine /æbəˈrɪdʒənɪ/ *n* [C] 澳大利亚〔亞〕土著人 Aodàlìyà tǔzhù rén.

abort /əˈbɔːt/ *v* [I, T] 1 流产〔產〕liúchǎn;堕胎 duòtāi. 2 夭折 yāozhé;取消 qǔxiāo: ~ *a space flight* 取消一次太空飞行. **abortion** /əˈbɔːʃn/ *n* [C, U] 流产〔產〕liúchǎn. **abortive** *adj* 失败的 shībàide.

abound /əˈbaʊnd/ *v* [I] (*in* /*with*) 多 duō;富于 fù yú.

about[1] /əˈbaʊt/ *prep* 1 有关〔關〕…(题目) yǒuguān: *a book ~ flowers* 一本关于花的书. 2 在…到处〔處〕zài dàochù: *walking ~ the town* 在镇上到处走走. 3 关心 guānxīn;从

A

〔從〕事于 cóngshì yú: *And while you're ~ it*, . . . 你正做的时候,… 4 [习语] **be about to do sth** 就要… jiùyào; 即将〔將〕… jíjiāng. **how/what about . . . ?** (a) (用于提出建议) …怎么〔麼〕样〔樣〕? … zěnmeyàng?: *How ~ some more tea?* 再来点茶怎么样? (b) (用于询问情况、信息) …怎么样? … zěnmeyàng: *What ~ the money—do we have enough?* 钱怎么样? 我们的钱够吗?

about[2] /ə'baʊt/ *adv* 1 大约 dàyuē: *It costs ~ £100*. 花费了大约 100 英镑. 2 到处〔處〕 dàochù: *The children were rushing ~*. 孩子们到处乱窜. 3 各处 gèchù: *papers lying ~ the room* 散在房间各处的报纸. 4 在周围〔圍〕活动〔動〕 zài zhōuwéi huódòng: *There was no one ~*. 周围没有人活动. **a,bout-'turn** *n* [C] (立场、观点等的)彻〔徹〕底转〔轉〕变〔變〕 chèdǐ zhuǎnbiàn.

above[1] /ə'bʌv/ *prep* 1 在…上面 zài…shàngmiàn; 高于 gāo yú: *fly ~ the clouds* 在云层上面飞行. 2 (数量、价格、重量等)大于 dà yú. 3 不屑于 búxiè yú; 不做 búzuò: *be ~ stealing* 不会偷窃. *be ~ suspicion* 无可怀疑. 4 [习语] **above all** 首先 shǒuxiān; 尤其重要的 yóuqí zhòngyào de. **above one's 'head** ⇨HEAD[1].

above[2] /ə'bʌv/ *adv* 1 在上面 zài shàngmiàn; 高于 gāo yú: *the shelf ~* 上面的架子. 2 (用于书籍等)在上文 zài shàngwén; 在前文 zài qiánwén.

abrasion /ə'breɪʒn/ *n* 1 [U] 磨损 mósǔn; 擦伤〔傷〕 cāshāng. 2 [C] 擦伤处〔處〕 cāshāngchù.

abrasive /ə'breɪsɪv/ *adj* 1 磨损的 mósǔnde; 粗糙的 cūcāode. 2 [喻]粗暴的 cūbàode: *an ~ manner* 粗暴的态度.

abreast /ə'brest/ *adv* 1 并〔並〕排 bìngpái; 并肩 bìngjiān. 2 [习语] **be/keep abreast of sth** 及时〔時〕了解(某事物) jíshí liǎojiě.

abridge /ə'brɪdʒ/ *v* [T] 删节〔節〕(书等) shānjié. **abridg(e)ment** *n* [C, U].

abroad /ə'brɔːd/ *adv* 在国〔國〕外 zài guówài; 去国外 qù guówài: *travel ~* 到国外旅行.

abrupt /ə'brʌpt/ *adj* 1 突然的 tūránde; 不意的 búyìde: *an ~ stop* 突然停止. 2 粗暴的 cūbàode; 不友好的 bù yǒuhǎode. **abruptly** *adv*. **abruptness** *n* [U].

abscess /'æbses/ *n* [C] 脓〔膿〕肿〔腫〕 nóngzhǒng.

abscond /əb'skɒnd/ *v* [I] [正式用语]潜〔潛〕逃 qiántáo.

absence /'æbsəns/ *n* 1 [U] 不在 búzài; 缺席 quēxí: *~ from school* 缺课. 2 [sing] 缺乏 quēfá; 没有 méiyǒu: *the ~ of information* 缺乏资料.

absent[1] /'æbsənt/ *adj* (*from*) 不在的 búzàide; 缺席的 quēxíde. **,absent-'minded** *adj* 心不在焉的 xīn bú zài yān de; 健忘的 jiànwàngde.

absent[2] /əb'sent/ *v* [正式用语] **~ oneself (from)** 未出席 wèi chūxí.

absentee /,æbsən'tiː/ *n* [C] 缺席者 quēxízhě.

absolute /'æbsəluːt/ *adj* 1 完全的 wánquánde: *~ trust* 充分的信任. 2 确〔確〕实〔實〕的 quèshíde: *~ proof* 确凿的证据. 3 独〔獨〕裁的 dúcáide: *an ~ ruler* 独裁的统治者. 4 独立的 dúlìde: *an ~ standard* 独立的标准. **absolutely** 1 完全地 wánquánde: *He's ~ly right*. 他完全正确. 2 /,æbsə'luːtlɪ/ [非正式用语](表示同意)当〔當〕然 dāngrán.

absolve /əb'zɒlv/ *v* [T] *from* / *of* [正式用语]免除 miǎnchú; 赦免 shèmiǎn.

absorb /əb'sɔːb/ *v* [T] 1 吸收 xīshōu. 2 吸引 xīyǐn: *~ed in her work* 全神贯注于工作. **absorbent** *adj* 能吸收的 néng xīshōu de. **absorption** /əb'sɔːpʃn/ *n* [U].

abstain /əb'steɪn/ *v* [I] 1 (*from*) 戒除… jièchú…; 避开〔開〕… bìkāi…. 2 弃〔棄〕权〔權〕 qìquán.

abstemious /əb'stiːmɪəs/ *adj* (饮食等)有节〔節〕制的 yǒu jiézhìde.

abstention /əb'stenʃn/ *n* [C, U] 弃〔棄〕权〔權〕 qìquán.

abstinence /'æbstɪnəns/ *n* [U] 戒除 jièchú; 戒酒 jièjiǔ.

abstract /'æbstrækt/ *adj* 1 抽象的 chōuxiàngde: *Beauty is ~*. 美是抽象的. 2 (艺术)抽象的 chōuxiàngde. 3 (名词)抽象的 chōuxiàngde. **abstract** *n* [C] (书籍、演说等的)摘要 zhāiyào.

absurd /əb'sɜːd/ *adj* 荒谬的 huāngmiùde; 可笑的 kěxiàode. **absurdity** *n* [C, U] [*pl* -ies]. **absurdly** *adv*.

abundance /ə'bʌndəns/ *n* [U, sing] 丰〔豐〕富 fēngfù. **abundant** /-ənt/ *adj*. **abundantly** *adv*.

abuse[1] /ə'bjuːz/ *v* [T] 1 滥〔濫〕用 lànyòng; 妄用 wàngyòng. 2 虐待 nüèdài. 3 辱骂 rǔmà.

abuse[2] /ə'bjuːs/ *n* 1 [U] 辱骂〔罵〕 rǔmà; 咒骂 zhòumà: *hurl ~ at sb* 辱骂某人. 2 [C, U] 滥〔濫〕用 lànyòng; 妄用 wàngyòng: *an ~ of power* 滥用权力. **abusive** *adj* 辱骂的 rǔmàde.

abysmal /ə'bɪzməl/ *adj* 很坏〔壞〕的 hěnhuàide: *an ~ failure* 彻底的失败. **abysmally** *adv*.

abyss /ə'bɪs/ *n* [C] 深渊〔淵〕 shēnyuān.

academic /,ækə'demɪk/ *adj* 1 学〔學〕校的

A

xuéxiàode；研究的 yánjiūde；教学的 jiàoxuéde. 2 学术〔術〕的 xuéshùde. **academic** *n* [C] 大学教师〔師〕dàxué jiàoshī. **academically** /-klɪ/ *adv*.

academy /əˈkædəmɪ/ *n* [C] [*pl* -ies] 1 专〔專〕门学〔學〕校 zhuānmén xuéxiào: *a music* ～ 音乐专科学校. 2 学会〔會〕xuéhuì.

accede /əkˈsiːd/ *v* [I] (*to*) [正式用语]答应〔應〕dāying；同意 tóngyì.

accelerate /əkˈseləreɪt/ *v* [I, T] (使)加速 jiāsù；变〔變〕快 biànkuài. **acceleration** /əkˌseləˈreɪʃn/ *n* [U]. **accelerator** *n* [C] (汽车的)油门 yóumén.

accent /ˈæksent；ˈæksənt/ *n* [C] 1 (个人、地方或民族的)口音 kǒuyīn. 2 重音符号〔號〕zhòngyīn fúhào. 3 强调 qiángdiào；重点〔點〕zhòngdiǎn. **accent** /ækˈsent/ *v* [T] 重读〔讀〕zhòngdú.

accentuate /əkˈsentʃʊeɪt/ *v* [T] 强调 qiángdiào；使明显 shǐ míngxiǎn；使突出 shǐ tūchū.

accept /əkˈsept/ *v* 1 [I, T] 接受 jiēshòu: ～ *a present* 接受一件礼品. 2 [T] 同意 tóngyì；承认〔認〕chéngrèn: ～ *the truth* 相信真理. **acceptable** *adj* 可接受的 kě jiēshòude；受欢〔歡〕迎的 shòu huānyíngde. **acceptance** *n* [U, C].

access /ˈækses/ *n* [U] (*to*) 1 通路 tōnglù. 2 接近或使用的机〔機〕会〔會〕jiējìn huò shǐyòng de jīhuì. **access** *v* [T] 从〔從〕(电子计算机)存取(信息) cóng cúnqǔ. **accessible** *adj* 易接近的 yì jiējìn de；易得到的 yì dédào de.

accession /ækˈseʃn/ *n* [U] 就高职〔職〕jiù gāozhí: *the King's* ～ *to the throne* 国王登基.

accessory /əkˈsesərɪ/ *n* [C] [*pl* -ies] 1 附件 fùjiàn；配件 pèijiàn: *car accessories* 汽车配件. 2 (亦作 accessary) [法律]从〔從〕犯 cóngfàn.

accident /ˈæksɪdənt/ *n* 1 [C] 事故 shìgù；偶然的事 ǒuránde shì. 2 [习语] **by accident** 偶然 ǒurán. **accidental** /ˌæksɪˈdentl/ *adj*. **accidentally** /-təlɪ/ *adv*.

acclaim /əˈkleɪm/ *v* [T] [正式用语] 欢〔歡〕呼 huānhū. **acclaim** *n* [U] 欢呼 huānhū；赞〔讚〕同 zàntóng.

acclimatize /əˈklaɪmətaɪz/ *v* [I, T] (*to*) 适〔適〕应〔應〕气〔氣〕候或环〔環〕境 shìyìng qìhòu huò huánjìng.

accolade /ˈækəleɪd；US ækəˈleɪd/ *n* [C] [正式用语]赞〔讚〕扬 zànyáng；赞同 zàntóng.

accommodate /əˈkɒmədeɪt/ *v* 1 [T] 为〔爲〕…提供住宿 wèi… tígòng zhùsù. 2 施恩惠于 shī ēnhuì yú. **accommodating** *adj* 乐〔樂〕于助人的 lè yú zhùrén de. **accommodation** *n* /əˌkɒməˈdeɪʃn/ *n* [U] (尤指供居住用的)房间 fángjiān.

accompaniment /əˈkʌmpənɪmənt/ *n* [C] 1 伴随物 bànsuíwù. 2 [音乐]伴奏 bànzòu；伴唱 bànchàng.

accompanist /əˈkʌmpənɪst/ *n* [C] 伴奏者 bànzòuzhě；伴唱者 bànchàngzhě.

accompany /əˈkʌmpənɪ/ *v* [*pt*, *pp* -ied] [T] 1 陪伴 péibàn. 2 伴随 bànsuí: *wind accompanied by rain* 风雨交加. 3 伴奏 bànzòu；伴唱 bànchàng.

accomplice /əˈkʌmplɪs；US əˈkɒm-/ *n* [C] 帮〔幫〕凶〔兇〕bāngxiōng；共犯 gòngfàn.

accomplish /əˈkʌmplɪʃ；US əˈkɒm-/ *v* [T] 完成 wánchéng；实〔實〕现 shíxiàn. **accomplished** *adj* 熟练〔練〕的 shúliànde；训练有素的 xùnliàn yǒusù de. **accomplishment** *n* 1 [U] 完成 wánchéng. 2 [C] 成就 chéngjiù；技艺〔藝〕jìyì: *Ability to play the piano well is quite an* ～. 弹得一手好钢琴确是一项成就.

accord /əˈkɔːd/ *n* [U] [习语] **in accord (with sth /sb)** 与〔與〕…一致 yǔ…yízhì. **of one's own accord** 自发〔發〕地 zìfāde；自愿〔願〕地 zìyuànde. **accord** *v* [I] [正式用语]与…一致 yǔ…yízhì.

accordance /əˈkɔːdəns/ *n* [习语] **in accordance with sth** 与〔與〕…一致 yǔ…yízhì；依照 yīzhào；根据〔據〕gēnjù.

accordingly /əˈkɔːdɪŋlɪ/ *adv* 照着 zhàozhe；相应〔應〕地 xiāngyìngde；因此 yīncǐ；所以 suǒyǐ.

according to /əˈkɔːdɪŋ tuː/ *prep* 1 按照…所述 ànzhào…suǒshù: *A*～ *to a recent report, people in Britain don't take enough exercise*. 根据最近报道，英国人体育活动做得不够. *A*～ *to my doctor, I ought to go on a diet*. 按照我的医生的要求，我应该继续节制饮食. 2 按照 ànzhào: *act* ～ *to one's principles* 按照自己的原则办事. 3 依…而定 yī…érdìng. *arranged* ～ *to size* 按大小顺序排列.

accordion /əˈkɔːdɪən/ *n* [C] 手风〔風〕琴 shǒufēngqín.

accost /əˈkɒst；US əˈkɔːst/ *v* [T] 与〔與〕(某不认识的人)搭讪 yǔ dāshàn.

account[1] /əˈkaʊnt/ *n* 1 [C] 报〔報〕告 bàogào；叙述 xùshù: *give an* ～ *of the meeting* 报道会议的情况. 2 [C] 账〔賬〕户 zhànghù: *open a bank* ～ 开立银行账户. 3 **accounts** [pl] 账目 zhàngmù. 4 [习语] **of great, no, etc. account** 非常重要，不重要 fēicháng zhòngyào, bú zhòngyào. **on account of sth** 因为〔爲〕yīnwèi. **on no account** 决不 juébù. **take account of sth, take sth into account** 考虑〔慮〕到 kǎolǜ dào.

A

account[2] /əˈkaʊnt/ *v* [短语动词] account for sth (a) 说明 shuōmíng; 解释〔釋〕jiěshì: *This* ~ *for his behaviour*. 这是他所作所为的一个说明. (b) 说明钱〔錢〕的开〔開〕支 shuōmíng qiánde kāizhī. accountable *adj* 应〔應〕负责任的 yīng fù zérènde.

accountant /əˈkaʊntənt/ *n* [C] 会〔會〕计 kuàijì. accountancy /-tənsɪ/ *n* [U] 会计工作 kuàijì gōngzuò. accounting *n* [U] 会计 kuàijì.

accredited /əˈkredɪtɪd/ *adj* 被正式认〔認〕可的 bèi zhèngshì rènkě de: *our* ~ *representative* 我们的正式代表.

accrue /əˈkruː/ *v* [I] [正式用语](尤指利息等)增长〔長〕zēngzhǎng.

accumulate /əˈkjuːmjʊleɪt/ *v* [I, T] 积〔積〕累 jīlěi; 积聚 jījù. accumulation /əˌkjuːmjʊˈleɪʃn/ *n* [C, U].

accurate /ˈækjʊrət/ *adj* 准确〔確〕的 zhǔnquède; 精密的 jīngmìde. accuracy /-rəsɪ/ *n* [U]. accurately *adv*.

accusation /ˌækjʊˈzeɪʃn/ *n* [C] 控告 kònggào; 谴责 qiǎnzé.

accuse /əˈkjuːz/ *v* [T] (*of*) 控告 kònggào: ~ *sb of theft* 控告某人偷窃. the accused *n* [C] [*pl* the accused] 被告 bèigào. accuser *n* [C].

accustom /əˈkʌstəm/ *v* [T] 使习〔習〕惯于 shǐ xíguàn yú. accustomed *adj* 惯常的 guànchángde.

ace /eɪs/ *n* [C] 1 扑〔撲〕克牌上的幺点〔點〕pūkèpái shàng de yāodiǎn. 2 [非正式用语] 专〔專〕家 zhuānjiā: *an* ~ *footballer* 技术精湛的足球运动员.

ache /eɪk/ *n* [C] [常用于复合词]疼痛 téngtòng: ˈ*headache* 头痛. ache *v* [I] 1 疼痛 téngtòng: *My head* ~*s*. 我头痛. 2 *for* / *to* 渴望 kěwàng: *He is aching for home*. 他正想家. ~ *to go home* 渴望回家.

achieve /əˈtʃiːv/ *v* [T] 完成 wánchéng; 达〔達〕到 dádào: ~ *one's aim* 达到目的. achievement *n* [C, U].

Achilles /əˈkɪliːz/ *n* [习语] Achilles' heel 致命的弱点〔點〕zhìmìngde ruòdiǎn. Achilles' tendon *n* [C] [解剖]跟腱 gēnjiàn.

acid /ˈæsɪd/ *n* 1 [C, U] [化学]酸 suān. 2 [习语] the ˈacid test [喻]严〔嚴〕峻的考验〔驗〕yánjùnde kǎoyàn. acid *adj* 1 酸的 suānde. 2 [喻]尖刻的 jiānkède; 讽〔諷〕刺的 fěngcìde. ˌacid ˈrain *n* [U] 酸雨 suānyǔ.

acknowledge /əkˈnɒlɪdʒ/ *v* [T] 1 承认〔認〕chéngrèn: *I* ~ *my mistake*. 我承认错误. 2 表示收到(信件等) biǎoshì shōudào. 3 表示已注意到(某人) biǎoshì yǐ zhùyì dào. 4 为〔爲〕(某事)表示感谢 wèi biǎoshì gǎnxiè. acknowledgement (亦作 acknowledgment) *n* [C, U].

acne /ˈæknɪ/ *n* [U] 粉刺 fěncì.

acorn /ˈeɪkɔːn/ *n* [C] 橡子 xiàngzi; 橡果 xiàngguǒ.

acoustic /əˈkuːstɪk/ *adj* 声〔聲〕音的 shēngyīnde. acoustics *n* 1 [pl] 音响〔響〕效果 yīnxiǎng xiàoguǒ. 2 [U] 声学〔學〕shēngxué.

acquaint /əˈkweɪnt/ *v* [T] *with* 使认〔認〕识〔識〕shǐ rènshi; 使熟悉 shǐ shúxī. acquaintance *n* 1 [C] 熟人 shúrén. 2 [U] (*with*) (稍稍的)熟悉 shúxī. 3 [习语] make sb's acquaintance 熟悉某人 shúxī mǒurén; 会〔會〕见 huìjiàn. acquainted *adj* (*with*) 熟悉(某人)的 shúxī de.

acquiesce /ˌækwɪˈes/ *v* [I] (*in*) [正式用语]默认〔認〕mòrèn. acquiescence *n* [U].

acquire /əˈkwaɪə(r)/ *v* [T] 获〔獲〕得 huòdé; 取得 qǔdé. acquisition /ˌækwɪˈzɪʃn/ *n* 1 [C] 获得物 huòdéwù. 2 [U] 获得 huòdé. acquisitive /əˈkwɪzətɪv/ *adj* 渴望获得的 kěwàng huòdé de.

acquit /əˈkwɪt/ *v* [-tt-] 1 [T] 宣告无〔無〕罪 xuāngào wúzuì. 2 ~ oneself 使(自己)作出某种〔種〕表现 shǐ zuòchū mǒuzhǒng biǎoxiàn: *He* ~*ted himself very well*. 他表现甚好. acquittal *n* [C, U].

acre /ˈeɪkə(r)/ *n* [C] 英亩〔畝〕yīngmǔ. acreage /ˈeɪkərɪdʒ/ *n* [U] 英亩数〔數〕yīngmǔshù.

acrid /ˈækrɪd/ *adj* 辣的 làde.

acrimonious /ˌækrɪˈməʊnɪəs/ *adj* [正式用语]尖刻的 jiānkède; 讥〔譏〕讽〔諷〕的 jīfěngde. acrimony /ˈækrɪmənɪ; *US* -məʊnɪ/ *n* [U].

acrobat /ˈækrəbæt/ *n* [C] 杂〔雜〕技演员 zájì yǎnyuán. acrobatic /ˌækrəˈbætɪk/ *adj*. acrobatics *n* [pl].

acronym /ˈækrənɪm/ *n* [C] 首字母缩写〔寫〕词 shǒuzìmǔ suōxiěcí.

across /əˈkrɒs; *US* əˈkrɔːs/ *adv*, *prep* 1 横过〔過〕héngguò; 越过 yuèguò: *swim* ~ *the lake* 横游这个湖. 2 在…那一边〔邊〕zài…nà yìbiān: *My house is just* ~ *the street*. 我家就在街的那一边.

acrylic /əˈkrɪlɪk/ *adj* 丙烯酸的 bǐngxīsuānde.

act[1] /ækt/ *v* 1 [I] 做 zuò; 干〔幹〕gàn; 作 zuò: *We must* ~ *quickly*. 我们必须赶快行动. 2 [I, T] 表演 biǎoyǎn; 扮演 bànyǎn. 3 [短语动词] act as sb / sth 充当〔當〕chōngdāng; 作为〔爲〕zuòwéi; 起…作用 qǐ…zuòyòng. acting *n* [U] 表演 biǎoyǎn. acting *adj* 代理的 dàilǐde: *the* ~*ing manager* 代经理.

act[2] /ækt/ *n* [C] 1 行为〔爲〕xíngwéi: *an* ~ *of kindness* 好意的行为. 2 行动〔動〕xíngdòng: *caught in the ~ of stealing* 行窃时被当场捉住. 3 法令 fǎlìng; 条〔條〕例 tiáolì: *A ~ of Parliament* 议院的法案. 4 [戏剧] 幕 mù. 5 简短的演出 jiǎnduǎnde yǎnchū: *a circus ~* 马戏表演. 6 [非正式用语] 装〔裝〕腔作势〔勢〕zhuāng qiāng zuò shì: *put on an ~* 装腔作势,炫耀自己. 7 [习语] an ˌact of ˈGod 不可抗拒力(如水灾等) bùkě kàngjù lì.

action /ˈækʃn/ *n* 1 [U] 行动〔動〕xíngdòng; 动作 dòngzuò: *take ~ to stop the rise in crime* 采取行动阻止犯罪的上升. 2 [C] 作为〔爲〕zuòwéi; 行为 xíngwéi. 3 [U] 情节〔節〕qíngjié; 细节 xìjié. 4 [U] 战〔戰〕斗〔鬥〕zhàndòu: *He was killed in ~.* 他阵亡了. 5 [C] 诉讼 sùsòng: *bring an ~ against sb* 对某人提出起诉. 6 [习语] into ˈaction 在运〔運〕转〔轉〕zài yùnzhuǎn. out of ˈaction 停止运转 tíngzhǐ yùnzhuǎn.

activate /ˈæktɪveɪt/ *v* [T] 使活动〔動〕shǐ huódòng; 触〔觸〕发〔發〕chùfā.

active /ˈæktɪv/ *adj* 1 积〔積〕极〔極〕的 jījíde; 活跃〔躍〕的 huóyuède; 活动〔動〕的 huódòngde. 2 [语法](动词)描述动作的 miáoshù dòngzuòde. the active *n* [sing] 描述动作的动词. actively *adv*.

activist /ˈæktɪvɪst/ *n* [C] 积〔積〕极〔極〕分子 jījífènzǐ.

activity /ækˈtɪvətɪ/ *n* [*pl* -ies] 1 [U] 活动〔動〕性 huódòngxìng; 繁忙 fánmáng: *a lot of ~ in the street* 街上很热闹. 2 [C, 尤作 pl] 活动 huódòng: *social activities* 社会活动.

actor /ˈæktə(r)/ *n* [C] (*fem* actress /ˈæktrɪs/) 演员 yǎnyuán.

actual /ˈæktʃʊəl/ *adj* 实〔實〕际〔際〕的 shíjìde; 真实的 zhēnshíde. actually /ˈæktʃʊlɪ/ *adv* 1 实际地 shíjìde: *what ~ly happened* 实际上发生的. 2 居然 jūrán: *He ~ly expected me to pay!* 他居然期望我付款!

acumen /əˈkjuːmen/ *n* [U] [正式用语]敏锐 mǐnruì; 聪〔聰〕明 cōngmíng.

acupuncture /ˈækjʊpʌŋktʃə(r)/ *n* [U] [医学]针刺 zhēncì; 针术〔術〕zhēnshù.

acute /əˈkjuːt/ *adj* [~r, ~st] 1 厉〔厲〕害的 lìhaide: *suffer ~ hardship* 遭遇严重困难. 2 敏锐的 mǐnruìde: *an ~ sense of hearing* 敏锐的听力. acute ˈaccent *n* [C] 重音符号〔號〕zhòngyīn fúhào. acute ˈangle *n* [C] 尖角 jiānjiǎo. acutely *adv*. acuteness *n* [U].

AD /ˌeɪˈdiː/ *abbr* 公元 gōngyuán.

ad /æd/ *n* [C] [非正式用语] (advertisement 的缩略语)广〔廣〕告 guǎnggào.

adamant /ˈædəmənt/ *adj* [正式用语]固执〔執〕的 gùzhíde

Adam's apple /ˈædəmz æpl/ *n* [C] 喉结 hóujié; 喉核 hóuhé.

adapt /əˈdæpt/ *v* [T] 使适〔適〕应〔應〕shǐ shìyìng. adaptable *adj* 能适应的 néng shìyìngde. adaptation /ædæpˈteɪʃn/ *n* [C, U] 适应 shìyìng; 适合 shìhé; 改编 gǎibiān: *an ~ of the play for television* 把戏剧改编为电视剧. adaptor *n* [C] 三通插头〔頭〕sāntōng chātóu.

add /æd/ *v* 1 [T] 加 jiā; 增加 zēngjiā: *~ the flour to the milk* 把面粉加进牛奶中. 2 [I, T] (*up*) 加起来〔來〕jiā qǐlái. 3 [T] 补〔補〕充说 bǔchōng shuō. 4 [短语动词] add up [非正式用语]可信的 kěxìnde: *It just doesn't ~ up.* 这简直不可相信. add up to sth 意味着 yìwèi zhe; 表示 biǎoshì; 说明 shuōmíng.

adder /ˈædə(r)/ *n* [C] 蝮蛇 fùshé.

addict /ˈædɪkt/ *n* [C] 1 癖嗜者 pìshìzhě; 有瘾的人 yǒu yǐn de rén. 2 …迷 …mí: *a TV ~* 电视迷. addicted /əˈdɪktɪd/ *adj* (*to*) 上了瘾的 shàngleyǐn de: *~ed to drugs* 吸毒成瘾的 addiction /əˈdɪkʃn/ *n* [U, C]. addictive /əˈdɪktɪv/ *adj* (使人)上瘾的 shàngyǐn de.

addition /əˈdɪʃn/ *n* 1 [U] 加 jiā; 加法 jiāfǎ. 2 [C] 附加物 fùjiāwù. 3 [习语] in addition (to sth/sb) 除…以外 chú…yǐwài. additional /-ʃənl/ *adj* 附加的 fùjiāde; 额外的 éwàide. additionally /-ʃənəlɪ/ *adv*.

additive /ˈædɪtɪv/ *n* [C] 添加物 tiānjiāwù; 添加剂〔劑〕tiānjiājì.

address /əˈdres; *US* ˈædres/ *n* [C] 1 通讯处〔處〕tōngxùnchù; 住址 zhùzhǐ. 2 致词 zhìcí. address *v* [T] 1 在(信封)上写〔寫〕姓名、住址 zài shàng xiě xìngmíng、zhùzhǐ. 2 向…致词 xiàng…zhìcí.

adept /ˈædept, əˈdept/ *adj* (*at* / *in*) 擅长〔長〕的 shànchángde; 熟练〔練〕的 shúliànde.

adequate /ˈædɪkwət/ *adj* 可胜〔勝〕任的 kě shèngrèn de; 充分的 chōngfènde. adequately *adv*.

adhere /ədˈhɪə(r)/ *v* [I] [正式用语] 1 (*to*) 黏着 niánzhuó. 2 *to* [喻] (a) 依照, 遵循(原则) yīzhào, zūnxún. (b) 坚〔堅〕持 jiānchí; 忠于 zhōngyú. adherent /ədˈhɪərənt/ *n* [C] 追随〔隨〕者 zhuīsuízhě; 依附者 yīfùzhě. adherence /-rəns/ *n* [U].

adhesive /ədˈhiːsɪv/ *adj* 黏着的 niánzhuóde; 有黏性的 yǒu niánxìng de. adhesion /ədˈhiːʒn/ *n* [U]. adhesive *n* [C, U] 胶〔膠〕 jiāo; 粘剂〔劑〕zhānjì.

ad hoc /ˌæd ˈhɒk/ *adj*, *adv* 特别的 tèbiéde; 特别地 tèbiéde.

adjacent /əˈdʒeɪsnt/ *adj* (*to*) 邻〔鄰〕接的 línjiēde; 邻近的 línjìnde.

adjective /ˈædʒɪktɪv/ *n* [C] [语法]形容词 xíngróngcí. adjectival /ˌædʒɪkˈtaɪvl/ *adj*.

A

adjoin /əˈdʒɔɪn/ *v* [I] [正式用语]相近 xiāngjìn；毗邻〔鄰〕pílín：～*ing rooms* 毗邻的房间.

adjourn /əˈdʒɜːn/ *v* [T] 休(会) xiū. **adjournment** *n* [C,U].

adjudicate /əˈdʒuːdɪkeɪt/ *v* [T,I] [正式用语]判决 pànjué；宣判 xuānpàn. **adjudication** /əˌdjuːdɪˈkeɪʃn/ *n* [U]. **adjudicator** *n* [C].

adjust /əˈdʒʌst/ *v* 1 [T] 校准 jiàozhǔn；调整 tiáozhěng. 2 [I, T] *to* 适〔適〕应〔應〕shìyìng. **adjustable** *adj*.

ad lib /ˌæd ˈlɪb/ *adj*, *adv* 即兴〔興〕的 jíxìngde；即兴地 jíxìngde. **ad lib** *v* [-bb-] 即兴演说 jíxìng yǎnshuō；即兴表演 jíxìng biǎoyǎn.

administer /ədˈmɪnɪstə(r)/ *v* [T] 1 支配 zhīpèi；管理 guǎnlǐ：～ *a hospital* 管理医院. 2 [正式用语]给予 jǐyǔ：～ *punishment* 给予惩罚. ～ *a drug* 施用药物. **administration** /ədˌmɪnɪˈstreɪʃn/ *n* 1 [U] 管理 guǎnlǐ；经〔經〕营〔營〕jīngyíng；行政 xíngzhèng. 2 [U] 提供 tígōng；施用 shīyòng. 3 (常作 the administration) [C] [尤用于美语]政府 zhèngfǔ：*the Bush A*～ 布什政府. **administrative** /ədˈmɪnɪstrətɪv; *US* -streɪtɪv/ *adj*. **administrator** /ədˈmɪnɪstreɪtə(r)/ *n* [C].

admirable /ˈædmərəbl/ *adj* 令人钦佩的 lìngrén qīnpèi de；极〔極〕好的 jíhǎode. **admirably** *adv*.

admiral /ˈædmərəl/ *n* [C] 海军〔軍〕上将〔將〕hǎijūn shàngjiàng.

admire /ədˈmaɪə(r)/ *v* [T] 赞〔讚〕赏 zànshǎng；钦佩 qīnpèi. **admiration** /ˌædməˈreɪʃn/ *n* [U] 赞赏 zànshǎng；钦佩 qīnpèi. **admirer** *n* [C]. **admiring** *adj* 钦佩的 qīnpèide：*admiring glances* 钦佩的目光.

admissible /ədˈmɪsəbl/ *adj* 1 [法律]容许提出的 róngxǔ tíchū de：～ *evidence* 容许提出的证据. 2 [正式用语]值得采〔採〕纳的 zhídé cǎinà de.

admission /ədˈmɪʃn/ *n* 1 [U] 准入 zhǔnrù；接纳 jiēnà. 2 [U] 入场费 rùchǎngfèi. 3 [C] 承认〔認〕chéngrèn.

admit /ədˈmɪt/ *v* [-tt-] [T] 1 允许进〔進〕入 yǔnxǔ jìnrù. 2 承认〔認〕chéngrèn：*I* ～ *that I was wrong*. 我承认自己错了. **admittance** *n* [U] 进入权〔權〕jìnrùquán. **admittedly** /ədˈmɪtɪdlɪ/ *adv* 公认地 gōngrènde.

admonish /ədˈmɒnɪʃ/ *v* [T] [正式用语]警告 jǐnggào；告诫 gàojiè.

ad nauseam /ˌædˈnɔːzɪæm/ *adv* 令人讨厌〔厭〕地 lìngrén tǎoyàn de：*She played the same record* ～. 她讨厌地老放同一张唱片.

ado /əˈduː/ *n* [U] 忙乱〔亂〕mángluàn；麻烦 máfan：*without further* ～ 没有更多麻烦地.

adolescent /ˌædəˈlesnt/ *adj*, *n* [C] 青少年 qīngshàonián. **adolescence** /-ˈlesns/ *n* [U].

adopt /əˈdɒpt/ *v* [T] 1 收养〔養〕(子女) shōuyǎng. 2 采〔採〕用 cǎiyòng. **adoption** /əˈdɒpʃn/ *n* [U,C]. **adoptive** *adj* 收养的 shōuyǎngde.

adore /əˈdɔː(r)/ *v* [T] 1 敬爱〔愛〕jìng'ài；崇拜 chóngbài. 2 [非正规用语]极〔極〕喜爱 jí xǐ'ài. **adorable** *adj* 可爱的 kě'àide：*an adorable child* 可爱的孩子. *an adorable puppy* 可爱的小狗. **adoration** /ˌædəˈreɪʃn/ *n* [U].

adorn /əˈdɔːn/ *v* [T] 装〔裝〕饰 zhuāngshì. **adornment** *n* [U].

adrenalin /əˈdrenəlɪn/ *n* [U] 肾〔腎〕上腺素 shènshàngxiànsù.

adrift /əˈdrɪft/ *adj* 漂流的 piāoliúde；漂泊的 piāobóde.

adulation /ˌædjʊˈleɪʃn; *US* ˌædʒʊˈl-/ *n* [U] [正式用语]谄媚 chǎnmèi；奉承 fèngcheng.

adult /ˈædʌlt; 亦作 əˈdʌlt/ *n* [C], *adj* 成人 chéngrén；成熟的动〔動〕物 chéngshúde dòngwù；成熟的 chéngshúde；成年的 chéngniánde. **adulthood** *n* [U] 成年 chéngnián.

adulterate /əˈdʌltəreɪt/ *v* [T] 搀〔攙〕假使不纯 chānjiǎ shǐ bù chún.

adultery /əˈdʌltərɪ/ *n* [U] 通奸 tōngjiān；私通 sītōng. **adulterer** /-tərə(r)/ *n* [C] (*fem* **adulteress** /-tərɪs/) 通奸者 tōngjiānzhě. **adulterous** /-tərəs/ *adj*.

advance[1] /ədˈvɑːns; *US* -ˈvæns/ *v* 1 [I,T] 前进〔進〕qiánjìn；推进 tuījìn. 2 预先垫〔墊〕付 yùxiān diànfù；赊借 shējiè. **advanced** *adj* 1 程度高的 chéngdù gāo de：～*d in years* 年长的. 2 高级的 gāojíde：～*d study* 高级研究. **advancement** *n* [U] 前进 qiánjìn；提升 tíshēng.

advance[2] /ədˈvɑːns; *US* -ˈvæns/ *n* 1 [C, U] 前进〔進〕qiánjìn；进展 jìnzhǎn. 2 [C] 预付的钱〔錢〕yùfùde qián. 3 **advances** [pl] (表示友好的)主动〔動〕姿态〔態〕zhǔdòng zītài. 4 [习语] **in advance** (**of sth**) 事先 shìxiān. **advance** *adj* 事先的 shìxiānde：*an* ～ *warning* 事先的警告.

advantage /ədˈvɑːntɪdʒ; *US* -ˈvæn-/ *n* 1 [C] 有利条〔條〕件 yǒulì tiáojiàn；优〔優〕势〔勢〕yōushì. 2 [U] 利益 lìyì. 3 [习语] **take advantage of sth** (充分)利用 lìyòng. **advantageous** /ˌædvənˈteɪdʒəs/ *adj* 有利的 yǒulìde；有用的 yǒuyòngde.

advent /ˈædvənt/ *n* **the advent** [sing] *of* (不寻常事物的)降临〔臨〕jiànglín；出现 chūxiàn.

adventure /ədˈventʃə(r)/ *n* 1 [C] 冒险〔險〕

màoxiǎn. 2 [U] 奇遇 qíyù; 历〔歷〕险 lìxiǎn. adventurer 冒险家 màoxiǎnjiā; 投机〔機〕者 tóujīzhě. adventurous *adj* 1 喜欢〔歡〕冒险的 xǐhuān màoxiǎn de. 2 惊〔驚〕险的 jīngxiǎnde.

adverb /ˈædvɜːb/ *n* [C] [语法]副词 fùcí. adverbial /ædˈvɜːbɪəl/ *adj*, *n* [C].

adversary /ˈædvəsərɪ; *US* -serɪ/ *n* [C] [*pl* -ies] [正式用语]敌〔敵〕人 dírén; 对〔對〕手 duìshǒu.

adverse /ˈædvɜːs/ *adj* 不利的 búlìde; 逆 nì: ~ *conditions* 不利条件. adversely *adv*. adversity /ədˈvɜːsətɪ/ *n* [C, U] [*pl* -ies] 逆境 nìjìng; 不幸 búxìng.

advert /ˈædvɜːt/ *n* [C] [非正式用语]广〔廣〕告 (advertisement 的缩略语) guǎnggào.

advertise /ˈædvətaɪz/ *v* [T] 做广〔廣〕告 zuò guǎnggào. advertisement /ədˈvɜːtɪsmənt; *US* ˌædvərˈtaɪzmənt/ *n* [C] 广告 guǎnggào. advertiser *n* [C]. advertising *n* [U].

advice /ədˈvaɪs/ *n* [U] 劝〔勸〕告 quàngào; 忠告 zhōnggào.

advise /ədˈvaɪz/ *v* [T] 1 劝〔勸〕告 quàngào; 建议〔議〕jiànyì. 2 (尤指商业上)通知 tōngzhī: ~ *sb of a delivery date* 通知某人发货日期. advisable *adj* 贤〔賢〕明的 xiánmíngde; 可取的 kěqǔde. adviser (亦作 advisor) *n* [C]. advisory *adj* 劝告的 quàngàode; 顾〔顧〕问的 gùwènde.

advocate /ˈædvəkət/ *n* [C] 倡导〔導〕者 chàngdǎozhě; 辩护〔護〕人 biànhùrén. advocate /ˈædvəkeɪt/ *v* [T] 提倡 tíchàng; 支持 zhīchí.

aerial /ˈeərɪəl/ *adj* 空气〔氣〕的 kōngqìde; 空中的 kōngzhōngde: *an* ~ *photograph* 从空中拍摄的照片. aerial *n* [C] (无线电)天线 tiānxiàn.

aerobatics /ˌeərəˈbætɪks/ *n* [pl] 特技飞〔飛〕行 tèjì fēixíng; 航空表演 hángkōng biǎoyǎn.

aerobics /eəˈrəubɪks/ *n* [亦作 sing, 用 pl v] 增氧健身法(如跑步、散步、游泳等) zēngyǎng jiànshēnfǎ.

aerodrome /ˈeərədrəum/ *n* [C] [旧词, 尤用于英国英语]小飞〔飛〕机〔機〕场〔場〕xiǎo fēijīchǎng.

aerodynamics /ˌeərəudaɪˈnæmɪks/ *n* [U] 空气〔氣〕动〔動〕力学〔學〕kōngqì dònglìxué. aerodynamic *adj*.

aeronautics /eərəˈnɔːtɪks/ *n* [U] 航空学〔學〕hángkōngxué; 航空术〔術〕hángkōngshù.

aeroplane /ˈeərəpleɪn/ *n* [C] 飞〔飛〕机〔機〕fēijī.

aerosol /ˈeərəsɒl; *US* -sɔːl/ *n* [C] 按钮式喷雾〔霧〕器 ànniǔshì pēnwùqì.

aerospace /ˈeərəuspeɪs/ *n* [U] 航空和宇宙航行空间 hángkōng hé yǔzhòu hángxíng kōngjiān.

aesthetic /iːsˈθetɪk; *US* esˈθetɪk/ *adj* 美学〔學〕的 měixuéde. aesthetically /-klɪ/ *adv*. aesthetics *n* [U] 美学 měixué.

afar /əˈfɑː(r)/ *adv* [习语] from aˈfar 从〔從〕远〔遠〕处〔處〕cóng yuǎnchù.

affable /ˈæfəbl/ *adj* 亲〔親〕切的 qīnqiède; 和蔼的 hé'ǎide. affably *adv*.

affair /əˈfeə(r)/ *n* 1 [C 常作 sing] 事件 shìjiàn. 2 [sing] 事 shì; 事情 shìqing. 3 affairs [pl] (a) 公众〔衆〕事务〔務〕gōngzhòng shìwù. (b) 个〔個〕人事务 gèrén shìwù. 4 [C] 桃色事件 táosè shìjiàn.

affect /əˈfekt/ *v* [T] 影响〔響〕yǐngxiǎng: *The cold climate* ~*ed his health*. 寒冷的气候影响了他的健康. affectation /ˌæfekˈteɪʃn/ *n* [C, U] 装〔裝〕模作样〔樣〕zhuāng mú zuò yàng; 造作 zàozuò. affected *adj* 假装的 jiǎzhuāngde; 做作的 zuòzuòde.

affection /əˈfekʃn/ *n* [U] 喜爱〔愛〕xǐ'ài; 慈爱 cí'ài. affectionate /-ʃənət/ *adj*. affectionately *adv*.

affidavit /ˌæfɪˈdeɪvɪt/ *n* [C] [法律]宣誓书〔書〕xuānshìshū.

affiliate /əˈfɪlɪeɪt/ *v* [I, T] (尤指团体、组织)(使)加入 jiārù; 接受为〔爲〕分支机〔機〕构〔構〕jiēshòu wéi fēnzhī jīgòu; 接受为会〔會〕员 jiēshòu wéi huìyuán. affiliation /əˌfɪlɪˈeɪʃn/ *n* [C, U].

affinity /əˈfɪnətɪ/ *n* [C, U] [*pl* -ies] 1 密切的关〔關〕系〔係〕mìqiède guānxì; 姻亲〔親〕关系 yīnqīn guānxì. 2 吸引力 xīyǐnlì.

affirm /əˈfɜːm/ *v* [T] [正式用语]断〔斷〕定 duàndìng; 肯定 kěndìng. affirmation /ˌæfəˈmeɪʃən/ [C, U]. affirmative *adj* (回答)肯定的 kěndìngde. affirmative *n* 1 [C] 肯定词 kěndìngcí; 肯定语 kěndìngyǔ. 2 [习语] in the affirmative [正式用语](回答)表示赞成 biǎoshì zànchéng.

affix[1] /əˈfɪks/ *v* [T] 附加 fùjiā; 贴上 tiēshàng.

affix[2] /ˈæfɪks/ *n* [C] 词缀 cízhuì.

afflict /əˈflɪkt/ *v* [T] 使痛苦 shǐ tòngkǔ; 使苦恼〔惱〕shǐ kǔnǎo. affliction /əˈflɪkʃn/ *n* [C, U] [正式用语]痛苦 tòngkǔ; 苦恼 kǔnǎo; 痛苦的原因 tòngkǔde yuányīn.

affluent /ˈæfluənt/ *adj* 富裕的 fùyùde. affluence /-luəns/ *n* [U].

afford /əˈfɔːd/ *v* [T] 1 (有足够的金钱、时间、空间等)能做 néngzuò. 2 不冒险〔險〕即能做 bú màoxiǎn jí néngzuò: *We can't* ~ *to lose such experienced workers*. 我们可损失不起这些有经验的工人.

A

affront /əˈfrʌnt/ *v* [T] 冒犯 màofàn；当〔當〕众〔衆〕侮辱 dāngzhòng wǔrǔ. **affront** *n* [C] 当众侮辱 dāngzhòng wǔrǔ.

afield /əˈfiːld/ *adv* [习语] **far afield** 远〔遠〕离〔離〕家乡〔鄉〕yuǎnlí jiāxiāng.

afloat /əˈfləʊt/ *adj* 1 漂浮的 piāofúde. 2 在船上 zài chuán shàng. 3 经〔經〕济〔濟〕上应〔應〕付自如的 jīngjì shàng yìngfù zìrú de.

afoot /əˈfʊt/ *adj* 在准〔準〕备〔備〕中的 zài zhǔnbèi zhōng de.

aforementioned /əˌfɔːˈmenʃənd/ (亦作 **aforesaid** /əˈfɔːsed/) *adj* [正式用语]上述的 shàngshùde.

afraid /əˈfreɪd/ *adj* 1 (*of* /*to*) 害怕 hàipà: ~ *of spiders* 害怕蜘蛛. 2 [习语] **I'm afraid** (用以表达可能令人不快的信息)糟糕! zāogāo! 对〔對〕不起 duìbùqǐ；遗憾 yíhàn: *I'm ~ we'll arrive late*. 糟糕，我们要晚到了.

afresh /əˈfreʃ/ *adv* 再 zài；重新 chóngxīn.

Africa /ˈæfrɪkə/ *n* [U] 非洲 Fēizhōu.

African /ˈæfrɪkən/ *adj* 非洲的 Fēizhōude. **African** *n* [C] 非洲人 Fēizhōurén.

after /ˈɑːftə(r)；*US* ˈæf-/ *prep* 1 在…之后〔後〕zài…zhīhòu: *leave ~ lunch* 午饭后离开. 2 (顺序)在…之后 zài…zhīhòu: *C comes ~ B in the alphabet*. 英语字母表上 C 排在 B 的后面. 3 由于 yóuyú. 4 追寻〔尋〕zhuīxún: *The police are ~ my brother*. 警察在追寻我的兄弟. 5 尽〔儘〕管 jǐnguǎn: *A~ everything I have done for you, you are leaving me now*. 尽管我为你做了这许多事，现在你还是要走了. 6 仿〔倣〕照 fǎngzhào: *a painting ~ Rembrandt* 一幅模仿伦勃朗的画. 7 [习语] ˌ**after** ˈ**all** 毕〔畢〕竟 bìjìng；终究 zhōngjiū. **after** *adv*, *conj* …之后… zhīhòu: *She died three days ~ (I had left)*. 三天后她死了(我走后三天她死了). ˈ**after-effect** *n* [C 常作 pl] 副作用 fùzuòyòng；后效 hòuxiào. ˈ**afterthought** *n* [C] 事后的想法 shìhòude xiǎngfǎ.

aftermath /ˈɑːftəmæθ；*Brit* 亦作 -mɑːθ/ *n* [C] (战争等的)后〔後〕果 hòuguǒ.

afternoon /ˌɑːftəˈnuːn；*US* ˌæf-/ *n* [U,C] 下午 xiàwǔ.

afterwards (*US* 亦作 **afterward**) /ˈɑːftəwədz；*US* ˌæf-/ *adv* 后〔後〕来〔來〕hòulái；以后 yǐhòu.

again /əˈgen, əˈgeɪn/ *adv* 1 再 zài: *try ~ later* 以后再试一次. 2 重又 chóngyòu. 3 另外 lìngwài；此外 cǐwài: *as many / much ~* 加倍 jiābèi. 4 [习语] **aˌgain and aˈgain** 再三地 zàisānde.

against /əˈgenst, əˈgeɪnst/ *prep* 1 接触〔觸〕jiēchù: *The ladder was leaning ~ the wall*. 梯子靠在墙上. 2 反对〔對〕fǎnduì: *swim ~ the current* 逆流游泳. 3 对比 duìbǐ；以…为〔爲〕背景 yǐ…wéi bèijǐng: *The trees were black ~ the sky*. 衬着天空，树是黑黝黝的. 4 防备〔備〕fángbèi: *an injection ~ measles* 麻疹的防预针.

age[1] /eɪdʒ/ *n* 1 [C,U] 年龄〔齡〕niánlíng. 2 [U] 老年 lǎonián: *Wisdom comes with ~*. 姜是老的辣. 3 [C] 时〔時〕代 shídài: *the Elizabethan ~* 伊丽莎白时代. 4 [C,常作 pl] [非正式用语]长〔長〕时间 cháng shíjiān: *waiting for ~s* 等候很久. 5 [习语] ˌ**be/** ˌ**come of** ˈ**age** 成年 chéngnián. ˌ**under** ˈ**age** 未成年 wèi chéngnián. ˈ**age-group** *n* [C] 同一年龄的人们 tóngyī niánlíng de rénmen. ˈ**age limit** *n* [C] (能做某种事情的)年龄限制 niánlíng xiànzhì. ˌ**age-**ˈ**old** *adj* 古老的 gǔlǎode；久远〔遠〕的 jiǔyuǎnde.

age[2] /eɪdʒ/ *v* [*pres part* **ageing** 或 **aging**, *pp* **aged** /eɪdʒd/] [I,T] 使变〔變〕老 shǐ biànlǎo；变老 biànlǎo. **aged** *adj* 1 /eɪdʒd/ …岁〔歲〕的 … suìde. 2 /ˈeɪdʒɪd/ 老的 lǎode；年老的 niánlǎode. **the aged** /ˈeɪdʒɪd / *n* [pl] 老人 lǎorén. **ageing** (亦作 **aging**) *n* [U] 变老 biànlǎo；变陈 biànchén. **ageing** *adj* 变老的 biànlǎode.

ageism /ˈeɪdʒɪzem/ *n* [U] 年龄〔齡〕歧视 niánlíngqíshì.

ageist (美语亦作 **agist**) /ˈeɪdʒɪst/ *adj* 年龄歧视的 niánlíng qíshì de；歧视老人的 qíshì lǎorén de: *What you said is positively~*. 你这么说对老人实在不公. **ageist** *n* [C] 年龄歧视者 niánlíng qíshì zhě；歧视老人者 qíshì lǎorén zhě.

agency /ˈeɪdʒənsɪ/ *n* [C] [*pl* -**ies**] 代理商 dàilǐshāng；机〔機〕构〔構〕jīgòu；社 shè: *a travel ~* 旅行社.

agenda /əˈdʒendə/ *n* [C] 议〔議〕事日程 yìshìrìchéng.

agent /ˈeɪdʒənt/ *n* [C] 1 代理人 dàilǐrén: *an estate ~* 房地产经纪人. 2 动〔動〕力 dònglì；动因 dòngyīn: *Rain and frost are ~s that wear away rocks*. 雨和霜是侵蚀岩石的自然力.

aggravate /ˈægrəveɪt/ *v* 1 [T] 使恶〔惡〕化 shǐ èhuà；使加剧〔劇〕shǐ jiājù. 2 [非正式用语] 使气〔氣〕恼〔惱〕shǐ qìnǎo: *an aggravating delay* 令人讨厌的延误. **aggravation** *n* [C, U].

aggregate /ˈægrɪgət/ *n* [C] 共计 gòngjì；合计 héjì.

aggression /əˈgreʃn/ *n* [U] 1 敌〔敵〕对〔對〕心理 díduì xīnlǐ. 2 敌对行为〔爲〕díduì xíngwéi；侵略 qīnlüè. **aggressor** /əˈgresə(r)/ *n* [C] 侵略者 qīnlüèzhě.

aggressive /əˈgresɪv/ *adj* 1 侵略的 qīnlüède. 2 有闯劲〔勁〕的 yǒu chuǎngjìn de: *an ～ salesman* 有闯劲的推销员. **aggressively** *adv*. **aggressiveness** *n* [U].

aggrieved /əˈgriːvd/ *adj* [正式用语]感到受委曲的 gǎndào shòu wěiqū de.

aggro /ˈægrəʊ/ *n* [C] [英俚]暴力扰〔擾〕乱〔亂〕bàolì rǎoluàn;闹事 nàoshì.

aghast /əˈgɑːst; *US* əˈgæst/ *adj* 吃惊〔驚〕的 chījīngde;吓〔嚇〕呆〔獃〕的 xiàdāide.

agile /ˈædʒaɪl; *US* ˈædʒl/ *adj* 敏捷的 mǐnjiéde;活泼〔潑〕的 huópode. **agility** /əˈdʒɪlətɪ/ *n* [U].

aging ⇨AGE².

agitate /ˈædʒɪteɪt/ *v* 1 [T] 鼓动〔動〕gǔdòng;激动 jīdòng. 2 [I] *for* / *against* 鼓吹… gǔchuī …. 3 [T] 摇动 yáodòng;搅〔攪〕动 jiǎodòng. **agitation** /ˌædʒɪˈteɪʃn/ *n* [U]. **agitator** *n* [C] 鼓动家 gǔdòngjiā.

AGM /ˌeɪ dʒiː ˈem/ *abbr* [尤用于英国英语] Annual General Meeting 年度大会〔會〕niándù dàhuì.

agnostic /ægˈnɒstɪk/ *n* [C], *adj* 不可知论〔論〕的 bùkězhīlùnde;不可知论者 bùkězhīlùnzhě.

ago /əˈgəʊ/ *adv* 以前 yǐqián: *The train left five minutes ～.* 火车在五分钟前开走了.

agog /əˈgɒg/ *adj* 渴望的 kěwàngde;焦急的 jiāojíde.

agonize /ˈægənaɪz/ *v* [I] (*over* / *about*) 感到焦虑〔慮〕gǎndào jiāolǜ. **agonized** *adj* 表示极〔極〕度痛苦的 biǎoshì jídù tòngkǔ de. **agonizing** *adj* 引起痛苦的 yǐnqǐ tòngkǔ de.

agony /ˈægənɪ/ *n* [U, C] [*pl* -ies] 极〔極〕度痛苦 jídù tòngkǔ. ˈ**agony aunt** *n* [C] [英国非正式用语,或谐谑]在报〔報〕纸上解答读〔讀〕者个〔個〕人问题的女性写〔寫〕作者 zài bàozhǐ shàng jiědá dúzhě gèrén wèntí de nǚxìng xiězuòzhě.

agrarian /əˈgreərɪən/ *adj* 耕地的 gēngdìde.

agree /əˈgriː/ *v* 1 [I] (*with*) 同意 tóngyì: *I ～ with you that money is the problem.* 我同意你的意见,问题是在钱上. 2 [I] *to* 应〔應〕允 yīngyǔn: *My boss ～d to let me go home early.* 老板允许我早一点回家. 3 [I, T] *on* 决定 juédìng. 4 [I, T] (*with*) 批准 pīzhǔn. 5 [I] 符合 fúhé: *The two descriptions do not ～.* 这两种描述不相符合. 6 [I] (*with*) [语法](动词等的性、数)一致 yízhì. 7 [习语] **be agreed** 达〔達〕成一致 dáchéng yízhì. 8 [短语动词] **agree with sb** (食物)适〔適〕合某人的健康 shìhé mǒurénde jiànkāng. **agreeable** *adj* 1 令人愉快的 lìngrén yúkuài de. 2 乐〔樂〕于同意的 lè yú tóngyì de. **agreeably** *adv*. **agreement** *n* 1 [C] 协〔協〕议〔議〕xiéyì;协定 xiédìng. 2 [U] 一致 yízhì: *The two sides failed to reach ～ment.* 双方未能达成一致.

agriculture /ˈægrɪkʌltʃə(r)/ *n* [U] 农〔農〕业〔業〕nóngyè. **agricultural** /ˌægrɪˈkʌltʃərəl/ *adj*.

aground /əˈgraʊnd/ *adv, adj* 搁浅〔淺〕(的) gēqiǎn.

ahead /əˈhed/ *adv* 向前 xiàngqián;在前 zàiqián: *go ～* 前进;继续下去. *plan ～* 未雨绸缪. **aˈhead of** *prep* 1 在…前面 zài…qiánmiàn;早于 zǎo yú;先于 xiān yú. 2 领先于 lǐngxiān yú: *be years ～ of one's rivals.* 比对手们领先数年.

aid /eɪd/ *n* 1 [U] 帮〔幫〕助 bāngzhù;援助 yuánzhù: *with the ～ of a friend* 在一个朋友的帮助下. 2 [C] 有帮助的物或人 yǒubāngzhùde wù huò rén: ˈ*teaching ～s* 教具 3 对〔對〕外国〔國〕的援助 duì wàiguóde yuánzhù. 4 [习语] **what is sth in aid of?** [非正式用语]那是干〔幹〕什〔甚〕么〔麼〕用的? nà shì gàn shénme yòng de? **aid** *v* 1 [T] [正式用语]帮〔幫〕助 bāngzhù;援助 yuánzhù. 2 [习语] **aid and aˈbet** [法律]伙同…作案 huǒtóng…zuò'àn;同谋 tóngmóu;怂〔慫〕恿〔慂〕犯罪 sǒngyǒng fànzuì. ˈ**aid flight** *n* [C] 援助物资班机〔機〕yuánzhù wùzī bānjī. **aid package** *n* [C] 一揽〔攬〕子援助计划〔劃〕yīlǎnzi yuánzhù jìhuà.

aide /eɪd/ *n* [C] (政府重要官员的)助手 zhùshǒu.

AIDS (亦作 **Aids**) /eɪdz/ *abbr* Acquired Immune Deficiency Syndrome 艾滋病 àizībìng.

ailing /ˈeɪlɪŋ/ *adj* 生病的 shēngbìngde. **ailment** /ˈeɪlmənt/ *n* [C] 病痛 bìngtòng.

aim /eɪm/ *v* 1 [I, T] (*at*) 瞄准〔準〕miáozhǔn. 2 [I] (*at* / *for*) 打算 dǎsuàn: *～ at increasing exports* 打算增加出口. 3 [T] (批评等)对〔對〕着 duìzhe: *My remarks were not ～ed at you.* 我的话不是对你的. **aim** *n* 1 [C] 目的 mùdì;志向 zhìxiàng: *Her ～ is to be famous.* 她立志成名. 2 [U] 瞄准 miáozhǔn. **aimless** *adj* 无〔無〕目的的 wú mùdì de. **aimlessly** *adv*.

ain't /eɪnt/ [用于非标准口语] 1 (short for) am /is/ are not: *Things ～ what they used to be.* 现在的情况可不一样了. 2 (short for) has /have not: *You ～ seen nothing yet.* 你什么也没看见.

air¹ /eə(r)/ *n* 1 [U] 空气〔氣〕kōngqì. 2 [U] 大气 dàqì: *travel by ～* 乘飞机旅行. 3 [C] 气派 qìpài;样〔樣〕子 yàngzi: *an ～ of importance* 煞有介事的神气. 4 [习语] **give oneself / put on ˈairs** 装〔裝〕腔作势〔勢〕zhuāngqiāng zuò shì. **in the ˈair** (a) (意见等)在流传〔傳〕中 zài liúchuán zhōng. (b) 未决定 wèi juédìng. ˌ**on the ˈair** 正在广〔廣〕播 zhèngzài

A

guǎngbō. ˌoff the ˈair 停止广播 tíngzhǐ guǎngbō. ˈair bag *n* [C] 安全气袋 ānquán qìdài;安全气囊 ānquán qìnáng. **airborne** /ˈeəbɔːn/ *adj* 1 空运〔運〕的 kōngyùnde. 2 (飞机)在飞〔飛〕行中的 zài fēixíng zhōng de. ˈ**air-conditioning** *n* [U] 空调 kōngtiáo. ˈ**air-conditioned** *adj*. ˈ**aircraft** *n* [C] [*pl* aircraft] 飞行器 fēixíngqì. ˈ**aircraft-carrier** *n* [C] 航空母舰〔艦〕hángkōngmǔjiàn. ˈ**airfield** *n* [C] 飞机〔機〕场〔場〕fēijīchǎng. ˈ**air force** *n* [C] 空军〔軍〕kōngjūn. ˈ**air-hostess** *n* [C] 客机上的女服务〔務〕员 kèjī shàng de nǚfúwùyuán;空中小姐 kōngzhōng xiǎojiě. ˈ**airlift** *n* [C] 空中补〔補〕给线〔綫〕kōngzhōng bǔjǐxiàn. ˈ**airlift** *v* [T] 用空中补给线运〔運〕输 yòng kōngzhōng bǔjǐxiàn yùnshū. ˈ**airline** *n* [C] 客机定期航线 kèjī dìngqī hángxiàn. ˈ**airliner** *n* [C] 大型客机 dàxíng kèjī. ˈ**airmail** *n* [U] 航空邮〔郵〕件 hángkōng yóujiàn. ˈ**airplane** /ˈeərpleɪn/ *n* [C] [美语] = AEROPLANE. ˈ**airport** *n* [C] 飞机场 fēijīchǎng. ˈ**air rage** *n* [U] 空中狂暴行为〔爲〕kōngzhōng kuángbào xíngwéi. ˈ**air raid** *n* [C] 空袭〔襲〕kōngxí. ˈ**airship** *n* [C] 飞艇 fēitǐng. ˈ**airspace** *n* [C] 领空 lǐngkōng. ˈ**airstrip** *n* [C] 飞机跑道 fēijī pǎodào. ˈ**air terminal** *n* [C] (航空运输的)市内终点〔點〕站 shìnèi zhōngdiǎnzhàn. ˈ**airtight** *adj* 密封的 mìfēngde. ˌ**air-to-ˈair** (火力攻击)空对〔對〕空的 kōngduìkōng de. **air traffic controller** *n* [C] 空中交通管制员 kōngzhōng jiāotōng guǎnzhìyuán. ˈ**airway** *n* [C] 航空线 hángkōngxiàn. ˈ**airworthy** *adj* (飞机等)适〔適〕航的 shìhángde.

air[2] /eə(r)/ *v* 1 [I, T] 晾晒〔曬〕liàngshài. 2 [T] 通空气〔氣〕tōngkōngqì;通风〔風〕tōngfēng. 3 [T] 发〔發〕表(意见) fābiǎo: ~ *one's views* 表示见解. **airing** *n* [sing] 晾晒: *give the blanket a good* ~ 把毯子好好晾晒一下. ˈ**airing-cupboard** *n* [C] 晾干〔乾〕橱 liànggānchú.

airless /ˈeəlɪs/ *adj* 新鲜空气〔氣〕不足的 xīnxiān kōngqì bùzú de.

airy /ˈeərɪ/ *adj* [-ier, -iest] 1 通气〔氣〕的 tōngqìde;通风〔風〕的 tōngfēngde. 2 轻〔輕〕率的 qīngshuàide;随〔隨〕便的 suíbiànde. **airily** *adv*.

aisle /aɪl/ *n* [C] (大厅中席位中间的)通道 tōngdào.

ajar /əˈdʒɑː(r)/ *adj* (门)微开〔開〕的 wēi kāi de.

akin /əˈkɪn/ *adj to* [正式用语]类〔類〕似的 lèisìde.

à la carte /ˌɑː lɑː ˈkɑːt/ *adj* (餐馆吃饭)点〔點〕菜的 diǎncàide.

alacrity /əˈlækrətɪ/ *n* [U] [正式用语]乐〔樂〕意 lèyì;欣然 xīnrán: *He accepted her offer with* ~. 他欣然接受了她的提议.

alarm /əˈlɑːm/ *n* 1 [U] 惊〔驚〕慌 jīnghuāng. 2 [C] 警报〔報〕jǐngbào: *a fire-*~ 火警. *sound / raise the* ~ 发警报. **alarm** *v* [T] 使忧〔憂〕虑〔慮〕shǐ yōulǜ;使惊慌 shǐ jīnghuāng. aˈ**larm clock** *n* [C] 闹〔鬧〕钟〔鐘〕nàozhōng. **alarming** *adj* 使人惊恐的 shǐ rén jīngkǒng de.

alas /əˈlæs/ *interj* [旧词或修辞](表示悲痛、怜悯等)哎哟! āiyō! 哎呀! āiyā!

albatross /ˈælbətrɒs/ *n* [C] 信天翁 xìntiānwēng.

albeit /ˌɔːlˈbiːɪt/ *conj* [旧词或正式用语]尽〔儘〕管 jǐnguǎn;即使 jíshǐ: *a useful,* ~ *brief, description* 尽管简短,但是有用的记述.

albino /ˌælˈbiːnəʊ; *US* -ˈbaɪ-/ *n* [C] [*pl* ~s] 白化病患者 báihuàbìng huànzhě;生白化病的动〔動〕物 shēng báihuàbìng de dòngwù.

album /ˈælbəm/ *n* [C] 1 相片册 xiàngpiàncè;集邮〔郵〕册 jíyóucè. 2 放唱时〔時〕间长〔長〕的唱片 fàngchàng shíjiān cháng de chàngpiàn.

alcohol /ˈælkəhɒl; *US* -hɔːl/ *n* [U] 酒精 jiǔjīng;酒 jiǔ. **alcoholic** /ˌælkəˈhɒlɪk; *US* -ˈhɔːl-/ *adj* 酒精的 jiǔjīngde;含酒精的 hán jiǔjīng de. **alcoholic** *n* [C] 酒鬼 jiǔguǐ. **alcoholism** *n* [U] 酗酒 xùjiǔ;酒精中毒 jiǔjīng zhòngdú.

alcove /ˈælkəʊv/ *n* [C] 壁龛〔龕〕bìkān.

ale /eɪl/ *n* [C, U] 浓〔濃〕啤酒 nóngpíjiǔ.

alert /əˈlɜːt/ *adj* 警惕的 jǐngtìde;提防的 dīfangde. **alert** *n* 1 [C] 警报〔報〕jǐngbào. 2 [习语] **on the aˈlert** 警惕 jǐngtì. **alert** *v* [T] 使警觉〔覺〕shǐ jǐngjué.

A level ⇨ A, a[1].

algae /ˈælgə; 亦作 ˈælgaɪ/ *n* [pl] 藻类〔類〕zǎolèi;海藻 hǎizǎo.

algebra /ˈældʒɪbrə/ *n* [U] 代数〔數〕dàishù.

alias /ˈeɪlɪəs/ *n* [C] 别名 biémíng;化名 huàmíng. **alias** *adv* 别名叫 biémíng jiào;化名叫 huàmíng jiào: *Joe Sykes,* ~ *John Smith* 乔·锡克斯,别名约翰·史密斯.

alibi /ˈælɪbaɪ/ *n* [C] 不在犯罪现场〔場〕bú zài fànzuì xiànchǎng.

alien /ˈeɪlɪən/ *n* [C] 1 外侨〔僑〕wàiqiáo;外国〔國〕人 wàiguórén. 2 外星人 wàixīngrén. **alien** *adj* 1 外国的 wàiguóde. 2 陌生的 mòshēngde.

alienate /ˈeɪlɪəneɪt/ *v* [T] 离〔離〕间 líjiàn;使疏远〔遠〕shǐ shūyuǎn. **alienation** /ˌeɪlɪəˈneɪʃn/ *n* [U].

alight[1] /əˈlaɪt/ *adj* 燃着的 ránzhede;点〔點〕亮的 diǎnliàngde.

alight[2] /əˈlaɪt/ *v* [I] [正式用语] 1 (从公共汽

车等)下来〔來〕xiàlái. 2 (鸟)飞〔飛〕落 fēiluò.

align /əˈlaɪn/ *v* 1 [T] 使成一直线〔綫〕shǐ chéng yī zhíxiàn. 2 ~ oneself with 与〔與〕…一致 yǔ… yízhì; 与…结盟 yǔ…jiéméng: *They ~ed themselves with the socialists*. 他们与社会主义者结成同盟. alignment *n* [C, U].

alike /əˈlaɪk/ *adj* 同样〔樣〕的 tóngyàngde; 相似的 xiāngsìde. alike *adv* 同样地 tóngyàngde; 相似地 xiāngsìde.

alimentary /ˌælɪˈmentərɪ/ *adj* 食物的 shíwùde; 消化的 xiāohuàde. the ˌalimentary caˈnal *n* [C] 消化道 xiāohuàdào.

alimony /ˈælɪmənɪ; *US* -məʊnɪ/ *n* [U] 离〔離〕婚后〔後〕付给配偶的生活费 líhūn hòu fùgěi pèi'ǒu de shēnghuófèi.

alive /əˈlaɪv/ *adj* 1 活的 huóde. 2 有活力的 yǒu huólìde; 有生气〔氣〕的 yǒu shēngqìde. 3 存在的 cúnzàide. 4 [习语] alive to sth 注意到 zhùyìdào; 意识〔識〕到 yìshídào. alive with sth 充满着…的 chōngmǎn zhe…de.

alkali /ˈælkəlaɪ/ *n* [C, U] [化学]碱 jiǎn.

all[1] /ɔːl/ *adj* 1 [与复数名词连用]全部的 quánbùde; 所有的 suǒyǒude: *A~ the people have come*. 所有的人都来了. 2 [与不可数名词连用]一切的 yíqiède; 整个〔個〕的 zhěnggède: *We have lost ~ the money*. 我们所有的钱都丢了. 3 任何的 rènhéde: *beyond ~ doubt* 毫无疑问.

all[2] /ɔːl/ *pron* 1 全部 quánbù; 大家 dàjiā; 全体〔體〕quántǐ: *They were ~ broken*. 它们全被打破了. 2 唯一的东西 wéiyīde dōngxi; 样〔樣〕样东西 yàngyàng dōngxi: *A~ I want is some peace!* 我只要求有一个安静点儿的环境! 3 [习语] all in ˈall 总〔總〕的来〔來〕说 zǒngde lái shuō. (ˌnot) at ˈall 根本(不) gēnběn: *I didn't enjoy it at ~*. 我一点儿也不喜欢它. in all 总共 zǒnggòng; 合计 héjì. ˌnot at ˈall (回答对方道谢)不谢 búxiè.

all[3] /ɔːl/ *adv* 1 完全地 wánquánde: *dressed ~ in black* 穿一身黑色服装. 2 (球赛得分等)双〔雙〕方相等 shuāngfāng xiāngděng; 各 gè: *The score was four ~*. 比分是四平. 3 [习语] all aˈlong [非正式用语]始终 shǐzhōng; 一直 yìzhí. all ˈin 精疲力竭 jīng pí lì jié. all over 到处〔處〕dàochù. all ˈright (亦作 alright [非正式用语]) (a) 赞同 zàntóng. (b) 安然无〔無〕恙 ānrán wúyàng. (c) (表示同意)好! hǎo; 可以 kěyǐ. all the better, harder, etc. 更好 gènghǎo; 更努力 gèng nǔlì: *We'll have to work ~ the harder when we get back from our holidays*. 我们休假回来后就得更加努力工作. all ˈthere 机〔機〕智的 jīzhìde. ˌall the ˈsame ⇨SAME. all too ⇨ TOO. be all for (doing) sth 完全赞成 wánquán zànchéng. be all the same to sb (对某人来说)无所谓 wú suǒwèi: *It's ~ the same to me when you go*. 你什么时候走, 我无所谓. not all that 不很 bùhěn. the ˌall-ˈclear *n* [C] 危险〔險〕已过〔過〕去的信号〔號〕wēixiǎn yǐ guòqùde xìnhào. ˌall-ˈin *adj* 包括一切的 bāokuò yíqiè de: *an ˌ~-in ˈprice* 一切在内的价格. ˈall out *adv* 全力以赴 quán lì yǐ fù: *The team is going ~ out to win*. 该队全力以赴争取胜利. *an ~ out effort* 最大的努力. ˌall-ˈrounder *n* [C] 多面手 duōmiànshǒu.

Allah /ˈælə/ *n* 安拉, 真主(伊斯兰教的主神) ānlā, zhēnzhǔ.

allay /əˈleɪ/ *v* [T] 减轻〔輕〕(恐惧等) jiǎnqīng.

allegation /ˌælɪˈgeɪʃn/ *n* [C] (无证据的)陈词 chéncí.

allege /əˈledʒ/ *v* [T] [正式用语]断〔斷〕言 duànyán; 宣称〔稱〕xuānchēng: *He ~s he was misled about the time*. 他宣称他是把时间弄错了. alleged *adj*. allegedly *adv*.

allegiance /əˈliːdʒəns/ *n* [U] 忠诚 zhōngchéng.

allegory /ˈælɪgərɪ; *US* ˈælɪgɔːrɪ/ *n* [C] [*pl* -ies] 寓言 yùyán; 讽〔諷〕喻 fěngyù. allegorical /ˌælɪˈgɒrɪkl; *US* ˌælɪˈgɔːrəkl/ *adj*.

alleluia /ˌælɪˈluːjə/ *n* [C], *interj* 哈利路亚〔亞〕(赞颂上帝用语) hālìlùyà.

allergy /ˈælədʒɪ/ *n* [C] [*pl* -ies] [医]过〔過〕敏症 guòmǐnzhèng. allergic /əˈlɜːdʒɪk/ *adj*.

alleviate /əˈliːvɪeɪt/ *v* [T] 减轻〔輕〕(痛苦等) jiǎnqīng. alleviation /əˌliːvɪˈeɪʃn/ *n* [U].

alley /ˈælɪ/ *n* [C] 1 小巷 xiǎoxiàng. 2 滚球戏〔戲〕等的球场〔場〕gǔnqiúxì děng de qiúchǎng.

alliance /əˈlaɪəns/ *n* [C] 联〔聯〕盟 liánméng; 同盟 tóngméng; 联合 liánhé.

allied /əˈlaɪd/ ⇨ALLY[2].

alligator /ˈælɪgeɪtə(r)/ *n* [C] 短吻鳄 duǎnwěn'è.

allocate /ˈæləkeɪt/ *v* [T] 分配 fēnpèi; 配给 pèijǐ. allocation /ˌæləˈkeɪʃn/ *n* [C, U].

allot /əˈlɒt/ *v* [-tt-] [T] 分配 fēnpèi; 拨〔撥〕给 bōgěi. allotment *n* [C] 1 部分 bùfen; 份额 fèn'é. 2 [尤用于英国英语]小块〔塊〕菜地 xiǎokuài càidì.

allow /əˈlaʊ/ *v* [T] 1 允许 yǔnxǔ: *You are not ~ed to smoke in this room*. 不允许你们在这间屋子里吸烟. 2 允给(钱、时间等) yǔngěi. 3 [短语动词] allow for sth 考虑〔慮〕到 kǎolǜ dào; 体〔體〕谅 tǐliàng: *~ for traffic delays* 考虑到交通上的耽搁. allowable *adj*. allowance *n* 1 [C] 津贴 jīntiē. 2 [习语] make allowance for sth 考虑到 kǎolǜ dào; 体谅 tǐliàng.

A

alloy /ˈælɔɪ/ *n* [C, U] 合金 héjīn.

allude /əˈluːd/ *v* [I] *to* [正式用语]提到 tídào;暗指 ànzhǐ. **allusion** /əˈluːʒn/ *n* [C] 提及 tíjí;暗指 ànzhǐ.

alluring /əˈlʊərɪŋ/ *adj* 诱人的 yòurénde;吸引人的 xīyǐnrénde;迷人的 mírénde.

ally[1] /ˈælaɪ/ *n* [C] [*pl* -ies] 同盟者 tóngméngzhě;盟国〔國〕 méngguó.

ally[2] /əˈlaɪ/ *v* [*pt*, *pp* -ied] [I, T] ~ oneself with/to 结盟 jiéméng;联〔聯〕姻 liányīn. **allied** *adj* (*to*) 有关〔關〕系〔係〕的 yǒu guānxì de; 有亲〔親〕缘关系的 yǒu qīnyuán guānxì de.

almanac /ˈɔːlmənæk; *US* ˈæl-/ *n* [C] 历〔曆〕书〔書〕 lìshū.

almighty /ˌɔːlˈmaɪtɪ/ *adj* [非正式用语]全能的 quánnéngde. **the Almighty** *n* [sing] 上帝 shàngdì.

almond /ˈɑːmənd/ *n* [C] 杏核 xìnghé;杏仁 xìngrén.

almost /ˈɔːlməʊst/ *adv* 几〔幾〕乎 jīhū;差不多 chàbùduō: ~ *everywhere* 几乎到处. ~ *impossible* 几乎不可能.

alms /ɑːmz/ *n* [pl] [旧词]施舍〔捨〕 shīshě;救济〔濟〕物 jiùjìwù.

aloft /əˈlɒft; *US* əˈlɔːft/ *adv* [正式用语]在高处〔處〕 zài gāochù.

alone /əˈləʊn/ *adj*, *adv* 1 孤独〔獨〕的 gūdúde; 孤独地 gūdúde: *living* ~ 孤独地生活. 2 仅〔僅〕 jǐn;只 zhǐ: *You* ~ *can help me*. 只有你能帮助我. 3 [习语] go it aˈlone 独〔獨〕自干〔幹〕 dúzì gàn.

along /əˈlɒŋ; *US* əˈlɔːŋ/ *prep* 1 沿着 yánzhe: *walk* ~ *the street* 沿着大街走. 2 挨着 āizhe: *a path* ~ *the river* 挨着河的一条小路. **along** *adv* 1 向前 xiàngqián: *Come* ~! 来吧! 2 和(别人)一起 hé yìqǐ: *Can I bring some friends* ~? 我能带朋友来吗? 3 [习语] along with sth 一道 yídào, 一起 yìqǐ. aˈlongside *adv*, *prep* 在旁 zài páng;靠近 kàojìn.

aloof /əˈluːf/ *adj* 孤僻的 gūpìde;冷淡的 lěngdànde. **aloofness** *n* [U].

aloud /əˈlaʊd/ *adv* 高声〔聲〕地 gāoshēngde;大声地 dàshēngde: *read the letter* ~ 大声读这封信.

alphabet /ˈælfəbet/ *n* [C] 字母表 zìmǔbiǎo. **alphabetical** /ˌælfəˈbetɪkl/ *adj* 按字母表顺序的 àn zìmǔbiǎo shùnxùde. **alphabetically** /-klɪ/ *adv*.

already /ˌɔːlˈredɪ/ *adv* 1 早已 zǎoyǐ: *I've* ~ *told them what happened*. 我早已把发生的事告诉他们了. 2 早得出乎预料 zǎo dé chū hū yùliào: *You are not leaving us* ~, *are you*? 你不会这么早就离开我们吧?

alright = ALL RIGHT (ALL[3]).

Alsatian /ælˈseɪʃn/ *n* [C] 艾尔〔爾〕萨〔薩〕星狗(一种大狼狗) ài'ěrsàxīnggǒu.

also /ˈɔːlsəʊ/ *adv* 也 yě.

altar /ˈɔːltə(r)/ *n* [C] 祭坛〔壇〕 jìtán.

alter /ˈɔːltə(r)/ *v* [I, T] 改变〔變〕 gǎibiàn;改做 gǎizuò. **alteration** /ˌɔːltəˈreɪʃn/ *n* [C, U].

alternate[1] /ɔːlˈtɜːnət; *US* ˈɔːltərnət/ *adj* 1 交替的 jiāotìde;轮〔輪〕流的 lúnliúde. 2 间隔的 jiàngéde: *on* ~ *days* 隔日. **alternately** *adv*.

alternate[2] /ˈɔːltəneɪt/ *v* [I, T] (*between*/*with*) 交替 jiāotì: *The weather will* ~ *between sunshine and rain*. 天气将时晴时雨. ˌalternating ˈcurrent *n* [U] 交流电〔電〕 jiāoliúdiàn. **alternation** /ˌɔːltəˈneɪʃn/ *n* [U, C].

alternative /ɔːlˈtɜːnətɪv/ *adj* 1 可供选〔選〕择〔擇〕的 kě gōng xuǎnzé de;可供替代的 kě gōng tìdài de: *an* ~ *means of transportation* 一种可供选择的交通工具. 2 非常规的 fēi chángguī de: ~ *medicine including homeopathy and acupuncture* 一种非常规的医学,包括顺势疗法和针刺疗法. **alternative ˈenergy** *n* [U] 替代能源 tìdài néngyuán. **alternative** *n* [C] 1 两种〔種〕或多种可能性之一 liǎngzhǒng huò duōzhǒng kěnéngxìng zhīyī. 2 两者选一 liǎngzhě xuǎn yī. **alternatively** *adv*.

although /ɔːlˈðəʊ/ *conj* 虽〔雖〕然 suīrán;尽〔儘〕管 jǐnguǎn;然而 rán'ér.

altitude /ˈæltɪtjuːd; *US* -tuːd/ *n* [C] (海拔)高度 gāodù.

alto /ˈæltəʊ/ *n* [C] [*pl* ~s] 1 男声最高音 nánshēng zuì gāoyīn;女低音 nǚ dīyīn. 2 中音乐〔樂〕器 zhōngyīn yuèqì: *an* ~-*saxophone* 中音萨克斯管.

altogether /ˌɔːltəˈgeðə(r)/ *adv* 1 完全 wánquán: *It is not* ~ *surprising that she failed the exam*. 她这次考试不及格一点不奇怪. 2 整个〔個〕说来〔來〕 zhěnggè shuō lái.

altruism /ˈæltruːɪzəm/ *n* [U] 利他主义〔義〕 lìtāzhǔyì. **altruist** /-ɪst/ *n* [C]. **altruistic** /ˌæltruːˈɪstɪk/ *adj*.

aluminium /ˌæljʊˈmɪnɪəm/ [美语 aluminum /əˈluːmɪnəm/] *n* [U] 铝 lǚ.

always /ˈɔːlweɪz/ *adv* 1 总〔總〕是 zǒngshì: *You should* ~ *use a seat-belt in a car*. 一坐上汽车就应该系好安全带. 2 永远〔遠〕 yǒngyuǎn: *I'll* ~ *love her*. 我永远爱她.

am[1] /æm/ ⇨BE.

am[2] /ˌeɪˈem/ *abbr* 上午 shàngwǔ.

amalgamate /əˈmælgəmeɪt/ *v* [I, T] 混合

hùnhé；合 并〔併〕hébìng. **amalgamation** /əˌmælgəˈmeɪʃn/ *n* [U,C].

amass /əˈmæs/ *v* [T] 积〔積〕聚 jījù.

amateur /ˈæmətə(r)/ *n* [C] 业〔業〕余〔餘〕爱〔愛〕好者 yèyú àihàozhě；业余活动〔動〕者 yèyú huódòngzhě. **amateurish** *adj* 不够熟练〔練〕的 búgòu shúliàn de.

amaze /əˈmeɪz/ *v* [T] 使惊〔驚〕奇 shǐ jīngqí：*~d at the news* 对这消息感到惊奇. **amazement** *n* [U]. **amazing** *adj*.

ambassador /æmˈbæsədə(r)/ *n* [C] 大使 dàshǐ.

amber /ˈæmbə(r)/ *n* [U] (a) 琥珀 hǔpò. (b) 淡黄色 dànhuángsè.

ambidextrous /ˌæmbɪˈdekstrəs/ *adj* 左右手都善于使用的 zuǒ yòu shǒu dōu shànyú shǐyòng de.

ambiguous /æmˈbɪgjʊəs/ *adj* 含糊的 hánhude. **ambiguity** /ˌæmbɪˈgjuːətɪ/ *n* [U, C] [*pl* -ies].

ambition /æmˈbɪʃn/ *n* (a) [U] 雄心 xióngxīn；野心 yěxīn. (b) [C] 抱负 bàofù：*achieve one's ~(s)* 实现自己的抱负. **ambitious** /-ʃəs/ *adj*.

amble /ˈæmbl/ *v* [I] 漫步 mànbù. **amble** *n* [sing].

ambulance /ˈæmbjʊləns/ *n* [C] 救护〔護〕车 jiùhùchē.

ambush /ˈæmbʊʃ/ *n* [U, C] 伏击〔擊〕fújī；**ambush** *v* [T] 伏击 fújī.

ameba [美语] = AMOEBA.

amen /ˌeɪˈmen, ɑːˈmen/ *interj* "阿门"(基督教祈祷结束时用语，意为"诚心所愿") āmen.

amenable /əˈmiːnəbl/ *adj* 能听〔聽〕教诲的 néng tīng jiàohuì de.

amend /əˈmend/ *v* [T] 改进〔進〕gǎijìn；修正 xiūzhèng. **amendment** *n* [C, U] 改变〔變〕gǎibiàn；改正 gǎizhèng.

amends /əˈmendz/ *n* [pl] [习语] **make amends (for sth)** 赔偿〔償〕péicháng；赔罪 péizuì；道歉 dàoqiàn.

amenity /əˈmiːnətɪ/ *n* [C] [*pl* -ies] 使人愉快的事物(如公园、商业中心等) shǐ rén yúkuài de shìwù.

America /əˈmerɪkə/ *n* 1 [U] 美国〔國〕Měiguó. 2 [U,C] 美洲 Měizhōu：*the Americas* 南北美洲.

American /əˈmerɪkən/ *adj* 美洲的 Měizhōude；(尤指)美国〔國〕的 Měiguóde. **American** *n* [C] 美洲人 Měizhōurén；(尤指)美国人 Měiguórén. **American ˈfootball** *n* [U] 美式橄榄球 měishì gǎnlǎnqiú.

amiable /ˈeɪmɪəbl/ *adj* 亲〔親〕切的 qīnqiède；和蔼的 hé'ǎide. **amiably** *adv*.

amicable /ˈæmɪkəbl/ *adj* 温柔的 wēnróude；友善的 yǒushànde：*reach an ~ agreement* 达成友好的协议. **amicably** *adv*.

amid /əˈmɪd/ (亦作 **amidst** /əˈmɪdst/) *prep* [旧词或正式用语]在…当〔當〕中 zài…dāngzhōng.

amiss /əˈmɪs/ *adj*, *adv* [旧词] 1 有差错的 yǒu chācuò de；错误地 cuòwùde；偏 piān；歪 wāi：*Something seems to be ~.* 似乎出了什么岔子了. 2 [习语] **take sth aˈmiss** 因某事而见怪 yīn mǒushì ér jiànguài.

ammonia /əˈməʊnɪə/ *n* [U] 氨 ān；阿摩尼亚〔亞〕āmóníyà.

ammunition /ˌæmjʊˈnɪʃn/ *n* [U] 军火 jūnhuǒ；弹〔彈〕药〔藥〕dànyào.

amnesia /æmˈniːzɪə; *US* -ˈniːʒə/ *n* [U] [医]健忘症 jiànwàngzhèng.

amnesty /ˈæmnəstɪ/ *n* [C] [*pl* -ies] 大赦 dàshè.

amoeba /əˈmiːbə/ *n* [C] [*pl* ~s 或 -ae /-biː/] 阿米巴变〔變〕形虫 āmǐbā biànxíngchóng. **amoebic** /-bɪk/ *adj*.

amok /əˈmɒk/ (亦作 **amuck** /əˈmʌk/) *adv* [习语]**run amok** ⇨ RUN[1].

among /əˈmʌŋ/ (亦作 **amongst** /əˈmʌŋst/) *prep* 1 在…中间 zài…zhōngjiān：*found it ~ a pile of papers* 在一堆报纸中间找到了它. 2 …之一… zhīyī：*~ the best in the world* 世界上最好的之一. 3 分到每个〔個〕成员 fēn dào měigè chéngyuán：*distribute the books ~ the class* 把书分给班上每一个人.

amorous /ˈæmərəs/ *adj* 色情的 sèqíngde；多情的 duōqíngde. **amorously** *adv*.

amount /əˈmaʊnt/ *n* [C] 总〔總〕数〔數〕zǒngshù：*a large ~ of money* 一大笔钱. **amount** *v* [I] *to* 等于 děngyú.

amp /æmp/ *n* [C] [非正式用语] short for AMPERE.

ampere /ˈæmpeə(r); *US* ˈæmpɪər/ *n* [C] 安培 ānpéi.

amphibian /æmˈfɪbɪən/ *n* [C] 两栖〔棲〕动〔動〕物 liǎngqī dòngwù. **amphibious** /-bɪəs/ *adj*.

amphitheatre [美语 -ter] /ˈæmfɪθɪətə(r)/ *n* [C] (圆形露天的)有梯式坐位的建筑〔築〕物 yǒu tīshì zuòwèi de jiànzhùwù.

ample /ˈæmpl/ *adj* 丰〔豐〕富的 fēngfùde；充分的 chōngfènde. **amply** *adv*.

amplify /ˈæmplɪfaɪ/ *v* [*pt*, *pp* -ied][T] 1 增强 zēngqiáng；放大 fàngdà：*~ the sound* 放大声音. 2 详述 xiángshù. **amplification** /ˌæmplɪfɪˈkeɪʃn/ *n* [U]. **amplifier** *n* [C] 放大器 fàngdàqì；扩〔擴〕音器 kuòyīnqì.

amputate /ˈæmpjʊteɪt/ *v* [I, T] 截肢 jiézhī. **amputation** /ˌæmpjʊˈteɪʃn/ *n* [C, U].

amuck /əˈmʌk/ *adv* ⇨AMOK.

A

amulet /ˈæmjʊlɪt/ *n* [C] 护〔護〕身符 hùshēnfú; 驱〔驅〕邪物 qūxiéwù.

amuse /əˈmjuːz/ *v* [T] 1 逗…笑 dòu…xiào. 2 使娱乐〔樂〕shǐ yúlè. **amusement** *n* 1 [C] 娱乐活动〔動〕yúlè huódòng. 2 [U] 娱乐 yúlè. **amusing** *adj* 逗乐的 dòulède.

an ⇨ A.

anachronism /əˈnækrənɪzəm/ *n* [C] 过〔過〕时〔時〕的人或事物 guòshíde rén huò shìwù.

anaconda /ˌænəˈkɒndə/ *n* [C](南美等地的)蟒蛇 mǎngshé.

anaemia /əˈniːmɪə/ *n* [U] 贫血症 pínxuèzhèng. **anaemic** /-mɪk/ *adj*.

anaesthesia /ˌænɪsˈθiːzɪə/ *n* [U] 麻木 mámù; 麻醉 mázuì. **anaesthetic** /ˌænɪsˈθetɪk/ *n* [C, U] 麻醉剂〔劑〕mázuìjì. **anaesthetist** /əˈniːsθətɪst/ *n* [C] 麻醉师〔師〕mázuìshī. **anaesthetize** /əˈniːsθətaɪz/ *v* [T] 使麻醉 shǐ mázuì.

anagram /ˈænəgræm/ *n* [C] (变换字母顺序构成的)变〔變〕形词 biànxíngcí: '*Stare*' *is an* ~ *of* '*tears*'. "stare"是"tears"的变形词.

analogy /əˈnælədʒɪ/ *n* [C] [*pl* -ies] 1 [C] 类〔類〕似 lèisì: *an* ~ *between the heart and a pump* 心脏同抽水机相类似. 2 [U] 类推 lèituī. **analogous** /-ləgəs/ *adj* 类似的 lèisìde.

analyse /ˈænəlaɪz/ *v* [T] 分析 fēnxī; 研究 yánjiū.

analysis /əˈnæləsɪs/ *n* [*pl* -yses /-əsiːz/] (a)[C, U]分析 fēnxī. (b) 分析结果 fēnxī jiéguǒ. **analyst** /ˈænəlɪst/ *n* [C] 1 分析者 fēnxīzhě; 化验〔驗〕员 huàyànyuán. 2 精神分析学〔學〕家 jīngshén fēnxīxuéjiā. **analytic** /ˌænəˈlɪtɪk/ (亦作 **analytical** /-kl/) *adj*.

analyze [美语] = ANALYSE.

anarchy /ˈænəkɪ/ *n* [U] 无〔無〕政府状〔狀〕态〔態〕wú zhèngfǔ zhuàngtài; 混乱〔亂〕hùnluàn. **anarchist** *n* [C] 无政府主义〔義〕者 wúzhèngfǔzhǔyìzhě.

anatomy /əˈnætəmɪ/ *n* [U, C][*pl* -ies] 解剖 jiěpōu; 解剖学〔學〕jiěpōuxué. **anatomical** /ˌænəˈtɒmɪkl/ *adj*.

ancestor /ˈænsestə(r)/ *n* [C] 祖先 zǔxiān. **ancestral** /ænˈsestrəl/ *adj* 祖传〔傳〕的 zǔchuánde; 祖先的 zǔxiānde. **ancestry** /-trɪ/ *n* [C] [*pl* -ies] 世系 shìxì; 家世 jiāshì.

anchor /ˈæŋkə(r)/ *n*[C] 锚 máo. **anchor** *v* [I, T] 用锚泊船 yòng máo bó chuán. **anchorage** *n* [C] 锚地 máodì.

anchovy /ˈæntʃəvɪ; *US* ˈæntʃəuvɪ/ *n* [C] [*pl* -ies] 鳀 tí.

ancient /ˈeɪnʃənt/ *adj* 1 古代的 gǔdàide; 古老的 gǔlǎode: ~ *Greece* 古希腊. 2 旧〔舊〕式的 jiùshìde; 旧的 jiùde.

ancillary /ænˈsɪlərɪ; *US* ˈænsəlerɪ/ *adj* 支援的 zhīyuánde; 帮〔幫〕助的 bāngzhùde.

and /ənd, ən; 强式: ænd/ *conj* 1 和 hé; 与〔與〕yǔ: *bread* ~ *butter* 面包和黄油. 2 然后〔後〕ránhòu; 随〔隨〕后 suíhòu: *She came in* ~ *then sat down*. 她走进来,然后坐下来. 3 那么〔麼〕nàmò; 于是 yúshì: *Work hard* ~ *you will succeed*. 努力干,你会成功的. 4 (表示继续)又 yòu; 加 jiā: *for hours* ~ *hours* 一连好多个钟头. 5 [非正式用语](在某些动词后面用以代替 to): *Try* ~ *come early*. 设法早点来.

anecdote /ˈænɪkdəut/ *n* [C] 轶事 yìshì; 趣闻〔聞〕qùwén.

anemia, anemic [美语] = ANAEMIA, ANAEMIC.

anemone /əˈnemənɪ/ *n* [C] 银莲〔蓮〕花 yínliánhuā.

anesthesia [美语] = ANAESTHESIA.

anew /əˈnjuː; *US* əˈnuː/ *adv* [常作修辞]再 zài; 重新 chóngxīn.

angel /ˈeɪndʒl/ *n* 1 天使 tiānshǐ; 安琪儿〔兒〕ānqí'ér. 2 天真可爱〔愛〕的人 tiānzhēn kě'ài de rén. **angelic** /ænˈdʒelɪk/ *adj*.

anger /ˈæŋgə(r)/ *n* [U] 愤怒 fènnù. **anger** *v* [T]激怒 jīnù; 使怒 shǐnù.

angle[1] /ˈæŋgl/ *n* 1 角 jiǎo. 2 角落 jiǎoluò. 3 [喻]观〔觀〕点〔點〕guāndiǎn; 看法 kànfǎ. 4 [习语] **at an ˈangle** 斜 xié; 倾斜 qīngxié. **angle** *v* [T] 1 斜放 xiéfàng; 斜移 xiéyí. 2 以某种观点报〔報〕道 yǐ mǒuzhǒng guāndiǎn bàodào.

angle[2] /ˈæŋgl/ *v* [I] 1 钓鱼 diàoyú. 2 *for* [非正式用语]使用花招得到某物 shǐyòng huāzhāo dédào mǒuwù: ~ *for compliments* 博取恭维. **angler** *n* [C]. **angling** *n* [U].

Anglican /ˈæŋglɪkən/ *n* [C], *adj* 英国〔國〕国教的 Yīngguó guójiàode;英国国教教徒 Yīngguó guójiào jiàotú.

Anglicize /ˈæŋglɪsaɪz/ *v* [T] 使英语化 shǐ Yīngyǔhuà.

Anglo- /ˈæŋgləu/ *prefix* 英国〔國〕Yīngguó; 英国的 Yīngguóde: *Anglo-American* 英美.

angry /ˈæŋgrɪ/ *adj* [-ier, -iest] 1 愤怒的 fènnùde. 2 肿〔腫〕痛发〔發〕炎的 zhǒngtòng fāyán de. **angrily** *adv*.

anguish /ˈæŋgwɪʃ/ *n* [U] 思想感情上极〔極〕度痛苦 sīxiǎng gǎnqíng shàng jídù tòngkǔ. **anguished** *adj*.

angular /ˈæŋgjulə(r)/ *adj* 1 有角的 yǒujiǎode. 2 骨瘦如柴的 gǔ shòu rú chái de.

animal /ˈænɪml/ *n* [C] 1 (a)动〔動〕物 dòngwù. (b)人以外的动物 rén yǐwài de dòngwù. 2 野蛮〔蠻〕而凶残〔殘〕的人 yěmán ér xiōngcánde rén. **animal** *adj* 1 动物的 dòngwùde. 2 肉体〔體〕的 ròutǐde. ˈ**animal rights** *n* [pl] 动物权〔權〕益 dòngwù quányì.

animate[1] /ˈænɪmət/ *adj* 有生命的 yǒu shēngmìng de; 有生气〔氣〕的 yǒu shēngqì de.

animate[2] /ˈænɪmeɪt/ *v* [T] 使有生命 shǐ yǒu shēngmìng; 使活泼〔潑〕shǐ huópo. **animated** *adj* 活生生的 huóshēngshēngde; 活跃〔躍〕的 huóyuède. ˌ**animated carˈtoon** 动〔動〕画〔畫〕片 dònghuàpiàn. **animation** /ˌænɪˈmeɪʃn/ *n* [U] 1 生气〔氣〕shēngqì; 活泼 huópo. 2 动画片制〔製〕作 dònghuàpiàn zhìzuò.

animosity /ˌænɪˈmɒsətɪ/ *n* [C, U] [*pl* -ies] 仇恨 chóuhèn; 憎恨 zènghèn.

ankle /ˈæŋkl/ *n* [C] 踝 huái.

annals /ˈænlz/ *n* [pl] 历〔歷〕史记载 lìshǐ jìzǎi.

annex /əˈneks/ *v* [T] 兼并〔併〕jiānbìng. **annexation** /ˌænekˈseɪʃn/ *n* [U, C].

annexe (美语 **annex**) /ˈænəks/ *n* [C] 附属〔屬〕建筑〔築〕物 fùshǔ jiànzhùwù: *the hospital* ～ 医院附属建筑物.

annihilate /əˈnaɪəleɪt/ *v* [T] 消灭〔滅〕xiāomiè; 歼〔殲〕灭 jiānmiè. **annihilation** /əˌnaɪəˈleɪʃn/ *n* [U].

anniversary /ˌænɪˈvɜːsərɪ/ *n* [C] [*pl* -ies] 周年纪念 zhōunián jìniàn: *a wedding* ～ 结婚周年纪念.

annotate /ˈænəteɪt/ *v* [T] 注释〔釋〕zhùshì. **annotation** /ˌænəˈteɪʃn/ *n* [C, U].

announce /əˈnaʊns/ *v* [T]宣布 xuānbù. **announcement** *n* [C] 宣布 xuānbù. **announcer** *n* [C] 电〔電〕台或电视台的播音员 diàntái huò diànshìtái de bōyīnyuán.

annoy /əˈnɔɪ/ *v* [T] 使烦恼 shǐ fánnǎo; 使生气〔氣〕shǐ shēngqì. **annoyance** *n* [C, U].

annual /ˈænjʊəl/ *adj* 1 每年的 měiniánde. 2 年度的 niándùde: ～ *income* 年度收入. **annual** *n* [C] 1 年刊 niánkān. 2 一年生植物 yìniánshēng zhíwù. **annually** *adv*.

annuity /əˈnjuːətɪ; *US* -ˈnuː-/ *n* [C] [*pl* -ies] 年金 niánjīn.

annul /əˈnʌl/ *v* [-ll-][T] 取消 qǔxiāo; 注销 zhùxiāo. **annulment** *n* [C, U].

anode /ˈænəʊd/ *n* [C] (电)阳〔陽〕极〔極〕yángjí.

anoint /əˈnɔɪnt/ *v* [T] 涂〔塗〕油于(一种宗教仪式) túyóu yú.

anomaly /əˈnɒməlɪ/ *n* [C] [*pl* -ies] 异〔異〕常 yìcháng; 反常 fǎncháng; 异态〔態〕yìtài. **anomalous** /-ləs/ *adj*.

anon[1] /əˈnɒn/ *abbr* anonymous 匿名的 nìmíngde.

anon[2] /əˈnɒn/ *adv* [旧词]立刻 lìkè.

anonymous /əˈnɒnɪməs/ *adj* 匿名的 nìmíngde; 无〔無〕名的 wúmíngde; 不知名的 bù zhīmíng de: *The author wishes to remain* ～. 作者希望匿名发表. **anonymity** /ˌænəˈnɪmətɪ/ *n* [U].

anorak /ˈænəræk/ *n* [C]带〔帶〕风〔風〕帽的厚夹克 dài fēngmào de hòu jiākè.

anorexia /ænəˈreksɪə/ *n* [U] 1 [医]厌〔厭〕食症 yànshízhèng 2 (亦作 **anorexia nervosa** /nɜːˈvəʊsə/)[医]神经〔經〕性食欲缺乏 shénjīngxìng shíyù quēfá. **anorexic** /-ˈreksɪk/ *adj*.

another /əˈnʌðə(r)/ *adj, pron* 1 再一 zàiyī: *have* ～ *cup of tea* 再来一杯茶. 2 别的 biéde: *Do that* ～ *time*. 别的时间做那件事. 3 类〔類〕似的 lèisìde: ～ *Einstein* 另一个爱因斯坦.

answer /ˈɑːnsə(r); *US* ˈænsər/ *n* [C] 1 答复〔復〕dáfù. 2 答案 dá'àn: *The* ～ *to 3 + 7 is 10*. 3+7 的答案是 10. **answer** *v* 1 [I, T] 答复 dáfù: *Think before you* ～. 想一想再答复. ～ *the phone* 接电话. ～ *the door* 听到敲门就去开. 2 [短语动词] **answer (sb) back** 向某人回嘴 xiàng mǒurén huízuǐ; 与〔與〕某人顶嘴 yǔ mǒurén dǐngzuǐ. **answer for sb / sth** (a) 对〔對〕…负责 duì…fùzé. (b) 讲〔講〕话支持 jiǎnghuà zhīchí. **answerable** *adj* 负责的 fùzéde: ～ *for one's actions* 对自己的行为负责.

ant /ænt/ *n* [C] 蚂蚁〔蟻〕mǎyǐ.

antagonism /ænˈtæɡənɪzəm/ *n* [U] 反对〔對〕fǎnduì; 不喜欢〔歡〕bù xǐhuān. **antagonist** /-nɪst/ *n* [C] 反对者 fǎnduìzhě. **antagonistic** /ænˌtæɡəˈnɪstɪk/ *adj*.

antagonize /ˌænˈtæɡənaɪz/ *v* [T] 引起…的反抗 yǐnqǐ…de fǎnkàng; 招怨 zhāoyuàn.

Antarctic /ˌænˈtɑːktɪk/ *adj* 南极〔極〕的 nánjíde. **the Antarctic** *n* [sing] 南极 nánjí.

antelope /ˈæntɪləʊp/ *n* [C] 羚羊 língyáng.

antenatal /ˌæntɪˈneɪtl/ *adj* (a) 产〔產〕前的 chǎnqiánde. (b) 孕妇〔婦〕的 yùnfùde: *an* ～ *clinic* 孕妇检查诊所.

antenna /ænˈtenə/ *n* [C] 1 [*pl* ～e /-niː/] 昆虫触〔觸〕角 kūnchóng chùjiǎo. 2 [*pl* ～s] [美语]天线〔綫〕tiānxiàn.

anthem /ˈænθəm/ *n* [C] 赞〔讚〕美诗 zànměishī; 圣〔聖〕歌 shènggē.

anthology /ˌænˈθɒlədʒɪ/ *n* [C] [*pl* -ies] 文集 wénjí; (尤指)诗集 shījí.

anthropology /ˌænθrəˈpɒlədʒɪ/ *n* [U] 人类〔類〕学〔學〕rénlèixué. **anthropologist** *n* [C].

anti- /ˌæntɪ/ *prefix* 反对〔對〕fǎnduì: ˌ*antiˈaircraft* 防空的;高射的.

antibiotic /ˌæntɪbaɪˈɒtɪk/ *n* [C], *adj* 抗生

A

素 kàngshēngsù; 抗菌的 kàngjūnde.

antibody /ˈæntɪbɒdɪ/ *n* [C] [*pl* -ies] 抗体〔體〕kàngtǐ.

anticipate /ænˈtɪsɪpeɪt/ *v* [T] 1 预期 yùqī; 预料 yùliào: *We ~ trouble.* 我们预料会发生麻烦. 2 预先处〔處〕理 yùxiān chǔlǐ. **anticipation** /ˌæntɪsɪˈpeɪʃn/ *n* [U].

anticlimax /ˌæntɪˈklaɪmæks/ *n* [C] 虎头〔頭〕蛇尾 hǔ tóu shé wěi.

anticlockwise /ˌæntɪˈklɒkwaɪz/ *adv, adj* 反时〔時〕钟〔鐘〕方向地(的) fǎn shízhōng fāngxiàng de.

antics /ˈæntɪks/ *n* [pl] 滑稽动〔動〕作 huájī dòngzuò: *the children's ~* 孩子们的滑稽动作.

anticyclone /ˌæntɪˈsaɪkləʊn/ *n* [C] 高气〔氣〕压〔壓〕区〔區〕gāo qìyā qū.

antidote /ˈæntɪdəʊt/ *n* [C] 解毒药〔藥〕jiědúyào.

antifreeze /ˈæntɪfriːz/ *n* [U] 抗冻〔凍〕剂〔劑〕kàngdòngjì.

antiquated /ˈæntɪkweɪtɪd/ *adj* 过〔過〕时〔時〕的 guòshíde; 老式的 lǎoshìde.

antique /ænˈtiːk/ *adj, n* [C] 古代的 gǔdàide; 古玩 gǔwán; 古物 gǔwù: *~ furniture* 古董家具.

antiquity /ænˈtɪkwətɪ/ *n* [*pl* -ies] 1 [U] 古代 gǔdài. 2 [C,常作 pl] 古代建筑〔築〕gǔdài jiànzhù; 古迹 gǔjì; 古代绘〔繪〕画〔畫〕gǔdài huìhuà 3 [U] 古老 gǔlǎo.

antiseptic /ˌæntɪˈseptɪk/ *n* [C], *adj* 防腐的 fángfǔde; 防腐剂〔劑〕fángfǔjì.

antisocial /ˌæntɪˈsəʊʃl/ *adj* 1 厌〔厭〕恶〔惡〕社交的 yànwù shèjiāo de. 2 反社会〔會〕的 fǎn shèhuì de.

antiterrorist /ˌæntɪˈterərɪst/ *n* [C] 反恐怖主义者 fǎn kǒngbù zhǔyìzhě. *adj* 反恐怖主义的 fǎn kǒngbù zhǔyìde.

antithesis /ænˈtɪθəsɪs/ *n* [C] [正式用语] [*pl* -ses /-siːz/] 对〔對〕立 duìlì; 对立面 duìlìmiàn.

antivirus /ˌæntɪˈvaɪərəs/ *adj* 防病毒的 fángbìngdúde.

antler /ˈæntlə(r)/ *n* [C] 鹿角 lùjiǎo.

antonym /ˈæntənɪm/ *n* [C] 反义〔義〕词 fǎnyìcí: *Hot is the ~ of cold.* hot 是 cold 的反义词.

anus /ˈeɪnəs/ *n* [C] [解剖]肛门 gāngmén.

anvil /ˈænvɪl/ *n* [C] 铁〔鐵〕砧 tiězhēn.

anxiety /æŋˈzaɪətɪ/ *n* [*pl* -ies] 1 [C,U] 忧〔憂〕虑〔慮〕yōulǜ. 2 [U] 渴望 kěwàng: *~ to please* 急于讨好.

anxious /ˈæŋkʃəs/ *adj* 1 忧〔憂〕虑〔慮〕的 yōulǜ de. 2 引起忧虑的 yǐnqǐ yōulǜ de: *an ~ time* 焦虑的时刻. 3 *for; to* 渴望 kěwàng; 急要 jíyào: *He's very ~ to meet you.* 他迫不及待地要见你. **anxiously** *adv*.

any /ˈenɪ/ *adj, pron* 1 不定量的 bú dìngliàngde: *Have you got ~ milk?* 你有牛奶吗? *I haven't read any book by Tolstoy.* 我没有读过托尔斯泰的作品. 2 任何的 rènhéde: *Take ~ card you like.* 你随意拿一张牌. **any** *adv* 丝毫 sīháo; 任何程度 rènhé chéngdù: *I can't run ~ faster.* 我跑得不能更快了.

anybody /ˈenɪbɒdɪ/ (亦作 **anyone** /ˈenɪwʌn/) *pron* 1 任何人 rènhé rén: *Did ~ see you?* 有人见到你吗? 2 许多人中之一 xǔduō rén zhōng zhīyī.

anyhow /ˈenɪhaʊ/ *adv* 1 (亦作 **anyway** /ˈenɪweɪ/) 无〔無〕论〔論〕如何 wúlùn rúhé: *It's too late now, ~.* 无论如何,现在是太晚了. 2 粗心大意地 cūxīn dàyìde: *do the work ~* 粗心大意地做工作.

anyone = ANYBODY.

anyplace /ˈenɪpleɪs/ [美语] = ANYWHERE.

anything /ˈenɪθɪŋ/ *pron* 1 任何(重要的)事物 rènhé shìwù: *Has ~ unusual happened?* 出了什么事吗? 2 无〔無〕论〔論〕什〔甚〕么〔麼〕wúlùn shénme: *I am so hungry; I'll eat ~!* 我饿得厉害;我什么都吃! 3 [习语]**anything but** 决不 juébù.

anyway /ˈenɪweɪ/ *adj* = ANYHOW 1.

anywhere /ˈenɪweə(r); *US* -hweər / *adv* 1 任何地方 rènhé dìfang. 2 [习语] **get anywhere** ⇨ GET.

aorta /eɪˈɔːtə/ *n* [C] 主动〔動〕脉〔脈〕zhǔdòngmài.

apart /əˈpɑːt/ *adv* 1 相隔 xiānggé; 相距 xiāngjù: *The houses are 500 metres ~.* 这些房子相隔 500 米. 2 分离〔離〕fēnlí; 分开〔開〕fēnkāi: *They are living ~.* 他们正分开居住. 3 拆开 chāikāi: *It fell ~.* 土崩瓦解. **apart from** *prep* 1 除去…外,都不 chúqù…wài,dōu bù 2 除去…外,还〔還〕有 chúqù…wài,háiyǒu.

apartheid /əˈpɑːthaɪt,-heɪt/ *n* [U] (南非)种〔種〕族隔离〔離〕政策 zhǒngzú gélí zhèngcè.

apartment /əˈpɑːtmənt/ *n* [C] 1 [美语]单〔單〕元房 dānyuánfáng; 公寓 gōngyù; 住宅楼〔樓〕zhùzháilóu. 2 一大间房子 yīdàjiān fángzi.

apathy /ˈæpəθɪ/ *n* [U] 冷淡 lěngdàn; 缺乏感情 quēfá gǎnqíng. **apathetic** /ˌæpəˈθetɪk/ *adj*.

ape /eɪp/ *n* [C] 无〔無〕尾猿 wúwěiyuán; 类〔類〕人猿 lèirényuán. **ape** *v* [T] 模仿〔倣〕mófǎng; 学〔學〕…的样〔樣〕xué…de yàng.

aperitif /əˈperətɪf; *US* əˌperəˈtiːf/ *n* [C] 开〔開〕胃酒 kāiwèijiǔ.

aperture /ˈæpətʃə(r)/ *n* [C] [正式用语]孔 kǒng; 眼 yǎn; (照相机镜头上的)孔径〔徑〕kǒngjìng.

apex /ˈeɪpeks/ *n* [C] [*pl* ~es 或 apices /ˈeɪpɪsiːz/] 顶点〔點〕dǐngdiǎn: *the ~ of a triangle* 三角形的顶点.

apiece /əˈpiːs/ *adv* 每个〔個〕měigè; 各 gè: *costing £1 ~* 每人花费一英镑.

aplomb /əˈplɒm/ *n* [U] 自信 zìxìn; 自恃 zìshì.

apologetic /əˌpɒləˈdʒetɪk/ *adj* 表示歉意的 biǎoshì qiànyì de. **apologetically** /-klɪ/ *adv*.

apologize /əˈpɒlədʒaɪz/ *v* [I]道歉 dàoqiàn: *I must ~ for being late*. 我必须道歉,我迟到了.

apology /əˈpɒlədʒɪ/ *n* [C] [*pl* -ies] **1** 道歉 dàoqiàn. **2** [习语] **an apology for sth** 聊以充数〔數〕的东西 liáoyǐ chōngshù de dōngxi.

apostle /əˈpɒsl/ *n* [C] **1** (基督教)使徒 shǐtú. **2** 改革家 gǎigéjiā.

apostrophe /əˈpɒstrəfɪ/ *n* [C] 撇号〔號〕piěhào; 省字号 shěngzìhào.

appal (美语亦作 **appall**) /əˈpɔːl/ *v* [-ll-][T] 使丧〔喪〕胆〔膽〕shǐ sàngdǎn; 使吃惊〔驚〕shǐ chījīng: *We were ~led at the news*. 我们听到这个消息大为吃惊. **appalling** *adj*.

apparatus /ˌæpəˈreɪtəs; *US* -ˈrætəs/ *n* [U, C] 仪〔儀〕器 yíqì; 设备〔備〕shèbèi.

apparent /əˈpærənt/ *adj* **1** 明显〔顯〕的 míngxiǎn de: *for no ~ reason* 没有什么明显的理由. **2** 表面上的 biǎomiàn shàng de: *an ~ lack of courage* 表面上的缺乏勇气. **apparently** *adv*.

apparition /ˌæpəˈrɪʃn/ *n* [C] 鬼怪 guǐguài.

appeal /əˈpiːl/ *v* [I] **1** (*for*) 呼吁〔籲〕hūyù; 要求 yāoqiú: *~ for help* 呼吁给予帮助. *~ for money* 呼吁资助. **2** [法律]上诉 shàngsù. **3** *to* 吸引 xīyǐn; 引起爱〔愛〕好 yǐnqǐ àihào: *The idea of camping does not ~ to me*. 出去野营的主意对我没有吸引力. **appeal** *n* **1** [C] 恳〔懇〕求 kěnqiú; 呼吁 hūyù. **2** [C] 上诉 shàngsù; 请求重作决定 qǐngqiú chóngzuò juédìng. **3** [U] 吸引力 xīyǐnlì: *ˈsex-~* 性感. **appealing** *adj* **1** 有感染力的 yǒu gǎnrǎnlì de; 吸引人的 xīyǐn rén de. **2** 使人怜〔憐〕悯的 shǐ rén liánmǐn de.

appear /əˈpɪə(r)/ *v* [I] **1** 出现 chūxiàn; 显〔顯〕露 xiǎnlù: *A ship ~ed on the horizon*. 一艘船出现在地平线上. **2** 来到 láidào. **3** 出版 chūbǎn: *Her latest book ~s in the spring*. 她的最新的一本书在春季出版. **4** [法律]出庭 chūtíng. **5** 看来 kànlái: *That explanation ~s (to be) reasonable*. 那个解释似乎是合理的. **appearance** *n* **1** [C] 出现 chūxiàn. **2** 外貌 wàimào; 外表 wàibiǎo; 衣着风〔風〕度 yīzhuó fēngdù: *an untidy ~ance* 衣冠不整. **3** [习语] ˌ**put in an apˈpearance** (尤指短时间)到场〔場〕dàochǎng. **to all apˈpearance** 就外表看 jiù wàibiǎo kàn.

appease /əˈpiːz/ *v* [T][正式用语]抚〔撫〕慰 fǔwèi. **appeasement** *n* [U].

append /əˈpend/ *v* [T][正式用语]附加 fùjiā; 附注〔註〕fùzhù. **appendage** *n* [C] 附属〔屬〕物 fùshǔwù; 附加物 fùjiāwù.

appendicitis /əˌpendəˈsaɪtɪs/ *n* [U] 阑尾炎 lánwěiyán.

appendix /əˈpendɪks/ *n* [C] **1** [*pl* -dices /-dɪsiːz/] 附录〔錄〕fùlù. **2** [*pl* ~es] 阑尾 lánwěi.

appetite /ˈæpɪtaɪt/ *n* [C, U] 食欲 shíyù; 欲〔慾〕望 yùwàng.

appetizer /ˈæpɪtaɪzə(r)/ *n* [C] 开〔開〕胃品 kāiwèipǐn. **appetizing** *adj* 开胃的 kāiwèide.

applaud /əˈplɔːd/ *v* **1** [I, T]鼓掌欢〔歡〕迎 gǔzhǎng huānyíng; 鼓掌赞成 gǔzhǎng zànchéng. **2** [T]赞成 zànchéng. **applause** /əˈplɔːz/ *n* [U].

apple /ˈæpl/ *n* [C] 苹〔蘋〕果 píngguǒ.

appliance /əˈplaɪəns/ *n* [C] 用具 yòngjù; 设备〔備〕shèbèi; 装〔裝〕置 zhuāngzhì.

applicable /əˈplɪkəbl 亦读 ˈæplɪkəbl/ *adj* (*to*) 合用的 héyòng de; 合适〔適〕的 héshì de.

applicant /ˈæplɪkənt/ *n* [C] 申请人 shēnqǐngrén; 请求者 qǐngqiúzhě.

application /ˌæplɪˈkeɪʃn/ *n* **1** [C, U] 请求 qǐngqiú; 申请表 shēnqǐngbiǎo: *an ~ (form) for a job* 求职申请表. **2** [U, C]应〔應〕用 yìngyòng: *the practical ~s of the invention* 该发明的实际应用. **3** [U]努力 nǔlì.

apply /əˈplaɪ/ *v* [*pt*, *pp* -ied] **1** [I] (*for*) 要求 yāoqiú; 申请 shēnqǐng: *~ for a job* 申请工作. *~ for a visa* 申请签证. **2** [I](*to*) 与〔與〕…有关〔關〕yǔ…yǒuguān; 适〔適〕用 shìyòng: *This rule does not ~ to you*. 这条规定对你不适用. **3** [T] 专〔專〕心致志于 zhuānxīn zhìzhì yú: *~ oneself / one's mind to the problem*. 专心致志于这个问题. **applied** *adj* 应〔應〕用的 yìngyòngde: *applied science* 应用科学.

appoint /əˈpɔɪnt/ *v* [T] **1** 任命 rènmìng. **2** [正式用语]约定 yuēdìng: *the time ~ed* 约定的时间. **appointment** *n* **1** (a) [C, U]任命 rènmìng. (b) [C] 职〔職〕位 zhíwèi. **2** [C, U]约会〔會〕yuēhuì.

appraise /əˈpreɪz/ *v*[T] [正式用语]估价〔價〕gūjià; 评价 píngjià; 鉴〔鑒〕定 jiàndìng. **appraisal** /əˈpreɪzl/ *n* [C, U].

appreciable /əˈpriːʃəbl/ *adj* 可以看到的 kěyǐ kàndào de; 可见的 kějiànde; 明显〔顯〕的 míngxiǎnde: *~ difference* 明显的差异. **appreciably** *adv*.

A

appreciate /əˈpriːʃɪeɪt/ *v* **1** [T] 欣赏 xīnshǎng: ~ *classical music* 欣赏古典音乐. **2** 感激 gǎnjī: *I really ~ all your help*. 我实在感激你们的一切帮助. **3** [T] 领会〔會〕lǐnghuì; 体〔體〕会 tǐhuì: *I ~ your problem, but am not able to help*. 我理解你的困难,但我帮不了你. **4** [I] (土地等)涨〔漲〕价〔價〕zhǎngjià. **appreciation** /əˌpriːʃɪˈeɪʃn/ *n* [U, C]. **appreciative** /-ʃətɪv/ *adj*.

apprehend /ˌæprɪˈhend/ *v* [T] [正式用语] **1** 逮捕 dàibǔ; 拘捕 jūbǔ. **2** 理解 lǐjiě; 明白 míngbai.

apprehension /ˌæprɪˈhenʃn/ *n* [U, C] 忧〔憂〕虑〔慮〕yōulǜ; 恐怕 kǒngpà. **apprehensive** /-ˈhensɪv/ *adj* 担〔擔〕心的 dānxīn de; 忧虑的 yōulǜ de.

apprentice /əˈprentɪs/ *n* [C] 学〔學〕徒 xuétú; 徒工 túgōng. **apprentice** *v* [T] (*to*) 使当〔當〕学徒 shǐ dāng xuétú: *He is ~d to a plumber*. 他给管子工当学徒. **apprenticeship** /əˈprentɪsʃɪp/ *n* [C, U] 学徒期 xuétúqī.

approach /əˈprəʊtʃ/ *v* **1** [I, T] 接近 jiējìn; 走近 zǒujìn. **2** [T] 要求 yāoqiú; 商洽 shāngqià: ~ *the manager for a pay rise* 要求经理提高工资. **3** [T] (着手)处〔處〕理 chǔlǐ; (开始)对〔對〕付 duìfù: *How shall I ~ this problem?* 我如何处理这个问题? **approach** *n* [C] **1** [usu sing] 接近 jiējìn. **2** 途径〔徑〕tújìng. **3** 方法 fāngfǎ. **approachable** *adj* 可接近的 kě jiējìn de; 谈得拢〔攏〕的 tándelǒngde.

appropriate[1] /əˈprəʊprɪət/ *adj* 合适〔適〕的 héshìde; 正确〔確〕的 zhèngquède. **appropriately** *adv*.

appropriate[2] /əˈprəʊprɪeɪt/ *v* [T] **1** 私占〔佔〕sīzhàn. **2** 拨〔撥〕作专〔專〕用 bō zuò zhuānyòng. **appropriation** /əˌprəʊprɪˈeɪʃn/ *n* [C, U].

approval /əˈpruːvl/ *n* [U] **1** 允许 yǔnxǔ; 批准 pīzhǔn; 赞同 zàntóng: *Your plans have my ~*. 我赞同你的计划. **2** [习语] **on approval** (商品)供试用,包退包换的 gòng shìyòng, bāotuì bāohuàn de.

approve /əˈpruːv/ *v* **1** [I] (*of*) 赞同 zàntóng. **2** [T] 同意 tóngyì. **approvingly** *adv*.

approximate[1] /əˈprɒksɪmət/ *adj* 近似的 jìnsì de; 约略的 yuēlüè de. **approximately** *adv*: ~*ly 1000 students* 大约 1,000 名学生.

approximate[2] /əˈprɒksɪmeɪt/ *v* [I] *to* 接近 jiējìn; 近似 jìnsì. **approximation** /əˌprɒksɪˈmeɪʃn/ *n* [C].

apricot /ˈeɪprɪkɒt/ *n* (a) [C] 杏 xìng. (b) [U] 杏黄色 xìnghuángsè.

April /ˈeɪprəl/ *n* [U, C] 四月 sìyuè: *on A~ the first*; [美语] *on A~ first* 在四月一日. *She was born in A~*. 她在四月出生. *last A~* 上个四月. *next A~* 下个四月.

apron /ˈeɪprən/ *n* [C] 围〔圍〕裙 wéiqún.

apt /æpt/ *adj* **1** 合适〔適〕的 héshìde; 妥当〔當〕的 tuǒdangde: *an ~ remark* 一番得体的话. **2** *to* 易于…的 yìyú…de; 倾向于…的 qīngxiàng yú…de: ~ *to be forgetful* 健忘的. **3** 伶俐的 línglìde; 聪〔聰〕明的 cōngmingde. **aptly** *adv*. **aptness** *n* [U].

aptitude /ˈæptɪtjuːd; *US* -tuːd/ *n* [C, U] 才能 cáinéng; 能力 nénglì.

Aqualung /ˈækwəlʌŋ/ *n* [C] (*P*) 水中呼吸器 shuǐzhōng hūxīqì.

aquarium /əˈkweərɪəm/ *n* [C] [*pl* ~s, ~ria /-rɪə/] 水族馆 shuǐzúguǎn; 养〔養〕鱼池 yǎngyúchí.

aquatic /əˈkwætɪk/ *adj* **1** 水产〔產〕的 shuǐchǎnde; 水生的 shuǐshēngde. **2** (运动)水上的 shuǐshàngde, 水中的 shuǐzhōngde.

aqueduct /ˈækwɪdʌkt/ *n* [C] 渡槽 dùcáo.

Arabic /ˈærəbɪk/ *adj* 阿拉伯的 Ālābóde. **Arabic** *n* [U] 阿拉伯语 Ālābóyǔ. **ˌArabic ˈnumeral** *n* [C] 阿拉伯数〔數〕字 Ālābó shùzì.

arable /ˈærəbl/ *adj* (土地)可耕的 kěgēngde.

arbitrary /ˈɑːbɪtrərɪ; *US* ˈɑːbɪtrerɪ/ *adj* **1** 任意的 rènyìde. **2** 专〔專〕断〔斷〕的 zhuānduànde. **arbitrarily** *adv*.

arbitrate /ˈɑːbɪtreɪt/ *v* [I, T] (*between*) 仲裁 zhòngcái; 公断〔斷〕gōngduàn. **arbitration** /ˌɑːbɪˈtreɪʃn/ *n* [U] 仲裁 zhòngcái; 公断 gōngduàn. **ˈarbitrator** *n* [C].

arc /ɑːk/ *n* [C] 弧 hú.

arcade /ɑːˈkeɪd/ *n* [C] 上有顶棚旁有商店的街道 shàng yǒu dǐngpéng páng yǒu shāngdiàn de jiēdào.

arch /ɑːtʃ/ *n* [C] 拱 gǒng; 桥〔橋〕洞 qiáodòng. **arch** *v* [I, T] 拱起 gǒngqǐ; 弯〔彎〕成弓形 wān chéng gōngxíng: *The cat ~ed its back*. 猫弓起了背.

archaeology /ˌɑːkɪˈɒlədʒɪ/ *n* [U] 考古学〔學〕kǎogǔxué. **archaeological** /ˌɑːkɪəˈlɒdʒɪkl/ *adj*. **archaeologist** *n* [C].

archaic /ɑːˈkeɪɪk/ *adj* (语言、词汇等)已废〔廢〕的 yǐfèide.

archangel /ˈɑːkeɪndʒl/ *n* [C] 大天使 dàtiānshǐ.

archbishop /ˌɑːtʃˈbɪʃəp/ *n* [C] 大主教 dàzhǔjiào.

archer /ˈɑːtʃə(r)/ *n* [C] 弓箭手 gōngjiànshǒu. **archery** *n* [U] 弓箭术〔術〕gōngjiànshù; 射术 shèshù.

archipelago /ˌɑːkɪˈpeləgəʊ/ *n* [C] [*pl* ~s, ~es] 群岛 qúndǎo.

architect /ˈɑːkɪtekt/ *n* [C] 建筑〔築〕师〔師〕jiànzhùshī; 设计师 shèjìshī. **architecture** /-tektʃə(r)/ *n* [U] 建筑学〔學〕jiànzhùxué; 建筑风〔風〕格 jiànzhù fēnggé. **architectural** /ˌɑːkɪˈtektʃərəl/ *adj*.

archives /ˈɑːkaɪvz/ *n* [pl] 档〔檔〕案(室) dàng'àn.

Arctic /ˈɑːktɪk/ *adj* 北极〔極〕的 běijíde. **the Arctic** *n* [sing] 北极 běijí.

ardent /ˈɑːdnt/ *adj* 热〔熱〕情的 rèqíngde; 热心的 rèxīnde. **ardently** *adv*.

arduous /ˈɑːdjʊəs; *US* -dʒʊ-/ *adj* 艰〔艱〕巨的 jiānjùde; 艰苦的 jiānkǔde. **arduously** *adv*.

are ⇨ BE.

area /ˈeərɪə/ *n* **1** [C, U] 面积〔積〕miànjī. **2** [C] 地区〔區〕dìqū; 区域 qūyù: *desert ~s* 沙漠地区. **3** [C] [喻] 范〔範〕围〔圍〕fànwéi; 领域 lǐngyù: *different ~s of human experience* 人类经验的不同领域.

arena /əˈriːnə/ *n* [C] **1** 竞〔競〕技场〔場〕jìngjìchǎng. **2** [喻] 比赛场所 bǐsài chǎngsuǒ: *in the political ~* 在政治舞台上.

aren't /ɑːnt/ are not ⇨ BE.

argue /ˈɑːgjuː/ *v* **1** [I] 不同意 bù tóngyì; 争论〔論〕zhēnglùn. **2** [I, T] *for* / *against* 为〔爲〕赞成(或反对)…而辩论 wèi zànchéng… ér biànlùn. **3** [T] [正式用语] 辩论 biànlùn: *The lawyers ~d the case.* 律师们就案件展开辩论. **arguable** /ˈɑːgjʊəbl/ *adj* 可争辩的 kě zhēngbiàn de. **arguably** *adv*.

argument /ˈɑːgjʊmənt/ *n* **1** [C] 不同意 bù tóngyì. **2** [C, U] 争论〔論〕zhēnglùn. **argumentative** /ˌɑːgjʊˈmentətɪv/ *adj* 爱〔愛〕争论的 ài zhēnglùn de.

aria /ˈɑːrɪə/ *n* [C] 咏叹〔嘆〕调 yǒngtàndiào.

arid /ˈærɪd/ *adj* **1** (土地) 干〔乾〕旱的 gānhàn de. **2** 枯燥的 kūzào de; 使人不感兴〔興〕趣的 shǐ rén bù gǎn xìngqù de.

arise /əˈraɪz/ *v* [*pt* **arose** /əˈrəʊz/, *pp* **arisen** /əˈrɪzn/] [I] 出现 chūxiàn; 发〔發〕生 fāshēng: *A difficulty has ~n.* 发生了困难.

aristocracy /ˌærɪˈstɒkrəsɪ/ *n* [C, 亦作 sing, 用 pl v] [*pl* -ies] 贵族(总称) guìzú. **aristocrat** /ˈærɪstəkræt; *US* əˈrɪst-/ *n* [C] 贵族 guìzú. **aristocratic** /ˌærɪstəˈkrætɪk; *US* əˌrɪstə-/ *adj*.

arithmetic /əˈrɪθmətɪk/ *n* [U] 算术〔術〕suànshù; 计算 jìsuàn. **arithmetical** /ˌærɪθˈmetɪkl/ *adj*.

ark /ɑːk/ *n* [C] (圣经) 诺亚〔亞〕方舟 Nuòyà fāngzhōu.

arm[1] /ɑːm/ *n* [C] **1** (a) 臂 bì. (b) 袖子 xiùzi. **2** 臂状〔狀〕物 bìzhuàngwù: *the ~s of a chair* 椅子的扶手. **3** 武装〔裝〕力量 wǔzhuāng lìliàng. **4** [习语] ˌ**arm in** ˈ**arm** 臂挽臂地 bìwǎnbìde. ˈ**armchair** *n* [C] 扶手椅 fúshǒuyǐ. ˈ**armpit** *n* [C] 腋窝〔窩〕yèwō.

arm[2] /ɑːm/ *v* **1** [I, T] 武装〔裝〕wǔzhuāng. **2** [习语] ˌ**armed to the** ˈ**teeth** 武装到牙齿〔齒〕wǔzhuāng dào yáchǐ. **the** ˌ**armed** ˈ**forces** *n* [pl] 军〔軍〕事力量 jūnshì lìliàng.

armada /ɑːˈmɑːdə/ *n* [C] 舰〔艦〕队〔隊〕jiànduì.

armadillo /ˌɑːməˈdɪləʊ/ *n* [C] [*pl* ~s] 犰狳 qiúyú.

armament /ˈɑːməmənt/ *n* **1** [C, 常用 pl] 兵器 bīngqì; 大炮 dàpào. **2** [U] 武装〔裝〕wǔzhuāng.

armistice /ˈɑːmɪstɪs/ *n* [C] 停战〔戰〕tíngzhàn; 休战 xiūzhàn.

armour (美语 -or) /ˈɑːmə(r)/ *n* [U] **1** 盔甲 kuījiǎ. **2** 装〔裝〕甲 zhuāngjiǎ. **armoured** (美语 -or-) *adj*. **armoury** (美语 -or-) *n* [C] [*pl* -ies] 军〔軍〕械库〔庫〕jūnxièkù.

arms /ɑːmz/ *n* [pl] **1** 武器 wǔqì. **2** [习语] **take up** ˈ**arms** [正式用语] 准〔準〕备〔備〕战〔戰〕斗〔鬥〕zhǔnbèi zhàndòu. (**be**) **up in** ˈ**arms** (**about** / **over sth**) 强烈反对〔對〕qiángliè fǎnduì. **the** ˈ**arms race** *n* [sing] 军〔軍〕备竞〔競〕赛 jūnbèi jìngsài.

army /ˈɑːmɪ/ *n* [*pl* -ies] **1** (a) [C] 陆〔陸〕军〔軍〕lùjūn. (b) **the army** [sing] 军队〔隊〕jūnduì; 部队 bùduì: *join the ~* 从军, 参军. **2** 群 qún; 大队〔隊〕dàduì: *an ~ of volunteers* 一群志愿者.

aroma /əˈrəʊmə/ *n* [C] 芳香 fāngxiāng. **aromatic** /ˌærəˈmætɪk/ *adj*.

arose /əˈrəʊz/ *pt* of ARISE.

around /əˈraʊnd/ *adv*, *prep* **1** 在…周〔週〕围〔圍〕zài…zhōuwéi: *The earth moves ~ the sun.* 地球围绕太阳旋转. **2** 四处〔處〕sìchù; 各处 gèchù: *walk ~ the exhibition* 在展览会的各处走走. **3** 到处 dàochù: *The children gathered ~.* 孩子们三五成群地聚在一起. **4** 可得到的 kě dédàode; 存在着的 cúnzàizhede: *Is anyone ~?* 有人吗? **5** 大约 dàyuē; 附近 fùjìn: *It's ~ six o'clock.* 大约六点钟.

arouse /əˈraʊz/ *v* [T] **1** [正式用语] 唤醒 huànxǐng. **2** 引起 yǐnqǐ: *~ suspicion* 引起怀疑.

arr *abbr* arrives 到达〔達〕dàodá.

arrange /əˈreɪndʒ/ *v* **1** [T] 筹〔籌〕备〔備〕chóubèi: *~ a holiday* 筹备过假日. **2** [I, T] 准〔準〕備 zhǔnbèi; 安排 ānpái: *We ~d to meet at one o'clock.* 我们安排一点钟见面. **3** [I, T] 商定 shāngdìng: *~ a loan* 商定一笔贷款. **4** 整理 zhěnglǐ; 排列 páiliè: *~ flowers* 整

理花束. 5 改编 gǎibiān. **arrangement** *n* 1 arrangements [pl] 准备 zhǔnbèi; 安排 ānpái. 2 [C] 商定 shāngdìng. 3 [C] 整理 zhěnglǐ; 改编 gǎibiān: *a flower ~ment* 插花. *an ~ment for piano* 一首改编的钢琴曲. 4 [U] 排列 páiliè.

array /əˈreɪ/ *n* [C] 大量 dàliàng; 一系列 yíxìliè.

arrears /əˈrɪəz/ *n* [pl] 1 欠款 qiànkuǎn. 2 [习语] be in arrears (with sth) 拖欠 tuōqiàn.

arrest /əˈrest/ *v* [T] 1 逮捕 dàibǔ. 2 [正式用语] 抑制 yìzhì; 阻止 zǔzhǐ. 3 吸引(注意) xīyǐn. **arrest** *n* 1 [C] 逮捕 dàibǔ. 2 [习语] under arrest 被逮捕 bèi dàibǔ.

arrival /əˈraɪvl/ *n* 1 [U] 到达〔達〕 dàodá; 抵达 dǐdá. 2 [C] 来者 láizhě; 来物 láiwù: *The new ~ (= baby) is a boy.* 生下的是个男孩子.

arrive /əˈraɪv/ *v* [I] 1 到达〔達〕 dàodá; 抵达 dǐdá: *~ home* 到家. 2 (时间)到来 dàolái: *The great day has ~d!* 伟大的日子来到了! 3 [短语动词] arrive at sth 达成 dáchéng; 得到 dédào; 作出(决定等) zuòchū: *~ at a decision* 作出决定.

arrogant /ˈærəgənt/ *adj* 傲慢的 àomànde; 自负的 zìfùde. **arrogance** /-gəns/ *n* [U]. **arrogantly** *adv*.

arrow /ˈærəʊ/ *n* [C] 1 箭 jiàn. 2 箭头〔頭〕标〔標〕志(➡) jiàntóu biāozhì.

arse /ɑːs/ *n* [C] [⚠俚语] 1 屁股 pìgu. 2 人 rén: *You stupid ~!* 你这笨蛋! **arse** *v* [短语动词] arse about /around [⚠英俚] 鬼混 guǐhùn.

arsenal /ˈɑːsənl/ *n* [C] 火药〔藥〕库 huǒyàokù; 军〔軍〕火库 jūnhuǒkù.

arsenic /ˈɑːsnɪk/ *n* [U] 砒霜 pīshuāng.

arson /ˈɑːsn/ *n* [U] 放火 fànghuǒ; 纵〔縱〕火 zònghuǒ.

art /ɑːt / *n* 1 [U] 美术〔術〕 měishù; 艺〔藝〕术 yìshù: *an ˈ~ gallery* 画廊. 2 arts [pl] 文科 wénkē. 3 [C, U] 诡计 guǐjì; 花招 huāzhāo.

artefact (亦作 artifact) /ˈɑːtɪfækt / *n* [C] 人工制〔製〕品 réngōngzhìpǐn.

artery /ˈɑːtərɪ/ *n* [C] [*pl* -ies] 1 动〔動〕脉〔脈〕 dòngmài. 2 主要道路或河流 zhǔyào dàolù huò héliú. **arterial** /ɑːˈtɪərɪəl/ *adj*.

artful /ˈɑːtfl/ *adj* 巧妙的 qiǎomiàode; 狡猾的 jiǎohuáde. **artfully** *adv*.

arthritis /ɑːˈθraɪtɪs/ *n* [U] 关〔關〕节〔節〕炎 guānjiéyán. **arthritic** /ɑːˈθrɪtɪk/ *adj*.

artichoke /ˈɑːtɪtʃəʊk/ *n* [C] 1 (亦作 globe ˈartichoke) 朝鲜蓟 cháoxiǎnjì. 2 (亦作 Jerusalem artichoke /dʒəˌruːsələm ˈɑːtɪtʃəʊk/) 菊芋 júyú.

article /ˈɑːtɪkl/ *n* [C] 1 物品 wùpǐn: *~s of clothing* 服装. 2 文章 wénzhāng. 3 [法律] 条〔條〕款 tiáokuǎn. 4 [语法] 冠词 guàncí.

articulate[1] /ɑːˈtɪkjʊlət/ *adj* 1 (人)说话表达〔達〕力强的 shuōhuà biǎodálì qiáng de. 2 发〔發〕音清晰的 fāyīn qīngxī de. **articulately** *adv*.

articulate[2] /ɑːˈtɪkjʊleɪt/ *v* [I, T] 1 清晰地发〔發〕音 qīngxīde fāyīn; 清楚地说话 qīngchǔde shuōhuà. 2 (用关节)连结 liánjiē. **articulated** *adj* (卡车)铰接式的 jiǎojiēshìde. **articulation** /ɑːˌtɪkjʊˈleɪʃn/ *n* [U].

artifact ⇨ARTEFACT.

artificial /ˌɑːtɪˈfɪʃl/ *adj* 1 人工的 réngōngde; 不真的 bù zhēn de. 2 矫〔矯〕揉造作的 jiǎoróuzàozuòde. **artificially** *adv*.

artillery /ɑːˈtɪlərɪ/ *n* [U] 大炮 dàpào; 炮兵 pàobīng.

artisan /ˌɑːtɪˈzæn; *US* ˈɑːrtɪzn/ *n* [C] [正式用语] 手艺〔藝〕人 shǒuyìrén; 技工 jìgōng.

artist /ˈɑːtɪst/ *n* [C] 1 艺〔藝〕术〔術〕家 yìshùjiā; 美术家 měishùjiā. 2 能手 néngshǒu. 3 = ARTISTE. **artistic** /ɑːˈtɪstɪk/ *adj* 1 有艺术性的 yǒu yìshùxìng de. 2 艺术的 yìshùde; 艺术家的 yìshùjiāde. **artistically** /-klɪ/ *adv*. **artistry** *n* [U] 艺术技巧 yìshù jìqiǎo.

artiste /ɑːˈtiːst/ *n* [C] 艺〔藝〕人 yìrén.

arty /ˈɑːtɪ/ *adj* [非正式用语, 贬] 冒充艺〔藝〕术〔術〕的 màochōng yìshù de.

as /əz; 强式: æz/ *prep* 1 如…一样〔樣〕 rú…yíyàng; 如…一般 rú…yìbān: *dressed as a policeman* 穿得像个警察. 2 有…的作用或身份 yǒu…de zuòyòng huò shēnfèn: *a career as a teacher* 教师职业. *treat as friends* 当作朋友对待. **as** *adv* **as . . . as** (用于比较) 如…一样 rú… yíyàng: *as tall as his father* 像他父亲一样高. *Run as fast as you can!* 你尽量快跑! **as** *conj* 1 当〔當〕 dāng; 在…的时〔時〕候 zài…de shíhòu: *I saw her as I was leaving.* 我离开的时候看见了她. 2 由于 yóuyú; 既然 jìrán: *As you were out, I left a message.* 由于你不在, 我留了个口信. 3 虽〔雖〕然 suīrán; 尽〔儘〕管 jǐnguǎn: *Young as I am, I know what I want to be.* 虽然我还年轻, 但我知道我要成为什么样的人. 4 按照 ànzhào; 如同 rútóng: *Do as I say.* 照我说的做. 5 [习语] **as for sb / sth, as to sth** 关〔關〕于 guānyú; 至于 zhìyú. **as from** [尤用于美语] **as of** 自…时间起 zì…shíjiān qǐ: *a new job as from Monday* 自星期一开始的新工作. **as if / though** 好像 hǎoxiàng; 似乎 sìhū. **as it is** 实〔實〕际〔際〕上 shíjìshang. **ˌas it ˈwere** 可以说 kěyǐ shuō; 在一定程度上 zài yídìng chéngdù shàng. **as much** 同样的事 tóngyàng de shì: *I thought as much.* 我已经料到了. **as per** 按照 àn zhào: *Work as per instruc-*

tions 按照指令工作.

asbestos /æsˈbestɒs/ *n* [U] 石棉 shímián; 石绒 shíróng.

ascend /əˈsend/ *v* 1 [I,T] [正式用语]登(山等) dēng;上升 shàngshēng. 2 [习语] **ascend the throne** [正式用语]登位(为帝或皇后) dēngwèi. **ascendancy** *n* [U] [正式用语] *n* [U] 优[優]势[勢] yōushì;权[權]势 quánshì. **ascendant** *n* [习语] **in the aˈscendant** 占有支配地位 zhànyǒu zhīpèi dìwèi.

ascent /əˈsent/ *n* [C] 上升 shàngshēng;上坡 shàngpō.

ascertain /ˌæsəˈteɪn/ *v* [T] [正式用语] 查明 chámíng;探查 tànchá.

ascribe /əˈskraɪb/ *v* [T] *to* 归[歸]因于 guīyīn yú;把…归于 bǎ…guīyú: ～ *failure to bad luck* 把失败归因于运气不好.

aseptic /ˌeɪˈseptɪk; *US* əˈsep-/ *adj* 无[無]病菌的 wú bìngjūn de;防腐的 fángfǔde.

asexual /ˌeɪˈsekʃʊəl/ *adj* 1 无[無]性的 wúxìngde. 2 无性欲[慾]的 wú xìngyù de.

ash[1] /æʃ/ *n* 1 [U] (亦作 **ashes**) [pl] 灰 huī; 灰烬[燼] huījìn. 2 [pl] 骨灰 gǔhuī. ˈ**ashtray** *n* [C] 烟灰碟 yānhuīdié.

ash[2] /æʃ/ *n*(a) [C] 桉树[樹] ānshù. (b) 桉树木 ānshùmù.

ashamed /əˈʃeɪmd/ *adj* 羞愧的 xiūkuìde;害臊的 hàisàode.

ashore /əˈʃɔː(r)/ *adv* 上岸 shàng'àn; 在岸上 zài ànshang.

Asia /ˈeɪʃə/ *n* [U] 亚[亞]洲 Yàzhōu

aside /əˈsaɪd/ *adv* 在旁边[邊] zài pángbiān;向旁边 xiàng pángbiān: *He laid the book* ～. 他把书放到一边. **aside** *n* [C] 旁白 pángbái.

ask /ɑːsk; *US* æsk/ *v* 1 [I,T] 问 wèn;询问 xúnwèn: *I ～ed him where he lived*. 我问他住在什么地方. "*What time is it?*" *she ～ed*. "现在几点钟?"她问道. 2 [I,T] 要求 yāoqiú;请求 qǐngqiú: *I ～ed them to close the door*. 我请他们关上窗. 3 [T] 邀请 yāoqǐng;请 qǐng: ～ *him to the party* 邀请他参加聚会. 4 [习语] ˈ**ask for it / trouble** [非正式用语]自找麻烦 zì zhǎo máfan. 5 [短语动词] **ask after sb** 问起某人健康情况 wènqǐ mǒurén jiànkāng qíngkuàng. **ask for sb / sth** 找某人 zhǎo mǒurén;要求某物 yāoqiú mǒuwù.

askance /əˈskɑːns/ *adv* [习语] **look askance at sb / sth** 斜视(表示怀疑) xiéshì.

askew /əˈskjuː/ *adv, adj* 歪斜 wāixié; 歪斜的 wāixiéde.

asleep /əˈsliːp/ *adj* 1 睡着了的 shuìzháolede. 2 (四肢)发[發]麻的 fāmá de.

asp /æsp/ *n* [C] 角蝰(一种北非的小毒蛇) jiǎokuí.

asparagus /əˈspærəgəs/ *n* [U] 芦[蘆]笋 lúsǔn; 石刀柏 shídāobǎi.

aspect /ˈæspekt/ *n* [C] 1 样[樣]子 yàngzi; 外貌 wàimào. 2 [正式用语](建筑物的)方向 fāngxiàng,方位 fāngwèi.

aspersion /əˈspɜːʃn; *US* -ʒn/ *n* [习语] **cast aspersions on sb / sth** ⇨ CAST[1].

asphalt /ˈæsfælt; *US* -fɔːlt/ *n* [U] 沥[瀝]青 lìqīng. **asphalt** *v* [T] 铺沥青于(马路) pū lìqīng yú; 铺沥青(路面) pū lìqīng.

asphyxiate /əsˈfɪksɪeɪt/ *v* [T] 使窒息 shǐ zhìxī; 掐死 qiāsǐ. **asphyxiation** /əsˌfɪksɪˈeɪʃn/ *n* [U].

aspirate /ˈæspərət/ *n* [C] [语音] "h" 音 "h" yīn. **aspirate** /ˈæspəreɪt/ *v* [T] 发[發] "h"音 fā "h"yīn.

aspire /əˈspaɪə(r)/ *v* [I] (*to*) 渴望 kěwàng. **aspiration** /ˌæspəˈreɪʃn/ *n* [C,U] 抱负 bàofù;渴望 kěwàng.

aspirin /ˈæsprɪn, æspərɪn/ *n* [C,U] *n* 阿斯匹林 āsīpīlín; 阿斯匹林药[藥]片 āsīpīlín yàopiàn.

ass[1] /æs/ *n* [C] 1 驴[驢] lǘ. 2 [非正式用语] 傻瓜 shǎguā.

ass[2] /æs/ *n* [C] [⚠美俚]屁股 pìgu.

assail /əˈseɪl/ *v* [T] [正式用语]攻击[擊] gōngjī. **assailant** *n* [C] 攻击者 gōngjīzhě.

assassin /əˈsæsɪn; *US* -sn/ *n* [C] 凶[兇]手 xiōngshǒu; 刺客 cìkè. **assassinate** /əˈsæsɪneɪt; *US* -sən-/ *v* [T] 暗杀[殺] ànshā;行刺 xíngcì. **assassination** /əˌsæsɪˈneɪʃn; *US* -səˈneɪʃn / *n* [U,C].

assault /əˈsɔːlt/ *n* [C,U] 袭[襲]击[擊] xíjī; 突击 tūjī. **assault** *v* [T] 袭击 xíjī.

assemble /əˈsembl/ *v* 1 [I,T] 聚集 jùjí; 聚合 jùhé. 2 [T] 装[裝]配 zhuāngpèi.

assembly /əˈsemblɪ/ *n* [*pl* -ies] 1 [C] 集会[會] jíhuì;集合 jíhé. 2 [U] 装[裝]配 zhuāngpèi. **asˈsembly line** *n* [C] 装配线[綫] zhuāngpèixiàn.

assent /əˈsent/ *n* [U] [正式用语]同意 tóngyì. **assent** *v* [I] (*to*) [正式用语]同意 tóngyì.

assert /əˈsɜːt/ *v* [T] 1 宣称[稱] xuānchēng; 断[斷]言 duànyán. 2 维护[護] wéihù. 3 ～ **oneself** 坚[堅]持 jiānchí;表明 biǎomíng. **assertion** /əˈsɜːʃn/ *n* [U,C]. **assertive** *adj* 断言的 duànyánde;过[過]分自信的 guòfèn zìxìn de.

assess /əˈses/ *v* [T] 1 估值 gūzhí; 确[確]定 quèdìng. 2 评价[價] píngjià. **assessment** *n* [C,U]. **assessor** *n* [C] 估价员 gūjiàyuán.

asset /ˈæset/ *n* [C] 1 宝[寶]贵的人才、性质或技能 bǎoguìde réncái、xìngzhì huò jìnéng. 2 [常作 pl] 财产[產] cáichǎn;资产 zīchǎn.

assign /əˈsaɪn/ *v* [T] 1 分配 fēnpèi;指派 zhǐ-

A

pài. 2 选〔選〕派 xuǎnpài. 3 确〔確〕定时〔時〕间或地点〔點〕 quèdìng shíjiān huò dìdiǎn. **assignment** *n* 1 [C] (分派的)任务〔務〕 rènwù; (指定的)作业〔業〕 zuòyè. 2 [U] 分配 fēnpèi; 指派 zhǐpài.

assimilate /əˈsɪməleɪt/ *v* 1 [T] 吸收 xīshōu. 2 [I, T] 归〔歸〕化 guīhuà: *immigrants ~d into the country they moved to* 移民归化在所移居的国家. **assimilation** /əˌsɪməˈleɪʃn/ *n* [U].

assist /əˈsɪst/ *v* [I, T] [正式用语]帮〔幫〕助 bāngzhù; 援助 yuánzhù. **assistance** *n* [U] [正式用语]帮助 bāngzhù. **assistant** *n* [C] 帮助者 bāngzhùzhě: *a ˈshop-~ant* 商店店员.

associate[1] /əˈsəʊʃieɪt/ *v* 1 [T] (*with*) 联〔聯〕合 liánhé; 联想 liánxiǎng: *Whisky is often ~d with Scotland*. 威士忌酒常常和苏格兰联系在一起. *the problems ~d with homelessness* 这些问题是同无家可归相联系的. 2 [I, T] *with* 结交 jiéjiāo; 支持 zhīchí: *~ with people one doesn't really like*. 同并不真正喜欢的人结交.

associate[2] /əˈsəʊʃiət/ *n* [C] 伙〔夥〕伴 huǒbàn; 同事 tóngshì: *business ~s* 业务上的伙伴.

association /əˌsəʊsiˈeɪʃn/ *n* 1 [C] 协〔協〕会〔會〕 xiéhuì; 社团〔團〕 shètuán. 2 联〔聯〕合 liánhé; 联结 liánjié. 3 [C] 联想 liánxiǎng. 4 [习语] in association with sb 与〔與〕…联合、结交 yǔ …liánhé、jiéjiāo. **AsˌsociationˈFootball** *n* [U] 英国〔國〕式足球 Yīngguóshì zúqiú.

assorted /əˈsɔːtɪd/ *adj* 各式各样〔樣〕的 gèshìgèyàngde; 什锦的 shíjǐnde. **assortment** /əˈsɔːtmənt/ *n* [C] 各式物品的配合 gèshì wùpǐn de pèihé.

assume /əˈsjuːm; *US* əˈsuːm/ *v* [T] 1 假定 jiǎdìng. 2 采〔採〕取 cǎiqǔ; 呈现出 chéngxiàn chū: *~ control* 承担管理. *~ a greater importance* 变得更加重要. 3 装〔裝〕出 zhuāngchū: *~ ignorance* 装出无知的样子. **assumption** /əˈsʌmpʃn/ *n* 1 [C] 假定之事 jiǎdìng zhī shì. 2 [U] 承担〔擔〕 chéngdān; 担任 dānrèn.

assurance /əˈʃɔːrəns; *US* əˈʃʊərəns/ *n* 1 [U] 自信 zìxìn; 把握 bǎwò. 2 [C] 承诺 chéngnuò; 保证〔證〕 bǎozhèng: *give an ~* 作出保证. 3 [U] [尤用于英国英语]保险〔險〕 bǎoxiǎn: *life ~* 人寿保险.

assure /əˈʃɔː(r); *US* əˈʃʊər/ *v* [T] 1 断〔斷〕言 duànyán: *I ~ you that the money will be safe with me*. 我向你保证,钱在我这里是安全的. 2 使确〔確〕信 shǐ quèxìn. 3 保险〔險〕(特指保人寿险) bǎoxiǎn. **assured** *adj* 自信的 zìxìnde; 有信心的 yǒu xìnxīn de.

asterisk /ˈæstərɪsk/ *n* [C] 星形符号 (*) xīngxíng fúhào.

astern /əˈstɜːn/ *adv* 在船尾部 zài chuán wěibù.

asteroid /ˈæstərɔɪd/ *n* [C] 小行星 xiǎo xíngxīng.

asthma /ˈæsmə; *US* ˈæzmə/ *n* [U] 气〔氣〕喘病 qìchuǎnbìng. **asthmatic** /ˌæsˈmætɪk; *US* æz-/ *adj*.

astonish /əˈstɒnɪʃ/ *v* [T] 使惊〔驚〕讶 shǐ jīngyà; 吃惊 chījīng. **astonishing** *adj* 惊讶的 jīngyàde. **astonishment** *n* [U].

astound /əˈstaʊnd/ *v* [T] 使震惊 shǐ zhènjīng.

astral /ˈæstrəl/ *adj* 星的 xīngde.

astray /əˈstreɪ/ *adv* 迷途 mítú.

astride /əˈstraɪd/ *adj*, *prep* 跨着的 kuàzhede; 跨着 kuàzhe.

astrology /əˈstrɒlədʒɪ/ *n* [U] 占星术〔術〕 zhānxīngshù. **astrological** /ˌæstrəˈlɒdʒɪkl/ *adj*. **astrologer** /-dʒə(r)/ *n* [C].

astronaut /ˈæstrənɔːt/ *n* [C] 宇宙航行员 yǔzhòu hángxíng yuán.

astronomy /əˈstrɒnəmɪ/ *n* [U] 天文学〔學〕 tiānwénxué. **astronomer** /-nəmə(r)/ *n* [C]. **astronomical** /ˌæstrəˈnɒmɪkl/ *adj* 1 天文学的 tiānwénxuéde. 2 [非正式用语]极〔極〕巨大的. jí jùdà de.

astute /əˈstjuːt; *US* əˈstuːt/ *adj* 机〔機〕敏的 jīmǐnde; 狡猾的 jiǎohuáde. **astutely** *adv*. **astuteness** *n* [U].

asylum /əˈsaɪləm/ *n* 1 [C] [旧]疯〔瘋〕人院 fēngrényuàn; 精神病院 jīngshénbìngyuàn. 2 [U] 避难〔難〕 bìnàn: *political ~* 政治避难.

at /ət; 强式:æt/ *prep* 1 在…里〔裡〕面或附近 zài lǐmiàn huò fùjìn: *at the station* 在火车站. *study languages at university* 在大学学习语言. 2 向着 xiàngzhe; 朝着 cháozhe: *look at her* 看着她. *guess at the meaning* 猜测含意. 3 (表示距离): *hold sth at arm's length*. 伸直手臂拿着某物. 4 (表示时间): *at 2 o'clock* (在)两点钟(的时候). 5 (表示年龄): *He got married at (the age of) 24*. 他 24 岁时结了婚。6 (表示状态): *at war* 正进行战争. 7 被 bèi: *shocked at the news* 被这些消息所震惊. 8 (表示速度、价钱等): *driving at 70 mph* 以每小时 70 英里的速度开车. *exports valued at £1 million* 价值 100 万英镑的出口货. 9 (用于形容词后表示能力): *good at music* 擅长音乐.

ate /et/ *pt* of EAT.

atheism /ˈeɪθiɪzəm/ *n* [U] 无〔無〕神论〔論〕 wúshénlùn. **atheist** /ˈeɪθiɪst/ *n* [C]. **atheistic** *adj*.

athlete /ˈæθliːt/ *n* [C] 体〔體〕育家 tǐyùjiā; 运〔運〕动〔動〕员 yùndòngyuán. **athletic** /æθˈletɪk/ *adj* 1 体育的 tǐyùde; 运动的 yùndòngde. 2 体格健壮〔壯〕的 tǐgé jiànzhuàngde. **athletics** *n* [U] 竞〔競〕技 jìngjì; 运动 yùndòng; 体育 tǐyù.

atlas /ˈætləs/ *n* [C] 地图〔圖〕集 dìtújí.

atmosphere /ˈætməsfɪə(r)/ *n* [sing] 1 the atmosphere 大气〔氣〕dàqì. 2 空气 kōngqì. 3 气氛 qìfèn. **atmospheric** /ætməsˈferɪk/ *adj* 大气的 dàqìde.

atoll /ˈætɒl/ *n* [C] 环〔環〕礁 huánjiāo.

atom /ˈætəm/ *n* [C] 1 原子 yuánzǐ. 2〔喻〕微粒 wēilì. **atomic** /əˈtɒmɪk/ *adj* 原子的 yuánzǐde. aˌtomic ˈbomb (亦作 ˈatom bomb) 原子弹〔彈〕yuánzǐdàn.

atrocious /əˈtrəʊʃəs/ *adj* 1 残〔殘〕忍的 cánrěnde; 万〔萬〕恶〔惡〕的 wàn'ède. 2 [非正式用语] 坏〔壞〕透了的 huài tòu le de: ~ *weather* 坏透了的天气. **atrociously** *adv*.

atrocity /əˈtrɒsətɪ/ *n* [*pl* -ies] 1 [C] 残〔殘〕暴的行为〔爲〕cánbàode xíngwéi. 2 [U] 恶〔惡〕毒 èdú; 残忍 cánrěn; 残暴 cánbào.

attach /əˈtætʃ/ *v* 1 [T] 系〔繫〕上 jìshàng; 附上 fùshàng; 加上 jiāshàng. 2 [T] 依附 yīfù; 参〔參〕加 cānjiā. 3 [I,T] *to* (使)与〔與〕…相关〔關〕连 yǔ…xiāngguānlián: ~ *importance to her speech* 认为她的话重要. 4 [习语] be attached to sb / sth 喜爱〔愛〕xǐ'ài; 依恋〔戀〕yīliàn. **attachment** *n* 1 [C] 附着物 fùzhuówù; 附件 fùjiàn. 2 [U] (*to*) 喜爱 xǐ'ài; 爱慕 àimù.

attaché /əˈtæʃeɪ; *US* ˌætəˈʃeɪ/ *n* [C] 大使馆馆员 dàshǐguǎn guǎnyuán. atˈtaché case *n* [C] 公文包 gōngwénbāo.

attack /əˈtæk/ *n* 1 [C,U] (a) 攻击〔擊〕gōngjī; 进〔進〕攻. jìngōng. (b) 非难〔難〕fēinàn; 抨击 pēngjī. 2 [C] 疾病的发〔發〕作 jíbìngde fāzuò. **attack** *v* 1 [I,T] 攻击 gōngjī; 进攻 jìngōng. 2 [T] 干〔幹〕劲〔勁〕十足地干 gànjìn shízú de gàn. **attacker** *n* [C].

attain /əˈteɪn/ *v* [T] [正式用语] 取得 qǔdé; 得到 dédào. **attainable** *adj*. **attainment** *n* 1 [U] 达〔達〕到 dádào; 得到 dédào. 2 [C] 造诣 zàoyì.

attempt /əˈtempt/ *v* [T] 尝〔嘗〕试 chángshì; 企图〔圖〕qǐtú: ~ *to escape* 企图逃跑. **attempt** *n* [C] 1 企图 qǐtú; 尝试 chángshì. 2 [习语] an attempt on sb's life 企图杀〔殺〕害某人 qǐtú shāhài mǒurén.

attend /əˈtend/ *v* 1 [T] 出席 chūxí; 到场〔場〕dàochǎng: ~ *a meeting* 出席会议. 2 [I] *to* 专〔專〕心 zhuānxīn; 注意 zhùyì. 3 [I] (*to*) [正式用语] 护〔護〕理 hùlǐ; 照顾 zhàogù. **attendance** *n* 1 [C,U] 到场 dàochǎng; 出席 chūxí. 2 [C] 出席人数〔數〕chūxí rénshù: *a large ~ance* 出席人数众多. **attendant** *n* [C] 服务〔務〕员 fúwùyuán.

attention /əˈtenʃn/ *n* [U] 1 注意 zhùyì: *pay* (或 *attract*) ~ 注意. 2 照料 zhàoliào; 关〔關〕心 guānxīn; 修理 xiūlǐ: *My old car needs some* ~. 我的旧汽车需要修理一下. 3 [军事] 立正 lìzhèng.

attentive /əˈtentɪv/ *adj* 注意的 zhùyìde; 专〔專〕心的 zhuānxīnde. **attentively** *adv*.

attest /əˈtest/ *v* [I,T] (*to*) [正式用语] 证〔證〕明 zhèngmíng.

attic /ˈætɪk/ *n* [C] 顶楼〔樓〕dǐnglóu; 阁楼 gélóu.

attitude /ˈætɪtjuːd; *US* -tuːd/ *n* [C] 1 态〔態〕度 tàidù; 看法 kànfǎ. 2 [正式用语] 姿势〔勢〕zīshì; 姿态 zītài.

attorney /əˈtɜːnɪ/ *n* [C] [美语] 律师〔師〕lǜshī.

attract /əˈtrækt/ *v* [T] 1 吸引 xīyǐn: *A magnet ~s steel*. 磁石吸引钢. 2 引起兴〔興〕趣、注意等 yǐnqǐ xìngqù、zhùyì děng; 招引 zhāoyǐn: *a window display that ~s customers* 吸引顾客注意的橱窗. 3 诱惑 yòuhuò; 有吸引力 yǒu xīyǐnlì. **attraction** /əˈtrækʃn/ *n* 1 [U] 吸引 xīyǐn; 吸引力 xīyǐnlì. 2 [C] 吸引人的事物 xīyǐn rén de shìwù. **attractive** *adj* 有吸引力的 yǒu xīyǐnlì de; 讨人喜欢〔歡〕的 tǎo rén xǐhuān de.

attribute /əˈtrɪbjuːt/ *v* [T] *to* 归〔歸〕因于 guī yīn yú: ~ *her success to hard work*. 她的成功是因为勤奋. **attribute** /ˈætrɪbjuːt/ *n* [C] 属〔屬〕性 shǔxìng; 性质〔質〕xìngzhì.

attributive /əˈtrɪbjʊtɪv/ *adj* [语法] 定语的 dìngyǔde.

aubergine /ˈəʊbəʒiːn/ *n* [C] 茄子 qiézi.

auburn /ˈɔːbən/ *adj* (尤指头发) 赭色的 zhěsède.

auction /ˈɔːkʃn/ *n* [C,U] 拍卖〔賣〕pāimài. **auction** *v* [T] 拍卖 pāimài. **auctioneer** /ˌɔːkʃəˈnɪə(r)/ *n* [C] 拍卖人 pāimàirén.

audacious /ɔːˈdeɪʃəs/ *adj* 大胆〔膽〕的 dàdǎnde; 鲁莽的 lǔmǎngde. **audaciously** *adv*. **audacity** /ɔːˈdæsətɪ/ *n* [U].

audible /ˈɔːdəbl/ *adj* 听〔聽〕得见的 tīng dé jiàn de. **audibly** *adv*.

audience /ˈɔːdɪəns/ *n* [C] 1 (聚集在一起的) 听〔聽〕众〔衆〕tīngzhòng. 2 (分散的) 听众 tīngzhòng. 3 接见 jiējiàn: *an ~ with the Queen* 王后接见.

audio /ˈɔːdɪəʊ/ *adj* 听〔聽〕觉〔覺〕的 tīngjuéde. ˈ**audiobook** *n* [C] 有声〔聲〕书〔書〕籍 yǒushēng shūjí; 有声读〔讀〕物 yǒushēng dúwù. ˌ**audio-ˈvisual** *adj* 听〔聽〕觉〔覺〕视觉的 tīngjué shìjuéde.

audit /ˈɔːdɪt/ *n* [C] 审〔審〕计 shěnjì; 查账〔賬〕cházhàng. **audit** *v* [T] 查账 cházhàng. **au-**

ditor *n* [C].

audition /ɔːˈdɪʃn/ *n* [C] 试听〔聽〕shìtīng;试演 shìyǎn. **audition** *v* [I,T] (使)试听 shìtīng;(使)试演 shìyǎn.

auditorium /ˌɔːdɪˈtɔːrɪəm/ *n* [C] 会〔會〕堂 huìtáng;礼〔禮〕堂 lǐtáng.

augment /ɔːgˈment/ *v* [T] [正式用语]增大 zēngdà;增加 zēngjiā.

augur /ˈɔːgə(r)/ *v* [习语] **augur ˈwell / ˈill for sb / sth** [正式用语]是好(坏)兆头〔頭〕shì hǎo zhàotóu.

August /ˈɔːgəst/ *n* [U,C] 八月 bāyuè.

august /ɔːˈgʌst/ *adj* 尊严〔嚴〕的 zūnyánde.

aunt / ɑːnt; *US* ænt/ [C] 姑母 gūmǔ;姨母 yímǔ;伯母 bómǔ;叔母 shūmǔ;舅母 jiùmǔ. **auntie** (亦作 **aunty**) *n* [C] [非正式用语] aunt 的昵称 aunt de nìchēng.

au pair /ˌəʊ ˈpeə(r)/ *n* [C] "互裨"(指帮助料理家务,换取食宿以学习语言的外国年轻人) hùbì.

aura /ˈɔːrə/ *n* [C] 气〔氣〕氛 qìfèn;氛围〔圍〕fènwéi.

aural /ˈɔːrəl,亦作 ˈaʊrəl/ *adj*. 耳的 ěrde;听〔聽〕觉〔覺〕的 tīngjuéde.

auspices /ˈɔːspɪsɪz/ *n* [pl] [习语] **under the auspices of sb / sth** [正式用语]在…的赞助下 zài…de zànzhù xià.

auspicious /ɔːˈspɪʃəs/ *adj* [正式用语]吉祥的 jíxiángde;繁荣〔榮〕的 fánróngde. **auspiciously** *adv*.

austere /ɒˈstɪə(r),亦作 ɔːˈstɪə(r)/ *adj* 1 简朴〔樸〕的 jiǎnpǔde 2 苦行的 kǔxíngde;严〔嚴〕格的 yángéde. **austerely** *adv*. **austerity** / ɒˈsterətɪ,亦作 ɔːˈsterətɪ/ *n* [C,U] [*pl* -ies].

Australia /ɒˈstreɪlɪə, ɔːˈstreɪlɪə/ *n* [U] 澳大利亚〔亞〕Aodàlìyà.

Australian /ɒˈstreɪlɪən, ɔːˈstreɪlɪən/ *adj* 澳大利亚〔亞〕的 Aodàlìyàde. **Australian** *n* [C] 澳大利亚人 Aodàlìyàrén.

authentic /ɔːˈθentɪk/ *adj* 真实〔實〕的 zhēnshíde;可靠的 kěkàode. **authentically** /-klɪ/ *adv*. **authenticate** *v* [T] 证〔證〕实 zhèngshí. **authenticity** *n* [U] 可靠性 kěkàoxìng;真实性 zhēnshíxìng.

author /ˈɔːθə(r)/ *n* [C] 1 作者 zuòzhě;作家 zuòjiā. 2 创〔創〕始人 chuàngshǐrén. **authoress** /ˈɔːθərɪs/ *n* [C] 女作者 nǚ zuòzhě;女作家 nǚ zuòjiā.

authoritative /ɔːˈθɒrətətɪv; *US* -teɪtɪv/ *adj* 1 有权〔權〕威的 yǒu quánwēi de. 2 命令的 mìnglìngde. **authoritatively** *adv*.

authority /ɔːˈθɒrətɪ/ *n* [*pl* -ies] 1 (a) [U] 权力 quánlì;威信 wēixìn. (b) [C] 当〔當〕局 dāngjú. 2 [C] 专〔專〕家 zhuānjiā: *She is an ~ on physics*. 她是物理专家.

authorize /ˈɔːθəraɪz/ *v* [T] 授权〔權〕shòuquán. **authorization** /ˌɔːθəraɪˈzeɪʃn; *US* -rɪˈz- / *n* [U].

autobiography /ˌɔːtəˌbaɪˈɒgrəfɪ/ *n* [C] [*pl* -ies] 自传〔傳〕zìzhuàn. **autobiographical** /ˌɔːtəbaɪəˈgræfɪkl/ *adj*.

autocrat /ˈɔːtəkræt/ *n* [C] (a) 专〔專〕制君主 zhuānzhì jūnzhǔ. (b) 独〔獨〕裁者 dúcáizhě. **autocratic** /ˌɔːtəˈkrætɪk/ *adj*.

autograph /ˈɔːtəgrɑːf; *US* -græf/ *n* [C] 亲〔親〕笔〔筆〕签〔簽〕名 qīnbǐ qiānmíng. **autograph** *v* [T] 签署 qiānshǔ.

automate /ˈɔːtəmeɪt/ *v* [T] 使自动〔動〕化 shǐ zìdònghuà.

automatic /ˌɔːtəˈmætɪk/ *adj* 1 (机器)自动〔動〕的 zìdòngde. 2 (动作)无〔無〕意识〔識〕的 wú yìshí de. **automatic** *n* [C] 小型自动武器 xiǎoxíng zìdòng wǔqì;自动机〔機〕器 zìdòng jīqì. **automatically** /-klɪ/ *adv*.

automation /ˌɔːtəˈmeɪʃn/ *n* [U] 自动〔動〕化 zìdònghuà;自动操作 zìdòng cāozuò.

automobile /ˈɔːtəməbiːl/ *n* [C] [尤用于美语]汽车 qìchē.

autonomous /ɔːˈtɒnəməs/ *adj* 自治的 zìzhìde;自主的 zìzhǔde. **autonomy** /-mɪ/ *n* [U] 自治 zìzhì. **auˌtonomous ˈregion** *n* [C] 自治区〔區〕zìzhìqū.

autopsy /ˈɔːtɒpsɪ/ *n* [C] [*pl* -ies] (医学)尸〔屍〕体〔體〕检〔檢〕验〔驗〕shītǐ jiǎnyàn.

autumn /ˈɔːtəm/ *n* [U,C] 秋季 qiūjì;秋天 qiūtiān. **autumnal** /ɔːˈtʌmnəl/ *adj*.

auxiliary /ɔːgˈzɪlɪərɪ/ *adj* 辅〔輔〕助的 fǔzhùde;协〔協〕助的 xiézhùde. **auxiliary** *n* [C] [*pl* -ies] 辅助者 fǔzhùzhě;助手 zhùshǒu;辅助物 fǔzhùwù. **auˌxiliary ˈverb** *n* [C] 助动〔動〕词 zhùdòngcí (如 "Do you know where he has gone?" 中的 "do" 和 "has")

avail /əˈveɪl/ *v* [正式用语] ~ **oneself of** 利用 lìyòng. **avail** *n* [习语] **of no avail** 无〔無〕用 wúyòng. **to no aˈvail, without aˈvail** 完全无用 wánquán wúyòng.

available /əˈveɪləbl/ *adj* 可获〔獲〕得的 kě huòdé de;可用的 kěyòng de: *There are no tickets* ~. 没有票了. **availability** /əˌveɪləˈbɪlətɪ/ *n* [U].

avalanche /ˈævəlɑːnʃ; *US* -læntʃ/ *n* [C] 1 雪崩 xuěbēng. 2 [喻] 大量涌来 dàliàng yǒnglái: *an ~ of letters* 大量信件涌来.

avarice /ˈævərɪs/ *n* [U] [正式用语]贪心 tānxīn. **avaricious** /ˌævəˈrɪʃəs/ *adj*.

avenge /əˈvendʒ/ *v* [T] 替…报〔報〕仇 tì…bàochóu: ~ *his father's death* 报了他的杀父之仇.

avenue /ˈævənjuː; *US* -nuː/ *n* [C] 1 林阴

〔陰〕道 línyīndào. 2［喻］方法 fāngfǎ；途径〔徑〕tújìng：*explore several ~s* 探索几种方法.

average /ˈævərɪdʒ/ *n* 1［C］平均数〔數〕píngjūnshù. 2［U］一般水准〔準〕yìbān shuǐzhǔn. **average** *adj* 平均的 píngjūnde：*the ~ age* 平均年龄. **average** *v* 1［I,T］平均为〔爲〕píngjūn wéi；求出…的平均数〔數〕qiúchū…de píngjūnshù. 2［T］平均做 píngjūnzuò：~ *200 miles a day* 平均一天 200 英里.

averse /əˈvɜːs/ *adj to*［正式用语］反对〔對〕的 fǎnduìde：*not ~ to new ideas* 不反对新的主意.

aversion /əˈvɜːʃn; *US* əˈvɜːʒn/ *n* 1［C,U］嫌恶〔惡〕xiánwù. 2［C］讨厌〔厭〕的人或事物 tǎoyànde rén huò shìwù.

avert /əˈvɜːt/ *v*［T］1 避开 bìkāi；防止 fángzhǐ. 2［非正式用语］转〔轉〕移(目光等) zhuǎnyí.

aviary /ˈeɪvɪərɪ; *US* -vɪerɪ/ *n*［C］［*pl* -ies］(大型)鸟舍 niǎoshè.

aviation /ˌeɪvɪˈeɪʃn/ *n*［U］航空 hángkōng；航空学〔學〕hángkōngxué；航空术〔術〕hángkōngshù.

avid /ˈævɪd/ *adj* 渴望的 kěwàngde. **avidly** *adv*.

avocado /ˌævəˈkɑːdəʊ/ *n*［C］［*pl* ~s］鳄梨 èlí.

avoid /əˈvɔɪd/ *v* 1［T］避免 bìmiǎn；逃避 táobì. 2 防止 fángzhǐ；阻止 zǔzhǐ. **avoidable** *adj* 可避免的 kě bìmiǎn de. **avoidance** *n*［U］.

avow /əˈvaʊ/ *v*［T］［正式用语］公开表示 gōngkāi biǎoshì.

await /əˈweɪt/ *v*［T］［正式用语］等待 děngdài；等候 děnghòu.

awake[1] /əˈweɪk/ *adj* 醒着的 xǐngzhede；醒来的 xǐngláide.

awake[2] /əˈweɪk/ *v*［*pt* **awoke** /əˈwəʊk/, *pp* **awoken** /əˈwəʊkən/］［I,T］醒 xǐng；唤醒 huànxǐng.

awaken /əˈweɪkən/ *v* 1［I,T］醒 xǐng；唤醒 huànxǐng. 2［T］激起 jīqǐ：~ *sb's interest* 引起某人兴趣. 3［短语动词］**awaken sb to sth** 使认〔認〕识〔識〕到 shǐ rènshi dào. **awakening** /-knɪŋ/ *n*［sing］认识 rènshi；意识 yìshí.

award /əˈwɔːd/ *v*［T］授予 shòuyǔ；判给 pàngěi：~ *her first prize* 授予她一等奖. **award** *n*［C］奖〔獎〕jiǎng；奖品 jiǎngpǐn：*an ~ for bravery* 勇敢奖.

aware /əˈweə(r)/ *adj of /that* 知道的 zhīdàode；意识到的 yìshídào de. **awareness** *n*［U］.

away /əˈweɪ/ *adv* 1 在远〔遠〕处〔處〕zài yuǎnchù；到远处 dào yuǎnchù. 2 继〔繼〕续〔續〕不断〔斷〕地 jìxù búduàn de：*He was working ~*. 他在继续不断地工作. 3（表示消失、减少）：*The water boiled ~*. 水被煮干了. 4［体育］在客场〔場〕zài kèchǎng：*play the next match ~* 打下一场客场比赛.

awe /ɔː/ *n*［U］敬畏 jìngwèi. **ˈawe-inspiring** *adj* 令人畏惧〔懼〕的 lìng rén wèijù de. **awesome** *adj* 可畏的 kěwèide.

awful /ˈɔːfl/ *adj* 1 可怕的 kěpàde：*an ~ accident* 可怕的事故. 2［非正式用语］糟糕的 zāogāode；极〔極〕度的 jídùde：~ *weather* 糟糕的天气. **awfully** *adv*［非正式用语］非常 fēicháng：~ *hot* 非常热.

awhile /əˈwaɪl; *US* əˈhwaɪl/ *adv* 片刻 piànkè.

awkward /ˈɔːkwəd/ *adj* 1 不灵〔靈〕活的 bù línghuó de；笨拙的 bènzhuóde. 2 难〔難〕使用的 nán shǐyòng de. 3 不方便的 bù fāngbiàn de；造成困难的 zàochéng kùnnande：*arrive at an ~ time* 在不方便的时候到达. 4 尴〔尷〕尬的 gāngàde：*an ~* **silence** 尴尬的沉默. **awkwardly** *adv*. **awkwardness** *n*［U］.

awning /ˈɔːnɪŋ/ *n*［C］雨棚 yǔpéng；凉棚 liángpéng.

awoke *pt* of AWAKE[2].

awoken *pp* of AWAKE[2].

axe（亦作，尤用于美语 **ax**）/æks/ *n*［C］1 斧 fǔ. 2［习语］ˌ**have an ˈaxe to grind** 别有用心 bié yǒu yòngxīn；另有企图〔圖〕lìng yǒu qǐtú. **axe** *v*［T］削减 xuējiǎn；解雇 jiěgù.

axiom /ˈæksɪəm/ *n*［C］公理 gōnglǐ. **axiomatic** /ˌæksɪəˈmætɪk/ *adj* 不言自喻的 bù yán zì yù de.

axis /ˈæksɪs/ *n*［C］［*pl* **axes** /ˈæksiːz/］1 轴 zhóu：*the earth's ~* 地轴. 2 轴线〔綫〕zhóuxiàn.

axle /ˈæksl/ *n*［C］轮〔輪〕轴 lúnzhóu.

aye（亦作 **ay**）/aɪ/ *interj*［废，方］是 shì. **aye** *n*［C］赞成票 zànchéngpiào.

azure /ˈæʒə(r)，亦作 ˈæzjʊə(r)/ *adj n*［U］天蓝〔藍〕色(的) tiānlánsè.

B b

B, b /biː/ *n*［C］［*pl* **B's, b's** /biːz/］英语的第二个〔個〕字母 Yīngyǔde dì'èrgè zìmǔ.

b *abbr* born 出生 chūshēng.

babble /ˈbæbl/ *v*［I］孩子般喋喋不休 háizibān diédié bù xiū. **babble** *n*［sing］.

babe /beɪb/ *n*［C］［古］婴儿〔兒〕yīng'ér.

baboon /bəˈbuːn; *US* bæ-/ *n*［C］狒狒 fèifèi.

baby /ˈbeɪbɪ/ *n*［C］［*pl* -bies］1 婴儿〔兒〕yīng'ér. 2［尤用于美国俚语］爱〔愛〕人 àirén.

babyish *adj* 幼儿的 yòu'érde；幼儿般的 yòu'érbānde；孩子气〔氣〕的 háiziqìde. ˈbabysit *v* [-tt-, *pt*, *pp* -sat] [I] 做临〔臨〕时〔時〕保姆 zuò línshí bǎomǔ. ˈbabysitter *n* [C].

bachelor /ˈbætʃələ(r)/ *n* [C] 1 单〔單〕身汉〔漢〕 dānshēnhàn. 2 Bachelor 学〔學〕士 xuéshì：*B～ of Arts / Science* 文学士 wénxuéshì/理学士 lǐxuéshì.

back[1] /bæk/ *n* [C] 1 背 bèi. 2 后〔後〕面 hòumiàn；背面 bèimiàn：*sit in the ～ of the car* 坐在汽车的后面. *the ～ of a cheque* 支票的背面. 3 椅背 yǐbèi. 4 [习语] ˌback to ˈfront 前后倒置 qiánhòu dàozhì. behind sb's ˈback 搞小动〔動〕作(背着某人说闲话) gǎo xiǎodòngzuò. get / put sb's ˈback up [非正式用语] 使某人生气〔氣〕 shǐ mǒurén shēngqì. get off sb's ˈback [非正式用语] 不再嘲笑某人 búzài cháoxiào mǒurén. put one's ˈback into sth 发〔發〕奋〔奮〕做某事 fāfèn zuò mǒushì；埋头〔頭〕做某事 máitóu zuò mǒushì. back *adj* 在后面的 zài hòumiàn de：*the ～ door* 后门 hòumén. ˈbackache *n* [U, C] 背痛 bèitòng. ˌbackˈbencher *n* [C] (英国)下(议)院后座议〔議〕员 xiàyuàn hòuzuò yìyuán. ˈbackbone *n* 1 [C] 脊椎骨 jǐzhuīgǔ. 2 [sing] [喻]骨干〔幹〕 gǔgàn；支柱 zhīzhù. 3 [U] [喻]刚〔剛〕强 gāngqiáng；坚〔堅〕毅 jiānyì. ˈback-breaking *adj* (工作)累死人的 lèisǐrénde. ˈbackground *n* 1 [sing] (a) 背景 bèijǐng；后景 hòujǐng. (b) [喻]有关〔關〕情况 yǒuguān qíngkuàng；背景 bèijǐng. 2 [C] 个〔個〕人经〔經〕历〔歷〕 gèrén jīnglì. ˈbackhand *n* [C] (网球等)反手击〔擊〕球 fǎnshǒu jīqiú. ˌbackˈhanded *adj* 1 反手击球的 fǎnshǒu jī qiú de. 2 讽〔諷〕刺挖苦的 fěngcì wākǔ de：*a ˌ～handed ˈcompliment* 带讽刺的恭维话. backless *adj*. ˈbacklog *n* [C] 积〔積〕压〔壓〕的工作 jīyāde gōngzuò. ˌback ˈnumber *n* [C] 过〔過〕期报〔報〕纸等 guòqī bàozhǐ děng. ˈbackpack *n* [C] [尤用于美语]帆布背包 fānbù bēibāo. ˈbackside *n* [C][非正式用语]屁股 pìgu. ˈbackstage *adv* 在后台 zài hòutái. ˈbackstroke *n* [U] 仰泳 yǎngyǒng. ˈbackwater *n* [C] 1 死水 sǐshuǐ；滞水 zhìshuǐ. 2 [喻]死气〔氣〕沉沉的地方 sǐqì chénchén de dìfang.

back[2] /bæk/ *adv* 1 向后〔後〕 xiàng hòu；在后面 zài hòumiàn：*Stand ～, please!* 请往后站! 2 返回 fǎnhuí：*put the book ～ on the shelf* 把书放回书架. 3 以前 yǐqián：*a few years ～* 几年以前. 4 回答 huídá；作为〔爲〕报〔報〕复〔復〕 zuòwéi bàofù：*I'll phone you ～*. 我会给你回电话. 5 [习语] ˌback and ˈforth 来〔來〕回地 láihuíde；反复〔復〕地 fǎnfùde. ˈbackbiting *n* [U] 背后说人坏〔壞〕话 bèihòu shuō rén huàihuà. ˈbackdate *v* [T] 回溯 huísù. ˈbackfire *v* [I] 1 (车辆)发〔發〕生逆火的响〔響〕声〔聲〕 fāshēng nìhuǒde xiǎngshēng. 2 [喻](计划等)失败 shībài. ˈbacklash *n* [sing] 强烈的反应〔應〕 qiángliède fǎnyìng.

back[3] /bæk/ *v* 1 [I, T] 倒退 dàotuì；使退后〔後〕 shǐ tuìhòu：*～ a car* (汽车)倒车. 2 [I] *onto* 背朝着 bèi cháo zhe：*The house ～s onto the park*. 这座房子背朝着公园. 3 [T] 支持 zhīchí；援助 yuánzhù. 4 下赌注于(某匹马) xià dǔzhù yú. 5 [T] 加于背面 jiā yú bèimiàn. 6 [短语动词] back ˈdown 放弃〔棄〕要求 fàngqì yāoqiú. back out (of sth) 收回(诺言等) shōuhuí. back sb / sth up (a) 支持某人 zhīchí mǒurén. (b) 证〔證〕实〔實〕 zhèngshí. (c) [电脑](为防止丢失)复〔複〕制〔製〕出备〔備〕用拷贝 fùzhì chū bèiyòng kǎobèi. backer *n* [C] (尤指财务上的)支持者 zhīchízhě. backing *n* [U] 1 支持 zhīchí；帮〔幫〕助 bāngzhù. 2 背衬〔襯〕 bèichèn. ˈbackup *n* 1 [U] 额外支持 éwài zhīchí. 2 [U, C] [电脑] 储备拷贝 chǔbèi kǎobèi.

backgammon /bækˈgæmən/ *n* [U] 十五子游戏〔戲〕 shíwǔzǐ yóuxì.

backward /ˈbækwəd/ *adj* 1 向后〔後〕的 xiànghòude：*a ～ glance* 向后的一瞥. 2 落后的 luòhòude：*a ～ child* 成长迟缓的孩子. backwards (亦作 backward) *adv* 1 向后地 xiànghòude. 2 倒 dào；反 fǎn：*say the alphabet ～(s)* 倒背字母表.

bacon /ˈbeɪkən/ *n* [U] 咸〔鹹〕肉 xiánròu；熏〔燻〕肉 xūnròu.

bacteria /bækˈtɪərɪə/ *n* [pl] [*sing* -ium /-ɪəm/] 细菌 xìjūn. bacterial /-rɪəl/ *adj*.

bad /bæd/ *adj* [worse /wɜːs/, worst /wɜːst/] 1 低劣的 dīliède：*a ～ actor* 蹩脚的演员. 2 坏〔壞〕的 huàide；不道德的 bú dàodéde. 3 使人不愉快的 shǐ rén bù yúkuài de：*～ news* 不好的消息. 4 严〔嚴〕重的 yánzhòngde；厉〔厲〕害的 lìhaide：*a ～ mistake* 严重的错误. *in a ～ mood* 心情很坏，爱生气. 5 (食物)腐坏〔壞〕的 fǔhuàide：*The fish has gone ～*. 这鱼坏了. 6 有病的 yǒubìngde：*a ～ back* 有病的背部. 7 有害的 yǒuhàide：*Smoking is ～ for you*. 吸烟对你有害. 8 [习语] be in sb's bad books ⇨BOOK[1]. be bad ˈluck 倒霉 dǎoméi；不幸 búxìng. ˌbad ˈblood 仇恨 chóuhèn；生气〔氣〕 shēngqì. go from ˌbad to ˈworse 愈来愈坏 yù lái yù huài. have a bad night ⇨NIGHT. not (so) ˈbad [非正式用语] 相当〔當〕好 xiāngdāng hǎo. too bad [非正式用语]可惜 kěxī；不幸 búxìng：*It's too ～ she is ill*. 不幸她病了. ˌbad ˈdebt *n* [C] (无法收回的)坏账〔賬〕 huàizhàng；呆账 dāizhàng. baddy *n* [C] [*pl* -ies] [非正式用语](小说、电影中的)反面人物 fǎnmiàn rénwù. ˌbad ˈlanguage *n* [U] 粗话 cūhuà；不礼〔禮〕貌的话 bù lǐmàode huà. badly *adv* (worse, worst) 1 很坏 hěnhuài;恶[惡]劣 èliè. 2 大大地 dàdàde;非常地 fēichángde: *~ly wounded* 伤得很重. *need some money ~ly* 很需要钱. 3 [习语] badly ˈoff 景况不好 jǐngkuàng bùhǎo;贫困 pínkùn. badness *n* [U]. ˈbad-tempered *adj* 脾气[氣]坏的 píqì huài de.

bade *pt* of BID 2.

badge /bædʒ/ *n* [C] 徽章 huīzhāng;证[證]章 zhèngzhāng;标[標]记 biāojì.

badger[1] /ˈbædʒə(r)/ *n* [C] 獾 huān.

badger[2] /ˈbædʒə(r)/ *v* [T] 烦扰[擾] fánrǎo;使困扰 shǐ kùnrǎo.

badminton /ˈbædmɪntən/ *n* [U] 羽毛球 yǔmáoqiú.

baffle /ˈbæfl/ *v* [T] 阻碍[礙] zǔ'ài;使困惑 shǐ kùnhuò.

bag[1] /bæg/ *n* [C] 1 袋 dài;包 bāo: *a paper ~* 纸袋. 2 bags [pl] *of* [非正式用语] 许多 xǔduō. 3 [习语] in the ˈbag [非正式用语] 十拿九稳[穩]的 shí ná jiǔ wěn de.

bag[2] /bæg/ *v* [-gg-] [T] 1 把…装[裝]进[進]袋 bǎ…zhuāngjìn dài. 2 捕杀[殺] bǔshā. 3 [非正式用语]要求拥[擁]有 yāoqiú yōngyǒu.

baggage /ˈbægɪdʒ/ *n* [U] = LUGGAGE. ˈbaggage reclaim *n* [C] (机场)取行李处[處] qǔxínglichù.

baggy /ˈbægɪ/ *adj* [-ier, -iest] 松[鬆]垂的 sōngchuíde: *~ trousers* 松垂的裤子.

bagpipes /ˈbægpaɪps/ *n* [pl] 风[風]笛 fēngdí.

bail[1] /beɪl/ *n* [U] (a) 保释[釋]金 bǎoshìjīn. (b) 保释 bǎoshì. bail *v* [短语动词] bail sb out (a) 交保证金释放某人 jiāo bǎozhèngjīn shìfàng mǒurén. (b) [喻] 帮[幫]助某人摆[擺]脱困难[難] bāngzhù mǒurén bǎituō kùnnan.

bail[2] (亦作 bale) /beɪl/ *v* [I, T] 将[將]船内的水舀出 jiāng chuán nèi de shuǐ yǎochū.

bail[3] /beɪl/ *n* [C] (板球)柱门[門]上的横木 zhùmén shàng de héngmù.

bailiff /ˈbeɪlɪf/ *n* [C] 1 法警 fǎjǐng. 2 (英国)地主代理人 dìzhǔ dàilǐrén.

bait /beɪt/ *n* [U] 1 饵 ěr. 2 [喻]诱惑物 yòuhuòwù. bait *v* [T] 1 装[裝]饵于 zhuāng ěr yú. 2 侮弄(某人) wǔnòng.

bake /beɪk/ *v* 1 [I, T] 烤 kǎo;烘 hōng;焙 bèi. 2 [I, T] 烧硬 shāoyìng;烤硬 kǎoyìng. 3 [I] [非正式用语] 非常炎热[熱] fēicháng yánrè: *It's baking (hot) today!* 今天热得厉害! baker *n* [C] 面[麵]包师[師]傅 miànbāo shīfù;bakery *n* [C] [*pl* -ies] 面包房 miànbāofáng. ˈbaking-powder *n* [U] 焙粉(化学膨松剂) bèifěn.

balance[1] /ˈbæləns/ *n* 1 [U] 平衡 pínghéng: *keep one's ~* 保持平衡. *lose one's ~* 失却平衡. 2 [C] 秤 chèng;天平 tiānpíng. 3 [U, sing] 和谐 héxié;协[協]调 xiétiáo: *a ~ between work and play* 工作和玩耍的平衡协调. 4 [C] 账目上的 余[餘]额 zhàngmù shàng de yú'é. 5 [C] 结欠 jiéqiàn. 6 [习语] in the balance 未定 wèidìng. on ˈbalance 总[總]的说来[來] zǒng de shuō lái. ˈbalance sheet *n* [C] 资产[產]负债表 zīchǎn fùzhàibiǎo

balance[2] /ˈbæləns/ *v* 1 (a) [T] 使(某物)平衡 shǐ pínghéng. (b) [I] (人)保持平衡 bǎochí pínghéng: *He ~d on the edge of the table*. 他在桌子边上保持平衡不倒. 2 [T] 使均衡 shǐ jūnhéng. 3 [T] 结算 jiésuàn;相抵 xiāngdǐ.

balcony /ˈbælkənɪ/ *n* [C] [*pl* -ies] 1 阳[陽]台[臺] yángtái. 2 (剧院)楼[樓]厅[廳] lóutīng.

bald /bɔːld/ *adj* 1 秃头[頭]的 tūtóude;秃的 tūde;无[無]毛的 wú máo de. 2 [喻]单[單]调的 dāndiàode;简单的 jiǎndānde: *a ~ statement* 枯燥无味的陈述. balding *adj* 变[變]秃的 biàntūde. baldly *adv*. baldness *n* [U].

bale[1] /beɪl/ *n* [C] 包 bāo;捆 kǔn.

bale[2] /beɪl/ *v* 1 = BAIL[2]. 2 [习语] bale out (of sth) 飞[飛]机[機]出事时[時]跳伞 fēijī chūshì shí tiàosǎn.

balk (亦作 baulk) /bɔːk/ *v* [I] (*at*) 犹[猶]豫 yóuyù;畏缩 wèisuō.

ball[1] /bɔːl/ *n* [C] 1 球 qiú;球戏[戲] qiúxì. 2 球状[狀]物 qiúzhuàngwù: *a ~ of wool* 一团毛线. 3 球形突出部分 qiúxíng tūchū bùfen: *the ~ of one's foot* 拇趾底部的肉球 mǔzhǐ dǐbùde ròuqiú. 4 [常作 pl] [非正式用语]睾丸 gāowán. 5 [习语] keep / start the ball rolling 继[繼]续[續] / 开[開]始活动[動] jìxù / kāishǐ huódòng. (be) on the ˈball [非正式用语]机[機]警的 jījǐngde;留心的 liúxīnde. ˈball game *n* 1 (a) [C] 球赛 qiúsài. (b) [U] [美语]棒球 bàngqiú. 2 [C] [非正式用语] 情况 qíngkuàng. ˈballpark *n* 1 [C] 棒球场[場] bàngqiúchǎng 2 大致范[範]围[圍] dàzhì fànwéi;大致程度 dàzhì chéngdù: *be in the (right) ballpark* 大致正确. *ballpark figure/estimate* 大概的数字/估计. ˈballpoint (亦作 ˌball-point ˈpen) *n* [C] 圆珠笔[筆] yuánzhūbǐ.

ball[2] /bɔːl/ *n* [C] 1 舞会[會] wǔhuì. 2 [习语] have a ˈball [非正式用语]痛快地玩 tòngkuàide wán. ˈballroom *n* [C] 舞厅[廳] wǔtīng.

ballad /ˈbæləd/ *n* [C] 民歌 míngē;歌谣 gēyáo.

ballast /ˈbæləst/ *n* [U] 1 压[壓]舱[艙]物 yācāngwù. 2 (气球)沙囊 shānáng.

ballerina /ˌbæləˈriːnə/ *n* [C] 芭蕾舞女演员 bāléiwǔ nǚ yǎnyuán.

B

ballet /ˈbæleɪ/ *n* 1 (a) [U] 芭蕾舞 bālěiwǔ. (b) [C] 芭蕾舞剧〔劇〕 bālěiwǔjù. 2 [C] 芭蕾舞团〔團〕 bālěiwǔtuán.

ballistics /bəˈlɪstɪks/ *n* [U] 弹〔彈〕道学〔學〕 dàndàoxué. **balˌlistic ˈmissile** *n* [C] 弹道导〔導〕弹 dàndào dǎodàn.

balloon /bəˈluːn/ *n* [C] 1 气〔氣〕球 qìqiú. 2 (亦作 **hot-ˈair balloon**) 热〔熱〕气球(飞行器) rèqìqiú. **balloon** *v* [I] 膨胀〔脹〕如气球 péngzhàng rú qìqiú. **balloonist** *n* [C] 热气球驾驶员 rè qìqiú jiàshǐyuán.

ballot /ˈbælət/ *n* 1 [C, U] 无〔無〕记名投票(用纸) wú jìmíng tóupiào. 2 [C] 票数〔數〕 piàoshù. **ballot** *v* 1 [I] 投票 tóupiào. 2 [T] 投票决定 tóupiào juédìng. **ˈballot-box** *n* [C] 票箱 piàoxiāng.

balm /bɑːm/ *n* [U, C] 1 止痛香油 zhǐtòng xiāngyóu. 2 [喻]安慰物 ānwèiwù. **balmy** *adj* [-ier, -iest] 1 (空气)温和的 wēnhéde. 2 疗〔療〕伤〔傷〕的 liáoshāngde. 3 [美语] = BARMY.

balsa /ˈbɔːlsə/ *n* [C, U] 西印度轻〔輕〕木(热带美洲的一种树木) xīyìndù qīngmù; 西印度轻木的木材 xīyìndù qīngmù de mùcái.

balustrade /ˌbæləˈstreɪd/ *n* [C] 栏〔欄〕杆 lángān.

bamboo /ˌbæmˈbuː/ *n* [C, U] 竹 zhú.

ban /bæn/ *v* [-nn-] [T] 禁止 jìnzhǐ. **ban** *n* [C] 禁令 jìnlìng.

banal /bəˈnɑːl; *US* ˈbeɪnl/ *adj* 枯燥无〔無〕味的 kūzào wúwèide; 平庸的 píngyōngde: ~ *remarks* 枯燥无味的话; 陈词滥调.

banana /bəˈnɑːnə; *US* bəˈnænə/ *n* [C] 香蕉 xiāngjiāo.

band /bænd/ *n* [C] 1 通俗乐〔樂〕队〔隊〕 tōngsú yuèduì. 2 (一)群 qún, (一)伙〔夥〕 huǒ: *a ~ of robbers* 一伙强盗. 3 带〔帶〕子 dàizi; 镶边〔邊〕 xiāngbiān. 4 范〔範〕围〔圍〕 fànwéi: *an income ~* 收入的幅度. **band** *v* [I] *together* 结伙 jiéhuǒ; 结合 jiéhé. **ˈbandstand** *n* [C] 室外音乐〔樂〕台〔臺〕 shìwài yīnyuètái. **ˈbandwagon** *n* [习语] **jump / climb on the ˈbandwagon** [非正式用语]赶〔趕〕浪头〔頭〕 gǎn làngtou.

bandage /ˈbændɪdʒ/ *n* [C] 绷带〔帶〕 bēngdài. **bandage** *v* [T] 用绷带扎〔紮〕绑 yòng bēngdài zābǎng.

bandit /ˈbændɪt/ *n* [C] 土匪 tǔfěi; 匪徒 fěitú.

bandy[1] /ˈbændɪ/ *v* [*pt*, *pp* -ied] 1 [习语] **bandy ˈwords** [旧]争吵 zhēngchǎo. 2 [短语动词] **bandy sth about** (漫不经心地)随〔隨〕便传〔傳〕播 suíbiàn chuánbō.

bandy[2] /ˈbændɪ/ *adj* [-ier, -iest] 膝外屈的 xī wài qū de.

bang /bæŋ/ *n* [C] 1 猛击〔擊〕 měngjī; 砰砰的声〔聲〕音 pēngpēngde shēngyīn. 2 [习语] **bang one's head against a brick wall** ⇨ HEAD[1]. **bang** *v* [I, T] 猛敲 měngqiāo; 砰然作声 pēngrán zuò shēng: *The door ~ed shut.* 门砰地关上了. *She ~ed her knee on the desk.* 她的膝盖撞到了书桌上. **bang** *adv* [非正式用语]正巧 zhèngqiǎo: ~ *in the middle* 正好在中间.

banger /ˈbæŋə(r)/ *n* [C] [英国非正式用语] 1 香肠〔腸〕 xiāngcháng. 2 鞭炮 biānpào. 3 破旧〔舊〕的汽车 pòjiùde qìchē.

bangle /ˈbæŋgl/ *n* [C] 手镯 shǒuzhuó; 脚镯 jiǎozhuó.

banish /ˈbænɪʃ/ *v* [T] 1 驱〔驅〕逐出境 qūzhú chūjìng; 放逐 fàngzhú. 2 消除(想法等) xiāochú. **banishment** *n* [U].

banister /ˈbænɪstə(r)/ *n* [C, pl] 栏〔欄〕杆小柱 lángān xiǎozhù; 楼〔樓〕梯扶手 lóutī fúshǒu.

banjo /bænˈdʒəʊ/ *n* [C] [*pl* ~s] 班卓琴 bānzhuóqín.

bank[1] /bæŋk/ *n* [C] 1 银行 yínháng. 2 库 kù: *a ˈblood-~* 血库. **bank** *v* 1 [T] 把(钱)存入银行 bǎ cúnrù yínháng. 2 [短语动词] **bank on sb / sth** 指望 zhǐwàng; 信赖 xìnlài. **ˈbank account** *n* [C] 银行账〔賬〕户 yínháng zhànghù. **ˈbank card** *n* [C] 银行卡 yínhángkǎ; (银行的)支票保付卡 zhīpiào bǎofù kǎ. **banker** *n* [C] 银行家 yínhángjiā. **ˌbank ˈholiday** *n* [C] 法定假日 fǎdìng jiàrì. **banking** *n* [U] 银行业〔業〕 yínhángyè. **ˈbanknote** *n* [C] 钞票 chāopiào.

bank[2] /bæŋk/ *n* [C] 1 河岸 hé'àn; 河边〔邊〕 hébiān. 2 堤 dī; 斜坡 xiépō. 3 雪堆 xuěduī; 云〔雲〕堆 yúnduī. **bank** *v* [I] 飞〔飛〕机〔機〕转〔轉〕弯〔彎〕时〔時〕倾斜行进〔進〕 fēijī zhuǎnwān shí qīngxié xíngjìn.

bank[3] /bæŋk/ *n* [C] (一)排 pái, (一)组 zǔ: *a ~ of switches* 一排电闸.

bankrupt /ˈbæŋkrʌpt/ *adj* 1 破产〔產〕了的 pòchǎnlede. 2 [喻] 完全缺乏的 wánquán quēfá de. **bankrupt** *n* [C] 破产者 pòchǎnzhě. **bankruptcy** /-rəpsɪ/ *n* [C, U] [*pl* -ies] 破产(事例) pòchǎn.

banner /ˈbænə(r)/ *n* [C] 旗 qí; (游行者手持的)横幅 héngfú.

banns /bænz/ *n* [pl] 教堂里〔裡〕的结婚预告 jiàotáng lǐde jiéhūn yùgào.

banquet /ˈbæŋkwɪt/ *n* [C] 宴会〔會〕 yànhuì.

bantam /ˈbæntəm/ *n* [C] 矮脚鸡〔鷄〕 ǎijiǎojī.

banter /ˈbæntə(r)/ *n* [U] 玩笑话 wánxiàohuà. **banter** *v* [I] 开〔開〕玩笑 kāiwánxiào; 戏〔戲〕弄 xìnòng.

baptism /ˈbæptɪzəm/ *n* 1 [C, U] 洗礼〔禮〕

xǐlǐ. 2 [习语] ˌbaptism of ˈfire (a) (兵士的)第一次经〔經〕历〔歷〕战〔戰〕争 dìyīcì jīnglì zhànzhēng. (b) 严〔嚴〕峻的考验〔驗〕 yánjùnde kǎoyàn. **baptize** /bæpˈtaɪz/ *v* [T] 给…施洗礼 gěi…shī xǐlǐ.

bar[1] /bɑː(r)/ *n* 1 [C] 棍 gùn; 棒 bàng; 杆 gān: *a steel* ～ 钢棒. *a* ～ *of chocolate* 一块条形巧克力. 2 [C] 门窗等的栅 ménchuāng děng de zhà: *be behind* ～*s* 在牢狱中. 3 [C] 酒吧间 jiǔbājiān; 餐柜〔櫃〕 cānguì. 4 [C] (颜色等形成的)条〔條〕纹 tiáowén; 带〔帶〕 dài. 5 [C] [喻] 障碍〔礙〕 zhàng'ài; 障碍物 zhàng'àiwù: *Poor health is a* ～ *to success*. 身体不好是成功的障碍. 6 [音乐] 小节〔節〕 xiǎojié. 7 [C] 法庭上的围〔圍〕栏〔欄〕 fǎtíng shàng de wéilán: *the prisoner at the* ～ 出庭受审的犯人. 8 **the bar** [sing, 亦作 sing, 用 pl v] 律师〔師〕的职〔職〕业〔業〕 lǜshīde zhíyè; 律师 lǜshī: *be called to the* ～ 成为律师. **bar code** *n* [C] 条形码 tiáoxíngmǎ. ˈ**bar code reader** *n* [C] 条形码阅读〔讀〕器 tiáoxíngmǎ yuèdúqì. ˈ**barman** *n* [C] (*fem* ˈ**barmaid**) 酒吧间招待员 jiǔbājiān zhāodàiyuán. ˈ**bartender** *n* [C] [尤用于美语] 酒吧间招待员 jiǔbājiān zhāodàiyuán.

bar[2] /bɑː(r)/ *v* [T] [-rr-] 1 闩(门等) shuān. 2 阻挡〔擋〕 zǔdǎng: ～ *the way* 挡路. 3 排斥 páichì; 不准 bùzhǔn: *She was* ～*red from* (*entering*) *the competition*. 不准她参加比赛.

bar[3] /bɑː(r)/ *prep* 1 除… chú…. 2 [习语] **bar none** 无〔無〕例外 wú lìwài.

barb /bɑːb/ *n* [C] 倒钩 dàogōu; 倒刺 dàocì. **barbed** *adj* 装〔裝〕倒钩的 zhuāng dàogōu de: ～*ed wire* 有刺铁丝(网).

barbarian /bɑːˈbeərɪən/ *adj*, *n* [C] 野蛮〔蠻〕的 yěmánde; 野蛮人 yěmánrén. **barbaric** /bɑːˈbærɪk/ *adj* 1 野蛮人的 yěmánrénde; 野蛮人似的 yěmánrénshìde. 2 粗野的 cūyěde. **barbarity** /bɑːˈbærətɪ/ *n* [C, U] [*pl* -ies] 野蛮 yěmán; 残〔殘〕暴 cánbào. **barbarous** /ˈbɑːbərəs/ *adj* 残暴的 cánbàode; 粗野的 cūyěde.

barbecue /ˈbɑːbɪkjuː/ *n* [C] 1 烤肉架 kǎoròujià. 2 烤肉野餐 kǎoròu yěcān. **barbecue** *v* [T] 烧烤 shāokǎo.

barber /ˈbɑːbə(r)/ *n* [C] 理发〔髮〕员 lǐfàyuán.

barbiturate /bɑːˈbɪtjʊrət/ *n* [C] (催眠等用的)巴比妥类〔類〕药物 bābǐtuǒ lèi yàowù.

bard /bɑːd/ *n* [C] [古] 诗人 shīrén.

bare /beə(r)/ *adj* [～r, ～st] 1 裸露的 luǒlùde. 2 空的 kōngde: ～ *cupboards* 空的碗柜. 3 最起码的 zuì qǐmǎde. **bare** *v* [T] 揭露 jiēlù; 揭开〔開〕 jiēkāi. ˈ**bareback** *adj*, *adv* (骑马)不用鞍(的) búyòng ān. **barefaced** *adj* 露骨的 lùgǔde; 公开〔開〕的 gōngkāide; 蛮〔蠻〕横的 mánhèngde. ˈ**barefoot** *adj*, *adv* 赤脚的 chìjiǎode. **barely** *adv* 仅〔僅〕仅 jǐnjǐn; 勉强 miǎnqiáng. **bareness** *n* [U].

bargain /ˈbɑːɡɪn/ *n* [C] 1 契约 qìyuē; 合同 hétong. 2 便宜货 piányìhuò; 廉价〔價〕品 liánjiàpǐn. 3 [习语] **into the bargain** [非正式用语] 另外 lìngwài; 另加 lìngjiā. **bargain** *v* 1 [I] 讲〔講〕价钱〔錢〕 jiǎng jiàqián. 2 [短语动词] **bargain for / on sth** [非正式用语] 预料 yùliào; 指望 zhǐwàng: *get more than you had* ～*ed for* 所得超过预料.

barge[1] /bɑːdʒ/ *n* [C] 驳船 bóchuán; 平底船 píngdǐchuán.

barge[2] /bɑːdʒ/ *v* [非正式用语] 1 [I] 猛撞 měngzhuàng; 冲 chōng. 2 [短语动词] **barge in** 粗暴地打断〔斷〕(谈话) cūbàode dǎ duàn.

baritone /ˈbærɪtəʊn/ *n* [C] 男中音 nánzhōngyīn.

bark[1] /bɑːk/ *n* [C] 犬吠 quǎnfèi. **bark** *v* 1 [I] (狗)叫 jiào. 2 [T] 咆哮地说话 páoxiàode shuōhuà: ～ *out orders* 咆哮地发出命令.

bark[2] /bɑːk/ *n* [U] 树〔樹〕皮 shùpí.

barley /ˈbɑːlɪ/ *n* [U] 大麦〔麥〕粒 dàmàilì; 大麦 dàmài.

barmy /ˈbɑːmɪ/ *adj* [-ier, -iest] [英国英语, 非正式用语] 傻〔傻〕呵呵的 shǎhēhēde; 疯〔瘋〕疯癫癫的 fēngfengdiāndiānde.

barn /bɑːn/ *n* [C] 谷〔穀〕仓〔倉〕 gǔcāng.

barnacle /ˈbɑːnəkl/ *n* [C] 藤壶〔壺〕(附在岩石、船底上的甲壳动物) ténghú.

barometer /bəˈrɒmɪtə(r)/ *n* [C] 气〔氣〕压〔壓〕计 qìyājì; 晴雨表 qíngyǔbiǎo: [喻] *a* ～ *of public feeling* 公众情绪的晴雨表.

baron /ˈbærən/ *n* [C] 1 (英国)男爵 nánjué. 2 工业〔業〕巨子 gōngyè jùzǐ; 大王 dàwáng. **baroness** *n* [C] 1 有男爵爵位的女人 yǒu nánjué juéwèi de nǚrén. 2 男爵夫人 nánjué fūrén. **baronet** /ˈbærənɪt/ *n* [C] (英国)从〔從〕男爵 cóngnánjué.

baroque /bəˈrɒk; *US* bəˈrəʊk/ *adj* (建筑等)巴罗〔羅〕克风〔風〕格的 bāluókè fēnggéde.

barrack /ˈbærək/ *v* [I, T] 嘲弄 cháonòng; 叫嚣 jiàoxiāo.

barracks /ˈbærəks/ *n* [C, sing 或 pl v] 营〔營〕房 yíngfáng.

barrage /ˈbærɑːʒ; *US* bəˈrɑːʒ/ *n* [C] 1 [军事] 弹〔彈〕幕射击〔擊〕 dànmù shèjī: [喻] *a* ～ *of complaints* 连珠炮似的牢骚. 2 坝〔壩〕 bà; 堰 yàn.

barrel /ˈbærəl/ *n* [C] 1 (a) 圆桶 yuántǒng. (b) 一圆桶的量 yì yuántǒng de liàng. 2 枪〔槍〕管 qiāngguǎn; 炮筒 pàotǒng. ˈ**barrel-organ** *n* [C] 手摇风〔風〕琴 shǒuyáofēngqín.

barren /ˈbærən/ *adj* 1 贫瘠的 pínjíde; 不毛的

B

bùmáode;不结果实〔實〕的 bù jié guǒshí de;不会〔會〕生育的 búhuì shēngyù de. 2 [喻]无〔無〕益的 wúyìde;无价〔價〕值的 wújiàzhí de;无兴〔興〕趣的 wú xìngqù de.

barricade /ˌbærɪˈkeɪd/ *n* [C] 路障 lùzhàng. **barricade** *v* [T] 在…设路障 zài…shè lùzhàng.

barrier /ˈbærɪə(r)/ *n* [C] 1 障碍〔礙〕物 zhàng'àiwù;栅栏〔欄〕zhàlan: [喻] ～*s to world peace* 世界和平的障碍. 2 人际〔際〕障碍物 rénjì zhàng'àiwù: *the language* ～ 人际语言障碍.

barring /ˈbɑːrɪŋ/ *prep* 如果没有 rúguǒméiyǒu.

barrister /ˈbærɪstə(r)/ *n* [C] (英国)律师〔師〕lǜshī.

barrow /ˈbærəʊ/ *n* 1 = WHEELBARROW (WHEEL). 2 手推车〔車〕shǒutuīchē.

barter /ˈbɑːtə(r)/ *v* [I, T] 货物交换 huòwù jiāohuàn. **barter** *n* [U].

base[1] /beɪs/ *n* [C] 1 基础〔礎〕jīchǔ;根基 gēnjī. 2 [喻]起点〔點〕qǐdiǎn. 3 主要成分 zhǔyào chéngfèn: *a drink with a rum* ～ 以兰姆酒为主要成分的饮料. 4 基地 jīdì;根据〔據〕地 gēnjùdì. **base** *v* [T] 1 *on* 把…作基础 bǎ…zuò jīchǔ: *a story* ～*d on real life* 以实际生活作基础的小说. 2 把…作生活或工作的基地 bǎ…zuò shēnghuó huò gōngzuòde jīdì: *a company* ～*d in Cairo* 设在开罗的一家公司. **baseless** *adj* 无〔無〕缘无故的 wúyuán wúgù de: ～*less fears* 无缘无故的恐惧〔懼〕. ˈ**base rate** *n* [C] 1 (央行的)基准(準)利率 jīzhǔn lìlǜ. 2 (一般银行的)基本利率 jīběn lìlǜ.

base[2] /beɪs/ *adj* [～r, ～st] 1 [正式用语]卑劣的 bēiliède;可鄙的 kěbǐde. 2 (金属) 低劣的 dīliède.

baseball /ˈbeɪsbɔːl/ *n* [U] 棒球 bàngqiú.

basement /ˈbeɪsmənt/ *n* [C] 底层〔層〕dǐcéng;地下室 dìxiàshì.

bases 1 *pl* of BASIS. 2 *pl* of BASE[1].

bash /bæʃ/ *v* [T] [非正式用语] 猛击〔擊〕měngjī;猛撞 měngzhuàng. **bash** *n* [C] 1 猛击 měngjī. 2 [习语] **have a bash at sth** [非正式用语]就…作一尝〔嘗〕试 jiù…zuò yī chángshì.

bashful /ˈbæʃfl/ *adj* 害羞的 hàixiūde;忸怩的 niǔníde. **bashfully** *adv*.

basic /ˈbeɪsɪk/ *adj* 基础〔礎〕的 jīchǔde;基本的 jīběnde: *the* ～ *facts* 基本事实. **basically** *adv* 基本地 jīběnde. **basics** *n* [pl] 要素 yàosù;要点〔點〕yàodiǎn.

basil /ˈbæzl/ *n* [U] (植物)罗〔羅〕勒 luōle.

basin /ˈbeɪsn/ *n* [C] 1 = WASH-BASIN (WASH[1]). 2 碗(盛粥等用) wǎn. 3 水洼 shuǐwā;水池 shuǐchí. 4 流域 liúyù.

basis /ˈbeɪsɪs/ *n* [C] [*pl* **bases** /ˈbeɪsiːz/] 1 基础〔礎〕jīchǔ: *arguments that have a firm* ～ 有事实为基础的论说. 2 基本原则 jīběn yuánzé: *a service run on a commercial* ～ 以商业原则管理的公用事业.

bask /bɑːsk; *US* bæsk/ *v* [I] (*in*) 取暖 qǔnuǎn: [喻] ～ *in sb's approval* 对于某人给予的赞扬感到乐滋滋的.

basket /ˈbɑːskɪt; *US* ˈbæs-/ *n* [C] 篮〔籃〕子 lánzi;筐 kuāng: *a* ˈ*shopping* ～ 购物篮子. **basketball** *n* [U] 篮〔籃〕球 lánqiú.

bass[1] /beɪs/ *n* [C] 1 男低音 nán dīyīn. 2 = DOUBLE BASS (DOUBLE[1]). **bass** *adj* 声〔聲〕音低沉的 shēngyīn dīchén de.

bass[2] /bæs/ *n* [C] 欧〔歐〕洲产〔產〕的鲈〔鱸〕鱼 Ouzhōu chǎn de lúyú.

bassoon /bəˈsuːn/ *n* [C] 巴松管 bāsōngguǎn;大管 dàguǎn;低音管 dīyīnguǎn.

bastard /ˈbɑːstəd; *US* ˈbæs-/ *n* [C] 1 私生子 sīshēngzǐ. 2 [贬,俚] 讨厌〔厭〕鬼 tǎoyànguǐ. 3 [俚]不幸的人 búxìngde rén: *The poor* ～ *has just lost his job*. 这个倒霉的人刚刚失去了工作.

baste[1] /beɪst/ *v* [T] 把油脂涂〔塗〕在(烤肉)上 bǎ yóuzhǐ tú zài…shàng.

baste[2] /beɪst/ *v* [T] 用长〔長〕针脚疏缝 yòng chángzhēnjiǎo shūféng.

bastion /ˈbæstɪən/ *n* [C] 1 棱堡 léngbǎo. 2 [喻](信仰、原则等的)堡垒〔壘〕bǎolěi.

bat[1] /bæt/ *n* [C] 1 球棒 qiúbàng;球拍 qiúpāi. 2 [习语] ˌ**off one's own** ˈ**bat** [非正式用语]独〔獨〕立地做某事 dúlìde zuò mǒushì. **bat** *v* [-tt-] [I] 用球棒、球拍打球 yòng qiúbàng qiúpāi dǎqiú. ˈ**batsman** *n* [C] (板球)击〔擊〕球手 jīqiúshǒu. **batter** *n* [C] (尤指棒球)击球员 jīqiúyuán.

bat[2] /bæt/ *n* [C] 蝙蝠 biānfú.

bat[3] /bæt/ *v* [-tt-] [习语] **not bat an** ˈ**eyelid** [非正式用语]处〔處〕之泰然 chǔ zhī tàirán.

batch /bætʃ/ *n* [C] 一批(人或物) yìpī.

bath /bɑːθ; *US* bæθ/ *n* [*pl* ～s /bɑːðz; *US* bæðz/] 1 [C] 洗澡缸 xǐzǎogāng. 2 [C] 洗澡 xǐzǎo;浴 yù. 3 **baths** [pl] 公共浴室 gōnggòng yùshì;澡堂 zǎotáng. **bath** *v* 1 [T] 为〔爲〕…洗澡 wèi…xǐzǎo. 2 [I] 洗澡 xǐzǎo. ˈ**bathrobe** *n* [C] 1 浴衣 yùyī. 2 [美语]晨衣 chényī. ˈ**bathroom** *n* [C] 1 浴室 yùshì. 2 [尤用于美语]厕所 cèsuǒ. ˈ**bath-tub** *n* [C] 浴缸 yùgāng;澡盆 zǎopén.

bathe /beɪð/ *v* 1 [I] [尤用于英国英语]下海游泳 xià hǎi yóuyǒng. 2 [I] [美语]洗澡 xǐzǎo. 3 [T] 用水洗 yòng shuǐ xǐ. **bathe** *n* [sing] 游泳 yóuyǒng. **bather** *n* [C] 洗澡的人 xǐzǎode rén.

batman /ˈbætmən/ *n* [C] [*pl* **-men** /-mən/] [英国英语]勤务〔務〕兵 qínwùbīng.

baton /ˈbætn, ˈbætɒn; *US* bəˈtɒn/ *n* [C] 1 (乐队指挥用)指挥棒 zhǐhuībàng. 2 警棍 jǐnggùn.

battalion /bəˈtæliən/ *n* [C] 营〔營〕(军事单位) yíng.

batten /ˈbætn/ *n* [C] 板条〔條〕 bǎntiáo. batten *v* [T] *down* 用压〔壓〕条压牢 yòng yātiáo yāláo.

batter[1] /ˈbætə(r)/ *v* [T] 连〔連〕续〔續〕猛击〔擊〕 liánxù měngjī; 打烂〔爛〕 dǎlàn. battered *adj* 破损的 pòsǔnde. battering-ram *n* [C] [军事]攻城槌 gōngchéngchuí.

batter[2] /ˈbætə(r)/ *n* [U] 面〔麵〕粉、鸡〔鷄〕蛋、牛奶等调成的糊状〔狀〕物(用以做蛋糕) miànfěn、jīdàn、niúnǎi děng tiáochéng de húzhuàngwù: *fish fried in* ~ 油煎鸡蛋面糊拖鱼.

battery /ˈbætəri/ *n* [C] [*pl* -ies] 1 电〔電〕池(组) diànchí. 2 炮兵连 pàobīnglián. 3 层〔層〕架式鸡〔鷄〕笼〔籠〕 céngjiàshì jīlóng. 4 (一)组 zǔ; (一)套 tào: *a* ~ *of cameras* 一套摄像管. *a* ~ *of tests* 一组测试.

battle /ˈbætl/ *n* 1 [C, U] 战〔戰〕役 zhànyì; 战斗〔鬥〕 zhàndòu. 2 [C] [喻]斗争 dòuzhēng: *a* ~ *of words* 论战; 舌战. battle *v* [I] 斗争 dòuzhēng; 战斗 zhàndòu: *battling against poverty* 向贫穷开战 xiàng pínqióng kāizhàn. ˈbattlefield *n* [C] 战场〔場〕 zhànchǎng; 疆场 jiāngchǎng. ˈbattleship *n* [C] 军〔軍〕舰〔艦〕 jūnjiàn.

battlements /ˈbætlmənts/ *n* [pl] 城垛 chéngduǒ.

batty /ˈbæti/ *adj* [-ier, -iest] [非正式用语] 疯〔瘋〕癫癫的 fēng diāndiān de.

bauble /ˈbɔːbl/ *n* [C] 小装〔裝〕饰品 xiǎo zhuāngshìpǐn.

baulk ⇨BALK.

bawdy /ˈbɔːdi/ *adj* [-ier, -iest] 淫秽〔穢〕的 yínhuìde; 猥亵的 wěixiède.

bawl /bɔːl/ *v* [I, T] 大喊 dàhǎn; 大叫 dàjiào.

bay[1] /beɪ/ *n* [C] 海湾〔灣〕 hǎiwān; 湾 wān.

bay[2] /beɪ/ *n* [C] (某种用途的)隔间 géjiān: *a* ˈ*loading* ~ 装货间. ˌbay ˈwindow *n* [C] (房间凸出部分的)凸窗 tūchuāng.

bay[3] /beɪ/ *v* [I] (猎犬)吠叫 fèijiào. bay *n* [习语] hold / keep sb / sth at ˈbay 不使(敌人等)走近 bùshǐ zǒujìn.

bay[4] (亦作 ˈbay-tree) /beɪ/ *n* [C] 月桂树〔樹〕 yuèguìshù.

bayonet /ˈbeɪənɪt/ *n* [C] (枪上的)刺刀 cìdāo. bayonet *v* [T] 用刺刀刺杀〔殺〕 yòng cìdāo cìshā.

bazaar /bəˈzɑː(r)/ *n* [C] 1 (东方国家)市场〔場〕 shìchǎng. 2 义〔義〕卖〔賣〕 yìmài.

bazooka /bəˈzuːkə/ *n* [C] 火箭筒 huǒjiàntǒng.

BBC /ˌbi bi ˈsiː/ *abbr* British Broadcasting Corporation 英国〔國〕广〔廣〕播公司 Yīngguó guǎngbō gōngsī.

BC /ˌbiː ˈsiː/ *abbr* (in the year) before the birth of Jesus Christ 公元前 gōngyuán qián.

be[1] /bɪ; 强式 biː/ *aux v* (第一人称单数现在时 am /əm, m; 强式 æm/; 第三人称单数现在时 is /s, z; 强式 ɪz /; 第一称复数现在时、第二人称单数和复数现在时、第三人称复数现在时 are /ə(r); 强式 ɑː(r)/; 第一人称单数过去时、第三人称单数过去时 was /wəz; 强式 wɒz; *US* wʌz/; 第一人称复数过去时、第二人称过去时、第三人称复数过去时 were /wə(r); 强式 wɜː(r)/; 现在分词 being /ˈbiːɪŋ/; 过去分词 been / biːn; (*US* 亦作) bɪn /) 1 [同现在分词连用, 构成各种进行时态]: *They are reading*. 他们正在阅读. 2 [同过去分词连用构成被动式]: *He was killed*. 他被杀死了. 3 [同动词不定式连用] (a) 必须 bìxū: *You are to report to the police at 10 o'clock*. 你必须在 10 点钟向警察报告. (b) 打算 dǎsuàn: *The president is to visit London in May*. 总统打算在五月访问伦敦.

be[2] /bɪ; 强式 biː/ *v* [现在时和过去时⇨BE[1]] [I] 1 (表示存在、发生)有 yǒu: *Is there a God?* 有上帝吗? 2 (表示地点): *The lamp is on the table*. 灯在桌子上. 3 (表示有特定的姓名、性质或情况): *This is Mrs Khan*. 这是卡恩夫人. *The film was very funny*. 这部电影很有趣. *Today is Monday*. 今天是星期一. *I'll be 35 next year*. 明年我 35 岁. 4 (表示所有): *The money's not yours*. 这钱不是你的. 5 成为〔爲〕 chéngwéi: *He wants to be a teacher*. 他想成为一名教师. 6 (表示价值、数字等的等同): *That will be £80.95*. 那将会是 80.95 英镑. 7 去 qù; 访问 fǎngwèn: *Have you been to college today?* 你今天上学去了吗? 8 [习语] be out in the open ⇨OPEN[1].

beach /biːtʃ/ *n* [C] 海滩〔灘〕 hǎitān. beach *v* [T] 使(船)冲〔沖〕向岸 shǐ chōngxiàng àn. ˈbeach-ball *n* [C] (海滩上玩的)沙滩球 shātānqiú. ˈbeachhead *n* [C] 滩头〔頭〕阵〔陣〕地 tāntóu zhèndì. ˈbeachwear *n* [U] 海滩装〔裝〕 hǎitānzhuāng.

beacon /ˈbiːkən/ *n* [C] 灯〔燈〕塔 dēngtǎ.

bead /biːd/ *n* 1 (a) [C] 念珠 niànzhū. (b) beads [pl] 珠子项链〔鏈〕 zhūzi xiàngliàn. 2 水珠 shuǐzhū: ~*s of sweat* 汗珠.

beady /ˈbiːdi/ *adj* [-ier, -iest] (眼睛)小而亮的 xiǎo ér liàng de.

beak /biːk/ *n* [C] 鸟喙 niǎohuì.

B

beaker /ˈbiːkə(r)/ *n* [C] 1 大酒杯 dà jiǔbēi. 2 烧〔燒〕杯 shāobēi.

beam /biːm/ *n* [C] 1 梁 liáng; 桁条〔條〕héngtiáo. 2 光束 guāngshù; 光柱 guāngzhù. 3 笑容 xiàoróng; 喜色 xǐsè. 4 飞〔飛〕机〔機〕导〔導〕航无〔無〕线〔綫〕电〔電〕射束 fēijī dǎoháng wúxiàndiàn shèshù. **beam** *v* 1 [I] 发〔發〕光 fāguāng; 发热〔熱〕fārè. 2 [I] 〔喻〕微笑 wēixiào. 3 [T] 定向发出(无线电节目等) dìngxiàng fāchū.

bean /biːn/ *n* [C] 1 (植物)豆 dòu; 豆粒 dòulì: ˈ*soya*- **~s** 大豆. ˈ*coffee*- *~s* 咖啡豆. 2 [习语] full of ˈbeans [非正式用语]精神旺盛 jīngshén wàngshèng. 兴〔興〕高采烈 xìng gāo cǎi liè.

bear[1] /beə(r)/ *n* [C] 熊 xióng.

bear[2] /beə(r)/ *v* [*pt* bore /bɔː(r)/, *pp* borne /bɔːn/] 1 [T] 携带〔帶〕xiédài; 负荷 fùhé. 2 [T] 承受 chéngshòu; 经〔經〕得起 jīngdeqǐ: *The ice is too thin to ~* **your weight.** 这冰太薄承受不住你的重量. 3 [T] 有 yǒu; 表现 biǎoxiàn: *The letter bore her signature*. 这封信有她的签名. 4 [T] 忍受 rěnshòu: **~ pain without complaining** 一声不哼地忍住疼痛. 5 长〔長〕出(花、果等) zhǎngchū. 6 [T] [正式用语]生育 shēngyù: **~ a child** 生孩子. 7 [T] [正式用语]对〔對〕…怀〔懷〕有(某种感情) duì…huáiyǒu: *I ~* **them no resentment.** 我不恨他们. 8 [I] 拐弯〔彎〕guǎiwān: *The road* **~s left.** 路向左拐弯. 9 [T] 适〔適〕宜于 shìyí yú; 堪 kān: *The plan will not ~* **close examination.** 这个计划经不起仔细审查. 10 [习语] bear the ˈbrunt of sth 首当〔當〕其冲〔衝〕shǒu dāng qí chōng: *~ the brunt of an attack / sb's anger* 首当其冲面对一次攻击(或某人的怒火). bear sth in mind ⇨MIND[1]. bear witness to sth [正式用语]构〔構〕成…的证〔證〕据〔據〕gòuchéng… de zhèngjù. bring sth to bear 施加 shījiā: *bring pressure to ~ on him to change his mind*. 对他施加压力使他改变主意. can't bear sb/sth 厌〔厭〕恶〔惡〕yànwù. 11 [短语动词] bear ˈdown on sb/sth 向…冲〔衝〕去 xiàng…chōngqù. bear sb/sth ˈout 帮〔幫〕助 bāngzhù; 证实〔實〕zhèngshí. bear ˈup (在困难中)挺得住 tǐngdezhù. ˈbear with sb 容忍 róngrěn. **bearable** *adj* 可以忍受的 kěyǐ rěnshòu de.

beard /bɪəd/ *n* [C] (下巴上的)胡〔鬍〕须〔鬚〕húxū. **bearded** *adj* 有胡须的 yǒu húxū de.

bearer /ˈbeərə(r)/ *n* [C] 1 带〔帶〕信人 dài xìn rén. 2 抬棺材的人 tái guāncai de rén. 3 持票(支票、票据)人 chí piào rén.

bearing /ˈbeərɪŋ/ *n* 1 [sing] [正式用语]举〔舉〕止 jǔzhǐ; 姿态〔態〕zītài. 2 [U] 关〔關〕系〔係〕guānxì; 联〔聯〕系 liánxì: *That has no ~* **on the subject.** 那同本题没有关系. 3 [C] 方位 fāngwèi; 方向 fāngxiàng. 4 bearings [pl] 对〔對〕自己处〔處〕境或环〔環〕境的认〔認〕识〔識〕duì zìjǐ chǔjìng huò huánjìng de rènshi: *get / lose one's ~s* 方向明; 迷失方向.

beast /biːst/ *n* [C] 1 [旧词或正式用语]四足兽〔獸〕sìzúshòu. 2 凶〔兇〕暴而残〔殘〕忍的人 xiōngbào ér cánrěn de rén. **beastly** *adj* [非正式用语]令人厌〔厭〕恶〔惡〕的 lìngrén yànwù de.

beat[1] /biːt/ *v* [*pt* beat, *pp* ~en /ˈbiːtn/] 1 [T] (接连地)打 dǎ; 击〔擊〕jī. 2 [T] 把…敲变〔變〕形 bǎ…qiāo biànxíng: **~ metal flat** 把金属敲平展. 3 [I,T] (有规则地)跳动〔動〕tiàodòng: *His heart was still* **~ing.** 他的心脏还在跳动. 4 [T] 搅〔攪〕拌 jiǎobàn: **~ eggs** 打鸡蛋. 5 [T] 胜〔勝〕shèng; 打败 dǎbài: *He* **~ me at chess.** 下国际象棋, 他赢了我. 6 [习语] ˌbeat about the ˈbush 旁敲侧击 páng qiāo cè jī. beat it [俚]走 zǒu; 滚 gǔn. beat a reˈtreat 匆匆撤退 cōngcōng chètuì. beat ˈtime (音乐)打拍子 dǎ pāizi. ˌoff the ˌbeaten ˈtrack 不落俗套 bú luò sútào; 不走老路 bù zǒu lǎolù. 7 [短语动词] beat down (太阳)火辣辣地照射 huǒ làlà de zhàoshè. beat sb down 杀〔殺〕…的价〔價〕shā…de jià. beat sb up 打伤〔傷〕某人 dǎshāng mǒurén. **beat** *adj* 筋疲力尽〔盡〕的 jīn pí lì jìn de: *I am dead ~*. 我完全筋疲力尽了. **beaten** *adj* 锤制〔製〕的 chuízhìde; 锤薄的 chuíbóde. **beater** *n* [C] 拍打器 pāidǎqì; 搅拌器 jiǎobànqì. **beating** *n* [C] 1 挨打 áidǎ. 2 失败 shībài; 溃败 kuìbài.

beat[2] /biːt/ *n* [C] 1 (接连地)打 dǎ; 敲 qiāo; 敲打声〔聲〕qiāodǎshēng: *the ~* **of a drum** 鼓声. 2 节〔節〕拍 jiépāi; 拍子 pāizi. 3 巡逻〔邏〕路线〔綫〕xúnluó lùxiàn.

beautician /bjuːˈtɪʃn/ *n* [C] 美容师〔師〕měiróngshī.

beautiful /ˈbjuːtɪfl/ *adj* 美的 měide; 美好的 měihǎode; 优〔優〕美的 yōuměide. **beautifully** *adv*. **beautify** /ˈbjuːtɪfaɪ/ *v* [*pt*, *pp* -ied] [T] 使美丽 shǐ měilì; 美化 měihuà; 化装〔裝〕huàzhuāng.

beauty /ˈbjuːtɪ/ *n* [*pl* -ies] 1 [U] 美丽〔麗〕měilì; 美 měi. 2 [C] 美人 měirén; 美好的事物 měihǎode shìwù. ˈbeauty salon (亦作 ˈbeauty parlour) *n* [C] 美容院 měiróngyuàn. ˈbeauty spot *n* [C] 风〔風〕景点〔點〕fēngjǐngdiǎn; 游览〔覽〕胜〔勝〕地 yóulǎn shèngdì.

beaver /ˈbiːvə(r)/ *n* [C] 河狸 hélí. **beaver** *v* [短语动词] beaver away [非正式用语, 尤用于英国英语]努力工作 nǔlì gōngzuò.

became *pt* of BECOME.

because /bɪˈkɒz; *US* -kɔːz/ *conj* 因为〔爲〕yīnwéi: *I did it ~ they asked me*. 我做了, 因为他们要我做. **because of** *prep* 因为 yīnwéi: *He couldn't walk fast ~ of his bad leg*. 他因为腿坏了, 走不快.

beckon /ˈbekən/ *v* [I, T] (用手势)招唤 zhāohuàn.

become /bɪˈkʌm/ *v* [*pt* became /bɪˈkeɪm/, *pp* become] [通常与形容词连用] 1 成为〔爲〕 chéngwéi; 变〔變〕得 biàndé: *They soon became angry*. 他们立刻发火了. ~ *a doctor* 成为一名医生. 2 [T] [正式用语]适〔適〕合 shìhé; 同…相称〔稱〕 tóng… xiāng chèn: *That hat ~s you*. 那顶帽子适合你戴. 3 [习语] what becomes of sb 某人情况怎样〔樣〕 mǒurén qíngkuàng zěnyàng. becoming *adj* [正式用语]好看的 hǎokànde; 引人注意的 yǐnrén zhùyì de.

bed[1] /bed/ *n* [C] 1 床〔牀〕 chuáng; 床铺 chuángpù. 2 (海)底 dǐ; (河)床 chuáng; (湖)底 dǐ. 3 底座 dǐzuò. 4 (花)坛〔壇〕 tán. 5 [习语] go to bed with sb [非正式用语]与〔與〕某人发〔發〕生性关〔關〕系〔係〕 yǔ mǒurén fāshēng xìng guānxì. ˈbedclothes *n* [pl] 床上用品 chuáng shàng yòngpǐn. ˈbedpan *n* [C] (病人在床上使用的)便盆 biànpén. ˈbedridden *adj* 卧病的 wòbìngde; 久病不起的 jiǔ bìng bù qǐ de. ˈbedroom *n* [C] 卧室 wòshì. ˈbedside *n* [sing] 床边〔邊〕 chuángbiān. ˌbedˈsitter (亦作 ˈbedsit) *n* [C] 卧室兼起居室 wòshì jiān qǐjūshì. ˈbedspread *n* [C] 床罩 chuángzhào. ˈbedstead *n* [C] 床架 chuángjià. ˈbedtime *n* [U] 上床时〔時〕间 shàng chuáng shíjiān.

bed[2] /bed/ *v* [-dd-] [T] 1 嵌 qiàn; 埋置 máizhì: *The brick are ~ded in the concrete*. 砖头埋放在水泥中. 2 栽 zāi; 种〔種〕 zhòng. 3 [非正式用语]发〔發〕生性关〔關〕系〔係〕 fāshēng xìng guānxì. 4 [短语动词] bed down 卧 wò. bed sb down 使舒服过〔過〕夜 shǐ shūfu guòyè. bedding *n* [U] 床上用品 chuáng shàng yòngpǐn.

bedlam /ˈbedləm/ *n* [U] 骚乱〔亂〕的情景 sāoluànde qíngjǐng.

bedraggled /bɪˈdrægld/ *adj* 湿〔濕〕漉漉的 shīlùlùde; 破烂〔爛〕的 pòlànde.

bee /biː/ *n* [C] 1 蜜蜂 mìfēng. 2 [习语] have a ˈbee in one's bonnet 钉住一件事想 dīngzhù yíjiànshì xiǎng. make a bee-line for sth/sb 直奔…而去 zhí bèn…ér qù. ˈbeehive *n* [C] 蜂房 fēngfáng; 蜂箱 fēngxiāng.

beech /biːtʃ/ *n* [C] 山毛榉〔櫸〕 shānmáojǔ.

beef /biːf/ *n* [U] 牛肉 niúròu. beef *v* [I] [俚]抱怨 bàoyuàn; 发〔發〕牢骚 fā láosāo. ˈbeefsteak *n* [U] 牛排 niúpái. beefy *adj* [-ier, -iest] [非正式用语]肌肉发达〔達〕的 jīròu fādá de; 粗壮〔壯〕的 cūzhuàngde.

been *pp* of BE.

beeper /ˈbiːpə(r)/ *n* [C] 寻〔尋〕呼机〔機〕 xúnhūjī.

beer /bɪə(r)/ *n* [U, C] 啤酒 píjiǔ. beery *adj* 啤酒似的 píjiǔ shì de; 带〔帶〕有啤酒味的 dàiyǒu píjiǔwèi de.

beet /biːt/ *n* [U, C] 1 甜菜 tiáncài; 糖萝〔蘿〕卜〔蔔〕 tángluóbo. 2 [美语]甜菜根 tiáncàigēn. ˈbeetroot *n* [U, C] 甜菜根 tiáncàigēn.

beetle /ˈbiːtl/ *n* [C] 甲虫 jiǎchóng.

befall /bɪˈfɔːl/ *v* [*pt* befell /bɪˈfel/, *pp* ~en /bɪˈfɔːlən/] [I, T] [古]临〔臨〕到…头〔頭〕上 líndào…tóu shàng; 发〔發〕生于 fāshēng yú.

befit /bɪˈfɪt/ *v* [-tt-] [T] [正式用语]适〔適〕合 shìhé; 适宜 shìyí. befitting *adj* 适宜的 shìyíde.

before /bɪˈfɔː(r)/ *prep* 1 (时间)在…之前 zài …zhīqián: *the day* ~ yesterday 前天. 2 (次序等)在…之前 zài…zhīqián: *B comes* ~ C in the alphabet. 在字母表上B在C的前面. before *adv* (表示时间)以前 yǐqián: *I've seen that film* ~. 我以前看过那部电影. before *conj* (时间)在…之前 zài…zhīqián: *Do it* ~ *you forget*. 记住做这件事.

beforehand /bɪˈfɔːhænd/ *adv* 预先 yùxiān; 事先 shìxiān.

befriend /bɪˈfrend/ *v* [T] 以朋友态〔態〕度对〔對〕待 yǐ péngyǒu tàidù duìdài.

beg /beg/ *v* [-gg-] 1 [I, T] (*for*) 乞讨(食物、钱〔錢〕等) qǐtǎo. 2 [I, T] 请求 qǐngqiú; 恳〔懇〕求 kěnqiú: *I* ~ you to stay. 我恳请你留下来. 3 [习语] I beg to differ. 我不同意. wǒ bù tóngyì. go ˈbegging (东西)没人要 méi rén yào. I beg your pardon (a) 请再说一遍 qǐng zài shuōyíbiàn. (b) 抱歉 bàoqiàn; 请原谅 qǐng yuánliàng.

beggar /ˈbegə(r)/ *n* [C] 乞丐 qǐgài.

begin /bɪˈgɪn/ *v* [-nn-; *pt* began /bɪˈgæn/, *pp* begun /bɪˈgʌn/] 1 [I, T] 开〔開〕始 kāishǐ: ~ to read a new book 开始读一本新书. *The film ~s at ten*. 电影10点钟开始. ~ *to feel ill* 开始觉得不舒服. 2 [习语] to begin with 首先 shǒuxiān; 第一 dìyī. beginner *n* [C] 初学〔學〕者 chūxuézhě; 生手 shēngshǒu. beginning *n* [C, U] 开端 kāiduān; 开始 kāishǐ.

begrudge /bɪˈgrʌdʒ/ *v* [T] 妒忌 dùjì: *I do not* ~ *them their success*. 我不妒忌他们的成功.

behalf /bɪˈhɑːf; US bɪˈhæf/ *n* [习语] on behalf of sb 代表… dàibiǎo…: *I am speaking on Ann's* ~. 我现在代表安说话.

behave /bɪˈheɪv/ *v* 1 [I] 举〔舉〕动〔動〕 jǔdòng; 表现 biǎoxiàn: ~ well 表现好. 2 ~ oneself 检〔檢〕点〔點〕自己的行为〔爲〕 jiǎndiǎn zìjǐde xíngwéi. behaviour (美语 -ior) *n* [U] 举止 jǔzhǐ; 行为 xíngwéi; (对人的)态〔態〕度 tàidù.

behead /bɪˈhed/ *v* [T] 砍(某人)的头〔頭〕 kǎn

B

…de tóu.

behind[1] /bɪˈhaɪnd/ *prep* 1 在…的后〔後〕面 zài…de hòumiàn: *Hide* ~ the tree. 藏到树后面. 2 不如 bùrú; 落后于 luòhòu yú: *He's* ~ the rest of the class. 他落后于班上的其他同学. 3 赞同 zàntóng; 支持 zhīchí. 4 作为〔爲〕…的原因 zuòwéi…de yuányīn; 引起 yǐnqǐ: *What's* ~ the smart suit, then? 那么, 穿得这么漂亮是为什么呢? **behind** *adv* 1 在…的后面 zài…de hòumiàn: *The children followed* ~ their parents. 孩子们跟在他们父母的后面. 2 留在原处〔處〕liú zài yuánchù: *stay* ~ after school. 放学后留在学校. 3 (*in/with*) 积〔積〕欠 jīqiàn; 未完成 wèi wánchéng: *be* ~ *with the rent* 积欠租金.

behind[2] /bɪˈhaɪnd/ *n* [C] [委婉, 非正式用语] 屁股 pìgu.

behindhand /bɪˈhaɪndhænd/ *adv* 落后〔後〕luòhòu; 耽误 dānwù: *be* ~ *with one's work* 未按时做完工作.

beige /beɪʒ/ *adj*, *n* [U] 灰棕色 huīzōngsè; 灰棕色的 huīzōngsède.

being[1] *present participle* of BE.

being[2] /ˈbiːɪŋ/ *n* 1 [U] 存在 cúnzài; 生存 shēngcún: *The society came into* ~ in 1990. 该协会成立于 1990 年. 2 [C] 人 rén: *human* ~s 人类.

belated /bɪˈleɪtɪd/ *adj* 来迟〔遲〕的 láichíde. **belatedly** *adv*.

belch /beltʃ/ *v* 1 [I] 打嗝 dǎgé; 打噎 dǎyē. 2 [T] 喷出, 冒出(烟等) pēnchū, màochū. **belch** *n* [C].

belfry /ˈbelfrɪ/ *n* [C] [*pl* -ies] (教堂的)钟〔鐘〕楼〔樓〕zhōnglóu; 钟塔 zhōngtǎ.

belief /bɪˈliːf/ *n* 1 [C] 信任 xìnrèn: ~ in his honesty 信任他的诚实. 2 [C] 信仰 xìnyǎng: *religous* ~s 宗教信仰.

believe /bɪˈliːv/ *v* 1 [T] 相信 xiāngxìn. 2 [T] 认〔認〕为〔爲〕rènwéi. 3 [I] (宗教)信仰 xìnyǎng. 4 [短语动词] believe in sb/sth (a) 相信(…的存在) xiāngxìn. (b) 相信(…的价值) xiāngxìn: *He* ~*s in getting plenty of exercise*. 他相信多做些体育运动有益处. **believable** *adj* 可以相信的 kěyǐ xiāngxìn de. **believer** *n* [C].

belittle /bɪˈlɪtl/ *v* [T] 轻〔輕〕视 qīngshì; 小看 xiǎokàn: *Don't* ~ *your achievements*. 别小看你的成就.

bell /bel/ *n* [C] 1 (a) 钟〔鐘〕zhōng; 铃 líng. (b) 门铃 ménlíng; 车铃 chēlíng. 2 钟形物 zhōngxíngwù. ˈ**bell-push** *n* [C] 电〔電〕铃按钮 diànlíng ànniǔ.

belligerent /bɪˈlɪdʒərənt/ *adj* 交战〔戰〕中的 jiāozhàn zhōng de; 好战的 hàozhànde.

bellow /ˈbeləʊ/ *v* [I, T] 吼叫 hǒujiào; 大声〔聲〕叫喊 dàshēng jiàohǎn.

bellows /ˈbeləʊz/ *n* [pl] (手用)风〔風〕箱 fēngxiāng.

belly /ˈbelɪ/ *n* [C] [*pl* -ies] 1 (a) 腹部 fùbù. (b) 胃 wèi. 2 物件的凸部 wùjiànde tūbù. ˈ**bellyache** *n* [C, U] [非正式用语] 胃痛 wèitòng. ˈ**bellyache** *v* [I] [非正式用语] 抱怨 bàoyuàn. ˈ**bellyful** *n* [C] [非正式用语] 饱量 bǎoliàng; 过〔過〕多 guòduō: *I've had a* ~*ful of your noise*. 我受不了你的吵闹.

belong /bɪˈlɒŋ; *US* -lɔːŋ/ *v* [I] 1 *to* 属〔屬〕于 shǔyú: *These books* ~ *to me*. 这些书是我的. 2 *to* 是…的一员 shì … de yìyuán: ~ *to a club* 是俱乐部的一个成员. 3 应〔應〕该在 yīnggāi zài: *The plates* ~ in this cupboard. 盘子应该放在这个碗柜里. **belongings** *n* [pl] 个〔個〕人所有物 gèrén suǒyǒuwù; 财物 cáiwù.

beloved *adj* 1 /bɪˈlʌvd/ 被热〔熱〕爱〔愛〕的 bèi rè'ài de: *He was* ~ *by all who knew him*. 所有认识他的人都喜爱他. 2 /bɪˈlʌvɪd/ 钟〔鍾〕爱的 zhōng'àide: *my* ~ *husband* 我所钟爱的丈夫. **beloved** /bɪˈlʌvɪd/ *n* [C] 被热爱的人 bèi rè'ài de rén.

below /bɪˈləʊ/ *prep*, *adv* 在, 到…的下面: zài, dào … de xiàmiàn: *We saw the ocean* ~. 我们看见了下面的海洋. *The temperature was* ~ *freezing-point*. 温度在零度点之下. *For details, see* ~. 详情请看下文.

belt /belt/ *n* [C] 1 腰带〔帶〕yāodài. 2 机〔機〕器皮带 jīqì pídài. 3 地带 dìdài; 区〔區〕qū: *the copper* ~ 产铜区. 4 [习语] below the belt [非正式用语] 不公正的 bù gōngzhèngde; 不公正地 bù gōngzhèng de. **belt** *v* 1 [T] 用带缚住 yòng dài fùzhù. 2 [T] [非正式用语] 用拳头〔頭〕打 yòng quántou dǎ. 3 [I] [非正式用语] 快速移动〔動〕kuàisù yídòng: ~ing along the road 在路上快速行驶. 4 [短语动词] belt up [俚] 保持安静 bǎochí ānjìng. **belting** *n* [C] [非正式用语] 用皮带抽打 yòng pídài chōudǎ.

bemoan /bɪˈməʊn/ *v* [T] [正式用语] 悲叹〔嘆〕bēitàn.

bench /bentʃ/ *n* 1 [C] 长〔長〕凳 chángdèng. 2 [C] (木工等的)工作台〔臺〕gōngzuòtái. 3 the bench [sing] (a) (法庭上的)法官席 fǎguānxí. (b) [亦作 sing, 用 pl v] 法官(总称) fǎguān.

bend /bend/ *v* [*pt*, *pp* bent /bent/] 1 [I, T] (使)弯〔彎〕曲 wānqū: ~ the wire 把金属线弄弯. 2 [I, T] (使)弯腰 wānyāo: ~ down and touch your toes 弯下腰来, 用手碰到脚尖. 3 [习语] be bent on (doing) sth 专〔專〕心致志于 zhuān xīn zhì zhì yú. bend over backwards 竭尽〔盡〕全力 jiéjìn quánlì. **bend** *n*

B

1 [C] 弯曲 wānqū; 弯曲处〔處〕wānqūchù: *a* ~ **in the road** 马路弯曲的地方. 2 the bends [pl] 潜〔潛〕水员病(潜水员过快地浮到水面时引起的疼痛) qiánshuǐyuánbìng. 3 [习语] round the bend [非正式用语]疯〔瘋〕狂 fēngkuáng.

beneath /bɪˈniːθ/ *prep, adv* [正式用语] 1 在下面 zài xiàmiàn. 2 不值得 bù zhí dé: ~ contempt 卑鄙到极点.

benefactor /ˈbenɪfæktə(r)/ *n* [C] 捐助人 juānzhùrén; 恩人 ēnrén. benefactress /-fæktrɪs/ *n* [C] 女捐助人 nǚ juānzhùrén; 女恩人 nǚ ēnrén.

beneficial /ˌbenɪˈfɪʃl/ *adj* 有益的 yǒuyìde; 有利的 yǒulìde.

beneficiary /ˌbenɪˈfɪʃərɪ; *US* -ˈfɪʃɪerɪ/ *n* [C] [*pl* -ies] (遗嘱等的)受益人 shòuyìrén.

benefit /ˈbenɪfɪt/ *n* 1 (a) [sing, U] 利益 lìyì; 好处〔處〕hǎochù; 帮〔幫〕助 bāngzhù: *have the ~ of a good education* 从良好教育获得的好处. (b) [C] 恩惠 ēnhuì; 益处 yìchù: *the ~s of modern medicine* 现代医学的恩惠. 2 [U, C] 补〔補〕助费 bǔzhùfèi; 救济〔濟〕金 jiùjìjīn: *sickness* ~ 疾病补助费. 3 [习语] for sb's benefit 为〔爲〕了帮助某人 wèile bāngzhù mǒurén. give sb the ˌbenefit of the ˈdoubt 在证〔證〕据〔據〕不足的情况下, 对某人的嫌疑作善意的解释 zài zhèngjù bùzú de qíngkuàng xià, duì mǒurén de xiányí zuò shànyìde jiěshì. benefit *v* 1 [T] 有益于 yǒuyì yú. 2 [I] 得益 déyì; 得到好处 dédào hǎochù.

benevolent /bɪˈnevələnt/ *adj* 仁慈的 réncíde; 慈善的 císhànde. benevolence /-ləns/ *n* [U].

benign /bɪˈnaɪn/ *adj* 1 慈祥的 cíxiángde; 宽厚的 kuānhòude. 2 (病)不危险〔險〕的 bù wēixiǎnde; 良性的 liángxìngde.

bent[1] *pt* of BEND.

bent[2] /bent/ *n* [C, 常作 sing] 才具 cáijù; 天赋 tiānfù: *have a ~ for language* 具有语言天赋.

bent[3] /bent/ *adj* [俚语, 尤用于英国英语] 1 不老实〔實〕的 bù lǎoshi de. 2 搞同性恋〔戀〕爱〔愛〕的 gǎo tóngxìng liàn'ài de.

bequeath /bɪˈkwiːð/ *v* [T] [正式用语]死后遗赠 sǐ hòu yízèng. bequest /bɪˈkwest/ *n* [C] [正式用语]遗赠物 yízèngwù; 遗产〔產〕yíchǎn.

berate /bɪˈreɪt/ *v* [T] [正式用语]严〔嚴〕责 yánzé; 骂 mà.

bereaved /bɪˈriːvd/ *adj* [正式用语]丧〔喪〕失亲〔親〕友的 sàngshī qīnyǒu de. bereavement /bɪˈriːvment / *n* [U, C].

bereft /bɪˈreft/ *adj of* [正式用语]失去…的 shīqù…de: ~ *of all hope* 丧失了一切希望.

beret /ˈbereɪ; *US* bəˈreɪ/ *n* [C] 贝雷帽(兵士戴的扁平帽子) bèiléimào.

berry /ˈberɪ/ *n* [C] [*pl* -ies] 浆〔漿〕果 jiāngguǒ: *black* ~ 黑刺莓.

berserk /bəˈsɜːk/ *adj* [习语] go berserk 狂怒 kuángnù. 发〔發〕狂 fākuáng.

berth /bɜːθ/ *n* [C] 1 (火车、船上的)卧铺〔舖〕wòpù. 2 停泊地 tíngbódì; 锚位 máowèi. berth *v* [I, T] (使)停泊 tíngbó.

beseech /bɪˈsiːtʃ/ *v* [*pt, pp* besought /bɪˈsɔːt/ 或~ed] [T] [正式用语]恳〔懇〕求 kěnqiú; 哀求 āiqiú.

beset /bɪˈset/ *v* [-tt-; *pt, pp* beset] [T] [正式用语][常用被动语态]困扰〔擾〕kùnrǎo: ~ *by problems* 被各种问题困扰.

beside /bɪˈsaɪd/ *prep* 1 在…旁边〔邊〕zài… pángbiān: *Sit* ~ me. 坐到我旁边来. 2 [习语] beˈside oneself 狂怒 kuángnù; 发〔發〕狂 fākuáng.

besides /bɪˈsaɪdz/ *prep* 除…之外 chú…zhīwài. besides *adv* 而且 érqiě; 还〔還〕有 háiyǒu.

besiege /bɪˈsiːdʒ/ *v* [T] 包围〔圍〕bāowéi; 围攻 wéigōng: [喻] *The Prime Minister was* ~d by reporters. 首相被记者包围.

bespoke /bɪˈspəʊk/ *adj* (衣裳等)定做的 dìngzuòde.

best[1] /best/ *adj* 1 最好的 zuìhǎode: *the* ~ dinner I've ever tasted 我所品尝过的最好的饭菜. 2 (健康情况)最好的 zuìhǎode: *She is very ill but always feels* ~ in the morning. 她病得很厉害, 但在早晨却往往觉得挺有精神. ˌbest ˈman *n* [C] 男傧〔儐〕相 nán bīnxiàng.

best[2] /best/ *adv* 1 最好地 zuìhǎode: *He works* ~ in the morning. 上午他工作效率最好. 2 最大程度地 zuìdà chéngdù de; 最 zuì: *I enjoyed her first book* ~. 我最欣赏他出版的第一本书. 3 [习语] as ˈbest one ˈcan 尽〔盡〕最大努力 jìn zuìdà nǔlì. ˌbest ˈseller *n* [C] 畅〔暢〕销书〔書〕chàngxiāoshū.

best[3] /best/ *n* [sing] 1 最好的事物 zuìhǎode shìwù: *want the* ~ for one's children 要给自己的孩子们弄到最好的. 2 最大努力 zuìdà nǔlì. 3 [习语] all the ˈbest [非正式用语](分别时用语)一切顺利! yíqiè shùnlì! at ˈbest 就最乐〔樂〕观〔觀〕的一面看 jiù zuì lèguānde yímiàn kàn. at its/one's best 处〔處〕在最好状〔狀〕态〔態〕chǔzài zuìhǎo zhuàngtài. the best of both worlds 两方面的优〔優〕点〔點〕liǎng fāngmiàn de yōudiǎn; 两全其美 liǎng quán qí měi. make the best of sth 随〔隨〕遇而安 suí yù ér ān.

bestial /ˈbestɪəl; *US* ˈbestʃəl/ *adj* 残〔殘〕忍

B

的 cánrěnde;野蛮〔蠻〕的 yěmánde. **bestiality** /ˌbestɪˈælətɪ; *US* ˌbestʃɪ-/ *n* [U].

bestow /bɪˈstəʊ/ *v* [T] 赠予 zèngyǔ;给予 jǐyǔ: ~ *an honour on her* 给她以荣誉.

bet /bet/ *v* [-tt-; *pt*, *pp* bet 或 betted] [I, T] 1 (用钱)打赌 dǎdǔ. 2 [非正式用语]敢断〔斷〕定 gǎn duàndìng: *I* ~ they'll come late. 我敢断定他们会迟到. **bet** *n* [C] (a) 打赌 dǎdǔ. (b) 赌注 dǔzhù. **better** *n* [C] 打赌者 dǎdǔzhě.

betray /bɪˈtreɪ/ *v* [T] 1 背叛 bèipàn;出卖〔賣〕chūmài. 2 泄漏(秘密等) xièlòu. 3 暴露 bàolù;表现 biǎoxiàn: *His face* ~ed his guilt. 他的表情显示出他是有罪的. **betrayal** /bɪˈtreɪəl/ *n* [C, U] 背叛 bèipàn;出卖 chūmài;背叛的事例 bèipànde shìlì. **betrayer** *n* [C] 背叛者 bèipànzhě.

betrothed /bɪˈtrəʊðd/ *adj* [正式用语]订了婚的 dìng le hūn de.

better[1] /ˈbetə(r)/ *adj* 1 较好的 jiàohǎode;更好的 gènghǎode: ~ weather than yesterday 比昨天好的天气. 2 (健康状况)好转〔轉〕的 hǎozhuǎnde: *She has been much* ~ since her operation. 自从她做了手术,身体好些了. 3 [习语] one's better ˈhalf [非正式用语,谐谑]自己的妻子或丈夫 zìjǐde qīzǐ huò zhàngfū.

better[2] /ˈbetə(r)/ *adv* 1 更好地 gènghǎode: *You play tennis* ~ than I do. 你网球打得比我好. 2 [习语] be better ˈoff 较富裕 jiào fùyù. had better 最好还〔還〕是 zuìhǎo háishì;还是…的好 háishì…de hǎo: *You'd* ~ *go soon*. 你最好马上就走. know better (than to do sth) 很明白(而不致于) hěn míngbai.

better[3] /ˈbetə(r)/ *n* [sing] 1 较好的事物 jiàohǎode shìwù: *I expected* ~ from him. 我期望他有较好的表现. 2 [习语] get the better of sb 打败 dǎbài;智胜〔勝〕zhìshèng.

better[4] /ˈbetə(r)/ *v* [T] 1 超过〔過〕chāoguò. 2 改善 gǎishàn: ~ oneself 改善自己的地位.

between /bɪˈtwiːn/ *prep* 1 (地点、时间)在…中间 zài…zhōngjiān: *Q comes* ~ P and R in the alphabet. 在字母表上,Q在P和R之间. *Children must go to school* ~ *5 and 16*. 5岁到16岁之间的儿童必须上学. 2 (表示关联、关系)在…之间 zài…zhījiān: *fly* ~ London and Paris 在伦敦和巴黎之间飞行. *the link* ~ *unemployment and crime* 失业和犯罪之间的联系. 3 由…分享,分担〔擔〕yóu…fēnxiǎng, fēndān: *We drank a bottle of wine* ~ us. 我们分享一瓶酒. 4 作为〔爲〕共同努力的结果 zuòwéi gòngtóng nǔlì de jiéguǒ: *B*~ them, they collected £500. 他们共同募集了500英镑. **between** *adv* 1 (亦作 in between) (时间或空间)在中间 zài zhōngjiān. 2 [习语] ˌfew and far beˈtween 稀少 xīshǎo;罕见 hǎnjiàn.

bevel /ˈbevl/ *v* [-ll-; 美语 -l-] [T] 斜截 xiéjié.

beverage /ˈbevərɪdʒ/ *n* [C] [正式用语]饮料(汽水、茶、酒等) yǐnliào.

bevy /ˈbevɪ/ *n* [C] [*pl* -ies] 大群 dàqún.

beware /bɪˈweə(r)/ *v* [I] (*of*) 谨防 jǐnfáng;当〔當〕心 dāngxīn: *B*~ *of the dog!* 当心狗!

bewilder /bɪˈwɪldə(r)/ *v* [T] 迷惑 míhuò;弄糊涂〔塗〕nòng hútu: ~*ed by the noise and lights* 被吵闹和光亮搞糊涂了. **bewildering** *adj*.

bewitch /bɪˈwɪtʃ/ *v* [T] 1 施魔力于 shī mólì yú. 2 使着迷 shǐ zháomí;使心醉 shǐ xīnzuì. **bewitching** *adj*.

beyond /bɪˈjɒnd/ *prep* 1 在,向…的那边〔邊〕zài, xiàng…de nàbiān: *The path continues* ~ the village. 这条小路延伸到村子的外边. 2 超出 chāochū: *What happened was* ~ my control. 发生的事是我控制不了的. 3 [习语] be beyond sb [非正式用语]某人所理解不了的 mǒurén suǒ lǐjiě bùliǎode. **beyond** *adv* 在远〔遠〕处〔處〕zài yuǎnchù;更远地 gèngyuǎnde.

bias /ˈbaɪəs/ *n* [U, C] 偏见 piānjiàn. **bias** *v* [-s-, -ss-] [T] [尤用于被动语态]以偏见影响〔響〕yǐ piānjiàn yǐngxiǎng: *a* ~*ed jury* 有偏见的陪审团.

bib /bɪb/ *n* [C] 1 (小孩的)围〔圍〕涎 wéixián. 2 裙的上部 qúnde shàngbù.

bible /ˈbaɪbl/ *n* 1 (a) the Bible [sing] (犹太教和基督教)圣〔聖〕经〔經〕shèngjīng. (b) 圣经的版本 shèngjīng de bǎnběn. 2 [C] [喻]有权〔權〕威的书 yǒu quánwēi de shū: *the gardeners'* ~ 园林方面的权威著作. **biblical** /ˈbɪblɪkl/ *adj*.

bibliography /ˌbɪblɪˈɒgrəfɪ/ *n* [C] [*pl* -ies] 书〔書〕目 shūmù;文献〔獻〕目录〔錄〕wénxiàn mùlù. **bibliographer** /-fə(r)/ *n* [C].

bicentenary /ˌbaɪˌsenˈtiːnərɪ; *US* -ˈsentənerɪ/ *n* [C] [*pl* -ies] 二百年(纪念) èrbǎinián.

bicentennial /ˌbaɪˌsenˈtenɪəl/ *adj* 二百年纪念的 èrbǎinián jìniàn de. **bicentennial** *n* [C] = BICENTENARY.

biceps /ˈbaɪseps/ *n* [C] [*pl* biceps] 二头〔頭〕肌 èrtóujī.

bicker /ˈbɪkə(r)/ *v* [I] 口角 kǒujiǎo;争吵 zhēngchǎo.

bicycle /ˈbaɪsɪkl/ *n* [C] 自行车 zìxíngchē;单

〔單〕车 dānchē. **bicycle** *v* [I] [旧]骑自行车 qí zìxíngchē.

bid /bɪd/ *v* [-dd-; *pt*, *pp* bid; 义项二中, *pt* bade /bæd/ , *pp* ~den /ˈbɪdn /] 1 [I, T] 出(价)购〔購〕买〔買〕chū gòumǎi. 2 [T] [古语或正式用语] (a) 命令 mìnglìng; 吩咐 fēnfù: *She bade me (to) come in*. 她命令我进去. (b) 说 shuō: ~ *sb farewell* 向某人说再见. **bid** *n* [C] 1 企图〔圖〕qǐtú; 努力 nǔlì: *a rescue* ~ 救援的图谋. 2 出价 chūjià. **bidder** *n* [C]. **bidding** *n* [U].

bide /baɪd/ *v* [习语] **bide one's time** 等待时〔時〕机〔機〕děngdài shíjī.

biennial /baɪˈenɪəl/ *adj* 1 两年一次的 liǎngnián yícì de. 2 延续〔續〕两年的 yánxù liǎngnián de.

bier /bɪə(r)/ *n* [C] 棺材架 guāncaijià.

bifocal /ˌbaɪˈfəʊkl/ *adj* (眼镜)双〔雙〕焦点〔點〕的 shuāng jiāodiǎn de. **bifocals** *n* [pl] 双焦点眼镜 shuāng jiāodiǎn yǎnjìng.

big /bɪg/ *adj* [~**ger**, ~**gest**] 1 大的 dàde; 重大的 zhòngdàde: ~ *feet* 大脚. *a* ~ *match* 重大比赛. 2 [非正式用语, 尤用于美国英语]大受欢〔歡〕迎的 dà shòu huānyíngde. 3 [习语] **a big noise / shot** [非正式用语]重要人物 zhòngyào rénwù. **big 'game** *n* [U] 大的猎〔獵〕物 dàde lièwù. **'big-head** *n* [C] [非正式用语]自高自大的人 zì gāo zì dà de rén. **'bigwig** *n* [C] [非正式用语]重要人物 zhòngyào rénwù.

bigamy /ˈbɪgəmɪ/ *n* [U] 重婚(罪) chónghūn. **'bigamist** *n* [C] 重婚罪犯 chónghūn zuìfàn. **bigamous** *adj*.

bigot /ˈbɪgət/ *n* [C] 执〔執〕拗的人 zhíniùde rén; 抱偏见的人 bào piānjiàn de rén. **bigoted** *adj* 执拗的 zhíniùde; 心胸狭窄的 xīnxiōng xiázhǎi de.

bike /baɪk/ *n* [C] [非正式用语] short for BICYCLE.

bikini /bɪˈkiːnɪ/ *n* [C] 三点〔點〕式女游泳衣 sāndiǎnshì nǚ yóuyǒngyī.

bilateral /ˌbaɪˈlætərəl/ *adj* 双〔雙〕边〔邊〕的 shuāngbiānde: *a* ~ *agreement* 双边协定.

bile /baɪl/ *n* [U] 胆〔膽〕汁 dǎnzhī.

bilge /bɪldʒ/ *n* [U] [俚]废〔廢〕话 fèihuà.

bilingual /ˌbaɪˈlɪŋgwəl/ *adj* 说两种〔種〕语言的 shuō liǎngzhǒng yǔyán de; 用两种语言写〔寫〕成的 yòng liǎngzhǒng yǔyán xiě chéng de.

bilious /ˈbɪlɪəs/ *adj* 恶〔噁〕心的 ěxinde.

bill[1] /bɪl/ *n* [C] 1 账〔賬〕单〔單〕zhàngdān. 2 [法律]议〔議〕案 yì'àn; 法案 fǎ'àn. 3 [美语]钞票 chāopiào; 纸币〔幣〕zhǐbì. 4 招贴 zhāotiē; 广〔廣〕告 guǎnggào; 传〔傳〕单 chuándān. 5 [习语] **fill/fit the 'bill** 符合需要 fúhé xūyào; 解决问题 jiějué wèntí. **bill** *v* [T] 1 向(某人)送账单 xiàng sòng zhàngdān; 向某人收…钱〔錢〕xiàng mǒurén shōu …qián. 2 宣布…扮演 xuānbù …bànyǎn: *He is* ~*ed to appear as Othello*. 宣布他扮演奥赛罗.

bill[2] /bɪl/ *n* [C] 鸟〔鳥〕嘴 niǎozuǐ.

billet /ˈbɪlɪt/ *n* [C] (军营以外的)部队〔隊〕宿舍 bùduì sùshè. **billet** *v* [T] 安顿〔頓〕(士兵)在军营〔營〕以外的地方住宿 āndùn zài jūnyíng yǐwài de dìfang zhùsù.

billiards /ˈbɪlɪədz/ *n* [用 sing v] 台球游戏〔戲〕táiqiú yóuxì; 弹〔彈〕子游戏 dànzǐ yóuxì.

billion /ˈbɪlɪən/ *pron*, *adj*, *n* 1 [C] 十亿〔億〕(的) shíyì. 2 [美国英语]万〔萬〕亿(的) wànyì.

billow /ˈbɪləʊ/ *n* [C] [喻]雾〔霧〕烟〔煙〕等波浪般滚滚向前的东〔東〕西 wù yān děng bōlàng bān gǔngǔn xiàngqián de dōngxi. **billow** *v* [I]波浪般滚动〔動〕bōlàng bān gǔndòng. **billowy** *adj*.

billy-goat /ˈbɪlɪ gəʊt/ *n* [C] 公山羊 gōng shānyáng.

bin /bɪn/ *n* [C] (贮藏食物、煤等的)箱子 xiāngzi.

binary /ˈbaɪnərɪ/ *adj* 二进〔進〕制的 èrjìnzhì de.

bind /baɪnd/ [*pt*, *pp* **bound** /baʊnd/] *v* 1 [T] (a) 捆 kǔn; 绑 bǎng: ~ *the prisoner's legs to the chair* 把犯人的双腿捆在椅子上. (b) [喻]使结合 shǐ jiéhé: *bound by friendship* 由于友谊而结合. 2 [T] 装〔裝〕订(书) zhuāngdìng: *a book bound in leather* 皮装书. 3 [T]使受诺言、法律等约束 shǐ shòu nuòyán、fǎlǜ děng yuēsù: ~ *her to secrecy* 使她答应保守秘密. 4 [I, T] 包扎〔紮〕bāozhā. **bind** *n* [sing] [非正式用语]令人厌〔厭〕烦的事物 lìng rén yànfán de shìwù. **binder** *n* [C] 1 活页夹 huóyèjiā. 2 装订工 zhuāngdìnggōng; 装订材料 zhuāngdìng cáiliào. **binding** *n* [C] 书〔書〕籍封面 shūjí fēngmiàn.

binge /bɪndʒ/ *n* [C][非正式用语] 1 狂欢〔歡〕作乐〔樂〕kuánghuān zuòlè. 2 无〔無〕节〔節〕制的狂热〔熱〕行为〔爲〕wú jiézhì de kuángrè xíngwéi: *a shopping* ~ 无节制的购物.

bingo /ˈbɪŋgəʊ/ *n* [U]宾〔賓〕戈(一种赌博游戏)bīngē.

binoculars /bɪˈnɒkjʊləz/ *n* [pl] (双筒)望远〔遠〕镜 wàngyuǎnjìng.

biochemistry /ˌbaɪəʊˈkemɪstrɪ/ *n* [U]生物化学〔學〕shēngwù huàxué. **biochemist** *n* [C] 生物化学家 shēngwù huàxué jiā.

biodegradable /ˌbaɪəʊdiˈgreɪdəbl/ *adj* 生物可降解的 shēngwù kějiàngjiě de.

biodiversity /ˌbaɪəʊdaɪˈvɜːsətɪ/ *n* [U] 生物多样〔樣〕性 shēngwù duōyàngxìng.

bioenergy /ˌbaɪəʊˈenədʒɪ/ *n* [U] 生物能

B

shēngwùnéng.

bioengineering /ˌbaɪəʊendʒɪˈnɪərɪŋ/ *n* [U] 生物工程(学) shēngwù gōngchéng.

biofuel /ˈbaɪəʊfjuːəl/ *n* [C] 生物燃料 shēngwù ránliào.

biography /baɪˈɒɡrəfɪ/ *n* [C] [*pl* -ies] 传〔傳〕记 zhuànjì. **biographer** /-fə(r)/ *n* [C] 传记作家 zhuànjì zuòjiā. **biographical** /ˌbaɪəˈɡræfɪkl/ *adj*.

biology /baɪˈɒlədʒɪ/ *n* [U] 生物学〔學〕shēngwùxué; 生态〔態〕学 shēngtàixué. **biological** /ˌbaɪəˈlɒdʒɪkl/ *adj*. **biologist** *n* [U] 生物学家 shēngwùxuéjiā; 生物学者 shēngwùxuézhě.

biosphere /ˈbaɪəʊsfɪə(r)/ *n* [C] 生物圈 shēngwùquān: *Society must learn to live sustainably in the* ～. 人类应学会与自然界和谐共存. *new methods of assessing the toxicity risks of releasing a substance into the* ～ 评估有毒物质排放可能对自然界造成的危害的新方法.

biotechnology /ˌbaɪəʊtekˈnɒlədʒɪ/ *n* [U] 生物技术〔術〕shēngwù jìshù.

bioterrorism /ˌbaɪəʊˈterərɪzəm/ *n* [U] 生物恐怖主义〔義〕shēngwù kǒngbù zhǔyì. **bioˈterrorist** *n* [C] 生物恐怖主义分子 shēngwù kǒngbù zhǔyì fènzǐ.

birch /bɜːtʃ/ *n* 1 [U,C] 桦〔樺〕huà; 白桦 báihuà; 桦木 huàmù. 2 **the birch** [sing] (鞭笞用的)桦条〔條〕huàtiáo.

bird /bɜːd/ *n* [C] 1 鸟 niǎo; 禽 qín. 2 [俚语,尤用于英国英语]年轻〔輕〕姑娘 niánqīng gūniang. ˈ**bird flu** *n* [U] 禽流感 qínliúgǎn. ˌ**bird of** ˈ**prey** *n* [C] 猛禽 měngqín.

biro /ˈbaɪərəʊ/ *n* [C] [*pl* ～s] (*P*) 圆珠笔〔筆〕yuánzhūbǐ.

birth /bɜːθ/ *n* 1 [C,U] 分娩 fēnmiǎn; 出生 chūshēng. 2 [U] 出身 chūshēn; 血统 xuètǒng. 3 [sing] 起源 qǐyuán. 4 [习语]**give birth (to sb/sth)** 分娩 fēnmiǎn. ˈ**birth control** *n* [C] 节〔節〕制生育(方法) jiézhì shēngyù. **birthday** *n* [C] 生日 shēngrì. ˈ**birthmark** *n* [C] 胎记 tāijì; 胎志 tāizhì. ˈ**birth rate** *n* [C] 出生率(每年的千分比) chūshēnglǜ.

biscuit /ˈbɪskɪt/ *n* [C]饼干〔乾〕bǐnggān.

bisect /ˌbaɪˈsekt/ *v* [T]把…分为〔爲〕二 bǎ…fēn wéi èr.

bishop /ˈbɪʃəp/ *n* [C] 1 (基督教)主教 zhǔjiào. 2 (国际象棋中的)象 xiàng. **bishopric** /-rɪk/ *n* [C] 主教职〔職〕位或管区〔區〕zhǔjiào zhíwèi huò guǎnqū.

bison /ˈbaɪsn/ *n* [C] [*pl* bison] 欧〔歐〕洲野牛 Ōuzhōu yěniú; 美洲水牛 Měizhōu shuǐniú.

bistro /ˈbiːstrəʊ/ *n* [C] [*pl* ～s] 小餐馆 xiǎo cānguǎn.

bit[1] *pt* of BITE.

bit[2] /bɪt/ *n* 1 [C]一点〔點〕yìdiǎn; 一些 yìxiē; 小片 xiǎopiàn: *a* ～ **of paper** 一点纸. 2 [习语] **a bit** (a) 有点儿〔兒〕yǒudiǎnr; 相当〔當〕xiāngdāng: *a* ～ *tired* 有点累. (b) 一点时〔時〕间或距离〔離〕yìdiǎn shíjiān huò jùlí: *Wait a* ～. 等一会儿. **bit by** ˈ**bit** 一点一点地 yìdiǎn yìdiǎn de; 慢慢地 mànmànde; 渐〔漸〕渐地 jiànjiànde. **do one's** ˈ**bit** [非正式用语] 尽〔盡〕自己的一份力量 jìn zìjǐde yífèn lìliàng. **every bit as good, bad, etc.** 完全好,坏〔壞〕等 wánquán hǎo, huài děng. **not a** ˈ**bit** 一点也不 yìdiǎn yě bù; 毫不 háo bù.

bit[3] /bɪt/ *n* [C] 1 马嚼子 Mǎjiáozi. 2 钻〔鑽〕头〔頭〕zuàntóu.

bit[4] /bɪt/ *n* [C][电子计算机](二进制数)位(有时译作"彼特") wèi.

bitch /bɪtʃ/ *n* 1 母狗 mǔgǒu. 2 [俚,贬]坏〔壞〕女人 huài nǚrén.

bite /baɪt/ *v* [*pt* bit /bɪt/, *pp* bitten /ˈbɪtn/] 1 [I,T] 咬 yǎo. 2 [I,T] (虫等)叮 dīng; 蜇 zhē. 3 [I] (鱼)吃饵 chī'ěr. 4 [I] 紧〔緊〕握 jǐn wò; 有效果 yǒu xiàoguǒ. 5 [习语] **bite sb's head off** [非正式用语]愤怒地顶撞某人 fènnùde dǐngzhuàng mǒurén. **bite off** ˌ**more than one can** ˈ**chew** 贪多嚼不烂〔爛〕tān duō jiáo bú làn. **bite** *n* 1 [C] (a) 咬 yǎo; 叮 dīng. (b) 咬下的一块〔塊〕yǎo xià de yíkuài. 2 [sing] [非正式用语](少量)食物 shíwù: *have a* ～ *to eat* 有点东西吃. 3 [C] 咬伤〔傷〕yǎoshāng; 蜇伤 zhēshāng. **biting** *adj* 尖厉〔厲〕刺人的 jiānlì cìrén de.

bitter /ˈbɪtə(r)/ *adj* 1 有苦味的 yǒu kǔwèi de. 2 愤恨的 fènhènde; 仇恨的 chóuhènde: ～ **enemies** 死敌. 3 辛酸的 xīnsuānde; 痛苦的 tòngkǔde. 4 严〔嚴〕寒的 yánhánde; 刺骨的 cìgǔde: *a* ～ **wind** 刺骨寒风. **bitter** *n* [U] [英国英语] 苦啤酒 kǔ píjiǔ. **bitterly** *adv*: ～*ly cold* 苦寒. ～*ly disappointed* 非常心酸的失望. **bitterness** *n* [U].

bitumen /ˈbɪtjʊmən; *US* bəˈtuːmən/ *n* [U] 沥〔瀝〕青 lìqīng.

bivouac /ˈbɪvʊæk/ *n* [C]露营〔營〕lùyíng. **bivouac** *v* [-ck-] [I] 露营 lùyíng.

bizarre /bɪˈzɑː(r)/ *adj* 异〔異〕乎寻〔尋〕常的 yì hū xúncháng de; 稀奇古怪的 xīqí gǔguài de.

blab /blæb/ *v* [-bb-] [I] [俚]泄露秘密 xièlù mìmì.

black /blæk/ *adj* 1 黑的 hēide; 漆黑的 qīhēide. 2 黑人的 hēirénde. 3 脏〔髒〕的 zāngde. 4 (咖啡)不加牛奶或奶油的 bùjiā niúnǎi huò nǎiyóu de. 5 没有希望的 méiyǒu xīwàng de: *The future looks* ～. 前途看来无望. 6 愤怒的 fènnùde: *a* ～ **look** 一脸怒气. 7 滑稽而嘲讽〔諷〕的 huájī ér cháofěng de. **black** *n* 1 [U] 黑色 hēisè. 2 [C] 黑人 hēirén. **black** *v* [T] 1 使黑 shǐ hēi; 弄黑 nòng hēi. 2 宣布不干〔幹〕(工作),不处〔處〕理(物资) xuānbù bú gàn, bú chǔlǐ:

The strikers ~ed the cargo. 罢工工人宣布拒绝装卸货物. 3 [短语动词] black 'out 失去知觉〔覺〕shīqù zhījué. black sth out 实〔實〕行灯〔燈〕火管制 shíxíng dēnghuǒ guǎnzhì. 'blackberry *n* [C] [*pl*. -ies] 黑莓 hēiméi. 'blackbird *n* [C] 乌〔烏〕鸫〔鶇〕wūdōng. 'blackboard *n* [C] 黑板 hēibǎn. ˌblack'currant *n* [C] 黑醋栗 hēicùlì. blacken *v* 1 [I,T] (使)变〔變〕黑 biànhēi. 2 [T] 破坏〔壞〕(名声等) pòhuài. black'eye *n* [C] 被打得发〔發〕青的眼圈 bèi dǎdé fāqīng de yǎnquān. 'blackhead *n* [C] 黑头〔頭〕粉刺 hēitóu fěncì. ˌblack 'ice *n* [U] 马路上察觉不出的冰 mǎlù shàng chájué bùchū de bīng. 'blackleg *n* [C] 罢〔罷〕工中擅自上工的人 bàgōng zhōng shànzì shànggōng de rén. 'blacklist *n* [C] 黑名单〔單〕hēi míngdān. 'blacklist *v* [T] 把…列入黑名单 bǎ…lièrù hēi míngdān. blackly *adv*. ˌblack 'magic *n* [U] 妖术〔術〕yāoshù; 巫术 wūshù. 'blackmail *n* [U] 1 敲诈 qiāozhà; 勒索 lèsuǒ. 2 威胁〔脅〕wēixié. 'blackmail *v* [T] 敲诈 qiāozhà; 勒索 lèsuǒ. 'blackmailer *n* [C]. ˌblack 'market *n* [C, 常作 sing] 黑市 hēishì. blackness *n* [U]. 'blackout *n* [C] 1 (战时)灯〔燈〕火管制 dēnghuǒ guǎnzhì. 2 停电〔電〕tíngdiàn. 3 临〔臨〕时记忆〔憶〕缺失 línshí jìyì quēshī; 临时眩晕 línshí xuànyùn. 4 (新闻等的)不准发〔發〕表 bùzhǔn fābiǎo: *a news ~out* 新闻封锁. ˌblack 'sheep *n* [C] 败家子 bàijiāzǐ. 'blacksmith /-smɪθ/ *n* [C] 铁匠 tiějiàng.

bladder /ˈblædə(r)/ *n* [C] 膀胱 pángguāng.

blade /bleɪd/ *n* [C] 1 刀刃 dāorèn; 刀口 dāokǒu; 刀片 dāopiàn. 2 桨〔槳〕片 jiǎngpiàn; 螺旋桨桨片 luóxuánjiǎng jiǎngpiàn. 3 草片 cǎopiàn.

blame /bleɪm/ *v* 1 [T] 责备〔備〕zébèi; 找…的差错 zhǎo…de chācuò. 2 [习语] be to blame (for sth) 应受责怪的 yīng shòu zéguàide. blame *n* [U] 责任 zérèn. blameless *adj* 无〔無〕可责难〔難〕的 wúkě zénàn de; 无过〔過〕错的 wú guòcuò de. blameworthy *adj* 该受责备的 gāi shòu zébèi de.

blanch /blɑːntʃ; *US* blæntʃ/ *v* [I,T] (使)变〔變〕白 biàn bái.

blancmange /bləˈmɒnʒ/ *n* [U] 牛奶冻 niúnǎidòng.

bland /blænd/ *adj* 1 温和的 wēnhéde; 和蔼的 hé'ǎide. 2 (食物)刺激性少的 cìjīxìng shǎo de. 3 枯燥乏味的 kūzào fáwèi de. blandly *adv*. blandness *n* [U].

blank /blæŋk/ *adj* 1 (纸)没有写〔寫〕字的 méiyǒu xiězì de, 白的 báide. 2 失色的 shīsède; 没有表情的 méiyǒu biǎoqíng de: *a ~ look* 茫然若失的样子. blank *n* [C] 1 空白 kòngbái. 2 空弹〔彈〕kōngdàn. ˌblank 'cheque *n* [C] 1 开〔開〕支票人已签〔簽〕字, 由收款人自填款数〔數〕的支票 kāi zhīpiào rén yǐ qiānzì, yóu shōukuǎnrén zì tián kuǎnshù de zhīpiào. 2 [喻] 自由处〔處〕理权〔權〕zìyóu chǔlǐquán. blankly *adv*. ˌblank 'verse *n* [U] 无〔無〕韵诗 wúyùnshī.

blanket /ˈblæŋkɪt/ *n* [C] 床单〔單〕chuángdān: [喻] *a ~ of snow* 一层雪. blanket *v* [T] 覆盖〔蓋〕fùgài. blanket *adj* 总〔總〕括的 zǒngkuòde: ~ *criticism* 总的批评.

blare /bleə(r)/ *v* [I,T] 发〔發〕出响〔響〕而刺耳的声〔聲〕音 fāchū xiǎng ér cì'ěrde shēngyīn. blare *n* [U].

blasé /ˈblɑːzeɪ; *US* blɑːˈzeɪ/ *adj* (因司空见惯而)无〔無〕动〔動〕于衷的 wú dòng yú zhōng de.

blaspheme /blæsˈfiːm/ *v* [I,T] 亵渎 xièdú. blasphemous /ˈblæsfəməs/ *adj*. blasphemy /ˈblæsfəmɪ/ *n* [C,U] [*pl* -ies].

blast /blɑːst; *US* blæst/ *n* [C] 1 爆炸气〔氣〕浪 bàozhà qìlàng. 2 一阵风〔風〕yízhèn fēng. 3 管乐〔樂〕器的声〔聲〕音 guǎnyuèqìde shēngyīn. 4 [习语] at full 'blast 全力地 quánlìde. blast *v* 1 [I,T] (用炸药)炸 zhà. 2 [短语动词] blast 'off (宇宙飞船等)发〔發〕射 fāshè. blast *interj* (表示厌烦)该死 gāisǐ. 'blastfurnace *n* [C] 鼓风炉〔爐〕gǔfēnglú; 高炉 gāolú. 'blast-off *n* [C] (宇宙飞船等的)发射 fāshè.

blatant /ˈbleɪtənt/ *adj* 厚颜的 hòuyánde; 炫耀的 xuànyàode; 显〔顯〕眼的 xiǎnyǎnde. blatantly *adv*.

blaze /bleɪz/ *n* 1 [C] (a) 火焰 huǒyàn; 火 huǒ. (b) 烈火 lièhuǒ. 2 [sing] 光辉〔輝〕guānghuī; 光彩 guāngcǎi: [喻] *a ~ of publicity* 大出风头. blaze *v* [I] 1 熊熊燃烧〔燒〕xióngxióng ránshāo. 2 闪〔閃〕耀 shǎnyào; 发〔發〕光彩 fā guāngcǎi. 3 (感情)激发 jīfā: *blazing with anger* 发怒 fānù. blazing *adj*.

blazer /ˈbleɪzə(r)/ *n* [C] 运〔運〕动〔動〕茄克 yùndòng jiākè.

bleach /bliːtʃ/ *v* [I,T] 漂白 piǎobái. bleach *n* [U] 漂白剂〔劑〕piǎobáijì.

bleak /bliːk/ *adj* (天气)阴〔陰〕冷的 yīnlěngde: *a ~ night* 阴冷的夜晚. [喻] *The future looks ~*. 前途看来是暗淡的. bleakly *adv*.

bleary /ˌblɪəˈriː/ *adj* [-ier, -iest] (眼睛)疲倦疼痛的 píjuàn téngtòng de.

bleat /bliːt/ *v* [I] *n* [C,U] (羊)叫 jiào.

bleed /bliːd/ *v* [*pt*, *pp* bled /bled/] 1 [I] 流血 liúxuè; 出血 chūxiě. 2 抽…的血 chōu…de xuè. 3 从〔從〕…抽出液体〔體〕或空气〔氣〕cóng…chōuchū yètǐ huò kōngqì.

blemish /ˈblemɪʃ/ *n* [C] 瑕疵 xiácī; 污点〔點〕

B

wūdiǎn. **blemish** *v* [T] 损害…的完美 sǔnhài … de wánměi; 玷污 diànwū: *His reputation has been ~ed*. 他的名声被玷污了.

blend /blend/ *v* 1 [I,T] 混合 hùnhé. 把…混成一体[體] bǎ …hùnchéng yìtǐ. 2 [短语动词] **blend in** 交融 jiāoróng. **blend** *n* [C] 混成品 hùnchéngpǐn; 混合物 hùnhéwù. **blender** *n* [C] [尤用于美国英语]榨汁机[機] zhàzhījī.

bless /bles/ *v* [*pt*, *pp* **~ed** /blest/] [T] 1 求上帝赐福于 qiú shàngdì cìfú yú. 2 使神圣[聖]化 shǐ shénshènghuà. **blessed** /ˈblesɪd/ *adj* 1 神圣的 shénshèngde. 2 幸运[運]的 xìngyùnde; 幸福的 xìngfúde. **blessing** *n* 1 [C] 幸事 xìngshì; 喜事 xǐshì. 2 [U] 同意 tóngyì; 允准 yǔnzhǔn. 3 [C] 上帝的赐福 shàngdìde cìfú.

blew /bluː/ *pt* of BLOW[1].

blight /blaɪt/ *n* 1 [U] 植物凋枯病. zhíwù diāokūbìng. 2 [C] 挫折 cuòzhé; 打击[擊] dǎjī. **blight** *v* [T] 挫折 cuòzhé; 损毁 sǔnhuǐ.

blind[1] /blaɪnd/ *adj* 1 瞎的 xiāde; 盲的 mángde. 2 (*to*) 视而不见的 shì ér bú jiàn de; 不想理解的 bù xiǎng lǐjiě de: *~ to the dangers involved* 看不到潜在的危险. 3 不合理的 bù hélǐ de; 无[無]理由的 wú lǐyóu de: ~ **obedience** 盲目的服从. 4 [习语] **as blind as a ˈbat** 完全看不见东西的 wánquán kànbújiàn dōngxi de. **blind ˈdrunk** [非正式用语]酩酊大醉 mǐngdǐng dàzuì. **the blind** *n* [pl] 盲人 mángrén. **ˌblind ˈalley** *n* [C] 1 死胡同 sǐ hútong. 2 [喻] 没有前途的事情 méiyǒu qiántúde shìqing. **blindly** *adv*. **blindness** *n* [U]. **ˈblind spot** *n* [C] 1 公路上司机[機]看不见的地方 gōnglù shàng sījī kànbújiàn de dìfang. 2 [喻](对某一领域的)无知 wúzhī; 不理解 bù lǐjiě.

blind[2] /blaɪnd/ *v* [T] 1 使失明 shǐ shīmíng. 2 [喻]使失去判断[斷]力 shǐ shīqù pànduànlì: **~ed by love** 被爱情所迷惑.

blind[3] /blaɪnd/ *n* [C] 窗帘 chuānglián.

blindfold /ˈblaɪndfəʊld/ *v* [T] 蒙住…的眼睛 méngzhù…de yǎnjīng. **blindfold** *n* [C] 障眼的蒙布或带[帶]子 zhàngyǎnde méngbù huò dàizi. **blindfold** *adj*, *adv* 眼睛被蒙住(的) yǎnjīng bèi méngzhù; 盲目的 mángmùde; 盲目地 mángmùde.

blink /blɪŋk/ *v* 1 [I,T] 眨眼睛 zhǎ yǎnjīng. 2 [I] (灯光等)闪烁[爍] shǎnshuò; 闪亮 shǎnliàng. 眨眼睛 zhǎ yǎnjīng. **blink** *n* 1 [C] 眨眼睛 zhǎ yǎnjīng; 一瞥 yìpiē. 2 [习语] **on the blink** [非正式用语](机器)坏[壞]了 huài le.

blinkers /ˈblɪŋkəz/ *n* [pl] (马的)眼罩 yǎnzhào.

bliss /blɪs/ *n* [U] 巨大的幸福 jùdàde xìngfú; 福 fú. **blissful** *adj*. **blissfully** *adv*.

blister /ˈblɪstə(r)/ *n* [C] 1 水疱 shuǐpào; 疱 pào. 2 (油漆表面等的)疱状[狀]突起 pàozhuàng tūqǐ. **blister** *v* [I,T] (使)起疱 qǐpào.

blithe /blaɪð/ *adj* 欢[歡]乐[樂]的 huānlède; 无[無]忧[憂]无虑[慮]的 wú yōu wú lǜ de.

blitz /blɪts/ *n* [C] 1 闪电[電]战[戰] shǎndiànzhàn; 猛烈的空袭[襲] měngliède kōngxí. 2 [喻]突击[擊] tūjī; 闪电式行动[動] shǎndiànshì xíngdòng.

blizzard /ˈblɪzəd/ *n* [C] 暴风[風]雪 bàofēngxuě.

bloated /ˈbləʊtɪd/ *adj* 肿[腫]胀[脹]的 zhǒngzhàngde.

blob /blɒb/ *n* [C] 一滴 yìdī; 一小团[團] yì xiǎo tuán.

bloc /blɒk/ *n* [C] 集团[團] jítuán.

block /blɒk/ *n* [C] 1 大块[塊] dàkuài: *a* ~ **of ice/stone** 大块冰/大石头. 2 (公寓、办公室等的)大楼[樓] dàlóu; 大厦[廈] dàshà: *a* **~of flats** 公寓大楼. 3 街区[區](四条街道当中的地区) jiēqū. 4 事物的聚集 shìwùde jùjí: *a* ~ **of theatre seats** 剧院内的座位划区. 5 障碍[礙]物 zhàng'àiwù; 阻碍 zǔ'ài. **block** *v* [T] 1 阻碍 zǔ'ài; 阻塞 zǔsè: *roads* **~ed by snow** 被雪阻塞的马路. 2 破坏[壞] pòhuài. **ˈblocking software** *n* [U] (网站)封闭软件 fēngbì ruǎnjiàn. **ˌblock ˈletters** (亦作 **ˌblock ˈcapitals**) *n* [pl] 大写[寫]字母 dàxiě zìmǔ.

blockade /blɒˈkeɪd/ *n* [C] 封锁 fēngsuǒ. **blockade** *v* [T] 封锁 fēngsuǒ.

blockage /ˈblɒkɪdʒ/ *n* [C] 阻塞物 zǔsèwù: *a ~ in a pipe* 堵塞在管道里的东西.

blog /blɒg/ *n* [C] 博客 bókè: *to keep/write a* ~ 写博客.

blogger /ˈblɒgə(r)/ *n* [C] 博主 bózhǔ; 写(寫)博客的人 xiě bókè de rén.

bloke /bləʊk/ *n* [C] [俚语]人 rén; 家伙(指男子) jiāhuo.

blond (亦指女人,通常用 **blonde**) /blɒnd/ *n* [C], *adj* 金发[髮]的(人) jīnfàde.

blood /blʌd/ *n* [U] 1 血 xuè; 血液 xuèyè. 2 [正式用语]家世 jiāshì; 家族 jiāzú; 血统 xuètǒng: *a woman of noble* ~ 贵族出身的妇女. 3 [习语] **make sb's ˈblood boil** 使发[發]怒 shǐ fānù. **make sb's ˈblood run cold** 使不寒而栗[慄] shǐ bù hán ér lì. **new/fresh ˈblood** 新鲜血液(指有新思想的新成员) xīnxiān xuèyè. **ˈblood bath** *n* [C] 血洗 xuèxǐ; 大屠杀[殺] dàtúshā. **ˈblood-curdling** *adj* 令人毛骨悚然的 lìng rén máo gǔ sǒng rán de. **ˈblood donor** *n* [C] 献[獻]血人 xiànxiěrén; 供血者 gōngxiězhě. **ˈblood group** (亦作 **ˈblood type**) *n* [C] 血型 xuèxíng. **ˈbloodhound** *n* [C] 一种[種]大警犬 yìzhǒng dàjǐngquǎn. **bloodless** *adj* 1 苍[蒼]白的 cāngbáide. 2 不流血的 bù liúxiěde; 兵不血刃的 bīng bú xuè rèn de. **blood poisoning** *n* [U] 血中毒 xuè zhòngdú. **ˈblood pressure** *n* [U] 血压[壓] xuèyā. **ˈbloodshed**

n [U] 流血 liúxuè; 杀戮 shālù. ˈ**bloodshot** *adj* (眼睛)充血的 chōngxiěde. ˈ**blood sports** *n* [pl] 可能流血的运〔運〕动〔動〕(如打猎、斗牛等) kěnéng liúxuè de yùndòng. ˈ**bloodstained** *adj* 沾染着血的 zhānrǎn zhe xiěde; **bloodstream** *n* [C] 血流 xuèliú. ˈ**bloodthirsty** *adj* 嗜血的 shìxuède; 残〔殘〕忍好杀的 cánrěn hàoshā de. ˈ**blood-vessel** *n* [C] 血管 xuèguǎn.

bloody /ˈblʌdɪ/ *adj* [-ier, -iest] **1** 血污的 xuèwūde; 染上血的 rǎn shàng xiě de. **2** 流血很多的 liúxuè hěnduō de; 伤〔傷〕亡很大的 shāngwáng hěndà de. **3** [⚠英国英语, 非正式用语](表示强调): *You ~ idiot!* 你这个大白痴! **bloody** *adv* [⚠英国英语, 非正式用语](表示强调): *too ~ quick* 特快. ˌ**bloody-ˈminded** *adj* [英国英语, 非正式用语]故意刁难〔難〕的 gùyì diāonàn de; 不易亲〔親〕近的 búyì qīnjìn de.

bloom /bluːm/ *n* **1** [C] 花 huā. **2** [习语] **in (full) bloom** 盛开〔開〕着花 shèngkāizhe huā. **bloom** *v* [I] **1** 开花 kāihuā. **2** 繁荣〔榮〕兴〔興〕旺 fánróng xīngwàng.

blossom /ˈblɒsəm/ *n* **1** [C] 花 huā; 果树〔樹〕花 guǒshùhuā. **2** [习语] **in (full) blossom** 正开〔開〕花 zhèng kāihuā. **blossom** *v* [I] **1** 开花 kāihuā. **2** [喻]繁荣〔榮〕发〔發〕达〔達〕 fánróng fādá.

blot /blɒt/ *n* [C] **1** 墨水渍 mòshuǐzì. **2** 污点〔點〕 wūdiǎn; 缺点 quēdiǎn: *a ~ on his character* 他性格上的一个缺点. **blot** *v* [-tt-] [T] **1** 涂〔塗〕污 túwū. **2** (用吸墨水纸)吸干〔乾〕(墨水) xīgān. **3** [短语动词] **blot sth out** 遮暗 zhē'àn; 把…弄模糊 bǎ …nòng móhu: *The cloud ~ted out the view.* 云遮住了视线. **blotter** *n* [C] 吸墨台 xīmòtái. **blotting-paper** *n* [U] 吸墨纸 xīmòzhǐ.

blotch /blɒtʃ/ *n* [C] (皮肤上的)红斑 hóngbān; 疹块〔塊〕 zhěnkuài.

blouse /blaʊz; *US* blaʊs/ *n* [C] 女式宽大短外套 nǚshì kuāndà duǎn wàitào.

blow[1] /bləʊ/ *v* [*pt* **blew** /bluː/, *pp* ~**n** /bləʊn/] **1** [I] (风)吹 chuī. **2** [I, T] (风)吹动〔動〕 chuī dòng: *The wind blew my hat off.* 风吹落了我的帽子. **3** [I, T] 吹气〔氣〕于 chuī qì yú; 充气于 chōng qì yú. **4** [T] 擤(鼻子) xǐng. **5** [T] 吹制〔製〕 chuīzhì: *~ bubbles* 吹泡泡. **6** [I, T] 吹响〔響〕乐〔樂〕器、号〔號〕角等 chuīxiǎng yuèqì, hàojiǎo děng. **7** [I, T] 烧〔燒〕断〔斷〕保险〔險〕丝 shāoduàn bǎoxiǎnsī: *A fuse has ~n.* 保险丝被烧断了. **8** [T] [非正式用语]挥〔揮〕霍 huīhuò. **9** [习语] **blow sb's ˈbrains out** [非正式用语]以枪〔槍〕弹〔彈〕射入头〔頭〕部杀〔殺〕死 yǐ qiāngdàn shèrù tóubù shāsǐ. **blow sb's mind** [俚语]使欣喜若狂 shǐ xīnxǐ ruò kuáng. **blow one's own ˈtrumpet** [非正式用语]自吹自擂 zìchuīzìléi. **10** [短语动词] **blow (sth) out** 吹熄 chuīxī: *~ out a candle* 吹熄蜡烛. **blow over** 平息 píngxī: *The argument will soon ~ over.* 争论会很快平息. **blow up** (a) 爆炸 bàozhà. (b) 突然而有力地开〔開〕始 tūrán ér yǒulìde kāishǐ: *A storm is ~ing up.* 一场暴风雨即将来临. (c) [非正式用语]发〔發〕脾气 fā píqì. **blow sth up** (a) 把…炸掉 bǎ… zhàdiào. (b) 充气 chōngqì: *~ up a tyre* 给轮胎打气. (c) 放大 fàngdà. ˈ**blowlamp** (亦作 ˈ**blowtorch**) *n* [C] 喷灯〔燈〕 pēndēng. ˈ**blow-out** *n* [C] **1** (汽车轮胎)突然漏气〔氣〕 tūrán lòuqì. **2** (油、汽井)突然井喷 tūrán jǐngpēn. **3** [俚]美餐 měicān. ˈ**blow-up** *n* [C] (照片)放大 fàngdà.

blow[2] /bləʊ/ *n* [C] 吹 chuī; 吹风〔風〕 chuīfēng: *Give your nose a good ~.* 好好擤一下你的鼻子.

blow[3] /bləʊ/ *n* [C] **1** 打 dǎ; 打击〔擊〕 dǎjī. **2** 精神上的打击 jīngshén shàng de dǎjī; 灾〔災〕祸〔禍〕 zāihuò. **3** [习语] **come to ˈblows** 动〔動〕手互殴〔毆〕 dòngshǒu hù ōu. ˌ**blow-by-ˈblow** *adj* 极〔極〕为〔為〕详细的 jíwéi xiángxìde.

blower /ˈbləʊə(r)/ *n* [C] **1** 风〔風〕箱 fēngxiāng; 吹风机〔機〕 chuīfēngjī. **2** [英国英语, 非正式用语]电〔電〕话 diànhuà.

blown /bləʊn/ *pp* of BLOW[1].

blubber /ˈblʌbə(r)/ *n* [U] 鲸脂 jīngzhī.

bludgeon /ˈblʌdʒən/ *v* [T] **1** 用重物打击〔擊〕 yòng zhòngwù dǎjī. **2** [喻]强迫某人做某事 qiǎngpò mǒurén zuò mǒushì.

blue /bluː/ *adj* **1** 蓝〔藍〕色的 lánsède; 青的 qīngde; 蔚蓝的 wèilánde. **2** [非正式用语]沮丧〔喪〕的 jǔsàngde; 郁闷的 yùmènde. **3** 色情的 sèqíngde; 粗鄙的 cūbǐde: *a ~ film* 色情电影. **blue** *n* **1** [U] 蓝色 lánsè; 青色 qīngsè. **2** **the blues** (a) [亦作 sing, 用 pl v]布鲁斯音乐〔樂〕(一种伤感的美国南方音乐) bùlǔsī yīnyuè. (b) [pl] [非正式用语]忧〔憂〕伤〔傷〕 yōushāng. **3** [习语] **out of the ˈblue** 出乎意料 chū hū yìliào; 蓦然 mòrán. ˈ**bluebell** 开〔開〕蓝色铃状〔狀〕花的植物 kāi lánsè língzhuànghuā de zhíwù. ˌ**blue-ˈblooded** *adj* 贵族出身的 guìzú chūshēn de. ˈ**bluebottle** *n* [C] 青蝇〔蠅〕 qīngyíng. ˌ**blue-ˈcollar** *adj* 体〔體〕力劳〔勞〕动〔動〕的 tǐlì láodòng de. ˈ**blueprint** *n* [C] 蓝图〔圖〕 lántú; 行动〔動〕计划〔劃〕 xíngdòng jìhuà. **bluish** /ˈbluːɪʃ/ *adj* 带〔帶〕蓝色的 dài lánsè de.

bluff[1] /blʌf/ *v* [I, T] 虚张〔張〕声〔聲〕势〔勢〕地诈骗 xū zhāng shēngshì de zhàpiàn. **bluff** *n* [C, U] 虚张声势的诈骗 xū zhāng shēngshì de zhàpiàn.

bluff[2] /blʌf/ *adj* (人)直率的 zhíshuàide.

blunder /ˈblʌndə(r)/ *n* [C] 因疏忽所犯的错

B

误 yīn shūhū suǒ fàn de cuòwù. **blunder** *v* [I] 1 犯愚蠢的错误 fàn yúchǔnde cuòwù. 2 瞎闯〔闖〕xiāchuǎng.

blunt /blʌnt/ *adj* 1 钝的 dùnde. 2 (人)生硬的 shēngyìngde; 直率的 zhíshuàide. **blunt** *v* [T] 使钝 shǐ dùn; 把…弄迟〔遲〕钝 bǎ…nòng chídùn. **bluntness** *n* [U].

blur /blɜː(r)/ *n* [C] 模糊不清的东西 móhu bùqīng de dōngxi; 模糊一片 móhu yípiàn. **blur** *v* [-rr-] [I, T] 使模糊 shǐ móhu; 变〔變〕模糊 biàn móhu.

blurb /blɜːb/ *n* [C] 书〔書〕籍护〔護〕封上的内容简介 shūjí hùfēng shàng de nèiróng jiǎnjiè.

blurt /blɜːt/ *v* [短语动词] **blurt sth out** 脱口漏出秘密 tuōkǒu lòuchū mìmì.

blush /blʌʃ/ *v* [I] (因羞愧等而)脸〔臉〕红 liǎn hóng. **blush** *n* [C].

bluster /ˈblʌstə(r)/ *v* [I] 1 (大风)狂吹 kuángchuī; 怒号〔號〕nùháo. 2 恫吓〔嚇〕dònghè; 大叫大嚷 dàjiào dàrǎng. **bluster** *n* [U]. **blustery** *adj* 狂风〔風〕大作的 kuángfēng dàzuò de.

boa /ˈbəʊə/ ˈ**boa constrictor** *n* [C] (南美)蟒蛇 mǎngshé; 王蛇 wángshé.

boar /bɔː(r)/ *n* [C] 1 公猪 gōngzhū. 2 野猪 yězhū.

board[1] /bɔːd/ *n* 1 [C] (a) 长〔長〕木板 chángmùbǎn: *a* ˈ*floor*~ 地板木板条. (b) 有专〔專〕门用途的木板 yǒu zhuānmén yòngtú de mùbǎn: *a* ˈ*notice*~ 公告牌. 2 [C] 棋盘〔盤〕qípán: *Chess is a* ˈ~ *game*. 国际象棋是棋类游戏. 3 [C] 委员会〔會〕wěiyuánhuì: *the* ~ *of directors* 董事会. 4 [U] (包饭的)伙食 huǒshí: *pay for* ~ *and lodging* 付膳宿费. 5 [习语] **above ˈboard** 坦诚的 tǎnchéngde. **aˌcross the ˈboard** 包括一切地 bāokuò yíqiè de; 全面地 quánmiànde: *an aˌcross-the-*~ ˈ*wage increase* 全面提高工资. **ˌgo by the ˈboard** 落空 luòkōng; 失去 shīqù. ˈ**on board** 在船上/飞〔飛〕机〔機〕上/火车上 zài chuánshàng/fēijīshàng/huǒchē shàng. **take sth on ˈboard** [非正式用语]接受某事物 jiēshòu mǒu shìwù.

board[2] /bɔːd/ *v* 1 [T] 用板盖〔蓋〕yòng bǎn gài; 加板 jiā bǎn: ~ *up a window* 用木板堵住窗户. 2[T] 登上(船、火车、公共汽车等) dēng shàng. 3 [I, T] 供应〔應〕伙食 gōngyìng huǒshí. **boarder** *n* [C] 寄宿学〔學〕校的小学生 jìsù xuéxiào de xiǎo xuésheng. ˈ**boarding card** *n* [C] 登机〔機〕卡 dēngjīkǎ; 登船卡 dēngchuánkǎ. ˈ**boarding-house** *n* [C] 供膳宿之私人住房 gōng shànsù zhī sīrén zhùfáng. ˈ**boarding-school** *n* [C] 寄宿学校 jìsù xuéxiào.

boast /bəʊst/ *v* 1 [I, T] (*about*/*of*) 自夸〔誇〕zìkuā: ~ *about one's new car* 夸耀自己的新汽车. 2 [T] 自豪地拥〔擁〕有 zìháode yōngyǒu: *The hotel* ~*s a fine swimming-pool*. 该饭店以其上乘之游泳池而自豪. **boast** *n* [C] 自吹自擂 zìchuī-zìléi. ˈ**boastful** *adj* 爱〔愛〕自夸的 ài zìkuā de. ˈ**boastfully** *adv*.

boat /bəʊt/ *n* [C] 1 小船 xiǎo chuán; 艇 tǐng: ˈ*rowing*-~ 划艇. 2 船 chuán. **boat** *v* [I] 乘船游玩 chéngchuán yóuwán: *go* ~*ing* (去)乘船玩. ˈ**boat-house** *n* [C] 船坞 chuánwù. ˈ**boat-train** *n* [C] 与〔與〕船联〔聯〕运〔運〕的火车〔車〕yǔ chuán liányùn de huǒchē.

boatswain (亦作 **bo'sn, bos'n, bo'sun**) /ˈbəʊsən/ *n* [C] 水手长〔長〕shuǐshǒuzhǎng.

bob[1] /bɒb/ *v* [-bb-] [I] 上下跳动〔動〕shàng xià tiàodòng: *a cork* ~*bing on the water* 浮子在水上上下浮动.

bob[2] /bɒb/ *v* [-bb-] [T] 给(妇女)剪短发〔髮〕gěi jiǎn duǎnfà. **bob** *n* [C] (女子的)短发式 duǎn fàshì.

bobbin /ˈbɒbɪn/ *n* [C] (纺织、缝纫等机器上绕线用的)筒管 tǒngguǎn, 筒子 tǒngzi.

bobsleigh /ˈbɒbsleɪ/ (亦作 **bobsled** /-sled/) *n* [C] 连〔連〕橇 liánqiāo.

bode /bəʊd/ *v* [习语] **bode ˈwell /ˈill (for sb/sth)** 主吉 zhǔ jí; 主凶〔兇〕zhǔ xiōng.

bodice /ˈbɒdɪs/ *n* [C] 连衣裙的上身 liányīqún de shàngshēn.

bodily /ˈbɒdəlɪ/ *adj* 身体〔體〕的 shēntǐde; 肉体的 ròutǐde. **bodily** *adv* 1 抓住整体 zhuāzhù zhěngtǐ. 2 全部地 quánbùde, 整体地 zhěngtǐde.

body /ˈbɒdɪ/ *n* [C] [*pl* **-ies**] 1 (a) 身体〔體〕shēntǐ; 躯〔軀〕体 qūtǐ. (b) 尸〔屍〕体 shītǐ. (c) 躯干〔幹〕(无头和四肢) qūgàn. 2 (物体的)身 shēn: *the* ~ *of a car* 汽车的车身. 3 团〔團〕体 tuántǐ: *a parliamentary* ~ 立法机构. 4 团 tuán; 片 piàn: *a* ~ *of water* 一潭水. 5 物体 wùtǐ: *heavenly bodies* 天体. ˈ**bodyguard** *n* [C] 警卫〔衛〕员 jǐngwèiyuán; 保镖 bǎobiāo. ˈ**bodywork** *n* [U] 汽车车身 qìchē chēshēn.

bog /bɒg/ *n* [C] 1 泥塘 nítáng; 沼泽〔澤〕zhǎozé. 2 [英国俚语]厕所 cèsuǒ. **bog** *v* [-gg-] [习语] **be /get bogged down** 使陷入泥沼, 不能动〔動〕弹〔彈〕shǐ xiànrù nízhǎo, bùnéng dòngtan: [喻] *get* ~*ged down in small details* 在细节问题上陷入僵局. **boggy** *adj*.

bogey = BOGY.

boggle /ˈbɒgl/ *v* [I] (*at*) [非正式用语]畏缩不前 wèisuō bù qián; 犹〔猶〕豫 yóuyù: *The mind* ~*s (at the idea)*. 心存犹豫.

bogus /ˈbəʊgəs/ *adj* 伪〔僞〕的 wěide; 伪造的 wěizàode.

bogy (亦作 **bogey**) /ˈbəʊgɪ/ *n* [C] [*pl* **-ies**]

妖怪 yāoguài.

boil[1] /bɔɪl/ *v* 1 [I, T] (使)沸腾 fèiténg: *The kettle is ~ing*. 壶开了. 2 [T]煮 zhǔ: *~ an egg* 煮蛋. 3 [I] 发〔發〕怒 fānù. 4 [习语] **boil ˈdry** 煮干〔乾〕zhǔ gān. 5 [短语动词] **boil away** 煮干 zhǔ gān. **boil down to sth** 归〔歸〕结起来是 guījié qǐlái shì; 问题是 wèntí shì: *It all ~s down to what you really want*. 问题是你真正想要什么. **boil over** (a) 沸溢 fèiyì. (b) 激动 jīdòng; 发怒 fānù. **boil** *n* [习语] **bring sth/come to the ˈboil** 把…煮开 bǎ…zhǔkāi. **boiling ˈhot** *adj* 滚烫〔燙〕的 gǔntàngde. **ˈboiling point** *n* [C] 沸点〔點〕fèidiǎn.

boil[2] /bɔɪl/ *n* [C] [医]疖〔癤〕jiē.

boiler /ˈbɔɪlə(r)/ *n* [C] 煮器(壶、锅等的泛称) zhǔqì; 锅〔鍋〕炉〔爐〕guōlú. **ˈboiler-suit** *n* [C] 连衫裤工作服 liánshānkù gōngzuòfú.

boisterous /ˈbɔɪstərəs/ *adj* (人)吵吵闹〔鬧〕闹的 chǎochǎo nàonào de, 兴〔興〕高采烈的 xìng gāo cǎi liè de.

bold /bəʊld/ *adj* 1 大胆〔膽〕的 dàdǎnde; 勇敢的 yǒnggǎnde. 2 无〔無〕耻的 wúchǐde; 无礼〔禮〕的 wúlǐde. 3 醒目的 xǐngmùde; 清楚的 qīngchude: *~ designs* 醒目的图样. **boldly** *adv*. **boldness** *n* [U].

bollard /ˈbɒləd/ *n* [C] 系〔繫〕缆〔纜〕柱 xìlǎnzhù; (行人安全岛顶端的)护〔護〕柱 hùzhù.

bolster /ˈbəʊlstə(r)/ *n* [C] 长〔長〕枕 chángzhěn. **bolster** *v* [T] (*up*) 支持 zhīchí; 加强 jiāqiáng; 鼓舞 gǔwǔ.

bolt /bəʊlt/ *n* [C] 1 插销 chāxiāo. 2 螺栓 luóshuān. 3 闪〔閃〕电〔電〕shǎndiàn. 4 逃跑 táopǎo: *make a ~ for it* 溜之大吉. **bolt** *v* 1 [I, T] 拴紧〔緊〕shuānjǐn. 2 [I] 马脱缰逃跑 mǎ tuōjiāng táopǎo. 3 [T] (*down*) 囫囵〔圇〕吞下 húlún tūnxià. **bolt** *adv*. [习语] **bolt ˈupright** 笔〔筆〕直地 bǐzhíde.

bomb /bɒm/ *n* 1 [C] 炸弹〔彈〕zhàdàn. 2 **the bomb** [sing] 原子弹 yuánzǐdàn. **bomb** *v* [T] 轰〔轟〕炸 hōngzhà; 投弹于 tóudàn yú. **bomber** *n* [C] 1 轰炸机〔機〕hōngzhàjī. 2 投弹手 tóudànshǒu. **bombshell** *n* [C] [非正式用语]令人大为〔爲〕震惊〔驚〕的意外事件 lìng rén dàwéi zhènjīng de yìwài shìjiàn. **ˈbomb shelter** *n* [C] 防空洞 fángkōngdòng; 防空掩体〔體〕fángkōng yǎntǐ.

bombard /bɒmˈbɑːd/ *v* [T] 1 炮击〔擊〕pàojī. 2 [喻]向…发〔發〕出连珠炮似的问题 xiàng…fāchū liánzhūpào shìde wèntí. **bombardment** *n* [C, U].

bona fide /ˌbəʊnə ˈfaɪdɪ/ *adj*, *adv* 真正的 zhēnzhèngde; 真正地 zhēnzhèngde.

bond /bɒnd/ *n* 1 [C] 结合 jiéhé; 连接 liánjiē: *~ of friendship* 友谊的结合. 2 [C] 契约 qìyuē. 3 [C] 债券 zhàiquàn. 4 **bonds** [pl] 镣铐 liàokào. **bond** *v* [T] 使结合 shǐ jiéhé.

bondage /ˈbɒndɪdʒ/ *n* [U] [旧词或正式用语]奴役 núyì; 束缚 shùfù.

bone /bəʊn/ *n* 1 [C, U] 骨骼 gǔgé. 2 [习语] **feel sth in one's bones** 确〔確〕有把握 què yǒu bǎwò. **have a ˈbone to pick with sb** 与〔與〕某人有争执〔執〕或怨恨 yǔ mǒurén yǒu zhēngzhí huò yuànhèn. **make no bones about (doing) sth** 毫不犹〔猶〕豫地做某事 háobù yóuyù de zuò mǒushì. **bone** *v* [T] 剔去…的骨 tīqù… de gǔ. **ˌbone-ˈdry** *adj* 干〔乾〕透了的 gāntòulede. **ˌbone-ˈidle** *adj* 极〔極〕懒的 jílǎnde.

bonfire /ˈbɒnfaɪə(r)/ *n* [C] 大篝火 dàgōuhuǒ.

bonnet /ˈbɒnɪt/ *n* [C] 1 汽车引擎盖子 qìchē yǐnqíng gàizi. 2 (有带子的)童帽 tóngmào, 女帽 nǚ mào.

bonny /ˈbɒnɪ/ *adj* [-ier, -iest] [褒,尤用于苏格兰]健康的 jiànkāngde; 强壮〔壯〕的 qiángzhuàngde.

bonus /ˈbəʊnəs/ *n* [C] 1 奖〔獎〕金 jiǎngjīn; 额外津贴 éwài jīntiē. 2 意外收益 yìwài shōuyì.

bony /ˈbəʊnɪ/ *adj* [-ier, -iest] 1 多骨的 duōgǔde: *The fish is ~*. 鱼的骨刺多. 2 瘦的 shòude; 骨头〔頭〕突出的 gútou tūchū de: *~ fingers* 皮包骨头的手指.

boo /buː/ *interj*, *n* [C] [*pl* ~s] 呸(表示嫌恶) pēi. **boo** *v* [I, T] 讥〔譏〕笑 jīxiào; 发〔發〕出呸的声〔聲〕音 fāchū pēide shēngyīn.

booby prize /ˈbuːbɪ praɪz/ *n* [C] 殿军奖〔獎〕diànjūn jiǎng.

booby trap /ˈbuːbɪ træp/ *n* [C] 陷阱 xiànjǐng. **booby-trap** *v* [-pp-] [T] 在…布〔佈〕陷阱 zài…bù xiànjǐng.

book[1] /bʊk/ *n* 1 [C] 书〔書〕shū; 书籍 shūjí. 2 本子 běnzi; 册 cè: *a ~ of stamps* 邮票册. 3 **books** [pl] 商业〔業〕账〔賬〕册 shāngyè zhàngcè. 4 [C] 篇 piān; 卷 juàn. 5 [习语] **be in sb's good /bad books** 得到(或得不到)某人的好感 dédào mǒurén de hǎogǎn. **ˈbookcase** *n* [C] 书橱 shūchú; 书柜〔櫃〕shūguì. **ˈbook club** *n* [C] 购〔購〕书会〔會〕gòushūhuì. **bookkeeping** *n* [U] 簿记 bùjì. **bookkeeper** *n* [C]. **bookmaker** *n* [C] (赛马等)登记赌注的人 dēngjì dǔzhù de rén. **ˈbookmark** *n* [C] 书签〔簽〕shūqiān. **ˈbookshop** *n* [C] 书店 shūdiàn. **ˈbookstall** *n* [C] 书摊〔攤〕shūtān; 书亭 shūtíng. **ˈbook token** *n* [C] (定额的)书籍预约证〔證〕shūjí yùyuēzhèng. **ˈbookworm** *n* [C] 极〔極〕爱〔愛〕读〔讀〕书的人 jí ài dúshū de rén.

book[2] /bʊk/ *v* 1 [I, T] 预定(车票等) yùdìng. 2 [T] (警察)登记(违章者) dēngjì: *be ~ed for speeding* 因超速行驶被警察登记. **book-**

B

able *adj* 可预约的 kě yùyuēde；可预订的 kě yùdìngde. **booking** *n* [C]. **booking-office** *n* [C] 售票处〔處〕 shòupiàochù.

bookie /ˈbʊkɪ/ *n* [C] [非正式用语] short for BOOKMAKER (BOOK[1]).

booklet /ˈbʊklɪt/ *n* [C] 小册子 xiǎocèzi；薄本书〔書〕 báoběnshū.

boom[1] /buːm/ *n* [C] (商业等的)景气〔氣〕 jǐngqì；繁荣〔榮〕 fánróng. **boom** *v* [I] 兴〔興〕旺 xīngwàng；迅速发〔發〕展 xùnsù fāzhǎn：*Sales are ~ing*. 销路正旺.

boom[2] /buːm/ *v* **1** [I] (大炮等)发〔發〕出隆隆声〔聲〕 fāchū lónglóng shēng. **2** [I, T] (*out*) 用低沉的声音说 yòng dīchénde shēngyīn shuō. **boom** *n* [C].

boom[3] /buːm/ *n* [C] **1** 帆的下桁 fānde xiàhéng. **2** 话筒吊杆〔桿〕 huàtǒng diàogān.

boomerang /ˈbuːməræŋ/ *n* [C] 飞〔飛〕镖(澳大利亚土著的武器,用曲形坚木制成,投出后可飞回原处) fēibiāo.

boon /buːn/ *n* [C] 恩惠 ēnhuì；裨益 bìyì.

boor /bʊə(r)/ *n* [C] 态〔態〕度粗鲁的人 tàidù cūlǔ de rén. **boorish** *adj*.

boost /buːst/ *v* [T] 增加(价值等) zēngjiā. **boost** *n* [C]. **booster** *n* [C] **1** 增强力量或提高价值的东西 zēngqiáng lìliàng huò tígāo jiàzhíde dōngxi. **2** 外加注射剂〔劑〕量 wàijiā zhùshè jìliàng.

boot /buːt/ *n* [C] **1** 靴 xuē. **2** 汽车的行李箱 qìchēde xínglixiāng. **3** [习语] **give sb/get the ˈboot** [非正式用语]解雇〔僱〕 jiěgù；被解雇 bèi jiěgù. **put the ˈboot in** [非正式用语]踢某人 tī mǒurén. **boot** *v* **1** [T] 踢人 tī rén. **2** [短语动词] **boot sb out (of sth)** [非正式用语]迫使某人离〔離〕开〔開〕工作或地方 pòshǐ mǒurén líkāi gōngzuò huò dìfang.

booth /buːð; *US* buːθ/ *n* [C] **1** 有篷的售货摊〔攤〕 yǒu péng de shòuhuòtān. **2** 隔开〔開〕的小间 gékāide xiǎojiān：*telephone ~* 电话间.

booze /buːz/ *n* [U] [非正式用语]酒 jiǔ. **booze** *v* [I] [非正式用语]饮酒 yǐnjiǔ. **boozer** *n* [C] [非正式用语] **1** 痛饮者 tòngyǐnzhě. **2** [英国英语]小酒店 xiǎo jiǔdiàn. **ˈbooze-up** *n* [C] [英国非正式用语]酒宴 jiǔyàn.

bop /bɒp/ *n* [C, U] [非正式用语]跳舞 tiàowǔ；随〔隨〕流行音乐〔樂〕跳舞 suí liúxíng yīnyuè tiàowǔ. **bop** *v* [-pp-] [I] [非正式英语] 随流行音乐跳舞 suí liúxíng yīnyuè tiàowǔ.

border /ˈbɔːdə(r)/ *n* [C] **1** 边〔邊〕界 biānjiè；国〔國〕界 guójiè. **2** 边 biān；边沿 biānyán. **3** (草坪边上的)狭长〔長〕花坛〔壇〕 xiácháng huātán. **border** *v* **1** [I, T] (*on*) 与〔與〕(国家)接界 yǔ jiējiè. **2** [短语动词] **border on sth** 近似 jìnsì：*a state of excitement ~ing on madness*. 近似于疯狂的激动状态. **ˈborderline** *n* [C] 边界线〔綫〕 biānjièxiàn. **ˈborderline** *adj* 两可间的 liǎngkějiānde：*a ~ line candidate* 可能及格也可能不及格的应试人.

bore[1] /bɔː(r)/ *v* [T] 厌〔厭〕烦 yànfán. **bore** *n* [C] 惹人厌烦的人或事物 rě rén yànfán de rén huò shìwù. **boredom** /-dəm/ *n* [U] 厌烦 yànfán；无〔無〕趣 wúqù. **boring** *adj* 烦人的 fánrénde；无兴〔興〕趣的 wú xìngqùde.

bore[2] /bɔː(r)/ *v* [I, T] 钻〔鑽〕孔 zuānkǒng；挖洞 wādòng. **bore** *n* [C] **1** 钻孔 zuànkǒng；洞 dòng. **2** 枪〔槍〕炮等的内膛、口径〔徑〕 qiāng pào děng de nèitáng、kǒujìng.

bore[3] /bɔː(r)/ *pt* of BEAR[2].

born /bɔːn/ *v* **be born** 出生 chūshēng；出世 chūshì：*He was ~ in 1954*. 他出生于 1954 年. **born** *adj* 有天生的某种〔種〕品质〔質〕的 yǒu tiānshēng de mǒuzhǒng pǐnzhìde：*be a ~ leader* 是个天生的领袖. **-born** [构成名词和形容词]具有某种出生时〔時〕国〔國〕籍的 jùyǒu mǒuzhǒng chūshēng shí guójí de：*Dutch ~* 在荷兰出生. ˌ**born-aˈgain** *adj* (在宗教信仰上)重生的 chóngshēngde；皈依的 guīyīde：*a ~-again ˈChristian* 重生的基督徒.

borne /bɔːn/ *pp* of BEAR[2].

borough /ˈbʌrə; *US* -rəʊ/ *n* [C] 城镇 chéngzhèn；大城镇的区〔區〕 dà chéngzhèn de qū.

borrow /ˈbɒrəʊ/ *v* [I, T] 借 jiè. **borrower** *n* [C].

bosom /ˈbʊzəm/ *n* [C] **1** [旧]胸 xiōng；(女性的)乳房 rǔfáng. **2 the bosom of sth** [sing] [旧]…的关〔關〕怀〔懷〕和保护〔護〕…de guānhuái hé bǎohù：*in the ~ of one's family* 在家庭的关怀和保护下. **bosom ˈfriend** *n* [C] 亲〔親〕密的朋友 qīnmìde péngyou.

boss /bɒs/ *n* [C] [非正式用语]工头〔頭〕 gōngtóu；老板〔闆〕 lǎobǎn. **boss** *v* [T] (*about/around*) [非正式用语] 指挥〔揮〕 zhǐhuī. **bossy** *adj* [-ier, -iest] 爱〔愛〕指手画〔畫〕脚的 ài zhǐshǒu huàjiǎo de.

botany /ˈbɒtənɪ/ *n* [U] 植物学〔學〕 zhíwùxué. **botanical** /bəˈtænɪkl/ *adj*. **botanist** *n* [C] 植物学家 zhíwùxuéjiā.

botch /bɒtʃ/ *v* [T] 笨手笨脚地弄坏〔壞〕 bènshǒu bènjiǎo de nòng huài. **botch** *n* [C] 粗劣的工作 cūliède gōngzuò.

both /bəʊθ/ *adj*, *pron* 两 liǎng；双〔雙〕 shuāng；两者 liǎngzhě：*B~ (the) books are expensive*. 两本书都很贵. *His parents are ~ dead*. 他的双亲都已亡故. **both** *adv* 不仅〔僅〕而且 bùjǐn érqiě：*She has houses in both London and Paris*. 她不仅在伦敦而且在巴黎也有房子.

bother /ˈbɒðə(r)/ *v* **1** [T] 烦扰〔擾〕 fánrǎo；

打扰 dǎrǎo: *Is something ~ing you?* 有什么事让你烦恼吗? 2 [I, T] 麻烦 máfán: *Don't ~ to stand up*. 别麻烦,不用站起来. **bother** *n* [sing] 麻烦事 máfánshì. **bothersome** *adj* 麻烦的 máfánde.

bottle /ˈbɒtl/ *n* 1 [C] (a) 瓶 píng. (b) 一瓶(的量) yìpíng. 2 [C] 奶瓶 nǎipíng. 3 [U] [英国俚语]勇气〔氣〕 yǒngqì. **bottle** *v* 1 [T] 把…装〔裝〕瓶 bǎ…zhuāng píng. 2 [短语动词] **bottle sth up** 抑制(强烈的感情) yìzhì. ˈ**bottle-neck** *n* [C] 1 交通容易阻塞的狭口 jiāotōng róngyì zǔsè de xiákǒu. 2 妨碍前进〔進〕的环〔環〕节〔節〕 fáng'ài qiánjìn de huánjié.

bottom /ˈbɒtəm/ *n* 1 [C, 常作 sing]底 dǐ, 底部 dǐbù. 2 [C] 屁股 pìgu. 3 [sing] (海、湖等的)底 dǐ. 4 [C, 常作 sing] 最后〔後〕部 zuìhòubù;最里〔裏〕面 zuìlǐmiàn: *at the ~ of the garden* 在花园的最后面. 5 [sing] (班级、组织等的)最低名次 zuìdī míngcì. 6 [习语] **at the bottom of sth** 是…的基本原因 shì…de jīběn yuányīn. **get to the ˈbottom of sth** 弄清真相 nòngqīng zhēnxiàng;盘〔盤〕根究底 pángēn jiūdǐ. **bottom** *v* [短语动词]**bottom out** 达〔達〕到低点〔點〕 dádào dīdiǎn. **bottomless** *adj* 很深的 hěnshēn de. **the ˌbottom ˈline** *n* [sing] [非正式用语]底细 dǐxì.

bough /baʊ/ *n* [C] 大树〔樹〕枝 dàshùzhī.

bought /bɔːt/ *pt, pp* of BUY.

boulder /ˈbəʊldə(r)/ *n* [C] 巨砾〔礫〕 jùlì.

bounce /baʊns/ *v* 1 [I, T] (球等)反跳 fǎntiào;弹〔彈〕起 tánqǐ. 2 [I, T] 跳上跳下 tiàoshàng tiàoxià. 3 [I, T] 冲〔衝〕 chōng: *She ~d into the room*. 她冲进了房间. 4 [I] [非正式用语](支票)因银行无〔無〕存款被拒付而退回. yīn yínháng wú cúnkuǎn bèi jùfù ér tuìhuí. **bounce** *n* [C] 球的弹跳 qiú de tántiào. **bouncer** *n* [C] (俱乐部等雇用的)驱〔驅〕逐捣乱〔亂〕者的壮〔壯〕汉〔漢〕 qūzhú dǎoluànzhěde zhuànghàn. **bouncing** *adj* 健壮的 jiànzhuàngde.

bound[1] *pt, pp* of BIND.

bound[2] /baʊnd/ *adj* 1 *to* (a) 一定的 yídìngde;必定的 bìdìngde: *He is ~ to win*. 他必定胜利. (b) (法律上、责任上)有义〔義〕务〔務〕的 yǒu yìwùde. 2 [习语] **bound ˈup in sth** 忙于 mángyú. **bound ˈup with sth** 与〔與〕…密切相关〔關〕 yǔ…mìqiè xiāngguān.

bound[3] /baʊnd/ *adj* (*for*) 正在到…去的 zhèngzài dào…qùde: *a ship ~ for Rotterdam* 开往鹿特丹的船.

bound[4] /baʊnd/ *v* [T] [通常用被动语态]形成…的疆界 xíngchéng… de jiāngjiè: *an airfield ~ed by woods* 四周是树林的飞机场.

bound[5] /baʊnd/ *v* [I] 跳跃〔躍〕 tiàoyuè;跳跃前进〔進〕 tiàoyuè qiánjìng. **bound** *n* [C].

boundary /ˈbaʊndrɪ/ *n* [C] [*pl* -ies] 边〔邊〕界 biānjiè;分界线〔綫〕 fēnjièxiàn.

boundless /ˈbaʊndlɪs/ *adj* 无〔無〕限的 wúxiànde.

bounds /baʊndz/ *n* [pl] 1 界限 jièxiàn;范〔範〕围〔圍〕 fànwéi. 2 [习语] **out of ˈbounds (to sb)** 不许(某人)进〔進〕入 bùxǔ jìnrù.

bounty /ˈbaʊntɪ/ *n* [*pl* -ies] 1 [U] [旧]慷慨 kāngkǎi. 2 [C] [旧]捐赠品 juānzèngpǐn;施舍〔捨〕品 shīshěpǐn. 3 [C] 奖〔獎〕金 jiǎngjīn. **bountiful** *adj* 慷慨的 kāngkǎide.

bouquet /bʊˈkeɪ, bəʊˈkeɪ/ *n* [C] 1 花束 huāshù. 2 [sing] 酒香 jiǔxiāng.

bourgeois /ˈbʊəʒwɑː, ˌbʊərˈʒwɑː/ *n* [C], *adj* 1 中产〔產〕阶〔階〕级的一员 zhōngchǎn jiējíde yìyuán;中产阶级的 zhōngchǎn jiējí de. 2 [贬]追求物质享受者 zhuīqiú wùzhì xiǎngshòuzhě;(人)追求物质〔質〕享受的 zhuīqiú wùzhì xiǎngshòu de. **bourgeoisie** /ˌbɔːʒwɑːˈziː, ˌbʊəʒwɑːˈziː/ *n* [sing, 亦作 sing 用 pl v] [贬]中产阶级 zhōngchǎn jiējí.

bout /baʊt/ *n* [C] 一回 yìhuí;一场〔場〕 yìchǎng;一阵〔陣〕 yízhèn;(疾病等的)发〔發〕作 fāzuò.

boutique /buːˈtiːk/ *n* [C] 小的时〔時〕装〔裝〕店 xiǎode shízhuāngdiàn.

bow[1] /baʊ/ *v* 1 [I, T] 鞠躬 jūgōng;欠身 qiànshēn. 2 [短语动词] **bow out (of sth)** 撤出 chèchū;退出 tuìchū. **bow to sth** 屈服 qūfú;服从〔從〕 fúcóng: *I ~ to your authority*. 我服从你的权力. **bow** *n* [C].

bow[2] /bəʊ/ *n* [C] 1 弓 gōng. 2 琴弓 qíngōng. 3 蝴蝶结 húdiéjié. ˌ**bow-ˈlegged** *adj* (人)有弓形腿的 yǒu gōngxíngtuǐ de. ˌ**bow-ˈtie** *n* [C] 蝴蝶结领结 húdiéjié lǐngjié. ˌ**bow ˈwindow** *n* [C] 凸肚窗 tūdùchuāng.

bow[3] /baʊ/ *n* [C] 船头〔頭〕 chuántóu.

bowel /ˈbaʊəl/ *n* [C, 常用 pl] 1 肠〔腸〕 cháng. 2 内部 nèibù;深处〔處〕 shēnchù: *in the ~s of the earth* 在地球内部.

bowl[1] /bəʊl/ *n* [C] 1 (a) 碗 wǎn. (b) 一碗的量 yìwǎnde liàng. 2 (某种东西的)碗状〔狀〕部分 wǎnzhuàng bùfen.

bowl[2] /bəʊl/ *v* 1 (a) [I, T] 在板球戏〔戲〕中投球给击〔擊〕球手 zài bǎnqiúxì zhōng tóuqiú gěi jīqiúshǒu. (b) [T] (*out*) (在板球戏中击中三柱门)迫使(击球员)退场〔場〕 pòshǐ tuìchǎng. 2 [I]玩草地滚木球戏 wán cǎodì gǔnmùqiúxì;玩地滚球戏 wán dìgǔnqiúxì. 3 [短语动词] **bowl sb over** (a) 击倒某人 jīdǎo mǒurén. (b) 使大吃一惊〔驚〕 shǐ dà chī yìjīng. **bowl** *n* 1 [C] (滚木球戏所用的)木球 mùqiú; (十柱保龄球戏所用的)球 qiú. 2 **bowls** [用 sing v] 滚木球戏 gǔnmùqiúxì.

bowler[1] /ˈbəʊlə(r)/ *n* [C] 玩滚木球戏者

B

wán gǔnmùqiúxì zhě.

bowler[2] (亦作 ˌbowler ˈhat) /ˈbəʊlə(r)/ *n* [C] 常礼〔禮〕帽 chánglǐmào.

bowling /ˈbəʊlɪŋ/ *n* [U] 保龄〔齡〕球戏〔戲〕bǎolíngqiúxì.

box[1] /bɒks/ *n* 1 [C] (a) 箱 xiāng; 盒 hé. (b) 一箱(或一盒)的量 yìxiāngde liàng. 2 [C] (a) 分隔间 fēngéjiān; 分隔区〔區〕域 fēngé qūyù: *a ~ in a theatre* 剧院里的包厢. (b) 特定用途的棚屋 tèdìng yòngtúde péngwū: *a ˈtelephone-~* 电话亭. 3 [C] (表格等上的)方格 fānggé. 4 **the box** [sing] [英国非正式用语]电〔電〕视机〔機〕diànshìjī. **box** *v* 1 [T] 把…装〔裝〕箱(或盒等) bǎ…zhuāng xiāng. 2 [短语动词] **box sb/sth in** 闭锁 bìsuǒ. ˈ**box number** *n* [C] 信箱号〔號〕码 xìnxiāng hàomǎ. ˈ**box office** *n* [C] (剧院等的)售票处〔處〕shòupiàochù.

box[2] /bɒks/ *v* [I, T] 与〔與〕…进〔進〕行拳击〔擊〕比赛 yǔ…jìnxíng quánjī bǐsài; 参〔參〕加拳击比赛 cānjiā quánjī bǐsài. **boxer** *n* [C] 1 拳击运〔運〕动〔動〕员 quánjī yùndòngyuán. 2 斗〔鬥〕拳狗 dòuquángǒu; 拳师〔師〕犬 quánshīquǎn. **boxing** *n* [U].

Boxing Day /ˈbɒksɪŋ deɪ/ *n* 节〔節〕礼〔禮〕日(圣诞节的次日,如为星期日,改为 12 月 27 日) jiélǐrì.

boy /bɔɪ/ *n* [C] 男孩子 nánháizi; 男青年 nán qīngnián. ˈ**boy-friend** *n* [C] 女孩子的男朋友 nǚháizide nánpéngyǒu. **boyhood** *n* [U] 男孩子的孩童时〔時〕代 nánháizide háitóng shídài. **boyish** *adj* 男孩子的 nánháizide; 适〔適〕于男孩子的 shìyú nánháizide; 男孩似的 nánhái shì de; 孩子气〔氣〕的 háiziqìde.

boycott /ˈbɔɪkɒt/ *v* [T] 联〔聯〕合抵制 liánhé dǐzhì. **boycott** *n* [C].

bra /brɑː/ *n* [C] 奶罩 nǎizhào; 胸罩 xiōngzhào.

brace /breɪs/ *v* 1 ~ **oneself** (**for/to**) 为〔爲〕(应付困难或不愉快的事情)作好准〔準〕备〔備〕wèi zuòhǎo zhǔnbèi. 2 [T] 使(手、脚等)牢置(以稳住身体) shǐ láozhì. 3 [T] 加固 jiāgù; 支撑 zhīchēng. **brace** *n* 1 [C] 牙科矫〔矯〕形钢〔鋼〕丝〔絲〕套 yákē jiǎoxíng gāngsītào. 2 [C] 拉条〔條〕lātiáo; 撑臂 chēngbì. 3 **braces** [pl] [英国英语] (裤子的)背带〔帶〕bēidài. **bracing** *adj* 令人振奋〔奮〕的 lìng rén zhènfèn de; 使人心旷〔曠〕神怡的 shǐ rén xīn kuàng shén yí de: *the bracing sea air* 使人精神爽快的海上空气.

bracelet /ˈbreɪslɪt/ *n* [C] 手镯 shǒuzhuó.

bracken /ˈbrækən/ *n* [U] 欧〔歐〕洲蕨 ōuzhōujué.

bracket /ˈbrækɪt/ *n* [C] 1 [通常为 pl] 括号〔號〕kuòhào. 2 托架 tuōjià. 3 等级段 děngjíduàn; 档〔檔〕次 dàngcì: *the* 20 – 30 *age* ~ 20 岁到 30 岁年龄段. **bracket** *v* [T] 1 给…套以括号 gěi…tàoyǐ kuòhào. 2 把…放在一起 bǎ…fàngzài yìqǐ.

brackish /ˈbrækɪʃ/ *adj* (水)微咸〔鹹〕的 wēixiánde.

brag /bræg/ *v* [-gg-] [I, T] 夸〔誇〕口 kuākǒu; 吹牛皮 chuīniúpí.

braid /breɪd/ *n* 1 [U] 编带〔帶〕biāndài; 辫 biàn. 2 [C] [美语] 发〔髮〕辫 fàbiàn; 辫子 biànzi. **braid** *v* [T] [美语] 把…编成辫子 bǎ…biānchéng biànzi.

braille /breɪl/ *n* [U] 布莱叶〔葉〕盲文 bùláiyè mángwén.

brain /breɪn/ *n* [C] 1 脑〔腦〕nǎo. 2 脑力 nǎolì; 智力 zhìlì: *have a good* ~ 智力好. 3 [非正式用语] 极〔極〕聪〔聰〕明的人 jí cōngmingde rén; 智者 zhìzhě. 4 [习语] **have sth on the brain** [非正式用语] 念念不忘 niànniàn búwàng. **brain** *v* [T] 猛击〔擊〕…的头〔頭〕部致死 měngjī…de tóubù zhìsǐ. ˈ**brain-child** *n* [sing] 新颖的主意 xīnyǐngde zhǔyì. ˈ**brain drain** *n* [C] 智囊流失 zhìnáng liúshī; 人才外流 réncái wàiliú. **brainless** *adj* 愚笨的 yúbènde. **brainstorm** *n* [C] [英国英语] 脑病暴发〔發〕nǎobìng bàofā. ˈ**brainwash** *v* [T] 对〔對〕…实〔實〕行洗脑 duì…shíxíng xǐ nǎo. ˈ**brainwave** *n* [C] [非正式用语] 突然想到的好主意 tūrán xiǎngdào de hǎo zhǔyì. **brainy** *adj* [-ier, -iest] [非正式用语] 聪〔聰〕明的 cōngmingde.

braise /breɪz/ *v* [T] (用文火)炖(肉等) dùn.

brake /breɪk/ *n* [C] 刹车 shāchē; 制动〔動〕器 zhìdòngqì. **brake** *v* [I, T] 用闸 yòngzhá; 刹车 shāchē; 刹住(车) shā zhù; 用闸使(车)放慢速度 yòng zhá shǐ fàngmàn sùdù.

bramble /ˈbræmbl/ *n* [C] 荆棘 jīngjí; 黑莓灌木丛〔叢〕hēiméi guànmùcóng.

bran /bræn/ *n* [U] 麸〔麩〕fū; 糠 kāng.

branch /brɑːntʃ; *US* bræntʃ/ *n* [C] 1 树〔樹〕枝 shùzhī. 2 支线〔綫〕zhīxiàn; 支路 zhīlù. 3 家族的支系 jiāzúde zhīxì; 分支机〔機〕构〔構〕fēnzhī jīgòu: *a* ~ **office** 分局; 分店. **branch** *v* 1 [I] 分支 fēnzhī; 分岔 fēnchà. 2 [短语动词] **branch ˈoff** 从大路转〔轉〕入小路 cóng dàlù zhuǎnrù xiǎolù. **branch ˈout** 扩〔擴〕充业〔業〕务〔務〕kuòchōng yèwù; 扩大活动〔動〕范〔範〕围〔圍〕kuòdà huódòng fànwéi.

brand /brænd/ *n* [C] 1 牌子 páizi: *the cheapest* ~ **of margarine** 人造黄油最便宜的一种品牌. 2 (独特的)一种〔種〕yìzhǒng; 一类〔類〕yílèi: *a strange* ~ **of humour** 一种离奇的幽默. 3 (牲畜身上标明其所有者的)烙印 làoyìn. **brand** *v* [T] 1 在…身上打烙印 zài…shēnshang dǎ làoyìn. 2 加污名于 jiā wūmíng yú: *He was* ~**ed** (**as**) **a thief.** 他被加上小偷的臭名. ˌ**brand-ˈnew** *adj* 全新的 quánxīnde.

brandish /ˈbrændɪʃ/ *v* [T] 挥〔揮〕舞 huīwǔ.

brandy /ˈbrændɪ/ *n* [C,U] [*pl* -ies] 白兰〔蘭〕地(酒) báilándì.

brash /bræʃ/ *adj* 爱〔愛〕表现自己的 ài biǎoxiàn zìjǐde; 自以为〔爲〕是的 zì yǐ wéi shì de.

brass /brɑːs; *US* bræs/ *n* **1** [U] 黄铜 huángtóng. **2** [U,C,通常为 pl] 黄铜器 huángtóngqì; 黄铜制〔製〕品 huángtóng zhìpǐn. **3 the brass** [sing,亦作 sing,用 pl v] (管弦乐队的)铜管乐〔樂〕组 tóngguǎnyuè zǔ; 铜管乐器 tóngguǎn yuèqì. **4** [U] [英国俚语]钱〔錢〕qián. ˌ**brass** ˈ**band** *n* [C] 铜管乐队〔隊〕tóngguǎn yuèduì.

brassière /ˈbræsɪə(r); *US* brəˈzɪər/ *n* [C] [正式用语] = BRA.

brat /bræt/ *n* [C] [贬]小孩 xiǎohái; 顽童 wántóng.

bravado /brəˈvɑːdəʊ/ *n* [U] 虚张〔張〕声〔聲〕势〔勢〕xū zhāng shēngshì.

brave /breɪv/ *adj* [~r, ~st] **1** 勇敢的 yǒnggǎnde. **2** 表现英勇的 biǎoxiàn yīngyǒngde. **brave** *v* [T] 勇敢地面对〔對〕(危险等) yǒnggǎnde miànduì. **bravely** *adv*. **bravery** /ˈbreɪvərɪ/ *n* [U].

bravo /ˌbrɑːˈvəʊ/ *interj*, *n* [C] [*pl* ~s] 好啊! hǎo'ā! 妙啊! miào'ā!

brawl /brɔːl/ *n* [C] 吵架 chǎojià. **brawl** *v* [I] 争吵 zhēngchǎo.

brawny /ˈbrɔːnɪ/ *adj* 强壮〔壯〕的 qiángzhuàngde; 肌肉发〔發〕达〔達〕的 jīròu fādá de.

bray /breɪ/ *n* [C] 驴〔驢〕叫声〔聲〕lǘ jiào shēng. *v* [I] (驴)叫 jiào; 发〔發〕出驴叫似的声〔聲〕音 fāchū lǘjiào shìde shēngyīn.

brazen /ˈbreɪzn/ *adj* 厚颜无〔無〕耻的 hòuyán wúchǐ de.

brazier /ˈbreɪzɪə(r)/ *n* [C] 火盆 huǒpén; 火钵 huǒbō.

breach /briːtʃ/ *n* **1** [C,U] 违〔違〕反 wéifǎn; 违背 wéibèi. **2** (友好关系的)破裂 pòliè. **3** [C] [正式用语](尤指墙上的)缺口 quēkǒu, 裂口 lièkǒu. **breach** *v* [T] **1** 违反(法律等) wéifǎn. **2** [正式用语]使有缺口 shǐ yǒu quēkǒu. ˌ**breach of the** ˈ**peace** *n* [C,常用 sing] [法律]扰〔擾〕乱〔亂〕治安 rǎoluàn zhì'ān.

bread /bred/ *n* [U] **1** 面〔麵〕包 miànbāo. **2** [俚]钱〔錢〕qián. **3** [习语] **on the** ˈ**breadline** 很穷〔窮〕hěnqióng. ˈ**breadcrumb** *n* [C,常用 pl] 面包屑 miànbāoxiè. ˈ**breadwinner** *n* [C] 养〔養〕家活口的人 yǎngjiā huókǒu de rén.

breadth /bredθ, bretθ/ *n* [U] **1** 宽度 kuāndù. **2** 广〔廣〕度 guǎngdù; 幅度 fúdù.

break[1] /breɪk/ *v* [*pt* **broke** /brəʊk/, *pp* **broken** /ˈbrəʊkən/] **1** [I,T] 打破 dǎpò; 断〔斷〕duàn: *Glass* ~**s easily.** 玻璃容易打破. ~ *a plate* 打破盘子. **2** [I,T] (使)分裂 fēnliè: ~ *open the boxes* 把箱子撬开. **3** [I,T] 破坏〔壞〕pòhuài: *My watch has broken*. 我的手表坏了. **4** [T] 违〔違〕反 wéifǎn; 违背(法律、诺言等) wéibèi. **5** [I] *off* 中止 zhōngzhǐ. **6** [T] 打断 dǎduàn: ~ *one's journey* 中断旅行. ~ *the silence* 打破沉默. **7** [I] 变〔變〕得光亮 biàndé guāngliàng; 开〔開〕始 kāishǐ: *Day was* ~*ing*. 天亮了. **8** [I,T] 削弱 xuēruò; (使)衰弱 shuāiruò: ~ *the power of the unions* 削弱了工会的力量. *His wife's death broke him*. 他妻子的去世使他身心受到摧残. **9** [T] 减弱(跌落的)效应〔應〕jiǎnruò xiàoyìng. **10** [T] (*of*) 使(某人)克服某种〔種〕习〔習〕惯 shǐ kèfú mǒuzhǒng xíguàn. **11** [I] (天气)突然变化 tūrán biànhuà. **12** [I,T] 传〔傳〕开 chuánkāi; 披露 pīlù. **13** [I] (男孩的嗓音由于青春期)变得低沉 biàndé dīchén. **14** [T] 打破(纪录) dǎpò. **15** [T] 译〔譯〕解(密码) yìjiě. **16** [习语] **break the** ˈ**back of sth** 完成某事的最主要或困难〔難〕部分 wánchéng mǒushì de zuì zhǔyào huò kùnnan bùfen. **break** ˈ**even** 不亏〔虧〕不赢 bù kuī bù yíng. **break fresh/new** ˈ**ground** 开辟〔闢〕新天地 kāipì xīn tiāndì. **break the** ˈ**ice** 打破沉默/僵局 dǎpò chénmò/jiāngjú. **break** ˈ**wind** [委婉]放屁 fàngpì. **make or break sb/sth** 使大成功或完全失败 shǐ dà chénggōng huò wánquán shībài. **17** [短语动词] **break away (from sb/sth)** 突然走开 tūrán zǒukāi; 脱离〔離〕(政党等) tuōlí. **break down** (a) (机器)坏〔壞〕huài. (b) 失败 shībài; 垮台 kuǎtái: *Talks between the two sides have broken down*. 双方谈判已经失败. (c) (精神)垮下来 kuǎ xiàlái. **break sth down** (a) 破坏 pòhuài: ~ *down resistance* 粉碎抵抗. (b) 分析 fēnxī; 分类〔類〕fēnlèi: ~ **down** *expenses* 把开支分成细类. **break in** (a) 破门而入 pò mén ér rù; 闯入 chuǎngrù. (b) (*on*) 打断 dǎduàn. **break sb/sth in** 训练〔練〕(某人) xùnliàn; 使(某物)合用 shǐ héyòng. **break into sth** (a) 破门而入 pò mén ér rù. (b) 突然…起来 tūrán…qǐlái: ~ **into laughter/ a run** 突然笑起来; 突然跑了起来. (c) 开始使用(存款) kāishǐ shǐyòng. **break off** 停止说话 tíngzhǐ shuōhuà. **break (sth) off** (使)折断 zhéduàn. **break sth off** 突然结束 tūrán jiéshù: *They've broken off their engagement*. 他们突然解除了婚约. **break out** (a) 暴发 bàofā: *Fire broke out*. 突然发生了火灾. (b) (*of*) 逃出监〔監〕狱 táochū jiānyù. (c) (*in*) 突然被…覆盖〔蓋〕tūrán bèi…fùgài: ~ *out in spots* 突然布满了斑点. **break through (sth)** (a) 突破 tūpò; 冲垮 chōngkuǎ. (b) (太阳)从〔從〕(云层中)露出 cóng lùchū. **break up** (a) (人群)四散走开 sìsàn zǒukāi. (b) 学〔學〕校期终放假 xuéxiào qīzhōng fàngjià. (c) (*with*) 关〔關〕系〔係〕结束 guānxì jiéshù. **break (sth) up** (a) 打碎 dǎsuì; 打破 dǎpò. (b) (使)结束 jiéshù:

B

Their marriage is ~ing up. 他们的婚姻结束了. breakable *adj*. 易碎的 yìsuìde. ˈbreakaway *adj* (人)脱离某党〔黨〕派、团〔團〕体〔體〕的 tuōlí mǒu dǎngpài、tuántǐ de. ˈbreak-in *n* [C]闯入 chuǎngrù. ˈbreak-out *n* [C] 越狱 yuèyù. breakthrough *n* [C] 新发明 xīn fāmíng;突破 tūpò. ˈbreakup *n* [C] (关系)结束 jiéshù.

break[2] /breɪk/ *n* [C] 1 破裂处〔處〕pòlièchù: *a ~ in a pipe* 管子上的一个裂口. 2 空间 kōngjiān;空隙 kòngxì. 3 (工作中间的)休息时〔時〕间 xiūxi shíjiān: *a ˈlunch-~* (工作中间的)吃饭时间. 4 中断〔斷〕zhōngduàn: *a ~ with tradition* 传统的中断. 5 [非正式用语]好运〔運〕气〔氣〕hǎo yùnqi. 6 [习语] break of day 破晓〔曉〕pòxiǎo;黎明 límíng. make a break for it (企图)逃跑 táopǎo.

breakage /ˈbreɪkɪdʒ/ *n* 1 [C] 破损物 pòsǔnwù. 2 [C, U] 破损 pòsǔn;损毁 sǔnhuǐ.

breakdown /ˈbreɪkdaʊn/ *n* [C] 1 (机械的)损坏〔壞〕sǔnhuài,故障 gùzhàng. 2 崩溃 bēngkuì;失败 shībài. 3 身体〔體〕(尤指精神上)衰弱 shēntǐ shuāiruò;垮下来〔來〕kuǎ xiàlái: *a ˌnervous ˈ~* 精神崩溃. 4 统计的分类〔類〕tǒngjìde fēnlèi: *a ~ of expenses* 开支的分类.

breaker /ˈbreɪkə(r)/ *n* [C] 1 碎浪 suìlàng;激浪 jīlàng. 2 打破者 dǎpòzhě;开〔開〕拓者 kāituòzhě: *a ˈlaw-~* 违〔違〕法者.

breakfast /ˈbrekfəst/ *n* [C, U] 早餐 zǎocān. breakfast *v* [I] 吃早饭 chī zǎofàn. breakfast ˈtelevision *n* [U] 早间电〔電〕视节〔節〕目 zǎojiān diànshì jiémù.

breakneck /ˈbreɪknek/ *adj* (速度)快到危险〔險〕程度的: kuàidào wēixiǎn chéngdù de: *at ~ speed* 以快到危险程度的速度.

breakwater /ˈbreɪkwɔːtə(r)/ *n* [C] 防浪堤 fánglàngdī.

breast /brest/ *n* [C] 1 乳房 rǔfáng. 2 [修辞]胸 xiōng. ˈbreastbone *n* [C] 胸骨 xiōnggǔ. ˈbreast-stroke *n* [U] 蛙泳 wāyǒng.

breath /breθ/ *n* 1 [U] 呼吸之空气〔氣〕hūxī zhī kōngqì;气息 qìxī. 2 [C] 一次吸气 yícì xīqì. 3 [sing] (空气的)轻〔輕〕微流通 qīngwēi liútōng. 4 [习语] get one's ˈbreath back 恢复〔復〕正常呼吸 huīfù zhèngcháng hūxī. out of breath 上气不接下气 shàngqì bù jiē xiàqì. take sb's breath away 使某人大吃一惊〔驚〕shǐ mǒurén dàchī yījīng. under one's breath 耳语 ěryǔ. breathless *adj* 1 上气不接下气的 shàngqì bù jiē xiàqì de. 2 (因害怕、激动等)透不过〔過〕气来〔來〕的 tòubúguòqìláide. breathlessly *adv*. ˈbreathtaking *adj* 惊〔驚〕人的 jīngrénde;惊险〔險〕的 jīngxiǎnde.

breathalyser (美语 -lyz-) /ˈbreθəlaɪzə(r)/ *n* [C] 测醉器(分析某人呼气,测定其酒醉程度) cèzuìqì.

breathe /briːð/ *v* 1 [I, T] 呼吸 hūxī. 2 [T] 低声〔聲〕,耳语地说 dīshēng, ěryǔ de shuō. 3 表明(感情等) biǎomíng. 4 [习语] breathe again (劳累、紧张后)静下心来〔來〕jìng xià xīn lái;宽心 kuānxīn;松〔鬆〕心 sōngxīn. breathe down sb's neck [非正式用语]紧〔緊〕盯(某人) jǐndīng. breather *n* [C] [非正式用语]短暂的休息 duǎnzànde xiūxi.

breeches /ˈbrɪtʃɪz/ *n* [pl] (膝下结扎的)短裤 duǎnkù.

breed /briːd/ *v* [*pt*, *pp* bred /bred/] 1 [T] 繁殖 fánzhí;育种〔種〕yùzhǒng: *~ horses (cattle)* 繁殖马匹(家畜). 2 [I] (动物)生育 shēngyù. 3 [T] 教养〔養〕jiàoyǎng;养育 yǎngyù: *a well-bred boy* 有教养的男孩子. 4 [T] 引起 yǐnqǐ;惹起 rěqǐ: *Dirt ~s disease*. 脏东西会引发疾病. breed *n* [C] 1 (动物)品种〔種〕pǐnzhǒng. 2 (人的)类〔類〕型 lèixíng: *a new ~ of manager* 新型的经理. breeder *n* [C] 饲养员 sìyǎngyuán. breeding *n* [U] 1 (动物的)繁殖 fánzhí. 2 教养 jiàoyǎng: *a man of good ~ing* 有教养的人.

breeze /briːz/ *n* [C, U] 微风〔風〕wēifēng. breeze *v* [短语动词] breeze in, out, etc [非正式用语]飘〔飄〕然而来、去等 piāorán ér lái、qù děng. breezy *adj* 1 惠风和畅的 huìfēng héchàng de. 2 活泼〔潑〕的 huópode. breezily *adv*.

brethren /ˈbreðrən/ *n* [pl] [旧]兄弟 xiōngdì.

brevity /ˈbrevətɪ/ *n* [U] [正式用语]短暂 duǎnzàn;短促 duǎncù: *the ~ of life* 生命的短暂.

brew /bruː/ *v* 1 [I, T] 沏 qī, 泡(茶等) pào;酿〔釀〕造(啤酒等) niàngzào. 2 [I] (不愉快的事)酝〔醞〕酿 yùnniàng, 形成 xíngchéng. brew *n* [C] 酿出的饮料 niàngchūde yǐnliào. brewer *n* [C]. brewery /ˈbruːərɪ/ *n* [C] [*pl* -ies] 啤酒厂〔廠〕píjiǔchǎng.

bribe /braɪb/ *n* [C] 贿赂 huìlù;行贿物 xínghuìwù. bribe *v* [T] 向…行贿 xiàng…xínghuì. bribery /ˈbraɪbərɪ/ *n* [U] 贿赂 huìlù.

bric-à-brac /ˈbrɪkəbræk/ *n* [U] (不值钱的)小装〔裝〕饰品 xiǎo zhuāngshìpǐn.

brick /brɪk/ *n* [C, U] 砖〔磚〕zhuān. brick *v* [短语动词] brick sth in / up 砌砖填补〔補〕(缺口等) qìzhuān tiánbǔ. ˈbricklayer *n* [C] 砌砖工人 qìzhuān gōngrén. ˈbrickwork *n* [U] 砖结构〔構〕zhuānjiégòu.

bridal /ˈbraɪdl/ *adj* 新娘的 xīnniángde;婚礼〔禮〕的 hūnlǐde.

bride /braɪd/ *n* [C] 新娘 xīnniáng;新婚妇〔婦〕女 xīnhūn fùnǚ. ˈbridegroom *n* [C] 新郎 xīnláng;新婚男子 xīnhūn nánzǐ. **bridesmaid** *n* [C] 女傧〔儐〕相 nǚ bīnxiàng.

bridge[1] /brɪʤ/ *n* [C] 1 桥〔橋〕 qiáo;桥梁 qiáoliáng. 2 [喻]提供联〔聯〕系〔繫〕的东西 tígōng liánxìde dōngxi. 3 (船上的)驾〔駕〕驶〔駛〕台 jiàshǐtái;桥楼〔樓〕 qiáolóu. 4 鼻梁 bíliáng. 5 (提琴等的)桥马 qiáomǎ. **bridge** *v* [T] 架桥于 jiàqiáo yú. **ˈbridgehead** *n* [C] [军事]桥头〔頭〕堡 qiáotóubǎo.

bridge[2] /brɪʤ/ *n* [U] 桥〔橋〕牌戏〔戲〕 qiáopáixì.

bridle /ˈbraɪdl/ *n* [C] 马勒 mǎlē;马笼〔籠〕头〔頭〕 mǎlóngtóu. **bridle** *v* 1 [T] 给(马)上笼头 gěi shàng lóngtóu. 2 [喻]抑制 yìzhì;约束 yuēshù: ~ *one's emotion* 控制情绪. 3 [I] 昂首收领表示愤怒 ángshǒu shōuhàn biǎoshì fènnù.

brief[1] /briːf/ *adj* 1 短暂〔暫〕的 duǎnzànde. 2 (用词)简短的 jiǎnduǎnde. 3 (衣服)短小的 duǎnxiǎode. 4 [习语] **in brief** 简言之 jiǎnyánzhī. **briefly** *adv*.

brief[2] /briːf/ *n* [C] 事先提供的背景材料、指示等 shìxiān tígōng de bèijǐng cáiliào、zhǐshì děng. **brief** *v* [T] 向…事先提供背景材料 xiàng… shìxiān tígōng bèijǐng cáiliào. **ˈbriefcase** *n* [C] 公事皮包 gōngshì píbāo.

briefs /briːfs/ *n* [pl] 三角裤 sānjiǎokù.

brigade /brɪˈgeɪd/ *n* [C] 1 (军事)旅 lǚ. 2 (执行一定任务的)队〔隊〕 duì: *the ˈfire-* ~ 消防队. **brigadier** /brɪgəˈdɪə(r)/ *n* [C] 旅长〔長〕 lǚzhǎng.

bright /braɪt/ *adj* [~er, ~est] 1 明亮的 míngliàngde;光辉〔輝〕的 guānghuīde. 2 (颜色)鲜亮的 xiānliàngde. 3 欢〔歡〕乐〔樂〕的 huānlède. 4 聪〔聰〕明的 cōngmingde. 5 (前途)大有希望的 dàyǒu xīwàng de: *The future looks* ~. 前途光明. **brighten** *v* [I,T] (使)发〔發〕亮 fāliàng. **brightly** *adv*. **brightness** *n* [U].

brilliant /ˈbrɪlɪənt/ *adj* 1 光辉的 guānghuīde;辉煌的 huīhuángde. 2 英明的 yīngmíngde. 3 [非正式用语]非常好的 fēicháng hǎo de. **brilliance** /-lɪəns/ *n* [U]. **brilliantly** *adv*.

brim /brɪm/ *n* [C] 1 杯边〔邊〕 bēibiān. 2 帽边 màobiān. **brim** *v* [-mm-] 1 [I] (*with*) 充满 chōngmǎn. 2 [短语动词] **brim over** 满溢 mǎnyì.

brine /braɪn/ *n* [U] 盐〔鹽〕水 yánshuǐ;咸〔鹹〕水 xiánshuǐ.

bring /brɪŋ/ *v* [*pt*, *pp* **brought** /brɔːt/] [T] 1 带〔帶〕来 dàilái;拿来 nálái: *B~ me my coat*. 把我的上衣拿来. *He brought his dog with him*. 他带着他的狗. 2 造成 zàochéng;产〔產〕生 chǎnshēng: *Spring ~s warm weather*. 春天带来温暖的天气. *The story brought tears to her eyes*. 这个故事使她泪水盈眶. 3 使达〔達〕到某种〔種〕状〔狀〕态〔態〕 shǐ dádào mǒuzhǒng zhuàngtài: *bring water to the boil* 把水烧开. 4 说服 shuōfú;劝〔勸〕使 quànshǐ: *I can't ~ myself to tell him*. 我鼓不起勇气来告诉他. 5 (*against*) [法律]提出 tíchū: ~ *a case against sb*. 对某人提出起诉. 6 [习语] **bring sth to a ˈhead** ⇨HEAD[1]. **bring sth to mind** ⇨MIND[1]. **bring sth into the open** ⇨OPEN[1]. 7 [短语动词] **bring sth about** 使某事发〔發〕生 shǐ mǒushì fāshēng. **bring sb/sth back** (a) 带回 dàihuí: *bring back a book* 带回一本书. *I brought the children back*. 我把孩子们带回来了. (b) 使回忆〔憶〕 shǐhuíyì. (c) 重新采〔採〕用 chóngxīn cǎiyòng: ~ *back hanging* 重新采用绞刑. **bring sth/sb down** (a) 使落下 shǐ luòxià;使倒下 shǐ dǎoxià: ~ *down the government* 推翻政府. *brought him down with a rugby tackle* 用橄榄球赛的抱人动作把他摔倒. (b) 减少 jiǎnshǎo: ~ *prices down* 降低物价. (c) 击〔擊〕落(飞机) jīluò;使(飞机)降落 shǐ jiàngluò. **bring sth forward** (a) 提前 tíqián: *The meeting has been brought forward*. 会议提前了. (b) 提出 tíchū. **bring sth/sb in** (a) 引进〔進〕 yǐnjìn;采用 cǎiyòng: ~ *in a new fashion* 引进新的式样. ~ *in a new legislation* 提出新的立法. (b) 为〔爲〕…提供利润 wèi… tígōng lìrùn. (c) 把…当〔當〕作顾〔顧〕问 bǎ… dāngzuò gùwèn: ~ *in a scientist to check pollution* 请一位科学家对污染治理提出意见. **bring sth off** [非正式用语]使成功 shǐ chénggōng. **bring sth on** 引起 yǐnqǐ;导〔導〕致 dǎozhì: *The rain brought on his cold*. 这场雨导致了他的感冒. **bring sb out** (a) 使罢〔罷〕工 shǐ bàgōng: *Union leaders brought out the workers*. 工会领导层发动工人罢工. (b) 使少腼腆 shǐ shǎo miǎntiǎn: *His first year at college brought him out a little*. 他在大学的头一年使他不怎么腼腆了. **bring sth out** (a) 使显〔顯〕出 shǐ xiǎnchū: ~ *out the meaning* 使意义明白表现出来. *brought out her kindness* 显出她的好意. (b) 生产 shēngchǎn;出版 chūbǎn: ~ *out a new type of computer* 推出一种新型的电子计算机. **bring sb round** (a) 使复〔復〕苏〔蘇〕 shǐ fùsū. (b) 说服 shuōfú. **bring sb up** 养〔養〕育 yǎngyù;教育 jiàoyù: *brought up to be polite* 养成懂礼貌. **bring sth up** (a) 使注意 shǐ zhùyì;提到 tídào: ~ *up the subject of salaries* 提到工资问题. (b) 呕〔嘔〕吐 ǒutù.

brink /brɪŋk/ *n* [C] 悬〔懸〕崖等的边〔邊〕沿 xuányá děng de biānyán: [喻] *on the ~ of war* 战争边缘.

brisk /brɪsk/ *adj* 活泼〔潑〕的 huópode;轻〔輕〕快的 qīngkuàide: *walk at a ~ pace* 轻快地

散步. **briskly** *adv*.

bristle /ˈbrɪsl/ *n* [C, U] 短而硬的毛 duǎn ér yìng de máo; 刷子的毛 shuāzide máo. **bristle** *v* [I] 1 (毛发等)直立 zhílì. 2 [喻]发〔發〕怒 fānù. 3 [短语动词] **bristle with sth** 丛〔叢〕生 cóngshēng; 重重 chóngchóng.

Britain /ˈbrɪtən/ *n* [U] 不列颠 Búlièdiān; 英国〔國〕Yīngguó.

British /ˈbrɪtɪʃ/ *adj* 1 大不列颠的 Dàbúlièdiānde; 英国〔國〕的 Yīngguóde; 英国人的 Yīngguórénde. 2 英联〔聯〕邦的 Yīngliánbāngde. **British** *n* [pl] the British (总称) 英国人 Yīngguórén.

brittle /ˈbrɪtl/ *adj* 易碎的 yìsuìde; 脆弱的 cuìruòde: ~ *glass* 易碎的玻璃.

broach /brəʊtʃ/ *v* [T] 开〔開〕始讨论〔論〕(问题等) kāishǐ tǎolùn.

broad /brɔːd/ *adj* 1 宽的 kuānde. 2 广〔廣〕阔的 guǎngkuòde: [喻] *a* ~ *range of subjects* 范围广阔的各种学科. 3 清楚的 qīngchude; 明显〔顯〕的 míngxiǎnde: *a* ~ *grin* 咧嘴一笑. 4 大概的 dàgàide; 概略的 gàilüède: *a* ~ *outline of a speech* 一篇演说的粗略的提纲. 5 (说话)方言性的 fāngyán xìng de; 口音重的 kǒuyīn zhòng de. 6 [习语] **in broad ˈdaylight** 在大白天 zài dàbáitiān. **broaden** *v* [I, T] 变〔變〕宽 biànkuān; 使更宽 shǐ gèng kuān. **broadly** *adv* 一般地 yībānde: ~*ly speaking* 一般地说. ˌ**broadˈminded** *adj* 能容纳不同意见的 néng róngnà bùtóng yìjiàn de.

broadband /ˈbrɔːdbænd/ *n* [U] 宽带〔帶〕kuāndài. **broadband** *adj* 宽带的 kuāndàide.

broadcast /ˈbrɔːdkɑːst; *US* -kæst/ *n* [C] 无〔無〕线〔綫〕电〔電〕或电视节〔節〕目 wúxiàndiàn huò diànshì jiémù. **broadcast** *v* [*pt*, *pp* **broadcast**] [I, T] 播出(无线电或电视节目) bōchū. **broadcaster** *n* [C]. **broadcasting** *n* [U].

broadside /ˈbrɔːdsaɪd/ *n* [C] 1 舷炮的齐〔齊〕射 xiánpàode qíshè. 2 [喻]连〔連〕珠炮似的攻讦或谴责 liánzhūpào shì de gōngjié huò qiǎnzé.

broccoli /ˈbrɒkəlɪ/ *n* [U] 硬花球花椰菜 yìnghuāqiúhuāyēcài; 花茎〔莖〕甘蓝〔藍〕huājìng gānlán.

brochure /ˈbrəʊʃə(r); *US* brəʊˈʃʊər/ *n* [C] (有某种信息或广告的)小册子 xiǎocèzi.

broil /brɔɪl/ *v* [T] [尤用于美国英语]烤(食物) kǎo.

broke[1] *pt* of BREAK[1].

broke[2] /brəʊk/ *adj* [非正式用语] 1 没有钱〔錢〕的 méiyǒu qián de. 2 [习语] **flat broke** 一个〔個〕钱〔錢〕也没有 yígè qián yě méiyǒu.

broken[1] *pp* of BREAK[1].

broken[2] /ˈbrəʊkən/ *adj* 1 不连续〔續〕的 bù liánxù de: ~ *sleep* 断断续续的睡眠. 2 (外语)说得不标〔標〕准〔準〕的 shuōde bù biāozhǔn de. 3 (人)因疾病或不幸而衰弱的 yīn jíbìng huò búxìng ér shuāiruò de. ˌ**broken ˈhome** *n* [C] 离〔離〕异〔異〕的家庭 líyì de jiātíng.

broker /ˈbrəʊkə(r)/ *n* [C] 股票经〔經〕纪人 gǔpiào jīngjìrén; 掮客 qiánkè.

brolly /ˈbrɒlɪ/ *n* [C] [*pl* **-ies**] [非正式用语, 尤用于英国英语]伞〔傘〕sǎn.

bronchial /ˈbrɒŋkɪəl/ *adj* 支气〔氣〕管的 zhīqìguǎnde.

bronchitis /brɒŋˈkaɪtɪs/ *n* [C] 支气〔氣〕管炎 zhīqìguǎnyán.

bronze /brɒnz/ *n* 1 [U] 青铜 qīngtóng. 2 [U] 青铜色 qīngtóngsè. 3 [C] 青铜器 qīngtóngqì; 青铜艺〔藝〕术〔術〕品 qīngtóng yìshùpǐn; 铜牌 tóngpái. **bronze** *v* [T] 上青铜色于 shàng qīngtóngsè yú. **bronze ˈmedal** *n* [C] (竞赛中的)铜牌 tóngpái.

brooch /brəʊtʃ/ *n* [C] 胸针 xiōngzhēn; 饰针 shìzhēn.

brood /bruːd/ *n* [C] 1 同窝〔窩〕幼鸟〔鳥〕tóngwō yòuniǎo. 2 [谐谑]一个〔個〕家庭的孩子 yígè jiātíng de háizi. **brood** *v* [I] 1 孵幼雏〔雛〕fū yòuchú. 2 沉思 chénsī; 忧〔憂〕思 yōusī: ~*ing over her problems* 苦思冥想她的问题. **broody** *adj* 1 (母鸡等)要孵小鸡〔鷄〕的 yào fū xiǎojī de. 2 好郁郁沉思的 hào yùyù chénsī de.

brook /brʊk/ *n* [C] 小河 xiǎohé; 溪 xī.

broom /bruːm/ *n* [C] 扫〔掃〕帚 sàozhou.

broth /brɒθ; *US* brɔːθ/ *n* [U] 肉汤 ròutāng.

brothel /ˈbrɒθl/ *n* [C] 妓院 jìyuàn.

brother /ˈbrʌðə(r)/ *n* [C] 1 兄弟 xiōngdì. 2 同胞 tóngbāo; 同事 tóngshì. 3 [*pl* **brethren** /ˈbreðrən/] (a) 修士 xūshì. (b) 同教会〔會〕的教友 tóng jiàohuìde jiàoyǒu. ˈ**brotherhood** 1 [U] 兄弟之情 xiōngdì zhī qíng. 2 社团〔團〕组织〔織〕shètuán zǔzhī; 社团组织成员 shètuán zǔzhī chéngyuán. ˈ**brother-in-law** *n* [C] [*pl* **~s-in-law**] 大伯 dàbó; 小叔 xiǎoshū; 内兄 nèixiōng; 内弟 nèidì; 姐夫 jiěfu; 妹夫 mèifu. **brotherly** *adj*.

brought /brɔːt/ *pt*, *pp* of BRING.

brow /braʊ/ *n* 1 额 é. 2 眉 méi; 眉毛 méimao. 3 通向坡顶的斜坡 tōngxiàng pōdǐng de xiépō.

browbeat /ˈbraʊbiːt/ *v* [*pt* **browbeat**, *pp* **~en** /-biːtn/] [T] 恫吓〔嚇〕dònghè.

brown /braʊn/ *n* [C, U], *adj* 褐色 hèsè; 棕色 zōngsè; 褐色的 hèsède; 棕色的 zōngsède. **brown** *v* [I] (使)变〔變〕成褐色或棕色 biànchéng hèsè huò zōngsè.

browse /braʊz/ *v* [I] 1 浏〔瀏〕览〔覽〕liúlǎn. 2 放牧 fàngmù. **browse** *n* [C, 常作 sing].

browser /ˈbraʊzə(r)/ *n* [C] 浏〔瀏〕览〔覽〕器

liúlǎnqì.

bruise /bruːz/ *n* [C] 青肿〔腫〕qīngzhǒng；伤〔傷〕痕 shānghén. **bruise** *v* 1 [T] 使青肿 shǐ qīngzhǒng；碰伤 pèngshāng. 2 [I] 伤成青肿 shāngchéng qīngzhǒng.

brunette /bruːˈnet/ *n* [C] 具深褐色头〔頭〕发〔髮〕的白种〔種〕女人 jù shēnhèsè tóufa de báizhǒng nǚrén.

brunt /brʌnt/ *n* [习语] bear the ˈbrunt of sth ⇨BEAR².

brush¹ /brʌʃ/ *n* [C] 1 刷子 shuāzi：*a tooth*~ 牙刷. 2 [sing] 刷 shuā. 3 [C] 争吵 zhēngchǎo；冲〔衝〕突 chōngtū：*a nasty* ~ *with his boss* 同他的老板大吵一架. 4 [U] 灌木丛〔叢〕guànmùcóng.

brush² /brʌʃ/ *v* [T] 1 刷 shuā. 2 轻〔輕〕触〔觸〕qīngchù；擦过〔過〕cāguò. 3 [短语动词] brush sth aside 不顾〔顧〕búgù；不理睬 bù lǐcǎi. brush sth up, brush up on sth 复〔復〕习〔習〕fùxí；温习 wēnxí：~ *up* (*on*) *your French* 复习你的法语.

brusque /bruːsk; *US* brʌsk/ *adj* 粗鲁的 cūlǔde；鲁莽的 lǔmǎngde. **brusquely** *adv*. **brusqueness** *n* [U].

Brussels sprout /ˌbrʌslz ˈspraʊt/ *n* [C] 球芽甘蓝〔藍〕qiúyá gānlán.

brutal /ˈbruːtl/ *adj* 野蛮〔蠻〕的 yěmánde；残〔殘〕忍的 cánrěnde. **brutality** /bruːˈtæləti/ *n* [C, U] [*pl* -ies]. **brutally** *adv*.

brute /bruːt/ *n* [C] 1 兽〔獸〕shòu；畜牲 chùsheng. 2 残〔殘〕忍的人 cánrěnde rén. **brute** *adj* 没有思想的 méiyǒu sīxiǎng de；身体〔體〕的 shēntǐde：~ *force* 蛮〔蠻〕力；暴力. **brutish** *adj* 野兽的 yěshòude；野蛮〔蠻〕的 yěmánde.

bubble /ˈbʌbl/ *n* [C] 1 空气〔氣〕中的气泡 kōngqì zhōng de qìpào. 2 液体〔體〕中的气泡 yètǐ zhōng de qìpào；泡沫 pàomò. **bubble** *v* [I] 1 冒泡 màopào. 2 [喻]充满快乐〔樂〕的情感 chōngmǎn kuàilède qínggǎn. ˈ**bubble gum** *n* [U] 泡泡糖 pàopàotáng. **bubbly** *adj* [-ier, -iest] 1 泡多的 pàoduōde；冒泡的 màopàode. 2 愉快的 yúkuàide；活泼〔潑〕的 huópode.

buck¹ /bʌk/ *n* [C] 雄鹿 xiónglù；公羊 gōngyáng；牡兔 mǔtù.

buck² /bʌk/ *v* 1 [I] (马)猛然弯〔彎〕背跃〔躍〕起 měngrán wānbèi yuèqǐ. 2 [短语动词] buck ˈup 快点〔點〕kuàidiǎn. buck (sb) up (使)精神振奋〔奮〕jīngshén zhènfèn.

buck³ /bʌk/ *n* [C] [美国非正式用语]美元 měiyuán.

buck⁴ /bʌk/ *n* the buck [sing] [非正式用语]责任 zérèn：*to pass the* ~ 推卸责任.

bucket /ˈbʌkɪt/ *n* [C] 1 水桶 shuǐtǒng；提桶 títǒng. 2 (亦作 bucketful) 一桶之量 yītǒng zhī liàng. **bucket** *v* [I] (*down*) [非正式用语](雨)倾盆地下 qīngpénde xià.

buckle /ˈbʌkl/ *n* [C] 扣子 kòuzi；带〔帶〕扣 dàikòu. **buckle** *v* 1 [I, T] 扣住 kòuzhù. 2 由于压〔壓〕力或热〔熱〕力而弯〔彎〕曲 yóuyú yālì huò rèlì ér wānqū. 3 [短语动词] buckle down (to sth) [非正式用语]开〔開〕始认〔認〕真地做 kāishǐ rènzhēn de zuò.

bud /bʌd/ *n* [C] 芽 yá. **bud** *v* [-dd-] [I] 发〔發〕芽 fāyá；萌芽 méngyá. **budding** *adj* 开〔開〕始发展的 kāishǐ fāzhǎn de.

Buddhism /ˈbʊdɪzəm/ *n* 佛教 fójiào；释〔釋〕教 shìjiào. **Buddhist** /ˈbʊdɪst/ *n* [C], *adj*.

buddy /ˈbʌdɪ/ *n* [C] [*pl* -ies] [非正式用语，尤用于美国英语]朋友 péngyou.

budge /bʌdʒ/ *v* [I, T] 移动〔動〕yídòng. *The stone won't* ~. 这石头移动不了.

budgerigar /ˈbʌdʒərɪgɑː(r)/ *n* [C] 小长〔長〕尾鹦〔鸚〕鹉〔鵡〕xiǎo chángwěi yīngwǔ.

budget /ˈbʌdʒɪt/ *n* [C] 预算 yùsuàn. **budget** *v* [I] (*for*) 为〔爲〕…编预算 wèi … biān yùsuàn. **budget** *adj* 廉价〔價〕的 liánjiàde：~ *holidays* 花钱不多的假期.

buff¹ /bʌf/ *n* [U] 暗黄色 ànhuángsè. **buff** *v* [T] 擦亮 cāliàng.

buff² /bʌf/ *n* [C] 迷 mí；爱〔愛〕好者 àihàozhě：*a computer* ~ 电脑迷.

buffalo /ˈbʌfələʊ/ *n* [C] [*pl* buffalo 或 ~es] 一种〔種〕大型野水牛 yìzhǒng dàxíng yě shuǐniú.

buffer /ˈbʌfə(r)/ *n* [C] 缓冲〔衝〕器 huǎnchōngqì.

buffet¹ /ˈbʊfeɪ; *US* bəˈfeɪ/ *n* [C] 1 (火车站等处的)食品饮料摊〔攤〕shípǐn yǐnliào tān. 2 自助餐 zìzhùcān.

buffet² /ˈbʌfɪt/ *v* [T] 推 tuī；打 dǎ：~*ed by the wind* 被风吹打.

buffoon /bəˈfuːn/ *n* [C] 小丑 xiǎochǒu.

bug /bʌg/ *n* [C] 1 小昆虫〔蟲〕xiǎo kūnchóng. 2 [非正式用语]病菌 bìngjūn；病菌引起的疾病 bìngjūn yǐnqǐ de jíbìng. 3 [非正式用语]癖 pǐ；狂 kuáng；迷 mí：*He's got the cooking* ~ ! 他迷上了烹饪! 4 [非正式用语](电子计算机等的)缺陷 quēxiàn. 5 [非正式用语]窃〔竊〕听〔聽〕器 qiètīngqì. **bug** *v* [-gg-] [T] 1 安装窃听器于 ānzhuāng qiètīngqìyú. 2 [非正式用语]烦扰〔擾〕fánrǎo.

bugbear /ˈbʌgbeə(r)/ *n* [C] 吓〔嚇〕人的事 xiàrénde shì；令人厌〔厭〕恶〔惡〕的事 lìng rén yànwùde shì.

bugger /ˈbʌgə(r)/ *n* [C] [⚠非正式用语，尤用于英国英语] 1 讨厌〔厭〕的人或事 tǎoyàn de rén huò shì. 2 人 rén；家伙 jiāhuo：*Poor* ~ ! *His wife left him last week*. 可怜的家伙，上周他的老婆抛弃了他. **bugger** *interj* [⚠非正式用语，尤用于英国英语](用于表示愤怒或厌恶)

B

他妈的 tāmāde.

bugle /ˈbjuːgl/ *n* [C] 喇叭 lǎba；号〔號〕角 hàojiǎo. **bugler** *n* [C].

build[1] /bɪld/ *v* [*pt*, *pp* built /bɪlt/] [T] 1 建筑〔築〕jiànzhù；造 zào. 2 发〔發〕展 fāzhǎn；建立 jiànlì；树〔樹〕立 shùlì：～ *a better future* 建立美好的未来. 3 [短语动词] **build on sth** 以…为〔爲〕基础〔礎〕yǐ…wéi jīchǔ. **build sth on sth** 依赖 yīlài；依靠 yīkào；指望 zhǐwàng. **build (sth) up** (使)增强 zēngqiáng；(使)增加 zēngjiā：*Traffic is ～ing up*. 交通量正在增加. ～ *up a business* 加强一家商号. **build sb/sth up** 大大赞〔讚〕扬〔揚〕dàdà zànyáng. **builder** *n* [C]. ˈ**build-up** *n* [C] 1 逐渐增加 zhújiàn zēngjiā；聚集 jùjí. 2 赞扬 zànyáng. ˌ**built-ˈin** *adj*. 内装〔裝〕的 nèizhuāngde. ˌ**built-ˈup** *adj*. 被建筑物覆盖〔蓋〕的 bèi jiànzhùwù fùgàide.

build[2] /bɪld/ *n* [U, C] 体〔體〕格 tǐgé.

building /ˈbɪldɪŋ/ *n* 1 [C] 建筑〔築〕物 jiànzhùwù. 2 [U] 建筑 jiànzhù, 建筑业 jiànzhùyè. ˈ**building society** *n* [C] [英国英语]房屋互助协〔協〕会〔會〕fángwū hùzhù xiéhuì.

bulb /bʌlb/ *n* [C] 1 电〔電〕灯〔燈〕泡 diàndēngpào. 2 鳞茎〔莖〕línjīng；球茎 qiújīng. **bulbous** *adj* 球茎状〔狀〕的 qiújīng zhuàng de.

bulge /bʌldʒ/ *v* [I] 膨胀 péngzhàng. **bulge** *n* [C] 膨胀 péngzhàng；肿〔腫〕胀 zhǒngzhàng.

bulk /bʌlk/ *n* 1 [U] (尤指巨大的)体〔體〕积〔積〕tǐjī；容积 róngjī. 2 [C] 巨大的外形或团〔團〕块〔塊〕jùdàde wàixíng huò tuánkuài. 3 **the bulk of sth** [sing] 大部分 dà bùfen. 4 [习语] **in ˈbulk** 大批 dàpī；大量 dàliàng. **bulky** *adj* [-ier, -iest] 体积大的 tǐjī dà de；笨大的 bèndàde.

bull /bʊl/ *n* [C] 1 (未阉割的)公牛 gōngniú. 2 雄性的象、鲸等大型动物 xióngxìngde xiàng, jīng děng dàxíng dòngwù. 3 [习语] **a bull in a ˈchina shop** 鲁莽而爱〔愛〕闯〔闖〕祸〔禍〕的人 lǔmǎng ér ài chuǎnghuò de rén. **take the bull by the ˈhorns** 大无〔無〕畏 dà wúwèi；不避艰〔艱〕险〔險〕búbì jiānxiǎn. ˈ**bulldog** *n* [C] 叭喇狗 bālǎgǒu. ˈ**bull's-eye** *n* [C] 靶的中心 bǎde zhōngxīn. ˈ**bullshit** *n* [U], *interj* [△俚]胡说 húshuō；废〔廢〕话 fèihuà.

bulldoze /ˈbʊldəʊz/ *v* [T] 1 用推土机〔機〕推或平整 yòng tuītǔjī tuī huò píngzhěng. 2 [喻]强迫(某人)做某事 qiángpò zuò mǒushì. **bulldozer** *n* [C] 推土机 tuītǔjī.

bullet /ˈbʊlɪt/ *n* [C] 枪〔槍〕弹〔彈〕qiāngdàn；子弹 zǐdàn. ˈ**bullet-proof** *adj* 防弹的 fángdànde：～*-proof glass* 防弹玻璃.

bulletin /ˈbʊlətɪn/ *n* [C] 公报〔報〕gōngbào.

bullion /ˈbʊlɪən/ *n* [U] 条〔條〕金 tiáojīn；条银 tiáoyín；块〔塊〕金 kuàijīn；块银 kuàiyín.

bullock /ˈbʊlək/ *n* [C] 阉〔閹〕公牛 yāngōngniú.

bully /ˈbʊlɪ/ *n* [C] [*pl* -ies] 恶〔惡〕霸 èbà；暴徒 bàotú. **bully** *v* [*pt*, *pp* -ied] [T] 欺侮 qīwǔ.

bulrush /ˈbʊlrʌʃ/ *n* [C] 芦〔蘆〕苇〔葦〕lúwěi.

bulwark /ˈbʊlwək/ *n* [C] 1 堡垒〔壘〕bǎolěi；防御〔禦〕工事 fángyù gōngshì. 2 [喻]屏藩 píngfān；保障 bǎozhàng.

bum[1] /bʌm/ *n* [C] [非正式用语, 尤用于英国英语]屁股 pìgu.

bum[2] /bʌm/ *n* [C] [非正式用语, 尤用于美语] 1 游民 yóumín；乞丐 qǐgài. 2 懒汉〔漢〕lǎnhàn. **bum** *v* [短语动词] **bum aˈround** 游手好闲 yóu shǒu hào xián.

bumble-bee /ˈbʌmblbiː/ *n* [C] 大蜂 dàfēng.

bump /bʌmp/ *v* 1 [I, T] 撞 zhuàng；撞击〔擊〕zhuàngjī：*I ～ed into the chair in the dark*. 黑暗中我撞着了椅子. 2 颠簸地行驶〔駛〕diānbǒde xíngshǐ：*The old bus ～ed along the mountain road*. 这辆旧公共汽车在山路上颠簸前进. 3 [短语动词] **bump into sb** [非正式用语]偶然遇到某人 ǒurán yùdào mǒurén. **bump sb off** [非正式用语]杀〔殺〕死某人 shāsǐ mǒurén. **bump sth up** [非正式用语]增加 zēngjiā. **bump** *n* [C] 1 撞 zhuàng；撞击 zhuàngjī；碰撞声〔聲〕pèngzhuàngshēng. 2 路面上的凹凸不平 lùmiàn shàng de āotūbùpíng. 3 (撞伤的)肿〔腫〕块〔塊〕zhǒngkuài. **bumpy** *adj* [-ier, -iest] 凹凸不平的 āotūbùpíngde.

bumper[1] /ˈbʌmpə(r)/ *n* [C] 汽车上的保险〔險〕杆〔桿〕qìchē shàng de bǎoxiǎngān.

bumper[2] /ˈbʌmpə(r)/ *adj* 大的 dàde；丰〔豐〕富的 fēngfùde：*a ～ harvest* 大丰收.

bumpkin /ˈbʌmpkɪn/ *n* [C] [常作贬]乡〔鄉〕下佬 xiāngxiàlǎo；乡下人 xiāngxiàrén.

bun /bʌn/ *n* [C] 1 小圆(甜)面〔麵〕包 xiǎo yuán miànbāo. 2 (尤指女人的)颈〔頸〕后〔後〕的发〔髮〕髻 jǐnghòude fàjì.

bunch /bʌntʃ/ *n* [C] 1 束 shù；串 chuàn：*a ～ of grapes* 一串葡萄；*a ～ of flowers* 一束花. 2 [非正式用语]一群 yìqún：*They're an interesting ～ of people*. 他们是一群有趣的人. **bunch** *v* [I, T] (*together* / *up*) 串成一串 chuànchéng yíchuàn；捆成一束 kǔnchéng yíshù.

bundle /ˈbʌndl/ *n* 1 [C] 捆 kǔn；包 bāo：*old clothes tied into a ～* 打成一捆的旧衣服. 2 **a bundle of sth** [sing] 一大堆 yídàduī：*He's a ～ of nerves*. 他神经非常紧张. **bundle** *v* 1 [T] (*up*) 打成捆 dǎchéng kǔn；打成包 dǎchéng bāo. 2 [I, T] 匆忙地走或放 cōngmángde zǒu huò fàng：*They ～d him into a taxi*. 他们匆匆忙忙地把他推进一辆出租车.

bung /bʌŋ/ *n* [C] 桶塞 tǒngsāi. **bung** *v* [T] 1 [英国英语, 非正式用语]扔 rēng; 抛 pāo. 2 (*up*) 塞住(孔洞) sāizhù.

bungalow /ˈbʌŋgələʊ/ *n* [C] 平房 píngfáng.

bungee /ˈbʌndʒiː/ *n* [C] 蹦极〔極〕bèngjí. ˈ**bungee jump** *n* [C] 蹦极跳 bèngjítiào. ˈ**bungee jumping** *n* [U] 蹦极运〔運〕动〔動〕bèngjí yùndòng.

bungle /ˈbʌŋgl/ *v* [I, T] 搞坏〔壞〕gǎohuài; 粗制〔製〕滥〔濫〕造 cūzhì lànzào.

bunion /ˈbʌnɪən/ *n* [C] 拇趾肿〔腫〕胀〔脹〕mǔzhǐ zhǒngzhàng.

bunk[1] /bʌŋk/ *n* [C] 1 (倚壁而设的)车、船上的床位 chē、chuán shàng de chuángwèi. 2 双〔雙〕层〔層〕单人床之一 shuāngcéng dānrénchuáng zhī yī.

bunk[2] /bʌŋk/ *n* [习语] **do a ˈbunk** [英国英语, 非正式用语]逃走 táozǒu.

bunker /ˈbʌŋkə(r)/ *n* [C] 1 煤舱〔艙〕méicāng. 2 [军事]地堡 dìbǎo. 3 高尔〔爾〕夫球场〔場〕上的沙坑 gāo'ěrfū qiúchǎng shàng de shākēng.

bunny /ˈbʌnɪ/ *n* [C] [*pl* **-ies**] 小兔子(儿童语) xiǎo tùzi.

buoy /bɔɪ/ *n* [C] 浮标〔標〕fúbiāo. **buoy** *v* [短语动词] **buoy sb/sth up** (a) (使)浮起 fúqǐ. (b) [喻]鼓舞 gǔwǔ; 使振作 shǐ zhènzuò.

buoyant /ˈbɔɪənt/ *adj* 1 有浮力的 yǒu fúlì de. 2 [喻]愉快的 yúkuàide; 轻〔輕〕松〔鬆〕的 qīngsōngde. 3 [喻](股票市场等)保持高价〔價〕的 bǎochí gāojià de. **buoyancy** /-ənsɪ/ *n* [U]. **buoyantly** *adv*.

burden /ˈbɜːdn/ *n* [C] 1 [正式用语]负担〔擔〕fùdān; 担子 dànzi. 2 [喻]重负 zhòngfù: *the ~ of taxation* 捐税的重负. **burden** *v* [T] 使负担 shǐ fùdān; 使负重担 shǐ fù zhòngdàn. **burdensome** /-səm/ *adj* 难〔難〕以负担的 nányǐ fùdān de.

bureau /ˈbjʊərəʊ; *US* bjʊˈrəʊ/ *n* [C] [*pl* ~**x** 或 ~**s** /-rəʊz/] 1 [英国英语]有抽屉的写〔寫〕字桌 yǒu chōutì de xiězìzhuō. 2 [美国英语]五斗橱 wǔdǒuchú. 3 [尤用于美国英语]局 jú; 司 sī; 处〔處〕chù; 所 suǒ. 4 所 suǒ; 社 shè; 室 shì.

bureaucracy /bjʊəˈrɒkrəsɪ/ [*pl* **-ies**] 1 (a) [U] 官僚(总称) guānliáo. (b) [C] 官僚制度 guānliáo zhìdù. 2 [U] [贬]官僚作风〔風〕guānliáo zuòfēng. **bureaucrat** /ˈbjʊərəkræt/ *n* [C] [常作贬]官僚 guānliáo. **bureauˈcratic** /ˌbjʊərəˈkrætɪk/ *adj*.

burglar /ˈbɜːglə(r)/ *n* [C] 破门入室的盗贼 pòmén rùshì de dàozéi. ˈ**burglar alarm** *n* [C] 防盗警报〔報〕器 fángdào jǐngbàoqì. ˈ**burglar-proof** *adj* 防贼的 fángzéide. **burglary** *n* [C, U] [*pl* **-ies**] 偷盗 tōudào. **burgle** (美语 **burglarize**) /ˈbɜːgl/ *v* [T] 偷盗 tōudào.

burial /ˈberɪəl/ *n* [C, U] 葬 zàng; 埋藏 máicáng.

burly /ˈbɜːlɪ/ *adj* [**-ier**, **-iest**] 强壮〔壯〕的 qiángzhuàngde; 壮实〔實〕的 zhuàngshide.

burn *v* [*pt*, *pp* ~**t** /bɜːnt/ 或 *US* ~**ed** /bɜːnd/] 1 [I] 烧〔燒〕shāo. 2 [T] 烧伤〔傷〕shāoshāng; 灼伤 zhuóshāng; 烧毁 shāohuǐ: ~ *old papers* 烧毁旧文件. 3 [T] 烧 shāo; 点〔點〕(烛、灯等) diǎn: ~ *coal in a fire* 在炉子里烧煤. 4 [I, T] (烹饪中)烧焦 shāojiāo: *Sorry, I've ~t the toast.* 很抱歉, 我把吐司烤焦了. 5 [I] (因窘迫而脸上)发〔發〕红 fāhóng. 6 [I] *with* 激怒 jīnù. 7 [短语动词] **burn (sth) down** 烧毁 shāohuǐ. **burn (itself) out** (因燃料耗完而)熄灭〔滅〕xīmiè. **burn oneself out** (因劳累过度而)精疲力竭 jīng pí lì jié, 损伤健康 sǔnshāng jiànkāng. **burn sth out** 烧毁 shāohuǐ: *the ~t-out wreck of a car* 被烧毁的汽车残骸. **burn** *n* [C] 烧伤 shāoshāng; 灼伤 zhuóshāng; 烙印 làoyìn. **burner** *n* [C] 燃烧器 ránshāoqì; 炉〔爐〕子 lúzi. **burning** *adj* 1 热〔熱〕切的 rèqiède: *a ~ing thirst* 热切的渴望; 灼热的干〔乾〕渴. ~ *desire* 炽烈的愿望. 2 非常重要的 fēicháng zhòngyào de; 紧〔緊〕迫的 jǐnpòde: *the ~ing question* 紧迫的问题.

burnish /ˈbɜːnɪʃ/ *v* [T] 擦亮 cāliàng.

burp /bɜːp/ *n* [C], *v* [I] [非正式用语]打嗝儿 dǎgér.

burrow /ˈbʌrəʊ/ *n* [C] 兔等的地洞 tù děng de dìdòng. **burrow** *v* [I, T] 打地洞 dǎ dìdòng; 掘(穴) jué.

bursar /ˈbɜːsə(r)/ *n* [C] 大学〔學〕等的财务〔務〕人员 dàxué děng de cáiwù rényuán. **bursary** *n* [C] [*pl* **-ies**] 奖〔獎〕学〔學〕金 jiǎngxuéjīn; 助学金 zhùxuéjīn.

burst /bɜːst/ *v* [*pt*, *pp* **burst**] 1 [I, T] (使)爆炸 bàozhà; 溃决 kuìjué; 胀破 zhàngpò: *The tyre ~ suddenly.* 轮胎突然爆裂了. *The river ~ its banks.* 河决堤了. 2 [I] (*with*) 满得快裂开〔開〕mǎnde kuài lièkāi: *She was ~ing with anger.* 她满腔怒火. 3 [习语] **be bursting to do sth** 急于要做某事 jíyú yào zuò mǒushì. **burst (sth) ˈopen** 猛地打开 měng de dǎkāi. 4 [短语动词] **burst in on sb/sth** 闯入 chuǎngrù; 插嘴 chāzuǐ. **burst into sth** 突然发〔發〕作 tūrán fāzuò: ~ *into tears* 突然哭了起来. ~ *into laughter* 突然笑了起来. **burst into, out of, etc sth** 突然猛烈移动〔動〕tūrán měngliè yídòng. **burst out** (a) 突然带〔帶〕感情地说 tūrán dài gǎnqíngde shuō. (b) 突然做某事 tūrán zuò mǒushì: ~ *out crying* 突然哭了起来. **burst** *n* [C] 1 爆炸 bàozhà; 爆裂 bàoliè. 2 短暂而猛烈的努力 duǎnzàn ér měngliède nǔlì: *a ~ of energy* 一股猛劲. 3 爆发 bàofā: *a ~ of gunfire* 一阵炮火射击.

B

bury /ˈberɪ/ *v* [*pt*, *pp* -ied] [T] 1 埋葬 máizàng; 葬 zàng. 2 埋藏 máicáng; 掩藏 yǎncáng: *buried treasure* 被埋藏的宝物. *She buried her face in her hands*. 她两手捂着脸. 3 ~ oneself in 专〔專〕心致志于 zhuān xīn zhì zhì yú. 4 [习语] ˌbury the ˈhatchet 停止争吵 tíngzhǐ zhēngchǎo.

bus /bʌs/ *n* [C] 公共汽车 gōnggòngqìchē. **bus** *v* [-s- 亦作 -ss-] [I, T] 乘公共汽车去 chéng gōnggòngqìchē qù. ˈ**bus station** *n* [C] 公共汽车总〔總〕站 gōnggòng qìchēzǒngzhàn. ˈ**bus stop** *n* [C] 公共汽车站 gōnggòng qìchēzhàn. ˈ**bus ticket** *n* [C] 公共汽车票 gōnggòng qìchēpiào.

bush /bʊʃ/ *n* 1 [C] 灌木 guànmù; 多枝矮树〔樹〕duōzhī ǎishù. 2 the bush [U] 澳大利亚〔亞〕未开〔開〕垦〔墾〕的土地 Àodàlìyà wèi kāikěn de tǔdì. ˈ**bushy** *adj* [-ier, -iest] 浓〔濃〕密的 nóngmìde: *~y eyebrows* 浓眉.

business /ˈbɪznɪs/ *n* 1 [U] 买〔買〕卖〔賣〕mǎimài; 商业〔業〕shāngyè; 贸易 màoyì. 2 [C] 商店 shāngdiàn; 商业企业 shāngyè qǐyè. 3 [C, U] 职〔職〕业〔業〕zhíyè. 4 [U] 任务〔務〕rènwù; 职〔職〕责 zhízé. 5 [U] 需要处〔處〕理的事 xūyào chùlǐ de shì. 6 [sing] 事务 shìwù; 事情 shìqing: *Let's forget the whole ~*. 我们把整个这件事都忘了吧. 7 [习语] get down to ˈbusiness 着手干〔幹〕正事 zhuóshǒu gàn zhèngshì. go out of ˈbusiness 破产〔產〕pòchǎn. have no ˈbusiness to do 无〔無〕权〔權〕做某事 wúquán zuò mǒushì. ˈ**business address** *n* [C] 办〔辦〕公地址 bàngōng dìzhǐ; 公司地址 gōngsī dìzhǐ. ˈ**business card** *n* [C] 名片 míngpiàn. **business deˈvelopment** *n* [U] 业〔業〕务〔務〕拓展 yèwù tuòzhǎn. **business ˈfailure** *n* [C, U] 倒闭 dǎobì; 倒闭的企业 dǎobì de qǐyè. **businesslike** *adj* 有效率的 yǒu xiàolǜ de; 有条〔條〕理的 yǒu tiáolǐ de. ˈ**businessman**, ˈ**businesswoman** *n* [C] 商人 shāngrén. ˈ**business model** *n* [C] 商业模式 shāngyè móshì. ˈ**business plan** *n* [C] 商业计划〔劃〕shāngyè jìhuà.

busker /ˈbʌskə(r)/ *n* [C] [非正式用语](演奏乐器的)街头〔頭〕艺〔藝〕人 jiētóu yìrén.

bust[1] /bʌst/ *v* [*pt*, *pp* bust 或 ~ed] [T] [非正式用语] 打破 dǎpò; 击〔擊〕破 jīpò. **bust** *adj* [非正式用语] 1 毁坏〔壞〕了的 huǐhuàilede. 2 [习语] go bust (企业)破产〔產〕pòchǎn.

bust[2] /bʌst/ *n* [C] 1 半身雕塑像 bànshēn diāosùxiàng. 2 妇〔婦〕女的胸部 fùnǚde xiōngbù.

bustle /ˈbʌsl/ *v* [I] 活跃〔躍〕huóyuè; 忙碌 mánglù. **bustle** *n* [U].

busy /ˈbɪzɪ/ *adj* [-ier, -iest] 1 繁忙的 fánmángde; 忙碌的 mánglùde. 2 没空的 méikòngde: *a* ~ day 忙碌的一天. 3 电〔電〕话占线〔綫〕diànhuà zhànxiàn. **busily** *adj*. **busy** *v* [*pt*, *pp* -ied] [T] ~ oneself 忙碌 mánglù.

but[1] /bət; 强式 bʌt/ *conj* 但 dàn.

but[2] /bət; 强式 bʌt/ *prep* 1 除了 chúle: *nothing to eat* ~ bread and cheese 除了面包和奶酪没有可吃的. 2 [习语] ˈbut for sb/sth 要不是 yàobúshì: *B ~ for your help we should not have finished on time*. 要不是你的帮助,我们就不能按时完成.

but[3] /bʌt, 亦作 bət/ *adv* [正式用语或旧词] 只 zhǐ; 仅〔僅〕仅 jǐnjǐn: *We can ~ try*. 我们只能试试看.

butcher /ˈbʊtʃə(r)/ *n* [C] 1 屠夫 túfū; 屠宰、卖〔賣〕肉的人 túzǎi、màiròu de rén. 2 残〔殘〕杀〔殺〕者 cánshāzhě. **butcher** *v* [T] 1 屠宰 túzǎi. 2 屠杀 túshā. **butchery** *n* [U] 屠杀 túshā.

butler /ˈbʌtlə(r)/ *n* [C] 男管家 nán guǎnjiā.

butt[1] /bʌt/ *n* [C] 1 枪〔槍〕托 qiāngtuō. 2 香烟未点〔點〕燃的一端 xiāngyān wèi diǎnrán de yìduān.

butt[2] /bʌt/ *n* [C] 大桶 dàtǒng.

butt[3] /bʌt/ *n* [C] 嘲笑的对〔對〕象 cháoxiàode duìxiàng.

butt[4] /bʌt/ *v* 1 [T] 用头〔頭〕顶撞 yòng tóu dǐngzhuàng. 2 [短语动词] butt in (on sb/sth) 插嘴 chāzuǐ; 打断〔斷〕说话 dǎduàn shuōhuà.

butter /ˈbʌtə(r)/ *n* [U] 黄油 huángyóu. **butter** *v* 1 [T] 涂〔塗〕黄油于 tú huángyóu yú. 2 [短语动词] butter sb up [非正式用语] 奉承 fèngcheng; 阿谀 ēyú. ˈ**buttercup** *n* [C] 毛茛属〔屬〕植物 máogènshǔ zhíwù. ˈ**butterscotch** *n* [U] 黄油硬糖 huángyóu yìngtáng.

butterfly /ˈbʌtəflaɪ/ *n* [C] [*pl* -ies] 蝴蝶 húdié.

buttock /ˈbʌtək/ *n* [C, 尤用 pl] 半边〔邊〕屁股 bànbiān pìgu.

button /ˈbʌtn/ *n* [C] 1 纽扣 niǔkòu. 2 按钮 ànniǔ. **button** *v* [I, T] 扣纽扣 kòu niǔkòu. ˈ**buttonhole** *n* [C] 1 纽孔 niǔkǒng; 纽眼 niǔyǎn. 2 戴在外衣翻领上的花 dài zài wàiyī fānlǐng shàng de huā. **buttonhole** *v* [T] 强留某人来倾听〔聽〕自己说话 qiángliú mǒurén lái qīngtīng zìjǐ shuōhuà.

buttress /ˈbʌtrɪs/ *n* [C] 扶垛 fúduò; 扶壁 fúbì. **buttress** *v* [T] 加强 jiāqiáng; 支持 zhīchí.

buxom /ˈbʌksəm/ *adj* (妇女)丰〔豐〕满的 fēngmǎnde; 健康的 jiànkāngde.

buy /baɪ/ *v* [*pt*, *pp* bought /bɔːt/] [T] 1 买〔買〕mǎi; 购〔購〕买 gòumǎi. 2 [非正式用语] 同意 tóngyì; 相信 xiāngxìn. 3 [短语动词] buy sb out (为控制某一企业)出钱[錢]使某人放弃[棄]其股份 chūqián shǐ mǒurén fàngqì qí gǔfèn. **buy** *n* [C] 买得的货物 mǎidéde huòwù: *a good* ~ 买得合算的东西. **buyer** *n* [C] (大商店中的)选[選]购[購]者 xuǎngòuzhě. **buy-to-'let** *n* 1 [U] (房产的)投资性购[購]买[買] tóuzīxìng gòumǎi. 2 [C] 投资型房产[產] tóuzīxíng fángchǎn.

buzz /bʌz/ *v* 1 [I] 嗡嗡叫 wēngwēngjiào. 2 [I] (*with*) 充满嘈杂[雜]的谈话声[聲] chōngmǎn cáozáde tánhuàshēng. 3 [I] 匆忙行走 cōngmáng xíngzǒu. 4 [T] 用蜂音电[電]铃叫(某人) yòng fēngyīn diànlíng jiào. 5 [短语动词] **buzz 'off** [非正式用语]离[離]开[開] líkāi. **buzz** *n* 1 [C] 嘁嘁喳喳声 qīqīchāchā shēng. 2 [sing] [非正式用语,尤用于美语]愉悦 yúyuè; 激动[動] jīdòng. 3 [习语] **give sb a 'buzz** [非正式用语]给(某人)打电话 gěi…dǎ diànhuà. **buzzer** *n* [C] 蜂音器 fēngyīnqì; 蜂音电[電]铃 fēngyīn diànlíng.

buzzard /'bʌzəd/ *n* [C] 鹰 yīng.

by[1] /baɪ/ *prep* 1 在…旁边[邊] zài…pángbiān; 靠近 kàojìn: *Sit by me*. 靠着我坐吧. 2 经[經] jīng; 由 yóu; 沿 yán: *Come in by the back door*. 由后门进来. 3 经过[過] jīngguò: *She walked by me*. 她从我身旁走过. 4 不迟[遲]于 bù chíyú: *finish the work by tomorrow* 不迟于明天完成这项工作. 5 在 zài: *The enemy attacked by night*. 敌人在夜间进攻. 6 由 yóu; 被 bèi; 通过某种[種]手段 tōngguò mǒuzhǒng shǒuduàn. *a play by Shaw* 肖伯纳的一个剧本. *pay by cheque* 用支票支付. *travel by train* 坐火车旅行. 7 由于 yóuyú; 因为[爲] yīnwéi: *meet by chance* 偶然相遇. 8 (表示接触身体的某一部分): *take sb by the hand* 拉住某人的手. 9 用…作标[標]准[準]或单[單]位 yòng…zuò biāozhǔn huò dānwèi: *get paid by the hour* 按小时付给工资. 10 (表示连续的单位)…接着… …jiēzhe…, …又… …yòu…: *The children came in two by two*. 孩子们两个两个地进入. 11 (表示长方形的面积): *a room 18 feet by 20 feet*. 18 英尺乘以 20 英尺的房间. 12 到…程度 dào…chéngdù. 13 按照 ànzhào; 根据[據] gēnjù: *By law, his parents should be informed*. 根据法律,应该通知他的父母.

by[2] /baɪ/ *adv* 1 经[經]过[過] jīngguò: *drive by* 开车经过. 2 在附近 zài fùjìn.

bye /baɪ/ (亦作 **bye-bye** /ˌbaɪ'baɪ/) *interj* [非正式用语]再见 zàijiàn.

by-election /'baɪɪlekʃn/ *n* [C] (议会的)补[補]缺选[選]举[舉] bǔquē xuǎnjǔ.

bygone /'baɪgɒn/ *adj* 过[過]去的 guòqùde; 以往的 yǐwǎngde: *in* ~ *days* 在往日. **bygones** *n* [习语] **let ˌbygones be 'bygones** 既往不咎 jì wǎng bù jiū; 让[讓]过去的事过去了吧 ràng guòqùde shì guòqù le ba.

by-law (亦作 **bye-law**) /'baɪlɔː/ *n* [C] 地方法规 dìfāng fǎguī.

bypass /'baɪpɑːs; *US* -pæs/ *n* [C] (绕过市镇的)迂回的旁道 yūhuíde pángdào; 旁路 pánglù. **bypass** *v* [T] 1 设旁道于 shè pángdào yú. 2 回避 huíbì; 躲开[開] duǒkāi: [喻] ~ *the problem* 回避问题.

by-product /'baɪprɒdʌkt/ *n* [C] 副产[產]品 fùchǎnpǐn.

bystander /'baɪstændə(r)/ *n* [C] 旁观[觀]者 pángguānzhě.

byte /baɪt/ *n* [C] (电子计算机)(二进制)字节[節] zìjié; (二进)位组 wèizǔ.

byword /'baɪwɜːd/ *n* [C] 1 (*for*) 绰号[號] chuòhào, 别称[稱] biéchēng. 2 俗语 súyǔ; 谚语 yànyǔ.

C c

C, c /siː/ [*pl* **C's, c's** /siːz/] 英语的第三个[個]字母 Yīngyǔde dìsāngè zìmǔ.

C *abbr* 1 Celsius (温度)摄[攝]氏的 shèshìde. 2 罗[羅]马数[數]字的 100 luómǎ shùzì de 100.

c *abbr* 1 cent(s). 2 century. 3 (亦作 **ca**)(尤用于日期前) about.

cab /kæb/ *n* [C] 1 出租汽车 chūzū qìchē; 计程汽车 jìchéng qìchē. 2 (机车等的)司机[機]室 sījīshì.

cabaret /'kæbəreɪ; *US* ˌkæbə'reɪ/ *n* [U, C] (餐馆等中的)歌舞表演 gēwǔ biǎoyǎn.

cabbage /'kæbɪdʒ/ *n* [C, U] 甘蓝[藍] gānlán; 卷[捲]心菜 juǎnxīncài; 洋白菜 yángbáicài.

cabin /'kæbɪn/ *n* [C] 1 船舱[艙] chuáncāng; 飞[飛]机[機]舱 fēijīcāng; 船的房舱 chuánde fángcāng. 2 小木屋 xiǎo mùwū. **'cabin crew** *n* [C, U] 空乘人员(指群体) kōngchéng rényuán. **'cabin cruiser** *n* [C] = CRUISER 2 (CRUISE).

cabinet /'kæbɪnɪt/ *n* [C] 1 柜[櫃]橱 guìchú. 2 **the Cabinet** [亦作 sing, 用 pl v] 内阁 nèigé.

cable /'keɪbl/ *n* 1 [C, U] 缆[纜] lǎn; 索 suǒ. 2 [C] 电[電]缆 diànlǎn. 3 [C] 电报[報] diànbào. **cable** *v* [T] 给…拍电报 gěi…pāi diànbào. **'cable-car** *n* [C] 电缆车 diànlǎnchē. **cable 'television** *n* [U] 有线[綫]电视 yǒuxiàn diànshì.

cache /kæʃ/ *n* [C] 隐[隱]藏物 yǐncángwù: *a drugs* ~ 隐藏的毒品.

cackle /'kækl/ *n* 1 [U] 母鸡[鷄]咯咯的叫声[聲] mǔjī gēgē de jiàoshēng. 2 [C] 咯咯的笑声 gēgē de xiàoshēng. **cackle** *v* [I] 1 (母鸡)

C

咯咯地叫 gēgēde jiào. 2 大声地笑 dàshēngde xiào.

cactus /ˈkæktəs/ *n* [C] [*pl* ～es, cacti /ˈkæktaɪ/] 仙人掌 xiānrénzhǎng.

cadet /kəˈdet/ *n* [C] 警校学〔學〕生 jǐngxiào xuéshēng; 军校学生 jūnxiào xuéshēng.

cadge /kædʒ/ *v* [I, T] [非正式用语] 乞求 qǐqiú; 乞讨 qǐtǎo: ～ *£5 from a friend* 向朋友乞求 5 英镑.

café /ˈkæfeɪ; *US* kæˈfeɪ/ *n* [C] 小餐馆 xiǎo cānguǎn.

cafeteria /ˌkæfəˈtɪərɪə/ *n* [C] 自助食堂 zìzhù shítáng; 自助餐馆 zìzhù cānguǎn.

caffeine /ˈkæfiːn/ *n* [U] 咖啡因 kāfēiyīn.

cage /keɪdʒ/ *n* [C] 笼〔籠〕子 lóngzi. **cage** *v* [T] 把…关〔關〕入笼子 bǎ…guānrù lóngzi.

cagey /ˈkeɪdʒɪ/ *adj* 保守秘密的 bǎoshǒu mìmì de.

cagoule /kəˈɡuːl/ *n* [C] 连帽防雨长〔長〕夹〔夾〕克衫 lián mào fángyǔ cháng jiākèshān.

cairn /keən/ *n* [C] (用作纪念或路标等的) 圆锥形石堆 yuánzhuīxíng shíduī.

cajole /kəˈdʒəʊl/ *v* [T] 哄骗〔騙〕 hǒngpiàn; 勾引 gōuyǐn; 引诱 yǐnyòu.

cake /keɪk/ *n* 1 [C, U] 饼 bǐng; 糕 gāo; 蛋糕 dàngāo. 2 [C] 饼状〔狀〕食物 bǐngzhuàng shíwù: ˈ*fish-～s* 鱼饼. 3 [C] 块〔塊〕kuài, 饼状物 bǐng zhuàng wù: *a* ～ *of soap* 一块肥皂. **cake** *v* [T] 把…沾上泥土等 bǎ… zhānshàng nítǔ děng.

calamity /kəˈlæmətɪ/ *n* [C] [*pl* -ies] 灾〔災〕难〔難〕 zāinàn; 灾祸〔禍〕 zāihuò; 祸患 huòhuàn.

calcium /ˈkælsɪəm/ *n* [U] 钙 gài.

calculate /ˈkælkjʊleɪt/ *v* 1 [I, T] 计算 jìsuàn; 核算 hésuàn: ～ *the cost* 计算成本. 2 [习语] **be calculated to do sth** 打算做某事 dǎsuàn zuò mǒushì: ～*d to attract attention* 目的是吸引注意力. **calculating** *adj* [贬] 阴〔陰〕谋的 yīnmóude; 有策略的 yǒu cèlüè de. **calculation** /ˌkælkjʊˈleɪʃn/ *n* [C, U]. **calculator** *n* [C] 计算机〔機〕 jìsuànjī.

calendar /ˈkælɪndə(r)/ *n* [C] 1 历〔曆〕书〔書〕 lìshū; 日历 rìlì; 周历 zhōulì; 月历 yuèlì. 2 历法 lìfǎ: *the Muslim* ～ 伊斯兰教历.

calf[1] /kɑːf; *US* kæf/ *n* [*pl* **calves** /kɑːvz; *US* kævz/] 1 [C] (a) 小牛 xiǎoniú; 犊子 dúzi. (b) 小海豹 xiǎo hǎibào; 小鲸 xiǎojīng. 2 (亦作 ˈ**calfskin**) 小牛皮 xiǎo niúpí.

calf[2] /kɑːf; *US* kæf/ *n* [C] [*pl* **calves** /kɑːvz; *US* kævz/] 腓 féi.

calibre (美语 -ber) /ˈkælɪbə(r)/ *n* 1 [U] 质〔質〕量 zhìliàng; 才干〔幹〕 cáigàn; 才能 cáinéng: *Her work is of the highest* ～. 她的工作质量最高. 2 [C] 口径〔徑〕 kǒujìng.

calipers = CALLIPERS.

call[1] /kɔːl/ *v* 1 [I, T] 大声〔聲〕说 dàshēng shuō; 叫 jiào; 喊 hǎn. 2 [T] 请来 qǐnglái; 传〔傳〕唤 chuánhuàn: ～ *the police* 请来警察. 3 [I] 访问 fǎngwèn; 拜访 bàifǎng. 4 [I, T] (给…) 打电〔電〕话 dǎ diànhuà. 5 [T] 召集 zhàojí; 宣布 xuānbù: ～ *a meeting* 召集会议. ～ *an election* 举行选举. ～ *a strike* 举行罢〔罷〕工. 6 [T] 把…叫做 bǎ… jiàozuò: *Her husband is* ～*ed Dick*. 她的丈夫名叫迪克. 7 [T] 认〔認〕为〔爲〕 rènwéi: *I* ～ *his behaviour very selfish*. 我认为他的行为很自私. 8 [T] 叫醒 jiàoxǐng: *Please* ～ *me at 7 o'clock*. 请七点钟叫醒我. 9 [习语] **call sb's bluff** 要某人摊〔攤〕牌 yào mǒurén tānpái. **call it a day** [非正式用语] (认为一天的工作量已做够) 决定停止做 juédìng tíngzhǐ zuò. **call sth to mind** ⇨ MIND[1]. **call sb ˈnames** 谩骂 mànmà. **call the ˈtune** [非正式用语] 定调子 dìng diàozi; 发〔發〕号〔號〕施令 fāhào shīlìng. 10 [短语动词] **call by** 顺便去一下 shùnbiàn qù yíxià. **call for sb/sth** (a) 去取(某物) qù qǔ; 去接(某人) qù jiē. (b) 需要 xūyào: *The problem* ～*s for immediate action*. 这个问题需要立即采取行动. **call sb in** 把…请来(提供帮助) bǎ… qǐnglái. **call sb/sth off** 命令(狗、士兵等)停止进〔進〕攻、搜寻〔尋〕 mìnglìng tíngzhǐ jìngōng、sōuxún. **call sth off** 取消(某活动) qǔxiāo: *The trip was* ～*ed off*. 旅行被取消了. **call on sb** 探望 tànwàng; 拜访 bàifǎng. **call on/upon sb** 正式邀请 zhèngshì yāoqǐng; 请求 qǐngqiú; 号召 hàozhào. **call sb out** (a) 紧〔緊〕急召唤 jǐnjí zhàohuàn: ～ *out the fire brigade* 把消防队叫来. (b) 命令罢工 mìnglìng bàgōng. **call sb up** (a) [尤用于美语] 给…打电话 gěi…dǎ diànhuà. (b) 命令…参〔參〕军 mìnglìng…cānjūn. **caller** *n* [C] 拜访的人 bàifǎng de rén; 打电话的人 dǎ diànhuà de rén. ˈ**call-up** *n* [U, C] (服兵役的) 征〔徵〕召令 zhēngzhàolìng.

call[2] /kɔːl/ *n* 1 [C] 喊 hǎn; 叫 jiào. 2 [C] (一次) 电〔電〕话通话 diànhuà tōnghuà. 3 [C] 鸟鸣 niǎomíng. 4 [C] 访问 fǎngwèn; 拜访 bàifǎng. 5 [C] 号〔號〕令 hàolìng; 传〔傳〕唤 chuánhuàn; 邀来 yāolái. 6 [U] 需要 xūyào; 要求 yāoqiú. 7 [习语] (**be**) **on call** (医生等) 随〔隨〕叫随到的 suí jiào suí dào de. ˈ**call-box** *n* [C] = TELEPHONE-BOX (TELEPHONE). ˈ**call centre** *n* [C] 电话服务〔務〕中心 diànhuà fúwù zhōngxīn. ˈ**call-girl** *n* [C] 电话应〔應〕召妓女 diànhuà yìngzhào jìnǚ.

calligraphy /kəˈlɪɡrəfɪ/ *n* [U] 书〔書〕法 shūfǎ.

calling /ˈkɔːlɪŋ/ *n* [C] 职〔職〕业〔業〕 zhíyè; 行业 hángyè.

callipers (亦作 **calipers**) /ˈkælɪpəz/ *n* [pl] 1 卡钳 kǎqián; 测径器 cèjìngqì. 2 支具(装于残

废人腿部) zhījù.

callous /ˈkæləs/ *adj* 残〔殘〕酷无〔無〕情的 cánkù wúqíng de.

callow /ˈkæləʊ/ *adj* [贬]稚嫩无〔無〕经〔經〕验〔驗〕的 zhìnèn wú jīngyàn de.

callus /ˈkæləs/ *n* [C] 胼胝 piánzhī.

calm /kɑːm; *US* kɑːlm/ *adj* 1 镇静的 zhènjìngde;沉着的 chénzhuóde. 2 (a) (海洋)风〔風〕平浪静的 fēngpíng làngjìng de. (b) (天气)无〔無〕风的 wúfēngde. **calm** *n* [U, C] 平静 píngjìng. **calm** *v* [I, T] (*down*) 平静下来〔來〕 píngjìng xiàlái;镇静下来 zhènjìng xiàlái;使平静 shǐ píngjìng;使镇静 shǐ zhènjìng. **calmly** *adv*. **calmness** *n* [U].

calorie /ˈkælərɪ/ *n* [C] 1 (热量单位)卡(路里)kǎ;小卡 xiǎokǎ. 2 卡(食物的热值)(路里)kǎ;大卡 dàkǎ.

calve /kɑːv; *US* kæv/ *v* [I] 生小牛(或小鹿等) shēng xiǎoniú.

calves /kɑːvz/ *pl* of CALF[1,2].

calypso /kəˈlɪpsəʊ/ *n* [C] [*pl* ~s] 加力骚(一种西印度群岛小调) jiālìsāo.

camber /ˈkæmbə(r)/ *n* [C] (道路等的)中凸形 zhōngtūxíng;起拱 qǐgǒng.

camcorder /ˈkæmkɔːdə(r)/ *n* [C] 摄〔攝〕像录〔錄〕像机〔機〕 shèxiàng lùxiàngjī.

came /keɪm/ *pt* of COME.

camel /ˈkæml/ *n* [C] 骆驼 luòtuo.

cameo /ˈkæmɪəʊ/ *n* [C] [*pl* ~s] 1 浮雕宝〔寶〕石 fúdiāo bǎoshí. 2 (文学、戏剧等的)小品 xiǎopǐn.

camera /ˈkæmərə/ *n* [C] 照相机〔機〕 zhàoxiàngjī;摄〔攝〕像机 shèxiàngjī;摄影机 shèyǐngjī. ˈ**camera phone** *n* [C] 可拍照手机 kě pāizhào shǒujī.

camouflage /ˈkæməflɑːʒ/ *n* [C, U] 伪〔僞〕装〔裝〕 wěizhuāng. **camouflage** *v* [T] 伪装 wěizhuāng;掩饰 yǎnshì.

camp /kæmp/ *n* [C] 1 营〔營〕 yíng;野营 yěyíng. 2 阵〔陣〕营 zhènyíng. **camp** *v* [I] 设营 shèyíng;营地度假 yíngdì dùjià: *We go ~ing every summer*. 我们每年夏天去野营. **camper** *n* [C] 野营者 yěyíngzhě;露营者 lùyíngzhě.

campaign /kæmˈpeɪn/ *n* [C] 1 运〔運〕动〔動〕 yùndòng: *an advertising* ~ 一系列广告活动. 2 战〔戰〕役 zhànyì. **campaign** *v* [I] 参〔參〕加运动 cānjiā yùndòng. **campaigner** *n* [C].

campus /ˈkæmpəs/ *n* [C] 校园〔園〕 xiàoyuán.

can[1] /kən; 强式 kæn/ *modal v* [否定式 cannot /ˈkænɒt/, 节略式 can't /kɑːnt; *US* kænt/, *pt* could /kəd; 强式 kʊd/, 否定式 could not, 节略式 couldn't /ˈkʊdnt/] 1 会〔會〕 huì: *C~ you ski?* 你会滑雪吗? 2 (与感官动词连用): *C~ you hear that cuckoo?* 你听见那杜鹃的咕咕叫声吗? 3 可以 kěyǐ. 4 (表示请求): *C~ you help me?* 请你帮个忙好吗? 5 (表示现在的可能性).

can[2] /kæn/ *n* [C] (a) (装食品或液体用的)金属〔屬〕罐 jīnshǔguàn;罐头〔頭〕 guàntou. (b) 罐头所装〔裝〕物品 guàntou suǒ zhuāng wùpǐn. **can** *v* [-nn-] [T] 把(食品等)装罐 bǎ zhuāng guàn. **cannery** *n* [C] [*pl* -ies] 罐头食品厂〔廠〕 guàntou shípǐn chǎng.

Canada /ˈkænədə/ *n* [U] 加拿大 Jiānádà.

Canadian /kəˈneɪdɪən/ *adj* 加拿大的 Jiānádàde. **Canadian** *n* [C] 加拿大人 Jiānádàrén.

canal /kəˈnæl/ *n* [C] 运〔運〕河 yùnhé;沟〔溝〕渠 gōuqú;水道 shuǐdào.

canary /kəˈneərɪ/ *n* [C] [*pl* -ies] 金丝雀 jīnsīquè.

cancel /ˈkænsl/ *v* [-ll-; *US* -l-] [T] 1 取消 qǔxiāo. 2 删去 shānqù;注销 zhùxiāo;作废〔廢〕 zuòfèi. 3 [短语动词] **cancel (sth) out** 势〔勢〕均力敌〔敵〕 shì jūn lì dí;抵消 dǐxiāo;使平衡 shǐ pínghéng. **cancellation** /ˌkænsəˈleɪʃn/ *n* [C, U].

cancer /ˈkænsə(r)/ *n* 1 [C, U] 癌症 áizhèng. 2 **Cancer** ⇨TROPIC. **cancerous** *adj* 癌的 áide;像癌的 xiàng'áide.

candid /ˈkændɪd/ *adj* 正直的 zhèngzhíde;坦率的 tǎnshuàide: *a ~ discussion* 坦率的讨论. **candidly** *adv*.

candidate /ˈkændɪdət; *US* -deɪt/ *n* [C] 1 候选〔選〕人 hòuxuǎnrén. 2 应〔應〕试人 yìngshìrén.

candied /ˈkændɪd/ *adj* (糕饼等面上)有一层〔層〕糖粒的 yǒu yìcéng tánglì de.

candle /ˈkændl/ *n* [C] 蜡〔蠟〕烛〔燭〕 làzhú. ˈ**candlestick** *n* [C] 烛台 zhútái.

candour (美语 -dor) /ˈkændə(r)/ *n* [U] 坦白 tǎnbái;爽直 shuǎngzhí.

candy /ˈkændɪ/ *n* [*pl* -ies (尤用于美语)] 1 [U] 糖果 tángguǒ;巧克力 qiǎokèlì. 2 [C] (一块)糖果 tángguǒ;(一块)巧克力 qiǎokèlì.

cane /keɪn/ *n* [C] 1 (a) [C] 竹等的茎〔莖〕 zhú děng de jīng. (b) [U] 竹料 zhúliào;藤料 téngliào. 2 [C] 竹竿(作支撑或手杖) zhúgān. 3 **the cane** [sing] (孩子所受的)鞭笞处〔處〕罚 biānchī chǔfá. **cane** *v* [T] 用藤鞭抽打 yòng téngbiān chōudǎ.

canine /ˈkeɪnaɪn/ *adj* 犬的 quǎnde;似犬的 sì quǎn de.

canister /ˈkænɪstə(r)/ *n* [C] 1 金属〔屬〕罐 jīnshǔguàn. 2 (榴)霰弹〔彈〕筒 sǎndàntǒng.

cannabis /ˈkænəbɪs/ *n* [U] 麻醉剂〔劑〕 mázuìjì;毒品 dúpǐn.

C

cannery ⇨CAN².

cannibal /ˈkænɪbl/ *n* [C] (a) 吃人肉的人 chī rénròu de rén. (b) 吃同类〔類〕肉的动〔動〕物 chī tónglèiròu de dòngwù. **cannibalism** /-bəlɪzəm/ *n* [U]. **cannibalize** /-bəlaɪz/ *v* [T] 拆取(机器等的)可用部件 chāiqǔ kěyòng bùjiàn.

cannon /ˈkænən/ *n* [C] [*pl* cannon] 1 大炮 dàpào; 加农〔農〕炮 jiānóngpào. 2 [C] 飞〔飛〕机〔機〕上的机〔機〕关〔關〕炮 fēijī shàng de jīguānpào.

cannot /ˈkænət/ ⇨CAN¹.

canoe /kəˈnuː/ *n* [C] 独〔獨〕木舟 dúmùzhōu; 轻〔輕〕舟 qīngzhōu. **canoe** *v* [I] 用独木舟载〔載〕运〔運〕yòng dúmùzhōu zàiyùn. **canoeist** *n* [C] 划独木舟者 huá dúmùzhōu zhě.

canon /ˈkænən/ *n* [C] 1 大教堂中有特殊任务的牧师〔師〕dà jiàotáng zhōng yǒu tèshū rènwù de mùshi. 2 [正式用语] 准〔準〕则 zhǔnzé; 标〔標〕准 biāozhǔn; 原则 yuánzé. **canonical** /kəˈnɒnɪkl/ *adj* 依照教规的 yīzhào jiàoguī de. **canonize** /ˈkænənaɪz/ *v* [T] 使(某人)成为〔爲〕圣〔聖〕徒 shǐ chéngwéi shèngtú. ˌ**canon** ˈ**law** *n* [U] 教(会法)规 jiàoguī.

canopy /ˈkænəpɪ/ *n* [C] [*pl* -ies] 1 床、王座等的罩篷(通常为布料) chuáng、wángzuò děng de zhào péng; 华〔華〕盖〔蓋〕huágài. 2 飞〔飛〕机〔機〕座舱〔艙〕罩 fēijī zuòcāng zhào.

can't cannot ⇨CAN¹.

cantankerous /kænˈtæŋkərəs/ *adj* 脾气〔氣〕坏〔壞〕的 píqì huài de; 爱〔愛〕争吵的 ài zhēngchǎo de.

canteen /kænˈtiːn/ *n* [C] 1 食堂 shítáng; 食品小卖〔賣〕部 shípǐn xiǎomàibù. 2 [英国英语] 餐具箱 cānjùxiāng.

canter /ˈkæntə(r)/ *n* [C, 常作 sing] (马的) 慢跑 mànpǎo. **canter** *v* [I, T] (马)慢跑 mànpǎo.

cantilever /ˈkæntɪliːvə(r)/ *n* [C] (建筑)悬〔懸〕臂 xuánbì; 悬臂梁 xuánbìliáng.

Cantonese /ˌkæntəˈniːz/ *adj* 广〔廣〕东〔東〕的 Guǎngdōngde; 广〔廣〕东〔東〕人的 Guǎngdōngrén de; 广〔廣〕东〔東〕话的 Guǎngdōnghuà de: ～ *cuisine* 粤菜. **Cantonese** *n* 1 [C] (*pl* ～) 广〔廣〕东〔東〕人 Guǎngdōngrén 2 [U] 广〔廣〕东〔東〕话 Guǎngdōnghuà; 粤语 Yuèyǔ.

canvas /ˈkænvəs/ *n* (a) [U] 粗帆布 cū fānbù. (b) [C] 油画〔畫〕布 yóuhuà bù; 油画 yóuhuà.

canvass /ˈkænvəs/ *v* [I, T] 四处〔處〕(对人们)进〔進〕行政治游说 sìchù jìnxíng zhèngzhì yóushuì. **canvasser** *n* [C].

canyon /ˈkænjən/ *n* [C] 峡〔峽〕谷 xiágǔ.

cap /kæp/ *n* [C] 1 便帽 biànmào; 制服帽 zhìfúmào. 2 盖〔蓋〕gài; 套 tào. **cap** *v* [-pp-] [T] 1 给…戴帽 gěi … dài mào; 给…加盖 gěi…jiāgài. 2 胜〔勝〕过〔過〕shèngguò; 凌驾〔駕〕língjià. 3 挑选〔選〕(运动员)进〔進〕全国〔國〕性运〔運〕动〔動〕队〔隊〕tiāoxuǎn jìn quánguóxìng yùndòngduì.

capability /ˌkeɪpəˈbɪlətɪ/ *n* [*pl* -ies] 1 [U] 能力 nénglì; 才能 cáinéng. 2 [常作 pl] 潜〔潛〕在能力 qiánzài nénglì.

capable /ˈkeɪpəbl/ *adj* 1 (*of*) 有做某事所必需的能力的 yǒu zuò mǒushì suǒ bìxū de nénglì de: *You are* ～ *of producing better work than this*. 你有能力把工作做得比这更好. 2 有才能的 yǒu cáinéng de, 聪〔聰〕明的 cōngmingde. **capably** *adv*.

capacity /kəˈpæsətɪ/ *n* [*pl* -ies] 1 [U] 容量 róngliàng; 容积〔積〕róngjī: *a hall with a seating* ～ *of 750* 有750个坐位的大厅. 2 [C, U] 能力 nénglì. 3 [C] 地位 dìwèi; 身份 shēnfèn; 资格 zīgé: *in my* ～ *as manager* 我作为经理的身份.

cape¹ /keɪp/ *n* [C] 披肩 pījiān; 斗篷 dǒupeng.

cape² /keɪp/ *n* [C] 海角 hǎijiǎo; 岬 jiǎ.

capillary /kəˈpɪlərɪ; *US* ˈkæpɪlerɪ/ *n* [C] [*pl* -ies] 毛细管 máoxìguǎn.

capital /ˈkæpɪtl/ *n* 1 [C] 首都 shǒudū. 2 [U] 资本 zīběn. 3 [C] (亦作 **capital letter**) 大写〔寫〕字母 dàxiě zìmǔ. 4 [习语] **make capital (out) of sth** 利用 lìyòng. **capital** *adj* 可处〔處〕死刑的 kě chǔ sǐxíng de.

capitalism /ˈkæpɪtəlɪzəm/ *n* [U] 资本主义〔義〕zīběnzhǔyì. **capitalist** /-lɪst/ *n* [C] 1 资本主义者 zīběnzhǔyìzhě. 2 资本家 zīběnjiā. **capitalist** *adj*.

capitalize /ˈkæpɪtəlaɪz/ *v* 1 [T] 用大写〔寫〕字母书〔書〕写 yòng dàxiě zìmǔ shūxiě. 2 [T] 使转〔轉〕作资本 shǐ zhuǎnzuò zīběn. 3 [短语动词] **capitalize on sth** 利用 lìyòng.

capitulate /kəˈpɪtʃʊleɪt/ *v* [I] (*to*) 投降 tóuxiáng. **capitulation** /kəˌpɪtʃʊˈleɪʃn/ *n* [U].

Capricorn ⇨TROPIC.

capsize /kæpˈsaɪz; *US* ˈkæpsaɪz/ *v* [I, T] (使船)倾覆 qīngfù.

capstan /ˈkæpstən/ *n* [C] 绞盘〔盤〕jiǎopán; 起锚机〔機〕qǐmáojī.

capsule /ˈkæpsjuːl; *US* ˈkæpsl/ *n* [C] 1 装〔裝〕一剂〔劑〕药的小囊 zhuāng yījì yào de xiǎonáng. 2 宇宙飞〔飛〕船密闭小舱〔艙〕yǔzhòu fēichuán mìbì xiǎocāng.

captain /ˈkæptɪn/ *n* [C] 1 (运动队) 队〔隊〕长〔長〕duìzhǎng. 2 (飞机的)机长 jīzhǎng; 舰〔艦〕长 jiànzhǎng. 3 连长 liánzhǎng. **captain** *v* [T] 做…的首领 zuò … de shǒulǐng.

C

caption /ˈkæpʃn/ *n* [C] (照片等的)说明 shuōmíng.

captivate /ˈkæptɪveɪt/ *v* [T] 迷住 mízhù; 强烈感染 qiángliè gǎnrǎn.

captive /ˈkæptɪv/ *n* [C], *adj* 被捉住的人或动〔動〕物 bèi zhuōzhù de rén huò dòngwù; 被俘虏〔虜〕的 bèi fúlǔ de; 被拴住的 bèi shuānzhù de. **captivity** /kæpˈtɪvətɪ/ *n* [U]俘虏 fúlǔ; 监禁 jiānjìn; 束缚 shùfù.

captor /ˈkæptə(r)/ *n* [C] 俘获〔獲〕(他人)者 fúhuòzhě; 捕获(猎物)者 bǔhuòzhě.

capture /ˈkæptʃə(r)/ *v* [T] 1 俘虏〔虜〕fúlǔ; 捕获〔獲〕bǔhuò. 2 夺〔奪〕得 duódé. 3 成功地拍摄〔攝〕chénggōngde pāishè. **capture** *n* 1 [U] 捕获 bǔhuò; 夺得 duódé. 2 [C] 被捕获者 bèi bǔhuò zhě; 战〔戰〕利品 zhànlìpǐn; 缴获品 jiǎohuòpǐn.

car /kɑː(r)/ *n* [C] 1 载客汽车〔車〕zàikè qìchē. 2 火车车厢 huǒchē chēxiāng: *a ˈdining-*～ 餐车. ˈ**car-boot sale** *n* [C] 户外旧〔舊〕货拍卖〔賣〕hùwài jiùhuò pāimài. ˈ**carjack** *v* [T] 劫车 jiéchē. ˈ**carjacker** *n* [C] 劫车人 jiéchērén; 车匪 chēfěi. ˈ**carjacking** *n* [C, U] 汽车劫持 qìchē jiéchí. ˈ**car park** *n* [C] 停车场〔場〕tíngchēchǎng.

carafe /kəˈræf/ *n* [C] (餐桌上的)饮料玻璃杯 yǐnliào bōlibēi.

caramel /ˈkærəmel/ *n* 1 [U] 酱〔醬〕色 jiàngsè. 2 [C] 一种〔種〕小糖果 yìzhǒng xiǎotángguǒ.

carat /ˈkærət/ *n* [C] 1 克拉(宝石重量单位) kèlā. 2 开〔開〕(金的纯度单位) kāi.

caravan /ˈkærəvæn/ *n* [C] 1 供住家用的汽车〔車〕拖车 gōng zhùjiā yòng de qìchē tuōchē. 2 大篷车 dàpéngchē. 3 (穿过沙漠的)商队〔隊〕shāngduì, 旅行队 lǚxíngduì.

carbohydrate /ˌkɑːbəʊˈhaɪdreɪt/ *n* [C, U] 碳水化合物 tànshuǐ huàhéwù.

carbon /ˈkɑːbən/ *n* 1 [U] (化学元素)碳 tàn. 2 [C] = CARBON COPY. 3 [C, U] = CARBON PAPER. ˌ**carbon** ˈ**copy** *n* [C] 复〔複〕写〔寫〕的副本 fùxiěde fùběn. ˌ**carbon** ˈ**footprint** *n* [C] 二氧化碳排放量 èryǎnghuàtàn páifàngliàng; 碳足迹 tànzújì. ˈ**carbon paper** *n* [C, U] 复写纸 fùxiězhǐ. ˈ**carbon** ˌ**tax** *n* [C] 碳排放税 tàn páifàng shuì, 烟〔烟〕尘〔塵〕排放税 yānchén páifàng shuì (对煤、石油等燃料征收的税).

carbuncle /ˈkɑːbʌŋkl/ *n* [C] 痈〔癰〕yōng.

carburettor /ˌkɑːbjʊˈretə(r)/ (美语 -t- / *US* ˈkɑːrbəreɪtər /) *n* [C] (汽车)汽化器 qìhuàqì.

carcass /ˈkɑːkəs/ *n* [C] 动〔動〕物尸〔屍〕体〔體〕dòngwù shītǐ.

card /kɑːd/ *n* [C, U] 1 卡片 kǎpiàn; 卡 kǎ. *a ˈmembership* ～ 会员卡. *a ˈpost*～ 明信片. 2 [C] = PLAYING-CARD (PLAY[2]). 3 [习语] lay / put one's ˈcards on the table 摊〔攤〕牌 tānpái; 公布自己的打算 gōngbù zìjǐde dǎsuàn. on the cards [非正式用语]多半 duōbàn; 可能的 kěnéng de.

cardboard /ˈkɑːdbɔːd/ *n* [U] 硬纸板 yìngzhǐbǎn.

cardiac /ˈkɑːdɪæk/ *adj* 心脏〔臟〕的 xīnzàngde.

cardigan /ˈkɑːdɪgən/ *n* [C] 羊毛衫 yángmáoshān; 羊毛背心 yángmáo bèixīn.

cardinal[1] /ˈkɑːdɪnl/ *adj* [正式用语]主要的 zhǔyàode; 基本的 jīběnde. **cardinal** (亦作 ˌ**cardinal** ˈ**number**) *n* [C] 基数〔數〕jīshù.

cardinal[2] /ˈkɑːdɪnl/ *n* [C] 红衣主教 hóngyīzhǔjiào; 枢〔樞〕机〔機〕主教 shūjīzhǔjiào.

care[1] /keə(r)/ *n* 1 [U] 小心 xiǎoxīn; 谨慎 jǐnshèn; 注意 zhùyì: *arrange the flowers with* ～ 仔细地插花. *Take* ～ *when crossing the road*. 过马路时要小心. 2 [U] 保护〔護〕bǎohù; 照管 zhàoguǎn: *The child was left in his sister's* ～. 孩子留给他的姐姐照管. 3 [C, U] 心事 xīnshì; 牵〔牽〕累 qiānlěi: *the* ～*s of a large family* 大家庭的牵累. 4 [习语] take care of oneself / sb / sth (a) 照看 zhàokàn; 照料 zhàoliào. (b) 负责 fùzé; 处〔處〕理 chǔlǐ. take sb into care 把(儿童等)交给地方当〔當〕局的福利院等照管 bǎ jiāogěi dìfāng dāngjú de fúlìyuàn děng zhàoguǎn. ˈ**carefree** *adj* 无〔無〕忧〔憂〕无虑〔慮〕的 wúyōu wúlǜ de. **careful** *adj* 1 (人)细心的 xìxīnde; 仔细的 zǐxìde. 2 细致的 xìzhìde. **carefulness** *n* [U]. **careless** *adj* 1 (人)粗心的 cūxīnde; 粗枝大叶的 cū zhī dà yè de. 2 由于粗心而引起的 yóuyú cūxīn ér yǐnqǐ de. 3 不介意的 bú jiè yì de; 不在乎的 bú zàihu de. **carelessly** *adj*. **carelessness** *n* [U].

care[2] /keə(r)/ *v* [I] 1 (*about*) 关〔關〕心 guānxīn; 担〔擔〕心 dānxīn: *I* ～ *about this country's future*. 我关心国家的未来. 2 *for; to* 喜爱〔愛〕xǐ'ài: *Would you* ～ *to go for a walk?* 出去散散步,好吗? 3 [短语动词] care for sb (a) 照管 zhàoguǎn. (b) 喜欢〔歡〕xǐhuan, 爱〔愛〕(某人) ài.

career /kəˈrɪə(r)/ *n* [C] 1 职〔職〕业〔業〕zhíyè. 2 生涯 shēngyá. **career** *v* [I] 飞〔飛〕跑 fēipǎo: ～ *down the hill* 飞奔下山.

caress /kəˈres/ *n* [C] 爱〔愛〕抚〔撫〕àifǔ. **caress** *v* [T] 爱抚 àifǔ; 抚摸 fǔmō.

caretaker /ˈkeəteɪkə(r)/ *n* [C] 看门人 kānménrén.

cargo /ˈkɑːgəʊ/ *n* [C, U] [*pl* ～es; 美语 ～s] (船或飞机上的)货物 huòwù.

caricature /ˌkærɪkəˈtʃʊə(r)/ *n* [C] 漫画〔畫〕mànhuà; 讽〔諷〕刺画 fěngcìhuà. **caricature** *v* [T] 用漫画表现 yòng mànhuà biǎoxiàn; 使

丑〔醜〕化 shǐ chǒuhuà.

carnage /ˈkɑːnɪdʒ/ *n* [U] 大屠杀〔殺〕dàtúshā；残〔殘〕杀 cánshā.

carnal /ˈkɑːnl/ *adj* [正式用语]肉体〔體〕的 ròutǐde；性欲的 xìngyùde；色情的 sèqíngde.

C

carnation /kɑːˈneɪʃn/ *n* [C] 麝香石竹 shèxiāng shízhú.

carnival /ˈkɑːnɪvl/ *n* [C] 狂欢〔歡〕节〔節〕kuánghuānjié.

carnivore /ˈkɑːnɪvɔː(r)/ *n* [C] 食肉动〔動〕物 shíròu dòngwù. **carnivorous** /kɑːˈnɪvərəs/ *adj*

carol /ˈkærəl/ *n* [C] 颂歌 sònggē；欢〔歡〕乐〔樂〕之歌 huānlè zhī gē；圣〔聖〕诞颂歌 shèngdàn sònggē.

carp[1] /kɑːp/ *n* [C] [*pl* **carp**] 鲤科的鱼 lǐkēde yú；鲤鱼 lǐyú.

carp[2] /kɑːp/ *v* [I] (*at* / *about*) 找岔子 zhǎo chàzi；挑剔 tiāoti.

carpenter /ˈkɑːpɪntə(r)/ *n* [C] 木工 mùgōng；木匠 mùjiàng. **carpentry** (/-trɪ/) *n* [U] 木工业〔業〕mùgōngyè.

carpet /ˈkɑːpɪt/ *n* [C] 地毯 dìtǎn. **carpet** *v* [T] 铺地毯(或地毯状物)于 pū dìtǎn yú.

carriage /ˈkærɪdʒ/ *n* **1** [C] (火车)客车厢 kèchēxiāng. **2** 马车 mǎchē. **3** [U] 运〔運〕输〔輸〕(费) yùnshū. **4** [C] (机器的)移动〔動〕承载部分 yídòng chéngzài bùfen：*a typewriter* ～ 打字机的滑动架. ˈ**carriageway** *n* [C] 车行道 chēxíngdào.

carrier /ˈkærɪə(r)/ *n* [C] **1** 运〔運〕货人 yùnhuòrén；运货公司 yùnhuò gōngsī. **2** 带〔帶〕菌者 dàijūnzhě. ˈ**carrier bag** *n* [C] (纸或塑料的)商品袋 shāngpǐndài.

carrot /ˈkærət/ *n* [C] 胡萝〔蘿〕卜〔蔔〕húluóbo.

carry /ˈkærɪ/ *v* [*pt*, *pp* -**ied**] **1** (a) 传〔傳〕送 chuánsòng；运〔運〕送 yùnsòng；携带〔帶〕xiédài：～ *the boxes upstairs* 把箱子搬到楼上. (b) 支撑 zhīchēng；支持 zhīchí：*The pillars* ～ *the whole roof*. 柱子支撑整个屋顶. **2** [T] 带有 dàiyǒu：*I never* ～ *much money*. 我身上从来不带很多的钱. **3** [T] (管道、电线等)传输 chuánshū. **4** 含有 hányǒu；使承担〔擔〕shǐ chéngdān：*Power carries great responsibility*. 权力本身是要承担很大责任的. **5** (报纸)刊登 kāndēng. **6** [T] [常用被动语态]投票通过〔過〕tóupiào tōngguò：*The proposal was carried*. 提议被通过. **7** [I] (声音)达〔達〕到 dá dào，传到(某种距离) chuándào：*His voice doesn't* ～ *very far*. 他的声音传不到很远. **8** [习语] **be/get carried away** 失去自制力 shīqù zìzhìlì. **9** [短语动词] **carry sth off** 赢得 yíngdé. **carry on** (**with/doing sth**) 继〔繼〕续〔續〕jìxù：～ *on reading* 继续阅读. **carry on** (**with sb**) [非正式用语]调情 tiáoqíng. **carry sth on** 参〔參〕加 cānjiā；进〔進〕行 jìnxíng. **carry sth out** 做 zuò；实〔實〕现 shíxiàn；完成 wánchéng：～ *out a plan* 完成计划. **carry sth through** 胜〔勝〕利完成 shènglì wánchéng. **carry sb through sth** 使渡过〔過〕难〔難〕关〔關〕shǐ dùguò nánguān.

cart /kɑːt/ *n* [C] **1** 马车 mǎchē. **2** [习语] **put the ˌcart before the ˈhorse** 本末倒置 běnmò dàozhì. **cart** *v* [T] **1** 用车运〔運〕送 yòng chē yùnsòng. **2** [非正式用语]携带〔帶〕xiédài：～ *parcels around* 提着小包到处走. ˈ**cart-horse** *n* [C] 担〔擔〕负沉重工作的壮〔壯〕马 dānfù chénzhòng gōngzuò de zhuàngmǎ. ˈ**cartwheel** *n* [C] (体操)侧手翻 cèshǒufān.

carte blanche /ˌkɑːt ˈblɒnʃ/ *n* [C] 全权〔權〕quánquán；自由处〔處〕理权 zìyóu chǔlǐquán.

cartilage /ˈkɑːtɪlɪdʒ/ *n* [U] 软骨 ruǎngǔ.

carton /ˈkɑːtn/ *n* [C] 纸板箱 zhǐbǎnxiāng；塑料箱 sùliàoxiāng.

cartoon /kɑːˈtuːn/ *n* [C] **1** 漫画〔畫〕mànhuà. **2** 卡通 kǎtōng；动〔動〕画片 dònghuàpiàn. **cartoonist** *n* [C] 漫画家 mànhuàjiā；动画片画家 dòng huàpiàn huàjiā.

cartridge /ˈkɑːtrɪdʒ/ *n* [C] **1** 子弹〔彈〕zǐdàn；弹筒 dàntǒng. **2** 唱机〔機〕的唱头〔頭〕chàngjīde chàngtóu. **3** 小的封闭容器 xiǎode fēngbì róngqì：*an ink* ～ 墨水瓶.

carve /kɑːv/ *v* [I, T] **1** 雕刻 diāokè；刻 kè；做雕刻工作 zuò diāokè gōngzuò：～ *one's initials on a tree* 把名字的首字母刻在树上. **2** 切(熟肉等) qiē. **3** [短语动词] **carve sth out** 努力创〔創〕建(事业等) nǔlì chuàngjiàn. **carver** *n* [C] 雕刻家 diāokèjiā；切肉人 qiēròurén. **carving** *n* [C] 雕刻品 diāokèpǐn. ˈ**carving knife** *n* [C] 切(熟)肉刀 qiēròudāo.

cascade /kæˈskeɪd/ *n* [C] 小瀑布 xiǎo pùbù；瀑布 pùbù. **cascade** *v* [I] 瀑布似地落下 pùbù sì de luòxià.

case[1] /keɪs/ *n* **1** [C] 情况 qíngkuàng；状〔狀〕况 zhuàngkuàng：*a clear* ～ *of blackmail* 明显的敲诈事例. *In most* ～*s*, *no extra charge is made*. 在大多数情况下不另付费. **2** **the case** [sing] 事实〔實〕shìshí；实情 shíqíng：*If that is the* ～, *you will have to work harder*. 果真如此，你就得更加努力工作. **3** [C] 病例 bìnglì. **4** [C] 案件 ànjiàn. **5** [C] (a) 诉讼 sùsòng. (b) [常作 sing] (辩论等中的)系列事实〔實〕xìliè shìshí. **6** [U, C] (语法)格 gé. **7** [习语] **a case in ˈpoint** 有关〔關〕的例证〔證〕yǒuguānde lìzhèng. **in ˈany case** 无〔無〕论〔論〕如何 wúlùn rúhé. **in case of sth** 如果 rúguǒ：*In* ～ *of emergency, phone the police*. 如有紧急情况，就给警方打电话. **in ˈthat**

case 假如那样〔樣〕jiǎrú nàyàng. (just) in case 以防万〔萬〕一 yǐ fáng wànyī: *Take an umbrella in ~ it rains*. 带一把伞,以防万一下雨. ˌcase ˈhistory *n* [C] 个〔個〕人档〔檔〕案 gèrén dàng'àn; 病历〔歷〕bìnglì.

case[2] /keɪs/ *n* [C] 1 箱子 xiāngzi; 袋子 dàizi; 套子 tàozi. 2 衣箱 yīxiāng. case *v* [T] 把…装〔裝〕箱 bǎ… zhuāngxiāng; 把…装盒 bǎ… zhuānghé.

cash /kæʃ/ *n* [U] 1 现金 xiànjīn; 现款 xiànkuǎn. 2 [非正式用语]钱〔錢〕qián; 款子 kuǎnzi. cash *v* 1 [T] 兑现 duìxiàn; 兑付 duìfù. 2[短语动词] cash in on sth 以…获〔獲〕利 yǐ… huòlì; 营〔營〕利 yínglì. ˈcash crop *n* [C] 商品作物 shāngpǐn zuòwù. ˈcash dispenser *n* [C] 自动〔動〕付款机〔機〕zìdòng fùkuǎnjī. ˈcash machine *n* [C] 取款机 qǔkuǎnjī. ˈcash register *n* [C] 现金收入记录〔錄〕机 xiànjīn shōurù jìlùjī.

cashew /ˈkæʃuː/ *n* [C] 腰果树 yāoguǒshù; 腰果 yāoguǒ.

cashier /kæˈʃɪə(r)/ *n* [C] 出纳员 chūnàyuán.

cashmere /ˈkæʃmɪə(r)/ *n* [U] 开〔開〕士米(一种细毛料) kāishìmǐ; 山羊绒 shānyángróng.

casing /ˈkeɪsɪŋ/ *n* [C] 包装〔裝〕bāozhuāng; 外壳〔殼〕wàiké; 套 tào.

casino /kəˈsiːnəʊ/ *n* [C] [*pl* ~s] 娱乐〔樂〕场〔場〕yúlèchǎng; 赌场 dǔchǎng.

cask /kɑːsk/ *n* [C] 木桶 mùtǒng.

casket /ˈkɑːskɪt; *US* ˈkæs-/ *n* [C] 1 精美的小盒子 jīngměide xiǎohézi; 首饰盒 shǒushìhé. 2 [美语]棺材 guāncái.

casserole /ˈkæsərəʊl/ *n* (a) [C] (烧菜用的)有盖〔蓋〕焙盘〔盤〕yǒugài bèipán; 蒸锅〔鍋〕zhēngguō. (b) [C, U] 用焙盘烧〔燒〕制〔製〕的食品 yòng bèipán shāozhì de shípǐn.

cassette /kəˈset/ *n* [C] 磁带〔帶〕盒 cídàihé; 照相软片盒 zhàoxiàng ruǎnpiàn hé.

cassock /ˈkæsək/ *n* [C] 教士穿的长〔長〕袍 jiàoshì chuān de chángpáo.

cast[1] /kɑːst; *US* kæst/ *v* [*pt*, *pp* cast] [T] 1 投 tóu; 掷〔擲〕zhì, 撒 sǎ: ~ *a net* 撒网. *Snakes ~ their skins*. 蛇蜕皮. [喻] *The tree ~ a long shadow*. 树木投下长长的树影. ~ *a glance at sb* 瞥了某人一眼. ~ *doubt on his claims* 对他的主张表示怀疑. 2 浇〔澆〕铸〔鑄〕jiāozhù: ~ *a statue* 浇铸铜像. 3 给(演员)选〔選〕派角色 gěi xuǎnpài juésè. 4 [习语] cast aspersions on sb/sth [正式用语] 诋毁 dǐhuǐ; 毁谤 huǐbàng. cast on eye/one's eyes over sth 迅速查看 xùnsù chákàn. cast light on sth ⇨LIGHT[1]. cast lots ⇨LOT[3]. 5 [短语动词] cast sb/sth aside 抛弃〔棄〕pāoqì. cast (sth) off 解缆〔纜〕放(船等) jiě lǎn fàng. cast sth off 抛弃 pāoqì. casting *n* [C] 铸〔鑄〕件 zhùjiàn; 铸造物 zhùzàowù. ˌcasting ˈvote *n* [C] 决定性的一票 juédìngxìng de yípiào. cast ˈiron *n* [U] 铸铁〔鐵〕zhùtiě; 生铁 shēngtiě. cast-iron *adj* 1 生铁造的 shēngtiě zào de. 2 [喻] 坚〔堅〕强的 jiānqiángde: *a ~-iron excuse* 无懈可击的理由. cast-off *n* [C, 常作 pl], *adj* 原主人不再穿的衣服 yuán zhǔrén búzài chuān de yīfu; (衣服)原主人不再穿的 yuán zhǔrén búzài chuān de.

cast[2] /kɑːst; *US* kæst/ *n* [C] 1 (戏剧等的)全体〔體〕演员 quántǐ yǎnyuán. 2 投 tóu; 掷〔擲〕zhì; 抛 pāo; 撒 sǎ. 3 (a) 铸〔鑄〕件 zhùjiàn; 模压〔壓〕品 múyāpǐn. (b) 铸型 zhùxíng; 模子 múzi.

castanets /ˌkæstəˈnets/ *n* [pl] 响〔響〕板(硬木或象牙的两片板,系于手指上,互击作响,配合音乐歌舞) xiǎngbǎn.

castaway /ˈkɑːstəweɪ/ *n* [C] 乘船遇难〔難〕的人 chéngchuán yùnàn de rén.

caste /kɑːst/ *n* [C] 种〔種〕姓(印度社会的等级之一) zhǒngxìng.

castigate /ˈkæstɪgeɪt/ *v* [T] [正式用语]申斥 shēnchì; 严〔嚴〕厉〔厲〕批评 yánlì pīpíng.

castle /ˈkɑːsl; *US* ˈkæsl/ *n* [C] 1 城堡 chéngbǎo. 2 (国际象棋)车 jū.

castor (亦作 caster) /kɑːstə(r); *US* ˈkæs-/ *n* [C] 1 (椅子等的)小脚轮〔輪〕xiǎo jiǎolún. 2 盛调味品的小瓶 chéng tiáowèipǐn de xiǎopíng. ˌcastor ˈsugar *n* [U] 细白砂糖 xì báishātáng.

castor oil /ˌkɑːstər ˈɔɪl; *US* ˈkæstər ɔɪl/ *n* [U] 蓖麻油 bìmáyóu.

castrate /kæˈstreɪt; *US* ˈkæstreɪt/ *v* [T] 阉〔閹〕割 yāngē. castration /kæˈstreɪʃn/ *n* [U].

casual /ˈkæʒʊəl/ *adj* 1 随〔隨〕便的 suíbiànde; 漫不经〔經〕心的 màn bù jīngxīn de: ~ *clothes* 便服. 2 偶然的 ǒuránde; 碰巧的 pèngqiǎode: *a ~ meeting* 偶然的相会,巧遇. 3 临〔臨〕时〔時〕的 línshíde: ~ *work* 临时工作. casually *adv*.

casualty /ˈkæʒʊəltɪ/ *n* [C] [*pl* -ies] 伤〔傷〕亡人员 shāngwáng rényuán.

cat /kæt/ *n* [C] (a) 猫 māo. (b) 猫科动〔動〕物 māokē dòngwù. ˈcat burglar *n* [C] 翻墙〔牆〕入室的窃〔竊〕贼 fānqiáng rùshì de qièzéi. ˈcatcall *n* [C] (表示不满的)尖厉〔厲〕口哨声〔聲〕jiānlì kǒushào shēng. ˈcatnap *n* [C] 小睡 xiǎoshuì; 假寐 jiǎmèi.

catacombs /ˈkætəkuːmz; *US* -kəʊmz/ *n* [pl] 地下墓穴 dìxià mùxué; 陵寝 língqǐn.

catalogue (美语亦作 -log) /ˈkætəlɒg; *US* -lɔːg/ *n* [C] (货品等)目录〔錄〕mùlù. catalogue *v* [T] 把…编入目录 bǎ … biānrù mùlù.

catalyst /ˈkætəlɪst/ *n* [C] [化学]催化剂〔劑〕cuīhuàjì.

C

catapult /ˈkætəpʌlt/ *n* [C] 弹〔彈〕弓 dàngōng. **catapult** *v* [T] 用弹弓射 yòng dàngōng shè; 如用弹弓射 rú yòng dàngōng shè.

cataract /ˈkætərækt/ *n* [C] **1** 大瀑布 dà pùbù. **2** 白内障 báinèizhàng.

C

catarrh /kəˈtɑː(r)/ *n* [U] 卡他 kǎtā; 黏膜炎 niánmóyán.

catastrophe /kəˈtæstrəfɪ/ *n* [C] 大灾〔災〕难〔難〕dàzāinàn; 大祸〔禍〕dàhuò. **catastrophic** /ˌkætəˈstrɒfɪk/ *adj*.

catch[1] /kætʃ/ *v* [*pt*, *pp* caught /kɔːt/] **1** [T] 接住 jiēzhù; 抓住 zhuāzhù: ～ *a ball* 接住球. **2** [T] 逮住 dǎizhù; 捕获〔獲〕bǔhuò: ～ *a thief* 逮住小偷. **3** [T] 撞见(某人)做某事(恶事) zhuàngjiàn zuò mǒushì: ～ *sb stealing* 撞见某人在偷东西. **4** [T] 赶〔趕〕上(火车等) gǎnshàng. **5** [I, T] 绊住 bànzhù; 挂住 guàzhù: *I caught my fingers in the door.* 我的手指夹在门缝里了. **6** [T] 感染到 gǎnrǎndào: ～ *a cold* 感冒, 伤风. **7** [T] 懂得 dǒngde; 了解 liáojiě; 听〔聽〕到(声音) tīngdào: *I didn't quite* ～ *your name.* 我没有听清你的名字. **8** [T] 打 dǎ; 击〔擊〕中 jīzhòng. **9** [习语] **be ˌcaught up in sth** 被卷〔捲〕入 bèi juǎnrù. **catch sb's atˈtention/ˈeye** 吸引某人注意 xīyǐn mǒurén zhùyì. **catch sb's fancy** ⇨ FANCY[1] **catch ˈfire** 着火 zháohuǒ. **catch sb napping** [非正式用语] 发〔發〕现…走神 fāxiàn … zǒushén. **catch sb red-ˈhanded** 当〔當〕场〔場〕抓住某人(做坏事) dāngchǎng zhuāzhù mǒurén. **catch sight of sb/sth** 瞥见 piējiàn. **10** [短语动词] **ˌcatch ˈon** [非正式用语] 流行 liúxíng; 时〔時〕髦 shímáo. **ˌcatch ˈon (to sth)** [非正式用语] 理解 lǐjiě. **ˌcatch sb ˈout** 证〔證〕明…无〔無〕知、错误 zhèngmíng … wúzhī、cuòwu. **ˌcatch ˈup (with sb)**, **ˌcatch sb ˈup** 赶上 gǎnshàng; 追上 zhuīshàng. **catch up on sth** 赶做 gǎnzuò. **catching** *adj* (疾病)传〔傳〕染性的 chuánrǎnxìngde. **ˈcatchment ˌarea** /ˈkætʃmənt/ *n* [C] 来源区〔區〕(某学校的生源区、某医院的病人来源区等) láiyuánqū. **catch-phrase** *n* [C] 时髦话 shímáohuà. **catchy** *adj* [-ier, -iest] (曲调)易记住的 yìjìzhùde.

catch[2] /kætʃ/ *n* [C] **1** 抓 zhuā; 接球 jiēqiú. **2** 捕获〔獲〕物 bǔhuòwù; 捕获量 bǔhuòliàng. **3** 窗钩 chuānggōu; 门扣 ménkòu. **4** 蹊跷〔蹺〕qīqiāo: *There must be a* ～ *in this somewhere.* 这里头一定有蹊跷.

categorical /ˌkætɪˈgɒrɪkl; *US* -ˈgɔːr-/ *adj* 无〔無〕条〔條〕件的 wútiáojiànde; 绝对〔對〕的 juéduìde. **categorically** /-klɪ/ *adv*.

category /ˈkætəgərɪ; *US* -gɔːrɪ/ *n* [C] [*pl* -ies] 种〔種〕类〔類〕zhǒnglèi; 类目 lèimù. **categorize** /-gəraɪz/ *v* [T] 把…分类 bǎ… fēnlèi.

cater /ˈkeɪtə(r)/ *v* [I] (*for*) **1** 供应〔應〕伙食 gōngyìng huǒshí. **2** 迎合 yínghé; 满足 mǎnzú: *television programmes* ～*ing for all tastes* 满足各种品味的电视节目. **caterer** *n* [C].

caterpillar /ˈkætəpɪlə(r)/ *n* [C] **1** 毛虫 máochóng. **2** (亦作 Caterpillar track) (*P*) 履带〔帶〕lǚdài.

catgut /ˈkætgʌt/ *n* [U] (用作小提琴弦、网球拍等)肠〔腸〕线〔綫〕chángxiàn.

cathedral /kəˈθiːdrəl/ *n* [C] 总〔總〕教堂 zǒngjiàotáng; 大教堂 dàjiàotáng.

cathode /ˈkæθəʊd/ *n* [C] [电]阴〔陰〕极〔極〕yīnjí.

catholic /ˈkæθəlɪk/ *adj* **1** Catholic = ROMAN CATHOLIC (ROMAN). **2** [正式用语] 普遍的 pǔbiànde; 广〔廣〕泛的 guǎngfànde: *have* ～ *tastes* 有广泛的兴趣. **Catholic** *n* [C] = ROMAN CATHOLIC (ROMAN). **Catholicism** /kəˈθɒləsɪzəm/ *n* [U] 天主教教义〔義〕、信仰 tiānzhǔjiào jiàoyì、xìnyǎng.

cattle /ˈkætl/ *n* [pl] 牛 niú.

catty /ˈkætɪ/ *adj* [-ier, -iest] 恶〔惡〕毒的 èdúde.

caught /kɔːt/ *pt*, *pp* of CATCH[1].

cauldron /ˈkɔːldrən/ *n* [C] 大锅〔鍋〕dàguō.

cauliflower /ˈkɒlɪflaʊə(r); *US* ˈkɔːlɪ-/ *n* [C, U] 菜花 càihuā.

cause /kɔːz/ *n* **1** [C, U] 原因 yuányīn; 起因 qǐyīn: *the* ～ *of the fire* 起火的原因. **2** [U] (*for*) 理由 lǐyóu: *have* ～ *for complaint* 有抱怨的理由. **3** [C] 事业〔業〕shìyè; 目标〔標〕mùbiāo: *the* ～ *of world peace* 世界和平事业. **cause** *v* [T] 是…的原因 shì…de yuányīn: *What* ～*d his death?* 他怎么死的?

causeway /ˈkɔːzweɪ/ *n* [C] (穿越湿地的)堤道 dīdào.

caustic /ˈkɔːstɪk/ *adj* **1** 腐蚀性的 fǔshíxìngde; 苛性的 kēxìngde: ～ *soda* 苛性钠. **2** [喻] (话语)讽〔諷〕刺的 fěngcìde; 刻薄的 kèbóde. **caustically** /-klɪ/ *adv*.

caution /ˈkɔːʃn/ *n* **1** [U] 小心 xiǎoxīn; 谨慎 jǐnshèn. **2** [C] 告诫 gàojiè; 警告 jǐnggào. **caution** *v* [T] 警告 jǐnggào. **cautionary** /ˈkɔːʃənərɪ; *US* -nerɪ/ *adj* 忠告的 zhōnggàode; 警告的 jǐnggàode.

cautious /ˈkɔːʃəs/ *adj* 小心的 xiǎoxīnde; 谨慎的 jǐnshènde. **cautiously** *adv*.

cavalcade /ˌkævlˈkeɪd/ *n* [C] 车队〔隊〕chēduì; 马帮 mǎbāng.

cavalry /ˈkævlrɪ/ *n* [C, 亦作 sing, 用 pl v] [*pl* -ies] 骑兵 qíbīng; 装〔裝〕甲兵 zhuāngjiǎbīng.

cave /keɪv/ *n* [C] 山洞 shāndòng; 窑洞 yáodòng; 地窖 dìjiào. **cave** *v* [短语动词] **cave in** 塌方 tāfāng; 坍陷 tānxiàn.

cavern /ˈkævən/ *n* [C] 大山洞 dà shāndòng;大洞穴 dà dòngxué. **cavernous** *adj* 大洞穴似的 dà dòngxué shì de;大而深的 dà ér shēn de.

caviare (亦作 **caviar**) /ˈkævɪɑː(r)/ *n* [U] 鱼子酱〔醬〕yúzǐjiàng.

cavity /ˈkævətɪ/ *n* [C] [*pl* -ies] [正式用语] 洞 dòng.

cayenne /keɪˈen/ (亦作 ˌcayenne ˈpepper) *n* [U] 辣椒 làjiāo.

CB /ˌsiː ˈbiː/ *abbr* citizens' band 民用电〔電〕台〔臺〕频带〔帶〕mínyòng diàntái píndài.

cc /ˌsiː ˈsiː/ *abbr* cubic centimetre 立方厘米 lìfāng límǐ.

CCTV /ˌsiː siː tiː ˈviː/ *abbr* closed-circuit television 闭路电〔電〕视 bìlù diànshì.

CD /ˌsiː ˈdiː/ *abbr* compact disc 激光唱盘〔盤〕jīguāng chàngpán. **CˈD burner** *n* [C] 光盘烧〔燒〕录〔錄〕机〔機〕guāngpán shāolùjī. **CˈD player** *n* [C] CD 播放机 CD bōfàngjī. **CD-ˈROM** *abbr* 只读〔讀〕光盘 zhǐdú guāngpán. **CD-ROM drive** *n* [C] 只读光盘驱〔驅〕动〔動〕器 zhǐdú guāngpán qūdòngqì. **CˈD writer** *n* [C] 光盘刻录机 guāngpán kèlùjī.

cease /siːs/ *v* [I,T] [正式用语]停止 tíngzhǐ. ˌ**cease-ˈfire** *n* [C] 停战〔戰〕协〔協〕定 tíngzhàn xiédìng. **ceaseless** *adj* 不停的 bùtíngde. **ceaselessly** *adv*.

cedar /ˈsiːdə(r)/ *n* (a) [C] 雪松 xuěsōng. (b) [U] 雪松木 xuěsōngmù.

ceiling /ˈsiːlɪŋ/ *n* [C] 1 天花板 tiānhuābǎn;顶篷 dǐngpéng. 2 最高限度 zuìgāo xiàndù: *price* (*wage*) ～ 物价(工资)最高限度.

celebrate /ˈselɪbreɪt/ *v* 1 [I,T] 庆〔慶〕祝 qìngzhù. 2 [T] [正式用语]歌颂 gēsòng;赞〔讚〕美 zànměi. **celebrated** 著名的 zhùmíngde;有名的 yǒumíngde. **celebration** /ˌselɪˈbreɪʃn/ *n* [C,U] 歌颂 gēsòng;赞美 zànměi.

celebrity /sɪˈlebrətɪ/ *n* [*pl* -ies] 1 [C] 著名人士 zhùmíng rénshì. 2 [U] 著名 zhùmíng;名声〔聲〕míngshēng.

celery /ˈselərɪ/ *n* [U] 芹菜 qíncài.

celestial /sɪˈlestɪəl; *US* -tʃl/ *adj* [非正式用语]天的 tiānde;天空的 tiānkōngde.

celibate /ˈselɪbət/ *adj* [C] 独〔獨〕身的 dúshēnde. **celibacy** /-bəsɪ/ *n* [U]. **celibate** *n* [C] 独身者 dúshēnzhě.

cell /sel/ *n* [C] 1 小房间〔間〕xiǎo fángjiān: *a prison* ～ 小牢房. 2 电〔電〕池 diànchí. 3 细胞 xìbāo. 4 (秘密组织等的)小组 xiǎozǔ.

cellar /ˈselə(r)/ *n* [C] 地窖 dìjiào: *a wine* ～ 酒窖.

cello /ˈtʃeləʊ/ *n* [C] [*pl* ～s] 大提琴 dàtíqín. **cellist** /ˈtʃelɪst/ *n* [C] 大提琴手 dàtíqínshǒu.

Cellophane /ˈseləfeɪn/ *n* [C] (*P*) 玻璃纸 bōlizhǐ;胶〔膠〕膜 jiāomó;赛璐玢 sàilùfēn.

cellular /ˈseljʊlə(r)/ *adj* 1 由细胞组成的 yóu xìbāo zǔchéng de. 2 (地毯等)织〔織〕得松〔鬆〕的 zhīdesōngde.

Celsius /ˈselsɪəs/ *adj*, *n* [U] 摄〔攝〕氏度(的) shèshìdù.

C

cement /sɪˈment/ *n* [U] 1 水泥 shuǐní. 2 结合剂〔劑〕jiéhéjì;黏固剂 niángùjì. **cement** *v* [T] 黏结 niánjiē;胶〔膠〕合 jiāohé.

cemetery /ˈsemətrɪ; *US* -terɪ/ *n* [C] [*pl* -ies] 墓地 mùdì.

cenotaph /ˈsenətɑːf; *US* -tæf/ *n* [C] (为战争中的牺牲者所立的)纪念碑 jìniànbēi.

censor /ˈsensə(r)/ *n* [C] 审〔審〕查官 shěncháguān;审查员 shěncháyuán. **censor** *v* [T] 审查 shěnchá; 检〔檢〕查 jiǎnchá. **censorship** *n* [U] 审查(制度) shěnchá;审查政策 shěnchá zhèngcè.

censure /ˈsenʃə(r)/ *v* [T][正式用语]指责 zhǐzé;非难〔難〕fēinàn. **censure** *n* [U].

census /ˈsensəs/ *n* [C] 人口调查 rénkǒu diàochá.

cent /sent/ *n* [C] 分(货币单位) fēn.

centaur /ˈsentɔː(r)/ *n* [C] [希腊神话]半人半马〔馬〕怪物 bànrén bànmǎ guàiwù.

centenarian /ˌsentɪˈneərɪən/ *n* [C], *adj* 百岁〔歲〕老人(的) bǎisuì lǎorén.

centenary /ˌsenˈtiːnərɪ; *US* ˈsentənerɪ/ *n* [C] [*pl* -ies] 百年纪念 bǎinián jìniàn.

centennial /senˈtenɪəl/ *n* [C] [美语]百年纪念 bǎinián jìniàn.

center [美语] = CENTRE.

centigrade /ˈsentɪgreɪd/ *adj*, *n* [U] = CELSIUS.

centimetre (美语 -meter) /ˈsentɪmiːtə(r)/ *n* [C] 公分 gōngfēn;厘米 límǐ.

centipede /ˈsentɪpiːd/ *n* [C] 蜈蚣 wúgōng.

central /ˈsentrəl/ *adj* 1 中央的 zhōngyāngde;中心的 zhōngxīnde. 2 最重要的 zuìzhòngyàode;主要的 zhǔyàode. ˌ**central ˈheating** *n* [U] 中央暖气〔氣〕系统 zhōngyāng nuǎnqì xìtǒng. **central ˈlocking** *n* [U] 中央门锁 zhōngyāng ménsuǒ. **centrally** *adv*.

centralize /ˈsentrəlaɪz/ *v* [I,T] (使)集中到中央 jízhōng dào zhōngyāng;由中央政府管理 yóu zhōngyāngzhèngfǔ guǎnlǐ. **centralization** /ˌsentrəlaɪˈzeɪʃn; *US* -lɪˈz-/ *n* [U].

centre /ˈsentə(r)/ *n* 1 [C] 中心 zhōngxīn;中央 zhōngyāng. 2 [C] 某种〔種〕活动〔動〕集中的地方 mǒuzhǒng huódòng jízhōng de dìfang: ˈ*a shopping* ～ 购物区. 3 人们兴〔興〕趣的集中点 rénmén xìngqù de jízhōngdiǎn: *the* ～ *of attention* 注意的中心. 4 (尤用 **the centre**) [sing] 政治上的中间立场〔場〕zhèngzhìshàng

C

de zhōngjiān lìchǎng. **centre** *v* [短语动词] centre (sth) on/around sb/sth 把…当〔當〕作中心 bǎ…dāngzuò zhōngxīn.

centrifugal /sen'trɪfjʊgl, 亦作 sen'trɪfjʊgl/ *adj* 离〔離〕心的 líxīnde: ~ *force* 离心力.

century /'sentʃərɪ/ *n* [C] [*pl* -ies] 1 一百年 yìbǎinián; 世纪 shìjì. 2 (板球的)一百分 yìbǎifēn.

ceramic /sɪ'ræmɪk/ *adj* 陶器的 táoqìde; 陶瓷的 táocíde. **ceramics** *n* 1 [U] 陶瓷艺〔藝〕术〔術〕 táocí yìshù. 2 [pl] 陶瓷制〔製〕品 táocí zhìpǐn.

cereal /'sɪərɪəl/ *n* [U, C] 1 谷〔穀〕类〔類〕粮〔糧〕食 gǔlèi liángshi. 2 谷类食品 gǔlèi shípǐn: '*breakfast* ~*s* 早餐麦片粥.

ceremonial /ˌserɪ'məʊnɪəl/ *adj* 礼〔禮〕仪〔儀〕的 lǐyíde: *a* ~ *occasion* 正式场合. **ceremonial** *n* [C, U] 礼仪 lǐyí; 仪式 yíshì. **ceremonially** /-nɪəlɪ/ *adv*.

ceremonious /ˌserɪ'məʊnɪəs/ *adj* 仪〔儀〕式隆重的 yíshì lóngzhòng de. **ceremoniously** *adv*.

ceremony /'serɪmənɪ; *US* -məʊnɪ/ *n* [*pl* -ies] 1 [C] 典礼〔禮〕 diǎnlǐ; 仪〔儀〕式 yíshì. 2 礼节〔節〕 lǐjié; 礼仪 lǐyí.

certain /'sɜːtn/ *adj* 1 确〔確〕定的 quèdìngde; 无〔無〕疑的 wúyíde. 2 (*to*) 一定的 yídìngde; 必然的 bìránde: *They're* ~ *to win the game*. 他们一定会打赢这场比赛. 3 某的 mǒude; 某种〔種〕的 mǒuzhǒngde; 某一的 mǒuyīde: *on* ~ *conditions* 在某些条件下. 4 一些的 yìxiēde; 一定的 yídìngde: *a* ~ *coldness in his attitude* 他的态度有些冷淡. 5 [习语] **make certain** 弄确实〔實〕 nòngquèshí: *Make* ~ *that no bones are broken*. 确定没有骨折. **certainly** *adv* 1 无疑 wúyí: *He will* ~*ly die*. 他一定会死的. 2 (回答疑问)好的 hǎode; 当〔當〕然可以 dāngrán kěyǐ. **certainty** *n* [*pl* -ies] 1 [U] 必然 bìrán; 确实 quèshí; 肯定 kěndìng. 2 [C] 必然的事 bìránde shì.

certificate /sə'tɪfɪkət/ *n* [C] 证〔證〕书〔書〕 zhèngshū; 执〔執〕照 zhí zhào: *a* '*birth* ~ 出生证明.

certify /'sɜːtɪfaɪ/ *v* [*pt*, *pp* -ied] [T] (正式)证〔證〕明 zhèngmíng: ~ *him dead* (*insane*) 证明他死亡(精神失常).

cessation /se'seɪʃn/ *n* [U, C] [正式用语]停止 tíngzhǐ.

cesspit /'sespɪt/ (亦作 **cesspool** /'sespuːl/) *n* [C] 污水坑 wūshuǐkēng; 粪〔糞〕坑 fènkēng.

CFC /ˌsiː'efsiː/ *abbr* chlorofluorocarbon 含氯氟烃〔烴〕hánlǜfútīng.

chafe /tʃeɪf/ *v* 1 [I] [T] 擦痛(皮肤等) cātòng. 2 [I] (*at*/*under*) 焦躁 jiāozào: ~ *at the delay* 因拖延而焦躁.

chaff /tʃɑːf; *US* tʃæf/ *n* [U] 谷〔穀〕壳〔殼〕 gǔké; 糠 kāng.

chagrin /'ʃægrɪn; *US* ʃə'griːn/ *n* [U] [正式用语]懊恼〔惱〕 àonǎo; 悔恨 huǐhèn.

chain /tʃeɪn/ *n* 1 [C, U] 链 liàn; 链条〔條〕 liàntiáo. 2 [C] 一连串 yìliánchuàn; 一系列 yíxìliè: *a* ~ *of mountains* 山脉, 山系. *a* ~ *of shops* 连锁店. *a* ~ *of events* 一系列事件. **chain** *v* [T] 用链条拴住 yòng liàntiáo shuānzhù; 束缚 shùfù. ˌ**chain re'action** *n* [C] 连锁反应〔應〕 liánsuǒ fǎnyìng. '**chain-smoke** [I, T] 一根接一根地吸烟 yìgēn jiē yìgēn de xīyān. '**chain-smoker** *n* [C]. '**chain-store** *n* [C] 连锁商店 liánsuǒ shāngdiàn.

chair /tʃeə(r)/ *n* 1 [C] 椅子 yǐzi. 2 **the chair** [sing] 会〔會〕议〔議〕主席职〔職〕位 huìyì zhǔxí zhíwèi; 会议主席 huìyì zhǔxí. 3 [C] 大学〔學〕教授的职位 dàxué jiàoshòu de zhíwèi. **chair** *v* [T] 任(会议)主席 rèn zhǔxí; 主持(会议) zhǔchí. '**chairman**, '**chairperson**, '**chairwoman** *n* [C] (会议)主席 zhǔxí.

chalet /'ʃæleɪ/ *n* [C] 1 瑞士山上的小木屋 Ruìshì shānshàng de xiǎomùwū. 2 木屋式别墅 mùwūshì biéshù.

chalk /tʃɔːk/ *n* (a) [U] 白垩〔堊〕 bái'è. (b) [C, U] 粉笔〔筆〕 fěnbǐ. **chalk** *v* 1 [I, T] 用粉笔写〔寫〕、画〔畫〕 yòng fěnbǐ xiě、huà. 2 [短语动词] **chalk sth up** 获〔獲〕得(成功) huòdé. **chalky** [-ier, -iest] 白垩的 bái'ède; 像白垩的 xiàng bái'è de.

challenge /'tʃælɪndʒ/ *n* [C] 1 艰〔艱〕难〔難〕的任务〔務〕 jiānnánde rènwù. 2 邀请比赛 yāoqǐng bǐsài; 挑战〔戰〕 tiǎozhàn. **challenge** *v* [T] 1 挑战 tiǎozhàn. 2 要求提出事实〔實〕(以证明一项声明) yāoqiú tíchū shìshí. **challenger** *n* [C]. **challenging** *adj* 挑战性的 tiǎozhànxìng de; 提出难题的 tíchū nántí de.

chamber /'tʃeɪmbə(r)/ *n* 1 (旧时的)房间〔間〕 fángjiān. 2 议〔議〕院 yìyuàn; 立法机〔機〕关〔關〕的会〔會〕议〔議〕厅〔廳〕 lìfǎ jīguān de huìyìtīng. 3 **chambers** [pl] 法官与律师〔師〕使用的套间 fǎguān yǔ lǜshī shǐyòngde tàojiān. 4 [C] (动植物体内的)腔 qiāng; 室 shì: *the* ~*s of the heart* 心腔(心房与心室). '**chambermaid** (旅馆)卧室女服务〔務〕员 wòshì nǚ fúwùyuán, 女招待 nǚzhāodài. '**chamber music** *n* [U] 室内乐〔樂〕 shìnèiyuè. **chamber of commerce** *n* [C] 商会 shānghuì.

chameleon /kə'miːlɪən/ *n* [C] 变〔變〕色蜥蜴 biànsè xīyì; 变色龙〔龍〕 biànsèlóng.

chamois /'ʃæmwɑː; *US* 'ʃæmɪ/ *n* [C] [*pl* chamois] 欧〔歐〕洲和高加索地区〔區〕的小羚羊 Ōuzhōu hé Gāojiāsuǒ dìqū de xiǎo língyáng. '**chamois leather** /'ʃæmɪ/ *n* [C, U] 羚羊皮 língyángpí.

champ[1] /tʃæmp/ *v* [I] 1 (马等)大声〔聲〕地嚼或咬 dàshēngde jiáo huò yǎo. 2 不耐烦 búnàifán;焦急 jiāojí.

champ[2] /tʃæmp/ *n* [C] [非正式用语] = CHAMPION.

champagne /ʃæmˈpeɪn/ *n* [C, U] 香槟〔檳〕酒 xiāngbīnjiǔ.

champion /ˈtʃæmpɪən/ *n* [C] 1 冠军 guànjūn. 2 战〔戰〕士 zhànshì;拥〔擁〕护〔護〕者 yōnghùzhě: *a ~ of women's rights* 妇女权利的拥护者. **champion** *v* [T] 支持 zhīchí;拥护 yōnghù;保卫〔衛〕bǎowèi. **championship** *n* 1 [C] 冠军赛 guànjūnsài;锦标〔標〕赛 jǐnbiāosài. 2 冠军的地位 guànjūnde dìwèi. 3 拥护 yōnghù;支持 zhīchí.

chance /tʃɑːns; *US* tʃæns/ *n* 1 [U] 机〔機〕会〔會〕jīhuì;幸运〔運〕xìngyùn;运气〔氣〕yùnqì. 2 [C, U] 可能性 kěnéngxìng: *no ~ of winning* 没有胜的可能. 3 [C] 机遇 jīyù;机会 jīhuì: *have a ~ to make an apology* 有机会道歉. 4 [习语] **by ˈchance** 偶然 ǒurán. **on the (off) chance** 抱着希望 bàozhe xīwàng. **take a ˈchance (on sth)** 冒险〔險〕màoxiǎn;投机 tóujī. **chance** *v* 1 [I] [正式用语] 碰巧 pèngqiǎo;偶然发〔發〕生 ǒurán fāshēng: *I ~d to be there.* 我碰巧在那里. 2 [T] 冒…的险 mào…de xiǎn. **chancy** *adj* [-ier, -iest] [非正式用语]冒险的 màoxiǎnde.

chancel /ˈtʃɑːnsl; *US* ˈtʃænsl/ *n* [C] (教堂东端的)圣〔聖〕坛〔壇〕shèngtán.

chancellor /ˈtʃɑːnsələ(r); *US* ˈtʃænsl-/ *n* [C] 1 (某些国家的)总〔總〕理 zǒnglǐ. 2 [英国英语] (某些大学的)名誉〔譽〕校长〔長〕míngyù xiàozhǎng. **Chancellor of the Exˈchequer** *n* [C] [英国英语]财政大臣 cáizhèng dàchén.

chandelier /ˌʃændəˈlɪə(r)/ *n* [C] 枝形吊灯 zhīxíng diàodēng.

change[1] /tʃeɪndʒ/ *v* 1 [I, T] 改变〔變〕gǎibiàn;变化 biànhuà: *Our plans have ~d.* 我们的计划改变了. *Water ~s into steam.* 水变成蒸汽. *~ one's attitude* 改变态度. 2 替换 tìhuàn;替代 tìdài;更换 gēnghuàn: *~ a light bulb* 换一个灯泡. 3 [I, T] 换衣服 huàn yīfu. 4 [I, T] 换车、船 huàn chē、chuán. 5 [T] 兑换 duìhuàn. 6 [习语] **change hands** 转〔轉〕手 zhuǎnshǒu. **change one's mind** 改变主意 gǎibiàn zhǔyì. **change one's tune** 改变态〔態〕度 gǎibiàn tàidù. 7 [短语动词] **ˌchange ˈover (from sth) (to sth)** 改变制度 gǎibiàn zhìdù. **changeable** *adj* 常变的 chángbiànde. **ˈchange-over** *n* [C] 制度的改变 zhìdùde gǎibiàn.

change[2] /tʃeɪndʒ/ *n* 1 [C, U] 改变〔變〕gǎibiàn. 2 [C] 替换物 tìhuànwù: *~ of clothes* 替换的衣服. *~ of name* 换用的名字. 3 [U] (a) 找头〔頭〕zhǎotou. (b) 零钱〔錢〕língqián. 4 [习语] **for a change** 为〔為〕了改变一下 wèile gǎibiàn yíxià.

channel /ˈtʃænl/ *n* [C] 1 水道 shuǐdào;河床 héchuáng;航道 hángdào. 2 海峡〔峽〕hǎixiá: *The English C~* 英吉利海峡. 3 路线〔綫〕lùxiàn;途径〔徑〕tújìng;系统 xìtǒng: *Your complaint must be made through the proper ~s.* 你的不满意见必须通过合适的途径提出. 4 电〔電〕视台〔臺〕diànshìtái. **channel** *v* [-ll-;美语亦作 -l-] [T] 1 在…形成水道 zài…xíngchéng shuǐdào. 2 引导〔導〕yǐndǎo:[喻] *~ all our resources into the new scheme* 把我们所有的资源都用到新的计划上. **ˈchannel changer** *n* [C] (电视机的)遥控器 yáokòngqì.

chant /tʃɑːnt/ *v* [I, T] 1 单〔單〕调地唱 dāndiàode chàng. 2 (有节奏地、反复地)唱或喊叫 chàng huò hǎnjiào. **chant** *n* [C].

chaos /ˈkeɪɒs/ *n* [U] 混乱〔亂〕hùnluàn;纷乱 fēnluàn. **chaotic** /keɪˈɒtɪk/ *adj*.

chap[1] /tʃæp/ *n* [C] [非正式用语,尤用于英国英语]家伙 jiāhuo;小伙子 xiǎohuǒzi.

chap[2] /tʃæp/ *v* [-pp-] [I, T] (使皮肤)粗糙 cūcāo,皲〔皸〕裂 jūnliè: *~ped lips* 皲裂的嘴唇.

chapel /ˈtʃæpl/ *n* [C] 1 学〔學〕校等的小教堂 xuéxiào děng de xiǎo jiàotáng. 2 教堂内的私人祈祷〔禱〕处〔處〕jiàotáng nèi de sīrén qídǎochù.

chaplain /ˈtʃæplɪn/ *n* [C] 军队〔隊〕、监〔監〕狱内之牧师〔師〕jūnduì、jiānyù nèi zhī mùshi.

chapter /ˈtʃæptə(r)/ *n* [C] 1 (书的)章 zhāng;回 huí. 2 时〔時〕期 shíqī;时代 shídài.

char[1] /tʃɑː(r)/ *v* [-rr-] [I, T] (使)烧〔燒〕焦 shāojiāo;(使)烧黑 shāohēi.

char[2] /tʃɑː(r)/ (亦作 **ˈcharwoman**) *n* [C] [英国英语]替人打扫〔掃〕清洁〔潔〕的女工 tì rén dǎsǎo qīngjié de nǚgōng.

character /ˈkærəktə(r)/ *n* 1 [U] (个人等的)天性 tiānxìng;性格 xìnggé;特性 tèxìng: *The ~ of the town has changed over the years.* 这些年来这个城镇的特性改变了. 2 [U] (事物的)性质〔質〕xìngzhì: *discussions that were confidential in ~* 属于机密性质的讨论. 3 [U] (a) 显〔顯〕著的特点〔點〕xiǎnzhùde tèdiǎn: *house with no ~* 无显著特点的房屋. (b) 道德的力量 dàodéde lìliàng: *a woman of ~* 品格高尚的女人. 4 [C] (戏剧、小说中的)人物 rénwù,角色 juésè. 5 [C] [非正式用语]人 rén;怪人 guàirén. 6 [C] 书〔書〕写〔寫〕或印刷符号 shūxiě huò yìnshuā fúhào;(汉)字 zì: *Chinese ~s* 汉字. 7 [习语] **in character** 与〔與〕自身特性相符 yǔ zìshēn tèxìng xiāngfú. **out of character** 与自身特性不相符 yǔ zìshēn tèxìng bù xiāngfú. **characterless** *adj* 无〔無〕特点的 wú tèdiǎn de;平常的 píngchángde.

characteristic /ˌkærəktəˈrɪstɪk/ *adj* 特有的 tèyǒude; 表示特征〔徵〕的 biǎoshì tèzhēng de. **characteristic** *n* [C] 特性 tèxìng; 特点〔點〕tèdiǎn. **characteristically** /-klɪ/ *adv*.

C

characterize /ˈkærəktəraɪz/ *v* [T] 1 描绘〔繪〕…的特征〔徵〕miáohuì…de tèzhēng. 2 成为〔爲〕…的特征 chéngwéi…de tèzhēng.

charade /ʃəˈrɑːd; *US* ʃəˈreɪd/ *n* 1 charades [用 sing v] 一种〔種〕猜字游戏〔戲〕yìzhǒng cāizì yóuxì. 2 荒唐而易被识〔識〕破的伪〔僞〕装〔裝〕huāngtáng ér yìbèi shípò de wěi zhuāng.

charcoal /ˈtʃɑːkəʊl/ *n* [U] 炭 tàn; 木炭 mùtàn; 炭笔〔筆〕tànbǐ.

charge[1] /tʃɑːdʒ/ *v* 1 [I, T] 要求支付(若干钱) yāoqiú zhīfù; 要价〔價〕yàojià: *They ~d me £50 for the repair*. 他们为这修理要我 50 英镑. 2 [T] (*to*) 把…记在账〔賬〕上 bǎ…jì zài zhàng shàng: *C~ it to his account*. 把它记在他的账上. 3 [T] (*with*) 控告 kònggào; 指控 zhǐkòng: *He was ~d with murder*. 他被控告有谋杀罪. 4 [I, T] 猛攻 měnggōng; 冲〔衝〕向 chōngxiàng. 5 [T] 给(电池等)充电〔電〕gěi chōngdiàn. 6 [T] (*with*) [尤用于被动语态]使充满 shǐ chōngmǎn: *a voice ~d with tension* 充满紧张的声音. 7 [T] (*with*) [正式用语]给以责任 gěi yǐ zérèn; 交付使命 jiāofù shǐmìng.

charge[2] /tʃɑːdʒ/ *n* 1 [C] 要价〔價〕yàojià. 2 [C] 控告 kònggào; 指控 zhǐkòng: *a ~ of murder* 控告谋杀. 3 [U] 主管 zhǔguǎn; 掌管 zhǎngguǎn: *take ~ of the department* 主管这个部门. 4 [C, U] 突然猛攻 tūrán měnggōng. 5 [C] 电〔電〕荷 diànhè; 充电 chōngdiàn. 6 [习语] **in charge (of sb/sth)** 主管 zhǔguǎn; 负责 fùzé.

chargé d'affaires /ˌʃɑːʒeɪ dæˈfeə(r)/ *n* [C] [*pl* **chargés d'affaires**] 代办〔辦〕dàibàn.

chariot /ˈtʃærɪət/ *n* [C] 古代双〔雙〕轮〔輪〕马拉战〔戰〕车 gǔdài shuānglún mǎlā zhànchē. **charioteer** /ˌtʃærɪəˈtɪə(r)/ *n* [C] 驾驶战车者 jiàshǐ zhànchē zhě.

charisma /kəˈrɪzmə/ *n* [U] 魅力 mèilì; 号〔號〕召力 hàozhàolì. **charismatic** /ˌkærəzˈmætɪk/ *adj*: *a ~tic politician* 有号召力的政治家.

charitable /ˈtʃærɪtəbl/ *adj* 1 慈善的 císhànde; 宽厚的 kuānhòude. 2 (有关)慈善机〔機〕构的 císhàn jīgòu de. **charitably** *adv*.

charity /ˈtʃærətɪ/ *n* [*pl* -ies] 1 [C] 慈善团〔團〕体〔體〕císhàn tuántǐ. 2 [U] 博爱〔愛〕bó'ài. 3 [U] 赈济〔濟〕款、物 zhènjì kuǎn、wù. ˈ**charity shop** *n* [C] (为慈善事业筹款的)旧〔舊〕货店 jiùhuòdiàn.

charlatan /ˈʃɑːlətən/ *n* [C] 冒充内行者 màochōng nèiháng zhě.

charm /tʃɑːm/ *n* 1 (a) [U] 吸引力 xīyǐnlì; 诱力 yòulì. (b) [C] 可爱〔愛〕之处〔處〕kě'ài zhī chù. 2 [C] 护〔護〕身符 hùshēnfú. 3 [C] 咒符 zhòufú; 咒语 zhòuyǔ. **charm** *v* [T] 1 吸引 xīyǐn; 使陶醉 shǐ táozuì. 2 对〔對〕…行魔法 duì…xíng mófǎ. **charming** *adj* 可爱的 kě'àide; 媚人的 mèirénde.

chart /tʃɑːt/ *n* 1 [C] 图〔圖〕tú; 图表 túbiǎo. 2 [C] 海图 hǎitú; 航线〔綫〕图 hángxiàntú. 3 **the charts** [pl] 流行音乐〔樂〕唱片每周畅〔暢〕销目录〔錄〕liúxíng yīnyuè chàngpiàn měizhōu chàngxiāo mùlù. **chart** *v* [T] 制〔製〕…的海图 zhì…de hǎitú.

charter /ˈtʃɑːtə(r)/ *n* [C] 1 君主或政府颁发〔發〕的特许状〔狀〕、凭〔憑〕照 jūnzhǔ huò zhèngfǔ bānfā de tèxǔzhuàng、píngzhào. 2 (飞机、船等)租赁 zūlìn: *a ˈ~ flight* 包租的班机. **charter** *v* [T] 租, 包(船、飞机等) zū, bāo. **chartered** *adj* 有特许状的 yǒu tèxǔzhuàng de: *a ˌ~ed acˈcountant* 有特许状的会计.

charwoman /ˈtʃɑːwʊmən/ *n* ⇨CHAR[2].

chase /tʃeɪs/ *v* [I, T] (*after*) 追逐 zhuīzhú; 追击〔擊〕zhuījī; 追赶〔趕〕zhuīgǎn; 追猎〔獵〕zhuīliè. **chase** *n* [C] 追逐 zhuīzhú; 追赶 zhuīgǎn; 追击 zhuījī.

chasm /ˈkæzəm/ *n* [C] 1 (地壳)陷窟 xiànkū, 断〔斷〕层〔層〕duàncéng, 裂口 lièkǒu. 2 [喻](感情、兴趣等)巨大分歧 jùdà fēnqí, 巨大差别 jùdà chābié.

chassis /ˈʃæsɪ/ *n* [C] [*pl* **chassis** /ˈʃæsɪz/] 汽车等的底盘〔盤〕qìchē děng de dǐpán.

chaste /tʃeɪst/ *adj* 1 纯洁〔潔〕的 chúnjiéde; 有道德的 yǒu dàodé de; 善良的 shànliángde. 2 贞洁的 zhēnjiéde. 3 (文风等)简洁朴〔樸〕实〔實〕的 jiǎnjié pǔshí de.

chasten /ˈtʃeɪsn/ *v* [T] [正式用语]惩〔懲〕戒 chěngjiè; 遏止 èzhǐ; 磨炼〔煉〕móliàn.

chastise /tʃæˈstaɪz/ *v* [T] [正式用语]严〔嚴〕惩〔懲〕yánchěng. **chastisement** *n* [U].

chastity /ˈtʃæstətɪ/ *n* [U] 贞洁〔潔〕zhēnjié; 纯洁 chúnjié; 高雅 gāoyǎ.

chat /tʃæt/ *n* [C] 闲〔閒〕谈 xiántán; 聊天 liáotiān. **chat** *v* [-tt-] 1 [I] 闲谈 xiántán; 聊天 liáotiān. 2 [短语动词] **chat sb up** [英国英语, 非正式用语]与〔與〕…搭讪 yǔ…dāshàn; 调情 tiáoqíng. ˈ**chatline** *n* [C] 闲聊电〔電〕话 xiánliáo diànhuà. ˈ**chat room** *n* [C] (网上)聊天室 liáotiānshì. ˈ**chat show** *n* [C] (电视)访谈节〔節〕目 fǎngtán jiémù. **chatty** *adj* [-ier, -iest] 爱〔愛〕闲聊的 ài xiánliáode.

chatter /ˈtʃætə(r)/ *v* [I] 1 喋喋不休 diédié bùxiū; 饶〔饒〕舌 ráoshé. 2 (鸟)啭〔囀〕鸣 zhuànmíng; (猴子)唧唧叫 jījījiào. 3 (牙齿)打战〔戰〕dǎzhàn. **chatter** *n* [C] 1 喋喋不休 diédié bùxiū;(牙齿)打战〔戰〕 dǎzhàn. 2 唧唧声〔聲〕 jījīshēng;啭〔囀〕鸣声 zhuànmíngshēng;(牙齿的)打战声 dǎzhànshēng. ˈ**chatterbox** *n* [C] 唠〔嘮〕唠叨叨的人 láoláodāodaode rén.

chauffeur /ˈʃəʊfə(r); *US* ʃəʊˈfɜːr/ *n* [C] 受雇的私人汽车司机〔機〕 shòugùde sīrén qìchē sījī. **chauffeur** *v* [T] 为〔爲〕…开〔開〕车 wèi … kāichē.

chauvinism /ˈʃəʊvɪnɪzəm/ *n* [U] 大国〔國〕主义〔義〕 dàguózhǔyì;本性别第一主义 běnxìngbié dìyī zhǔyì. **chauvinist** /-ɪst/ *n* [C]. **chauvinistic** /ˌʃəʊvɪˈnɪstɪk/ *adj*.

cheap /tʃiːp/ *adj* 1 便宜的 piányìde;廉价〔價〕的 liánjiàde. 2 低劣的 dīliède;劣质〔質〕的 lièzhìde: ~ *and nasty* 质量低劣的. 3 粗鄙的 cūbǐ de;不正当〔當〕的 bú zhèngdāng de: *a ~ joke* 粗鄙的玩笑. **cheapen** *v* [I, T] (使)成为〔爲〕便宜 chéngwéi piányì. **cheaply** *adv*. **cheapness** *n* [U].

cheat /tʃiːt/ *v* 1 [I] 欺诈 qīzhà;欺骗〔騙〕 qīpiàn: ~ *in an examination* 考试作弊. 2 [短语动词] **cheat sb (out) of sth** 从〔從〕某人骗取某物 cóng mǒurén piànqǔ mǒuwù. **cheat** *n* [C] 骗子 piànzi.

check[1] /tʃek/ *v* 1 (a) [I, T] 检〔檢〕查 jiǎnchá;核对〔對〕 héduì. (b) 审〔審〕查 shěnchá;核查 héchá. 2 [T] 制止 zhìzhǐ;控制 kòngzhì: ~ *the enemy's progress* 制止敌人的前进. 3 [短语动词] **check in** (住旅馆或登飞机等)办〔辦〕理登记手续〔續〕 bànlǐ dēngjì shǒuxù. **check out** 付账〔賬〕后〔後〕离〔離〕开〔開〕旅馆 fùzhàng hòu líkāi lǚguǎn. **check up on sth** (或美语) **check sth out** 检查 jiǎnchá. ˈ**check-in** *n* [C] (机场的)登机〔機〕登记处〔處〕 dēngjī dēngjìchù. ˈ**check-out** *n* [C] (超级市场的)付款处 fùkuǎnchù. ˈ**checkpoint** *n* [C] 边〔邊〕防检查站 biānfáng jiǎncházhàn. **check-up** *n* [C] 体〔體〕格检查 tǐgé jiǎnchá.

check[2] /tʃek/ *n* 1 [C] 检〔檢〕查 jiǎnchá. 2 [U] 控制 kòngzhì: *hold/keep one's emotions in ~* 控制情绪. 3 [sing] (国际象棋)将〔將〕 jiāng. 4 [C] [美语](饭馆的)账〔賬〕单〔單〕 zhàngdān. 5 [C] [美语] = CHEQUE.

check[3] /tʃek/ *n* [U, C] 方格图〔圖〕案 fānggé tú'àn.

checkered [美语] = CHEQUERED.

checkmate /ˈtʃekmeɪt/ *n* [U] 1 (国际象棋)将〔將〕死王棋的局面 jiāngsǐ wángqíde júmiàn. 2 [喻]彻〔徹〕底失败 chèdǐ shībài.

cheek /tʃiːk/ *n* 1 [C] 面颊〔頰〕 miànjiá;脸〔臉〕蛋儿 liǎndànr. 2 [U] 厚脸皮 hòu liǎnpí;没礼〔禮〕貌 méi lǐmào. **cheek** *v* [T] 无〔無〕礼地对〔對〕…说 wúlǐde duì…shuō. **cheeky** *adj* [-ier, -iest] 无礼的 wúlǐde. **cheekily** *adv*.

cheer[1] /tʃɪə(r)/ *v* 1 [I, T] 欢〔歡〕呼 huānhū;喝彩 hècǎi. 2 [T] 使高兴〔興〕 shǐ gāoxìng;振奋〔奮〕 zhènfèn: ~*ing news* 振奋人心的消息. 3 [短语动词] **cheer (sb) up** (使)高兴起来 gāoxìng qǐlái.

cheer[2] /tʃɪə(r)/ *n* 1 [C] 欢〔歡〕呼 huānhū;喝彩 hècǎi. 2 [U] [古] 高兴〔興〕 gāoxìng. 3 **cheers** [pl] (祝酒)祝你健康 zhù nǐ jiànkāng. **cheerful** /ˈtʃɪəfl/ *adj* 高兴的 gāoxìngde. **cheerfully** *adv*. **cheerless** *adj* 不快乐〔樂〕的 bú kuàilède;阴〔陰〕暗的 yīn'ànde.

cheerio /ˌtʃɪərɪˈəʊ/ *interj* [英国非正式用语] 再见 zàijiàn.

cheery /ˈtʃɪərɪ/ *adj* [-ier, -iest] 活泼〔潑〕的 huópode;喜气〔氣〕洋洋的 xǐqì yángyáng de. **cheerily** *adv*.

cheese /tʃiːz/ *n* [C, U] 乳酪 rǔlào;干〔乾〕酪 gānlào. ˈ**cheesecake** *n* [C, U] 干酪饼 gānlàobǐng. ˈ**cheesecloth** *n* [U] 粗布 cūbù;干酪包布 gānlào bāobù. ˌ**cheesed** ˈ**off** *adj* [英国非正式用语] 厌〔厭〕烦的 yànfánde;恼〔惱〕怒的 nǎonùde.

cheetah /ˈtʃiːtə/ *n* [C] 猎〔獵〕豹 lièbào.

chef /ʃef/ *n* [C] 男厨师〔師〕长〔長〕 nán chúshīzhǎng.

chemical /ˈkemɪkl/ *adj* 化学〔學〕的 huàxuéde;用化学方法得到的 yòng huàxué fāngfǎ dédào de. **chemical** *n* [C] 化学制〔製〕品 huàxué zhìpǐn. **chemically** /-klɪ/ *adv*.

chemist /ˈkemɪst/ *n* [C] 1 药剂〔劑〕师〔師〕 yàojìshī;药剂商 yàojìshāng;化妆〔妝〕品商 huàzhuāngpǐnshāng. 2 化学〔學〕家 huàxuéjiā;化学师 huàxuéshī.

chemistry /ˈkemɪstrɪ/ *n* [U] 化学〔學〕 huàxué.

cheque /tʃek/ *n* [C] 支票 zhīpiào. ˈ**chequebook** *n* [C] 支票簿 zhīpiàobù. **cheque card** *n* [C] (银行)支票保付限额卡 zhīpiào bǎofù xiàn'é kǎ.

chequered /ˈtʃekəd/ *adj* 盛衰无〔無〕常的 shèng shuāi wúcháng de: *a ~ history* 盛衰无常的历史.

cherish /ˈtʃerɪʃ/ *v* [T] [正式用语] 1 爱〔愛〕护〔護〕 àihù. 2 抱有(希望) bàoyǒu;怀〔懷〕有(情感) huáiyǒu: ~*ed memories* 怀念.

cherry /ˈtʃerɪ/ *n* [C] [*pl* -ies] 樱桃 yīngtao.

cherub /ˈtʃerəb/ *n* [C] 1 [*pl* ~im /-ɪm/] 天使 tiānshǐ. 2 [*pl* ~s] 美丽〔麗〕可爱〔愛〕的小孩子 měilì kě'ài de xiǎoháizi.

chess /tʃes/ *n* [U] 国〔國〕际〔際〕象棋 guójì xiàngqí.

chest /tʃest/ *n* 1 [C] 胸腔 xiōngqiāng. 2 [C] 箱子 xiāngzi;柜〔櫃〕子 guìzi. 3 [习语] ˌ**get sth off one's** ˈ**chest** [非正式用语]把话倾吐出来 bǎ huà qīngtù chūlái. ˌ**chest of** ˈ**drawers** *n* [C] 衣柜 yīguì;五斗橱 wǔdǒuchú.

C

chestnut /ˈtʃesnʌt/ *n* [C] 栗 lì;栗树〔樹〕lìshù. **chestnut** *adj* 红褐色的 hónghèsède.

chew /tʃuː/ *v* **1** [I, T] 嚼 jiáo;咀嚼 jǔjué. **2** [短语动词] **chew sth over** [非正式用语]深思 shēnsī;考虑〔慮〕kǎolǜ. **chew** *n* [C] 咀嚼 jǔjué. ˈ**chewing-gum** *n* [C] 橡皮糖 xiàngpítáng;口香糖 kǒuxiāngtáng. **chewy** *adj* [-ier, -iest].

C

chic /ʃiːk/ *adj* 时〔時〕髦的 shímáode.

chick /tʃɪk/ *n* [C] 小鸡〔鷄〕xiǎojī;小鸟 xiǎoniǎo.

chicken /ˈtʃɪkɪn/ *n* (a) [C] 小鸡〔鷄〕xiǎojī;小鸟 xiǎoniǎo. (b) [U] 鸡肉 jīròu. **chicken** *adj* 〔俚〕胆〔膽〕怯的 dǎnqiède;软〔軟〕弱的 ruǎnruòde. **chicken** *v* [短语动词] **chicken out (of sth)** [非正式用语]因胆小而放弃〔棄〕做 yīn dǎnxiǎo ér fàngqì zuò. ˈ**chickenpox** /-pɒks/ *n* [U] 水痘 shuǐdòu.

chicory /ˈtʃɪkərɪ/ *n* [U] (a) 菊苣(蔬菜) jújù. (b) 菊苣粉(与咖啡同用) jújùfěn.

chief /tʃiːf/ *n* [C] 领袖 lǐngxiù;首领 shǒulǐng. **chief** *adj* **1** 主要的 zhǔyàode;首要的 shǒuyàode. **2** 首席的 shǒuxíde;最高的 zuìgāode. **chief** ˈ**constable** *n* [C] [英国英语](郡等的)警察局长〔長〕jǐngchájúzhǎng. **chiefly** *adv* 大半 dàbàn;主要 zhǔyào. **-in-ˈchief** [用于复合词]最高的 zuìgāode: *the Commander-in-*~ 统帅,总司令.

chieftain /ˈtʃiːftən/ *n* [C] 首领 shǒulǐng;酋长〔長〕qiúzhǎng.

child /tʃaɪld/ *n* [C] [*pl* **children** /ˈtʃɪldrən/] **1** 儿〔兒〕童 értóng;小孩 xiǎohái. **2** 儿子 érzi;女儿 nǚ'ér. ˈ**childbirth** *n* [U] 分娩 fēnmiǎn;生产〔產〕shēngchǎn ˈ**childhood** *n* [U] 幼年 yòunián;童年 tóngnián;童年时〔時〕代 tóngnián shídài. **childish** *adj* (成年人)幼稚的 yòuzhìde,傻〔儍〕气〔氣〕的 shǎqìde. **childless** *adj* 无〔無〕子女的 wú zǐnǚ de. ˈ**childlike** *adj* 孩子般天真的 háizibān tiānzhēnde. ˈ**child-minder** *n* [C] 代人照看孩子者 dài rén zhàokàn háizǐ zhě.

chill /tʃɪl/ *v* **1** [I, T] 使寒冷 shǐ hánlěng;变〔變〕冷 biànlěng;感到寒冷 gǎndào hánlěng. **2** [T] 使害怕 shǐ hàipà. **chill** *n* **1** [sing] 冷飕〔颼〕飕 lěng sōusōu. **2** [C] 着凉 zháoliáng;感冒 gǎnmào. **chilly** *adj* [-ier, -iest] **1** 寒冷的 hánlěngde;感到寒冷的 gǎndào hánlěngde. **2** [喻]不友善的 bù yǒushàn de;冷淡的 lěngdànde.

chilli (美语 **chili**) /ˈtʃɪlɪ/ *n* [C, U] [*pl* ~**es**] 干〔乾〕辣椒 gānlàjiāo. ˌ**chilli con** ˈ**carne** *n* [C, U] 墨西哥辣味牛肉末 mòxīgē làwèi niúròumò.

chime /tʃaɪm/ *n* [C] 编钟〔鐘〕biānzhōng;一套编钟的谐和的钟声〔聲〕yítào biānzhōng de xiéhéde zhōngshēng. **chime** *v* [I, T] (乐钟)鸣响〔響〕míngxiǎng.

chimney /ˈtʃɪmnɪ/ *n* [C] 烟囱 yāncōng;烟筒 yāntong. ˈ**chimney-pot** *n* [C] 烟囱管帽 yāncōng guǎnmào. ˈ**chimney-stack** *n* [C] 丛〔叢〕烟囱(有几个顶管的烟囱) cóngyāncōng. ˈ**chimney-sweep** *n* [C] 打扫〔掃〕烟囱的工人 dǎsǎo yāncōngde gōngrén.

chimp /tʃɪmp/ *n* [C] [非正式用语]黑猩猩 hēixīngxīng.

chimpanzee /ˌtʃɪmpənˈziː, -pæn-/ *n* [C] 黑猩猩 hēixīngxīng.

chin /tʃɪn/ *n* [C] 颏 kē;下巴 xiàba.

china /ˈtʃaɪnə/ *n* [U] (a) 瓷 cí. (b) 瓷器 cíqì.

China /ˈtʃaɪnə/ *n* 中国〔國〕Zhōngguó; **People's Republic of China** 中华〔華〕人民共和国 zhōnghuá Rénmín Gònghéguó.

Chinese /ˌtʃaɪˈniːz/ *n* **1** [U]中文 zhōngwén. **2** [C] [*pl* **Chinese**] 中国〔國〕人 zhōngguórén. **Chinese** *adj* 中国的 zhōngguóde;中国人的 zhōngguóréndе;中文的 zhōngwénde.

chink[1] /tʃɪŋk/ *n* [C] 裂缝 lièfèng;裂口 lièkǒu.

chink[2] /tʃɪŋk/ *n* [C], *v* [I] (金属、玻璃等)丁当〔當〕声〔聲〕dīng dāngshēng;作丁当声 zuò dīngdāngshēng.

chip /tʃɪp/ *n* [C] **1** [常作 pl] (土豆)薄片 bópiàn: *fish and* ˈ~*s* 油炸的鱼和土豆片. **2** (a) 碎片 suìpiàn;片屑 piànxiè. (b) (破损的)缺口 quēkǒu. **3** (赌博中代替钱的)塑料筹〔籌〕码 sùliào chóumǎ. **4** 集成电〔電〕路片 jíchéng diànlùpiàn;芯片 xīnpiàn. **5** [习语] **have a** ˈ**chip on one's shoulder** [非正式用语]认〔認〕为〔爲〕受到不公平对〔對〕待而怀〔懷〕恨或忿〔憤〕怒 rènwéi shòudào bùgōngpíng duìdài ér huáihèn huò fènnù. **chip** *v* [-pp-] **1** [I, T] (使)形成缺口 xíngchéng quēkǒu. **2** [短语动词] **chip** ˈ**in (with sth)** [非正式用语] (a) 插嘴 chāzuǐ;打断〔斷〕别人的话 dǎduàn biérénde huà: *She* ~*ped in with a couple of useful comments*. 她插进一两句很有用的话. (b) 捐(款) juān;凑(钱) còu.

chiropodist /kɪˈrɒpədɪst/ *n* [C] 替人治疗〔療〕脚病的人 tì rén zhìliáo jiǎobìng de rén. **chiropody** /-dɪ/ *n* [U].

chirp /tʃɜːp/ *v* [I], *n* [C] (小鸟)嘁嘁喳喳地叫 qīqīchāchāde jiào;小鸟嘁嘁喳喳的叫声〔聲〕xiǎoniǎo qīqīchāchāde jiàoshēng. **chirpy** *adj* [-ier, -iest] [英国非正式用语]活泼〔潑〕的 huópode;快活的 kuàihuode.

chisel /ˈtʃɪzl/ *n* [C] 凿〔鑿〕子 záozi;錾子 zànzi. **chisel** *v* [-ll-, 美语亦作 -l-] [T] 凿 záo;雕 diāo.

chit /tʃɪt/ *n* [C] 欠条〔條〕qiàntiáo;欠款单〔單〕据〔據〕qiànkuǎn dānjù.

chivalry /ˈʃɪvlrɪ/ *n* [U] **1** 中世纪的骑士制度

zhōngshìjìde qíshì zhìdù. 2 帮助弱者和妇〔婦〕女的慈爱〔愛〕精神 bāngzhù ruòzhě hé fùnǚ de cí'ài jīngshén. **chivalrous** /ˈʃɪvlrəs/ *adj*.

chlorine /ˈklɔːriːn/ *n* [U] [化学]氯 lǜ.

chloro-fluorocarbon /ˌklɔːrəˌflʊərəʊˈkɑːbən/ *n* [C] = CFC.

chlorophyll /ˈklɒrəfɪl; *US* ˈklɔːr-/ *n* [U] 叶〔葉〕绿素 yèlǜsù.

chocolate /ˈtʃɒklət/ *n* (a) [U] 巧克力 qiǎokèlì; 朱古力 zhūgǔlì. (b) [C] 夹〔夾〕心巧克力糖 jiāxīn qiǎokèlìtáng. (c) [U] 巧克力饮料 qiǎokèlì yǐnliào. **chocolate** *adj* 赭色的 zhěsède.

choice /tʃɔɪs/ *n* 1 [C] 选〔選〕择〔擇〕 xuǎnzé. 2 [U] 选择的权〔權〕利或可能 xuǎnzéde quánlì huò kěnéng: *I had no ~ but to leave*. 我没有选择的权利,只得离开. 3 [C] 选择的种〔種〕类〔類〕 xuǎnzéde zhǒnglèi: *a large ~ of restaurants* 很多可供选择的餐馆. 4 [C] 被选中的人或物 bèi xuǎnzhòng de rén huò wù: *I don't like his ~ of friends*. 我不喜欢他选中的朋友. **choice** *adj* 上等的 shàngděngde; 优〔優〕质〔質〕的 yōuzhìde: *~ fruit* 上等水果.

choir /ˈkwaɪə(r)/ *n* [C] (a) (教会的)歌唱队〔隊〕 gēchàngduì; 唱诗班 chàngshībān. (b) 歌唱队的席位 gēchàngduìde xíwèi.

choke /tʃəʊk/ *v* 1 [I, T] 闷塞 mēnsāi. 2 [T] 堵塞 dǔsè; 阻塞 zǔsè: *The drains are ~d with dead leaves*. 水沟被枯叶堵塞. 3 [短语动词] **choke sth back** 忍住 rěnzhù; 抑制 yìzhì. **choke** *n* [C] (机械)阻气〔氣〕门 zǔqìmén; 阻气门开〔開〕关〔關〕 zǔqìmén kāiguān.

cholera /ˈkɒlərə/ *n* [U] 霍乱〔亂〕 huòluàn.

cholesterol /kəˈlestərɒl/ *n* [U] (生化)胆〔膽〕固醇 dǎngùchún.

choose /tʃuːz/ *v* [*pt* **chose** /tʃəʊz/, *pp* **chosen** /ˈtʃəʊzn/] 1 [I, T] 选〔選〕择〔擇〕 xuǎnzé; 挑选 tiāoxuǎn: *You can't have all of the sweets, you must ~ one*. 你不能把糖都吃了,你必须挑选一个. 2 选定 xuǎndìng; 决定 juédìng: *She chose to become a doctor*. 她决定当医生.

chop /tʃɒp/ *v* [-pp-] [T] 劈 pī; 砍 kǎn; 剁 duò. **chop** *n* [C] 1 砍 kǎn; 劈 pī; 剁 duò. 2 排骨 páigǔ.

chopper /ˈtʃɒpə(r)/ *n* [C] 1 斧头〔頭〕 fǔtóu; 屠刀 túdāo; 砍刀 kǎndāo. 2 [非正式用语] 直升机〔機〕 zhíshēngjī.

choppy /ˈtʃɒpɪ/ *adj* [-ier, -iest] (海)波涛〔濤〕汹涌的 bōtāo xiōngyǒng de.

chopsticks /ˈtʃɒpstɪks/ *n* [pl] 筷子 kuàizi.

choral /ˈkɔːrəl/ *adj* 合唱队〔隊〕的 héchàngduìde; 合唱的 héchàngde.

chord /kɔːd/ *n* [C] 1 (音乐)和弦 héxián; 和音 héyīn. 2 (数学)弦 xián.

chore /tʃɔː(r)/ *n* [C] 日常工作 rìcháng gōngzuò; 琐碎烦人的杂〔雜〕务〔務〕 suǒsuì fánrén de záwù.

choreography /ˌkɒrɪˈɒgrəfɪ; *US* ˌkɔːrɪ-/ *n* [U] 舞蹈设计 wǔdǎo shèjì. **choreographer** /-fə(r)/ *n* [C].

chorister /ˈkɒrɪstə(r)/ *n* [C] 唱诗班歌手 chàngshībān gēshǒu.

chorus /ˈkɔːrəs/ *n* [C] 1 合唱队〔隊〕 héchàngduì; 合唱 héchàng. 2 (歌的)合唱句 héchàngjù; 合唱部分 héchàng bùfen. 3 齐〔齊〕声〔聲〕 qíshēng: *a ~ of approval* 齐声赞同. **chorus** *v* [T] 合唱 héchàng; 齐声地说 qíshēngde shuō.

chose *pt* of CHOOSE.

chosen *pp* of CHOOSE.

Christ /kraɪst/ (亦作 ˌ**Jesus** ˈ**Christ** /ˈdʒiːzəs/) *n* [sing] 基督 Jīdū.

christen /ˈkrɪsn/ *v* [T] 1 为〔爲〕…施洗礼〔禮〕 wèi…shī xǐlǐ; 洗礼时〔時〕命名 xǐlǐshí mìngmíng. 2 [喻]首次使用 shǒucì shǐyòng. **christening** *n* [C].

Christendom /ˈkrɪsndəm/ *n* [sing] [正式用语]全体〔體〕基督教徒 quántǐ Jīdūjiàotú.

Christian /ˈkrɪstʃən/ *n* [C] 基督教徒 Jīdūjiàotú. **Christian** *adj* 1 基督教的 Jīdūjiàode. 2 表现基督精神的 biǎoxiàn Jīdū jīngshén de; 仁慈的 réncíde. **Christianity** /ˌkrɪstɪˈænətɪ/ *n* [U] 基督教 Jīdūjiào. ˈ**Christian name** *n* [C] 教名 jiàomíng.

Christmas /ˈkrɪsməs/ (亦作 ˌ**Christmas** ˈ**Day**) *n* [U, C] 圣〔聖〕诞节〔節〕 Shèngdànjié.

chrome /krəʊm/ *n* [U] 铬黄 gèhuáng.

chromium /ˈkrəʊmɪəm/ *n* [U] 铬 gè.

chromosome /ˈkrəʊməsəʊm/ *n* [C] 染色体〔體〕 rǎnsètǐ.

chronic /ˈkrɒnɪk/ *adj* 1 (疾病)慢性的 mànxìngde. 2 [英国非正式用语]很坏〔壞〕的 hěnhuàide. **chronically** /-klɪ/ *adv*.

chronicle /ˈkrɒnɪkl/ *n* [C] 年代纪 niándàijì; 编年史 biānniánshǐ. **chronicle** *v* [T] 把…载入编年史 bǎ…zǎirù biānniánshǐ.

chronology /krəˈnɒlədʒɪ/ *n* [*pl* -ies] 1 [U] 年代学〔學〕 niándàixué. 2 [C] 年表 niánbiǎo. **chronological** /ˌkrɒnəˈlɒdʒɪkl/ *adj* 按时〔時〕间顺序的 àn shíjiān shùnxù de. **chronologically** /-klɪ/ *adv*.

chrysalis /ˈkrɪsəlɪs/ *n* [C] 蛹 yǒng.

chrysanthemum /krɪˈsænθəməm/ *n* [C] 菊花 júhuā.

chubby /ˈtʃʌbɪ/ *adj* [-ier, -iest] 微胖的 wēipàngde; 丰〔豐〕满的 fēngmǎnde.

chuck[1] /tʃʌk/ *v* [T] [非正式用语] 1 扔 rēng; 抛 pāo. 2 丢弃〔棄〕 diūqì; 放弃 fàngqì: *She's just ~ed her boyfriend*. 她刚刚甩掉

了她的男朋友.

chuck[2] /tʃʌk/ *n* [C] 1 车床〔牀〕的夹〔夾〕盘〔盤〕chēchuángde jiāpán. 2 夹头〔頭〕jiātóu.

chuckle /ˈtʃʌkl/ *v* [I] 抿着嘴轻〔輕〕声〔聲〕地笑 mǐnzhe zuǐ qīngshēngde xiào. **chuckle** *n* [C].

C

chum /tʃʌm/ *n* [C] [过时非正式用法]朋友 péngyou. **chummy** *adj* [-ier, -iest] 亲〔親〕密的 qīnmìde, 友好的 yǒuhǎode.

chump /tʃʌmp/ *n* [C] 1 [非正式用语]笨蛋 bèndàn. 2 厚肉块〔塊〕hòu ròukuài.

chunk /tʃʌŋk/ *n* [C] 1 厚块〔塊〕hòukuài. 2 [非正式用语]相当〔當〕大的数〔數〕量 xiāngdāng dà de shùliàng. **chunky** *adj* [-ier, -iest] 短粗的 duǎncūde.

church /tʃɜːtʃ/ *n* 1 [C] 基督教教堂 Jīdūjiào jiàotáng. 2 **Church** [C] 基督教教会〔會〕或教派 Jīdūjiào jiàohuì huò jiàopài: *the Anglican C~* 圣公会. 3 **the Church** [sing] 基督教牧师〔師〕的职〔職〕位 Jīdūjiào mùshi de zhíwèi; 神职 shénzhí: *go into/enter the C~* 担任神职. **ˈchurchyard** *n* [C] 教堂的墓地 jiàotángde mùdì.

churn /tʃɜːn/ *n* [C] 1 (制黄油用的)搅〔攪〕乳器 jiǎorǔqì. 2 大的盛奶罐 dàde chéngnǎiguàn. **churn** *v* 1 [T] 用搅乳器搅(乳等)(以制黄油) yòng jiǎorǔqì jiǎo. 2 [I, T] 剧〔劇〕烈搅拌 jùliè jiǎobàn. 3 [短语动词] **churn sth out** [非正式用语]粗制〔製〕滥造 cūzhì lànzào.

chute /ʃuːt/ *n* [C] 滑运〔運〕道 huáyùndào.

chutney /ˈtʃʌtnɪ/ *n* [U] 水果辣椒等混合制〔製〕成的辣酱〔醬〕shuǐguǒ làjiāo děng hùnhé zhìchéng de làjiàng.

cider /ˈsaɪdə(r)/ *n* [U] 苹〔蘋〕果酒 píngguǒjiǔ.

cigar /sɪˈgɑː(r)/ *n* [C] 雪茄烟 xuějiāyān.

cigarette /ˌsɪgəˈret; US ˈsɪgərət/ *n* [C] 香烟 xiāngyān; 纸烟 zhǐyān; 卷〔捲〕烟 juǎnyān.

cinder /ˈsɪndə(r)/ *n* [C, 常作 pl] 炉〔爐〕渣 lúzhā; 煤渣 méizhā.

cinema /ˈsɪnəmə; ˈsɪnəmɑː/ *n* 1 [C] 电〔電〕影院 diànyǐngyuàn. 2 [sing] 电影 diànyǐng; 电影工业〔業〕diànyǐng gōngyè.

cinnamon /ˈsɪnəmən/ *n* [U] 肉桂 ròuguì.

cipher (亦作 **cypher**) /ˈsaɪfə(r)/ *n* 1 [C, U] 密码 mìmǎ. 2 [C] [喻, 贬]不重要的人 bú zhòngyào de rén; 无〔無〕价〔價〕值的东西 wú jiàzhí de dōngxi.

circa /ˈsɜːkə/ *prep* [与年代连用]大约 dàyuē: *born ~ 150 BC* 约生于公元前 150 年.

circle /ˈsɜːkl/ *n* [C] 1 圆 yuán; 圆周 yuánzhōu. 2 圆形物 yuánxíngwù; 环〔環〕huán; 圈 quān. 3 圈子 quānzi; 集团〔團〕jítuán; 界 jiè: *our ~ of friends* 我们交游的朋友. 4 楼〔樓〕厅〔廳〕(剧场的二楼厅坐) lóutīng. **circle** *v* [I, T] 环绕〔繞〕huánrào; 盘〔盤〕旋 pánxuán.

circuit /ˈsɜːkɪt/ *n* [C] 1 圈道 quāndào; 环〔環〕行道 huánxíngdào: *a racing ~* 赛车道. 2 电〔電〕路 diànlù. 3 巡回〔迴〕旅行 xúnhuí lǚxíng: *a lecture ~* 巡回讲学旅行. **circuitous** /sɜːˈkjuːɪtəs/ *adj* 迂回的 yūhuíde; 绕〔繞〕行的 ràoxíngde: *a ~ous route* 迂回路线.

circular /ˈsɜːkjʊlə(r)/ *adj* 1 圆形的 yuánxíngde. 2 环〔環〕绕〔繞〕的 huánràode: *a ~ route* 环行路. **circular** *n* [C] 通知 tōngzhī; 通告 tōnggào; 通函 tōnghán.

circulate /ˈsɜːkjʊleɪt/ *v* [I, T] 1 循环〔環〕xúnhuán; 流通 liútōng. 2 流传〔傳〕liúchuán; 传播 chuánbō. **circulation** /ˌsɜːkjʊˈleɪʃn/ *n* 1 [C, U] 血液循环 xuèyè xúnhuán. 2 [U] (a) 传播 chuánbō: *the ~ of news* 消息的传播 (b) 流通 liútōng: *There are only a few of the new coins in ~.* 只有少数新的硬币在使用. 3 [C] 报〔報〕纸等的发〔發〕行量 bàozhǐ děng de fāxíngliàng.

circumcise /ˈsɜːkəmsaɪz/ *v* 环〔環〕割…的包皮 huángē …de bāopí. **circumcision** /ˌsɜːkəmˈsɪʒn/ *n* [C, U].

circumference /sɜːˈkʌmfərəns/ *n* [C] (a) 圆周 yuánzhōu. (b) 周围长〔長〕度 zhōuwéi chángdù: *the earth's ~* 地球的周长.

circumflex /ˈsɜːkəmfleks/ *n* [C] 元音字母上的声〔聲〕调符号〔號〕(如法语 rôle 上的 ˆ) yuányīn zìmǔ shàng de shēngdiào fúhào.

circumnavigate /ˌsɜːkəmˈnævɪgeɪt/ *v* [T] [正式用语]环〔環〕航 huánháng; 环球航行 huánqiú hángxíng. **circumnavigation** /ˌsɜːkəmˌnævɪˈgeɪʃn/ *n* [C, U].

circumspect /ˈsɜːkəmspekt/ *adj* 谨慎小心的 jǐnshèn xiǎoxīn de.

circumstance /ˈsɜːkəmstəns/ *n* 1 [C, 常作 pl]情况 qíngkuàng; 形势〔勢〕xíngshì; 环〔環〕境 huánjìng: *the ~s of his death* 他死亡时的情况. 2 **circumstances** [pl] 经〔經〕济〔濟〕状〔狀〕况 jīngjì zhuàngkuàng. 3 [习语] **in/under the circumstances** 在此种〔種〕情况下 zài cǐzhǒng qíngkuàng xià. **in/under no circumstances** 决不 juébù.

circumstantial /ˌsɜːkəmˈstænʃl/ *adj* 1 (证据)间接的 jiànjiēde. 2 (描述)详细的 xiángxìde; 详尽〔盡〕的 xiángjìnde.

circus /ˈsɜːkəs/ *n* [C] 1 马戏〔戲〕表演 mǎxì biǎoyǎn. 2 [英国英语](用于地名)几〔幾〕条〔條〕街道交叉处〔處〕的广〔廣〕场〔場〕jǐtiáo jiēdào jiāochāchù de guǎngchǎng: *Piccadilly C~* (伦敦)皮卡迪利广场.

cistern /ˈsɪstən/ *n* [C] (厕所等的)水箱 shuǐxiāng; 水槽 shuǐcáo.

cite /saɪt/ *v* [T] [正式用语]1 引用 yǐnyòng; 举〔舉〕例 jǔlì. 2 [法律]传〔傳〕讯 chuánxùn. **citation** /saɪˈteɪʃn/ *n* (a) [U] 引用 yǐnyòng; 引证〔證〕yǐnzhèng. (b) [C] 引文 yǐnwén.

C

citizen /ˈsɪtɪzn/ *n* [C] 1 公民 gōngmín. 2 市民 shìmín;城市居民 chéngshì jūmín. ˌ**citizens' ˈband** *n* [sing] 民用波段 mínyòng bōduàn. **citizenship** *n* [U] 公民或市民身份 gōngmín huò shìmín shēnfèn;公民的权〔權〕利和义〔義〕务〔務〕gōngmínde quánlì hé yìwù.

citric acid /ˌsɪtrɪk ˈæsɪd/ *n* [U] 柠〔檸〕檬酸 níngméngsuān.

citrus /ˈsɪtrəs/ *n* [C] 柑桔〔橘〕属〔屬〕植物 gānjúshǔ zhíwù: ~ *fruit* 柑桔属水果.

city /ˈsɪtɪ/ *n* [*pl* -ies] 1 [C] (a) 都市 dūshì;城市 chéngshì;享有特别自治权〔權〕之城市 xiǎngyǒu tèbié zìzhìquán zhī chéngshì. (b) [亦作 sing,用 pl v]全市居民 quánshì jūmín. 2 the City [sing]英国〔國〕伦〔倫〕敦之金融中心 Yīngguó Lúndūn zhī jīnróng zhōngxīn. **city aˈcademy** *n* [C] (英国) 城市学〔學〕院 chéngshì xuéyuàn.

civic /ˈsɪvɪk/ *adj* 城市的 chéngshìde;市民的 shìmínde.

civil /ˈsɪvl/ *adj* 1 公民的 gōngmínde. 2 民用的 mínyòngde; 平民的 píngmínde. 3 文明的 wénmíngde;有礼〔禮〕貌的 yǒu lǐmào de;客气〔氣〕的 kèqìde. ˌ**civil engiˈneering** *n* [U] 土木工程 tǔmùgōngchéng. **civility** /sɪˈvɪlətɪ/ [*pl* -ies][正式用语] 1 [U]礼貌 lǐmào;客气 kèqì. 2 [C,常用 pl]礼仪〔儀〕lǐyí;客套 kètào. **civilly** /ˈsɪvəlɪ/ *adj*. ˌ**civil ˈpartnership** *n* [C] (同性恋者的)民事伴侣关〔關〕系〔係〕mínshì bànlǚ guānxì. **civil rights** *n* [pl] 公民权〔權〕gōngmínquán. ˌ**civil ˈservant** *n* [C] 文职〔職〕公务〔務〕员 wénzhí gōngwùyuán. **the ˌCivil ˈService** *n* [sing] (a) 文职政府部门 wénzhí zhèngfǔ bùmén. (b)[用 sing 或 pl v] (总称)文职公务员 wénzhí gōngwùyuán. ˌ**civil ˈwar** *n* [C,U]内战〔戰〕nèizhàn.

civilian /sɪˈvɪlɪən/ *n*[C], *adj* 平民 píngmín;老百姓 lǎobǎixìng; 平民的 píngmínde; 民用的 mínyòngde; 民间的 mínjiānde.

civilization /ˌsɪvəlaɪˈzeɪʃn; *US* -əlɪˈz-/ *n* 1 [U] 开〔開〕化 kāihuà;教化 jiàohuà. 2[C] 文明 wénmíng; 文化 wénhuà.

civilize /ˈsɪvəlaɪz/ *v* [T] 1 使文明 shǐ wénmíng: *a ~d society* 文明社会. 2 教导〔導〕jiàodǎo;教育 jiàoyù.

clad /klæd/ *adj* [旧词或正式用语]穿…衣服的 chuān…yīfúde.

claim /kleɪm/ *v*[T] 1 宣称〔稱〕xuānchēng; 声〔聲〕言 shēngyán: *He ~s to be a British citizen*. 他声称是一位英国公民. 2 对〔對〕(权利)提出要求 duì tíchū yāoqiú. 3[正式用语](灾难等)造成…后〔後〕果 zàochéng…hòuguǒ: *The earthquake ~ed thousands of lives*. 这次地震造成成千上万人死亡. **claim** *n* 1 [C] 声称 shēngchēng; 断〔斷〕言 duànyán. 2 [C]权〔權〕利要求 quánlì yāoqiú: *an insurance ~* 保险索赔. 3 权利 quánlì. **claimant** *n* [C] 根据〔據〕权利提出法律上的要求的人 gēnjù quánlì tíchū fǎlǜ shàng de yāoqiú de rén.

clairvoyance /kleəˈvɔɪəns/ *n* [U] 洞察力 dòngchálì. **clairvoyant** /-ənt/ *n* [C], *adj* 有洞察力的人 yǒu dòngchálì de rén; (人)有洞察力的 yǒu dòngchálì de.

clam /klæm/ *n* [C]. **clam** *v* [-mm-] [短语动词] **clam up** 变〔變〕为〔爲〕沉默 biànwéi chénmò.

clamber /ˈklæmbə(r)/ *v* [I] 攀登 pāndēng; 爬 pá.

clammy /ˈklæmɪ/ *adj* [-ier, -iest] (天气)炎热〔熱〕而潮湿〔濕〕的 yánrè ér cháoshī de.

clamour (美语 -or) /ˈklæmə(r)/ *n* [C, U] 喧闹 xuānnào; 吵嚷 chǎorǎng. **clamour** *v* [I] (*for*) 吵吵闹闹地要求 chǎochǎonàonàode yāoqiú.

clamp /klæmp/ *n* [C] 螺丝钳 luósīqián. **clamp** *v* [T] 1 用螺丝钳夹〔夾〕yòng luósīqián jiā. 2[短语动词] **clamp down on sb / sth** 取缔 qǔdì; 压〔壓〕制 yāzhì. ˈ**clamp-down** *n* [C].

clan /klæn/ *n* [C] 氏族 shìzú; 苏〔蘇〕格兰〔蘭〕高地人的氏族 sūgélángāodìrén de shìzú.

clandestine /klænˈdestɪn/ *adj* [正式用语] 秘密的 mìmìde; 私下的 sīxiàde.

clang /klæŋ/ *n* [C] 铿〔鏗〕锵〔鏘〕声〔聲〕kēngqiāngshēng. **clang** *v* [I, T] (使)发〔發〕铿锵声 fā kēngqiāngshēng.

clank /klæŋk/ *n* [C] (金属链相击的)丁当〔當〕声〔聲〕dīngdāngshēng. **clank** *v* [I, T] (使)发〔發〕丁当声 fā dīngdāngshēng.

clap /klæp/ *v* [-pp-] 1 [I, T] 拍手喝彩 pāishǒu hècǎi. 2 用手轻〔輕〕拍 yòng shǒu qīngpāi. 3[非正式用语]猛推(入狱) měngtuī. **clap** *n* [C] 1 拍手喝彩(声) pāishǒu hècǎi. 2 霹雳〔靂〕声〔聲〕pīlìshēng. ˌ**clapped ˈout** *adj* [英国非正式用语]破旧〔舊〕不堪的 pòjiù bùkān de: *a ~ped out old car* 一辆破旧不堪的汽车.

claret /ˈklærət/ *n* [U, C] 法国〔國〕波尔〔爾〕多红葡萄酒 Fǎguó pō'ěrduō hóngpútáojiǔ. **claret** *adj* 紫红色的 zǐhóngsède.

clarify /ˈklærɪfaɪ/ *v* [*pt*, *pp* -ied] [T] 使清晰明了 shǐ qīngxī míngliǎo. **clarification** /ˌklærɪfɪˈkeɪʃn/ *n* [U].

clarinet /ˌklærɪˈnet/ *n* [C] 单〔單〕簧管 dānhuángguǎn. **clarinettist** *n* [C] 单簧管演奏者 dānhuángguǎn yǎnzòuzhě.

clarity /ˈklærətɪ/ *n* [U] 清澈 qīngchè; 明晰 míngxī.

clash /klæʃ/ *v* 1 [I] 发〔發〕生冲〔衝〕突 fāshēng chōngtū; 争论〔論〕zhēnglùn. 2 [I]不协〔協〕调 bù xiétiáo; 不一致 bù yízhì. 3 [I] (事情)发生时〔時〕间上的冲突 fāshēng shíjiān shàng de chōngtū. 4 [I, T]发出刺耳的冲击〔擊〕

声〔聲〕fāchū cì'ěrde chōngjīshēng. **clash** *n* [C] 1 抵触〔觸〕dǐchù;不一致 bù yízhì. 2 碰撞声 pèngzhuàngshēng.

clasp /klɑːsp; *US* klæsp/ *n* [C] 1 扣子 kòuzi; 扣紧〔緊〕物(如书夹子等) kòujǐnwù. 2 紧握 jǐnwò; 拥〔擁〕抱 yōngbào. **clasp** *v* [T] 1 拥抱 yōngbào. 2 扣住 kòuzhù.

C

class /klɑːs; *US* klæs/ *n* 1 (a) [C]阶〔階〕级 jiējí: *the middle ~es* 中等阶级. (b)[U] 阶级制度 jiējí zhìdù. 2 [C](a) (学校的)年级 niánjí. (b)课 kè;上课 shàngkè. 3[C](质量的)等级 děngjí. 4[U][非正式用语]优〔優〕雅 yōuyǎ; 精致〔緻〕jīngzhì. **class** *v* [T]把…分入某等级 bǎ…fēnrù mǒuděngjí. ˈ**classroom** *n* [C]教室 jiàoshì. **classy** *adj* [-ier, -iest][非正式用语]时〔時〕髦的 shímáode;漂亮的 piàoliàngde.

classic /ˈklæsɪk/ *adj* 1 典型的 diǎnxíngde: *a ~ example* 典型的例子. 2 第一流的 dìyīliúde;最优〔優〕秀的 zuìyōuxiùde: *a ~ film* 第一流的影片. **classic** *n* 1 [C]文豪 wénháo; 艺〔藝〕术〔術〕大师〔師〕yìshù dàshī; 名著 míngzhù. 2 **classics** [用 sing v] 古希腊〔臘〕、罗〔羅〕马〔馬〕的语文和文学〔學〕经〔經〕典 gǔxīlà、luómǎ de yǔwén hé wénxué jīngdiǎn; 古希腊、罗马文学、语文研究 gǔxīlà、luómǎ wénxué、yǔwén yánjiū.

classical /ˈklæsɪkl/ *adj* 1 古希腊〔臘〕罗〔羅〕马〔馬〕风〔風〕格的 gǔxīlà luómǎ fēnggéde. 2 传〔傳〕统的 chuántǒngde. 3(音乐)古典的 gǔdiǎnde. **classically** /-klɪ/ *adv*.

classify /ˈklæsɪfaɪ/ *v* [*pt*, *pp* -ied][T] 把…分类〔類〕bǎ…fēnlèi. 把…分等级 bǎ… fēn děngjí. **classification** /ˌklæsɪfɪˈkeɪʃn/ *n* [C,U]. **classified** *adj* 机〔機〕密的 jīmìde; 保密的 bǎomìde.

clatter /ˈklætə(r)/ *n* [sing](物体碰击的)卡嗒声〔聲〕kādāshēng. **clatter** *v* [I]发〔發〕出卡嗒声 fāchū kādāshēng.

clause /klɔːz/ *n* [C] 1[语法]子句 zǐjù; 从〔從〕句 cóngjù. 2 [法律]条〔條〕款 tiáokuǎn.

claustrophobia /ˌklɔːstrəˈfəʊbɪə/ *n* [U] 幽闭恐怖 yōubì kǒngbù.

claw /klɔː/ *n* [C] 1 爪 zhǎo; 脚爪 jiǎozhǎo. 2 蟹等的钳、螯 xiè děng de qián、áo. 3 爪形器具 zhuǎxíng qìjù. **claw** *v* [I,T] (*at*) 用爪抓 yòng zhǎo zhuā; 搔 sāo.

clay /kleɪ/ *n* [U] 黏土 niántǔ; 泥土 nítǔ.

clean[1] /kliːn/ *adj* 1 清洁〔潔〕的 qīngjiéde; 干〔乾〕净的 gānjìngde. 2 没有用过〔過〕的 méiyǒu yòngguò de: *a ~ piece of paper* 一张没有用过的纸. 3 纯洁的 chúnjiéde; 清白的 qīngbáide: *a ~ joke* 文雅的玩笑. 4 匀称〔稱〕的 yúnchènde; 规则的 guīzéde: *a ~ cut* 干净利落的切削. 5[习语] **make a clean** ˈ**breast of sth** 彻〔徹〕底坦白 chèdǐ tǎnbái. **clean** *adv*. 1 彻底地 chèdǐde; 完全地 wánquánde: *I ~ forgot it*. 我把它完全忘了. 2 [习语] **come clean** 全盘〔盤〕招供 quánpán zhāogòng. ˌ**clean-**ˈ**cut** *adj* 1 轮〔輪〕廓鲜明的 lúnkuò xiānmíng de. 2 整洁的 zhěngjiéde. ˌ**clean-**ˈ**shaven** *adj* 脸〔臉〕刮得光光的 liǎn guā de guāngguāng de.

clean[2] /kliːn/ *v* 1 [T]使干〔乾〕净 shǐ gānjìng. 2 [短语动词]**clean sb out** [非正式用语]耗尽〔盡〕…的钱〔錢〕财 hàojìn…de qiáncái. **clean sth out** 打扫〔掃〕干净 dǎsǎo gānjìng;打扫内部 dǎsǎo nèibù. **clean (sth) up** (a) 清除(污物等) qīngchú. (b)[非正式用语]赚钱 zhuànqián. **clean sth up** 清除不法现象 qīngchú bùfǎ xiànxiàng. **clean** *n* [sing] 打扫 dǎsǎo; 清洁〔潔〕qīngjié. **cleaner** *n* [C] 1 清洁工 qīngjiégōng; 清洁器 qīngjiéqì: *a* ˈ*vacuum-~* 真空吸尘器. 2 干洗店 gānxǐdiàn.

cleanliness /ˈklenlɪnəs/ *n* [U] 清洁〔潔〕qīngjié;干〔乾〕净 gānjìng.

cleanly /ˈkliːnlɪ/ *adv* 利落地 lìluode.

cleanse /klenz/ *v* [T] 使纯洁〔潔〕shǐ chúnjié; 净化 jìnghuà. **cleanser** *n* [C]清洁剂〔劑〕qīngjiéjì.

clear[1] /klɪə(r)/ *adj* 1 清澈的 qīngchède; 透明的 tòumíngde: *~ glass* 透明的玻璃. 2 清楚的 qīngchude: *a ~ explanation of the problems* 对问题的清楚的解释. 3 明显〔顯〕的 míngxiǎnde; 不含糊的 bù hánhude: *a ~ case of cheating* 明显的诈骗案. 4 明确〔確〕的 míngquède;无〔無〕疑的 wúyíde: *I'm not ~ about what I should do*. 我不明确我应该做什么. 5 无障碍〔礙〕的 wú zhàng'ài de; 无阻的 wúzǔde. 6 (*of*) 不接触〔觸〕…的 bù jiēchù…de. 7 晴朗的 qínglǎngde: *a ~ sky* 晴朗的天空. 8 无瑕疵的 wú xiácīde: *~ skin* 光洁的皮肤. 9 清白的 qīngbáide; 无罪的 wúzuìde: *a ~ conscience* 清白的良心. 10 (钱数等)整整的 zhěngzhěngde; 净的 jìngde: *~ profit* 净利. 11 [习语] **make sth /oneself** ˈ**clear** 把…表达〔達〕清楚 bǎ…biǎodá qīngchu. **clear** *n* [习语] **in the** ˈ**clear** [非正式用语]无危险〔險〕的 wú wēixiǎnde; 清白无辜的 qīngbái wúgū de. **clear** *adv* 1 清楚地 qīngchude;清晰地 qīngxīde: *I can hear you loud and ~*. 我能听清楚你响亮的声音. 2 十分地 shífēnde; 完全地 wánquánde: *The prisoner got ~ away*. 这囚徒逃得无影无踪. 3 不阻碍 bù zǔ'ài: *Stand ~ of the door*. 别站在那里挡着门. 4[习语]**keep/stay/steer clear of sb/sth** 避开〔開〕bìkāi; 躲开 duǒkāi. ˌ**clear-**ˈ**cut** *adj* 容易理解的 róngyì lǐjiěde; 不含混的 bù hánhùnde. ˌ**clear-**ˈ**headed** *adj* 头〔頭〕脑〔腦〕清楚的 tóunǎo qīngchude. **clearly** *adv* 清楚地

qīngchude；明显地 míngxiǎnde. ˌclear-ˈsighted *adj* 理解清楚的 lǐjiě qīngchude；思维清楚的 sīwéi qīngchude.

clear[2] /klɪə(r)/ *v* 1 [T]清除 qīngchú；扫〔掃〕清 sǎoqīng. 2 [T]越过〔過〕而未触〔觸〕及 yuèguò ér wèi chùjí：*The horse ～ed the fence*. 马跃过栅栏. 3 [I](雾霭)逐渐消散 zhújiàn xiāosàn. 4 [T] 批准 pīzhǔn. 5 [T] (*of*)宣告…无〔無〕罪 xuāngào…wúzuì. 6 [习语] **clear the ˈair** 消除恐惧〔懼〕、猜疑气〔氣〕氛 xiāochú kǒngjù、cāiyí qìfēn. 7 [短语动词] **clear (sth) away** 清除 qīngchú. **clear off** [非正式用语](从…)走开〔開〕zǒukāi，溜掉 liūdiào. **clear out (of)** [非正式用语]离〔離〕开 líkāi. **clear sth out** 清理 qīnglǐ；出空 chūkōng：～ *out the cupboards* 清理碗橱. **clear up** (天气)晴朗起来 qínglǎng qǐlái. **clear (sth) up** 使整洁〔潔〕shǐ zhěngjié. **clear sth up** 澄清 chéngqīng；解除 jiěchú：～ *up a mystery* 消除疑团.

clearance /ˈklɪərəns/ *n* 1 [C,U]清除 qīngchú；清理 qīnglǐ；出清 chūqīng. 2 [C,U] 净空 jìngkōng：～ *under a bridge* 桥下的净空. 3 [U]许可 xǔkě.

clearing /ˈklɪərɪŋ/ *n* [C] 林中空地 línzhōng kòngdì.

cleavage /ˈkliːvɪdʒ/ *n* [C] 1 (妇女两乳之间的)胸槽 xiōngcáo. 2 [正式用语]分裂 fēnliè；开〔開〕裂 kāiliè.

clef /klef/ *n* [C] 音乐〔樂〕谱号〔號〕yīnyuè pǔhào.

clemency /ˈklemənsɪ/ *n* [U] [正式用语]仁慈 réncí.

clench /klentʃ/ *v* [T] 紧〔緊〕握 jǐnwò；压〔壓〕紧 yājǐn：～ *one's fist* 攥紧拳头.

clergy /ˈklɜːdʒɪ/ *n* [pl]正式委任的牧师〔師〕、教士 zhèngshì wěirèn de mùshi、jiàoshì. **clergyman** /ˈklɜːdʒɪmən/ *n* [C] 牧师 mùshi；教士 jiàoshì.

clerical /ˈklerɪkl/ *adj* 1 办〔辦〕事员的 bànshìyuánde. 2 牧师的 mùshide；教士的 jiàoshìde.

clerk /klɑːk; *US* klɜːrk/ *n* [C] 职〔職〕员 zhíyuán；办〔辦〕事员 bànshìyuán；秘书〔書〕mìshū.

clever /ˈklevə(r)/ *adj* 1 聪〔聰〕明的 cōngmingde；伶俐的 línglìde. 2 精巧的 jīngqiǎode；机〔機〕敏的 jīmǐnde. **cleverly** *adv*. **cleverness** *n* [U].

cliché /ˈkliːʃeɪ; *US* kliːˈʃeɪ/ *n* [C] 陈腐思想 chénfǔ sīxiǎng；陈词滥〔濫〕调 chéncí làndiào.

click /klɪk/ *n* [C] 卡嗒声〔聲〕(类似钥匙在锁中转动的声音) kādā shēng. **click** *v* 1 [I,T] 发〔發〕卡嗒声 fā kādāshēng. 2 [I] [非正式用语]突然变〔變〕得明白 tūrán biànde míngbai. **click** *v* 点〔點〕击〔擊〕diǎnjī：～ **on the icon** 点击该图标. ～ **the left mouse button** 点击鼠标左键.

client /ˈklaɪənt/ *n* [C] 1 律师〔師〕等的当〔當〕事人、委托人 lǜshī děng de dāngshìrén、wěituōrén. 2 商店顾〔顧〕客 shāngdiàn gùkè.

clientele /ˌkliːənˈtel; *US* ˌklaɪən-/ *n* [sing][用 sing 或 pl v] [集合名词]顾〔顧〕客 gùkè；当〔當〕事人 dāngshìrén.

cliff /klɪf/ *n* [C] 悬〔懸〕崖 xuányá；(尤指海边的)峭壁 qiàobì.

climactic /ˌklaɪˈmæktɪk/ *adj* [正式用语]形成高潮的 xíngchéng gāocháo de.

climate /ˈklaɪmɪt/ *n* 1 [C,U] 气〔氣〕候 qìhòu. 2 [C]社会〔會〕趋〔趨〕势〔勢〕shèhuì qūshì. **climatic** /ˌklaɪˈmætɪk/ *adj*. ˈ**climate change** *n* [U] 气〔氣〕候变〔變〕化 qìhòu biànhuà.

climax /ˈklaɪmæks/ *n* [C] 顶点〔點〕dǐngdiǎn；小说等的高潮 xiǎoshuō děng de gāocháo. **climax** *v* [I,T](使)达〔達〕到高潮 dádào gāocháo.

climb /klaɪm/ *v* 1 [I,T] 攀登 pāndēng；爬 pá. 2 [I]攀爬 pānpá：～ *out of the lorry* 爬出卡车. 3 [I](飞机)爬升 páshēng. 4 [I](植物)攀缘向上 pānyuán xiàngshàng. 5 [习语] **climb on the bandwagon** ⇨BAND. 6 [短语动词] **climb down** [非正式用语]认〔認〕错 rèncuò. **climb** *n* [C] 1 攀登 pāndēng；爬升 páshēng. 2 攀登的地方 pāndēngde dìfang；山坡 shānpō. ˈ**climb-down** *n* [C] 认错 rèncuò. **climber** *n* [C] 1 攀登者 pāndēngzhě. 2 攀缘植物 pānyuán zhíwù.

clinch /klɪntʃ/ *v* [T] 1 [非正式用语]确〔確〕定 quèdìng；决定 juédìng. 2 拥〔擁〕抱 yōngbào. **clinch** *n* [C] 拥抱 yōngbào.

cling /klɪŋ/ *v* [*pt*, *pp* **clung** /klʌŋ/] [I]抱紧〔緊〕bàojǐn；坚〔堅〕守 jiānshǒu. ˈ**cling film** *n* [U] 保鲜纸 bǎoxiānzhǐ. 保鲜膜 bǎoxiānmó.

clinic /ˈklɪnɪk/ *n* [C] 诊所 zhěnsuǒ；门诊所 ménzhěnsuǒ：*a children's* ～ 儿童诊所. **clinical** *adj* 1 临〔臨〕床〔牀〕的 línchuángde；临诊的 línzhěnde. 2 冷静的 lěngjìngde. 3 (房间或建筑物)简朴〔樸〕的 jiǎnpǔde；朴素的 pǔsùde.

clink /klɪŋk/ *n* [C] 丁当〔當〕声〔聲〕dīngdāngshēng. **clink** *v* [I,T]丁当作响〔響〕dīngdāng zuòxiǎng；使作丁当声 shǐ zuò dīngdāngshēng.

clip[1] /klɪp/ *n* [C] 回形针 huíxíngzhēn；夹〔夾〕子 jiāzi：*a paper*-～ 回形针. **clip** *v* [-pp-] [I, T] 夹住 jiāzhù；钳牢 qiánláo. ˈ**clipboard** *n* [C]带〔帶〕夹〔夾〕子的写〔寫〕字板 dài jiāzide xiězìbǎn.

clip[2] /klɪp/ *v* [-pp-] [T] 1 剪短 jiǎnduǎn；剪整齐〔齊〕jiǎn zhěngqí. 2 [非正式用语]猛击〔擊〕měngjī；痛打 tòngdǎ. **clip** *n* [C] 1 剪 jiǎn；剪短 jiǎnduǎn；修剪 xiūjiǎn. 2 [非正式用语]猛打 měngdǎ. **clippers** *n* [pl] 剪刀 jiǎn-

C

dāo；修剪器 xiūjiǎnqì. **clipping** *n* [C] 1 剪下物 jiǎnxiàwù. 2 [尤用于美语]剪报〔報〕jiǎnbào.

clique /kliːk/ *n* [C][常作贬]派系 pàixì；小集团〔團〕xiǎojítuán.

C

cloak /kləʊk/ *n* [C] 1 斗篷 dǒu peng；大氅 dàchǎng. 2[sing][喻]遮盖物 zhēgàiwù：*a ~ of secrecy* 笼罩着神秘气氛. **cloak** *v* [T] 掩盖 yǎngài；包藏 bāocáng. ˈ**cloakroom** *n* [C] 1 衣帽间 yīmàojiān. 2[英国英语，委婉]厕所 cèsuǒ.

clock /klɒk/ *n* 1[C] 时〔時〕钟〔鐘〕shízhōng. 2[习语] **put/turn the clock back** 倒退 dàotuì. **round the ˈclock** 连续〔續〕一昼〔晝〕夜 liánxù yí zhòuyè；日夜不停地 rìyè bùtíngde. **clock** *v* 1 [T]测量…的时间 cèliáng…de shíjiān. 2[短语动词]**clock in / out** (用自动计时钟)记录〔錄〕上(下)班时间 jìlù shàngbān shíjiān. **clock sth up** 达〔達〕到（某一时间、速度）dádào. ˈ**clockwise** *adv, adj* 顺时针方向(的) shùn shízhēn fāngxiàng. ˈ**clockwork** *n* [U] 1 钟表机〔機〕械 zhōngbiǎo jīxiè；发〔發〕条〔條〕装〔裝〕置 fātiáo zhuāngzhì. 2[习语] **like ˈclockwork** 顺利地 shùnlìde.

clod /klɒd/ *n* [C] 土块〔塊〕tǔkuài；泥块 níkuài.

clog[1] /klɒg/ *n* [C] 木底鞋 mùdǐxié.

clog[2] /klɒg/ [-gg-] [I,T](*up*)阻塞 zǔsè；填塞 tiánsè.

cloister /ˈklɔɪstə(r)/ *n* [C] 回廊 huíláng；走廊 zǒuláng. **cloistered** *adj* 隐〔隱〕居的 yǐnjūde.

clone /kləʊn/ *n* (生物)无〔無〕性繁殖(系) wúxìng fánzhí；克隆 kèlóng. **clone** *v* [I,T] (使)无性繁殖 wúxìng fánzhí；克隆 kèlóng.

close[1] /kləʊz/ *v* 1 [I,T]关〔關〕guān；闭 bì；合起 héqǐ：*~ the door* 关门. *The shop ~s at 5pm*. 这家商店下午五时停止营业. 2[I,T] (使)终止 zhōngzhǐ；(使)停止 tíngzhǐ：*~ a meeting* 结束会议. 3[习语] **close one's ˈeyes to sth** 无〔無〕视 wúshì. 4[短语动词] ˈ**close down** (电台、电视台)停止广〔廣〕播 tíngzhǐ guǎngbō. **close (sth) down** 歇业〔業〕xiēyè. **close in (on sb/sth)** 迫近 pòjìn；包围〔圍〕bāowéi. **close** *n* [sing][正式用语](时间或活动的)结束 jiéshù：*at the ~ of the day* 在黄昏时候. ˌ**closed-ˌcircuit ˈtelevision** *n* [U] 闭路电〔電〕视 bìlù diànshì. ˈ**closed-down** *n* [C] 关闭 guānbì. **closed ˈshop** *n* [C](根据劳资协议)只雇用工会〔會〕会员的企业 zhǐ gùyòng gōnghuì huìyuánde qǐyè.

close[2] /kləʊs/ *adj* [~r, ~st] 1 接近的 jiējìnde. 2(a)关〔關〕系〔係〕接近的 guānxì jiējìnde：*~ relatives* 近亲.(b)亲〔親〕密的 qīnmìde：*a ~ friend* 亲密的朋友. 3 严〔嚴〕密的 yánmìde；彻〔徹〕底的 chèdǐde：*~ inspection* 严密的审查. 4 比分接近的 bǐfēn jiējìnde：*a ~ race* 势均力敌的竞赛. 5 闷热〔熱〕的 mēnrède. 6[习语] **a ˌclose ˈcall/ˈshave** 幸免于难〔難〕xìngmiǎn yú nàn. **close** *adv* 紧〔緊〕密地 jǐnmìde：*follow ~ behind* 紧跟在后面. ˌ**close-ˈfitting** *adj* (衣服)紧身的 jǐnshēnde. ˌ**close-ˈknit** *adj* (人群)紧密结合的 jǐnmì jiéhéde. **closely** *adv*. **closeness** *n* [U]. ˌ**close-ˈset** *adj* 紧靠在一起的 jǐnkào zài yìqǐ de：ˌ*~-set ˈeyes* 靠在一起的眼睛. ˈ**close-up** *n* [C] (照相等的)特写〔寫〕镜头〔頭〕tèxiě jìngtóu.

close[3] /kləʊs/ *n* [C] 1 (不通行的)死路 sǐlù. 2(大教堂等的)围〔圍〕地 wéidì，院子 yuànzi.

closet /ˈklɒzɪt/ *n* [C] [尤用于美语]小储藏室 xiǎo chǔcángshì. **closet** *adj* 秘密的 mìmìde. **closet** *v* [T]把…关〔關〕在小房间里〔裏〕bǎ…guān zài xiǎo fángjiān lǐ.

closure /ˈkləʊʒə(r)/ *n* [C,U] 关〔關〕闭〔閉〕guānbì：*the ~ of a factory* 工厂的关闭.

clot /klɒt/ *n* [C] 1 血等的凝块〔塊〕xuè děng de níngkuài；泥块 níkuài. 2[英国非正式用语]傻〔傻〕子 shǎzi；蠢人 chǔnrén. **clot** *v* [-tt-] [I,T](使)(血等)凝块 níngkuài.

cloth /klɒθ; *US* klɔːθ/ *n* (a) [U] *n* (棉花、羊毛等的)布，织〔織〕物 bù, zhīwù. (b)[C] 布块 bùkuài：*a table ~* 桌布.

clothe /kləʊð/ *v*[T] 供给…衣穿 gōngjǐ…yī chuān.

clothes /kləʊðz; *US* kləʊz/ *n* [pl] 衣服 yīfu；服装〔裝〕fúzhuāng. ˈ**clothes-horse** *n*[C] (尤指室内的)晾衣架 liàngyījià. ˈ**clothes-line** *n* [C] 晾衣绳〔繩〕liàngyīshéng. ˈ**clothes-peg** *n* [C] (晾衣用的)衣夹〔夾〕yījiā.

clothing /ˈkləʊðɪŋ/ *n* [U] [集合名词]衣服 yīfu.

cloud /klaʊd/ *n* 1[C,U] 云〔雲〕yún. 2[C](空中成团的)尘〔塵〕chén，烟 yān. 3[C][喻]引起悲伤〔傷〕、恐惧〔懼〕之物 yǐnqǐ bēishāng、kǒngjù zhī wù：*the ~s of war* 战云. 4[习语] **under a ˈcloud** 名誉〔譽〕扫〔掃〕地 míngyù sǎodì；受嫌疑 shòu xiányí. **cloud** *v* 1 [I,T]变〔變〕得不清楚 biàndé bù qīngchu；使不清楚 shǐ bù qīngchu：*The sky ~ed over*. 天空阴云密布. 2 [T]使混乱〔亂〕shǐ hùnluàn **cloudy** *adj* [-ier, -iest] 1 有云的 yǒuyúnde；阴〔陰〕的 yīnde. 2 含糊的 hánhude；混浊〔濁〕的 hùnzhuóde.

clout /klaʊt/ *v* [T][非正式用语]敲击〔擊〕qiāojī；掌击 zhǎngjī. **clout** *n* [非正式用语] 1 [C]敲击 qiāojī；掌击 zhǎngjī. 2 [U]影响〔響〕yǐngxiǎng；门路 ménlù.

clove[1] /kləʊv/ *n* [C] 丁香 dīngxiāng.

clove[2] /kləʊv/ *n* [C] 小鳞茎〔莖〕xiǎo línjīng：*a ~ of garlic* 一瓣蒜.

clover /ˈkləʊvə(r)/ *n* [C, U] 三叶〔葉〕草 sānyècǎo.

clown /klaʊn/ *n* [C] (a)(马戏等)小丑 xiǎochǒu; 丑角 chǒujué. (b)行动〔動〕像小丑的人 xíngdòng xiàng xiǎochǒu de rén. **clown** *v* [I] 做出小丑似的行为〔爲〕 zuòchū xiǎochǒu shì de xíngwéi.

club /klʌb/ *n* [C] 1(a)俱乐〔樂〕部 jùlèbù; 会〔會〕huì; 社 shè. (b)俱乐部的会所 jùlèbùde huìsuǒ. 2 棍棒 gùnbàng. 3 高尔〔爾〕夫球球棒 gāo'ěrfūqiú qiúbàng. 4(纸牌)梅花 méihuā. **club** *v* [-bb-] 1 [T]用棍棒打 yòng gùnbàng dǎ. 2[短语动词]**club together** 凑钱〔錢〕 còuqián; 分摊〔攤〕费用 fēntān fèiyòng.

cluck /klʌk/ *v* [I], *n* [C] 咯咯叫 gēgē jiào; 咯咯声〔聲〕 gēgēshēng.

clue /kluː/ *n* [C] 1 线〔綫〕索 xiànsuǒ. 2[习语]**not have a ˈclue** [非正式用语]一无〔無〕所知 yī wú suǒ zhī. **clueless** *adj* [非正式用语, 贬]愚蠢的 yúchǔnde.

clump[1] /klʌmp/ *n* [C] (树、灌木)丛〔叢〕 cóng.

clump[2] /klʌmp/ *v* [I] 用沉重的脚步行走 yòng chénzhòngde jiǎobù xíngzǒu.

clumsy /ˈklʌmzɪ/ *adj* [-ier, -iest] 1 笨拙的 bènzhuóde. 2 不好使用的 bùhǎo shǐyòng de. 3 不灵〔靈〕活的 bù línghuóde. **clumsily** *adv*. **clumsiness** *n* [U].

clung /klʌŋ/ *pt*, *pp* of CLING.

cluster /ˈklʌstə(r)/ *n* [C] 一串 yíchuàn; 一簇 yícù; 一组 yìzǔ. **cluster** *v* [I] 群集 qúnjí; 丛〔叢〕生 cóngshēng.

clutch[1] /klʌtʃ/ *v* [I, T] 抓住 zhuāzhù; 攫住 juézhù. **clutch** *n* 1 [C] 抓 zhuā; 攫 jué. 2 **clutches** [pl][非正式用语]控制 kòngzhì: *be in sb's ~es* 在某人的控制下. 3 [C]离〔離〕合器 líhéqì.

clutch[2] /klʌtʃ/ *n* [C] 一窝蛋 yìwōdàn.

clutter /ˈklʌtə(r)/ *n* [U] 零乱〔亂〕 língluàn; 杂〔雜〕乱 záluàn. **clutter** *v*[T] 把…弄乱 bǎ… nòngluàn.

cm *abbr* [*pl* **cm** 或 **~s**] centimetre(s) 厘〔釐〕米 límǐ.

CND /ˌsiː en ˈdiː/ *abbr* Campaign for Nuclear Disarmament 核裁军运〔運〕动〔動〕 hécáijūn yùndòng.

Co. *abbr* company 公司 gōngsī.

c/o /ˌsiːˈəʊ/ *abbr* (信封上用语) care of 由…转〔轉〕交 yóu…zhuǎnjiāo.

coach[1] /kəʊtʃ/ *n* [C] 1 长途公共汽车 chángtú gōnggòng qìchē. 2 铁〔鐵〕路客车 tiělù kèchē. 3 公共马车 gōnggòng mǎchē.

coach[2] /kəʊtʃ/ *v* [T] 辅导〔導〕 fǔdǎo; 训练〔練〕 xùnliàn. **coach** *n* [C] 私人教师〔師〕 sīrén jiàoshī; 体〔體〕育教练 tǐyù jiàoliàn.

coagulate /ˌkəʊˈægjʊleɪt/ *v* [I, T] 使凝结 shǐ níngjié; 凝结 níngjié.

coal /kəʊl/ *n* [C, U] 煤 méi. ˈ**coal-face** *n* [C] 采〔採〕煤工作面 cǎiméi gōngzuòmiàn. ˈ**coal-field** *n* [C] 煤田 méitián; 产〔產〕煤区〔區〕 chǎnméiqū. ˈ**coal-mine** *n* [C] 煤矿〔礦〕 méikuàng. ˈ**coal-miner** *n* [C] 煤矿工人 méikuàng gōngrén.

coalesce /ˌkəʊəˈles/ *v* [I][正式用语]接合 jiēhé; 结合 jiéhé.

coalition /ˌkəʊəˈlɪʃn/ *n* [C] (政党等)联〔聯〕盟 liánméng.

coarse /kɔːs/ *adj* [~r, ~st] 1 粗的 cūde; 粗糙的 cūcāode. 2(语言等)粗俗的 cūsúde; 粗鲁的 cūlǔde. **coarsely** *adv*. **coarsen** /ˈkɔːsn/ *v* [I, T] 变〔變〕粗 biàn cū; 使粗 shǐ cū. **coarseness** *n*[U].

coast /kəʊst/ *n* [C] 1 海岸 hǎi'àn; 海滨〔濱〕 hǎibīn. 2 [习语]**the ˌcoast is ˈclear** [非正式用语]危险〔險〕已过〔過〕 wēixiǎn yǐguò. **coast** *v* [I]顺坡滑行 shùn pō huáxíng. **coastal** *adj*. ˈ**coastguard** *n* [C, 亦作 sing, 用 pl v]海岸警卫〔衛〕队〔隊〕 hǎi'àn jǐngwèiduì. ˈ**coastline** *n* [C]海岸线〔綫〕 hǎi'ànxiàn.

coat /kəʊt/ *n* [C] 1 外套 wàitào; 上衣 shàngyī. 2 动〔動〕物皮毛 dòngwù pímáo. 3 涂〔塗〕层〔層〕 túcéng; 膜 mó: *a ~ of paint* 一层漆. **coat** *v* [T] 涂以油漆等 tú yǐ yóuqī děng. ˈ**coat-hanger** *n* [C]衣架 yījià. **coating** *n* [C] 涂层 túcéng. ˌ**coat of ˈarms** *n* [C]盾形纹章 dùnxíng wénzhāng.

coax /kəʊks/ *v*[T] 1 劝〔勸〕诱 quànyòu. 2[短语动词]**coax sth out of/from sb** 哄出 hǒngchū; 诱出 yòuchū.

cob /kɒb/ *n* [C] 1 矮脚马 ǎijiǎomǎ. 2 雄天鹅 xióng tiān'é. 3 CORN-COB (CORN[1]).

cobble[1] /ˈkɒbl/ *n* [C] (亦作 ˈ**cobblestone**)(铺路等用的)大鹅卵石 dà éluǎnshí; 圆石块〔塊〕 yuánshíkuài. **cobbled** *adj*.

cobble[2] /ˈkɒbl/ *v* [短语动词]**cobble sth together** 草率地拼凑起来 cǎoshuàide pīncòu qǐlái.

cobbler /ˈkɒblə(r)/ *n* [C] 修鞋匠 xiūxiéjiàng.

cobra /ˈkəʊbrə/ *n* [C] 眼镜蛇 yǎnjìngshé.

cobweb /ˈkɒbweb/ *n* [C] 蜘蛛网〔網〕 zhīzhūwǎng.

cocaine /kəʊˈkeɪn/ *n* [U] 可卡因 kěkǎyīn.

cock[1] /kɒk/ *n* [C] 雄禽 xióngqín; 公鸡〔鷄〕 gōngjī.

cock[2] /kɒk/ *n* [C] 1 开〔開〕关〔關〕 kāiguān; 龙〔龍〕头〔頭〕 lóngtóu; 旋塞 xuánsāi. 2(枪的)击〔擊〕铁〔鐵〕 jītiě.

cock[3] /kɒk/ *v*[T] 1 使翘〔翹〕起 shǐ qiàoqǐ; 竖〔豎〕起 shùqǐ: *The horse ~ed its ears.*

马竖起了耳朵. 2 扳起(枪)的击〔擊〕铁〔鐵〕 bānqǐ de jītiě. 3 [短语动词]cock sth up[英国非正式用语]把…弄糟 bǎ… nòngzāo. 'cock-up *n* [C][英国非正式用语]大错 dàcuò.

cockatoo /ˌkɒkəˈtuː/ *n* [C] [*pl* ~s] 白鹦 báiyīng.

C

cockerel /ˈkɒkərəl/ *n* [C] 小公鸡〔鷄〕 xiǎo gōngjī.

cock-eyed /ˈkɒkaɪd/ *adj* [非正式用语] 1 斜的 xiéde;歪的 wāide. 2 荒谬的 huāngmiùde: *a ~ plan* 荒谬的计划.

cockle /ˈkɒkl/ *n*[C] 鸟蛤 niǎogé.

cockney /ˈkɒknɪ/ *n* (a)[C]伦〔倫〕敦东区〔區〕佬 Lúndūn dōngqūlǎo;伦敦佬 Lúndūnlǎo. (b)[U] 伦敦土话 Lúndūn tǔhuà;伦敦东区土话 Lúndūn dōngqū tǔhuà.

cockpit /ˈkɒkpɪt/ *n* [C] (小型飞机飞行员的)坐舱〔艙〕 zuòcāng.

cockroach /ˈkɒkrəʊtʃ/ *n* [C] 蟑螂 zhāngláng.

cocksure /ˌkɒkˈʃɔː(r); *US* -ˈʃʊər/ *adj* [非正式用语]过〔過〕于自信的 guòyú zìxìn de; 自以为〔爲〕是的 zì yǐ wéi shì de.

cocktail /ˈkɒkteɪl/ *n* [C] 1 鸡〔鷄〕尾酒 jīwěijiǔ. 2 水果、贝类〔類〕开〔開〕胃品 shuǐguǒ、bèilèi kāiwèipǐn: *a ˌprawn ˈ~* 大虾冷盘.

cocky /ˈkɒkɪ/ *adj* [-ier, -iest][非正式用语]自以为〔爲〕是的 zì yǐ wéi shì de.

cocoa /ˈkəʊkəʊ/ *n* (a) [U] 可可粉 kěkěfěn. (b)[U, C]可可茶 kěkěchá.

coconut /ˈkəʊkənʌt/ *n* [C, U] 椰子果 yēziguǒ.

cocoon /kəˈkuːn/ *n* [C] 茧〔繭〕 jiǎn.

cod /kɒd/ *n* (a)[C] [*pl* **cod**] 鳕 xuě. (b) (作为食物的)鳕鱼肉 xuěyúròu.

coddle /ˈkɒdl/ *v*[T] 娇〔嬌〕养〔養〕 jiāoyǎng;溺爱〔愛〕 nì'ài.

code /kəʊd/ *n* 1[C] 规则 guīzé; 准则 zhǔnzé: *a ~ of behaviour* 行为准则. 2[C, U]代号〔號〕 dàihào; 密码 mìmǎ: *break the ~ the enemy use to send messages* 破译敌人写信用的密码. 3 [C](用机器发出的)电〔電〕码 diànmǎ. **code** *v* [T] 把…译〔譯〕成密码. bǎ…yìchéng mìmǎ.

coed /kəʊˈed/ *n* [C] [美国非正式用语]男女同校大学〔學〕的女生 nánnǚ tóngxiào dàxuéde nǚshēng. **coed** *adj* [非正式用语]男女合校的 nánnǚ héxiàode.

coeducation /ˌkəʊˌedʒʊˈkeɪʃn/ *n* [U] 男女同校 nán nǚ tóngxiào. **coeducational** *adj*.

coerce /kəʊˈɜːs/ *v* [T] [正式用语] 强迫 qiángpò;胁〔脅〕迫 xiépò; 迫使 pòshǐ. **coercion** /kəʊˈɜːʃn/ *n* [U]. **coercive** *adj*.

coexist /ˌkəʊɪgˈzɪst/ *v* [I] 共存 gòngcún. **coexistence** *n* [U](国与国的)共存 gòngcún: *peaceful ~ence* 和平共处.

coffee /ˈkɒfɪ; *US* ˈkɔːfɪ/ *n* (a) [U] 咖啡豆 kāfēidòu; 咖啡 kāfēi. (b) 咖啡茶 kāfēichá.

coffer /ˈkɒfə(r)/ *n* 1 [C] (盛金钱的)保险〔險〕箱 bǎoxiǎnxiāng. 2 **coffers** [pl] [正式用语]金库 jīnkù.

coffin /ˈkɒfɪn/ *n* [C] 棺材 guāncai; 棺木 guānmù.

cog /kɒg/ *n* [C] 1 齿〔齒〕轮〔輪〕的轮牙 chǐlúnde lúnyá. 2 [习语] **a cog in a machine** 不重要但又不可少的人 bú zhòngyào dàn yòu bùkěshǎo de rén. **ˈcog-wheel** *n* [C]嵌齿轮 qiànchǐlún.

cogent /ˈkəʊdʒənt/ *adj* [正式用语] (论据等)强有力的 qiángyǒulìde; 有说服力的 yǒu shuōfúlì de.

cognac /ˈkɒnjæk/ *n* [U] 法国〔國〕白兰〔蘭〕地酒 Fǎguó báilándìjiǔ.

cohabit /ˌkəʊˈhæbɪt/ *v*[I][正式用语]男女姘居 nánnǚ pīnjū. **cohabitation** /ˌkəʊhæbɪˈteɪʃn/ *n* [U].

cohere /ˌkəʊˈhɪə(r)/ *v* [I] [正式用语] 1 黏着 niánzhuó; 黏合 niánhé. 2 (思想等) 连贯 liánguàn; 前后〔後〕一致 qiánhòu yízhì. **coherent** /-ˈhɪərənt/ *adj* (思想、语言等)连贯的 liánguànde; 清楚的 qīngchude. **coherence** /-rəns/ *n* [U]. **coherently** *adv*.

cohesion /ˌkəʊˈhiːʒn/ *n* [U] 内聚性 nèijùxìng; 内聚力 nèijùlì. **cohesive** /-ˈhiːsɪv/ *adj*.

coil /kɔɪl/ *v*[I, T] 盘〔盤〕绕〔繞〕 pánrào;缠绕 chánrào. **coil** *n* [C] 1 一卷 yìjuǎn; 一圈 yìquān; 盘绕物 pánràowù. 2 线〔綫〕圈 xiànquān. 3 子宫节〔節〕育环〔環〕 zǐgōng jiéyùhuán.

coin /kɔɪn/ *n* [C] 铸〔鑄〕币〔幣〕 zhùbì; 硬币 yìngbì. **coin** *v* [T] 1 铸造(硬币) zhùzào. 2 杜撰(新字、词) dùzhuàn. **coinage** /ˈkɔɪnɪdʒ/ *n* [U] 硬币币制 yìngbì bìzhì.

coincide /ˌkəʊɪnˈsaɪd/ *v* [I] 1 (事情)同时〔時〕发〔發〕生 tóngshí fāshēng. 2 (意见)一致 yízhì. 3 (物体)位置重合 wèizhì chónghé.

coincidence /ˌkəʊˈɪnsɪdəns/ *n* [C, U] 符合 fúhé; 巧合 qiǎohé; 巧合的事例 qiǎohéde shìlì: *It was pure ~ that we were both travelling on the same plane.* 我们乘同一架飞机旅行纯然是一种巧合. **coincidental** /ˌkəʊˌɪnsɪˈdentl/ *adj* 巧合的 qiǎohéde.

coke /kəʊk/ *n* [U] 焦 jiāo; 焦炭 jiāotàn.

colander (亦作 **cullender**) /ˈkʌləndə(r)/ *n* [C] 滤〔濾〕器 lǜqì; 滤锅〔鍋〕 lǜguō.

cold[1] /kəʊld/ *adj* 1 冷的 lěngde;寒冷的 hánlěngde. 2(食品)未热〔熱〕过〔過〕的 wèi règuòde; 热过后〔後〕变〔變〕冷的 règuòhòu biàn lěngde. 3 冷淡的 lěngdànde; 不热情的 bú rèqíngde: *a ~ stare* 冷淡的凝视. *a ~ welcome*

冷淡的接待. 4 失去知觉〔覺〕的 shīqù zhījuéde: *knock sb out* ～ 把某人打晕. 5［习语］get/have cold 'feet［非正式用语］害怕 hàipà; 临〔臨〕阵退缩 línzhèn tuìsuō. give sb/get the cold 'shoulder （被）冷落 lěngluò. in cold'blood 残〔殘〕酷的 cánkùde; 无〔無〕情的 wúqíngde: *kill sb in* ～ *blood* 残酷地杀害某人. pour / throw cold'water on sth 对〔對〕…泼〔潑〕冷水 duì…pō lěngshuǐ. ˌcold-'blooded *adj* 1 (动物)冷血的 lěngxuède. 2 残酷无情的 cánkù wúqíng de. ˌcold 'hearted *adj* 无情的 wúqíngde. coldly *adv*. coldness *n* [U]. ˌcold 'war *n* [sing] 冷战〔戰〕lěngzhàn.

cold[2] /kəʊld/ *n* 1[U] 寒冷 hánlěng. 2 [C, U] 伤〔傷〕风〔風〕shāngfēng; 感冒 gǎnmào. 3［习语］(be left) out in the cold 不被理睬 bú bèi lǐcǎi.

coleslaw /ˈkəʊlslɔː/ *n* [U] 酸卷〔捲〕心菜丝（一种生拌凉菜）suān juǎnxīncài sī.

collaborate /kəˈlæbəreɪt/ *v*[I] 1 协〔協〕作 xiézuò; 合作 hézuò. 2 (*with*)(同敌人)勾结 gōujié. collaboration /kəlæbəˈreɪʃn/ *n* [U]. collaborator *n*[C].

collage /ˈkɒlɑːʒ; *US* kəˈlɑːʒ/ *n* [C] 抽象派的拼贴画〔畫〕chōuxiàngpàide pīntiēhuà.

collapse /kəˈlæps/ *v* 1 [I] 倒坍 dǎotān: *The building* ～*d in the earthquake*. 该建筑物在地震中倒坍. 2 [I] 晕倒 yūndǎo. 3 [I] 垮下来 kuǎxiàlái. 4 [I, T]折叠起来 zhédiéqǐlái: *The table* ～*s to fit into the cupboard*. 桌子折叠起来装进了壁橱. collapse *n* [sing]: *the* ～ *of the company* 这家公司的垮台. collapsible *adj* 可折叠的 kě zhédié de.

collar /ˈkɒlə(r)/ *n* [C] 1 领子 lǐngzi. 2(狗等的)围〔圍〕脖 wéibó, 颈〔頸〕圈 jǐngquān. collar *v*[T] 扭住…的领口 niǔzhù…de lǐngkǒu. ˈcollar-bone *n* [C] 锁骨 suǒgǔ.

collate /kəˈleɪt/ *n* [U] 校勘 jiàokān.

collateral /kəˈlætərəl/ *n* [U] 担〔擔〕保品 dānbǎopǐn.

colleague /ˈkɒliːg/ *n* [C] 同事 tóngshì; 同僚 tóngliáo.

collect /kəˈlekt/ *v* 1 [I, T] 聚集 jùjí; 收集 shōují: ～ *the empty glasses* 收集空玻璃杯. *A crowd* ～*ed at the scene of the accident*. 出事现场聚集了一群人. 2 [I] (为了爱好)积〔積〕攒(邮票等) jīzǎn. 3 [I, T] (*for*)募捐 mùjuān: ～ *money for charity* 为慈善事业募捐. 4 [T]接 jiē: ～ *a child from school* 从学校接孩子. 5 [T]使(自己)镇定下来〔來〕shǐ zhèndìng xiàlái. collect *adj*, *adv* [美语](电话)由受话人付费(的) yóu shòuhuàrén fùfèi. collected *adj* 镇定的 zhèndìngde; 泰然的 tàiránde. collection /kəˈlekʃn/ 1 [U] 收集 shōují. 2 [C] 一批收集的东西 yìpī shōujíde dōngxi. 3 [C] 募集的钱〔錢〕mùjíde qián. collective *adj* 集体〔體〕的 jítǐde; 共同的 gòngtóngde. collectively *adv*. collector *n* [C] 收藏家 shōucángjiā: *a* ˈ*ticket-*～*or* 入场券收藏家.

college /ˈkɒlɪdʒ/ *n* [C] 1(独立的)学〔學〕院 xuéyuàn; 综合大学中的学院 zōnghé dàxué zhōng de xuéyuàn. 2 学会〔會〕xuéhuì; 社团〔團〕shètuán: *the Royal C*～ *of Surgeons* 皇家外科医生学会.

collide /kəˈlaɪd/ *v* [I] (*with*) 1 猛冲〔衝〕měngchōng. 2 冲突 chōngtū; 抵触〔觸〕dǐchù.

collier /ˈkɒlɪə(r)/ *n* [C] 煤矿〔礦〕工人 méikuàng gōngrén.

colliery /ˈkɒlɪərɪ/ *n* [C] [*pl* -ies] 煤矿〔礦〕méikuàng.

collision /kəˈlɪʒn/ *n* [C, U] 碰 pèng; 撞 zhuàng; 冲〔衝〕突 chōngtū; 抵触〔觸〕dǐchù.

colloquial /kəˈləʊkwɪəl/ *adj* 口语的 kǒuyǔde; 会〔會〕话的 huìhuàde. colloquialism *n* [C] 口语 kǒuyǔ; 口语词 kǒuyǔcí. colloquially *adv*.

collude /kəˈluːd/ *v*[I] (*with*)[正式用语]勾结 gōujié. collusion /kəˈluːʒn/ *n* [U].

colon[1] /ˈkəʊlən/ *n* [C] 冒号〔號〕(:) màohào.

colon[2] /ˈkəʊlən/ *n* [C]结肠〔腸〕jiécháng.

colonel /ˈkɜːnl/ *n* [C]陆〔陸〕军(或美国空军)上校 lùjūn shàngxiào.

colonial /kəˈləʊnɪəl/ *adj* 殖民地的 zhímíndìde; 关〔關〕于殖民的 guānyú zhímín de. colonial *n* [C] 殖民地居民 zhímíndì jūmín. colonialism *n* [U] 殖民主义〔義〕zhímínzhǔyì. colonialist *n*[C], *adj*.

colonist /ˈkɒlənɪst/ *n* [C] 殖民地开〔開〕拓者 zhímíndì kāituòzhě.

colonize /ˈkɒlənaɪz/ *v*[T] 在…开〔開〕拓殖民地 zài…kāituò zhímíndì. colonization /ˌkɒlənaɪˈzeɪʃn; *US* -nɪˈz-/ *n*[U].

colonnade /ˌkɒləˈneɪd/ *n* [C] 一列柱子 yíliè zhùzi.

colony /ˈkɒlənɪ/ *n* [C] [*pl* -ies] 1 殖民地 zhímíndì. 2 殖民队〔隊〕zhímínduì.

color [美语] = COLOUR[1,2].

colossal /kəˈlɒsl/ *adj* 庞〔龐〕大的 pángdàde.

colossus /kəˈlɒsəs/ *n* [C] [*pl* -lossi /-lɒsaɪ/ 或 ～es] 1 巨像 jùxiàng. 2 巨人 jùrén.

colour[1] /ˈkʌlə(r)/ *n* 1(a) [U] 颜色 yánsè; 色彩 sècǎi; 彩色 cǎisè. (b) [C](某一种)色 sè. 2[U] 红晕 hóngyùn; 血色 xuèsè; 脸〔臉〕色 liǎnsè. 3 colours [pl](a)(作为团体、队、学校

C

C

标志的)徽章 huīzhāng. (b)船旗 chuánqí;团〔團〕旗 tuánqí. 4 生动〔動〕的细节〔節〕shēngdòngde xìjié;兴〔興〕趣 xìngqù. 5 [习语] off colour [非正式用语]身体〔體〕不舒服 shēntǐ bù shūfu. with ˌflying ˈcolours 成功地 chénggōngde. ˈcolour bar *n* [C]对〔對〕有色人种〔種〕的歧视 duì yǒusè rénzhǒng de qíshì;种族隔离〔離〕zhǒngzú gélí. ˌcolour-ˈblind *adj* 色盲的 sèmángde. colourful *adj* 1 颜色鲜艳〔艷〕的 yánsè xiānyànde. 2 有趣的 yǒuqùde;刺激性的 cìjīxìngde. colourless *adj* 1 无〔無〕色的 wúsède. 2 平淡无趣的 píngdàn wúqù de. ˈcolour supplement *n*[C][英国英语](报纸等的)彩色增刊 cǎisè zēngkān.

colour² /ˈkʌlə(r)/ *v* 1 [T] 给…着色 gěi…zhuósè;染色 rǎnsè. 2 [I]脸〔臉〕红 liǎnhóng. 3 [T]影响〔響〕yǐngxiǎng. 4[短语动词] colour sth in 给…着色 gěi…zhuósè. coloured *adj* 1 有某种〔種〕颜色的 yǒu mǒuzhǒng yánsè de;彩色的 cǎisède. 2 有色人种的 yǒusè rénzhǒng de. colouring *n* 1 [U](a) 颜色 yánsè. (b)肤〔膚〕色 fūsè. 2 [C, U] 食物色料 shíwù sèliào.

colt /kəʊlt/ *n* [C] 小公马 xiǎo gōngmǎ.

column /ˈkɒləm/ *n* [C] 1 (a)柱 zhù. (b)柱状〔狀〕物 zhùzhuàngwù: *a ~ of smoke* 烟柱. 2 纵〔縱〕列 zòngliè. 3(a) (报纸的)专〔專〕栏〔欄〕zhuānlán. (b)(印刷物上的)栏 lán. columnist /-nɪst/ *n* [C](报纸的)专栏作家 zhuānlán zuòjiā.

coma /ˈkəʊmə/ *n* [C] 昏迷 hūnmí.

comb /kəʊm/ *n* [C] 1 梳 shū. 2 [常作 sing] (头发的)梳理 shūlǐ: *give one's hair a ~* 梳理头发. 3 *n* [C, U] = HONEYCOMB (HONEY). comb *v*[T] 1 梳(头发) shū. 2 彻〔徹〕底搜查 chèdǐ sōuchá.

combat /ˈkɒmbæt/ *n* [C, U], *v* [I, T]战〔戰〕斗〔鬥〕zhàndòu;搏斗 bódòu. combatant /-bətənt/ *n* [C] 战斗者 zhàndòuzhě. combatant *adj* 战斗的 zhàndòude.

combination /ˌkɒmbɪˈneɪʃn/ *n* 1[U] 联〔聯〕合 liánhé;结合 jiéhé;合并〔併〕hébìng: *a ~ of traditional and modern architecture* 传统建筑同现代建筑的结合. 2[U] 结合、合并的行为〔為〕jiéhé、hébìngde xíngwéi. 3[C] 保险〔險〕柜〔櫃〕的暗码〔碼〕bǎoxiǎnguìde ànmǎ.

combine¹ /kəmˈbaɪn/ *v*[I, T] 联〔聯〕合 liánhé;连结 liánjié.

combine² /ˈkɒmbaɪn/ *n* [C] 集团〔團〕jítuán;联〔聯〕合企业〔業〕liánhé qǐyè. ˌcombine ˈharvester *n* [C] 联合收割机〔機〕liánhéshōugējī;康拜因 kāngbàiyīn.

combustible /kəmˈbʌstəbl/ *adj* 易燃的 yìránde;可燃的 kěránde.

combustion /kəmˈbʌstʃən/ *n* [U] 燃烧〔燒〕ránshāo.

come /kʌm/ *v* [*pt* came /keɪm/ , *pp* come] [I] 1 (a)来 lái: *~ and talk to me* 来同我谈谈. (b)来到 láidào;到达〔達〕dàodá. 2 行进〔進〕(一定距离) xíngjìn: *We have ~ thirty miles since lunch.* 午饭后我们走了30英里. 3 达到 dádào;至 zhì: *The path ~s right up to the gate.* 这条小路一直通到大门口. 4 发〔發〕生 fāshēng: *Christmas ~s once a year.* 每年有一次圣诞节. 5 存在 cúnzài;被供应〔應〕bèi gōngyìng: *This dress ~s in several different colours.* 这衣服有几种不同颜色可供应. 6 成为〔為〕chéngwéi: *~ loose* 变松了. 7 (*to*)开〔開〕始 kāishǐ: *~ to realize the truth* 开始了解真相. 8 (*to/into*)达到(某种状态等) dádào: *~ to an end* 结束. 9 [习语] come to grips with sth ⇨ GRIP. come to a ˈhead ⇨ HEAD¹. come loose ⇨ LOOSE. come to nothing 终未实〔實〕现 zhōng wèi shíxiàn. come out into the open ⇨ OPEN. come what ˈmay 不管发生什〔甚〕么〔麼〕事 bùguǎn fāshēng shénme shì. how come (...)? [非正式用语]…怎么回事? …zěnme huíshì? …怎么搞的? … zěnme gǎode? to come 将〔將〕要到来的 jiāngyào dàolái de: *for several years to ~* 在未来的几年里. 10 [短语动词] come aˈbout 发生 fāshēng. come across sb/sth 偶然遇到 ǒurán yùdào;偶然找到 ǒurán zhǎodào. come aˈlong (a)来到 láidào;出现 chūxiàn: *When the right job ~s along, she will take it.* 有合适的工作机会,她就会工作的. (b)进〔進〕展 jìnzhǎn;进行 jìnxíng: *Her work is coming along nicely.* 她的工作进展顺利. (c) = COME ON (c). come aˈpart 裂开 lièkāi;破碎 pòsuì. come at sb(with sth) 袭〔襲〕击〔擊〕xíjī: *He came at me with a knife.* 他拿着一把小刀向我刺来. come back 回来 huílái. come ˈback (to sb)被回想起来 bèi huíxiǎng qǐlái. come before sb/sth 被…处〔處〕理 bèi…chǔlǐ. come between A and B 介入 jièrù;干涉 gānshè. ˈcome by sth 获〔獲〕得 huòdé: *Good jobs are hard to ~ by these days.* 这些日子很难获得好的工作岗位. come ˈdown (a)倒塌 dǎotā. (b)(雨等)降下 jiàngxià;(物价)下跌 xiàdiē. (c)作出决定 zuòchū juédìng. come down to sb (传统、故事等)流传〔傳〕到 liúchuán dào. come down to sth (a) 下垂到 xiàchuí dào;达到 dádào: *Her hair ~s down to her waist.* 她的头发下垂到腰部. (b)可归〔歸〕结为 kě guījié wéi;实〔實〕质〔質〕上意味着 shízhì shàng yìwèizhe: *What it ~s down to is that if your work doesn't improve you'll have to leave.* 这实质上意味着如果你的工作没有改进,你就得离开. come in (a) (潮)涨〔漲〕zhǎng. (b)流行起来 liúxíng qǐlái. (c) (钱)到手 dàoshǒu;被收入 bèi shōurù. (d)起作用 qǐ zuòyòng: *Where do I ~ in?* 我在哪里发挥作用? **come in for sth** 挨āi;遭受 zāoshòu. **come into sth** 继〔繼〕承 jìchéng. **come of sth** 是…的结果 shì…de jiéguǒ. **come off** (a)能被除掉 néng bèi chúdiào: *Will these dirty marks come off?* 这些污痕能被除掉吗? (b)发生 fāshēng;举〔舉〕行 jǔxíng: *Did your holiday ~ off?* 你休过假了吗? (c) (计划等)成功 chénggōng: *The experiment did not ~ off.* 试验没有成功. **come off (sth)** (a) 从〔從〕…分开 cóng…fēnkāi: *The button has ~ off my coat.* 我外套上的纽扣掉下来了. (b)从…跌下 cóng…diēxià. **come on** (a) (演员)登场〔場〕dēngchǎng. (b) = COME ALONG(b). (c)(表示激、挑战等)快点〔點〕kuàidiǎn: *C~ on, if we don't hurry we'll be late.* 快点,如果我们不加快,就要迟到了. (d)(雨、夜、病等)开始 kāishǐ: *I think he has a cold coming on.* 我想他感冒了. **come 'out** (a)出现 chūxiàn: *The rain stopped and the sun came out.* 雨停了,太阳出来了. (b)被知道 bèi zhīdào;出版 chūbǎn: *The truth came out eventually.* 真相最终被披露出来. (c)(工人)罢〔罷〕工 bàgōng. (d) (照片等)清楚地显〔顯〕露 qīngchude xiǎnlù. **come 'out (of sth)** 从…除去 cóng…chúqù. *Will the stains ~ out?* 污渍能除掉吗? **come out in sth** (皮肤等)发出(丘疹等) fāchū: *~ out in a rash* 发皮疹. **come out with sth** 说出 shuōchū: *~ out with the strangest remarks* 说出最奇怪的话. **come over** (a)从远〔遠〕处来 cóng yuǎnchù lái: *~ over to Scotland for a holiday* 来苏格兰度假. (b)传〔傳〕达 chuándá: *Your position didn't really ~ over in your speech.* 你的讲话并没有真实地传达出你的立场. **come over sb** (某种感觉等)支配(某人) zhīpèi: *A feeling of dizziness came over him.* 他感到一阵头晕. **come 'round** (a)绕〔繞〕道而行 ràodào ér xíng. (b)访问 fǎngwèn: *C~ round to my place for the evening.* 晚上来我们家坐坐. (c) 到来 dàolái;再度来临〔臨〕zàidù láilín: *Christmas seems to ~ round quicker every year.* 圣诞节似乎一年比一年来得快. (d)苏〔蘇〕醒 sūxǐng. (e)改变〔變〕意见 gǎibiàn yìjiàn. **come 'through** (消息等)传来 chuánlái. **come through (sth)** 经〔經〕历〔歷〕疾病而康复〔復〕jīnglì jíbìng ér kāngfù;躲过〔過〕(伤害) duǒguò. **come 'to** = COME ROUND (d). **ˌcome to 'sth** 总〔總〕计 zǒngjì;达到 dádào: *The bill came to £20.* 账单总计 20 英镑. **come to sb** (思想等)来到某人脑〔腦〕子里〔裡〕láidào mǒurén nǎozi lǐ: *The idea came to me in a dream.* 这个主意是我在一个梦里想出来的. **come under sth** (a) 归〔歸〕入(某一种类) guīrù. (b)受到(影响等) shòudào: *~ under her influence* 受她的影响. **come 'up** (a) (植物等)长〔長〕出地面 zhǎngchū dìmiàn. (b) 被提到 bèi tídào: *The question hasn't ~ up yet.* 这个问题还没有提到. (c)发生 fāshēng: *A couple of problems have ~ up so I'll be late home from work.* 发生了一些问题,我下班回家要晚. **come up against sb/sth** 碰到(困难等) pèngdào;与〔與〕…相撞 yǔ…xiāngzhuàng. **come up (to sth)** 达到 dádào: *The water came up to my waist.* 水深齐我的腰. **come up with sth** 产〔產〕生 chǎnshēng;找到 zhǎodào: *~ up with a solution.* 找到解决办法. **come upon sb/sth** 无〔無〕意中遇到、发现 wúyì zhōng yùdào、fāxiàn: *~ upon a group of children playing* 无意中碰到一群正在玩的孩子. **come-back** *n* [C, 常作 sing]恢复 huīfù; 复原 fùyuán. **come-down** *n* [C, 常作 sing]落泊 luòbó; 失势〔勢〕shīshì. **coming** *adj* 未来的 wèilái de: *in the coming months* 在今后的几个月里. **coming** *n* 1[sing] 来临〔臨〕láilín: *the coming of spring* 春天的来到. 2[习语] **ˌcomings and 'goings** 来来往往 láiláiwǎngwǎng.

comedian /kəˈmiːdɪən/ *n* [C] 1 (*fem* **comedienne** /kəˌmiːdɪˈen/) 喜剧〔劇〕演员 xǐjù yǎnyuán. 2 丑角式人物 chǒujuéshì rénwù.

comedy /ˈkɒmədɪ/ *n* [*pl* -ies] 1 [C] 喜剧〔劇〕xǐjù;喜剧片 xǐjùpiàn. 2[U]喜剧成分 xǐjù chéngfèn;喜剧性 xǐjùxìng.

comet /ˈkɒmɪt/ *n* [C] 彗星 huìxīng.

comfort /ˈkʌmfət/ *n* 1[U] 舒适〔適〕shūshì;安逸 ānyì. 2[U] 安慰 ānwèi: *words of ~* 安慰的话. 3 [sing]给予安慰的人或物 gěiyǔ ānwèide rén huò wù. 4 [C, 常作 pl]使生活愉快、身体〔體〕舒适的东西 shǐ shēnghuó yúkuài、shēntǐ shūshì de dōngxi. **comfort** *v* [T] 安慰 ānwèi. **comfortable** /ˈkʌmftəbl; *US* -fərt-/ *adj* 1 使身体舒适的 shǐ shēntǐ shūshì de: *a ~able chair* 舒适的椅子. 2 轻〔輕〕松〔鬆〕的 qīngsōngde: *a ~able job* 轻松的工作. 3 [非正式用语]富裕的 fùyùde; 小康的 xiǎokāngde. 4 充裕的 chōngyùde. **comfortably** *adv*.

comic /ˈkɒmɪk/ *adj* 1 滑稽的 huájī de;使人发〔發〕笑的 shǐ rén fāxiào de. 2 喜剧〔劇〕的 xǐjùde. **comic** *n* [C] 1 喜剧演员 xǐjù yǎnyuán. 2 连环〔環〕漫画〔畫〕杂〔雜〕志〔誌〕liánhuán mànhuà zázhì. **comical** *adj* 使人发笑的 shǐ rén fāxiào de. **comic 'strip** *n* [C] 连环漫画 liánhuán mànhuà.

comma /ˈkɒmə/ *n* [C] 逗点〔點〕dòudiǎn.

command /kəˈmɑːnd; *US* -ˈmænd / *v* 1

C

[I, T] 命令 mìnglìng. 2 [T]应〔應〕得 yīngdé; 博得 bódé: ~ *respect* 博得尊敬. 3 [T] 管辖 guǎnxiá: ~ *a regiment* 管辖一个团. 4 [T]俯视 fǔshì: *a ~ing position over the valley* 一个控制着这山谷的阵地. **command** *n* 1 [C] 命令 mìnglìng. 2 [U]控制 kòngzhì, 指挥 zhǐhuī: *in ~ of a ship* 指挥一艘军舰. 3 **Command** [C]部队〔隊〕bùduì; 军区〔區〕jūnqū. 4 [U, sing] 掌握 zhǎngwò; 运〔運〕用能力 yùnyòng nénglì: *a good ~ of French* 对法语的掌握和运用能力.

C

commandant /ˌkɒmənˈdænt/ *n* [C] 司令 sīlìng; 指挥官 zhǐhuīguān.

commandeer /ˌkɒmənˈdɪə(r)/ *v* [T] 征〔徵〕用 zhēngyòng.

commander /kəˈmɑːndə(r); *US* -ˈmæn-/ *n* [C] 1 指挥官 zhǐhuīguān; 司令 sīlìng. 2 海军中校 hǎijūn zhōngxiào.

commandment /kəˈmɑːndmənt; *US* -ˈmænd-/ *n* [C] 戒律 jièlǜ.

commando /kəˈmɑːndəʊ; *US* -ˈmæn-/ *n* [C][*pl* **~s** 或 **~es**] 突击〔擊〕队〔隊〕tūjīduì; 突击队员 tūjī duìyuán.

commemorate /kəˈmeməreɪt/ *v* [T] 纪念 jìniàn. **commemoration** /kəˌmeməˈreɪʃn/ *n* [C, U]. **commemorative** /-rətɪv/ *adj*.

commence /kəˈmens/ *v* [I, T][正式用语]开〔開〕始 kāishǐ. **commencement** *n* [U].

commend /kəˈmend/ *v*[T] [正式用语] 1 称〔稱〕赞〔讚〕chēngzàn; 表扬〔揚〕biǎoyáng. 2 ~ **oneself to** 给…以好印象 gěi…yǐ hǎo yìnxiàng. **commendable** *adj* 值得称赞的 zhídé chēngzàn de; 值得表扬的 zhídébiǎoyáng de. **commendation** /ˌkɒmenˈdeɪʃn/ *n* [U, C].

commensurate /kəˈmenʃərət/ *adj* (*with*) [正式用语]相称〔稱〕的 xiāngchènde; 相当〔當〕的 xiāngdāngde: *pay ~ with the importance of the job* 按工作的重要性付酬.

comment /ˈkɒment/ *n* [C, U] 评论〔論〕pínglùn; 批评 pīpíng. **comment** *v*[I] (*on*) 评论 pínglùn.

commentary /ˈkɒməntrɪ; *US* -terɪ/ *n* [*pl* **-ies**] 1 [C, U] 广〔廣〕播实〔實〕况报〔報〕导〔導〕guǎngbō shíkuàng bàodǎo: *a ~ on a football match* 足球比赛的广播实况报导. 2 [C]集注 jízhù; 集释 jíshì.

commentate /ˈkɒmənteɪt/ *v* [I] 评论〔論〕pínglùn. **commentator** *n* [C].

commerce /ˈkɒmɜːs/ *n* [U] 贸易 màoyì.

commercial /kəˈmɜːʃl/ *adj* 1 贸易的 màoyìde; 商业〔業〕的 shāngyède. 2 以获〔獲〕利为〔爲〕目的的 yǐ huòlì wéi mùdì de. 3(电视、广播)由广告收入支付的 yóu guǎnggào shōurù zhīfù de. **commercial** *n* [C] 电〔電〕视或无〔無〕线电广〔廣〕告 diànshì huò wúxiàndiàn guǎnggào. **commercialized** *adj* 以获利为目的的 yǐ huòlì wéi mùdì de. **commercially** /-ʃəlɪ/ *adv* **comˌmercial ˈtraveller** *n* [C] 旅行推销员 lǚxíng tuīxiāoyuán.

commiserate /kəˈmɪzəreɪt/ *v*[I] (*with*) [正式用语]表示同情 biǎoshì tóngqíng; 表示怜〔憐〕悯 biǎoshì liánmǐn: *I ~d with her on the loss of her job*. 我对她失去工作表示慰问. **commiseration** /kəˌmɪzəˈreɪʃn/ *n* [C, U].

commission /kəˈmɪʃn/ *n* 1 [C]任务〔務〕rènwu; 所托〔託〕之事 suǒ tuō zhī shì. 2 [C, U] 佣金 yōngjīn; 回扣 huíkòu. 3 [C] 考察团〔團〕kǎochátuán; 调查团 diàochátuán; 委员会〔會〕wěiyuánhuì. 4 [C] 军事任职〔職〕令 jūnshì rènzhílìng. **commission** *v*[T] 1 委任 wěirèn; 委托 wěituō; 任命 rènmìng. 2 授予(某人)军事任职令 shòuyǔ jūnshì rènzhílìng.

commissionaire /kəˌmɪʃəˈneə(r)/ *n* [C] [尤用于英国英语](剧院、旅馆等)穿制服的守门人 chuān zhìfú de shǒuménrén.

commissioner /kəˈmɪʃənə(r)/ *n* [C] 1 专〔專〕员 zhuānyuán; 委员 wěiyuán. 2 政府高级代表 zhèngfǔ gāojí dàibiǎo; 高级专员 gāojí zhuānyuán.

commit /kəˈmɪt/ *v* [-tt-] [T] 1 犯(罪行等) fàn; 干〔幹〕(坏事) gàn. 2 (*to*) 承诺做(某事) chéngnuò zuò: *The government has ~ted itself to fighting inflation*. 政府承诺要同通货膨胀作斗争. 3 ~ **oneself** 坚〔堅〕定地表明态〔態〕度 jiāndìngde biǎomíng tàidù. 4 把…送进〔進〕(监狱或医院) bǎ… sòngjìn. **commitment** *n* 1[C]所承诺之事 suǒ chéngnuò zhī shì. 2 [U] 献〔獻〕身 xiànshēn; 忠诚 zhōngchéng.

committee /kəˈmɪtɪ/ *n* [C, 亦作 sing, 用 pl v]委员会〔會〕wěiyuánhuì.

commodity /kəˈmɒdətɪ/ *n* [C] [*pl* **-ies**] 日用品 rìyòngpǐn; 商品 shāngpǐn.

common[1] /ˈkɒmən/ *adj* 1 普通的 pǔtōngde; 一般的 yìbānde. 2 公共的 gōnggòngde; 共有的 gòngyǒude: *a ~ interest* 共同利益. *~ knowledge* 众〔衆〕所周〔週〕知的事. 3 [贬](人)粗鲁的 cūlǔde; 粗俗的 cūsúde. **ˌcommon ˈground** *n*[U] (观点、目标等的)共同基础〔礎〕gòngtóng jīchǔ. **ˌcommon ˈlaw** *n* [U](尤指英国的)不成文法 bùchéngwénfǎ. **ˈcommon-law** *adj*. **commonly** *adv*. **the ˌCommon ˈMarket** *n* [sing]欧〔歐〕洲经〔經〕济〔濟〕共同体〔體〕Ōuzhōu Jīngjì Gòngtóngtǐ. **ˈcommonplace** *adj* 普通的 pǔtōngde. **ˌcommon ˈsense** *n* [U] (由实际生活经验得来的)常识〔識〕chángshí.

common[2] /ˈkɒmən/ *n* 1[C] 公地 gōngdì. 2 [习语]**have sth in common** 有共同之处〔處〕yǒu gòngtóng zhī chù. **in common with sb/**

sth 与〔與〕…一样〔樣〕 yǔ…yíyàng.

commoner /ˈkɒmənə(r)/ *n* [C] 平民 píngmín.

Commons /ˈkɒmənz/ *n* the Commons [sing, 亦作 sing, 用 pl v] 英国〔國〕下议〔議〕院 Yīngguó xiàyìyuàn; 英国下议院议员 Yīngguó xiàyìyuàn yìyuán.

commonwealth /ˈkɒmənwelθ/ *n* **1** [C] 联〔聯〕邦 liánbāng: *the C～ of Australia* 澳大利亚联邦. **2 the Commonwealth** [sing] 英联邦 yīngliánbāng.

commotion /kəˈməʊʃn/ *n* [sing, U] 混乱〔亂〕 hùnluàn; 动〔動〕乱 dòngluàn; 骚〔騷〕乱 sāoluàn.

communal /ˈkɒmjʊnl/ *adj* 公共的 gōnggòngde.

commune[1] /ˈkɒmjuːn/ *n* [C] **1** 公社 gōngshè. **2**(法国等)最小行政区〔區〕 zuìxiǎo xíngzhèngqū.

commune[2] /kəˈmjuːn/ *v* [I] *with* (感情上)融为〔爲〕一体〔體〕 róngwéi yìtǐ; 谈心 tánxīn: ～ *with nature* 沉浸于大自然中.

communicate /kəˈmjuːnɪkeɪt/ *v* **1** [I, T] 传〔傳〕达〔達〕 chuándá; 传送(消息等) chuánsòng. **2** [T] 传染(疾病) chuánrǎn. **3** [I](房间)相通 xiāngtōng: *a communicating door* 通房间的门. **communication** /kəˌmjuːneˈkeɪʃn/ *n* **1** [U] 传达 chuándá; 传播 chuánbō. **2**[C][正式用语]信 xìn; 电〔電〕话 diànhuà. **3 communications** [pl] 通讯工具 tōngxùn gōngjù; 交通(工具) jiāotōng. **communicative** /-kətɪv; *US* -keɪtɪv/ *adj* 愿意提供信息的 yuànyì tígōng xìnxī de; 爱〔愛〕说话的 ài shuōhuà de.

communion /kəˈmjuːnɪən/ *n* [U] **1** [正式用语](思想、感情等)交流 jiāoliú. **2 Communion** (基督教)圣〔聖〕餐 shèngcān.

communiqué /kəˈmjuːnɪkeɪ; *US* kəˌmjuːnəˈkeɪ/ *n* [C] 公报〔報〕 gōngbào.

communism /ˈkɒmjʊnɪzəm/ *n* [U] (a)共产〔產〕主义〔義〕 gòngchǎnzhǔyì. (b) **Communism** 共产主义学〔學〕说 gòngchǎnzhǔyì xuéshuō; 共产主义运〔運〕动〔動〕 gòngchǎnzhǔyì yùndòng; 共产主义制度 gòngchǎnzhǔyì zhìdù. **communist** /-nɪst/ *n* [C], *adj*.

community /kəˈmjuːnətɪ/ *n* [C] [*pl* -ies] **1**[C] **the community** [sing] 社会〔會〕 shèhuì; 社区〔區〕 shèqū. **2**[C, 亦作 sing, 用 pl v] 团〔團〕体〔體〕 tuántǐ; 社团 shètuán. **3**[U] 共有 gòngyǒu; 共同性 gòngtóngxìng; 一致 yízhì. **community charge** *n* [sing] 成人税(英国的一种地方税) chéngrénshuì.

commute /kəˈmjuːt/ *v* **1** [I](尤指在市区和郊区之间)乘公交车辆上下班 chéng gōngjiāo chēliàng shàngxiàbān. **2** [T]减轻〔輕〕(刑罚) jiǎnqīng. **commuter** *n* [C](尤指在市区和郊区之间)乘公交车辆上下班的人 chéng gōngjiāo chēliàng shàngxiàbān de rén.

compact[1] /kəmˈpækt/ *adj* 紧〔緊〕密的 jǐnmìde; 紧凑的 jǐncòude. ˌ**compact** ˈ**disc** *n* [C]激光唱片 jīguāng chàngpiàn; (信息容量极大的)光盘〔盤〕 guāngpán. **compactly** *adv*. **compactness** *n* [U].

compact[2] /ˈkɒmpækt/ *n* [C] 连镜小粉盒 liánjìng xiǎo fěnhé.

companion /kəmˈpænɪən/ *n* [C] 同伴 tóngbàn. **companionship** *n* [U]伴侣关〔關〕系〔係〕 bànlǚ guānxì.

company /ˈkʌmpənɪ/ *n* [*pl* -ies] **1** [C] 公司 gōngsī. **2** [C]一群一起工作的人 yìqún yìqǐ gōngzuò de rén: *an opera* ～ 歌剧团. **3** [U] 陪伴 péibàn: *He is good / bad* ～. 他是令人愉快/不愉快的伴侣. **4** [U]一群人 yìqúnrén; 客人 kèren. **5** [U] 伙〔夥〕伴 huǒbàn: *That girl keeps very bad* ～. 那女孩同坏人交往. **6** [C] (步兵)连 lián.

comparable /ˈkɒmprəbl/ *adj* 可比较的 kě bǐjiào de; 类〔類〕似的 lèisìde.

comparative /kəmˈpærətɪv/ *adj* **1** 比较的 bǐjiàode; 比较上的 bǐjiào shàng de. **2** 比较而言的 bǐjiào ér yán de: *living in* ～ *comfort* 比较舒适的生活. **3**[语法]比较级的 bǐjiàojíde: '*Better*' *is the* ～ *form of* '*good*'. "better"是"good"的比较级. **comparative** *n* [C] [语法](形容词和副词的)比较级 bǐjiàojí. **comparatively** *adv*.

compare /kəmˈpeə(r)/ *v* **1** [T] (*with*/*to*) 比较 bǐjiào; 对〔對〕照 duìzhào: ～ *the results of one test with the results of another* 把一次试验和另一次试验的结果进行比较. **2** [T] (*A to B*) 比拟〔擬〕 bǐnǐ. **3** [I] (*with*) 比得上 bǐdéshàng. **4**[习语] **compare** ˈ**notes** 交换意见 jiāohuàn yìjiàn.

comparison /kəmˈpærɪsn/ *n* **1** [C, U] 比较 bǐjiào; 对〔對〕照 duìzhào. **2** [U] 相似 xiāngsì: *There is no* ～ *between them*. 两者不可同日而语. **3** [习语] **by/in comparison** (**with sb/sth**) 与〔與〕…比较起来 yǔ…bǐjiào qǐlái.

compartment /kəmˈpɑːtmənt/ *n* [C] 分隔间〔間〕 fēngéjiān; 火车车厢的分隔间 huǒchē chēxiāng de fēngéjiān.

compass /ˈkʌmpəs/ *n* **1** [C] 指南针 zhǐnánzhēn. **2 compasses** [pl] 圆规 yuánguī. **3** [C] [正式用语]界限 jièxiàn; 范〔範〕围〔圍〕 fànwéi: *beyond the* ～ *of the human mind* 超出了人类智力的范围.

compassion /kəmˈpæʃn/ *n* [U] 怜〔憐〕悯 liánmǐn; 同情 tóngqíng. **compassionate** /-ʃənət/ *adj* 表示怜悯的 biǎoshì liánmǐnde, 表示同情的 biǎoshì tóngqíngde. **compassionately** *adv*.

C

compatible /kəmˈpætəbl/ *adj* (思想、人、原则等)可和谐共存的 kě héxié gòngcún de;相容的 xiāngróng de. **compatibility** /kəmˌpætəˈbɪlətɪ/ *n* [U].

compatriot /kəmˈpætrɪət; *US* -ˈpeɪt-/ *n* [C] 同胞 tóngbāo.

compel /kɒmˈpel/ *v* [-ll-] [T] [正式用语]强迫 qiǎngpò; 迫使 pòshǐ. **compelling** *adj* 令人信服的 lìng rén xìnfú de.

compensate /ˈkɒmpenseɪt/ *v* [I, T] (*for*) 赔偿〔償〕péicháng; 补〔補〕偿 bǔcháng. **compensation** /ˌkɒmpenˈseɪʃn/ *n* 1 [U] 赔偿 péicháng. 2 [U, C]赔偿物 péichángwù; 赔偿费 péichángfèi.

compère /ˈkɒmpeə(r)/ *n* [C] 表演节〔節〕目主持人 biǎoyǎn jiémù zhǔchí rén. **compère** *v* [T] 主持(演出) zhǔchí.

compete /kəmˈpiːt/ *v* [I] 比赛 bǐsài: ~ *against* / *with other* 与别人比赛.

competence /ˈkɒmpɪtəns/ *n* [U] 1 能力 nénglì;胜〔勝〕任 shèngrèn. 2[正式用语]权〔權〕能 quánnéng; 权限 quánxiàn. **competent** /-tənt/ *adj* 能胜任的 néng shèngrèn de; 有权能的 yǒu quánnéng de. **competently** *adv*.

competition /ˌkɒmpəˈtɪʃn/ *n* 1 [C]比赛会〔會〕bǐsàihuì: *a photography* ~ 摄影比赛会. 2 [U]比赛 bǐsài; 竞〔競〕争 jìngzhēng. **competitive** /kɒmˈpetətɪv/ *adj* 1 竞争的 jìngzhēngde. 2 好竞争的 hào jìngzhēngde.

competitor /kəmˈpetɪtə(r)/ *n* [C] 竞〔競〕争者 jìngzhēngzhě; 比赛者 bǐsàizhě; 敌〔敵〕手 díshǒu.

compile /kəmˈpaɪl/ *v* [T] 编辑〔輯〕biānjí;编写〔寫〕biānxiě. **compilation** /ˌkɒmpɪˈleɪʃn/ *n* 1 [U]编辑 biānjí;汇〔匯〕编 huìbiān. 2 [C]编辑物 biānjíwù. **compiler** *n* [C].

complacent /kəmˈpleɪsnt/ *adj* [常作贬]自满的 zìmǎnde. **complacency** /-snsɪ/ *n* [U]. **complacently** *adv*.

complain /kəmˈpleɪn/ *v* [I] 不满意 bù mǎnyì; 埋怨 mányuàn; 抱怨 bàoyuàn; 诉苦 sùkǔ: ~ *about the food* 对食物表示不满.

complaint /kəmˈpleɪnt/ *n* 1 [C, U] 抱怨 bàoyuàn; 叫屈 jiàoqū. 2 [C]疾病 jíbìng.

complement /ˈkɒmplɪmənt/ *n* [C] 1 补〔補〕足物 bǔzúwù; 补充物 bǔchōngwù: *Wine is the perfect* ~ *to a meal*. 吃饭有酒,再好不过. 2 定额 dìng'é. 3[语法]补〔補〕足语 bǔzúyǔ: *In 'I'm unhappy', 'unhappy' is the* ~. 在"I'm unhappy"这个句子里,"unhappy"是补足语. **complement** *v* [T] 补足 bǔzú; 补充 bǔchōng. **complementary** /ˌkɒmplɪˈmentrɪ/ *adj* 互为〔爲〕补充的 hùwéi bǔchōng de.

complete /kəmˈpliːt/ *adj* 1 完全的 wánquánde; 全部的 quánbùde. 2 完成的 wánchéngde; 结束了的 jiéshùlede. 3 彻〔徹〕底的 chèdǐde; 完完全全的 wánwánquánquánde: *a* ~ *surprise* 十足的意外. **complete** *v* [T] 1 完成 wánchéng;结束 jiéshù. 2 填写〔寫〕(表格) tiánxiě. **completely** *adv* 完全地 wánquánde; 彻底地 chèdǐde. **completeness** *n* [U]. **completion** /kəmˈpliːʃn/ *n* [U].

complex[1] /ˈkɒmpleks; *US* kəmˈpleks/ *adj* 复〔複〕杂〔雜〕的 fùzáde. **complexity** /kəmˈpleksətɪ/ *n* [C, U] [*pl* -ies].

complex[2] /ˈkɒmpleks/ *n* [C] 1 复〔複〕合体〔體〕fùhétǐ: *a sports* ~ 体育中心. 2 变〔變〕态〔態〕心理 biàntài xīnlǐ.

complexion /kəmˈplekʃn/ *n* [C] 1 肤〔膚〕色 fūsè: *a dark* (*fair*) ~ 黑色(淡色)肤色. 2 [常作 sing]情况 qíngkuàng; 局面 júmiàn.

compliance /kəmˈplaɪəns/ *n* [U][正式用语]顺从〔從〕shùncóng; 依从 yīcóng. **compliant** /-ənt/ *adj* 依从的 yīcóngde;屈从的 qūcóngde.

complicate /ˈkɒmplɪkeɪt/ *v*[T] 使复〔複〕杂〔雜〕shǐ fùzá; 使麻烦 shǐ máfan. **complicated** *adj* 结构〔構〕复杂的 jiégòu fùzá de; 困难〔難〕的 kùnnande. **complication** /ˌkɒmplɪˈkeɪʃn/ *n* [C]使情况更加困难的事物 shǐ qíngkuàng gèngjiā kùnnan de shìwù.

complicity /kəmˈplɪsətɪ/ *n* [U][正式用语]同谋关〔關〕系〔係〕tóngmóu guānxì;共犯关系 gòngfàn guānxì.

compliment /ˈkɒmplɪmənt/ *n* 1 [C]敬意 jìngyì; 赞〔讚〕扬〔揚〕zànyáng. 2 **compliments** [pl][正式用语]问候 wènhòu;致意 zhìyì. **compliment** /-ment/ *v* [T]恭维 gōngwei; 称〔稱〕赞 chēngzàn. **complimentary** /ˌkɒmplɪˈmentrɪ/ *adj* 1 恭维的 gōngweide; 表示钦羡的 biǎoshì qīnxiàn de. 2 赠送的 zèngsòngde: ~*ary tickets* 招待券.

comply /kəmˈplaɪ/ *v* [*pt*, *pp* -ied] [I] (*with*)[正式用语]照做 zhàozuò; 遵守 zūnshǒu.

component /kəmˈpəʊnənt/ *n* [C] 组成部分 zǔchéng bùfēn; 成分 chéngfèn. **component** *adj*.

compose /kəmˈpəʊz/ *v* 1 [I, T]创〔創〕作(音乐等)chuàngzuò. 2 ~ **oneself** 使自己镇定下来 shǐ zìjǐ zhèndìng xiàlái. 3[习语]**be composed of sb/sth** 由…组成 yóu… zǔchéng. **composed** *adj* 镇定的 zhèndìngde. **composer** *n* [C] 作曲家 zuòqǔjiā.

composite /ˈkɒmpəzɪt/ *n* 合成物 héchéngwù; 复〔複〕合材料 fùhé cáiliào. **composite** *adj* 合成的 héchéngde; 复合的 fùhéde; 混成的 hùnchéngde.

composition /ˌkɒmpəˈzɪʃn/ *n* 1 [C]作品

zuòpǐn；乐〔樂〕曲 yuèqǔ. 2 写〔寫〕作 xiězuò；作曲 zuòqǔ. 3 [C] 作文 zuòwén. 4 [U] 构〔構〕成 gòuchéng；成分 chéngfèn: *the chemical ~ of the soil* 土壤的化学成分.

compost /ˈkɒmpɒst/ *n* [U] 堆肥 duīféi；混合肥料 hùnhé féiliào.

composure /kəmˈpəʊʒə(r)/ *n* [U][正式用语]沉着 chénzhuó；镇静 zhènjìng.

compound[1] /ˈkɒmpaʊnd/ *n* [C] 1 混合物 hùnhéwù；化合物 huàhéwù. 2 [语法]复〔複〕合词 fùhécí. **compound** *adj*. ˌ**compound ˈinterest** *n* [U]复利 fùlì.

compound[2] /kəmˈpaʊnd/ *v* [T][正式用语] 1 使混合 shǐ hùnhé；使化合 shǐ huàhé: *~ several chemicals* 化合几种化学制品. 2 使恶〔惡〕化 shǐ èhuà.

compound[3] /ˈkɒmpaʊnd/ *n* [C] 院子 yuànzi.

comprehend /ˌkɒmprɪˈhend/ *v* [T][正式用语] 1 了〔瞭〕解 liǎojiě；领会〔會〕 lǐnghuì. 2 包括 bāokuò；包含 bāohán.

comprehension /ˌkɒmprɪˈhenʃn/ *n* 1 [U] 理解力 lǐjiělì. 2 [C] 理解练〔練〕习〔習〕 lǐjiě liànxí. **comprehensible** /-ˈhensəbl/ *adj* 能理解的 néng lǐjiě de.

comprehensive /ˌkɒmprɪˈhensɪv/ *adj* 1 包罗〔羅〕广〔廣〕泛的 bāoluó guǎngfàn de: *a ~ description* 综合性的描述. 2 [英国英语](教育)综合的 zōnghéde. **comprehensive school** *n* [C][英国英语]综合学〔學〕校 zōnghé xuéxiào.

compress /kəmˈpres/ *v* [T] 1 压〔壓〕缩 yāsuō. 2 使精炼〔煉〕 shǐ jīngliàn. **compression** /-ˈpreʃn/ *n* [U].

comprise /kəmˈpraɪz/ *v* [T] 包含 bāohán；包括 bāokuò.

compromise /ˈkɒmprəmaɪz/ *n* [C, U] 妥协〔協〕 tuǒxié；折衷 zhézhōng. **compromise** *v* 1 [I]妥协 tuǒxié. 2 [T]使遭受损害 shǐ zāoshòu sǔnhài；危及 wēijí.

compulsion /kəmˈpʌlʃn/ *n* 1 [U] 强制 qiángzhì；强迫 qiǎngpò. 2 [C] 冲〔衝〕动〔動〕 chōngdòng.

compulsive /kəmˈpʌlsɪv/ *adj* 1 入迷的 rùmíde；上瘾〔癮〕的 shàngyǐnde: *a ~ liar* 说谎成癖的人. 2(书、影片等)极〔極〕有趣的 jí yǒuqùde.

compulsory /kəmˈpʌlsərɪ/ *adj* 义〔義〕务〔務〕的 yìwùde；强制的 qiángzhìde.

compunction /kəmˈpʌŋkʃn/ *n* [U][正式用语]内疚 nèijiù.

compute /kəmˈpjuːt/ *v* [T][正式用语]计算 jìsuàn. **computation** /ˌkɒmpjuːˈteɪʃn/ *n* [U, C] 计算 jìsuàn.

computer /kəmˈpjuːtə(r)/ *n* [C] 电〔電〕子计算机〔機〕 diànzǐ jìsuànjī. **computerize** *v* [T]用电子计算机操作 yòng diànzǐ jìsuànjī cāozuò. **computerization** /kəmˌpjuːtəraɪˈzeɪʃn; *US* -rɪˈz-/ *n* [U]. **computer-ˈliterate** *adj* 懂计算机的 dǒng jìsuànjī de；熟悉计算机工作原理的 shúxī jìsuànjī gōngzuò yuánlǐ de.

comrade /ˈkɒmreɪd; *US* -ræd/ *n* [C] 1 同志 tóngzhì. 2 [旧]朋友 péngyou；伙〔夥〕伴 huǒbàn. **comradeship** *n* [U].

Con /kɒn/ *abbr* [英国政治] Conservative (party) 保守党〔黨〕 Bǎoshǒudǎng.

con /kɒn/ *v* [-nn-] [T][非正式用语]欺骗 qīpiàn；诈骗 zhàpiàn. **con** *n* [C] 诡计 guǐjì；骗局 piànjú. ˈ**con man** *n* [C] 骗钱〔錢〕的人 piànqiánde rén.

concave /ˈkɒŋkeɪv/ *adj* 凹的 āode.

conceal /kənˈsiːl/ *v* [T] 隐〔隱〕藏 yǐncáng；隐瞒 yǐnmán. **concealment** *n* [U].

concede /kənˈsiːd/ *v* 1 [T]承认〔認〕…为〔爲〕真 chéngrèn…wéizhēn. 2 [I, T]承认比赛等失败 chéngrèn bǐsài děng shībài. 3 [T] 让〔讓〕予 ràngyǔ.

conceit /kənˈsiːt/ *n* [U] 自负 zìfù；自高自大 zì gāo zì dà；骄〔驕〕傲 jiāo'ào. **conceited** *adj*.

conceive /kənˈsiːv/ *v* [I, T] 1 (*of*)想出(主意) xiǎngchū. 2 怀〔懷〕孕 huáiyùn. **conceivable** *adj* 可以相信的 kěyǐ xiāngxìn de；可以想像的 kěyǐ xiǎngxiàng de. **conceivably** *adv*.

concentrate /ˈkɒnsntreɪt/ *v* 1 [I] (*on*)集中注意力于 jízhōng zhùyìlì yú；全神贯注于 quán shén guàn zhù yú: *~ on one's work* 全神贯注于工作. 2 [I, T]集中 jízhōng. 3 [T]浓〔濃〕缩 nóngsuō；提浓 tínóng. **concentrate** *n* [C, U]浓缩物 nóngsuōwù.

concentration /ˌkɒnsnˈtreɪʃn/ *n* 1 [U]专〔專〕心 zhuānxīn. 2 [C]集中的人或物 jízhōngde rén huò wù. **concenˈtration camp** *n* [C] 集中营〔營〕 jízhōngyíng.

concentric /kənˈsentrɪk/ *adj* (圆)同心的 tóngxīnde.

concept /ˈkɒnsept/ *n* [C] 概念 gàiniàn；思想 sīxiǎng.

conception /kənˈsepʃn/ *n* 1 (a) [U] 概念的形成 gàiniànde xíngchéng. (b) [C] 概念 gàiniàn；想法 xiǎngfǎ. 2 [U]怀〔懷〕孕 huáiyùn.

concern[1] /kənˈsɜːn/ *v* 1 [T]担〔擔〕心 dānxīn；记挂〔掛〕 jìguà: *I am ~ed about her safety*. 我担心她的安全. 2 **~ oneself with** 忙于 mángyú. 3 [T]对〔對〕…有重要性 duì…yǒu zhòngyàoxìng；影响〔響〕 yǐngxiǎng. 4 [T] 涉及 shèjí. 5 [习语] **as far as sb/sth is concerned** 就…而言 jiù…ér yán: *As far as I'm ~ed, it doesn't matter what you do*. 就我来说，

你做什么都没有关系. **concerning** *prep* 关〔關〕于 guānyú.

concern[2] /kən'sɜːn/ *n* 1 [U] 担〔擔〕心 dānxīn; 忧〔憂〕虑〔慮〕yōulǜ. 2 关〔關〕切的事 guānqiède shì. 3 [C] 商行 shāngháng; 企业〔業〕qǐyè: *a profitable* ~ 赚钱的企业.

C

concert /'kɒnsət/ *n* 1 [C] 音乐〔樂〕会〔會〕yīnyuèhuì. 2 [习语] **in 'concert** (a) 现场〔場〕演出音乐会 xiànchǎng yǎnchū yīnyuèhuì. (b) [正式用语] 合作 hézuò.

concerted /kən'sɜːtɪd/ *adj* 商定的 shāngdìngde; 一致的 yízhìde: *make a* ~ *effort* 齐心协力.

concertina /ˌkɒnsə'tiːnə/ *n* [C] 六角手风〔風〕琴 liùjiǎo shǒufēngqín. **concertina** *v* [I] 折起 zhéqǐ.

concerto /kən'tʃeətəʊ, -'tʃɜːt-/ *n* [C] [*pl* ~s] 协〔協〕奏曲 xiézòuqǔ.

concession /kən'seʃn/ *n* 1 (a) [U] 让〔讓〕步 ràngbù. (b) [C] 让与〔與〕物 ràngyǔwù. 2 [C] 特许权〔權〕tèxǔquán: *a* ~ *to drill for oil* 钻探石油的特许权.

conciliate /kən'sɪlɪeɪt/ *v* [T] [正式用语] 安抚〔撫〕ānfǔ; 劝〔勸〕慰 quànwèi. **conciliation** /kənˌsɪlɪ'eɪʃn/ *n* [U]. **conciliatory** /kən'sɪlɪətərɪ; *US* -ɪetɔːrɪ/ *adj* 抚慰的 fǔwèide.

concise /kən'saɪs/ *adj* 简明的 jiǎnmíngde; 简要的 jiǎnyàode: *a* ~ *report* 简要的报告. **concisely** *adv*. **conciseness** *n* [U].

conclude /kən'kluːd/ *v* 1 [I,T] [常为正式用语] 结束 jiéshù. 2 [T] 推论〔論〕出 tuīlùn chū: *The jury* ~*d that he was guilty*. 陪审团断定他有罪. 3 [T] 安排 ānpái; 缔结 dìjié: ~ *an agreement* 缔结协定. **conclusion** /-'kluːʒn/ *n* [C] 1 结束 jiéshù; 终了 zhōngliǎo 2 决定 juédìng; 解决 jiějué. **conclusive** /-'kluːsɪv/ (证据等) 令人信服的 lìng rén xìnfú de. **conclusively** *adv*.

concoct /kən'kɒkt/ *v* [T] 1 调合 tiáohé; 混合 hùnhé. 2 编造(故事等) biānzào. **concoction** /-'kɒkʃn / *n* 1 [C] 混合物 hùnhéwù; 调制〔製〕物 tiáozhìwù. 2 [U] 混合 hùnhé.

concord /'kɒŋkɔːd/ *n* [U] [正式用语] 和谐 héxié; 一致 yízhì.

concourse /'kɒŋkɔːs/ *n* [C] 群集场〔場〕所 qúnjí chǎngsuǒ.

concrete /'kɒŋkriːt/ *n* [U] 混凝土 hùnníngtǔ. **concrete** *v* [T] 浇〔澆〕混凝土于 jiāo hùnníngtǔ yú. **concrete** *adj* 1 有形的 yǒuxíngde. 2 具体〔體〕的 jùtǐde; 明确〔確〕的 míngquède: *a* ~ *suggestion* 具体的建议.

concur /kən'kɜː(r)/ *v* [-rr-] [I] [正式用语] 1 同意 tóngyì; 赞〔讚〕成 zànchéng. 2 同时〔時〕发〔發〕生 tóngshí fāshēng. **concurrence** /-'kʌrəns / *n* [U]. **concurrent** /-'kʌrənt/ *adj* 同时的 tóngshíde; 兼任的 jiānrènde. **concurrently** *adv*.

concuss /kən'kʌs/ *v* [T] 使(脑)震伤〔傷〕shǐ zhènshāng. **concussion** /-'kʌʃn/ *n* [U].

condemn /kən'dem/ *v* [T] 1 谴责 qiǎnzé. 2 *to* (a) [法律] 给…判刑 gěi…pànxíng: *He was* ~*ed to death*. 他被判死刑. (b) 迫使接受不愉快的事物 pòshǐ jiēshòu bù yúkuàide shìwù: ~*ed to a job she hates* 被迫做她讨厌的工作. 3 宣告(建筑物)不宜使用 xuāngào bùyí shǐyòng. **condemnation** /ˌkɒndem'neɪʃn/ *n* [U,C].

condense /kən'dens/ *v* 1 [I,T] (a) (使)(液体)浓〔濃〕缩 nóngsuō. (b) (气体、水汽等) 冷凝 lěngníng. 2 [T] 缩短 suōduǎn; 压〔壓〕缩 yāsuō: ~ *a speech* 压缩讲话. **condensation** /ˌkɒnden'seɪʃn / *n* [U] 1 凝结 níngjié; 冷凝 lěngníng. 2 蒸汽凝结成的水滴 zhēngqì níngjié chéng de shuǐdī. **condenser** *n* [C].

condescend /ˌkɒndɪ'send/ *v* [I] (*to*) [贬] 俯就 fǔjiù; 屈尊 qūzūn; 俯允 fǔyǔn: *The manager* ~*ed to talk to the workers*. 经理放下架子同工人们谈话. **condescending** *adj*. **condescension** /-'senʃn/ *n* [U].

condiment /'kɒndɪmənt/ *n* [C] 调味品 tiáowèipǐn; 作料 zuóliào.

condition[1] /kən'dɪʃn/ *n* 1 [sing] 状〔狀〕况 zhuàngkuàng; 状态〔態〕zhuàngtài: *a car in good* ~ 车况良好的汽车. 2 **conditions** [pl] 环〔環〕境 huánjìng; 情形 qíngxíng. 3 [C] (a) 条〔條〕件 tiáojiàn: *One of the* ~*s of the job is that you can drive*. 这个工作岗位的条件之一是会开车. (b) (合同等上的) 条件 tiáojiàn. 4 [U] 健康 jiànkāng: *be out of* ~ 健康状况不佳. 5 [C] 病 bìng. 6 [习语] **on condition that** 在…条件下 zài… tiáojiàn xià.

condition[2] /kən'dɪʃn/ *v* [T] 1 决定 juédìng; 支配 zhīpèi. 2 训练〔練〕xùnliàn; 使适〔適〕应〔應〕shǐ shìyìng. **conditioner** *n* [C] 护〔護〕发〔髮〕剂〔劑〕hùfàjì. **conditioning** *n* [U].

conditional /kən'dɪʃənl/ *adj* 1 (*on*) 附有条〔條〕件的 fù yǒu tiáojiàn de; 视…而定的 shì …ér dìng de: *Payment is* ~ *on satisfactory completion of the work*. 完满完成工作才付酬. 2 [语法] (子句) 条件的 tiáojiànde. **conditionally** /-ʃənəlɪ/ *adv*.

condolence /kən'dəʊləns/ [U,C 尤作 pl] 吊唁 diàoyàn; 吊慰 diàowèi; 慰问 wèiwèn.

condom /'kɒndəm/ *n* [C] 避孕套 bìyùntào.

condone /kən'dəʊn/ *v* [T] 宽恕 kuānshù; 原谅 yuánliàng.

conducive /kən'djuːsɪv; *US* -'duːs-/ *adj to* 有益于…的 yǒuyì yú…de; 有助于…的 yǒuzhù yú… de: ~ *to health* 有益于健康.

conduct[1] /kən'dʌkt/ *v* **1** [T] 组织〔織〕zǔzhi；指导〔導〕zhǐdǎo；进〔進〕行 jìnxíng：～ *a survey* 进行调查. **2** ～ **oneself** [正式用语]表现 biǎoxiàn；为〔爲〕人 wéirén. **3** [I,T]指挥(乐队等) zhǐhuī. **4** [T]传〔傳〕导(热、电等) chuándǎo. **conduction** /-'dʌkʃn/ *n* [U](热、电的)传导 chuándǎo. **conductor** *n* [C] **1** (乐队等的)指挥 zhǐhuī. **2** (*fem* **conductress** /-'dʌktrɪs/) [英国英语]公共汽车〔車〕售票员 gōnggòngqìchē shòupiàoyuán. **3** 导体〔體〕dǎotǐ.

conduct[2] /'kɒndʌkt/ *n* [U] **1** 行为〔爲〕xíngwéi；举〔舉〕动〔動〕jǔdòng；品行 pǐnxíng. **2** 处〔處〕理方法 chǔlǐ fāngfǎ.

cone /kəʊn/ *n* [C] **1** (a)圆锥体〔體〕yuánzhuītǐ. (b)圆锥形的东〔東〕西 yuánzhuīxíngde dōngxi：*an ice-cream* ～ 蛋卷冰淇淋. **2** (松树等的)球果 qiúguǒ.

confection /kən'fekʃən/ *n* [C][正式用语]糖果 tángguǒ；点〔點〕心 diǎnxīn. **confectioner** /-ʃənə(r)/ *n* [C]制〔製〕造、销售糖果点心的人 zhìzào、xiāoshòu tángguǒ diǎnxīn de rén. **confectionery** *n* [U] 糖果点心 tángguǒ diǎnxīn.

confederacy /kən'fedərəsɪ/ *n* [C] [*pl* -ies] 邦联〔聯〕bānglián；同盟 tóngméng；联盟 liánméng.

confederate /kən'fedərət/ *n* [C] 同盟者 tóngméngzhě；同盟国〔國〕tóngméngguó；同谋 tóngmóu；同伙〔夥〕tónghuǒ.

confederation /kənˌfedə'reɪʃn/ *n* [C] 同盟 tóngméng；联〔聯〕盟 liánméng；邦联 bānglián.

confer /kən'fɜː(r)/ *v*[-rr-][正式用语] **1** [I] (*with*) 协〔協〕商 xiéshāng. **2** [T] (*on*)授予 shòuyǔ：～ *authority on sb* 授予某人权〔權〕力.

conference /'kɒnfərəns/ *n* [C] **1** 会〔會〕议〔議〕huìyì；大会 dàhuì. **2**[习语] **in conference** 正开〔開〕正式会议 zhèngkāi zhèngshì huìyì. **'conference call** *n* [C] 电〔電〕话会议 diànhuà huìyì.

confess /kən'fes/ *v*[I,T] **1** 承认〔認〕(做错) chéngrèn. **2**(尤指罗马天主教)向神父忏〔懺〕悔 xiàng shénfù chànhuǐ. **confession** /-'feʃn/ *n* [C,U] **1** 招供 zhāogòng；交代 jiāodài；坦白 tǎnbái. **2** 忏悔 chànhuǐ. **confessional** /-'feʃənl/ *n* [C] 忏悔室(神父听取忏悔处) chànhuǐshì.

confetti /kən'fetɪ/ *n* [用 sing v] (婚礼中投掷的)五彩纸屑 wǔcǎi zhǐxiè.

confidant /ˌkɒnfɪ'dænt/ (*fem* **-dante** /kɒnfɪ'dænt/) *n* [C] 知心人 zhīxīnrén.

confide /kən'faɪd/ *v* **1**[T]向…吐露秘密 xiàng…tǔlù mìmì. **2** [短语动词] **confide in sb** 向信任的人吐露秘密 xiàng xìnrènde rén tǔlù mìmì.

confidence /'kɒnfɪdəns/ *n* **1**[U] 信任 xìnrèn. **2**[U]信心 xìnxīn；自信 zìxìn. **3** [C]秘密话 mìmìhuà. **4**[习语] **in (strict) confidence** 作为〔爲〕秘密 zuòwéi mìmì. **take sb into one's confidence** 把某人作为知心人 bǎ mǒurén zuòwéi zhīxīnrén. **confident** /-dənt/ *adj* 确〔確〕信的 quèxìnde；有把握的 yǒu bǎwò de. **confidently** *adv*.

confidential /ˌkɒnfɪ'denʃl/ *adj* **1** 机〔機〕密的 jīmìde；秘密的 mìmìde. **2** 信任的 xìnrènde；心腹的 xīnfùde. **confidentiality** /-ˌdenʃɪ'ælətɪ/ *n* [U]. **confidentially** /-ʃəlɪ/ *adv*.

configuration /kənˌfɪgə'reɪʃn; *US* -ˌfɪgjʊ'reɪʃn/ *n* [正式用语]配置 pèizhì；布〔佈〕局 bùjú.

confine /kən'faɪn/ *v* [T] **1** (*to*) 限制 xiànzhì；控制 kòngzhì：*The illness was* ～*d to the village*. 这种疾病被控制在这个村的范围里. **2** 禁闭 jìnbì：～*d to bed with a fever* 因发烧而卧床. **confined** *adj* (空间)有限的 yǒuxiànde；狭〔狹〕窄的 xiázhǎide. **confinement** *n* **1**[U] 监〔監〕禁 jiānjìn；禁闭 jìnbì. **2** [C,U] 分娩 fēnmiǎn. **confines** /'kɒnfaɪnz/ *n* [pl] [正式用语]界限 jièxiàn；边〔邊〕界 biānjiè.

confirm /kən'fɜːm/ *v* [T] **1** 证〔證〕实〔實〕zhèngshí：*The announcement* ～*ed my suspicions*. 这个通告证实了我的怀疑. **2** 确〔確〕定 quèdìng：*Please write to* ～ *the details*. 请把细节写明确. **3** [通常用被动语态] (基督徒)施坚〔堅〕信礼〔禮〕(使成为教徒) shī jiānxìnlǐ. **confirmation** /ˌkɒnfə'meɪʃn/ *n* [C,U]. **confirmed** *adj* 确定的 quèdìngde；坚〔堅〕定的 jiāndìngde：*a* ～*ed bachelor* 抱独身主义的单身汉.

confiscate /'kɒnfɪskeɪt/ *v*[T] 没收(私人财产) mòshōu. **confiscation** /ˌkɒnfɪ'skeɪʃn/ *n* [C,U].

conflagration /kɒnflə'greɪʃn/ *n* [C][正式用语]大火灾〔災〕dà huǒzāi.

conflict /'kɒnflɪkt/ *n* [C,U] **1** 战〔戰〕斗〔鬥〕zhàndòu；斗争 dòuzhēng. **2** (意见)分歧 fēnqí. **conflict** /kən'flɪkt/ *v* [I] 抵触〔觸〕dǐchù；冲〔衝〕突 chōngtū.

conform /kən'fɔːm/ *v* [I] **1** (*to*)遵守(规则、标准等) zūnshǒu. **2** (*with* /*to*) 符合 fúhé. **conformist** *n* [C]遵纪守法者 zūnjì shǒufǎzhě. **conformity** *n* [U].

confound /kən'faʊnd/ *v* [T] [旧词,正式用语]使困惑和惊〔驚〕奇 shǐ kùnhuò hé jīngqí.

confront /kən'frʌnt/ *v* [T] **1** (*with*)使面临〔臨〕(困难等) shǐ miànlín. **2** 使面对〔對〕(令人不愉快的事物) shǐ miànduì. **3** 面对 miànduì；对抗 duìkàng. **confrontation** /ˌkɒnfrʌn'teɪʃn/ *n* [C,U]对抗 duìkàng.

confuse /kən'fjuːz/ *v* **1**[T]弄错 nòngcuò：

You have ~d him and/with his brother. 你把他和他的兄弟搞混了. 2 使糊涂〔塗〕shǐ hútu: *I am ~d*. 我弄糊涂了. 3 使模糊不清 shǐ móhu bùqīng. **confusion** /-ˈfjuːʒn/ *n* [U].

C

congeal /kənˈdʒiːl/ *v* [I,T] (使)冻结 dòngjié; (使)凝结 níngjié.

congenial /kənˈdʒiːnɪəl/ *adj* 1 令人愉快的 lìng rén yúkuàide: *a ~ atmosphere* 令人愉快的气氛. 2 情投意合的 qíng tóu yì hé de. **congenially** *adv*.

congenital /kənˈdʒenɪtl/ *adj* (疾病等)先天的 xiāntiānde.

congested /kənˈdʒestɪd/ *adj* 拥〔擁〕挤〔擠〕的 yōngjǐde: *streets ~ with traffic* 车流拥挤的街道. **congestion** /-ˈdʒestʃən/ *n* [U].

conglomerate /kənˈglɒmərət/ *n* [C] 联〔聯〕合大企业〔業〕liánhé dà qǐyè. **conglomeration** /kənˌglɒməˈreɪʃn/ *n* [C] 聚集物 jùjíwù; 混合体〔體〕hùnhétǐ.

congratulate /kənˈgrætʃuleɪt/ *v* [T] 祝贺 zhùhè; 庆〔慶〕贺 qìnghè: *~ sb on good exam results* 祝贺某人考试成绩优秀. **congratulations** /kənˌgrætʃuˈleɪʃnz/ *interj* 祝贺你! zhùhènǐ!

congregate /ˈkɒŋgrɪgeɪt/ *v* [I] 集合 jíhé. **congregation** /ˌkɒŋgrɪˈgeɪʃn/ *n* [C] 教堂会〔會〕众〔衆〕jiàotáng huìzhòng. **congregational** *adj*.

congress /ˈkɒŋgres; *US* -grəs/ *n* [C, 亦作 sing, 用 pl v] 1 代表会〔會〕议〔議〕dàibiǎo huìyì. 2 Congress (美国等)议会 yìhuì. **congressional** /kənˈgreʃənl/ *adj*. ˈ**Congressman**, ˈ**Congresswoman** *n* [C] (美国国会)男女议员 nánnǚ yìyuán.

congruent /ˈkɒŋgruənt/ *adj* (三角形)全等的 quánděngde; 迭合的 diéhéde.

congruous /ˈkɒŋgruəs/ *adj* [正式用语]适〔適〕合的 shìhéde.

conical /ˈkɒnɪkl/ *adj* 圆锥形的 yuánzhuīxíngde.

conifer /ˈkɒnɪfə(r), 亦作 ˈkəun-/ *n* [C]针叶〔葉〕树〔樹〕zhēnyèshù. **coniferous** / kəˈnɪfərəs; *US* kəuˈn- / *adj*.

conjecture /kənˈdʒektʃə(r)/ *v* [I,T] [正式用语]猜想 cāixiǎng; 猜测 cāicè; 推测 tuīcè. **conjecture** *n* [C,U][正式用语]推测 tuīcè. **conjectural** *adj*.

conjugal /ˈkɒndʒugl/ *adj* [正式用语]婚姻的 hūnyīnde; 夫妇〔婦〕关〔關〕系〔係〕的 fūfù guānxì de; 夫妇的 fūfùde.

conjunction /kənˈdʒʌŋkʃn/ *n* 1 [C] [语法] 连词 liáncí. 2 [C,U][正式用语]联〔聯〕合 liánhé; 接合 jiēhé; 连接 liánjiē. 3 [习语]**in conjunction with sb/sth** 与〔與〕…共同 yǔ…gòngtóng.

conjure /ˈkʌndʒə(r)/ *v* 1 [I] 变〔變〕戏〔戲〕法 biànxìfǎ; 施魔术〔術〕shī móshù. 2 [短语动词] **conjure sth up** 使呈现于脑〔腦〕际〔際〕shǐ chéngxiàn yú nǎojì. **conjurer** (亦作 **conjuror**) *n* [C] 变戏法者 biàn xìfǎzhě.

conk /kɒŋk/ *v* [短语动词]**conk out** [非正式用语] (a)(机器)停止运〔運〕转〔轉〕tíngzhǐ yùnzhuǎn: *His old car has ~ed out*. 他的那辆老车开不动了. (b)(人)筋疲力尽〔盡〕jīn pí lì jìn; 入睡 rùshuì; 死去 sǐqù.

connect /kəˈnekt/ *v* 1 [I,T]连结 liánjié; 连接 liánjiē: *~ two wires* 把两条电线连接起来. 2 [T]联〔聯〕想 liánxiǎng.

connection (英国英语亦作 **connexion**) /kəˈnekʃn/ *n* 1 (a)[U] 连接 liánjiē; 连结 liánjié. (b)[C] 连结点〔點〕liánjiédiǎn; 关〔關〕系〔係〕guānxì. 2 [C] (火车、飞机等)联运〔運〕liányùn. 3[C, 常用 pl](生意上的)熟人 shúrén. 4 [习语] **in connection with sb/sth** 关于 guānyú.

connive /kəˈnaɪv/ *v*[I] (*at*)默许 mòxǔ; 纵〔縱〕容 zòngróng. **connivance** *n* [U].

connoisseur /ˌkɒnəˈsɜː(r)/ *n* [C] 鉴〔鑒〕赏家 jiànshǎngjiā; 鉴定家 jiàndìngjiā; 行家 hángjiā; 内行 nèiháng.

connotation /ˌkɒnəˈteɪʃn/ *n* [C, 尤作 pl] 言外之意 yán wài zhī yì: *Be careful not to use slang words that have obscene ~s*. 当心别使用含有下流的言外之意的俚语词.

conquer /ˈkɒŋkə(r)/ *v* [T]1 攻取 gōngqǔ; 攻克 gōngkè. 2 战〔戰〕胜〔勝〕zhànshèng; 克服 kèfú: [喻] *You must ~ your fear of driving*. 你必须克服你对开车的害怕情绪. **conqueror** *n* [C].

conquest /ˈkɒŋkwest/ *n* 1 [U] 征服 zhēngfú. 2 [C] 征服地 zhēngfúdì; 掠取物 lüèqǔwù.

conscience /ˈkɒnʃəns/ *n* 1 [C,U] 是非感 shìfēigǎn; 良心 liángxīn: *have a clear ~* 问心无愧. *have a guilty ~* 感到内疚. 2 [习语] **(have sth) on one's conscience** 因某事而感到内疚 yīn mǒushì ér gǎndào nèijiù.

conscientious /ˌkɒnʃɪˈenʃəs/ *adj* (人、行为)小心谨慎的 xiǎoxīn jǐnshèn de. **conscientiously** *adv*. **conscientiousness** *n* [U].

conscious /ˈkɒnʃəs/ *adj* 1 清醒的 qīngxǐngde. 2 (*of*) 知道的 zhīdàode; 觉〔覺〕察的 juécháde. 3 故意的 gùyìde: *make a ~ effort* 刻意. **consciously** *adv*. **consciousness** *n* [U]: *regain ~ness after an accident* 事故之后恢复了知觉.

conscript /kənˈskrɪpt/ *v* [T] 征〔徵〕募 zhēngmù; 征召 zhēngzhào. **conscript** /ˈkɒnskrɪpt/ *n* [C] 应〔應〕征士兵 yìngzhēng shìbīng. **conscription** /-ˈskrɪpʃn/ *n* [U].

consecrate /ˈkɒnsɪkreɪt/ *v* [T] 1 把…奉为

〔爲〕神圣〔聖〕bǎ… fèngwéi shénshèng；使成为神圣 shǐ chéngwéi shénshèng：～ *a church* 主持教堂的奉献礼. 2 把…放着做祭祀用 bǎ… fàngzhe zuò jìsì yòng. **consecration** /ˌkɒnsɪˈkreɪʃn/ *n* [U].

consecutive /kənˈsekjʊtɪv/ *adj* 连续〔續〕的 liánxùde；连贯的 liánguànde；顺序的 shùnxùde. **consecutively** *adv*.

consensus /kənˈsensəs/ *n* [C, U] 一致 yízhì；合意 héyì.

consent /kənˈsent/ *v* [I] (*to*) 同意 tóngyì；赞成 zànchéng. **consent** *n* [U] 同意 tóngyì；赞成 zànchéng；允许 yǔnxǔ.

consequence /ˈkɒnsɪkwəns; *US* -kwens/ *n* 1 [C] 结果 jiéguǒ；后〔後〕果 hòuguǒ：*the political ～s of the decision* 这个决定的政治后果. 2 [U] [正式用语]重要(性) zhòngyào；重大 zhòngdà：*It is of no ～*. 那没有什么重要.

consequent /ˈkɒnsɪkwənt/ *adj* [正式用语] 随〔隨〕之发〔發〕生的 suí zhī fāshēng de. **consequently** *adv* 因而 yīn'ér；所以 suǒyǐ.

consequential /ˌkɒnsɪˈkwenʃl/ *adj* [正式用语] 1 随〔隨〕之发〔發〕生的 suí zhī fāshēng de. 2 重要的 zhòngyàode.

conservation /ˌkɒnsəˈveɪʃn/ *n* [U] 1 保存 bǎocún；保护〔護〕bǎohù. 2 对〔對〕自然环〔環〕境的保护 duì zìrán huánjìngde bǎohù. **conservationist** *n* [C] 自然环境保护者 zìrán huánjìng bǎohùzhě.

conservative /kənˈsɜːvətɪv/ *adj* 1 保守的 bǎoshǒude；守旧〔舊〕的 shǒujiùde. 2 **Conservative** 英国〔國〕保守党〔黨〕的 Yīngguó Bǎoshǒudǎng de. 3 谨慎的 jǐnshènde；稳〔穩〕当〔當〕的 wěndangde：*a ～ estimate* 稳妥的估计. **conservative** *n* [C] 1 保守主义〔義〕者 bǎoshǒuzhǔyìzhě. 2 **Conservative** 英国保守党人 Yīngguó Bǎoshǒudǎngrén. **conservatively** *adv*. **the Conˈservative Party** *n* [sing] [英国政治]英国保守党 Yīngguó Bǎoshǒudǎng. **conservatism** /-tɪzəm/ *n* [U].

conservatory /kənˈsɜːvətrɪ; *US* -tɔːrɪ/ *n* [C] [*pl* -ies] 1 (培养植物的)暖房 nuǎnfáng，温室 wēnshì. 2 艺〔藝〕术〔術〕学〔學〕校 yìshù xuéxiào.

conserve /kənˈsɜːv/ *v* [T] 保存 bǎocún；保藏 bǎocáng. **conserve** /ˈkɒnsɜːv/ *n* [C, U] [正式用语]果酱〔醬〕guǒjiàng；蜜饯〔餞〕mìjiàn.

consider /kənˈsɪdə(r)/ *v* [T] 1 想 xiǎng；考虑〔慮〕kǎolǜ. 2 认〔認〕为〔爲〕rènwéi；以为 yǐwéi：*We ～ this (to be) very important*. 我们认为这很重要. 3 顾〔顧〕及 gùjí；体〔體〕谅 tǐliàng：～ *the feelings of others* 体谅别人的感情. **considered** *adj* 经〔經〕过〔過〕深思熟虑的 jīngguò shēnsī shúlǜde：*a ～ed opinion* 经过反复考虑的意见.

considerable /kənˈsɪdərəbl/ *adj* 相当〔當〕大的 xiāngdāng dà de. **considerably** /-əblɪ/ *adv* 相当大地 xiāngdāng dà de：*It's considerably colder today*. 今天冷得多了.

considerate /kənˈsɪdərət/ *adj* 体〔體〕贴别人的 tǐtiē biérén de. **considerately** *adv*.

consideration /kənˌsɪdəˈreɪʃn/ *n* 1 [U] 考虑〔慮〕kǎolǜ. 2 [U] (对别人的)体〔體〕贴 tǐtiē. 3 [C] 要考虑的事 yào kǎolǜ de shì：*Cost is just one of the ～s*. 费用仅仅是要考虑的因素之一. 4 [C] [正式用语]报〔報〕酬 bàochóu. 5 [习语] **take sth into consideration** 考虑某事 kǎolǜ mǒushì.

considering /kənˈsɪdərɪŋ/ *prep, conj* 考虑〔慮〕到 kǎolǜdào；就…而论〔論〕jiù…ér lùn：*She's very active, ～ her age*. 考虑到她的年龄，她是很积极的.

consign /kənˈsaɪn/ *v* [T] 1 运〔運〕送(货物) yùnsòng. 2 [正式用语]交付 jiāofù；把…委托〔託〕给 bǎ…wěi tuō gěi：～ *the boy to his brother's care* 把男孩子托付给他的兄弟照顾. **consignment** *n* 1 [U] 交付 jiāofù；托付 tuōfù. 2 [C] 托付物 tuōfùwù.

consist /kənˈsɪst/ *v* [I] [短语动词] **consist of** 由…组成 yóu…zǔchéng；由…构〔構〕成 yóu…gòuchéng：*a meal ～ing of soup and bread* 一顿有汤和面包的饭. **consist in** 以…为〔爲〕主要成分 yǐ…wéi zhǔyào chéngfèn.

consistency /kənˈsɪstənsɪ/ *n* 1 [U] 一致性 yízhìxìng；连贯性 liánguànxìng. 2 [C, U] [*pl* -ies] (尤指液体的)浓〔濃〕度 nóngdù；稠度 chóudù；密度 mìdù.

consistent /kənˈsɪstənt/ *adj* 1 [褒](行为等)始终如一的 shǐzhōng rúyīde. 2 (*with*) 与〔與〕…一致的 yǔ…yízhìde：*injuries ～ with the accident* 与这次事故相符的受伤情况. **consistently** *adv*.

consolation /ˌkɒnsəˈleɪʃn/ *n* 1 [U] 安慰 ānwèi；慰藉 wèijiè：*a few words of ～* 几句安慰的话. 2 [C] 安慰的人或物 ānwèide rén huò wù.

console[1] /kənˈsəʊl/ *v* [T] 安慰 ānwèi；慰问 wèiwèn.

console[2] /ˈkɒnsəʊl/ *n* [C] (电子设备的)控制盘〔盤〕kòngzhìpán.

consolidate /kənˈsɒlɪdeɪt/ *v* [I, T] 1 巩〔鞏〕固 gǒnggù；加强 jiāqiáng. 2 [商]把…合为〔爲〕一体〔體〕bǎ… héwéi yìtǐ：～ *all his debts* 把他所有的债务合并起来. **consolidation** /kənˌsɒlɪˈdeɪʃn/ *n* [C, U].

consonant /ˈkɒnsənənt/ *n* [C] (a) 辅音 fǔyīn. (b) 辅音字母 fǔyīn zìmǔ

consort[1] /ˈkɒnsɔːt/ *n* [C] 帝王的夫或妻 dìwángde fū huò qī；配偶 pèi'ǒu.

consort[2] /kənˈsɔːt/ *v* [I] (*with*) [常作贬]

C

陪伴 péibàn；结交 jiéjiāo：~*ing with criminals* 结交犯罪分子.

consortium /kən'sɔːtɪəm；*US* -'sɔːrʃɪəm/ *n* [*pl* -tia /-tɪə；*US* -ʃɪə/] [C] [用 sing 或 pl v] 国〔國〕际〔際〕财团〔團〕guójì cáituán.

C

conspicuous /kən'spɪkjuəs/ *adj* 明显〔顯〕的 míngxiǎnde；引人注目的 yǐn rén zhùmù de. **conspicuously** *adv*.

conspiracy /kən'spɪrəsɪ/ *n* [*pl* -ies] 1 [U] 阴〔陰〕谋 yīnmóu；密谋 mìmóu. 2 [C] 同谋 tóngmóu；共谋 gòngmóu.

conspire /kən'spaɪə(r)/ *v* [I] 1 (*with*；*against*) 密商 mìshāng；阴〔陰〕谋 yīnmóu；密谋 mìmóu：~ *to kill the king* 密谋弄死国王. *He* ~*d with others against the government*. 他与别人密谋反对政府. 2 (*against*) 协〔協〕力 xiélì；联〔聯〕合 liánhé：*Circumstances* ~*d against them*. 种种对他们不利的情况凑在了一起. **conspirator** /kən'spɪrətə(r)/ *n* [C] 阴谋家 yīnmóujiā；共谋者 gòngmóuzhě.

constable /'kʌnstəbl；*US* 'kɒn-/ *n* [C] [英国旧词] 警察 jǐngchá. **constabulary** /kən'stæbjʊlərɪ；*US* -lerɪ/ *n* [C, 亦作 sing, 用 pl v] [*pl* -ies] 警察 jǐngchá；保安队〔隊〕bǎo'ānduì.

constant /'kɒnstənt/ *adj* 1 经〔經〕常的 jīngchángde；经久的 jīngjiǔde；不变〔變〕的 búbiànde；不断〔斷〕的 búduànde：~ *noise* 不断的噪音. 2 持久不变〔變〕的 chíjiǔ búbiàn de：*a* ~ *temperature* 恒温. **constancy** *n* [U].

constellation /ˌkɒnstə'leɪʃn/ *n* [C] 星座 xīngzuò.

consternation /ˌkɒnstə'neɪʃn/ *n* [U] 惊〔驚〕恐 jīngkǒng；惊愕 jīng'è.

constipated /'kɒnstɪpeɪtɪd/ *adj* 便秘的 biànmìde. **constipation** /ˌkɒnstɪ'peɪʃn/ *n* [U] 便秘 biànmì.

constituency /kən'stɪtʃʊənsɪ/ *n* [C] [用 sing 或 pl v] [C] [*pl* -ies] 选〔選〕区〔區〕xuǎnqū；全体〔體〕选民 quántǐ xuǎnmín.

constituent /kən'stɪtʃʊənt/ *adj* 1 组成的 zǔchéngde. 2 (大会等)有宪〔憲〕法制订权〔權〕的 yǒu xiànfǎ zhìdìngquán de. **constituent** *n* [C] 1 选〔選〕民 xuǎnmín；选举〔舉〕人 xuǎnjǔrén. 2 成分 chéngfèn；要素 yàosù.

constitute /'kɒnstɪtjuːt/ *v* [T] 1 组成 zǔchéng；构〔構〕成 gòuchéng：*Twelve months* ~ *a year*. 一年有 12 个月. 2 是 shì：*The decision to build the road* ~*s a real threat to the countryside*. 修建这条路的决定是对农村的真正的威胁.

constitution /ˌkɒnstɪ'tjuːʃn；*US* -'tuːʃn/ *n* 1 [C] 宪〔憲〕法 xiànfǎ. 2 [C] (人的)体〔體〕格 tǐgé；体质〔質〕tǐzhì；素质 sùzhì：*a strong* ~ 强壮的体格. 3 [C] (事物的)构〔構〕造 gòuzào；组成(方式) zǔchéng. **constitutional** *adj* 符合宪法的 fúhé xiànfǎ de. **constitutionally** /-əlɪ/ *adv*.

constrain /kən'streɪn/ *v* [T] [正式用语]强迫 qiǎngpò；强使 qiǎngshǐ：*I felt* ~*ed to obey*. 我觉得非遵命不可.

constraint /kən'streɪnt/ *n* 1 [C] 限制性的事物 xiànzhìxìngde shìwù：*One of the* ~*s on the project will be the money available*. 这项工程遇到的制约之一是可动用的资金问题. 2 [U]约束 yuēshù；强制 qiángzhì.

constrict /kən'strɪkt/ *v* [T] 使收缩 shǐ shōusuō；压〔壓〕缩 yāsuō：*a tight collar* ~*ing the neck* 卡着脖子的衣领. **constriction** /kən'strɪkʃn/ *n* 1 [U] 压缩 yāsuō. 2 [C] 压缩的事物 yāsuōde shìwù：[喻] *the* ~*ions of prison life* 牢狱生活中的种种约束.

construct /kən'strʌkt/ *v* [T] 建造 jiànzào；建筑〔築〕jiànzhù.

construction /kən'strʌkʃn/ *n* 1 [U] 建设 jiànshè；建造 jiànzào, 建筑〔築〕jiànzhù：*The new bridge is still under* ~. 新桥仍在建筑中. 2 [C] 结构〔構〕jiégòu；建筑物 jiànzhùwù.

constructive /kən'strʌktɪv/ *adj* 有帮〔幫〕助的 yǒu bāngzhù de；有用的 yǒuyòngde：~ *suggestions* 有用的建议.

consul /'kɒnsl/ *n* [C] 领事 lǐngshì. **consular** /'kɒnsjʊlə(r)；*US* -sel-/ *adj* 领事的 lǐngshìde；领事职〔職〕权〔權〕的 lǐngshì zhíquán de. **consulate** / 'kɒnsjʊlət / *n* [C] 领事馆 lǐngshìguǎn.

consult /kən'sʌlt/ *v* 1 [T] 请教 qǐngjiào；咨询 zīxún；查阅 cháyuè：~ *the doctor about a sore throat* 为喉咙疼去看医生. 2 [I] (*with*) 商量 shāngliáng：~ *with one's friend* 同朋友商量.

consultant /kən'sʌltənt/ *n* [C] 1 顾〔顧〕问 gùwèn. 2 [英国英语]会〔會〕诊医〔醫〕师〔師〕huìzhěn yīshī：*a* ~ *surgeon* 会诊外科医师.

consultation /ˌkənsəl'teɪʃn/ *n* 1 [U] 咨询 zīxún；磋商 cuōshāng. 2 [C] (磋商)会〔會〕议〔議〕huìyì；会诊 huìzhěn.

consume /kən'sjuːm；*US* -'suːm/ *v* [T] 1 消耗 xiāohào：*Some types of car* ~ *less petrol than others*. 某些类型的汽车比其他汽车汽油消耗得少. 2 (火等)烧〔燒〕毁〔燬〕shāohuǐ；毁灭〔滅〕huǐmiè. 3 [正式用语] 吃光 chīguāng；喝光 hēguāng. **consuming** *adj* 强烈的 qiángliède：*a* ~ *passion* 强烈的情绪.

consumer /kən'sjuːmə(r)；*US* -suː-/ *n* [C] 消费者 xiāofèizhě；用户 yònghù. **consumer durables** = DURABLES (DURABLE). **consumer goods** *n* [pl] 生活资料 shēnghuó zīliào；消费品 xiāofèipǐn.

consummate /ˈkɒnsəmeɪt/ *v* [T] 1 [正式用语]使完善 shǐ wánshàn. 2 (初次同房而)完(婚) wán. **consummation** /kɒnsəˈmeɪʃn/ *n* [C, U].

consumption /kənˈsʌmpʃn/ *n* [U] (a) 消费 xiāofèi: *This food is not fit for human* ~. 这种食物不适合人吃. (b) 消耗量 xiāohàoliàng: *measure a car's fuel* ~. 测量汽车的燃料消耗量.

contact /ˈkɒntækt/ *n* 1 [U] 接触〔觸〕jiēchù: *Her hand came into* ~ *with a hot surface*. 她的手接触到一个热的表面. 2 [U] 联〔聯〕络 liánluò: *Stay in* ~ *with your parents*. 同你的父母保持联络. 3 [C] 会〔會〕晤 huìwù; 联系〔係〕liánxì: *a job involving* ~*s with other companies* 一个要同其他公司进行联系的工作岗位. 4 [C] (能提供帮助的)熟人 shúrén: *He has several* ~*s in the building trade*. 他在建筑行业有若干关系户. 5 [C] (电)接点〔點〕jiēdiǎn. **contact** /ˈkɒntækt, kənˈtækt/ *v* [T] (用电话、信等)同…联系 tóng…liánxì: *Where can I* ~ *you next week?* 下周同你联系, 你在哪里? ˈ**contact lens** *n* [C] 隐〔隱〕形眼镜 yǐnxíng yǎnjìng.

contagious /kənˈteɪdʒəs/ *adj* 1 (a) (疾病)接触传染的 jiēchù chuánrǎn de. (b) (人)患接触传染病的 huàn jiēchù chuánrǎnbìng de. 2 感染性的 gǎnrǎnxìngde: *contagious laughter* 有感染力的笑(声).

contain /kənˈteɪn/ *v* [T] 1 容纳 róngnà; 包含 bāohán: *A bottle* ~*s two litres of milk*. 一瓶盛两升牛奶. 2 控制 kòngzhì; 抑制 yìzhì: *trying to* ~ *her anger* 控制她不发脾气.

container /kənˈteɪnə(r)/ *n* [C] 1 容器 róngqì: *a* ~ *for sugar* 糖瓶. 2 集装〔裝〕箱 jízhuāngxiāng.

contaminate /kənˈtæmɪneɪt/ *v* [T] 弄脏〔髒〕nòng zāng; 污染 wūrǎn: ~*d food* 被污染的食物. **contamiˈnation** /kənˌtæmɪˈneɪʃn/ *n* [U].

contemplate /ˈkɒntempleɪt/ *v* [T] 1 沉思 chénsī; 打算 dǎsuàn: ~ *visiting London* 打算访问伦敦. 2 [正式用语]注视 zhùshì: ~ *a picture* 注视一幅画. **contemplation** /ˌkɒntəmˈpleɪʃn/ *n* [U] 注视 zhùshì; 沉思 chénsī. **contemplative** /kənˈtemplətɪv/ *adj* 沉思的 chénsīde.

contemporary /kənˈtemprərɪ; *US* -pərerɪ/ *adj* 1 当〔當〕代的 dāngdàide. 2 同时〔時〕代的 tóngshídàide: *a play by Shakespeare accompanied by* ~ *music* 有同时代音乐伴奏的莎士比亚戏剧. **contemporary** *n* [C] [*pl* -ies] 同时代的人 tóngshídàide rén: *Shakespeare and his contemporaries* 莎士比亚以及他的同时代人.

contempt /kənˈtempt/ *n* [U] (*for*) 1 蔑视 mièshì: *feel* ~ *for people who are cruel to animals* 鄙视那些虐待动物的人. 2 不顾〔顧〕búgù: *her* ~ *for the risks* 她的置危险于不顾. **contemptible** /-əbl/ *adj* 可鄙视的 kě bǐshìde; 卑鄙的 bēibǐde. **conˌtempt of ˈcourt** *n* [U] 蔑视法庭 mièshì fǎtíng. **contemptuous** /-tʃʊəs/ *adj* 鄙视的 bǐshìde.

contend /kənˈtend/ *v* 1 [I] *with* / *against* 斗〔鬥〕争 dòuzhēng; 竞〔競〕争 jìngzhēng. 2 争论〔論〕zhēnglùn; 主张 zhǔzhāng: ~ *that the theory was wrong* 认为这种理论是错误的. **contender** *n* [C] 竞争者 jìngzhēngzhě; 对〔對〕手 duìshǒu.

content[1] /kənˈtent/ *adj* 满意的 mǎnyìde; 甘愿〔願〕的 gānyuànde: ~ *to stay at home* 满足于呆在家里. **content** *n* [U] 满意 mǎnyì; 满足 mǎnzú. **content** *v* [T] 使满意 shǐ mǎnyì. **contented** *adj* 心满意足的 xīn mǎn yì zú de; 满意的 mǎnyìde. **contentedly** *adv*. **contentment** *n* [U] 满意 mǎnyì.

content[2] /ˈkɒntent/ *n* 1 **contents** [pl] 内容 nèiróng; 容纳物 róngnàwù: *the* ~*s of her bag* 她提包里装的东西. 2 **contents** [pl] (书籍)目录〔錄〕mùlù. 3 [sing] (书籍)内容 nèiróng. 4 [sing] 容量 róngliàng: *the silver* ~ *of a coin* 一个硬币的银含量.

contention /kənˈtenʃn/ *n* 1 [U] 争论〔論〕zhēnglùn. 2 [C] 论点〔點〕lùndiǎn. **contentious** /-ʃəs/ *adj* 好争论的 hào zhēnglùn de; 引起争论的 yǐnqǐ zhēnglùn de.

contest[1] /ˈkɒntest/ *n* [C] 争夺〔奪〕zhēngduó; 竞〔競〕争 jìngzhēng; 比赛 bǐsài.

contest[2] /kənˈtest/ *v* [T] 1 争论〔論〕zhēnglùn; 争议〔議〕zhēngyì. 2 参〔參〕加(竞争) cānjiā: ~ *an election* 参加竞选 **contestant** *n* [C] 竞争者 jìngzhēngzhě.

context /ˈkɒntekst/ *n* [C, U] 1 上下文 shàngxiàwén. 2 (事情的)来龙〔龍〕去脉〔脈〕lái lóng qù mài.

continent /ˈkɒntɪnənt/ *n* 1 [C] 大陆〔陸〕dàlù; 大洲 dàzhōu. 2 **the Continent** [sing] 欧〔歐〕洲大陆 Ōuzhōu dàlù. **continental** /ˌkɒntɪˈnentl/ *adj* 1 大陆的 dàlùde; 大陆性的 dàlùxìngde. 2 (亦作 **Continental**) 欧洲大陆的 Ōuzhōu dàlù de: *a* ~*al holiday* 欧洲大陆的假日.

contingency /kənˈtɪndʒənsɪ/ *n* [C] [*pl* -ies] 偶然事件 ǒurán shìjiàn: *prepared for every* ~ 以防万一.

contingent[1] /kənˈtɪndʒənt/ *n* [C] 1 分遣部队〔隊〕fēnqiǎn bùduì; 分遣舰队 fēnqiǎn jiànduì. 2 构〔構〕成一个〔個〕大集团〔團〕的一批人

C

gòuchéng yígè dà jítuán de yìpīrén.

contingent[2] /kənˈtɪndʒənt/ *adj* 不可预料的 bùkě yùliào de.

continual /kənˈtɪnjʊəl/ *adj* 频繁的 pínfánde;不断〔斷〕的 búduànde: ~ *rain* 不停的雨. ~ *interruptions* 不停的打断. **continually** *adv* 不断地 búduànde;一再地 yízàide.

continuation /kənˌtɪnjʊˈeɪʃn/ *n* 1 [U, sing] 继〔繼〕续〔續〕jìxù. 2 [C] 延续部分 yánxù bùfen: *This road is a* ~ *of the motorway*. 这条路是高速公路的延伸.

continue /kənˈtɪnjuː/ *v* [I, T] 1 (使)继〔繼〕续〔續〕向前 jìxù xiàngqián: ~ *up the hill* 继续上山. 2 (使)继续存在、发〔發〕生 jìxù cúnzài、fāshēng: ~ *running* 继续跑. ~*d her visits to the hospital* 她继续去医院. 3 恢复〔復〕huīfù.

continuity /ˌkɒntɪˈnjuːətɪ/ *n* [U] 1 继〔繼〕续〔續〕性 jìxùxìng. 2 连贯性 liánguànxìng: *The story lacks* ~. 这故事缺乏连贯性.

continuous /kənˈtɪnjʊəs/ *adj* 继〔繼〕续〔續〕的 jìxùde;连续的 liánxùde: *a* ~ *line* 连续不断的线. *a* ~ *noise* 不断的噪音. *a* ~ *flow* 不断的涨潮. **continuously** *adv*. **conˈtinuous tense** *n* [语法]进〔進〕行时〔時〕态〔態〕jìnxíng shítài.

contort /kənˈtɔːt/ *v* [T] 扭弯〔彎〕niǔ wān;弄歪 nòng wāi: *a face* ~*ed with pain* 因痛苦而扭曲的脸. **contortion** /kənˈtɔːʃn/ *n* [C, U].

contour /ˈkɒntʊə(r)/ *n* [C] 轮〔輪〕廓 lúnkuò;外形 wàixíng. **ˈcontour line** (地图的)等高线〔綫〕děnggāoxiàn.

contraband /ˈkɒntrəbænd/ *n* [U] 走私货 zǒusīhuò.

contraception /ˌkɒntrəˈsepʃn/ *n* [U] 避孕法 bìyùnfǎ. **contraceptive** /-ˈseptɪv/ *n* [C], *adj* 避孕药 bìyùnyào;避孕器具 bìyùn qìjù;避孕的 bìyùnde.

contract[1] /ˈkɒntrækt/ *n* [C, U] 合同 hétong;契约 qìyuē: *a* ~ *between a person and his/her employer* 一个人同其雇主所订的合同. *The builder is under* ~ *to finish the house by the end of June*. 按照合同,营造商应在六月底以前建造完这房子. **contractual** /kənˈtræktʃʊəl/ *adj* 契约性的 qìyuēxìngde;契约的 qìyuēde.

contract[2] /kənˈtrækt/ *v* 1 [I, T] 订约 dìngyuē: ~ *with the firm to supply goods* 同这家商号订供货合同. 2 [T] 生(病) shēng. 3 [T] [正式用语]负(债) fù. 4 [短语动词] **contract out (of sth)** 退出(…的)合同 tuìchū hétong.

contract[3] /kənˈtrækt/ *v* [I, T] 缩小 suōxiǎo: *Metal* ~*s when it cools*. 金属遇冷时收缩. **contraction** /kənˈtrækʃn/ *n* 1 [U] 收缩 shōusuō;缩短 suōduǎn. 2 缩写〔寫〕式 suōxiěshì: '*Can't*' *is a* ~*ion of* '*cannot*'. "can't" 是 "cannot" 的缩写式. 3 (分娩前的)子宫收缩 zǐgōng shōusuō.

contradict /ˌkɒntrəˈdɪkt/ *v* [T] 1 反驳〔駁〕fǎnbó;否认〔認〕fǒurèn;驳斥 bóchì: *Don't* ~ *your mother*. 不要同你母亲顶嘴. 2 同…矛盾 tóng…máodùn;同…抵触〔觸〕tóng…dǐchù: *Her account* ~*s what you said*. 她的叙述同你说的有矛盾. **contradiction** *n* [C, U]. **contradictory** *adj* 矛盾的 máodùnde;对〔對〕立的 duìlìde: ~*ory accounts of the accident* 有关这次事故的互相矛盾的报道.

contraflow /ˈkɒntrəfləʊ/ *n* [C, U] (车辆)逆行 nìxíng.

contralto /kənˈtræltəʊ/ *n* [C, U] 女低音 nǚdīyīn.

contraption /kənˈtræpʃn/ *n* [C] [非正式用语]新发〔發〕明的玩意儿〔兒〕xīn fāmíng de wán yìr;奇特的装〔裝〕置 qítède zhuāngzhì.

contrary[1] /ˈkɒntrərɪ; US -trerɪ/ *adj* (*to*) 相反的 xiāngfǎnde;相对〔對〕的 xiāngduìde;对抗的 duìkàngde: ~ *to what you believe* 同你认为的相反.

contrary[2] /ˈkɒntrərɪ; US -trerɪ/ *n* 1 **the contrary** [sing] 相反 xiāngfǎn: *The* ~ *is true*. 恰恰相反. 2 [习语] **on the ˈcontrary** 恰恰相反 qiàqià xiāngfǎn: *I've never said I don't like music; on the* ~, *I like it a lot*. 我从未说过我不爱音乐,恰恰相反,我很爱音乐. **to the ˈcontrary** 相反的(地) xiāngfǎnde: *I shall continue to believe this until I get proof to the* ~. 我将对此深信不疑,除非我得到相反的证据.

contrary[3] /kənˈtreərɪ/ *adj* [非正式用语]乖戾的 guāilìde: *Don't be so* ~! 别这样别扭! **contrariness** *n* [U].

contrast /kənˈtrɑːst/ *v* 1 [T] 使对〔對〕比 shǐ duìbǐ. 2 [I] 形成对照 xíngchéng duìzhào: *the* ~*ing cultures of Africa and Europe* 非洲和欧洲形成对照的文化. **contrast** /ˈkɒntrɑːst/ *n* [C, U] 明显〔顯〕的差别 míngxiǎnde chābié.

contravene /ˌkɒntrəˈviːn/ *v* [T] 违〔違〕反 wéifǎn;触〔觸〕犯 chùfàn. **contravention** /ˌkɒntrəˈvenʃn/ *n* [C, U].

contribute /kənˈtrɪbjuːt/ *v* 1 [I, T] (*to/towards*) 贡献〔獻〕gòngxiàn;捐助 juānzhù. 2 [I] (*to*) 促成 cùchéng: ~ *to her success* 促成她的成功. 3 [I, T] 投稿 tóugǎo. **contribution** /ˌkɒntrɪˈbjuːʃn/ *n* [C, U]. **contributor** *n* [C] 捐助者 juānzhùzhě;投稿者 tóugǎozhě. **contributory** /kənˈtrɪbjʊtərɪ/ *adj*.

contrite /ˈkɒntraɪt/ *adj* 痛悔的 tònghuǐde. **contritely** *adv*. **contrition** /kənˈtrɪʃn/ *n* [U].

contrive /kənˈtraɪv/ *v* [T] **1** 设法 shèfǎ: ~ *to live on a small income* 靠微薄收入,精打细算过日子. **2** 发〔發〕明 fāmíng;谋划〔劃〕móuhuà;设计 shèjì: ~ *a way of avoiding paying tax* 谋划避税. **contrivance** *n* **1** [U] 发明 fāmíng;设计 shèjì. **2** [C] 发明物 fāmíngwù.

control /kənˈtrəʊl/ *n* **1** [U] 控制(能力) kòngzhì;指挥(能力)zhǐhuī;支配(能力) zhīpèi: *She lost* ~ *of the car on the ice*. 她在冰上开车时,控制不住汽车. **2** [C] 控制手段 kòngzhì shǒuduàn: ~*s on pollution* 控制污染的手段. **3** [C] (鉴定实验结果的)对〔對〕照标〔標〕准〔準〕duìzhào biāozhǔn. **4** [常作 pl] 操纵〔縱〕装〔裝〕置 cāozòng zhuāngzhì. **5** [习语] **be in control (of sth)** 掌管着… zhǎngguǎnzhe…; 控制着 kòngzhìzhe. **out of conˈtrol** 失去控制 shīqù kòngzhì: *The car went out of* ~. 汽车失去了控制. **under control** 被控制 bèi kòngzhì: *The fire was brought under* ~. 火势得到控制. **control** *v* [-ll-] [T] **1** 控制 kòngzhì;支配 zhīpèi: ~ *one's temper* 控制自己不发脾气. **2** 管理(交通、物价等) guǎnlǐ. **3** 检〔檢〕查 jiǎnchá: *inspections to* ~ *quality* 质〔質〕量检查. **controller** *n* [C] 管理员 guǎnlǐyuán;部门负责人 bùmén fùzérén.

controversy /ˈkɒntrəvɜːsɪ, kənˈtrɒvəsɪ/ *n* [*pl* -ies] [C, U] 论〔論〕战〔戰〕lùnzhàn: ~ *over the building of a new motorway* 关于修建新高速公路的公开辩论. **controversial** /ˌkɒntrəˈvɜːʃl/ *adj* 引起争论的 yǐnqǐ zhēnglùn de. **controversially** *adv*.

conundrum /kəˈnʌndrəm/ *n* [C, 常作 sing] **1** (以双关语作答案的)谜语 míyǔ. **2** 谜似的难〔難〕题 míshìde nántí.

conurbation /kɒnɜːˈbeɪʃn/ *n* [C] (连带卫星城镇和市郊的)大都市 dà dūshì;集合城市 jíhé chéngshì.

convalesce /ˌkɒnvəˈles/ *v* [I] 痊愈〔癒〕quányù;恢复〔復〕健康 huīfù jiànkāng. **convalescence** *n* [sing, U] 恢复健康 huīfù jiànkāng;恢复期 huīfùqī. **convalescent** *n* [C], *adj* 恢复健康的人 huīfù jiànkāng de rén. 恢复健康的 huīfù jiànkāng de.

convene /kənˈviːn/ *v* [I, T] 召集 zhàojí;召唤 zhàohuàn;集合 jíhé. **convener** (亦作 -**venor**) *n* [C] 召集人 zhàojírén.

convenience / kənˈviːnɪəns/ *n* **1** [U] 便利 biànlì;方便 fāngbiàn. **2** [C] 便利的设施 biànlìde shèshī: *Central heating is one of the* ~*s of modern houses*. 集中供暖是现代化房屋的便利设施之一.

convenient /kənˈviːnɪənt/ *adj* 便利的 biànlìde;方便的 fāngbiànde;近便的 jìnbiànde: *a* ~ *place to stay* 停留的近便地方. **conveniently** *adv*.

convent /ˈkɒnvənt; *US* -vent/ *n* [C] 女修道院 nǚ xiūdàoyuàn.

convention /kənˈvenʃn/ *n* **1** [C] 会〔會〕议〔議〕huìyì;大会 dàhuì;全国〔國〕性大会 quánguóxìng dàhuì: *a scientists'* ~ 科学家大会. **2** (a) [U] 习〔習〕俗 xísú. (b) [C] 惯例 guànlì;常规 chángguī: *the* ~*s of international trade* 国际贸易惯例. **3** [C] 协〔協〕定 xiédìng;公约 gōngyuē. **conventional** *adj* 惯例的 guànlìde;常规的 chángguīde;传〔傳〕统的 chuántǒngde. **conventionally** *adv*.

converge /kənˈvɜːdʒ/ *v* [I] (线、移动物体等)会〔會〕聚 huìjù;集中 jízhōng: *a village where two roads* ~ 两条公路会聚处的一个村庄. **convergence** *n* [U]. **convergent** *adj*.

conversant /kənˈvɜːsnt/ *adj with* 精通的 jīngtōngde;熟悉的 shúxīde: ~ *with modern teaching methods* 精通现代教学法.

conversation /ˌkɒnvəˈseɪʃn/ *n* **1** [U] 谈话 tánhuà: *the art of* ~ 谈话的艺术. **2** [C] 会〔會〕话 huìhuà: *hold a* ~ 举行非正式会谈. **conversational** *adj* 会话的 huìhuàde;谈话的 tánhuàde: *a* ~*al tone* 谈话的语调. *a* ~*al style* 谈话的文体.

converse[1] /kənˈvɜːs/ *v* [I] (*with*) [正式用语]谈话 tánhuà.

converse[2] /ˈkɒnvɜːs/ **the converse** *n* [sing] 相反的事物 xiāngfǎnde shìwù;反面说法 fǎnmiàn shuōfǎ: *The* ~ *is true*. 实际情况相反. **converse** *adj* 相反的 xiāngfǎnde. **conversely** *adv*.

conversion /kənˈvɜːʃn; *US* kənˈvɜːrʒn/ *n* [C, U]变〔變〕换 biànhuàn;转〔轉〕变 zhuǎnbiàn;(宗教、政党等)皈依 guīyī;改变 gǎibiàn;兑换 duìhuàn: *the* ~ *of the barn into a house* 把谷仓改成人住的房子.

convert[1] /kənˈvɜːt/ *v* [I, T] **1** 转〔轉〕变〔變〕zhuǎnbiàn;变换 biànhuàn;兑换 duìhuàn: ~ *a house into flats* 把一所房子改建成几套公寓房间. **2** 使改变信仰 shǐ gǎibiàn xìnyǎng: ~ *him to Christianity* 使他改信基督教. **convertible** /-əbl/ *adj* 可改变的 kě gǎibiàn de;可变换的 kě biànhuàn de. **convertible** *n* [C] 折篷汽车 zhépéng qìchē.

convert[2] /ˈkɒnvɜːt/ *n* [C] 皈依宗教者 guīyī zōngjiào zhě;改变〔變〕宗教信仰者 gǎibiàn zōngjiào xìnyǎng zhě.

convex /ˈkɒnveks/ *adj* 凸的 tūde;凸面的 tūmiànde: *a* ~ *mirror* 凸面镜.

convey /kənˈveɪ/ *v* [T] **1** 运〔運〕送 yùnsòng, 搬运 bānyùn: *goods* ~*ed by rail* 由铁

C

C

路运送的货物.2 (*to*) 转〔轉〕达〔達〕zhuǎndá；传〔傳〕达(思想、感情等) chuándá：*She ~ed her fears to her friends*. 她向朋友们表达了自己的恐惧心情. **conveyance** *n* [C, U] 运输〔輸〕yùnshū；搬运 bānyùn；运输工具 yùnshū gōngjù. **conveyancing** *n* [U] [法律]产〔產〕权〔權〕转让〔讓〕chǎnquán zhuǎnràng. **conveyor** (亦作 **-veyer**) *n* [C] 运送者 yùnsòngzhě；运送设备〔備〕yùnsòng shèbèi. **con'veyor belt** *n* [C] 传送带〔帶〕chuánsòngdài.

convict /kən'vɪkt/ *v* [T] 证〔證〕明…有罪 zhèngmíng…yǒu zuì；宣判…有罪 xuānpàn…yǒu zuì：*She was ~ed of theft*. 她被宣判犯有盗窃罪. **convict** /'kɒnvɪkt/ *n* [C] 罪犯 zuìfàn.

conviction /kən'vɪkʃn/ *n* [C, U] 1 定罪 dìngzuì；证〔證〕明有罪 zhèngmíng yǒu zuì. 2 深信 shēnxìn；确〔確〕信 quèxìn：*a ~ that what she said was true* 对她所说属实的深信不疑.

convince /kən'vɪns/ *v* [T] (*of*) 使信服 shǐ xìnfú；使确〔確〕信 shǐ quèxìn：*I ~d her that I was right*. 我使她确信我是对的. *~ sb of the truth* 使某人相信事实. **convincing** *adj* 有说服力的 yǒu shuōfúlì de；使人深信的 shǐ rén shēnxìn de：*a convincing argument* 有说服力的论据. **convincingly** *adv*.

convivial /kən'vɪvɪəl/ *adj* 愉快的 yúkuàide：*a ~ person/evening* 愉快的人；愉快的夜晚. **conviviality** /kənˌvɪvɪ'ælətɪ/ *n* [U].

convoluted /'kɒnvəluːtɪd/ *adj* 1 扭曲的 niǔqūde；盘〔盤〕绕〔繞〕的 pánràode. 2 [喻]复〔複〕杂〔雜〕难〔難〕懂的 fùzá nándǒng de.

convolution /ˌkɒnvə'luːʃn/ *n* [C, 常作 pl] 扭曲 niǔqū；盘〔盤〕绕〔繞〕pánrào：[喻] *the ~s of the plot* 情节的错综复杂.

convoy /'kɒnvɔɪ/ *n* [C] (a) 车队〔隊〕chēduì；船队 chuánduì. (b) 被护〔護〕航的船队 bèi hùháng de chuánduì. **convoy** *v* [T] (军舰等) 为〔爲〕…护航 wèi…hùháng.

convulse /kən'vʌls/ *v* [T] 使剧〔劇〕烈震动〔動〕shǐ jùliè zhèndòng；摇动 yáodòng：*a city ~d by riots* 被骚乱震憾的城市. **convulsion** /-'vʌlʃn/ *n* [C] 1 [常作 pl] 惊〔驚〕厥 jīngjué；抽搐 chōuchù. 2 动乱〔亂〕dòngluàn. **convulsive** *adj*.

coo /kuː/ *v* 1 [I] (鸽)咕咕叫 gūgūjiào. 2 [T] 柔情地说 róuqíngde shuō. **coo** *n* [C].

cook /kʊk/ *v* 1 (a) [I, T] 烹调 pēngtiáo；烧〔燒〕shāo；煮 zhǔ：*~ breakfast/dinner* 做早饭；做饭. (b) [I] 被煮 bèi zhǔ；被烧 bèi shāo. 2 [T] [非正式用语,贬]窜〔竄〕改(账目等) cuàngǎi：*~ the figures* 窜改数字. **cook** *n* [C] 厨师〔師〕chúshī. **cooker** *n* [C] 炊具 chuījù. **cookery** *n* [U] 烹调艺〔藝〕术〔術〕pēngtiáo yìshù. **cooking** *n* [U] 烹调 pēngtiáo.

cookie /'kʊkɪ/ *n* [C] [美语] 1 饼干〔乾〕bǐnggān. 2 人 rén；家伙 jiāhuo：*a tough ~* 厉害的家伙.

cool[1] /kuːl/ *adj* 1 凉的 liángde；凉快的 liángkuàide：*It feels ~ in the shade*. 背阴处是凉爽的. 2 沉着的 chénzhuóde；冷静的 lěngjìngde：*stay ~ in spite of danger* 遇险不惊. 3 冷淡的 lěngdànde：*He was ~ about the suggestion*. 他对这建议不感兴趣. 4 [非正式用语](表示数量很大)足足的 zúzúde，整整的 zhěngzhěngde：*a ~ five million pounds!* 足足五百万英镑! 5 [非正式用语]绝妙的 juémiàode；顶刮刮的 dǐngguāguāde：*real ~ music* 真正绝妙的音乐. **cool** *n* 1 **the cool** [sing] 凉快的空气〔氣〕liángkuaide kōngqì；凉快的地方 liángkuaide dìfang；凉快 liángkuai：*sitting in the ~* 坐在凉快的地方. 2 [习语] **keep/lose one's cool** [非正式用语]保持冷静；bǎochí lěngjìng；失去冷静 shīqù lěngjìng. ˌ**cool-'headed** *adj* 头〔頭〕脑〔腦〕冷静的 tóunǎo lěngjìng de. **coolly** *adv*. **coolness** *n* [U].

cool[2] /kuːl/ *v* [I, T] 1 (*down / off*) (使)变〔變〕凉 biàn liáng：*have a drink to ~ down* 喝杯饮料凉快凉快. 2 [短语动词] **cool down / off** 冷静下来 lěngjìng xiàlái.

coop /kuːp/ *n* [C] 笼〔籠〕lóng；鸡〔鷄〕笼 jīlóng. **coop** *v* [短语动词] **coop up** 禁闭 jìnbì：*prisoners ~ed up in cells* 关在单人牢房里的囚犯.

co-operate /kəʊ'ɒpəreɪt/ *v* [I] 协〔協〕作 xiézuò；合作 hézuò：*They ~ on the project*. 他们在这个科研项目上合作. **co-operation** /kəʊˌɒpə'reɪʃn/ *n* [U] 1 合作 hézuò；协作 xiézuò. 2 协助 xiézhù. **co-operative** / -pərətiv/ *adj* 1 合办〔辦〕的 hébànde. 2 乐〔樂〕意合作的 lèyì hézuò de. **co-operative** *n* [C] 合作社 hézuòshè；合作农〔農〕场〔場〕hézuò nóngchǎng.

co-opt /kəʊ'ɒpt/ *v* [T] (委员会)增选〔選〕某人为〔爲〕成员 zēngxuǎn mǒurén wéi chéngyuán.

co-ordinate[1] /ˌkəʊ'ɔːdɪneɪt/ *v* [T] (*with*) 使协〔協〕调 shǐ xiétiáo：*~ efforts to get the project finished* 同心协力完成这一工程. **co-ordination** /ˌkəʊˌɔːdɪ'neɪʃn/ *n* [U]. **co-ordinator** *n* [C].

co-ordinate[2] /ˌkəʊ'ɔːdɪnət/ *n* 1 [C] (图表上的)坐标〔標〕zuòbiāo. 2 **co-ordinates** [pl] 配套衣服 pèitào yīfu.

cop[1] /kɒp/ *n* [C] [俚语]警察 jǐngchá.

cop[2] /kɒp/ *v* [-pp-] [T] [俚语] 1 忍受 rěnshòu；挨 āi：*~ a bang on the head* 头上挨

了一下.2［短语动词］cop out［贬］逃避(做…) táobì. 'cop-out *n*［C］［俚语,贬］逃避(的借口) táobì.

cope /kəup/ *v*［I］(*with*) 对〔對〕付 duìfu;妥善处〔處〕理 tuǒshàn chǔlǐ: *She couldn't ~ with all her work*. 她不能妥善处理自己的全部工作.

copier ⇨COPY².

copious /'kəupɪəs/ *adj*［正式用语］丰〔豐〕富的 fēngfùde;富饶〔饒〕的 fùráode: *a ~ supply* 丰富的供应. copiously *adv*.

copper¹ /'kɒpə(r)/ *n* 1［U］铜 tóng: *~ wire* 铜线. 2［U］紫铜色 zǐtóngsè. 3［C］铜币〔幣〕tóngbì.

copper² /'kɒpə(r)/ *n*［C］［俚］警察 jǐngchá.

copse /kɒps/ *n*［C］小灌木林 xiǎo guànmùlín;矮树〔樹〕林 ǎi shùlín.

copulate /'kɒpjuleɪt/ *v*［I］(*with*)［正式用语］(尤指动物)交配 jiāopèi;交媾 jiāogòu. copulation /ˌkɒpju'leɪʃn/ *n*［U］.

copy¹ /'kɒpɪ/ *n*［C］［*pl* -ies］1 抄本 chāoběn;副本 fùběn;复〔複〕制〔製〕品 fùzhìpǐn;(电影)拷贝 kǎobèi: *Put a ~ of the letter in the file*. 把这封信的一份副本放进档案. 2 一本 yìběn;一册 yícè;一份 yífèn: *The library has two copies of this book*. 这图书馆有两本这种书. 'copycat *n*［C］［非正式用语,贬］模仿他人者 mófǎng tārén zhě.

copy² /'kɒpɪ/ *v*［*pt, pp* -ied］1［T］(a) 抄写〔寫〕chāoxiě: *He wrote the sentence on the blackboard and told the children to ~ it into their books*. 他把这个句子写在黑板上,让孩子们抄写到自己的本子上. (b) 复〔複〕制〔製〕fùzhì: *~ a document on the photocopier* 在影印机上复印一份文件. 2［T］模仿 mófǎng: *The teacher told the class to ~ his movements*. 教师让班上的学生模仿他的动作. 3［I］抄袭〔襲〕(考试中作弊) chāoxí. copier *n*［C］复印机〔機〕fùyìnjī.

copyright /'kɒpɪraɪt/ *n*［U, C］版权〔權〕bǎnquán. copyright *v*［T］保护〔護〕…的版权 bǎohù…de bǎnquán.

coral /'kɒrəl; *US* 'kɔːrəl/ *n*［U］珊瑚 shānhú. coral *adj* 用珊瑚制〔製〕造的 yòng shānhú zhìzào de.

cord /kɔːd/ *n* 1［C, U］粗线〔綫〕cūxiàn;细绳〔繩〕xìshéng;索 suǒ. 2［C］人体〔體〕的带〔帶〕状〔狀〕部分 réntǐde dàizhuàng bùfen: *the vocal ~s* 声带. 'cordless telephone *n*［C］无〔無〕绳电〔電〕话 wúshéng diànhuà.

cordial¹ /'kɔːdɪəl; *US* 'kɔːrdʒəl/ *adj* 热〔熱〕诚的 rèchéngde;衷心的 zhōngxīnde;亲〔親〕切的 qīnqiède: *a ~ welcome/smile* 亲切的欢迎(微笑). cordially *adv*.

cordial² /'kɔːdɪəl/ *n*［U］［英国英语］(不含酒精的)甜饮料 tián yǐnliào: *lime ~* 酸橙汁饮料.

cordon /'kɔːdn/ *n*［C］警戒线〔綫〕jǐngjièxiàn;警卫〔衛〕圈 jǐngwèiquān: *a police ~* 警察的封锁线. cordon *v*［短语动词］cordon off 用警戒线围〔圍〕住 yòng jǐngjièxiàn wéizhù: *The army ~ed off the area*. 军队警戒了这个地区.

corduroy /'kɔːdərɔɪ/ *n*［U］灯芯绒 dēngxīnróng: *~ trousers* 灯芯绒裤子.

core /kɔː(r)/ *n*［C］1 果实〔實〕的心 guǒshíde xīn. 2 核心 héxīn;精髓 jīngsuí: *the ~ of the problem* 问题的核心. 3［习语］to the 'core 彻〔徹〕底 chèdǐ: *shocked to the ~* 大吃一惊. core *v*［T］挖去…的果心 wāqù…de guǒxīn.

cork /kɔːk/ *n* 1［U］软木 ruǎnmù: *~ table mats* 软木桌垫. 2［C］软木塞 ruǎnmùsāi. cork *v*［T］塞住(瓶子等) sāizhù. 'corkscrew *n*［C］瓶塞钻〔鑽〕píngsāizuàn.

corn¹ /kɔːn/ *n* 1［U］谷〔穀〕物 gǔwù;五谷 wǔgǔ. 2［尤用于美语］玉米 yùmǐ. corn-cob *n*［C］玉米穗轴 yùmǐ suìzhóu. 'cornflour *n*［U］玉米粉 yùmǐfěn. ˌcorn on the 'cob *n*［C］(煮熟的)玉米棒子 yùmǐ bàngzi.

corn² /kɔːn/ *n*［C］鸡〔鷄〕眼 jīyǎn;钉胼 dīngpián.

cornea /'kɔːnɪə/ *n*［C］(眼球上的)角膜 jiǎomó.

corned beef /ˌkɔːnd 'biːf/ *n*［U］咸〔鹹〕牛肉 xián niúròu.

corner /'kɔːnə(r)/ *n*［C］1 角 jiǎo. 2 冷僻地方 lěngpì dìfang;角落 jiǎoluò. 3 地区〔區〕dìqū: *from all ~s of the earth* 从世界各地 4［非正式用语］困境 kùnjìng. 5［习语］turn the 'corner 渡过〔過〕难〔難〕关〔關〕dùguò nánguān. corner *v* 1［T］把…逼入困境 bǎ…bīrù kùnjìng;使走投无〔無〕路 shǐ zǒutóuwúlù: *~ed by the police* 被警察逼得走投无路. 2［I］转〔轉〕弯〔彎〕zhuǎnwān: *a car designed for fast ~ing* 设计成可快速转弯的汽车.

cornet /'kɔːnɪt/ *n*［C］1 (乐器)短号〔號〕duǎnhào. 2 (盛冰淇淋等的)锥形鸡〔鷄〕蛋卷 zhuīxíng jīdànjuǎn.

cornice /'kɔːnɪs/ *n*［C］(建筑)上楣(柱) shàngméi;檐口 yánkǒu.

corny /'kɔːnɪ/ *adj*［-ier, -iest］老一套的 lǎoyítàode;多愁善感的 duōchóu shàngǎn de.

coronary /'kɒrənrɪ; *US* 'kɔːrənerɪ/ *adj* 冠状〔狀〕动〔動〕脉〔脈〕的 guānzhuàng dòngmài de. coronary *n*［C］［*pl* -ies］(亦作 coronary thrombosis) 冠状动脉血栓形成 guānzhuàng dòngmài xuèshuān xíngchéng.

coronation /ˌkɒrə'neɪʃn; *US* ˌkɔːr-/ *n*［C］

C

加冕典礼〔禮〕jiāmiǎn diǎnlǐ.

coroner /ˈkɒrənə(r); *US* ˈkɔːr-/ *n* [C] [英国英语]验〔驗〕尸官 yànshīguān.

coronet /ˈkɒrənet; *US* ˈkɔːr-/ *n* [C] (贵族戴的)小冠冕 xiǎo guānmiǎn.

corporal[1] /ˈkɔːpərəl/ *adj* 肉体〔體〕的 ròutǐde; 身体的 shēntǐde: ~ *punishment* 肉刑 ròuxíng; 体罚 tǐfá.

corporal[2] /ˈkɔːpərəl/ *n* [C] (军队)下士 xiàshì.

corporate /ˈkɔːpərət/ *adj* 1 社团〔團〕的 shètuánde; 法人的 fǎrénde. 2 共同的 gòngtóngde; 全体〔體〕的 quántǐde: ~ *responsibility* 共同的责任.

corporation /ˌkɔːpəˈreɪʃn/ *n* [C, 亦作 sing, 用 pl v] 1 市镇自治机〔機〕关〔關〕shì zhèn zìzhì jīguān 2 法人 fǎrén; 公司 gōngsī; 社团〔團〕shètuán.

corps /kɔː(r)/ *n* [C] [*pl* **corps** /kɔːz/] 1 兵团〔團〕bīngtuán; 军 jūn. 2 技术〔術〕兵种〔種〕jìshù bīngzhǒng; 特殊兵种 tèshū bīngzhǒng: *the Medical C* ~ 医疗队. 3 (从事某种活动的)团 tuán; 组 zǔ: *the diplomatic* ~ 外交使团

corpse /kɔːps/ *n* [C] 尸〔屍〕体〔體〕shītǐ, 死尸 sǐshī.

corpulent /ˈkɔːpjʊlənt/ *adj* [正式用语]肥胖的 féipàngde.

corpuscle /ˈkɔːpʌsl/ *n* [C] 血球(白血球或红血球) xuèqiú.

corral /kəˈrɑːl/ *n* [C] 畜栏〔欄〕xùlán. **corral** *v* [-ll-; 美语 -l-] [T] 把…关〔關〕进〔進〕畜栏 bǎ…guānjìn xùlán.

correct[1] /kəˈrekt/ *adj* 1 正确〔確〕的 zhèngquède: *the* ~ *answer* 正确的答案. *the* ~ *way to do it* 做此事的正确方法. 2 恰当〔當〕的 qiàdàngde; 端正的 duānzhèngde. **correctly** *adv*. **correctness** *n* [U].

correct[2] /kəˈrekt/ *v* [T] 1 改正 gǎizhèng; 修正 xiūzhèng: ~ *sb's spelling* 改正某人的拼写. 2 纠正 jiūzhèng: *glasses to* ~ *your eyesight* 纠正视力的眼镜. **correction** /kəˈrekʃn/ *n* 1 [C] 修改之处〔處〕xiūgǎi zhī chù; 改正的东西 gǎizhèngde dōngxi: *corrections written in red ink* 用红墨水书写的修改之处. 2 [U] 改正 gǎizhèng; 纠正 jiūzhèng. 3 惩〔懲〕罚 chéngfá. **corrective** *n* [C], *adj* 纠正物 jiūzhèngwù; 改正的 gǎizhèngde.

correlate /ˈkɒrəleɪt; *US* ˈkɔːr-/ *v* [I, T] (*with*) (使)相互关〔關〕联〔聯〕xiānghù guānlián: *The results of the two tests do not* ~. 这两种试验的结果并不相互关联. **correlation** /ˌkɒrəˈleɪʃn/ *n* [sing, U] 相互关系〔係〕xiānghù guānxì.

correspond /ˌkɒrɪˈspɒnd; *US* ˌkɔːr-/ *v* [I] 1 (*with* / *to*) 符合 fúhé; 一致 yízhì: *Your account doesn't* ~ *with hers*. 你的叙述同她的不一致. 2 (*with*) 通信 tōngxìn. **corresponding** *adj* 相等的 xiāngděngde; 相称〔稱〕的 xiāngchèngde; 相当〔當〕的 xiāngdāngde. **correspondingly** *adv*.

correspondence /ˌkɒrɪˈspɒndəns; *US* ˌkɔːr-/ *n* 1 [C, U] 符合 fúhé; 一致 yízhì; 相似 xiāngsì: *a close* ~ *between the two texts* 两种文本的极其相似. 2 [U] 通信 tōngxìn; 信件 xìnjiàn. **correspondent** *n* [C] 1 通信者 tōngxìnzhě. 2 (新闻)通讯员 tōngxùnyuán; 记者 jìzhě.

corridor /ˈkɒrɪdɔː(r); *US* kɔːr-/ *n* [C] 走廊 zǒuláng; 通路 tōnglù; 回〔迴〕廊 huíláng.

corroborate /kəˈrɒbəreɪt/ *v* [T] 巩〔鞏〕固(信仰) gǒnggù; 证〔證〕实〔實〕zhèngshí: *I can* ~ *what she said*. 我能证实她说的话. **corroboration** /kəˌrɒbəˈreɪʃn/ *n* [U].

corrode /kəˈrəʊd/ *v* [I, T] 腐蚀 fǔshí; 侵蚀 qīnshí. **corrosion** /kəˈrəʊʒn/ *n* [U] (a) 腐蚀 fǔshí; 侵蚀 qīnshí. (b) 锈〔鏽〕xiù; 铁〔鐵〕锈 tiěxiù. **corrosive** /kəˈrəʊsɪv/ *n* [C], *adj* 腐蚀剂〔劑〕fǔshíjì; 腐蚀的 fǔshíde.

corrugated /ˈkɒrəgeɪtɪd; *US* ˈkɔːr-/ *adj* 皱〔皺〕的 zhòude; 起皱的 qǐzhòude: ~ *iron* 瓦楞铁. ~ *cardboard* 瓦楞纸.

corrupt /kəˈrʌpt/ *adj* 1 堕落的 duòluòde; 邪恶〔惡〕的 xié'ède; 不道德的 bú dàodé de: *a* ~ *society* / *mind* 邪恶的社会/心. 2 贪污的 tānwūde; 腐败的 fǔbàide: *a* ~ *business deal* 营私舞弊的买卖. **corrupt** *v* [I, T] (使)腐败 fǔbài; 贿赂 huìlù: ~*ing young people* 道德败坏的年轻人. **corruption** / kəˈrʌpʃn / *n* [U]. **corruptly** *adv*.

corset /ˈkɔːsɪt/ *n* [C] 妇〔婦〕女紧〔緊〕身胸衣 fùnǚ jǐnshēn xiōngyī.

cortege /kɔːˈteɪʒ/ *n* [C] (送葬人的)行列 hángliè; 随〔隨〕从〔從〕们 suícóngmén.

cosh /kɒʃ/ *n* [C] [英国俚语](用以打人的)内装〔裝〕金属〔屬〕的橡皮棒 nèizhuāng jīnshǔ de xiàngpíbàng.

cosmetic /kɒzˈmetɪk/ *n* [C] 化妆〔妝〕品 huàzhuāngpǐn. **cosmetic** *adj* 1 化妆用的 huàzhuāng yòng de. 2 [喻, 常贬]粉饰用的. fěnshì yòng de: *These are just* ~ *improvements to the system, they do not really change anything*. 这些不过是对这个系统所作的一些装饰门面的改进, 没有任何真正的改变.

cosmic /ˈkɒzmɪk/ *adj* 宇宙的 yǔzhòude.

cosmonaut /ˈkɒzmənɔːt/ *n* [C] (前苏联的)宇航员 yǔhángyuán, 航天员 hángtiānyuán.

cosmopolitan /ˌkɒzməˈpɒlɪtən/ *adj* 1 全世界的 quánshìjiède: *a* ~ *gathering* 世界性集会. 2 [褒]世界主义〔義〕的 shìjièzhǔyìde; 四海为

C

〔爲〕家的 sìhǎi wéijiā de.

cosmos /ˈkɒzmɒs/ *n* the cosmos 宇宙 yǔzhòu.

cost[1] /kɒst; *US* kɔːst/ *n* **1** [C, U] 费用 fèiyòng: *the high ~ of repairs* 高昂的修理费. **2** [sing, U] 代价〔價〕dàijià: *the ~ of victory* 胜利的代价. **3 costs** [pl] [法律]诉讼费 sùsòngfèi. **4** [习语] **at ˈall costs** 不惜任何代价 bùxī rènhé dàijià. **to one's ˈcost** 吃了苦头〔頭〕之后〔後〕才… chī le kǔtou zhīhòu cái…. **costly** *adj* [-ier, -iest] **1** 费用高的 fèiyòng gāo de; 贵重的 guìzhòngde. **2** 代价大的 dàijià dà de: *a ~ly mistake* 代价大的错误.

cost[2] /kɒst; *US* kɔːst/ *v* [*pt*, *pp* cost, 第三义项 **costed**] **1** [I] 价〔價〕钱〔錢〕为〔爲〕jiàqián wéi: *shoes ~ing £20* 20 英镑一双的鞋. **2** [I] 代价为 dàijià wéi: *a mistake that ~ him his life* 一个使他付出了自己生命的错误. **3** [T] [商]估计…的价钱 gūjì…de jiàqián. **costing** *n* [C, U] [商]估价 gūjià; 成本计算 chéngběn jìsuàn.

co-star /ˈkəʊstɑː(r)/ *n* [C] (电影等中与其他明星)联〔聯〕衔合演明星 liánxián héyǎn míngxīng. **co-star** *v* [-rr-] [I] (与其他明星)联衔主演 liánxián zhǔyǎn.

costume /ˈkɒstjuːm; *US* -tuːm/ *n* **1** [C, U] 服装〔裝〕式样〔樣〕fúzhuāng shìyàng. **2** [C] 化妆〔妝〕服 huàzhuāngfú; 戏〔戲〕服 xìfú.

cosy /ˈkəʊzɪ/ *adj* [-ier, -iest] 温暖而舒适〔適〕的 wēnnuǎn ér shūshìde; 安逸的 ānyìde: *a ~ room / feeling* 舒适的房间/感觉. [喻] *a ~ little talk* 轻松的闲谈. **cosily** *adv*. **cosiness** *n* [U]. **cosy** *n* [C] [*pl* -ies] (茶壶等的)保暖罩 bǎonuǎnzhào

cot /kɒt/ *n* [C] **1** [英国英语]儿〔兒〕童床〔牀〕értóngchuáng. **2** [美国英语](船等上的)简单〔單〕的窄床 jiǎndānde zhǎichuáng.

cottage /ˈkɒtɪdʒ/ *n* [C] 村舍 cūnshè; 小屋 xiǎowū.

cotton[1] /ˈkɒtn/ *n* [U] **1** 棉花 miánhua; 棉 mián. **2** 棉线〔綫〕miánxiàn: *a ~ dress* 棉布衣服. ˌ**cotton ˈwool** *n* [U] 脱脂棉 tuōzhīmián.

cotton[2] /ˈkɒtn/ *v* [短语动词] **cotton on (to sth)** [非正式用语]明白 míngbai; 领会〔會〕lǐnghuì; 领悟 lǐngwù.

couch[1] /kaʊtʃ/ *n* [C] 长〔長〕沙发〔發〕cháng shāfā.

couch[2] /kaʊtʃ/ *v* [T] (*in*) [正式用语]表达〔達〕biǎodá: *a reply ~ed in friendly terms* 措辞友好的答复.

cougar /ˈkuːɡə(r)/ *n* [C] (尤用于美国英语) = PUMA.

cough /kɒf/ *v* **1** [I] 咳嗽 késou: *The smoke made me ~.* 这烟呛得我咳嗽. **2** [T] (*up*) 咳出 kéchū. **cough** *n* **1** [C] 咳嗽 késou; 咳嗽声〔聲〕késoushēng. **2** [sing] 咳嗽病 késoubìng.

could[1] /kəd; 强式 kʊd/ *modal v* (否定式 **could not**, 缩略式 **couldn't** /ˈkʊdnt/) **1** (用于请求)可以 kěyǐ: *C~ I use your phone?* 我可以用一下你的电话吗? **2** (表示结果): *We were so tired, we ~ have slept for days.* 我们疲倦得能一下子睡上几天. **3** (表示可能性)可能 kěnéng: *You ~ be right.* 你可能是对的. **4** (表示建议): *You ~ ask her to go with you.* 你不妨要求她同你一起去.

could[2] *pt* of CAN[1].

couldn't could not. ⇨COULD[1].

council /ˈkaʊnsl/ *n* [C, 亦作 sing, 用 pl v] 市、镇议〔議〕会〔會〕shì、zhèn yìhuì; 政务〔務〕会 zhèngwùhuì; 会议 huìyì; 委员会 wěiyuánhuì; 理事会 lǐshìhuì: *a ~ meeting* 理事会会议. ˈ**council house** 市议会所有的房产〔產〕shìyìhuì suǒyǒude fángchǎn. **councillor** (美语 **councilor**) /ˈkaʊnsələ(r)/ *n* [C] 地方议会议员 dìfāng yìhuì yìyuán.

counsel /ˈkaʊnsl/ *n* **1** [U] 忠告 zhōnggào; 劝〔勸〕告 quàngào; 建议〔議〕jiànyì. **2** [C] [*pl* **counsel**] 律师〔師〕lǜshī. **counsel** *v* [-ll-; 美语 -l-] [T] [正式用语]忠告 zhōnggào; 劝告 quàngào: *He ~ed her to leave.* 他劝她离开. **counsellor** (美语 **counselor**) *n* [C] **1** 顾〔顧〕问 gùwèn. **2** [美语]律师 lǜshī.

count[1] /kaʊnt/ *v* **1** [I] 数〔數〕shǔ; 计数 jìshù; 点〔點〕数目 diǎn shùmù: *C~ from 1 to 10.* 从一数到十. **2** [T] (*up*) 点…的数目 diǎn…de shùmù: *~ the people in the room* 点房间里的人数. **3** [T] 把…算入 bǎ…suànrù: *ten people ~ing Ann* 把安算在内,十个人. **4** [T] 认〔認〕为〔爲〕rènwéi; 看作 kànzuò: *~ oneself lucky* 认为自己幸运. **5** [I] (a) 重要 zhòngyào; 有考虑〔慮〕价〔價〕值 yǒu kǎolǜ jiàzhí: *Every minute ~s.* 每一分钟都重要. (b) 有效 yǒuxiào: *That goal didn't ~ because the game was over.* 那个进球被认为无效,因为比赛已经结束. **6** [短语动词] **count (sth) against sb** 认为是不利于…的 rènwéi shì búlìyú…de: *Will my past mistakes ~ against me?* 我过去的错误还会对我有不利影响吗? **count on sb** 依靠 yīkào; 指望 zhǐwàng: *I am ~ing on you to help.* 我正依靠你来帮我. **count sb/sth out** (a) 点…的数 diǎn… de shù. (b) 把…不计在内 bǎ…bú jì zài nèi: *C~ me out, I'm not going.* 别算我,我不去. **countable** *adj* 可数的 kěshǔde: *'House' is a ~able noun.* "house"是可数名词. ˈ**countdown** *n* [C] (火箭发射等的)倒读〔讀〕数 dào dúshù.

C

count[2] /kaʊnt/ *n* [C] **1** 点〔點〕diǎn;数〔數〕shǔ;得数 déshù: *There were 50, at the last* ～. 最后一次点数是 50. **2** [法律]被控告事项 bèi kònggào shìxiàng: *a* ～ *of robbery* 抢劫罪状. **3** [习语] **keep/lose 'count of sth** 知道…的确〔確〕切数目 zhīdào…de quèqiè shùmù;不知道…的确切数目 bù zhīdào…de quèqiè shùmù.

count[3] /kaʊnt/ *n* [C] (法国、意大利等)伯爵 bójué.

countenance /ˈkaʊntɪnəns/ *n* **1** [C] [正式用语]面目 miànmù;面部表情 miànbùbiǎoqíng;面容 miànróng;脸〔臉〕色 liǎnsè. **2** [U] 赞助 zànzhù,支持 zhīchí;鼓励〔勵〕gǔlì: *give / lend* ～ *to a plan* 支持一项计划. **countenance** *v* [T] [正式用语]支持 zhīchí;赞成 zànchéng: *I cannot* ～ *violence*. 我不能支持暴力.

counter[1] /ˈkaʊntə(r)/ *n* [C] 柜〔櫃〕台〔臺〕guìtái.

counter[2] /ˈkaʊntə(r)/ *n* [C] **1** 游戏〔戲〕等记分用的筹〔籌〕码〔碼〕yóuxì děng jìfēn yòng de chóumǎ. **2** (讨价还价的)本钱〔錢〕běnqián;有利条〔條〕件 yǒulì tiáojiàn: *a bargaining* ～ 讨价还价的有利资本.

counter[3] /ˈkaʊntə(r)/ *adv to* 相反地 xiāngfǎnde;违〔違〕反 wéifǎn;与〔與〕…背道而驰 yǔ…bèi dào ér chí: *Her theories ran* ～ *to the evidence*. 她的理论同事实根据背道而驰.

counter[4] /ˈkaʊntə(r)/ *v* [I,T] (*with*) 反对〔對〕fǎnduì;反击〔擊〕fǎnjī: ～ *his arguments with her own opinion* 用她自己的意见来反击他的说法.

counter- /ˈkaʊntə(r)-/ (用于复合词) **1** 反 fǎn;逆 nì: ˌ～-*proˈductive*. 有碍于进展的. **2** 回报〔報〕huíbào: ˈ～-*attack* 反攻,反击. **3** 对〔對〕应〔應〕duìyìng: ˈ～*part* 配对物或人;对应物或人.

counteract /ˌkaʊntəˈrækt/ *v* [T] 抵抗 dǐkàng;抵制 dǐzhì;阻碍〔礙〕zǔ'ài;抵消 dǐxiāo: *try to* ～ *the bad influence of TV* 企图抵销电视的负面影响.

counter-attack /ˈkaʊntər əˈtæk/ *n* [C], *v* [I] 反攻 fǎngōng;反击〔擊〕fǎnjī.

counterbalance /ˈkaʊntəbæləns/ *n* [C] 平衡 pínghéng;抗衡 kànghéng;平衡力 pínghénglì. **counterbalance** /ˌkaʊntəˈbæləns/ *v* [T] 使平衡 shǐ pínghéng;抵消 dǐxiāo.

counter-espionage /ˌkaʊntər ˈespɪənɑːʒ/ *n* [U] 反间谍活动〔動〕fǎn jiàndié huódòng.

counterfeit /ˈkaʊntəfɪt/ *n* [C], *adj* 伪〔僞〕造物 wěizàowù;伪造的 wěizàode;假冒的 jiǎmàode;仿〔倣〕造的 fǎngzàode: ～ *banknotes* 假钞票. **counterfeit** *v* [T] 伪造 wěizào;仿造 fǎngzào. **counterfeiter** *n* [C] 伪造货币〔幣〕的人 wěizào huòbìde rén.

counterfoil /ˈkaʊntəfɔɪl/ *n* [C] (支票、收据等的)存根 cúngēn.

countermand /ˌkaʊntəˈmɑːnd; *US* -ˈmænd/ *v* [T] 取消 qǔxiāo,改变〔變〕(命令等) gǎibiàn.

counterpart /ˈkaʊntəpɑːt/ *n* [C] 对〔對〕应〔應〕物或人 duìyìng wù huò rén;配对人或物 pèiduì rén huò wù.

counter-productive /ˌkaʊntə prəˈdʌktɪv/ *adj* 产〔產〕生相反效果的 chǎnshēng xiāngfǎn xiàoguǒ de: *Her anger was* ～: *it just made him refuse to help at all*. 她的发脾气效果适得其反:使他干脆拒绝帮助.

countersign /ˈkaʊntəsaɪn/ *v* [T] 连署 liánshǔ;会〔會〕签〔簽〕huìqiān;副署 fùshǔ.

countess /ˈkaʊntɪs/ *n* [C] **1** 伯爵夫人 bójué fūrén. **2** 女伯爵 nǚ bójué.

countless /ˈkaʊntlɪs/ *adj* 无〔無〕数〔數〕的 wúshùde;数不清的 shǔbùqīngde: *I have been there* ～ *times*. 我到过那里无数次.

country /ˈkʌntrɪ/ *n* [*pl* -**ies**] **1** [C] 国〔國〕家 guójiā. **2 the country** [sing] 国民 guómín: *a politician loved by the whole* ～. 受全体国民爱戴的政治家. **3 the country** [sing] 农〔農〕村 nóngcūn: ～ *life / people* 农村生活;农民. **4** [习语] **go to the country** (政府)举〔舉〕行大选〔選〕jǔxíng dàxuǎn.

countryman /ˈkʌntrɪmən/ (*fem* **countrywoman** /ˈkʌntrɪwʊmən/) *n* [C] **1** 农〔農〕村人 nóngcūnrén;农民 nóngmín. **2** 同胞 tóngbāo.

countryside /ˈkʌntrɪsaɪd/ **the countryside** *n* [sing] 农〔農〕村 nóngcūn;乡〔鄉〕村 xiāngcūn.

county /ˈkaʊntɪ/ *n* [C] [*pl* -**ies**] 郡 jùn;县〔縣〕xiàn.

coup /kuː/ *n* [C] [*pl* ～**s** /kuːz/] **1** 突然而成功的行动〔動〕tūrán ér chénggōng de xíngdòng: *This deal was a* ～ *for her*. 这笔交易是她的一次成功的行动. **2** (亦作 **coup d'état** /kuːdeɪˈtɑː/) 政变〔變〕zhèngbiàn.

couple[1] /ˈkʌpl/ *n* [C] **1** 一对〔對〕yíduì;一双〔雙〕yìshuāng: *a married* ～ 夫妇. **2** [习语] **a couple of** [非正式用语]几〔幾〕个〔個〕jǐgè: *a* ～ *of drinks / days* 几份饮料;几天.

couple[2] /ˈkʌpl/ *v* (*with*) **1** [T] 使连接 shǐ liánjiē;使接合 shǐ jiēhé. **2** [T] 把…联〔聯〕系〔係〕起来 bǎ… liánxì qǐlái: *His illness,* ～*d with his lack of money, prevented him leaving*. 他生病,加之缺钱,就走不了啦. **3** [I] [古语或修辞]性交 xìngjiāo.

coupon /ˈkuːpɒn/ *n* [C] **1** 证〔證〕明持券人有某种〔種〕权〔權〕利的卡片、票、证 zhèngmíng chíquànrén yǒu mǒuzhǒng quánlì de kǎpiàn、piào、 zhèng. 2 (从报刊上剪下的)参〔參〕赛表 cānsàibiǎo;订货单〔單〕 dìnghuòdān.

courage /ˈkʌrɪdʒ/ *n* [U] 勇气〔氣〕 yǒngqì;胆〔膽〕量 dǎnliàng: *show ~ in a battle* 在战斗中表现英勇无畏. **courageous** /kəˈreɪdʒəs/ *adj*. **courageously** *adv*.

courgette /kʊəˈʒet/ *n* [C] 密生西葫芦〔蘆〕(蔬菜) mìshēng xīhúlu.

courier /ˈkʊrɪə(r)/ *n* [C] 1 旅游服务〔務〕员 lǚyóu fúwùyuán;导〔導〕游 dǎoyóu. 2 信使 xìnshǐ;送急件的人 sòng jíjiàn de rén.

course[1] /kɔːs/ *n* 1 [C] 行进〔進〕方向 xíngjìn fāngxiàng;路线〔綫〕 lùxiàn: *the ~ of a river* 河流所经区域. *the ~ of an aircraft* 飞机的航线 2 [C] (常用于复合词)运〔運〕动〔動〕场〔場〕所 yùndòng chǎngsuǒ: *a golf-~* 高尔夫球场. *a race ~* 跑道. 3 [sing] 进〔進〕展 jìnzhǎn;进程 jìnchéng: *the ~ of history* 历史的进程. 4 [C] 课程 kèchéng;学〔學〕程 xuéchéng: *a French ~* 法语课程. 5 [C] [医]疗〔療〕程 liáochéng: *a ~ of injections* 一个疗程的注射. 6 [C] 一道菜 yídàocài: *the fish ~* 鱼菜. 7 [习语] **(as) a matter of course** 当〔當〕然之事 dāngrán zhī shì;自然之事 zìrán zhī shì. **in the course of** 在…的过程中 zài…de guòchéng zhōng. **in ˌdue ˈcourse** 及时〔時〕地 jíshíde;在适〔適〕当〔當〕的时候 zài shìdàngde shíhòu. **of course** 当然 dāngrán;自然 zìrán. **run/take its ˈcourse** 持续〔續〕到自然结束 chíxù dào zìrán jiéshù. **ˈcourse book** *n* [C] 教科书〔書〕 jiàokēshū;课本 kèběn. **ˈcoursework** *n* [U] 课程作业〔業〕 kèchéng zuòyè.

course[2] /kɔːs/ *v* [I] [正式用语](液体)流淌 liútǎng: *The blood ~d round his veins*. 血液在他的血管里流淌.

court[1] /kɔːt/ *n* 1 [C, U] 法院 fǎyuàn;法庭 fǎtíng. 2 **the court** [sing] (法庭的)出庭人员 chūtíng rényuán;审〔審〕判人员 shěnpàn rényuán. 3 [C, U] 宫廷 gōngtíng;朝廷 cháotíng;宫廷人员 gōngtíng rényuán;朝廷人员 cháotíng rényuán. 4 [C] (常用于复合词)球场〔場〕 qiúchǎng: *a tennis ~* 网球场. 5 [C] (亦作 **ˈcourtyard**) 庭院 tíngyuàn.

court[2] /kɔːt/ *v* 1 [旧] (a) [T] 讨好 tǎohǎo;求爱〔愛〕 qiú'ài. (b) [I] (情侣)谈恋〔戀〕爱 tán liàn'ài. 2 [T] [常贬]奉承 fèngcheng: *~ sb's favour* 奉承某人. 3 [T] 冒…的危险〔險〕 mào …de wēixiǎn;导〔導〕致 dǎozhì: *~ disaster* 导致灾难.

courteous /ˈkɜːtɪəs/ *adj* 有礼〔禮〕貌的 yǒu lǐmào de;殷勤的 yīnqínde: *a ~ person* 有礼貌的人. *a ~ request* 有礼貌的请求.

courtesy /ˈkɜːtəsɪ/ *n* [*pl* -ies] 1 [U] 礼〔禮〕貌 lǐmào;谦恭 qiāngōng. 2 [C] 有礼貌的言行 yǒu lǐmàode yánxíng. 3 [习语] **by courtesy of** 蒙…的好意 méng… de hǎoyì;蒙…的允许 méng… de yǔnxǔ.

courtier /ˈkɔːtɪə(r)/ *n* [C] 廷臣 tíngchén;朝臣 cháochén.

court martial /ˌkɔːt ˈmɑːʃl/ *n* [C] [*pl* **courts martial**] 军事法庭 jūnshì fǎtíng;军事审〔審〕判 jūnshì shěnpàn. **court martial** *v* [-ll-; *US* -l-] [T] (*for*) 军事审判(某人) jūnshì shěnpàn.

courtship /ˈkɔːtʃɪp/ *n* [C, U] 求爱〔愛〕 qiú'ài;求婚 qiúhūn;求爱期间 qiú'ài qījiān.

courtyard /ˈkɔːtjɑːd/ = COURT[1](5).

cousin /ˈkʌzn/ *n* [C] 堂、表兄弟 táng、biǎo xiōngdì;堂、表姐妹 táng、biǎo jiěmèi.

cove /kəʊv/ *n* [C] 小海湾〔灣〕 xiǎo hǎiwān.

cover[1] /ˈkʌvə(r)/ *v* 1 [T] (*up/over*) 遮盖〔蓋〕 zhēgài;遮掩 zhēyǎn;保护〔護〕 bǎohù: *~ a table with a cloth* 给桌子铺上台布. *~ one's face* 遮住脸. *~ (up) the body* 盖住尸体. 2 [T] (*in/ with*) [尤用于被动语态]落满 luòmǎn;盖满 gàimǎn: *hills ~ed with snow* 盖了一层雪的小山. *boots ~ed in mud* 沾满泥土的靴子. 3 [T] 行过〔過〕(路程) xíngguò: *~ 100 miles in a day* 一天 100 英里. 4 [T] (钱)够用于 gòu yòng yú: *Will £20 ~ your expenses?* 20 英镑够你花销吗? 5 [T] 包括 bāokuò;包含 bāohán: *His researches ~ed a wide field*. 他的研究包括很广的范围. 6 (记者)采〔採〕访(某事件) cǎifǎng: *I've been asked to ~ the election*. 我被要求采访选举. 7 [I] (*for*) 代替(某人)工作 dàitì gōngzuò. 8 [T] 枪〔槍〕口对〔對〕准〔準〕(某人) qiāngkǒu duìzhǔn: *We've got him ~ed*. 我们用枪对准了他. 9 [习语] **cover one's tracks** 掩盖行踪 yǎngài xíngzōng. 10 [短语动词] **cover up** [贬]掩饰 yǎnshì;遮掩 zhēyǎn. **cover up for sb** 为〔為〕…遮掩 wèi…zhēyǎn. **coverage** *n* [U] 新闻报〔報〕导〔導〕 xīnwén bàodǎo. **covered** *adj* (*in/with*) 盖满…的 gàimǎn… de: *trees ~ed in blossom* 繁花满枝的树木. **ˈcover-up** *n* [C] [贬]遮掩 zhēyǎn;掩饰 yǎnshì.

cover[2] /ˈkʌvə(r)/ *n* 1 [C] (a) 套子 tàozi: *a chair ~* 椅套. (b) 盖〔蓋〕子 gàizi;顶子 dǐngzi. 2 [C] (书、杂志)封面 fēngmiàn;封底 fēngdǐ. 3 [U] 庇护〔護〕所 pìhùsuǒ;隐蔽处〔處〕 yǐnbìchù: *seek ~ under some trees* 在树下找一个隐蔽的地方. 4 **the covers** [pl] 床〔牀〕罩 chuángzhào;被子 bèizi. 5 [常用 sing] (*for*) 掩护〔護〕 yǎnhù;假身份 jiǎ shēnfen: *a business that is a ~ for drug dealing* 用作掩护毒品交易的一家商行. 6 [U] 防护 fánghù;掩护 yǎnhù: *Aircraft gave the infantry ~*. 飞机掩护步兵. 7 [U] 保险〔險〕 bǎoxiǎn. 8 [C] 包皮 bāopí;封皮 fēngpí;信封 xìnfēng. 9 [习语] **under cover of** 在…掩护下 zài…yǎnhù

C

xià;趁着 chènzhe: *under ~ of darkness* 在黑暗的掩护下. **covering letter** *n* [C] 附信 fùxìn;附函 fùhán.

covert /ˈkʌvət; *US* ˈkəʊvɜːt/ *adj* 隐〔隱〕蔽的 yǐnbìde;暗地里〔裏〕的 àndìlǐde,偷偷摸摸的 tōutōumōmōde: *a ~ glance* 偷偷的一瞥. *a ~ threat* 隐蔽的威胁.

C

cow[1] /kaʊ/ *n* [C] 1 母牛 mǔniú;奶牛 nǎiniú. 2 (象、鲸、犀牛等)母兽〔獸〕mǔshòu. 3 [贬,俚语]女人 nǚrén: *You silly ~!* 你这蠢女人! ˈ**cowboy** *n* [C] 1 (美国西部)牛仔 niúzǎi. 2 [英国非正式用语]不老实〔實〕的建筑〔築〕商、管子工 bù lǎoshide jiànzhùshāng、guǎnzigōng.

cow[2] /kaʊ/ *v* [T] 吓〔嚇〕唬 xiàhu;威胁〔脅〕wēixié: *He was ~ed into giving them all his money.* 他被吓得把钱都给了他们.

coward /ˈkaʊəd/ *n* [C] [贬]胆〔膽〕小者 dǎnxiǎozhě;懦夫 nuòfū. **cowardly** *adj* [贬]怯懦的 qiènuòde;胆小的 dǎnxiǎode: *a ~ attack* 怯懦的进攻. **cowardice** /-dɪs/ *n* [U] [贬]胆小 dǎnxiǎo;怯懦 qiènuò.

cower /ˈkaʊə(r)/ *v* [I] 畏缩 wèisuō;抖缩 dǒusuō.

cowl /kaʊl/ *n* [C] 1 僧衣的头〔頭〕巾 sēngyīde tóujīn. 2 烟囱帽 yāncōngmào.

cox /kɒks/ (亦作[非正式用语] **coxswain** /ˈkɒksn/) *n* [C] 赛船的舵手 sàichuánde duòshǒu. **cox** *v* [I, T] 做赛船的舵手 zuò sàichuánde duòshǒu.

coy /kɔɪ/ *adj* 1 怕羞的 pàxiūde;装〔裝〕着怕羞的 zhuāngzhe pàxiū de: *a ~ smile* 忸怩的一笑. 2 不愿〔願〕表态〔態〕的 búyuàn biǎotài de: *She was a little ~ about her past.* 她不愿评说自己的过去. **coyly** *adv*. **coyness** *n* [U].

coyote /ˈkɔɪəʊt; *US* ˈkaɪəʊt/ *n* [C] (北美西部的一种小狼)丛〔叢〕林狼 cónglínláng,郊狼 jiāoláng.

crab /kræb/ *n* (a) [C] 蟹 xiè. (b) 蟹肉 xièròu.

crabby /ˈkræbɪ/ *adj* [-ier, -iest] [非正式用语]脾气〔氣〕坏〔壞〕的 píqì huài de;烦躁的 fánzàode: *in a ~ mood* 心情烦躁.

crack[1] /kræk/ *n* [C] 1 裂缝 lièfèng: *a ~ in a cup* 杯子上的裂缝. *a ~ in the ice* 冰上的裂缝. 2 破裂声〔聲〕pòlièshēng;爆裂声 bàolièshēng: *the ~ of a whip* 抽鞭子的噼啪声. *the ~ of a rifle* 枪声. 3 (砰的)一击〔擊〕yìjī: *a ~ on the head* 迎头一击. 4 [非正式用语]俏皮话 qiàopíhuà;笑话 xiàohua: *She made a ~ about his baldness.* 她对他的秃顶开了一个玩笑. 5 [习语] **the crack of** ˈ**dawn** [非正式用语]破晓〔曉〕pòxiǎo. **crack** *adj* 第一流的 dìyīliúde: *She's a ~ shot.* 她是一名神枪手.

crack[2] /kræk/ *v* 1 [I, T] 使破裂 shǐ pòliè;裂开〔開〕lièkāi: *~ a plate* 把盘子碰裂. 2 [I, T] (使)噼啪作响〔響〕pīpā zuòxiǎng: *~ a whip* 噼噼啪啪地抽鞭子. 3 [T] 砸开 zákāi;砸碎 zásuì: *~ a safe* 砸开保险箱. *~ nuts* 把胡桃砸开. 4 [T] 猛击〔擊〕měngjī: *~ one's head on the door* 把头撞在门上. 5 [I, T] (使)停止抵抗 tíngzhǐ dǐkàng;屈服 qūfú: *She finally ~ed and told the truth.* 最后她屈服了,招了供. 6 [T] [非正式用语]解决(难题等) jiějué: *~ a code* 破译密码. 7 [I] (声音)变〔變〕哑〔啞〕biàn yǎ;(男孩声音)变粗 biàn cū. 8 [T] (非正式用语)说(笑话) shuō. 9 [习语] **get** ˈ**cracking** [非正式用语]开始繁忙 kāishǐ fánmáng. 10 [短语动词] **crack down** (**on sb / sth**) 对〔對〕…采〔採〕取严〔嚴〕厉〔厲〕措施 duì…cǎiqǔ yánlì cuòshī: *~ down on crime* 严厉打击犯罪. **crack up** [非正式用语](身体或精神上)垮掉 kuǎdiào. ˈ**crack-down** *n* [C] 镇压〔壓〕zhènyā: *a police ~-down on vandalism* 警方对破坏公共财产行为的打击措施. **cracked** *adj* [非正式用语]有点〔點〕疯〔瘋〕狂的 yǒu diǎn fēngkuángde: *You must be ~ed to drive so fast!* 你疯了,开这么快的车!

crack[3] /kræk/ *n* [U] [俚]强效纯可卡因 qiángxiào chún kěkǎyīn;快克 kuàikè;霹雳〔靂〕pīlì.

cracker /ˈkrækə(r)/ *n* [C] 1 (常与奶酪一起吃的)薄脆饼干〔乾〕báocuì bǐnggān. 2 鞭炮 biānpào;爆竹 bàozhú. 3 彩包爆竹(宴会等上的娱乐用品) cǎibāo bàozhú.

crackers /ˈkrækəz/ *adj* [英国非正式用语]发〔發〕疯〔瘋〕的 fāfēngde.

crackle /ˈkrækl/ *v* [I] 噼啪作响〔響〕pīpā zuòxiǎng: *Dry leaves ~d under our feet.* 枯树叶被我们踩得吱吱作响. **crackle** *n* [sing, U] 噼啪声〔聲〕pīpāshēng;爆裂声 bàolièshēng.

crackpot /ˈkrækpɒt/ *n* [C] [非正式用语]怪人 guàirén;疯〔瘋〕子 fēngzi.

cradle /ˈkreɪdl/ *n* [C] 1 摇篮 yáolán. 2 [喻]策源地 cèyuándì;发〔發〕源地 fāyuándì: *the ~ of Western culture* 西方文化的发源地. 3 摇篮形支架 yáolánxíng zhījià. **cradle** *v* [T] 把…放在摇篮里〔裡〕bǎ… fàngzài yáolán lǐ;把…放在摇篮形支架上 bǎ…fàngzài yáolánxíng zhījià shàng.

craft /krɑːft; *US* kræft/ *n* 1 [C] 工艺〔藝〕gōngyì;手艺 shǒuyì;手工业〔業〕shǒugōngyè: *the potter's ~* 制陶手艺. 2 [C] [*pl* **craft**] 船 chuán;小船 xiǎo chuán;飞〔飛〕行器 fēixíngqì;宇宙飞船 yǔzhòu fēichuán. 3 [U] [正式用语,贬]诡计 guǐjì;手腕 shǒuwàn. **-craft** (用于复合词): *handi~* 手工业. *needle~* 刺绣技艺. **craftsman** *n* [C] [*pl* **-men**] 手艺人 shǒuyìrén;工匠 gōngjiàng;名匠 míngjiàng. **crafts-**

manship *n* [U] 手艺 shǒuyì;技艺 jìyì.

crafty /ˈkrɑːftɪ; *US* ˈkræftɪ/ *adj* [-ier, -iest] 狡猾的 jiǎohuáde;诡计多端的 guǐjì duōduān de. **craftily** *adv*. **craftiness** *n* [U].

crag /kræg/ *n* [C] 岩 yán;峭壁 qiàobì;危岩 wēiyán. **craggy** *adj* [-ier, -iest] 1 峻峭的 jùnqiàode. 2 (人脸)多皱〔皺〕纹的 duō zhòuwén de.

cram /kræm/ *v* [-mm-] 1 [T] (*in/into/with*) 塞进 sāijìn;塞满 sāimǎn: ~ *clothes into the suitcase* 把衣服塞进箱子. ~ *the file with papers* 把文件塞进文件夹. 2 [I] (*for*) 为〔爲〕考试而死记硬背 wèi kǎoshì ér sǐjì yìngbèi.

cramp[1] /kræmp/ *n* [C, 常用 pl, U] (肌肉)痉〔痙〕挛〔攣〕jìngluán;抽筋 chōujīn.

cramp[2] /kræmp/ *v* 1 [T] [常用被动语态]束缚 shùfù: *feel ~ed by the rules* 感觉受到规则的束缚. 2 [习语] **cramp sb's style** [非正式用语]限制某人的正常自由 xiànzhì mǒurénde zhèngcháng zìyóu. **cramped** *adj* 狭〔狹〕窄的 xiázhǎide: ~ *conditions* 狭窄的环境.

crampon /ˈkræmpɒn/ *n* [C] (登冰山用的)鞋底铁〔鐵〕钉 xiédǐ tiědīng.

cranberry /ˈkrænbərɪ; *US* -berɪ/ *n* [C] 蔓越桔〔橘〕(酸果蔓的果实) mànyuèjú.

crane[1] /kreɪn/ *n* [C] 1 鹤 hè. 2 起重机〔機〕qǐzhòngjī;吊车〔車〕diàochē.

crane[2] /kreɪn/ *v* [I, T] 伸(颈) shēn: *Children ~d to see the animals*. 孩子们伸长脖子观看动物.

cranium /ˈkreɪnɪəm/ *n* [C] [*pl* ~s 或 **crania** /ˈkreɪnɪə/] [解剖]头〔頭〕盖〔蓋〕tóugài;脑〔腦〕壳〔殼〕nǎoké;头盖骨 tóugàigǔ. **cranial** *adj*.

crank[1] /kræŋk/ *n* [C] 曲柄 qūbǐng. **crank** *v* [T] (*up*) 用曲柄启〔啓〕动〔動〕或转〔轉〕动 yòng qūbǐng qǐdòng huò zhuàndòng: ~ *the engine* 用曲柄启动发动机. ˈ**crankshaft** *n* [C] 曲轴 qūzhóu.

crank[2] /kræŋk/ *n* [C] [贬]怪人 guàirén;脾气〔氣〕古怪的人 píqì gǔguài de rén. **cranky** *adj* [-ier, -iest] [非正式用语,贬] 1 (人)古怪的 gǔguàide. 2 [美语]脾气〔氣〕坏〔壞〕的 píqì huài de.

cranny /ˈkrænɪ/ *n* [C] 1 (墙壁等上的)裂缝 lièfèng. 2 [习语] **every nook and cranny** ⇨ NOOK.

crap /kræp/ *v* [-pp-] [I] [俚语⚠]拉屎 lāshǐ. **crap** *n* (⚠) 1 [U] 屎 shǐ. 2 [sing] 拉屎 lāshǐ. 3 [U] 胡扯 húchě;废〔廢〕话 fèihuà;废物 fèiwù. **crappy** *adj* [-ier, -iest] [俚语]蹩脚的 biéjiǎode;没价值的 méi jiàzhí de.

crash[1] /kræʃ/ *n* [C] 1 [常作 sing] 坠〔墜〕地撞击〔擊〕声〔聲〕zhuìdì zhuàngjīshēng;突然坠落 tūrán zhuìluò: *The dishes fell with a ~ to the floor*. 盘碟哗啦一声摔到地上. 2 事故 shìgù;撞车〔車〕事故 zhuàngchē shìgù: *a car ~* 汽车撞车事故. 3 倒闭 dǎobì;垮台〔臺〕kuǎtái. **crash** *adj* 速成的 sùchéngde: *a ~ course in French* 法语速成课程. **crash** *adv* 砰地一声 pēngde yìshēng. ˈ**crash-helmet** *n* [C] (摩托车驾驶者用的)防撞头〔頭〕盔 fángzhuàng tóukuī. ˌ**crash-ˈland** *v* [I, T] (飞机失控而)猛撞降落 měngzhuàng jiàngluò. ˌ**crash-ˈlanding** *n* [C] 猛撞降落 měngzhuàng jiàngluò.

crash[2] /kræʃ/ *v* 1 [I, T] (使)哗〔嘩〕啦一声落下 huālā yìshēng luòxià;撞击〔擊〕zhuàngjī: *The tree ~ed through the window*. 树倒进了窗里. 2 [I, T] (使)碰撞 pèngzhuàng: ~ *the car* (*into a wall*) 把车撞(到墙上)了. 3 [I] 发〔發〕出巨声〔聲〕fāchū jùshēng: *The thunder ~ed*. 雷声隆隆. 4 [I, T] (使)猛冲〔衝〕měngchōng: *an elephant ~ing through the trees* 一头在树丛中猛冲直闯的象. 5 [I] (企业等)倒闭 dǎobì.

crass /kræs/ *adj* [非正式用语,贬] 1 愚钝的 yúdùnde;无〔無〕知的 wúzhīde. 2 (愚蠢、无知等)极〔極〕度的 jídùde, 非常的 fēichángde: ~ *stupidity* 极度的愚蠢.

crate /kreɪt/ *n* [C] 板条〔條〕箱 bǎntiáoxiāng;柳条箱 liǔtiáoxiāng. **crate** *v* [T] 用板条箱装〔裝〕yòng bǎntiáoxiāng zhuāng.

crater /ˈkreɪtə(r)/ *n* [C] 1 火山口 huǒshānkǒu. 2 弹〔彈〕坑 dànkēng.

cravat /krəˈvæt/ *n* [C] 旧〔舊〕式领带〔帶〕jiùshì lǐngdài.

crave /kreɪv/ *v* [T] (*for*) 恳〔懇〕求 kěnqiú;渴望 kěwàng: ~ *for a cigarette* 非常想抽支烟. **craving** *n* [C].

crawl /krɔːl/ *v* [I] 1 爬行 páxíng;匍匐前进〔進〕púfú qiánjìn: *The baby ~ed along the floor*. 婴儿在地板上爬. 2 缓慢地行进 huǎnmàn de xíngjìn: *traffic ~ing into London* 缓慢地驶进伦敦的车流. 3 *with* [尤用于进行时态]爬满 pámǎn;充斥着(爬虫) chōngchìzhe: *a floor ~ing with ants* 爬满蚂蚁的地板. 4 *to* [非正式用语]奉承 fèngcheng;巴结 bājie. 5 [习语] **make one's flesh crawl** ⇨ FLESH. **crawl** *n* 1 [C] 爬行 páxíng;爬 pá;蠕动〔動〕rúdòng. 2 **the crawl** [sing] 自由泳 zìyóuyǒng;爬泳 páyǒng. **crawler** *n* [非正式用语,贬]马屁精 mǎpìjīng.

crayon /ˈkreɪən/ *n* [C] 粉笔〔筆〕fěnbǐ;蜡〔蠟〕笔 làbǐ;颜色笔 yánsèbǐ. **crayon** *v* [T] 用粉笔等画〔畫〕yòng fěnbǐ děng huà.

craze /kreɪz/ *n* [C] (a) (一时的)狂热〔熱〕kuángrè. (b) 风〔風〕靡一时〔時〕的事物 fēngmǐ yìshí de shìwù;红极〔極〕一时的人 hóngjí yìshí de rén.

crazed /kreɪzd/ *adj* (*with*) 疯〔瘋〕狂的 fēngkuángde；非常兴〔興〕奋〔奮〕的 fēicháng xìngfèn de.

crazy /ˈkreɪzɪ/ *adj* [-ier,-iest] 1 狂热〔熱〕的 kuángrède；热衷于 rèzhōng yú：～ *about football* 热衷于足球. 2 [非正式用语]疯〔瘋〕狂的 fēngkuángde. 3 [非正式用语]愚蠢的 yúchǔnde；糊涂〔塗〕的 hútude：*a* ～ *idea* 愚蠢的主意 **crazily** *adv*. **craziness** *n* [U].

C

creak /kriːk/ *v* [I], *n* [C] 吱吱嘎嘎(地响) zhīzhīgāgā：*The branches* ～*ed in the wind*. 树枝被风刮得吱吱嘎嘎地响. **creaky** *adj* [-ier,-iest] 吱吱响〔響〕的 zhīzhī xiǎng de.

cream /kriːm/ *n* 1 [U] 乳脂 rǔzhǐ；奶油 nǎiyóu. 2 [U] 奶油状〔狀〕物 nǎiyóu zhuàng wù：ˈ*furniture* ～ 家具蜡 3 **the cream** [sing] 精华〔華〕jīnghuá；最精彩的部分 zuìjīngcǎide bùfen：*the* ～ *of society* 社会中坚. 4 [U] 奶油色 nǎiyóusè；米色 mǐsè. **cream** *adj* 奶油色的 nǎiyóusède；米色的 mǐsède. **cream** *v* [T] 1 从〔從〕(牛奶中)提取奶油 cóng tíqǔ nǎiyóu. 2 把(马铃薯等)搅〔攪〕拌成糊 bǎ jiǎobàn chéng hú. 3 [短语动词] **cream off** 取出最好部分 qǔchū zuìhǎo bùfen. **creamy** *adj* [-ier,-iest] 奶油似的 nǎiyóu sì de；含奶油的 hán nǎiyóu de.

crease /kriːs/ *n* [C] 1 (衣服、纸等的)折缝 zhéfèng；皱〔皺〕痕 zhòuhén. 2 皮肤〔膚〕上的皱纹 pífū shàng de zhòuwén 3 (板球)球员位置的白线〔綫〕qiúyuán wèizhì de báixiàn. **crease** *v* [I,T] (使)起折痕 qǐ zhéhén.

create /krɪˈeɪt/ *v* [T] 1 创〔創〕造 chuàngzào；创作 chuàngzuò. 2 产〔產〕生 chǎnshēng；造成 zàochéng；引起 yǐnqǐ：～ *problems* 引起问题.

creation /krɪˈeɪʃn/ *n* 1 [U] 创〔創〕造 chuàngzào；创作 chuàngzuò：*the* ～ *of the world* 世界的创造. 2 (亦作 Creation) [U] 天地万〔萬〕物 tiāndì wànwù；宇宙 yǔzhòu. 3 [C] 创作物 chuàngzuòwù.

creative /krɪˈeɪtɪv/ *adj* 1 有创〔創〕造力的 yǒu chuàngzàolì de；有创造性的 yǒu chuàngzàoxìng de：*a* ～ *person who writes and paints* 一个又写又画，有创造性的人. 2 创作的 chuàngzuòde：*the* ～ *act* 创作的节目. **creatively** *adv*. **creativity** /ˌkriːeɪˈtɪvətɪ/ *n* [U].

creator /krɪˈeɪtə(r)/ *n* 1 [C] 创〔創〕造者 chuàngzàozhě；创作者 chuàngzuòzhě：*the* ～ *of this novel* 这本小说的创作者. 2 **the Creator** [sing] 上帝 shàngdì；造物主 zàowùzhǔ.

creature /ˈkriːtʃə(r)/ *n* [C] 动〔動〕物 dòngwù；人 rén：*all God's* ～*s* 人和动物.

crèche /kreɪʃ/ *n* [C] 日托托儿〔兒〕所 rìtuō tuō'érsuǒ.

credentials /krɪˈdenʃlz/ *n* [pl] 1 信任状〔狀〕xìnrènzhuàng；证〔證〕书〔書〕zhèngshū. 2 资格 zīgé：*Does she have the* ～ *for this demanding work?* 她有资格做这种要求很高的工作吗？

credible /ˈkredəbl/ *adj* 可信任的 kě xìnrèn de；可靠的 kěkàode：*a* ～ *story* 可信的描述. *a* ～ *explanation* 可靠的解释. **credibility** /ˌkredəˈbɪlətɪ/ *n* [U] 可信 kěxìn. **credibly** /-əblɪ/ *adv* 可信地 kěxìnde.

credit[1] /ˈkredɪt/ *n* 1 赊购〔購〕(制度) shēgòu：*buy a car on* ～ 赊购一辆汽车. 2 信誉〔譽〕xìnyù：*have good* ～ 信誉好. *have poor* ～ 信誉不好. 3 [U] (银行)存款 cúnkuǎn. 4 [C] (银行)信用贷款 xìnyòng dàikuǎn. 5 [C] (簿记)贷方 dàifāng. 6 [U] 相信 xiāngxìn：*give* ～ *to his story* 相信他的话. 7 [U] 赞〔讚〕扬〔揚〕zànyáng：*get/be given all the* ～ *for sth* 为…大受赞扬. 8 [sing] *to* 增光的人或事物 zēngguāngde rén huò shìwù：*She's a* ～ *to her family*. 她为家庭增光. 9 [C] [美语] 学〔學〕分 xuéfēn. 10 [习语] **be to sb's credit** 为〔爲〕某人带〔帶〕来荣〔榮〕誉 wèi mǒurén dàilái róngyù. ˈ**credit card** *n* [C] 信用卡 xìnyòngkǎ；记账〔賬〕卡 jìzhàngkǎ. ˈ**credit crunch** *n* [C] 信贷紧〔緊〕缩 xìndài jǐnsuō. ˈ**credit-worthy** *adj* 值得提供信贷的 zhídé tígōng xìndài de. ˈ**credit-worthiness** *n* [U].

credit[2] /ˈkredɪt/ *v* [T] 1 (*with*) 认〔認〕为〔爲〕…有… rènwéi…yǒu…：*I* ～*ed you with more sense*. 我认为你不糊涂. 2 把…记入贷方 bǎ…jìrù dàifāng. 3 相信 xiāngxìn：*Would you* ～ *it?* 你相信吗？

creditable /ˈkredɪtəbl/ *adj* 值得赞〔讚〕扬〔揚〕的(虽不完美) zhídé zànyángde：*a* ～ *piece of work* 值得称赞的作品. **creditably** *adv*.

creditor /ˈkredɪtə(r)/ *n* [C] 债权〔權〕人 zhàiquánrén.

credulous /ˈkredjʊləs; *US* -dʒə-/ *adj* 轻〔輕〕信的 qīngxìnde. **credulity** /krɪˈdjuːlətɪ/ *n* [U].

creed /kriːd/ *n* [C] 信条〔條〕xìntiáo；教义〔義〕jiàoyì.

creek /kriːk; *US* krɪk/ *n* [C] 1 [英国英语] 小湾〔灣〕xiǎowān；小港 xiǎogǎng. 2 [美语]小河 xiǎohé.

creep /kriːp/ *v* [I] [*pt*, *pp* **crept** /krept/] 1 爬行 páxíng；匍匐而行 púfú ér xíng；缓慢移行 huǎnmàn yíxíng；悄悄移行 qiāoqiāo yíxíng：*The thief crept along the corridor*. 小偷悄悄地在走廊里走. [喻] *Old age is* ～*ing up on me*. 老年正悄悄向我走近. 2 (植物等)匍匐 púfú；蔓生 mànshēng. 3 [习语] **make one's flesh creep** ⇨ FLESH. **creep** *n* 1 [C] [非正

式用语,贬]讨厌〔厭〕的人 tǎoyànde rén;奴颜卑膝的人 núyán bēixī de rén. 2 [习语] **give sb the creeps** [非正式用语]使恐惧〔懼〕shǐ kǒngjù;使厌恶〔惡〕shǐ yànwù. **creeper** *n* [C] 匍匐植物 púfú zhíwù.

creepy /ˈkriːpɪ/ *adj* [-ier, -iest] [非正式用语]令人毛骨悚然的 lìng rén máogǔ sǒngrán de: *a ~ house/atmosphere* 令人毛骨悚然的屋子/气氛.

creepy-crawly /ˌkriːpɪˈkrɔːlɪ/ *n* [C] [非正式用语,尤用于谐谑]爬虫 páchóng;蜘蛛 zhīzhū.

cremate /krɪˈmeɪt/ *v* [T] 焚(尸) fén. **cremation** /-ˈmeɪʃn/ *n* [C,U] 焚尸〔屍〕fénshī. 火葬 huǒzàng. **crematorium** /ˌkreməˈtɔːrɪəm/ *n* [C] [*pl* ~s 或 -oria /-ɔːrɪə/] 焚尸炉〔爐〕fénshīlú;火化场〔場〕huǒhuàchǎng.

creosote /ˈkrɪəsəʊt/ *n* [U] 杂〔雜〕酚油(木材防腐剂) záfēnyóu.

crepe (亦作 **crêpe**) /kreɪp/ *n* [U] 1 绉〔縐〕布 zhòubù;绉纸 zhòuzhǐ: *a ~ blouse* 绉布罩衫 2 绉胶〔膠〕zhòujiāo. 3 薄烤饼 báokǎobǐng.

crept /krept/ *pt*, *pp* of CREEP.

crescendo /krɪˈʃendəʊ/ *n* [C] [*pl* ~s] 1 (音乐)渐强 jiànqiáng. 2 [喻]向高潮渐进〔進〕xiàng gāocháo jiànjìn. **crescendo** *adj*, *adv* 渐强的(地) jiànqiángde: *a ~ passage* 渐强的乐节.

crescent /ˈkreznt, ˈkresnt/ *n* [C] 1 月牙 yuèyá;新月 xīnyuè;新月状〔狀〕物 xīnyuè zhuàng wù. 2 新月形排房 xīnyuè xíng páifáng.

cress /kres/ *n* [U] 水芹 shuǐqín.

crest /krest/ *n* [C] 1 鸟禽等的冠 niǎo qín děng de guān. 2 (a) (小山的)山顶 shāndǐng. (b) 浪峰 làngfēng 3 (盾形纹章上方的)饰章 shìzhāng. 4 盔上的羽毛饰 kuī shàng de yǔmáoshì. **crest** *v* [T] 达〔達〕到…的顶端 dádào…de dǐngduān.

crestfallen /ˈkrestfɔːlən/ *adj* 沮丧〔喪〕的 jǔsàngde.

cretin /ˈkretɪn/ *n* [C] 1 [蔑△]笨蛋 bèndàn. 2 [医]白痴〔癡〕báichī.

crevasse /krɪˈvæs/ *n* [C] 裂隙 lièxì;冰川的裂隙 bīngchuānde lièxì.

crevice /ˈkrevɪs/ *n* [C] (岩石、墙等)裂缝 lièfèng.

crew /kruː/ *n* [C] 1 全体〔體〕船员 quántǐ chuányuán;全体空勤人员 quántǐ kōngqín rényuán;上述工作人员(不包括高级职员) shàngshù gōngzuò rényuán. 2 同事们 tóngshìmen;一起工作的人们 yìqǐ gōngzuò de rénmen;一帮人 yìbāngrén: *a camera ~* 摄影组. **crew** *v* [I, T] 以船员身份操作 yǐ chuányuán shēnfen cāozuò.

crib[1] /krɪb/ *n* [C] 1 婴儿〔兒〕小床〔牀〕yīng'ér xiǎochuáng. 2 (牲口的)饲料槽 sìliàocáo.

crib[2] /krɪb/ *n* [C] 1 剽窃〔竊〕piāoqiè;抄袭〔襲〕chāoxí: *The teacher said my exam answer was a ~.* 老师说我的考试答案是抄来的. 2 用来帮助理解的东西(如学外语用的对照译文) yònglái bāngzhù lǐjiě de dōngxi. **crib** *v* [-bb-] [I,T] 剽窃 piāoqiè;抄袭 chāoxí.

crick /krɪk/ *n* [sing] (颈部等的)痛性痉〔痙〕挛〔攣〕tòngxìng jìngluán.

cricket[1] /ˈkrɪkɪt/ *n* [U] 板球(运动) bǎnqiú: *a ~ match* 板球比赛. **cricketer** *n* [C] 板球选〔選〕手 bǎnqiú xuǎnshǒu.

cricket[2] /ˈkrɪkɪt/ *n* [C] 蟋蟀 xīshuài.

cried /kraɪd/ *pt*, *pp* of CRY².

cries /kraɪz/ 1 *3rd pers sing pres t* of CRY². 2 *pl* of CRY¹.

crime /kraɪm/ *n* 1 [C] 罪 zuì;罪行 zuìxíng: *commit a ~* 犯罪. 2 [U] 犯罪行为〔爲〕fànzuì xíngwéi. 3 **a crime** [sing] 愚蠢或可耻的行为 yúchǔn huò kěchǐde xíngwéi: *It's a ~ to waste money like that.* 那样浪费金钱真是罪过. **criminal** /ˈkrɪmɪnl/ *adj* 1 犯罪的 fànzuìde;刑事上的 xíngshì shàng de: *a ~ offence* 刑事犯罪. *~ law* 刑法. 2 愚蠢的 yúchǔnde;无〔無〕耻的 wúchǐde: *It's ~ not to use your talents fully.* 不充分发挥你的才能真是罪过. **criminal** *n* [C] 罪犯 zuìfàn. **criminally** /-nəlɪ/ *adv*.

crimson /ˈkrɪmzn/ *n* [U], *adj* 深红(的) shēnhóng;绯红(的) fēihóng.

cringe /krɪndʒ/ *v* [I] 1 畏缩 wèisuō. 2 (*to/before*) 卑躬屈膝 bēi gōng qū xī: *Don't always ~ to the boss.* 对老板别总是卑躬屈膝.

crinkle /ˈkrɪŋkl/ *n* [C] 皱〔皺〕折 zhòuzhé. **crinkle** *v* [I,T] (使)起皱 qǐ zhòu: *~d paper* 皱纸.

cripple /ˈkrɪpl/ *n* [C] 残〔殘〕疾人 cánjírén;跛子 bǒzi. **cripple** *v* [T] [通常用被动语态] 1 使跛 shǐ bǒ;使残疾 shǐ cánjí: *~d by a back injury* 背部受伤致残. 2 [喻]严〔嚴〕重削弱 yánzhòng xuēruò;损坏〔壞〕sǔnhuài: *~d by debt* 深受债务之害.

crisis /ˈkraɪsɪs/ *n* [C] [*pl* **crises** /-siːz/] 转〔轉〕折点〔點〕zhuǎnzhédiǎn;危急存亡关〔關〕头〔頭〕wēijí cúnwáng guāntóu;危机〔機〕wēijī: *an economic ~* 经济危机. *a country in ~* 处于危急存亡关头的国家.

crisp /krɪsp/ *adj* 1 (a) (尤指食物)脆的 cuìde;易碎的 yìsuìde: *a ~ biscuit* 脆饼干. *~ snow* 风干的积雪. (b) (尤指水果蔬菜)鲜脆的 xiāncuìde: *a ~ lettuce* 鲜脆的莴苣 (c) (尤指纸)挺括的 tǐngkuòde: *~ banknotes* 挺括的钞票. 2 (天气)干〔乾〕冷的 gānlěngde: *a ~ winter morning* 一个干冷的冬日早晨. 3 (说

C

C

话、行为等)干脆的 gāncuìde;干净利落的 gānjìng lìluò de:*a ~ reply* 干净利落的答复. **crisp** *n* [C,通常作 pl] 油炸马〔馬〕铃薯片(袋装) yóuzhá mǎlíngshǔpiàn. **crisp** *v* [I,T] (使)发〔發〕脆 fā cuì. **crisply** *adv*. **crispness** *n* [U]. **crispy** *adj* [-ier, -iest] [非正式用语] (食物)脆的 cuìde;(水果、蔬菜)鲜脆的 xiāncuìde.

criss-cross /ˈkrɪskrɒs/ *adj* 十字形的 shízìxíngde;交叉的 jiāochāde:*a ~ pattern* 十字形花样. **criss-cross** *v* [I,T] 在…上画〔畫〕十字形图〔圖〕案 zài…shàng huà shízìxíng tú'àn:*roads ~ing the country* 全国纵横交错的公路.

criterion /kraɪˈtɪərɪən/ *n* [C] [*pl* -ria /-rɪə/] 判断〔斷〕的标〔標〕准〔準〕 pànduànde biāozhǔn.

critic /ˈkrɪtɪk/ *n* [C] **1** 批评家 pīpíngjiā;评论〔論〕家 pínglùnjiā;文艺〔藝〕评论家 wényì pínglùnjiā:*The ~s liked the play*. 评论家们喜欢这个戏剧. **2** 批评缺点〔點〕错误的人 pīpíng quēdiǎn cuòwù de rén.

critical /ˈkrɪtɪkl/ *adj* **1** 批评(缺点、错误)性的 pīpíngxìngde:*a ~ remark* 批评的话. **2** (尤指文艺方面)评论〔論〕性的 pínglùnxìngde:*a ~ review* 评论性期刊. **3** 紧〔緊〕急的 jǐnjíde:*a ~ decision* 紧急决定. **critically** /-ɪklɪ/ *adv* 紧急地 jǐnjíde:*~ly ill* 病得危急.

criticism /ˈkrɪtɪsɪzəm/ *n* **1** (a) [U] (对文学、书籍等的)评论〔論〕 pínglùn:*literary ~* 文学评论. (b) [C] 评论文章 pínglùn wénzhāng. **2** (a) [U] (对缺点、错误的)批评 pīpíng:*I can't stand her constant ~*. 我受不了她的不断的批评. (b) [C] 批评的话 pīpíngde huà.

criticize /ˈkrɪtɪsaɪz/ *v* **1** [I,T] 批评(…的缺点错误) pīpíng:*Don't ~ my work*. 不要批评我的工作. **2** [T] 评论〔論〕(文艺等) pínglùn.

critique /krɪˈtiːk/ *n* [C] 评论〔論〕文章 pínglùn wénzhāng:*The book contains a ~ of her ideas*. 这本书里有一篇关于她的思想的评论文章.

croak /krəʊk/ *n* [C] (蛙等)呱呱叫声〔聲〕 guāguājiàoshēng. **croak** *v* **1** [I] 呱呱地叫 guāguāde jiào. **2** [I,T] 用嘶哑〔啞〕的声音说 yòng sīyǎde shēngyīn shuō.

crockery /ˈkrɒkərɪ/ *n* [U] 陶器 táoqì;瓦器 wǎqì.

crocodile /ˈkrɒkədaɪl/ *n* [C] **1** 鳄鱼 èyú. **2** [非正式用语]两人一排的学〔學〕生行列 liǎngrén yìpái de xuéshēng hángliè. **3** [习语] **crocodile tears** 鳄鱼的眼泪〔淚〕 èyúde yǎnlèi;假慈悲 jiǎ cíbēi.

crocus /ˈkrəʊkəs/ *n* [C] 藏红花 zànghónghuā.

croissant /ˈkrwʌsɒŋ; *US* krʌˈsɒŋ/ *n* [C] 羊角面〔麵〕包 yángjiǎo miànbāo.

crony /ˈkrəʊnɪ/ *n* [C] [*pl* -ies] [贬]朋友 péngyou;伙〔夥〕伴 huǒbàn.

crook /krʊk/ *n* [C] **1** [非正式用语]骗子 piànzi;流氓 liúmáng. **2** 弯〔彎〕曲处〔處〕 wānqūchù. 牧羊人用的弯柄杖 mùyángrén yòng de wānbǐngzhàng. **crook** *v* [T] 使(手指、手臂等)弯曲 shǐ wānqū.

crooked /ˈkrʊkɪd/ *adj* **1** 弯〔彎〕曲的 wānqūde;扭曲的 niǔqūde:*a ~ line* 弯曲的线. **2** 欺诈的 qīzhàde;不正当〔當〕的 bú zhèngdàngde:*a ~ politician* 狡猾的政客. **crookedly** *adv*.

crop[1] /krɒp/ *n* [C] **1** (农作物等)一熟 yìshú;收成 shōuchéng:*a good ~ of wheat* 麦子的好收成. **2 crops** [pl] 作物 zuòwù;庄〔莊〕稼 zhuāngjia. **3** [sing] *of* 一批 yìpī;一群 yìqún:*a new ~ of problems* 一大堆新问题.

crop[2] /krɒp/ *v* [-pp-] [T] **1** 剪短(头发、马尾等) jiǎnduǎn. **2** (牲畜)咬掉(草等)的顶端 yǎodiào de dǐngduān;啃吃(青草) kěnchī. **3** [短语动词] **crop up** 突然发〔發〕生、出现 tūrán fāshēng、chūxiàn:*A new problem has ~ped up*. 突然发生了新的问题.

croquet /ˈkrəʊkeɪ; *US* krəʊˈkeɪ/ *n* [U] 槌球游戏〔戲〕 chuíqiú yóuxì.

cross[1] /krɒs; *US* krɔːs/ *n* **1** [C] 十字形记号〔號〕 shízìxíng jìhào. **2** (a) **the Cross** [sing] 耶稣被钉死的十字架 Yēsū bèi dīngsǐ de shízìjià. (b) [C] (作为基督徒标志的)十字架 shízìjià (c) [C] (基督教牧师的)划〔劃〕十字动〔動〕作 huà shízì dòngzuò. **3** [正式用语]苦难〔難〕 kǔnàn;忧〔憂〕伤〔傷〕 yōushāng:*We all have our ~ to bear*. 每个人都要承受苦难. **4** (a) (动植物的)杂〔雜〕种〔種〕 zázhǒng. (b) 两种事物的混合 liǎngzhǒng shìwùde hùnhé.

cross[2] /krɒs; *US* krɔːs/ *v* **1** [I,T] 横穿 héngchuān;横过〔過〕 héngguò;横渡 héngdù:*a bridge ~ing the road* 横穿过公路的一座桥梁. **2** [T] 使交叉 shǐ jiāochā:*~ one's arms* 抱着双臂. **3** [T] 划〔劃〕横线〔綫〕于 huà héngxiàn yú:*~ a cheque* 在支票上划双线(表示只能用记入银行账户来兑付). **4** [I] (行人)对〔對〕面而过 duìmiàn ér guò;(邮寄信件)相互错过 xiānghù cuòguò:*The letters ~ed in the post*. 信件在邮寄中互相错过. **5** [T] 阻挠〔撓〕 zǔnáo;反对 fǎnduì:*You shouldn't ~ her in business*. 你不应在事业上阻挠她. **6** [T] (*with*) 使杂〔雜〕交 shǐ zájiāo:*~ different varieties of rose* 使不同品种的玫瑰杂交. **7 ~ oneself** 在胸前画〔畫〕十字 zài xiōngqián huà shízì. **8** [习语] **cross one's mind** (想法等)浮现心头〔頭〕 fúxiàn xīntóu. **9** [短语动词] **cross sth off /out /through** 划掉 huàdiào:*~ her name off the list* 从名单上划掉她的名字. *~ his name out* 划掉他的名字.

cross[3] /krɒs; US krɔːs/ *adj* 1 生气〔氣〕的 shēngqìde: *I was ~ with him for being late*. 因为他迟到,我生气了. *She's ~ about this*. 她为此而生气. 2 (风)逆的 nìde: *a ~ breeze* 逆的微风. crossly *adv*. crossness *n* [U].

crossbow /ˈkrɒsbəʊ; US ˈkrɔːs-/ *n* [C] 十字弓 shízìgōng; 弩 nǔ.

crossbred /ˈkrɒsbred; US ˈkrɔːs-/ *adj* 杂〔雜〕交的 zájiāode; 杂种〔種〕的 zázhǒngde: *a ~ horse* 杂交马.

crossbreed /ˈkrɒsbriːd; US krɔːs-/ *n* [C] (动植物)杂〔雜〕种〔種〕 zázhǒng.

cross-check /ˌkrɒs ˈtʃek; US ˌkrɔːs/ *v* [I, T] (从不同角度或以不同资料)反复〔復〕核对〔對〕 fǎnfù héduì. cross-check /ˈkrɒstʃek/ *n* [C] 反复核对 fǎnfù héduì.

cross country /ˌkrɒs ˈkʌntrɪ; US krɔːs/ *adj*, *adv* 横穿全国〔國〕的(地) héngchuān quánguó de; 越野的(地) yuèyěde: *a ~ race* 越野赛跑.

cross-examine /ˌkrɒs ɪgˈzæmɪn; US ˌkrɔːs/ *v* [T] 盘〔盤〕问 pánwèn. cross-examiˈnation *n* [C, U] 盘问 pánwèn.

cross-eyed /ˈkrɒsaɪd; US ˈkrɔːs-/ *adj* 内斜视的 nèixiéshìde; 斗〔鬥〕鸡〔鷄〕眼的 dòujīyǎnde.

crossfire /ˈkrɒsfaɪə(r); US ˈkrɔːs-/ *n* [U] 交叉火力 jiāochā huǒlì.

crossing /ˈkrɒsɪŋ; US ˈkrɔːs-/ *n* [C] 1 交叉点〔點〕 jiāochādiǎn; 十字路口 shízì lùkǒu. 2 (公路与铁路的)平交道口 píngjiāo dàokǒu 3 横渡 héngdù; 横穿 héngchuān: *a stormy ~ of the Atlantic* 暴风雨中横渡大西洋.

cross-legged /ˌkrɒs ˈlegd; US ˌkrɔːs/ *adv* 盘〔盤〕着腿 pánzhetuǐ; 跷〔蹺〕着二郎腿 qiàozhe èrlángtuǐ: *sitting ~* 跷着二郎腿坐着.

cross-piece /ˈkrɒspiːs; US ˈkrɔːs-/ *n* [C] (结构、工具等上的)横杆 hénggān; 横档〔檔〕 héngdàng.

cross purposes /ˌkrɒs ˈpɜːpəsɪz; US ˌkrɔːs/ *n* [习语] at cross ˈpurposes 互相误解 hùxiāng wùjiě; 有矛盾 yǒu máodùn.

cross-reference /ˌkrɒs ˈrefrəns; US ˌkrɔːs/ *n* [C] 相互参〔參〕照 xiānghù cānzhào; 互见〔見〕条〔條〕目 hùjiàn tiáomù.

crossroads /ˈkrɒsrəʊdz; US ˈkrɔːs-/ *n* [C] [*pl* crossroads] 1 十字路口 shízì lùkǒu; (多条道路的)交叉路口 jiāochā lùkǒu. 2 [习语] at a/the ˈcrossroads 处〔處〕于抉择〔擇〕的紧〔緊〕要关〔關〕头〔頭〕 chǔyú juézéde jǐnyào guāntóu.

cross-section /ˌkrɒs ˈsekʃn; US ˌkrɔːs/ *n* [C] 1 横断〔斷〕面 héngduànmiàn; 截面 jiémiàn; 断面图〔圖〕 duànmiàntú. 2 [喻]样〔樣〕品 yàngpǐn; 典型 diǎnxíng: *a ~ of society* 社会的缩影.

crosswalk /ˈkrɒswɔːk/ *n* [C] 过〔過〕街人行道 guòjiē rénxíngdào.

crossword /ˈkrɒswɜːd; US ˈkrɔːs-/ *n* [C] 一种〔種〕纵〔縱〕横填字字谜 yìzhǒng zònghéng tiánzì zìmí.

crotch /krɒtʃ/ *n* [C] 人体〔體〕两腿分叉处〔處〕 réntǐ liǎngtuǐ fēnchàchù; 胯部 kuàbù; 裤裆〔襠〕 kùdāng.

crouch /kraʊtʃ/ *v* [I] 蹲伏 dūnfú: *~ on the floor* 蹲伏在地板上. crouch *n* [sing] 蹲伏(姿势) dūnfú.

croupier /ˈkruːpɪeɪ; US -pɪər/ *n* [C] 赌台管理员 dǔtái guǎnlǐyuán.

crow[1] /krəʊ/ *n* 1 [C] 鸦 yā; 乌鸦 wūyā. 2 [习语] as the ˈcrow flies 笔〔筆〕直地 bǐzhíde: *It's ten miles away, as the ~ flies*. 直线距离 10 英里. ˈcrow's-feet *n* [pl] 眼睛外角的皱〔皺〕纹 yǎnjīng wàijiǎo de zhòuwén. ˈcrow's-nest *n* [C] 桅上瞭望台 wéi shàng liàowàngtái.

crow[2] /krəʊ/ *v* [I] 1 (公鸡)啼 tí. 2 (*over*) 得意洋洋 déyì yángyáng: *~ing over her profits* 为她的利润得意洋洋. crow *n* [通常 sing] 鸡〔鷄〕啼声〔聲〕 jītíshēng

crowbar /ˈkrəʊbɑː(r)/ *n* [C] 撬棍 qiàogùn.

crowd /kraʊd/ *n* [C, 亦作 sing, 用 pl v] 1 人群 rénqún: *a ~ of tourists* 一群游客. 2 [非正式用语] 一伙〔夥〕 yìhuǒ; 一帮 yìbāng: *the golfing ~* 打高尔夫球的一帮人. crowd *v* 1 [I] 群聚 qúnjù; 拥〔擁〕挤〔擠〕 yōngjǐ: *~ around the stage* 聚集在舞台周围. 2 [T] 拥过〔過〕 yōngguò; 挤满 jǐmǎn: *Tourists ~ed the beach*. 旅游者挤满了海滩. 3 [T] [非正式用语] 催逼(某人) cuībī. crowded *adj* 挤满人的 jǐmǎn rén de: *a ~ room* 挤满人的房间.

crown[1] /kraʊn/ *n* 1 [C] 王冠 wángguān; 冕 miǎn. 2 the Crown [sing] 王权〔權〕 wángquán. 3 [C] 顶部 dǐngbù; 帽顶 màodǐng.

crown[2] /kraʊn/ *v* [T] 1 为〔爲〕…加冠 wèi…jiāguān; 为…加冕 wèi… jiāmiǎn. 2 (*with*) [通常为被动语态] (a) [正式用语] 占据〔據〕…的顶部 zhànjù…de dǐngbù: *a hill ~ed with a wood* 顶部长满了树的小山. (b) 圆满地结束 yuánmǎnde jiéshù: *a project ~ed with success* 圆满成功的工程. 3 [习语] to crown it ˈall 更糟糕的是 gèng zāogāo de shì. crowning *adj* 登峰造极〔極〕的 dēng fēng zào jí de: *a ~ing achievement* 空前的成功.

crucial /ˈkruːʃl/ *adj* 决定性的 juédìngxìngde; 紧〔緊〕要关〔關〕头〔頭〕的 jǐnyào guāntóu de: *a ~ decision* 关键性的决定 crucially /-ʃəlɪ/ *adv*.

crucifix /ˈkruːsɪfɪks/ *n* [C] 耶稣钉在十字架

上的图〔圖〕像 Yēsū dīng zài shízìjià shang de túxiàng.

crucifixion /ˌkruːsɪˈfɪkʃn/ *n* [C, U] 在十字架上钉死的刑罚 zài shízìjià shang dīngsǐ de xíngfá.

crucify /ˈkruːsɪfaɪ/ *v* [*pt*, *pp* -ied] [T] 1 把…钉死在十字架上 bǎ…dīngsǐ zài shízìjià shang. 2 [非正式用语]诋毁 dǐhuǐ;虐待 nüèdài

crude /kruːd/ *adj* 1 天然的 tiānránde;未加工的 wèi jiāgōng de: ~ *oil* 原油,石油. 2 (a) 粗制〔製〕的 cūzhìde;粗糙的 cūcāode: ~ *tools* 粗糙的工具. (b) 粗鲁的 cūlǔde;粗鄙的 cūbǐde: ~ *jokes* 粗俗的笑话. **crudely** *adv*.

cruel /kruːəl/ *adj* 1 (人)残〔殘〕忍的 cánrěnde;残酷的 cánkùde. 2 残暴的 cánbàode;无〔無〕情的 wúqíngde: ~ *treatment* 残忍的处理. **cruelly** *adv*. **cruelty** *n* 1 [U] 残忍 cánrěn;残暴 cánbào. 2 [C, 常用 pl] [*pl* -ies] 残忍的行为〔爲〕 cánrěnde xíngwéi. **cruelty-free** *adj* (对动物)不残忍的 bù cánrěn de.

cruet /ˈkruːɪt/ *n* [C] (餐桌上的)调味品瓶 tiáowèipǐnpíng.

cruise /kruːz/ *v* [I] 1 巡航 xúnháng;巡游 xúnyóu. 2 (汽车、飞机等)以最节〔節〕省燃料的速度行进〔進〕 yǐ zuì jiéshěng ránliào de sùdù xíngjìn: ~ *along at 50 miles per hour* 以每小时 50 英里的经济速度行驶. **cruise** *n* [C] 乘船巡游 chéng chuán xúnyóu. **cruiser** *n* [C] 1 巡洋舰〔艦〕 xúnyángjiàn. 2 (有住宿设备的)机〔機〕动〔動〕游艇 jīdòng yóutǐng. ˈ**cruise missile** *n* [C] 巡航导〔導〕弹〔彈〕 xúnháng dǎodàn

crumb /krʌm/ *n* [C] 1 面〔麵〕包屑 miànbāoxiè;糕饼屑 gāobǐngxiè. 2 一点〔點〕点 yīdiǎndiǎn;少许 shǎoxǔ.

crumble /ˈkrʌmbl/ *v* 1 [I, T] 弄碎 nòng suì;破碎 pòsuì;碎裂 suìliè: *material that* ~*s easily* 容易破碎的材料. 2 [I] [喻]灭〔滅〕亡 mièwáng;消失 xiāoshī: *Their marriage* ~*d*. 他们的婚姻结束了. **crumbly** *adj* [-ier, -iest] 易碎的 yìsuìde;易摧毁的 yì cuīhuǐ de.

crumple /ˈkrʌmpl/ *v* (*up*) 1 [I, T] 起皱〔皺〕 qǐzhòu;把…弄皱 bǎ…nòng zhòu: *material that* ~*s easily* 容易起皱的材料. 2 [I] [喻]垮掉 kuǎdiào: *Her resistance* ~*d*. 她的抵抗结束了. ˈ**crumple zone** *n* [C] (汽车)防撞压〔壓〕损区〔區〕 fángzhuàng yāsǔnqū.

crunch /krʌntʃ/ *v* 1 [T] (*up*) 嘎嘎吱吱地咬嚼 gāgā zhīzhī de yǎojiáo. 2 [I, T] 压〔壓〕碎 yāsuì;嘎嘎吱吱地被压碎 gāgāzhīzhīde bèi yāsuì: *The snow* ~*ed under our feet*. 我们踩着积雪嘎吱作响. **crunch** *n* [sing] 1 嘎吱作响〔響〕地咀嚼 gāzhīzuòxiǎngde jǔjué;嘎吱嘎吱的声〔聲〕音 gāzhīgāzhīde shēngyīn. 2 **the crunch** [非正式用语]危急关〔關〕头〔頭〕 wēijí guāntóu: *when the* ~ *comes* 到了危急关头的时候.

crusade /kruːˈseɪd/ *n* [C] (*for* / *against*) 讨伐 tǎofá;运〔運〕动〔動〕 yùndòng. **crusade** *v* [I] 参〔參〕加某种〔種〕运动 cānjiā mǒuzhǒng yùndòng. **crusader** *n* [C].

crush[1] /krʌʃ/ *v* 1 [T] 压〔壓〕坏〔壞〕 yā huài: *Her hand was* ~*ed by the heavy door*. 她的手被很重的门轧伤了. 2 [T] 压碎 yā suì. 3 [I, T] (使)起皱〔皺〕 qǐzhòu: *clothes* ~*ed in a suitcase* 在小提箱里弄皱的衣服. 4 [T] 压垮 yā kuǎ;制服 zhìfú. 5 [I] 挤〔擠〕入 jǐrù: *Crowds* ~*ed into the theatre*. 人群挤进剧场. **crushing** *adj* 1 压倒的 yādǎode;决定性的 juédìngxìngde: *a* ~*ing defeat* 彻〔徹〕底的失败. 2 羞辱性的 xiūrǔxìngde: *a* ~*ing remark* 让人受不了的话.

crush[2] /krʌʃ/ *n* 1 [sing] 拥〔擁〕挤〔擠〕的人群 yōngjǐde rénqún. 2 [C] (*on*) 短暂的热〔熱〕爱〔愛〕 duǎnzàn de rè'ài.

crust /krʌst/ *n* [C, U] 1 面〔麵〕包、饼等的皮 miànbāo、bǐng děng de pí. 2 硬外皮 yìngwàipí;外壳〔殼〕 wàiké: *the earth's* ~ 地壳 **crusty** *adj* [-ier, -iest] 1 有硬皮的 yǒu yìngpí de;像外壳的 xiàng wàikéde: ~*y bread* 有硬皮的面包. 2 [非正式用语]脾气〔氣〕坏〔壞〕的 píqì huài de.

crustacean /krʌˈsteɪʃn/ *n* [C] 甲壳〔殼〕纲〔綱〕动〔動〕物 jiǎkégāng dòngwù.

crutch /krʌtʃ/ *n* [C] 1 (跛子用的)拐杖 guǎizhàng. 2 [喻]支撑物 zhīchēngwù;给予帮〔幫〕助或支持的人 gěiyú bāngzhù huò zhīchí de rén. 3 = CROTCH.

crux /krʌks/ *n* [C] 难〔難〕题 nántí;症〔癥〕结 zhēngjié.

cry[1] /kraɪ/ *n* [*pl* -ies] 1 [C] 叫喊 jiàohǎn;喊 hǎn: *a* ~ *for help* 呼救. 2 [sing] 一阵哭 yìzhènkū: *have a good* ~ 痛哭一阵. 3 [C] 鸟〔鳥〕等动〔動〕物的叫声〔聲〕 niǎo děng dòngwùde jiàoshēng: *the* ~ *of the thrush* 歌鸫的叫声. 4 [习语] **a far cry from** 大不相同 dà bù xiāngtóng.

cry[2] /kraɪ/ *v* [*pt*, *pp* -ied] 1 [I] (*for*; *over*; *with*) 哭 kū;哭泣 kūqì: ~ *with pain* 痛得哭起来. *He was* ~*ing for his mother*. 他哭着要妈妈. 2 [I] (人、动物因疼痛、恐惧而)大叫 dàjiào: ~ *out in surprise* 惊叫起来. 3 [I, T] 叫喊 jiàohǎn;大声〔聲〕地说 dàshēngde shuō: '*Get out!*' *he cried*. "滚出去!"他大声喊道. 4 [短语动词] **cry off** 取消(约会等) qǔxiāo. **cry out for** 迫切需要 pòqiè xūyào. ˈ**cry-baby** *n* [C] 爱〔愛〕哭的人 ài kū de rén.

crypt /krɪpt/ *n* [C] 教堂的地下室 jiàotángde dìxiàshì.

cryptic /ˈkrɪptɪk/ *adj* 有隐〔隱〕义〔義〕的 yǒu yǐnyì de.

crystal /ˈkrɪstl/ *n* 1 (a) [U] 水晶 shuǐjīng; 石英晶体〔體〕 shíyīng jīngtǐ (b) [C] 水晶石 shuǐ jīngshí; 水晶饰品 shuǐjīng shìpǐn. 2 [U] 晶质〔質〕玻璃 jīngzhì bōli. 3 [C] 结晶体〔體〕 jiéjīngtǐ: *salt* ～*s* 盐的结晶体 4 [C] [美语]表〔錶〕蒙子 biǎoméngzi. **crystalline** *adj* 1 水晶的 shuǐjīngde; 水晶似的 shuǐjīng shì de. 2 [正式用语]清澈透明的 qīngchè tòumíng de: ～ *water* 清澈透明的水. **crystallize** *v* 1 [I, T] (使)结晶 jiéjīng. 2 [I, T] [喻](使想法、计划等)明确而具体化 míngquè ér jùtǐhuà 3 [T] 蜜饯〔餞〕(水果) mìjiàn.

CT /ˌsiː ˈtiː/ *abbr* computerized tomography X 射线〔綫〕电〔電〕子计算机〔機〕断〔斷〕层〔層〕扫〔掃〕描 X shèxiàn diànzǐjìsuànjī duàncéng sǎomiáo.

cub /kʌb/ *n* [C] 幼狐 yòuhú; 幼兽〔獸〕 yòushòu.

cubby-hole /ˈkʌbɪ həʊl/ *n* [C] 围〔圍〕起来的小天地 wéi qǐlái de xiǎotiāndì.

cube /kjuːb/ *n* [C] 1 立方体〔體〕 lìfāngtǐ. 2 [数学]立方 lìfāng. **cub** *v* [T] [尤用被动语态] 自乘三次 zìchéng sāncì: *3* ～*d is 27*. 3 的立方是 27. **cubic** /ˈkjuːbɪk/ *adj* 1 立方形的 lìfāngxíngde; 立方体的 lìfāngtǐde. 2 立方的 lìfāngde: *a* ～ *metre* 1 立方米.

cubicle /ˈkjuːbɪkl/ *n* [C] 大房间中用帷幕等隔开〔開〕的小室 dà fángjiān zhōng yòng wéimù děng gékāi de xiǎoshì.

cuckoo /ˈkʊkuː/ *n* [C] 杜鹃 dùjuān; 布谷〔穀〕鸟 bùgǔniǎo.

cucumber /ˈkjuːkʌmbə(r)/ *n* [C, U] 黄瓜 huángguā.

cud /kʌd/ *n* [U] 反刍〔芻〕的食物 fǎnchúde shíwù.

cuddle /ˈkʌdl/ *v* 1 [T] 拥〔擁〕抱 yōngbào; 怀〔懷〕抱 huáibào: ～ *a child* 抱着一个孩子. 2 [短语动词] **cuddle up** 贴身而卧 tiēshēn ér wò; 蜷曲着身子 quánqūzhe shēnzi: *She* ～*d up to her father*. 她偎依着爸爸. **cuddle** *n* [C] 拥抱 yōngbào; 搂〔摟〕抱 lǒubào. **cuddly** *adj* [-ier, -iest] [非正式用语]引人搂抱的 yǐnrén lǒubào de.

cudgel /ˈkʌdʒəl/ *n* [C] 1 短粗的棍棒 duǎncūde gùnbàng. 2 [习语] **take up the cudgels** 保卫〔衛〕 bǎowèi; 维护〔護〕 wéihù. **cudgel** *v* [-ll-; 美语 -l-] [T] 用短粗的棍棒打 yòng duǎncūde gùnbàng dǎ.

cue[1] /kjuː/ *n* [C] 1 [戏剧]尾白 wěibái; 提示 tíshì: *The actor came in on* ～. 演员按提示走上了舞台. 2 暗示 ànshì.

cue[2] /kjuː/ *n* [C] (台球戏中的)弹〔彈〕子棒 dànzǐbàng.

cuff[1] /kʌf/ *n* [C] 1 袖口 xiùkǒu. 2 [习语] **off the ˈcuff** 即兴〔興〕地 jíxìngde; 非正式地 fēi zhèngshì de. **ˈcuff-link** *n* [C] (衬衫袖口的)链扣 liànkòu.

cuff[2] /kʌf/ *v* [T] 掌击〔擊〕 zhǎngjī; 打…一巴掌 dǎ… yìbāzhang. **cuff** *n* [C].

cuisine /kwɪˈziːn/ *n* [U] 烹饪 pēngrèn; 烹饪法 pēngrènfǎ.

cul-de-sac /ˈkʌl də sæk/ *n* [C] 死胡同 sǐhútòng; 死巷 sǐxiàng.

culinary /ˈkʌlɪnərɪ; *US* -nerɪ/ *adj* 烹饪的 pēngrènde; 烹饪用的 pēngrèn yòng de.

cullender /ˈkʌləndə(r)/ *n* [C] = COLANDER.

culminate /ˈkʌlmɪneɪt/ *v* [I] *in* 达〔達〕到顶点〔點〕 dádào dǐngdiǎn; 告终 gàozhōng: ～ *in success* 以成功告终. **culmination** /ˌkʌlmɪˈneɪʃn/ *n* [sing] 顶点 dǐngdiǎn; 结果 jiéguǒ.

culpable /ˈkʌlpəbl/ *adj* 应〔應〕受责备〔備〕的 yīn shòu zébèi de. **culpability** *n* [U]. **culpably** *adv*.

culprit /ˈkʌlprɪt/ *n* [C] 犯过〔過〕错的人 fàn guòcuò de rén.

cult /kʌlt/ *n* [C] 1 宗教崇拜 zōngjiào chóngbài; 迷信 míxìn. 2 崇拜 chóngbài; 狂热〔熱〕 kuángrè. 3 时〔時〕尚 shíshàng; 时髦 shímáo: *a* ～ *film* 时髦影片.

cultivate /ˈkʌltɪveɪt/ *v* [T] 1 耕作(土地) gēngzuò. 2 培植(作物) péizhí. 3 培养〔養〕péiyǎng: ～ *her interest in literature* 培养她对文学的兴趣. 4 努力获〔獲〕得(某人)的友谊 nǔlì huòdé de yǒuyì. **cultivated** *adj* 有教养的 yǒu jiàoyǎng de; 有修养的 yǒu xiūyǎng de; 举〔舉〕止文雅的 jǔzhǐ wényǎ de. **cultivation** /ˌkʌltɪˈveɪʃn/ *n* [C].

culture /ˈkʌltʃə(r)/ *n* 1 [U] 文化(文学、艺术等及文艺修养) wénhuà. 2 [U, C] 文明(艺术、思想等的特定表现) wénmíng: *Greek* ～ 希腊文明. 3 [U] (作物等的)栽培 zāipéi; 养〔養〕殖 yǎngzhí. 4 [生物](为研究用的)培养细胞组织〔織〕 péiyǎng xìbāo zǔzhi. **cultural** *adj* 文化的 wénhuàde; 文化上的 wénhuà shàng de. **cultured** *adj* (人)有文化修养的 yǒu wénhuà xiūyǎng de. **ˈculture shock** *n* [C] 文化冲〔衝〕击〔擊〕(首次接触异国文化时的困惑、不安的感觉) wénhuà chōngjī; 文化震惊〔驚〕 wénhuà zhènjīng.

cumbersome /ˈkʌmbəsəm/ *adj* 1 笨重的 bènzhòngde; 不便携〔攜〕带〔帶〕的 búbiàn xiédài de. 2 行动〔動〕缓慢的 xíngdòng huǎnmàn de; 效率低的 xiàolǜ dī de.

cumulative /ˈkjuːmjʊlətɪv; *US* -leɪtɪv/ *adj* 累积〔積〕的 lěijīde; 累加的 lěijiāde.

cunning /ˈkʌnɪŋ/ *adj* 狡猾的 jiǎohuáde; 精巧的 jīngqiǎode: *a* ～ *trick* 狡猾的骗局. **cunning** *n* [U] 狡猾 jiǎohuá; 精巧 jīngqiǎo. **cunningly** *adv*.

cunt /kʌnt/ *n* [C] [蔑⚠俚] 1 阴〔陰〕道 yīn-

C

dào;女性阴部 nǚxìng yīnbù. 2[贬]讨厌〔厭〕鬼 tǎoyànguǐ.

cup[1] /kʌp/ *n* [C] 1 杯 bēi. 2 杯中之物 bēi zhōng zhī wù. 3 奖〔獎〕杯 jiǎngbēi;优〔優〕胜〔勝〕杯 yōushèngbēi. 4 杯状〔狀〕物 bēizhuàngwù 5[习语] not sb's cup of ˈtea [非正式用语] 不是某人所喜爱〔愛〕的 búshì mǒurén suǒ xǐ'ài de. **cupful** *n* [C] 一杯的量 yībēide liàng.

cup[2] /kʌp/ *v* [-pp-] [T] 用(两手)做成杯形 yòngzuòchéng bēixíng; 把…放入杯形物中 bǎ …fàngrù bēixíngwù zhōng: ～ *one's chin in one's hands* 用两手托着下巴.

cupboard /ˈkʌbəd/ *n* [C] 柜〔櫃〕橱 guìchú.

curable /ˈkjʊərəbl/ *adj* 可以医〔醫〕好的 kěyǐ yīhǎo de.

curate /ˈkjʊərət/ *n* [C] 副牧师〔師〕fùmùshi.

curative /ˈkjʊərətɪv/ *adj* 治病的 zhìbìngde; 有疗〔療〕效的 yǒu liáoxiào de.

curator /kjʊəˈreɪtə(r); *US* ˈkjʊərətər/ *n* [C] (博物馆、美术馆等的)馆长〔長〕guǎnzhǎng.

curb /kɜːb/ *n* [C] 1 (*on*) 控制 kòngzhì;抑制 yìzhì;约束 yuēshù. 2 马嚼子 mǎjiáozi. 3[尤用于美语] = KERB. **curb** *v* [T] 1 控制 kòngzhì;抑制 yìzhì: ～ *one's joy* 控制喜悦之情. 2 (用马嚼子)勒住(马) lèzhù.

curd /kɜːd/ *n* 1[C,常用 pl]凝乳 níngrǔ. 2[U] 凝乳样〔樣〕的东西 níngrǔyàngde dōngxi: ˌ*lemon*-ˈ～ 柠檬乳糕.

curdle /ˈkɜːdl/ *v* [I,T] (使)凝结 níngjié.

cure /kjʊə(r)/ *v* [T] 1 (*of*) 治愈〔癒〕zhìyù: ～*d of a serious illness* 治愈一种严重疾病. 2 消除 xiāochú: *a policy to* ～ *inflation* 消除通货膨胀的政策. 3 改正 gǎizhèng;矫〔矯〕正 jiǎozhèng: ～ *sb of an obsession* 打消了某人心头的块垒. 4(用腌、熏等方法)加工处〔處〕理(肉、鱼等) jiāgōng chǔlǐ. **cure** *n* 1[C,常用 sing]治愈 zhìyù;痊愈 quányù. 2 [C]疗〔療〕法 liáofǎ;药〔藥〕物 yàowù: *a* ～ *for arthritis* 关节炎的疗法.

curfew /ˈkɜːfjuː/ *n* [C] 宵禁 xiāojìn.

curio /ˈkjʊərɪəʊ/ *n* [C] [*pl* ～s] 珍奇小物品 zhēnqí xiǎo wùpǐn.

curiosity /ˌkjʊərɪˈɒsətɪ/ *n* [*pl* -ies] 1 [U] 好奇 hàoqí;好奇心 hàoqíxīn. 2 [C]奇异〔異〕的东西 qíyìde dōngxi;珍品 zhēnpǐn.

curious /ˈkjʊərɪəs/ *adj* 1 好奇的 hàoqíde; 爱〔愛〕打听〔聽〕的 ài dǎtīng de: ～ *about how a machine works* 很想知道机器是如何运转的. 2[贬]爱管闲事的 ài guǎn xiánshì de. 3 稀奇古怪的 xīqí gǔguài de;不寻〔尋〕常的 bù xúncháng de. **curiously** *adv*.

curl /kɜːl/ *n* [C] 卷〔捲〕毛 juǎnmáo;卷曲物 juǎnqūwù;螺旋形物 luóxuánxíngwù;卷发〔髮〕juǎnfà. **curl** *v* 1 [I,T](使)卷曲 juǎnqū. 2 [I] 形成卷曲 xíngchéng juǎnqū 盘〔盤〕绕〔繞〕pánrào: *a plant* ～*ing round a post* 盘绕着柱子的植物. 3[短语动词] curl up (躺或坐)蜷曲着身体〔體〕quánqūzhe shēntǐ. **curly** *adj* [-ier, -iest] 有卷毛的 yǒu juǎnmáo de;有卷发的 yǒu juǎnfà de.

currant /ˈkʌrənt/ *n* [C] 1 无〔無〕核小葡萄干〔乾〕wúhé xiǎo pútaogān. 2(用于构成复合词)醋栗 cùlì;醋栗树〔樹〕cùlìshù: *black* ～*s* (黑)茶藨子.

currency /ˈkʌrənsɪ/ *n* [*pl* -ies] 1 [C,U]通货 tōnghuò; 货币〔幣〕huòbì. 2 [U] 通用 tōngyòng;流通 liútōng.

current[1] /ˈkʌrənt/ *adj* 1 当〔當〕前的 dāngqiánde;现今的 xiànjīnde;现行的 xiànxíngde: ～ *affairs* 时事. 2 通用的 tōngyòngde;流行的 liúxíngde. ˌ**current acˈcount** *n* [C] 活期存款(账户) huóqī cúnkuǎn. **currently** *adv* 当前 dāngqián;现今 xiànjīn.

current[2] /ˈkʌrənt/ *n* 1 [C]流 liú;水流 shuǐliú; 气〔氣〕流 qìliú. 2 [U, sing] 电〔電〕流 diànliú. 3 [C]趋〔趨〕势〔勢〕qūshì; 倾向 qīngxiàng; 潮流 cháoliú.

curriculum /kəˈrɪkjʊləm/ *n* [C] [*pl* ～s 或 -la /-lə/] 学〔學〕校的课程 xuéxiàode kèchéng. **curriculum vitae** /ˈviːtaɪ/ *n* [C] 简短的履历〔歷〕书〔書〕jiǎnduǎnde lǚlìshū.

curry[1] /ˈkʌrɪ/ *n* [C, U] [*pl* -ies] 咖喱 gālí; 咖喱食品 gālí shípǐn. **curried** *adj* (肉等)加咖喱的 jiā gālí de.

curry[2] /ˈkʌrɪ/ *v* [*pt*, *pp* -ied] [习语] curry favour (with sb) 求宠〔寵〕qiúchǒng; 献〔獻〕媚 xiànmèi;拍马屁 pāi mǎpì.

curse[1] /kɜːs/ *n* 1 [C] 咒骂(语) zhòumà. 2 [sing] 咒语 zhòuyǔ;诅咒 zǔzhòu: *The witch put a* ～ *on him*. 女巫念咒语诅咒他. 3 [C] 祸〔禍〕因 huòyīn;祸根 huògēn.

curse[2] /kɜːs/ *v* 1 [I,T] 咒骂 zhòumà: *cursing her bad luck* 咒骂她的运气不佳. 2 [T] 诅咒 zǔzhòu. 3 [T] *with* [通常用被动语态]被…所苦 bèi…suǒ kǔ;因…遭殃 yīn… zāoyāng: *a man* ～*d with arthritis* 一个因关节炎而痛苦不堪的男人. **cursed** /ˈkɜːsɪd/ *adj* 可恨的 kěhènde;讨厌〔厭〕的 tǎoyànde: *a* ～*d nuisance* 讨厌的东西.

cursor /ˈkɜːsə(r)/ *n* [C] [电子计算机]光标〔標〕guāngbiāo.

cursory /ˈkɜːsərɪ/ *adj* [常作贬]草草的 cǎocǎode;粗略的 cūlüède. **cursorily** *adv*.

curt /kɜːt/ *adj* 草率的 cǎoshuàide; 简短的 jiǎnduǎnde: *a* ～ *refusal* 草率的拒绝. **curtly** *adv*. **curtness** *n* [U].

curtail /kɜːˈteɪl/ *v* [T] 截短 jiéduǎn;缩短 suōduǎn;削减 xuējiǎn: ～ *sb's activities* 减少某人的活动. **curtailment** *n* [C, U] 缩短

suōduǎn;缩减 suōjiǎn;减少 jiǎnshǎo.

curtain /ˈkɜːtn/ *n* [C] **1** 帘〔簾〕lián;窗帘 chuānglián: *draw the ~s* 拉上窗帘. **2** [C] (舞台的)幕 mù. **3** [C]遮蔽物 zhēbìwù;保护〔護〕物 bǎohùwù: *a ~ of mist* 一层薄雾. **4** **curtains** [pl] (*for*) [非正式用语]完蛋 wándàn;死 sǐ: *It's ~ for us if they find out what you've done!* 要是他们发现你干的这些事,我们就完蛋了. **curtain** *v* [T] 给…装〔裝〕上帘子 gěi… zhuāngshàng liánzi.

curtsey (亦作 **curtsy**) /ˈkɜːtsɪ/ *n* [C] [*pl* ~**s**, **-ies**] 西方女子的屈膝礼〔禮〕 xīfāng nǚzǐ de qūxīlǐ. **curtsey** (亦作 **curtsy**) *v* [*pt*, *pp* ~**ed** 或**-ied**] [I] 行屈膝礼 xíng qūxīlǐ.

curve /kɜːv/ *n* [C] 曲线〔綫〕qūxiàn. **curve** *v* **1** [I, T] 弄弯〔彎〕nòng wān;(使)成曲线 chéng qūxiàn. **2** [I] 沿曲线运〔運〕动〔動〕yán qūxiàn yùndòng.

cushion /ˈkʊʃn/ *n* [C] **1** 垫〔墊〕子 diànzi;座垫 zuòdiàn;靠垫 kàodiàn. **2** 垫状〔狀〕物 diànzhuàngwù: *a ~ of air* 气垫. **cushion** *v* [T] **1** 使减少震动〔動〕shǐ jiǎnshǎo zhèndòng;缓和…的冲〔衝〕击〔擊〕huǎnhé…de chōngjī. **2** (*from*) 使免遭不愉快 shǐ miǎnzāo bù yúkuài.

cushy /ˈkʊʃɪ/ *adj* [**-ier**, **-iest**] [常作贬](工作岗位等)舒适〔適〕的 shūshìde;安逸的 ānyìde;不费心劳神的 bú fèixīn láoshén de.

custard /ˈkʌstəd/ *n* [C, U] 牛奶蛋糊 niúnǎi dànhú.

custodian /kəˈstəʊdɪən/ *n* [C] 保管人 bǎoguǎnrén;监〔監〕护〔護〕人 jiānhùrén;公共建筑〔築〕的看守人 gōnggòngjiànzhùde kānshǒurén

custody /ˈkʌstədɪ/ *n* [U] **1** 保管 bǎoguǎn;保护〔護〕bǎohù;监〔監〕护 jiānhù: *~ of her child* 对她的孩子的监护. **2** 监禁 jiānjìn;拘留 jūliú: *be in ~* 被拘留;被监禁.

custom /ˈkʌstəm/ *n* **1** [U]习〔習〕俗 xísú;惯例 guànlì. **2** [C]习惯 xíguàn: *ancient ~s* 古代的习惯. **3** [U] (顾客的)光顾〔顧〕guānggù. **customary** /-mərɪ; *US* -merɪ/ *adj* 按照习惯的 ànzhào xíguàn de;通常的 tōngchángde. ˌ**custom-ˈbuilt**, ˌ**custom-ˈmade** *adj* 定做的 dìngzuòde;定制〔製〕的 dìngzhìde.

customer /ˈkʌstəmə(r)/ *n* [C] 顾〔顧〕客 gùkè.

customs /ˈkʌstəms/ *n* [pl] **1** 关〔關〕税 guānshuì. **2** **Customs** 海关 hǎiguān.

cut[1] /kʌt/ *v* [**-tt-**; *pt*, *pp* **cut**] **1** [I, T]割 gē;切 qiē;剪 jiǎn;砍 kǎn;削 xiāo: *I ~ my hand with a knife.* 我用一把小刀把手割破了. **2** [T] (a) (*off*) 割出 gēchū;切出 qiēchū: *~ (off) a piece of cake* 切出一块蛋糕 (b) 切开〔開〕qiēkāi: *~ the cake* 把蛋糕切开. **3** [T]剪短 jiǎn duǎn;切短 qiē duǎn: *~ sb's hair* 把某人的头发剪短. **4** [I] (a) (小刀等)可用以切、割 kěyòngyǐ qiē、gē. (b) (织物等)可被切、割 kě bèi qiē、gē. **5** [T] 使疼痛、痛苦 shǐ téngtòng、tòngkǔ: *His remarks ~ me deeply.* 他的话很使我伤心. **6** [T] (线)与〔與〕(另一线)相交 yǔ xiāngjiāo. **7** [T]减少 jiǎnshǎo: *~ taxes* 减税. **8** (a) [T] 去除(影片、磁带等的一部分) qùchú: *~ some scenes from a film* 去掉影片的某些镜头. (b) [I] 停止(拍摄、录音) tíngzhǐ. **9** [T] [非正式用语]旷〔曠〕课 kuàngkè;不到场〔場〕bú dàochǎng. **10** [习语] **cut and dried** 现成的 xiànchéngde;事先准〔準〕备〔備〕好的 shìxiān zhǔnbèi hǎo de. **cut both / two ˈways** 有弊亦有利 yǒubì yì yǒulì;两方面都说得通 liǎng fāngmiàn dōu shuōdétōng. **cut ˈcorners** 抄近路 chāo jìnlù;走捷径〔徑〕zǒu jiéjìng. **cut sb dead** 不理睬(某人) bù lǐcǎi. **cut it ˈfine** (时间、金钱等)几〔幾〕乎不留余〔餘〕地 jīhū bùliú yúdì. **cut ˈloose** [非正式用语]无〔無〕约束 wú yuēshù. **cut one's ˈlosses** 趁损失不大赶〔趕〕紧〔緊〕丢手 chèn sǔnshī búdà gǎnjǐn diūshǒu. ˌ**cut no ˈice (with sb)** 对〔對〕…不发〔發〕生影响〔響〕duì… bù fāshēng yǐngxiǎng. **cut sb to the ˈquick** 伤〔傷〕害某人的感情 shānghài mǒurén de gǎnqíng. **cut sb short** 使停止(说话等) shǐ tíngzhǐ;打断〔斷〕(谈话等) dǎduàn. **11** [短语动词] **cut across sth** (a) 抄近路穿过〔過〕chāo jìnlù chuānguò. (b) 与〔與〕(通常的分类)不符 yǔ bùfú: *~ across social barriers* 超越社会壁垒. **cut sth back, cut back (on sth)** (a)修剪 xiūjiǎn;截短 jiéduǎn. (b)减少 jiǎnshǎo: *~ back (on) the number of workers* 减少工人人数. **cut down** 砍倒 kǎndǎo: *~ down a tree* 把树砍倒. **cut sth down, cut down on (sth)** 减少 jiǎnshǎo: *~ down on one's smoking* 减少吸烟. **cut ˈin (on)** (a) 打断(谈话等) dǎduàn. (b) 插进〔進〕(另一辆车的前面) chājìn. **cut sb ˈoff** 打断(谈话) dǎduàn: *be ~ off while talking on the phone* 正打着电话,线路断了. **cut sb/sth off** 停止供应〔應〕tíngzhǐ gōngyìng: *~ off the gas* 停止供应煤气. **cut sth off** (a) 切除 qiēchú (b) 阻断 zǔduàn: *~ off their retreat* 阻断他们的退路. (c) 孤立 gūlì: *a town ~ off by floods* 被洪水包围的城镇. **cut sth open** 弄破 nòng pò;弄开 nòng kāi. **cut out** (发动机等)停止运〔運〕转〔轉〕tíngzhǐ yùnzhuǎn. **cut sth out** (a) 切除 qiēchú;(b) 切出 qiēchū;剪出 jiǎnchū: *~ out a dress* 裁出一件衣服. (c) 省略 shěnglüè. (d) [非正式用语]停止做、使用 tíngzhǐ zuò、shǐyòng: *~ out cigarettes* 戒烟. **(not) be cut out for / to be sth** (没)有当〔當〕…的能力 yǒu dāng…de nénglì: *I'm not ~ out to be a teacher.* 我当不了教师. **cut up** (a)切碎 qiēsuì;割碎 gēsuì. (b) [非正式用语]使伤〔傷〕心 shǐ shāngxīn. ˈ**cut-back** *n* [C] 削减 xuējiǎn.

C

'cut-out *n* [C] 1 用纸剪的图〔圖〕样〔樣〕yòng zhǐ jiǎn de túyàng. 2 断流器 duànliúqì; 保险〔險〕装〔裝〕置 bǎoxiǎn zhuāngzhì. **ˌcut-'price** *adj* 减价〔價〕的 jiǎnjiàde; 便宜的 piányide.

cut² /kʌt/ *n* [C] 1 切口 qiēkǒu; 伤〔傷〕口 shāngkǒu. 2(刀等的)砍 kǎn; 击〔擊〕jī. 3 切 qiē; 割 gē; 剪 jiǎn; 砍 kǎn; 削 xiāo; 截 jié: *Your hair needs a* ~ 你的头发该剪了. 4 (*in*) 削减 xuējiǎn; 缩短 suōduǎn; 删节〔節〕shānjié: *a* ~ *in taxes* 减税. 5 切除 qiēchú; 删除 shānchú: *make some* ~*s in the film* 对这影片作一些删剪. 6 切下的部分 qiēxiàde bùfen: *a* ~ *of beef* 一块牛肉. 7 剪裁式样〔樣〕jiǎncái shìyàng; 发〔髮〕式 fàshì: *a suit with a loose* ~ 宽松式样的西服. 8[非正式用语]份额 fèn'é: *a* ~ *of the profits* 利润的一个份额. 9[习语] **a cut above sb/sth** 优〔優〕于 yōuyú.

cute /kju:t/ *adj* 1 漂亮的 piàoliàngde; 逗人喜爱〔愛〕的 dòu rén xǐ'ài de. 2[非正式用语, 尤用于美语]机〔機〕灵〔靈〕的 jīling de; 聪〔聰〕明的 cōngmingde. **cutely** *adv*. **cuteness** *n* [U].

cuticle /'kju:tɪkl/ *n* [C] 指甲根部的表皮 zhǐjia gēnbù de biǎopí.

cutlery /'kʌtlərɪ/ *n* [U] 刀叉餐具 dāo chā cānjù.

cutlet /'kʌtlɪt/ *n* [C] 肉片 ròupiàn; 鱼片 yúpiàn; 炸肉排 zhá ròupái.

cutter /'kʌtə(r)/ *n* [C] 1 从〔從〕事切、割、剪、削的人 cóngshì qiē、gē、jiǎn、xiāo de rén. 切割机〔機〕器 qiēgē jīqì. 2 **cutters** [pl] (尤用于构成复合词)切割工具 qiēgē gōngjù. 3 独〔獨〕桅帆船 dúwéi fānchuán.

cut-throat /'kʌtθrəʊt/ *adj* 残〔殘〕酷的 cánkùde.

cutting¹ /'kʌtɪŋ/ *adj* (话语等)尖刻的 jiānkède; 刻薄的 kèbóde.

cutting² /'kʌtɪŋ/ *n* [C] 1 剪报〔報〕jiǎnbào. 2(公路、铁路等的)路堑 lùqiàn. 3(供扦插用的)插枝 chāzhī; 插条〔條〕chātiáo.

cv /ˌsi: 'vi:/ *abbr* curriculum vitae (求职者等写的)简历〔歷〕jiǎnlì.

cyanide /'saɪənaɪd/ *n* [U] 氰化物 qínghuàwù.

cybercafé /'saɪbəˌkæfeɪ/ *n* [C] 网〔網〕吧 wǎngbā.

cyberspace /'saɪbəspeɪs/ *n* [U] 网〔網〕络空间 wǎngluò kōngjiān.

cycle /'saɪkl/ *n* [C] 1 循环〔環〕xúnhuán; 周〔週〕期 zhōuqī; 周转〔轉〕zhōuzhuǎn: *the* ~ *of the seasons* 四季循环. 2[非正式用语]摩托车〔車〕mótuōchē; 自行车 zìxíngchē. **cycle** *v* [I] 乘自行车 chéng zìxíngchē. **cyclical** /'sɪklɪkl/ *adj* 循环的 xúnhuánde; 周期的 zhōuqīde; 轮〔輪〕转的 lúnzhuànde. **cyclist** *n* [C] 骑自行车的人 qí zìxíngchē de rén.

cyclone /'saɪkləʊn/ *n* [C] 旋风〔風〕xuànfēng; 气〔氣〕旋 qìxuán. **cyclonic** /saɪ'klɒnɪk/ *adj*.

cygnet /'sɪgnɪt/ *n* [C] 小天鹅 xiǎo tiān'é.

cylinder /'sɪlɪndə(r)/ *n* [C] 1 圆柱 yuánzhù; 圆柱体〔體〕yuánzhùtǐ. 2 汽缸 qìgāng. **cylindrical** /sɪ'lɪndrɪkl/ *adj* 圆柱形的 yuánzhùxíngde.

cymbal /'sɪmbl/ *n* [C] [音乐]铙〔鐃〕钹 náobó; 镲 chǎ.

cynic /'sɪnɪk/ *n* [C] 认〔認〕为〔爲〕人的动〔動〕机〔機〕皆自私的人 rènwéi rénde dòngjī jiē zìsīde rén. **cynical** *adj* 不信世间有真诚善意的 búxìn shìjiān yǒu zhēnchéng shànyì de: *a* ~*al remark* 愤世嫉俗的话. **cynically** /-klɪ/ *adv*. **cynicism** /'sɪnɪsɪzəm/ *n* [U] 愤世嫉俗的观点〔點〕、态〔態〕度 fènshì jísúde guāndiǎn、tàidù.

cypher /'saɪfə(r)/ *n* [C] = CIPHER.

cypress /'saɪprəs/ *n* [C] 柏属〔屬〕植物 bǎishǔ zhíwù.

cyst /sɪst/ *n* [C] [生物]胞 bāo; 囊 náng.

cystitis /sɪ'staɪtɪs/ *n* [U] [医]膀胱炎 pángguāngyán.

czar, czarina = TSAR, TSARINA.

D d

D, d /di:/ [*pl* **D's, d's** /di:z/] 1 英语的第四个〔個〕字母 Yīngyǔde dìsìgè zìmǔ. 2 罗马数〔數〕字的 500 Luómǎ shùzìde 500.

d. *abbr* died 死亡 sǐwáng: *d.* 1924 死于 1924 年.

'd = HAD 或 WOULD: *I'd, she'd*.

dab /dæb/ *v* [-bb-] [T] 轻〔輕〕拍 qīngpāi; 轻敲 qīngqiāo; 轻搽 qīngchá: ~ *one's face dry* 轻轻把脸擦干. **dab** *n* [C] (涂上的)小量(颜色等) xiǎoliàng.

dabble /'dæbl/ *v* 1 [I] (*in*) 涉猎〔獵〕shèliè; 把…作为〔爲〕业〔業〕余〔餘〕爱〔愛〕好 bǎ…zuòwéi yèyú àihào. 2 [T] 用(手、脚等)嬉水 yòng xìshuǐ.

dachshund /'dækshʊnd/ *n* [C] 达〔達〕克斯猎〔獵〕狗 dákèsī liègǒu. (德国种的小猎狗).

dad /dæd/ *n* [C] [非正式用语]爸爸 bàba.

daddy /'dædɪ/ *n* [C] [*pl* -ies] (儿童用语)爸爸 bàba.

daffodil /'dæfədɪl/ *n* [C] 黄水仙 huángshuǐxiān.

daft /dɑ:ft/ *adj* [非正式用语]傻〔傻〕的 shǎde; 愚笨的 yúbènde.

dagger /'dægə(r)/ *n* [C] 短剑〔劍〕duǎnjiàn; 匕首 bǐshǒu.

daily /ˈdeɪlɪ/ *adj*, *adv* 每天的 měitiānde;每天地 měitiānde. **daily** *n* [C] [*pl* **-ies**] 日报〔報〕rìbào.

dainty /ˈdeɪntɪ/ *adj* [**-ier**, **-iest**] 秀丽〔麗〕的 xiùlìde;优〔優〕雅的 yōuyǎde;精致〔緻〕的 jīngzhìde;精巧的 jīngqiǎode. **daintily** *adv*.

dairy /ˈdeərɪ/ *n* [C] [*pl* **-ies**] **1** 牛奶房 niúnǎifáng;牛奶场〔場〕niúnǎichǎng;制〔製〕酪场 zhìlàochǎng. **2** 牛奶及乳品店 niúnǎi jí rǔpǐn diàn. ˈ**dairy cattle** *n*[U] 奶牛 nǎiniú.

daisy /ˈdeɪzɪ/ *n* [C] [*pl* **-ies**] 雏〔雛〕菊 chújú.

dale /deɪl/ *n* [C] [诗]山谷 shāngǔ.

dam /dæm/ *n* [C] 水坝〔壩〕shuǐbà;水堤 shuǐdī. **dam** *v* [**-mm-**] [T] **1** 在…筑〔築〕坝 zài…zhù bà. **2**[喻]控制 kòngzhì;抑制 yìzhì.

damage /ˈdæmɪdʒ/ *n* **1** [U] 损坏〔壞〕sǔnhuài;损失 sǔnshī;毁坏 huǐhuài;破坏 pòhuài: *The fire caused great* ~. 火灾造成巨大损失. **2 damages** [pl] [法律]损失赔偿〔償〕金 sǔnshī péichángjīn. **damage** *v* [T] 损坏 sǔnhuài;毁坏 huǐhuài.

dame /deɪm/ *n* [C] **1** 夫人 fūrén;贵夫人 guìfūrén: *D~ Janet Baker* 珍妮特·贝克夫人. **2** [美国俚语]女人 nǚrén.

damn /dæm/ *interj* [非正式用语](表示厌烦、忿怒等)该死! gāisǐ! 讨厌〔厭〕! tǎoyàn! **damn** *v* [T] **1**(上帝)罚…入地狱 fá…rù dìyù;诅咒 zǔzhòu. **2** 谴责 qiǎnzé;指责 zhǐzé. **damn** *n* [习语] **not care/give a damn** [非正式用语]毫无〔無〕价〔價〕值 háo wú jiàzhí;根本不值得 gēnběn bùzhídé. **damnation** /-ˈneɪʃn/ *n* [U] 罚入地狱 fárù dìyù;毁灭〔滅〕huǐmiè.

damned /dæmd/ *adj* [非正式用语](表示厌恶)讨厌〔厭〕的 tǎoyànde,该死的 gāisǐde;十足的 shízúde,完全的 wánquánde: *You* ~ *fool!* 你这十足的傻瓜! **damned** *adv* [非正式用语]非常 fēicháng: ~ *lucky* 非常幸运.

damp[1] /dæmp/ *adj* 潮湿〔濕〕的 cháoshīde: *a* ~ *cloth* 一块潮湿的布. **damp** *n* [U] 潮湿 cháoshī. **dampness** *n* [U].

damp[2] /dæmp/ *v* [T] **1** 使潮湿〔濕〕shǐ cháoshī. **2**(亦作 **dampen** /ˈdæmpən/) 使沮丧〔喪〕shǐ jǔsàng;减少 jiǎnshǎo;降低 jiàngdī: ~ *his enthusiasm* 给他的热情泼冷水. **3**[短语动词] **damp sth down** 减弱火势〔勢〕jiǎnruò huǒshì.

damper /ˈdæmpə(r)/ *n* [C] **1** 令人扫〔掃〕兴〔興〕的人或事 lìng rén sǎoxìng de rén huò shì: *put a* ~ *on the party* 使聚会大为扫兴. **2** 风〔風〕挡〔擋〕fēngdǎng;气〔氣〕流调节〔節〕器 qìliú tiáojiéqì.

damson /ˈdæmzn/ *n* [C] 布拉斯李 bùlāsīlǐ;布拉斯李树〔樹〕bùlāsīlǐ shù.

dance /dɑːns/ *n* [C] **1** 舞蹈 wǔdǎo;跳舞 tiàowǔ. **2** 舞会〔會〕wǔhuì. **dance** *v* **1** [I]跳舞 tiàowǔ. **2** [T] 跳(某一种舞) tiào. **dancer** *n* [C]. **dancing** *n* [U]: *a dancing teacher* 舞蹈教师.

dandelion /ˈdændɪlaɪən/ *n* [C] 蒲公英 púgōngyīng.

dandruff /ˈdændrʌf/ *n* [U] 头〔頭〕垢 tóugòu;头皮屑 tóupíxiè.

danger /ˈdeɪndʒə(r)/ *n* **1**[U] 危险〔險〕wēixiǎn. **2** [C]危险的事物 wēixiǎnde shìwù;危险人物 wēixiǎn rénwù. **3**[习语] **in danger** 在危险中 zài wēixiǎn zhōng. **out of danger** 脱离〔離〕危险 tuōlí wēixiǎn. **dangerous** *adj* 危险的 wēixiǎnde. **dangerously** *adv*.

dangle /ˈdæŋgl/ *v* [I,T] (使)悬〔懸〕垂 xuánchuí;(使)悬荡〔蕩〕xuándàng.

dank /dæŋk/ *adj* 湿〔濕〕冷的 shīlěngde;阴〔陰〕湿的 yīnshīde: *a* ~ *cellar/cave* 阴湿的地窖(洞穴).

dare[1] /deə(r)/ *modal v* [*pres tense*, *all persons* **dare**, *neg* **dare not** 或 **daren't** /deənt/] 敢 gǎn: *I* ~*n't ask him*. 我不敢问他. *D~ we try again?* 我们敢再试一试吗?

dare[2] /deə(r)/ *v* **1** [T] *to* 向…挑战〔戰〕xiàng…tiǎozhàn;激 jī: *I* ~ *you to jump off the tree*. 你要有种就从树上跳下来. **2**[I] (*to*)敢 gǎn: *No one* ~*d* (*to*) *speak*. 没有一个人敢说话. **dare** *n* [习语] **do sth for a dare** 因为〔爲〕受到激将〔將〕才做某事 yīnwéi shòudào jījiàng cái zuò mǒushì. ˈ**daredevil** *n* [C] 鲁莽大胆〔膽〕的人 lǔmǎng dàdǎn de rén.

daring /ˈdeərɪŋ/ *adj* 大胆的 dàdǎnde;鲁莽的 lǔmǎngde. **daringly** *adv*.

dark[1] /dɑːk/ *adj* **1** 黑暗的 hēi'ànde;暗的 ànde: *a* ~ *night* 一个黑暗的夜晚. *a* ~ *room* 一个黑暗的房间. **2**(颜色)深色的 shēnsède;暗色的 ànsède: ~ *blue* 深蓝色. **3**(肤色)黑色的 hēisède;浅〔淺〕黑的 qiǎnhēide. **4**(对事物的看法)悲观〔觀〕的 bēiguānde;忧〔憂〕伤〔傷〕的 yōushāngde: *look on the* ~ *side of things* 看事物的阴暗面. **5**[习语] **a ˌdark ˈhorse** 黑马 hēimǎ;竞〔競〕争中出人意料的胜〔勝〕利者 jìngzhēng zhōng chū rén yì liào de shènglìzhě. **darken** *v* [I,T] (使)变〔變〕黑 biànhēi;(使)变暗 biàn'àn. **darkly** *adv*. **darkness** *n* [U].

dark[2] /dɑːk/ *n* [U] **1** 黑暗 hēi'àn: *sit in the* ~ 坐在黑暗中. **2**[习语] **after dark** 黄昏后〔後〕huánghūn hòu. **before dark** 天黑以前 tiānhēi yǐqián. **be in the dark** 不知道 bù zhīdào;蒙在鼓里〔裡〕méng zài gǔlǐ. **keep sb in the dark** 对〔對〕某人保密 duì mǒu rén bǎomì.

darling /ˈdɑːlɪŋ/ *n* [C] 心爱〔愛〕的人 xīn'àide rén.

darn /dɑːn/ *v* [I,T] 织〔織〕补〔補〕zhībǔ: ~

D

sb's socks 织补某人的袜子. darn *n* [C] 织补处〔處〕zhībǔchù.

dart[1] /dɑːt/ *n* 1 [C] 飞〔飛〕镖 fēibiāo. 2 darts [用 sing v]掷〔擲〕镖游戏〔戲〕zhì biāo yóuxì.

dart[2] /dɑːt/ *v* [I] 突进〔進〕tūjìn;急冲〔衝〕jíchōng.

dash[1] /dæʃ/ *n* [C] 1 猛冲〔衝〕měngchōng: *make a ~ for the bus* 为赶上公共汽车而猛跑了一阵. 2 少量的搀〔攙〕和物 shǎoliàngde chānhéwù: *a ~ of pepper* 加一点胡椒. 3 破折号〔號〕pòzhéhào. 'dashboard *n* [C] (汽车上的)仪〔儀〕表〔錶〕板 yíbiǎobǎn.

D

dash[2] /dæʃ/ *v* 1 [I]猛冲〔衝〕měngchōng: *~ across the road* 冲过公路. 2 [T]猛掷〔擲〕měngzhì. 3 [T] 破坏〔壞〕(某人的希望) pòhuài. dashing *adj* 闯劲〔勁〕很大的 chuǎngjìn hěndà de;精神抖擞〔擻〕的 jīngshén dǒusǒu de.

data /'deɪtə/ *n* [U] 事实〔實〕资料 shìshí zīliào;已知材料 yǐzhī cáiliào;供电〔電〕子计算机〔機〕程序用的资料 gōng diànzǐjìsuànjī chéngxù yòng de zīliào. 'database *n* [C] 数〔數〕据〔據〕库 shùjùkù;资料库 zīliàokù. data 'processing *n* [U] 数〔數〕据〔據〕处〔處〕理 shùjù chǔlǐ. data pro'tection *n* [U] (涉及个人隐私权的)数据保护〔護〕shùjù bǎohù. data re'trieval *n* [U] 数据检〔檢〕索 shùjù jiǎnsuǒ. data se'curity *n* [U] 数据安全 shùjù ānquán. data 'storage *n* [U] 数据存储 shùjù cúnchǔ.

date[1] /deɪt/ *n* [C] 1 日期 rìqī;日子 rìzi: *His ~ of birth is 18 May 1930*. 他是 1930 年 5 月 18 日出生的. 2[非正式用语] (a) (男女间的)约会〔會〕yuēhuì. (b) [尤用于美语]约会的异〔異〕性对〔對〕象 yuēhuìde yìxìng duìxiàng. 3[习语] (be / go) out of date 过〔過〕时〔時〕的 guòshíde;陈旧〔舊〕的 chénjiùde. to date 到此时为〔爲〕止 dào cǐshí wéizhǐ. be up to date 现代的 xiàndàide. bring up to date 使成为现代的 shǐ chéngwéi xiàndài de.

date[2] /deɪt/ *v* 1 [T]注明…的日期 zhùmíng…de rìqī: *The letter was ~d 23 July*. 这封信注明的日期是 7 月 23 日. 2 [I] *from / back to* 自…时〔時〕代至今 zì…shídài zhì jīn;属〔屬〕于…时代 shǔyú…shídài: *The church ~s from the twelfth century*. 这座教堂早在 12 世纪就建成了. 3 [I]过〔過〕时 guòshí. 4 [T] [非正式用语,尤用于美语]与〔與〕(异性朋友)约会〔會〕yǔ yuēhuì. dated / 'deɪtɪd/ *adj* 过时的 guòshíde.

date[3] /deɪt/ *n* [C] 海枣〔棗〕hǎizǎo;枣椰子 zǎoyēzi.

daub /dɔːb/ *v* [T] 涂〔塗〕抹 túmǒ;乱〔亂〕画〔畫〕luànhuà.

daughter /'dɔːtə(r)/ *n* [C] 女儿〔兒〕nǚ'ér. 'daughter-in-law [*pl* ~s-in-law] 儿媳 érxí.

daunting /'dɔːntɪŋ/ *adj* 气〔氣〕馁的 qìněide.

dawdle /'dɔːdl/ *v* [I] 游荡〔蕩〕yóudàng;胡混 húhùn.

dawn /dɔːn/ *n* 1 [C,U] 黎明 límíng;破晓〔曉〕pòxiǎo. 2 [sing] [喻]开〔開〕始 kāishǐ;发〔發〕生 fāshēng: *the ~ of civilization* 文明的发端. dawn *v* [I] 1 破晓 pòxiǎo. 2 (*on*) 渐被理解 jiàn bèi lǐjiě: *The truth began to ~ on him*. 他开始明白了真相.

day /deɪ/ *n* 1 [C] 天 tiān; 日 rì;一昼〔晝〕夜 yízhòuyè. 2 [C,U]白天 báitiān;白昼 báizhòu. 3 [C]工作日 gōngzuòrì. 4 [C,U]时〔時〕代 shídài: *in the ~s of the Roman Empire* 在罗马帝国时代. 5[习语] any day (now) 不久 bùjiǔ;很快 hěnkuài. day and night ⇨NIGHT. day in, day out, day after day 一天又一天 yìtiān yòu yìtiān. sb/sth's days are numbered …的日子不长〔長〕了(指快死或快失败) …de rìzi bùchángle. make sb's day [非正式用语]使某人非常高兴〔興〕shǐ mǒurén fēicháng gāoxìng. one day (过去)某一天 mǒuyìtiān;(将来)有一天 yǒu yìtiān. 'day break *n* [U]黎明 límíng. 'daydream *v* [I] *n* [C] (做)白日梦〔夢〕báirìmèng. 'day job *n* [C] 本职〔職〕工作 běnzhí gōngzuò. 'daylight *n* [U] 1 日光 rìguāng. 2 黎明 límíng. 'daytime 白天 báitiān. 'day trader *n* [C] 做当〔當〕日买〔買〕进〔進〕卖〔賣〕出股票交易的人 zuò dàngrì mǎijìn màichū gǔpiào jiāoyì de rén. 'day trading *n* [U] 当日买进卖出股票交易 dàngrì mǎijìn màichū gǔpiào jiāoyì.

daze /deɪz/ *v* [T] 使茫然 shǐ mángrán;使发〔發〕昏 shǐ fāhūn. daze *n* [习语] in a daze 迷乱〔亂〕míluàn;茫然 mángrán.

dazzle /'dæzl/ *v* [T] 1 使目眩 shǐ mùxuàn;耀(眼) yào. 2 使惊〔驚〕奇 shǐ jīngqí.

dB *abbr* decibel(s) 分贝(音强单位) fēnbèi.

DDT /ˌdiː diː 'tiː/ *n* [U]滴滴涕(杀虫剂) dīdītì.

dead /ded/ *adj* 1(人、动植物)死的 sǐde. 2(语言、习惯等)废〔廢〕弃〔棄〕了的 fèiqìlede. 3(身体的一部分)被冻得麻木的 bèi dòng de mámù de. 4 完全的 wánquánde;绝对〔對〕的 juéduìde;突然的 tūránde: *a ~ stop* 突然的停止. 5 停止运〔運〕转〔轉〕的 tíngzhǐ yùnzhuǎn de: *The telephone went ~*. 电话打不通了. 6 停止活动〔動〕的 tíngzhǐ huódòng de: *The town is ~ after 10 o'clock*. 十点钟以后,这个城镇就全都入睡了. 7 [喻](颜色)晦暗的 huì'ànde;(声音)低沉的 dīchénde. 8 [习语] a dead 'loss [俚]无〔無〕用的人或物 wúyòngde rén huò wù. dead *adv* 全然 quánrán;绝对 juéduì: *~ certain* 绝对有把握. *~ accurate* 完全准确. the dead *n* [pl] 死人 sǐrén. ˌdead 'end *n* [C] (路等的)尽〔盡〕头〔頭〕jìntóu;死巷 sǐxiàng;绝境 juéjìng. 'deadline *n* [C] 最后〔後〕期限 zuìhòu qīxiàn: *meet a ~line* 如期. *miss a ~line*

超过期限.

deaden /ˈdedn/ *v* [T] 闷抑(声音等) mēnyì；使缓和 shǐ huǎnhé；使失去光泽〔澤〕shǐ shīqù guāngzé.

deadlock /ˈdedlɒk/ *n* [C, U] 僵持 jiāngchí；僵局 jiāngjú.

deadly /ˈdedlɪ/ *adj* [-ier, -iest] 1 致命的 zhìmìngde：*a* ~ *poison* 致命的毒药. 2 令人厌〔厭〕烦的 lìng rén yànfán de；枯燥的 kūzàode. **deadly** *adv* [非正式用语]极〔極〕其 jíqí：~ *serious* 极其严重.

deaf /def/ *adj* 1 聋〔聾〕的 lóngde. 2 *to* 不愿〔願〕听〔聽〕的 búyuàn tīng de. **the deaf** *n* [pl] 聋人 lóngrén. ˌ**deaf-and-ˈdumb** *adj* 聋哑〔啞〕的 lóngyǎde. ˌ**deafˈmute** *n* [C] 聋哑人 lóngyǎrén. **deafness** *n* [U].

deafen /ˈdefn/ *v* [T] 使难〔難〕以听〔聽〕到声〔聲〕音 shǐ nányǐ tīngdào shēngyīn：~*ed by the noise* 被噪音吵得几乎听不见别的声音.

deal[1] /diːl/ *n* [习语] **a good / great deal** 大量 dàliàng：*a good* ~ *of money* 大量金钱/ *I see him a great* ~. 我常常看见他.

deal[2] /diːl/ *n* [C] 1(商业)协〔協〕议〔議〕xiéyì. 2(牌戏)发〔發〕牌 fāpái.

deal[3] /diːl/ *v* [*pt*, *pp* ~t /delt/] 1 [I, T] (牌戏)发〔發〕牌 fāpái；发(牌) fā. 2 [T] 给予 jǐyǔ. 3[短语动词] **deal in sth** 买〔買〕卖〔賣〕(货物) mǎimài；经〔經〕营〔營〕jīngyíng：~ *in second-hand cars* 经营旧汽车. **deal with sb** 用…做买卖 yòng… zuò mǎimài. **deal with sth** (a) 处〔處〕理 chǔlǐ. (b) 关〔關〕于 guānyú；讨论〔論〕tǎolùn：*a book* ~*ing with Africa* 一本关于非洲的书. **dealer** *n* [C] 1(牌戏)发牌的人 fāpáide rén. 2 商人 shāngrén. **dealings** *n* [pl] 交易 jiāoyì；交往 jiāowǎng：*have* ~*ings with sb* 同某人有交往.

dean /diːn/ *n* [C] 1 主任牧师〔師〕(主管几个牧区) zhǔrèn mùshi. 2(大学)系主任 xìzhǔrèn.

dear /dɪə(r)/ *adj* 1 亲〔親〕爱〔愛〕的 qīn'àide；可爱的 kě'àide. 2 亲爱的(信件开头的套语) qīn'àide：*D*~ *Madam* 亲爱的女士. *D*~ *Sir* 亲爱的先生. 3[英国英语]昂贵的 ángguìde；索价〔價〕高的 suǒjià gāo de. 4 (*to*)可贵的 kěguìde. **dear** *adv* 高价地 gāojiàde. **dear** *n* [C] 1 可爱的人 kě'àide rén；亲爱的人 qīn'àide rén. 2(对人的称呼)亲爱的 qīn'àide：'*Yes*, ~.' "好,亲爱的." **dear** *interj* (表示惊讶、伤感等)呵! hē! 哎呀! āiyā! *Oh* ~! 呵,哎呀! *D*~ *me!* 哎呀,我的天啊! **dearly** *adv* 1 非常 fēicháng. 2[喻]代价很高地 dàijià hěngāo de.

dearth /dɜːθ/ *n* [sing] (*of*) [正式用语]缺乏 quēfá；不足 bùzú.

death /deθ/ *n* 1 [C]死亡 sǐwáng；死 sǐ. 2 [U] 生命的结束 shēngmìngde jiéshù；死亡状〔狀〕态〔態〕sǐwáng zhuàngtài. 3 [sing] [喻]破灭〔滅〕pòmiè；毁灭 huǐmiè：*the* ~ *of one's hopes* 希望的破灭. 4[习语] **bored/sick, etc to death of sth** 对〔對〕某事厌〔厭〕烦得要死 duì mǒushì yànfánde yàosǐ. **put sb to death** 杀〔殺〕死 shāsǐ；处〔處〕死 chǔsǐ. **deathly** *adj*, *adv* 死一般的(地) sǐyìbānde. ˈ**death penalty** *n* [sing] 死刑 sǐxíng. ˈ**death-trap** *n* [C]危险〔險〕场〔場〕所 wēixiǎn chǎngsuǒ；危险车辆 wēixiǎn chēliàng. ˈ**death-warrant** *n* [C] 死刑执〔執〕行令 sǐxíng zhíxínglìng.

débâcle /deɪˈbɑːkl/ *n* [C] 溃败 kuìbài；崩溃 bēngkuì.

debase /dɪˈbeɪs/ *v* [T] 降低…的身份 jiàngdī…de shēnfen；使贬值 shǐ biǎnzhí. **debasement** *n* [U].

debate /dɪˈbeɪt/ *n* [C, U] 争论〔論〕zhēnglùn；辩论 biànlùn；讨论 tǎolùn. **debate** *v* [I, T] 辩论 biànlùn；争论 zhēnglùn；讨论 tǎolùn；思考 sīkǎo. **debatable** *adj* 争论中的 zhēnglùn zhōng de；成问题的 chéng wèntí de；可争论的 kě zhēnglùn de.

debauched /dɪˈbɔːtʃt/ *adj* [正式用语]道德败坏〔壞〕的 dàodé bàihuài de；堕落的 duòluòde. **debauchery** /-tʃərɪ/ *n* [U] 放纵〔縱〕行为〔爲〕fàngzòng xíngwéi.

debilitating /dɪˈbɪlɪteɪtɪŋ/ *adj* 使衰弱的 shǐ shuāiruò de：*a* ~ *illness* 使人虚弱的疾病.

debit /ˈdebɪt/ *n* [C] (会计)借方 jièfāng. **debit** *v* [T] 将〔將〕…记入借方 jiāng…jìrù jièfāng. ˈ**debit card** *n* [C] 借记卡 jièjìkǎ；扣账〔賬〕卡 kòuzhàngkǎ.

debris /ˈdeɪbriː; *US* dəˈbriː/ *n* [U] 碎片 suìpiàn.

debt /det/ *n* 1 [C] 欠款 qiànkuǎn. 2 [U]负债状〔狀〕态〔態〕fùzhài zhuàngtài：*be in* ~ 负债. *be out of* ~ 不负债. 3 [C, U]恩情 ēnqíng；人情债 rénqíng zhài. **debtor** *n* [C] 债务人 zhàiwùrén；欠债人 qiànzhàirén.

début /ˈdeɪbjuː; *US* dɪˈbjuː/ *n* [C] (演员、音乐家)首次演出 shǒucì yǎnchū：*make one's* ~ 作首次演出.

decade /ˈdekeɪd; *US* dɪˈkeɪd/ *n* [C] 十年 shínián.

decadent /ˈdekədənt/ *adj* 堕〔墮〕落的 duòluòde：~ *behaviour* 颓废的行为. ~ *society* 颓废的社会. **decadence** /-dəns/ *n* [U].

decaffeinated /ˌdiːˈkæfɪneɪtɪd/ *adj* (咖啡)脱咖啡因的 tuō kāfēiyīn de.

decant /dɪˈkænt/ *v* [T] 把(酒等)注入另一容器 bǎ zhùrù lìngyī róngqì. **decanter** *n* [C] 倾析器 qīngxīqì.

decapitate /dɪˈkæpɪteɪt/ *v* [T] [正式用语]杀〔殺〕…的头〔頭〕shā…de tóu.

decay /dɪˈkeɪ/ *v* 1 [I, T] (使)腐烂〔爛〕fǔlàn；

(使)衰退 shuāituì. 2[I]衰弱 shuāiruò. **decay** *n* [U] 腐朽 fǔxiǔ; 腐烂 fǔlàn; 衰微 shuāiwēi: *tooth* ～ 龋齿; 蛀牙; 虫〔蟲〕牙.

deceased /dɪˈsiːst/ **the deceased** *n* [C] [*pl* **the deceased**] [正式用语](新近的)死者 sǐzhě.

deceit /dɪˈsiːt/ *n* [U, C] 欺骗 qīpiàn; 欺诈 qīzhà; 欺骗行为〔為〕 qīpiàn xíngwéi. **deceitful** *adj* 1 惯于欺骗的 guànyú qīpiàn de. 2 有意欺骗的 yǒuyì qīpiàn de: ～*ful words* 骗人的话. **deceitfully** *adv*. **deceitfulness** *n* [U].

D

deceive /dɪˈsiːv/ *v* [T] 欺骗 qīpiàn; 诓骗 kuāngpiàn. **deceiver** *n* [C].

December /dɪˈsembə(r)/ *n* 十二月 shí'èryuè. (用法举例见 *April*).

decent /ˈdiːsnt/ *adj* 1 正当〔當〕的 zhèngdàngde; 合适〔適〕的 héshìde; 尊重人的 zūnzhòng rén de: *wear* ～ *clothes to the party* 穿像样的衣服去参加这次聚会. 2 文雅的 wényǎde; 受人尊重的 shòu rén zūnzhòng de: ～ *behaviour* 文雅的举止. **decency** /ˈdiːsnsɪ/ *n* [U]. **decently** *adv*.

deception /dɪˈsepʃn/ *n* 1 [U]欺骗 qīpiàn; 诓骗 kuāngpiàn; 蒙蔽 méngbì: *obtain sth by* ～ 骗得某物. 2 [C] 诡计 guǐjì; 骗术〔術〕 piànshù.

deceptive /dɪˈseptɪv/ *adj* 骗人的 piàn rén de; 靠不住的 kàobúzhùde: *a* ～ *appearance* 骗人的外表. **deceptively** *adv*.

decibel /ˈdesɪbel/ *n* [C] 分贝(测量音强的单位) fēnbèi.

decide /dɪˈsaɪd/ *v* 1 [I] 决定 juédìng; 决意 juéyì: *I* ～*d to leave*. 我决意离开. 2 [T]使决意 shǐ juéyì. 3 [T]解决(问题等) jiějué; 裁决 cáijué. **decided** *adj* 1 明显〔顯〕的 míngxiǎnde; 明确〔確〕的 míngquède. 2 (人)坚〔堅〕决的 jiānjuéde; 果断〔斷〕的 guǒduànde. **decidedly** *adv* 明确地 míngquède.

deciduous /dɪˈsɪdjʊəs/ *adj* (树木)每年落叶〔葉〕的 měinián luòyè de.

decimal /ˈdesɪml/ *adj* 十进〔進〕法的 shíjìnfǎde: ～ *currency* 十进制货币. **decimal** *n* [C] 小数〔數〕 xiǎoshù; 十进小数 shíjìn xiǎoshù. **decimalize** /-məlaɪz/ *v* [I, T] 把…改为〔為〕十进制 bǎ…gǎiwéi shíjìnzhì. **decimalization** /ˌdesɪməlaɪˈzeɪʃn; *US* -lɪˈz-/ *n* [U]. ˌ**decimal** ˈ**point** *n* [C] 小数〔數〕点〔點〕 xiǎoshùdiǎn; 10.25 十点二五.

decimate /ˈdesɪmeɪt/ *v* [T] 1 大批杀〔殺〕死或毁坏〔壞〕 dàpī shāsǐ huò huǐhuài. 2[喻]减少 jiǎnshǎo; 降低 jiàngdī.

decipher /dɪˈsaɪfə(r)/ *v* [T] 译〔譯〕解(密码等) yìjiě.

decision /dɪˈsɪʒn/ *n* 1 [C, U]决定 juédìng; 判断〔斷〕 pànduàn: *come to / reach / make a* ～ 作出决定. 2 [U]果断 guǒduàn; 坚〔堅〕定 jiāndìng. **decisive** /dɪˈsaɪsɪv/ *adj* 1 有明确〔確〕结果的 yǒu míngquè jiéguǒ de. 2 果断的 guǒduànde. **decisively** *adv*. **decisiveness** *n* [U].

deck[1] /dek/ *n* [C] 1 甲板 jiǎbǎn; 舱〔艙〕面 cāngmiàn; 公共汽车〔車〕的层〔層〕面 gōnggòngqìchēde céngmiàn. 2 (录音机的)走带〔帶〕机〔機〕构〔構〕 zǒudài jīgòu. 3 一副纸牌 yífù zhǐpái. ˈ**deck-chair** *n* [C] 折叠〔疊〕帆布躺椅 zhédié fānbù tǎngyǐ.

deck[2] /dek/ *v* [T] (*out*) 装〔裝〕饰 zhuāngshì; 打扮 dǎbàn: *streets* ～*ed out with flags* 挂着许多旗子的街道.

declare /dɪˈkleə(r)/ *v* [I, T] 1 宣告 xuāngào; 宣布〔佈〕 xuānbù; 声〔聲〕明 shēngmíng. 2 断〔斷〕言 duànyán; 宣称〔稱〕 xuānchēng. 3 申报〔報〕(应纳税物品) shēnbào: *Have you anything to* ～? 你有什么要申报的吗? **declaration** /ˌdekləˈreɪʃn/ *n* [C].

decline[1] /dɪˈklaɪn/ *n* [C, U] 下降 xiàjiàng; 衰退 shuāituì; 减弱 jiǎnruò: *a* ～ *in population* 人口减少.

decline[2] /dɪˈklaɪn/ *v* 1 [I]减少 jiǎnshǎo; 衰退 shuāituì. 2 [I, T] 拒绝 jùjué.

decode /ˌdiːˈkəʊd/ *v* [T] 译〔譯〕(电报) yì.

decompose /ˌdiːkəmˈpəʊz/ *v* [I, T] (使)腐败 fǔbài; (使)腐烂〔爛〕 fǔlàn. **decomposition** /ˌdiːkɒmpəˈzɪʃn/ *n* [U].

décor /ˈdeɪkɔː(r); *US* deɪˈkɔːr/ *n* [U, sing] (房间、家具等的)装〔裝〕饰风〔風〕格 zhuāngshì fēnggé.

decorate /ˈdekəreɪt/ *v* 1 [T] 装〔裝〕饰 zhuāngshì; 装潢 zhuānghuáng. 2 [I, T]给(房间)贴壁纸 gěi tiē bìzhǐ; 油漆(建筑物等) yóuqī 3 [T]授勋〔勳〕章给… shòu xūnzhāng gěi…: ～*d for bravery* 因英勇而被授勋. **decoration** /ˌdekəˈreɪʃn/ *n* 1 [U]装〔裝〕饰 zhuāngshì; 装潢 zhuānghuáng. 2 [C] 装饰品 zhuāngshìpǐn: *Christmas decorations* 圣诞节装饰品. 3 [C] 勋章 xūnzhāng; 奖〔獎〕章 jiǎngzhāng. **decorative** /ˈdekərətɪv; *US* -ret-/ *adj* 可作装饰的 kě zuò zhuāngshì de. **decorator** *n* [C] 贴壁纸工人 tiē bìzhǐ gōngrén; (墙壁)油漆工 yóuqīgōng.

decoy /ˈdiːkɔɪ/ *n* [C] 1(诱擒鸟兽用的)引诱物 yǐnyòuwù; 囮子 ézi. 2[喻]诱人入圈套的人或东西 yòurén rù quāntào de rén huò dōngxi.

decrease /dɪˈkriːs/ *v* [I, T] (使)减小 jiǎnxiǎo; (使)减少 jiǎnshǎo: *Sales are decreasing*. 销量减少. **decrease** /ˈdiːkriːs/ *n* [U, C] 减小 jiǎnxiǎo; 减少 jiǎnshǎo; 减少量 jiǎnshǎoliàng; 减小额 jiǎnxiǎo'é: *a small* ～ *in sales* 销售稍有减少.

decree /dɪˈkriː/ *n* [C] 1 法令 fǎlìng; 政令

zhènglìng: *by royal* ~ 诏书,敕令. 2[法律]判决 pànjué. *v* [T] 颁布[佈](法令) bānbù;下令 xiàlìng.

decrepit /dɪˈkrepɪt/ *adj* 老弱的 lǎoruòde;衰老的 shuāilǎode.

decrypt /dɪˈkrɪpt/ *v* [T] 解密 jiěmì.

dedicate /ˈdedɪkeɪt/ *v* [T] *to* 1 奉献[獻] fèngxiàn;贡献 gòngxiàn. 2(作者)题献词于(作品) tí xiàncí yú. **dedicated** *adj* 专[專]心致志的 zhuān xīn zhì zhì de. **dedication** /ˌdedɪˈkeɪʃn/ *n* [C,U].

deduce /dɪˈdjuːs/ *v* [T] 演绎[繹] yǎnyì;推演 tuīyǎn;推论[論] tuīlùn.

deduct /dɪˈdʌkt/ *v* [T] 扣除 kòuchú;减去 jiǎnqù: ~ *£50 from her salary* 从她工资中扣掉 50 英镑.

deduction /dɪˈdʌkʃn/ *n* [U,C] 1 扣除 kòuchú;扣除量 kòuchúliàng;回扣 huíkòu: *tax ~s* 减税额 2 演绎[繹] yǎnyì; 推论[論] tuīlùn;用演绎推得的结论 yòng yǎnyì tuīdéde jiélùn.

deed /diːd/ *n* [C] 1[正式用语]行为[爲] xíngwéi;行动[動] xíngdòng. 2[法律]契约 qìyuē.

deem /diːm/ *v* [T]认[認]为[爲] rènwéi.

deep[1] /diːp/ *adj* 1 深的 shēnde: *a ~ river* 水深的河. *a hole one metre ~* 一米深的洞. 2[喻]严[嚴]肃[肅]的 yánsùde: *a ~ book* 严肃的书. 3(声音)深沉的 shēnchénde. 4 (颜色)深色的 shēnsède;浓[濃]色的 nóngsède;(感情)深厚的 shēnhòude;深切的 shēnqiède: ~ *hatred* 深仇大恨. 5(睡眠)深沉的 shēnchénde. 6 *in* 专[專]心于 zhuānxīn yú: ~ *in thought* 陷入沉思. ~ *in a book* 专心致志于读一本书. 7[习语] **go off the ˈdeep end** 大发[發]脾气[氣] dàfā píqì. **in deep water** 遇到麻烦 yùdào máfan. **deeply** *adv* 深入地 shēnrùde;深刻地 shēnkède;深厚地 shēnhòude: *~ly hurt by your remarks* 被你的话深深地伤害.

deep[2] /diːp/ *adv* 深 shēn. **ˌdeep-ˈfreeze** *n* [C] 以极[極]低温度快速冷藏的冷藏箱 yǐ jídī wēndù kuàisù lěngcáng de lěngcángxiāng. **ˌdeep-ˈrooted** [喻]根深蒂固的 gēn shēn dì gù de: ~*-rooted suspicions* 根深蒂固的猜疑. **ˌdeep-ˈseated** *adj* 由来已久的 yóulái yǐjiǔ de; 根深蒂固的 gēn shēn dì gù de: ~*-seated fears* 由来已久的恐惧.

deepen /ˈdiːpən/ *v* [I,T] 加深 jiāshēn;深化 shēnhuà;深入 shēnrù.

deep-vein thrombosis /ˌdiːpveɪn θrɒmˈbəʊsɪs/ *n* [U] 深静脉[脈]血栓症 shēnjìngmài xuèshuānzhèng;深层[層]静脉栓塞 shēncéng jìngmài shuānsāi;经[經]济[濟]舱[艙]综合征[徵] jīngjìcāng zōnghézhēng.

deer /dɪə(r)/ *n* [C] [*pl* ~]鹿 lù. ⇨DOE, STAG.

deface /dɪˈfeɪs/ *v* [T] 损伤[傷]…的外貌 sǔnshāng…de wàimào.

defame /dɪˈfeɪm/ *v* [T] [正式用语]破坏[壞]…的名誉[譽] pòhuài…de míngyù;诽谤 fěibàng. **defamation** /ˌdefəˈmeɪʃn/ *n* [U].

default /dɪˈfɔːlt/ *v* [I] 拖欠 tuōqiàn;不履行 bù lǚxíng;不出庭 bù chūtíng. **default** *n* [U] 拖欠 tuōqiàn;不履行 bù lǚxíng;违[違]约 wéiyuē;不出庭 bù chūtíng: *win a game by* ~ 因对手未出场而赢得比赛. **defaulter** *n* [C] 拖欠者 tuōqiànzhě;缺席者 quēxízhě;违约者 wéiyuēzhě.

defeat /dɪˈfiːt/ *v* [T] 1 打败 dǎbài;战[戰]胜[勝] zhànshèng;击[擊]败 jībài. 2 使失败 shǐ shībài;使落空 shǐ luòkōng: *Our hopes were ~ed*. 我们的希望破灭了. **defeat** *n* [C,U]击败 jībài;失败 shībài.

defect[1] /ˈdiːfekt/ *n* [C] 毛病 máobìng;缺点[點] quēdiǎn;不足之处[處] bùzú zhī chù. **defective** /dɪˈfektɪv/ *adj*.

defect[2] /dɪˈfekt/ *v* [I] 背叛 bèipàn;逃跑 táopǎo;开[開]小差 kāi xiǎochāi. **defection** /dɪˈfekʃn/ *n* [C,U]. **defector** *n* [C] 背叛者 bèipànzhě;逃兵 táobīng.

defence (美语 **-fense**) /dɪˈfens/ *n* 1 [U]防卫[衛] fángwèi;保卫 bǎowèi;防护[護] fánghù. 2 [C] 防务[務] fángwù;防御[禦]物 fángyùwù: *the country's ~s* 这个国家的防务. 3 [C,U] [法律](a)辩护 biànhù;答辩 dábiàn. (b) **the defence** (用 sing 或 pl v) 被告律师 bèigào lǜshī. **defenceless** *adj* 无[無]防御的 wú fángyù de;没有保护的 méiyǒu bǎohù de.

defend /dɪˈfend/ *v* [T] 1 (*from* / *against*) 保卫[衛] bǎowèi;防御[禦] fángyù. 2 为[爲]…辩护[護] wèi…biànhù; 为…答辩 wèi…dábiàn: ~ *a decision* 为一项决定辩护. **defendant** *n* [C] [法律]被告 bèigào. **defender** *n* [C] 1 *n* [C]防御者 fángyùzhě;保护人 bǎohùrén. 2(体育)防守队[隊]员 fángshǒu duìyuán. **defensible** /dɪˈfensəbl/ *adj* 能防御的 néng fángyù de;能辩护的 néng biànhù de.

defensive /dɪˈfensɪv/ *adj* 防卫[衛]用的 fángwèi yòng de. **defensive** *n* [习语] **on the defensive** 准[準]备[備]好辩护[護]自己 zhǔnbèi hǎo biànhù zìjǐ. **defensively** *adv*.

defer /dɪˈfɜː(r)/ *v*[-rr-] 1 [I] *to* 听[聽]从[從] tīngcóng;遵从 zūncóng: *I ~ to her experience*. 我尊重她的体验. 2 [T] 推迟[遲] tuīchí: ~ *payment* 推迟支付. **deference** /ˈdefərəns/ *n* [U] 听从 tīngcóng;依从 yīcóng;尊重 zūnzhòng.

defiance /dɪˈfaɪəns/ *n* [U] 蔑视 mièshì;违[違]抗 wéikàng;不服从[從] bù fúcóng: *in ~ of my orders* 蔑视我的命令. **defiant** /-ənt/

D

adj 挑战〔戰〕的 tiǎozhànde；违抗的 wéikàngde. **defiantly** *adv*.

deficiency /dɪˈfɪʃnsɪ/ *n* [C, U] [*pl* -ies] 缺乏 quēfá；缺少 quēshǎo；不足 bùzú. **deficient** /-ʃnt/ *adj* 缺少的 quēshǎode；不足的 bùzúde：～ *in vitamins* 缺少维生素.

deficit /ˈdefɪsɪt/ *n* [C] 空额 kòng'é；赤字 chìzì.

defile /dɪˈfaɪl/ *v* [T] 弄脏〔髒〕nòng zāng；污损 wūsǔn.

D

define /dɪˈfaɪn/ *v* [T] **1** 解释〔釋〕jiěshì；给…下定义〔義〕gěi…xià dìngyì. **2** 明确〔確〕表示 míngquè biǎoshì：～ *a judge's powers* 明确规定法官的权力. **definable** *adj* 可限定的 kě xiàndìng de；可下定义的 kě xià dìngyì de.

definite /ˈdefɪnət/ *adj* 确〔確〕切的 quèqiède；明确的 míngquède. ˌ**definite** ˈ**article** *n* [C] 定冠词 dìngguàncí. **definitely** *adv* **1** 确切地 quèqiède；明确地 míngquède：～*ly not true* 毫无疑问不是真的. **2**[非正式用语](用于回答问题)当〔當〕然 dāngrán.

definition /ˌdefɪˈnɪʃn/ *n* **1** [C](词的)释〔釋〕义〔義〕shìyì. **2** [U]清晰(度)qīngxī：*The photograph lacks* ～. 这张照片不清晰.

definitive /dɪˈfɪnətɪv/ *adj* 决定的 juédìngde；最后〔後〕的 zuìhòude；权〔權〕威性的 quánwēixìngde.

deflate /dɪˈfleɪt/ *v* [T] **1** 使(轮胎等)瘪下去 shǐ biě xiàqù. **2**[喻]降低(重要性) jiàngdī. **3** /ˌdiːˈfleɪt/ 紧〔緊〕缩(通货) jǐnsuō. **deflation** / dɪˈfleɪʃn / *n* [U].

deflect /dɪˈflekt/ *v* [I, T] (使)偏斜 piānxié：～ *a bullet* 把一颗子弹打偏了. ～ *a criticism* 批评得不对路. **deflection** /dɪˈflekʃn/ *n* [C, U].

deform /dɪˈfɔːm/ *v* [T] 损坏〔壞〕…的形象 sǔnhuài…de xíngxiàng；使成畸形 shǐ chéng jīxíng：*a* ～*ed foot* 畸形脚. **deformity** *n* [C, U] [*pl* -ies].

defraud /dɪˈfrɔːd/ *v* [T] 欺骗 qīpiàn；欺诈 qīzhà：～ *him of £100* 骗了他100英镑.

defrost /ˌdiːˈfrɒst; *US* -ˈfrɔːst/ *v* [T] 除去…的冰霜 chúqù…de bīngshuāng；使不结冰 shǐ bù jiébīng.

deft /deft/ *adj* (*at*) (尤指手)灵〔靈〕巧的 língqiǎode；熟练〔練〕的 shúliànde. **deftly** *adv*. **deftness** *n* [U].

defunct /dɪˈfʌŋkt/ *adj* [正式用语]不再使用的 búzài shǐyòng de；失效的 shīxiàode.

defuse /ˌdiːˈfjuːz/ *v* [T] **1** 去掉(炸弹等)的信管 qùdiào de xìnguǎn. **2**[喻]缓和 huǎnhé；平息 píngxī.

defy /dɪˈfaɪ/ *v* [*pt*, *pp* -ied] [T] **1** 公然反抗 gōngrán fǎnkàng；蔑视 mièshì；拒绝服从〔從〕jùjué fúcóng. **2** 激(某人)做某事 jī zuò mǒushì. **3** 使…简直不可能 shǐ jiǎnzhí bù kěnéng：～ *description* 无法描述.

degenerate /dɪˈdʒenəreɪt/ *v* [I] 衰退 shuāituì；变〔變〕坏〔壞〕biànhuài；退化 tuìhuà. **degenerate** /-nərət / *adj* 堕〔墮〕落的 duòluòde；颓废〔廢〕的 tuífèide.

degrade /dɪˈɡreɪd/ *v* [T] 使降低身份 shǐ jiàngdī shēnfèn；使丢脸〔臉〕shǐ diūliǎn：～ *oneself by cheating* 因欺骗而丢脸. **degradation** /ˌdeɡrəˈdeɪʃn / *n* [U].

degree /dɪˈɡriː/ *n* [C] **1** 程度 chéngdù：*a high* ～ *of accuracy* 高度精确. *not in the slightest* ～ *interested* 一点不感兴趣. **2**(温度的)度数〔數〕dùshù：*ten* ～*s Celsius* (*10°C*) 摄氏十度. **3**(角的)度数 dùshù：*an angle of 30* ～*s* (*30°*)三十度的角. **4** 学〔學〕位 xuéwèi；学衔 xuéxián. **5**[习语] **by de**ˈ**grees** 逐渐地 zhújiànde.

dehydrate /ˌdiːhaɪˈdreɪt/ *v* [T] 使(食品)脱水 shǐ tuōshuǐ.

de-ice /ˌdiːˈaɪs/ *v* [T] 除去…上的冰 chúqù…shang de bīng.

deign /deɪn/ *v* [T] 屈尊 qūzūn；垂顾〔顧〕chuígù：*She didn't* ～ *to speak to me*. 她不屑于同我说话.

deity /ˈdeɪətɪ/ *n* [C] [*pl* -ies] 神 shén；女神 nǚshén.

dejected /dɪˈdʒektɪd/ *adj* 沮丧〔喪〕的 jǔsàngde；情绪低落的 qíngxù dīluò de. **dejection** /-kʃn/ *n* [U].

delay /dɪˈleɪ/ *v* [I, T] **1** 延缓 yánhuǎn；耽搁〔擱〕dānge：*I was* ～*ed by the traffic*. 路上车子拥挤，我被耽搁了. **2** 推迟〔遲〕tuīchí；延期 yánqī. **delay** *n* [C, U] 延缓 yánhuǎn；耽搁 dānge；延迟 yánchí；延迟的事例 yánchíde shìlì.

delectable /dɪˈlektəbl/ *adj* [正式用语](尤指食物)使人愉快的 shǐ rén yúkuài de；美味的 měiwèide.

delegate[1] /ˈdelɪɡət/ *n* [C] 代表 dàibiǎo.

delegate[2] /ˈdelɪɡeɪt / *v* [T] 委派…为〔為〕代表 wěipài…wéi dàibiǎo；授权〔權〕shòuquán. **delegation** /ˌdelɪˈɡeɪʃn/ *n* **1** [U] 委派 wěipài；派遣 pàiqiǎn. **2** [C] 代表团〔團〕dàibiǎotuán.

delete /dɪˈliːt/ *v* [T] 删除(文字) shānchú；擦去(字迹) cāqù. **deletion** /dɪˈliːʃn/ *n* [C, U].

deliberate[1] /dɪˈlɪbərət/ *adj* **1** 故意的 gùyìde；蓄意的 xùyìde；存心的 cúnxīnde：*a* ～ *insult* 故意的侮辱. **2**(行动、语言上)从〔從〕容的 cóngróngde；谨慎的 jǐnshènde. **deliberately** *adv*.

deliberate[2] /dɪˈlɪbəreɪt/ *v* [I, T] (*about*/ *on*) [正式用语]仔细考虑〔慮〕zǐxì kǎolǜ；商议〔議〕shāngyì.

deliberation /dɪˌlɪbəˈreɪʃn/ *n* **1** [C, U] 细想

xìxiǎng. 2 [U] 谨慎 jǐnshèn;审慎 shěnshèn.

delicacy /ˈdelɪkəsɪ/ *n* [*pl* -ies] 1 [U]精美 jīngměi;细致 xìzhì;纤〔纖〕弱 xiānruò;优〔優〕美 yōuměi;浅〔淺〕淡 qiǎndàn;微妙 wēimiào;棘手 jíshǒu;灵〔靈〕敏 língmǐn;精密 jīngmì. 2 [C]精美的食品 jīngměide shípǐn: *a local* ~ 当地的精美食品.

delicate /ˈdelɪkət/ *adj* 1 细软〔軟〕的 xìruǎnde;纤〔纖〕细的 xiānxìde;柔嫩的 róunènde;精美的 jīngměide;雅致的 yǎzhìde. 2(颜色)浅〔淺〕淡的 qiǎndànde;柔和的 róuhéde. 3 娇〔嬌〕嫩的 jiāonènde;脆弱的 cuìruòde;难〔難〕办〔辦〕的 nánbànde: *a* ~ *vase* 容易碰坏的花瓶. *a* ~ *situation* 棘手的局面. 4 病弱的 bìngruòde: *in* ~ *health* 身体虚弱. 5 灵〔靈〕敏的 língmǐnde: *a* ~ *instrument* 精密仪器. **delicately** *adv*.

delicatessen /ˌdelɪkəˈtesn/ *n* [C] 熟食店(尤指出售较少见的或进口食品者) shúshídiàn.

delicious /dɪˈlɪʃəs/ *adj* 美味的 měiwèide;可口的 kěkǒude.

delight[1] /dɪˈlaɪt/ *n* 1 [U]高兴〔興〕 gāoxìng;快乐〔樂〕 kuàilè: *take* ~ *in being a parent* 享受做父母的快乐. 2[C] 乐事 lèshì. **delightful** *adj*. **delightfully** *adv*.

delight[2] /dɪˈlaɪt/ *v* 1 [T]使高兴〔興〕shǐ gāoxìng;使快乐〔樂〕 shǐ kuàile. 2 [I] 感到快乐、高兴 gǎndào kuàilè、gāoxìng: *She* ~*s in working hard*. 她以努力工作为乐. 3[习语] **be delighted** 感到很高兴 gǎndào hěn gāoxìng.

delinquent /dɪˈlɪŋkwənt/ *adj*, *n* [C] 做坏〔壞〕事的(人) zuò huàishì de. **delinquency** /-kwənsɪ/ *n* [C, U] [*pl* -ies] 为〔爲〕非作歹 wéi fēi zuò dǎi;过〔過〕失 guòshī.

delirious /dɪˈlɪrɪəs/ *adj* 1 神志昏迷的 shénzhì hūnmí de. 2[喻]发〔發〕狂的 fākuángde;极〔極〕度兴〔興〕奋〔奮〕的 jídù xìngfèn de. **deliriously** *adv*.

delirium /dɪˈlɪrɪəm/ *n* [U] 1 神志昏迷 shénzhì hūnmí;说胡话 shuō húhuà. 2[喻]极〔極〕度兴〔興〕奋〔奮〕 jídù xīngfèn.

deliver /dɪˈlɪvə(r)/ *v* 1 [I, T]投递〔遞〕(信件、货物等) tóudì: ~ *milk* 送牛奶. ~ *newspapers* 送报纸. 2 [T]发〔發〕表 fābiǎo: ~ *a lecture* 发表演说. 3 [T]给产〔產〕妇〔婦〕接生(婴儿) gěi chǎnfù jiēshēng. 4[习语] **deliver the goods** ⇨GOODS.

delivery /dɪˈlɪvərɪ/ *n* [*pl* -ies] 1 [C, U](信件,货物等)投递〔遞〕 tóudì. 2 [C]分娩 fēnmiǎn: *The mother had an easy* ~. 母亲顺利分娩. 3 [C, sing, U] 演讲〔講〕的风〔風〕格 yǎnjiǎngde fēnggé. 4[习语] **take delivery (of sth)** 收(货) shōu;提取(货物) tíqǔ.

delta /ˈdeltə/ *n* [C] (河流的)三角洲 sānjiǎozhōu.

delude /dɪˈluːd/ *v* [T] 欺骗 qīpiàn;哄骗 hǒngpiàn.

deluge /ˈdeljuːdʒ/ *n* [C] 1 暴雨 bàoyǔ. 2[喻]洪水般的泛滥〔濫〕 hóngshuǐ bān de fànlàn: *a* ~ *of letters* 信件纷至沓来. **deluge** *v* [T] 使泛滥 shǐ fànlàn;使满溢 shǐ mǎnyì: ~*d with questions* 问题不断涌来.

delusion /dɪˈluːʒn/ *n* [C, U] 误会〔會〕 wùhuì: *under the* ~ *that he is Napoleon* 把他误认成拿破仑.

deluxe /dɪˈlʌks/ *adj* 豪华〔華〕的 háohuáde;高级的 gāojíde: *a* ~ *hotel* 一家豪华饭店.

delve /delv/ *v* [I] *in/into* 探究 tànjiū;钻〔鑽〕研 zuānyán: ~ *into the past* 探索过去.

Dem *abbr* Democrat(ic) (美国)民主党〔黨〕人 Mínzhǔdǎng rén; 民主党的 Mínzhǔdǎngde.

demand[1] /dɪˈmɑːnd; *US* dɪˈmænd/ *n* 1 [C] 要求 yāoqiú;要求的事物 yāoqiúde shìwù: *the workers' ~s for higher pay* 工人们关于增加工资的要求. 2 [U] 需要 xūyào;需求 xūqiú: *no* ~ *for history graduates* 对历史专业的毕业生没有需求. *Our goods are in great* ~. 我们的货物需求量很大. 3[习语] **on demand** 一经〔經〕要求 yìjīng yāoqiú.

demand[2] /dɪˈmɑːnd; *US* dɪˈmænd/ *v* [T] 1 要求 yāoqiú. 2[正式用语]需要 xūyào: *work* ~*ing great care* 需要很细心地做的工作. **demanding** *adj* (a) 费力的 fèilìde;需要技能的 xūyào jìnéng de: *a* ~*ing job* 一个需要技能的工作岗位. (b)要求别人努力工作的 yāoqiú biérén nǔlì gōngzuò de: *a* ~*ing boss* 一个要求很严的老板.

demarcate /ˈdiːmɑːkeɪt/ *v* [T] 给…划〔劃〕界 gěi…huàjiè. **demarcation** /ˌdiːmɑːˈkeɪʃn/ *n* [U, C].

demean /dɪˈmiːn/ *v* [T] [正式用语] ~ **oneself** 降低自己的身份 jiàngdī zìjǐ de shēnfèn.

demeanour (美语 -or) /dɪˈmiːnə(r)/ *n* [C, 通常用 sing] 行为〔爲〕 xíngwéi;举〔舉〕止 jǔzhǐ.

demented /dɪˈmentɪd/ *adj* 发〔發〕狂的 fākuángde.

demilitarize /ˌdiːˈmɪlɪtəraɪz/ *v* [T] 使非军事化 shǐ fēi jūnshìhuà.

demise /dɪˈmaɪz/ *n* [sing] 1[正式用语]死亡 sǐwáng. 2[喻]终止 zhōngzhǐ;失败 shībài.

demist /ˌdiːˈmɪst/ *v* [T] 除去(汽车挡风玻璃等上的)雾〔霧〕水 chúqù wùshuǐ.

democracy /dɪˈmɒkrəsɪ/ *n* [*pl* -ies] 1 [C, U]民主国〔國〕 mínzhǔguó;民主政体〔體〕 mínzhǔ zhèngtǐ;民主政治 mínzhǔ zhèngzhì. 2 [U]民主 mínzhǔ;民主精神 mínzhǔjīngshén.

democrat /ˈdeməkræt/ *n* [C] 1 民主主义〔義〕者 mínzhǔzhǔyìzhě. 2 **Democrats** [美语]民主党〔黨〕人 Mínzhǔdǎng rén. **democratic**

D

/ˌdeməˈkrætɪk / *adj* 民主的 mínzhǔde；支持民主的 zhīchí mínzhǔ de. **democratically** *adv*.

demolish /dɪˈmɒlɪʃ/ *v* [T] **1** 拆毁(旧建筑) chāihuǐ. **2**[喻]推翻(论据、理论等) tuīfān. **demolition** /ˌdeməˈlɪʃn/ *n* [C,U].

demon /ˈdiːmən/ *n* [C] **1** 恶〔惡〕魔 èmó；恶鬼 èguǐ. **2**[正式用语]精力过〔過〕人的人 jīnglì guòrén de rén；技艺〔藝〕高超的人 jìyì gāochāo de rén. **demonic** /diːˈmɒnɪk/ *adj*.

D

demonstrable /ˈdemənstrəbl；*US* dɪˈmɒnstrəbl/ *adj* 可证〔證〕明的 kě zhèngmíng de. **demonstrably** *adv*.

demonstrate /ˈdemənstreɪt/ *v* **1**[T]论〔論〕证〔證〕lùnzhèng；证明 zhèngmíng. **2** [I]参〔參〕加示威 cānjiā shìwēi. **demonstrator** *n* [C] **1** 示威者 shìwēizhě. **2** 示范〔範〕者 shìfànzhě.

demonstration /ˌdemənˈstreɪʃn/ *n* **1** [C, U]论〔論〕证〔證〕lùnzhèng；证明 zhèngmíng. **2** 示威 shìwēi. **demonstrative** /dɪˈmɒnstrətɪv/ *adj* **1** 感情外露的 gǎnqíng wàilùde. **2**[语法](代名词)指示的 zhǐshìde.

demoralize /dɪˈmɒrəlaɪz；*US* -ˈmɔːr-/ *v* [T]使泄气〔氣〕shǐ xièqì；使士气低落 shǐ shìqì dīluò：*~d unemployed school-leavers* 对前途失去信心的失业辍学生.

demote /ˌdiːˈməʊt/ *v* [T] 使降级 shǐ jiàngjí.

demure /dɪˈmjʊə(r)/ *adj* 娴静的 xiánjìngde；严〔嚴〕肃〔肅〕的 yánsùde；害羞的 hàixiūde：*a ~ young woman* 娴静的年轻女人 **demurely** *adv*.

den /den/ *n* [C] **1** 兽〔獸〕穴 shòuxué；窝〔窩〕wō. **2**[非正式用语](小而安静的)私人的工作室 sīrénde gōngzuòshì.

denationalize /ˌdiːˈnæʃənəlaɪz/ *v* [T] 使非国〔國〕有化 shǐ fēi guóyǒuhuà；使私有化 shǐ sīyǒuhuà. **denationalization** /ˌdiːˌnæʃənəlaɪˈzeɪʃn；*US* -lɪˈz-/ *n* [U].

denial /dɪˈnaɪəl/ *n* **1** 否认〔認〕fǒurèn；否定 fǒudìng. **2** [C,U] 拒绝 jùjué；拒绝一项请求 jùjué yíxiàng qǐngqiú.

denigrate /ˈdenɪgreɪt/ *v* [T] 贬低 biǎndī；轻〔輕〕视 qīngshì.

denim /ˈdenɪm/ *n* **1** [U]斜纹粗棉布 xiéwén cū miánbù. **2 denims** [pl] (尤指蓝色的)斜纹粗棉布的工装〔裝〕裤 xiéwén cū miánbùde gōngzhuāngkù.

denomination /dɪˌnɒmɪˈneɪʃn/ *n* [C] **1** 教派 jiàopài. **2**(度量衡、货币等的)单〔單〕位 dānwèi. **denominational** *adj* 教派的 jiàopàide.

denominator /dɪˈnɒmɪneɪtə(r)/ *n* [C]分母 fēnmǔ.

denote /dɪˈnəʊt/ *v* [T] **1** 是…的符号〔號〕shì…de fúhào；是…的名称〔稱〕shì… de míngchēng. **2** 指示 zhǐshì；表示 biǎoshì：*His silence ~d criticism*. 他的沉默表示了他的指责.

denounce /dɪˈnaʊns/ *v* [T] 谴责 qiǎnzé；斥责 chìzé：*~ sb as a spy* 谴责某人是间谍.

dense /dens/ *adj* [~r, ~st] **1**(人、物)密集的 mìjíde：*~ traffic* 密集的车流. **2**(液体、蒸气等)浓〔濃〕密的 nóngmìde：*a ~ fog* 浓雾. **3** [非正式用语]愚笨的 yúbènde. **densely** *adv*.

density /ˈdensətɪ/ *n* [*pl* -ies] **1** [U]稠密度 chóumìdù. **2** [C,U] [物理] 密度 mìdù.

dent /dent/ *n* [C]凹部 āobù；凹痕 āohén. **dent** *v* [T] 使出现凹痕 shǐ chūxiàn āohén.

dental /ˈdentl/ *adj* (为)牙齿〔齒〕的 yáchǐde.

dentist /ˈdentɪst/ *n* [C]牙医〔醫〕yáyī. **dentistry** *n* [U] 牙科 yákē.

denunciation /dɪˌnʌnsɪˈeɪʃn/ *n* [C,U] 谴责 qiǎnzé；斥责 chìzé.

deny /dɪˈnaɪ/ *v* [*pt*, *pp* -ied] [T] **1** 否认〔認〕fǒurèn；否定 fǒudìng. **2** 拒绝一项要求 jùjué yíxiàng yāoqiú.

deodorant /ˌdiːˈəʊdərənt/ *n* [C,U] 除臭剂〔劑〕chúchòujì.

dep *abbr* departs 离〔離〕开〔開〕líkāi.

depart /dɪˈpɑːt/ *v* [I] 离〔離〕开〔開〕líkāi；启〔啓〕程 qǐchéng：*The train ~s from platform 3*. 火车从第三站台开出. *~ from the truth* 背离事实.

department /dɪˈpɑːtmənt/ *n* [C] (行政、企业、大学等的)部，司，局，处〔處〕，科，系 bù, sī, jú, chù, kē, xì. **deˈpartment store** *n* [C] (大型)百货商店 bǎihuò shāngdiàn.

departure /dɪˈpɑːtʃə(r)/ *n* [C,U] 离〔離〕开〔開〕líkāi；启〔啓〕程 qǐchéng. **deˈparture lounge** *n* [C] 候机〔機〕室 hòujīshì.

depend /dɪˈpend/ *v* [I] **1** *on* (a) (为生存而)依赖 yīlài：*Children ~ on their parents*. 儿童依赖父母(而生活). (b)信任 xìnrèn；相信 xiāngxìn：*You can ~ on John not to be late*. 你可以相信约翰不会迟到. **2** *on* 视…而定 shì…ér dìng：*Our success ~s on how hard we work*. 我们的成功决定于我们努力得如何. **dependable** *adj* 可靠的 kěkàode：*a ~able friend* 可靠的朋友.

dependant (亦作，尤用于美语 -ent) /dɪˈpendənt / *n* [C] 被赡养〔養〕者 bèi shànyǎng zhě.

dependence /dɪˈpendəns/ *n* [U] **1** 依靠 yīkào；依赖 yīlài：*~ on drugs* 毒瘾. *~ on foreign imports* 依赖外国进口. **2** 信赖 xìnlài；信任 xìnrèn.

dependent /dɪˈpendənt/ *adj* **1** 依靠的 yīkàode；依赖的 yīlàide：*~ on her parents* 依靠她的父母. **2** 取决于 qǔjué yú：*~ on your passing the exam* 取决于你考试合格. **de-**

pendent *n* [C] [尤用于美语]被赡养〔養〕者 bèi shànyǎng zhě.

depict /dɪˈpɪkt/ *v* [T] 描绘〔繪〕miáohuì;描写〔寫〕miáoxiě. **depiction** /-kʃn/ *n* [U,C].

deplete /dɪˈpliːt/ *v* [T] 耗尽〔盡〕hàojìn;大量消耗 dàliàng xiāohào: *Our food supplies are badly ~d.* 我们的食物已消耗殆尽. **depletion** /-iːʃn/ *n* [U].

deplore /dɪˈplɔː(r)/ *v* [T] 强烈反对〔對〕qiángliè fǎnduì. **deplorable** *adj* 糟糕的 zāogāode; 应〔應〕受谴责的 yīng shòu qiǎnzé de.

deploy /dɪˈplɔɪ/ *v* [I,T] 部署(军队) bùshǔ; 调度(军队) diàodù.

deport /dɪˈpɔːt/ *v* [T] 把(外国人)驱〔驅〕逐出境 bǎ qūzhú chūjìng. **deportation** /ˌdiːpɔːˈteɪʃn/ *n* [C,U].

depose /dɪˈpəʊz/ *v* [T] 废〔廢〕黜 fèichù.

deposit[1] /dɪˈpɒzɪt/ *n* 1 [C] 存款 cúnkuǎn. 2 [C]定金 dìngjīn. 3 [C]押金 yājīn. 4 [C,U] (河流的)沉淀〔澱〕物 chéndiànwù. **deˈposit account** *n* [C] 定期存款账〔賬〕户 dìngqī cúnkuǎn zhànghù.

deposit[2] /dɪˈpɒzɪt/ *v* [T] 1[正式用语]放 fàng;置 zhì. 2(河流等)淤积〔積〕(泥沙等)yūjī. 3 存(款)于银行 cún yú yínháng;存放(贵重物品等) cúnfàng.

depot /ˈdepəʊ; *US* ˈdiːpəʊ/ *n* 1 (a) 仓〔倉〕库 cāngkù. (b)(公共汽车等的)车〔車〕库 chēkù. 2[美语](火车、公共汽车)车站 chēzhàn.

depraved /dɪˈpreɪvd/ *adj* 堕〔墮〕落的 duòluòde;道德败坏〔壞〕的 dàodé bàihuài de. **depravity** /dɪˈprævətɪ/ *n* [U,C].

deprecate /ˈdeprəkeɪt/ *v* [T] [正式用语]对〔對〕…表示不赞成 duì…biǎoshì bú zànchéng.

depreciate /dɪˈpriːʃɪeɪt/ *v* [I]贬值 biǎnzhí; 降价〔價〕jiàngjià. **depreciation** /dɪˌpriːʃɪˈeɪʃn/ *n* [C,U].

depress /dɪˈpres/ *v* [T]1 使沮丧〔喪〕shǐ jǔsàng;使消沉 shǐ xiāochén: *feel very ~ed* 感到非常伤心. 2 降低…的价〔價〕值 jiàngdī…de jiàzhí: ~ *prices* 降价. 3[正式用语]压〔壓〕下 yāxià;按下 ànxià. **depressing** *adj* 压抑的 yāyìde: *a ~ing film* 使人感到压抑的影片.

depression /dɪˈpreʃn/ *n* 1 [U]沮丧〔喪〕jǔsàng;消沉 xiāochén. 2 [C] 萧〔蕭〕条〔條〕时〔時〕期 xiāotiáo shíqī. 3 [C] 凹陷 āoxiàn;凹地 āodì. 4 [C] [气象]低气〔氣〕压〔壓〕dīqìyā.

deprive /dɪˈpraɪv/ *v* [T] *of* 剥夺〔奪〕bōduó;使丧〔喪〕失 shǐ sàngshī: ~ *people of freedom* 剥夺人民的自由. **deprivation** /ˌdeprɪˈveɪʃn/ *n* [C,U]. **deprived** *adj* 贫困的 pínkùnde.

Dept *abbr* Department 司 sī;局 jú;科 kē;(学校的)系 xì.

depth /depθ/ *n* 1 [C,U]深 shēn;深度 shēndù;厚度 hòudù. 2 [U] 深奥 shēnʼào;深沉 shēnchén;深厚 shēnhòu: *a writer of great* ~ 极有悟性的作家. 3[习语] in ˈdepth 详细地 xiángxìde;彻〔徹〕底地 chèdǐde. out of one's depth (a) 在超过〔過〕自己身高的水中 zài chāoguò zìjǐ shēngāo de shuǐ zhōng. (b) 非…所能理解 fēi…suǒ néng lǐjiě.

deputation /ˌdepjʊˈteɪʃn/ *n* [C] [用 sing 或 pl v] 代表团〔團〕dàibiǎotuán.

deputize /ˈdepjʊtaɪz/ *v* [I] 担〔擔〕任代表 dānrèn dàibiǎo: ~ *for the manager* 充当经理的代表.

deputy /ˈdepjʊtɪ/ *n* [C] [*pl* -ies] 1 副手 fùshǒu. 2 代表 dàibiǎo;代理人 dàilǐrén.

derail /dɪˈreɪl/ *v* [T] 使(火车)出轨 shǐ chūguǐ. **derailment** *n* [C,U].

deranged /dɪˈreɪndʒd/ *adj* 精神错乱〔亂〕的 jīngshén cuòluàn de;疯〔瘋〕狂的 fēngkuángde.

derelict /ˈderəlɪkt/ *adj* 被抛弃〔棄〕的 bèi pāoqìde: *a* ~ *house* 被遗弃的房屋. **dereliction** /ˌderəˈlɪkʃn/ *n* [U].

derision /dɪˈrɪʒn/ *n* [U] 嘲笑 cháoxiào.

derisory /dɪˈraɪsərɪ/ *adj* 微不足道得可笑的 wēi bù zú dào dé kěxiào de.

derivation /ˌderɪˈveɪʃn/ *n* [C,U] 词源 cíyuán. **derivative** /dɪˈrɪvətɪv/ *adj*, *n* [C] 衍生的 yǎnshēngde;派生的 pàishēngde;派生词 pàishēngcí.

derive /dɪˈraɪv/ *v* 1 [T]得到 dédào;取得 qǔdé: ~ *pleasure from something* 从某事得到乐趣. 2 [I] *from* 起源于 qǐyuán yú: *words ~d from Latin* 起源于拉丁语的词.

derogatory /dɪˈrɒgətrɪ; *US* -tɔːrɪ/ *adj* 贬抑的 biǎnyìde;毁损的 huǐsǔnde.

derrick /ˈderɪk/ *n* [C] 1(船用)起重摇臂吊杆〔桿〕qǐzhòng yáobì diàogǎn. 2(油井)井架 jǐngjià.

descend /dɪˈsend/ *v* 1 [I,T][正式用语]下降 xiàjiàng;下来 xiàlái. 2[习语] be descended from sb/sth 是…的后〔後〕代 shì…de hòudài. 3[短语动词] descend on sb/sth 突然访问 tūrán fǎngwèn 袭〔襲〕击〔擊〕xíjī. **deˈscendant** *n* [C] 后裔 hòuyì;后代 hòudài;子孙〔孫〕zǐsūn: *the ~ants of Queen Victoria* 维多利亚女王的后代.

descent /dɪˈsent/ *n* 1 [C,常作 sing] 下降 xiàjiàng;降下 jiàngxià. 2 [C]斜坡 xiépō;下坡 xiàpō. 3 [U]出身 chūshēn;血统 xuètǒng: *of French* ~ 法国血统.

describe /dɪˈskraɪb/ *v* [T] 1 描述 miáoshù;描绘〔繪〕miáohuì;形容 xíngróng. 2[正式用语]画〔畫〕huà: ~ *a circle* 画一个圆圈.

description /dɪˈskrɪpʃn/ *n* 1 [C,U] 描写〔寫〕miáoxiě;描述 miáoshù;叙述 xùshù. 2 [C] 种〔種〕类〔類〕zhǒnglèi: *boots of every* ~ 所

D

有种类的靴子. **descriptive** /dɪˈskrɪptɪv/ *adj* 描写的 miáoxiěde.

desecrate /ˈdesəkreɪt/ *v* [T] 亵〔褻〕渎〔瀆〕xièdú; 污辱 wūrǔ. **desecration** /ˌdesɪˈkreɪʃn/ *n* [U].

desegregate /ˌdiːˈsegrɪgeɪt/ *v* [T] 废〔廢〕除…的种族隔离〔離〕fèichú…de zhǒngzú gélí: *~ schools* 废除学校的种族隔离. **desegregation** /ˌdiːˌsegrɪˈgeɪʃn/ *n* [U].

desert[1] /dɪˈzɜːt/ *v* 1 [T] 丢弃〔棄〕diūqì; 离〔離〕开〔開〕líkāi. 2 [T]背弃 bèiqì; 置…于不顾〔顧〕zhì…yú búgù: *~ one's family* 置家庭于不顾. 3 [I, T] 开小差 kāi xiǎochāi. **deserter** *n* 逃兵 táobīng. **desertion** /dɪˈzɜːʃn/ *n* [C, U].

desert[2] /ˈdezət/ *n* [C, U] 沙漠 shāmò; 不毛之地 bùmáo zhī dì. ˌ**desert** ˈ**island** *n* [C] 荒无〔無〕人烟〔煙〕的热〔熱〕带〔帶〕岛屿〔嶼〕huāng wú rén yān de rèdài dǎoyǔ.

deserts /dɪˈzɜːts/ *n* [pl] 应〔應〕得的赏罚 yīngdéde shǎngfá: *get one's just ~* 得到应得的赏罚.

deserve /dɪˈzɜːv/ *v* [T] 应〔應〕得 yīngdé; 应受 yīngshòu; 值得 zhídé: *She ~d to win.* 她的获胜是应该的.

design /dɪˈzaɪn/ *n* 1 (a) [C]设计图〔圖〕shèjìtú. (b) [U] 设计制〔製〕图术〔術〕shèjì zhìtú shù. 2 [C]装〔裝〕饰图案 zhuāngshì tú'àn. 3 [U](机器、建筑物等的)设计 shèjì. 4 [C, U]计划〔劃〕jìhuà; 图谋 túmóu. **design** *v* [T] 1 打…的图样 dǎ… de túyàng. 2 打算 dǎsuàn; 计划 jìhuà: *a room ~ed for the children* 打算给孩子们用的房间. **designer** *n* [C]. **designer** ˈ**drug** *n* [C] 策划药〔藥〕(一种毒品) cèhuàyào.

designate /ˈdezɪgneɪt/ *v* [T] 1 指派 zhǐpài; 选〔選〕派 xuǎnpài. 2 标〔標〕出 biāochū; 指明 zhǐmíng.

desirable /dɪˈzaɪərəbl/ *adj* 值得弄到手的 zhídé nòngdào shǒu de; 值得做的 zhídé zuò de. **desirability** /dɪˌzaɪərəˈbɪlətɪ/ *n* [U].

desire /dɪˈzaɪə(r)/ *n* 1 [C, U]愿〔願〕望 yuànwàng; 心愿 xīnyuàn: *no ~ to be rich / for wealth* 不想发财. 2 [C]想望的事物 xiǎngwàngde shìwù. **desire** *v* [T] [正式用语]想望 xiǎngwàng; 希望 xīwàng.

desist /dɪˈzɪst/ *v* [I] (*from*) [正式用语]停止(做…) tíngzhǐ.

desk /desk/ *n* [C]写〔寫〕字台〔臺〕xiězìtái; 办〔辦〕公桌 bàngōngzhuō. ˈ**desktop** *n* [C] 1 桌面 zhuōmiàn; 台式 táishì: *desktop computer / machine* 台式计算机/台式机. 2 台式计算机〔機〕táishì jìsuànjī. 3 (计算机屏幕上的)桌面 zhuōmiàn. ˌ**desk-top** ˈ**publishing** *n* [U] 桌面出版(使用电子计算机和激光印刷机编写、印刷书籍等) zhuōmiàn chūbǎn.

desolate /ˈdesələt/ *adj* 1 荒芜〔蕪〕的 huāngwúde; 无〔無〕人居住的 wúrén jūzhù de. 2 孤寂的 gūjìde; 凄凉的 qīliángde. **desolation** /ˌdesəˈleɪʃn/ *n* [U].

despair /dɪˈspeə(r)/ *n* [U] 绝望 juéwàng. **despair** *v* [I] (*of*) 绝望 juéwàng; 丧〔喪〕失信心 sàngshī xìnxīn: *~ of ever getting better* 对病情好转已不抱希望.

despatch = DISPATCH.

desperate /ˈdespərət/ *adj* 1 绝望的 juéwàngde; 不顾〔顧〕一切的 búgù yíqiè de. 2 孤注一掷〔擲〕的 gū zhù yí zhì de: *a ~ attempt to save her* 孤注一掷去救她. 3 极〔極〕需要的 jí xūyào de: *~ for money* 极需要钱. 4 危急的 wēijíde: *a ~ situation* 危急的形势. **desperately** *adv*. **desperation** /ˌdespəˈreɪʃn/ *n* [U].

despicable /dɪˈspɪkəbl/ *adj* 可鄙的 kěbǐde; 卑鄙的 bēibǐde.

despise /dɪˈspaɪz/ *v* [T] 鄙视 bǐshì; 看不起 kànbùqǐ.

despite /dɪˈspaɪt/ *prep* 尽〔儘〕管 jǐnguǎn: *still a clear thinker, ~ his old age* 尽管年纪大了, 他仍然是一位头脑清楚的思想家.

despondent /dɪˈspɒndənt/ *adj* 沮丧〔喪〕的 jǔsàngde; 失望的 shīwàngde. **despondency** /-dənsɪ/ *n* [U]. **despondently** *adv*.

despot /ˈdespɒt/ *n* [C] 专〔專〕制统治者 zhuānzhì tǒngzhìzhě; 暴君 bàojūn. **despotic** /dɪˈspɒtɪk/ *adj* 暴君的 bàojūnde; 暴虐的 bàonüède.

dessert /dɪˈzɜːt/ *n* [C]甜食(正餐的最后一道菜) tiánshí. **des**ˈ**sert-spoon** *n* [C] 点〔點〕心匙 diǎnxīnchí; 中匙 zhōngchí.

destination /ˌdestɪˈneɪʃn/ *n* [C] 目的地 mùdìdì.

destined /ˈdestɪnd/ *adj* 1 打算使成为〔爲〕的 dǎsuàn shǐ chéngwéi de; 注定的 zhùdìngde: *~ to become famous* 注定要成名. 2 *for* 去到某一目的地的 qùdào mǒuyí mùdìdìde.

destiny /ˈdestɪnɪ/ *n* [*pl* -ies] 1 [C]天命 tiānmìng; 定数〔數〕dìngshù. 2 [U] 命运〔運〕mìngyùn.

destitute /ˈdestɪtjuːt; *US* -tuːt/ *adj* 赤贫的 chìpínde. **destitution** /ˌdestɪˈtjuːʃn; *US* -ˈtuː-/ *n* [U].

destroy /dɪˈstrɔɪ/ *v* [T] 1 破坏〔壞〕pòhuài; 毁坏 huǐhuài; 摧毁 cuīhuǐ. 2 杀〔殺〕死(动物)(因其生病不能保留) shāsǐ. **destroyer** *n* [C] (a) 破坏者 pòhuàizhě; 起破坏作用的东西 qǐ pòhuài zuòyòng de dōngxi. (b) 驱〔驅〕逐舰〔艦〕qūzhújiàn.

destruction /dɪˈstrʌkʃn/ *n* [U] 破坏〔壞〕pòhuài; 毁灭〔滅〕huǐmiè. **destructive** /-ktɪv/

adj 破坏的 pòhuàide；破坏成性的 pòhuài chéngxìngde.

detach /dɪˈtætʃ/ *v* [T] 分开〔開〕fēnkāi；拆开 chāikāi. **detached** *adj* (a)（房屋）独〔獨〕立的 dúlìde.（b）超然的 chāoránde；公正的 gōngzhèngde. **detachment** *n* (a) [U] 超然 chāorán；公正 gōngzhèng.（b）[C] 分遣队〔隊〕fēnqiǎnduì；支队 zhīduì.

detail[1] /ˈdiːteɪl; *US* dɪˈteɪl/ *n* [C, U] 细节〔節〕xìjié；详情 xiángqíng：*describe sth in* ～ 详细描述某事.

detail[2] /ˈdiːteɪl; *US* dɪˈteɪl/ *v* [T] **1** 详细叙述 xiángxì xùshù；细说 xìshuō. **2** 派遣 pàiqiǎn.

detain /dɪˈteɪn/ *v* [T] 扣留 kòuliú；拘留 jūliú；耽搁 dānge. **detainee** /ˌdiːteɪˈniː/ *n* [C]（尤指因政治原因）被拘留者 bèi jūliú zhě.

detect /dɪˈtekt/ *v* [T] 发〔發〕现 fāxiàn；发觉〔覺〕fājué；侦察 zhēnchá. **detection** *n* [U]. **detective** *n* [C]（尤指警方的）侦查员 zhēncháyuán. **detector** *n* [C] 探测器 tàncèqì.

detention /dɪˈtenʃn/ *n* **1** [U] 拘留 jūliú；关〔關〕押 guānyā. **2**（处罚学生的）课后〔後〕留校 kèhòu liúxiào.

deter /dɪˈtɜː(r)/ *v* [-rr-] [T] (*from*) 阻止 zǔzhǐ；使不敢 shǐ bùgǎn；吓〔嚇〕住 xiàzhù.

detergent /dɪˈtɜːdʒənt/ *n* [C, U] 去垢剂〔劑〕qùgòujì；清洁〔潔〕剂 qīngjiéjì.

deteriorate /dɪˈtɪərɪəreɪt/ *v* [I] 恶〔惡〕化 èhuà；败坏〔壞〕bàihuài：*His health* ～*d*. 他的健康状况恶化. **deterioration** /dɪˌtɪərɪəˈreɪʃn/ *n* [U].

determination /dɪˌtɜːmɪˈneɪʃn/ [U, C] **1** 决心 juéxīn：*a* ～ *to improve one's English* 提高英语水平的决心. **2** 决定 juédìng.

determine /dɪˈtɜːmɪn/ *v* **1** [T] 是…的决定因素 shì …de juédìng yīnsù：*Our living standards are* ～*d by our income*. 我们的收入决定了我们的生活水平. **2** [T] 查明 cháming：～ *what happened* 查明发生的事. **3** [T] 决定 juédìng：～ *party policy* 决定党的政策. **4** [T] [正式用语] 决心(做) juéxīn. **determined** *adj* 决意的 juéyìde：～*d to win* 决心取胜.

deterrent /dɪˈterənt; *US* -ˈtɜː-/ *n* [C] 威慑〔懾〕因素 wēishè yīnsù：*the nuclear* ～ 核威慑.

detest /dɪˈtest/ *v* [T] 痛恨 tònghèn；憎恶〔惡〕zèngwù. **detestable** *adj* 令人厌〔厭〕恶的 lìng rén yànwù de.

dethrone /dɪˈθrəʊn/ *v* [T] 废〔廢〕黜 fèichù.

detonate /ˈdetəneɪt/ *v* [I, T]（使）爆炸 bàozhà. **detonation** /ˌdetəˈneɪʃn/ *n* [C, U] **detonator** *n* [C] 起爆剂〔劑〕qǐbàojì；雷管 léiguǎn.

detour /ˈdiːtʊə(r); *US* dɪˈtʊər/ *n* [C] 弯〔彎〕路 wānlù；绕〔繞〕道 ràodào：*make a* ～ *round the floods* 围着洪水绕道走.

detract /dɪˈtrækt/ *v* [I] *from* 贬低 biǎndī；减损(价值、名誉等) jiǎnsǔn.

detriment /ˈdetrɪmənt/ *n* [U] 损害 sǔnhài；损伤〔傷〕sǔnshāng：*to the* ～ *of her health* 损害她的健康. *without* ～ *to her health* 不损害她的健康. **detrimental** /ˌdetrɪˈmentl/ *adj* (*to*) 有害的 yǒuhàide；有损的 yǒusǔnde.

deuce /djuːs; *US* duːs/ *n* [C]（网球赛中的）40 平 sìshí píng.

devalue /ˌdiːˈvæljuː/ *v* [T] 使(货币)贬值 shǐ biǎnzhí. **devaluation** /ˌdiːvæljʊˈeɪʃn/ *n* [C, U].

devastate /ˈdevəsteɪt/ *v* [T] 破坏〔壞〕pòhuài；摧毁 cuīhuǐ：[喻] ～*d by his death* 因他的死而痛不欲生. **devastation** /ˌdevəˈsteɪʃn/ *n* [U].

develop /dɪˈveləp/ *v* **1** [I, T]（使）成长〔長〕chéngzhǎng；发〔發〕展 fāzhǎn：*The argument* ～*ed into a fight*. 辩论发展成打斗. **2** [I, T] 显〔顯〕现(出) xiǎnxiàn；显露(出) xiǎnlù；开〔開〕始患(病) kāishǐ huàn：～ *a cough* 患咳嗽. **3** [T] [摄影] 使显影 shǐ xiǎnyǐng；显(影) xiǎn. **4** [T] 开发〔發〕利用(土地) kāifā lìyòng. **developer** *n* [C] 房地产〔產〕投资开发者 fángdìchǎn tóuzī kāifā zhě；房地产投资开发公司 fángdìchǎn tóuzī kāifā gōngsī. **development** *n* [U] (a) 发展 fāzhǎn；成长〔長〕chéngzhǎng；显影 xiǎnyǐng；开发 kāifā. (b) 新事件 xīn shìjiàn；新形势〔勢〕xīn xíngshì. (c) 新开发地 xīn kāifādì.

deviate /ˈdiːvɪeɪt/ *v* [I] *from* 偏离〔離〕piānlí；背离 bèilí. **deviation** /ˌdiːvɪˈeɪʃn/ *n* [C, U].

device /dɪˈvaɪs/ *n* [C] **1** 装〔裝〕置 zhuāngzhì；设备〔備〕shèbèi；器具 qìjù. **2** 手段 shǒuduàn；策略 cèlüè；诡计 guǐjì.

devil /ˈdevl/ *n* [C] **1 the Devil** 魔王 mówáng；撒旦 sādàn. **2** 魔鬼 móguǐ；恶〔惡〕魔 èmó. **3** [非正式用语] 调皮鬼 tiáopíguǐ；捣蛋鬼 dǎodànguǐ. **4** [习语] **devil's ˈadvocate** 故意反对〔對〕以引发〔發〕讨论〔論〕的人 gùyì fǎnduì yǐ yǐnfā tǎolùn de rén.

devious /ˈdiːvɪəs/ *adj* 狡猾的 jiǎohuáde；不正当〔當〕的 bú zhèngdàng de；歪门斜道的 wāimén xiédào de.

devise /dɪˈvaɪz/ *v* [T] 设计 shèjì；想出 xiǎngchū.

devoid /dɪˈvɔɪd/ *adj of* 缺乏的 quēfáde；没有的 méiyǒude：～ *of any ability* 没有一点能力的.

devolution /ˌdiːvəˈluːʃn; *US* ˌdev-/ *n* [U]（中央政府向地方政府的）权〔權〕力下放 quánlì xiàfàng.

D

devote /dɪˈvəʊt/ *v* [T] *to* 把…奉献〔獻〕给… bǎ…fèngxiàn gěi…. **devoted** *adj* (*to*) 热〔熱〕心的 rèxīnde; 忠诚的 zhōngchéngde; 虔诚的 qiánchéngde. **devotee** /ˌdevəˈtiː/ *n* [C] 热心的人 rèxīnde rén; 信徒 xìntú. **devotion** /dɪˈvəʊʃn/ *n* (a) [U] 忠诚 zhōngchéng; 献身 xiànshēn; 热〔熱〕爱〔愛〕rè'ài. (b) [C, 常作 pl] 祈祷〔禱〕qídǎo.

devour /dɪˈvaʊə(r)/ *v* [T] 1 狼吞虎咽地吃 láng tūn hǔ yàn de chī. 2[喻] 挥霍 huīhuò; 耗尽〔盡〕hàojìn; 吸引 xīyǐn; 毁灭〔滅〕huǐmiè: *forests ~ed by fire* 大火毁灭了的森林.

devout /dɪˈvaʊt/ *adj* 1 虔诚的 qiánchéngde; 虔敬的 qiánjìngde. 2 诚恳〔懇〕的 chéngkěnde; 衷心的 zhōngxīnde.

dew /djuː; *US* duː/ *n* [U] 露水 lùshuǐ; 露 lù. **dewy** *adj*. ˈ**dewdrop** *n* [C] 露珠 lùzhū.

dexterity /ˌdekˈsterətɪ/ *n* [U] (手)灵〔靈〕巧的 língqiǎode; 敏捷的 mǐnjiéde. **dexterous, dextrous** /ˈdekstrəs/ *adj*.

diabetes /ˌdaɪəˈbiːtɪz/ *n* [U] 糖尿病 tángniàobìng. **diabetic** /ˌdaɪəˈbetɪk/ *adj*, *n* [C] 糖尿病的 tángniàobìngde; 糖尿病人 tángniàobìng rén.

diabolical /ˌdaɪəˈbɒlɪkl/ *adj* 1 凶〔兇〕暴的 xiōngbàode; 残暴的 cánbàode. 2[非正式用语] 糟透的 zāotòude: ~ *weather* 糟透了的天气.

diagnose /ˌdaɪəgˈnəʊz/ *v* [T] 诊断〔斷〕(疾病) zhěnduàn; 对〔對〕(错误等)作判断 duì zuò pànduàn. **diagnosis** /ˌdaɪəgˈnəʊsɪs/ *n* [C, U] [*pl* **-noses** / -siːz/] 诊断 zhěnduàn; 判断 pànduàn. **diagnostic** /ˌdaɪəgˈnɒstɪk/ *adj*.

diagonal /daɪˈægənl/ *n* [C], *adj* 对〔對〕角线〔綫〕duìjiǎoxiàn; 对角线的 duìjiǎoxiànde. **diagonally** *adv*.

diagram /ˈdaɪəgræm/ *n* [C] 图〔圖〕解 tújiě. **diagramatic** /ˌdaɪəgrəˈmætɪk/ *adj*.

dial /ˈdaɪəl/ *n* [C] 1 表〔錶〕面 biǎomiàn; 钟〔鐘〕面 zhōngmiàn; 罗〔羅〕盘〔盤〕面板 luópán miànbǎn. 2(电话)拨〔撥〕号〔號〕盘〔盤〕bōhàopán. **dial** *v* [-ll-; *US* -l-] [I, T] 给…打电〔電〕话 gěi…dǎ diànhuà; 拨(电话号码) bō. **dialling tone** *n* [C] (电话)拨号音 bōhàoyīn.

dialect /ˈdaɪəlekt/ *n* [C, U] 方言 fāngyán: *the Yorkshire* ~ 约克郡方言.

dialogue (美语 **-log**) /ˈdaɪəlɒg; *US* -lɔːg/ *n* 1 [U] (国家、组织之间的)对〔對〕话 duìhuà: ~ *between the superpowers* 超级大国之间的对话. 2 [C, U] (戏剧中的)对白 duìbái; (生活中的)谈话 tánhuà.

dialysis /daɪˈælɪsɪs/ *n* [U] 血液透析 xuèyè tòuxī.

diameter /daɪˈæmɪtə(r)/ *n* [C] (圆的)直径〔徑〕zhíjìng.

diametrically /ˌdaɪəˈmetrɪklɪ/ *adv* 完全地 wánquánde; 全然地 quánránde: ~ *opposed* 完全相反.

diamond /ˈdaɪəmənd/ *n* 1 [C, U] 金刚〔剛〕石 jīngāngshí; 钻〔鑽〕石 zuànshí. 2 [C] 菱形 língxíng. 3 [C] (纸牌)方块〔塊〕牌 fāngkuàipái. ˌ**diamond** ˈ**jubilee** *n* [C] (重大事件的)六十周〔週〕年纪念 liùshí zhōunián jìniàn.

diaper /ˈdaɪəpə(r); *US* 亦作 ˈdaɪpər/ *n* [C] [美语] 一次性尿布 yícìxìng niàobù.

diaphragm /ˈdaɪəfræm/ *n* [C] 1 [解剖] 膈 gé. 2 膜片 mópiàn; 振动〔動〕膜 zhèndòngmó.

diarrhoea (美语 **-rrhea**) /ˌdaɪəˈrɪə/ *n* [U] 腹泻〔瀉〕fùxiè; 泻肚 xièdù.

diary /ˈdaɪərɪ/ *n* [C] [*pl* **-ies**] 日记 rìjì; 日记簿 rìjìbù: *keep a* ~ 保持记日记.

dice /daɪs/ *n* [C] [*pl* **dice**] 骰子 shǎizi. **dice** *v* [T] 1 将〔將〕…(食物)切成小方块〔塊〕jiāng…qiē chéng xiǎofāngkuài. 2[习语] **dice with** ˈ**death** 冒生命危险〔險〕mào shēngmìng wēixiǎn.

dictate /dɪkˈteɪt; *US* ˈdɪkteɪt/ *v* [I, T] 1 (使)听〔聽〕写〔寫〕tīngxiě. 2 命令 mìnglìng; 支配 zhīpèi. **dictation** /-ˈteɪʃn/ *n* 1 [U] 听写 tīngxiě. 2 [C] 听写的一段文字 tīngxiěde yíduàn wénzì.

dictator /ˌdɪkˈteɪtə(r); *US* ˈdɪkteɪtər/ *n* [贬] 独〔獨〕裁者 dúcáizhě. **dictatorial** /ˌdɪktəˈtɔːrɪəl/ *adj*. **dictatorship** *n* [C, U] 独裁政府 dúcái zhèngfǔ; 独裁国〔國〕家 dúcái guójiā; 专〔專〕政 zhuānzhèng.

diction /ˈdɪkʃn/ *n* [U] 措辞 cuòcí; 用词风〔風〕格 yòng cí fēnggé.

dictionary /ˈdɪkʃənrɪ; *US* -nerɪ/ *n* [C] [*pl* **-ies**] 词典 cídiǎn; 字典 zìdiǎn.

did *pt* of DO.

didn't did not. ⇨DO.

die[1] /daɪ/ *n* [C] 印模 yìnmó; 冲模 chòngmó; 钢〔鋼〕型 gāngxíng.

die[2] /daɪ/ *v* [*pres part* **dying** /ˈdaɪɪŋ/] [I] 1 死 sǐ; 死亡 sǐwáng. 2[喻] 消亡 xiāowáng; 灭〔滅〕亡 mièwáng; 消失 xiāoshī: *love that will never* ~ 永不消亡的爱情. 3 *for*; *to* 渴望 kěwàng; 切望 qièwàng: *dying for a drink* 渴得要命. *dying to tell her* 急着想告诉她. 4[习语] **die laughing** [非正式用语] 差点〔點〕笑死 chàdiǎn xiàosǐ. 5 [短语动词] **die away** 变〔變〕弱 biànruò; 逐渐消失 zhújiàn xiāoshī. **die out** 死光 sǐguāng; 绝种〔種〕juézhǒng; 灭绝 mièjué.

diesel /ˈdiːzl/ *n* 1 [C] 内燃机〔機〕车〔車〕nèirán jīchē; 柴油车 cháiyóuchē. 2 (亦作 ˈ**diesel oil**) 柴油 cháiyóu. ˈ**diesel engine** *n* [C] 内燃机 nèiránjī.

diet /ˈdaɪət/ *n* 1 [C, U] 日常饮食 rìcháng yǐnshí; 日常食物 rìcháng shíwù. 2 [C] 减肥饮食 jiǎnféi yǐnshí: *be/go on a* ~ 实行减肥节食.

diet *v* [I] 吃减肥饮食 chī jiǎnféi yǐnshí.

differ /ˈdɪfə(r)/ *v* [I] 1 (*from*) 不相同 bù xiāngtóng. 2 意见不一致 yìjiàn bù yízhì: *I am sorry to ~ with you on that.* 我很抱歉，在这个问题上我同你意见不一致. **difference** /ˈdɪfrəns/ *n* 1 [C, U] 差别 chābié; 差异〔異〕chāyì: *the ~ in their ages* 他们年龄的差异. 2 [sing] 差距 chājù; 差额 chā'é: *The ~ between 7 and 18 is 11.* 7 和 18 的差数是 11. 3 [C] 意见分歧 yìjiàn fēnqí. 4 [习语] **not make any / the slightest difference** 不重要 bú zhòngyào; 不要紧〔緊〕bú yàojǐn.

different /ˈdɪfrənt/ *adj* 1 (*from*; [非正式用语] *to*; [美语] *than*) 不同的 bùtóngde; 相异〔異〕的 xiāngyìde. 2 分别的 fēnbiéde; 各别的 gèbiéde: *several ~ people* 几个各不相同的人.

differentiate /ˌdɪfəˈrenʃɪeɪt/ *v* [I, T] *between A and B; A from B* 区〔區〕别 qūbié; 区分 qūfēn.

difficult /ˈdɪfɪkəlt/ *adj* 1 困难〔難〕的 kùnnande; 难的 nánde: *find sth ~ to understand* 发现某事难以理解. 2 (人) 难对〔對〕付的 nán duìfu de. **difficulty** *n* [*pl* -ies] 1 [C] 难懂的事物 nándǒngde shìwù. 2 [U] 困难 kùnnan; 困难性 kùnnanxìng.

diffident /ˈdɪfɪdənt/ *adj* 缺乏信心的 quēfá xìnxīn de; 羞怯的 xiūquède. **diffidence** /-dəns/ *n* [U].

diffuse /dɪˈfjuːz/ *v* [I, T] (使)(光线)漫射 mànshè. **diffuse** /dɪˈfjuːs/ *adj* 1 扩〔擴〕散的 kuòsànde; 散开的 sànkāide: *~ light* 漫射光. 2 冗长〔長〕的 rǒngchángde. **diffusion** /-uːʒn/ *n* [U].

dig[1] /dɪg/ *n* [C] 1 推 tuī; 刺 cì: *a ~ in the ribs* 对肋骨部位的一杵. 2 挖苦 wākǔ; 讽〔諷〕刺话 fěngcìhuà: *That was a ~ at Ray.* 那是对莱的挖苦. 3 考古挖掘 kǎogǔ wājué. 4 **digs** [pl] [英国英语] 住宿处〔處〕zhùsùchù.

dig[2] /dɪg/ *v* [-gg-; *pt*, *pp* dug /dʌg/] 1 [I, T] 掘 jué; 掘进〔進〕juéjìn; 挖(洞) wā. 2 [T] 掘取 juéqǔ: *~ potatoes* 挖马铃薯. 3 [短语动词] **dig sb/sth out (of sth)** (a) 从〔從〕…挖出 cóng…wāchū. (b) [非正式用语] 找出 zhǎochū. **dig sth up** 挖出 wāchū; 找出 zhǎochū.

digest[1] /dɪˈdʒest, daɪ-/ *v* 1 (a) [T] 消化(食物) xiāohuà. (b) [I] (食物) 被消化 bèi xiāohuà. 2 [T] 领会〔會〕lǐnghuì; 透彻〔徹〕了〔瞭〕解 tòuchè liáojiě; 融会贯通 róng huì guàn tōng.

digest[2] /ˈdaɪdʒest/ *n* [C] 摘要 zhāiyào; 文摘 wénzhāi.

digit /ˈdɪdʒɪt/ *n* [C] 1 数〔數〕字(0 到 9 中的任何一个数字) shùzì. 2 [正式用语] 手指 shǒuzhǐ; 脚趾 jiǎozhǐ. **digital** *adj* 数字的 shùzìde; 计数的 jìshùde: *~al watch* 数字显示式手表. *~al camera* 数码相机〔機〕. *~al television* 数字电〔電〕视.

dignified /ˈdɪgnɪfaɪd/ *adj* 高贵的 gāoguìde; 尊贵的 zūnguìde.

dignitary /ˈdɪgnɪtərɪ; US -terɪ/ *n* [C] [*pl* -ies] [正式用语] 职〔職〕位高的人 zhíwèi gāo de rén.

dignity /ˈdɪgnətɪ/ *n* 1 [U] (态度、举止等的) 庄〔莊〕严〔嚴〕zhuāngyán; 尊严 zūnyán. 2 高贵 gāoguì; 尊贵 zūnguì. 3 [习语] **beneath one's dignity** 有失身份 yǒu shī shēnfen.

digress /daɪˈgres/ *v* [I] (*from*) 离〔離〕题 lítí. **digression** /-ˈgreʃn/ *n* [U, C].

digs ⇨ DIG[1] 4.

dike (亦作 **dyke**) /daɪk/ *n* [C] 1 堤 dī; 堤防 dīfáng; 堰 yàn. 2 排水道 páishuǐdào; 沟〔溝〕gōu; 渠 qú.

dilapidated /dɪˈlæpɪdeɪtɪd/ *adj* (建筑物) 破旧〔舊〕的 pòjiùde; 坍坏〔壞〕的 tānhuàide.

dilate /daɪˈleɪt/ *v* [I, T] (尤指眼睛)(使) 扩〔擴〕大 kuòdà; (使) 张〔張〕大 zhāngdà.

dilemma /dɪˈlemə/ *n* [C] 进〔進〕退两难〔難〕的境地 jìntuì liǎng nán de jìngdì; 困境 kùnjìng.

diligent /ˈdɪlɪdʒənt/ *adj* 勤奋〔奮〕的 qínfènde; 勤勉的 qínmiǎnde: *a ~ worker* 勤奋的工人. **diligence** /-dʒəns/ *n* [U]. **diligently** *adv*.

dilute /daɪˈljuːt/ *v* [T] (*with*) 使变〔變〕淡 shǐ biàndàn; 冲淡 chōngdàn; 稀释〔釋〕xīshì. **dilution** /-ˈluːʃn/ *n* [U, C].

dim /dɪm/ *adj* [~mer, ~mest] 1 暗的 ànde; 暗淡的 àndànde; 不明亮的 bù míngliàng de: *in a ~ light* 在暗淡的光线中. 2 看不清楚的 kàn bù qīngchu de; 模糊的 móhude. 3 [喻] 不清晰的 bù qīngxīde: *~ memories* 模糊的记忆. 4 [非正式用语] 迟〔遲〕钝的 chídùnde. 5 [习语] **take a dim view of sth** 对〔對〕…抱悲观〔觀〕、怀〔懷〕疑态〔態〕度 duì…bào bēiguān、huáiyí tàidù. **dim** *v* [-mm-] [I, T] (使) 变〔變〕暗淡 biàn àndàn; (使) 变模糊 biàn móhu. **dimly** *adv*. **dimness** *n* [U].

dime /daɪm/ *n* [C] (美国、加拿大) 一角钱〔錢〕硬币〔幣〕yìjiǎoqián yìngbì.

dimension /dɪˈmenʃn/ *n* 1 [C] 长〔長〕度 chángdù; 宽度 kuāndù; 高度 gāodù. 2 **dimensions** [pl] 规模 guīmó; 程度 chéngdù; 大小 dàxiǎo: *the ~s of the problem* 问题的程度. 3 [C] [喻] 方面 fāngmiàn. **dimensional** /-ʃənəl/ (构成复合形容词) …维的 …wéide: *two-~al* 二维的.

diminish /dɪˈmɪnɪʃ/ *v* [I, T] 减小 jiǎnxiǎo; 减少 jiǎnshǎo; 缩小 suōxiǎo: *Our chances of success are ~ing.* 我们成功的机会正在减少.

diminutive /dɪˈmɪnjʊtɪv/ *adj* 微小的 wēi-

D

xiǎode.

dimple /ˈdɪmpl/ *n* [C] 酒窝〔窩〕jiǔwō；笑窝 xiàowō；笑靥〔靨〕xiàoyè.

din /dɪn/ *n* [U, sing] 喧闹声〔聲〕xuānnào-shēng；嘈杂〔雜〕声 cáozáshēng. **din** *v* [-nn-] [短语动词] **din sth into sb** 反复〔復〕告诉（某人）fǎnfù gàosù.

dine /daɪn/ *v* 1 [I] [正式用语]吃饭 chīfàn；进〔進〕餐 jìncān. 2 [短语动词] **dine out** （尤指在餐馆、饭店）外出进餐 wàichū jìncān. ˈ**dining-car** *n* [C] （火车）餐车〔車〕cānchē. ˈ**dining-room** *n* [C] 餐室 cānshì；餐厅〔廳〕cāntīng.

D

dinghy /ˈdɪŋgɪ/ *n* [C] [*pl* -ies] 小艇 xiǎo-tǐng；橡皮筏 xiàngpífá.

dingy /ˈdɪndʒɪ/ *adj* [-ier, -iest] 脏〔髒〕的 zāngde；褴〔襤〕褛〔褸〕的 lánlǚde；邋遢的 lātā-de. **dinginess** *n* [U].

dinner /ˈdɪnə(r)/ *n* [C, U] 正餐 zhèngcān. ˈ**dinner-jacket** *n* [C] 男式晚礼〔禮〕服 nánshì wǎnlǐfú.

dinosaur /ˈdaɪnəsɔː(r)/ *n* [C] 恐龙〔龍〕kǒnglóng.

diocese /ˈdaɪəsɪs/ *n* [C] 主教管区〔區〕zhǔ-jiào guǎnqū.

dip /dɪp/ *v* [-pp-] 1 [T] 沾 zhān；蘸 zhàn；浸 jìn. 2 [I] 落下 luòxià：*The sun ~ped below the horizon*. 太阳落到地平线下面. 3 [T] 把（光束）调低 bǎ tiáodī：~ *the headlights of a car* 把汽车前灯的远光调为近光. 4 [短语动词] **dip into sth** (a) 动〔動〕用（储蓄等）dòng-yòng. (b) 随〔隨〕便翻阅 suíbiàn fānyuè. **dip** *n* 1 [C] 沾 zhān；蘸 zhàn；浸 jìn. 2 [C] 短时〔時〕的游泳 duǎnshíde yóuyǒng. 3 [C, U] 奶油沙司 nǎiyóu shāsī. 4 [C] 下坡 xiàpō.

diphtheria /dɪfˈθɪərɪə/ *n* [U] [医]白喉 bái-hóu.

diphthong /ˈdɪfθɒŋ; *US* -θɔːŋ/ *n* [C] 双〔雙〕元音 shuāngyuányīn；复〔複〕合元音 fùhé yuányīn.

diploma /dɪˈpləʊmə/ *n* [C] 毕〔畢〕业〔業〕证〔證〕书〔書〕bìyè zhèngshū；文凭〔憑〕wénpíng.

diplomacy /dɪˈpləʊməsɪ/ *n* [U] 1 外交 wài-jiāo. 2 外交手腕 wàijiāo shǒuwàn；交际〔際〕手腕 jiāojì shǒuwàn.

diplomat /ˈdɪpləmæt/ *n* [C] 外交家 wàijiāo-jiā；外交人员 wàijiāo rényuán；外交官 wàijiāo-guān. **diplomatic** /dɪpləˈmætɪk/ *adj* 1 外交的 wàijiāode；外交上的 wàijiāo shangde：*work in the ~ic service* 外交部门的工作. 2 有手腕的 yǒu shǒuwàn de；策略的 cèlüède. **diplomatically** *adv*.

dire /ˈdaɪə(r)/ *adj* 可怕的 kěpàde；悲惨〔慘〕的 bēicǎnde.

direct[1] /dɪˈrekt, daɪ-/ *adj* 1 笔〔筆〕直的 bǐ-zhíde；笔直前进〔進〕的 bǐzhí qiánjìn de：*a ~ route* 笔直的路 2 直系〔係〕的 zhíxìde；直接的 zhíjiēde：*a ~ result* 直接的结果. 3 直率的 zhíshuàide；直截了当〔當〕的 zhíjiéliǎodàngde；坦白的 tǎnbáide. 4 正好的 zhènghǎode：*the ~ opposite* 正好相反. **direct** *adv* 径〔徑〕直地 jìngzhíde；直接地 zhíjiēde：*travel ~ to Rome* 直接去罗马. **direct** ˈ**current** *n* [U] 直流电〔電〕zhíliúdiàn. **direct** ˈ**debit** *n* [C] （会计）直接借记 zhíjiē jièjì. **directness** *n* [U]. **direct** ˈ**object** *n* [C] [语法]直接宾〔賓〕语 zhí-jiē bīnyǔ. **direct** ˈ**speech** *n* [U] [语法]直接引语 zhíjiē yǐnyǔ.

direct[2] /dɪˈrekt, daɪ-/ *v* [T] 1 指引 zhǐyǐn；指点〔點〕zhǐdiǎn：*Can you ~ me to the station, please?* 请问到车站怎么走? 2 指导〔導〕zhǐdǎo；管理 guǎnlǐ；支配 zhīpèi：~ *a project* 监督一个工程. ~ *a film* 导演一部影片. 3 把…对〔對〕准〔準〕某一目标〔標〕bǎ…duì-zhǔn mǒu yí mùbiāo；使转〔轉〕向 shǐ zhuǎn-xiàng：~ *one's attention to a more important matter* 把注意力转向更重要的问题. 4 [正式用语]命令 mìnglìng；指示 zhǐshì.

direction /dɪˈrekʃn, daɪ-/ *n* 1 [C] 方向 fāngxiàng；方位 fāngwèi：*run off in the opposite ~* 向相反的方向逃走. 2 **directions** [pl] 说明 shuōmíng；指引 zhǐyǐn. 3 [U] 管理 guǎnlǐ；指挥〔揮〕zhǐhuī：*under my ~* 在我的指导下.

directive /dɪˈrektɪv, daɪ-/ *n* [C] [正式用语]指示 zhǐshì；命令 mìnglìng.

directly /dɪˈrektlɪ, daɪ-/ *adv* 1 直接地 zhí-jiēde；正好地 zhènghǎode. 2 立即 lìjí；马上 mǎ-shàng. **directly** *conj* 一当〔當〕yìdāng：*I came ~ I knew*. 我一知道就来了.

director /dɪˈrektə(r), daɪ-/ *n* [C] 1 董事 dǒngshì；处〔處〕长〔長〕chùzhǎng；署长 shǔ-zhǎng；总〔總〕监〔監〕zǒngjiān. 2 导〔導〕演 dǎo-yǎn；指挥〔揮〕zhǐhuī. **directorship** *n* [U] 董事、导演等的职〔職〕位 dǒngshì、dǎoyǎn děng de zhíwèi.

directory /dɪˈrektərɪ, daɪ-/ *n* [C] [*pl* -ies] 1 名录〔錄〕（姓名地址录、电话号码簿等）mínglù：*a telephone ~* 电话号码簿. 2 （计算机中的）目录 mùlù.

dirt /dɜːt/ *n* [U] 1 脏〔髒〕物 zāngwù；污垢 wūgòu. 2 [非正式用语]下流话 xiàliúhuà；丑〔醜〕闻 chǒuwén. 3 [非正式用语]粪〔糞〕便 fènbiàn：*dog ~ on my shoe* 我鞋上的狗屎. **dirt** ˈ**cheap** *adj* [非正式用语]非常便宜的 fēicháng piányì de.

dirty /ˈdɜːtɪ/ *adj* [-ier, -iest] 1 脏〔髒〕的 zāngde：~ *water* 脏水. 2 残〔殘〕忍的 cán-rěnde；不公正的 bù gōngzhèng de：*a ~ trick* 鬼把戏. 3 下流的 xiàliúde；色情的 sè-qíngde：*a ~ joke* 下流的玩笑. 4 不许可的 bù xǔkěde：*give sb a ~ look* 给某人不许可的眼

色.dirty *v* [*pt*, *pp* -ied] [T] 弄脏 nòng zāng. **dirty 'bomb** *n* [C] (有放射性微粒的) 脏弹〔彈〕zāngdàn.

disable /dɪs'eɪbl/ *v* [T] 使无〔無〕能力 shǐ wú nénglì; 使伤〔傷〕残〔殘〕shǐ shāngcán. **disability** /ˌdɪsə'bɪlətɪ/ *n* [*pl* -ies] **1** [C] 导〔導〕致无〔無〕能力的事物 dǎozhì wú nénglìde shìwù; 残〔殘〕疾 cánjí. **2** [U] [正式用语] 伤〔傷〕残 shāngcán; 残废〔廢〕cánfèi. **disabled** *adj*. **disablement** *n* [U].

disabuse /ˌdɪsə'bjuːz/ *v* [T] *of* 使省悟 shǐ xǐngwù.

disadvantage /ˌdɪsəd'vɑːntɪdʒ; *US* -væn-/ *n* [C] **1** 不利条〔條〕件 búlì tiáojiàn. **2** [习语] **to sb's disadvantage** [正式用语] 对〔對〕某人不利 duì mǒurén búlì. **disadvantaged** *adj* 下层〔層〕社会〔會〕的 xiàcéng shèhuì de. **disadvantageous** /ˌdɪsædvɑːn'teɪdʒəs; *US* -væn- / *adj*.

disagree /ˌdɪsə'griː/ *v* [I] **1** 不同意 bù tóngyì: *I ~ with you*. 我不同意你的意见. *I ~ with what you say*. 我不同意你所说的. **2** 不一致 bù yízhì; 不符 bùfú. **3** [短语动词] **disagree with sb** (食物)使感到不舒服 shǐ gǎndào bù shūfu. **disagreeable** *adj* 令人不快的 lìng rén búkuài de. **disagreement** *n* [C, U] 意见不一致 yìjiàn bù yízhì.

disappear /ˌdɪsə'pɪə(r)/ *v* [I] **1** 不见 bújiàn. **2** 消失 xiāoshī. **disappearance** *n* [C, U].

disappoint /ˌdɪsə'pɔɪnt/ *v* [T] 使失望 shǐ shīwàng. **disappointed** *adj* 失望的 shīwàngde; 沮丧〔喪〕的 jǔsàngde. **disappointing** *adj*. **disappointingly** *adv*. **disappointment** *n* **1** [U] 失望 shīwàng; 扫〔掃〕兴〔興〕sǎoxìng. **2** [C] 令人失望的人或事物 lìng rén shīwàngde rén huò shìwù.

disapprove /ˌdɪsə'pruːv/ *v* [I] (*of*) 不赞〔讚〕成 bú zànchéng; 不同意 bù tóngyì. **disapproval** *n* [U].

disarm /dɪs'ɑːm/ *v* **1** [T] 缴…的械 jiǎo…de xiè; 解除武装〔裝〕jiěchú wǔzhuāng. **2** [I] (国家)裁军 cáijūn. **3** [T] 使消除怒气〔氣〕、敌〔敵〕意等 shǐ xiāochú nùqì、díyì děng. **disarmament** *n* [U] 裁军 cáijūn.

disarray /ˌdɪsə'reɪ/ *n* [U] [正式用语] 混乱〔亂〕hùnluàn; 紊乱 wěnluàn: *in ~* 混乱地; 凌乱地.

disassociate = DISSOCIATE.

disaster /dɪ'zɑːstə(r); *US* -'zæs-/ *n* [C] 灾〔災〕难〔難〕zāinàn; 祸〔禍〕患 huòhuàn. **disastrous** /dɪ'zɑːstrəs; *US* -'zæs- / *adj*. **disastrously** *adv*.

disband /dɪs'bænd/ *v* [I, T] 解散 jiěsàn; 遣散 qiǎnsàn.

disbelieve /ˌdɪsbɪ'liːv/ *v* [T] 不相信 bù xiāngxìn; 怀〔懷〕疑 huáiyí. **disbelief** /-bɪ'liːf/ *n* [U] 不信 bú xìn; 怀疑 huáiyí.

disc (亦作, 尤用于美语 **disk**) /dɪsk / *n* [C] **1** 圆盘〔盤〕yuánpán; 圆面 yuánmiàn; 圆板 yuánbǎn. **2** 椎间盘 zhuījiānpán: *a slipped ~* 脱出的椎间盘. **'disc jockey** *n* [C] 广〔廣〕播电〔電〕台〔臺〕或迪斯科舞厅〔廳〕流行音乐〔樂〕唱片播放及介绍人 guǎngbōdiàntái huò dísikē wǔtīng liúxíng yīnyuè chàngpiàn bōfàng jí jièshào rén.

discard /dɪ'skɑːd/ *v* [T] 抛弃〔棄〕pāoqì; 遗弃 yíqì.

discern /dɪ'sɜːn/ *v* [T] [正式用语] 看出 kànchū; 辨出 biànchū. **discernible** *adj*. **discerning** *adj* [褒] 有眼力的 yǒu yǎnlì de. **discernment** *n* [U] 敏锐 mǐnruì; 精明 jīngmíng.

discharge /dɪs'tʃɑːdʒ/ *v* **1** [T] 释〔釋〕放 shìfàng; 允许离〔離〕开〔開〕yǔnxǔ líkāi. **2** [T] [正式用语] 履行(义务) lǚxíng. **3** [I, T] 排出(液体、气体等) páichū. **4** [T] (从船上)卸(货) xiè. **5** [T] [正式用语] 偿〔償〕付(债款) chángfù. **discharge** /'dɪstʃɑːdʒ / *n* **1** [U] 释放 shìfàng; 排出 páichū; 卸货 xièhuò; 放出 fàngchū. **2** [U, C] 流出物 liúchūwù, 排泄物 páixièwù.

disciple /dɪ'saɪpl/ *n* [C] 信徒 xìntú; 门徒 méntú; 追随〔隨〕者 zhuīsuízhě.

discipline /'dɪsɪplɪn/ *n* **1** (a) [U] (为服从、自我控制等而进行的) 训练〔練〕xùnliàn. (b) [U] 纪律 jìlǜ; 风〔風〕纪 fēngjì. **2** [U] 惩〔懲〕罚 chéngfá; 处〔處〕罚 chǔfá. **3** [C] [正式用语] 学〔學〕科 xuékē. **discipline** *v* [T] **1** 训导〔導〕xùndǎo. **2** 惩罚 chéngfá.

disclaim /dɪs'kleɪm/ *v* [T] [正式用语] 否认〔認〕(有…责任) fǒurèn.

disclose /dɪs'kləʊz/ *v* [T] (a) 透露 tòulù; 泄露 xièlòu. (b) 使显〔顯〕露 shǐ xiǎnlù. **disclosure** /-'kləʊʒə(r)/ *n* [U, C].

disco /'dɪskəʊ/ *n* [C] (亦作 **discotheque** /'dɪskətek/) *n* [C] [*pl* ~s] 迪斯科舞厅〔廳〕dísikē wǔtīng; 迪斯科舞会〔會〕dísikē wǔhuì.

discolour (美语 -or) /dɪs'kʌlə(r)/ *v* [I, T] (使)变〔變〕色 biànsè; (使)变污 biànwū. **discoloration** / ˌdɪskʌlə'reɪʃən / *n* [C, U].

discomfort /dɪs'kʌmfət/ *n* (a) [U] 不舒服 bù shūfu. (b) [C] 使人不舒服的事物 shǐ rén bù shūfu de shìwù.

disconcert /ˌdɪskən'sɜːt/ *v* [T] 使不安 shǐ bù'ān; 使仓〔倉〕惶失措 shǐ cānghuáng shīcuò.

disconnect /ˌdɪskə'nekt/ *v* [T] *A* (*from B*) 拆开〔開〕chāikāi; 断〔斷〕开 duànkāi; 使分离〔離〕shǐ fēnlí. **disconnected** *adj* (说话、写作) 不连贯的 bù liánguàn de; 凌乱〔亂〕的 língluànde; 无〔無〕条〔條〕理的 wú tiáolǐ de.

disconsolate /dɪs'kɒnsələt/ *adj* [正式用语] 忧〔憂〕郁〔鬱〕的 yōuyùde; 不愉快的 bù yú-

D

kuài de. **disconsolately** *adv*.

discontent /ˌdɪskən'tent/ *n* [U] (*with*) 不满意 bù mǎnyì. **discontented** *adj* 不满意的 bù mǎnyì de.

discontinue /ˌdɪskən'tɪnjuː/ *v* [T] [正式用语] 停止 tíngzhǐ; 中止 zhōngzhǐ; 中断〔斷〕 zhōngduàn.

discord /'dɪskɔːd/ *n* **1** [U] 不和 bùhé; 争吵 zhēngchǎo. **2** (a) [U] (音乐) 不协〔協〕和 bù xiéhé. (b) [C] (音乐) 不协和和弦 bù xiéhé héxián. **discordant** /dɪ'skɔːdənt/ *adj*.

D

discotheque = DISCO.

discount[1] /'dɪskaʊnt/ *n* [C] (价格) 折扣 zhékòu. **'discount card** *n* [C] 打折卡 dǎzhékǎ; 优〔優〕惠卡 yōuhuìkǎ.

discount[2] /dɪs'kaʊnt; *US* 'dɪskaʊnt/ *v* [T] 不信 búxìn; 看轻〔輕〕 kànqīng.

discourage /dɪ'skʌrɪdʒ/ *v* [T] **1** 使泄气〔氣〕 shǐ xièqì; 使失掉信心 shǐ shīdiào xìnxīn; 使沮丧〔喪〕 shǐ jǔsàng: *~d by failure* 因失败而失掉信心. **2** 劝〔勸〕阻 quànzǔ: *~ children from smoking* 劝阻孩子们不要吸烟. **discouragement** *n* [U, C].

discourse /'dɪskɔːs/ *n* [C, U] [正式用语] 演说 yǎnshuō; 讲〔講〕话 jiǎnghuà.

discourteous /dɪs'kɜːtɪəs/ *adj* [正式用语] 不客气〔氣〕的 bú kèqi de; 不礼〔禮〕貌的 bù lǐmào de. **discourteously** *adv*. **discourtesy** /-'kɜːtəsɪ/ *n* [U].

discover /dɪ'skʌvə(r)/ *v* [T] **1** 发〔發〕现 fāxiàn; 第一次了〔瞭〕解 dìyīcì liǎojiě. **2** 了解到 liǎojiě dào; 认〔認〕识〔識〕到 rènshi dào; 找到 zhǎodào. **discoverer** *n* [C]. **discovery** /dɪ'skʌvərɪ/ *n* [*pl* **-ies**] **1** [U] 发现 fāxiàn. **2** [C] 被发现的事物 bèi fāxiàn de shìwù.

discredit /dɪs'kredɪt/ *v* [T] **1** 败坏〔壞〕…的名声〔聲〕 bàihuài…de míngshēng. **2** 使不可置信 shǐ bùkě zhìxìn. **discredit** *n* [U] 丧〔喪〕失信誉〔譽〕 sàngshī xìnyù; 丧失名声 sàngshī míngshēng.

discreet /dɪ'skriːt/ *adj* 谨慎的 jǐnshènde; 思虑〔慮〕周全的 sīlǜ zhōuquán de. **discreetly** *adv*.

discrepancy /dɪ'skrepənsɪ/ *n* [C, U] [*pl* **-ies**] 不一致 bù yízhì; 差异〔異〕 chāyì; 不符 bùfú.

discretion /dɪ'skreʃn/ *n* [U] **1** 明智 míngzhì. **2** 处〔處〕理权〔權〕 chǔlǐquán: *use your own ~* 你自行决定.

discriminate /dɪ'skrɪmɪneɪt/ *v* [I] **1** (*between*) 区〔區〕别 qūbié; 区分 qūfēn; 辨别 biànbié. **2** *against / in favour of* 歧视(或优待) qíshì. **discriminating** *adj*. **discrimination** /dɪˌskrɪmɪ'neɪʃn/ *n* [U].

discus /'dɪskəs/ *n* [C] [体育] 铁〔鐵〕饼 tiěbǐng.

discuss /dɪ'skʌs/ *v* [T] 讨论 tǎolùn; 商讨 shāngtǎo. **discussion** *n* [C, U].

disdain /dɪs'deɪn/ *n* [U] 蔑视 mièshì; 轻〔輕〕视 qīngshì. **disdain** *v* [T] **1** 蔑视 mièshì; 轻视 qīngshì. **2** 不屑做(某事) bú xiè zuò. **disdainful** *adj*.

disease /dɪ'ziːz/ *n* [C, U] 疾病 jíbìng; 病 bìng. **diseased** *adj* 生病的 shēngbìngde; 有病的 yǒubìngde.

disembark /ˌdɪsɪm'bɑːk/ *v* [I] (*from*) 离〔離〕船上岸 lí chuán shàng'àn; 下飞〔飛〕机〔機〕 xià fēijī; 下公共汽车 xià gōnggòngqìchē. **disembarkation** /ˌdɪsembɑː'keɪʃn/ *n* [U].

disenchanted /ˌdɪsɪn'tʃɑːntɪd; *US* -'tʃænt-/ (*with*) 对〔對〕…失去好感的 duì…shīqù hǎogǎn de.

disentangle /ˌdɪsɪn'tæŋgl/ *v* [T] **1** 解开〔開〕…的结 jiěkāi…de jié. **2** (*from*) 使摆〔擺〕脱 shǐ bǎituō.

disfigure /dɪs'fɪgə(r); *US* -gjər/ *v* [T] 损毁…的容貌 sǔnhuǐ…de róngmào; 破…的相 pò…de xiàng; 破坏〔壞〕…的外形 pòhuài…de wàixíng. **disfigurement** *n* [C, U].

disgorge /dɪs'gɔːdʒ/ *v* [I, T] (使) 流出 liúchū; (使) 倒出 dàochū.

disgrace /dɪs'greɪs/ *n* **1** [U] 耻辱 chǐrǔ; 丢脸〔臉〕 diūliǎn. **2** [sing] 使人丢脸的事 shǐ rén diūliǎn de shì; 使人丢脸的人 shǐ rén diūliǎn de rén. **disgrace** *v* [T] 使丢脸 shǐ diūliǎn; 使蒙受耻辱 shǐ méngshòu chǐrǔ. **disgraceful** *adj* 可耻的 kěchǐde; 不名誉〔譽〕的 bù míngyù de.

disgruntled /dɪs'grʌntld/ *adj* 不满意的 bù mǎnyì de; 不高兴〔興〕的 bù gāoxìng de.

disguise /dɪs'gaɪz/ *v* [T] **1** 把…假装〔裝〕起来 bǎ…jiǎzhuāng qǐlái; 把…假扮起来 bǎ…jiǎbàn qǐlái. **2** 掩饰 yǎnshì; 隐〔隱〕蔽 yǐnbì: *~ one's anger* 按捺住怒火. **disguise** *n* **1** [C] (供穿戴的) 伪〔僞〕装品 wěizhuāngpǐn. **2** [U] 伪装 wěizhuāng; 假扮 jiǎbàn; 掩饰 yǎnshì.

disgust /dɪs'gʌst/ *n* [U] 厌〔厭〕恶〔惡〕 yànwù; 讨厌 tǎoyàn. **disgust** *v* [T] 使厌恶 shǐ yànwù. **disgusted** *adj* 感到厌恶的 gǎndào yànwù de. **disgusting** 令人厌恶的 lìng rén yànwù de.

dish /dɪʃ/ *n* **1** [C] 盘〔盤〕 pán; 碟 dié **2** [C] 菜肴 càiyáo. **3 the dishes** [pl] 全部餐具 quánbù cānjù. **dish** *v* [短语动词] **dish sth out** 大量分发〔發〕 dàliàng fēnfā: *~ out leaflets* 分发传单. *~ out compliments* 大加赞扬. **dish sth up** 把(食物)装〔裝〕盘上菜 bǎ zhuāng pán shàngcài. **'dishcloth** *n* [C] 洗碟布 xǐdiébù. **'dishwasher** 洗碗机〔機〕 xǐwǎnjī.

dishearten /dɪs'hɑːtn/ *v* [T] 使失去希望或信心 shǐ shīqù xīwàng huò xìnxīn.

dishevelled (美语 -l-) /dɪˈʃevld/ *adj* (衣服、头发)散乱〔亂〕的 sǎnluànde;不整洁〔潔〕的 bù zhěngjié de.

dishonest /dɪsˈɒnɪst/ *adj* 不诚实〔實〕的 bù chéngshí de;不老实的 bù lǎoshi de. **dishonestly** *adv*. **dishonesty** *n* [U].

dishonour (美语 -or) /dɪsˈɒnə(r)/ *n* [U, sing] [正式用语]耻辱 chǐrǔ;不光彩 bù guāngcǎi;不名誉〔譽〕 bù míngyù. **dishonour** *v* [T] [正式用语] 1 使受耻辱 shǐ shòu chǐrǔ;使丢脸〔臉〕 shǐ diūliǎn;使不光彩 shǐ bù guāngcǎi. 2 (银行)拒付(票据) jùfù. **dishonourable** *adj* 不明誉的 bù míngyù de;可耻的 kěchǐde.

disillusion /ˌdɪsɪˈluːʒn/ *v* [T] 使醒悟 shǐ xǐngwù;使幻想破灭〔滅〕 shǐ huànxiǎng pòmiè. **disillusioned** *adj*. **disillusionment** *n* [U].

disinclined /ˌdɪsɪnˈklaɪnd/ *adj* (*for*, *to*) 不愿〔願〕的 búyuànde;不喜欢〔歡〕的 bù xǐhuān de: ~ *for study* 不愿学习. ~ *to leave* 不愿离开.

disinfect /ˌdɪsɪnˈfekt/ *v* [T] 给…消毒 gěi…xiāodú;杀〔殺〕死…的细菌 shāsǐ…de xìjūn: ~ *a wound* 给伤口消毒. **disinfectant** *n* [U, C] 消毒剂〔劑〕 xiāodújì.

disinformation /dɪsˌɪnfəˈmeɪʃn/ *n* [U] (尤指来自政府的)假情报〔報〕 jiǎ qíngbào;假消息 jiǎ xiāoxi.

disinherit /ˌdɪsɪnˈherɪt/ *v* [T] 剥夺〔奪〕…的继〔繼〕承权〔權〕 bōduó…de jìchéngquán.

disintegrate /dɪsˈɪntɪɡreɪt/ *v* [I] 瓦解 wǎjiě;崩溃 bēngkuì. **disintegration** /dɪsˌɪntɪˈɡreɪʃn/ *n* [U].

disinterested /dɪsˈɪntrəstɪd/ *adj* 无〔無〕私的 wúsīde;无偏见的 wú piānjiàn de.

disjointed /dɪsˈdʒɔɪntɪd/ *adj* (言语、思想等) 不连贯的 bù liánguàn de;没有条〔條〕理的 méiyǒu tiáolǐ de.

disk /dɪsk/ *n* [C] 1 [尤用于美语] = DISC. 2 (电子计算机)磁盘〔盤〕 cípán. ˈ**disk drive** *n* [C] 磁盘驱〔驅〕动〔動〕器 cípán qūdòngqì.

diskette /dɪsˈket/ *n* [C] 软磁盘〔盤〕 ruǎncípán.

dislike /dɪsˈlaɪk/ *v* [T] 不喜欢〔歡〕 bù xǐhuān;不爱〔愛〕 bú ài;厌〔厭〕恶〔惡〕 yànwù. **dislike** *n* 1 [U] 不喜欢 bù xǐhuān;厌恶 yànwù. 2 不喜欢的对〔對〕象 bù xǐhuānde duìxiàng.

dislocate /ˈdɪsləkeɪt; *US* -ləʊ-/ *v* [T] 1 使(骨骼)脱位 shǐ tuōwèi;使离〔離〕开〔開〕原位 shǐ líkāi yuánwèi. 2 使(交通等)紊乱〔亂〕 shǐ wěnluàn. **dislocation** /ˌdɪsləˈkeɪʃn; *US* -ləʊ-/ *n* [U, C].

dislodge /dɪsˈlɒdʒ/ *v* [T] (从固定位置上)强行移开〔開〕 qiángxíng yíkāi.

disloyal /dɪsˈlɔɪəl/ *adj* 不忠诚的 bù zhōngchéng de. **disloyally** *adv*. **disloyalty** *n* [U].

dismal /ˈdɪzməl/ *adj* 忧〔憂〕愁的 yōuchóude;阴〔陰〕沉的 yīnchénde. **dismally** *adv*.

dismantle /dɪsˈmæntl/ *v* [T] 拆散 chāisàn: ~ *a machine* 拆机器. ~ *an engine* 拆发动机.

dismay /dɪsˈmeɪ/ *n* [U] 灰心 huīxīn;惊〔驚〕愕 jīng'è. **dismay** *v* [T] 使灰心 shǐ huīxīn;使沮丧〔喪〕 shǐ jǔsàng.

dismember /dɪsˈmembə(r)/ *v* [T] 1 肢解 zhījiě. 2 瓜分(国家) guāfēn.

dismiss /dɪsˈmɪs/ *v* [T] 1 解雇 jiěgù;开〔開〕除 kāichú;免职〔職〕 miǎnzhí. 2 解散 jiěsàn;让〔讓〕…离〔離〕开 ràng…líkāi;遣散 qiǎnsàn. 3 不考虑〔慮〕 bù kǎolǜ;消除(念头等) xiāochú. 4 [法律]驳回(上诉等) bóhuí. **dismissal** *n* [U, C].

disobedient /ˌdɪsəˈbiːdɪənt/ *adj* 不服从〔從〕的 bù fúcóng de;不顺从的 bú shùncóng de. **disobedience** /-əns/ *n* [U]. **disobediently** *adv*.

disobey /ˌdɪsəˈbeɪ/ *v* [I, T] 不服从〔從〕(某人、法律等) bù fúcóng.

disorder /dɪsˈɔːdə(r)/ *n* 1 [U] 混乱〔亂〕 hùnluàn;杂〔雜〕乱 záluàn. 2 [C, U] 骚乱 sāoluàn;骚动〔動〕 sāodòng. 3 [C, U] (身、心)失调 shītiáo. **disorder** *v* [T] 使混乱 shǐ hùnluàn;使失调 shǐ shītiáo;扰〔擾〕乱 rǎoluàn. **disorderly** *adj*.

disorganize /ˌdɪsˈɔːɡənaɪz/ *v* [T] 打乱〔亂〕 dǎluàn.

disorientate /dɪsˈɔːrɪənteɪt/ (亦作,尤用于美国英语 **disorient** /dɪsˈɔːrɪənt/) *v* [T] 使迷失方向 shǐ míshī fāngxiàng;使迷惘 shǐ míwǎng. **disorientation** / dɪsˌɔːrɪənˈteɪʃn / *n* [U].

disown /dɪsˈəʊn/ *v* [T] 声〔聲〕明与〔與〕…脱离〔離〕关〔關〕系〔係〕 shēngmíng yǔ…tuōlí guānxì.

disparaging /dɪˈspærɪdʒɪŋ/ *adj* 贬低的 biǎndīde;轻〔輕〕蔑的 qīngmiède.

disparate /ˈdɪspərət/ *adj* [正式用语]完全不相同的 wánquán bù xiāngtóng de;不能比拟〔擬〕的 bùnéng bǐnǐ de. **disparity** /dɪˈspærətɪ/ *n* [C, U] [*pl* -ies] 不同 bùtóng;悬〔懸〕殊 xuánshū.

dispassionate /dɪˈspæʃənət/ *adj* 不动〔動〕感情的 búdòng gǎnqíng de;冷静的 lěngjìngde;公平的 gōngpíngde. **dispassionately** *adv*.

dispatch (亦作 **despatch**) /dɪˈspætʃ/ *v* [T] 1 派遣 pàiqiǎn;发〔發〕送 fāsòng. 2 迅速办〔辦〕理 xùnsù bànlǐ;了结 liǎojié. **dispatch** (亦作 **despatch**) *n* 1 [U] [正式用语]派遣 pàiqiǎn;发送 fāsòng. 2 [C] (发送的)信件 xìnjiàn;报〔報〕告 bàogào. 3 [U] [正式用语]迅速 xùnsù.

dispel /dɪˈspel/ *v* [-ll-] [T] 消除 xiāochú: ~ *doubts* 解除疑虑.

D

dispense /dɪˈspens/ *v* [T] 1 [正式用语]分配 fēnpèi;分发〔發〕fēnfā. 2 配(药) pèi;配(方) pèi;发(药) fā. 3 [短语动词] **dispense with sth** 省掉 shěngdiào;免除 miǎnchú. **dispensary** /dɪˈspensərɪ/ *n* [C] [*pl* -ies] 药〔藥〕房 yàofáng. **dispensation** /ˌdɪspenˈseɪʃn/ *n* [正式用语] 1 [U] 分配 fēnpèi;分发 fēnfā. 2 [U, C] 特许 tèxǔ.

disperse /dɪˈspɜːs/ *v* [I, T] (使)散开〔開〕sànkāi;(使)疏开 shūkāi;(使)分散 fēnsàn. **dispersal** *n* [U].

D

dispirited /dɪˈspɪrɪtɪd/ *adj* 没精打采的 méi jīng dǎ cǎi de;垂头〔頭〕丧〔喪〕气〔氣〕的 chuí tóu sàng qì de.

displace /dɪsˈpleɪs/ *v* [T] 1 转〔轉〕移 zhuǎnyí;移置 yízhì. 2 取代 qǔdài;撤换 chèhuàn. **displacement** *n* [U].

display /dɪˈspleɪ/ *v* [T] 展览〔覽〕zhǎnlǎn;陈列 chénliè. **display** *n* [C] 展览 zhǎnlǎn;陈列 chénliè;展览品 zhǎnlǎnpǐn;陈列品 chénlièpǐn.

displease /dɪsˈpliːz/ *v* [T] 使不愉快 shǐ bù yúkuài;使不高兴〔興〕shǐ bù gāoxìng;冒犯 màofàn;使生气〔氣〕shǐ shēngqì. **displeasure** /dɪsˈpleʒə(r)/ *n* [U] 生气 shēngqì;不愉快 bù yúkuài.

dispose /dɪˈspəʊz/ *v* [短语动词] **dispose of sth** 处〔處〕理 chǔlǐ;处置 chǔzhì;除去 chúqù. **disposable** /dɪˈspəʊzəbl/ *adj* 1 (用毕)可任意处置的 kě rènyì chǔzhì de: ~ *nappies* 用毕扔掉的尿布. 2 可自由使用的 kě zìyóu shǐyòng de: ~ *income* 可自由使用的收入. **disposal** *n* 1 [U] 处理 chǔlǐ;处置 chǔzhì. 2 [习语] **at one's disposal** 由某人支配 yóu mǒurén zhīpèi. **disposed** *adj* 1 (*to*) 愿〔願〕意的 yuànyìde. 2 [习语] **well / favourably disposed towards sb/sth** 认〔認〕为〔爲〕…很好 rènwéi…hěnhǎo. **disposition** /ˌdɪspəˈzɪʃn/ *n* [U] [正式用语](人的)气〔氣〕质〔質〕qìzhì;性情 xìngqíng.

dispossess /ˌdɪspəˈzes/ *v* [T] (*of*) 剥夺〔奪〕bōduó.

disproportionate /ˌdɪsprəˈpɔːʃənət/ *adj* 不相称〔稱〕的 bù xiāngchèn de;不匀称的 bù yúnchèn de. **disproportionately** *adv*.

disprove /ˌdɪsˈpruːv/ *v* [T] 证〔證〕明…为〔爲〕错误 zhèngmíng…wéi cuòwù;证明…为伪〔僞〕zhèngmíng…wéi wěi.

dispute /dɪˈspjuːt/ *n* [C, U] 争执〔執〕zhēngzhí;争论〔論〕zhēnglùn. **dispute** *v* 1 [T] 就…发〔發〕生争论 jiù…fāshēng zhēnglùn;对〔對〕…表示异〔異〕议〔議〕duì…biǎoshì yìyì. 2 [I] (*with*) 争论 zhēnglùn.

disqualify /dɪsˈkwɒlɪfaɪ/ *v* [*pt*, *pp* -ied] [T] (*from*) 使(某人)无〔無〕资格(做某事) shǐ wú zīgé. **disqualification** /dɪsˌkwɒlɪfɪˈkeɪʃn/ *n* [U, C].

disquiet /dɪsˈkwaɪət/ *n* [U] [正式用语]不安 bù'ān;焦虑〔慮〕jiāolǜ. **disquiet** *v* [T] [正式用语]使忧〔憂〕虑 shǐ yōulǜ.

disregard /ˌdɪsrɪˈgɑːd/ *v* [T] 不理 bùlǐ;不顾〔顧〕búgù;漠视 mòshì. **disregard** *n* [U] 漠视 mòshì;忽视 hūshì.

disrepair /ˌdɪsrɪˈpeə(r)/ *n* [U] 破损 pòsǔn;失修 shīxiū.

disrepute /ˌdɪsrɪˈpjuːt/ *n* [U] 声〔聲〕名狼藉 shēngmíng lángjí: *bring the sport into* ~ 使这项运动声名狼藉. **disreputable** /dɪsˈrepjʊtəbl/ *adj* 名声不好的 míngshēng bùhǎo de: *a* ~ *nightclub* 名声不好的夜总会.

disrespect /ˌdɪsrɪˈspekt/ *n* [U] 无〔無〕礼〔禮〕wúlǐ;失敬 shījìng;粗鲁 cūlǔ. **disrespectful** *adj*.

disrupt /ˌdɪsˈrʌpt/ *v* [T] 使混乱〔亂〕shǐ hùnluàn;破坏〔壞〕pòhuài: ~ *a public meeting* 破坏公共集会. **disruption** /-ˈrʌpʃn/ *n* [C, U]. **disruptive** *adj* 破坏性的 pòhuàixìngde;制〔製〕造混乱的 zhìzào hùnluàn de: *a* ~*ive influence* 破坏性的影响.

dissatisfy /dɪˈsætɪsfaɪ/ *v* [*pt*, *pp* -ied] [T] 使不满 shǐ bùmǎn;使不高兴〔興〕shǐ bù gāoxìng. **dissatisfaction** /ˌdɪˌsætɪsˈfækʃn/ *n* [U]. **dissatisfied** *adj*.

dissect /dɪˈsekt/ *v* [T] 解剖 jiěpōu. **dissection** /dɪˈsekʃn/ *n* [U, C].

disseminate /dɪˈsemɪneɪt/ *v* [T] [正式用语]散布 sànbù;传〔傳〕播 chuánbō. **dissemination** /dɪˌsemɪˈneɪʃn/ *n* [U].

dissension /dɪˈsenʃn/ *n* [U, C] 意见分歧 yìjiàn fēnqí;激烈争吵 jīliè zhēngchǎo.

dissent /dɪˈsent/ *n* [U] 不同意 bù tóngyì;异〔異〕义〔義〕yìyì. **dissent** *v* [I] (*from*) [正式用语]不同意 bù tóngyì;持不同意见 chí bùtóng yìjiàn. **dissenter** *n* [C] 持不同意见者 chí bùtóng yìjiàn zhě.

dissertation /ˌdɪsəˈteɪʃn/ *n* [C] (*on*) 长〔長〕篇论〔論〕文 chángpiān lùnwén;专〔專〕题演讲 zhuāntí yǎnjiǎng.

disservice /dɪsˈsɜːvɪs/ *n* [C, 常作 sing] 帮〔幫〕倒忙行为〔爲〕bāng dàománg xíngwéi: *do sb a* ~ 给某人帮倒忙.

dissident /ˈdɪsɪdənt/ *n* [C] 持不同政见者 chí bùtóng zhèngjiàn zhě.

dissimilar /dɪˈsɪmələ(r)/ *adj* 不同的 bùtóngde;不一样〔樣〕的 bù yíyàng de. **dissimilarity** /ˌdɪsɪmɪˈlærətɪ/ *n* [U, C] [*pl* -ies].

dissipated /ˈdɪsɪpeɪtɪd/ *adj* 放荡〔蕩〕的 fàngdàngde;浪荡的 làngdàngde.

dissociate /dɪˈsəʊʃɪeɪt/ (亦作 **disassociate** /ˌdɪsəˈsəʊʃɪeɪt/) *v* [T] 1 ~ **oneself from** 否认〔認〕同…有关〔關〕系〔係〕fǒurèn tóng…yǒu guānxì. 2 *A from B* 使分离〔離〕shǐ fēnlí;使

无〔無〕关系 shǐ wú guānxì. **dissociation** /dɪˌsəʊsɪˈeɪʃn/ *n* [U].

dissolve /dɪˈzɒlv/ *v* 1 [I] 液化 yèhuà; 融化 rónghuà: *Salt ~s in water*. 盐融于水. 2 [T] 使液化 shǐ yèhuà; 使融化 shǐ rónghuà. 3 [T] 使解散 shǐ jiěsàn; 使终结 shǐ zhōngjié: ~ *parliament* 解散议会. 4 [习语] dissolve into tears/laughter 情不自禁地流泪(或大笑起来) qíng bù zì jīn de liúlèi. **dissolution** /ˌdɪsəˈluːʃn/ *n* [C, U] (婚姻、会议等)终止 zhōngzhǐ; 结束 jiéshù.

dissuade /dɪˈsweɪd/ *v* [T] (*from*) 劝〔勸〕阻 quànzǔ: ~ *sb from leaving* 劝某人不要离去.

distance /ˈdɪstəns/ *n* 1 [C, U] 距离〔離〕 jùlí. 2 [U] (时间或空间)远〔遠〕 yuǎn, 遥远 yáoyuǎn. 3 [C, U] 远处〔處〕 yuǎnchù: *listen from a* ~ 从远处听. 4 [习语] go the distance 自始至终地坚〔堅〕持 zì shǐ zhì zhōng de jiānchí. **distance** *v* [T] (*from*) 对〔對〕…冷淡 duì…lěngdàn. ˈ**distance learning** *n* [U] 远程学〔學〕习〔習〕 yuǎnchéng xuéxí.

distant /ˈdɪstənt/ *adj* 1 远〔遠〕隔的 yuǎngéde; 远处〔處〕的 yuǎnchùde; 久远的 jiǔyuǎnde. 2 不密切的 bú mìqiè de; 关〔關〕系〔係〕不亲〔親〕近的 guānxì bù qīnjìn de; 不亲密的 bù qīnmì de: *a* ~ *cousin* 远房表兄弟. 3 冷淡的 lěngdànde. **distantly** *adv*.

distaste /dɪsˈteɪst/ *n* [U, sing] 不喜欢〔歡〕 bù xǐhuān; 讨厌〔厭〕 tǎoyàn. **distasteful** *adj* 讨厌的 tǎoyànde; 不合口味的 bù hé kǒuwèi de.

distil (美语 distill) /dɪˈstɪl/ *v* [-ll-] [T] 1 (*from*) (a) 蒸馏 zhēngliú. (b) 用蒸馏法制〔製〕造(威士忌酒等) yòng zhēngliú fǎ zhìzào. 2 (*from*) 取自 qǔzì: *advice ~led from years of experience* 多年经验凝结成的忠告. **distillation** /ˌdɪstɪˈleɪʃn/ *n* [U]. **distillery** *n* [C] (威士忌酒等的)酒厂〔廠〕 jiǔchǎng.

distinct /dɪˈstɪŋkt/ *adj* 1 不同的 bùtóngde; 各别的 gèbiéde. 2 清晰的 qīngxīde. **distinctly** *adv*.

distinction /dɪˈstɪŋkʃn/ *n* 1 [C, U] (*between A and B*) 区〔區〕分 qūfēn; 区别 qūbié. 2 [U] 卓著 zhuózhù; 卓越 zhuóyuè. 3 [C] 荣〔榮〕誉〔譽〕称〔稱〕号〔號〕 róngyù chēnghào.

distinctive /dɪˈstɪŋktɪv/ *adj* 有特色的 yǒu tèsè de; 特别的 tèbiéde. **distinctively** *adv*.

distinguish /dɪˈstɪŋgwɪʃ/ *v* 1 [I, T] (*between*) *A and B*; *A from B* 区〔區〕别 qūbié; 分别 fēnbié; 辨别 biànbié. 2 [T] *A* (*from B*) (a) 显〔顯〕示(两者)的区别 xiǎnshì de qūbié. (b) 为〔爲〕…的特征〔徵〕 wéi…de tèzhēng. 3 [T] 看清 kànqīng; 听〔聽〕出 tīngchū. 4 ~ oneself 使杰〔傑〕出 shǐ jiéchū; 使著名 shǐ zhùmíng. **distinguishable** *adj*. **distinguished** *adj* 杰出的 jiéchūde.

distort /dɪˈstɔːt/ *v* [T] 1 弄歪 nòng wāi. 2 歪曲 wāiqū; 曲解 qūjiě: ~ *the facts* 歪曲事实. **distortion** /dɪˈstɔːʃn/ *n* [C, U].

distract /dɪˈstrækt/ *v* [T] 分散(注意力) fēnsàn. **distracted** *adj* 心神烦乱〔亂〕的 xīnshén fánluàn de. **distraction** /dɪˈstrækʃn/ *n* 1 [C, U] 分散注意力的事物(如噪音等) fēnsàn zhùyìlì de shìwù. 2 [C] 消遣 xiāoqiǎn; 娱乐〔樂〕 yúlè.

distraught /dɪˈstrɔːt/ *adj* 心烦意乱〔亂〕的 xīnfán yì luàn de; 极其烦恼〔惱〕的 jíqí fánnǎo de.

distress /dɪˈstres/ *n* [U] 1 悲痛 bēitòng; 忧〔憂〕伤〔傷〕 yōushāng; 痛苦 tòngkǔ; 贫苦 pínkǔ. 2 危难〔難〕 wēinàn: *a ship in* ~ 处于危险中的船. **distress** *v* [T] 使痛苦 shǐ tòngkǔ; 使悲痛 shǐ bēitòng. **distressing** *adj* 令人痛苦的 lìng rén tòngkǔ de; 令人悲痛的 lìng rén bēitòng de: *~ing news* 令人伤心的消息.

distribute /dɪˈstrɪbjuːt/ *v* [T] 1 分发〔發〕 fēnfā; 分配 fēnpèi; 发行 fāxíng. 2 散布〔佈〕 sànbù; 使分布 shǐ fēnbù. **distribution** /ˌdɪstrɪˈbjuːʃn/ *n* [C, U] 分布 fēnbù; 分配 fēnpèi. **distriˈbution list** *n* [C] 分发列表 fēnfā lièbiǎo; 通讯组列表 tōngxùnzǔ lièbiǎo. **distributor** /dɪˈstrɪbjʊtə(r)/ *n* [C] 1 批发商 pīfāshāng; 批发公司 pīfā gōngsī. 2 (供电)分配器 fēnpèiqì; 配电〔電〕盘〔盤〕 pèidiànpán.

district /ˈdɪstrɪkt/ *n* [C] 区〔區〕(行政单位) qū.

distrust /dɪsˈtrʌst/ *v* [T] 不信任 bú xìnrèn; 疑惑 yíhuò. **distrust** *n* [U, sing] 不信任 bú xìnrèn; 怀〔懷〕疑 huáiyí. **distrustful** *adj*.

disturb /dɪˈstɜːb/ *v* [T] 1 打扰〔擾〕 dǎrǎo; 扰乱〔亂〕 rǎoluàn; 打断〔斷〕 dǎduàn. 2 使烦恼〔惱〕 shǐ fánnǎo; 使心神不安 shǐ xīnshénbù'ān. **disturbance** *n* 1 [C, U] 打扰 dǎrǎo. 2 [C] 骚动〔動〕 sāodòng; 骚乱 sāoluàn. **disturbed** *adj* 有精神病的 yǒu jīngshénbìng de.

disunity /dɪsˈjuːnətɪ/ *n* [U] [正式用语]不团〔團〕结 bù tuánjié; 不和 bùhé.

disuse /dɪsˈjuːs/ *n* [U] 废〔廢〕弃〔棄〕 fèiqì; 搁置不用 gēzhì búyòng: *fall into* ~ 废而不用. **disused** /-ˈjuːzd/ *adj*.

ditch /dɪtʃ/ *n* [C] 排水沟〔溝〕 páishuǐgōu; 沟 gōu; 沟渠 gōuqú. **ditch** *v* [T] [非正式用语]断〔斷〕绝同(某人)的关〔關〕系〔係〕 duànjué tóng de guānxi: *She ~ed her boyfriend*. 她甩掉了她的男朋友.

dither /ˈdɪðə(r)/ *v* [I] 踌〔躊〕躇 chóuchú; 犹〔猶〕豫 yóuyù.

ditto /ˈdɪtəʊ/ *n* [C] [*pl* ~s] (用于表示避免重复)同上 tóngshàng; 同前 tóngqián.

ditty /ˈdɪtɪ/ *n* [C] [*pl* -ies] 小调 xiǎodiào;

D

小曲 xiǎoqǔ.

divan /dɪˈvæn; *US* ˈdaɪvæn/ *n* [C] 无〔無〕靠背的长〔長〕沙发〔發〕 wú kàobèi de cháng shāfā.

dive /daɪv/ *v* [*pt*, *pp* **dived**; *US* 亦作 *pt* **dove** /dəʊv/] [I] **1** 跳水 tiàoshuǐ. **2** 潜〔潛〕水 qiǎnshuǐ. **3** (飞机)俯冲〔衝〕 fǔchōng; 突然下降 tūrán xiàjiàng. **4** 奔向 bēnxiàng; 冲向 chōngxiàng: ~ *under the bed* 钻到床下. **5** [短语动词] **dive into sth** 全身心投入 quánshēnxīn tóurù. **dive** *n* [C] **1** 跳水 tiàoshuǐ. **2** 低级夜总〔總〕会〔會〕 dījí yèzǒnghuì; 下等酒吧 xiàděng jiǔbā. **diver** *n* [C] 潜水员 qiǎnshuǐyuán. **ˈdiving-board** *n* [C] 跳水板 tiàoshuǐbǎn.

diverge /daɪˈvɜːdʒ/ *v* [I] 岔开〔開〕 chàkāi; 分歧 fēnqí; 背驰 bèichí. **divergence** /-dʒəns/ *n* [C, U]. **divergent** /-dʒənt/ *adj*.

diverse /daɪˈvɜːs/ *adj* 多种〔種〕多样〔樣〕的 duōzhǒng duōyàng de: ~ *interests* 多种多样的兴趣. **diversity** *n* [U, sing] 差异〔異〕 chāyì; 多样性 duōyàngxìng.

diversify /ˌdaɪˈvɜːsɪfaɪ/ *v* [*pt*, *pp* **-ied**] [I, T] (使)多样化 duōyànghuà. **diversification** /daɪˌvɜːsɪfɪˈkeɪʃn/ *n* [U].

diversion /daɪˈvɜːʃn; *US* -vɜːrʒn/ *n* **1** [C] 用以转〔轉〕移视线〔綫〕的事物(或假象) yòng yǐ zhuǎnyí shìxiàn de shìwù: *create a* ~ 制造一个假象. **2** [C] 改道 gǎidào; 临〔臨〕时〔時〕绕〔繞〕行路 línshí ràoxínglù. **3** [U, C] 转〔轉〕向 zhuǎnxiàng: *the* ~ *of a river* 河流的改道. **diversionary** *adj*: ~*ary tactics* 转移注意力的策略.

divert /ˌdaɪˈvɜːt/ *v* [T] (*from*, *to*) **1** 使转〔轉〕向 shǐ zhuǎnxiàng; 使改道 shǐ gǎidào: ~ *traffic* 使车辆绕行. ~ *money to education* 把钱改用到教育上. **2** 使得到消遣 shǐ dédào xiāoqiǎn; 给…娱乐〔樂〕 gěi… yúlè.

divide /dɪˈvaɪd/ *v* **1** [I, T] 分 fēn; 划〔劃〕分 huàfēn. **2** [I, T] (使)意见分歧 yìjiàn fēnqí. **3** [T] *by* [数学]除(尽) chú: *30* ~*d by 6 is 5*. 30 除以 6 得 5. **divide** *n* [C] 分水岭〔嶺〕 fēnshuǐlǐng; 分界线〔綫〕 fēnjièxiàn. **dividers** *n* [pl] 两脚规 liǎngjiǎoguī; 分线规 fēnxiànguī.

dividend /ˈdɪvɪdənd/ *n* [C] 红利 hónglì; 股息 gǔxī.

divine[1] /dɪˈvaɪn/ *adj* **1** 神的 shénde; 神样〔樣〕的 shényàngde. **2** [非正式用语]极〔極〕好的 jíhǎode. **divinely** *adv*. **divinity** /dɪˈvɪnətɪ/ *n* **1** [U] 神学〔學〕 shénxué. **2** [U] 神性 shénxìng; 神威 shénwēi. **3** [C] 神 shén; 女神 nǚshén.

divine[2] /dɪˈvaɪn/ *v* [T] [正式用语]凭〔憑〕猜测发〔發〕现 píng cāicè fāxiàn.

divisible /dɪˈvɪzəbl/ *adj* 可除尽〔盡〕的 kě chújìn de: *4 is* ~ *by 2*. 4 可用 2 除.

division /dɪˈvɪʒn/ *n* **1** [U] 分开〔開〕 fēnkāi; 分割 fēngē. **2** [C] 分成的一部分 fēnchéngde yíbùfen. **3** [C] (机构的组成部分)部 bù; 处〔處〕 chù; 室 shì: *the sales* ~ 销售部. **4** [C, U] 意见分歧 yìjiàn fēnqí. **5** [U] [数学]除(法) chú. **6** [C] [尤用于英国英语](议会)分组表决 fēnzǔ biǎojué. **7** [C] (比赛的)级 jí; 组 zǔ. **divisional** /-ʒənl/ *adj*.

divisive /dɪˈvaɪsɪv/ *adj* 引起分歧的 yǐnqǐ fēnqí de; 造成不和的 zàochéng bùhé de.

divorce /dɪˈvɔːs/ *n* **1** [C, U] 离〔離〕婚 líhūn. **2** [C] 分离 fēnlí; 脱离 tuōlí. **divorce** *v* **1** [T] 判…离婚 pàn…líhūn: ~ *sb* 判某人离婚. *get* ~*d* 离婚了. **2** [T] *from* 使分离 shǐ fēnlí; 使脱离 shǐ tuōlí. **divorcee** /dɪˌvɔːˈsiː/ *n* [C] 离了婚的人 lílehūnde rén.

divulge /daɪˈvʌldʒ/ *v* [T] 泄露(秘密) xièlòu.

DIY /ˌdiː aɪ ˈwaɪ/ *n* [U] 自己动〔動〕手 (do it yourself, 指自己修理、自己粉刷装饰房间等) zìjǐ dòngshǒu.

dizzy /ˈdɪzɪ/ *adj* [**-ier**, **-iest**] **1** 眩晕的 xuànyùnde. **2** 使人眩晕的 shǐ rén xuànyùnde: ~ *heights* 使人眩晕的高处. **dizzily** *adv*. **dizziness** *n* [U].

DJ /ˌdiː ˈdʒeɪ/ *abbr* [非正式用语] **1** dinner jacket 晚礼〔禮〕服 wǎnlǐfú. **2** disc jockey 无〔無〕线〔綫〕电〔電〕唱片音乐〔樂〕节〔節〕目广〔廣〕播员 wúxiàndiàn chàngpiàn yīnyuè jiémù guǎngbōyuán.

DNA /ˌdiː en ˈeɪ/ *abbr deoxyribonucleic acid* 脱氧核糖核酸(基因的基本成分) tuō yǎng hétáng hésuān.

do[1] /duː/ *aux v* [否定式 **do not**, 缩略式 **don't** /dəʊnt/; 第三人称单数现在式 **does** /dəz; 强式 dʌz/, 否定式 **does not**, 缩略式 **doesn't** /ˈdʌznt/; 过去式 **did** /dɪd/, 否定式 **did not**, 缩略式 **didn't**; 过去分词 **done** /dʌn/] **1** (a) [用于动词前, 构成否定句和疑问句]: *I don't like fish*. 我不喜欢鱼. *Do you believe him?* 你相信他吗? (b) [用于句尾, 构成疑问]: *You live in Hastings, don't you?* 你住在黑斯丁斯, 是吗? **2** [用于加强语气]: *He ˈdoes look tired*. 他确实看上去疲倦了. *Do shut up!* 快闭嘴! **3** [用于避免动词的重复]: *She runs faster than I do*. 她比我跑得快.

do[2] /duː/ *v* [第三人称单数现在式 **does** /dʌz/, 过去式 **did** /dɪd/, 过去分词 **done** /dʌn/] **1** [T] 做 zuò; 干〔幹〕 gàn: *What are you doing now?* 现在你在做什么? **2** [T] 制〔製〕造 zhìzào; 生产〔產〕 shēngchǎn: *do a drawing* 画画. *do science at school* 在学校学习. **3** [T] 解答 jiědá; 解决 jiějué: *do a puzzle* 解决

难题. 4 [T] 整理 zhěnglǐ; 使整洁〔潔〕 shǐ zhěngjié: *do one's hair* 做头发. *do the cooking* 做饭. 5 [I, T] 做 zuò; 表现 biǎoxiàn: *do as you please* 你愿意怎么做就怎么做吧. *do one's best* 尽最大努力. 6 [T] 行经〔經〕(若干距离) xíngjīng: *How many miles did you do?* 你走了多少英里? 7 [I, T] (*for*) 合适〔適〕 héshì; 足够 zúgòu; 行 xíng: *'Can you lend me some money?' 'Yes—will £10 do (for you)?'* "你能借给我一些钱吗?" "可以——10 英镑行吗?" 8 [I] (生活、工作等方面) 进〔進〕展 jìnzhǎn: *She's doing well at school.* 她在学校学得很好. 9 [T] 欺骗 qīpiàn: *You've been done!* 你受骗了! 10 [习语] **be/have to do with sb/sth** 与〔與〕…有关〔關〕 yǔ…yǒuguān: *The letter is to do with the trip to France.* 这封信同法国之行有关. ˌ**how do you** ˈ**do?** (用于被介绍给某人时的客套话) 你好 nǐhǎo. **what do you do (for a living)?** 你做什么〔麼〕工作? nǐ zuò shénme gōngzuò? 11 [短语动词] **do away with oneself/sb** 杀〔殺〕死自己(或某人) shāsǐ zìjǐ. **do away with sth** [非正式用语] 去掉 qùdiào; 废〔廢〕除 fèichú. **do sb/sth down** [非正式用语] 贬低 biǎndī. **do for sb** 为〔爲〕…做家务〔務〕工作 wèi…zuò jiāwù gōngzuò. **do for sb/sth** [非正式用语] [通常用被动语态] 杀〔殺〕死 shāsǐ; 使毁灭〔滅〕 shǐ huǐmiè: *If we can't borrow the money, we're done for.* 如果我们借不到这笔钱, 我们就完蛋了. **do for sth** [非正式用语] 设法得到 shèfǎ dédào: *What will you do for lunch?* 你们午饭怎么办? **do sb** ˈ**in** [非正式用语] (a) 杀死 shāsǐ; (b) 使精疲力竭 shǐ jīn pí lì jié: *You look done in!* 你看起来是精疲力竭了! **do sth out** [非正式用语] 打扫〔掃〕、清理(房间、柜橱等) dǎsǎo、qīnglǐ. **do sb out of sth** [非正式用语] (尤指用欺骗手法) 阻止某人得到某事物 zǔzhǐ mǒurén dédào mǒu shìwù. **do sb** ˈ**over** [非正式用语] 痛打 tòngdǎ; 打伤〔傷〕 dǎshāng. **do (sth) up** 扎〔紮〕 zā; 缚 fù; 捆 kǔn; 扣 kòu. **do sth up** 整修 zhěngxiū; 装〔裝〕饰 zhuāngshì. **do with sth** 想要 xiǎngyào; 需要 xūyào: *I could do with a cold drink.* 我想要一份冷饮. **do sth with oneself** 使(有益地)度过〔過〕时〔時〕间 shǐ dùguò shíjiān; 使忙碌 shǐ mánglù: *What does Simon do with himself at weekends?* 西蒙周末忙些什么呢? **do sth with sth** 放 fàng; 隐〔隱〕藏 yǐncáng; 使用 shǐyòng: *What have you done with my keys?* 你把我的钥匙放哪里去了? **do without (sb/sth)** 没有…而设法对〔對〕付过去 méiyǒu…ér shèfǎ duìfù guòqù. ˌ**do-**ˈ**gooder** *n* [C] [常贬] 不现实〔實〕的慈善家 bú xiànshíde císhànjiā; 空想的社会〔會〕改良家 kōngxiǎngde shèhuì gǎiliángjiā.

do[3] /duː/ *n* [C] [*pl* **dos** 或 **do's** /duːz/] 1 [英国非正式用语] 社交聚会〔會〕 shèjiāo jùhuì. 2 [习语] **do's and don'ts** / ˌduːzenˈdəʊntz / 规则 guīzé.

docile /ˈdəʊsaɪl; *US* ˈdɒsl/ *adj* 容易驯服的 róngyì xùnfú de; 容易管教的 róngyì guǎnjiào de; 驯良的 xùnliáng de.

dock[1] /dɒk/ *n* [C] 船坞 chuánwù; 码头〔頭〕 mǎtóu. **dock** *v* 1 [I, T] (使)(船)进〔進〕港、船坞 jìn gǎng、chuánwù 2 [I] (宇宙飞行器) 在外层〔層〕空间对〔對〕接 zài wàicéng kōngjiān duìjiē. **docker** *n* [C] 码头工人 mǎtóu gōngrén. ˈ**dockland** *n* [U, C] 港区〔區〕陆〔陸〕域 gǎngqū lùyù. ˈ**dockyard** *n* [C] 造船所 zàochuánsuǒ; 修船厂〔廠〕 xiūchuánchǎng.

dock[2] /dɒk/ *n* [C] 刑事法庭的被告席 xíngshì fǎtíng de bèigàoxí.

dock[3] /dɒk/ *v* [T] 1 剪短(动物的尾巴) jiǎnduǎn. 2 从〔從〕工资中扣除(一定数额) cóng gōngzī zhōng kòuchú.

doctor /ˈdɒktə(r)/ *n* [C] 1 医〔醫〕生 yīshēng. 2 博士 bóshì. **doctor** *v* [T] 1 窜〔竄〕改 cuàngǎi: ~ *the figures* 窜改数字. 2 阉割(猫、狗等) yāngē. **doctorate** /-tərət/ *n* [C] 博士学〔學〕位 bóshì xuéwèi; 博士衔 bóshì xián.

doctrinaire /ˌdɒktrɪˈneə(r)/ *adj* [正式用语, 贬] 空谈理论〔論〕的 kōngtán lǐlùn de; 教条〔條〕主义〔義〕的 jiàotiáozhǔyì de: ~ *attitudes* 教条主义的态度.

doctrine /ˈdɒktrɪn/ *n* [C, U] 教条〔條〕 jiàotiáo; 教义〔義〕 jiàoyì; 主义 zhǔyì. **doctrinal** /dɒkˈtraɪnl; *US* ˈdɒktrɪnl/ *adj*.

document /ˈdɒkjʊmənt/ *n* [C] 文献〔獻〕 wénxiàn; 文件 wénjiàn. **document** /-ment/ *v* [T] 用文件证〔證〕明 yòng wénjiàn zhèngmíng; 为〔爲〕…提供文件 wèi…tígōng wénjiàn. **documentation** /ˌdɒkjʊ-menˈteɪʃn/ *n* [U] (提供或使用的) 文件证据〔據〕 wénjiàn zhèngjù.

documentary /dɒkjʊˈmentrɪ/ *n* [C] [*pl* **-ies**] 记录〔錄〕影片 jìlù yǐngpiàn; 记实〔實〕性影片 jìshíxìng yǐngpiàn; (广播、电视等) 记实节〔節〕目 jìshí jiémù. **documentary** *adj* 文件的 wénjiànde: ~ *evidence* 书面证明.

dodge /dɒdʒ/ *v* 1 [I, T] 闪开 shǎnkāi; 躲闪 duǒshǎn. 2 [T] 躲避 duǒbì. **dodge** *n* [C] 1 躲闪 duǒshǎn; 闪开 shǎnkāi. 2 托词 tuōcí; 妙计 miàojì. **dodger** *n* [C] 油滑的人 yóuhuáde rén. **dodgy** /ˈdɒdʒɪ/ *adj* [非正式用语] 狡猾的 jiǎohuáde; 冒险〔險〕的 màoxiǎnde.

doe /dəʊ/ *n* [C] 雌鹿 cílù; 雌兔 cítù.

does ⇨ DO[1,2].

doesn't does not. ⇨ DO[1].

dog[1] /dɒg; *US* dɔːg/ *n* [C] 1 (a) 狗 gǒu (b) 雄狗 xiónggǒu. 2 **the dogs** 赛狗会〔會〕(赌博) sàigǒuhuì. 3 [习语] **a** ˌ**dog in the** ˈ**manger** 占

D

〔佔〕着茅坑不拉屎的人 zhànzhe máokēng bù lāshǐ de rén. **a dog's life** 困苦的生活 kùnkǔde shēnghuó. **go to the 'dogs** (国家或组织)衰败 shuāibài. **'dog-collar** *n* [C] **1** 狗项圈 gǒuxiàngquān. **2** 牧士领(钮扣钉在颈后的白色硬立领) mùshìlǐng. **'dog-eared** *adj* (书)翻旧〔舊〕了的 fānjiùlede. **'doghouse** *n* [C] **1** [美语]狗窝〔窩〕gǒuwō. **2** [习语] **in the doghouse** [非正式用语]失宠〔寵〕的 shīchǒngde; 丢脸〔臉〕的 diūliǎnde. **dog-tired** *adj* [非正式用语]很累的 hěnlèide.

dog[2] /dɒg; *US* dɔːg/ *v* [-gg-] [T] 尾随〔隨〕wěisuí: [喻] *~ged by illness* 疾病缠身.

dogged /ˈdɒgɪd/ *adj* 顽强的 wánqiángde; 顽固的 wángùde. **doggedly** *adv*.

dogma /ˈdɒgmə; *US* dɔːg-/ *n* [C, U] (尤指宗教的)教理 jiàolǐ; 教条〔條〕jiàotiáo; 教义〔義〕jiàoyì. **dogmatic** /dɒgˈmætɪk; *US* dɔːg-/ *adj* 武断〔斷〕的 wǔduànde; 固执〔執〕己见的 gùzhí jǐjiàn de. **dogmatically** /-klɪ/ *adv*.

do-gooder ⇨ DO².

dogsbody /ˈdɒgzbɒdɪ; *US* dɔːg-/ *n* [C] [*pl* -ies] [英国非正式用语]勤杂〔雜〕工 qínzágōng.

doldrums /ˈdɒldrəmz/ *n* [习语] **in the 'doldrums 1** 悲哀的 bēi'āide; 沮丧〔喪〕的 jǔsàngde. **2** 停滞〔滯〕的 tíngzhìde; 萧〔蕭〕条〔條〕的 xiāotiáode.

dole /dəʊl/ *n* **the dole** [sing] [英国非正式用语]失业〔業〕救济〔濟〕金 shīyè jiùjìjīn: *be on the ~* 靠失业救济金生活. *go on the ~* 开始领失业救济金. **dole** *v* [短语动词] **dole sth out** 少量发〔發〕放(救济金、救济品等) shǎoliàng fāfàng.

doleful /ˈdəʊlfl/ *adj* 悲哀的 bēi'āide; 不高兴〔興〕的 bù gāoxìngde. **dolefully** *adv*.

doll /dɒl; *US* dɔːl/ *n* [C] 玩偶 wán'ǒu; 洋娃娃 yángwáwa. **doll** *v* [短语动词] **doll oneself up** [非正式用语]打扮得漂漂亮亮 dǎbànde piàopiaoliàngliang.

dollar /ˈdɒlə(r)/ *n* [C] **1** 元(美国、加拿大、澳大利亚等国的货币单位) yuán. **2** 一元钞票 yìyuán chāopiào; 一元硬币〔幣〕yìyuán yìngbì.

dollop /ˈdɒləp/ *n* [C] [非正式用语] (软而不成形的)一团〔團〕(尤指食物) yìtuán.

dolphin /ˈdɒlfɪn/ *n* [C] 海豚 hǎitún.

domain /dəʊˈmeɪn/ *n* [C] [正式用语] **1** (活动、知识的)范〔範〕围〔圍〕fànwéi, 领域 lǐngyù. **2** 势〔勢〕力范围 shìlì fànwéi; 领地 lǐngdì. **3** (计算机)域 yù. **do'main name** *n* [C] (计算机网络)域名 yùmíng.

dome /dəʊm/ *n* [C] 圆屋顶 yuánwūdǐng; 穹顶 qióngdǐng. **domed** *adj* 圆屋顶形的 yuánwūdǐngxíngde.

domestic /dəˈmestɪk/ *adj* **1** 家的 jiāde; 家庭的 jiātíngde; 家里〔裏〕的 jiālǐde: *~ duties* 家庭责任. **2** 本国〔國〕的 běnguóde: *~ policies* 国内政策. **3** (动物)驯〔馴〕养〔養〕的(非野生的) xùnyǎngde. **domestic** (亦作 **domestic 'help**) *n* [C] 用人 yòngren. **domesticated** *adj* **1** (动物)驯化的 xùnhuàde. **2** (人)喜爱〔愛〕家务〔務〕劳〔勞〕动〔動〕和家庭生活的 xǐ'ài jiāwù láodòng hé jiātíng shēnghuó de. **domestic 'science** *n* [U] = HOME ECONOMICS.

dominant /ˈdɒmɪnənt/ *adj* 支配的 zhīpèide; 统治的 tǒngzhìde: *a ~ position* 统治地位. **dominance** /-nəns/ *n* [U].

dominate /ˈdɒmɪneɪt/ *v* **1** [I, T] 支配 zhīpèi; 统治 tǒngzhì. **2** [T] 在…中占首要地位 zài …zhōng zhàn shǒuyào dìwèi. **3** [T] 俯瞰 fǔkàn; 俯视 fǔshì: *The castle ~s the whole city.* 城堡俯瞰全城. **domination** /ˌdɒmɪˈneɪʃn/ *n* [U].

domineering /ˌdɒmɪˈnɪərɪŋ/ *adj* 盛气〔氣〕凌人的 shèng qì líng rén de; 作威作福的 zuò wēi zuò fú de.

dominion /dəˈmɪnɪən/ *n* **1** [U] [正式用语]统治 tǒngzhì; 支配 zhīpèi; 管辖 guǎnxiá. **2** [C] 领土 lǐngtǔ; 版图〔圖〕bǎntú; 疆土 jiāngtǔ.

domino /ˈdɒmɪnəʊ/ *n* [*pl* ~es] **1** [C] 多米诺骨牌 duōmǐnuò gǔpái. **2 dominoes** [用 sing v] 多米诺骨牌戏〔戲〕duōmǐnuò gǔpáixì.

don /dɒn/ *n* [C] [英国英语]大学〔學〕教师〔師〕dàxué jiàoshī.

donate /dəʊˈneɪt; *US* ˈdəʊneɪt/ *v* [T] (*to*) 捐赠 juānzèng; 捐献〔獻〕juānxiàn. **donation** /dəʊˈneɪʃn/ *n* [C, U].

done[1] *pt* of DO¹,².

done[2] /dʌn/ *adj* **1** 完毕〔畢〕的 wánbìde; 完成的 wánchéngde. **2** (食物)煮熟的 zhǔshúde. **3** 合乎规矩的 héhū guījù de.

donkey /ˈdɒŋkɪ/ *n* [C] **1** 驴〔驢〕lǘ. **2** [习语] **'donkey's years** [非正式用语]很久 hěnjiǔ; 多年 duōnián.

donor /ˈdəʊnə(r)/ *n* [C] 捐献〔獻〕者 juānxiànzhě; 赠与〔與〕者 zèngyǔzhě: *a blood-~* 输血人.

don't do not. ⇨ DO¹.

doodle /ˈduːdl/ *v* [I] 心不在焉地乱〔亂〕涂〔塗〕xīn bú zài yān de luàntú. **doodle** *n* [C].

doom /duːm/ *n* [U] 毁灭〔滅〕huǐmiè; 死亡 sǐwáng; 厄运〔運〕èyùn. **doomed** *adj* (坏事)注定要发〔發〕生的 zhùdìng yào fāshēng de: *be ~ed to die* 注定要死. *be ~ed to failure* 注定要失败. **doomsday** /ˈduːmzdeɪ/ *n* [sing] 世界末日 shìjiè mòrì.

door /dɔː(r)/ *n* [C] **1** 门 mén. **2** = DOORWAY. **3** [习语] **ˌdoor-to-'door** 挨家挨户的 āijiā āihù de: *a ˌ~-to-~ 'salesman* 挨家挨

户走的推销员. next ˈdoor (to sb/sth) 在隔壁 zài gébì; 到隔壁 dào gébì: *go next ~ to borrow some milk* 到隔壁去借一些牛奶. (be) on the ˈdoor (为公共集会等)把门(如收票等) bǎmén. out of ˈdoors 在户外 zài hùwài; 在室外 zài shìwài. ˈdoorbell *n* [C] 门铃 ménlíng. ˈdoorstep *n* [C] 门前台阶〔階〕 ménqián táijiē. ˈdoorway *n* [C] 门道 méndào; 出入口 chūrùkǒu.

dope /dəʊp/ *n* [非正式用语] 1 [U] 毒品 dúpǐn; 麻醉品 mázuìpǐn. 2 [C] 笨蛋 bèndàn. **dope** *v* [T] 给…毒品服 gěi…dúpǐn fú. **dopey** (亦作 dopy) *adj* [非正式用语] 1 (如麻醉后)昏昏沉沉的 hūnhunchénchénde. 2 迟〔遲〕钝的 chídùnde; 愚笨的 yúbènde.

dormant /ˈdɔːmənt/ *adj* 休眠的 xiūmiánde; 暂〔暫〕死的 zànsǐde: *a ~ volcano* 暂死的火山, 休眠的火山.

dormitory /ˈdɔːmɪtrɪ; *US* -ˈtɔːrɪ/ *n* [C] [*pl* -ies] 集体〔體〕寝室 jítǐ qǐnshì; (集体)宿舍 sùshè.

dormouse /ˈdɔːmaʊs/ *n* [C] [*pl* dormice /ˈdɔːmaɪs/] 榛睡鼠 zhēnshuìshǔ.

dosage /ˈdəʊsɪdʒ/ *n* [C, 常用 sing] 剂〔劑〕量 jìliàng.

dose /dəʊs/ *n* [C] 1 (药的)一剂〔劑〕 yíjì; 一服 yífù. 2 (苦事的)一次 yícì; 一番 yìfān: *a ~ of flu* 患一次流行性感冒. **dose** *v* [T] (*with*) 给…服药〔藥〕 gěi…fúyào.

doss /dɒs/ *v* [短语动词] doss down [英国俚语]在可以凑合的地方过〔過〕夜 zài kěyǐ còuhé de dìfang guòyè. ˈdoss-house *n* [C] [英国俚语]廉价〔價〕小旅店 liánjià xiǎo lǚdiàn.

dossier /ˈdɒsɪeɪ; *US* 亦作 ˈdɔːsɪər/ *n* [C] 一宗档〔檔〕案材料 yìzōng dàng'àn cáiliào.

dot /dɒt/ *n* [C] 1 小圆点〔點〕 xiǎoyuándiǎn. 2 [习语] on the dot 准〔準〕时〔時〕地 zhǔnshíde. **dot** *v* [-tt-] [T] 1 打圆点于 dǎ yuándiǎn yú. 2 [通常为被动语态] 布〔佈〕满 bùmǎn; 散布于 sànbù yú: *The sky was ~ted with stars.* 繁星满天. ˈdot-com *n* [C] 网〔網〕络公司 wǎngluò gōngsī.

dotage /ˈdəʊtɪdʒ/ *n* [习语] in one's dotage 老年昏愦 lǎonián hūnkuì.

dote /dəʊt/ *v* [I] *on* 过〔過〕分喜爱〔愛〕 guòfèn xǐ'ài: *~ on a child* 溺爱孩子.

dotty /ˈdɒtɪ/ *adj* [-ier, -iest] [英国非正式用语]半痴〔癡〕的 bànchīde.

double[1] /ˈdʌbl/ *adj* 1 加倍的 jiābèide; 两倍的 liǎngbèide: *Her income is ~ what it was a year ago.* 她的收入是一年前的两倍. 2 双〔雙〕的 shuāngde; 双重的 shuāngchóngde: *~ door* 双重门. '*Otter*' *is spelt with a ~ 't'.* "otter" 的拼写中有两个"t". 3 双人的 shuāngrénde: *a ~ bed* 双人床. ˌdouble-ˈbass *n* [C] 低音提琴 dīyīn tíqín. ˌdouble ˈchin *n* [C] 双下巴 shuāngxiàba. ˌdouble-ˈdealing *n* [U] 两面派行为〔爲〕 liǎngmiànpài xíngwéi. ˌdouble-ˈdecker *n* [C] 双层〔層〕公共汽车〔車〕 shuāngcéng gōnggòngqìchē. ˌdouble ˈDutch *n* [U] [英国非正式用语]莫名其妙的话 mò míng qí miào de huà; 难〔難〕以理解的语言 nányǐ lǐjiě de yǔyán.

double[2] /ˈdʌbl/ *adv* 双〔雙〕倍 shuāngbèi; 成两部分 chéng liǎng bùfen: *fold a blanket ~* 把毯子对折叠起. ˌdouble-ˈbarrelled *adj* (枪)双管的 shuāngguǎnde. ˌdouble-ˈbook *v* [I, T] 为〔爲〕(同一机票、旅馆房间等)接受两家预订 wéi jiēshòu liǎngjiā yùdìng. ˌdouble-ˈbreasted *adj* (上衣)双排纽扣的 shuāngpái niǔkòu de. ˌdouble-ˈcheck *v* [I, T] 从〔從〕两方面查对〔對〕 cóng liǎng fāngmiàn cháduì. ˈdouble-click *v* [T, I] 双击〔擊〕 shuāngjī. ˌdouble-ˈcross *v* [T] [非正式用语]欺骗 qīpiàn; 叛卖〔賣〕 pànmài. ˌdouble-ˈedged *adj* [喻](评语)模棱两可的 móléng liǎngkě de; 可作两种〔種〕解释〔釋〕的 kězuò liǎngzhǒng jiěshìde. ˌdouble-ˈglazing *n* [U] (窗户的)双层〔層〕玻璃 shuāngcéng bōli. ˌdouble-ˈjointed *adj* (手指、手臂等)可前弯〔彎〕也可后〔後〕弯的 kě qiánwān yě kě hòuwān de. ˌdouble-ˈquick *adj*, *adv* [非正式用语]非常快的(地) fēicháng kuàide.

double[3] /ˈdʌbl/ *n* [C] 1 两倍 liǎngbèi: *He's paid ~ for the same job.* 做同样的工作, 他的报酬比别人多出一倍. 2 与〔與〕另一人极〔極〕其相似的人 yǔ lìngyìrén jíqí xiāngsìde rén. 3 doubles [pl] (体育比赛)双〔雙〕打 shuāngdǎ. 4 [习语] at the double [非正式用语]迅速地 xùnsùde.

double[4] /ˈdʌbl/ *v* 1 [I, T] 使加倍 shǐ jiābèi; 成倍 chéngbèi. 2 [T] 把…对〔對〕折 bǎ…duìzhé. 3 [短语动词] double as sb 兼任(某工作) jiānrèn. double as sth 兼作某物使用 jiānzuò mǒuwù shǐyòng. double back 往回走 wǎnghuí zǒu. double (sb) up (使)弯〔彎〕身 wānshēn: *be ~d up with laughter* 笑得直不起身子.

doubly /ˈdʌblɪ/ *adv* [用于形容词前]双〔雙〕倍地 shuāngbèide: *make ~ sure* 要加倍注意.

doubt /daʊt/ *n* 1 [C, U] 怀〔懷〕疑 huáiyí; 疑惑 yíhuò; 疑问 yíwèn. 2 [习语] in ˈdoubt 不能肯定的 bùnéng kěndìng de. ˌno ˈdoubt 十有八九 shí yǒu bā jiǔ. without doubt 无〔無〕疑地 wúyíde. **doubt** *v* [I, T] 怀〔懷〕疑 huáiyí; 不相信…是真的 bù xiāngxìn…shì zhēn de. **doubtful** *adj* 1 疑惑的 yíhuòde; 怀疑的 huáiyíde. 2 不大可能的 búdà kěnéng de. **doubtless** *adv* 大概 dàgài; 很可能 hěn kěnéng.

dough /dəʊ/ *n* [U] 1 揉好的生面〔麵〕 róuhǎode shēngmiàn. 2 [俚]钱〔錢〕 qián. ˈdoughnut *n* [C] 炸面圈 zhá miànquān.

D

douse (亦作 **dowse**) /daʊs/ *v* [T] **1** 浇〔澆〕水在…上 jiāo shuǐ zài… shàng. **2** 熄(灯) xī.

dove[1] /dʌv/ *n* [C] **1** 鸽 gē. **2** [喻]从〔從〕事和平运〔運〕动〔動〕的人 cóngshì hépíng yùndòng de rén. **dovecote** /ˈdʌvkɒt, 亦作 ˈdʌvkəʊt/ 鸽棚 gēpéng;鸽房 gēfáng.

dove[2] [美语] *pt* of DIVE.

dovetail /ˈdʌvteɪl/ *n* [C] 鸠尾榫 jiūwěisǔn;楔形榫 xiēxíngsǔn. **dovetail** *v* **1** [T] 用鸠尾榫接合 yòng jiūwěisǔn jiēhé. **2** [I] [喻]和…吻合 hé…wěnhé.

D

dowdy /ˈdaʊdɪ/ *adj* [-ier, -iest] (人)衣着过〔過〕时〔時〕的 yīzhuó guòshí de.

down[1] /daʊn/ *adv* **1** 向下 xiàngxià;在下面 zài xiàmiàn: *jump* ~ 跳下. **2** 向地面 xiàng dìmiàn: *knock sb* ~ 把某人打倒下. **3** (a) 往较次要的地方 wǎng jiàocìyàode dìfang: *move* ~ *from London* 从伦敦迁出. (b) 向南方 xiàng nánfāng. **4** (程度等)由高到低 yóu gāo dào dī;(数量等)由大到小 yóu dà dào xiǎo: *calm* ~ 平静下来. *settle* ~ 安静下来. *Prices are down*. 物价下降. **5** (写)到纸上 dào zhǐshàng: *Copy this* ~. 把这个复印下来. *Take this* ~. 把这个写下来. **6** [习语] **be/go down with sth** 患…病 huàn…bìng. **down ˈunder** [非正式用语]在澳大利亚〔亞〕zài Àodàlìyà. **down with sb/sth** 打倒 dǎdǎo: *D~ with fascism!* 打倒法西斯! **ˈdown-and-out** *n* [C] 穷〔窮〕困潦倒的人 qióngkùn liáodǎo de rén. **ˌdown-to-ˈearth** *adj* 务〔務〕实〔實〕的 wùshíde;实际〔際〕的 shíjìde.

down[2] /daʊn/ *prep* **1** 在下面 zài xiàmiàn;往下 wǎngxià;向下 xiàngxià: *roll* ~ *the hill* 滚下山来. **2** 沿着 yánzhe: *live* ~ *the street* 顺街道住着.

down[3] /daʊn/ *adj* **1** 向下的 xiàngxiàde: *the* ~ *escalator* 下行自动扶梯. **2** 沮丧〔喪〕的 jǔsàngde: *feel* ~ 感到沮丧. **3** 停工的 tínggōngde;关〔關〕闭的 guānbìde: *The computer is* ~ *again*. 电脑又死机了. **ˌdown ˈpayment** (分期付款的)初付款额 chūfù kuǎn'é.

down[4] /daʊn/ *v* [T] **1** 吞下 tūnxià;(大口地)喝下 hēxià. **2** 击〔擊〕倒 jīdǎo.

down[5] /daʊn/ *n* [U] 绒毛 róngmáo;羽绒 yǔróng;茸毛 róngmáo: *duck* ~ 鸭绒.

downcast /ˈdaʊnkɑːst/ *adj* **1** (人)垂头〔頭〕丧〔喪〕气〔氣〕的 chuí tóu sàng qì de;消沉的 xiāochénde. **2** (眼睛)往下看的 wǎng xià kàn de.

downfall /ˈdaʊnfɔːl/ *n* [sing] 垮台 kuǎtái;衰落 shuāiluò;垮台、衰落的原因 kuǎtái、shuāiluò de yuányīn.

downgrade /ˌdaʊnˈgreɪd/ *v* [T] 使降级 shǐ jiàngjí;降低…的重要性 jiàngdī…de zhòngyàoxìng.

downhearted /ˌdaʊnˈhɑːtɪd/ *adj* 消沉的 xiāochénde;沮丧〔喪〕的 jǔsàngde.

downhill /daʊnˈhɪl/ *adv* **1** 向坡下 xiàng pōxià. **2** [习语] **go downhill** 恶〔惡〕化 èhuà;衰退 shuāituì.

Downing Street /ˈdaʊnɪŋ striːt/ *n* [sing] (a) (英国伦敦的)唐宁〔寧〕街(英国首相官邸所在地) Tángníngjiē. (b) [喻]英国〔國〕首相 Yīngguó shǒuxiàng. 英国政府 Yīngguó zhèngfǔ.

download /ˈdaʊnləʊd/ *v* [T] 下载〔載〕xiàzài.

downpour /ˈdaʊnpɔː(r)/ *n* [C] 倾盆大雨 qīngpén dàyǔ.

downright /ˈdaʊnraɪt/ *adj* 彻〔徹〕头〔頭〕彻尾的 chè tóu chè wěi de;十足的 shízúde: *a* ~ *lie* 彻头彻尾的谎话. **downright** *adv* 彻底地 chèdǐde;完全地 wánquánde: ~ *rude* 无礼透顶.

downs /daʊnz/ *n* **the downs** [pl] 丘陵地 qiūlíngdì;开〔開〕阔的高地 kāikuòde gāodì.

downstairs /ˌdaʊnˈsteəz/ *adv* 往楼〔樓〕下 wǎng lóuxià;在楼下 zài lóuxià;往楼下的 wǎng lóuxià de;在楼下的 zài lóuxià de.

downstream /daʊnˈstriːm/ *adv* 顺流地 shùnliúde.

downtown /ˈdaʊntaʊn/ *adv, adj* [尤用于美国英语]在城市的商业〔業〕区〔區〕(的) zài chéngshìde shāngyèqū. 往城市的商业区(的) wǎng chéngshìde shāngyèqū.

downtrodden /ˌdaʊnˈtrɒdn/ *adj* 受压〔壓〕制的 shòu yāzhìde: ~ *workers* 受压制的工人.

downward /ˈdaʊnwəd/ *adj* 向下的 xiàng xià de. **downwards** (亦作 **downward**) *adv* 向下地 xiàng xià de.

dowry /ˈdaʊərɪ/ *n* [C] [*pl* -ies] 嫁妆〔妝〕jiàzhuang.

dowse = DOUSE.

doz *abbr* dozen (一)打 dá;十二个〔個〕shí'èrgè.

doze /dəʊz/ *v* [I] 打盹儿〔兒〕dǎdǔnr;打瞌睡 dǎ kēshuì. **doze** *n* [C, 常用 sing] 小睡 xiǎoshuì;打盹儿 dǎ dǔnr. **dozy** *adj* [-ier, -iest] **1** 昏昏欲睡的 hūnhūn yù shuì de. **2** [非正式用语]笨的 bènde.

dozen /ˈdʌzn/ *n* [*pl* ~s 或与数字连用时 **dozen**] **1** (一)打 dá;十二个〔個〕shí'èrgè. **2** [习语] **talk, etc nineteen to the dozen** 不停地谈 bùtíngde tán.

Dr *abbr* **1** Doctor 博士 bóshì;医〔醫〕生 yīshēng. **2** (用于街名) Drive 路 lù;大道 dàdào.

drab /dræb/ *adj* [~ber, ~best] 单〔單〕调的 dāndiàode;没有兴〔興〕趣的 méiyǒu xìngqù de. **drabness** *n* [U].

draft /drɑːft; *US* dræft/ *n* **1** [C] 草案

cǎo'àn. 2 [C] 汇〔匯〕票 huìpiào. 3 the draft [sing] [美语] = CALL-UP (CALL[1]). 4 [C] [美语] ⇨ DRAUGHT. **draft** *v* [T] 1 起草 qǐcǎo. 2 派遣 pàiqiǎn. 3 [美语] 征〔徵〕召…入伍 zhēngzhào… rùwǔ. **draftsman** *n* [C] [*pl* -men] 1 法案起草人 fǎ'àn qǐcǎo rén. 2 [美语] = DRAUGHTSMAN (DRAUGHT).

drafty /ˈdrɑːftɪ/ *adj* [美语] = DRAUGHTY (DRAUGHT).

drag /dræg/ *v* [-gg-] 1 [T] 拖 tuō; 拉 lā; 拽 zhuài. 2 [I] 吃力而慢吞吞地移动〔動〕 chīlì ér màntūntūnde yídòng. 3 [T] 迫使去某处〔處〕 pòshǐ qù mǒuchù: *She ~ged herself out of bed*. 她颇不情愿地从床上爬了起来. 4 [I] (时间)缓慢地过〔過〕去 huǎnmànde guòqù. 5 [T] 用拖网〔網〕捕捞〔撈〕 yòng tuōwǎng bǔlāo. 6 [习语] **drag one's ˈfeet/ˈheels** 故意拖沓 gùyì tuōtà. 7 [短语动词] **drag on** 拖延 tuōyán; 使拖延 shǐ tuōyán. **drag sth out** 拖延 tuōyán; 拖长〔長〕 tuōcháng. **drag sth out of sb** 迫使某人说出情况 pòshǐ mǒurén shuōchū qíngkuàng. **drag sth up** 说起令人不愉快的事情 shuōqǐ lìng rén bù yúkuài de shìqing. **drag** *n* 1 [sing] [俚]令人厌〔厭〕倦的人、事物 lìng rén yànjuànde rén、shìwù. 2 [U] [俚]男人穿的女子服装〔裝〕 nánrén chuān de nǚzǐ fúzhuāng: *in* ~ (男人)穿着女子服装的 3 [C] [俚](香烟的)一吸 yìxī. 4 [sing] *on* [非正式用语]累赘 léizhui.

dragon /ˈdrægən/ *n* [C] 1 龙〔龍〕 lóng. 2 老悍妇〔婦〕 lǎohànfù.

drain /dreɪn/ *n* 1 [C] 排水管 páishuǐguǎn; 排水沟〔溝〕 páishuǐgōu; 阴〔陰〕沟 yīngōu; 排水设备〔備〕 páishuǐ shèbèi. 2 [习语] **a drain on sth** 消耗 xiāohào; 耗竭 hàojié: *a ~ on one's resources* 财力的耗竭. **(go) down the drain** 浪费掉 làngfèidiào. **drain** *v* 1 [I, T] (*away/off; from*) 使(液体)流出 shǐ liúchū; 流掉 liúdiào; 排出 páichū: *The water ~ed away*. 水流掉了. *She ~ed the oil from the engine*. 她把引擎中的油排了出来. 2 [T] 喝光(杯中的酒、水) hēguāng. 3 [I, T] (使)流干〔乾〕 liúgān; (使)滴干 dīgān: *leave the dishes to ~* 让盘子控干. 4 [T] 使身体〔體〕虚弱 shǐ shēntǐ xūruò; 使变〔變〕穷〔窮〕 shǐ biàn qióng. **drainage** *n* 1 [U] 排水系统 páishuǐ xìtǒng. 2 排水 páishuǐ; 放水 fàngshuǐ. **ˈdraining-board** (美语 **ˈdrain-board**) *n* [C] (洗涤池边上的)滴水板 dīshuǐbǎn. **ˈdrain-pipe** *n* [C] (排泄屋顶雨水的)排水管 páishuǐguǎn.

drake /dreɪk/ *n* [C] 雄鸭 xióngyā.

drama /ˈdrɑːmə/ *n* 1 [C] (一出)戏〔戲〕 xì. 2 [U] 戏剧〔劇〕 xìjù: *Elizabethan* ~ 伊丽莎白时代的戏剧. 3 [C, U] 一系列戏剧性事件 yíxìliè xìjùxìng shìjiàn. **dramatic** /drəˈmætɪk/ *adj* 1 戏剧性的 xìjùxìngde; 激动〔動〕人心的 jīdòng rénxīn de. 2 戏剧的 xìjùde. **dramatically** /-klɪ/ *adv*. **dramatics** /drəˈmætɪks/ *n* [U] 1 [用 sing v] 演剧活动〔動〕 yǎnjù huódòng; 戏剧作品 xìjù zuòpǐn. 2 [pl] [贬]戏剧性的行为〔為〕 xìjùxìngde xíngwéi. **dramatist** /ˈdræmətɪst/ *n* [C] 剧作家 jùzuòjiā. **dramatize** /ˈdræmətaɪz/ *v* [T] 1 把(小说等)改编为戏剧 bǎ gǎibiānwéi xìjù. 2 使(事情)更具刺激性 shǐ gèng jù cìjīxìng **dramatization** /ˌdræmətaɪˈzeɪʃn/ *n* [C, U]: *a ~tization of the novel* 小说改编成的戏剧.

drank /dræŋk/ *pt* of DRINK.

drape /dreɪp/ *v* [T] 1 把(布等)随〔隨〕便地悬〔懸〕挂〔掛〕 bǎ suíbiànde xuánguà. 2 (*in / with*) 用布遮盖〔蓋〕、装〔裝〕饰 yòng bù zhēgài、zhuāngshì. 3 *round/ over* 伸开〔開〕手或脚放在…上 shēnkāi shǒu huò jiǎo fàng zài…shàng. **drape** *n* [C, 常作 pl] [美语]帘 lián. **draper** *n* [C] [英国英语]布商 bùshāng. **drapery** *n* [*pl* -ies] 1 [C, U] 打摺的装饰织〔織〕物 dǎzhěde zhuāngshì zhīwù. 2 [U] [英国英语]布业〔業〕 bùyè; [总称]布 bù.

drastic /ˈdræstɪk/ *adj* 严〔嚴〕厉〔厲〕的 yánlìde; 严重的 yánzhòngde: *a ~ shortage of food* 食物严重缺乏. **drastically** / -klɪ / *adv*.

draught /drɑːft/ (美语 **draft** /dræft/) *n* 1 [C] 气〔氣〕流 qìliú. 2 [C] 一饮的量 yìyǐnde liàng. 3 [习语] **on draught** (啤酒等)取自桶中的 qǔ zì tǒng zhōng de; 散装〔裝〕的 sǎnzhuāngde. **draught** *adj* 1 (啤酒等)散装的 sǎnzhuāngde. 2 (牲畜)拖重物的 tuō zhòngwù de; 役用的 yìyòngde. **draughtsman** (美语 **draftsman**) *n* [C] [*pl* -men] 1 起草人 qǐcǎorén; 制〔製〕图〔圖〕员 zhìtúyuán. 2 长〔長〕于描绘〔繪〕的美术〔術〕家 chángyú miáohuìde měishùjiā. **draughty** *adj* [-ier, -iest] 有穿堂风〔風〕的 yǒu chuāntángfēng de.

draughts /drɑːfts/ *n* [用 sing v] 国〔國〕际〔際〕跳棋 guójì tiàoqí.

draw[1] /drɔː/ *v* [*pt* **drew** /druː/, *pp* ~**n** /drɔːn/] 1 [I, T] 画〔畫〕(画) huà. 2 [I] 移动〔動〕 yídòng; 行进〔進〕 xíngjìn: *The train drew into the station*. 火车进了站. 3 [T] 拖 tuō; 拉 lā: *The horse drew the coach along*. 马拉着公共马车前进. ~ *the curtains* 拉开窗帘; 拉上窗帘. 4 [T] *from / out of* 拔(出) bá: ~ *a gun from one's pocket* 从衣袋里拔出枪来. 5 [T] 吸引 xīyǐn; 招引 zhāoyǐn: ~ *a crowd* 招引了一大群人. 6 [T] 提取 tíqǔ; 汲取 jíqǔ; 领取 lǐngqǔ: ~ *water from a well* 从井中汲水. ~ *one's salary* 领取工资. 7 [T] 推断〔斷〕出 tuīduànchū; 作出 zuòchū; 形成 xíngchéng: ~ *a conclusion* 作出结论. ~ *a comparison* 形成比较. 8 [I, T] 打成平

局 dàchéng píngjú；不分胜〔勝〕负 bù fēn shèngfù：*The match was ~n*. 比赛打平. 9 [I, T] 吸(气) xī. 10 [I, T] (*from*) 抽签〔簽〕chōuqiān：~ *the winning ticket* 抽了张中彩票. 11 [习语] draw a ˈblank 没有找到人或物 méiyǒu zhǎodào rén huò wù. draw lots ⇨ LOT³. draw the line at sth 拒绝(做某事) jùjué. 12 [短语动词] draw back (from sth/doing sth) (尤因无把握)取消 qǔxiāo，撤回 chèhuí. draw in (白昼)变〔變〕短 biàn duǎn. draw sb in, draw sb into sth 诱使某人参〔參〕加 yòushǐ mǒurén cānjiā. draw on 临〔臨〕近 línjìn；接近 jiējìn. draw on sth 利用 lìyòng；凭〔憑〕píng；靠 kào：~ *on sb's experience* 利用某人的经验. draw out (白昼)变长〔長〕biànchána. draw sb out 引(某人)畅〔暢〕谈 yǐn chàngtán. draw sth out 拉长(讨论等) lācháng. draw up (车辆)停下 tíngxià. draw oneself up 笔〔筆〕直地站立 bǐzhíde zhànlì. draw sth up 写〔寫〕出 xiěchū；草拟〔擬〕出 cǎonǐchū.

draw² /drɔː/ *n* [C] 1 (比赛的)平局 píngjú. 2 [常为 sing] 抽签〔簽〕chōuqiān. 3 [常为 sing] 有吸引力的人或事物 yǒu xīyǐnlì de rén huò shìwù.

drawback /ˈdrɔːbæk/ *n* [C] 障碍〔礙〕zhàng'ài；不利 búlì.

drawer /drɔː(r)/ *n* [C] 抽屉 chōuti.

drawing /ˈdrɔːɪŋ/ *n* 1 [C] 图〔圖〕画〔畫〕túhuà；素描画 sùmiáohuà. 2 [U] 绘〔繪〕画(艺术) huìhuà；制〔製〕图(技巧) zhìtú. ˈdrawing-pin *n* [C] 图钉 túdīng. ˈdrawing-room *n* [C] [旧] 客厅〔廳〕kètīng.

drawl /drɔːl/ *v* [I, T] 慢吞吞地说 màntūntūnde shuō. drawl *n* [sing].

drawn¹ /drɔːn/ *pp* of DRAW¹.

drawn² /drɔːn/ *adj* (人、人脸)憔悴的 qiáocuìde.

dread /dred/ *v* [T] 畏惧〔懼〕wèijù；深惧 shēnjù. dread *n* [U] 恐怖 kǒngbù；害怕 hàipà；担〔擔〕忧〔憂〕dānyōu. dreaded *adj* 畏惧的 wèijùde；非常可怕的 fēicháng kěpàde. dreadful *adj* 糟透的 zāotòude；非常可怕的 fēicháng kěpà de. dreadfully *adv* 可怕地 kěpàde；非常 fēicháng；极〔極〕其 jíqí.

dream /driːm/ *n* 1 [C] 梦〔夢〕mèng. 2 [C] 梦想 mèngxiǎng；空想 kōngxiǎng：*his ~ of becoming president* 他当总统的梦想. 3 [sing] [非正式用语]美妙的事物 měimiàode shìwù. dream *v* [*pt*, *pp* ~t /dremt/ 或，尤用于美语 ~ed] 1 [I, T] 做梦 zuò mèng；梦见 mèngjiàn；梦到 mèngdào. 2 [I, T] 想像 xiǎngxiàng；幻想 huànxiǎng. 3 [习语] not dream of sth/doing sth 不考虑〔慮〕做某事 bù kǎolǜ zuò mǒushì；决不做某事 jué bú zuò mǒushì：*I wouldn't ~ of allowing you to pay*. 我决不让你付账. 4 [短语动词] dream sth up 想入非非 xiǎngrù fēifēi. dream *adj* [非正式用语]极〔極〕好的 jíhǎode：*a ~ house* 极好的房子. dreamer *n* [C] 1 做梦的人 zuòmèngde rén. 2 [贬] 空想家 kōngxiǎngjiā. dreamless *adj* (睡眠)无〔無〕梦的 wúmèngde. dreamlike *adj* 似梦的 sìmèngde；奇异〔異〕的 qíyìde. dreamy *adj* [-ier, -iest] 1 (人)心不在焉的 xīn bú zài yān de. 2 模糊的 móhude. 3 轻〔輕〕松〔鬆〕恬静的 qīngsōng tiánjìng de. dreamily *adv*.

dreary /ˈdrɪərɪ/ *adj* [-ier, -iest] 沉闷的 chénmènde；阴〔陰〕沉的 yīnchénde. drearily /-rəlɪ/ *adv*. dreariness *n* [U].

dredge /dredʒ/ *v* 1 [T] 疏浚(河道) shūjùn. 2 [短语动词] dredge sth up 重提不愉快的旧〔舊〕事 chóngtí bù yúkuàide jiùshì. dredger *n* [C] 挖泥船 wāníchuán；疏浚船 shūjùnchuán.

dregs /dregz/ *n* [pl] 1 残〔殘〕渣 cánzhā；渣滓 zhāzi；糟粕 zāopò. 2 [贬]废〔廢〕料 fèiliào；渣滓 zhāzi：*the ~ of society* 社会渣滓.

drench /drentʃ/ *v* [T] 使淋透 shǐ líntòu；使湿〔濕〕透 shǐ shītòu：*We were ~ed in the rain*. 我们被雨淋透.

dress¹ /dres/ *n* 1 [C] 女服 nǚfú. 2 [U] 服装〔裝〕fúzhuāng：*formal ~* 礼服. dressmaker *n* [C] 裁缝 cáifeng；(尤指)女裁缝 nǚ cáifeng. ˈdress rehearsal *n* [C] (戏剧)彩排 cǎipái.

dress² /dres/ *v* 1 [I, T] 穿衣 chuān yī；给…穿衣 gěi…chuān yī. 2 [I] 穿上晚礼〔禮〕服 chuān shàng wǎnlǐfú：~ *for dinner* 穿晚礼服赴宴. 3 [T] 装〔裝〕饰 zhuāngshì：~ *a shop window* 布置商店橱窗. 4 [T] 清洗敷裹(伤口) qīngxǐ fūguǒ. 5 [T] (为烹调)加工(禽、畜等) jiāgōng；(加佐料)制〔製〕作 zhìzuò. 6 [习语] dressed to ˈkill [非正式用语]穿着引人注目(尤指异性) chuānzhuó yǐnrén zhùmù. 7 [短语动词] dress sb down 痛斥 tòngchì. dress up (a) 穿上盛装 chuān shàng shèngzhuāng. (b) (尤指儿童)化装〔裝〕huàzhuāng.

dresser /ˈdresə(r)/ *n* [C] [尤用于英国英语] 食具柜〔櫃〕shíjùguì.

dressing /ˈdresɪŋ/ *n* 1 [C, U] (医用)敷料 fūliào. 2 [C, U] (拌色拉的)调味汁 tiáowèizhī. ˈdressing-gown *n* [C] (罩于睡衣外的)晨衣 chényī. ˈdressing-table *n* [C] 梳妆〔妝〕台 shūzhuāngtái.

drew /druː/ *pt* of DRAW².

dribble /ˈdrɪbl/ *v* 1 [I] 流口水 liú kǒushuǐ. 2 [I, T] (使)液体〔體〕点〔點〕滴流淌 yètǐ diǎndī liútǎng. 3 [I, T] (足球)短传〔傳〕duǎn chuán. dribble *n* [C, 常作 sing].

dried /draɪd/ *pt*, *pp* of DRY.

drier ⇨ DRY.

drift /drɪft/ *v* [I] 1 漂流 piāoliú；飘〔飄〕

piāo. 2 (人)漂泊 piāobó; 游荡〔蕩〕yóudàng. **drift** *n* 1 [U] 漂流 piāoliú; 飘 piāo. 2 [C] 风〔風〕吹积〔積〕的雪堆 fēng chuī jī de xuěduī. 3 [C, U] [喻]趋〔趨〕势〔勢〕qūshì; 倾向 qīngxiàng; 动〔動〕向 dòngxiàng. 4 [sing] 大概意思 dàgài yìsi; 要旨 yàozhǐ: *the ~ of his arguments* 他的话的主要内容. **drifter** *n* [C] 流浪者 liúlàngzhě.

drill[1] /drɪl/ *n* [C] 钻〔鑽〕zuàn; 钻头〔頭〕zuàntóu. **drill** *v* [I, T] 钻孔 zuān kǒng; 在…上钻孔 zài…shang zuān kǒng.

drill[2] /drɪl/ *n* 1 [C] 操练〔練〕cāoliàn; 练习〔習〕liànxí: *pronunciation ~s* 发音操练. 2 [U] (士兵的)训练方法 xùnliàn fāngfǎ. 3 [C] 紧〔緊〕急措施 jǐnjí cuòshī: *a fire ~* 消防措施. **drill** *v* [I, T] 训练 xùnliàn; 操练 cāoliàn.

drily ⇨DRY.

drink /drɪŋk/ *v* [*pt* **drank** /dræŋk/, *pp* **drunk** /drʌŋk/] 1 [I, T] 饮 yǐn; 喝 hē. 2 [I] 饮酒 yǐnjiǔ; 喝酒 hējiǔ. 3 [习语] **drink sb's health** [正式用语]向某人祝酒 xiàng mǒurén zhùjiǔ. **drink like a fish** [非正式用语]豪饮 háoyǐn. 4 [短语动词] **drink sth in** 全神贯注地看或听〔聽〕quán shén guàn zhù de kàn huò tīng. **drink to sb/sth** 向…祝酒 xiàng…zhùjiǔ; 为〔爲〕…干〔乾〕杯 wèi…gānbēi. **drink** *n* [C, U] 1 饮料 yǐnliào. 2 酒 jiǔ. **drinkable** *adj*. **drinker** *n* [C] 酒徒 jiǔtú.

drip /drɪp/ *v* [-pp-] [I, T] 1 (使)滴下 dīxià. 2 [习语] ˌ**dripping** ˈ**wet** 全部湿〔濕〕透 quánbù shītòu. **drip** *n* [C] 1 滴下的液体〔體〕dīxiàde yètǐ. 2 [医]滴注器 dīzhùqì. 3 [俚]呆子 dāizi. ˌ**drip-**ˈ**dry** *adj* (衣服无须绞干)能滴干〔乾〕的 néng dīgān de. **dripping** *n* [U] (烤肉上滴下的)油滴 yóudī.

drive[1] /draɪv/ *v* [*pt* **drove** /drəʊv/, *pp* **~n** /ˈdrɪvn/] 1 [I, T] 驾(车) jià. 2 [T] 驾车送(人) jiàchē sòng. 3 [T] 驱〔驅〕赶〔趕〕(牲畜或人) qūgǎn. 4 [T] 驱动〔動〕(机器) qūdòng. 5 [T] 猛击〔擊〕(球) měngjī; 猛抽(球) měngchōu. 6 [T] 打 dǎ; 敲 qiāo: *~ nails into wood* 把钉子敲进木头. 7 [T] 逼迫 bīpò; 迫使 pòshǐ: *You are driving me mad!* 你逼我发疯! 8 [习语] **be driving at** 要说 yào shuō; 意指 yìzhǐ: *What are you driving at?* 你要说的是什么? **drive a hard** ˈ**bargain** 坚〔堅〕持苛刻的条〔條〕件 jiānchí kēkède tiáojiàn. ˈ**drive-in** (顾客无须下车即可得到服务的)"免下车"餐馆、剧场〔場〕、银行、邮〔郵〕局 "miǎn xiàchē" cānguǎn、jùchǎng、yínháng、yóujú; 有"免下车"服务〔務〕设施的 yǒu "miǎnxiàchē" fúwù shèshī de. **driver** *n* [C] 赶车者 gǎnchēzhě; 驾驶员 jiàshǐyuán. ˈ**driving-licence** (美语 **driver's licence**) *n* [C] 驾驶执〔執〕照 jiàshǐ zhízhào. ˈ**driving test** (美语 **driver's test**) *n* [C] 驾车考试 jiàchē kǎoshì; 路考 lùkǎo.

drive[2] /draɪv/ *n* 1 [C] 驾车〔車〕旅行 jiàchē lǚxíng. 2 [C] (美语常为 ˈ**drive-way**) (通向一所房屋的)私人车道 sīrén chēdào. 3 [C] (高尔夫球等)猛击〔擊〕měngjī; 猛抽 měngchōu. 4 [U] 干〔幹〕劲〔勁〕gànjìn; 魄力 pòlì. 5 [C] 欲望 yùwàng; 冲〔衝〕动〔動〕chōngdòng. 6 [C] 运〔運〕动 yùndòng: *an* ˈ*export ~* 出口运动.

drivel /ˈdrɪvl/ *n* [U] 幼稚无〔無〕聊的话 yòuzhì wúliáo de huà.

drizzle /ˈdrɪzl/ *n* [U] 蒙蒙细雨 méngméng xìyǔ. **drizzle** *v* [I] (与 it 连用)下蒙蒙细雨 xià méngméng xìyǔ.

drone /drəʊn/ *v* 1 [I] 发〔發〕出嗡嗡声〔聲〕fāchū wēngwēngshēng. 2 [短语动词] **drone on** 用单〔單〕调沉闷的声调说话 yòng dāndiào chénmèn de shēngdiào shuōhuà. **drone** *n* 1 [sing] 低沉的嗡嗡声 dīchénde wēngwēngshēng. 2 [C] 雄蜂 xióngfēng.

drool /druːl/ *v* [I] 1 滴口水 dī kǒushuǐ; 垂涎 chuíxián. 2 (*over*) [非正式用语]过〔過〕分地表示兴〔興〕奋〔奮〕guòfènde biǎoshì xīngfèn.

droop /druːp/ *v* [I] (因衰弱而)下垂 xiàchuí; 低垂 dīchuí.

drop[1] /drɒp/ *v* [-pp-] 1 [I, T] (使)滴下 dīxià; (使)落下 luòxià. 2 [I] 减弱 jiǎnruò; 降低 jiàngdī. 3 [T] (*off*) 使下车 shǐ xiàchē. 4 [T] (*from*) 使退出 shǐ tuìchū; 开除 kāichú: *He's been ~ped from the team*. 他被队里开除了. 5 [T] [非正式用语]寄(信) jì; 不经〔經〕意地说出 bù jīngyì de shuōchū. 6 [T] 停止做 tíngzhǐ zuò; 停止讨论〔論〕tíngzhǐ tǎolùn. 7 [习语] **drop sb a line** [非正式用语]给某人写〔寫〕一短信 gěi mǒurén xiě yī duǎnxìn. 8 [短语动词] **drop back** 落后〔後〕luòhòu. **drop by/in/round, drop in on sb** 顺便访问 shùnbiàn fǎngwèn; 偶然访问 ǒurán fǎngwèn. **drop off** (a) 睡着 shuìzháo; 入睡 rùshuì. (b) 逐渐减少 zhújiàn jiǎnshǎo. **drop out (of sth)** (a) 退学〔學〕tuìxué. (b) 退出(活动) tuìchū. ˈ**drop-out** *n* [C] 退学学生 tuìxué xuéshēng. **droppings** *n* [pl] (鸟、兽等的)粪〔糞〕fèn.

drop[2] /drɒp/ *n* 1 [C] 滴 dī. 2 **drops** [pl] (药)滴剂〔劑〕dījì. 3 [C] 水果硬糖 shuǐguǒ yìngtáng. 4 [sing] 倾斜或垂直的距离〔離〕qīngxié huò chuízhí de jùlí: *a ~ of 500 metres* 垂直距离 500 米. 5 [sing] [喻]减少 jiǎnshǎo: *a ~ in price* 减价. 6 [习语] **at the** ˌ**drop of a** ˈ**hat** 毫不迟〔遲〕疑地 háo bù chíyí de.

drought /draʊt/ *n* [C, U] 干〔乾〕旱 gānhàn.

drove[1] /drəʊv/ *pt* of DRIVE[1].

drove[2] /drəʊv/ *n* [C] 大群 dàqún: *~s of visitors* 一大群一大群的访问者.

drown /draʊn/ *v* 1 [I, T] (使)淹死 yānsǐ. 2 [T] (*out*) (声音)压〔壓〕过〔過〕yāguò. 3 [习语] **drown one's** ˈ**sorrows** 借酒浇〔澆〕愁 jiè

D

jiǔ jiāo chóu.

drowsy /ˈdraʊzɪ/ *adj* [-ier, -iest] 昏昏欲睡的 hūnhūn yù shuì de. **drowsily** *adv*. **drowsiness** *n* [U].

drudge /drʌdʒ/ *n* [C] 做苦工的人 zuò kǔgōng de rén. **drudgery** /-ərɪ/ *n* [U] 苦工 kǔgōng;重活 zhònghuó;单〔單〕调乏味的工作 dāndiào fáwèi de gōngzuò.

drug /drʌg/ *n* [C] **1** 药〔藥〕yào;药物 yàowù. **2** 麻醉药 mázuìyào;成瘾〔癮〕性毒品 chéngyǐnxìng dúpǐn: *He's on ~s*. 他吸毒成瘾. **drug** *v* [-gg-] [T] **1** 搀〔攙〕毒药于(食物、饮料) chān dúyào yú. **2** 用药使…麻醉 yòng yào shǐ…mázuì. ˈ**drug addict** *n* [C] 吸毒者 xīdúzhě;瘾君子 yǐnjūnzǐ. ˈ**drug dealer** *n* [C], ˈ**drug pusher** *n* [C] 贩毒者 fàndúzhě;毒贩 dúfàn. ˈ**drug store** *n* [C] [美语]杂〔雜〕货店 záhuòdiàn.

drum /drʌm/ *n* [C] **1** 鼓 gǔ. **2** 圆桶 yuántǒng: *an oil ~* 油桶. **drum** *v* [-mm-] **1** [I] 打鼓 dǎ gǔ. **2** [I, T] (用手指等)连续〔續〕地叩击〔擊〕 liánxùde kòujī. **3** [短语动词] **drum sth into sb** 反复〔復〕向某人灌输某事物 fǎnfù xiàng mǒurén guànshū mǒushìwù. **drum sth up** 竭力争取 jiélì zhēngqǔ;招徕(顾客等) zhāolái. **drummer** *n* [C] 鼓手 gǔshǒu. **drumstick** *n* [C] 鼓槌 gǔchuí.

drunk[1] *pp* of DRINK.

drunk[2] /drʌŋk/ *adj* 酒醉的 jiǔzuìde. **drunk** (亦作 **drunkard** /-əd/) *n* [C] 醉汉〔漢〕zuìhàn;酒鬼 jiǔguǐ. **drunken** *adj* **1** 显〔顯〕出酒力的 xiǎnchū jiǔlì de. **2** 酒醉的 jiǔzuìde. **drunkenly** *adv*. **drunkenness** *n* [U].

dry /draɪ/ *adj* [**drier**, **driest**] **1** 干〔乾〕的 gānde;干燥的 gānzàode: *a ~ cloth* 干布. *~ paint* 干了的油漆. *~ weather* 干燥的天气. **2** (酒)不甜的 bùtiánde. **3** (幽默)冷面滑稽的 lěngmiàn huájī de;冷嘲的 lěngcháode. **4** 枯燥乏味的 kūzào fáwèi de: *a ~ speech* 枯燥乏味的讲话. **drier** (亦作 **dryer**) /ˈdraɪə(r)/ *n* [C] 干燥器 gānzàoqì: *a clothes drier* 干衣机. **dry** *v* [*pt*, *pp* **dried**] **1** [I, T] (使)干 gān. **2** [短语动词] **dry (sth) out** (使)干透 gāntòu. **dry up** (a) (供应)停止 tíngzhǐ. (b) (忘记要说的话而)说不下去 shuō bú xiàqù. **dry (sth) up** 擦干(碗、碟等) cā gān. ˌ**dry-ˈclean** *v* [T] 干洗 gānxǐ. ˌ**dry-ˈcleaner** *n* [C]. ˌ**dry-ˈcleaning** *n* [U]. ˌ**dry ˈdock** *n* [C] 干船坞 gān chuánwù. **dryly** (亦作 **drily**) /ˈdraɪlɪ/ *adv*. **dryness** *n* [U]. ˌ**dry ˈrot** *n* [U] (植物)干腐病 gānfǔbìng.

dual /ˈdjuːəl; *US* ˈduːəl/ *adj* 双〔雙〕的 shuāngde;二重的 èrchóngde;二体〔體〕的 èrtǐde. ˌ**dual ˈcarriageway** *n* [C] (有中央分隔带的)双车〔車〕道 shuāngchēdào.

dub /dʌb/ *v* [-bb-] [T] **1** 给…起绰号〔號〕gěi…qǐ chuòhào. **2** 译〔譯〕制〔製〕(影片)yìzhì.

dubious /ˈdjuːbɪəs; *US* ˈduː-/ *adj* 引起怀〔懷〕疑的 yǐnqǐ huáiyí de. **dubiously** *adv*.

duchess /ˈdʌtʃɪs/ *n* [C] **1** 公爵夫人 gōngjué fūrén. **2** 女公爵 nǚ gōngjué.

duchy /ˈdʌtʃɪ/ *n* [C] [*pl* **-ies**] 公爵、女公爵领地 gōngjué、nǚ gōngjué lǐngdì.

duck[1] /dʌk/ *n* [*pl* **duck** 或 **~s**] **1** (a) [C] 鸭 yā. (b) [C] 雌鸭 cíyā. (c) [U] 鸭肉 yāròu. **2** [C] (板球)零分 língfēn.

duck[2] /dʌk/ *v* **1** [I, T] 突然低下(头) tūrán dīxià. **2** [T] 把(某人)暂按入水中 bǎ zàn ànrù shuǐ zhōng. **3** [I, T] (*out of*) 逃避责任 táobì zérèn.

duckling /ˈdʌklɪŋ/ *n* [C] 小鸭 xiǎoyā;幼鸭 yòuyā.

duct /dʌkt/ *n* [C] (输送液体或气体的)导〔導〕管 dǎoguǎn;管道 guǎndào.

dud /dʌd/ *n* [C], *adj* [非正式用语]不中用的东西 bù zhōngyòng de dōngxi;无〔無〕价〔價〕值的东西 wú jiàzhí de dōngxi;不中用的 bù zhōngyòng de;无价值的 wú jiàzhí de: *a ~ cheque* 无用的支票.

due /djuː; *US* duː/ *adj* **1** 应〔應〕支付的 yīng zhīfù de. **2** 预定应到的 yùdìng yīngdào de;预期的 yùqīde: *The train is ~ (to arrive) at 1:30*. 列车一点半钟到站. **3** 适〔適〕当〔當〕的 shìdàngde;正当的 zhèngdāngde. **4** *to* 由于 yóuyú: *His success is ~ to hard work*. 他由于努力而获得成功. **due** *adv* (罗盘指针)正(南、北等) zhèng: *~ east* 正东. **due** *n* **1** [sing] 应得的事物 yīngdéde shìwù. **2** **dues** [pl] 应缴款 yīng jiǎo kuǎn;会〔會〕费 huìfèi.

duel /ˈdjuːəl; *US* ˈduːəl/ *n* [C] **1** (旧时的)决斗〔鬥〕juédòu. **2** (双方的)斗争 dòuzhēng. **duel** *v* [-ll-; 美语 -l-] [I] 决斗 juédòu.

duet /djuːˈet; *US* duːˈet/ *n* [C] 二重唱 èrchóngchàng;二重奏 èrchóngzòu.

duffle-coat (亦作 **duffel-coat**) /ˈdʌflkəʊt/ *n* [C] 粗呢上衣 cūní shàngyī.

dug /dʌg/ *pt*, *pp* of DIG[2].

dug-out /ˈdʌgaʊt/ *n* [C] **1** 独〔獨〕木舟 dúmùzhōu. **2** 地下掩蔽部 dìxià yǎnbìbù.

duke /djuːk; *US* duːk/ *n* [C] 公爵 gōngjué. **dukedom** *n* [C] **1** 公爵爵位 gōngjué juéwèi. **2** 公爵领地 gōngjué lǐngdì.

dull /dʌl/ *adj* **1** 阴〔陰〕暗的 yīn'ànde. **2** 迟〔遲〕钝的 chídùnde. **3** 沉闷的 chénmènde;令人厌〔厭〕烦的 lìng rén yànfán de. **4** 钝的 dùnde: *a ~ knife* 一把钝刀. *a ~ ache* 隐痛. **dull** *v* [I, T] (使)变〔變〕钝 biàn dùn. **dullness** *n* [U]. **dully** /ˈdʌllɪ/ *adv*.

duly /ˈdjuːlɪ; *US* ˈduːlɪ/ *adj* 适〔適〕当〔當〕地 shìdàngde;按时〔時〕地 ànshíde.

dumb /dʌm/ *adj* **1** 哑〔啞〕的 yǎde;不能说话

的 bùnéng shuōhuà de. 2 不愿〔願〕说话的 búyuàn shuōhuà de；沉默的 chénmòde. 3［非正式用语，贬］愚笨的 yúbènde；蠢的 chǔnde. dumbly *adv*. dumbness *n* [U].

dumbfounded /dʌmˈfaʊndɪd/ *adj* 惊〔驚〕得说不出话的 jīngde shuōbùchū huà de.

dummy /ˈdʌmɪ/ *n* [C] [*pl* -ies] 1（服装店的）人体〔體〕模型 réntǐ móxíng. 2［英国英语］（哄婴儿的）橡皮奶头〔頭〕xiàngpí nǎitóu. ˌdummy ˈrun *n* [C] 演习〔習〕yǎnxí；排演 páiyǎn.

dump /dʌmp/ *v* [T] 1 倒掉 dàodiào；扔掉 rēngdiào. 2 随〔隨〕便放置 suíbiàn fàngzhì. 3［贬］向国〔國〕外倾销 xiàng guówài qīngxiāo. dump *n* [C] 1 堆垃圾的地方 duī lājī de dìfang；垃圾堆 lājīduī. 2 军需品堆集处〔處〕jūnxūpǐn duījíchù. 3［非正式用语，贬］丑〔醜〕陋的处〔處〕所 chǒulòude chùsuǒ. 4［习语］down in the dumps 不高兴〔興〕的 bù gāoxìng de；沮丧〔喪〕的 jǔsàngde. ˈdumper truck *n* [C] 自动〔動〕卸货卡车 zìdòng xièhuò kǎchē.

dumpling /ˈdʌmplɪŋ/ *n* [C] 水果布丁 shuǐguǒ bùdīng.

dumpy /ˈdʌmpɪ/ *adj* [-ier, -iest] 矮而胖的 ǎi ér pàng de.

dunce /dʌns/ *n* [C] [贬] 笨人 bènrén；笨学〔學〕生 bènxuésheng.

dune /djuːn; *US* duːn/（亦作 ˈsand-dune）*n* [C]（风吹积成的）沙丘 shāqiū.

dung /dʌŋ/ *n* [U]（牲畜的）粪〔糞〕fèn；粪肥 fènféi.

dungarees /ˌdʌngəˈriːz/ *n* [pl] 粗布工作服 cūbù gōngzuòfú.

dungeon /ˈdʌndʒən/ *n* [C] 土牢 tǔláo；地牢 dìláo.

dunk /dʌŋk/ *v* [T]（吃前）把…在汤〔湯〕等中浸一浸 bǎ…zài tāng děng zhōng jìnyíjìn.

duo /ˈdjuːəʊ; *US* ˈduːəʊ/ *n* [C] [*pl* ~s] 一对〔對〕表演者 yíduì biǎoyǎnzhě.

dupe /djuːp; *US* duːp/ *v* [T] 欺骗 qīpiàn；诈骗 zhàpiàn. dupe *n* [C] 受骗者 shòupiànzhě.

duplex /ˈdjuːpleks; *US* ˈduː-/ *n* [C] [美语] 1 联〔聯〕式房屋 liánshì fángwū. 2 占〔佔〕两层〔層〕楼〔樓〕的公寓套房 zhàn liǎngcénglóu de gōngyù tàofáng.

duplicate[1] /ˈdjuːplɪkeɪt; *US* ˈduːpləkeɪt/ *v* [T] 复〔複〕写〔寫〕fùxiě；复制〔製〕fùzhì. duplication /ˌdjuːplɪˈkeɪʃn; *US* ˌduːpləˈkeɪʃn/ *n* [U]. duplicator *n* [C] 复印机〔機〕fùyìnjī.

duplicate[2] /ˈdjuːplɪkət; *US* ˈduːpləkət/ *adj* 完全一样〔樣〕的 wánquán yíyàng de. duplicate *n* 1 [C] 完全一样的东西 wánquán yíyàngde dōngxi. 2［习语］in duplicate 一式两份地 yíshì liǎngfèn de.

durable /ˈdjʊərəbl; *US* ˈdʊ-/ *adj* 耐用的 nàiyòngde. durables *n* [pl] 耐用品 nàiyòngpǐn.

duration /djʊˈreɪʃn; *US* dʊ-/ *n* [U] 持续〔續〕时〔時〕间 chíxù shíjiān.

duress /djʊˈres; *US* dʊ-/ *n* [U] 威胁〔脅〕wēixié；强迫 qiǎngpò：*under* ~ 在被胁迫的情况下.

during /ˈdjʊərɪŋ; *US* ˈdʊ-/ *prep* 1 在…期间 zài…qījiān. 2 在…的时〔時〕候（在…期间的某个时候）zài …de shíhòu：*He died* ~ *the night*. 他在夜里死了.

dusk /dʌsk/ *n* [U] 黄昏 huánghūn，薄暮 bómù. dusky *adj* [-ier, -iest] 暗淡的 àndànde；暗黑的 ànhēide.

dust /dʌst/ *n* [U] 灰尘〔塵〕huīchén；尘土 chéntǔ；尘埃 chén'āi. dust *v* [T] 1 去掉…上的尘土 qùdiào… shàng de chéntǔ. 2 撒粉状〔狀〕物于… sǎ fěnzhuàngwù yú… ˈdustbin *n* [C] 垃圾箱 lājīxiāng. ˈdust bowl *n* [C] 干〔乾〕旱不毛的地区〔區〕gānhàn bù máo de dìqū. ˈdust-cart *n* [C] 垃圾车〔車〕lājīchē. duster *n* [C] 揩布 kāibù；抹布 mǒbù. ˈdust-jacket *n* [C] 书〔書〕的护〔護〕封 shūde hùfēng. ˈdustman /-mən/ *n* [C] [*pl* -men] 倒垃圾工 dào lājī gōng. dustpan *n* [C] 畚箕 běnjī. dust-sheet *n* [C]（家具的）防尘套 fángchén tào. dusty *adj* [-ier, -iest] 灰尘覆盖〔蓋〕的 huīchén fùgàide.

Dutch /dʌtʃ/ *adj* 1 荷兰〔蘭〕的 Hélánde；荷兰人的 Hélánrénde；荷兰语的 Hélányǔde；2［习语］go Dutch（with sb）平摊〔攤〕费用 píngtān fèiyòng.

duty /ˈdjuːtɪ; *US* ˈduːtɪ/ *n* [C, U] [*pl* -ies] 1 责任 zérèn；本分 běnfèn；义〔義〕务〔務〕yìwù. 2 税 shuì：ˈ*customs duties* 关税. 3［习语］on duty 上班 shàngbān；值班 zhíbān. off duty 下班 xiàbān. dutiful *adj* 恭敬的 gōngjìngde；孝敬的 xiàojìngde. dutifully *adv*. ˌduty-ˈfree *adj*, *adv*（货物）免关〔關〕税的（地）miǎn guānshuì de.

duvet /ˈdjuːveɪ/ *n* [C] 褥垫〔墊〕rùdiàn.

DVD /ˌdiː viː ˈdiː/ *abbr* digital video disc 数〔數〕字式激光视盘〔盤〕shùzìshì jīguāng shìpán. DVˈD player *n* [C] DVD 播放机〔機〕DVD bōfàngjī.

DVT /diː viː ˈtiː/ *abbr* deep-vein thrombosis 深静脉〔脈〕血栓症 shēnjìngmài xuèshuānzhèng；深层〔層〕静脉栓塞 shēncéng jìngmài shuānsāi；经〔經〕济〔濟〕舱〔艙〕综合征〔徵〕jīngjìcāng zōnghézhēng.

dwarf /dwɔːf/ *n* [C] [*pl* ~s] 矮人 ǎirén；矮小的动〔動〕植物 ǎixiǎode dòngzhíwù. dwarf *v* [T] 使显〔顯〕得矮小 shǐ xiǎnde ǎixiǎo.

dwell /dwel/ *v* [*pt*, *pp* dwelt /dwelt/] 1 [I] [旧词或修辞] 居住（于某地）jūzhù. 2［短语动词］dwell on sth 细思 xìsī；详述 xiángshù；详

D

论〔論〕xiánglùn. **dweller** *n* [C] (用于复合词) 居住者 jūzhùzhě; 居民 jūmín: ˈ*city-~ers* 城市居民. **dwelling** *n* [C] [正式用语] 住处〔處〕zhùchù; 住宅 zhùzhái; 寓所 yùsuǒ.

dwindle /ˈdwɪndl/ *v* [I] 缩小 suōxiǎo; 减少 jiǎnshǎo.

dye /daɪ/ *v* [*pres part* ~ing] [T] 使…染色 shǐ…rǎnsè. **dye** *n* [C, U] 染料 rǎnliào. ˌ**dyed-in-the-**ˈ**wool** *adj* 死心塌地的 sǐ xīn tā dì de.

dying ⇨ DIE².

dyke = DIKE.

dynamic /daɪˈnæmɪk/ *adj* **1** 动〔動〕力的 dònglìde. **2** 精力充沛的 jīnglì chōngpèi de; 精悍的 jīnghànde. **dynamically** /-klɪ/ *adv*. **dynamics** *n* [U] [用 sing v] 力学〔學〕lìxué; 动力学 dònglìxué. **dynamism** /ˈdaɪnəmɪzəm/ *n* [U] 活力 huólì; 干〔幹〕劲〔勁〕gànjìn.

dynamite /ˈdaɪnəmaɪt/ *n* [U] **1** 炸药〔藥〕zhàyào. **2** [喻] 具有爆炸性的事物 jùyǒu bàozhàxìngde shìwù; 轰〔轟〕动〔動〕一时〔時〕的人物 hōngdòng yìshí de rénwù. **dynamite** *v* [T] 用炸药爆炸 yòng zhàyào bàozhà.

dynamo /ˈdaɪnəməʊ/ *n* [C] [*pl* ~s] 发〔發〕电〔電〕机〔機〕fādiànjī.

dynasty /ˈdɪnəstɪ; *US* ˈdaɪ-/ *n* [C] [*pl* -ies] 朝代 cháodài; 王朝 wángcháo.

dysentery /ˈdɪsəntrɪ; *US* -terɪ/ *n* [U] 痢疾 lìji.

dyslexia /dɪsˈleksɪə; *US* -ˈlekʃə/ *n* [U] [医] 诵读〔讀〕困难〔難〕sòngdú kùnnan. **dyslexic** /-ˈleksɪk/ *n* [C], *adj* 诵读困难患者 sòngdú kùnnan huànzhě; 诵读困难的 sòngdú kùnnan de.

E e

E, e /iː/ *n* [C] [*pl* **E's, e's** /iːz/] 英语的第五个〔個〕字母 Yīngyǔde dìwǔgè zìmǔ. ˈ**E number** *n* [C] E 数〔數〕(食品添加剂的代号) Eshù.

E *abbr* **1** (尤用于电器插头) earth. **2** east(ern): *E Sussex* 东苏萨克斯.

each /iːtʃ/ *adj* 每一 měiyī; 各 gè; 各自的 gèzìde: *a ring on ~ finger* 每个〔個〕指头上戴着一个戒指. **each** *pron* 每个 měigè; 各个 gègè: *~ of the girls* 每个女孩. **each** *adv* 各个地 gègède; 分别地 fēnbiéde: *They cost £10 each*. 它们每个的价钱为 10 英镑. **each** ˈ**other** [只用作动词或介词的宾语] 互相 hùxiāng: *Paul and Sue helped ~ other*. 保罗和苏互相帮助.

eager /ˈiːgə(r)/ *adj* (*for*; *to*) 渴望的 kěwàngde; 热〔熱〕切的 rèqiède: *~ for success* 渴望成功. **eagerly** *adv*. **eagerness** *n* [U].

eagle /ˈiːgl/ *n* [C] 鹰 yīng. ˌ**eagle-**ˈ**eyed** *adj* 目光锐利的 mùguāng ruìlì de; 注意到细微末节〔節〕的 zhùyì dào xìwēi mòjié de.

ear¹ /ɪə(r)/ *n* **1** [C] 耳朵 ěrduo. **2** [sing] 听〔聽〕觉〔覺〕tīngjué: *She has a good ~ for music*. 她对音乐有很好的听觉. **3** [习语] **(be) all ears** 专〔專〕心倾听 zhuānxīn qīngtīng. **(be) up to one's** ˈ**ears in sth** 忙于 mángyú; 深深卷〔捲〕入 shēnshēn juǎnrù. ˈ**earache** *n* [U, sing] 耳中疼痛 ěr zhōng téngtòng. ˈ**ear-drum** *n* [C] 耳膜 ěrmó; 鼓膜 gǔmó. ˈ**ear-ring** *n* [C] 耳环〔環〕ěrhuán. ˈ**earshot** *n* [U] [习语] **out of earshot** 在听力范〔範〕围〔圍〕之外 zài tīnglì fànwéi zhī wài. **within earshot** 在听力范围之内 zài tīnglì fànwéi zhī nèi.

ear² /ɪə(r)/ *n* [C] 穗 suì.

earl /ɜːl/ *n* [C] (*fem* **countess**) (英国)伯爵 bójué. **earldom** *n* [C] 伯爵爵位 bójué juéwèi; 伯爵领地 bójué lǐngdì.

early /ˈɜːlɪ/ *adj*, *adv* [-ier, -iest] **1** 在开〔開〕始阶〔階〕段 zài kāishǐ jiēduàn; 在初期 zài chūqī; 早期的 zǎoqīde: *in the ~ morning* 在清晨. **2** 提早 tízǎo; 提早的 tízǎode: *The bus arrived ~*. 公共汽车提早到达. **3** [习语] **at the earliest** 作为〔爲〕最早日期 zuòwéi zuìzǎo rìqī. **an** ˈ**early bird** [谑] 早到者 zǎodàozhě; 早起者 zǎoqǐzhě. **early closing day** *n* [C] [英国英语] (商店每周一次的) 提早打烊日 tízǎo dǎyàng rì. **early** ˈ**warning system** *n* [C] (雷达) 预警系〔係〕统 yùjǐng xìtǒng.

earmark /ˈɪəmɑːk/ *v* [T] 指定…作特殊用途 zhǐdìng … zuò tèshū yòngtú: *money ~ed for research* 供研究用的专款.

earn /ɜːn/ *v* **1** [I, T] 赚得 zhuàndé; 挣得 zhèngdé. **2** [T] 赢得 yíngdé; 博得 bódé. **earner** *n* [C]. **earnings** *n* [pl] 挣得的钱〔錢〕zhèngdéde qián.

earnest /ˈɜːnɪst/ *adj* 认〔認〕真的 rènzhēnde; 坚〔堅〕决的 jiānjuéde. **earnest** *n* [习语] **in earnest** 坚决地 jiānjuéde; 认真地 rènzhēnde. **earnestly** *adv*. **earnestness** *n* [U].

earth /ɜːθ/ *n* **1** (通常用 **the earth**) [sing] 世界 shìjiè; 地球 dìqiú. **2** [sing] 大地 dàdì; 地面 dìmiàn. **3** [U] 土 tǔ; 泥 ní. **4** [C] 野兽〔獸〕的洞穴 yěshòude dòngxué. **5** [C, 常为 sing] [尤用于英国英语] (电) 地线〔綫〕dìxiàn. **6** [习语] **charge, cost, etc the earth** [非正式用语] 要付很多钱〔錢〕yào fù hěnduō qián. **how, why, etc on** ˈ**earth** [非正式用语] [用于加强语气] 究竟 jiūjìng; 到底 dàodǐ: *What on ~ are you doing?* 你究竟在做什么? **earth** *v* [T] [英国英语] [通常用被动语态] (电) 把…接

地 bǎ … jiēdì. **earthly** *adj* 1 尘〔塵〕世的 chénshìde; 世俗的 shìsúde. 2 [非正式用语] 可能的 kěnéngde: *no ~ly use* 毫无用处. **earthquake** /ˈɜːθkweɪk/ *n* [C] 地震 dìzhèn. ˈ**earthworm** *n* [C] 蚯蚓 qiūyǐn. **earthy** *adj* 1 泥土的 nítǔde; 泥土似的 nítǔshìde. 2 不文雅的 bù wényǎde; 粗俗的 cūsúde: *an ~y sense of humour* 粗俗的幽默感.

earthenware /ˈɜːθnweə(r)/ *n* [U] 陶器 táoqì.

ease /iːz/ *n* [U] 1 容易 róngyi; 不费力 bú fèilì: *do sth with ~* 轻而易举地做某事. 2 舒适〔適〕shūshì. 3 [习语] **at (one's) ease** 安适 ānshì. **ease** *v* 1 [I, T] (使)变〔變〕得容易 biànde róngyì; 减轻〔輕〕…的痛苦 jiǎnqīng … de tòngkǔ 2 [I, T] 缓和 huǎnhé; 放松〔鬆〕fàngsōng. 3 [T] 缓慢地移动〔動〕huǎnmànde yídòng: *~ the injured man out of the car* 慢慢地把这个受伤的人抬出车子. 4 [短语动词] ˌ**ease** ˈ**off** /ˈ**up** 放松 fàngsōng; 缓和 huǎnhé.

easel /ˈiːzl/ *n* [C] 画〔畫〕架 huàjià; 黑板架 hēibǎnjià.

east /iːst/ *n* [sing] 1 **the east** 东 dōng; 东方 dōngfāng. 2 **the East** (a) 亚〔亞〕洲国家 Yàzhōu guójiā; (尤指)中国 Zhōngguó、日本 Rìběn. (b) 欧〔歐〕洲以东地区〔區〕Ōuzhōu yǐ dōng dìqū: *the Middle E~* 中东. (c) (某一国家的)东部地区 dōngbù dìqū. **east** *adj* 1 在东方的 zài dōngfāng de; 向东方的 xiàng dōngfāng de. 2 (风)来〔來〕自东方的 lái zì dōngfāng de. **east** *adv* 向东方 xiàng dōngfāng. **east-bound** /ˈiːstbaʊnd/ *adj* 向东行的 xiàng dōng xíng de. **easterly** /ˈiːstəlɪ/ *adj*, *adv* 1 在东方(的) zài dōngfāng; 向东方(的) xiàng dōngfāng. 2 (风)来自东方(的) lái zì dōngfāng. **eastern** /ˈiːstən/ (亦作 **Eastern**) *adj* (世界或某一国家)东部地区的 dōngbù dìqū de. **eastward** /ˈiːstwəd/ *adj* 向东方的 xiàng dōngfāng de. **eastward(s)** *adv*.

Easter /ˈiːstə(r)/ *n* 耶稣复〔復〕活节〔節〕Yēsū fùhuójié.

easy /ˈiːzɪ/ *adj* [-ier, -iest] 1 容易的 róngyìde. 2 舒适〔適〕的 shūshìde; 安心的 ānxīnde; 自在的 zìzàide. **easily** /ˈiːzəlɪ/ *adv* 1 容易地 róngyìde; 不费力地 bú fèilì de. 2 无〔無〕疑地 wúyíde: *easily the best* 无疑是最好的. **easy** *adv* [习语] **go easy on sb** 温和地对〔對〕待(某人) wēnhéde duìdài. **go easy on sth** 有节〔節〕制地使用(某物) yǒu jiézhìde shǐyòng: *Go ~ on the milk*. 牛奶要省着点喝. **take it/things easy** 不拼命工作 bù pīnmìng gōngzuò; 放松〔鬆〕fàngsōng. ˌ**easy** ˈ**chair** *n* [C] 安乐〔樂〕椅 ānlèyǐ. **easy**ˈ**going** *adj* 随〔隨〕遇而安的 suíyù ér'ān de; 脾气〔氣〕随和的 píqì suíhé de.

eat /iːt/ *v* [*pt* **ate** /et; *US* eɪt/, *pp* **~en** /ˈiːtn/] 1 [I, T] 吃 chī. 2 [习语] **eat one's heart out** 忧〔憂〕伤〔傷〕的 yōushāngde; 沮丧〔喪〕的 jǔsàngde. ˌ**eat one's** ˈ**words** 承认〔認〕自己说错话 chéngrèn zìjǐ shuō cuòhuà. 3 [短语动词] **eat sth away** 逐渐毁掉 zhújiàn huǐdiào. **eat into sth** (a) 毁掉 huǐdiào; 侵蚀 qīnshí. (b) 消耗掉(时间、供应等) xiāohàodiào. **eatable** *adj* 可吃的 kěchīde; 可食用的 kě shíyòng de. **eater** *n* [C] 惯于吃…的人 guàn yú chī … de rén: *a big ~er* 食量大的人.

eaves /iːvz/ *n* [pl] 屋檐 wūyán.

eavesdrop /ˈiːvzdrɒp/ *v* [-pp-] [I] (*on*) 偷听〔聽〕tōutīng; 窃〔竊〕听 qiètīng.

e-banking /ˈiːbæŋkɪŋ/ *n* [U] 电〔電〕子银行业〔業〕务〔務〕diànzǐ yínháng yèwù; 网〔網〕上银行服务 wǎngshàng yínháng fúwù.

ebb /eb/ *v* [I] 1 退潮 tuìcháo; 落潮 luòcháo. 2 [喻]衰退 shuāituì; 衰落 shuāiluò; 减少 jiǎnshǎo. **ebb** (常作 **the ebb**) [sing] 落潮 luòcháo; 退潮 tuìcháo.

ebony /ˈebənɪ/ *n* [U] 乌〔烏〕木 wūmù; 黑檀 hēitán. **ebony** *adj* 乌黑发〔發〕亮的 wūhēi fāliàng de.

e-book /ˈiːbʊk/ *n* [C] 电〔電〕子书〔書〕籍 diànzǐ shūjí; 电子读〔讀〕物 diànzǐ dúwù.

eccentric /ɪkˈsentrɪk/ *adj* 1 (人、行为举止)古怪的 gǔguàide, 不正常的 bú zhèngcháng de, 偏执〔執〕的 piānzhíde. 2 (圆)不同心的 bù tóngxīn de. **eccentric** *n* [C] 古怪的人 gǔguàide rén. **eccentricity** /ˌeksenˈtrɪsətɪ/ *n* [C, U] [*pl* **-ies**] 古怪 gǔguài; 怪僻 guàipì.

ecclesiastical /ɪˌkliːzɪˈæstɪkl/ *adj* (基督教)教会〔會〕的 jiàohuìde; 传〔傳〕教士的 chuánjiàoshìde.

echo /ˈekəʊ/ *n* [C] [*pl* **~es**] 回声〔聲〕huíshēng; 反响〔響〕fǎnxiǎng. **echo** *v* 1 [I] 产〔產〕生回响 chǎnshēng huíxiǎng. 2 [T] 重复〔複〕(他人的话) chóngfù; 同意(他人的话) tóngyì.

éclair /ɪˈkleə(r); eɪˈkleə(r)/ *n* [C] 巧克力包奶油的小蛋糕 qiǎokèlì bāo nǎiyóu de xiǎodàngāo.

eclipse /ɪˈklɪps/ *n* [C] 1 日食 rìshí. 2 月食 yuèshí. **eclipse** *v* [T] [喻](通过比较)使暗淡 shǐ àndàn; 使失色 shǐ shīsè.

ecology /iːˈkɒlədʒɪ/ *n* [U] 生态〔態〕学〔學〕shēngtàixué. **ecological** /ˌiːkəˈlɒdʒɪkl/ *adj*. **ecologist** /-dʒɪst/ *n* [C] 生态学研究者 shēngtàixué yánjiūzhě; 生态学家 shēngtàixuéjiā.

e-commerce /iːˈkɒmɜːs/ *n* [U] 电〔電〕子商务〔務〕diànzǐ shāngwù.

economic /ˌiːkəˈnɒmɪk, ˌekə-/ *adj* 1 经〔經〕济〔濟〕上的 jīngjìshangde; 经济学〔學〕的

jīngjìxuéde. 2 有利可图〔圖〕的 yǒulì kětú de. **economical** *adj* 节〔節〕约的 jiéyuēde. **economically** /-klɪ/ *adv*.

economics /ˌiːkəˈnɒmɪks, ˌekə-/ *n* [U] [用 sing v] 经〔經〕济〔濟〕学〔學〕 jīngjìxué. **economist** /iːˈkɒnəmɪst/ *n* [C] 经济学家 jīngjìxuéjiā; 经济学研究者 jīngjìxué yánjiūzhě.

economize /ɪˈkɒnəmaɪz/ *v* [I] 节〔節〕约 jiéyuē; 节省 jiéshěng.

economy /ɪˈkɒnəmɪ/ *n* [*pl* -ies] 1 (常用 the economy) [C] (国家的)经〔經〕济〔濟〕体〔體〕系 jīngjì tǐxì. 2 [C, U] 节〔節〕约 jiéyuē; 节省 jiéshěng. **economy** *adj* 便宜的 piányìde; 经济的 jīngjìde: ~ *class air travel* 飞机旅行的经济舱. **eˈconomy-class syndrome** *n* [U] 经济舱〔艙〕综合征〔徵〕 jīngjìcāng zōnghézhēng; 深静脉〔脈〕血栓症 shēnjìngmài xuèshuānzhèng; 深层〔層〕静脉栓塞 shēncéng jìngmài shuānsāi.

ecotourism /ˈiːkəʊˌtʊərɪzəm/ *n* [U] 生态〔態〕旅游 shēngtài lǚyóu.

ecotourist /ˈiːkəʊˌtʊərɪst/ *n* [C] 生态〔態〕旅游度假者 shēngtài lǚyóu dùjiàzhě.

ecstasy /ˈekstəsɪ/ *n* [C, U] [*pl* -ies] 1 狂喜 kuángxǐ; 心醉神迷 xīnzuì shénmí. 2 **Ecstasy** *n* [U] 摇头〔頭〕丸 yáotóuwán. **ecstatic** /ɪkˈstætɪk/ *adj*. **ecstatically** /-klɪ/ *adv*.

eddy /ˈedɪ/ *n* [C] [*pl* -ies] (空气、水等)旋涡〔渦〕 xuánwō; 涡流 wōliú. **eddy** [*pt*, *pp* -ied] [I] 旋转〔轉〕 xuánzhuàn; 起旋涡 qǐ xuánwō.

edge /edʒ/ *n* [C] 1 边〔邊〕 biān; 边缘 biānyuán: *the* ~ *of the bed* 床边. 2 刀口 dāokǒu; 锋 fēng. 3 [习语] **have the edge on/over sb/sth** 比…略胜〔勝〕一筹〔籌〕 bǐ … lüèshèng yìchóu. **on ˈedge** 紧张的 jǐnzhāngde; 不安的 bù'ānde. **take the edge off sth** 减弱 jiǎnruò. **edge** *v* 1 [T] 给…加上边 gěi… jiā shàng biān. 2 [I, T] (使)徐徐移动〔動〕 xúxú yídòng: *She* ~*d* (*her way*) *along the cliff*. 她在悬崖上慢慢移动. **edging** *n* [C, U] 边缘 biānyuán. **edgy** *adj* [非正式用语] 紧张的 jǐnzhāngde; 不安的 bù'ānde.

edible /ˈedɪbl/ *adj* 可以食用的 kěyǐ shíyòng de.

edit /ˈedɪt/ *v* [T] 1 编辑(他人作品) biānjí. 2 编辑(报纸、书等) biānjí. 3 剪辑 jiǎnjí. **editor** *n* [C] 编辑 biānjí.

edition /ɪˈdɪʃn/ *n* [C] 1 版本 bǎnběn: *a paperback* ~ 纸面平装版. 2 (书、报等的)一次印刷数〔數〕 yícì yìnshuāshù.

editorial /ˌedɪˈtɔːrɪəl/ *adj* 编辑的 biānjíde; 编者的 biānzhěde. **editorial** *n* [C] 社论〔論〕 shèlùn.

educate /ˈedʒʊkeɪt/ *v* [T] 教育 jiàoyù; 培养〔養〕 péiyǎng. **education** /ˌedʒʊˈkeɪʃən/ *n* [U] 1 教育 jiàoyù. 2 修养〔養〕 xiūyǎng; 教养 jiàoyǎng. **educational** /ˌedʒʊˈkeɪʃənl/ *adj*.

EEC /ˌiː iː ˈsiː/ *abbr* European Economic Community (the Common Market) 欧〔歐〕洲经〔經〕济〔濟〕共同体〔體〕(共同市场) Ōuzhōu jīngjì gòngtóngtǐ.

eel /iːl/ *n* [C] 鳝 shàn; 鳗 mán.

eerie, eery /ˈɪərɪ/ *adj* [-ier, -iest] 引起恐惧〔懼〕的 yǐnqǐ kǒngjù de; 奇怪的 qíguàide. **eerily** /ˈɪərəlɪ/ *adv*.

effect /ɪˈfekt/ *n* 1 [C, U] 结果 jiéguǒ; 效果 xiàoguǒ. 2 [C] 印象 yìnxiàng. 3 **effects** [pl] [正式用语](个人)财产〔產〕 cáichǎn; 所有物 suǒyǒuwù. 4 [习语] **bring / put sth into effect** 实〔實〕行 shíxíng; 使生效 shǐ shēngxiào. **in effect** (a) 事实〔實〕上 shìshí shàng; 实〔實〕际〔際〕上 shíjì shàng. (b) 正在实行 zhèngzài shíxíng. **take effect** 生效 shēngxiào. **effect** *v* [T] [正式用语]使发〔發〕生 shǐ fāshēng.

effective /ɪˈfektɪv/ *adj* 1 有效的 yǒuxiàode: *the most* ~ *method* 最有效的方法. 2 实〔實〕际〔際〕的 shíjìde; 事实上的 shìshí shàng de: *the club's* ~ *membership* 俱乐部实际上的会员. **effectively** *adv*. **effectiveness** *n* [U].

effectual /ɪˈfektʃʊəl/ *adj* [正式用语]有效的 yǒuxiàode: *an* ~ *remedy* 有效药品.

effeminate /ɪˈfemɪnət/ *adj* [贬](男人)女人气〔氣〕的 nǚrénqìde; 无〔無〕大丈夫气概的 wú dàzhàngfu qìgài de.

effervesce /ˌefəˈves/ *v* [I] 冒气〔氣〕泡 mào qìpào. **effervescence** /-ˈvesns/ *n* [U] 1 冒泡 màopào; 起沫 qǐmò. 2 欢〔歡〕腾 huānténg. **effervescent** /-ˈvesnt/ *adj*.

efficient /ɪˈfɪʃnt/ *adj* 1 能胜〔勝〕任的 néng shèngrèn de: *an* ~ *manager* 能干的经理. 2 (机器等)效率高的 xiàolǜ gāo de. **efficiency** /-ʃnsɪ/ *n* [U]. **efficiently** *adv*.

effigy /ˈefɪdʒɪ/ *n* [C] [*pl* -ies] 肖像 xiāoxiàng; 模拟〔擬〕像 mónǐxiàng.

effort /ˈefət/ *n* 1 [U] 力量和精力的使用 lìliàng hé jīnglì de shǐyòng: *a waste of time and* ~ 时间和精力的浪费. 2 [C] 努力尝〔嘗〕试 nǔlì chángshì; 企图〔圖〕 qǐtú: *make an* ~ *to escape* 企图逃跑. **effortless** *adj* 不需要努力的 bù xūyào nǔlì de; 不费力的 bú fèilì de. **effortlessly** *adv*.

effrontery /ɪˈfrʌntərɪ/ *n* [U] 厚颜 hòuyán; 无〔無〕耻 wúchǐ.

effusive /ɪˈfjuːsɪv/ *adj* 过〔過〕分热〔熱〕情的 guòfèn rèqíng de. **effusively** *adv*.

EFL /ˌiː ef ˈel/ *abbr* English as a Foreign Language 非母语英语课程 fēi mǔyǔ yīngyǔ kèchéng.

eg /ˌiː ˈdʒiː/ *abbr* 例如 lìrú.

egg[1] /eg/ *n* 1 [C] 蛋 dàn. 2 [C, U] 食用蛋

shíyòngdàn. 3 [C] 卵细胞 luǎn xìbāo. 4 [习语] ˌput all one's ˌeggs in one ˈbasket 孤注一掷〔擲〕gū zhù yí zhì. ˈegg-cup *n* [C] (吃煮鸡蛋用的)蛋杯 dànbēi. ˈegghead *n* [C] [非正式用语,贬]自以为〔爲〕有大学〔學〕问的人 zì yǐwéi yǒu dà xuéwèn de rén ˈegg-plant *n* [C, U] [尤用于美语]茄子 qiézi.

egg[2] /eg/ *v* [短语动词] egg sb on 鼓励〔勵〕gǔlì; 怂〔慫〕恿 sǒngyǒng.

ego /ˈegəʊ, ˈiːgəʊ/ *n* [C] [*pl* ~s] 自我 zìwǒ; 自尊 zìzūn; 自负 zìfù.

egocentric /ˌegəʊˈsentrik; *US* ˌiːg-/ *adj* 利已的 lìjǐde; 自我中心的 zìwǒ zhōngxīn de.

egoism /ˈegəʊɪzəm; *US* ˈiːg-/ *n* [U] 自我主义〔義〕zìwǒzhǔyì; 利己主义 lìjǐzhǔyì; 自私自利 zìsī zìlì. egoist /-ɪst/ *n* [C] 自我主义者 zìwǒzhǔyìzhě. egotistic /ˌegəˈtɪstɪk; *US* ˌiːg-/ (亦作 egotistical) *adj*.

egotism /ˈegəʊtɪzəm; *US* ˈiːg-/ *n* [U] 自我中心 zìwǒ zhōngxīn; 利己主义〔義〕lìjǐzhǔyì. egotist /-tɪst/ *n* [C] 自私自利者 zìsī zìlì zhě. egotistic /ˌegəˈtɪstɪk; *US* ˌiːg-/ (亦作 egotistical) *adj*.

eiderdown /ˈaɪdədaʊn/ *n* [C] 鸭绒被 yāróngbèi; 鸭绒垫〔墊〕yāróngdiàn.

eight /eɪt/ *pron*, *adj*, *n* [C] 八 bā; 八个〔個〕bāgè. eighth /eɪtθ/ *pron*, *adj* 第八 dìbā; 第八个 dìbā gè. eighth *pron*, *n* [C] 八分之一 bāfēn zhī yī.

eighteen /ˌeɪˈtiːn/ *pron*, *adj*, *n* [C] 十八 shíbā; 十八个〔個〕shíbāgè. eighteenth /ˌeɪˈtiːnθ/ *pron*, *adj* 第十八 dìshíbā; 第十八个 dìshíbā gè. eighteenth *pron*, *n* [C] 十八分之一 shíbāfēn zhī yī.

eighty /ˈeɪtɪ/ *pron*, *adj*, *n* [C] [*pl* -ies] 八十 bāshí; 八十个〔個〕bāshígè. eightieth *pron*, *adj* 第八十 dìbāshí; 第八十个 dì bāshí gè. eightieth *pron*, *n* [C] 八十分之一 bāshífēn zhī yī.

either /ˈaɪðə(r), ˈiːðər/ *adj*, *pron* (两者中)任一的 rènyīde; 两者之一 liǎngzhě zhī yī: *park on ~ side of the road* 把车停在马路的哪一边都可以. either *adv*, *conj* 1 [与两个否定动词连用]也 yě: *I don't like the red tie and I don't like the blue one ~.* 我不喜欢红领带,也不喜欢蓝领带. 2 either ... or... (表示两者挑一)或者 huòzhě; 要么 yàomò: *You can ~ write or phone for the book.* 你可以写信或者打电话要这本书.

eject /ɪˈdʒekt/ *v* [T] (*from*) 排出 páichū; 弹〔彈〕射出 tánshè chū. ejection /ɪˈdʒekʃn/ *n* [U]. ejector seat *n* [C] (飞机)弹射坐椅 tánshè zuòyǐ.

eke /iːk/ *v* [短语动词] eke sth out 竭力维持(生计) jiélì wéichí; 设法过〔過〕(活) shèfǎ guò.

elaborate /ɪˈlæbərət/ *adj* 复〔複〕杂〔雜〕的 fùzáde; 详尽〔盡〕的 xiángjìnde. elaborate /ɪˈlæbəreɪt/ *v* [I, T] (*on*) 详细说明 xiángxì shuōmíng. elaborately *adv*.

elapse /ɪˈlæps/ *v* [I] [正式用语](时间)流逝 liúshì.

elastic /ɪˈlæstɪk/ *adj* 1 弹〔彈〕性的 tánxìngde; 有伸缩性的 yǒu shēnsuōxìng de. 2 [喻]可伸缩的 kě shēnsuō de; 灵〔靈〕活的 línghuóde: *Our plans are fairly ~.* 我们的计划相当灵活. elastic *n* [U] 弹性织〔織〕物 tánxìng zhīwù. eˌlastic ˈband *n* [C] 橡皮圈 xiàngpíquān. elasticity /ˌelæˈstɪsətɪ, ˌiːl-/ *n* [U].

elated /ɪˈleɪtɪd/ *adj* (*at* / *by*) 欢〔歡〕欣鼓舞的 huānxīn gǔwǔ de; 兴〔興〕高采烈的 xìng gāo cǎi liè de. elation /ɪˈleɪʃn/ *n* [U].

elbow /ˈelbəʊ/ *n* [C] (a) 肘 zhǒu. (b) 衣服的肘部 yīfude zhǒubù. elbow *v* [短语动词] elbow sb aside 用肘推 yòng zhǒu tuī; 用肘挤〔擠〕yòng zhǒu jǐ. elbow one's way 挤进〔進〕jǐjìn; 挤过〔過〕jǐguò. ˈelbow-grease *n* [U] [非正式用语]苦差使 kǔchāishi; 重活 zhònghuó. ˈelbow-room *n* [U] [非正式用语]活动〔動〕余〔餘〕地 huódòng yúdì.

elder[1] /ˈeldə(r)/ *adj* 年长〔長〕的 niánzhǎngde: *my ~ brother* 我的哥哥. elder *n* 1 my, etc elder [sing] 年龄〔齡〕较大的人 niánlíng jiàodà de rén. 2 [C] 长〔長〕者 zhǎngzhě; 前辈 qiánbèi. 3 [C] (某些基督教会的)长老 zhǎnglǎo. elderly *adj* 过〔過〕了中年的 guòle zhōngnián de; 上了年纪的 shàngle niánjì de. ˌelder ˈstatesman *n* [C] 政界元老 zhèngjiè yuánlǎo.

elder[2] /ˈeldə(r)/ *n* [C] [植物]接骨木 jiēgǔmù.

eldest /ˈeldɪst/ *adj*, *n* [C] (三人或三人以上的人中)年龄〔齡〕最大的(人) niánlíng zuìdà de.

elect /ɪˈlekt/ *v* [T] 1 选〔選〕举〔舉〕xuǎnjǔ. 2 [非正式用语]决定 juédìng. *They ~ed to stay.* 他们决定留下来. elect *adj* [正式用语]选出而未上任的 xuǎnchū ér wèi shàngrèn de: *president-~* 当选(尚未上任)总统. elector *n* [C] 有选举权〔權〕的人 yǒu xuǎnjǔquán de rén. electoral /ɪˈlektərəl/ *adj* 选举的 xuǎnjǔde. electorate /ɪˈlektərət / *n* [C, 亦作 sing, 用 pl v] [总称]选举人 xuǎnjǔrén; 选民 xuǎnmín.

election /ɪˈlekʃn/ *n* [C, U] 选〔選〕举〔舉〕xuǎnjǔ.

electric /ɪˈlektrɪk/ *adj* 1 电〔電〕的 diànde; 电动〔動〕的 diàndòngde; 发〔發〕电的 fādiànde: *an ~ fire* 家用电炉. 2 [喻]高度刺激的 gāodù cìjī de. electrical *adj* 由电发生的 yóu diàn fāshēng de; 与〔與〕电有关〔關〕的 yǔ diàn

E

yǒuguān de. **electrically** /-klɪ/ *adv*. the eˌlectric ˈ**chair** *n* [sing] [尤用于美语]电椅 diànyǐ. eˌlectric ˈ**shock** *n* [C] 触〔觸〕电 chù-diàn.

electrician /ɪˌlekˈtrɪʃn/ *n* [C] 电〔電〕工 diàngōng.

electricity /ɪˌlekˈtrɪsətɪ/ *n* [U] 1 电〔電〕diàn; 电能 diànnéng. 2 电力供应〔應〕diànlì gōngyìng: *Don't waste* ~. 别浪费电.

electrify /ɪˈlektrɪfaɪ/ *v* [*pt*, *pp* -ied] [T] 1 向…供电〔電〕xiàng … gōngdiàn. 2 [喻]使激动〔動〕shǐ jīdòng; 使震惊〔驚〕shǐ zhènjīng.

E

electrocute /ɪˈlektrəkjuːt/ *v* [T] 用电〔電〕刑处〔處〕死 yòng diànxíng chǔsǐ. **electrocution** /ɪˈlektrəˈkjuːʃn/ *n* [U].

electrode /ɪˈlektrəʊd/ *n* [C] 电〔電〕极〔極〕diànjí.

electron /ɪˈlektrɒn/ *n* [C] 电〔電〕子 diànzǐ. **electronic** /ˌɪlekˈtrɒnɪk/ *adj* 1 电子的 diànzǐde; 用电子操纵〔縱〕的 yòng diànzǐ cāozòng de: *an* ~ *calculator* 电子计算器. 2 电子器件的 diànzǐ qìjiàn de. **electronically** /-klɪ/ *adv*. **electronics** /ˌɪlekˈtrɒnɪks/ *n* [U] [用 sing v] 电子学〔學〕diànzǐxué.

elegant /ˈelɪgənt/ *adj* 雅致的 yǎzhìde; 优〔優〕美的 yōuměide. **elegance** /-gəns/ *n* [U]. **elegantly** *adv*.

element /ˈelɪmənt/ *n* 1 [C] (*in* / *of*) 组成部分 zǔchéng bùfen: *Justice is only one* ~ *in good government*. 公正只是仁政的一个要素. 2 [C, 常为 sing] 少量 shǎoliàng: *an* ~ *of truth in their story* 他们的话中的一点道理. 3 [C] (化学)元素 yuánsù. 4 the **elements** [pl] 大自然的力量 dà zìránde lìliàng; 坏〔壞〕天气〔氣〕huài tiānqì. 5 **elements** [pl] 原理 yuánlǐ; 基础〔礎〕jīchǔ. 6 [C] 电〔電〕阻丝(电热壶等的供热部分) diànzǔsī. 7 [习语] **in one's** ˈ**element** 处〔處〕于适〔適〕宜环〔環〕境之中 chǔyú shìyí huánjìng zhī zhōng; 得其所 dé qí suǒ. **out of one's** ˈ**element** 处于不适宜环境之中 chǔyú bú shìyí huánjìng zhī zhōng; 不得其所 bù dé qí suǒ.

elementary /ˌelɪˈmentərɪ/ *adj* 1 基本的 jīběnde; 初级的 chūjíde; 基础〔礎〕的 jīchǔde: ~ *maths* 基础数学. 2 简单〔單〕的 jiǎndānde: ~ *question* 简单的问题. **eleˈmentary ˌschool** *n* [C] [美语]小学〔學〕xiǎoxué.

elephant /ˈelɪfənt/ *n* [C] 象 xiàng; 大象 dàxiàng.

elevate /ˈelɪveɪt/ *v* [T] [正式用语] 1 升高 shēnggāo; 抬起 táiqǐ. 2 提高(思想等) tígāo.

elevation /ˌelɪˈveɪʃn/ *n* 1 [sing] 提高 tígāo; 提升 tíshēng. 2 [C] 海拔 hǎibá. 3 [C] (建筑物) 正视图〔圖〕zhèngshìtú.

elevator /ˈelɪveɪtə(r)/ *n* [C] 1 [美语]电〔電〕梯 diàntī. 2 斗式皮带输送机〔機〕dǒushì pídài shūsòngjī.

eleven /ɪˈlevn/ *pron*, *adj*, *n* [C] 11 shíyī; 11 个〔個〕shíyīgè. **elevenses** /-zɪz/ *n* [U] [用 sing v]上午 11 时〔時〕用的茶点〔點〕shàngwǔ shíyīshí yòng de chádiǎn. **eleventh** / ɪˈlevnθ / *pron*, *adj* 第 11 (个) dìshíyī. **eleventh** *pron*, *n* [C] 十一分之一 shíyīfēn zhī yī.

elf /elf/ *n* [C] [*pl* **elves** / elvz /] (民间故事中喜与人捣乱的)小精灵〔靈〕xiǎo jīnglíng.

elicit /ɪˈlɪsɪt/ *v* [T] (*from*) [正式用语]引出 yǐnchū; 诱出(想了解的情况等) yòuchū.

eligible /ˈelɪdʒəbl/ *adj* (*for*; *to*) 合格的 hégéde; 适〔適〕宜的 shìyíde; 符合要求的 fúhé yāoqiú de. **eligibility** /ˌelɪdʒəˈbɪlətɪ/ *n* [U].

eliminate /ɪˈlɪmɪneɪt/ *v* [T] 消灭〔滅〕xiāomiè; 消除 xiāochú. **elimination** /ɪˌlɪmɪˈneɪʃn/ *n* [U].

élite /eɪˈliːt/ *n* [C] 社会〔會〕精英 shèhuì jīngyīng. **élitism** /-ɪzəm/ *n* [U] [常贬]精英主义〔義〕jīngyīngzhǔyì; 精英统治 jīngyīng tǒngzhì. **élitist** /-tɪst/ *n* [C], *adj*.

elk /elk/ *n* [C] 麋 mí.

ellipse /ɪˈlɪps/ *n* [C] 椭〔橢〕圆 tuǒyuán. **elliptical** /ɪˈlɪptɪkl/ *adj*.

elm /elm/ *n* (a) [C] (亦作 ˈ**elm tree**) 榆 yú. (b) [U] 榆木 yúmù.

elocution /ˌeləˈkjuːʃn/ *n* [U] 演说术〔術〕yǎnshuōshù; 演讲〔講〕技巧 yǎnjiǎng jìqiǎo.

elongate /ˈiːlɒŋgeɪt; *US* ɪˈlɔːŋ-/ *v* [T] 伸长〔長〕shēncháng; 拉长 lācháng; 延长 yáncháng.

elope /ɪˈləʊp/ *v* [I] 私奔 sībēn. **elopement** *n* [C, U].

eloquence /ˈeləkwəns/ *n* [U] 雄辩 xióngbiàn; 口才 kǒucái. **eloquent** /-ənt/ *adj*. **eloquently** *adv*.

else /els/ *adv* 1 另外 lìngwài; 其他 qítā: *Have you anything* ~ *to do?* 你还有其他事要做吗? *We went to the cinema and nowhere* ~. 我们去了电影院,没有去其他地方. 2 [习语] **or else** 否则 fǒuzé: *Run or* ~ *you'll be late*. 快跑,否则你就晚了. **elsewhere** /ˌelsˈweə(r); *US* -ˈhweər / *adv* 在别处〔處〕zài biéchù; 向别处 xiàng biéchù.

ELT /ˌiː el ˈtiː/ *abbr* English Language Teaching 英语教学〔學〕Yīngyǔ jiàoxué.

elucidate /ɪˈluːsɪdeɪt/ *v* [T] [正式用语]阐〔闡〕明 chǎnmíng; 解释 jiěshì.

elude /ɪˈluːd/ *v* [T] 1 逃避 táobì; 躲避 duǒbì; 避开〔開〕bìkāi. 2 不为〔爲〕…所记得 bù wéi… suǒ jìde. **elusive** /ɪˈluːsɪv/ *adj* 难〔難〕以捉摸的 nán yǐ zhuōmō de; 难以记忆〔憶〕

的 nán yǐ jìyì de；难以形容的 nán yǐ xíngróng de.

elves *pl* of ELF.

emaciated /ɪˈmeɪʃɪeɪtɪd/ *adj* 消瘦的 xiāoshòude；憔悴的 qiáocuìde.

email /ˈiːmeɪl/ *n* 电〔電〕子函件 diànzǐ hánjiàn. **email** *v* [T] 给…发电子函件 gěi…fā diànzǐ hánjiàn ˈ**email address** *n* [C] 电邮〔郵〕地址 diànyóu dìzhǐ.

emanate /ˈeməneɪt/ *v* [I] *from* [正式用语]散发〔發〕sànfā；发射 fāshè.

emancipate /ɪˈmænsɪpeɪt/ *v* [T] (尤指政治上或社会问题上)解放 jiěfàng. **emancipation** /ɪˌmænsɪˈpeɪʃn/ *n* [U].

embalm /ɪmˈbɑːm; *US* 亦作 -ˈbɑːlm/ *v* [T] (用化学药剂)对〔對〕(尸体)作防腐处〔處〕理 duì zuò fángfǔ chǔlǐ.

embankment /ɪmˈbæŋkmənt/ *n* [C] 堤岸 dī'àn；路堤 lùdī.

embargo /ɪmˈbɑːgəʊ/ *n* [C] [*pl* ~es /-gəʊz/] (*on*) 禁止贸易令 jìnzhǐ màoyì lìng. **embargo** *v* [*pt*, *pp* ~ed /-gəʊd/] [T] 禁止(贸易) jìnzhǐ.

embark /ɪmˈbɑːk/ *v* 1 [I] 上船 shàngchuán. 2 [短语动词] **embark on / upon sth** 从〔從〕事 cóngshì；开〔開〕始 kāishǐ. **embarkation** /ˌembɑːˈkeɪʃn/ *n* [U, C].

embarrass /ɪmˈbærəs/ *v* [T] 使为〔爲〕难〔難〕shǐ wéinán；使尴〔尷〕尬 shǐ gāngà；使难为情 shǐ nánwéiqíng：*His smile ~ed her*. 他微微一笑倒使她感到很尴尬. **embarrassing** *adj*：*an ~ing mistake* 使人难堪的错误. **embarrassingly** *adv*. **embarrassment** *n* [U, C].

embassy /ˈembəsɪ/ *n* [C] [*pl* -ies] 大使馆 dàshǐguǎn.

embed /ɪmˈbed/ *v* [-dd-] [T] (*in*) [常用被动语态]把…嵌入 bǎ … qiànrù；把…放入 bǎ … fàngrù.

embellish /ɪmˈbelɪʃ/ *v* [T] 1 (*with*) [常用被动语态]美化 měihuà；装〔裝〕饰 zhuāngshì. 2 给(叙述)添加细节〔節〕gěi tiānjiā xìjié. **embellishment** *n* [C, U].

ember /ˈembə(r)/ *n* [C, 常用 pl] 余〔餘〕烬〔燼〕yújìn.

embezzle /ɪmˈbezl/ *v* [I, T] 盗用 dàoyòng；贪污 tānwū.

embitter /ɪmˈbɪtə(r)/ *v* [T] [常用被动语态]激怒 jīnù；使愤怒 shǐ fènnù.

emblem /ˈembləm/ *n* [C] 象征〔徵〕xiàngzhēng；标〔標〕志 biāozhì：*The dove is an ~ of peace*. 鸽子是和平的象征.

embody /ɪmˈbɒdɪ/ *v* [*pt*, *pp* -ied] [T] (*in*) [正式用语]体〔體〕现 tǐxiàn；使具体化 shǐ jùtǐhuà. **embodiment** *n* [sing]：*She is the embodiment of honesty*. 她是诚实的化身.

embossed /ɪmˈbɒst; *US* -ˈbɔːst/ *adj* 1 (表面)有浮雕图〔圖〕案的 yǒu fúdiāo tú'àn de. 2 (图案)凸起的 tūqǐde，隆起的 lóngqǐde.

embrace /ɪmˈbreɪs/ *v* 1 [I, T] 拥〔擁〕抱 yōngbào. 2 [T] [正式用语]欣然接受(主意、宗教等) xīnrán jiēshòu. 3 [T] [正式用语]包含 bāohán；包括 bāokuò. **embrace** *n* [C] 拥抱 yōngbào：*a loving* ~ 爱的拥抱.

embroider /ɪmˈbrɔɪdə(r)/ *v* 1 [I, T] 在…上刺绣〔繡〕zài … shàng cìxiù；在…上绣花 zài… shàng xiùhuā. 2 [T] 渲染 xuànrǎn. **embroidery** *n* [U].

embryo /ˈembrɪəʊ/ *n* [C] [*pl* ~s /-əʊz/] 1 胚胎 pēitāi；胚 pēi 2 [习语] **in** ˈ**embryo** 在未成熟时〔時〕期 zài wèi chéngshú shíqī. **embryonic** /ˌembrɪˈɒnɪk/ *adj*.

emerald /ˈemərəld/ *n* [C] 绿宝〔寶〕石 lǜbǎoshí. **emerald** *adj* 鲜绿色的 xiānlǜsède；翠绿色的 cuìlǜsède.

emerge /ɪˈmɜːdʒ/ *v* [I] 1 出现 chūxiàn；浮现 fúxiàn. 2 (事实等)被知晓〔曉〕bèi zhīxiǎo. **emergence** /-dʒəns/ *n* [U]. **emergent** /-dʒənt/ *adj* 新出现的 xīn chūxiàn de；发〔發〕展的 fāzhǎnde. **emerging** ˈ**market** *n* [C] 新兴〔興〕市场〔場〕xīnxīng shìchǎng.

emergency /ɪˈmɜːdʒənsɪ/ *n* [C, U] [*pl* -ies] 紧〔緊〕急情况 jǐnjí qíngkuàng；突发〔發〕事件 tūfā shìjiàn.

emigrate /ˈemɪgreɪt/ *v* [I] 移居国〔國〕外 yíjū guówài. **emigrant** /ˈemɪgrənt/ *n* [C] 移居外国〔國〕的人 yíjū wàiguó de rén；移民 yímín. **emigration** /ˌemɪˈgreɪʃn/ *n* [U].

eminent /ˈemɪnənt/ *adj* (人)著名的 zhùmíngde；卓越的 zhuóyuède. **eminence** /-əns/ *n* [U]. **eminently** *adv* [正式用语]非常 fēicháng；明显〔顯〕地 míngxiǎnde：~*ly qualified* 非常胜任的.

emir /eˈmɪə(r)/ *n* [C] 埃米尔〔爾〕(某些穆斯林国家统治者的称号) āimǐ'ěr. **emirate** /ˈemɪəreɪt/ *n* [C] 埃米尔的管辖地 āimǐ'ěrde guǎnxiádì；埃米尔的职〔職〕位 āimǐ'ěrde zhíwèi.

emit /ɪˈmɪt/ *v* [-tt-] [T] [正式用语]散发〔發〕sànfā；发射 fāshè：~ *heat* 散发热. **emission** /ɪˈmɪʃn/ *n* [U, C].

emoticon /ɪˈmɒtɪkɒn/ *n* [C] 表情符 biǎoqíngfú；情感图〔圖〕标〔標〕qínggǎn túbiāo.

emotion /ɪˈməʊʃn/ *n* [C, U] 情绪 qíngxù；情感 qínggǎn. **emotional** /-ʃənl/ *adj* 1 情感的 qínggǎnde；情绪的 qíngxùde. 2 激起情感的 jīqǐ qínggǎn de；激动〔動〕人心的 jīdòng rénxīn de：*an ~al speech* 激动人心的演说. 3 表现(强烈)感情的 biǎoxiàn gǎnqíng de. **emotional quotient** *n* [U] 情商 qíngshāng. **emotionally** *adv*.

E

emotive /ɪˈməʊtɪv/ *adj* 激动〔動〕情感的 jīdòng qínggǎn de.
emperor /ˈempərə(r)/ *n* [C] 皇帝 huángdì.
emphasis /ˈemfəsɪs/ *n* [C, U] [*pl* -ases /-əsiːz/] **1** 强调 qiángdiào. **2** 强语气〔氣〕qiáng yǔqì. **emphasize** /-əsaɪz/ *v* [T] 强调 qiángdiào. **emphatic** /ɪmˈfætɪk/ *adj* 强调的 qiángdiàode; 加强语气的 jiāqiáng yǔqì de. **emphatically** /-klɪ/ *adv*.
empire /ˈempaɪə(r)/ *n* [C] 帝国〔國〕dìguó.
empirical /ɪmˈpɪrɪkəl/ *adj* (知识)以经〔經〕验〔驗〕(或观察)为〔爲〕依据〔據〕的 yǐ jīngyàn wéi yījù de; 经验主义〔義〕的 jīngyànzhǔyìde.
employ /ɪmˈplɔɪ/ *v* [T] **1** 雇用 gùyòng. **2** [正式用语]使用 shǐyòng; 用 yòng. **employable** *adj* 达〔達〕到受雇条〔條〕件的 dádào shòugù tiáojiàn de. **employee** /ˌemplɔɪˈiː; 亦作 ˌɪmplɔɪˈiː/ *n* [C] 雇工 gùgōng; 受雇者 shòugùzhě; 雇员 gùyuán. **employer** *n* [C] 雇主 gùzhǔ. **employment** *n* [U] **1** 职〔職〕业〔業〕zhíyè; 付酬的工作 fùchóude gōngzuò. **2** 雇用 gùyòng.
empower /ɪmˈpaʊə(r)/ *v* [T] [正式用语] [常用被动语态]授权〔權〕给 shòuquán gěi.
empress /ˈemprɪs/ *n* [C] 女皇 nǚhuáng; 皇后 huánghòu.
empty /ˈemptɪ/ *adj* [-ier, -iest] **1** 空的 kōngde. **2** 无〔無〕价〔價〕值的 wú jiàzhí de; 无意义〔義〕的 wú yìyì de: ~ *promises* 无价值的许诺. **empties** *n* [pl] 空桶 kōngtǒng; 空瓶 kōngpíng; 空箱 kōngxiāng. **emptiness** /-tɪnɪs/ *n* [U]. **empty** *v* [*pt*, *pp* -ied] [I, T] (使)成为〔爲〕空的 chéngwéi kōng de. ˌ**empty-ˈhanded** *adj* 空手的 kōngshǒude; 一无〔無〕所获〔獲〕的 yì wú suǒ huò de. ˌ**empty-ˈheaded** *adj* 傻的 shǎde; 愚蠢的 yúchǔnde.
emu /ˈiːmjuː/ *n* [C] (澳洲产的)鸸鹋 érmiáo.
emulate /ˈemjʊleɪt/ *v* [T] [正式用语]同…竞〔競〕争 tóng … jìngzhēng; 努力赶上或超过〔過〕nǔlì gǎnshàng huò chāoguò. **emulation** /ˌemjʊˈleɪʃn/ *n* [U].
emulsion /ɪˈmʌlʃn/ *n* [C, U] 乳胶〔膠〕rǔjiāo; 乳剂〔劑〕rǔjì.
enable /ɪˈneɪbl/ *v* [T] *to* 使能够 shǐ nénggòu.
enamel /ɪˈnæml/ *n* [U] **1** 釉药〔藥〕yòuyào; 珐琅〔瑯〕fàláng; 搪瓷 tángcí. **2** 珐琅质〔質〕fàlángzhì. **enamel** *v* [-ll-; 美语亦作 -l-] [T] 涂〔塗〕瓷釉于… tú cíyòu yú….
enamoured (美语 -ored) /ɪˈnæməd / *adj* *of* 迷恋〔戀〕于…的 míliàn yú … de.
enchant /ɪnˈtʃɑːnt/ *v* [T] 使喜悦 shǐ xǐyuè; 使心醉 shǐ xīnzuì. **enchanted** /-ɪd/ *adj* 着了魔的 zháolèmóde. **enchanting** *adj* 迷人的 mírénde; 醉人的 zuìrénde. **enchantment** *n* [U, C].
encircle /ɪnˈsɜːkl/ *v* [T] 包围〔圍〕bāowéi; 环〔環〕绕〔繞〕huánrǎo.
enclave /ˈenkleɪv/ *n* [C] 飞〔飛〕地(国境内属于另一国的一块领土) fēidì.
enclose /ɪnˈkləʊz/ *v* [T] **1** 把…围〔圍〕起来〔來〕bǎ … wéi qǐlái. **2** 把…封入(信封) bǎ … fēngrù. **enclosure** /ɪnˈkləʊʒə(r)/ *n* [C] **1** (四周有围墙等的)围场〔場〕wéichǎng. **2** (信内的)附件 fùjiàn.
encore /ˈɒŋkɔː(r)/ *interj*, *n* [C] 再来〔來〕一个〔個〕! zài lái yígè! 重演 chóngyǎn; 重唱 chóngchàng.
encounter /ɪnˈkaʊntə(r)/ *v* [T] [正式用语]遇到 yùdào; 意外地遇到(朋友) yìwàide yùdào. **encounter** *n* [C] 意外的相见 yìwàide xiāngjiàn; 不愉快的相遇 bù yúkuài de xiāngyù.
encourage /ɪnˈkʌrɪdʒ/ *v* [T] 鼓励〔勵〕gǔlì; 支持 zhīchí: *They ~d him to come*. 他们鼓励他来. **encouragement** *n* [U, C]. **encouraging** *adj*: *encouraging news* 鼓舞人心的消息.
encroach /ɪnˈkrəʊtʃ/ *v* [I] (*on*) [正式用语]侵犯 qīnfàn; 侵占〔佔〕qīnzhàn: ~ *on sb's right* 侵犯某人的权利.
encrypt /enˈkrɪpt/ *v* [T] 加密 jiāmì.
encyclopedia (亦作 -paedia) /ɪnˌsaɪkləˈpiːdɪə/ *n* [C] 百科全书〔書〕bǎikēquánshū. **encyclopedic** (亦作 -paedic /-ˈpiːdɪk/) *adj* 广〔廣〕博的 guǎngbó de.
end /end/ *n* [C] **1** 末尾 mòwěi; 末端 mòduān; 尽〔盡〕头〔頭〕jìntóu: *at the ~ of the street* 在街道的尽头. *at the ~ of the war* 在战争结束时. **2** 剩余〔餘〕部分 shèngyú bùfen; 残〔殘〕余部分 cányú bùfen: *cigarette ~s* 香烟头. **3** 目的 mùdì; 目标〔標〕mùbiāo: *with this ~ in view* 以此为目标. **4** [习语] **in the ˈend** 最后〔後〕zuìhòu; 终于 zhōngyú. **make ends meet** 量入为〔爲〕出 liàng rù wéi chū. **no ˈend of sth** [非正式用语]无〔無〕数〔數〕wúshù; 大量 dàliàng. **on ˈend** (a) 直立 zhílì; 竖〔豎〕着 shùzhe. (b) 连续〔續〕地 liánxùde: *rain for days on ~* 连续几天地下雨. **put an end to sth** 停止 tíngzhǐ; 结束 jiéshù. **end** *v* **1** [I, T] 结束 jiéshù; 使结束 shǐ jiéshù. **2** [短语动词] **end up** 结束 jiéshù; 告终 gàozhōng. **ending** *n* [C] 词尾 cíwěi; 结尾 jiéwěi; 结局 jiéjú. **endless** /-lɪs/ *adj* 无止境的 wú zhǐjìng de; 无穷〔窮〕的 wúqióngde; 没完的 méiwánde. **endlessly** *adv*.
endanger /ɪnˈdeɪndʒə(r)/ *v* [T] 危及 wēijí; 危害 wēihài.
endear /ɪnˈdɪə(r)/ *v* [T] *to* [正式用语]使受喜欢〔歡〕shǐ shòu xǐhuan. **endearment** *n* [C,

U] 亲〔親〕爱〔愛〕的表示 qīn'àide biǎoshì.

endeavour (美语 -vor) /ɪnˈdevə(r)/ *v* [I] *to* [正式用语]努力 nǔlì; 力图〔圖〕 lìtú. **endeavour** *n* [正式用语] 1 [C] 尝〔嘗〕试 chángshì. 2 [U] 努力 nǔlì; 尽〔盡〕力 jìnlì.

endemic /enˈdemɪk/ *adj* [正式用语] (尤指疾病)流行于某地方的 liúxíng yú mǒu dìfang de.

endorse /ɪnˈdɔːs/ *v* [T] 1 赞〔讚〕同 zàntóng; 支持 zhīchí. 2 背签〔簽〕(支票) bèiqiān. 3 [常用被动语态](驾驶员执照)被写〔寫〕上违〔違〕章记录〔錄〕 bèi xiěshàng wéizhāng jìlù. **endorsement** *n* [C, U].

endow /ɪnˈdaʊ/ *v* [T] 1 捐款 juānkuǎn; 资助 zīzhù. 2 [习语] **be endowed with sth** 有…的天赋 yǒu … de tiānfù. **endowment** *n* [C, U].

endure /ɪnˈdjʊə(r); *US* -ˈdʊər/ *v* 1 [T] 忍耐 rěnnài; 忍受 rěnshòu. 2 [I] 持久 chíjiǔ; 持续〔續〕 chíxù. **endurance** *n* [U] 忍耐力 rěnnàilì. **enduring** *adj* 持久的 chíjiǔde; 耐久的 nàijiǔde.

enemy /ˈenəmɪ/ *n* [*pl* -ies] 1 [C] 敌〔敵〕人 dírén. 2 **the enemy** [sing] [用 sing 或 pl v] 敌军 díjūn; 敌国〔國〕 díguó.

energy /ˈenədʒɪ/ *n* 1 [U] 活力 huólì; 劲〔勁〕 jìn. 2 **energies** [pl] (人的)精力 jīnglì; 能力 nénglì. 3 [U] 能 néng; 能量 néngliàng: *atomic* ~ 原子能. **energetic** /ˌenəˈdʒetɪk/ *adj* 精力旺盛的 jīnglì wàngshèng de. **energetically** /-klɪ/ *adv*.

enforce /ɪnˈfɔːs/ *v* [T] 强迫服从〔從〕 qiángpò fúcóng; 实〔實〕施 shíshī. **enforceable** *adj*. **enforcement** *n* [U].

engage /ɪnˈgeɪdʒ/ *v* 1 [T] [正式用语]雇用 gùyòng; 聘 pìn. 2 [T] [正式用语]吸引 xīyǐn; 占〔佔〕用(注意力等) zhànyòng. 3 [I, T] (使机器部件)啮〔嚙〕合 nièhé. 4 [短语动词] **engage (sb) in sth** 使从〔從〕事 shǐ cóngshì; 使参〔參〕加 shǐ cānjiā. **engaged** *adj* 1 已订婚的 yǐ dìnghūn de. 2 (电话线等)被占用的 bèi zhànyòng de; 使用中的 shǐyòng zhōng de; 忙的 mángde; 从事…的 cóngshì … de. **engagement** *n* [C] 1 订婚 dìnghūn. 2 约会〔會〕 yuēhuì. 3 [正式用语]交战〔戰〕 jiāozhàn. **engaging** *adj* 可爱〔愛〕的 kě'àide; 迷人的 mírénde.

engine /ˈendʒɪn/ *n* [C] 1 发〔發〕动〔動〕机〔機〕 fādòngjī; 引擎 yǐnqíng. 2 火车头〔頭〕 huǒchētóu. **ˈengine-driver** *n* [C] 火车司机 huǒchē sījī.

engineer /ˌendʒɪˈnɪə(r)/ *n* [C] 1 工程师〔師〕 gōngchéngshī. 2 (操纵发动机的)技工 jìgōng. **engineer** *v* [T] 策划〔劃〕 cèhuà. **engineering** *n* [U] 工程 gōngchéng; 工程师行业〔業〕 gōngchéngshī hángyè.

England /ˈɪŋglənd/ *n* 英格兰〔蘭〕 Yīnggélán.

English /ˈɪŋglɪʃ/ *n* 1 [U] 英语 Yīngyǔ. 2 **the English** [pl] 英国〔國〕人 Yīngguórén. **English** *adj* 英国的 Yīngguóde; 英国人的 Yīngguórén de; 英语的 Yīngyǔde. **Englishman** /-mən/ [*pl* -men], **Englishwoman** [*pl* -women] *n* [C] 英国人 Yīngguórén.

engrave /ɪnˈgreɪv/ *v* [T] 1 *A on B* / *B* (*with A*) 在…上雕刻 zài … shàng diāokè. 2 [习语] **be engraved on sb's mind, memory, etc** 铭刻于心 míngkè yú xīn; 铭记 míngjì. **engraver** *n* [C]. **engraving** *n* 1 [C] 雕版印刷品 diāobǎn yìnshuāpǐn. 2 [U] 雕刻品 diāokèpǐn.

engross /ɪnˈgrəʊs/ *v* [T] [常用被动语态]全神贯注于 quán shén guàn zhù yú: *~ed in her work* (她)全神贯注于工作.

engulf /ɪnˈgʌlf/ *v* [T] 使陷入 shǐ xiànrù; 使消失 shǐ xiāoshī: *The hotel was ~ed in flames*. 饭店陷入一片火海.

enhance /ɪnˈhɑːns; *US* -ˈhæns/ *v* [T] 提高(质量) tígāo. **enhancement** *n* [U, C].

enigma /ɪˈnɪgmə/ *n* [C] 神秘的事物 shénmìde shìwù; 谜 mí. **enigmatic** /ˌenɪgˈmætɪk/ *adj*. **enigmatically** /-klɪ/ *adv*.

enjoy /ɪnˈdʒɔɪ/ *v* [T] 1 欣赏 xīnshǎng; 喜爱〔愛〕 xǐ'ài. 2 享受 xiǎngshòu; 享有 xiǎngyǒu. 3 ~ **oneself** 生活快乐〔樂〕 shēnghuó kuàilè. **enjoyable** *adj* 有乐趣的 yǒu lèqù de; 能使人快乐的 néng shǐ rén kuàilè de. **enjoyably** *adv*. **enjoyment** *n* [U, C].

enlarge /ɪnˈlɑːdʒ/ *v* 1 [I, T] 变〔變〕大 biàndà; 增大 zēngdà; 扩〔擴〕大 kuòdà; 放大 fàngdà. 2 [短语动词] **enlarge on sth** [正式用语] 详述 xiángshù. **enlargement** *n* [C, U].

enlighten /ɪnˈlaɪtn/ *v* [T] 启〔啓〕发〔發〕 qǐfā; 开〔開〕导〔導〕 kāidǎo. **enlightenment** *n* [U].

enlist /ɪnˈlɪst/ *v* 1 [I, T] 征〔徵〕募 zhēngmù; (使)服兵役 fú bīngyì. 2 谋取 móuqǔ; 罗〔羅〕致 luózhì. **enlistment** *n* [U, C].

enormity /ɪˈnɔːmətɪ/ *n* [*pl* -ies] 1 [C, U] [正式用语] 穷〔窮〕凶极〔極〕恶〔惡〕 qióng xiōng jí è; 无〔無〕法无天 wúfǎ wútiān. 2 [U] 庞〔龐〕大 pángdà; 巨大 jùdà.

enormous /ɪˈnɔːməs/ *adj* 庞〔龐〕大的 pángdàde; 巨大的 jùdàde. **enormously** *adv* 极〔極〕大地 jídàde; 巨大地 jùdàde.

enough /ɪˈnʌf/ *adj, pron* 足够的 zúgòude, 充足的 chōngzúde; 足够 zúgòu; 充分 chōngfèn: *Is £100 ~?* 100 英镑够吗? **enough** *adv* 1 足够地 zúgòude; 充分地 chōngfènde: *not old* ~ 年纪不够大. 2 [习语] **oddly, strangely, etc enough** 说来奇怪 shuō lái qíguài.

enquire, enquiry ⇨INQUIRE, INQUIRY.

E

enraged /ɪnˈreɪdʒd/ *adj* 勃然大怒的 bórán dànù de.

enrich /ɪnˈrɪtʃ/ *v* [T] **1** (*with*) 使丰〔豐〕富 shǐ fēngfù; 加料于 jiāliào yú; 增进〔進〕zēngjìn: *soil ~ed with fertilizer* 施用了肥料的土壤. **2** 使富有 shǐ fùyǒu; 使富裕 shǐ fùyù. **enrichment** *n* [C, U].

enrol (亦作,尤用于美语 **-ll**) /ɪnˈrəʊl/ *v* [-ll-] [I, T] 招收 zhāoshōu; (使)入学〔學〕rùxué; 注册 zhùcè. **enrolment** *n* [U, C].

en route /ˌɒn ˈruːt/ *adv* [法语] 在途中 zài tú zhōng.

ensemble /ɒnˈsɒmbl/ *n* [C] **1** 全体〔體〕quántǐ; 总〔總〕体 zǒngtǐ. **2** 演唱组 yǎnchàngzǔ; 演奏组 yǎnzòuzǔ.

ensign /ˈensən, 亦作 ˈensaɪn/ *n* [C] **1** 军舰〔艦〕旗 jūnjiànqí. **2** (美国)海军少尉 hǎijūn shàowèi.

ensue /ɪnˈsjuː; *US* -ˈsuː/ *v* [I] 跟着发〔發〕生 gēnzhe fāshēng; 结果产〔產〕生 jiéguǒ chǎnshēng; 结果是 jiéguǒ shì.

ensure (美语 **insure**) /ɪnˈʃɔː(r); *US* ɪnˈʃʊər/ *v* [T] 保证〔證〕bǎozhèng; 担〔擔〕保 dānbǎo.

entail /ɪnˈteɪl/ *v* [T] 需要 xūyào: *Your plan ~s a lot of work*. 你的计划需要大量的工作.

entangled /ɪnˈtæŋgld/ *adj* (*in*) 缠〔纏〕住的 chánzhùde. **entanglement** *n* [C, U].

enter /ˈentə(r)/ *v* **1** [I, T] 进〔進〕jìn; 入 rù. **2** [T] 加入 jiārù; 参〔參〕加 cānjiā: *~ university* 进入大学. **3** [T] 登录〔錄〕(细节) dēnglù. **4** [I, T] 参加(竞赛、考试等) cānjiā. **5** [短语动词] **enter into sth** (a) 开〔開〕始从〔從〕事 kāishǐ cóngshì. (b) 构〔構〕成…的一部分 gòuchéng … de yíbùfen. **enter on / upon sth** [正式用语]开始 kāishǐ; 着手 zhuóshǒu.

enterprise /ˈentəpraɪz/ *n* **1** [C] 新计划〔劃〕xīn jìhuà; 艰〔艱〕巨的计划 jiānjùde jìhuà. **2** [U] 勇气〔氣〕yǒngqì; 进〔進〕取心 jìnqǔxīn; 事业〔業〕心 shìyèxīn. **3** [C] 商业企业 shāngyè qǐyè: *private ~* 私人企业. **enterprising** *adj* 有进〔進〕取心的 yǒu jìnqǔxīn de; 有事业心的 yǒu shìyèxīn de.

entertain /ˌentəˈteɪn/ *v* **1** [I, T] 使娱乐〔樂〕shǐ yúlè; 使有兴〔興〕趣 shǐ yǒu xìngqù. **2** [I, T] 招待 zhāodài; 款待 kuǎndài. **3** [T] 怀〔懷〕有 huáiyǒu; 持有 chíyǒu; 准〔準〕备〔備〕考虑〔慮〕zhǔnbèi kǎolǜ: *~ an idea* 怀有想法. **entertainer** *n* [C] 表演者 biǎoyǎnzhě. **entertaining** *adj* 娱乐的 yúlède; 有趣的 yǒuqùde. **entertainment** *n* **1** [U] 招待 zhāodài; 款待 kuǎndài; 娱乐 yúlè. **2** [C] 表演 biǎoyǎn; 文娱节〔節〕目 wényú jiémù.

enthral (亦作 **enthrall**, 尤用于美语) /ɪnˈθrɔːl/ *v* [-ll-] [T] 迷住 mízhù.

enthuse /ɪnˈθjuːz; *US* -ˈθuːz/ *v* [I] (*about / over*) 表现出热〔熱〕情 biǎoxiànchū rèqíng; 津津乐〔樂〕道 jīnjīn lèdào.

enthusiasm /ɪnˈθjuːzɪæzəm; *US* -ˈθuː-/ *n* [U] 热〔熱〕情 rèqíng; 热心 rèxīn; 积〔積〕极〔極〕性 jījíxìng. **enthusiast** / -æst / *n* [C] 热心人 rèxīnrén; 热情者 rèqíngzhě. **enthusiastic** / ɪnˌθjuːzɪˈæstɪk; *US* -ˌθuː-/ *adj* 热心的 rèxīnde; 热情的 rèqíngde. **enthusiastically** /-klɪ/ *adv*.

entice /ɪnˈtaɪs/ *v* [T] 诱惑 yòuhuò; 怂〔慫〕恿〔慂〕sǒngyǒng. **enticement** *n* [C, U].

entire /ɪnˈtaɪə(r)/ *adj* 全部的 quánbùde; 完全的 wánquánde; 完整的 wánzhěngde. **entirely** *adv*. **entirety** /ɪnˈtaɪərətɪ/ *n* [U].

entitle /ɪnˈtaɪtl/ *v* [T] **1** 给(书)题名 gěi tímíng. **2** *to* 给予…权〔權〕利 jǐyǔ … quánlì. **entitlement** *n* [U, C].

entity /ˈentətɪ/ *n* [C] [*pl* **-ies**] [正式用语] 存在 cúnzài; 实〔實〕体〔體〕shítǐ.

entourage /ˌɒntʊˈrɑːʒ/ *n* [C, 亦作 sing, 用 pl v] 随〔隨〕行人员 suíxíng rényuán; 扈从〔從〕hùcóng.

entrance[1] /ˈentrəns/ *n* **1** [C] 入口 rùkǒu; 门口 ménkǒu. **2** [C, U] 进〔進〕入 jìnrù. **3** [U] 进入权〔權〕jìnrùquán.

entrance[2] /ɪnˈtrɑːns; *US* -ˈtræns/ *v* [T] 使入迷 shǐ rùmí; 使快乐〔樂〕shǐ kuàilè: *~d by the music* 被音乐迷住了.

entrant /ˈentrənt/ *n* [C] 刚〔剛〕就业〔業〕者 gāng jiùyè zhě; 参〔參〕加竞〔競〕赛者 cānjiā jìngsài zhě.

entreat /ɪnˈtriːt/ *v* [T] [正式用语]恳〔懇〕求 kěnqiú; 央求 yāngqiú. **entreaty** *n* [C, U] [*pl* **-ies**] 恳求 kěnqiú.

entrenched /ɪnˈtrentʃt/ *adj* (主意等)确〔確〕立了的 quèlìlede.

entrepreneur /ˌɒntrəprəˈnɜː(r)/ *n* [C] 企业〔業〕家 qǐyèjiā.

entrust /ɪnˈtrʌst/ *v* [T] *with*; *to* 委托 wěituō; 托管 tuōguǎn: *~ the job to him* 把这工作委托给他. *~ him with the job* 委托给他这项工作.

entry /ˈentrɪ/ *n* [*pl* **-ies**] **1** [C] 进〔進〕入 jìnrù. **2** [U] 进入权〔權〕jìnrùquán. **3** [C] 入口 rùkǒu; 门口 ménkǒu. **4** 条〔條〕目 tiáomù; 项目 xiàngmù; 词条 cítiáo: *dictionary entries* 词典词条. **ˈentry visa** *n* [C] 入境签〔簽〕证〔證〕rùjìng qiānzhèng.

enumerate /ɪˈnjuːməreɪt; *US* ɪˈnuː-/ *v* [T] 数〔數〕shǔ; 点〔點〕diǎn. **enumeration** /ɪˌnjuːməˈreɪʃn; *US* ɪˌnuː-/ *n* [U].

enunciate /ɪˈnʌnsɪeɪt/ *v* [I, T] (清晰地)发〔發〕音 fāyīn; 念〔唸〕字 niànzì; (清晰地)发(音) fā; 念(字) niàn.

envelop /ɪnˈveləp/ *v* [T] 包 bāo; 裹 guǒ;

封 fēng：*~ed in fog* 被雾遮蔽. **envelopment** *n* [U].

envelope /ˈenvələʊp, 亦作 ˈɒn-/ *n* [C] 信封 xìnfēng.

enviable /ˈenvɪəbl/ *adj* 值得羡慕的 zhídé xiànmù de；引起妒忌的 yǐnqǐ dùjì de.

envious /ˈenvɪəs/ *adj* 妒忌的 dùjìde. **enviously** *adv*.

environment /ɪnˈvaɪərənmənt/ *n* [C, U] 环〔環〕境 huánjìng. **environmental** /ɪnˌvaɪərənˈmentl/ *adj*. **environmentalist** /ɪnˌvaɪərənˈmentəlɪst/ *n* [C] 环境保护〔護〕论〔論〕者 huánjìng bǎohùlùn zhě.

envisage /ɪnˈvɪzɪdʒ/ *v* [T] 期望 qīwàng；设想 shèxiǎng.

envoy /ˈenvɔɪ/ *n* [C] **1** 使节〔節〕shǐjié；代表 dàibiǎo；使者 shǐzhě. **2** (外交)公使 gōngshǐ.

envy /ˈenvɪ/ *n* **1** [U] 妒忌 dùjì；羡慕 xiànmù. **2** [习语] **the envy of sb** 某人羡慕的事物 mǒurén xiànmù de shìwù. **envy** *v* [*pt*, *pp* **-ied**] [T] 妒忌 dùjì；羡慕 xiànmù.

enzyme /ˈenzaɪm/ *n* [C] 酶 méi.

epaulette (亦作 **epaulet**，尤用于美语) /ˈepəlet/ *n* [C] 肩章 jiānzhāng.

ephemeral /ɪˈfemərəl/ *adj* 短暂〔暫〕的 duǎnzànde.

epic /ˈepɪk/ *n* [C] 史诗 shǐshī. **epic** *adj* 宏大的 hóngdàde；规模大的 guīmó dà de；场〔場〕面大的 chǎngmiàn dà de.

epidemic /ˌepɪˈdemɪk/ *n* [C] 流行病 liúxíngbìng.

epilepsy /ˈepɪlepsɪ/ *n* [U] 癫痫〔癇〕diānxián；羊痫疯〔瘋〕yángxiánfēng. **epileptic** /ˌepɪˈleptɪk/ *adj*, *n* [C].

epilogue /ˈepɪlɒg/ (美语 **-log** /-lɔːg/) *n* [C] (书或剧本)结尾部分 jiéwěi bùfen；尾声〔聲〕wěishēng；跋 bá.

episode /ˈepɪsəʊd/ *n* [C] **1** 一系列事件中的一个〔個〕事件 yíxìliè shìjiàn zhōng de yígè shìjiàn；一段时〔時〕间(的经历) yíduàn shíjiān. **2** (电视等的)连续〔續〕剧〔劇〕的一集 liánxùjùde yìjí.

epitaph /ˈepɪtɑːf; *US* -tæf/ *n* [C] 墓志铭 mùzhìmíng.

epithet /ˈepɪθet/ *n* [C] 表示性质〔質〕、特征〔徵〕的形容词 biǎoshì xìngzhì、tèzhēng de xíngróngcí.

epitome /ɪˈpɪtəmɪ/ *n* [C] 概括 gàikuò；缩影 suōyǐng；集中体〔體〕现 jízhōng tǐxiàn：*She is the ~ of kindness*. 她是和善的象征. **epitomize** /ɪˈpɪtəmaɪz/ *v* [T] 为〔為〕…的缩影 wéi … de suōyǐng；集中体现 jízhōng tǐxiàn.

epoch /ˈiːpɒk; *US* ˈepək/ *n* [C] 新纪元 xīnjìyuán；新时〔時〕代 xīnshídài.

EQ /ˈiː kjuː/ *abbr* emotional quotient 情商 qíngshāng.

equable /ˈekwəbl/ *adj* 稳〔穩〕定的 wěndìngde；变〔變〕化小的 biànhuà xiǎo de：*an ~ climate* 稳定的气候. *an ~ temper* 温和的性情.

equal /ˈiːkwəl/ *adj* **1** 相等的 xiāngděngde；相同的 xiāngtóngde. **2** *to* 胜〔勝〕任的 shèngrènde：*~ to the task* 胜任这项任务. **equal** *n* [C] 相等的事物 xiāngděngde shìwù；匹敌〔敵〕者 pǐdízhě. **equal** *v* [-ll-；美语 -l-] 相等于 xiāngděng yú. **equality** /ɪˈkwɒlətɪ/ *n* [U] 相等 xiāngděng. **equalize** *v* [I, T] 变〔變〕成相等 biànchéng xiāngděng；使相等 shǐ xiāngděng. **equally** *adv* **1** 相等地 xiāngděngde. **2** 同样〔樣〕地 tóngyàngde.

equate /ɪˈkweɪt/ *v* [T] 同等对〔對〕待 tóngděng duìdài：*You cannot ~ these two systems of government*. 不能把这两种政府体系等同起来.

equation /ɪˈkweɪʒn/ *n* [C] 方程式 fāngchéngshì；等式 děngshì.

equator /ɪˈkweɪtə(r)/ *n* **the equator** [sing] 赤道 chìdào. **equatorial** /ekwəˈtɔːrɪəl/ *adj*.

equestrian /ɪˈkwestrɪən/ *adj* 骑马的 qímǎde；马术〔術〕的 mǎshùde.

equilibrium /ˌiːkwɪˈlɪbrɪəm, 亦作 ˌek-/ *n* [U] [正式用语]平衡 pínghéng；均衡 jūnhéng.

equinox /ˈiːkwɪnɒks, 亦作 ˈek-/ *n* [C] (天文)昼〔晝〕夜平分时〔時〕zhòuyè píngfēnshí.

equip /ɪˈkwɪp/ *v* [-pp-] [T] (*with*) 装〔裝〕备〔備〕zhuāngbèi；配备 pèibèi. **equipment** *n* [U] 装备 zhuāngbèi；设备 shèbèi：*office ~ment* 办公室设备.

equitable /ˈekwɪtəbl/ *adj* 公正的 gōngzhèngde；公平的 gōngpíngde：*an ~ tax system* 公正的税收制度. **equitably** *adv*.

equity /ˈekwətɪ/ *n* **1** [U] [正式用语]公平 gōngpíng；公道 gōngdào. **2 equities** [pl] 无〔無〕固定利息之股票 wú gùdìng lìxī zhī gǔpiào.

equivalent /ɪˈkwɪvələnt/ *adj*, *n* [C] 相等的 xiāngděngde；相同的 xiāngtóngde；等同物 děngtóngwù.

equivocal /ɪˈkwɪvəkl/ *adj* [正式用语]暧〔曖〕昧的 àimèide；可疑的 kěyíde；不明确〔確〕的 bù míngquè de：*an ~ answer* 不明确的回答. **equivocate** /ɪˈkwɪvəkeɪt/ *v* [I] [正式用语]含糊其词 hánhu qící.

era /ˈɪərə/ *n* [C] 时〔時〕代 shídài；历〔歷〕史时期 lìshǐ shíqī.

eradicate /ɪˈrædɪkeɪt/ *v* [T] 根除 gēnchú；消除 xiāochú. **eradication** /ɪˌrædɪˈkeɪʃn/ *n* [U].

erase /ɪˈreɪz; *US* -s/ *v* [T] 擦掉 cādiào；抹掉 mǒdiào：[喻] *~ the event from his memory* 从他的记忆里消除这件事. **eraser** *n*

E

[C] [尤用于美语]擦除器 cāchúqì；橡皮 xiàngpí；黑板擦 hēibǎncā.

erect /ɪˈrekt/ *v* [T] 1 [正式用语]建造 jiànzào；建立 jiànlì. 2 架设 jiàshè；竖〔豎〕立 shùlì：～ *a tent* 架设帐篷. **erect** *adj* 直立的 zhílìde；竖直的 shùzhíde：*stand* ～ 直立. **erection** /ɪˈrekʃn/ *n* 1 [U] 直立 zhílì；建立 jiànlì；建造 jiànzào. 2 [C] [正式用语]建筑〔築〕物 jiànzhùwù. 3 [C] (男人阴茎的)勃起 bóqǐ. **erectness** *n* [U].

E

erode /ɪˈrəʊd/ *v* [T] [常用被动语态](海水、风等)腐蚀 fǔshí；侵蚀 qīnshí. **erosion** /ɪˈrəʊʒn/ *n* [U].

erotic /ɪˈrɒtɪk/ *adj* (引起)性欲〔慾〕的 xìngyùde；(引起)性爱〔愛〕的 xìng'ài de.

err /ɜː(r)；*US* eər/ *v* [I] [正式用语]犯错误 fàn cuòwù；弄错 nòng cuò.

errand /ˈerənd/ *n* [C] 差使(如购物等) chāishi.

erratic /ɪˈrætɪk/ *adj* 无〔無〕规律的 wú guīlǜ de；不可靠的 bù kěkàode. **erratically** /-klɪ/ *adv*.

erroneous /ɪˈrəʊnɪəs/ *adj* [正式用语]错误的 cuòwùde；不正确〔確〕的 bú zhèngquè de.

error /ˈerə(r)/ *n* 1 [C] 错误 cuòwù. 2 [U] 弄错 nòng cuò：*do it in* ～ 做错.

erudite /ˈeruːdaɪt/ *adj* [正式用语]有学〔學〕问的 yǒu xuéwèn de；博学的 bóxuéde.

erupt /ɪˈrʌpt/ *v* [I] 1 (火山)喷发〔發〕pēnfā. 2 爆发 bàofā：*Fighting* ～*ed on the street*. 街上爆发了打斗. **eruption** /ɪˈrʌpʃn/ *n* [C, U].

escalate /ˈeskəleɪt/ *v* [I, T] 升级 shēngjí；使升级 shǐ shēngjí. **escalation** /ˌeskəˈleɪʃn/ *n* [U, C].

escalator /ˈeskəleɪtə(r)/ *n* [C] 自动〔動〕楼〔樓〕梯 zìdòng lóutī.

escapade /ˈeskəpeɪd/ *n* [C]. 越轨〔軌〕行为〔爲〕yuèguǐ xíngwéi.

escape /ɪˈskeɪp/ *v* 1 [I] (*from*) 逃跑 táopǎo；逃脱 táotuō；逃亡 táowáng. 2 [I] (*from*) (气体、液体等)漏出 lòuchū；流出 liúchū. 3 [I, T] 逃避 táobì；避免 bìmiǎn. 4 [T] 被忘记 bèi wàngjì：*His name* ～*s me*. 我忘记了他的名字. **escape** *n* 1 [C, U] 逃跑 táopǎo；逃脱 táotuō. 2 [C] 逸出 yìchū；漏出 lòuchū. **escapism** *n* [U] 逃避现实〔實〕táobì xiànshí. **escapist** *adj*, *n* [C].

escort /ˈeskɔːt/ *n* [C] 护〔護〕卫〔衛〕者 hùwèizhě；护送者 hùsòngzhě；护航舰〔艦〕hùhángjiàn；护航机〔機〕hùhángjī. **escort** /ɪˈskɔːt/ *v* [T] 护送 hùsòng；护卫 hùwèi.

e-shopping /ˈiːʃɒpɪŋ/ *n* [U] 网〔網〕上购〔購〕物 wǎngshàng gòuwù.

esophagus [美语] = OESOPHAGUS.

esoteric /ˌesəʊˈterɪk, ˌiːsəʊ-/ *adj* [正式用语]奥秘的 àomìde；深奥的 shēn'àode.

especially /ɪˈspeʃəlɪ/ *adv* 1 特别 tèbié：*I love the country*, ～ *in spring*. 我喜欢农村，特别是在春天. 2 主要地 zhǔyàode；在很大程度上 zài hěndà chéngdù shàng：*This is* ～ *true of old people*. 这主要适用于老年人.

espionage /ˈespɪənɑːʒ/ *n* [U] 间谍活动〔動〕jiàndié huódòng.

essay /ˈeseɪ/ *n* [C] 文章 wénzhāng；小品文 xiǎopǐnwén；随笔 suíbǐ. **essayist** *n* [C] 小品文作家 xiǎopǐnwén zuòjiā；随笔作家 suíbǐ zuòjiā.

essence /ˈesns/ *n* 1 [U] 本质〔質〕běnzhì；实〔實〕质 shízhì. 2 [C, U] 香精 xiāngjīng；香料 xiāngliào. 3 [习语] in ˈ**essence** 实质上 shízhìshàng；本质上 běnzhìshàng.

essential /ɪˈsenʃl/ *adj* 1 最重要的 zuì zhòngyào de；必需的 bìxūde. 2 基本的 jīběnde：*an* ～ *part of the English character* 英国人的民族性的基本部分. **essential** *n* [C, 常为 pl] 本质 běnzhì；要素 yàosù. **essentially** *adv* 基本上 jīběnshàng；本质上 běnzhìshàng.

establish /ɪˈstæblɪʃ/ *v* [T] 1 建立 jiànlì；创〔創〕立 chuànglì. 2 使开〔開〕业〔業〕shǐ kāiyè；使立足 shǐ lìzú. 3 证〔證〕实〔實〕zhèngshí. **establishment** *n* 1 [U] 建立 jiànlì；设立 shèlì. 2 [C] [正式用语]建立的机〔機〕构〔構〕(如军事机构、行政机关等) jiànlìde jīgòu；公司 gōngsī；企业〔業〕qǐyè. 3 **the establishment** [sing] [尤用于英国英语，常贬]统治集团〔團〕tǒngzhì jítuán；权〔權〕势〔勢〕集团 quánshì jítuán.

estate /ɪˈsteɪt/ *n* 1 [C] 地产〔產〕dìchǎn. 2 [C] [尤用于英国英语]有大片建筑〔築〕物的地区〔區〕yǒu dàpiàn jiànzhùwù de dìqū：*a housing* ～ 住宅区. 3 [U, C] [法律]财产 cáichǎn；产业〔業〕chǎnyè. **estate agent** *n* [C] 房地产经〔經〕纪人 fángdìchǎn jīngjìrén. **estate car** *n* [C] 旅行轿〔轎〕车 lǚxíng jiàochē；客货两用轿车 kèhuò liǎngyòng jiàochē.

esteem /ɪˈstiːm/ *n* [正式用语] [U] 尊重 zūnzhòng；尊敬 zūnjìng. **esteem** *v* [T][正式用语] 尊敬 zūnjìng；尊重 zūnzhòng.

esthetic [美语] = AESTHETIC.

estimate /ˈestɪmeɪt/ *v* [T] 1 估计 gūjì；估量 gūliàng；估价〔價〕gūjià. 2 评价 píngjià. **estimate** / ˈestɪmət / *n* [C]估计 gūjì；估量 gūliàng；估价 gūjià. **estimation** / ˌestɪˈmeɪʃn / *n* [U] 判断〔斷〕pànduàn；看法 kànfǎ.

estuary /ˈestʃʊərɪ；*US* -ʊerɪ/ *n* [C] [*pl* -ies] 河口湾〔灣〕hékǒuwān；江口湾 jiāngkǒuwān.

etc /ɪt ˈsetərə, et-/ *abbr* 等等 děngděng.

etch /etʃ/ *v* [I, T] 蚀刻 shíkè. **etching** *n* 1 [U] 蚀刻法 shíkèfǎ. 2 [C] 蚀刻画〔畫〕shíkè huà.

eternal /ɪˈtɜːnl/ *adj* **1** 永久的 yǒngjiǔde；永存的 yǒngcúnde；不朽的 bùxiǔde. **2** [非正式用语]不停的 bùtíngde：～ *fighting* 不停的战斗. **eternally** /-nəlɪ/ *adv*.

eternity /ɪˈtɜːnətɪ/ *n* **1** [U] [正式用语]永恒 yǒnghéng；无〔無〕穷〔窮〕wúqióng；来生 láishēng. **2** [常为 sing] [非正式用语]无穷无尽〔盡〕的一段时〔時〕间 wúqióng wújìn de yíduàn shíjiān.

ether /ˈiːθə(r)/ *n* [U] 醚 mí；乙醚 yǐmí. **ethereal** /ɪˈθɪərɪəl/ *adj* 轻〔輕〕飘的 qīngpiāode.

ethic /ˈeθɪk/ *n* **1** [sing] 伦〔倫〕理 lúnlǐ：*the Christian* ～ 基督教伦理观. **2 ethics** (a) [pl] 道德规范〔範〕dàodé guīfàn. (b) [用 sing v] 伦理学〔學〕lúnlǐxué. **ethical** *adj* **1** 道德的 dàodéde. **2** 合乎道德的 héhū dàodé de. **ethically** *adv*.

ethnic /ˈeθnɪk/ *adj* 种〔種〕族的 zhǒngzúde；部落的 bùluòde. **ethnically** /-klɪ/ *adv*.

etiquette /ˈetɪket/ *n* [U] 礼〔禮〕节〔節〕lǐjié；礼仪〔儀〕lǐyí.

etymology /ˌetɪˈmɒlədʒɪ/ *n* [U] 词源学〔學〕cíyuánxué.

EU /iːˈjuː/ *abbr* European Union 欧〔歐〕盟 Ōuméng.

eucalyptus /ˌjuːkəˈlɪptəs/ *n* [C] 桉树〔樹〕ānshù.

euphemism /ˈjuːfəmɪzəm/ *n* [C, U] 委婉法 wěiwǎnfǎ；婉言法 wǎnyánfǎ：'*Pass away*' *is a* ～ *for* '*die*'. "pass away (逝世)"是 "die (死)"的委婉说法.

euphoria /juːˈfɔːrɪə/ *n* [U] 异〔異〕常欣快 yìcháng xīnkuài. **euphoric** /juːˈfɒrɪk; *US* -ˈfɔːr-/ *adj*.

euro /ˈjʊərəʊ/ *n* [C] 欧〔歐〕元 ōuyuán.

Europe /ˈjʊərəp/ *n* [U] 欧〔歐〕洲 Ōuzhōu.

European /ˌjʊərəˈpɪən/ *adj* 欧〔歐〕洲的 Ōuzhōude. **European** *n* 欧洲人 Ōuzhōurén. **European Central ˈBank** *n* [U] 欧洲中央银行 Ōuzhōu Zhōngyāng Yínháng. **European ˈParliament** *n* [U] 欧洲议〔議〕会 Ōuzhōu Yìhuì. **European ˈUnion** *n* [U] 欧洲联〔聯〕盟 Ōuzhōu Liánméng.

eurosceptic /ˈjʊərəʊˌskeptɪk/ *n* [C] 对〔對〕欧〔歐〕盟持怀〔懷〕疑态〔態〕度者 duì Ōuméng chí huáiyí tàidù zhě. **eurosceptic** *adj* 对欧盟持怀疑态度的 duì Ōuméng chí huáiyí tàidù de.

eurozone /ˈjʊərəʊzəʊn/ *n* [U] 欧〔歐〕元区〔區〕Ōuyuánqū.

euthanasia /ˌjuːθəˈneɪzɪə; *US* -ˈneɪʒə/ *n* [U] 安乐〔樂〕死术〔術〕ānlèsǐshù.

evacuate /ɪˈvækjʊeɪt/ *v* [T] 撤离〔離〕chèlí；疏散 shūsàn：～ (*children from*) *the city* (把孩子们)撤离城市. **evacuation** /ɪˌvækjʊˈeɪʃn/ *n* [C, U].

evade /ɪˈveɪd/ *v* [T] **1** 躲避 duǒbì；逃避 táobì：～ (*answering*) *a question* 逃避(回答)问题. **2** 躲开〔開〕duǒkāi.

evaluate /ɪˈvæljʊeɪt/ *v* [T] 估…的价〔價〕gū…de jià；定…的值 dìng… de zhí. **evaluation** /ɪˌvæljʊˈeɪʃn/ *n* [C, U].

evangelical /ˌiːvænˈdʒelɪkl/ *adj* 福音的 fúyīnde；合乎福音的 héhū fúyīn de.

evangelist /ɪˈvændʒəlɪst/ *n* [C] **1** 福音作者之一 fúyīn zuòzhě zhī yī. **2** 福音传〔傳〕道者 fúyīn chuándào zhě. **evangelistic** /ɪˌvændʒəˈlɪstɪk/ *adj*.

evaporate /ɪˈvæpəreɪt/ *v* **1** [I, T] (使)蒸发〔發〕掉 zhēngfādiào. **2** [I] 消失 xiāoshī. **evaporation** /ɪˌvæpəˈreɪʃn/ *n* [U].

evasion /ɪˈveɪʒn/ *n* [C, U] 逃避 táobì；躲避 duǒbì. **evasive** /ɪˈveɪsɪv/ *adj* 回避的 huíbìde；躲避的 duǒbìde. **evasively** *adv*.

eve /iːv/ *n* [C] [C, 常为 sing] **1** (节日的)前夕 qiánxī；前夜 qiányè. **2** (重大事件的)前夕 qiánxī；前夜 qiányè：*on the* ～ *of the election* 选举前夕.

even[1] /ˈiːvn/ *adv* **1** 甚至…(也) shènzhì…；连…都 lián… dōu：*Anyone can understand this*, ～ *a child*. 任何人都会懂这个道理，连孩子也会懂的. **2** 甚至(比…)还〔還〕shènzhì hái：*You know* ～ *less than I do*. 你甚至比我知道得还少. **3** [习语] **even if / though** 即使 jíshǐ；纵〔縱〕使 zòngshǐ：*I'll get there*, ～ *if I have to walk*. 即使不得不走路，我也会到那里的. **ˌeven ˈnow/ˈso/ˈthen** 尽〔儘〕管情况如此 jǐnguǎn qíngkuàng rúcǐ：*I told him, but* ～ *then he didn't believe me*. 我告诉了他，尽管如此，他还是不相信我.

even[2] /ˈiːvn/ *adj* **1** 平的 píngde；平滑的 pínghuáde；平坦的 píngtǎnde：*an* ～ *surface* 平坦的表面. **2** 有规律的 yǒu guīlǜde；稳〔穩〕定的 wěndìngde：*an* ～ *temperature* 稳定的温度. **3** (数量、距离等)相等的 xiāngděngde. **4** (数字)双〔雙〕数〔數〕的 shuāngshùde. **5** 均衡的 jūnhéngde；对〔對〕等的 duìděngde：*The two teams are very* ～. 这两个队旗鼓相当. **6** [习语] **get even with sb** 报〔報〕复〔復〕某人 bàofù mǒurén. **on an even keel** 稳定 wěndìng. **even** *v* [短语动词] **even (sth) out** 使平 shǐ píng；拉平 lā píng. **even (sth) up** 扯平 chě píng；使相等 shǐ xiāngděng. **ˌeven-handed** *adj* 公正的 gōngzhèngde. **evenly** *adv*. **evenness** *n* [U]. **eventempered** *adj* 性情平和的 xìngqíng pínghé de.

evening /ˈiːvnɪŋ/ *n* [C, U] 晚上 wǎnshàng；傍晚 bàngwǎn；黄昏 huánghūn. **ˈevening dress** *n* **1** [U] 夜礼〔禮〕服 yèlǐfú. **2** [C] 女装〔裝〕晚礼

服 nǚzhuāng wǎnlǐfú.

event /ɪˈvent/ *n* [C] 1 事件 shìjiàn;事变〔變〕shìbiàn;大事 dàshì. 2 比赛项目 bǐsài xiàngmù. 3 [习语] **at ˈall event** 无〔無〕论〔論〕如何 wúlùn rúhé;不管怎样〔樣〕bùguǎn zěnyàng. **in the event of sth** [正式用语]倘若 tǎngruò;万〔萬〕一 wànyī. **eventful** /-fl/ *adj* 充满大事的 chōngmǎn dàshì de;发〔發〕生许多有趣事件的 fāshēng xǔduō yǒuqù shìjiàn de.

eventual /ɪˈventʃuəl/ *adj* 最后〔後〕的 zuìhòude;结果的 jiéguǒde. **eventuality** /ɪˌventʃuˈælətɪ/ *n* [C] [*pl* **-ies**] [正式用语]可能发〔發〕生的事 kěnéng fāshēng de shì;可能的结果 kěnéngde jiéguǒ. **eventually** *adv* 最后〔後〕zuìhòu;终于 zhōngyú: *They ~ly agreed to pay the bill*. 他们终于同意付账.

ever /evə(r)/ *adv* 1 在任何时〔時〕候 zài rènhé shíhòu: *Nothing ~ happens here*. 这里平静无事. *Do you ~ wish you were rich?* 你有时希望发财吗? *the best work you've ~ done* 你做过的最好的工作. 2 **ever-** (构成复合词)总〔總〕是 zǒngshì;不断〔斷〕地 búduànde: *the ~-increasing number of students* 不断增加的学生数目. 3 究竟 jiūjìng;到底 dàodǐ: *What ~ do you mean?* 你到底是什么意思? 4 [习语] **for ever** ⇨FOREVER. **ever since** 自从〔從〕…以来〔來〕zìcóng …yǐlái: *She's liked reading ~ since she was a child*. 她从儿童时期就喜欢读书. **ever so / such** [非正式用语]非常 fēicháng: *~ so rich* 非常富有.

evergreen /ˈevəgriːn/ *n* [C], *adj* 常绿植物 chánglǜ zhíwù;常绿树〔樹〕chánglǜshù;(树)常绿的 chánglǜde.

everlasting /ˌevəˈlɑːstɪŋ; *US* -ˈlæst-/ *adj* 永久的 yǒngjiǔde;永恒的 yǒnghéngde.

every /ˈevrɪ/ *adj* 1 每一的 měiyīde;每个〔個〕的 měigède: *E~ child passed the exam*. 每个孩子都考试及格. 2 一切可能的 yíqiè kěnéng de: *You have ~ reason to be satisfied*. 你有充分理由感到满足. 3 每…中的 měi …zhōng de: *She phones ~ week*. 她每周打电话. 4 [习语] **every other** 每隔 měi gé: *~ other day* 每隔一天. **ˈeverybody** (亦作 **ˈeveryone**) *pron* 每个人 měigèrén. **ˈeveryday** *adj* 日常的 rìchángde;普通的 pǔtōngde;每天的 měitiānde. **ˈeverything** *pron* 所有事物 suǒyǒu shìwù: *E~thing was destroyed*. 一切都被摧毁了. **ˈeverywhere** *adv* 到处〔處〕dàochù.

evict /ɪˈvɪkt/ *v* [T] 驱〔驅〕逐 qūzhú. **eviction** /-kʃn/ *n* [C, U].

evidence /ˈevɪdəns/ *n* [U] 1 (尤用于法律)证〔證〕据〔據〕zhèngjù. 2 [习语] **in evidence** 明显〔顯〕的 míngxiǎnde;显而易见的 xiǎn ér yì jiàn de.

evident /ˈevɪdənt/ *adj* 明白的 míngbaide;显〔顯〕然的 xiǎnránde;明显的 míngxiǎnde. **evidently** *adv*.

evil /ˈiːvl/ *adj* 坏〔壞〕的 huàide;邪恶〔惡〕的 xié'ède;有害的 yǒuhàide. **evil** *n* 1 [U] 邪恶 xié'è;罪恶 zuì'è. 2 [C] 坏〔壞〕事 huàishì;恶行 èxíng. **evilly** /-vəlɪ/ *adv*.

evocative /ɪˈvɒkətɪv/ *adj* 引起…的 yǐnqǐ… de;唤起…的 huànqǐ … de: *an ~ picture* 勾起往日之情的图画.

evoke /ɪˈvəʊk/ *v* [T] 引起 yǐnqǐ;唤起 huànqǐ.

evolution /ˌiːvəˈluːʃn; *US* ˌev-/ *n* [U] 进〔進〕化 jìnhuà;进化论〔論〕jìnhuàlùn.

evolve /ɪˈvɒlv/ *v* [I, T] 发〔發〕展 fāzhǎn;使发展 shǐ fāzhǎn.

ewe /juː/ *n* [C] 母羊 mǔyáng.

exacerbate /ɪgˈzæsəbeɪt/ *v* [T] [正式用语] 使恶〔惡〕化 shǐ èhuà.

exact[1] /ɪgˈzækt/ *adj* 正确〔確〕的 zhèngquède;确切的 quèqiède;精确的 jīngquède: *the ~ time* 精确的时间. **exactitude** /-ɪtjuːd; *US* -tuːd/ *n* [U] 正确性 zhèngquèxìng. **exactly** *adv* 1 正确地 zhèngquède;精确地 jīngquède. 2 (用于回答)确实〔實〕如此 quèshí rúcǐ,一点〔點〕不错 yìdiǎn búcuò. **exactness** *n* [U].

exact[2] /ɪgˈzækt/ *v* [T] [正式用语]强求 qiángqiú;坚〔堅〕持 jiānchí: *~ obedience* 强求服从. **exacting** *adj* 需付出极〔極〕大努力的 xū fùchū jídà nǔlì de;需要小心细致〔緻〕的 xūyào xiǎoxīn xìzhì de.

exaggerate /ɪgˈzædʒəreɪt/ *v* [I, T] 夸〔誇〕大 kuādà;夸张〔張〕kuāzhāng. **exaggeration** /ɪgˌzædʒəˈreɪʃn/ *n* [C, U].

exam /ɪgˈzæm/ *n* [C] [非正式用语]考试 kǎoshì (examination 的缩略).

examination /ɪgˌzæmɪˈneɪʃn/ *n* 1 [C] 考试 kǎoshì. 2 [U, C] 仔细观〔觀〕察 zǐxì guānchá.

examine /ɪgˈzæmɪn/ *v* [T] 1 仔细观〔觀〕察 zǐxì guānchá. 2 考试 kǎoshì. **examiner** *n* [C] 主考人 zhǔkǎorén.

example /ɪgˈzɑːmpl; *US* -ˈzæm-/ *n* [C] 1 例子 lìzi;例证〔證〕lìzhèng: *a fine ~ of Norman architecture* 诺曼底建筑的一个杰出的例子. 2 范〔範〕例 fànlì;榜样〔樣〕bǎngyàng: *His bravery is an ~ to us all*. 他的英勇是我们所有人的榜样. 3 [习语] **for example** 例如 lìrú;举〔舉〕例来〔來〕说 jǔlì lái shuō: *Many women, Alison for ~, have a job and a family*. 许多妇女,例如阿里森,都有工作和家庭. **make an example of sb** 惩〔懲〕罚…以儆戒别人 chéngfá… yǐ jǐngjiè biérén.

exasperate /ɪgˈzɑːspəreɪt/ *v* [T] 激怒 jīnù;

使恼〔惱〕火 shǐ nǎohuǒ. **exasperation** /ɪgˌzæspəˈreɪʃn/ *n* [U].

excavate /ˈekskəveɪt/ *v* [T] 挖掘 wājué;挖出 wāchū: ~ *a hole* 挖一个洞. ~ *a buried city* 挖掘一座被埋藏的城市. **excavation** /ˌekskəˈveɪʃn/ *n* [C,U]. **excavator** *n* [C] 挖掘者 wājuézhě;挖土机〔機〕wātǔjī;电〔電〕铲〔鏟〕diànchǎn.

exceed /ɪkˈsiːd/ *v* [T] **1** 比…大 bǐ … dà;大于 dàyú. **2** 超出(规定) chāochū: ~ *the speed limit* 超出规定的最高速度. **exceedingly** *adv* [正式用语]极〔極〕端地 jíduānde;非常 fēicháng.

excel /ɪkˈsel/ *v* [-ll-] [I] *at/in* 突出 tūchū;超常 chāocháng;优〔優〕于 yōuyú;杰〔傑〕出 jiéchū.

Excellency /ˈeksələnsɪ/ *n* [C] [*pl* -ies] 阁下 géxià.

excellent /ˈeksələnt/ *adj* 优〔優〕秀的 yōuxiùde;杰〔傑〕出的 jiéchūde; **excellence** /-ləns/ *n* [U]. **excellently** *adv*.

except /ɪkˈsept/ *prep* 除…之外 chú … zhīwài: *The shop is open every day ~ Sunday*. 这家商店除星期日外,每天营业. **except** *v* [T] [正式用语][常用被动语态]除去 chúqù;除掉 chúdiào.

exception /ɪkˈsepʃn/ *n* **1** [C] 除外 chúwài;例外 lìwài: *All the students did well, with the ~ of Jo, who failed*. 所有孩子都考得很好,只有乔是例外,他不及格. **2** [习语] **make an exception (of sb/sth)** 把…作为〔爲〕例外 bǎ … zuòwéi lìwài. **take exception to sth** 生气〔氣〕shēngqì 不悦 búyuè. **exceptional** /-ʃənl/ *adj* 异〔異〕常的 yìchángde;优〔優〕越的 yōuyuède. **exceptionally** /-ʃənəlɪ/ *adv*.

excerpt /ˈeksɜːpt/ *n* [C] 摘录〔錄〕zhāilù;节〔節〕录 jiélù.

excess /ɪkˈses/ *n* **1** [sing] *of* 超过〔過〕量 chāoguòliàng. **2 excesses** [pl] [正式用语]暴行 bàoxíng. **3** [习语] **in excess of sth** 超过 chāoguò. **to excess** 过度 guòdù;过多 guòduō: *drink to* ~ 饮酒过度. **excess** /ˈekses/ *adj* 额外的 éwàide;附加的 fùjiāde: ~ *baggage* 超重行李. **excessive** *adj* 过多的 guòduōde;过分的 guòfènde. **excessively** *adv*.

exchange /ɪksˈtʃeɪndʒ/ *v* [T] 交换 jiāohuàn;兑换 duìhuàn: ~ *pounds for dollars* 以英镑兑换美元. **exchange** *n* **1** [C,U] 交换 jiāohuàn;互换 hùhuàn;交易 jiāoyì. **2** 兑换 duìhuàn. [C] 争吵 zhēngchǎo. **3** [C] 交易所 jiāoyìsuǒ: *the* ˈ*Stock E~* 证券交易所. **4** = TELEPHONE EXCHANGE (TELEPHONE). **exchange rate** *n* [C] (外汇)兑换率 duìhuànlǜ.

exchequer /ɪksˈtʃekə(r)/ *n* **the Exchequer** [sing] [英国英语](英国)财政部 cáizhèngbù: *the Chancellor of the E~* 英国财政大臣.

excise /ˈeksaɪz/ *n* [U] 国〔國〕内货物税 guónèi huòwùshuì.

excite /ɪkˈsaɪt/ *v* [T] **1** 刺激 cìjī;使激动〔動〕shǐ jīdòng. **2** 引起 yǐnqǐ;激发〔發〕jīfā. **excitable** *adj* 易激动〔動〕的 yì jīdòng de;易兴〔興〕奋〔奮〕的 yì xīngfèn de. **excited** *adj* 激动的 jīdòngde;兴奋的 xìngfènde. **excitedly** *adv*. **excitement** *n* [U,C]. **exciting** *adj* 令人激动的 lìng rén jīdòng de;令人兴奋的 lìng rén xīngfèn de.

exclaim /ɪkˈskleɪm/ *v* [I,T] 呼叫 hūjiào;呼喊 hūhǎn;惊〔驚〕叫 jīngjiào. **exclamation** /ˌekskləˈmeɪʃn/ *n* [C] 呼喊 hūhǎn;惊叫 jīngjiào;感叹〔嘆〕词 gǎntàncí. **exclamation mark** (美语 **exclamation point**) *n* [C] 惊叹号〔號〕(!) jīngtànhào.

exclude /ɪkˈskluːd/ *v* [T] **1** 把…排斥在外 bǎ … páichì zàiwài;不包括 bù bāokuò. **2** 不予考虑〔慮〕bùyǔ kǎolǜ: ~ *the idea of failure* 不考虑失败的可能性. **exclusion** /-luːʒn/ *n* [U].

exclusive /ɪkˈskluːsɪv/ *adj* **1** (团体)不轻〔輕〕易吸收新会〔會〕员的 bù qīngyì xīshōu xīnhuìyuán de. **2** 为〔爲〕少数〔數〕富人服务〔務〕的 wèi shǎoshù fùrén fúwù de. **3** (报导)独〔獨〕家发〔發〕表的 dújiā fābiǎo de. **exclusively** *adv* 仅〔僅〕仅 jǐnjǐn.

excommunicate /ˌekskəˈmjuːnɪkeɪt/ *v* [T] (基督教)开〔開〕除…的教籍 kāichú … de jiàojí;把…逐出教门 bǎ … zhúchū jiàomén. **excommunication** /ˌekskəˌmjuːnɪˈkeɪʃn/ *n* [U,C].

excrement /ˈekskrɪmənt/ *n* [U] [正式用语]粪〔糞〕便 fènbiàn.

excrete /ɪkˈskriːt/ *v* [T] 排泄(身体废物) páixiè.

excruciating /ɪkˈskruːʃɪeɪtɪŋ/ *adj* (痛苦)难〔難〕忍受的 nán rěnshòu de. **excruciatingly** *adv*.

excursion /ɪkˈskɜːʃn; *US* -ɜːrʒn/ *n* [C] 远足 yuǎnzú;短途旅行 duǎntú lǚxíng.

excuse /ɪkˈskjuːs/ *n* [C] 借〔藉〕口 jièkǒu;理由 lǐyóu. **excusable** /ɪkˈskjuːzəbl/ *adj* 可原谅的 kě yuánliàng de. **excuse** /ɪkˈskjuːz/ *v* [T] **1** 原谅 yuánliàng. **2** (*from*) 给…免去(责任等) gěi … miǎnqù. **3** 为〔爲〕…辩解 wèi … biànjiě: *Nothing can ~ such rudeness*. 无法为这种粗鲁行为辩解. **4** [习语] **excuse me** (a) (用作打断对方谈话或表示不同意的道歉语)对〔對〕不起 duìbùqǐ. (b) [美语]请再说一遍 qǐng zài shuō yíbiàn.

execute /ˈeksɪkjuːt/ *v* [T] **1** [正式用语]执〔執〕行 zhíxíng;实〔實〕行 shíxíng;实施 shíshī: ~ *a plan* 实施一项计划. **2** 将〔將〕…处〔處〕死

jiāng … chūsǐ. **execution** /ˌeksɪˈkjuːʃn/ *n* **1** [U] [正式用语]实行 shíxíng；实施 shíshī；完成 wánchéng. **2** [C, U] 死刑 sǐxíng. **executioner** /ˌeksɪˈkjuːʃənə(r)/ *n* [C] 行刑人 xíngxíngrén.

executive /ɪgˈzekjʊtɪv/ *adj* 执〔執〕行的 zhíxíngde；实〔實〕行的 shíxíngde；经〔經〕营〔營〕管理的 jīngyíng guǎnlǐ de. **executive** *n* **1** [C] (企业组织的)经营管理人员 jīngyíng guǎnlǐ rényuán. **2 the executive** [sing] 政府行政部门 zhèngfǔ xíngzhèng bùmén.

E

executor /ɪgˈzekjʊtə(r)/ *n* [C] 指定的遗嘱执〔執〕行人 zhǐdìngde yízhǔ zhíxíngrén.

exemplify /ɪgˈzemplɪfaɪ/ *v* [*pt*, *pp* -ied] [T] 举〔舉〕例说明 jǔlì shuōmíng；作为〔爲〕…的例证〔證〕 zuòwéi … de lìzhèng. **exemplification** /ɪgˌzemplɪfɪˈkeɪʃn/ *n* [U, C].

exempt /ɪgˈzempt/ *adj* (*from*) 被免除(责任、义务等)的 bèi miǎnchú de. **exempt** *v* [T] (*from*) 免除 miǎnchú；豁免 huòmiǎn. **exemption** /ɪgˈzempʃn/ *n* [U, C].

exercise /ˈeksəsaɪz/ *n* **1** [U] 运〔運〕动〔動〕 yùndòng：*Jogging is good* ～. 慢跑是好的运动. **2** [C] 练〔練〕习〔習〕 liànxí；训练 xùnliàn：*maths* ～*s* 数学练习. **3** [U] 行使 xíngshǐ；运用 yùnyòng：*the* ～ *of authority* 权力的运用. **exercise** *v* **1** [I, T] 锻炼〔煉〕 duànliàn；训练 xùnliàn. **2** [T] 行使 xíngshǐ；运用 yùnyòng. ˈ**exercise book** *n* [C]练习簿 liànxíbù.

exert /ɪgˈzɜːt/ *v* [T] **1** 发〔發〕挥 fāhuī；行使 xíngshǐ；运〔運〕用 yùnyòng 施加 shījiā：～ *pressure on sb to do sth* 对某人施加压力使其做某事. **2** ～ **oneself** 努力 nǔlì；尽〔盡〕力 jìnlì. **exertion** /ɪgˈzɜːʃn; *US* -ɜːrʒn/ *n* [C, U].

exhale /eksˈheɪl/ *v* [I, T]呼气〔氣〕 hūqì. **exhalation** /ˌekshəˈleɪʃn/ *n* [C, U].

exhaust /ɪgˈzɔːst/ *v* [I, T] **1** 使精疲力竭 shǐ jīng pí lì jié. **2** 耗尽〔盡〕 hàojìn；用完 yòngwán. **exhaust** *n* (a) [C] 排气〔氣〕管 páiqìguǎn. (b) [U] (排出的)废〔廢〕气 fèiqì. **exhausted** *adj* 精疲力竭的 jīng pí lì jié de. **exhaustion** /ɪgˈzɔːstʃən/ *n* [U]. **exhaustive** *adj* 全面彻〔徹〕底的 quánmiàn chèdǐ de.

exhibit /ɪgˈzɪbɪt/ *v* [T] **1** [正式用语]显〔顯〕示 xiǎnshì；表现 biǎoxiàn. **2** 展出 zhǎnchū；陈列 chénliè. **exhibit** *n* [C] **1** 陈列品 chénlièpǐn；展览〔覽〕品 zhǎnlǎnpǐn. **2** [法律](法庭上出示的)证〔證〕据〔據〕 zhèngjù. **exhibitor** *n* [C] 展出者 zhǎnchūzhě.

exhibition /ˌeksɪˈbɪʃn/ *n* **1** [C] 展览〔覽〕会〔會〕 zhǎnlǎnhuì **2** [C] [常为 sing] 表现 biǎoxiàn；显〔顯〕示 xiǎnshì：*an* ～ *of bad manner* 没有礼貌的表现. **exhibitionism** /-ʃənɪzəm/ *n* [U] 出风〔風〕头〔頭〕 chūfēngtou；风头主义〔義〕 fēngtóuzhǔyì. **exhibitionist** *n* [C].

exhilarate /ɪgˈzɪləreɪt/ *v* [T] [常用被动语态]使振奋〔奮〕 shǐ zhènfèn；使高兴〔興〕 shǐ gāoxìng. **exhilaration** /ɪgˌzɪləˈreɪʃn/ *n* [U].

exhort /ɪgˈzɔːt/ *v* [T] [正式用语]敦促 dūncù；劝〔勸〕告 quàngào；规劝 guīquàn：～ *him to try harder* 劝他再加劲. **exhortation** /ˌegzɔːˈteɪʃn/ *n* [C, U].

exile /ˈeksaɪl/ *n* **1** [U] 流放 liúfàng；放逐 fàngzhú：*live in* ～ 过流放生活. **2** [C] 被流放者 bèi liúfàngzhě. **exile** *v* [T] 流放 liúfàng；放逐 fàngzhú.

exist /ɪgˈzɪst/ *v* [I] 有 yǒu；存在 cúnzài；生存 shēngcún. **existence** *n* **1** [U] 存在 cúnzài：*believe in the* ～*ence of God* 相信上帝的存在. **2** [sing] 生存方式 shēngcún fāngshì：*a miserable* ～*ence* 凄惨的生活. **existent** *adj* [正式用语]存在的 cúnzàide；实〔實〕在的 shízàide.

exit /ˈeksɪt/ *n* [C] **1** 出口 chūkǒu；太平门〔門〕 tàipíngmén. **2** 出去 chūqù；离〔離〕去 líqù；(演员的)退场〔場〕 tuìchǎng. **exit** *v* [I] 出去 chūqù；离去 líqù；(演员)退场 tuìchǎng. ˈ**exit visa** *n* [C] 出境签〔簽〕证〔證〕 chūjìng qiānzhèng.

exonerate /ɪgˈzɒnəreɪt/ *v* [T] [正式用语]使免受责备〔備〕 shǐ miǎnshòu zébèi. **exoneration** /ɪgˌzɒnəˈreɪʃn/ *n* [U].

exorbitant /ɪgˈzɔːbɪtənt/ *adj* 价〔價〕格高昂的 jiàgé gāo'áng de. **exorbitantly** *adv*.

exorcize /ˈeksɔːsaɪz/ *v* [T] (用祷告等)驱〔驅〕除(妖魔) qūchú. **exorcism** /-sɪzəm/ *n* [U, C]. **exorcist** *n* [C].

exotic /ɪgˈzɒtɪk/ *adj* **1** 外国〔國〕种〔種〕的 wàiguó zhǒng de；外国传〔傳〕入的 wàiguó chuánrù de：～ *fruits* 外国水果. **2** 奇异〔異〕的 qíyìde；吸引人的 xīyǐn rén de.

expand /ɪkˈspænd/ *v* **1** [I, T] (使)扩〔擴〕大 kuòdà；(使)膨胀〔脹〕 péngzhàng；(使)扩张〔張〕 kuòzhāng：*Metal* ～*s when heated*. 金属受热就膨胀. **2** [短语动词] **expand on sth** 详述 xiángshù；充分叙述 chōngfèn xùshù.

expanse /ɪkˈspæns/ *n* [C] (陆地、海洋等的)广〔廣〕阔〔闊〕地区〔區〕 guǎngkuò dìqū.

expansion /ɪkˈspænʃn/ *n* [U] 扩〔擴〕张〔張〕 kuòzhāng；扩大 kuòdà；膨胀〔脹〕 péngzhàng. **expansionism** /-ʃənɪzəm/ *n* [U] [尤用于贬](领土、事业等的)扩张主义 kuòzhāng zhǔyì；扩张政策 kuòzhāng zhèngcè. **expansionist** *adj*.

expansive /ɪkˈspænsɪv/ *adj* (人)爱〔愛〕说的 àishuōde；豪爽的 háoshuǎngde；开〔開〕朗的 kāilǎngde.

expatriate /eksˈpætrɪət; *US* -ˈpeɪt-/ *n* [C] 移居国〔國〕外的人 yíjū guówài de rén；移民

yímín.

expect /ɪkˈspekt/ *v* 1 [T] 预期 yùqī; 期望 qīwàng. 2 [习语] **be expecting** 怀〔懷〕孕 huáiyùn. **expectancy** *n* [U] [正式用语] 期待 qīdài; 期望 qīwàng. **expectant** *adj* 1 期待的 qīdàide; 期望的 qīwàngde. 2 怀孕的 huáiyùnde. **expectation** /ˌekspekˈteɪʃn/ *n* [C,U] 期待 qīdài; 预期 yùqī.

expedient /ɪkˈspiːdɪənt/ *adj*, *n* [C] [正式用语] 权〔權〕宜之计的 quányí zhī jì de; 合算的 hésuànde; 紧〔緊〕急的办〔辦〕法 jǐnjíde bànfǎ; 权宜之计 quányí zhī jì.

expedition /ˌekspɪˈdɪʃn/ *n* [C] (a) 远〔遠〕征 yuǎnzhēng; 探险〔險〕 tànxiǎn; 考察 kǎochá. (b) 远征队〔隊〕 yuǎnzhēngduì; 探险队 tànxiǎnduì; 考察队 kǎocháduì.

expel /ɪkˈspel/ *v* [-ll-] [T] 1 驱〔驅〕逐 qūzhú; 开〔開〕除 kāichú. 2 排出 páichū: ~ *air from the lungs* 从肺里排出空气.

expend /ɪkˈspend/ *v* [T] [正式用语] 消费 xiāofèi; 花费 huāfèi; 用尽〔盡〕 yòngjìn. **expendable** *adj* [正式用语] 可消费的 kě xiāofèi de; 为〔爲〕达〔達〕到某种目的可被牺〔犧〕牲的 wèi dádào mǒuzhǒng mùdì kě bèi xīshēng de.

expenditure /ɪkˈspendɪtʃə(r)/ *n* [U,C] 1 消费量 xiāofèiliàng; 支出额 zhīchū'é. 2 花费 huāfèi; 支出 zhīchū; 消费 xiāofèi; 使用 shǐyòng.

expense /ɪkˈspens/ *n* 1 [U,C] 消费 xiāofèi; 花费 huāfèi; 支出 zhīchū. 2 **expenses** [pl] 开〔開〕支 kāizhī; 经〔經〕费 jīngfèi: *travelling* ~*s* 旅行开支. 3 [习语] **at sb's expense** (a) 由某人付款 yóu mǒurén fùkuǎn. (b) (玩笑) 取笑某人 qǔxiào mǒurén.

expensive /ɪkˈspensɪv/ *adj* 花费的 huāfèide; 昂贵的 ángguìde; 花钱〔錢〕多的 huāqián duō de. **expensively** *adv*.

experience /ɪkˈspɪərɪəns/ *n* 1 [U] 体〔體〕验〔驗〕 tǐyàn; 经〔經〕验 jīngyàn: *learn by* ~ 从经验中学习. 2 [C] 经历〔歷〕 jīnglì; 阅历 yuèlì: *a happy* ~ 一段幸福的经历. **experience** *v* [T] 体验 tǐyàn; 经历 jīnglì; 感受 gǎnshòu: ~ *difficulty* 经受困难. ~ *pain* 感受痛苦. **experienced** *adj* 经验丰〔豐〕富的 jīngyàn fēngfù de.

experiment /ɪkˈsperɪmənt/ *n* [C,U] (尤指科学上的) 实〔實〕验〔驗〕 shíyàn; 试验 shìyàn. **experiment** *v* [I] 做实验 zuò shíyàn; 进〔進〕行试验 jìnxíng shìyàn. **experimental** /ɪkˌsperɪˈmentl/ *adj* 实验(性)的 shíyànde; 用实验的 yòng shíyàn de. **experimentation** /ɪkˌsperɪmenˈteɪʃn/ *n* [U].

expert /ˈekspɜːt/ *n* [C] 专〔專〕家 zhuānjiā; 能手 néngshǒu. **expert** *adj* 有经〔經〕验〔驗〕的 yǒu jīngyàn de; 熟练〔練〕的 shúliànde. **expertly** *adv*.

expertise /ˌekspɜːˈtiːz/ *n* [U] 专〔專〕门知识〔識〕 zhuānmén zhīshi; 专门技能 zhuānmén jìnéng.

expire /ɪkˈspaɪə(r)/ *v* [I] 1 满期 mǎnqī; 到期 dàoqī: *My passport has* ~*d*. 我的护照到期了. 2 [旧词, 正式用语] 死 sǐ. **expiry** /ɪkˈspaɪərɪ/ *n* [U] 满期 mǎnqī.

explain /ɪkˈspleɪn/ *v* 1 [I,T] 解释〔釋〕 jiěshì; 阐〔闡〕明 chǎnmíng; 说明 shuōmíng. 2 说明…的理由 shuōmíng … de lǐyóu; 为〔爲〕…辩解 wèi … biànjiě: ~ *one's behaviour* 为其行为辩解. 3 [短语动词] **explain sth away** 对〔對〕…进〔進〕行解释以消除指责 duì … jìnxíng jiěshì yǐ xiāochú zhǐzé. **explanation** /ˌekspləˈneɪʃn/ *n* 1 [C] (为解释所作的) 陈述 chénshù. 2 [U] 解释 jiěshì; 说明 shuōmíng. **explanatory** /ɪkˈsplænətrɪ; *US* -tɔːrɪ/ *adj* (陈述) 用作解释的 yòng zuò jiěshì de.

explicit /ɪkˈsplɪsɪt/ *adj* 1 (陈述等) 清楚的 qīngchǔde; 明确〔確〕的 míngquède. 2 (人) 直言的 zhíyánde; 坦率的 tǎnshuàide. **explicitly** *adv*. **explicitness** *n* [U].

explode /ɪkˈspləʊd/ *v* 1 [I,T] (使) 爆炸 bàozhà; (使) 爆发〔發〕 bàofā. 2 [I] (人) 感情发作 gǎnqíng fāzuò.

exploit[1] /ɪkˈsplɔɪt/ *v* [T] 1 剥削 bōxuē. 2 开〔開〕拓 kāituò; 开发〔發〕 kāifā; 开采〔採〕 kāicǎi: ~ *oil reserves* 开发石油资源. **exploitation** /ˌeksplɔɪˈteɪʃn/ *n* [U].

exploit[2] /ˈeksplɔɪt/ *n* [C] 英雄行为〔爲〕 yīngxióng xíngwéi.

explore /ɪkˈsplɔː(r)/ *v* [T] 1 考察 kǎochá; 勘察 kānchá. 2 探索 tànsuǒ; 探究 tànjiū: ~ *different possibilities* 探索不同的可能性. **exploration** /ˌekspləˈreɪʃn/ *n* [U,C]. **exploratory** /ɪkˈsplɒrətrɪ; *US* -tɔːrɪ/ *adj* 探索的 tànsuǒde. **explorer** *n* [C] 考察者 kǎocházhě; 勘察者 kāncházhě.

explosion /ɪkˈspləʊʒn/ *n* [C] 1 爆炸声〔聲〕 bàozhàshēng; 爆炸 bàozhà; 爆发〔發〕 bàofā. 2 感情爆发 gǎnqíng bàofā. 3 激增 jīzēng: *the population* ~ 人口激增.

explosive /ɪkˈspləʊsɪv/ *n* [C], *adj* 炸药〔藥〕 zhàyào; 爆炸的 bàozhàde; 爆炸性的 bàozhàxìngde; 爆发〔發〕(性)的 bàofāde. **explosively** *adv*.

exponent /ɪkˈspəʊnənt/ *n* [C] (信仰等的) 支持者 zhīchízhě; 鼓吹者 gǔchuīzhě.

export /ɪkˈspɔːt/ *v* [I,T] 出口 chūkǒu; 输出 shūchū. **export** /ˈekspɔːt/ *n* 1 [U] 出口 chūkǒu; 出口企业〔業〕 chūkǒu qǐyè. 2 [C] 出口品 chūkǒupǐn. **exporter** *n* [C] 出口国〔國〕 chūkǒuguó; 出口商 chūkǒushāng; 输出者 shūchūzhě.

expose /ɪkˈspəʊz/ *v* [T] 1 使暴露 shǐ bàolù.

E

2 揭发〔發〕jiēfā；揭露 jiēlù. 3 使曝光 shǐ bàoguāng. exposure /ɪkˈspəʊʒə(r)/ *n* [U,C].

expound /ɪkˈspaʊnd/ *v* [T] [正式用语]详述 xiángshù；陈述 chénshù：～ *a theory* 详述一种理论.

express[1] /ɪkˈspres/ *v* [T] 1 表示 biǎoshì；表白 biǎobái：～ *an opinion* 陈述意见. 2 ～ **oneself** 表达自己的思想感情 biǎodá zìjǐ de sīxiǎng gǎnqíng.

express[2] /ɪkˈspres/ *adj* 1 快的 kuàide；特快的 tèkuàide：*an* ～ *letter* 快信. 2 [正式用语] 明白表示的 míngbái biǎoshì de：*his* ～ *wish* 他的明确的愿望. **express** *adv* 以快邮〔郵〕寄送 yǐ kuàiyóu jìsòng. **express** (亦作 **express train**) *n* [C] 特快列车 tèkuài lièchē. **expressly** *adv* 明确〔確〕地 míngquède. **expressway** *n* [C] [美语]高速公路 gāosù gōnglù.

expression /ɪkˈspreʃn/ *n* 1 [C, U] 表示 biǎoshì；表达〔達〕biǎodá. 2 [C] 词语 cíyǔ：*a polite* ～ 礼貌用语. 3 [C] 表情 biǎoqíng：*an angry* ～ 愤怒的表情. 4 [U] (表演时的)感情 gǎnqíng. **expressionless** *adj* 无〔無〕表情的 wú biǎoqíng de.

expressive /ɪkˈspresɪv/ *adj* 富于表情的 fù yú biǎoqíng de. **expressively** *adv*. **expressiveness** *n* [U].

expropriate /eksˈprəʊprɪeɪt/ *v* [T] [正式用语] 征用 zhēngyòng；没收 mòshōu.

expulsion /ɪkˈspʌlʃn/ *n* [C, U] 驱〔驅〕除 qūchú；开〔開〕除 kāichú.

exquisite /ekˈskwɪzɪt；亦作 ɪkˈskwɪzɪt/ *adj* 优〔優〕美的 yōuměide；精巧的 jīngqiǎode. **exquisitely** *adv*.

extend /ɪkˈstend/ *v* 1 [I] 延伸 yánshēn；伸展 shēnzhǎn：*The park* ～*s to the river*. 公园延伸到河边. 2 [T] 扩〔擴〕展 kuòzhǎn；扩大 kuòdà：～ *the house* 扩展房屋. 3 [T] 伸出 shēnchū；伸开〔開〕shēnkāi. 4 [T] [正式用语]给予 jǐyǔ；提供 tígōng：～ *an invitation* 发出邀请.

extension /ɪkˈstenʃn/ *n* 1 [U] 扩〔擴〕大 kuòdà；伸展 shēnzhǎn；延伸 yánshēn. 2 [C] 附加部分 fùjiā bùfēn；增设部分 zēngshè bùfēn：*a new* ～ *to the hospital* 医院新扩建部分. 3 [C] 电〔電〕话分机〔機〕diànhuà fēnjī.

extensive /ɪkˈstensɪv/ *adj* 广〔廣〕大的 guǎngdàde；广泛的 guǎngfànde；数〔數〕量大的 shùliàng dà de. **extensively** *adv*.

extent /ɪkˈstent/ *n* [U] 1 广〔廣〕度 guǎngdù；长〔長〕度 chángdù；范〔範〕围〔圍〕fànwéi：*the* ～ *of the damage* 破坏的范围. 2 [sing] 程度 chéngdù：*to some* ～ 在某种程度上.

extenuating /ɪkˈstenjʊeɪtɪŋ/ *adj* [正式用语]情有可原的 qíng yǒu kě yuán de：～ *circumstances* 情有可原的实际情况.

exterior /ekˈstɪərɪə(r)/ *n* [C] 外部 wàibù；外表 wàibiǎo. **exterior** *adj* 外部的 wàibùde；外面的 wàimiànde；外部来〔來〕的 wàibù lái de.

exterminate /ɪkˈstɜːmɪneɪt/ *v* [T] 灭〔滅〕绝 mièjué；根除 gēnchú. **extermiˈnation** /ɪkˌstɜːmɪˈneɪʃn/ *n* [C, U].

external /ekˈstɜːnl, ɪkˈstɜːnl/ *adj* 外面的 wàimiànde；外部的 wàibùde：～ *injuries* 外伤. **externally** / -nəlɪ/ *adv*.

extinct /ɪkˈstɪŋkt/ *adj* 1 消灭〔滅〕了的 xiāomièlede；灭绝了的 mièjuélede. 2 (火山)熄灭了的 xīmièlede. **extinction** / ɪkˈstɪŋkʃn / *n* [U] 消灭 xiāomiè；熄灭 xīmiè；灭绝 mièjué.

extinguish /ɪkˈstɪŋgwɪʃ/ *v* [T] 1 [正式用语] 熄灭〔滅〕(火) xīmiè；扑〔撲〕灭 pūmiè. 2 熄灭(希望等) xīmiè. **extinguisher** = FIRE EXTINGUISHER (FIRE[1]).

extol /ɪkˈstəʊl/ *v* [-ll-] [T] [正式用语]颂扬〔揚〕sòngyáng；赞〔讚〕扬 zànyáng.

extort /ɪkˈstɔːt/ *v* [T] 强取 qiángqǔ；勒索 lèsuǒ. **extortion** /ɪkˈstɔːʃn/ *n* [U,C] **extortionate** /-ʃənət / *adj* [贬](要求)过〔過〕分的 guòfènde；(价格)昂贵的 ángguìde.

extra /ˈekstrə/ *adj* 额外的 éwàide；附加的 fùjiāde：～ *pay* 额外报酬. **extra** *adv* 1 非常 fēicháng；特别地 tèbiéde；格外 géwài：*an* ～ *strong box* 特别结实的箱子. 2 另外 lìngwài；另加 lìngjiā：*price £1 .75, postage* ～ 货价 1.75 英镑，外加邮资. **extra** *n* [C] 1 额外的东西 éwàide dōngxī. 2 (群众场面的)临〔臨〕时〔時〕演员 línshí yǎnyuán. 3 报〔報〕纸号〔號〕外 bàozhǐ hàowài.

extract /ɪkˈstrækt/ *v* [T] 1 拔出 báchū；用力取出 yònglì qǔchū. 2 索得 suǒdé：～ *money from sb* 从某人索得钱. 3 榨取(液汁) zhàqǔ. **extract** /ˈekstrækt/ *n* [C] 1 (书、影片等的)摘录〔錄〕zhāilù；选〔選〕辑 xuǎnjí. 2 提出物 tíchūwù；精 jīng；汁 zhī：*beef* ～ 牛肉汁. **extraction** /ɪkˈstrækʃn / *n* 1 [C, U]：*the* ～*ion of information* 探听消息. *the* ～*ion of a tooth* 拔牙. 2 [U] 血统 xuètǒng；出身 chūshēn：*of French* ～*ion* 法国血统的.

extra-curricular /ˌekstrəkəˈrɪkjələ(r)/ *adj* 课外的 kèwàide.

extradite /ˈekstrədaɪt/ *v* [T] 引渡(罪犯) yǐndù. **extradition** /ekstrə ˈdɪʃn/ *n* [U,C].

extra-marital /ˌekstrəˈmærɪtl/ *adj* (性关系)婚外的 hūnwàide.

extraneous /ɪkˈstreɪnɪəs/ *adj* [正式用语]无〔無〕关〔關〕的 wúguānde.

extraordinary /ɪkˈstrɔːdnrɪ；*US* -dənerɪ/ *adj* 1 非常的 fēichángde；特别的 tèbiéde；非凡的 fēifánde：～ *beauty* 出众的美丽. 2 令人惊〔驚〕讶的 lìng rén jīngyà de. **extraordinarily**

adv.

extrapolate /ɪkˈstræpəleɪt/ *v* [I,T] [正式用语]推断〔斷〕tuīduàn;推知 tuīzhī;进〔進〕行推断 jìnxíng tuīduàn. **extrapolation** /ɪkˌstræpəˈleɪʃn/ *n* [U].

extraterrestrial /ˌekstrətəˈrestrɪəl/ *adj* 地球外的 dìqiú wài de;来自地球外的 láizì dìqiú wài de.

extravagant /ɪkˈstrævəgənt/ *adj* 1 奢侈的 shēchǐde;浪费的 làngfèide. 2 (思想、行为等)过〔過〕分的 guòfènde;过度的 guòdùde. **extravagance** /-gəns/ *n* [C,U]. **extravagantly** *adv*.

extravaganza /ɪkˌstrævəˈgænzə/ *n* [C] 铺张〔張〕华〔華〕丽〔麗〕的娱乐〔樂〕表演 pūzhāng huálì de yúlè biǎoyǎn.

extreme /ɪkˈstriːm/ *adj* 1 极〔極〕度的 jídùde;极大的 jídàde: *in ~ pain* 在极度痛苦中. 2 在尽〔盡〕头〔頭〕的 zài jìntóu de;末端的 mòduānde: *the ~ north of the country* 这个国家的最北部. 3 [常贬] 偏激的 piānjīde;走极端的 zǒu jíduān de: *~ opinions* 偏激的意见. **extreme** *n* [C] 1 极端 jíduān: *Love and hate are ~s*. 爱和恨是两个极端. 2 最大程度 zuìdà chéngdù: *the ~s of heat in the desert* 沙漠中的酷热. **extremely** *adv* 非常 fēicháng.

extremist /ɪkˈstriːmɪst/ *n* [C], *adj* [常贬] (政治上的)极〔極〕端主义〔義〕者 jíduānzhǔyìzhě;(政治上)极端主义的 jíduānzhǔyìde.

extremity /ɪkˈstremətɪ/ *n* [*pl* -ies] 1 [sing] [正式用语]极〔極〕度 jídù. 2 (a) [C] [正式用语]尽〔盡〕头〔頭〕jìntóu;末端 mòduān. (b) **extremities** [pl] (人体的)肢 zhī.

extricate /ˈekstrɪkeɪt/ *v* [T] 使摆〔擺〕脱 shǐ bǎituō.

extrovert /ˈekstrəvɜːt/ *n* [C] 活泼〔潑〕愉快的人 huópo yúkuài de rén.

exuberant /ɪgˈzjuːbərənt; *US* -ˈzuː-/ *adj* 精力充沛的 jīnglì chōngpèi de;活泼〔潑〕的 huópode. **exuberance** / -əns / *n* [U]. **exuberantly** *adv*.

exude /ɪgˈzjuːd; *US* -ˈzuːd/ *v* [正式用语] 1 [I,T] (使)缓慢流出 huǎnmàn liúchū;(使)渗〔滲〕出 shènchū. 2 [T] 充分显〔顯〕露(感情) chōngfèn xiǎnlù: *~ happiness* 喜气洋洋.

exult /ɪgˈzʌlt/ *v* [I] [正式用语]欢〔歡〕欣鼓舞 huānxīn gǔwǔ;狂喜 kuángxǐ. **exultant** *adj*. **exultation** /ˌegzʌlˈteɪʃn/ *n* [U].

eye /aɪ/ *n* 1 [C] 眼睛 yǎnjing. 2 [sing] 眼力 yǎnlì;判断〔斷〕pànduàn: *have a good ~ for detail* 有明察细部的敏锐眼力. 3 [C] 针眼 zhēnyǎn. 4 [C] (台风的)风〔風〕眼 fēngyǎn. 5 [习语] **(be) all ˈeyes** 目不转〔轉〕睛地看 mù bù zhuǎn jīng de kàn. **in the eyes of sb/sth** 在…看来 zài … kànlái. **make ˈeyes at sb** [非正式用语]含情脉〔脈〕脉地看 hánqíngmòmòde kàn. **with one's ˈeyes open** 有意识〔識〕地 yǒu yìshi de. **eye** *v* [T] 注视 zhùshì;审〔審〕视 shěnshì. **ˈeyeball** *n* [C] 眼球 yǎnqiú. **ˈeyebrow** *n* [C] 眉毛 méimáo. **ˈeyelash** *n* [C] 睫毛 jiémáo. **ˈeyelid** *n* [C] 眼睑〔瞼〕yǎnjiǎn. **ˈeyeopener** *n* [C,常为 sing] 令人瞠目的事物 lìng rén chēngmù de shìwù;发〔發〕人深省的事物 fā rén shēn xǐng de shìwù. **ˈeyesight** *n* [U] 视力 shìlì;目力 mùlì. **ˈeyesore** 丑〔醜〕东西 chǒudōngxi;丑陋的高层〔層〕建筑〔築〕chǒulòude gāocéng jiànzhù. **ˈeyewitness** *n* = WITNESS 1.

F f

F, f /ef/ *n* [C] [*pl* F's, f's /efs/] 英语的第六个〔個〕字母 Yīngyǔde dìliùgè zìmǔ.

F *abbr* Fahrenheit.

fable /ˈfeɪbl/ *n* 1 [C] 寓言 yùyán. 2 [C,U] 传〔傳〕说 chuánshuō;神话 shénhuà. **fabled** *adj* 传说的 chuánshuōde;因寓言而著称〔稱〕的 yīn yùyán ér zhùchēng de.

fabric /ˈfæbrɪk/ *n* 1 [C,U] 织〔織〕物 zhīwù;布 bù. 2 **the fabric (of sth)** [sing] (某物的)构〔構〕造 gòuzào,结构 jiégòu: *the ~ of society* 社会结构. *the ~ of a building* 建筑物的构造.

fabricate /ˈfæbrɪkeɪt/ *v* [T] 1 捏造 niēzào;编造(谎言等) biānzào. 2 制〔製〕造 zhìzào;建造 jiànzào;装〔裝〕配 zhuāngpèi. **fabrication** /ˌfæbrɪˈkeɪʃn/ *n* [C,U].

fabulous /ˈfæbjʊləs/ *adj* 1 [非正式用语]极〔極〕好的 jíhǎode. 2 巨大的 jùdàde: *~ wealth* 巨大的财富. 3 传〔傳〕说中的 chuánshuō zhōng de;神话中的 shénhuà zhōng de: *~ monsters* 神话中的怪物. **fabulously** *adv* 极 jí: *~ly rich* 极富.

facade /fəˈsɑːd/ *n* [C] 1 建筑〔築〕物的正面 jiànzhùwùde zhèngmiàn. 2 [喻]门面 ménmiàn;假象 jiǎxiàng: *behind a ~ of respectability* 在正派、体面的假象的后面.

face /feɪs/ *n* [C] 1 脸〔臉〕liǎn;面孔 miànkǒng. 2 表情 biǎoqíng. 3 表面 biǎomiàn;正面 zhèngmiàn: *the north ~ of the mountain* 山脉的北坡. 4 [习语] **face to face (with sb/sth)** 面对〔對〕着的 miàn duìzhe de. **make/pull ˈfaces / a ˈface** 做鬼脸 zuò guǐliǎn;做怪相 zuò guàixiàng. **to sb's ˈface** 当〔當〕面地 dāng miàn de;坦率地 tǎnshuàide. **face** *v* 1 [I,T] 面向 miànxiàng;朝向 cháoxiàng. 2 [T] 正视 zhèngshì;有信心地面对 yǒu xìnxīn de miànduì;蔑视 mièshì: *~ danger* 蔑视危险. 3 [T] 需要

…加以注意 xūyào…jiāyǐ zhùyì：*the problems that ~ the government* 政府面临的问题. 4 [T] 抹盖[蓋] mǒgài；覆盖 fùgài. 5 [习语] **face the ˈmusic** [非正式用语]为[爲]错误决定或行动[動]而接受批评 wèi cuòwù juédìng huò xíngdòng ér jiēshòu pīpíng. 6 [短语动词] **face up to sth** 勇敢地接受或对付 yǒnggǎnde jiēshòu huò duìfu. **ˈface-cloth** *n* [C] 洗脸毛巾 xǐliǎn máojīn. **faceless** *adj* 无[無]个[個]性的 wú gèxìng de；身份不明的 shēnfèn bùmíng de. **facelift** 1 整容 zhěngróng. 2 [喻]（建筑物等的）翻新 fānxīn；整修 zhěngxiū. **ˌface ˈvalue** *n* 1 [C, U]（钞票、邮票等的）票面价[價]值 piàomiàn jiàzhí. 2 [习语] **take sth at ˈface value** 相信…真像其表面所显[顯]示的 xiāngxìn…zhēnxiàng qí biǎomiàn suǒ xiǎnshì de.

facet /ˈfæsɪt/ *n* [C] 1（宝石等的）琢面 zhuómiàn. 2（问题等的）一个[個]方面 yígè fāngmiàn.

facetious /fəˈsiːʃəs/ *adj* 幽默的 yōumòde；(尤指不分场合地)爱[愛]开[開]玩笑的 ài kāi wánxiào de. **facetiously** *adv*.

facial /ˈfeɪʃl/ *adj* 面部的 miànbùde；面部用的 miànbù yòng de.

facile /ˈfæsaɪl; *US* ˈfæsl/ *adj* [常为贬]草草写[寫]成的 cǎocǎo xiěchéng de；随[隨]口说出的 suí kǒu shuōchū de：~ *comments* 信口开河的评说.

facilitate /fəˈsɪlɪteɪt/ *v* [T] [正式用语] 使变[變]得容易 shǐ biànde róngyì；使便利 shǐ biànlì.

facility /fəˈsɪlətɪ/ *n* [*pl* -ies] 1 [C, 常为 pl] 设备[備] shèbèi；设施 shèshī：ˈ*sports facilities* 体育设施, 运动器材. 2 [U, sing] 技能 jìnéng；技巧 jìqiǎo：*a ~ for learning languages* 学习语言的技巧.

facsimile /fækˈsɪməlɪ/ *n* [C] 摹真本 mózhēnběn；传[傳]真 chuánzhēn.

fact /fækt/ *n* 1 [C] 事实[實] shìshí. 2 [U] 实情 shíqíng；真相 zhēnxiàng；实际[際] shíjì. [习语] **the ˌfacts of ˈlife** 性生活常识[識] xìng shēnghuó chángshí. **in ˈfact** 事实上 shìshíshàng.

faction /ˈfækʃn/ *n* [C]（尤指政治上的）宗派 zōngpài；派系 pàixì；小集团[團] xiǎo jítuán.

factor /ˈfæktə(r)/ *n* [C] 因素 yīnsù；要素 yàosù：*a major ~ in making a decision* 制定一项决定的主要因素.

factory /ˈfæktərɪ/ *n* [C] [*pl* -ies] 工厂[廠] gōngchǎng；制[製]造厂 zhìzàochǎng.

factual /ˈfæktʃuəl/ *adj* 事实[實]的 shìshíde；根据[據]事实的 gēnjù shìshí de. **factually** *adv*.

faculty /ˈfæklti/ *n* [C] [*pl* -ies] 1 才能 cáinéng；本领 běnlǐng；能力 nénglì：*her mental faculties* 她的智力. 2 (a)（大学的）系科 xìkē；学[學]院 xuéyuàn. (b) [亦作 sing, 用 pl v] 系科、学院的全体[體]教员 xìkē、xuéyuàn de quántǐ jiàoyuán.

fade /feɪd/ *v* 1 [I, T]（使）褪色 tuìsè；（使）不新鲜 bù xīnxiān. 2 [I] (*away*) 逐渐消失 zhújiàn xiāoshī. 3 [短语动词] **fade away**（人）衰弱 shuāiruò；死亡 sǐwáng.

faeces /ˈfiːsiːz/ [pl] [正式用语] 粪[糞]便 fènbiàn.

fag /fæg/ *n* 1 [C] [英国非正式用语]香烟 xiāngyān. 2 [C] [非正式用语, 贬, 尤用于美语] 搞男性同性恋[戀]的人 gǎo nánxìng tóngxìngliàn de rén. **fagged out** /fægd/ *adj* [非正式用语]非常疲劳的 fēicháng píláo de.

Fahrenheit /ˈfærənhaɪt/ *n* [U] 华[華]氏温度计 huáshì wēndùjì.

fail /feɪl/ *v* 1 [I, T] 失败 shībài. 2 [T] 评定（学生等）不及格 píngdìng bù jígé. 3 [I, T] 不足 bùzú；歉收 qiànshōu；使失望 shǐ shīwàng：*The crops ~ed because of drought.* 因干旱而粮食歉收. *All his friends ~ed him.* 所有的朋友都使他失望. 4 [I]（健康、视力等）衰弱 shuāiruò；衰退 shuāituì. 5 [I] 忘记 wàngjì；疏忽 shūhu：~ *to keep an appointment* 未能履行约会. 6 [I] 破产[產] pòchǎn：*The company ~ed.* 公司破产了. **fail** *n* 1 [C]（考试）不及格 bù jígé. 2 [习语] **without ˈfail** 必定 bìdìng.

failing /ˈfeɪlɪŋ/ *n* [C] 缺点[點] quēdiǎn；弱点 ruòdiǎn. **failing** *prep* 如果…不发[發]生 rúguǒ…bù fāshēng. 如果…不可能 rúguǒ…bù kěnéng.

failure /ˈfeɪljə(r)/ *n* 1 [U] 失败 shībài. 2 [C] 失败者 shībàizhě；失败的事物 shībài de shìwù. 3 [C, U] 疏忽 shūhu；没做到 méi zuòdào. *His ~ to help us was disappointing.* 他没有帮助我们, 真使人失望. 4 [C, U] 故障 gùzhàng；失灵[靈] shīlíng：*engine ~* 发动机故障. *heart ~* 心脏衰竭.

faint /feɪnt/ *adj* 1 微弱的 wēiruòde；不清楚的 bù qīngchu de：~ *sound* 微弱的声音. 2（想法等）模糊的 móhude；不明确[確]的 bù míngquè de：*a ~ hope* 渺茫的希望. 3（人）将[將]要昏晕[暈]的 jiāngyào hūnyùn de. **faint** *v* [I] 昏厥 hūnjué. **faint** *n* [C] 昏厥 hūnjué. **ˌfaint-ˈhearted** *adj* 怯懦的 qiènuòde；优[優]柔寡断[斷]的 yōuróu guǎ duàn de. **faintly** *adv*. **faintness** *n* [U].

fair[1] /feə(r)/ *adj* 1 公正的 gōngzhèngde；公平的 gōngpíngde；诚实[實]的 chéngshíde：*a ~ decision* 公正的决定. 2 相当[當]好的 xiāngdāng hǎo de：*a ~ chance of success* 相当好的成功机会. 3（天气）晴朗的 qínglǎngde. 4（肤色）白皙的 báixīde；（头发）金色的 jīnsède：*a ˌ~-ˈhaired boy* 金色头发的男孩. 5 干[乾]净的 gānjìngde；清楚的 qīngchude：*a ~ copy*

清楚的副件.6［习语］fair ˈplay 公平对［對］待 gōngpíng duìdài. fair *adv* 1 公平地 gōngpíngde;公正地 gōngzhèngde. 2［习语］fair enough 行! xíng! 说得对 shuōdeduì. fair ˈtrade *n*［U］公平贸［貿］易 gōngpíng màoyì. fairly *adv* 1 相当 xiāngdāng: *~ly easy* 相当容易.2 公正地 gōngzhèngde;诚实地 chéngshíde. fairness *n*［U］.

fair[2] /feə(r)/ *n*［C］1 公共露天游乐［樂］场［場］gōnggòng lùtiān yóulèchǎng. 2 农贸市场 nóngmào shìchǎng. 3 商品展览［覽］会［會］shāngpǐn zhǎnlǎnhuì;商品交易会 shāngpǐn jiāoyìhuì: *a book ~* 图书展览会 ˈfairground *n*［C］流动表演场［場］地 liúdòng biǎoyǎn chǎngdì.

fairy /ˈfeərɪ/ *n*［C］［*pl* -ies］仙女 xiānnǚ;小妖精 xiǎoyāojing. ˈfairy story, ˈfairy-tale *n*［C］1 神话 shénhuà;童话 tónghuà. 2 谎言 huǎngyán.

fait accompli /ˌfeɪt əˈkɒmpliː; *US* əkɒmˈpliː/ *n*［C］［法语］既成事实［實］jìchéng shìshí.

faith /feɪθ/ *n* 1［U］信心 xìnxīn;信任 xìnrèn. 2［U, sing］宗教信仰 zōngjiào xìnyǎng. 3［C］宗教 zōngjiào: *the Jewish ~* 犹太教.4［习语］in good faith 诚实［實］地 chéngshíde.

faithful /ˈfeɪθfl/ *adj* 1（*to*）忠实［實］的 zhōngshíde;守信的 shǒuxìnde. 2 准［準］确［確］的 zhǔnquède: *a ~ description* 准确的描述. the faithful *n*［pl］虔诚的教徒 qiánchéngde jiàotú. faithfully /-fəlɪ/ *adv*. faithfulness *n*［U］.

fake /feɪk/ *n*［C］1 假货 jiǎhuò;伪［僞］品 wěipǐn. 2 骗子 piànzi;伪造者 wěizàozhě. fake *v*［T］1 伪造 wěizào. 2 假装［裝］jiǎzhuāng.

falcon /ˈfɔːlkən; *US* ˈfælkən/ *n*［C］猎［獵］鹰 lièyīng.

fall[1] /fɔːl/ *v*［*pt* fell /fel/, *pp* ~en /ˈfɔːlən/］［I］1 落下 luòxià;跌落 diēluò: *Leaves ~ in autumn*. 秋天叶落. *~ off a ladder* 从梯子上跌落.2 倒下 dǎoxià;倒坍 dǎotān;垮台［臺］kuǎtái: *The tree fell* (*down*) *in the storm*. 这棵树在暴风雨中倒下了.3 垂下 chuíxià: *Her hair ~s over her shoulders*. 她的头发垂到双肩.4（温度、价格等）下跌 xiàdiē: *The temperature fell sharply*. 温度剧烈下降.5（土地）下斜 xiàxié. 6 垮台 kuǎtái: *The government fell after the revolution*. 革命后这个政府垮台了.7 阵亡 zhènwáng;（城市）失陷 shīxiàn. 8 成为［爲］chéngwéi: *~ asleep* 睡着了. *~ into disuse* 废弃不用了.9（日子）适［適］逢 shìféng: *Christmas ~s on a Friday this year*. 今年圣诞节适逢星期五.10［习语］fall flat 达［達］不到预想效果 dábúdào yùxiǎng xiàoguǒ. fall foul of sb/sth 同…冲［衝］突 tóng … chōngtū;同…争吵 tóng … zhēngchǎo. fall in love with sb 与［與］…相爱［愛］yǔ … xiāng'ài. fall on one's feet ⇨ FOOT. fall short of sth 达不到 dábúdào;不符合 bù fúhé. 11［短语动词］fall apart 破碎 pòsuì;互解 hùjiě. fall back 退却 tuìquè;后［後］退 hòutuì. fall back on sth 求助于 qiúzhù yú;依靠 yīkào. fall behind (sb/sth) 落后［後］于 luòhòu yú;跟不上 gēnbúshàng. fall behind with sth 拖欠未付(租金等) tuōqiàn wèifù. fall for sb［非正式用语］爱［愛］上 àishàng;迷上 míshàng. fall for sth［非正式用语］受…的骗 shòu … de piàn;上…的当［當］shàng … de dàng. fall in 倒坍 dǎotān: *The roof fell in*. 屋顶倒坍了. fall off 减少 jiǎnshǎo;缩小 suōxiǎo. fall on sb/sth (a) 由…负担［擔］yóu … fùdān. (b)（眼睛）被引向 bèi yǐn xiàng. fall out (with sb) 同…争吵 tóng … zhēngchǎo. fall through 失败 shībài: *The business deal fell through*. 交易失败.

fall[2] /fɔːl/ *n*［C］1 落下 luòxià;跌倒 diēdǎo;垂下 chuíxià. 2 降落量 jiàngluòliàng: *a heavy ~ of snow* 很大的降雪量.3 落差 luòchā;降落距离［離］jiàngluò jùlí. 4（亦作 falls［pl］）瀑布 pùbù. 5［美语］秋季 qiūjì.

fallacy /ˈfæləsɪ/ *n*［C, U］［*pl* -ies］谬论［論］miùlùn;谬见 miùjiàn. fallacious /fəˈleɪʃəs/ *adj*［正式用语］谬误的 miùwùde.

fallen *pp* of FALL[1].

fallible /ˈfæləbl/ *adj* 易犯错误的 yì fàn cuòwù de;错误难［難］免的 cuòwù nánmiǎn de. fallibility /ˌfæləˈbɪlətɪ/ *n*［U］.

fallout /ˈfɔːlaʊt/ *n*［U］放射性尘［塵］埃 fàngshèxìng chén'āi.

fallow /ˈfæləʊ/ *adj*（土地）休闲的 xiūxiánde.

false /fɔːls/ *adj* 1 错误的 cuòwùde;不正确［確］的 bú zhèngquè de. 2 假的 jiǎde;人工的 réngōngde;人造的 rénzàode: *~ teeth* 假牙.3 欺诈的 qīzhàde;不忠诚的 bù zhōngchéngde: *a ~ friend* 不可靠的朋友. 4［习语］a false aˈlarm 假警报［報］jiǎ jǐngbào. a false ˈstart (a)（赛跑中的）抢［搶］跑 qiǎngpǎo;偷跑 tōupǎo. (b) 失败的开［開］端 shībàide kāiduān. on/under false pretences 冒充某人以行骗 màochōng mǒurén yǐ xíngpiàn. falsehood /ˈfɔːlshʊd/ *n*［C, U］谎言 huǎngyán;说谎 shuōhuǎng. falsely *adv*. falseness *n*［U］.

falsify /ˈfɔːlsɪfaɪ/ *v*［*pt*, *pp* -ied］［T］窜［竄］改 cuàngǎi;伪［僞］造 wěizào. falsification /ˌfɔːlsɪfɪˈkeɪʃn/ *n*［C, U］.

falter /ˈfɔːltə(r)/ *v*［I］1 蹒跚 pánshān;踉跄［蹌］liàngqiàng;犹［猶］豫 yóuyù. 2 支吾 zhīwú. falteringly *adv*.

fame /feɪm/ *n*［U］名声［聲］míngshēng;声誉［譽］shēngyù. famed *adj* 有名的 yǒumíngde.

familiar /fəˈmɪliːə(r)/ *adj* 1（*to*）为［爲］…

所熟悉的 wèi … suǒ shúxī de；常见的 chángjiànde；听〔聽〕惯的 tīngguànde. 2 *with* 熟悉的 shúxīde；通晓〔曉〕的 tōngxiǎode. 3 随〔隨〕便的 suíbiànde；友好的 yǒuhǎode；亲〔親〕密的 qīnmìde. **familiarity** /fəˌmɪlɪˈærətɪ/ *n* [C, U] [*pl* -ies]. **familiarly** *adv*.

familiarize /fəˈmɪlɪəraɪz/ *v* [T] *with* 使熟悉 shǐ shúxī.

family /ˈfæməlɪ/ *n* [*pl* -ies] 1 [C, 亦作 sing, 用 pl v] (a) 家 jiā；家庭 jiātíng. (b) 家庭成员及关〔關〕系〔係〕密切的亲〔親〕戚 jiātíng chéngyuán jí guānxì mìqiè de qīnqi. 2 [C, U, 亦作 sing, 用 pl v] 子女 zǐnǚ. 3 [C, 亦作 sing, 用 pl v]家族 jiāzú；氏族 shìzú. 4 [C] (动植物) 科 kē；语族 yǔzú：*the cat* ～ 猫科. ˌ**family** ˈ**planning** *n* [U] 计划〔劃〕生育 jìhuà shēngyù. ˌ**family** ˈ**tree** *n* [C] 家系 jiāxì；家谱 jiāpǔ.

F

famine /ˈfæmɪn/ *n* [C, U] 饥〔饑〕荒 jīhuāng.

famished /ˈfæmɪʃt/ *adj* [非正式用语]挨饿的 āi'ède.

famous /ˈfeɪməs/ *adj* 著名的 zhùmíngde；有名的 yǒumíngde. **famously** *adv* 很好 hěnhǎo：*They get on ～ly*. 他们过得很好.

fan[1] /fæn/ *n* [C] 风〔風〕扇 fēngshàn；扇子 shànzi. **fan** *v* [-nn-] 1 [T] 向…扇〔搧〕风 xiàng …shān fēng. 2 [短语动词] **fan out** 成扇形展开〔開〕 chéng shànxíng zhǎnkāi：*The troops ～ned out across the field*. 部队在田野上成扇形展开. ˈ**fan belt** *n* [C] (汽车发动机散热风扇上用的)风扇皮带〔帶〕 fēngshàn pídài.

fan[2] /fæn/ *n* [C] 狂热〔熱〕爱〔愛〕好者 kuángrè àihào zhě：*football ～s* 足球迷. ˈ**fan mail** *n* [U] 狂热者寄出的信(如影迷寄给电影明星的信) kuángrèzhě jìchū de xìn.

fanatic /fəˈnætɪk/ *n* [C] 狂热〔熱〕者 kuángrèzhě：*a religious* ～ 宗教狂. **fanatical** *adj* 狂热的 kuángrède. **fanatically** /-klɪ/ *adv*. **fanaticism** /-tɪsɪzəm/ *n* [U].

fanciful /ˈfænsɪfl/ *adj* 1 (人)爱〔愛〕空想的 ài kōngxiǎng de. 2 不真实〔實〕的 bù zhēnshí de；奇异〔異〕的 qíyìde：～ *ideas* 奇异的想法. **fancifully** *adv*.

fancy[1] /ˈfænsɪ/ *n* [*pl* -ies] 1 [C] (*for*) 爱〔愛〕好 àihào；喜爱 xǐ'ài：*a* ～ *for some cake* 对蛋糕的喜爱. 2 [U] 想像力 xiǎngxiànglì. 3 [C] 模糊的想法 móhude xiǎngfǎ. 4 [习语] **catch/take sb's fancy** 中某人的意 zhòng mǒurén de yì；吸引某人 xīyǐn mǒurén. **take a fancy to sb** 喜欢〔歡〕上某人 xǐhuān shàng mǒurén. **fancy** *v* [*pt*, *pp* -ied] [T] 1 [非正式用语]想要 xiǎngyào：*I* ～ *a cup of tea*. 我想要一杯茶. 2 [非正式用语]喜爱 xǐ'ài：*I think she fancies you*. 我想她喜欢你. 3 认〔認〕为〔爲〕 rènwéi；相信 xiāngxìn. 4 (表示惊讶)：*F*～ *that!* 真想不到!

fancy[2] /ˈfænsɪ/ *adj* 1 有装〔裝〕饰的 yǒu zhuāngshì de；颜色鲜艳〔艷〕的 yánsè xiānyàn de：～ *cakes* 花哨的蛋糕. 2 越轨的 yuèguǐde；异〔異〕想天开〔開〕的 yì xiǎng tiān kāi de：～ *ideas* 奇特的想法. ˌ**fancy** ˈ**dress** *n* [U] (化装舞会等上的)化装服饰 huàzhuāng fúshì.

fanfare /ˈfænfeə(r)/ *n* [C] 嘹亮的喇叭声〔聲〕 liáoliàngde lǎbāshēng.

fang /fæŋ/ *n* [C] 尖牙 jiānyá.

fanny /ˈfænɪ/ *n* [C] [*pl* -ies] 1 [英国英语 ⚠ 俚]女性生殖器 nǚxìng shēngzhíqì. 2 [俚, 尤用于美语]屁股 pìgu.

fantasize /ˈfæntəsaɪz/ *v* [I, T] (*about*) 想像 xiǎngxiàng；幻想 huànxiǎng.

fantastic /fænˈtæstɪk/ *adj* 1 [非正式用语]极〔極〕好的 jíhǎode：*a* ～ *party* 极好的聚会. 2 [非正式用语]非常大的 fēicháng dà de. 3 奇异〔異〕的 qíyìde；古怪的 gǔguàide. 4 (主意)不现实〔實〕的 bú xiànshí de. **fantastically** /-klɪ/ *adv*.

fantasy /ˈfæntəsɪ/ *n* [C, U] [*pl* -ies] 幻想 huànxiǎng；想像 xiǎngxiàng；荒诞的念头〔頭〕 huāngdànde niàntou：*childhood ～ies* 童年幻想.

FAQ /ef eɪ ˈkjuː, fæk/ *n* [C] frequently asked questions (计算机)常见问题解答 chángjiàn wèntí jiědá

far[1] /fɑː(r)/ *adv* [～**ther** /ˈfɑːðə(r)/ 或 **further** /ˈfɜːðə(r)/, ～**thest** /ˈfɑːðɪst/ 或 **furthest** /ˈfɜːðɪst/] 1 远〔遠〕 yuǎn；遥远地 yáoyuǎnde：*How far is it to London?* 到伦敦有多远? 2 到很大程度 dào hěndà chéngdù；远远 yuǎnyuǎn：*fallen* ～ *behind with his work* 工作远没有完成. 3 很 hěn：～ *richer* 富有得多. 4 [习语] **as/so far as, in so far as** 就… jiù…：*As* ～ *as I know, they're still coming*. 就我所知道的, 他们还是要来的. **far from doing sth** 非但不 fēidàn bù：*F*～ *from hating the music, I love it*. 我不但不讨厌, 而且爱音乐. **far from sth** 完全不 wánquán bù：*The work is* ～ *from easy*. 这工作决不是容易的. **go** ˈ**far** (钱)可买〔買〕很多东西 kě mǎi hěnduō dōngxi. **go** ˈ**far, go a long** ˈ**way** (人)非常成功 fēicháng chénggōng. **go too** ˈ**far** 做得过〔過〕分 zuòde guòfèn. ˈ**so far** 到目前为〔爲〕止 dào mùqián wéizhǐ. ˈ**far-away** *adj* 1 遥远的 yáoyuǎnde. 2 (眼神)恍惚的 huǎnghūde. **far-**ˈ**fetched** 牵〔牽〕强的 qiānqiángde. ˌ**far-**ˈ**reaching** *adj* 有广〔廣〕泛影响〔響〕的 yǒu guǎngfàn yǐngxiǎng de：*a* ～*-reaching decision* 有广泛影响的决定. ˌ**far-**ˈ**sighted** *adj* 有远见的 yǒu yuǎnjiàn de；深谋远虑〔慮〕的 shēn móu yuǎn lǜ de.

far[2] /fɑː(r)/ *adj* [～**ther** /ˈfɑːðə(r)/ 或 **further** /ˈfɜːðə(r)/, ～**thest** /ˈfɑːðɪst/ 或 **fur-**

thest /ˈfɜːðɪst /] 1 较远〔遠〕的 jiàoyuǎnde: *the ~ end of the street* 在街的那一头. *on the ~ right* 持极右观点. 2 [旧词或正式用语] 遥远的 yáoyuǎnde: *a ~ country* 遥远的国家. the Far ˈEast *n* [sing] 远东 yuǎndōng.

farce /fɑːs/ *n* 1 (a) [C] 笑剧〔劇〕xiàojù; 滑稽戏〔戲〕huájìxì. (b) [U] 滑稽戏剧 huájì xìjù. 2 [C] 一系列可笑的事物 yíxìliè kěxiào de shìwù. farcical *adj*.

fare /feə(r)/ *n* [C] 车〔車〕费 chēfèi; 船费 chuánfèi: *bus ~s* 公共汽车费. fare *v* [I] [正式用语] 进〔進〕展 jìnzhǎn: *~ well* 情况很好. *~ badly* 情况很糟.

farewell /ˌfeəˈwel/ *interj*, *n* [C] [旧词语或正式用语] 再见 zàijiàn.

farm /fɑːm/ *n* [C] 农〔農〕场〔場〕nóngchǎng; 农庄〔莊〕nóngzhuāng. farm *v* [I, T] 种〔種〕植 zhòngzhí; 养〔養〕殖 yǎngzhí. farmer *n* [C] 农场主 nóngchǎngzhǔ. farm-hand *n* [C] 农场工人 nóngchǎng gōngrén. farmyard *n* [C] 农场场院 nóngchǎng chángyuàn.

fart /fɑːt/ *v* [I] [⚠] 放屁 fàngpì. fart *n* [C] [⚠] 放屁 fàngpì; [俚, 贬] 讨厌〔厭〕的家伙 tǎoyànde jiāhuo.

farther, farthest *adv*, *adj* ⇨FAR.

fascinate /ˈfæsɪneɪt/ *v* [T] 使神魂颠倒 shǐ shénhún diāndǎo; 迷住 mízhù. fascinating *adj*. fascination /ˌfæsɪˈneɪʃn / *n* [U, C].

fascism (亦作 Fascism) /ˈfæʃɪzəm/ *n* [U] 法西斯主义〔義〕fǎxīsīzhǔyì. fascist (亦作 Fascist) *adj*, *n* [C].

fashion /ˈfæʃn/ *n* 1 [sing] 方式 fāngshì; 样〔様〕子 yàngzi: *walk in a strange ~* 走路样子古怪. 2 [C, U] (服装等) 流行式样 liúxíng shìyàng: *wearing the latest ~* 穿最新款式的服装. 3 [习语] after a ˈfashion 勉强 miǎnqiǎng; 马〔馬〕马虎虎 mǎmǎhūhū. in fashion 时〔時〕新的 shíxīnde; 时髦的 shímáode. out of fashion 不合时尚的 bùhé shíshàng de. fashion *v* [T] 使成形 shǐ chéngxíng.

fashionable /ˈfæʃnəbl/ *adj* 1 时〔時〕髦的 shímáode. 2 高档〔檔〕的 gāodàngde: *a ~ restaurant* 高档饭馆.

fast[1] /fɑːst; *US* fæst/ *adj* 1 快的 kuàide; 迅速的 xùnsùde: *~ cars* 开得快的汽车. 2(钟表) 偏快的 piānkuàide. fast *adv* 快地 kuàide; 迅速地 xùnsùde. fast ˈfood *n* [U] 快餐食品 kuàicān shípǐn.

fast[2] /fɑːst; *US* fæst/ *adj* 1 牢固的 láogùde; 紧〔緊〕的 jǐnde. 2 不褪色的 bú tuìsè de. 3 [习语] stand fast ⇨STAND[2]. fast *adv* 1 牢固地 láogùde; 紧紧地 jǐnjǐnde. 2 [习语] fast asleep 熟睡 shúshuì.

fast[3] /fɑːst; *US* fæst/ *v* [I] 禁食 jìnshí; 斋〔齋〕戒 zhāijiè. fast *n* [C] 斋戒期 zhāijièqī.

fasten /ˈfɑːsn; *US* ˈfæsn/ *v* 1 [I, T] 扎〔紮〕牢 zāláo; 扣紧〔緊〕kòujǐn; 闩牢 shuānláo: *~ your seat-belt* 系好你的安全带. 2[短语动词] *fasten on sth* 抓住 zhuāzhù; 捉住 zhuōzhù; 注意 zhùyì. fasten sth on sth 集中(注意力、思想等)于… jízhōng yú…. fastener, fastening *n* [C] 紧〔緊〕固件 jǐngùjiàn; 扣件 kòujiàn; 扣拴物 kòushuānwù: *a ˈzip-~er* 拉链.

fastidious /fəˈstɪdɪəs, fæ-/ *adj* 难〔難〕讨好的 nán tǎohǎo de; 爱〔愛〕挑剔的 ài tiāotì de. fastidiously *adv*.

fat[1] /fæt/ *adj* [-ter, -test] 1 (人体) 胖的 pàngde. 2 厚的 hòude; 宽阔的 kuānkuòde: *a ~ book* 一本厚书. 3[非正式用语] 大量的 dàliàngde: *~ profits* 巨利. fatness *n* [U].

fat[2] /fæt/ *n* 1 [U] (动物的) 皮下脂肪 píxià zhīfáng. 2 [C, U] (烹饪用) 植物油 zhíwùyóu, 动〔動〕物油 dòngwù yóu.

fatal /ˈfeɪtl/ *adj* 1 致命的 zhìmìngde: *a ~ accident* 人命事故. 2 灾〔災〕难〔難〕性的 zāinànxìngde: *a ~ mistake* 灾难性的错误. fatally *adv*.

fatalism /ˈfeɪtəlɪzəm/ *n* [U] 宿命论〔論〕sùmìnglùn. fatalist *n* [C].

fatality /fəˈtælətɪ/ *n* [*pl* -ies] 1 [C] (事故或暴力造成的) 死亡 sǐwáng. 2 [U] 天数〔數〕tiānshù; 命中注定 mìng zhōng zhùdìng.

fate /feɪt/ *n* 1 [U] 命运〔運〕mìngyùn; 天数〔數〕tiānshù. 2 [C] 未来〔來〕的吉凶〔兇〕wèiláide jíxiōng; 死亡 sǐwáng. fateful *adj* 重要的 zhòngyàode: *that ~ day* 那重要的一天.

father /ˈfɑːðə(r)/ *n* 1 [C] 父亲〔親〕fùqin; 爸爸 bàba. 2 [C, 常作 pl] 祖先 zǔxiān. 3 [C] 先驱〔驅〕xiānqū; 鼻祖 bízǔ; 元老 yuánlǎo: *city ~s* 市元老. 4 [C] 神父 shénfù; 教士 jiàoshì. 5 Father [sing] 上帝 shàngdì. father *v* [T] 当〔當〕…的父亲 dāng…de fùqin. ˌFather ˈChristmas *n* [C] 圣〔聖〕诞老人 shèngdàn lǎorén. ˈfather-in-law *n* [C] [*pl* ~s-in-law] 岳父 yuèfù; 公公(丈夫的父亲) gōnggong. ˈfatherland *n* [C] 祖国〔國〕zǔguó. fatherly *adj* 父亲的 fùqinde; 慈父般的 cífùbānde.

fathom /ˈfæðəm/ *n* [C] 㖊〔噚〕(测量水深的单位, 约合 1.8 米或 6 英尺) xún. fathom *v* [T] 充分了〔瞭〕解 chōngfèn liáojiě. fathomless *adj* 深不可测的 shēn bù kěcè de; 无〔無〕法理解的 wúfǎ lǐjiě de.

fatigue /fəˈtiːg/ *n* 1[U] 疲劳〔勞〕píláo; 劳累 láolèi. 2 [U] (金属材料) 疲劳 píláo. fatigues [pl] (士兵做杂役时穿的) 工作服 gōngzuòfú, 劳动服 láodòngfú. fatigue *v* [T] [正式用语] 使疲劳 shǐ píláo.

fatten /ˈfætn/ *v* [I, T] (使) 长〔長〕肥 zhǎngféi; 发〔發〕财 fācái; 使肥沃 shǐ féiwò.

F

fatty /ˈfæti/ *adj* [-ier, -iest] 含脂肪的 hán zhīfáng de; 含过〔過〕多脂肪的 hán guòduō zhīfáng de. **fatty** *n* [C] [*pl* -ies] [非正式用语, 贬]胖子 pàngzi.

fatuous /ˈfætʃuəs/ *adj* 愚昧的 yúmèide; 蠢的 chǔnde: ~ *remarks* 蠢话.

faucet /ˈfɔːsɪt/ *n* [C] [美语]水龙〔龍〕头〔頭〕shuǐlóngtóu; 开〔開〕关〔關〕kāiguān; 旋塞 xuánsāi.

fault /fɔːlt/ *n* 1 [sing] 过〔過〕错 guòcuò; 错误〔誤〕的责任 cuòwùdezérèn: *It was Pat's* ~. 这是帕特的过错. 2 [C] 错误 cuòwù; 缺点〔點〕quēdiǎn; 故障 gùzhàng: *an electrical* ~ 电路故障. 3 [C] (地质)断〔斷〕层〔層〕duàncéng. 4 [习语] **at fault** 出毛病 chū máobìng; 有故障 yǒu gùzhàng. **fault** *v* [T] 找出…的缺点 zhǎo chū…de quēdiǎn: *I cannot* ~ *her performance*. 她的表演我找不出毛病. **faultless** *adj* 完美无〔無〕缺的 wánměi wúquē de. **faultlessly** *adv*. **faulty** *adj* (尤指机器)出了故障的 chūle gùzhàng de.

fauna /ˈfɔːnə/ *n* [U] 动〔動〕物群(同一地区或同一时代) dòngwùqún.

faux pas /ˌfəʊˈpɑː/ *n* [C] [*pl* faux pas /-ˈpɑːz/] [法语]失态〔態〕shītài.

favour (美语 -or) /ˈfeɪvə(r)/ *n* 1 [U] 喜爱〔愛〕xǐ'ài; 赞同 zàntóng: *look with* ~ *on the idea* 赞同一个主意. 2 [U] 偏爱 piān-ài; 偏袒 piāntǎn: *show* ~ *to sb* 偏爱某人. 3 [C] 善意的行为〔爲〕shànyìde xíngwéi; 恩惠 ēnhuì: *Do me a* ~ *and lend me your pen*. 劳驾把你的钢笔借我用一用. 4 [习语] **be out of ˈfavour with sb** 不受某人赞同 búshòu mǒurén zàntóng. **in favour of sb/sth** 支持某人(或某事) zhīchí mǒurén. **in sb's favour** 对〔對〕某人有利 duì mǒurén yǒulì. **favour** *v* [T] 1 支持 zhīchí. 2 偏爱 piān'ài. **favourable** *adj* 1 赞成的 zànchéngde. 2 有帮助的 yǒu bāngzhù de; 适〔適〕宜的 shìyíde. **favourably** *adv*.

favourite (美语 favor-) /ˈfeɪvərɪt/ *n* 1 [C] 特别受喜爱〔愛〕的人或物 tèbié shòu xǐ'ài de rén huò wù. 2 **the favourite** [sing] (比赛中)最有希望获〔獲〕胜〔勝〕者 zuìyǒu xīwàng huòshèngzhě. **favourite** *adj* 最喜爱的 zuìxǐ'àide. **favouritism** /-ɪzəm/ *n* [U] 偏爱 piān'ài.

fawn[1] /fɔːn/ *n* [C] 幼鹿 yòulù. **fawn** *adj* 浅〔淺〕黄褐色的 qiǎnhuánghèsède.

fawn[2] /fɔːn/ *v* [短语动词] **fawn on sb** 奉承 fèngcheng; 讨好 tǎohǎo.

fax /fæks/ *n* [C] 传〔傳〕真件 chuánzhēnjiàn. **fax** *v* [T] 用传真机〔機〕传送 yòng chuánzhēnjī chuán sòng. **ˈfax machine** *n* [C] 传真机 chuánzhēnjī. **ˈfax modem** *n* [C] 传真调制解调器 chuánzhēn tiáozhìjiětiáoqì.

FBI /ˌef biː ˈaɪ/ *abbr* **the FBI** [美语] Federal Bureau of Investigation (美国)联〔聯〕邦调查局 liánbāng diàochájú.

fear /fɪə(r)/ *n* 1 [C, U] 恐惧〔懼〕kǒngjù; 害怕 hàipà. 2 [U] 可能性 kěnéngxìng: *There's no* ~ *of me going*. 没有我去的可能性(我不会去的) 3 [习语] **in ˌfear of one's ˈlife** 担〔擔〕心自己的安全 dānxīn zìjǐde ānquán. **ˌno ˈfear** [非正式用语]当〔當〕然不! dāngrán bù! **fear** *v* 1 [T] 害怕 hàipà; 惧怕 jùpà. 2 [I] *for* 担心 dānxīn; 担忧〔憂〕dānyōu: ~ *for one's life* 担心生命安全. **fearful** *adj* 1 害怕的 hàipàde; 惧怕的 jùpàde. 2 令人极〔極〕其不快的 lìng rén jíqí búkuài de. 3 [非正式用语]极大的 jí dàde: *a* ~*ful mess* 一片混乱. **fearless** *adj* 不怕的 búpàde; 无〔無〕畏的 wúwèide. **fearlessly** *adv*.

feasible /ˈfiːzəbl/ *adj* 可行的 kěxíngde; 可做的 kězuòde. **feasibility** /ˌfiːzəˈbɪləti/ *n* [U].

feast /fiːst/ *n* [C] 1 筵席 yánxí; 宴会〔會〕yànhuì. 2 宗教节〔節〕日 zōngjiào jiérì. **feast** *v* 1 [I] 参〔參〕加宴会 cānjiā yànhuì. 2 [T] 宴请 yànqǐng. 3 [习语] **feast one's eyes on sth** 饱看 bǎokàn.

feat /fiːt/ *n* [C] 功绩 gōngjì.

feather /ˈfeðə(r)/ *n* [C] 1 羽毛 yǔmáo. 2 [习语] **a ˈfeather in one's cap** 引以为〔爲〕荣〔榮〕的事物 yǐn yǐ wéi róng de shìwù. **feather** *v* [T] 1 用羽毛覆盖〔蓋〕yòng yǔmáo fùgài; 给…装上羽毛 gěi… zhuāngshàng yǔmáo. 2 [习语] **feather one's ˈnest** 营〔營〕私 yíngsī; 自肥 zìféi. **ˌfeather ˈbed** *n* [C] 羽毛褥垫〔墊〕yǔmáo rùdiàn. **featherly** *adj* 轻〔輕〕而软〔軟〕的 qīng ér ruǎn de.

feature /ˈfiːtʃə(r)/ *n* [C] 1 特征〔徵〕tèzhēng: *an important* ~ *of city life* 城市生活的一个重要特征. 2 **features** 脸〔臉〕的一部分(如口、眼等) liǎnde yí bùfen. 3 (报纸上的)特写〔寫〕tèxiě. 4 故事片 gùshìpiàn; 艺〔藝〕术〔術〕片 yìshùpiàn. **feature** *v* 1 [T] 给…以显〔顯〕著地位 gěi…yǐ xiǎnzhù dìwèi; 由…主演 yóu…zhǔyǎn. 2 [I] *in* 起重要作用 qǐ zhòngyào zuòyòng; 作为主要角色 zuòwéi zhǔyào juésè. **featureless** *adj* 平凡的 píngfánde; 不吸引人的 bù xīyǐn rén de.

February /ˈfebruəri; *US* -ueri/ *n* [U, C] 二月 èryuè. (参见 April 词条的用法例证)

feces [美语] = FAECES.

fed /fed/ *pt, pp* of FEED.

federal /ˈfedərəl/ *adj* 1 联〔聯〕邦制的 liánbāngzhìde. 2 联邦政府的 liánbāng zhèngfǔ de.

federation /ˌfedəˈreɪʃn/ *n* [C] 1 联〔聯〕邦 liánbāng. 2 (社会团体的)联合会〔會〕liánhéhuì.

fed up /ˌfed ˈʌp/ *adj* [非正式用语]极〔極〕其厌〔厭〕倦的 jíqí yànjuàn de.

fee /fiː/ *n* [C] **1**(考试的)报〔報〕名费 bàomíngfèi; (俱乐部的)入会〔會〕费 rùhuìfèi: *entrance* ～ 入会费. **2** [常为 pl] 劳〔勞〕务〔務〕费 láowùfèi.

feeble /ˈfiːbl/ *adj* [～r, ～st] 虚弱的 xūruòde; 无〔無〕力的 wúlìde. ˌ**feeble-ˈminded** 弱智的 ruòzhìde. **feebly** /-blɪ/ *adv*.

feed /fiːd/ *v* [*pt*, *pp* **fed** /fed/] **1** [T] 喂 wèi;饲 sì. **2** [I] (*on*) (尤指动物)吃 chī. **3** [T] *A with B*; *B to A* 以…供给… yǐ…gōngjǐ…;供料给… gōngliào gěi…. **feed** *n* **1** [C] (动物或婴儿的)一餐 yìcān; 一顿 yídùn. **2** [U] 饲料 sìliào. **3** [C] (机器的)进〔進〕料管 jìnliàoguǎn; 进料槽 jìnliàocáo. ˈ**feedback** *n* [U] 反馈 fǎnkuì; 用户反应〔應〕 yònghù fǎnyìng.

feel /fiːl/ *v* [*pt*, *pp* **felt** /felt/] **1** [T] 触〔觸〕chù;摸 mō;摸索 mōsuǒ. **2** [T] 感知 gǎnzhī; 觉〔覺〕得 juédé; 感觉 gǎnjué: ～ *the pain* 感觉到疼痛. ～ *concern* 感到忧虑. **3** [常与形容词连用](**a**) (表示某种状态): ～ *happy* 感到愉快. ～ *tired* 觉得累了. (**b**) (表示具有某种性质): *These shoes* ～ *tight*. 这些鞋穿上去有些紧. **4** [T] 遭受…的苦 zāoshòu…de kǔ: ～ *the cold* 挨冻. **5** [T] 认〔認〕为〔爲〕 rènwéi; 相信 xiāngxìn: *He felt he would succeed*. 他认为他会成功. **6**[习语] **feel like** (**doing**) **sth** 想要做 xiǎngyào zuò: ～ *like* (*having*) *a drink* 想喝点东西. **7** [短语动词] **feel for sb** 同情 tóngqíng. **feel** *n* [sing] **1** 触 chù;摸 mō. **2** 感知 gǎnzhī; 感觉 gǎnjué. **3**(对…的)总〔總〕的印象 zǒng de yìnxiàng.

feeler /ˈfiːlə(r)/ *n* [C] **1** 触〔觸〕角 chùjiǎo; 触须〔鬚〕 chùxū. **2** [习语] **put out feelers** 作试探 zuò shìtàn.

feeling /ˈfiːlɪŋ/ *n* **1** [C] 感觉〔覺〕 gǎnjué; 感触〔觸〕 gǎnchù. **2** [U] 知觉 zhījué. **3** [C, 常为 sing]预感 yùgǎn; 模糊的想法 móhude xiǎngfǎ: *a* ～ *that something awful is going to happen*. 可怕的事情就要发生的预感. **4** [sing] 意见 yìjiàn. **5** [U] 同情 tóngqíng; 体〔體〕谅 tǐliàng. **6 feelings** [pl] 情绪 qíngxù. **7** [习语] **bad/ill feeling** 反感 fǎngǎn; 愤慨 fènkǎi.

feet /fiːt/ *n pl* of FOOT.

feign /feɪn/ *v* [T] [正式用语]假装〔裝〕 jiǎzhuāng; 冒充 màochōng.

feint /feɪnt/ *n* [C, U] 假象 jiǎxiàng; 佯攻 yánggōng. **feint** *v* [I] 佯(攻) yáng; 假装〔裝〕 jiǎzhuāng.

felicity /fəˈlɪsətɪ/ *n* [U] [正式用语]幸福 xìngfú; 快乐〔樂〕 kuàilè.

feline /ˈfiːlaɪn/ *adj* 猫的 māode; 猫一样〔樣〕的 māo yíyàng de.

fell[1] /fel/ *pt* of FALL[1].

fell[2] /fel/ *n* [C] (英格兰北部的)荒野 huāngyě, 沼泽〔澤〕地 zhǎozédì.

fell[3] /fel/ *v* [T] **1** 砍倒(树) kǎndǎo. **2** 击〔擊〕倒(某人) jīdǎo.

fellow /ˈfeləʊ/ *n* [C] **1**[旧词,非正式用语]男人 nánrén; 小伙子 xiǎohuǒzi. **2** [常为 pl]伙伴 huǒbàn: ˈ*school* ～*s* 同学. **fellow** *adj* 同类〔類〕的 tónglèide; 同种〔種〕的 tóngzhǒngde: *one's* ～ *men* 同胞. **fellowship** *n* **1** [U] 交情 jiāoqing; 友谊 yǒuyí. **2** [C] 团〔團〕体〔體〕 tuántǐ; 协〔協〕会〔會〕 xiéhuì. **3** [C] (学院中)董事的职〔職〕位 dǒngshìde zhíwèi, 研究员的职位 yánjiūyuánde zhíwèi.

felony /ˈfelənɪ/ *n* [C, U] [*pl* **-ies**] [法律]重罪 zhòngzuì. **felon** /ˈfelən/ *n* [C] 重罪犯 zhòngzuìfàn.

felt[1] /felt/ *pt*, *pp* of FEEL.

felt[2] /felt/ *n* [U] 毡 zhān. ˌ**felt-tip ˈpen** (亦作 ˌ**felt-ˈtip**) *n* [C] (书写标签等用的)毡制〔製〕粗头〔頭〕笔〔筆〕 zhānzhì cūtóubǐ.

female /ˈfiːmeɪl/ *adj* **1** 雌的 cíde;女性的 nǚxìngde. **2**(植物)雌性的 cíxìngde. **3** (机械) 阴〔陰〕的 yīnde; 内的 nèide. **female** *n* [C] 妇〔婦〕女 fùnǚ; 雌性动〔動〕物 cíxìng dòngwù.

feminine /ˈfemənɪn/ *adj* **1** 女性的 nǚxìngde; 妇〔婦〕女的 fùnǚde. **2** [语法]阴〔陰〕性的 yīnxìngde. **femininity** /ˌfeməˈnɪnətɪ/ *n* [U] 女人气〔氣〕质〔質〕 nǚrén qìzhì.

feminism /ˈfemɪnɪzəm/ *n* [U] 男女平等主义〔義〕 nánnǚ píngděng zhǔyì. **feminist** *n* [C], *adj*.

fen /fen/ *n* [C] 沼泽〔澤〕 zhǎozé.

fence[1] /fens/ *n* [C] 篱〔籬〕笆 líba; 栅栏〔欄〕 zhàlan. *v* [T] *in*/*off* 把…用篱笆围〔圍〕起来〔來〕 bǎ… yòng líba wéi qǐlái; 把…用篱笆分开〔開〕 bǎ…yòng líba fēnkāi. **fencing** *n* [U] 筑〔築〕栅栏的材料 zhù zhàlan de cáiliào.

fence[2] /fens/ *v* [I] **1** 击〔擊〕剑〔劍〕 jījiàn. **2** 搪塞 tángsè;模棱两可 móléng liǎngkě. **fencing** *n* [U] 击剑 jījiàn.

fend /fend/ *v* [短语动词] **fend for oneˈself** 照料自己 zhàoliào zìjǐ. **fend sb/sth off** 挡〔擋〕开〔開〕 dǎngkāi; 避开 bìkāi.

ferment[1] /fəˈment/ *v* [I, T] **1**(使)发〔發〕酵 fājiào. **2**(使)激动〔動〕 jīdòng. **fermentation** /fɜːmenˈteɪʃn/ *n* [U].

ferment[2] /ˈfɜːment/ *n* [U] 骚动〔動〕 sāodòng.

fern /fɜːn/ *n* [C, U] (植物)蕨类〔類〕 juélèi.

ferocious /fəˈrəʊʃəs/ *adj* 凶〔兇〕猛的 xiōngměngde; 凶残〔殘〕的 xiōngcánde; 凶恶〔惡〕的 xiōng'ède. **ferociously** *adv*.

F

ferocity /fəˈrɒsətɪ/ *n* [U] 凶〔兇〕猛 xiōngměng; 凶恶〔惡〕xiōng'è.

ferret /ˈferɪt/ *n* [C] 白鼬 báiyòu; 雪貂 xuědiāo. **ferret** *v* 1 [I] (*about*) [非正式用语] 搜寻 sōuxún. 2 [短语动词] **ferret sth out** [非正式用语]搜出 sōuchū.

ferry (亦作 ˈ**ferry-boat**) /ˈferɪ/ *n* [C] [*pl* **-ies**] 渡船 dùchuán. **ferry** *v* [*pt*, *pp* **-ied**] [T] 渡运〔運〕(人、货等) dùyùn.

fertile /ˈfɜːtaɪl; *US* ˈfɜːrtl/ *adj* 1 (土地、土壤)肥沃的 féiwòde; 富饶〔饒〕的 fùráode; 多产〔產〕的 duōchǎnde. 2 (人)创〔創〕造力丰〔豐〕富的 chuàngzàolì fēngfù de; 想像力丰富的 xiǎngxiànglì fēngfù de. 3 (植物)能结果实〔實〕的 néng jiē guǒshí de; (动物)能产仔的 néng chǎnzǎi de. **fertility** /fəˈtɪlətɪ/ *n* [U].

fertilize /ˈfɜːtəlaɪz/ *v* [T] 使肥沃 shǐ féiwò. **fertilization** /ˌfɜːtəlaɪˈzeɪʃn; *US* -lɪˈz-/ *n* [U]. **fertilizer** *n* [C, U] 肥料 féiliào.

fervent /ˈfɜːvənt/ *adj* 热〔熱〕情的 rèqíngde; 热烈的 rèliède: ~ *belief* 强烈的信仰. ~ *supporter* 热情的支持者. **fervently** *adv*.

fervour (美语-or) /ˈfɜːvə(r)/ *n* [U] 炽〔熾〕热〔熱〕chìrè; 热情 rèqíng; 热烈 rèliè.

fester /ˈfestə(r)/ *v* [I] 1 (伤口)感染 gǎnrǎn; 化脓〔膿〕huànóng. 2 [喻]恶〔惡〕化 èhuà.

festival /ˈfestəvl/ *n* [C] 1 表演会〔會〕期 biǎoyǎn huìqī; 音乐〔樂〕节〔節〕yīnyuèjié; 戏〔戲〕剧〔劇〕节 xìjùjié. 2 节日 jiérì.

festive /ˈfestɪv/ *adj* 欢〔歡〕乐〔樂〕的 huānlède.

festivity /feˈstɪvətɪ/ *n* [U, C] [*pl* **-ies**] 欢〔歡〕庆〔慶〕huānqìng; 欢乐〔樂〕huānlè.

fetch /fetʃ/ *v* [T] 1 接来 jiēlái; 请来 qǐnglái; 取来 qǔlái: ~ *the children* (*from school*) (从学校)接孩子. 2 (货物)售得(价钱) shòudé: *The vase* ~*ed* £*1000*. 这花瓶卖了一千英镑.

fête /feɪt/ *n* [C] (为筹集基金等而举行的)室外游〔遊〕乐〔樂〕会〔會〕shìwài yóulèhuì. **fête** *v* [T] [常用被动语态]款待 kuǎndài; 盛宴招待 shèngyàn zhāodài.

fetish /ˈfetɪʃ/ *n* [C] 迷恋〔戀〕物 míliànwù.

fetter /ˈfetə(r)/ *n* [C] 1 脚镣 jiǎoliào. 2 [喻][常用 pl] 羁绊 jībàn; 束缚 shùfù: *the* ~*s of government controls* 政府控制的束缚. **fetter** *v* [T] 1 为〔爲〕…上脚镣 wèi…shàng jiǎoliào. 2[喻]束缚 shùfù; 拘束 jūshù.

fetus [美语] = FOETUS.

feud /fjuːd/ *n* [C] 长〔長〕期不和 chángqī bùhé. **feud** *v* [I] 长期争吵 chángqī zhēngchǎo.

feudal /ˈfjuːdl/ *adj* 封建的 fēngjiànde; 封建制度的 fēngjiàn zhìdù de. **feudalism** /-dəlɪzəm/ *n* [U].

fever /ˈfiːvə(r)/ *n* 1 [C, U] 发〔發〕烧〔燒〕fāshāo; 热〔熱〕度 rèdù. 2 [U] 热病 rèbìng. 3 [sing] 狂热 kuángrè; 兴〔興〕奋〔奮〕xīngfèn: *in a* ~ *of impatience* 急不可耐. **feverish** *adj* 1 发烧的 fāshāode; 发热的 fārède. 2 极〔極〕度兴奋的 jídù xīngfèn de. **feverishly** *adv*.

few /fjuː/ *adj* 1 **a few** 少数〔數〕的 shǎoshùde; 不多的 bùduōde; 有些 yǒuxiē. 2 (不与 a 连用)很少的 hěnshǎode; 几〔幾〕乎没有的 jīhū méiyǒu de: *F*~ *people live to be 100*. 很少有人活到 100 岁.

fiancé /fɪˈɒnseɪ; *US* ˌfiːɑːnˈseɪ/ *n* [C] (*fem* **fiancée**) *n* [C] 未婚夫 wèihūnfū.

fiasco /fɪˈæskəʊ/ *n* [C] [*pl* **~s**, 美语亦作 **~es**] 惨〔慘〕败 cǎnbài; 大败 dàbài.

fib /fɪb/ *n* [C] [非正式用语]小小的谎话 xiǎoxiǎode huǎnghuà. **fib** *v* [**-bb-**] 撒小谎 sā xiǎohuǎng. **fibber** *n* [C].

fibre (美语 **fiber**) /ˈfaɪbə(r)/ *n* 1 [C] 纤〔纖〕维 xiānwéi: *muscle* ~*s* 肌肉纤维. 2 [U] 纤维物质〔質〕xiānwéi wùzhì; 纤维质料 xiānwéi zhìliào. 3 [U] (人的)性格 xìnggé: *strong moral* ~ 高尚的道德品质. ˈ**fibreglass** (美语 ˈ**fiber-**) *n* [U] 玻璃纤维 bōli xiānwéi; 玻璃棉 bōlimián. **fibrous** /-brəs/ *adj* 纤维构〔構〕成的 xiānwéi gòuchéng de; 纤维状〔狀〕的 xiānwéizhuàngde.

fickle /ˈfɪkl/ *adj* 易变〔變〕的 yìbiànde; 无〔無〕常的 wúchángde.

fiction /ˈfɪkʃn/ *n* 1 [U] 虚构〔構〕xūgòu; 杜撰 dùzhuàn. 2 [C, U] 小说 xiǎoshuō; 虚构性的陈述 xūgòuxìngde chénshù. **fictional** /-ʃənl/ *adj*.

fictitious /fɪkˈtɪʃəs/ *adj* 虚构〔構〕的 xūgòude; 杜撰的 dùzhuànde.

fiddle /ˈfɪdl/ *n* [C] 1 [俚]欺骗行为〔爲〕qīpiàn xíngwéi. 2 [非正式用语]小提琴 xiǎotíqín. **fiddle** *v* 1 [I] *with* 无〔無〕目的地拨〔撥〕弄 wú mùdì de bōnòng. 2 [T] [非正式用语]篡改(账目) cuàngǎi; 以欺骗手段得到 yǐ qīpiàn shǒuduàn dédào. 3 [I] 拉小提琴 lā xiǎotíqín. **fiddler** *n* [C] 1 小提琴手 xiǎotíqínshǒu. 2 弄虚作假者 nòng xū zuò jiǎ zhě. **fiddling** *adj* 微不足道的 wēi bù zú dào de; 无足轻重的 wú zú qīng zhòng de. **fiddly** *adv* 费事的 fèishìde; 不便使用的 búbiàn shǐyòng de.

fidelity /fɪˈdelətɪ; *US* faɪ-/ *n* [U] 1 忠诚 zhōngchéng; 忠实〔實〕zhōngshí. 2 精确〔確〕jīngquè; 逼真 bīzhēn.

fidget /ˈfɪdʒɪt/ *v* [I] 坐立不安 zuò lì bù'ān; 烦躁 fánzào. **fidget** *n* [C] 烦躁不安的人 fánzào bù'ān de rén. **fidgety** *adj*.

field[1] /fiːld/ *n* 1 [C] 田野 tiányě; 田地 tiándì. 2 [C] 场〔場〕地 chǎngdì; 空地 kòngdì: *a*

ˈ*football* ~ 足球场. ˈ*oil* ~ 油田. ˈ*battle* ~ 战场. 3 [C] (学术研究等)界 jiè; 领域 lǐngyù. 4 [C] (某种力效应的)场 chǎng: *a magnetic* ~ 磁场. ˈ**field-day** *n* [习语] **have a field-day** 特别有趣 tèbié yǒuqù; 获〔獲〕得重大成功 huòdé zhòngdà chénggōng. ˌ**field ˈmarshal** *n* [C] (英国) 陆〔陸〕军元帅〔帥〕 lùjūn yuánshuài.

field[2] /fiːld/ *v* 1 [I,T] (板球等)截(球) jié; 守(球) shǒu. 2 [T] 使(球队)上场〔場〕 shǐ shàngchǎng. 3 [T] 巧妙地对〔對〕付(问题) qiǎomiàode duìfu. **fielder** *n* [C] (板球等)外场员 wàichǎngyuán, 守队〔隊〕队员 shǒuduì duìyuán.

fiend /fiːnd/ *n* [C] 1 非常坏〔壞〕的人 fēicháng huàide rén. 2 渴望某种〔種〕事物的人 kěwàng mǒuzhǒng shìwù de rén: *a health* ~ 极注意身体健康的人. **fiendish** *adj*. **fiendishly** *adv* 很 hěn; 极〔極〕度地 jídùde.

fierce /fɪəs/ *adj* [~r, ~st] 1 凶〔兇〕猛的 xiōngměngde; 愤怒的 fènnùde. 2 狂热〔熱〕的 kuángrède; 强烈的 qiángliède: ~ *heat* 酷热. ~ *opposition* 强烈的反对. **fiercely** *adv*. **fierceness** *n* [U].

fiery /ˈfaɪərɪ/ *adj* [-ier, -iest] 1 火焰的 huǒyánde; 燃烧〔燒〕着的 ránshāozhede; 火一般的 huǒ yìbān de; 火热〔熱〕的 huǒrède. 2 (人)易怒的 yìnùde; 脾气〔氣〕暴躁的 píqì bàozào de. **fierily** /-rəlɪ/ *adv*.

fifteen /ˌfɪfˈtiːn/ *pron, adj, n* [C] 十五 shíwǔ; 十五个〔個〕 shíwǔgè. **fifteenth** /ˌfɪfˈtiːnθ/ *pron, adj* 第十五 dìshíwǔ; 第十五个 dìshíwǔgè. **fifteenth** *pron, n* [C] 十五分之一 shíwǔfēn zhī yī.

fifth /fɪfθ/ *pron, adj* 第五 dìwǔ; 第五个〔個〕 dìwǔgè; 第五的 dìwǔde. **fifth** *pron, n* [C] 五分之一 wǔfēn zhī yī.

fifty /ˈfɪftɪ/ *pron, adj, n* [C] [*pl* -ies] 五十 wǔshí; 五十个〔個〕 wǔshígè. **fiftieth** *pron, adj* 第五十 dìwǔshí; 第五十个 dìwǔshígè; 第五十的 dìwǔshíde. **fiftieth** *pron, n* [C] 五十分之一 wǔshífēn zhī yī.

fig /fɪg/ *n* [C] 1 无〔無〕花果 wúhuāguǒ; 无花果树〔樹〕 wúhuāguǒshù. 2 [习语] **not care / give a ˈfig (about sth)** 不在乎 búzàihu.

fig *abbr* 1 figure: *See fig 3* 参见图 3. 2 figurative.

fight /faɪt/ *v* [*pt, pp* **fought** /fɔːt/] 1 [I, T] 打架 dǎjià; 打仗 dǎzhàng: [喻] ~ *against poverty* 与贫困作斗争. 2 [T] 打(仗) dǎ. 3 [I] 争吵 zhēngchǎo; 争论〔論〕 zhēnglùn. 4 [短语动词] **fight back** (a) 抵抗 dǐkàng. (b) 为〔為〕恢复〔復〕原来状〔狀〕态〔態〕而奋〔奮〕斗〔鬥〕 wèi huīfù yuánlái zhuàngtài ér fèndòu. **fight sb/sth off** 击〔擊〕退 jītuì; 竭力摆〔擺〕脱 jiélì bǎituō: ~ *off an attacker* 击退来犯的人. ~ *a cold* 治愈感冒. **fight sth out** 通过斗争解决争吵 tōngguò dòuzhēng jiějué zhēngchǎo. **fight** *n* 1 [C] 战〔戰〕斗 zhàndòu; 搏斗 bódòu. 2 [U] 战斗的愿〔願〕望 zhàndòude yuànwàng; 战斗力 zhàndòulì. **fighter** *n* [C] 1 战士 zhànshì; 兵士 bīngshì; 拳击手 quánjīshǒu. 2 战斗机 zhàndòujī.

figment /ˈfɪgmənt/ *n* [C] 想像的事 xiǎngxiàngde shì; 虚构〔構〕的事 xūgòude shì: *a* ~ *of her imagination* 她想像中的事物.

figurative /ˈfɪgjərətɪv/ *adj* (词语)比喻的 bǐyùde. **figuratively** *adv*.

figure /ˈfɪgə(r); *US* ˈfɪgjər/ *n* 1 [C] 数〔數〕字 shùzì. 2 [C]价〔價〕格 jiàgé. 3 [C] 体〔體〕形 tǐxíng; 风〔風〕姿 fēngzī; 人影 rényǐng: *a* ~ *approaching in the darkness* 黑暗中走来的一个人影. *a good* ~ 苗条的身材. 4[C] 人物 rénwù: *an important* ~ *in history* 历史上的重要人物. 5 [C]画〔畫〕像 huàxiàng; 塑像 sùxiàng. 6 [C] 图〔圖〕形 túxíng; 图表 túbiǎo; 图解 tújiě. 7 **figures** [pl] 算术〔術〕 suànshù; 计算 jìsuàn. **figure** *v* 1 [I] (*in*) 出现 chūxiàn; 露头〔頭〕角 lù tóujiǎo. 2 [尤用于美语]认〔認〕为〔為〕 rènwéi. 3 [I] [非正式用语](与 *it* 或 *that* 连用)是很可能的 shì hěn kěnéng de: *That* ~*s*. 那是很可能的. 4 [短语动词] **figure on sth** [美语]计划〔劃〕 jìhuà; 指望 zhǐwàng. **figure sth out** 想出 xiǎngchū; 计算出 jìsuànchū. ˈ**figure-head** *n* [C] 挂〔掛〕名首脑〔腦〕 guàmíng shǒunǎo. ˌ**figure of ˈspeech** *n* [C] 比喻 bǐyù.

filament /ˈfɪləmənt/ *n* [C] 细丝〔絲〕 xìsī; 灯〔燈〕丝 dēngsī.

file[1] /faɪl/ *n* [C] 锉 cuò; 锉刀 cuòdāo. **file** *v* [T] 锉 cuò; 锉平 cuò píng; 锉光 cuò guāng: ~ *one's fingernails* 把指甲锉光. **filings** /ˈfaɪlɪŋz/ *n* [pl] 锉屑 cuòxiè.

file[2] /faɪl/ *n* [C] 1 文件夹〔夾〕 wénjiànjiā; 公文箱 gōngwénxiāng; 卷宗 juànzōng. 2 档〔檔〕案 dàng'àn. 3 (电子计算机)文件 wénjiàn. 4 [习语] **on file** 存档 cúndàng. **file** *v* 1 [T] 把…归〔歸〕档 bǎ…guīdàng. 2 [I,T] (*for*) 提出申请 tíchū shēnqǐng; 起诉 qǐsù: ~ *for divorce* 起诉要求离婚. ˈ**filing cabinet** *n* [C] 文件柜〔櫃〕 wénjiànguì.

file[3] /faɪl/ *n* [C] 纵〔縱〕列 zòngliè. **file** *v* [I] 成纵队〔隊〕前进〔進〕 chéng zòngduì qiánjìn: ~ *out of the room* 从房里鱼贯而出.

fill /fɪl/ *v* 1 [I,T] 装〔裝〕满 zhuāngmǎn; 注满 zhùmǎn; 充满 chōngmǎn. 2 [T] 担〔擔〕任(职务) dānrèn; 派人担任 pàirén dānrèn: ~ *a vacancy* 补上空缺. 3 [T] 履行(职能等) lǚxíng. 4[短语动词] **fill in (for sb)** 暂代 zàn dài. **fill sth in** (美语亦作) **fill sth out** 填写〔寫〕 tiánxiě: ~ *in a form* 填写表格. **fill**

out 扩〔擴〕大 kuòdà; 变〔變〕胖 biàn pàng. fill sth up 装〔裝〕满 zhuāng mǎn; 满 mǎn. fill *n* [习语] one's fill of sth (a) 吃饱喝足的量 chībǎo hē zú de liàng. (b) 忍受的限度 rěnshòude xiàndù: *I've had my ~ of your rudeness!* 你的粗暴我受够了! filler *n* [C] 填补〔補〕物 tiánbǔwù. filling *n* [C] (牙科医生用的)填补物 tiánbǔwù. 'filling station *n* [C] 加油站 jiāyóuzhàn.

fillet /ˈfɪlɪt/ *n* [C] 肉片 ròupiàn; 鱼片 yúpiàn. fillet *v* [T] (把鱼、肉)切成片 qiē chéng piàn.

film /fɪlm/ *n* 1 [C] 影片 yǐngpiàn; 电〔電〕影 diànyǐng. 2 [C, U] (摄影)胶〔膠〕卷〔捲〕jiāojuǎn; 软片 ruǎnpiàn. 3 [C, 常为 sing] 薄膜 bómó; 膜 mó; 薄层〔層〕bócéng: *a ~ of oil* 一层油. film *v* [I, T] (把…)拍成电影 pāichéng diànyǐng. 'film star *n* [C] 电影明星 diànyǐng míngxīng.

filter /ˈfɪltə(r)/ *n* [C] 1 滤〔濾〕器 lǜqì. 2 滤光器 lǜguāngqì; 滤色器 lǜsèqì. filter *v* 1 [I, T] (使)滤过〔過〕lǜguò. 2 [I] 慢慢传〔傳〕开〔開〕mànmàn chuánkāi; 慢慢通过 mànmàn tōngguò; 慢慢流过 mànmàn liúguò.

filth /fɪlθ/ *n* [U] 1 污秽〔穢〕wūhuì; 污物 wūwù. 2 淫猥 yínwěi. filthy *adj* [-ier, -iest].

fin /fɪn/ *n* [C] 1 鳍 qí. 2 鳍状〔狀〕的东〔東〕西 qízhuàngde dōngxi; (飞机)直尾翅 zhíwěichì.

final /ˈfaɪnl/ *adj* 1 最后〔後〕的 zuìhòude; 最终的 zuìzhōngde. 2 确〔確〕定性的 quèdìngxìngde; 决定性的 juédìngxìngde. 3 [习语] final straw ⇨STRAW. final *n* [C] 1 决赛 juésài: *the tennis ~s* 网球决赛. 2 finals [pl] (大学)期终考试 qīzhōng kǎoshì. finalist /-nəlɪst/ *n* [C] 决赛选〔選〕手 juésài xuǎnshǒu. finalize /-nəlaɪz/ *v* [T] 把…最后定下来 bǎ… zuìhòu dìng xiàlái. finally /-nəlɪ/ *adv* 1 最后地 zuìhòude; 最终地 zuìzhōngde. 2 决定性地 juédìngxìngde: *settle the matter ~ly* 彻底解决这个问题.

finale /fɪˈnɑːlɪ; *US* -ˈnælɪ/ *n* [C] (音乐)终曲 zhōngqǔ; 末乐〔樂〕章 mò yuèzhāng; (戏剧)终场〔場〕zhōngchǎng.

finance /ˈfaɪnæns, fɪˈnæns/ *n* 1 [U] 财政 cáizhèng; 金融 jīnróng: *an expert in ~* 财政专家. 2 [U] (工程项目、计划等所需的)资金 zījīn: *obtain ~ from the bank* 从银行获得资金. 3 finances [pl] (个人、公司等)可动〔動〕用的钱〔錢〕kě dòngyòng de qián; 财源 cáiyuán. finance *v* [T] 为〔爲〕…提供资金 wèi …tígōng zījīn. financial /faɪˈnænʃl, fɪˈnæ-/ *adj*. financially *adv*. financier /faɪˈnænsɪə(r); *US* ˌfɪnənˈsɪər/ *n* [C] 金融家 jīnróngjiā.

finch /fɪntʃ/ *n* [C] 雀科鸣〔鳴〕禽 quèkē míngqín.

find /faɪnd/ *v* [*pt*, *pp* found /faʊnd/] [T] 1 找到 zhǎodào; 寻〔尋〕得 xúndé. 2 意外发〔發〕现 yìwài fāxiàn. 3 找回(丢失的物或人) zhǎohuí. 4 设法获〔獲〕得 shèfǎ huòdé: *~ time to study* 挤出时间学习. 5 感到 gǎndào; 认〔認〕为〔爲〕rènwéi: *I ~ it difficult to understand him.* 我觉得了解他是困难的. 6 自然地到达〔達〕zìránde dàodá: *Water always ~s its own level.* 水总会自成水平面. 7 发现…的存在 fāxiàn…de cúnzài: *Tigers are found in India.* 印度有老虎. 8 [法律] 判决 pànjué; 裁决 cáijué: *~ her innocent* 判她无罪. 9 [习语] find fault with sth/sb 找岔子 zhǎochàzi; 抱怨 bàoyuàn. 10 [短语动词] find sth out 找出 zhǎochū; 查明 chámíng: *~ out when the next train leaves* 查明下一趟火车何时开出. find *n* [C] (有价值或有趣的)发现物 fāxiànwù. finder *n* [C]. finding *n* [C, 常作 pl] 1 调查研究的结果 diàochá yánjiū de jiéguǒ. 2 [法律]判决 pànjué; 裁决 cáijué.

fine[1] /faɪn/ *adj* [~r, ~st] 1 可爱〔愛〕的 kě'àide; 美好的 měihǎo de: *a ~ view* 美好的景色. 2 身体〔體〕健康的 shēntǐ jiànkāng de. 3 (天气)晴朗的 qínglǎngde. 4 颗粒微小的 kēlì wēixiǎo de: *~ powder* 细粉末. 5 纤〔纖〕巧的 xiānqiǎode; 精制〔製〕的 jīngzhìde. 6 细微难〔難〕察的 xìwēi nánchá de: *a ~ distinction* 细微难察的差别. fine *adv* 很好 hěnhǎo. fine 'art *n* [U] (亦作 the fine 'arts [pl]) 美艺〔藝〕术〔術〕(绘画、雕塑、诗歌、音乐等) měi yìshù. finely *adv* 1 很好 hěnhǎo; 极〔極〕好 jíhǎo. 2 细小地 xìxiǎode: *~ly cut meat* 切得很细的肉. fineness *n* [U].

fine[2] /faɪn/ *n* [C] 罚款 fákuǎn; 罚金 fájīn. fine *v* [T] 处〔處〕以罚金 chǔyǐ fájīn.

finery /ˈfaɪnərɪ/ *n* [U] 华丽〔麗〕的服饰 huálìde fúshì.

finesse /fɪˈnes/ *n* [U] 手腕 shǒuwàn; 策略 cèlüè.

finger /ˈfɪŋgə(r)/ *n* [C] 1 手指 shǒuzhǐ. 2 (手套的)套手指部分 tào shǒuzhǐ bùfen. 3 [习语] get, put, etc one's 'finger out (不再懒惰)开〔開〕始努力工作 kāishǐ nǔlì gōngzuò. put one's finger on sth 确〔確〕切指出 quèqiè zhǐchū. finger *v* [T] 用手指触〔觸〕、碰 yòng shǒuzhǐ chù、pèng. 'fingernail *n* [C] 指甲 zhǐjia. 'fingerprint *n* [C] 指纹印 zhǐwényìn; 手印 shǒuyìn. 'fingertip *n* [C] 1 指尖 zhǐjiān. 2 [习语] have sth at one's 'fingertips 熟知某事物 shúzhī mǒu shìwù.

finish /ˈfɪnɪʃ/ *v* 1 [I, T] 完成 wánchéng; 结束 jiéshù. 2 [T] 吃完 chīwán; 饮完 yǐnwán; 耗尽〔盡〕hàojìn. 3 [T] 使完美 shǐ wánměi; 使完善 shǐ wánshàn. 4 [短语动词] finish sb/sth off

杀〔殺〕死 shāsǐ; 毁灭〔滅〕 huǐmiè. **finish with sb/sth** 与〔與〕…断〔斷〕绝关〔關〕系〔係〕 yǔ… duànjué guānxi. **finish** *n* **1** [C] 最后〔後〕部分 zuìhòu bùfen. **2** [C, U] 完善 wánshàn; 完美 wánměi: *a highly polished* ~ 精心修饰后的完美.

finite /ˈfaɪnaɪt/ *adj* **1** 有限的 yǒuxiànde. **2** [语法]限定的 xiàndìngde: '*Is*' *and* '*was*' *are* ~ *forms of* '*be*'. "is" 和 "was" 是 "be" 的限定形式.

fir (亦作 ˈ**fir-tree**) /fɜː(r)/ *n* [C] 冷杉 lěngshān. ˈ**fir-cone** *n* [C] 冷杉球果 lěngshān qiúguǒ.

fire[1] /ˈfaɪə(r)/ *n* **1** [U] 火 huǒ. **2** (a) [C] 失火 shīhuǒ; 火灾〔災〕 huǒzāi: *forest* ~*s* 森林火灾. (b) [U] 失火造成的破坏〔壞〕 shīhuǒ zàochéngde pòhuài. **3** [C] 炉〔爐〕火 lúhuǒ: *light a* ~ 生炉子. **4** [C] 取暖装〔裝〕置 qǔnuǎn zhuāngzhì: *a gas* ~ 煤气取暖炉. **5** [U](枪炮的)开〔開〕火 kāihuǒ. **6** [习语] **on fire** 着火 zháohuǒ; 起火 qǐhuǒ. **under** ˈ**fire** 遭射击〔擊〕 zāo shèjī. ˈ**fire-alarm** *n* [C] 火警 huǒjǐng. ˈ**firearm** *n* [C, 常为 pl] 火器(步枪、手枪等) huǒqì. **the** ˈ**fire brigade** *n* [sing] 消防队〔隊〕 xiāofángduì. ˈ**fire-drill** *n* [C, U] 消防演习〔習〕 xiāofáng yǎnxí. ˈ**fire-engine** *n* [C] 救火车〔車〕 jiùhuǒchē. ˈ**fire-escape** *n* [C] (建筑物外面的)太平梯 tàipíngtī. ˈ**fire extinguisher** *n* [C] 灭〔滅〕火器 mièhuǒqì. ˈ**fire-fighter** *n* [C] 消防队员 xiāofáng duìyuán. **fireguard** *n* [C] 炉栏〔欄〕 lúlán. **fireman** /-mən/ *n* [C] [*pl* **-men**] 消防队员 xiāofáng duìyuán. ˈ**fireplace** *n* [C] 壁炉〔爐〕 bìlú. ˈ**fireproof** *v* [T], *adj* 使防火 shǐ fánghuǒ; 防火的 fánghuǒde; 耐火的 nàihuǒde. ˈ**fireside** *n* [C, 常为 sing] (壁)炉边〔邊〕 lúbiān. ˈ**fire station** *n* [C] 消防站 xiāofángzhàn. ˈ**firewall** *n* [C] (计算机病毒)防火墙〔牆〕 fánghuǒqiáng. ˈ**firewood** *n* [U] 木柴 mùchái. ˈ**firework** *n* [C] 焰火 yànhuǒ.

fire[2] /ˈfaɪə(r)/ *v* **1** [I, T] 开〔開〕火 kāihuǒ; (枪等)射击〔擊〕 shèjī; 开(枪、炮) kāi; 射出(子弹等) shèchū. **2** [T] [非正式用语]开除(雇员等) kāichú. **3** [T] 激起 jīqǐ; 激发〔發〕 jīfā: ~ *sb's imagination* 激发某人的想像力. **4** [T] (在窑内)烧〔燒〕制〔製〕(陶器等) shāozhì. ˈ**firing-line** *n* [sing] 火线〔綫〕 huǒxiàn. ˈ**firing-squad** *n* [C, U] 行刑队〔隊〕 xíngxíngduì.

firm[1] /fɜːm/ *adj* **1** 结实〔實〕的 jiēshide; 坚〔堅〕硬的 jiānyìngde. **2** 牢固的 láogùde. **3** 坚定的 jiāndìngde. **4**(人的动作)沉稳〔穩〕的 chénwěnde. **5** [习语] **stand firm** ⇨ STAND[2] 8. **firm** *v* [I, T] 使坚定 shǐ jiāndìng; 使牢固 shǐ láogù; 变〔變〕坚定 biànjiāndìng; 变牢固 biàn láogù. **firmly** *adv* 坚定地 jiāndìngde; 稳固地 wěngùde. **firmness** *n* [U].

firm[2] /fɜːm/ *n* [C] 商号〔號〕 shānghào; 商行 shāngháng.

first[1] /fɜːst/ *adj* **1** 第一的 dìyīde; 首要的 shǒuyàode. **2**[习语] **at first** ˈ**sight** 乍看之下 zhà kàn zhī xià. **first** ˈ**thing** 首先 shǒuxiān; 立即 lìjí; 首先要做的事 shǒuxiān yàozuò de shì. ˌ**first** ˈ**aid** *n* [U] (对病人的)急救 jíjiù. ˌ**first** ˈ**class** *n* [U] (火车的)头〔頭〕等车〔車〕厢 tóuděngchēxiāng; (轮船等的)头等舱〔艙〕 tóuděngcāng. ˈ**first-class** *adj, adv* 头等车厢(或舱)的 tóuděngchēxiāngde; 乘头等车厢(或舱) chéng tóuděngchēxiāng. ˌ**first** ˈ**floor** *n* [C] **1** [英国英语]二(层)楼 èrlóu. **2** [美语]底层 dǐcéng; 一(层)楼 yīlóu. ˌ**first** ˈ**hand** *adj, adv* (资料等)第一手的 dìyīshǒude; 直接的 zhíjiēde; 直接地 zhíjiēde. **firstly** *adv* (列举论点等)首先 shǒuxiān, 第一 dìyī. ˈ**first name** *n* [C] 教名 jiàomíng; 名字 míngzi. **the** ˌ**first** ˈ**person** *n* [sing] [语法]第一人称〔稱〕 dìyī rénchēng. **first-rate** *adj* 第一流的 dìyīliúde.

first[2] /fɜːst/ *adv* **1** 第一 dìyī; 最初 zuìchū; 最先 zuìxiān: *She spoke* ~. 她第一个讲话. **2** 第一次 dìyīcì: *when I* ~ *came to London* 当我第一次来到伦敦. **3** 宁〔寧〕可 nìngkě; 宁愿〔願〕 nìngyuàn.

first[3] /fɜːst/ *n, pron* **1 the first** [sing] 第一个〔個〕人(或物) dìyīgèrén: *the* ~ *to leave* 离开的第一个人. **2** [C] [非正式用语]重要的新成就 zhòngyàode xīn chéngjiù. **3** [C] (大学考试成绩的)优〔優〕等 yōuděng. **4**[习语] **at** ˈ**first** 最初 zuìchū; 当〔當〕初 dāngchū.

fish /fɪʃ/ *n* [*pl* **fish** 或 ~**es**] **1** [C] 鱼 yú. **2** [U] 鱼肉 yúròu: ~ *and chips* 鱼和炸土豆片. **fish** *v* **1** [I] 捕鱼 bǔyú; 钓鱼 diàoyú. **2** [短语动词] **fish for sth** 转〔轉〕弯〔彎〕抹角地引出 zhuǎn wān mò jiǎo de yǐnchū. **fish sth out (of sth)** 从〔從〕…掏出 cóng… tāochū: *He* ~*ed a coin out of his pocket*. 他从口袋里掏出一个硬币. **fisherman** /ˈfɪʃəmən/ *n* [C] [*pl* **-men**] 渔民 yúmín; 渔夫 yúfū. **fishery** *n* [C, 常作 pl] [*pl* **-ies**] 渔场〔場〕 yúchǎng. **fishing** *n* [U] 钓鱼 diàoyú; 捕鱼 bǔyú: *go* ~*ing* 出去钓鱼. ˈ~*ing-rod* 钓竿. **fishmonger** /ˈfɪʃmʌŋgə(r)/ *n* [C] 鱼商 yúshāng. **fishy** *adj* [-ier, -iest] **1** 像鱼的 xiàng yú de. **2** [非正式用语]可疑的 kěyíde: *a* ~*y story* 可疑的说法.

fission /ˈfɪʃn/ *n* [U] (尤指原子)裂变〔變〕 lièbiàn: *nuclear* ~ (核)裂变 lièbiàn.

fissure /ˈfɪʃə(r)/ *n* [C] (岩石等的)裂缝 lièfèng.

fist /fɪst/ *n* [C] 拳 quán; 拳头〔頭〕 quántou.

F

fistful *n* [C] 一把 yìbǎ.

fit[1] /fɪt/ *v* [-tt-] 1 [I, T] (使)适〔適〕合 shìhé: *These shoes don't* ~ (*me*). 这双鞋(大小)不适合(我). 2 [T] 试穿(衣服) shìchuān: *have a new coat* ~*ted* 试穿一件新上衣. 3 [T]安装〔裝〕ānzhuāng; 装置 zhuāngzhì: ~ *a new window* 安装新窗户. 4 [T] 使符合 shǐ fúhé; 使适应〔應〕shǐ shìyìng: *make the punishment* ~ *the crime* 按罪量刑. 5[短语动词] fit sb in 安排时〔時〕间见某人 ānpái shíjiān jiàn mǒurén. fit sth in 插入 chārù. fit in (with sb/sth) 相合 xiānghé; 合得来 hédelái. fit sb/sth out 装备〔備〕zhuāngbèi; 配备 pèibèi. fit *n* [C] 合身 héshēn; 适合 shìhé: *a tight* ~ 贴身. fitted *adj* 按放置位置定做的 àn fàngzhì wèizhì dìngzuò de: ~*ted carpets/cupboard* 按放置位置定做的地毯(碗橱). fitter *n* [C] 1 装配工 zhuāngpèigōng. 2 剪裁并〔並〕试样的裁缝 jiǎncái bìng shìyàng de cáifeng.

fit[2] /fɪt/ *adj*. [~ter, ~test] 1 适〔適〕合的 shìhéde; 适宜的 shìyíde; 恰当〔當〕的 qiàdàngde; 正当的 zhèngdàngde: *not* ~ *to eat* 不适宜食用. *Do as you think* ~. 你认为怎样合适就怎样办. 2 健康的 jiànkāngde; 强健的 qiángjiànde. 3 *to* 齐〔齊〕备〔備〕的 qíbèide; 就要…的 jiùyào…de: *laughing* ~ *to burst* 笑不可支. fitness *n* [U] 1 健康 jiànkāng. 2 *for*; *to* 适合 shìhé; 恰当 qiàdàng.

fit[3] /fɪt/ *n* [C] 1 (病的)发〔發〕作 fāzuò; 歇斯底里发作 xiēsīdǐlǐ fāzuò; 痉〔痙〕挛〔攣〕jìngluán. 2 (感情的)突发 tūfā; (活动的)一阵紧〔緊〕张〔張〕yízhèn jǐnzhāng: *a* ~ *of anger* 勃然大怒. *a* ~ *of enthusiasm* 一阵热情. 3 [习语] by / in ˌfits and ˈstarts 一阵一阵地 yízhènyízhènde. have / throw a ˈfit (a) 痉挛 jìngluán; 昏厥 hūnjué. (b) [非正式用语]震惊〔驚〕zhènjīng; 愤怒 fènnù. fitful /-fl/ *adj* 间歇的 jiànxiēde. fitfully /-fəlɪ/ *adv*.

fitting /ˈfɪtɪŋ/ *adj* 适〔適〕合的 shìhéde; 恰当〔當〕的 qiàdàngde. fitting *n* [C] 1 [常作 pl] 零件 língjiàn; 配件 pèijiàn: *electrical* ~*s* 电气配件. 2 [常作 pl] 搬家时〔時〕可移走的装〔裝〕置 bānjiāshí kě yízǒude zhuāngzhì.

five /faɪv/ *pron*, *adj*, *n* [C] 五 wǔ; 五个〔個〕wǔgè. fiver /-ə(r)/ [英国非正式用语] 五英镑 wǔ yīngbàng; 五英镑钞票 wǔ yīngbàng chāopiào.

fix[1] /fɪks/ *v* [T] 1 使固定 shǐ gùdìng; 安装〔裝〕ānzhuāng; 安置 ānzhì. 2 盯住 dīngzhù; 凝视 níngshì; 吸引(注意) xīyǐn. 3 安排 ānpái: ~ *a date for a meeting* 安排会议的日期. 4 修理 xiūlǐ. 5 整理 zhěnglǐ; 收拾 shōushi: ~ *one's hair* 梳头. 6 [尤用于美语]准〔準〕备〔備〕(饮食) zhǔnbèi. 7 用不正当〔當〕手段操纵〔縱〕yòng bú zhèngdàng shǒuduàn cāozòng. 8 [短语动词] fix on sb / sth 选〔選〕定 xuǎndìng. fix sb up (with sth) 为〔爲〕…安排好… wèi…ānpái hǎo…. fixation /fɪkˈseɪʃn/ *n* [C] 不健康的依恋〔戀〕bú jiànkāngde yīliàn.

fix[2] /fɪks/ *n* [C] [常作 sing] 1 窘境 jiǒngjìng; 困境 kùnjìng. 2 方位 fāngwèi. 3 [俚]吸毒者的毒品注射 xīdúzhě de dúpǐn zhùshè.

fixture /ˈfɪkstʃə(r)/ *n* [C] 1 [常作 pl] (房屋内的)固定装〔裝〕置(如浴缸等) gùdìng zhuāngzhì. 2 已确〔確〕定日期的体〔體〕育项目 yǐ quèdìng rìqī de tǐyù xiàngmù.

fizz /fɪz/ *v* [I] (液体冒气泡时)嘶嘶作响〔響〕sīsī zuò xiǎng. fizz *n* [U] 液体〔體〕起气泡 yètǐ qǐ qìpào. fizzy *adj* [-ier, -iest].

fizzle /ˈfɪzl/ *v* [I] 1 发〔發〕微弱的嘶嘶声〔聲〕fā wēiruòde sīsīshēng. 2 [短语动词] fizzle out 结果不妙 jiéguǒ búmiào.

flab /flæb/ *n* [U] [非正式用语]松〔鬆〕弛的肌肉 sōngchí de jīròu. flabby *adj* [-ier, -iest] 1 (肌肉)不结实〔實〕的 bù jiēshi de; 松弛的 sōngchíde. 2 [喻]软弱的 ruǎnruòde. flabbiness *n* [U].

flabbergasted /ˈflæbəgɑːstɪd; *US* -gæst-/ *adj* 感到震惊〔驚〕的 gǎndào zhènjīng de.

flag[1] /flæg/ *n* [C] 旗 qí. flag *v* [-gg-] [短语动词] flag sth down 打信号〔號〕使(车辆)停下 dǎ xìnhào shǐ tíngxià. ˈflagship *n* [C] 1 旗舰〔艦〕qíjiàn. 2 [喻](同类事物中的)佼佼者 jiǎojiǎozhě.

flag[2] /flæg/ *v* [-gg-] [I] 变〔變〕弱 biànruò: *Interest is* ~*ging*. 兴趣正在低落下来. *Enthusiasm is* ~*ging*. 热情正在减退.

flagon /ˈflægən/ *n* [C] 大肚酒瓶 dàdù jiǔpíng.

flagrant /ˈfleɪgrənt/ *adj* 明目张〔張〕胆〔膽〕的 míng mù zhāng dǎn de; 公然的 gōngránde: ~ *disobedience* 公然抗拒. flagrantly *adv*.

flagstone /ˈflægstəʊn/ *n* [C] (铺地、铺路用)石板 shíbǎn.

flair /fleə(r)/ *n* [U, sing] 天赋 tiānfù; 资质〔質〕zīzhì; 才能 cáinéng: *She has a* ~ *for languages*. 她有语言天赋.

flake /fleɪk/ *n* [C] 薄片 bópiàn: ˈ*snow*~*s* 雪片. flake *v* [I] 1 雪片似地落下 xuěpiàn shìde luòxià. 2 [短语动词] flake out [非正式用语](因疲倦而)倒下 dǎoxià. flaky *adj* [-ier, -iest] 由一片片组成的 yóu yípiànpiàn zǔchéng de; 易剥落的 yì bōluò de.

flamboyant /flæmˈbɔɪənt/ *adj* 1 (人)爱〔愛〕炫耀的 ài xuànyào de. 2 艳〔艶〕丽〔麗〕的

yànlìde；灿〔燦〕烂〔爛〕的 cànlànde. **flamboyance** /-əns/ *n* [U]. **flamboyantly** *adv*.

flame /fleɪm/ *n* [C, U] 火焰 huǒyàn；火舌 huǒshé：*The house was in ~s*. 房屋着火了. **flame** *v* [I] **1** 发〔發〕出火焰 fāchū huǒyàn；燃烧〔燒〕ránshāo. **2** 呈火红色 chéng huǒhóngsè；发光 fāguāng. **flaming** *adj* 猛烈的 měngliède；激烈的 jīliède：*a flaming argument* 激烈的争论.

flamingo /flə'mɪŋgəʊ/ *n* [C] [*pl* ~s] 火烈鸟〔鳥〕huǒlièniǎo.

flammable /'flæməbl/ *adj* 易燃的 yìránde.

flan /flæn/ *n* [C] 果酱〔醬〕饼 guǒjiàngbǐng.

flank /flæŋk/ *n* [C] **1** 胁〔脇〕xié；胁腹 xiéfù. **2** [军事]侧翼 cèyì. **flank** *v* [T] 位于…的侧翼 wèiyú… de cèyì；包抄…的侧翼 bāochāo…de cèyì.

flannel /'flænl/ *n* **1** [U] 法兰〔蘭〕绒 fǎlánróng. **2 flannels** [pl] （男式）法兰绒裤子 fǎlánróng kùzi. **3** ⇨FACE-CLOTH (FACE).

flap /flæp/ *n* [C] **1**（口子的）覆盖〔蓋〕物（袋盖、信封口盖等）fùgàiwù. **2** 拍打 pāidǎ；拍击〔擊〕pāijī；拍打声〔聲〕pāidǎshēng. **3**（飞机）襟翼 jīnyì. **4** [习语] **be in / get into a flap** [非正式用语]慌乱〔亂〕huāngluàn；神经〔經〕紧〔緊〕张〔張〕shénjīng jǐnzhāng. **flap** *v* [-pp-] **1** [I, T]（使）上下左右拍动 shàngxià zuǒyòu pāidòng；挥〔揮〕动〔動〕huīdòng；摆〔擺〕动 bǎidòng：*sails ~ping in the wind* 在风中扑动的船帆. **2** [I, T] 轻〔輕〕轻拍打 qīngqīng pāidǎ：~ *the flies away* 把苍蝇赶走. *The bird ~ped its wing*. 鸟儿轻轻拍动翅膀. **3** [I] [非正式用语]激动 jīdòng；忧〔憂〕虑〔慮〕yōulǜ.

flare[1] /fleə(r)/ *v* **1** [I] 熊熊地燃烧〔燒〕xióngxióngde ránshāo. **2** [短语动词] **flare up** (a) 突然燃烧 tūrán ránshāo. (b) [喻]（暴烈行为等）突然爆发〔發〕tūrán bàofā. **flare** *n* [C] **1** [常作 sing] 摇曳的火焰 yáoyède huǒyàn；闪烁〔爍〕的火光 shǎnshuòde huǒguāng. **2** 闪光信号〔號〕装〔裝〕置 shǎnguāng xìnhào zhuāngzhì；闪光信号 shǎnguāng xìnhào. '**flare-up** *n* [C] **1** 突然发光 tūrán fāguāng；突然燃烧 tūrán ránshāo. **2** [喻]爆发暴力事件 bàofā bàolì shìjiàn.

flare[2] /fleə(r)/ *v* [I, T]（使）底部变〔變〕宽 dǐbù biànkuān：*a ~d skirt* 下摆宽大的衬衫. **flare** *n* [C] 逐渐变宽 zhújiàn biànkuān.

flash /flæʃ/ *n* **1** [C] 闪光 shǎnguāng；闪烁〔爍〕shǎnshuò：*a ~ of lightning* 一道闪电. [喻] *a ~ of inspiration* 灵感的闪现. **2** [C, U]（摄影）闪光灯〔燈〕shǎnguāngdēng. **3** [习语] **in a flash** 转〔轉〕瞬间 zhuǎnshùnjiān；一刹那 yíshànà. **flash** *adj* [非正式用语]华〔華〕而不实〔實〕的 huá ér bù shí de；俗艳〔豔〕的 súyànde. **flash** *v* **1** [I, T]（使）闪光 shǎnguāng；闪耀 shǎnyào；闪烁〔爍〕shǎnshuò. **2** [I] 闪现 shǎnxiàn；掠过〔過〕心头〔頭〕lüèguò xīntóu. **3** [T]（通过电视、卫星等）传〔傳〕送（新闻、信息等）chuánsòng. **4** [I] 飞〔飛〕驰 fēichí；掠过〔過〕lüèguò：*The train ~ed past us*. 火车从我们身旁飞驰而过. '**flashback** *n* [C]（电影等的）闪回（镜头）shǎnhuí. '**flashbulb** *n* [C] 闪光灯〔燈〕泡 shǎnguāng dēngpào. '**flashlight** *n* [C] **1** = FLASH 2. **2** [尤用于美语]手电〔電〕筒 shǒudiàntǒng. **flashy** *adj* [-ier, -iest] 俗艳的 súyànde：~*y clothes* 华丽而俗气的衣裳. **flashily** *adv*.

flask /flɑːsk; *US* flæsk/ *n* [C] **1** 细颈〔頸〕瓶 xìjǐngpíng. **2** 热〔熱〕水瓶 rèshuǐpíng. **3** = HIP-FLASK (HIP).

flat[1] /flæt/ *n* [C] [尤用于英国英语][亦作 **apartment**，尤用于美语]（用作住家的在同层楼上的）一套房间〔間〕yítào fángjiān.

flat[2] /flæt/ *adj* [~ter, ~test] **1** 平的 píngde；平坦的 píngtǎnde；扁平的 biǎnpíngde. **2** 平展的 píngzhǎnde；平伸的 píngshēnde：*lying ~ on her back*（她）平躺着. **3** 浅〔淺〕的 qiǎnde：*a ~ dish* 浅盘子. **4** 枯燥的 kūzàode；乏味的 fáwèide. **5**（电池）电〔電〕用完了的 diàn yòng wán le de. **6**（轮胎）没有气〔氣〕了的 méiyǒu qì le de. **7**（饮料）没有气泡了的 méiyǒu qìpào le de. **8** 绝对〔對〕的 juéduìde：*a ~ refusal* 断然拒绝. **9**（价格等）固定的 gùdìngde：*a ~ rate* 固定收费率. **10** [音乐]降音的 jiàngyīnde. **flat** *adv* **1** 平坦地 píngtǎnde；平直地 píngzhíde. **2** 恰好 qiàhǎo；正好 zhènghǎo：*in 10 seconds ~* 正好 10 秒钟. **3** [音乐]降音地 jiàngyīnde. **4** [习语] **flat 'out** [非正式用语]竭尽〔盡〕全力 jié jìn quánlì. ˌ**flat-'footed** *adj* 有扁平足的 yǒu biǎnpíngzú de. '**flatpack** *n* [C] 组装〔裝〕式 zǔzhuāngshì；扁平组件包装 biǎnpíng zǔjiàn bāozhuāng：*flatpack furniture* 组装式家具.

flat[3] /flæt/ *n* **1** [sing] 平坦部分 píngtǎn bùfen. **2** [C, 常作 pl] 平地 píngdì；浅〔淺〕滩〔灘〕qiǎntān：'*mud ~s* 泥泞的浅滩. **3** [C] [音乐]降半音 jiàngbànyīn. **4** [C] [尤用于美语]没有气〔氣〕了的轮〔輪〕胎 méiyǒu qì le de lúntāi.

flatten /'flætn/ *v* [I, T] 把…弄平 bǎ… nòngpíng；变〔變〕平 biànpíng.

flatter /'flætə(r)/ *v* [T] **1** 阿谀 ēyú；奉承 fèngcheng. **2** [常用被动语态]使高兴〔興〕shǐ gāoxìng. **3**（肖像、画等）胜〔勝〕过〔過〕（真人、真物）shèngguò. **flatterer** *n* [C]. **flattery** *n* [U] 捧场〔場〕的话 pěngchǎngde huà.

flaunt /flɔːnt/ *v* [T] 夸〔誇〕耀 kuāyào；夸示 kuāshì：~ *one's wealth* 炫耀财富.

F

flautist /ˈflɔːtɪst/ *n* [C] 笛手 díshǒu.

flavour (美语 -or) /ˈfleɪvə(r)/ *n* 1 [U] 味 wèi: *add salt to improve the* ~ 加盐以提味. 2 [C] 风(風)味 fēngwèi; 情味 qíngwèi; 风(風)韵 fēngyùn: *six* ~*s of ice-cream* 六味冰淇淋. 3 [C,U] 特点(點) tèdiǎn. **flavour** *v* [T] 给…调味 gěi…tiáowèi; 给…增添风趣 gěi…zēngtiān fēngqù. **flavouring** *n* [C,U] 调味品 tiáowèipǐn. **flavourless** *adj*.

flaw /flɔː/ *n* [C] 瑕疵 xiácī; 缺点(點) quēdiǎn. **flaw** *v* [T] 使有缺点 shǐ yǒu quēdiǎn. **flawless** *adj* 无(無)缺点的 wú quēdiǎn de; 完美的 wánměide. **flawlessly** *adv*.

flax /flæks/ *n* [U] 亚(亞)麻 yàmá. **flaxen** /flæksn/ *adj* (头发)亚麻色的 yàmásède; 淡黄色的 dànhuángsède.

F

flea /fliː/ *n* [C] 蚤 zǎo.

fleck /flek/ *n* [C] 斑点(點) bāndiǎn; 微粒 wēilì. **fleck** *v* [T] 使有斑点 shǐ yǒu bāndiǎn.

flee /fliː/ *v* [*pt*, *pp* **fled** /fled/] [I,T] (*from*) 迅速离(離)开(開) xùnsù líkāi; 逃 táo; 逃走 táozǒu.

fleece /fliːs/ *n* [C] (未剪下的)羊毛 yángmáo. **fleece** *v* [T] 敲诈 qiāozhà; 诈取 zhàqǔ. **fleecy** *adj* 羊毛似的 yángmáo shì de; 羊毛制(製)的 yángmáo zhì de.

fleet /fliːt/ *n* [C] 1 舰(艦)队(隊) jiànduì. 2 船队 chuánduì; 机(機)群 jīqún; 汽车(車)队 qìchēduì.

fleeting /ˈfliːtɪŋ/ *adj* 飞(飛)逝的 fēishìde; 短暂的 duǎnzànde: *a* ~ *glimpse* 瞟一眼.

flesh /fleʃ/ *n* 1 [U] 肉 ròu. 2 [U] 果肉 guǒròu. 3 **the flesh** [sing] 肉体(體)(与精神、灵魂相对而言) ròutǐ. 4 [习语] **in the flesh** 本人 běnrén; 在实(實)际(際)生活中 zài shíjì shēnghuó zhōng. **make one's flesh crawl / creep** 令人毛骨悚然 lìng rén máo gǔ sǒngrán. **one's ˌown ˌflesh and ˈblood** 亲(親)骨肉 qīngǔròu. **fleshy** *adj* 肥胖的 féipàngde.

flew /fluː/ *pt* of FLY[1].

flex[1] /fleks/ *n* [C, U] (电)花线(綫) huāxiàn; 皮线 píxiàn.

flex[2] /fleks/ *v* [T] 屈曲(四肢) qūqū; 活动(動)(肌肉) huódòng.

flexible /ˈfleksəbl/ *adj* 1 易弯(彎)曲的 yì wānqū de; 柔软(軟)的 róuruǎnde. 2 灵(靈)活的 línghuóde; 能适(適)应(應)的 néng shìyìng de: ~ *plans* 灵活的计划. **flexibility** /ˌfleksəˈbɪlətɪ/ *n* [U].

flexitime /ˈfleksɪtaɪm/, **flextime** /ˈfleks-taɪm/ *n* [U] 弹(彈)性工作时(時)间 tánxìng gōngzuò shíjiān.

flick /flɪk/ *n* [C] 1 轻(輕)打 qīngdǎ; 轻弹(彈) qīngtán. 2 抖 dǒu: *with a* ~ *of the wrist* 手腕一抖. **flick** *v* 1 [T] 轻打 qīngdǎ; 轻拍 qīngpāi; 轻弹 qīngtán. 2 [短语动词] **flick through sth** 快速地翻阅 kuàisùde fānyuè.

flicker /ˈflɪkə(r)/ *v* [I] 1 (光、焰等)闪烁(爍) shǎnshuò, 摇曳 yáoyè. 2 (希望等)闪现 shǎnxiàn. 3 (轻微地)颤动(動) chàndòng; 摆(擺)动 bǎidòng. **flicker** *n* [C, 常作 sing] 1 闪烁 shǎnshuò; 摇曳 yáoyè. 2 [喻]闪现 shǎnxiàn.

flier (亦作 **flyer**) /ˈflaɪə(r)/ *n* [C] 飞(飛)行员 fēixíngyuán.

flight[1] /flaɪt/ *n* 1 [U] 飞(飛)行 fēixíng; 飞翔 fēixiáng: *the development of* ~ 飞行的发展. 2 [C] (a) 空中旅行 kōngzhōng lǚxíng; (b) 航班 hángbān: ~ *number BA4793 from London* 从伦敦来的 BA4793 航班. 3 [C] 一群飞鸟(鳥) yìqún fēiniǎo; 一群飞机(機) yìqún fēijī. 4 [C] (两层楼之间的)一段楼(樓)梯 yíduàn lóutī. 5 [习语] **ˈflight attendant** *n* [C](飞机)乘务(務)员 chéngwùyuán. **a flight of ˈfancy** 异(異)想天开(開) yì xiǎng tiān kāi. **ˈflight path** *n* [C] (飞机的)飞行路线(綫) fēixíng lùxiàn.

flight[2] /flaɪt/ *n* [C, U] 逃跑 táopǎo.

flimsy /ˈflɪmzɪ/ *adj* [-ier, -iest] 1 轻(輕)而薄的 qīng ér bó de; 容易损坏(壞)的 róngyì sǔnhuài de. 2 [喻]脆弱的 cuìruòde: *a* ~ *excuse* 站不住脚的借口. **flimsily** *adv*.

flinch /flɪntʃ/ *v* [I] 退缩 tuìsuō; 畏缩 wèisuō.

fling /flɪŋ/ *v* [*pt*, *pp* **flung** /flʌŋ/] [T] 1 掷(擲) zhì; 抛 pāo; 扔 rēng; 猛烈移动(動) měngliè yídòng. 2 [短语动词] **fling oneself into sth** 投身于工作 tóushēn yú gōngzuò. **fling** *n* [C] 1 抛 pāo; 掷 zhì; 扔 rēng. 2 一时(時)的放纵(縱)行乐(樂) yìshíde fàngzòng xínglè: *have a* ~ *after the exams* 考试以后纵情玩了一阵. 3 奔放的苏(蘇)格兰(蘭)舞蹈 bēnfàngde sūgélán wǔdǎo.

flint /flɪnt/ *n* 1 [C, U] 燧石 suìshí; 打火石 dǎhuǒshí. 2 [C] (打火机)电(電)石 diànshí.

flip /flɪp/ *v* [-pp-] 1 [T] 捻掷(擲) niǎnzhì: ~ *a coin* 捻掷硬币. 2 [I] [非正式用语]发(發)怒 fānù. **flip** *n* [C] 弹 tán; 抛 pāo; 轻(輕)击(擊) qīngjī. **ˈflip chart** *n* [C] 活动(動)挂(掛)图(圖) huódòng guàtú; 翻纸板 fānzhǐbǎn.

flippant /ˈflɪpənt/ *adj* 无(無)礼(禮)的 wúlǐde; 不客气(氣)的 bú kèqì de. **flippancy** /-ənsɪ/ *n* [U]. **flippantly** *adv*.

flipper /ˈflɪpə(r)/ *n* [C] 1 (某些海中动物的)鳍状(狀)肢 qízhuàngzhī. 2 橡皮脚掌(游泳用) xiàngpí jiǎozhǎng; 足蹼 zúpǔ.

flirt /flɜːt/ *v* [I] 1(*with*) 调情 tiáoqíng; 卖(賣)俏 màiqiào. 2 *with* 对…偶尔(爾)想想而已 duì…ǒu'ěr xiǎngxiǎng éryǐ. **flirt** *n* [C] 调情者 tiáoqíngzhě. **flirtation** /flɜːˈteɪʃn/ *n* [C, U]. **flirtatious** /flɜːˈteɪʃəs/ *adj* 爱(愛)

调情的 ài tiáoqíngde；轻〔輕〕佻的 qīngtiāode.

flit /flɪt/ *v* [-tt-] [I] 掠过〔過〕lüèguò；飞〔飛〕过 fēiguò.

float /fləʊt/ *v* **1** [I, T] 漂浮 piāo fú；浮 fú；使漂浮 shǐ piāofú；使浮 shǐ fú. **2** [T] 提出(意见、计划等) tíchū. **3** 筹〔籌〕资开〔開〕办〔辦〕(公司等) chóuzī kāibàn. **4** [I, T] (货币)币值浮动〔動〕bìzhí fúdòng；使币值浮动 shǐ bìzhí fúdòng. **float** *n* [C] **1** (常用于在水中承载较重物品的)漂浮物 piāofúwù. **2** (游行时装载展品的)低架平板车〔車〕dījià píngbǎnchē. **3** (商店的)日常零钱〔錢〕rìcháng língqián. **floating** *adj* 不固定的 bú gùdìng de；浮动〔動〕的 fúdòngde.

flock /flɒk/ *n* [C] **1** (鸟、兽等)群 qún. **2** 一群人 yìqúnrén. **3** 基督教会〔會〕的会众〔衆〕Jīdūjiàohuì de huìzhòng. **flock** *v* [I] 成群行动〔動〕chéngqún xíngdòng；蜂拥〔擁〕fēngyōng：*Crowds ~ed to the football match*. 一群一群的人蜂拥去看足球比赛.

flog /flɒg/ *v* [-gg-] [T] **1** 鞭打 biāndǎ；抽打 chōudǎ. **2** [俚]卖〔賣〕mài. **3** [习语] ˌ**flog a dead ˈhorse** [非正式用语]浪费精力 làngfèi jīnglì. ˌ**flog sth to ˈdeath** [非正式用语]"炒冷饭""chǎo lěngfàn". **flogging** *n* [C, U] 抽打 chōudǎ.

flood /flʌd/ *n* [C] **1** 洪水 hóngshuǐ；水灾〔災〕shuǐzāi. **2** [喻]大量 dàliàng：*a ~ of tears* 泪流满面. *a ~ of letters* 信件雪片飞来. **flood** *v* [I, T] **1** 淹没 yānmò；泛滥〔濫〕fànlàn. **2** 充满 chōngmǎn；充斥 chōngchì：[喻] *A sense of relief ~ed over her*. 她深感宽慰. **3** [短语动词] **flood in** 大量涌来 dàliàng yǒnglái. ˈ**flood-tide** *n* [C, U] 涨〔漲〕潮 zhǎngcháo.

floodlight /ˈflʌdlaɪt/ *n* [C, 常作 pl] 泛光灯〔燈〕fànguāngdēng. **floodlight** *v* [*pt*, *pp* **floodlit** /-lɪt/] [T] 用泛光照亮 yòng fànguāng zhàoliàng.

floor /flɔː(r)/ *n* **1** [C] 地面 dìmiàn；地板 dìbǎn. **2** [C] (海洋、山洞等的)底 dǐ. **3** [C] 楼〔樓〕层〔層〕lóucéng：*I live on the fourth ~*. 我住在五楼. **4** [C, 常作 sing] (某些活动的)场〔場〕地 chǎngdì：*the dance ~* 舞池. *the factory / shop ~* 车间. **5** [习语] ˌ**take the ˈfloor** (在辩论中)发〔發〕言 fāyán. **floor** *v* [T] **1** 在…上铺地板 zài…shàng pū dìbǎn；在…上铺地面 zài…shàng pū dìmiàn. **2** 击〔擊〕败 jībài，把…打倒在地 bǎ…dǎdǎo zài dì. **3** (问题等)难〔難〕倒 nándǎo，使困惑 shǐ kùnhuò. ˈ**floor-board** *n* [C] 做地板用的木板 zuò dìbǎn yòng de mùbǎn. ˈ**floor show** *n* [C] 夜总〔總〕会〔會〕的文娱〔娛〕表演 yèzǒnghuìde wényú biǎoyǎn.

flop /flɒp/ *v* [-pp-] [I] **1** 笨拙地移动〔動〕或倒下 bènzhuóde yídòng huò dǎoxià；无〔無〕奈地移动或躺下 wúnàide yídòng huò tǎngxià：*~ exhausted into a chair* 精疲力竭噗地一下坐到椅子上. **2** [非正式用语](书、电影)失败 shībài. **flop** *n* [C] **1** [常作 sing] 拍击〔擊〕pāijī；拍击声〔聲〕pāijīshēng；重坠〔墜〕声 zhòngzhuìshēng；重坠 zhòngzhuì. **2** [非正式用语](书、电影等的)失败 shībài. **floppy** *adj* [-ier, -iest] 松〔鬆〕软地下垂的 sōngruǎnde xiàchuí de；耷拉着的 dālazhede；松软的 sōngruǎnde：*a ~py hat* 松软的帽子. ˌ**floppy ˈdisk** *n* [C] [电子计算机] 软磁盘 ruǎn cípán.

flora /ˈflɔːrə/ *n* [pl, U] 某一地区〔區〕或某一时〔時〕期的植物群 mǒuyī dìqū huò mǒuyī shíqī de zhíwùqún.

floral /ˈflɔːrəl/ *adj* 花的 huāde.

florid /ˈflɒrɪd; *US* ˈflɔːrɪd/ *adj* **1** [常贬]过〔過〕分华〔華〕丽〔麗〕的 guòfèn huálì de；过分装〔裝〕饰的 guòfèn zhuāngshì de. **2** (人脸)发〔發〕红的 fāhóngde.

florist /ˈflɒrɪst; *US* ˈflɔːr-/ *n* [C] 花商 huāshāng.

flotation /fləʊˈteɪʃn/ *n* [C, U] (企业的)筹〔籌〕资开〔開〕办〔辦〕chóuzī kāibàn.

flotilla /fləˈtɪlə/ *n* [C] 小舰〔艦〕队〔隊〕xiǎo jiànduì；小船队 xiǎo chuánduì.

flounce /flaʊns/ *v* [I] 愤然离〔離〕去 fènrán líqù：*She ~d out of the room*. 她愤怒地走出房间.

flounder /ˈflaʊndə(r)/ *v* [I] **1** (陷入水中等时)挣扎 zhēngzhá；(肢体)乱〔亂〕动〔動〕luàndòng. **2** [喻]错乱地做事 cuòluànde zuò shì；胡乱说话 húluàn shuōhuà.

flour /ˈflaʊə(r)/ *n* [U] 面〔麵〕粉 miànfěn.

flourish /ˈflʌrɪʃ/ *v* **1** [I] 繁荣〔榮〕fánróng；兴〔興〕旺 xīngwàng；兴盛 xīngshèng：*Her business is ~ing*. 她生意兴隆. **2** [I] 健壮〔壯〕地生长 jiànzhuàngde shēngzhǎng. **3** [T] 挥舞 huīwǔ：*~ a pen* 挥舞着笔. **flourish** *n* [C, 常作 sing] **1** 挥舞 huīwǔ. **2** 高昂的乐〔樂〕段 gāo'ángde yuèduàn.

flout /flaʊt/ *v* [T] 藐视 miǎoshì；轻〔輕〕视 qīngshì.

flow /fləʊ/ *v* [I] **1** (液体)流 liú，流通 liútōng：[喻] *Keep the traffic ~ing*. 保持车辆畅行无阻. **2** (潮)涨〔漲〕zhǎng. **3** (头发)飘〔飄〕垂 piāochuí，飘拂 piāofú. **4** [短语动词] **flow from sth** 来〔來〕自 láizì；产〔產〕生于 chǎnshēng yú. **flow** *n* **1** [C, 常作 sing] 流通 liútōng；水流 shuǐliú；持续〔續〕供应〔應〕chíxù gōngyìng. **2** (常作 **the flow**) [sing] 涨潮 zhǎngcháo.

flower /ˈflaʊə(r)/ *n* **1** [C] 花 huā；花卉 huāhuì. **2** [sing] [修辞]精华〔華〕jīnghuá：*the ~ of the nation's youth* 全国青年的精华. **flower** *v* [I] 开〔開〕花 kāihuā. ˈ**flower-bed**

F

n [C] 花坛〔壇〕huātán. ˈ**flowerpot** *n* [C] 花盆 huāpén. **flowery** *adj* **1** 多花的 duōhuāde. **2** (语言)词藻华丽〔麗〕的 cízǎo huálì de: *a ~y speech* 词藻华丽的演说.

flown /fləʊn/ *pp* of FLY[1].

flu /fluː/ *n* [U] [非正式用语]流行性感冒 liúxíng xìng gǎnmào.

fluctuate /ˈflʌktʃʊeɪt/ *v* [I] **1** (物价等)涨〔漲〕落 zhǎngluò; 起落 qǐluò; 波动〔動〕bōdòng. **2** (态度)动摇不定 dòngyáo búdìng. **fluctuation** /ˌflʌktʃʊˈeɪʃn/ *n* [C, U].

fluent /ˈfluːənt/ *adj* **1** (人)说话流利的 shuōhuà liúlì de: *He's ~ in Spanish*. 他西班牙语说得很流利. **2** (演说等)流畅〔暢〕的 liúchàngde: *speak ~ English* 英语说得很流畅. **fluency** /-ənsɪ/ *n* [U]. **fluently** *adv*.

F

fluff /flʌf/ *n* [U] **1** (毛织品上的)绒毛 róngmáo. **2** (幼兽身上的)软毛 ruǎnmáo. **fluff** *v* [T] **1** 抖开〔開〕dǒu kāi; 抖松〔鬆〕dǒu sōng: *~ up a pillow* 抖松枕头. **2** [非正式用语]把…弄糟 bǎ…nòng zāo: *He ~ed his exams*. 他考试考糟了. **fluffy** *adj* [-ier, -iest] 软而轻〔輕〕的 ruǎn ér qīng de; 毛绒绒的 máoróngróngde: *a ~y cat* 毛绒绒的猫.

fluid /ˈfluːɪd/ *adj* **1** 流动〔動〕的 liúdòngde. **2** (思想等)不固定的 bú gùdìng de, 易变〔變〕的 yìbiànde. **fluid** *n* [C, U] 流体〔體〕liútǐ; 液 yè.

fluke /fluːk/ *n* [C, 常作 sing]侥〔僥〕倖的成功 jiǎoxìngde chénggōng.

flung /flʌŋ/ *pt*, *pp* of FLING.

fluorescent /flʊəˈresnt; *US* flʊəˈr-/ *adj* 荧〔熒〕光的 yíngguāngde; 发〔發〕荧光的 fā yíngguāng de.

fluoride /ˈflɔːraɪd; *US* ˈflʊər-/ *n* [U] 氟化物 fúhuàwù.

flurry /ˈflʌrɪ/ *n* [C] [*pl* -ies] **1** 阵风〔風〕zhènfēng; 一阵雪 yízhèn xuě. **2** [喻]活动〔動〕的突然发〔發〕生 huódòngde tūrán fāshēng: *a ~ of activity* 一阵活动. *a ~ of excitement* 一阵紧张. **flurry** *v* [*pt*, *pp* -ied] [T] 使混乱〔亂〕shǐ hùnluàn; 使慌乱 shǐ huāngluàn.

flush[1] /flʌʃ/ *n* **1** [sing] 急流 jíliú; (厕所的)冲水 chōngshuǐ. **2** [C, 常作 sing] (脸)红晕 hóngyùn. **3** [C, 常作 sing] 突然的激动〔動〕tūránde jīdòng. **flush** *v* **1** [I, T] (脸)发〔發〕红 fā hóng; 使(脸)发红 shǐ fā hóng. **2** [T] 冲洗 chōngxǐ: *~ the toilet* 冲洗马桶. **flushed** *adj* 得意的 déyìde.

flush[2] /flʌʃ/ *adj* **1** 齐〔齊〕平的 qípíngde. **2** [非正式用语]富有的 fùyǒude.

fluster /ˈflʌstə(r)/ *v* [T] 使慌张〔張〕shǐ huāngzhāng; 使慌乱〔亂〕shǐ huāngluàn. **fluster** *n* [sing] 慌张 huāngzhāng.

flute /fluːt/ *n* [C] 长〔長〕笛 chángdí.

flutter /ˈflʌtə(r)/ *v* **1** [I, T] (鸟)振翼 zhènyì; 拍翅 pāichì; 振〔翼〕zhèn; 拍〔翅〕pāi. **2** [I, T] 颤动〔動〕chàndòng; 使颤动 shǐ chàndòng: *curtains ~ing in the breeze* 在微风中颤动的窗帘. **3** [I] (心脏)不规则地跳动 bù guīzé de tiàodòng. **flutter** *n* **1** [C, 常作 sing] 颤动 chàndòng. **2** [sing] 焦急 jiāojí.

flux /flʌks/ *n* [U] (不断的)变〔變〕动〔動〕biàndòng: *in a state of ~* 处于不断变化之中.

fly[1] /flaɪ/ *v* [*pt* **flew** /fluː/, *pp* **flown** /fləʊn/] **1** [I] 飞〔飛〕fēi; 飞翔 fēixiáng; 乘飞机〔機〕旅行 chéng fēijī lǚxíng. **2** [T] 驾驶(飞机) jiàshǐ. **3** [I] 飞跑 fēipǎo: *It's late, I must ~*. 已经晚了,我必须快跑. **4** [T] 升(旗) shēng. **5** [习语] **fly in the face of sth** 与〔與〕…相违〔違〕背 yǔ…xiāng wéibèi; 反对〔對〕fǎnduì. **fly into a ˈpassion, ˈrage, ˈtemper, etc** 勃然大怒 bórán dànù. ˈ**fly-by-wire** *n* [U] 线〔綫〕控飞行 xiànkòng fēixíng; 线传〔傳〕飞控 xiànchuán fēikòng. ˈ**fly-drive** *adj* 陆〔陸〕空联〔聯〕游的 lùkōng liányóu de. ˌ**flying ˈsaucer** *n* [C] 飞碟 fēidié; 不明飞行物 bùmíng fēixíngwù. ˈ**flying squad** *n* [C] (警察局处理危急犯罪的)闪电〔電〕行动〔動〕队〔隊〕shǎndiàn xíngdòng duì. ˌ**flying ˈstart** *n* [C] 很好的开〔開〕端 hěnhǎode kāiduān. ˌ**flying ˈvisit** *n* [C] (短暂的)闪电式访问 shǎndiànshì fǎngwèn.

fly[2] /flaɪ/ *n* [C] [*pl* **flies**] **1** 苍〔蒼〕蝇〔蠅〕cāngying. **2** (作钓饵用的)苍蝇 cāngying, 假蝇 jiǎyíng. ˈ**fly-on-the-wall** *adj* (影视制作)非常逼真的 fēicháng bīzhēnde; 非常自然的 fēicháng zìránde.

fly[3] /flaɪ/ *n* [C, 常作 pl] [*pl* **flies**] 裤子上拉链的遮盖〔蓋〕kùzi shàng lāliànde zhēgài.

flyer = FLIER.

flyleaf /ˈflaɪliːf/ *n* [C] [*pl* -leaves /-liːvz/] (书的)扉页 fēiyè; 飞〔飛〕页 fēiyè.

flyover /ˈflaɪəʊvə(r)/ *n* [C] (公路上的)陆〔陸〕桥〔橋〕lùqiáo, 立交桥 lìjiāoqiáo.

foal /fəʊl/ *n* [C] 小马 xiǎomǎ; 驹〔駒〕jū.

foam /fəʊm/ *n* [U] 泡沫 pàomò. **foam** *v* [I] 起泡沫 qǐ pàomò; 发〔發〕出泡沫 fāchū pàomò. ˌ**foam ˈrubber** *n* [U] 海绵橡胶〔膠〕hǎimián xiàngjiāo; 泡沫橡胶 pàomò xiàngjiāo.

fob /fɒb/ *v* [-bb-] [短语动词] **fob sb off (with) sth** 搪塞 tángsè: *He ~bed me off with a weak excuse*. 他用很勉强的借口搪塞我.

focus /ˈfəʊkəs/ *n* [C] **1** 焦点〔點〕jiāodiǎn. **2** [常作 sing] (兴趣等的)集中点 jízhōng diǎn, 中心 zhōngxīn: *the ~ of attention* 注意的中心. **3** [习语] **in focus** 清晰的 qīngxīde; 焦点

对〔對〕准〔準〕的 jiāodiǎn duìzhǔn de. **out of focus** 不清晰的 bù qīngxī de; 焦点未对准的 jiāodiǎn wèi duìzhǔn de. **focus** *v* [-s- 或 -ss-] 1 [I, T] 调节〔節〕(…的)焦距 tiáojié jiāojù. 2 [T] (*on*) 集中(注意) jízhōng.

fodder /ˈfɒdə(r)/ *n* [U] 粗饲料 cū sìliào; 草料 cǎoliào.

foe /fəʊ/ *n* [C] [正式用语或旧词]敌〔敵〕人 dírén.

foetus /ˈfiːtəs/ *n* [C] 胎儿〔兒〕tāi'ér; 胎 tāi.

fog /fɒg; *US* fɔːg/ *n* 1 [U] 雾〔霧〕wù: *I couldn't see through the ~.* 有雾,我看不见. 2 [C, U] [摄影](底片、照片上的)灰雾 huīwù. **fog** *v* [-gg-] [I, T] (被、以)雾气笼〔籠〕罩 wùqì lǒngzhào: *The window has ~ged up.* 窗玻璃上满是雾气. ˈ**fogbound** 因雾受阻的 yīn wù shòu zǔ de. **foggy** *adj* [-ier, -iest] 雾蒙蒙的 wùméngméngde: *a ~gy night* 雾蒙蒙的夜. ˈ**fog-horn** *n* [C] 雾角(警告浓雾的号角) wùjiǎo. ˈ**fog-lamp** *n* [C] (汽车在雾中使用的)雾灯〔燈〕wùdēng.

foil[1] /fɔɪl/ *n* 1 [U] 金属〔屬〕薄片 jīnshǔ báopiàn; 箔 bó: *tin ~* 锡纸. 2 [C] 陪衬〔襯〕物 péichènwù; 陪衬者 péichènzhě.

foil[2] /fɔɪl/ *v* [T] 挫败 cuòbài.

foist /fɔɪst/ *v* [短语动词] **foist sth on sb** 把…强加给… bǎ…qiángjiā gěi….

fold[1] /fəʊld/ *v* 1 [T] 折叠 zhédié: *~ a letter* 折信. 2 [I] 可被折叠 kě bèi zhédié: *a ~ing bed* 折叠床. 3 [I] (企业)停业〔業〕tíngyè; 倒闭 dǎobì. 4 [习语] **fold one's arms** 双〔雙〕臂在胸前交叉 shuāngbì zài xiōngqián jiāochā. **fold** *n* [C] 1 褶 zhě. 2 褶痕 zhěhén. **folder** *n* [C] (硬纸)文件夹〔夾〕wénjiànjiā.

fold[2] /fəʊld/ *n* [C] 羊栏〔欄〕yánglán.

foliage /ˈfəʊlɪɪdʒ/ *n* [U] [正式用语]树〔樹〕或植物的叶〔葉〕子的总〔總〕称〔稱〕shù huò zhíwù de yèzi de zǒngchēng.

folk /fəʊk/ *n* 1 [pl] 人们〔們〕rénmen. 2 **folks** [pl] [非正式用语]家属〔屬〕jiāshǔ; 亲〔親〕属 qīnshǔ: *the ~s at home* 家里的人. 3 [U] 民间音乐〔樂〕mínjiānyīnyuè. ˈ**folk-dance** *n* [C] 民间舞 mínjiānwǔ; 民间舞的音乐 mínjiānwǔde yīnyuè. ˈ**folklore** /ˈfəʊklɔː(r)/ *n* [U] 民俗 mínsú; 民俗学〔學〕mínsúxué. ˈ**folk-music** *n* [U] (亦作 ˈ**folk-song** [C]) 民间音乐 mínjiānyīnyuè; 民歌 míngē.

follow /ˈfɒləʊ/ *v* 1 [I] 跟随〔隨〕gēnsuí. 2 [T] 沿着(路等) yánzhe. 3 [T] 遵照…行事 zūnzhào…xíngshì: *~ her advice* 听从她的劝告. 4 [T] 从〔從〕事(工作、行业等) cóngshì: *~ a career in law* 做法律工作. 5 [T] 对〔對〕…有兴〔興〕趣 duì… yǒu xìngqù: *~ all the football news* 关心所有足球新闻. 6 [I, T] 理解 lǐjiě; 懂 dǒng: *I don't ~ (your meaning).* 我不懂(你的意思). 7 [I] 作为〔爲〕…的必然结果 zuòwéi…de bìrán jiéguǒ; 因…而起 yīn…érqǐ: *It ~s from what you say that...* 按你所说,则必然会…. 8 [T] 听〔聽〕着别人的朗读〔讀〕跟着阅读(文字) tīngzhe biérén de lǎngdú gēnzhe yuèdú. 9 [习语] **as follows** (用于列举)如下 rúxià. **follow in** ˌ**sb's** ˈ**footsteps** 效法他人 xiàofǎ tārén. **follow one's** ˈ**nose** 由本能指引 yóu běnnéng zhíyǐn. **follow** ˈ**suit** 仿〔倣〕效榜样〔樣〕fǎngxiào bǎngyàng. 10 [短语动词] **follow sth through** 进〔進〕行到底 jìnxíng dàodǐ; 坚〔堅〕持完成 jiānchí wánchéng. **follow sth up** (a) 采〔採〕取进一步行动〔動〕cǎiqǔ jìnyíbù xíngdòng: *~ up a suggestion* 建议之后采取行动. (b) 追查 zhuīchá: *~ up a clue* 追查线索. **follower** *n* [C] 支持者 zhīchízhě; 追随〔隨〕者 zhuīsuízhě. ˈ**follow-up** *n* [C] 后〔後〕续〔續〕行动 hòuxù xíngdòng: *~-up visit* 后续访问.

following /ˈfɒləʊɪŋ/ *adj* 1 接着的 jiēzhede. 2 下列的 xiàliède; 下述的 xiàshùde. *Answer the ~ questions.* 回答下列问题. **following** *n* [sing] 一批支持者 yìpī zhīchízhě. **following** *prep* 在…之后〔後〕zài… zhī hòu; 由于 yóuyú.

folly /ˈfɒlɪ/ *n* [*pl* -ies] 1 [U] 愚蠢 yúchǔn; 笨拙 bènzhuó. 2 [C] 笨事 bènshì; 傻〔傻〕主意 shǎ zhǔyì.

fond /fɒnd/ *adj* 1 *of* 喜欢〔歡〕…的 xǐhuan… de; 喜爱〔愛〕…的 xǐ'ài…de. 2 深情的 shēnqíngde: *a ~ embrace* 深情的拥抱. 3 (愿望等)热〔熱〕切而很难〔難〕实〔實〕现的 rèqiè ér hěnnán shíxiàn de: *~ belief* 难以实现的信念. *~ wish* 美梦. **fondly** *adv*. **fondness** *n* [U].

fondle /ˈfɒndl/ *v* [T] 爱〔愛〕抚〔撫〕àifǔ; 抚弄 fǔnòng.

font /fɒnt/ *n* [C] (基督教)洗礼〔禮〕盘〔盤〕xǐlǐpán.

food /fuːd/ *n* 1 [U] 食物 shíwù: *a shortage of ~* 食物短缺. 2 [C] (某种)食品 shípǐn: *health ~s* 保健食品. 3 [习语] **food for** ˈ**thought** 发〔發〕人深思的事 fā rén shēnsī de shì. ˈ**foodstuff** *n* [C] 食物 shíwù.

fool /fuːl/ *n* [C] 1 [贬]傻〔傻〕子 shǎzi; 笨蛋 bèndàn. 2 [习语] **make a** ˈ**fool of oneself** 做蠢事出丑〔醜〕zuò chǔnshì chūchǒu. **fool** *v* 1 [I] 干〔幹〕蠢事 gàn chǔnshì: *Stop ~ing around.* 别胡混了. 2 [T] 欺骗 qīpiàn. 3 [I] 玩弄 wánnòng; 戏〔戲〕弄 xìnòng. **fool** *adj* [非正式用语,贬]愚蠢的 yúchǔnde: *some ~ politician* 一些愚蠢的政客. **foolhardy** /-hɑːdɪ/ *adj* 有勇无〔無〕谋的 yǒu yǒng wú móu de. **foolish** *adj* 愚蠢的 yúchǔnde. **fool-**

ishly *adv*. foolishness *n* [U]. ˈ**foolproof** /-pruːf/ *adj* 不会〔會〕出毛病的 búhuì chū máobìng de: *a ~proof plan* 万全之策.

foot /fʊt/ *n* [*pl* **feet** /fiːt/] **1** [C] 脚 jiǎo; 足 zú. **2** [C] 英尺 yīngchǐ. **3** [sing] 下端 xiàduān: *at the ~ of the stairs* 在楼梯的下端. **4** [习语] **fall / land on one's ˈfeet** 逢凶〔兇〕化吉 féng xiōng huà jí; 化险〔險〕为〔爲〕夷 huà xiǎn wéi yí. **on foot** 步行 bùxíng. **put one's ˈfeet up** 休息 xiūxi. **put one's ˈfoot down** 坚〔堅〕决压〔壓〕制 jiānjué yāzhì. **put one's ˈfoot in it** 说错话shuō cuòhuà; 做错事 zuò cuòshì. **foot** *v* [习语] **foot the ˈbill** 付账〔賬〕fùzhàng; 付钱〔錢〕fùqián. ˈ**football** *n* **1** [C] 足球 zúqiú; 橄榄〔欖〕球 gǎnlǎnqiú. **2** 足球赛 zúqiúsài; 橄榄球赛 gǎnlǎnqiúsài. **footballer** *n* [C]. ˈ**football pools** *n* [pl] 足球赛赌博 zúqiúsài dǔbó. ˈ**foothill** *n* [C, 常作 pl] 山麓小丘 shānlù xiǎoqiū. ˈ**foothold** *n* [C] **1** (攀登时可踩脚的)立足处〔處〕lìzúchù. **2** [喻]立足点〔點〕lìzúdiǎn; 据〔據〕点 jùdiǎn. ˈ**footnote** *n* [C] 脚注〔註〕jiǎozhù. **footpath** *n* [C] 人行道 rénxíngdào. **footprint** *n* [C, 常作 pl] 足迹 zújì; 脚印 jiǎoyìn. **footstep** *n* [C, 常作 pl] 脚步声〔聲〕jiǎobùshēng; 脚印 jiǎoyìn. **footwear** *n* [U] (总称)鞋类〔類〕xiélèi.

footing /ˈfʊtɪŋ/ *n* [sing] **1** 站稳〔穩〕zhànwěn. **2** 关〔關〕系〔係〕guānxi: *on an equal ~* 处于平等的关系.

for /fə(r); 强读 fɔː(r)/ *prep* **1** (表示接受某事物的人)给…的 gěi…de. **2** (表示目的或功能)为〔爲〕了 wèile: *go ~ a walk* 去散步. *What's this machine ~?* 这机器做什么用的? **3** (表示目的地、目标或原因): *Is this the train ~ York?* 这火车是开往约克郡的吗? *books ~ children* 儿童读物. **4** (表示为了帮助…)为 wèi: *What can I do ~ you?* 有什么要我帮忙的吗? **5** 以…为代价〔價〕yǐ…wéi dàijià; 作为…的报酬 zuòwéi…de bàochóu; 作为…的惩〔懲〕罚 zuòwéi…de chéngfá: *buy a book ~ £15* 花 15 英镑买一本书. **6** 用以取代 yòngyǐ qǔdài: *change one's car ~ a new one* 给自己换一辆新车. **7** 支持 zhīchí: *Are you ~ or against nuclear arms?* 你赞成还是反对核武器? **8** 代表 dàibiǎo; 意为 yìwéi: *Speak ~ yourself!* 谈你自己的看法吧! *Red is ~ danger*. 红色意为危险. **9** (用于动词后面)为得到(某事物) wèi dédào: *pray ~ peace* 祈祷和平. **10** 对〔對〕于 duìyú; 关〔關〕于 guānyú: *anxious ~ his safety* 担心他的安全. **11** 因为 yīnwéi: *famous ~ its church* 由于它的教堂而出名. **12** (表示距离或一段时间): *walk ~ three miles* 步行三英里. *stay ~ a few days* 逗留几天. **13** (用于形容词后面)考虑〔慮〕到 kǎolǜdào: *She is tall ~ her age*. 考虑到她的年龄,她的身材是高的. **14** (用于引导词组): *It's impossible ~ me to continue*. 我是不可能继续下去了.

forage /ˈfɒrɪdʒ; *US* ˈfɔːr-/ *v* [I] (*for*) 搜寻〔尋〕sōuxún.

foray /ˈfɒreɪ; *US* ˈfɔːreɪ/ *n* [C] 突袭〔襲〕tūxí; 突进〔進〕tūjìn: [喻] *the company's first ~ into the computer market* 这家公司首次打进电子计算机市场.

forbear = FOREBEAR.

forbearance /fɔːˈbeərəns/ *n* [U] [正式用语]克制 kèzhì; 宽容 kuānróng.

forbid /fəˈbɪd/ *v* [*pt* **forbade** /fəˈbæd; *US* fəˈbeɪd/ 或 **forbad** /fəˈbæd/ *pp* **~den** /fəˈbɪdn/] [T] **1** (*to*) 禁止 jìnzhǐ: *I ~ you to go*. 我禁止你去. **2** 不准 bùzhǔn: *Smoking is ~den*. 不许吸烟. **Forbidden ˈCity** *n* 紫禁城 Zǐjìnchéng. **forbidding** *adj* 严〔嚴〕峻的 yánjùnde.

force /fɔːs/ *n* **1** [U] 力量 lìliàng; 力 lì; 暴力 bàolì. **2** [C, U] 影响〔響〕yǐngxiǎng; 实〔實〕力 shílì: *economic ~s* 经济实力. **3** [C, U] (产生运动的)力 lì: *the ~ of gravity* 地心吸力. **4** [C] (风、雨等大自然的)威力 wēilì: *the ~s of nature* 大自然的威力. **5** [C] 部队〔隊〕bùduì; 队伍 duìwu: *the poˈlice ~* 警察部队. *a sales ~* 销售队伍. **6** [U] 权〔權〕威 quánwēi: *the ~ of the law* 法律的权威. **7** [习语] **bring sth / come into ˈforce** (使)开〔開〕始实〔實〕施 kāishǐ shíshī. **in ˈforce** (a) (人)众〔衆〕多的 zhòngduōde. (b) (法律等)在实施中 zài shíshī zhōng. **force** *v* [T] **1** (*to*) 强迫 qiǎngpò; 迫使 pòshǐ: *~ him to talk* 强迫他说. **2** 用力使(某物)移动〔動〕yònglì shǐ yídòng. **3** 用力打开〔開〕yònglì dǎkāi: *~ (open) a door* 用力把门打开. **4** 勉强产〔產〕生 miǎnqiáng chǎnshēng: *~ a smile* 强作笑颜. **forceful** /-fl/ *adj* 强有力的 qiáng yǒulì de; 有说服力的 yǒu shuōfúlì de. **forcefully** /-fəlɪ/ *adv*. **forcible** /ˈfɔːsəbl/ *adj* 用强力的 yòng qiáng lì de. **forcibly** *adv*.

forceps /ˈfɔːseps/ *n* [pl] (医用)镊〔鑷〕子 nièzi; (医用)钳子 qiánzi.

ford /fɔːd/ *n* [C] 津 jīn; 可涉水而过〔過〕的地方 kě shèshuǐ ér guò de dìfang. **ford** *v* [T] 徒涉 túshè.

fore /fɔː(r)/ *adj* 前部的 qiánbùde: *a cat's ~ legs* 猫的前腿. **fore** *n* [习语] **be / come to the fore** 是重要的 shì zhòngyàode; 成为〔爲〕重要的 chéngwéi zhòngyàode.

forearm /ˈfɔːrɑːm/ *n* [C] 前臂 qiánbì.

forebear (亦作 **forbear**) /ˈfɔːbeə(r)/ *n* [C, 常作 pl] [正式用语]祖先 zǔxiān.

foreboding /fɔːˈbəʊdɪŋ/ *n* [C, U] (对不幸之

F

事的)预感 yùgǎn.

forecast /ˈfɔːkɑːst; *US* -kæst/ *v* [*pt*, *pp* ~ 或 ~**ed**] [T] 预报〔報〕yùbào; 预测 yùcè. **forecast** *n* [C] 预告 yùgào; 预报 yùbào: *weather* ~ 天气预报.

forecourt /ˈfɔːkɔːt/ *n* [C] 前院 qiányuàn.

forefather /ˈfɔːfɑːðə/ *n* [C, 常作 pl] 祖先 zǔxiān.

forefinger /ˈfɔːfɪŋgə(r)/ *n* [C] 食指 shízhǐ.

forefront /ˈfɔːfrʌnt/ *n* [sing] 最前列 zuì qiánliè; 最重要的地位 zuì zhòngyàode dìwèi: *in the* ~ *of space research* 空间研究的最前沿.

foregone /ˈfɔːgɒn; *US* -ˈgɔːn/ *adj* [习语] **a foregone conclusion** 预料的必然结果 yùliàode bìrán jiéguǒ.

foreground /ˈfɔːgraʊnd/ *n* [sing] **1** (景物、图画等的)前景 qiánjǐng: *in the* ~ 在前景中. **2** [喻]最令人瞩〔矚〕目的地位 zuì lìng rén zhǔmù de dìwèi.

forehand /ˈfɔːhænd/ *n* [C], *adj* (网球等)正手打 zhèngshǒu dǎ; 正手打的 zhèngshǒu dǎ de.

forehead /ˈfɒrɪd, 亦作 ˈfɔːhed; *US* ˈfɔːrɪd/ *n* [C] 额 é.

foreign /ˈfɒrən; *US* ˈfɔːr-/ *adj* **1** (a) 外国〔國〕的 wàiguóde; 在外国的 zài wàiguó de; 从〔從〕外国来〔來〕的 cóng wàiguó lái de. (b) 有关〔關〕外国的 yǒuguān wàiguó de: ~ *policy* 外交政策. **2** *to* [正式用语]非…所固有的 fēi…suǒ gùyǒu de: ~ *to his nature* 同他的本性格格不入. **3** [正式用语]外来的 wàiláide; 异〔異〕质〔質〕的 yìzhìde: *a* ~ *body in the eye* 眼睛里的异物. **foreigner** *n* [C] 外国人 wàiguórén. **foreign exˈchange** *n* [U] 国际〔際〕汇〔匯〕兑 guójì huìduì; 外汇 wàihuì.

foreman /ˈfɔːmən/ *n* [C] [*pl* -**men** /-mən/, *fem* **forewoman** /-wʊmən/, *pl* -**women** /-wɪmɪn/] **1** 工头〔頭〕gōngtóu; 领班 lǐngbān. **2** 陪审〔審〕长〔長〕péishěnzhǎng.

foremost /ˈfɔːməʊst/ *adj* 最重要的 zuì zhòngyào de; 第一流的 dìyīliúde.

forensic /fəˈrensɪk; *US* -zɪk/ *adj* 法庭的 fǎtíngde: ~ *medicine* 法医学.

forerunner /ˈfɔːrʌnə(r)/ *n* [C] 前征〔徵〕qiánzhēng; 先驱〔驅〕xiānqū.

foresee /fɔːˈsiː/ *v* [*pt* **foresaw** /fɔːˈsɔː/, *pp* ~**n** /fɔːˈsiːn/] [T] 预见 yùjiàn: ~ *difficulties* 预见到种种困难. **foreseeable** /-əbl/ *adj* **1** 可以预见到的 kěyǐ yùjiàn dào de. **2** [习语] **in the foreˌseeable ˈfuture** 在可预见的将〔將〕来〔來〕zài kě yùjiàn de jiānglái.

forest /ˈfɒrɪst; *US* ˈfɔːr-/ *n* [C, U] 森林 sēnlín; 森林地带〔帶〕sēnlín dìdài. **forestry** *n* [U] 林业〔業〕línyè; 林学〔學〕línxué.

forestall /fɔːˈstɔːl/ *v* [T] (先发制人地)预先阻止 yùxiān zǔzhǐ.

foretell /fɔːˈtel/ *v* [*pt*, *pp* **foretold** /fɔːˈtəʊld/] [T] [正式用语]预言 yùyán; 预告 yùgào.

forever /fəˈrevə(r)/ *adv* **1** (亦作 **for ever**) 永远〔遠〕yǒngyuǎn: *I'll love you* ~! 我永远爱你! [非正式用语] *It takes her* ~ *to get dressed*. 她穿衣打扮得花老半天时间. **2** 常常 chángcháng: *He is* ~ *complaining*. 他老是埋怨.

forewarn /fɔːˈwɔːn/ *v* [T] (*of*) 预先警告 yùxiān jǐnggào: ~ *him of the danger* 警告他有危险.

foreword /ˈfɔːwɜːd/ *n* [C] 序 xù; 前言 qiányán.

forfeit /ˈfɔːfɪt/ *v* [T] (因受罚等而)失去 shīqù. **forfeit** *n* [C] (因受罚等而)丧〔喪〕失的东西 sàngshīde dōngxi.

forgave *pt* of FORGIVE.

forge[1] /fɔːdʒ/ *n* [C] 锻工车〔車〕间 duàngōng chējiān; 铁〔鐵〕工厂〔廠〕tiěgōngchǎng; 铁匠店 tiějiàngdiàn. **forge** *v* [T] **1** 锻造 duànzào; 打(铁等) dǎ. **2** [喻]使形成 shǐ xíngchéng; 制〔製〕作 zhìzuò: ~ *a friendship* 缔造友谊. ~ *a link* 建立联系. **3** 伪〔偽〕造 wěizào: ~ *banknotes* 伪造纸币. **forger** *n* [C] 伪造者 wěizàozhě. **forgery** /-ərɪ/ *n* [*pl* -**ies**] **1** [U] 伪造 wěizào. **2** [C] 伪造品 wěizàopǐn; 赝品 yànpǐn.

forge[2] /fɔːdʒ/ *v* [短语动词] **forge ahead** 快速前进〔進〕kuàisù qiánjìn.

forget /fəˈget/ *v* [*pt* **forgot** /fəˈgɒt/, *pp* **forgotten** /fəˈgɒtn/] [I, T] **1** 忘记(某事) wàngjì: *Don't* ~ *to post the letters*. 别忘记寄这些信. **2** 不以…为〔為〕意 bùyǐ…wéi yì; 不再思念 búzài sīniàn: *Let's* ~ *our differences*. 让我们把分歧置诸脑后. **forgetful** /-fl/ *adj* 健忘的 jiànwàngde.

forgive /fəˈgɪv/ *v* [*pt* **forgave** /fəˈgeɪv/, *pp* ~**n** /fəˈgɪvn/] [T] 原谅 yuánliàng; 宽恕 kuānshù: *She forgave him his rudeness*. 她原谅了他的粗鲁. **forgivable** *adj* 可原谅的 kě yuánliàng de. **forgiveness** *n* [U]. **forgiving** *adj* 宽容的 kuānróngde.

forgo /fɔːˈgəʊ/ *v* [*pt* **forwent** /fɔːˈwent/, *pp* **forgone** /fɔːˈgɒn; *US* -ˈgɔːn/] [T] 放弃〔棄〕fàngqì; 摒绝 bìngjué.

forgot *pt* of FORGET.

forgotten *pp* of FORGET.

fork /fɔːk/ *n* [C] **1** (a) 餐叉 cānchā; (b) 叉 chā. **2** (a) (路的)分岔 fēnchà; (树)分叉 fēnchà. (b) 岔路 chàlù; 叉枝 chàzhī. **fork** *v* **1** [T] 叉 chā; 叉起 chāqǐ. **2** [I] (路等)分岔 fēnchà, 分叉 fēnchà. **3** [I] (人)拐弯〔彎〕(向左或右) guǎiwān. **4** [短语动词] **fork out (sth)**

F

[非正式用语](不情愿地)付出(钱) fùchū. **forked** *adj* 分叉的 fēnchàde. ˌ**fork-lift** ˈ**truck** *n* [C] 叉车[車] chāchē; 铲[鏟]车 chǎnchē.

forlorn /fəˈlɔːn/ *adj* 悲惨[慘]的 bēicǎnde; 可怜[憐]的 kěliánde; 孤苦伶仃的 gūkǔ língdīng de. **forlornly** *adv*.

form[1] /fɔːm/ *n* 1 [C, U] 形状[狀] xíngzhuàng; 外貌 wàimào. 2 [C] 体[體]制 tǐzhì; 种[種]类[類] zhǒnglèi; 类型 lèixíng: *different ~s of government* 不同的政体. 3 [C, U] [语法]词形 cíxíng; 词的发[發]音 cíde fāyīn: *The plural ~ of 'goose' is 'geese'.* "goose" 的复数词形是 "geese". 4 [C] 表格 biǎogé: *application ~s* 申请表. 5 [C] [英国英语](学校的)年级 niánjí. 6 [U] 形式 xíngshì: *~ and content* 形式和内容. 7 [习语] on ˈ**form** 竞[競]技状[狀]态[態]良好 jìngjì zhuàngtài liánghǎo. **off** ˈ**form** 竞技状态不佳 jìngjì zhuàngtài bùjiā. **formless** *adj* 无[無]形状的 wú xíngzhuàng de.

form[2] /fɔːm/ *v* 1 [T] 使形成 shǐ xíngchéng; 制[製]作 zhìzuò. 2 组成 zǔchéng; 建立 jiànlì: *~ a government* 组成政府. 3 [T] 是…的组成部分 shì…de zǔchéng bùfen: *It ~s part of the course.* 它构成了课程的一部分. 4 [I, T] 排列 páiliè; 把…编排成 bǎ…biānpái chéng: *~ a line* 排成队列.

formal /ˈfɔːml/ *adj* 1 (a) 正式的 zhèngshìde; 庄[莊]重的 zhuāngzhòngde: *a ~ dinner* 正式的晚餐. (b) (衣服或词语)正式场[場]合使用的 zhèngshì chǎnghé shǐyòng de. 2 整齐[齊]的 zhěngqíde; 有条[條]理的 yǒu tiáolǐ de: *~ gardens* 用有规则的几何图形构成的花园. 3 官方的 guānfāngde; 正式的 zhèngshìde: *a ~ declaration of war* 正式宣战. **formality** /fɔːˈmælətɪ/ *n* [*pl* -ies] 1 [U] 繁文缛节[節] fán wén rù jié. 2 [C] 手续[續] shǒuxù: *a legal ~ity* 法律手续. **formalize** *v* [T] 使(计划等)形成文字 shǐ xíngchéng wénzì. **formally** *adv*.

format /ˈfɔːmæt/ *n* [C] 大小 dàxiǎo; 形式 xíngshì; 总[總]体[體]安排 zǒngtǐ ānpái. **format** *v* [-tt-] [T] (电子计算机)为[爲]…编排格式 wéi…biānpái géshì.

formation /fɔːˈmeɪʃn/ *n* 1 [U] 形成 xíngchéng. 2 [C, U] 构[構]造 gòuzào; 排列 páiliè.

formative /ˈfɔːmətɪv/ *adj* 影响[響]…发[發]展的 yǐngxiǎng…fāzhǎn de: *a child's ~ years* 儿童性格形成的时期.

former /ˈfɔːmə(r)/ *adj* 以前的 yǐqiánde; 从[從]前的 cóngqiánde: *the ~ President* 前任总统. **the former** *pron* 前者 qiánzhě. **formerly** *adv* 从前 cóngqián; 以前 yǐqián.

formidable /ˈfɔːmɪdəbl/ *adj* 1 可怕的 kěpàde: *a ~ opponent* 可怕的敌手. 2 难[難]以对[對]付的 nányǐ duìfu de: *a ~ task* 艰难的任务. 3 优[優]秀的 yōuxiùde; 杰[傑]出的 jiéchūde. **formidably** /-əblɪ/ *adv*.

formula /ˈfɔːmjʊlə/ *n* [C] [*pl* ~s, 或作为科技用语 -mulae /-mjʊliː/] 1 公式 gōngshì; 程式 chéngshì: *a chemical ~* 化学式. 2 方案 fāng'àn; 计划[劃] jìhuà: *a peace ~* 和平方案. 3 俗套话 sútàohuà: *'How do you do' is a social ~.* "How do you do" 是一句社交俗套话. 4 配方 pèifāng.

formulate /ˈfɔːmjʊleɪt/ *v* [T] 1 制定 zhìdìng: *~ a rule* 制定规则. 2 精确[確]地表达[達] jīngquède biǎodá. **formulation** /ˌfɔːmjʊˈleɪʃn/ *n* [C, U].

forsake /fəˈseɪk/ *v* [*pt* **forsook** /fəˈsʊk/; *pp* ~n /fəˈseɪkən/] [T] [正式用语]抛弃[棄] pāoqì; 遗弃 yíqì.

fort /fɔːt/ *n* [C] 堡垒[壘] bǎolěi; 要塞 yàosài.

forte /ˈfɔːteɪ; *US* fɔːrt/ *n* [C] 长[長]处[處] chángchù; 特长 tècháng: *Singing is not my ~.* 唱歌不是我的特长.

forth /fɔːθ/ *adv* 1 [正式用语]向前方 xiàng qiánfāng; 向前 xiàngqián. 2 [习语] **and** (ˌ**so on and**) ˈ**so forth** 等等 děngděng.

forthcoming /fɔːθˈkʌmɪŋ/ *adj* 1 即将[將]发[發]生的 jíjiāng fāshēng de; 即将出现的 jíjiāng chūxiàn de. 2 现有的 xiànyǒude; 唾手可得的 tuò shǒu kě dé de; 现成的 xiànchéngde: *The money was not ~.* 没有现成的钱. 3 愿[願]意帮助的 yuànyì bāngzhù de.

fortieth ⇨ FORTY.

fortify /ˈfɔːtɪfaɪ/ *v* [*pt*, *pp* -ied] [T] 1 (*against*) 防卫[衛](某地) fángwèi. 2 强化 qiánghuà: *cereal fortified with extra vitamins* 用额外维生素增强营养的麦片. **fortification** /fɔːtɪfɪˈkeɪʃn/ *n* 1 [U] 防卫 fángwèi; 强化 qiánghuà. 2 [C, 常作 pl] 防御[禦]工事 fángyù gōngshì.

fortnight /ˈfɔːtnaɪt/ *n* [C] [尤用于英国英语]两星期 liǎng xīngqī. **fortnightly** *adj*, *adv* 每两周的 měi liǎngzhōu de; 每两周地 měi liǎngzhōu de.

fortress /ˈfɔːtrɪs/ *n* [C] 要塞 yàosài; 堡垒[壘] bǎolěi.

fortuitous /fɔːˈtjuːɪtəs; *US* -ˈtuː-/ *adj* [正式用语]偶然发[發]现的 ǒurán fāxiàn de.

fortunate /ˈfɔːtʃənət/ *adj* 幸运[運]的 xìngyùnde; 吉利的 jílìde. **fortunately** *adv*.

fortune /ˈfɔːtʃuːn/ *n* 1 [C, U] 好运[運] hǎoyùn; 坏[壞]运 huàiyùn; 机[機]会[會] jīhuì. 2 [C] 命运 mìngyùn: *tell sb's ~* 给某人算命. 3 [C] 大量资财 dàliàng zīcái: *cost a ~* 花费大

量钱财. ˈfortune-teller *n* [C] 算命先生 suànmìng xiānsheng.

forty /ˈfɔːtɪ/ *pron*, *adj*, *n* [C] [*pl* -ies] 四十 sìshí; 四十个〔個〕sìshígè. **fortieth** /-tɪəθ/ *pron*, *adj* 第四十 dìsìshí; 第四十个 dìsìshígè. **fortieth** *pron*, *n* [C] 四十分之一 sìshí fēn zhī yī.

forum /ˈfɔːrəm/ *n* [C] 论〔論〕坛〔壇〕lùntán.

forward[1] /ˈfɔːwəd/ *adj* 1 向前的 xiàngqiánde; 在前部的 zài qiánbù de: ~ *movements* 向前运动. 2 未来〔來〕的 wèiláide: ~ *planning* 对未来的计划. 3 (庄稼、儿童等)早熟的 zǎoshúde. 4 孟浪的 mènglàngde; 冒失的 màoshīde. **forward** *n* [C] (足球等)前锋 qiánfēng. **forward** *v* 1 [T] (信等)转〔轉〕寄 zhuǎnjì; 转交 zhuǎnjiāo. 2 发〔發〕送(货物等) fāsòng. 3 助长〔長〕zhùzhǎng; 促进〔進〕cùjìn: ~ *her career* 促进她的事业. **forwardness** *n* [U] 冒失 màoshi; 鲁莽 lǔmǎng.

forward[2] /ˈfɔːwəd/ *adv* (亦作 **forwards**) 向前 xiàngqián; 向未来〔來〕xiàng wèilái: *take a step* ~ 向前迈进一步. **forward-looking** *adj* 有现代思想的 yǒu xiàndài sīxiǎng de.

forwent *pt* of FORGO.

fossil /ˈfɒsl/ *n* [C] 化石 huàshí. **fossilize** /-səlaɪz/ *v* [I, T] 1 成化石 chéng huàshí; 使成化石 shǐ chéng huàshí. 2 [喻](思想等)僵化 jiānghuà; 使(思想等)僵化 shǐ jiānghuà.

foster /ˈfɒstə(r); *US* ˈfɔː-/ *v* [T] 1 培养〔養〕péiyǎng; 促进〔進〕cùjìn. 2 领养(孩子) lǐngyǎng. **foster-** (用于复合词)通过〔過〕领养而产〔產〕生家庭关〔關〕系〔係〕的 tōngguò lǐngyǎng ér chǎnshēng jiātíng guānxì de: ~*-parent* 养父母. ~*-child* 养子;养女.

fought /fɔːt/ *pt*, *pp* of FIGHT.

foul /faʊl/ *adj* 1 恶〔惡〕臭的 èchòude; 难〔難〕闻〔聞〕的 nánwénde; 腐败的 fǔbàide. 2 令人不愉快的 lìng rén bù yúkuài de: *a* ~ *temper* 坏脾气. 3 (语言)下流的 xiàliúde; 辱骂性的 rǔmàxìngde. 4 (天气)暴风〔風〕雨的 bàofēngyǔde. **foul** *n* [C] [体育]犯规 fànguī. **foul** *v* 1 [T] 弄脏〔髒〕nòng zāng; 污染 wūrǎn. 2 [I, T] [体育](比赛中)(对…)犯规 fànguī. 3 [短语动词] **foul sth up** [非正式用语]把…搞糟 bǎ…gǎo zāo. ˌ**foul** ˈ**play** *n* [U] 1 [体育]不合体〔體〕育道德的行为〔爲〕bùhé tǐyù dàodé de xíngwéi. 2 (导致谋杀的)暴行 bàoxíng.

found[1] /faʊnd/ *pt*, *pp* of FIND.

found[2] /faʊnd/ *v* [T] 1 建立 jiànlì; 设立 shèlì: ~ *a hospital* 建立一所医院. 2 [常用被动语态]把…建立在 bǎ…jiànlì zài: *a novel* ~*ed on facts* 根据事实写成的小说. **founder** *n* [C] 创〔創〕建者 chuàngjiànzhě.

foundation /faʊnˈdeɪʃn/ *n* 1 [U] (学校等)创〔創〕建 chuàngjiàn; 建立 jiànlì. 2 [C] (慈善事业等的)基金 jījīn. 3 [C, 常作 pl] 地基 dìjī; 房基 fángjī. 4 [C, U] 基础〔礎〕jīchǔ.

founder /ˈfaʊndə(r)/ *v* [I] 1 (船)沉没 chénmò. 2 [喻](计划等)失败 shībài.

foundry /ˈfaʊndrɪ/ *n* [C] [*pl* -ies] 铸〔鑄〕工车〔車〕间 zhùgōng chējiān; 铸工厂〔廠〕zhùgōngchǎng.

fount /faʊnt/ *n* [C] (*of*) [修辞]源泉 yuánquán; 源头〔頭〕yuántóu: *the* ~ *of all wisdom* 一切智慧的源泉.

fountain /ˈfaʊntɪn/ *n* [C] 1 (水池中的)人造喷泉 rénzào pēnquán. 2 (液体的)喷出 pēnchū. ˈ**fountain-pen** *n* [C] 自来〔來〕水笔〔筆〕zìláishuǐbǐ.

four /fɔː(r)/ *pron*, *adj*, *n* [C] 1 四 sì; 四个〔個〕sìgè. 2 [习语] **on all** ˈ**fours** 爬 pá; 匍匐 púfú. **fourth** /fɔːθ/ *pron*, *adj* 1 第四 dìsì; 第四个 dìsìgè. 2 [美语] ⇨QUARTER.

fourteen /ˌfɔːˈtiːn/ *pron*, *adj*, *n* [C] 十四 shísì; 十四个〔個〕shísìgè. **fourteenth** /ˌfɔːˈtiːnθ/ *pron*, *adj* 第十四 dìshísì; 第十四个 dìshísìgè. **fourteenth** *pron*, *n* [C] 十四分之一 shísìfēn zhī yī.

fowl /faʊl/ [*pl* **fowl** 或 ~**s**] 1 [C] 鸡〔鷄〕jī. 2 [U] (食用的)禽肉 qínròu.

fox /fɒks/ *n* [C] 狐 hú. **fox** *v* [T] 迷惑 míhuò; 欺骗 qīpiàn. ˈ**fox-hunting** *n* [U] 猎〔獵〕狐 lièhú.

foyer /ˈfɔɪeɪ; *US* ˈfɔɪər/ *n* [C] (剧院的)门厅〔廳〕méntīng.

fraction /ˈfrækʃn/ *n* [C] 1 [数学]分数〔數〕fēnshù. 2 小部分 xiǎo bùfen; 片断〔斷〕piànduàn: *a* ~ *of a second* 瞬间. **fractional** /-ʃənl/ *adj* 微不足道的 wēi bù zú dào de.

fracture /ˈfræktʃə(r)/ *n* [C, U] 断〔斷〕裂 duànliè; 折断 zhéduàn; 骨折 gǔzhé. **fracture** *v* [I, T] (使)断裂 duànliè; (使)折断 zhéduàn.

fragile /ˈfrædʒaɪl; *US* -dʒl/ *adj* 1 易断〔斷〕的 yìduànde; 易损坏〔壞〕的 yì sǔnhuài de. 2 [非正式用语]虚弱的 xūruòde; 不健康的 bú jiànkāng de. **fragility** /frəˈdʒɪlətɪ/ *n* [U].

fragment /ˈfrægmənt/ *n* [C] 碎片 suìpiàn; 碎块〔塊〕suìkuài; 片断〔斷〕piànduàn. **fragment** /frægˈment/ *v* [I, T] (使)裂成碎片 lièchéng suìpiàn. **fragmentary** *adj* 不完整的 bù wánzhěng de. **fragmentation** /ˌfrægmenˈteɪʃn/ *n* [U].

fragrance /ˈfreɪgrəns/ *n* [C, U] 香味 xiāngwèi; 香气〔氣〕xiāngqì. **fragrant** /-grənt/ *adj* 香的 xiāngde; 芬芳的 fēnfāngde.

frail /freɪl/ *adj* 虚弱的 xūruòde. **frailty** *n* [*pl* -ies] 1 [U] 虚弱 xūruò. 2 [C] (性格上的)弱点〔點〕ruòdiǎn.

frame /freɪm/ *n* [C] 1 (窗、画等的)框 kuàng; 框架 kuàngjià. 2 构〔構〕架 gòujià; 骨架 gǔjià; 结构 jiégòu. 3 [常作 pl] 眼镜架 yǎnjìngjià. 4 [常作 sing] (人或动物的)骨骼 gǔgé. 5 (电影的)画〔畫〕面 huàmiàn; 镜头〔頭〕jìngtóu. 6 [习语] **a frame of 'mind** 精神状〔狀〕态〔態〕jīngshén zhuàngtài; 心情 xīnqíng. **frame** *v* [T] 1 给…装〔裝〕框架 gěi…zhuāng kuàngjià. 2 说出 shuōchū; 表达〔達〕biǎodá. 3 [非正式用语]诬陷 wūxiàn; 陷害 xiànhài. **'framework** *n* [C] 1 框架 kuàngjià. 2 准〔準〕则 zhǔnzé; 观〔觀〕点〔點〕guāndiǎn.

France /frɑːns/ *n* [U] 法国〔國〕Fǎguó.

franchise /'fræntʃaɪz/ *n* 1 **the franchise** [sing] 公民权〔權〕gōngmínquán; 选〔選〕举〔舉〕权 xuǎnjǔquán. 2 [C] 特许经〔經〕销权 tèxǔ jīngxiāoquán.

F

frank[1] /fræŋk/ *adj* 坦率的 tǎnshuàide; 坦白的 tǎnbáide. **frankly** *adv*. **frankness** *n* [U].

frank[2] /fræŋk/ *v* [T] 在(信件)上盖〔蓋〕印表示邮〔郵〕资已付 zài shàng gài yìn biǎoshì yóuzī yǐfù.

frankfurter /'fræŋkfɜːtə(r)/ *n* [C] 一种〔種〕小的熏〔燻〕香肠〔腸〕yìzhǒng xiǎo de xūn xiāngcháng.

frantic /'fræntɪk/ 1 疯〔瘋〕狂地害怕 fēngkuángde hàipà; 发〔發〕狂地焦虑〔慮〕fākuángde jiāolǜ. 2 紧〔緊〕张〔張〕而纷乱〔亂〕的 jǐnzhāng ér fēnluàn de: *a ~ search* 狂乱的搜查. **frantically** /-klɪ/ *adv*.

fraternal /frə'tɜːnl/ *adj* 兄弟般的 xiōngdìbānde; 兄弟的 xiōngdìde. **fraternally** /-nəlɪ/ *adv*.

fraternity /frə'tɜːnətɪ/ *n* [*pl* -ies] 1 [U] 兄弟般情谊 xiōngdìbān qíngyì. 2 [C] 趣味相投的人 qùwèi xiāngtóu de rén; 兄弟会〔會〕xiōngdìhuì; 行会 hánghuì. 3 [C] [美语]男大学〔學〕生联〔聯〕谊会 nán dàxuéshēng liányìhuì.

fraternize /'frætənaɪz/ *v* [I] (*with*) 亲〔親〕善 qīnshàn; 友善 yǒushàn: *~ with the enemy* 与敌人亲善. **fraternization** /frætənaɪ'zeɪʃn; *US* -nɪ'z-/ *n* [U].

fraud /frɔːd/ *n* 1 [C, U] 诈骗 zhàpiàn; 欺诈行为〔爲〕qīzhà xíngwéi. 2 [C] 骗子 piànzi. **fraudulent** /'frɔːdjʊlənt; *US* -dʒʊ-/ *adj* 欺骗性的 qīpiànxìngde; 骗来〔來〕的 piànláide.

fraught /frɔːt/ *adj* 1 *with* 充满的 chōngmǎnde: *~ with danger* 充满危险. 2 忧〔憂〕虑〔慮〕的 yōulǜde; 担〔擔〕心的 dānxīnde.

fray /freɪ/ *v* [I, T] 1 (织物等)磨损 mósǔn; 磨破(织物等) mópò. 2 [喻]使紧〔緊〕张〔張〕shǐ jǐnzhāng: *~ed nerves* 紧张的神经.

freak /friːk/ *n* [C] 1 怪诞的行为〔爲〕或事 guàidànde xíngwéi huò shì: *a ~ storm* 极不寻常的暴风雨. 2 背离〔離〕社会〔會〕习〔習〕俗的人 bèilí shèhuì xísú de rén. 3 [非正式用语] …迷 …mí: *a jazz ~* 爵士乐迷. **freakish** *adj* 怪诞的 guàidànde.

freckle /'frekl/ *n* [C, 常作 pl] 雀斑 quèbān; (皮肤上的)斑点〔點〕bāndiǎn. **freckled** *adj*.

free /friː/ *adj* [~r /-ə(r)/, ~st /-ɪst/] 1 (人)不受监〔監〕禁的 búshòu jiānjìn de, 可自由行动〔動〕的 kě zìyóu xíngdòng de. 2 不受控制、约束的 búshòu kòngzhì、yuēshù de: *a ~ press* 享有新闻自由的报业. 3 松〔鬆〕开〔開〕的 sōng kāi de; 未固定的 wèi gùdìng de: *the ~ end of a rope* 绳子的松开的一头. 4 不受阻的 bú shòuzǔ de; 通畅的 tōngchàngde: *a ~ flow of water* 水流通畅. 5 *from/of* 摆〔擺〕脱了…的 bǎituō le…de; 没有…的 méiyǒu …de: *~ from pain* 无痛苦的. *~ from blame* 不受责备的. 6 免费的 miǎnfèide. 7 不包括的 bù bāokuò de: *tax ~* 不包括税. 8 (a) 未被占〔佔〕用的 wèi bèi zhànyòng de; 空闲〔閒〕的 kòngxiánde: *a ~ seat* 空坐位. (b) (人)空闲的 kòngxiánde. 9 [习语] **free and easy** 不拘礼节〔節〕的 bùjū lǐjié de; 轻〔輕〕松的 qīngsōngde. **a free 'hand** 准许愿〔願〕做什么〔麼〕就做什么 zhǔnxǔ yuàn zuò shénme jiù zuò shénme: *get/have a ~ hand* 被准许自由行动. **free** *adv* 1 免费地 miǎnfèide. 2 松开地 sōngkāide; 不固定地 bú gùdìng de. 3 [习语] **make free with sth** 擅自使用 shànzì shǐyòng. **free** *v* [T] 使自由 shǐ zìyóu; 解放 jiěfàng; 使摆脱 shǐ bǎituō. **ˌfree 'enterprise** *n* [U] 自由企业〔業〕制 zìyóu qǐyè zhì. **'free-for-all** *n* [C] (争吵等)在场〔場〕者都参〔參〕加的 zàichǎngzhě dōu cānjiā de. **'free-hand** *adj*, *adv* 徒手画〔畫〕的(地) túshǒu huà de. **'freelance** /-lɑːns; *US* -læns/ *n* [C], *adj*, *adv* 自由职〔職〕业者 zìyóu zhíyè zhě; 自由职业者做的 zìyóu zhíyèzhě zuò de; 作为〔爲〕自由职业者 zuòwéi zìyóu zhíyè zhě. **'free-lance** *v* [I] 当〔當〕自由职业者 dāng zìyóu zhíyè zhě. **ˌfree-'range** *adj* (鸡蛋)由自由放养〔養〕的鸡〔鷄〕产〔產〕下的 yóu zìyóu fàngyǎng de jī chǎn xià de. **free speech** *n* [U] 言论〔論〕自由 yánlùn zìyóu. **free 'trade** *n* [U] 自由贸易 zìyóu màoyì. **'freeway** *n* [C] [美语]高速公路 gāosù gōnglù. **ˌfree 'will** *n* [U] 1 自由选〔選〕择〔擇〕zìyóu xuǎnzé. 2 自由意志 zìyóu yìzhì; 自由意志论〔論〕zìyóu yìzhì lùn.

freedom /'friːdəm/ *n* 1 [U] 自由 zìyóu. 2 [C, U] (*of*) 自由权〔權〕zìyóuquán: *~ of worship* 敬神自由.

freeze /friːz/ *v* [*pt* **froze** /frəʊz/, *pp* **frozen** /'frəʊzn/] 1 [I, T] (尤指水)结冰 jiébīng; 冻结 dòngjié; 使(水)结冰 shǐ jiébīng. 2

[I] [与 it 连用] (天气)冰冷 bīnglěng; 酷寒 kùhán: *It's freezing today*. 今天冰冷冰冷的. **3** [I] 感到极〔極〕冷 gǎndào jílěng. **4** [T] 冷冻(食物) lěngdòng: *frozen peas* 冻豆. **5** [I, T] (因恐惧等)呆〔獃〕住 dāizhù; 使突然停住 shǐ tūrán tíngzhù: ~ *with terror* 吓得呆住了. **6** [T] 冻结(工资、物价等) dòngjié. **7** [习语] **ˌfreeze to ˈdeath** 冻死 dòngsǐ. **8** [短语动词] **freeze over** 被冰覆盖〔蓋〕 bèi bīng fùgài. **freeze up** 冻住 dòngzhù. **freeze** *n* [C] **1** 严〔嚴〕寒期 yánhánqī. **2** (工资、物价等的)冻结 dòngjié. **freezer** *n* [C] 大型冰箱 dàxíng bīngxiāng. **ˈfreezing-point** *n* [U, C] (尤指水的)冰点〔點〕 bīngdiǎn.

freight /freɪt/ *n* [U] (运输的)货物 huòwù. **freight** *v* [T] 运〔運〕输(货物) yùnshū. **freighter** *n* [C] 货船 huòchuán; 运输机〔機〕 yùnshūjī.

French /frentʃ/ *n* **1** [U] 法语 Fǎyǔ. **2 the French** [pl] 法国人 Fǎguórén. **French** *adj* 法国的 Fǎguóde; 法国人的 Fǎguórénde; 法语的 Fǎyǔde. **ˌFrench ˈfries** *n* [pl] [尤用于美语] 法式炸土豆条 fǎshì zhá tǔdòutiáo. **ˌFrench ˈwindow** *n* [C, 常作 pl] 落地长〔長〕窗 luòdì chángchuāng.

frenzy /ˈfrenzɪ/ *n* [sing, U] 疯〔瘋〕狂的激动〔動〕 fēngkuángde jīdòng. **frenzied** /ˈfrenzɪd/ *adj*.

frequency /ˈfriːkwənsɪ/ *n* [*pl* **-ies**] **1** [U] 重复〔複〕发〔發〕生率 chóngfù fāshēnglǜ. **2** [C] (无线电波)频率 pínlǜ.

frequent[1] /ˈfriːkwənt/ *adj* 时〔時〕常发〔發〕生的 shícháng fāshēng de. **frequently** *adv*.

frequent[2] /frɪˈkwent/ *v* [T] 常到(某地) chángdào; 常去 chángqù.

fresco /ˈfreskəʊ/ *n* [C] [*pl* **~s** 或 **~es**] 湿〔濕〕壁画〔畫〕 shī bìhuà.

fresh /freʃ/ *adj* **1** 新的 xīnde; 新颖的 xīnyǐngde: *make a ~ start* 重新开始. **2** 新鲜的 xīnxiānde: ~ *bread* 新鲜的面包. **3** (食物)鲜的(非罐装或冷冻的) xiānde. **4** (水)淡的 dànde. **5** (天气)冷而有风〔風〕的 lěng ér yǒu fēng de. **6** (颜色)明亮的 míngliàngde. **7** 精神饱满的 jīngshén bǎomǎn de. **8** [非正式用语] (对异性)鲁莽的 lǔmǎngde. **9** *from / out of* 刚〔剛〕离〔離〕开〔開〕(某地)的 gāng líkāi de: *students ~ from college* 刚出大学校门的学生们. **fresh** *adv* [常与过去分词连用]新近地 xīnjìnde: ~ *painted* 新近油漆的. **freshness** *n* [U]. **ˈfresh water** *adj* 来〔來〕自淡水的 láizì dànshuǐ de; 淡水的 dànshuǐde; 生活于淡水的 shēnghuó yú dànshuǐ de; 含淡水的 hán dànshuǐ de.

freshen /ˈfreʃn/ *v* **1** [T] 使新鲜 shǐ xīnxian. **2** [I] (风)增强 zēngqiáng. **3** [短语动词] **freshen (oneself) up** 梳洗打扮 shūxǐ dǎbàn.

fret[1] /fret/ *v* [-tt-] [I, T] (*about*) (使)烦躁 fánzào. **fretful** /-fl/ *adj* 烦躁的 fánzàode; 抱怨的 bàoyuànde. **fretfully** *adv*.

fret[2] /fret/ *n* [C] (吉他等弦乐器上的)品 pǐn, 柱 zhù, 桥〔橋〕 qiáo.

friar /ˈfraɪə(r)/ *n* [C] 天主教托钵修会〔會〕修士 tiānzhǔjiào tuōbō xiūhuì xiūshì.

friction /ˈfrɪkʃn/ *n* **1** [U] 摩擦 mócā. **2** [C, U] 不和 bùhé; 倾轧〔軋〕 qīngyà.

Friday /ˈfraɪdɪ/ *n* 星期五 xīngqī wǔ. (用法举例参见 Monday)

fridge /frɪdʒ/ *n* [C] 电〔電〕冰箱 diànbīngxiāng.

fried /fraɪd/ *pt*, *pp* of FRY.

friend /frend/ *n* [C] **1** 朋友 péngyou; 友人 yǒurén. **2** 赞助者 zànzhùzhě; 支持者 zhīchízhě: *a ~ of the arts* 美术的赞助者. **3** [习语] **be friends (with sb)** 与〔與〕…友好 yǔ…yǒuhǎo. **make friends (with sb)** 与…交朋友 yǔ…jiāo péngyou. **friendless** *adj* 没有朋友的 méiyǒu péngyou de. **friendly** *adj* [**-ier, -iest**] **1** 友好的 yǒuhǎode. **2** (比赛等)友谊的 yǒuyìde. **friendliness** *n* [U]. **friendship** *n* [C, U] 友好的关〔關〕系〔係〕 yǒuhǎode guānxì.

frieze /friːz/ *n* [C] [建筑](墙顶的)横饰带〔帶〕 héngshìdài.

frigate /ˈfrɪgət/ *n* [C] (小型)快速护〔護〕航舰〔艦〕 kuàisù hùhángjiàn.

fright /fraɪt/ *n* [C, U] 惊〔驚〕恐 jīngkǒng; 惊吓〔嚇〕 jīngxià.

frighten /ˈfraɪtn/ *v* [T] 使惊〔驚〕恐 shǐ jīngkǒng; 吓〔嚇〕唬 xiàhu. **frightened** *adj* 害怕的 hàipàde. **frightening** *adj* 令人惊恐的 lìng rén jīngkǒng de. **frighteningly** *adv*.

frightful /ˈfraɪtfl/ *adj* **1** 令人厌〔厭〕恶〔惡〕的 lìng rén yànwù de. **2** [非正式用语]极〔極〕度的 jídùde; 极糟的 jízāode. **frightfully** /-fəlɪ/ *adv* [非正式用语]非常 fēicháng; 极 jí.

frigid /ˈfrɪdʒɪd/ *adj* **1** 寒冷的 hánlěngde. **2** (妇女)性感缺失的 xìnggǎn quēshī de. **frigidity** /frɪˈdʒɪdətɪ/ *n* [U]. **frigidly** *adv*.

frill /frɪl/ *n* [C] **1** (服装)褶边〔邊〕 zhěbiān; 饰边 shìbiān. **2** [常作 pl] [喻]虚饰 xūshì; 矫〔矯〕饰 jiǎoshì; 装〔裝〕腔作势〔勢〕 zhuāng qiāng zuò shì. **frilly** *adj*.

fringe /frɪndʒ/ *n* [C] **1** (妇女发式)前刘〔劉〕海 qián liúhǎi. **2** 缘饰 yuánshì; 蓬边〔邊〕 péngbiān; 毛边 máobiān. **3** 边缘 biānyuán: *on the ~ of the forest* 在森林的边缘. *on the ~ of the crowd* 在人群的边缘.

frisk /frɪsk/ *v* **1** [I] 欢〔歡〕跃〔躍〕 huānyuè; 跳跳蹦蹦 tiàotiào bèngbèng. **2** [T] 搜查(某人是否身上有武器) sōuchá. **frisky** *adj* [**-ier, -iest**] 活泼〔潑〕的 huópode.

fritter[1] /ˈfrɪtə(r)/ *v* [短语动词] **fritter sth**

away 浪费(尤指金钱或时间) làngfèi.

fritter[2] /ˈfrɪtə(r)/ *n* [C] (果馅、肉馅)油煎饼 yóu jiānbǐng.

frivolous /ˈfrɪvələs/ *adj* 轻〔輕〕薄的 qīngbóde; 轻浮的 qīngfúde. **frivolity** /frɪˈvɒlətɪ/ *n* [*pl* -ies] 1 [U] 轻薄的举〔舉〕动〔動〕qīngbóde jǔdòng. 2 [C] 无〔無〕聊的活动或话语 wúliáode huódòng huò huàyǔ. **frivolously** *adv*.

frizzy /ˈfrɪzɪ/ *adj* (头发)有小鬈曲的 yǒu xiǎo quánqū de.

fro /frəʊ/ *adv* [习语] to and fro ⇨ TO[3].

frog /frɒg; US frɔːg/ *n* [C] 青蛙 qīngwā. ˈ**frogman** /-mən/ *n* [C] [*pl* -men] (使用蛙式潜水装备进行水下作业的)蛙人 wārén.

frolic /ˈfrɒlɪk/ *v* [*pt*, *pp* ~ked] [I] 嬉戏〔戲〕xīxì; 打打闹闹 dǎdǎnàonào. **frolic** *n* [sing] 欢〔歡〕乐〔樂〕huānlè; 嬉戏 xīxì.

F

from /frəm; 强式 frɒm/ *prep* 1 (表示起点) 从〔從〕cóng: *go ~ London to Oxford* 从伦敦去牛津. 2 (表示时间的开始)从 cóng: *on holiday ~ 1 May* 从5月1日开始度假. 3 (表示施予者)来〔來〕自 láizì: *a letter ~ my brother* 我兄弟的来信. 4 (表示来源)来自 láizì; 用 yòng: *quotations ~ Shakespeare* 引自莎士比亚的文句. 5 (表示距离)离〔離〕lí; 距 jù: *ten miles ~ the sea* 离海10英里. 6 (表示下限)从 cóng: *Tickets cost ~ £3 to £12*. 门票从3英镑到12英镑. 7 (表示制作所用材料)用 yòng: *Wine is made ~ grapes*. 酒是用葡萄制造的. 8 (表示分开、除去等)从 cóng: *take the money ~ my purse* 从我的钱包拿出钱. 9 (表示保护或防止): *save a boy ~ drowning* 救了一个要淹死的男孩. *prevent sb ~ sleeping* 不让某人睡着. 10 (表示理由或原因): *suffer ~ cold and hunger* 饥寒交迫. 11 (表示变化): *~ bad to worse* 每况愈下. 12 考虑〔慮〕到(某事物) kǎolǜdào: *reach a decision ~ the evidence* 根据证据作出决定.

front /frʌnt/ *n* 1 [尤作 the front] [sing] 正面 zhèngmiàn; 前面 qiánmiàn: *the ~ of a building* 建筑物的正面. 2 the front [sing] 海边〔邊〕道路 hǎibiān dàolù. 3 the front [sing] 前线〔綫〕qián xiàn; 战〔戰〕线 zhànxiàn. 4 [sing] (常为假装的)外表 wàibiǎo: *put on a brave ~* 装作勇敢的样子. 5 [C] [气象]锋 fēng. 6 [sing] [非正式用语]起掩蔽作用的人或物 qǐ yǎnbì zuòyòngde rén huò wù. 7 [C] (某一)领域 lǐngyù: *on the financial ~* 在财政方面. 8 [习语] in front 在最前面的位置 zài zuì qiánmiàn de wèizhi; 在前面 zài qiánmiàn. in front of (a) 在…的前面 zài…de qiánmiàn. (b) 当〔當〕(某人的)面 dāng miàn. **front** *v* [I, T] 面对〔對〕miànduì; 朝 cháo: *hotels that ~ onto the sea* 朝着海的旅馆. **frontage** /-ɪdʒ/ *n* [C] 土地或建筑〔築〕物的正面宽度 tǔdì huò jiànzhùwù de zhèngmiàn kuāndù. **frontal** *adj* 正面的 zhèngmiànde; 从〔從〕正面的 cóng zhèngmiàn de; 在正面的 zài zhèngmiàn de. the ˌfront ˈline *n* [C] 前线〔綫〕qiánxiàn. ˌ**front-ˈpage** *adj* (新闻等)头〔頭〕版上的 tóubǎn shàng de.

frontier /ˈfrʌntɪə(r); US frʌnˈtɪər/ *n* [C] 1 国〔國〕界 guójiè; 边〔邊〕界 biānjiè. 2 [pl] 尖端 jiānduān: *the ~s of science* 科学尖端.

frost /frɒst; US frɔːst/ *n* 1 [C, U] 冰点〔點〕以下的气〔氣〕候 bīngdiǎn yǐxià de qìhòu; 严〔嚴〕寒 yánhán. 2 [U] 霜 shuāng. **frost** *v* 1 [T] 结霜于 jié shuāng yú. 2 [T] 使(玻璃)具有无〔無〕光泽〔澤〕的表面 shǐ jùyǒu wú guāngzé de biǎomiàn. 3 [T] [尤用于美语]撒糖粒于(糕饼) sǎ tánglì yú. 4 [短语动词] frost over /up 结霜 jié shuāng. ˈ**frost-bite** *n* [C] 冻伤〔傷〕dòngshāng. ˈ**frost-bitten** 冻伤的 dòngshāngde. **frosty** *adj* [-ier, -iest] 1 霜冻的 shuāngdòngde; 严寒的 yánhánde. 2 [喻]冷若冰霜的 lěng ruò bīngshuāng de; 冷淡的 lěngdànde: *a ~y welcome* 冷淡的接待.

froth /frɒθ; US frɔːθ/ *n* [U] 1 泡沫 pàomò. 2 [贬]空谈 kōngtán; 浅〔淺〕薄而空洞的主意 qiǎnbó ér kōngdòng de zhǔyi; 迷人而无〔無〕价〔價〕值的事物 mírén ér wú jiàzhí de shìwù. **froth** *v* [I] 起泡沫 qǐ pàomò. **frothy** *adj* [-ier, -iest] 泡沫状〔狀〕的 pàomò zhuàng de; 有泡沫的 yǒu pàomò de.

frown /fraʊn/ *v* 1 [I] 皱〔皺〕眉(表示不满等) zhòu méi. 2 [短语动词] frown on /upon sth 不赞成 bú zànchéng. **frown** *n* [C]: *with a ~ on his face* 他愁眉不展的样子.

froze *pt* of FREEZE.

frozen *pp* of FREEZE.

frugal /ˈfruːgl/ *adj* 1 经〔經〕济〔濟〕的 jīngjìde; 俭〔儉〕朴〔樸〕的 jiǎnpǔde. 2 花钱〔錢〕少的 huāqián shǎo de; 小的 xiǎode: *a ~ supper* 一顿凑合的晚饭.

fruit /fruːt/ *n* 1 [C, U] 水果 shuǐguǒ. 2 [C] [生物]果实〔實〕guǒshí. 3 [尤用 the fruits] [pl] 艰〔艱〕苦工作的成果 jiānkǔ gōngzuò de chéngguǒ. **fruitful** *adj* [喻]有成果的 yǒu chéngguǒ de. **fruitless** *adj* [喻]徒劳〔勞〕的 túláode; 无〔無〕成果的 wú chéngguǒ de. **fruity** *adj* [-ier, -iest] 1 水果的 shuǐguǒ de; 像水果的 xiàng shuǐguǒ de. 2 [非正式用语](声音)圆润的 yuánrùnde.

fruition /fruːˈɪʃn/ *n* [习语] come to fruition [正式用语](希望、计划等)实〔實〕现 shíxiàn; 完成 wánchéng.

frustrate /frʌˈstreɪt; US ˈfrʌstreɪt/ *v* [T] 1 阻挠〔撓〕(某人做某事) zǔnáo; 使灰心 shǐ huīxīn; 使恼〔惱〕怒 shǐ nǎonù. 2 挫败 cuòbài；使受挫折 shǐ shòu cuòzhé. **frustrated** *adj* 失意的 shīyìde；失望的 shīwàngde. **frustration** /frʌˈstreɪʃn/ *n* [U, C].

fry /fraɪ/ *v* [*pt*, *pp* fried /fraɪd/] [I, T] 油煎 yóujiān；油炸 yóuzhá；油炒 yóuchǎo. **ˈfrying-pan**（美语 **ˈfry-pan**）*n* [C] 1 煎锅〔鍋〕jiānguō. 2 [习语] **out of the ˈfrying-pan into the ˈfire** 跳出油锅又落火坑 tiàochū yóuguō yòu luò huǒkēng.

ft *abbr* feet; foot.

FTP *abbr* 文件传〔傳〕输〔輸〕协〔協〕议〔議〕wénjiàn chuánshū xiéyì. *vt* (pp ～ing, pt ～'d or ～ed) 传〔傳〕输〔輸〕chuánshū.

fuck /fʌk/ *v* [I, T] [⚠俚] 1 (与…)性交 xìngjiāo. 2 (用于表示愤怒、恼怒等)诅咒 zǔzhòu: *F～ (it)!* 他妈的! 3 [短语动词] **fuck ˈoff** 滚开〔開〕gǔnkāi. **fuck** *n* [C] [⚠俚]性交 xìngjiāo. **ˌfuck-ˈall** *n* [U] [⚠俚] 一点〔點〕儿〔兒〕也不 yìdiǎnr yě bù；绝不 juébù. **ˈfucking** *adv*, *adj* [⚠俚](用于表示愤怒、恼怒等)该死(的) gāisǐ；讨厌〔厭〕的 tǎoyànde.

fudge[1] /fʌdʒ/ *n* [U] 一种〔種〕牛奶软糖 yìzhǒng niúnǎi ruǎntáng.

fudge[2] /fʌdʒ/ *v* [T] [非正式用语] 回〔迴〕避 huíbì.

fuel /ˈfjuːəl/ *n* [U] 燃料 ránliào. **fuel** *v* [-ll-；美语 -l-] [T] 1 对〔對〕…供给燃料 duì… gōngjǐ ránliào. 2 为〔爲〕…火上加油 wèi… huǒ shàng jiāyóu: *to ～ inflation* 为通货膨胀火上加油.

fugitive /ˈfjuːdʒətɪv/ *n* [C] (*from*) 逃亡者 táowángzhě: *～ from famine* 逃(饥)荒者.

fulfil（美语 **fulfill**）/fʊlˈfɪl/ *v* [-ll-] [T] 1 完成 wánchéng；履行(任务、职责、诺言等) lǚxíng. 2 **～ oneself** 充分发〔發〕挥自己的才能 chōngfèn fāhuī zìjǐ de cáinéng. **fulfilment** *n* [U].

full /fʊl/ *adj* 1 满的 mǎnde；充满的 chōngmǎnde: *a ～ bottle* 装满瓶的. 2 吃饱了的 chībǎolede. 3 完全的 wánquánde；无〔無〕省略的 wú shěnglüè de. 4 丰〔豐〕满的 fēngmǎnde；又胖又圆的 yòupàng yòuyuán de: *a ～ figure* 丰满的身材. *a ～ face* 胖圆脸〔臉〕. 5 (衣服)宽松〔鬆〕的 kuān sōng de: *a ～ skirt* 宽松的衬衫. 6 *of* 只想某事物的 zhǐxiǎng mǒu shìwùde: [贬] *He's ～ of himself* 他只想自己. 7 [习语] (at) **full speed / pelt / tilt** 全速 quán sù. **in full** 完全地 wánquánde；无省略地 wú shěnglüè de. **to the ˈfull** 充分地 chōngfènde；彻〔徹〕底地 chèdǐde: *enjoy life to the ～* 充分享受. **full** *adv* 1 正好 zhènghǎo；直接 zhíjiē: *hit him ～ in the face* 正打着他的脸. 2 非常 fēicháng；十分 shífēn. **ˌfull-ˈboard** *n* [U] (旅馆提供的)全食宿 quán shísù. **ˌfull-ˈlength** *adj* 1 全身的 quánshēnde；全长〔長〕的 quánchángde. 2 未经〔經〕删节〔節〕的 wèi jīng shānjié de. **ˌfull ˈmoon** *n* [C] 满月 mǎnyuè. **fullness**（亦作 **fulness**）*n* [U]. **ˌfull-ˈscale** *adj* 1 与〔與〕原物同样〔樣〕大小的 yǔ yuánwù tóngyàng dàxiǎo de. 2 完全的 wánquánde；详尽〔盡〕的 xiángjìnde: *a ～-scale inquiry* 全面调查. **ˌfullˈstop**（亦作 **full point**）*n* [C] 1 (标点符号)句点〔點〕jùdiǎn. 2 [习语] **come to a fullstop** 完全停止 wánquán tíngzhǐ. **ˌfull-ˈtime** *adj*, *adv* 全部工作时〔時〕间工作的(地) quánbù gōngzuò shíjiān gōngzuò de. **fully** *adv* 1 完全地 wánquánde；充分地 chōngfènde. 2 至少 zhìshǎo: *The journey took ～y two hours.* 行程至少 2 小时.

fumble /ˈfʌmbl/ *v* [I] 笨手笨脚地做 bènshǒu bènjiǎo de zuò.

fume /fjuːm/ *n* [C, 常作 pl] (气味浓烈的)烟 yān；汽 qì. **fume** *v* [I] 1 熏〔燻〕xūn；冒烟 màoyān；冒汽 màoqì. 2 [喻]发〔發〕怒 fānù.

fun /fʌn/ *n* [U] 1 玩笑 wánxiào；乐〔樂〕趣 lèqù. 2 滑稽 huájì. 3 [习语] **for ˈfun** 闹着玩儿〔兒〕地 nào zhe wánr de. **in ˈfun** 开〔開〕个〔個〕玩笑似地 kāi gè wánxiào shì de. **make fun of sb/sth** 拿(某人或某事)开玩笑 ná kāi wánxiào. **ˈfun-fair** *n* [C] 公共露天游〔遊〕乐〔樂〕场〔場〕gōnggòng lùtiān yóulèchǎng.

function /ˈfʌŋkʃn/ *n* [C] 1 职〔職〕责 zhízé；作用 zuòyòng；功能 gōngnéng. 2 正式社会〔會〕集会 zhèngshì shèhuì jíhuì. **function** *v* [I] 起作用 qǐ zuòyòng；运〔運〕行 yùnxíng: *The lift doesn't ～.* 电梯坏了. **functional** /-ʃənl/ *adj* 1 实〔實〕用的 shíyòngde. 2 有功能的 yǒu gōngnéng de；在工作的 zài gōngzuò de.

fund /fʌnd/ *n* [C] 1 专〔專〕款 zhuānkuǎn；基金 jījīn. 2 蕴藏 yùncáng: *a large ～ of experience* 丰富的经验. **fund** *v* [T] 资助 zīzhù.

fundamental /ˌfʌndəˈmentl/ *adj* 基础〔礎〕的 jīchǔde；作为〔爲〕起点〔點〕的 zuòwéi qǐdiǎn de；十分重要的 shífēn zhòngyào de. **fundamental** *n* [C, 常作 pl] 基本原则 jīběn yuánzé；基本原理 jīběn yuánlǐ. **fundamentalism** /-təlɪzəm/ *n* [U] 基要主义(认为《圣经》、《古兰经》等的经文翔实无误) jīyào zhǔyì. **fundamentalist** *n* [C], *adj*. **fundamentally** /-təlɪ/ *adv*.

funeral /ˈfjuːnərəl/ *n* [C] 丧〔喪〕葬 sāngzàng；葬礼〔禮〕zànglǐ.

fungus /ˈfʌŋgəs/ *n* [C, U] [*pl* -gi /-gaɪ；亦作 -dʒaɪ / 或 ～es /-gəsɪz/] 真菌 zhēnjūn.

funnel /ˈfʌnl/ *n* [C] 1 漏斗 lòudǒu. 2 (轮船等的)烟囱 yāncōng. **funnel** *v* [-ll-；*US* -l-] [I, T] (使)汇〔匯〕集 huìjí；(使)流经〔經〕漏斗 liújīng lòudǒu.

F

funny /ˈfʌnɪ/ *adj* [-ier, -iest] 1 可笑的 kěxiàode; 有趣的 yǒuqùde. 2 奇特的 qítède. **funnily** *adv*. ˈ**funny-bone** *n* [C] 麻筋儿〔兒〕(肘端神经敏感处) máJīnr.

fur /fɜː(r)/ *n* 1 [U] (兽类)软〔軟〕毛 ruǎnmáo. 2 [C] 毛皮 máopí; 毛皮衣 máopíyī. 3 (锅、壶等中的)水垢 shuǐgòu. **furry** *adj* [-ier, -iest] 毛皮的 máopíde; 像毛皮的 xiàng máopíde; 穿毛皮的 chuān máopí de.

furious /ˈfjʊərɪəs/ *adj* 1 狂怒的 kuángnùde. 2 猛烈的 měngliède; 强烈的 qiángliède: *a ~ storm* 猛烈的暴风雨.

furlong /ˈfɜːlɒŋ; *US* -lɔːŋ/ *n* [C] 弗隆(=201 米) fúlóng.

furnace /ˈfɜːnɪs/ *n* [C] 炉〔爐〕子 lúzi; 熔炉 rónglú.

G

furnish /ˈfɜːnɪʃ/ *v* [T] 1 用家具装〔裝〕备〔備〕(房子) yòng jiājù zhuāngbèi. 2 [正式用语]供应〔應〕gōngyìng. **furnishings** *n* [pl] 家具 jiājù; 设备〔備〕shèbèi; 陈设 chénshè.

furniture /ˈfɜːnɪtʃə(r)/ *n* [U] 家具 jiājù.

furrier /ˈfʌrɪə(r)/ *n* [C] 皮货商 píhuòshāng; 毛皮加工制〔製〕作者 máopí jiāgōng zhìzuòzhě.

furrow /ˈfʌrəʊ/ *n* [C] 1 犁沟〔溝〕lígōu. 2 (面部)皱〔皺〕纹 zhòuwén. **furrow** *v* [T] 使起皱纹 shǐ qǐ zhòuwén: *a ~ed brow* 布满皱纹的前额.

furry /ˈfɜːrɪ/ ⇨ FUR.

further /ˈfɜːðə(r)/ *adv* 1 (表示空间或时间的距离)更远〔遠〕地: gèngyuǎnde: *It is not safe to go any ~*. 走更远就不安全了. 2 此外 cǐwài; 而且 érqiě: *F~, it has come to my attention* ... 此外,我已注意到…. 3 进〔進〕一步地 jìnyíbùde. **further** *adj* 1 (空间或时间的距离)更远的 gèngyuǎnde. 2 更多的 gèngduōde; 进一步的 jìnyíbùde; 另外的 lìngwàide: *~ information* 更多的信息. **further** *v* [T] 促进 cùjìn; 推进 tuījìn; 助长〔長〕zhùzhǎng. **furtherance** *n* [U] [正式用语]促进 cùjìn; 推动〔動〕tuīdòng. ˌ**further eduˈcation** *n* [U] (为成年人的)继〔繼〕续〔續〕教育 jìxù jiàoyù; 进修 jìnxiū. **furthermore** *adv* 而且 érqiě; 此外 cǐwài. **furthermost** *adj* 最远的 zuìyuǎnde.

furthest /ˈfɜːðɪst/ *adj*, *adv* ⇨ FAR.

furtive /ˈfɜːtɪv/ *adj* 偷偷摸摸的 tōutōumōmōde; 鬼鬼祟祟的 guǐguǐsuìsuìde. **furtively** *adv*. **furtiveness** *n* [U].

fury /ˈfjʊərɪ/ *n* [U, C] 狂怒 kuángnù; 暴怒 bàonù.

fuse[1] /fjuːz/ *n* [C] 保险〔險〕丝 bǎoxiǎnsī. **fuse** *v* [I, T] 1 (使电器等)因保险丝熔断而中断工作 yīn bǎoxiǎnsī róngduàn ér zhōngduàn gōngzuò: *~ the lights* 因保险熔断,电灯不亮了. 2 熔化 rónghuà; 熔接 róngjiē.

fuse[2] /fjuːz/ *n* [C] 1 导〔導〕火线〔綫〕dǎohuǒxiàn; 导爆线 dǎobàoxiàn. 2 (美语亦作 **fuze**) 引信 yǐnxìn; 信管 xìnguǎn.

fuselage /ˈfjuːzəlɑːʒ; *US* -sə-/ *n* [C] 飞〔飛〕机〔機〕机身 fēijī jīshēn.

fusion /ˈfjuːʒn/ *n* [C, U] 熔合 rónghé; 熔接 róngjiē.

fuss /fʌs/ 1 [U, sing] 大惊〔驚〕小怪 dà jīng xiǎo guài. 2 [习语] **make a fuss of sb** 娇〔嬌〕养〔養〕某人 jiāoyǎng mǒurén; 过〔過〕分体〔體〕贴某人 guòfèn tǐtiē mǒurén. **fuss** [I] 大惊小怪 dà jīng xiǎo guài; 小题大作 xiǎo tí dà zuò. **fussy** *adj* [-ier, -iest] 1 (*about*) 过分注重细节〔節〕的 guòfèn zhùzhòng xìjié de. 2 大惊小怪的 dà jīng xiǎo guài de. 3 (服装等)过分装〔裝〕饰的 guòfèn zhuāngshì de. **fussily** *adv*.

futile /ˈfjuːtaɪl; *US* -tl/ *adj* 无〔無〕效的 wúxiàode; 无用的 wúyòngde: *a ~ attempt* 枉费心机的企图. **futility** /fjuːˈtɪlətɪ/ *n* [U].

future /ˈfjuːtʃə(r)/ *n* 1 **the future** [sing] 将〔將〕来〔來〕jiānglái; 未来 wèilái: *in the ~* 在将来. 2 [C] 前途 qiántú; 前景 qiánjǐng: *The company's ~ is uncertain*. 这家公司前景不明. 3 [U] 成功的可能 chénggōngde kěnéng: *There is no ~ in this job*. 这个工作没有前途. 4 [习语] **in future** 在将来 zài jiānglái. **future** *adj* 将来的 jiāngláide.

futuristic /ˌfjuːtʃəˈrɪstɪk/ *adj* 未来〔來〕派的 wèiláipàide.

fuzz /fʌz/ *n* [U] 茸毛 róngmáo; 绒毛 róngmáo. **fuzzy** *adj* [-ier, -iest] 1 (毛发)卷曲的 juǎnqūde. 2 (布等)柔软的 róuruǎnde; 绒毛似的 róngmáoshìde. 3 (形状、轮廓)模糊的 móhude. **fuzzily** *adv*. **fuzziness** *n* [U].

G g

G, g /dʒiː/ *n* [C] [*pl* **G's, g's** /dʒiːz/] 英语的第七个〔個〕字母 Yīngyǔde dìqīgè zìmǔ.

g *abbr* gram(s) 克(重量单位) kè: *500g* 500 克.

gabardine (亦作 **gaberdine**) /ˈgæbədiːn; ˌgæbəˈdiːn/ *n* 1 [U] 华〔華〕达〔達〕呢 huádání. 2 [C] 华达呢雨衣 huádání yǔyī.

gabble /ˈgæbl/ *v* [I, T] 急促而不清楚地说话 jícù ér bù qīngchu de shuōhuà. **gabble** *n* [U] 急促不清的话 jícù bùqīng de huà.

gable /ˈgeɪbl/ *n* [C] 山墙〔牆〕shānqiáng.

gad /gæd/ *v* [-dd-] [短语动词] **gad about/around** [非正式用语] 闲〔閒〕逛 xiánguàng; 游〔遊〕荡〔蕩〕yóudàng; 漫游 mànyóu.

gadget /ˈgædʒɪt/ *n* [C] 小巧的机〔機〕械 xiǎoqiǎode jīxiè. 小装〔裝〕置 xiǎozhuāngzhì.

gadgetry *n* [U] (总称)小巧机械 xiǎoqiǎo jīxiè, 精巧装置 jīngqiǎo zhuāngzhì.

Gaelic *n* [U], *adj* **1** /ˈgeɪlɪk/ 爱〔愛〕尔〔爾〕兰〔蘭〕盖〔蓋〕尔语 Ài'ěrlán Gài'ěryǔ. 爱尔兰盖尔人的 Ài'ěrlán Gài'ěrrén de. **2** /ˈgælɪk, 亦作 ˈgeɪlɪk/ 苏〔蘇〕格兰盖尔语 Sūgélán Gài'ěryǔ; 苏格兰盖尔人的 Sūgélán Gài'ěrrén de.

gaffe /gæf/ *n* [C] 失礼〔禮〕 shīlǐ; 失言 shīyán; 失态〔態〕 shītài.

gag /gæg/ *n* [C] **1** 塞口物 sāikǒuwù. **2** 笑话 xiàohuà; 插科打诨 chākē dǎhùn. **gag** *v* [-gg-] [T] 塞住…的嘴 sāizhù…de zuǐ.

gaga /ˈgɑːgɑː/ *adj* [非正式用语]老朽的 lǎoxiǔde; 老糊涂〔塗〕的 lǎo hútu de.

gage [美语] = GAUGE.

gaggle /ˈgægl/ *n* [C] **1** (鹅)群 qún. **2** 嘈杂〔雜〕的人群 cáozáde rénqún.

gaiety /ˈgeɪətɪ/ *n* [U] 高兴〔興〕 gāoxìng; 快乐〔樂〕 kuàilè.

gaily /ˈgeɪlɪ/ *adv* 快乐〔樂〕地 kuàilède; 娱乐地 yúlède.

gain[1] /geɪn/ *v* **1** [I, T] 获〔獲〕得(所需之物) huòdé: ~ *experience* 取得经验. ~ *an advantage* 取得优势. **2** 增加(速度、重量等) zēngjiā. **3** (钟、表)走快 zǒukuài: *My watch ~s two minutes a day*. 我的手表一天快两分钟. **4** [习语] **gain ground** ⇨ GROUND[1]. **gain ˈtime** 赢得时〔時〕间 yíngdé shíjiān; 借故拖延时间 jiègù tuōyán shíjiān. **5** [短语动词] **gain on sb/sth** (赛跑等中)逼近 bījìn.

gain[2] /geɪn/ *n* [C, U] 增加 zēngjiā; 增进〔進〕 zēngjìn. **gainful** *adj* 有收益的 yǒu shōuyìde: *~ful employment* 有报酬的工作.

gait /geɪt/ *n* [C] 步态〔態〕 bùtài; 马的步法 mǎde bùfǎ.

gala /ˈgɑːlə/ *n* [C] 盛会〔會〕 shènghuì; 节〔節〕日 jiérì; 庆〔慶〕祝 qìngzhù.

galaxy /ˈgæləksɪ/ *n* [*pl* **-ies**] **1** [C] [天文] 星系 xīngxì. **2 the Galaxy** [sing] [天文]银河系 yínhéxì. **3** [喻]一群(精英) yìqún: *a ~ of famous singers* 一群著名歌星. **galactic** /gəˈlæktɪk/ *adj*.

gale /geɪl/ *n* [C] **1** 大风〔風〕 dàfēng. **2** 一阵喧闹 yízhèn xuānnào.

gall[1] /gɔːl/ *n* [U] **1** = BILE. **2** 厚颜 hòuyán. **ˈgall-bladder** *n* [C] 胆〔膽〕囊 dǎnnáng. **ˈgallstone** *n* [C] 胆石 dǎnshí.

gall[2] /gɔːl/ *v* [T] 使恼〔惱〕怒 shǐ nǎonù; 使烦恼 shǐ fánnǎo.

gallant /ˈgælənt/ *adj* **1** 勇敢的 yǒnggǎnde. **2** 对〔對〕妇女献〔獻〕殷勤的 duì fùnǚ xiàn yīnqín de. **gallantly** *adv*. **gallantry** *n* [U].

galleon /ˈgælɪən/ *n* [C] (15—17 世纪)西班牙帆船 Xībānyá fānchuán.

gallery /ˈgælərɪ/ *n* [C] [*pl* **-ies**] **1** 画〔畫〕廊 huàláng; 美术〔術〕品陈列室 měishùpǐn chénlièshì. **2** (教堂、大厅等沿内壁凸出的)廊台〔臺〕 lángtái. **3** (剧场)顶层〔層〕楼〔樓〕座 dǐngcéng lóuzuò. **4** (矿井)水平巷道 shuǐpíng hàngdào.

galley /ˈgælɪ/ *n* [C] **1** (从前的)桨〔槳〕帆并用大木船 jiǎngfān bìngyòng dà mùchuán. **2** 船上厨房 chuán shàng chúfáng.

gallivant /ˌgælɪˈvænt, ˈgælɪvænt/ *v* [短语动词] **gallivant about** [非正式用语]游〔遊〕荡〔蕩〕 yóudàng; 闲逛 xiánguàng.

gallon /ˈgælən/ *n* [C] 加仑〔侖〕(液量单位, = 4.5 升) jiālún.

gallop /ˈgæləp/ *n* [C] (马等)飞〔飛〕跑 fēipǎo: *at full ~* 以最快速度. **gallop** *v* **1** [I, T] (使马)飞跑 fēipǎo. **2** [I] [非正式用语] 急速行动〔動〕 jísù xíngdòng.

gallows /ˈgæləuz/ *n* [常与 sing v 连用]绞刑架 jiǎoxíngjià; 绞台〔臺〕 jiǎotái.

galore /gəˈlɔː(r)/ *adv* 许多 xǔduō; 大量 dàliàng; 丰〔豐〕盛 fēngshèng: *prizes ~* 大量战利品.

galvanize /ˈgælvənaɪz/ *v* [T] **1** 给(铁)镀锌 gěi dùxīn. **2** (*into*) 使振奋〔奮〕 shǐ zhènfèn; 激起 jīqǐ.

gambit /ˈgæmbɪt/ *n* [C] **1** 开〔開〕局让〔讓〕棋法(国际象棋中开头作出牺牲以取得优势的下法) kāijú ràngqífǎ. **2** [喻] 第一步行动〔動〕 dìyībù xíngdòng.

gamble /ˈgæmbl/ *v* [I] **1** 赌博 dǔbó. **2** [短语动词] **gamble on sth** 投机〔機〕 tóujī; 冒险〔險〕 màoxiǎn. **gamble** *n* [C] 投机 tóujī; 冒险 màoxiǎn. **gambler** *n* [C] 赌博者 dǔbózhě; 投机者 tóujīzhě. **gambling** *n* [U].

gambol /ˈgæmbl/ *v* (-ll-; 美语亦作 -l-) [I] 蹦跳 bèngtiào; 嬉戏〔戲〕 xīxì.

game[1] /geɪm/ *n* **1** [C] 游戏〔戲〕 yóuxì; 运〔運〕动〔動〕 yùndòng. **2 games** [pl] 运动会〔會〕 yùndònghuì; 竞〔競〕技会 jìngjìhuì. **3** [C] (比赛中的)一局 yìjú; 一场〔場〕 yìchǎng; 一盘〔盤〕 yìpán. **4** [C] 游戏器具 yóuxì qìjù; 比赛用具 bǐsài yòngjù. **5** [C] [非正式用语] 计策 jìcè; 花招 huāzhāo. **6** [C] [非正式用语] 活动 huódòng; 行当〔當〕 hángdàng: *Politics is a power ~*. 政治是权力活动. **7** [U] 猎〔獵〕物 lièwù; 野味 yěwèi. **8** [习语] **give the ˈgame away** 泄露秘密 xièlòu mìmì; 暴露意图〔圖〕 bàolù yìtú. **(be) ˌoff one's ˈgame** 发〔發〕挥失常 fāhuī shīcháng; 状〔狀〕态〔態〕不佳 zhuàngtài bùjiā. **ˈgamekeeper** *n* [C] 猎场看守人 lièchǎng kānshǒurén. **ˈgame show** *n* [C] (电视)有奖〔獎〕游戏节〔節〕目 yǒujiǎng yóuxì jiémù. **ˈgames console** *n* [C] (小型)游戏机〔機〕 yóuxìjī.

game[2] /geɪm/ *adj* 勇敢的 yǒnggǎnde; 雄纠纠的 xióngjiūjiūde. **gamely** *adv*.

gammon /ˈgæmən/ *n* [U] 熏〔燻〕猪腿 xūnzhūtuǐ; 腌腿 yāntuǐ.

G

gamut /ˈgæmət/ *n* the gamut [sing] 整个〔個〕范〔範〕围〔圍〕zhěnggè fànwéi.

gander /ˈgændə(r)/ *n* [C] 雄鹅 xióng'é.

gang /gæŋ/ *n* [C, 亦作 sing, 用 pl v] **1** 一群罪犯 yìqún zuìfàn; 一队〔隊〕工人 yíduì gōngrén. **2** 一群年轻人(通常为男人) yìqún niánqīngrén. **gang** *v* [短语动词] gang up (on sb) 结成一帮(反对某人) jiéchéng yìbāng.

gangling /ˈgæŋglɪŋ/ *adj* (人)细长〔長〕的 xìchángde, 瘦长难〔難〕看的 shòucháng nánkàn de.

gangrene /ˈgæŋgriːn/ *n* [U] (医学)坏〔壞〕疽 huàijū. **gangrenous** /ˈgæŋgrɪnəs/ *adj*.

gangster /ˈgæŋstə(r)/ *n* [C] (一帮中的一个)匪徒 fěitú.

gangway /ˈgæŋweɪ/ *n* [C] **1**(船)跳板 tiàobǎn. **2**(坐位中间的)通道 tōngdào.

G

gaol (美语通常作 jail) /dʒeɪl/ *n* [C, U] 监〔監〕狱 jiānyù. **goal** (美语通常作 jail) *v* [T] 监禁 jiānjìn. **goaler** (美语通常作 jailer) *n* [C] 监狱看守 jiānyù kānshǒu.

gap /gæp/ *n* [C] **1** 裂口 lièkǒu; 缺口 quēkǒu. **2** (时间上的)间隙 jiànxì: ~ *between school and university* 在高中毕业到上大学之间的间隙. **3** [喻] 缺失 quēshī: ~*s in one's knowledge* 知识上的缺失.

gape /geɪp/ *v* [I] **1** 目瞪口呆地凝视 mù dèng kǒu dāi de níngshì. **2** 张开〔開〕zhāngkāi; 裂开 lièkāi: *a gaping hole* 裂口. **gape** *n* [C] 目瞪口呆的凝视 mù dèng kǒu dāi de níngshì.

garage /ˈgærɑːʒ, ˈgærɪdʒ; *US* gəˈrɑːʒ/ *n* [C] **1** 汽车〔車〕房 qìchēfáng. **2** 汽车修理站 qìchēxiūlǐzhàn. **garage** *v* [T] 把(汽车)送入汽车房或修理站 bǎ sòngrù qìchēfáng huò xiūlǐzhàn. **garage ˈstart-up** *n* [C] (计算机、网络行业)车库〔庫〕起步公司 chēkù qǐbù gōngsī; 家庭创〔創〕业〔業〕公司 jiātíng chuàngyè gōngsī.

garbage /ˈgɑːbɪdʒ/ *n* [U] [尤用于美语] 垃圾 lājī; 污物 wūwù. **ˈgarbage can** *n* [C] [美语] 垃圾箱 lājīxiāng; 垃圾桶 lājītǒng.

garbled /ˈgɑːbld/ *adj* 零星而混乱〔亂〕的 língxīng ěr hùnluàn de: *a ~ message* 零星而混乱的信息.

garden /ˈgɑːdn/ *n* **1** [C, U] 花园〔園〕huāyuán; 菜园 càiyuán. **2 gardens** [pl] 公园 gōngyuán. **garden** *v* [I] 从〔從〕事园艺〔藝〕cóngshì yuányì. **ˈgarden centre** *n* [C] (兼售园艺工具等的)花卉商店 huāhuì shāngdiàn. **gardener** *n* [C] 园林工人 yuánlín gōngrén. **gardening** *n* [U]. **garden party** *n* [C] 花园招待会〔會〕huāyuán zhāodàihuì.

gargle /ˈgɑːgl/ *v* [I] 漱喉 shùhóu; 漱口 shùkǒu. **gargle** *n* **1** [C] 漱口剂〔劑〕shùkǒujì. **2** [sing] 漱口 shùkǒu; 漱喉 shùhóu.

gargoyle /ˈgɑːgɔɪl/ *n* [C] (建筑)滴水嘴(常作怪兽状) dīshuǐzuǐ.

garish /ˈgeərɪʃ/ *adj* 耀眼的 yàoyǎnde; 炫目的 xuànmùde. **garishly** *adv*.

garland /ˈgɑːlənd/ *n* [C] 花环〔環〕huāhuán, 花冠 huāguān. **garland** *v* [T] 用花环装饰 yòng huāhuán zhuāngshì.

garlic /ˈgɑːlɪk/ *n* [U] 大蒜 dàsuàn.

garment /ˈgɑːmənt/ *n* [C] [正式用语](一件)衣服(长袍、外套) yīfu.

garnish /ˈgɑːnɪʃ/ *v* [T] 加饰菜于(食品) jiā shìcài yú. **garnish** *n* [C] 饰菜 shìcài.

garret /ˈgærət/ *n* [C] 阁楼〔樓〕gélóu.

garrison /ˈgærɪsn/ *n* [C, 亦作 sing, 用 pl v] 卫〔衛〕戍部队〔隊〕wèishù bùduì; 警卫部队 jǐngwèi bùduì. **garrison** *v* [T] 卫戍 wèishù, 守卫(城市) shǒuwèi.

garrulous /ˈgærələs/ *adj* [正式用语] 饶〔饒〕舌的 ráoshéde; 喋喋不休的 diédié bùxiū de.

garter /ˈgɑːtə(r)/ *n* [C] 吊袜〔襪〕带〔帶〕diàowàdài.

gas /gæs/ *n* [*pl* ~es; 美语亦作 ~ses] **1** [C, U] 气〔氣〕体〔體〕qìtǐ. **2** [U] 可燃气 kěránqì; 煤气 méiqì; 沼气 zhǎoqì. **3** [U] [美语, 非正式用语] 汽油 qìyóu. **gas** *v* [-ss-] [T] 用毒气杀〔殺〕死(某人) yòng dúqì shā sǐ. **ˈgasbag** *n* [C] [非正式用语, 贬] 饶〔饒〕舌的人 ráoshéde rén. **gaseous** /ˈgæsɪəs, ˈgeɪsɪəs/ *adj* 气体的 qìtǐde; 气体似的 qìtǐshìde. **ˈgas-fitter** *n* [C] 煤气设备〔備〕安装〔裝〕工 méiqì shèbèi ānzhuānggōng. **ˈgaslight** *n* [C, U] 煤气灯〔燈〕méiqìdēng. **ˈgasman** /-mæn/ *n* [C] [*pl* -men /-men/] [非正式用语] 煤气表〔錶〕抄表员 méiqìbiǎo chāobiǎoyuán. **ˈgas mask** *n* [C] 防毒面具 fángdú miànjù. **ˈgas station** *n* [C] [美语] (汽车)加油站 jiāyóuzhàn. **gassy** *adj* [-ier, -iest] 气体的 qìtǐde; 气体似的 qìtǐshìde; 充满气体的 chōngmǎn qìtǐ de: ~*sy beer* 气很足的啤酒. **ˈgaswork** *n* [C] [*pl* gasworks] 煤气厂〔廠〕méiqìchǎng.

gash /gæʃ/ *n* [C] (*in*) 深而长〔長〕的切口 shēn ér cháng de qiēkǒu; 深而长的伤〔傷〕口 shēn ér cháng de shāngkǒu. **gash** *v* [T] 划〔劃〕开 huákāi.

gasket /ˈgæskɪt/ *n* [C] 垫〔墊〕圈 diànquān; 垫片 diànpiàn.

gasoline (亦作 gasolene) /ˈgæsəliːn/ *n* [U] [美语] 汽油 qìyóu.

gasp /gɑːsp/ *v* **1** [I] 喘气〔氣〕chuǎnqì; 透不过〔過〕气 tòu bú guò qì. **2** [T] 气喘吁吁地说 qìchuǎn xūxū de shuō: ~ *a reply* 气喘吁吁地回答. **gasp** *n* [C] 气喘 qìchuǎn.

gastric /ˈgæstrɪk/ *adj* 胃部的 wèibùde: ~ *ulcers* 胃溃疡〔瘍〕.

gastro-enteritis /ˌgæstrəʊˌentəˈraɪtɪs/ *n* [U] 胃肠〔腸〕炎 wèicháng yán.

gate /geɪt/ *n* [C] **1** 门〔門〕mén; 大门 dàmén; 篱〔籬〕笆门 líbamén. **2** (飞机场登机的)入口 rùkǒu. **3** (运动会等)观〔觀〕众〔衆〕人数〔數〕guānzhòng rénshù; 门票收入 ménpiào shōurù. ˈ**gatecrash** *v* [I, T]擅自进〔進〕入 shànzì jìnrù; 无〔無〕票入场〔場〕wúpiào rùchǎng. ˈ**gatecrasher** *n* [C]. ˈ**gatepost** *n* [C]门柱 ménzhù. ˈ**gateway** *n*[C] **1** 门口 ménkǒu; 入口 rùkǒu. **2** [常作 sing] *to* [喻]途径〔徑〕tújìng; 手段 shǒuduàn: *the* ~ *to success* 成功的途径.

gâteau /ˈgætəʊ; *US* gæˈtəʊ/ *n*[C] [*pl* ~x 或~s] 大奶油蛋糕 dà nǎiyóu dàngāo.

gather /ˈgæðə(r)/ *v* **1** [I, T](使)聚集 jùjí, (使)集拢〔攏〕jílǒng. **2** [T]采〔採〕集 cǎijí; 收集(花、果等) shōují. **3** [T] 积〔積〕聚 jījù; 积累 jīlěi: ~ *information* 积累资料. **4** [T] 猜想 cāixiǎng; 推测 tuīcè: *I* ~ *she's looking for a job*. 我推测, 她在找工作做. **5** [T]增加 zēngjiā: ~ *speed* 增加速度. **6** [T]在(衣服上)打褶子 zài dǎ zhězi. **gathering** *n* [C]集会〔會〕jíhuì.

gauche /gəʊʃ/ *adj* 不善交际〔際〕的 búshàn jiāojì de; 粗鲁的 cūlǔde.

gaudy /ˈgɔːdɪ/ *adj* [**-ier**, **-iest**] [贬]炫丽〔麗〕的 xuànlìde. **gaudily** *adv*.

gauge(美语亦作 **gage**) /geɪdʒ/ *n* [C] **1** 计量器 jìliàngqì: *a patrol* ~ 汽油计量器. **2** (铁道)轨距 guǐjù. **3** (金属板等的)厚度 hòudù; (钢丝等的)直径〔徑〕zhíjìng. **4** [喻]估计 gūjì: *a* ~ *of her progress* 对她的进步的估计. **gauge** *v* [T] **1** 精确〔確〕测量 jīngquè cèliáng. **2** [喻]估计 gūjì; 评价〔價〕píngjià.

gaunt /gɔːnt/ *adj* (人)憔悴的 qiáocuìde; 瘦弱的 shòuruòde. **gauntness** *n* [U].

gauntlet /ˈgɔːntlɪt/ *n* [C] 防护〔護〕手套 fánghù shǒutào.

gauze /gɔːz/ *n* [U] 薄纱 bóshā; 罗〔羅〕luó; 网〔網〕纱 wǎngshā; 纱布 shābù.

gave /geɪv/ *pt* of GIVE[1].

gawky /ˈgɔːkɪ/ *adj* [**-ier**, **-iest**] (尤指身材高的人)粗笨难〔難〕看的 cūbèn nánkàn de. **gawkiness** *n* [U].

gawp /gɔːp/ *v* [I] [非正式用语]呆头〔頭〕呆脑〔腦〕地凝视 dāitóu dāinǎo de níngshì.

gay /geɪ/ *adj* **1** 同性恋〔戀〕的 tóngxìngliànde. **2** 快乐〔樂〕的 kuàilède; 愉快的 yúkuàide: ~ *laughter* 欢乐的笑声. ~ *colours* 鲜艳的旗帜. **gay** *n*[C] 搞同性恋的人 gǎo tóngxìngliàn de rén.

gaze /geɪz/ *v* [I] (*at*)注视 zhùshì; 凝视 níngshì. **gaze** *n*[sing] 注视 zhùshì; 凝视 níngshì.

gazelle /gəˈzel/ *n* [C] 小羚羊 xiǎolíngyáng; 瞪羚 dènglíng.

gazette /gəˈzet/ *n* [C] (政府等)公报〔報〕gōngbào.

gazump /gəˈzʌmp/ *v* [T] [英国非正式用语, 贬][常用被动语态]向…抬高房价〔價〕敲诈 xiàng…tái gāo fángjià qiāozhà.

GB /ˌdʒiː ˈbiː/ *abbr* = Great Britain.

GCSE /ˌdʒiː siː es ˈiː/ *n* [C] [英国英语]普通中等教育证〔證〕书〔書〕pǔtōng zhōngděng jiàoyù zhèngshū. (General Certificate of Secondary Education); 普通中等教育证书考试 pǔtōng zhōngděng jiàoyù zhèngshū kǎoshì.

gear /gɪə(r)/ *n* **1**[C, U]齿〔齒〕轮〔輪〕chǐlún, 传〔傳〕动〔動〕装〔裝〕置 chuándòng zhuāngzhì; (排)挡〔擋〕dǎng: *The car has five* ~*s*. 这汽车有五个挡. *change* ~ 换挡. **2**[U] 设备〔備〕shèbèi: *camping* ~ 野营用具. **3**[U]装置 zhuāngzhì: *the landing-*~ *of an aircraft* 飞机着陆装置. **gear** *v* [短语动词] **gear sb to/towards sth** 调节〔節〕…以适〔適〕应〔應〕… tiáojié…yǐ shìyìng…: *The whole city is* ~*ed to the needs of tourists*. 整个城市都来适应旅游者的需要. **gear (sb) up (for/to sth)** (为…)做好准〔準〕备〔備〕zuòhǎo zhǔnbèi. ˈ**gearbox** *n* [C] 齿轮箱 chǐlúnxiāng; 变〔變〕速箱 biànsùxiāng. ˈ**gear-lever**; ˈ**gear-stick**(美语常作 **gearshift**) *n* [C] 变速装置 biànsù zhuāngzhì.

geese /giːs/ *n pl* of GOOSE.

gelatine /ˌdʒeləˈtiːn; -ˌtɪn/ (亦作 **gelatin** /-ˌtɪn/, 尤用于美语) *n* [U] 明胶〔膠〕míngjiāo; 动〔動〕物胶 dòngwùjiāo.

gelignite /ˈdʒelɪgnaɪt/ *n* [U] 葛里炸药 gělǐ zhàyào.

gem /dʒem/ *n* [C] **1** 宝〔寶〕石 bǎoshí. **2** 难〔難〕能可贵的人 nán néng kěguìde rén; 珍贵的物品 zhēnguìde wùpǐn.

gender /ˈdʒendə(r)/ *n* [C, U] **1**[语法](名词、代名词的)性 xìng. **2**[正式用语](生理上的)性 xìng.

gene /dʒiːn/ *n* [C] [生物]基因 jīyīn.

genealogy /ˌdʒiːnɪˈælədʒɪ/ *n* [*pl* **-ies**] **1** [U]家系学〔學〕jiāxìxué; 系谱学 xìpǔxué. **2**[C] 系谱图〔圖〕xìpǔtú; 系统图 xìtǒngtú. **genealogical** /ˌdʒiːnɪəˈlɒdʒɪkl/ *adj*.

general /ˈdʒenrəl/ *adj* **1** 普遍的 pǔbiànde; 全面的 quánmiànde: *of* ~ *interest* 普遍有兴趣的. **2** 一般的 yìbānde: ~ *knowledge* 一般的知识. **3** 总〔總〕的 zǒngde; 概括的 gàikuòde: ~ *impressions* 总的印象. **4**[习语] **in** ˈ**general** 一般地 yìbānde; 大体〔體〕上 dàtǐshàng. **general** *n* [C] 将〔將〕军 jiāngjūn. **general anaesˈthetic** *n* [C] 全身麻醉 quánshēn mázuì. **general eˈlection** *n* [C] 大选〔選〕dàxuǎn; 普选 pǔxuǎn. **generality** /ˌdʒenəˈrælətɪ/ *n* [*pl* **-ies**] **1**[C]笼〔籠〕统的表述 lǒngtǒngde biǎoshù. **2**[U]一般性 yìbān-

G

xìng; 普通性 pǔtōngxìng. **generally** *adv* 1 一般地 yìbānde; 通常 tōngcháng: *I ~ly get up early*. 我通常起得很早. 2 被大多数〔數〕人 bèi dàduōshù rén: *The plan was ~ly welcomed*. 这项计划受到大多数人的欢迎. 3 一般地 yìbānde; 概括地 gàikuòde: *~ly speaking* 一般地说. ˌ**general pracˈtitioner** *n* [C] (非专科的)普通医〔醫〕生 pǔtōng yīshēng. ˌ**general ˈstrike** *n* [C] 总罢〔罷〕工 zǒngbàgōng.

generalize /ˈdʒenrəlaɪz/ *v* [I] 概括 gàikuò; 归〔歸〕纳 guīnà. **generalization** /ˌdʒenrəlaɪˈzeɪʃn; *US* -lɪˈz-/ *n* [C, U] 概括 gàikuò; 推论〔論〕 tuīlùn.

generate /ˈdʒenəreɪt/ *v* [T] 使产〔產〕生 shǐ chǎnshēng; 使发〔發〕生 shǐ fāshēng: ~ *electricity* 发电. **generative** /ˈdʒenərətɪv/ *adj* 有生产力的 yǒu shēngchǎnlì de. **generator** *n* [C] 发电〔電〕机〔機〕 fādiànjī.

generation /ˌdʒenəˈreɪʃn/ *n* 1[C]代 dài; 一代 yídài; 辈〔輩〕 bèi; 世代 shìdài. 2[C](家史中的)一代人 yídàirén. 3[U]发〔發〕生 fāshēng: *the ~ of heating* 产生热.

generic /dʒɪˈnerɪk/ *adj* [正式用语]一般的 yìbānde; 普通的 pǔtōngde. **generically** /-klɪ/ *adv*.

generous /ˈdʒenərəs/ *adj* 1 慷慨的 kāngkǎide: *He's ~ with his money*. 他用钱慷慨. 2 丰〔豐〕盛的 fēngshèngde; 丰富的 fēngfùde. **generosity** /ˌdʒenəˈrɒsətɪ/ *n* [U]. **generously** *adv*.

genetic /dʒɪˈnetɪk/ *adj* 发〔發〕生的 fāshēngde; 遗传〔傳〕学〔學〕的 yíchuánxuéde. **genetically** /-klɪ/ *adv*. **genetically modified** 转〔轉〕基因的 zhuǎnjīyīn de; 基因改造的 jīyīn gǎizào de. **genetics** *n* [与 sing v 连用]遗传学 yíchuánxué.

genial /ˈdʒiːnɪəl/ *adj* 和蔼的 hé'ǎide; 亲〔親〕切的 qīnqiède; 友好的 yǒuhǎode. **genially** *adv*.

genital /ˈdʒenɪtl/ *adj* 生殖器的 shēngzhíqìde. **genitals** *n* [pl] 生殖器 shēngzhíqì; 外阴〔陰〕部 wàiyīnbù.

genius /ˈdʒiːnɪəs/ *n* 1(a)[U]天才 tiāncái. (b)[C] 天才人物 tiāncái rénwù. 2[sing]才华〔華〕 cáihuá; 天资 tiānzī; 天赋 tiānfù: *have a ~ for languages* 在语言上有天赋.

genocide /ˈdʒenəsaɪd/ *n* [U] 种〔種〕族灭〔滅〕绝 zhǒngzú mièjué; 灭绝种族的屠杀〔殺〕 mièjué zhǒngzú de túshā.

genome /ˈdʒiːnəʊm/ *n* [U] 基因组 jīyīnzǔ.

genre /ˈʒɑːnrə/ *n* [正式用语]种〔種〕 zhǒng; 类〔類〕 lèi; 样〔樣〕式 yàngshì.

gent /dʒent/ *n* 1 [C] [非正式用语或谑]绅士 shēnshì; 假绅士 jiǎ shēnshì; 人 rén; 家伙 jiāhuo. 2 **the Gents** [非正式英国英语][常用 sing v] 男公共厕所 nán gōnggòngcèsuǒ.

genteel /dʒenˈtiːl/ *adj* 彬彬有礼〔禮〕的 bīnbīn yǒulǐ de; 过〔過〕分礼貌的 guòfèn lǐmào de.

gentile /ˈdʒentaɪl/ *n* [C], *adj* 非犹〔猶〕太人 fēi yóutài rén; 非犹太人的 fēi yóutàirén de.

gentle /ˈdʒentl/ *adj* [~r /-lə(r)/, ~st /-lɪst/] 文雅的 wényǎde; 有礼〔禮〕貌的 yǒu lǐmào de. **gentleness** *n* [U]. **gently** /-lɪ/ *adv*.

gentleman /ˈdʒentlmən/ *n* [C][*pl* -men /-mən/] 1 有教养〔養〕的人 yǒu jiàoyǎng de rén; 有礼〔禮〕貌的人 yǒu lǐmào de rén. 2(对男子的尊称)先生 xiānsheng. 3[旧]绅士 shēnshì; 有钱〔錢〕有社会〔會〕地位的人 yǒu qián yǒu shèhuì dìwèi de rén. **gentlemanly** *adj* [正式用语或旧词]绅士风〔風〕度的 shēnshì fēngdù de.

gentry /ˈdʒentrɪ/ *n* **the gentry** [pl] (仅次于贵族的)中上阶〔階〕级 zhōng shàng jiējí.

genuine /ˈdʒenjʊɪn/ *adj* 真正的 zhēnzhèngde; 名副其实〔實〕的 míng fù qí shí de. **genuinely** *adv*. **genuineness** *n* [U].

genus /ˈdʒiːnəs/ *n* [C] [*pl* **genera** /ˈdʒenərə/] (生物分类)属〔屬〕 shǔ.

geography /dʒɪˈɒgrəfɪ/ *n* [U] 1 地理学〔學〕 dìlǐxué. 2 位置 wèizhì; 地形 dìxíng. 布〔佈〕局 bùjú. **geographer** /-fə(r)/ *n* [C]地理学家 dìlǐxuéjiā. **geographical** /ˌdʒɪəˈgræfɪkl/ *adj*. **geographically** /-klɪ/ *adv*.

geology /dʒɪˈɒlədʒɪ/ *n* [U] 1 地质〔質〕学〔學〕 dìzhìxué. 2 (某地的)地质 dìzhì. **geological** /dʒɪəˈlɒdʒɪkl/ *adj*. **geologically** /-klɪ/ *adv*. **geologist** /dʒɪˈɒlədʒɪst/ *n* [C] 地质学家 dìzhìxuéjiā.

geometry /dʒɪˈɒmətrɪ/ *n* [U] 几〔幾〕何学〔學〕 jǐhéxué. **geometric** /dʒɪəˈmetrɪk/ (亦作 **geometrical**) *adj*.

geranium /dʒəˈreɪnɪəm/ *n* [C] 天竺葵 tiānzhúkuí.

geriatrics /ˌdʒerɪˈætrɪks/ *n* [U] 老年病学〔學〕 lǎoniánbìngxué. **geriatric** *adj*.

germ /dʒɜːm/ *n* 1[C]微生物 wēishēngwù; 病菌 bìngjūn. 2[sing] *of* 开〔開〕始 kāishǐ; 发〔發〕端 fāduān; 萌芽 méngyá: *the ~ of an idea* 一个主意的萌发.

German /ˈdʒɜːmən/ *n* 1[U]德语 Déyǔ. 2[C] 德国〔國〕人 Déguórén. **German** *adj* 德国的 Déguóde; 德国人的 Déguórénde; 德语的 Déyǔde. ˌ**German ˈmeasles** *n* [U] [医]风〔風〕疹 fēngzhěn.

Germany /ˈdʒɜːmənɪ/ *n* [U] 德国〔國〕 Déguó.

germinate /ˈdʒɜːmɪneɪt/ *v* [I, T] (使种子)

发〔發〕芽 fāyá. **germination** /ˌdʒɜːmɪˈneɪʃn/ *n* [U].

gerund /ˈdʒerənd/ *n* [C][语法]动〔動〕名词 dòngmíngcí.

gestation /dʒeˈsteɪʃn/ *n* [U] 妊娠 rènshēn; 怀〔懷〕孕 huáiyùn.

gesticulate /dʒɪˈstɪkjʊleɪt/ *v* [I] [正式用语]打手势〔勢〕 dǎ shǒushì; (说话时)做手势 zuò shǒushì. **gesticulation** /dʒeˌstɪkjʊˈleɪʃn/ *n*[C,U].

gesture /ˈdʒestʃə(r)/ *n* [C] 1 姿势〔勢〕 zīshì; 手势 shǒushì. 2[喻]姿态〔態〕 zītài; 表示 biǎoshì: *a ~ of support* 支持的姿态 . *a ~ of defiance* 对抗的表示.

get /get/ *v* [-tt-; *pt*, *pp* got /gɒt /; *US pp* gotten / ˈgɒtn /] 1 [T]得到 dédào; 获〔獲〕得 huòdé: *~ a new car* 得到一辆新车. 2 [T]收到 shōudào: *~ a letter* 收到一封信. 3 [T]取来 qǔlái; 拿来 nálái: *G~ your coat*. 把你的外套拿来. 4 [T]使受惩〔懲〕处〔處〕 shǐ shòu chéngchǔ: *~ six months* 判刑六个月. 5 [T]乘(交通工具) chéng: *~ a plane to Rome* 乘飞机去罗马. 6 [T]使遭受病痛 shǐ zāoshòu bìngtòng: *~ the flu* 得了流感. *~ a headache* 头痛. 7 [T]准〔準〕备〔備〕(饭食) zhǔnbèi. 8 [T](a)俘获 fúhuò; 抓到 zhuādào: *The police got the robber*. 警方抓到了强盗. (b)杀〔殺〕死 shāsǐ; 惩罚 chéngfá: *I'll ~ you for that!* 这件事我可饶不了你. 9 [I,T](使)成为〔爲〕 chéngwéi: *~ wet* 弄湿. *~ dressed* 梳装打扮好. *~ a box open* 把箱子打开. *~ your hair cut* 理理你的发. *He got killed in a car accident*. 他在一次车祸中丧生. 10 [I](a)有机〔機〕会〔會〕 yǒu jīhuì; 设法 shèfǎ; 能够 nénggòu: *~ to know someone* 有机会认识某人. (b)开〔開〕始做某事 kāishǐ zuò mǒushì: *We soon got talking*. 我们很快就谈了起来. 11 [T]使做某事 shǐ zuò mǒushì: *I can't ~ her to understand*. 我没法让她了解. *He got me to help him with his homework*. 他让我在他做家庭作业时帮帮他. 12 [I,T](使)移动〔動〕(有时是艰难地) yídòng: *~ off the bus* 下公共汽车. *We can't ~ the piano downstairs*. 我们没法把钢琴弄到楼下去. *~ a message to sb* 给某人传个口信. 13 [I] *to* 到达〔達〕 dàodá: *~ home early* 很早就到家. *What time did you ~ to London?* 你什么时候到达伦敦的? 14 [T] [非正式用语]了〔瞭〕解 liáojiě: *I don't ~ you*. 我不了解你. 15 [T][非正式用语]使困惑 shǐ kùnhuò; 使迷惑 shǐ míhuò: *That's got you!* 你被弄糊涂〔塗〕了! 16 [T] 使苦恼〔惱〕 shǐ kǔnǎo: *Loud pop music really ~s me*. 吵人的通俗音乐把我害苦了. 17 [习语] **get somewhere** (或 **anywhere**) [非正式用语](使)有一些进〔進〕展 yǒu yìxiē jìnzhǎn; (使)有一些成就 yǒu yìxiē chéngjiù **get nowhere** [非正式用语](使)无〔無〕进展 wú jìnzhǎn; (使)徒劳〔勞〕túláo. **get to grips** ⇨GRIP. 18 [短语动词] **get (sth) aˈcross (to sb)** (使某事)被了解 bèi liáojiě. **get aˈhead (of sb)** (使)走在(某人)前面 zǒu zài qiánmiàn; (使)领先(某人) lǐngxiān. **get aˈlong** = GET ON WITH (a). **get aˈlong (with sb)** = GET ON (WITH SB). **ˈget at sb** [非正式用语]批评 pīpíng; 指责 zhǐzé: *Stop ~ting at me!* 别再数落我! **get at sth** (a) 够得着某物 gòudezháo mǒuwù. (b)发〔發〕现 fāxiàn; 查明 chámíng: *~ at the truth* 发现真相. **be getting at sth** 意指 yìzhǐ; 暗指 ànzhǐ: *What are you ~ting at?* 你倒底什么意思? **get aˈway** (a) 逃走 táozǒu: *Two prisoners got away*. 两名囚犯逃走了. (b) 度假 dùjià: *~ away for two weeks in France*. 在法国度假两个星期. **get away with sth** 做成(某种坏事而未受惩处) zuòchéng: *~ away with cheating* 作弊得逞. **get by** 勉强过〔過〕活 miǎnqiǎng guòhuó: *~ by on a small salary* 靠微薄的薪水糊口. **get sb ˈdown** [非正式用语]使沮丧〔喪〕 shǐ jǔsàng. **get sth down** 费力地吞下 fèilìde tūnxià. **get down to sth** 开始认真做某事 kāishǐ rènzhēn zuò mǒushì: *~ down to work* 开始认真工作. *~ down to business* 开始办正经事. **get in** 到达 dàodá: *The train got in late*. 列车晚点到达. **get sb in** 请某人来服务〔務〕 qǐng mǒurén lái fúwù: *~ someone in to fix the TV* 请某人来修电视. **get sth in** 得到…的供应〔應〕 dédào…de gōngyìng: *~ some coal in for the winter* 得到一些过冬用的煤. **get in with sb** [非正式用语](为得到好处而)结交某人 jiéjiāo mǒurén. **get into sth** (a) (使)陷入(某种状态) xiànrù: *~ into trouble* 陷入困境. (b) (使)染上(某种习惯) rǎnshàng: *~ into the habit of rising at 6 a.m.* 养成六点钟起床的习惯. *Don't ~ into drugs!* 别随随便便吸起毒来. (c) 对〔對〕…产〔產〕生兴〔興〕趣 duì…chǎnshēng xìngqù: *I can't ~ into this book*. 这本书不吸引我. (d) 开始 kāishǐ: *~ into a fight* 打起来. *~ into a conversation* 谈了起来. (e) 着手某种〔種〕事业〔業〕 zhuóshǒu mǒuzhǒng shìyè: *~ into journalism* 开始从事新闻事业. **get (sb) ˈoff** (使某人)离〔離〕去 líqù; (使某人)出发 chūfā: *~ children off to school* 打发孩子们去上学. **get (sb) off (with sth)** (使某人)逃脱重罚 táotuō zhòngfá: *He got off with just a fine*. 他被从轻发落,罚款了事. **get on (with sb)** (与某人)关〔關〕系〔係〕很好 guānxì hěnhǎo: *We don't ~ on*. 我们关系不好. *Do you ~ on with your boss?* 你和

G

你的上司关系好吗? get on (with sth) (a) 进〔進〕展 jìnzhǎn; 进步 jìnbù: *How are you ~ting on with your new job?* 你的新工作做得怎样? (b) 继〔繼〕续〔續〕jìxù: *G~ on with your work*. 继续做你的工作. be getting on [非正式用语] (a) 上了年纪 shàngle niánjì. (b) 晚的 wǎnde: *It's ~ting on, so I must go home*. 天晚了,我得回家了. get ˈout (a) 逃走 tǎozǒu. (b) 泄露 xièlòu: *The secret got out*. 秘密泄露了. get out of sth / doing sth (使)逃避(该做的事) táobì; (使)规避(该做的事) guībì. get over sth (a) (从震惊等中)恢复〔復〕过来 huīfù guòlái: *I haven't got over my mother's death*. 我自母亲去世以后心情一直一蹶不振. (b)克服 kèfú; 战〔戰〕胜〔勝〕zhànshèng: *~ over one's shyness* 克服羞怯心理. get sth over (to sb) 把…向某人讲〔講〕清楚 bǎ… xiàng mǒurén jiǎng qīngchǔ. get sth over (with) [非正式用语]熬过 áoguò; 结束 jiéshù: *I'm glad I've got my exams over with*. 我很高兴,我把考试熬过去了. get round sb 用奉承等说服 yòng fèngcheng děng shuōfú: *She knows how to ~ round her father*. 她知道怎样去哄得她父亲依顺她. get round sth 回〔迴〕避(法律、规章等) huíbì. get round to sth/doing sth(处理完其他事情后)终于能做某事 zhōngyú néng zuò mǒushì. get through 用完 yòngwán: *~ through £100 a week* 一星期花掉 100 英镑. get through (sth) 通过(考试等) tōngguò. get through (to sb) (通过电话等)同…联〔聯〕系〔繫〕tóng…liánxì. get (sth) ˈthrough to sb 使某人理解(某事) shǐ mǒurén lǐjiě: *I just can't ~ through to them (that this is wrong)*. 我没法使他们理解(这是错误的). get toˈgether (with sb) 会面 huìmiàn: *~ together for a drink* 聚一聚喝上一杯. get up (a) 起床〔牀〕qǐchuáng. (b) 起立 qǐlì. get up to sth (a) 达到 dádào: *~ up to page ten* (学或阅读)到第十页. (b) 做(某种顽皮、意外的事) zuò: *What have you been ~ting up to?* 你在搞什么名堂? ˈgetaway *n* [C] 逃跑 táopǎo: *a fast ~away* 急速逃逸 jísù táoyì. ˈget-together *n*[C] [非正式用语]社交聚会 shèjiāo jùhuì. ˈgetup *n* [C][非正式用语]服装〔裝〕fúzhuāng; 穿戴 chuāndài. ˌget-up-and-ˈgo *n* [C] [非正式用语]干〔幹〕劲〔勁〕gànjìn;进取心 jìnqǔxīn.

geyser /ˈgiːzə(r); *US* ˈgaɪzər/ *n* [C] 喷出喷柱的温泉 pēnchū pēn zhù de wēnquán.

ghastly /ˈgɑːstlɪ; *US* ˈgæstlɪ/ *adj* [-ier, -iest] 1 可怕的 kěpàde; 恐怖的 kǒngbùde: *a ~ accident* 可怕的事故. 2[非正式用语]极〔極〕坏〔壞〕的 jíhuàide; 糟糕透了的 zāogāotòulede: *a ~ mistake* 糟透了的错误. 3 苍〔蒼〕白的 cāngbáide.

ghetto /ˈgetəʊ/ *n* [C] [*pl* ~s] [常贬](美国的)少数民族居住区〔區〕shǎoshù mínzú jūzhùqū. ˈghetto blaster *n* [C] [非正式用语]大型收录〔錄〕机〔機〕dàxíng shōulùjī.

ghost /gəʊst/ *n* 1 [C]鬼魂 guǐhún; 幽灵〔靈〕yōulíng. 2 [sing] [喻]一点〔點〕点 yìdiǎndiǎn; 一丝 yìsī: *the ~ of a chance* 很少的一点机会. 3[习语] give up the ˈghost 死 sǐ. ghostly *adj* 鬼的 guǐde; 鬼一样〔樣〕的 guǐ yíyàng de. ˈghost town *n* [C] 被废〔廢〕弃〔棄〕的城镇 bèi fèiqìde chéngzhèn. ˈghost-writer *n* [C] 代人写〔寫〕作的人 dài rén xiězuò de rén; 捉刀人 zhuōdāorén.

GI /ˌdʒiː ˈaɪ/ *n* [C] 美国〔國〕陆〔陸〕军士兵 měiguó lùjūn shìbīng.

giant /ˈdʒaɪənt/ *n* [C] (*fem* ~ess)(神话故事中的)巨人 jùrén. giant *adj* 特大的 tèdàde.

gibberish /ˈdʒɪbərɪʃ/ *n* [U] 无〔無〕意义〔義〕的谈话 wú yìyì de tánhuà.

gibbon /ˈgɪbən/ *n* [C] 长〔長〕臂猿 chángbìyuán.

gibe (亦作 jibe) /dʒaɪb/ *v* [I] (*at*) 嘲弄 cháonòng; 嘲笑 cháoxiào. gibe (亦作 jibe) *n* [C] 嘲笑话 cháoxiàohuà; 嘲弄话 cháonònghuà.

giblets /ˈdʒɪblɪts/ *n* [pl] (鸡鸭等作食用的)内脏〔臟〕nèizàng.

giddy /ˈgɪdɪ/ *adj* [-ier,-iest] 使人头〔頭〕晕的 shǐ rén tóuyūnde. giddiness *n* [U].

gift /gɪft/ *n* [C] 1 赠品 zèngpǐn; 礼〔禮〕物 lǐwù. 2 天赋 tiānfù; 才能 cáinéng: *a ~ for languages* 语言的天赋. 3[习语] the gift of the ˈgab 口才 kǒucái; 辩才 biàncái. gifted *adj* 有天赋的 yǒu tiānfù de.

gig /gɪg/ *n* [C] [非正式用语]爵士乐〔樂〕队〔隊〕等的特约演奏 juéshì yuèduì děng de tèyuē yǎnzòu.

gigantic /dʒaɪˈgæntɪk/ *adj* 巨大的 jùdàde; 庞〔龐〕大的 pángdàde.

giggle /ˈgɪgl/ *v* [I] (*at*) 咯咯地笑 gēgēde xiào; 傻〔傻〕笑 shǎxiào. giggle *n* 1 [C] 傻笑 shǎxiào. 2 [sing] [非正式用语]娱〔娛〕乐〔樂〕yúlè; 趣事 qùshì.

gild /gɪld/ *v* [T] 包金箔于 bāo jīnbó yú; 涂〔塗〕金色于 tú jīnsè yú.

gill[1] /gɪl/ *n* [C,常作 pl] (鱼的)腮 sāi.

gill[2] /dʒɪl/ *n* [C] 吉尔〔爾〕(液量单位, $=\frac{1}{4}$ 品脱) jí'ěr.

gilt /gɪlt/ *n* [U] 镀金用的材料 dùjīn yòng de cáiliào.

gimmick /ˈgɪmɪk/ *n* [C] 骗人的花招 piànrénde huāzhāo; 鬼把戏〔戲〕guǐbǎxì. gimmicky *adj*.

gin /dʒɪn/ *n* [U] 杜松子酒 dùsōngzǐjiǔ.

ginger /ˈdʒɪndʒə(r)/ *n* [U] 1 生姜〔薑〕shēngjiāng；姜 jiāng. 2 姜黄色 jiānghuángsè. **ginger** *v* [短语动词] **ginger sb / sth up** 使有活力 shǐ yǒu huólì；使兴〔興〕奋〔奮〕shǐ xīngfèn. **ginger-ˈale, ginger-ˈbeer** *n* [U] 姜味汽水 jiāngwèi qìshuǐ. **ˈgingerbread** *n* [U] 姜味饼 jiāngwèibǐng.

gingerly /ˈdʒɪndʒəlɪ/ *adv* 小心谨慎地 xiǎoxīn jǐnshèn de；犹〔猶〕豫地 yóuyùde.

gipsy = GYPSY.

giraffe /dʒɪˈrɑːf; US dʒəˈræf/ *n* [C] 长〔長〕颈〔頸〕鹿 chángjǐnglù.

girder /ˈgɜːdə(r)/ *n* [C] (建筑)大梁 dàliáng.

girdle /ˈgɜːdl/ *n* [C] 1 腰带〔帶〕yāodài. 2(妇女的)紧〔緊〕身胸衣 jǐnshēn xiōngyī. **girdle** *v* [T] [修辞]围〔圍〕绕〔繞〕wéirào；束 shù：*a lake ~d with trees* 树木环绕的湖泊.

girl /gɜːl/ *n* [C] 女孩子 nǚháizi；姑娘 gūniang；女儿〔兒〕nǚ'ér. **ˈgirlfriend** *n* [C] 1(男人的)情人 qíngrén，情妇〔婦〕qíngfù. 2 女朋友 nǚ péngyou. **Girl ˈGuide** *n* [C] 女童子军 nǚ tóngzǐjūn. **girlhood** *n* [U] 少女时〔時〕期 shàonǚ shíqī. **girlish** *adj* 少女的 shàonǚde；少女似的 shàonǚshìde；适〔適〕合于女子的 shìhé yú nǚzǐ de.

giro /ˈdʒaɪrəʊ/ *n* [*pl* ~s] 1 [U,C]银行或邮〔郵〕局间的直接转〔轉〕账〔賬〕制度 yínháng huò yóujújiānde zhíjiē zhuǎnzhàng zhìdù. 2 [C] [英国英语](政府支付社会保障金的)直接转账支票 zhíjiē zhuǎnzhàng zhīpiào.

girth /gɜːθ/ *n* 1 [C,U] [正式用语](物体的)围〔圍〕长〔長〕wéicháng. 2(马的)肚带〔帶〕dùdài.

gist /dʒɪst/ *n* **the gist** [sing] 要旨 yàozhǐ：*Tell me the ~ of what he said.* 告诉我他说话的要点.

give[1] /gɪv/ *v* [*pt* **gave** /geɪv/, *pp* **given** /ˈgɪvn/] 1 [T] 给 gěi：*~ her a cheque* 给她一张支票. *Have you been ~n the book you need?* 你需要的书给你了吗? 2 [T] *for* 付给 fùgěi：*I gave (her) £500 for the car.* 我用 500 英镑买了(她的)这辆车. 3 [T] 提供 tígōng：*a book giving information on schools* 提供各学校信息的书. 4 [T] 允许(有) yǔnxǔ：*~ her a week to decide* 允许她有一周的时间作出决定. 5 [T] 给…造成 gěi…zàochéng：*~ trouble* 带来麻烦. *Does your back ~ you pain?* 你背痛吗? 6 [T] 发〔發〕出(笑声、呻吟等) fāchū. 7 [T] 作 zuò；用言词表示 yòng yáncí biǎoshì：*~ an account of one's journey* 报告此行经过. *She gave a speech to parliament.* 她在议会发表演说. 8 [T] 表演(戏剧等) biǎoyǎn：*~ a poetry reading* 表演诗朗诵. 9 [T] 作出(动作) zuòchū：*~ a wave* 挥手示意. *He gave the door a kick.* 他朝门上踢了一脚. 10[T] (作为主人)举〔舉〕办〔辦〕(宴会等) jǔbàn. 11[I] 压〔壓〕弯〔彎〕yāwān；伸展 shēnzhǎn：*The plank gave a little when I stepped on it.* 这块板子,我一踏上去,就弯下去了一点. 12[习语] **ˌgive and ˈtake** 互相让〔讓〕步 hùxiāng ràngbù；互相迁〔遷〕就 hùxiāng qiānjiù：*You have to ~ and take in a marriage.* 夫妻双方都要互相迁就. **give ground** ⇨ GROUND[1]. **give or take sth** [非正式用语]相差不到… xiāngchā búdào：*It takes an hour to get to Hastings, ~ or take a few minutes.* 到黑斯丁斯要一个小时,快慢相差不到几分钟. **give sb sth on a plate**⇨PLATE. 13[短语动词] **give sth away** 赠送 zèngsòng. **give sth/sb away** 泄露 xièlòu：*~ away secrets* 泄露秘密. **give sth back (to sb), give sb back sth** 把某物归〔歸〕还〔還〕给某人 bǎ mǒuwù guīhuán gěi mǒurén：*~ the book back (to him)* 还书(给他). *~ him back the book* 还给他书. **give ˈin (to sb/sth)** 投降 tóuxiáng；屈服 qūfú. **give sth off** 发出(气味等) fāchū. **give ˈout** (a) 用完 yòngwán；筋疲力尽〔盡〕jīn pí lì jìn. (b) (发动机等)停止运〔運〕转〔轉〕tíngzhǐ yùnzhuǎn. **give sth out** 分发 fēnfā：*~ out prizes* 分发奖品. *~ out leaflets* 分发小册子. **give over (doing sth)** [非正式用语]停止(做某事) tíngzhǐ. **give sb up** (a)对〔對〕…不再抱有希望 duì…búzài bàoyǒu xīwàng：*The doctors have ~n him up.* 医生们已对他不再抱有希望. (b) 不再同…交往 búzài tóng…jiāowǎng. **give (sth) up** 停止做… tíngzhǐ zuò…：*She has ~n up trying to change him.* 她已不再试图改变他了. **give sth up** (a) 不再做 búzài zuò；不再拥〔擁〕有 búzài yōngyǒu：*I've ~n up smoking.* 我戒烟了. *I gave up my job.* 我辞职了. (b) 把…让给… bǎ…rànggěi…：*He gave up his seat to the old man.* 他把坐位让给这位老人. **give sb/sth up** 将…交出 jiāng…jiāochū. **give oneself up** 投降 tóuxiáng：*He gave himself up to the police.* 他向警方投降. **given** *adj* 商定的 shāngdìngde：*at the ~n time* 在商定的时间. **given** *prep* 考虑〔慮〕到 kǎolǜdào：*He runs very fast, ~n his size.* 考虑到他的身材,他是跑得很快的. **ˈgive-away** *n* [C] [非正式用语] (a)赠品 zèngpǐn. (b) 泄露出秘密的某种事物 xièlòu chū mìmì de mǒuzhǒng shìwù.

give[2] /gɪv/ *n* 1 [U] 延展性 yánzhǎnxìng：*This rope has too much ~ in it.* 这绳子延展性太大. 2[习语] **ˌgive and ˈtake** 迁〔遷〕就 qiānjiù；妥协〔協〕tuǒxié：*There must be ~ and take in a marriage.* 婚姻必须互相迁就妥协.

glacial /ˈgleɪsɪəl; *US* ˈgleɪʃl/ *adj* 冰的 bīngde; 冰河期的 bīnghéqīde.

glacier /ˈglæsɪə(r); *US* ˈgleɪʃər/ *n* [C]冰川 bīngchuān; 冰河 bīnghé.

glad /glæd/ *adj* [~der, ~dest] 1 高兴〔興〕的 gāoxìngde; 乐〔樂〕意的 lèyìde. 2[旧]令人愉快的 lìng rén yúkuài de: ~ *news* 好消息. **gladden** /ˈglædn/ *v* [T] 使高兴 shǐ gāoxìng; 使快乐 shǐ kuàilè. **gladly** *adv* 乐意地 lèyìde; 情愿〔願〕地 qíngyuànde. **gladness** *n* [U].

glade /gleɪd/ *n* [C] [修辞]林间空地 línjiān kòngdì.

gladiator /ˈglædɪeɪtə(r)/ *n* [C] (古罗马)斗〔鬥〕士 dòushì, 斗剑〔劍〕士 dòujiànshì.

glamour (美语亦作 -or) /ˈglæmə(r)/ *n* [U] 1 魅力 mèilì. 2 性感的女性美 xìnggǎnde nǚxìngměi. **glamorize** *v* [T] 使有魅力 shǐ yǒu mèilì; 美化 měihuà. **glamorous** *adj*.

glance /glɑːns; *US* glæns/ *v* [I] 1 扫〔掃〕视 sǎoshì; 看一眼 kàn yìyǎn. 2[短语动词] **glance off sth** 擦过〔過〕cāguò; 掠过 lüèguò. **glance** *n*[C] 1 一瞥 yìpiē; 扫视 sǎoshì. 2[习语] **at a glance** 看一眼 kàn yì yǎn.

gland /glænd/ *n* [C] [解剖]腺 xiàn. **glandular** /-jʊlə(r); *US* -ʒʊlə(r)/ *adj*.

glare /gleə(r)/ *v* [I] 1 (*at*) 怒视 nùshì; 瞪视 dèngshì. 2 闪耀 shǎnyào. **glare** *n* 1 [C] 怒视 nùshì; 瞪视 dèngshì. 2 [U] 令人不快的耀眼的光 lìng rén búkuài de yàoyǎn de guāng. **glaring** /ˈgleərɪŋ/ *adj* 1 耀眼的 yàoyǎnde; 刺目的 cìmùde. 2 愤怒的 fènnùde. 3 显〔顯〕眼的 xiǎnyǎnde: *a glaring mistake* 显著的错误.

glass /glɑːs; *US* glæs/ *n* 1 [U] 玻璃 bōli. 2 [C] 玻璃杯 bōlibēi; 一杯(的容量) yìbēi: *a* ~ *of milk* 一杯牛奶. 3 **glasses** [pl] 眼镜 yǎnjìng. ˈ**glasshouse** *n* [C] (栽培植物用的)玻璃暖房 bōli nuǎnfáng; 温室 wēnshì. **glassware** /-weə(r)/ *n* [U] 玻璃制〔製〕品 bōli zhìpǐn; 料器 liàoqì. **glassworks** *n* [C][用 sing 或 pl v] 玻璃(工)厂〔廠〕bōli chǎng. **glassy** *adj* [-ier, -iest] 1 光滑的 guānghuáde; 光亮的 guāngliàngde. 2[喻]没有表情的 méiyǒu biǎoqíng de: *a* ~*y stare* 呆滞的凝视.

glaze /gleɪz/ *v* 1 [T] 装〔裝〕玻璃于 zhuāng bōli yú: ~ *a window* 给窗户装玻璃. 2[T] 上釉于 shàng yòu yú; 上光于 shàng guāng yú: ~ *pottery* 给陶瓷器上釉. 3[短语动词] **glaze over** (眼)变〔變〕呆滞〔滯〕biàn dāizhì. **glaze** *n* [C,U] 釉彩 yòucǎi; 釉面 yòumiàn. **glazier** /ˈgleɪzɪə(r); *US* -ʒər/ *n* [C] 装玻璃工人 zhuāng bōli gōngrén.

gleam /gliːm/ *n* [C] 1 微光 wēiguāng; 闪光 shǎnguāng. 2[喻]短暂而微弱的闪现 duǎnzàn ér wēiruò de shǎnxiàn: *a* ~ *of hope* 一线希望. **gleam** *v* [I] 闪烁〔爍〕shǎnshuò.

glean /gliːn/ *v* [T] 搜集(资料、新闻等) sōují.

glee /gliː/ *n* [U] (*at*) 高兴〔興〕gāoxìng; 快乐〔樂〕kuàilè. **gleeful** /-fl/ *adj*. **gleefully** *adv*.

glen /glen/ *n* [C] (尤指苏格兰和爱尔兰的)峡〔峽〕谷 xiágǔ.

glib /glɪb/ *adj* [~ber, ~best] [贬]圆滑的 yuánhuáde; 流利的 liúlìde: *a* ~ *answer* 圆滑的回答. **glibly** *adv*. **glibness** *n* [U].

glide /glaɪd/ *v* [I] 1 滑动〔動〕huádòng; 滑行 huáxíng. 2(飞机)滑翔 huáxiáng. **glide** *n* [C] 滑动 huádòng; 滑行 huáxíng. **glider** *n* [C] 滑翔机〔機〕huáxiángjī. **gliding** *n* [U] 滑翔运〔運〕动 huáxiáng yùndòng.

glimmer /ˈglɪmə(r)/ *v* [I] 发〔發〕微光 fā wēiguāng. **glimmer** *n* [C] 1 微光 wēiguāng. 2[喻]少许 shǎoxǔ; 微量 wēiliàng: *a* ~ *of interest* 一点兴趣.

glimpse /glɪmps/ *n* [C] 一瞥 yìpiē; 一看 yíkàn: *catch a* ~ *of the secret papers* 瞥见了秘密文件. **glimpse** *v* [T] 瞥见 piējiàn.

glint /glɪnt/ *v* [I] 闪烁〔爍〕shǎnshuò; 发〔發〕微光 fā wēiguāng. **glint** *n* [C] 闪光 shǎnguāng; 闪烁 shǎnshuò.

glisten /ˈglɪsn/ *v* [I] (尤指湿润表面)反光 fǎnguāng, 闪耀 shǎnyào.

glitter /ˈglɪtə(r)/ *v* [I] 闪闪发〔發〕光 shǎnshǎn fāguāng: ~*ing jewels* 闪亮的宝石. **glitter** *n* [U] 1 闪光 shǎnguāng. 2[喻]诱惑力 yòuhuòlì; 吸引力 xīyǐnlì: *the* ~ *of show business* 演艺业的诱惑力.

gloat /gləʊt/ *v* [I] (*over*) 对〔對〕(自己的胜利等)洋洋得意 duì yángyáng déyì; 对(别人的失败等)幸灾〔災〕乐〔樂〕祸〔禍〕duì xìng zāi lè huò. **gloatingly** *adv*.

global /ˈgləʊbl/ *adj* 1 全世界的 quánshìjiède; 全球的 quánqiúde. 2 综合的 zōnghéde; 概括的 gàikuòde. **globally** /-bəlɪ/ *adv*. **global eˈconomy** *n* [C] 世界经〔經〕济〔濟〕shìjiè jīngjì; 全球化经济 quán-qiú-huà jīng-jì. **global poˈsitioning system** *n* [C] 全球定位系统 quánqiú dìngwèi xìtǒng. **global ˈvillage** *n* [C] 地球村 dìqiúcūn. **global ˈwarming** *n* [U] 全球变〔變〕暖 quánqiú biànnuǎn.

globe /gləʊb/ *n* 1 [C] 地球仪〔儀〕dìqiúyí. 2 **the globe** [sing] 地球 dìqiú.

globule /ˈglɒbjuːl/ *n* [C] [正式用语]小滴 xiǎodī.

gloom /gluːm/ *n* [U] 1 黑暗 hēi'àn; 阴〔陰〕暗 yīn'àn. 2 忧〔憂〕愁 yōuchóu; 忧郁〔鬱〕yōuyù. **gloomy** *adj* [-ier, -iest] 1 黑暗的 hēi'ànde. 2 郁闷的 yùmènde. **gloomily** /-ɪlɪ/ *adv*.

glorify /ˈglɔːrɪfaɪ/ *v* [*pt*, *pp* -ied] [T] 1 美化 měihuà: *His cottage is only a glorified* *barn*. 他的小别墅只不过是一间稍加装饰的谷仓而已. 2 崇拜(上帝) chóngbài; 赞〔讚〕美(上帝) zànměi. **glorification** /ˌglɔːrɪfɪˈkeɪʃn/ *n* [U].

glorious /ˈglɔːrɪəs/ *adj* 1 光荣〔榮〕的 guāngróngde: *a ~ victory* 光荣的胜利. 2 辉煌的 huīhuángde; 壮〔壯〕丽〔麗〕的 zhuànglìde. **gloriously** *adv*.

glory /ˈglɔːrɪ/ *n* [*pl* -ies] 1 [U] 光荣〔榮〕 guāngróng; 荣誉〔譽〕 róngyù. 2 [U] (对上帝的) 赞〔讚〕美 zànměi; 崇拜 chóngbài: *~ to God* 赞美上帝. 3 [U] 壮〔壯〕丽 zhuànglì: *the ~ of a sunset* 落日的壮丽. 4 [C] 值得称〔稱〕赞的事 zhídé chēngzàn de shì; 自豪的原因 zìháode yuányīn: *the glories of ancient Rome* 值得古罗马骄傲的事物. **glory** *v* [*pt*, *pp* -ied] [I] *in* 骄〔驕〕傲 jiāo'ào; 自豪 zìháo.

gloss[1] /glɒs/ *n* [U, sing] 1 光泽〔澤〕 guāngzé; 光滑 guānghuá. 2 [喻] 虚饰 xūshì; 假象 jiǎxiàng. **gloss** *v* [短语动词] **gloss over sth** 掩饰 yǎnshì; 遮掩 zhēyǎn. **ˈgloss paint** *n* [U] 清漆 qīngqī; 有光涂〔塗〕料 yǒu guāng túliào. **glossy** *adj* [-ier, -iest] 光滑的 guānghuáde; 光泽的 guāngzéde: *~y magazines* 用有光纸印刷的杂志.

gloss[2] /glɒs/ *n* [C] 注释〔釋〕 zhùshì. **gloss** *v* [T] 注释 zhùshì.

glossary /ˈglɒsərɪ/ *n* [C] [*pl* -ies] 词汇〔彙〕表 cíhuìbiǎo.

glove /glʌv/ *n* [C] 手套 shǒutào.

glow /gləʊ/ *v* [I] 1 (无火焰地) 发〔發〕光 fāguāng, 发热〔熱〕 fārè: *~ing coal* 灼热的煤. 2 (脸) 发红 fāhóng, 发热 fārè. 3 (色彩) 鲜艳〔艷〕夺〔奪〕目 xiānyàn duómù. **glow** *n* [sing] 光辉 guānghuī: *the ~ of a sunset* 落日的光辉. **glowing** *adj* 热烈赞扬〔揚〕的 rèliè zànyáng de: *a ~ing report* 热情赞扬的报告.

glower /ˈglaʊə(r)/ *v* [I] (*at*) 怒视 nùshì; 沉着脸〔臉〕 chéngzheliǎn.

glucose /ˈgluːkəʊs/ *n* [U] 葡萄糖 pútáotáng.

glue /gluː/ *n* [U, C] 胶〔膠〕 jiāo; 胶水 jiāoshuǐ. **glue** *v* [T] 1 粘贴 zhāntiē; 胶合 jiāohé. 2 [习语] **glued to sth** [非正式用语] 紧〔緊〕附于 jǐnfùyú: *They were ~d to the television*. 他们电视看个没完. **glue-sniffing** *n* [U] (为获得麻醉和迷幻效果的) 吸胶毒 xījiāodú.

glum /glʌm/ *adj* [~mer, ~mest] 忧〔憂〕郁〔鬱〕的 yōuyùde; 阴〔陰〕郁的 yīnyùde. **glumly** *adv*.

glut /glʌt/ *n* [C, 常作 sing] 过〔過〕量供应〔應〕 guòliàng gōngyìng.

glutton /ˈglʌtn/ *n* [C] 1 贪食者 tānshízhě; 好食者 hàoshízhě. 2 [非正式用语] 承受力强的人 chéngshòulì qiáng de rén: *a ~ for punishment* 不怕罚的人. **gluttonous** /-tənəs/ *adj* 贪吃的 tānchīde; 贪心的 tānxīnde. **gluttony** *n* [U] 贪食 tānshí; 暴食 bàoshí.

glycerine /ˈglɪsəriːn/ (美语 **glycerin** /-rɪn/) *n* [U] 甘油 gānyóu.

gm *abbr* gram(s) 克 kè.

GM /dʒiː ˈem/ *abbr* genetically modified 转〔轉〕基因的 zhuǎnjīyīn de; 基因改造的 jīyīn gǎizào de.

gnarled /nɑːld/ *adj* (树干等) 扭曲的 niǔqūde.

gnash /næʃ/ *v* [T] 咬(牙) yǎo.

gnat /næt/ *n* [C] 咬人的小昆虫〔蟲〕 yǎoréndexiǎokūnchóng.

gnaw /nɔː/ *v* [I, T] 1 咬 yǎo; 啃 kěn; 啮〔嚙〕 niè. 2 [喻] 折磨 zhémó: *guilt ~ing at his conscience* 折磨着他的良心的负疚感.

gnome /nəʊm/ *n* [C] 1 (故事中的) 土地神 tǔdìshén. 2 (花园中的) 土地神塑像 túdìshén sùxiàng.

go[1] /gəʊ/ *v* [第三人称单数现在时 **goes** /gəʊz/, *pt* **went** /went/, *pp* **gone** /gɒn; *US* gɔːn/] [I] 1 (a) 去 qù: *go home* 回家. *go for a walk* 去散步. *go on holiday* 去度假. *go to the cinema* 去看电影. (b) 行进〔進〕 xíngjìn: *go five miles to get a doctor* 行五英里去请一位医生. 2 离〔離〕开〔開〕 líkāi: *It's time for us to go*. 我们该走了. 3 伸展 shēnzhǎn; 达〔達〕到 dádào: *This road goes to London*. 这条路通到伦敦. 4 *to* 经〔經〕常去某处〔處〕 jīngcháng qù mǒuchù: *go to school* 上学. *go to church* (去教堂) 做礼拜. 5 (经常) 被放置 bèi fàngzhì: *The book goes on the shelf*. 书放在书架上. 6 插入 chārù; 嵌入 qiànrù: *This key won't go (in the lock)*. 这把钥匙插不进(锁). 7 进展 jìnzhǎn: *How are things going?* 事情进展得如何? *The party went very well*. 聚会进行得很好. 8 工作 gōngzuò: *This clock doesn't go*. 这钟不走了. 9 (尤用于命令) 开始 kāishǐ: *One, two, three, go!* 一、二、三、开始! 10 发〔發〕某种〔種〕声〔聲〕音 fā mǒuzhǒng shēngyīn: *The bell went at 3 p.m.* 这钟下午三时鸣响. *The clock goes 'tick-tock'*. 这钟嘀嗒嘀嗒地响. 11 用某种言辞〔辭〕表达 yòng mǒuzhǒng yáncí biǎodá; 有某种调子 yǒu mǒuzhǒng diàozi: *How does the poem go?* 这诗是怎么写的? *How does the song go?* 这歌是怎么唱的? 12 成为〔爲〕 chéngwéi: *go from bad to worse* 每况愈下. *go to sleep* 入睡. *go mad* 疯了. *go blind* 瞎了. 13 处于某种状〔狀〕态〔態〕 chǔyú mǒuzhǒng zhuàngtài: *go hungry* 饿了. *go armed* 武装起来. 14 (a) 丧〔喪〕失 sàngshī; 用光 yòngguāng: *Supplies of coal*

G

went very quickly. 存煤很快用光. (b) (*to*, *for*) 卖〔賣〕出 màichū: *The car went to a dealer for £500*. 这辆车以500英镑卖给了一个商人. 15 恶〔惡〕化 èhuà; 衰退 shuāituì; 停止运〔運〕转〔轉〕 tíngzhǐ yùnzhuǎn: *My sight is going*. 我的视力在衰退. *The car battery has gone*. 汽车电池用完了. 16 (时间)过〔過〕去 guòqù: *two hours to go before lunch* 吃午饭还有两个小时. 17 [习语] **'anything goes** [非正式用语] 无〔無〕论〔論〕什〔甚〕么〔麽〕事件都有可能 wúlùn shénme shìjiàn dōuyǒu kěnéng. **be going to do sth** (a) 打算 dǎsuàn; 计划〔劃〕 jìhuà: *We are going to sell our house*. 我们打算出售我们的房子. (b) 可能 kěnéng; 将〔將〕要 jiāngyào: *It's going to rain*. 将要下雨. **go and do sth** [非正式用语] 做蠢事、错事等 zuò chǔnshì、cuòshì děng: *That stupid girl went and lost her watch*. 那个傻姑娘把手表弄丢了. **go to seed** ⇨ SEED. **go to waste** ⇨ WASTE². **there goes sth** (用于表示失去某事物的遗憾): *There goes my chance of getting the job*. 我获得这份工作的机会是没有了. 18 [短语动词] **go a'bout** 四处走动〔動〕 sìchù zǒudòng. **go about sth** 着手 zhuóshǒu; 开始做 kāishǐ zuò: *How do you go about writing a novel?* 你怎样着手写小说? **go after sb/sth** 追逐 zhuīzhú; 追求 zhuīqiú. **go against sb/sth** (a) 反对〔對〕 fǎnduì: *Don't go against my wishes*. 不要同我的愿望作对. (b) 对某人不利 duì mǒurén búlì: *The verdict went against him*. 裁决对他不利. **go a'head** 进行 jìnxíng; 发生 fāshēng: *The tennis match went ahead in spite of the bad weather*. 尽管天气不好, 网球比赛照样进行. **go a'long** 进行 jìnxíng. **go a'long with sb/sth** (a) 同行 tóngxíng; 一起 yìqǐ. (b) 同意 tóngyì: *Will they go along with the plan?* 他们会同意这项计划吗? **go at sb/sth** (a) 攻击〔擊〕某人 gōngjī mǒurén. (b) 努力做某事 nǔlì zuò mǒushì. **go 'away** (a) 离开 líkāi. (b) 消失 xiāoshī: *Has the pain gone away?* 疼痛消失了吗? **go 'back** (a) 返回 fǎnhuí. (b) 向后〔後〕伸展 xiànghòu shēnzhǎn; 追溯 zhuīsù: *Our family goes back 300 years*. 我们的家系可以追溯到300年前. **go back on sth** 违〔違〕背(诺言等) wéibèi: *go back on one's word* 违背诺言. **go 'by** (时间)过去 guòqù; 流逝 liúshì: *The days go by so slowly*. 日子过得很慢. **'go by sth** 遵循 zūnxún: *I always go by what my doctor says*. 我总是按照医生的话去做. **go 'down** (a) (船等)下沉 xiàchén. (b) (太阳、月亮等)落下 luòxià. (c) (食物)咽〔嚥〕下 yànxià. (d) (海、风等)宁〔寧〕静下来 níngjìng xiàlái. (e) (物价、温度等)下降 xiàjiàng. **go 'down (in sth)** 被写〔寫〕下 bèi xiěxià; 被记录〔錄〕 bèi jìlù: *Her name will go down in history*. 她的名字将永垂史册. **go down well (with sb)** 被接受 bèi jiēshòu; 受欢〔歡〕迎 shòu huānyíng. **go down badly (with sb)** 不被接受 bú bèi jiēshòu; 不受欢迎 bú shòu huānyíng. **go down with sth** 患 huàn; 感染上 gǎnrǎnshàng: *go down with flu* 得了流感. **go for sb/sth** (a) 去拿 qù ná; 去买〔買〕 qù mǎi; 去请 qù qǐng. (b) 攻击 gōngjī: *The dog went for him*. 狗向他扑过去. (c) 适〔適〕用于 shì yòng yú: *What she said goes for me too*. 她说的也适用于我. (d) [非正式用语] 喜欢 xǐhuān; 倾心于 qīnxīn yú. **go 'in** (a) 进入 jìnrù. (b) (太阳、月亮等)被云〔雲〕层〔層〕遮蔽 bèi yúncéng zhēbì. **go in for sth** (a) 参〔參〕加(比赛等) cānjiā. (b) 爱〔愛〕好(业余活动等) àihào: *go in for golf* 喜爱高尔〔爾〕夫球运动. **go into sth** (a) (汽车等)撞上 zhuàngshàng. (b) 参加(某团体等) cānjiā: *go into the Army* 参军. (c) 调查 diàochá; 研究 yánjiū: *go into (the) details* 调查详细情况. (d) 开始 kāishǐ: *go into a long explanation* 开始大作解释. **go 'off** (a) 爆炸 bàozhà; 被发射 bèi fāshè. (b) (食物等)腐败变〔變〕质〔質〕 fǔbài biànzhì: *The milk has gone off*. 牛奶坏了. (c) 进行 jìnxíng: *The party went off well*. 舞会开得很成功. **go off sb/sth** 不再喜爱 búzài xǐ'ài. **go 'on** (a) (时间)过去 guòqù. (b) (灯)点〔點〕亮 diǎn liàng; (自来水等)开始供应〔應〕 kāishǐ gōngyìng. (c) 继〔繼〕续〔續〕 jìxù: *The meeting went on for hours*. 会议连续开了几个小时. (d) 发生 fāshēng: *What's going on here?* 这里发生了什么事? **go 'on (about sb/sth)** 没完没了地讲〔講〕 méiwán méiliǎo de jiǎng. **go 'on (at sb)** 责骂 zémà; 批评 pīpíng. **go 'on (with sth/ doing sth)** 继续 jìxù. **go on to sth/to do sth** 转入 zhuǎn rù; 进而讨论(另一问题等) jìn ér tǎolùn. **go 'out** (a) 外出娱〔娛〕乐〔樂〕 wàichū yúlè; 外出交际〔際〕 wàichū jiāojì: *I don't go out much at weekends*. 周末我不大出去活动. (b) (火、灯等)熄灭〔滅〕 xīmiè. (c) 过时 guòshí; 不流行 bù liúxíng. **go 'out (together), go out with sb** [非正式用语] 与〔與〕…谈恋〔戀〕爱或有性关〔關〕系〔係〕 yǔ…tán liàn'ài huò yǒu xìng guānxī. **go over sth** 仔细察看 zǐxì chákàn; 检〔檢〕查 jiǎnchá. **go 'round** (a) 满足人人的需要 mǎnzú rénrénde xūyào: *There aren't enough apples to go round*. 没有足够的苹果人人都分到. (b) 绕〔繞〕路走 ràolù zǒu. **go round (to)** 访问 fǎngwèn: *We're going round to see Sarah*. 我们去访问莎拉. **go round with sb** 经常与…结伴 jīngcháng yǔ…jiébàn. **go 'through** 完成 wánchéng; 谈妥 tántuǒ: *The deal didn't go through*. 生意没有谈成. **go through sth** (a) 详细讨论〔論〕 xiángxì tǎolùn. (b) 检查 jiǎnchá; 审〔審〕查 shěnchá: *go through the papers* 检查证件. (c) 遭受 zāoshòu; 经受 jīngshòu. (d) 用完(钱) yòngwán. **go through with sth** 完成(尤指令人讨厌或艰难的事) wánchéng. **go to/towards sth** 有助于 yǒu zhù yú; 贡献〔獻〕给 gòngxiàn gěi: *All profits go to charity*. 全部收益捐给慈善事业. **go 'under** (a) 沉没 chénmò. (b) [喻]失败 shībài. **go 'up** (a) 上升 shàngshēng; 增长〔長〕 zēngzhǎng. (b) 被建成 bèi jiànchéng. (c) 被炸毁 bèi zhàhuǐ; 被烧〔燒〕毁 bèi shāohuǐ: *The petrol station went up in flames*. 汽油站被大火烧毁. (d) (价格)上涨〔漲〕 shàngzhǎng. **go up sth** 攀登 pāndēng. **go with sb** (a) 和…一起存在 hé…yìqǐ cúnzài. (b) 和…谈恋爱 hé…tán liàn'ài. **go together, go with sth** 与…相配 yǔ…xiāngpèi; 与…协〔協〕调 yǔ…xiétiáo: *Do green curtains go with a pink carpet?* 绿窗帘同粉红的地毯是否相配? **go without (sth)** 没有…而将就对〔對〕付 méiyǒu…ér jiāngjiu duìfu: *go without food for four days* 忍饥挨饿四天. **'go-ahead** *n* **the go-ahead** [sing] 准许 zhǔnxǔ; 许可 xǔkě. **'go-ahead** *adj* 有进取心的 yǒu jìnqǔxīn de. **ˌgo-'slow** *n* [C] 怠工 dàigōng.

go[2] /gəʊ/ *n* [*pl* ~es /gəʊz/] 1 [C] (游戏中)轮〔輪〕到的机〔機〕会〔會〕 lúndàode jīhuì. 2 [C]尝〔嘗〕试 chángshì: '*I can't lift this box*.' '*Let me have a go*.' "我抬不起这箱子." "我来试一试." 3[U][非正式用语]精力 jīnglì: *He's full of* ~. 他精力充沛. 4[习语] **be on the 'go** [非正式用语]非常活跃〔躍〕 fēicháng huóyuè; 忙碌 mánglù. **it's all 'go** [非正式用语]很忙碌 hěn mánglù. **make a 'go of sth** [非正式用语]使成功、美满 shǐ chénggōng、měimǎn.

goad /gəʊd/ *v* 1 [T] (*into*) 招惹 zhāorě: *He ~ed me into an angry reply*. 他招惹得我回答时没有好气. 2[短语动词] **goad sb on** 驱〔驅〕使(做) qūshǐ. **goad** *n* [C] (赶家畜用的)刺棒 cìbàng.

goal /gəʊl/ *n* [C] 1(a) (足球等)球门〔門〕 qiúmén. (b) 得分 défēn. 2[喻]目的 mùdì; 目标〔標〕 mùbiāo. **'goal-keeper** *n*[C] (足球等)守门员 shǒuményuán. **'goal-post** *n*[C] 球门柱 qiú ménzhù.

goat /gəʊt/ *n* [C] 1 山羊 shānyáng. 2 [习语] **get sb's 'goat** [非正式用语]惹怒某人 rěnù mǒurén.

gobble[1] /'gɒbl/ *v* [I, T] 狼吞虎咽〔嚥〕 láng tūn hǔ yàn.

gobble[2] /'gɒbl/ *v* [I], *n* [C] 发〔發〕公火鸡〔鷄〕叫声〔聲〕 fā gōng huǒjī jiàoshēng; 公火鸡叫声 gōng huǒjī jiàoshēng.

go-between /'gəʊbɪtwiːn/ *n* [C] 中间人 zhōngjiānrén; 媒人 méirén.

goblet /'gɒblɪt/ *n* [C] 高脚无〔無〕把手酒杯 gāojiǎo wú bǎshǒu jiǔbēi.

goblin /'gɒblɪn/ *n* [C] (神话故事中的)小妖精 xiǎo yāojing.

god /gɒd/ *n* 1 [C]神 shén. 2 **God** [sing] (基督教、天主教、犹太教和伊斯兰教的)上帝 Shàngdì, 天主 tiānzhǔ, 主 zhǔ, 真主 zhēnzhǔ. 3[C] 极〔極〕受崇敬的人或物 jí shòu chóngjìng de rén huò wù. 4 **the gods** [pl] (剧院)最高楼〔樓〕座 zuìgāo lóuzuò. 5[习语]**God willing** (表示但愿事情能如愿)如上帝许可 rú Shàngdì xǔkě. **'godchild** *n* [C] 教子 jiàozǐ; 教女 jiàonǚ. **'god-daughter** *n* [C] 教女 jiàonǚ. **'godson** *n* [C] 教子 jiàozǐ. **goddess** /'gɒdɪs/ *n* [C] 女神 nǚshén. **'godfather** *n* [C] 教父 jiàofù. **'godmother** *n* [C] 教母 jiàomǔ. **'godparent** *n* [C] 教父 jiàofù; 教母 jiàomǔ. **'god-fearing** *adj* 虔诚的 qiánchéngde. **'godforsaken** (地方)凄凉的 qīliángde. **godless** *adj* 不信神的 bú xìnshén de; 邪恶〔惡〕的 xié'ède. **'godlike** *adj* 上帝般的 Shàngdìbānde; 如神的 rúshénde. **godly** *adj* [-ier, -iest] 虔诚的 qiánchéngde. **godliness** *n* [U]. **'godsend** *n* [C] 天赐之物 tiān cì zhī wù; 令人喜出望外的事物 lìng rén xǐ chū wàng wài de shìwù.

goggle /'gɒgl/ *v* [I] (*at*) 瞪视 dèngshì. **goggles** *n* [pl] 风〔風〕镜 fēngjìng; 护〔護〕目镜 hùmùjìng.

going /'gəʊɪŋ/ *n* 1 [sing] 离〔離〕去 líqù. 2 [U]工作或行驶的速度 gōngzuò huò xíngshǐ de sùdù: *It was good ~ to get to York so quickly*. 这样快到达约克郡,速度相当可以了. **going** *adj* [习语] **a ˌgoing con'cern** 兴〔興〕隆昌盛的企业〔業〕 xīnglóng chāngshèng de qǐyè. **the ˌgoing 'rate** 时〔時〕价〔價〕 shíjià.

go-kart /'gəʊkɑːt/ *n* [C] 微型竞〔競〕赛汽车〔車〕 wēixíng jìngsài qìchē.

gold /gəʊld/ *n* 1 [U]黄金 huángjīn; 金 jīn. 2 [U]金饰品 jīnshìpǐn; 金币〔幣〕 jīnbì. 3 [U, C]金黄色 jīnhuángsè. 4[C] [体育]金质〔質〕奖〔獎〕章 jīnzhì jiǎngzhāng. **goldfish** *n* [C] [*pl* **goldfish**] 金鱼 jīnyú. **ˌgold 'foil** (亦作 **ˌgold-'leaf**) *n* [U] 金叶〔葉〕 jīnyè. **ˌgold 'medal** *n* [C] 金质奖章 jīnzhì jiǎngzhāng. **'gold-mine** *n* [C] 1 金矿〔礦〕 jīnkuàng. 2[喻]繁荣〔榮〕的企业〔業〕 fánróngde qǐyè. **'gold-rush** *n* [C]淘金热〔熱〕 táojīnrè. **'goldsmith** *n* [C] 金匠 jīnjiàng.

golden /'gəʊldən/ *adj* 1 金的 jīnde; 像黄金的 xiàng huángjīnde. 2 极〔極〕好的 jíhǎode: *a ~ opportunity* 极好的机会. 3[习语] **a golden handshake** 大笔〔筆〕的退职〔職〕金 dàbǐde tuìzhíjīn. **golden jubilee** *n* [C] 五十周年纪念 wǔshí zhōunián jìniàn. **ˌgolden 'rule** *n* [C] 为〔爲〕人准〔準〕则 wéi rén zhǔnzé.

G

golf /gɒlf/ *n* [U] 高尔〔爾〕夫球戏〔戲〕gāo'ěrfūqiúxì. ˈ**golf ball** 高尔夫球 gāo'ěrfūqiú. ˈ**golf club** *n* [C] 高尔夫球俱乐〔樂〕部 gāo'ěrfūqiú jùlèbù; 高尔夫球场〔場〕及会〔會〕所 gāo'ěrfū qiúchǎng jí huìsuǒ. ˈ**golf-club** *n* [C] 高尔夫球棍 gāo'ěrfū qiúgùn. ˈ**golf-course** *n* [C] 高尔夫球场 gāo'ěrfū qiúchǎng. **golfer** *n* [C] 打高尔夫球的人 dǎ gāo'ěrfūqiú de rén.

gone /gɒn/ *pp* of GO[1].

gong /gɒŋ/ *n* [C] 锣〔鑼〕luó.

gonorrhoea (亦作 **gonorrhea**) /ˌgɒnəˈrɪə/ *n* [U] 淋病 línbìng.

good[1] /gʊd/ *adj* [**better** /ˈbetə(r)/, **best** /best/] **1** 好的 hǎode; 出色的 chūsède: *very ~ exam results* 出色的考试成绩. **2** 使人愉快的 shǐ rén yúkuài de; 悦人的 yuèrénde: *~ news* 喜讯. *~ weather* 好天气. *a ~ time* 好时光. **3** 能干〔幹〕的 nénggànde: *a ~ teacher* 能干的老师. *~ at languages* 擅长语言. **4** 有道德的 yǒu dàodéde: *~ deeds* 合乎道德的行为. **5**(尤指儿童)守规矩的 shǒu guīju de. **6** 有益的yǒuyìde; 适〔適〕合的 shìhéde: *Milk is ~ for you.* 牛奶对你有益. **7** 仁慈的 réncíde; 和善的 héshànde: *They were very ~ to her when she was ill.* 她有病时他们待她很好. **8** 充分的 chōngfènde; 透彻〔徹〕的 tòuchède: *a ~ sleep* 酣睡. **9** **good for sth** (a) (对一定数额)可以信赖的 kěyǐ xìnlàide: *My credit is ~ for £500.* 我凭我的信用可贷款 500 英镑. (b) 有效的 yǒuxiàode: *tickets ~ for three months* 有效期为三个月的票. (c) 能维持(一段时间)的 néng wéichí de: *The car's ~ for a few months yet.* 这辆车还能开几个月. **10**(用于打招呼和告别): *G~ morning.* 早安. *G~ afternoon.* 下午好;再见. **11** **a good...** (a) 许多 xǔduō; 大量 dàliàng: *a ~ many people* 许许多多的人. (b) 十足的 shízúde; 至少的 zhìshǎode: *a ~ three miles to the station* 离车站至少三英里. **12**(用于感叹句): *G~ Heavens!* 天哪! **13**(用于表示赞同)好! hǎo: '*I've finished!*' '*G~!*' "我完成了!" "好!" **14** [习语] **a good deal** ⇨ DEAL[1]. **a good** ˈ**job** [非正式用语]幸运〔運〕事 xìngyùnshì. **a good many** ⇨ MANY. **all in good time** 来得及 láidejí; 快了 kuàile; 别急 biéjí. **as good as** 几〔幾〕乎 jīhū: *as ~ as finished* 几乎完成. **as good as gold** 表现很好的 biǎoxiàn hěnhǎo de. **be a good thing** (a) 值得庆〔慶〕幸的事 zhídé qìngxìng de shì. (b) 好主意 hǎo zhǔyi. **do sb a good turn** 做有益于某人的事 zuò yǒuyìyú mǒurén de shì. **for good measure** 作为〔為〕外加的东西 zuòwéi wàijiāde dōngxi; 另外 lìngwài. **good and** [非正式用语]完全地 wánquánde: *I won't go until I'm ~ and ready.* 我要完全准备好了才去. **good for** ˈ**sb**, ˈ**you**, ˈ**them, etc** [非正式用语](用于表示赞许)真行 zhēnxíng; 真棒 zhēnbàng. **good** ˈ**grief** [非正式用语](用于表示惊讶等强烈感情)哎呀! āiyā! 天哪! tiānna! ˌ**good** ˈ**luck** (用于祝贺)好运道 hǎo yùndao; 成功 chénggōng. **have a good mind to do sth** 很乐〔樂〕意做某事 hěn lèyì zuò mǒushì. **have a good night** ⇨ NIGHT. **in good time** 及早 jízǎo. **make good** 成功 chénggōng. ˈ**good-for-nothing** *n* [C], *adj* 没有用处〔處〕的人 méiyǒu yòngchù de rén; 懒汉〔漢〕lǎnhàn. ˌ**Good** ˈ**Friday** *n* [U, C] (基督教)受难〔難〕节〔節〕(复活节前的星期五) shòunànjié. ˌ**good-**ˈ**humoured** *adj* 脾气〔氣〕好的 píqi hǎo de; 心情好的 xīnqíng hǎo de; ˌ**good-**ˈ**looking** *adj* 好看的 hǎokànde; 漂亮的 piàoliang de. ˌ**good-**ˈ**natured** *adj* 性情温和的 xìngqíng wēnhé de. ˌ**good** ˈ**sense** *n* [U] 理智 lǐzhì. ˌ**good-**ˈ**tempered** *adj* 脾气好的 píqi hǎo de.

good[2] /gʊd/ *n* [U] **1** 好事 hǎoshì; 善 shàn: *~ and evil* 善与恶. **2** 好处〔處〕hǎochù; 益处 yìchù: *It's for your own ~.* 那是为了你好. **3**[习语] **be no / not much** ˈ**good** 没(或没有多大)用 méi yòng: *It's no ~ talking to them.* 同他们说没用. **do (sb)** ˈ**good** 对…有好处 duì…yǒu hǎochù: *Drinking the medicine will do you ~.* 喝这药水会对你有好处. **for** ˈ**good** 永久地 yǒngjiǔde. **up to no** ˈ**good** 做坏〔壞〕事 zuò huàishì.

goodbye /ˌgʊdˈbaɪ/ *interj*, *n* [C] 再见! zàijiàn! 告别 gàobié.

goodness /ˈgʊdnɪs/ *n* [U] **1** 优〔優〕良 yōuliáng; 善良 shànliáng. **2**(食物的)养〔養〕分 yǎngfèn: *Brown bread is full of ~.* 黑面包营养丰富. **3**(用于表示惊讶、宽慰、烦恼等的词语中): *My ~!* 我的天哪! *For ~' sake!* 看在老天爷的份上!

goods /gʊdz/ *n* [pl] **1** 货物 huòwù; 动〔動〕产〔產〕dòngchǎn: *electrical ~* 电器商品. **2** (火车的)运〔運〕货 yùnhuò: *a ~ train* 货运列车. **3**[习语] **come up with/deliver the goods** [非正式用语]履行诺言 lǚxíng nuòyán.

goodwill /ˌgʊdˈwɪl/ *n* [U] **1** 亲〔親〕善 qīnshàn; 友好 yǒuhǎo. **2**(商店企业等)信誉〔譽〕xìnyù; [会计]商誉 shāngyù.

goody /ˈgʊdɪ/ *n* [C] [*pl* **-ies**] [非正式用语] **1**[常作 pl] 好吃的东西 hǎochī de dōngxi; 好东西 hǎo dōngxi. **2**(书、电影等中的)正面人物 zhèngmiàn rénwù.

goose /guːs/ *n* [*pl* **geese** /giːs/] **1** [C]鹅 é. **2** [C]母鹅 mǔ'é. **3** [U]鹅肉 éròu. ˈ**goose-flesh** *n*[U] (亦作 ˈ**goose-pimples** [pl]) (因恐惧、寒冷等引起的)鸡〔鷄〕皮疙瘩 jīpí gēda.

gooseberry /ˈgʊzbərɪ; *US* ˈguːsberɪ/ *n* [C] [*pl* **-ies**] [植物]醋栗 cùlì; 醋栗果实〔實〕cùlì guǒshí.

gorge[1] /gɔːdʒ/ *n* [C] 山峡〔峽〕shānxiá; 峡谷 xiágǔ.

gorge[2] /gɔːdʒ/ *v* [I, T] ~ (oneself) (on) 狼吞虎咽〔嚥〕láng tūn hǔ yàn.

gorgeous /ˈgɔːdʒəs/ *adj* 1[非正式用语]令人十分愉快的 lìng rén shífēn yúkuài de;极〔極〕好的 jíhǎode. 2 吸引人的 xīyǐn rén de; 华〔華〕丽〔麗〕的 huálìde. **gorgeously** *adv*.

gorilla /gəˈrɪlə/ *n* [C] 大猩猩 dàxīngxīng.

gorse /gɔːs/ *n* [U] (植物)荆豆 jīngdòu.

gory /ˈgɔːrɪ/ *adj* [-ier, -iest] 血淋淋的 xiělínlínde; 沾满血的 zhānmǎnxiěde: *a ~ film* 充满血肉横飞镜头的影片.

gosh /gɒʃ/ *interj* [非正式用语](表示惊讶)天哪! tiānna! 哎呀! āiyā!

gosling /ˈgɒzlɪŋ/ *n* [C] 小鹅 xiǎo'é.

gospel /ˈgɒspl/ *n* 1(《圣经》) (a) the Gospel [sing] 耶稣生平及其教导〔導〕Yēsū shēngpíng jíqí jiàodǎo. (b) Gospel [C] (基督教)《新约》四福音书〔書〕之一《Xīnyuē》sìfúyīnshū zhī yī. 2 [U]绝对〔對〕真理 juéduì zhēnlǐ.

gossamer /ˈgɒsəmə(r)/ *n* [U] 蛛丝 zhūsī; 游〔遊〕丝 yóusī.

gossip /ˈgɒsɪp/ *n* 1 [U]流言飞语 liúyán fēiyǔ. 2 [C]爱〔愛〕传〔傳〕流言飞语的人 ài chuán liúyán fēiyǔ de rén. **gossip** *v* [I] 传播流言飞语 chuánbō liúyán fēiyǔ.

got *pt, pp* of GET.

gotten [美语] *pp* of GET.

gouge /gaʊdʒ/ *n* [C] 半圆凿〔鑿〕bànyuánzáo. **gouge** *v* 1 [T]在…上凿孔 zài…shàng záokǒng. 2 [短语动词] gouge sth out 挖出 wāchū.

goulash /ˈguːlæʃ/ *n* [C, U] 菜炖〔燉〕牛肉 càidùn niúròu.

gourd /gʊəd/ *n* [C] 1 葫芦〔蘆〕húlu; 葫芦属〔屬〕植物 húlushǔ zhíwù. 2 葫芦制〔製〕成的容器 húlu zhìchéng de róngqì.

gourmet /ˈgʊəmeɪ/ *n* [C] 美食家 měishíjiā.

gout /gaʊt/ *n* [U] [医]痛风〔風〕tòngfēng.

govern /ˈgʌvn/ *v* 1 [I, T]统治 tǒngzhì; 管理 guǎnlǐ. 2[T]控制 kòngzhì; 抑制 yìzhì; 影响〔響〕yǐngxiǎng; 支配 zhīpèi: *The law of supply and demand ~s the prices of goods*. 供求规律支配着物价. **governing** /ˈgʌvənɪŋ/ *adj* 统治的 tǒngzhìde; 管理的 guǎnlǐde: *the ~ing body of a school* 学校的管理机构.

governess /ˈgʌvənɪs/ *n* [C](住在学生家的)家庭女教师〔師〕jiātíng nǚjiàoshī.

government /ˈgʌvənmənt/ *n* 1 [C, 亦作 sing 用 pl v] 政府 zhèngfǔ; 内阁 nèigé. 2 [U]政治 zhèngzhì; 政体〔體〕zhèngtǐ: *democratic ~* 民主政治.

governor /ˈgʌvənə(r)/ *n* [C] 1 省长〔長〕shěngzhǎng;(美国)州长 zhōuzhǎng. 2 学〔學〕校等主管人员 xuéxiào děng zhǔguǎn rényuán; 管理者 guǎnlǐzhě; 理事 lǐshì: *a prison ~* 典狱长. *a school ~* 校长.

gown /gaʊn/ *n* [C] 1 妇〔婦〕女的正式服装〔裝〕fùnǚde zhèngshì fúzhuāng. 2 教授、法官等的礼〔禮〕服 jiàoshòu、fǎguān děng de lǐfú.

GP /ˌdʒiː ˈpiː/ *abbr* general practitioner 普通医〔醫〕生(通治各科疾病) pǔtōng yīshēng.

GPS /dʒiː piː ˈes/ *abbr* global positioning system 全球定位系统 quánqiú dìngwèi xìtǒng.

grab /græb/ *v* [-bb-] [I, T] 攫取 juéqǔ; 抓取 zhuāqǔ. **grab** *n* [C] 1 攫取 juéqǔ; 掠夺〔奪〕lüèduó. 2[习语] up for ˈgrabs [非正式用语] 可得的 kědéde; 易得的 yìdéde.

grace /greɪs/ *n* 1 [U]优〔優〕美 yōuměi; 优雅 yōuyǎ; 雅致〔緻〕yǎzhì. 2 [U]宽限(期) kuānxiàn: *give sb a week's ~* 给某人一个星期的宽限. 3 [U]善意 shànyì; 恩惠 ēnhuì. 4 [U, C] (宗教)饭前饭后〔後〕的感恩祷〔禱〕告 fànqián fànhòu de gǎn'ēn dǎogào. 5 [U](宗教)上帝的恩典 Shàngdìde ēndiǎn. 6[习语] with (a) bad grace 勉强地 miǎnqiǎngde. with (a) good grace 欣然 xīnrán. **grace** *v* [T] [正式用语]1 修饰 xiūshì; 使优美 shǐ yōuměi. 2 给…增光 gěi…zēngguāng; 使…有荣〔榮〕耀 shǐ…yǒu róngyào: *The Queen is gracing us with her presence*. 女王的光临使我们深感荣耀. **graceful** /-fl/ *adj* 优美的 yōuměide; 雅致的 yǎzhìde: *a ~ful dancer* 姿态优美的舞蹈家. **gracefully** *adv*. **graceless** *adj* 不优美的 bù yōuměide; 粗野的 cūyěde.

gracious /ˈgreɪʃəs/ *adj* 1 亲〔親〕切的 qīnqiède; 和善的 héshànde; 仁慈的 réncíde. 2 奢华〔華〕的 shēhuáde: *~ living* 奢侈的生活. **graciously** *adv*. **graciousness** *n* [U].

grade /greɪd/ *n* [C] 1 等级 děngjí; 级别 jíbié: *different ~s of pay* 工资的不同等级. 2 学校给的分数、等级 xuéxiào gěi de fēnshù、děngjí. 3(美国学校的)年级 niánjí. 4[美语]坡度 pōdù. 5[习语] make the ˈgrade [非正式用语]达〔達〕到要求的标〔標〕准〔準〕dádào yāoqiú de biāozhǔn. **grade** *v*[T] 给…分等 gěi…fēnděng; 给…批分数〔數〕gěi…pī fēnshù. ˈ**grade school** *n* [C] [美语]小学〔學〕xiǎoxué.

gradient /ˈgreɪdɪənt/ *n* [C] 坡度 pōdù; 斜度 xiédù.

gradual /ˈgrædʒʊəl/ *adj* 逐渐的 zhújiànde. **gradually** /-dʒʊlɪ/ *adv*.

graduate[1] /ˈgrædʒʊət/ *n* [C] 1 大学〔學〕毕〔畢〕业〔業〕生 dàxué bìyèshēng. 2 [美语]毕业生 bìyèshēng.

graduate[2] /ˈgrædʒʊeɪt/ *v* 1 [I] (a)接受学〔學〕位 jiēshòu xuéwèi: *~ in law* 获法学学

位.(b)[美语]毕〔畢〕业〔業〕bìyè. 2[T]给…分等 gěi…fēn děng;刻度数〔數〕于 kè dùshù yú. 3[I]升级 shēngjí. **graduation** /ˌgrædʒʊˈeɪʃn/ *n* 1[U]授予学位(典礼) shòuyǔ xuéwèi; 毕业(典礼) bìyè. 2 刻度线〔綫〕kèdùxiàn.

graffiti /grəˈfiːtɪ/ *v* [pl, U] (墙壁等处的)乱〔亂〕涂〔塗〕luàntú.

graft[1] /grɑːft; *US* græft/ *n* [C] 1 接穗 jiēsuì. 2[医学]移植物 yízhíwù; 移植片 yízhípiàn. **graft** *v* [T] 将〔將〕…嫁接于 jiāng…jiàjiē yú

graft[2] /grɑːft; *US* græft/ *n* [U] [英国英语] 艰〔艱〕巨的工作 jiānjùde gōngzuò.

grain /greɪn/ *n* 1 (a) [U] 谷〔穀〕物 gǔwù; 谷类〔類〕gǔlèi. (b) [C] 谷粒 gǔlì. 2[C]粒子 lìzi; 细粒 xìlì: *~s of sand* 沙粒. 3 [C][喻]少量 shǎoliàng; 一点〔點〕yìdiǎn: *a ~ of truth* 一点真实性. 4[U,C] 木纹 mùwén. [习语] **be/go against the ˈgrain** 格格不入 gégé búrù. **take sth with a grain of salt**⇨SALT.

gram (亦作 **gramme**) /græm/ *n* [C](重量单位)克 kè.

grammar /ˈgræmə(r)/ *n* [C,U] 语法 yǔfǎ; 语法书〔書〕yǔfǎshū. **grammarian** /grəˈmeərɪən/ *n* [C]语法学〔學〕家 yǔfǎxuéjiā. **ˈgrammar school** *n* [C] 文法学校(16 世纪前后教授文化课程而非技术课程) wénfǎ xuéxiào. **grammatical** /grəˈmætɪkl/ *adj* 语法的 yǔfǎde; 合乎语法的 héhū yǔfǎde. **grammatically** /-klɪ/ *adv*.

gramophone /ˈgræməfəʊn/ *n* [C] [旧] 留声〔聲〕机〔機〕liúshēngjī.

granary /ˈgrænərɪ/ *n* [C][*pl* -ies] 谷〔穀〕仓〔倉〕gǔcāng; 粮仓 liángcāng.

grand /grænd/ *adj* 1 宏伟〔偉〕的 hóngwěide; 壮〔壯〕丽〔麗〕的 zhuànglìde: *a ~ palace* 宏伟的宫殿. 2 [常作贬]傲慢的 àomànde; 自负的 zìfùde; 重要的 zhòngyàode. 3[非正式用语]快乐〔樂〕的 kuàilède; 称〔稱〕心的 chènxīnde: *We had a ~ time.* 我们过得很愉快. 4 总〔總〕括的 zǒngkuòde; 最终的 zuìzhōngde: *the ~ total* 总额. **grand** *n* [C] 1 [*pl* grand] [俚]一千美元 yìqiān měiyuán; 一千英镑 yìqiān yīngbàng. 2 平台〔臺〕式钢〔鋼〕琴 píngtáishì gāngqín. **grandly** *adv* ˌ**grand ˈpiano** *n* [C] 平台式钢琴 píngtáishì gāngqín. **ˈgrandstand** *n* [C] 大看台 dà kàntái.

grand- (用于复合词,表示亲属关系)祖…zǔ…,外祖… wàizǔ…,孙〔孫〕… sūn…, 外孙… wàisūn…. **ˈgrandchild** [*pl* -children] 孙子 sūnzi; 孙女 sūnnǚ; 外孙 wàisūn; 外孙女 wàisūnnǚ. **ˈgranddaughter** *n* [C] 孙女 sūnnǚ;外孙女 wàisūnnǚ. **ˈgrandfather** *n* [C] 祖父 zǔfù; 外祖父 wàizǔfù. **ˈgrandfather clock** *n* [C] 落地式大摆〔擺〕钟〔鐘〕luòdìshì dà bǎizhōng. **ˈgrandmother** *n* [C] 祖母 zǔmǔ; 外祖母 wàizǔmǔ. **ˈgrandparent** *n* [C] 祖父 zǔfù; 外祖父 wàizǔfù; 祖母 zǔmǔ; 外祖母 wàizǔmǔ. **ˈgrandson** *n* [C] 孙子 sūnzi;外孙 wàisūn.

grand-dad (亦作 **grandad**) /ˈgrændæd/ *n* [英国非正式用语]祖父 zǔfù; 外祖父 wàizǔfù.

grandeur /ˈgrændʒə(r)/ *n* [U] 壮〔壯〕观〔觀〕zhuàngguān; 宏伟〔偉〕hóngwěi.

grandiose /ˈgrændɪəʊs/ *adj* [常作贬]过〔過〕分华〔華〕丽〔麗〕的 guòfèn huálì de.

grandma /ˈgrænmɑː/ *n* [C] [非正式用语]祖母 zǔmǔ; 外祖母 wàizǔmǔ.

grandpa /ˈgrænpɑː/ *n* [C] [非正式用语]祖父 zǔfù; 外祖父 wàizǔfù.

granite /ˈgrænɪt/ *n* [U] 花岗〔崗〕石 huāgāngshí.

granny (亦作 **grannie**) /ˈgrænɪ/ *n* [C][*pl* -ies][非正式用语]祖母 zǔmǔ. **ˈgranny flat** *n* [C][非正式用语]老奶奶(住的)套间 lǎonǎinai tàojiān.

grant /grɑːnt/ *v* [T] 1[正式用语]同意给予 tóngyì gěiyǔ; 允许 yǔnxǔ: *~ sb's request* 允许某人的请求. 2 [正式用语]承认〔認〕(…是真的) chéngrèn. 3 [习语] **take sb/sth for ˈgranted** (因视作当然而)对〔對〕…不予重视 duì…bùyǔ zhòngshì. **take sth for ˈgranted** 认为〔爲〕…理所当〔當〕然 rènwéi…lǐ suǒ dāng rán. **grant** *n* [C] 拨〔撥〕款 bōkuǎn; 授予物 shòuyǔwù.

granulated /ˈgrænjʊleɪtɪd/ *adj* (糖)砂状〔狀〕的 shāzhuàngde.

granule /ˈgrænjuːl/ *n* [C] 细粒 xìlì.

grape /greɪp/ *n* [C] 葡萄 pútáo. **ˈgrape-vine** *n* 1 [C]葡萄藤 pútáoténg. 2 [sing] [喻]小道消息 xiǎodào xiāoxi: *heard about it on the ~-vine* 从小道消息听到.

grapefruit /ˈgreɪpfruːt/ *n* [C] [*pl* grapefruit 或 ~s] 葡萄柚 pútáoyòu.

graph /grɑːf; *US* græf/ *n* [C] 曲线〔綫〕图〔圖〕qūxiàntú; 图表 túbiǎo. **ˈgraph paper** *n* [U] 方格纸 fānggézhǐ; 坐标〔標〕纸 zuòbiāozhǐ.

graphic /ˈgræfɪk/ *adj* 1 图〔圖〕示的 túshìde; 图解的 tújiěde: *~ design* 平面造型设计. 2 (描写)详细的 xiángxìde; 生动〔動〕的 shēngdòngde; 鲜明的 xiānmíngde. **graphically** /-klɪ/ *adv* 生动地 shēngdòngde; 鲜明地 xiānmíngde: *~ally described* 生动地描写的. **graphics** *n* [pl] 书〔書〕画〔畫〕刻印作品 shūhuà kèyìn zuòpǐn.

graphite /ˈgræfaɪt/ *n* [U] [化学]石墨 shímò.

grapple /ˈgræpl/ *v* [I] (*with*) 1 格斗〔鬥〕gédòu; 扭打 niǔdǎ. 2 [喻]尽〔盡〕力解决(问题) jìnlì jiějué.

grasp /grɑːsp; *US* græsp/ *v* [T] 1 抓住 zhuāzhù; 抓紧〔緊〕zhuājǐn. 2 领会〔會〕lǐnghuì;

掌握 zhǎngwò. 3[短语动词] **grasp at sth** 抓住 zhuāzhù; 攫取 juéqǔ: ~ *at an opportunity* 抓住机会. **grasp** *n* [C, 常作 sing] 1 抓 zhuā. 2 了〔瞭〕解 liáojiě. **grasping** *adj* [贬]贪财的 tāncáide.

grass /grɑːs; *US* græs/ *n* 1 [U] 草 cǎo; 青草 qīngcǎo. 2[C]禾本科植物 héběnkē zhíwù. 3 [U]草地 cǎodì; 牧场〔場〕mùchǎng: *Don't walk on the* ~. 别在草地上行走. 4 [U][俚]大麻 dàmá. 5[C][英国俚语]向警方告密的人 xiàng jǐngfāng gàomìde rén. 6[习语] (**not**) **let the grass grow under one's feet** (别)坐失良机〔機〕zuò shī liángjī. **grass** *v* 1[T] 使长〔長〕满草 shǐ zhǎngmǎn cǎo. 2 [I][英国俚语] 向警方告密 xiàng jǐngfāng gàomì. ˌ**grass** ˈ**roots** *n* [pl] 基层〔層〕jīcéng; 基层群众〔衆〕jīcéng qúnzhòng. **grassy** *adj* [-ier, -iest] 生满草的 shēngmǎn cǎo de; 多草的 duōcǎode.

grasshopper /ˈgrɑːshɒpə(r); *US* ˈgræs-/ *n* [C] 蚱蜢 zhàměng.

grate[1] /greɪt/ *n* [C] 炉〔爐〕格 lúgé; 炉篦 lúbì.

grate[2] /greɪt/ *v* 1 [T]擦碎 cāsuì; 磨碎 mósuì: ~ *cheese* 磨碎干酪. 2 [I]擦响〔響〕cāxiǎng. 3 [I] (*on*) [喻]使烦躁 shǐ fánzào: ~ *on sb's nerves* 使某人神经不安. **grater** *n* [C] (擦食物的)擦子 cāzi. **grating** *adj* 令人气〔氣〕恼〔惱〕的 lìng rén qìnǎo de.

grateful /ˈgreɪtfl/ *adj* 感激的 gǎnjīde; 感谢的 gǎnxiède: *I'm* ~ *to you for your help*. 我感谢你的帮助. **gratefully** /-fəlɪ/ *adv*.

gratify /ˈgrætɪfaɪ/ *v* [*pt*, *pp* -ied] [T] [正式用语]使快意 shǐ kuàiyì; 使满意 shǐ mǎnyì. **gratification** /ˌgrætɪfɪˈkeɪʃn/ *n* [U, C]. **gratifying** *adj* [正式用语]令人快意的 lìng rén kuàiyì de.

grating /ˈgreɪtɪŋ/ *n* [C] (门、窗等)格 gé, 栅 shān.

gratitude /ˈgrætɪtjuːd; *US* -tuːd/ *n* [U] 感激 gǎnjī; 感恩 gǎn'ēn: *feel* ~ 感激.

gratuitous /grəˈtjuːɪtəs; *US* -tuː-/ *adj* [正式用语,贬]无〔無〕故的 wúgùde; 无理的 wúlǐde: ~ *violence on television* 电视节目中不必要的暴力场面. **gratuitously** *adv*.

gratuity /grəˈtjuːətɪ; *US* -ˈtuː-/ *n* [C] [*pl* -ies] 1 小账〔賬〕xiǎozhàng; 小费 xiǎofèi. 2 [英国英语]退职〔職〕金 tuìzhíjīn.

grave[1] /greɪv/ *n* [C] 墓 mù; 坟墓 fénmù. ˈ**gravestone** *n* [C] 墓碑 mùbēi. ˈ**graveyard** *n* [C] 墓地 mùdì.

grave[2] /greɪv/ *adj* [~r, ~st] 严〔嚴〕重的 yánzhòngde: *a* ~ *situation* 严重的局势. **gravely** *adv*.

gravel /ˈgrævl/ *n* [U] 砾〔礫〕lì; 砾石 lìshí. **gravel** *v* [-ll-; 美语亦作 -l-] [T] 铺以砾石 pū yǐ lìshí. **gravelly** /ˈgrævəlɪ/ *adj* 1 砂砾多的 shālì duō de. 2[喻](声音)粗重而沙哑〔啞〕的 cūzhòng ér shāyǎ de.

gravitate /ˈgrævɪteɪt/ *v* [I] *towards* / *to* 受吸引 shòu xīyǐn; 倾向 qīngxiàng. **gravitation** /grævɪˈteɪʃn/ *n* [U].

gravity /ˈgrævətɪ/ *n* [U] 1 地球引力 dìqiú yǐnlì. 2 严〔嚴〕重性 yánzhòngxìng: *the* ~ *of the situation* 形势的严重性.

gravy /ˈgreɪvɪ/ *n* [U] 肉汁 ròuzhī.

gray /greɪ/ (尤用于美语) = GREY.

graze[1] /greɪz/ *v* 1 [I] (牲畜)吃草 chīcǎo. 2 [T] 放牧 fàngmù.

graze[2] /greɪz/ *v* [T] 1 擦去…的皮 cāqù…de pí. 2 擦过〔過〕cāguò. **graze** *n* [C] 擦破处〔處〕cāpòchù.

grease /griːs/ *n* [U] 1 动〔動〕物脂肪 dòngwù zhīfáng; 熔化的动物脂肪 rónghuàde dòngwù zhīfáng. 2 油脂状〔狀〕物 yóuzhī zhuàng wù. **grease** *v* [T] 1 涂〔塗〕油脂于 tú yóuzhī yú. 2 [习语] **grease sb's palm** [非正式用语]向…行贿 xiàng…xínghuì. **like greased lightning** [非正式用语]闪电〔電〕似地 shǎndiànshìde; 飞〔飛〕快地 fēikuàide. ˌ**grease-proof** ˈ**paper** *n* [U] 防油纸 fáng yóu zhǐ. **greasy** *adj* [-ier, -iest] 油污的 yóuwūde; 涂有油脂的 tú yǒu yóuzhīde. **greasily** *adv*.

great /greɪt/ *adj* 1 (体积、数量、程度)超过〔過〕一般标〔標〕准〔準〕的 chāoguò yìbān biāozhǔn de; 巨大的 jùdàde; 非常的 fēichángde: *of* ~ *importance* 非常重要的. 2 伟〔偉〕大的 wěidàde: *a* ~ *artist* 伟大的艺术家. 3[非正式用语]美妙的 měimiàode: *a* ~ *time on holiday* 假日过得非常快活. 4 [非正式用语]绝妙的 juémiàode; 极〔極〕好的 jíhǎode: *What a* ~ *idea!* 这主意妙极了! 5 精神非常好的 jīngshén fēicháng hǎode; 健康的 jiànkāngde: *I feel* ~ *today*. 我今天精神好极了. 6[非正式用语](用于表示强调)多么〔麼〕duōme: *Look at that* ~ *big tree!* 瞧那棵好大的树! 7[习语] **a great deal**⇨DEAL[1]. **a great many**⇨MANY. ˌ**Great** ˈ**Britain** *n* [sing] 大不列颠岛(包括英格兰、威尔士和苏格兰) Dàbúlièdiāndǎo. **greatly** *adv* [正式用语]非常 fēicháng. **greatness** *n* [U].

great- (用于复合词,表示隔两代)曾 zēng: ~ *uncle* 伯(或叔)祖父. ˌ~-ˈ*grandson* 曾孙;曾外孙.

greed /griːd/ *n* [U] (*for*) 贪心 tānxīn; 贪婪 tānlán. **greedy** *adj* [-ier, -iest] 贪吃的 tānchīde; 贪婪的 tānlánde. **greedily** *adv*.

green[1] /griːn/ *adj* 1 绿的 lǜde; 青的 qīngde. 2(水果)未熟的 wèishúde. 3(脸色)发〔發〕青的 fāqīngde; 苍〔蒼〕白的 cāngbáide. 4[非正式用

G

语]没有经[經]验[驗]的 méiyǒu jīngyàn de；易受骗的 yì shòupiàn de. 5 嫉妒的 jìdùde：～ *with envy* 十分妒忌. 6(尤指政治上)关[關]心环[環]境保护[護]的 guānxīn huánjìng bǎohù de. 7[习语] **give sb the green 'light** [非正式用语]允许某人做… yǔnxǔ mǒurén zuò…. **get the green light** [非正式用语]被允许做… bèi yǔnxǔ zuò…. **ˌgreen 'belt** *n* [C] (城市周围等的)绿化地带[帶] lǜhuā dìdài；绿带 lǜdài. **ˌgreen 'fingers** *n* [pl] [非正式用语]园[園]艺[藝]技能 yuányì jìnéng. **'greengrocer** *n* [C] [英国英语]蔬菜水果零售商 shūcài shuǐguǒ língshòushāng. **'greenhouse** *n* [C] 温室 wēnshì. **'greenhouse effect** *n* [sing] 温室效应[應] wēnshì xiàoyìng. **greenhouse 'gas** *n* [C] 温室气[氣]体[體] wēnshì qìtǐ. **greenness** *n* [U].

green[2] /griːn/ *n* 1 [C,U] 绿色 lǜsè；青色 qīngsè. 2 **greens** [pl] 蔬菜 shūcài. 3 [C] 草地 cǎodì；草坪 cǎopíng：*the village* ～ 村中公有草地. 4 [C]高尔[爾]夫球场[場]球洞四周的草地 gāo'ěrfū qiúchǎng qiúdòng sìzhōu de cǎodì.

G

greenery /ˈgriːnəri/ *n* [U] 草木 cǎomù；绿叶[葉] lǜyè.

greet /griːt/ *v* [T] 1 迎接 yíngjiē；欢[歡]迎 huānyíng. 2(被眼、耳)察觉[覺] chájué；呈现 chéngxiàn. **greeting** *n* [C] 问候 wènhòu；招呼 zhāohu.

gregarious /grɪˈgeəriəs/ *adj* 1 爱[愛]群居的 ài qúnjū de；合群的 héqúnde. 2 群居的 qúnjūde.

grenade /grɪˈneɪd/ *n* [C] 手榴弹[彈] shǒuliúdàn.

grew /gruː/ *pt* of GROW.

grey (亦作 **gray**，尤用于美语) /greɪ/ *adj* 1 灰色的 huīsède. 2 头[頭]发[髮]灰白的 tóufa huībáide. **grey** *n* [U,C] 灰色 huīsè. **grey** *v* [I] 成灰色 chéng huīsè. **'grey matter** *n* [C] [非正式用语]智力 zhìlì；脑[腦] nǎo.

greyhound /ˈgreɪhaʊnd/ *n* [C] 跑狗(一种身体细长而善跑的赛狗) pǎogǒu.

grid /grɪd/ *n* [C] 1 格子 gézi；格栅 gézhà：*a 'cattle*-～ 牲口栅栏. 2 (a)网[網]格 wǎnggé. (b) 地图[圖]的坐标[標]方格 dìtúde zuòbiāo fānggé. 3 高压[壓]输电[電]线[綫]路网 gāoyā shūdiàn xiànlùwǎng.

gridlock /ˈgrɪdlɒk/ *n* [U] (十字路口的)交通大堵塞 jiāotōng dà dǔsè. **'gridlocked** *adj* 交通全面堵塞的 jiāotōng quánmiàn dǔsè de；堵得不能动[動]的 dǔ de bùnéng dòng de.

grief /griːf/ *n* 1 [U] (*at* / *over*) 悲伤[傷] bēishāng；悲痛 bēitòng. 2 [C]产[產]生悲痛的缘由 chǎnshēng bēitòngde yuányóu. 3 [习语] **come to 'grief** 以失败告终 yǐ shībài gàozhōng；出事故 chū shìgù.

grievance /ˈgriːvns/ *n* [C] (*against*) 冤情 yuānqíng；苦情 kǔqíng.

grieve /griːv/ *v* [正式用语] 1 [I]感到悲痛 gǎndào bēitòng；伤[傷]心 shāngxīn. 2 [T]使悲痛 shǐ bēitòng；使伤心 shǐ shāngxīn.

grill /grɪl/ *n* [C] 1(烤食物用的)烤架 kǎojià. 2 炙 zhì；烤的肉类[類]食品 kǎode ròulèi shípǐn：*a mixed* ～ 什锦烤肉. **grill** *v* 1 [I, T]炙 zhì；烤(食品) kǎo. 2 [T] 对[對]…严[嚴]加盘[盤]问 duì…yánjiā pánwèn.

grille (亦作 **grill**) /grɪl/ *n* [C] 铁[鐵]栅 tiězhà；邮[郵]局柜[櫃]台[臺]上的铁栅 yóujú guìtái shàng de tiězhà.

grim /grɪm/ *adj* [～**mer**，～**mest**] 1 讨厌[厭]的 tǎoyànde；糟糕的 zāogāode：～ *news* 糟糕的消息. 2 严[嚴]厉[厲]的 yánlìde；严格的 yángéde. **grimly** *adv*.

grimace /grɪˈmeɪs；US ˈgrɪməs/ *n* [C] 怪脸[臉] guàiliǎn；怪相 guàixiàng. **grimace** *v* [I] 做怪脸 zuò guàiliǎn；做怪相 zuò guàixiàng.

grime /graɪm/ *n* [U] (积于表面的)尘[塵]垢 chéngòu. **grimy** *adj* [**-ier**, **-est**].

grin /grɪn/ *v* [**-nn-**][I] 1 露齿[齒]而笑 lù chǐ-ér xiào. 2[习语] **grin and 'bear it** 逆来顺受 nì lái shùn shòu. **grin** *n* [C]露齿的笑 lù chǐ de xiào.

grind /graɪnd/ *v* [*pt*, *pp* **ground** /graʊnd/] [T] 1 磨碎 mósuì；碾碎 niǎnsuì：～ *corn into flour* 磨谷成粉. 2 磨光 móguāng；磨快 mókuài：～ *a knife* 磨小刀. 3 用力擦 yònglì cā；用力压[壓] yònglì yā：～ *one's teeth* 咬牙切齿. 4 [习语] **grind to a halt** 慢慢停下来 mànmàn tíng xiàlái. 5[短语动词] **grind sb down** 虐待 nüèdài；折磨 zhémó. **grind** *n* [sing] 1 磨 mó. 2[非正式用语]苦差使 kǔchāishi. **grinder** *n* [C] 磨床[牀] móchuáng；磨工 mógōng. **'grindstone** *n* [C] 磨石 móshí.

grip /grɪp/ *v* [**-pp-**] 1 [I,T] 紧[緊]握 jǐnwò；抓紧 zhuājǐn. 2 [T] [喻]抓住…的注意 zhuāzhù …de zhùyì：*a* ～*ping film* 吸引人的电影. **grip** *n* 1[sing] 紧握 jǐnwò；紧夹[夾] jǐnjiā. 2 [C]夹子 jiāzi. 3 [C] [美语]手提包 shǒutíbāo；旅行包 lǚxíngbāo. 4 [习语] **come/get to grips with sth** (认真)对[對]付(问题等) duìfu.

grisly /ˈgrɪzli/ *adj* 可怕的 kěpàde.

gristle /ˈgrɪsl/ *n* [U] (肉食中的)软[軟]骨 ruǎngǔ.

grit /grɪt/ *n* [U] 1 粗砂 cūshā；砂砾[礫] shālì. 2 刚[剛]毅 gāngyì；勇气[氣] yǒngqì；坚[堅]忍 jiānrěn. **grit** *v* [**-tt-**] [T] 1 铺砂砾于(冰冻的路面等) pū shālì yú. 2 [习语] **grit one's teeth** (a) 咬紧[緊]牙 yǎo jǐn yá. (b) [喻]咬紧牙关[關]坚[堅]决… yǎo jǐn yáguān jiānjué…. **gritty** *adj* [**-ier**，**-iest**].

groan /grəʊn/ *v* [I]，*n* [C] 呻吟 shēnyín：

She ~ed with pain. 她痛苦得呻吟起来.

grocer /ˈgrəʊsə(r)/ *n* [C] 杂〔雜〕货商 záhuòshāng; 食品商 shípǐnshāng. **groceries** *n* [pl] 食品杂货 shípǐn záhuò.

groggy /ˈgrɒgɪ/ *adj* [-ier, -iest] 身体〔體〕虚弱的 shēntǐ xūruò de.

groin /grɔɪn/ *n* [C] 腹股沟〔溝〕fùgǔgōu.

groom /gruːm/ *n* [C] **1** 马夫 mǎfū. **2** 新郎 xīnláng. **groom** *v* [T] **1** 饲养〔養〕(马) sìyǎng. **2** 使为〔爲〕某工作做准〔準〕备〔備〕shǐ wèi mǒu gōngzuò zuò zhǔnbèi. **groomed** *adj* 穿戴整洁〔潔〕的 chuāndài zhěngjié de: *a well- ~ed young man* 衣冠楚楚的年轻人.

groove /gruːv/ *n* [C] **1** 槽 cáo; 沟〔溝〕gōu. **2** [习语] **get into / be stuck in a groove** 成为〔爲〕习〔習〕惯 chéngwéi xíguàn. **grooved** *adj* 有槽的 yǒucáode.

grope /grəʊp/ *v* **1** [I]触〔觸〕摸 chùmō; 暗中摸索 ànzhōng mōsuǒ: *~ for one's glasses* 摸索自己的眼镜. **2** [T][非正式用语, 贬](调情时)抚〔撫〕摸(…的身体) fǔmō.

gross[1] /grəʊs/ *n* [C] [*pl* **gross**] (商业用语)罗〔羅〕luó(=144个或12打).

gross[2] /grəʊs/ *adj* **1** 非常胖的 fēicháng pàngde. **2** 粗俗的 cūsúde. **3** 显〔顯〕著的 xiǎnzhùde: *~ injustice* 显著的不公. **4** 总〔總〕的 zǒngde; 毛的 máode: *~ income* 毛收入(即税前收入). **gross** *v* [T] 获〔獲〕得…毛收入 huòdé… máo shōurù. **grossly** *adv*. **grossness** *n* [U].

grotesque /grəʊˈtesk/ *adj* 奇形怪状〔狀〕的 qí xíng guài zhuàng de; 奇异〔異〕的 qíyìde. **grotesquely** *adv*.

grotto /ˈgrɒtəʊ/ *n* [C] [*pl* **~es** 或 **~s**] 洞 dòng; 穴 xué.

ground[1] /graʊnd/ *n* **1 the ground** [sing] 地面 dìmiàn: *fall to the ~* 掉到地上. **2** [U]地面上的区〔區〕域、距离〔離〕dìmiàn shàng de qūyù、jùlí. **3** [U]土地 tǔdì; 土壤 tǔrǎng: *stony ~* 多石地. *marshy ~* 沼泽地. **4** [C]场〔場〕地 chǎngdì: *a football ~* 足球场. *a play ~* (学校的)操场. **5 grounds** [pl] (建筑物周围的)场地 chǎngdì, 庭院 tíngyuàn: *the palace ~s* 王宫庭院. **6** [U] [喻](兴趣、讨论等的)领域 lǐngyù; 范〔範〕围〔圍〕fànwéi: *The programme covered a lot of ~.* 这一计划包括了多方面的内容. *common ~ between the two sides* 双方的共同点. **7**[C, 尤作 pl] 理由 lǐyóu: *~s for divorce* 离婚的理由. **8 grounds** [pl] 渣滓 zhāzǐ; 沉积〔積〕物 chénjīwù: *ˈcoffee- ~s* 咖啡渣. **9** [习语] **gain / make up ground (on sb / sth)** 追上 zhuī shàng: [喻] *gain ~ on one's competitors* 追上对手. **get off the ground** 有一个〔個〕好的开〔開〕始 yǒu yígè hǎode kāishǐ. **give / lose ˈground (to sb / sth)** 失利 shīlì. **hold/keep/stand one's ˈground** 坚〔堅〕持立场 jiānchí lìchǎng. ˌ**ground ˈfloor** *n* [sing] [英国英语] (建筑物的)一楼〔樓〕yīlóu, 一层〔層〕yīcéng. **groundless** *adj* 没有理由的 méiyǒu lǐyóu de: *~less fears* 没有理由的害怕. ˈ**groundsheet** *n* [C] (防止睡袋受潮的)铺地防潮布 pūdì fángcháobù. ˈ**groundwork** *n* [U] 基础〔礎〕工作 jīchǔ gōngzuò.

ground[2] /graʊnd/ *v* **1** [I, T] (使)船搁〔擱〕浅〔淺〕chuán gēqiǎn. **2** [T] 使(飞机)停飞〔飛〕shǐ tíngfēi. **3** [短语动词] **ground sb in sth** 给(某人)…基础〔礎〕训练〔練〕gěi… jīchǔ xùnliàn. **ground sth on sth** 使基于 shǐ jīyú. **grounding** *n* [sing] 基础训练 jīchǔ xùnliàn.

ground[3] /graʊnd/ *pt, pp* of GRIND.

group /gruːp/ *n* [C, 亦作 sing, 用 pl v] 群 qún; 批 pī. **group** *v* [I, T] (把…)分组 fēnzǔ.

grouse[1] /graʊs/ *n* [C] [*pl* **grouse**] 松鸡〔鷄〕sōngjī.

grouse[2] /graʊs/ *v* [I] [非正式用语]埋怨 mányuàn; 发〔發〕牢骚 fā láosāo. **grouse** *n* [C] 牢骚 láosāo.

grove /grəʊv/ *n* [C] 树〔樹〕丛〔叢〕shùcóng; 小树林 xiǎoshùlín.

grovel /ˈgrɒvl/ *v* [-ll-; 美语 -l-] [贬]卑躬屈节〔節〕bēi gōng qū jié.

grow /grəʊ/ *v* [*pt* **grew** /gruː/, *pp* **~n** /grəʊn/] **1** [I] 增大 zēngdà. **2** [I, T] (使)生长〔長〕shēngzhǎng: *Plants ~ from seeds.* 植物是从种子生长起来的. *~ a beard* 蓄须. **3** [通常与形容词连用]成为〔爲〕chéngwéi; 变〔變〕得 biàndé: *~ older* 变老. **4** [短语动词] **grow on sb** 引起…的爱〔愛〕好 yǐnqǐ…de àihào: *The picture will ~ on you.* 这图画会引起你的喜爱. **grow out of sth (a)** 长大得穿不上(某一衣服等) zhǎngdàdé chuānbúshàng. **(b)** 长大得不宜 zhǎngdàdé bùyí: *~ out of playing with toys* 长大, 不玩玩具了. **grow up (a)** 成年 chéngnián. **(b)** 开〔開〕始存在 kāishǐ cúnzài: *A warm friendship grew up between them.* 他们之间发展起了亲密的友谊.

growl /graʊl/ *v* [I], *n* [C] (动物)嗥叫 háojiào; (雷)轰〔轟〕鸣〔鳴〕hōngmíng: *The dog ~ed at the burglars.* 那狗向小偷汪汪直叫.

grown /grəʊn/ *adj* 成年的 chéngniánde; 成熟的 chéngshúde. ˌ**grown ˈup** *adj* 成年的 chéngniánde; 成熟的 chéngshúde. ˈ**grown-up** *n* [C] 成年人 chéngniánrén.

growth /grəʊθ/ *n* **1** [U] 生长〔長〕shēngzhǎng; 发〔發〕展 fāzhǎn. **2** 生长物 shēngzhǎngwù: *three days' ~ of beard* 长了三天的胡子. **3** [C] [医]瘤 liú.

G

grub[1] /grʌb/ *n* 1 [C] (动物)蛴〔蠐〕螬 qícáo. 2 [U] [俚]食物 shíwù.

grub[2] /grʌb/ *v* [-bb-] [I] 掘地(掘出某物) juédì.

grubby /ˈgrʌbɪ/ *adj* [-ier, -iest] 污秽〔穢〕的 wūhuìde.

grudge /grʌʤ/ *v* [T] 吝惜 lìnxī; 不愿〔願〕给 búyuàn gěi; 不愿接受 búyuàn jiēshòu: *I ~ paying so much for such bad goods*. 对这么糟的食物我不愿付很多钱. **grudge** *n* [C] 恶〔惡〕意 èyì; 怨恨 yuànhèn; 忌妒 jìdù: *have a ~ against sb* 怀恨某人. **grudgingly** *adv*.

gruelling (美语 **grueling**) /ˈgruːəlɪŋ/ *adj* 累垮人的 lèikuǎ rén de.

gruesome /ˈgruːsəm / *adj* 可怕的 kěpàde; 讨厌〔厭〕的 tǎoyànde. **gruesomely** *adv*.

G

gruff /grʌf/ *adj* 粗暴的 cūbàode; 不友好的 bùyǒuhǎode. **gruffly** *adv*. **gruffness** *n* [U].

grumble /ˈgrʌmbl/ *v* [I] 埋怨 mányuàn; 发〔發〕牢骚 fā láosāo. **grumble** *n* [C] 埋怨 mányuàn; 牢骚 láosāo.

grumpy /ˈgrʌmpɪ/ *adj* [-ier, -iest] 脾气〔氣〕坏〔壞〕的 píqi huài de. **grumpily** *adv*.

grunt /grʌnt/ *v* [I] (a) (猪等)作呼噜声〔聲〕zuò hūlu shēng. (b) (人)发〔發〕哼哼声 fā hēnghēng shēng. **grunt** *n* [C] (猪等的)呼噜声 hūlu shēng; (人的)哼哼声 hēnghēng shēng.

guarantee /ˌgærənˈtiː/ *n* [C] 1 保证〔證〕(书) bǎozhèng: *The repairs to this watch are covered by the ~*. 这表保修. 2 担〔擔〕保 dānbǎo. **guarantee** *v* [T] 1 为〔爲〕…担保 wèi … dānbǎo. 2 保证 bǎozhèng: *We cannot ~ that train will arrive on time*. 我们不能保证火车会正点到达.

guarantor /ˌgærənˈtɔː(r)/ *n* [C] [法律]担〔擔〕保人 dānbǎorén; 保证〔證〕人 bǎozhèngrén; 保人 bǎo rén.

guard /gɑːd/ *n* 1 [U] 警惕 jǐngtì; 警戒 jǐngjiè: *a soldier on ~* 担任警戒的士兵. 2 [C] 警卫〔衛〕人员 jǐngwèi rényuán. 3 **the guard** [C, 亦作 sing, 用 pl v] 卫队〔隊〕wèiduì: *the ~ of honour* 仪仗队. 4 [英国英语]列车长〔長〕lièchēzhǎng. 5 [C] (尤用于复合词)防护〔護〕器 fánghùqì: *ˈfire-~* 挡火板. **guard** *v* 1 [T] 保护 bǎohù. 2 [T] 看守(某人) kānshǒu; 监〔監〕视 jiānshì. 3 [短语动词] **guard against sth** 防止 fángzhǐ; 防范〔範〕fángfàn: *~ against disease* 防病. **guarded** *adj* 谨慎的 jǐnshènde; 小心提防着的 xiǎoxīn dīfáng zhe de.

guardian /ˈgɑːdɪən/ *n* [C] 保护〔護〕人 bǎohùrén; 监〔監〕护人 jiānhùrén. **guardianship** *n* [U] 监护人的职责 jiānhùrénde zhízé.

guerrilla (亦作 **guerilla**) /gəˈrɪlə/ *n* [C] 游击〔擊〕队〔隊〕员 yóujīduìyuán.

guess /ges/ *v* 1 [I, T] 猜想 cāixiǎng; 推测 tuīcè. 2 [T] [非正式用语, 尤用于美语]认〔認〕为〔爲〕rènwéi; 想 xiǎng. **guess** *n* [C] 1 (*at*) 猜想 cāixiǎng. 2 猜想出的意见 cāixiǎng chū de yìjiàn. ˈ**guesswork** *n* [U] 猜想 cāixiǎng; 推测 tuīcè.

guest /gest/ *n* [C] 1 旅客 lǚkè. 2 (应邀吃饭、看戏等的)客人 kèrén. 3 客串演员 kèchuàn yǎnyuán. 4 [习语] **be my ˈguest** [非正式用语]请便! qǐngbiàn! ˈ**guest-house** *n* [C] 小旅馆 xiǎo lǚguǎn.

guffaw /gəˈfɔː/ *v* [I] *n* [C] 大笑 dàxiào; 狂笑 kuángxiào.

guidance /ˈgaɪdns/ *n* [U] 指导〔導〕zhǐdǎo; 指引 zhǐyǐn; 忠告 zhōnggào.

guide /gaɪd/ *n* [C] 1 领路人 lǐnglùrén; 向〔嚮〕导〔導〕xiàngdǎo. 2 影响行为〔爲〕的人或物 yǐngxiǎng xíngwéi de rén huò wù. 3 (亦作 ˈ**guidebook**) (介绍某一地方的)指南 zhǐnán. 4 手册 shǒucè: *a ~ to plants* 花木手册. 5 **Guide** 女童子军 nǚ tóngzǐjūn. **guide** *v* [T] 为…领路 wèi … lǐnglù; 指引 zhǐyǐn. ˌ**guided** ˈ**missile** *n* [C] 导弹〔彈〕dǎodàn. ˈ**guide-line** [C, 常作 pl] 指导方针 zhǐdǎo fāngzhēn; 指导原则 zhǐdǎo yuánzé.

guild /gɪld/ *n* [C] 行会〔會〕hánghuì; 同业〔業〕公会 tóngyè gōnghuì.

guile /gaɪl/ *n* [U] 诡计 guǐjì.

guillotine /ˈgɪlətiːn/ *n* [C] 1 断〔斷〕头〔頭〕台〔臺〕duàntóutái. 2 (切纸用)裁刀 cáidāo. 3 [喻, 英国英语, 政治]议〔議〕会〔會〕截止辩论〔論〕以付表决法 yìhuì jiézhǐ biànlùn yǐ fù biǎojuéfǎ. **guillotine** *v* [T] 在断头台上处〔處〕决 zài duàntóutái shàng chǔjué; 切开〔開〕qiēkāi.

guilt /gɪlt/ *n* [U] 1 内疚 nèijiù. 2 罪责 zuìzé. **guilty** *adj* [-ier, -iest] 1 有罪的 yǒuzuìde. 2 内疚的 nèijiùde; 自觉〔覺〕有罪的 zìjué yǒuzuì de. **guiltily** *adv*.

guinea /ˈgɪnɪ/ *n* [C] (尤用于过去的英国)21 先令(£1.05) èrshíyī xiānlìng.

guinea-pig /ˈgɪnɪ pɪg/ *n* [C] 1 [动物]豚鼠 túnshǔ. 2 供试验〔驗〕用的人 gōng shìyàn yòng de rén.

guise /gaɪz/ *n* [C] [正式用语]外表 wàibiǎo.

guitar /gɪˈtɑː(r)/ *n* [C] [音乐]六弦琴 liùxiánqín; 吉他 jítā. **guitarist** *n* [C].

gulf /gʌlf/ *n* [C] 1 海湾〔灣〕hǎiwān: *the G~ of Mexico* 墨西哥湾. 2 (*between*) [喻]深刻的分歧 shēnkède fēnqí.

gull /gʌl/ *n* [C] (海)鸥〔鷗〕ōu.

gullet /ˈgʌlɪt/ *n* [C] 咽喉 yānhóu.

gullible /ˈgʌləbl/ *adj* 容易上当〔當〕受骗的 róngyì shàngdàng shòupiàn de.

gulp /gʌlp/ *v* [T] 吞食 tūnshí. **gulp** *n* [C] 吞食 tūnshí.

gum[1] /gʌm/ *n* [C, 常作 pl] 牙床〔牀〕yáchuáng;齿〔齒〕龈 chǐyín.

gum[2] /gʌm/ *n* 1 [U] 树〔樹〕胶〔膠〕shùjiāo. 2 [U] 口香糖 kǒuxiāngtáng;橡皮糖 xiàngpítáng. 3 [C] 果味糖果 guǒwèi tángguǒ. **gum** *v* [-mm-] [T] 用树胶粘 yòng shùjiāo zhān;涂〔塗〕树胶于 tú shùjiāo yú. ˈ**gumboot** *n* [C] 齐〔齊〕膝胶靴 qí xī jiāoxuē. **gummy** *adj* [-ier, -iest] 黏性的 niánxìngde. ˈ**gum-tree** *n* [C] 胶树 jiāoshù.

gun /gʌn/ *n* [C] 炮 pào;枪〔槍〕qiāng. **gun** *v* [-nn-] [短语动词] **gun sb down** 向…开〔開〕枪 xiàng…kāiqiāng. **gun for sb** [非正式用语] 伺机〔機〕攻击〔擊〕sìjī gōngjī. ˈ**gunboat** *n* [C] 炮艇 pàotǐng. **gunfire** *n* [C] 炮火 pàohuǒ;火器射击 huǒqì shèjī. **gunman** /-mən/ *n* [C] [*pl* **-men** /-mən/] 持枪歹徒 chíqiāng dǎitú;枪手 qiāngshǒu. **gunner** /ˈgʌnə(r)/ *n* [C] 炮手 pàoshǒu. ˈ**gunpoint** *n* [习语] **at** ˈ**gunpoint** 在枪口威胁〔脅〕下 zài qiāngkǒu wēixié xià. ˈ**gunpowder** *n* [U] 炸药〔藥〕zhàyào. ˈ**gunshot** *n* 1 [C] 枪炮射击 qiāngpào shèjī. 2 [U] 射程 shèchéng. **gunsmith** *n* [C] 枪炮匠 qiāngpàojiàng;枪炮工 qiāngpàogōng.

gurgle /ˈgɜːgl/ *v* [I] *n* [C] (发)汩汩流水声〔聲〕gǔgǔ liúshuǐ shēng.

gush /gʌʃ/ *v* [I] 1 涌出 yǒngchū;喷出 pēnchū: *blood ~ing from a wound* 伤口涌出的血. 2 [贬] 滔滔不绝地说 tāotāo bùjué de shuō. **gush** *n* [sing] 迸发〔發〕bèngfā. **gushing** *adj*.

gust /gʌst/ *n* [C] 阵风〔風〕zhènfēng. **gusty** *adj* [-ier, -iest].

gut /gʌt/ *n* 1 **guts** [pl] [非正式用语] (a) 内脏〔臟〕nèizàng. (b) [喻](机器等的)主要部分 zhǔyào bùfen. 2 **guts** [pl] [非正式用语] 勇气〔氣〕yǒngqì;决心 juéxīn. 3 肠〔腸〕cháng. 4 [C] 肠线〔綫〕chángxiàn. **gut** *v* [-tt-] [T] 1 取出(鱼等)内脏 qǔchū nèizàng. 2 损毁…内部装〔裝〕置 sǔnhuǐ… nèibù zhuāngzhì: *a house ~ted by fire* 被烧毁了内部装置的房子. **gut** *adj* 发〔發〕自内心深处〔處〕的 fā zì nèixīn shēnchù de;直觉〔覺〕的 zhíjuéde: *a ~ reaction* 本能的反应.

gutter /ˈgʌtə(r)/ *n* 1 [C] 檐槽 yáncáo. 2 **the gutter** [sing] [喻]贫贱〔賤〕pínjiàn. **the** ˈ**gutter press** *n* [sing] [贬]低级趣味报〔報〕纸 dījí qùwèi bàozhǐ.

guy[1] /gaɪ/ *n* [C] 1 [非正式用语]人 rén;家伙 jiāhuo. 2 盖〔蓋〕伊·福克斯的模拟〔擬〕像(每年11月15日盖伊·福克斯日被示众后烧毁) gàiyī·fúkèsīde mónǐ xiàng.

guy[2] /gaɪ/ *n* [C] 牵〔牽〕索 qiānsuǒ;稳〔穩〕索 wěnsuǒ.

guzzle /ˈgʌzl/ *v* [I, T] [非正式用语]大吃大喝 dàchī dàhē.

gym /dʒɪm/ *n* [C] [非正式用语] 1 [C] 体〔體〕育馆 tǐyùguǎn. 2 [U] 体操 tǐcāo. ˈ**gym-shoes** *n* [C] (橡皮底帆布面的)运〔運〕动〔動〕鞋 yùndòngxié.

gymkhana /dʒɪmˈkɑːnə/ *n* [C] 赛马 sàimǎ.

gymnasium /dʒɪmˈneɪzɪəm/ *n* [C] 体〔體〕育馆 tǐyùguǎn.

gymnast /ˈdʒɪmnæst/ *n* [C] 体〔體〕操家 tǐcāojiā.

gymnastics /dʒɪmˈnæstɪks/ *n* [pl] 体〔體〕操 tǐcāo. **gymnastic** *adj*.

gynaecology (美语 **gynec-**) /gaɪnəˈkɒlədʒɪ/ *n* [U] 妇〔婦〕科学〔學〕fùkēxué. **gynaecological** (美语 **gynec-**) /ˌgaɪnəkəˈlɒdʒɪkl/ *adj*. **gynaecologist** (美语 **gynec-**) *n* [C] 妇科医〔醫〕生 fùkē yīshēng.

gypsy (亦作 **gipsy**) /ˈdʒɪpsɪ/ *n* [C] [*pl* **-ies**] 吉卜赛人 jíbǔsàirén.

gyrate /ˌdʒaɪˈreɪt; *US* ˈdʒaɪreɪt/ *v* [I] 旋转〔轉〕xuánzhuǎn. **gyration** /ˌdʒaɪˈreɪʃn/ *n* [C, U].

H

H h

H, h /eɪtʃ/ *n* [C] [*pl* **H's, h's** /ˈeɪtʃɪz/] 英语的第八个〔個〕字母 Yīngyǔde dìbāgè zìmǔ.

haberdasher /ˈhæbədæʃə(r)/ *n* [C] 1 [英国英语] [C] 零星服饰针线〔綫〕商 língxīng fúshì zhēnxiàn shāng. 2 [美语] 男子服装〔裝〕商 nánzǐ fúzhuāngshāng. **haberdashery** *n* [U] 零星服饰针线 língxīng fúshì zhēnxiàn.

habit /ˈhæbɪt/ *n* 1 [C, U] 习〔習〕惯 xíguàn;习性 xíxìng: *Smoking is a bad ~.* 吸烟是坏习惯. 2 [C] 修道士或修女穿的衣服 xiūdàoshì huò xiūnǚ chuānde yīfu. 3 [习语] **make a habit of (doing) sth** 经〔經〕常做… jīngcháng zuò ….

habitable /ˈhæbɪtəbl/ *adj* 可居住的 kě jūzhù de.

habitat /ˈhæbɪtæt/ *n* [C] (动植物的)生境 shēngjìng, 栖〔棲〕息地 qīxīdì.

habitation /ˌhæbɪˈteɪʃn/ *n* [U] 居住 jūzhù: *houses fit for ~* 适宜居住的房屋.

habitual /həˈbɪtʃʊəl/ *adj* 1 惯常的 guànchángde;通常的 tōngchángde. 2 习〔習〕惯的 xíguànde: *a ~ smoker* 有烟瘾〔癮〕的人. **habitually** *adv*.

hack[1] /hæk/ *v* [I, T] 劈 pī;砍 kǎn. ˈ**hacksaw** *n* [C] 钢〔鋼〕锯 gāngjù;弓锯 gōngjù.

hack[2] /hæk/ *n* [C] 雇佣文人 gùyōng wénrén.

hacker /ˈhækə(r)/ *n* [C] 私自存取电〔電〕子计算机〔機〕资料的人 sīzì cúnqǔ diànzǐ jìsuànjī zīliào de rén.

hackneyed /ˈhæknɪd/ *adj* (词语等)陈腐的 chénfǔde.

had /hæd/ *pt*, *pp* of HAVE.

haddock /ˈhædək/ *n* [C, U] [*pl* haddock] 黑线〔綫〕鳕 hēixiànxuě.

hadn't /ˈhædnt/ had not. ⇨HAVE.

haemophilia (亦作 hem-, 尤用于美语) /ˌhiːməˈfɪlɪə/ *n* [U] 血友病 xuèyǒubìng. **haemophiliac** (亦作 hem-, 尤用于美语) / -lɪæk/ *n* [C] 血友病人 xuèyǒubìng rén.

haemorrhage (亦作 hem-, 尤用于美语) /ˈhemərɪdʒ/ *n* [C, U] 大出血 dà chūxiě.

haemorrhoids (亦作 hem-, 尤用于美语) /ˈhemərɔɪdz/ *n* [pl] [医]痔 zhì.

hag /hæg/ *n* [C] [贬]丑〔醜〕老妇〔婦〕 chǒulǎofù.

haggard /ˈhægəd/ *adj* 憔悴的 qiáocuìde; 枯槁的 kūgǎode.

haggis /ˈhægɪs/ *n* [C, U] (苏格兰食品)肉馅羊肚 ròuxiàn yángdǔ.

H

haggle /ˈhægl/ *v* [I] (*over* / *about*) 讨价〔價〕还〔還〕价 tǎojià huánjià.

hail[1] /heɪl/ *n* 1 [U] 冰雹 bīngbáo; 雹子 báozi. 2 [sing] [喻](冰雹般)一阵 yízhèn: *a ~ of bullets* 一阵弹雨. **hail** *v* 1 [I] (与 it 连用) 下雹 xià báo. 2 [I, T] [喻] 落下 luòxià. ˈ**hailstone** *n* [C] 冰雹 bīngbáo; 雹子 báozi. ˈ**hailstorm** *n* [C] 雹暴 báobào.

hail[2] /heɪl/ *v* 1 [T] 向…打招呼 xiàng…dǎ zhāohu. 2 [T] 示意(出租车)停下 shìyì tíngxià. 3 [T] 热〔熱〕情赞〔讚〕扬〔揚〕 rèqíng zànyáng: *They ~ed him as their hero.* 他们赞颂他是他们的英雄. 4 [I] *from* 来自 láizì.

hair /heə(r)/ *n* 1 (a) [C] 毛 máo. (b) [U] 头〔頭〕发〔髮〕 tóufa. 2 [习语] (by) a ˌ**hair's ˈbreadth** (以)极〔極〕短的距离〔離〕 jíduǎnde jùlí. **make one's hair stand on end** 使某人毛骨悚然 shǐ mǒurén máo gǔ sǒngrán. ˈ**haircut** *n* [C] 理发 lǐfà. ˈ**hair-do** *n* [C] [*pl* -dos] [非正式用语](女子的)做发 zuò fà; (女子)发式 fàshì. ˈ**hairdresser** *n* [C] 理发(女发)师〔師〕 lǐfàshī. ˈ**hair-grip** *n* [C] 小发夹〔夾〕 xiǎo fàjiā. ˈ**hair-line** *n* [C] 1 (前额)发际〔際〕线〔綫〕 fàjìxiàn. 2 [喻]细线 xìxiàn: *a ~-line ˈcrack* 裂缝. ˈ**hairpin** *n* [C] 发夹 fàjiā; 发卡 fàqiǎ. ˌ**hairpin ˈbend** *n* [C] (道路的)U字形急转〔轉〕弯〔彎〕 U zìxíng jízhuǎnwān. ˈ**hair-raising** *adj* 令人毛骨悚然的 lìng rén máo gǔ sǒngrán de. ˈ**hairstyle** 发式 fàshì. **hairy** *adj* [-ier, -iest] 1 毛的 máode; 像毛一样〔樣〕的 xiàng máo yíyàng de; 长〔長〕满毛的 zhǎng mǎn máo de. 2 [俚]惊〔驚〕险〔險〕的 jīngxiǎnde; 令人毛骨悚然的 lìng rén máo gǔ sǒngrán de. **hairiness** *n* [U].

hale /heɪl/ *adj* [习语] **hale and hearty** 矍铄〔鑠〕的 juéshuòde; 健壮〔壯〕的 jiànzhuàngde.

half[1] /hɑːf; *US* hæf/ *n* [C] [*pl* **halves** /hɑːvz; *US* hævz/] 1 一半 yíbàn; $\frac{1}{2}$. 2 半票 bànpiào; (饮料的)半杯 bànbēi: *Two halves to the station, please.* 买两张到火车站的半票. 3 (体育比赛或音乐会的)半场〔場〕 bànchǎng. 4 [习语] **go ˈhalves (with) sb** 与〔與〕某人均摊〔攤〕费用 yǔ mǒurén jūntān fèiyòng.

half[2] /hɑːf; *US* hæf/ *adj* 1 一半的 yíbànde: *~ an hour* 半小时. 2 [习语] **half past ˈone, ˈtwo, etc**, [美语] **half after ˈone, ˈtwo, etc** 一点〔點〕、两点(等)三十分 yìdiǎn、liǎngdiǎn sānshí fēn. **half** *pron* 一半 yíbàn: *H~ of the money is hers.* 这钱的一半是她的. ˌ**half-and-ˈhalf** *adj* 一半…一半…的 yíbàn…yíbàn…de. ˌ**half ˈboard** *n* [U] 半膳宿(旅馆供应早餐及晚餐) bàn shànsù. **half-caste** (亦作 **half-breed**) *n* [C], *adj* 混血儿〔兒〕 hùnxuè'r; 混血的 hùnxuède. **half-mast** *n* [习语] **at half-mast** (旗)升半的 shēng bàn de. **half-ˈterm** *n* [C] 期中假(学期中间的假日) qīzhōngjià. ˌ**half-ˈtime** *n* [U] (体育比赛上下半场中间的)中场〔場〕休息 zhōngchǎng xiūxi. ˌ**half-ˈway** *adv*, *adj* 在中途(的) zài zhōngtú; 半路上(的) bànlùshàng. ˈ**half-wit** *n* [C] 笨蛋 bèndàn; 傻〔儍〕瓜 shǎguā. ˌ**half-ˈwitted** *adj*.

half[3] /hɑːf; *US* hæf/ *adv* 1 一半地 yíbànde: *~ full* 半满. 2 部分地 bùfende: *~ cooked* 没有完全煮熟的. 3 [非正式用语]几〔幾〕乎 jīhū: *They felt ~ dead.* 他们筋疲力尽. 4 [习语] **not half** [俚]非常 fēicháng: '*Do you like ice-cream?*' '*Not ~.*' "你爱吃冰淇淋吗?""非常爱吃." ˌ**half-ˈbaked** *adj* [非正式用语]愚蠢的 yúchǔnde. ˌ**half-ˈhearted** *adj* 兴〔興〕趣不大的 xìngqù búdà de; 不热〔熱〕心的 bú rèxīn de.

hall /hɔːl/ *n* [C] 1 门厅〔廳〕 méntīng; 过〔過〕道 guòdào. 2 礼〔禮〕堂 lǐtáng; 会〔會〕堂 huìtáng; 大厅 dàtīng. 3 大学〔學〕生宿舍 dàxuéshēng sùshè: *a ~ of residence* 大学宿舍.

hallelujah = ALLELUIA.

hallmark /ˈhɔːmɑːk/ *n* [C] 1 金银纯度标〔標〕记 jīnyín chúndù biāojì. 2 [喻]特点〔點〕 tèdiǎn; 特征〔徵〕 tèzhēng.

hallo (亦作 **hello, hullo**) /həˈləʊ/ *n* [C], *interj* [*pl* ~s] (用于打招呼、引起注意或表示惊讶)喂! wèi! 你好! nǐhǎo! 嘀! hē! 嘿! hēi!

Hallowe'en /ˌhæləʊˈiːn/ *n* [U]十月三十一日(万圣节前夕) shíyuè sānshíyīrì.

hallucination /həˌluːsɪˈneɪʃn/ *n* [C, U] 幻觉〔覺〕 huànjué.

halo / ˈheɪləʊ/ *n* [C] [*pl* ~es] 1 (绘于神像

头上的)光环〔環〕 guānghuán. 2 (日、月)晕 yùn.

halt /hɔːlt/ *v* [I,T] (使)停止前进〔進〕 tíngzhǐ qiánjìn. **halt** *n* [sing, C] 停止 tíngzhǐ: *The train came to a ~ outside the station.* 火车在站外停了下来.

halter /ˈhɔːltə(r)/ *n* [C] (马)笼〔籠〕头〔頭〕 lóngtóu; 缰绳〔繩〕 jiāngshéng.

halting /ˈhɔːltɪŋ/ *adj* 踌〔躊〕躇的 chóuchúde; 迟〔遲〕疑不决的 chíyí bù jué de. **haltingly** *adv*.

halve /hɑːv; *US* hæv/ *v* [T] 1 把…等分为〔爲〕两半 bǎ…děngfēn wéi liǎngbàn. 2 把…减少一半 bǎ…jiǎnshǎo yíbàn: ~ *the cost* 把费用减少一半.

halves *n pl* of HALF[1].

ham /hæm/ *n* 1 (a) [C] 火腿 huǒtuǐ. (b) [U] 火腿肉 huǒtuǐròu. 2 [C] [俚]拙劣的演员 zhuóliède yǎnyuán. 3 [C] 业〔業〕余〔餘〕无〔無〕线〔綫〕电〔電〕爱〔愛〕好者 yèyú wúxiàndiàn àihàozhě. **ham** *v* [-mm-] [I,T] [俚]过〔過〕火地表演某一角色 guòhuǒde biǎoyǎn mǒuyī juésè. ˌ**ham-ˈfisted** *adj* [贬]笨手笨脚地 bènshǒu bènjiǎo de.

hamburger /ˈhæmbɜːgə(r)/ *n* [C] 面〔麵〕包片夹〔夾〕牛肉饼 miànbāopiàn jiā niúròubǐng; 汉〔漢〕堡包 hànbǎobāo.

hamlet /ˈhæmlɪt/ *n* [C] 小村庄〔莊〕 xiǎocūnzhuāng.

hammer /ˈhæmə(r)/ *n* [C] 1 锤 chuí; 榔头〔頭〕 lángtou. 2 (钢琴)音锤 yīnchuí. **hammer** *v* 1 [I,T] 锤击〔擊〕 chuíjī; 锤打 chuídǎ. 2 [T] [非正式用语]击败 jībài; 打垮 dǎkuǎ. 3 [短语动词] **hammer away at sth** 致力于 zhìlì yú; 埋头于 máitóu yú: ~ *away at a problem* 苦苦研究一个问题. **hammer sth out** 经〔經〕详细讨论〔論〕得出一致意见 jīng xiángxì tǎolùn déchū yízhì yìjiàn.

hammock /ˈhæmək/ *n* [C] 吊床〔牀〕 diàochuáng.

hamper[1] /ˈhæmpə(r)/ *v* [T] 阻碍〔礙〕 zǔ'ài; 妨碍 fáng'ài; 牵〔牽〕制 qiānzhì.

hamper[2] /ˈhæmpə(r)/ *n* [C] (携带食品用的)有盖〔蓋〕篮〔籃〕子 yǒu gài lánzi.

hamster /ˈhæmstə(r)/ *n* [C] 仓〔倉〕鼠 cāngshǔ.

hand[1] /hænd/ *n* 1 [C] 手 shǒu. 2 a **hand** [sing] 帮〔幫〕助 bāngzhù: *Can you give me a ~ with the washing-up?* 你帮我洗洗餐具吧. 3 [C] (钟表等的)指针 zhǐzhēn: *hour ~* 时针. 4 [C] 工人 gōngrén: *a farm-~* 农场工人. 5 [C] (纸牌戏中的)一手牌 yìshǒupái. 6 [sing] 字迹 zìjì; 手迹 shǒujì. 7 [sing] 鼓掌 gǔzhǎng. 8 [习语] **at first ˈhand** 直接 zhíjiē. **at second ˈhand** 间接 jiàn jiē. **at ˈhand** 在附近 zài fùjìn. **by ˈhand** (a) 用手工 yòng shǒugōng. (b) 由专〔專〕人递〔遞〕送(非邮寄) yóu zhuānrén dìsòng. ˌ**hand in ˈhand** (a) 手拉手 shǒu lā shǒu. (b) [喻]密切关〔關〕联〔聯〕地 mìqiè guānlián de. **have / take a hand in sth** 起一份作用 qǐ yífèn zuòyòng. **have one's hands full** 很忙 hěnmáng. **in ˈhand** (a) 被拥〔擁〕有 bèi yōngyǒu; 待使用 dài shǐyòng. (b) 在控制下 zài kòngzhì xià: *The situation is well in ~.* 局势得到了很好的控制. (c) 在进〔進〕行中 zài jìnxíng zhōng: *the job in ~* 正在进行的工作. **in sb's ˈhands** 在某人控制、照管下 zài mǒurén kòngzhì、zhàoguǎn xià. **out of sb's hands** 不在某人控制、照管下 bú zài mǒurén kòngzhì、zhàoguǎn xià. **off one's ˈhands** 不再由某人负责 búzài yóu mǒurén fùzé. **on one's ˈhands** 由某人负责 yóu mǒurén fùzé. **on ˈhand** 现有 xiànyǒu; 在手头〔頭〕 zài shǒutóu. **on the ˈone hand ... on the ˈother (hand)** (用于表示两种相反的意见)一方面…,另一方面… yì fāngmiàn…, lìng yì fāngmiàn…. **out of ˈhand** (a) 失去控制 shīqù kòngzhì. (b) 不假思索地 bùjiǎ sīsuǒ de. **ˈhandbag** *n* [C] (女式)手提包 shǒutíbāo. **ˈhandbook** *n* [C] 手册 shǒucè; 便览〔覽〕 biànlǎn; 指南 zhǐnán. **ˈhandbrake** *n* [C] (汽车等的)手闸 shǒuzhá; 手刹车 shǒu shāchē. **ˈhandcuff** *v* [T] 给…带〔帶〕上手铐 gěi…dàishàng shǒukào. **ˈhandcuffs** *n* [pl] 手铐 shǒukào. **handful** *n* 1 [C] 一把(的量) yìbǎ. 2 [sing] 少数〔數〕 shǎoshù; 少量 shǎoliàng. 3 [sing] [非正式用语]难〔難〕控制的人或动〔動〕物 nán kòngzhì de rén huò dòngwù. **ˈhandheld deˌvice** *n* [C] 便携〔攜〕设备〔備〕 biànxié shèbèi. ˌ**hand-ˈpicked** *adj* 精选〔選〕的 jīngxuǎnde. **ˈhands-free** *adj* (电话)免提的 miǎntí de. **ˈhandshake** *n* [C] 握手 wòshǒu. **ˈhandstand** *n* [C] [体育]手倒立 shǒu dàolì. **ˈhandwriting** *n* [U] 手写〔寫〕 shǒuxiě; 笔〔筆〕迹 bǐjì.

hand[2] /hænd/ *v* 1 [T] 传〔傳〕递〔遞〕 chuándì; 交 jiāo; 给 gěi: *Please ~ me that book.* 请把那本书递给我. 2 [习语] **hand sb sth on a plate** ⇨PLATE. 3 [短语动词] **hand sth down (to sb)** 把(习惯、知识等)传〔傳〕给下一代 bǎ chuángěi xiàyídài. **hand sth in (to sb)** 交上 jiāoshàng; 呈送 chéngsòng: ~ *in homework* 交上家庭作业. **hand sth on (to sb)** 转〔轉〕交 zhuǎnjiāo; 传送 chuánsòng. **hand sth out (to sb)** (a) 分发〔發〕给 fēnfā gěi; 散发给 sànfā gěi. (b) 施舍〔捨〕给 shīshě gěi. **hand sb/sth over (to sb)** 交出 jiāochū; 移交 yíjiāo: ~ *a prisoner to the authorities* 把一个囚犯交给当局. **ˈhand-out** *n* [C] 1 施舍(物) shīshě. 2 传单〔單〕 chuándān; 分发的印刷品、资料等 fēnfā de yìnshuāpǐn、zīliào děng.

handicap /ˈhændɪkæp/ *n* [C] 1 (身体或智力上的)残〔殘〕疾 cánjí; 障碍〔礙〕 zhàng'ài. 2 障碍 zhàng'ài. 3 给予优〔優〕者的不利条〔條〕件以使竞〔競〕赛机〔機〕会〔會〕相等 jǐyǔ yōuzhě de búlì

H

tiáojiàn yǐ shǐ jìngsài jīhuì xiāngděng. **handicap** *v* [-pp-] [T] 使不利 shǐ búlì. **handicapped** *adj* (身体或智力上)有残疾的 yǒu cánjí de.

handicraft /ˈhændɪkrɑːft; *US* -kræft/ *n* [C] 手工业〔業〕 shǒugōngyè;手艺〔藝〕 shǒuyì;手工艺品 shǒugōngyìpǐn.

handiwork /ˈhændɪwɜːk/ *n* [U] **1** 手工 shǒugōng;手工制〔製〕品 shǒugōng zhìpǐn. **2** (某人)所做事物 suǒzuò shìwù.

handkerchief /ˈhæŋkətʃɪf/ *n* [C] 手帕 shǒupà.

handle /ˈhændl/ *n* [C] 把手 bǎshǒu;柄 bǐng. **handle** *v* **1** [T] 抓住 zhuāzhù;摸 mō;触〔觸〕 chù;弄 nòng. **2** [T] 处〔處〕理 chǔlǐ;管理 guǎnlǐ: ～ *a situation* 对付局势. **3** [I, T] 操纵〔縱〕 cāozòng;操作(交通工具等) cāozuò: *This car ～s well*. 这辆车很好开. ˈ**handlebars** *n* [pl] (自行车等的)把手 bǎshǒu. **handler** *n* [C] (警犬等的)训练〔練〕员 xùnliànyuán.

handsome /ˈhænsəm/ *adj* **1** (尤指男人)漂亮的 piàoliàngde;清秀的 qīngxiùde. **2** 慷慨的 kāngkǎide;大方的 dàfangde. **handsomely** *adv*.

H

handy /ˈhændɪ/ *adj* [-ier, -iest] **1** 容易掌握的 róngyì zhǎngwò de;使用方便的 shǐyòng fāngbiàn de. **2** 近便的 jìnbiande;手边〔邊〕的 shǒubiānde. **3** (人)手灵〔靈〕巧的 shǒu língqiǎo de. **4** [习语] **come in** ˈ**handy** 派得上用处〔處〕 pàideshàng yòngchù. **handily** *adv*. ˈ**handyman** *n* [C] [*pl* **-men**] 善于做零碎修理活的人 shànyú zuò língsuì xiūlǐhuó de rén.

hang[1] /hæŋ/ *v* [*pt*, *pp* **hung** /hʌŋ/;下列第二义项,～ed] **1** [I, T] 挂〔掛〕 guà;悬〔懸〕挂 xuánguà. **2** [T]吊死 diàosǐ;绞死 jiǎosǐ. **3** [T] 把(墙纸)贴于墙〔牆〕上 bǎ tiē yú qiángshàng. **4** [I, T] (把)肉挂起来(晾晒)到可以食用 ròu guà qǐlái dào kěyǐ shíyòng. **5** [短语动词] **hang about / around** 闲呆着 xiándāizhe. **hang back** 不情愿〔願〕做某事 bù qíngyuàn zuò mǒushì. **hang on** (a) 紧〔緊〕紧握住 jǐnjǐn wòzhù. (b) [非正式用语]等待片刻 děngdài piànkè. **hang on to sth** (a) 紧紧抓住 jǐnjǐn zhuāzhù. (b) [非正式用语]保有 bǎoyǒu. **hang up** 挂〔掛〕断〔斷〕电〔電〕话 guàduàn diànhuà. **be / get hung up** [俚]忧〔憂〕虑〔慮〕 yōulǜ;着急 zháojí. ˈ**hang-gliding** *n* [U] 悬挂式滑翔运〔運〕动〔動〕 xuánguàshì huáxiáng yùndòng. **hanging** *n* **1** [U, C] 绞死 jiǎosǐ. **2 hangings** [pl] 悬挂物(如帷幕等) xuánguàwù. ˈ**hangman** *n* [C] [*pl* **-men**] 执〔執〕行绞刑的刽〔劊〕子手 zhíxíng jiǎoxíngde guìzishǒu. ˈ**hang-up** *n* [C] [俚]烦恼〔惱〕 fánnǎo.

hang[2] /hæŋ/ *n* [习语] **get the hang of sth** 熟悉…的做法 shúxī … de zuòfǎ.

hangar /ˈhæŋə(r)/ *n* [C] 飞〔飛〕机〔機〕库〔庫〕 fēijīkù.

hanger /ˈhæŋə(r)/ *n* [C] 挂〔掛〕钩 guàgōu: *a* ˈ*coat*-～ 衣架. ˌ**hanger-**ˈ**on** *n* [C] [*pl* **～s-on**] [贬]为〔爲〕讨便宜而与〔與〕人交好者 wèi tǎo piányì ér yǔ rén jiāohǎo zhě.

hangover /ˈhæŋəʊvə(r)/ *n* [C] **1** (酗酒后的)宿醉 sùzuì. **2** 遗留物 yíliúwù.

hanker /ˈhæŋkə(r)/ *v* [I] *after / for* 渴望 kěwàng. **hankering** *n* [C].

hanky /ˈhæŋkɪ/ *n* [C] [*pl* **-ies**] [非正式用语] 手帕 shǒupà.

haphazard /hæpˈhæzəd/ *adj* 杂〔雜〕乱〔亂〕的 záluànde;任意的 rènyìde. **haphazardly** *adv*.

happen /ˈhæpən/ *v* [I] **1** 发〔發〕生 fāshēng. **2** 偶然 ǒurán: *I ～ed to be out when he called*. 他打电话时我碰巧出去了. **3** [短语动词] **happen on sb / sth** [正式用语]偶然发现 ǒurán fāxiàn. **happening** *n* [C] 事件 shìjiàn.

happy /ˈhæpɪ/ *adj* [-ier, -iest] **1** 幸福的 xìngfúde;幸运〔運〕的 xìngyùnde. **2** [正式用语] 愉快的 yúkuàide: *I shall be ～ to accept your invitation*. 我们欣然接受你的邀请. **3** (言语、行为等)恰当〔當〕的 qiàdàngde;巧妙的 qiǎomiàode. **4** (用于表示祝贺)快乐〔樂〕的 kuàilède: *H～ birthday!* 祝你生日快乐! **5** [习语] **a happy** ˈ**medium** 中庸之道 zhōngyōng zhī dào;折中办〔辦〕法 zhézhōng bànfǎ. **happily** *adv*. **happiness** *n* [U]. ˌ**happy-go-**ˈ**lucky** *adj* 无〔無〕忧〔憂〕无虑〔慮〕的 wúyōu wúlǜ de.

harangue /həˈræŋ/ *n* [C] 长〔長〕篇的训斥性演说 chángpiānde xùnchìxìng yǎnshuō. **harangue** *v* [T] (向…)作冗长的训斥性演说 zuò rǒngchángde xùnchìxìng yǎnshuō.

harass /ˈhærəs; *US* həˈræs/ *v* [T] 使烦恼〔惱〕 shǐ fánnǎo;折磨 zhémó;骚扰〔擾〕 sāorǎo. **harassment** *n* [U].

harbour (美语 **-or**) /ˈhɑːbə(r)/ *n* [C] 港 gǎng;港湾〔灣〕 gǎngwān;港口 gǎngkǒu. **harbour** *v* [T] **1** 隐〔隱〕匿 yǐnnì;包庇 bāobì. **2** 心怀〔懷〕 xīnhuái;怀有 huáiyǒu: ～ *secret fears* 心怀不外露的恐惧.

hard[1] /hɑːd/ *adj* **1** 坚〔堅〕硬的 jiānyìngde;坚固的 jiāngùde: *as ～ as rock* 坚如磐石. **2** 困难〔難〕的 kùnnande: *a ～ exam* 困难的考试. **3** 辛苦的 xīnkǔde;费力的 fèilìde: ～ *work* 费力的工作. *a ～ worker* 辛苦的工人. **4** 难忍的 nánrěnde;艰〔艱〕难的 jiānnánde: *I had a ～ childhood*. 我的童年是很艰苦的. **5** (天气)严〔嚴〕厉〔厲〕的 yánlìde;严酷的 yánkùde: *a ～ winter* 严冬. **6** (人)严厉的 yánlìde;苛刻的 kēkède. **7** [习语] ˌ**hard and** ˈ**fast** (规则等)硬性的 yìngxìngde;不容改变〔變〕的 bùróng gǎibiàn de. **hard** ˈ**at it** 拼死拼活地工作 pīnsǐ pīnhuó de gōngzuò. hard facts 准〔準〕确〔確〕的信息 zhǔnquède xìnxī. ˌhard ˈluck (用于对不幸表示同情)真倒霉! zhēn dǎoméi! ˌhard of ˈhearing 耳背 ěrbèi. ˈhardback *n* [C] 硬皮书〔書〕yìngpíshū. hardboard *n* [U] 硬纸板 yìng zhǐbǎn. ˌhard ˈcash *n* [U] 现金 xiànjīn; 现款 xiànkuǎn. ˌhard ˈcopy *n* [U] (电子计算机)硬拷贝 yìng kǎobèi; 复〔複〕印文本 fùyìn wénběn. ˈhard core *n* [sing] 中坚力量 zhōngjiān lìliàng; 骨干〔幹〕gǔgàn. ˌhard ˈcurrency *n* [U, C] 硬通货 yìngtōnghuò. hard ˈdisk *n* [C] 硬盘〔盤〕yìngpán. hard drive *n* [C] 硬盘〔盤〕驱〔驅〕动〔動〕器 yìngpán qūdòngqì. ˌhard ˈdrug *n* [C] 硬毒品 yìng dúpǐn; 易成瘾的烈性毒品(如海洛因等) yì chéngyǐn de lièxìng dúpǐn. ˌhard-ˈheaded *adj* 讲〔講〕究实〔實〕际〔際〕的 jiǎngjiū shíjì de; 不易激动〔動〕的 búyì jīdòng de. ˌhard-ˈhearted *adj* 硬心肠〔腸〕的 yìng xīncháng de; 冷酷的 lěngkùde. ˌhard ˈlabour *n* [U] 苦工 kǔgōng; 苦役 kǔyì. ˌhard-ˈline *adj* 不妥协〔協〕的 bù tuǒxié de; 立场〔場〕强硬的 lìchǎng qiángyìng de. ˌhard ˈshoulder *n* [C] (高速路旁供紧急情况下车辆离开车道停车用的)硬质〔質〕路肩 yìngzhì lùjiān. ˈhardware *n* [U] 1 五金制〔製〕品 wǔjīn zhìpǐn. 2 (电子计算机)硬件 yìngjiàn. ˌhard ˈwater *n* [U] 硬水(含钙镁等矿物质多、易生水垢的水) yìngshuǐ. ˈhardwood *n* [U] 硬木(如橡木等) yìngmù.

hard[2] /hɑːd/ *adv* 1 努力地 nǔlìde; 尽〔盡〕力地 jìnlìde: *try* ~ 努力干. *push* ~ 用力推. 2 重重地 zhòngzhòngde; 猛烈地 měngliède: *raining* ~ 下大雨. 3 困难〔難〕地 kùnnande: *my* ˈ*~-earned money* 我的血汗钱. 4 [习语] be hard ˈput (to it) (to do sth) (做某事)有很大困难 yǒu hěndà kùnnan. be hard to say 很难估计 hěnnán gūjì. be hard ˈup 缺钱〔錢〕quē qián. hard ˈdone by 被不公正对〔對〕待 bèi bù gōngzhèng duìdài. hard on sb / sth [正式用语]紧〔緊〕接…之后〔後〕jǐnjiē…zhī hòu. take sth hard 因某事而心烦意乱〔亂〕yīn mǒushì ér xīnfán yìluàn. ˌhard-ˈboiled *adj* (蛋)煮得老的 zhǔdé lǎo de. hard-ˈpressed *adj* 处〔處〕境困难的 chǔjìng kùnnan de. ˌhard-ˈwearing *adj* (衣服等)经〔經〕穿的 jīngchuānde.

harden /ˈhɑːdn/ *v* 1 [I,T] (使)变〔變〕硬 biàn yìng; (使)变强壮〔壯〕biàn qiángzhuàng. 2 [T] (*to*) 使对〔對〕…变得冷酷无〔無〕情 shǐ duì… biànde lěngkù wúqíng.

hardly /ˈhɑːdlɪ/ *adv* 1 刚〔剛〕刚 gānggāng; 简直不 jiǎnzhí bù: *I* ~ *know him*. 不怎么认识他. 2 决不 juébù: *You can* ~ *expect me to lend you money again*. 你别想我再借给你钱. 3 几〔幾〕乎没有 jīhū méiyǒu; 几乎不 jīhū bù: ~ *ever* 很少.

hardship /ˈhɑːdʃɪp/ *n* [C, U] 苦难〔難〕kǔnàn; 困苦 kùnkǔ.

hardy /ˈhɑːdɪ/ *adj* [-ier, -iest] 耐劳〔勞〕的 nàiláode; 能吃苦的 néng chīkǔ de. hardiness *n* [U].

hare /heə(r)/ *n* [C] 野兔 yětù. hare *v* [I] 飞〔飛〕跑 fēipǎo. ˈhare-brained *adj* 愚蠢的 yúchǔnde.

harem /ˈhɑːriːm; *US* ˈhærəm/ *n* [C] (伊斯兰教徒)女眷居住的内室 nǚjuàn jūzhùde nèishì; (伊斯兰教徒的)妻妾 qīqiè.

hark /hɑːk/ *v* 1 [I] [古]听〔聽〕tīng. 2 [短语动词] hark back (to sth) 回到原题 huídào yuántí.

harm /hɑːm/ *n* [U] 1 损害 sǔnhài; 伤〔傷〕害 shānghài. 2 [习语] out of harm's way 在安全的地方 zài ānquánde dìfang. harm *v* [T] 损害 sǔnhài; 损伤 sǔnshāng. harmful *adj* 有害的 yǒuhàide. harmless *adj* 1 无〔無〕害的 wúhàide. 2 无恶〔惡〕意的 wú èyì de.

harmonica /hɑːˈmɒnɪkə/ *n* [C] = MOUTH-ORGAN (MOUTH[1]).

harmonize /ˈhɑːmənaɪz/ *v* [I,T] 1 (使)协〔協〕调 xiétiáo: *colours that* ~ *well* 很协调的几种颜色. 2 [音乐] 用和声〔聲〕唱或演奏 yòng héshēng chàng huò yǎnzòu.

harmony /ˈhɑːmənɪ/ *n* [*pl* -ies] 1 [U] 一致 yízhì; 融洽 róngqià: *live together in perfect* ~ 非常融洽地生活在一起. 2 [C,U] 协〔協〕调 xiétiáo; 融和 rónghé: *the* ~ *of colour* 色彩的协调. 3 [C,U] 和声〔聲〕héshēng; 和声学〔學〕héshēngxué. harmonious /hɑːˈməʊnɪəs/ *adj*.

harness /ˈhɑːnɪs/ *n* [C,U] 1 挽具 wǎnjù; 马具 mǎjù. 2 降落伞等的背带〔帶〕jiàngluòsǎn děng de bēidài: *a parachute* ~ 降落伞的背带. harness *v* [T] 1 给…上挽具 gěi… shàng wǎnjù. 2 治理(河流等) zhìlǐ; 利用 lìyòng.

harp /hɑːp/ *n* [C] 竖〔豎〕琴 shùqín. harp *v* [短语动词] harp on (about) sth 唠〔嘮〕唠叨叨地说 lāolaodāodāode shuō. harpist *n* [C] 竖琴师〔師〕shùqínshī.

harpoon /hɑːˈpuːn/ *n* [C] 鱼叉 yúchā; 标〔標〕枪〔槍〕biāoqiāng. harpoon *v* [T] 用鱼叉叉 yòng yúchā chā.

harpsichord /ˈhɑːpsɪkɔːd/ *n* [C] 拨〔撥〕弦古钢〔鋼〕琴 bōxián gǔgāngqín.

harrowing /ˈhærəʊɪŋ/ *adj* 折磨人的 zhémó rén de; 使人痛苦的 shǐ rén tòngkǔ de.

harsh /hɑːʃ/ *adj* 1 粗糙的 cūcāode. 2 严〔嚴〕厉〔厲〕的 yánlìde: *a* ~ *punishment* 严厉的处罚. harshly *adv*. harshness *n* [U].

harvest /ˈhɑːvɪst/ *n* [C] (a) 收获〔獲〕shōuhuò; 收获季节〔節〕shōuhuò jìjié. (b) 收成 shōucheng; 收获量 shōuhuòliàng: *a good wheat* ~ 小麦丰收. harvest *v* [T] 收割 shōugē; 收获 shōuhuò.

has /hæz/ ⇨HAVE.

H

hash /hæʃ/ *n* 1 [U] 回锅〔鍋〕肉丁 huíguō ròudīng. 2 [习语] **make a hash of sth** [非正式用语]把…弄糟 bǎ…nòng zāo.

hashish /ˈhæʃiːʃ, ˈhæʃɪʃ/ *n* [U] 大麻麻醉剂〔劑〕 dàmá mázuìjì.

hasn't /ˈhæznt/ has not. ⇨HAVE.

hassle /ˈhæsl/ *n* [C, U] [非正式用语]困难〔難〕 kùnnan; 麻烦 máfan. **hassle** *v* [T] [非正式用语]不断〔斷〕打扰〔擾〕 búduàn dǎrǎo; 使烦恼〔惱〕 shǐ fánnǎo.

haste /heɪst/ *n* [U] 急速 jísù; 仓〔倉〕促 cāngcù.

hasten /ˈheɪsn/ *v* 1 [I] 急忙 jímáng; 赶〔趕〕快 gǎnkuài; 急忙说 jímáng shuō: *I ~ to say that your child is safe.* 我急忙补充说你的孩子安然无恙. 2 [T] 催促 cuīcù; 使赶快 shǐ gǎnkuài.

hasty /ˈheɪstɪ/ *adj* 1 急速的 jísùde; 匆促的 cōngcùde; 仓〔倉〕促的 cāngcùde: *a ~ meal* 急速的用餐. 2 (人)草率的 cǎoshuàide; 轻〔輕〕率的 qīngshuàide: *too ~ in deciding to get married* 太草率地决定结婚. **hastily** *adv*.

hat /hæt/ *n* [C]1 帽子 màozi. 2 [习语] **take one's hat off to sb** 向…致敬 xiàng…zhìjìng. ˈ**hat trick** *n* [C] 连续〔續〕三次取胜〔勝〕 liánxù sāncì qǔshèng.

hatch[1] /hætʃ/ *v* 1 [I, T] (使)孵出 fūchū: *The chicks have ~ed (ˈout).* 小鸡孵出来了. 2 [T] 策划〔劃〕 cèhuà; 计划 jìhuà.

hatch[2] /hætʃ/ *n* [C] (a) 地板上的开〔開〕口 dìbǎn shàng de kāikǒu; 舱〔艙〕口 cāngkǒu. (b) (地板开口、舱口等的)盖〔蓋〕 gài.

hatchback /ˈhætʃbæk/ *n* [C] 仓〔倉〕门式后〔後〕背车〔車〕身小轿〔轎〕车 cāngménshì hòubèi chēshēn xiǎojiàochē.

hatchet /ˈhætʃɪt/ *n* [C] 短柄小斧 duǎnbǐng xiǎofǔ.

hatchway/ˈhætʃweɪ/ *n* [C] = HATCH²(a).

hate /heɪt/ *v* [T] 1 恨 hèn; 憎恨 zènghèn; 讨厌〔厭〕 tǎoyàn. 2 [非正式用语]抱歉 bàoqiàn; 遗憾 yíhàn: *I ~ to trouble you.* 真抱歉, 麻烦你了. 3 [习语] ˌ**hate sb's ˈguts** [非正式用语]对〔對〕某人恨之入骨 duì mǒurén hèn zhī rù gǔ. **hate** *n* [U] 憎恨 zènghèn; 憎恶〔惡〕 zèngwù. **hateful** *adj* 非常讨厌的 fēicháng tǎoyàn de. **hatefully** *adv*.

hatred /ˈheɪtrɪd/ *n* [U] (*for / of*) 仇恨 chóuhèn; 憎恨 zènghèn.

haughty /ˈhɔːtɪ/ *adj* [-ier, -iest] 傲慢的 àomànde; 骄〔驕〕傲的 jiāo'àode. **haughtily** *adv* **haughtiness** *n* [U].

haul /hɔːl/ *v* [I, T] 用力拉 yònglì lā; 拖 tuō. **haul** *n* [C] 1 拖 tuō; 拉 lā. 2 拖运〔運〕的距离〔離〕 tuōyùnde jùlí. 3 捕获〔獲〕量 bǔhuòliàng. **haulage** *n* [U] 货运 huòyùn.

haunch /hɔːntʃ/ *n* [C, 常作 pl] (人的)腿臀部 tuǐtúnbù.

haunt /hɔːnt/ *v* [T] 1 (鬼魂)常出没于 cháng chūmò yú: *a ~ed house* 闹鬼的屋子. 2 常去 cháng qù; 常到 cháng dào. 3(思想等) 萦〔縈〕绕〔繞〕 yíngrǎo: *The memory still ~s me.* 往事仍萦绕在我的心头. **haunt** *n* [C] 常去的地方 cháng qù de dìfang.

have[1] /həv, əv, v; 强式 hæv/ *aux v* [第三人称单数现在时 **has** / həz, əz, s, z; 强式 hæz/, *pt* **had** /həd, əd, d; 强式 hæd/, *pp* **had** /hæd/] 1 (用于构成完成时态)已经〔經〕 yǐjīng: *I ~ / I've finished.* 我完成了. *She has / She's gone.* 她走了. 2 [习语] **had I, he, she, etc.** 如果我, 他, 她等… rúguǒ wǒ, tā, tā děng …: *Had I known, ...* 如果我知道, …

have[2] (英国英语 **have got**) /hæv/ *v* [T] 1 有 yǒu; 据〔據〕有 jùyǒu: *He has / has got a house in London.* 他在伦敦有一所房子. *Has she (got)/ Does she ~ blue eyes?* 她的眼睛是蓝色的吗? 2 感受 gǎnshòu; 怀〔懷〕有 huáiyǒu: *I ~ no doubt that you are right.* 我不怀疑你是正确的. *Have you (got) any idea where he lives?* 你知道他住在哪里吗? 3 患(病)huàn: ~ *a headache* 患头痛. 4 [习语] **have it ˈin for sb** [非正式用语]总〔總〕想与〔與〕某人过〔過〕不去 zǒngxiǎng yǔ mǒurén guòbúqù. **have (got) to (do sth)** 必须 bìxū: *I've got to go now.* 我现在就得走了. 5 [短语动词] **have sth on** 穿着 chuānzhe; 戴着 dàizhe. **have sth on sb** [非正式用语]有(信息)表明某人做了错事 yǒu biǎomíng mǒurén zuòle cuòshì.

have[3] /hæv/ *v* [T] [在否定句和疑问句中常与 *do* 连用] 1 做 zuò; 进〔進〕行 jìnxíng; 从〔從〕事 cóngshì: ~ *a swim* 游泳. ~ *a walk* 散步. 2 吃 chī; 喝 hē; 吸烟 xī yān: ~ *breakfast* 吃早餐. ~ *a cigarette* 吸烟. 3 接受 jiēshòu; 体〔體〕验〔驗〕 tǐyàn: *I've had a letter from my aunt.* 我收到了姑母的来信. ~ *a good holiday* 假期过得很愉快. 4 生育 shēngyù; 产〔產〕生 chǎnshēng: ~ *a baby* 生孩子. [喻] ~ *a good effect* 产生好的作用. 5 使(某事被做) shǐ: *You should ~ your hair cut.* 你该理发了. 6 遭受…的后〔後〕果 zāoshòu…de hòuguǒ: *They had their house burgled.* 他们家被盗了. 7 允许 yǔnxǔ: *I won't ~ such behaviour here.* 我不许在这里胡作非为. 8 请…来做客 qǐng…lái zuòkè: *We're having friends round for dinner.* 我们把朋友们请来吃饭. 9 [非正式用语]欺骗 qīpiàn: *You've been had!* 你上当受骗了! 10 [习语] **have**

ˈhad it [非正式用语] 不能继〔繼〕续〔續〕做某事 bùnéng jìxù zuò mǒushì. ˈhave it (that) 坚〔堅〕持说 jiānchí shuō; 说 shuō: *Rumour has it that* ... 有谣言说⋯. 11 [短语动词] **have sb ˈon** 欺哄 qīhǒng; 捉弄 zhuōnòng. **have sth ˈout** 把⋯除去 bǎ⋯chúqù; 拔除 báchú: ~ *a tooth out* 拔掉一颗牙齿. **have sth ˈout (with sb)** 通过〔過〕争论〔論〕解决同某人的某事 tōngguò zhēnglùn jiějué tóng mǒurén de mǒushì. **have sb ˈup (for sth)** [非正式用语][尤用于被动语态]使某人上法庭受审〔審〕 shǐ mǒurén shàng fǎtíng shòushěn: *He was had up for robbery*. 他因抢劫被送上法庭.

haven /ˈheɪvn/ *n* [C] [喻]安全处〔處〕所 ānquán chùsuǒ; 避难〔難〕所 bìnànsuǒ.

haven't /ˈhævnt/ have not. ⇨HAVE.

haversack /ˈhævəsæk/ *n* [C] 帆布背包 fānbù bēibāo.

havoc /ˈhævək/ *n* [U] 大灾〔災〕难〔難〕 dàzāinàn; 浩劫 hàojié.

hawk /hɔːk/ *n* [C] 1 鹰 yīng; 隼 sǔn. 2 [喻]主战〔戰〕分子 zhǔzhàn fènzǐ.

hay /heɪ/ *n* [U] 干〔乾〕草(饲料) gāncǎo. ˈ**hay fever** *n* [U] [医学]枯草热〔熱〕 kūcǎorè; 花粉热 huāfěnrè. ˈ**haystack** *n* 干草堆 gāncǎoduī. ˈ**haywire** *adj* [习语] **go haywire** 乱〔亂〕七八糟 luànqībāzāo; 杂〔雜〕乱不堪 záluàn bùkān.

hazard /ˈhæzəd/ *n* [C] (*to*) 危险〔險〕 wēixiǎn; 危害 wēihài. **hazard** *v* [T] 1 使冒危险 shǐ mào wēixiǎn. 2 斗胆〔膽〕提出 dǒudǎn tíchū. **hazardous** *adj* 危险的 wēixiǎnde; 冒险的 màoxiǎnde. **hazardous ˈwaste** *n* [C, U] 危险废〔廢〕物 wēixiǎn fèiwù; 有害健康的垃圾 yǒuhài jiànkāng de lājī.

haze /heɪz/ *n* [U] 1 薄雾〔霧〕 bówù; 霾 mái. 2 [喻]困惑 kùnhuò; 糊涂〔塗〕 hútu.

hazel /ˈheɪzl/ *n* [C] 榛 zhēn. **hazel** *adj* (尤指眼睛) 淡褐色的 dànhèsède.

hazy /ˈheɪzɪ/ *adj* [-ier, -iest] 1 雾〔霧〕蒙蒙的 wùméngméngde. 2 模糊的 móhude; 困惑的 kùnhuòde: ~ *memories* 模糊的记忆. **hazily** *adv* **haziness** *n* [U].

H-bomb /ˈeɪtʃ bɒm/ *n* [C] 氢〔氫〕弹〔彈〕 qīngdàn.

he /hiː/ *pron* [用于作动词的主语] 1 (代表男人或雄性动物)他 tā; 它 tā: *I spoke to John before he left*. 约翰离开以前,我和他说过话. 2 (不论性别的)一个人 yígèrén; 任何人 rènhérén: *Anyone can learn a foreign language, if he wants to*. 任何人只要想学,都可以学外语.

head[1] /hed/ *n* 1 [C] 头〔頭〕 tóu. 2 [C] 头脑〔腦〕 tóunǎo; 才智 cáizhì; 理解力 lǐjiělì: *The thought never entered my* ~. 我从来没有这个想法. 3 [sing] 天资 tiānzī: *a good* ~ *for figures* 数学天才. 4 **heads** [用 sing v] (硬币的有头像的)正面 zhèngmiàn. 5 **a head** [sing] 每人 měirén: *dinner at £15 a* ~ 每人 15 英镑的客饭. 6 [C] 头状〔狀〕物 tóuzhuàngwù: *the* ~ *of a pin* 针头. *the* ~ *of a hammer* 锤头. 7 [C, 常作 sing] 顶端 dǐngduān: *at the* ~ *of the page* 在这一页的顶端. 8 [C] 较重要的一端 jiào zhòngyào de yìduān: *at the* ~ *of the table* 在桌子的上首. *the* ~ *of a bed* 床头. 9 [C] 领导〔導〕人 lǐngdǎorén; 统治者 tǒngzhìzhě: ~*s of government* 政府首脑. 10 [sing] 前部 qiánbù: *at the* ~ *of the queue* 在排成的长队的前列. 11 [sing] 水压〔壓〕 shuǐyā; 水头 shuǐtóu; 水的落差 shuǐde luòchā. 12 [习语] **above / over one's ˈhead** 太高深而难〔難〕以理解 tài gāoshēn ér nányǐ lǐjiě. **bang / hit one's head against a brick wall** 以头碰壁,试图〔圖〕干〔幹〕不可能成功的事 yǐ tóu pèngbì, shìtú gàn bù kěnéng chénggōng de shì. **bring sth to a ˈhead** 使达〔達〕到危急关〔關〕头 shǐ dádào wēijí guāntóu. **come to a ˈhead** 迫近紧要关头 pòjìn jǐnyào guāntóu. **go to one's ˈhead** (a) (酒)上头 shàng tóu; 使头晕 shǐ tóuyūn. (b) (胜利等)引起骄〔驕〕傲 yǐnqǐ jiāo'ào. **have one's ˈhead screwed on** 精明能干〔幹〕 jīngmíng nénggàn; 有见识〔識〕 yǒu jiànshi. **head ˈfirst** (a) 头朝下(跌下去) tóu cháoxià: *fall* ~ *first down the stairs* 一个倒栽葱,从楼梯上跌了下去. (b) 仓〔倉〕促地 cāngcùde; 匆匆 cōngcōng. **head over ˈheels** (a) 向前翻跟斗 xiàngqián fān gēndǒu. (b) 完全地 wánquánde: ~ *over heels in love* 深陷爱河. **keep one's ˈhead** 保持镇静 bǎochí zhènjìng. **lose one's ˈhead** 张〔張〕皇失措 zhānghuáng shīcuò. **laugh, scream, etc one's ˈhead off** [非正式用语]大笑不止 dàxiào bùzhǐ; 拼命地喊叫 pīnmìngde hǎnjiào. **put our / your / their ˈheads together** 大家一起商量 dàjiā yìqǐ shāngliang; 集思广〔廣〕益 jí sī guǎng yì. ˈ**headache** *n* [C] 1 头痛 tóutòng. 2 [喻]麻烦事 máfanshì; 难〔難〕题 nántí. ˈ**headhunt** *v* [T] 物色(人才) wùsè; 猎〔獵〕头 liètóu. ˈ**headhunter** *n* [C] 猎頭人 liètóurén; 獵头 liètóu. ˈ**headland** *n* [C] 陆〔陸〕岬 lùjiǎ; 海角 hǎijiǎo. ˈ**headlight** (亦作 ˈ**headlamp**) *n* [C] (车辆的)前灯〔燈〕 qiándēng. ˈ**headline** *n* 1 [C] (报纸的)标〔標〕题 biāotí. 2 **the headlines** [pl] (广播、电视的)内容提要 nèiróng tíyào. **headˈmaster** (*fem* **headˈmistress**) *n* [C] 校长〔長〕 xiàozhǎng. ˌ**head-ˈon** *adj, adv* 迎面的(地) yíngmiànde: *The cars crashed* ~-ˈ*on*. 两辆汽车迎面相撞. ˈ**headphones** *n* [pl] 耳机〔機〕 ěrjī. ˌ**headˈquarters** *n* [用 sing 或 pl v] 总〔總〕部 zǒngbù. ˈ**head-rest** *n* [C] (某些座椅上的)头靠 tóukào. ˈ**headroom** *n* [U] (汽车等)车身内

H

部高度 chēshēn nèibù gāodù. ˈ**headstone** *n* [C] 墓碑 mùbēi. ˈ**headway** *n* [习语] **make headway** 前进〔進〕qiánjìn;取得进展 qǔdé jìnzhǎn.

head[2] /hed/ *v* **1** [T] (a) 位于(…)前部 wèiyú qiánbù;位于(…)顶端 wèiyú dǐngduān: ~ *the procession* 在队伍的前列. ~ *the list* 在名单的前列. (b) 主管 zhǔguǎn;领导〔導〕lǐngdǎo: ~ *the government* 领导政府. **2** [I] 朝着特定方向前进〔進〕cháozhe tèdìng fāngxiàng qiánjìn: ~ *south* 朝南行. ~ *for home* 往家去. **3** [T] (足球)顶(球) dǐng. **4** [短语动词] **head sb off** 上前拦〔攔〕住使转〔轉〕变〔變〕方向 shàng qián lánzhù shǐ zhuǎnbiàn fāngxiàng. **head sth off** 阻止 zǔzhǐ.

heading /ˈhedɪŋ/ *n* [C] 标〔標〕题 biāotí.

headlong /ˈhedlɒŋ; *US* -lɔːŋ/ *adj*, *adv* **1** 头〔頭〕向前的 tóu xiàngqián de;头向前地 tóu xiàngqiánde. **2** 轻〔輕〕率地 qīngshuàide: *rush ~ into a decision* 轻率地作出决定.

headstrong /ˈhedstrɒŋ; *US* -strɔːŋ/ *adj* 任性的 rènxìngde;顽固的 wángùde.

heady /ˈhedɪ/ *adj* [-ier, -iest] **1** (酒)易醉的 yìzuìde. **2** [喻](成就等)令人兴〔興〕奋〔奮〕的 lìng rén xīngfèn de.

heal /hiːl/ *v* [I, T] 痊愈〔癒〕quányù;治愈 zhìyù.

health /helθ/ *n* [U] **1** 健康状〔狀〕况 jiànkāng zhuàngkuàng: *be in good* ~ 很健康. *be in poor* ~ 不健康. **2** 健康 jiànkāng. **healthy** *adj* [-ier, -iest] **1** 健康的 jiànkāngde. **2** 有益于健康的 yǒu yì yú jiànkāng de: *a ~y climate* 有益于健康的气候. **3** 表示健康的 biǎoshì jiànkāng de: *a ~y appetite* 好胃口. [喻] *~y profits* 可观的利润. **healthily** *adv*.

heap /hiːp/ *n* [C] **1** 堆 duī;一堆 yìduī: *a ~ of books* 一堆书. *a ~ of sand* 一堆沙. **2 heaps** [pl] [非正式用语]大量 dàliàng;许多 xǔduō: *~s of time* 大量时间. **heap** *v* [T] 堆积〔積〕duījī;装〔裝〕载 zhuāngzài: ~ *food on one's plate* 把食品装在盘子里.

hear /hɪə(r)/ *v* [*pt*, *pp* ~**d** /hɜːd/] **1** [I, T] 听〔聽〕见 tīngjiàn. **2** [T] 注意听 zhùyì tīng;认〔認〕真听 rènzhēn tīng: *You're not to go, do you ~ me?* 你不要去,听见了吗? **3** 听说 tīngshuō: *I hear she's leaving.* 我听说她要离开. **4** [T] [法律]开〔開〕审〔審〕kāishěn. **5** [习语] **Hear! Hear!** (用于在会议上表示同意)说得对〔對〕! 说得对! Shuōdeduì! Shuōdeduì! **6** [短语动词] **hear from sb** 从〔從〕某人获〔獲〕悉 cóng mǒurén huòxī. **hear of sb / sth** 听说 tīngshuō;得知 dézhī: *I've never ~d of the place.* 我从来没有听说过这个地方. **not ˈhear of sth** 不允许 bù yǔnxǔ;不予考虑〔慮〕bùyǔ kǎolǜ: *He wouldn't ~ of my walking home alone.* 他不准我独〔獨〕自走回家. **hear sb out** 听完某人的话 tīng wán mǒurén de huà.

hearing /ˈhɪərɪŋ/ *n* **1** [U] 听〔聽〕力 tīnglì. **2** [U] 听力所及的距离〔離〕tīnglì suǒjí de jùlí: *He's out of* ~. 他在(我们互相)叫得应的距离以外. **3** [C] (尤指辩护时)被倾听(申诉)的机〔機〕会〔會〕bèi qīngtīng de jīhuì: *get a fair* ~ 获得公正地申诉的机会. **4** [C] [法律]开〔開〕庭审〔審〕理(案件) kāitíng shěnlǐ. ˈ**hearing-aid** *n* [C] 助听器 zhùtīngqì.

hearsay /ˈhɪəseɪ/ *n* [U] 谣言 yáoyán;传〔傳〕闻 chuánwén.

hearse /hɜːs/ *n* [C] 柩车 jiùchē.

heart /hɑːt/ *n* [C] **1** 心脏〔臟〕xīnzàng;心 xīn. **2** 感情 gǎnqíng;爱〔愛〕心 àixīn;内心 nèixīn;心地 xīndì. **3** 中心 zhōngxīn. **4** 心状〔狀〕物 xīnzhuàngwù. **5** (纸牌花色)桃 táo. **6** [习语] **break sb's / one's ˈheart** 使伤〔傷〕心 shǐ shāngxīn. **by ˈheart** 靠记忆〔憶〕kào jìyì: *learn / know a poem by* ~ 背诵一首诗. **from the (bottom of one's) heart** 真诚地 zhēnchéngde;从〔從〕内心 cóng nèixīn. **not have the ˈheart to do sth** 不忍心做某事 bù rěnxīn zuò mǒushì. **take ˈheart** 鼓起勇气〔氣〕gǔqǐ yǒngqì;受到鼓励〔勵〕shòudào gǔlì. **lose ˈheart** 失去勇气 shīqù yǒngqì;丧〔喪〕失信心 sàngshī xìnxīn. **take sth to ˈheart** 关〔關〕注某事 guānzhù mǒushì;把某事放在心上 bǎ mǒushì fàng zài xīn shàng. ˈ**heartache** *n* [U, C] 痛心 tòngxīn;伤心 shāngxīn. ˈ**heart attack** *n* [C] 心脏病发〔發〕作 xīnzàngbìng fāzuò. ˈ**heartbeat** *n* [C] 心跳 xīntiào;心搏 xīnbó. ˈ**heart-breaking** *adj* 伤心的 shāngxīnde;令人心碎的 lìng rén xīnsuì de. ˈ**heart-broken** *adj* 心碎的 xīnsuìde;断〔斷〕肠〔腸〕的 duànchángde. ˈ**heartburn** *n* [U] [医学]胃灼热〔熱〕wèi zhuórè. ˈ**heartfelt** *adj* 衷心的 zhōngxīnde;诚挚〔摯〕的 chéngzhìde. ˈ**heartless** *adj* 残〔殘〕忍的 cánrěnde. ˈ**heartlessly** *adv*. ˈ**heart-rending** *adj* 令人心碎的 lìng rén xīnsuì de. ˌ**heart-to-ˈheart** *n* [C] 真诚的谈心 zhēnchéng de tánxīn.

hearten /ˈhɑːtn/ *v* [T] 鼓励〔勵〕gǔlì;激励 jīlì.

hearth /hɑːθ/ *n* [C] 壁炉〔爐〕bìlú;壁炉地面 bìlú dìmiàn.

hearty /ˈhɑːtɪ/ *adj* [-ier, -iest] **1** 衷心的 zhōngxīnde;热〔熱〕忱的 rèchénde: *a ~ welcome* 衷心的欢迎. **2** 强烈的 qiángliède;尽〔盡〕情的 jìnqíngde. **3** 丰〔豐〕盛的 fēngshèngde;胃口好的 wèikǒu hǎo de. **4** 健壮〔壯〕的 jiànzhuàngde. **heartily** *adv* **1** 热忱地 rèchénde;衷心地 zhōngxīnde. **2** 非常 fēicháng: *I'm heartily sick of this wet weather.* 我非常厌恶这种潮湿天气.

heat[1] /hiːt/ *n* **1** [U] 热〔熱〕rè;热度 rèdù. **2**

炎热的天气〔氣〕 yánrède tiānqì；暑热 shǔrè. 3 [U] [喻] 愤怒 fènnù；激情 jīqíng. 4 [C] (比赛的)预赛 yùsài. 5 [习语] **be on heat**, (美语) **be in heat** (母畜)发〔發〕情 fāqíng. ˈ**heatwave** *n* [C] [气象]热浪期 rèlàngqī.

heat[2] /hiːt/ *v* [I, T] 变〔變〕热〔熱〕 biànrè；使热 shǐ rè. **heated** *adj* 愤怒的 fènnùde；热烈的 rèliède: *a ~ed argument* 热烈的争论. **heater** *n* [C] 供热装〔裝〕置 gōngrè zhuāngzhì；加热器 jiārèqì. **heating** *n* [U] 暖气〔氣〕 nuǎnqì.

heath /hiːθ/ *n* [C] 石南丛〔叢〕生的荒地 shínán cóngshēng de huāngdì.

heathen /ˈhiːðn/ *n* [C] 1 [旧]异〔異〕教徒(基督教徒、犹太教徒、伊斯兰教徒以外的人) yìjiàotú. 2 [非正式用语] 野蛮〔蠻〕人 yěmánrén.

heather /ˈheðə(r)/ *n* [U] 石南属〔屬〕植物 shínánshǔ zhíwù.

heave /hiːv/ *v* [*pt*, *pp* ~d; 第六义项 **hove** /həʊv/] 1 [I, T] 用力举〔舉〕起 yònglì jǔqǐ. 2 [T] 掷〔擲〕(重物) zhì. 3 [T] 说出 shuōchū；发〔發〕出 fāchū: ~ *a sigh of relief* 如释〔釋〕重负地舒一口气〔氣〕. 4 [I] 使起伏 shǐ qǐfú. 5 [I] 呕〔嘔〕吐 ǒutù；恶〔惡〕心 ěxīn. 6 [习语] ˌ**heave** ˈ**to** (船)顶风〔風〕停航 dǐngfēng tíngháng.

heaven /ˈhevn/ *n* 1 [sing] 天国〔國〕 tiānguó；天堂 tiāntáng. 2 **Heaven** [sing] 上帝 shàngdì. 3 [U, C] 极〔極〕乐〔樂〕之地 jílè zhī dì. 4 **the heavens** [pl] 天空 tiānkōng. 5 [习语] (**Good**) ˈ**Heavens!** (表示惊讶)天哪! tiān na! **heavenly** *adj* 1 天国的 tiānguóde；天堂的 tiāntángde. 2 [非正式用语]天堂般的 tiāntángbānde；非常可爱〔愛〕的 fēicháng kě'ài de. ˌ**heavenly** ˈ**body** *n* [C] [天文]天体〔體〕 tiāntǐ.

heavy /ˈhevɪ/ *adj* [-ier, -iest] 1 重的 zhòngde. 2 大量的 dàliàngde；猛烈的 měngliède: ~ *rain* 大雨. *a ~ smoker* 吸烟多的人. 3 繁忙的 fánmángde: *a very ~ day* 繁忙的一天. *a very ~ schedule* 活动繁多的日程. 4 (工作)繁重的 fánzhòngde；费力的 fèilìde. 5 (食物)难〔難〕消化的 nán xiāohuà de. 6 (音乐等)沉闷的 chénmènde；乏味的 fáwèide. 7 沉痛的 chéntòngde；悲伤〔傷〕的 bēishāngde: *a ~ heart* 沉痛的心情. 8 [习语] **heavy going** 困难〔難〕的 kùnnande；令人厌〔厭〕烦的 lìng rén yànfán de. **make heavy weather of sth** 把…弄得比实〔實〕际〔際〕困难 bǎ…nòngde bǐ shíjì kùnnan. **heavily** *adv*: *drink heavily* 酗酒. *sleep heavily* 酣睡. **heaviness** *n* [U]. **heavy** *n* [C] [*pl* -ies] [非正式用语]膀粗腰圆的贴身保镖 bǎng cū yāo yuán de tiēshēn bǎobiāo. ˌ**heavy-**ˈ**duty** *adj* 结实〔實〕而耐穿的 jiēshi ér nàichuān de. ˌ**heavy** ˈ**industry** *n* [C] 重工业〔業〕 zhònggōngyè. ˈ**heavyweight** *n* [C] 1 重量级拳击〔擊〕手 zhòngliàngjí quánjīshǒu. 2 大人物 dàrénwù；要人 yàorén.

heckle /ˈhekl/ *v* [I, T] 当〔當〕众〔衆〕诘问 dāngzhòng jiéwèn. **heckler** /ˈheklə(r)/ *n* [C].

hectare /ˈhekteə(r)/ *n* [C] 公顷(一万平方米) gōngqǐng.

hectic /ˈhektɪk/ *adj* 闹〔鬧〕哄哄的 nàohōnghōngde；兴〔興〕奋〔奮〕的 xīngfènde: *lead a ~ life* 生活闹哄哄的.

he'd /hiːd/ 1 he had ⇨HAVE. 2 he would. ⇨WILL[1], WOULD[1].

hedge /hedʒ/ *n* [C] 1 树〔樹〕篱〔籬〕 shùlí. 2 [喻]障碍〔礙〕 zhàng'ài；障碍物 zhàng'àiwù: *a ~ against inflation* 反通货膨胀的手段. **hedge** *v* 1 [T] 用树篱围〔圍〕住 yòng shùlí wéizhù；设障碍于 shè zhàng'ài yú. 2 躲闪 duǒshǎn；推诿 tuīwěi. 3 [习语] ˌ**hedge one's** ˈ**bets** 脚踏两只〔隻〕船 jiǎotà liǎngzhī chuán；骑墙〔牆〕 qíqiáng. ˈ**hedgerow** *n* [C] 灌木树篱 guànmù shùlí.

hedgehog /ˈhedʒhɒg; *US* -hɔːg/ *n* [C] 刺猬 cìwèi.

heed /hiːd/ *v* [T] [正式用语]注意 zhùyì；留意 liúyì. **heed** *n* [U] [正式用语]注意 zhùyì: *take ~ of her advice* 留心她的劝告. **heedless** *adj* (*of*) 不注意的 bú zhùyì de.

heel[1] /hiːl/ *n* [C] 1 (a) 脚后〔後〕跟 jiǎohòugēn；踵 zhǒng. (b) 袜〔襪〕后跟 wàhòugēn；鞋后跟 xiéhòugēn. 2 鞋后掌(指后跟高出的部分) xié hòuzhǎng. 3 [习语] **at / on sb's heels** 紧〔緊〕跟某人后面 jǐngēn mǒurén hòumiàn. **come to** ˈ**heel** (a) 服从〔從〕 fúcóng. (b) (狗)紧跟主人 jǐngēn zhǔrén. ˌ**down at** ˈ**heel** 衣衫褴〔襤〕褛〔褸〕的 yīshān lánlǚ de；邋遢的 lātade. **heel** *v* [T] 修理(鞋的)后跟 xiūlǐ hòugēn.

heel[2] /hiːl/ *v* [I] (*over*) (船)倾侧 qīngcè.

hefty /ˈheftɪ/ *adj* [-ier, -iest] [非正式用语] 大的 dàde；重的 zhòngde.

heifer /ˈhefə(r)/ *n* [C] 小母牛 xiǎomǔniú.

height /haɪt/ *n* 1 (a) [U, C] (自底至顶的)高度 gāodù. (b) [U] 高 gāo. 2 [C, U] (表示某物与地面或海平面距离的)高度 gāodù: *gain ~* 升高. *lose ~* 损失高度. 3 [C, 尤作 pl] 高地 gāodì；高处〔處〕 gāochù. 4 [sing] 最高程度 zuìgāo chéngdù；顶点〔點〕 dǐngdiǎn: *the ~ of folly* 愚蠢之至. *the ~ of summer* 盛夏.

heighten /ˈhaɪtn/ *v* [I, T] (使)提高 tígāo；(使)加强 jiāqiáng.

heir /eə(r)/ *n* [C] 继〔繼〕承人 jìchéngrén. **heiress** /ˈeərɪs, eəˈres/ *n* [C] 女继承人 nǚjìchéngrén. **heirloom** /ˈeəluːm/ *n* [C] 传〔傳〕家宝〔寶〕 chuánjiābǎo；祖传物 zǔchuánwù.

held /held/ *pt*, *pp* of HOLD[1].

helicopter /ˈhelɪkɒptə(r)/ *n* [C] 直升机

H

〔機〕zhíshēngjī. helicopter 'gunship *n* [C] 武装〔裝〕直升机 wǔzhuāng zhíshēngjī.

helium /'hiːlɪəm/ *n* [U] 氦 hài.

hell /hel/ *n* 1 [sing] 地狱 dìyù; 阴〔陰〕间 yīnjiān. 2 [U, C] 苦境 kǔjìng; 极〔極〕大的困苦 jídàde kùnkǔ. 3 [U] [俚](表示愤怒或加强语气): *Who the ~ is he?* 到底他是谁? 4 [习语] for the 'hell of it [非正式用语] 仅〔僅〕仅为了取乐〔樂〕jǐnjǐn wèile qǔlè. give sb 'hell [非正式用语] 给某人吃苦头〔頭〕gěi mǒurén chī kǔtóu. like 'hell (a) [非正式用语](用于加强语气): *drive like ~* 拼命地开(车). (b) [俚, 讽] 绝不 juébù. hellish *adj* [非正式用语] 讨厌〔厭〕的 tǎoyànde; 可憎的 kězèngde.

he'll /hiːl/ he will. ⇨ WILL[1].

hello = HALLO.

helm /helm/ *n* [C] 1 舵 duò; 舵柄 duòbǐng; 舵轮〔輪〕duòlún. 2 [习语] at the helm 掌握 zhǎngwò; 领导〔導〕lǐngdǎo.

helmet /'helmɪt/ *n* [C] 头〔頭〕盔 tóukuī; 安全帽 ānquánmào.

H

help[1] /help/ *v* 1 [I, T] 帮〔幫〕助 bāngzhù; 援助 yuánzhù; 救助 jiùzhù: *They ~ed me (to) lift the boxes.* 他们帮我抬箱子. *H~! I'm stuck!* 救命啊! 我陷进去出不来了. 2 [T] ~ oneself / sb (to) 给…夹〔夾〕菜 gěi…jiā cài; 给…斟饮料 gěi…zhēn yǐnliào. 3 [习语] can / could not help (doing) sth 忍不住 rěnbúzhù; 避免不了 bìmiǎnbùliǎo. 4 [短语动词] help (sb) 'out 帮助…摆〔擺〕脱困难〔難〕bāngzhù…bǎituō kùnnan. helper *n* [C] 帮助者 bāngzhùzhě; 帮手 bāngshǒu. helping *n* [C] (食物的)一份 yífèn; 一客 yíkè.

help[2] /help/ *n* 1 [U] 帮〔幫〕助 bāngzhù; 救助 jiùzhù. 2 [C] 帮助者 bāngzhùzhě; 帮手 bāngshǒu; 帮助的东西 bāngzhùde dōngxi: *She's a great ~ to me.* 她帮了我很大的忙. 3 [C] 佣人 yòngrén. helpful *adj* 有用的 yǒuyòngde. helpfully *adv*. helpfulness *n* [U]. helpless *adj* 无〔無〕助的 wúzhùde; 无依无靠的 wú yī wú kào de. helplessly *adv*. helplessness *n* [U].

hem /hem/ *n* [C] (衣服等)折边〔邊〕zhébiān. hem *v* [-mm-] 1 [T] 给…缝边 gěi…féng biān; 给…镶边 gěi…xiāng biān. 2 [短语动词] hem sb in 包围〔圍〕bāowéi; 禁闭 jìnbì. 'hemline *n* [C] (衣服的)下摆〔擺〕xiàbǎi.

hemisphere /'hemɪsfɪə(r)/ *n* [C] 1 半球 bànqiú. 2 (地球的)半球 bànqiú: *the Northern ~* 北半球.

hemo- = HAEMO-.

hemp /hemp/ *n* [U] 1 大麻 dàmá. 2 由大麻制〔製〕成的麻醉剂〔劑〕yóu dàmá zhìchéngde mázuìjì.

hen /hen/ *n* [C] 1 母鸡〔鷄〕mǔjī. 2 母禽 mǔqín. 'henpecked *adj* [非正式用语](男人)怕老婆的 pà lǎopo de.

hence /hens/ *adv* [正式用语] 1 从〔從〕此时〔時〕cóng cǐshí. 2 因此 yīncǐ; 由此 yóucǐ. henceforth /ˌhens'fɔːθ/ (亦作 henceforward) *adv* [正式用语] 今后〔後〕jīnhòu; 从此 cóngcǐ.

henchman /'hentʃmən/ *n* [C] [*pl* -men] 亲〔親〕信 qīnxìn; 仆〔僕〕从〔從〕púcóng.

henna /'henə/ *n* [U] [植物] 散沫花 sànmòhuā; 散沫花染剂〔劑〕sànmòhuā rǎnjì.

her /hɜː(r)/ *pron* [用作动词或介词的宾语] 她 tā: *I love ~.* 我爱她. *Give it to ~.* 把它交给她. her *adj* 她的 tāde: *That's ~ book, not yours.* 那是她的书, 不是你的. hers /hɜːz/ *pron* 她的 tāde: *Is that ~s?* 那是她的吗?

herald /'herəld/ *n* [C] 1 (从前的)传〔傳〕令官 chuánlìngguān. 2 先驱〔驅〕xiānqū; 预兆 yùzhào. herald *v* [T] 预示…的来到 yùshì…de láidào. heraldry /'herəldrɪ/ *n* [U] 纹章学〔學〕wénzhāngxué.

herb /hɜːb; *US* ɜːrb/ *n* [C] 草本植物 cǎoběn zhíwù; 药〔藥〕草 yàocǎo; 香草 xiāngcǎo. herbal *adj* 药草的 yàocǎode. herbalist *n* [C] 种〔種〕草药的人 zhòng cǎoyào de rén; 卖〔賣〕草药的人 mài cǎoyào de rén.

herbaceous /hɜː'beɪʃəs; *US* ɜːr-/ *adj* (植物)草本的 cǎoběnde. herˌbaceous 'border *n* [C] 种〔種〕植多年生花草的花坛〔壇〕zhòngzhí duōniánshēng huācǎo de huātán.

herd /hɜːd/ *n* [C] 兽〔獸〕群 shòuqún; 牲口群 shēngkouqún. herd *v* [T] 把…驱〔驅〕赶〔趕〕到一起 bǎ…qūgǎndào yìqǐ: *prisoners ~ed onto a train* 被驱赶上火车的囚犯们. herdsman /-mən/ *n* [C] [*pl* -men] 牧人 mùrén; 牧工 mùgōng.

here /hɪə(r)/ *adv* 1 这〔這〕里〔裏〕zhèlǐ; 向这里 xiàng zhèlǐ; 在这里 zài zhèlǐ; 到这里 dào zhèlǐ: *I live ~.* 我住在这里. *Come ~.* 到这里来. 2 在这点〔點〕上 zài zhèdiǎn shàng: *H~ the speaker paused.* 演讲人说到这一点时停了一下. 3 [习语] ˌhere and 'there 各处〔處〕gèchù; 到处 dàochù. here's to sb/sth (用于敬酒时)祝…健康 zhù…jiànkāng, 祝…成功 zhù…chénggōng, 为〔爲〕…干〔乾〕杯 wèi…gānbēi. neither ˌhere nor 'there 不相干的 bù xiānggān de; 与〔與〕题目不相关〔關〕yǔ tímù bù xiāngguān. ˌhere a'bouts *adv* 在这附近 zài zhè fùjìn. ˌhere'in *adv* [正式用语] 在这里 zài zhèlǐ; 在本文件中 zài běn wénjiàn zhōng. ˌhere'with *adv* [正式用语] 与此一道 yǔ cǐ yídào.

hereafter /ˌhɪər'ɑːftə(r); *US* -'æf-/ *adv* [正式用语] 此后〔後〕cǐhòu; 今后 jīnhòu. the hereafter *n* [sing] 死后(灵魂)的生活 sǐhòu de shēnghuó.

hereditary /hɪˈredɪtrɪ; *US* -terɪ/ *adj* 世袭〔襲〕的 shìxíde;遗传〔傳〕的 yíchuánde.

heredity /hɪˈredətɪ/ *n* [U] 遗传〔傳〕yíchuán.

heresy /ˈherəsɪ/ *n* [C,U] [*pl* -ies] 异〔異〕端 yìduān;异教 yìjiào. **heretic** /ˈherətɪk/ *n* [C] 持异端论〔論〕者 chí yìduānlùn zhě;异教徒 yìjiàotú. **heretical** /hɪˈretɪkl/ *adj*.

heritage /ˈherɪtɪdʒ/ *n* [C,常作 sing] 传〔傳〕统 chuántǒng;遗产〔產〕yíchǎn.

hermit /ˈhɜːmɪt/ *n* [C] 隐〔隱〕士 yǐnshì;独〔獨〕居修道士 dújū xiūdàoshì.

hernia /ˈhɜːnɪə/ *n* [U] [医学]疝 shàn.

hero /ˈhɪərəʊ/ *n* [C] [*pl* ~es] **1** 英雄 yīngxióng;勇士 yǒngshì. **2** (小说、戏剧等中的)男主人公 nánzhǔréngōng. **heroic** /hɪˈrəʊɪk/ *adj* 英雄的 yīngxióngde;英勇的 yīngyǒngde. **heroically** /-klɪ/ *adv*. **heroics** *n* [pl] (常指哗众取宠的)英雄辞〔辭〕令 yīngxióng cílìng;(炫耀性的)豪壮〔壯〕行为〔爲〕háozhuàng xíngwéi. **heroine** /ˈherəʊɪn/ *n* [C] 女英雄 nǚ yīngxióng;(小说、戏剧等的)女主人公 nǚ zhǔréngōng. **heroism** /ˈherəʊɪzəm/ *n* [U] 英雄行为 yīngxióng xíngwéi;英勇 yīngyǒng.

heroin /ˈherəʊɪn/ *n* [U] (药)海洛因 hǎiluòyīn.

herpes /ˈhɜːpiːz/ *n* [U] [医]疱疹 pàozhěn.

herring /ˈherɪŋ/ *n* [C] 鲱鱼 fēiyú. ˈ**herringbone** *n* [U] 人字形图〔圖〕案 rénzìxíng tú'àn.

hers ⇨HER.

herself /həˈself/ *pron* **1** [反身]她自己 tā zìjǐ: *She ˈhurt* ~. 她伤了自己. *She ˌbought* ~ *a new ˈdress*. 她给自己买了一件新衣服. **2** (用于加强语气)她亲〔親〕自 tā qīnzì;她本人 tā běnrén: *She told me the news* ~. 她亲自告诉我这个消息. **3** [习语] (**all**) **by herˈself** (a) 她单〔單〕独〔獨〕地 tā dāndúde. (b) 她独力地 tā dúlìde.

he's /hiːz/ **1** he is. ⇨BE. **2** he has. ⇨HAVE.

hesitant /ˈhezɪtənt/ *adj* 犹〔猶〕豫的 yóuyùde;踌〔躊〕躇的 chóuchúde. **hesitancy** *n* [U].

hesitate /ˈhezɪteɪt/ *v* [I] 犹〔猶〕豫 yóuyù;踌〔躊〕躇 chóuchú. **hesitation** /ˌhezɪˈteɪʃn/ *n* [U,C].

heterosexual /ˌhetərəˈsekʃʊəl/ *adj* 异〔異〕性爱〔愛〕的 yìxìngài de.

het up /ˌhetˈʌp/ *adj* [非正式用语]心急火燎的 xīn jí huǒ liǎo de.

hexagon /ˈheksəgən; *US* -gɒn/ *n* [C] 六边〔邊〕形 liùbiānxíng.

heyday /ˈheɪdeɪ/ *n* [sing] 全盛时〔時〕期 quánshèng shíqī.

hiatus /haɪˈeɪtəs/ *n* [常作 sing] 脱漏 tuōlòu;间断〔斷〕jiànduàn.

hibernate /ˈhaɪbəneɪt/ *v* [I] (动物)冬眠 dōngmián. **hibernation** /ˌhaɪbəˈneɪʃn/ *n* [U].

hiccup (亦作 **hiccough**) /ˈhɪkʌp/ *n* [C] **1** 打呃 dǎ'è. **2** [非正式用语]小问题 xiǎo wèntí. **hiccup** *v* [I] 打呃 dǎ'è.

hide[1] /haɪd/ *v* [*pt* **hid** /hɪd/, *pp* **hidden** /ˈhɪdn/] **1** [T] 隐〔隱〕藏 yǐncáng;遮掩 zhēyǎn. **2** 躲藏 duǒcáng. ˈ**hide-out** (美语亦作 ˈ**hideaway**) *n* [C] 躲藏处〔處〕duǒcángchù;隐藏处 yǐncángchù: *a terrorist* ~*-out* 恐怖分子的黑窝. ˈ**hiding** *n* [U] [习语] ˌ**go into ˈhiding** 躲藏起来 duǒcáng qǐlái. ˌ**come out of ˈhiding** 从躲藏处出来 cóng duǒcángchù chūlái. **in ˈhiding** 躲藏着 duǒcángzhe. ˈ**hiding-place** *n* [C] 隐藏处 yǐncángchù.

hide[2] /haɪd/ *n* [C] 兽〔獸〕皮 shòupí.

hideous /ˈhɪdɪəs/ *adj* 丑〔醜〕陋的 chǒulòude;可怕的 kěpàde. **hideously** *adv*.

hiding[1] ⇨HIDE[1].

hiding[2] /ˈhaɪdɪŋ/ *n* [C] 痛打 tòngdǎ;鞭打 biāndǎ.

hierarchy /ˈhaɪərɑːkɪ/ *n* [C] [*pl* -ies] 等级森严〔嚴〕的组织〔織〕děngjí sēnyánde zǔzhi.

hi-fi /ˈhaɪfaɪ/ *n* [C], *adj* [非正式用语] (HIGH FIDELITY (HIGH[1]) 的缩略)高保真音响〔響〕(的) gāobǎozhēn yīnxiǎng.

high[1] /haɪ/ *adj* **1** (a) 高的 gāode: *a* ~ *fence* 高围墙. (b) 有某一高度的 yǒu mǒu yī gāodù de: *The wall is six feet* ~. 这墙六英尺高. **2** 在正常之上的 zài zhèngcháng zhī shàng de: *a* ~ *price* 高物价. **3** 巨大的 jùdàde;强烈的 qiángliède: *a* ~ *degree of accuracy* 高度准确. **4** 高尚的 gāoshàngde;崇高的 chónggāode: *have* ~ *ideals* 有崇高的理想. **5** 有利的 yǒulìde: *have a* ~ *opinion of her* 对她有好评. **6** 重要的 zhòngyàode: *a* ~ *official* 高级官员. **7** 尖声〔聲〕的 jiānshēngde. **8** 全盛的 quánshèngde: ~ *summer* 盛夏. **9** (食物)开〔開〕始变〔變〕质〔質〕的 kāishǐ biànzhì de. **10** (*on*) [非正式用语]被毒品麻醉了的 bèi dúpǐn mázuì le de. **11** (汽车等变速器的挡)高速的 gāosùde;高的 gāode. **12** [习语] **be / get on one's ˌhigh ˈhorse** [非正式用语]摆〔擺〕架子 bǎi jiàzi;神气〔氣〕活现 shénqì huóxiàn. ˌ**high and ˈdry** 孤立无〔無〕援 gūlì wúyuán;处〔處〕于困境 chǔyú kùnjìng. ˈ**high time** 应〔應〕该马上做某事的时〔時〕候 yīnggāi mǎshàng zuò mǒushì de shíhòu: *It's* ~ *time you cleaned the car*. 你该擦洗车了. ˈ**highbrow** *adj*, *n* [C] [有时贬]文化修养〔養〕很高的(人) wénhuà xiūyǎng hěngāo de. ˌ**high-ˈclass** *adj* 高级的 gāojíde. ˌ**High Comˈmissioner** *n* [C] 高级专〔專〕员(英联邦国家间互相派驻的外交代表) gāojí zhuānyuán. ˌ**High ˈCourt** *n* [C] (审理民

H

事案件的)最高法院 zuìgāo fǎyuàn. ˌ**higher edu'cation** *n* [U] 高等教育 gāoděng jiàoyù. ˌ**high fi'delity** *adj*, *n* [C] 高保真音响〔響〕(的) gāo bǎozhēn yīnxiǎng. ˌ**high-'flier** *n* [C] 有抱负的人 yǒu bàofù de rén. ˌ**high-'grade** *adj* 高级的 gāojíde; 优〔優〕质的 yōuzhìde. ˌ**high-'handed** *adj* 专横的 zhuānhèngde. **the 'high jump** *n* [sing] [运动]跳高 tiàogāo. **'highlands** /-ləndz/ *n* [pl] 山岳地带〔帶〕shānyuè dìdài; 高原地区〔區〕gāoyuán dìqū. ˌ**high-'level** *adj* (会议等)由高阶〔階〕层〔層〕人士进〔進〕行的 yóu gāo jiēcéng rénshì jìnxíng de. **the 'high life** *n* [sing] 上层社会〔會〕的豪华〔華〕生活 shàngcéng shèhuì de háohuá shēnghuó. ˌ**high-'minded** *adj* 思想高超的 sīxiǎng gāochāo de. ˌ**high-'powered** *adj* 精力充沛的 jīnglì chōngpèi de; 能力很强的 nénglì hěnqiáng de. ˌ**high 'profile** ⇨ PROFILE. **'high-rise** *adj* (建筑物)高层的 gāocéngde. **'high school** *n* [C](尤指美国的)中学(学生年龄约为 15—18 岁) zhōngxué. **the ˌhigh 'seas** *n* [pl] 公海 gōnghǎi. ˌ**high 'season** *n* [U] (旅游等的)旺季 wàngjì. ˌ**high-'spirited** *adj* 活泼〔潑〕的 huópo de; 兴〔興〕高采烈的 xìng gāo cǎi liè de. **'high spot** *n* [C] (事物的)最突出或最精彩部分 zuì tūchū huò zuì jīngcǎi bùfen. **'high street** *n* [C] (市镇的)主要街道 zhǔyào jiēdào. ˌ**high 'tea** *n* [U] [英国英语] 傍晚茶(傍晚吃的茶点) bàngwǎnchá. ˌ**high tech'nology** *n* [U] 高技术〔術〕gāo jìshù. ˌ**high-'tech** *adj* [非正式用语] 高技术的 gāo jìshù de. **'highway** *n* [C] 公路 gōnglù. **'highwayman** *n* [C] [*pl* -men] (旧时的)拦〔攔〕路抢〔搶〕劫的强盗 lánlù qiǎngjié de qiángdào.

high² /haɪ/ *n* [C] **1** 高水平 gāo shuǐpíng; 最高水平 zuìgāo shuǐpíng: *profits reached a new* ~ 利润达到新的最高水平. **2** [非正式用语]强烈的快感 qiángliède kuàigǎn: *on a* ~ 享受快感.

high³ /haɪ/ *adv* 高高地 gāogāode; 向高处〔處〕xiàng gāochù; 高度地 gāodùde.

highlight /ˈhaɪlaɪt/ *n* [C] **1** (事物的)最有趣部分 zuì yǒuqù bùfen. **2** [常作 pl] (a) (画等)最亮部 zuì liàng bù. (b) (头发上)发〔發〕亮的浅〔淺〕色部分 fāliàng de qiǎnsè bùfen. **highlight** *v* [T] 使注意力集中于 shǐ zhùyìlì jízhōng yú.

highly /ˈhaɪlɪ/ *adv* **1** 高度地 gāodùde; 非常 fēicháng: *a* ~ *amusing film* 非常有趣的影片. **2** 非常赞〔讚〕许的 fēicháng zànxǔ de: *think* ~ *of sb* 赞赏某人. ˌ**highly-'strung** *adj* 易激动〔動〕的 yì jīdòng de; 神经〔經〕紧〔緊〕张的 shénjīng jǐnzhāng de.

Highness /ˈhaɪnɪs/ *n* [C] 王室成员的尊称〔稱〕wángshì chéngyuán de zūnchēng: *His / Her (Royal)* ~ 殿下.

hijack /ˈhaɪdʒæk/ *v* [T] 劫持 jiéchí; 劫机〔機〕jiéjī. **hijacker** *n* [C].

hike /haɪk/ *n* [C], *v* [I] 远〔遠〕足 yuǎnzú; 长〔長〕途徒步旅行 chángtú túbù lǚxíng. **hiker** *n* [C].

hilarious /hɪˈleərɪəs/ *adj* 狂欢〔歡〕的 kuánghuānde; 热〔熱〕闹的 rènàode. **hilariously** *adv*. **hilarity** /hɪˈlærətɪ/ *n* [U] 欢闹 huānnào; 热闹 rènào.

hill /hɪl/ *n* [C] **1** 小山 xiǎoshān; 丘陵 qiūlíng; 山坡 shānpō. **2** 坡 pō. **'hillside** *n* [C] (小山的)山腰 shānyāo; 山坡 shānpō. **'hilltop** *n* [C] 小山山顶 xiǎoshān shāndǐng. **hilly** *adj* 丘陵的 qiūlíngde; 多坡的 duōpōde.

hilt /hɪlt/ *n* [C] **1** 剑〔劍〕柄 jiànbǐng. **2** [习语] (**up**) **to the 'hilt** 彻〔徹〕底地 chèdǐde; 完全地 wánquánde: *We support you to the* ~. 我们完全支持你.

him /hɪm/ *pron* [he 的宾格] 他 tā: *I love* ~. 我爱他. *Give it to* ~. 把它给他.

himself /hɪmˈself/ *pron* **1** 他自己 tā zìjǐ: *He 'cut* ~. 他割伤了自己. **2** (用于加强语气)他亲〔親〕自 tā qīnzì; 他本人 tā běnrén: *He told me the news* ~. 他亲自告诉我这个消息. **3** [习语] (**all**) **by him'self** (a) 单〔單〕独〔獨〕地 dāndúde. (b) 独立地 dúlìde.

hind¹ /haɪnd/ *adj* 后〔後〕面的 hòumiànde; 后部的 hòubùde: *the* ~ *legs of a horse* 马的两条后腿. ˌ**hind'quarters** *n* [pl] (牲畜的)半边〔邊〕胴体〔體〕的后半部 bànbiān tóngtǐde hòu bànbù.

hind² /haɪnd/ *n* [C] 雌马鹿 cí mǎlù.

hinder /ˈhɪndə(r)/ *v* [T] 阻碍〔礙〕zǔ'ài; 阻止 zǔzhǐ: ~ *sb from working* 阻止某人工作. **hindrance** /ˈhɪndrəns/ *n* [C] 起妨碍作用的人或事物 qǐ fáng'ài zuòyòng de rén huò shìwù; 障碍物 zhàng'àiwù; 障碍 zhàng'ài.

hindsight /ˈhaɪndsaɪt/ *n* [U] 事后〔後〕的聪〔聰〕明 shìhòu de cōngmíng.

Hindu /ˌhɪnˈduː; *US* ˈhɪnduː/ *n* [C] 印度教教徒 yìndùjiào jiàotú. **Hindu** *adj* 印度教的 yìndùjiàode. **Hinduism** /ˈhɪnduːɪzəm/ *n* [U] 印度教 yìndùjiào.

hinge /hɪndʒ/ *n* [C] 铰链 jiǎoliàn; 合页 héyè. **hinge** *v* **1** [T] 给…安铰链 gěi…ān jiǎoliàn. **2** [短语动词] **hinge on sth** 取决于 qǔjué yú: *Everything* ~*s on the result of these talks*. 一切取决于谈判的结果.

hint /hɪnt/ *n* [C] **1** 暗示 ànshì; 示意 shìyì. **2** 线〔綫〕索 xiànsuǒ; 细微的迹象 xìwēide jìxiàng: *a* ~ *of sadness in his voice* 他声音中些许的哀伤. **3** 建议〔議〕jiànyì: *helpful* ~*s* 有益的建议. **hint** *v* [I, T] *at* 暗示 ànshì.

hip /hɪp/ *n* [C] 臀部 túnbù. **'hip-flask** *n* [C] (可放在裤子后袋的)小酒瓶 xiǎo jiǔpíng.

hippie (亦作 hippy) /ˈhɪpɪ/ *n* [C] [*pl* -ies] 嬉皮士(反对正常的社会价值观者) xīpíshì.

hippo /ˈhɪpəʊ/ *n* [C] [*pl* ~s] [非正式用语] 河马 (HIPPOPOTAMUS 的缩略) hémǎ.

hippopotamus /ˌhɪpəˈpɒtəməs/ *n* [C] [*pl* -muses 或 -mi /-maɪ/] 河马 hémǎ.

hire /ˈhaɪə(r)/ *v* [T] 1 租用 zūyòng: ~ *a car for a week* 租一星期汽车. 2 雇用(某人) gùyòng. 3 [短语动词] **hire sth out** 租出 zūchū. **hire** *n* [U] 出租 chūzū: *bicycles for* ~ 供出租的自行车. ˌ**hire-ˈpurchase** *n* [U] [英国英语]分期付款购〔購〕买〔買〕(法) fēnqī fùkuǎn gòumǎi.

his /hɪz/ *adj* 他的 tāde: *That's ~ book, not yours.* 那是他的书,不是你的. **his** *pron* 他的 tāde: *Is that ~?* 那是他的吗?

hiss /hɪs/ *v* [I, T] 发〔發〕嘶嘶声〔聲〕 fā sīsīshēng;发嘘声反对〔對〕 fā xūshēng fǎnduì. **hiss** *n* [C] 嘘声 xūshēng;嘶嘶声 sīsīshēng.

historian /hɪˈstɔːrɪən/ *n* [C] 历〔歷〕史学〔學〕家 lìshǐxuéjiā.

historic /hɪˈstɒrɪk; US -ˈstɔːr-/ *adj* 有历〔歷〕史意义〔義〕的 yǒu lìshǐ yìyì de: *a(n) ~ event* 有历史意义的事件.

historical /hɪˈstɒrɪkl; US -ˈstɔːr-/ *adj* 历〔歷〕史的 lìshǐde: ~ *novels* 历史小说. ~ *research* 历史研究. **historically** /-klɪ/ *adv*.

history /ˈhɪstrɪ/ *n* [*pl* -ies] 1 [U] 历〔歷〕史学〔學〕 lìshǐxué;历史 lìshǐ. 2 [C] 过〔過〕去事件的记载 guòqù shìjiàn de jìzǎi;沿革 yángé. 3 [C] 某人或某物的事件记载 mǒurén huò mǒuwù de shìjiàn jìzǎi: *his medical ~* 他的病历. 4 [习语] **make ˈhistory** 开〔開〕创〔創〕历史的新篇章 kāichuàng lìshǐde xīn piānzhāng. **go down in ˈhistory** 载入史册 zǎirù shǐcè.

hit[1] /hɪt/ *v* [-tt-; *pt, pp* hit] [T] 1 (a) (用某物)打 dǎ;打击〔擊〕 dǎjī: *He ~ me with a stick.* 他用棍子打我. (b) (使)碰撞 pèngzhuàng: *The car ~ a tree.* 汽车撞到了树上. 2 对〔對〕…有不良影响〔響〕 duì…yǒu bùliáng yǐngxiǎng: *The new law will ~ the poor.* 新的法律对穷人不利. 3 到达〔達〕 dàodá;找到 zhǎodào: ~ *the right road* 找到正确的路. 4 [习语] **hit it ˈoff** [非正式用语] 相处〔處〕很好 xiāngchǔ hěnhǎo. **hit one's head against a brick wall** ⇨ HEAD[1]. **hit the nail on the ˈhead** 说中 shuō zhòng;打中要害 dǎ zhòng yàohài. **hit the ˈroof** [非正式用语] 发〔發〕脾气〔氣〕 fā píqi;暴跳如雷 bào tiào rú léi. **hit the ˈsack** [非正式用语] 上床睡觉〔覺〕 shàng chuáng shuìjiào. 5 [短语动词] **hit back (at sb)** 回击 huíjī. **hit on / upon sth** 偶然想起 ǒurán xiǎngqǐ. **hit out (at sb)** 挥拳猛击 huīquán měngjī;猛烈抨击 měngliè pēngjī. ˌ**hit-and-ˈrun** *adj* (车祸)肇事人逃逸的 zhàoshìrén táoyì de.

hit[2] /hɪt/ *n* [C] 1 打 dǎ;打击〔擊〕 dǎjī. 2 轰〔轟〕动〔動〕一时〔時〕的人或事物 hōngdòng yìshí de rén huò shìwù;成功 chénggōng: *Her new play is a great ~.* 她的新剧本轰动一时. ˈ**hit list** *n* [C] [非正式用语] 黑名单〔單〕 hēimíngdān. ˈ**hit man** *n* [C] [非正式用语,尤用于美语]职〔職〕业〔業〕杀〔殺〕手 zhíyè shāshǒu. ˈ**hit parade** *n* [C] 畅〔暢〕销流行音乐〔樂〕唱片目录〔錄〕 chàngxiāo liúxíng yīnyuè chàngpiàn mùlù.

hitch /hɪtʃ/ *v* 1 [I, T] 免费搭乘汽车〔車〕 miǎnfèi dāchéng qìchē: ~ *round Europe* 沿途搭乘便车周游欧洲. 2 钩住 gōuzhù;拴住 shuānzhù. 3 [短语动词] **hitch sth up** 急速拉起(自己的衣服) jísù lāqǐ. **hitch** *n* [C] 1 小困难〔難〕xiǎo kùnnan. 2 急拉 jílā;急推 jítuī. 3 索结 suǒjié. ˈ**hitch-hike** *v* [I] 搭便车旅行 dā biànchē lǚxíng. ˈ**hitch-hiker** *n* [C].

hitherto /ˌhɪðəˈtuː/ *adv* [正式用语]到目前为〔為〕止 dào mùqián wéizhǐ;迄今 qìjīn.

HIV /ˌeɪtʃ aɪ ˈviː/ *abbr* human immunodeficiency virus 人体〔體〕免疫缺损病毒 réntǐ miǎnyì quēsǔn bìngdú;艾滋病病毒 àizībìng bìngdú.

hive /haɪv/ *n* [C] 1 蜂箱 fēngxiāng. 2 [喻]充满喧闹繁忙的人群的处〔處〕所 chōngmǎn xuānnào fánmáng de rénqún de chùsuǒ: *a ~ of activity* 紧张繁忙的场所. **hive** *v* [短语动词] **hive sth off** 使(下属单位等)分立出来 shǐ fēnlì chūlái.

HMS /ˌeɪtʃ em ˈes/ *abbr* (用于英国军舰名称前) Her /His Majesty's Ship (英国)皇家海军 huángjiā hǎijūn.

hoard /hɔːd/ *n* [C] 秘藏的钱〔錢〕财 mìcángde qiáncái. **hoard** *v* [T] 积〔積〕攒 jīzǎn;积聚 jījù.

hoarding /ˈhɔːdɪŋ/ *n* [C] [英国英语](张贴广告的)广〔廣〕告牌 guǎnggàopái.

hoarse /hɔːs/ *adj* [~r, ~st] (声音)嘶哑〔啞〕的 sīyǎde. **hoarsely** *adv*. **hoarseness** *n* [U].

hoax /həʊks/ *n* [C] 戏〔戲〕弄 xìnòng. **hoax** *v* [T] 欺骗 qīpiàn;戏弄 xìnòng.

hob /hɒb/ *n* [C] (火炉顶部的)搁架 gējià.

hobble /ˈhɒbl/ *v* [I] 跛行 bǒxíng;蹒跚 pánshān.

hobby /ˈhɒbɪ/ *n* [C] [*pl* -ies] 业〔業〕余〔餘〕爱〔愛〕好 yèyú àihào;癖好 pǐhào.

hobnail boot /ˈhɒbneɪl/ *n* [C] (鞋底钉有防磨损的平头钉的)粗重靴子 cūzhòng xuēzi.

hockey /ˈhɒkɪ/ *n* [U] 曲棍球 qūgùnqiú.

hod /hɒd/ *n* [C] (建筑工人使用的)砖〔磚〕斗 zhuāndǒu.

hoe /həʊ/ *n* [U] 锄头〔頭〕 chútou. **hoe** *v* [I, T] 用锄干〔幹〕活 yòng chú gànhuó;用锄(为作

H

物)松〔鬆〕土、间苗等 yòng chú sōngtǔ、jiànmiáo děng.

hog /hɒg; *US* hɔːg/ *n* [C] **1** 阉过〔過〕的公猪 yānguòde gōngzhū. **2** [非正式用语]肮〔骯〕脏〔髒〕、贪婪、贪吃的人 āngzāng、tānlán、tānchī de rén. **hog** *v* [-gg-] [T] [喻]多占〔佔〕duōzhàn.

Hogmanay /ˈhɒgməneɪ/ *n* [U] (苏格兰)除夕 chúxī;大年夜 dàniányè.

hoist /hɔɪst/ *v* [T] 升〔昇〕起 shēngqǐ;扯起 chěqǐ;绞起 jiǎoqǐ. **hoist** *n* **1** [C] 起重机〔機〕qǐzhòngjī;升降机 shēngjiàngjī. **2** [sing] 向上拉 xiàng shàng lā;向上推 xiàng shàng tuī.

hold[1] /həʊld/ *v* [*pt, pp* **held** /held/] **1** [T] 握 wò;拿 ná;抓住 zhuāzhù. **2** [T] 使保持某一姿势〔勢〕shǐ bǎochí mǒuyi zīshì: *H~ your head up!* 抬起头! **3** [T] 支持 zhīchí: *That branch won't ~ you.* 那树枝吃不消你. **4** [T] 扣留 kòuliú;拘留 jūliú: *H~ the thief until the police come.* 扣住这小偷,等警察来. **5** [I] 保持坚〔堅〕定 bǎochí jiāndìng;保持不变〔變〕bǎochí búbiàn: *How long will this fine weather ~?* 这好天气会保持多久? **6** [T] (汽车等)贴住(道路等) tiēzhù. **7** [T] 装〔裝〕得下 zhuāngdexià;容得下 róngdexià: *This barrel ~s 25 litres.* 这桶能装25升. **8** [T] 守住 shǒuzhù. **9** [T] 拥〔擁〕有 yōngyǒu;据〔據〕有 jùyǒu;持有 chíyǒu: *~ 25 shares* 拥有25股. **10** [T] 拥有(职位) yōngyǒu: *~ the post of Prime Minister* 担任首相职位. **11** [T] 吸引…的注意或兴〔興〕趣 xīyǐn…de zhùyì huò xìngqù. **12** [T] 认〔認〕为〔爲〕rènwéi. **13** [T] 召开〔開〕(会议) zhàokāi. **14** [T] 相信 xiāngxìn: *I ~ you responsible for the accident.* 我认为你应对这次事故负责. **15** [习语] **hold sb / sth at bay** ⇨ BAY[3]. **hold one's ˈbreath** (因恐惧或激动等)屏息 bǐngxī;暂时〔時〕停止呼吸 zànshí tíngzhǐ hūxī. **hold the ˈfort** 暂时代理 zànshí dàilǐ. **hold ˈgood** 有效 yǒuxiào;适〔適〕用 shìyòng. **hold one's ˈground** ⇨ GROUND[1]. **ˈhold it** [非正式用语] 就这〔這〕样〔樣〕! jiù zhèyàng! 别动〔動〕! bié dòng! 等一等! děngyìděng! **hold the ˈline** 请别挂〔掛〕电〔電〕话 qǐng bié guà diànhuà. **hold one's ˈown (against sb)** 不被(某人)击〔擊〕败 bú bèi jībài. **ˌhold one's ˈtongue** 不说什〔甚〕么〔麼〕bùshuō shénme;保持沉默 bǎochí chénmò. **there's no ˈholding sb** (由于性格倔强等)简直拦〔攔〕不住某人 jiǎnzhí lánbúzhù mǒurén. **16** [短语动词] **hold sth against sb** 因…而歧视(某人) yīn…ér qíshì;因…而对〔對〕(某人)抱成见 yīn…ér duì bào chéngjiàn. **hold ˈback** 踌〔躊〕躇 chóuchú. **hold sb / sth back** (a) 控制 kòngzhì: *~ back the crowd* 控制群众. (b) 保守秘密 bǎoshǒu mìmì. **ˈhold sb down** 限制某人的自由 xiànzhì mǒurén de zìyóu. **hold sth down** (a) 压〔壓〕低 yādī: *~ down prices* 压低价格. (b) 保有(工作等) bǎoyǒu. **hold ˈforth (on sth)** 滔滔不绝地讲〔講〕tāotāo bùjué de jiǎng. **hold ˈoff** (雨等)被推迟〔遲〕bèi tuīchí. **hold sb / sth off** 抵挡〔擋〕住(进攻) dǐdǎng zhù. **hold off (doing) sth** 推迟 tuīchí. **hold ˈon** (a) 等一下 děng yíxià. (b) 坚〔堅〕持 jiānchí;忍住 rěnzhù. **hold sth on** 固定住 gùdìng zhù. **hold on to sth** 保持 bǎochí. **hold ˈout** (a) 维持 wéichí;继〔繼〕续〔續〕生存或运〔運〕行 jìxù shēngcún huò yùnxíng. (b) 抵抗 dǐkàng. **hold sth out** 提出 tíchū;提供 tígōng. **hold out for sth** 坚决要求 jiānjué yāoqiú. **hold sth over** 推迟 tuīchí. **hold sb to sth** 使遵守(诺言等) shǐ zūnshǒu. **hold sb / sth up** (a) 举〔舉〕出…为榜样〔樣〕jǔchū…wéi bǎngyàng. (b) 延迟 yánchí;停止 tíngzhǐ: *Our flight was held up by fog.* 我们的航班因雾而推迟. **hold up sth** 抢〔搶〕劫(银行等) qiǎngjié. **ˈhold-up** *n* [C] **1** 交通阻塞 jiāotōng zǔsè. **2** 抢劫 qiǎngjié.

hold[2] /həʊld/ *n* **1** [sing] 抓 zhuā;握 wò;掌握 zhǎngwò. **2** [C] (摔跤等)擒拿法 qínnáfǎ. **3** [C] 用以把握的东西 yòngyǐ bǎwò de dōngxi;支撑点〔點〕zhīchēngdiǎn. **4** [sing] 影响〔響〕yǐngxiǎng;力量 lìliàng. **5** [习语] **catch, take, etc hold of sb/ sth** 控制 kòngzhì;掌握 zhǎngwò. **get hold of sb / sth** [非正式用语] (a) 找到并使用 zhǎodào bìng shǐyòng. (b) 联〔聯〕系〔繫〕(某人) liánxì;找到(某人) zhǎodào.

hold[3] /həʊld/ *n* [C] 货舱〔艙〕huòcāng;底层〔層〕舱 dǐcéngcāng.

holdall /ˈhəʊldɔːl/ *n* [C] 手提旅行包 shǒutí lǚxíngbāo.

holder /ˈhəʊldə(r)/ *n* [C] **1** 持有者 chíyǒuzhě;占〔佔〕有者 zhànyǒuzhě: *ticket-~* 持票人. **2** 支托物 zhītuōwù;手把 shǒubà;柄 bǐng.

holding /ˈhəʊldɪŋ/ *n* [C] 拥〔擁〕有物(如土地等) yōngyǒuwù.

hole /həʊl/ *n* **1** [C] 洞 dòng;孔 kǒng: *a ~ in the road* 道路上的一个坑洼. *a ~ in the wall* 墙上的一个洞. **2** [C] (a) 兽〔獸〕穴 shòuxué. (b) [喻,非正式用语]狭〔狹〕窄、黑暗、令人厌〔厭〕恶〔惡〕的处〔處〕所 xiázhǎi、hēi'àn、lìng rén yànwù de chùsuǒ. **3** [sing] [俚]困境 kùnjìng;窘境 jiǒngjìng: *be in a ~* 处于困境. **4** [C] (高尔夫球)球穴 qiúxué. **5** [习语] **make a hole in sth** [非正式用语]大量耗费 dàliàng hàofèi. **hole** *v* (a) [T] 打洞于 dǎdòng yú;穿孔于 chuānkǒng yú. (b) [I,T] (*out*) (高尔夫球等)击〔擊〕球入洞 jīqiú rù dòng. **6** [短语动词] **hole up** [俚]躲藏 duǒcáng. **hole-in-the-ˈwall** *n* [C] 取款机〔機〕qǔkuǎnjī.

holiday /ˈhɒlədeɪ/ *n* [C] **1** 假日 jiàrì;节〔節〕日 jiérì. **2** [习语] **on ˈholiday** 度假 dùjià. **holi-**

day *v* [I] 度假 dùjià. ˈholiday-maker *n* [C] 度假的人 dùjiàde rén.

holiness /ˈhəʊlɪnɪs/ *n* [U] 1 神圣〔聖〕shénshèng. 2 His / Your Holiness 陛下(对罗马教皇的尊称) bìxià.

hollow /ˈhɒləʊ/ *adj* 1 空的 kōngde; 中空的 zhōngkōngde. 2 凹陷的 āoxiànde; 凹的 āode: ～ *cheeks* 凹陷的双颊. 3 (声音)空洞的 kōngdòngde; 沉重的 chénzhòngde. 4 [喻] 虚假的 xūjiǎde: ～ *words* 虚假的言语. ～ *pleasures* 空欢喜. hollow *n* [C] 坑 kēng; 洞 dòng. hollow *v* [T] (*out*) 挖空 wā kōng; 使成凹形 shǐ chéng āoxíng.

holly /ˈhɒlɪ/ *n* [C,U] (植物)冬青 dōngqīng; 冬青树〔樹〕枝 dōngqīng shùzhī.

holocaust /ˈhɒləkɔːst/ *n* [C] 大破坏〔壞〕dà pòhuài; 大屠杀〔殺〕dà túshā.

holster /ˈhəʊlstə(r)/ *n* [C] 手枪〔槍〕皮套 shǒuqiāng pítào.

holy /ˈhəʊlɪ/ *adj* [-ier,-iest] 1 上帝的 shàngdìde; 与〔與〕宗教有关〔關〕的 yǔ zōngjiào yǒuguān de. 2 圣〔聖〕洁〔潔〕的 shèngjiéde: *live a* ～ *life* 过圣洁的生活. the Holy ˈSpirit (亦作 the Holy ˈGhost) *n* [sing] (基督教)圣灵〔靈〕shènglíng.

homage /ˈhɒmɪdʒ/ *n* [U] [正式用语] 尊敬 zūnjìng; 敬重 jìngzhòng.

home[1] /həʊm/ *n* 1 [C,U] 家 jiā. 2 [C] 老人院 lǎorényuàn; 儿〔兒〕童养〔養〕育院 értóng yǎngyùyuàn. 3 (动植物的)生息地 shēngxīdì. 4 [sing] 发〔發〕祥地 fāxiángdì: *Greece is the* ～ *of democracy*. 希腊是民主的发祥地. 5 [U] (赛跑等的)终点〔點〕zhōngdiǎn. 6 [习语] at home (a) 在家 zài jiā. (b) 舒适〔適〕shūshì; 无〔無〕拘束 wú jūshù: *Make yourself at* ～! 请别拘束! a ˌhome ˈtruth 令人不愉快的事实〔實〕lìng rén bù yúkuài de shìshí. ˌHome ˈCounties *n* [pl] 英国〔國〕伦〔倫〕敦周围〔圍〕各郡 Yīngguó Lúndūn zhōuwéi gèjùn. ˌhome ecoˈnomics *n* [用 sing v] 家政学〔學〕jiāzhèngxué. ˌhome-ˈgrown *adj* (食品等)本国产〔產〕的 běnguó chǎn de; 自家园〔園〕子产的 zìjiā yuánzi chǎn de. ˌhome ˈhelp *n* [C] 家庭用人 jiātíng yòngren. ˈhomeland *n* [C] 1 祖国 zǔguó. 2 [常作 pl] (南非的)"黑人家园" hēirén jiāyuán. ˌhomeland seˈcurity *n* [U] [美语] 国〔國〕土安全 guótǔ ānquán. homeless *adj* 无家的 wújiāde. ˌhome-ˈmade *adj* 家里〔裏〕做的 jiālǐ zuò de. the ˈHome Office *n* [sing] (英国)内政部 Nèizhèngbù. ˈhome page *n* [C] 主页〔頁〕zhǔyè. home ˈshopping *n* [U] 家居购〔購〕物 jiājū gòuwù. ˈhomesick *adj* 想家的 xiǎngjiāde. ˈhomesickness *n* [U]. homeward *adj* 归〔歸〕家的 guījiāde. homewards *adv* 向家 xiàngjiā. ˈhomework *n* [U] 1 (学生的)家庭作业〔業〕jiātíng zuòyè. 2 [喻] (会议、讨论等之前的)准〔準〕备〔備〕工作(如看资料等) zhǔnbèi gōngzuò.

home[2] /həʊm/ *adj* 1 家庭的 jiātíngde; 家用的 jiāyòngde; 在家里〔裏〕进〔進〕行的 zài jiālǐ jìnxíng de. 2 国〔國〕内的 guónèide: ～ *news* 国内新闻. 3 [体育] 主场〔場〕的 zhǔchǎngde: *a* ～ *match* 主场比赛.

home[3] /həʊm/ *adv* 1 在家 zài jiā; 回家 huí jiā: *on her way* ～ 在她回家的路上. 2 中目标〔標〕zhòng mùbiāo; 彻〔徹〕底 chèdǐ; 深深地 shēnshēnde: *drive a nail* ～ 把钉子钉到头儿. 3 [习语] bring sth ˈhome to sb 使某人充分了〔瞭〕解某事 shǐ mǒurén chōngfèn liǎojiě mǒushì. come ˈhome to sb 使某人完全理解 shǐ mǒurén wánquán lǐjiě. home and ˈdry 安全地大功告成 ānquánde dà gōng gào chéng. ˈhome-coming *n* [C,U] (长期外出后的)回(到)家 huí jiā.

home[4] /həʊm/ *v* [短语动词] home in (on sth) 准〔準〕确〔確〕地朝向、移向(某物) zhǔnquède cháoxiàng、yíxiàng.

homely /ˈhəʊmlɪ/ *adj* [-ier,-iest] 1 [褒,尤用于英国英语] 简朴〔樸〕的 jiǎnpǔde; 家常的 jiāchángde. 2 [美语,贬] (人)不好看的 bù hǎokàn de; 相貌平平的 xiàngmào píngpíng de. homeliness *n* [U].

homeopathy /həʊmɪˈɒpəθɪ/ *n* [U] [医] 顺势〔勢〕疗〔療〕法 shùnshì liáofǎ. homeopathic /ˌhəʊmɪəˈpæθɪk/ *adj*.

homicide /ˈhɒmɪsaɪd/ *n* [U] 杀〔殺〕人 shārén. homicidal /ˌhɒmɪˈsaɪdl/ *adj*.

homing /ˈhəʊmɪŋ/ *adj* 1 (鸽)有归〔歸〕家性的 yǒu guījiāxìng de. 2 (武器)自导〔導〕引的 zìdǎoyǐnde; 导航的 dǎohángde.

homogeneous /ˌhəʊməˈdʒiːnɪəs/ *adj* 由同类〔類〕部分组成的 yóu tónglèi bùfen zǔchéng de.

homogenized /həˈmɒdʒənaɪzd/ *adj* (牛奶)均质〔質〕的 jūnzhìde.

homonym /ˈhɒmənɪm/ *n* [C] 同形异〔異〕义〔義〕词 tóngxíng yìyì cí; 同音异义词 tóngyīn yìyì cí.

homosexual /ˌhɒməˈsekʃʊəl/ *adj*, *n* [C] 同性恋〔戀〕的 tóngxìngliànde; 同性恋者 tóngxìngliànzhě. homosexuality /ˌhɒməsekʃʊˈælətɪ/ *n* [U].

honest /ˈɒnɪst/ *adj* 1 (人)诚实〔實〕的 chéngshíde; 正直的 zhèngzhíde. 2 显〔顯〕出诚意的 xiǎnchū chéngyì de; 由诚意产〔產〕生的 yóu chéngyì chǎnshēng de: *give an* ～ *opinion* 提出诚实的意见. honestly *adv* 1 诚实地 chéngshíde. 2 (用以加强语气)实在 shízài; 的确〔確〕díquè; 真个〔個〕zhēngè. honesty *n* [U].

honey /ˈhʌnɪ/ *n* 1 [U] 蜂蜜 fēngmì; 蜜 mì. 2

H

[C] [非正式用语,尤用于美语]亲〔親〕爱〔愛〕的人 qīn'àide rén; 宝〔寶〕贝儿〔兒〕 bǎobèir. 'honeycomb /-kəʊm/ *n* [C, U] 巢脾 cháopǐ; 蜂房 fēngfáng. 'honeysuckle /-sʌkl/ *n* [U] [植物]忍冬属〔屬〕 rěndōngshǔ.

honeymoon /ˈhʌnɪmuːn/ *n* [C] 1 蜜月 mìyuè. 2[喻] 共同事业〔業〕中关〔關〕系〔係〕和谐的阶〔階〕段 gòngtóng shìyè zhōng guānxì héxié de jiēduàn. **honeymoon** *v* [I] 度蜜月 dù mìyuè.

honk /hɒŋk/ *n* [C] *v* [I] 汽车喇叭声〔聲〕 qìchē lǎbashēng; 汽车喇叭响〔響〕 qìchē lǎba xiǎng.

honorary /ˈɒnərərɪ; *US* -rerɪ/ *adj* 1 (学位、等级等)作为〔爲〕荣〔榮〕誉〔譽〕而授予的 zuòwéi róngyù ér shòuyǔ de; 名誉的 míngyùde. 2 (工作职位)无〔無〕报〔報〕酬的 wú bàochóu de; 义〔義〕务〔務〕的 yìwùde: ~ *president* 义务会长.

honour (美语 -or) /ˈɒnə(r)/ *n* 1 [U, sing] 荣〔榮〕誉〔譽〕 róngyù; 光荣 guāngróng: *a great ~ to be invited* 承蒙邀请备感荣幸. 2 [U] 正义〔義〕感 zhèngyìgǎn; 道义 dàoyì; 廉耻 liánchǐ: *a man of ~* 有节操的人. 3 [U] 崇敬 chóngjìng; 尊敬 zūnjìng. 4 [sing] 带来光荣的人或事物 dàilái guāngróngde rén huò shìwù: *You are an ~ to your school.* 你是你的学校的光荣. 5 **honours** [pl] 大学〔學〕荣誉学位课程(的优等成绩) dàxué róngyù xuéwèi kèchéng. 6 **your / his / her Honour** [sing] (对法官的尊称)法官大人 fǎguān dàrén. **honour** *v* [T] 1 尊敬 zūnjìng; 尊重 zūnzhòng. 2 实〔實〕践〔踐〕(协议等) shíjiàn.

honourable (美语 -nor-) /ˈɒnərəbl/ *adj* 1 光荣〔榮〕的 guāngróngde; 荣誉〔譽〕的 róngyùde. 2 **the honourable** (对某些高级官员的尊称) 阁下 géxià. **honourably** *adv*.

hood /hʊd/ *n* [C] 1 (连在外衣等上的)风〔風〕帽 fēngmào; 兜帽 dōumào. 2 (汽车、婴儿车等上的)折合式车篷 zhéhéshì chēpéng. 3 [美语]汽车发〔發〕动〔動〕机〔機〕罩盖〔蓋〕 qìchē fādòngjī zhàogài. **hooded** *adj* 带风帽的 dài fēngmào de.

hoodwink /ˈhʊdwɪŋk/ *v* [T] 欺诈(某人) qīzhà; 哄骗(某人) hǒngpiàn.

hoof /huːf/ *n* [C] [*pl* ~s 或 **hooves** /huːvz/] 蹄 tí.

hook /hʊk/ *n* [C] 1 钩 gōu; 挂〔掛〕钩 guàgōu. 2 (拳击)肘弯〔彎〕击〔擊〕 zhǒuwānjī. 3 [习语] **off the 'hook** (a) (电话听筒)未挂上 wèi guàshàng. (b) [非正式用语]脱离〔離〕困境 tuōlí kùnjìng: *let / get sb off the ~* 使某人脱离困境. **hook** *v* [T] 1 钩住 gōuzhù; 用钩连结 yòng gōu liánjié. 2 把…弯成钩状〔狀〕 bǎ…wānchéng gōuzhuàng. **hooked** *adj* 1 钩状的 gōuzhuàngde. 2 [习语] **be hooked on sth** (吸毒)成瘾〔癮〕 chéngyǐn.

hooligan /ˈhuːlɪgən/ *n* [C] 流氓 liúmáng; 恶〔惡〕少 èshào. **hooliganism** *n* [U].

hoop /huːp/ *n* [C] 箍 gū.

hooray = HURRAH.

hoot /huːt/ *n* [C] 1 猫头〔頭〕鹰叫声〔聲〕 māotóuyīng jiàoshēng. 2 汽车〔車〕喇叭声 qìchē lǎbashēng. 3 表示不同意的叫声 biǎoshì bù tóngyì de jiàoshēng. 4 [习语] **not care/give a hoot/two hoots** [非正式用语]毫不在乎 háo bù zàihu. **hoot** *v* 1 [I] (猫头鹰)叫 jiào; (汽车喇叭)鸣响〔響〕 míngxiǎng. 2 [T] 使(喇叭)鸣响 shǐ míngxiǎng. **hooter** *n* [C] [尤用于英国英语]警笛 jǐngdí; 汽笛 qìdí.

Hoover /ˈhuːvə(r)/ *n* [C] [*P*] 胡佛牌真空吸尘〔塵〕器 Húfúpái zhēnkōng xīchénqì; 真空吸尘器 zhēnkōng xīchénqì. **hoover** *v* [I, T] 用真空吸尘器吸(…的)尘 yòng zhēnkōng xīchénqì xī chén.

hooves /huːvz/ *pl* of HOOF.

hop[1] /hɒp/ *v* [-pp-] [I] 1 (a) (人)单〔單〕脚跳 dānjiǎotiào. (b) (鸟、兽)齐〔齊〕足跳 qízútiào. 2[非正式用语]快速行走 kuàisù xíngzǒu; 跳 tiào: ~ *on a bus* 跳上一辆公共汽车. 3 [习语] **hop it** [俚]走开〔開〕 zǒukāi; 离〔離〕开 líkāi. **hop** *n* [C] 1 跳跃 tiàoyuè; 短距离跳 duǎn jùlí tiào; 单脚跳 dānjiǎotiào. 2 [非正式用语] (长距离飞行中的)一段旅程 yīduàn lǚchéng.

hop[2] /hɒp/ *n* [C] 蛇麻草 shémácǎo.

hope /həʊp/ *n* 1 [C, U] 希望 xīwàng. 2 [C] 寄予希望的人或物 jìyǔ xīwàng de rén huò wù. 3 [习语] **be beyond hope** (成功、痊愈等)毫无〔無〕希望 háo wú xīwàng. **hope** *v* [I, T] 希望 xīwàng: *I ~ (that) you win.* 我希望你赢. **hopeful** *adj* 有希望的 yǒu xīwàng de. **hopefully** *adv* 1 抱有希望地 bàoyǒu xīwàng de. 2 但愿〔願〕 dànyuàn; 作为〔爲〕希望 zuòwéi xīwàng: *H~fully she'll be here soon.* 但愿她马上就来到这里. **hopeless** *adj* 1 不给人希望的 bù gěi rén xīwàng de. 2 (*at*) [非正式用语]不行的 bùxíngde; 无〔無〕能的 wúnéngde: *~less at maths* 在数学上无能. **hopelessly** *adv*. **hopelessness** *n* [U].

horde /hɔːd/ *n* [C] 群 qún: *~s of football fans* 一帮足球迷.

horizon /həˈraɪzn/ *n* 1 **the horizon** [sing] 地平线〔綫〕 dìpíngxiàn. 2 [C] [喻]眼界 yǎnjiè; 视野 shìyě: *Travel broadens one's ~s.* 旅行可以开阔人们的视野.

horizontal /ˌhɒrɪˈzɒntl; *US* ˌhɔːr-/ *adj* 平的 píngde; 水平的 shuǐpíngde. **horizontal** *n* [sing] 水平线〔綫〕 shuǐpíngxiàn; 水平位置 shuǐpíng wèizhi. **horizontally** /-təlɪ/ *adv*.

hormone /ˈhɔːməʊn/ *n* [C] 荷尔〔爾〕蒙 hé'ěrméng; 激素 jīsù.

horn /hɔːn/ *n* 1 (a) [C] (兽)角 jiǎo. (b) [U] 角质〔質〕物 jiǎozhìwù. 2 [C] 喇叭 lǎba; 管

H

guǎn；号〔號〕hào：*a French* ˈ~ 法国号. 3 [C]（汽车等的）喇叭 lǎba. **horny** *adj* [-ier, -iest] 1 角制〔製〕的 jiǎozhìde；像角一样〔樣〕坚〔堅〕硬的 xiàng jiǎo yíyàng jiānyìng de. 2 [俚] 欲火中烧〔燒〕的 yùhuǒ zhōng shāo de.

hornet /ˈhɔːnɪt/ *n* [C] 大黄蜂 dà huángfēng.

horoscope /ˈhɒrəskəʊp; *US* ˈhɔːr-/ *n* [C] 根据〔據〕星象算命 gēnjù xīngxiàng suànmìng.

horrendous /hɒˈrendəs/ *adj* 可怕的 kěpàde；骇人的 hàirénde：~ *colours* 使人吃惊的颜色. ~ *clothes* 令人惊讶的衣服.

horrible /ˈhɒrəbl; *US* ˈhɔːr-/ *adj* 1 可怕的 kěpàde；恐怖的 kǒngbùde：*a* ~ *crime* 骇人听〔聽〕闻的罪行. 2 [非正式用语]讨厌〔厭〕的 tǎoyànde：~ *weather* 讨厌的天气. **horribly** *adv*.

horrid /ˈhɒrɪd; *US* ˈhɔːrɪd/ *adj* [非正式用语]讨厌〔厭〕的 tǎoyànde.

horrific /həˈrɪfɪk/ *adj* 非常可怕的 fēicháng kěpàde. **horrifically** *adv*.

horrify /ˈhɒrɪfaɪ; *US* ˈhɔːr-/ *v* [*pt*, *pp* -ied] [T] 使恐怖 shǐ kǒngbù；使害怕 shǐ hàipà：*horrified by his death* 对他的死感到震惊.

horror /ˈhɒrə(r); *US* ˈhɔːr-/ *n* 1 [C, U] 恐怖 kǒngbù；极〔極〕端厌〔厭〕恶〔惡〕jíduān yànwù. 2 [C] [非正式用语]小讨厌（指调皮捣蛋的小孩）xiǎo tǎoyàn. **horror** *adj* 意在引起恐怖的 yì zài yǐnqǐ kǒngbù de：*a* ~ *story* 恐怖故事. *a* ~ *film* 恐怖电影. **horror-stricken**（亦作 **-struck**）*adj* 惊〔驚〕恐万〔萬〕状〔狀〕的 jīngkǒng wàn zhuàng de.

hors d'oeuvre /ˌɔːˈdɜːvrə; *US* -ˈdɜːv/ *n* [C] 餐前的开〔開〕胃小吃 cānqiánde kāiwèi xiǎochī.

horse /hɔːs/ *n* [C] 1 马〔馬〕mǎ. 2 [习语] **(straight) from the horse's ˈmouth**（情报）直接来自参〔參〕予者的 zhíjiē láizì cānyǔzhě de. **horse** *v* [短语动词] **horse about / around** [非正式用语] 哄闹 hōngnào；胡闹 húnào. ˈ**horseplay** *n* [U] 闹腾 nàoteng；胡闹 húnào. ˈ**horsepower** *n* [U] 马力 mǎlì. ˈ**horseshoe** *n* [C] 马蹄铁〔鐵〕mǎtítiě.

horseback /ˈhɔːsbæk/ *n* [习语] **on ˈhorseback** 骑着马〔馬〕qízhe mǎ. **horseback** *adv*, *adj* [尤用于美语]：~ *riding* 骑马.

horticulture /ˈhɔːtɪkʌltʃə(r)/ *n* [U] 园〔園〕艺〔藝〕yuányì. **horticultural** /ˌhɔːtɪˈkʌltʃərəl/ *adj*.

hose[1] /həʊz/（亦作 **hose-pipe**）*n* [C, U] 输水软管 shūshuǐ ruǎnguǎn. **hose** *v* [T] (*down*) 用水管冲洗 yòng shuǐguǎn chōngxǐ；用水管浇〔澆〕yòng shuǐguǎn jiāo.

hose[2] /həʊz/ *n* [pl] 长〔長〕统袜〔襪〕chángtǒngwà；短统袜 duǎntǒngwà.

hosiery /ˈhəʊzɪərɪ; *US* ˈhəʊʒərɪ/ *n* [U] 针织〔織〕业〔業〕zhēnzhīyè.

hospice /ˈhɒspɪs/ *n* [C] 晚期病人收容所 wǎnqī bìngrén shōuróngsuǒ.

hospitable /həˈspɪtəbl; 亦作 ˈhɒspɪtəbl/ *adj* 1 (*to* / *toward*) 好客的 hàokède；招待周到的 zhāodài zhōudào de. 2（地方、处所）使人乐〔樂〕于居住的 shǐ rén lèyú jūzhù de. **hospitably** *adv*.

hospital /ˈhɒspɪtl/ *n* [C] 医〔醫〕院 yīyuàn. **hospitalize** *v* [T] 使住院 shǐ zhùyuàn.

hospitality /ˌhɒspɪˈtælətɪ/ *n* [U] 好客 hàokè；殷勤 yīnqín.

host[1] /həʊst/ *n* [C] 1 主人 zhǔrén. 2（电视、广播节目的）主持人 zhǔchírén. **host** *v* [T] 作…的主持人 zuò…de zhǔchírén；在…作主持人 zài…zuò zhǔchírén.

host[2] /həʊst/ *n* [C] 许多 xǔduō；一大群 yídàqún：*a* ~ *of different reasons* 种种不同的原因.

hostage /ˈhɒstɪdʒ/ *n* [C] 人质〔質〕rénzhì.

hostel /ˈhɒstl/ *n* [C]（为学生、无家者提供膳宿的）寄宿舍 jìsùshè.

hostess /ˈhəʊstɪs/ *n* [C] 1 女主人 nǚzhǔrén；女主持人 nǚzhǔchírén. 2 女服务〔務〕员 nǚfúwùyuán；女招待 nǚzhāodài.

hostile /ˈhɒstaɪl; *US* -tl/ *adj* (*to*/ *toward*) 1 不友好的 bù yǒuhǎo de. 2 敌〔敵〕方的 dífāngde：~ *aircraft* 敌机.

hostility /hɒˈstɪlətɪ/ *n* 1 [U] 敌〔敵〕意 díyì；敌视 díshì. 2 **hostilities** [pl] 战〔戰〕争 zhànzhēng；战争行动〔動〕zhànzhēng xíngdòng.

hot /hɒt/ *adj* [~ter, ~test] 1 热〔熱〕的 rède. 2 辣的 làde：~ *spices* 辣的调味品. ~ *curry* 辛辣的咖喱. 3 强烈的 qiángliède；猛烈的 měngliède；暴躁的 bàozàode：*He has a* ~ *temper*. 他脾气暴躁. 4（消息等）新近的 xīnjìnde；刚〔剛〕刚的 gānggāngde. 5 [习语] **be in / get into hot water** [非正式用语]惹上严〔嚴〕重的麻烦 rě shàng yánzhòng de máfan. **hot ˈair** [非正式用语]空话 kōnghuà；夸〔誇〕夸其谈 kuākuā qí tán. **(be) hot on sb's ˈheels / ˈtracks/ ˈtrail** 紧〔緊〕跟某人 jǐngēn mǒurén. **not so hot** [非正式用语]并不怎么〔麼〕好 bìng bù zěnme hǎo. **hot** *v* [-tt-] [短语动词] **hot up** [非正式用语]变〔變〕得激动〔動〕起来〔來〕biànde jīdòng qǐlái；加剧〔劇〕jiājù. ˌ**hot-ˈblooded** *adj* 易怒的 yìnùde；感情强烈的 gǎnqíng qiángliè de. ˈ**hot-desking** *n* [U] 办〔辦〕公桌轮〔輪〕用制 bàngōngzhuō lúnyòngzhì. ˌ**hot ˈdog** *n* [C] 热〔熱〕狗 règǒu；红肠〔腸〕面〔麵〕包 hóngcháng miànbāo. ˌ**hotˈfoot** *adv* 匆忙地 cōngmángde；火烧〔燒〕火燎地 huǒ shāo huǒ liǎo de. ˈ**hothead** *n* [C] 鲁莽的人 lǔmǎngde rén；容易头〔頭〕脑〔腦〕发〔發〕热的人

H

róngyì tóunǎo fārè de rén. ˌ**hot-ˈheaded** *adj*. ˈ**hothouse** *n* [C] 温室 wēnshì; 暖房 nuǎnfáng. ˈ**hot line** (政府首脑间的)热线〔綫〕rèxiàn. ˈ**hotly** *adv* **1** 热烈地 rèliède. **2** 紧〔緊〕紧地 jǐnjǐnde: *~ly pursued* 紧追. ˌ**hot-ˈtempered** *adj* 脾气〔氣〕暴躁的 píqi bàozào de.

hotel /həʊˈtel/ *n* [C] 旅馆 lǚguǎn. **hotelier** /-lɪə(r), -lɪeɪ; *US* ˌhəʊtelˈjeɪ / *n* [C] 旅馆老板 lǚguǎn lǎobǎn.

hound /haʊnd/ *n* [C] 猎〔獵〕狗 liègǒu; 赛狗 sàigǒu. **hound** *v* [T] 追逼 zhuībī; 困扰〔擾〕kùnrǎo; 追逐 zhuīzhú: *~ed by the newspapers* 被记者纠缠.

hour /aʊə(r)/ *n* **1** [C] 小时〔時〕xiǎoshí. **2** [C] 钟〔鐘〕点〔點〕(指 24 小时中的正 1 点、正 2 点等) zhōngdiǎn: *Trains leave on the ~.* 列车每个钟点的整点开出一趟. **3 hours** [pl] (工作等的)固定时间 gùdìng shíjiān: *Office ~s are from 9 am to 5 pm*. 办公时间为上午 9 时到下午 5 时. **4** [C, 常作 sing] (大约一小时的作某种用途的)时间 shíjiān: *a long lunch ~* 很长的午餐时间. **5** [C] 一小时的行程 yì xiǎoshí de xíngchéng: *London is only two ~s away*. 到伦敦只不过两小时的行程. **6** [习语] **at the eˌleventh ˈhour** 在最后〔後〕时刻 zài zuìhòu shíkè.

hourly /ˈaʊəlɪ/ *adv* **1** 每小时〔時〕地 měixiǎoshíde. **2** 按每工作一小时 àn měi gōngzuò yìxiǎoshí: *be paid ~* 按每工作小时付酬. **hourly** *adj* **1** 每小时的 měixiǎoshíde: *an ~ bus service* 每小时开一班车的公共汽车. **2** 按小时计算的 àn xiǎoshí jìsuàn de.

house[1] /haʊs/ *n* [C] [*pl* **~s** /ˈhaʊzɪz/] **1** (a) 房屋 fángwū. (b) 同住一所房屋的人们 tóng zhù yìsuǒ fángwū de rénmén: *Be quiet or you'll wake the whole ~!* 请安静,不然你们会把全屋子的人都吵醒! **2** 为〔爲〕所提到的用途建筑〔築〕的房舍 wèi suǒ tídào de yòngtú jiànzhù de fángshè: *an ˈopera-~* 歌剧院. *a ˈhen-~* 鸡舍. **3** 学〔學〕校为体〔體〕育比赛等分的组 xuéxiào wèi tǐyù bǐsài děng fēn de zǔ. **4** (常作 **House**) 议〔議〕院 yìyuàn; 议院大楼〔樓〕yìyuàn dàlóu: *the ˌH~s of ˈParliament* 国会两院. *the ˌH~ of ˌRepreˈsentatives* 众议院. **5** 企业〔業〕机〔機〕构 qǐyè jīgòu: *a publishing ~* 出版社. **6** (常作 **House**) 家族 jiāzú; 贵族 guìzú; 王族 wángzú. **7** [常作 sing] (剧院等的)观〔觀〕众〔衆〕guānzhòng: *a full ~* 客满. **8** [习语] **bring the ˈhouse down** [非正式用语]博得全场〔場〕喝彩 bódé quánchǎng hècǎi. **on the ˈhouse** 由店家出钱〔錢〕yóu diànjiā chūqián; 免费 miǎnfèi. ˈ**house-bound** *adj* (因病等)出不了门的 chūbùliǎo mén de. ˈ**house-breaking** *n* [U] (为图谋不轨而)破门入屋 pò mén rù wū. ˈ**housekeeper** *n* [C] 女管家 nǚguǎnjiā. ˈ**housekeeping** *n* [U] **1** 料理家务〔務〕liàolǐ jiāwù; 管家 guǎnjiā. **2** 家务开〔開〕支 jiāwù kāizhī. ˈ**housemaster** (*fem* ˈ**housemistress**) *n* [C] (寄宿学校的)舍监〔監〕shèjiān. **the House of Lords** [英国英语]贵族院 guìzúyuàn; 上议院 shàngyìyuàn. ˈ**house-proud** *adj* 热中于美化家庭的 rèzhōngyú měihuà jiātíng de. ˈ**housewife** *n* [C] [*pl* **housewives** /-waɪvz/] 家庭妇〔婦〕女 jiātíng fùnǚ. ˈ**housework** *n* [U] 家务劳〔勞〕动〔動〕jiāwù láodòng.

house[2] /haʊz/ *v* [T] 供给…房子住 gōngjǐ…fángzi zhù.

household /ˈhaʊshəʊld/ *n* **1** [C] 一家人 yìjiārén; 家庭 jiātíng. **2** [习语] **a ˌhousehold ˈname /ˈword** 家喻户晓〔曉〕的人(或事物) jiā yù hù xiǎo de rén.

housing /ˈhaʊzɪŋ/ *n* **1** [U] 住房 zhùfáng. **2** [C] (机器等的)遮盖〔蓋〕物 zhēgàiwù.

hove ⇨HEAVE.

hovel /ˈhɒvl; *US* ˈhʌvl/ *n* [C] [贬]陋屋 lòuwū; 棚 péng; 茅屋 máowū.

hover /ˈhɒvə(r); *US* ˈhʌvər/ *v* [I] **1** (鸟等)盘〔盤〕旋 pánxuán; 翱翔 áoxiáng. **2** (人)徘徊 páihuái; 彷徨 pánghuáng. **hovercraft** *n* [C] [*pl* **hovercraft**] 气〔氣〕垫〔墊〕船 qìdiànchuán.

how /haʊ/ *adv* **1** (用于问句) (a) 如何 rúhé; 怎样〔樣〕zěnyàng: *H~ is this word spelt?* 这个词怎样拼? (b) 健康情况怎样 jiànkāng qíngkuàng zěnyàng: *H~ are you?* 你身体怎样? (c) (与形容词或副词连用)何种〔種〕程度 hézhǒng chéngdù: *H~ old is he?* 他多大岁数? **2** (用于感叹句,形容程度)多么〔麽〕duōme, 真 zhēn: *H~ hot it is!* 天气多么热呀! **how** *conj* 怎样 zěnyàng; 如何 rúhé: *He told me ~ to get to the station*. 他告诉我到车站怎么走.

however /haʊˈevə(r)/ *adv* **1** 无〔無〕论〔論〕如何 wúlùn rúhé; 不管怎样〔樣〕bùguǎn zěnyàng: *He'll never succeed, ~ hard he tries*. 不管他如何努力,都成功不了. **2** (用于评说前述事实)然而 rán'ér, 不过〔過〕búguò, 仍然 réngrán: *She felt ill; she went to work, ~*. 她觉得不舒服,然而她仍然去工作. **3** (用于问句,表示惊讶)究竟怎样〔樣〕jiūjìng zěnyàng, 到底如何 dàodǐ rúhé: *H~ did you get here without a car?* 没有开汽车,你到底是怎么到这里来的? **however** *conj* 无论以何种〔種〕方式 wúlùn yǐ hézhǒng fāngshì: *H~ I thought about the problem, I couldn't work out an answer*. 我翻来覆去地思考这个问题,怎么也想不出个办法.

howl /haʊl/ *v* [I] *n* [C] 发〔發〕出吼叫 fāchū

hǒujiào；吼叫 hǒujiào.

HQ /ˌeɪtʃ ˈkjuː/ *abbr* headquarters 总〔總〕部 zǒngbù.

hr *abbr* [*pl* **hrs**] hour 小时〔時〕xiǎoshí.

HR /eɪtʃ ˈɑː(r)/ *abbr* human resources 人力资源 rénlì zīyuán.

HRH /ˌeɪtʃ ɑː(r) ˈeɪtʃ/ *abbr* His /Her Royal Highness 殿下 diànxià.

HTML /ˌeitʃ tiː em ˈel/ *abbr* hypertext markup language 超文本标〔標〕记语言 chāowénběn biāojì yǔyán.

hub /hʌb/ *n* [C] **1** 轮〔輪〕毂 lúngǔ. **2** [喻]活动〔動〕中心 huódòng zhōngxīn. ˈ**hub-cap** *n* [C] (汽车的)毂盖〔蓋〕gǔgài.

hubbub /ˈhʌbʌb/ *n* [U] [sing] 吵闹 chǎonào；喧哗〔嘩〕xuānhuá.

huddle /ˈhʌdl/ *v* **1** [I,T] 挤〔擠〕成一团〔團〕jǐchéng yìtuán. **2** [短语动词] **huddle up** (身体)缩成一团 suōchéng yìtuán. **huddle** *n* [C] 杂〔雜〕乱〔亂〕的一团 záluànde yìtuán.

hue[1] /hjuː/ *n* [C] [正式用语] 颜色 yánsè；色度 sèdù.

hue[2] /hjuː/ *n* [习语] ˌ**hue and** ˈ**cry** 公众〔衆〕抗议〔議〕的愤怒喊叫声〔聲〕gōngzhòng kàngyì de fènnù hǎnjiàoshēng.

huff /hʌf/ *n* [sing] 愤怒 fènnù: *be in a* ～ 发脾气.

hug /hʌg/ *v* [-gg-] [T] **1** 紧〔緊〕抱 jǐnbào；拥〔擁〕抱 yōngbào. **2** 紧靠 jǐnkào；紧挨 jǐn'āi: *The boat* ～*ged the shore*. 小艇紧靠着岸. **hug** *n* [C] 拥抱 yōngbào: *give sb a* ～ 拥抱某人.

huge /hjuːdʒ/ *adj* 巨大的 jùdàde；庞〔龐〕大的 pángdàde. **hugely** *adv* 非常地 fēichángde.

hulk /hʌlk/ *n* [C] **1** 废〔廢〕船 fèichuán. **2** 巨大笨重的人或物 jùdà bènzhòng de rén huò wù. **hulking** *adj* 巨大而笨重的 jùdà ér bènzhòng de.

hull /hʌl/ *n* [C] 船体〔體〕chuántǐ.

hullo = HALLO.

hum /hʌm/ *v* [-mm-] **1** [I] 发〔發〕哼哼声〔聲〕fā hēnghēng shēng. **2** [I,T] 哼(曲子) hēng: ～ *a tune* 哼一个曲调. **3** [I] 活跃〔躍〕huóyuè；忙碌 mánglù. **hum** *n* [C] 哼哼声 hēnghēng shēng；嗡嗡声 wēngwēng shēng.

human /ˈhjuːmən/ *adj* **1** 人的 rénde；人类〔類〕的 rénlèide. **2** 有人性的 yǒu rénxìng de；有人情味的 yǒu rénqíngwèi de. **human** (亦作 **human** ˈ**being**) *n* [C] 人 rén. **humanly** 人力所及地 rénlì suǒ jí de: *do all that is* ～*ly possible* 尽人力之所及. ˌ**human** ˈ**rights** *n* [pl] 人权〔權〕rénquán. **human resources** *n* [pl] 人力资源 rénlì zīyuán.

humane /hjuːˈmeɪn/ *adj* **1** 仁慈的 réncíde；人道的 réndàode. **2** 使少受痛苦的 shǐ shǎoshòu tòngkǔ de: ～ *killing of animals* 无痛宰杀动物. **humanely** *adv*.

humanity /hjuːˈmænətɪ/ *n* [U] **1** 人类〔類〕rénlèi. **2** 仁慈 réncí；仁爱〔愛〕rén'ài.

humble /ˈhʌmbl/ *adj* [～r, ～st] **1** 谦卑的 qiānbēide；恭顺的 gōngshùnde. **2** 地位低下的 dìwèi dīxià de；微贱〔賤〕的 wēijiànde. **3** 简陋的 jiǎnlòude: *my* ～ *home* 我的简陋的家. **humble** *v* [T] 使卑下 shǐ bēixià；贬抑 biǎnyì. **humbly** *adv*.

humdrum /ˈhʌmdrʌm/ *adj* 单〔單〕调的 dāndiàode；枯燥的 kūzàode.

humid /ˈhjuːmɪd/ *adj* (尤指空气)潮湿〔濕〕的 cháoshīde. **humidity** /hjuːˈmɪdətɪ/ *n* [U] 湿气〔氣〕shīqì；湿度 shīdù.

humiliate /hjuːˈmɪlɪeɪt/ *v* [T] 羞辱 xiūrǔ；使丢脸〔臉〕shǐ diūliǎn. **humiliating** *adj*: *a humiliating defeat* 丢脸的失败. **humiliation** /hjuːˌmɪlɪˈeɪʃn/ *n* [C,U].

humility /hjuːˈmɪlətɪ/ *n* [U] 谦卑 qiānbēi；谦恭 qiāngōng.

humorist /ˈhjuːmərɪst/ *n* [C] 幽默家 yōumòjiā；幽默作家 yōumò zuòjiā.

humorous /ˈhjuːmərəs/ *adj* 幽默的 yōumòde；有幽默感的 yǒu yōumògǎn de. **humorously** *adv*.

humour (美语 -or) /ˈhjuːmə(r)/ *n* [U] 幽默 yōumò；诙谐 huīxié: *a sense of* ～ 幽默感. **humour** *v* [T] 迁〔遷〕就 qiānjiù；使满足 shǐ mǎnzú.

hump /hʌmp/ *n* [C] 圆形隆起物 yuánxíng lóngqǐwù；驼峰 tuófēng. **hump** *v* [T] [非正式用语] 费力地扛、搬运〔運〕fèilì de káng、bānyùn.

hunch /hʌntʃ/ *n* [C] [非正式用语] 基于直觉〔覺〕的想法 jīyú zhíjué de xiǎngfǎ；预感 yùgǎn. **hunch** *v* [T] 弓起(肩和背) gōngqǐ. ˈ**hunchback** *n* [C] 驼背 tuóbèi；驼背的人 tuóbèide rén. ˈ**hunchbacked** *adj*.

hundred /ˈhʌndrəd/ *pron*, *adj*, *n* [C] 一百 yìbǎi；一百个〔個〕yìbǎigè: *one, two, etc* ～ 一百，二百…. ～*s of people* 好几百人. **hundredth** /-dθ/ *pron*, *adj* 第一百 dìyībǎi. **hundredth** *pron*, *n* [C] 百分之一 bǎifēn zhī yī.

hundredweight /ˈhʌndrədweɪt/ *n* [C] [*pl* **hundredweight**] 英担〔擔〕(衡名，约合 50.8 千克) yīngdàn.

hung /hʌŋ/ *pt*, *pp* of HANG[1].

hunger /ˈhʌŋgə(r)/ *n* **1** [U] 饿 è. **2** [sing] *for* [喻]渴望 kěwàng. **hunger** *v* [短语动词] **hunger for / after sth** 热〔熱〕望 rèwàng；渴望 kěwàng. ˈ**hunger strike** 绝食 juéshí.

hungry /ˈhʌŋgrɪ/ *adj* [-ier, -iest] 饥〔饑〕饿的 jī'ède. **hungrily** *adv*.

hunk /hʌŋk/ *n* [C] 厚块〔塊〕hòukuài；大块

H

dàkuài: *a ~ of bread* 一大块面包.

hunt /hʌnt/ *v* [I, T] 1 打猎〔獵〕 dǎliè; 猎取 lièqǔ. 2 (*for*) 搜寻〔尋〕 sōuxún. 3 [短语动词] **hunt sb down** 搜寻…直到找到 sōuxún… zhídào zhǎodào. **hunt** *n* 1 [sing] 狩猎 shǒuliè; 搜寻 sōuxún. 2 猎狐队〔隊〕 lièhúduì. **hunter** *n* [C] 猎人 lièrén.

hurdle /ˈhɜːdl/ *n* [C] 1 跳栏〔欄〕 tiàolán. 2 [喻]障碍〔礙〕 zhàng'ài.

hurl /hɜːl/ *v* [T] 猛掷〔擲〕 měngzhì; 猛投 měngtóu: [喻] *~ insults at sb* 恶狠狠地辱骂某人.

hurly-burly /ˈhɜːlɪbɜːlɪ/ *n* [sing] 喧嚣 xuānxiāo; 喧哗〔嘩〕 xuānhuá.

hurrah /hʊˈrɑː/ (亦作 **hurray, hooray** /hʊˈreɪ/) *interj, n* [C] (表示高兴、赞许等)好哇! hǎowa!

hurricane /ˈhʌrɪkən; US -keɪn/ *n* [C] 飓风〔風〕 jùfēng.

hurry /ˈhʌrɪ/ *v* [*pt, pp* -ied] 1 [I, T] (使)赶〔趕〕紧〔緊〕 gǎnjǐn; 匆忙 cōngmáng. 2 [短语动词] **hurry (sb) up** (使)赶紧 gǎnjǐn; (使)赶快 gǎnkuài: *H~ up! It's late.* 快一些! 已经晚了. **hurried** *adj* 匆促做成的 cōngcù zuòchéng de. **hurriedly** *adv*. **hurry** *n* 1 [U] 匆忙 cōngmáng; 仓〔倉〕促 cāngcù. 2 [习语] **in a ˈhurry** (a) 匆忙 cōngmáng. (b) 急于 jíyú; 渴望 kěwàng.

hurt /hɜːt/ *v* [*pt, pp* **hurt**] 1 [I, T] (使)受伤〔傷〕痛 shòu shāngtòng: *He ~ himself.* 他把自己弄伤了. *I ~ my hand.* 我弄伤了手. 2 [T] 伤…的感情 shāng…de gǎnqíng; 使痛心 shǐ tòngxīn. 3 损害 sǔnhài: *It wouldn't ~ (you) to say sorry.* 道一声歉(对你)没有损害. **hurt** *n* [C, U] 伤害 shānghài; 感情伤害 gǎnqíng shānghài. **hurtful** *adj*. **hurtfully** *adv*.

hurtle /ˈhɜːtl/ *v* [I] 猛冲〔衝〕 JP]měngchōng; 飞〔飛〕驰 fēichí.

husband /ˈhʌzbənd/ *n* [C] 丈夫 zhàngfu.

hush /hʌʃ/ *v* 1 [I, T] (使)静下来 jìng xiàlái. 2 [短语动词] **hush sth up** 不使(某事)张扬〔揚〕 bù shǐ zhāngyáng. **hush** *n* [U, sing] 沉默 chénmò; 寂静 jìjìng.

husk /hʌsk/ *n* [C] 荚〔莢〕 jiá; 外果壳〔殼〕 wàiguǒké. **husk** *v* [T] 去…的荚 qù…de jiá; 去…的壳 qù…de ké.

husky[1] /ˈhʌskɪ/ *adj* [-ier, -iest] (声音)沙哑〔啞〕的 shāyǎde. **huskily** *adv*.

husky[2] /ˈhʌskɪ/ *n* [C][*pl* -ies] 爱〔愛〕斯基摩种〔種〕狗 àisījīmó zhǒng gǒu.

hustle /ˈhʌsl/ *v* [T] 1 乱〔亂〕推 luàntuī. 2 (*into*) 催促 cuīcù: *~ sb into a decision* 催某人作出决定. **hustle** *n* [U] 忙碌 mánglù; 奔忙 bēnmáng. **hustler** /ˈhʌslə(r)/ *n* [C] [美国俚语]妓女 jìnǚ.

hut /hʌt/ *n* [C] 小棚屋 xiǎopéngwū.

hutch /hʌtʃ/ *n* [C] 兔箱 tùxiāng; 兔笼〔籠〕 tùlóng.

hyacinth /ˈhaɪəsɪnθ/ *n* [C] [植物]风〔風〕信子 fēngxìnzǐ.

hyaena = HYENA.

hybrid /ˈhaɪbrɪd/ *n* [C] (动植物)杂〔雜〕种〔種〕 zázhǒng.

hydrant /ˈhaɪdrənt/ *n* [C] (尤指街上的)取水管 qǔshuǐguǎn.

hydraulic /haɪˈdrɔːlɪk/ *adj* 水力的 shuǐlìde; 液力的 yèlìde; 液压〔壓〕的 yèyāde.

hydroelectric /ˌhaɪdrəʊɪˈlektrɪk/ *adj* 水力发〔發〕电〔電〕的 shuǐlì fādiàn de.

hydrofoil /ˈhaɪdrəfɔɪl/ *n* [C] 水翼艇 shuǐyìtǐng.

hydrogen /ˈhaɪdrədʒən/ *n* [U] 氢〔氫〕气〔氣〕 qīngqì. **hydrogen bomb** *n* [C] 氢弹〔彈〕 qīngdàn.

hyena (亦作 **hyaena**) /haɪˈiːnə/ *n* [C] 鬣狗 liègǒu.

hygiene /ˈhaɪdʒiːn/ *n* [U] 卫〔衛〕生 wèishēng. **hygienic** /haɪˈdʒiːnɪk; US -dʒɪˈen-/ *adj* 卫生的 wèishēngde. **hygienically** *adv*.

hymn /hɪm/ *n* [C] (颂扬上帝的)赞〔讚〕美诗 zànměishī; 圣〔聖〕歌 shènggē.

hyperactive /ˌhaɪpə(r)ˈæktɪv/ *adj* 活动〔動〕过〔過〕强的 huódòng guòqiáng de; 活动亢进〔進〕的 huódòng kàngjìn de.

hypermarket /ˈhaɪpəmɑːkɪt/ *n* [C] [英国英语]大型超级市场〔場〕 dàxíng chāojí shìchǎng.

hypertext /ˈhaɪpətekst/ *n* [U] 超文本 chāowénběn. **hypertext ˈmarkup language** *n* [U] 超文本标〔標〕记语言 chāowénběn biāojì yǔyán.

hyphen /ˈhaɪfn/ *n* [C] 连字号〔號〕 liánzìhào. **hyphenate** /ˈhaɪfəneɪt/ *v* [T] 用连字号连接 yòng liánzìhào liánjiē.

hypnosis /hɪpˈnəʊsɪs/ *n* [C] 催眠状〔狀〕态〔態〕 cuīmián zhuàngtài. **hypnotic** /hɪpˈnɒtɪk/ *adj*. **hypnotism** /ˈhɪpnətɪzəm/ *n* [U] 催眠 cuīmián; 催眠状态 cuīmián zhuàngtài. **hypnotist** /ˈhɪpnətɪst/ *n* [C]. **hypnotize** /ˈhɪpnətaɪz/ *v* [T] 为〔爲〕…催眠 wèi…cuīmián.

hypochondriac /ˌhaɪpəˈkɒndrɪæk/ *n* [C] 过〔過〕分担〔擔〕心自己健康的人 guòfèn dānxīn zìjǐ jiànkāng de rén.

hypocrisy /hɪˈpɒkrəsɪ/ *n* [C, U] [*pl* -ies] 伪〔僞〕善 wěishàn; 虚伪 xūwěi. **hypocrite** /ˈhɪpəkrɪt/ *n* [C] 伪君子 wěijūnzǐ. **hypocritical** /ˌhɪpəˈkrɪtɪkl/ *adj*.

hypodermic /ˌhaɪpəˈdɜːmɪk/ *n* [C], *adj* 皮下注射器针头〔頭〕(的) píxià zhùshèqì zhēntóu.

hypotenuse /ˌhaɪˈpɒtənjuːz; *US* -tənuːs/ *n* [C] [数学]弦 xián;斜边[邊] xiébiān.

hypothesis /ˌhaɪˈpɒθəsɪs/ *n* [C] [*pl* -theses /-siːz/] (逻辑)前提 qiántí;假说 jiǎshuō. **hypothetical** /ˌhaɪpəˈθetɪkl/ *adj* 假设的 jiǎshède.

hysteria /hɪˈstɪərɪə/ *n* [U] 1 歇斯底里 xiēsīdǐlǐ;癔病 yìbìng. 2 狂热[熱] kuángrè. **hysterical** /hɪˈsterɪkl/ *adj*. **hysterics** /hɪˈsterɪks/ *n* [pl] 癔病发[發]作 yìbìng fāzuò.

I i

I, i[1] /aɪ/ *n* [C] [*pl* I's, i's /aɪz/] 1 英语的第九个[個]字母 Yīngyǔde dìjiǔgè zìmǔ. 2 罗马数[數]字 1 Luómǎ shùzì yī.

I[2] /aɪ/ *pron* 我 wǒ.

ice[1] /aɪs/ *n* 1 [U] 冰 bīng. 2 [C] 一份冰淇淋 yífèn bīngqílín. 3 [习语] **put sth on ice** 延迟[遲] yánchí;把…暂时[時]搁起 bǎ…zànshí gēqǐ. **iceberg** /ˈaɪsbɜːg/ *n* [C] 冰山 bīngshān;流冰 liúbīng. ˈ**icebox** *n* [C] 1 (内有冰块以冷藏食物的)冰箱 bīngxiāng. 2 [尤用于美语]电[電]冰箱 diànbīngxiāng. ˌ**ice-**ˈ**cream** [尤用于美语] /*US* ˈaɪskriːm / *n* [C,U] (一份)冰淇淋 bīngqílín. ˈ**ice hockey** *n* [U] 冰球 bīngqiú. ˌ**ice** ˈ**lolly** *n* [C] 冰棍 bīnggùn. ˈ**ice-skate** *n* [C] 冰鞋 bīngxié. ˈ**ice-skate** *v* [I] 溜冰 liūbīng;滑冰 huábīng.

ice[2] /aɪs/ *v* 1 [T] 使凉 shǐ liáng;冰镇 bīngzhèn. 2 [T] 在(糕饼等上)滚糖霜 zài gǔn tángshuāng. 3 [短语动词] **ice (sth) over/up** 冰覆盖[蓋]着 bīng fùgàizhe;结冰 jiébīng.

icicle /ˈaɪsɪkl/ *n* [C] 冰柱 bīngzhù.

icing /ˈaɪsɪŋ/ *n* [C] (糕饼表层上的)糖霜 tángshuāng,糖衣 tángyī,酥皮 sūpí.

icy /ˈaɪsɪ/ *adj* [-ier, -iest] 1 冰冷的 bīnglěngde. 2 盖[蓋]着冰的 gàizhebīngde. 3 [喻] 冷冰冰的 lěngbīngbīngde;不友好的 bù yǒuhǎo de: *an* ~ *stare* 冷冰冰的盯视. **icily** *adv*.

I'd /aɪd/ = 1 I had. ⇨HAVE. 2 I would. ⇨WILL[1], WOULD[1].

idea /aɪˈdɪə/ *n* [C] 1 计划[劃] jìhuà;主意 zhǔyi;打算 dǎsuàn: *That's a good* ~! 这是个好主意! 2 [U, sing] 想像 xiǎngxiàng. 3 [C] 意见 yìjiàn;信念 xìnniàn. 4 [U, sing] 认[認]为[爲]某事可能发[發]生的感觉[覺] rènwéi mǒushì kěnéng fāshēng de gǎnjué: *I've an* ~ *it will rain*. 我预感天会下雨. 5 **the idea** [sing] 目的 mùdì;目标[標] mùbiāo. 6 [习语] **get the i'dea** 理解 lǐjiě. **have no i'dea** 不知道 bù zhīdào: *He has no* ~ *how to manage people*. 他完全不知道如何管理人. **not have the first idea about sth** 完全不知道 wánquán bù zhīdào.

ideal /aɪˈdɪəl/ *adj* 1 完美的 wánměide;理想的 lǐxiǎngde: ~ *weather* 理想的天气. 2 想像中的 xiǎngxiàng zhōng de;空想的 kōngxiǎngde: *in an* ~ *world* 在想像的世界. **ideal** *n* [C] 1 理想的人或事物 lǐxiǎngde rén huò shìwù. 2 [常作 pl]行为[爲]的高标[標]准[準] xíngwéide gāo biāozhǔn. **ideally** *adv* 1 理想地 lǐxiǎngde: ~*ly suited to the job* 最适合这项工作. 2 最理想的是 zuì lǐxiǎng de shì.

idealist /aɪˈdɪəlɪst/ *n* [C] 理想主义[義]者 lǐxiǎngzhǔyìzhě. **idealism** *n* [U]. **idealistic** /ˌaɪdɪəˈlɪstɪk/ *adj*.

idealize /aɪˈdɪəlaɪz/ *v* [T] 使理想化 shǐ lǐxiǎnghuà. **idealization** /aɪˌdɪəlaɪˈzeɪʃn / *n* [U,C].

identical /aɪˈdentɪkl/ *adj* 1 同一的 tóngyīde. 2 (*to/with*) 完全相似的 wánquán xiāngsì de;完全相同的 wánquán xiāngtóng de: ~ *twins* 同卵双[雙]生. **identically** *adv*.

identify /aɪˈdentɪfaɪ/ *v* [*pt*, *pp* -ied] 1 [T] 认[認]出 rènchū;识[識]别 shíbié: *Can you* ~ *the man who attacked you?* 你能认出打你的人吗? 2 [短语动词] **identify (oneself) with sb/sth** 和…打成一片 hé…dǎchéng yípiàn. **identify with sb** 了[瞭]解某人的感情 liǎojiě mǒurén de gǎnqíng. **identification** /aɪˌdentɪfɪˈkeɪʃn/ *n* [U] 1 认出 rènchū;识别 shíbié. 2 身份证[證]明 shēnfèn zhèngmíng.

identity /aɪˈdentətɪ/ *n* [*pl* -ies] 1 [C,U] 身份 shēnfèn;个[個]性 gèxìng;特性 tèxìng: *the* ~ *of the thief* 窃贼身份. 2 [U] 同一 tóngyī;一致 yízhì. **i'dentity theft** *n* [U] 身份盗[盜]窃[竊] shēnfèn dàoqiè.

ideology /ˌaɪdɪˈɒlədʒɪ/ *n* [C,U] [*pl* -ies] 思想 sīxiǎng;思想体[體]系 sīxiǎng tǐxì;意识[識]形态[態] yìshìxíngtài. **ideological** /ˌaɪdɪəˈlɒdʒɪkl / *adj*.

idiocy /ˈɪdɪəsɪ/ *n* [*pl* -ies] 1 [U] 极[極]端愚笨 jíduān yúbèn;白痴[癡] báichī. 2 [C] 极愚蠢的言行 jí yúchǔn de yánxíng.

idiom /ˈɪdɪəm/ *n* [C] 习[習]语 xíyǔ;成语 chéngyǔ;惯用语 guànyòngyǔ: '*Pull your socks up*' *is an* ~ *meaning* '*improve your behaviour*'. "pull your socks up" 是一个习语,意为"加紧努力". **idiomatic** /ˌɪdɪəˈmætɪk/ *adj* (语言)自然而正确[確]的 zìrán ér zhèngquè de.

idiosyncrasy /ˌɪdɪəˈsɪŋkrəsɪ/ *n* [C] [*pl* -ies] (人的)特性 tèxìng;癖性 pǐxìng. **idiosyn'cratic** /ˌɪdɪəsɪŋˈkrætɪk / *adj*.

idiot /ˈɪdɪət/ *n* [C] 1 [非正式用语]傻[儍]子 shǎzi. 2 [旧]白痴[癡] báichī. **idiotic** /ˌɪdɪˈɒtɪk/ *adj* 愚蠢的 yúchǔnde.

idle /ˈaɪdl/ *adj* [～r, ～st] 1 (a) 不工作的 bù gōngzuò de. (b) 不使用的 bù shǐyòngde: *The machines are lying* ～. 这些机器闲置不用. 2 懒惰的 lǎnduòde. 3 无〔無〕用的 wúyòngde: ～ *gossip* 无聊的闲话. ～ *promises* 无用的诺言. **idle** *v* 1 [I] 无所事事 wú suǒ shì shì; 浪费时〔時〕间 làngfèi shíjiān. 2 [I] (发动机)空转〔轉〕 kōngzhuàn. 3 [短语动词] **idle sth away** 浪费(时间) làngfèi. **idleness** *n* [U]. **idly** *adv*.

idol /ˈaɪdl/ *n* [C] 1 偶像 ǒuxiàng. 2 宠〔寵〕儿 chǒng'ér; 宠物 chǒngwù; 崇拜的对〔對〕象 chóngbàide duìxiàng. **idolize** /ˈaɪdəlaɪz/ *v* [T] 崇拜 chóngbài.

idyllic /ɪˈdɪlɪk; *US* aɪˈd-/ *adj* 质〔質〕朴〔樸〕宜人的 zhìpǔ yírén de.

ie /ˌaɪ ˈiː/ *abbr* (拉丁文) id est 即 jí: *They arrived on the next day, ie Monday*. 他们在第二天即星期一抵达.

if /ɪf/ *conj* 1 假使 jiǎshǐ; 如果 rúguǒ: *She will help you if you ask her*. 如果你要求, 她会帮助你. 2 是否 shìfǒu: *Do you know if he's working today?* 你知道他今天工作吗? 3 当〔當〕dāng: *If you mix yellow and blue, you get green*. 把黄色同蓝色混合起来, 就成绿色. 4 (用于表示情感的动词或形容词后面): *I'm sorry if I'm disturbing you*. 很抱歉, 打扰你了. 5 虽〔雖〕然 suīrán; 尽〔儘〕管 jǐnguǎn: *The hotel was good value, if a little expensive*. 这家旅馆值得住, 尽管房价贵了一点. 6 [习语] **if I were ˈyou** (用于引出劝告): *If I were you, I'd look for a new job*. 要是我是你, 我就另找工作了. **if ˈonly** (用于表示强烈的愿望)要是…多好 yàoshì…duōhǎo: *If only I were rich!* 我要是发财多好! **if** *n* [C] 1 不确〔確〕定的事 bú quèdìng de shì; 疑问 yíwèn: *If he wins, but it's a big if*. 如果他获胜, 但是他能否获胜还是个大疑问. 2 [习语] **ˌifs and ˈbuts** 故意拖延的借〔藉〕口 gùyì tuōyán de jièkǒu.

igloo /ˈɪgluː/ *n* [C] [*pl* ～s] 爱〔愛〕斯基摩人用雪块〔塊〕砌成的小屋 àisījīmórén yòng xuěkuài qìchéng de xiǎowū.

ignite /ɪgˈnaɪt/ *v* [I, T] 点〔點〕燃 diǎnrán; 使燃烧〔燒〕 shǐ ránshāo. **ignition** /ɪgˈnɪʃn/ *n* 1 [C] (机械)发〔發〕火装〔裝〕置 fā huǒ zhuāngzhì. 2 [U] 点火 diǎnhuǒ; 着火 zháohuǒ.

ignorant /ˈɪgnərənt/ *adj* 无〔無〕知的 wúzhīde. **ignorance** /-rəns/ *n* [U]. **ignorantly** *adv*.

ignore /ɪgˈnɔː(r)/ *v* [T] 不顾〔顧〕 búgù; 不理 bùlǐ.

ill /ɪl/ *adj* 1 有病的 yǒubìngde; 不健康的 bú jiànkāng de. 2 坏〔壞〕的 huàide; 恶〔惡〕劣的 èliède: ～ *feeling* 愤怒; 妒忌. 3 [习语] **be taken ill** 生病 shēngbìng. **ill** *n* [正式用语] 1 恶行 èxíng; 伤〔傷〕害 shānghài. 2 [C, 常作 pl] 困难〔難〕 kùnnan; 不幸 búxìng. **ill** *adv* 1 坏〔壞〕 huài; 恶劣地 èliède: *an* ˌ～-*written* ˈ*book* 一本写得很不好的书. 2 不利地 búlìde: *think* ～ *of sb* 对某人没有好感. 3 几〔幾〕乎不 jīhū bù: *We can* ～ *afford the time*. 我们花不起这个时间. 4 [习语] **ˌill at ˈease** 不舒服 bù shūfu; 不安 bù'ān. **ˌill-adˈvised** *adj* 不明智的 bù míngzhìde. **ˌill-ˈbred** *adj* 没有教养〔養〕的 méiyǒu jiàoyǎng de. **ˌill-ˈnatured** *adj* 脾气〔氣〕坏的 píqi huài de. **ˌill-ˈtreat** *v* [T] 虐待 nüèdài. **ˌill-ˈtreatment** *n* [U]. **ˌill ˈwill** *n* [U] 恶意 èyì.

I'll /aɪl/ I will⇨WILL¹.

illegal /ɪˈliːgl/ *adj* 非法的 fēifǎde; 违〔違〕法的 wéifǎde; 不合法的 bù héfǎ de. **illegality** /ˌɪlɪˈgæləti/ *n* [U, C]. **illegally** /-gəlɪ/ *adv*. **illegal ˈimmigrant** *n* [C] 非法移民者 fēifǎ yímínzhě; 非法滞〔滯〕留者 fēifǎ zhìliúzhě.

illegible /ɪˈledʒəbl/ *adj* (字迹)难〔難〕以辨认〔認〕的 nányǐ biànrèn de; 字迹不清的 zìjī bùqīng de.

illegitimate /ˌɪlɪˈdʒɪtɪmət/ *adj* 1 (孩子)非婚生的 fēi hūnshēng de; 私生的 sīshēngde. 2 违〔違〕法的 wéifǎde; 非法的 fēifǎde. **illegitimately** *adv*.

illicit /ɪˈlɪsɪt/ *adj* 违〔違〕法的 wéifǎde. **illicitly** *adv*.

illiterate /ɪˈlɪtərət/ *n* [C], *adj* 文盲(的) wénmáng. **illiteracy** /-rəsɪ/ *n* [U].

illness /ˈɪlnɪs/ *n* 1 [U] 生病 shēngbìng. 2 [C] 某种〔種〕疾病 mǒuzhǒng jíbìng.

illogical /ɪˈlɒdʒɪkl/ *adj* 不合逻〔邏〕辑的 bùhé luójí de; 悖理的 bèilǐde; 无〔無〕缘由的 wú yuányóu de. **illogicality** /ɪˌlɒdʒɪˈkæləti/ *n* [C, U]. **illogically** *adv*.

illuminate /ɪˈluːmɪneɪt/ *v* [T] 1 照亮 zhàoliàng; 照明 zhàomíng; 阐〔闡〕明 chǎnmíng. 2 用灯〔燈〕装〔裝〕饰 yòng dēng zhuāngshì. 3 (尤指旧时)用金色等鲜明色彩装饰(书) yòng jīnsè děng xiānmíng sècǎi zhuāngshì. **illuminating** *adj* 富于启〔啓〕发〔發〕性的 fù yú qǐfāxìngde: *an illuminating lecture* 富有启发性的讲课. **illumination** /ɪˌluːmɪˈneɪʃn/ *n* 1 [U] 照明 zhàomíng; 照亮 zhàoliàng. 2 **illuminations** [pl] [英国英语] (城市大街上的)灯彩装饰 dēngcǎi zhuāngshì.

illusion /ɪˈluːʒn/ *n* [C] 1 错误的观〔觀〕念 cuòwù de guānniàn; 幻想 huànxiǎng. 2 幻觉〔覺〕 huànjué: *an optical* ～ 光幻觉; 视错觉. **illusory** /ɪˈluːsərɪ/ *adj* 虚幻的 xūhuànde; 幻觉的 huànjuéde; 迷惑人的 míhuò rén de.

illustrate /ˈɪləstreɪt/ *v* [T] 1 配以插图〔圖〕 pèi yǐ chātú: ～ *a book* 给一本书配插图. 2 举

〔舉〕例或以图表说明 jǔlì huò yǐ túbiǎo shuōmíng. **illustration** /ˌɪlə'streɪʃn/ *n* 1 [C] 插图 chātú. 2 [C] 例证〔證〕lìzhèng. 3 [U] 作插图 zuò chātú; 图解 tújiě; 举例说明 jǔlì shuōmíng. **illustrative** /'ɪləstrətɪv; *US* ɪ'lʌs-/ *adj* 用作例证的 yòng zuò lìzhèng de. **illustrator** *n* [C] 插图作者 chātú zuòzhě.

illustrious /ɪ'lʌstrɪəs/ *adj* 著名的 zhùmíngde. **illustriously** *adv*.

I'm /aɪm/ I am ⇨BE.

image /'ɪmɪdʒ/ *n* [C] 1 心目中的形象 xīnmù zhōng de xíngxiàng. 2 (个人、公司等给予公众的)总〔總〕的印象 zǒngde yìnxiàng. 3 (镜中的)映像 yìngxiàng; (拍照的)影像 yǐngxiàng. 4 (某物的)像 xiàng; 木像 mùxiàng; 石像 shíxiàng. 5 [习语] **be the (living/spitting) image of sb** [非正式用语]同某人一模一样〔樣〕tóng mǒurén yìmóyíyàng. **imagery** *n* [U] 形象化描述 xíngxiànghuà miáoshù.

imaginary /ɪ'mædʒɪnərɪ; *US* -ənerɪ/ *adj* 虚构〔構〕的 xūgòude; 假想的 jiǎxiǎngde.

imagine /ɪ'mædʒɪn/ *v* [T] 1 想像 xiǎngxiàng; 设想 shèxiǎng: *Can you ~ life without electricity?* 你能想像没有电的生活吗? 2 料想 liàoxiǎng; 以为〔爲〕yǐwéi: *I ~ he will be there*. 我以为他会在那里. **imaginable** *adj* 可以想像得到的 kěyǐ xiǎngxiàng dédào de. **imagination** /ɪˌmædʒɪ'neɪʃn/ *n* 1 [U, C] 想像力 xiǎngxiànglì. 2 [U] 想像出的事物 xiǎngxiàngchūde shìwù. **imaginative** /ɪ'mædʒɪnətɪv; *US* -əneɪtɪv/ *adj* 想像的 xiǎngxiàngde; 有想像力的 yǒu xiǎngxiànglì de.

imbalance /ˌɪm'bæləns/ *n* [C] 不平衡 bù pínghéng.

imbecile /'ɪmbəsiːl; *US* -sl/ *n* [C] 1 [非正式用语]笨人 bènrén; 蠢货 chǔnhuò. 2 [旧词]低能儿〔兒〕dīnéng'ér. **imbecile** *adj* 愚蠢的 yúchǔnde.

imbue /ɪm'bjuː/ *v* [T] *with* [正式用语]使充满(情绪、精神等) shǐ chōngmǎn.

imitate /'ɪmɪteɪt/ *v* [T] 1 模仿〔倣〕mófǎng; 仿效 fǎngxiào. 2 模拟〔擬〕mónǐ. **imitative** /'ɪmɪtətɪv; *US* -teɪtɪv/ *adj* 模仿的 mófǎngde; 模拟的 mónǐde. **imitator** *n* [C].

imitation /ˌɪmɪ'teɪʃn/ *n* 1 [C] 仿〔倣〕制〔製〕品 fǎngzhìpǐn; 赝品 yànpǐn. 2 [U] 模仿 mófǎng; 仿效 fǎngxiào; 学〔學〕样〔樣〕xuéyàng. **imitation** *adj* 假的 jiǎde; 人造的 rénzàode: *~ jewels* 人造宝石.

immaculate /ɪ'mækjʊlət/ *adj* 纯洁〔潔〕的 chúnjiéde; 无〔無〕瑕疵的 wú xiácī de. **immaculately** *adv*.

immaterial /ˌɪmə'tɪərɪəl/ *adj* 1 (*to*) 不重要的 bú zhòngyào de. 2 非物质〔質〕的 fēi wùzhì de; 无〔無〕形的 wúxíngde.

immature /ˌɪmə'tjʊə(r); *US* -tʊər/ *adj* 1 (所作所为)不老练〔練〕的 bù lǎoliànde. 2 未成熟的 wèi chéngshú de; 未完成的 wèi wánchéng de. **immaturity** *n* [U].

immeasurable /ɪ'meʒərəbl/ *adj* 大得不可计量的 dàdé bùkě jìliàng de; 无〔無〕比的 wúbǐde.

immediate /ɪ'miːdɪət/ *adj* 1 立即的 lìjíde: *take ~ action* 立即采取行动. 2 最接近的 zuì jiējìn de; 紧〔緊〕靠的 jǐnkàode: *in the ~ future* 在最近的将来.

immediately /ɪ'miːdɪətlɪ/ *adv* 1 立即 lìjí. 2 紧〔緊〕靠地 jǐnkàode; 直接地 zhíjiēde: *the years ~ after the war* 战后最初几年. **immediately** *conj* [尤用于英国英语]一…(就…) yī…: *I recognized her ~ I saw her*. 我一看见她就认出她来了.

immense /ɪ'məns/ *adj* 广〔廣〕大的 guǎngdàde; 巨大的 jùdàde. **immensely** *adv* 非常 fēicháng: *I enjoyed the film ~ly*. 我非常喜欢这部电影. **immensity** *n* [U].

immerse /ɪ'mɜːs/ *v* [T] 1 (*in*) 使浸没 shǐ jìnmò. 2 **~ oneself (in)** 使沉浸于 shǐ chénjìn yú; 使专〔專〕心于 shǐ zhuānxīn yú: *~ oneself in one's work* 沉浸于工作之中. *~d in thought* 陷入沉思之中. **immersion** /ɪ'mɜːʃn; *US* -ʒn/ *n* [U]. **im'mersion heater** *n* [C] 浸没式加热〔熱〕器 jìnmòshì jiārèqì.

immigrant /'ɪmɪgrənt/ *n* [C] 移民 yímín; 侨〔僑〕民 qiáomín. **immigration** /ˌɪmɪ'greɪʃn/ *n* [U] 侨居 qiáojū.

imminent /'ɪmɪnənt/ *adj* 迫近的 pòjìnde; 紧〔緊〕迫的 jǐnpòde. **imminently** *adv*.

immobile /ɪ'məʊbaɪl; *US* -bl/ *adj* 固定的 gùdìngde; 不动〔動〕的 búdòngde. **immobility** /ˌɪmə'bɪlətɪ/ *n* [U]. **immobilize** /ɪ'məʊbəlaɪz/ *v* [T] 使不动 shǐ búdòng; 使固定 shǐ gùdìng. **immobilizer** *n* [C] (汽车防盗)止动装〔裝〕置 zhǐdòng zhuāngzhì.

immoral /ɪ'mɒrəl; *US* ɪ'mɔːrəl/ *adj* 1 不道德的 bú dàodé de; 邪恶〔惡〕的 xié'ède. 2 (在性问题上)不道德的 bú dàodé de. **immorality** /ˌɪmə'rælətɪ/ *n* [U].

immortal /ɪ'mɔːrtl/ *adj* 1 不死的 bùsǐde; 长〔長〕生的 chángshēngde. 2 不朽的 bùxiǔde; 流芳百世的 liúfāng bǎishì de. **immortal** *n* [C] 永生不朽者 yǒngshēng bùxiǔ zhě. **immortality** /ˌɪmɔː'tælətɪ/ *n* [U]. **immortalize** /-təlaɪz/ *v* [T] 使不朽 shǐ bùxiǔ: *~ized in a novel* 在一本小说中成为不朽的人物.

immune /ɪ'mjuːn/ *adj* 1 (*to / against*) 对〔對〕…有免疫力的 duì… yǒu miǎnyìlì de: *~ to smallpox* 对天花有免疫力. 2 (*to*) 不受影响〔響〕的 búshòu yǐngxiǎng de: *~ to criticism* 不为批评所动摇. **immunity** *n* [U]. **immunize** /'ɪmjʊnaɪz/ *v* [T] (*against*) 使对…有

I

免疫力 shǐ duì…yǒu miǎnyìlì. **immunization** /ˌɪmjʊnaɪˈzeɪʃn; *US* -nɪˈz- / *n* [U,C].

imp /ɪmp/ *n* [C] 1 小魔鬼 xiǎomóguǐ. 2 小淘气〔氣〕xiǎotáoqì; 顽童 wántóng.

impact /ˈɪmpækt/ *n* 1 [U] 碰撞 pèngzhuàng; 撞击〔擊〕zhuàngjī; 撞击力 zhuàngjīlì: *The bomb exploded on* ～. 炸弹一碰撞就爆炸了. 2 [C, 常作 sing] (*on*) (对…的)强烈影响〔響〕qiángliè yǐngxiǎng: *the* ～ *of computers on industry* 电子计算机对工业的影响. **impact** /ɪmˈpækt/ *v* [T] 挤〔擠〕满 jǐmǎn.

impair /ɪmˈpeə(r)/ *v* [T] 损害 sǔnhài; 削弱 xuēruò: *Loud noise can* ～ *your hearing*. 强烈的噪音会损害听力.

impale /ɪmˈpeɪl/ *v* [T] (*on*) (以尖物)刺穿 cìchuān, 刺住 cìzhù: ～*d on a spear* 用矛戳起的.

impart /ɪmˈpɑːt/ *v* [T] [正式用语]传〔傳〕授 chuánshòu; 告知 gàozhī.

impartial /ɪmˈpɑːʃl/ *adj* 公正的 gōngzhèngde; 公平的 gōngpíngde: *A judge must be* ～. 法官必须公正. **impartiality** /ˌɪmˌpɑːʃɪˈælətɪ/ *n* [U].

impassable /ɪmˈpɑːsəbl; *US* -ˈpæs-/ *adj* (道路等)不能通行的 bùnéng tōngxíng de.

impassioned /ɪmˈpæʃnd/ *adj* 充满热〔熱〕情的 chōngmǎn rèqíng de; 激动〔動〕的 jīdòngde: *an* ～ *appeal* 热情的呼吁.

impassive /ɪmˈpæsɪv/ *adj* 冷淡的 lěngdànde. **impassively** *adv*.

impatient /ɪmˈpeɪʃnt/ *adj* 1 不耐烦的 bú nàifán de; 急躁的 jízàode. 2 切望的 qièwàngde: ～ *to leave school* 迫不及待地要离开学校. **impatience** /ɪmˈpeɪʃns/ *n* [U]. **impatiently** *adv*.

impeccable /ɪmˈpekəbl/ *adj* 无〔無〕瑕疵的 wú xiácī de. **impeccably** *adv*.

impede /ɪmˈpiːd/ *v* [T] 妨碍〔礙〕fáng'ài; 阻碍 zǔ'ài.

impediment /ɪmˈpedɪmənt/ *n* [C] 1 障碍〔礙〕物 zhàng'àiwù. 2 残〔殘〕疾 cánjí; 口吃 kǒuchī.

impending /ɪmˈpendɪŋ/ *adj* 即将〔將〕发〔發〕生的 jíjiāng fāshēng de: ～ *disaster* 即将发生的灾祸.

impenetrable /ɪmˈpenɪtrəbl/ *adj* 1 穿不进〔進〕的 chuān bú jìn de; 刺不进的 cì bú jìn de. 2 费解的 fèijiěde; 不能理解的 bùnéng lǐjiě de.

imperative /ɪmˈperətɪv/ *adj* 紧〔緊〕急的 jǐnjíde; 必要的 bìyàode. **imperative** *n* [C] [语法] 祈使语气〔氣〕qíshǐyǔqì. **imperatively** *adv*.

imperfect /ɪmˈpɜːfɪkt/ *adj* 不完整的 bù wánzhěng de; 不完美的 bù wánměi de. **imperfect** *n* the imperfect [sing] [语法]未完成过〔過〕去时〔時〕(动词) wèiwánchéng guòqùshí. **imperfection** /ˌɪmpəˈfekʃn/ *n* 1 [U] 不完美 bù wánměi. 2 [C] 缺点〔點〕quēdiǎn; 瑕疵 xiácī. **imperfectly** *adv*.

imperial /ɪmˈpɪərɪəl/ *adj* 帝国〔國〕的 dìguóde; 皇帝的 huángdìde. **imperialism** *n* [U] 帝国主义〔義〕dìguózhǔyì. **imperialist** *n* [C], *adj*. **imperially** *adv*.

impersonal /ˌɪmˈpɜːsənl/ *adj* 1 不受个〔個〕人感情影响〔響〕的 búshòu gèrén gǎnqíng yǐngxiǎng de; 没有人情味的 méiyǒu rénqíngwèi de: *a large* ～ *organization* 一个庞大的没有人情味的组织. 2 不特指某个人的 bú tèzhǐ mǒugèrén de. **impersonally** /-nəlɪ/ *adv*.

impersonate /ɪmˈpɜːsəneɪt/ *v* [T] 假冒(某人) jiǎmào. **impersonation** /ɪmˌpɜːsəˈneɪʃn/ *n* [C, U].

impertinent /ɪmˈpɜːtɪnənt/ *adj* 不礼〔禮〕貌的 bù lǐmào de; 不客气〔氣〕的 bú kèqi de. **impertinence** /-nəns/ *n* [U, sing]. **impertinently** *adv*.

impervious /ɪmˈpɜːvɪəs/ *adj* (*to*) 1 (材料)透不过〔過〕的 tòubúguòde; 穿不过的 chuānbúguòde. 2 [喻]无〔無〕动〔動〕于衷的 wú dòng yú zhōng de; 不受影响〔響〕的 búshòu yǐngxiǎng de: ～ *to criticism* 对批评无动于衷.

impetuous /ɪmˈpetʃʊəs/ *adj* 鲁莽的 lǔmǎngde; 轻〔輕〕举〔舉〕妄动〔動〕的 qīng jǔ wàng dòng de.

impetus /ˈɪmpɪtəs/ *n* 1 [U, sing] 促进〔進〕cùjìn; 推动〔動〕tuīdòng; 激励〔勵〕jīlì: *give a fresh* ～ *to trade* 进一步推进贸易. 2 [U] 动力 dònglì; 推动力 tuīdònglì.

impinge /ɪmˈpɪndʒ/ *v* [I] *on* [正式用语]起作用 qǐ zuòyòng; 影响〔響〕yǐngxiǎng.

implacable /ɪmˈplækəbl/ *adj* 不变〔變〕的 búbiànde; 不能安抚〔撫〕的 bùnéng ānfǔ de.

implant /ɪmˈplɑːnt; *US* -ˈplænt/ *v* [T] (*in* /*into*) 灌输 guànshū; 使树〔樹〕立 shǐ shùlì: ～ *ideas in sb's mind* 给某人灌输思想.

implement[1] /ˈɪmplɪment/ *v* [T] 贯彻〔徹〕guànchè; 履行 lǚxíng. **implementation** /ˌɪmplɪmenˈteɪʃn/ *n* [U].

implement[2] /ˈɪmplɪmənt/ *n* [C] 工具 gōngjù; 器具 qìjù.

implicate /ˈɪmplɪkeɪt/ *v* [T] (*in*) 使(某人)牵〔牽〕连于罪行之中 shǐ qiānlián yú zuìxíng zhī zhōng.

implication /ˌɪmplɪˈkeɪʃn/ *n* 1 [C, U] 暗示 ànshì; 含意 hányì. 2 [U] 牵〔牽〕连(于罪行) qiānlián.

implicit /ɪmˈplɪsɪt/ *adj* 1 暗示的 ànshìde; 含蓄的 hánxùde. 2 无〔無〕疑的 wúyíde; 无保留的

wú bǎoliú de: ~ *trust* 无保留的信任. **implicitly** *adv*.

implore /ɪmˈplɔː(r)/ *v* [T] 恳〔懇〕求 kěnqiú; 乞求 qǐqiú: *They ~d her to stay*. 他们恳求她留下来不要走. **imploringly** *adv*.

imply /ɪmˈplaɪ/ *v* [*pt*, *pp* -ied] [T] **1** 暗示 ànshì; 含有…的意思 hán yǒu…de yìsi: *Are you ~ing that I stole your watch?* 你的意思是我偷了你的手表? **2** 必然包含 bìrán bāohán.

impolite /ˌɪmpəˈlaɪt/ *adj* 不客气〔氣〕的 bú kèqi de. **impolitely** *adv*. **impoliteness** *n* [U].

import /ɪmˈpɔːt/ *v* [T] 进〔進〕口 jìnkǒu. **import** /ˈɪmpɔːt/ *n* **1** [U] 进口 jìnkǒu; 进口生意 jìnkǒu shēngyì. **2** 进口货 jìnkǒuhuò. **3** [U] [正式用语] 重要(性) zhòngyào. **importation** /ˌɪmpɔːˈteɪʃn/ *n* [U, C]. **importer** *n* [C] 进口商 jìnkǒushāng.

important /ɪmˈpɔːtnt/ *adj* **1** 重要的 zhòngyàode; 重大的 zhòngdàde: *an ~ decision* 重要的决定. **2** (人)有权〔權〕力的 yǒu quánlì de. **importance** /-tns/ *n* [U]. **importantly** *adv*.

impose /ɪmˈpəʊz/ *v* **1** [T] (*on*) 征〔徵〕(税等) zhēng. **2** [T] (*on*) 把…强加于 bǎ…qiángjiā yú. **3** [短语动词] **impose on sb** 占〔佔〕…的便宜 zhàn…de piányi. **imposing** *adj* 壮〔壯〕丽〔麗〕的 zhuànglìde; 堂皇的 tánghuángde. **imposition** /ˌɪmpəˈzɪʃn/ *n* [U, C].

impossible /ɪmˈpɒsəbl/ *adj* **1** 不可能的 bù kěnéng de. **2** 无〔無〕法忍受的 wúfǎ rěnshòu de: *an ~ situation* 不能忍受的局面. **impossibility** /ɪmˌpɒsəˈbɪlətɪ/ *n* [U, C]. **impossibly** *adv*.

impostor /ɪmˈpɒstə(r)/ *n* [C] 冒名顶替者 màomíng dǐngtìzhě.

impotent /ˈɪmpətənt/ *adj* **1** 无〔無〕力的 wúlìde; 软〔軟〕弱无能的 ruǎnruò wúnéng de. **2** [医学] 阳〔陽〕萎的 yángwěide. **impotence** /-təns/ *n* [U].

impound /ɪmˈpaʊnd/ *v* [T] 没收 mòshōu.

impoverish /ɪmˈpɒvərɪʃ/ *v* [T] 使穷〔窮〕困 shǐ qióngkùn.

impracticable /ɪmˈpræktɪkəbl/ *adj* 不能实〔實〕行的 bùnéng shíxíng de; 行不通的 xíngbùtōngde.

impractical /ɪmˈpræktɪkl/ *adj* 不现实〔實〕的 bú xiànshí de; 不切实际〔際〕的 bú qiè shíjì de.

imprecise /ˌɪmprɪˈsaɪs/ *adj* 不精确〔確〕的 bù jīngquè de; 不准〔準〕确的 bù zhǔnquè de.

impregnable /ɪmˈpregnəbl/ *adj* 坚〔堅〕不可摧的 jiān bù kě cuī de: *an ~ fort* 坚不可摧的堡垒.

impregnate /ˈɪmpregneɪt; *US* ɪmˈpreg-/ *v* [T] 灌注 guànzhù; 浸透 jìntòu: *cloth ~d with perfume* 浸过香水的布.

impresario /ˌɪmprɪˈsɑːrɪəʊ/ *n* [C] [*pl* ~s] (歌舞剧团等的)经〔經〕理 jīnglǐ.

impress /ɪmˈpres/ *v* [T] **1** 使钦佩 shǐ qīnpèi: *Her honesty ~ed me*. 我钦佩她的诚实. **2** *on* 使铭记 shǐ míngjì: ~ *on him the importance of hard work* 使他铭记努力工作的重要. **3** 印 yìn; 盖〔蓋〕印 gàiyìn.

impression /ɪmˈpreʃn/ *n* [C] **1** 印象 yìnxiàng: *create a good ~* 创造一个好的印象. **2** (不清晰的)想法 xiǎngfǎ; 感觉〔覺〕gǎnjué: *My general ~ was that she seemed a nice woman*. 我的总的感觉是她似乎是一个很好的女人. **3** (对某人言谈举止的)滑稽的模仿〔倣〕huájīde mófǎng. **4** 印记 yìnjì; 压〔壓〕痕 yāhén. **5** [习语] **be under the impression that...** 有…(通常为错误的)想法 yǒu…xiǎngfǎ. **impressionable** /-ʃənəbl/ *adj* 易受影响〔響〕的 yìshòu yǐngxiǎng de. **impressionism** /-ʃənɪzəm/ *n* [U] (绘画的)印象主义〔義〕yìnxiàngzhǔyì; 印象派 yìnxiàngpài.

impressive /ɪmˈpresɪv/ *adj* 感人的 gǎnrénde; 给人深刻印象的 gěi rén shēnkè yìnxiàng de; 令人钦佩的 lìng rén qīnpèi de. *an ~ building* 给人印象深刻的建筑物. **impressively** *adv*.

imprint /ɪmˈprɪnt/ *v* [T] 印 yìn; 铭刻 míngkè: [喻] *details ~ed on his memory* 他所记得的详情. **imprint** /ˈɪmprɪnt/ *n* [C] **1** 印 yìn; 印记 yìnjì. **2** [喻] 持久的影响〔響〕chíjiǔde yǐngxiǎng.

imprison /ɪmˈprɪzn/ *v* [T] 监〔監〕禁 jiānjìn; 关〔關〕押 guānyā. **imprisonment** *n* [U].

improbable /ɪmˈprɒbəbl/ *adj* 不大可能的 bú dà kěnéng de; 不大可能是真的 bú dà kěnéng shì zhēn de. **improbability** /ɪmˌprɒbəˈbɪlətɪ/ *n* [C, U] [*pl* -ies]. **improbably** *adv*.

impromptu /ɪmˈprɒmptjuː; *US* -tuː/ *adj*, *adv* 无〔無〕准〔準〕备〔備〕的(地) wú zhǔnbèi de; 即兴〔興〕的(地) jíxìngde: *an ~ speech* 即席演讲.

improper /ɪmˈprɒpə(r)/ *adj* **1** 不正确〔確〕的 bú zhèngquè de: ~ *use of a word/drug* 用字(药)不正确. **2** 不适〔適〕当〔當〕的 bú shìdàng de; 不合适的 bù héshì de: ~ *behaviour* 不适当的举止. ~ *dress* 不适当的衣服. **3** 不道德的 bú dàodé de; 不正派的 bú zhèngpài de; 不合礼〔禮〕仪〔儀〕的 bùhé lǐyí de: *make ~ suggestions* 提出不礼貌的建议. **improperly** *adv*.

improve /ɪmˈpruːv/ *v* [I, T] 改进〔進〕gǎijìn; 改善 gǎishàn. **improvement** *n* **1** [C, U] 改进

gǎijìn;改良 gǎiliáng. 2 [C] 改进措施 gǎijìn cuòshī;(改进某事物所作的)修改 xiūgǎi: *home ~ments* 住宅装修.

improvise /ˈɪmprəvaɪz/ *v* [I, T] 1 临〔臨〕时〔時〕凑成 línshí còuchéng. 2 即席创〔創〕作 jíxí chuàngzuò;即席演奏 jíxí yǎnzòu. **improvisation** /ˌɪmprəvaɪˈzeɪʃn / *n* [U, C].

impudent /ˈɪmpjʊdənt/ *adj* 厚颜无〔無〕耻的 hòuyán wúchǐ de. **impudence** /-əns/ *n* [U]. **impudently** *adv*.

impulse /ˈɪmpʌls/ *n* 1 [C, U] 冲〔衝〕动〔動〕chōngdòng. 2 冲力 chōnglì; 推力 tuīlì: *an electrical ~* 电脉冲 diànmàichōng. 3 [习语] **on impulse** 一时〔時〕冲动 yìshí chōngdòng.

impulsive /ɪmˈpʌlsɪv/ *adj* 凭〔憑〕感情冲〔衝〕动〔動〕行事的 píng gǎnqíng chōngdòng xíngshì de. **impulsively** *adv*. **impulsiveness** *n* [U].

impunity /ɪmˈpjuːnətɪ/ *n* [习语] **with impunity** 不受惩〔懲〕罚 búshòu chéngfá.

impure /ɪmˈpjʊə(r)/ *adj* 1 不纯的 bùchúnde. 2 [旧]不道德的 bú dàodé de. **impurity** *n* [C, U] [*pl* -ies].

in[1] /ɪn/ *adv* 1 (指位置)进〔進〕jìn;入 rù: *He opened the bedroom door and went in.* 他打开卧室的门走了进去. 2 在家里〔裡〕zài jiālǐ;在工作处〔處〕所 zài gōngzuò chùsuǒ: *Nobody was in when we called.* 我们打过电话可屋里没有人. 3 (火车、公共汽车等)在站里 zài zhànlǐ. 4 (海潮)上涨〔漲〕或处〔處〕于最高点〔點〕shàngzhǎng huò chǔyú zuìgāodiǎn. 5 收到 shōudào: *Competition entries should be in by 31 May.* 参赛者名单须在5月31日前交来. 6 流行 liúxíng;时〔時〕兴〔興〕shíxīng: *Miniskirts are in again.* 超短裙又流行了. 7 当〔當〕选〔選〕dāngxuǎn;执〔執〕政 zhízhèng: *Labour came in after the war.* 战后工党执政. 8 [体育] (a) 轮〔輪〕到击〔擊〕球 lúndào jīqiú. (b) (球)在界内 zài jiènèi. 9 [习语] **be in for sth** [非正式用语]注定要遭受 zhùdìng yào zāoshòu. **be/get in on sth** [非正式用语]参〔參〕与〔與〕某事 cānyǔ mǒushì. **be (well) ˈin with sb** [非正式用语]与某人(非常)友好 yǔ mǒurén yǒuhǎo. **have (got) it ˈin for sb** [非正式用语]伺机〔機〕报〔報〕复〔復〕某人 sìjī bàofù mǒurén. **in-** *adj* 1 [非正式用语]流行的 liúxíngde;时髦的 shímáode: *the in-thing* 时髦的事情. *the in-place* 众人喜欢的地方. 2 小圈子里〔裡〕的 xiǎoquānzǐ lǐ de: *an in-joke* 小圈子里的笑话.

in[2] /ɪn/ *prep* 1 (表示地点)在…里〔裡〕面 zài…lǐmiàn;在…之内 zài…zhī nèi: *Rome is in Italy.* 罗马在意大利. *play in the street* 在街上玩. *lying in bed* 躺在床上. *a pen in his pocket* 他口袋里的一支笔. 2 (表示运动)入…中 rù…zhōng: *Throw it in the fire.* 把它扔到火里. 3 在(一段时间) zài: *in June* 在六月. 4 过〔過〕…之久 guò…zhī jiǔ: *Lunch will be ready in an hour.* 过一个小时午饭就准备好了. 5 构〔構〕成(某事物的)整体〔體〕或部分 gòuchéng zhěngtǐ huò bùfen: *seven days in a week* 七天是一星期. 6 (表示比率)…比… …bǐ…: *a slope of 1 in 5* 一比五的坡度. 7 穿…衣服的 chuān…yīfu de: *the woman in white* 白衣女人. 8 (表示环境): *go out in the cold* 冒着寒冷外出. 9 (表示状态、情况): *in a mess* 乱七八糟. *in love* 相爱. 10 (表示形式、安排等): *a story in three parts* 由三部分组成的故事. 11 (表示媒体、手段等): *speak in English* 说英语. *write in ink* 用墨水写. 12 在…方面 zài…fāngmiàn: *lacking in courage* 缺乏勇气. *3 metres in length* 长三米. 13 (表示某人的职业): *a career in journalism* 新闻生涯. 14 [习语] **in that** 因为〔爲〕yīnwèi: *The chemical is dangerous in that it can kill.* 化学物品是危险的因为它能致命.

in[3] /ɪn/ *n* [习语] **the ins and outs** 详情 xiángqíng;细节〔節〕xìjié.

inability /ˌɪnəˈbɪlətɪ/ *n* [U] (*to*) 无〔無〕技能 wú jìnéng; 无力量 wú lìliàng.

inaccessible /ˌɪnækˈsesəbl/ *adj* 达〔達〕不到的 dá búdào de;难〔難〕接近的 nán jiējìn de;难得到的 nán dédào de.

inaccurate /ɪˈnækjərət/ *adj* 不正确〔確〕的 bú zhèngquè de. **inaccuracy** /-jərəsɪ/ *n* [U, C] [*pl* -ies]. **inaccurately** *adv*.

inadequate /ɪnˈædɪkwət/ *adj* 不够格的 bú gòugé de:不能胜〔勝〕任的 bùnéng shèngrèn de. **inadequately** *adv*.

inadmissible /ˌɪnədˈmɪsəbl/ *adj* (法律上)不许可的 bù xǔkě de: *~ evidence* 不能承认的证据.

inadvertent /ˌɪnədˈvɜːtənt/ *adj* [正式用语]不经〔經〕心的 bù jīngxīn de;因疏忽造成的 yīn shūhū zàochéng de. **inadvertently** *adv*.

inalienable /ɪnˈeɪlɪənəbl/ *adj* [正式用语]不可剥夺〔奪〕的 bùkě bōduó de;不可让〔讓〕与〔與〕的 bùkě ràngyǔ de.

inane /ɪˈneɪn/ *adj* 愚蠢的 yúchǔnde. **inanely** *adv*.

inanimate /ɪnˈænɪmət/ *adj* 无〔無〕生命的 wú shēngmìng de: *A rock is an ~ object.* 岩石是无生命的东西.

inapplicable /ɪnˈæplɪkəbl, 亦作 ˌɪnəˈplɪkəbl/ *adj* (*to*) 不适〔適〕用的 bú shìyòng de.

inappropriate /ˌɪnəˈprəʊprɪət/ *adj* 不适〔適〕当〔當〕的 bú shìdàng de. **inappropriately** *adv*.

inapt /ɪnˈæpt/ *adj* 不适〔適〕当〔當〕的 bú shìdàng de;不合适的 bù héshì de: *~ remarks*

不适当的话.

inarticulate /ˌɪnɑːˈtɪkjʊlət/ *adj* 1 口齿〔齒〕不清的 kǒuchǐ bùqīng de. 2 (话语)没有表达〔達〕清楚的 méiyǒu biǎodá qīngchǔ de.

inasmuch as /ˌɪnəzˈmʌtʃ əz/ *conj* [正式用语]在…的范〔範〕围〔圍〕内 zài…de fànwéi nèi; 由于 yóuyú; 因为〔爲〕yīnwèi.

inaudible /ɪnˈɔːdəbl/ *adj* (声音)听〔聽〕不见的 tīng bú jiàn de.

inaugural /ɪˈnɔːgjʊrəl/ *adj* 就职〔職〕的 jiùzhíde; 开〔開〕幕的 kāimùde; 开始的 kāishǐde: *an* ～ *speech* 就职(开幕)演说.

inaugurate /ɪˈnɔːgjʊreɪt/ *v* [T] 1 为〔爲〕…举〔舉〕行就职〔職〕典礼〔禮〕wèi…jǔxíng jiùzhí diǎnlǐ. 2 为(展览会等)揭幕 wèi jiēmù. 3 开〔開〕创〔創〕kāichuàng. **inauguration** /ɪˌnɔːgjʊˈreɪʃn/ *n* [C,U].

inborn /ˌɪnˈbɔːn/ *adj* 生来的 shēngláide.

in-box /ˌɪnˈbɒks/ *n* [C] 收件箱 shōujiànxiāng.

inbred /ˌɪnˈbred/ *adj* 1 生来的 shēngláide. 2 近亲〔親〕繁殖的 jìnqīn fánzhí de. **inbreeding** /ˈɪnbriːdɪŋ/ *n* [U] 近亲繁殖 jìnqīn fánzhí.

in-built /ˌɪnˈbɪlt/ *adj* ⇨ BUILT-IN (BUILD).

Inc /ɪŋk/ *abbr* [美语] Incorporated 股份有限公司 gǔfèn yǒuxiàn gōngsī.

incalculable /ɪnˈkælkjʊləbl/ *adj* 无〔無〕数〔數〕的 wúshùde; 数不清的 shǔ bùqīng de.

incapable /ɪnˈkeɪpəbl/ *adj of* 无〔無〕能力的 wú nénglì de; 不会〔會〕的 búhuìde. 不能的 bùnéngde: ～ *of telling a lie* 不会说谎.

incapacitate /ˌɪnkəˈpæsɪteɪt/ *v* [T] 使无〔無〕能力 shǐ wú nénglì. **incapacity** /-sətɪ/ *n* [U] 无能力 wú nénglì.

incarcerate /ɪnˈkɑːsəreɪt/ *v* [T] [正式用语] 监〔監〕禁 jiānjìn. **incarceration** /ɪnˌkɑːsəˈreɪʃn/ *n* [U].

incarnation /ˌɪnkɑːˈneɪʃn/ *n* 1 [C] (象征某种品质的)典型人物 diǎnxíng rénwù; 化身 huàshēn. 2 (神灵等的)化身 huàshēn.

incendiary /ɪnˈsendɪərɪ; *US* -dɪerɪ/ *adj* 1 引起燃烧〔燒〕的 yǐnqǐ ránshāo de: *an* ～ *bomb* 燃烧弹. 2 煽动〔動〕性的 shāndòngxìngde: *an* ～ *speech* 煽动性的演说. **incendiary** *n* [C] [*pl* -ies] 燃烧弹〔彈〕ránshāodàn.

incense[1] /ˈɪnsens/ *n* [U] (点燃用的)香 xiāng.

incense[2] /ɪnˈsens/ *v* [T] 激怒 jīnù; 触〔觸〕怒 chùnù.

incentive /ɪnˈsentɪv/ *n* [C,U] (*to*) 激励某人做某事的事物 jīlì mǒurén zuò mǒushì de shìwù.

incessant /ɪnˈsesnt/ *adj* 连续〔續〕的 liánxùde; 不停的 bùtíngde. **incessantly** *adv*.

incest /ˈɪnsest/ *n* [U] 乱〔亂〕伦〔倫〕luànlún. **incestuous** /ɪnˈsestjʊəs; *US* -tʃʊəs/ *adj*.

inch /ɪntʃ/ *n* [C] 1 英寸 yīngcùn. 2 少量 shǎoliàng, 一点〔點〕点 yìdiǎndiǎn: *He escaped death by an* ～. 他差一点儿死了. 3 [习语] **every inch** 在各方面 zài gèfāngmiàn; 完全 wánquán; 彻〔徹〕底 chèdǐ. **within an inch of sth** 差一点儿〔兒〕chà yīdiǎnr. **inch** *v* [短语动词] **inch (sth) forward, past, etc** 使缓慢地移动〔動〕shǐ huǎnmànde yídòng.

incidence /ˈɪnsɪdəns/ *n* [C] 发〔發〕生率 fāshēnglǜ; 发生的方式 fāshēngde fāngshì: *a high* ～ *of crime* 犯罪的高发生率.

incident /ˈɪnsɪdənt/ *n* [C] 1 事情 shìqing; 小事 xiǎoshì. 2 事件 shìjiàn; 事变〔變〕shìbiàn: *border* ～*s* 边境事件.

incidental /ˌɪnsɪˈdentl/ *adj* 1 零星的 língxīngde; 次要的 cìyàode: ～ *expenses* 杂费. 2 伴随〔隨〕的 bànsuíde: ～ *music for a film* 电影配乐. **incidentally** /-tlɪ/ *adv* (为了引导刚刚想起要说的一件事)顺便说一下 shùnbiàn shuō yíxià.

incinerate /ɪnˈsɪnəreɪt/ *v* [T] 把…烧〔燒〕成灰 bǎ…shāochéng huī; 焚化 fénhuà. **incineration** /ɪnˌsɪnəˈreɪʃn/ *n* [U]. **incinerator** *n* [C] 焚化炉〔爐〕fénhuàlú.

incipient /ɪnˈsɪpɪənt/ *adj* [正式用语]开〔開〕始的 kāishǐde; 早期的 zǎoqīde.

incision /ɪnˈsɪʒn/ *n* 1 [C] (尤指开刀后的)切口 qiēkǒu. 2 [U] 切开〔開〕qiēkāi; 切入 qiērù.

incisive /ɪnˈsaɪsɪv/ *adj* 尖锐的 jiānruìde; 直接的 zhíjiēde: ～ *questions* 尖锐的问题. **incisively** *adv*.

incisor /ɪnˈsaɪzə(r)/ *n* [C] 门牙 ményá.

incite /ɪnˈsaɪt/ *v* [T] 1 激励〔勵〕jīlì; 煽动〔動〕shāndòng: ～ *workers to riot* 煽动工人骚乱. 2 制〔製〕造 zhìzào; 引起 yǐnqǐ: ～ *violence* 制造暴力事件. **incitement** *n* [U,C].

inclination /ˌɪnklɪˈneɪʃn/ *n* 1 [C,U] 倾向 qīngxiàng; 爱〔愛〕好 àihào: *I have no* ～ *to leave*. 我不想离开. 2 [C] 趋〔趨〕势〔勢〕qūshì. 3 [U] 倾角 qīngjiǎo; 斜角 xiéjiǎo.

incline[1] /ɪnˈklaɪn/ *v* 1 [I] *towards* 倾斜 qīngxié. 2 [T] 屈身 qūshēn; 低头〔頭〕dītóu. 3 [T] *towards* [正式用语]说服(某人)做某事 shuōfú zuò mǒushì; 影响〔響〕yǐngxiǎng. 4 [I] *to/towards* [正式用语]倾向于 qīngxiàng yú; 喜欢〔歡〕xǐhuān: *He* ～*s to laziness*. 他爱懒散. **inclined** *adj* (*to*) 1 想以某种方式行事 xiǎngyǐ mǒuzhǒng fāngshì xíngshì. 2 倾向于…的 qīngxiàng yú…de: *She's* ～*d to be depressed*. 她老爱郁郁寡欢.

incline[2] /ˈɪnklaɪn/ *n* [C] 斜坡 xiépō.

include /ɪnˈkluːd/ *v* [T] 1 包括 bāokuò; 包含 bāohán: *Prices* ～ *delivery*. 价钱包括送货. 2 使成为〔爲〕整体〔體〕的一部分 shǐ chéngwéi

I

zhěngtǐde yíbùfen: ~ *Chris in the team* 把克雷斯吸收到队里. **inclusion** /ɪnˈkluːʒn/ *n* [U]. **inclusive** /ɪnˈkluːsɪv/ *adj* 一切包括在内的 yíqiè bāokuò zàinèide.

incognito /ˌɪnkɒgˈniːtəʊ; *US* ɪŋˈkɒgnətəʊ/ *adj, adv* 化名的(地) huàmíngde: *travel* ~ 化名旅行.

incoherent /ˌɪnkəʊˈhɪərənt/ *adj* 语无〔無〕伦〔倫〕次的 yǔ wú lúncì de; 难〔難〕懂的 nándǒngde. **incoherence** /-əns/ *n* [U]. **incoherently** *adv*.

income /ˈɪnkʌm/ *n* [C, U] 收入 shōurù; 所得 suǒdé. ˈ**income tax** *n* [U] 所得税 suǒdéshuì.

incoming /ˈɪnkʌmɪŋ/ *adj* 1 进〔進〕来的 jìnláide: ~ *mail* 进来的邮件. 2 新当〔當〕选的 xīn dāngxuǎnde; 新任命的 xīn rènmìngde: *the* ~ *president* 新当选的总统.

incomparable /ɪnˈkɒmprəbl/ *adj* (好、大等)无〔無〕比的 wúbǐde.

incompatible /ˌɪnkəmˈpætəbl/ *adj* 不相容的 bù xiāngróng de; 不能共存的 bùnéng gòngcún de: *Smoking is* ~ *with good health*. 吸烟与健康不相容. **incompatibility** /ˌɪŋkəmˌpætəˈbɪlətɪ/ *n* [U].

incompetent /ɪnˈkɒmpɪtənt/ *adj* 不胜〔勝〕任的 bú shèngrèn de; 不够格的 bú gòugé de. **incompetence** /-əns/ *n* [U].

incomplete /ˌɪnkəmˈpliːt/ *adj* 不完全的 bù wánquán de; 不完善的 bù wánshàn de. **incompletely** *adv*.

incomprehensible /ˌɪnˌkɒmprɪˈhensəbl/ *adj* 不能理解的 bùnéng lǐjiě de. **incomprehension** /-ˈhenʃn/ *n* [U] 不理解 bù lǐjiě.

inconceivable /ˌɪnkənˈsiːvəbl/ *adj* 1 [非正式用语]难〔難〕以相信的 nányǐ xiāngxìn de. 2 不能想像的 bùnéng xiǎngxiàng de.

inconclusive /ˌɪnkənˈkluːsɪv/ *adj* 非结论〔論〕性 fēi jiélùnxìng de; 无〔無〕最后〔後〕结果的 wú zuìhòu jiéguǒ de: ~ *evidence* 无说服力的证据.

incongruous /ɪnˈkɒŋgrʊəs/ *adj* 不适〔適〕宜的 bú shìyí de; 不协〔協〕调的 bù xiétiáo de: *Modern buildings look* ~ *in an old village*. 现代化的建筑与古老的农村看上去很不协调. **incongruity** /ˌɪŋkɒŋˈgruːətɪ/ *n* [U, C] [*pl* -ies].

inconsiderate /ˌɪnkənˈsɪdərət/ *adj* 不替别人着想的 bútì biérén zhuóxiǎng de; 不体〔體〕谅别人的 bù tǐliàng biérén de. **inconsiderately** *adv*.

inconsistent /ˌɪnkənˈsɪstənt/ *adj* (*with*) 矛盾的 máodùnde; 不协〔協〕调的 bù xiétiáo de; 反复〔復〕无〔無〕常的 fǎnfù wúcháng de. **inconsistency** /-tənsɪ/ *n* [C, U] [*pl* -ies]. **inconsistently** *adv*.

inconspicuous /ˌɪnkənˈspɪkjʊəs/ *adj* 不显〔顯〕著的 bù xiǎnzhù de; 不引人注意的 bù yǐnrén zhùyì de. **inconspicuously** *adv*.

incontinent /ɪnˈkɒntɪnənt/ *adj* (大小便)失禁的 shījìnde. **incontinence** /-nəns/ *n* [U].

incontrovertible /ˌɪŋkɒntrəˈvɜːtəbl/ *adj* 无〔無〕可否认〔認〕的 wúkě fǒurèn de.

inconvenience /ˌɪnkənˈviːnɪəns/ *n* [C, U] 不方便 bù fāngbiàn; 烦扰〔擾〕fánrǎo; 不方便之事 bù fāngbiàn zhī shì. **inconvenience** *v* [T] 打扰 dǎrǎo; 使感到不方便 shǐ gǎndào bù fāngbiàn. **inconvenient** /-ənt/ *adj* 不方便的 bù fāngbiàn de. **inconveniently** *adv*.

incorporate /ɪnˈkɔːpəreɪt/ *v* [T] 使并〔併〕入 shǐ bìngrù; 包含 bāohán; 吸收 xīshōu: ~ *your ideas in the new plan* 把你的想法吸收到新的计划中. **incorporated** *adj* [美语]组成公司的 zǔchéng gōngsī de; 组成社团〔團〕的 zǔchéng shètuán de. **incorporation** /ɪnˌkɔːpəˈreɪʃn/ *n* [U].

incorrect /ˌɪnkəˈrekt/ *adj* 不正确〔確〕的 bú zhèngquè de; 错误的 cuòwùde. **incorrectly** *adv*. **incorrectness** *n* [U].

incorrigible /ɪnˈkɒrɪdʒəbl; *US* -ˈkɔːr-/ *adj* (人)不可救药〔藥〕的 bùkě jiùyào de; (毛病)难〔難〕以改正的 nányǐ gǎizhèng de.

increase[1] /ɪnˈkriːs/ *v* [I, T] 增加 zēngjiā; 增长〔長〕zēngzhǎng. **increasingly** *adv* 愈来愈 yù lái yù; 日益 rìyì: *increasingly difficult* 愈来愈困难.

increase[2] /ˈɪnkriːs/ *n* [C, U] 增加量 zēngjiāliàng.

incredible /ɪnˈkredəbl/ *adj* 1 难〔難〕以置信的 nányǐ zhìxìn de. 2 [非正式用语]惊〔驚〕人的 jīngrénde. **incredibly** *adv*.

incredulous /ɪnˈkredjʊləs; *US* -dʒuːl/ *adj* 不相信的 bù xiāngxìn de; 表示怀〔懷〕疑的 biǎoshì huáiyí de. **incredulity** /ˌɪŋkrɪˈdjuːlətɪ; *US* -ˈduː-/ *n* [U]. **incredulously** *adv*.

increment /ˈɪnkrəmənt/ *n* [C] 增值 zēngzhí; (薪金等的)增额 zēng'é.

incriminate /ɪnˈkrɪmɪneɪt/ *v* [T] 控告 kònggào; 显〔顯〕示(某人)有罪 xiǎnshì yǒuzuì.

incubate /ˈɪnkjʊbeɪt/ *v* [I, T] 孵(卵) fū; 孵化 fūhuà. **incubation** /ˌɪnkjʊˈbeɪʃn/ *n* 1 [U] 孵卵 fūluǎn; 孵化 fūhuà. 2 [C] (亦作 **incubation period**) [医](传染病的)潜〔潛〕伏期 qiánfúqī. **incubator** *n* [C] 1 孵化器 fūhuàqì. 2 早产〔產〕婴儿〔兒〕保育箱 zǎochǎn yīng'ér bǎoyùxiāng.

incumbent /ɪnˈkʌmbənt/ *adj on* [正式用语]负有责任的 fùyǒu zérèn de; 义〔義〕不容辞〔辭〕的 yì bù róng cí de. **incumbent** *n* [C] 任职〔職〕者 rènzhízhě.

I

incur /ɪnˈkɜː(r)/ *v* [-rr-] [T] 招致 zhāozhì; 遭受 zāoshòu: ~ *large debts* 负债累累.

incurable /ɪnˈkjʊərəbl/ *adj* 医〔醫〕不好的 yī bùhǎo de. **incurable** *n* [C] 医不好的病人 yī bùhǎo de bìngrén. **incurably** *adv*.

incursion /ɪnˈkɜːʃn; *US* -ʒn/ *n* [C] [正式用语]突然袭〔襲〕击〔擊〕 tūrán xíjī; 入侵 rùqīn; 侵犯 qīnfàn.

indebted /ɪnˈdetɪd/ *adj* 蒙恩的 méng'ēnde; 感激的 gǎnjīde: ~ *to him for his help* 很感激他的帮助.

indecent /ɪnˈdiːsnt/ *adj* 1 下流的 xiàliúde; 粗鄙的 cūbǐde; 猥亵的 wěixiède. 2 不合适〔適〕的 bù héshì de; 不对〔對〕的 búduìde. **indecency** /-nsɪ/ *n* [U]. **indecently** *adv*.

indecision /ˌɪndɪˈsɪʒn/ *n* [U] 优〔優〕柔寡断〔斷〕 yōuróu guǎduàn; 犹〔猶〕豫 yóuyù.

indecisive /ˌɪndɪˈsaɪsɪv/ *adj* 1 优〔優〕柔寡断〔斷〕的 yōuróu guǎduàn de. 2 非决定性的 fēi juédìngxìng de. **indecisively** *adv*.

indeed /ɪnˈdiːd/ *adv* 1 真正地 zhēnzhèngde; 当〔當〕然 dāngrán: '*Did he complain?*' '*I~ he did.*' "他埋怨了吗?" "他当然埋怨了." 2 (与 very 连用, 以加强语气) 确〔確〕实〔實〕 quèshí; 实在 shízài: *Thank you very much ~.* 确实非常感谢你. 3 (表示惊讶、兴趣)哦! ó!: '*She thinks she got the job.*' '*Does she ~!*' "她认为她得到了这个工作." "哦!"

indefensible /ˌɪndɪˈfensəbl/ *adj* 无〔無〕法防御〔禦〕的 wúfǎ fángyù de; 无法辩护〔護〕的 wúfǎ biànhù de: ~ *rudeness* 无可辩解的粗暴表现.

indefinable /ˌɪndɪˈfaɪnəbl/ *adj* 难〔難〕下定义〔義〕的 nánxià dìngyì de; 难以用言语表达〔達〕的 nányǐ yòng yányǔ biǎodá de.

indefinite /ɪnˈdefɪnət/ *adj* 1 模糊的 móhude; 不明确〔確〕的 bù míngquè de. 2 无〔無〕定限的 wú dìngxiàn de: *an ~ period of time* 一段长短不确定的时间. **inˌdefinite ˈarticle** *n* [C] [语法]不定冠词 búdìngguàncí. **indefinitely** *adv*: *The meeting was postponed ~ly.* 会议无限期推迟.

indelible /ɪnˈdeləbl/ *adj* 去不掉的 qùbúdiàode; 擦不掉的 cābúdiàode. **indelibly** *adv*.

indelicate /ɪnˈdelɪkət/ *adj* [正式用语, 常作委婉]不文雅的 bù wényǎ de; 粗野的 cūyěde; 令人窘迫的 lìng rén jiǒngpò de.

indemnify /ɪnˈdemnɪfaɪ/ *v* [*pt*, *pp* -ied] [T] 赔偿〔償〕 péicháng; 补〔補〕偿 bǔcháng.

indemnity /ɪnˈdemnətɪ/ *n* [*pl* -ies] 1 [U] 保障 bǎozhàng; 保护〔護〕 bǎohù. 2 [C] 赔偿〔償〕 péicháng; 补〔補〕偿 bǔcháng.

indent /ɪnˈdent/ *v* [I, T] 缩格书〔書〕写〔寫〕 suōgé shūxiě. **indentation** /ˌɪndenˈteɪʃn/ 1 [C, U] 缩格书写 suōgé shūxiě. 2 [C] 凹陷 āoxiàn; 缺口 quēkǒu: *the ~ations of the coastline* 海岸线的犬牙交错.

independent /ˌɪndɪˈpendənt/ *adj* 1 独〔獨〕立的 dúlìde: *an ~ nation* 独立国家 2 (*of*) 自立的 zìlìde; 不需外援的 bù xū wàiyuán de. 3 能独立工作的 néng dúlì gōngzuò de; 自信的 zìxìnde. **independent** *n* [C] 无〔無〕党〔黨〕派人士 wú dǎngpài rénshì. **independence** /-əns/ *n* [U]: *independence from one's parents* 不依赖父母. **independently** *adv*.

indescribable /ˌɪndɪˈskraɪbəbl/ *adj* 难〔難〕以形容的 nányǐ xíngróng de. **indescribably** *adv*.

indestructible /ˌɪndɪˈstrʌktəbl/ *adj* 破坏〔壞〕不了的 pòhuài bùliǎo de.

index /ˈɪndeks/ *n* [C] [*pl* ~es; 义项 2 ~es 或 indices /ˈɪndɪsiːz/] 1 (a) (书末的)索引 suǒyǐn. (b) (图书馆等的)卡片索引 kǎpiàn suǒyǐn: *a ˈcard ~* 卡片索引. 2 (物价等的)指数〔數〕 zhǐshù: *the cost-of-living ~* 生活(费用)指数. **index** *v* [T] 为〔爲〕…编索引 wèi… biān suǒyǐn; 把…编入索引 bǎ… biānrù suǒyǐn. **ˈindex finger** *n* [C] 食指 shízhǐ.

India /ˈɪndɪə/ *n* [U] 印度 Yìndù.

Indian *adj* 印度的 Yìndùde. **Indian** *n* [C] 印度人 Yìndùrén.

indicate /ˈɪndɪkeɪt/ *v* 1 [T] 指示 zhǐshì; 指出 zhǐchū; 表示 biǎoshì. 2 [I, T] 发〔發〕出改变〔變〕行车〔車〕方向信号〔號〕 fāchū gǎibiàn xíngchē fāngxiàng xìnhào. **indication** /ˌɪndɪˈkeɪʃn/ *n* 1 [U] 指示 zhǐshì; 指出 zhǐchū; 表示 biǎoshì. 2 [C, U] 作出某种〔種〕指示的言语、标〔標〕记等 zuòchū mǒuzhǒng zhǐshì de yányǔ、biāojì děng. **indicative** /ɪnˈdɪkətɪv/ *adj* *of* 标示的 biāoshìde; 指示的 zhǐshìde; 暗示的 ànshìde; 象征〔徵〕的 xiàngzhēngde. **indicator** *n* [C] 1 (仪器上的)指针 zhǐzhēn; 指示器 zhǐshìqì; 记录〔錄〕器 jìlùqì. 2 (车辆上的)变〔變〕向指示灯〔燈〕 biànxiàng zhǐshìdēng.

indict /ɪnˈdaɪt/ *v* [T] (*for*) [法律]控告 kònggào; 对〔對〕…起诉 duì… qǐsù: *~ed for murder* 被控告谋杀. **indictable** *adj* (罪行) 可招致起诉的 kě zhāozhì qǐsù de: *an ~able offence* 可提起公诉的罪行. **indictment** *n* [C, U].

indifferent /ɪnˈdɪfrənt/ *adj* 1 (*to*) 不感兴〔興〕趣的 bù gǎn xìngqù de; 不关〔關〕心的 bù guānxīn de. 2 质〔質〕量不高的 zhìliàng bùgāo de: *an ~ meal* 一顿凑合饭. **indifference** /-frəns/ *n* [U]. **indifferently** *adv*.

indigenous /ɪnˈdɪdʒɪnəs/ *adj* (*to*) 土生土长〔長〕的 tǔ shēng tǔ zhǎng de; 本土的 běntǔde: *Kangaroos are ~ to Australia.* 袋鼠产于澳大利亚.

I

indigestion /ˌɪndɪˈdʒestʃən/ *n* [U] 消化不良 xiāohuà bùliáng; 消化不良症 xiāohuà bùliáng zhèng.

indignant /ɪnˈdɪgnənt/ *adj* 愤慨的 fènkǎide; 义〔義〕愤的 yìfènde. **indignantly** *adv*. **indignation** /ˌɪndɪgˈneɪʃn/ *n* [U].

indignity /ɪnˈdɪgnətɪ/ *n* [C, U] [*pl* -ies] 无〔無〕礼〔禮〕wúlǐ; 侮辱 wǔrǔ.

indirect /ˌɪndɪˈrekt, -daɪˈr-/ *adj* 1 迂回〔迴〕的 yūhuíde: *an ~ route* 迂回路线. 2 间接的 jiànjiēde: *an ~ answer* 间接的回答. 3 非直接相关〔關〕的 fēi zhíjiē xiāngguān de; 次要的 cìyàode: *an ~ cause* 次要的原因. **indirectly** *adv*. ˌ**indirect** ˈ**object** *n* [C] [语法] 间接宾〔賓〕语 jiànjiē bīnyǔ: *In 'Give him the book.' 'him' is the ~ object.* 在"Give him the book"的句子中,"him"是间接宾语. ˌ**indirect** ˈ**speech** *n* [U] [语法] 间接引语 jiànjiē yǐnyǔ: *In ~ speech, 'He said, "I will come."' becomes 'He said he would come.'* 如果用间接引语,'He said, "I will come."'就成了'He said he would come.' ˈ**indirect tax** *n* [C] 间接税 jiànjiēshuì.

indiscreet /ˌɪndɪˈskriːt/ *adj* 不慎重的 bú shènzhòng de; 轻〔輕〕率 qīngshuài. **indiscreetly** *adv*. **indiscretion** /ˌɪndɪˈskreʃn/ *n* 1 [U] 不慎重 búshènzhòng; 轻率 qīngshuài. 2 [C] 不检〔檢〕点〔點〕的言行 bùjiǎndiǎnde yánxíng.

indiscriminate /ˌɪndɪˈskrɪmɪnət/ *adj* 不加区〔區〕别的 bùjiā qūbié de: *~ praise* 一味恭维. **indiscriminately** *adv*.

indispensable /ˌɪndɪˈspensəbl/ *adj* 必需的 bìxūde; 必不可少的 bì bù kě shǎo de.

indisposed /ˌɪndɪˈspəʊzd/ *adj* [正式用语] 1 有病的 yǒubìngde; 不舒服的 bù shūfu de. 2 不愿〔願〕的 búyuànde: *~ to help* 不愿帮助.

indisputable /ˌɪndɪˈspjuːtəbl/ *adj* 无〔無〕可争辩的 wú kě zhēngbiàn de. **indisputably** *adv*.

indistinguishable /ˌɪndɪˈstɪŋgwɪʃəbl/ *adj* (*from*) 区〔區〕分不出的 qūfēn bù chū de; 难〔難〕分辨的 nán fēnbiàn de: *~ from her sister* 分辨不出她和她的姐姐.

individual /ˌɪndɪˈvɪdʒʊəl/ *adj* 1 单〔單〕独〔獨〕的 dāndúde; 个〔個〕别的 gèbiéde. 2 个人的 gèrénde; 个体〔體〕的 gètǐde. **individual** *n* [C] 个人 gèrén. **individuality** /ˌɪndɪˌvɪdʒʊˈælətɪ/ *n* [U] 个性 gèxìng. **individually** *adv*.

indoctrinate /ɪnˈdɒktrɪneɪt/ *v* [T] (*with*) [常作贬] 向(某人)灌输(某种思想) xiàng guànshū. **indoctrination** /ɪnˌdɒktrɪˈneɪʃn/ *n* [U].

indolent /ˈɪndələnt/ *adj* [正式用语] 懒惰的 lǎnduòde. **indolence** /-ləns/ *n* [U].

indoor /ˈɪndɔː(r)/ *adj* 在室内的 zài shìnèi de; 在屋内的 zài wūnèi de. **indoors** /ˌɪnˈdɔːz/ *adv* 在屋里〔裡〕zài wūlǐ; 进〔進〕屋里 jìn wūlǐ.

induce /ɪnˈdjuːs; US -duːs/ *v* [T] 1 劝〔勸〕诱 quànyòu; 促使 cùshǐ. 2 造成 zàochéng; 导〔導〕致 dǎozhì. 3 用药〔藥〕为〔爲〕(孕妇)催生 yòng yào wèi cuīshēng. **inducement** *n* [C, U] 引诱 yǐnyòu; 刺激 cìjī: *a pay rise as an ~ment to work harder* 用来激励人们努力工作的增加工资.

induction /ɪnˈdʌkʃn/ *n* 1 [U, C] 就职〔職〕jiùzhí. 2 [U] [逻辑] 归〔歸〕纳法 guīnàfǎ. 3 [U] (对孕妇的)催产〔產〕cuīchǎn.

indulge /ɪnˈdʌldʒ/ *v* 1 [I] (*in*) 让〔讓〕自己尽〔盡〕情享受某事物 ràng zìjǐ jìnqíng xiǎngshòu mǒu shìwù; 沉迷于 chénmí yú; 纵〔縱〕情于 zòngqíng yú. 2 [T] 满足(欲望) mǎnzú. 3 [T] 放纵 fàngzòng. **indulgence** *n* 1 [C] 嗜好 shìhào; 着迷的事物 zháomíde shìwù. 2 [U] 沉溺 chénnì; 纵容 zòngróng; 娇〔嬌〕惯 jiāoguàn. **indulgent** *adj* 放纵的 fàngzòngde; 沉溺的 chénnìde.

industrial /ɪnˈdʌstrɪəl/ *adj* 工业〔業〕的 gōngyède. inˌ**dustrial** ˈ**action** *n* [U] 劳〔勞〕工行动〔動〕(如怠工、罢工等) láogōng xíngdòng. **industrialism** *n* [U] 工业主义〔義〕(以大工业为主的体制) gōngyèzhǔyì. **industrialist** *n* [C] 实〔實〕业家 shíyèjiā. **industrialize** *v* [I, T] (使)工业化 gōngyèhuà. **industrially** *adv*.

industrious /ɪnˈdʌstrɪəs/ *adj* 勤奋〔奮〕的 qínfènde; 勤劳〔勞〕的 qínláode.

industry /ˈɪndəstrɪ/ *n* [*pl* -ies] 1 [C, U] 工业〔業〕gōngyè; 产〔產〕业 chǎnyè; 行业 hángyè: *the steel ~* 钢铁工业. 2 [U] [正式用语] 勤奋〔奮〕qínfèn.

inebriated /ɪˈniːbrɪeɪtɪd/ *adj* [正式用语或谑] 喝醉的 hēzuìde.

inedible /ɪnˈedɪbl/ *adj* [正式用语] 不能食用的 bùnéng shíyòng de.

ineffective /ˌɪnɪˈfektɪv/ *adj* 无〔無〕效的 wúxiàode; 不起作用的 bùqǐ zuòyòng de. **ineffectively** *adv*. **ineffectiveness** *n* [U].

ineffectual /ˌɪnɪˈfektʃʊəl/ *adj* 无〔無〕效的 wúxiàode; 不成功的 bù chénggōng de: *an ~ attempt* 徒然的尝试. **ineffectually** *adv*.

inefficient /ˌɪnɪˈfɪʃnt/ *adj* 1 (人)无〔無〕能的 wúnéngde; 不称〔稱〕职〔職〕的 bú chènzhí de. 2 (机器等)无效的 wúxiàode; 效率低的 xiàolǜ dī de. **inefficiency** /-nsɪ/ *n* [U]. **inefficiently** *adv*.

ineligible /ɪnˈelɪdʒəbl/ *adj* (*for*) 不合格的 bù hégé de: *~ for the job* 没有资格做这项

工作.

inept /ɪˈnept/ *adj* 1 (*at*) 不熟练〔練〕的 bù shúliàn de;不擅长的 bù shàncháng de. 2 不合时〔時〕宜的 bùhé shíyí de. **ineptitude** /ɪˈneptɪtjuːd; *US* -tuːd / *n* [U].

inequality /ˌɪnɪˈkwɒlətɪ/ *n* [C, U] [*pl* -ies] 不平等 bù píngděng;不平衡 bù pínghéng.

inert /ɪˈnɜːt/ *adj* 1 无〔無〕活动〔動〕能力的 wú huódòng nénglì de. 2 呆滞〔滯〕的 dāizhìde;迟〔遲〕钝的 chídùnde.

inertia /ɪˈnɜːʃə/ *n* [U] 1 呆滞〔滯〕dāizhì;迟〔遲〕钝 chídùn. 2 [物理]惯性 guànxìng.

inescapable /ˌɪnɪˈskeɪpəbl/ *adj* 逃避不了的 táobì bùliǎo de.

inevitable /ɪnˈevɪtəbl/ *adj* 1 不可避免的 bùkě bìmiǎn de. 2 [非正式用语]照例必有的 zhàolì bì yǒu de: *a tourist with his ~ camera* 照例携有照相机的游客. **inevitability** /ɪnˌevɪtəˈbɪlətɪ/ *n* [U]. **inevitably** *adv*.

inexact /ˌɪnɪgˈzækt/ *adj* 不精确〔確〕的 bù jīngquè de;不准〔準〕确的 bù zhǔnquè de.

inexcusable /ˌɪnɪkˈskjuːzəbl/ *adj* 不可原谅的 bùkě yuánliàng de: ~ *rudeness* 不可宽恕的粗鲁行为.

inexpensive /ˌɪnɪkˈspensɪv/ *adj* 花费不大的 huāfèi búdà de;廉价〔價〕的 liánjiàde.

inexperience /ˌɪnɪkˈspɪərɪəns/ *n* [U] (*in*) 缺乏经〔經〕验〔驗〕quēfá jīngyàn. **inexperienced** *adj*.

inexplicable /ˌɪnɪkˈsplɪkəbl/ *adj* 费解的 fèijiěde;不能说明的 bùnéng shuōmíng de.

inextricable /ˌɪnɪkˈstrɪkəbl, ɪnˈekstrɪkəbl/ *adj* 无〔無〕法逃离〔離〕的 wúfǎ táolí de;解不开〔開〕的 jiě bùkāi de;分不开的 fēn bùkāi de.

infallible /ɪnˈfæləbl/ *adj* 1 不会〔會〕犯错误的 búhuì fàn cuòwù de: *Nobody is ~.* 没有人不犯错误. 2 绝对〔對〕可靠的 juéduì kěkào de: *an ~ method* 绝对可靠的方法. **infallibility** /ɪnˌfæləˈbɪlətɪ/ *n* [U].

infamous /ˈɪnfəməs/ *adj* 邪恶〔惡〕的 xié'è-de;可耻的 kěchǐde. **infamy** /ˈɪnfəmɪ/ *n* [C, U] [*pl* -ies] 声〔聲〕名狼藉 shēngmíng lángjí;无耻的行为〔爲〕wúchǐde xíngwéi.

infancy /ˈɪnfənsɪ/ *n* [U] 1 婴儿〔兒〕yīng'ér;婴儿期 yīng'érqī. 2 [喻]初期阶〔階〕段 chūqī jiēduàn: *The project is still in its ~.* 这个项目仍然是在初期阶段.

infant /ˈɪnfənt/ *n* [C] 婴儿〔兒〕yīng'ér.

infantile /ˈɪnfəntaɪl/ *adj* 婴儿〔兒〕的 yīng'érde;幼稚的 yòuzhìde;孩子气〔氣〕的 háiziqìde: ~ *behaviour* 孩子气的行为.

infantry /ˈɪnfəntrɪ/ *n* [U] [用 sing 或 pl v] 步兵 bùbīng.

infatuated /ɪnˈfætʃueɪtɪd/ *adj* (*with*) 迷恋〔戀〕某人的 míliàn mǒurén de. **infatuation** /ɪnˌfætʃʊˈeɪʃn/ *n* [U, C].

infect /ɪnˈfekt/ *v* [T] (*with*) 1 传〔傳〕染 chuánrǎn. 2 [喻]受影响〔響〕shòu yǐngxiǎng;受感染 shòu gǎnrǎn. **infection** /ɪnˈfekʃn/ *n* 1 [C] 传染病 chuánrǎnbìng. 2 [U] 传染 chuánrǎn: *danger of ~ion* 传染的危险. **infectious** /ɪnˈfekʃəs/ *adj* 1 (疾病)传染的 chuánrǎnde. 2 [喻]有感染力的 yǒu gǎnrǎnlì de: *~ious laughter* 有感染力的笑声.

infer /ɪnˈfɜː(r)/ *v* [T] [-rr-] (*from*) 推论〔論〕tuīlùn;推断〔斷〕tuīduàn: *What can be ~red from the election results?* 从选举结果能作出什么推断呢? **inference** /ˈɪnfərəns/ *n* [C, U].

inferior /ɪnˈfɪərɪə(r)/ *adj* (*to*) 劣质〔質〕的 lièzhìde;差的 chàde;下等的 xiàděngde. **inferior** *n* [C] 地位低的人 dìwèi dī de rén;能力低的人 nénglì dī de rén. **inferiority** /ɪnˌfɪərɪˈɒrətɪ; *US* -ˈɔːr- / *n* [U]. **inferiˈority complex** *n* [C] 自卑感 zìbēigǎn.

infernal /ɪnˈfɜːnl/ *adj* 1 阴〔陰〕间的 yīnjiānde;地狱的 dìyùde. 2 [非正式用语]可恨的 kěhènde.

inferno /ɪnˈfɜːnəʊ/ *n* [C] [*pl* ~s] 1 毁灭〔滅〕性大火(的地方) huǐmièxìng dàhuǒ. 2 地狱般的地方 dìyùbānde dìfang.

infertile /ˌɪnˈfɜːtaɪl; *US* -tl/ *adj* 贫瘠的 pínjíde;不毛的 bùmáode: ~ *land* 不毛之地.

infest /ɪnˈfest/ *v* [T] (*with*) (昆虫等)大批出现于 dàpī chūxiàn yú: *a dog ~ed with fleas* 身上满是跳蚤的狗.

infidelity /ˌɪnfɪˈdelətɪ/ *n* [C, U] [*pl* -ties] 不忠诚 bù zhōngchéng;背信 bèixìn;(夫妻间的)不忠 bù zhōng.

infighting /ˈɪnfaɪtɪŋ/ *n* [U] [非正式用语]暗斗〔鬥〕àndòu.

infiltrate /ˈɪnfɪltreɪt/ *v* [T] 悄悄穿越 qiāoqiāo chuānyuè;使(思想)渗〔滲〕透 shǐ shèntòu. **infiltration** /ˌɪnfɪlˈtreɪʃn/ *n* [U]. **infiltrator** *n* [C].

infinite /ˈɪnfɪnət/ *adj* 无〔無〕限的 wúxiànde;无穷〔窮〕的 wúqióngde. **infinitely** *adv*.

infinitive /ɪnˈfɪnətɪv/ *n* [C] [语法]不定式 búdìngshì.

infinity /ɪnˈfɪnətɪ/ *n* [U] 无〔無〕穷〔窮〕wúqióng.

infirm /ˌɪnˈfɜːm/ *adj* 体〔體〕弱的 tǐruòde;年老体衰的 niánlǎo tǐshuāi de. **infirmity** *n* [C, U] [*pl* -ties].

infirmary /ɪnˈfɜːmərɪ/ *n* [C] [*pl* -ies] 医〔醫〕院 yīyuàn.

inflame /ɪnˈfleɪm/ *v* [T] 激怒 jīnù;使极〔極〕度激动〔動〕shǐ jídù jīdòng. **inflamed** *adj* (身体的一部分)发〔發〕炎的 fāyánde.

I

inflammable /ɪnˈflæməbl/ *adj* 易燃的 yìránde.

inflammation /ˌɪnfləˈmeɪʃn/ *n* [C,U] 发〔發〕炎 fāyán.

inflammatory /ɪnˈflæmətrɪ; *US* -tɔːrɪ/ *adj* 煽动〔動〕性的 shāndòngxìngde: ～ *remarks* 煽动性的话.

inflate /ɪnˈfleɪt/ *v* 1 [I,T] (轮胎、气球等)充气〔氣〕chōngqì;使膨胀〔脹〕shǐ péngzhàng. 2 [T] [喻]使骄〔驕〕傲 shǐ jiāo'ào;使自高自大 shǐ zìgāo zì dà: *an ～d ego* 自高自大的虚荣心. 3 [I,T] (使)通货膨胀 tōnghuò péngzhàng. **inflation** /ɪnˈfleɪʃn/ *n* [U] 1 充气 chōngqì. 2 通货膨胀 tōnghuò péngzhàng. **inflationary** /ɪnˈfleɪʃnrɪ; *US* -nerɪ/ *adj* 通货膨胀的 tōnghuò péngzhàng de;造成通货膨胀的 zàochéng tōnghuò péngzhàng de.

inflection (亦作 **inflexion**) /ɪnˈflekʃn/ *n* [C,U] 1 [语法]词形变〔變〕化 cíxíng biànhuà;屈折形式 qūzhé xíngshì. 2 变〔變〕音 biànyīn;转〔轉〕调 zhuǎndiào.

inflexible /ɪnˈfleksəbl/ *adj* 1 不可弯〔彎〕曲的 bùkě wānqū de. 2 [喻]坚〔堅〕定的 jiāndìngde;固执〔執〕的 gùzhíde. **inflexibility** /ɪnˌfleksəˈbɪlətɪ/ *n* [U]. **inflexibly** *adv*.

inflict /ɪnˈflɪkt/ *v* [T] (*on*) 使遭受(痛苦等) shǐ zāoshòu. **infliction** /ɪnˈflɪkʃn/ *n* [U,C].

influence /ˈɪnflʊəns/ *n* 1 [U] 影响〔響〕力 yǐngxiǎnglì;感化力 gǎnhuàlì. 2 [C] 有影响的人或事 yǒu yǐngxiǎng de rén huò shì: *She's a bad ～ on me*. 她是个对我有坏影响的人. 3 [U] 权〔權〕力 quánlì;权势〔勢〕quánshì: *Can you use your ～ to get me a job?* 你能使用权力为我谋到工作吗? 4 [习语] **under the ˈinfluence** [正式用语或谑]喝醉酒 hē zuì jiǔ. **influence** *v* [T] 影响 yǐngxiǎng.

influential /ˌɪnflʊˈenʃl/ *adj* 有权〔權〕势〔勢〕的 yǒu quánshì de.

influenza /ˌɪnflʊˈenzə/ *n* [U] [正式用语]流行性感冒 liúxíngxìng gǎnmào.

influx /ˈɪnflʌks/ *n* [C] 涌进〔進〕yǒngjìn: *an ～ of tourists* 大批游客涌进.

inform /ɪnˈfɔːm/ *v* 1 [T] 通知 tōngzhī;告诉 gàosù. 2 [I] *against* /*on* [法律]告发〔發〕gàofā. **informant** /-ənt/ *n* [C] 提供消息或情报〔報〕的人 tígōng xiāoxi huò qíngbào de rén. **informed** *adj* 见闻广〔廣〕的 jiànwén guǎng de. **informer** *n* [C] 告发人 gàofārén.

informal /ˌɪnˈfɔːml/ *adj* 1 非正规的 fēi zhèngguī de;非正式的 fēi zhèngshì de;不拘礼〔禮〕节〔節〕的 bùjū lǐjié de;日常的 rìchángde: ～ *clothes* 便服. 2 (词语)非正式使用的 fēi zhèngshì shǐyòng de. **informality** /ˌɪnfɔːˈmælətɪ/ *n* [U]. **informally** *adv*.

information /ˌɪnfəˈmeɪʃn/ *n* [U] (*on* / *about*) 通知 tōngzhī;报〔報〕告 bàogào;消息 xiāoxi;情报 qíngbào. **inforˈmation eˌconomy** *n* [C] 信息经〔經〕济〔濟〕xìnxī jīngjì;知识经〔經〕济〔濟〕zhīshí jīngjì. **inforˈmation pack** *n* [C] 整套资料 zhěngtào zīliào. **inforˈmation retrieval** *n* [U] 信息检〔檢〕索 xìnxī jiǎnsuǒ;情报检索 qíngbào jiǎnsuǒ. **inforˈmation science** *n* [U] 信息科学〔學〕xìnxī kēxué. **information ˈsuperhighway** *n* [C] 信息高速公路 xìnxī gāosù gōnglù. **inforˈmation system** *n* [C] 信息系统 xìnxī xìtǒng. **inforˈmation technology** *n* [U] 信息技术〔術〕xìnxī jìshù.

informative /ɪnˈfɔːmətɪv/ *adj* 提供消息、情报〔報〕的 tígōng xiāoxi、qíngbào de.

infra-red /ˌɪnfrə ˈred/ *adj* 红外线〔綫〕的 hóngwàixiànde.

infrequent /ɪnˈfriːkwənt/ *adj* 不常发〔發〕生的 bùcháng fāshēng de;稀罕的 xīhande. **infrequency** /-kwənsɪ/ *n* [U]. **infrequently** *adv*.

infringe /ɪnˈfrɪndʒ/ *v* 1 [T] 违〔違〕反(规则等) wéifǎn;触〔觸〕犯 chùfàn. 2 [I] *on* 侵犯 qīnfàn;侵害 qīnhài: ～ *on the rights of other people* 侵犯其他人的权利. **infringement** *n* [C,U].

infuriate /ɪnˈfjʊərɪeɪt/ *v* [T] 激怒 jīnù.

infuse /ɪnˈfjuːz/ *v* 1 [T] [正式用语]向…灌输 xiàng… guànshū;使获〔獲〕得 shǐ huòdé: ～ *the workers with energy* 鼓舞工人的干劲. ～ *energy into the workers* 使工人有干劲. 2 [I,T] 泡(茶) pào;浸渍 jìnzì;浸液 jìnyè. **infusion** /ɪnˈfjuːʒn/ *n* [C,U] 浸渍 jìnzì;浸液 jìnyè.

ingenious /ɪnˈdʒiːnɪəs/ *adj* 1 (人)机〔機〕灵〔靈〕的 jīlingde. 2 制〔製〕作精巧的 zhìzuò jīngqiǎo de;灵巧的 língqiǎode. **ingeniously** *adv*. **ingenuity** /ˌɪndʒɪˈnjuːətɪ; *US* -ˈnuː-/ *n* [U].

ingot /ˈɪŋgət/ *n* [C] 锭 dìng;铸〔鑄〕块〔塊〕zhùkuài.

ingrained /ˌɪnˈgreɪnd/ *adj* (习惯等)根深蒂固的 gēn shēn dì gù de.

ingratiate /ɪnˈgreɪʃɪeɪt/ *v* [T] [正式用语,贬] ～ **oneself** (**with**) 使得到…的欢〔歡〕心 shǐ dédào…de huānxīn. **ingratiating** *adj*.

ingratitude /ɪnˈgrætɪtjuːd; *US* -tuːd/ *n* [U] 忘恩负义〔義〕wàng ēn fù yì.

ingredient /ɪnˈgriːdɪənt/ *n* [C] 混合物的组成部分 hùnhéwùde zǔchéng bùfen;配料 pèiliào: *the ～s of a cake* 蛋糕的成分.

inhabit /ɪnˈhæbɪt/ *v* [T] 居住于 jūzhù yú. **inhabitant** /-ənt/ *n* [C] 居民 jūmín.

inhale /ɪnˈheɪl/ *v* [I,T] 吸气〔氣〕xīqì. **inhaler** *n* [C] 吸入器 xīrùqì.

inherent /ɪnˈhɪərənt,-ˈher-/ *adj* 内在的 nèizàide;固有的 gùyǒude: ～ *weaknesses in* *a design* 设计本身的弱点.

inherit /ɪnˈherɪt/ *v* [T] 1 继〔繼〕承 jìchéng. 2 经〔經〕遗传〔傳〕而得(特性等) jīng yíchuán ér dé. **inheritance** *n* 1 [U] 继承 jìchéng. 2 [C] 继承物 jìchéngwù; 遗产〔產〕yíchǎn. **inheritor** *n* [C] 继承人 jìchéngrén; 后〔後〕继者 hòujìzhě.

inhibit /ɪnˈhɪbɪt/ *v* [T] (*from*) 禁止 jìnzhǐ; 阻止 zǔzhǐ; 抑制 yìzhì. **inhibited** *adj* 拘谨的 jūjǐnde; 不能自然地表达〔達〕感情的 bùnéng zìránde biǎodá gǎnqíng de. **inhibition** /ˌɪnhɪˈbɪʃn/ *n* [C, U] 压〔壓〕抑 yāyì.

inhospitable /ˌɪnhɒˈspɪtəbl/ *adj* 不适〔適〕于居住的 bú shìyú jūzhù de: *an ~ climate* 不适宜居住的气候; 气候恶劣.

inhuman /ˌɪnˈhjuːmən/ *adj* 野蛮〔蠻〕的 yěmánde; 残〔殘〕暴的 cánbàode; 无〔無〕情的 wúqíngde. **inhumanity** /ˌɪnhjuːˈmænətɪ/ *n* [U, C] [*pl* -ies].

inhumane /ˌɪnhjuːˈmeɪn/ *adj* 无〔無〕人道的 wú réndào de; 残〔殘〕忍的 cánrěnde. **inhumanely** *adv*.

inimitable /ɪˈnɪmɪtəbl/ *adj* 不能模仿的 bùnéng mófǎng de; 无〔無〕与〔與〕伦〔倫〕比的 wú yǔ lún bǐ de.

initial /ɪˈnɪʃl/ *adj* 最初的 zuìchūde; 开〔開〕始的 kāishǐde. **initial** *n* [C, 常作 pl] 人名的首字母 rénmíngde shǒuzìmǔ. **initial** *v* [-ll-; 美语常作-l-] [I, T] 签〔簽〕署姓名首字母(于) qiānshǔ xìngmíng shǒuzìmǔ. **initially** /-ʃəlɪ/ *adv* 开始 kāishǐ; 最初 zuìchū.

initiate /ɪˈnɪʃɪeɪt/ *v* [T] 1 [正式用语]创〔創〕始 chuàngshǐ; 着手 zhuóshǒu; 发〔發〕动〔動〕fādòng. 2 (*into*) 介绍(某人)为〔爲〕(会员等) jièshào wéi. **initiate** /ɪˈnɪʃɪət/ *n* [C] 新入会〔會〕的人 xīn rùhuì de rén. **initiation** /ɪˌnɪʃɪˈeɪʃn/ *n* [U].

initiative /ɪˈnɪʃətɪv/ *n* 1 [C] 主动〔動〕的行动 zhǔdòng de xíngdòng. 2 **the initiative** [sing] 主动权〔權〕zhǔdòngquán. 3 [U] 主动性 zhǔdòngxìng: *do sth on one's own ~* 主动做某事. 4 [习语] **take the initiative** 采〔採〕取主动 cǎiqǔ zhǔdòng; 首先采取行动 shǒuxiān cǎiqǔ xíngdòng.

inject /ɪnˈdʒekt/ *v* [T] 1 注射 zhùshè: *~ a drug into sb* (或 *~ sb with a drug*) 为某人注射药液. 2 (*into*) [喻]注入(新事物) zhùrù: *~ new life into the team* 为该队增添了生气. **injection** /ɪnˈdʒekʃn/ *n* [C, U].

injunction /ɪnˈdʒʌŋkʃn/ *n* [C] [正式用语] 法院的强制令 fǎyuànde qiángzhìlìng.

injure /ˈɪndʒə(r)/ *v* [T] 伤〔傷〕害 shānghài; 损害 sǔnhài. **injured** *adj* 受伤害的 shòu shānghài de; 被触〔觸〕怒的 bèi chùnù de. **the injured** *n* [pl] 受伤者 shòushāngzhě.

injury /ˈɪndʒərɪ/ *n* [*pl* -ies] 1 [U] 伤〔傷〕害 shānghài; 损害 sǔnhài. 2 [C] (a) (对身体的)伤害 shānghài. (b) (对感情的)伤害 shānghài.

injustice /ɪnˈdʒʌstɪs/ *n* 1 [U] 非正义〔義〕fēi zhèngyì; 不公正 bùgōngzhèng. 2 [C] 非正义的行为〔爲〕fēi zhèngyì de xíngwéi. 3 [习语] **do sb an inˈjustice** 对〔對〕某人不公平 duì mǒurén bù gōngpíng; 冤枉某人 yuānwàng mǒurén.

ink /ɪŋk/ *n* [U, C] 墨水 mòshuǐ; 油墨 yóumò. **inky** *adj* 黑的 hēide.

inkling /ˈɪŋklɪŋ/ *n* [sing] 模糊的想法 móhude xiǎngfǎ.

inland /ˈɪnlənd/ *adj* 内地的 nèidìde; 内陆〔陸〕的 nèilùde: *~ lakes* 内陆湖. **inland** /ˌɪnˈlænd/ *adv* 向内地 xiàng nèidì. **the ˌInland ˈRevenue** *n* [sing] (英国)税务〔務〕局 shuìwùjú.

in-laws /ˈɪnlɔːz/ *n* [pl] [非正式用语]姻亲〔親〕yīnqīn.

inlet /ˈɪnlet/ *n* [C] 海湾〔灣〕hǎiwān; 小港 xiǎogǎng.

inmate /ˈɪnmeɪt/ *n* [C] 同住者(同狱犯人等) tóngzhùzhě.

inmost /ˈɪnməʊst/ *adj* 1 最内的 zuìnèide; 最深处〔處〕的 zuì shēnchù de. 2 [喻]内心深处的 nèixīn shēnchù de: *~ thoughts* 内心深处的思想.

inn /ɪn/ *n* [C] 小旅馆 xiǎo lǚguǎn; 小客栈〔棧〕xiǎo kèzhàn. **ˈinn-keeper** *n* [C] 小旅馆老板〔闆〕xiǎo lǚguǎn lǎobǎn.

innards /ˈɪnədz/ *n* [pl] 1 内脏〔臟〕nèizàng. 2 内部结构〔構〕nèibù jiégòu; 内部机〔機〕件 nèibù jījiàn.

innate /ɪˈneɪt/ *adj* 天生的 tiānshēngde; 固有的 gùyǒude. **innately** *adv*.

inner /ˈɪnə(r)/ *adj* 1 内部的 nèibùde; 里〔裡〕面的 lǐmiànde. 2 (感情)内心的 nèixīnde. **innermost** /-məʊst/ *adj* 内心深处〔處〕的 nèixīn shēnchù de: *her ~most feelings* 她内心深处的感情.

innings /ˈɪnɪŋz/ *n* [C] [*pl* **innings**] 1 [板球]局 jú; 回合 huíhé. 2 [习语] **have had a good ˈinnings** [英国非正式用语]一生幸福而长〔長〕寿〔壽〕yīshēng xìngfú ér chángshòu. **inning** *n* [C] [棒球]局 jú; 回合 huíhé.

innocent /ˈɪnəsnt/ *adj* 1 无〔無〕罪的 wúzuìde. 2 无害的 wúhàide: *~ fun* 无害的玩笑. 3 天真的 tiānzhēnde; 单〔單〕纯的 dānchúnde. 4 无知的 wúzhīde; 轻〔輕〕易信任别人的 qīngyì xìnrèn biérén de. **innocence** /-sns/ *n* [U]. **innocently** *adv*.

innocuous /ɪˈnɒkjʊəs/ *adj* 无〔無〕害的 wúhàide: *an ~ remark* 不得罪人的话.

innovate /ˈɪnəveɪt/ *v* [I] 创〔創〕新 chuàngxīn; 革新 géxīn. **innovation** /ˌɪnəˈveɪʃn/ *n*

1 [U] 创新 chuàngxīn; 改革 gǎigé. 2 [C] 新主意 xīn zhǔyi; 新方法 xīn fāngfǎ. **innovative** /ˈɪnəvətɪv/ (亦作 **innovatory** /ˌɪnəˈveɪtərɪ/) *adj*. **innovator** *n* [C] 改革者 gǎigézhě.

innuendo /ˌɪnjʊˈendəʊ/ *n* [C, U] [*pl* ~es /-z/] 影射 yǐngshè; 暗讽〔諷〕 ànfěng.

innumerable /ɪˈnjuːmərəbl; *US* ɪˈnuː-/ *adj* 数〔數〕不清的 shǔ bùqīng de.

inoculate /ɪˈnɒkjʊleɪt/ *v* [T] 给…接种〔種〕(疫苗) gěi…jiēzhòng; 给…作预防注射 gěi…zuò yùfáng zhùshè: ~ *sb against cholera* 给某人打针预防霍乱. **inoculation** /ɪˌnɒkjʊˈleɪʃn/ *n* [C, U].

inoffensive /ˌɪnəˈfensɪv/ *adj* 不触〔觸〕犯人的 bú chùfàn rén de; 不粗野的 bù cūyě de.

inopportune /ˌɪnˈɒpətʃuːn; *US* -tuːn/ *adj* [正式用语] 不合适〔適〕的 bù héshì de; 不合时〔時〕宜的 bùhé shíyí de: *an* ~ *remark* 不合时宜的话. *an* ~ *time* 不合适的时候. **inopportunely** *adv*.

inordinate /ɪnˈɔːdɪnət/ *adj* [正式用语] 过〔過〕度的 guòdùde; 极〔極〕度的 jídùde. **inordinately** *adv*.

I

inorganic /ˌɪnɔːˈgænɪk/ *adj* 无〔無〕机〔機〕的 wújīde: *Rocks and minerals are* ~. 岩石和矿物是无机的.

input /ˈɪnpʊt/ *n* 1 [U] 输入 shūrù. 2 [C] 输入信息 shūrù xìnxī. **input** *v* [-tt-; *pt*, *pp* **input** 或 **~ted**] [T] 把…输入电子计算机〔機〕 bǎ…shūrù diànzǐjìsuànjī.

inquest /ˈɪnkwest/ *n* [C] 审〔審〕讯 shěnxùn; 审问 shěnwèn.

inquire (亦作 **enquire**) /ɪnˈkwaɪə(r)/ *v* 1 [T] 询问 xúnwèn. 2 [I] (*about*) 打听〔聽〕 dǎting: ~ *about trains to Oxford* 打听去牛津的火车. 3 [习语] **inquire after sb** 问候 wènhòu; 问好 wènhǎo. **inquire into sth** 调查 diàochá. **inquiring** *adj* 爱〔愛〕打听的 ài dǎting de; 好询问的 hào xúnwèn de: *an inquiring mind* 爱探索的头脑.

inquiry (亦作 **enquiry**) /ɪnˈkwaɪərɪ; *US* ˈɪnkwərɪ/ *n* [*pl* **-ies**] 1 [C] 质〔質〕询 zhìxún; 调查 diàochá. 2 [U] 询问 xúnwèn; 打听〔聽〕 dǎting.

inquisition /ˌɪnkwɪˈzɪʃn/ *n* [C] [正式用语] 彻〔徹〕底调查 chèdǐ diàochá.

inquisitive /ɪnˈkwɪzətɪv/ *adj* 爱〔愛〕打听〔聽〕别人事情的 ài dǎting biérén shìqing de. **inquisitively** *adv*.

inroads /ˈɪnrəʊdz/ *n* [pl] 1 (对一个国家的) 突然袭〔襲〕击〔擊〕 tūrán xíjī. 2 [习语] **make inroads into/on sth** 消耗 xiāohào; 花费 huāfèi: *make* ~ *into one's savings* 耗去大量的储蓄.

insane /ɪnˈseɪn/ *adj* 疯〔瘋〕狂的 fēngkuángde. **insanely** *adv*. **insanity** /ɪnˈsænətɪ/ *n* [U].

insatiable /ɪnˈseɪʃəbl/ *adj* 无〔無〕法满足的 wúfǎ mǎnzú de.

inscribe /ɪnˈskraɪb/ *v* [T] 题写〔寫〕 tíxiě: ~ *words on a tombstone* 在墓碑上题字. **inscription** /ɪnˈskrɪpʃn/ *n* [C] 铭文 míngwén; 题字 tízì; 题词 tící.

inscrutable /inˈscruːtəbl/ *adj* 不可理解的 bùkě lǐjiě de; 谜一样〔樣〕的 mí yīyàng de.

insect /ˈɪnsekt/ *n* [C] 昆虫 kūnchóng. **insecticide** /ɪnˈsektɪsaɪd/ *n* [C, U] 杀〔殺〕虫剂〔劑〕 shāchóngjì.

insecure /ˌɪnsɪˈkjʊə(r)/ *adj* 1 不安全的 bù ānquán de; 不可靠的 bù kěkào de. 2 得不到信任的 débúdào xìnrèn de. **insecurely** *adv*. **insecurity** *n* [U].

insensible /ɪnˈsensəbl/ *adj* [正式用语] 1 失去知觉〔覺〕的 shīqù zhījué de. 2 (*of*) 不知道的 bù zhīdào de. 3 (*to*) 感觉〔覺〕不到的 gǎnjué búdào de: ~ *to pain* 感觉不到痛. **insensibility** /ɪnˌsensəˈbɪlətɪ/ *n* [U].

insensitive /ɪnˈsensətɪv/ *adj* 不敏感的 bù mǐngǎn de; 不灵〔靈〕敏的 bù língmǐn de. **insensitively** *adv*. **insensitivity** /ɪnsensəˈtɪvətɪ/ *n* [U].

inseparable /ɪnˈseprəbl/ *adj* 分不开〔開〕的 fēn bùkāi de; 不可分割的 bùkě fēngē de: ~ *friends* 形影不离的好友.

insert /ɪnˈsɜːt/ *v* [T] 插入 chārù: ~ *a key in a lock* 把钥匙插进锁里. **insert** /ˈɪnsɜːt/ *n* [C] 插入物 chārùwù; 插页 chāyè. **insertion** /ɪnˈsɜːʃn/ *n* [C, U].

inset /ˈɪnset/ *n* [C] (大地图上的)小插图〔圖〕 xiǎochātú; 图表 túbiǎo.

inshore /ˈɪnʃɔː(r)/ *adj*, *adv* 靠海岸的 kào hǎi'àn de; 沿海岸的 yán hǎi'àn de; 沿海岸 yán hǎi'àn.

inside[1] /ɪnˈsaɪd/ *n* 1 [C, 常作 sing] 里〔裡〕面 lǐmiàn; 内部 nèibù. 2 [sing] (亦作 **insides** [pl]) [非正式用语] 肠〔腸〕胃 chángwèi; 肚子 dùzi. 3 [习语] ˌ**inside** ˈ**out** (a) 里面朝外 lǐmiàn cháowài. (b) 彻〔徹〕底地 chèdǐde: *know sth* ~ *out* 非常熟悉某事. **on the inˈside** 熟悉内幕的 shúxī nèimù de. **inside** *adj* 1 里面的 lǐmiànde; 内幕的 nèimùde. 2 有内应〔應〕的 yǒu nèiyìng de; 内部人干〔幹〕的 nèibù rén gàn de: *The robbery was an* ~ *job*. 这劫案是内部人干的. **insider** *n* [C] (社团等)内部的人 nèibùde rén. **inˌsider** ˈ**dealing** (亦作 **inˌsider** ˈ**trading**) *n* [U] 内幕交易 nèimù jiāoyì.

inside[2] /ɪnˈsaɪd/ (尤用于美语 **inside of**) *prep* 1 在…里〔裡〕面 zài…lǐmiàn; 到…里面 dào…lǐmiàn: *come* ~ *the house* 到屋里来.

2(时间)在…之内 zài…zhī nèi: ~ *a year* 一年之内. **inside** *adv* 1 在里面 zài lǐmiàn; 到屋里 dào wūlǐ: *go* ~ 走进屋里. 2[俚]在监〔監〕牢里 zài jiānláo lǐ.

insidious /ɪnˈsɪdɪəs/ *adj* 暗中为〔爲〕害的 ànzhōng wéihài de; 阴〔陰〕险〔險〕的 yīnxiǎnde. **insidiously** *adv*.

insight /ˈɪnsaɪt/ *n* [C,U] 洞悉 dòngxī; 洞察 dòngchá; 见识〔識〕jiànshi: ~*s into his character* 深刻了解他的性格.

insignia /ɪnˈsɪgnɪə/ *n* [pl] 权〔權〕威或荣〔榮〕誉〔譽〕的标〔標〕识〔識〕quánwēi huò róngyù de biāoshí.

insignificant /ˌɪnsɪgˈnɪfɪkənt/ *adj* 无〔無〕价〔價〕值的 wú jiàzhí de; 无足轻〔輕〕重的 wú zú qīng zhòng de. **insignificance** /-kəns/ *n* [U]. **insignificantly** *adv*.

insincere /ˌɪnsɪnˈsɪə(r)/ *adj* 不真诚的 bù zhēnchéng de; 虚假的 xūjiǎde. **insincerely** *adv*. **insincerity** /-ˈserətɪ/ *n* [U].

insinuate /ɪnˈsɪnjʊeɪt/ *v* [T] 1 含沙射影地说 hán shā shè yǐng de shuō. 2 *into* [正式用语]使迂回〔迴〕地挤〔擠〕入 shǐ yūhuí de jǐrù. **insinuation** /ɪnˌsɪnjʊˈeɪʃn/ *n* [C,U].

insipid /ɪnˈsɪpɪd/ *adj* 1 [贬] 无〔無〕味的 wúwèide. 2 [喻]枯燥乏味的 kūzào fáwèi de; 单〔單〕调的 dāndiàode. **insipidly** *adv*.

insist /ɪnˈsɪst/ *v* [I,T] (*on*) 1 坚〔堅〕决要求 jiānjué yāoqiú: ~ *on going with sb* 坚决要求同某人一起去. ~ *that she (should) stop* 坚决要求她停下来. 2 坚决认〔認〕为〔爲〕jiānjué rènwéi; 坚决地宣布 jiānjuéde xuānbù: *He* ~*s that he is innocent*. 他坚决认为他是无罪的. **insistent** *adj* 坚持的 jiānchíde. **insistence** *n* [U].

insofar as /ˌɪnsəˈfɑːr əz/ = AS FAR AS (FAR[1]).

insolent /ˈɪnsələnt/ *adj* (*to*) 蛮〔蠻〕横的 mánhèngde; 粗鲁的 cūlǔde. **insolence** /-əns/ *n* [U].

insoluble /ɪnˈsɒljʊbl/ *adj* 1 不能溶解的 bùnéng róngjiě de; 难〔難〕溶解的 nán róngjiě de. 2 [喻](问题等)不能解决的 bùnéng jiějué de.

insolvent /ɪnˈsɒlvənt/ *n* [C], *adj* 无〔無〕偿〔償〕债能力的人 wú chángzhài nénglì de rén; (人)无偿债能力的 wú chángzhài nénglì de. **insolvency** /-ənsɪ/ *n* [U].

insomnia /ɪnˈsɒmnɪə/ *n* [U] 失眠 shīmián; 失眠症〔癥〕shīmiánzhèng. **insomniac** /-nɪæk/ *n* [C] 失眠者 shīmiánzhě.

inspect /ɪnˈspekt/ *v* [T] 检〔檢〕查 jiǎnchá; 审〔審〕查 shěnchá. **inspection** /ɪnˈspekʃn/ *n* [C,U]. **inspector** *n* [C] 1 检查员 jiǎncháyuán; 督学〔學〕dūxué. 2 [英国英语]警察巡官 jǐngchá xúnguān.

inspire /ɪnˈspaɪə(r)/ *v* [T] 1 鼓舞 gǔwǔ; 激励〔勵〕jīlì. 2 激起 jīqǐ; 唤起 huànqǐ: ~ *sb with confidence* (或 ~ *confidence in sb*) 唤起某人的信心. **inspiration** /ˌɪnspəˈreɪʃn/ *n* 1 [U] 灵〔靈〕感 línggǎn. 2 [C] 鼓舞人心的人或事 gǔwǔ rénxīnde rén huò shì. 3[非正式用语]好主意 hǎo zhǔyi; 灵机〔機〕妙算 língjī miàosuàn. **inspired** *adj* 有灵感的 yǒu línggǎn de. **inspiring** *adj*.

instability /ˌɪnstəˈbɪlətɪ/ *n* [U] 不稳〔穩〕定性 bù wěndìngxìng.

install (美语亦作 instal) /ɪnˈstɔːl/ *v* [T] 1 安装〔裝〕(机器等) ānzhuāng. 2 [正式用语]任命 rènmìng; 使就职〔職〕shǐ jiùzhí. 3 [正式用语]安置 ānzhì; 安顿 āndùn. **installation** /ˌɪnstəˈleɪʃn/ *n* [U,C].

instalment (美语常作 -ll-) /ɪnˈstɔːlmənt/ *n* [C] 1 分期连载〔載〕、连演的一个部分 fēnqī liánzǎi、liányǎn de yīgè bùfen: *a television series in six* ~*s* 六集的电视连续剧. 2 分期付款的一期付款 fēnqī fùkuǎn de yī qī fùkuǎn.

instance /ˈɪnstəns/ *n* [C] 1 例子 lìzi; 实〔實〕例 shílì. 2[习语] **for instance** 例如 lìrú.

instant /ˈɪnstənt/ *n* [C, 常作 sing] 1 时〔時〕刻 shíkè. 2 瞬息 shùnxī; 霎时 shàshí: *I'll be there in an* ~. 我立刻就来. **instant** *adj* 1 立即的 lìjíde; 紧〔緊〕迫的 jǐnpòde: *an* ~ *success* 立即(获得的)成功. 2(食物)速溶的 sùróngde; 配制〔製〕好的 pèizhì hǎo de: ~ *coffee* 速溶咖啡. **instantly** *adv* 立刻 lìkè; 马上 mǎshàng. **instant messaging** *n* [C] 即时〔時〕通信 jíshí tōngxìn.

instantaneous /ˌɪnstənˈteɪnɪəs/ *adj* 瞬间的 shùnjiānde; 即刻的 jíkède. **instantaneously** *adv*.

instead /ɪnˈsted/ *adv* 代替 dàitì; 顶替 dǐngtì: *Bill was ill so I went* ~. 比尔病了,就由我去了. **instead of** *prep* 代替 dàitì; 而不是 ér búshì: *drink tea* ~ *of coffee* 喝茶而不是喝咖啡.

instep /ˈɪnstep/ *n* [C] 脚背 jiǎobèi.

instigate /ˈɪnstɪgeɪt/ *v* [T] 煽动〔動〕shāndòng; 挑动 tiǎodòng: ~ *a strike* 挑动罢工. ~ *a riot* 煽动骚乱. **instigation** /ˌɪnstɪˈgeɪʃn/ *n* [U]. **instigator** *n* [C].

instil (美语 instill) /ɪnˈstɪl/ *v* [-ll-] [T] (*in/into*) 灌输(思想) guànshū.

instinct /ˈɪnstɪŋkt/ *n* [C,U] 本能 běnnéng. **instinctive** /ɪnˈstɪŋktɪv/ *adj* 本能的 běnnéngde: *an* ~*ive fear of fire* 天生怕火. **instinctively** *adv*.

institute /ˈɪnstɪtjuːt; *US* -tuːt/ *n* [C] 学〔學〕会〔會〕xuéhuì; 协〔協〕会 xiéhuì; 学院 xuéyuàn; 研究所 yánjiūsuǒ. **institute** *v* [T] [正式用语]着手 zhuóshǒu; 实〔實〕行 shíxíng.

I

institution /ˌɪnstɪˈtjuːʃn; *US* -tuːʃn/ *n* 1 [U] 建立 jiànlì;制定 zhìdìng. 2 [C]公共机〔機〕构〔構〕或其建筑〔築〕物 gōnggòng jīgòu huò qí jiànzhùwù. 3 [C] 制度 zhìdù;惯例 guànlì. **institutional** /-ʃənl/ *adj*. **institutionalize** /-ʃənəlaɪz/ *v* [T] 1 使制度化 shǐ zhìdùhuà. 2 使收容于社会〔會〕福利机构 shǐ shōuróng yú shèhuì fúlì jīgòu.

instruct /ɪnˈstrʌkt/ *v* [T] 1 教 jiāo;教育 jiàoyù. 2 指导〔導〕zhǐdǎo;指示 zhǐshì: ~ *the child not to go out* 嘱咐孩子不要走出去. 3 (尤用于法律)通知 tōngzhī. **instructive** *adj* 提供丰〔豐〕富知识〔識〕的 tígōng fēngfù zhīshi de. **instructor** *n* [C] 教员 jiàoyuán;指导者 zhǐdǎozhě.

instruction /ɪnˈstrʌkʃn/ *n* 1 [U] 教育 jiàoyù;指导〔導〕zhǐdǎo. 2 [C] 命令 mìnglìng. 3 **instructions** [pl] 用法说明 yòngfǎ shuōmíng;操作指南 cāozuò zhǐnán: *follow the ~s on a tin of paint* 按照颜料桶上的说明操作.

instrument /ˈɪnstrʊmənt/ *n* [C] 1 仪〔儀〕器 yíqì;器具 qìjù;器械 qìxiè. 2 乐〔樂〕器 yuèqì. **instrumental** /ˌɪnstrʊˈmentl/ *adj* 1 *in* 起作用的 qǐ zuòyòng de;有助于…的 yǒu zhùyú …de: *You were ~al in his promotion.* 他的提升,你是出了力的. 2 用乐器演奏的 yòng yuèqì yǎnzòu de;为〔爲〕乐器谱写〔寫〕的 wèi yuèqì pǔxiě de. **instrumentalist** /ˌɪnstrʊˈmentəlɪst/ *n* [C] 乐器演奏者 yuèqì yǎnzòuzhě.

insubordinate /ˌɪnsəˈbɔːdɪnət/ *adj* 不服从〔從〕的 bù fúcóng de;不听〔聽〕话的 bù tīnghuà de. **insubordination** /ˌɪnsəˌbɔːdɪˈneɪʃn/ *n* [C, U].

insufferable /ɪnˈsʌfrəbl/ *adj* 难〔難〕以忍受的 nányǐ rěnshòu de: ~ *behaviour* 令人难以忍受的行为.

insufficient /ˌɪnsəˈfɪʃnt/ *adj* 不足的 bùzúde;不够的 búgòude. **insufficiency** /-ʃnsɪ/ *n* [U]. **insufficiently** *adv*.

insular /ˈɪnsjʊlə(r); *US* -sələr/ *adj* 1 [贬] 思想狭〔狹〕窄的 sīxiǎng xiázhǎi de. 2 岛屿〔嶼〕的 dǎoyǔde. **insularity** /ˌɪnsjʊˈlærətɪ; *US* -səˈl-/ *n* [U].

insulate /ˈɪnsjʊleɪt; *US* -səl-/ *v* [T] 1 使绝缘 shǐ juéyuán;使绝热〔熱〕shǐ juérè: ~*d wires* 绝缘电线. 2 [喻]使隔离〔離〕(以免遭受不愉快) shǐ gélí. **insulation** /ˌɪnsjʊˈleɪʃn; *US* -səˈl-/ *n* [U] 绝缘 juéyuán;绝缘材料 juéyuáncáiliào.

insult /ɪnˈsʌlt/ *v* [T] 侮辱 wǔrǔ;凌辱 língrǔ. **insult** /ˈɪnsʌlt/ *n* [C] 侮辱的言词或行为〔爲〕wǔrǔde yáncí huò xíngwéi. **insulting** *adj*.

insurance /ɪnˈʃɔːrəns; *US* -ˈʃʊər-/ *n* 1 [U] (a) 保险〔險〕bǎoxiǎn. (b) 保险费 bǎoxiǎnfèi;保险金额 bǎoxiǎn jīn'é. 2 [C] [喻]安全保障 ānquán bǎozhàng.

insure /ɪnˈʃɔː(r); *US* ɪnˈʃʊər/ *v* [T] 1 给…上保险〔險〕gěi…shàng bǎoxiǎn: ~ *a car against fire/theft* 给汽车投保火险/盗险. 2 [美语] = ENSURE.

insurgent /ɪnˈsɜːdʒənt/ *adj* 暴动〔動〕的 bàodòngde;起义〔義〕的 qǐyìde;造反的 zàofǎnde. **insurgent** *n* [C] 暴动者 bàodòngzhě;起义者 qǐyìzhě.

insurmountable /ˌɪnsəˈmaʊntəbl/ *adj* [正式用语](问题、困难等)解决不了的 jiějué bùliǎo de;克服不了的 kèfú bùliǎo de.

insurrection /ˌɪnsəˈrekʃn/ *n* [C, U] 暴动〔動〕bàodòng;起义 qǐyì;造反 zàofǎn.

intact /ɪnˈtækt/ *adj* 未受损的 wèishòusǔnde;完整的 wánzhěngde.

intake /ˈɪnteɪk/ *n* 1 (a) [U] (机器等的液体、气体的)吸入 xīrù;纳入 nàrù. (b) [C] (液体等的)入口 rùkǒu. 2 [C, U] (人员的)吸收量 xīshōuliàng: *last year's ~ of students* 去年的新生数量.

intangible /ɪnˈtændʒəbl/ *adj* 1 难〔難〕以捉摸的 nányǐ zhuōmó de: *an ~ air of sadness* 说不出的凄惨气氛. 2 [商业](资产等)无〔無〕形的 wúxíng de: *the ~ value of a good reputation* 良好商誉的无形价值.

integer /ˈɪntɪdʒə(r)/ *n* [C] 整数〔數〕zhěngshù.

integral /ˈɪntɪgrəl/ *adj* 构〔構〕成整体〔體〕所必需的 gòuchéng zhěngtǐ suǒ bìxū de: *an ~ part of the plan* 计划的一个组成部分. **integrally** *adv*.

integrate /ˈɪntɪgreɪt/ *v* 1 [T] (*into/with*) 使一体〔體〕化 shǐ yìtǐhuà. 2 [I, T] (在种族、宗教等方面)使取消隔离〔離〕shǐ qǔxiāo gélí. **integration** /ˌɪntɪˈgreɪʃn/ *n* [U].

integrity /ɪnˈtegrətɪ/ *n* [U] 1 诚实〔實〕chéngshí;正直 zhèngzhí. 2 完整 wánzhěng;完全 wánquán.

intellect /ˈɪntəlekt/ *n* [U] 智力 zhìlì;才智 cáizhì. **intellectual** /ˌɪntɪˈlektʃʊəl/ *adj* 1 智力的 zhìlìde;理智的 lǐzhìde. 2 观〔觀〕念(而非实际问题)的 guānniànde. **intellectual** *n* [C] 知识〔識〕分子 zhīshi fènzǐ. **intellectually** *adv*.

intelligence /ɪnˈtelɪdʒəns/ *n* 1 [U] 智力 zhìlì;理解力 lǐjiělì. 2 (a) [U] (有关敌方的)情报〔報〕qíngbào. (b) [sing] [用 sing 或 pl v] 情报人员 qíngbào rényuán. **intelligent** /-dʒənt/ *adj* 聪〔聰〕颖的 cōngyǐngde. **intelligently** *adv*.

intelligible /ɪnˈtelɪdʒəbl/ *adj* 可理解的 kě lǐjiě de;明白的 míngbaide. **intelligibility** /ɪnˌtelɪdʒəˈbɪlətɪ/ *n* [U]. **intelligibly** *adv*.

I

intend /ɪnˈtend/ *v* [T] 打算 dǎsuàn;想要 xiǎngyào: *I ~ to leave soon*. 我打算很快就离开.

intense /ɪnˈtens/ *adj* 1 强烈的 qiángliède; 剧〔劇〕烈的 jùliède: ~ *heat* 酷热. ~ *anger* 勃然大怒. 2 (人)认〔認〕真的 rènzhēnde;热〔熱〕情的 rèqíngde. **intensely** *adv*. **intensify** /-sɪfaɪ/ *v* [*pt*, *pp* -ied] [I, T] 加强 jiāqiáng;加剧〔劇〕jiājù. **intensification** /ɪnˌtensɪfɪˈkeɪʃn/ *n* [U]. **intensity** *n* [U] 强烈 qiángliè;剧烈 jùliè;强度 qiángdù.

intensive /ɪnˈtensɪv/ *adj* 加强的 jiāqiángde;深入细致的 shēnrù xìzhì de;彻〔徹〕底的 chèdǐde: *an ~ search* 彻底的搜查. **intensively** *adv*.

intent[1] /ɪnˈtent/ *adj* 1 专〔專〕心的 zhuānxīnde;专注的 zhuānzhùde: *an ~ look/gaze* 专心致志的样子;目不转睛的注视. 2 *on* 下决心的 xià juéxīn de;坚〔堅〕决的 jiānjuéde: ~ *on becoming manager* 一心想成为经理. **intently** *adv*.

intent[2] /ɪnˈtent/ *n* 1 [U] (尤指法律)目的 mùdì;意图〔圖〕yìtú: *shoot with ~ to kill* 蓄意射杀. 2 [习语] **to all intents (and purposes)** 在一切重要方面 zài yíqiè zhòngyào fāngmiàn;实〔實〕际〔際〕上 shíjìshàng.

intention /ɪnˈtenʃn/ *n* [C, U] 意图〔圖〕yìtú;目的 mùdì. **intentional** /-ʃənl/ *adj* 有意的 yǒuyìde;故意的 gùyìde. **intentionally** *adv*.

inter /ɪnˈtɜː(r)/ *v* [-rr-] [T] [正式用语]埋葬 máizàng.

interact /ˌɪntərˈækt/ *v* [I] (*with*) 1 互相作用 hùxiāng zuòyòng;互相影响〔響〕hùxiāng yǐngxiǎng. 2 (人)互相联〔聯〕系〔繫〕hùxiāng liánxì. **interaction** /-ˈækʃn/ *n* [U, C]. **interactive** *adj* 1 互相作用的 hùxiāng zuòyòng de;互相影响的 hùxiāng yǐngxiǎng de. 2 [计算机]交互的 jiāohùde;人机〔機〕对〔對〕话的 rén jī duìhuà de.

intercept /ˌɪntəˈsept/ *v* [T] 拦〔攔〕截 lánjié;截击〔擊〕jiéjī;截断〔斷〕jiéduàn. **interception** /-ˈsepʃn/ *n* [U].

interchange /ˌɪntəˈtʃeɪndʒ/ *v* [I, T] 交换 jiāohuàn;互换 hùhuàn. ˈ**interchange** *n* 1 [C, U] 交换 jiāohuàn;互换 hùhuàn. 2 [C] (高速公路的)立体〔體〕交叉道 lìtǐ jiāochādào. **interchangeable** *adj*.

inter-city /ˌɪntəˈsɪtɪ/ *adj* (高速运输)城市间的 chéngshìjiānde;市际〔際〕间的 shìjìjiānde.

intercom /ˈɪntəkɒm/ *n* [C] 内部通话系统 nèibù tōnghuà xìtǒng;内部通话设备〔備〕nèibù tōnghuà shèbèi.

intercontinental /ˌɪntəˌkɒntɪˈnentl/ *adj* 洲际〔際〕的 zhōujìde: ~ *flights* 洲际飞行.

intercourse /ˈɪntəkɔːs/ *n* [U] [正式用语] 1 ⇨SEXUAL INTERCOURSE (SEXUAL). 2 交际〔際〕jiāojì;往来 wǎnglái.

interest /ˈɪntrəst/ *n* 1 [U, sing] (*in*) 兴〔興〕趣 xìngqù;好奇心 hàoqíxīn: *lose ~* 对…失去兴趣. *take an ~ in art* 对艺术感兴趣. 2 [U] 吸引力 xīyǐnlì;趣味 qùwèi: *an idea of ~ to us* 我们感兴趣的一个主意. 3 [C] 爱〔愛〕好的事物 àihàode shìwù: *His great ~ is football*. 他的一大爱好是足球. 4 [C, 常作 pl] 利益 lìyì;好处〔處〕hǎochù: *It is in your ~(s) to work hard*. 勤奋努力是对你有好处的. 5 [U] 利息 lìxī: *borrow money at a high rate of ~* 高利率借款. 6 [C, 常作 pl] 股份 gǔfèn. 7 [C, 常作 pl] 行业〔業〕hángyè. 8 [习语] **in the interests of sth** 为〔爲〕了某事(起见) wèile mǒushì. **interest** *v* [T] 使发〔發〕生兴趣 shǐ fāshēng xìngqù. **interested** *adj* 1 (*in*) (对某事)感兴趣的 gǎn xìngqù de: *be ~ed in history* 对历史感兴趣. 2 有(利害)关〔關〕系〔係〕的 yǒu guānxi de. **interesting** *adj* 引起兴趣的 yǐnqǐ xìngqù de.

interface /ˈɪntəfeɪs/ *n* [U] (计算机)界面 jièmiàn;接口 jiēkǒu.

interfere /ˌɪntəˈfɪə(r)/ *v* [I] 1 (*in*) 干预(他人的事) gānyù;干涉 gānshè. 2 *with* (a) (未得允许)摆〔擺〕弄 bǎinòng;损害 sǔnhài. (b) 妨碍〔礙〕fáng'ài;妨害 fánghài. 3 *with* (a) 干扰〔擾〕或妨碍某人 gānrǎo huò fáng'ài mǒurén. (b) [英国英语,婉]性骚扰 xìngsāorǎo;性攻击〔擊〕xìnggōngjī. **interference** *n* [U] 1 干预 gānyù;干涉 gānshè;妨碍 fáng'ài;性攻击 xìnggōngjī. 2 [无线电]干扰 gānrǎo.

interim /ˈɪntərɪm/ *adj* 临〔臨〕时〔時〕的 línshíde;暂时的 zànshíde: ~ *arrangements* 临时安排. **interim** *n* [习语] **in the interim** 在其间 zài qíjiān.

interior /ɪnˈtɪərɪə(r)/ *n* 1 [C] 内部 nèibù;里〔裏〕面 lǐmiàn. 2 **the interior** [sing] 内地 nèidì;内陆〔陸〕nèilù. **interior** *adj* 1 在内的 zàinèide;内部的 nèibùde. 2 内政的 nèizhèngde;内务〔務〕的 nèiwùde.

interjection /ˌɪntəˈdʒekʃn/ *n* [C] [语法]感叹〔嘆〕词 gǎntàncí.

interlock /ˌɪntəˈlɒk/ *v* [I, T] (使)连锁 liánsuǒ;(使)连结 liánjié.

interlude /ˈɪntəluːd/ *n* [C] 两事件中间的时〔時〕间 liǎng shìjiàn zhōngjiān de shíjiān;幕间 mùjiān.

intermarry /ˌɪntəˈmærɪ/ *v* [*pt*, *pp* -ied] [I] (指不同种族、宗教等)通婚 tōnghūn. **intermarriage** /-ˈmærɪdʒ/ *n* [U].

intermediary /ˌɪntəˈmiːdɪərɪ; *US* -dɪerɪ/ *n* [C] [*pl* -ies] 中间人 zhōngjiānrén;调解人 tiáojiěrén.

intermediate /ˌɪntəˈmiːdɪət/ *adj* 1 居间的

I

jūjiānde. 2 中级的 zhōngjíde: *an* ~ *course* 中级的课程.

interminable /ɪnˈtɜːmɪnəbl/ *adj* [常作贬] 无[無]休止的 wú xiūzhǐ de; 持续[續]过[過]长[長]的 chíxù guòcháng de. **interminably** *adv*.

intermission /ˌɪntəˈmɪʃn/ *n* [C, U] 间歇 jiànxiē; 幕间休息 mùjiān xiūxi.

intermittent /ˌɪntəˈmɪtənt/ *adj* 间歇的 jiànxiēde; 断[斷]断续[續]续的 duànduànxùxùde: ~ *rain* 时下时停的雨. **intermittently** *adv*.

intern[1] /ɪnˈtɜːn/ *v* [T] (尤指战时)拘留 jūliú; 扣押 kòuyā. **internment** *n* [U].

intern[2] /ˈɪntɜːn/ *n* [C] [美语] 实[實]习[習]医[醫]师[師] shíxí yīshī.

internal /ɪnˈtɜːnl/ *adj* 1 内部的 nèibùde; 在内部的 zài nèibùde: ~ *injuries* 内伤. 2 国[國]内的 guónèide; 内政的 nèizhèngde: ~ *trade* 国内贸易. **internally** *adv*.

international /ˌɪntəˈnæʃnəl/ *adj* 国[國]际[際]的 guójìde; 世界(性)的 shìjiède. **international** *n* [C] (a) (体育)国际比赛 guójì bǐsài. (b) 国际比赛选[選]手 guójì bǐsài xuǎnshǒu. **internationally** *adv*.

I

Internet /ˈɪntənet/ *n* [U] 因特网[網] Yīntèwǎng: *to be on the* ~ 正在上网. ˌ**Internet** ˈ**banking** *n* [U] 网[網]上银行 wǎngshàng yínháng. **Internet** ˈ**café** *n* [C] 网吧 wǎngbā. ˈ**Internet connection** *n* [C] 因特网联[聯]接 Yīntèwǎng liánjiē. **Internet** ˈ**Service Provider** *n* [C] 因特网服务[務]提供者 Yīntèwǎng fúwù tígōngzhě. **Internet** ˈ**shopping** *n* [U] 网上购[購]物 wǎngshàng gòuwù.

interplay /ˈɪntəpleɪ/ *n* [U] 相互影响[響] xiānghù yǐngxiǎng; 相互作用 xiānghù zuòyòng.

interpret /ɪnˈtɜːprɪt/ *v* 1 [T] 解释[釋] jiěshì; 说明 shuōmíng. 2 [T] *as* 理解 lǐjiě; 了[瞭]解 liǎojiě: ~ *his silence as an admission of guilt* 认为他的沉默是承认有罪. 3 [I,T] 口译[譯] kǒuyì. **interpretation** /ɪnˌtɜːprɪˈteɪʃn/ *n* [U,C] 说明 shuōmíng; 解释 jiěshì. **interpreter** *n* [C] 口译者 kǒuyìzhě; 译员 yìyuán.

interrogate /ɪnˈterəgeɪt/ *v* [T] 审[審]问 shěnwèn; 盘[盤]问 pánwèn. **interrogation** /ɪnˌterəˈgeɪʃn/ *n* [C, U]. **interrogator** *n* [C].

interrogative /ˌɪntəˈrɒgətɪv/ *adj* [语法]用于疑问句的 yòng yú yíwènjù de: ~ *pronouns/adverbs* 疑问代词; 疑问副词(例如 *who, why*). **interrogative** *n* [C] 疑问词 yíwèncí.

interrupt /ˌɪntəˈrʌpt/ *v* 1 [I,T] 打断[斷]讲[講]话 dǎduàn jiǎnghuà. 2 [T] 中断 zhōngduàn; 中止 zhōngzhǐ: ~ *a journey* 中断旅行. **interruption** /-ˈrʌpʃn/ *n* [C,U].

intersect /ˌɪntəˈsekt/ *v* 1 [I,T] (直线、道路等)相交 xiāngjiāo; 交叉 jiāochā. 2 [T] 横切 héngqiē; 横断[斷] héngduàn. **intersection** /-ˈsekʃn/ *n* 1 [U] 横切 héngqiē; 横断 héngduàn. 2 [C] 交叉路口 jiāochā lùkǒu; 十字路口 shízì lùkǒu.

intersperse /ˌɪntəˈspɜːs/ *v* [T] 散布 sànbù; 散置 sànzhì.

interval /ˈɪntəvl/ *n* [C] 1 (a) (两件事的)间隔时[時]间 jiàngé shíjiān. (b) 间隔空间 jiàngé kōngjiān. 2 [英国英语] (戏剧等的)幕间休息 mùjiān xiūxi.

intervene /ˌɪntəˈviːn/ *v* [I] [正式用语] 1 (*in*) 干预 gānyù; 干涉 gānshè. 2 (时间)介于 jièyú. 3 (事件)干扰[擾] gānrǎo; 阻挠[撓] zǔnáo. **intervening** *adj* 发[發]生于其间的 fāshēng yú qíjiān de: *in the intervening years* 发生在这几年. **intervention** /-ˈvenʃn/ *n* [C,U].

interview /ˈɪntəvjuː/ *n* [C] (*with*) 面试 miànshì; 面谈 miàntán. **interview** *v* [T] 采[採]访 cǎifǎng; 访问 fǎngwèn. **interviewer** *n* [C] 主持面试者 zhǔchí miànshìzhě; 采访者 cǎifǎngzhě.

intestate /ɪnˈtesteɪt/ *adj* [法律]未留遗嘱[囑]的 wèi liú yízhǔ de: *die* ~ 死时未留遗嘱.

intestine /ɪnˈtestɪn/ *n* [C, 尤作 pl] 肠[腸] cháng. **intestinal** *adj*.

intimacy /ˈɪntɪməsɪ/ *n* 1 [U] 亲[親]密 qīnmì; 亲近 qīnjìn. 2 **intimacies** [pl] 接吻 jiēwěn; 爱[愛]抚[撫] àifǔ.

intimate[1] /ˈɪntɪmət/ *adj* 1 亲[親]密的 qīnmìde: *They are* ~ *friends*. 他们是知己. 2 私人的 sīrénde; 个[個]人的 gèrénde: ~ *details of her life* 她生活中的隐私. 3 精通的 jīngtōngde: *an* ~ *knowledge of Greek* 对希腊语的精通. **intimately** *adv*.

intimate[2] /ˈɪntɪmeɪt/ *v* [T] [正式用语]宣布[佈] xuānbù; 通知 tōngzhī; 暗示 ànshì. **intimation** /ˌɪntɪˈmeɪʃn/ *n* [C,U].

intimidate /ɪnˈtɪmɪdeɪt/ *v* [T] 恫吓[嚇] dònghè; 威胁[脅] wēixié. **intimidation** /ɪnˌtɪmɪˈdeɪʃn/ *n* [U].

into /ˈɪntə, 元音前读作 ˈɪntuː/ *prep* 1 进[進]入 jìnrù; 到…里[裏]面 dào…lǐmiàn. 2 触[觸]及(某人、某物) chùjí: *A lorry drove* ~ *a line of cars*. 一辆卡车撞上一排汽车. 3 持续[續]到 chíxù dào: *work long* ~ *the night* 一直工作到深夜. 4(表示形式的变化): *Cut the paper* ~ *strips*. 把纸裁成条. 5(表示情况或行动的变化): *frighten sb* ~ *submission* 威逼某人顺从. 6(用以表示数学的)除 chú: 5 ~ 25 = 5. 5 除 25 等于 5. 7 [习语] **be into sth** [非

正式用语]对〔對〕…很有兴〔興〕趣 duì…hěn yǒu xìngqù.

intolerable /ɪnˈtɒlərəbl/ *adj* 无〔無〕法容忍的 wúfǎ róngrěn de; 不能忍受的 bùnéng rěnshòu de. **intolerably** *adv*.

intolerant /ɪnˈtɒlərənt/ *adj* 不容忍的 bù róngrěn de. **intolerance** /-rəns/ *n* [U].

intonation /ˌɪntəˈneɪʃn/ *n* [C,U] 语调 yǔdiào; 声〔聲〕调 shēngdiào.

intoxicate /ɪnˈtɒksɪkeɪt/ *v* [T] [正式用语] 1 使喝醉 shǐ hē zuì. 2[喻]使陶醉 shǐ táozuì: *~d with success* 为成功所陶醉. **intoxication** /ɪnˌtɒksɪˈkeɪʃn/ *n* [U].

intransitive /ɪnˈtrænsətɪv/ *adj* [语法](动词)不及物的 bùjíwùde.

in-tray /ˈɪn treɪ/ *n* [C] (办公室中存放待处理的信件等的)文件盘〔盤〕 wénjiànpán.

intrepid /ɪnˈtrepɪd/ *adj* [尤作修辞]勇敢的 yǒnggǎnde; 无〔無〕畏的 wúwèide: ~ *explorers* 无畏的探险者. **intrepidly** *adv*.

intricate /ˈɪntrɪkət/ *adj* 错综复〔複〕杂〔雜〕的 cuòzōng fùzá de. **intricacy** /-kəsɪ/ *n* [*pl* -ies] 1 [U] 错综复杂 cuòzōng fùzá. 2 [C,常作 pl]错综复杂的事物 cuòzōng fùzá de shìwù. **intricately** *adv*.

intrigue /ɪnˈtriːg/ *v* 1 [T] 引起…的兴〔興〕趣或好奇心 yǐnqǐ…de xìngqù huò hàoqíxīn: *be ~d by a story* 被一个故事迷住. 2 [I] 策划〔劃〕阴〔陰〕谋 cèhuà yīnmóu; 施诡计 shī guǐjì. **intrigue** /ˈɪntriːg, ɪnˈtriːg/ *n* 1 [U] 密谋 mìmóu. 2 [C]阴谋 yīnmóu. **intriguing** *adj* 引人入胜〔勝〕的 yǐn rén rù shèng de.

intrinsic /ɪnˈtrɪnsɪk, -zɪk/ *adj* (价值、性质)固有的 gùyǒude; 内在的 nèizàide. **intrinsically** /-klɪ/ *adv*.

introduce /ˌɪntrəˈdjuːs; US -ˈduːs/ *v* [T] 1 (*to*) 介绍相识〔識〕 jièshào xiāngshí; 引见 yǐnjiàn: *I ~d Paul to Sarah*. 我把保罗介绍给萨拉. 2 引进〔進〕 yǐnjìn; 采〔採〕用 cǎiyòng: ~ *computers into schools* 将计算机引进学校. 3 宣布〔佈〕并〔並〕介绍(细节) xuānbù bìng jièshào.

introduction /ˌɪntrəˈdʌkʃn/ *n* 1 [C,U] 介绍相识〔識〕 jièshào xiāngshí. 2 [C] (a) 引言 yǐnyán; 序言 xùyán. (b) 入门(书) rùmén. 3 [U] 初次投入使用 chūcì tóurù shǐyòng.

introductory /ˌɪntrəˈdʌktərɪ/ *adj* 导〔導〕言的 dǎoyánde; 序言的 xùyánde.

introspection /ˌɪntrəˈspekʃn/ *n* [U] 反省 fǎnxǐng; 内省 nèixǐng. **introspective** /-ˈspektɪv/ *adj*.

introvert /ˈɪntrəvɜːt/ *n* [C] 内向性格的人 nèixiàng xìnggé de rén. **introverted** *adj*.

intrude /ɪnˈtruːd/ *v* [I] *on* 闯入 chuǎngrù; 侵入 qīnrù. **intruder** *n* [C] 闯入者 chuǎngrùzhě; 入侵者 rùqīnzhě. **intrusion** /ɪnˈtruːʒn/ *n* [C,U]. **inˈtruder alarm** *n* [C] 防盗警报〔報〕器 fángdào jǐngbàoqì. **intrusive** /ɪnˈtruːsɪv/ *adj* 闯入的 chuǎngrùde; 侵入的 qīnrùde.

intuition /ˌɪntjuːˈɪʃn; US -tu-/ *n* 1 [U] 直觉〔覺〕 zhíjué; 直觉力 zhíjuélì. 2 [C] 直觉知识〔識〕 zhíjué zhīshi. **intuitive** /ɪnˈtjuːɪtɪv; US -ˈtuː-/ *adj*. **intuitively** *adv*.

inundate /ˈɪnʌndeɪt/ *v* [T] 1 淹没 yānmò; 泛滥〔濫〕 fànlàn. 2 [喻]压〔壓〕倒 yādǎo: *~d with replies* 回应的信件如雪片纷飞.

invade /ɪnˈveɪd/ *v* [T] 1 侵略 qīnlüè; 侵入 qīnrù; 侵犯 qīnfàn. 2 [喻]蜂拥〔擁〕而至 fēng yōng ér zhì: *Fans ~d the football pitch*. 球迷们拥进了足球场. **invader** *n* [C]. **invasion** /ɪnˈveɪʒn/ *n* [C,U].

invalid[1] /ɪnˈvælɪd/ *adj* 无〔無〕效的 wúxiàode; 作废〔廢〕的 zuòfèide: *an ~ argument / passport* 无效的辩论; 作废的护照. **invalidate** *v* [T] 使无效 shǐ wúxiào; 使作废 shǐ zuòfèi. **invalidation** /ɪnˌvælɪˈdeɪʃn/ *n* [U].

invalid[2] /ˈɪnvəlɪd, -liːd/ *n* [C] 病人 bìngrén; 病弱者 bìngruòzhě; 伤〔傷〕残〔殘〕者 shāngcánzhě. **invalid** *v* [短语动词] **invalid sb out (of sth)** (因病)使退役 shǐ tuìyì.

invaluable /ɪnˈvæljʊəbl/ *adj* 无〔無〕价〔價〕的 wújiàde; 非常宝〔寶〕贵的 fēicháng bǎoguì de.

invariable /ɪnˈveərɪəbl/ *adj* 不变〔變〕的 búbiànde; 永不变的 yǒng búbiàn de. **invariably** *adv* 不变地 búbiànde; 永恒地 yǒnghéngde: *He's invariably late*. 他总是迟到.

invasion ⇨ INVADE.

invective /ɪnˈvektɪv/ *n* [U] [正式用语]抨击〔擊〕 pēngjī; 谩骂 mànmà.

invent /ɪnˈvent/ *v* [T] 1 发〔發〕明 fāmíng; 创〔創〕造 chuàngzào: *Who ~ed television?* 谁发明了电视? 2 虚构〔構〕 xūgòu; 捏造 niēzào: ~ *an excuse* 捏造借口. **invention** /ɪnˈvenʃn/ *n* 1 [U] 发明 fāmíng; 创造 chuàngzào. 2 [C] 发明物 fāmíngwù. **inventive** *adj* 有发明才能的 yǒu fāmíng cáinéng de; 善于创造的 shànyú chuàngzào de. **inventor** *n* [C].

inventory /ˈɪnvəntrɪ; US -tɔːrɪ/ *n* [C] [*pl* -ies] 详细目录〔錄〕 xiángxì mùlù; 存货清单〔單〕 cúnhuò qīngdān; 存货盘〔盤〕存 cúnhuò páncún.

inverse /ˌɪnˈvɜːs/ *adj* (位置、关系等)相反的 xiāngfǎnde; 反向的 fǎnxiàngde. **inverse** /ˈɪnvɜːs/ *n* **the inverse** [sing] 相反 xiāngfǎn; 反面 fǎnmiàn.

invert /ɪnˈvɜːt/ *v* [T] 倒转〔轉〕 dàozhuǎn; 倒置 dàozhì. **inversion** /ɪnˈvɜːʃn; US ɪnˈvɜːrʒn/ *n* [U, C]. **inverted commas** *n* [pl] [英国英语] = QUOTATION-MARKS (QUOTATION).

I

invest /ɪnˈvest/ *v* 1 [I,T] (*in*) 投资 tóuzī: ~ (*money*) *in shares* 股票(金钱)投资. 2 [T] *in* 投入(时间、精力等) tóurù: ~ *one's time in learning French* 花时间学习法语. 3 [I] *in* [非正式用语]购〔購〕买〔買〕(价钱高的有用之物) gòumǎi: ~ *in a new car* 花一笔钱买辆新汽车. 4 [T] (*with*) [正式用语]授予 shòuyǔ. **investment** *n* 1 [U] 投资 tóuzī. 2 [C] 投资额 tóuzī'é. 3 [C] 接受投资的企业 jiēshòu tóuzī de qǐyè. **investor** *n* [C].

investigate /ɪnˈvestɪgeɪt/ *v* [I,T] 调查 diàochá; 调查研究 diàochá yánjiū: ~ *a murder* 调查谋杀案. **investigation** /ɪnˌvestɪˈgeɪʃn/ *n* [C,U]. **investigative** /-gətɪv; *US* -geɪtɪv/ *adj* 调查的 diàocháde. **investigator** *n* [C].

investiture /ɪnˈvestɪtʃə(r); *US* -tʃʊər/ *n* [C] 授权〔權〕(仪式) shòuquán; 授爵(仪式) shòujué; 授职〔職〕(仪式) shòuzhí.

inveterate /ɪnˈvetərət/ *adj* [贬](指恶习)根深蒂固的 gēn shēn dì gù de: *an* ~ *liar* / *smoker* 积习难改的说谎者;烟瘾很大的人.

invigilate /ɪnˈvɪdʒɪleɪt/ *v* [I,T] [英国英语]监〔監〕考 jiānkǎo. **invigilator** *n* [C].

invigorate /ɪnˈvɪgəreɪt/ *v* [T] 使生气〔氣〕勃勃 shǐ shēngqì bóbó; 使精力充沛 shǐ jīnglì chōngpèi. **invigorating** *adj*: *an invigorating walk* 令人爽快的散步.

invincible /ɪnˈvɪnsəbl/ *adj* 不可战〔戰〕胜〔勝〕的 bùkě zhànshèng de; 不能征服的 bù néng zhēngfú de.

inviolable /ɪnˈvaɪələbl/ *adj* [正式用语]不可侵犯的 bùkě qīnfàn de; 不可违〔違〕背的 bùkě wéibèi de: ~ *rights* 不可侵犯的权利.

inviolate /ɪnˈvaɪələt/ *adj* (*from*) [正式用语]不受侵犯的 bú shòu qīnfàn de; 未遭损害的 wèi zāo sǔnhài de.

invisible /ɪnˈvɪzəbl/ *adj* (*to*) 看不见的 kàn bú jiàn de; 无〔無〕形的 wúxíngde. **invisibility** /ɪnˌvɪzəˈbɪlətɪ/ *n* [U]. **invisibly** *adv*.

invite /ɪnˈvaɪt/ *v* [T] 1 (*to/for*) 邀请 yāoqǐng: ~ *sb to/for dinner* 邀请某人吃饭. 2 请求 qǐngqiú; 要求 yāoqiú; 征〔徵〕求 zhēngqiú. 3 引起 yǐnqǐ; 招致 zhāozhì: ~ *criticism* 招致批评. **invitation** /ˌɪnvɪˈteɪʃn/ *n* 1 [U] 邀请 yāoqǐng. 2 [C] 请求去(或来)某处 qǐngqiú qù mǒuchù: *an invitation to a party* 宴会请帖. **inviting** *adj* 动〔動〕人的 dòngrénde. **invitingly** *adv*.

invoice /ˈɪnvɔɪs/ *n* [C] 发〔發〕票 fāpiào; 发货清单〔單〕 fāhuò qīngdān. **invoice** *v* [T] 开〔開〕发票给(某人) kāi fāpiào gěi.

invoke /ɪnˈvəʊk/ *v* [T] [正式用语] 1 以…为〔爲〕行动〔動〕依据〔據〕 yǐ…wéi xíngdòng yījù. 2 祈求(上帝、法律等)帮〔幫〕助 qíqiú bāngzhù. 3 (用法术)召唤 zhàohuàn. **invocation** /ˌɪnvəˈkeɪʃn/ *n* [C,U] 祷〔禱〕告祈求 dǎogào qíqiú; 恳〔懇〕求帮助 kěnqiú bāngzhù.

involuntary /ɪnˈvɒləntrɪ; *US* -terɪ/ *adj* 无〔無〕意的 wúyìde; 非本意的 fēi běnyì de: *an* ~ *movement* 不自觉的动作. **involuntarily** /-trəlɪ; *US* ɪnˌvɒlənˈterəlɪ/ *adv*.

involve /ɪnˈvɒlv/ *v* [T] 1 需要 xūyào; 使…成为〔爲〕必要条〔條〕件(或结果) shǐ…chéngwéi bìyào tiáojiàn: *The job* ~*d me/my living in London*. 工作需要我住在伦敦. 2 包含 bāohán; 包括 bāokuò. 3 *in* 使陷入 shǐ xiànrù; 使卷〔捲〕入 shǐ juǎnrù. **involved** *adj* 1 复〔複〕杂〔雜〕的 fùzáde. 2 (a) (*in*) 有关〔關〕的 yǒuguānde. (b) (*with*) 有密切关系〔係〕的 yǒu mìqiè guānxì de. **involvement** *n* [U,C].

invulnerable /ɪnˈvʌlnərəbl/ *adj* 不能伤〔傷〕害的 bùnéng shānghài de; 不能损害的 bùnéng sǔnhàide.

inward /ˈɪnwəd/ *adj* 1 内部的 nèibùde; 内在的 nèizàide: ~ *thoughts* 内心的思想. 2 向内的 xiàngnèide. **inward** (亦作 **inwards**) *adv* 1 向内 xiàngnèi. 2 向着心灵〔靈〕 xiàng zhe xīnlíng. **inwardly** *adv* 在内心 zài nèixīn; 精神上 jīngshén shàng.

iodine /ˈaɪədiːn; *US* -daɪn/ *n* [U] 碘 diǎn.

ion /ˈaɪən; *US* 亦读 ˈaɪɒn/ *n* [C] 离〔離〕子 lízǐ. **ionize** *v* [I,T] (使)电〔電〕离 diànlí.

iota /aɪˈəʊtə/ *n* [sing] 极〔極〕少量 jí shǎoliàng.

IOU /ˌaɪ əʊ ˈjuː/ *n* [C] [非正式用语]借据〔據〕 jièjù.

IQ /ˌaɪ ˈkjuː/ *n* [C] 智商 zhìshāng: *have a high/low IQ* 智商高/低.

irate /aɪˈreɪt/ *adj* [正式用语]发〔發〕怒的 fānùde; 愤怒的 fènnùde. **irately** *adv*.

Ireland /ˈaɪələnd/ *n* 爱尔〔爾〕兰〔蘭〕岛 Ài'ěrlándǎo.

iridescent /ˌɪrɪˈdesnt/ *adj* [正式用语]彩虹色的 cǎihóngsède.

iris /ˈaɪərɪs/ *n* [C] 1 虹膜 hóngmó. 2 鸢尾属植物 yuānwěishǔ zhíwù.

irk /ɜːk/ *v* [T] 使厌〔厭〕烦 shǐ yànfán; 使苦恼〔惱〕 shǐ kǔnǎo. **irksome** /ˈɜːksəm/ *adj* 令人厌烦的 lìng rén yànfán de.

iron[1] /ˈaɪən; *US* ˈaɪərn/ *n* 1 [U] 铁〔鐵〕 tiě: *an* ~ *bridge/gate* 铁桥;铁门. 2 [C] 熨斗 yùndǒu. 3 **irons** [pl] 镣铐 liàokào. 4 [U] 坚〔堅〕强 jiānqiáng; 刚〔剛〕强 gāngqiáng: *have a will of* ~ / *an* ~ *will* 有钢铁般的意志. 5 [习语] **have many, etc irons in the fire** 同时〔時〕参〔參〕与〔與〕许多活动〔動〕 tóngshí cānyù xǔduō huódòng. **the ˌIron ˈCurtain** *n* [sing] 铁幕 tiěmù. **ironmonger** /ˈaɪənmʌŋgə(r)/ *n* [C] [英国英语]五金商 wǔjīnshāng.

iron[2] /ˈaɪən; US ˈaɪərn/ *v* 1 [I,T] 熨 yùn; 熨平 yùnpíng. 2 [短语动词] iron sth out 消除(困难〔難〕等) xiāochú. ironing *n* [U] 1 熨烫〔燙〕yùntàng. 2 要熨的衣物 yào yùn de yīwù: *do the ~ing* 熨衣服. ˈironing-board *n* [C] 熨衣板 yùnyībǎn.

ironic /aɪˈrɒnɪk/ (亦作 ironical /-kl/) *adj* 讽〔諷〕刺的 fěngcìde; 反语的 fǎnyǔde. ironically /-klɪ/ *adv*.

irony /ˈaɪərənɪ/ *n* [*pl* -ies] 1 [U] 反话 fǎnhuà; 冷嘲 lěngcháo. 2 [U,C] 出乎意料的事情 chū hū yìliào de shìqing; 讽刺性的事件(情况等) fěngcìxìngde shìjiàn.

irrational /ɪˈræʃənl/ *adj* 没有道理的 méiyǒu dàolǐ de; 荒谬的 huāngmiùde: *an ~ fear of water* 没有道理的怕水. irrationally /-nəlɪ/ *adv*.

irreconcilable /ɪˌrekənˈsaɪləbl/ *adj* [正式用语]不能和解的 bùnéng héjiě de; 相对〔對〕立的 xiāng duìlì de.

irregular /ɪˈregjʊlə(r)/ *adj* 1 不平坦的 bù píngtǎn de; 不整齐〔齊〕的 bù zhěngqí de: *an ~ surface* 不整齐的外表. 2 不规则的 bù guīzé de. 3 [语法]不规则(变化)的 bù guīzé de: *~ verbs* 不规则动词. irregularity /ɪˌregjʊˈlærətɪ/ *n* [C,U] [*pl* -ies]. irregularly *adv*.

irrelevant /ɪˈreləvənt/ *adj* 离〔離〕题的 lítíde; 不相干的 bù xiānggān de. irrelevance /-əns/ *n* [U].

irreparable /ɪˈrepərəbl/ *adj* (损失、伤害等)不能弥〔彌〕补〔補〕的 bùnéng míbǔ de; 无〔無〕可挽救的 wú kě wǎnjiù de.

irreplaceable /ˌɪrɪˈpleɪsəbl/ *adj* 不能替代的 bùnéng tìdài de.

irrepressible /ˌɪrɪˈpresəbl/ *adj* 不能抑制的 bùnéng yìzhì de; 不能控制的 bùnéng kòngzhì de.

irreproachable /ˌɪrɪˈprəʊtʃəbl/ *adj* [正式用语]无〔無〕可指责的 wú kě zhǐzé de; 无过〔過〕失的 wú guòshī de.

irresistible /ˌɪrɪˈzɪstəbl/ *adj* (强大得)不可抵抗的 bùkě dǐkàng de; 不能压〔壓〕制的 bùnéng yāzhì de. irresistibly *adv*.

irrespective /ˌɪrɪˈspektɪv/ irrespective of *prep* 不考虑〔慮〕的 bù kǎolǜ de; 不顾〔顧〕的 búgùde: *buy it now, ~ of the cost* 不考虑价钱,现在就买它.

irresponsible /ˌɪrɪˈspɒnsəbl/ *adj* 无〔無〕责任感的 wú zérèngǎn de; 不负责任的 bú fù zérèn de. irresponsibility /ˌɪrɪˌspɒnsəˈbɪlətɪ/ *n* [U]. irresponsibly *adv*.

irreverent /ɪˈrevərənt/ *adj* 不虔诚的 bù qiánchéng de; 不尊敬的 bù zūnjìng de. irreverence /-əns/ *n* [U]. irreverently *adv*.

irrevocable /ɪˈrevəkəbl/ *adj* [正式用语]不可改变〔變〕的 bùkě gǎibiàn de; 不可取消的 bùkě qǔxiāo de: *an ~ decision* 最后决定.

irrigate /ˈɪrɪgeɪt/ *v* [T] 灌溉(田地) guàngài. irrigation /ˌɪrɪˈgeɪʃn/ *n* [U].

irritable /ˈɪrɪtəbl/ *adj* 急躁的 jízàode; 易怒的 yìnùde. irritability /ˌɪrɪtəˈbɪlətɪ/ *n* [U]. irritably *adv*.

irritate /ˈɪrɪteɪt/ *v* [T] 1 激怒 jīnù; 使烦躁 shǐ fánzào. 2 使(身体某部分)感到不适 shǐ gǎndào búshì. irritation /ˌɪrɪˈteɪʃn/ *n* [U,C].

is ⇨ BE.

Islam /ɪzˈlɑːm; US ˈɪslɑːm/ *n* 1 [U] 伊斯兰〔蘭〕教 Yīsīlánjiào. 2 [sing] (总称)伊斯兰教徒 Yīsīlánjiàotú; 穆斯林 mùsīlín. Islamic /ɪzˈlæmɪk; US ɪsˈlɑːmɪk/ *adj*.

island /ˈaɪlənd/ *n* [C] 1 岛 dǎo; 岛屿〔嶼〕dǎoyǔ. 2 = TRAFFIC ISLAND (TRAFFIC). islander *n* [C] 岛民 dǎomín.

isle /aɪl/ *n* [C] (尤用于诗歌和专有名词中)岛 dǎo.

isn't /ˈɪznt/ is not. ⇨BE.

isolate /ˈaɪsəleɪt/ *v* [T] 隔离〔離〕gélí; 孤立 gūlì. isolated *adj* 隔离的 gélíde; 孤立的 gūlìde: *an ~d cottage* 孤立的小屋. isolation /ˌaɪsəˈleɪʃn/ *n* [U].

ISP /aɪ es ˈpiː/ *abbr* Internet Service Provider 因特网〔網〕服务〔務〕提供者 Yīntèwǎng fúwù tígōngzhě.

issue /ˈɪʃuː, ˈɪsjuː/ *n* 1[C] 议〔議〕题 yìtí; 争端 zhēngduān. 2[C] (杂志等的)期号〔號〕qīhào. 3 [U] 分发〔發〕fēnfā; 发出 fāchū. 4 [sing] [正式用语]结果 jiéguǒ. 5 [U] [法律]子女 zǐnǚ. 6 [习语] (the matter, point, etc) at issue 争议(或讨论)中的 zhēngyì zhōng de. issue *v* [正式用语] 1 [T] 公布〔佈〕gōngbù: *~ a statement* 发表声明. 2[T] 供给 gōngjǐ; 分配 fēnpèi: *~ weapons* 提供武器. 3 [I] 流出 liúchū.

it /ɪt/ *pron* (用作动词的主语或宾语或用于介词之后) 1 (a) 它(指东西、动物) tā: *Where's my book? Have you seen ~?* 我的书在哪儿? 你看见它没有? (b) 他(尤指性别不详的婴儿) tā. 2 (用以确定人的身份): '*Who's that?*' '*It's the postman.*' "是谁?" "是邮递员." 3(作主语或宾语的先行代词): *It's nice to see you.* 见到你很高兴. 4(指时间、距离或天气时作句中主语): *It's 12 o'clock.* 十二点钟. *It's raining.* 下雨了. 5(用以强调句中的任何部分): *It was work that exhausted him.* 是工作使他疲劳不堪. 6 [习语] this/that is ˈit (a) 这〔這〕(或那)正是所需要的 zhè zhèng shì suǒ xūyào de. (b) 这(或那)正是原因 zhè zhèng shì yuányīn. (c) 这(或那)就是终结 zhè jiù shì zhōngjié: *That's it, then —we've lost the match*. 到此为止——这场比赛我们已经输了. **its** /ɪts/ *adj* 它的 tāde;他的 tāde: *its tail* 它的尾巴.

IT /aɪ ˈtiː/ *abbr* information technology 信息技术〔術〕xìnxī jìshù.

Italian /ɪˈtæljən/ *adj* 意大利的 Yìdàlìde. **Italian** *n* 1 [C] 意大利人 Yìdàlìrén. 2 [U] 意大利语 Yìdàlìyǔ.

italic /ɪˈtælɪk/ *adj* (印刷字母)斜体〔體〕的 xiétǐde: *This is ~ type*. 这是斜体. **italics** *n* [pl] 斜体字母 xiétǐ zìmǔ.

Italy /ˈɪtəlɪ/ *n* [U] 意大利 Yìdàlì.

itch /ɪtʃ/ *n* 1 [C,常作 sing] 痒〔癢〕yǎng. 2 [sing]渴望 kěwàng: *have an ~ to travel* 渴望旅行. **itch** *v* 1 [I] 发〔發〕痒 fāyǎng. 2 [I] *for /to* [非正式用语]渴望 kěwàng. **itchy** *adj* 1 发痒的 fāyǎngde: *an ~y shirt* 使人穿上瘙痒的衬衫. 2[习语] (get/have) **itchy feet** [非正式用语]渴望旅行 kěwàng lǚxíng.

it'd /ˈɪtəd/ 1 it had. ⇨HAVE. 2 it would. ⇨WILL[1], WOULD[1].

item /ˈaɪtəm/ *n* [C] 1 条〔條〕款 tiáokuǎn;项目 xiàngmù. 2(新闻)一条 yìtiáo. **itemize** *v* [T] 分项记载 fēnxiàng jìzǎi;逐条列出 zhútiáo lièchū.

itinerant /aɪˈtɪnərənt/ *adj* [正式用语]巡回〔迴〕的 xúnhuíde: *an ~ preacher* 巡回传教士.

itinerary /aɪˈtɪnərərɪ; *US* -rerɪ/ *n* [C] [*pl* -ies] 旅行计划〔劃〕lǚxíng jìhuà;旅程 lǚchéng.

it'll /ˈɪtl/ it will. ⇨WILL[1].

its ⇨IT.

it's /ɪts/ 1 it is. ⇨ BE. 2 it has. ⇨ HAVE.

itself /ɪtˈself/ *pron* 1 [反身]它自己 tā zìjǐ;它本身 tā běnshēn: *My dog hurt ~*. 我的狗伤了它自己. 2(用于加强语气): *The name ~ sounds foreign*. 这名字本身听起来就陌生. 3 [习语] (all) **by itˈself** (a) 自动〔動〕地 zìdòngde. (b) 独〔獨〕自地 dúzìde.

ITV /ˌaɪ tiː ˈviː/ *abbr* Independent Television 独〔獨〕立电〔電〕视公司 dúlì diànshì gōngsī.

I've /aɪv/ I have. ⇨ HAVE.

IVF /ˌaɪ viː ˈef/ *abbr* in-vitro fertilization 体〔體〕外受精 tǐwài shòujīng.

ivory /ˈaɪvərɪ/ *n* [U] 1 象牙 xiàngyá;长〔長〕牙 chángyá. 2 象牙色 xiàngyásè;乳白色 rǔbáisè. 3 [习语] **an ˌivory ˈtower** 象牙塔 xiàngyátǎ.

ivy /ˈaɪvɪ/ *n* [U] 常春藤 chángchūnténg.

J j

J, j /dʒeɪ/ *n* [C] [*pl* **J's, j's** /dʒeɪz/] 英语的第十个〔個〕字母 Yīngyǔde dìshígè zìmǔ.

jab /dʒæb/ *v* [-bb-] [I,T] 刺 cì;戳 chuō;猛击〔擊〕měngjī. **jab** *n* [C] 1 猛刺 měngcì;猛戳 měngchuō;猛击 měngjī. 2 [非正式用语]打针 dǎzhēn;注射 zhùshè.

jabber /ˈdʒæbə(r)/ *v* [I,T] 急促而激动〔動〕地说 jícù ér jīdòngde shuō. **jabber** *n* [U] 喋喋不休 diédié bùxiū.

jack[1] /dʒæk/ *n* [C] 1 起重器 qǐzhòngqì;千斤顶 qiānjīndǐng. 2(纸牌中的)杰克(介于 10 点和王后之间) jiékè.

jack[2] /dʒæk/ *v* [短语动词] **jack sth in** [俚]停止(工作等) tíngzhǐ;放弃〔棄〕fàngqì. **jack sth up** (用千斤顶)顶起 dǐngqǐ.

jacket /ˈdʒækɪt/ *n* [C] 1 短上衣 duǎn shàngyī;夹〔夾〕克 jiākè. 2(罐、管等的)保护〔護〕罩 bǎohùzhào;隔离〔離〕罩 gélízhào. 3(土豆的)皮 pí. 4 (书的)护〔護〕封 hùfēng.

jack-knife /ˈdʒæknaɪf/ *n* [C] [*pl* -knives] (可放袋内的)大折刀 dà zhédāo. **jack-knife** *v* [I] (尤指铰接车辆)发〔發〕生弯〔彎〕折 fāshēng wānzhé.

jackpot /ˈdʒækpɒt/ *n* [C] (游戏等)大笔〔筆〕收入 dàbǐ shōurù;巨额奖〔獎〕金 jù'é jiǎngjīn.

Jacuzzi /dʒəˈkuːzɪ/ *n* [C] (*P*)(一种漩水)浴缸 yùgāng.

jade /dʒeɪd/ *n* [U] 翡翠 fěicuì;玉 yù;硬玉 yìngyù.

jaded /ˈdʒeɪdɪd/ *adj* 精疲力竭的 jīng pí lì jié de.

jagged /ˈdʒægɪd/ *adj* 边〔邊〕缘不整齐〔齊〕的 biānyuán bù zhěngqí de;参差不齐的 cēncī bù qí de.

jaguar /ˈdʒægjʊə(r)/ *n* [C] 美洲虎 měizhōuhǔ;美洲豹 měizhōubào.

jail = GAOL.

jam[1] /dʒæm/ *n* [U] 果酱〔醬〕guǒjiàng.

jam[2] /dʒæm/ *v* [-mm-] 1 [T] 把…塞入 bǎ…sāirù;使挤〔擠〕满 shǐ jǐmǎn: *~ clothes into a suitcase* 把衣服塞进箱子里. 2 [I,T] (机器等)发〔發〕生故障 fāshēng gùzhàng: *The window ~med*. 窗户卡住了. 3 [T] 堵塞(道路或地区) dǔsè;阻塞 zǔsè. 4[T] (无线电)干扰〔擾〕gānrǎo. 5 [短语动词] **jam sth on** 猛踩(制动器) měngcǎi;急拉 jílā. **jam** *n* [C] 1 拥〔擁〕挤 yōngjǐ;堵塞 dǔsè: *a traffic ~* 交通堵塞. 2 [非正式用语]困境 kùnjìng;窘境 jiǒngjìng: *be in a ~* 陷入困境.

jangle /ˈdʒæŋgl/ *v* [I,T] (使)发〔發〕出刺耳

J

的金属〔屬〕声〔聲〕 fāchū cì'ěrde jīnshǔshēng. **jangle** *n* [sing] 刺耳的金属声 cì'ěrde jīnshǔshēng.

janitor /ˈdʒænɪtə(r)/ *n* [C] [美语]看门人 kānménrén;管门人 guǎnménrén.

January /ˈdʒænjʊərɪ; *US* -jʊerɪ/ *n* [U, C] 一月 yīyuè.

Japan /dʒəˈpæn/ *n* [U] 日本 Rìběn.

Japanese /ˌdʒæpəˈniːz/ *adj* 日本的 Rìběnde. **Japanese** *n* 1 [C] 日本人 Rìběnrén. 2 [U] 日语 Rìyǔ.

jar[1] /dʒɑː(r)/ *n* [C] 1 罐子 guànzi;坛〔罎〕子 tánzi;广〔廣〕口瓶 guǎngkǒupíng. 2 一罐(或一坛)之量 yīguàn zhī liàng: *a* ～ *of honey* 一瓶蜂蜜.

jar[2] /dʒɑː(r)/ *v* [-rr-] 1 [I] (*on*) 有不愉快的感觉〔覺〕 yǒu bù yúkuài de gǎnjué: *Her singing really* ～*s on my nerves*. 她的歌声确实使我的神经受到刺激. 2 [I] (*with*) 不和谐 bù héxié;不一致 bù yīzhì. 3 [T] 震伤〔傷〕 zhènshāng;震动〔動〕 zhèndòng. **jarring** *adj*.

jargon /ˈdʒɑːgən/ *n* [U] 行话 hánghuà;切口 qièkǒu: *medical* ～ 医学用语.

jaundice /ˈdʒɔːndɪs/ *n* [U] 黄疸 huángdǎn. **jaundiced** *adj* 妒忌的 dùjìde;怨恨的 yuànhènde;猜疑的 cāiyíde: *a* ～*d opinion* 带怨恨的偏见.

jaunt /dʒɔːnt/ *n* [C] 短途游览〔覽〕 duǎntú yóulǎn: *go on a* ～ 作短途游览.

javelin /ˈdʒævlɪn/ *n* [C] 标〔標〕枪〔槍〕 biāoqiāng.

jaw /dʒɔː/ *n* 1 [C] 颌 hé: *the lower/upper* ～ 下/上颌. 2 [sing] 下颌 xiàhé;下巴 xiàba. 3 **jaws** [pl] 口部 kǒubù;嘴 zuǐ: [喻] *escape from the* ～*s of death* 逃脱险境. 4 **jaws** [pl] (工具、机器等)夹住东西的部分 jiā zhù dōngxi de bùfen. ˈ**jaw-bone** *n* [C] 下颌骨 xiàhégǔ.

jazz /dʒæz/ *n* [U] 爵士乐〔樂〕 juéshìyuè. **jazz** *v* 1 [T] 用爵士乐风〔風〕格演奏 yòng juéshìyuè fēnggé yǎnzòu. 2 [短语动词] **jazz sth up** 使…有生气〔氣〕 shǐ…yǒu shēngqì. **jazzy** *adj* [-ier, -iest] [非正式用语] 1 爵士乐的 juéshìyuède. 2 鲜明的 xiānmíngde;花哨的 huāshaode: *a* ～*y tie* 花哨的领带.

jealous /ˈdʒeləs/ *adj* 1 妒忌的 dùjìde: *a* ～ *husband* 爱妒忌的丈夫. 2 (*of*) 羡慕的 xiànmùde. 3 精心守护〔護〕的 jīngxīn shǒuhù de: ～ *of one's rights* 珍惜自己的权利. **jealously** *adv*. **jealousy** *n* [U, C] [*pl* -ies].

jeans /dʒiːnz/ *n* [pl] 牛仔裤 niúzǎikù.

Jeep /dʒiːp/ *n* [C] (*P*)吉普车 jípǔchē.

jeer /dʒɪə(r)/ *v* [I, T] (*at*) 嘲笑 cháoxiào;嘲弄 cháonòng. **jeer** *n* [C] 讥〔譏〕笑的言语 jīxiàode yányǔ;奚落人的话 xīluò rén de huà.

jelly /ˈdʒelɪ/ *n* [*pl* -ies] 1 [U, C] 果(子)冻 guǒdòng. 2 [U] 果酱〔醬〕 guǒjiàng: *blackcurrant* ～ 黑醋栗果酱. ˈ**jellyfish** *n* [C] [*pl* **jellyfish** 或～**es**] 水母 shuǐmǔ;海蜇 hǎizhé.

jeopardize /ˈdʒepədaɪz/ *v* [T] 使陷险〔險〕境 shǐ xiàn xiǎnjìng;危及 wēijí. **jeopardy** /-pədɪ/ *n* [习语] **in jeopardy** 处〔處〕于失败(受损失等)的险境 chǔyú shībàide xiǎnjìng: *The success of our plan has been put in jeopardy*. 我们的计划已面临失败的危险.

jerk /dʒɜːk/ *n* [C] 1 急动〔動〕 jídòng;急拉 jílā. 2 [非正式用语,贬] 蠢人 chǔnrén. **jerk** *v* [I, T] (使)猛然一动 měngrán yīdòng;急拉 jílā. **jerky** *adj* [-ier, -iest] 忽动忽停的 hūdòng hūtíng de.

jersey /ˈdʒɜːzɪ/ *n* [C] 毛织〔織〕紧〔緊〕身套衫 máozhī jǐnshēn tàoshān.

jest /dʒest/ *n* 1 [C] 玩笑 wánxiào;笑话 xiàohuà. 2 [习语] **in jest** 开〔開〕玩笑地 kāi wánxiào de. **jest** *v* [I] [正式用语]说笑话 shuō xiàohuà;开玩笑 kāi wánxiào.

jet[1] /dʒet/ *n* [C] 1 喷气〔氣〕式飞〔飛〕机〔機〕 pēnqìshì fēijī. 2 (a)喷射 pēnshè. (b) 喷射口 pēnshèkǒu;喷嘴 pēnzuǐ. **jet** *v* [-tt-] [I] 乘喷气式飞机 chéng pēnqìshì fēijī. ˈ**jet engine** *n* [C] 喷气发〔發〕动〔動〕机 pēnqì fādòngjī. ˈ**jet lag** *n* [U] 喷气机飞行时〔時〕差反应〔應〕 pēnqìjī fēixíng shíchā fǎnyìng. **the** ˈ**jet set** *n* [sing] (乘喷气式飞机周游世界的)喷气式飞机阶〔階〕层〔層〕 pēnqìshì fēijī jiēcéng. ˈ**jet ski** *n* [C] 喷气式滑水车〔車〕 pēnqìshì huáshuǐchē. ˈ**jet-ski** *v* [I] 做喷气式滑水 zuò pēnqìshì huáshuǐ. ˈ**jet-skiing** *n* [U] 喷气式滑水 pēnqìshì huáshuǐ.

jet[2] /dʒet/ *n* [U] 煤玉 méiyù;黑玉 hēiyù. **jet-**ˈ**black** *adj* 乌黑发〔發〕亮的 wūhēi fāliàng de.

jettison /ˈdʒetɪsn/ *v* [T] 丢弃〔棄〕 diūqì;抛弃 pāoqì.

jetty /ˈdʒetɪ/ *n* [C] [*pl* -ies] 防波堤 fángbōdī;码头〔頭〕 mǎtóu.

Jew /dʒuː/ *n* [C] 犹〔猶〕太人 Yóutàirén;犹太教徒 Yóutài jiàotú.

jewel /ˈdʒuːəl/ *n* [C] 1 宝〔寶〕石 bǎoshí. 2 (手表内的)宝石轴承 bǎoshí zhóuchéng. 3 [喻] 受珍重的人或物 shòu zhēnzhòng de rén huò wù. **jeweller** (美语 -l-) *n* [C] 宝石商 bǎoshíshāng;珠宝商 zhūbǎoshāng;宝石匠 bǎoshíjiàng. **jewellery** (亦作 **jewelry**) /-rɪ/ *n* [U] 珠宝 zhūbǎo;首饰〔飾〕 shǒushì.

jibe = GIBE.

jiffy /ˈdʒɪfɪ/ *n* [C] [*pl* -ies] [非正式用语] 瞬间 shùnjiān;一会〔會〕儿〔兒〕 yīhuìr.

jig /dʒɪg/ *n* [C] 吉格舞 jígéwǔ;吉格舞曲 jígé

J

wǔqǔ. **jig** *v* [-gg-] **1** [I] 跳吉格舞 tiào jígé-wǔ. **2** [I,T] 上下急动〔動〕shàngxià jídòng; 急速颠簸 jísù diānbǒ.

jiggle /ˈdʒɪgl/ *v* [I,T] [非正式用语]轻〔輕〕快地左右(或上下)移动〔動〕qīngkuàide zuǒyòu yídòng.

jigsaw /ˈdʒɪgsɔː/ *n* [C] (亦作 ˈ**jigsaw puzzle**) 拼图〔圖〕玩具 pīntú wánjù.

jilt /dʒɪlt/ *v* [T] 抛弃〔棄〕(情人) pāoqì; 遗弃 yíqì.

jingle /ˈdʒɪŋgl/ *n* **1** [sing] (硬币、小铃、钥匙等碰击时发出的)丁当〔當〕声〔聲〕dīngdāng-shēng. **2**[C](广告)押韵的短诗或短歌 yāyùnde duǎnshī huò duǎngē. **jingle** *v* [I,T] (使)发〔發〕出丁当声 fāchū dīngdāngshēng.

jinx /dʒɪŋks/ *n* [C,常作 sing] 不祥的人或物 bùxiángde rén huò wù.

jive /dʒaɪv/ *n* [sing] (常作 **the jive**) 摇摆〔擺〕乐〔樂〕yáobǎiyuè; 摇摆舞 yáobǎiwǔ.

job /dʒɒb/ *n* [C] **1** 职〔職〕业〔業〕zhíyè; 职位 zhíwèi. **2** (一件)工作 gōngzuò. **3** 难〔難〕做的工作 nánzuòde gōngzuò: *Finding a flat to rent was quite a* ～. 找一套出租的公寓房可不是件容易的事. **4** [常作 sing] 职责 zhízé; 作用 zuòyòng: *It is not my* ～ *to do this*. 做这件事不是我分内的事. **5** [非正式用语]犯罪行为〔爲〕(尤指盗窃) fànzuì xíngwéi. **6** [习语] **just the** ˈ**job** [非正式用语]正是想要的 zhèng shì xiǎngyàode. **make a bad, good, etc job of sth** 将某事做坏〔壞〕、做好等 jiāng mǒushì zuò huài、zuò hǎo děng. **jobless** *adj* 失业的 shīyède. **job sharing** *n* [C] 一工分做制(两人分时做一份工作) yì gōng fēn zuò zhì.

jockey[1] /ˈdʒɒkɪ/ *n* [C] 职〔職〕业〔業〕赛马骑师〔師〕zhíyè sàimǎ qíshī.

jockey[2] /ˈdʒɒkɪ/ *v* [短语动词] **jockey for sth** 用手段获〔獲〕取(利益、好处等) yòng shǒuduàn huòqǔ: ～ *for position* 用计谋获得职位.

jog /dʒɒg/ *v* [-gg-] **1** [T] 轻〔輕〕推 qīngtuī; 轻撞 qīngzhuàng. **2** [I] 慢跑 mànpǎo. **3** [习语] **jog sb's memory** 唤起某人的记忆〔憶〕huànqǐ mǒurénde jìyì. **4** [短语动词] **jog along/on** 持续〔續〕而缓慢地进〔進〕行 chíxù ér huǎnmànde jìnxíng. **jog** *n* [sing] **1** 轻推 qīngtuī; 轻撞 qīngzhuàng. **2** 慢跑 mànpǎo. **jogger** *n* [C] 慢跑的人 mànpǎode rén.

join /dʒɔɪn/ *v* **1** [T] 连接 liánjiē; 接合 jiēhé. **2** [I,T] (与)会〔會〕合 huìhé; 相聚 xiāngjù: *The two roads* ～ *here*. 两条路在这里连接. *Please* ～ *us for a drink*. 请和我们一起喝点. **3** [T] 参〔參〕加 cānjiā; 加入 jiārù: ～ *a club* 加入俱乐部. **4** [习语] **join** ˈ**forces (with sb)** 联〔聯〕合以达〔達〕到共同的目的 liánhé yǐ dádào gòngtóngde mùdì. **5**[短语动词] **join in (sth)** 参〔參〕加(活动) cānjiā. **join** *n* [C] 连接处〔處〕liánjiēchù.

joiner /ˈdʒɔɪnə(r)/ *n* [C] 细木工人 xìmù gōngrén. **joinery** *n* [C] 细木工的工作(或制品) xìmùgōngde gōngzuò.

joint[1] /dʒɔɪnt/ *n* [C] **1** 关〔關〕节〔節〕guānjié. **2** 连接处〔處〕liánjiēchù; 接合点〔點〕jiēhé-diǎn: *the* ～*s of a pipe* 管道的接口. **3** 大块〔塊〕肉 dàkuài ròu. **4**[俚,贬]下流场〔場〕所(酒馆、赌场等) xiàliú chǎngsuǒ. **5**[俚]含大麻的香烟 hán dàmá de xiāngyān.

joint[2] /dʒɔɪnt/ *adj* 共有的 gòngyǒude; 共同做的 gòngtóng zuò de: ～ *responsibility* 共同的责任. *a* ～ *account* 共同账户. **jointly** *adv*.

joist /dʒɔɪst/ *n* [C] 小梁〔樑〕xiǎoliáng; (地板等的)托梁 tuōliáng.

joke /dʒəʊk/ *n* [C] 笑话 xiàohuà; 玩笑 wánxiào. **joke** *v* [I] 开〔開〕玩笑 kāi wánxiào. **joker** *n* [C] **1** 喜开玩笑的人 xǐ kāi wánxiào de rén. **2**(纸牌)百搭(可作任何点数的牌或王牌) bǎidā. **jokingly** *adv* 开玩笑地 kāi wánxiào de.

jolly /ˈdʒɒlɪ/ *adj* [-ier, -iest] 高兴〔興〕的 gāoxìngde; 愉快的 yúkuàide. **jolly** *adv* [英国非正式用语]很 hěn; 非常 fēicháng: *a* ～ *good teacher* 一位非常好的老师.

jolt /dʒəʊlt/ *v* [I,T] (使)颠簸 diānbǒ; 颠簸而行 diānbǒ ér xíng. **jolt** *n* [C,常作 sing] 颠簸 diānbǒ; 震动〔動〕zhèndòng.

jostle /ˈdʒɒsl/ *v* [I,T] 推撞 tuīzhuàng; 拥〔擁〕挤〔擠〕yōngjǐ.

jot /dʒɒt/ *v* [-tt-] [短语动词] **jot sth down** 草草记下 cǎocǎo jì xià. **jotter** *n* [C] 笔〔筆〕记本 bǐjìběn; 记事本 jìshìběn.

journal /ˈdʒɜːnl/ *n* [C] **1** 日报〔報〕rìbào; 期刊 qīkān; 杂〔雜〕志〔誌〕zázhì. **2** 日志 rìzhì; 日记 rìjì. **journalism** /-nəlɪzəm/ *n* [C] 新闻工作 xīnwén gōngzuò. **journalist** *n* [C] 新闻工作者 xīnwén gōngzuò zhě; 新闻记者 xīnwén jìzhě.

journey /ˈdʒɜːnɪ/ *n* [C] 旅行 lǚxíng. **journey** *v* [I] [正式用语] 旅行 lǚxíng.

jovial /ˈdʒəʊvɪəl/ *adj* 和蔼快活的 hé'ǎi kuàihuó de; 愉快的 yúkuàide.

joy /dʒɔɪ/ *n* **1** [U] 快乐〔樂〕kuàilè; 喜悦 xǐyuè. **2**[C] 乐事 lèshì. **joyful** *adj* 充满欢〔歡〕乐的 chōngmǎn huānlè de; 使人高兴〔興〕的 shǐ rén gāoxìng de. **joyfully** *adv*. **joyous** *adj* [修辞] 充满欢乐的 chōngmǎn huānlè de. **joyously** *adv*.

jubilant /ˈdʒuːbɪlənt/ *adj* [正式用语](尤指由于成功)欢〔歡〕欣的 huānxīnde; 欣喜的 xīnxǐde. **jubilation** /ˌdʒuːbɪˈleɪʃn/ *n* [U] 欢欣 huānxīn; 欢腾 huānténg.

jubilee /ˈdʒuːbɪliː/ *n* [C] (有特定意义的)周

〔週〕年纪念 zhōunián jìniàn.

Judaism /ˈdʒuːdeɪɪzəm; *US* -dɪɪzəm/ *n* [U] 犹〔猶〕太教 Yóutàijiào; 犹太人的文化 Yóutàirén de wénhuà.

judge /dʒʌdʒ/ *n* [C] 1 法官 fǎguān; 审〔審〕判员 shěnpànyuán. 2 裁判员 cáipànyuán; 评判人 píngpànrén. 3 鉴〔鑒〕赏家 jiànshǎngjiā; 鉴定人 jiàndìngrén: *She's a good ~ of character.* 她是一位善于鉴别人的个性的人. **judge** *v* [I, T]. 1 审判 shěnpàn; 审理 shěnlǐ. 2 断〔斷〕定 duàndìng; 判断 pànduàn.

judgement (尤用于法律 **judgment**) /ˈdʒʌdʒmənt/ *n* 1 [C] 意见 yìjiàn: *make a fair ~ of his character* 对他的品格作出公正的评价. 2 [C, U] (法官或法庭的)判决 pànjué; 裁决 cáijué: *The court has still to pass ~.* 法庭仍需作出判决. 3 [U] 判断〔斷〕力 pànduànlì.

judicial /dʒuːˈdɪʃl/ *adj* 法庭的 fǎtíngde; 法官的 fǎguānde; 审〔審〕判的 shěnpànde.

judiciary /dʒuːˈdɪʃərɪ; *US* -ʃɪerɪ/ *n* [C, 亦作 sing, 用 pl v] [*pl* -ies] (总称)法官 fǎguān.

judicious /dʒuːˈdɪʃəs/ *adj* [正式用语]有见识〔識〕的 yǒu jiànshide; 明智的 míngzhìde. **judiciously** *adv*.

judo /ˈdʒuːdəʊ/ *n* [U] (日本)柔道 róudào.

jug /dʒʌg/ *n* [C] [英国英语] 1 壶〔壺〕hú; 罐 guàn. 2 一壶(或一罐)的容量 yìhúde róngliàng: *a ~ of milk* 一罐牛奶.

juggernaut /ˈdʒʌgənɔːt/ *n* [C] [英国英语] 重型货车 zhòngxíng huòchē.

juggle /ˈdʒʌgl/ *v* [I, T] 1(用球等)玩杂〔雜〕耍 wán záshuǎ; 变〔變〕戏〔戲〕法 biàn xìfǎ. 2 (*with*) 耍花招 shuǎ huāzhāo; 欺骗 qīpiàn: *juggling (with) the figures* 篡改数字. **juggler** *n* [C].

juice /dʒuːs/ *n* [U, C] 果汁 guǒzhī; 菜汁 càizhī; 肉汁 ròuzhī. **juicy** *adj* [-ier, -iest] 1 多汁的 duōzhīde. 2 [非正式用语]有趣的(尤指丑事) yǒuqùde.

juke-box /ˈdʒuːkbɒks/ *n* [C] (投币式)自动〔動〕唱机〔機〕zìdòng chàngjī.

July /dʒuːˈlaɪ/ *n* [U, C] 七月 qīyuè.

jumble /ˈdʒʌmbl/ *v* [T] (*up*) 使混杂〔雜〕shǐ hùnzá. **jumble** *n* 1 [sing] 杂乱〔亂〕的一堆 záluànde yìduī; 混乱 hùnluàn. 2 [U] [英国英语]廉卖〔賣〕的旧〔舊〕杂物 lián mài de jiù záwù. ˈ**jumble sale** *n* [C] [英国英语](为慈善筹款)旧杂物义〔義〕卖 jiù záwù yìmài.

jumbo /ˈdʒʌmbəʊ/ *adj* [非正式用语]特大的 tèdàde; 巨大的 jùdàde. **jumbo** *n* [C] [*pl* ~s] (亦作 **jumbo** ˈ**jet**) 大型喷气〔氣〕式客机〔機〕dàxíng pēnqìshì kèjī.

jump[1] /dʒʌmp/ *v* 1 [I] 跳 tiào; 跳跃〔躍〕tiàoyuè: *~ up in the air* 向上跳起来. 2[T] 跳过〔過〕tiàoguò; 跃过 yuèguò: *~ a wall* 跳过一堵墙. 3 [I] 迅速而突然行动〔動〕xùnsù ér tūrán xíngdòng: *The loud bang made me ~.* 砰的一声巨响吓我一跳. 4 [I] 暴涨〔漲〕bàozhǎng; 猛增 měngzēng: *Prices ~ed by 60% last year.* 物价去年暴涨 60%. 5 [T] [非正式用语]突然攻击〔擊〕tūrán gōngjī. 6[习语] **jump on the bandwagon** ⇨ BAND. **jump the gun** 抢〔搶〕先做某事 qiǎngxiān zuò mǒushì. **jump the queue** 在未轮〔輪〕到前抢〔搶〕先获〔獲〕得某物 zài wèi lúndào qián qiǎngxiān huòdé mǒuwù. **jump to conˈclusions** 匆匆作出结论 cōngcōng zuòchū jiélùn. 7 [短语动词] **jump at sth** 迫不及待地抓住 pò bù jí dài de zhuāzhù. **jumper** *n* [C].

jump[2] /dʒʌmp/ *n* [C] 1 跳 tiào; 跳跃〔躍〕tiàoyuè. 2(需跳越的)障碍〔礙〕物 zhàngˈàiwù. 3 (*in*) 猛增 měngzēng; 暴涨〔漲〕bàozhǎng: *a huge ~ in profits* 利润大增. **jumpy** *adj* [-ier, -iest] [非正式用语]神经〔經〕质〔質〕的 shénjīngzhìde; 焦虑〔慮〕的 jiāolǜde.

jumper /ˈdʒʌmpə(r)/ *n* [C] [英国英语] = JERSEY

junction /ˈdʒʌŋkʃn/ *n* [C] (公路、铁路的)交叉点〔點〕jiāochādiǎn; 交叉口 jiāochākǒu.

juncture /ˈdʒʌŋktʃə(r)/ *n* [习语] **at this juncture** [正式用语]在此时〔時〕zài cǐshí.

June /dʒuːn/ *n* [U, C] 六月 liùyuè.

jungle /ˈdʒʌŋgl/ *n* [C, U] 丛〔叢〕林 cónglín, 密林 mìlín.

junior /ˈdʒuːnɪə(r)/ *adj* 1(*to*) 地位(或等级)较低的 dìwèi jiàodī de. 2 **Junior** [尤用于美语](父子同名时,用于儿子姓名之后). 3 [英国英语](7 至 11 岁)儿〔兒〕童的 értóngde: *a ~ school* 小学. **junior** *n* 1 [C] 地位(或等级)较低者 dìwèi jiàodī zhě. 2 [sing] 较年幼者 jiào niányòu zhě: *He is three years her ~.* 他比她小三岁.

junk /dʒʌŋk/ *n* [U] 废〔廢〕弃〔棄〕的旧〔舊〕物 fèiqìde jiùwù; 无〔無〕价〔價〕值的东西 wú jiàzhí de dōngxi. ˈ**junk food** *n* [U] [非正式用语, 贬]劣等食物 lièděng shíwù. ˈ**junk mail** *n* [U] 垃圾邮〔郵〕件 lājī yóujiàn.

jurisdiction /ˌdʒʊərɪsˈdɪkʃn/ *n* [U] 司法 sīfǎ; 司法权〔權〕sīfǎquán.

juror /ˈdʒʊərə(r)/ *n* [C] 陪审〔審〕员 péishěnyuán.

jury /ˈdʒʊərɪ/ *n* [C, 亦作 sing, 用 pl v] [*pl* -ies] 1 陪审〔審〕团〔團〕péishěntuán. 2 (比赛的)评判委员会〔會〕píngpàn wěiyuánhuì.

just[1] /dʒʌst/ *adj* 公平的 gōngpíngde; 公正的 gōngzhèngde: *a ~ decision* 公正的决定. **justly** *adv*.

just[2] /dʒʌst/ *adv* 1 刚〔剛〕才 gāngcái; 方才 fāngcái: *I've ~ had dinner.* 我刚吃过饭. 2 正好 zhènghǎo; 恰好 qiàhǎo: *It's ~ 2 o'clock.* 现在是两点正. *Put it ~ here.* 把

它就放在这里. 3 just as (a) 正如 zhèngrú; 如同 rútóng: *Leave everything* ~ *as you find it*. 让一切保持原样. (b) 正当〔當〕…的时〔時〕候 zhèngdāng…de shíhòu: *She arrived* ~ *as I did*. 我到达时她也到了. 4 仅〔僅〕仅 jǐnjǐn; 几〔幾〕乎不 jīhū bù: *I can only* ~ *reach the shelf*. 我刚能够着架子. 5 此时〔時〕cǐshí; 那时 nàshí: *We're* ~ *leaving*. 我们正要离开. 6 just about/going to do sth (表示即将): *The clock is* ~ going to strike 12. 钟即将敲响 12 点. 7 只管 zhǐguǎn: *Why not* ~ *wait and see?* 为什么不等着看呢? 8 仅 jǐn: *There is* ~ *one way of saving him*. 只有一个办法能救他. 9 (请求注意): *J*~ *listen to me!* 听听我的! 10 [习语] just about 几乎 jīhū. just 'now (a) 此时 cǐshí; 现在 xiànzài: *I can't do it* ~ now. 我现在不能做这件事. (b) 刚才 gāngcái: *I saw him* ~ *now*. 我刚才看见他了.

justice /ˈdʒʌstɪs/ *n* 1 [U] 正义〔義〕zhèngyì; 公正 gōngzhèng; 公平 gōngpíng. 2 [U] 司法 sīfǎ; 审〔審〕判 shěnpàn: *a court of* ~ 法庭. 3 [C] 法官 fǎguān: *the Lord Chief J*~ 首席法官. ˌJustice of the ˈPeace *n* [C] 治安官 zhì'ānguān.

justify /ˈdʒʌstɪfaɪ/ *v* [*pt*, *pp* -ied] [T] 1 证明…是正当〔當〕的或有理的 zhèngmíng…shì zhèngdàngde huò yǒulǐde. 2 为〔爲〕…的正当理由 wéi…de zhèngdàng lǐyóu. justifiable /ˌdʒʌstɪˈfaɪəbl/ *adj* 可证明为正当的 kě zhèngmíng wéi zhèngdàng de; 有理由的 yǒu lǐyóu de. justifiably *adv*. justification /ˌdʒʌstɪfɪˈkeɪʃn/ *n* [U,C] (*for*) 正当的理由 zhèngdàngde lǐyóu.

jut /dʒʌt/ *v* [-tt-] [短语动词] jut out 突出 tūchū; 伸出 shēnchū.

juvenile /ˈdʒuːvənaɪl/ *n* [C] [正式用语或法律]少年 shàonián. juvenile *adj* 1 [正式用语或法律]少年的 shàoniánde; 适〔適〕合于少年的 shìhé yú shàonián de. 2 [贬]幼稚的 yòuzhìde; 不成熟的 bù chéngshúde. juvenile deˈlinquent *n* [C] 少年犯 shàoniánfàn.

juxtapose /ˌdʒʌkstəˈpəʊz/ *v* [T] [正式用语] 把…并〔並〕列 bǎ…bìngliè; 把…并置 bǎ…bìngzhì. juxtaposition /ˌdʒʌkstəpəˈzɪʃn/ *n* [U].

K k

K, k /keɪ/ *n* [C] [*pl* K's, k's /keɪz/] 英语的第十一个〔個〕字母 Yīngyǔde dìshíyīgè zìmǔ.

K /keɪ/ *abbr* [计算机] kilobyte.

kaleidoscope /kəˈlaɪdəskəʊp/ *n* 1 [C] 万〔萬〕花筒 wànhuātǒng. 2 [sing] 千变〔變〕万化 qiānbiànwànhuà.

kangaroo /ˌkæŋgəˈruː/ *n* [C] [*pl* ~s] 袋鼠 dàishǔ.

karate /kəˈrɑːtɪ/ *n* [U] 空手道(日本式徒手武术) kōngshǒudào.

kebab /kɪˈbæb/ *n* [C] 烤肉串 kǎoròuchuàn.

keel /kiːl/ *n* (船)龙〔龍〕骨 lónggǔ. keel *v* [短语动词] keel over 1 (船)倾覆 qīngfù; 翻倒 fāndǎo. 2 倒下 dǎoxià.

keen /kiːn/ *adj* 1 (a) *on* 热〔熱〕中于 rèzhōng yú: *He's very* ~ *on tennis*. 他很喜欢打网球. (b) *on* 喜欢〔歡〕某人 xǐhuān mǒurén. 2(指感觉、头脑、感性)灵〔靈〕敏的 língmǐnde; 敏捷的 mǐnjiéde; 强烈的 qiángliède. 3(风)刺骨的 cìgǔde. keenly *adv*.

keep[1] /kiːp/ *v* (*pt*, *pp* kept /kept/) 1 [I,T] (使)保持某状〔狀〕态〔態〕(或某地位) bǎochí mǒu zhuàngtài: *K*~ (*them*) *quiet!* (让他们)保持安静! *K*~ *off the grass!* 勿踏草地! 2 [I] (*on*) *doing* 继〔繼〕续〔續〕做某事 jìxù zuò mǒushì; 重复〔復〕做某事 chóngfù zuò mǒushì: *He* ~*s* (*on*) *interrupting me*. 他总是打扰我. 3 [T]保有 bǎoyǒu: *Here's £5 — you can* ~ *the change*. 这是五英镑——零钱不用找了. 4 [T] *from* 阻止 zǔzhǐ: ~ *him from leaving* 不让他离开. 5 [T] 延误 yánwù; 耽搁 dānge: *You're very late— what kept you?* 你太晚了——是什么事给耽误了? 6 [T] 拥〔擁〕有 yōngyǒu; 经营〔營〕jīngyíng: ~ *a shop* 经营商店. 7 [T] 保守(秘密) bǎoshǒu. 8 [I] (指食物)保存好 bǎocún hǎo: *Milk doesn't* ~ *in hot weather*. 牛奶不能在热天保存. 9 [I] 处〔處〕于健康状态 chǔyú jiànkāng zhuàngtài: *Is she* ~*ing well?* 她的身体好吗? 10 [T] (a) 记入 jìrù: ~ *a diary* 记日记. (b)记录〔錄〕jìlù: ~ *an account* 记账. 11 [T] 经济〔濟〕上支持 jīngjì shàng zhīchí. 12 [T] 履行 lǚxíng; 遵守 zūnshǒu: ~ *a promise* 遵守诺言. 13 [习语] keep abreast of sth ⇨ ABREAST. keep sb at arm's length 与〔與〕某人保持距离〔離〕yǔ mǒurén bǎochí jùlí. keep the ball rolling ⇨ BALL[1]. keep sb/sth at bay ⇨ BAY[3]. keep sb company 陪伴某人 péibàn mǒurén. keep count of sth ⇨ COUNT[2]. keep one's ˈdistance (from sb/sth) (a) (与某人、某物)保持距离 bǎochí jùlí. (b) (对人、事)冷淡 lěngdàn. keep an ˈeye on sb/sth 照料(某人、某物) zhàoliào. keep one's fingers crossed 祈求成功 qíqiú chénggōng: *Good luck with your exam— we're* ~*ing our fingers crossed for you*. 祝你考试好运,我们为你祈求成功. keep one's ground ⇨ GROUND[1]. keep one's ˈhair/ˈshirt on [非正式用语]不生气〔氣〕bù shēngqì. keep one's head ⇨ HEAD[1]. keep one's head above water 未举〔舉〕债 wèi jǔzhài；未陷入困境 wèi xiànrù kùnjìng. keep sth in mind ⇨ MIND[1]. keep sb in the dark⇨DARK[2]. ˌkeep it ˈup 继续保持 jìxù bǎochí. keep one's ˈmouth shut 保持缄默 bǎochí jiānmò. keep an open mind ⇨ OPEN[1]. keep pace (with sb/sth) (与某人、某物)并〔並〕驾齐〔齊〕驱〔驅〕bìng jià qí qū. ˌkeep the ˈpeace (a) 维持秩序 wéichí zhìxù. (b) 维持治安 wéichí zhì'ān. keep quiet about sth, keep sth quiet (对某事)缄默不语 jiānmò bù yǔ. keep a straight ˈface 绷着脸〔臉〕běng zhe liǎn；忍住不笑 rěn zhù bú xiào. keep a tight ˈrein on sb/sth (对某人、某事)严〔嚴〕加约束 yán jiā yuēshù. keep one's wits about one ⇨WIT. 14 [短语动词] keep at sth 继续做 jìxù zuò. keep (sb/sth) away (from sb/sth) 不接近 bù jiējìn；远〔遠〕离 yuǎnlí. keep sth back (from sb) 隐〔隱〕瞒(某事) yǐnmán. keep sb ˈdown 压〔壓〕制 yāzhì. keep sth ˈdown 控制 kòngzhì；压缩 yāsuō. keep sth from sb 不将〔將〕某事告诉某人 bù jiāng mǒushì gàosu mǒurén. keep in with sb 与(某人)保持友谊 yǔ bǎochí yǒuyí. keep on about sth⇨ ON[1]. keep ˈon (at sb) (about sth) 唠〔嘮〕叨 láodao. keep ˈout (of sth) 不进〔進〕入 bú jìnrù. keep ˈout of sth 避开〔開〕bìkāi. keep to sth (a) 不偏离 bù piānlí；不离开 bù líkāi：～ *to the path* 不偏离轨道. ～ *to the point* [喻]不要离题. (b) 遵循 zūnxún；遵守 zūnshǒu. keep oneˌself to oneˈself 不与人交往 bù yǔ rén jiāowǎng. keep sth to oneˈself 不把(某事)告诉别人 bù bǎ…gàosu biérén. keep sth up (a) 使(某物)不落下 shǐ bú luòxià. (b) 使保持高水平 shǐ bǎochí gāo shuǐpíng：～ *prices up* 使物价居高不下. ～ *one's spirits up* [喻] 保持高昂的情绪. (c) 继续 jìxù：*Do you still* ～ *up your French?* 你仍在学法语吗？(d) 维修 wéixiū；保养〔養〕bǎoyǎng. keep ˈup (with sb/sth) 跟上 gēnshàng；同步前进 tóngbù qiánjìn.

keep[2] /kiːp/ *n* 1 [U] 生活费 shēnghuófèi；(食物等)生活必需品 shēnghuó bìxūpǐn：*earn one's* ～ 谋生. 2 [习语] for ˈkeeps [非正式用语]永远〔遠〕地 yǒngyuǎnde.

keeper /ˈkiːpə(r)/ *n* [C] 1(动物园的)饲养〔養〕员 sìyǎngyuán. 2 (尤用以构成复合词)管理人 guǎnlǐrén；经〔經〕营〔營〕者 jīngyíngzhě：*a ˈshop*～ 店主.

keeping /ˈkiːpɪŋ/ *n* [习语] in sb's keeping 由某人保管 yóu mǒurén bǎoguǎn：*The keys are in his* ～. 钥匙由他保管. in/out of keeping with sth 一致 yízhì；不一致 bù yízhì.

keepsake /ˈkiːpseɪk/ *n* [C] 纪念品 jìniànpǐn.

kennel /ˈkenl/ *n* 1 [C] 狗舍 gǒushè；狗窝〔窩〕gǒuwō. 2 kennels [用 sing 或 pl v] 养〔養〕狗场〔場〕yǎnggǒuchǎng.

kept *pt*, *pp* of KEEP[1].

kerb (亦作 curb, 尤用于美语) /kɜːb/ *n* [C] (人行道的)边〔邊〕石 biānshí.

kernel /ˈkɜːnl/ *n* [C] 1(果)核 hé；(果)仁 rén；(谷)粒 lì. 2 [喻]核心 héxīn；中心 zhōngxīn.

kestrel /ˈkestrəl/ *n* [C] 红隼 hóngsǔn.

ketchup /ˈketʃəp/ *n* [U] 番茄酱〔醬〕fānqiéjiàng.

kettle /ˈketl/ *n* [C] (烧水用的)壶〔壺〕hú.

key[1] /kiː/ *n* [C] 1 钥〔鑰〕匙 yàoshi. 2 [常作 sing] (*to*) [喻]关〔關〕键〔鍵〕guānjiàn：*Diet and exercise are the* ～ *to good health*. 规定食物和锻炼运动是身体健康的关键. 3 答案 dá'àn；题解 tíjiě. 4(打字机、钢琴等)键盘〔盤〕jiànpán. 5(音乐)调 diào：*in the* ～ *of G* G 调. key *adj* 极〔極〕重要的 jí zhòngyào de：*a* ～ *position* 重要的位置. ˈkeyboard *n* [C] (打字机等)键盘 jiànpán. ˈkeyboard *v* [T] 用键盘把…输入计算机〔機〕yòng jiànpán bǎ… shūrù jìsuànjī. ˈkeyhole *n* [C] 锁〔鎖〕孔 suǒkǒng. ˈkeynote *n* [C] (演说等)要旨 yàozhǐ. ˈkey-ring *n* [C] 钥匙圈 yàoshiquān.

key[2] /kiː/ *v* [T] (*in*) (计算机)用键盘〔盤〕输入 yòng jiànpán shūrù. keyed up *adj* 激动〔動〕的 jīdòngde；紧〔緊〕张的 jǐnzhāngde.

kg *abbr* kilogram(s).

khaki /ˈkɑːkɪ/ *adj* 土黄色的 tǔhuángsède.

kibbutz /kɪˈbʊts/ *n* [C] [*pl* ～im /kɪbʊˈtsiːm/] 基布兹(以色列的合作农场或居留地) jībùzī.

kick[1] /kɪk/ *v* 1 [T] 踢 tī. 2 [I] 蹬 dēng；跺 duò. 3 [I] (枪)反冲〔衝〕fǎnchōng. 4 [习语] ˌkick the ˈbucket [俚]死亡 sǐwáng. kick the habit [非正式用语]戒烟 jièyān；戒酒 jièjiǔ. 5 [短语动词] kick against sth 反对〔對〕fǎnduì. kick ˈoff 开〔開〕始 kāishǐ. kick sb out (of sth) [非正式用语]驱〔驅〕逐某人 qūzhú mǒurén. ˈkick-off *n* [C] (足球比赛的)开球 kāiqiú.

kick[2] /kɪk/ *n* 1 [C] 踢 tī：*give sb a* ～ 踢某人一脚. 2 [C] [非正式用语]快感 kuàigǎn；乐〔樂〕趣 lèqù：*She gets her* ～*s from skiing*. 她从滑雪中得到极大乐趣. 3 [U, sing] [非正式用语]精力 jīnglì；气〔氣〕力 qìlì.

kid[1] /kɪd/ *n* 1 [C] [非正式用语]小孩 xiǎohái；年轻〔輕〕人 niánqīngrén. 2 (a) [C] 小山羊 xiǎo shānyáng. (b) [U] 小山羊皮革 xiǎo shānyáng pígé.

kid[2] /kɪd/ *v* [-dd-] [I, T] [非正式用语]欺骗 qīpiàn；哄骗 hǒngpiàn.

kidnap /ˈkɪdnæp/ *v* [-pp-；美语-p-] [T] 诱拐 yòuguǎi；绑架 bǎngjià. kidnapper *n* [C].

kidney /ˈkɪdnɪ/ *n* 1 [C] 肾〔腎〕shèn；肾脏〔臟〕shènzàng. 2 [U, C] (用作食物的)腰子 yāozi.

kill /kɪl/ *v* 1 (a) [I] 致死 zhìsǐ. (b) [T] 杀〔殺〕死 shāsǐ：[喻] *He'll* ～ *me if he*

K

finds me here. 他要是发现我在这儿,会非常生气. 2 [T] [非正式用语]使受伤〔傷〕(或受痛苦) shǐ shòushāng: *My feet are ~ing me*. 我的脚疼极了. 3 [T] 终止 zhōngzhǐ: *~ sb's love* 使某人失去爱情. 4 [习语] **kill ˌtwo ˌbirds with ˌone ˈstone** 一箭双〔雙〕雕 yí jiàn shuāng diāo. **kill** *n* 1 [C] 杀死 shāsǐ. 2 [常作 sing] 被杀死的动〔動〕物 bèi shāsǐ de dòngwù. **killer** *n* [C]. **killing** *n* 1 [C] 杀死 shāsǐ. 2 [习语] **ˌmake a ˈkilling** [非正式用语]财运〔運〕亨通 cáiyùn hēngtōng. **ˈkilljoy** *n* [C] [贬]令人扫〔掃〕兴〔興〕的人 lìng rén sǎoxìng de rén.

kiln /kɪln/ *n* [C]窑〔窰〕yáo.

kilo /ˈkiːləʊ/ *n* [C] [*pl* ~s] 公斤 gōngjīn; 千克 qiānkè.

kilobyte /ˈkɪləbaɪt/ *n* [C] (计算机)千字节〔節〕(1个千字节实为1024个字节) qiānzìjié.

kilogram (亦作-**gramme**) /ˈkɪləgræm/ *n* [C] 公斤 gōngjīn; 千克 qiānkè.

kilometre (美语-**meter**) /ˈkɪləmiːtə(r), kɪˈlɒmɪtə(r)/ *n* [C] 公里 gōnglǐ; 千米 qiānmǐ.

kilowatt /ˈkɪləwɒt/ *n* [C] 千瓦 qiānwǎ.

K

kilt /kɪlt/ *n* [C] (苏格兰男子穿的)短褶裙 duǎnzhěqún.

kind[1] /kaɪnd/ *n* 1 [C]种〔種〕类 zhǒnglèi: *two ~s of fruit* 两种水果. 2 [习语] **in kind** (a) 以货代款 yǐ huò dài kuǎn. (b) [喻]以同样〔樣〕方式 yǐ tóngyàng fāngshì. **a kind of** [非正式用语](用以表示不肯定): *I had a ~ of feeling this might happen*. 我隐隐约约地感到这事可能发生.

kind[2] /kaɪnd/ *adj* 亲〔親〕切的 qīnqiède; 友好的 yǒuhǎode. **ˌkind-ˈhearted** *adj* 仁慈的 réncíde; 好心的 hǎoxīnde. **kindly** *adj* [-ier, -iest] [非正式用语]友好的 yǒuhǎode; 亲切的 qīnqiède. **kindly** *adv* 1 亲切地 qīnqiède; 和蔼地 hé'ǎide. 2(礼貌用语)请 qǐng: *K~ly leave me alone!* 请别打扰我! 3[习语] **not take kindly to sb/sth** 不喜欢〔歡〕某人(或某物) bù xǐhuān mǒurén. **kindness** *n* 1 [U] 亲切 qīnqiè; 和蔼 hé'ǎi. 2[C] 好心的行为〔爲〕 hǎoxīnde xíngwéi.

kindergarten /ˈkɪndəgɑːtn/ *n* [C] 幼儿〔兒〕园〔園〕 yòu'éryuán.

kindle /ˈkɪndl/ *v* 1 [I, T] 点〔點〕燃 diǎnrán. 2 [T] [喻]激起(感情) jīqǐ.

kindred /ˈkɪndrɪd/ *adj* [习语] **a kindred ˈspirit** 意气〔氣〕相投的人 yìqì xiāngtóu de rén.

king /kɪŋ/ *n* [C] 1 国〔國〕王 guówáng. 2 最重要者 zuì zhòngyào zhě. 3(国际象棋)王 wáng. 4 纸牌 K zhǐpái K. **ˈking-size** (亦作-**sized**) *adj* 比正常大的 bǐ zhèngcháng dà de; 特大的 tèdàde: *a ~-size bed* 特大的床.

kingdom /ˈkɪŋdəm/ *n* [C] 1 王国〔國〕 wángguó. 2 (自然三界之一)界 jiè: *the animal, plant and mineral ~s* 动物、植物和矿物三界.

kink /kɪŋk/ *n* [C] 1(绳、索等)纽结 niǔjié. 2 [常作贬]乖僻 guāipì; 奇想 qíxiǎng. **kink** *v* [I, T] (使)扭结 niǔjié. **kinky** *adj* [-ier, -iest] [非正式用语](尤指性行为)变〔變〕态〔態〕的 biàntàide.

kiosk /ˈkiːɒsk/ *n* [C] (出售报纸等)售货亭 shòuhuòtíng.

kipper /ˈkɪpə(r)/ *n* [C] 腌或熏〔燻〕的鲱鱼 yān huò xūn de fēiyú.

kiss /kɪs/ *v* [I, T] 吻 wěn; 接吻 jiēwěn. **kiss** *n* [C] 吻 wěn. **the kiss of ˈlife** *n* [sing] 人工呼吸 réngōng hūxī.

kit /kɪt/ *n* 1 [C] 成套工具 chéngtào gōngjù: *a first-ˈaid ~* 一套急救用品. 2 [C, U] (士兵、运动员的)衣物和装〔裝〕备〔備〕 yīwù hé zhuāngbèi. 3 [C] 配套元件 pèitào yuánjiàn. **kit** *v* [-tt-] [短语动词] **kit sb out/up** (**with sth**) 给…装备… gěi…zhuāngbèi….

kitchen /ˈkɪtʃɪn/ *n* [C] 厨〔廚〕房 chúfáng.

kite /kaɪt/ *n* [C] 风〔風〕筝 fēngzheng.

kith /kɪθ/ *n* [习语] **ˌkith and ˈkin** /kɪn/ 亲〔親〕友 qīnyǒu.

kitten /ˈkɪtn/ *n* [C] 小猫〔貓〕 xiǎomāo.

kitty /ˈkɪtɪ/ *n* [C] [*pl* -**ies**] (共同凑集的)一笔〔筆〕钱〔錢〕 yì bǐ qián.

kiwi /ˈkiːwiː/ *n* [C] 1 几〔幾〕维(新西兰的一种不能飞的鸟) jǐwéi. 2 **Kiwi** [非正式用语]新西兰〔蘭〕人 Xīnxīlánrén.

km *abbr* [*pl* **km** 或~**s**] kilometre(s).

knack /næk/ *n* [sing] 诀窍〔竅〕 juéqiào; 技巧 jìqiǎo.

knackered /ˈnækəd/ *adj* [英俚]筋疲力尽〔盡〕的 jīn pí lì jìn de.

knead /niːd/ *v* [T] 1 揉(面团) róu; 捏〔揑〕 niē. 2 按摩(肌肉) ànmó.

knee /niː/ *n* [C] 1 (a) 膝 xī; 膝盖〔蓋〕 xīgài. (b) (裤子等的)膝部 xībù. 2 [习语] **bring sb to his/her ˈknees** 迫使某人屈服 pò shǐ mǒurén qūfú. **ˈkneecap** *n* [C] 膝盖骨 xīgàigǔ; 髌〔髕〕骨 bìngǔ. **ˌknee-ˈdeep** *adj* 深及膝的 shēn jí xī de.

kneel /niːl/ *v* [*pt*, *pp* **knelt** /nelt/或尤用于美语 ~**ed**] [I] 跪下 guìxià; 屈膝 qūxī.

knew *pt* of KNOW.

knickers /ˈnɪkəz/ *n* [pl] (女用)内裤〔褲〕 nèikù.

knick-knack /ˈnɪknæk/ *n* [C, 尤作 pl] 小装〔裝〕饰品 xiǎo zhuāngshìpǐn.

knife /naɪf/ *n* [C] [*pl* **knives** /naɪvz/] (有柄的)刀 dāo. **knife** *v* [I] 用刀刺(人) yòng dāo cì. **ˈknife-edge** *n* [习语] **on a knife-edge** (指重要情况、结果)极〔極〕不肯定 jí bù kěndìng.

knight /naɪt/ *n* [C] 1 爵士(其名前冠以 Sir) juéshì. 2 骑士 qíshì. 3(国际象棋的)马〔馬〕 mǎ. **knight** *v* [T] 封…为〔爲〕爵士 fēng…wéi juéshì. **knighthood** /-hʊd/ *n* [C, U] 爵士(或骑士)的地位、身份 juéshìde dìwèi、shēnfen.

knit /nɪt/ *v* [-tt-; *pt*, *pp* ~ted; 用于下述第二义项时常作 **knit**] [I, T] **1** 编织〔織〕(衣物等) biānzhī; 针织 zhēnzhī. **2** 牢固地结合 láogùde jiéhé; 紧〔緊〕密地结合 jǐnmìde jiéhé: *a closely-~ family* 关系密切的家庭. **knitting** *n* [C] 编织物 biānzhīwù. **ˈknitting-needle** *n* [C] 编结针 biānjiézhēn, 织针 zhīzhēn.

knives *pl* of KNIFE.

knob /nɒb/ *n* [C] **1** (a) (门、抽屉等) 圆形把手 yuánxíng bǎshǒu. (b) (收音机的) 旋钮 xuánniǔ. **2** 圆形物 yuánxíngwù: *a ~ of butter* 一块黄油. **knobbly** /-blɪ/ *adj* [-ier, -iest] 多节〔節〕的 duō jiéde; 多疙瘩的 duō gēda de: *~bly knees* 长着很多疙瘩的膝盖.

knock[1] /nɒk/ *v* **1** (a) [T] 敲 qiāo; 击〔擊〕jī; 打 dǎ. (b) [I] 敲击(某物)出声〔聲〕qiāojī chū shēng: *~ on the door* 敲门. **2** [T] [非正式用语] 批评 pīpíng. **3** [短语动词] **knock about with sb** [非正式用语] 常与〔與〕某人作伴 cháng yǔ mǒurén zuò bàn. **knock sb/sth about** 粗暴对待某人(或某事) cūbào duìdài mǒurén. **knock sth back** [非正式用语] 很快喝掉 hěnkuài hēdiào. **knock sb down** 打倒 dǎdǎo; 击倒 jīdǎo: *She was ~ed down by a bus.* 她被公共汽车撞倒了. **knock sth down** 拆除(建筑) chāichú. **knock sth/sb down** (迫使)减(价) jiǎn. **knock off** (sth) [非正式用语] 停止(工作) tíngzhǐ: *When do you ~ off?* 你什么时候下班? **knock sth off** (a) 减价〔價〕jiǎnjià: *~ £20 off the price* 减价 20 英镑. (b) [俚] 偷 tōu. **knock sb out** (a) 击昏某人 jī hūn mǒurén. (b) 使筋疲力尽〔盡〕shǐ jīn pí lì jìn. **knock sb out (of sth)** 淘汰某人 táotài mǒurén. **knock sth up** 匆匆做(某事) cōngcōng zuò: *~ up a meal* 匆匆做好一顿饭. **knocker** *n* [C] 门环〔環〕ménhuán. ˌ**knock-ˈkneed** *adj* 膝外翻的 xīwàifānde. ˌ**knock-ˈon effect** *n* [C] 间接结果 jiànjiē jiéguǒ. **ˈknock-out** *n* [C] **1** 击倒对〔對〕手的一击 jīdǎo duìshǒu de yìjī. **2** 淘汰赛 táotàisài. **3** [非正式用语] 引人注目的人(或物) yǐn rén zhùmù de rén.

knock[2] /nɒk/ *n* [C] **1** 敲击〔擊〕声〔聲〕qiāojīshēng. **2** [非正式用语] 不幸的经〔經〕历〔歷〕búxìng de jīnglì.

knot[1] /nɒt/ *n* [C] **1** (绳索等的) 结 jié. **2** 扭结 niǔjié; 纠结 jiūjié. **3** (木材的) 节〔節〕jié; 节疤 jiébā. **4** 一小群人 yìxiǎoqún rén. **knot** *v* [-tt-] **1** [I, T] 打结 dǎjié; 缠〔纏〕结 chánjié. **2** [T] 打结系〔繫〕牢 dǎjié jìláo. **knotty** *adj* [-ier, -iest] **1** (木材) 多节的 duōjiéde. **2** 棘手的 jíshǒude: *a ~ty problem* 难以解决的问题.

knot[2] /nɒt/ *n* [C, 常作 pl] 节〔節〕(速度单位, 为每小时一海里) jié.

know /nəʊ/ *v* [*pt* **knew** /njuː; *US* nuː/, *pp* ~n /nəʊn/] **1** [I, T] 知道 zhīdào; 懂得 dǒngdé. **2** [T] 认〔認〕识〔識〕rènshi. **3** [T] 熟悉(某地) shúxī. **4** [T] 认〔認〕出 rènchū; 识别 shíbié: *I'll ~ her when I see her.* 我看到她时, 就会认出她. **5** [T] 通晓〔曉〕(语言) tōngxiǎo; 掌握(技能) zhǎngwò; 会〔會〕huì. **6** [T] 经〔經〕历〔歷〕jīnglì; 体〔體〕验〔驗〕tǐyàn: *a man who has ~n poverty* 经历贫困的人. **7** [习语] **be known as sb/sth** 以…著称〔稱〕yǐ…zhùchēng. **know sb by sight** 面熟 miànshú. **know one's own ˈmind** 有自己的想法 yǒu zìjǐ de xiǎngfǎ. **8** [短语动词] **know about sth** 了〔瞭〕解(某事) liǎojiě; 知道(某事) zhīdào. **know of sb/sth** 知道(某人或某事)的情况 zhīdào … de qíngkuàng: *I ~ of the book but I've not read it.* 我听说过这本书, 但我没读过. **ˈknow-how** *n* [U] [非正式用语] 实〔實〕践知识 shíjiàn zhīshi; 技能 jìnéng.

knowing /ˈnəʊɪŋ/ *adj* 心照不宣的 xīn zhào bù xuān de; 会〔會〕意的 huìyìde: *a ~ look* 露出了解内情的样子. **knowingly** *adv* **1** 故意地 gùyìde. **2** 会意地 huìyìde.

knowledge /ˈnɒlɪdʒ/ *n* **1** [U] 了〔瞭〕解 liǎojiě; 理解 lǐjiě. **2** [U, sing] (个人的) 知识〔識〕zhīshi; 学〔學〕识 xuéshí: *a ~ of French* 法语知识. **3** [U] 学问 xuéwèn; 知识 zhīshi. **knowledgeable** /-əbl/ *adj* 知识渊〔淵〕博的 zhīshi yuānbó de. **ˈknowledge economy** *n* [U] 知识经〔經〕济〔濟〕zhīshi jīngjì.

known *pp* of KNOW.

knuckle /ˈnʌkl/ *n* [C] 指节〔節〕zhǐjié. **knuckle** *v* [短语动词] **knuckle under** [非正式用语] 屈服 qūfú.

koala /kəʊˈɑːlə/ *n* [C] [动物] (澳洲) 树〔樹〕袋熊 shùdàixióng.

Koran /kəˈrɑːn; *US* -ˈræn/ *n* **the Koran** [sing] (伊斯兰教) 《古兰〔蘭〕经〔經〕》(一译《可兰经》) 《Gǔlánjīng》.

kosher /ˈkəʊʃə(r)/ *adj* (食物) 合礼〔禮〕的 (符合犹太教规) hélǐde; 洁〔潔〕净〔淨〕的 jiéjìngde.

kowtow /ˌkaʊˈtaʊ/ *v* [I] (*to*) 叩头〔頭〕kòutóu; 磕头 kētóu; 卑躬屈膝 bēi gōng qū xī.

kph /ˌkeɪ piː ˈeɪtʃ/ *abbr* kilometres per hour 公里/小时〔時〕gōnglǐ/xiǎoshí; 千米/小时 qiānmǐ/xiǎoshí.

L l

L, l /el/ *n* [C] [*pl* **L's, l's** /elz/] **1** 英语的第十二个〔個〕字母 Yīngyǔde dìshí'èrgè zìmǔ. **2** 罗〔羅〕马〔馬〕数〔數〕字的 50 Luómǎ shùzì de 50.

L *abbr* **1** Lake. **2** (尤用于电器插头) live (connection).

l *abbr* **1** line. **2** litre(s).

Lab /læb/ *abbr* (英国政治) Labour (Party)

工党〔黨〕Gōngdǎng.

lab /læb/ *n* [C] [非正式用语]实〔實〕验〔驗〕室 shíyànshì.

label /ˈleɪbl/ *n* [C] **1** 标〔標〕签〔籤〕biāoqiān; 签条〔條〕qiāntiáo. **2**[喻](用以描述人或事物)称〔稱〕号〔號〕chēnghào. **label** *v* [-ll-; 美语 -l-] [T] **1** 贴标签于 tiē biāoqiān yú. **2**[喻]把…归〔歸〕类〔類〕bǎ… guīlèi; 把…称为〔爲〕bǎ… chēngwéi: *They ~led her (as) a liar*. 他们把她说成说谎者.

labor (美语) = LABOUR. **labor union** (美语) = TRADE UNION (TRADE[1]).

laboratory /ləˈbɒrətrɪ; *US* ˈlæbrətɔːrɪ/ *n* [C] [*pl* -ies] 实〔實〕验〔驗〕室 shíyànshì.

laborious /ləˈbɔːrɪəs/ *adj* (工作等)吃力的 chīlìde; 艰〔艱〕苦的 jiānkǔde. **laboriously** *adv*.

labour[1] (美语-or) /ˈleɪbə(r)/ *n* **1** [U] 劳〔勞〕动〔動〕láodòng. **2** [C, 常作 pl] 工作 gōngzuò; 任务〔務〕rènwu. **3**[U] 劳工 láogōng. **4** [U, sing] 分娩 fēnmiǎn: *a woman in ~* 分娩中的妇女. **5 Labour** [sing] (英国政治)[用 sing 或 pl v] 工党〔黨〕Gōngdǎng. **the ˈLabour Party** *n* [sing] (英国政治)工党 Gōngdǎng.

labour[2] (美语 -or) /ˈleɪbə(r)/ *v* **1** [I] 劳〔勞〕动〔動〕láodòng; 工作 gōngzuò; 努力 nǔlì. **2** [I] 努力地做 nǔlìde zuò. **3** [习语] **ˈlabour the point** 一再重复〔複〕yí zài chóngfù; 一再解释〔釋〕yí zài jiěshì. **4**[短语动词] **labour under sth** 因…而苦恼〔惱〕yīn… ér kǔnǎo. **labourer** (美语-bor-) *n* [C] 劳动者 láodòngzhě; 工人 gōngrén.

labyrinth /ˈlæbərɪnθ/ *n* [C] 迷宫 mígōng; 曲径〔徑〕qūjìng.

lace /leɪs/ *n* **1** [U] (网眼)花边〔邊〕huābiān; 透孔织〔織〕品 tòukǒng zhīpǐn. **2** [C]鞋带〔帶〕xiédài; 带 dài. **lace** *v* **1** [I, T] 用带子束紧〔緊〕yòng dàizi shù jǐn. **2** [T] (*with*)搀〔攙〕酒于(饮料) chān jiǔ yú.

lacerate /ˈlæsəreɪt/ *v* [T] [正式用语]划〔劃〕破(肌肉等) huápò; 撕裂 sīliè. **laceration** /ˌlæsəˈreɪʃn/ *n* [C, U].

lack /læk/ *v* **1** [T] 没有 méiyǒu; 缺少 quēshǎo. **2** [习语] **be ˈlacking** 缺乏 quēfá. **be ˈlacking in sth** 不足 bùzú. **lack** *n* [U, sing] 缺乏 quēfá; 短缺 duǎnquē: *a ~ of money* 缺钱.

lackadaisical /ˌlækəˈdeɪzɪkl/ *adj* 无〔無〕精打采的 wú jīng dǎ cǎi de; 不热〔熱〕心的 bú rèxīn de.

laconic /ləˈkɒnɪk/ *adj* [正式用语]简洁〔潔〕的 jiǎnjiéde; 精练〔練〕的 jīngliànde. **laconically** /-klɪ/ *adv*.

lacquer /ˈlækə(r)/ *n* [U] **1** 漆 qī. **2** [旧]发〔髮〕胶〔膠〕fàjiāo. **lacquer** *v* [T] 用漆涂〔塗〕yòng qī tú; 喷发胶于 pēn fàjiāo yú.

lacy /ˈleɪsɪ/ *adj* [-ier, -iest] 花边〔邊〕的 huābiānde; 似花边的 sì huābiān de; 透孔织〔織〕物的 tòukǒng zhīwù de.

lad /læd/ *n* [C] **1** 男孩子 nánháizi; 男青年 nán qīngnián. **2** [非正式用语]活泼〔潑〕(或大胆、鲁莽)的男子 huópo de nánzǐ: *He's a bit of a ~*. 他是个有点莽撞的小伙子. **the lads** [pl] [非正式用语]伙〔夥〕伴 huǒbàn; 家〔傢〕伙 jiāhuo: *He's gone out with the ~s*. 他和伙伴们出去了.

ladder /ˈlædə(r)/ *n* [C] **1** 梯子 tīzi. **2** (长统袜上的)抽丝〔絲〕chōusī. **3**[喻](事业等)阶〔階〕梯 jiētī: *climb up the social ~* 攀登社会阶梯. **ladder** *v* [I, T] (长统袜)抽丝 chōusī.

laden /ˈleɪdn/ *adj* (*with*) 装〔裝〕满的 zhuāngmǎnde; 满载的 mǎnzàide.

ladle /ˈleɪdl/ *n* [C] 长〔長〕柄勺〔杓〕chángbǐngsháo; 勺子 sháozi. **ladle** *v* [T] (用勺)盛 chéng, 舀 yǎo.

lady /ˈleɪdɪ/ *n* [C] [*pl* -ies] **1**(尤作礼貌用语)女士 nǚshì; 夫人 fūrén; 小姐 xiǎojiě. **2** 举〔舉〕止文雅的女子 jǔzhǐ wényǎ de nǚzǐ; 淑女 shūnǚ. **3**(尤指旧时)贵族夫人 guìzú fūrén; 贵族小姐 guìzú xiǎojiě. **4 Lady** (对贵族妻子的尊称)夫人 fūrén. **5 the Ladies** [pl] [常用 sing v] [英国, 非正式用语]女厕〔廁〕所 nǚcèsuǒ. **ˈladylike** *adj* 淑女的 shūnǚde; 文雅的 wényǎde. **ˈladyship** *n* (尤用 **Ladyship**) [C] (用作尊称)夫人 fūrén; 小姐 xiǎojiě: *her L~ship* 夫人; 小姐.

lag[1] /læg/ *v* [-gg-] [I] (*behind*) 走得慢 zǒu de màn; 落后〔後〕luòhòu.

lag[2] /læg/ *v* [-gg-] [T] 给(水管等)装〔裝〕绝缘材料 gěi zhuāng juéyuán cáiliào. **lagging** *n* [U] 绝缘材料 juéyuán cáiliào.

lager /ˈlɑːgə(r)/ *n* [C, U] (一杯或一瓶)贮〔貯〕藏啤酒 zhùcáng píjiǔ.

lagoon /ləˈguːn/ *n* [C] 泻〔瀉〕湖 xièhú; 礁湖 jiāohú; 咸〔鹹〕水湖 xiánshuǐhú.

laid *pt, pp* of LAY[1].

lain *pp* of LIE[2].

lair /leə(r)/ *n* [C] 兽〔獸〕穴 shòuxuè; 兽窝〔窩〕shòuwō.

laity /ˈleɪətɪ/ *n* **the laity** [sing] [用 sing 或 pl v] 俗人 súrén.

lake /leɪk/ *n* [C] 湖 hú.

lamb /læm/ *n* **1** (a) [C] 小羊 xiǎoyáng; 羔羊 gāoyáng. (b) [U] 小羊肉 xiǎoyángròu; 羔羊肉 gāoyángròu. **2** [C] [非正式用语]温顺的人 wēnshùnde rén; 可亲〔親〕的人 kěqīnde rén.

lame /leɪm/ *adj* **1** 跛的 bǒde; 瘸的 quéde. **2** (借口)蹩脚的 biéjiǎode; 不能说服人的 bùnéng shuōfú rén de. **3** [习语] **a ˌlame ˈduck** (a) 处〔處〕于困境的人(或组织等) chǔyú kùnjìng de rén. (b) [尤用于美语](任期将满的)官员

L

guānyuán. **lame** *v* [T] 使跛 shǐ bǒ. **lameness** *n* [C].

lament /lə'ment/ *v* [I, T] 悲痛 bēitòng; 哀悼 āidào. **lament** *n* [C] 挽〔輓〕歌 wǎngē; 挽诗 wǎnshī. **lamentable** /'læməntəbl/ *adj* 可悲的 kěbēide; 令人惋惜的 lìng rén wǎnxī de. **lamentably** *adv*.

laminated /'læmɪneɪtɪd/ *adj* 由薄片组成的 yóu bópiàn zǔchéng de.

lamp /læmp/ *n* [C] 灯〔燈〕dēng. **'lamp-post** *n* [C] 路灯柱 lùdēngzhù. **'lampshade** *n* [C] 灯罩 dēngzhào.

lance[1] /lɑːns; *US* læns/ *n* [C] (旧时)骑兵用的长〔長〕矛 qíbīng yòng de chángmáo.

lance[2] /lɑːns; *US* læns/ *v* [T] 用刀割开〔開〕yòng dāo gēkāi.

land[1] /lænd/ *n* **1** [U] 陆〔陸〕地 lùdì. **2** [U] 土地 tǔdì; 田地 tiándì: *work on the* '~ 务农. **3** [有时作 **lands**] [U, pl] 地产〔產〕dìchǎn. **4** [C] [修辞]国〔國〕家 guójiā. **5** [习语] **see, etc how the 'land lies** 了〔瞭〕解情况 liǎojiě qíngkuàng. **landed** *adj* 有土地的 yǒu tǔdì de. **'land-locked** *adj* 陆围〔圍〕的 lùwéide; 内陆的 nèilùde. **'landmark** *n* [C] **1** 路标〔標〕lùbiāo; 地标 dìbiāo. **2** [喻]里程碑 lǐchéngbēi. **'landowner** *n* [C] 土地所有者 tǔdì suǒyǒuzhě. **'landslide** *n* [C] **1** 山崩 shānbēng; 地滑 dìhuá; 崩塌 bēngtā. **2** [喻](选举中)压〔壓〕倒多数〔數〕的选〔選〕票 yādǎo duōshù de xuǎnpiào; 一边〔邊〕倒的胜〔勝〕利 yìbiān dǎo de shènglì.

land[2] /lænd/ *v* **1** [I, T] 上岸 shàng àn; 登陆〔陸〕dēng lù; 下船 xià chuán. **2** [I, T] (飞机)着陆 zhuó lù. **3** [T] [非正式用语]获〔獲〕得 huòdé: ~ *a job* 得到一份工作. **4** [习语] **land on one's feet** ⇨ FOOT. **5** [短语动词] **land sb/oneself in sth** [非正式用语]使(某人或自己)陷入困境 shǐ xiànrù kùnjìng. **land up** [非正式用语]最终达〔達〕到 zuìzhōng dádào; 最后〔後〕处〔處〕于 zuìhòu chǔyú: ~ *up in gaol* 结果入狱. **land sb with sth** [非正式用语]要(某人)承担〔擔〕(责任等) yào chéngdān.

landfill /'lændfɪl/ *n* **1** [U] 垃圾填埋 lājī tiánmái. **2** [C] 垃圾填埋场〔場〕lājī tiánmáichǎng. **'landfill site** *n* [C] 垃圾填埋场 lājī tiánmáichǎng.

landing /'lændɪŋ/ *n* [C] **1** 登陆〔陸〕dēnglù; 着陆 zhuólù: *a* ˌ*crash-* ~ 紧急着陆. **2** 楼〔樓〕梯平台〔臺〕lóutī píngtái. **3** (亦作 **'landing-place**) 码头〔頭〕mǎtóu; 浮动〔動〕码头 fúdòng mǎtóu. **'landing-craft** *n* [C] 登陆艇 dēnglùtǐng. **'landing-gear** *n* [U] = UNDERCARRIAGE. **'landing-stage** *n* [C] 码头 mǎtóu; 浮动码头 fúdòngmǎtóu.

landlady /'lændleɪdɪ/ *n* [C] [*pl* **-ies**] **1** 女房东 nǚ fángdōng. **2** (酒店、寄宿舍的)女店主 nǚ diànzhǔ.

landlord /'lændlɔːd/ *n* [C] **1** 地主 dìzhǔ; 房东 fángdōng. **2**(酒店、寄宿舍的)店主 diànzhǔ.

landscape /'lændskeɪp/ *n* [C] **1** 风〔風〕景 fēngjǐng; 景色 jǐngsè. **2** 风景画〔畫〕fēngjǐnghuà. **landscape** *v* [T] 对〔對〕…作景观〔觀〕美化 duì…zuò jǐngguān měihuà.

lane /leɪn/ *n* [C] **1** 小径〔徑〕xiǎojìng; 小路 xiǎolù. **2** (用作路名)巷 xiàng; 胡同 hútòng: *Mill* ~ 米尔巷. **3** 车〔車〕道 chēdào: *a four-* ~ *motorway* 四车道高速公路. **4**(船或飞机的)航道 hángdào, 航线〔綫〕hángxiàn. **5** (比赛用的)跑道 pǎodào; 泳道 yǒngdào.

language /'læŋgwɪdʒ/ *n* **1** [U] 语言 yǔyán. **2** [C] (集团、国家、民族等的)语言 yǔyán; 部落语 bùluòyǔ: *the English* ~ 英语. **3** [U] 表达〔達〕方式 biǎodá fāngshì. **4** [U] 术〔術〕语 shùyǔ; 行话 hánghuà: *medical* ~ 医学用语. **5** [C, U] 符号〔號〕fúhào; 标〔標〕志〔誌〕biāozhì: *a computer* ~ 计算机用语. *body* ~ 身势语. **'language laboratory** *n* [C] 语言实〔實〕验〔驗〕室 yǔyán shíyànshì.

languid /'læŋgwɪd/ *adj* [正式用语]没精打采的 méi jīng dǎ cǎi de; 倦怠的 juàndàide. **languidly** *adv*.

languish /'læŋgwɪʃ/ *v* [I] [正式用语] **1** 变〔變〕得衰弱无〔無〕力 biànde shuāiruò wúlì. **2** *in* 受苦 shòukǔ; 受折磨 shòu zhémó: ~ *in poverty* 在贫穷中挣扎.

lank /læŋk/ *adj* **1** (头发)平直的 píngzhíde. **2** (人)瘦长〔長〕的 shòuchángde.

lanky /'læŋkɪ/ *adj* [**-ier, -iest**] 瘦长〔長〕的 shòuchángde.

lantern /'læntən/ *n* [C] 灯〔燈〕笼〔籠〕dēnglóng; 提灯 tídēng.

lap[1] /læp/ *n* [C] (人坐着时)自腰至膝的大腿前部 zì yāo zhì xī de dàtuǐ qiánbù: *a baby on his* ~ 坐在他腿上的婴儿. **'lap dance** *n* [C] 腿上艳〔艷〕舞 tuǐshàng yànwǔ. **'lap dancer** *n* [C] 腿上艳舞女郎 tuǐshàng yànwǔ nǚláng. **lap dancing** *n* [U] 腿上艳舞 tuǐshàng yànwǔ. **'laptop** *n* [C] 便携式计算机〔機〕biànxiéshì jìsuànjī.

lap[2] /læp/ *n* [C] (跑道的)一圈 yìquān. **lap** *v* [**-pp-**] [T] (在跑道上)比(某人)领先一圈 bǐ… lǐngxiān yìquān.

lap[3] /læp/ *v* [**-pp-**] **1** [T] 舔 tiǎn; 舔食 tiǎnshí. **2** [I] (水)发〔發〕出轻〔輕〕轻的拍打声〔聲〕fāchū qīngqīngde pāidǎ shēng. **3** [短语动词] **lap sth up** [非正式用语]接受(夸奖等) jiēshòu.

lapel /lə'pel/ *n* [C] (大衣的)翻领 fānlǐng.

lapse /læps/ *n* [C] **1** 小错 xiǎocuò; 记错 jìcuò. **2** (时间)流逝 liúshì. **lapse** *v* [I] **1** (*from, into*) 失足 shīzú; 堕落 duòluò: *a* ~*d Catholic* 叛教的天主教徒. **2** *into* 陷入

L

(或进入)某种〔種〕状〔狀〕态〔態〕 xiànrù mǒuzhǒng zhuàngtài: ~ *into sleep* 入睡. 3 (时间)流逝 liúshì. 4 [法律](权利)丧〔喪〕失 sàngshī; 失效 shīxiào.

larch /lɑːtʃ/ *n* [C] 落叶〔葉〕松 luòyèsōng.

lard /lɑːd/ *n* [U] 猪油 zhūyóu.

larder /ˈlɑːdə(r)/ *n* [C] 食橱 shíchú; 食物贮〔貯〕藏室 shíwù zhùcángshì.

large /lɑːdʒ/ *adj* [~r, ~st] 1 大的 dàde. 2 [习语] (as) large as ˈlife [谑]本人 běnrén; 本身 běnshēn. by and ˈlarge 大体〔體〕上 dàtǐ shàng; 一般而论〔論〕 yì bān ér lùn. **large** *n* [习语] at ˈlarge (a) 自由的 zìyóude. (b) 一般 yìbān: *the country at* ~ 一般的国家. **largely** *adv* 在很大程度上 zài hěndà chéngdù shàng; 主要地 zhǔyàode. ˈ**large-scale** *adj* 1 大规模的 dàguīmóde: *a* ~*-scale search* 大规模搜查. 2 大比例尺的 dà bǐlìchǐ de.

lark[1] /lɑːk/ *n* [C] 小鸣禽 xiǎomíngqín.

lark[2] /lɑːk/ *n* [C, 常作 sing][非正式用语]嬉戏〔戲〕 xīxì; 玩笑 wánxiào. **lark** *v* [I] *about/around* [非正式用语]嬉戏 xīxì; 取笑 qǔxiào.

larva /ˈlɑːvə/ *n* [C] [*pl* ~e /-viː/] 幼虫 yòuchóng.

larynx /ˈlærɪŋks/ *n* [C] [*pl* larynges /læˈrɪndʒiːz/] 喉 hóu. **laryngitis** /ˌlærɪnˈdʒaɪtɪs/ *n* [U] 喉炎 hóuyán.

L

lascivious /ləˈsɪvɪəs/ *adj* [正式用语]好色的 hàosède; 猥亵〔褻〕的 wěixiède.

laser /ˈleɪzə(r)/ *n* [C] 激光 jīguāng; 激光器 jīguāngqì.

lash[1] /læʃ/ *n* [C] 1 鞭子 biānzi; 鞭鞘 biānshāo. 2 = EYELASH (EYE).

lash[2] /læʃ/ *v* 1 [I, T] 鞭打 biāndǎ; 抽打 chōudǎ. 2 [I, T](动物尾巴)甩动〔動〕 shuǎidòng; 摆〔擺〕动 bǎidòng. 3 [T](用绳等)绑紧〔緊〕 bǎngjǐn. 4 [短语动词] lash out (a) (*against/at*) 猛击〔擊〕 měngjī; 猛烈抨击 měngliè pēngjī. (b) (*on*) [非正式用语]花大量的钱〔錢〕 huā dàliàngde qián.

lashings /ˈlæʃɪŋz/ *n* [pl] [英国非正式用语] 大量 dàliàng: ~ *of cream* 大量的奶油.

lass /læs/ *n* [C] [尤用于苏格兰和英国北部, 非正式用语]少女 shàonǚ; 小姑娘 xiǎogūniang.

lasso /læˈsuː/ *n* [C] [*pl* ~s 或 ~es] 套索 tàosuǒ. **lasso** *v* [T] 用套索捕捉 yòng tàosuǒ bǔzhuō.

last[1] /lɑːst; *US* læst/ *adj* 1 最后〔後〕的 zuìhòude: *December is the* ~ *month of the year*. 十二月是一年的最后一个月份. 2 最近的 zuìjìnde; 刚〔剛〕过〔過〕去的 gāng guòqù de: ~ *night* 昨晚. 3 唯一剩下的 wéiyī shèngxià de; 最终的 zuìzhōngde: *This is our* ~ *bottle of milk*. 这是我们最后的一瓶牛奶. 4 极〔極〕少可能的 jíshǎo kěnéng de; 最不适〔適〕当〔當〕的 zuì bú shìdàng de: *She's the* ~ *person to trust with a secret*. 她是最不可能保密的人. 5 [习语] be on one's/its last ˈlegs 危殆 wēidài; 糟糕 zāogāo. have the last ˈlaugh 获〔獲〕得最后胜〔勝〕利 huòdé zuìhòu shènglì. have, etc the last ˈword (辩论中)作最后一次发〔發〕言 zuò zuìhòu yícì fāyán. in the /as a last reˈsort 作为〔爲〕最后手段 zuòwéi zuìhòu shǒuduàn. the ˌlast ˈditch 最后拼〔拚〕搏 zuìhòu pīnbó: *a* ˌ~*-*ˈ*ditch attempt* 最后的努力. the last straw ⇨ STRAW. the last ˈword (in sth) 最新的(或最时髦的)事物 zuìxīn de shìwù: *This car is the* ~ *word in luxury*. 这种汽车是最新的豪华车. **last** *n* 1 the last 最后的人(或事物) zuìhòu de rén; 最后提到的人(或事物) zuìhòu tí dào de rén. 2 [习语] at (long) ˈlast 终于 zhōngyú. **lastly** *adv* 最后一点〔點〕 zuìhòu yìdiǎn; 最后 zuìhòu.

last[2] /lɑːst; *US* læst/ *adv* 1 最后〔後〕 zuìhòu. 2 最近一次 zuìjìn yícì; 上次 shàngcì.

last[3] /lɑːst; *US* læst/ *v* 1 [I] 延续〔續〕 yánxù; 持续 chíxù. 2 [I, T] 足够维持 zúgòu wéichí: *enough food to* ~ *two days* 足够维持两天的食物. **lasting** *adj* 持久的 chíjiǔde.

latch /lætʃ/ *n* [C] 1 门闩 ménshuān. 2 碰锁〔鎖〕 pèngsuǒ; 弹〔彈〕簧锁 tánhuángsuǒ. **latch** *v* 1 [I, T] 用门闩拴住 yòng ménshuān shuān zhù; 用碰锁锁住 yòng pèngsuǒ suǒ zhù. 2 [短语动词] latch on to sb [非正式用语]缠〔纏〕住不放 chán zhù bú fàng.

late /leɪt/ *adj* [~r, ~st] 1 迟〔遲〕的 chíde: *The train is* ~. 火车晚点. 2 晚的 wǎnde: *in the* ~ *afternoon* 在下午晚些时候. 3 最近的 zuìjìnde: *the* ~*st news* 最新消息. 4 已故的 yǐgùde: *her* ~ *husband* 她已故的丈夫. 5 [习语] at the ˈlatest 至迟 zhì chí; 最晚 zuì wǎn. **late** *adv* 1 迟 chí: *get up* ~ 起床晚. 2 接近末期 jiējìn mòqī: *as* ~ *as the 1970's* 直到 20 世纪 70 年代. **lately** *adv* 近来 jìnlái; 不久前 bùjiǔ qián.

latent /ˈleɪtnt/ *adj* 潜〔潛〕在的 qiánzàide; 不明显〔顯〕的 bù míngxiǎn de: ~ *talent* 潜在的才能.

lateral /ˈlætərəl/ *adj* 侧面的 cèmiànde; 从〔從〕侧面的 cóng cèmiàn de; 向侧面的 xiàng cèmiàn de.

lathe /leɪð/ *n* [C] 车〔車〕床〔牀〕 chēchuáng.

lather /ˈlɑːðə(r); *US* ˈlæð-/ *n* [U] (肥皂)泡沫 pàomò. **lather** *v* 1 [I] 起泡沫 qǐ pàomò. 2 [T] 涂〔塗〕以皂沫 tú yǐ zàomò.

Latin /ˈlætɪn; *US* ˈlætn/ *adj*, *n* [U] 拉丁语的 Lādīngyǔde; 拉丁语 Lādīngyǔ. ˌ**Latin Aˈmerica** *n* 拉丁美洲 Lādīngměizhōu. ˌ**Latin Aˈmerican** *n* [C], *adj*.

latitude /ˈlætɪtjuːd; *US* -tuːd/ *n* 1 [U] 纬〔緯〕

度 wěidù. 2 [U] (言论、行动的)自由 zìyóu.

latter /ˈlætə(r)/ *adj* 后〔後〕期的 hòuqīde; 末尾的 mòwěide: *the ~ part of her life* 她的晚年. **the latter** *pron* (已提到的两者中的)后者 hòuzhě. ˌ**latter-ˈday** *adj* 近代的 jìndài-de; 当〔當〕今的 dāngjīnde. **latterly** *adv* 近来 jìnlái; 最近 zuìjìn.

lattice /ˈlætɪs/ *n* [C,U] (板条制成的)格子架 gézijià.

laugh /lɑːf; *US* læf/ *v* 1 [I]笑 xiào; 发〔發〕笑 fāxiào. 2 [习语] **be no laughing matter** 不是开〔開〕玩笑的事 búshì kāi wánxiào de shì. **laugh one's head off** ⇨ HEAD[1]. 3 [短语动词] **laugh at sb/sth** 取笑 qǔxiào; 嘲笑 cháo-xiào. **laugh** *n* [C] 1 笑 xiào; 笑声〔聲〕 xiào-shēng. 2 [非正式用语]引人发笑的事 yǐn rén fāxiào de shì; 笑柄 xiàobǐng. **laughable** *adj* 可笑的 kěxiàode; 荒唐的 huāngtángde. **laugh-ably** *adv*. ˈ**laughing-stock** *n* [C, 常作 sing] 笑柄 xiàobǐng. **laughter** *n* [U] 笑 xiào; 笑声 xiàoshēng.

launch[1] /lɔːntʃ/ *v* [T] 1 使(新船)下水 shǐ xiàshuǐ. 2 发〔發〕射(火箭) fāshè. 3 开〔開〕始 kāishǐ; 开办〔辦〕 kāibàn: *~ a new business* 创办新商行. 4 [短语动词] **launch (out) into sth** 开始从〔從〕事 kāishǐ cóngshì; 积〔積〕极〔極〕投入 jījí tóurù: *~ out into a new career* 开始从事新的事业. **launch** *n* [C] (船)下水 xià-shuǐ; 发射 fāshè. ˈ**launching pad** *n* [C] (航天器等的)发射台〔臺〕 fāshètái.

launch[2] /lɔːntʃ/ *n* [C] 大汽艇 dà qìtǐng.

launder /ˈlɔːndə(r)/ *v* [T] [正式用语]洗熨(衣服) xǐ yùn.

launderette /ˌlɔːnˈdret, ˌlɔːndəˈret/ *n* [C] (设有投币洗衣机的)自助洗衣店 zhìzhù xǐyī-diàn.

laundromat /ˈlɔːndrəmæt/ *n* [C] (*P*) [尤用于美语]自助洗衣店 zhìzhù xǐyīdiàn.

laundry /ˈlɔːndrɪ/ *n* [*pl* -ies] 1 [C] 洗衣店 xǐyīdiàn. 2 [U]所洗的衣物 suǒxǐde yīwù; 待洗的衣物 dàixǐde yīwù.

laurel /ˈlɒrəl; *US* ˈlɔːrəl/ *n* [C] 月桂属〔屬〕植物 yuèguìshǔ zhíwù; 月桂树〔樹〕 yuèguìshù.

lava /ˈlɑːvə/ *n* [U] 熔岩 róngyán.

lavatory /ˈlævətrɪ; *US* -tɔːrɪ/ *n* [C] [*pl* -ies] 盥洗室 guànxǐshì; 厕〔廁〕所 cèsuǒ.

lavender /ˈlævəndə(r)/ *n* [U] 1 薰衣草 xūnyīcǎo. 2 淡紫色 dànzǐsè.

lavish /ˈlævɪʃ/ *adj* 1 慷慨的 kāngkǎide. 2 大量的 dàliàngde: *a ~ meal* 丰盛的饭菜. **lav-ish** *v* [短语动词] **lavish sth on sb** 慷慨地给予 kāngkǎide jǐyǔ. **lavishly** *adv*.

law /lɔː/ *n* 1 (a) [C] 法律 fǎlǜ. (b) (亦作 **the law**) [U] 法 fǎ; 法律 fǎlǜ; 法规 fǎguī; 法令 fǎlìng: *Murder is against the ~.* 谋杀是违法的. 2 [C] 法则 fǎzé; 定律 dìnglǜ: *the ~s of physics* 物理学定律. 3 **the law** [sing] [非正式用语]警方 jǐngfāng; 警察 jǐngchá. 4 [习语] **be a law unto oneˈself** (无视惯例)自行其是 zì xíng qí shì. **law and ˈorder** 法治 fǎzhì. ˈ**law-abiding** *adj* 守法的 shǒufǎde. ˈ**law-court** *n* [C] 法院 fǎyuàn; 法庭 fǎtíng. **lawful** *adj* 1 合法的 héfǎde; 法定的 fǎdìngde. 2 法律承认〔認〕的 fǎlǜ chéngrèn de. **lawfully** *adv*. **lawless** *adj* 未实〔實〕施法律的 wèi shíshī fǎlǜ de. **lawlessness** *n* [C]. ˈ**lawsuit** *n* [C] 诉讼 sùsòng.

lawn /lɔːn/ *n* [C, U] 草地 cǎodì; 草坪 cǎo-píng. ˈ**lawn-mower** *n* [C] 割草机〔機〕 gē-cǎojī. ˌ**lawn ˈtennis** [正式用语] = TENNIS.

lawyer /ˈlɔːjə(r)/ *n* [C] 律师〔師〕 lǜshī.

lax /læks/ *adj* 疏忽的 shūhude; 不严〔嚴〕格的 bù yángéde. **laxity** *n* [U].

laxative /ˈlæksətɪv/ *n* [C], *adj* 泻〔瀉〕药〔藥〕 xièyào; 缓泻的 huǎnxiède.

lay[1] /leɪ/ *v* [*pt*, *pp* **laid** /leɪd/] 1 [T] 放 fàng; 放置 fàngzhì: *~ a book on the table* 把书放在桌上. 2 [T] 把…放在适〔適〕当〔當〕位置 bǎ…fàng zài shìdàng wèizhì: *~ the table* (饭前)摆好餐具. 3 [T] [正式用语]使…减轻〔輕〕 shǐ … jiǎnqīng; 缓解 huǎnjiě: *~ sb's fears* 消除某人的恐惧. 4 [I, T] (鸟、虫等)产〔產〕(卵) chǎn. 5 [T] [⚠俚语] [尤作被动语态] 性交 xìngjiāo. 6 [习语] **lay sth ˈbare** 揭露 jiēlù; 揭发〔發〕 jiēfā: *~ bare one's feelings* 表露感情. **lay the ˈblame on sb** 把…归〔歸〕咎于某人 bǎ…guījiù yú mǒurén. **lay claim to sth** 声〔聲〕称〔稱〕有 shēngchēng yǒu; 拥〔擁〕有 yōngyǒu. **lay down the ˈlaw** 以权〔權〕威资格说话 yǐ quánwēi zīgé shuōhuà. **lay down one's life** [修辞]献〔獻〕身 xiànshēn; 献出生命 xiànchū shēngmìng. **lay a ˈfinger on sb** 伤〔傷〕害 shānghài. **lay it ˈon (ˈthick)** [非正式用语]夸大 kuādà. **lay sb ˈlow** 使衰弱 shǐ shuāi-ruò. **lay oneself ˈopen to sth** 使自己遭到(指责等) shǐ zìjǐ zāodào. **lay sth ˈwaste** [正式用语]摧毁 cuīhuǐ; 毁坏〔壞〕 huǐhuài. 7 [短语动词] **lay into sb/sth** [非正式用语]痛打 tòngdǎ; (用言语)攻击〔擊〕 gōngjī. **lay ˈoff (sth)** [非正式用语]不再做(有害的事) búzài zuò; 不再使用 búzài shǐyòng. **lay sb ˈoff** 解雇〔僱〕 jiěgù. **lay sth ˈon (a)** 供应〔應〕(煤气、水等) gōngyìng. (b)[非正式用语]提供(某物) tígōng: *~ on a party* 为社交聚会准备茶点. **lay sb ˈout** 打昏 dǎhūn. **lay sth ˈout (a)** 展示 zhǎnshì. (b)布〔佈〕置 bùzhì; 设计 shèjì: *a well laid out garden* 设计得精美的花园. **lay sb ˈup** 使卧床〔牀〕 shǐ wòchuáng: *be laid up with flu* 因患流感而卧床. ˌ**laid-ˈback** *adj* [俚语]松〔鬆〕弛的 sōngchíde; 悠闲〔閒〕的 yōuxiánde. ˈ**lay-off** *n* [C] 解雇 jiěgù. ˈ**lay-out** *n* [C] 安排

L

ānpái;设计 shèjì.

lay[2] *pt* of LIE[2].

lay[3] /leɪ/ *adj* 1 世俗的 shìsúde;非神职〔職〕的 fēi shénzhí de. 2 外行的 wàihángde;非专〔專〕业〔業〕的 fēi zhuānyè de. ˈ**layman** /-mən/ *n* [C] 俗人 súrén;外行 wàiháng.

layabout /ˈleɪəbaʊt/ *n* [C][英国,非正式用语]不务〔務〕正业〔業〕的人 bú wù zhèngyè de rén;游手好闲〔閑〕的人 yóu shǒu hào xián de rén.

lay-by /ˈleɪ baɪ/ *n* [C] [英国英语]路旁停车〔車〕场〔場〕 lùpáng tíngchēchǎng.

layer /ˈleɪə(r)/ *n* [C] 层〔層〕 céng: *a ~ of dust* 一层灰尘. *~s of clothing* 几层衣服.

layman ⇨LAY[3].

laze /leɪz/ *v* [I] 懒散 lǎnsǎn;混日子 hùn rìzi.

lazy /ˈleɪzɪ/ *adj* [-ier, -iest] 1 懒惰的 lǎnduòde;怠惰的 dàiduòde. 2 懒洋洋的 lǎnyángyángde;无〔無〕精打采的 wú jīng dǎ cǎi de. **lazily** *adv*. **laziness** *n* [U].

lb *abbr* [*pl* **lb, lbs**] pound (weight) 磅(重量单位) bàng.

LD /ˌel ˈdiː/ *abbr* laser disc 激光视盘〔盤〕 jīguāng shìpán.

lead[1] /liːd/ *v* [*pt*, *pp* **led** /led/] 1 [T] (a) 给…引路 gěi…yǐnlù. (b) 带〔帶〕领 dàilǐng: *~ a blind person* 搀扶一位盲人. 2 [T]影响〔響〕 yǐngxiǎng: *What led you to this conclusion?* 你是怎样得出这个结论的? 3 [I](道路)通 tōng;达〔達〕 dá. 4 [I] *to* 导〔導〕致某种〔種〕结果 dǎozhì mǒuzhǒng jiēguǒ: *a mistake that led to his death* 导致他死亡的一个错误. 5 [T]过〔過〕(某种生活) guò: *~ a miserable existence* 过悲惨的生活. 6 [I, T]领导 lǐngdǎo;领先 lǐngxiān. 7 [I, T] 率领 shuàilǐng;指挥 zhǐhuī: *~ a team of scientists* 领导一科学家小组. 8 [习语]**lead sb astray** 将〔將〕某人引入歧途 jiāng mǒurén yǐnrù qítú. **lead the ˈway** 引路 yǐnlù;带路 dàilù. 9 [短语动词] **lead sb on** 使误入歧途 shǐ wùrù qítú. **lead up to sth** 作为〔爲〕…的准〔準〕备〔備〕 zuòwéi… de zhǔnbèi. **leader** *n* [C] 领导 lǐngdǎo;领袖 lǐngxiù. **leadership** *n* [U] 领导地位 lǐngdǎo dìwèi;领导能力 lǐngdǎo nénglì. **leading** *adj* 最重要的 zuì zhòngyào de. ˌ**leading** ˈ**article** *n* [C] (报纸的)社论〔論〕 shèlùn. ˌ**leading** ˈ**question** *n* [C] 诱导性问题 yòudǎoxìng wèntí.

lead[2] /liːd/ *n* 1 [U, sing] 带〔帶〕领 dàilǐng;领导〔導〕 lǐngdǎo;指引 zhǐyǐn: *follow sb's ~* 跟着某人学. 2 [sing] 领先地位 lǐngxiān dìwèi: *a ~ of ten metres* 领先十米. 3 **the lead** [sing] 首位 shǒuwèi: *take the ~* 夺得领先地位. 4 [C] 主角 zhǔjué;扮演主角的演员 bànyǎn zhǔjué de yǎnyuán. 5 [C] 牵〔牽〕狗的绳〔繩〕索(或带子) qiān gǒu de shéngsuǒ. 6 [C] 导线〔綫〕 dǎoxiàn;引线 yǐnxiàn. 7 [C] 线索 xiànsuǒ.

lead[3] /led/ *n* 1 [U] 铅 qiān. 2 [C, U] 铅笔〔筆〕心 qiānbǐxīn. **leaden** *adj* 1 沉重的 chénzhòngde;缓慢的 huǎnmànde;沉闷的 chénmènde. 2 铅灰色的 qiānhuīsède;暗灰色的 ànhuīsède.

leaf /liːf/ *n* [*pl* **leaves** /liːvz/] 1 [C] 叶〔葉〕 yè;叶子 yèzi. 2 [C] (书刊等的)张〔張〕(即正反两页) zhāng. 3 [U] 金属〔屬〕薄片 jīnshǔ báopiàn;(金、银)箔 bó: *gold-~* 金箔. 4 [C] (活边桌的)折面或活面 zhémiàn huò huómiàn. 5 [习语] **take a leaf out of sb's ˈbook** 模仿某人 mófǎng mǒurén;仿效某人的举〔擧〕止 fǎngxiào mǒurén de jǔzhǐ. **leaf** *v* [短语动词] **leaf through sth** 匆匆翻阅 cōngcōng fānyuè;草草浏〔瀏〕览〔覽〕 cǎocǎo liúlǎn. **leafy** *adj* [-ier, -iest].

leaflet /ˈliːflɪt/ *n* [C] 散页印刷品 sǎnyè yìnshuāpǐn;传〔傳〕单 chuándān.

league /liːg/ *n* [C] 1 同盟 tóngméng;联〔聯〕盟 liánméng. 2 (体育俱乐部)联合会〔會〕 liánhéhuì;社团〔團〕 shètuán;协〔協〕会 xiéhuì. 3 [非正式用语]等级 děngjí;范〔範〕畴〔疇〕 fànchóu: *They're not in the same ~.* 他们不属于同一级别. 4 [习语] **in league (with sb)** 勾结 gōujié;共谋 gòngmóu.

leak /liːk/ *n* [C] 1 (a) 漏洞 lòudòng;漏隙 lòuxì. (b) 泄出物 xièchūwù. 2 [喻]泄漏 xièlòu: *a security ~* 保安上的泄密. **leak** *v* 1 [I] (a) (容器)漏 lòu. (b) (液体、气体)渗〔滲〕漏 shènlòu; 泄漏 xièlòu. 2 [T] 泄漏(消息等) xièlòu;透露 tòulù. **leakage** / ˈliːkɪdʒ / *n* [C, U] 渗漏 shènlòu;泄露 xièlòu;渗漏量 shènlòuliàng. **leaky** *adj* [-ier, -iest].

lean[1] /liːn/ *v* [*pt*, *pp* **~t** /lent/ 或尤用于美语 **~ed** /liːnd/] 1 [I] 倾斜 qīngxié;弯〔彎〕曲 wānqū;屈身 qūshēn. 2 [I, T] *against/on* (使)倚靠 yǐkào: *~ a ladder against a wall* 把梯子靠在墙上. 3 [短语动词] **lean on sb** [非正式用语,尤用于美语]威胁〔脅〕(某人) wēixié;恐吓〔嚇〕 kǒnghè. **lean (up)on sb** 依靠 yīkào. **lean towards sth** 倾向 qīngxiàng. **leaning** *n* [C] 倾向 qīngxiàng;爱〔愛〕好 àihào: *political ~ings* 政治倾向.

lean[2] /liːn/ *adj* 1 (人、动物)瘦的 shòude. 2 (肉)脂肪少的 zhīfáng shǎo de;无〔無〕脂肪的 wú zhīfáng de. 3 产〔產〕量低的 chǎnliàng dī de: *~ years* 歉收年.

leap /liːp/ *v* [*pt*, *pp* **~t** /lept/或尤用于美语 **~ed** / liːpt /] [I] 1 跳 tiào;跳跃〔躍〕 tiàoyuè. 2 急速移动〔動〕 jísù yídòng; 冲〔衝〕 chōng;窜〔竄〕 cuàn: *~ into the car* 一头钻进汽车. 3 [短语动词] **leap at sth** 迫不及待地接受 pò bù jí dài de jiēshòu: *She ~t at the chance.* 她赶紧抓住这个机会. **leap** *n* [C] 1

L

跳 tiào；跳跃 tiàoyuè. 2 激增 jīzēng；骤变〔變〕zhòubiàn. 3［习语］by ˌleaps and ˈbounds 非常迅速 fēicháng xùnsù. ˈleap-frog *n*［U］跳背游戏〔戲〕tiào bèi yóuxì. ˈleap-frog *v*［-gg-］［I，T］（做跳背游戏）跳过〔過〕tiàoguò. ˈleap year *n*［C］闰年 rùnnián.

learn /lɜːn/ *v*［*pt*，*pp* ~t /lɜːnt/ 或尤用于美语 ~ed /lɜːnd/］1［I，T］学〔學〕xué；学习〔習〕xuéxí：~ *Dutch* 学荷兰语. ~（*how*）*to swim* 学游泳. 2［T］记住 jìzhù：~ *a poem* 把一首诗背下来. 3［I，T］（*of*/*about*）获〔獲〕悉 huòxī；得知 dézhī：~ *of sb's death* 听说某人死了. **learned** /ˈlɜːnɪd/ *adj* 有学问的 yǒu xuéwèn de；博学的 bóxuéde. **learner** *n*［C］. **learning** *n*［U］学问 xuéwèn；知识〔識〕zhīshi；学识 xuéshí.

lease /liːs/ *n*［C］（土地或房屋的）租约 zūyuē；租契 zūqì. **lease** *v*［T］出租 chūzū；租得 zūdé. ˈ**leasehold** *n*［U］，*adj* 租赁（的）zūlìn.

leash /liːʃ/ *n*［C］= LEAD[2] 5.

least /liːst/ *pron*，*adj* 最小（的）zuìxiǎo；最少（的）zuìshǎo：*She gave*（*the*）~ *of all towards the present*. 她提供的礼品最少. **least** *adv* 1 最小 zuìxiǎo；最少 zuìshǎo：*the* ~ *expensive hotel* 最便宜的旅馆. 2［习语］at least（a）至少 zhìshǎo：*at* ~ *three months* 至少三个月.（b）无〔無〕论〔論〕如何 wúlùn rúhé：*at* ~ *she's reliable* 无论如何她很可靠. ˌnot in the ˈleast 绝对〔對〕不 juéduì bù；一点〔點〕也不 yìdiǎn yě bù. not least 尤其 yóuqí；特别 tèbié.

leather /ˈleðə(r)/ *n*［U］皮革 pígé；皮革制〔製〕品 pígé zhìpǐn. **leathery** *adj* 似皮革的 sìpígéde.

leave[1] /liːv/ *v*［*pt*，*pp* left /left/］1［I，T］离〔離〕开〔開〕líkāi. 2［T］使…处〔處〕于某状〔狀〕态〔態〕shǐ…chǔyú mǒu zhuàngtài：~ *the window open* 让窗户敞着. 3［T］遗忘 yíwàng；丢下 diūxià：*I left my umbrella at home*. 我把雨伞落在家里了. 4［T］留下 liúxià：*Blood* ~*s a stain*. 血留下污迹. 5［T］遗留 yíliú；遗赠 yízèng. 6［T］委托 wěituō；交给 jiāogěi：*We left him to do the cooking*. 我们把做饭的事交给他了. 7［T］（数学）剩余〔餘〕shèngyú；剩下 shèngxià：*7 from 10* ~*s 3*. 10 减 7 得 3. 8［习语］leave/let sb/sth aˈlone/ˈbe 不打扰〔擾〕bù dǎrǎo；不干预 bù gānyù. leave ˈgo/ˈhold（of sth）松〔鬆〕开 sōngkāi. leave it at ˈthat［非正式用语］到此为〔為〕止 dào cǐ wéi zhǐ. leave sb in the lurch 抛弃〔棄〕（某人）于困境 pāoqì…yú kùnjìng. leave well alone ⇨ WELL[3]. 9［短语动词］leave sb/sth behind 忘记带〔帶〕wàngjì dài；遗落 yíluò. leave off（doing）sth［非正式用语］停止某事 tíngzhǐ mǒushì；停止做某事 tíngzhǐ zuò mǒushì. leave sb/sth out 不包括 bù bāokuò.

leave[2] /liːv/ *n*［U］1 假 jià；假期 jiàqī：*a few days* ~ 几天假期. 2［正式用语］许可 xǔkě；准许 zhǔnxǔ. 3［习语］take ˌleave of one's ˈsenses［修辞或戏谑］发〔發〕疯〔瘋〕fāfēng.

leaves *pl* of LEAF.

lecherous /ˈletʃərəs/ *adj*［贬］好色的 hàosède；纵〔縱〕欲〔慾〕的 zòngyùde.

lectern /ˈlektən/ *n*［C］（教堂中的）读〔讀〕经〔經〕台〔臺〕dújīngtái；讲〔講〕台 jiǎngtái.

lecture /ˈlektʃə(r)/ *n*［C］讲〔講〕课 jiǎngkè；演讲 yǎnjiǎng. **lecture** *v* 1［I］讲课 jiǎngkè；演讲 yǎnjiǎng. 2［T］责骂 zémà；训斥 xùnchì. **lecturer** *n*［C］讲师〔師〕jiǎngshī. **lectureship** *n*［C］讲师的职〔職〕位 jiǎngshīde zhíwèi.

led *pt*，*pp* of LEAD[1].

ledge /ledʒ/ *n*［C］岩石架 yánshíjià；壁架 bìjià；架状〔狀〕突出物 jiàzhuàng tūchūwù.

ledger /ˈledʒə(r)/ *n*［C］分类〔類〕账〔賬〕fēnlèizhàng.

lee /liː/ *n*［sing］［正式用语］避风〔風〕处〔處〕bìfēngchù；背风处 bèifēngchù.

leech /liːtʃ/ *n*［C］1 水蛭 shuǐzhì；蚂蟥 mǎhuáng. 2［喻，贬］吸血鬼 xīxuèguǐ；榨取他人脂膏者 zhàqǔ tārén zhīgāo zhě.

leek /liːk/ *n*［C］韭葱 jiǔcōng.

leer /lɪə(r)/ *n*［C，常作 sing］（表示恶意、挑逗的）一瞥 yìpiē；睨视 nìshì. **leer** *v*［I］（*at*）投以（恶意、挑逗的）一瞥 tóu yǐ…yìpiē；睨视 nìshì.

left[1] *pt*，*pp* of LEAVE[1]. **left-ˈluggage office** *n*［C］［英国英语］（火车站等的）行李寄存处〔處〕xíngli jìcúnchù. ˈ**left-overs** *n*［pl］剩余〔餘〕物 shèngyúwù；残〔殘〕羹剩饭 cán gēng shèng fàn.

left[2] /left/ *adj*，*adv* 左边〔邊〕的 zuǒbiānde；左侧的 zuǒcède；向左 xiàngzuǒ；在左边 zài zuǒbiān. **left** *n* 1［U］左边 zuǒbiān；左侧 zuǒcè. 2 the left［sing］［用 sing 或 pl v］（a）（政党的）左翼 zuǒyì.（b）左派人士 zuǒpài rénshì. ˈ**left-click** *v* 左击〔擊〕zuǒjī：~*-click on the icon* 左击该图标. ~*-click the mouse* 左击鼠标键. ˈ**left-hand** *adj* 左边的 zuǒbiānde；左侧的 zuǒcède. ˌ**left-ˈhanded** *adj* 惯用左手的 guàn yòng zuǒshǒu de；左撇子的 zuǒpiězide. **leftist** *n*［C］，*adj* 左派 zuǒpài；左派的 zuǒpàide. the ˌleft ˈwing *n*［sing］［用 sing 或 pl v］左翼 zuǒyì. **left-wing** *adj*：~*-wing policies* 左倾政策.

leg /leg/ *n*［C］1（a）腿 tuǐ.（b）动〔動〕物的腿（用作食物）dòngwù de tuǐ.（c）裤腿 kùtuǐ：*a trouser* ~ 一条裤腿. 2（桌、椅等的）腿 tuǐ. 3 一段行程 yíduàn xíngchéng. 4［习语］not have a ˌleg to ˈstand on［非正式用语］（论点）站不住

L

脚 zhàn bú zhù jiǎo;缺乏根据〔據〕quēfá gēnjù.

legacy /ˈlegəsɪ/ *n* [C] [*pl* -ies] 1 遗赠的财物 yízèng de cáiwù;遗产〔產〕yíchǎn. 2 [喻]遗留之物 yíliú zhī wù

legal /ˈli:gl/ *adj* 1 法律的 fǎlǜde;法定的 fǎdìngde: *my ~ adviser* 我的法律顾问. 2 合法的 héfǎde;法律认〔認〕可的 fǎlǜ rènkě de. **legality** /li:ˈgæləti/ *n* [U] 合法 héfǎ;依法 yīfǎ. **legally** /ˈli:gəlɪ/ *adv*.

legalistic /li:gəˈlɪstɪk/ *adj* [常作贬]墨守法规的 mò shǒu fǎguī de;条〔條〕文主义〔義〕的 tiáowén zhǔyì de.

legalize /ˈli:gəlaɪz/ *v* [T] 使合法化 shǐ héfǎhuà.

legend /ˈledʒənd/ *n* 1 (a) [C] 传〔傳〕说 chuánshuō;传奇 chuánqí. (b) [U] 民间传说 mínjiān chuánshuō; 传奇文学〔學〕chuánqí wénxué. 2 [C] [非正式用语]传奇人物 chuánqí rénwù;传奇事件 chuánqí shìjiàn: *He has become a ~ in his own lifetime*. 他成为他那个时代的传奇人物. 3 [C] (地图、图片等的)图〔圖〕例 túlì,说明 shuōmíng. **legendary** /ˈledʒəndrɪ; *US* -derɪ/ *adj* 著名的 zhùmíngde;有名的 yǒumíngde.

legible /ˈledʒəbl/ *adj* 易读〔讀〕的 yìdúde;(字迹、印刷等)清楚的 qīngchude. **legibly** *adv*.

legion /ˈli:dʒən/ *n* [C] 1 古罗〔羅〕马军团〔團〕gǔluómǎ jūntuán. 2 众〔衆〕多 zhòngduō;大批 dàpī. **legion** *adj* [修辞]众多的 zhòngduōde;大批的 dàpīde. **legionary** /ˈli: dʒənərɪ; *US* -nerɪ/ *n* [C] [pl -ies], *adj* 古罗马军团成员 gǔluómǎ jūntuán chéngyuán;军团的 jūntuánde.

legislate /ˈledʒɪsleɪt/ *v* [I] 立法 lìfǎ. **legislation** /ˌledʒɪsˈleɪʃn/ *n* [U] 1 立法 lìfǎ. 2 法律 fǎlǜ;法规 fǎguī. **legislator** *n* [C].

legislative /ˈledʒɪslətɪv; *US* -leɪtɪv/ *adj* 立法的 lìfǎde: *a ~ assembly* 立法会议.

legislature /ˈledʒɪslətʃə(r) 或 ˈledʒɪsleɪtʃə(r)/ *n* [C,亦作 sing,用 pl v] [正式用语]立法机〔機〕关〔關〕lìfǎ jīguān;立法团〔團〕体〔體〕lìfǎ tuántǐ.

legitimate /lɪˈdʒɪtɪmət/ *adj* 1 合法的 héfǎde. 2 合法婚姻所生的 héfǎ hūnyīn suǒ shēng de. 3 合理的 hélǐde: *a ~ excuse* 合乎情理的理由. **legitimacy** /-məsɪ/ *n* [U].

legless /ˈleglɪs/ *adj* [俚语]大醉 dàzuì.

leisure /ˈleʒə(r); *US* ˈli:ʒər/ *n* [U] 1 空闲〔閒〕kòngxián;闲暇 xiánxiá. 2 [习语] **at one's ˈleisure** 有空时〔時〕yǒukòng shí;方便时 fāngbiàn shí. **leisured** *adj* 有空闲的 yǒu kòngxián de. **leisurely** *adv*, *adj* 不慌不忙(的) bùhuāng bùmáng;从〔從〕容(的) cóngróng: *a ~ly walk* 漫步.

lemon /ˈlemən/ *n* 1 (a) [C,U] 柠〔檸〕檬 níngméng. (b) [C] 柠檬树〔樹〕níngméngshù. 2 [U] 柠檬黄 níngménghuáng;淡黄色 dànhuángsè.

lemonade /ˌleməˈneɪd/ *n* [C,U] 柠〔檸〕檬汽水 níngméng qìshuǐ.

lend /lend/ *v* [*pt*, *pp* **lent** /lent/] [T] 1 (*to*) 借出 jièchū;把…借给 bǎ…jiègěi: *He lent him the money*. 他借给他钱. *He lent it to him*. 他把它借给他. 2 (*to*) [正式用语]提供 tígōng;添加 tiānjiā: *Her presence lent dignity to the occasion*. 她的出席给这场合增添了尊严. 3 **lend itself to** 适〔適〕合于 shìhé yú. 4 [习语] **lend (sb) a hand** 帮〔幫〕助(某人) bāngzhù. ˈ**lending rate** *n* [C] 贷款利率 dàikuǎn lìlǜ.

length /leŋθ 或 leŋkθ/ *n* 1 [U] 长〔長〕cháng;长度 chángdù. 2 [U,C] 一段时〔時〕间 yíduàn shíjiān. 3 [C] (作度量单位之物的)长度 chángdù: *swim two ~s of the pool* 在游泳池游了一个来回. 4 [C] 一段 yíduàn;一节〔節〕yìjié: *a ~ of wire* 一段电线. 5 [习语] **at length** (a) [正式用语]最终 zuìzhōng; 终于 zhōngyú. (b) 详尽〔盡〕地 xiángjìnde. **go to any, some, great, etc ˈlengths (to do sth)** (为达到目的)不遗余〔餘〕力 bù yí yú lì;不顾〔顧〕一切 búgù yíqiè. **lengthen** *v* [I,T] (使)变〔變〕长 biàncháng;(使)延长 yáncháng. ˈ**lengthways** (亦作 ˈ**lengthwise**) *adv* 纵〔縱〕长地 zòngchángde;纵向地 zòngxiàngde. **lengthy** *adj* [-ier, -iest] 很长的 hěnchángde.

lenient /ˈli:nɪənt/ *adj* 宽大的 kuāndàde;宽厚的 kuānhòude. **leniency** /-ənsɪ/ *n* [U]. **leniently** *adv*.

lens /lenz/ *n* [C] 1 透镜 tòujìng;镜片 jìngpiàn. 2 (眼球的)晶状〔狀〕体〔體〕jīngzhuàngtǐ.

Lent /lent/ *n* [U] (基督教)四旬斋〔齋〕sìxúnzhāi;大斋节〔節〕dàzhāijié.

lent *pt*, *pp* of LEND.

lentil /ˈlentl/ *n* [C] 小扁豆 xiǎobiǎndòu.

leopard /ˈlepəd/ *n* [C] 豹 bào. **leopardess** /ˌlepəˈdes/ *n* [C] 母豹 mǔbào.

leotard /ˈli:ətɑ:d/ *n* [C] (杂技、舞蹈演员等的)紧〔緊〕身连衣裤 jǐnshēn liányīkù.

leper /ˈlepə(r)/ *n* [C] 1 麻风〔風〕病患者 máfēngbìng huànzhě. 2 [喻]被排斥的人 bèi páichì de rén.

leprosy /ˈleprəsɪ/ *n* [U] 麻风〔風〕病 máfēngbìng.

lesbian /ˈlezbɪən/ *n* [C] 同性恋〔戀〕女子 tóngxìngliàn nǚzǐ. **lesbian** *adj* 女性同性恋的 nǚxìng tóngxìngliàn de.

less /les/ *adj*, *pron* 较少的 jiàoshǎode;更少的 gèngshǎode: *~ to do than I thought* 做的事比我想的要少一些. **less** *adv*. 1 较少地 jiàoshǎode;更少地 gèngshǎode: *It rains ~ here*. 这里的降雨量较少. 2 [习语] **even/much/still less** 更不用说 gèng búyòng shuō;更何况 gèng hékuàng. **less and less** 越来越小

地 yuè lái yuè xiǎo de；越来越少地 yuè lái yuè shǎo de. **no less (than)** 多达〔達〕duōdá. **less** *prep* 先扣除 xiān kòuchú；减去 jiǎnqù：*£1000 a month ～ tax*. 扣除税款一月 1000 英镑.

lessen /ˈlesn/ *v* [I, T] (使)减少 jiǎnshǎo；(使)变〔變〕少 biànshǎo.

lesser /ˈlesə(r)/ *adj* 1 较小的 jiàoxiǎode；更少的 gèngshǎode. 2 [习语] **the ˌlesser of two ˈevils** 两害取其轻〔輕〕liǎng hài qǔ qí qīng.

lesson /ˈlesn/ *n* [C] 1 一节〔節〕课 yìjiékè；一堂课 yìtángkè：*piano ～s* 钢琴课. 2 经〔經〕验〔驗〕jīngyàn；教训 jiàoxùn：*Let this be a ～ to you!* 把这件事当作你的教训吧!

lest /lest/ *conj* [正式用语]为〔爲〕了不使 wèile bùshǐ；免得 miǎndé.

let /let/ *v* [-tt-; *pt*, *pp* **let**] [T] 1 允许 yúnxǔ；让〔讓〕ràng：*We ～ him leave*. 我们让他走了. 2 允许进〔進〕入 yúnxǔ jìnrù；通过〔過〕tōngguò：*～ sb into the house* 允许某人进屋. 3(用于祈使句)：*Let's go!* 我们走吧! 4 出租(房屋) chūzū. 5 [习语] **let alone** 更不必说 gèng búbì shuō：*We cannot even pay our bills, ～ alone make a profit*. 我们甚至连账都付不起,更不必说赚钱了. **let sb/sth alone/be** ⇨LEAVE[1]. **let the ˈcat out of the bag** 泄露秘密 xièlòu mìmì. **let sth ˈdrop** 说出 shuōchū；吐露 tǔlù. **let fly (at sb/sth)** 飞〔飛〕掷〔擲〕fēizhì；攻击〔擊〕gōngjī. **let sb/sth go, let ˈgo of sb/sth** 松〔鬆〕开〔開〕sōngkāi；释〔釋〕放 shìfàng. **ˌlet oneself ˈgo** (a) 尽〔盡〕情 jìnqíng；放纵〔縱〕fàngzòng. (b) 不再整齐〔齊〕búzài zhěngqí；不再谨慎 búzài jǐnshèn. **let one's ˈhair down** [非正式用语]放松一下 fàngsōng yí xià. **let sb ˈhave it** [俚]打击(某人) dǎjī；惩〔懲〕罚(某人) chéngfá. **let sb know (about sth)** 告诉 gàosu；通知 tōngzhī. **let off ˈsteam** [非正式用语]宣泄(精力或情感) xuānxiè. **let the ˈside down** 不帮〔幫〕助 bù bāngzhù；使失望 shǐ shīwàng. **let sleeping dogs ˈlie** 别惹事生非 bié rě shì shēng fēi. **let sth ˈslide** 放任 fàngrèn；听〔聽〕其自然 tīng qí zìrán. **let sth slip** (a) 错过 cuòguò；放过 fàngguò. (b) 无〔無〕意中吐露 wúyì zhōng tǔlù. **let us ˈsay** 例如 lìrú；譬如 pìrú. **let well alone** ⇨WELL[3]. 6 [短语动词] **let sb down** 使失望 shǐ shīwàng. **let sth down** (a) 放长〔長〕(衣服) fàngcháng. (b) 放掉(车胎等的)气〔氣〕fàngdiào qì. **let sb/oneself in for sth** 使陷入(困境) shǐ xiànrù；惹起(麻烦) rě qǐ. **let sb in on/into sth** [非正式用语]让〔讓〕(某人)知道(秘密) ràng…zhīdào. **let sb off (with sth)** 不惩罚 bù chéngfá；从轻〔輕〕处〔處〕理 cóng qīng chǔlǐ. **let sb off (sth)** 不强迫(某人)做(某事) bù qiǎngpò…zuò. **let sth off** 放(枪、炮、烟火等) fàng. **let ˈon** [非正式用语]泄露秘密 xièlòu mìmì：*Don't ～ on that you know*. 别把你知道的秘密泄露出去. **let sth out** (a) 放宽 fàngkuān；放大(衣服) fàngdà. (b) 发〔發〕出(叫喊) fāchū. **let ˈup** 减弱 jiǎnruò；停止 tíngzhǐ：*The rain began to ～ up*. 雨开始小了. **ˈlet-down** *n* [C] 失望 shīwàng；沮丧〔喪〕jǔsàng. **ˈlet-up** *n* [C, U] 减弱 jiǎnruò；缓和 huǎnhé；放松 fàngsōng.

lethal /ˈliːθl/ *adj* 致命的 zhìmìngde；致死的 zhìsǐde.

lethargy /ˈleθədʒɪ/ *n* [U] 无〔無〕生气〔氣〕wú shēngqì；无兴〔興〕趣 wú xìngqù. **lethargic** /ləˈθɑːdʒɪk/ *adj*.

let's let us. ⇨LET 3.

letter /ˈletə(r)/ *n* 1 [C] 信 xìn；函件 hánjiàn. 2 [C] 字母 zìmǔ. **ˈletter-bomb** *n* [C] 信件炸弹〔彈〕xìnjiàn zhàdàn. **ˈletter-box** *n* [C] 1[英国英语]信箱 xìnxiāng. 2 邮〔郵〕筒 yóutǒng. **lettering** *n* [U] 字母 zìmǔ；字 zì.

lettuce /ˈletɪs/ *n* [C, U] 莴〔萵〕苣 wōjù；生菜 shēngcài.

leukaemia (美语-kem-) /luːˈkiːmɪə/ *n* [U] 白血病 báixuèbìng.

level[1] /ˈlevl/ *adj* 1 水平的 shuǐpíngde；平的 píngde. 2 (*with*) 等高的 děnggāode；同等的 tóngděngde：*Wales drew ～ early in the game*. 比赛初期威尔士队打了个平局. 3 [习语] **do one's level ˈbest** 全力以赴 quán lì yǐ fù. **ˌlevel-ˈcrossing** *n* [C] (公路和铁路的)平面交叉处〔處〕píngmiàn jiāochāchù；(平交)道口 dàokǒu. **ˌlevel-ˈheaded** *adj* 头〔頭〕脑〔腦〕冷静的 tóunǎo lěngjìng de；清醒的 qīngxǐngde.

level[2] /ˈlevl/ *n* 1 [C] 水平线〔綫〕shuǐpíngxiàn；水平面 shuǐpíngmiàn. 2 [C] (测量的)数〔數〕量 shùliàng；强度 qiángdù；数值 shùzhí：*a high ～ of output* 高生产率. 3 [U] 等级 děngjí；水平 shuǐpíng：*talks at management ～* 管理人员的商谈.

level[3] /ˈlevl/ *v* [-ll-; 美语-l-] [T] 1 使成水平状〔狀〕态〔態〕shǐ chéng shuǐpíng zhuàngtài. 2 摧毁(建筑等) cuīhuǐ；夷平 yípíng. 3 (*at*) 瞄准〔準〕miáozhǔn；对〔對〕准 duìzhǔn. 4 [短语动词] **level off/out** (a) (飞机在着陆前或在爬升、俯冲后)水平飞〔飛〕行 shuǐpíng fēixíng. (b) [喻] 呈平稳〔穩〕状态 chéng píngwěn zhuàngtài：*Prices ～led off*. 物价趋稳. **level with sb** [非正式用语]坦诚待人 tǎn chéng dài rén.

lever /ˈliːvə(r)/ *n* [C] 1 杆〔桿〕gǎn；杠〔槓〕杆 gànggǎn. 2 控制杆 kòngzhìgǎn；操作杆 cāozuògǎn. 3[喻](施加影响的)手段 shǒuduàn；方法 fāngfǎ. **lever** *v* [T] (用杠杆)撬动〔動〕qiàodòng：*L～ it into position*. 用杠杆将其移入位置. **leverage** /-ərɪdʒ/ *n* [U] 1 杠杆作用 gànggǎn zuòyòng. 2 [喻]影响〔響〕yǐngxiǎng；力量 lìliàng.

levy /ˈlevɪ/ *v* [*pt*, *pp* **-ied**] [T] 征〔徵〕收

L

zhēngshōu;征集 zhēngjí: ~ *a tax* 征税. **levy** *n* [C] [*pl* -ies] 征收额 zhēngshōu'é;税款 shuìkuǎn.

lewd /ljuːd; *US* luːd/ *adj* 淫荡[蕩]的 yíndàngde;猥亵[褻]的 wěixiède: ~ *jokes* 下流的笑话.

liability /ˌlaɪə'bɪlətɪ/ *n* [*pl* -ies] **1** [U] 义[義]务[務] yìwù;责任 zérèn. **2 liabilities** [pl] 债务 zhàiwù. **3** [C] [非正式用语]不利 búlì;妨碍[礙] fáng'ài: *An old car is a* ~. 旧车是个累赘.

liable /'laɪəbl/ *adj* **1** *to* 有…倾向的 yǒu…qīngxiàng de: ~ *to make mistakes* 可能出差错. **2** *to* 可能遭受的 kěnéng zāoshòu de: *be* ~ *to flu in winter* 冬天易患流感. **3** 应[應]负责的 yīng fùzé de: ~ *for debts* 应对债务负责.

liaise /lɪ'eɪz/ *v* [I] 取得联[聯]系[繫] qǔdé liánxì;做联系人 zuò liánxì rén.

liaison /lɪ'eɪzn; *US* 'lɪəzɒn/ *n* **1** [U] 联[聯]络 liánluò. **2** [C] 私通 sītōng.

liar /'laɪə(r)/ *n* [C] 说谎的人 shuōhuǎngde rén.

libel /'laɪbl/ *n* [U, C] 诽谤 fěibàng. **libel** *v* [-ll-;美语 -l-] [T] (发表文章等)诽谤 fěibàng. **libellous** (美语 **libelous**) /-bələs/ *adj*.

liberal /'lɪbərəl/ *adj* **1** 宽容的 kuānróngde;大度的 dàdùde. **2** 慷慨的 kāngkǎide;大方的 dàfangde: *a* ~ *supply* 大量的供应. **3** (教育)扩[擴]展知识[識]的 kuòzhǎn zhīshi de. **liberalism** *n* [C] 自由主义[義] zìyóu zhǔyì. **liberalize** /'lɪbrəlaɪz/ *v* [T] 使自由化 shǐ zìyóuhuà: ~*ize shop opening hours* 使营业时间不固定. **liberally** *adv*. **the 'Liberal Party** *n* [sing] (英国政治)自由党[黨] Zìyóudǎng.

liberate /'lɪbəreɪt/ *v* [T] [正式用语]解放 jiěfàng;使获[獲]自由 shǐ huò zìyóu. **liberated** *adj* 解放的 jiěfàngde. **liberation** /ˌlɪbə'reɪʃn/ *n* [U].

liberty /'lɪbətɪ/ *n* [*pl* -ies] **1** [U] [正式用语]自由 zìyóu;自主 zìzhǔ. **2** [C, U] [正式用语]自由权[權] zìyóuquán. **3** [习语] **at liberty** 自由的 zìyóude;获[獲]许可的 huò xǔkě de. **take the liberty of doing sth** 擅自做某事 shànzì zuò mǒushì;冒昧做某事 màomèi zuò mǒushì.

library /'laɪbrərɪ; *US* -brerɪ/ *n* [C] [*pl* -ies] 图[圖]书[書]馆 túshūguǎn. **librarian** /laɪ'breərɪən/ *n* [C] 图书馆长[長] túshūguǎnzhǎng.

lice *pl* of LOUSE.

licence (美语 **license**) /'laɪsns/ *n* [C, U] 执[執]照 zhízhào;许可证[證] xǔkězhèng.

license (亦作 **licence**) /'laɪsns/ *v* [T] 给(某人)执[執]照(或许可证) gěi…zhízhào;准许 zhǔnxǔ. **licensee** /ˌlaɪsən'siː/ *n* [C] 领有执照者 lǐng yǒu zhízhào zhě.

lick /lɪk/ *v* [T] **1** 舔 tiǎn: *The dog ~ed its paw*. 狗舔爪子. **2** [非正式用语]打败 dǎbài. **3** (波浪)轻[輕]拍 qīngpāi;(火焰)触[觸]及 chùjí. **4** [习语] **lick one's lips** ⇨LIP. **lick** *n* **1** [C] 舔 tiǎn. **2** [sing] 少许 shǎoxǔ.

licorice [美语] = LIQUORICE.

lid /lɪd/ *n* [C] **1** 盖[蓋]子 gàizi. **2** = EYELID (EYE).

lie[1] /laɪ/ *v* [*pt*, *pp* ~d, *pres p* lying] [I] 说谎 shuōhuǎng. **lie** *n* [C] 谎言 huǎngyán;假话 jiǎhuà.

lie[2] /laɪ/ *v* [*pt* lay /leɪ/ , *pp* lain /leɪn/, *pres p* lying] [I] **1** 躺 tǎng;平卧 píngwò. **2** 平放 píngfàng. **3** 处[處]于某种[種]状[狀]态[態] chǔyú mǒuzhǒng zhuàngtài: *machines lying idle* 闲置的机器. **4** 位于 wèiyú: *The town ~s on the coast*. 这座城镇位于海滨. **5** 展现 zhǎnxiàn;伸展 shēnzhǎn: *The valley lay before us*. 山谷展现在我们面前. **6** (抽象事物)存在 cúnzài;在于 zàiyú: *It does not ~ within my power to help you*. 要帮助你实在是超出了我的能力范围. **7** [习语] **lie in 'wait (for sb)** 隐[隱]蔽 yǐnbì. **lie 'low** [非正式用语]不出声[聲] bù chūshēng;隐藏 yǐncáng. **not take sth lying 'down** 不甘忍受侮辱 bùgān rěnshòu wǔrǔ. **8** [短语动词] **lie behind sth** 是某事的原因或理由 shì mǒushìde yuányīn huò lǐyóu. **lie down** 躺着 tǎngzhe;躺下 tǎngxià. **lie with sb** [正式用语]是(某人)的义[義]务[務]、责任 shì…de yìwù、zérèn: *The final decision ~s with the director*. 最后的决定由主任做主. **lie** *n* [sing] **1** 状态 zhuàngtài;位置 wèizhi. **2** [习语] **the ˌlie of the 'land** (a) 地形地貌 dìxíng dìmào. (b) [喻]事态 shìtài. **'lie-down** *n* [sing] [非正式用语]小睡 xiǎoshuì;小憩 xiǎoqì. **'lie-in** *n* [sing] [非正式用语]睡懒觉[覺] shuì lǎn jiào.

lieutenant /lef'tenənt; *US* luː't-/ *n* [C] 陆[陸]军[軍]中尉 lùjūn zhōngwèi;海军上尉 hǎijūn shàngwèi.

life /laɪf/ *n* [*pl* lives /laɪvz/] **1** [U] 生命 shēngmìng. **2** [U] 生物 shēngwù: *Is there ~ on Mars?* 火星上有生物吗? **3** [U] 人生 rénshēng: *He expects a lot from* ~. 他对生活所求很多. **4** [C] 人 rén: *Many lives were lost*. 许多人丧生. **5** [C] 一生 yìshēng;终身 zhōngshēn: *She spent her whole ~ in Canada*. 她在加拿大度过一生. **6** [U] (亦作 **life sentence**) [非正式用语]终身监[監]禁 zhōngshēn jiānjìn;无[無]期徒刑 wúqī túxíng. **7** 社交活动[動] shèjiāo huódòng: *Join the navy and see ~!* 参加海军,可增广见识. **8** [U] 活力 huólì;精力 jīnglì: *full of* ~ 充满活力. **9** [C, U] 生活方式 shēnghuó fāngshì: *city* ~ 城市生活方式. **10** [C] 传[傳]记 zhuànjì: *a*

L

~ *of Dante* 但丁传. 11 [U] (美术创作中的)实〔實〕物 shíwù; 活体〔體〕模型 huótǐ móxíng: *a portrait drawn from* ~ 以真人作模特儿的画像. 12 [C] 寿〔壽〕命 shòumìng; 有效期 yǒuxiàoqī: *a battery with a* ~ *of three years* 寿命为三年的电池. 13 [习语] **come to 'life** 表现生气〔氣〕或活力 biǎoxiàn shēngqì huò huólì. **for the 'life of one** [非正式用语] 无〔無〕论〔論〕怎样〔樣〕努力 wúlùn zěnyàng nǔlì. **the life and soul of the party** [非正式用语] (聚会等的)最活跃〔躍〕的人物 zuì huóyuè de rénwù. **not on your 'life** [非正式用语] 当〔當〕然不 dāngrán bù. **take one's life in one's hands** 冒生命危险〔險〕 mào shēngmìng wēixiǎn. **take sb's 'life** 杀〔殺〕死某人 shāsǐ mǒurén. **'lifebelt** (亦作 **lifebuoy**) *n* [C] 救生带〔帶〕 jiùshēngdài; 救生圈 jiùshēngquān. **'life-boat** *n* [C] 救生艇 jiùshēngtǐng; 救生船 jiùshēngchuán. **'life cycle** *n* [C] [生物] 生活周〔週〕期 shēnghuó zhōuqī; 生活史 shēnghuóshǐ: *the* ~ *cycle of a frog* 蛙的生活周期. **'life-guard** *n* [C] 救生员 jiùshēngyuán. **'life-jacket** *n* [C] 救生衣 jiùshēngyī. **lifeless** *adj* 1 死的 sǐde. 2 无生气的 wú shēngqì de; 沉闷的 chénmènde. **'lifelike** *adj* 逼真的 bīzhēnde; 栩栩如生的 xǔxǔ rú shēng de: *a* ~*like painting* 栩栩如生的绘画. **'life line** *n* [C] 1 救生索 jiùshēngsuǒ. 2 [喻] 生命线〔綫〕 shēngmìngxiàn. **'lifelong** *adj* 毕〔畢〕生的 bìshēngde; 终身的 zhōngshēnde. **'life-size(d)** *adj* 与〔與〕真人(或实物)一样〔樣〕大小的 yǔ zhēnrén yíyàng dà xiǎo de. **'life-span** *n* [C] 寿〔壽〕命 shòumìng; 生命期限 shēngmìng qīxiàn; 使用期 shǐyòngqī. **'life-style** *n* [C] 生活方式 shēnghuó fāngshì. **'lifetime** *n* [C] 一生 yìshēng; 终身 zhōngshēn.

lift /lɪft/ *v* 1 [T] 举〔舉〕起 jǔqǐ; 抬起 táiqǐ. 2 [T] 使高兴〔興〕 shǐ gāoxìng: *The news* ~*ed her spirits*. 这个消息让她精神振奋. 3 [I] (云、雾等)消失 xiāoshī; 消散 xiāosàn. 4 [T] 撤销 chèxiāo; 解除 jiěchú. 5 [T] [非正式用语] 偷 tōu. 6 [习语] **not lift a finger** [非正式用语] 不帮〔幫〕忙 bù bāngmáng. 7 [短语动词] **lift off** (航天器)发〔發〕射 fāshè; 起飞〔飛〕 qǐfēi; 升空 shēngkōng. **lift** *n* 1 [sing] 举 jǔ; 抬 tái. 2 [C] 电〔電〕梯 diàntī; 升降机〔機〕 shēngjiàngjī. 3 [C] 免费搭车〔車〕 miǎnfèi dāchē; 搭便车 dā biànchē: *a* ~ *to the station* 搭便车去车站. 4 [sing] 鼓舞 gǔwǔ; 振奋〔奮〕 zhènfèn. **'lift-off** *n* [C, U] (航天器)发射 fāshè; 升空 shēngkōng; 起飞 qǐfēi.

ligament /ˈlɪgəmənt/ *n* [C] 韧〔韌〕带〔帶〕 rèndài.

light[1] /laɪt/ *n* 1 [U] 光 guāng; 光线〔綫〕 guāngxiàn: *the* ~ *of the sun* 阳光. 2 [C] 光源 guāngyuán; 电〔電〕灯〔燈〕 diàndēng. 3 [C] 点〔點〕火物 diǎnhuǒwù; 火焰 huǒyàn. 4 [U] 了〔瞭〕解 liǎojiě; 领悟 lǐngwù. 5 [sing] (观察人、物的)角度 jiǎodù; 眼光 yǎnguāng: *see things in a good* ~ 从适当的角度看事物. 6 [习语] **bring sth/come to 'light** 揭露(某事) jiēlù; 暴露 bàolù. **cast /shed/throw light on sth** 使某事清楚些 shǐ mǒushì qīngchu xiē. **in the light of sth** 考虑〔慮〕到某事 kǎolǜ dào mǒushì: *in the* ~ *of this news* 考虑到这条新闻. **light at the end of the tunnel** 历〔歷〕尽〔盡〕艰〔艱〕辛后〔後〕的成功(或幸福等) lì jìn jiānxīn hòu de chénggōng; 苦尽甘来 kǔ jìn gān lái. **'light bulb** = BULB 1. **'lighthouse** *n* [C] 灯塔 dēngtǎ. **'light-year** *n* 1 [C] 光年 guāngnián. 2 [常作 pl] [非正式用语] 长〔長〕期 chángqī.

light[2] /laɪt/ *adj* 1(地方)明亮的 míngliàngde: *a* ~ *room* 明亮的房间. 2 淡色的 dànsède; 浅〔淺〕色的 qiǎnsède: ~*-blue eyes* 淡蓝色的眼睛.

light[3] /laɪt/ *v* [*pt*, *pp* lit /lɪt/ 或 lighted] 1 [I, T] 点〔點〕燃 diǎnrán; 点 diǎn. 2 [T] 开〔開〕(灯) kāi. 3 [T] 提供光源 tígōng guāngyuán: *a castle lit by coloured lights* 彩色灯照亮的城堡. 4 [短语动词] **light up** [非正式用语] 点(烟)吸起来 diǎn…xī qǐlái. **light (sth) up** 容光焕发〔發〕 róngguāng huànfā. **light sth up** 照亮某物 zhàoliàng mǒuwù: *The fire lit up the whole sky*. 火光照亮了整个天空. **lighting** *n* [U] 照明设备〔備〕 zhàomíng shèbèi.

light[4] /laɪt/ *adj* 1 轻〔輕〕的 qīngde; 不重的 búzhòngde. 2 少量的 shǎoliàngde; (比平均重量)轻的 qīngde: ~ *rain* 小雨. 3 轻柔的 qīngróude: *a* ~ *touch* 轻轻的一碰. 4 容易做的 róngyì zuò de: ~ *work* 轻活儿. 5 轻松〔鬆〕的 qīngsōngde: ~ *reading* 消遣读物. 6 不严〔嚴〕厉〔厲〕的 bù yánlì de: *a* ~ *attack of the flu* 轻度流感. 7 (食物)易消化的 yì xiāohuà de. 8 (睡眠)不沉的 bùchénde; 不熟的 bùshúde. 9 (饮料)酒精含量低的 jiǔjīng hánliàng dī de; 淡味的 dànwèide. 10 [习语] **make light of sth** 轻视 qīngshì; 视…为〔爲〕微不足道 shì…wéi wēi bù zú dào. **ˌlight-ˈfingered** *adj* [非正式用语] 惯窃〔竊〕的 guànqiède. **ˌlight-ˈheaded** *adj* 眩晕的 xuányūnde. **ˈlight-hearted** *adj* 轻松愉快的 qīngsōng yúkuài de. **ˌlight ˈindustry** *n* [C] 轻工业〔業〕 qīnggōngyè. **lightly** *adv* 1 轻轻地 qīngqīngde. 2 轻率地 qīngshuàide. 3 [习语] **get off ˈlightly** [非正式用语] 逃避重罚 táobì zhòngfá. **lightness** *n* [U]. **ˈlightweight** *n* [C] 1 (体重为 59—61 千克的)轻量级拳击〔擊〕手 qīngliàngjí quánjīshǒu. 2 [非正式用语] 无〔無〕足轻重的人 wú zú qīng zhòng de rén.

light[5] /laɪt/ *v* [*pt*, *pp* lit /lɪt/ 或 lighted] [正式用语] [短语动词] **light on/upon sb/sth** 偶遇某人(或某事) ǒu yù mǒurén.

L

lighten[1] /ˈlaɪtn/ *v* [I,T] 减轻〔輕〕 jiǎnqīng; 变〔變〕轻 biànqīng.

lighten[2] /ˈlaɪtn/ *v* [I,T] (使)变〔變〕得明亮 biàn de míngliàng.

lighter /ˈlaɪtə(r)/ *n* [C] 打火机〔機〕 dǎhuǒjī.

lightning /ˈlaɪtnɪŋ/ *n* [U] 闪电〔電〕 shǎndiàn. **lightning** *adj* 闪电般的 shǎndiànbānde; 快速的 kuàisùde: *at ~ speed* 闪电般的速度. ˈ**lightning conductor** (美语 **lightning rod**) *n* [C] 避雷针 bìléizhēn.

like[1] /laɪk/ *v* [T] **1** 喜欢〔歡〕 xǐhuān; 喜爱〔愛〕 xǐ'ài. **2** [用于否定句] 愿〔願〕意 yuànyì: *I didn't ~ to stop you.* 我不愿意阻止你. **3** (与 should 或 would 连用, 表示愿望或选择): *Would you ~ a cup of tea?* 你要不要来一杯茶? *I'd ~ to think about it.* 我愿意考虑考虑. **4** [习语] **if you like** (作表示同意或建议的礼貌用语). **not like the look / sound of sth** 对〔對〕某事有不好的印象 duì mǒushì yǒu bùhǎode yìnxiàng. **likeable** (亦作 **likable**) *adj* 讨人喜欢的 tǎo rén xǐhuān de. **likes** *n* [pl] [习语] ˌ**likes and** ˈ**dislikes** 好恶〔惡〕 hàowù; 爱憎 àizēng.

like[2] /laɪk/ *prep* **1** 像 xiàng; 像…一样〔樣〕 xiàng… yíyàng: *a hat ~ mine* 和我那顶一样的帽子. **2** 符合(某人或某事物的)特点〔點〕 fúhé… tèdiǎn: *It's just ~ him to be rude.* 像他那样的人才会无礼. **3** 像(某人或某事)一样 xiàng… yíyàng: *behave ~ children* 举止像孩子. *drink ~ a fish* 大口大口地喝. **4** 例如 lìrú; 比如 bǐrú: *sports, ~ football and hockey* 体育项目, 比如足球和曲棍球. **5** [习语] **like** ˈ**anything** [非正式用语] 以全力 yǐ quánlì. **like** *conj* [非正式用语] **1** 像…那样 xiàng… nàyàng: *No one sings ~ she did.* 唱歌谁也比不上她. **2** (尤用于美语) 好像 hǎoxiàng.

like[3] /laɪk/ *adj* 相似的 xiāngsìde; 相同的 xiāngtóngde. **like** *n* [sing] 相似的人(或事物) xiāngsìde rén: *music, painting and the ~* 音乐、绘画等等. ˌ**like-**ˈ**minded** *adj* 志趣相投的 zhìqù xiāngtóu de.

likelihood /ˈlaɪklɪhʊd/ *n* [U] 可能(性) kěnéng.

likely /ˈlaɪklɪ/ *adj* [-ier, -iest] **1** 预期的 yùqīde; 可能的 kěnéngde: *~ to rain* 像要下雨. **2** [习语] **a** ˈ**likely story** [反语](用以表示对某人的话不相信)说得倒像是真的 shuōde dào xiàng shì zhēnde. **likely** *adv* [习语] **as** ˌ**likely as** ˈ**not, most/very** ˈ**likely** (很)可能 kěnéng. **not** ˈ**likely** [非正式用语]决不可能 jué bù kěnéng.

liken /ˈlaɪkən/ *v* [T] *to* [正式用语]把…比做 bǎ… bǐzuò.

likeness /ˈlaɪknɪs/ *n* [C, U] 相像 xiāngxiàng; 相似 xiāngsì: *a family ~* 家族特征.

likewise /ˈlaɪkwaɪz/ *adv* 同样〔樣〕地 tóngyàngde; 照样地 zhàoyàngde.

liking /ˈlaɪkɪŋ/ *n* [习语] **have a liking for sth** 喜爱〔愛〕 xǐ'ài. **to sb's liking** [正式用语] 合某人意 hé mǒurén yì.

lilac /ˈlaɪlək/ *n* **1** [C] 丁香 dīngxiāng. **2** [U] 淡紫色 dànzǐsè.

lilt /lɪlt/ *n* [sing] (说话时声音的)抑扬〔揚〕顿挫 yìyáng dùncuò. **lilting** *adj*.

lily /ˈlɪlɪ/ *n* [C] [*pl* **-ies**] 百合 bǎihé; 百合花 bǎihéhuā.

limb /lɪm/ *n* [C] **1** 肢 zhī; 臂 bì; 腿 tuǐ; 翼 yì. **2** (树的)主枝 zhǔzhī. **3** [习语] **out on a** ˈ**limb** [非正式用语]处〔處〕于孤立无〔無〕援的境地 chǔyú gūlì wúyuán de jìngdì.

limber /ˈlɪmbə(r)/ *v* [短语动词] ˌ**limber** ˈ**up** (运动前)做准〔準〕备〔備〕活动〔動〕 zuò zhǔnbèi huódòng.

limbo /ˈlɪmbəʊ/ *n* [习语] **in limbo** 处〔處〕于不定(或中间)状〔狀〕态〔態〕 chǔyú búdìng zhuàngtài: *The company is in ~.* 公司处于不稳定状态.

lime[1] /laɪm/ *n* [U] 石灰 shíhuī. ˈ**limestone** *n* [U] 石灰岩 shíhuīyán.

lime[2] /laɪm/ *n* [C] 椴树〔樹〕 duànshù.

lime[3] /laɪm/ *n* [C] 酸橙树〔樹〕 suānchéngshù; 酸橙 suānchéng.

limelight /ˈlaɪmlaɪt/ *n* **the limelight** [sing] 公众〔衆〕注意中心 gōngzhòng zhùyì zhōngxīn.

limerick /ˈlɪmərɪk/ *n* [C] 五行打油诗 wǔháng dǎyóushī.

limit /ˈlɪmɪt/ *n* [C] **1** 界线〔綫〕 jièxiàn; 界限 jièxiàn. **2** 最大限度 zuìdà xiàndù; 限量 xiànliàng. **3** [习语] **(be) the limit** [俚]能忍受的极〔極〕限 néng rěnshòu de jíxiàn. ˌ**off** ˈ**limits** [美语] = OUT OF BOUNDS (BOUNDS). **within** ˈ**limits** 有限度地 yǒu xiàndù de: *You are free to spend money, within ~s.* 你在一定范围内可自由地花钱. **limit** *v* [T] 限制 xiànzhì; 限定 xiàndìng. **limitation** /ˌlɪmɪˈteɪʃn/ *n* **1** [U] 限制 xiànzhì; 限定 xiàndìng. **2** [C] 局限 júxiàn; 限制因素 xiànzhì yīnsù. **limited** *adj* **1** 有限的 yǒuxiànde; 少的 shǎode; 小的 xiǎode. **2** (企业等)有限责任的 yǒuxiàn zérèn de. **limitless** *adj* 无〔無〕限制的 wú xiànzhì de; 无限度的 wú xiàndù de; 无界限的 wú jièxiàn de.

limousine /ˈlɪməziːn/ *n* [C] (前后座间用玻璃隔开的)豪华〔華〕轿〔轎〕车 háohuá jiàochē.

limp[1] /lɪmp/ *v* [I] 跛行 bǒxíng; 蹒跚 pánshān. **limp** *n* [sing] 跛行 bǒxíng.

limp[2] /lɪmp/ *adj* 柔软的 róuruǎnde; 软弱的 ruǎnruòde. **limply** *adv*. **limpness** *n* [U].

linchpin /ˈlɪntʃpɪn/ *n* [C] **1** 制轮〔輪〕楔 zhìlúnxiē. **2** [喻]关〔關〕键性人物(或事物) guānjiàn xìng rénwù.

L

line[1] /laɪn/ *n* 1 [C] (a) 线〔綫〕xiàn;线条〔條〕xiàntiáo. (b) [常作 pl] (皮肤上的)纹 wén: *the ~s on his face* 他脸上的皱纹. 2 [C] 界线 jièxiàn;边〔邊〕界 biānjiè: *~s marking a tennis court* 网球场的场界. 3 [C] (军事)防线 fángxiàn. 4 [C] (人或物的)行 háng,排 pái,列 liè: *customers standing in (a) ~.* 顾客排成队. 5 [C,常作 sing] 家系 jiāxì;家族 jiāzú. 6 [C] (a) 字行 zìháng. (b) lines [pl] 台〔臺〕词 táicí. 7 [C] [非正式用语] 短简 duǎnjiǎn;便条〔條〕biàntiáo. 8 [C] 线 xiàn;绳〔繩〕shéng;索 suǒ. 9 [C] 电〔電〕话线 diànhuàxiàn: *Our firm has 20 ~s.* 我们公司有 20 条电话线路. 10 [C] (铁路的)轨道 guǐdào;线路 xiànlù. 11 lines [pl] 外形 wàixíng;轮〔輪〕廓 lúnkuò. 12 [C] (行动、行为、思想的)方针 fāngzhēn,路线 lùxiàn: *a new ~ of research* 一种新的研究方针. 13 [sing] 方向 fāngxiàng;路线 lùxiàn: *the ~ of gunfire* 炮火射击路线. 14 [C] 运〔運〕输公司 yùnshū gōngsī: *a 'shipping ~* 航运公司. 15 [sing] (a) 行业〔業〕hángyè: *a job in the banking ~* 在银行的工作. (b) (产品的)类〔類〕别 lèibié;种〔種〕类 zhǒnglèi: *a new ~ in coats* 一种新款式的大衣. 16 [习语] **in line for sth** 有可能获〔獲〕得 yǒu kěnéng huòdé. **in line with sth** 与〔與〕…一致 yǔ…yízhì. **(put sth) on the 'line** [非正式用语] 冒风〔風〕险〔險〕mào fēngxiǎn. **on the right 'lines** 正确〔確〕的 zhèngquède. **out of 'line (with sb/sth)** (a) 不成一直线 bùchéng yìzhíxiàn. (b) 出格 chūgé. **'line-drawing** *n* [C] (用钢笔、铅笔)线条画〔畫〕xiàntiáohuà. **'line-printer** *n* [C] (计算机)行式打印机〔機〕hángshì dǎyìnjī.

line[2] /laɪn/ *v* [T] 1 用线〔綫〕标〔標〕示 yòng xiàn biāoshì;划〔劃〕线于 huà xiàn yú: *~d paper* 印有横格的纸. 2 沿…排列成行 yán… páiliè chéngháng: *a road ~d with trees* 树木成行的道路. 3 [短语动词] **line (sb) up** (使) 排成行 pái chéngháng. **line sth up** [非正式用语] 安排(某事) ānpái;组织〔織〕zǔzhī. **'line-up** *n* [C] 1 (等待检查的)一排人 yìpái rén. 2 (同一目的)一组人 yìzǔ rén;(同一用途的)一批东西 yìpī dōngxi.

line[3] /laɪn/ *v* [T] 1 加衬〔襯〕里〔裏〕于 jiā chènlǐ yú: *fur-~d gloves* 毛皮里的手套. 2 [习语] **line one's (own) pocket(s)** 以钱〔錢〕装〔裝〕入私囊(尤指来路不正的钱) yǐ qián zhuāngrù sīnáng.

linear /ˈlɪnɪə(r)/ *adj* 1 线〔綫〕的 xiànde;直线的 zhíxiànde. 2 长〔長〕度的 chángdùde: *~ measurement* 长度.

linen /ˈlɪnɪn/ *n* [U] 亚〔亞〕麻布 yàmábù;亚麻制〔製〕品 yàmá zhìpǐn.

liner[1] /ˈlaɪnə(r)/ *n* [C] 班轮〔輪〕bānlún;邮〔郵〕轮 yóulún.

liner[2] /ˈlaɪnə(r)/ *n* [C] (用于构成复合词)衬〔襯〕里〔裏〕chènlǐ;衬垫〔墊〕chèndiàn: *bin-~s* (衬在垃圾桶内的)垃圾塑料袋.

linesman /ˈlaɪnzmən/ *n* [C] [*pl* -men] (球赛中的)边〔邊〕线〔綫〕裁判员 biānxiàn cáipànyuán;巡边员 xúnbiānyuán.

linger /ˈlɪŋgə(r)/ *v* [I] 逗留 dòuliú;徘徊 páihuái. **lingering** *adj* 逗留的 dòuliúde;拖延的 tuōyánde: *a ~ illness* 久病不愈.

lingerie /ˈlænʒəriː; *US* ˌlɑːndʒəˈreɪ/ *n* [U] [正式用语] 女内衣 nǚ nèiyī.

linguist /ˈlɪŋgwɪst/ *n* [C] 1 通晓〔曉〕数〔數〕国〔國〕语言的人 tōngxiǎo shùguó yǔyán de rén. 2 语言学〔學〕家 yǔyánxuéjiā. **linguistic** /lɪŋˈgwɪstɪk/ *adj* 语言的 yǔyánde;语言学的 yǔyánxuéde. **linguistics** *n* [用 sing v] 语言学 yǔyánxué.

liniment /ˈlɪnɪmənt/ *n* [C,U] 搽剂〔劑〕(指去痛剂) chájì;擦剂 cājì.

lining /ˈlaɪnɪŋ/ *n* [C,U] 衬〔襯〕里〔裏〕chènlǐ;里子 lǐzi: *a fur ~* 毛皮里.

link /lɪŋk/ *n* [C] 1 联〔聯〕系〔繫〕liánxì;关〔關〕系〔係〕guānxì. 2 (链的)环〔環〕huán,圈 quān. 3 链〔鏈〕接 liànjiē. **link** *v* 1 [T] 连接 liánjiē;联系 liánxì. 2 [短语动词] **link (sth) up (with sth)** 将〔將〕…连接起来 jiāng… liánjiē qǐlái. 3 (计算机网络)链接点 liànjiēdiǎn.

lino /ˈlaɪnəʊ/ *n* [U] [非正式用语] short for LINOLEUM.

linoleum /lɪˈnəʊlɪəm/ *n* [U] (亚麻)油地毡〔氈〕yóudìzhān.

lint /lɪnt/ *n* [U] (作绷带等用的)纱布 shābù.

lion /ˈlaɪən/ *n* [C] 1 狮〔獅〕子 shīzi. 2 [习语] **the 'lion's share (of sth)** 最大部分 zuìdà bùfen. **lioness** *n* [C] 母狮 mǔshī.

lip /lɪp/ *n* 1 [C] 嘴唇 zuǐchún. 2 [C] (器皿的)边〔邊〕biān. 3 [U] [俚] 唐突无〔無〕礼〔禮〕的话 tángtū wúlǐ de huà. 4 [习语] **lick/smack one's lips** [非正式用语] 舔嘴唇(表示满意、渴望等) tiǎn zuǐchún. **one's lips are sealed** 闭口不谈 bìkǒu bù tán. **'lip-read** *v* [*pt*, *pp* 'lip-read /-red/] [I,T] 观〔觀〕察(说话人)嘴唇动〔動〕作来理解(话意) guānchá…zuǐchún dòngzuò lái lǐjiě;唇读〔讀〕chúndú. **'lip-reading** *n* [U]. **'lip-service** *n* [习语] **give/pay 'lip-service to sth** 口惠而实〔實〕不至 kǒuhuì ér shí búzhì. **'lipstick** *n* [C,U] 口红 kǒuhóng;唇膏 chúngāo.

liqueur /lɪˈkjʊə(r); *US* lɪˈkɜːr/ *n* [C,U] (通常指甜的)烈性酒 lièxìngjiǔ.

liquid /ˈlɪkwɪd/ *n* [C,U] 液体〔體〕yètǐ. **liquid** *adj* 1 液体的 yètǐde. 2 清澈的 qīngchède: *~ blue eyes* 水汪汪的蓝眼睛. 3 (声音)清脆的 qīngcuìde;流畅〔暢〕的 liúchàngde. 4 易变〔變〕为〔爲〕现金的 yì biànwéi xiànjīn de: ~

L

assets 流动资产.

liquidate /ˈlɪkwɪdeɪt/ *v* [T] **1** [非正式用语] 除掉(某人)(尤指杀掉) chúdiào. **2** 清算(破产的企业等) qīngsuàn; 清理 qīnglǐ. **liquidation** /ˌlɪkwɪˈdeɪʃn/ *n* [U].

liquidize /ˈlɪkwɪdaɪz/ *v* [T] 将〔將〕(水果、蔬菜等)榨成汁 jiāng…zhà chéng zhī. **liquidizer** (尤用于美语 **blender**) *n* [C] (电动的)果汁机〔機〕guǒzhījī.

liquor /ˈlɪkə(r)/ *n* [U] [尤用于美语]烈性酒 lièxìngjiǔ. ˈ**liquor store** *n* [C] [美语] 酒店 jiǔdiàn.

liquorice /ˈlɪkərɪs, -ɪʃ/ *n* [U] 甘草 gāncǎo.

lisp /lɪsp/ *v* [I, T] 用咬舌音说(将/s/音读作/θ/) yòng yǎoshéyīn shuō. **lisp** *n* [sing] 咬舌儿〔兒〕yǎoshér.

list[1] /lɪst/ *n* [C] 一览〔覽〕表 yìlǎnbiǎo; 名单〔單〕míngdān; 目录〔錄〕mùlù; 表 biǎo. **list** *v* [T] 把…列入表册(目录、名册) bǎ…lièrù biǎocè; 把…造表 bǎ…zàobiǎo; 把…编目录〔錄〕bǎ…biān mùlù.

list[2] /lɪst/ *v* [I] (尤指船只)倾侧 qīngcè; 倾斜 qīngxié. **list** *n* [sing] (船)倾侧 qīngcè; 倾斜 qīngxié.

listen /ˈlɪsn/ *v* [I] **1** (*to*) 听〔聽〕tīng; 倾听 qīngtīng: *L~ carefully to what I'm saying*. 仔细听我说话. **2** (*to*) 听从〔從〕tīngcóng; 听信 tīngxìn: *I warned you, but you wouldn't ~*. 我提醒过你, 可你不听. **3** [短语动词] **listen ˈin (to sth)** (a) 收听电〔電〕台〔臺〕广〔廣〕播 shōutīng diàntái guǎngbō. (b) 偷听(谈话) tōutīng. **listener** *n* [C].

listless /ˈlɪstlɪs/ *adj* 无〔無〕精打采的 wú jīng dǎ cǎi de; 倦怠的 juàndàide. **listlessly** *adv*.

lit *pt, pp* of LIGHT[3,5].

liter [美语] = LITRE.

literacy /ˈlɪtərəsɪ/ *n* [U] 读〔讀〕写〔寫〕能力 dú xiě nénglì.

literal /ˈlɪtərəl/ *adj* **1** 照字面的 zhào zìmiàn de; 原义〔義〕的 yuányìde. **2** 逐字的 zhúzìde: *a ~ translation* 逐字翻译(或直译). **literally** *adv* **1** [非正式用语] (用以加强语气): *I was ~ly bored to tears*. 我真的十分厌烦. **2** 逐字地 zhúzìde: *translate ~ly* 逐字翻译.

literary /ˈlɪtərərɪ; *US* ˈlɪtərerɪ/ *adj* 文学〔學〕的 wénxuéde; 作家的 zuòjiāde.

literate /ˈlɪtərət/ *adj* **1** 有读〔讀〕写〔寫〕能力的 yǒu dú xiě nénglì de. **2** 有文化的 yǒu wénhuà de; 有教养〔養〕的 yǒu jiàoyǎng de.

literature /ˈlɪtrətʃə(r); *US* -tʃʊər/ *n* [U] **1** 文学〔學〕wénxué; 文学作品 wénxué zuòpǐn. **2** (某学科的)文献〔獻〕wénxiàn. **3** [非正式用语] 印刷品 yìnshuāpǐn; 宣传〔傳〕品 xuānchuánpǐn.

lithe /laɪð/ *adj* [正式用语](人等)柔软的 róuruǎnde; 易弯〔彎〕曲的 yì wānqū de.

litigation /ˌlɪtɪˈgeɪʃn/ *n* [U] 诉讼 sùsòng; 打官司 dǎ guānsi.

litre /ˈliːtə(r)/ *n* [C] 升(容量单位) shēng.

litter /ˈlɪtə(r)/ *n* **1** [U] 废〔廢〕弃〔棄〕物(如纸屑、瓶子等) fèiqìwù. **2** [C] (一胎生下的)小动〔動〕物 xiǎo dòngwù; 一窝〔窩〕yìwō. **litter** *v* [T] 乱〔亂〕扔杂〔雜〕物于 luàn rēng záwù yú; 使凌乱 shǐ língluàn. ˈ**litterbin** *n* [C] 废物箱 fèiwùxiāng.

little[1] /ˈlɪtl/ *adj* **1** 小的 xiǎode: *~ cups* 小杯子. **2** (距离、时间)短的 duǎnde: *wait a ~ while* 等一小会儿. **3** 微不足道的 wēi bù zú dào de: *a ~ mistake* 小错. **4** 幼小的 yòuxiǎode.

little[2] /ˈlɪtl/ *adj* [**less, least**] 小量的 xiǎoliàngde; 不足的 bùzúde: *I have very ~ time to spare*. 我没有多余的时间. **little** *pron* [U], *n* 少量 shǎoliàng: *I understood ~ of what she said*. 她说的我只听懂一点. **little** *adv* **1** 稍许 shāoxǔ; 些少 xiēshǎo: *I slept very ~ last night*. 昨晚我睡得很少. *L~ does he know what trouble he's in*. 他对自己所处的困境一无所知. **2** [习语] ˌ**little by ˈlittle** 逐渐地 zhújiànde.

little[3] /ˈlɪtl/ *pron, adj* 少量 shǎoliàng; 些微 xiēwēi: *a ~ sugar* 少许糖. **a little** *adv* 有些 yǒuxiē; 有几〔幾〕分 yǒu jǐfēn: *a ~ afraid* 有点怕.

live[1] /lɪv/ *v* **1** [I] 活着 huózhe. **2** [I] 活 huó; 生存 shēngcún: *The doctors don't think he'll ~*. 医生认为他不能活了. **3** [I] 居住 jūzhù: *~ in Leeds* 住在里兹. **4** [I, T] 生活 shēnghuó; 过〔過〕活 guòhuó: *~ happily* 过幸福生活. **5** [I] 享受生活乐〔樂〕趣 xiǎngshòu shēnghuó lèqù. **6** [习语] **live beˌyond/withˌin one's ˈmeans** 入不敷出 rù bù fū chū; 量入为〔爲〕出 liàng rù wéi chū. **live from ˌhand to ˈmouth** 仅〔僅〕能餬口 jǐn néng húkǒu. **live it ˈup** [非正式用语]享乐 xiǎnglè. **7** [短语动词] **live sth ˈdown** 以某种〔種〕方式生活使忘却(过去的丑行等) yǐ mǒuzhǒng fāngshì shēnghuó shǐ wàngquè. **live for sth** 以…为生活目标〔標〕yǐ…wéi shēnghuó mùbiāo. **live in/out** 寄宿在工作处〔處〕jìsù zài gōngzuòchù; 不寄宿在工作处 bú jìsù zài gōngzuòchù. **live off sb** 依赖…生活 yīlài…shēnghuó. **live on** 继〔繼〕续〔續〕活着 jìxù huózhe. **live on sth** (a) 以某物为主食 yǐ mǒuwù wéi zhǔshí. (b) 靠(某种经济来源)生活 kào…shēnghuó. **live through sth** 经〔經〕历〔歷〕…而未死 jīnglì…ér wèisǐ: *~ through two wars* 经历过两次战争而幸存. **live together** 同居 tóngjū. **live up to sth** 符合(某种标准) fúhé: *The new house ~d up to my expectations*. 新房子符合我的期望. **live with sb** 同居 tóngjū. **live with sth** 接受 jiēshòu; 容忍 róngrěn.

L

live[2] /laɪv/ *adj* 1 活的 huóde；有生命的 yǒu shēngmìng de. 2 点〔點〕燃着的 diǎnránzhede；发〔發〕着光的 fāzheguāngde：～ *coals* 燃烧着的煤. 3 未爆炸的 wèi bàozhà de；未点火的 wèi diǎnhuǒ de：*a* ～ *bomb* 未爆炸的炸弹. 4（电线）带〔帶〕电〔電〕的 dàidiànde；通电的 tōngdiànde. 5（广播）现场〔場〕直播的 xiànchǎng zhíbō de；实〔實〕况转〔轉〕播的 shíkuàng zhuǎnbō de. 6（当前）重要的 zhòngyàode；令人关〔關〕切的 lìng rén guānqiè de：*a* ～ *issue* 当前的大问题.

livelihood /ˈlaɪvlɪhʊd/ *n* [C, 常作 sing] 生活 shēnghuó；生计 shēngjì.

lively /ˈlaɪvlɪ/ *adj* [-ier, -iest] 1 充满生气〔氣〕的 chōngmǎn shēngqì de；精力充沛的 jīnglì chōngpèi de. 2（颜色）鲜明的 xiānmíngde；鲜艳〔艷〕的 xiānyànde. **liveliness** *n* [U].

liven /ˈlaɪvn/ *v* [短语动词] ˌ**liven (sb/sth)** ˈ**up**（使某人或某物）有生气〔氣〕 yǒu shēngqì；（使）活跃〔躍〕 huóyuè.

liver /ˈlɪvə(r)/ *n* 1 [C] 肝脏〔臟〕 gānzàng. 2 [U]（牛、鸡等供食用的）肝 gān.

lives *pl* of LIFE.

livestock /ˈlaɪvstɒk/ *n* [U] 家畜 jiāchù；牲畜 shēngchù.

livid /ˈlɪvɪd/ *adj* 1 [非正式用语]大怒的 dànùde. 2 铅色的 qiānsède；青灰色的 qīnghuīsède.

living[1] /ˈlɪvɪŋ/ *adj* 1 活的 huóde；活着的 huózhede. 2 尚在使用的 shàng zài shǐyòng de：*a* ～ *language* 现用的语言. 3 [习语] **be the living image of sb** ⇨ IMAGE. **within/in** ˌ**living** ˈ**memory** 在当〔當〕今人的记忆〔憶〕中 zài dāngjīn rén de jìyì zhōng. **the living** *n* [pl] 活着的人 huózhede rén.

living[2] /ˈlɪvɪŋ/ *n* 1 [sing] 生计 shēngjì. 2 [U] 生活方式 shēnghuó fāngshì：*a low standard of* ～ 低水准的生活. ˈ**living-room** *n* [C] 起居室 qǐjūshì；客厅〔廳〕 kètīng.

lizard /ˈlɪzəd/ *n* [C] 蜥蜴 xīyì.

load /ləʊd/ *n* 1 [C] 负荷 fùhè；负载 fùzài. 2 [C]（尤用于构成复合词）装〔裝〕载量 zhuāngzàiliàng：*coach-* ～*s of tourists* 一车一车的游客. 3 [C]（机器等的）负载 fùzài；负荷 fùhè. 4 [C] [喻]（责任、忧虑等的）沉重感 chénzhònggǎn. 5 **loads (of)** [pl] [非正式用语]大量 dàliàng：～*s of money* 很多钱. **load** *v* 1 [I, T] 装载 zhuāngzài；（使）负荷 fùhè：～ *cargo onto a ship* 装船. 2 [T] (a) 把弹〔彈〕药〔藥〕装入（枪炮）bǎ dànyào zhuāngrù. (b) 把胶〔膠〕卷〔捲〕装入（照相机）bǎ jiāojuǎn zhuāngrù. **loaded** *adj* 1 载重的 zàizhòngde；装着货的 zhuāngzhehuòde. 2 [俚]富有的 fùyǒude；有钱〔錢〕的 yǒuqiánde. 3 [习语] **a** ˌ**loaded** ˈ**question** 别有用心的问题 biéyǒu yòngxīn de wèntí.

loaf[1] /ləʊf/ *n* [*pl* **loaves** /ləʊvz/] [C] 大面〔麵〕包 dà miànbāo.

loaf[2] /ləʊf/ *v* [I] (*about/around*) [非正式用语]虚度光阴〔陰〕 xūdù guāngyīn；游手好闲〔閒〕 yóu shǒu hào xián.

loan /ləʊn/ *n* 1 [C] 借出物 jièchūwù；贷款 dàikuǎn. 2 [U] 借出 jièchū. 3 [习语] **on loan** 借来的 jièláide. **loan** *v* [T] [尤用于美语或英国正式用语]借出 jièchū.

loath（亦作 **loth**）/ləʊθ/ *adj to* [正式用语]不愿〔願〕意的 bú yuànyì de.

loathe /ləʊð/ *v* [T] 憎恨 zēnghèn；厌〔厭〕恶〔惡〕 yànwù. **loathing** *n* [U] 憎恨 zēnghèn；厌〔厭〕恶〔惡〕 yànwù. **loathsome** /-səm/ *adj* 讨厌的 tǎoyànde；令人厌恶的 lìng rén yànwù de.

loaves *pl* of LOAF[1].

lob /lɒb/ *v* [-bb-] [I, T]（打网球、板球时）吊高球 diào gāoqiú. **lob** *n* [C]（网球）高球 gāoqiú；（板球）低手球 dīshǒuqiú.

lobby /ˈlɒbɪ/ *n* [*pl* -ies] 1 [C]（旅馆、戏院的）大厅〔廳〕 dàtīng；门厅 méngtīng. 2 [C, 亦作 sing, 用 pl v] 院外活动〔動〕集团〔團〕 yuànwài huódòng jítuán：*the anti-nuclear* ～ 反核院外活动集团. **lobby** *v* [*pt*, *pp* -ied] [I, T] 对〔對〕（议员等）游说支持或反对某法案 duìyóushuì zhīchí huò fǎnduì mǒu fǎ'àn.

lobe /ləʊb/ *n* [C] 耳垂 ěrchuí.

lobster /ˈlɒbstə(r)/ *n* 1 [C] 龙〔龍〕虾〔蝦〕 lóngxiā. 2 [U]（作食物的）龙虾肉 lóngxiāròu.

local /ˈləʊkl/ *adj* 1 地方的 dìfāngde；本地的 běndìde：～ *news* 本地新闻. 2 局部的 júbùde：*a* ～ *anaesthetic* 局部麻醉. **local** *n* [C] 1 [常作 pl] 本地人 běndìrén；当〔當〕地人 dāngdìrén. 2 [英国非正式用语]当地酒店 dāngdì jiǔdiàn. **locally** *adv*.

locality /ləʊˈkælətɪ/ *n* [C] [*pl* -ies] 地区〔區〕 dìqū；地点〔點〕 dìdiǎn；现场〔場〕 xiànchǎng.

localize /ˈləʊkəlaɪz/ *v* [T] 使局部化 shǐ júbùhuà；使具有地方性 shǐ jùyǒu dìfāngxìng：～ *a disease* 使疾病限于局部.

locate /ləʊˈkeɪt; *US* ˈləʊkeɪt/ *v* [T] 1 找出…的位置 zhǎochū…de wèizhi. 2 [常作被动语态]把…设置在 bǎ…shèzhì zài；使…坐落于 shǐ…zuòluò yú：*Our offices are* ～*d in Paris*. 我们的办事处设置在巴黎. **location** /ləʊˈkeɪʃn/ *n* 1 [C] 位置 wèizhi. 2 [习语] **on location** 拍摄〔攝〕外景 pāishè wàijǐng.

loch /lɒk/ *n* [C] [苏格兰英语]湖 hú：*L*～ *Ness* 内斯湖.

lock[1] /lɒk/ *n* 1 [C] 锁 suǒ. 2 [C]（运河的）水闸 shuǐzhá. 3 [习语] ˌ**lock, stock and** ˈ**barrel** 全部 quánbù；完全 wánquán. ˈ**locksmith** *n* [C] 锁匠 suǒjiàng.

lock[2] /lɒk/ *v* [I, T] 1 锁 suǒ；锁上 suǒshàng. 2（使）卡住 kǎzhù；刹住 shāzhù. 3 [短语动词] **lock sth away** 将〔將〕（某物）锁藏 jiāng

L

…suǒ cáng. **lock sb in/out** 将某人锁在某处〔處〕jiāng mǒurén suǒ zài mǒuchù；把某人关〔關〕在门外 bǎ mǒurén guān zài ménwài. **lock (sth) up** 上锁 shàng suǒ；关锁（房门）guān suǒ. **lock sb up** 将某人监〔監〕禁 jiāng mǒurén jiānjìn；送…进〔進〕精神病院 sòng… jìn jīngshénbìngyuàn.

lock[3] /lɒk/ *n* [C] 一绺头〔頭〕发〔髮〕yìliǔ tóufa.

locker /ˈlɒkə(r)/ *n* [C]（公共场所供存放衣物用的）小橱柜〔櫃〕xiǎo chúguì.

locket /ˈlɒkɪt/ *n* [C] 盒式项链坠〔墜〕（用以藏照片等）héshì xiàngliànzhuì.

locomotive /ˈləʊkəməʊtɪv/ *n* [C]［正式用语］机〔機〕车〔車〕jīchē；火车头〔頭〕huǒchētóu.

locust /ˈləʊkəst/ *n* [C] 蝗虫 huángchóng.

lodge[1] /lɒdʒ/ *n* [C] **1**（花园宅第大门口的）小屋 xiǎowū. **2** 乡〔鄉〕间小舍 xiāngjiān xiǎoshè：*a hunting* ～ 打猎时用的小屋.

lodge[2] /lɒdʒ/ *v* **1** [I] 租住（某人）房屋 zū zhù fángwū. **2** [T] 供（某人）住宿 gòng… zhùsù. **3** [I, T] *in*（使）射入 shèrù；嵌入 qiànrù；埋入 máirù：*The bullet (was)* ～*d in his arm*. 子弹射入他的手臂. **4** [T] 提出（申诉、抗议等）tíchū：～ *a complaint* 提出控告. **lodger** *n* [C] 房客 fángkè；租住者 zūzhùzhě.

lodging /ˈlɒdʒɪŋ/ *n* **1** [U] 寄宿 jìsù；借宿 jièsù. **2 lodgings** [pl] 寄宿舍 jìsùshè；公寓房间（有别于旅馆）gōngyù fángjiān.

loft /lɒft; *US* lɔːft/ *n* [C]（存放东西的）阁楼〔樓〕gélóu；顶楼 dǐnglóu.

lofty /ˈlɒftɪ; *US* ˈlɔːftɪ/ *adj* [-ier, -iest] **1**（思想等）高尚的 gāoshàngde. **2** [修辞] 极〔極〕高的 jígāode. **3** [贬] 高傲的 gāo'àode.

log[1] /lɒg; *US* lɔːg/ *n* [C] 原木 yuánmù；圆材 yuáncái.

log[2] /lɒg; *US* lɔːg/ *n* [C] **1** 航海（或飞行）日志〔誌〕hánghǎi rìzhì. **2** 机〔機〕动〔動〕车车主登记册 jīdòngchē chēzhǔ dēngjìcè. **log** *v* [-gg-] [T] **1** 把…载入航海（或飞行）日志 bǎ… zǎirù hánghǎi rìzhì. **2** [习语] **log in/on** [计] 登记（接通数据库等作联机存取）dēngjì. **log out/off** [计] 注销（关闭数据库等结束联机存取）zhùxiāo.

loggerheads /ˈlɒgəhedz/ *n* [习语] **at loggerheads (with sb)** 不和 bùhé；相争〔爭〕xiāngzhēng.

logic /ˈlɒdʒɪk/ *n* [U] **1** 逻〔邏〕辑学〔學〕luójìxué；论〔論〕理学 lùnlǐxué. **2** 逻辑性 luójìxìng；条〔條〕理性 tiáolǐxìng：*There's no* ～ *in what he says*. 他讲的话没有逻辑性. **logical** /ˈlɒdʒɪkl/ *adj* 符合逻辑的 fúhé luójì de. **logically** /-klɪ/ *adv*.

loins /lɔɪnz/ *n* [pl] 腰 yāo；腰部 yāobù.

loiter /ˈlɔɪtə(r)/ *v* [I] 闲〔閒〕逛 xiánguàng；消磨时〔時〕光 xiāomó shíguāng.

loll /lɒl/ *v* [I] **1** 懒洋洋地呆着 lǎnyángyángde dāizhe. **2** [短语动词] **loll out**（舌头）伸出 shēnchū.

lollipop /ˈlɒlɪpɒp/ *n* [C] 棒糖 bàngtáng；冰棍 bīnggùn.

lolly /ˈlɒlɪ/ *n* [*pl* -ies] [英国英语] **1** [C] [非正式用语] 棒糖 bàngtáng；冰棍 bīnggùn. **2** [U] [俚] 钱〔錢〕qián.

lone /ləʊn/ *adj* [常作修辞] 孤独〔獨〕的 gūdúde；孤单〔單〕的 gūdānde.

lonely /ˈləʊnlɪ/ *adj* [-ier, -iest] **1** 孤独〔獨〕的 gūdúde；寂寞的 jìmòde. **2**（地方）偏僻的 piānpìde；人迹稀少的 rénjì xīshǎo de. **loneliness** *n* [U].

lonesome /ˈləʊnsəm/ *adj* [尤用于美语] 孤寂的 gūjìde；寂寞的 jìmòde.

long[1] /lɒŋ; *US* lɔːŋ/ *adj* [～er /-ŋgə(r)/, ～est /-ŋgɪst/] **1**（空间、时间）长〔長〕的 chángde：*a* ～ *journey* 长途旅行. *800 metres* ～ 800 米长. **2** [习语] **go a long way** ⇨ FAR[1] **in the ˈlong run** 最后〔後〕zuìhòu；终于 zhōngyú. **ˌlong in the ˈtooth** [谑]（人）年老的 niánlǎode. **not by a ˈlong chalk/shot** 完全不 wánquán bù. **ˌlong-ˈdistance** *adj, adv* 长距离〔離〕的 chángjùlíde；长距离 chángjùlí. **ˈlong drink** *n* [C] 大杯饮料（用高脚杯盛的啤酒）dàbēi yǐnliào. **ˈlong-range** *adj* 长期的 chángqīde；长远〔遠〕的 chángyuǎnde：*a* ～*-range weather forecast* 远期天气预报. **ˌlong-ˈsighted** *adj* 远视的 yuǎnshìde. **ˌlong-ˈterm** *adj* 长期的 chángqīde. **ˈlong wave** *n* [U] 长波 chángbō. **ˌlong-ˈwinded** *adj* 喋喋不休的 diédié bùxiū de；冗长的 rǒngchángde.

long[2] /lɒŋ; *US* lɔːŋ/ *n* **1** [U] 长〔長〕时〔時〕间 chángshíjiān：*This won't take* ～. 这要不了多久. *I hope to see you before* ～. 我希望不久就能见到你. **2** [习语] **the ˌlong and (the) ˈshort of it** 总〔總〕的意思 zǒngde yìsi.

long[3] /lɒŋ; *US* lɔːŋ/ *adv* [～er /-ŋgə(r)/, ～est /-ŋgɪst/] **1** 长〔長〕期地 chángqīde；长久 chángjiǔ：*Were you in Rome* ～? 你在罗马呆的时间长吗? *I shan't be* ～. 我用不了很久时间. **2** 很久地 hěnjiǔde：～ *ago* 很久以前. **3** 始终 shǐzhōng；一直 yìzhí：*all day* ～ 整天. **4** [习语] **as/so long as** 只要 zhǐyào；如果 rúguǒ. **no longer/not any longer** 不再 búzài. **ˌlong-playing ˈrecord** *n* [C] 密纹唱片 mìwén chàngpiàn. **ˌlong-ˈstanding** *adj* 长期存在的 chángqī cúnzài de：*a* ˌ～*-standing arˈrangement* 长期安排. **ˌlong-ˈsuffering** *adj* 长期忍受的 chángqī rěnshòu de.

long[4] /lɒŋ; *US* lɔːŋ/ *v* [I] *for; to* 渴望 kěwàng；非常想有（某事物）fēicháng xiǎng yǒu：～ *for the holidays* 盼望放假. **longing** *n*

L

[C, U], *adj* 渴望(的) kěwàng; 热〔熱〕望(的) rèwàng. **longingly** *adv*.

longitude /ˈlɒndʒɪtjuːd; *US* -tuːd/ *n* [C] 经〔經〕度 jīngdù.

loo /luː/ *n* [C] [*pl* ~s] [英国非正式英语]厕所 cèsuǒ.

look[1] /lʊk/ *v* **1** [I] (*at*) 看 kàn; 瞧 qiáo. **2** [常与形容词连用]看上去 kàn shàng qù; 像是 xiàng shì: ~ *sad* 面带忧伤. **3** [I] 面向 miànxiàng; 朝向 cháoxiàng: *The house ~s east*. 这房子朝东. **4** [I, T] 留心 liúxīn; 注意 zhùyì: *L~ where you're going!* 瞧, 你到哪里去了! **5** [习语] **look one's ˈbest** 使人看上去最美(或最吸引人) shǐ rén kàn shàng qù zuìměi. **look daggers at sb** 怒目而视 nù mù ér shì. **look down one's ˈnose at sb/sth** 轻〔輕〕视(或蔑视)某人(或某事) qīngshì mǒurén. **ˌLook ˈhere!** (用以表示抗议或叫某人注意). **look like sb/sth, look as if** 看着像是 kànzhe xiàng shì: *She ~ed as if she was asleep*. 她看着像是睡着了. *It ~s like rain*. 天像是要下雨. **look ˈsharp** 赶〔趕〕快 gǎnkuài. **never/not look ˈback** [非正式用语]一直顺利 yìzhí shùnlì. **not be much to ˈlook at** [非正式用语]其貌不扬〔揚〕qí mào bù yáng. **not look oneˈself** 看起来和往常不一样〔樣〕(健康) kàn qǐlái hé wǎngcháng bù yíyàng. **6** [短语动词] **look ˈafter sb/sth** 照料 zhàoliào; 照顾〔顧〕zhàogù. **look aˈhead** 向前看 xiàngqián kàn; 为〔爲〕将〔將〕来打算 wèi jiānglái dǎsuàn. **look at sth** 检〔檢〕查(某事物) jiǎnchá; 考虑〔慮〕kǎolǜ: *I'll ~ at your proposal tomorrow*. 明天我要考虑你的建议. **look ˈback (on sth)** 回顾 huígù; 追想 zhuīxiǎng. **look down on sb/sth** [非正式用语]轻视 qīngshì; 看不起 kàn bù qǐ. **look for sb/sth** 寻〔尋〕找 xúnzhǎo; 期望 qīwàng. **look forward to sth** (喜滋滋地)盼望 pànwàng; 期待 qīdài. **look ˈin (on sb)** (顺道)访问 fǎngwèn; 看望 kànwàng. **look into sth** 调查 diàochá; 考查 kǎochá. **look ˈon** 旁观〔觀〕pángguān. **look on sth as sth** 将某事物看作他事物 jiāng mǒushìwù kàn zuò tā shìwù. **look ˈout** 小心 xiǎoxīn; 当〔當〕心 dāngxīn. **look out for sb/sth** 留心 liúxīn; 留神 liúshén. **look out onto sth** 俯视 fǔshì. **look over sth** 检查 jiǎnchá; 查看 chákàn. **look round sth** 观光 guānguāng; 游览〔覽〕yóulǎn. **look through sth** 快速检查 kuàisù jiǎnchá; 快速阅读〔讀〕kuàisù yuèdú. **look to sb for sth/to do sth** 依赖(某人) yīlài; 指望(某人) zhǐwàng. **look ˈup** [非正式用语]好转〔轉〕hǎozhuǎn; 改善 gǎishàn. **look sb up** [非正式用语]拜访 bàifǎng; 探访 tànfǎng. **look sth up** (在词典、参考书中)查阅 cháyuè. **look up to sb** 尊敬(某人) zūnjìng; 钦佩 qīnpèi. **look** *interj* (用以唤起某人听要说的话). **ˈlook-in** *n* [习语] **(not) give sb/get a look-in** [非正式用语](不)给某人参〔參〕加的机〔機〕会〔會〕gěi mǒurén cānjiā de jīhuì; (不)给某人成功的机会 gěi mǒurén chénggōng de jīhuì. **ˈlook-out** *n* [C] **1** 岗〔崗〕哨 gǎngshào; 观察所 guāncháсuǒ. **2** 岗哨(指人) gǎngshào; 守望员 shǒuwàngyuán. **3** [习语] **be ˈsb's look-out** [非正式用语]为某人的责任 wéi mǒurén de zérèn: *If you want to waste your money, that's your ~-out*. 假如你乱花钱, 那是你的事.

look[2] /lʊk/ *n* **1** [C, 常作 sing] 看 kàn; 望 wàng: *Take a ~ at this*. 请看一看这个. **2** [C] 表情 biǎoqíng; 外表 wàibiǎo: *I don't like the ~ of him*. 我不喜欢他的外表. **3 looks** [pl] 容貌 róngmào; 美貌 měimào: *She's got her father's good ~s*. 她有她父亲那样俊秀的容貌.

loom[1] /luːm/ *n* [C] 织〔織〕布机〔機〕zhībùjī.

loom[2] /luːm/ *v* [I] 隐〔隱〕约地出现 yǐnyuēde chūxiàn: *The outline of a ship ~ed through the fog*. 船的轮廓透过雾气隐约出现. *Her problems ~ed large in her mind*. [喻]她面临的诸多问题涌上心头.

loop /luːp/ *n* [C] **1** 环〔環〕形 huánxíng. **2** (线、绳等打成的)圈 quān; 环 huán. **loop** *v* **1** [I, T] (使)成环 chénghuán; (使)成圈 chéngquān. **2** [T] 打环扣住 dǎ huán kòuzhù; 缠〔纏〕绕〔繞〕chánrào.

loophole /ˈluːphəʊl/ *n* [C] (法律等的)漏洞 lòudòng: *tighten up ~s in the law* 堵塞法律的漏洞.

loose /luːs/ *adj* [~r, ~st] **1** 自由的 zìyóude; 不受束缚的 búshòu shùfù de: *The dog is too dangerous to be set ~*. 这条狗不拴太危险了. **2** 不牢固的 bù láogù de: *a ~ tooth* 松动的牙齿. **3** 未系〔繫〕在一起的 wèi xì zài yìqǐ de: *~ sheets of paper* 散页纸. **4** (衣服)宽松〔鬆〕的 kuānsōngde. **5** 不精确〔確〕的 bù jīngquède: *a ~ translation* 不精确的译文. **6** [旧词]放荡〔蕩〕的 fàngdàngde. **7** [习语] **at a loose ˈend**(美语亦作 **at loose ends**) 无〔無〕事做 wúshì zuò. **come/work ˈloose** (扣件等)松开〔開〕sōngkāi, 不牢固 bù láogù. **loosely** *adv*. **loosen** /ˈluːsn/ *v* [I, T] 使松 shǐ sōng; 变〔變〕松 biàn sōng; 放松 fàng sōng.

loot /luːt/ *n* [U] 掠夺〔奪〕物 lüèduówù; 战〔戰〕利品 zhànlìpǐn; 赃〔贓〕物 zāngwù. **loot** *v* [I, T] 掠夺 lüèduó; 抢〔搶〕劫 qiǎngjié.

lop /lɒp/ *v* [-pp-] [T] 剪去 jiǎnqù; 砍掉(树枝等) kǎndiào.

lop-sided /ˌlɒp ˈsaɪdɪd/ *adj* (两侧)不平衡的 bù pínghéng de, 不匀称〔稱〕的 bù yúnchen de.

lord /lɔːd/ *n* **1** [C] 君主 jūnzhǔ. **2** (the) **Lord** [sing] 上帝 Shàngdì; 基督 Jīdū. **3** (a) [C] 贵族 guìzú. (b) **the Lords** [sing] [用 sing 或 pl v] 上议〔議〕院 shàngyìyuàn; 上议院议员

L

shàngyìyuàn yìyuán. 4 Lord [C] [英国英语] (对某些高级官员的尊称): *L~ Mayor* 市长. 5 [C] (表示惊讶等): *Good L~!* 天哪! **lordly** *adj* 高傲的 gāo'àode; 不可一世的 bù kě yí shì de. **lordship** *n* [C] 大人 dàrén; 阁下 géxià; 爵爷〔爺〕 juéyé.

lorry /ˈlɒrɪ; *US* ˈlɔːrɪ/ *n* [C] [*pl* -ies] 运〔運〕货汽车〔車〕 yùnhuò qìchē; 卡车 kǎchē.

lose /luːz/ *v* [*pt*, *pp* **lost** /lɒst; *US* lɔːst/] 1 [T] 遗失 yíshī; 丢失 diūshī: *~ one's keys* 丢了钥匙. 2 [T] 失去 shīqù; 丧〔喪〕失 sàngshī: *~ one's job* 失业. 3 [T] 不再有(或保持) búzài yǒu: *~ interest in sth* 对某事失去兴趣. *~ weight* (人)减轻体重. 4 [I, T] 未赢得 wèi yíngdé: *~ a game* 比赛输了. 5 [I, T] (钟、表)慢(若干时间) màn. 6 **~ oneself in** 入迷 rùmí; 专〔專〕心于 zhuānxīn yú. 7 [T] [非正式用语] 使(某人)不明白 shǐ… bù míngbai: *I'm afraid you've lost me.* 对不起, 我不明白了. 8 [T] 浪费(时间或机会) làngfèi. 9 [习语] **lose count of sth** ⇨COUNT. **lose ˈface** 丢脸〔臉〕 diūliǎn; 丧失声〔聲〕誉〔譽〕 sàngshī shēngyù. **lose ground** ⇨GROUND[1]. **lose one's head** ⇨HEAD[1]. **lose ˈheart** ⇨HEART. **lose one's ˈheart to sb** 爱〔愛〕上 ài shàng. **lose sight of sb/sth** (a) 看不见某人(或某事物) kànbújiàn mǒurén. (b) 忽略(某事) hūlüè. **lose touch (with sb)** 失去(和某人的)联〔聯〕系〔繫〕 shīqù liánxì. **lose one's way** 迷路 mílù. **lose weight** ⇨WEIGHT. 10 [短语动词] **lose ˈout** 不成功 bù chénggōng. **loser** *n* [C].

loss /lɒs; *US* lɔːs/ *n* 1 [U] 遗失 yíshī; 损失 sǔnshī; 丧〔喪〕失 sàngshī: *~ of blood* 失血. 2 [C] (a) 损失的人(或物) sǔnshī de rén: *heavy ~ of life* 一生的重大损失. (b) (生意)亏〔虧〕损 kuīsǔn. 3 [习语] **at a ˈloss** 茫然不知所措 mángrán bùzhī suǒ cuò; 困惑 kùnhuò.

lost[1] *pt*, *pp* of LOSE.

lost[2] /lɒst; *US* lɔːst/ *adj* 1 迷失的 míshīde; 迷路的 mílùde. 2 遗失的 yíshīde; 丧〔喪〕失的 sàngshīde. 3 [习语] **a lost ˈcause** 已失败的计划〔劃〕 yǐ shībài de jìhuà.

lot[1] /lɒt/ *pron* **a lot, lots** [非正式用语] 大量 dàliàng; 许多 xǔduō. **a lot of** (亦作[非正式用语] **lots of**) *adj* 大量 dàliàng; 许多 xǔduō: *a ~ of people* 许多人. **the ˈlot** *n* [sing] [用 sing 或 pl v] [非正式用语] 全部 quánbù; 全体〔體〕 quántǐ.

lot[2] /lɒt/ *adv* **a lot** [非正式用语] 1 [与形容词或副词连用] 很 hěn; 非常 fēicháng: *I feel a ~ better.* 我感到好多了. 2 [与动词连用] (a) 很 hěn; 非常 fēicháng. (b) 时〔時〕常 shícháng.

lot[3] /lɒt/ *n* 1 [C, 亦作 sing 用 pl v] (人或物的)组 zǔ, 批 pī, 套 tào: *the next ~ of students* 下一批学生. 2 [C] (拍卖的)(一)件 jiàn, (一)批 pī. 3 [C] 地皮 dìpí; 一块〔塊〕地 yíkuàidì. 4 [sing] 命运〔運〕 mìngyùn; 运气〔氣〕 yùnqi. 5 [习语] **cast/draw ˈlots** 抽签〔簽〕 chōuqiān; 抓阄〔鬮〕 zhuājiū.

loth = LOATH.

lotion /ˈləʊʃn/ *n* [C, U] (外用)药〔藥〕液 yàoyè; (化妆用的)润肤〔膚〕液 rùnfūyè; 洗剂〔劑〕 xǐjì.

lottery /ˈlɒtərɪ/ *n* [C] [*pl* -ies] 抽彩给奖〔獎〕法 chōucǎi gěijiǎng fǎ.

loud /laʊd/ *adj* 1 高声〔聲〕的 gāoshēngde; 响〔響〕亮的 xiǎngliàngde. 2 (颜色)刺眼的 cìyǎnde. **loud** *adv* 大声地 dàshēngde. **loudly** *adv*. **loudness** *n* [U]. ˌ**loudˈspeaker** *n* [C] 扬〔揚〕声器 yángshēngqì.

lounge /laʊndʒ/ *v* [I] (懒洋洋地)坐着(或站着) zuòzhe. **lounge** *n* [C] 1 [英国英语]起居室 qǐjūshì. 2 候机〔機〕室 hòujīshì. ˈ**lounge bar** *n* [C] [英国英语]豪华〔華〕酒吧 háohuá jiǔbā.

louse /laʊs/ *n* [C] [*pl* **lice** /laɪs/] 虱〔蝨〕 shī.

lousy /ˈlaʊzɪ/ *adj* [-ier, -iest] 1 [非正式用语]极〔極〕坏〔壞〕的 jíhuàide: *a ~ holiday* 极糟的假日. 2 多虱〔蝨〕的 duōshīde.

lout /laʊt/ *n* [C] 粗鲁的人 cūlǔde rén. **loutish** *adj*.

lovable /ˈlʌvəbl/ *adj* 可爱〔愛〕的 kě'àide; 讨人喜欢〔歡〕的 tǎo rén xǐhuān de.

love /lʌv/ *n* 1 [U] 热〔熱〕爱〔愛〕 rè'ài; 喜爱 xǐ'ài. 2 [U] 性爱 xìng'ài; 恋〔戀〕爱 liàn'ài: *He's in ~.* 他在热恋中. 3 [U, sing] 酷爱 kù'ài: *a ~ of books* 酷爱书籍. 4 [C] 招人喜爱的人(或物) zhāo rén xǐ'ài de rén. 5 [U] (网球比赛)零分 língfēn. 6 [习语] ˌ**give/**ˌ**send sb one's ˈlove** 向某人致意 xiàng mǒurén zhìyì. **make love (to sb)** 性交 xìngjiāo. **there's little/no ˈlove lost between A and B** (他们之间)没有好感 méiyǒu hǎogǎn; 互相厌〔厭〕恶〔惡〕 hùxiāng yànwù. **love** *v* [T] 1 爱 ài; 热爱 rè'ài: *~ one's wife* 爱妻子. 2 喜欢〔歡〕 xǐhuān; 爱好 àihào: *I ~ cakes.* 我爱吃蛋糕. ˈ**love-affair** *n* [C] 风〔風〕流韵〔韻〕事 fēngliú yùnshì; 性关〔關〕系〔係〕 xìng guānxì.

lovely /ˈlʌvlɪ/ *adj* [-ier, -iest] 1 美丽〔麗〕的 měilìde; 可爱〔愛〕的 kě'àide: *a ~ woman* 可爱的女人. 2 令人愉快的 lìng rén yúkuài de: *a ~ holiday* 愉快的假日. **loveliness** *n* [U].

lover /ˈlʌvə(r)/ *n* [C] 1 (婚外恋的)情人 qíngrén. 2 爱〔愛〕好者 àihàozhě; 热〔熱〕爱者 rè'àizhě: *a ~ of music* 音乐爱好者.

loving /ˈlʌvɪŋ/ *adj* 爱〔愛〕的 àide; 表示爱的 biǎoshì ài de. **lovingly** *adv*.

low[1] /ləʊ/ *adj* 1 低的 dīde; 矮的 ǎide: *a ~ wall* 矮墙. 2 低于通常水平的 dī yú tōngcháng shuǐpíng de: *~ prices* 低价格. 3 (重要性或质

量)低的 dīde,差的 chàde. 4 粗俗的 cūsúde;卑劣的 bēiliède: *keep ~ company* 结交庸俗的朋友. 5 (声音)低沉的 dīchénde. 6 小声〔聲〕的 xiǎoshēngde;(声音)不大的 búdàde. 7 衰弱的 shuāiruòde;消沉的 xiāochénde: *feel ~* 情绪低落. 8 不赞成的 bú zànchéng de;不同意的 bù tóngyì de: *have a ~ opinion of him* 对他评价很低. 9 (变速器)低挡〔擋〕的 dīdǎngde. 10 [习语] **at a low 'ebb** 处〔處〕于低潮 chǔyú dīcháo;情况不佳 qíngkuàng bùjiā. **be/run 'low (on sth)** (供应品)几〔幾〕乎耗尽〔盡〕 jīhū hàojìn. **'low-down** *n* [习语] **give sb/get the low-down on sb/sth** [非正式用语]告诉某人真相 gàosu mǒurén zhēnxiàng;获〔獲〕得实〔實〕情 huòdé shíqíng. **'low-down** *adj* [非正式用语]卑鄙的 bēibǐde. **ˌlow-'key** (亦作 **ˌlow-'keyed**) *adj* 低调的 dīdiàode;克制的 kèzhìde. **lowlands** /ˈləʊləndz/ *n* [pl] 低地 dīdì. **lowness** *n* [U]. **ˌlow 'profile** ⇨ PROFILE. **ˌlow-'spirited** *adj* 无〔無〕精打采的 wú jīng dǎ cǎi de;消沉的 xiāochénde.

low[2] /ləʊ/ *adv* 在(或向)低水平 zài dī shuǐpíng: *aim/shoot ~* 向低处瞄准/射击.

low[3] /ləʊ/ *n* [C] 低水平 dī shuǐpíng: *Shares reached a new ~ yesterday.* 昨天股票跌到新的低价.

lower /ˈləʊə(r)/ *adj* 较低的 jiàodīde;较下的 jiàoxiàde: *the ~ lip* 下唇. **lower** *v* 1 [T] (使)降低 jiàngdī;降下 jiàngxià: *~ a flag* 降旗. 2 [I,T] 减低 jiǎndī;减少 jiǎnshǎo: *~ the price* 降低价格. 3 ~ **oneself** 贬低身份 biǎndī shēnfen. **ˌlower 'class** *n* [C] 下层〔層〕阶〔階〕级 xiàcéng jiējí. **ˌlower-'class** *adj*.

lowly /ˈləʊlɪ/ *adj* [-ier, -iest] [旧]谦虚的 qiānxūde;谦卑的 qiānbēide.

loyal /ˈlɔɪəl/ *adj* (*to*) 忠诚的 zhōngchéngde;忠贞的 zhōngzhēnde: *~ supporters* 忠实的拥护者. *~ to one's country* 忠于国家. **loyally** *adv*. **loyalty** *n* [*pl* -ies] 1 [U] 忠诚 zhōngchéng. 2 [C, 常作 pl] 向…效忠的义〔義〕务〔務〕 xiàng … xiàozhōngde yìwù. **'loyalty card** *n* [C] 联〔聯〕名卡 liánmíngkǎ;(鼓励顾客再次光临的)忠诚卡 zhōngchéngkǎ;积〔積〕分奖〔獎〕励〔勵〕卡 jīfēn jiǎnglìkǎ.

lozenge /ˈlɒzɪndʒ/ *n* [C] 1 糖锭 tángdìng;锭剂〔劑〕 dìngjì. 2 菱形 língxíng.

LP /ˌel ˈpiː/ *abbr* long-playing (record). ⇨ LONG[3].

Ltd *abbr* Limited. = LIMITED 2 (LIMIT).

lubricate /ˈluːbrɪkeɪt/ *v* [T] 加润滑油于 jiā rùnhuáyóu yú;使润滑 shǐ rùnhuá. **lubrication** /ˌluːbrɪˈkeɪʃn/ *n* [U].

lucid /ˈluːsɪd/ *adj* [正式用语] 1 明白的 míngbaide;易懂的 yìdǒngde. 2 清醒的 qīngxǐngde;头〔頭〕脑〔腦〕清楚的 tóunǎo qīngchu de. **lucidity** /luːˈsɪdətɪ/ *n* [U]. **lucidly** *adv*.

luck /lʌk/ *n* [U] 1 运〔運〕气〔氣〕 yùnqi. 2 幸运 xìngyùn;好运 hǎoyùn. 3 [习语] **be ˌdown on one's 'luck** [非正式用语]背运之时〔時〕 bèiyùn zhī shí. **be in/out of 'luck** 走运 zǒuyùn;不走运 bù zǒuyùn. **lucky** *adj* [-ier, -iest] 幸运的 xìngyùnde;好运的 hǎoyùnde. **luckily** *adv*.

lucrative /ˈluːkrətɪv/ *adj* 可获〔獲〕利的 kě huòlì de;赚钱〔錢〕的 zhuànqiánde.

ludicrous /ˈluːdɪkrəs/ *adj* 荒唐的 huāngtángde;可笑的 kěxiàode. **ludicrously** *adv*.

lug /lʌg/ *vt* [-gg-] [T] (用力)拉 lā,拖 tuō.

luggage /ˈlʌgɪdʒ/ *n* [U] 行李 xíngli.

lukewarm /ˌluːkˈwɔːm/ *adj* 1(指液体)不冷不热〔熱〕的 bùlěng búrè de;温热的 wēnrède. 2 [喻]不热情的 bú rèqíng de;冷淡的 lěngdànde.

lull /lʌl/ *v* [T] 使安静 shǐ ānjìng: *~ a baby to sleep* 哄婴儿入睡. **lull** *n* [C, 常作 sing] 间歇 jiànxiē.

lullaby /ˈlʌləbaɪ/ *n* [C] [*pl* -ies] 摇篮〔籃〕曲 yáolánqǔ;催眠曲 cuīmiánqǔ.

lumbago /lʌmˈbeɪgəʊ/ *n* [U] 腰痛 yāotòng.

lumber[1] /ˈlʌmbə(r)/ *n* [U] 1[尤用于英国英语]旧〔舊〕家〔傢〕具 jiù jiājù. 2 [尤用于美语] = TIMBER 1. **lumber** *v* [T] (*with*) [非正式用语]给…负担〔擔〕 gěi… fùdān;给…不便 gěi … búbiàn: *They've ~ed me with the washing-up again.* 他们再次给我增加洗餐具的负担. **'lumberjack** *n* [C] 伐木工人 fámù gōngrén;木材加工工人 mùcái jiāgōng gōngrén.

lumber[2] /ˈlʌmbə(r)/ *v* [I] 笨重地移动〔動〕 bènzhòngde yídòng.

luminous /ˈluːmɪnəs/ *adj* 发〔發〕光的 fāguāngde;发亮的 fāliàngde.

lump[1] /lʌmp/ *n* [C] 1 堆 duī;团〔團〕 tuán;块〔塊〕 kuài: *a ~ of coal* 一块煤. 2 肿〔腫〕块 zhǒngkuài;隆起 lóngqǐ. 3 [习语] **have a lump in one's throat** (因激动等而形成的)哽咽 gěngyè. **lump** *v* [T] (*together*) 把…混为〔爲〕一谈 bǎ… hùn wéi yì tán. **'lump sum** *n* [C] 一次总〔總〕付的款 yícì zǒng fù de kuǎn. **lumpy** *adj* [-ier, -iest].

lump[2] /lʌmp/ *v* [习语] **'lump it** [非正式用语]勉强接受不想要(或讨厌)的事物 miǎnqiǎng jiēshòu bù xiǎngyàode shìwù.

lunacy /ˈluːnəsɪ/ *n* [U] 疯〔瘋〕狂 fēngkuáng;精神错乱〔亂〕 jīngshén cuòluàn.

lunar /ˈluːnə(r)/ *adj* 月的 yuède;月球的 yuèqiúde.

lunatic /ˈluːnətɪk/ *n* [C] 1[非正式用语]极〔極〕愚蠢的人 jí yúchǔnde rén. 2 [旧]疯〔瘋〕子 fēngzi;精神失常者 jīngshén shīcháng zhě. **lunatic** *adj* [非正式用语]极愚蠢的 jí yúchǔnde.

ˈ**lunatic asylum** *n* [C] [旧]精神病院 jīngshénbìngyuàn.

lunch /lʌntʃ/ *n* [C, U] 午餐 wǔcān. **lunch** *v* [I] [正式用语]进〔進〕午餐 jìn wǔcān; 吃午饭 chī wǔfàn.

luncheon /ˈlʌntʃən/ *n* [C, U] [正式用语] = LUNCH.

lung /lʌŋ/ *n* [C] 肺 fèi.

lunge /lʌndʒ/ *n* [C], *v* [I] 前冲〔衝〕qiánchōng; 刺 cì; 戳 chuō.

lurch /lɜːtʃ/ *n* [C, 常作 sing] 突然倾斜 tūrán qīngxié. **lurch** *v* [I] 蹒跚 pánshān; 跌跌撞撞 diēdiē zhuàngzhuàng.

lure /lʊə(r)/ *n* [C, 常作 sing] 诱惑物 yòuhuòwù: *the* ～ *of adventure* 冒险的诱惑. **lure** *v* [T] 吸引 xīyǐn; 诱惑 yòuhuò: ～ *sb into a trap* 引诱某人上圈套.

lurid /ˈlʊərɪd/ *adj* **1** 耀眼的 yàoyǎnde. **2** [喻] 耸〔聳〕人听〔聽〕闻的 sǒng rén tīng wén de: ～ *details of the murder* 凶杀案惊人的详情.

lurk /lɜːk/ *v* [I] 潜〔潛〕伏 qiánfú; 埋伏 máifú.

luscious /ˈlʌʃəs/ *adj* (味道)香甜的 xiāngtiánde.

lush /lʌʃ/ *adj* 茂盛的 màoshèngde; 繁密的 fánmìde.

lust /lʌst/ *n* [C] **1** (强烈的)性欲〔慾〕xìngyù. **2** (*for*) 渴望 kěwàng; 物欲 wùyù. **lust** *v* [I] *after/for* 对〔對〕…有强烈的欲望 duì…yǒu qiángliè de yùwàng; 渴望 kěwàng; 贪求 tānqiú. **lustful** *adj*.

lustre (美语 **luster**) /ˈlʌstə(r)/ *n* [U] **1** 光泽〔澤〕guāngzé; 光辉 guānghuī. **2** [喻]光荣〔榮〕guāngróng; 荣耀 róngyào.

lusty /ˈlʌstɪ/ *adj* 健壮〔壯〕的 jiànzhuàngde; 精力充沛的 jīnglì chōngpèi de.

luxuriant /lʌgˈʒʊərɪənt/ *adj* 茂盛的 màoshèngde; 繁茂的 fánmàode. **luxuriance** /-əns/ *n* [U]. **luxuriantly** *adv*.

luxurious /lʌgˈʒʊərɪəs/ *adj* 非常舒适〔適〕的 fēicháng shūshì de; 奢华〔華〕的 shēhuáde. **luxuriously** *adv*.

luxury /ˈlʌkʃərɪ/ *n* [*pl* -**ies**] **1** [U] 奢侈 shēchǐ: *a life of* ～ 奢侈的生活. **2** [C] 奢侈品 shēchǐpǐn.

lying ⇨LIE[1,2].

lynch /lɪntʃ/ *v* [T] 以私刑处〔處〕死 yǐ sīxíng chǔsǐ.

lyric /ˈlɪrɪk/ *adj* (诗)抒情的 shūqíngde. **lyric** *n* **1** 抒情诗 shūqíngshī. **2 lyrics** [pl] 歌词 gēcí. **lyrical** /-kl/ *adj* **1** = LYRIC. **2** 狂热〔熱〕的 kuángrède. **lyrically** /-klɪ/ *adv*.

M

M m

M, m /em/ *n* [C] [*pl* **M's, m's** /emz/] **1** 英语的第十三个〔個〕字母 Yīngyǔde dìshísāngè zìmǔ. **2** 罗〔羅〕马数〔數〕字的 1000 Luómǎ shùzì de 1000. **3** 高速公路 gāosù gōnglù: *take the M1 to London* 取道 1 号高速公路去伦敦.

m *abbr* **1** metre(s). **2** mile(s). **3** million.

ma /mɑː/ *n* [C] [非正式用语]妈 mā; 妈妈 māma.

ma'am /mæm, 或罕读 mɑːm/ *n* [sing] (对女王、贵妇人等的尊称)夫人 fūrén; 女士 nǚshì.

mac /mæk/ *n* [C] [英国非正式用语] short for MACKINTOSH.

macabre /məˈkɑːbrə/ *adj* 可怕的 kěpàde; 令人毛骨悚然的 lìng rén máo gǔ sǒngrán de.

macaroni /ˌmækəˈrəʊnɪ/ *n* [U] 通心粉 tōngxīnfěn; 通心面〔麵〕tōngxīnmiàn.

mace[1] /meɪs/ *n* [C] 权〔權〕杖 quánzhàng.

mace[2] /meɪs/ *n* [U] 肉豆蔻干〔乾〕皮(用作食物香料) ròudòukòu gānpí.

Mach /mɑːk, mæk/ *n* [U] 马赫(飞行速度与音速之比) mǎhè: ～ *2* 两倍于音速.

machete /məˈtʃetɪ, -ˈʃetɪ/ *n* [C] (拉丁美洲人使用的)大砍刀 dà kǎndāo.

machine /məˈʃiːn/ *n* [C] **1** 机〔機〕器 jīqì; 机械 jīxiè. **2** (操纵政党的)核心组织〔織〕héxīn zǔzhī: *the party* ～ 党的核心组织. **machine** *v* [T] 用机器制〔製〕造(或切削等) yòng jīqì zhìzào. **maˈchine-gun** *n* [C] 机枪〔槍〕jīqiāng. **maˌchine-ˈreadable** *adj* [计]机器可读〔讀〕的 jīqì kědú de. **maˈchinery** *n* [U] **1** (总称)机器 jīqì; 机械 jīxiè. **2** (机器的)转〔轉〕动〔動〕部分 zhuàndòng bùfen. **3** 组织 zǔzhī; 机构〔構〕jīgòu: *the* ～ *of government* 政府机构. **maˈchine tool** *n* [C] 机床〔牀〕jīchuáng. **maˈchinist** *n* [C] 机械工 jīxiègōng; 机械师〔師〕jīxièshī.

macho /ˈmætʃəʊ/ *adj* [非正式用语, 尤作贬] 大男子气〔氣〕的 dà nánzǐqì de.

mackerel /ˈmækrəl/ *n* [C] [*pl* **mackerel**] 鲭 qīng.

mackintosh /ˈmækɪntɒʃ/ *n* [C] [英国英语] 雨衣 yǔyī.

mad /mæd/ *adj* [～**der**, ～**dest**] **1** 疯〔瘋〕的 fēngde; 精神失常的 jīngshén shīcháng de. **2** [非正式用语]极〔極〕愚蠢的 jí yúchǔn de; 疯狂的 fēngkuángde. **3** *about* 狂热〔熱〕的 kuángrède; 着迷的 zháomíde: *He's* ～ *about football*. 他对足球很入迷. **4** (*at*) [非正式用语]愤怒的 fènnùde; 狂怒的 kuángnùde: *You're driving me* ～*!* 你要逼我发疯了! **5** [非正式用语]非常激动〔動〕的 fēicháng jīdòng de: *in a* ～

rush 狂奔.6[习语] like ˈmad [非正式用语]非常 fēicháng;很快地 hěnkuàide. mad ˈkeen (on sb/sth) [非正式用语]很着迷 hěn zháomí. madly *adv* 1 疯狂地 fēngkuángde: *rush about ~ly* 狂奔. 2 [非正式用语]极端地 jíduānde: *~ly in love* 热恋 ˈmadman, ˈmadwoman *n* [C] 疯子 fēngzi;狂人 kuángrén. madness *n* [U].

madam /ˈmædəm/ *n* Madam [sing] [正式用语](对妇女的尊称)夫人 fūrén;女士 nǚshì.

madden /ˈmædn/ *v* [T] 激怒 jīnù;使狂怒 shǐ kuángnù.

made *pt*, *pp* of MAKE[1].

Madonna /məˈdɒnə/ *n* 1 the Madonna [sing] 圣〔聖〕母马利亚〔亞〕Shèngmǔ Mǎlìyà. 2 madonna [C] 圣母像 shèngmǔ xiàng.

madrigal /ˈmædrɪgl/ *n* [C] (无伴奏的合唱)歌曲 gēqǔ;牧歌 mùgē.

maestro /ˈmaɪstrəʊ/ *n* [C] [*pl* ~s 或 -stri /-strɪ/] 大师〔師〕(用以称作曲家、指挥家、音乐教师) dàshī.

magazine /ˌmægəˈziːn; *US* ˈmægəziːn/ *n* [C] 1 杂〔雜〕志〔誌〕zázhì;期刊 qīkān. 2 弹〔彈〕盒 dànhé;弹仓〔倉〕dàncāng.

magenta /məˈdʒentə/ *adj*, *n* [U] 洋红色的 yánghóngsède;洋红色 yánghóngsè;洋红染料 yánghóng rǎnliào.

maggot /ˈmægət/ *n* [C] 蛆 qū.

magic /ˈmædʒɪk/ *n* [U] 1 魔法 mófǎ;巫术〔術〕wūshù. 2 戏〔戲〕法 xìfǎ;魔术 móshù. 3 [喻]魔力 mólì;魅力 mèilì. magic *adj* 1 用魔法的 yòng mófǎ de;用巫术的 yòng wūshù de. 2 [俚]绝妙的 juémiàode. magical /-kl/ *adj* 神秘的 shénmìde;奇妙的 qímiàode. magically /-klɪ/ *adv*. magician /məˈdʒɪʃn/ *n* [C] 魔术师〔師〕móshùshī.

magistrate /ˈmædʒɪstreɪt/ *n* [C] 地方法官 dìfāng fǎguān.

maglev /ˈmæglev/ *n* [U, C] 磁悬〔懸〕浮 cíxuánfú: *The Shanghai ~ is German-built.* 上海的磁悬浮交通系统是德国制造的. a ~ train 磁悬浮列车.

magnanimous /mægˈnænɪməs/ *adj* [正式用语]慷慨的 kāngkǎide;宽宏大量的 kuānhóng dàliàng de. magnanimity /ˌmægnəˈnɪmətɪ/ *n* [U]. magnanimously *adv*.

magnate /ˈmægneɪt/ *n* [C] 富豪 fùháo;巨头〔頭〕jùtóu;大企业〔業〕家 dà qǐyèjiā.

magnesium /mægˈniːzɪəm; *US* mægˈniːʒəm/ *n* [U] 镁 měi.

magnet /ˈmægnɪt/ *n* [C] 1 磁铁〔鐵〕cítiě;磁石 císhí. 2 [喻]有吸引力的人(或物) yǒu xīyǐnlì de rén. magnetic /mægˈnetɪk/ *adj* 1 有磁性的 yǒu cíxìng de. 2 [喻]有吸引力的 yǒu xīyǐnlì de. magnetically /-klɪ/ *adv*. magnetic ˈnorth *n* [U] 磁北 cíběi. magnetic ˈtape *n* [U, C] 磁带〔帶〕cídài. magnetism /ˈmægnɪtɪzəm/ *n* 1 磁性 cíxìng;磁力 cílì. 2 [喻]人的魅力 rén de mèilì;人的吸引力 rén de xīyǐnlì. magnetize *v* [T] 使磁化 shǐ cíhuà;使生磁性 shǐ shēng cíxìng.

magnificent /mægˈnɪfɪsnt/ *adj* 壮〔壯〕丽〔麗〕的 zhuànglìde;宏伟〔偉〕的 hóngwěide. magnificence /-sns/ *n* [U]. magnificently *adv*.

magnify /ˈmægnɪfaɪ/ *v* [*pt*, *pp* -ied] [T] 1 放大 fàngdà;扩〔擴〕大 kuòdà. 2 [正式用语]夸〔誇〕大 kuādà;夸张〔張〕kuāzhāng: ~ *the dangers* 夸大危险. magnification /ˌmægnɪfɪˈkeɪʃn/ *n* [U] 放大 fàngdà;放大率 fàngdàlǜ. magnifying glass *n* [C] 放大镜 fàngdàjìng.

magnitude /ˈmægnɪtjuːd; *US* -tuːd/ *n* [U] 1 [正式用语]大小 dà xiǎo. 2 重要性 zhòngyàoxìng;重要 zhòngyào.

magpie /ˈmægpaɪ/ *n* [C] 鹊〔鵲〕què;喜鹊 xǐquè.

mahogany /məˈhɒgənɪ/ *n* [U] 桃花心木 táohuāxīnmù;红木 hóngmù.

maid /meɪd/ *n* [C] 女仆〔僕〕nǚpú;保姆 bǎomǔ.

maiden /ˈmeɪdn/ *n* [C] [古]少女 shàonǚ;未婚女子 wèihūn nǚzǐ. maiden *adj* 1 首次的 shǒucìde: *a ship's ~ voyage* 轮船的首航. 2 老处〔處〕女的 lǎo chǔnǚ de. ˈmaiden name *n* [C] (女子的)娘家姓 niángjia xìng.

mail /meɪl/ *n* [U] 1 邮〔郵〕政 yóuzhèng. 2 邮件 yóujiàn;信件 xìnjiàn;邮包 yóubāo. **mail** *v* [T] [尤用于美语]邮寄 yóujì. ˈmailbox *n* [C] [美语] = LETTERBOX 2 (LETTER). ˈmailman /-mæn/ *n* [C] [美语] = POSTMAN (POST[1]). ˈmail order *n* [U] 邮购〔購〕yóugòu. ˈmailshot *n* [C] (a) (寄给客户的)广〔廣〕告材料 guǎnggào cáiliào. (b) 邮寄广告材料(给客户) yóujì guǎnggào cáiliào.

maim /meɪm/ *v* [T] 使残废〔廢〕shǐ cánfèi.

main[1] /meɪn/ *adj* 1 主要的 zhǔyàode;最重要的 zuì zhòngyào de: *the ~ purpose of the meeting* 会议的首要目的. 2 [习语] in the main 大体〔體〕上 dàtǐ shàng. ˈmainframe *n* [C] [计]主机〔機〕zhǔjī. ˈmainland *n* [sing] 大陆〔陸〕dàlù. mainly *adv* 主要地 zhǔyàode. ˈmainspring *n* [C] 1 (钟表的)主发〔發〕条〔條〕zhǔ fātiáo. 2 [正式用语,喻]主要动〔動〕机 zhǔyào dòngjī;主要原因 zhǔyào yuányīn. ˈmainstay *n* [C] 主要依靠 zhǔyào yīkào;支柱 zhīzhù. ˈmainstream *n* [sing] 主流 zhǔliú;主要倾向 zhǔyào qīngxiàng.

main[2] /meɪn/ *n* 1 [C] (自来水、煤气等的)总〔總〕管道 zǒngguǎndào;干〔幹〕线〔綫〕gànxiàn. 2 the mains (供应建筑物的)水源 shuǐyuán;煤气〔氣〕源 méiqìyuán;电〔電〕源 diànyuán.

M

maintain /meɪnˈteɪn/ *v* [T] 1 维持 wéichí; 保持 bǎochí: ~ *peaceful relations* 保持和平关系. 2 赡养〔養〕 shànyǎng; 扶养 fúyǎng. 3 保养 bǎoyǎng; 维修 wéixiū: ~ *a car* 保养汽车. 4 坚〔堅〕持 jiānchí; 断〔斷〕言 duànyán: ~ *one's innocence* 坚持自己无辜. **maintenance** /ˈmeɪntənəns/ *n* [U] 1 维持 wéichí; 赡养 shànyǎng. 2 [英国英语]赡养费 shànyǎngfèi.

maisonette /ˌmeɪzəˈnet/ *n* [C] (占有两层楼的)公寓套房 gōngyù tàofáng.

maize /meɪz/ *n* [U] 玉米 yùmǐ.

majesty /ˈmædʒəstɪ/ *n* [*pl* -ies] 1 Majesty [C] (对帝王、王后的尊称): *Good morning, Your M*~. 陛下, 早安. *His M*~ 陛下. 2 [U] 威严〔嚴〕 wēiyán; 庄〔莊〕严 zhuāngyán. **majestic** /məˈdʒestɪk/ *adj*. **majestically** /-klɪ/ *adv*.

major[1] /ˈmeɪdʒə(r)/ *adj* 主要的 zhǔyàode; (较)重要的 zhòngyàode: *a* ~ *road* 干道; 要道. **major** *v* [I] *in* 主修(科目) zhǔxiū: ~ *in French* 主修法语.

major[2] /ˈmeɪdʒə(r)/ *n* [C] 陆〔陸〕军少校 lùjūn shàoxiào.

majority /məˈdʒɒrətɪ; US -ˈdʒɔːr-/ *n* [*pl* -ies] 1 [sing] [用 sing 或 pl v] 大多数〔數〕 dà duōshù; 多数 duōshù 2 [C] 超过〔過〕对〔對〕方的票数 chāoguò duìfāng de piàoshù: *win by a* ~ *of 9 votes* 超过对方 9 票获胜. 3 [sing] 法定年龄〔齡〕 fǎdìng niánlíng.

make[1] /meɪk/ *v* [*pt, pp* made /meɪd/] 1 [T] 建造 jiànzào; 制〔製〕造 zhìzào: ~ *bread* 做面包. ~ *a lot of noise* 造成很大噪音. 2 [T] 引起 yǐnqǐ; 产〔產〕生 chǎnshēng: ~ *trouble* 引起麻烦. 3 [T] 使成为〔為〕 shǐ chéngwéi; 变〔變〕成 biànchéng: *The news made her happy*. 这消息使她很高兴. 4 [T] (a) 使发〔發〕生 shǐ fāshēng: *Can you* ~ *this door shut?* 你能关上门吗? (b) 使做某事 shǐ zuò mǒushì: ~ *sb jump* 使某人跳起来. 5 [T] 选〔選〕举〔舉〕 xuǎnjǔ; 委派 wěipài: *They made me the manager*. 他们委派我做经理. 6 [T] 足以成为 zú yǐ chéngwéi; 可发展为 kě fāzhǎn wéi: *She will* ~ *a brilliant doctor*. 她将来可以成为技艺精湛的医生. 7 [T] 赚得 zhuàndé; 获〔獲〕得 huòdé: ~ *a profit* 获利. 8 [T] 计算 jìsuàn; 估计 gūjì: *What do you* ~ *the time?* 你估计现在几点钟? 9 [T] 等于 děngyú; 合计 héjì: *Two and two* ~ *four*. 2 加 2 等于 4. 10 [T] 保持(某一速度) bǎochí; 达〔達〕到 dádào: ~ *the station on time* 按时到达火车站. 11 [I] 表现出要做 biǎoxiàn chū yàozuò: *She made (as if) to hit him*. 她做出要打他的样子. 12 [习语] **make (sth)ˈdo, make do with sth** 将〔將〕就 jiāngjiu; 凑〔湊〕合 còuhe. **ˈmake ˌit** [非正式用语]成功 chénggōng; 达到预定目标〔標〕 dádào yùdìng mùbiāo. **make up ground** ⇨ GROUND[1]. 13 [短语动词] **make after sb/sth** 追捕 zhuībǔ; 追赶〔趕〕 zhuīgǎn. **make for sb/sth** (a) 走向 zǒuxiàng; 移向 yíxiàng. (b) 有助于 yǒu zhù yú: *Does exercise* ~ *for good health?* 锻炼有益于健康吗? **make A into B** 使变为 shǐ biàn wéi; 转〔轉〕变为 zhuǎnbiàn wéi: ~ *water into wine* 把水变成酒. **make sth of sb/sth** 理解 lǐjiě; 明白 míngbai: *What do you* ~ *of this sentence?* 你明白这个句子的意思吗? **make ˈoff** [非正式用语]匆匆离〔離〕开〔開〕 cōngcōng líkāi; 逃走 táozǒu. **make off with sth** 携…而逃 xié…értáo. **make ˈout** [非正式用语]尽〔盡〕力应〔應〕付 jìnlì yìngfù: *How are you making out in your new job?* 新工作你对付得还可以吗? **make sth out** (a) 填写〔寫〕 tiánxiě; 写出 xiěchū: ~ *out a cheque* 开支票. (b) 辨认〔認〕出 biànrèn chū: *I can't* ~ *out his writing*. 我辨认不出他的笔迹. **make sb/sth out** [用于否定句和疑问句]理解 lǐjiě; 了〔瞭〕解 liǎojiě: *I just can't* ~ *her out*. 我的确不了解她. **make out that, make oneself/sb/sth out to be** 声〔聲〕称〔稱〕 shēngchēng: *He* ~*s himself out to be cleverer than he is*. 他把自己说得比实际聪明. **make (sb/oneself) up** 为…化妆〔妝〕 wèi…huàzhuāng. **make sth up** (a) 补〔補〕足 bǔzú; 弥〔彌〕补 míbǔ: *We need £5 to* ~ *up the sum*. 我们需要五英镑以补足总数. (b) 捏〔揑〕造 niēzào; 虚〔虛〕构〔構〕 xūgòu: *a made-up story* 编造的故事. (c) 组成 zǔchéng; 构成 gòuchéng: *Bodies are made up of cells*. 身体是由细胞组成的. (d) 把…制成(衣服) bǎ…zhìchéng. (e) 铺(床) pū. **make up (for sth)** 补偿〔償〕 bǔcháng; 弥补 míbǔ. **make up to sb** 讨好 tǎohǎo; 奉承 fèngcheng. **make it up to sb** 补偿某人损失 bǔcháng mǒurén sǔnshī. **make (it) ˈup (with sb)** 与〔與〕…和解 yǔ…héjiě. **make-believe** *n* [U] 假装〔裝〕 jiǎzhuāng: *a world of* ~*-believe* 幻想世界. **make-up** *n* 1 [U] 化妆品 huàzhuāngpǐn. 2 [sing] (a) 性格 xìnggé; 气〔氣〕质〔質〕 qìzhì: *There is no jealousy in his* ~*-up*. 他的品性中没有忌妒. (b) 组成 zǔchéng; 构成 gòuchéng: *the* ~*-up of the new committee* 新委员会的人员组成.

make[2] /meɪk/ *n* [C] 1 牌子 páizi; 样〔樣〕式 yàngshì: *a* ~ *of car* 汽车的牌子. 2 [习语] **on the ˈmake** [非正式用语]追求利益 zhuīqiú lìyì.

maker /ˈmeɪkə(r)/ *n* 1 [C] 制〔製〕造者 zhìzàozhě; 制作者 zhìzuòzhě: *a film-*~ 电影制片人. 2 **the / our Maker** [sing] [宗教]上帝 Shàngdì.

makeshift /ˈmeɪkʃɪft/ *adj* 权〔權〕宜的 quányíde;(临时)代用的 dàiyòngde.

making /ˈmeɪkɪŋ/ *n* [习语] **be the making of sb** 使成功 shǐ chénggōng;使顺利 shǐ shùnlì. **have the makings of sth** 具备〔備〕所需的素质〔質〕 jùbèi suǒxūde sùzhì.

maladjusted /ˌmæləˈdʒʌstɪd/ *adj* (人)不适〔適〕应〔應〕环〔環〕境的 bú shìyìng huánjìng de;心理失调的 xīnlǐ shītiáo de.

malaria /məˈleərɪə/ *n* [U] 疟〔瘧〕疾 nüèji.

male /meɪl/ *adj* 1 男的 nánde;雄的 xióngde. 2 (植物)雄的 xióngde. 3 (工具零件等)阳〔陽〕的 yángde. **male** *n* [C] 男人 nánrén;雄性动〔動〕物 xióngxìng dòngwù. **male ˈchauvinist** *n* [C] [贬]大男子主义〔義〕 dà nánzǐ zhǔyì.

malevolent /məˈlevələnt/ *adj* [正式用语] 恶〔惡〕意的 èyìde;恶毒的 èdúde. **malevolence** /-ləns/ *n* [U]. **malevolently** *adv*.

malformation /ˌmælfɔːˈmeɪʃn/ *n* [U,C] 畸形 jīxíng. **malformed** /-ˈfɔːmd/ *adj*.

malfunction /ˌmælˈfʌŋkʃn/ *v* [I] [正式用语](机器)发〔發〕生故障 fāshēng gùzhàng;运〔運〕转〔轉〕不正常 yùnzhuǎn bú zhèngcháng. **malfunction** *n* [C,U].

malice /ˈmælɪs/ *n* [U] 恶〔惡〕意 èyì;怨恨 yuànhèn. **malicious** /məˈlɪʃəs/ *adj*. **maliciously** *adv*.

malignant /məˈlɪgnənt/ *adj* 1 恶〔惡〕意的 èyìde;恶毒的 èdúde. 2 (疾病)恶性的 èxìngde,致命的 zhìmìngde. **malignantly** *adv*.

mall /mæl, mɔːl/ *n* [C] [尤用于美语]商店大街 shāngdiàn dàjiē;(车辆不得入内的)商店区〔區〕 shāngdiànqū.

malleable /ˈmælɪəbl/ *adj* (金属)可锻的 kěduànde;有延展性的 yǒu yánzhǎnxìng de.

mallet /ˈmælɪt/ *n* [C] 木槌 mùchuí.

malnutrition /ˌmælnjuːˈtrɪʃn; *US* -nuː-/ *n* [U] 营〔營〕养〔養〕不良 yíngyǎng bù liáng.

malt /mɔːlt/ *n* [U] 麦〔麥〕芽 màiyá.

maltreat /ˌmælˈtriːt/ *v* [T] [正式用语]虐待 nüèdài. **maltreatment** *n* [U].

mamba /ˈmæmbə/ *n* [C] 曼巴(非洲黑色或绿色毒蛇) mànbā.

mamma /ˈmɑːmə/ *n* [C] [美语,非正式用语] 妈妈 māma.

mammal /ˈmæml/ *n* [C] 哺乳动〔動〕物 bǔrǔ dòngwù.

mammoth /ˈmæməθ/ *n* [C] 猛犸(已绝种的古代大象) měngmǎ. **mammoth** *adj* [非正式用语]巨大的 jùdàde.

man[1] /mæn/ *n* [*pl* **men** /men/] 1 [C] 男人 nánrén;男子 nánzǐ. 2 [C] 人(指男人或女人) rén: *All men must die*. 所有人都得死. 3 [U] 人类〔類〕 rénlèi: *the origins of* ～ 人类的起源. 4 [C,常作 pl] 雇员 gùyuán;下属〔屬〕 xiàshǔ: *officers and men* 官兵. 5 丈夫 zhàngfu;男情人 nán qíngrén: ～ *and wife* 夫妻. 6 [C] 男子汉〔漢〕 nánzǐhàn;大丈夫气〔氣〕概 dà zhàngfū qìgài: *Don't give up, be a* ～! 别认输,要做个大丈夫! 7 [C] 棋子 qízǐ. 8 [习语] **be one's own ˈman** 能做主 néng zuòzhǔ. **the ˌman in the ˈstreet** 普通人 pǔtōngrén. **ˌman to ˈman** 真诚地 zhēnchéngde;公开〔開〕地 gōngkāide. **to a ˈman** 毫无〔無〕例外 háo wú lìwài. **ˈmanhole** *n* [C] 人孔 rénkǒng;检〔檢〕修孔 jiǎnxiūkǒng. **ˈmanhood** *n* [U] (男性的)成年 chéngnián;男子的气质〔質〕 nánzǐ de qìzhì. **ˌman-ˈmade** *adj* 人造的 rénzàode;人工的 réngōngde. **ˈmanpower** *n* [U] 人力 rénlì;劳〔勞〕动〔動〕力 láodònglì. **ˈmanslaughter** *n* [U] 过〔過〕失杀〔殺〕人 guòshī shārén.

man[2] /mæn/ *v* [-nn-] [T] 为〔爲〕…提供服务〔務〕(或操作)人员 wèi…tígōng fúwù rényuán: ～ *a boat* 为一艘船配备船员.

manacle /ˈmænəkl/ *n* [C,常作 pl] 手铐 shǒukào;脚镣 jiǎoliào. **manacle** *v* [T] 给…上手铐(或脚镣) gěi…shàng shǒukào;束缚 shùfù.

manage /ˈmænɪdʒ/ *v* 1 [T] 负责 fùzé;经〔經〕营〔營〕 jīngyíng;管理 guǎnlǐ. 2 [I,T] (a) 做成(某事)zuòchéng: *How did the prisoners* ～ *to escape?* 犯人是怎样设法逃跑的? (b) [I] 过〔過〕活 guòhuó: *I can only just* ～ *on my wages*. 我靠工资仅够维持生活. **manageable** *adj* 易管理的 yì guǎnlǐ de;易处〔處〕理的 yì chǔlǐ de.

management /ˈmænɪdʒmənt/ *n* 1 [U] 管理 guǎnlǐ;经〔經〕营〔營〕 jīngyíng: *problems caused by bad* ～ 经营不善引起的问题. 2 [C,亦作 sing,用 pl v] (企业等)管理人员 guǎnlǐ rényuán;资方 zīfāng. 3 [U] [正式用语]手段 shǒuduàn;手腕 shǒuwàn.

manager /ˈmænɪdʒə(r)/ *n* [C] 经〔經〕理 jīnglǐ;管理人 guǎnlǐrén. **manageress** /ˌmænɪdʒəˈres/ *n* [C] 女经理 nǚ jīnglǐ;女管理人 nǚ guǎnlǐrén. **managerial** /ˌmænəˈdʒɪərɪəl/ *adj* 经理的 jīnglǐde;管理人的 guǎnlǐrénde.

Mandarin /ˈmændərɪn/ *n* [U] 普通话 pǔtōnghuà; 国语 guóyǔ.

mandate /ˈmændeɪt/ *n* [C,常作 sing] 授权〔權〕shòuquán. **mandatory** /ˈmændətərɪ; *US* -tɔːrɪ/ *adj* [正式用语] 依法的 yīfǎde;强制的 qiángzhìde.

mandolin /ˈmændəlɪn, ˌmændəˈlɪn/ *n* [C] 曼陀林(乐器) màntuólín.

mane /meɪn/ *n* [C] (马、狮等的)鬃 zōng.

maneuver = MANOEUVER.

manful /ˈmænfl/ *adj* 勇敢的 yǒnggǎnde;坚〔堅〕定的 jiāndìngde. **manfully** *adv*.

manger /ˈmeɪndʒə(r)/ *n* [C] (牛、马的)食槽 shícáo.

M

mangle /ˈmæŋgl/ *v* [T] [常作被动语态]严〔嚴〕重损伤〔傷〕 yánzhòng sǔnshāng;损毁 sǔnhuǐ.

mango /ˈmæŋgəʊ/ *n* [C] [*pl* ～es 或 ～s] 芒果 mángguǒ;芒果树〔樹〕 mángguǒshù.

mangy /ˈmeɪndʒɪ/ *adj* [-ier, -iest] 褴〔襤〕褛〔褸〕的 lánlǚde.

manhandle /ˈmænhændl/ *v* [T] 1 用人力移动〔動〕 yòng rénlì yídòng. 2 粗暴地对〔對〕待 cūbàode duìdài.

mania /ˈmeɪnɪə/ *n* 1 [C, U] (*for*) 癖好 pǐhào;狂热〔熱〕 kuángrè: *a ～ for motor bikes* 对摩托车的狂热. 2 [U] [医学]躁狂 zàokuáng. **maniac** /-nɪæk/ *n* [C] 1 躁狂(症)者 zàokuángzhě;疯〔瘋〕子 fēngzi;狂人 kuángrén. 2 入迷的人 rùmíde rén;有癖者 yǒupǐzhě. **maniacal** /məˈnaɪəkl/ *adj*.

manicure /ˈmænɪkjʊə(r)/ *n* [C, U] 修剪指甲 xiūjiǎn zhǐjia. **manicure** *v* [T] 给…修剪指甲 gěi… xiūjiǎn zhǐjia. **manicurist** *n* [C].

manifest /ˈmænɪfest/ *adj* [正式用语]明白的 míngbaide;明显〔顯〕的 míngxiǎnde. **manifest** *v* [T] [正式用语]显示 xiǎnshì;表明 biǎomíng: *The disease ～ed itself*. 症状已出现. **manifestation** /ˌmænɪfeˈsteɪʃn/ *n* [C, U]. **manifestly** *adv*.

manifesto /ˌmænɪˈfestəʊ/ *n* [C] [*pl* ～s 或 ～es] 宣言 xuānyán;声〔聲〕明 shēngmíng.

manifold /ˈmænɪfəʊld/ *adj* [正式用语]各种〔種〕各样〔樣〕的 gèzhǒng gèyàng de;多种的 duōzhǒngde. **manifold** *n* [C] 歧管 qíguǎn;多支管 duōzhīguǎn.

manipulate /məˈnɪpjʊleɪt/ *v* [T] 1 (熟练地)操作 cāozuò;使用 shǐyòng. 2 (巧妙地或不正当地)控制 kòngzhì;操纵〔縱〕 cāozòng;影响〔響〕 yǐngxiǎng. **manipulation** /məˌnɪpjʊˈleɪʃn/ *n* [C, U]. **manipulative** /-lətɪv; *US* -leɪtɪv/ *adj*.

mankind /ˌmænˈkaɪnd/ *n* [U] 人类〔類〕 rénlèi.

manly /ˈmænlɪ/ *adj* [-ier, -iest] [褒]有男子气〔氣〕概的 yǒu nánzǐ qìgài de.

manner /ˈmænə(r)/ *n* 1 [sing] [正式用语] 方式 fāngshì;方法 fāngfǎ: *in a friendly ～* 友好的态度. 2 [sing] 态〔態〕度 tàidù;举〔舉〕止 jǔzhǐ: *I don't like your ～*. 我不喜欢你的态度. 3 **manners** [pl] 礼〔禮〕貌 lǐmào;规矩 guīju: *good ～s* 有礼貌. 4 [习语] **all manner of sb/sth** [正式用语] 各种〔種〕各样〔樣〕的 gèzhǒng gèyàng de. **in a manner of speaking** 可以说 kěyǐ shuō;在某种意义〔義〕上 zài mǒuzhǒng yìyì shàng. **-mannered** (用以构成复合形容词)有…态度的 yǒu…tàidù de;有…举止的 yǒu… jǔzhǐ de: *well-ˈ～ed* 有礼貌的.

mannerism /ˈmænərɪzəm/ *n* [C] (言谈举止的)特殊习〔習〕惯 tèshū xíguàn.

manoeuvre (美语 **maneuver**) /məˈnuːvə(r)/ *n* 1 [C] (a) 熟练〔練〕的动〔動〕作 shúliànde dòngzuò. (b) [喻]巧计 qiǎojì;花招 huāzhāo. 2 **manoeuvres** [pl] (大规模)演习〔習〕 yǎnxí. **manoeuvrable** (美语 **maneuverable**) *adj* 可移动的 kě yídòng de;可演习的 kě yǎnxí de;机〔機〕动的 jīdòngde. **manoeuvre** (美语 **maneuver**) *v* 1 [I, T] 运〔運〕用技巧移动 yùnyòng jìqiǎo yídòng. 2 [T] (巧妙地)操纵〔縱〕 cāozòng.

manor /ˈmænə(r)/(亦作 **manor house**) *n* [C] 庄〔莊〕园〔園〕主宅第 zhuāngyuánzhǔ zháidì.

mansion /ˈmænʃn/ *n* [C] 大厦 dàshà;宅第 zháidì;官邸 guāndǐ.

mantelpiece /ˈmæntlpiːs/ *n* [C] 壁炉〔爐〕台〔臺〕 bìlútái.

mantle /ˈmæntl/ *n* 1 [C] (a) 斗篷 dǒupéng;披风〔風〕 pīfēng. (b) [喻]覆盖〔蓋〕物 fùgàiwù: *a ～ of snow* 一层雪. 2 [sing] *of* [修辞] (重要工作的)责任 zérèn: *take on the ～ of supreme power* 担当最高权力的重任.

manual /ˈmænjʊəl/ *adj* 手工的 shǒugōngde;用手操作的 yòng shǒu cāozuò de. **manual** *n* [C] 手册 shǒucè;指南 zhǐnán. **manually** *adv*.

manufacture /ˌmænjʊˈfæktʃə(r)/ *v* [T] (大量)制〔製〕造 zhìzào. **manufacture** *n* [U] 制造 zhìzào. **manufacturer** *n* [C].

manure /məˈnjʊə(r)/ *n* [U] 粪〔糞〕肥 fènféi;肥料 féiliào.

manuscript /ˈmænjʊskrɪpt/ *n* [C] 1 手稿 shǒugǎo;原稿 yuángǎo. 2 手写〔寫〕本 shǒuxiěběn.

many /ˈmenɪ/ *adj, pron* 1 许多的 xǔduōde;多的 duōde;许多人(或物) xǔduō rén: *～ people* 很多人. *～ of the students* 许多学生. 2 **many a** [与单数名词连用]许多 xǔduō: *～ a mother* 很多母亲. 3 [习语] **a good/great many** 很多 hěnduō;许多 xǔduō. **have had ˌone too ˈmany** [非正式用语]有点〔點〕醉 yǒu diǎn zuì.

map /mæp/ *n* [C] 1 地图〔圖〕 dìtú. 2 [习语] **put sth on the ˈmap** 使出名 shǐ chūmíng;赋予…重要性 fùyǔ… zhòngyàoxìng. **map** *v* [-pp-] [T] 绘〔繪〕制〔製〕…地图 huìzhì… dìtú.

mar /mɑː(r)/ *v* [-rr-] [T] [正式用语]毁坏〔壞〕 huǐhuài;损坏 sǔnhuài: *a mistake that ～red his career* 毁掉他事业的错误.

marathon /ˈmærəθən; *US* -θɒn/ *n* [C] 马拉松赛跑(全长约 42 千米或 26 英里) mǎlāsōng sàipǎo. **marathon** *adj* [喻]有耐力的 yǒu nàilì de;马拉松式的 mǎlāsōngshìde: *a ～ speech lasting five hours* 持续五小时的马拉松式演

说.

marauding /mə'rɔːdɪŋ/ *adj* 抢〔搶〕劫的 qiǎngjiéde;劫掠的 jiélüède.

marble /'mɑːbl/ *n* 1 [U] 大理石 dàlǐshí. 2 (a) [C] (儿童玩的玻璃的)弹〔彈〕子 dànzi. (b) marbles [pl] 弹子游戏〔戲〕dànzi yóuxì.

March /mɑːtʃ/ *n* [U,C] 三月 sānyüè.

march /mɑːtʃ/ *v* 1 [I] (齐步)前进〔進〕qiánjìn;行进 xíngjìn. 2 [T] 使行进 shǐ xíngjìn;使前进 shǐ qiánjìn: *They ~ed the prisoner away*. 他们令犯人齐步走. **march** *n* 1 [C] 行军 xíngjūn;行进 xíngjìn. 2 [C] 进行曲 jìnxíngqǔ. 3 [C] 游行 yóuxíng;游行示威 yóuxíng shìwēi. 4 [sing] *of* [喻]进展 jìnzhǎn;进行 jìnxíng: *the ~ of time* 时间的推移.

marchioness /ˌmɑːʃə'nes/ *n* [C] 1 侯爵夫人 hóujué fūrén. 2 女侯爵 nǚ hóujué.

mare /meə(r)/ *n* [C] 母马 mǔmǎ;牝驴〔驢〕pìnlǘ.

margarine /ˌmɑːdʒə'riːn; *US* 'mɑːrdʒərɪn/ *n* [U] 人造黄油 rénzào huángyóu.

margin /'mɑːdʒɪn/ *n* [C] 1 页边〔邊〕空白 yèbiān kòngbái. 2 边 biān;缘 yuán. 3 (a) 差数〔數〕chāshù;差距 chājù: *a ~ of six votes* 六票之差. (b) 余〔餘〕地 yúdì. **marginal** /-nl/ *adj* 很少的 hěnshǎode;很小的 hěnxiǎode: *a ~al increase* 稍微增加. **marginally** /-nəlɪ/ *adv*.

marijuana /ˌmærɪjʊ'ɑːnə, ˌmærɪ'wænə/ *n* [U] 大麻 dàmá;大麻叶〔葉〕和花 dàmáyè hé huā;大麻烟 dàmáyān.

marina /mə'riːnə/ *n* [C] 小艇船坞〔塢〕xiǎotǐng chuánwù;游艇停泊港 yóutǐng tíngbógǎng.

marinade /ˌmærɪ'neɪd/ *n* [C,U] (酒、香料等配成的)腌泡汁 yānpàozhī. **marinade** (亦作 **marinate** /'mærɪneɪt/) *v* [T] (用腌泡汁)腌泡 yānpào;浸泡 jìnpào.

marine /mə'riːn/ *adj* 1 海的 hǎide;海产〔產〕的 hǎichǎnde;海中的 hǎizhōngde: *~ life* 海生生物. 2 海运〔運〕的 hǎiyùnde;船只〔隻〕的 chuánzhīde. **marine** *n* [C] 海军陆〔陸〕战〔戰〕队〔隊〕士兵 hǎijūn lùzhànduì shìbīng. **ma'rine re'serve** *n* [C] 海洋(自然)保护〔護〕区〔區〕hǎi-yáng bǎohù qū.

mariner /'mærɪnə(r)/ *n* [C] [旧或正式用语] 水手 shuǐshǒu.

marionette /ˌmærɪə'net/ *n* [C] 牵〔牽〕线〔綫〕木偶 qiānxiàn mù'ǒu.

marital /'mærɪtl/ *adj* 婚姻的 hūnyīnde;夫妻的 fūqīde.

maritime /'mærɪtaɪm/ *adj* 1 海上的 hǎishàngde;航海的 hánghǎide;海事的 hǎishìde. 2 近海的 jìnhǎide;沿海的 yánhǎide.

mark[1] /mɑːk/ *n* [C] 1 (a) 痕迹 hénjì;斑点〔點〕bāndiǎn;污点 wūdiǎn: *dirty ~s on my new shirt* 我的新衬衫上的污迹. (b) 特征〔徵〕tèzhēng;胎记 tāijì: *a birth ~* 胎痣. 2 (书写或印刷的)符号〔號〕fúhào: *ˌpunctu'ation ~s* 标点符号. 3 痕迹 hénjì;迹象 jìxiàng: *~s of old age* 老年的标志. *a ~ of respect* 敬意. 4 (评定工作或品行等用的)数〔數〕字或字母符号 shùzì huò zìmǔ fúhào: *top ~s* 最高分. 5 Mark (与数字连用表示机器等的)型 xíng;式 shì: *a M~ 2 Ford Escort* 福特埃斯科特 II 型轿车. 6 [习语] be ˌquick/slow off the 'mark 不失时〔時〕机〔機〕地开〔開〕始 bùshī shíjī de kāishǐ;慢吞吞地开始 màntūntūnde kāishǐ. ˌmake one's 'mark (in sth) 出名 chūmíng;成功 chénggōng. 'up to the 'mark 达〔達〕到要求的标〔標〕准〔準〕dádào yāoqiú de biāozhǔn.

mark[2] /mɑːk/ *v* 1 [I,T] 作记号〔號〕(或符号) zuò jìhào;留痕迹(于) liú hénjì: *You've ~ed the table*. 你给这张桌子留下了痕迹. 2 [T] 表示 biǎoshì;表明 biǎomíng: *This cross ~s the place where she died*. 这个十字符号表明她死去的地点. *His death ~ed the end of an era*. 他的逝世标志着一个时代的结束. 3 [T] 给…评分 gěi…píngfēn;给…评成绩 gěi…píng chéngjì. 4 [T] 用记号表示 yòng jìhào biǎoshì: *documents ~ed 'secret'* 标明"机密"的文件. 5 [T] [正式用语]注意 zhùyì;留心 liúxīn: *~ my words* 留心听我说的话. 6 [T] 为〔爲〕…的特征〔徵〕wéi…de tèzhēng: *qualities that ~ a leader* 表示领袖特征的品质. 7 [T] (体育)盯住(对方队员) dīngzhù. 8 [习语] mark 'time 等待时〔時〕机〔機〕děngdài shíjī. 9 [短语动词] mark sth down /up 减价〔價〕jiǎnjià;加价 jiājià. mark sth off/out 以界线〔綫〕隔开〔開〕yǐ jièxiàn gékāi;划〔劃〕线分出 huàxiàn fēnchū. mark sb out for sth 选〔選〕出 xuǎnchū;选定 xuǎndìng. **marked** *adj* 易见的 yìjiànde;清楚的 qīngchude: *a ~ed improvement* 明显的改进. **markedly** /'mɑːkɪdlɪ/ *adv*. **marker** *n* [C] 1 作记号的人 zuò jìhào de rén;作记号的工具 zuò jìhào de gōngjù. 2 打分数〔數〕的人 dǎ fēnshù de rén. 3 标〔標〕示物 biāoshìwù;(标示位置的)旗(或杆) qí. **marking** *n* [C,常作 pl] (兽皮、鸟羽等的)斑纹 bānwén;斑点〔點〕bāndiǎn. **'mark-up** *n* [C,常作 sing] (为确定售价而增加的)成本加价率 chéngběn jiājiàlǜ.

market /'mɑːkɪt/ *n* 1 [C] 市场〔場〕shìchǎng;集市 jíshì. 2 [C,常作 sing] 行情 hángqíng: *The coffee ~ was steady*. 咖啡行情稳定. 3 [sing,U] (*for*) 需求 xūqiú: *a good ~ for cars* 良好的汽车销路. 4 [C] 推销地区〔區〕tuīxiāo dìqū: *foreign ~* 国外推销市场. 5 the market [sing] 买〔買〕者和卖〔賣〕者 mǎizhě hé màizhě. 6 [习语] in the market for sth [非正式用语]想买进〔進〕xiǎng mǎijìn. on/onto the 'market 待售 dàishòu;出售 chūshòu: *a product not yet on the ~* 尚未上市

M

的产品. *new goods coming onto the* ～ 上市的新商品. **market** *v* [T] 销售 xiāoshòu; 出售 chūshòu. **marketable** *adj*. ˌ**market** ˈ**garden** *n* [C] [英国英语] 蔬菜农[農]场[場] shūcài nóngchǎng. **marketing** *n* [U] 销售部门 xiāoshòu bùmén; 市场推广[廣]部 shìchǎng tuīguǎng bù. ˈ**market-place** *n* 1 [C] 集市 jíshì; 市场 shìchǎng. 2 **the market-place** [sing] 商业[業]活动[動] shāngyè huódòng. ˌ**market reˈsearch** *n* [U] 市场调查 shìchǎng diàochá. ˌ**market ˈsurvey** *n* [C] 市场[場]调查 shìchǎng diàochá.

marksman /ˈmɑːksmən/ *n* [C] [*pl* -men /-mən/] 射击[擊]能手 shèjī néngshǒu; 神射手 shénshèshǒu.

marmalade /ˈmɑːməleɪd/ *n* [U] 橘子酱[醬] júzijiàng; 橙子酱 chéngzijiàng.

maroon[1] /məˈruːn/ *adj*, *n* [C] 褐红色的 hèhóngsède; 褐红色 hèhóngsè.

maroon[2] /məˈruːn/ *v* [T] 将[將](某人)放逐到荒岛(或渺无人烟的地方) jiāng…fàngzhú dào huāngdǎo.

marquee /mɑːˈkiː/ *n* [C] 大帐[帳]篷 dà zhàngpeng.

marquis (亦作 **marquess**) /ˈmɑːkwɪs/ *n* [C] (英国的)侯爵 hóujué.

marriage /ˈmærɪdʒ/ *n* [U, C] 结婚 jiéhūn; 婚姻 hūnyīn. **marriageable** *adj* (年龄)适[適]宜结婚的 shìyí jiéhūn de; 达[達]到结婚年龄[齡]的 dádào jiéhūn niánlíng de.

marrow[1] /ˈmærəʊ/ *n* [C, U] 西葫芦[蘆] xīhúlu.

marrow[2] /ˈmærəʊ/ *n* [U] 髓 suí; 骨髓 gǔsuí.

marry /ˈmærɪ/ *v* [*pt*, *pp* -ied] 1 [I, T] 结婚 jiéhūn; 嫁 jià; 娶 qǔ. 2 [T] 为[爲]…主持婚礼[禮] wèi … zhǔchí hūnlǐ: *Which priest is going to* ～ *them?* 哪位牧师来为他们主持婚礼? 3 [T] (*off*) 嫁(女) jià: *They married* (*off*) *their daughter to a rich banker*. 他们把女儿嫁给一位富有的银行家. **married** *adj* 1 (*to*) 结婚的 jiéhūnde; 已婚的 yǐhūnde. 2 婚姻的 hūnyīnde: *married life* 婚姻生活.

marsh /mɑːʃ/ *n* [C, U] 沼泽[澤](地带) zhǎozé; 湿[濕]地 shīdì. **marshy** *adj* [-ier, -iest].

marshal[1] /ˈmɑːʃl/ *n* [C] 1 元帅[帥] yuánshuài; 高级军官 gāojí jūnguān. 2 司仪[儀] sīyí; 典礼[禮]官 diǎnlǐguān. 3 [美语] 执[執]法官 zhífǎguān; 治安官 zhì'ānguān.

marshal[2] /ˈmɑːʃl/ *v* [-ll-; 美语 -l-] [T] 1 整理 zhěnglǐ; 安排 ānpái. 2 (按礼仪)引导[導] yǐndǎo.

marsupial /mɑːˈsuːpɪəl/ *adj*, *n* [C] 有袋动[動]物的 yǒu dài dòngwù de; 有袋动物(如袋鼠等) yǒu dài dòngwù.

martial /ˈmɑːʃl/ *adj* [正式用语] 军事的 jūnshìde; 战[戰]争的 zhànzhēngde. **martial** ˈ**arts** *n* [pl] 武术[術](如柔道、空手道) wǔshù. ˌ**martial** ˈ**law** *n* [U] 军事管制 jūnshì guǎnzhì.

martin /ˈmɑːtɪn; *US* -tn/ *n* [C] 圣[聖]马丁鸟 shèngmǎdīng niǎo; 燕科小鸟 yànkē xiǎoniǎo.

martyr /ˈmɑːtə(r)/ *n* [C] 烈士 lièshì; 殉道者 xùndàozhě. **martyr** *v* [T] 使殉难[難] shǐ xùnnàn; 处[處]死(坚持某种信仰者) chǔsǐ. **martyrdom** /ˈmɑːtədəm/ *n* [U, C] 殉难 xùnnàn; 殉道 xùndào.

marvel /ˈmɑːvl/ *n* [C] 令人惊[驚]奇的事 lìng rén jīngqí de shì: *the* ～*s of modern science* 现代科学的奇迹. **marvel** *v* [-ll-; 美语 -l-] [T] *at* [正式用语] 对[對]…感到惊讶 duì…gǎndào jīngyà. **marvellous** (美语 -**velous**) /ˈmɑːvələs/ *adj* 极[極]好的 jíhǎode; 绝妙的 juémiàode. **marvellously** (美语 -**velously**) *adv*.

Marxism /ˈmɑːksɪzəm/ *n* [U] 马克思主义[義] Mǎkèsī zhǔyì. **Marxist** /-sɪst/ *n* [C], *adj*.

marzipan /ˈmɑːzɪpæn/ *n* [U] 杏仁蛋白糊 xìngrén dànbáihú.

mascara /mæˈskɑːrə; *US* -ˈskærə/ *n* [U] 染睫毛膏 rǎn jiémáo gāo.

mascot /ˈmæskət, -skɒt/ *n* [C] 吉祥的人(或动物、东西) jíxiángde rén.

masculine /ˈmæskjʊlɪn/ *adj* 1 男性的 nánxìngde. 2 阳[陽]性的 yángxìngde. **masculinity** /ˌmæskjʊˈlɪnətɪ/ *n* [U] 男性 nánxìng; 阳性 yángxìng.

mash /mæʃ/ *v* [T] 把…捣成糊状[狀] bǎ…dǎochéng húzhuàng. **mash** *n* [U] [非正式用语] 土豆泥 tǔdòuní.

mask /mɑːsk; *US* mæsk/ *n* [C] 面具 miànjù; 面罩 miànzhào: [喻] *His behaviour is really a* ～ *for his shyness*. 他的行为实际上是用来遮掩他腼腆的性格的. **mask** *v* [T] 用面具遮住(脸) yòng miànjù zhēzhù; 遮盖 zhēgài. **masked** *adj* 戴面具的 dài miànjù de; 戴面罩的 dài miànzhào de: ～*ed robbers* 戴面具的盗贼.

masochism /ˈmæsəkɪzəm/ *n* [U] 受虐狂 shòunüèkuáng; 性受虐狂 xìngshòunüèkuáng. **masochist** /-kɪst/ *n* [C]. **masochistic** /ˌmæsəˈkɪstɪk/ *adj*.

mason /ˈmeɪsn/ *n* [C] 石工 shígōng; 石匠 shíjiàng; 泥瓦工 níwǎgōng. **masonry** /-sənrɪ/ *n* [U] 砖[磚]石建筑[築] zhuānshí jiànzhù; 水泥砖石结构[構] shuǐní zhuānshí jiégòu.

masquerade /ˌmɑːskəˈreɪd; *US* ˌmæsk-/ *v* [I] (*as*) 乔[喬]装[裝] qiáozhuāng; 伪[僞]装 wěizhuāng: ～ *as a police officer* 假冒警官. **masquerade** *n* [C] 伪装 wěizhuāng; 假扮 jiǎbàn.

Mass (亦作 mass) /mæs/ *n* [U,C] (天主教的)弥〔彌〕撒 mísa.

mass /mæs/ *n* 1 [C] 块〔塊〕kuài, 堆 duī; 团〔團〕tuán: *a* ~ *of earth* 土块. 2 [C] 大量 dàliàng; 大宗 dàzōng: *a* ~ *of tourists* 大批游客. 3 [U] [物理] (物体的)质〔質〕量 zhìliàng. 4 **the masses** [pl] 群众〔衆〕qúnzhòng; 民众 mínzhòng. **mass** *v* [I,T] (使)集合 jíhé: *The general ~ed his troops for the attack.* 将军集合部队准备进攻. **the ˌmass ˈmedia** *n* [pl] 大众传〔傳〕播媒介 dàzhòng chuánbō méijiè; 大众传播工具 dàzhòng chuánbō gōngjù. **ˌmass-proˈduce** *v* [T] 大量生产〔產〕dàliàng shēngchǎn. **ˌmass proˈduction** *n* [U].

massacre /ˈmæsəkə(r)/ *n* [C] 大屠杀〔殺〕dàtúshā. **massacre** *v* [T] 大规模屠杀 dà guīmó túshā.

massage /ˈmæsɑːʒ; *US* məˈsɑːʒ/ *n* [C,U] 按摩 ànmó; 推拿 tuīná. **massage** *v* [T] 给…按摩 gěi…ànmó; 给…推拿 gěi…tuīná.

masseur /mæˈsɜː(r)/ *n* [C] (*fem* **masseuse** /mæˈsɜːz/) 按摩师〔師〕ànmóshī.

massive /ˈmæsɪv/ *adj* 大而重的 dà ér zhòng de; 巨大的 jùdàde. **massively** *adv*.

mast /mɑːst; *US* mæst/ *n* [C] 1 船桅 chuánwéi; 桅杆 wéigān; 樯〔檣〕qiáng. 2 天线〔綫〕塔 tiānxiàntǎ.

master[1] /ˈmɑːstə(r); *US* ˈmæs-/ *n* [C] 1 主人 zhǔrén; 雇主 gùzhǔ. 2 男户主 nán hùzhǔ. 3 船长〔長〕chuánzhǎng. 4 (狗、马等的)男主人 nán zhǔrén. 5 [尤用于英国英语]男教师〔師〕nán jiàoshī. 6 **Master** 硕士 shuòshì: *a ˌM~ of ˈArts/ˈSciences* 文学硕士; 理学硕士. 7 大师 dàshī. 8 *of* [正式用语]专〔專〕家 zhuānjiā; 行家 hángjiā. 9 原版影片 yuánbǎn yǐngpiàn; 原版磁带〔帶〕yuánbǎn cídài: *the* ~ *copy* 原版拷贝. **master** *adj* 1 技术〔術〕熟练〔練〕的 jìshù shúliàn de; 精通的 jīngtōngde: *a* ~ *carpenter* 手艺高明的木工. 2 总〔總〕体〔體〕的 zǒngtǐde: *a* ~ *plan* 总体规划. **ˈmastermind** *v* [T] 策划〔劃〕cèhuà; 操纵〔縱〕cāozòng. **ˈmastermind** *n* [C] 才子 cáizǐ; 决策者 juécèzhě. **ˌMaster of ˈCeremonies** *n* [C] 司仪〔儀〕sīyí; 典礼〔禮〕官 diǎnlǐguān. **ˈmasterpiece** *n* [C] 杰〔傑〕作 jiézuò; 名著 míngzhù.

master[2] /ˈmɑːstə(r); *US* ˈmæs-/ *v* [T] 1 控制 kòngzhì; 制服 zhìfú. 2 掌握 zhǎngwò; 精通 jīngtōng: ~ *a foreign language* 掌握一门外语.

masterful /ˈmɑːstəfl; *US* ˈmæs-/ *adj* 专〔專〕横的 zhuānhèngde; 能控制别人的 néng kòngzhì biérén de. **masterfully** /-fəlɪ/ *adv*.

masterly /ˈmɑːstəlɪ; *US* ˈmæs-/ *adj* 熟练〔練〕的 shúliànde; 巧妙的 qiǎomiàode.

mastery /ˈmɑːstərɪ/ *n* [U] 1 熟练〔練〕shúliàn; 精通 jīngtōng. 2 控制 kòngzhì.

masturbate /ˈmæstəbeɪt/ *v* [I] 手淫 shǒuyín. **masturbation** /ˌmæstəˈbeɪʃn/ *n* [U].

mat[1] /mæt/ *n* [C] 1 席〔蓆〕子 xízi; 垫〔墊〕子 diànzi. 2 (花瓶、盘等的)小垫 xiǎodiàn. **mat** *v* [-tt-] [I,T] (使)缠〔纏〕结 chánjié: *~ted hair* 缠结在一起的头发.

mat[2] = MATT.

matador /ˈmætədɔː(r)/ *n* [C] 斗〔鬥〕牛士 dòuniúshì.

match[1] /mætʃ/ *n* [C] 火柴 huǒchái. **ˈmatchbox** *n* [C] 火柴盒 huǒcháihé.

match[2] /mætʃ/ *n* 1 [C] 比赛 bǐsài; 竞〔競〕赛 jìngsài: *a ˈfootball* ~ 足球比赛. 2 [sing] 对〔對〕手 duìshǒu; 敌〔敵〕手 díshǒu: *He's no* ~ *for her at tennis.* 在网球上他不是她的对手. 3 [C] 婚姻 hūnyīn: *They made a good* ~. 他们成就了美满的婚姻. 4 [sing] 相配的物 xiāngpèi de wù: *The carpets and curtains are a perfect* ~. 地毯和窗帘很匹配. **match** *v* 1 [I,T] 相配 xiāngpèi: *The carpets and the curtains* ~ *perfectly.* 地毯和窗帘十分相称. 2 [T] (a) 比得上 bǐ dé shàng. (b) 使相当〔當〕shǐ xiāngdāng; 使相等 shǐ xiāngděng. **matchless** *adj* [正式用语] 无〔無〕比的 wúbǐde; 无双〔雙〕的 wúshuāngde. **ˈmatchmaker** *n* [C] 媒人 méirén.

mate /meɪt/ *n* [C] 1 朋友 péngyǒu; 伙伴 huǒbàn; 同事 tóngshì: *He's gone out with his ~s.* 他和朋友出去了. *a flat-*~ 同住一单元的人. 2 [英俚](用作对男子的称呼)老兄 lǎoxiōng. 3 (商船的)大副 dàfù. 4 兽〔獸〕的配偶 shòu de pèi'ǒu. 5 助手 zhùshǒu: *a plumber's* ~ 管子工的助手. **mate** *v* [I,T] (*with*) (鸟、兽)(使)交配 jiāopèi.

material /məˈtɪərɪəl/ *n* 1 [C,U] 材料 cáiliào; 原料 yuánliào. 2 [U,C] 布料 bùliào. 3 [U] 资料 zīliào: ~ *for a newspaper article* 写报纸文章的素材. **material** *adj* 1 物质〔質〕的 wùzhìde. 2 肉体〔體〕的 ròutǐde; 身体需要的 shēntǐ xūyào de: ~ *comforts* 身体的享乐. 3 [尤用于法律] 重要的 zhòngyàode: ~ *evidence* 重要证据.

materialism /məˈtɪərɪəlɪzəm/ *n* [U] 1 唯物主义〔義〕wéiwùzhǔyì; 唯物论〔論〕wéiwùlùn. 2 [常作贬]实〔實〕利主义 shílì zhǔyì; 物质〔質〕主义 wùzhì zhǔyì. **materialist** /-lɪst/ *n* [C]. **materialistic** /məˌtɪərɪəˈlɪstɪk/ *adj*.

materialize /məˈtɪərɪəlaɪz/ *v* [I] 1 成为〔爲〕事实〔實〕chéngwéi shìshí; 实现 shíxiàn. 2 具体〔體〕化 jùtǐhuà; 实体化 shítǐhuà.

maternal /məˈtɜːnl/ *adj* 1 母亲〔親〕的 mǔqīnde; 似母亲的 sìmǔqīnde. 2 母系的 mǔxìde; 母方的 mǔfāngde: *a* ~ *grandfather* 外祖

M

父.

maternity /məˈtɜːnətɪ/ *n* [U] 母亲〔親〕身份 mǔqīn shēnfen; 母性 mǔxìng. **maternity** *adj* 产〔產〕妇〔婦〕的 chǎnfùde; 孕妇的 yùnfùde: *a ~ hospital* 产科医院. *~ leave* 产假.

math /mæθ/ *n* [美语][用 sing v] short for MATHEMATICS.

mathematics /ˌmæθəˈmætɪks/ *n* [用 sing v] 数〔數〕学〔學〕 shùxué. **mathematical** /-ɪkl/ *adj*. **mathematically** /-klɪ/ *adv*. **mathematician** /ˌmæθəməˈtɪʃn/ *n* [C] 数学家 shùxuéjiā.

maths /mæθs/ *n* [英国英语][用 sing v] short for MATHEMATICS.

matinée (美语亦作 **matinee**) /ˈmætneɪ, ˈmætɪneɪ; *US* ˌmætnˈeɪ/ *n* [C] (电影院、剧院的)下午场〔場〕 xiàwǔchǎng.

matriarch /ˈmeɪtrɪɑːk/ *n* [C] 女家长〔長〕 nǚ jiāzhǎng; 女族长 nǚ zúzhǎng. **matriarchal** /ˌmeɪtrɪˈɑːkl/ *adj*.

matriculate /məˈtrɪkjʊleɪt/ *v* [I] 被录〔錄〕取入学〔學〕 bèi lùqǔ rùxué; 注册入学 zhùcè rùxué. **matriculation** /məˌtrɪkjʊˈleɪʃn/ *n* [U].

matrimony /ˈmætrɪmənɪ; *US* -məʊnɪ/ *n* [U] [正式用语]婚姻 hūnyīn; 婚姻生活 hūnyīn shēnghuó. **matrimonial** /ˌmætrɪˈməʊnɪəl/ *adj*.

matron /ˈmeɪtrən/ *n* [C] **1** (旧时)护〔護〕士长〔長〕 hùshìzhǎng. **2** 女总〔總〕管 nǚ zǒngguǎn; 女舍监〔監〕 nǚ shèjiān. **3** (已婚的、仪表庄重的)中年妇〔婦〕女 zhōngnián fùnǚ. **matronly** *adj* 似中年妇女的 sì zhōngnián fùnǚ de; 庄〔莊〕重的 zhuāngzhòngde.

matt (亦作 **mat**, 美语亦作 **matte**) /mæt/ *adj* (表面)粗糙的 cūcāode; 无〔無〕光泽〔澤〕的 wú guāngzé de.

matter[1] /ˈmætə(r)/ *n* **1** [C] 事情 shìqing; 问题 wèntí: *an important business ~* 重要的商业问题. **2** [U] 物质〔質〕 wùzhì: *The universe is composed of ~.* 宇宙是由物质组成的. **3** [U] 材料 cáiliào; 物品 wùpǐn: *reading ~* 读物. **4** [习语] **as a matter of fact** (用于加强语气)事实〔實〕上 shìshí shàng; 其实 qíshí. **for ˈthat matter** 就那件事而论〔論〕 jiù nàjiànshì ér lùn. **(as) a matter of ˈcourse** (作为)理所当〔當〕然的事 lǐ suǒ dāngrán de shì; (按照)常规 chángguī. **(be) the matter (with sb/sth)** [非正式用语](不幸、痛苦等的)原因 yuányīn; 理由 lǐyóu: *What's the ~ with her?* 她怎么啦? *Is anything the ~?* 怎么啦? **a matter of ˈhours, ˈminutes, etc** 不多于 bù duōyú; 至多 zhìduō. **a matter of oˈpinion** 看法不同的问题 kànfǎ bùtóng de wèntí. **(be) a matter of (doing) sth** 取决于某事的问题(或情况) qǔjué yú mǒushì de wèntí: *Teaching isn't just a ~ of good communication.* 教学的好坏不仅仅取决于有良好的思想沟通. **no matter who, what, etc** 无〔無〕论〔論〕谁 wúlùn shuí; 无论什么〔麼〕 wúlùn shénme: *Don't believe him, no ~ what he says.* 无论他说什么, 都别相信. **ˌmatter-of-ˈfact** *adj* 不动〔動〕情感的 búdòng qínggǎn de; 不加想像的 bù jiā xiǎngxiàng de.

matter[2] /ˈmætə(r)/ *v* [I] 关〔關〕系〔係〕重要 guānxì zhòngyào: *It doesn't ~.* 没关系.

matting /ˈmætɪŋ/ *n* [U] 粗糙编织〔織〕物 cūcāo biānzhīwù; 地席〔蓆〕 dìxí.

mattress /ˈmætrɪs/ *n* [C] 床〔牀〕垫〔墊〕 chuángdiàn.

mature /məˈtjʊə(r); *US* -ˈtʊər/ *adj* **1** 成熟的 chéngshúde. **2** 深思熟虑〔慮〕的 shēnsī shúlǜ de. **3** (葡萄酒或干酪)成熟的 chéngshúde. **mature** *v* [I, T] (使)成熟 chéngshú. **maturity** *n* [U].

maul /mɔːl/ *v* [T] 伤〔傷〕害 shānghài; 虐打 nüèdǎ: *~ed by a lion* 受到狮子伤害.

mausoleum /ˌmɔːsəˈliːəm/ *n* [C] 陵墓 língmù.

mauve /məʊv/ *adj*, *n* [U] 淡紫色的 dànzǐsède; 淡紫色 dànzǐsè.

maxim /ˈmæksɪm/ *n* [C] 格言 géyán; 箴言 zhēnyán.

maximize /ˈmæksɪmaɪz/ *v* [T] 使增加到最大限度 shǐ zēngjiā dào zuìdà xiàndù.

maximum /ˈmæksɪməm/ *n* [C, 常作 sing] [*pl* **maxima** /-mə/] 最大量 zuìdàliàng; 最大限度 zuìdà xiàndù; 极〔極〕限 jíxiàn. **maximum** *adj* 最大的 zuìdàde; 最大限度的 zuìdà xiàndù de: *the ~ load a lorry can carry* 卡车的最大载重量. *make ~ use of the room* 最大限度利用这个房间.

May /meɪ/ *n* [U, C] 五月 wǔyuè.

may /meɪ/ *modal v* [否定式 **may not**, 罕, 缩略式 **mayn't** /meɪnt/; *pt* **might** /maɪt/, 否定式 **might not**, 罕, 缩略式 **mightn't** /ˈmaɪtnt/] **1** (用以表示可能): *This coat ~ be Sarah's.* 这件大衣可能是萨拉的. *He ~ have forgotten to come.* 他可能忘记来了. **2** [正式用语](用以表示允许): *M~ I sit down?* 我可以坐下吗? **3** (用以表示希望): *M~ you both be very happy!* 祝你们二位幸福!

maybe /ˈmeɪbiː/ *adv* 大概 dàgài; 或许 huòxǔ.

mayonnaise /ˌmeɪəˈneɪz; *US* ˈmeɪəneɪz/ *n* [U] (用蛋黄、油、醋等制成的)蛋黄酱〔醬〕 dànhuángjiàng.

mayor /meə(r); *US* ˈmeɪər/ *n* [C] 市长〔長〕 shìzhǎng. **mayoress** /meəˈres; *US* ˈmeɪərəs/

n [C] 1 女市长 nǚ shìzhǎng. 2 市长夫人 shìzhǎng fūrén.

maze /meɪz/ *n* [C] 迷宫 mígōng.

MBA /ˌem biː ˈeɪ/ *abbr* Master of Business Administration 工商管理学硕士 gōngshāng guǎnlǐ xué shuòshì.

MC /ˌem ˈsiː/ *abbr* 1 Master of Ceremonies 司仪〔儀〕sīyí；典礼〔禮〕官 diǎnlǐguān. 2 [美语] Member of Congress 国〔國〕会〔會〕议〔議〕员 guóhuì yìyuán.

m-commerce /emˈkɒmɜːs/ *n* [U] 移动〔動〕(电子)商务〔務〕yídòng shāngwù.

MD /ˌem ˈdiː/ *abbr* Doctor of Medicine 医〔醫〕学〔學〕博士 yīxué bóshì.

me /miː/ *pron* (用作动词或介词的宾语)我 wǒ: *Don't hit* ～. 别打我. *Give it to* ～. 给我.

meadow /ˈmedəʊ/ *n* [C, U] 草地 cǎodì；牧场〔場〕mùchǎng.

meagre (美语 **meager**) /ˈmiːgə(r)/ *adj* 少量的 shǎoliàngde；不足的 bùzúde；贫乏的 pínfáde: *a* ～ *income* 微薄的收入. **meagrely** *adv*. **meagreness** *n* [U].

meal[1] /miːl/ *n* [C] 1 一餐 yìcān；一顿(饭) yídùn. 2 饭食 fànshí.

meal[2] /miːl/ *n* [U] 粗粉 cūfěn: ˈ*oat* ～ 燕麦〔麥〕片.

mean[1] /miːn/ *v* [*pt, pp* ～t /ment/] [T] 1 意指 yìzhǐ；意谓 yìwèi: *What does this word* ～? 这个词是什么意思? 2 (符号、标志)象征〔徵〕xiàngzhēng: *A green light* ～*s* '*go*'. 绿灯表示"通行". 3 造成(某种结果)zàochéng: *This will* ～ *more work*. 这将意味着有更多的工作. 4 意欲 yìyù；打算 dǎsuàn: *What do you* ～ *by coming so late?* 你干什么这么晚才来? *Sorry, I* ～*t to tell you earlier*. 对不起，我是要早点告诉你的. *Don't laugh! I* ～ *it!* 别笑! 我真是这个意思! 5 *to* 对〔對〕…重要 duì …zhòngyào: *Your friendship* ～*s a lot to me*. 你的友谊对我很重要. 6 [习语] **be meant to** 必须 bìxū；应〔應〕该 yīnggāi: *You're* ～*t to pay before you come in*. 你进来之前得先付款. **mean ˈbusiness** 是认〔認〕真的 shì rènzhēn de. **ˈmean well** 出于好心 chū yú hǎoxīn；怀〔懷〕有好意 huáiyǒu hǎoyì. **meaning** *n* 1 [U, C] 意义〔義〕yìyì；意思 yìsi. 2 [U] 目的 mùdì: *My life has lost all* ～*ing*. 我的生活已毫无目的. **meaningful** *adj* 富有意义的 fùyǒu yìyì de；意味深长〔長〕的 yìwèi shēncháng de. **meaningless** *adj* 无〔無〕意义的 wú yìyì de.

mean[2] /miːn/ *adj* 1 吝啬〔嗇〕的 lìnsède；自私的 zìsīde. 2 不善良的 bú shànliángde. 3 [尤用于美语]脾气〔氣〕坏〔壞〕的 píqì huài de；恶〔惡〕毒的 èdúde. 4 [习语] **no mean** [褒](表演者等)很好的 hěnhǎode: *He's no mean tennis player*. 他是个网球高手. **meanness** *n* [U].

mean[3] /miːn/ *n* [C] [数学]平均数〔數〕píngjūnshù；平均值 píngjūnzhí；中数 zhōngshù. **mean** *adj*.

meander /mɪˈændə(r)/ *v* [I] 1 (河川)蜿蜒而流 wānyán ér liú. 2 漫步 mànbù；闲〔閒〕荡〔蕩〕xiándàng.

means[1] /miːnz/ *n* [用 sing 或 pl v] 1 方法 fāngfǎ；手段 shǒuduàn: *find a* ～ *of improving the standard of education* 找到改进教育标准的方法. 2 [习语] **by ˈall means** [正式用语]当〔當〕然可以 dāngrán kěyǐ. **by means of sth** [正式用语] 用某办〔辦〕法 yòng mǒu bànfǎ. **by ˈno means** [正式用语]绝不 juébù.

means[2] /miːnz/ *n* [pl] 金钱〔錢〕jīnqián；财富 cáifù: *a man of* ～ 富有的人. **ˈmeans test** *n* [C] (对申请补助者所作的)家庭经〔經〕济〔濟〕情况调查 jiātíng jīngjì qíngkuàng diàochá.

meant *pt, pp* of MEAN[1].

meantime /ˈmiːntaɪm/ *n* [习语] **in the ˈmeantime** 在此期间 zài cǐ qījiān；同时〔時〕tóngshí. **meantime** *adv* 其间 qíjiān；同时 tóngshí.

meanwhile /ˈmiːnwaɪl; *US* -hwaɪl/ *adv* 其间 qíjiān；同时〔時〕tóngshí.

measles /ˈmiːzlz/ *n* [用 sing v] 麻疹 mázhěn.

measure[1] /ˈmeʒə(r)/ *v* [T] 1 量 liáng；测量 cèliáng: ～ *a piece of wood* 测量一块木头. 2 为〔為〕(某长度、体积等) wéi: *The room* ～*s 5 metres across*. 这房间宽 5 米. 3 [短语动词] **measure sth out** 量取(一定量) liángqǔ. **measure up (to sth)** 符合标〔標〕准〔準〕fúhé biāozhǔn. **measured** *adj* 慎重的 shènzhòngde. **measurement** *n* 1 [U] 测量 cèliáng；量度 liángdù. 2 [C] 宽度 kuāndù；长〔長〕度 chángdù.

measure[2] /ˈmeʒə(r)/ *n* 1 (a) [U, C] 计量制度 jìliàng zhìdù；度量法 dùliàngfǎ. (b) [C] 计量单〔單〕位 jìliàng dānwèi: *The metre is a* ～ *of length*. 米是长度单位. 2 [C] 量具 liángjù；量器 liángqì: *a* ˈ*tape*-～ 卷尺；皮尺. 3 [sing] *of* (判断事物的)尺度 chǐdù；标〔標〕准〔準〕biāozhǔn: *a* ～ *of his anger* 他气愤的程度. 4 [sing] *of* [正式用语]程度 chéngdù；地步 dìbù: *a* ～ *of success* 一定程度的成功. 5 [C, 常作 pl] 措施 cuòshī；办〔辦〕法 bànfǎ: *The government is taking* ～*s to reduce crime*. 政府正采取措施遏止犯罪活动. 6 [习语] **ˌmade-to-ˈmeasure** 定做(衣服) dìngzuò. **get / take the measure of sb** 判断某人的性格(或能力) pànduàn mǒurén de xìnggé.

meat /miːt/ *n* 1 [U, C] (可食用的)肉 ròu. 2 [U] [喻]实〔實〕质〔質〕shízhì: *There's not much* ～ *in his argument*. 他的论点没有

什么实质性的东西. meaty *adj* [-ier, -iest].

mechanic /mɪˈkænɪk/ *n* [C] 技工 jìgōng; 机〔機〕械工 jīxiègōng; 机修工 jīxiūgōng. mechanical *adj* 1 机械的 jīxiède; 机械制〔製〕造的 jīxiè zhìzào de. 2 机械似的 jīxièshìde; 呆板的 dāibǎnde. mechanically /-klɪ/ *adv*.

mechanics /mɪˈkænɪks/ *n* 1 [用 sing v] 力学〔學〕 lìxué; 机〔機〕械学 jīxièxué. 2 the mechanics [pl] (a) 机件 jījiàn; 工作部件 gōngzuò bùjiàn. (b) [喻] (制作的)过〔過〕程 guòchéng.

mechanism /ˈmekənɪzəm/ *n* [C] 1 机〔機〕械装〔裝〕置 jīxiè zhuāngzhì. 2 [喻]手法 shǒufǎ; 技巧 jìqiǎo.

mechanize /ˈmekənaɪz/ *v* [T] 使机〔機〕械化 shǐ jīxièhuà. mechanization /ˌmekənaɪˈzeɪʃn; *US* -nɪˈz-/ *n* [U].

medal /ˈmedl/ *n* [C] 奖〔獎〕章 jiǎngzhāng; 勋〔勳〕章 xūnzhāng; 纪念章 jìniànzhāng. medallist (美语 medalist) /ˈmedəlɪst/ *n* [C] 奖章(或勋章)获〔獲〕得者 jiǎngzhāng huòdézhě.

medallion /mɪˈdælɪən/ *n* [C] 大奖〔獎〕章 dà jiǎngzhāng; 大纪念章 dà jìniànzhāng; (奖章形的)圆形装〔裝〕饰〔飾〕(物) yuánxíng zhuāngshì.

meddle /ˈmedl/ *v* [I] [贬]干涉 gānshè; 干预 gānyù. meddler *n* [C].

media /ˈmiːdɪə/ *n* the media [pl] 传〔傳〕播工具 chuánbō gōngjù; 传播媒介 chuánbō méijiè.

mediaeval = MEDIEVAL.

mediate /ˈmiːdɪeɪt/ *v* [I] (*between*) 调停 tiáotíng; 斡旋 wòxuán. mediation /ˌmiːdɪˈeɪʃn/ *n* [U]. mediator *n* [C].

medic /ˈmedɪk/ *n* [C] [非正式用语]医〔醫〕科学〔學〕生 yīkē xuéshēng; 医生 yīshēng.

medical /ˈmedɪkl/ *adj* 1 医〔醫〕学〔學〕的 yīxuéde; 医术〔術〕的 yīshùde. 2 内科的 nèikēde. medical *n* [C] 体〔體〕格检〔檢〕查 tǐgé jiǎnchá. medically /-klɪ/ *adv*.

Medicare /ˈmedɪkeə(r)/ *n* [U] (美国)老年保健医〔醫〕疗(制度) lǎonián bǎojiàn yīliáo.

medication /ˌmedɪˈkeɪʃn/ *n* [C,U] 药〔藥〕物 yàowù; 药品 yàopǐn; 药剂〔劑〕 yàojì.

medicinal /məˈdɪsɪnl/ *adj* 治疗〔療〕的 zhìliáode; 药〔藥〕用的 yàoyòngde.

medicine /ˈmedsn; *US* ˈmedɪsn/ *n* 1 [U] 医〔醫〕学〔學〕 yīxué; 医术〔術〕 yīshù; 内科学 nèikēxué. 2 [C,U] 药〔藥〕 yào; 内服药 nèifúyào. 3 [习语] a dose/taste of one's own medicine 以牙还〔還〕牙 yǐ yá huán yá. ˈmedicine-man *n* [C] = WITCH-DOCTOR (WITCH).

medieval (亦作 mediaeval) /ˌmedɪˈiːvl; *US* ˌmiːd- / *adj* 中世纪的 zhōngshìjìde; 中古的 zhōnggǔde.

mediocre /ˌmiːdɪˈəʊkə(r)/ *adj* 平庸的 píngyōngde; 平常的 píngchángde. mediocrity /ˌmiːdɪˈɒkrətɪ/ *n* [U,C] [*pl* -ies].

meditate /ˈmedɪteɪt/ *v* [I] (*on*) 深思 shēnsī; 沉思 chénsī. meditation /ˌmedɪˈteɪʃn/ *n* [U,C].

medium /ˈmiːdɪəm/ *n* [C] [*pl* media /ˈmiːdɪə/ 或 ~s; 用于下列第四义项 ~s] 1 媒介 méijiè: *an effective advertising* ~ 有效的广告宣传工具. 2 中间物 zhōngjiānwù. 3 借〔藉〕以生存之物 jiè yǐ shēngcún zhī wù; 环〔環〕境 huánjìng. 4 灵〔靈〕媒 língméi; 巫师〔師〕 wūshī. medium *adj* 中间的 zhōngjiānde; 中等的 zhōngděngde. ˈmedium wave *n* [U] [无线电]中波 zhōngbō.

meek /miːk/ *adj* 温顺的 wēnshùnde; 驯服的 xùnfúde. meekly *adv*. meekness *n* [U].

meet[1] /miːt/ *v* [*pt*, *pp* met /met/] 1 [I,T] 会〔會〕面 huìmiàn: *Let's* ~ *again soon*. 我们不久再相会. 2 [I,T] 结识〔識〕 jiéshí; 引见 yǐnjiàn. 3 [T] [喻] 经〔經〕历〔歷〕(不愉快的事) jīnglì: ~ *one's death* 死亡. 4 [T] 迎接 yíngjiē. 5 [I,T] 接触〔觸〕 jiēchù: *Their hands met*. 他们的手相触. 6 [T] 满足 mǎnzú; 符合 fúhé: ~ *sb's wishes* 满足某人的愿望. 7 [T] 支付 zhīfù. 8 [习语] meet sb half-ˈway 妥协〔協〕 tuǒxié. there is more to sb/sth than meets the eye 某人(或某事)比原想的复〔複〕杂〔雜〕(或有趣) mǒurén bǐ yuán xiǎng de fùzá. 9 [短语动词] meet with sb [美语]与〔與〕…会晤 yǔ…huìwù. meet with sth 经历(某事) jīnglì: ~ *with difficulties / an accident* 遇到困难; 遇到意外.

meet[2] /miːt/ *n* [C] 1 [尤用于英国英语](猎人和猎犬在猎狐前的)集合 jíhé. 2 [尤用于美语]运〔運〕动〔動〕会〔會〕yùndònghuì.

meeting /ˈmiːtɪŋ/ *n* [C] 集会〔會〕 jíhuì; 会议〔議〕 huìyì.

megabyte /ˈmegəbaɪt/ *n* [C] 兆字节〔節〕 zhàozìjié.

megaphone /ˈmegəfəʊn/ *n* [C] 扩〔擴〕音器 kuòyīnqì; 喇叭筒 lǎbatǒng.

megapixel /ˈmegəˌpɪksel/ *n* [C] 百万像素 bǎiwàn xiàngsù.

melancholy /ˈmelənkɒlɪ/ *n* [U] 忧〔憂〕郁〔鬱〕 yōuyù; 悲哀 bēi'āi. melancholic /ˌmelənˈkɒlɪk/ *adj*. melancholy *adj* 忧郁的 yōuyùde; 悲哀的 bēi'āide.

mellow /ˈmeləʊ/ *adj* 1 熟透的 shútòude. 2 (颜色)丰〔豐〕富的 fēngfùde. 3 成熟的 chéngshúde. mellow *v* [I,T] (使)成熟 chéngshú. mellowness *n* [U].

melodrama /ˈmelədrɑːmə/ *n* [C,U] 1 情节〔節〕剧〔劇〕 qíngjiéjù. 2 情节剧式的事件(或行为等) qíngjiéjù shì de shìjiàn. melodramatic /ˌmelədrəˈmætɪk/ *adj*. melodramatically /-klɪ/ *adv*.

M

melody /ˈmelədɪ/ *n* [C] [*pl* -ies] 曲调 qǔdiào；歌曲 gēqǔ. **melodic** /mɪˈlɒdɪk/ *adj* 曲调的 qǔdiàode. **melodious** /mɪˈləʊdɪəs/ *adj* 音调悦耳的 yīndiào yuè'ěr de；音调优〔優〕美的 yīndiào yōuměi de.

melon /ˈmelən/ *n* [C] 瓜 guā.

melt /melt/ *v* 1 [I,T] (使)融化 rónghuà；(使)熔化 rónghuà：*The sun ~ed the snow*. 太阳把雪融化了. 2 [I] (*away*) 融掉 róngdiào；消失 xiāoshī. 3 [I,T] (使人的感情)软化 ruǎnhuà. 4 [短语动词] **melt sth down** (重新)熔化 rónghuà；熔毁 rónghuǐ. ˈ**meltdown** *n* [C] (核反应堆核心遇热的)熔毁 rónghuǐ. ˈ**melting-pot** *n* [C] 1 大量多国〔國〕移民聚居的地方 dàliàng duōguó yímín jùjū de dìfang. 2 [习语] **in the melting-pot** 在改变〔變〕中 zài gǎibiàn zhōng.

member /ˈmembə(r)/ *n* [C] 1 (团体、组织等的)成员 chéngyuán；会〔會〕员 huìyuán. 2 [正式用法] 身体〔體〕的一部分 shēntǐde yíbùfen；肢体 zhītǐ. ˌ**Member of ˈParliament** *n* [C] 下院议〔議〕员 xiàyuàn yìyuán. **membership** *n* 1 [U] 会员资格 huìyuán zīgé；会员身份 huìyuán shēnfen. 2 [sing] [用 sing 或 pl v] 会员(或成员)人数〔數〕huìyuán rénshù.

membrane /ˈmembreɪn/ *n* [C,U] 膜 mó；薄膜 bómó.

memento /mɪˈmentəʊ/ *n* [C] [*pl* ~s 或 ~es] 纪念品 jìniànpǐn.

memo /ˈmeməʊ/ *n* [C] [*pl* ~s] [非正式用语] short for MEMORANDUM.

memoir /ˈmemwɑː(r)/ *n* **memoirs** [pl] 自传〔傳〕zìzhuàn；回忆〔憶〕录〔錄〕huíyìlù.

memorable /ˈmemərəbl/ *adj* 值得纪念的 zhídé jìniàn de；值得注意的 zhídé zhùyì de. **memorably** *adv*.

memorandum /ˌmeməˈrændəm/ *n* [C] [*pl* -da /-də/ 或 ~s] 非正式的商业〔業〕文件 fēizhèngshìde shāngyè wénjiàn.

memorial /məˈmɔːrɪəl/ *n* [C] 纪念物 jìniànwù；纪念碑 jìniànbēi.

memorize /ˈmeməraɪz/ *v* [T] 熟记 shújì；记住 jìzhù.

memory /ˈmemərɪ/ *n* [*pl* -ies] 1 [C,U] 记忆〔憶〕jìyì；记忆力 jìyìlì：*He's got a good ~*. 他的记忆力好. 2 [C] 记忆的事 jìyì de shì：*memories of childhood* 对童年的回忆. 3 [U] 记忆所及的时〔時〕期 jìyì suǒjí de shíqī；记忆的范〔範〕围〔圍〕jìyì de fànwéi. 4 [U] 对〔對〕死者的记忆 duì sǐzhě de jìyì. 5 [C] [计]存储器 cúnchǔqì. 6 [习语] **in memory of sb** 为〔爲〕纪念某人 wèi jìniàn mǒurén. ˈ**memory stick** *n* [C] 记忆〔憶〕棒 jìyìbàng.

men *pl* of MAN[1].

menace /ˈmenəs/ *n* 1 [C,U] 威胁〔脅〕wēixié；恐吓〔嚇〕kǒnghè. 2 [sing] [非正式用语]讨厌〔厭〕的人(或东西) tǎoyànde rén. **menace** *v* [T] 威胁 wēixié；恐吓 kǒnghè. **menacingly** *adv*.

menagerie /mɪˈnædʒərɪ/ *n* [C] 动〔動〕物园〔園〕dòngwùyuán；(笼中的)野生动物 yěshēng dòngwù.

mend /mend/ *v* 1 [T] 修理 xiūlǐ；修补〔補〕xiūbǔ. 2 [I] 恢复〔復〕健康 huīfù jiànkāng；痊愈〔癒〕quányù. 3 [习语] **mend one's ˈways** 改变〔變〕作风〔風〕gǎibiàn zuòfēng. **mend** *n* 1 [C] 修补过〔過〕的地方 xiūbǔ guò de dìfang；补丁 bǔdīng. 2 [习语] **on the ˈmend** [非正式用语]在康复中 zài kāngfù zhōng.

menial /ˈmiːnɪəl/ *adj* [常作贬](工作)不体〔體〕面的 bù tǐmiàn de；乏味的 fáwèide.

meningitis /ˌmenɪnˈdʒaɪtɪs/ *n* [U] 脑〔腦〕(脊)膜炎 nǎomóyán.

menopause /ˈmenəpɔːz/ *n* **the menopause** [sing] 绝经〔經〕(期) juéjīng.

menstruate /ˈmenstrʊeɪt/ *v* [I] [正式用语]行经〔經〕xíngjīng；月经来潮 yuèjīng láicháo. **menstrual** /-strʊəl/ *adj*. **menstruation** /ˌmenstrʊˈeɪʃn/ *n* [U].

mental /ˈmentl/ *adj* 1 精神的 jīngshénde；心理的 xīnlǐde：*a ~ illness* 精神病. *make a ~ note of sth* 把某事记在脑子里. 2 精神病的 jīngshénbìngde：*a ~ patient / hospital* 精神病人；精神病院. 3 [非正式用语,贬] 疯〔瘋〕的 fēngde. **mentally** /-təlɪ/ *adv* 精神上 jīngshén shàng；心理上 xīnlǐ shàng：*~ly ill* 精神上有病的.

mentality /menˈtælətɪ/ *n* [*pl* -ies] 1 [C] 思想方法 sīxiǎng fāngfǎ. 2 [U] [正式用语]智力 zhìlì；智能 zhìnéng.

menthol /ˈmenθɒl/ *n* [U] 薄荷醇 bòhechún.

mention /ˈmenʃn/ *v* 1 [T] 说到 shuōdào；写〔寫〕到 xiědào；提及 tíjí. 2 [习语] **don't ˈmention it** (用以表示不必道谢). **not to mention** 更不必说 gèng búbì shuō. **mention** *n* [C, U] 简述 jiǎnshù.

menu /ˈmenjuː/ *n* [C] 菜单〔單〕càidān.

MEP /ˌem iː ˈpiː/ *abbr* Member of the European Parliament 欧〔歐〕洲议〔議〕会〔會〕议员 Ouzhōu yìhuì yìyuán.

mercantile /ˈmɜːkəntaɪl; *US* -tiːl, -tɪl/ *adj* [正式用语]贸易的 màoyìde；商业〔業〕的 shāngyède；商人的 shāngrénde.

mercenary /ˈmɜːsɪnərɪ; *US* -nerɪ/ *adj* 惟利是图〔圖〕的 wéilì shì tú de；为〔爲〕钱〔錢〕的 wèiqiánde. **mercenary** *n* [C] [*pl* -ies] 外国〔國〕雇佣兵 wàiguó gùyōngbīng.

merchandise /ˈmɜːtʃəndaɪz/ *n* [U] [正式用语]商品 shāngpǐn；货物 huòwù.

merchant /ˈmɜːtʃənt/ *n* [C] 商人 shāngrén. **merchant** *adj* 商人的 shāngrénde；商业〔業〕的 shāngyède：*the ~ navy* 商船. ˌ**merchant ˈbank** *n* [C] 商业银行 shāngyè yínháng.

mercury /ˈmɜːkjʊrɪ/ *n* [U] 汞 gǒng；水银

M

shuǐyín. **mercurial** /mɜːˈkjʊrɪəl/ *adj* [正式用语](人或情绪)多变〔變〕的 duōbiànde;无〔無〕常的 wúchángde.

mercy /ˈmɜːsɪ/ *n* [*pl* -ies] 1 [U] 仁慈 réncí;宽恕 kuānshù. 2 [C] 幸运〔運〕xìngyùn. 3 [习语] **at the mercy of sb/sth** 任凭〔憑〕…的摆〔擺〕布 rènpíng…de bǎibù;受…的支配 shòu…de zhīpèi. **merciful** *adj* 仁慈的 réncíde;宽恕的 kuānshùde. **mercifully** *adv*. **merciless** *adj* 不宽容的 bù kuānróng de;不仁慈的 bù réncí de. **mercilessly** *adv*.

mere /mɪə(r)/ *adj* 仅〔僅〕仅的 jǐnjǐnde;仅只的 jǐnzhǐde:*She's a ~ child*. 她只不过是个孩子. **merely** *adv* 仅 jǐn;只 zhǐ;不过 bùguò.

merge /mɜːdʒ/ *v* 1 [I, T] (使)合并〔併〕hébìng;兼并 jiānbìng:*The two companies ~d*. 这两家公司合并了. 2 [I] (*into*) 渐渐消失 jiànjiàn xiāoshī;渐渐变〔變〕化 jiànjiàn biànhuà:*Day ~d into night*. 日尽夜至. **merger** *n* [C] (两公司)合并 hébìng;归〔歸〕并 guībìng.

meridian /məˈrɪdɪən/ *n* [C] 子午线〔綫〕zǐwǔxiàn;经〔經〕线 jīngxiàn.

meringue /məˈræŋ/ *n* 1 [U] (蛋白和糖混合烤成的)酥皮 sūpí. 2 [C] 蛋白酥皮饼 dànbái sūpíbǐng.

merit /ˈmerɪt/ *n* 1 [U] 值得称〔稱〕赞〔讚〕(或奖励)的品质〔質〕zhídé chēngzàn de pǐnzhì. 2 [C, 常作 pl] 值得称赞(或奖励)的事情(或行为等) zhídé chēngzàn de shìqing. **merit** *v* [T] [正式用语]值得 zhídé.

mermaid /ˈmɜːmeɪd/ *n* [C] (传说中的)美人鱼 měirényú.

merry /ˈmerɪ/ *adj* [-ier, -iest] 1 [旧]愉快的 yúkuàide;欢〔歡〕乐〔樂〕的 huānlède. 2 [非正式用语]微醉的 wēizuìde. **merrily** *adv*. **merriment** *n* [U]. ˈ**merry-go-round** *n* [C] = ROUNDABOUT 2.

mesh /meʃ/ *n* [C, U] 网〔網〕状〔狀〕物 wǎngzhuàngwù. **mesh** *v* [I] (齿轮)啮〔嚙〕合 nièhé:[喻] *Their opinions don't really ~*. 他们的意见并不协调一致.

mesmerize /ˈmezməraɪz/ *v* [T] 吸引住(某人) xīyǐn zhù.

mess[1] /mes/ *n* 1 [C, 常作 sing] 脏〔髒〕乱〔亂〕状〔狀〕态〔態〕zāng luàn zhuàngtài. 2 [sing] 困难〔難〕状态 kùnnan zhuàngtài;凌乱状态 língluàn zhuàngtài:*My life's in a ~*. 我的生活杂乱无章. **mess** *v* [非正式用语][短语动词] **mess about / around** (a) 胡闹 húnào. (b) 瞎忙 xiāmáng. **mess sb about/around** 粗鲁地对〔對〕待某人 cūlǔde duìdài mǒurén. **mess sth up** (a) 把…弄乱 bǎ…nòngluàn. (b) 弄糟 nòngzāo. **messy** *adj* [-ier, -iest].

mess[2] /mes/ *n* [C] (军人的)食堂 shítáng.

message /ˈmesɪdʒ/ *n* 1 [C] 消息 xiāoxi;信息 xìnxī. 2 [sing] 启〔啓〕示 qǐshì;教训 jiàoxùn;中心思想 zhōngxīn sīxiǎng. 3 [习语] **get the** ˈ**message** [非正式用语]明白 míngbai;领会〔會〕lǐnghuì. **messenger** /ˈmesɪndʒə(r)/ *n* [C] 送信者 sòngxìnzhě;报〔報〕信者 bàoxìnzhě.

messiah /mɪˈsaɪə/ *n* 1 [C] (常大写)弥〔彌〕赛亚〔亞〕(犹太人盼望的复国救主) Mísàiyà. 2 **the Messiah** [sing] 耶稣基督 Yēsū Jīdū.

met *pt, pp* of MEET[1].

metabolism /məˈtæbəlɪzəm/ *n* [U] 新陈代谢 xīn chén dàixiè. **metabolic** /ˌmetəˈbɒlɪk/ *adj*.

metal /ˈmetl/ *n* [C, U] 金属〔屬〕jīnshǔ. **metallic** /mɪˈtælɪk/ *adj*.

metaphor /ˈmetəfə(r)/ *n* [C, U] 隐〔隱〕喻(如 'She has a heart of stone.') yǐnyù. **metaphorical** /ˌmetəˈfɒrɪkl; *US* -ˈfɔːr- / *adj*. **metaphorically** / -klɪ / *adv*.

mete /miːt/ *v* [短语动词] **mete sth out (to sb)** [正式用语]给予(惩罚、奖励) jǐyǔ.

meteor /ˈmiːtɪə(r)/ *n* [C] 流星 liúxīng. **meteoric** /ˌmiːtɪˈɒrɪk; *US* -ˈɔːr-/ *adj* 1 流星的 liúxīngde. 2 [喻]迅速的 xùnsùde:*a ~ic rise to fame* 迅速出名. **meteorite** / ˈmiːtɪəraɪt / *n* [C]陨星 yǔnxīng.

meteorology /ˌmiːtɪəˈrɒlədʒɪ/ *n* [U] 气〔氣〕象学〔學〕qìxiàngxué. **meteorological** /-rəˈlɒdʒɪkl/ *adj*. **meteorologist** *n* [C] 气象学家 qìxiàngxuéjiā.

meter[1] /ˈmiːtə(r)/ *n* [C] 计 jì;仪〔儀〕yí;表〔錶〕biǎo:*a gas ~* 煤气表.

meter[2] [美语] = METRE.

method /ˈmeθəd/ *n* 1 [C] 方法 fāngfǎ;办〔辦〕法 bànfǎ. 2 [U] 条〔條〕理 tiáolǐ;秩序 zhìxù. **methodical** /mɪˈθɒdɪkl/ *adj* 有条理的 yǒu tiáolǐ de;井井有条的 jǐngjǐng yǒu tiáo de. **methodically** /-klɪ/ *adv*.

methodology /ˌmeθəˈdɒlədʒɪ/ *n* [C, U] [*pl* -ies] 一套方法 yítào fāngfǎ.

meticulous /mɪˈtɪkjʊləs/ *adj* 谨小慎微的 jǐn xiǎo shèn wēi de;极〔極〕注意细节〔節〕的 jí zhùyì xìjié de. **meticulously** *adv*.

metre[1] /ˈmiːtə(r)/ *n* [C] (公制长度单位)米 mǐ;公尺 gōngchǐ. **metric** /ˈmetrɪk/ *adj* (公制长度单位)米的 mǐde. **metrication** /ˌmetrɪˈkeɪʃn / *n* [U] 采〔採〕用公制 cǎiyòng gōngzhì;改为〔爲〕公制 gǎi wéi gōngzhì. **the** ˈ**metric system** *n* [sing] 十进〔進〕制 shíjìnzhì;公制 gōngzhì;米制 mǐzhì.

metre[2] /ˈmiːtə(r)/ *n* [C, U] (诗的)韵〔韻〕律 yùnlǜ;格律 gélǜ.

metropolis /məˈtrɒpəlɪs/ *n* [C] 大城市 dà chéngshì;首都 shǒudū;首府 shǒufǔ. **metro-**

M

politan /ˌmetrəˈpɒlɪtən/ *adj*.

mettle /ˈmetl/ *n* [U] 1 耐力 nàilì; 勇气〔氣〕yǒngqì. 2 [习语] put sb on his /her mettle 激励〔勵〕某人尽〔盡〕最大努力 jīlì mǒurén jìn zuìdà nǔlì.

mews /mjuːz/ *n* [C] [*pl* mews] (马厩改建的)住房 zhùfáng.

miaow /miːˈaʊ/ *n* [C] 喵(猫叫声) miāo. miaow *v* [I] 喵喵叫 miāomiāojiào.

mice *pl* of MOUSE.

mickey /ˈmɪkɪ/ *n* [习语] take the mickey (out of sb) [非正式用语]嘲笑 cháoxiào; 取笑 qǔxiào.

micro /ˈmaɪkrəʊ/ *n* [C] [*pl* ~s] [非正式用语]short for MICROCOMPUTER.

microbe /ˈmaɪkrəʊb/ *n* [C] 微生物 wēishēngwù; 细菌 xìjūn.

microchip /ˈmaɪkrəʊtʃɪp/ *n* [C] 集成电〔電〕路 jíchéng diànlù.

microcomputer /ˌmaɪkrəʊkəmˈpjuːtə(r)/ *n* [C] 微型(电子)计算机〔機〕wēixíng jìsuànjī.

microcosm /ˈmaɪkrəʊkɒzəm/ *n* [C] 微观〔觀〕世界 wēiguān shìjiè; 小天地 xiǎo tiāndì; 小宇宙 xiǎo yǔzhòu.

microfilm /ˈmaɪkrəʊfɪlm/ *n* [C, U] 缩微胶〔膠〕卷〔捲〕suōwēi jiāojuǎn. microfilm *v* [T] 用缩微胶卷拍摄〔攝〕yòng suōwēi jiāojuǎn pāishè.

microphone /ˈmaɪkrəfəʊn/ *n* [C] 麦〔麥〕克风〔風〕màikèfēng; 扩〔擴〕音器 kuòyīnqì; 话筒 huàtǒng.

microscope /ˈmaɪkrəskəʊp/ *n* [C] 显〔顯〕微镜 xiǎnwēijìng. microscopic /ˌmaɪkrəˈskɒpɪk/ *adj* 1 极〔極〕小的 jíxiǎode; 微小的 wēixiǎode. 2 显微镜的 xiǎnwēijìngde; 用显微镜的 yòng xiǎnwēijìngde.

microwave /ˈmaɪkrəweɪv/ (亦作 ˌmicrowave ˈoven) *n* [C] 微波炉〔爐〕wēibōlú.

mid- /mɪd/ *prefix* 在中间 zài zhōngjiān: ~-*morning* 上午的中段时间. ~-*air* 天空.

midday /ˌmɪdˈdeɪ/ *n* [U] 正午 zhèngwǔ; 中午 zhōngwǔ.

middle /ˈmɪdl/ *n* the middle [sing] 中间 zhōngjiān; 中部 zhōngbù; 中央 zhōngyāng. middle *adj* 中间的 zhōngjiānde; 中部的 zhōngbùde; 中央的 zhōngyāngde. middle ˈage *n* [U] 中年 zhōngnián. ˌmiddle-ˈaged *adj*. the ˌMiddle ˈAges *n* [pl] 中世纪 zhōngshìjì. the ˌmiddle ˈclass *n* [C] 中产〔產〕阶〔階〕级 zhōngchǎn jiējí. ˌmiddle-ˈclass *adj*. the ˌMiddle ˈEast *n* [sing] 中东 zhōngdōng. ˈmiddleman *n* [C] [*pl* -men /-men /] 经〔經〕纪人 jīngjìrén; 掮客 qiánkè. ˌmiddle-of-the-ˈroad *adj* 温和路线〔綫〕的 wēnhé lùxiàn de; 不极〔極〕端的 bù jíduān de.

middling /ˈmɪdlɪŋ/ *adj* (质量等)中等的 zhōngděngde; 普通的 pǔtōngde.

midge /mɪdʒ/ *n* [C] 蠓 měng; 摇蚊 yáowén.

midget /ˈmɪdʒɪt/ *n* [C] 侏儒 zhūrú; 矮人 ǎirén. midget *adj* 极〔極〕小的 jíxiǎode.

Midlands /ˈmɪdləndz/ *n* the Midlands [用 sing 或 pl v] 英格兰〔蘭〕中部地区〔區〕Yīnggélán zhōngbù dìqū.

midnight / ˈmɪdnaɪt / *n* [U] 午夜 wǔyè; 子夜 zǐyè; 夜半 yèbàn.

midriff /ˈmɪdrɪf/ *n* [C] 腹部 fùbù.

midst /mɪdst/ *n* [习语] in the midst of sth 在…之中 zài…zhī zhōng.

midway /ˌmɪdˈweɪ/ *adv, adj* 中途(的) zhōngtú: ~ *between Paris and Rome* 巴黎至罗马的中途.

midwife /ˈmɪdwaɪf/ *n* [C] [*pl* -wives /-waɪvz/] 助产〔產〕士 zhùchǎnshì; 接生婆 jiēshēngpó. midwifery /ˈmɪdwɪfərɪ; *US* -waɪf-/ *n* [U] 产科学〔學〕chǎnkēxué; 助产学 zhùchǎnxué; 助产士的职〔職〕业〔業〕zhùchǎnshìde zhíyè.

might[1] /maɪt/ *modal v* [否定式 might not, 缩略式 mightn't /ˈmaɪtnt /] 1 (表示可能): *He ~ be at home, but I doubt it*. 他也许在家,但是我说不准. 2 (用以表示许可): *M~ I make a suggestion?* 我可以提个建议吗? 3 (用于婉转的请求或吁请): *You ~ at least offer to help!* 你至少可以帮个忙吧!

might[2] *pt* of MAY.

might[3] /maɪt/ *n* [U] 力量 lìliang; 威力 wēilì; 权〔權〕力 quánlì. mighty *adj* [-ier, -iest] [正式用语] 1 强有力的 qiáng yǒulì de; 权力大的 quánlì dà de. 2 巨大的 jùdàde; 浩大的 hàodàde: *the ~y oceans* 汪洋大海. mightily *adv*. mighty *adv* [非正式用语,尤用于美语]非常 fēicháng; 很 hěn: *~y good* 很好.

migraine /ˈmiːgreɪn, ˈmaɪgreɪn/ *n* [U, C] 偏头〔頭〕痛 piāntóutòng.

migrate /maɪˈgreɪt; *US* ˈmaɪgreɪt/ *v* [I] (*from, to*) 1 移居 yíjū; 迁〔遷〕移 qiānyí. 2 (候鸟等的)迁徙 qiānxǐ; 移栖 yíqī. migrant /ˈmaɪgrənt/ *n* [C] 移居者 yíjūzhě; 迁移动〔動〕物 qiānyí dòngwù; 候鸟 hòuniǎo. migration /maɪˈgreɪʃn/ *n* [C, U]. migratory /ˈmaɪgrətrɪ, maɪˈgreɪtərɪ; *US* ˈmaɪgrətɔːrɪ/ *adj*.

mike /maɪk/ *n* [C] [非正式用语] short for MICROPHONE.

mild /maɪld/ *adj* 1 温和的 wēnhéde; 温柔的 wēnróude: *a ~ punishment / climate* 轻微的惩罚; 温和的气候. 2 (味道)淡的 dànde; 不强烈的 bù qiángliè de. mildly *adv*. mildness *n* [U].

mildew /ˈmɪldjuː; *US* -duː/ *n* [U] 霉 méi;

M

霉菌 méijūn.

mile /maɪl/ *n* [C] 英里 yīnglǐ. **mileage** /-ɪdʒ/ *n* 1 [C, U] 英里数〔數〕yīnglǐshù. 2 [U] [喻,非正式用语] 利益 lìyì; 好处〔處〕hǎochù: *The unions are getting a lot of ~ out of the manager's mistakes.* 联合会从经理的错误中得到许多好处. ˈ**milestone** *n* [C] 1 里程碑 lǐchéngbēi. 2 [喻] 历〔歷〕史上的重大事件 lìshǐ shàng de zhòngdà shìjiàn. **milometer** (亦作 **mileometer**) /maɪˈlɒmɪtə(r)/ *n* [C] 计程器 jìchéngqì.

militant /ˈmɪlɪtənt/ *n* [C], *adj* 好斗〔鬥〕(的) hàodòu; 好战〔戰〕(的) hàozhàn. **militancy** /-tənsɪ/ *n* [U].

military /ˈmɪlɪtrɪ; *US* -terɪ/ *adj* 军人的 jūnrénde; 军事的 jūnshìde. **the military** *n* [用 sing 或 pl v] 军人 jūnrén; 陆〔陸〕军 lùjūn; 武装〔裝〕部队〔隊〕wǔzhuāng bùduì.

militate /ˈmɪlɪteɪt/ *v* [I] *against* [正式用语] 发〔發〕生作用 fāshēng zuòyòng; 产〔產〕生影响〔響〕chǎnshēng yǐngxiǎng.

militia /mɪˈlɪʃə/ *n* [C, 亦作 sing, 用 pl v] 民兵组织〔織〕mínbīng zǔzhī; 全体〔體〕民兵 quántǐ mínbīng; (在紧急情况下召集的) 国〔國〕民军 guómínjūn.

milk /mɪlk/ *n* [U] 1 奶 nǎi; 牛奶 niúnǎi; 羊奶 yángnǎi. 2 (植物、果实的) 乳液 rǔyè: *coconut ~* 椰子汁. **milk** *v* 1 [I, T] 挤〔擠〕奶 jǐ nǎi. 2 [T] [喻] 榨取 zhàqǔ; 骗取 piànqǔ. ˈ**milkman** /-mən/ *n* [C] 送牛奶的人 sòng niúnǎi de rén. **milk shake** *n* [C] 奶昔 (牛奶和冰淇淋等混合后搅打至起泡的饮料) nǎixī. **milky** *adj* [-ier, -iest] 1 乳的 rǔde; 似乳的 sìrǔde. 2 含乳的 hánrǔde; 乳制〔製〕的 rǔzhìde. **the ˌMilky ˈWay** *n* [sing] = GALAXY 2.

M

mill[1] /mɪl/ *n* [C] 1 磨粉机〔機〕mòfěnjī; 磨粉厂〔廠〕mòfěnchǎng. 2 磨碎机 mòsuìjī; 碾磨机 niǎnmòjī: *a ˈpepper-~* 胡椒研磨器. 3 工厂〔廠〕gōngchǎng: *a ˈpaper-~* 造纸厂. 4 [习语] **put sb/go through the ˈmill** 经〔經〕受严〔嚴〕格的训练〔練〕jīngshòu yángé de xùnliàn; 经受磨炼〔煉〕jīngshòu móliàn. **miller** *n* [C] 磨坊主 mòfángzhǔ; 磨粉厂主 mòfěnchǎngzhǔ. ˈ**millstone** *n* [C] 1 磨石 mòshí; 磨盘〔盤〕mòpán. 2 [喻] 重负 zhòngfù; 重担 zhòngdàn: *His debts are a ~stone round his neck.* 他欠的债像是在脖子上套着个磨盘.

mill[2] /mɪl/ *v* 1 [T] 碾碎 niǎnsuì; 磨细 mòxì. 2 [短语动词] **mill about / around** 绕〔繞〕圈子转〔轉〕rào quānzi zhuàn; 乱〔亂〕转 luànzhuàn.

millennium /mɪˈlenɪəm/ *n* [*pl* **-nia** /-nɪə/ 或 **~s**] 1 [C] 一千年 yìqiānnián; 千年间 qiānniánjiān. 2 **the millennium** [sing] 美满时〔時〕期 měimǎn shíqī; 太平盛世 tàipíng shèngshì.

millepede (亦作 **millipede**) /ˈmɪlɪpiːd/ *n* [C] 马陆〔陸〕mǎlù; 千足虫 qiānzúchóng.

millet /ˈmɪlɪt/ *n* [U] 1 黍 shǔ; 稷 jì. 2 小米 xiǎomǐ.

milli- /ˈmɪlɪ/ *prefix* (公制的) 千分之一 qiānfēn zhī yī: ˈ*~metre* 毫米.

milliner /ˈmɪlɪnə(r)/ *n* [C] 女帽商 nǚmàoshāng; 妇〔婦〕女服饰商 fùnǚ fúshìshāng. **millinery** *n* [U] 女帽 nǚmào; 女帽业〔業〕nǚmàoyè.

million /ˈmɪljən/ *pron, adj, n* [C] 1 百万〔萬〕bǎiwàn. 2 [非正式用语] 许多 xǔduō: *~s of things to do* 有许多事情要做. **millionaire** /ˌmɪljəˈneə(r)/ *n* [C] (*fem* **millionairess** /ˌmɪljəˈneəres/) 百万富翁 bǎiwàn fùwēng; 大富翁 dà fùwēng. **millionth** *pron, adj* 第一百万(的) dìyìbǎiwàn. **millionth** *pron, n* [C] 百万分之一 bǎiwànfēn zhī yī.

millipede = MILLEPEDE.

milometer ⇨ MILE.

mime /maɪm/ *n* 1 [U] 哑〔啞〕剧〔劇〕yǎjù. 2 [C] 哑剧演员 yǎjù yǎnyuán. **mime** *v* [I, T] 以哑剧的形式表演 yǐ yǎjùde xíngshì biǎoyǎn.

mimic /ˈmɪmɪk/ *v* [*pt, pp* **~ked**] [T] 1 模仿…以取笑 mófǎng…yǐ qǔxiào. 2 (物) 酷似 kùsì. **mimic** *n* [C] 善于模仿的人 shànyú mófǎng de rén. **mimicry** *n* [U] 模仿 mófǎng; 酷似 kùsì.

minaret /ˌmɪnəˈret/ *n* [C] (清真寺旁的) 尖塔 jiāntǎ.

mince /mɪns/ *v* 1 [T] 切碎 qiēsuì; 剁碎 duòsuì. 2 [习语] **not mince one's ˈwords** 直言不讳〔諱〕zhíyán bú huì. **mince** *n* [U] 切碎的肉 qiēsuìde ròu. ˈ**mincemeat** *n* [U] 1 百果馅 bǎiguǒxiàn. 2 [习语] **make mincemeat of sb** 彻〔徹〕底击〔擊〕败 chèdǐ jībài; 彻底驳倒 chèdǐ bódǎo.

mind[1] /maɪnd/ *n* 1 [U] 智力 zhìlì; 悟性 wùxing: *The idea never entered my ~.* 我从未有过这样的主意. *She has a brilliant ~.* 她头脑聪明. 2 [U] 记忆〔憶〕jìyì: *My ~ has gone blank!* 我的脑子里成了一片空白. 3 [C] 有才智的人 yǒu cáizhì de rén: *one of the greatest ~s this century* 本世纪才智出众的人之一. 4 [习语] **be in two ˈminds about sth** 犹〔猶〕豫不决 yóuyù bùjué; 三心二意 sān xīn èr yì. **be / take a load / weight off sb's mind** 使…如释〔釋〕重负 shǐ…rú shì zhòngfù. **be on one's mind, have sth on one's mind** (使某人) 为〔爲〕…担〔擔〕忧〔憂〕wèi…dānyōu. **be ˌout of one's mind** [非正式用语] 发〔發〕疯〔瘋〕fāfēng. **bear/keep sth in ˈmind** 记住某事 jìzhù mǒushì. **bring / call sth to mind** 想起某事 xiǎngqǐ mǒushì. **have a (good) mind to do sth** [非正式用语] 想做某事 xiǎngzuò mǒushì. **in one's mind's ˈeye** 在想像中 zài xiǎngxiàng zhōng. **make up one's mind** 决定 juédìng; 决心 juéxīn. **put/set/ turn one's mind**

to sth 专〔專〕心于某事 zhuānxīn yú mǒushì. **take one's mind off sth** 转〔轉〕移对〔對〕某事的注意 zhuǎnyí duì mǒushì de zhùyì. **to ˈmy mind** 照我的想法 zhào wǒde xiǎngfǎ.

mind[2] /maɪnd/ *v* **1** [I,T] 介意 jièyì;反对〔對〕fǎnduì: *Do you ~ if I open the window?* 我打开窗户你不反对吧? **2** [T] 照看 zhàokàn: *~ the baby* 照料婴儿. **3** [I,T] 留心 liúxīn;留神 liúshén: *M~ you don't fall!* 小心,别摔跤. **4** [习语] **ˌmind one's ˌown ˈbusiness** 管自己的事 guǎn zìjǐ de shì;少管闲〔閒〕事 shǎo guǎn xiánshì. **mind one's step** ⇨ STEP[1]. **ˌmind ˈyou, mind** 请注意 qǐng zhùyì: *She's still ill, ~ you, but at least she's getting better.* 她仍在生病,请注意,但无论如何她渐渐痊愈了. **ˌnever ˈmind** 不必担〔擔〕心 búbì dānxīn. **5** [短语动词] **ˌmind ˈout** [非正式用语] 当〔當〕心 dāngxīn;小心 xiǎoxīn. **minder** *n* [C] 照料者 zhàoliàozhě;看守人 kānshǒurén: *a ˈchild-~er* 照看孩子的人.

mindful /ˈmaɪndfl/ *adj* *of* [正式用语]留意的 liúyìde;注意的 zhùyìde.

mindless /ˈmaɪndlɪs/ *adj* **1** 不用脑〔腦〕子的 búyòng nǎozi de. **2** [贬]没头〔頭〕脑的 méi tóunǎo de;愚笨的 yúbènde.

mine[1] /maɪn/ *pron* 我的 wǒde: *Is this book yours or ~?* 这本书是你的还是我的?

mine[2] /maɪn/ *n* [C] **1** 矿〔礦〕kuàng;矿井 kuàngjǐng;矿山 kuàngshān. **2** 地雷 dìléi;水雷 shuǐléi. **3** [习语] **a mine of information** 知识〔識〕的宝〔寶〕库 zhīshi de bǎokù. **mine** *v* **1** [I, T] (*for*) 开〔開〕矿 kāikuàng;采〔採〕矿 cǎikuàng;采掘 cǎijué. **2** [T] 在…埋地雷 zài … mái dìléi;布水雷 bù shuǐléi. **ˈmine-detector** *n* [C] 探雷器 tànléiqì. **ˈminefield** *n* [C] **1** 布雷区〔區〕bùléiqū. **2** 危险〔險〕形势〔勢〕wēixiǎn xíngshì. **miner** *n* [C] 矿工 kuànggōng. **ˈminesweeper** *n* [C] 扫〔掃〕雷舰〔艦〕sǎoléijiàn.

mineral /ˈmɪnərəl/ *n* [C, U] 矿〔礦〕物 kuàngwù. **mineral** *adj* 含矿物的 hán kuàngwù de;矿物的 kuàngwùde. **ˈmineral water** *n* [U] 矿泉水 kuàngquánshuǐ.

mineralogy /ˌmɪnəˈrælədʒɪ/ *n* [U] 矿〔礦〕物学〔學〕kuàngwùxué. **mineralogist** *n* [C] 矿物学家 kuàngwùxuéjiā.

mingle /ˈmɪŋgl/ *v* [I, T] *with* (使)混合 hùnhé.

mini- /ˈmɪnɪ/ *prefix* 表示"极〔極〕小的"、"极短的"等 biǎoshì "jíxiǎode"、"jíduǎnde" děng: *a ˈ~bus* 微型公共汽车.

miniature /ˈmɪnətʃə(r); *US* ˈmɪnɪətʃʊər/ *adj* 小型的 xiǎoxíngde;微型的 wēixíngde. **miniature** *n* [C] 微型人像画〔畫〕wēixíng rénxiànghuà. **miniaturize** *v* [T] 使小型化 shǐ xiǎoxínghuà;使微型化 shǐ wēixínghuà.

minimal /ˈmɪnɪməl/ *adj* 最小的 zuìxiǎode;最低限度的 zuìdī xiàndù de.

minimize /ˈmɪnɪmaɪz/ *v* [T] 使减到最小量 shǐ jiǎn dào zuìxiǎoliàng;使减到最低程度 shǐ jiǎn dào zuìdī chéngdù.

minimum /ˈmɪnɪməm/ *n* [C, 常作 sing] [*pl* **minima** /-mə/] 最小量 zuì xiǎoliàng;最低限度 zuìdī xiàndù. **minimum** *adj* 最小的 zuìxiǎode;最低限度的 zuìdī xiàndù de: *the ~ age* 最低年龄.

mining /ˈmaɪnɪŋ/ *n* [U] 采〔採〕矿〔礦〕cǎikuàng.

minion /ˈmɪnɪən/ *n* [C] [贬]惟命是从〔從〕的奴仆〔僕〕wéi mìng shì cóng de núpú.

minister /ˈmɪnɪstə(r)/ *n* [C] **1** 部长〔長〕bùzhǎng;大臣 dàchén. **2** (基督教)牧师〔師〕mùshi. **minister** *v* [I] *to* [正式用语]给予援助 jǐyǔ yuánzhù;给予照料 jǐyǔ zhàoliào. **ministerial** /ˌmɪnɪˈstɪərɪəl/ *adj*.

ministry /ˈmɪnɪstrɪ/ *n* [*pl* -ies] **1** [C] (政府的)部 bù. **2** (全体)牧师〔師〕mùshi. **3 the ministry** [sing] 牧师职〔職〕位(或职责、任期) mùshi zhíwèi: *enter the ~* 从事牧师工作.

mink /mɪŋk/ *n* **1** [C] 貂 diāo. **2** [U] 貂皮 diāopí.

minor /ˈmaɪnə(r)/ *adj* 较小的 jiàoxiǎode;次要的 cìyàode: *~ problems* 次要问题. *a ~ illness* 小病. **minor** *n* [C] [法律]未成年人 wèichéngniánrén.

minority /maɪˈnɒrətɪ; *US* -ˈnɔːr-/ *n* [*pl* -ies] **1** [C] (a) [亦作 sing, 用 pl v] (尤指投票)少数〔數〕shǎoshù. (b) 少数民族 shǎoshù mínzú. **2** [U] [法律]未成年 wèi chéngnián.

minster /ˈmɪnstə(r)/ *n* [C] 大教堂 dà jiàotáng.

minstrel /ˈmɪnstrəl/ *n* [C] (中世纪的)吟游歌手 yínyóu gēshǒu.

mint[1] /mɪnt/ *n* **1** [U] 薄荷 bòhe;薄荷属〔屬〕植物 bòheshǔ zhíwù. **2** [U, C] short for PEPPERMINT.

mint[2] /mɪnt/ *n* **1** [C] 铸〔鑄〕币〔幣〕厂〔廠〕zhùbìchǎng. **2** [sing] [非正式用语]巨款 jùkuǎn: *make / earn a ~* 赚了好多钱. **3** [习语] **in mint condition** 崭新的 zhǎnxīnde. **mint** *v* [T] 铸造(硬币) zhùzào.

minuet /ˌmɪnjʊˈet/ *n* [C] 小步舞 xiǎobùwǔ;小步舞曲 xiǎobùwǔqǔ.

minus /ˈmaɪnəs/ *prep* **1** 减(去) jiǎn: *15 ~ 6 equals 9.* 15 减 6 等于 9. **2** 零下 língxià: *~ 3 degrees Celsius.* 零下 3 摄氏度 (−3°C). **3** [非正式用语]无〔無〕wú;没有 méiyǒu. **minus** *adj* 负的 fùde. **minus** (亦作 **minus sign**) *n* [C] [数学]减号〔號〕jiǎnhào;负号(−) fùhào.

M

minute[1] /ˈmɪnɪt/ *n* 1 (a) [C] 分(一小时的六十分之一) fēn. (b) [sing] 片刻 piànkè; 瞬间 shùnjiān: *I'll be with you in a ~.* 我很快就会和你在一起. 2 [C] 分(角的度量单位,六十分之一度) fēn. 3 **minutes** [pl] 会〔會〕议〔議〕记录〔錄〕 huìyì jìlù. 4 [习语] **the minute / moment (that)** 一…就… yī … jiù…. **minute** *v* [T] 将〔將〕…记入会议记录 jiāng … jìrù huìyì jìlù.

minute[2] /maɪˈnjuːt; *US* -ˈnuːt/ *adj* [~r, ~st] 微小的 wēixiǎode; 极〔極〕小的 jíxiǎode. **minutely** *adv*.

minutiae /maɪˈnjuːʃɪiː; *US* mɪˈnuː-/ *n* [pl] 微小的细节〔節〕 wēixiǎode xìjié.

miracle /ˈmɪrəkl/ *n* 1 (a) [C] 奇迹 qíjì. (b) [sing] [非正式用语,喻] 惊〔驚〕人的奇事 jīng rén de qíshì: *It's a ~ we weren't all killed.* 我们大家没有被害真是不可思议. 2 [C] *of* 惊人的事例 jīng rén de shìlì: *a ~ of modern science* 现代科学的一大奇迹. **miraculous** /mɪˈrækjʊləs/ *adj*.

mirage /ˈmɪrɑːʒ, mɪˈrɑːʒ/ *n* [C] 海市蜃楼〔樓〕 hǎi shì shèn lóu; 蜃景 shènjǐng.

mire /ˈmaɪə(r)/ *n* [U] 泥潭 nítán; 沼泽〔澤〕 zhǎozé; 泥沼 nízhǎo.

mirror /ˈmɪrə(r)/ *n* [C] 镜 jìng. **mirror** *v* [T] 反射 fǎnshè; 映照 yìngzhào.

misadventure /ˌmɪsədˈventʃə(r)/ *n* [C, U] [正式用语]不幸 búxìng; 灾〔災〕祸〔禍〕 zāihuò; 不幸事故 búxìng shìgù.

misappropriate /ˌmɪsəˈprəʊprɪeɪt/ *v* [T] 滥〔濫〕用 lànyòng; 误用 wùyòng: *~ sb's money* 盗用他人的金钱.

misbehave /ˌmɪsbɪˈheɪv/ *v* [I] 行为〔爲〕不端 xíngwéi bùduān; 举〔舉〕止不当〔當〕 jǔzhǐ búdàng. **misbehaviour** (美语 -ior) *n* [U].

miscalculate /ˌmɪsˈkælkjʊleɪt/ *v* [I, T] 误算 wùsuàn; 算错 suàncuò. **miscalculation** /ˌmɪskælkjʊˈleɪʃn/ *n* [C, U].

miscarriage /ˌmɪsˈkærɪdʒ, ˈmɪskærɪdʒ/ *n* [C, U] 流产〔產〕 liúchǎn; 小产 xiǎochǎn. **miscarriage of ˈjustice** *n* [C] 审〔審〕判不公 shěnpàn bùgōng; 误审 wùshěn; 误判 wùpàn.

miscarry /ˌmɪsˈkærɪ/ *v* [*pt*, *pp* -ied] [I] 1 流产〔產〕 liúchǎn; 小产 xiǎochǎn. 2 (计划等)失败 shībài.

miscellaneous /ˌmɪsəˈleɪnɪəs/ *adj* 各种〔種〕各样〔樣〕的 gèzhǒng gèyàng de; 不同种类〔類〕的 bùtóng zhǒnglèi de.

miscellany /mɪˈselənɪ; *US* ˈmɪsəleɪnɪ/ *n* [C] [*pl* -ies] 杂〔雜〕集 zájí.

mischance /ˌmɪsˈtʃɑːns; *US* -ˈtʃæns/ *n* [C, U] [正式用语]不幸 búxìng; 厄运〔運〕 èyùn.

mischief /ˈmɪstʃɪf/ *n* [U] 1 恶〔惡〕作剧〔劇〕 èzuòjù; 顽皮 wánpí; 淘气〔氣〕 táoqì. 2 [习语] **do sb / oneself a ˈmischief** [非正式用语,谑]伤〔傷〕害某人(或自己) shānghài mǒurén. **mischievous** /-tʃɪvəs/ *adj* 1 顽皮的 wánpíde; 淘气的 táoqìde. 2 有害的 yǒuhàide. **mischievously** *adv*.

misconception /mɪskənˈsepʃn/ *n* [C, U] 误解 wùjiě.

misconduct /ˌmɪsˈkɒndʌkt/ *n* [U] [正式用语]不端行为〔爲〕 bùduān xíngwéi.

misdeed /ˌmɪsˈdiːd/ *n* [C, 常作 pl] [正式用语]恶〔惡〕行 èxíng; 罪行 zuìxíng.

miser /ˈmaɪzə(r)/ *n* [C] 守财奴 shǒucáinú; 吝啬〔嗇〕鬼 lìnsèguǐ. **miserly** *adj*.

miserable /ˈmɪzrəbl/ *adj* 1 悲惨〔慘〕的 bēicǎnde; 不幸的 búxìngde. 2 使人难〔難〕受(或痛苦)的 shǐ rén nánshòu de: *~ weather* 令人难受的天气. 3 粗劣的 cūliède; 贫乏的 pínfáde: *earn a ~ wage* 赚得微薄的工资. **miserably** *adv*.

misery /ˈmɪzərɪ/ *n* [*pl* -ies] 1 [U, C] 痛苦 tòngkǔ; 苦难〔難〕 kǔnàn. 2 [英国非正式用语] 总〔總〕发〔發〕牢骚的人 zǒng fā láosāo de rén.

misfire /ˌmɪsˈfaɪə(r)/ *v* [I] 1 (枪等)走火 zǒuhuǒ; 不发〔發〕火 bù fāhuǒ; 射不出 shè bùchū. 2 [喻,非正式用语](计划等)未产〔產〕生预期效果 wèi chǎnshēng yùqī xiàoguǒ; 未能奏效 wèinéng zòuxiào.

misfit /ˈmɪsfɪt/ *n* [C] 不适〔適〕应〔應〕环〔環〕境的人 bú shìyìng huánjìng de rén; 不适应工作的人 bú shìyìng gōngzuò de rén.

misfortune /ˌmɪsˈfɔːtʃuːn/ *n* [C, U] 不幸 búxìng; 灾〔災〕祸〔禍〕 zāihuò.

misgiving /ˌmɪsˈgɪvɪŋ/ *n* [U, C, 尤作 pl] [正式用语]疑虑〔慮〕 yílǜ; 担〔擔〕忧〔憂〕 dānyōu.

misguided /ˌmɪsˈgaɪdɪd/ *adj* 举〔舉〕措失当〔當〕(或愚蠢)的 jǔcuò shīdàng de.

mishap /ˈmɪshæp/ *n* [C, U] (不严重的)不幸事故 búxìng shìgù.

misjudge /ˌmɪsˈdʒʌdʒ/ *v* [T] 对〔對〕…判断〔斷〕错误 duì … pànduàn cuòwù; 把…估计错误 bǎ … gūjì cuòwù: *~ sb / sb's character* 对某人的品德看法不公正.

mislay /ˌmɪsˈleɪ/ *v* [*pt*, *pp* **mislaid** /-ˈleɪd/] [T] 误置 wùzhì; 误放 wùfàng.

mislead /ˌmɪsˈliːd/ *v* [*pt*, *pp* **misled** /-ˈled/] [T] 使产〔產〕生错误想法(或印象) shǐ chǎnshēng cuòwù xiǎngfǎ.

mismanage /ˌmɪsˈmænɪdʒ/ *v* [T] 管理不善 guǎnlǐ búshàn; 处〔處〕置失当〔當〕 chǔzhì shīdàng. **mismanagement** *n* [U].

misprint /ˈmɪsprɪnt/ *n* [C] 印刷错误 yìnshuā cuòwù; 排版错误 páibǎn cuòwù.

misrepresent /ˌmɪsˌreprɪˈzent/ *v* [T] 误传〔傳〕 wùchuán; 歪曲 wāiqū. **misrepresen-**

tation /-zen'teɪʃn/ *n* [C, U].

Miss /mɪs/ *n* [C] (对未婚女子的称呼)小姐 xiǎojiě: ~ *Smith* 史密斯小姐.

miss /mɪs/ *v* **1** [I, T] 未击〔擊〕中 wèi jī-zhòng; 未抓住 wèi zhuāzhù; 未达〔達〕到 wèi dádào: ~ *the ball* / *the train* 未击中(或未接住)球; 没赶上火车. **2** [T] 未看见 wèi kàn-jiàn; 未听〔聽〕见 wèi tīngjiàn. **3** [T] 因…不在而感到惋惜 yīn … búzài ér gǎndào wǎnxī: *I'll* ~ *you when you go*. 你走了,我会怀念你. **4** [短语动词] **miss sb / sth out** 不包括某人(或某事) bù bāokuò mǒurén. **miss 'out (on sth)** 错过〔過〕获〔獲〕利机〔機〕会〔會〕cuò-guò huòlì jīhuì. **miss** *n* [C] **1** 击不中 jī bú-zhòng; 失误 shīwù. **2** [习语] **give sth a 'miss** 避开〔開〕bìkāi. **missing** *adj* 找不到的 zhǎo bú dào de; 失去的 shīqùde.

missile /'mɪsaɪl; *US* 'mɪsl/ *n* [C] **1** 导〔導〕弹〔彈〕dǎodàn; 飞〔飛〕弹 fēidàn: *nuclear* ~*s* 核导弹. **2** 发〔發〕射(或投掷)之物(或武器) fāshè zhī wù.

mission /'mɪʃn/ *n* [C] **1** 代表团〔團〕dàibiǎo-tuán; 外交使团 wàijiāoshǐtuán: *a trade* ~ *to China* 派往中国的商务代表团. **2** 特殊任务〔務〕tèshū rènwù; 特殊使命 tèshū shǐmìng: *her* ~ *in life* 她的天职. **3** 传〔傳〕教地区〔區〕chuánjiào dìqū. **missionary** /'mɪʃənrɪ; *US* -nerɪ/ *n* [C] [*pl* **-ies**] 传教士 chuán-jiàoshì.

misspell /ˌmɪs'spel/ *v* [*pt*, *pp* **-spelt** /-'spelt/ 或尤用于美语 **~ed**] [T] 拼写〔寫〕错 pīnxiě cuò. **misspelling** *n* [U, C].

misspent /ˌmɪs'spent/ *adj* 滥〔濫〕用的 làn-yòngde; 浪费的 làngfèide: *his* ~ *youth* 他虚度的青春.

mist /mɪst/ *n* [U, C] **1** 薄雾〔霧〕bówù: *hills covered in* ~ 薄雾笼罩的群山. **2** [喻] 迷雾 míwù: *lost in the* ~*s of time* 湮没在时间的迷雾中. **mist** *v* [短语动词] ˌ**mist 'over** 蒙上薄雾 méng shàng bówù: *His glasses* ~*ed over*. 他的眼镜被蒙上了一层水汽. **misty** *adj* [**-ier**, **-iest**] **1** 充满雾气〔氣〕的 chōngmǎn wùqì de; 薄雾笼〔籠〕罩的 bówù lǒngzhào de: *a* ~*y morning* 薄雾笼罩的早晨. **2** [喻]不清楚的 bù qīngchu de; 朦胧〔朧〕的 ménglóngde.

mistake /mɪ'steɪk/ *n* [C] **1** 错误 cuòwù; 过〔過〕失 guòshī. **2** [习语] **by mi'stake** 错误地 cuòwùde. **mistake** *v* [*pt* **mistook** /mɪ-'stʊk/, *pp* ~**n** / mɪs'teɪkən /] **1** [T] 弄错 nòngcuò; 误解 wùjiě; 误会〔會〕wùhuì. **2** *for* 把…误认〔認〕为〔爲〕bǎ … wù rènwéi: *People often* ~ *Jill for her twin sister*. 人们常把吉尔当成她的孪生妹妹. **mistaken** *adj* 错误的 cuòwùde; 不正确的 bú zhèngquè de: ~*n beliefs* 错误的信念. **mistakenly** *adv*.

mistletoe /'mɪsltəʊ/ *n* [U] [植物]槲寄生(用作圣诞节的装饰物) hújìshēng.

mistress /'mɪstrɪs/ *n* [C] **1** 女主人 nǚ zhǔ-rén; 主妇〔婦〕zhǔfù. **2** (狗、马等的)女主人 nǚ zhǔrén. **3** [尤用于英国英语](中小学的)女教师〔師〕nǚ jiàoshī. **4** 情妇 qíngfù.

mistrust /ˌmɪs'trʌst/ *v* [T] 不信任 bú xìn-rèn; 不相信 bù xiāngxìn. **mistrust** *n* [U] 不信任 bú xìnrèn; 不相信 bù xiāngxìn. **mis-trustful** *adj*.

misty ⇨MIST.

misunderstand /ˌmɪsˌʌndə'stænd/ *v* [*pt*, *pp* **-stood** /-'stʊd/] [T] 误解 wùjiě; 误会〔會〕wùhuì: *He misunderstood the instructions and got lost*. 他对操作指南理解错误而不知所措. **misunderstanding** *n* [C, U] 误会 wùhuì; 误解 wùjiě.

misuse /ˌmɪs'ju:z/ *v* [T] **1** 误用 wùyòng; 滥〔濫〕用 lànyòng: ~ *one's time* 虚度光阴. **2** 虐待 nüèdài: *He felt* ~*d by the company*. 他觉得受到公司苛待. **misuse** /ˌmɪs'ju:s/ *n* [C, U].

mitigate /'mɪtɪgeɪt/ *v* [T] [正式用语]使和缓 shǐ héhuǎn; 使减轻〔輕〕shǐ jiǎnqīng. **miti-gating** *adj* 使(某事)似乎不太严〔嚴〕重 shǐ sìhū bú tài yánzhòng: *There were mitigating circumstances to explain her bad behaviour*. 她行为不端,但在一定程度上情有可原. **mitigation** /ˌmɪtɪ'geɪʃn/ *n*.

mitre (美语 **miter**) /'maɪtə(r)/ *n* [C] 主教冠 zhǔjiàoguān.

mitten /'mɪtn/ (亦作 **mitt** /mɪt/) *n* [C] 连指手套(四指相连与拇指分开) liánzhǐ shǒutào.

mix /mɪks/ *v* **1** [I, T] 混合 hùnhé; 搀〔攙〕和 chānhuo: ~ *flour and water to make paste* 把面和水和成面团. *Oil and water don't* ~. 油和水不能溶合. **2** [I] (人)交往 jiāowǎng; 相处〔處〕xiāngchǔ: *He finds it hard to* ~. 他感到很难与人相处. **3** [习语] **be / get mixed 'up in sth** [非正式用语]使发〔發〕生牵〔牽〕连 shǐ fāshēng qiānlián; 使卷〔捲〕入 shǐ juǎnrù. **4** [短语动词] **mix sb / sth up** 混淆某人(或某事)与〔與〕他人(或他事) hùn xiáo mǒurén yǔ tārén: *I got her* ~*ed up with her sister*. 我把她和她的妹妹弄混了. **mix** *n* [C, U] 混合 hùnhé; 结合 jiéhé: *a* '*cake* ~ 蛋糕混合料. **mixed** *adj* **1** 混合的 hùnhéde; 搀和的 chānhuode. **2** 男女混合的 nán nǚ hùnhé de: *a* ~*ed school* 男女生混合学校. **mixer** *n* [C] 混合者 hùnhézhě. '**mix-up** *n* [C] [非正式用语]混乱〔亂〕hùnluàn; 杂〔雜〕乱 záluàn.

mixture /'mɪkstʃə(r)/ *n* [C] 混合物 hùnhé-wù: *a* ~ *of fear and sadness* 恐惧中带着

M

忧伤.

mm *abbr* [*pl* mm 或～s] millimetre(s).

moan /məʊn/ *v* [I] **1** 发〔發〕出呻吟声〔聲〕 fāchū shēnyínshēng. **2** (*about*) [非正式用语]抱怨 bàoyuàn; 发牢骚 fā láosāo: *He's always ～ing about having no money*. 他总是抱怨没有钱. **moan** *n* [C].

moat /məʊt/ *n* [C] (城堡的)护〔護〕城河 hùchénghé; 城壕 chéngháo.

mob /mɒb/ *n* [C] **1** 暴民 bàomín; 乌〔烏〕合之众〔衆〕 wū hé zhī zhòng. **2**[俚](罪犯等的)一伙〔夥〕 yìhuǒ; 一群 yìqún. **mob** *v* [-bb-] [T] (出于好奇、愤怒等)成群围〔圍〕住 chéngqún wéizhù: *a film star ～bed by his fans* 被影迷团团围住的电影明星.

mobile /ˈməʊbaɪl; *US* -bl/ *adj* (可)动〔動〕的 dòngde; 易于移动的 yìyú yídòng de. **mobile** *n* [C] 风〔風〕动饰物(用金属等组成的悬挂饰物,可随风而动) fēng dòng shìwù. **mobile ˈphone** *n* [C] 移动电〔電〕话 yídòng diànhuà; 手机〔機〕 shǒujī. **mobility** /məʊˈbɪlətɪ/ *n* [U].

mobilize /ˈməʊbɪlaɪz/ *v* [I, T] 动〔動〕员 dòngyuán; 调动 diàodòng.

moccasin /ˈmɒkəsɪn/ *n* [C] 软皮(平底)鞋 ruǎn píxié.

mock[1] /mɒk/ *v* [I, T] 嘲弄 cháonòng; 嘲笑 cháoxiào: *a ～ing smile* 嘲弄的微笑. **mockery** *n* **1** [U] 嘲弄 cháonòng;嘲笑 cháoxiào. **2** [sing] 恶〔惡〕例 èlì; 可蔑视之例 kě mièshì zhī lì: *a ～ of justice* 蔑视正义的恶例. **3** [习语] **make a mockery of sth** 使某事显〔顯〕得荒谬 shǐ mǒushì xiǎnde huāngmiù.

mock[2] /mɒk/ *adj* 模拟〔擬〕的 mónǐde; 非真实〔實〕的 fēi zhēnshí de: *a ～ battle* 模拟战争.

modal /ˈməʊdl /(亦作 **modal auˈxiliary**) *n* [C] [语法]情态〔態〕助动〔動〕词 (如 *can, may, should*) qíngtài zhùdòngcí.

mode /məʊd/ *n* [C] [正式用语]方法 fāngfǎ; 方式 fāngshì.

model[1] /ˈmɒdl/ *n* [C] **1** 模型 móxíng: *a ～ of the new airport* 新机场模型. **2**(产品的)设计 shèjì; 型号〔號〕 xínghào: *This car is our latest ～*. 这辆汽车是我们最新的型号. **3** 模范〔範〕 mófàn; 典型 diǎnxíng: *a ～ wife* 模范妻子. **4** (艺术家、摄影家用的)模特儿〔兒〕 mótèr. **5** 时〔時〕装〔裝〕模特儿 shízhuāng mótèr: *a ˈfashion ～* 时装模特儿.

model[2] /ˈmɒdl/ *v* [-ll-, 美语 -l-] **1** [I, T] (用泥、蜡等)塑造 sùzào; 做…的模型 zuò … de móxíng. **2** [I, T] 当〔當〕模特儿〔兒〕 dāng mótèr; 展示(服装等) zhǎnshì. **3** [T] *on* 以…作榜样〔樣〕 yǐ … zuò bǎngyàng: *He ～s himself on his uncle*. 他以他的叔叔为榜样.

modem /ˈməʊdem/ *n* [C] 调制解调器 tiáozhìjiětiáoqì.

moderate[1] /ˈmɒdərət/ *adj* 适〔適〕度的 shìdùde; 适中的 shìzhōngde. **moderate** *n* [C] (政治上)稳〔穩〕健派 wěnjiànpài; 温和派 wēnhépài. **moderately** *adv* 不过〔過〕分地 bú guòfènde: *only ～ly successful* 稍有成功.

moderate[2] /ˈmɒdəreɪt/ *v* [I] 和缓 héhuǎn; 节〔節〕制 jiézhì; 减轻〔輕〕 jiǎnqīng.

moderation /ˌmɒdəˈreɪʃn/ *n* [U] **1** 适〔適〕度 shìdù; 温和 wēnhé. **2** [习语] **in moderation** 适度地 shìdùde: *drink whisky in ～* 适量喝点威士忌.

modern /ˈmɒdn/ *adj* **1** 现代的 xiàndàide; 近代的 jìndàide. **2** 最新的 zuìxīnde; 新式的 xīnshìde. **modernize** /ˈmɒdənaɪz/ *v* [I, T] (使)现代化 xiàndàihuà. **modernization** /ˌmɒdənaɪˈzeɪʃn; *US* -nɪˈz-/ *n* [U].

modest /ˈmɒdɪst/ *adj* **1** 谦虚的 qiānxūde; 谦逊〔遜〕的 qiānxùnde. **2** 适〔適〕度的 shìdùde; 不大的 búdàde: *a ～ salary* 不高的工资. **3** 羞怯的 xiūqiède; 检〔檢〕点〔點〕的 jiǎndiǎnde: *～ behaviour* 行为检点. **modestly** *adv*. **modesty** *n* [U].

modify /ˈmɒdɪfaɪ/ *v* [*pt, pp* -ied] [T] **1** 修改 xiūgǎi; 更改 gēnggǎi. **2** 减轻〔輕〕 jiǎnqīng; 缓和 huǎnhé; 降低 jiàngdī: *～ one's demands* 降低要求. **3** [语法](尤指形容词或副词)修饰 xiūshì: *In the phrase 'the red car', 'red' modifies 'car'*. 在"the red car"这一词组中,"red"修饰"car". **modification** /ˌmɒdɪfɪˈkeɪʃn/ *n* [C, U].

module /ˈmɒdjuːl; *US* -dʒuːl/ *n* [C] **1** (标准的)建筑〔築〕部件 jiànzhù bùjiàn; 预制〔製〕件 yùzhìjiàn. **2** (航天器的)舱〔艙〕 cāng. **3** (主修课程的)单〔單〕元 dānyuán: *the biology ～ in the science course* 科学课程中的生物学单元. **modular** /-jʊlə(r); *US* -dʒʊ- / *adj*.

mohair /ˈməʊheə(r)/ *n* [U] 马海毛 mǎhǎimáo; 马海毛织〔織〕物 mǎhǎimáo zhīwù.

Mohammedan = MUHAMMADAN (MUHAMMAD).

moist /mɔɪst/ *adj* 潮湿〔濕〕的 cháoshīde; 湿润的 shīrùnde. **moisten** /ˈmɔɪstn/ *v* [I, T] 变〔變〕(潮)湿 biàn shī; 弄湿 nòng shī. **moisture** /ˈmɔɪstʃə(r)/ *n* [U] 潮气〔氣〕 cháoqì; 湿气 shīqì; 水气 shuǐqì.

molar /ˈməʊlə(r)/ *n* [C] 臼齿〔齒〕 jiùchǐ; 磨牙 móyá.

mold [美语] = MOULD.

molder [美语] = MOULDER.

mole[1] /məʊl/ *n* [C] 痣 zhì.

mole[2] /məʊl/ *n* [C] **1** 鼹鼠 yǎnshǔ. **2** [非正式用语]内奸 nèijiān. **ˈmolehill** *n* [C] 鼹鼠丘 yǎnshǔ qiū.

molecule /ˈmɒlɪkjuːl/ *n* [C] 分子 fēnzǐ. **molecular** /məˈlekjʊlə(r)/ *adj*.

molest /məˈlest/ *v* [T] 1 骚扰〔擾〕sāorǎo; 干扰 gānrǎo. 2 对〔對〕(妇女、儿童)作性骚扰 duì …zuò xìngsāorǎo.

mollusc (美语亦作 **mollusk**) /ˈmɒləsk/ *n* [C] 软〔軟〕体〔體〕动〔動〕物(如牡蛎、蜗牛等) ruǎntǐ dòngwù.

molt [美语] = MOULT.

molten /ˈməʊltən/ *adj* 熔化的 rónghuàde; 熔融的 róngróngde: ~ *rock* / *steel* 熔化的岩石;熔化的钢.

moment /ˈməʊmənt/ *n* 1 [C] 瞬间 shùnjiān; 片刻 piànkè. 2 [sing] 就在那时〔時〕jiù zài nàshí. 3 [U] [正式用语]重要 zhòngyào: *a matter of great* ~ 最重要的一件事. 4 [习语] **the moment (that)** ⇨ MINUTE[1]. **momentary** /-məntrɪ/ *adj* 片刻的 piànkède; 短暂的 duǎnzànde; 瞬间的 shùnjiānde. **momentarily** / *US* ˌməʊmənˈterəlɪ/ *adv* 1 片刻地 piànkède; 短暂地 duǎnzànde. 2[尤用于美语]立即 lìjí; 即刻 jíkè.

momentous /məˈmentəs; məʊˈm-/ *adj* 重要的 zhòngyàode; 重大的 zhòngdàde.

momentum /məˈmentəm, məʊˈm-/ *n* [U] 1 [物理]动〔動〕量 dòngliàng. 2[喻]冲〔衝〕力 chōnglì;动力 dònglì: *The demands for reform are slowly gathering* ~. 改革的要求正慢慢加强.

monarch /ˈmɒnək/ *n* [C] 君主 jūnzhǔ; 国〔國〕王 guówáng; 女王 nǚwáng; 皇帝 huángdì; 女皇 nǚhuáng. **monarchy** *n* [*pl* -ies] 1 [U] 君主政体〔體〕jūnzhǔ zhèngtǐ; 君主制 jūnzhǔzhì. 2 [C] 君主国 jūnzhǔguó.

monastery /ˈmɒnəstrɪ; *US* -terɪ/ *n* [C] [*pl* -ies] 隐〔隱〕修院 yǐnxiūyuàn; 寺院 sìyuàn.

monastic /məˈnæstɪk/ *adj* 隐〔隱〕修院的 yǐnxiūyuànde; 寺院的 sìyuànde.

Monday /ˈmʌndɪ/ *n* [U, C] 星期一 xīngqīyī: *They're coming on* ~. 他们星期一来. *last* / *next* ~ 上星期一;下星期一. *The museum is closed on* ~*s*. 博物馆每星期一闭馆.

monetary /ˈmʌnɪtrɪ; *US* -terɪ/ *adj* 钱〔錢〕的 qiánde; 货币〔幣〕的 huòbìde.

money /ˈmʌnɪ/ *n* [U] 1 货币〔幣〕(硬币和纸币) huòbì; 钱〔錢〕qián. 2 财富 cáifù; 财产〔產〕cáichǎn. 3 [习语] **get one's money's worth** 花得上算 huā de shàng suàn. ˈ**money-box** *n* [C] 扑〔撲〕满 pūmǎn; 钱箱 qiánxiāng.

mongrel /ˈmʌŋgrəl/ *n* [C] 杂〔雜〕种〔種〕狗 zázhǒnggǒu.

monitor /ˈmɒnɪtə(r)/ *n* [C] 1 监〔監〕听〔聽〕器 jiāntīngqì; 监视器 jiānshìqì; 监测器 jiāncèqì: *a heart* ~ 心脏监测器. 2 (对外国广播的)监听员 jiāntīngyuán. 3 (电视台选播用的)监视屏 jiānshìpíng. 4 [计]监控荧〔熒〕光屏(或装置) jiānkòng yíngguāngpíng. 5 (学校的)班长〔長〕bānzhǎng; 级长 jízhǎng. **monitor** *v* [T] 监听 jiāntīng; 监视 jiānshì; 监测 jiāncè.

monk /mʌŋk/ *n* [C] 修道士 xiūdàoshì; 僧侣 sēnglǚ.

monkey /ˈmʌŋkɪ/ *n* [C] 1 猴 hóu; 猿 yuán. 2 [非正式用语] 顽童 wántóng. **monkey** *v* [短语动词] **monkey about** / **around** [非正式用语]调皮 tiáopí; 捣蛋 dǎodàn.

mono /ˈmɒnəʊ/ *adj*, *n* [U] 单〔單〕声〔聲〕道的 dānshēngdàode; 单声道录〔錄〕放音 dānshēngdào lù fàng yīn: *a recording in* ~ 单声道录音.

monochrome /ˈmɒnəkrəʊm/ *adj* 单〔單〕色的 dānsède; 黑白的 hēibáide.

monocle /ˈmɒnəkl/ *n* [C] 单〔單〕眼镜 dān yǎnjìng.

monogamy /məˈnɒgəmɪ/ *n* [U] 一夫一妻(制) yìfū yìqī. **monogamous** /-məs/ *adj*.

monogram /ˈmɒnəgræm/ *n* [C] 字母组合图〔圖〕案 zìmǔ zǔhé tú'àn.

monologue (美语亦作 **monolog**) /ˈmɒnəlɒg; *US* -lɔːg/ *n* [C] [戏剧]独〔獨〕白 dúbái; 滔滔不绝的话 tāotāo bù jué de huà.

monopoly /məˈnɒpəlɪ/ *n* [C] [*pl* -ies] 垄〔壟〕断〔斷〕权〔權〕lǒngduànquán; 专〔專〕卖〔賣〕权 zhuānmàiquán; 专利权 zhuānlìquán: [喻] *A good education should not be the* ~ *of the rich*. 良好的教育不应是富人独占的事. **monopolize** *v* [T] 垄断 lǒngduàn.

monorail /ˈmɒnəʊreɪl/ *n* [U] 单〔單〕轨 dānguǐ; 单轨铁路 dānguǐ tiělù.

monosyllable /ˈmɒnəsɪləbl/ *n* [C] 单〔單〕音节〔節〕词 dānyīnjié cí. **monosyllabic** /ˌmɒnəsɪˈlæbɪk/ *adj*.

monotonous /məˈnɒtənəs/ *adj* 单〔單〕调的 dāndiàode; 无〔無〕变〔變〕化的 wú biànhuà de: *a* ~ *voice* 单调的声音. **monotonously** *adv*. **monotony** /-tənɪ/ *n* [U].

monsoon /ˌmɒnˈsuːn/ *n* [C] 季风〔風〕jìfēng; (西南季风带来的)雨季 yǔjì.

monster /ˈmɒnstə(r)/ *n* [C] 1 (巨大、丑陋、可怕的)怪物 guàiwù. 2 残忍的人 cánrěnde rén; 恶〔惡〕人 èrén. 3 巨大的东西 jùdàde dōngxi: *The new house is a real* ~. 新房子是个庞然大物.

monstrous /ˈmɒnstrəs/ *adj* 1 巨大的 jùdàde; 丑〔醜〕陋的 chǒulòude. 2 令人震惊〔驚〕的 lìng rén zhènjīng de; 畸形的 jīxíngde. **monstrosity** /mɒnˈstrɒsətɪ/ *n* [C] [*pl* -ies] 巨大而丑陋的东西 jùdà ér chǒulòu de dōngxi. **monstrously** *adv*.

month /mʌnθ/ *n* [C] 月 yuè; 一个〔個〕月的时〔時〕间 yígèyuède shíjiān. **monthly** *adv*,

M

adj 1 每月(的) měiyuè; 每月一次(的) měiyuè yícì. 2 一个月内有效(的) yígèyuè nèi yǒuxiào. **monthly** *n* [C] [*pl* -ies] 月刊 yuèkān.

monument /ˈmɒnjʊmənt/ *n* [C] 1 纪念碑 jìniànbēi; 纪念馆 jìniànguǎn; 纪念像 jìniànxiàng. 2 历〔歷〕史遗迹 lìshǐ yíjì; 遗址 yízhǐ. **monumental** /ˌmɒnjʊˈmentl/ *adj* 1 纪念物的 jìniànwùde. 2 巨大而难〔難〕忘的 jùdà ér nánwàng de. 3 极〔極〕大的 jídàde.

moo /muː/ *n* [C] 哞(牛叫声) mōu. **moo** *v* [I] (牛) 哞哞地叫 mōumōude jiào.

mood[1] /muːd/ *n* [C] 1 心境 xīnjìng; 情绪 qíngxù: *in a good* ~ 情绪好. 2 生气〔氣〕shēngqì; 情绪不好 qíngxù bùhǎo. **moody** *adj* [-ier, -iest] 心情多变〔變〕的 xīnqíng duōbiàn de; 喜怒无〔無〕常的 xǐ nù wúcháng de. **moodily** *adv*.

mood[2] /muːd/ *n* [C] [语法]语气〔氣〕yǔqì: *the subjunctive* ~ 虚拟语气.

moon[1] /muːn/ *n* 1 **the moon** [sing] 月亮 yuèliàng; 月球 yuèqiú. 2 [C] 行星的卫〔衛〕星 xíngxīngde wèixīng. 3 [习语] **over the ˈmoon** [非正式用语]非常快乐〔樂〕fēicháng kuàilè. **ˈmoonbeam** *n* [C] (一道)月光 yuèguāng. **ˈmoon cake** *n* [C] 月饼〔餅〕yuèbǐng. **ˈMoon ˌFestival** *n* [C] 中秋节〔節〕zhōngqiūjié. **ˈmoonlight** *n* [U] 月光 yuèguāng. **ˈmoonlight** *v* [*pt*, *pp* -lighted] [I] (尤指夜晚)做兼职〔職〕工作 zuò jiānzhí gōngzuò.

moon[2] /muːn/ *v* [I] (*about* /*around*) 闲逛 xiánguàng; 懒散度日 lǎnsǎn dùrì.

moor[1] /mɔː(r); *US* mʊər/ *n* [C, 尤作 pl] 沼泽〔澤〕zhǎozé; 高沼 gāozhǎo; 荒野 huāngyě; 旷〔曠〕野 kuàngyě: *walk on the* ~*s* 在野外散步. **ˈmoorland** /-lənd/ *n* [U, C] 高沼地 gāozhǎodì.

moor[2] /mɔː(r); *US* mʊər/ *v* [I, T] (使)停泊 tíngbó. **mooring** *n* 1 **moorings** [pl] 系〔繫〕泊设备〔備〕xìbó shèbèi. 2 [C] 停泊处〔處〕tíngbóchù.

moose /muːs/ *n* [C] [*pl* **moose**] [美语]麋 mí; 驼鹿 tuólù.

mop /mɒp/ *n* [C] 1 拖把 tuōbǎ. 2 蓬乱〔亂〕的头〔頭〕发〔髮〕péngluànde tóufa. **mop** *v* [-pp-] 1 [T] 用拖把拖洗 yòng tuōbǎ tuōxǐ. 2 [短语动词] **mop sth up** 擦掉 cādiào.

mope /məʊp/ *v* [I] 忧〔憂〕郁〔鬱〕yōuyù; 闷闷不乐〔樂〕mènmèn bú lè.

moped /ˈməʊped/ *n* [C] 机〔機〕动〔動〕脚踏车〔車〕jīdòng jiǎotàchē; 摩托自行车 mótuō zìxíngchē.

moral[1] /ˈmɒrəl; *US* ˈmɔːr-/ *adj* 1 道德的 dàodéde: *a drop in* ~ *standards* 道德标准下降. 2 有道德的 yǒu dàodé de; 品行端正的 pǐnxíng duānzhèng de. **morally** *adv*. **ˌmoral ˈsupport** *n* [U] 道义〔義〕上的支持 dàoyì shàng de zhīchí; 精神支持 jīngshén zhīchí.

moral[2] /ˈmɒrəl; *US* ˈmɔːr-/ *n* 1 [C] 教训 jiàoxun; 寓意 yùyì. 2 **morals** [pl] 行为〔爲〕准〔準〕则 xíngwéi zhǔnzé; 道德规范〔範〕dàodé guīfàn.

morale /məˈrɑːl; *US* -ˈræl/ *n* [U] 士气〔氣〕shìqì; 精神状〔狀〕态〔態〕jīngshén zhuàngtài.

morality /məˈrælətɪ/ *n* [*pl* -ies] 1 [U] 道德 dàodé; 美德 měidé. 2 [C] 道德体〔體〕系 dàodé tǐxì.

moralize /ˈmɒrəlaɪz; *US* ˈmɔːr-/ *v* [I] (*about* / *on*) [贬]说教 shuōjiào; 训导〔導〕xùndǎo.

morbid /ˈmɔːbɪd/ *adj* 病态〔態〕的 bìngtàide; 忧〔憂〕郁〔鬱〕的 yōuyùde. **morbidly** *adv*.

more /mɔː(r)/ *adj*, *pron* 更大的 gèngdàde; 更多的 gèngduōde; 较大 jiàodà; 较多 jiàoduō: *I need* ~ *time*. 我还需要些时间. ~ *people* 更多的人. *Please tell me* ~. 请再告诉我一些. **more** *adv* 1 (用以构成两个音节以上形容词或副词的比较级)更 gèng: ~ *expensive* 更昂贵. *talk* ~ *quietly* 更轻声地谈话. 2 更加 gèng jiā; 更甚 gèng shèn: *You need to sleep* ~. 你需要更多的睡眠. 3 再 zài: *I'll go there once* ~. 我要再去那里一次. 4 [习语] **ˌmore and ˈmore** 越来越 yuè lái yuè. **ˌmore or ˈless** (a) 几〔幾〕乎 jīhū. (b) 大约 dàyuē: *£20*, ~ *or less* 大约 20 英镑.

moreover /mɔːˈrəʊvə(r)/ *adv* [正式用语]而且 érqiě; 此外 cǐwài.

morgue /mɔːg/ *n* [C] [尤用于美语]陈尸〔屍〕所 chénshīsuǒ; 停尸房 tíngshīfáng.

morning /ˈmɔːnɪŋ/ *n* [C, U] 1 早晨 zǎochén; 上午 shàngwǔ. 2 [习语] **in the ˈmorning** 次日上午 cìrì shàngwǔ: *see him in the* ~ 明天上午见他. **ˈmorning dress** *n* [U] 常礼〔禮〕服 chánglǐfú.

moron /ˈmɔːrɒn/ *n* [C] [非正式用语]傻〔傻〕子 shǎzi; 蠢人 chǔnrén. **moronic** /məˈrɒnɪk/ *adj*.

morose /məˈrəʊs/ *adj* 忧〔憂〕愁的 yōuchóude; 脾气〔氣〕不好的 píqì bùhǎo de; 孤僻的 gūpìde. **morosely** *adv*.

morphine /ˈmɔːfiːn/ *n* [U] 吗啡 mǎfēi.

Morse /mɔːs/ (亦作 **ˌMorse ˈcode**) *n* [U] 莫尔〔爾〕斯电〔電〕码 Mò'ěrsī diànmǎ.

morsel /ˈmɔːsl/ *n* [C] (*of*) (尤指食物)一小块〔塊〕yìxiǎokuài; 少量 shǎoliàng.

mortal /ˈmɔːtl/ *adj* 1 终有一死的 zhōng yǒu yì sǐ de. 2 致死的 zhìsǐde; 致命的 zhìmìngde: *a* ~ *wound* 致命的创伤. 3 极〔極〕大的 jídàde; 极度的 jídùde: *in* ~ *fear* 在极度的恐惧中. **mortal** *n* [C] 人 rén. **mortality** /mɔːˈtælətɪ/ *n* [U] 1 不免一死 bùmiǎn yì sǐ. 2 死亡率 sǐwánglǜ. **mortally** /-təlɪ/ *adv* 1 致命

M

地 zhìmìngde：～*ly wounded* 受致命伤．2 极 jí：～*ly offended* 极为震怒．

mortar[1] /ˈmɔːtə(r)/ *n* [U] 砂浆〔漿〕shājiāng；灰浆 huījiāng.

mortar[2] /ˈmɔːtə(r)/ *n* [C] **1** 迫击〔擊〕炮 pǎijīpào. **2** 臼 jiù；研钵 yánbō.

mortgage /ˈmɔːgɪdʒ/ *n* [C] **1** 抵押 dǐyā；抵押契据〔據〕dǐyā qìjù. **2** 抵押借款 dǐyā jièkuǎn. **mortgage** *v* [T] 抵押(房产等) dǐyā.

mortify /ˈmɔːtɪfaɪ/ *v* [*pt*, *pp* **-ied**] [T] [常作被动语态] 使羞辱 shǐ xiūrǔ；使难〔難〕堪 shǐ nánkān. **mortification** /ˌmɔːtɪfɪˈkeɪʃn/ *n* [U].

mortuary /ˈmɔːtʃərɪ; *US* ˈmɔːtʃʊərɪ/ *n* [C] [*pl* **-ies**] 停尸〔屍〕房 tíngshīfáng；(医院的)太平间 tàipíngjiān.

mosaic /məʊˈzeɪɪk/ *n* [C, U] 马赛克 mǎsàikè；镶嵌图〔圖〕案 xiāngqiàn tú'àn；镶嵌画〔畫〕xiāngqiànhuà.

Moslem = MUSLIM.

mosque /mɒsk/ *n* [C] 清真寺 qīngzhēnsì.

mosquito /məsˈkiːtəʊ/ *n* [C] [*pl* ～**es**] 蚊 wén.

moss /mɒs; *US* mɔːs/ *n* [U] 苔藓 táixiǎn. **mossy** *adj* [-ier, -iest].

most /məʊst/ *adj*, *pron* **1** 最大的 zuìdàde；最多的 zuìduōde；最高程度的 zuìgāo chéngdù de；最多数〔數〕zuìduōshù；最大量 zuìdàliàng：*Who will get the* ～ *votes?* 谁会得票最多？*He ate the* ～. 他吃得最多. **2** 大部分(的) dà bùfen；大多数(的) dà duōshù：*M*～ *people must pay the new tax*. 大多数人必须纳新税. **3** [习语] ˈ**at (the) most** 至多 zhìduō；不超过〔過〕bù chāoguò. **most** *adv* **1** (用以构成两个以上音节形容词和副词的最高级)：*the* ～ *expensive car* 最昂贵的汽车. **2** 最 zuì：*Children need* ～ *sleep*. 儿童最需要睡眠. **3** 很 hěn；非常 fēicháng：*a* ～ *interesting talk* 十分有趣的谈话. **4** [习语] **most likely** ⇨LIKELY. **mostly** *adv* 主要地 zhǔyàode；大体〔體〕dàtǐ.

motel /məʊˈtel/ *n* [C] 汽车〔車〕旅馆 qìchēlǚguǎn.

moth /mɒθ; *US* mɔːθ/ *n* [C] 蛾 é. ˈ**mothball** *n* [C] 卫〔衛〕生球 wèishēngqiú；樟脑〔腦〕丸 zhāngnǎowán. ˈ**moth-eaten** *adj* **1** 虫蛀的 chóngzhùde；虫坏〔壞〕的 chónghuàide. **2** [喻] 破旧〔舊〕的 pòjiùde；破烂〔爛〕的 pòlànde.

mother /ˈmʌðə(r)/ *n* [C] **1** 母亲〔親〕mǔqīn. **2** 妇〔婦〕女宗教团〔團〕体〔體〕的女主持人 fùnǚ zōngjiào tuántǐ de nǚ zhǔchírén. **mother** *v* [T] **1** 像母亲般照管(或关怀) xiàng mǔqīn bān zhàoguǎn. **2** 溺爱〔愛〕nì'ài. ˈ**mother country** *n* [C] 祖国〔國〕zǔguó. **motherhood** *n* [U]. ˈ**mother-in-law** *n* [C] [*pl* ～**s-in-law**] 岳母 yuèmǔ；婆母 pómǔ. **motherly** *adv* 母亲般地 mǔqīnbānde. **mother** ˈ**tongue** *n* [C] 母语 mǔyǔ.

motif /məʊˈtiːf/ *n* [C] (文艺作品的)主题 zhǔtí；主旨 zhǔzhǐ.

motion /ˈməʊʃn/ *n* **1** [U] 运〔運〕动〔動〕yùndòng；移动 yídòng；动态〔態〕dòngtài. **2** [C] 动作 dòngzuò；姿态 zītài：*signal with a* ～ *of the hand* 手势. **3** [C] 动议〔議〕dòngyì；提议 tíyì. **4** [习语] **go through the motions** [非正式用语]装〔裝〕装样〔樣〕子 zhuāngzhuāng yàngzi；敷衍了事 fūyǎn liǎoshì. **put / set sth in** ˈ**motion** 使某物开〔開〕始运转〔轉〕(或工作) shǐ mǒuwù kāishǐ yùnzhuǎn. **motion** *v* [I, T] *to* (向…)做手势〔勢〕zuò shǒushì；以姿势示意 yǐ zīshì shìyì. **motionless** *adj* 不动的 búdòngde；静止的 jìngzhǐde.

motivate /ˈməʊtɪveɪt/ *v* [T] **1** 构〔構〕成(行为)的动〔動〕机〔機〕gòuchéng … de dòngjī；使产〔產〕生动机 shǐ chǎnshēng dòngjī. **2** 使欲做某事 shǐ yù zuò mǒushì. **motivation** /ˌməʊtɪˈveɪʃn/ *n* [C, U].

motive /ˈməʊtɪv/ *n* [C] 动〔動〕机〔機〕dòngjī；(行动的)缘由 yuányóu.

motor /ˈməʊtə(r)/ *n* [C] **1** 发〔發〕动〔動〕机〔機〕fādòngjī；马达〔達〕mǎdá：*an electric* ～ 电动机. **2** [英旧或谑]汽车〔車〕qìchē. **motor** *adj* **1** 有发动机的 yǒu fādòngjī de：～ *vehicles* 机动车辆. **2** 机动车辆的 jīdòng chēliàng de：～ *racing* 汽车比赛. **motor** *v* [I] [英旧]乘汽车 chéng qìchē. ˈ**motor bike** *n* [C] [非正式用语] = MOTORCYCLE. **motorcade** /ˈməʊtəkeɪd/ *n* [C] 一长〔長〕列汽车 yìchánglié qìchē. ˈ**motor car** *n* [C] [英国正式用语] = CAR. ˈ**motor cycle** *n* [C] 摩托车 mótuōchē. **motorist** *n* [C] 开〔開〕汽车的人 kāi qìchē de rén. **motorize** *v* [T] [常作被动语态]给…装〔裝〕发动机 gěi … zhuāng fādòngjī. ˈ**motor-scooter** *n* [C] = SCOOTER 1. **motorway** *n* [C] 高速公路 gāosù gōnglù. **motorway** ˈ**service area, motorway** ˈ**services** *n* [C] 高速公路服务〔務〕区〔區〕gāosù gōnglù fúwùqū.

motto /ˈmɒtəʊ/ *n* [C] [*pl* ～**es**] 座右铭 zuòyòumíng；箴言 zhēnyán；格言 géyán (例如 'Live each day as it comes.'"有一天过一天".).

mould[1] /məʊld/ *n* [C] 模子 múzi；模型 múxíng；铸〔鑄〕模 zhùmú. **mould** *v* [T] **1** 使成形 shǐ chéngxíng；用模子制〔製〕作 yòng múzi zhìzuò. **2** [喻]影响〔響〕yǐngxiǎng；塑造 sùzào：～ *sb's character* 塑造某人的性格.

mould[2] /məʊld/ *n* [U] 霉 méi；霉菌 méijūn. **mouldy** *adj* [-ier, -iest].

moulder /ˈməʊldə(r)/ *v* [I] 碎裂 suìliè；崩

M

塌 bēngtā；腐烂〔爛〕fǔlàn.

moult /məʊlt/ *v* [I] 1 (鸟)换羽 huànyǔ. 2 (猫狗)脱毛 tuōmáo.

mound /maʊnd/ *n* [C] 1 小丘 xiǎoqiū；小山岗〔崗〕xiǎoshāngǎng. 2 堆 duī；垛 duò.

mount[1] /maʊnt/ *v* 1 [I, T] 登上 dēng shàng: *slowly ~ the stairs* 慢步登上楼梯. 2 [I, T] 骑上(马) qí shàng；为〔爲〕(某人)备〔備〕马 wèi … bèi mǎ. 3 [I] 增加 zēngjiā: *~ing costs* 日益增多的费用. 4 [T] 安装〔裝〕ānzhuāng；裱贴 biǎotiē: *~ pictures* 裱画. 5 [T] 组织〔織〕zǔzhi；开〔開〕始 kāishǐ: *~ an exhibition* 举办展览. **mount** *n* [C] 承载物(如马等) chéngzàiwù.

mount[2] /maʊnt/ *n* [C] (用于地名)山 shān；峰 fēng.

mountain /ˈmaʊntɪn; *US* -ntn/ *n* 1 [C] 山 shān；山岳 shānyuè. 2 [sing] 大量 dàliàng: *a ~ of work* 大量的工作. 3 [习语] **make a ˌmountain out of a ˈmolehill** 小题大做 xiǎo tí dà zuò. **ˈmountain bike** *n* [C] 山地车〔車〕shāndìchē. **mountaineer** /ˌmaʊntɪˈnɪə(r); *US* -ntn-/ *n* [C] 爬山能手 páshān néngshǒu；登山运〔運〕动〔動〕员 dēngshān yùndòngyuán. **mountaineering** *n* [U]. **mountainous** *adj* 1 多山的 duōshānde. 2 巨大的 jùdàde: *~ous waves* 巨浪.

mourn /mɔːn/ *v* [I, T] (*for*) (对死者)感到悲痛 gǎndào bēitòng；表示哀悼 biǎoshì āidào. **mourner** *n* [C]. **mournful** *adj* 悲哀的 bēi'āide；令人悲痛的 lìng rén bēitòngde. **mourning** *n* [U] 1 哀痛 āitòng；哀悼 āidào. 2 丧〔喪〕服 sāngfú.

mouse /maʊs/ *n* [C] [*pl* **mice** /maɪs/] 1 鼠 shǔ. 2 胆小的人 dǎnxiǎo de rén. 3 [计]鼠标〔標〕shǔbiāo. **ˈmouse mat** *n* [C] 鼠标垫〔墊〕shǔbiāodiàn. **mousy** /ˈmaʊsɪ/ *adj* [-ier, -iest] [贬] 1 (毛发)灰褐色的 huīhèsède. 2 (人)胆小的 dǎnxiǎode；羞怯的 xiūqiède.

mousse /muːs/ *n* [U, C] 奶油冻 nǎiyóudòng.

moustache /məˈstɑːʃ/ (美语 **mustache** /ˈmʌstæʃ/) *n* [C] 髭 zī.

mouth[1] /maʊθ/ *n* [C] [*pl* **~s** /maʊðz/] 1 嘴 zuǐ；口 kǒu. 2 口状〔狀〕物 kǒuzhuàngwù；(江河的)出口 chūkǒu: *the ~ of the cave* 洞口. **mouthful** *n* 1 [C] 一口(的量) yìkǒu. 2 [sing] [非正式用语，谑]长〔長〕而拗口的词语 cháng ér àokǒu de cíyǔ. **ˈmouth-organ** *n* [C] 口琴 kǒuqín. **ˈmouthpiece** *n* [C] 1 (乐器的)吹口 chuīkǒu；(电话的)送话口 sònghuàkǒu. 2 代言人 dàiyánrén；喉舌 hóushé. **ˈmouthwatering** *adj* [褒]令人垂涎的 lìng rén chuíxián de；诱人食欲〔慾〕的 yòu rén shíyù de.

mouth[2] /maʊð/ *v* [I, T] 不出声〔聲〕地说 bù chū shēng de shuō.

movable /ˈmuːvəbl/ *adj* 可动〔動〕的 kědòngde；活动的 huódòngde.

move[1] /muːv/ *v* 1 [I, T] 改变〔變〕位置 gǎibiàn wèizhì；移动〔動〕yídòng: *Don't ~ while I'm taking the photo.* 我拍照时别动. 2 [I] (*from*, *to*) 搬家 bānjiā；迁〔遷〕居 qiānjū: *They are moving (house) soon.* 他们不久就要搬家. 3 [I] 进〔進〕步 jìnbù: *The company has ~d ahead of the competition.* 公司在竞争中已走在前头. 4 [T] 感动 gǎndòng: *~d by a sad film* 为一部悲惨的影片所感动. 5 [T] (在会议上)提议〔議〕tíyì. 6 [习语] **move ˈhouse** 搬家 bānjiā. 7 [短语动词] **move in / out** 迁〔遷〕入 qiānrù；迁出 qiānchū. **move off** (尤指车辆)出发〔發〕chūfā；起程 qǐchéng.

move[2] /muːv/ *n* [C] 1 一步棋 yíbùqí: *It's your ~!* 该你走了! 2 步骤 bùzhòu. 3 [习语] **get a ˈmove on** [非正式用语]赶〔趕〕快 gǎnkuài. **make a ˈmove** (a) 起程 qǐchéng. (b) 采〔採〕取行动〔動〕cǎiqǔ xíngdòng. **on the ˈmove** 在移动中 zài yídòng zhōng.

movement /ˈmuːvmənt/ *n* 1 [C, U] 动〔動〕dòng；运〔運〕动 yùndòng；活动 huódòng. 2 [C, 亦作 sing，用 pl v] (有共同目标或原则的)团〔團〕体〔體〕tuántǐ；(这种团体开展的)运动 yùndòng: *the peace ~* 和平运动. 3 [C] 乐〔樂〕章 yuèzhāng.

movie /ˈmuːvɪ/ *n* [尤用于美语] 1 [C] 电〔電〕影 diànyǐng. 2 **the movies** [pl] 电影院 diànyǐngyuàn；电影业〔業〕diànyǐngyè；电影界 diànyǐngjiè.

mow /məʊ/ *v* [*pt* **~ed**, *pp* **~n** /məʊn/ 或 **~ed**] [T] 1 (用刈草机)割 gē，刈 yì. 2 [短语动词] **mow sb down** 大量杀〔殺〕死(人) dàliàng shāsǐ. **mower** *n* [C] = LAWN MOWER (LAWN).

MP /ˌem ˈpiː/ *abbr*, *n* [C] Member of Parliament (英国)下院议〔議〕员 xiàyuàn yìyuán.

mpg /ˌem piː ˈdʒiː/ *abbr* miles per gallon 英里/加仑〔侖〕(每加仑汽油所行驶英里数) yīnglǐ/jiālún.

mph /ˌem piː ˈeɪtʃ/ *abbr* miles per hour 英里/小时〔時〕(每小时所行驶英里数) yīnglǐ/xiǎoshí.

MP3 player /ˌem piː ˈθriː ˌpleɪə(r)/ *n* [C] MP3 播放器 bōfàngqì.

MPV /em piː ˈviː/ *abbr* multi-purpose vehicle 多功能商务〔務〕车〔車〕duōgōngnéng shāngwùchē.

Mr /ˈmɪstə(r)/ *abbr* (用在男子的姓、姓名或职务之前)先生 xiānsheng.

Mrs /ˈmɪsɪz/ *abbr* (用在已婚女子的夫姓或丈夫的姓名之前)夫人 fūrén.

Ms /mɪz/ *abbr* (用在已婚或未婚女子的姓或姓

名之前)女士 nǚshì.

Mt *abbr* mount[2]: *Mt Everest* 埃佛勒斯峰(即:珠穆朗玛峰).

much[1] /mʌtʃ/ *adj, pron* 1 大量(的) dàliàng; 多的 duōde; 许多 xǔduō: *I haven't got ~ money*. 我的钱不多. *There's too ~ salt in this pie*. 馅饼里的盐太多了. *How ~ is it?* 多少钱? 2 [习语] **not much of a** 不太好的 bú tài hǎo de: *It isn't ~ of a car*. 它算不上一辆好车.

much[2] /mʌtʃ/ *adv* 1 很 hěn; 非常 fēicháng; 在很大程度上 zài hěndà chéngdù shàng: *work ~ harder* 更加努力地工作. *He isn't in the office ~*. 他不常在办公室. *I would very ~ like to come*. 我很愿意来. 2 [习语] **much as** 尽〔儘〕管 jǐnguǎn; 虽〔雖〕然 suīrán: *M~ as I want to stay, I must go now*. 虽然我想要留下,可现在必须走了. ˌ**much the** ˈ**same** 情况大致相同 qíngkuàng dàzhì xiāngtóng.

muck /mʌk/ *n* [U] 1 粪〔糞〕 fèn; 粪肥 fènféi. 2 [非正式用语]脏〔髒〕物 zāngwù; 污秽〔穢〕 wūhuì. **muck** *v* [短语动词] **muck about/around** [英国非正式用语]混日子 hùn rìzi. **muck in** [英国非正式用语]同工作 tóng gōngzuò: *If we all ~ in we'll soon get the job done*. 如果我们一块儿干,很快就会把工作做完了. **muck sth up** [非正式用语,尤用于英国英语] (a) 弄脏 nòng zāng. (b) 弄糟 nòng zāo. **mucky** *adj* [-ier, -iest].

mucous /ˈmjuːkəs/ *adj* 黏液的 niányède; 似黏液的 sìniányède. ˌ**mucous** ˈ**membrane** *n* [C] 黏膜 niánmó.

mucus /ˈmjuːkəs/ *n* [U] (黏膜分泌的)黏液 niányè.

mud /mʌd/ *n* [U] 泥 ní. **muddy** *adj* [-ier, -iest]. ˈ**mudguard** *n* [C] (自行车等的)挡〔擋〕泥板 dǎngníbǎn.

muddle /ˈmʌdl/ *n* [C, 常作 sing] 混乱〔亂〕 hùnluàn; 凌乱 língluàn. **muddle** *v* 1 [T] 把…混在一起 bǎ … hùn zài yìqǐ; 弄乱 nòng luàn. 2 [短语动词] **muddle along** [贬]混日子 hùn rìzi. **muddle through** [尤作谑]胡乱应〔應〕付过〔過〕去 húluàn yìngfù guòqù; 混过去 hùn guòqù.

muesli /ˈmjuːzlɪ/ *n* [U] (由谷物、坚果、干果等制成的)早餐食品 zǎocān shípǐn.

muffle /ˈmʌfl/ *v* [T] 1 包住(某物)使其声〔聲〕音低沉 bāozhù … shǐ qí shēngyīn dīchén. 2 (为保暖用头巾、围巾)包 bāo, 裹 guǒ. **muffler** *n* [C] 1 [旧]围〔圍〕巾 wéijīn. 2 [美语]消声〔聲〕器 xiāoshēngqì.

mug[1] /mʌg/ *n* [C] 1 (a) (圆筒形有柄的)大杯 dàbēi. (b) 一大杯的容量 yídàbēide róngliàng. 2 [俚] 脸〔臉〕 liǎn.

mug[2] /mʌg/ *n* [C] [俚]愚人 yúrén; 容易受骗的人 róngyì shòupiàn de rén.

mug[3] /mʌg/ *v* [-gg-] [T] [非正式用语]行凶〔兇〕抢〔搶〕劫 xíngxiōng qiǎngjié. **mugger** *n* [C]. **mugging** *n* [C, U].

muggy /ˈmʌgɪ/ *adj* [-ier, -iest] (天气)闷热〔熱〕而潮湿〔濕〕的 mēnrè ér cháoshī de.

Muhammad /məˈhæmɪd/ *n* 穆罕默德(伊斯兰教创始人) Mùhǎnmòdé. **Muhammadan** (亦作 **Muhammedan, Mohammedan**) /-ən/ *adj, n* [C] 伊斯兰〔蘭〕教徒(的). Yīsīlánjiàotú.

mulberry /ˈmʌlbrɪ; *US* -berɪ/ *n* [C] [*pl* -ies] 桑树〔樹〕 sāngshù; 桑葚 sāngshèn.

mule /mjuːl/ *n* [C] 骡 luó. **mulish** *adj* 顽固的 wángùde; 执〔執〕拗的 zhíniùde.

mull[1] /mʌl/ *v* [T] (加糖、香料等)将〔將〕(葡萄酒)制〔製〕成热〔熱〕饮 jiāng … zhìchéng rèyǐn.

mull[2] /mʌl/ [短语动词] **mull sth over** 仔细考虑〔慮〕 zǐxì kǎolǜ; 反复〔復〕思考 fǎnfù sīkǎo: *Give me time to ~ my decision over*. 给我时间仔细考虑我的决定. *~ over what to do* 仔细考虑做什么.

multilateral /ˌmʌltɪˈlætərəl/ *adj* 多边〔邊〕的 duōbiānde; 多国〔國〕的 duōguóde; 多方面的 duōfāngmiànde.

multimedia /ˌmʌltɪˈmiːdɪə/ *n* 多媒体〔體〕(的采用) duōméitǐ.

multinational /ˌmʌltɪˈnæʃnəl/ *adj* 多国〔國〕的 duōguóde. **multinational** *n* [C] 跨国公司 kuàguó gōngsī.

multiple /ˈmʌltɪpl/ *adj* 多个〔個〕(或多部分、多种)的 duōgède; 由多个(或多部分、多种)组成的 yóu duōgè zǔchéng de. **multiple** *n* [C] [数学]倍数〔數〕 bèishù: *28 is a ~ of 7*. 28 是 7 的倍数. **multiple choice** *adj* (试题)多项(答案供)选〔選〕择〔擇〕的 duōxiàng xuǎnzé de. ˌ**multiple scle**ˈ**rosis** /skləˈrəʊsɪs/ *n* [U] 多发〔發〕性硬化(症) duōfāxìng yìnghuà.

multiply /ˈmʌltɪplaɪ/ *v* [*pt, pp* -ied] [I, T] 1 [数学]乘 chéng: *6 multiplied by 5 is 30*. 6 乘 5 等于 30. 2 增加 zēngjiā; 增多 zēngduō. 3 增殖 zēngzhí; 繁殖 fánzhí: *Rabbits ~ quickly*. 兔子繁殖很快. **multiplication** /ˌmʌltɪplɪˈkeɪʃn/ *n* [U, C].

multi-purpose /ˌmʌltɪˈpɜːpəs/ *adj* 多用途的 duōyòngtúde.

multitude /ˈmʌltɪtjuːd; *US* -tuːd/ *n* [C] [正式用语] 多数〔數〕 duōshù; 大批 dàpī.

mum[1] /mʌm/ *n* [C] [非正式用语]妈妈 māma.

mum[2] /mʌm/ *adj* 1 沉默的 chénmòde. 2 [习语] ˌ**mum's the** ˈ**word** [英国非正式用语]别说出去 bié shuō chūqù.

mumble /ˈmʌmbl/ *v* [I, T] 含糊地说 hánhude shuō; 咕哝〔噥〕gūnong.

mummify /ˈmʌmɪfaɪ/ *v* [*pt*, *pp* -ied] [T] 将〔將〕(尸体)制〔製〕成木乃伊 jiāng … zhìchéng mùnǎiyī.

mummy[1] /ˈmʌmɪ/ *n* [C] [*pl* -ies] (用作儿语)妈妈 māma.

mummy[2] /ˈmʌmɪ/ *n* [C] [*pl* -ies] 木乃伊 mùnǎiyī: *an Egyptian* ～ 埃及木乃伊.

mumps /mʌmps/ *n* [用 sing v] 腮腺炎 sāixiànyán.

munch /mʌntʃ/ *v* [I, T] 用力咀嚼 yònglì jǔjué.

mundane /mʌnˈdeɪn/ *adj* 平凡的 píngfánde; 平淡的 píngdànde.

municipal /mjuːˈnɪsɪpl/ *adj* 市的 shìde; 市政的 shìzhèngde. **municipality** /mjuːˌnɪsɪˈpælətɪ/ *n* [C] [*pl* -ies] 自治市 zìzhìshì; 市政当〔當〕局 shìzhèng dāngjú.

munitions /mjuːˈnɪʃnz/ *n* [pl] 军需品 jūnxūpǐn; 军火 jūnhuǒ.

mural /ˈmjʊərəl/ *n* [C] 壁画〔畫〕bìhuà.

murder /ˈmɜːdə(r)/ *n* 1 [C, U] 谋杀〔殺〕móushā; 谋杀案 móushā'àn. 2 [U] [喻,非正式用语]极〔極〕艰〔艱〕难〔難〕(或不愉快)的经〔經〕历 jí jiānnánde jīnglì: *Climbing that hill was* ～. 爬那座山真是活受罪. **murder** *v* [T] 谋杀 móushā. **murderer** *n* [C] 谋杀犯 móushāfàn; 凶〔兇〕手 xiōngshǒu. **murderess** *n* [C] 女谋杀犯 nǚ móushāfàn; 女凶手 nǚ xiōngshǒu. **murderous** *adj* 杀人的 shārénde; 蓄意谋杀的 xùyì móushā de: *a* ～*ous attack* 凶狠的袭击.

murky /ˈmɜːkɪ/ *adj* [-ier, -iest] 阴〔陰〕暗的 yīn'ànde; 昏暗的 hūn'àndе: ～ *streets* 昏暗的街道.

murmur /ˈmɜːmə(r)/ *n* [C] 1 (低沉、连续而不清的)细声〔聲〕xìshēng. 2 低语声 dīyǔshēng. 3 小声的抱怨 xiǎoshēngde bàoyuàn. **murmur** *v* 1 [I] 发〔發〕连续〔續〕而低沉声 fā liánxù ér dīchén shēng. 2 低声说 dīshēng shuō.

muscle /ˈmʌsl/ *n* 1 [C, U] 肌肉 jīròu. 2 [U] [喻]力量 lìliàng. **muscle** *v* [短语动词] **muscle in (on sth)** [非正式用语,贬]强行挤〔擠〕入以便分享利益 qiángxíng jǐrù yǐbiàn fēnxiǎng lìyì.

muscular /ˈmʌskjʊlə(r)/ *adj* 1 肌肉的 jīròude. 2 肌肉发〔發〕达〔達〕的 jīròu fādá de.

museum /mjuːˈzɪəm/ *n* [C] 博物馆 bówùguǎn.

mushroom /ˈmʌʃrʊm; *US* -ruːm/ *n* [C] 蘑菇 mógu; 食用伞〔傘〕菌 shíyòng sǎnjùn; 蕈 xùn. **mushroom** *v* [I] 迅速增长〔長〕xùnsù zēngzhǎng; 迅速蔓延 xùnsù mànyán.

music /ˈmjuːzɪk/ *n* [U] 1 音乐〔樂〕yīnyuè. 2 乐曲 yuèqǔ: *a piece of* ～ 一首乐曲. 3 乐谱 yuèpǔ. **musical** /-kl/ *adj* 1 音乐的 yīnyuède. 2 爱〔愛〕好音乐的 àihào yīnyuè de; 精于音乐的 jīng yú yīnyuè de. **musical** *n* [C] 音乐喜剧〔劇〕yīnyuè xǐjù. **musically** /-klɪ/ *adv*.

musician /mjuːˈzɪʃn/ *n* [C] 音乐〔樂〕家 yīnyuèjiā; 作曲家 zuòqǔjiā.

Muslim /ˈmʊzlɪm; *US* ˈmʌzləm/ (亦作 **Moslem** /ˈmɒzləm/) *n* [C] 穆斯林 Mùsīlín; 伊斯兰〔蘭〕教信徒 Yīsīlánjiào xìntú. **Muslim** (亦作 **Moslem**) *adj* 穆斯林的 Mùsīlínde; 伊斯兰教信徒的 Yīsīlánjiào xìntú de.

muslin /ˈmʌzlɪn/ *n* [U] 平纹细布 píngwén xìbù.

mussel /ˈmʌsl/ *n* [C] 贻贝 yíbèi; 壳菜 kécài; 淡菜 dàncài.

must /məst; 强式 mʌst/ *modal v* [否定式 **must not**, 缩略式 **mustn't** /ˈmʌsnt/] 1 (表示必要): *You* ～ *finish your work before you go*. 你走以前必须完成你的工作. *Visitors* ～ *not feed the birds*. 参观者不得喂鸟. 2 (表示必定): *You* ～ *be tired after your journey*. 旅行后你一定累了. **must** *n* [C] [非正式用语]必须做(或看)的事 bìxū zuò de shì: *If you like her acting then her new film is a* ～. 你如果喜欢她的演技,那么她的新影片是一定要看的.

mustache [美语] = MOUSTACHE.

mustard /ˈmʌstəd/ *n* [U] 芥 jiè; 芥末 jièmò.

muster /ˈmʌstə(r)/ *v* [I, T] 集合 jíhé; 召集 zhàojí.

musty /ˈmʌstɪ/ *adj* [-ier, -iest] 霉的 méide; 有霉味的 yǒu méiwèi de; 霉烂〔爛〕而潮湿〔濕〕的 méilàn ér cháoshī de.

mutation /mjuːˈteɪʃn/ *n* [C, U] 变〔變〕化 biànhuà; 变异〔異〕biànyì; 突变 tūbiàn; 转〔轉〕变 zhuǎnbiàn.

mute /mjuːt/ *adj* 沉默的 chénmòde; 无〔無〕声〔聲〕的 wúshēngde. **mute** *n* [C] 1 [旧]哑〔啞〕巴 yǎba. 2 弱音器 ruòyīnqì. **muted** *adj* (声音)减弱的 jiǎnruòde; 轻〔輕〕轻的 qīngqīngde; (颜色)不耀眼的 bú yàoyǎn de: ～*d colours* 各种柔和的颜色.

mutilate /ˈmjuːtɪleɪt/ *v* [T] 使损伤〔傷〕shǐ sǔnshāng; 使伤残〔殘〕shǐ shāngcán; 使残缺 shǐ cánquē. **mutilation** /ˌmjuːtɪˈleɪʃn/ *n* [C, U].

mutiny /ˈmjuːtɪnɪ/ *n* [C, U] [*pl* -ies] (水手对上级的)反叛 fǎnpàn; 哗〔嘩〕变〔變〕huábiàn; 叛变 pànbiàn. **mutineer** /ˌmjuːtɪˈnɪə(r)/ *n* [C] 反叛者 fǎnpànzhě; 叛变者 pànbiànzhě. **mutinous** /-nəs/ *adj* 反叛的 fǎnpànde. **mutiny** *v* [*pt*, *pp* -ied] [I] 反叛 fǎnpàn; 叛变 pànbiàn.

mutter /ˈmʌtə(r)/ *v* [I, T] 小声〔聲〕而含糊

M

不清地说 xiǎoshēng ér hánhu bùqīng de shuō; 咕哝〔噥〕gūnong. **mutter** *n* [C, 常作 sing] 轻〔輕〕声低语 qīngshēng dīyǔ; 含糊不清的声音 hánhu bùqīng de shēngyīn.

mutton /ˈmʌtn/ *n* [U] 羊肉 yángròu.

mutual /ˈmjuːtʃʊəl/ *adj* 1 相互的 xiānghùde; 彼此的 bǐcǐde: *~ affection* 相互间的爱慕. 2 共同的 gòngtóngde; 共有的 gòngyǒude: *our ~ friend / interests* 我们共同的朋友/利益. **mutually** /-ʊəlɪ/ *adv*.

muzzle /ˈmʌzl/ *n* [C] 1 (a) (狗等的)鼻口部分 bí kǒu bùfen. (b) (防动物咬人的)口套 kǒutào. 2 枪〔槍〕口 qiāngkǒu; 炮口 pàokǒu. **muzzle** *v* [T] 1 给(狗等)戴口套 gěi … dài kǒutào. 2 [喻] 禁止…自由发〔發〕表意见 jìnzhǐ … zìyóu fābiǎo yìjiàn.

my /maɪ/ *adj* 1 我的 wǒde: *Where's my hat?* 我的帽子在哪儿? 2 (用于称呼): *Yes, my dear.* 是的,我亲爱的. 3 [用于感叹语]: *My goodness!* 天哪!

myopia /maɪˈəʊpɪə/ *n* [U] 近视 jìnshi. **myopic** /-ˈɒpɪk/ *adj*.

myriad /ˈmɪrɪəd/ *n* [C] 无〔無〕数〔數〕wúshù; 极〔極〕大数量 jídà shùliàng.

myself /maɪˈself/ *pron* 1 (用于反身): *I've cut ~.* 我伤了自己. 2 (用于加强语气): *I said so ~.* 我自己这样说过. 3 [习语] (all) by myˈself (a) 独〔獨〕自 dúzì. (b) 独力地 dúlìde.

mysterious /mɪˈstɪərɪəs/ *adj* 1 神秘的 shénmìde; 不可思议〔議〕的 bùkě sīyì de; 难〔難〕解的 nánjiěde: *her ~ disappearance* 她神秘的失踪. 2 保密的 bǎomìde: *He's been very ~ and not told anyone his plans.* 他很会保密,不告诉任何人他的计划. **mysteriously** *adv*.

mystery /ˈmɪstərɪ/ *n* [*pl* -ies] 1 [C] 神秘的事物 shénmìde shìwù; 不可思议〔議〕的事物 bùkě sīyì de shìwù: *Her disappearance is a real ~.* 她的失踪真是不可思议的事. 2 [U] 神秘 shénmì; 秘密 mìmì.

mystic /ˈmɪstɪk/ (亦作 **mystical** /ˈmɪstɪkl/) *adj* 秘教的 mìjiàode; 神秘的 shénmìde; 玄妙的 xuánmiàode; 不可思议〔議〕的 bùkě sīyì de. **mystic** *n* [C] 神秘主义〔義〕者 shénmìzhǔyìzhě. **mysticism** /ˈmɪstɪsɪzəm/ *n* [U] 神秘主义 shénmìzhǔyì.

mystify /ˈmɪstɪfaɪ/ *v* [*pt*, *pp* -ied] [T] 使困惑不解 shǐ kùnhuò bùjiě; 使迷惑 shǐ míhuò.

mystique /mɪˈstiːk/ *n* [C, 常作 sing] 神秘性 shénmìxìng.

myth /mɪθ/ *n* 1 (a) [C] 神话 shénhuà: *one of many ~s about the creation of the world* 关于创世的许多神话之一. (b) [U] 神话(总称) shénhuà. 2 [C] 虚构〔構〕的人(或事) xūgòu de rén. **mythical** /-ɪkl/ *adj* 1 存在于神话中的 cúnzài yú shénhuà zhōng de. 2 虚构的 xūgòude; 想像的 xiǎngxiàngde.

mythology /mɪˈθɒlədʒɪ/ *n* [U] 1 神话(总称) shénhuà: *Greek ~* 希腊神话. 2 神话学〔學〕shénhuàxué. **mythological** /ˌmɪθəˈlɒdʒɪkl/ *adj* 神话(中)的 shénhuàde; 神话学(上)的 shénhuàxuéde.

N n

N, n /en/ *n* [C] [*pl* N's, n's /enz/] 英语的第十四个〔個〕字母 Yīngyǔde dìshísìgè zìmǔ.

N *abbr* 1 north(ern): *N Yorkshire* 北约克郡. 2 neutral (connection) (尤用于电器插头上)不带〔帶〕电的(接线) bú dàidiàn de.

nab /næb/ *v* [-bb-] [T] [英国非正式用语] 逮住 dǎizhù; 抓住 zhuāzhù; 捉住 zhuōzhù.

nag[1] /næg/ *v* [-gg-] [I, T] (*at*) 指责不休 zhǐzé bùxiū; 不断〔斷〕地批评 búduànde pīpíng.

nag[2] /næg/ *n* [C] [非正式用语] 老马 lǎomǎ.

nail /neɪl/ *n* [C] 1 钉子 dīngzi. 2 指甲 zhǐjia; 趾甲 zhǐjiǎ. **nail** *v* [T] 1 钉牢 dīngláo; 钉住 dīngzhù. 2 [非正式用语] 抓住 zhuāzhù; 逮住 dǎizhù. 3 [短语动词] nail sb down 迫使某人说明其打算 pòshǐ mǒurén shuōmíng qí dǎsuàn.

naive (亦作 **naïve**) /naɪˈiːv/ *adj* 天真的 tiānzhēnde. **naively** *adv*. **naivety** *n* [U].

naked /ˈneɪkɪd/ *adj* 1 裸体〔體〕的 luǒtǐde. 2 无〔無〕遮蔽的 wú zhēbì de: *a ~ light* 没有灯罩的灯. 3 [习语] with the naked ˈeye 用肉眼 yòng ròuyǎn. **nakedly** *adv*. **nakedness** *n* [U].

name /neɪm/ *n* 1 [C] 名字 míngzi; 名称〔稱〕míngchēng: *My ~ is Tim.* 我的名字叫蒂姆. 2 [sing] 名誉〔譽〕míngyù; 名声〔聲〕míngshēng: *a ~ for being lazy* 由于懒惰而出名. 3 [C] 名人 míngrén: *the big ~s in show business* 演艺业的名人. 4 [习语] in the name of sb/sth (a) 代表某人(某事) dàibiǎo mǒurén. (b) 凭〔憑〕借…的权〔權〕威 píngjiè… de quánwēi: *I arrest you in the ~ of the law.* 我依法逮捕你. make a ˈname for oneself 成名 chéngmíng; 出名 chūmíng. take sb's name in vain 滥〔濫〕用某人的名义〔義〕lànyòng mǒurén de míngyì. **name** *v* [T] 1 (*after*; 美语 *for*) 给…命名 gěi…mìngmíng; 给…取名 gěi…qǔmíng: *The child was ~d after his father.* 那孩子是按他父亲的名字取的名. 2 说出…的名字 shuōchū…de míngzi. 3 说定 shuōdìng; 确定 quèdìng: *~ the day for the party* 说定聚会的日期. ˈ**name-dropping** *n* [U] (在谈话中)提起名人(暗示与之相识)以提高身价〔價〕的行为〔爲〕tíqǐ míngrén yǐ tígāo

N

shēnjià de xíngwéi. **nameless** *adj* 1 无〔無〕名的 wúmíngde;不知名的 bù zhīmíng de. 2 不可名状〔狀〕的 bùkě míngzhuàng de;难〔難〕以形容的 nán yǐ xíngróng de. ˈ**namesake** *n* [C] 同名(或同姓、同姓名)的人 tóngmíng de rén.

namely /ˈneɪmlɪ/ *adv* 即 jí;就是 jiùshì: *Only one child was missing, ~ John.* 只有一个孩子不在场,就是约翰.

nanny /ˈnænɪ/ *n* [C] [*pl* -ies] (照看小孩的)保姆 bǎomǔ.

nanny-goat /ˈnænɪ gəʊt/ *n* [C] 雌山羊 cí shānyáng.

nanotechnology /ˈnænəʊtekˌnɒlədʒɪ/ *n* [U] 纳米技术〔術〕nàmǐjìshù.

nap[1] /næp/ *n* [C] 小睡 xiǎoshuì;打盹 dǎdǔn. **nap** *v* [-pp-] [I] 小睡 xiǎoshuì;打盹 dǎdǔn.

nap[2] /næp/ *n* [U] (织物表面的)绒毛 róngmáo.

napalm /ˈneɪpɑːm/ *n* [U] 凝固汽油 nínggù qìyóu.

nape /neɪp/ *n* [C, 常作 sing] 项(颈的后部) xiàng.

napkin /ˈnæpkɪn/ *n* [C] 餐巾 cānjīn.

nappy /ˈnæpɪ/ *n* [C] [*pl* -ies] 尿布 niàobù.

narcissus /nɑːˈsɪsəs/ *n* [C] (*pl* ~es /nɑːˈsɪsəsɪz/ 或 narcissi /nɑːˈsɪsaɪ/) 水仙属〔屬〕shuǐxiānshǔ;水仙 shuǐxiān.

narcotic /nɑːˈkɒtɪk/ *n* [C], *adj* 麻醉剂〔劑〕mázuìjì;麻醉的 mázuìde.

narrate /nəˈreɪt; *US* ˈnæreɪt/ *v* [T] 讲〔講〕(故事) jiǎng;叙述 xùshù. **narration** /nəˈreɪʃn/ *n* [C, U]. **narrator** *n* [C] 讲述者 jiǎngshùzhě;叙述者 xùshùzhě.

narrative /ˈnærətɪv/ *n* 1 [C] 故事 gùshi. 2 [U] 叙述 xùshù;讲〔講〕述 jiǎngshù.

narrow /ˈnærəʊ/ *adj* 1 狭〔狹〕窄的 xiázhǎide;狭小的 xiáxiǎode: *a ~ road* 窄路. 2 小的 xiǎode;有限的 yǒuxiànde: *a ~ circle of friends* 交游不广. 3 勉强的 miǎnqiǎngde: *a ~ escape* 死里逃生. 4 偏狭的 piānxiáde;狭隘的 xiá'àide: *a ~ mind* 小心眼;心胸狭窄. **narrow** *v* [I, T] (使)变〔變〕狭 biànxiá;(使)变窄 biànzhǎi. **narrowly** *adv* 仅〔僅〕仅 jǐnjǐn;勉强地 miǎnqiǎngde: *~ly escape* 勉强地逃脱. ˌ**narrow-**ˈ**minded** *adj* 气〔氣〕量小的 qìliàng xiǎo de;心胸狭窄的 xīnxiōng xiázhǎi de. **narrowness** *n* [U].

nasal /ˈneɪzl/ *adj* 鼻的 bíde;鼻音的 bíyīnde.

nasturtium /nəˈstɜːʃəm; *US* næ-/ *n* [C] 旱金莲 hànjīnlián.

nasty /ˈnɑːstɪ; *US* ˈnæ-/ *adj* [-ier, -iest] 1 令人作呕〔嘔〕的 lìng rén zuò'ǒu de;令人不快的 lìng rén búkuài de: *a ~ smell* 难闻的气味. 2 不善良的 bú shànliáng de;恶〔惡〕意的 èyìde: *a ~ person* 恶人. 3 疼痛的 téngtòngde;严〔嚴〕重的 yánzhòngde: *a ~ injury* 重伤. **nastily** *adv*. **nastiness** *n* [U].

nation /ˈneɪʃn/ *n* [C] 民族 mínzú;国〔國〕家 guójiā;国民 guómín. ˌ**nation-**ˈ**wide** *adv*, *adj* 全国范〔範〕围〔圍〕(的) quánguó fànwéi;全国性(的) quánguóxìng.

national /ˈnæʃnəl/ *adj* 1 民族的 mínzúde;国〔國〕家的 guójiāde;国民的 guómínde: *local and ~ news* 地方和全国新闻. 2 国有的 guóyǒude;国立的 guólìde;国营〔營〕的 guóyíngde. **national** *n* [C] (某国的)公民 gōngmín;国民 guómín. ˌ**national** ˈ**anthem** *n* [C] 国歌 guógē. ˌ**National** ˈ**Health Service** *n* [sing] (英国)国民保健署 Guómín Bǎojiànshǔ. **nationalism** *n* [U] 1 民族主义〔義〕mínzú zhǔyì;国家主义 guójiā zhǔyì. 2 政治独〔獨〕立运〔運〕动〔動〕zhèngzhì dúlì yùndòng. **nationalist** *adj*, *n* [C]. **nationally** *adv*. ˌ**national** ˈ**service** *n* [U] 义务〔務〕兵役 yìwù bīngyì.

nationality /ˌnæʃəˈnælətɪ/ *n* [U, C] [*pl* -ies] 国〔國〕籍 guójí: *a person with French ~* 一位法国籍的人士.

nationalize /ˈnæʃnəlaɪz/ *v* [T] 使国〔國〕有化 shǐ guóyǒuhuà;收归〔歸〕国有 shōu guī guóyǒu. **nationalization** /ˌnæʃnəlaɪˈzeɪʃn; *US* -lɪˈz-/ *n* [U].

native /ˈneɪtɪv/ *n* [C] 1 本地人 běndìrén;本国〔國〕人 běnguórén. 2 [尤作蔑] 土著 tǔzhù;土人 tǔrén. 3 当〔當〕地土生动〔動〕物或植物 dāngdì tǔshēng dòngwù huò zhíwù. **native** *adj* 1 出生地的 chūshēngdìde: *my ~ city* 我的故里. 2 (动植物)当地土生的 dāngdì tǔshēng de.

nativity /nəˈtɪvətɪ/ *n* **the Nativity** [sing] 耶稣基督的诞生 Yēsū Jīdū de dànshēng.

NATO /ˈneɪtəʊ/ *abbr* North Atlantic Treaty Organization 北大西洋公约组织〔織〕Běidàxīyáng Gōngyuē Zǔzhī.

natural /ˈnætʃrəl/ *adj* 1 自然的 zìránde;与〔與〕自然有关〔關〕的 yǔ zìrán yǒuguān de;天然的 tiānránde: *the earth's ~ resources* 地球的自然资源. 2 本能的 běnnéngde: *It's ~ for a bird to fly.* 鸟生来就会飞. 3 生来就有的 shēnglái jiù yǒu de: *a ~ artist* 天生的艺术家. 4 意料中的 yìliào zhōng de;正常的 zhèngchángde: *It's only ~ you're upset.* 你心烦,那是很自然的. 5 不夸〔誇〕张的 bù kuāzhāng de;不做作的 bú zuòzuo de. **natural** *n* [C] 天生具有某种〔種〕才能的人 tiānshēng jùyǒu mǒuzhǒng cáinéng de rén: *That dancer is a ~.* 那位舞蹈演员是天生的料子. ˌ**natural** ˈ**history** *n* [U] 博物学〔學〕bówùxué. **natural** ˈ**wastage** *n* [U] (离职退休等引起的)自然减员 zìrán jiǎnyuán.

naturalist /ˈnætʃrəlɪst/ *n* [C] 博物学〔學〕家

N

bówùxuéjiā.

naturalize /ˈnætʃrəlaɪz/ *v* [T] 使加入国〔國〕籍 shǐ jiārù guójí; 使归〔歸〕化 shǐ guīhuà. **naturalization** /ˌnætʃrəlaɪˈzeɪʃn; *US* -lɪˈz-/ *n* [U].

naturally /ˈnætʃrəlɪ/ *adv* **1** 天生地 tiānshēngde: *She's ~ musical*. 她天生喜爱音乐. **2** 当〔當〕然 dāngrán: *N~, I'll help you*. 当然,我要帮助你. **3** 自然地 zìránde: *behave ~* 举止自然. **4** 非人为〔爲〕地 fēi rénwéi de.

nature /ˈneɪtʃə(r)/ *n* **1** [U] 自然界 zìránjiè; 大自然 dàzìrán: *Animals and plants are all part of ~*. 动物和植物是自然界的一部分. **2** [U] 简朴〔樸〕生活 jiǎnpǔ shēnghuó: *go back to ~* 回到自然的生活. **3** [C, U] 本性 běnxìng; 天性 tiānxìng: *It's her ~ to be kind*. 和蔼是她的天性. *the ~ of language* 语言的特征. **4** [sing] 种〔種〕类〔類〕zhǒnglèi; 类型 lèixíng: *changes of that ~* 那种类型的种种变化.

naught /nɔːt/ *n* [古] **1** 无〔無〕wú; 无物 wúwù. **2** [习语] **ˌcome to ˈnaught** 失败 shībài: *All his plans came to ~*. 他所有的计划都失败了.

naughty /ˈnɔːtɪ/ *adj* [-ier, -iest] **1** 顽皮的 wánpíde; 不听〔聽〕话的 bù tīnghuà de. **2** 下流的 xiàliúde; 猥亵〔褻〕的 wěixiède. **naughtily** *adv*. **naughtiness** *n* [U].

nausea /ˈnɔːsɪə; *US* ˈnɔːʒə/ *n* [U] 恶〔惡〕心 ěxīn; 作呕〔嘔〕zuò'ǒu. **nauseate** /ˈnɔːsɪeɪt; *US* ˈnɔːz-/ *v* [T] 使恶心 shǐ ěxīn; 使作呕 shǐ zuò'ǒu. **nauseous** *adj*.

nautical /ˈnɔːtɪkl/ *adj* 航海的 hánghǎide; 船舶的 chuánbóde; 海员的 hǎiyuánde. **ˌnautical ˈmile** *n* [C] 海里(约 6080 英尺或 1852 米) hǎilǐ.

naval /ˈneɪvl/ *adj* 海军的 hǎijūnde.

nave /neɪv/ *n* [C] (教堂的)中殿 zhōngdiàn.

navel /ˈneɪvl/ *n* [C] 肚脐〔臍〕dùqí.

navigable /ˈnævɪgəbl/ *adj* (江河、海洋等)可通航的 kě tōnghángde; 可航行的 kě hángxíngde.

navigate /ˈnævɪgeɪt/ *v* [I, T] 导〔導〕航 dǎoháng; 领航 lǐngháng. **navigation** /ˌnævɪˈgeɪʃn/ *n* [U]. **navigator** *n* [C].

navy /ˈneɪvɪ/ *n* [C] 海军 hǎijūn. **ˌnavy ˈblue** *adj* 海军蓝〔藍〕hǎijūnlán.

NB /ˌen ˈbiː/ *abbr* note carefully 注意 zhùyì; 留心 liúxīn.

near[1] /nɪə(r)/ *adj* **1** (空间、时间)近的 jìnde: *The house is ~ (to) the station*. 这房子离车站很近. **2** 关〔關〕系〔係〕近的 guānxì jìn de; 关系密切的 guānxì mìqiè de: *~ relations* 近亲. **3** [习语] **a near ˈthing** 几〔幾〕乎失败或造成灾〔災〕祸〔禍〕的事 jīhū shībài huò zàochéng zāihuò de shì. **near** *v* [I, T] 靠近 kàojìn; 接近 jiējìn: *The ship is ~ing land*. 船正在接近陆地. **nearness** *n* [U]. **ˈnearside** *adj, n* [sing] 左边〔邊〕的 zuǒbiānde; 左边 zuǒbiān. **ˌnear-ˈsighted** = SHORT-SIGHTED (a) (SHORT[1]).

near[2] /nɪə(r)/ *prep* (距离、时间)靠近 kàojìn; 接近 jiējìn: *Bradford is ~ Leeds*. 布雷德福靠近利兹. **near** *adv* **1** 在近处〔處〕zài jìnchù. **2** [习语] **nowhere ˈnear** 离〔離〕得远〔遠〕lí de yuǎn. **near ˈby** *adv* 在附近 zài fùjìn: *They live ~ by*. 他们住在附近. **ˈnearby** *adj* 不远的 bùyuǎnde. **nearly** *adv* **1** 几〔幾〕乎 jīhū; 很接近地 hěn jiējìn de. **2** [习语] **not nearly** 相差很远 xiāngchà hěnyuǎn: *not ~ly enough money* 钱远远不够.

neat /niːt/ *adj* **1** 整齐〔齊〕的 zhěngqíde; 安排有序的 ānpái yǒuxù de. **2** 灵〔靈〕巧的 língqiǎode; 巧妙的 qiǎomiàode: *a ~ answer to the problem* 巧妙的回答问题. **3** [非正式用语]绝妙的 juémiàode: *a ~ idea* 好的主意. **4** (酒)不搀〔攙〕水的 bù chān shuǐ de; 纯的 chúnde. **neatly** *adv*. **neatness** *n* [U].

necessary /ˈnesəsərɪ; *US* -serɪ/ *adj* 必要的 bìyàode; 必需的 bìxūde; 必须的 bìxūde: *Have you made the ~ arrangements?* 你已经作出必要的安排了吗? **necessarily** /ˌnesəˈserəlɪ/ *adv* 必定 bìdìng; 必然地 bìránde: *Tall men aren't necessarily strong*. 高大的人未必就强壮.

necessitate /nɪˈsesɪteɪt/ *v* [T] [正式用语] 使成为必需 shǐ chéngwéi bìxū.

necessity /nɪˈsesətɪ/ *n* [*pl* -ies] **1** [U] 必要(性) bìyào; 需要 xūyào. **2** [C] 必需品 bìxūpǐn: *Food is a ~ of life*. 食物为生活的必需品.

neck /nek/ *n* [C] **1** (a) 颈〔頸〕jǐng; 脖子 bózi. (b) (衣服的)领圈 lǐngquān; 领口 lǐngkǒu. **2** (物的)颈状〔狀〕部位 jǐngzhuàng bùwèi; 狭〔狹〕长〔長〕部分 xiácháng bùfen: *the ~ of a bottle* 瓶颈. **3** [习语] **ˌneck and ˈneck** (竞赛等)并〔並〕驾齐〔齊〕驱〔驅〕bìng jià qí qū; 不分上下 bùfēn shàngxià. **risk/save one's ˈneck** 冒着危险〔險〕màozhe wēixiǎn; 保住性命 bǎozhù xìngmìng. **up to one's neck in sth** 深深陷入(或卷入) shēnshēn xiànrù. **neck** *v* [I] [非正式用语] 拥〔擁〕抱亲〔親〕吻 yōngbào qīnwěn. **necklace** /ˈneklɪs/ *n* [C] 项链 xiàngliàn. **ˈnecktie** *n* [C] [旧或美语] = TIE[2] 1.

nectar /ˈnektə(r)/ *n* [U] 花蜜 huāmì.

née /neɪ/ *adj* (用于已婚妇女姓名之后,娘家姓氏之前): *Mrs Jane Smith, ~ Brown* 娘家姓布朗的简·史密斯夫人.

need[1] /niːd/ *modal v* (*pres tense all per-*

sons need，否定式 need not 或 needn't /ˈniːdnt/）（表示必要）：*You ~n't finish that work today*. 你今天不必把那件工作做完.

need² /niːd/ *v* [T] 1 需要 xūyào；要 yào：*That dog ~s a bath*. 那狗该洗澡了. 2（表示必要）：*You ~ to work harder!* 你一定要努力工作!

need³ /niːd/ *n* 1 [sing, U] 需要 xūyào；必要 bìyào：*There's a ~ for more engineers*. 这里需要更多的工程师. *There's no ~ to start yet*. 现在还不必动身. 2 **needs** [pl] 必需品 bìxūpǐn：*My ~s are few*. 我没什么需要. 3 [U] 贫穷〔窮〕 pínqióng；不幸 búxìng：*in ~* 处于贫困中. 4 [习语] **if need be** 需要的话 xūyào de huà. **needless** *adj* 1 不需要的 bù xūyào de；不必要的 bú bìyào de. 2 [习语] ˌ**needless to ˈsay** 不用说 búyòng shuō. **needlessly** *adv*. **needy** *adj* [-ier, -iest] 贫穷的 pínqióngde.

needle /ˈniːdl/ *n* [C] 1 针 zhēn；缝衣针 féngyīzhēn. 2 = KNITTING-NEEDLE (KNIT). 3（注射器的）针头〔頭〕 zhēntóu. 4（唱机的）唱针 chàngzhēn. **needle** *v* [T] [非正式用语]烦扰〔擾〕 fánrǎo；（用话）刺激 cìjī. ˈ**needlework** *n* [U] 缝纫 féngrèn；刺绣 cìxiù.

negation /nɪˈgeɪʃn/ *n* [U] [正式用语]否定 fǒudìng；否认〔認〕 fǒurèn.

negative /ˈnegətɪv/ *adj* 1 否定的 fǒudìngde；否认〔認〕的 fǒurènde. 2 消极〔極〕的 xiāojíde；无〔無〕助益的 wú zhùyì de：*~ criticism* 消极的批评. 3 [数学]负的 fùde. 4 [电]阴〔陰〕极的 yīnjíde；负极的 fùjíde. **negative** *n* [C] 1 否定词 fǒudìngcí；否定语 fǒudìngyǔ. 2（摄影）底片 dǐpiàn. 3 [习语] **in the ˈnegative** 否定的（地）fǒudìngde；否认的（地）fǒurènde. **negatively** *adv*.

neglect /nɪˈglekt/ *v* [T] 1 忽视 hūshì；忽略 hūlüè：*~ one's work* 忽视工作. 2 未做 wèizuò；忘记做 wàngjì zuò：*He ~ed to write*. 他忘了写信. **neglect** *n* [U] 忽略 hūlüè；疏忽 shūhu；疏漏 shūlòu. **neglectful** *adj* [正式用语]疏忽的 shūhude；不注意的 bú zhùyì de.

négligé（亦作 **negligee**）/ˈneglɪʒeɪ；*US* ˌneglɪˈʒeɪ/ *n* [C] 轻〔輕〕而薄的女晨衣 qīng ér bó de nǚ chényī.

negligent /ˈneglɪdʒənt/ *adj* 疏忽的 shūhude；玩忽的 wánhūde. **negligence** /-dʒəns/ *n* [U]. **negligently** *adv*.

negligible /ˈneglɪdʒəbl/ *adj* 不重要的 bú zhòngyào de；极〔極〕小的 jíxiǎode；微不足道的 wēi bù zú dào de.

negotiable /nɪˈgəʊʃɪəbl/ *adj* 1 可谈判的 kě tánpàn de；可磋商的 kě cuōshāng de. 2（支票等）可兑换现金的 kě duìhuàn xiànjīn de；可转〔轉〕让〔讓〕的 kě zhuǎnràng de. 3（道路、河流等）可穿越的 kě chuānyuè de；可通行的 kě tōngxíng de.

negotiate /nɪˈgəʊʃɪeɪt/ *v* 1 [I, T] 谈判 tánpàn；协〔協〕商 xiéshāng；洽谈 qiàtán. 2 [T] 越过〔過〕（障碍）yuèguò；超越 chāoyuè. **negotiation** /nɪˌgəʊʃɪˈeɪʃn/ *n* [C, U]. **negotiator** *n* [C] 谈判人 tánpànrén；洽谈人 qiàtánrén.

Negress /ˈniːgres/ *n* [C] [有时作蔑]女黑人 nǚ hēirén.

Negro /ˈniːgrəʊ/ *n* [C] [*pl* ~es] [有时作蔑] 黑人 hēirén；黑种〔種〕人 hēizhǒngrén.

neigh /neɪ/ *v* [I], *n* [C]（马）嘶叫 sījiào；马的嘶叫声〔聲〕 mǎde sījiàoshēng.

neighbour（美语 -or）/ˈneɪbə(r)/ *n* [C] 1 邻〔鄰〕居 línjū；邻人 línrén. 2 邻国〔國〕 línguó；邻近的人（或物）línjìnde rén. **neighbourhood** *n* [C] 1 地区〔區〕 dìqū；邻近地区 línjìn dìqū. 2 [习语] **in the neighbourhood of** 大约 dàyuē. **neighbouring** *adj* 邻近的 lín jìnde；附近的 fùjìnde：*~ing towns* 邻近的城市. **neighbourliness** *n* [U] 睦邻 mùlín；友善 yǒushàn；亲〔親〕切 qīnqiè. **neighbourly** *adj* 睦邻的 mùlínde；友善的 yǒushànde.

neither /ˈnaɪðə(r), ˈniːðə(r)/ *adj, pron* 两者皆非的 liǎngzhě jiē fēi de：*N~ boy is to blame*. 两个男孩都不应责怪. *I chose ~ of them*. 这两个我都不要. **neither** *adv, conj* 1 也不 yěbù：*She doesn't like Mozart and ~ do I*. 她不喜欢莫扎特的作品，我也不喜欢. *I've never been to Paris and ~ has she*. 我从未去过巴黎，她也没去过. 2 [习语] **neither...nor** 既不…也不 jì bù…yě bù：*N~ his sister nor his brother was invited*. 他妹妹和他弟弟均未受到邀请.

neon /ˈniːɒn/ *n* [U] 氖 nǎi.

nephew /ˈnevjuː, ˈnefjuː/ *n* [C] 侄子 zhízi；外甥 wàisheng.

nepotism /ˈnepətɪzəm/ *n* [U] 裙带〔帶〕关〔關〕系〔係〕 qúndài guānxi；任人唯亲〔親〕 rèn rén wéi qīn.

nerve /nɜːv/ *n* 1 [C] 神经〔經〕 shénjīng. 2 **nerves** [pl] [非正式用语]神经质〔質〕 shénjīngzhì；神经紧〔緊〕张〔張〕 shénjīng jǐnzhāng；神经过〔過〕敏 shénjīng guòmǐn：*He has ~s of steel*. 他沉得住气. 3 [U] 胆〔膽〕量 dǎnliàng；勇气〔氣〕 yǒngqì：*lose one's ~* 失去勇气. 4 [sing] 无〔無〕礼〔禮〕 wúlǐ；放肆〔肆〕 fàngsì：*She had the ~ to say I was cheating!* 她竟敢说我作弊，太放肆了. 5 [习语] **get on sb's ˈnerves** [非正式用语]烦扰〔擾〕某人 fánrǎo mǒurén. ˈ**nerve-racking** *adj* 使人心烦的 shǐ rén xīnfán de.

nervous /ˈnɜːvəs/ *adj* 1 神经〔經〕的 shénjīngde. 2 神经质〔質〕的 shénjīngzhìde；神经紧〔緊〕张〔張〕的 shénjīng jǐnzhāng de. ˌ**nervous**

ˈbreakdown *n* [C] 神经衰弱 shénjīng shuāiruò. nervously *adv*. nervousness *n* [U]. ˈnervous system *n* [C] 神经系统 shénjīng xìtǒng.

nervy /ˈnɜːvɪ/ *adj* [英国非正式用语] 神经〔經〕质〔質〕的 shénjīngzhìde; 神经紧〔緊〕张〔張〕的 shénjīng jǐnzhāng de.

nest /nest/ *n* [C] 1 (鸟的)巢 cháo; 窝〔窩〕wō. 2 一组(或一套)相似物件 yìzǔ xiāngsì wùjiàn. **nest** *v* [I] 做窝 zuò wō; 筑〔築〕巢 zhù cháo. ˈ**nest-egg** *n* [C] 储备〔備〕金 chǔbèijīn.

nestle /ˈnesl/ *v* 1 [I] (舒适地)安顿下来〔來〕āndùn xiàlái: ~ (*down*) *among the cushions* 舒适地倚在靠垫上. 2 [T] 偎依 wēiyī: *She ~d her head on his shoulder*. 她把头偎依在他的肩上.

nestling /ˈnestlɪŋ/ *n* [C] 雏〔雛〕鸟 chúniǎo.

net[1] /net/ *n* [C, U] 网〔網〕wǎng; 网状〔狀〕物 wǎngzhuàngwù: ˈ*fishing-~s* 鱼网. **net** *v* [-tt-] [T] 用网捕捉 yòng wǎng bǔzhuō. **the Net** 因特网 Yīntèwǎng. ˈ**netball** *n* [U] 无〔無〕挡〔擋〕板篮〔籃〕球 wú dǎngbǎn lánqiú. ˈ**network** *n* [C] 1 网状系统(如公路网) wǎngzhuàng xìtǒng. 2 联〔聯〕络网 liánluòwǎng. 3 广〔廣〕播网 guǎngbōwǎng; 电〔電〕视网 diànshìwǎng.

net[2] (亦作 **nett**) /net/ *adj* 净〔淨〕的 jìngde; 纯的 chúnde: ~ *profit* 纯利. **net** *v* [-tt-] [T] 净得 jìngdé; 净赚 jìngzhuàn.

netting /ˈnetɪŋ/ *n* [U] 网〔網〕wǎng; 网状〔狀〕(织)物 wǎngzhuàngwù.

nettle /ˈnetl/ *n* [C] 荨〔蕁〕麻 xúnmá.

network ⇨ NET[1].

neurology /njʊəˈrɒlədʒɪ; *US* nʊ-/ *n* [U] 神经〔經〕病学〔學〕shénjīngbìngxué. **neurologist** *n* [C] 神经病学家 shénjīngbìngxuéjiā.

neurosis /njʊəˈrəʊsɪs; *US* nʊ-/ *n* [C] [*pl* -oses /-əʊsiːz/] 神经〔經〕机〔機〕能病 shénjīng jīnéng bìng; 神经官能症 shénjīng guānnéng zhèng.

neurotic /njʊəˈrɒtɪk; *US* nʊ-/ *adj* 神经〔經〕机〔機〕能病的 shénjīng jīnéng bìng de; 神经官能症的 shénjīng guānnéng zhèng de. **neurotic** *n* [C] 神经官能症患者 shénjīng guānnéng zhèng huànzhě.

neuter /ˈnjuːtə(r); *US* ˈnuː-/ *adj* [语法]中性的 zhōngxìngde. **neuter** *v* [T] 阉割 yāngē.

neutral /ˈnjuːtrəl; *US* ˈnuː-/ *adj* 1 中立的 zhōnglìde. 2 中性的 zhōngxìngde: *a dull ~ colour* 暗淡的颜色. 3 (汽车排挡)空挡〔擋〕的 kōngdǎngde. **neutral** *n* 1 [C] 中立者 zhōnglìzhě; 中立国〔國〕zhōnglìguó. 2 [U] 空挡位置 kōngdǎng wèizhi. **neutrality** /njuːˈtrælətɪ; *US* nuː-/ *n* [U] 中立 zhōnglì. **neutralize** *v* [T] 使无〔無〕效 shǐ wúxiào; 中和 zhōnghé: *~ize a poison* 解毒.

neutron /ˈnjuːtrɒn; *US* ˈnuː-/ *n* [C] 中子 zhōngzǐ.

never /ˈnevə(r)/ *adv* 从〔從〕未 cóng wèi; 永不 yǒng bù; 未曾 wèi céng: *I've ~ been to Wales*. 我从未去过威尔士.

nevertheless /ˌnevəðəˈles/ *adv, conj* [正式用语] 虽〔雖〕然如此 suīrán rúcǐ; 不过〔過〕búguò; 仍然 réngrán: *He was old and poor, but ~ he was happy*. 他年老而且贫穷,但仍然很快乐.

new /njuː; *US* nuː/ *adj* 1 新的 xīnde: *a ~ film* 新影片. 2 新发〔發〕现的 xīn fāxiàn de; 生疏的 shēngshūde: *learn ~ words* 学习生词. 3 (*to*) 不熟悉的 bù shúxī de: *I'm ~ to this town*. 我不熟悉这个城市. 4 转〔轉〕换的 zhuǎnhuànde: *get a ~ job* 换个新工作. 5 重新的 chóngxīnde; 重新开〔開〕始的 chóngxīn kāishǐ de: *start a ~ life* 开始新生活. 6 [习语] **new blood** ⇨ BLOOD. **a ˌnew lease of ˈlife** (病愈或烦恼消除后)愉快和更有生气〔氣〕的新生活 yúkuài hé gèng yǒu shēngqì de xīn shēnghuó. **new-** *prefix* [构成复合形容词]新近的 xīnjìnde: ~*-born* 新生的. ˈ**newcomer** *n* [C] 新来的人 xīnláide rén. **newly** *adv* 新近 xīnjìn; 最近 zuìjìn: *a ~ly married couple* 新婚夫妇. ˈ**newly-weds** *n* [pl] 新婚夫妇〔婦〕xīnhūn fūfù. ˌ**new ˈmoon** *n* [C] 新月 xīnyuè. **newness** *n* [U]. **new ˈyear** *n* [U, C] 新年 xīnnián.

news /njuːz; *US* nuːz/ *n* 1 [U] 新闻 xīnwén; 新闻报〔報〕道 xīnwén bàodào: *Here's some good ~!* 有好新闻了. 2 **the news** [sing] (电台、电视的)定时〔時〕新闻广〔廣〕播 dìngshí xīnwén guǎngbō. ˈ**newsagent** (美语 ˈ**newsdealer**) *n* [C] 报刊经〔經〕销人 bàokān jīngxiāorén. ˈ**newsflash** *n* [C] (电台、电视台播送的)简明新闻(尤指重要新闻) jiǎnmíng xīnwén. **newspaper** /ˈnjuːspeɪpə(r); *US* ˈnuːz-/ *n* [C] 报纸 bàozhǐ; 报 bào.

newt /njuːt, *US* nuːt/ *n* [C] 蝾〔蠑〕螈 róngyuán.

next /nekst/ *adj* 1 紧〔緊〕接在后〔後〕的 jǐn jiē zài hòu de; 其次的 qícìde: *the ~ name on the list* 名单上的下一个名字. 2 接下去的 jiēxiàqùde: ~ *Thursday* 下星期四. **next** *adv* 在这〔這〕(或那)之后 zài zhè zhīhòu: *What are you going to do ~?* 下一步你要做什么? ˌ**next ˈdoor** *adv* 隔壁 gébì. ˌ**next of ˈkin** /ˈkɪn/ *n* [用 sing 或 pl v] 近亲〔親〕jìnqīn; 至亲 zhìqīn. **next to** *prep* 1 在…旁边〔邊〕zài … pángbiān; 在…附近 zài … fùjìn: *Come and sit ~ to me*. 过来,坐在我旁边. 2 几〔幾〕乎 jīhū: *say ~ to nothing* 几乎什么

N

也没说. *in ~ to no time* 几乎马上 jīhū mǎshàng.

NHS /ˌen eɪtʃ ˈes/ *abbr* National Health Service (英国)国[國]民保健署 Guómín Bǎojiànshǔ.

nib /nɪb/ *n* [C] (钢)笔[筆]尖 bǐjiān.

nibble /ˈnɪbl/ *v* [I,T] 一点[點]一点地咬 yìdiǎn yìdiǎn de yǎo;轻[輕]咬 qīngyǎo. **nibble** *n* [C] 小口的咬 xiǎokǒude yǎo;轻咬 qīngyǎo.

nice /naɪs/ *adj* [~r, ~st] 1 令人愉快的 lìng rén yúkuài de;宜人的 yírénde: *a ~ day* 美好的一天. 2 友好的 yǒuhǎode;亲[親]切的 qīnqiède. 3 [反语]坏[壞]的 huàide: *You've got us into a ~ mess!* 你使我们陷入困境了. 4 需慎重的 xū shènzhòng de;细微的 xìwēide: *a ~ distinction* 细微的区别. 5 [习语] nice and ... [非正式用语][用在形容词前]宜人地 yírénde: *It's ~ and quiet here*. 这里清静宜人. **nicely** *adv* 1 愉快地 yúkuàide;美好地 měihǎode. 2 [非正式用语]很好 hěnhǎo: *The patient is doing ~ly*. 那病人好得很快. **niceness** *n* [U].

nicety /ˈnaɪsətɪ/ *n* [C,常作 pl] [*pl* -ies] 细微的区[區]别 xìwēide qūbié: *niceties of meaning* 意义上的细微区别.

niche /niːʃ, nɪtʃ/ *n* [C] 1 壁龛[龕] bìkān. 2 [喻]适[適]当[當]的位置(或职业等) shìdàngde wèizhi.

nick[1] /nɪk/ *n* [C] 1 小切口 xiǎo qiēkǒu;刻痕 kèhén. 2 [习语] in good, bad, etc ˈnick [英俚]情况好(或坏等) qíngkuàng hǎo. in the ˌnick of ˈtime 正是时[時]候 zhèng shì shíhòu;不迟[遲] bùchí. **nick** *v* [T] 在…上切口 zài…shàng qiēkǒu;刻痕于 kèhén yú.

nick[2] /nɪk/ *n* the nick [sing] [英俚]监[監]狱 jiānyù;警察局 jǐngchájú. **nick** *v* [T] 1 [英俚]逮捕 dàibǔ. 2 [英国非正式用语]偷 tōu.

nickel /ˈnɪkl/ *n* 1 [U] 镍 niè. 2 [C] (美国或加拿大的)五分镍币[幣] wǔfēn nièbì.

nickname /ˈnɪkneɪm/ *n* [C] 绰号[號] chuòhào;诨名 húnmíng. **nickname** *v* [T] 给…起绰号 gěi…qǐ chuòhào.

nicotine /ˈnɪkətiːn/ *n* [U] 尼古丁 nígǔdīng.

niece /niːs/ *n* [C] 侄女 zhínǚ;甥女 shēngnǚ.

night /naɪt/ *n* 1 [C,U] 夜 yè;夜晚 yèwǎn;夜间 yèjiān. 2 [习语] at/by night 在夜里 zài yèlǐ. have a good/bad ˈnight (夜里)睡得好 shuì de hǎo;睡得不好 shuì de bùhǎo. ˌnight and ˈday, ˌday and ˈnight 日日夜夜 rìrì yèyè;夜以继[繼]日 yè yǐ jì rì. ˈ**night-club** *n* [C] 夜总[總]会[會] yèzǒnghuì. ˈ**night-dress** (亦作 nightie [非正式用语] /ˈnaɪtɪ/) *n* [C] (妇女或女孩的)睡衣 shuìyī. ˈ**nightfall** *n* [U] 黄昏 huánghūn;傍晚 bàngwǎn. ˈ**night-life** *n* [U] 夜生活 yèshēnghuó. **nightly** *adv, adj* 夜间(的) yèjiān;每夜(发生、做)(的) měiyè. ˈ**nightmare** *n* [C] 1 恶[惡]梦[夢] èmèng. 2 [非正式用语]非常可怕的经[經]历[歷] fēicháng kěpàde jīnglì;不愉快的经历 bù yúkuài de jīnglì. ˌ**night-ˈwatchman** *n* [C] [*pl* -men] 守夜人 shǒuyèrén;值夜者 zhíyèzhě.

nightingale /ˈnaɪtɪŋgeɪl; *US* -tŋg-/ *n* [C] 夜莺[鶯] yèyīng.

nil /nɪl/ *n* [U] 无[無] wú;零 líng.

nimble /ˈnɪmbl/ *adj* [~r, ~st] 1 敏捷的 mǐnjiéde;灵[靈]活的 línghuóde;迅速的 xùnsùde. 2 [喻](头脑)聪[聰]明的 cōngmingde;敏锐的 mǐnruìde. **nimbly** *adv*.

nine /naɪn/ *pron, adj, n* [C] 九(的) jiǔ. **ninth** /naɪnθ/ *pron, adj* 第九(的) dìjiǔ. **ninth** *n* [C], *pron* 九分之一 jiǔfēn zhī yī.

nineteen /ˌnaɪnˈtiːn/ *pron, adj, n* [C] 十九(的) shíjiǔ. **nineteenth** /ˌnaɪnˈtiːnθ/ *pron, adj* 第十九(的) dìshíjiǔ. **nineteenth** *pron, n* [C] 十九分之一 shíjiǔfēn zhī yī.

ninety /ˈnaɪntɪ/ *pron, adj, n* [C] [*pl* -ies] 九十(的) jiǔshí. **ninetieth** /ˈnaɪntɪəθ/ *pron, adj* 第九十(的) dìjiǔshí. **ninetieth** *pron, n* [C] 九十分之一 jiǔshífēn zhī yī.

nip /nɪp/ *v* [-pp-] 1 [T] 夹[夾]住 jiāzhù;掐住 qiāzhù;咬住 yǎozhù;捏[揑]住 niēzhù. 2 [I] [非正式用语]快速行动[動] kuàisù xíngdòng;急忙 jímáng: *I'll just ~ along to the shops*. 我要赶紧去商店. 3 [习语] nip sth in the bud 把…消灭[滅]于萌芽状[狀]态[態] bǎ…xiāomiè yú méngyá zhuàngtài. **nip** *n* [C] 1 [常作 sing] 夹 jiā;捏 niē;咬 yǎo. 2 (烈酒)少量 shǎoliàng. 3 [习语] a ˈnip in the air 刺骨的寒气[氣] cìgǔde hánqì.

nipple /ˈnɪpl/ *n* [C] 1 奶头[頭] nǎitóu. 2 橡皮奶头 xiàngpí nǎitóu.

nippy /ˈnɪpɪ/ *adj* [-ier, -iest] [非正式用语] 1 寒冷的 hánlěngde. 2 敏捷的 mǐnjiéde: *a ~ little car* 速度快的小汽车.

nit /nɪt/ *n* [C] 1 (寄生虫等的)卵 luǎn. 2 [非正式用语,尤用于英国英语] = NITWIT.

nitrogen /ˈnaɪtrədʒən/ *n* [U] 氮 dàn.

nitroglycerine (亦作 -glycerin, 尤用于美语) /ˌnaɪtrəʊˈglɪsəriːn; *US* -rɪn/ *n* [U] 硝化甘油 xiāohuàgānyóu.

nitwit /ˈnɪtwɪt/ *n* [C] [非正式用语]傻[儍]瓜 shǎguā;笨人 bènrén.

No (亦作 no) *abbr* [*pl* ~s] number.

no /nəʊ/ *adj* 1 没有 méiyǒu: *She had ~ money*. 她没有钱. 2 (表示禁止): *No smoking*. 禁止吸烟. 3 (表示与所说的事相反): *He's no fool*. 他可不是傻子. **no** *interj* (表示否定): '*Would you like a drink?*' '*No thanks.*' "你想喝点什么?""不,谢谢." no *adv* 不 bù: *He's feeling no better*. 他不觉得有所好转. **no** *n* [C] [*pl* ～es] 1 投反对〔對〕票者 tóu fǎnduìpiào zhě. 2 不 bù; 否定 fǒudìng; 没有 méiyǒu. ˌ**no-claims** ˈ**bonus** *n* [C] 保险〔險〕金(尤指汽车保险金)优〔優〕惠 bǎoxiǎnjīn yōuhuì. ˌ**no-**ˈ**go area** *n* [C] 禁区〔區〕jìnqū. ˈ**no man's land** *n* [U] (战争中双方阵前的)无〔無〕人地带〔帶〕wúrén dìdài. **no one** = NOBODY.

nobility /nəʊˈbɪlətɪ/ *n* 1 [U] 高贵 gāoguì; 高贵的出身(或地位) gāoguìde chūshēn; 高尚的思想 gāoshàngde sīxiǎng. 2 **the nobility** [sing] [用 sing 或 pl v] 贵族 guìzú.

noble /ˈnəʊbl/ *adj* [～r, ～st] 1 贵族的 guìzúde; 高贵的 gāoguìde. 2 高尚的 gāoshàngde; 崇高的 chónggāode: *a ～ leader* 伟大的领袖. 3 给人深刻印象的 gěi rén shēnkè yìnxiàng de; 卓越的 zhuóyuède. **noble** *n* [C] 贵族 guìzú; 贵族的成员 guìzúde chéngyuán. ˈ**nobleman** (*fem* ˈ**noblewoman**) *n* [C] 贵族 guìzú. **nobly** *adv*.

nobody /ˈnəʊbədɪ/ (亦作 **no one** /ˈnəʊwʌn/) *pron* 没有人 méiyǒu rén; 无〔無〕人 wúrén: *N～ came to see me*. 没人来看我. **nobody** *n* [C] [*pl* -ies] 无足轻〔輕〕重的人 wú zú qīng zhòng dè rén; 小人物 xiǎorénwù.

nocturnal /nɒkˈtɜːnl/ *adj* 夜间的 yèjiānde; 在夜间的 zài yèjiān de; 夜间发〔發〕生的 yèjiān fāshēng de: *Owls are ～*. 猫头鹰是夜间出没的.

nod /nɒd/ *v* [-dd-] 1 [I, T] 点〔點〕头〔頭〕(表示同意或打招呼) diǎntóu. 2 [短语动词] **nod off** [非正式用语]打瞌睡 dǎ kēshuì; 睡着 shuìzháo. **nod** *n* [C, 常作 sing] 点头 diǎntóu; 瞌睡 kēshuì.

noise /nɔɪz/ *n* [C, U] 噪声〔聲〕zàoshēng; 噪音 zàoyīn; 嘈杂〔雜〕声 cáozáshēng. **noisy** *adj* [-ier, -iest] 嘈杂的 cáozáde; 喧闹〔鬧〕的 xuānnàode; 充满噪声的 chōngmǎn zàoshēng de. **noisily** *adv*.

nomad /ˈnəʊmæd/ *n* [C] 游牧部落的人 yóumù bùluò de rén; 流浪者 liúlàngzhě. **nomadic** /nəʊˈmædɪk/ *adj*.

nominal /ˈnɒmɪnl/ *adj* 1 名义〔義〕上的 míngyìshàngde; 有名无〔無〕实〔實〕的 yǒumíng wúshí de: *the ～ ruler of the country* 名义上的国家统治者. 2 很少的 hěnshǎode: *a ～ rent* 象征性房租. 3 [语法]名词性的 míngcíxìngde. **nominally** /-nəlɪ/ *adv*.

nominate /ˈnɒmɪneɪt/ *v* [T] 提名 tímíng; 推荐〔薦〕tuījiàn. **nomination** /ˌnɒmɪˈneɪʃn/ *n* [C, U].

nominee /ˌnɒmɪˈniː/ *n* [C] 被提名者 bèi tímíng zhě; 被任命者 bèi rènmìng zhě.

non- /nɒn/ *prefix* 无〔無〕wú; 非 fēi; 不 bù. ˌ**non-com**ˈ**missioned** *adj* 未受军官衔〔銜〕的 wèishòu jūnguānxián de; 无委任状〔狀〕的 wú wěirènzhuàng de; 未受任命的 wèishòu rènmìng de. ˌ**non-com**ˈ**mittal** /kəˈmɪtl/ *adj* 不表态〔態〕的 bù biǎotài de; 不表明意见的 bù biǎomíng yìjiàn de. ˌ**non-con**ˈ**formist** *adj*, *n* [C] 不遵照社会〔會〕常规的(人) bù zūnzhào shèhuì chángguī de. ˌ**non-**ˈ**fiction** *n* [U] (非小说类)写〔寫〕实〔實〕文学〔學〕xiěshí wénxué. ˌ**non-**ˈ**stick** *adj* (锅)不粘食物的 bùzhān shíwù de. ˌ**non-**ˈ**stop** *adv*, *adj* 中途不停(的) zhōngtú bùtíng; 直达〔達〕(的) zhídá: *a ～-stop train* 直达火车.

nonchalant /ˈnɒnʃələnt/ *adj* 不感兴〔興〕趣的 bù gǎn xìngqù de; 不热〔熱〕心的 bú rèxīn de. **nonchalance** /-ləns/ *n* [U]. **nonchalantly** *adv*.

nondescript /ˈnɒndɪskrɪpt/ *adj* 平常的 píngchángde; 没有特征〔徵〕的 méiyǒu tèzhēng de.

none /nʌn/ *pron* 没有一个〔個〕měiyǒu yígè; 全无〔無〕quánwú: *N～ of them has/have come back yet*. 他们当中还没有一个人回来. **none** *adv* 1 **none the** 毫不 háo bù; 毫无 háo wú: *～ the worse for this experience* 这经验一点都不差. 2 **none too** 不很 bù hěn; 不太 bú tài: *～ too happy* 不太高兴. ˌ**none the** ˈ**less** *adv* 尽〔儘〕管如此 jǐnguǎn rúcǐ; 依然 yīrán; 然而 rán'ér: *She may be ill but she got the work done ～ the less*. 她也许病了,可是她把工作做完了.

nonentity /nɒˈnentətɪ/ *n* [C] [*pl* -ies] 无〔無〕足轻〔輕〕重的人 wú zú qīng zhòng de rén.

nonplussed /ˌnɒnˈplʌst/ *adj* 惊〔驚〕讶的 jīngyàde; 困惑的 kùnhuòde.

nonsense /ˈnɒnsns; *US* -sens/ *n* 1 [U] 无〔無〕意义〔義〕的词语 wú yìyì de cíyǔ. 2 [U, sing] 废〔廢〕话 fèihuà; 胡说 húshuō; 糊涂〔塗〕想法 hútu xiǎngfǎ. **nonsensical** /nɒnˈsensɪkl/ *adj* 愚蠢的 yúchǔnde; 荒谬的 huāngmiùde.

noodle /ˈnuːdl/ *n* [C, 常作 pl] 面〔麵〕条〔條〕miàntiáo.

nook /nʊk/ *n* [C] 1 隐〔隱〕蔽处〔處〕yǐnbìchù; 幽深处 yōushēnchù; 角落 jiǎoluò. 2 [习语] **every** ˌ**nook and** ˈ**cranny** 到处 dàochù.

noon /nuːn/ *n* [U] 中午 zhōngwǔ; 正午 zhèngwǔ.

no-one, no one = NOBODY.

noose /nuːs/ *n* [C] 索套 suǒtào; 活结 huójié; 活套 huótào.

nor /nɔː(r)/ *conj*, *adv* (用在 *neither* 或 *not* 之后)也不 yě bù; 也没有 yě méiyǒu: *Neither Chris ～ his sister wanted to come*. 克里斯和他妹妹都不想来. *He can't see, ～*

can he hear. 他看不见,也听不见.

norm /nɔːm/ *n* [C] 标[標]准[準] biāozhǔn;规范[範] guīfàn.

normal /ˈnɔːml/ *adj* 正常的 zhèngchángde;正规的 zhèngguīde;常态[態]的 chángtàide. **normal** *n* [U] 正常 zhèngcháng;常态 chángtài. **normality** /nɔːˈmælətɪ/ (亦作 **normalcy**, 尤用于美语 /ˈnɔːmlsɪ/) *n* [U] 正常 zhèngcháng;常态 chángtài. **normally** /-məlɪ/ *adv*.

north /nɔːθ/ *n* [sing] 1 **the north** 北 běi;北方 běifāng. 2 **the North** 北部 běibù. **north** *adj* 1 北方的 běifāngde;在北方的 zài běifāngde;向北的 xiàngběide. 2 (风)来自北方的 lái zì běifāng de. **north** *adv* 在北方 zài běifāng;向北方 xiàng běifāng. ˌ**north-ˈeast** *n* [sing], *adj*, *adv* (地区、方向等)东北 dōngběi. ˌ**north-ˈeastern** *adj*. **northerly** /ˈnɔːðəlɪ/ *adv*, *adj* 1 向北(的) xiàngběi;在北方(的) zài běifāng. 2 (风)来自北方(的) lái zì běifāng. **northern** /ˈnɔːðən/ *adj* 北方的 běifāngde;在北方的 zài běifāngde. **northerner** *n* [C] 北方人 běifāngrén. **northward** /ˈnɔːθwəd/ *adj* 向北的 xiàngběide. **northward(s)** *adv*. ˌ**north-ˈwest** *n* [sing], *adj*, *adv* (地区、方向等)西北 xīběi. ˌ**north-ˈwestern** *adj*.

N

Nos *abbr* numbers.

nose[1] /nəʊz/ *n* 1 [C] 鼻子 bízi. 2 [C] 鼻状[狀]物(如飞机机头) bízhuàngwù. 3 [sing] (a) 嗅觉[覺] xiùjué. (b) *for* [非正式用语]觉察力 juéchálì: *a ~ for a good story* 善于发现好题材. 4 [习语] **get up sb's ˈnose** [俚]使人恼[惱]怒 shǐ rén nǎonù. **poke/stick one's nose into sth** [非正式用语]干预(别人的事) gānyù;管闲[閑]事 guǎn xiánshì. **under sb's nose** [非正式用语]就在某人面前 jiù zài mǒurén miànqián. ˈ**nosebleed** *n* [C] 鼻出血 bí chūxuě. ˈ**nosedive** *n* [C], *v* [I] (飞机的)俯冲[衝] fǔchōng: [喻] *Prices have taken a ~dive*. 价格已暴跌.

nose[2] /nəʊz/ *v* 1 [I,T] (使)缓慢前进[進] huǎnmàn qiánjìn. 2 [短语动词] **nose about/around** 打听[聽]某事 dǎtīng mǒushì: *He's been nosing around in my department*. 他在我的部门里到处打听.

nosey (亦作 **nosy**) /ˈnəʊzɪ/ *adj* [-ier, -iest] [非正式用语,贬]好打听[聽]的 hào dǎtingde;爱[愛]管闲[閑]事的 àiguǎn xiánshì de. ˌ**Nosey ˈParker** *n* [C] [英国非正式用语,贬]爱打听消息的人 ài dǎting xiāoxi de rén;好管闲事的人 hàoguǎn xiánshì de rén.

nostalgia /nɒˈstældʒə/ *n* [U] 恋[戀]旧[舊] liànjiù;怀[懷]旧 huáijiù. **nostalgic** /-dʒɪk/ *adj* 恋旧的 liànjiùde;怀旧的 huáijiùde.

nostril /ˈnɒstrəl/ *n* [C] 鼻孔 bíkǒng.

not /nɒt/ (常略作 -n't /nt/) *adv* 1 (用以构成否定式): *She did ~ see him*. 她没见到他. *He warned me ~ to be late*. 他警告我不要迟到. *Don't be late!* 别迟到! 2 [习语] **not only... (but) also** (用于进一步强调某人或某事): *She's ~ only my sister but also my best friend*. 她不仅是我的妹妹,还是我最好的朋友. ˈ**not that** 并不是说 bìng búshì shuō: *I asked him to visit me — ~ that I like him, you understand*. 我要他来看我——并不是说我喜欢他,你是了解的.

notable /ˈnəʊtəbl/ *adj* 值得注意的 zhídé zhùyì de;显[顯]著的 xiǎnzhùde. **notable** *n* [C] 名人 míngrén;要人 yàorén. **notably** *adv* 特别地 tèbiéde;特殊地 tèshūde.

notary /ˈnəʊtərɪ/ *n* [C] [*pl* -ies] ˌ**notary ˈpublic** 公证[證]人 gōngzhèngrén;公证员 gōngzhèngyuán.

notation /nəʊˈteɪʃn/ *n* [C,U] (数学、音乐等用的)一套符号[號] yítào fúhào.

notch /nɒtʃ/ *n* [C] (V字形)切口 qiēkǒu;刻痕 kèhén. **notch** *v* [T] 1 在…上刻V形痕 zài…shàng kè Vxínghén. 2 [短语动词] **notch sth up** 赢得 yíngdé;获[獲]得 huòdé: *~ up a victory* 获胜.

note /nəʊt/ *n* 1 [C] 笔[筆]记 bǐjì;摘记 zhāijì: *take ~s at a lecture* 课上记笔记. 2 [C] 短笺[箋] duǎnjiān;便条[條] biàntiáo: *Leave a ~ about it on his desk*. 请在他桌上留个有关这件事的便条. 3 [C] 注释[釋] zhùshì;注解 zhùjiě. 4 [C] 纸币[幣] zhǐbì: ˈ*bank ~s* 钞票. 5 [C] (a) 单[單]音 dānyīn. (b) 音符 yīnfú. 6 [sing] 声[聲]音 shēngyīn: *a ~ of bitterness in his voice* 他的声调中带有悲伤. 7 [U] 重要 zhòngyào: *a family of ~* 显要之家. 8 [习语] **take note of sth** 注意 zhùyì;留意 liúyì. **note** *v* [T] 1 注意 zhùyì. 2 (*down*) 记录[錄] jìlù. ˈ**notebook** *n* [C] 笔记本 bǐjìběn;记事本 jìshìběn. **notebook comˈputer** *n* [C] 笔记本电[電]脑[腦] bǐjìběn diànnǎo. **noted** *adj* 著名的 zhùmíngde. ˈ**notepaper** *n* [C] 信纸 xìnzhǐ. ˈ**noteworthy** *adj* 值得注意的 zhídé zhùyì de;显[顯]著的 xiǎnzhùde.

nothing /ˈnʌθɪŋ/ *pron* 1 没有东西 méiyǒu dōngxi;没有什么[麼] méiyǒu shénme: *I've had ~ to eat since lunch*. 从午饭到现在我什么都没吃. '*You've hurt your arm*.' '*It's ~*.' "你伤了自己的胳膊." "没什么." 2 [习语] **for ˈnothing** (a) 免费 miǎnfèi: *He did the job for ~*. 他无偿地干了那份工作. (b) 无[無]结果 wú jiéguǒ;徒劳[勞] túláo. **have nothing to ˈdo with sb/sth** 自己与[與]…无[無]关[關] zìjǐ yǔ…wúguān. ˈ**nothing but** 仅[僅]仅 jǐnjǐn;只不过[過] zhǐ bú guò: *~ but* *the best* 最好的. **nothing (else) 'for it (but)** 没有别的办〔辦〕法 méiyǒu biéde bànfǎ: *There's ~ for it but to work late tonight*. 除了深夜工作没有别的办法. **nothing like** [非正式用语] (a) 完全不像 wánquán búxiàng: *She's ~ like her sister*. 她完全不像她的妹妹. (b) 绝对〔對〕不 juéduì bù: *This is ~ like as good*. 绝对没有这样好.

notice /ˈnəʊtɪs/ *n* **1** [C] 布告 bùgào; 公告 gōnggào; 启〔啟〕事 qǐshì. **2** [U] 警告 jǐnggào; 通知 tōngzhī; 预告 yùgào: *give her a month's ~ to leave* 通知她一个月后解雇. *at short ~* 提前很短时〔時〕间通知. **3** [习语] **bring sth/come to sb's notice** 引起某人对〔對〕…的注意 yǐnqǐ mǒurén duì…de zhùyì. **take no notice of sb/sth** 不注意 bú zhùyì; 不理会〔會〕 bù lǐhuì. **notice** *v* [I, T] 注意到 zhùyì dào; 察觉〔覺〕到 chájué dào. **noticeable** *adj* 明显〔顯〕的 míngxiǎnde; 显著的 xiǎnzhùde. **noticeably** *adv*.

notify /ˈnəʊtɪfaɪ/ *v* [*pt*, *pp* -ied] [T] (*of*) 报〔報〕告 bàogào; 通知 tōngzhī: *~ the police of the accident* 向警方报告出了事故. **notification** /ˌnəʊtɪfɪˈkeɪʃn/ *n* [U, C].

notion /ˈnəʊʃn/ *n* [C] 概念 gàiniàn; 观〔觀〕念 guānniàn.

notorious /nəʊˈtɔːrɪəs/ *adj* 臭名昭著的 chòumíng zhāozhù de; 声〔聲〕名狼藉的 shēngmíng lángjí de: *a ~ murder* 声名狼藉的谋杀案. **notoriety** /ˌnəʊtəˈraɪətɪ/ *n* [U] 臭名 chòumíng; 恶〔惡〕名 èmíng. **notoriously** *adv*.

nougat /ˈnuːgɑː, ˈnʌgət; *US* ˈnuːgət/ *n* [U] 牛轧糖(用花生等做成的糖果) niúzhátáng.

nought /nɔːt/ *n* [C] 零 líng.

noun /naʊn/ *n* [C] [语法]名词 míngcí.

nourish /ˈnʌrɪʃ/ *v* [T] **1** 养〔養〕育 yǎngyù. **2** [正式用语, 喻] 怀〔懷〕有(希望等) huáiyǒu. **nourishment** *n* [U] 食物 shíwù.

novel[1] /ˈnɒvl/ *n* [C] 小说 xiǎoshuō. **novelist** /ˈnɒvəlɪst/ *n* [C] 小说家 xiǎoshuōjiā.

novel[2] /ˈnɒvl/ *adj* 新奇的 xīnqíde; 新的 xīnde: *a ~ idea* 新的观念.

novelty /ˈnɒvltɪ/ *n* [*pl* -ies] **1** [U] 新颖 xīnyǐng; 新奇 xīnqí. **2** [C] 新奇的事物 xīnqíde shìwù. **3** [C] (廉价的)小玩具 xiǎo wánjù; 小装〔裝〕饰品 xiǎo zhuāngshìpǐn.

November /nəʊˈvembə(r)/ *n* [U, C] 十一月 shíyīyuè.

novice /ˈnɒvɪs/ *n* [C] **1** 新手 xīnshǒu; 生手 shēngshǒu; 初学〔學〕者 chūxuézhě. **2** 见习〔習〕修士(或修女) jiànxí xiūshì.

now /naʊ/ *adv* **1** (a) 现在 xiànzài; 目前 mùqián: *Where are you living ~?* 你现在住在什么地方? (b) 立刻 lìkè; 马上 mǎshàng: *Start writing ~*. 立刻开始写. **2** (用于引起注意): *N~ stop quarrelling and listen!* 别吵了, 听我说! **3** [习语] **(every) now and then/again** 有时〔時〕 yǒushí: *He visits me every ~ and then*. 他有时来看我. **now** *conj* (*that*) 既然 jìrán; 由于 yóuyú: *N~ (that) you're here, let's begin*. 既然你已经来了, 那就开始吧!

nowadays /ˈnaʊədeɪz/ *adv* 现在 xiànzài; 现今 xiànjīn: *She doesn't go out much ~*. 她现在不参加社交活动.

nowhere /ˈnəʊweə(r); *US* -hweər/ *adv* **1** 任何地方都不 rènhé dìfang dōu bù: *There is ~ interesting to visit in this town*. 这座城市没有有趣的地方可以参观. **2** [习语] **get nowhere** ⇨GET.

noxious /ˈnɒkʃəs/ *adj* [正式用语]有害的 yǒuhàide; 有毒的 yǒudúde.

nozzle /ˈnɒzl/ *n* [C] 管嘴 guǎnzuǐ; 喷嘴 pēnzuǐ.

nuance /ˈnjuːɑːns; *US* ˈnuː-/ *n* [C] (意义、意见、颜色等)细微差别 xìwēi chābié.

nuclear /ˈnjuːklɪə(r); *US* ˈnuː-/ *adj* 核的 héde; (使用)核能的 hénéngde. ˌ**nuclear** ˈ**energy** *n* [U] 核能 hénéng; 核动〔動〕力 hédònglì. ˌ**nuclear reˈactor** *n* [C] 核反应〔應〕堆 héfǎnyìngduī.

nucleus /ˈnjuːklɪəs; *US* ˈnuː-/ *n* [C] [*pl* **nuclei** /-klɪaɪ/] **1** (a) [物理]核 hé; 原子核 yuánzǐhé. (b) [生物]细胞核 xìbāohé. **2** 核心 héxīn; 中心 zhōngxīn: *These books form the ~ of the library*. 这些书成为图书馆的主要部分.

nude /njuːd; *US* nuːd/ *adj* 裸体〔體〕的 luǒtǐde. **nude** *n* **1** [C] 裸体画〔畫〕 luǒtǐhuà. **2** [习语] **in the nude** 未穿衣的 wèi chuān yī de; 赤裸裸的 chìluǒluǒde. **nudism** /-ɪzəm/ *n* [U] 裸体主义〔義〕 luǒtǐ zhǔyì. **nudist** *n* [C]. **nudity** *n* [U].

nudge /nʌdʒ/ *v* [T] 用肘轻〔輕〕推(以引起注意) yòng zhǒu qīngtuī. **nudge** *n* [C] (以肘)轻推 qīngtuī.

nugget /ˈnʌgɪt/ *n* [C] **1** 金属〔屬〕块〔塊〕(尤指天然金块) jīnshǔ kuài. **2** [喻]有价〔價〕值的消息(或情报) yǒujiàzhíde xiāoxi.

nuisance /ˈnjuːsns; *US* ˈnuː-/ *n* [C, 常作 sing] 讨厌〔厭〕的人 tǎoyànde rén; 讨厌的东西 tǎoyànde dōngxi; 恼〔惱〕人的事 nǎorénde shì.

null /nʌl/ *adj* [习语] **null and void** [法律]无〔無〕约束力的 wú yuēshùlì de; 无效的 wúxiàode. **nullify** /ˈnʌlɪfaɪ/ *v* [*pt*, *pp* -fied] [T] 使无效 shǐ wúxiào; 使无约束力 shǐ wú yuēshùlì.

numb /nʌm/ *adj* 麻木的 mámùde; 失去感觉〔覺〕的 shīqù gǎnjué de: *~ with cold/shock*

冻僵的;惊呆的. **numb** *v* [T] 使麻木 shǐ mámù;使失去知觉 shǐ shīqù zhījué. **numbness** *n* [U].

number /ˈnʌmbə(r)/ *n* [C] **1** 数〔數〕字 shùzì;数目 shùmù;号〔號〕码 hàomǎ: *3, 13 and 103 are ~s.* 3、13 和 103 都是数字. **2** 数量 shùliàng;数额 shù'é: *a large ~ of people* 很多人. *A ~ of books are missing.* 一些图书丢失了. **3** (期刊等的)一期 yìqī. **4** 一段舞 yíduàn wǔ;一首歌 yìshǒu gē. **number** *v* [T] **1** 给…编号 gěi…biānhào: *~ the pages* 编页码. **2** 总〔總〕共 zǒnggòng;计有 jìyǒu: *The crowd ~ed over 3000.* 总共三千多人. **3** *among* 包括 bāokuò: *I ~ her among my friends.* 我把她算作朋友.

numeral /ˈnjuːmərəl; *US* ˈnuː-/ *n* [C] 数〔數〕字 shùzì.

numerate /ˈnjuːmərət; *US* ˈnuː-/ *adj* 识〔識〕数〔數〕的 shíshùde;有计算能力的 yǒu jìsuàn nénglì de.

numerical /njuːˈmerɪkl; *US* nuː-/ *adj* 数〔數〕字的 shùzìde;用数字表示的 yòng shùzì biǎoshì de. **numerically** /-klɪ/ *adv*.

numerous /ˈnjuːmərəs; *US* ˈnuː-/ *adj* [正式用语]许多的 xǔduōde: *on ~ occasions* 许多次.

nun /nʌn/ *n* [C] 修女 xiūnǚ;尼姑 nígū. **nunnery** *n* [C] [*pl* -ies] 女修道院 nǚxiūdàoyuàn;尼姑庵 nígū'ān.

nurse /nɜːs/ *n* [C] 护〔護〕士 hùshì. **nurse** *v* [T] **1** 看护 kānhù;护理(病人等) hùlǐ. **2** 哺乳 bǔrǔ;给(婴儿)喂奶 gěi…wèinǎi. **3** 培养〔養〕péiyǎng;特别照料 tèbié zhàoliào: *~ young plants* 培育幼苗. **4** 怀〔懷〕有 huáiyǒu: *~ feelings of revenge* 心存报复. **nursing** *n* [U] 护理 hùlǐ. ˈ**nursing-home** *n* [C] (私立的)小医〔醫〕院 xiǎo yīyuàn.

nursery /ˈnɜːsərɪ/ *n* [C] [*pl* -ies] **1** 保育室 bǎoyùshì;托儿〔兒〕所 tuō'érsuǒ;儿童室 értóngshì. **2** 苗圃 miáopǔ. ˈ**nursery rhyme** *n* [C] 儿歌 érgē;童谣〔謠〕tóngyáo. ˈ**nursery school** *n* [C] 幼儿园〔園〕yòu'éryuán.

nurture /ˈnɜːtʃə(r)/ *v* [T] [正式用语] **1** 养〔養〕育 yǎngyù;教育 jiàoyù;教养 jiàoyǎng. **2** 培养 péiyǎng;培育 péiyù.

nut /nʌt/ *n* [C] **1** 坚〔堅〕果 jiānguǒ. **2** 螺母 luómǔ;螺帽 luómào. **3** [俚,贬]疯〔瘋〕子 fēngzi. **4** [习语] ˌ**off one's** ˈ**nut** [俚]疯狂的 fēngkuángde. ˈ**nut-case** *n* [C] [俚]疯狂的人 fēngkuángde rén. ˈ**nutcrackers** *n* [pl] 坚果钳 jiānguǒqián. ˈ**nutshell** *n* [习语] (**put sth) in a nutshell** 简括地(说) jiǎnkuòde. **nutty** *adj* [-ier, -iest] **1** 坚果味的 jiānguǒwèide. **2** [俚]疯狂的 fēngkuángde.

nutmeg /ˈnʌtmeg/ *n* [U, C] 肉豆蔻(树) ròudòukòu;肉豆蔻末 ròudòukòumò.

nutrient /ˈnjuːtrɪənt; *US* ˈnuː-/ *n* [C] 营〔營〕养〔養〕yíngyǎng;滋养 zīyǎng.

nutrition /njuːˈtrɪʃn; *US* nuː-/ *n* [U] 营〔營〕养〔養〕yíngyǎng;滋养 zīyǎng. **nutritional** /-ʃənl/ *adj*. **nutritious** /-ʃəs/ *adj* 有营养的 yǒu yíngyǎngde;滋养的 zīyǎngde.

nuts /nʌts/ *adj* [俚]发〔發〕疯〔瘋〕的 fāfēngde;疯狂的 fēngkuángde.

nuzzle /ˈnʌzl/ *v* [I, T] (用鼻子)轻〔輕〕触〔觸〕qīngchù;轻擦 qīngcā.

nylon /ˈnaɪlɒn/ *n* [U] 尼龙〔龍〕nílóng.

nymph /nɪmf/ *n* [C] (希腊、罗马神话中居于山林、河上的)小仙女 xiǎo xiānnǚ.

O o

O, o /əʊ/ *n* [C] [*pl* **O's, o's** /əʊz/] **1** 英语的第十五个〔個〕字母 Yīngyǔ de dìshíwǔgè zìmǔ. **2** (说电话号码时的)零 líng.

OA /ˌəʊ ˈeɪ/ *abbr* office automation 办〔辦〕公自动〔動〕化 bàngōng zìdònghuà.

oaf /əʊf/ *n* [C] 蠢人 chǔnrén;白痴〔癡〕báichī.

oak /əʊk/ *n* **1** [C] 栎〔櫟〕树〔樹〕yuèshù;橡树 xiàngshù. **2** [U] 栎木 yuèmù;橡木 xiàngmù.

OAP /ˌəʊ eɪ ˈpiː/ *abbr* old-age pensioner [英国非正式用语]领养〔養〕老金的人 lǐng yǎnglǎojīn de rén.

oar /ɔː(r)/ *n* **1** [C] 桨〔槳〕jiǎng;橹 lǔ. **2** [习语] **put/stick one's** ˈ**oar in** [非正式用语]干涉 gānshè;干预 gānyù.

oasis /əʊˈeɪsɪs/ *n* [C] [*pl* **oases** /-siːz/] (沙漠中的)绿洲 lǜzhōu.

oath /əʊθ/ *n* [C] [*pl* **~s** /əʊðz/] **1** 誓言 shìyán;誓约 shìyuē. **2** 诅咒语 zǔzhòuyǔ. **3** [习语] **be on/under** ˈ**oath** (在法庭上)宣过〔過〕誓要说实〔實〕话 xuān guò shì yàoshuō shíhuà.

oats /əʊts/ *n* [pl] 燕麦〔麥〕yànmài. ˈ**oatmeal** *n* [U] 燕麦片 yànmàipiàn.

obedient /əˈbiːdɪənt/ *adj* 服从〔從〕的 fúcóngde;顺从的 shùncóngde. **obedience** /-əns/ *n* [U]. **obediently** *adv*.

obelisk /ˈɒbəlɪsk/ *n* [C] 方尖碑 fāngjiānbēi;方尖塔 fāngjiāntǎ.

obese /əʊˈbiːs/ *adj* [正式用语](人)非常肥胖的 fēicháng féipàng de. **obesity** *n* [U].

obey /əˈbeɪ/ *v* [I, T] 服从〔從〕fúcóng;听〔聽〕从 tīngcóng.

obituary /əˈbɪtʃʊərɪ; *US* -tʃʊerɪ/ *n* [C] [*pl* -ies] 讣告 fùgào.

object[1] /ˈɒbdʒɪkt/ *n* [C] **1** 实〔實〕物 shíwù;物体〔體〕wùtǐ. **2** *of* (行动、情感等的)对〔對〕象

duìxiàng；客体 kètǐ：*an ~ of pity* 可怜的人(或物). 3 目的 mùdì：*Our ~ is to win*. 我们的目的是要获胜. 4 [语法]宾〔賓〕语(如例句 *Give him the money* 中的 *him* 和 *the money*) bīnyǔ. 5 [习语] **money, etc is no object** 钱〔錢〕等不成问题 qián děng bùchéng wèntí.

object[2] /əbˈdʒekt/ *v* [I] (*to*) 反对〔對〕 fǎnduì；不赞成 bú zànchéng.

objection /əbˈdʒekʃn/ *n* 1 [C, U] 厌〔厭〕恶〔惡〕 yànwù；反对〔對〕 fǎnduì. 2 [C] 反对的理由 fǎnduìde lǐyóu. **objectionable** /-ʃənəbl/ *adj* 令人不快的 lìng rén búkuài de. **objectionably** *adv*.

objective /əbˈdʒektɪv/ *adj* 1 客观〔觀〕的 kèguānde；无〔無〕偏见的 wú piānjiàn de；不带〔帶〕感情的 búdài gǎnqíng de：*an ~ report* 客观的报道. 2 [哲学]客观存在的 kèguān cúnzài de；真实〔實〕的 zhēnshíde. **objective** *n* [C] 目标〔標〕 mùbiāo；目的 mùdì. **objectively** *adv* 客观地 kèguānde；无偏见地 wú piānjiàn de. **objectivity** /ˌɒbdʒekˈtɪvətɪ/ *n* [U].

obligation /ˌɒblɪˈgeɪʃn/ *n* [C, U] 1 义〔義〕务〔務〕 yìwù；责任 zérèn. 2 [习语] **be under no obligation to do sth** 没有义务 méiyǒu yìwù；没有道义责任 méiyǒu dàoyì zérèn.

obligatory /əˈblɪgətrɪ; *US* -tɔːrɪ/ *adj* (法律上或道义上)必须的 bìxūde；强制的 qiángzhìde.

oblige /əˈblaɪdʒ/ *v* 1 [T] *to* [常作被动语态] 要求(某人)做 yāoqiú… zuò；强使 qiángshǐ：*They were ~d to sell the house*. 他们被迫卖掉房子. 2 [I, T] 帮〔幫〕忙 bāngmáng：*Could you ~ me by closing the door?* 你能帮我把门关上吗? 3 [习语] **much obliged, I'm much obliged to you** [旧]多谢 duōxiè. **obliging** *adj* 乐〔樂〕于助人的 lèyú zhùrén de. **obligingly** *adv*.

oblique /əˈbliːk/ *adj* 1 斜的 xiéde；倾斜的 qīngxiéde. 2 [喻]间接的 jiànjiēde：*an ~ reference* 拐弯抹角的提到. **obliquely** *adv*.

obliterate /əˈblɪtəreɪt/ *v* [T] 抹掉 mǒdiào；涂〔塗〕去 túqù. **obliteration** /əˌblɪtəˈreɪʃn/ *n* [U].

oblivion /əˈblɪvɪən/ *n* [U] 遗忘 yíwàng；忘却 wàngquè.

oblivious /əˈblɪvɪəs/ *adj of/to* 未觉〔覺〕察的 wèi juéchá de；不注意的 bú zhùyì de：~ *of the news* 不注意新闻. ~ *to his problems* 未觉察到他的问题.

oblong /ˈɒblɒŋ; *US* ˈɒblɔːŋ/ *n* [C], *adj* 长〔長〕方形 chángfāngxíng；长方形的 chángfāngxíngde.

obnoxious /əbˈnɒkʃəs/ *adj* 非常不快的 fēicháng búkuài de；讨厌〔厭〕的 tǎoyàn de；可憎的 kězèngde.

oboe /ˈəʊbəʊ/ *n* [C] 双〔雙〕簧管 shuānghuángguǎn. **oboist** *n* [C] 双簧管吹奏者 shuānghuángguǎn chuīzòuzhě.

obscene /əbˈsiːn/ *adj* 猥亵〔褻〕的 wěixiède；淫秽〔穢〕的 yínhuìde；下流的 xiàliúde. **obscenely** *adv*. **obscenity** /əbˈsenətɪ/ *n* [C, U] [*pl* -**ies**] 淫秽的语言(或行为) yínhuìde yǔyán.

obscure /əbˈskjʊə(r)/ *adj* 1 不易看清的 búyì kànqīng de；费解的 fèijiěde. 2 不著名的 bú zhùmíng de：*an ~ poet* 不著名的诗人. **obscure** *v* [T] 使不分明 shǐ bù fēnmíng；遮掩 zhēyǎn：*a hill ~d by fog* 被雾遮住的小山. **obscurely** *adv*. **obscurity** *n* [U] 不明 bùmíng；费解 fèijiě；无〔無〕闻 wúwén.

observance /əbˈzɜːvəns/ *n* 1 [U] (法律、习俗等的)遵守 zūnshǒu；奉行 fèngxíng；(节日的)纪念 jìniàn. 2 [C] 宗教仪〔儀〕式 zōngjiào yíshì；庆〔慶〕祝典礼〔禮〕 qìngzhù diǎnlǐ.

observant /əbˈzɜːvənt/ *adj* 善于观〔觀〕察的 shànyú guānchá de；观察力敏锐的 guānchálì mǐnruì de.

observation /ˌɒbzəˈveɪʃn/ *n* 1 [U] 观〔觀〕察 guānchá；注意 zhùyì：*a doctor's ~ of a patient* 医生对病人的观察. 2 [U] 观察力 guānchálì：*keen powers of ~* 敏锐的观察力. 3 [C] 评论〔論〕 pínglùn；言论 yánlùn. 4 [习语] **under obserˈvation** 在观察中 zài guānchá zhōng；在监〔監〕视中 zài jiānshì zhōng.

observatory /əbˈzɜːvətrɪ; *US* -tɔːrɪ/ *n* [C] [*pl* -**ies**] 天文台〔臺〕 tiānwéntái；观〔觀〕象台 guānxiàngtái；气〔氣〕象台 qìxiàngtái.

observe /əbˈzɜːv/ *v* [T] 1 看到 kàndào；注意到 zhùyì dào；观〔觀〕察 guānchá. 2 [正式用语]遵守(规则、法律等) zūnshǒu；奉行 fèngxíng. 3 [正式用语]庆〔慶〕祝 qìngzhù；过〔過〕(节日、生日等) guò. 4 [正式用语]评论〔論〕 pínglùn；评说 píngshuō. **observer** *n* [C] 1 观察者 guāncházhě；遵守者 zūnshǒuzhě；评论者 pínglùnzhě. 2 (会议等的)观察员 guāncháyuán；旁听〔聽〕者 pángtīngzhě.

obsess /əbˈses/ *v* [T] [常用被动语态]使困扰〔擾〕 shǐ kùnrǎo；使心神不宁〔寧〕 shǐ xīnshén bùníng；使着迷 shǐ zháomí：*be ~ed by the fear of death* 受着死亡恐惧的困扰. **obsession** /əbˈseʃn/ *n* 1 [U] 困扰 kùnrǎo；着迷 zháomí；分神 fēnshén. 2 [C] 萦〔縈〕绕〔繞〕于心的事 yíngrǎo yú xīn de shì；强迫观〔觀〕念 qiángpò guānniàn. **obsessive** *adj* 萦绕于心的 yíngrǎo yú xīn de；强迫性的 qiángpòxìngde.

obsolescent /ˌɒbsəˈlesnt/ *adj* 逐步废〔廢〕弃〔棄〕的 zhúbù fèiqì de；即将〔將〕过〔過〕时〔時〕的 jíjiāng guòshí de. **obsolescence** /-ˈlesns/ *n* [U].

obsolete /ˈɒbsəliːt/ *adj* 不再使用的 búzài shǐyòng de；过〔過〕时〔時〕的 guòshíde.

obstacle /ˈɒbstəkl/ *n* [C] [常作喻]障碍〔礙〕(物) zhàng'ài；妨碍 fáng'ài：*an ~ to world*

O

peace 世界和平的障碍.

obstetrics /əbˈstetrɪks/ *n* [用 sing *v*] 产〔產〕科学〔學〕chǎnkēxué. **obstetrician** /ˌɒbstəˈtrɪʃn/ *n* [C] 产科医〔醫〕生 chǎnkē yīshēng.

obstinate /ˈɒbstənət/ *adj* 1 顽固的 wángùde;倔强的 juéjiàngde;固执〔執〕的 gùzhíde. 2 顽强的 wánqiángde;不易去除的 búyì qùchú de;难〔難〕治的 nánzhìde: ~ *stains* 去不掉的污迹. **obstinacy** /-nəsɪ/ *n* [U]. **obstinately** *adv*.

obstreperous /əbˈstrepərəs/ *adj* 喧闹〔鬧〕的 xuānnàode;喧哗〔嘩〕的 xuānhuáde: *a class full of ~ children* 有许多喧闹儿童的班级.

obstruct /əbˈstrʌkt/ *v* [T] 1 阻塞 zǔsè;堵塞 dǔsè: ~ *a road* 阻塞道路. 2 妨碍〔礙〕fáng'ài;阻挠〔撓〕zǔnáo: ~ *justice* 阻挠执法. **obstruction** /-kʃn/ *n* 1 [U] 阻碍 zǔ'ài;障碍 zhàng'ài;妨碍 fáng'ài. 2 [C] 障碍物 zhàng'àiwù;阻塞物 zǔsèwù. **obstructive** *adj* 阻碍的 zǔ'àide;阻挠的 zǔnáode.

obtain /əbˈteɪn/ *v* [T] [正式用语]得到 dédào;获〔獲〕得 huòdé: *Where can I ~ the book?* 我在哪里可以买到这本书? **obtainable** *adj*.

obtrusive /əbˈtruːsɪv/ *adj* 显〔顯〕眼的 xiǎnyǎnde;突出的 tūchūde: *a modern house which is ~ in an old village* 在古老乡村中一所刺眼的现代化房子. **obtrusively** *adv*.

obtuse /əbˈtjuːs/ *adj* 1 [正式用语,贬]迟〔遲〕钝的 chídùnde;愚笨的 yúbènde. 2 [数学]钝角的 dùnjiǎode. **obtusely** *adv*. **obtuseness** *n* [U].

O

obverse /ˈɒbvɜːs/ *n* [常用 sing] [正式用语] 1 (钱币的)正面 zhèngmiàn. 2 对〔對〕立面 duìlìmiàn.

obvious /ˈɒbvɪəs/ *adj* 明显〔顯〕的 míngxiǎnde;显然的 xiǎnránde;明白的 míngbaide. **obviously** *adv*.

occasion /əˈkeɪʒn/ *n* 1 [C] 时〔時〕刻 shíkè;时候 shíhòu;场〔場〕合 chǎnghé. 2 [C] 特殊事件 tèshū shìjiàn;庆〔慶〕典 qìngdiǎn. 3 [U, sing] [正式用语]理由 lǐyóu;原因 yuányīn: *I have had no ~ to visit them recently*. 我最近不需要去看他们. 4 [习语] **on ocˈcasion** 有时 yǒushí. **occasion** *v* [T] [正式用语]引起 yǐnqǐ;惹起 rěqǐ.

occasional /əˈkeɪʒənl/ *adj* 偶然的 ǒuránde;偶尔〔爾〕的 ǒu'ěrde: *an ~ drink/visit* 偶尔喝的酒;偶然的拜访. **occasionally** /-nəlɪ/ *adv*.

occidental /ˌɒksɪˈdentl/ *adj* [正式用语]西方的 xīfāngde;西方国〔國〕家的 xīfāng guójiā de.

occult /ɒˈkʌlt; *US* əˈ-/ *n* **the occult** [sing] 超自然的 chāo zìrán de;有魔力的 yǒu mólì de. **occult** *adj*.

occupant /ˈɒkjʊpənt/ *n* [C] 居住者 jūzhùzhě;占〔佔〕用者 zhànyòngzhě. **occupancy** /-pənsɪ/ *n* [U] 居住 jūzhù;占用 zhànyòng;占用期 zhànyòngqī.

occupation /ˌɒkjʊˈpeɪʃn/ *n* 1 [C] 工作 gōngzuò;职〔職〕业〔業〕zhíyè. 2 [C] 日常事务〔務〕rìcháng shìwù;消遣 xiāoqiǎn. 3 [U] 占据〔據〕zhànjù;占领 zhànlǐng. **occupational** /-ʃənl/ *adj* 职业的 zhíyède;职业引起的 zhíyè yǐnqǐ de.

occupy /ˈɒkjʊpaɪ/ *v* [*pt*, *pp* -ied] [T] 1 占〔佔〕用 zhànyòng;占有 zhànyǒu. 2 占领 zhànlǐng;侵占 qīnzhàn. 3 占(空间、时间、头脑) zhàn;填满 tiánmǎn. 4 担〔擔〕任(职务) dānrèn. 5 ~ **oneself** 忙于 mángyú. **occupier** *n* [C] 居住人 jūzhùrén;占用者 zhànyòngzhě.

occur /əˈkɜː(r)/ *v* [-rr-] [I] 1 发〔發〕生 fāshēng: *The accident ~red in the rain*. 事故发生在下雨天. 2 被发现 bèi fāxiàn;存在 cúnzài: *Poverty ~s in every country*. 每个国家都存在贫穷. 3 *to* 想到 xiǎngdào;想起 xiǎngqǐ: *It never ~red to me that I should tell you*. 我从未想到我应当告诉你. **occurrence** /əˈkʌrəns/ *n* 1 [C] 事件 shìjiàn;事情 shìqing. 2 [U] [正式用语]事情发生的情况 shìqing fāshēng de qíngkuàng.

ocean /ˈəʊʃn/ *n* **Ocean** [C] 洋 yáng;海洋 hǎiyáng: *the Pacific O~* 太平洋. **oceanic** /ˌəʊʃɪˈænɪk/ *adj*.

o'clock /əˈklɒk/ *adv* (说钟点时与数字连用) …点〔點〕钟〔鐘〕…diǎnzhōng: *It's 5 ~*. 现在是5点钟.

octagon /ˈɒktəgən; *US* -gɒn/ *n* [C] 八边〔邊〕形 bābiānxíng;八角形 bājiǎoxíng. **octagonal** /ɒkˈtægənl/ *adj*.

octane /ˈɒkteɪn/ *n* [U] 辛烷 xīnwán.

octave /ˈɒktɪv/ *n* [C] [音乐]八度 bādù;八度音 bādùyīn;八度音程 bādù yīnchéng.

October /ɒkˈtəʊbə(r)/ *n* [U, C] 十月 shíyuè.

octopus /ˈɒktəpəs/ *n* [C] 章鱼 zhāngyú.

odd /ɒd/ *adj* 1 奇怪的 qíguàide;不寻〔尋〕常的 bù xúncháng de. 2 奇数〔數〕的 jīshùde: *1 and 5 are ~ numbers*. 1和5是奇数. 3 单〔單〕的 dānde: *an ~ sock/shoe* 单只的袜子;单只的鞋. 4 稍多于 shāoduō yú: *30-~ years* 三十多年. 5 [习语] **odd man/one ˈout** 与〔與〕众〔衆〕不同的人(或物) yǔ zhòng bùtóng de rén. **oddity** *n* [*pl* -ties] 1 [U] 奇特 qítè;奇怪 qíguài. 2 [C] 怪人 guàirén;怪事 guàishì. ˌ**odd ˈjobs** *n* [pl] 零工 línggōng. **odd ˈjob man** *n* [C] 打零工者 dǎ línggōng zhě;打短工者 dǎ duǎngōng zhě. **oddly** *adv* 奇特地 qítède;奇

怪地 qíguàide.

oddment /ˈɒdmənt/ *n* [C] 剩余〔餘〕物 shèngyúwù.

odds /ɒdz/ *n* [pl] **1** 可能性 kěnéngxìng; 机〔機〕会〔會〕jīhuì: *The ~ are she'll win*. 可能她赢. **2** [习语] **be at odds** 不和 bùhé; 意见不一致 yìjiàn bù yízhì. **it makes no ˈodds** 无〔無〕关〔關〕紧〔緊〕要 wúguān jǐnyào. **ˌodds and ˈends** *n* [pl] [英国非正式用语]零星杂〔雜〕物 língxīng záwù.

ode /əʊd/ *n* [C] (通常为长篇的)颂诗 sòngshī; 颂歌 sònggē.

odious /ˈəʊdɪəs/ *adj* [正式用语]可憎的 kězèngde; 可恨的 kěhènde.

odour (美语 **odor**) /ˈəʊdə(r)/ *n* [C] [正式用语](香的或臭的)气〔氣〕味 qìwèi.

oesophagus /ɪˈsɒfəgəs/ *n* [C] [医学]食管 shíguǎn; 食道 shídào.

of /əv; 强式 ɒv/ *prep* **1** 属〔屬〕于 shǔyú: *a friend of mine* 我的朋友. *the lid of the box* 箱子的盖. **2** 来自 lái zì; 居住于 jūzhù yú: *the miners of Wales* 威尔士的矿工. **3** 由…创〔創〕作的 yóu…chuàngzuò de: *the works of Shakespeare* 莎士比亚的著作. **4** 关〔關〕于 guānyú: *a picture of sb* 某人的像. **5** (表示制作某物的材料): *a dress of silk* 丝绸连衣裙. **6** (表示某种关系): *a lover of music* 爱好音乐的人. *the support of the voters* 选民的支持. **7** (表示数量或内容): *40 litres of petrol* 40升汽油. *a bottle of lemonade* 一瓶汽水. **8** (表示部分): *a member of the team* 队员. **9** (表示空间或时间的距离): *20 kilometres south of Paris* 巴黎以南20公里. **10** (用于日期): *the first of May* 五月一日. **11** (表示原因): *die of cancer* 死于癌症. **12** (表示除去、剥夺等): *rob sb of sth* 抢去某人的东西. **13** [旧]经〔經〕常(在某时)发〔發〕生 jīngcháng fāshēng: *go for a walk of an evening* 通常晚上去散步.

off[1] /ɒf; *US* ɔːf/ *adv* **1** 离〔離〕开〔開〕líkāi; 距 jù; 离 lí; 到 dào: *The town is still 5 miles ~*. 那小城还在五英里以外. **2** (表示除掉或分离): *take one's hat ~* 摘帽. **3** 出发〔發〕chūfā: *He's ~ to France today*. 他今天出发去法国. **4** [非正式用语]取消 qǔxiāo: *The wedding is ~*. 婚礼取消了. **5** 切断〔斷〕qiēduàn; 停止 tíngzhǐ: *The electricity is ~*. 电停了. **6** 关〔關〕掉 guāndiào; 不用 búyòng: *The radio is ~*. 收音机已关掉. **7** (餐馆的某种菜肴)不再供应〔應〕búzài gōngyìng: *The soup is ~*. 汤已售完. **8** 不工作 bù gōngzuò: *take the day ~* 休假一天. **9** [习语] **ˌoff and ˈon, ˌon and ˈoff** 有时〔時〕yǒushí.

off[2] /ɒf; *US* ɔːf/ *adj* **1** [非正式用语]不礼〔禮〕貌的 bù lǐmào de; 不友好的 bù yǒuhǎo de: *He can be a bit ~ sometimes*. 他有时会有点不礼貌. **2** (食物)不新鲜 bù xīnxiān: *The milk is ~*. 牛奶已变质. **3** [非正式用语]不佳的 bùjiāde; 倒霉的 dǎoméide: *an ˈ~-day* 倒霉的日子. **4** 萧〔蕭〕条〔條〕的 xiāotiáode: *the ˈ~-season* 淡季. **5** [习语] **on the ˈoff-chance** 极〔極〕小的可能性 jíxiǎode kěnéngxìng: *I went to his house on the ~-chance (that he'd be at home)*. 我抱着万一他在家的想法,去他家了.

off[3] /ɒf; *US* ɔːf/ *prep* **1** 离〔離〕开〔開〕líkāi; 从〔從〕…向下 cóng…xiàngxià: *fall ~ a ladder* 从梯子上跌下来. *take a packet ~ the shelf* 从架上取下一小包. [喻] *We're getting ~ the subject*. 我们离题了. **2** (尤指道路)通向 tōngxiàng; 从…分岔 cóng…fēnchà: *a lane ~ the main road* 可从大路进入的一条小路. **3** 离… lí…: *a house ~ the high street* 离大街不远的一所房子. **4** [非正式用语]不想要 bù xiǎngyào; 不需要 bù xūyào: *~ one's food* 不想吃东西. *He's ~ drugs now*. 他现在戒毒了.

offal /ˈɒfl; *US* ˈɔːfl/ *n* [U] (食用的)动〔動〕物内脏〔臟〕dòngwù nèizàng; 下水 xiàshui.

offence (美语 **-ense**) /əˈfens/ *n* **1** [C] 犯法 fànfǎ; 罪行 zuìxíng. **2** [U] 冒犯 màofàn; 得罪 dézuì: *I didn't mean to give ~*. 我并不是有意得罪你. *He's quick to take ~*. 他动不动就生气.

offend /əˈfend/ *v* **1** [T] 伤〔傷〕…的感情 shāng…de gǎnqíng; 冒犯 màofàn. **2** [T] 使不快 shǐ búkuài: *ugly buildings that ~ the eye* 刺眼的难看建筑物. **3** [I] *against* [正式用语]犯过〔過〕错 fàn guò cuò; 犯罪 fànzuì. **offender** *n* [C] 犯法者 fànfǎzhě; 犯罪者 fànzuìzhě. **offending** *adj* 冒犯的 màofànde; 得罪的 dézuìde; 使不快的 shǐ búkuài de; 犯法的 fànfǎde.

offensive /əˈfensɪv/ *adj* **1** 冒犯的 màofànde; 唐突的 tángtūde: *~ language* 无礼语言. **2** [正式用语]攻击〔擊〕性的 gōngjīxìngde; 进〔進〕攻的 jìngōngde: *~ weapons* 进攻性武器. **offensive** *n* [C] **1** 进攻 jìngōng; 攻势〔勢〕gōngshì. **2** [习语] **go on/take the offensive** 开〔開〕始攻击 kāishǐ gōngjī. **offensively** *adv*. **offensiveness** *n* [U].

offer /ˈɒfə(r); *US* ˈɔːf-/ *v* **1** [T] 给予 jǐyǔ; 提供 tígōng: *They ~ed him a good job*. 他们给他一份好工作. **2** [I, T] 表示愿〔願〕意做 biǎoshì yuànyì zuò; 给(某物) gěi: *I ~ed to go first*. 我表示要第一个去. **3** [T] [正式用语]给予 jǐyǔ: *The job ~s good chances of promotion*. 这份工作有好的晋升机会. **offer** *n* [C] **1** 提议〔議〕tíyì; 建议 jiànyì. **2** 给予物 jǐyǔwù;提供物 tígōngwù. **offering** *n* [C] 捐献〔獻〕物 juānxiànwù;捐助物 juānzhùwù.

offhand /ˌɒfˈhænd; *US* ˌɔːf-/ *adj* (行为)随便的 suíbiànde;无〔無〕礼〔禮〕的 wúlǐde. **offhand** *adv* 不假思索地 bù jiǎ sīsuǒde: *I can't give you an answer* ~. 我不能即刻给你回答.

office /ˈɒfɪs; *US* ˈɔːfɪs/ *n* 1 [C] 办〔辦〕公室 bàngōngshì;办公楼〔樓〕bàngōnglóu. 2 [C] (有特定用途的)办事处 bànshìchù;事务〔務〕所 shìwùsuǒ;营〔營〕业〔業〕所 yíngyèsuǒ: *a ˈticket* ~ 售票处. 3 **Office** [sing] (政府部门的)部 bù;局 jú;厅〔廳〕tīng: *The Foreign O*~ 外交部. 4 [C, U] 公职〔職〕gōngzhí;官职 guānzhí: *the* ~ *of president* 总统职位.

officer /ˈɒfɪsə(r); *US* ˈɔːf-/ *n* [C] 1 军官 jūnguān: *an* ~ *in the navy* 海军军官. 2 (政府的)官员 guānyuán: *a customs* ~ 海关官员. 3 (男、女)警察 jǐngchá;警官 jǐngguān.

official /əˈfɪʃl/ *adj* 1 公务〔務〕的 gōngwùde;公职〔職〕的 gōngzhíde;职权〔權〕的 zhíquánde. 2 官方的 guānfāngde;正式的 zhèngshìde: *an* ~ *statement* 官方声明. **official** *n* [C] 官员 guānyuán. **officialdom** /-dəm/ *n* [U] [用 sing, 或 pl v][正式用语,常作贬]官员(总称) guānyuán. **officially** /-ʃəlɪ/ *adv* 公务(或公职)上 gōngwù shàng;正式地 zhèngshìde.

officiate /əˈfɪʃɪeɪt/ *v* [I] (*at*) 执〔執〕行职〔職〕务〔務〕zhíxíng zhíwù;主持 zhǔchí.

officious /əˈfɪʃəs/ *adj* [贬]爱〔愛〕发〔發〕号〔號〕施令的 ài fā hào shī lìng de;好管闲〔閒〕事的 hào guǎn xiánshì de. **officiously** *adv*. **officiousness** *n* [U].

O

offing /ˈɒfɪŋ; *US* ˈɔːf-/ *n* [习语] **in the offing** [非正式用语]即将〔將〕发〔發〕生 jíjiāng fāshēng.

off-licence /ˈɒf laɪsns/ *n* [C] [英国英语]持有外卖〔賣〕酒类〔類〕执〔執〕照的酒店 chíyǒu wàimài jiǔlèi zhízhào de jiǔdiàn.

offline /ɒfˈlaɪn/ *adj*, *adv* 脱机〔機〕的 tuōjīde.

off-peak /ˌɒf ˈpiːk; *US* ˌɔːf/ *adj* 非高峰(时间)的 fēi gāofēng de: ~ *travel* 淡季旅行.

off-putting /ˌɒf ˈpʊtɪŋ; *US* ˌɔːf/ *adj* [尤用于英国英语,非正式用语]令人厌〔厭〕恶〔惡〕的 lìng rén yànwù de;令人气〔氣〕恼〔惱〕的 lìng rén qìnǎo de: *His manner is very* ~. 他的举止使人难堪.

offset /ˈɒfset; *US* ˈɔːf-/ *v* [-tt-; *pt*, *pp* **offset**] [T] 补〔補〕偿〔償〕bǔcháng;抵消 dǐxiāo: *increase prices to* ~ *higher costs* 提高售价以补偿较高的成本.

offshoot /ˈɒfʃuːt; *US* ˈɔːf-/ *n* [C] 枝条〔條〕zhītiáo;枝杈 zhīchà;枝子 zhīzi: [喻] *the* ~ *of a large organization* 一个大机构的分支机构.

offshore /ˌɒfˈʃɔː(r); *US* ˌɔːf- / *adv*, *adj* 1 离〔離〕岸(的) lí'àn: ~ *breezes* 离岸微风. 2 近海的 jìnhǎide: *an* ~ *ˈoil rig* 近海的石油钻塔.

offside /ˌɒfˈsaɪd; *US* ˌɔːf-/ *adj*, *adv* 越位(的) yuèwèi. **offside** *n* [sing], *adj* 右侧(的) yòucè.

offspring /ˈɒfsprɪŋ; *US* ˈɔːf-/ *n* [C] [*pl* **offspring**] [正式用语]子女 zǐnǚ;子孙 zǐsūn;(动物的)崽 zǎi.

off-white /ˌɒf ˈwaɪt; *US* ˌɔːf ˈhwaɪt/ *adj* 灰白色的 huībáisède;米色的 mǐsède.

often /ˈɒfn, ˈɒftən; *US* ˈɔːfn/ *adv* 1 时〔時〕常 shícháng;常常 chángcháng: *We* ~ *go there*. 我们时常去那里. 2 通常 tōngcháng: *Old houses are* ~ *damp*. 旧房子大都潮湿. 3 [习语] **as ˌoften as ˈnot, more ˌoften than ˈnot** 往往 wǎngwǎng. **ˌevery so ˈoften** 有时 yǒushí.

ogle /ˈəʊgl/ *v* [I, T] (*at*) [贬]挑逗地注视 tiǎodòude zhùshì;做媚眼 zuò mèiyǎn.

ogre /ˈəʊgə(r)/ *n* 1(童话中)吃人的妖魔 chī rén de yāomó. 2 [喻]可怕的人 kěpàde rén: *Our teacher is a real* ~. 我们的老师是个十足的恶魔. **ogress** /ˈəʊgres/ *n* 吃人女妖 chī rén nǚyāo.

oh /əʊ/ *interj* (表示惊奇、恐惧等): *Oh dear!* 啊呀!

oil /ɔɪl/ *n* 1 [U] 油 yóu;石油 shíyóu;汽油 qìyóu. 2 **oils** [pl] 油画〔畫〕颜料 yóuhuà yánliào. **oil** *v* [T] 给…加润滑油 gěi…jiā rùnhuáyóu. **ˈoil-colour** *n* [C, U] 油画颜料 yóuhuà yánliào. **ˈoilfield** *n* [C] 油田 yóutián. **ˈoil-painting** *n* [C] 油画作品(或艺术) yóuhuà zuòpǐn. **ˈoil rig** *n* [C] 石油钻〔鑽〕塔 shíyóu zuàntǎ;油井设备〔備〕yóujǐng shèbèi. **ˈoilskin** *n* [C, U] 防水油布 fángshuǐ yóubù;油布雨衣 yóubù yǔyī. **ˈoil-slick** *n* [C] (海面)浮油 fúyóu. **ˈoil well** *n* [C] 油井 yóujǐng. **oily** *adj* [-ier, -iest] 1 油的 yóude;似油的 sìyóude;涂〔塗〕油的 túyóude. 2 [贬]油滑的 yóuhuáde;谄媚的 chǎnmèide.

ointment /ˈɔɪntmənt/ *n* [C, U] 软膏 ruǎngāo;油膏 yóugāo.

OK (亦作 **okay**) /ˌəʊˈkeɪ/ *adj*, *adv* [非正式用语]好 hǎo;不错 búcuò: *Was your holiday OK?* 你的假日过得好吗? **OK** *interj* [非正式用语](表示同意): *OK, I'll do it*. 好吧,我会做的. **OK** *v* [T] [非正式用语]同意 tóngyì;认〔認〕可 rènkě: *I'll OK the plan if you make a few changes*. 你如果作些改动,我将同意这项计划. **OK** *n* [C] [非正式用语]同意 tóngyì;允许 yǔnxǔ: *give a plan the OK* 批准一项计划.

old /əʊld/ *adj* 1 (指年龄)…岁〔歲〕的… suìde:

He's 40 years ～. 他四十岁了. *How* ～ *are you?* 你多大岁数了? **2** 年老的 niánlǎode;老的 lǎode: *an* ～ *man* 老人. **3** 很久的 hěnjiǔde;陈旧〔舊〕的 chénjiùde: ～ *shoes* 旧鞋. **4** 古老的 gǔlǎode;旧时〔時〕的 jiùshīde: ～ *habits* 旧习惯. **5** 熟悉的 shúxīde;认〔認〕识〔識〕的 rènshide: *an* ～ *friend* 老朋友. **6** 以前的 yǐqiánde;从〔從〕前的 cóngqiánde: ～ *boys/girls* 男校友;女校友. **7** [习语] **(be) an old hand (at sth)** 老手 lǎoshǒu;有经〔經〕验者 yǒu jīngyànzhě. **old 'hat** 老式的 lǎoshìde;过〔過〕时的 guòshíde. **an old 'wives' tale** 陈腐的观〔觀〕念 chénfǔde guānniàn;愚蠢的想法 yúchǔnde xiǎngfǎ. **the old** *n* [pl] 老人 lǎorén. **ˌold age 'pension** *n* [C] 养〔養〕老金 yǎnglǎojīn. **ˌold-age 'pensioner** *n* [C] 领养老金的人 lǐng yǎnglǎojīn de rén. **ˌold-'fashioned** *adj* **1** 过时的 guòshíde;老式的 lǎoshìde. **2** 守旧的 shǒujiùde;保守的 bǎoshǒude. **old 'maid** *n* [C] [非正式用语,贬]老处〔處〕女 lǎo chǔnǚ. **old 'master** *n* [C] 大画〔畫〕家 dà huàjiā;大画家的作品 dà huàjiā de zuòpǐn.

olden /ˈəʊldən/ *adj* [古]古时〔時〕的 gǔshíde;往昔的 wǎngxīde: *in the* ～ *days* 往昔.

olive /ˈɒlɪv/ *n* **1** [C] 橄榄〔欖〕gǎnlǎn. **2** [U] 橄榄色 gǎnlǎnsè. **'olive-branch** *n* [C] 橄榄枝(和平的象征) gǎnlǎnzhī.

ombudsman /ˈɒmbʊdzmən, -mæn/ *n* [C] [*pl* **-men**/ -mən/] 调查官 diàocháguān;巡视官(指调查公民对政府、渎职官员所提控告的特派员) xúnshìguān.

omelette /ˈɒmlɪt/ *n* [C] 煎蛋卷 jiāndànjuǎn;炒蛋 chǎodàn.

omen /ˈəʊmen/ *n* [C] 预兆 yùzhào;征〔徵〕兆 zhēngzhào.

ominous /ˈɒmɪnəs/ *adj* 不祥的 bùxiángde;不吉的 bùjíde. **ominously** *adv*.

omission /əˈmɪʃn/ *n* **1** [U] 省略 shěnglüè;删节〔節〕shānjié;排除 páichú. **2** [C] 省略(或删节、遗漏)的东西 shěnglüède dōngxi.

omit /əˈmɪt/ *v* [-tt-] [T] **1** 不包括 bùbāokuò;省略 shěnglüè;删节〔節〕shānjié;排除 páichú. **2** (*to*) [正式用语]疏忽 shūhu;忘记做 wàngjì zuò: *I* ～*ted to mention his age*. 我忘了提到他的年龄.

omnibus /ˈɒmnɪbəs/ *n* [C] **1** 选〔選〕集 xuǎnjí;汇〔彙〕编 huìbiān. **2** (广播、电视)综合节〔節〕目 zōnghé jiémù. **3** [旧,正式用语]公共汽车〔車〕gōnggòng qìchē.

omnipotent /ɒmˈnɪpətənt/ *adj* [正式用语]有无〔無〕限权〔權〕力的 yǒu wúxiàn quánlì de. **omnipotence** /-təns/ *n* [U].

omniscient /ɒmˈnɪsɪənt/ *adj* [正式用语]无〔無〕所不知的 wú suǒ bù zhī de;全知的 quánzhīde. **omniscience** /-əns/ *n* [U].

omnivorous /ɒmˈnɪvərəs/ *adj* [正式用语](动物)杂〔雜〕食的 záshíde.

on[1] /ɒn/ *adv* **1** (表示继续、进展): *They wanted the band to play on*. 他们要乐队继续演奏下去. **2** (表示在空间、时间中的进展): *walk on to the bus-stop* 走着去公共汽车站. *from that day on* 从那天起. **3** (衣服)穿上 chuānshang;戴上 dàishang: *Put your coat on*. 穿上你的大衣. *He had nothing on*. 他没穿衣服. **4** 接通 jiētōng: *The electricity is on*. 通电了. **5** 使用中 shǐyòng zhōng: *The radio is on*. 收音机开着. **6** (按计划将)发〔發〕生 fāshēng: *Is the strike still on?* 罢工仍将举行吗? *What's on at the cinema?* 电影院上演什么? *Have you got anything on for this evening?* 你今晚有什么安排吗? **7** 在…里〔裡〕zài…lǐ: *get on the bus* 上了公共汽车. **8** 向前地 xiàngqiánde: *crash head-on* 迎头撞上. **9** [习语] **be 'on** [非正式用语]认〔認〕可的 rènkěde: *Such bad behaviour isn't on*. 这样的不良行为不能接受. **be/go/ keep on about sth** [非正式用语]唠〔嘮〕叨 láodao. **on and off** ⇨ OFF[1]. **ˌon and 'on** 不停地 bùtíngde.

on[2] /ɒn/ *prep* **1** 在…上 zài…shàng: *a picture on the wall* 墙上的画. **2** 支撑 zhīchēng;依附于 yīfù yú: *a roof on the house* 房顶. **3** 在…里〔裏〕zài…lǐ: *on the train* 在火车上. **4** 有 yǒu;身上带〔帶〕着 shēnshàng dàizhe: *Have you got any money on you?* 你带着钱吗? **5** (表示时间): *on Sunday* 在星期日. *on 1 May* 在五月一日. **6** 就在某时〔時〕(之后) jiù zài mǒushí: *on arriving home* 一到家. **7** 关〔關〕于 guānyú: *a lecture on Bach* 有关巴赫的讲演. **8** (表示集团的成员): *on the committee* 在委员会中. **9** 借〔藉〕助于 jièzhù yú;用 yòng: *Most cars run on petrol*. 大多数汽车行驶靠汽油. *speak on the telephone* 在电话中说. **10** (表示方向): *march on Rome* 向罗马进发. **11** 靠近 kàojìn: *a town on the coast* 沿海的市镇. **12** (表示原因): *arrested on a charge of theft* 因偷窃被捕. **13** 经〔經〕济〔濟〕上依靠 jīngjì shàng yīkào: *live on a student grant* 靠助学金生活. **14** (表示有关费用): *a tax on beer* 啤酒税. **15** (表示活动或状态): *go to Paris on business* 出差去巴黎. *on fire* 着火.

once /wʌns/ *adv* **1** 一次 yícì;一回 yìhuí: *I've only been there* ～. 我只去过那里一次. **2** 曾经〔經〕céngjīng;一度 yídù: *She* ～ *lived in Zambia*. 她曾在赞比亚住过. **3** [习语] **at 'once (a)** 立刻 lìkè;马上 mǎshàng. **(b)** 同时〔時〕tóngshí: *Don't all speak at* ～! 不要大家同时说! **ˌonce and for 'all** 最终地 zuìzhōngde. **ˌonce in a blue 'moon** [非正式用语]极〔極〕少 jíshǎo. **(every) ˌonce in a**

ˈwhile 偶尔〔爾〕ǒu'ěr. once ˈmore 再一次 zài yícì. ˌonce or ˈtwice 一两次 yìliǎngcì. ˌonce upon a ˈtime (用于童话开头)从〔從〕前 cóngqián. once *conj* 一旦… yídàn…: *O~ you know how, it's easy*. 你一旦知道如何,就容易了.

oncoming /ˈɒnkʌmɪŋ/ *adj* 即将〔將〕来临〔臨〕的 jíjiāng láilín de;接近的 jiējìnde.

one[1] /wʌn/ *pron, adj* 1 一(个) yī;(数字) 1 yī. 2 某一 mǒuyī: *~ day* 一天. *The winner is ~ Mrs West from Hull*. 获胜者是来自赫尔的威斯特夫人. 3 (与 the other 或 another 连用表示对比). 4 同一 tóngyī: *They all went off in ~ direction*. 他们都往同一方向去了. 5 [习语] be at ˈone [正式用语]一致 yízhì. I, he/she, etc for one 我(或他、她等)就是 wǒ jiùshì: *I for ~ don't like it*. 我个人不喜欢它. ˌone or ˈtwo 几〔幾〕个〔個〕jǐgè. one ˈup on sb [非正式用语]略胜〔勝〕一筹〔籌〕lüè shèng yì chóu. one *n* [C] (数字)1 yī. ˌone-ˈoff *adj, n* [C] 一次性的 yícìxìngde;一次性事物 yícìxìng shìwù. ˌone-parent ˈfamily *n* [C] 单〔單〕亲〔親〕家庭 dānqīn jiātíng. ˌone-ˈsided *adj* 1 (思想)不公正的 bù gōngzhèng de: *a ˌ~-sided ˈargument* 片面的论点. 2 (体育)力量悬〔懸〕殊的 lìliàng xuánshū de. one-stop ˈshopping *n* [U] 一站式购〔購〕物 yīzhànshì gòuwù. ˌone-to-ˈone *adv, adj* 一对〔對〕一(的) yī duì yī;一比一(的) yī bǐ yī: *a ~-to-~ relationship* 一对一的关系. ˌone-ˈway *adv, adj* 单行(的) dānxíng;单程(的) dānchéng: *a ~-way street* 单行道.

O

one[2] /wʌn/ *pron* 1 (用于代替名词) *The blue hat is the ~ I like best*. 这顶蓝帽子是我最喜欢的. *The small car is just as fast as the big ~*. 这辆小汽车像那辆大汽车一样快. 2 *of* (表示一组中的一个): *He is not ~ of my customers*. 他不是我的顾客. 3 [正式用语]任何人 rènhérén: *O~ cannot always find the time for reading*. 人们不一定能经常找到读书的时间. ˌone aˈnother 互相 hùxiāng: *They don't like ~ another*. 他们彼此不喜欢.

onerous /ˈɒnərəs, ˈəʊn-/ *adj* [正式用语]艰〔艱〕巨的 jiānjùde;繁重的 fánzhòngde.

oneself /wʌnˈself/ *pron* 1 (用于反身): *ˈwash ~* 洗澡. 2 (用于加强语气): *One could arrange it all ~*. 谁都能自己安排好. 3 [习语] (all) by oneˈself (a) 单〔單〕独〔獨〕dāndú;独自 dúzì. (b) 靠自己 kào zìjǐ.

ongoing /ˈɒngəʊɪŋ/ *adj* 继〔繼〕续〔續〕的 jìxùde: *~ research* 持续的研究.

onion /ˈʌnɪən/ *n* [C,U] 洋葱 yángcōng.

online /ɒnˈlaɪn/ *adj, adv* 联〔聯〕机〔機〕的(地) liánjīde. ˌonline ˈbanking *n* [U] 网〔網〕上银行 wǎngshàng yínháng. ˌonline ˈgaming *n* [U] 联〔聯〕机〔機〕游〔遊〕戏〔戲〕liánjī yóuxì 网〔網〕络游〔遊〕戏〔戲〕wǎngluò yóuxì 在线〔綫〕游〔遊〕戏〔戲〕zàixiàn yóuxì. ˌonline ˈshopping *n* [U] 网〔網〕上购〔購〕物 wǎngshàng gòu wù.

onlooker /ˈɒnlʊkə(r)/ *n* [C] 旁观〔觀〕者 pángguānzhě.

only[1] /ˈəʊnlɪ/ *adj* 1 唯一的 wéiyīde;仅〔僅〕有的 jǐnyǒude: *Jane was the ~ person able to do it*. 简是唯一能做那事的人. 2 [非正式用语]最好的 zuìhǎode: *He's the ~ person for the job*. 他是最适合做这一工作的人.

only[2] /ˈəʊnlɪ/ *adv* 1 只 zhǐ;仅〔僅〕仅 jǐnjǐn. 2 [习语] only ˈjust 几〔幾〕乎不 jīhū bù: *We ~ just caught the train*. 我们差点没赶上火车. only too ⇨ TOO.

only[3] /ˈəʊnlɪ/ *conj* [非正式用语]可是 kěshì;但是 dànshì: *I'd love to come, ~ I have to work*. 我很愿意来,可是我还得工作.

onrush /ˈɒnrʌʃ/ *n* [sing] [正式用语]猛冲〔衝〕měngchōng;奔流 bēnliú.

onset /ˈɒnset/ *n* [sing] 开〔開〕始(尤指不愉快的事) kāishǐ.

onshore /ˈɒnʃɔː(r)/ *adv, adj* 向岸(的) xiàng'àn;向陆〔陸〕(的) xiànglù: *~ winds* 向岸风.

onslaught /ˈɒnslɔːt/ *n* [C] (*on*) 猛攻 měnggōng.

onto (亦作 on to) /ˈɒntə/ *prep* 1 到…上 dào…shàng: *climb ~ a horse* 骑上马. 2 [习语] be onto sb 追查某人的违〔違〕法活动〔動〕zhuīchá mǒurén de wéifǎ huódòng. be onto sth 有能导〔導〕致重要发〔發〕现的信息(或证据) yǒu néng dǎozhì zhòngyào fāxiàn de xìnxī.

onus /ˈəʊnəs/ *n* [sing] [正式用语]责任 zérèn;职〔職〕责 zhízé.

onward /ˈɒnwəd/ *adj* 向前的 xiàngqiánde;前进〔進〕的 qiánjìnde: *an ~ movement* 前移. onward (亦作 onwards) *adv*: *move ~s* 向前移动.

ooze /uːz/ *v* 1 [I] (浓液)慢慢流出 mànmàn liúchū. 2 [I,T] 使(某物)慢慢流出 shǐ…mànmàn liúchū: [喻] *She ~d charm*. 她浑身透着迷人的气息. ooze *n* [U] 软泥 ruǎnní;淤泥 yūní.

opal /ˈəʊpl/ *n* [C] 蛋白石 dànbáishí.

opaque /əʊˈpeɪk/ *adj* 1 不透光的 bú tòuguāng de;不透明的 bú tòumíng de. 2 (语言、写作等)难〔難〕理解的 nán lǐjiě de.

open[1] /ˈəʊpən/ *adj* 1 开〔開〕着的 kāizhede: *leave the door ~* 让门开着. 2 敞开的 chǎngkāide;未围〔圍〕起的 wèi wéiqǐ de;开阔

的 kāikuòde：～ *field* 田野. 3 营〔營〕业〔業〕(或办公) 的 yíngyède：*Are the shops ～ yet?* 商店都营业了吗? 4 展开的 zhǎnkāide；伸开的 shēnkāide：*The flowers were all ～.* 花儿都开了. 5 未系〔繫〕住的 wèi jìzhù de；松〔鬆〕开的 sōngkāide：*an ～ shirt* 没系纽扣的衬衫. 6 无〔無〕遮盖〔蓋〕的 wú zhēgài de；无覆盖的 wú fùgài de：*an ～ car* 敞篷汽车. 7 公开的 gōngkāide；开放的 kāifàngde. 8 众〔衆〕所周知的 zhòng suǒ zhōu zhī de；不保密的 bù bǎomì de：*an ～ secret* 公开的秘密. 9 愿〔願〕意谈的 yuànyì tán de；诚实〔實〕的 chéngshíde. 10 未决定的 wèi juédìng de：*leave the matter ～* 此事尚无定论. 11 *to* (a) 乐〔樂〕意接受 lèyì jiēshòu：～ *to new ideas* 乐于接受新意见. (b) 容易受到 róngyì shòudào：～ *to criticism* 易受批评. 12 [习语] **have/ keep an open 'mind** 愿考虑〔慮〕别人的意见 yuàn kǎolǜ biérén de yìjiàn. **in the open 'air** 在户外 zài hùwài. **with open 'arms** 热〔熱〕情地 rèqíngde. **the open** *n* [sing] 1 户外 hùwài；野外 yěwài；露天 lùtiān. 2 [习语] **bring sth/be/come (out) in(to) the open** 公开(秘密等) gōngkāi：*bring the truth out into the ～* 公开事实真相. *a problem which is out in the ～* 众所周知的问题. **ˌopen-'air** *adj* 户外的 hùwàide；露天的 lùtiānde. **ˌopen-and-'shut** *adj* 明显〔顯〕的 míngxiǎnde；显然的 xiǎnránde. **ˌopen 'cheque** *n* [C] 非划〔劃〕线〔綫〕支票 fēi huàxiàn zhīpiào；普通支票 pǔtōng zhīpiào. **ˌopen-'ended** *adj* 无限制的 wú xiànzhì de. **ˌopen-'handed** *adj* 慷慨的 kāngkǎide. **openly** *adv* 公开地 gōngkāide；公然地 gōngránde. **ˌopen-'minded** *adj* 能接受新思想的 néng jiēshòu xīnsīxiǎng de. **openness** *n* [U] 真诚 zhēnchéng. **ˌopen-'plan** *adj* 开敞布置的 kāichǎng bùzhì de. **'open-work** *n* [U] 透雕细工 tòudiāo xìgōng；网〔網〕状〔狀〕细工 wǎngzhuàng xìgōng.

open[2] /'əʊpən/ *v* 1 [I, T] 开〔開〕kāi；打开 dǎkāi；张〔張〕开 zhāngkāi：*The door ～ed.* 门开了. *Please ～ a window.* 请打开窗. 2 [T] 在…上开孔 zài…shang kāikǒng；开辟〔闢〕通道 kāipì tōngdào：～ *a new road through the forest* 开辟一条穿过森林的新路. 3 [I, T] (使)展开 zhǎnkāi；(使)张开 zhāngkāi：～ *a book* 打开书. 4 [T] 开始 kāishǐ：～ *a bank account* 在银行开户. 5 [I, T] (使)开张 kāizhāng；营〔營〕业〔業〕yíngyè：*When does the bank ～?* 银行什么时间办公? 6 [习语] **open one's/sb's eyes** 使某人了〔瞭〕解(…) shǐ mǒurén liǎojiě；使某人看清(…) shǐ mǒurén kànqīng. **open 'fire** 开火 kāihuǒ. 7 [短语动词] **open up** [非正式用语] 畅谈 chàngtán. **open (sth) up** (使某物)供开发〔發〕gōng kāifā；开业 kāiyè：～ *up possibilities* 开发可用的东西. **opener** /'əʊpnə(r)/ *n* [C] (用以构成复合词)开启〔啟〕工具 kāiqǐ gōngjù：*'tin-～er* 开听器.

opening /'əʊpnɪŋ/ *n* [C] 1 (通道的)口子 kǒuzi；洞 dòng；孔 kǒng. 2 [常作 sing] 开〔開〕始 kāishǐ；开端 kāiduān. 3 [sing] 开 kāi；张〔張〕开 zhāngkāi：*the ～ of the new library* 新图书馆的开张. 4 (职位的)空缺 kòngquē. **opening** *adj* 首先的 shǒuxiānde；开头〔頭〕的 kāitóude：*her ～ words* 她的开场白.

opera /'ɒprə/ *n* [C] 歌剧〔劇〕gējù. **operatic** /ˌɒpə'rætɪk/ *adj*.

operate /'ɒpəreɪt/ *v* 1 [I, T] 操作 cāozuò；操纵〔縱〕cāozòng；开〔開〕动〔動〕kāidòng：～ *a machine* 开动机器. 2 [I] 有效 yǒuxiào；起作用 qǐ zuòyòng. 3 [I, T] 经〔經〕营〔營〕jīngyíng；管理 guǎnlǐ. 4 [I] 动手术〔術〕dòng shǒushù. **operable** /'ɒpərəbl/ *adj* 可动手术的 kědòng shǒushù de. **'operating-theatre** *n* [C] 手术室 shǒushùshì.

operation /ˌɒpə'reɪʃn/ *n* 1 [U] 操作 cāozuò；运〔運〕转〔轉〕yùnzhuǎn；作业〔業〕zuòyè：*the ～ of the controls* 操纵装置的运转. 2 [C] 活动〔動〕huódòng；行动 xíngdòng：*a rescue ～* 救援活动. 3 [C] [医学] 手术〔術〕shǒushù. 4 [C] 公司 gōngsī. 5 [C, 常作 pl] 作战〔戰〕行动 zuòzhàn xíngdòng；军事行动 jūnshì xíngdòng. 6 [习语] **in(to) operation** 工作中 gōngzuò zhōng；操作中 cāozuò zhōng；运转中 yùnzhuǎn zhōng：*put our plans into ～* 把我们的计划付诸实施. **operational** /-ʃənl/ *adj* [正式用语] 1 操作的 cāozuòde；手术的 shǒushùde；军事行动的 jūnshì xíngdòng de；公司的 gōngsīde. 2 即可使用的 jíkě shǐyòng de.

operative /'ɒpərətɪv; *US* -reɪt-/ *adj* [正式用语] 操作的 cāozuòde；使用着的 shǐyòngzhede；有效的 yǒuxiàode：*The law becomes ～ in July.* 此法令自 7 月起生效. **operative** *n* [C] [正式用语] 技工 jìgōng；工人 gōngrén.

operator /'ɒpəreɪtə(r)/ *n* [C] 操作者 cāozuòzhě；电〔電〕话接线〔綫〕员 diànhuà jiēxiànyuán.

operetta /ˌɒpə'retə/ *n* [C] 小歌剧〔劇〕xiǎo gējù；轻〔輕〕歌剧 qīng gējù.

opinion /ə'pɪnɪən/ *n* 1 [C] 意见 yìjiàn；看法 kànfǎ；主张〔張〕zhǔzhāng：*In my ～, the price is too high.* 我的意见是价格太高. *his ～ of the new manager* 他对新经理的看法. 2 [U] 舆论〔論〕yúlùn：*public ～* 公众舆论. 3 [C] (专业的)评估 pínggū，意见 yìjian：*a doctor's ～* 医生的诊断. **opinionated** /-eɪtɪd/ *adj* 固执己见的 gùzhí jǐjiàn de.

opium /'əʊpɪəm/ *n* [U] 鸦片 yāpiàn.

opponent /ə'pəʊnənt/ *n* [C] 对〔對〕手 duì-

O

shǒu;敌〔敵〕手 díshǒu;(争论的)对方 duìfāng.

opportune /ˈɒpətjuːn; *US* -tuːn/ *adj* [正式用语] 1 (时间)合适〔適〕的 héshìde;恰好的 qiàhǎode. 2 (行动)及时〔時〕的 jíshíde;适时的 shìshíde.

opportunism /ˌɒpəˈtjuːnɪzəm; *US* -ˈtuːn-/ *n* [U] [正式用语,贬]机〔機〕会〔會〕主义〔義〕 jīhuì zhǔyì. **opportunist** /-ɪst/ *n* [C].

opportunity /ˌɒpəˈtjuːnətɪ; *US* -ˈtuːn-/ *n* [C,U] [*pl* -ies] 机〔機〕会〔會〕 jīhuì;时〔時〕机 shíjī.

oppose /əˈpəʊz/ *v* [T] 反对〔對〕 fǎnduì;反抗 fǎnkàng;抵制 dǐzhì. **opposed** *adj* 1 *to* 反对的 fǎnduìde;对抗的 duìkàngde: *He is ~d to our plans*. 他反对我们的计划. 2 [习语] **as opposed to** 与〔與〕…对照(或对比) yǔ…duìzhào.

opposite /ˈɒpəzɪt/ *adj* 1 对〔對〕面的 duìmiànde;相对的 xiāngduìde: *the house ~ (to) mine* 我住所对面的那所房子. 2 相反的 xiāngfǎnde;完全不同的 wánquán bùtóng de: *in the ~ direction* 朝相反的方向. **opposite** *prep, adv* 在对面 zài duìmiàn;面对 miànduì: *~ the station* 在车站的对面. *the person sitting ~* 坐在对面的那个人. **opposite** *n* [C] 反义〔義〕词 fǎnyìcí;对立物 duìlìwù. **one's ˌopposite ˈnumber** *n* [C] (在另一部门中工作或职位)与〔與〕自己相当〔當〕的人 yǔ zìjǐ xiāngdāng de rén: *the President's ~ number from France* 这位会长的法国对应人物.

O **opposition** /ˌɒpəˈzɪʃn/ *n* 1 [U] 反对〔對〕 fǎnduì;敌〔敵〕对 díduì;抵抗 dǐkàng;对抗 duìkàng: *strong ~ to the new law* 对新法律的强烈反对. 2 [sing, 亦作 sing, 用 pl v] (a) 反对派 fǎnduìpài;对手 duìshǒu. (b) **the Opposition** [尤用于英国英语]反对党〔黨〕 fǎnduìdǎng.

oppress /əˈpres/ *v* [T] 1 压〔壓〕迫 yāpò;压制 yāzhì. 2 使烦恼〔惱〕 shǐ fánnǎo;使忧〔憂〕虑〔慮〕 shǐ yōulǜ: *~ed by the heat* 因暑热而烦闷. **oppression** /əˈpreʃn/ *n* [U, C]. **oppressive** *adj* 1 不公正的 bù gōngzhèngde;暴虐的 bàonüède. 2 难〔難〕以忍受的 nán yǐ rěnshòu de;令人烦恼的 lìng rén fánnǎo de: *~ive heat* 难忍的暑热. **oppressor** *n* [C] 压迫者 yāpòzhě;压制者 yāzhìzhě.

opt /ɒpt/ *v* 1 [T] *to* 选〔選〕择〔擇〕 xuǎnzé: *He ~ed to go to Paris*. 他选择了去巴黎. 2 [短语动词] **opt for sth** 选择 xuǎnzé: *~ for that plan* 选择那项计划. **opt out (of sth)** 决定不参〔參〕加 juédìng bù cānjiā.

optic /ˈɒptɪk/ *adj* [正式用语]视觉〔覺〕的 shìjuéde;眼睛的 yǎnjīngde: *the ~ nerve* 视觉神经. **optical** /-kl/ *adj* 视觉的 shìjuéde. ˌ**optical ilˈlusion** *n* [C] 视错觉 shìcuòjué;光幻觉 guānghuànjué. **optician** /ɒpˈtɪʃn/ *n* [C] 眼镜制〔製〕造者 yǎnjìng zhìzàozhě;眼镜商 yǎnjìngshāng.

optimism /ˈɒptɪmɪzəm/ *n* [U] 乐〔樂〕观〔觀〕 lèguān;乐观主义〔義〕 lèguān zhǔyì. **optimist** /-mɪst/ *n* [C]. **optimistic** /ˌɒptɪˈmɪstɪk/ *adj*.

optimize /ˈɒptɪmaɪz/ *v* [T] 使尽〔盡〕可能完善 shǐ jìnkěnéng wánshàn;最有效地进〔進〕行 zuì yǒuxiàode jìnxíng.

optimum /ˈɒptɪməm/ *adj* [正式用语]最佳的 zuìjiāde;最适〔適〕宜的 zuì shìyí de: *the ~ price* 最适宜的价格.

option /ˈɒpʃn/ *n* 1 [U] 选〔選〕择〔擇〕自由 xuǎnzé zìyóu;选择权〔權〕 xuǎnzéquán. 2 [C] 可选择的事物 kě xuǎnzé de shìwù. **optional** /-ʃənl/ *adj* 可选择的 kě xuǎnzé de;随〔隨〕意的 suíyìde.

opulent /ˈɒpjʊlənt/ *adj* [正式用语]富裕的 fùyùde;富有的 fùyǒude. **opulence** /-ləns/ *n* [U].

or /ɔː(r)/ *conj* 1 (表示选择): *Is it green or blue?* 它是绿的还是蓝的? *Do you want tea, coffee or milk?* 你要喝茶、咖啡还是牛奶? 2 否则 fǒuzé;要不然 yàobùrán: *Turn the heat down or the cake will burn*. 把热度调低,要不然糕饼要糊了. 3 换句话说 huàn jù huà shuō: *It weighs one pound, or about 450 grams*. 它重一磅,也就是说大约 450 克. 4 [习语] **or ˈelse** [非正式用语](用以表示威胁)否则后〔後〕果不妙 fǒuzé hòuguǒ búmiào: *Do it, or else I'll hit you!* 你去干,不然我要打你. **or so** 左右 zuǒyòu;大约 dàyuē: *We stayed there an hour or so*. 我们在那里停留了一小时左右.

oral /ˈɔːrəl/ *adj* 1 口头〔頭〕的 kǒutóude;口述的 kǒushùde: *an ~ test* 口试. 2 口的 kǒude;口用的 kǒuyòngde: *~ medicine* 口服药. **oral** *n* [C] 口试 kǒushì. **orally** *adv*.

orange /ˈɒrɪndʒ; *US* ˈɔːr-/ *n* [C] 柑橘 gānjú;橙 chéng. **orange** *adj* 橙黄色 chénghuángsè;橘黄色 júhuángsè.

orang-utan (亦作 **orang-outan**) /ɔːˌræŋuːˈtæn; *US* əˌræŋəˈtæn / (亦作 **orang-outang** / -uːˈtæŋ /) *n* [C] 猩猩 xīngxing.

orator /ˈɒrətə(r); *US* ˈɔːr-/ *n* [C] [正式用语]演说者 yǎnshuōzhě. **oratory** /ˈɒrətrɪ; *US* ˈɔːrətɔːrɪ/ *n* [U] 演讲〔講〕术〔術〕 yǎnjiǎngshù;雄辩术 xióngbiànshù.

orbit /ˈɔːbɪt/ *n* [C] 1 (天体的)轨道 guǐdào. 2 [喻]势〔勢〕力范〔範〕围〔圍〕 shìlì fànwéi. **orbit** *v* [I,T] 环〔環〕绕〔繞〕(天体等)的轨道运〔運〕行 huánrào… de guǐdào yùnxíng. **orbital** /-tl/ *adj*.

orchard /ˈɔːtʃəd/ *n* [C] 果园〔園〕guǒyuán.

orchestra /ˈɔːkɪstrə/ *n* [C, 亦作 sing 用 pl v] 管弦乐〔樂〕队〔隊〕guǎnxiányuèduì. **orchestral** /ɔːˈkestrəl/ *adj*. **orchestrate** /-streɪt/ *v* [T] **1** 把…谱写〔寫〕成管弦乐曲 bǎ…pǔxiě chéng guǎnxiányuèqǔ. **2** 精心安排 jīngxīn ānpái. **orchestration** /ˌɔːkɪˈstreɪʃn/ *n* [C, U].

orchid /ˈɔːkɪd/ *n* [C] 兰〔蘭〕科植物 lánkē zhíwù; 兰花 lánhuā.

ordain /ɔːˈdeɪn/ *v* [T] **1** 委任(某人)为〔爲〕牧师〔師〕wěirèn…wéi mùshi. **2** [正式用语](上帝、法律等)命令 mìnglìng.

ordeal /ɔːˈdiːl, ˈɔːdiːl/ *n* [C] 苦难〔難〕经〔經〕历〔歷〕kǔnàn jīnglì; 折磨 zhémó.

order[1] /ˈɔːdə(r)/ *n* **1** [U] 次序 cìxù; 顺序 shùnxù: *names in alphabetical ～* 按字母顺序排列的名字. *arranged in ～ of size* 按大小排列的. **2** [U] 整齐〔齊〕zhěngqí; 有条〔條〕理 yǒu tiáolǐ. **3** [U] 工作状〔狀〕况 gōngzuò zhuàngkuàng: *The machine is out of ～.* 机器出故障了. **4** [U] 治安 zhì'ān; 秩序 zhìxù. **5** [C] 命令 mìnglìng; 指示 zhǐshì. **6** [C] (a) 定购〔購〕dìnggòu; 定货 dìnghuò; 定单〔單〕dìngdān: *Send the shop your ～ for books.* 把你的订书单送到商店. (b) 交付的货 jiāofùde huò: *Your ～ will arrive tomorrow.* 你的货明天到. **7** [C] 汇〔匯〕票 huìpiào. **8** [U] (会议、议会等的)程序 chéngxù; 规程 guīchéng: *a point of ˈ～* 程序问题. **9** [C] [正式用语] 种〔種〕类〔類〕zhǒnglèi: *skills of the highest ～* 最高技巧. **10** [C] 勋〔勳〕章 xūnzhāng: *～s and medals* 勋章和奖章. **11** [习语] **in ˈorder** 处〔處〕于良好状态〔態〕chǔyú liánghǎo zhuàngtài: *Your passport is in ～.* 你的护照仍然有效. **in the order of** [正式用语] 大约 dàyuē: *It will cost in the ～ of £60.* 它大约值 60 英镑. **in order that** [正式用语] 为〔爲〕了 wèile. **in order to do sth** 为了做某事 wèile zuò mǒushì. **on ˈorder** 已定购(货尚未到) yǐ dìnggòu. **take (holy) orders** 任圣〔聖〕职〔職〕rèn shèngzhí.

order[2] /ˈɔːdə(r)/ *v* **1** [T] 命令 mìnglìng; 指示 zhǐshì; 吩咐 fēnfù: *He ～ed the soldiers to attack.* 他命令士兵发动进攻. **2** [I, T] 定购〔購〕dìnggòu; 预定 yùdìng: *to ～ a new carpet* 定购一块新地毯. **3** [T] [正式用语] 布置 bùzhì. **4** [短语动词] **order sb about** 不断〔斷〕驱〔驅〕使某人做事 búduàn qūshǐ mǒurén zuòshì.

orderly /ˈɔːdəlɪ/ *adj* **1** 有条〔條〕理的 yǒu tiáolǐ de; 整齐〔齊〕的 zhěngqíde. **2** 守秩序的 shǒu zhìxù de; 品行良好的 pǐnxíng liánghǎo de: *an ～ crowd* 守秩序的群众. **orderliness** *n* [U]. **orderly** *n* [C] [*pl* -ies] (医院的)勤杂〔雜〕工 qínzágōng; 护〔護〕理员 hùlǐyuán.

ordinal /ˈɔːdɪnl; *US* -dənl/ (亦作 ˌordinal ˈnumber) *n* [C] 序数〔數〕(如 *first, second, third*) xùshù.

ordinary /ˈɔːdənrɪ; *US* ˈɔːrdənerɪ/ *adj* **1** 普通的 pǔtōngde; 平常的 píngchángde. **2** [习语] **out of the ˈordinary** 例外的 lìwàide; 特殊的 tèshūde. **ordinarily** /-rəlɪ; *US* ˌɔːrdnˈerəlɪ/ *adv* 通常地 tōngchángde; 惯常地 guànchángde.

ordination /ˌɔːdɪˈneɪʃn; *US* ˌɔːdnˈeɪʃn/ *n* [C, U] (牧师等职位的)任命仪〔儀〕式 rènmìng yíshì.

ore /ɔː(r)/ *n* [U, C] 矿〔礦〕石 kuàngshí; 矿砂 kuàngshā.

organ[1] /ˈɔːgən/ *n* [C] **1** 器官 qìguān: *The eye is the ～ of sight.* 眼睛是视觉器官. **2** 机〔機〕构〔構〕jīgòu; 机关〔關〕jīguān: *Parliament is an ～ of government.* 议会是一个治国机构. **3** [正式用语] 新闻媒介 xīnwén méijiè; 机关报〔報〕jīguānbào.

organ[2] /ˈɔːgən/ *n* [C] 风琴 fēngqín; 管风琴 guǎnfēngqín. **organist** *n* [C] 风琴演奏者 fēngqín yǎnzòuzhě; 风琴手 fēngqínshǒu.

organic /ɔːˈgænɪk/ *adj* **1** 生物体〔體〕的 shēngwùtǐde; 有机〔機〕体的 yǒujītǐde; 有机物的 yǒujīwùde. **2** 施用有机肥料(或有机农药)的 shīyòng yǒujī féiliào de. **3** [正式用语] 有机的 yǒujīde; 有组织〔織〕的 yǒu zǔzhī de; 建制的 jiànzhìde. **organically** /-klɪ/ *adv*.

organism /ˈɔːgənɪzəm/ *n* [C] **1** (微小的)生物 shēngwù; 有机〔機〕体〔體〕yǒujītǐ. **2** [正式用语] 有机组织〔織〕yǒujī zǔzhī.

organization /ˌɔːgənaɪˈzeɪʃn; *US* -nɪˈz-/ *n* **1** [C] 组织〔織〕zǔzhī; 机〔機〕构〔構〕jīgòu. **2** [U] 组织的活动〔動〕zǔzhīde huódòng.

organize /ˈɔːgənaɪz/ *v* [T] **1** 为〔爲〕…做准〔準〕备〔備〕wèi…zuò zhǔnbèi: *～ a party* 筹备宴会. **2** 组织〔織〕zǔzhī; 把…编组 bǎ…biānzǔ: *～ one's time* 安排某人的时间.

orgasm /ˈɔːgæzəm/ *n* [C] 性高潮 xìnggāocháo.

orgy /ˈɔːdʒɪ/ *n* [C] [*pl* -ies] 狂欢〔歡〕kuánghuān; 纵〔縱〕酒 zòngjiǔ; 纵欲〔慾〕zòngyù.

orient /ˈɔːrɪənt/ *n* **the Orient** [sing] [正式用语或修辞] 东方国〔國〕家 dōngfāng guójiā. **oriental** /ˌɔːrɪˈentl/ *adj* 东方国家的 dōngfāng guójiā de; 来自东方国家的 láizì dōngfāng guójiā de.

orientate /ˈɔːrɪənteɪt/ (尤用于美语 **orient** /ˈɔːrɪent/) *v* **1** [T] (*towards*) [常作被动语态] 以…为〔爲〕目的 yǐ…wéi mùdì; 使朝向 shǐ cháoxiàng: *Our company is ～d towards exports.* 我公司的方向是出口. **2** ～

O

oneself 使自己熟悉环〔環〕境 shǐ zìjǐ shúxī huánjìng. **orientation** /ˌɔːrɪənˈteɪʃn/ *n* [U, C].

orifice /ˈɒrɪfɪs/ *n* [C] [正式用语](身体的)外孔 wàikǒng;外口 wàikǒu.

origin /ˈɒrɪdʒɪn/ *n* 1 [C, U] 起源 qǐyuán;来源 láiyuán;开〔開〕端 kāiduān. 2 [C, 尤作 pl] 出身 chūshēn;血统 xuètǒng: *of Polish* ~ 波兰血统.

original /əˈrɪdʒənl/ *adj* 1 最初的 zuìchūde;最早的 zuìzǎode. 2 (a) [常作褒]创〔創〕新的 chuàngxīnde;新颖的 xīnyǐngde: ~ *designs* 创新的设计. (b) 有创见的 yǒu chuàngjiàn de;创造性的 chuàngzàoxìngde: *an* ~ *thinker* 有创见的思想家. 3 非模仿的 fēi mófǎng de. **original** *n* **the original** [C] 原作 yuánzuò;原文 yuánwén;原型 yuánxíng;原物 yuánwù. **originality** /əˌrɪdʒəˈnælətɪ/ *n* [U] 创新 chuàngxīn;独〔獨〕创性 dúchuàngxìng. **originally** /-nəlɪ/ *adv* 1 独创地 dúchuàngde. 2 最初 zuìchū;起先 qǐxiān: *His shirt was* ~*ly white*. 他的衬衫原先是白的.

originate /əˈrɪdʒɪneɪt/ *v* [I, T] [正式用语] 开〔開〕始 kāishǐ;发〔發〕端 fāduān. **originator** *n* [C].

ornament /ˈɔːnəmənt/ *n* 1 [C] 装〔裝〕饰物 zhuāngshìwù;点〔點〕缀品 diǎnzhuìpǐn. 2 [U] [正式用语]装饰 zhuāngshì;点缀 diǎnzhuì. **ornament** /-ment/ *v* [T] 装饰 zhuāngshì;点缀 diǎnzhuì. **ornamental** /ˌɔːnəˈmentl/ *adj*.

ornate /ɔːˈneɪt/ *adj* 装〔裝〕饰华〔華〕丽〔麗〕的 zhuāngshì huálì de;过〔過〕分修饰的 guòfèn xiūshì de. **ornately** *adv*.

O

ornithology /ˌɔːnɪˈθɒlədʒɪ/ *n* [U] 鸟类〔類〕学〔學〕niǎolèixué. **ornithologist** *n* [C].

orphan /ˈɔːfn/ *n* [C] 孤儿〔兒〕gū'ér. **orphan** *v* [T] 使成孤儿 shǐ chéng gū'ér. **orphanage** /ˈɔːfənɪdʒ/ *n* [C] 孤儿院 gū'éryuàn.

orthodox /ˈɔːθədɒks/ *adj* 公认〔認〕的 gōngrènde;普遍赞〔讚〕同的 pǔbiàn zàntóng de. **orthodoxy** *n* [U, C] [*pl* -ies].

orthography /ɔːˈθɒgrəfɪ/ *n* [U] [正式用语] 正字法 zhèngzìfǎ;拼字法 pīnzìfǎ.

orthopaedics (亦作 -pedics) /ˌɔːθəˈpiːdɪks/ *n* [用 sing v] 矫〔矯〕形外科 jiǎoxíng wàikē;整形外科 zhěngxíng wàikē. **orthopaedic** (亦作 -pedic) *adj*.

oscillate /ˈɒsɪleɪt/ *v* [I] [正式用语] 1 摆〔擺〕动〔動〕bǎidòng. 2 [喻](感情、想法等)波动 bōdòng;犹〔猶〕豫 yóuyù. **oscillation** /ˌɒsɪˈleɪʃn/ *n* [U, C] [正式用语].

ostensible /ɒˈstensəbl/ *adj* [正式用语](理由)表面的 biǎomiànde;假装〔裝〕的 jiǎzhuāngde. **ostensibly** *adv*.

ostentation /ˌɒstenˈteɪʃn/ *n* [U] [贬](对财富、知识等的)夸〔誇〕耀 kuāyào;卖〔賣〕弄 màinòng. **ostentatious** /-ʃəs/ *adj*.

ostracize /ˈɒstrəsaɪz/ *v* [T] [正式用语]排斥 páichì;摈〔擯〕弃〔棄〕bìngqì.

ostrich /ˈɒstrɪtʃ/ *n* [C] 鸵鸟 tuóniǎo.

other /ˈʌðə(r)/ *adj* 1 另外的 lìngwàide;其他的 qítāde: *Tim, John and two* ~ *students were there*. 蒂姆、约翰和另外两位学生都在那里. 2 (两个中的)另一个〔個〕lìng yígè: *Pull the cork out with your* ~ *hand*. 用你另一只手拔瓶塞. 3 其余〔餘〕的 qíyúde;剩下的 shèngxiàde: *The* ~ *teachers are from Brunei*. 其余的教师都是文莱人. **others** *pron* 1 另外的人(或物) lìngwàide rén;其他的人(或物) qítāde rén. 2 其余的人(或物) qíyúde rén;剩下的人(或物) shèngxiàde rén: *I went swimming while the* ~*s played tennis*. 我去游泳,其余的人打网球. **other than** *prep* 除了 chúle: *She never speaks to me* ~ *than to ask for something*. 她除了向我要东西,从来不跟我说话.

otherwise /ˈʌðəwaɪz/ *adv* 1 [正式用语]用别的方法 yòng biéde fāngfǎ;不同地 bùtóngde. 2 除此之外 chú cǐ zhī wài;在其他方面 zài qítā fāngmiàn: *The rent is high, but* ~ *the room is satisfactory*. 租金是贵,但房子令人满意. **otherwise** *conj* 否则 fǒuzé: *We must run,* ~ *we'll be late*. 我们必须跑着去,否则要晚了.

otter /ˈɒtə(r)/ *n* [C] 水獭 shuǐtǎ.

ouch /aʊtʃ/ *interj* (表示突然疼痛): *O* ~! *That hurt!* 哎哟! 疼!

ought /ɔːt/ *modal v* (否定式 **ought not** 或 **oughtn't** /ˈɔːtnt/) **to** 1 (表示责任或义务): *You* ~ *to say you're sorry*. 你应该说声对不起. 2 (表示劝告): *You* ~ *to see a doctor about that cough*. 你应该去找医生看看你的咳嗽. 3 (表示可能性): *She started early, so she* ~ *to be here by now*. 她动身早,现在该到这儿了.

ounce /aʊns/ *n* 1 [C] 盎司($\frac{1}{16}$磅,等于 28.35 克) àngsī. 2 [sing] [非正式用语]少量 shǎoliàng;一点〔點〕yìdiǎn.

our /ɑː(r), ˈaʊə(r)/ *adj* 我们的 wǒménde: ~ *house* 我们的房子. **ours** /ɑːz, ˈaʊəz/ *pron* 我们的 wǒménde: *That's* ~*s*. 那是我们的.

ourselves /ɑːˈselvz, aʊəˈselvz/ *pron* 1 (反身代词): *We dried* ~. 我们自己擦干了身体. 2 (用于强调): *We saw the crash* ~. 我们亲眼看见了撞车. 3 [习语] (all) by our'selves (a) 我们单〔單〕独〔獨〕地 wǒmen dāndúde. (b) 靠我们自己 kào wǒmen zìjǐ.

oust /aʊst/ *v* [T] (*from*) [正式用语]免职〔職〕miǎnzhí;罢〔罷〕黜 bàchù.

out /aʊt/ *adv* 1 离〔離〕开〔開〕líkāi;不在里〔裏〕面 búzài lǐmiàn: *go ~ for some fresh air* 出去呼吸新鲜空气. 2 不在家 búzài jiā;不在工作单〔單〕位(或办公室) búzài gōngzuò dānwèi: *I phoned her but she was ~.* 我给她打电话,可是她不在. 3 (表示远离陆地、城镇等): *The boats were all ~ at sea.* 船都已出海. 4 不隐〔隱〕蔽 bù yǐnbì;显〔顯〕露 xiǎnlù: *The secret is ~.* 那秘密泄露了. 5 不再流行 búzài liúxíng: *Short skirts are ~.* 短裙不时兴了. 6 (潮汐)退潮 tuìcháo. 7 在罢〔罷〕工中 zài bàgōng zhōng: *The teachers are ~ again.* 教师又罢工了. 8 (火、灯等)熄灭〔滅〕xīmiè. 9 到底 dàodǐ;全部 quánbù: *I'm tired ~.* 我已筋疲力尽. 10 大声〔聲〕地 dàshēngde: *shout ~* 大声喊. 11 (表示差错): *I'm ~ in my calculations.* 我的计算有误. 12 [体育] (a) 出局 chūjú. (b) (球)出界 chūjiè. 13 [习语] **be out to do sth** 努力想做某事 nǔlì xiǎngzuò mǒushì: *I'm not ~ to change the world!* 我并不想要改变世界! ˌ**out-and-ˈout** *adj* 完全的 wánquánde;彻〔徹〕头〔頭〕彻尾的 chè tóu chè wěi de. **out of** *prep* 1 离开 líkāi;在外 zài wài: *Fish cannot live ~ of water.* 鱼离了水就不能活. 2 离开(某处) líkāi: *walk ~ of the room* 从房间里走出来. 3 (表示动机或原因): *They helped us ~ of kindness.* 他们出于好意帮助我们. 4 从〔從〕…中 cóng…zhōng: *in nine cases ~ of ten* 十之八九. 5 用 yòng: *made ~ of wood* 用木头做的. 6 没有 méiyǒu;缺乏 quēfá: *~ of breath* 喘不过气来. 7 (不处于所示的情况): *~ of order* 坏了;发生故障;出毛病;弄乱. 8 以…为〔為〕起源 yǐ… wéi qǐyuán: *a story ~ of a book* 一本书中的故事. 9 离 lí;距 jù: *a mile ~ of Hull* 距赫尔一英里.

outboard /ˈaʊtbɔːd/ *adj* 舷外的 xiánwàide;尾挂〔掛〕的 wěiguàde: *an* ˌ*~ ˈmotor* 舷外发动机.

outbreak /ˈaʊtbreɪk/ *n* [C] 爆发〔發〕bàofā;突然发生 tūrán fāshēng: *the ~ of war* 战争的爆发.

outbuilding /ˈaʊtbɪldɪŋ/ *n* [C] 附属〔屬〕建筑〔築〕物 fùshǔ jiànzhùwù.

outburst /ˈaʊtbɜːst/ *n* [C] (怒气等)发〔發〕作 fāzuò;迸发 bèngfā.

outcast /ˈaʊtkɑːst; *US* -kæst/ *n* [C] 被(家庭、社会)抛弃〔棄〕的人 bèi pāoqìde rén;被逐出的人 bèi zhúchūde rén.

outcome /ˈaʊtkʌm/ *n* [C, 常作 sing] 效果 xiàoguǒ;结果 jiéguǒ.

outcrop /ˈaʊtkrɒp/ *n* [C] [地质](岩层等)露头〔頭〕lùtóu;露出地表 lòuchū dìbiǎo.

outcry /ˈaʊtkraɪ/ *n* [C] [*pl* -ies] 强烈抗议〔議〕(或反对) qiángliè kàngyì.

outdated /ˌaʊtˈdeɪtɪd/ *adj* 过〔過〕时〔時〕的 guòshíde;老式的 lǎoshìde;已废〔廢〕弃〔棄〕的 yǐ fèiqì de.

outdo /ˌaʊtˈduː/ *v* [第三人称单数现在时 **-does** /-ˈdʌz/, *pt* **-did** /-ˈdɪd/, *pp* **-done** /-ˈdʌn/] [T] 比…做得多(或做得好) bǐ …zuò de duō;胜〔勝〕过〔過〕shèngguò;超过 chāoguò: *She tries to ~ her friends at games.* 她试图在体育活动中胜过她的朋友.

outdoor /ˈaʊtdɔː(r)/ *adj* 户外的 hùwàide;露天的 lùtiānde. **outdoors** /ˌaʊtˈdɔːz/ *adv* 在户外 zài hùwài;在露天 zài lùtiān.

outer /ˈaʊtə(r)/ *adj* 1 外面的 wàimiànde;外部的 wàibùde: *~ walls* 外墙. 2 远〔遠〕离〔離〕内部(或中心)的 yuǎnlí nèibù de: *the ~ suburbs* 远郊. **outermost** *adj* 最外面的 zuì wàimiàn de;远离中心的 yuǎnlí zhōngxīn de. ˌ**outer ˈspace** = SPACE 5.

outfit /ˈaʊtfɪt/ *n* [C] 1 全套装〔裝〕备〔備〕quántào zhuāngbèi;全部用品 quánbù yòngpǐn;全套工具 quántào gōngjù. 2 [非正式用语]组织〔織〕zǔzhī. **outfitter** *n* [C] 服装商店 fúzhuāng shāngdiàn;服装商 fúzhuāngshāng.

outflank /ˌaʊtˈflæŋk/ *v* [T] (对敌人)翼侧包抄 yìcè bāochāo.

outgoing /ˈaʊtgəʊɪŋ/ *adj* 1 外出的 wàichūde;离〔離〕去的 líqùde: *the ~ president* 将离任的总统. 2 友好的 yǒuhǎode. **outgoings** *n* [pl] 支出 zhīchū;开〔開〕支 kāizhī.

outgrow /ˌaʊtˈgrəʊ/ *v* [*pt* **-grew** /-ˈgruː/, *pp* **-grown** /-ˈgrəʊn/] [T] 1 长〔長〕大而穿不下(原有的衣服) zhǎng dà ér chuān bú xià. 2 因年长而放弃〔棄〕(坏习惯等) yīn niánzhǎng ér fàngqì.

outhouse /ˈaʊthaʊs/ *n* [C] [*pl* ~s /-haʊzɪz/] 附属〔屬〕建筑〔築〕物 fùshǔ jiànzhùwù.

outing /ˈaʊtɪŋ/ *n* [C] 远〔遠〕足 yuǎnzú;短途旅行 duǎntú lǚxíng.

outlandish /aʊtˈlændɪʃ/ *adj* [尤作贬]怪异〔異〕的 guàiyìde;奇特的 qítède: *~ clothes* 奇装异服. **outlandishly** *adv*.

outlaw /ˈaʊtlɔː/ *n* [C] (旧时)不法之徒 bùfǎ zhī tú;歹徒 dǎitú;逃犯 táofàn. **outlaw** *v* [T] 宣布…非法 xuānbù… fēifǎ: *~ the sale of guns* 宣布出售枪支非法.

outlay /ˈaʊtleɪ/ *n* [C] 费用 fèiyòng;支出 zhīchū.

outlet /ˈaʊtlet/ *n* [C] 1 出口 chūkǒu;排放孔 páifàngkǒng;出路 chūlù. 2 [喻]发〔發〕泄〔洩〕(感情、精力等的)途径〔徑〕fāxiè tújìng: *sport is an ~ for energy* 运动是释放精力的途径.

outline /ˈaʊtlaɪn/ *n* [C] 1 轮〔輪〕廓 lúnkuò;外形 wàixíng. 2 大纲〔綱〕dàgāng;纲要 gāngyào: *an ~ of the plans* 计划纲要.

O

outline *v* [T] 概述 gàishù.

outlive /ˌaʊtˈlɪv/ *v* [T] 比…活得久 bǐ…huó de jiǔ: ~ *one's children* 比自己的孩子活得久.

outlook /ˈaʊtlʊk/ *n* [C] **1** (对生活的)看法 kànfǎ;观〔觀〕点〔點〕guāndiǎn;态〔態〕度 tàidù. **2** 展望 zhǎnwàng;前景 qiánjǐng.

outlying /ˈaʊtlaɪɪŋ/ *adj* 远〔遠〕离〔離〕中心的 yuǎnlí zhōngxīn de;远离城市的 yuǎnlí chéngshì de: ~ *villages* 偏僻的乡村.

outmoded /ˌaʊtˈməʊdɪd/ *adj* 过〔過〕时〔時〕的 guòshíde;不流行的 bù liúxíng de.

outnumber /ˌaʊtˈnʌmbə(r)/ *v* [T] 在数〔數〕量上超过〔過〕zài shùliàng shàng chāoguò.

out of date ⇨ DATE[1].

outpatient /ˈaʊtpeɪʃnt/ *n* [C] 门诊病人 ménzhěn bìngrén.

outpost /ˈaʊtpəʊst/ *n* [C] **1** 前哨 qiánshào. **2** 边〔邊〕远〔遠〕居民区〔區〕biānyuǎn jūmín qū.

output /ˈaʊtpʊt/ *n* [sing] **1** 产〔產〕量 chǎnliàng. **2** (信息等的)输出 shūchū.

outrage /ˈaʊtreɪdʒ/ *n* **1** [C, U] 暴行 bàoxíng;暴虐 bàonüè. **2** [C] 激起民愤的行为〔爲〕jīqǐ mínfèn de xíngwéi. **3** [U] 义〔義〕愤 yìfèn;愤慨 fènkǎi. **outrage** *v* [T] 激怒 jīnù. **outrageous** /aʊtˈreɪdʒəs/ *adj* **1** 骇人的 hàirénde. **2** 不寻〔尋〕常的 bù xúncháng de. **outrageously** *adv*.

outright /ˈaʊtraɪt/ *adv* **1** 坦率地 tǎnshuàide;诚实〔實〕地 chéngshíde: *I told him* ~ *what I thought*. 我把我的想法坦率地告诉了他. **2** 立即 lìjí: *be killed* ~ 立即毕命. **3** 完全地 wánquánde;彻〔徹〕底地 chèdǐde: *He won* ~. 他获得全胜. **outright** *adj* 毫无〔無〕疑义〔義〕的 háo wú yíyì de;清楚的 qīngchude: *the* ~ *winner* 毫无疑问的获胜者.

outset /ˈaʊtset/ *n* [习语] **at/from the outset** 开〔開〕始 kāishǐ, 开端 kāiduān;从〔從〕一开始 cóng yì kāishǐ.

outshine /ˌaʊtˈʃaɪn/ *v* [*pt*, *pp* **outshone** /-ˈʃɒn/] [T] [喻]比…光亮 bǐ…guāngliàng;比…出色 bǐ…chūsè: *She* ~*s all her friends at games*. 她在体育比赛中比她的所有朋友更出色.

outside /ˌaʊtˈsaɪd/ *n* [C, 常作 sing] 外部 wàibù;外面 wàimiàn: *the* ~ *of the house* 房子外部. **outside** /ˈaʊtsaɪd/ *adj* **1** 外面的 wàimiànde;在外面的 zài wàimiàn de;对〔對〕着外面的 duìzhe wàimiàn de. **2** 局外的 júwàide;外界的 wàijiède: ~ *help* 外援. **3** 非常小的 fēicháng xiǎo de: *an* ~ *chance* 微乎其微的机会. **outside** *adv* 在外面 zài wàimiàn;向外面 xiàng wàimiàn;在户外 zài hùwài: *Please wait* ~. 请在外面等候. **outside** (亦作 **outside of**, 尤用于美语) *prep* **1** 在…的外面 zài …de wàimiàn;向…的外面 xiàng…de wàimiàn: ~ *the bank* 在银行外面. **2** 超出…的范〔範〕围〔圍〕chāochū…de fànwéi: ~ *my areas of responsibility* 超出我的责任范围. **3** 除了 chúle: *no interests* ~ *his work* 他除了工作没有别的兴趣.

outsider /ˌaʊtˈsaɪdə(r)/ *n* [C] **1** 外人 wàirén;局外人 júwàirén;组织〔織〕之外的人 zǔzhī zhī wài de rén. **2** 不大可能获〔獲〕胜〔勝〕的选手(或赛马) búdà kěnéng huòshèng de xuǎnshǒu.

outsize /ˈaʊtsaɪz/ *adj* (尤指衣服)大于标〔標〕准〔準〕尺寸的 dàyú biāozhǔn chǐcùn de;特大的 tèdàde.

outskirts /ˈaʊtskɜːts/ *n* [pl] 市郊 shìjiāo;郊区〔區〕jiāoqū.

outsmart /ˌaʊtˈsmɑːt/ *v* [T] 比…精明 bǐ… jīngmíng;智胜〔勝〕zhìshèng.

outspoken /ˌaʊtˈspəʊkən/ *adj* 直言的 zhíyánde;坦率的 tǎnshuàide.

outstanding /ˌaʊtˈstændɪŋ/ *adj* **1** 杰〔傑〕出的 jiéchūde;优〔優〕秀的 yōuxiùde. **2** 显〔顯〕著的 xiǎnzhùde;突出的 tūchūde. **3** (报酬、工作等)未偿〔償〕付的 wèi chángfù de;未完成的 wèi wánchéng de. **outstandingly** *adv*.

outstay /ˌaʊtˈsteɪ/ *v* [习语] **outstay one's welcome** 做客时〔時〕间过〔過〕久 zuòkè shíjiān guòjiǔ.

outstrip /ˌaʊtˈstrɪp/ *v* [**-pp-**] [T] 胜〔勝〕过〔過〕shèngguò;超过 chāoguò: *Demand is* ~*ping production*. 需求正在超过生产能力.

outward /ˈaʊtwəd/ *adj* **1** (旅行)外出的 wàichūde;出外的 chūwàide: *the* ~ *flight* 飞出的航班. **2** 外面的 wàimiànde;在外面的 zài wàimiàn de: *an* ~ *appearance* 外表. **outward** (亦作 **outwards**) *adv* 向外 xiàngwài;离〔離〕家 líjiā. **outwardly** *adv* 表面上 biǎomiàn shang;外表上 wàibiǎo shang.

outweigh /ˌaʊtˈweɪ/ *v* [T] 在重要性方面超过〔過〕zài zhòngyàoxìng fāngmiàn chāoguò.

outwit /ˌaʊtˈwɪt/ *v* [**-tt-**] [T] 智胜〔勝〕zhìshèng.

outworn /ˌaʊtˈwɔːn/ *adj* 不能再用的 bùnéng zàiyòng de;旧〔舊〕式的 jiùshìde.

oval /ˈəʊvl/ *n* [C], *adj* 卵形(的) luǎnxíng;椭圆形(的) tuǒyuánxíng.

ovary /ˈəʊvərɪ/ *n* [C] [*pl* **-ies**] [解剖]卵巢 luǎncháo.

ovation /əʊˈveɪʃn/ *n* [C] 热〔熱〕烈欢〔歡〕迎(或鼓掌) rèliè huānyíng;欢呼 huānhū.

oven /ˈʌvn/ *n* [C] 烤炉〔爐〕kǎolú;烤箱 kǎoxiāng.

over[1] /ˈəʊvə(r)/ *prep* **1** 在…上面 zài… shàngmiàn;覆盖〔蓋〕在…上面 fùgài zài… shàngmiàn: *spill oil* ~ *one's clothes* 把油溅到自己的衣服上. **2** 在…的上方 zài…de

O

shàngfāng；高于 gāoyú：*They held an umbrella ~ her*．他们给她撑着一把伞．3 (a) 从〔從〕…的一边〔邊〕到另一边 cóng… de yìbiān dào lìng yìbiān：*a bridge ~ the river* 一座桥横跨河上．(b) 在…另一边 zài… lìng yìbiān. (c) 越过〔過〕yuèguò：*jump ~ the wall* 跳过墙．4 遍及各处〔處〕(或大部分) biànjí gèchù：*travel all ~ Africa* 游遍非洲．5 多于 duōyú；超过 chāoguò：*wait for ~ an hour* 等了一个多小时．6 (表示控制、掌握等)：*rule ~ an empire* 统治一个帝国．7 在…期间 zài… qījiān：*discuss it ~ lunch* 吃午饭时讨论此事．8 因为〔爲〕yīnwéi；由于 yóuyú：*an argument ~ money* 因钱而引起的争论．9 以 yǐ；借 jiè：*hear it ~ the radio/telephone* 从无线电广播(或电话)中听到这件事．10 [习语] **ˌover and aˈbove** 另外 lìngwài. **over one's ˈhead** ⇨ HEAD[1].

over[2] /ˈəʊvə(r)/ *adv* 1 (倒)下 xià；(掉)下 xià；翻转〔轉〕过〔過〕来 fānzhuǎn guòlái：*knock a vase ~* 把花瓶打翻．2 从〔從〕一边〔邊〕到另一边 cóng yìbiān dào lìng yìbiān：*turn a page ~* 翻过一页．3 穿过〔過〕(街道、开阔地等) chuānguò；横过 héngguò：*Take this letter ~ to the post office*．把这封信送到对面邮局去．4 [尤用于美语]再 zài；又 yòu：*do it ~* 再做一次．5 余〔餘〕下 yúxià：*the food left ~* 剩下的食物．6 加上 jiā shàng；…多… duō：*children of 14 and ~* 十四岁和十四岁以上的少年．7 结束 jiéshù；完结 wánjié：*The meeting is ~*．会议结束了．8 全部遮盖〔蓋〕quánbù zhēgài：*paint sth ~* 把某物全部涂上颜料．9 [习语] (**all**) **over aˈgain** 再一次 zài yícì. **ˌover and ˌover aˈgain** 一再 yízài；多次 duōcì.

over[3] /ˈəʊvə(r)/ *n* [C] (板球)(投手的)一轮〔輪〕投球数〔數〕(一次连续投 6 个球) yìlún tóuqiúshù.

over- *prefix* 1 在上 zài shàng；越过〔過〕yuèguò：*~land* 经由陆路的．*~head* 头顶上的；上空的．2 过多 guòduō：*~eat* 吃得过多．*~work* 工作时间过长．

overall[1] /ˌəʊvərˈɔːl/ *adj*, *adv* 包括一切的 bāokuò yíqiè de；全部的 quánbùde；总〔總〕共 zǒnggòng：*the ~ cost* 全部成本．

overall[2] /ˈəʊvərɔːl/ *n* 1 [C] [英国英语]罩衫 zhàoshān；罩衣 zhàoyī. 2 **overalls** [pl] [英国英语]工装〔裝〕裤 gōngzhuāngkù.

overawe /ˌəʊvərˈɔː/ *v* [T] [常作被动语态] 使(某人)敬畏 shǐ jìngwèi；慑〔懾〕服 shèfú.

overbalance /ˌəʊvəˈbæləns/ *v* [I] 失去平衡 shīqù pínghéng；跌倒 diēdǎo.

overbearing /ˌəʊvəˈbeərɪŋ/ *adj* [贬]专〔專〕横的 zhuānhèngde；跋扈的 báhùde；盛气〔氣〕凌人的 shèng qì líng rén de. **overbearingly** *adv*.

overboard /ˈəʊvəbɔːd/ *adv* 自船边〔邊〕缘落入水中 zì chuán biānyuán luòrù shuǐ zhōng；向舷外 xiàng xiánwài.

overcast /ˌəʊvəˈkɑːst; *US* -ˈkæst/ *adj* (天空)阴〔陰〕的 yīnde, 多云〔雲〕的 duōyúnde.

overcharge /ˌəʊvəˈtʃɑːdʒ/ *v* [I, T] 要价〔價〕过〔過〕高 yào jià guògāo.

overcoat /ˈəʊvəkəʊt/ *n* [C] 大衣 dàyī.

overcome /ˌəʊvəˈkʌm/ *v* [*pt* -came /-ˈkeɪm/, *pp* -come] [T] 1 击〔擊〕败 jībài；战〔戰〕胜〔勝〕zhànshèng；制伏 zhìfú. 2 使软弱 shǐ ruǎnruò；使失去控制力 shǐ shīqù kòngzhìlì：~ *by/with sadness* 因忧伤而不能自持．

overcrowded /ˌəʊvəˈkraʊdɪd/ *adj* 过〔過〕度拥〔擁〕挤〔擠〕的 guòdù yōngjǐ de. **overcrowding** /-dɪŋ/ *n* [U].

overdo /ˌəʊvəˈduː/ *v* [第三人称单数现在时 -does /-ˈdʌz/, *pt* -did /-ˈdɪd/, *pp* -done /-ˈdʌn/] 1 [T] 把…做得过〔過〕分 bǎ… zuòde guòfèn. 2 [习语] **overˈdo it** 工作过度 gōngzuò guòdù.

overdose /ˈəʊvədəʊs/ *n* [C, 常作 sing] (药物)过〔過〕量 guòliàng.

overdraft /ˈəʊvədrɑːft; *US* -dræft/ *n* [C] 透支 tòuzhī；透支额 tòuzhī'é.

overdrawn /ˌəʊvəˈdrɔːn/ *adj* 1 (人)有透支的 yǒu tòuzhī de. 2 (账户)透支的 tòuzhīde.

overdrive /ˈəʊvədraɪv/ *n* [C, U] (汽车的)超速挡〔擋〕chāosùdǎng.

overdue /ˌəʊvəˈdjuː; *US* -ˈduː/ *adj* (到期)未付款的 wèi fùkuǎn de；未到达〔達〕的 wèi dàodá de；延误〔誤〕的 yánwùde.

overflow /ˌəʊvəˈfləʊ/ *v* [I, T] 1 溢出 yìchū；泛滥〔濫〕fànlàn：*The river has ~ed its banks*．河水漫过堤岸．2 超过〔過〕…的范〔範〕围〔圍〕chāoguò … de fànwéi. **overflow** /ˈəʊvəfləʊ/ *n* [C] 1 [常作 sing] 溢出物 yìchūwù. 2 溢流管 yìliúguǎn.

overgrown /ˌəʊvəˈgrəʊn/ *adj* (野草等)蔓生的 mànshēngde.

overhang /ˌəʊvəˈhæŋ/ *v* [*pt*, *pp* -hung /-ˈhʌŋ/] [I, T] 悬〔懸〕于…之上 xuán yú… zhī shàng；突出于…之上 tūchū yú … zhī shàng. **overhang** /ˈəʊvəhæŋ/ *n* [C, 常作 sing]悬垂(或突出)部分 xuánchuí bùfen.

overhaul /ˌəʊvəˈhɔːl/ *v* [T] 彻〔徹〕底检〔檢〕修 chèdǐ jiǎnxiū；大修 dàxiū：~ *the engine* 检修发动机. **overhaul** /ˈəʊvəhɔːl/ *n* [C, 常作 sing] 彻底检修 chèdǐ jiǎnxiū；大修 dàxiū.

overhead /ˈəʊvəhed/ *adj* 在头〔頭〕顶上的 zài tóudǐng shang de；离〔離〕地面的 lí dìmiàn de：~ *wires* 架空线. **overhead** /ˌəʊvəˈhed/ *adv* 在头顶上 zài tóudǐng shang；在空中 zài

O

kōngzhōng: *aircraft flying* ～ 在空中飞行的飞机.

overheads /ˈəʊvəhedz/ *n* [pl] (企业等的)经〔經〕费(如房租、工资、保险等) jīngfèi.

overhear /ˌəʊvəˈhɪə(r)/ *v* [*pt*, *pp* -heard /-ˈhɜːd/] [T] 无〔無〕意中听〔聽〕到 wúyì zhōng tīngdào; 偷听到 tōutīngdào.

overjoyed /ˌəʊvəˈdʒɔɪd/ *adj* 极〔極〕高兴〔興〕的 jí gāoxìng de.

overland /ˈəʊvəlænd/ *adv*, *adj* 横越陆〔陸〕地(的) héngyuè lùdì; 经〔經〕由陆路(的) jīng yóu lùlù.

overlap /ˌəʊvəˈlæp/ *v* [-pp-] [I, T] (与某物)部分重叠〔疊〕bùfen chóngdié: [喻] *These two subjects* ～. 这两个学科交叉重叠. **overlap** /ˈəʊvəlæp/ *n* [C, U] 重叠部分 chóngdié bùfen.

overleaf /ˌəʊvəˈliːf/ *adv* 在(纸的)背面 zài bèimiàn.

overload /ˌəʊvəˈləʊd/ *v* [T] **1** 使超载 shǐ chāozài; 使过〔過〕载 shǐ guòzài. **2** 使(电路等)超负荷 shǐ chāo fùhé.

overlook /ˌəʊvəˈlʊk/ *v* [T] **1** 俯视 fǔshì; 俯瞰 fǔkàn. **2** 忽略 hūlüè; 忽视 hūshì. **3** 宽恕 kuānshù: ～ *a fault* 宽容错误.

overmanned /ˌəʊvəˈmænd/ *adj* 人手过〔過〕多的 rénshǒu guòduō de; 人浮于事的 rén fú yú shì de. **overmanning** /-nɪŋ/ *n* [U].

overnight /ˌəʊvəˈnaɪt/ *adv* **1** 在晚上 zài wǎnshang; 在夜里 zài yèlǐ: *stay* ～ 过夜. **2** [非正式用语]很快 hěnkuài; 突然 tūrán: *become a success* ～ 一下子成功. **overnight** /ˈəʊvənaɪt/ *adj*: *an* ～ *bag* (短途旅行用的)小旅行袋.

overpass /ˈəʊvəpɑːs; *US* -pæs/ *n* [C] [尤用于美语]立交桥〔橋〕lìjiāoqiáo.

overpower /ˌəʊvəˈpaʊə(r)/ *v* [T] 以较强力量打败 yǐ jiàoqiáng lìliàng dǎbài; 制服 zhìfú. **overpowering** *adj* 太强的 tàiqiángde; 力量极〔極〕大的 lìliàng jídà de: *an* ～*ing smell* 浓烈的臭味.

overrate /ˌəʊvəˈreɪt/ *v* [T] 对〔對〕…估计过〔過〕高 duì…gūjì guògāo.

overreach /ˌəʊvəˈriːtʃ/ *v* ～ **oneself** 因不自量力而失败 yīn bú zì liàng lì ér shībài.

over-react /ˌəʊvərɪˈækt/ *v* [I] 反应〔應〕过〔過〕火 fǎnyìng guòhuǒ; 反应过激 fǎnyìng guòjī.

override /ˌəʊvəˈraɪd/ *v* [*pt* -rode /-ˈrəʊd/, *pp* -ridden /-ˈrɪdn/] [T] **1** 不理会〔會〕(某人意见等) bù lǐhuì; 不顾〔顧〕búgù. **2** 比…更重要 bǐ…gèng zhòngyào. **overriding** *adj* 首要的 shǒuyàode.

overrule /ˌəʊvəˈruːl/ *v* [T] 否决 fǒujué; 驳回 bóhuí.

overrun /ˌəʊvəˈrʌn/ *v* [*pt* -ran /-ˈræn/, *pp* -run] **1** [T] 侵占〔佔〕qīnzhàn; 横行于 héngxíng yú: *a house* ～ *by insects* 满屋昆虫. **2** [I, T] 超越(时限) chāoyuè: *The meeting might* ～. 会议也许超过了原定时间.

overseas /ˌəʊvəˈsiːz/ *adj*, *adv* (在)海外的 hǎiwàide; (在)国〔國〕外的 guówàide; (向或来自)外国的 wàiguóde; 在(或向)海外 zài hǎiwài; 在(或向)国外 zài guówài.

oversee /ˌəʊvəˈsiː/ *v* [*pt* -saw /-ˈsɔː/, *pp* -seen /-ˈsiːn/] [T] 监〔監〕视 jiānshì; 监督 jiāndū. **ˈoverseer** /ˈəʊvəsɪə(r)/ *n* [C].

overshadow /ˌəʊvəˈʃædəʊ/ *v* [T] **1** 给…遮暗 gěi…zhē'àn; 使阴〔陰〕暗 shǐ yīn'àn. **2** [喻] 使黯然失色 shǐ ànrán shīsè; 使不快 shǐ búkuài.

overshoot /ˌəʊvəˈʃuːt/ *v* [*pt*, *pp* -shot /-ˈʃɒt/] [T] 超过〔過〕(目标) chāoguò.

oversight /ˈəʊvəsaɪt/ *n* [C, U] 失察 shīchá; 疏忽 shūhu.

oversleep /ˌəʊvəˈsliːp/ *v* [*pt*, *pp* -slept /-ˈslept/] [I] 睡得过〔過〕久 shuì de guòjiǔ; 睡过头〔頭〕shuìguòtóu.

overspill /ˈəʊvəspɪl/ *n* [U] [尤用于英国英语]城市过〔過〕剩人口的迁〔遷〕移 chéngshì guòshèng rénkǒu de qiānyí.

overstep /ˌəʊvəˈstep/ *v* [-pp-] [T] 超越(正常或容许的范围) chāoyuè.

overt /ˈəʊvɜːt; *US* əʊˈvɜːrt/ *adj* [正式用语] 公开〔開〕的 gōngkāide: ～ *hostility* 公然的敌意. **overtly** *adv*.

overtake /ˌəʊvəˈteɪk/ *v* [*pt* -took /-ˈtʊk/, *pp* -taken /-ˈteɪkən/] **1** [I, T] 追上 zhuī shàng; 超越 chāoyuè. **2** [T] (不愉快的事)突然降临〔臨〕tūrán jiànglín.

overthrow /ˌəʊvəˈθrəʊ/ *v* [*pt* -threw /-ˈθruː/, *pp* -thrown /-ˈθrəʊn/] [T] 推翻 tuīfān; 打倒 dǎdǎo. **overthrow** /ˈəʊvəθrəʊ/ *n* [C].

overtime /ˈəʊvətaɪm/ *n* [U], *adv* 加班 jiābān; 加班时〔時〕间 jiābān shíjiān; 超时地 chāoshíde; 在加班时间内 zài jiābān shíjiān nèi.

overtone /ˈəʊvətəʊn/ *n* [C, 常作 pl] 弦外之音 xián wài zhī yīn; 暗示 ànshì.

overture /ˈəʊvətjʊə(r)/ *n* **1** [C] (歌剧等的)序曲 xùqǔ; 前奏曲 qiánzòuqǔ. **2** [习语] **make overtures to sb** (向某人)做出友好表示 zuò chū yǒuhǎo biǎoshì.

overturn /ˌəʊvəˈtɜːn/ *v* **1** [I, T] 翻倒 fāndǎo; 倾覆 qīngfù; 翻转〔轉〕fānzhuǎn. **2** [T] 否决 fǒujué; 驳回 bóhuí. **3** [T] 推翻 tuīfān; 颠覆 diānfù.

overview /ˈəʊvəvjuː/ *n* [C] 概述 gàishù; 概观〔觀〕gàiguān.

overweight /ˌəʊvəˈweɪt/ *adj* (人)体〔體〕重超常的 tǐzhòng chāocháng de; 肥胖的 féipàngde.

overwhelm /ˌəʊvəˈwelm; *US* -ˈhwelm/ *v*

O

[T] 1 [常作被动语态]使无〔無〕助 shǐ wúzhù；使焦虑〔慮〕shǐ jiāolǜ：*~ed by sorrow* 不胜悲伤. 2 击〔擊〕败 jībài；压〔壓〕倒 yādǎo；制服 zhìfú.

overwork /ˌəʊvəˈwɜːk/ *v* 1 [I, T] (使)工作过〔過〕度 gōngzuò guòdù；(使)过分劳〔勞〕累 guòfèn láolèi. 2 [T] 对〔對〕…使用过度 duì…shǐyòng guòdù.

overwrought /ˌəʊvəˈrɔːt/ *adj* 神经〔經〕紧〔緊〕张〔張〕的 shénjīng jǐnzhāng de；忧〔憂〕虑〔慮〕的 yōulǜde；不安的 bù'ānde.

ovulate /ˈɒvjuleɪt/ *v* [I] [医学]排卵 páiluǎn；产〔產〕卵 chǎnluǎn. **ovulation** /ˌɒvjuˈleɪʃn/ *n* [U].

ovum /ˈəʊvəm/ *n* [C] [*pl* **ova** /ˈəʊvə/] [生物]卵子 luǎnzǐ；卵细胞 luǎnxìbāo.

ow /aʊ/ *interj* (表示疼痛)：*Ow! That hurt!* 啊唷! 痛!

owe /əʊ/ *v* [T] 1 欠(债等) qiàn：*I ~ him £10*. 我欠他 10 英镑. 2 to 把…归〔歸〕功于 bǎ… guīgōng yú：*She ~s her success to hard work*. 她把成功归因于努力工作. 3 对〔對〕…感激 duì…gǎnjī.

owing /ˈəʊɪŋ/ *adj* 未付的 wèifùde. **owing to** *prep* 由于 yóuyú.

owl /aʊl/ *n* [C] 猫头〔頭〕鹰 māotóuyīng.

own[1] /əʊn/ *adj*, *pron* 1 自己的 zìjǐde；属〔屬〕于自己的 shǔyú zìjǐ de：*his ~ room* 他自己的房间. *a room of his ~* 他自己的房间. 2 [习语] **get one's ˈown back (on sb)** [非正式用语]报〔報〕复〔復〕bàofù. **(all) on one's ˈown** (a) 独〔獨〕自 dúzì. (b) 独力地 dúlìde.

own[2] /əʊn/ *v* [T] 1 有 yǒu；拥〔擁〕有 yōngyǒu：*~ a house* 拥有一所房子. 2 [短语动词] **own up (to sth)** [非正式用语]承认〔認〕有错 chéngrèn yǒucuò. **owner** *n* [C]. **ownership** *n* [U].

ox /ɒks/ *n* [C] [*pl* **~en** /ˈɒksn/] 牛 niú；(去势的)公牛 gōngniú.

oxygen /ˈɒksɪdʒən/ *n* [U] 氧 yǎng；氧气〔氣〕yǎngqì. **ˈoxygen bar** *n* [C] 氧吧 yǎngbā.

oyster /ˈɔɪstə(r)/ *n* [C] 蚝〔蠔〕háo；牡蛎〔蠣〕mǔlì. **ˈoyster-catcher** *n* [C] 蛎鹬 lìyù.

oz *abbr* [*pl* **oz** 或 **ozs**] ounce(s).

ozone /ˈəʊzəʊn/ *n* [U] 1 臭氧 chòuyǎng. 2 [非正式用语]清新空气〔氣〕qīngxīn kōngqì. **ˈozone depletion** *n* [U] 臭氧层〔層〕损耗 chòuyǎngcéng sǔnhào；臭氧层破坏〔壞〕chòuyǎngcéng pòhuài. **ozone-ˈfriendly** *adj* 不损臭氧层的 bù sǔn chòuyǎngcéng de. **ˈozone hole** *n* [C] 臭氧层空洞 chòuyǎngcéng kōngdòng. **ˈozone layer** *n* [U] 臭氧层 chòuyǎngcéng.

P p

P, p /piː/ *n* [C] [*pl* **P's, p's** /piːz/] 英语的第十六个〔個〕字母 Yīngyǔ de dìshíliùgè zìmǔ.

P *abbr* 1 [英国非正式用语] penny; pence. 2 [*pl* **pp**] page.

pa /pɑː/ *n* [C] [非正式用语]爸爸 bàba.

pace /peɪs/ *n* 1 [C] 一步 yíbù；一步的距离〔離〕yíbù de jùlí. 2 [sing] (走或跑的)速度 sùdù. 3 [U] 进步(或发展)的速度 jìnbùde sùdù. **pace** *v* 1 [I, T] 慢步行走 mànbù xíngzǒu；踱方步 duó fāngbù. 2 [T] 为〔爲〕…定速度 wèi…dìng sùdù. 3 [动词短语] **pace sth off/out** 步测 bùcè. **ˈpace maker** *n* [C] (心脏)起搏器 qǐbóqì.

pacifism /ˈpæsɪfɪzəm/ *n* [U] 和平主义〔義〕hépíng zhǔyì；反战〔戰〕主义 fǎnzhàn zhǔyì. **pacifist** /-ɪst/ *n* [C].

pacify /ˈpæsɪfaɪ/ *v* [*pt*, *pp* **-ied**] [T] 抚〔撫〕慰 fǔwèi；使平静 shǐ píngjìng；使息怒 shǐ xīnù. **pacification** /ˌpæsɪfɪˈkeɪʃn/ *n* [U].

pack[1] /pæk/ *n* [C] 1 包 bāo；包裹 bāoguǒ. 2 [尤用于美语]小包(或袋) xiǎobāo；小盒(或箱) xiǎohé. 3 (野兽的)一群 yìqún：*a ~ of wolves* 一群狼. 4 (人或物的)一伙〔夥〕yìhuǒ，一帮〔幫〕yìbāng：*a ~ of fools/lies* 一伙傻子；一派谎言. 5 (纸牌的)一副 yífù.

pack[2] /pæk/ *v* 1 [I, T] 把…装〔裝〕入(箱、盒等) bǎ…zhuāngrù：*~ clothes in a bag* 把衣物装入袋子里. 2 [T] 用…包(或垫) yòng…bāo；用…充填 yòng…chōngtián：*glass ~ed in paper* 用纸包垫的玻璃. 3 [I, T] (*into*) (物)塞满 sāimǎn；(人)挤〔擠〕满 jǐmǎn：*Crowds ~ed (into) the theatre*. 人群挤进剧院. 4 [短语动词] **pack sth in** [非正式用语]停止做某事 tíngzhǐ zuò mǒushì. **pack sb off** [非正式用语]打发〔發〕某人 dǎfa mǒurén. **pack up** [非正式用语] (a) 结束工作 jiéshù gōngzuò. (b) (机器)出故障 chū gùzhàng. **pack (sth) up** 整理(行装)并〔並〕离〔離〕开〔開〕某地 zhěnglǐ…bìng líkāi mǒudì. **packed** *adj* 拥〔擁〕挤的 yōngjǐde；挤满的 jǐmǎnde.

package /ˈpækɪdʒ/ *n* [C] 1 包裹 bāoguǒ. 2 [美语]小包(或袋) xiǎobāo. 3 (亦作 **ˈpackage deal**) 一揽〔攬〕子交易 yìlǎnzi jiāoyì. **package** *v* [T] 将〔將〕…包装〔裝〕(如为出售) jiāng…bāozhuāng. **ˈpackage holiday/tour** *n* [C] (由旅行社代办的)包价〔價〕旅游 bāojià lǚyóu；一揽子旅游 yìlǎnzi lǚyóu. **package ˈtourist** *n* [C] 包价旅游游客 bāojià lǚyóu yóukè.

packet /ˈpækɪt/ *n* 1 [C] 小包(或盒、袋) xiǎobāo：*a ~ of cigarettes* 一小包香烟. 2 [sing] [非正式用语]大笔〔筆〕款项 dàbǐ kuǎnxiàng.

packing /ˈpækɪŋ/ *n* [U] **1** (货物)包装〔裝〕bāozhuāng; 包装法 bāozhuāngfǎ. **2** 包装材料 bāozhuāng cáiliào.

pact /pækt/ *n* [C] 协〔協〕定 xiédìng; 契约 qìyuē; 条〔條〕约 tiáoyuē; 公约 gōngyuē.

pad[1] /pæd/ *n* [C] **1** 垫〔墊〕diàn; 衬〔襯〕垫 chèndiàn; 护〔護〕垫 hùdiàn. **2** 拍纸簿 pāizhǐbù; 便笺〔箋〕本 biànjiānběn. **3** (航天器等的)发〔發〕射台〔臺〕fāshètái; 直升机〔機〕起落处〔處〕zhíshēngjī qǐluòchù. **4** [俚]住处 zhùchù. **5** (狗、狐等的)肉趾 ròuzhǐ.

pad[2] /pæd/ *v* [-dd-] **1** [T] (用软物)填塞 tiánsāi; 覆盖〔蓋〕fùgài; 垫〔墊〕(或衬) diàn. **2** [短语动词] **pad sth out** (用多余的内容)拉长〔長〕lācháng. **padding** *n* [U] **1** (软的)垫料 diànliào; 衬〔襯〕料 chènliào. **2** (书等的)凑篇幅的材料 còu piānfu de cáiliào.

pad[3] /pæd/ *v* [-dd-] [短语动词] **pad about, along, etc** 放轻〔輕〕脚步走 fàngqīng jiǎobù zǒu.

paddle[1] /ˈpædl/ *n* [C] 短桨〔槳〕duǎnjiǎng. **paddle** *v* [I, T] 用桨划 yòng jiǎng huá.

paddle[2] /ˈpædl/ *v* [I] 涉水 shèshuǐ; 蹚水 tāngshuǐ. **paddle** *n* [sing] 涉水 shèshuǐ; 蹚水 tāngshuǐ.

paddock /ˈpædək/ *n* [C] (放牧、驯马等的)小围〔圍〕场〔場〕xiǎo wéichǎng.

paddy (亦作 **ˈpaddy-field**) /ˈpædɪ/ *n* [C] [*pl* **-ies**] 稻田 dàotián.

padlock /ˈpædlɒk/ *n* [C] 挂〔掛〕锁 guàsuǒ; 扣锁 kòusuǒ. **padlock** *v* [T] 用挂锁锁 yòng guàsuǒ suǒ.

P

paediatrics /ˌpiːdɪˈætrɪks/ *n* [用 sing v] 儿〔兒〕科学〔學〕érkēxué. **paediatrician** /ˌpiːdɪəˈtrɪʃn/ *n* [C] 儿科医〔醫〕师〔師〕érkē yīshī; 儿科学家 érkēxuéjiā.

pagan /ˈpeɪgən/ *n* [C] 异〔異〕教徒 yìjiàotú. **pagan** *adj* 异教徒的 yìjiàotúde. **paganism** *n* [U].

page[1] /peɪdʒ/ *n* [C] **1** (书等的)页 yè. **2** (纸的)张〔張〕zhāng.

page[2] (亦作 **ˈpage-boy**) /peɪdʒ/ *n* [C] **1** 男侍 nánshì. **2** (婚礼上的)男傧〔儐〕相 nán bīnxiàng.

page[3] *v* [T] **1** 用寻〔尋〕呼机〔機〕发〔發〕信息给 yòng xúnhūjī fā xìnxī gěi. **2** 用寻呼机呼唤 yòng xúnhūjī hūhuàn; 呼 hū.

pageant /ˈpædʒənt/ *n* [C] **1** 露天演出的历〔歷〕史剧〔劇〕lùtiān yǎnchū de lìshǐjù. **2** 壮〔壯〕丽〔麗〕的场〔場〕面 zhuànglìde chǎngmiàn. **pageantry** *n* [U] 盛况 shèngkuàng.

pager /ˈpeɪdʒə(r)/ *n* [C] 寻〔尋〕呼机〔機〕xúnhūjī; 呼机 hūjī.

pagoda /pəˈgəudə/ *n* [C] (印度、东亚的)塔 tǎ; 宝〔寶〕塔 bǎotǎ.

paid *pt, pp* of PAY[1].

pail /peɪl/ *n* [C] 桶 tǒng.

pain /peɪn/ *n* **1** [U] 痛苦 tòngkǔ: *cry with* ~ 疼得大叫. **2** [C] (身体某部分的)疼痛 téngtòng: *a* ~ *in her leg* 她的腿痛. **3** [C] [非正式用语]令人厌〔厭〕烦的人(或事) lìng rén yànfán de rén. **4** [习语] **a pain in the neck** [非正式用语]令人厌烦的人(或事) lìng rén yànfán de rén. **pain** *v* [T] 使痛苦 shǐ tòngkǔ. **pained** *adj* 痛苦的 tòngkǔde; 难〔難〕过〔過〕的 nánguòde: *a* ~*ed look* 一副痛苦相. **painful** *adj* 疼痛的 téngtòngde; 痛苦的 tòngkǔde. **painless** *adj* 不痛的 bútòngde.

pains /peɪnz/ *n* [pl] [习语] **take (great)/be at pains to do sth** 尽〔盡〕力去做 jìnlì qù zuò. **ˈpainstaking** *adj* 十分小心的 shífēn xiǎoxīn de; 仔细的 zǐxìde.

paint /peɪnt/ *n* **1** [U] 油漆 yóuqī; 涂〔塗〕料 túliào. **2** **paints** [pl] (一套)管装〔裝〕的颜料 guǎnzhuāngde yánliào. **paint** *v* **1** [I, T] (用颜料)画〔畫〕huà: ~ *flowers* 画花卉. **2** [T] 油漆 yóuqī; 涂饰〔飾〕túshì: ~ *the door* 油漆门. **3** [T] [喻]描写〔寫〕miáoxiě; 描绘〔繪〕miáohuì. **4** [习语] **paint the ˈtown red** [非正式用语]饮酒作乐〔樂〕yǐnjiǔ zuòlè; 狂欢〔歡〕kuánghuān. **painting** *n* **1** [U] 涂色 túsè; 油漆 yóuqī; 油漆技巧 yóuqī jìqiǎo; 绘画 huìhuà. **2** [C] 图〔圖〕画 túhuà. **ˈpaintwork** *n* [U] 已涂颜料的表面 yǐtú yánliào de biǎomiàn.

painter /ˈpeɪntə(r)/ *n* [C] **1** 画〔畫〕家 huàjiā. **2** 油漆工 yóuqīgōng; 粉刷工 fěnshuāgōng.

pair /peə(r)/ *n* **1** [C] 一双〔雙〕yìshuāng; 一对〔對〕yíduì; 一副 yífù: *a* ~ *of shoes* 一双鞋. **2** [C] (由两个相同部分组成的)一把 yìbǎ; 一条〔條〕yìtiáo: *a* ~ *of trousers / scissors* 一条裤子; 一把剪刀. **3** [C, 亦作 sing, 用 pl v] 两个〔個〕关〔關〕系〔係〕密切的人(如一对夫妇、一对情侣) liǎnggè guānxì mìqiè de rén. **pair** *v* [I, T] (*off*) (使)成对 chéngduì; (使)成双 chéngshuāng: ~ (*off*) *a pile of socks* 使一堆袜子成为一双一双的袜子.

pajamas [美语] = PYJAMAS.

pal /pæl/ *n* [C] [非正式用语]朋友 péngyǒu.

palace /ˈpælɪs/ *n* [C] 王宫 wánggōng; 宫殿 gōngdiàn; 豪华〔華〕住宅 háohuá zhùzhái.

palaeontology /ˌpælɪɒnˈtɒlədʒɪ/ (亦作 **paleon-** /ˌpeɪl-/, 尤用于美语) *n* [U] 古生物学〔學〕gǔshēngwùxué. **palaeontologist** (亦作 **paleon-**, 尤用于美语) / -dʒɪst / *n* [C].

palatable /ˈpælətəbl/ *adj* **1** 可口的 kěkǒude; 美味的 měiwèide. **2** [喻]合意的 héyìde; 认〔認〕可的 rènkěde: *The truth is not always very* ~. 事实真相并不尽如人意.

palate /ˈpælət/ *n* [C] **1** 腭 è. **2** [常作 sing] 味觉〔覺〕wèijué.

palatial /pəˈleɪʃl/ *adj* 像宫殿的 xiàng gōngdiàn de；壮〔壯〕丽〔麗〕的 zhuànglìde：*a* ～ *hotel* 富丽堂皇的旅馆．

palaver /pəˈlɑːvə(r)；*US* -ˈlæv-/ *n* [U, sing] [非正式用语]烦恼〔惱〕fánnǎo；忙乱〔亂〕mángluàn.

pale[1] /peɪl/ *adj* [～r，～st] 1 (脸色)苍〔蒼〕白的 cāngbáide. 2 (颜色)浅〔淺〕的 qiǎnde；暗淡的 àndànde：～ *blue eyes* 淡蓝色的眼睛. **pale** *v* [I] 1 变〔變〕苍白 biàn cāngbái. 2 相形失色 xiāng xíng shīsè；相形见绌 xiāng xíng jiàn chù：*Compared to your problems mine* ～ *into insignificance*. 我的问题和你的相比就显得微不足道了. **paleness** *n* [U].

pale[2] /peɪl/ *n* [习语] **beˌyond the ˈpale** 越轨的 yuèguǐde：*Your remarks are beyond the* ～. 你的话出格了.

paleo- = PALAEO-.

palette /ˈpælət/ *n* [C] 调色板 tiáosèbǎn.

paling /ˈpeɪlɪŋ/ *n* [C] 栅栏〔欄〕zhàlan；木栅 mùzhà.

pall[1] /pɔːl/ *v* [I] 生厌〔厭〕shēngyàn；乏味 fáwèi；厌烦 yànfán.

pall[2] /pɔːl/ *n* [C] 1 棺罩 guānzhào；柩衣 jiùyī. 2 [常作 sing] [喻](阴暗色的)遮盖〔蓋〕物 zhēgàiwù：*a* ～ *of smoke* 一片浓烟. **ˈpallbearer** *n* [C] (出殡时)抬棺者 táiguānzhě.

pallet /ˈpælɪt/ *n* [C] (移动或堆放货物的)托盘〔盤〕tuōpán；集装〔裝〕架 jízhuāngjià；货板 huòbǎn.

pallid /ˈpælɪd/ *adj* 苍〔蒼〕白的 cāngbáide；无〔無〕血色的 wú xuèsè de. **pallor** /ˈpælə(r)/ *n* [U].

palm[1] /pɑːm/ *n* [C] 手掌 shǒuzhǎng；手心 shǒuxīn. **palm** *v* [短语动词] **palm sth off (on sb)** [非正式用语]将〔將〕(自己不想要的东西)劝〔勸〕说别人接受 jiāng…quànshuō biérén jiēshòu：*She always* ～*s off her old clothes on me*. 她总是哄骗我接受她不穿了的旧衣服. **ˈpalmtop** *n* [C] 掌上电〔電〕脑〔腦〕zhǎngshàng diànnǎo.

palm[2] (亦作 **ˈpalm-tree**) /pɑːm/ *n* [C] 棕榈树〔樹〕zōnglǘshù.

palmist /ˈpɑːmɪst/ *n* [C] 看手相者 kànshǒuxiàngzhě. **palmistry** *n* [U] 手相术〔術〕shǒuxiàngshù.

palpable /ˈpælpəbl/ *adj* [正式用语]明显〔顯〕的 míngxiǎnde；明白的 míngbaide. **palpably** /-əblɪ/ *adv*.

palpitate /ˈpælpɪteɪt/ *v* [I] 1 (心脏)急速地跳动〔動〕jísùde tiàodòng. 2 (人)颤抖 chàndǒu. **palpitation** /ˌpælpɪˈteɪʃn/ *n* [U,C,常作 pl].

paltry /ˈpɔːltrɪ/ *adj* [-ier，-iest] 没价〔價〕值的 méi jiàzhí de；微不足道的 wēi bù zú dào de.

pamper /ˈpæmpə(r)/ *v* [T] 纵〔縱〕容 zòngróng；娇〔嬌〕养〔養〕jiāoyǎng.

pamphlet /ˈpæmflɪt/ *n* [C] 小册子 xiǎocèzi.

pan[1] /pæn/ *n* [C] 1 平底锅〔鍋〕píngdǐguō；盘〔盤〕状〔狀〕器皿 pánzhuàng qìmǐn：*a ˈfrying-*～ 煎锅. 2 盆状器皿 pénzhuàng qìmǐn：*a toilet* ～ 卫生间马桶. **pan** *v* [-nn-] 1 [I] (*for*) (用淘盘)淘(金等) táo. 2 [T] [非正式用语]严〔嚴〕厉〔厲〕地批评 yánlìde pīpíng. 3 [短语动词] **pan out** [喻](事情)发〔發〕展 fāzhǎn；结果 jiéguǒ：*How did things* ～ *out?* 事情的结果怎么样？

pan[2] /pæn/ *v* [-nn-] [I,T] (为拍摄全景或动景)向左或向右移动〔動〕(摄影机) xiàng zuǒ huò xiàng yòu yídòng；摇镜头〔頭〕yáo jìngtóu.

panacea /ˌpænəˈsɪə/ *n* [C] 治百病的药〔藥〕zhìbǎibìngde yào；万〔萬〕灵〔靈〕药 wànlíngyào.

panache /pæˈnæʃ；*US* pə-/ *n* [U] 神气〔氣〕十足 shénqì shízú；炫耀 xuànyào.

pancake /ˈpæŋkeɪk/ *n* [C] 烙饼 làobǐng；薄饼 báobǐng.

pancreas /ˈpæŋkrɪəs/ *n* [C] 胰 yí；胰腺 yíxiàn.

panda /ˈpændə/ *n* [C] 大熊猫 dà xióngmāo；大猫熊 dà māoxióng.

pandemonium /ˌpændɪˈməʊnɪəm/ *n* [U] 大混乱〔亂〕dà hùnluàn；喧闹〔鬧〕xuānnào.

pander /ˈpændə(r)/ *v* [短语动词] **pander to sb/sth** 迎合(他人的低级趣味等) yínghé：*newspapers that* ～ *to the public's interest in violence* 迎合公众对暴力的兴趣的报纸.

pane /peɪn/ *n* [C] (窗上的)单〔單〕块〔塊〕玻璃 dānkuài bōli.

panel /ˈpænl/ *n* [C] 1 镶板 xiāngbǎn；嵌板 qiànbǎn. 2 控制板 kòngzhìbǎn；仪〔儀〕表〔錶〕板 yíbiǎobǎn. 3 (广播、电视中)座谈小组 zuòtán xiǎozǔ；答问小组 dáwèn xiǎozǔ. **panel** *v* [-ll-；*US* -l-] [T] (用镶板)镶嵌 xiāngqiàn. **panelling** (美语 -l-) *n* [U] 镶板细工 xiāngbǎn xìgōng；镶板饰面 xiāngbǎn shìmiàn.

pang /pæŋ/ *n* [C] 一阵剧〔劇〕痛 yízhèn jùtòng；悲痛 bēitòng.

panic /ˈpænɪk/ *n* [U,C] 惊〔驚〕慌 jīnghuāng；恐慌 kǒnghuāng. **panic** *v* [-ck-] [I] 受惊 shòujīng；惊慌 jīnghuāng. **ˈpanic ˌbuying** *n* [U] 抢〔搶〕购〔購〕qiǎnggòu. **panicky** *adj* [非正式用语]惊恐的 jīngkǒngde；惊恐引起的 jīngkǒng yǐnqǐ de. **ˈpanic-stricken** *adj* 惊慌失措的 jīnghuāng shīcuò de；万〔萬〕分恐慌的 wànfēn kǒnghuāng de.

pannier /ˈpænɪə(r)/ *n* [C] (自行车两侧的)

P

挂〔掛〕篮〔籃〕guàlán;挂包 guàbāo.

panorama /ˌpænəˈrɑːmə; *US* -ˈræmə/ *n* [C] 全景 quánjǐng. **panoramic** /-ˈræmɪk/ *adj*.

pansy /ˈpænzɪ/ *n* [C] [*pl* -ies] 1 三色堇 sānsèjǐn. 2 [非正式用语,贬]女性化的男子 nǚxìnghuàde nánzǐ;同性恋〔戀〕男子 tóngxìngliàn nánzǐ.

pant /pænt/ *v* [I] 气〔氣〕喘 qìchuǎn;喘息 chuǎnxī. **pant** *n* [C] 喘息 chuǎnxī;气喘 qìchuǎn.

panther /ˈpænθə(r)/ *n* [C] 豹 bào;黑豹 hēibào.

panties /ˈpæntɪz/ *n* [pl] [非正式用语](女用)紧〔緊〕身短衬〔襯〕裤 jǐnshēn duǎnchènkù.

pantomime /ˈpæntəmaɪm/ *n* [C, U] (圣诞节期间演出的)童话剧〔劇〕tónghuàjù.

pantry /ˈpæntrɪ/ *n* [C] [*pl* -ies] 食品(储藏)室 shípǐnshì.

pants /pænts/ *n* [pl] 1 [英国英语](男用的、女用的)内裤 nèikù. 2 [尤用于美语]裤子 kùzi.

papa /pəˈpɑː; *US* ˈpɑːpə/ *n* [C] [旧,非正式用语](儿语)爸爸 bàba.

papal /ˈpeɪpl/ *adj* 教皇的 jiàohuángde.

paper /ˈpeɪpə(r)/ *n* 1 [U] 纸 zhǐ. 2 [C] 报〔報〕纸 bàozhǐ. 3 **papers** [pl] 文件 wénjiàn. 4 [C] 试卷 shìjuàn. 5 [C] 文章 wénzhāng;论〔論〕文 lùnwén. **paper** *v* [T] 用壁纸裱糊(墙壁) yòng bìzhǐ biǎohú. ˈ**paperback** *n* [C] (书)平装〔裝〕本 píngzhuāngběn;纸面本 zhǐmiànběn. ˈ**paper-boy**, ˈ**paper-girl** *n* [C] 送报男孩 sòngbào nánhái;送报女孩 sòngbào nǚhái. ˈ**paper-clip** *n* [C] 回〔迴〕形针 huíxíngzhēn. **paperweight** *n* [C] 镇纸 zhènzhǐ. ˈ**paperwork** *n* [U] 文书〔書〕工作 wénshū gōngzuò.

paprika /ˈpæprɪkə; *US* pəˈpriːkə/ *n* [U] 辣椒粉 làjiāofěn.

par /pɑː(r)/ *n* 1 [sing] (高尔夫球)规定击〔擊〕球次数〔數〕(18 个穴共 72 次) guīdìng jīqiú cìshù;标〔標〕准〔準〕杆〔桿〕数 biāozhǔn gānshù. 2 [习语] **below** ˈ**par** [非正式用语]一般水平以下 yìbān shuǐpíng yǐxià;不佳的 bùjiāde. **on a par with sb/sth** 与〔與〕…同等重要 yǔ… tóngděng zhòngyào;与…同水平 yǔ… tóng shuǐpíng.

parable /ˈpærəbl/ *n* [C] (尤指《圣经》中的)寓言故事 yùyán gùshi.

parachute /ˈpærəʃuːt/ *n* [C] 降落伞〔傘〕jiàngluòsǎn. **parachute** *v* [I, T] 跳伞 tiàosǎn;用降落伞空投 yòng jiàngluòsǎn kōngtóu. **parachutist** *n* [C] 跳伞者 tiàosǎnzhě.

parade /pəˈreɪd/ *n* [C] 1 (部队的)检〔檢〕阅 jiǎnyuè. 2 游行 yóuxíng. **parade** *v* 1 [I, T] (为检阅等)集合(部队) jíhé. 2 [I] 游行 yóuxíng;列队〔隊〕行进〔進〕lièduì xíngjìn. 3 [T] 炫耀 xuànyào;展示 zhǎnshì: ~ *one's wealth* 炫耀个人的财富.

paradise /ˈpærədaɪs/ *n* 1 [U] 天堂 tiāntáng;天国〔國〕tiānguó. 2 [C, 常作 sing, U] 乐〔樂〕园〔園〕lèyuán;乐土 lètǔ.

paradox /ˈpærədɒks/ *n* [C] 似非而是的隽语 sì fēi ér shì de juànyǔ;似矛盾而可能正确〔確〕的说法 sì máodùn ér kěnéng zhèngquè de shuōfǎ. **paradoxical** /ˌpærəˈdɒksɪkl/ *adj*. **paradoxically** /-klɪ/ *adv*.

paraffin /ˈpærəfɪn/ *n* [U] 煤油 méiyóu.

paragon /ˈpærəgən; *US* -gɒn/ *n* [C] (*of*) 典范〔範〕diǎnfàn;完人 wánrén: *She is a ~ of virtue*. 她是美德的典范.

paragraph /ˈpærəgrɑːf; *US* -græf/ *n* [C] (文章的)段落 duànluò;节〔節〕jié.

parakeet /ˈpærəkiːt/ *n* [C] 长〔長〕尾鹦鹉 chángwěi yīngwǔ.

parallel /ˈpærəlel/ *adj* 1 平行的 píngxíngde. 2 [喻]类〔類〕似的 lèisìde. **parallel** *n* 1 [C, U] 类似的人(或事) lèisìde rén. 2 [C] 对〔對〕比 duìbǐ;比较 bǐjiào: *draw a ~ between A and B* 把 A 和 B 作一比较. **parallel** *v* [T] 与〔與〕…相当〔當〕yǔ… xiāngdāng;与…相似 yǔ… xiāngsì.

parallelogram /ˌpærəˈleləgræm/ *n* [C] 平行四边〔邊〕形 píngxíng sìbiānxíng.

paralyse (美语 **-lyze**) /ˈpærəlaɪz/ *v* [T] 1 使麻痹 shǐ mábì;使瘫〔癱〕痪 shǐ tānhuàn. 2 [喻]使不能正常活动〔動〕shǐ bùnéng zhèngcháng huódòng;使丧〔喪〕失作用力 shǐ sàngshī zuòyònglì: *The city was ~d by the railway strike*. 铁路罢工使该市陷于瘫痪.

paralysis /pəˈræləsɪs/ *n* [U] 1 麻痹 mábì;瘫〔癱〕痪 tānhuàn. 2 [喻](活动、工作等)瘫痪 tānhuàn. **paralytic** /ˌpærəˈlɪtɪk/ *adj* 1 麻痹的 mábìde;瘫痪的 tānhuànde. 2 [英俚]酩酊大醉的 mǐngdǐng dàzuìde. **paralytic** *n* [C] 麻痹症患者 mábìzhèng huànzhě;瘫痪病人 tānhuàn bìngrén.

parameter /pəˈræmɪtə(r)/ *n* [C, 常作 pl] 起限定作用的因素 qǐ xiàndìng zuòyòng de yīnsù;界限 jièxiàn.

paramilitary /ˌpærəˈmɪlɪtrɪ; *US* -terɪ/ *adj* 准军事的 zhǔnjūnshìde;辅助军事的 fǔzhù jūnshì de.

paramount /ˈpærəmaʊnt/ *adj* [正式用语]最重要的 zuì zhòngyào de;首要的 shǒuyàode.

paranoia /ˌpærəˈnɔɪə/ *n* [U] 妄想狂 wàngxiǎngkuáng;偏执〔執〕狂 piānzhíkuáng;多疑症 duōyízhèng. **paranoid** /ˈpærənɔɪd/ *n* [C], *adj* 有妄想狂的(人) yǒu wàngxiǎngkuáng de;有偏执狂的(人) yǒu piānzhíkuáng de;多疑的(人) duōyíde.

parapet /ˈpærəpɪt/ *n* [C] (屋顶、桥梁等边缘的)矮护〔護〕墙〔牆〕ǎihùqiáng.

paraphernalia /ˌpærəfəˈneɪlɪə/ *n* [U] (个

人的)随〔隨〕身物品 suíshēn wùpǐn.

paraphrase /ˈpærəfreɪz/ *v* [T], *n* [C] 将〔將〕…释〔釋〕义〔義〕jiāng…shìyì;将…意译〔譯〕jiāng…yìyì;(对一段文字的)释义 shìyì;意译 yìyì.

parasite /ˈpærəsaɪt/ *n* [C] **1** 寄生物(如寄生虫、寄生植物) jìshēngwù. **2** [喻]靠他人为〔爲〕生的人 kào tārén wéishēng de rén. **parasitic** /ˌpærəˈsɪtɪk/ *adj*.

parasol /ˈpærəsɒl; *US* -sɔːl/ *n* [C] 阳〔陽〕伞〔傘〕yángsǎn.

paratroops /ˈpærətruːps/ *n* [pl] 伞〔傘〕兵部队〔隊〕sǎnbīng bùduì. **paratrooper** /-pə(r)/ *n* [C].

parcel /ˈpɑːsl/ *n* [C] 包 bāo;包裹 bāoguǒ. **parcel** *v* [-ll-; *US* -l-] [短语动词] **parcel sth out** 将〔將〕…分成若干部分 jiāng…fēnchéng ruògān bùfen. **parcel sth up** 将…打包 jiāng…dǎbāo.

parched /pɑːtʃt/ *adj* **1** 干〔乾〕透的 gāntòude;干枯的 gānkūde. **2** [非正式用语]口渴的 kǒukěde.

parchment /ˈpɑːtʃmənt/ *n* [U] **1** 羊皮纸 yángpízhǐ. **2** 仿羊皮纸 fǎng yángpízhǐ.

pardon /ˈpɑːdn/ *n* [C, U] **1** 原谅 yuánliàng;宽恕 kuānshù. **2** 赦免 shèmiǎn. **pardon** *v* [T] 原谅 yuánliàng;宽恕 kuānshù. **pardon** *interj* (用以请求某人重复所说). **pardonable** *adj* 可原谅的 kě yuánliàng de;可宽恕的 kě kuānshù de.

pare /peə(r)/ *v* [T] **1** 剥 bō;削 xiāo;剥去(外皮) bōqù. **2** [短语动词] **pare sth down** 削减某物 xuējiǎn mǒuwù.

parent /ˈpeərənt/ *n* [C] 父亲〔親〕fùqīn;母亲 mǔqīn. **parental** /pəˈrentl/ *adj*.

parenthesis /pəˈrenθəsɪs/ *n* [C] [*pl* -eses /-əsiːz/] **1** 插入成分 chārù chéngfen;插入句 chārùjù;插入词 chārùcí. **2** [常作 pl] 圆括号〔號〕yuánkuòhào.

parish /ˈpærɪʃ/ *n* [C] 教区〔區〕jiàoqū. **parishioner** /pəˈrɪʃənə(r)/ *n* [C] 教区居民(经常上教堂礼拜者) jiàoqū jūmín.

parity /ˈpærətɪ/ *n* [U] [正式用语]相等 xiāngděng;对〔對〕等 duìděng.

park /pɑːk/ *n* [C] 公园〔園〕gōngyuán. **park** *v* [I, T] 停放(车辆) tíngfàng. **park-and-ˈride** *n* **1** [U] (火车站、公共汽车站等为驾车者提供的)停车〔車〕换乘公共车辆〔輛〕方式 tíngchē huànchéng gōnggòng chēliàng fāngshì. **2** [C] 停车换乘公共车辆处 tíngchē huànchéng gōnggòng chēliàng chù. **ˈparking-meter** *n* [C] 停车计时〔時〕收费器 tíngchē jìshí shōufèiqì. **ˈparkland** *n* [U] 有树〔樹〕木的开〔開〕阔草地 yǒu shùmù de kāikuò cǎodì.

parliament /ˈpɑːləmənt/ *n* [C, 亦作 sing, 用 pl v] 议〔議〕会〔會〕yìhuì;国〔國〕会 guóhuì. **parliamentary** /ˌpɑːləˈmentrɪ/ *adj*.

parlour (美语 -lor) /ˈpɑːlə(r)/ *n* [C] **1** (旧时)客厅〔廳〕kètīng;会〔會〕客室 huìkèshì. **2** [尤用于美语]店 diàn;馆 guǎn: *an ice-ˈcream* ~ 冷饮店.

parochial /pəˈrəʊkɪəl/ *adj* **1** [正式用语]教区〔區〕的 jiàoqūde. **2** [喻,贬]偏狭〔狹〕的 piānxiáde;狭隘的 xiá'àide: *a* ~ *attitude* 偏狭的态度. **parochially** *adv*.

parody /ˈpærədɪ/ *n* [*pl* -ies] **1** [C, U] (诙谐)模仿诗文 mófǎng shīwén. **2** [C] 拙劣的模仿 zhuōliède mófǎng: *a* ~ *of justice* 假装公正. **parody** *v* [*pt*, *pp* -ied] [T] 通过〔過〕模仿嘲弄 tōngguò mófǎng cháonòng.

parole /pəˈrəʊl/ *n* [U] (刑满前)有条〔條〕件释〔釋〕放 yǒutiáojiàn shìfàng;假释 jiǎshì. **parole** *v* [T] 假释 jiǎshì.

paroxysm /ˈpærəksɪzəm/ *n* [C] [正式用语] (愤怒、疼痛等的)发〔發〕作 fāzuò;阵发 zhènfā.

parquet /ˈpɑːkeɪ; *US* pɑːrˈkeɪ/ *n* [U] 拼花地板 pīnhuā dìbǎn.

parrot /ˈpærət/ *n* [C] 鹦鹉 yīngwǔ. **parrot** *v* [T] 鹦鹉学〔學〕舌般地重复〔複〕yīngwǔ xuéshébānde chóngfù.

parry /ˈpærɪ/ *v* [*pt*, *pp* -ied] [T] 挡〔擋〕开〔開〕dǎngkāi;避开 bìkāi. **parry** *n* [C] 挡开 dǎngkāi;避开 bìkāi.

parsimonious /ˌpɑːsɪˈməʊnɪəs/ *adj* [正式用语,贬]过〔過〕于节〔節〕俭〔儉〕的 guòyú jiéjiǎn de;吝啬的 lìnsède.

parsley /ˈpɑːslɪ/ *n* [U] (皱叶)欧〔歐〕芹 ōuqín;荷兰〔蘭〕芹 hélánqín.

parsnip /ˈpɑːsnɪp/ *n* [C, U] 欧〔歐〕洲防风〔風〕(根长,黄色,可食) Ōuzhōu fángfēng.

parson /ˈpɑːsn/ *n* [C] 教区〔區〕牧师〔師〕jiàoqū mùshi. **parsonage** /-ɪdʒ/ *n* [C] (教区)牧师住所 mùshi zhùsuǒ.

part[1] /pɑːt/ *n* [C] **1** (*of*) 部分 bùfen: *We spent* (*a*) ~ *of our holiday in Paris.* 我们的假期部分是在巴黎度过的. **2** (机器的)部件 bùjiàn: *spare* ~*s* 备件. **3** (国家、市镇的)地区〔區〕dìqū. **4** 等份中的一份 děngfèn zhōng de yífèn;…分之一 …fēn zhī yī. **5** [常作 sing] (活动中个人的)作用 zuòyòng;份儿〔兒〕fènr;(戏剧、电影中的)角色 juésè. **6** [音乐]部 bù;声〔聲〕部 shēngbù;段 duàn. **7** [习语] **for the ˈmost part** 多半 duōbàn;通常 tōngcháng. **for ˈmy, ˈhis/ˈher, etc part** 就我(或他、她等)来说 jiù wǒ lái shuō. **in ˈpart** 在某种〔種〕程度上 zài mǒuzhǒng chéngdù shàng. **on sb's part** 由某人做出 yóu mǒurén zuòchū. **take part (in sth)** 参〔參〕加 cānjiā;参与〔與〕cānyù. **take sb's part** 支持某人(如在辩论中) zhīchí mǒurén. **part** *adv* 部分地 bùfende. **partly** *adv* 在一定程度上 zài yídìng chéngdù shàng;不完全地 bù wánquán de. **ˌpart of ˈspeech** *n* [C]

P

［语法］词类［類］(如名词、动词等) cílèi；词性 cíxìng. ˌpart-ˈtime *adj*, *adv* 部分时［時］间工作(的) bùfen shíjiān gōngzuò；兼职［職］(的) jiānzhí.

part[2] /pɑːt/ *v* **1** [I, T] 分开［開］fēnkāi；分离［離］fēnlí：*The clouds ~ed*. 云散开了. *~ two people* 把两人拉开. **2** [T] 将［將］(头发) 梳成分头［頭］jiāng… shūchéng fēntóu. **3** [习语] **part ˈcompany (with sb/sth)** (a) 分手 fēnshǒu；各奔东西 gè bèn dōng xī. (b) 与［與］…意见不合 yǔ… yìjiàn bùhé. **4** [短语动词] **part with sth** 放弃［棄］某物 fàngqì mǒuwù：*She'll never ~ with the family jewels*. 她永远不会变卖家中的珠宝. **parting** *n* **1** [U, C] 离别 líbié；分手 fēnshǒu. **2** [C] (头发的)分缝 fēnfèng.

partial /ˈpɑːʃl/ *adj* **1** 不完全的 bù wánquán de；部分的 bùfende：*only a ~ success* 仅部分成功. **2** (*towards*) 偏向的 piānxiàngde；偏心的 piānxīnde；偏袒的 piāntǎnde. **3** *to* 偏爱［愛］的 piān'àide：*He's (rather) ~ to cakes*. 他特别爱吃蛋糕. **partiality** /ˌpɑːʃɪˈælətɪ/ *n* **1** [U] 偏向 piānxiàng；偏袒 piāntǎn. **2** [C, 常作 sing] 偏爱 piān'ài；特别喜爱 tèbié xǐ'ài. **partially** /ˈpɑːʃəlɪ/ *adv* 不完全地 bù wánquán de；部分地 bùfende.

participate /pɑːˈtɪsɪpeɪt/ *v* [I] (*in*) 参［參］加 cānjiā；参与［與］cānyù. **participant** /-pənt/ *n* [C] 参加者 cānjiāzhě. **participation** /pɑːˌtɪsɪˈpeɪʃn/ *n* [U].

participle /ˈpɑːtɪsɪpl/ *n* [C] [语法]分词 fēncí：'*Hurrying*' *and* '*hurried*' *are the present and past ~s of* '*hurry*'. hurrying 和 hurried 是 hurry 的现在分词和过去分词.

particle /ˈpɑːtɪkl/ *n* [C] **1** 粒子 lìzǐ；微粒 wēilì. **2** [语法]小品词 xiǎopǐncí.

particular /pəˈtɪkjʊlə(r)/ *adj* **1** 个［個］别的 gèbiéde：*in this ~ case* 在此个别情况下. **2** 特殊的 tèshūde；特别的 tèbiéde：*of ~ interest* 特殊的兴趣. **3** (*about*) 非常讲［講］究的 fēicháng jiǎngjiu de；难［難］以满足的 nányǐ mǎnzú de. **4** [习语] **in parˈticular** 特别地 tèbiéde；尤其 yóuqí：*I like these flowers in ~*. 我尤其喜欢这些花. **particular** *n* [C, 常作 pl] 信息 xìnxī；细节［節］xìjié. **particularly** *adv* 尤其 yóuqí；特别地 tèbiéde.

partisan /ˌpɑːtɪˈzæn；*US* ˈpɑːrtɪzn/ *n* [C] **1** 热［熱］情而盲目的支持者 rèqíng ér mángmù de zhīchízhě. **2** 敌［敵］后［後］游击［擊］队［隊］员 díhòu yóujīduìyuán. **partisan** *adj* 盲从［從］的 mángcóngde；偏袒的 piāntǎnde.

partition /pɑːˈtɪʃn/ *n* [C] **1** (房子中的)隔断［斷］géduàn；隔墙［牆］géqiáng. **2** 分割 fēngē；分裂(国家) fēnliè. **partition** *v* **1** [T] 把…分成部分 bǎ… fēnchéng bùfen；分割 fēngē. **2** [短语动词] **partition sth off** 分隔 fēngé；隔开［開］gékāi.

partner /ˈpɑːtnə(r)/ *n* [C] **1** 合伙［夥］人 héhuǒrén；股东 gǔdōng；伙伴 huǒbàn. **2** (跳舞、打球等的)同伴 tóngbàn；搭档［檔］dādàng. **3** 配偶 pèi'ǒu；情人 qíngrén. **partner** *v* [T] 做…的同伴(或搭档) zuò… de tóngbàn. **partnership** *n* **1** [U] 合伙人身份 héhuǒrén shēnfen；合股 hégǔ；合伙经［經］营［營］héhuǒ jīngyíng. **2** [C] 合伙企业［業］héhuǒ qǐyè.

partridge /ˈpɑːtrɪdʒ/ *n* [C] 山鹑 shānchún.

party /ˈpɑːtɪ/ *n* [C] [*pl* -ies] **1** 社交聚会［會］shèjiāo jùhuì：*a birthday ~* 生日宴会. **2** 党［黨］dǎng；政党 zhèngdǎng；党派 dǎngpài. **3** (一起工作、同行的)组 zǔ；团［團］tuán；队［隊］duì：*a ~ of tourists* 旅游团. **4** [法律](契约中的)一方 yìfāng. **5** [习语] **be (a) party to sth** 参［參］与［與］cānyù；支持 zhīchí. **the ˌparty ˈline** *n* [sing] 政党的路线［綫］zhèngdǎngde lùxiàn.

pass[1] /pɑːs；*US* pæs/ *v* **1** [I, T] 经［經］过［過］jīngguò；穿过 chuānguò；越过 yuèguò：*~ the house* 经过这所房子. **2** [I, T] 沿…行进［進］yán… xíngjìn：*He ~ed through Oxford on his way to London*. 他在去伦敦的路上经过牛津. **3** [T] 将［將］…递［遞］给某人 jiāng… dìgěi mǒurén：*Please ~ me the butter*. 请把黄油递给我. **4** [I, T] 传(球给己方队员) chuán. **5** [I] 改变［變］…的状［狀］况 gǎibiàn… de zhuàngkuàng. **6** (a) [I] (时间)消逝 xiāoshì；过去 guòqù. (b) [T] 消磨(时间) xiāomó. **7** [I] 结束 jiéshù；完结 wánjié：*wait for the storm to ~* 等待暴风雨过去. **8** (a) [I, T] 考及格 kǎo jígé. (b) [T] 通过(考试、检查) tōngguò. **9** [T] 表决通过(法规等) biǎojué tōngguò. **10** [I] 许可 xǔkě：*I don't like it but I'll let it ~*. 我不喜欢，但就让它过去吧. **11** [T] 宣布 xuānbù：*~ (a) sentence on a prisoner* 对犯人宣判. **12** [习语] **pass the time of ˈday (with sb)** 与［與］…互相寒暄 yǔ… hùxiāng hánxuān. **pass ˈwater** [正式用语]排尿 pái niào. **13** [短语动词] **pass aˈway** [婉]死 sǐ. **pass by sb/sth** 走过 zǒuguò；经过 jīngguò. **pass sb/sth by** 不注意某人(或某事) bú zhùyì mǒurén；忽视某人(或某事) hūshì mǒurén. **pass for sb/sth** 被认［認］为［爲］某人(或某物) bèi rènwéi mǒurén：*He could ~ for a Frenchman*. 他可能被当成法国人. **pass ˈoff** (事情)发［發］生并［並］完成 fāshēng bìng wánchéng. **pass sb/sth off as sb/sth** 冒充某人(某物) màochōng mǒurén. **pass ˈon** = PASS AWAY. **pass sth on (to sb)** 把某物交给(某人) bǎ mǒuwù jiāogěi. **pass ˈout** 昏厥 hūnjué. **pass sb over** (在提升、任命时)对［對］(某人)不加考虑［慮］duì… bù-

P

jiā kǎolǜ. **pass over sth** 忽略某事 hūlüè mǒushì. **pass sth up** 放弃〔棄〕fàngqì；放过(机会等) fàngguò. ˌ**passer-ˈby** *n* [C] [*pl* **passers-by**] 过路人 guòlùrén.

pass[2] /pɑːs; *US* pæs/ *n* [C] 1 考试及格 kǎoshì jígé. 2 通行证〔證〕tōngxíngzhèng；出入证 chūrùzhèng. 3 [体育]传〔傳〕球 chuán qiú. 4 关〔關〕隘 guān'ài；山口 shānkǒu. 5 [习语] **make a pass at sb** [非正式用语]向某人调情 xiàng mǒurén tiáoqíng.

passable /ˈpɑːsəbl; *US* ˈpæs-/ *adj* 1 (道路等)可通行的 kě tōngxíng de. 2 尚可的 shàngkěde；过〔過〕得去的 guòdeqùde.

passage /ˈpæsɪdʒ/ *n* 1 [C] 通道 tōngdào；走廊 zǒuláng. 2 [C, 常作 sing] 通路 tōnglù：*clear a ~ through the crowd* 在人群中挤出一条通路. 3 [U] 过〔過〕guò；经〔經〕过 jīngguò：*the ~ of time* 时间的推移. 4 [C] 旅程 lǚchéng；旅行 lǚxíng；旅费 lǚfèi. 5 [C] (书、讲话等的)一段 yíduàn；一节〔節〕yìjié.

passenger /ˈpæsɪndʒə(r)/ *n* [C] 乘客 chéngkè；旅客 lǚkè.

passing /ˈpɑːsɪŋ; *US* ˈpæsɪŋ/ *adj* 短暂的 duǎnzànde：*a ~ thought* 一时的念头. **passing** *n* [U] 1 经〔經〕过〔過〕jīngguò. 2 (a) [正式用语]末尾 mòwěi. (b) [婉]去世 qùshì. 3 [习语] **in passing** 顺便地 shùnbiànde；附带〔帶〕地 fùdàide.

passion /ˈpæʃn/ *n* 1 [U, C] 强烈的情感(如爱、恨、怒) qiángliède qínggǎn. 2 [U] 强烈的情欲 qiángliède qíngyù. 3 [sing] *for* 酷爱〔愛〕kù'ài：*a ~ for books* 很喜欢书籍. **passionate** /ˈpæʃənət/ *adj* 感情强烈的 gǎnqíng qiángliè de. **passionately** *adv*.

passive /ˈpæsɪv/ *adj* 1 被动〔動〕的 bèidòngde；消极〔極〕的 xiāojíde. 2 [语法]被动语态〔態〕的(如'She *was bitten* by a dog.'中的动词形式) bèidòng yǔtài de. **the passive** *n* [sing] 被动语态 bèidòng yǔtài. ˌ**passive ˈsmoking** *n* [U] 被动〔動〕吸烟 bèidòng xīyān. **passively** *adv*. **passiveness** *n* [U].

Passover /ˈpɑːsəʊvə(r); *US* ˈpæs-/ *n* [U] (犹太人的)逾越节〔節〕yúyuèjié.

passport /ˈpɑːspɔːt; *US* ˈpæs-/ *n* [C] 1 护〔護〕照 hùzhào. 2 [喻](获得某物的)手段 shǒuduàn；保障 bǎozhàng.

password /ˈpɑːswɜːd; *US* ˈpæs-/ *n* [C] 口令 kǒulìng；(计算机)密码 mìmǎ. ˌ**password-proˈtected** *adj* 有密码保护〔護〕的 yǒu mìmǎ bǎohù de.

past[1] /pɑːst; *US* pæst/ *adj* 1 过〔過〕去的 guòqùde；以前的 yǐqiánde：*in ~ years* 在过去的年月. 2 [语法](动词形式)过去(时)的 guòqùde：*the ~ tense* 过去时. *a ~ participle* 过去分词. **past** *n* [sing] 1 **the past** 过去 guòqù；昔时〔時〕xīshí. 2 经〔經〕历〔歷〕jīnglì；过去的生活 guòqùde shēnghuó.

past[2] /pɑːst; *US* pæst/ *prep* 1 (时间)晚于 wǎnyú；在…之后〔後〕zài…zhī hòu：*~ midnight* 半夜以后. 2 在…的更远〔遠〕处〔處〕zài…de gèngyuǎnchù；另一边〔邊〕lìng yìbiān：*She walked ~ the church* 她走过那座教堂. 3 (在兴趣、能力方面)超过〔過〕chāoguò：*I'm ~ caring what happens*. 我不再关注发生什么事情. 4 [习语] ˈ**past it** [非正式用语]无〔無〕法做年轻〔輕〕时〔時〕能做的事的 wúfǎ zuò niánqīngshí néngzuòde shì de；(因年老等而)不能工作的 bùnéng gōngzuò de. **past** *adv* 经〔經〕过 jīngguò.

pasta /ˈpæstə; *US* ˈpɑːstə/ *n* [U] 意大利面〔麵〕食(如通心粉、细面条等) Yìdàlì miànshí.

paste /peɪst/ *n* 1 [U, C] 面〔麵〕团〔團〕miàntuán. 2 [U] 糨糊 jiànghu. 3 [U] (尤用于构成复合词)肉酱〔醬〕ròujiàng；鱼酱 yújiàng：*fish ~* 鱼酱. **paste** *v* [T] (用浆糊)贴 tiē；粘 zhān.

pastel /ˈpæstl; *US* pæˈstel/ *adj* (色彩)柔和的 róuhéde；淡的 dànde. **pastel** *n* [C] 1 彩色粉笔〔筆〕cǎisè fěnbǐ；蜡〔蠟〕笔 làbǐ. 2 彩色粉笔画〔畫〕cǎisè fěnbǐhuà；蜡笔画 làbǐhuà.

pasteurize /ˈpɑːstʃəraɪz; *US* ˈpæs-/ *v* [T] (用巴氏杀菌法)对〔對〕(牛奶等)消毒 duì…xiāodú.

pastille /ˈpæstɪl; *US* pæˈstiːl/ *n* [C] (药的)锭剂〔劑〕dìngjì；糖锭 tángdìng.

pastime /ˈpɑːstaɪm; *US* ˈpæs-/ *n* [C] 消遣 xiāoqiǎn；娱乐〔樂〕yúlè.

pastor /ˈpɑːstə(r); *US* ˈpæs-/ *n* [C] (基督教的)牧师〔師〕mùshi.

pastoral /ˈpɑːstərəl; *US* ˈpæs-/ *adj* 1 牧师〔師〕的 mùshide；牧师工作的 mùshi gōngzuò de. 2 乡〔鄉〕村生活的 xiāngcūn shēnghuó de；田园〔園〕风〔風〕光的 tiányuán fēngguāng de.

pastry /ˈpeɪstrɪ/ *n* [*pl* -ies] 1 [U] 油酥面〔麵〕团〔團〕yóusū miàntuán；油酥皮 yóusūpí. 2 [C] 酥皮糕点〔點〕sūpí gāodiǎn.

pasture /ˈpɑːstʃə(r); *US* ˈpæs-/ *n* [C, U] 牧场〔場〕mùchǎng；牧地 mùdì.

pasty[1] /ˈpeɪstɪ/ *adj* [-ier, -iest] 苍〔蒼〕白的 cāngbáide；不健康的 bú jiànkāng de：*a ~ white skin* 苍白的皮肤.

pasty[2] /ˈpæstɪ/ *n* [C] [*pl* -ies] (肉等的)馅饼 xiànbǐng.

pat[1] /pæt/ *v* [-tt-] [T] (用掌)轻〔輕〕拍 qīngpāi. **pat** *n* [C] 1 轻拍 qīngpāi. 2 (黄油等的)小块〔塊〕xiǎokuài.

pat[2] /pæt/ *adj* 过〔過〕快的 guòkuàide；轻〔輕〕易的 qīngyìde：*a ~ answer* 脱口而出的回答.

patch /pætʃ/ *n* [C] 1 补〔補〕丁 bǔding. 2 (与周围颜色等不同的)斑 bān；块〔塊〕kuài. 3 (保护受伤眼睛的)眼罩 yǎnzhào. 4 一小块地 yìxiǎokuài dì：*a ˈcabbage ~* 洋白菜菜地. 5 [习语] **not be a patch on sb/sth** [非正式用语]远〔遠〕不如某人(或某物) yuǎn bùrú mǒurén.

patch *v* [T] 1 修补 xiūbǔ. 2 [短语动词] **patch sth up** (a) 修理 xiūlǐ; 快修 kuàixiū. (b) 调停(争执) tiáotíng. ˈ**patchwork** *n* 1 [U] (由形形色色的小布片拼缝而成的)拼缝物 pīnféngwù. 2 [C, 常作 sing] 拼凑的东西 pīncòude dōngxi. **patchy** *adj* [-ier, -iest] 质〔質〕量不一致的 zhìliàng bù yízhì de; 不均匀的 bù jūnyún de.

pâté /ˈpæteɪ; *US* pɑːˈteɪ/ *n* [U] 肉酱〔醬〕ròujiàng; 鱼酱 yújiàng.

patent[1] /ˈpeɪtnt, 亦读 ˈpætnt; *US* ˈpætnt/ *adj* 清楚的 qīngchude; 显〔顯〕著的 xiǎnzhùde. **patently** *adv* 明显地 míngxiǎnde.

patent[2] /ˈpætnt, 亦读 ˈpeɪtnt; *US* ˈpætnt/ *n* [C] 专〔專〕利 zhuānlì; 专利权〔權〕zhuānlìquán; 专利证书〔書〕zhuānlì zhèngshū. **patent** *adj* 受专利保护〔護〕的 shòu zhuānlì bǎohù de. **patent** *v* [T] 取得…的专利权 qǔdé…de zhuānlìquán. **patent** ˈ**leather** *n* [U] 漆皮 qīpí.

paternal /pəˈtɜːnl/ *adj* 1 父亲〔親〕的 fùqīnde; 父亲般的 fùqīnbānde. 2 父系的 fùxìde: *my ~ grandfather* 我的祖父. **paternally** *adv*.

paternity /pəˈtɜːnətɪ/ *n* [U] 父亲〔親〕身份 fùqin shēnfen.

path /pɑːθ; *US* pæθ/ *n* [C] [*pl* **~s** /pɑːðz; *US* pæðz/] 1 (亦作 ˈ**pathway**) 小路 xiǎolù; 小径〔徑〕xiǎojìng. 2 路线〔綫〕lùxiàn; 轨道 guǐdào.

pathetic /pəˈθetɪk/ *adj* 1 可怜〔憐〕的 kěliánde; 可悲的 kěbēide: *a ~ sight* 悲惨的景象. 2 [非正式用语]不足的 bùzúde; 微弱的 wēiruòde: *a ~ attempt* 不充分的尝试. **pathetically** /-klɪ/ *adv*.

pathology /pəˈθɒlədʒɪ/ *n* [U] 病理学〔學〕bìnglǐxué. **pathological** /ˌpæθəˈlɒdʒɪkl/ *adj* 1 病理学的 bìnglǐxuéde. 2 疾病的 jíbìngde; 由疾病引起的 yóu jíbìng yǐnqǐ de. 3 [非正式用语]无〔無〕道理的 wú dàolǐ de; 病态〔態〕的 bìngtàide. **pathologist** *n* [C] 病理学家 bìnglǐxuéjiā.

pathos /ˈpeɪθɒs/ *n* [U] [正式用语](文学作品、演讲等)激起怜〔憐〕悯(或同情)的因素 jīqǐ liánmǐnde yīnsù.

patience /ˈpeɪʃns/ *n* [U] 1 容忍 róngrěn; 忍耐 rěnnài. 2 耐心 nàixīn; 耐性 nàixìng; 忍耐力 rěnnàilì. 3 单〔單〕人纸牌戏〔戲〕dānrén zhǐpáixì.

patient[1] /ˈpeɪʃnt/ *adj* 有耐性的 yǒu nàixìng de; 容忍的 róngrěnde; 忍耐的 rěnnàide. **patiently** *adv*.

patient[2] /ˈpeɪʃnt/ *n* [C] 病人 bìngrén.

patio /ˈpætɪəʊ/ *n* [C] [*pl* **~s**] (连接房屋并铺有地面的)露台〔臺〕lùtái; 平台(作户外休息、用餐处) píngtái.

patriarch /ˈpeɪtrɪɑːk; *US* ˈpæt-/ *n* [C] 1 (男性)家长〔長〕jiāzhǎng; 族长 zúzhǎng. 2 Patriarch (东正教的)高级主教 gāojí zhǔjiào. **patriarchal** /ˌpeɪtrɪˈɑːkl; *US* ˌpæt-/ *adj*.

patriot /ˈpætrɪət; *US* ˈpeɪt-/ *n* [C] 爱〔愛〕国〔國〕者 àiguózhě. **patriotic** /ˌpætrɪˈɒtɪk; *US* ˌpeɪt-/ *adj*. **patriotically** /-klɪ/ *adv*. **patriotism** *n* [U].

patrol /pəˈtrəʊl/ *v* [-ll-] [I, T] (在某地区等)巡逻〔邏〕xúnluó; 巡查 xúnchá. **patrol** *n* 1 [U] 巡逻 xúnluó; 巡查 xúnchá: *soldiers on ~* 在巡逻中的士兵. 2 [C] 巡逻者 xúnluózhě; 巡逻队〔隊〕xúnluóduì.

patron /ˈpeɪtrən/ *n* [C] 1 赞助人 zànzhùrén; 资助人 zīzhùrén: *a wealthy ~ of the arts* 艺术方面的富有的赞助人. 2 [正式用语]老主顾〔顧〕lǎo zhǔgù; 顾客 gùkè. **patronage** /ˈpætrənɪdʒ; *US* ˈpeɪt-/ *n* [U] 1 资助 zīzhù; 赞助 zànzhù: *her ~age of the arts* 她对艺术方面的赞助. *his ~age of the shop* 他对这家商店的光顾. 2 (重要职务的)任命权〔權〕rènmìngquán. ˌ**patron** ˈ**saint** *n* [C] 守护〔護〕神 shǒuhùshén.

patronize /ˈpætrənaɪz; *US* ˈpeɪt-/ *v* [T] 1 以屈尊俯就的态〔態〕度对〔對〕待 yǐ qūzūn fǔjiù de tàidù duìdài. 2 [正式用语](经常)光顾〔顧〕guānggù; 惠顾 huìgù. **patronizing** *adj*.

patter[1] /ˈpætə(r)/ *v* [I], *n* [sing] 发〔發〕出轻〔輕〕快的脚步声〔聲〕或拍打声 fāchū qīngkuài de jiǎobùshēng huò pāidǎshēng; 轻快的脚步声或拍打声 qīngkuàide jiǎobùshēng huò pāidǎshēng.

patter[2] /ˈpætə(r)/ *n* [U] (演员、推销员的)顺口溜 shùnkǒuliū.

pattern /ˈpætn/ *n* [C] 1 图〔圖〕案 tú'àn; 花样〔樣〕huāyàng. 2 形式 xíngshì; 模式 móshì; 方式 fāngshì: *the usual ~ of events* 事件的通常形式. 3 模型 móxíng; 样式 yàngshì; 说明 shuōmíng: *a knitting ~* 编织样式. **pattern** *v* [T] *on* [常用被动语态]仿制〔製〕fǎngzhì; 仿造 fǎngzào: *The tax system is ~ed on the one used in Sweden.* 税务制度是仿效瑞典使用的一种税制. **patterned** *adj* 有图案的 yǒu tú'àn de; 带〔帶〕花样的 dài huāyàng de.

paucity /ˈpɔːsətɪ/ *n* [sing] [正式用语]少量 shǎoliàng; 不足 bùzú.

paunch /pɔːntʃ/ *n* [C] 大肚子 dàdùzi.

pauper /ˈpɔːpə(r)/ *n* [C] 穷〔窮〕人 qióngrén; 贫民 pínmín.

pause /pɔːz/ *n* [C] 中止 zhōngzhǐ; 暂停 zàntíng: *a ~ in the conversation* 交谈中的停顿. **pause** *v* [I] 中止 zhōngzhǐ; 暂停 zàntíng: *He ~d a minute before finishing his* *speech*. 在结束讲话之前他稍作停顿.

pave /peɪv/ *v* 1 [T] (用石、砖)铺(路) pū;铺砌 pūqì. 2 [习语] ˌpave the ˈway (for sth) 为〔爲〕…做准〔準〕备〔備〕 wèi…zuò zhǔnbèi;创〔創〕造条〔條〕件 chuàngzào tiáojiàn. ˈpaving stone *n* [C] 铺路石 pūlùshí.

pavement /ˈpeɪvmənt/ *n* [C] 人行道 rénxíngdào.

pavilion /pəˈvɪlɪən/ *n* [C] 1 [英国英语](运动场旁的)休息室 xiūxishì. 2 (展览会的)大帐篷 dà zhàngpéng.

paw /pɔː/ *n* [C] 爪子 zhuǎzi. paw *v* 1 [I,T] (*at*) 用爪子抓 yòng zhuǎzi zhuā;扒 bā. 2 [T] (人)粗鲁地摸弄 cūlǔde mōnòng.

pawn[1] /pɔːn/ *n* [C] 1(西洋象棋)兵 bīng;卒 zú. 2[喻]被人利用的人 bèi rén lìyòng de rén;马前卒 mǎqiánzú.

pawn[2] /pɔːn/ *v* [T] 典当〔當〕 diǎndàng;抵押 dǐyā. ˈpawnbroker *n* [C] 当铺老板 dàngpù lǎobǎn;典当业〔業〕者 diǎndàngyèzhě.

pay[1] /peɪ/ *v* [*pt*, *pp* paid /peɪd/] 1 [I,T] 付钱〔錢〕给 fùqián gěi: ～ *him for the bread* 付给了他面包钱. 2 [T] 还〔還〕 huán;偿〔償〕还 chánghuán: ～ *the rent* 缴租. 3 [I,T] 有利 yǒulì;有收益 yǒu shōuyì: *It* ～*s to be honest*. 诚实不吃亏. 4 [T] 给予 jǐyǔ;致以 zhìyǐ;进〔進〕行 jìnxíng: ～*attention to sth* 对某事注意. ～ *a visit* 拜访. 5 [习语] pay lip-service to sth⇨LIP. pay through the ˈnose (for sth) 为〔爲〕…花钱过〔過〕多 wèi…huāqián guòduō. pay one's way 挣钱维持生活 zhèngqián wéichí shēnghuó. put ˈpaid to sth 毁掉某物 huǐdiào mǒuwù. 6 [短语动词] pay sb back (sth) 还(钱)给某人 huán…gěi mǒurén. pay sb back (for sth) 惩〔懲〕罚某人 chéngfá mǒurén;报〔報〕复〔復〕 bàofù. pay for sth 为…吃苦(或受惩罚) wèi…chīkǔ. pay off [非正式用语] 取得成功 qǔdé chénggōng. pay sb off (a) 付清工资解雇(某人) fùqīng gōngzī jiěgù. (b) [非正式用语]贿赂某人 huìlù mǒurén. pay sth off 全部偿还 quánbù chánghuán. pay sth out (a) 付出(钱) fùchū. (b) 放松〔鬆〕(绳等) fàngsōng. pay up 付清欠款 fùqīng qiànkuǎn. ˌpaid-ˈup *adj* 已付清的 yǐ fùqīng de;已缴款的 yǐ jiǎokuǎn de. payable *adj* 应〔應〕付的 yīngfùde;可支付的 kě zhīfù de. payee /peɪˈiː/ *n* [C] 收款人 shōukuǎnrén. payer *n* [C] 付款人 fùkuǎnrén;交款人 jiāokuǎnrén. payment *n* 1 [U] 支付 zhīfù;付款 fùkuǎn. 2 [C] 支付的款项 zhīfùde kuǎnxiàng. ˈpay-off *n* [C] [非正式用语] 1 贿赂 huìlù. 2 报偿 bàocháng;结果 jiéguǒ. pay-per-ˈview *n* [U] (电视)按次付费服务〔務〕 àn cì fùfèi fúwù. ˈpay station *n* [C] 电〔電〕话亭 diànhuàtíng. ˈpay television, ˈpay TV *n* [U] 收费电视 shōufèi diànshì.

pay[2] /peɪ/ *n* [U] 工资 gōngzī;薪金 xīnjīn. ˈpayload *n* [C] 酬载 chóuzài. ˈpaypacket *n* [C] 工资袋 gōngzīdài. ˈpay phone *n* [C] (投币式)公用电〔電〕话 gōngyòng diànhuà. ˈpayroll *n* [C] 工资(或薪水)名单〔單〕 gōngzī míngdān.

PC /piː ˈsiː/ *abbr* 1 personal computer 个〔個〕人计算机〔機〕 gèrén jìsuànjī. 2 politically correct 政治上正确〔確〕 zhèngzhìshàng zhèngquè;政治立场〔場〕正确 zhèngzhì lìchǎng zhèngquè.

PDF /ˌpiː diː ˈef/ *abbr* Portable Document Format [U] 可移植文档〔檔〕格式 kěyízhí wéndàng géshì;PDF 格式 géshì;[C] PDF 文件 wénjiàn.

PE /ˌpiː ˈiː/ *abbr* physical education 体〔體〕育 tǐyù: *a PE lesson at school* 学校的体育课.

pea /piː/ *n* [C] 豌豆 wāndòu.

peace /piːs/ *n* 1 [U] 和平 hépíng. 2 the peace [sing] 安定 āndìng;治安 zhì'ān: *break/disturb the* ～ 破坏治安;扰乱治安. 3 [U] 和睦 hémù;友好 yǒuhǎo. 4 [U] 安静 ānjìng;平静 píngjìng. 5 [习语]make one's peace with sb 与〔與〕某人和解(尤指主动道歉) yǔ mǒurén héjiě. peaceable *adj* 不争吵的 bù zhēngchǎo de. peaceful *adj* 1 和平的 hépíngde. 2 安静的 ānjìngde;安宁〔寧〕的 ānníngde. peacefully *adv*. peacefulness *n* [U]. ˈpeace-keeping force *n* [C] 维持和平部队〔隊〕 wéichí hépíng bùduì;维和部队 wéihé bùduì. ˈpeacetime *n* [U] 和平时〔時〕期 hépíng shíqī.

peach /piːtʃ/ *n* [C] 桃 táo. peach *adj* 桃色的 táosède.

peacock /ˈpiːkɒk/ *n* [C] (雄)孔雀 kǒngquè.

peahen /ˈpiːhen/ *n* [C] 雌孔雀 cíkǒngquè.

peak /piːk/ *n* [C] 1 山峰 shānfēng. 2 最高点〔點〕 zuìgāodiǎn;顶峰 dǐngfēng: *Sales reached a new* ～ in May. 五月份的销售额达到了新的高峰. 3 帽舌 màoshé. peak *adj* 最大值的 zuìdàzhíde;高峰的 gāofēngde: ～ *hours* 高峰时间. peak *v* [I] 达〔達〕到高峰 dádào gāofēng;达到最大值 dádào zuìdàzhí. peaked *adj* 有峰的 yǒufēngde;有帽舌的 yǒu màoshé de.

peal /piːl/ *n* [C] 1 响〔響〕亮的铃声〔聲〕(或钟声) xiǎngliàngde língshēng. 2 洪亮的响声 hóngliàngde xiǎngshēng: ～*s of laughter/thunder* 一阵大笑声;雷声隆隆. peal *v* [I] (钟或铃)大声鸣响 dàshēng míngxiǎng.

peanut /ˈpiːnʌt/ *n* 1 [C] 花生 huāshēng;落花生 luòhuāshēng. 2 peanuts [pl] [俚]小数〔數〕额(尤指钱) xiǎoshù'é.

pear /peə(r)/ *n* [C] 梨 lí.

pearl /pɜːl/ *n* [C] 珍珠 zhēnzhū.

peasant /ˈpeznt/ *n* [C] 1(某些国家的)农〔農〕民 nóngmín. 2 [非正式用语,贬]举〔舉〕止粗鲁的人 jǔzhǐ cūlǔ de rén. peasantry *n* [sing] [用 sing 或 pl v] (总称)农民 nóngmín.

peat /piːt/ *n* [U] 泥煤 níméi;泥炭 nítàn;泥炭

块〔塊〕nítànkuài. **peaty** *adj*.

pebble /ˈpebl/ *n* [C] 卵石 luǎnshí; 小圆石 xiǎoyuánshí. **pebbly** *adj*.

peck /pek/ *v* **1** [I,T] (指鸟)啄 zhuó; 鹐 qiān. **2** [T] [非正式用语] 匆匆轻〔輕〕吻 cōngcōng qīng wěn. **peck** *n* [C] **1** 啄 zhuó; 鹐 qiān; 啄痕 zhuóhén; 鹐伤〔傷〕qiānshāng. **2** [非正式用语] 匆匆一吻 cōngcōng yì wěn.

peckish /ˈpekɪʃ/ *adj* [非正式用语] (有点)饿的 ède.

peculiar /pɪˈkjuːlɪə(r)/ *adj* **1** 奇怪的 qíguàide; 古怪的 gǔguàide. **2** [非正式用语] 不舒服的 bù shūfu de. **3** (*to*) 特有的 tèyǒude; 独〔獨〕特的 dútède: *an accent ~ to the West of the country* 该国西部独特的口音. **peculiarity** /pɪˌkjuːlɪˈærətɪ/ *n* [*pl* -ies] **1** [C] 怪异〔異〕的性质〔質〕guàiyìde xìngzhì; 怪癖 guàipǐ. **2** [C] 怪异的东西 guàiyìde dōngxi. **3** [U] 特质 tèzhì; 独特性 dútèxìng. **peculiarly** *adv* **1** 古怪地 gǔguàide. **2** 特殊地 tèshūde.

pedagogue (美语 -gog) /ˈpedəgɒg/ *n* [C] **1** [古或非正式用语] 教师〔師〕jiàoshī. **2** [贬] 严〔嚴〕厉〔厲〕的教师 yánlìde jiàoshī. **pedagogy** /ˈpedəgɒdʒɪ/ *n* [U] [正式用语] 教学〔學〕法 jiàoxuéfǎ. **pedagogic** /ˌpedəˈgɒdʒɪk/ (亦作 **pedagogical** /-ɪkl/) *adj*. **pedagogically** /-klɪ/ *adv*.

pedal /ˈpedl/ *n* [C] (自行车等的) 脚蹬 jiǎodēng; 踏板 tàbǎn. **pedal** *v* [-ll-; 美语亦作 -l-] [I,T] 踩踏板 cǎi tàbǎn; 踩踏板驱〔驅〕动〔動〕(或操作) cǎi tàbǎn qūdòng.

pedant /ˈpednt/ *n* [C] [贬] 书〔書〕呆〔獃〕子 shūdāizi; 学〔學〕究 xuéjiū. **pedantic** /pɪˈdæntɪk/ *adj*. **pedantically** /-klɪ/ *adv*.

peddle /ˈpedl/ *v* [I,T] 沿街叫卖〔賣〕yánjiē jiàomài; 挨户兜售 āihù dōushòu. **peddler** *n* [C] **1** [美语] = PEDLAR. **2** 贩毒者 fàndúzhě.

pedestal /ˈpedɪstl/ *n* [C] **1** 基座 jīzuò; 柱脚 zhùjiǎo; 柱基 zhùjī. **2** [习语] **put sb on a ˈpedestal** (尤指盲目地) 崇拜某人 chóngbài mǒurén.

pedestrian /pɪˈdestrɪən/ *n* [C] 行人 xíngrén; 步行者 bùxíngzhě. **pedestrian** *adj* **1** 平淡的 píngdànde; 乏味的 fáwèide. **2** 行人的 xíngrénde; 为〔為〕行人的 wèi xíngrén de. **peˌdestrian ˈcrossing** *n* [C] 人行横道 rénxíng héngdào.

pediatrics [美语] = PAEDIATRICS.

pedigree /ˈpedɪgriː/ *n* **1** [C] 世系 shìxì. **2** [U] 门第 méndì; 出身 chūshēn. **pedigree** *adj* (动物) 纯种〔種〕的 chúnzhǒngde.

pedlar /ˈpedlə(r)/ *n* [C] (挨户兜售的) 小贩 xiǎofàn; (沿街叫卖的) 货郎 huòláng.

pee /piː/ *v* [I] [俚] 撒尿 sā niào. **pee** *n* [俚] **1** [U] 尿 niào. **2** [sing] 撒尿 sā niào.

peek /piːk/ *v* [I], *n* [C] (*at*) 偷看 tōukàn; 窥视 kuīshì.

peel /piːl/ *v* **1** [T] 削(或剥)去…的皮 xiāoqù…de pí: *~ the potatoes* 削土豆皮. **2** [I] 剥落 bōluò; 脱落 tuōluò: *The paint is ~ing*. 油漆在剥落. **3** [短语动词] **peel (sth) off** [非正式用语] 脱掉(衣服) tuōdiào. **peel** *n* [U] (水果等的) 皮 pí: *lemon ~* 柠檬皮.

peep[1] /piːp/ *v* [I], *n* [sing] (*at*) 偷看 tōukàn; 窥视 kuīshì.

peep[2] /piːp/ *n* **1** [C] 唧唧声〔聲〕jījīshēng; 啾啾声 jiūjiūshēng. **2** [sing] [非正式用语] 人语声 rényǔshēng; 人声 rénshēng.

peer[1] /pɪə(r)/ *n* [C] **1** (英国) 有(公、侯、伯、子、男) 爵位的贵族 yǒu juéwèide guìzú: *Dukes and earls are ~s*. 公爵和伯爵是贵族. **2** [常作 pl] 同龄〔齡〕人 tónglíngrén. **peerage** *n* **1 the peerage** [sing] 贵族 guìzú. **2** [C] 贵族爵位 guìzú juéwèi. **peeress** *n* [C] **1** 女贵族 nǚ guìzú. **2** 贵族的夫人 guìzúde fūrén. **ˈpeer group** *n* [C] 同辈群体〔體〕tóngbèi qúntǐ.

peer[2] /pɪə(r)/ *v* [I] (*at*) 仔细看 zǐxì kàn.

peeved /piːvd/ *adj* [非正式用语] 生气〔氣〕的 shēngqìde. **peevish** /ˈpiːvɪʃ/ *adj* 易怒的 yìnùde; 脾气坏〔壞〕的 píqì huài de. **peevishly** *adv*.

peg /peg/ *n* [C] **1** (木、金属、塑料的) 钉 dīng; 栓 shuān; 挂〔掛〕钉 guàdīng; 销子 xiāozi. **2** = CLOTHES-PEG (CLOTHES). **peg** *v* [-gg-] **1** [T] 用钉(或桩等)固定 yòng dīng gùdìng. **2** [T] [常用被动语态] 固定(或维持)在某水平上 gùdìng zài mǒu shuǐpíng shàng: *Pay increases have been ~ged at five per cent*. 工资增长率已限定在百分之五. **3** [短语动词] **peg out** [非正式用语] 死 sǐ.

pejorative /pɪˈdʒɒrətɪv; *US* -ˈdʒɔːr-/ *adj* [正式用语] 贬损的 biǎnsǔnde; 贬抑的 biǎnyìde.

Pekinese /ˌpiːkɪˈniːz/ *n* [C] 狮〔獅〕子狗 shīzigǒu; 哈巴狗 hǎbagǒu.

pelican /ˈpelɪkən/ *n* [C] 鹈鹕 tíhú; 淘河 táohé. **ˌpelican ˈcrossing** *n* [C] (行人穿越马路时可自行按亮红灯使车辆停下的) 自控人行横道 zìkòng rénxínghéngdào.

pellet /ˈpelɪt/ *n* [C] **1** 小球 xiǎoqiú; 小团〔團〕xiǎotuán; 小丸 xiǎowán. **2** 小弹〔彈〕丸 xiǎo dànwán.

pelmet /ˈpelmɪt/ *n* [C] 窗帘〔簾〕盒 chuāngliánhé.

pelt[1] /pelt/ *v* **1** [T] (*with*) 连续〔續〕地投掷〔擲〕liánxùde tóuzhì. **2** [I] (*down*) (雨) 下得很大 xià de hěndà. **3** [习语] (at) **full pelt** ⇨ FULL.

pelt[2] /pelt/ *n* [C] 毛皮 máopí.

pelvis /ˈpelvɪs/ *n* [C] [解剖] 骨盆 gǔpén. **pelvic** /-vɪk/ *adj*.

P

pen[1] /pen/ *n* [C] 笔〔筆〕(如钢笔、圆珠笔等) bǐ. **pen** *v* [-nn-] [T] [正式用语] 写〔寫〕(信等) xiě. ˈ**pen-friend** *n* [C] 笔友 bǐyǒu. ˈ**penknife** *n* [C] [*pl* -**knives**] 小折〔摺〕刀 xiǎo zhédāo. ˈ**pen-name** *n* [C] 笔名 bǐmíng.

pen[2] /pen/ *n* [C] 1 (家畜的)栏〔欄〕lán; 圈 juàn; 槛〔檻〕jiàn. **pen** *v* [-nn-] [T] (*up/in*) 将〔將〕…关〔關〕入圈(或栏)中 jiāng…guānrù juàn zhōng.

penal /ˈpiːnl/ *adj* 处〔處〕罚的 chǔfáde; 刑罚的 xíngfáde.

penalize /ˈpiːnəlaɪz/ *v* [T] [常用被动语态] 1 (因违法)处〔處〕罚 chǔfá; (因比赛犯规)判罚 pànfá. 2 使处于不利地位 shǐ chǔyú búlì dìwèi.

penalty /ˈpenltɪ/ *n* [C] [*pl* -**ies**] 1 处〔處〕罚 chǔfá; 刑罚 xíngfá; 惩〔懲〕罚 chéngfá: *the* ˈ*death* ~ 死刑. 2 [体育] (对犯规者的)处罚(如罚球或罚下场等) chǔfá. 3 (行为或处境造成的)不利 búlì; 不便 búbiàn. ˈ**penalty kick** *n* [C] (足球)罚点〔點〕球 fá diǎnqiú.

penance /ˈpenəns/ *n* [U,C] (表示悔过的)自我惩〔懲〕罚 zìwǒ chéngfá.

pence *pl* of PENNY.

penchant /ˈpɒnʃɒn; *US* ˈpentʃənt/ *n* [sing] *for* [正式用语] 爱〔愛〕好 àihào.

pencil /ˈpensl/ *n* [C] 铅笔〔筆〕qiānbǐ. **pencil** *v* [-ll-; 美语-l-] 1 [T] 用铅笔写〔寫〕(或画等) yòng qiānbǐ xiě. 2 [短语动词] **pencil sth in** 用铅笔(暂时)添入 yòng qiānbǐ tiānrù.

pendant /ˈpendənt/ *n* [C] (项链上的)垂饰 chuíshì; 挂〔掛〕件 guàjiàn.

pending /ˈpendɪŋ/ *adj* [正式用语] 1 未决定的 wèi juédìng de; 待决的 dàijuéde. 2 即将〔將〕发〔發〕生的 jíjiāng fāshēng de; 迫近的 pòjìnde. **pending** *prep* [正式用语] 直至 zhízhì.

pendulum /ˈpendjʊləm; *US* -dʒʊləm/ *n* [C] 摆〔擺〕bǎi; 摆锤 bǎichuí.

penetrate /ˈpenɪtreɪt/ *v* 1 [I,T] 进〔進〕入 jìnrù; 穿过〔過〕chuānguò: *The snow* ~*d his shoes through holes*. 雪渗入他的鞋缝里. 2 [T] [喻] 看穿 kànchuān; 透过 tòuguò: ~ *the disguise* 看穿伪装. **penetrating** *adj* 1 (声音)响〔響〕亮的 xiǎngliàngde. 2 有洞察力的 yǒu dòngchálì de; 敏锐的 mǐnruìde. **penetration** /ˌpenɪˈtreɪʃn/ *n* [U].

penguin /ˈpeŋgwɪn/ *n* [C] 企鹅 qǐ'é.

penicillin /ˌpenɪˈsɪlɪn/ *n* [U] 青霉素 qīngméisù; 盘〔盤〕尼西林 pánníxīlín.

peninsula /pəˈnɪnsjʊlə; *US* -nsələ/ *n* [C] 半岛〔島〕bàndǎo. **peninsular** *adj*.

penis /ˈpiːnɪs/ *n* [C] 阴〔陰〕茎〔莖〕yīnjīng.

penitent /ˈpenɪtənt/ *adj* 悔过〔過〕的 huǐguòde; 后〔後〕悔的 hòuhuǐde. **penitence** /-təns/ *n* [U].

penitentiary /ˌpenɪˈtenʃərɪ/ *n* [C] [*pl* -**ies**] [美语] 监〔監〕狱 jiānyù.

pennant /ˈpenənt/ *n* [C] (船上用作航海信号等的)长〔長〕三角旗 chángsānjiǎoqí.

penniless /ˈpenɪlɪs/ *adj* 身无〔無〕分文的 shēn wú fēnwén de; 一贫如洗的 yì pín rú xǐ de.

penny /ˈpenɪ/ *n* [C] [*pl* **pence** /pens/ 或 **pennies**] 1 便士 (英国硬币, 自 1971 年实行十进位制后, 其值为一英镑的百分之一) biànshì. 2 便士(英国硬币, 1971 年以前其值为一先令的 $\frac{1}{12}$) biànshì. 3 [习语] **the penny (has) dropped** [尤用于英国英语, 非正式用语] 原来〔來〕如此 yuánlái rúcǐ; 恍然大悟 huǎngrán dàwù: *I had to explain the problem to him several times before the* ~ *dropped*. 那问题我给他解释了好几次, 最后他才明白.

pension[1] /ˈpenʃn/ *n* [C,U] 养〔養〕老金 yǎnglǎojīn; 退休金 tuìxiūjīn; 抚〔撫〕恤金 fǔxùjīn. **pension** *v* [短语动词] **pension sb off** 发〔發〕给…养老金使其退休 fāgěi…yǎnglǎojīn shǐ qí tuìxiū. **pensionable** *adj* 可领取养老金(或退休金、抚恤金)的 kě lǐngqǔ yǎnglǎojīn de. **pensioner** *n* [C] 领退休金(或养老金、抚恤金)的人 lǐng tuìxiūjīn de rén.

pension[2] /ˈpɒnsɪɒn/ *n* [C] (法国等的)私人小旅店 sīrén xiǎo lǚdiàn.

pensive /ˈpensɪv/ *adj* 沉思的 chénsīde; 忧〔憂〕虑〔慮〕的 yōulǜde. **pensively** *adv*.

pentagon /ˈpentəgən; *US* -gɒn/ *n* 1 [C] 五角形 wǔjiǎoxíng; 五边〔邊〕形 wǔbiānxíng. 2 **the Pentagon** [sing] [用 sing 或 pl v] 五角大楼〔樓〕(美国国防部办公大楼) Wǔjiǎo Dàlóu. **pentagonal** /penˈtægənl/ *adj*.

pentathlon /penˈtæθlən/ *n* [C] 五项全能运〔運〕动〔動〕(跑步、骑马、游泳、击剑、射击) wǔxiàng quánnéng yùndòng.

penthouse /ˈpenthaʊs/ *n* [C] (高楼的)顶层〔層〕房子 dǐngcéng fángzi.

pent up /ˌpent ˈʌp/ *adj* (感情)不流露的 bù liúlù de; 被压〔壓〕抑的 bèi yāyì de: ~ *anger* 强忍的怒火.

penultimate /penˈʌltɪmət/ *adj* 倒数〔數〕第二的 dàoshǔ dì'èr de.

penury /ˈpenjʊrɪ/ *n* [U] [正式用语] 贫穷〔窮〕pínqióng.

people /ˈpiːpl/ *n* 1 [pl] 人 rén: *How many* ~ *were at the party?* 这次聚会来了多少人? 2 [C] 民族 mínzú; 种〔種〕族 zhǒngzú: *the* ~*s of Asia* 亚洲各民族. 3 [pl] (生活在某地的)人们〔們〕rénmén: *the* ~ *of London* 伦敦居民. 4 **the people** [pl] 普通人 pǔtōngrén; 平民 píngmín; 民众〔衆〕mínzhòng. **people** *v* [T] 使住(满)人 shǐ zhù rén.

People's Liberation Army *n* 人民解放军 Rénmínjiěfàngjūn.

People's Republic of China 中华〔華〕人民共和国 Zhōnghuá Rénmín Gònghéguó.

P

pep /pep/ *n* [U] [非正式用语]精力 jīnglì;活力 huólì. **pep** *v* [-pp-] [短语动词]**pep sb/sth up** [非正式用语]使某人活跃〔躍〕(或精力充沛) shǐ mǒurén huóyuè;使振奋〔奮〕 shǐ zhènfèn. ˈ**pep pill** *n* [C] 兴〔興〕奋丸 xīngfènwán;兴奋片(尤指安非他明) xīngfènpiàn. ˈ**pep talk** *n* [C] 鼓励〔勵〕的讲〔講〕话 gǔlìde jiǎnghuà;激励性讲话 jīlìxìng jiǎnghuà.

pepper /ˈpepə(r)/ *n* **1** [U] 胡椒粉 hújiāofěn. **2** [C] 辣椒 làjiāo: *green* ~*s* 绿辣椒. **pepper** *v* [T] **1** 在…上撒胡椒粉 zài…shàng sǎ hújiāofěn. **2** (*with*) 不断〔斷〕打击〔擊〕 búduàn dǎjī. ˌ**peppercorn** ˈ**rent** *n* [C] 极〔極〕低的租金 jídīde zūjīn.

peppermint /ˈpepəmɪnt/ *n* **1** [U] (胡椒)薄荷 bòhe. **2** [C] (胡椒)薄荷糖 bòhetáng.

per /pə(r); 强式 pɜː(r)/ *prep* 每 měi;每一 měiyī: *£60* ~ *day* 每天 60 英镑. ˌ**per** ˈ**annum** /ˈænəm/ *adv* 每年 měinián. ˌ**per** ˈ**cent** *adv* 每一百中 měiyìbǎi zhōng;百分之… bǎifēnzhī…: *a five* ~ *cent wage increase* 工资增加百分之五. ˌ**per** ˈ**se** /ˌpɜː ˈseɪ/ *adv* 本身 běnshēn.

per se ⇨PER.

perambulator /pəˈræmbjʊleɪtə(r)/ *n* [C] [英国非正式用语]手推童车〔車〕 shǒutuī tóngchē;婴儿〔兒〕车 yīng'érchē.

perceive /pəˈsiːv/ *v* [T] [正式用语]意识〔識〕到 yìshì dào;察觉〔覺〕 chájué;理解 lǐjiě.

percentage /pəˈsentɪdʒ/ *n* **1** [C] 百分比 bǎifēnbǐ;百分率 bǎifēnlǜ. **2** [亦作 sing, 用 pl v] 比例 bǐlì;部分 bùfen: *pay a* ~ *of one's earnings in tax* 按自己收入的比例纳税.

P

perceptible /pəˈseptəbl/ *adj* [正式用语]可感知的 kě gǎnzhī de;可觉〔覺〕察的 kě juéchá de: *a* ~ *change in colour* 看得出的颜色变化. **perceptibly** *adv*.

perception /pəˈsepʃn/ *n* [正式用语] **1** [U] 感知能力 gǎnzhī nénglì;认〔認〕识〔識〕能力 rènshi nénglì. **2** [C] 看法 kànfǎ;理解 lǐjiě.

perceptive /pəˈseptɪv/ *adj* [正式用语]观〔觀〕察敏锐的 guānchá mǐnruì de;善于理解的 shànyú lǐjiě de. **perceptively** *adv*.

perch[1] /pɜːtʃ/ *n* [C] **1** (鸟类的)栖〔棲〕息处〔處〕 qīxīchù. **2** [非正式用语]高座 gāozuò;高位 gāowèi. **perch** *v* **1** [I] (鸟)栖息 qīxī. **2** [I] 坐(在高处或窄处) zuò. **3** [I, T] 把…置于(高处或险处) bǎ…zhìyú.

perch[2] /pɜːtʃ/ *n* [C] [*pl* **perch**] 鲈〔鱸〕 lú.

percolate /ˈpɜːkəleɪt/ *v* **1** [I, T] (水经咖啡)渗〔滲〕透 shèntòu;过〔過〕滤〔濾〕 guòlǜ. **2** [I] *through* (消息等)传〔傳〕播 chuánbō;扩〔擴〕散 kuòsàn. **percolator** *n* [C] 过滤式咖啡壶〔壺〕 guòlǜshì kāfēihú.

percussion /pəˈkʌʃn/ *n* [U] 打击〔擊〕乐〔樂〕器 dǎjī yuèqì.

peremptory /pəˈremptərɪ; US ˈperəmptɔːrɪ/ *adj* [正式用语]专〔專〕横的 zhuānhèngde;霸道的 bàdàode. **peremptorily** /-trəlɪ; US -tɔːrəlɪ/ *adv*.

perennial /pəˈrenɪəl/ *adj* **1** 持久的 chíjiǔde;长〔長〕久的 chángjiǔde. **2** 一再的 yízàide;反复〔復〕的 fǎnfùde: *a* ~ *problem* 一再出现的问题. **3** (植物)多年生的 duōniánshēngde. **perennial** *n* [C] 多年生植物 duōniánshēng zhíwù. **perennially** *adv*.

perfect[1] /ˈpɜːfɪkt/ *adj* **1** 完美的 wánměide;无〔無〕瑕的 wúxiáde;优〔優〕异〔異〕的 yōuyìde: ~ *weather* 美好的天气. **2** 最好的 zuìhǎode;理想的 lǐxiǎngde: *the* ~ *example* 最好的事例. **3** 完备〔備〕的 wánbèide;完全的 wánquánde: *a* ~ *set of teeth* 一副完整的牙齿. **4** 准〔準〕确〔確〕的 zhǔnquède: *The dress is a* ~ *fit*. 那件连衣裙很合身. **5** [非正式用语]全部的 quánbùde: *a* ~ *stranger* 完全陌生的人. **6** [语法]完成时〔時〕的(如 *have eaten*) wánchéngshíde. **perfectly** *adv* 完美地 wánměide;完全地 wánquánde.

perfect[2] /pəˈfekt/ *v* [T] 使完美 shǐ wánměi;使完善 shǐ wánshàn;使完备〔備〕 shǐ wánbèi. **perfectible** *adj* 可使之完美的 kě shǐ zhī wánměide;可完善的 kě wánshàn de.

perfection /pəˈfekʃn/ *n* [U] **1** 完善(指过程) wánshàn;完满 wánmǎn. **2** 完美(指状况) wánměi;完善 wánshàn: *The part of 'Macbeth' suited him to* ~. "麦克白"这个角色对他最适合了. **perfectionist** /-ʃənɪst/ *n* [C] 完美主义〔義〕者 wánměi zhǔyì zhě;至善论〔論〕者 zhì shàn lùn zhě.

perfidious /pəˈfɪdɪəs/ *adj* [正式用语]背信弃〔棄〕义〔義〕的 bèi xìn qì yì de;不忠的 bùzhōngde.

perforate /ˈpɜːfəreɪt/ *v* [T] **1** 在…上穿孔 zài…shàng chuānkǒng;在…上打眼 zài…shàng dǎyǎn. **2** 在(纸)上打齿〔齒〕孔 zài…shàng dǎ chǐkǒng. **perforation** /ˌpɜːfəˈreɪʃn/ *n* [C, U].

perform /pəˈfɔːm/ *v* **1** [T] 做 zuò;履行 lǚxíng;执〔執〕行 zhíxíng: ~ *a task* 执行任务. **2** [I, T] 表演 biǎoyǎn;演奏 yǎnzòu;演出 yǎnchū. **3** [I] 工作 gōngzuò;运〔運〕转〔轉〕 yùnzhuǎn: *This new car* ~*s well*. 这辆新汽车性能好. **performance** *n* **1** [U] 执行 zhíxíng;履行 lǚxíng;工作 gōngzuò. **2** [C] 表演 biǎoyǎn;演出 yǎnchū. **performer** *n* [C] 表演者 biǎoyǎnzhě;演出者 yǎnchūzhě.

perfume /ˈpɜːfjuːm; US pərˈfjuːm/ *n* [C, U] 香水 xiāngshuǐ;香味 xiāngwèi. **perfume** /pəˈfjuːm/ *v* [T] 使带〔帶〕香味 shǐ dài xiāngwèi.

perfunctory /pəˈfʌŋktərɪ/ *adj* [正式用语] 敷衍的 fūyǎnde;马虎的 mǎhude;例行的 lìxíngde. **perfunctorily** /-trəlɪ; *US* -tɔːrəlɪ/ *adv*.

perhaps /pəˈhæps, 亦读 præps/ *adv* 也许 yěxǔ;大概 dàgài;可能 kěnéng: *P~ the weather will improve tomorrow*. 明天天气可能好转.

peril /ˈperəl/ *n* [正式用语] **1** [U](严重的)危险〔險〕wēixiǎn. **2** [C] 危险的事物 wēixiǎnde shìwù. **perilous** *adj*. **perilously** *adv*.

perimeter /pəˈrɪmɪtə(r)/ *n* [C] 周边〔邊〕zhōubiān;周长〔長〕zhōucháng;边缘 biānyuán.

period /ˈpɪərɪəd/ *n* [C] **1** (一段)时〔時〕间 shíjiān;时期 shíqī. **2**(学校的)课 kè;课时 kèshí. **3** 月经〔經〕yuèjīng. **4** [尤用于美语]句号〔號〕jùhào;句点〔點〕jùdiǎn. **periodic** /ˌpɪərɪˈɒdɪk/ *adj* 周期的 zhōuqīde;定期的 dìngqīde. **periodical** /-kl/ *n* [C] 期刊 qīkān. **periodically** /-klɪ/ *adv* 周期地 zhōuqīde;定期地 dìngqīde.

peripatetic /ˌperɪpəˈtetɪk/ *adj* [正式用语] 到处〔處〕走的 dàochù zǒu de;(因工作而)流动〔動〕的 liúdòngde.

periphery /pəˈrɪfərɪ/ *n* [C] [*pl* -ies] [正式用语]外围〔圍〕wàiwéi;边〔邊〕缘 biānyuán. **peripheral** /-əl/ *adj* [正式用语]外围的 wàiwéide;边缘的 biānyuánde:[喻] ~ *topics* 无关紧要的话题.

periscope /ˈperɪskəʊp/ *n* [C] 潜〔潛〕望镜 qiánwàngjìng.

perish /ˈperɪʃ/ *v* [I] **1**[正式用语]毁灭〔滅〕huǐmiè;死亡 sǐwáng. **2** 凋谢 diāoxiè;腐烂〔爛〕fǔlàn. **perishable** *adj* (食物)易腐烂的 yì fǔlàn de;易坏〔壞〕的 yìhuàide. **perishables** *n* [pl] 易腐烂的食物 yì fǔlànde shíwù. **perishing** *adj* [非正式用语,尤用于英国英语]极〔極〕冷的 jílěngde.

perjure /ˈpɜːdʒə(r)/ *v* ~ **oneself** (在法庭上)作伪〔僞〕证 zuò wěizhèng. **perjury** *n* [U].

perk[1] /pɜːk/ *v* [短语动词]**perk (sb/sth) up** 使振作 shǐ zhènzuò;使活跃〔躍〕shǐ huóyuè. **perky** *adj* [-ier, -iest] 活跃的 huóyuède;生气〔氣〕勃勃的 shēngqì bóbó de.

perk[2] /pɜːk/ *n* [C,常作 pl] [非正式用语]额外收入(如奖金、小费、津贴等) éwài shōurù.

perm /pɜːm/ *n* [C] [非正式用语] 烫〔燙〕发〔髮〕tàngfà. **perm** *v* [T] 烫(发) tàng.

permanent /ˈpɜːmənənt/ *adj* 永久的 yǒngjiǔde; 永恒的 yǒnghéngde. **permanence** /-nəns/ *n* [U]. **permanently** *adv*.

permeate /ˈpɜːmɪeɪt/ *v* [I, T] (*through*) [正式用语]弥〔彌〕漫 mímàn;遍布 biànbù;充满 chōngmǎn. **permeable** /ˈpɜːmɪəbl/ *adj* [正式用语]可渗〔滲〕入的 kě shènrù de;可渗透的 kě shèntòu de.

permissible /pəˈmɪsəbl/ *adj* [正式用语] 容许的 róngxǔde;许可的 xǔkěde;可准许的 kě zhǔnxǔ de. **permissibly** /-əblɪ/ *adv*.

permission /pəˈmɪʃn/ *n* [U] 允许 yǔnxǔ;许可 xǔkě;准许 zhǔnxǔ.

permissive /pəˈmɪsɪv/ *adj* 纵〔縱〕容的 zòngróngde;放任的 fàngrènde: *the ~ society* 放任的社会. **permissiveness** *n* [U].

permit /pəˈmɪt/ *v* [-tt-] [T] [正式用语]允许 yǔnxǔ;许可 xǔkě. **permit** /ˈpɜːmɪt/ *n* [C] 许可证〔證〕xǔkězhèng;通行证 tōngxíngzhèng.

permutation /ˌpɜːmjuːˈteɪʃn/ *n* [C] [正式用语]排列 páiliè;置换 zhìhuàn.

pernicious /pəˈnɪʃəs/ *adj* [正式用语]有害的 yǒuhàide;恶〔惡〕性的 èxìngde.

pernickety /pəˈnɪkətɪ/ *adj* [非正式用语,常作贬]吹毛求疵的 chuī máo qiú cī de.

perpendicular /ˌpɜːpənˈdɪkjʊlə(r)/ *adj* **1** 直立的 zhílìde. **2** 垂直的 chuízhíde;成直角的 chéng zhíjiǎo de. **perpendicular** *n* [C, U] 垂直线〔綫〕chuízhíxiàn;垂直 chuízhí.

perpetrate /ˈpɜːpɪtreɪt/ *v* [T] [正式用语]犯(罪等) fàn. **perpetrator** *n* [C].

perpetual /pəˈpetʃʊəl/ *adj* **1** 永久的 yǒngjiǔde;永恒的 yǒnghéngde. **2** 反复〔復〕的 fǎnfùde;不断〔斷〕的 búduànde: *their ~ complaints* 他们无休止的抱怨. **perpetually** /-tʃʊəlɪ/ *adv*.

perpetuate /pəˈpetʃʊeɪt/ *v* [T] [正式用语] 使永久 shǐ yǒngjiǔ;使永恒 shǐ yǒnghéng;使持续〔續〕shǐ chíxù.

perplex /pəˈpleks/ *v* [T] 使困惑 shǐ kùnhuò;使迷惑 shǐ míhuò: *They were all ~ed by her behaviour*. 她的行为使他们大惑不解. *a ~ing problem* 一个复杂的问题. **perplexity** /-ətɪ/ *n* [U] 困惑 kùnhuò;茫然 mángrán.

persecute /ˈpɜːsɪkjuːt/ *v* [T] (因宗教信仰、政治等原因)迫害 pòhài. **persecution** /ˌpɜːsɪˈkjuːʃn/ *n* [C, U]. **persecutor** *n* [C].

persevere /ˌpɜːsɪˈvɪə(r)/ *v* [I] (*in/with*) 坚〔堅〕持不懈 jiānchí bú xiè;坚持做(某事) jiānchí zuò: *You need to ~ with your studies if you want to pass your exams*. 要想通过考试,你必须锲而不舍地学习. **perseverance** *n* [U].

persist /pəˈsɪst/ *v* [I] **1** (*in/with*) 坚〔堅〕持不懈 jiānchí bú xiè;执〔執〕意 zhíyì: *He will ~ in thinking I don't like him*. 他会坚持认为我不喜欢他. **2** 持续〔續〕chíxù;存留 cúnliú: *Fog will ~ in most areas*. 大部分地区将持续有雾. **persistence** *n* [U]. **persistent** *adj* 持续的 chíxùde;一再出现的 yízài chūxiàn de: *~ent warnings/attacks* 一再警告;不停的进攻. **persistently** *adv*.

person /ˈpɜːsn/ *n* [C] [*pl* **people** /ˈpiːpl/

P

或作正式用语时复数为 persons〕1 人 rén: *You're just the ~ we need.* 你正是我们需要的人. 2〔语法〕人称〔稱〕 rénchēng: *the first ~* 第一人称. *the second ~* 第二人称. *the third ~* 第三人称. 3〔习语〕in 'person 亲〔親〕自 qīnzì; 本人 běnrén: *The actress will be there in ~.* 女演员将亲自去那里.

personable /ˈpɜːsənəbl/ *adj* 英俊的 yīngjùnde; 美貌的 měimàode; 风〔風〕度好的 fēngdù hǎo de: *a ~ young woman* 漂亮年轻的妇女.

personal /ˈpɜːsənl/ *adj* 1 个〔個〕人的 gèrénde: *~ belongings* 私人物品. 2 私人的 sīrénde: *receive a ~ phone call at work* 工作时接私人电话. 3 攻击〔擊〕人的 gōngjī rén de: *~ remarks* 批评个人的言词. 4 人身的 rénshēnde; 身体〔體〕的 shēntǐde: *~ cleanliness* 身体的清洁卫生. **personally** /ˈpɜːsənəlɪ/ *adv* 1 就个人而言 jiù gèrén ér yán: *P~ly, I think you're crazy!* 就我个人来说, 我认为你疯了. 2 亲〔親〕自 qīnzì. 3 私下地 sīxiàde. **personal comˈputer** *n* [C] 个人计算机〔機〕 gèrén jìsuànjī. ˌ**personal ˈpronoun** *n* [C]〔语法〕人称〔稱〕代词 rénchēng dàicí.

personality /ˌpɜːsəˈnælətɪ/ *n* [*pl* -ies] 1 [C, U] 个〔個〕性 gèxìng: *a strong ~* 坚强的个性. 2 [C] (尤指娱乐、体育界的)名人 míngrén: *a television ~* 电视人物.

personify /pəˈsɒnɪfaɪ/ *v* [*pt, pp* -ied] [T] 1 将〔將〕…人格化 jiāng… réngéhuà; 将…拟〔擬〕人化 jiāng… nǐrénhuà. 2 是…的化身 shì …de huàshēn: *She personifies kindness.* 她是仁慈的化身. **personification** /pəˌsɒnɪfɪˈkeɪʃn/ *n* [U, C].

P

personnel /ˌpɜːsəˈnel/ *n* 1 [pl] 职〔職〕员 zhíyuán; 人员 rényuán. 2 [U] 人事部门 rénshì bùmén: *a ~ manager* 人事部主任.

perspective /pəˈspektɪv/ *n* 1 [U] 透视法 tòushìfǎ. 2 [U]〔喻〕(观察问题的)视角 shìjiǎo. 3〔习语〕in perspective 用透视法的(地) yòng tòushìfǎ de: *get / see one's problems in ~* 正确看待问题.

Perspex /ˈpɜːspeks/ *n* [U] (*P*) 有机〔機〕玻璃(一种高强度透明塑料) yǒujī bōlí.

perspire /pəˈspaɪə(r)/ *v* [I]〔正式用语〕出汗 chū hàn; 流汗 liú hàn. **perspiration** /ˌpɜːspəˈreɪʃn/ *n* [U].

persuade /pəˈsweɪd/ *v* [T] 1 说服(某人) shuōfú; 劝〔勸〕说 quànshuō: *They ~d him to try again.* 他们劝他再试一次. 2〔正式用语〕使相信 shǐ xiāngxìn; 使信服 shǐ xìnfú.

persuasion /pəˈsweɪʒn/ *n* 1 [U] 说服 shuōfú; 劝〔勸〕服 quànfú. 2 [C] 信念 xìnniàn; 信仰 xìnyǎng.

persuasive /pəˈsweɪsɪv/ *adj* 有说服力的 yǒu shuōfúlì de; 令人信服的 lìng rén xìnfú de: *She can be very ~ when she wants.* 她提出要求时, 很有说服力. **persuasively** *adv*.

pert /pɜːt/ *adj* 无〔無〕礼〔禮〕的 wúlǐde; 冒失的 màoshide: *a ~ reply* 无礼的回答. **pertly** *adv*. **pertness** *n* [U].

pertain /pəˈteɪn/ *v* [I] *to*〔正式用语〕有关〔關〕 yǒuguān; 从〔從〕属〔屬〕 cóngshǔ; 附属 fùshǔ.

pertinent /ˈpɜːtɪnənt; *US* ˈpɜːtənənt/ *adj*〔正式用语〕有关〔關〕的 yǒuguānde; 相关的 xiāngguānde.

perturb /pəˈtɜːb/ *v* [T]〔正式用语〕使不安 shǐ bù'ān; 使烦恼〔惱〕 shǐ fánnǎo.

peruse /pəˈruːz/ *v* [T]〔正式用语〕仔细阅读〔讀〕 zǐxì yuèdú. **perusal** *n* [C, U].

pervade /pəˈveɪd/ *v* [T]〔正式用语〕弥〔彌〕漫 mímàn; 遍及 biànjí.

pervasive /pəˈveɪsɪv/ *adj* 弥〔彌〕漫的 mímànde; 遍布的 biànbùde.

perverse /pəˈvɜːs/ *adj* 1 (人)坚〔堅〕持错误〔誤〕的 jiānchí cuòwù de; 背理的 bèilǐde; 不合常情的 bùhé chángqíng de. 2(行为)任性的 rènxìngde; 不讲〔講〕理的 bù jiǎnglǐ de. **perversely** *adv*. **perversity** *n* [U].

perversion /pəˈvɜːʃn; *US* -ʒn/ *n* 1 [U] 变〔變〕错 biàncuò; 反常 fǎncháng: *the ~ of truth* 歪曲事实. 2[C, U] 性欲〔慾〕反常(或倒错) xìngyù fǎncháng; 性变态〔態〕 xìngbiàntài.

pervert[1] /pəˈvɜːt/ *v* [T] 1 误用 wùyòng; 滥〔濫〕用 lànyòng: *~ the course of justice* 滥用司法程序. 2 使入邪路 shǐ rù xiélù; 使反常 shǐ fǎncháng; 使变〔變〕坏〔壞〕 shǐ biànhuài.

pervert[2] /ˈpɜːvɜːt/ *n* [C] 堕落者 duòluòzhě; 反常者 fǎnchángzhě; 性变〔變〕态〔態〕者 xìngbiàntàizhě.

pessimism /ˈpesɪmɪzəm/ *n* [U] 悲观〔觀〕 bēiguān; 悲观主义〔義〕 bēiguān zhǔyì. **pessimist** /-mɪst/ *n* [C]. **pessimistic** /ˌpesɪˈmɪstɪk/ *adj*.

pest /pest/ *n* [C] 1 害兽〔獸〕 hàishòu; 害虫 hàichóng; 有害生物 yǒuhài shēngwù. 2〔非正式用语〕讨厌〔厭〕的人 tǎoyànde rén.

pester /ˈpestə(r)/ *v* [T] 不断〔斷〕打扰〔擾〕 búduàn dǎrǎo; 纠缠〔纏〕 jiūchán.

pesticide /ˈpestɪsaɪd/ *n* [C, U] 杀〔殺〕虫剂〔劑〕 shāchóngjì; 农〔農〕药〔藥〕 nóngyào.

pestle /ˈpesl/ *n* [C] (捣研用的)杵 chǔ.

pet /pet/ *n* [C] 1 玩赏动〔動〕物 wánshǎng dòngwù; 宠〔寵〕物 chǒngwù. 2 宠儿〔兒〕 chǒng'ér; 宝〔寶〕贝 bǎobèi. **pet** *v* [-tt-] 1 [T] 宠爱〔愛〕 chǒng'ài; 抚〔撫〕摸 fǔmō. 2 [I] 亲〔親〕吻和爱抚 qīnwěn hé àifǔ. ˈ**pet name** *n* [C] 爱称〔稱〕 àichēng; 昵〔暱〕称 nìchēng.

petal /ˈpetl/ *n* [C] 花瓣 huābàn.

peter /ˈpiːtə(r)/ *v* [短语动词] peter out 逐渐减少 zhújiàn jiǎnshǎo; 逐渐消失 zhújiàn xiāoshī.

petition /pəˈtɪʃn/ *n* [C] 1 请愿〔願〕书〔書〕qǐngyuànshū. 2 [法律](向法院递交的)诉状〔狀〕sùzhuàng. **petition** *v* [I,T] [正式用语]正式请求 zhèngshì qǐngqiú; 请愿 qǐngyuàn.

petrify /ˈpetrɪfaɪ/ *v* [*pt*, *pp* -ied] 1 [T] [常作被动语态]使吓〔嚇〕呆 shǐ xiàdāi; 使惊〔驚〕呆 shǐ jīngdāi. 2 [I,T] 使石化 shǐ shíhuà.

petrol /ˈpetrəl/ *n* [U] 汽油 qìyóu. ˈ**petrol station** *n* [C] 汽车〔車〕加油站 qìchē jiāyóuzhàn.

petroleum /pəˈtrəʊlɪəm/ *n* [U] 石油 shíyóu.

petticoat /ˈpetɪkəʊt/ *n* [C] 衬〔襯〕裙 chènqún.

petty /ˈpetɪ/ *adj* [-ier, -iest] 1 小的 xiǎode; 不重要的 bú zhòngyào de: ~ *details* 细节. 2 琐碎的 suǒsuìde; 小气〔氣〕的 xiǎoqìde. **pettiness** *n* [U]. ˌ**petty** ˈ**cash** *n* [U] 小额现金 xiǎo'é xiànjīn. ˌ**petty** ˈ**officer** *n* [C] 海军军士 hǎijūn jūnshì.

petulant /ˈpetjʊlənt; *US* -tʃʊ-/ *adj* 任性的 rènxìngde; 脾气〔氣〕坏〔壞〕的 píqì huài de. **petulance** /-ləns/ *n* [U]. **petulantly** *adv*.

pew /pjuː/ *n* [C] 教堂长〔長〕椅 jiàotáng chángyǐ.

pewter /ˈpjuːtə(r)/ *n* [U] 白镴 báilà.

phallus /ˈfæləs/ *n* [C] (某些宗教作为生殖力象征的)阴〔陰〕茎〔莖〕图〔圖〕像 yīnjīngtúxiàng. **phallic** /ˈfælɪk/ *adj*.

phantom /ˈfæntəm/ *n* [C] 1 鬼魂 guǐhún; 幽灵〔靈〕yōulíng. 2 不真实〔實〕(或想像)的事物 bù zhēnshí de shìwù.

Pharaoh /ˈfeərəʊ/ *n* [C] (古埃及君王称号)法老 Fǎlǎo.

pharmaceutical /ˌfɑːməˈsjuːtɪkl; *US* -ˈsuː-/ *adj* 制〔製〕药〔藥〕的 zhìyàode; 配药的 pèiyàode.

pharmacist /ˈfɑːməsɪst/ *n* [C] 药〔藥〕剂〔劑〕师〔師〕yàojìshī; 药商 yàoshāng.

pharmacy /ˈfɑːməsɪ/ *n* [*pl* -ies] 1 [U] 药〔藥〕剂〔劑〕学〔學〕yàojìxué; 制〔製〕药学 zhìyàoxué; 配药学 pèiyàoxué. 2 [C] 药店 yàodiàn; 药房 yàofáng.

phase /feɪz/ *n* [C] 1 阶〔階〕段 jiēduàn; 时〔時〕期 shíqī. 2 (指月亮)位相 wèixiàng; 盈亏〔虧〕(新月、满月等) yíngkuī. **phase** *v* 1 [T] 按阶段计划〔劃〕(或实行、安排) àn jiēduàn jìhuà. 2 [短语动词] **phase sth in/out** 逐步采〔採〕用(或引入) zhúbù cǎiyòng; 逐步停止使用 zhúbù tíngzhǐ shǐyòng.

PhD /ˌpiː eɪtʃ ˈdiː/ *abbr* Doctor of Philosophy 哲学〔學〕博士 zhéxué bóshì.

pheasant /ˈfeznt/ *n* 1 [C] 雉 zhì. 2 [U] 雉肉 zhìròu.

phenomenal /fəˈnɒmɪnl/ *adj* 非凡的 fēifánde; 不寻〔尋〕常 bù xúncháng de: ~ *success* 非常成功. **phenomenally** /-nəlɪ/ *adv*: ~*ly successful* 非常成功的.

phenomenon /fəˈnɒmɪnən; *US* -nɒn/ *n* [C] [*pl* -mena /-mɪnə/] 1 现象 xiànxiàng. 2 非凡的人 fēifánde rén; 奇迹〔跡〕qíjì.

philanthropy /fɪˈlænθrəpɪ/ *n* [U] 慈善事业〔業〕císhàn shìyè; 慈善性捐赠 císhànxìng juānzèng. **philanthropic** /ˌfɪlənˈθrɒpɪk/ *adj*. **philanthropist** /fɪˈlænθrəpɪst/ *n* [C].

philately /fɪˈlætəlɪ/ *n* [U] 集邮〔郵〕jíyóu.

philistine /ˈfɪlɪstaɪn; *US* -stiːn/ *n* [C] 讨厌〔厭〕艺〔藝〕术〔術〕的人 tǎoyàn yìshù de rén; 无〔無〕教养〔養〕的人 wú jiàoyǎng de rén.

philosopher /fɪˈlɒsəfə(r)/ *n* [C] 1 研究哲学〔學〕者 yánjiū zhéxué zhě; 哲学教师〔師〕zhéxué jiàoshī. 2 [非正式用语]善于思考的人 shànyú sīkǎo de rén.

philosophy /fɪˈlɒsəfɪ/ *n* [*pl* -ies] 1 [U] 哲学〔學〕zhéxué. 2 [C] 哲学思想 zhéxué sīxiǎng; 哲学体〔體〕系 zhéxué tǐxì. **philosophical** /ˌfɪləˈsɒfɪkl/ *adj* 1 哲学的 zhéxuéde. 2 达〔達〕观〔觀〕的 dáguānde; 泰然自若的 tàirán zìruò de. **philosophically** /-klɪ/ *adv*. **philosophize** /-faɪz/ *v* [I] 哲学家似地思考(或推理、辩论) zhéxuéjiā shì de sīkǎo.

phishing /ˈfɪʃɪŋ/ *n* [U] 网〔網〕络钓鱼〔魚〕wǎngluò diàoyú(一种网络诈骗手段).

phlegm /flem/ *n* [U] 1 痰 tán. 2 [旧,正式用语]冷静 lěngjìng. **phlegmatic** /flegˈmætɪk/ *adj* 冷静的 lěngjìngde; 沉着的 chénzhuóde. **phlegmatically** /-klɪ/ *adv*.

phobia /ˈfəʊbɪə/ *n* [C] 恐惧〔懼〕kǒngjù; 憎恶〔惡〕zēngwù.

phone /fəʊn/ *n* [C], *v* [I, T] short for TELEPHONE. ˈ**phone book** *n* [C] ⇨TELEPHONE DIRECTORY (TELEPHONE). ˈ**phonebox** (亦作 ˈ**phone booth**) *n* [C] = TELEPHONE-BOX (TELEPHONE). ˈ**phone card** *n* [C] 电话(储金)卡 diànhuàkǎ. ˈ**phone-in** *n* [C] (电台或电视台的)听〔聽〕(或观)众〔衆〕通过〔過〕电〔電〕话的直播节〔節〕目(向主持人提问或交谈) tīngzhòng tōngguò diànhuà de zhíbō jiémù. ˈ**phone number** = TELEPHONE NUMBER (TELEPHONE).

phonetic /fəˈnetɪk/ *adj* [语言]语音的 yǔyīnde. **phonetically** /-klɪ/ *adv*. **phonetician** /ˌfəʊnɪˈtɪʃn/ *n* [C] 语音学〔學〕家 yǔyīnxuéjiā. **phonetics** *n* [用 sing v] 语音学 yǔyīnxué.

phoney (亦作 **phony**) /ˈfəʊnɪ/ *adj* [-ier, -iest] [非正式用语,贬]假的 jiǎde; 伪〔僞〕造的 wěizàode. **phoney** (亦作 **phony**) *n* [C] 假冒者 jiǎmàozhě; 假货 jiǎhuò; 赝品 yànpǐn.

phonology /fəˈnɒlədʒɪ/ *n* [U] [语言]音系学

〔學〕 yīnxìxué；音位学 yīnwèixué；音韵〔韻〕学 yīnyùnxué：*English* ～ 英语语音体系. **phonological** /ˌfəʊnəˈlɒdʒɪkl/ *adj*.

phosphorescence /ˌfɒsfəˈresns/ *n* [U] 磷光 línguāng；磷火 línhuǒ. **phosphorescent** /-ˈresnt/ *adj* 在黑暗中发〔發〕光的 zài hēi'àn zhōng fāguāng de.

phosphorus /ˈfɒsfərəs/ *n* [U] 磷 lín.

photo /ˈfəʊtəʊ/ *n* [C] [*pl* ～s] [非正式用语] short for PHOTOGRAPH. ˌ**photo ˈfinish** *n* [C] (比赛者到达终点时十分接近，需用照片来判断结果的)摄〔攝〕影定名次 shèyǐng dìng míngcì.

photocopy /ˈfəʊtəʊkɒpɪ/ *n* [C] [*pl* -ies] 摄〔攝〕影复〔複〕制〔製〕品 shèyǐng fùzhìpǐn；复印件 fùyìnjiàn；照相复制本 zhàoxiàng fùzhìběn. **photocopy** *v* [*pt*, *pp* -ied] 摄影复制 shèyǐng fùzhì；复印 fùyìn；照相复印 zhàoxiàng fùyìn；影印 yǐngyìn. **photocopier** /-pɪə(r)/ *n* [C] 摄影复制机〔機〕 shèyǐng fùzhìjī；复印机 fùyìnjī；影印机 yǐngyìnjī.

photogenic /ˌfəʊtəʊˈdʒenɪk/ *adj* 适〔適〕于拍照的 shì yú pāizhào de；上相的 shàngxiàngde；上镜的 shàngjìngde.

photograph /ˈfəʊtəgrɑːf; *US* -græf/ *n* [C] 照片 zhàopiàn；相片 xiàngpiàn. **photograph** *v* [T] 给…拍照 gěi…pāizhào. **photographer** /fəˈtɒgrəfə(r)/ *n* [C] 摄〔攝〕影师〔師〕 shèyǐngshī；摄影者 shèyǐngzhě. **photographic** /ˌfəʊtəˈgræfɪk/ *adj*. **photography** /fəˈtɒgrəfɪ/ *n* [U] 摄影 shèyǐng；摄影术〔術〕 shèyǐngshù.

P

phrasal /ˈfreɪzl/ *adj* 短语的 duǎnyǔde；词组的 cízǔde；片语的 piànyǔde. ˌ**phrasal ˈverb** *n* [C] 短语动〔動〕词 duǎnyǔ dòngcí：'*Blow up*' *and* '*look forward to*' *are* ～ *verbs*. blow up 和 look forward to 是短语动词.

phrase /freɪz/ *n* [C] 1 一组字 yìzǔ zì. 2 [语法]短语 duǎnyǔ；词组 cízǔ；片语 piànyǔ. **phrase** *v* [T] 用词或词组表达〔達〕 yòng cí huò cízǔ biǎodá：*a badly* ～*d example* 措辞不当的例子. ˈ**phrase-book** *n* [C] (供到国外旅游用的)外语常用语手册 wàiyǔ chángyòngyǔ shǒucè.

phraseology /ˌfreɪzɪˈɒlədʒɪ/ *n* [U] 措辞〔辭〕 cuòcí；用语 yòngyǔ.

physical /ˈfɪzɪkl/ *adj* 1 身体〔體〕的 shēntǐde；肉体的 ròutǐde：～ *exercise* 体育活动. ～ *education* 体育. 2 物质〔質〕的 wùzhìde：*the* ～ *world* 物质世界. 3 自然规律的 zìrán guīlǜ de；按自然法则的 àn zìrán fǎzé de：*a* ～ *impossibility* 自然法则上不可能的事. 4 自然(界)的 zìránde：～ *geography* 自然地理学. **physically** /-klɪ/ *adv*.

physician /fɪˈzɪʃn/ *n* [C] 医〔醫〕生 yīshēng；内科医生 nèikē yīshēng.

physicist /ˈfɪzɪsɪst/ *n* [C] 物理学〔學〕家 wùlǐxuéjiā.

physics /ˈfɪzɪks/ *n* [U] 物理 wùlǐ；物理学〔學〕 wùlǐxué.

physiology /ˌfɪzɪˈɒlədʒɪ/ *n* [U] 生理学〔學〕 shēnglǐxué. **physiological** /ˌfɪzɪəˈlɒdʒɪkl/ *adj*. **physiologist** *n* [U] 生理学家 shēnglǐxuéjiā.

physiotherapy /ˌfɪzɪəʊˈθerəpɪ/ *n* [U] 物理疗〔療〕法 wùlǐliáofǎ；理疗 lǐliáo. **physiotherapist** *n* [C].

physique /fɪˈziːk/ *n* [C] 体〔體〕格 tǐgé；体形 tǐxíng.

piano /pɪˈænəʊ/ *n* [C] [*pl* ～s] 钢〔鋼〕琴 gāngqín. **pianist** /ˈpɪənɪst/ *n* [C] 钢琴家 gāngqínjiā；钢琴演奏者 gāngqín yǎnzòuzhě.

piccolo /ˈpɪkələʊ/ *n* [C] [*pl* ～s] 短笛 duǎndí.

pick[1] /pɪk/ *v* [T] 1 选〔選〕择〔擇〕 xuǎnzé；挑选 tiāoxuǎn. 2 采〔採〕摘 cǎizhāi；采集 cǎijí：～ *strawberries* 摘草莓. 3 除掉 chúdiào. 4 从〔從〕…去掉某物 cóng…qùdiào mǒuwù：～ *one's teeth* 剔牙. 5 寻〔尋〕衅〔釁〕 xúnxìn；找茬儿〔兒〕 zhǎochár. 6 拨〔撥〕开〔開〕(锁) bōkāi. 7 扎(或掘、挖、凿)成(洞等) zhāchéng. 8(鸟)叼起 diāoqǐ；啄起 zhuóqǐ. 9[习语]**pick and ˈchoose** 挑挑拣拣 tiāotiāo jiǎnjiǎn. **pick sb's ˈbrains** 利用(或抄袭)别人的成果 lìyòng biérén de chéngguǒ；借问问题以获〔獲〕取有用的信息 jiè wèn wèntí yǐ huòqǔ yǒuyòng de xìnxī. **pick holes in sth** 找毛病 zhǎo máobìng. **pick sb's ˈpocket** 扒窃〔竊〕 páqiè. 10 [短语动词] **pick at sth** 一点〔點〕一点地吃(食物) yìdiǎn yìdiǎn de chī. **pick on sb** 选〔選〕中某人惩〔懲〕罚(或责怪等) xuǎnzhòng mǒurén chéngfá：*He's always* ～*ing on me*. 他总是责备我. **pick sb/sth out** (a) 挑选出某人(或某物) tiāoxuǎn chū mǒurén. (b) 分辨出某人(或某物) fēnbiàn chū mǒurén. **pick up** (a) 好转〔轉〕 hǎozhuǎn；改善 gǎishàn. (b) 重新开始 chóngxīn kāishǐ. **pick sb up** (a) (用汽车)搭载某人 dāzài mǒurén. (b) [非正式用语，贬]偶然结识〔識〕某人 ǒurán jiéshí mǒurén. (c) 拘留 jūliú；逮捕 dàibǔ. **pick sth up** (a) 举〔舉〕起 jǔqǐ；拿起 náqǐ；拾起 shíqǐ. (b) 学〔學〕会〔會〕(技术、外语等) xuéhuì. (c) 得(病) dé；染(疾病) rǎn. (d) 收集 shōují. (e)收听〔聽〕到 shōutīng dào. **picker** *n* [C] 采摘者 cǎizhāizhě；采集者 cǎijízhě；采摘机〔機〕(或工具) cǎizhāijī. **pickings** *n* [pl] 利润 lìrùn；(来得容易的)不义〔義〕之财 búyì zhī cái. ˈ**pickpocket** *n* [C] 扒手 páshǒu. ˈ**pick-up** *n* [C] 1 拾音器 shíyīnqì；电〔電〕唱头〔頭〕 diànchàngtóu. 2 轻〔輕〕型小货车〔車〕 qīngxíng xiǎo huòchē. 3 [非正式用语，贬]偶然结识〔識〕的人 ǒurán jiéshí de rén.

pick[2] /pɪk/ *n* [sing] 1 挑选〔選〕 tiāoxuǎn；选择〔擇〕 xuǎnzé：*take your* ～ 你自己选. 2 **the pick of sth** 精华〔華〕 jīnghuá.

pick[3] /pɪk/ (亦作 **pickaxe**，美语 **pickax** /ˈpɪkæks/) *n* [C] 镐 gǎo；丁字镐 dīngzìgǎo.

picket /ˈpɪkɪt/ *n* [C] (罢工时，守在工作地点门口阻止他人上班的)纠察队〔隊〕员 jiūchá duìyuán；纠察队 jiūcháduì. **picket** *v* [I,T] (罢工时)设置纠察队 shèzhì jiūcháduì：～ *a factory* 在工厂设置纠察队.

pickle /ˈpɪkl/ *n* 1 (a) [U] (腌肉、泡菜等的)盐〔鹽〕卤〔鹵〕 yánlǔ；腌汁 yānzhī. (b) [C,U] 腌菜 yāncài. 2 [sing] [非正式用语]处〔處〕境困难〔難〕(或不愉快) chǔjìng kùnnan：*in a* ～ 在困境中. **pickle** *v* [T] (用腌汁)腌渍 yānzì. **pickled** *adj* [非正式用语]醉的 zuìde.

picnic /ˈpɪknɪk/ *n* [C] 野餐 yěcān. **picnic** *v* [-ck-] [I]. **picnicker** *n* [C] 野餐者 yěcānzhě.

pictorial /pɪkˈtɔːrɪəl/ *adj* 用图〔圖〕表示的 yòng tú biǎoshì de；有图片的 yǒu túpiàn de.

picture /ˈpɪktʃə(r)/ *n* 1 [C] (a) 绘〔繪〕画〔畫〕 huìhuà；图〔圖〕画 túhuà. (b) 照片 zhàopiàn；相片 xiàngpiàn. (c) 电〔電〕视图像 diànshì túxiàng. 2 [英国英语，旧] (a) [C] 影片 yǐngpiàn；电影 diànyǐng. (b) **the pictures** [pl] 电影院 diànyǐngyuàn：*go to the* ～*s* 去看电影. 3 [C] (心目中的)形象 xíngxiàng. 4 [C] 描述 miáoshù；叙述 xùshù. 5 [习语] **be/put sb in the ˈpicture** (使某人)了〔瞭〕解实〔實〕情 liǎojiě shíqíng. **be the picture of health, happiness, etc** 看上去很健康(或愉快等) kàn shàng qù hěn jiànkāng. **get the ˈpicture** [非正式用语]明白 míngbai；理解 lǐjiě. **picture** *v* [T] 1 想像 xiǎngxiàng：*He* ～*d himself as a rich man*. 他想像自己是个富人. 2 画 huà；拍摄〔攝〕 pāishè.

picturesque /ˌpɪktʃəˈresk/ *adj* 1 美如画〔畫〕的 měi rú huà de：*a* ～ *fishing village* 风景如画的渔村. 2 (语言)生动〔動〕的 shēngdòngde；绘〔繪〕声〔聲〕绘色的 huì shēng huì sè de.

pidgin /ˈpɪdʒɪn/ *n* [C] (在贸易、交往中形成的不同语种的)混杂〔雜〕语 hùnzáyǔ，不纯正的语言 bù chúnzhèng de yǔyán.

pie /paɪ/ *n* [C,U] (肉或水果的)馅饼 xiànbǐng；肉馅排 ròuxiànpái；果馅排 guǒxiànpái.

piebald /ˈpaɪbɔːld/ *adj* (马)有黑白斑的 yǒu hēibáibān de.

piece[1] /piːs/ *n* [C] 1 块〔塊〕 kuài；片 piàn；段 duàn. 2 部件 bùjiàn. 3 件 jiàn；个〔個〕 gè：*a* ～ *of furniture* 一件家具. [喻] *a* ～ *of news/advice* 一则新闻；一个忠告. 4 (艺术品、音乐等的)幅 fú；篇 piān；首 shǒu. 5 棋子 qízǐ：*a chess* ～ (国际象棋)棋子. 6 硬币〔幣〕 yìngbì：*a ten-pence* ～ 十便士的硬币. 7 [习语] **give sb a piece of one's ˈmind** [非正式用语]直言 zhíyán；坦诚相告 tǎnchéng xiānggào. **go to ˈpieces** 失去自制力 shīqù zìzhìlì. **in one ˈpiece** 未受伤〔傷〕的 wèi shòushāng de. **a ˌpiece of ˈcake** [非正式用语]容易的事 róngyìde shì. **ˈpiece-work** *n* [U] 计件工作 jìjiàn gōngzuò.

piece[2] /piːs/ *v* [短语动词] **piece sth together** 拼合 pīnhé；拼凑 pīncòu；组装〔裝〕 zǔzhuāng.

piecemeal /ˈpiːsmiːl/ *adv* 一件一件地 yíjiàn yíjiàn de；一块〔塊〕一块地 yíkuài yíkuài de：*work done* ～ 逐个地做完的工作.

pier /pɪə(r)/ *n* [C] 1 码头〔頭〕 mǎtóu；突堤 tūdī. 2 桥〔橋〕墩 qiáodūn.

pierce /pɪəs/ *v* 1 [I,T] 刺入 cìrù；刺透 cìtòu；刺穿 cìchuān. 2 [T] [喻](声、光等)进〔進〕入 jìnrù；透入 tòurù. **piercing** *adj* 1 (声音)尖锐的 jiānruìde；刺耳的 cì'ěrde. 2 (眼睛)敏锐的 mǐnruìde；锐利的 ruìlìde. 3 (风)刺骨的 cìgǔde；凛冽的 lǐnliède. **piercingly** *adv*.

piety /ˈpaɪətɪ/ *n* [U] 虔诚 qiánchéng；虔敬 qiánjìng.

pig /pɪg/ *n* [C] 1 猪 zhū. 2 [非正式用语，贬]贪心(或肮脏、粗野)的人 tānxīnde rén. 3 [习语] **make a ˈpig of oneself** [非正式用语]吃得(或喝得)太多 chīde tàiduō. **piggy** *n* [C] [*pl* **-ies**] [非正式用语](儿语)小猪 xiǎozhū. **ˈpiggy bank** *n* [C] 扑〔撲〕满 pūmǎn；(猪形)储蓄罐 chǔxùguàn. **ˌpigˈheaded** *adj* 顽固的 wángùde；固执〔執〕的 gùzhíde. **ˈpigsty** *n* [C] [*pl* **-ies**] 1 猪圈 zhūjuàn. 2 [非正式用语]肮〔骯〕脏〔髒〕地方 āngzāng dìfang. **ˈpigtail** *n* [C] 辫子 biànzi.

pigeon /ˈpɪdʒɪn/ *n* [C] 1 鸽子 gēzi. 2 [非正式用语]责任 zérèn：*That's not my* ～. 那不是我的事. **ˈpigeon-hole** *n* [C] 信件架 xìnjiànjià；文件格 wénjiàngé. **pigeon-hole** *v* [T] 1 把…分类〔類〕(或归档) bǎ…fēnlèi. 2 把…搁置一边〔邊〕 bǎ…gēzhì yìbiān. **ˈpigeon-toed** *adj* 足内翻的 zúnèifānde；内八字的 nèibāzìde.

piglet /ˈpɪglɪt/ *n* [C] 小猪 xiǎozhū.

pigment /ˈpɪgmənt/ *n* 1 [C,U] 颜料 yánliào. 2 [U] 色素 sèsù. **pigmentation** /ˌpɪgmenˈteɪʃn/ *n* [U] 色素沉着 sèsù chénzhuó.

pigmy = PYGMY.

pike[1] /paɪk/ *n* [C] [*pl* **pike**] 狗鱼 gǒuyú.

pike[2] /paɪk/ *n* [C] 长〔長〕矛 chángmáo.

pilchard /ˈpɪltʃəd/ *n* [C] 沙丁鱼 shādīngyú.

pile[1] /paɪl/ *n* [C] 1 堆 duī：*a* ～ *of papers* 一堆纸. 2 [常作 pl] [非正式用语]大量 dàliàng；许多 xǔduō：～*s of work* 大量工作. 3 [习语] **make a ˈpile** [非正式用语]赚钱〔錢〕 zhuànqián；发〔發〕财 fācái. **pile** *v* 1 [T] 堆积〔積〕 duījī；堆放 duīfàng：～ *the books on the table* 把书堆放在桌子上. 2 [T] 将〔將〕(某物)堆在某

物上 jiāng…duī zài mǒuwù shang: *The table was ~d high with boxes*. 桌子上高高地摞着盒子. 3 [I] *into/out of* 蜂拥[擁]而入 fēngyōng ér rù; 蜂拥而出 fēngyōng ér chū. 4 [短语动词] **pile up** (a) 增多 zēngduō: *The work is piling up*. 工作越积越多. (b) (车辆)互相碰撞 hùxiāng pèng zhuàng. **'pile-up** *n* [C] 几[幾]辆车相撞 jǐliàng chē xiāngzhuàng.

pile[2] /paɪl/ *n* [C] (房屋、桥梁等的)桩[樁] zhuāng.

pile[3] /paɪl/ *n* [U] (织物、地毯的)绒面 róngmiàn; 绒毛 róngmáo; 绒头[頭] róngtóu.

piles /paɪlz/ *n* [pl] = HAEMORRHOIDS.

pilfer /ˈpɪlfə(r)/ *v* [I, T] 小偷小摸 xiǎotōu xiǎomō.

pilgrim /ˈpɪlgrɪm/ *n* [C] 朝圣[聖]者 cháoshèngzhě; 香客 xiāngkè. **pilgrimage** /-ɪdʒ/ *n* [C, U] 朝圣 cháoshèng.

pill /pɪl/ *n* 1 [C] 药[藥]丸 yàowán; 药片 yàopiàn. 2 **the pill** [sing] 口服避孕药 kǒufú bìyùnyào.

pillage /ˈpɪlɪdʒ/ *v* [I, T] [正式用语](尤指战争中的)抢[搶]劫 qiǎngjié; 掠夺[奪] lüèduó.

pillar /ˈpɪlə(r)/ *n* [C] 1 支柱 zhīzhù; 柱子 zhùzi. 2 重要成员 zhòngyào chéngyuán; 积[積]极[極]支持者 jījí zhīchízhě. **'pillar-box** *n* [C] 邮[郵]筒 yóutǒng; 信筒 xìntǒng.

pillion /ˈpɪlɪən/ *n* [C] 摩托车[車]后[後]座 mótuōchē hòuzuò.

pillory /ˈpɪlərɪ/ *v* [*pt*, *pp* -ied] [T] [正式用语]公开[開]攻击[擊] gōngkāi gōngjī.

P

pillow /ˈpɪləʊ/ *n* [C] 枕头[頭] zhěntou. **pillow** *v* [T] 把(头)枕在 bǎ… zhěn zài. **'pillowcase** (亦作 **'pillowslip**) *n* [C] 枕套 zhěntào.

pilot /ˈpaɪlət/ *n* [C] 1 驾驶员 jiàshǐyuán; 飞[飛]行员 fēixíngyuán. 2 领港员 lǐnggǎngyuán; 领航员 lǐnghángyuán. **pilot** *adj* 试验[驗]性的 shìyànxìngde; 试点[點]的 shìdiǎnde: *a* ˈ~ *scheme* 试验性计划. **pilot** *v* [T] 驾驶 jiàshǐ; 引航 yǐnháng. **'pilot-light** *n* [C] (煤气灶具等用于引火的)常燃火苗 chángrán huǒmiáo.

pimp /pɪmp/ *n* [C] 拉皮条[條]的男人 lāpítiáode nánrén.

pimple /ˈpɪmpl/ *n* [C] 丘疹 qiūzhěn; 小脓[膿]疱 xiǎo nóngpào. **pimply** *adj*.

pin[1] /pɪn/ *n* [C] 大头[頭]针 dàtóuzhēn. **'pincushion** *n* [C] 针垫[墊] zhēndiàn. **'pinpoint** *v* [T] 准[準]确[確]描述(或确定) zhǔnquè miáoshù. **ˌpins and 'needles** *n* [pl] 发[發]麻 fāmá; 针刺感 zhēncìgǎn. **'pin-stripe** *n* (布上的)细条[條]子 xìtiáozi.

pin[2] /pɪn/ *v* [-nn-] [T] 1 (用大头针等)别住 biézhù, 钉住 dìngzhù. 2 使不能行动[動] shǐ bùnéng xíngdòng. 3 *on* 将[將]某事(如责怪、希望等)附加在某人身上 jiāng mǒushì fùjiā zài mǒurén shēn shàng. 4 [短语动词] **pin sb down** 强使承担 qiángshǐ chéngdān. **pin sth down** 明确[確]说明某事 míngquè shuōmíng mǒushì: *The nature of beauty is difficult to ~ down*. 美的性质是很难确切说清楚的. **'pin-up** *n* [C] (钉在墙上的美人等的)画[畫]像 huàxiàng; 照片 zhàopiàn.

PIN /pɪn/ *abbr* personal identification number 个[個]人识[識]别码[碼] gèrén shíbiémǎ.

pinafore /ˈpɪnəfɔː(r)/ *n* [C] 连胸围[圍]裙 lián xiōng wéiqún.

pincer /ˈpɪnsə(r)/ *n* 1 **pincers** [pl] 钳子 qiánzi. 2 [C] 螯 áo.

pinch /pɪntʃ/ *v* 1 [T] 捏 niē; 拧[擰] níng; 掐 qiā. 2 [I] 挤[擠]痛 jǐ tòng; 夹[夾]痛 jiā tòng: *These shoes ~*. 这双鞋挤脚. 3 [T] [非正式用语] 偷取 tōuqǔ. **pinch** *n* 1 [C] 捏 niē; 拧 níng; 掐 qiā. 2 [C] (一)撮 cuō; 少量 shǎoliàng: *a ~ of salt* 一撮盐. 3 **the pinch** [sing] 拮据 jiéjū: *feel the ~* 感到手头拮据. 4 [习语] **at a 'pinch** 必要时[時] bìyàoshí. **take sth with a pinch of salt** ⇨ SALT.

pine[1] /paɪn/ *n* 1 [C] (亦作 **'pine tree**) 松树[樹] sōngshù. 2 [U] 松木 sōngmù.

pine[2] /paɪn/ *v* [I] (*for*; *to*) 1 (因生离死别而)痛苦 tòngkǔ: ~ *for one's lover* 苦思自己的情人. 2 渴望 kěwàng.

pineapple /ˈpaɪnæpl/ *n* [C, U] 凤[鳳]梨 fènglí; 菠萝[蘿] bōluó.

ping /pɪŋ/ *v* [I], *n* [C] 发[發]出砰(或铛等)的响[響]声[聲] fāchū pēngde xiǎngshēng; 砰 pēng; 铛[鐺] dāng.

ping-pong /ˈpɪŋpɒŋ/ *n* [U] = TABLE TENNIS (TABLE).

pinion[1] /ˈpɪnɪən/ *v* [T] 绑住(人的双臂) bǎngzhù.

pinion[2] /ˈpɪnɪən/ *n* [C] 小齿[齒]轮[輪] xiǎo chǐlún; 副齿轮 fù chǐlún.

pink /pɪŋk/ *adj* 粉红色的 fěnhóngsède; 淡红色的 dànhóngsède. **pink** *n* 1 [U] 粉红色 fěnhóngsè. 2 [C] 石竹 shízhú. 3 [习语] **in the pink** 健康状[狀]况很好的 jiànkāng zhuàngkuàng hěnhǎo de.

pinnacle /ˈpɪnəkl/ *n* [C] 1 (建筑上的)小尖塔 xiǎo jiāntǎ; 尖顶 jiāndǐng. 2 尖锥形岩石 jiānzhuīxíng yánshí. 3 [常作 sing] [喻] 顶峰 dǐngfēng: *the ~ of her career* 她事业的顶峰.

pinpoint ⇨ PIN[1].

pin-stripe ⇨ PIN[1].

pint /paɪnt/ *n* [C] 1 品脱(液量或干量单位, 作液量单位时等于$\frac{1}{8}$加仑, 或 0.568 升) pǐntuō. 2 一品脱啤酒(或牛奶) yìpǐntuō píjiǔ.

Pinyin /pɪnˈjɪn/ *n* [U] 拼音 pīnyīn.

pioneer /ˌpaɪəˈnɪə(r)/ *n* [C] 1 拓荒者 tuòhuāngzhě;开〔開〕发〔發〕者 kāifāzhě. 2 先驱〔驅〕者 xiānqūzhě;创〔創〕始人 chuàngshǐrén;先锋 xiānfēng. **pioneer** *v* [T] 当〔當〕拓荒者 dāng tuòhuāngzhě;当先驱者 dāng xiānqūzhě.

pious /ˈpaɪəs/ *adj* 虔诚的 qiánchéngde;虔敬的 qiánjìngde. **piously** *adv*.

pip[1] /pɪp/ *n* [C] (苹果、桔子、葡萄等的)种〔種〕子 zhǒngzi.

pip[2] /pɪp/ *n* **the pips** [pl] (广播中的)报〔報〕时〔時〕信号〔號〕bàoshí xìnhào.

pip[3] /pɪp/ *v* [-pp-] [习语]**pip sb at the post** 在最后〔後〕一刻击〔擊〕败 zài zuìhòu yíkè jībài.

pipe[1] /paɪp/ *n* 1 [C] 管子 guǎnzi. 2 [C] 烟斗 yāndǒu. 3 [C]管乐〔樂〕器 guǎnyuèqì. 4 **pipes** [pl] = BAGPIPES. ˈ**pipe-dream** *n* [C] 白日梦〔夢〕báirìmèng;不能实〔實〕现的计划〔劃〕(或希望等) bùnéng shíxiàn de jìhuà. ˈ**pipeline** *n* 1 [C] (长距离输送油、气等的)管道 guǎndào. 2 [习语]**in the** ˈ**pipeline** 在准〔準〕备〔備〕中 zài zhǔnbèi zhōng;即将〔將〕发〔發〕生 jíjiāng fāshēng.

pipe[2] /paɪp/ *v* 1 [T] 用管道输〔輸〕送(水、煤气等) yòng guǎndào shūsòng. 2[I,T] 用管乐〔樂〕器吹奏 yòng guǎnyuèqì chuīzòu. 3 [短语动词] **pipe down** [非正式用语]安静〔靜〕下来〔來〕ānjìng xiàlái;停止讲〔講〕话 tíngzhǐ jiǎnghuà. **pipe up** [非正式用语](突然)开〔開〕始说 kāishǐ shuō. **piped music** *n* [U] 在公共场〔場〕所连续〔續〕播放的轻〔輕〕音乐 zài gōnggòng chǎngsuǒ liánxù bōfàng de qīngyīnyuè.

piper /ˈpaɪpə(r)/ *n* [C] 吹奏者 chuīzòuzhě.

piping /ˈpaɪpɪŋ/ *n* [U] 管道 guǎndào;管道系统 guǎndào xìtǒng. **piping** *adj* (人声)尖声〔聲〕的 jiānshēngde. **piping** ˈ**hot** *adj* (食物)滚〔滾〕烫的 gǔntàngde.

piquant /ˈpiːkənt/ *adj* 1 辛辣的 xīnlàde;开〔開〕胃的 kāiwèide. 2 刺激的 cìjīde;振奋〔奮〕的 zhènfènde. **piquancy** /-ənsɪ/ *n* [U]. **piquantly** *adv*.

pique /piːk/ *n* [U] (因自尊心受到伤害的)激怒 jīnù;生气〔氣〕shēngqì. **pique** *v* [T] [常用被动语态]伤〔傷〕害…的自尊心 shānghài…de zìzūnxīn.

piracy /ˈpaɪərəsɪ/ *n* [U] 1 海上掠夺〔奪〕hǎishàng lüèduó;海盗行为〔爲〕hǎidào xíngwéi. 2 侵犯版权〔權〕qīnfàn bǎnquán;非法翻印 fēifǎ fānyìn.

piranha /pɪˈrɑːnjə/ *n* [C] 比拉鱼(南美淡水中出产的食肉小鱼) bǐlāyú;水虎鱼 shuǐhǔyú.

pirate /ˈpaɪərət/ *n* [C] 1(尤指旧时)海盗 hǎidào;(海上)掠夺〔奪〕者 lüèduózhě. 2 侵犯版权〔權〕者 qīnfàn bǎnquán zhě. **pirate** *v* [T] 非法翻印 fēifǎ fānyìn;盗用 dàoyòng.

pirouette /ˌpɪrʊˈet/ *n* [C] (芭蕾舞的)单〔單〕足(或单脚尖)旋转〔轉〕dānzú xuánzhuǎn. **pirouette** *v* [I] 用单足(或单脚尖)旋转 yòng dānzú xuánzhuǎn.

piss /pɪs/ *v* [⚠俚] 1 [I] 撒尿 sāniào. 2 [短语动词]**piss off** [尤用于英国英语]滚开〔開〕gǔnkāi. **piss** *n* [⚠俚] 1 尿 niào. 2 [习语]**take the piss (out of sb)** 取笑(某人) qǔxiào. **pissed** *adj* [英国 ⚠俚语]喝醉的 hēzuìde.

pistol /ˈpɪstl/ *n* [C] 手枪〔槍〕shǒuqiāng.

piston /ˈpɪstən/ *n* [C] 活塞 huósāi.

pit /pɪt/ *n* 1 [C] 坑 kēng;深坑 shēnkēng. 2 [C] 矿〔礦〕井 kuàngjǐng;坑道 kēngdào: *a* ˈ*gravel-* ~ 采石场. 3 [C]煤矿 méikuàng. 4 [C] (动物身体上的)凹部 āobù;窝〔窩〕wō: *the* ~ *of the stomach* 胸口(或心窝). 5[C] (天花留下的)麻点〔點〕mádiǎn;痘痕 dòuhén. 6 [C] 乐〔樂〕池 yuèchí. 7 **the pits** [pl] (赛车道旁的)检〔檢〕修加油站 jiǎnxiū jiāyóuzhàn. 8 [习语]**be the pits** [非正式用语]极〔極〕坏〔壞〕jíhuài;最糟糕 zuì zāogāo. **pit** *v* [-tt-] 1 [T] 使留下麻点 shǐ liúxià mádiǎn;使有凹陷 shǐ yǒu āoxiàn. 2 [短语动词]**pit sb/sth against sb** 使某人(或某事)与〔與〕他人较量 shǐ mǒurén yǔ tārén jiàoliàng.

pitch[1] /pɪtʃ/ *n* 1 [C] (足球、板球等)球场〔場〕qiúchǎng. 2 [U] 声〔聲〕音的高低度 shēngyīnde gāodīdù. 3 [sing] 程度 chéngdù;强度 qiángdù: *The excitement reached a high* ~. 高度兴奋. 4 [C] [尤用于英国英语](商贩的)摊〔攤〕位 tānwèi. 5 [C]商品推销员的用语 shāngpǐn tuīxiāoyuán de yòngyǔ: *a clever sales* ~ 精明的推销用语.

pitch[2] /pɪtʃ/ *v* 1 [T] 投 tóu;掷〔擲〕zhì;扔 rēng;抛 pāo. 2 [I,T] (使向前或向外)跌倒 diēdǎo. 3 [I] (船、飞机)颠簸 diānbǒ. 4 [T]搭(帐篷) dā;扎〔紮〕(营) zhā. 5 [T] (音乐)定…的音调 dìng…de yīndiào. 6 [T] 以某水平表达〔達〕yǐ mǒu shuǐpíng biǎodá. 7 [短语动词]**pitch in** (a) 使劲〔勁〕干〔幹〕shǐjìn gàn. (b)协〔協〕力相助 xiélì xiāngzhù. **pitch into sb** [非正式用语]猛烈攻击〔擊〕某人 měngliè gōngjī mǒurén. **pitched** ˈ**battle** *n* [C] 对〔對〕阵战〔戰〕duìzhènzhàn. ˈ**pitchfork** *n* [C] 干〔乾〕草叉 gāncǎochā.

pitch[3] /pɪtʃ/ *n* [U] 沥〔瀝〕青 lìqīng. ˌ**pitch-**ˈ**black** *adj* 乌〔烏〕黑的 wūhēide;漆黑的 qīhēide.

pitcher[1] /ˈpɪtʃə(r)/ *n* [C] 1[尤用于英国英语](双柄的)大罐 dàguàn;大壶〔壺〕dàhú. 2 [美语]罐 guàn.

pitcher[2] /ˈpɪtʃə(r)/ *n* [C] (棒球的)投手 tóushǒu.

piteous /ˈpɪtɪəs/ *adj* [正式用语]可怜〔憐〕的 kěliánde;值得同情的 zhíde tóngqíng de: *a* ~ *cry* 令人怜悯的哭声. **piteously** *adv*.

pitfall /ˈpɪtfɔːl/ *n* [C] 意想不到的困难〔難〕(或危险) yìxiǎng bú dào de kùnnan.

pith /pɪθ/ *n* [U] (木)髓 suí. **pithy** *adj*

P

[-ier, -iest] 1 简练〔練〕的 jiǎnliànde: ～ *remarks* 简要的评论. 2 多髓的 duōsuǐde. pithily *adv*.

pitiable /ˈpɪtɪəbl/ *adj* 1 可怜〔憐〕的 kěliánde; 令人怜悯〔憫〕的 lìng rén liánmǐn de. 2 可鄙的 kěbǐde. pitiably *adv*.

pitiful /ˈpɪtɪfl/ *adj* 1 可怜〔憐〕的 kěliánde; 令人同情的 lìng rén tóngqíng de. 2 可鄙的 kěbǐde. pitifully *adv*.

pitiless /ˈpɪtɪlɪs/ *adj* 无〔無〕情的 wúqíngde; 无怜〔憐〕悯〔憫〕心的 wú liánmǐnxīn de; 残〔殘〕酷的 cánkùde. pitilessly *adv*.

pittance /ˈpɪtns/ *n* [常作 sing] 微薄的收入 wēibóde shōurù.

pity /ˈpɪtɪ/ *n* 1 [U] 怜〔憐〕悯〔憫〕 liánmǐn; 同情 tóngqíng. 2 [sing] 可悲的事 kěbēide shì; 遗憾的事 yíhànde shì: *It's a ～ (that) the weather isn't better*. 天气不见好, 真遗憾. 3 [习语] ˌmore's the ˈpity [非正式用语] 真不幸 zhēn búxìng. take ˈpity on sb 出于同情而帮〔幫〕助某人 chūyú tóngqíng ér bāngzhù mǒurén. pity *v* [*pt*, *pp* -ied] [T] 同情 tóngqíng; 怜悯 liánmǐn.

pivot /ˈpɪvət/ *n* 1 枢〔樞〕轴〔軸〕 shūzhóu; 支点〔點〕 zhīdiǎn; 中心点 zhōngxīndiǎn. 2 [喻] 中心人物 zhōngxīn rénwù; 关〔關〕键人物 guānjiàn rénwù; 中枢 zhōngshū; 要点 yàodiǎn. pivot *v* [I] 在枢轴上转〔轉〕动〔動〕 zài shūzhóu shàng zhuàndòng. pivotal *adj*.

pixel /ˈpɪksel/ *n* [C] 像素 xiàngsù.

pixie (亦作 pixy) /ˈpɪksɪ/ *n* [C] [*pl* -ies] 小精灵〔靈〕 xiǎo jīnglíng; 小仙子 xiǎo xiānzǐ.

P

pizza /ˈpiːtsə/ *n* [C, U] 比萨〔薩〕饼(涂有奶酪、番茄酱的意大利式烘饼) bǐsàbǐng.

placard /ˈplækɑːd/ *n* [C] 布告 bùgào; 招贴 zhāotiē; 海报〔報〕 hǎibào.

placate /pləˈkeɪt; *US* ˈpleɪkeɪt/ *v* [T] 使息怒 shǐ xīnù; 抚〔撫〕慰 fǔwèi.

place[1] /pleɪs/ *n* 1 [C] 城 chéng; 镇 zhèn; 村 cūn: *Canada is a big ～*. 加拿大是个大地方. 2 [C] (作特定用途的) 建筑〔築〕物或场〔場〕所 jiànzhùwù huò chǎngsuǒ: *a ˈmeeting-～* 会面地点. 3 [C] 地方 dìfang; 场所 chǎngsuǒ; 所在地 suǒzàidì. 4 [C] 坐位 zuòwèi; 位置 wèizhi. 5 [sing] (社会) 地位 dìwèi; 等级 děngjí; 身份 shēnfen. 6 [C] 职〔職〕位 (或职务) zhíwèi; 学〔學〕习〔習〕的机〔機〕会〔會〕 xuéxíde jīhuì: *get a ～ at university* 得到在大学学习的机会. 7 [C] 恰当〔當〕(或合适) 的位置 qiàdàngde wèizhi: *Put everything away in the right ～*. 把东西放到该放的地方去. 8 [C, 常作 sing] (竞赛中获胜者的) 名次 míngcì. 9 [sing] (辩论等的) 层〔層〕次 céngcì; 步骤 bùzhòu: *in the first ～* 第一点. 10 [C, 常作 sing] [非正式用语] 家 jiā: *come to my ～* 到我家来. 11 Place [sing] [尤用于英国英语] (用于广场或较短的街道的名称). 12 [C] (在餐桌上为某人) 摆〔擺〕好餐具 bǎihǎo cānjù: *lay / set a ～* 摆上一套餐具. 13 [习语] all ˈover the place [非正式用语] (a) 到处〔處〕 dàochù. (b) 凌乱〔亂〕 língluàn. in / out of place (a) 在平常(或应在)的位置 zài píngchángde wèizhi; 不在平常(或应在)的位置 búzài píngchángde wèizhi. (b) 合适〔適〕的 héshìde; 不合适的 bù héshì de: *His remarks were out of ～*. 他的话不合时宜. in place of sb / sth 代替某人(或某物) dàitì mǒurén: *Machines can do this job in ～ of people*. 机器能代替人做这项工作. put sb in his / her ˈplace 使某人安分 shǐ mǒurén ānfèn. take ˈplace 发〔發〕生 fāshēng. take the place of sb / sth 代替某人(或某物) dàitì mǒurén.

place[2] /pleɪs/ *v* [T] 1 放置 fàngzhì. 2 任命 rènmìng. 3 (向某公司) 发〔發〕出 (定单) fāchū. 4 认〔認〕出 rènchū: *I know her face, but I can't ～ her*. 她的面孔我很熟, 但记不清她是谁了. placement *n* [U] 放置 fàngzhì; 安置 ānzhì; 辨认 biànrèn.

placenta /pləˈsentə/ *n* [C] [*pl* -tae /-tiː/ 或 ～s] [解剖] 胎盘〔盤〕 tāipán.

placid /ˈplæsɪd/ *adj* 平静的 píngjìngde; 平和的 pínghéde. placidly *adv*.

plagiarize /ˈpleɪdʒəraɪz/ *v* [T] 抄袭〔襲〕(他人的作品、学说等) chāoxí; 剽窃〔竊〕 piáoqiè. plagiarism /-rɪzəm/ *n* [C, U].

plague /pleɪg/ *n* 1 [C, U] 瘟疫 wēnyì. 2 [C] [喻] 麻烦 máfan; 祸〔禍〕患 huòhuàn: *a ～ of locusts* 蝗灾. plague *v* [T] (*with*) 烦扰〔擾〕 fánrǎo: *They ～d him with questions*. 他们用种种问题使他烦恼.

plaice /pleɪs/ *n* [C, U] [*pl* plaice] 鲽 dié.

plaid /plæd/ *n* [C, U] (苏格兰高地人用的) 长〔長〕披肩 cháng pījiān.

plain[1] /pleɪn/ *adj* 1 无〔無〕装〔裝〕饰〔飾〕的 wú zhuāngshì de; 朴〔樸〕素的 pǔsùde; 简单〔單〕的 jiǎndānde. 2 清楚的 qīngchude; 明白的 míngbaide; 易懂的 yìdǒngde. 3 (人、言行等) 真诚的 zhēnchéngde; 坦率的 tǎnshuàide. 4 不漂亮的 bú piàoliàng de; 不好看的 bù hǎokàn de: *a ～ girl* 不漂亮的女孩. 5 [习语] ˌplain ˈsailing 轻〔輕〕而易举〔舉〕的行动〔動〕 qīng ér yì jǔ de xíngdòng; 十分顺利 shífēn shùnlì. plain *adv* 清楚地 qīngchude; 完全地 wánquánde. ˈplain-clothes *adj* (尤指警察) 便衣的 biànyīde. plainly *adv*. plainness *n* [U]. ˈplain-ˌspoken *adj* 说话坦率的 shuōhuà tǎnshuài de; 直言的 zhíyánde.

plain[2] /pleɪn/ *n* [C] 平原 píngyuán; 平地 píngdì.

plaintiff /ˈpleɪntɪf/ *n* [C] [法律] 原告 yuángào.

plaintive /ˈpleɪntɪv/ *adj* 哀伤〔傷〕的 āishāngde；悲哀的 bēi'āide. **plaintively** *adv*.

plait /plæt/ *v* [T] 把…编成辫 bǎ…biānchéng biàn. **plait** *n* [C] 发〔髮〕辫 fàbiàn；辫状〔狀〕物 biànzhuàngwù.

plan /plæn/ *n* [C] 1 计划〔劃〕jìhuà；规划 guīhuà；方案 fāng'àn：*make ~s for the holidays* 作度假计划. 2(机器部件的)图〔圖〕解 tújiě. 3(建筑、城市、花园等)平面图 píngmiàntú. **plan** *v* [-nn-] [I, T] 订计划 dìng jìhuà. **planner** *n* [C] 设计者 shèjìzhě；策划者 cèhuàzhě.

plane[1] /pleɪn/ *n* [C] 1 = AEROPLANE. 2 [几何]平面 píngmiàn. 3 [喻](思想、存在等的)水平 shuǐpíng；程度 chéngdù；阶〔階〕段 jiēduàn. **plane** *adj* 平的 píngde；平面的 píngmiànde.

plane[2] /pleɪn/ *n* [C] 刨子 bàozi；木工刨 mùgōngbào. **plane** *v* [T] 刨平 bào píng；刨光 bào guāng.

plane[3] /pleɪn/ (亦作 'plane-tree) *n* [C] 悬〔懸〕铃木(树) xuánlíngmù.

planet /ˈplænɪt/ *n* [C] 行星 xíngxīng. **planetary** /-trɪ/ *adj*.

plank /plæŋk/ *n* [C] 厚(木)板 hòubǎn. **planking** *n* [U] 板材 bǎncái；地板 dìbǎn.

plankton /ˈplæŋktən/ *n* [U] 浮游生物 fúyóu shēngwù.

plant[1] /plɑːnt; *US* plænt/ *n* 1 [C] 植物 zhíwù. 2 [U](用于工业生产中的)机〔機〕器 jīqì；设备〔備〕shèbèi. 3 工厂〔廠〕gōngchǎng.

plant[2] /plɑːnt; *US* plænt/ *v* [T] 1 种〔種〕植 zhòngzhí；栽种 zāizhòng. 2 使固定 shǐ gùdìng；插 chā；放置 fàngzhì. 3 (*on*) [非正式用语]栽(赃) zāi. 4 [非正式用语]使(某人)秘密加入一集团〔團〕shǐ…mìmì jiārù yì jítuán；安插(间谍等) ānchā. **planter** *n* [C] (农场的)种植者 zhòngzhízhě；经〔經〕营〔營〕者 jīngyíngzhě.

plantation /plænˈteɪʃn/ *n* [C] 种〔種〕植园〔園〕zhòngzhíyuán；大农〔農〕场〔場〕dà nóngchǎng.

plaque[1] /plɑːk; *US* plæk/ *n* [C] (装于墙上作饰物、纪念物的石质或金属等制的)饰〔飾〕板 shìbǎn.

plaque[2] /plɑːk; *US* plæk/ *n* [U] [医学]牙斑 yábān；齿〔齒〕菌斑 chǐjūnbān.

plasma /ˈplæzmə/ *n* [U] 血浆〔漿〕xuèjiāng.

plaster /ˈplɑːstə(r); *US* ˈplæs-/ *n* 1 [U] 灰泥 huīní. 2[U] (亦作 ˌplaster of ˈParis) 熟石膏 shúshígāo；烧〔燒〕石膏 shāoshígāo：*Her leg is still in ~.* 她的腿至今仍打着石膏. 3 [C, U] 橡皮膏 xiàngpígāo. **plaster** *v* [T] 1 在…上抹灰泥 zài…shàng mǒ huīní. 2 厚厚地涂〔塗〕抹 hòuhòude túmǒ：*hair ~ed with oil* 抹油的头发. ˈ**plaster cast** *n* [C] 1 石膏绷带〔帶〕shígāo bēngdài. 2 石膏模型 shígāo móxíng. **plastered** *adj* [俚]醉的 zuìde. **plasterer** *n* [C] 抹灰工 mǒhuīgōng；粉刷工 fěnshuāgōng.

plastic /ˈplæstɪk/ *n* [U, C] 塑料 sùliào. **plastic** *adj* 1 塑料的 sùliàode. 2 可塑的 kěsùde. **plasticity** /plæˈstɪsətɪ/ *n* [U]. ˌ**plastic** ˈ**surgery** *n* [U] 整形外科 zhěngxíng wàikē.

plasticine (亦作 **Plasticine**) /ˈplæstɪsiːn/ *n* [U] 橡皮泥 xiàngpíní；彩泥 cǎiní.

plate /pleɪt/ *n* 1 [C] (a) 盘〔盤〕子 pánzi；碟子 diézi. (b) 一盘食物 yìpán shíwù. 2 [U] 金的(或银的)餐具 jīnde cānjù. 3 [C] 金属〔屬〕镀层〔層〕jīnshǔ dùcéng. 4 [C] (a) (金属等制的印刷用的)版 bǎn；印版 yìnbǎn. (b)(书籍的)整版插图〔圖〕zhěngbǎn chātú. 5 [习语] **hand/give sb sth on a** ˈ**plate** 把某物奉送某人 bǎ mǒuwù fèngsòng mǒurén；乐〔樂〕意地给某人某物 lèyìde gěi mǒurén mǒuwù. **on one's** ˈ**plate** [非正式用语]要做的工作(或要办的事) yàozuòde gōngzuò：*I've got a lot on my ~ at the moment.* 目前我有很多事要做. **plate** *v* [T] 镀上(尤指镀金、镀银) dù shàng. ˌ**plate** ˈ**glass** *n* [U] 厚玻璃板 hòu bōlibǎn.

plateau /ˈplætəʊ; *US* plæˈtəʊ/ *n* [C] [pl ~s 或 -eaux /-təʊz/] 1 高原 gāoyuán. 2 (上升或发展后的)稳〔穩〕定状〔狀〕态〔態〕wěndìng zhuàngtài：*prices have reached a ~* 物价趋于平稳.

platform /ˈplætfɔːm/ *n* [C] 1(火车站的)月台〔臺〕yuètái；站台 zhàntái. 2 讲〔講〕台 jiǎngtái；舞台 wǔtái；戏〔戲〕台 xìtái. 3 (政党在选举前发表的)政纲〔綱〕zhènggāng；纲领 gānglǐng. 4 (计算机)平台 píngtái.

plating /ˈpleɪtɪŋ/ *n* [U] (金或银等的)镀层〔層〕dùcéng.

platinum /ˈplætɪnəm/ *n* [U] 铂 bó；白金 báijīn.

platitude /ˈplætɪtjuːd; *US* -tuːd/ *n* [C] [正式用语]陈词滥〔濫〕调 chéncí làndiào.

platonic /pləˈtɒnɪk/ *adj* (两人的爱或友谊)亲〔親〕密的 qīnmìde；纯友谊的 chún yǒuyí de.

platoon /pləˈtuːn/ *n* [C] [军事]排 pái.

platter /ˈplætə(r)/ *n* [C] 1 大浅〔淺〕盘〔盤〕dàqiǎnpán. 2[英古语](木制的)盘 pán；碟 dié.

platypus /ˈplætɪpəs/ *n* [C] ˌ**duck-billed** ˈ**platypus** 鸭〔鴨〕嘴兽〔獸〕yāzuǐshòu.

plausible /ˈplɔːzəbl/ *adj* 似乎有理的 sìhū yǒulǐ de；似乎正确〔確〕的 sìhū zhèngquè de. **plausibly** *adv*.

play[1] /pleɪ/ *n* 1 [U] 游戏〔戲〕yóuxì；玩耍 wánshuǎ. 2 [U] (体育等的)比赛(作风) bǐsài；运〔運〕动〔動〕(表现) yùndòng. 3 [C] 剧〔劇〕本 jùběn；戏剧 xìjù. 4 [U] 轻〔輕〕快的活动(或移动) qīngkuàide huódòng：*the ~ of sunlight on water* 阳光在水面上闪烁. 5 [U] 自由活动(空间) zìyóu huódòng：*a lot of ~ in the rope* 绳子可以大大放开. 6 [习语] **bring sth/come into** ˈ**play** (使某事)发〔發〕生影响〔響〕(或作用)

P

fāshēng yǐngxiǎng. **a play on 'words** = PUN. **'play-act** *v* [I] 做作 zuòzuò; 假装〔裝〕jiǎzhuāng. **'playboy** *n* [C] (尤指年轻的)寻〔尋〕欢〔歡〕作乐〔樂〕的男子 xún huān zuò lè de nánzi; 花花公子 huāhuā gōngzǐ. **'playground** *n* [C] 游戏场〔場〕yóuxìchǎng; (学校的)操场 cāochǎng. **'playgroup** *n* [C] (学龄前的)幼儿〔兒〕学〔學〕校 yòu'ér xuéxiào. **'playhouse** *n* [C] = THEATRE. **'playmate** *n* [C] 游戏伙〔夥〕伴 yóuxì huǒbàn. **'play-pen** *n* [C] (供婴儿在内玩的携带式)游戏围〔圍〕栏〔欄〕yóuxì wéilán. **'plaything** *n* [C] **1** 玩具 wánjù. **2** [喻] 被玩弄的人 bèi wánnòngde rén. **playwright** /'pleɪraɪt/ *n* [C] 剧作家 jùzuòjiā.

play² /pleɪ/ *v* **1** [I] 玩 wán; 游戏〔戲〕yóuxì. **2** [I, T] (*at*) 装〔裝〕扮 zhuāngbàn; 假装 jiǎzhuāng. **3** [I, T] 参〔參〕加(比赛等) cānjiā; 同(某人)比赛 tóng…bǐsài. **4** [T] (板球、足球等)踢 tī; 传〔傳〕chuán. **5** [I, T] (a) 下(棋) xià; 移动〔動〕(棋子) yídòng. (b) (纸牌)出牌 chūpái. **6** [I, T] 演奏(乐器) yǎnzòu. **7** [T] (唱片等)播放 bōfàng. **8** [T] 上演(戏剧) shàngyǎn; 扮演(角色) bànyǎn. **9** [T] [非正式用语]以某种〔種〕方式表现 yǐ mǒuzhǒng fāngshì biǎoxiàn: ~ *the fool* 做蠢事. ~ (*it*) *safe* 持慎重态度. **10** [T] (*on*) 开〔開〕(玩笑) kāi; 逗弄 dòunòng: ~ *a joke/trick on sb* 开(某人)玩笑; 作弄某人. **11** [T] 将〔將〕…对〔對〕准〔準〕(某处) jiāng…duìzhǔn: ~ *water on a burning building* 向燃烧的建筑物上喷水. **12** [I] 轻〔輕〕快地活动(或移动) qīngkuàide huódòng: *sunlight ~ing on the lake* 湖面上闪动的阳光. **13** [习语] **play 'ball** [非正式用语]合作 hézuò. **play sth by 'ear** 临〔臨〕机〔機〕应〔應〕变〔變〕lín jī yìngbiàn: *We'll ~ it by ear depending on the weather*. 我们将依据天气情况临时作出决定. **play one's 'cards right** 做事精明 zuò shì jīngmíng; 处〔處〕理得当〔當〕chǔlǐ dédàng. **play it 'cool** [非正式用语]泰然处〔處〕之 tàirán chǔ zhī. **play for 'time** (以拖延的手段)争取时〔時〕间 zhēngqǔ shíjiān. **play the 'game** 办〔辦〕事公道 bànshì gōngdào; 为〔爲〕人正直 wéi rén zhèngzhí. **play gooseberry** [非正式用语]不知趣的第三者 bùzhīqùde dìsānzhě. **play hell with sth** [非正式用语]给某事造成麻烦 gěi mǒushì zàochéng máfan. **play into sb's 'hands** 做有利于(对手)的蠢事 zuò yǒulì yú…de chǔnshì. **play a part (in sth)** 参〔參〕加 cānjiā; 对某事起作用 duì mǒushì qǐ zuòyòng. **play second 'fiddle (to sb)** 居次位 jū cìwèi. **14** [短语动词] **play a'long (with sb/sth)** 假装与〔與〕某人合作 jiǎzhuāng yǔ mǒurén hézuò; 假意参与某事 jiǎyì cānyù mǒushì. **'play at sth** (a) 敷衍地做 fūyǎnde zuò. (b) **what sb is playing at** (表示愤怒)某人在搞什么〔麼〕名堂 mǒurén zài gǎo shénme míngtang. **play sth 'back** 播放(已录制的录音带、录像带等) bōfàng. **play sth 'down** 减低…的重要性 jiǎndī…de zhòngyàoxìng. **play sb off against sb else** 使双〔雙〕方互斗〔鬥〕以坐收渔利 shǐ shuāngfāng hùdòu yǐ zuò shōu yúlì. **play on sth** 利用(他人的情感或弱点) lìyòng. **play (sb) up** 给…带〔帶〕来痛苦(或麻烦) gěi…dàilái tòngkǔ. **play sth up** 使…显〔顯〕得重要 shǐ…xiǎnde zhòngyào. **play up to sb** 迎合 yínghé; 讨好 tǎohǎo. **play with sth** 不认〔認〕真地考虑〔慮〕(意见等) bú rènzhēnde kǎolǜ. **'play-back** *n* [U] (录音、录像的)播放 bōfàng. **'playing-card** *n* [C] 纸牌 zhǐpái; 扑〔撲〕克牌 pūkèpái. **'playing-field** *n* [C] 球场〔場〕qiúchǎng; 运〔運〕动场 yùndòngchǎng. **'play-off** *n* [C] (平局后的)延长〔長〕赛 yánchángsài; 加赛 jiāsài.

player /'pleɪə(r)/ *n* [C] **1** 游戏〔戲〕的人 yóuxìde rén; 运〔運〕动〔動〕员 yùndòngyuán. **2** 演奏者 yǎnzòuzhě: *a 'trumpet* ~ 吹奏小号的人. **3** 演员 yǎnyuán.

playful /'pleɪfl/ *adj* **1** 爱〔愛〕玩的 àiwánde; 顽皮的 wánpíde. **2** 开〔開〕玩笑的 kāi wánxiào de; 闹〔鬧〕着玩的 nàozhewánde. **playfully** *adv*. **playfulness** *n* [U].

plaza /'plɑːzə; *US* 'plæzə/ *n* [C] (城市中的)广〔廣〕场〔場〕guǎngchǎng; 集市 jíshì.

PLC (亦作 **plc**) /ˌpiː el 'siː/ *abbr* (*Brit*) Public Limited Company (英国)股份公开〔開〕有限公司 Gǔfèn Gōngkāi Yǒuxiàn Gōngsī.

plea /pliː/ *n* [C] **1** [正式用语] 恳〔懇〕求 kěnqiú; 请求 qǐngqiú: ~*s for mercy* 恳求宽恕. **2** [法律](被告在法庭上所作的)答辩 dábiàn; 申诉 shēnsù.

plead /pliːd/ *v* [*pt*, *pp* ~ed; *US* pled /pled/] **1** [I] (*with*) 再三恳〔懇〕求(或请求) zàisān kěnqiú. **2** [T] [法律]承认〔認〕chéngrèn; 认(罪) rèn. **3** [I] *for* [法律](律师)(在法庭上为原告或被告)提出申诉 tíchū shēnsù; 答辩 dábiàn; 辩护〔護〕biànhù. **4** [T] 提出…为〔爲〕借〔藉〕口 tíchū…wéi jièkǒu.

pleasant /'pleznt/ *adj* **1** 令人愉快的 lìng rén yúkuài de; 可喜的 kěxǐde. **2** 友好的 yǒuhǎode; 友善的 yǒushànde. **pleasantly** *adv*. **pleasantness** *n* [U].

pleasantry /'plezntrɪ/ *n* [C] [*pl* -ies] [正式用语]有礼〔禮〕貌的话 yǒu lǐmàode huà; 客气〔氣〕话 kèqìhuà.

please /pliːz/ *interj* (用于客气的请求): *Come in*, ~. 请进. **please** *v* **1** [I, T] (使)高兴〔興〕gāoxìng; (使)满意 mǎnyì. **2** [I] 选〔選〕择〔擇〕xuǎnzé; 想要 xiǎngyào: *He does as he ~s*. 他喜欢怎么做就怎么做. **pleased** *adj* 高兴的 gāoxìngde; 满意的 mǎnyìde: *She was very ~d with her exam results*. 她对考试结果非常满意. **pleasing** *adj* (*to*) 令人高兴的 lìng rén gāoxìng de; 合意的 héyìde.

pleasure /'pleʒə(r)/ *n* **1** [U] 愉快 yúkuài; 高

P

兴〔興〕gāoxìng；满足 mǎnzú. 2 [C] 乐〔樂〕事 lèshì；快事 kuàishì：*It's a ～ to help you*. 帮助你是件乐事. **pleasurable** /-ərəbl/ *adj* [正式用语]令人愉快的 lìng rén yúkuài de；使人高兴的 shǐ rén gāoxìng de. ˈ**pleasure-boat** *n* [C] 游船 yóuchuán；游艇 yóutǐng.

pleat /pliːt/ *n* [C] 褶 zhě. **pleat** *v* [T] 给…打褶 gěi…dǎzhě.

plectrum /ˈplektrəm/ *n* [C] [*pl* ～s 或 -tra /-trə/] (弹奏弦乐器用的)拨〔撥〕子 bōzi；琴拨 qínbō.

pled [美语] *pt, pp* of PLEAD.

pledge /pledʒ/ *n* [C] 1 誓言 shìyán；誓约 shìyuē；诺言 nuòyán；保证〔證〕bǎozhèng. 2 抵押品 dǐyāpǐn；典当〔當〕物 diǎndàngwù. 3 (表示爱情的)信物 xìnwù. **pledge** *v* [T] 1 保证给予 bǎozhèng jǐyǔ；许诺 xǔnuò；发〔發〕誓 fāshì. 2 保证做某事 bǎozhèng zuò mǒushì：*The government has ～d itself to fight poverty*. 政府已承诺与贫困作斗争.

plenary /ˈpliːnərɪ/ *adj* (会议)全体〔體〕出席的 quántǐ chūxí de：*a ～ session* 全体会议.

plentiful /ˈplentɪfl/ *adj* 大量的 dàliàngde；丰〔豐〕富的 fēngfùde：*a ～ supply* 丰富的供应. **plentifully** *adv*.

plenty /ˈplentɪ/ *pron* (*of*) 丰〔豐〕富 fēngfù；充足 chōngzú；大量 dàliàng：*There's ～ of time before the train goes*. 这趟火车距发车还有很多时间.

pleurisy /ˈplʊərəsɪ/ *n* [U] 胸膜炎 xiōngmóyán.

pliable /ˈplaɪəbl/ *adj* 1 易弯〔彎〕的 yìwānde；柔韧〔韌〕的 róurènde. 2 [喻]易受影响〔響〕的 yìshòu yǐngxiǎng de. **pliability** /ˌplaɪəˈbɪlətɪ/ *n* [U].

pliant /ˈplaɪənt/ *adj* 1 易弯〔彎〕的 yìwānde；柔韧〔韌〕的 róurènde. 2 [喻]易受影响〔響〕的 yì shòu yǐngxiǎng de.

pliers /ˈplaɪəz/ *n* [pl] 钳子 qiánzi；老虎钳 lǎohǔqián.

plight /plaɪt/ *n* [sing] [正式用语]困境 kùnjìng；苦境 kǔjìng.

plimsoll /ˈplɪmsəl/ *n* [C] 橡皮底帆布鞋 xiàngpídǐ fānbùxié.

Plimsoll line /ˈplɪmsəl/ *n* [C] (船的)载〔載〕重线〔綫〕标〔標〕志 zàizhòngxiàn biāozhì；载货吃水线 zàihuò chīshuǐxiàn.

plinth /plɪnθ/ *n* [C] (柱、雕像的)底座 dǐzuò；柱基 zhùjī；基座 jīzuò.

plod /plɒd/ *v* [-dd-] 1 沉重缓慢地走 chénzhòng huǎnmàn de zǒu. 2 孜孜从〔從〕事 zīzī cóngshì；辛苦工作 xīnkǔ gōngzuò. **plodder** *n* [C] 做事慢条〔條〕斯理的人 zuò shì màntiáo sīlǐ de rén.

plonk[1] /plɒŋk/ *v* [T] (*down*) [非正式用语]重重放下(某物) zhòngzhòng fàngxià：*P～ it (down) on the chair*. 把它砰的一声扔到椅子上.

plonk[2] /plɒŋk/ *n* [U] [非正式用语，尤用于英国英语]廉价〔價〕酒 liánjiàjiǔ；劣质〔質〕酒 lièzhìjiǔ.

plop /plɒp/ *n* [C] 扑〔撲〕通声〔聲〕pūtōngshēng；啪嗒声 pādāshēng. **plop** *v* [-pp-] [I] 扑通落下 pūtōng luòxià.

plot[1] /plɒt/ *n* [C] 小块〔塊〕土地 xiǎokuài tǔdì. **plot** *v* [-tt-] [T] 1 在图〔圖〕上标〔標〕出(飞机、船的)位置 zài tú shàng biāochū…wèizhì. 2 (在图上连接标定的点)绘〔繪〕成(曲线) huìchéng.

plot[2] /plɒt/ *n* [C] 1 密谋 mìmóu；阴〔陰〕谋 yīnmóu. 2 (故事的)情节〔節〕qíngjié. **plot** *v* [-tt-] [I, T] 密谋 mìmóu；策划〔劃〕cèhuà. **plotter** *n* [C].

plough (美语 **plow**) /plaʊ/ *n* [C] 犁 lí. **plough** (美语 **plow**) *v* 1 [I, T] 犁(地) lí；耕(地) gēng. 2 [短语动词] **plough sth back** 把(利润)再投资 bǎ…zài tóuzī. **plough into sth** 猛撞某物 měng zhuàng mǒuwù. **plough (one's way) through sth** 费力通过〔過〕fèilì tōngguò；艰〔艱〕苦前进〔進〕jiānkǔ qiánjìn.

ploy /plɔɪ/ *n* [C] 策略 cèlüè；手段 shǒuduàn.

pluck /plʌk/ *v* [T] 1 拔 bá；摘 zhāi；采〔採〕cǎi：*～ flowers/fruit* 摘花；采果. 2 拔去…的毛 báqù…de máo. 3 (*at*) 拉 lā；拖 tuō；抽 chōu；扯 chě. 4 弹〔彈〕tán；拨〔撥〕(乐器的弦) bō. 5 [习语] **pluck up ˈcourage** 鼓起勇气〔氣〕gǔ qǐ yǒngqì. **pluck** *n* [U] 勇气 yǒngqì；胆〔膽〕量 dǎnliàng. **plucky** *adj* [-ier, -iest] 勇敢的 yǒnggǎnde；有胆量的 yǒu dǎnliàng de.

plug /plʌg/ *n* [C] 1 塞子 sāizi；栓 shuān. 2 插头〔頭〕chātóu；插塞 chāsāi. 3 [非正式用语](广播、电视的)推销广〔廣〕告 tuīxiāo guǎnggào. **plug** *v* [-gg-] [T] 1 用…塞住 yòng…sāi zhù；堵塞 dǔsè. 2 [非正式用语]大肆宣传〔傳〕dàsì xuānchuán；大做广告 dà zuò guǎnggào. 3 [短语动词] **plug away (at sth)** 孜孜工作 zīzī gōngzuò；苦干〔幹〕kǔgàn. **plug sth in** (插上插头)接通(电源) jiētōng. ˈ**plug-hole** *n* [C] (洗脸池等的)排水孔 páishuǐkǒng.

plum /plʌm/ *n* [C] 李子 lǐzi；梅子 méizi. **plum** *adj* [非正式用语]最好的 zuìhǎode；称〔稱〕心的 chènxīnde：*a ～ job* 美差.

plumage /ˈpluːmɪdʒ/ *n* [U] (鸟的)全身羽毛 quánshēn yǔmáo；羽衣 yǔyī.

plumb /plʌm/ *v* [T] 1 探究 tànjiū；探索 tànsuǒ. 2 [习语] **plumb the depths of sth** 到达〔達〕…的最低点〔點〕dàodá…de zuì dīdiǎn. **plumb** *adv* 恰恰 qiàqià；正 zhèng：*～ in the middle* 在正中间. ˈ**plumb-line** *n* [C] 铅垂线〔綫〕qiānchuíxiàn.

plumber /ˈplʌmə(r)/ *n* [C] 管子工 guǎnzigōng；水暖工 shuǐnuǎngōng.

P

plumbing /ˈplʌmɪŋ/ *n* [U] 1(建筑物的)管道设备〔備〕(或装置) guǎndào shèbèi; 水暖设备 shuǐnuǎn shèbèi. 2 管子工(或水暖工)的工作 guǎnzigōngde gōngzuò.

plume /pluːm/ *n* [C] 1 羽毛 yǔmáo; (尤指色彩鲜艳的)大(或长)羽 dàyǔ. 2 羽状〔狀〕物 yǔzhuàngwù: *a ~ of smoke* 一缕烟.

plummet /ˈplʌmɪt/ *v* [I] 快速落下 kuàisù luòxià; 陡直落下 dǒuzhí luòxià: *House prices have ~ed.* 房价大跌.

plump[1] /plʌmp/ *adj* 肥胖的 féipàngde; 丰〔豐〕满的 fēngmǎnde. **plump** *v* [短语动词] **plump up** (使)长〔長〕胖 zhǎng pàng; (使)变〔變〕丰满 biàn fēngmǎn. **plumpness** *n* [U].

plump[2] /plʌmp/ *v* [短语动词] **plump (oneself/sb/sth) down** (沉重或突然)倒下 dǎoxià; 落下 luòxià. **plump for sb/sth** 选〔選〕择〔擇〕 xuǎnzé; 支持 zhīchí. **plump** *n* [C, 常作 sing] (突然沉重的)坠〔墜〕落(的声音) zhuìluò.

plunder /ˈplʌndə(r)/ *v* [I, T] (尤指战时)抢〔搶〕劫 qiǎngjié; 掠夺〔奪〕 lüèduó. **plunder** *n* [U] 1 抢劫 qiǎngjié; 掠夺 lüèduó. 2 赃〔贓〕物 zāngwù; 掠夺物 lüèduówù.

plunge /plʌndʒ/ *v* [I, T] (使…)突然前倾(或向下) tūrán qiánqīng: *The car ~d into the river.* 汽车冲入河中. *He ~d his hands into his pockets.* 他把手插进口袋里. **plunge** *n* 1 [C, 常作 sing] (向前或向下的)冲〔衝〕 chōng; 投 tóu; 猛跌 měngdiē; 骤降 zhòujiàng. 2 [习语] **take the ˈplunge** 决意冒险〔險〕 juéyì màoxiǎn; 采〔採〕取决定性步骤 cǎiqǔ juédìngxìng bùzhòu. **plunger** *n* [C]柱塞 zhùsāi; 活塞 huósāi.

P

pluperfect /ˌpluːˈpɜːfɪkt/ *n* **the pluperfect** [sing] [语法]过〔過〕去完成时〔時〕 guòqù wánchéngshí.

plural /ˈplʊərəl/ *n* [常作 sing], *adj* [语法] 复〔複〕数〔數〕(的) fùshù: *The ~ of 'child' is 'children'.* child 的复数是 children.

plus /plʌs/ *prep* 1 加 jiā; 加上 jiāshàng: *One ~ two equals three.* 一加二等于三. 2 在零以上 zài líng yǐshàng. 3[非正式用语]和 hé. **plus** *adj* 在零以上的 zài líng yǐshàng de; 正的 zhèngde. **plus** (亦作 **plus sign**) *n* [C] 1 加号〔號〕 jiāhào; 正号(+) zhènghào. 2 [非正式用语]有利因素 yǒulì yīnsù.

plush /plʌʃ/ *adj* 豪华〔華〕的 háohuáde; 漂亮的 piàoliàngde.

plutonium /pluːˈtəʊnɪəm/ *n* [U] [化学]钚 bù.

ply[1] /plaɪ/ *n* [U] 1(布的)厚度 hòudù; (木的)层〔層〕 céng; (绳的)股 gǔ. 2(胶合板的)层 céng. **ˈplywood** *n* [U] 胶〔膠〕合板 jiāohébǎn.

ply[2] /plaɪ/ *v* [*pt*, *pp* **plied**] 1 [I, T] (船等沿某航线)定期航行 dìngqī hángxíng: *ferries that ~ between the islands* 定期在两岛间航行的渡船. 2 [习语] **ply one's ˈtrade** 从〔從〕事(熟练)工作 cóngshì…gōngzuò. 3 [短语动词] **ply sb with sth** (a) 不断〔斷〕供给(食物和饮料) búduàn gōngjǐ. (b) 不断提出(问题) búduàn tíchū.

PM /ˌpiː ˈem/ *abbr* [非正式用语, 尤用于英国英语]Prime Minister 首相.

pm /ˌpiː ˈem/ *abbr* afternoon 下午 xiàwǔ.

pneumatic /njuːˈmætɪk/ *adj* 1 由压〔壓〕缩空气〔氣〕推动〔動〕(或操作)的 yóu yāsuō kōngqì tuīdòng de: *a ~ drill* 风钻. 2 充气的 chōngqìde: *a ~ tyre* 气胎. **pneumatically** /-klɪ/ *adv*.

pneumonia /njuːˈməʊnɪə/ *n* [U] 肺炎 fèiyán.

PO /ˌpiː ˈəʊ/ *abbr* 1 Post Office 邮〔郵〕政局 yóuzhèngjú. 2 postal order 邮政汇〔匯〕票 yóuzhèng huìpiào.

poach[1] /pəʊtʃ/ *v* 1 [I, T](侵入他人地界)偷猎〔獵〕 tōuliè; 偷捕 tōubǔ. 2 [T] [喻]窃〔竊〕取 qièqǔ; 盗用 dàoyòng; 侵犯 qīnfàn. **poacher** *n* [C].

poach[2] /pəʊtʃ/ *v* [T] 水煮(荷包蛋、鱼等) shuǐzhǔ.

pock /pɒk/ *n* [C] **ˈpock-mark** (出天花后留下的)痘痕 dòuhén; 麻子 mázi. **ˈpock-marked** *adj* 有痘痕的 yǒu dòuhén de; 有麻子的 yǒu mázi de.

pocket /ˈpɒkɪt/ *n* [C] 1 (a) 衣袋 yīdài; 口袋 kǒudài. (b) (汽车门、衣箱等内侧的)口袋 kǒudài. 2(孤立的)小群体〔體〕(或地区) xiǎo qúntǐ: *~s of resistance* 孤军抵抗地区. 3 [常作 sing]钱〔錢〕 qián; 财力 cáilì: *within reach of everyone's ~* 为每个人财力所及. 4[习语] **ˌout of ˈpocket** 因…赔钱 yīn…péiqián. **pocket** *v* [T] 1 把…放入衣袋 bǎ…fàngrù yīdài. 2 把…据〔據〕为〔爲〕己有 bǎ…jù wéi jǐ yǒu. **pocket** *adj* 袖珍的 xiùzhēnde: *a ~ calculator* 袖珍计算器. **ˈpocket-book** *n* [C] 小笔〔筆〕记本 xiǎo bǐjìběn. **ˈpocket-money** *n* [U] 零用钱 língyòngqián.

pod /pɒd/ *n* [C] 豆荚〔莢〕 dòujiá; 荚 jiá. **pod** *v* [-dd-] [T] 剥出(豆等) bōchū.

podcast /ˈpɒdkɑːst/ *n* [C] 播客 bōkè.

podgy /ˈpɒdʒɪ/ *adj* [-ier, -iest] 矮胖的 ǎipàngde.

poem /ˈpəʊɪm/ *n* [C] 诗 shī; 韵文 yùnwén.

poet /ˈpəʊɪt/ *n* [C] 诗人 shīrén. **ˌPoet ˈLaureate** /ˈlɒrɪət; *US* ˈlɔːr-/ *n* [C] 桂冠诗人(正式任命为英国王室成员, 为特定场合作诗) guìguān shīrén.

poetic /pəʊˈetɪk/ (亦作 **poetical** /-ɪkl/) *adj* 1 有诗意的 yǒu shīyì de; 优〔優〕美的 yōuměide. 2 诗的 shīde; 韵文的 yùnwénde. **poet-**

ically /-klɪ/ *adv*.

poetry /ˈpəʊɪtrɪ/ *n* [U] 1 诗 shī. 2 诗意 shīyì: *the ~ of dance* 舞蹈的诗意.

poignant /ˈpɔɪnjənt/ *adj* 痛苦的 tòngkǔde; 伤〔傷〕心的 shāngxīnde; 辛酸的 xīnsuānde: *~ memories* 辛酸的回忆. **poignancy** /-jənsɪ/ *n* [U]. **poignantly** *adv*.

point[1] /pɔɪnt/ *n* 1 [C] 尖 jiān; 尖端 jiānduān: *the ~ of a pin/pencil* 针尖; 铅笔尖. 2 [C] 岬角 jiǎjiǎo. 3 [C] (书写、印刷用的)点〔點〕(如句点、小数点等) diǎn. 4 [C] 地点 dìdiǎn; 时〔時〕刻 shíkè. 5 [C] (进展的)程度 chéngdù; (温度的)度 dù: *ˈboiling-~* 沸点. 6 [C] 罗〔羅〕经〔經〕点(罗盘上的 32 个刻度之一) luójīngdiǎn. 7 [C] (作计量、记分单位的)点(或分) diǎn: *We won the game by six ~s.* 我们以六分胜了这一局. 8 [C] (表示意见、事项等的)点 diǎn; 条〔條〕 tiáo; 项 xiàng: *the main ~s of a story* 故事要点. 9 **the point** [sing] 要点 yàodiǎn; 核心问题 héxīn wèntí: *come to/get to the ~* 谈到正题(或关键问题). *see/miss the ~ of a joke* 明白笑话的寓意; 不明白笑话的寓意. 10 [U] 目的 mùdì; 理由 lǐyóu: *There's no ~ in going now.* 没有理由现在去. 11 [C] 特点 tèdiǎn; 特征〔徵〕 tèzhēng: *Tidiness is not his strong ~.* 他不讲究整洁. 12 [C] 插座 chāzuò. 13 **points** [pl] [英国英语](铁路的)道岔 dàochà. 14 [习语] **beside the ˈpoint** 离〔離〕题的 lítíde; 不相关〔關〕的 bù xiāngguān de. **make a point of doing sth** 打定主意做某事 dǎdìng zhǔyi zuò mǒushì; 总〔總〕是要做某事 zǒng shì yàozuò mǒushì. **on the point of doing sth** 正要做某事时〔時〕 zhèngyào zuò mǒushì shí. **a point of ˈview** 看法 kànfǎ; 观〔觀〕点 guāndiǎn. **take sb's ˈpoint** 领会〔會〕某人的论〔論〕点 lǐnghuì mǒurén de lùndiǎn. **to the ˈpoint** 中肯的(地) zhòngkěnde; 切题的(地) qiètíde.

point[2] /pɔɪnt/ *v* 1 [I] (*at/to*) 指出 zhǐchū; 指明 zhǐmíng. 2 [T] *at* 对〔對〕准〔準〕 duìzhǔn; 瞄准 miáozhǔn: *~ a gun at sb* 用枪瞄准某人. 3 [T] (用水泥等)勾(砖石墙等的)砌缝 gōu qìfèng. 4 [短语动词] **point sth out** 使注意 shǐ zhùyì. ˌ**point-and-ˈclick** *adj* 点〔點〕选〔選〕式的 diǎnxuǎnshìde. **pointed** *adj* 1 尖的 jiānde; 有尖头〔頭〕的 yǒu jiāntóu de. 2 [喻]有针对性的 yǒu zhēnduìxìng de; 直截了当〔當〕的 zhíjiéliǎodàng de: *~ remarks* 一针见血的话. **pointedly** *adv*.

point-blank /ˌpɔɪnt ˈblæŋk/ *adj*, *adv* 1 近距离〔離〕平射的(地) jìn jùlí píngshè de. 2 [喻] 直截了当〔當〕的(地) zhíjié-liǎodàng de; 断〔斷〕然的(地) duànránde: *He refused ~.* 他直截了当地拒绝了.

pointer /ˈpɔɪntə(r)/ *n* [C] 1 指物棒 zhǐwùbàng; 指示棒 zhǐshìbàng. 2 (仪表、刻度上的)指针 zhǐzhēn. 3 主意 zhǔyi; 意见 yìjiàn. 4 (短毛)猎〔獵〕犬 lièquǎn.

pointless /ˈpɔɪntlɪs/ *adj* 无〔無〕意义〔義〕的 wú yìyì de; 无目的的 wú mùdì de; 无用的 wúyòngde. **pointlessly** *adv*.

poise /pɔɪz/ *n* [U] 1 平衡 pínghéng; 均衡 jūnhéng. 2 [喻]泰然自若 tàirán zìruò; 自信 zìxìn. **poise** *v* [I,T] (使)平衡 pínghéng; 保持平衡 bǎochí pínghéng. **poised** *adj* 1 (*to*; *for*) 准〔準〕备〔備〕好行动〔動〕的 zhǔnbèi hǎo xíngdòng de. 2 [喻]镇定的 zhèndìngde; 镇静的 zhènjìngde.

poison /ˈpɔɪzn/ *n* [C] 毒药〔藥〕 dúyào; 毒物 dúwù. **poison** *v* [T] 1 给…服毒药 gěi…fú dúyào; 毒死 dúsǐ; 放毒 fàngdú. 2 [喻]破坏〔壞〕 pòhuài; 毁坏 huǐhuài. **poisonous** *adj*.

poke /pəʊk/ *v* [I,T] 1 (用棍棒等)捅 tǒng; 戳 chuō; 拨〔撥〕 bō. 2 猛推 měng tuī; 插入 chārù; 刺 cì. 3 [习语] **poke ˈfun at sb** 嘲弄某人 cháonòng mǒurén. **poke one's nose into sth** ⇨ NOSE[1]. **poke** *n* [C] 捅 tǒng; 戳 chuō; 拨 bō.

poker[1] /ˈpəʊkə(r)/ *n* [C] 拨〔撥〕火棒 bōhuǒbàng; 通条〔條〕 tōngtiáo.

poker[2] /ˈpəʊkə(r)/ *n* [U] 扑〔撲〕克牌戏〔戲〕 pūkèpáixì.

poky /ˈpəʊkɪ/ *adj* [-ier, -iest] [非正式用语, 贬]小的 xiǎode; 狭〔狹〕小的 xiáxiǎode.

polar /ˈpəʊlə(r)/ *adj* 1 地极〔極〕的 dìjíde; 近地极的 jìndìjíde. 2 [正式用语]完全相反的 wánquán xiāngfǎn de. ˈ**polar bear** *n* [C] 北极熊 běijíxióng. **polarity** /pəˈlærətɪ/ *n* [U] [正式用语] (性质、倾向等的)正好相反 zhènghǎo xiāngfǎn.

polarize /ˈpəʊləraɪz/ *v* [I,T] (使人、观点)两极〔極〕化 liǎngjíhuà: *an issue that ~d opinions* 造成意见对立的问题. **polarization** /ˌpəʊləraɪˈzeɪʃn; US -rɪˈz-/ *n* [U].

pole[1] /pəʊl/ *n* [C] 1 地极〔極〕 dìjí: *the North/South P~* 北极; 南极. 2 电〔電〕极 diànjí; 磁极 cíjí. 3 [习语] **be ˈpoles apart** 完全相反 wánquán xiāngfǎn.

pole[2] /pəʊl/ *n* [C] 杆 gān; 竿 gān; 棒 bàng; 篙 gāo. ˈ**pole-vault** *n* [C] 撑竿跳高 chēng gān tiàogāo.

polecat /ˈpəʊlkæt/ *n* [C] 鸡〔鷄〕貂 jīdiāo; 臭鼬(产于北美) chòuyòu.

police /pəˈliːs/ *n* (**the**) **police** [pl] 警察 jǐngchá; 警方 jǐngfāng; 警察部门 jǐngchá bùmén. **police** *v* [T] 维持…的治安 wéichí…de zhì'ān; 守卫〔衛〕 shǒuwèi. **poˈlice force** *n* [C] (国家、地区的)警察 jǐngchá. **poˈliceman**, **poˈlice-officer**, **poˈlicewoman** *n* [C] 男警察 nán jǐngchá; (男或女)警察 jǐngchá; 女警察 nǚ jǐngchá. **poˈlice station** *n* [C] 警察分局 jǐngchá fēnjú; 派出所 pàichūsuǒ.

P

policy /ˈpɒləsɪ/ *n* [C] [*pl* -ies] **1** 政策 zhèngcè;方针 fāngzhēn: *the Government's foreign* ~ 政府外交政策. **2** 保险〔險〕单〔單〕bǎoxiǎndān.

polio /ˈpəʊlɪəʊ/ *n* [U] 小儿〔兒〕麻痹症〔癥〕xiǎo'ér mábìzhèng;脊髓灰质〔質〕炎 jǐsuǐ huīzhìyán.

polish /ˈpɒlɪʃ/ *v* [T] **1** 磨光 mó guāng;擦亮 cā liàng. **2**(*up*) [喻]润饰 rùnshì;修改 xiūgǎi. **3** [短语动词]**polish sth off** (迅速地)完成 wánchéng;匆匆做完 cōngcōng zuòwán. **polish** *n* **1**[U] 擦光剂〔劑〕cāguāngjì;上光剂 shàngguāngjì. **2**[sing]磨光 mó guāng;擦亮 cā liàng;修饰 xiūshì. **3** [U] [喻]优〔優〕雅 yōuyǎ;完美 wánměi. **polished** *adj* 优美的 yōuměide;文雅的 wényǎde.

polite /pəˈlaɪt/ *adj* 有礼〔禮〕貌的 yǒu lǐmào de;文雅的 wényǎde. **politely** *adv*. **politeness** *n* [U].

political /pəˈlɪtɪkl/ *adj* **1** 国〔國〕家的 guójiāde;政府的 zhèngfǔde. **2** 政治的 zhèngzhìde;政党〔黨〕的 zhèngdǎngde. **3** 关〔關〕心政治的 guānxīn zhèngzhì de;对〔對〕政治感兴〔興〕趣的 duì zhèngzhì gǎn xìngqù de. **politically** /-klɪ/ *adv*. **politically correct** 政治上正确〔確〕zhèngzhìshàng zhèngquè;政治立场〔場〕正确 zhèngzhì lìchǎng zhèngquè. **politically incorrect** 政治上不正确 zhèngzhìshàng bù zhèngquè;政治立场不正确 zhèngzhì lìchǎng bù zhèngquè.

politician /ˌpɒləˈtɪʃn/ *n* [C] 政治家 zhèngzhìjiā;政客 zhèngkè.

politics /ˈpɒlətɪks/ *n* **1** [亦作 sing, 用 pl v] 政治活动〔動〕zhèngzhì huódòng;政治事务〔務〕zhèngzhì shìwù. **2** [pl] 政治观〔觀〕点〔點〕zhèngzhì guāndiǎn. **3** [用 sing v] 政治学〔學〕zhèngzhìxué.

polka /ˈpɒlkə; *US* ˈpəʊlkə/ *n* [C] 波尔〔爾〕卡舞 bō'ěrkǎwǔ;波尔卡舞曲 bō'ěrkǎ wǔqǔ.

poll /pəʊl/ *n* **1** [C] 民意测验〔驗〕(或调查) mínyì cèyàn. **2** [C] 选〔選〕举〔舉〕xuǎnjǔ. **3** [sing] (投的)票数〔數〕piàoshù. **poll** *v* [T] **1** 获〔獲〕得(若干选票) huòdé. **2** 对〔對〕…作民意测验 duì …zuò mínyì cèyàn. ˈ**polling-booth** (亦作 ˈ**polling-station**) *n* [C] 投票站 tóupiàozhàn. **poll tax** *n* [sing] [非正式用语] = COMMUNITY CHARGE (COMMUNITY).

pollen /ˈpɒlən/ *n* [U] 花粉 huāfěn.

pollinate /ˈpɒləneɪt/ *v* [T] 给…传〔傳〕授花粉 gěi…chuánshòu huāfěn. **pollination** /ˌpɒləˈneɪʃn/ *n* [U].

pollute /pəˈluːt/ *v* [T] 弄脏〔髒〕nòng zāng;污染 wūrǎn: ~*d water* 被污染的水. **pollution** /pəˈluːʃn/ *n* [U].

polo /ˈpəʊləʊ/ *n* [U] 马球 mǎqiú. ˈ**polo neck** *n* [C] 高圆翻领 gāo yuán fānlǐng.

polyester /ˌpɒlɪˈestə(r); *US* ˈpɒliːestər/ *n* [U] 聚酯纤〔纖〕维 jùzhǐ xiānwéi.

polygamy /pəˈlɪgəmɪ/ *n* [U] 一夫多妻 yìfū duōqī.

polygon /ˈpɒlɪgən; *US* -gɒn/ *n* [C] 多边〔邊〕形 duōbiānxíng;多角形 duōjiǎoxíng.

polystyrene /ˌpɒlɪˈstaɪriːn/ *n* [U] 聚苯乙烯 jùběnyǐxī.

polytechnic /ˌpɒlɪˈteknɪk/ *n* [C] 理工学〔學〕院 lǐgōngxuéyuàn.

polythene /ˈpɒlɪθiːn/ *n* [U] [化学]聚乙烯 jùyǐxī.

polyunsaturated /ˌpɒlɪʌnˈsætʃəreɪtɪd/ *adj* 多不饱和的 duōbùbǎohéde.

pomegranate /ˈpɒmɪgrænɪt/ *n* [C] 石榴(树) shíliu.

pomp /pɒmp/ *n* [U] (典礼等的)盛况 shèngkuàng;盛大的仪〔儀〕式 shèngdàde yíshì.

pompous /ˈpɒmpəs/ *adj* 自负〔負〕的 zìfùde;自大的 zìdàde. **pomposity** /pɒmˈpɒsətɪ/ *n* [U]. **pompously** *adv*.

poncho /ˈpɒntʃəʊ/ *n* [C] [*pl* ~s] 斗篷 dǒupeng.

pond /pɒnd/ *n* [C] 池塘 chítáng.

ponder /ˈpɒndə(r)/ *v* [I, T] 深思 shēnsī;仔细考虑〔慮〕zǐxì kǎolǜ.

ponderous /ˈpɒndərəs/ *adj* [正式用语] **1** 笨重的 bènzhòngde. **2**(文章、讲话)沉闷的 chénmènde,生硬的 shēngyìngde;乏味的 fáwèide. **ponderously** *adv*.

pong /pɒŋ/ *v* [I], *n* [C] [英国非正式用语]难〔難〕闻的气〔氣〕味 nánwénde qìwèi.

pontoon[1] /pɒnˈtuːn/ *n* [C] (架设浮桥用的)浮舟 fúzhōu;(作浮桥用的)平底船 píngdǐchuán.

pontoon[2] /pɒnˈtuːn/ *n* [U] [英国英语](二十一点)牌戏〔戲〕páixì.

pony /ˈpəʊnɪ/ *n* [C] [*pl* -ies] 小马 xiǎomǎ. ˈ**pony-tail** *n* [C] 马尾辫(一种发型) mǎwěibiàn.

poodle /ˈpuːdl/ *n* [C] 鬈毛狗 quánmáogǒu.

pool[1] /puːl/ *n* [C] **1** 水塘 shuǐtáng. **2** (液体等的)一滩〔灘〕yìtān: *a* ~ *of blood* 血泊. **3** = SWIMMING-POOL (SWIM).

pool[2] /puːl/ *n* **1** [C] (几个人或机构集中起来使用的)共用物(如共用款、共用物资等) gòngyòngwù;共用人员 gòngyòng rényuán: *a* ˈ*typing* ~ 打字小组. **2** [U] [尤用于美语]落袋台〔臺〕球戏〔戲〕luòdài táiqiúxì. **3 the pools** [pl] = FOOTBALL POOLS (FOOT). **pool** *v* [T] 把…集中一起用 bǎ…jízhōng yìqǐ yòng;共用 gòngyòng.

poor /pɔː(r); *US* pʊə(r)/ *adj* **1** 贫穷〔窮〕的 pínqióngde;贫困的 pínkùnde. **2** 贫乏的 pínfáde;缺少的 quēshǎode: *a* ~ *crop* 歉收. **3** 劣质〔質〕的 lièzhìde: ~ *soil* 贫瘠的土壤. **4** 值得

P

同情的 zhíde tóngqíng de；可怜〔憐〕的 kěliánde：*P～ Lisa is ill*. 不幸的莉萨病了. **poorness** *n* [U].

poorly /ˈpɔːlɪ; *US* ˈpʊərlɪ/ *adj* [非正式用语] 身体〔體〕不适〔適〕的 shēntǐ búshì de；健康不佳的 jiànkāng bùjiā de. **poorly** *adv* 拙劣地 zhuōliède；不足地 bùzúde.

pop[1] /pɒp/ *n* **1** [C] 短促爆裂声〔聲〕 duǎncù bàolièshēng. **2** [U] [非正式用语] 含气〔氣〕饮料(如汽水、啤酒等) hánqì yǐnliào. **pop** *adv* 砰的一声 pēngde yìshēng.

pop[2] /pɒp/ *n* [C] [非正式用语] 爸爸 bàba.

pop[3] /pɒp/ *n* [U] [非正式用语] 流行音乐〔樂〕 liúxíng yīnyuè；流行歌曲 liúxíng gēqǔ：*a ～ singer / group* 流行歌曲歌手；流行音乐乐队.

pop[4] /pɒp/ *v* [-pp-] **1** [I, T] (使)发〔發〕短促爆裂声〔聲〕 fā duǎncù bàolièshēng. **2** [I] 来去匆匆 lái qù cōngcōng：*She's just ～ped out to the shops*. 她刚才急匆匆地去商店了. **3** [短语动词] **pop up** (意外地)出现 chūxiàn. ˈ**popcorn** *n* [U] 爆玉米花 bào yùmǐhuā. ˈ**pop-eyed** *adj* (因惊讶而)睁大眼睛的 zhēng dà yǎnjīng de.

pope /pəʊp/ *n* [C] (天主教的)教皇 jiàohuáng.

poplar /ˈpɒplə(r)/ *n* [C] 杨〔楊〕树〔樹〕 yángshù.

poppy /ˈpɒpɪ/ *n* [C] [*pl* -ies] 罂粟 yīngsù.

populace /ˈpɒpjʊləs/ *n* **the populace** [sing] [正式用语] 平民 píngmín；百姓 bǎixìng.

popular /ˈpɒpjʊlə(r)/ *adj* **1** 多数〔數〕人喜爱〔愛〕的 duōshù rén xǐ'ài de；流行的 liúxíngde. **2** 民众〔衆〕的 mínzhòngde；大众的 dàzhòngde. **3** 通俗的 tōngsúde；普及的 pǔjíde. **popularity** /ˌpɒpjʊˈlærətɪ/ *n* [U]. **popularize** *v* [T] 使受大家喜欢〔歡〕 shǐ shòu dàjiā xǐhuan. **popularly** *adv*.

populate /ˈpɒpjʊleɪt/ *v* [T] [常用被动语态] 居住于 jūzhù yú.

population /ˌpɒpjʊˈleɪʃn/ *n* [C] 人口(数) rénkǒu.

porcelain /ˈpɔːsəlɪn/ *n* [U] 瓷 cí；瓷器 cíqì.

porch /pɔːtʃ/ *n* [C] 门廊 ménláng.

porcupine /ˈpɔːkjʊpaɪn/ *n* [C] 豪猪 háozhū；箭猪 jiànzhū.

pore[1] /pɔː(r)/ *n* [C] 毛孔 máokǒng.

pore[2] /pɔː(r)/ *v* [短语动词] **pore over sth** 钻〔鑽〕研 zuānyán；仔细阅读〔讀〕 zǐxì yuèdú.

pork /pɔːk/ *n* [U] 猪肉 zhūròu.

porn /pɔːn/ *n* [U] [非正式用语] short for PORNOGRAPHY.

pornography /pɔːˈnɒgrəfɪ/ *n* [U] 色情作品(书刊、影片等) sèqíng zuòpǐn. **pornographic** /ˌpɔːnəˈgræfɪk/ *adj*.

porous /ˈpɔːrəs/ *adj* 能渗〔滲〕透的 néng shèntòu de；渗水的 shènshuǐde；透气〔氣〕(或风、光)的 tòuqìde.

porpoise /ˈpɔːpəs/ *n* [C] 鼠海豚 shǔhǎitún；海豚 hǎitún.

porridge /ˈpɒrɪdʒ; *US* ˈpɔːr-/ *n* [U] 粥 zhōu；麦〔麥〕片粥 màipiànzhōu.

port[1] /pɔːt/ *n* [C] **1** 港 gǎng；港口 gǎngkǒu. **2** 港市 gǎngshì；口岸 kǒu'àn.

port[2] /pɔːt/ *n* [U] (船、飞机的)左舷 zuǒxián.

port[3] /pɔːt/ *n* [U] 波尔〔爾〕图〔圖〕葡萄酒(产自葡萄牙，深红色) bō'ěrtú pútáojiǔ.

portable /ˈpɔːtəbl/ *adj* 手提式的 shǒutíshìde；便于携带〔帶〕的 biànyú xiédài de.

portal /ˈpɔːtl/ *n* [C] **1** (宏伟的)正门 zhèngmén；入口 rùkǒu. **2** (计算机网络)门户网〔網〕站 ménhù wǎngzhàn；门户站点〔點〕 ménhù zhàndiǎn.

porter /ˈpɔːtə(r)/ *n* [C] **1**(火车站等的)搬运〔運〕工 bānyùngōng. **2**(旅馆等的)守门人 shǒuménrén.

portfolio /pɔːtˈfəʊlɪəʊ/ *n* [C] [*pl* ～s] **1** 公事包 gōngshìbāo；文件夹〔夾〕 wénjiànjiā. **2**(个人等所有的)投资组合 tóuzī zǔhé. **3** 部长(或大臣)的职〔職〕位或职责 bùzhǎngde zhíwèi huò zhízé.

porthole /ˈpɔːthəʊl/ *n* [C] (船、飞机的)舷窗 xiánchuāng.

portion /ˈpɔːʃn/ *n* [C] **1** 部分 bùfen；一份 yífèn. **2**(食物的)一份 yífèn；一客 yíkè. **portion** *v* [短语动词] **portion sth out** 将〔將〕…分成份 jiāng…fēnchéng fèn.

portly /ˈpɔːtlɪ/ *adj* [-ier, -iest] 胖的 pàngde；发〔發〕福的 fāfúde.

portrait /ˈpɔːtreɪt, -trɪt/ *n* [C] **1** 肖像 xiàoxiàng；画〔畫〕像 huàxiàng. **2** 描写〔寫〕 miáoxiě；描绘〔繪〕 miáohuì.

portray /pɔːˈtreɪ/ *v* [T] **1** 画〔畫〕(人物、风景等) huà；为〔為〕…画像 wèi…huàxiàng. **2** 描述 miáoshù；描写〔寫〕 miáoxiě. **3** 扮演 bànyǎn. **portrayal** *n* [C, U].

pose /pəʊz/ *v* **1** [I] (*for*) (画像、拍照前)摆〔擺〕姿势〔勢〕 bǎi zīshì. **2** [I] *as* 假装〔裝〕 jiǎzhuāng；冒充 màochōng. **3** [T] 引起(问题) yǐnqǐ. **4** [T] [正式用语] 提出 tíchū. **pose** *n* [C] **1** 姿势〔勢〕 zīshì；姿态〔態〕 zītài. **2** 装腔作势 zhuāngqiāng zuòshì. **poser** *n* [C] 难〔難〕题 nántí.

posh /pɒʃ/ *adj* [非正式用语] 漂亮的 piàoliàngde；豪华〔華〕的 háohuáde.

position /pəˈzɪʃn/ *n* **1** [C, U] 位置 wèizhì；方位 fāngwèi. **2** [C] (人或物)被安置的方式 bèi ānzhìde fāngshì；姿势〔勢〕 zīshì：*lie in a comfortable ～* 舒服地躺着. **3** [C] 态〔態〕度 tàidù；看法 kànfǎ. **4** [C] 处〔處〕境 chǔjìng；状〔狀〕况 zhuàngkuàng：*I am not in a ～ to help you*. 我无力帮助你. **5** [C] [正式用语] 工作 gōngzuò. **6** [C] 地位 dìwèi；等级 děngjí. **7** [习

P

语]in position 在适〔適〕当〔當〕的位置 zài shìdàngde wèizhi. position *v* [T] 安置 ānzhì;安放 ānfàng.

positive /ˈpɒzətɪv/ *adj* 1 明确〔確〕的 míngquède;确定的 quèdìngde: ~ *proof* 确凿的证据. 2 有把握的 yǒu bǎwò de;确信的 quèxìnde: *I'm* ~ *he's here*. 我确信他在这里. 3 有用的 yǒuyòngde;有帮〔幫〕助的 yǒu bāngzhù de. 4 [数学]正的 zhèngde. 5(电)正的 zhèngde;正极〔極〕的 zhèngjíde. 6 [非正式用语]完全的 wánquánde;真实〔實〕的 zhēnshíde: *a* ~ *pleasure* 十足的乐事. **positively** *adv* 确定地 quèdìngde;确实地 quèshíde.

possess /pəˈzes/ *v* [T] 1 拥〔擁〕有 yōngyǒu. 2 [尤作被动语态](感情)控制 kòngzhì;支配 zhīpèi: ~*ed by jealousy* 妒火中烧. **possessor** *n* [C] [正式用语]拥有者 yōngyǒuzhě;所有人 suǒyǒurén.

possession /pəˈzeʃn/ *n* 1 [U] 持有 chíyǒu;具有 jùyǒu;拥〔擁〕有 yōngyǒu. 2 [C, 尤作 pl] 财产〔產〕cáichǎn;所有物 suǒyǒuwù.

possessive /pəˈzesɪv/ *adj* 1 不愿〔願〕与〔與〕人分享的 búyuàn yǔ rén fēnxiǎng de. 2[语法]所有格的 suǒyǒugéde: '*Yours*' *is a* ~ *pronoun*. yours 是物主代词. **possessively** *adv*. **possessiveness** *n* [U].

possibility /ˌpɒsəˈbɪlətɪ/ *n* [*pl* -ies] 1 [U] 可能 kěnéng;可能性 kěnéngxìng. 2 [C] 可能的事 kěnéngde shì;可能发〔發〕生的事 kěnéng fāshēng de shì.

possible /ˈpɒsəbl/ *adj* 1 可能的 kěnéngde;可能存在的 kěnéng cúnzài de. 2 合理的 hélǐde;可接受的 kě jiēshòu de. **possible** *n* [C] 可能的候选〔選〕人 kěnéngde hòuxuǎnrén;可能适〔適〕合的物 kěnéng shìhé de wù. **possibly** *adv* 1 大概 dàgài;也许 yěxǔ. 2 合理地 hélǐde: *I'll come as soon as I* ~ *can*. 我尽可能早来.

post[1] /pəʊst/ *n* 1 [U] 邮〔郵〕政 yóuzhèng;邮递〔遞〕yóudì. 2 [C, U] 信件 xìnjiàn;包裹 bāoguǒ;邮件 yóujiàn. **post** *v* [T] 投寄 tóujì;邮寄 yóujì. ˈ**post-box** *n* [C] 邮筒 yóutǒng;邮政信箱 yóuzhèng xìnxiāng. ˈ**postcard** *n* [C] 明信片 míngxìnpiàn. ˈ**post-code** *n* [C] 邮政编码 yóuzhèng biānmǎ. ˌ**post**ˈ**haste** *adv* [正式用语]急速地 jísùde. ˈ**postman** /-mən/ [*pl* -men] *n* [C] 邮递员 yóudìyuán. ˈ**postmark** *n* [C] 邮戳 yóuchuō. ˈ**post-office** *n* [C] 邮政局 yóuzhèngjú. ˈ**post-office box, P**ˈ**O box** *n* [C] 邮政专〔專〕用信箱 yóuzhèng zhuānyòng xìnxiāng.

post[2] /pəʊst/ *n* 1 [C](木、金属等的)柱 zhù;支柱 zhīzhù;标〔標〕杆 biāogān. 2[sing](速度比赛的)起点〔點〕标 qǐdiǎnbiāo;终点标 zhōngdiǎnbiāo. **post** *v* [T] 1 张〔張〕贴(公告等) zhāngtiē. 2 公开〔開〕宣布 gōngkāi xuānbù.

post[3] /pəʊst/ *n* [C] 1 工作 gōngzuò;职〔職〕业〔業〕zhíyè. 2 岗〔崗〕位 gǎngwèi;哨所 shàosuǒ. **post** *v* [T] 1 委派 wěipài;任命 rènmìng. 2 布置(岗哨等) bùzhì.

postage /ˈpəʊstɪdʒ/ *n* [U] 邮〔郵〕费 yóufèi;邮资 yóuzī. ˈ**postage stamp** *n* [C] = STAMP 1.

postal /ˈpəʊstl/ *adj* 邮〔郵〕政的 yóuzhèngde;邮递〔遞〕的 yóudìde;邮务〔務〕的 yóuwùde. ˈ**postal order** *n* [C] 邮政汇〔匯〕票 yóuzhèng huìpiào.

post-date /ˌpəʊstˈdeɪt/ *v* [T] 在(支票等)上填写〔寫〕比实〔實〕际〔際〕晚的日期 zài…shang tiánxiě bǐ shíjì wǎn de rìqī.

poster /ˈpəʊstə(r)/ *n* [C] 招贴 zhāotiē;广〔廣〕告画〔畫〕guǎnggàohuà;海报〔報〕hǎibào.

posterior /pɒˈstɪərɪə(r)/ *adj* [正式用语](时间、次序上)较后〔後〕的 jiàohòude.

posterity /pɒˈsterətɪ/ *n* [U] [正式用语]后〔後〕代 hòudài;子孙 zǐsūn;后世 hòushì.

postgraduate /ˌpəʊstˈgrædʒʊət/ *adj* 研究生的 yánjiūshēngde. **postgraduate** *n* [C] 研究生 yánjiūshēng.

posthumous /ˈpɒstjʊməs; *US* ˈpɒstʃəməs/ *adj* 死后〔後〕的 sǐhòude;身后的 shēnhòude. **posthumously** *adv*.

post-mortem /ˌpəʊst ˈmɔːtəm/ *n* [C] 1 验〔驗〕尸〔屍〕yànshī;尸体〔體〕解剖 shītǐ jiěpōu. 2 [非正式用语]事后〔後〕剖析 shìhòu pōuxī.

postpone /pəˈspəʊn/ *v* [T] 推迟〔遲〕tuīchí;延期 yánqī: *The match was* ~*d because of the rain*. 比赛因雨延期. **postponement** *n* [C, U].

postscript /ˈpəʊsskrɪpt/ *n* [C] (信末签名后的)附笔〔筆〕fùbǐ;又及 yòují.

posture /ˈpɒstʃə(r)/ *n* 1 [U] 姿势〔勢〕zīshì;姿态〔態〕zītài. 2 [C] 态度 tàidù.

posy /ˈpəʊzɪ/ *n* [C] [*pl* -ies] 小花束 xiǎo huāsù.

pot[1] /pɒt/ *n* 1 [C] (a) 罐 guàn;锅〔鍋〕guō;壶〔壺〕hú. (b) 一罐之物 yíguàn zhī wù;一锅之量 yìguō zhī liàng. 2 [U] [俚]大麻(烟) dàmá. 3 pots [pl] [非正式用语]大量 dàliàng: ~*s of money* 大笔钱. 4 [习语] **go to** ˈ**pot** [非正式用语]被损坏〔壞〕bèi sǔnhuài;被毁掉 bèi huǐdiào. **take** ˌ**pot** ˈ**luck** 有什么〔麼〕吃什么 yǒu shénme chī shénme;吃便饭 chī biànfàn. ˌ**pot-**ˈ**bellied** *adj* [非正式用语]大腹便便的 dà fù piánpián de. ˈ**pot-hole** *n* [C] 1 锅穴 guōxué;瓯〔甌〕穴 ōuxué. 2(路面的)坑洼〔窪〕kēngwā. ˈ**pot-shot** *n* [C] 任意射击〔擊〕rènyì shèjī;盲目射击 mángmù shèjī.

pot[2] /pɒt/ *v* [-tt-] [T] 把(植物)栽种〔種〕在花盆里〔裏〕bǎ…zāizhòng zài huāpén lǐ. **pot-**

P

ted *adj* 1(熟肉、熟鱼)放入罐内保存的 fàngrù guànnèi bǎocún de. 2(书等)节〔節〕略的 jiélüède.

potassium /pəˈtæsɪəm/ *n* [U] 钾 jiǎ.

potato /pəˈteɪtəʊ/ *n* [C, U] [*pl* ~es] 马铃薯 mǎlíngshǔ;土豆 tǔdòu.

potent /ˈpəʊtnt/ *adj* 强有力的 qiáng yǒulì de; 有效的 yǒuxiàode: ~ *arguments/drugs* 有说服力的论据;很有效的药物. **potency** /-tnsɪ/ *n* [U]. **potently** *adv*.

potential /pəˈtenʃl/ *adj* 可能的 kěnéngde; 可能存在的 kěnéng cúnzài de. **potential** *n* [U] 潜〔潛〕在性 qiánzàixìng;可能性 kěnéngxìng. **potentiality** /pəˌtenʃɪˈælətɪ/ *n* [C, U] [*pl* -ies] [正式用语]潜力 qiánlì;潜在性 qiánzàixìng. **potentially** /-ʃəlɪ/ *adv*.

potion /ˈpəʊʃn/ *n* [C] (有药效、有毒性、有魔力的)饮料 yǐnliào.

potter[1] /ˈpɒtə(r)/ *v* [短语动词] **potter about/around** 轻〔輕〕松〔鬆〕地做琐碎的事 qīngsōngde zuò suǒsuìde shì;慢条〔條〕斯理地干〔幹〕活 màntiáo sīlǐ de gànhuó.

potter[2] /ˈpɒtə(r)/ *n* [C] 陶工 táogōng;制〔製〕陶工人 zhì táo gōngrén. **pottery** *n* [*pl* -ies] 1 [U] 陶器 táoqì. 2 [C] 陶器制〔製〕造厂〔廠〕 táoqì zhìzàochǎng.

potty[1] /ˈpɒtɪ/ *adj* [-ier, -iest] [英国非正式用语]愚蠢的 yúchǔnde;疯〔瘋〕癫的 fēngdiānde.

potty[2] /ˈpɒtɪ/ *n* [C] [*pl* -ies] (儿童的)便盆 biànpén;夜壶〔壺〕 yèhú.

pouch /paʊtʃ/ *n* [C] 1 小袋 xiǎo dài. 2(袋鼠等的)育儿〔兒〕袋 yù'érdài.

poultry /ˈpəʊltrɪ/ *n* 1 [pl] 家禽 jiāqín. 2[U] 家禽肉 jiāqínròu.

pounce /paʊns/ *v* [I] (*on*) 1 猛扑〔撲〕 měng pū;突然袭〔襲〕击〔擊〕 tūrán xíjī. 2 [喻]渴望抓住 kěwàng zhuāzhù: *She ~d on the chance to go abroad*. 她巴不得抓住机会到国外去.

pound[1] /paʊnd/ *n* [C] 1(英)镑(英国货币单位,合 100 便士) bàng. 2 镑(爱尔兰等国的货币单位) bàng. 3 磅(重量单位,合 16 盎司或 0.454 千克) bàng.

pound[2] /paʊnd/ *n* [C] (收留走失狗、猫以待认领的)待领处〔處〕 dàilǐngchù.

pound[3] /paʊnd/ *v* 1 [I, T] 连续〔續〕重击〔擊〕 liánxù zhòngjī. 2 [T] 捣碎 dǎosuì;把…捣成粉 bǎ…dǎochéng fěn. 3 [I] (心脏)剧〔劇〕烈地跳动〔動〕jùliède tiàodòng.

pour /pɔː(r)/ *v* 1 [I, T] (液体)不断〔斷〕流动〔動〕 búduàn liúdòng. 2 [I] (雨)倾盆而下 qīngpén ér xià. 3 [I] (人)不断地涌现 búduànde yǒngxiàn: *In summer tourists ~ into London*. 在夏季游客拥入伦敦. 4 [习语] **pour cold water on sth** ⇨ COLD[1]. 5 [短语动词] **pour sth out** 倾吐 qīngtǔ; 倾诉 qīngsù: ~ *out one's troubles* 倾诉苦恼.

pout /paʊt/ *v* [I] 撅嘴 juēzuǐ. **pout** *n* [C, 常作 sing] 撅嘴 juēzuǐ.

poverty /ˈpɒvətɪ/ *n* [U] 贫穷〔窮〕 pínqióng; 贫困 pínkùn. ˈ**poverty-stricken** *adj* 贫困不堪的 pínkùn bùkān de;极〔極〕贫穷的 jí pínqióng de.

powder /ˈpaʊdə(r)/ *n* [C, U] 粉末 fěnmò; 粉 fěn. **powder** *v* [T] 往…上搽粉 wǎng…shàng cāfěn. **powdered** *adj* (成)粉状〔狀〕的 fěnzhuàngde. ˈ**powder-room** *n* [C] 女盥洗室 nǚ guànxǐshì;女厕所 nǚ cèsuǒ. **powdery** *adj* 粉的 fěnde;粉状的 fěnzhuàngde.

power /ˈpaʊə(r)/ *n* 1 [U] (人的)能力 nénglì. 2 [U] (亦作 **powers**) [pl] 体〔體〕力 tǐlì;智力 zhìlì: *the ~ of speech* 说话能力. 3 [U] 力 lì;力量 lìliàng. 4 [U] (a) 操纵〔縱〕力 cāozònglì;影响〔響〕力 yǐngxiǎnglì. (b) 政权〔權〕 zhèngquán;统治 tǒngzhì: *The Conservative Party came to ~ in 1979*. 保守党于 1979 年上台执政. 5 [C, U] 职〔職〕权 zhíquán;权力 quánlì;权限 quánxiàn. 6 [C] 很有权力(或影响)的人(或国家等) hěn yǒu quánlìde rén: *a world ~* 世界大国. 7 [U] 动〔動〕力 dònglì: *nuclear ~* 核动力. **power** *v* [T] 给…提供动力 gěi …tígōng dònglì: *~ed by electricity* 用电作动力. ˈ**power drill** *n* [C] 电〔電〕钻〔鑽〕 diànzuàn. ˈ**power point** *n* [C] 电源插座 diànyuán chāzuò. ˈ**power-station** *n* [C] 发〔發〕电站 fādiànzhàn;发电厂〔廠〕 fādiànchǎng.

powerful /ˈpaʊəfl/ *adj* 强大的 qiángdàde; 强有力的 qiáng yǒulì de. **powerfully** *adv*.

powerless /ˈpaʊəlɪs/ *adj* 无〔無〕权〔權〕力的 wú quánlì de;无力量的 wú lìliàng de: ~ *to act* 无力行动. **powerlessness** *n* [U].

pp *abbr* pages.

PR /ˌpiː ˈɑː(r)/ *abbr* public relations 公关〔關〕活动〔動〕 gōngguān huódòng.

practicable /ˈpræktɪkəbl/ *adj* 能实〔實〕行的 néng shíxíngde;可行的 kěxíngde: ~ *ideas* 切实可行的意见. **practicability** /ˌpræktɪkəˈbɪlətɪ/ *n* [U].

practical /ˈpræktɪkl/ *adj* 1 实〔實〕践〔踐〕的 shíjiànde;实际〔際〕的 shíjìde. 2 切合实际的 qièhé shíjì de: ~ *clothing for wearing in bad weather* 适于坏天气穿的衣服. 3 (人)心灵〔靈〕手巧的 xīnlíng shǒuqiǎo de. 4 讲〔講〕求实际的 jiǎngqiú shíjì de. **practicality** /ˌpræktɪˈkælətɪ/ *n* [C, U] [*pl* -ies]. ˌ**practical** ˈ**joke** *n* [C] 恶〔惡〕作剧〔劇〕 èzuòjù. **practically** /-klɪ/ *adv* 1 几〔幾〕乎 jīhū: ~ *no time left* 几乎没有时间了. 2 实际地 shíjìde.

P

practice /ˈpræktɪs/ *n* 1 [U] 实〔實〕行 shíxíng；实践〔踐〕shíjiàn：*put a plan into* ～ 实行一项计划. 2 [C, U]（经常反复的）练〔練〕习〔習〕liànxí. 3 [C, U] 惯例 guànlì；常规 chángguī：*standard* ～ 一般惯例. 4 (a) [U]（医生或律师的）工作 gōngzuò. (b) [C]（医生）诊所 zhěnsuǒ；（律师）事务〔務〕所 shìwùsuǒ. 5 [习语] ˌin / ˌout of ˈpractice 勤于实践 qín yú shíjiàn；疏于实践 shū yú shíjiàn.

practise（美语 -ice）/ˈpræktɪs/ *v* 1 [I, T] 练〔練〕习〔習〕liànxí；实〔實〕习 shíxí：～ *the piano* 练习弹钢琴. 2 [T] 惯做 guàn zuò；常为〔爲〕cháng wéi. 3 [I, T] (*as*) 以（医生或律师）为业〔業〕yǐ wéi yè. 4 [T] 积〔積〕极〔極〕从〔從〕事 jījí cóngshì：～ *one's religion* 实践自己的信仰. 5 [习语] ˌpractise what one ˈpreaches 身体〔體〕力行 shēn tǐ lì xíng. **practised** *adj* 有经〔經〕验〔驗〕的 yǒu jīngyàn de；熟练〔練〕的 shúliànde.

practitioner /prækˈtɪʃənə(r)/ *n* [C] 1 习〔習〕艺〔藝〕者 xíyìzhě. 2 从〔從〕业〔業〕者 cóngyèzhě；（尤指）行医〔醫〕者 xíngyīzhě.

pragmatic /prægˈmætɪk/ *adj* 讲〔講〕究实〔實〕际〔際〕的 jiǎngjiu shíjì de；重实效的 zhòng shíxiào de；实事求是的 shí shì qiú shì de.

prairie /ˈpreərɪ/ *n* [C]（北美洲的）大草原 dàcǎoyuán.

praise /preɪz/ *v* [T] 1 赞〔讚〕扬〔揚〕zànyáng；称〔稱〕赞 chēngzàn. 2 [宗教] 颂扬（上帝）sòngyáng；赞美 zànměi. **praise** *n* [U] 颂扬 sòngyáng；赞美 zànměi. ˈ**praiseworthy** *adj* 值得赞扬的 zhíde zànyáng de；可嘉的 kějiāde.

pram /præm/ *n* [C] 手推童车 shǒutuī tóngchē；婴儿〔兒〕车 yīng'érchē.

P

prance /prɑːns; *US* præns/ *v* [I] 1（马）腾〔騰〕跃〔躍〕téngyuè. 2 雀跃 quèyuè；欣喜地跳跃 xīnxǐde tiàoyuè.

prank /præŋk/ *n* [C] 恶〔惡〕作剧〔劇〕èzuòjù；玩笑 wánxiào.

prattle /ˈprætl/ *v* [I] 闲〔閒〕聊 xiánliáo；絮絮叨叨地说 xùxùdāodāode shuō. **prattle** *n* [U] 闲话 xiánhuà；闲聊 xiánliáo.

prawn /prɔːn/ *n* [C] 对〔對〕虾〔蝦〕duìxiā；明虾 míngxiā.

pray /preɪ/ *v* [I] 1 祈祷〔禱〕qídǎo；祷告 dǎogào. 2 [非正式用语] 祈求 qíqiú；恳〔懇〕求 kěnqiú：*I just* ～ *he won't get hurt*. 我仅祈求他别受伤.

prayer /preə(r)/ *n* 1 [U] 祈祷〔禱〕qídǎo；祷告 dǎogào. 2 [C] 祈祷文 qídǎowén. 3 [C]（宗教的）祈祷式 qídǎoshì.

PRC /ˌpiː ɑː(r) ˈsiː/ *abbr* People's Republic of China 中华〔華〕人民共和国〔國〕Zhōnghuá Rénmín Gònghéguó.

preach /priːtʃ/ *v* 1 [I, T] 布道 bùdào；讲〔講〕道 jiǎngdào. 2 [T] 劝〔勸〕说 quànshuō. 3 [I]（进行道德等的）说教 shuōjiào. **preacher** *n* [C].

preamble /priːˈæmbl/ *n* [C, U]（尤指正式文件的）序言 xùyán；绪论〔論〕xùlùn.

precarious /prɪˈkeərɪəs/ *adj* 不稳〔穩〕定的 bù wěndìng de；不安全的 bù ānquán de. **precariously** *adv*.

precaution /prɪˈkɔːʃn/ *n* [C] 预防 yùfáng：*take* ～*s against illness* 预防疾病. **precautionary** *adj*.

precede /prɪˈsiːd/ *v* [T]（时间、位置或顺序上）在…之前 zài…zhī qián；先于 xiānyú. **preceding** *adj* 在前的 zàiqiánde；在先的 zàixiānde.

precedence /ˈpresɪdəns/ *n* [U] [正式用语]（在顺序、时间、重要程度上）领先 lǐngxiān；居前 jūqián：*take* ～ *over all others* 领先于所有其他人.

precedent /ˈpresɪdənt/ *n* [C, U] [正式用语] 先例 xiānlì；（法律）判例 pànlì：*set a* ～ 创先例.

precinct /ˈpriːsɪŋkt/ *n* 1 [C] [英国英语]（市镇中作特定用途的）区〔區〕域 qūyù：*a* ˈ*shopping* ～ 商业区. 2 [C]（市、县等的）区 qū. 3 **precincts** [pl]（由建筑物、围墙、教堂等围成的）场〔場〕地 chǎngdì；区域 qūyù.

precious /ˈpreʃəs/ *adj* 1 宝〔寶〕贵的 bǎoguìde；珍贵的 zhēnguìde. 2 [贬]（语言、风格等）矫〔矯〕揉造作的 jiǎo róu zào zuò de；过〔過〕分讲〔講〕究的 guòfèn jiǎngjiu de. **precious** *adv* [非正式用语] 很 hěn；非常 fēicháng：～ *little time* 极少的时间.

precipice /ˈpresɪpɪs/ *n* [C] 悬〔懸〕崖 xuányá；峭壁 qiàobì.

precipitate /prɪˈsɪpɪteɪt/ *v* [T] 1 [正式用语] 使突然发〔發〕生 shǐ tūrán fāshēng；使迅速发生 shǐ xùnsù fāshēng：*Illness* ～*d her death*. 疾病加速了她的死亡. 2 [化学] 使沉淀〔澱〕shǐ chéndiàn. **precipitate** *n* [C, U] [化学] 沉淀物 chéndiànwù. **precipitate** /prɪˈsɪpɪtət/ *adj* 急促的 jícùde. **precipitation** /prɪˌsɪpɪˈteɪʃn/ *n* [U] 1 沉淀 chéndiàn. 2 急促 jícù. 3（雨、雪等）降落 jiàngluò.

precipitous /prɪˈsɪpɪtəs/ *adj* [正式用语] 陡峭的 dǒuqiàode；险〔險〕峻的 xiǎnjùnde.

précis /ˈpreɪsiː; *US* preɪˈsiː/ *n* [C] [*pl* **précis** /-iːz/]（演说、文章的）摘要 zhāiyào；梗概 gěnggài；大意 dàyì.

precise /prɪˈsaɪs/ *adj* 1 准〔準〕确〔確〕的 zhǔnquède. 2 精确的 jīngquède. 3 精细的 jīngxìde. **precisely** *adv* 1 精确地 jīngquède. 2（用以表示同意）对〔對〕duì.

precision /prɪˈsɪʒn/ *n* [U] 精确〔確〕（性）jīngquè；精密（度）jīngmì.

preclude /prɪˈkluːd/ *v* [T] (*from*) [正式

用语]阻止 zǔzhǐ;妨碍〔礙〕fáng'ài.

precocious /prɪˈkəʊʃəs/ *adj* (儿童的智力等)过〔過〕早发〔發〕育的 guòzǎo fāyù de;早熟的 zǎoshúde. **precociousness** *n* [U].

preconceived /ˌpriːkənˈsiːvd/ *adj* (看法、观点等)事先形成的 shìxiān xíngchéng de. **preconception** /-ˈsepʃn/ *n* [C] 事先形成的观〔觀〕点〔點〕shìxiān xíngchéng de guāndiǎn;先入之见 xiān rù zhī jiàn.

precursor /ˌpriːˈkɜːsə(r)/ *n* [C] [正式用语] 前兆 qiánzhào;先兆 xiānzhào.

predatory /ˈpredətrɪ; *US* -tɔːrɪ/ *adj* (动物)食肉的 shíròude. **predator** /-tə(r)/ *n* [C] 食肉动〔動〕物 shíròu dòngwù.

predecessor /ˈpriːdɪsesə(r); *US* ˈpredə-/ *n* [C] (职务或职位的) 前任 qiánrèn.

predestined /priːˈdestɪnd/ *adj* 命定的 mìngdìngde;宿命的 sùmìngde.

predicament /prɪˈdɪkəmənt/ *n* [C] (为难的)处〔處〕境 chǔjìng;困境 kùnjìng.

predicate /ˈpredɪkət/ *n* [C] [语法]谓语(如 "Life is short." 中的 "is short" 是谓语) wèiyǔ.

predicative /prɪˈdɪkətɪv; *US* ˈpredɪkeɪtɪv/ *adj* [语法]表语的 biǎoyǔde;谓语性的 wèiyǔxìngde.

predict /prɪˈdɪkt/ *v* [T] 预言 yùyán;预示 yùshì;预料 yùliào. **predictable** *adj* 可预言的 kě yùyán de;可预示的 kě yùshì de. **prediction** /-ˈdɪkʃn/ *n* **1** [U] 预言 yùyán;预料 yùliào. **2** [C] 预言(或预料)的事物 yùyánde shìwù.

predispose /ˌpriːdɪˈspəʊz/ *v* [T] [正式用语]事先影响〔響〕shìxiān yǐngxiǎng;使预先有倾向 shǐ yùxiān yǒu qīngxiàng. **predisposition** /-dɪspəˈzɪʃn/ *n* [C].

predominant /prɪˈdɒmɪnənt/ *adj* [正式用语]有势〔勢〕力的 yǒu shìlì de;重要的 zhòngyàode;显〔顯〕著的 xiǎnzhùde. **predominance** /-nəns/ *n* [U]. **predominantly** *adv* 主要地 zhǔyàode.

predominate /prɪˈdɒmɪneɪt/ *v* [I] [正式用语] **1** 支配 zhīpèi;统治 tǒngzhì. **2** (数量等)占〔佔〕优〔優〕势〔勢〕zhàn yōushì.

pre-eminent /ˌpriːˈemɪnənt/ *adj* [正式用语]卓越的 zhuóyuède;杰〔傑〕出的 jiéchūde. **pre-eminence** /-nəns/ *n* [U]. **pre-eminently** *adv*.

preen /priːn/ *v* **1** [I, T] (鸟)用喙整理(羽毛) yòng huì zhěnglǐ. **2** [喻] ~ **oneself** 打扮 dǎbàn.

prefabricated /ˌpriːˈfæbrɪkeɪtɪd/ *adj* (房屋、墙等)预制〔製〕的 yùzhìde.

preface /ˈprefɪs/ *n* [C] 序言 xùyán;前言 qiányán. **preface** *v* [T] (*with*) [正式用语] 作为〔爲〕…的开〔開〕端 zuòwéi…de kāiduān.

prefect /ˈpriːfekt/ *n* [C] **1** (学校的)级长〔長〕jízhǎng,班长 bānzhǎng. **2** (法国地区的)最高行政长官 zuìgāo xíngzhèng zhǎngguān.

prefer /prɪˈfɜː(r)/ *v* [-rr-] [T] **1** 宁〔寧〕可 nìngkě;更喜欢〔歡〕gèng xǐhuān: *I ~ tea to coffee.* 我喜欢茶,不喜欢咖啡. **2** [习语] **prefer ˈcharges** [法律](对某人)提出控告 tíchū kònggào. **preferable** /ˈprefrəbl/ *adj* 更合意的 gèng héyì de;更适〔適〕宜的 gèng shìyí de. **preferably** *adv*.

preference /ˈprefrəns/ *n* **1** [U, sing] (*for*) 更加的喜爱〔愛〕gèngjiāde xǐ'ài;偏爱 piān'ài. **2** [C] 偏爱物 piān'àiwù. **3** [U] 优〔優〕先 yōuxiān;优待 yōudài;优惠 yōuhuì.

preferential /ˌprefəˈrenʃl/ *adj* 优〔優〕先的 yōuxiānde;优待的 yōudàide;特惠的 tèhuìde: *get ~ ˈtreatment* 受优待.

prefix /ˈpriːfɪks/ *n* [C] 前缀(如 *pre-*, *un-*) qiánzhuì. **prefix** *v* [T] 加前缀于 jiā qiánzhuì yú.

pregnant /ˈpregnənt/ *adj* **1** 怀〔懷〕孕的 huáiyùnde;妊娠的 rènshēnde. **2** [喻]富有意义〔義〕的 fùyǒu yìyì de: *a ~ ˈpause* 意味深长的停顿. **pregnancy** /-nənsɪ/ *n* [U, C] [*pl* -ies].

prehistoric /ˌpriːhɪˈstɒrɪk; *US* -tɔːrɪk/ *adj* 史前的 shǐqiánde. **prehistory** /ˌpriːˈhɪstrɪ/ *n* [U].

prejudge /ˌpriːˈdʒʌdʒ/ *v* [T] [正式用语](未了解全部情况)对〔對〕…预先作出判断〔斷〕duì…yùxiān zuòchū pànduàn.

prejudice /ˈpredʒʊdɪs/ *n* **1** [C, U] 偏见 piānjiàn;成见 chéngjiàn. **2** [U] [法律]损害 sǔnhài;侵害 qīnhài. **prejudice** *v* [T] **1** 使抱偏见 shǐ bào piānjiàn;使有成见 shǐ yǒu chéngjiàn. **2** 使受到损害 shǐ shòudào sǔnhài;侵害 qīnhài. **prejudicial** /ˌpredʒʊˈdɪʃl/ *adj*.

preliminary /prɪˈlɪmɪnərɪ; *US* -nerɪ/ *adj* 起始的 qǐshǐde;初步的 chūbùde: *a ~ study / report* 初步研究/报道. **preliminary** *n* [C] [*pl* -ies] [常作 pl] 初步的行动〔動〕chūbùde xíngdòng.

prelude /ˈpreljuːd/ *n* [C] **1** 前奏 qiánzòu;序幕 xùmù. **2** 前奏曲 qiánzòuqǔ.

premarital /ˌpriːˈmærɪtl/ *adj* 婚前的 hūnqiánde: ~ *sex* 婚前的性行为.

premature /ˈpremətjʊə(r); *US* ˌpriːməˈtʊər/ *adj* 提前的 tíqiánde;过〔過〕早的 guòzǎode;未到期的 wèi dàoqī de: ~ *birth* 早产. **prematurely** *adv*.

premeditated /ˌpriːˈmedɪteɪtɪd/ *adj* 预先考虑〔慮〕的 yùxiān kǎolǜ de;预先计划〔劃〕的 yùxiān jìhuà de;预谋的 yùmóude: ~ *murder* 谋杀.

premier /ˈpremɪə(r); *US* ˈpriːmɪər/ *n* [C] 总〔總〕理 zǒnglǐ;首相 shǒuxiàng. **premier**

adj 首要的 shǒuyàode；首位的 shǒuwèide. premiership *n* [U].

première /ˈpremɪeə(r)；*US* prɪˈmɪər/ *n* [C] (戏剧或电影的)首次公演 shǒucì gōngyǎn.

premise /ˈpremɪs/ *n* [C] [正式用语]前提 qiántí.

premises /ˈpremɪsɪz/ *n* [pl] 房屋连地基 fángwū lián dìjī：*The company is looking for larger* ～. 该公司正在寻找较大的办公地址.

premium /ˈpriːmɪəm/ *n* [C] 1 保险〔險〕费 bǎoxiǎnfèi. 2 额外费用 éwài fèiyòng；津贴 jīntiē. ˈPremium Bond *n* [C] (英国)(有奖无息的)储蓄债券 chǔxù zhàiquàn.

premonition /ˌpreməˈnɪʃn, ˌpriː-/ *n* [C] (不祥的)预感 yùgǎn；预兆 yùzhào.

preoccupation /ˌpriːɒkjuˈpeɪʃn/ *n* 1 [U] 先占〔佔〕xiānzhàn. 2 [C] 令人全神贯注的事物 lìng rén quán shén guàn zhù de shìwù.

preoccupy /priːˈɒkjupaɪ/ *v* [*pt*，*pp* -ied] [T] 使全神贯注 shǐ quán shén guàn zhù.

preparation /ˌprepəˈreɪʃn/ *n* 1 [U]准〔準〕备〔備〕zhǔnbèi；预备 yùbèi：*work done without* ～ 无准备而完成的工作. 2 [C，常作 pl] 准备工作 zhǔnbèi gōngzuò. 3 [C] (配制的)制〔製〕剂〔劑〕zhìjì；配制品 pèizhìpǐn.

preparatory /prɪˈpærətrɪ；*US* -tɔːrɪ/ *adj* 预备〔備〕的 yùbèide；准〔準〕备的 zhǔnbèide. preˈparatory school *n* [C] 1 (英国)私立小学〔學〕sīlì xiǎoxué. 2 (美国，通常为私立)大学预科学校 dàxué yùkē xuéxiào.

prepare /prɪˈpeə(r)/ *v* 1 [I，T] 预备〔備〕yùbèi；准〔準〕备 zhǔnbèi. 2 [习语] be prepared to do sth 愿〔願〕意做某事 yuànyì zuò mǒushì.

preposition /ˌprepəˈzɪʃn/ *n* [C][语法]介词(如 *in*，*from*，*to*) jiècí；前置词 qiánzhìcí. prepositional /-ʃənl/ *adj*.

preposterous /prɪˈpɒstərəs/ *adj* 反常的 fǎnchángde；荒谬的 huāngmiùde. preposterously *adv*.

prerogative /prɪˈrɒgətɪv/ *n* [C] 特权〔權〕tèquán.

Presbyterian /ˌprezbɪˈtɪərɪən/ *n* [C]，*adj* 长〔長〕老会〔會〕教友 Zhǎnglǎohuì jiàoyǒu；长老制的 zhǎnglǎozhìde.

prescribe /prɪˈskraɪb/ *v* [T] 1 吩咐使用 fēnfù shǐyòng：～ *medicine* 开药方. 2 [正式用语]规定 guīdìng；指定 zhǐdìng.

prescription /prɪˈskrɪpʃn/ *n* 1 [C] (a) 药〔藥〕方 yàofāng；处〔處〕方 chǔfāng. (b) 处方上开〔開〕的药 chǔfāng shàng kāi de yào. 2 [U] 开处方 kāi chǔfāng.

prescriptive /prɪˈskrɪptɪv/ *adj* [正式用语]规定的 guīdìngde；指定的 zhǐdìngde.

presence /ˈprezns/ *n* [U] 1 出席 chūxí；在场〔場〕zàichǎng. 2 仪〔儀〕表 yíbiǎo；风〔風〕度 fēngdù.

present[1] /ˈpreznt/ *adj* 1 出席的 chūxíde；在场〔場〕的 zàichǎngde：*Were you* ～ *at the meeting when the news was announced?* 宣布这消息时你在会场吗？2 现存的 xiàncúnde；现有的 xiànyǒude：*the* ～ *government* 现政府. 3 [语法]现在时〔時〕的 xiànzàishíde：*the* ～ *tense* 一般现在时. *a* ～ *participle* 现在分词. present *n* 1 the present [sing] 现在 xiànzài；目前 mùqián. 2 [习语] at ˈpresent 现在 xiànzài.

present[2] /ˈpreznt/ *n* [C] 礼〔禮〕物 lǐwù；赠品 zèngpǐn.

present[3] /prɪˈzent/ *v* [T] 1 (*with*，*to*) 赠送 zèngsòng；授予 shòuyǔ：～ *her with a book* 赠她一本书. ～ *it to her* 把它赠给她. 2 (*to*) 引见 yǐnjiàn；介绍 jièshào. 3 提出 tíchū；提供 tígōng. 4 ～ oneself (a) 出现 chūxiàn；出席 chūxí. (b) (机会)产〔產〕生 chǎnshēng：*The opportunity may not* ～ *itself again*. 机会不会再有. 5 显〔顯〕示 xiǎnshì. 6 公演(戏剧等) gōngyǎn. 7 (在广播、电视中)主持播出(节目) zhǔchí bōchū. presenter *n* [C] (广播、电视)节〔節〕目主持人 jiémù zhǔchírén.

presentable /prɪˈzentəbl/ *adj* 拿得出去的 nádechūqùde；体〔體〕面的 tǐmiànde；像样〔樣〕的 xiàngyàngde. presentably *adv*.

presentation /ˌpreznˈteɪʃn；*US* ˌpriːzen-/ *n* 1 [U] 赠送 zèngsòng；引见 yǐnjiàn；提出 tíchū；出席 chūxí. 2 [U] 表现 biǎoxiàn；呈现 chéngxiàn. 3 [C] 礼〔禮〕物 lǐwù；赠品 zèngpǐn.

presently /ˈprezntlɪ/ *adv* 1 不久 bùjiǔ：*I'll see you* ～. 我过不久就去看你. 2 [尤用于美语]现在 xiànzài.

preservative /prɪˈzɜːvətɪv/ *n* [C]，*adj* 防腐剂〔劑〕fángfǔjì；防腐的 fángfǔde.

preserve /prɪˈzɜːv/ *v* [T] 1 保护〔護〕bǎohù；维护 wéihù. 2 保护(某人) bǎohù. 3 (用干燥、冷冻法等)保存(食物) bǎocún. preservation /ˌprezəˈveɪʃn/ *n* [U]. preserve *n* [C，常作 pl，U] 蜜饯〔餞〕mìjiàn；果酱〔醬〕guǒjiàng.

preside /prɪˈzaɪd/ *v* [I] (*over* / *at*) 主持(会议) zhǔchí；作(会议)主席 zuò zhǔxí.

presidency /ˈprezɪdənsɪ/ *n* [*pl* -ies] 1 the presidency [sing] 总〔總〕统(或国家主席、院长、校长、总裁、会长等)的职〔職〕位 zǒngtǒngde zhíwèi. 2 [C] 上述各职位的任期 shàngshù gè zhíwèi de rènqī.

president /ˈprezɪdənt/ *n* [C] 1 总〔總〕统 zǒngtǒng；国〔國〕家主席 guójiā zhǔxí. 2 (政府部门)首长〔長〕shǒuzhǎng；(社会团体的)会〔會〕长 huìzhǎng；校长 xiàozhǎng；院长 yuànzhǎng. presidential /ˌprezɪˈdenʃl/ *adj*.

press[1] /pres/ *v* 1 [T] 压〔壓〕yā；按 àn；挤〔擠〕jǐ. 2 [T] 压平 yā píng；熨平 yùn píng. 3

P

[T] 榨取(汁等) zhàqǔ. 4 催促 cuīcù; 敦促 dūncù. 5 [I] (人群)拥〔擁〕挤 yōngjǐ; 推进〔進〕tuījìn: *The crowd ~ed forward.* 人群拥挤着向前进. 6 [习语] **be pressed for sth** 缺少 quēshǎo; 缺乏 quēfá: *be ~ed for time* 时间紧迫. 7 [短语动词] **press for sth** 急切要求 jíqiè yāoqiú. **press on (with sth)** 坚〔堅〕持 jiānchí. **pressing** *adj* 紧〔緊〕迫的 jǐnpòde; 急迫的 jípòde: *~ing business* 急事.

press[2] /pres/ *n* 1 [C, 常作 sing] 压〔壓〕yā; 按 àn; 挤〔擠〕jǐ; 熨 yùn. 2 [C] 压榨机〔機〕yāzhàjī. 3 **the press** [sing] [用 sing 或 pl v] 新闻界 xīnwénjiè; 报〔報〕界 bàojiè; 记者 jìzhě. 4 [sing] 报道 bàodào; 评论〔論〕pínglùn: *The film got a good ~.* 该影片受到舆论界的好评. ˈ**press conference** *n* [C] 记者招待会〔會〕jìzhě zhāodàihuì.

pressure /ˈpreʃə(r)/ *n* 1 [C, U] 压〔壓〕力 yālì: *the ~ of her hand on his head* 她的手紧按他的头部. 2 [C, U] 气〔氣〕压 qìyā: *air ~* 气压. 3 [U] (施加的)压力 yālì. 4 [U] 困扰〔擾〕kùnrǎo; 忧〔憂〕虑〔慮〕yōulǜ: *The ~ of work is making her ill.* 工作的忧虑使她生了病. ˈ**pressure-cooker** *n* [C] 压力锅〔鍋〕yālìguō. ˈ**pressure group** *n* [C] 压力集团〔團〕yālì jítuán.

pressurize /ˈpreʃəraɪz/ *v* [T] 1 (*into*) 迫使(某人)做某事 pòshǐzuò mǒushì. 2 使(飞机座舱等)保持恒定气〔氣〕压〔壓〕shǐbǎochí héngdìng qìyā.

prestige /preˈstiːʒ/ *n* [U] 威信 wēixìn; 威望 wēiwàng; 声〔聲〕望 shēngwàng. **prestigious** /-ˈstɪdʒəs/ *adj* 有威信的 yǒu wēixìn de; 有声望的 yǒu shēngwàng de.

presumably /prɪˈzjuːməblɪ; US -ˈzuː-/ *adv* 可假定地 kě jiǎdìng de; 据〔據〕推测 jù tuīcè; 大概 dàgài.

presume /prɪˈzjuːm; US -ˈzuːm/ *v* 1 [T] 假定 jiǎdìng; 假设 jiǎshè; 推测 tuīcè. 2 [I] [正式用语] 冒昧(做) màomèi; 敢于 gǎnyú: *I wouldn't ~ to advise you.* 我不敢向你提出劝告.

presumption /prɪˈzʌmpʃn/ *n* 1 [C] 假定 jiǎdìng; 假设 jiǎshè; 推测 tuīcè. 2 [U] [正式用语] 无〔無〕理 wúlǐ; 傲慢 àomàn; 放肆 fàngsì.

presumptuous /prɪˈzʌmptʃuəs/ *adj* 自行其是的 zì xíng qí shì de; 胆〔膽〕大妄为〔爲〕的 dǎn dà wàng wéi de.

presuppose /ˌpriːsəˈpəuz/ *v* [T] [正式用语] 1 预先假定 yùxiān jiǎdìng; 推测 tuīcè; 预料 yùliào. 2 以…为〔爲〕先决条〔條〕件 yǐ…wéi xiānjué tiáojiàn. **presupposition** /-sʌpəˈzɪʃn/ *n* [C, U].

pretence (美语 -tense) /prɪˈtens/ *n* [C, U] 假装〔裝〕jiǎzhuāng; 做作 zuòzuo: *a ~ of grief* 伤心的假象.

pretend /prɪˈtend/ *v* [I, T] 假装〔裝〕jiǎzhuāng; 佯装 yángzhuāng.

pretension /prɪˈtenʃn/ *n* [U, C, 尤作 pl] 自称〔稱〕zìchēng; 自命 zìmìng.

pretentious /prɪˈtenʃəs/ *adj* 自负的 zìfùde; 自命不凡的 zìmìng bùfán de. **pretentiously** *adv*. **pretentiousness** *n* [U].

pretext /ˈpriːtekst/ *n* [C] 借〔藉〕口 jièkǒu; 托词 tuōcí.

pretty /ˈprɪtɪ/ *adj* [-ier, -iest] 漂亮的 piàoliàngde; 标〔標〕致〔緻〕的 biāozhìde; 可爱〔愛〕的 kě'àide: *a ~ girl* 可爱的女孩子. **prettily** *adv*. **prettiness** *n* [U]. **pretty** *adv* 1 相当〔當〕xiāngdāng: *I'm ~ sure he came back.* 我非常肯定他回来了. 2 [习语] **pretty well** 几〔幾〕乎 jīhū.

prevail /prɪˈveɪl/ *v* [I] [正式用语] 1 流行 liúxíng; 盛行 shèngxíng. 2 获〔獲〕胜〔勝〕huòshèng. 3 [短语动词] **prevail on / upon sb to do sth** 劝〔勸〕说 quànshuō; 说服 shuōfú. **prevailing** *adj* 1 流行的 liúxíngde; 盛行的 shèngxíngde; 普遍的 pǔbiànde. 2 (风)常刮的 chángguāde.

prevalent /ˈprevələnt/ *adj* [正式用语]普遍的 pǔbiànde; 流行的 liúxíngde; 盛行的 shèngxíngde. **prevalence** /-ləns/ *n* [U].

prevent /prɪˈvent/ *v* [T] 阻止 zǔzhǐ; 妨碍〔礙〕fáng'ài; 防止 fángzhǐ. **prevention** /-ˈvenʃn/ *n* [U]. **preventive** *adj* 预防的 yùfángde; 防止的 fángzhǐde: *~ive medicine* 预防医学.

preview /ˈpriːvjuː/ *n* [C] 预演 yùyǎn; 预映 yùyìng; 预展 yùzhǎn. **preview** *v* [T] 预演 yùyǎn; 预映 yùyìng; 预展 yùzhǎn.

previous /ˈpriːvɪəs/ *adj* 以前的 yǐqiánde; 先前的 xiānqiánde: *the ~ day* 前一天. **previously** *adv*.

prey /preɪ/ *n* [U] 被捕食的动〔動〕物 bèi bǔshí de dòngwù; 捕获〔獲〕物 bǔhuòwù. **prey** *v* [习语] **prey on sb's ˈmind** 烦扰〔擾〕某人 fánrǎo mǒurén. **prey on sth** 捕食(动物) bǔshí.

price /praɪs/ *n* 1 [C] 价〔價〕格 jiàgé; 价钱〔錢〕jiàqian. 2 [sing] 代价 dàijià: *a small ~ to pay for freedom* 以小的代价换取自由. **price** *v* [T] 给…定价 gěi…dìngjià. ˈ**price increase** *n* [C] 价格上涨〔漲〕jiàgé shàngzhǎng. **priceless** *adj* 1 无〔無〕价的 wújiàde; 极〔極〕贵重的 jí guìzhòng de. 2 [非正式用语] 极有趣的 jí yǒuqù de; 十分荒唐的 shífēn huāngtáng de. ˈ**price list** *n* [C] 价目表 jiàmùbiǎo.

prick[1] /prɪk/ *v* 1 [T] 刺 cì; 扎 zhā; 戳 chuō. 2 [I, T] 引起刺痛 yǐnqǐ cìtòng; 感到刺痛 gǎndào cìtòng. 3 [习语] **prick up one's ears** (a) (马、狗等)竖〔豎〕起耳朵 shùqǐ ěrduo. (b) (人)突然注意听〔聽〕tūrán zhùyì tīng.

P

prick[2] /prɪk/ *n* [C] **1** 小洞 xiǎodòng；刺痕 cìhén；刺孔 cìkǒng. **2** 刺痛 cìtòng. **3** [⚠俚] (a) 屌 diǎo；阴〔陰〕茎〔莖〕yīnjīng. (b) [贬] 蠢人 chǔnrén.

prickle /ˈprɪkl/ *n* [C] **1** (植物的)刺 cì；(动物的)皮刺 pící. **2** 针刺般的感觉〔覺〕zhēncìbānde gǎnjué. **prickle** *v* [I, T] (使)感到刺痛 gǎndào cìtòng. **prickly** *adj* [-ier, -iest] **1** 多刺的 duōcìde. **2** [非正式用语] 易怒的 yìnùde.

pride /praɪd/ *n* **1** [U] (a) 自豪 zìháo；得意 déyì. (b) [sing] 引以自豪的人(或事物) yǐn yǐ zìháo de rén: *Their daughter was their ~ and joy*. 他们的女儿使他们引以自豪和愉快. **2** [U] 自尊 zìzūn. **3** [U] 骄〔驕〕傲 jiāo'ào；傲慢 àomàn；自大 zìdà. **4** [C] 狮〔獅〕群 shīqún. **pride** *v* [短语动词] **pride oneself on sth** 以…自豪 yǐ… zìháo.

priest /priːst/ *n* [C] 司铎〔鐸〕sīduó；司祭 sījì；教士 jiàoshì；牧师〔師〕mùshi；神父 shénfù. **the priesthood** *n* [sing] 司铎(或司祭、牧师、神父等)的职〔職〕位 sīduóde zhíwèi.

prig /prɪg/ *n* [C] [贬] 自以为〔爲〕道德高尚的人 zì yǐwéi dàodé gāoshàng de rén. **priggish** *adj*.

prim /prɪm/ *adj* [~mer, ~mest] 一本正经〔經〕的 yī běn zhèngjīng de；拘谨的 jūjǐnde: *~ and proper* 一本正经的；循规蹈矩的.

primary /ˈpraɪmərɪ; *US* -merɪ/ *adj* **1** 最初的 zuìchūde；最早的 zuìzǎode；初级的 chūjíde. **2** 首要的 shǒuyàode；主要的 zhǔyàode. **primarily** /ˈpraɪmerəlɪ; *US* praɪˈmerəlɪ/ *adv* 主要地 zhǔyàode. **primary** *n* [C] [*pl* -ies] (美国为大选推举候选人的)初选〔選〕chūxuǎn. **primary ˈcolour** *n* [C] 原色 yuánsè；基色(指能混合生成其他各种颜色的红、黄和蓝三色之一) jīsè. **ˈprimary school** *n* [C] **1** (英国)小学〔學〕(5 至 11 岁儿童) xiǎoxué. **2** (美国)初等学校(6 至 9 岁儿童) chūděng xuéxiào.

P

primate[1] /ˈpraɪmeɪt/ *n* [C] 灵〔靈〕长〔長〕目动〔動〕物 língzhǎngmù dòngwù.

primate[2] /ˈpraɪmeɪt/ *n* [C] 大主教 dàzhǔjiào；首席主教 shǒuxí zhǔjiào.

prime[1] /praɪm/ *adj* **1** 主要的 zhǔyàode；首要的 shǒuyàode. **2** 最好的 zuìhǎode；第一流的 dìyīliúde. ˌ**prime ˈminister** *n* [C] 首相 shǒuxiàng；总〔總〕理 zǒnglǐ.

prime[2] /praɪm/ *n* [sing] 最好部分 zuìhǎo bùfen: *in the ~ of life* 正在壮年.

prime[3] /praɪm/ *v* [T] **1** 在…上涂〔塗〕底色(或底漆) zài … shàng tú dǐsè. **2** 事先为〔爲〕…提供情况(或消息等) shìxiān wèi… tígōng qíngkuàng.

primer /ˈpraɪmə(r)/ *n* [C] 底漆 dǐqī；底层〔層〕涂〔塗〕料 dǐcéng túliào.

primeval (亦作 **-aeval**) /praɪˈmiːvl/ *adj* 原始的 yuánshǐde；远〔遠〕古的 yuǎngǔde.

primitive /ˈprɪmɪtɪv/ *adj* **1** 原始的 yuánshǐde；上古的 shànggǔde；早期的 zǎoqīde: *~ tribes* 原始部落. **2** 简单〔單〕的 jiǎndānde；古老的 gǔlǎode. **primitively** *adv*.

primrose /ˈprɪmrəuz/ *n* [C] 报〔報〕春花 bàochūnhuā.

prince /prɪns/ *n* [C] **1** 王子 wángzǐ；王孙〔孫〕wángsūn；亲〔親〕王 qīnwáng. **2** (小国的)君主 jūnzhǔ. **princely** *adj* **1** 王子的 wángzǐde；王侯的 wánghóude. **2** 豪华〔華〕的 háohuáde；慷慨的 kāngkǎide.

princess /prɪnˈses/ *n* [C] **1** 公主 gōngzhǔ. **2** 王妃 wángfēi.

principal /ˈprɪnsəpl/ *adj* 主要的 zhǔyàode；首要的 shǒuyàode；最重要的 zuì zhòngyào de. **principal** *n* [C] **1** 校长〔長〕xiàozhǎng；院长 yuànzhǎng. **2** [常作 sing] 本金 běnjīn；资本 zīběn. **principally** /-plɪ/ *adv* 主要地 zhǔyàode.

principality /ˌprɪnsɪˈpælətɪ/ *n* [C] [*pl* -ies] 公国〔國〕gōngguó；侯国 hóuguó.

principle /ˈprɪnsəpl/ *n* **1** [C] 原理 yuánlǐ；原则 yuánzé: *the ~ of justice* 公正的原则. **2** [C, U] (行为)准〔準〕则 zhǔnzé. **3** [习语] **in principle** 原则上 yuánzé shàng. **on principle** 根据〔據〕行为〔爲〕准则 gēnjù xíngwéi zhǔnzé；按照原则 ànzhào yuánzé.

print[1] /prɪnt/ *v* **1** [T] (a) 印在(纸)上 yìn zàishàng. (b) 印刷(书等) yìnshuā. **2** [I, T] 用印刷体〔體〕写〔寫〕yòng yìnshuātǐ xiě. **3** [T] 从〔從〕(底片)印出 cóngyìnchū. **printer** *n* [C] **1** 印刷工人 yìnshuā gōngrén；印刷商 yìnshuāshāng. **2** (计算机)打印机〔機〕dǎyìnjī. **ˈprintout** *n* [C, U] 打印输出 dǎyìn shūchū.

print[2] /prɪnt/ *n* **1** [U] 印刷字体〔體〕yìnshuā zìtǐ. **2** [C] 印痕 yìnhén；印记 yìnjì: *ˈfinger~s* 指印；指纹. **3** [C] 印出的图〔圖〕片 yìnchūde túpiàn；版画〔畫〕bǎnhuà. **4** [C] (由底片印出的)照片 zhàopiàn. **5** [习语] **in/out of print** (书)已印好的 yǐyìnhǎode, 可买〔買〕到的 kě mǎidào de；(书)已售完的 yǐ shòuwán de, 绝版的 juébǎnde.

prior /ˈpraɪə(r)/ *adj* 较早的 jiàozǎode；在前的 zàiqiánde；更重要的 gèng zhòngyào de: *a ~ engagement* 优先的约会. **ˈprior to** *prep* 在…之前 zài…zhī qián.

priority /praɪˈɒrətɪ; *US* -ˈɔːr-/ *n* [*pl* -ies] **1** [U] 优〔優〕先权〔權〕yōuxiānquán；优先 yōuxiān. **2** [C] 优先考虑〔慮〕的事 yōuxiān kǎolǜ de shì.

prise (亦作 **prize**, 尤用于美语) /praɪz/ *v* [T] 撬 qiào；撬起 qiàoqǐ；撬动〔動〕qiàodòng.

prism /ˈprɪzəm/ *n* [C] 棱〔稜〕镜 léngjìng；三棱镜 sānléngjìng.

prison /ˈprɪzn/ *n* [C, U] 监〔監〕狱 jiānyù；牢

房 láofáng. **prisoner** *n* [C] 犯人 fànrén; 囚犯 qiúfàn. ˌ**prisoner of** ˈ**war** *n* [C] 战〔戰〕俘 zhànfú.

privacy /ˈprɪvəsɪ, ˈpraɪv-/ *n* [U] (不受干扰的)独〔獨〕处〔處〕dúchǔ; 隐〔隱〕居 yǐnjū.

private /ˈpraɪvɪt/ *adj* 1 私人的 sīrénde; 私有的 sīyǒude; 私用的 sīyòngde; 个〔個〕人的 gèrénde. 2 不公开〔開〕的 bù gōngkāi de; 秘密的 mìmìde. 3 与〔與〕工作无〔無〕关〔關〕的 yǔ gōngzuò wúguān de. 4 私营〔營〕的 sīyíngde; 民间的 mínjiānde; 私立的 sīlìde: *a ~ school* 私立学校. 5 清静的 qīngjìngde. **private** *n* 1 [C] 士兵 shìbīng. 2 [习语] **in private** 私下地 sīxiàde. **privately** *adv*.

privatize /ˈpraɪvɪtaɪz/ *v* [T] 使私有化 shǐ sīyǒuhuà. **privatization** /ˌpraɪvɪtaɪˈzeɪʃn; *US* -tɪˈz-/ *n* [U].

privet /ˈprɪvɪt/ *n* [U] 水蜡〔蠟〕树〔樹〕shuǐlàshù.

privilege /ˈprɪvəlɪdʒ/ *n* 1 [C,U] 特权〔權〕tèquán; 特别待遇 tèbié dàiyù. 2 [C] 特殊的荣〔榮〕幸 tèshūde róngxìng: *a ~ to hear him sing* 听他歌唱不胜荣幸. **privileged** *adj* 享有特权的 xiǎngyǒu tèquán de.

prize[1] /praɪz/ *n* [C] 奖〔獎〕品 jiǎngpǐn; 奖金 jiǎngjīn; 奖赏 jiǎngshǎng. **prize** *adj* 获〔獲〕奖的 huòjiǎngde; 该得奖的 gāi déjiǎngde: *~ cattle* 优选的牛. **prize** *v* [T] 重视 zhòngshì; 珍视 zhēnshì.

prize[2] [尤用于美语] = PRISE.

pro[1] /prəʊ/ *n* [习语] **the** ˌ**pros and** ˈ**cons** /ˈkɒnz/ 赞成和反对〔對〕的论〔論〕点〔點〕zànchéng hé fǎnduì de lùndiǎn.

pro[2] /prəʊ/ *n* [C] [*pl* ~s] [非正式用语] short for PROFESSIONAL.

pro- /prəʊ/ *prefix* 亲〔親〕qīn; 赞〔讚〕成 zànchéng: *pro-American* 亲美的. **pro-aˈbortion** *adj* 赞成堕胎的 zànchéng duòtāi de. **pro-ˈchoice** *adj* 赞成堕胎的 zànchéng duòtāi de. **pro-ˈlife** *adj* 反堕胎的 fǎn duòtāide; 反安乐〔樂〕死的 fǎn ānlèsǐ de.

probability /ˌprɒbəˈbɪlətɪ/ *n* [*pl* -ies] 1 [U, sing] 可能性 kěnéngxìng: *There is little ~ that you will win*. 你不大可能取胜. 2 [C] (很)可能有的事 kěnéng yǒu de shì; 可能出现的结果 kěnéng chūxiàn de jiéguǒ. 3 [习语] **in** ˌ**all proba**ˈ**bility** 多半 duōbàn; 很可能 hěn kěnéng.

probable /ˈprɒbəbl/ *adj* 很可能发〔發〕生的 hěn kěnéng fāshēng de; 很可能成为〔爲〕事实〔實〕的 hěn kěnéng chéngwéi shìshí de. **probably** *adv*.

probation /prəˈbeɪʃn; *US* prəʊ-/ *n* [U] 1 缓刑 huǎnxíng: *a ~ officer* 缓刑监视官. 2 试用(期) shìyòng.

probe /prəʊb/ *v* [I, T] 1 细查 xìchá. 2 探查 tànchá; 探测 tàncè. **probe** *n* [C] 1 (医生用的)探子 tànzi; 探针 tànzhēn. 2 (*into*) 深入调查 shēnrù diàochá. 3 (航天)探测器 tàncèqì.

problem /ˈprɒbləm/ *n* [C] 问题 wèntí; 难〔難〕题 nántí. **problematic** /ˌprɒbləˈmætɪk/ *adj* 成问题的 chéng wèntí de; 疑难的 yínánde.

procedure /prəˈsiːdʒə(r)/ *n* [C, U] 程序 chéngxù; 手续〔續〕shǒuxù; 步骤 bùzhòu. **procedural** *adj*.

proceed /prəˈsiːd; *US* prəʊ-/ *v* [I] 1 (*to*) 继〔繼〕续〔續〕进〔進〕行 jìxù jìnxíng; 继续下去 jìxù xiàqù. 2 [正式用语]前进 qiánjìn; 行进 xíngjìn.

proceedings /prəˈsiːdɪŋz/ *n* [pl] [正式用语] 1 诉讼(程序) sùsòng. 2 (会议)议〔議〕程 yìchéng.

proceeds /ˈprəʊsiːdz/ *n* [pl] 收入 shōurù; 收益 shōuyì.

process /ˈprəʊses; *US* ˈprɒses/ *n* 1 [C] 步骤 bùzhòu; 程序 chéngxù. 2 [C] 方法 fāngfǎ; 工艺〔藝〕流程 gōngyì liúchéng. 3 [习语] **in the process of doing sth** 在…的进〔進〕程中 zài…de jìnchéng zhōng. **process** *v* [T] 1 加工贮〔貯〕藏(食物) jiāgōng zhùcáng. 2 冲〔沖〕洗(摄影胶片) chōngxǐ. 3 审〔審〕查 shěnchá; 处〔處〕理 chǔlǐ: *~ an application* 审查申请书. 4 (用计算机)处理 chǔlǐ.

procession /prəˈseʃn/ *n* [C] (人、车等的)行列 hángliè; 队〔隊〕伍 duìwǔ.

proclaim /prəˈkleɪm/ *v* [T] [正式用语]宣告 xuāngào; 宣布 xuānbù; 声〔聲〕明 shēngmíng. **proclamation** /ˌprɒkləˈmeɪʃn/ *n* 1 [C] 公告 gōnggào; 布告 bùgào; 声明 shēngmíng. 2 [U] 宣告 xuāngào; 公布 gōngbù; 声明 shēngmíng.

procure /prəˈkjʊə(r)/ *v* [T] [正式用语]取得 qǔdé; 获〔獲〕得 huòdé.

prod /prɒd/ *v* [-dd-] 1 [I, T] 刺 cì; 戳 chuō; 捅 tǒng. 2 [T] [喻]激励〔勵〕jīlì; 促使 cùshǐ. **prod** *n* [C].

prodigal /ˈprɒdɪgl/ *adj* [正式用语,贬]挥霍的 huīhuòde; 浪费的 làngfèide; 奢侈的 shēchǐde.

prodigious /prəˈdɪdʒəs/ *adj* 巨大的 jùdàde; 大得惊〔驚〕人的 dàde jīngrén de. **prodigiously** *adv*.

prodigy /ˈprɒdɪdʒɪ/ *n* [C] [*pl* -ies] 奇才 qícái; 天才 tiāncái.

produce /prəˈdjuːs; *US* -ˈduːs/ *v* [T] 1 引起 yǐnqǐ; 产〔產〕生 chǎnshēng. 2 制〔製〕造 zhìzào; 生产 shēngchǎn. 3 拿出 náchū; 出示 chūshì. 4 上演 shàngyǎn; 上映 shàngyìng; 播放 bōfàng. **produce** /ˈprɒdjuːs; *US* -duːs/ *n* [U] 产品 chǎnpǐn; 农〔農〕产品 nóngchǎnpǐn.

producer /prəˈdjuːsə(r); *US* -ˈduː- / *n* [C]

P

1 制〔製〕片人 zhìpiànrén; 制作人 zhìzuòrén; 舞台〔臺〕监〔監〕督 wǔtái jiāndū. 2 生产〔產〕者 shēngchǎnzhě; 制造者 zhìzàozhě.

product /ˈprɒdʌkt/ *n* [C] 1 产〔產〕品 chǎnpǐn; 产物 chǎnwù. 2 结果 jiéguǒ; 成果 chéngguǒ. 3 [数学] (乘)积〔積〕 jī. ˌ**product** ˈ**recall** *n* [C] 产〔產〕品召回 chǎnpǐn zhāohuí.

production /prəˈdʌkʃn/ *n* 1 [U] 生产〔產〕 shēngchǎn; 制〔製〕造 zhìzào. 2 [U] 产量 chǎnliàng. 3 [C] 上演的戏〔戲〕 shàngyǎnde xì; 上映的影片 shàngyìngde yǐngpiàn; 播放的电视节〔節〕目 bōfàngde diànshì jiémù.

productive /prəˈdʌktɪv/ *adj* 1 多产〔產〕的 duōchǎnde; 有生产力的 yǒu shēngchǎnlì de. 2 富有成效的 fùyǒu chéngxiào de; 得益的 déyìde: *a ~ meeting* 富有成效的会议. **productively** *adv*.

productivity /ˌprɒdʌkˈtɪvətɪ/ *n* [U] 生产〔產〕率 shēngchǎnlǜ.

profane /prəˈfeɪn; *US* prəʊ-/ *adj* [正式用语] 1 渎〔瀆〕神的 dúshénde; 亵〔褻〕渎的 xièdúde. 2 下流的 xiàliúde: *~ language* 下流语言. 3 世俗的 shìsúde. **profane** *v* [T] [正式用语] 亵渎 xièdú; 玷污 diànwū. **profanely** *adv*. **profanity** /preˈfænətɪ; *US* prəʊ-/ *n* [C,U] [*pl* -ies] 亵渎语言(或行为) xièdú yǔyán.

profess /prəˈfes/ *v* [T] [正式用语] 1 自称〔稱〕 zìchēng; 声〔聲〕称 shēngchēng; 伪〔僞〕称 wěichēng: *I don't ~ to be an expert*. 我不自认为是个专家. 2 公开〔開〕表明 gōngkāi biǎomíng. 3 宣称信仰 xuānchēng xìnyǎng. **professed** *adj* 1 自称的 zìchēngde; 声称的 shēngchēngde; 伪称的 wěichēngde. 2 公开表示的 gōngkāi biǎoshì de; 公开承认〔認〕的 gōngkāi chéngrèn de.

profession /prəˈfeʃn/ *n* [C] 1 职〔職〕业〔業〕 zhíyè. 2 表白 biǎobái; 表示 biǎoshì.

professional /prəˈfeʃənl/ *adj* 1 职〔職〕业〔業〕的 zhíyède; 职业上的 zhíyè shàng de. 2 内行的 nèihángde. 3 专〔專〕业的 zhuānyède; 非业余〔餘〕的 fēi yèyú de: *a ~ actor* 专业演员. **professional** *n* [C] 专业人员 zhuānyè rényuán. **professionalism** *n* [U] 专业技能 zhuānyè jìnéng; 职业特性 zhíyè tèxìng. **professionally** /-ʃənəlɪ/ *adv*.

professor /prəˈfesə(r)/ *n* [C] (大学)教授 jiàoshòu. **professorial** /ˌprɒfɪˈsɔːrɪəl/ *adj*. **professorship** *n* [C] 教授职〔職〕位 jiàoshòu zhíwèi.

proffer /ˈprɒfə(r)/ *v* [T] [正式用语] 提供 tígōng; 提出 tíchū.

proficient /prəˈfɪʃnt/ *adj* 熟练〔練〕的 shúliànde; 精通的 jīngtōngde. **proficiency** /-nsɪ/ *n* [U]. **proficiently** *adv*.

profile /ˈprəʊfaɪl/ *n* [C] 1 (面部的)侧面(像) cèmiàn. 2 传〔傳〕略 zhuànlüè; 人物简介 rénwù jiǎnjiè. 3 [习语] **a** ˌ**high** /ˌ**low** ˈ**profile** 引人注目 yǐn rén zhùmù; 不引人注目 bù yǐn rén zhùmù.

profit /ˈprɒfɪt/ *n* 1 [C, U] 利润 lìrùn; 赢利 yínglì. 2 [U] [正式用语] 利益 lìyì. **profit** *v* [I] *from* / *by* 有益 yǒuyì; 获〔獲〕利 huòlì. **profitable** *adj* 1 可获利的 kě huòlì de. 2 [喻] 有益的 yǒuyìde: *a ~ discussion* 有益的讨论. **profitably** *adv*. ˈ**profit** ˌ**warning** *n* [C] 盈利预警 yínglì yùjǐng.

profound /prəˈfaʊnd/ *adj* [正式用语] 1 深的 shēnde; 极〔極〕度的 jídùde: *a ~ effect* 极大的效应. 2 知识〔識〕渊〔淵〕博的 zhīshi yuānbóde; 思想深邃的 sīxiǎng shēnsuì de. **profoundly** *adv* 深深地 shēnshēnde.

profuse /prəˈfjuːs/ *adj* [正式用语] 极〔極〕其丰〔豐〕富的 jí qí fēngfù de; 大量的 dàliàngde. **profusely** *adv*. **profusion** /-ˈfjuːʒn/ *n* [sing, U] [正式用语] 大量 dàliàng; 丰富 fēngfù: *a ~ of flowers* 许多的鲜花.

program /ˈprəʊgræm; *US* -grəm/ *n* [C] 1 [计] 程序 chéngxù; 编码指令 biānmǎ zhǐlìng. 2 [美语] = PROGRAMME. **program** *v* [-mm-; 美语亦作 -m-] [T] 1 为〔爲〕…编制〔製〕程序 wèi…biānzhì chéngxù. 2 [美语] = PROGRAMME. **programmer** (美语亦作 **programer**) *n* [C] [计] 程序编制员 chéngxù biānzhìyuán.

programme /ˈprəʊgræm/ *n* [C] 1 (广播、电视) 节〔節〕目 jiémù. 2 计划〔劃〕 jìhuà; 方案 fāng'àn; 安排 ānpái: *a ~ of modernization* 现代化计划. 3 节目单〔單〕 jiémùdān; 课程 kèchéng; (教学)大纲〔綱〕 dàgāng. **programme** *v* [T] 计划 jìhuà; 安排 ānpái.

progress /ˈprəʊgres; *US* ˈprɒg-/ *n* [U] 1 前进〔進〕 qiánjìn; 行进 xíngjìn. 2 改进 gǎijìn; 发〔發〕展 fāzhǎn. 3 [习语] **in progress** 进行中 jìnxíng zhōng. **progress** /prəˈgres/ *v* [I] 前进 qiánjìn; 改进 gǎijìn.

progression /prəˈgreʃn/ *n* 1 [U] 前进〔進〕 qiánjìn; 进展 jìnzhǎn. 2 [C] 连续〔續〕 liánxù; 一系列 yíxìliè.

progressive /prəˈgresɪv/ *adj* 1 先进〔進〕的 xiānjìnde; 改革的 gǎigéde. 2 渐〔漸〕进的 jiànjìnde; 累进的 lěijìnde. **progressive** *n* [C] 进步人士 jìnbù rénshì; 改革派人士 gǎigépài rénshì. **progressively** *adv*.

prohibit /prəˈhɪbɪt; *US* prəʊ-/ *v* [T] [正式用语] 1 禁止 jìnzhǐ. 2 阻止 zǔzhǐ.

prohibition /ˌprəʊhɪˈbɪʃn; *US* ˌprəʊəˈbɪʃn/ *n* 1 [U] 禁止 jìnzhǐ; 阻止 zǔzhǐ. 2 [C] 禁令 jìnlìng; 禁律 jìnlǜ.

prohibitive /prəˈhɪbətɪv; *US* prəʊ-/ *adj* 1 (价格)高得买〔買〕不起的 gāode mǎibùqǐ de. 2 禁止的 jìnzhǐde; 禁止性的 jìnzhǐxìngde. pro-

P

hibitively *adv*.

project[1] /ˈprɒdʒekt/ *n* [C] 计划〔劃〕 jìhuà; 规划 guīhuà; 工程 gōngchéng; 事业〔業〕 shìyè.

project[2] /prəˈdʒekt/ *v* 1 [T] 设计 shèjì; 规划〔劃〕 guīhuà; 计划 jìhuà. 2 [T] 预计 yùjì; 推断〔斷〕 tuīduàn: ~ *the population growth* 预测人口的增加. 3 [T] *on*(*to*) 投射(光、影像等) tóushè; 放映 fàngyìng. 4 [T] 向他人表现(某人、某事或自己)以产〔產〕生好的印象 xiàng tārén biǎoxiàn yǐ chǎnshēng hǎode yìnxiàng. 5 [I] 伸出 shēnchū; 突出 tūchū.

projectile /prəˈdʒektaɪl/ *n* [C] 抛射物 pāoshèwù; 发〔發〕射物 fāshèwù; 射弹〔彈〕(如子弹、炮弹) shèdàn.

projection /prəˈdʒekʃn/ *n* 1 [U] 设计 shèjì; 规划〔劃〕 guīhuà; 投射 tóushè. 2 [C] 凸出物 tūchūwù. 3 [C] 预测 yùcè; 推断〔斷〕 tuīduàn.

projector /prəˈdʒektə(r)/ *n* [C] (电影)放映机〔機〕 fàngyìngjī; 幻灯 huàndēng.

proletariat /ˌprəʊlɪˈteərɪət/ *n* the proletariat [sing] [用 sing 或 pl v] 无〔無〕产〔產〕阶〔階〕级 wúchǎn jiējí; 工人阶级 gōngrén jiējí.

proliferate /prəˈlɪfəreɪt; *US* prəʊ-/ *v* [I] (数量)激增 jīzēng. **proliferation** /prəˌlɪfəˈreɪʃn; *US* prəʊ-/ *n* [U].

prolific /prəˈlɪfɪk/ *adj* (作家、艺术家等)多创〔創〕作的 duō chuàngzuò de.

prologue (美语亦作 -log) /ˈprəʊlɒg; *US* -lɔːg/ *n* [C] 1 序诗 xùshī; 开〔開〕场〔場〕白 kāichǎngbái. 2 (一系列事件的)开端 kāiduān; 序幕 xùmù.

prolong /prəˈlɒŋ; *US* -ˈlɔːŋ/ *v* [T] 延长〔長〕 yáncháng; 延伸 yánshēn. **prolonged** *adj* 持续〔續〕很久的 chíxù hěnjiǔ de; 长时〔時〕间的 cháng shíjiān de.

promenade /ˌprɒməˈnɑːd; *US* -ˈneɪd/ *n* [C] 散步场〔場〕所 sànbù chǎngsuǒ.

prominent /ˈprɒmɪnənt/ *adj* 1 (指人)著名的 zhùmíngde; 重要的 zhòngyàode. 2 显〔顯〕著的 xiǎnzhùde. 3 突出的 tūchūde; 凸出的 tūchūde. **prominence** *n* 1 [U] 突出 tūchū; 显著 xiǎnzhù; 卓越 zhuóyuè. 2 [C] [正式用语]突出物 tūchūwù; 突出部分 tūchū bùfen. **prominently** *adv*.

promiscuous /prəˈmɪskjʊəs/ *adj* [贬]性关〔關〕系〔係〕随便的 xìngguānxì suíbiàn de. **promiscuity** /ˌprɒmɪˈskjuːətɪ/ *n* [U]. **promiscuously** *adv*.

promise /ˈprɒmɪs/ *n* 1 [C] 承诺 chéngnuò; 允诺 yǔnnuò; 诺言 nuòyán. 2 [U] 成功(或成果、成绩)的征〔徵〕兆 chénggōngde zhēngzhào: *His work shows great* ~. 他的作品大有前途. **promise** *v* 1 [I, T] 允诺 yǔnnuò; 答应〔應〕 dāying. 2 [T] 使…很有可能 shǐ…hěnyǒu kěnéng: *It ~s to be a hot day*. 天气可望转热. **promising** *adj* 有希望的 yǒu xīwàng de; 有前途的 yǒu qiántú de.

promontory /ˈprɒməntrɪ; *US* -tɔːrɪ/ *n* [C] [*pl* -ies] 海角 hǎijiǎo; 岬 jiǎ.

promote /prəˈməʊt/ *v* [T] 1 提升 tíshēng; 晋升 jìnshēng. 2 促进〔進〕 cùjìn; 鼓励〔勵〕 gǔlì; 支持 zhīchí. 3 宣传〔傳〕 xuānchuán; 推销 tuīxiāo. **promoter** *n* [C] 创〔創〕办〔辦〕人 chuàngbànrén; 赞助人 zànzhùrén.

promotion /prəˈməʊʃn/ *n* [C, U] 1 提升 tíshēng; 晋升 jìnshēng. 2 (商品等的)宣传〔傳〕 xuānchuán; 推销 tuīxiāo.

prompt[1] /prɒmpt/ *adj* 迅速的 xùnsùde; 及时〔時〕的 jíshíde: *a* ~ *reply* 及时的答复. **promptly** *adv*. **promptness** *n* [U].

prompt[2] /prɒmpt/ *v* 1 [T] 促使 cùshǐ; 激励〔勵〕 jīlì. 2 [I, T] (为演员)提词 tící; 提白 tíbái. **prompt** *n* [C] (给演员)提词 tící; 提白 tíbái. **prompter** *n* [C] 提词员 tícíyuán.

prone /prəʊn/ *adj* 1 *to* 有…倾向的 yǒu…qīngxiàng de; 易于…的 yìyú…de: ~ *to infection* 易受感染. ˈ*accident*-~ 易出事故. 2 俯卧的 fǔwòde.

prong /prɒŋ; *US* prɔːŋ/ *n* [C] (叉的)尖齿〔齒〕 jiānchǐ.

pronoun /ˈprəʊnaʊn/ *n* [C] [语法]代词(如 *it*, *hers* 等) dàicí.

pronounce /prəˈnaʊns/ *v* [T] 1 发〔發〕…的音 fā…de yīn. 2 [正式用语]宣称〔稱〕 xuānchēng; 宣告 xuāngào. **pronounced** *adj* 明显〔顯〕的 míngxiǎnde; 显著的 xiǎnzhùde. **pronouncement** *n* [C] 声〔聲〕明 shēngmíng; 公告 gōnggào.

pronunciation /prəˌnʌnsɪˈeɪʃn/ *n* 1 [U] 发〔發〕音 fāyīn; 发音法 fāyīnfǎ. 2 [C] 读〔讀〕法 dúfǎ.

proof[1] /pruːf/ *n* 1 [C, U] 证〔證〕据〔據〕 zhèngjù; 证物 zhèngwù; 证言 zhèngyán. 2 [U] 证明 zhèngmíng; 证实〔實〕 zhèngshí; 验〔驗〕证 yànzhèng. 3 [C, 尤作 pl] 校样〔樣〕 jiàoyàng. 4 [U] (酒的)标〔標〕准〔準〕酒精度 biāozhǔn jiǔjīngdù.

proof[2] /pruːf/ *adj* (用以构成复合词)抗…的 kàng…de; 防…的 fáng…de; 耐…的 nài…de: ˌ*bullet*-~ ˈ*glass* 防弹玻璃. ˈ*water*~ 防水.

prop[1] /prɒp/ *n* [C] 1 支柱 zhīzhù; 支撑物 zhīchēngwù. 2 [喻]支持者 zhīchízhě; 后〔後〕盾 hòudùn. **prop** *v* [-pp-] [T] 支持 zhīchí; 支撑 zhīchēng.

prop[2] /prɒp/ *n* [C, 常作 pl] (舞台)道具 dàojù.

propaganda /ˌprɒpəˈgændə/ *n* [U] 宣传〔傳〕 xuānchuán; 传播 chuánbō.

propagate /ˈprɒpəgeɪt/ *v* 1 [I, T] 繁殖 fánzhí; 增殖 zēngzhí. 2 [T] [正式用语]传〔傳〕播 chuánbō: ~ *ideas* 传播观点. **propagation**

P

/ˌprɒpəˈgeɪʃn/ *n* [U].

propel /prəˈpel/ *v* [-ll-] [T] 推进〔進〕tuījìn; 推动〔動〕tuīdòng. **propeller** *n* [C] (轮船、飞机上的)螺旋桨〔槳〕luóxuánjiǎng; 推进器 tuījìnqì.

propensity /prəˈpensətɪ/ *n* [C] [*pl* -ies] (*for* / *to*) [正式用语]倾向 qīngxiàng; 习〔習〕性 xíxìng.

proper /ˈprɒpə(r)/ *adj* 1 正确〔確〕的 zhèngquède; 适〔適〕当〔當〕的 shìdàngde. 2 可敬的 kějìngde; 体〔體〕面的 tǐmiànde. 3 真的 zhēnde; 真实〔實〕的 zhēnshíde: *We've not had a ~ holiday in years.* 多年来我们没有过真正的假日. 4 本身的 běnshēnde: *There is a small hall and the concert hall ~.* 音乐厅主体建筑附有一间小厅. **properly** *adv* 正确地 zhèngquède. ˈ**proper name** (亦作 ˈ**proper noun**) *n* [C] [语法]专〔專〕有名词 zhuānyǒu míngcí.

property /ˈprɒpətɪ/ *n* [*pl* -ies] 1 [U] 财产〔產〕cáichǎn; 资产 zīchǎn; 所有物 suǒyǒuwù. 2 [C, U] 房地产 fángdìchǎn. 3 [C, 尤作 pl] 特性 tèxìng; 性质〔質〕xìngzhì: *the chemical properties of the metal* 金属的化学特性.

prophecy /ˈprɒfəsɪ/ *n* [*pl* -ies] 1 [U] 预言能力 yùyán nénglì. 2 [C] 预言 yùyán.

prophesy /ˈprɒfəsaɪ/ *v* [*pt*, *pp* -ied] [I, T] 预言 yùyán; 预告 yùgào.

prophet /ˈprɒfɪt/ *n* [C] 1 预言家 yùyánjiā; 预言者 yùyánzhě. 2 (宗教)先知 xiānzhī. **prophetic** /prəˈfetɪk/ *adj*.

propitious /prəˈpɪʃəs/ *adj* [正式用语]有利的 yǒulìde; 合适〔適〕的 héshìde.

P

proportion /prəˈpɔːʃn/ *n* 1 [C] 部分 bùfen; 份儿〔兒〕fènr. 2 [U] 比例 bǐlì; 比 bǐ. 3 **proportions** [pl] 大小 dàxiǎo; 面积〔積〕miànjī; 容积 róngjī; 体〔體〕积 tǐjī: *trade of substantial ~s* 大量的贸易. 4 [习语] **in proportion to sth** 与〔與〕…成比例 yǔ…chéng bǐlì: *paid in ~ to the work done* 报酬与工作量成比例. **proportional** *adj* 成比例的 chéngbǐlìde.

proposal /prəˈpəʊzl/ *n* [C] 1 计划〔劃〕jìhuà; 方案 fāng'àn. 2 求婚 qiúhūn.

propose /prəˈpəʊz/ *v* 1 [T] 提议〔議〕tíyì; 建议 jiànyì. 2 [T] 打算 dǎsuàn; 计划〔劃〕jìhuà. 3 [I, T] (*to*) 求婚 qiúhūn.

proposition /ˌprɒpəˈzɪʃn/ *n* [C] 1 观〔觀〕点〔點〕guāndiǎn; 见解 jiànjiě; 主张〔張〕zhǔzhāng. 2 (尤指商业)提议〔議〕tíyì; 建议 jiànyì. 3 [非正式用语] 要处〔處〕理的事 yào chǔlǐde shì. **proposition** *v* [T] 向…提出猥亵〔褻〕的要求 xiàng… tíchū wěixiè de yāoqiú.

proprietary /prəˈpraɪətrɪ; *US* -terɪ/ *adj* 独〔獨〕家制〔製〕造和销售的 dújiā zhìzào hé xiāoshòu de; 专〔專〕利的 zhuānlìde.

proprietor /prəˈpraɪətə(r)/ *n* [C] (*fem* -tress /-trɪs/) 所有人 suǒyǒurén; 业〔業〕主 yèzhǔ.

propriety /prəˈpraɪətɪ/ *n* [U] [正式用语]正当〔當〕(或得体)的行为〔爲〕zhèngdàngde xíngwéi; 礼〔禮〕貌 lǐmào.

propulsion /prəˈpʌlʃn/ *n* [U] 推进〔進〕tuījìn; 推进力 tuījìnlì.

pro rata /ˌprəʊ ˈrɑːtə/ *adv*, *adj* [正式用语] 成比例(的) chéng bǐlì.

prosaic /prəˈzeɪɪk/ *adj* 乏味的 fáwèide; 单〔單〕调的 dāndiàode.

proscribe /prəˈskraɪb; *US* prəʊ-/ *v* [T] [正式用语]禁止 jìnzhǐ.

prose /prəʊz/ *n* [U] 散文 sǎnwén.

prosecute /ˈprɒsɪkjuːt/ *v* [I, T] 对〔對〕…提起公诉 duì…tíqǐ gōngsù; 告发〔發〕gàofā; 检〔檢〕举〔舉〕jiǎnjǔ. **prosecution** /ˌprɒsɪˈkjuːʃn/ *n* 1 [C, U] 起诉 qǐsù; 告发 gàofā; 检举 jiǎnjǔ. 2 **the prosecution** [sing] [用 sing 或 pl v] 原告 yuángào; 代表原告的律师 dàibiǎo yuángào de lǜshī. **prosecutor** *n* [C] [尤用于美语].

prospect[1] /ˈprɒspekt/ *n* 1 [U] (*of*) 期望 qīwàng; 指望 zhǐwàng. 2 [C, U] 将〔將〕要发〔發〕生的事 jiāngyào fāshēng de shì; 期望中的事 qīwàng zhōng de shì. 3 **prospects** [pl] 成功的机〔機〕会〔會〕chénggōngde jīhuì.

prospect[2] /prəˈspekt; *US* ˈprɒs-/ *v* [I] (*for*) 勘探 kāntàn; 勘察 kānchá. **prospector** *n* [C].

prospective /prəˈspektɪv/ *adj* 预期的 yùqīde; 未来的 wèiláide.

prospectus /prəˈspektəs/ *n* [C] 章程 zhāngchéng; 简章 jiǎnzhāng; 简介 jiǎnjiè; 说明书〔書〕shuōmíngshū.

prosper /ˈprɒspə(r)/ *v* [I] 兴〔興〕旺 xīngwàng; 繁荣〔榮〕fánróng; 成功 chénggōng. **prosperity** /prɒˈsperətɪ/ *n* [U] 成功 chénggōng; 富足 fùzú. **prosperous** /ˈprɒspərəs/ *adj* 成功的 chénggōngde; 繁荣的 fánróngde.

prostitute /ˈprɒstɪtjuːt; *US* -tuːt/ *n* [C] 妓女 jìnǚ; 娼妓 chāngjì; 男妓 nánjì. **prostitute** *v* [T] 滥〔濫〕用(才能等) lànyòng; (为图利)糟蹋(自己) zāotà. **prostitution** /ˌprɒstɪˈtjuːʃn; *US* -ˈtuːʃn/ *n* [U].

prostrate /ˈprɒstreɪt/ *adj* 俯卧的 fǔwòde; 卧倒的 wòdǎode. **prostrate** /prɒˈstreɪt; *US* ˈprɒstreɪt/ *v* ~ **oneself** 使俯卧 shǐ fǔwò; 使拜倒 shǐ bàidǎo.

protagonist /prəˈtægənɪst/ *n* [C] 1 [正式用语](戏剧等的)主角 zhǔjué, 主人公 zhǔréngōng. 2 (运动等的)提倡者 tíchàngzhě; 拥〔擁〕护〔護〕者 yōnghùzhě.

protect /prəˈtekt/ *v* [T] 保护〔護〕bǎohù; 防护 fánghù. **protection** /prəˈtekʃn/ *n* 1 [U]

保护 bǎohù；防护 fánghù. 2 [C] 防护物 fánghùwù. **protective** *adj* 1 保护的 bǎohùde；防护的 fánghùde. 2 (*towards*) (对人)关〔關〕切保护的 guānqiè bǎohù de；有保护愿〔願〕望的 yǒu bǎohù yuànwàng de. **protector** *n* [C] 保护者 bǎohùzhě；保护装〔裝〕置 bǎohù zhuāngzhì.

protectorate /prəˈtektərət/ *n* [C] 受保护〔護〕国〔國〕(或领地) shòu bǎohùguó.

protégé /ˈprɒtɪʒeɪ; US ˌprəʊtɪˈʒeɪ/ *n* [C] 被保护〔護〕人 bèi bǎohù rén.

protein /ˈprəʊtiːn/ *n* [C,U] 蛋白质〔質〕dànbáizhì；朊 ruǎn.

protest[1] /ˈprəʊtest/ *n* [C, U] 抗议〔議〕kàngyì；抗议书〔書〕kàngyìshū；抗议活动〔動〕kàngyì huódòng.

protest[2] /prəˈtest/ *v* 1 [I,T] (*about* / *against* / *at*) 抗议〔議〕kàngyì；反对〔對〕fǎnduì；提出异〔異〕议 tíchū yìyì. 2 [T] 申明 shēnmíng；声〔聲〕言 shēngyán. 他严正申明自己无罪. **protester** *n* [C].

Protestant /ˈprɒtɪstənt/ *n* [C], *adj* 新教徒 xīnjiàotú；新教(徒)的 xīnjiàode.

protocol /ˈprəʊtəkɒl; US -kɔːl/ *n* [U] 礼〔禮〕仪〔儀〕lǐyí；外交礼节〔節〕wàijiāo lǐjié.

proton /ˈprəʊtɒn/ *n* [C] 质〔質〕子 zhìzǐ.

prototype /ˈprəʊtətaɪp/ *n* [C] 原型 yuánxíng.

protracted /prəˈtræktɪd; US prəʊ-/ *adj* 延长〔長〕的 yánchángde；拖延的 tuōyánde.

protractor /prəˈtræktə(r); US prəʊ- / *n* [C] 量角器 liángjiǎoqì；分度规 fēndùguī.

protrude /prəˈtruːd; US prəʊ-/ *v* [I, T] (使)伸出 shēnchū；(使)突出 tūchū. **protrusion** /-truːʒn/ *n* [C,U].

protuberance /prəˈtjuːbərəns; US prəʊˈtuː-/ *n* [C] [正式用语]隆起物 lóngqǐwù；凸出物 tūchūwù.

proud /praʊd/ *adj* 1 感到自豪的 gǎndào zìháo de；得意的 déyìde. 2 有自尊心的 yǒu zìzūnxīn de. 3 骄〔驕〕傲的 jiāo'àode；妄自尊大的 wàng zì zūn dà de；自负的 zìfùde. **proudly** *adv*.

prove /pruːv/ *v* [*pp* ~d; *US* ~n /ˈpruːvn/] 1 [T] 证〔證〕明 zhèngmíng；证实〔實〕zhèngshí. 2 被发〔發〕现(是) bèi fāxiàn；表现出 biǎoxiàn chū: *The attempts ~d to be useless*. 这些尝试证实是无用的.

proverb /ˈprɒvɜːb/ *n* [C] 谚语(如 *A stitch in time saves nine*.) yànyǔ；格言 géyán. **proverbial** /prəˈvɜːbɪəl/ *adj* 1 谚语的 yànyǔde；谚语所表达〔達〕的 yànyǔ suǒ biǎodá de. 2 众〔衆〕所周知的 zhòng suǒ zhōu zhī de.

provide /prəˈvaɪd/ *v* 1 [T] (*for*) 供给 gōngjǐ；供应〔應〕gōngyìng；提供 tígōng. 2 [短语动词] **provide for sb** 供应…所需 gōngyìng …suǒ xū. **provide for sth** (为某事可能发生) 预先准〔準〕备〔備〕yùxiān zhǔnbèi.

provided /prəˈvaɪdɪd/ (亦作 **providing** /prəˈvaɪdɪŋ/) *conj* (*that*) 在…条〔條〕件下 zài…tiáojiàn xià；除非 chúfēi；假如 jiǎrú.

providence /ˈprɒvɪdəns/ *n* [U] 天道 tiāndào；天意 tiānyì；天命 tiānmìng. **providential** /ˌprɒvɪˈdenʃl/ *adj* [正式用语]幸运〔運〕的 xìngyùnde.

province /ˈprɒvɪns/ *n* 1 [C] 省 shěng；行政区〔區〕xíngzhèngqū. 2 **the provinces** [pl] 首都以外的地方 shǒudū yǐwài de dìfāng；外省 wàishěng；外地 wàidì. 3 [sing] [正式用语](知识、责任的)范〔範〕围〔圍〕fànwéi. **provincial** *adj* 1 省的 shěngde；行政区的 xíngzhèngqūde；首都以外的 shǒudū yǐwài de. 2 偏狭〔狹〕的 piānxiáde；守旧〔舊〕的 shǒujiùde. **provincial** *n* [C] 外省人 wàishěngrén；外地人 wàidìrén；地方居民 dìfāng jūmín.

provision /prəˈvɪʒn/ *n* 1 [U] 供给 gōngjǐ；供应〔應〕gōngyìng；提供 tígōng. 2 [U] (*for*) 准〔準〕备〔備〕zhǔnbèi；预备 yùbèi. 3 **provisions** [pl] 食品的供应 shípǐnde gōngyìng. 4 [C] (法律文件中的)条〔條〕款 tiáokuǎn；规定 guīdìng.

provisional /prəˈvɪʒənl/ *adj* 临〔臨〕时〔時〕的 línshíde；暂时性的 zànshíxìngde. **provisionally** /-nəlɪ/ *adv*.

provocation /ˌprɒvəˈkeɪʃn/ *n* 1 [U] 激怒 jīnù；挑衅〔釁〕tiǎoxìn；刺激 cìjī. 2 [C] 挑衅性的事 tiǎoxìnxìngde shì；激怒人的事 jīnù rén de shì.

provocative /prəˈvɒkətɪv/ *adj* 1 激怒的 jīnùde；挑衅〔釁〕的 tiǎoxìnde；刺激的 cìjīde. 2 引起色欲的 yǐnqǐ sèyù de；挑逗的 tiǎodòude. **provocatively** *adv*.

provoke /prəˈvəʊk/ *v* [T] 1 激怒 jīnù；对〔對〕…挑衅〔釁〕duì…tiǎoxìn. 2 激起 jīqǐ；引起(感情等) yǐnqǐ.

prow /praʊ/ *n* [C] 船首 chuánshǒu.

prowess /ˈpraʊɪs/ *n* [U] [正式用语]高超的技艺〔藝〕gāochāode jìyì；杰〔傑〕出的才能 jiéchūde cáinéng.

prowl /praʊl/ *v* [I,T] (*about* / *around*) (为觅食、偷窃等)潜〔潛〕行 qiánxíng. **prowl** *n* [习语] **be on the prowl** 徘徊 páihuái；潜行 qiánxíng.

proximity /prɒkˈsɪmətɪ/ *n* [U] [正式用语] 邻〔鄰〕近 línjìn；接近 jiējìn. **proˈximity card** *n* [C] 感应〔應〕卡 gǎnyìngkǎ.

proxy /ˈprɒksɪ/ *n* [*pl* -ies] 1 [U] 代理权〔權〕dàilǐquán；代理投票 dàilǐ tóupiào. 2 [C] 代理人 dàilǐrén；代表 dàibiǎo.

prude /pruːd/ *n* [C] [贬]过〔過〕分拘谨的人 guòfèn jūjǐn de rén；(对性问题)故作正经〔經〕的人 gùzuò zhèngjing de rén. **prudish** *adj*.

prudent /ˈpruːdnt/ *adj* 谨慎的 jǐnshènde；慎重的 shènzhòngde. **prudence** /-dns/ *n* [U].

P

prudently *adv*.

prune[1] /pruːn/ *n* [C] 梅干〔乾〕méigān;梅脯 méifǔ.

prune[2] /pruːn/ *v* [T] 1 修剪(树枝等) xiūjiǎn. 2 [喻]删除 shānchú;除去 chúqù.

pry /praɪ/ *v* [*pt*, *pp* **pried** /praɪd/] [I] (*into*) 刺探(他人私事) cìtàn;打听〔聽〕dǎting.

PS /ˌpiː ˈes/ *abbr* (at the end of a letter) postscript.

psalm /sɑːm/ *n* [C] 圣〔聖〕诗 shèngshī;赞〔讚〕美诗 zànměishī;圣歌 shènggē.

pseudonym /ˈsjuːdənɪm; *US* ˈsuːdənɪm/ *n* [C] 假名 jiǎmíng;笔〔筆〕名 bǐmíng.

psyche /ˈsaɪkɪ/ *n* [C] 心灵〔靈〕xīnlíng;灵魂 línghún.

psychedelic /ˌsaɪkɪˈdelɪk/ *adj* 1 (药物)引起幻觉〔覺〕的 yǐnqǐ huànjué de. 2 (色彩等)产〔產〕生迷幻效果的 chǎnshēng míhuàn xiàoguǒ de.

psychiatry /saɪˈkaɪətrɪ; *US* sɪ-/ *n* [U] 精神病学〔學〕jīngshénbìngxué;精神病治疗〔療〕jīngshénbìng zhìliáo. **psychiatric** /ˌsaɪkɪˈætrɪk/ *adj*. **psychiatrist** *n* [C] 精神科医〔醫〕生 jīngshénkē yīshēng;精神病学家 jīngshénbìngxuéjiā.

psychic /ˈsaɪkɪk/ *adj* 1 有超自然力的 yǒu chāo zìránlì de. 2 (亦作 **psychical** /-kɪkl/) (a) 灵〔靈〕魂的 línghúnde;心灵的 xīnlíngde. (b) 超自然的 chāo zìrán de.

psychoanalysis /ˌsaɪkəʊəˈnæləsɪs/ *n* [U] 精神分析(治疗法) jīngshén fēnxī;心理分析(治疗法) xīnlǐ fēnxī. **psychoanalyse** /ˌsaɪkəʊˈænəlaɪz/ *v* [T] 给(某人)作精神(或心理)分析 gěizuò jīngshén fēnxī;用精神(或心理)分析法治疗〔療〕yòng jīngshén fēnxīfǎ zhìliáo. **psychoanalyst** /ˌsaɪkəʊˈænəlɪst/ *n* [C] 精神分析学〔學〕家 jīngshénfēnxīxuéjiā;心理分析学家 xīnlǐfēnxīxuéjiā.

psychology /saɪˈkɒləʤɪ/ *n* [U] 心理学〔學〕xīnlǐxué. **psychological** /ˌsaɪkəˈlɒʤɪkl/ *adj*. **psychologist** *n* [C] 心理学家 xīnlǐxuéjiā.

psychopath /ˈsaɪkəʊpæθ/ *n* [C] 精神变〔變〕态〔態〕者 jīngshénbiàntàizhě;精神病患者 jīngshénbìng huànzhě. **psychopathic** /ˌsaɪkəʊˈpæθɪk/ *adj*.

pt *abbr* 1 part. 2 pint. 3 point. 4 port.

PTO /ˌpiː tiː ˈəʊ/ *abbr* (at the bottom of a page, etc) please turn over 见下页 jiàn xiàyè.

pub /pʌb/ *n* [C] 酒店 jiǔdiàn;酒吧 jiǔbā.

puberty /ˈpjuːbətɪ/ *n* [U] 青春期 qīngchūnqī;发〔發〕育期 fāyùqī.

pubic /ˈpjuːbɪk/ *adj* 阴〔陰〕部的 yīnbùde;近阴部的 jìn yīnbù de.

public /ˈpʌblɪk/ *adj* 1 公众〔衆〕的 gōngzhòngde. 2 公用的 gōngyòngde;公共的 gōngòngde: ~ *money* 公款. *a* ~ *library* 公共图书馆. 3 公开〔開〕的 gōngkāide;众所周知的 zhòng suǒ zhōu zhī de. 4 [习语] **in the public ˈeye** 众所熟知的 zhòng suǒ shú zhī de;公众常见的 gōngzhòng chángjiàn de. **public** *n* 1 **the public** [sing] [用 sing 或 pl v] (a) 公众 gōngzhòng;民众 mínzhòng. (b) 一群人 yìqún rén: *the reading* ~ 读者大众. 2 [习语] **in public** 公开地 gōngkāide;公然 gōngrán. **ˌpublic ˈbar** *n* [C] [英国英语](酒店、旅馆里供应便宜饮品的)酒吧 jiǔbā. **ˌpublic ˈcompany, ˌpublic ˈlimited company** *n* [C] 公开招股公司 gōngkāi zhāogǔ gōngsī. **ˌpublic conˈvenience** *n* [C] [英国英语]公共厕所 gōnggòng cèsuǒ. **ˌpublic ˈhouse** *n* [C] [正式用语] = PUB. **publicly** *adv*. **ˌpublic reˈlations** *n* 1 [U] 公关〔關〕工作(或活动) gōngguān gōngzuò. 2 [pl] 公共关系〔係〕gōnggòng guānxi. **ˌpublic ˈschool** *n* [C] (英国)公学〔學〕(私立付费学校,寄宿制) gōngxué.

publication /ˌpʌblɪˈkeɪʃn/ *n* 1 [U] 出版 chūbǎn;刊印 kānyìn. 2 [C] 出版物 chūbǎnwù.

publicity /pʌbˈlɪsətɪ/ *n* [U] 1 广〔廣〕告 guǎnggào;宣传〔傳〕xuānchuán. 2 众所周知 zhòng suǒ zhōu zhī.

publicize /ˈpʌblɪsaɪz/ *v* [T] 宣传〔傳〕xuānchuán;使引人注意 shǐ yǐn rén zhùyì.

publish /ˈpʌblɪʃ/ *v* [T] 1 出版(书、期刊等) chūbǎn;发〔發〕行 fāxíng. 2 公布 gōngbù;发布 fābù. **publisher** *n* [C] 出版者 chūbǎnzhě;出版商 chūbǎnshāng;出版公司 chūbǎn gōngsī.

pucker /ˈpʌkə(r)/ *v* [I, T] (使)起皱〔皺〕qǐzhòu;(使)成褶 chéngzhě.

pudding /ˈpʊdɪŋ/ *n* [C, U] 1 甜点〔點〕心 tiándiǎnxīn;(一道)甜食 tiánshí. 2 布丁(用面粉等烘烤或蒸煮做成的甜食品) bùdīng.

puddle /ˈpʌdl/ *n* [C] 水坑 shuǐkēng;小水潭 xiǎo shuǐtán.

puff[1] /pʌf/ *v* 1 [I, T] 一阵阵地吹(或喷) yízhènzhènde chuī. 2 [I, T] 一口口地吸烟(或喷烟) yìkǒukǒude xīyān. 3 [I] 喘息 chuǎnxī. 4 [短语动词] **puff** (**sth**) **out** / **up** 膨胀〔脹〕péngzhàng. **puffed** *adj* [非正式用语]呼吸困难〔難〕的 hūxī kùnnan de;气〔氣〕喘吁吁的 qìchuǎn xūxū de.

puff[2] /pʌf/ *n* [C] 吹 chuī;呼 hū;喷 pēn;(空气、烟雾等)一股 yìgǔ. **ˌpuff ˈpastry** *n* [U] (做饼、糕用的)油酥面〔麵〕团〔團〕yóusū miàntuán. **puffy** *adj* [-ier, -iest] 膨胀〔脹〕的 péngzhàngde.

puffin /ˈpʌfɪn/ *n* [C] 海鹦(产于北大西洋的海鸟,喙大而色艳) hǎiyīng;角嘴海雀 jiǎozuǐhǎiquè.

pull[1] /pʊl/ *v* **1** [I, T] 拉 lā; 拖 tuō; 牵〔牽〕qiān: ~ *the cart up the hill* 把大车拉上小山. ~ *the plug out* 拔掉塞子. **2** [T] 用力移动〔動〕yònglì yídòng; 拔出 báchū; 抽出 chōuchū: ~ (*out*) *a tooth* 拔牙. **3** [T] 拉伤〔傷〕lāshāng; 扭伤 niǔshāng: ~ *a muscle* 扭伤肌肉. **4** [习语] **pull faces / a face** ⇨FACE. **pull a 'fast one (on sb)** [非正式用语]欺骗〔騙〕qīpiàn; 欺诈 qīzhà. **pull one's finger out** ⇨FINGER. **pull sb's 'leg** [非正式用语]开〔開〕…的玩笑 kāi…de wánxiào. **pull one's 'socks up** [非正式用语]努力改进〔進〕nǔlì gǎijìn. **pull sth to 'pieces** 苛刻地批评 kēkède pīpíng. **pull one's weight** 尽〔盡〕应〔應〕尽之力 jìn yīngjìn zhī lì. **5** [短语动词] **pull away** (车辆)开始开动 kāishǐ kāidòng. **pull sth down** 拆毁(如旧建筑物) chāihuǐ; 拆掉 chāidiào. **pull in** (a) (火车)进站 jìnzhàn, 到站 dàozhàn. (b) (车辆)停下 tíngxià. **pull sth off** [非正式用语]成功 chénggōng; 做成某事 zuòchéng mǒushì. **pull out** (车辆)驶出 shǐchū; 打斜 dǎxié. **pull (sb / sth) out (of sth)** (使某人或某事)从〔從〕…中退出 cóng…zhōng tuìchū: ~ *out of a race* 退出比赛. **pull over** (车辆)靠边〔邊〕(停下) kàobiān. **pull (sb) through** (使某人)恢复〔復〕健康 huīfù jiànkāng. **pull together** 同心协〔協〕力 tóngxīn xiélì. **pull oneself together** 控制自己(或感情) kòngzhì zìjǐ. **pull up** (车辆)停下 tíngxià. **pull sb up** [非正式用语]责备〔備〕zébèi; 训斥 xùnchì.

pull[2] /pʊl/ *n* **1** [C] 拉 lā; 拖 tuō; 牵〔牽〕qiān. **2** [sing] 力 lì; 引力 yǐnlì: *the ~ of the river current* 河水激流的冲力. **3** [U] [非正式用语] 影响〔響〕(力) yǐngxiǎng. **4** [sing] 持续〔續〕的努力 chíxùde nǔlì: *a hard ~ to the top of the hill* 为爬到山顶所作的艰苦努力.

pullet /ˈpʊlɪt/ *n* [C] 小母鸡〔鷄〕xiǎo mǔjī.

pulley /ˈpʊlɪ/ *n* [C] 滑轮〔輪〕huálún; 滑车 huáchē.

pullover /ˈpʊləʊvə(r)/ *n* [C] (毛衣等)套头〔頭〕衫 tàotóushān.

pulp /pʌlp/ *n* [U] **1** 果肉 guǒròu. **2** 纸浆〔漿〕zhǐjiāng. **pulp** *v* [T] 使成浆状〔狀〕shǐ chéng jiāngzhuàng.

pulpit /ˈpʊlpɪt/ *n* [C] (教堂的)讲〔講〕坛〔壇〕jiǎngtán; 布道坛 bùdàotán.

pulsate /pʌlˈseɪt; *US* ˈpʌlseɪt/ *v* [I] 有规律地跳动〔動〕yǒu guīlǜ de tiàodòng; 搏动 bódòng; 颤动 chàndòng. **pulsation** /-ˈseɪʃn/ *n* [C, U].

pulse /pʌls/ *n* **1** [C, 常作 sing] 脉搏 màibó. **2** [sing] (音乐的)节〔節〕拍 jiépāi. **pulse** *v* [I] (有规律地)跳动 tiàodòng; 搏动 bódòng.

pulverize /ˈpʌlvəraɪz/ *v* [T] **1** 把…研磨成粉 bǎ…yánmó chéng fěn; 粉碎 fěnsuì. **2** 摧毁 cuīhuǐ; 毁灭〔滅〕huǐmiè.

puma /ˈpjuːmə/ *n* [C] 美洲狮〔獅〕měizhōu shī.

pump /pʌmp/ *n* [C] 泵 bèng; 抽水(或气)机〔機〕chōushuǐjī; 唧筒 jītǒng. **pump** *v* **1** [T] 用泵抽出(或压入)(气体、液体等) yòng bèng chōuchū: *The heart ~s blood around the body.* 心脏把血液压送至全身. **2** [I] 似唧筒般运〔運〕作 sì jītǒngbān yùnzuò; 跳动〔動〕tiàodòng. **3** [T] [非正式用语]盘〔盤〕诘(信息) pánjié; 追问 zhuīwèn.

pumpkin /ˈpʌmpkɪn/ *n* [C, U] 南瓜 nánguā; 倭瓜 wōguā.

pun /pʌn/ *n* [C] 双关〔關〕语(如 'The soldier laid down his *arms*.') shuāngguānyǔ. **pun** *v* [-nn-] [I] 用双关语 yòng shuāngguānyǔ.

punch[1] /pʌntʃ/ *v* [T] 用拳猛击〔擊〕yòng quán měngjī. **punch** *n* **1** [C] 一拳 yìquán; 一击 yìjī. **2** [U] [非正式用语, 喻] 力量 lìliàng; 活力 huólì. **ˈpunch-up** *n* [C] 打架 dǎjià; 打斗〔鬥〕dǎdòu.

punch[2] /pʌntʃ/ *n* [C] 打孔器 dǎkǒngqì; 穿孔机〔機〕chuānkǒngjī; 冲〔衝〕床 chòngchuáng. **punch** *v* [T] (用打孔器)在…上打孔 zài…shang dǎ kǒng; (用冲床)冲 chòng.

punch[3] /pʌntʃ/ *n* [U] (用酒、果汁、糖、香料等搀和的)混合饮料 hùnhé yǐnliào.

punctual /ˈpʌŋktʃʊəl/ *adj* 准〔準〕时〔時〕的 zhǔnshíde; 即时的 jíshíde; 守时的 shǒushíde. **punctuality** /ˌpʌŋktʃʊˈælətɪ/ *n* [U]. **punctually** *adv*.

punctuate /ˈpʌŋktʃʊeɪt/ *v* **1** [I, T] 加标〔標〕点〔點〕(于) jiā biāodiǎn. **2** [T] (*with / by*) [常用被动语态]不时〔時〕打断〔斷〕bùshí dǎduàn. **punctuation** /ˌpʌŋktʃʊˈeɪʃn/ *n* [U] 标点法 biāodiǎnfǎ.

puncture /ˈpʌŋktʃə(r)/ *n* [C] 小孔 xiǎo kǒng; (车胎等的)穿孔 chuānkǒng. **puncture** *v* [I, T] (轮胎)被刺穿 bèi cìchuān; 穿孔 chuānkǒng.

pungent /ˈpʌndʒənt/ *adj* (气味、味道)有刺激性的 yǒu cìjīxìng de; 刺鼻的 cìbíde; 辣的 làde.

punish /ˈpʌnɪʃ/ *v* [T] **1** 处〔處〕罚 chǔfá; 惩〔懲〕罚 chéngfá. **2** [非正式用语]粗暴地对〔對〕待 cūbàode duìdài. **punishing** *adj* 使人筋疲力尽〔盡〕的 shǐ rén jīn pí lì jìn de; 吃力的 chīlìde. **punishment** *n* **1** [U] 处罚 chǔfá; 惩罚 chéngfá. **2** [C] 受罚 shòufá; 刑罚 xíngfá.

punitive /ˈpjuːnɪtɪv/ *adj* [正式用语]处〔處〕罚的 chǔfáde; 刑罚的 xíngfáde; 严〔嚴〕厉〔厲〕的 yánlìde.

punk /pʌŋk/ *n* **1** [U] (亦作 **punk ˈrock**) 朋客(一种摇滚乐, 自 20 世纪 70 年代末期起流行) péngkè. **2** [C] (亦作 **punk ˈrocker**) 朋客摇滚〔滾〕乐〔樂〕迷 péngkè yáogǔnyuèmí.

punnet /ˈpʌnɪt/ *n* [C] 水果篮〔籃〕子 shuǐguǒ

lánzi.

punt /pʌnt/ *n* [C] (用篙撑的)方头〔頭〕平底船 fāngtóu píngdǐchuán. **punt** *v* [I] 用篙撑方头平底船 yòng gāo chēng fāngtóu píngdǐchuán.

punter /ˈpʌntə(r)/ *n* [C] [英国非正式用语] 1 (对赛马)下赌注的人 xià dǔzhù de rén. 2 顾〔顧〕客 gùkè.

puny /ˈpjuːnɪ/ *adj* [-ier, -iest] 弱小的 ruòxiǎode;微弱的 wēiruòde.

pup /pʌp/ *n* [C] 1 =PUPPY. 2 幼小动〔動〕物(如小海豹) yòuxiǎo dòngwù.

pupil[1] /ˈpjuːpl/ *n* [C] 学〔學〕生 xuésheng;小学生 xiǎoxuésheng.

pupil[2] /ˈpjuːpl/ *n* [C] 瞳孔 tóngkǒng.

puppet /ˈpʌpɪt/ *n* [C] 1 木偶 mù'ǒu. 2 傀儡 kuǐlěi.

puppy /ˈpʌpɪ/ *n* [C] [*pl* -ies] 小狗 xiǎo gǒu;幼犬 yòuquǎn.

purchase /ˈpɜːtʃəs/ *v* [T] [正式用语]购〔購〕买〔買〕gòumǎi. **purchase** *n* [正式用语] 1 [U] 购买 gòumǎi. 2 [C] 购买之物 gòumǎi zhī wù. **purchaser** *n* [C] 购买人 gòumǎirén;买主 mǎizhǔ.

pure /pjʊə(r)/ *adj* [~r, ~st] 1 纯粹的 chúncuìde;不搀〔攙〕杂〔雜〕的 bù chānzá de. 2 无〔無〕有害物质〔質〕的 wú yǒuhài wùzhì de;洁〔潔〕净〔淨〕的 jiéjìngde. 3 无罪的 wúzuìde;无错的 wúcuòde. 4 (声音)清晰的 qīngxīde. 5 完全的 wánquánde;十足的 shízúde: *They met by ~ chance*. 他们相遇纯属巧合. 6 纯理论〔論〕的 chún lǐlùn de;非实〔實〕用的 fēi shíyòng de: *~ science* 理论科学. **purely** *adv* 完全地 wánquánde;仅〔僅〕仅 jǐnjǐn.

purée /ˈpjʊəreɪ; *US* pjʊəˈreɪ/ *n* [U, C] (蔬菜、水果等制成的)泥 ní;酱〔醬〕jiàng.

purgatory /ˈpɜːgətrɪ; *US* -tɔːrɪ/ *n* [U] 1 (天主教教义中的)炼〔煉〕狱 liànyù. 2 [喻]暂时〔時〕受苦的地方 zànshí shòukǔ de dìfang;一时的受难 yìshíde shòunàn.

purge /pɜːdʒ/ *v* [T] 1 (*of* / *from*) 清洗(党员) qīngxǐ;清除(异己) qīngchú: *~ a party of extremists*, *~ extremists from the party* 把极端主义者清除出党. 2 (*of* / *from*) 使洁〔潔〕净〔淨〕shǐ jiéjìng;使净化 shǐ jìnghuà. **purge** *n* [C] 清洗 qīngxǐ;清除 qīngchú.

purify /ˈpjʊərɪfaɪ/ *v* [*pt*, *pp* -ied] [T] 净〔淨〕化 jìnghuà;使纯净 shǐ chúnjìng. **purification** /ˌpjʊərɪfɪˈkeɪʃn/ *n* [U].

purist /ˈpjʊərɪst/ *n* [C] (语言、艺术等方面的)纯粹主义〔義〕者 chúncuì zhǔyì zhě.

puritan /ˈpjʊərɪtən/ *adj*, *n* [C] 1 [常作贬] 道德上极〔極〕拘谨的(人) dàodé shàng jí jūjǐn de;禁欲〔慾〕的(人) jìnyùde. 2 Puritan 清教徒(的) qīngjiàotú. **puritanical** /ˌpjʊərɪˈtænɪkl/ *adj* [常作贬].

purity /ˈpjʊərətɪ/ *n* [U] 纯净〔淨〕chúnjìng;纯正 chúnzhèng;纯洁〔潔〕chúnjié.

purl /pɜːl/ *n* [U] (编织中的)反针 fǎnzhēn. **purl** *v* [I, T] 用反针编织〔織〕yòng fǎnzhēn biānzhī.

purple /ˈpɜːpl/ *adj* 紫色的 zǐsède.

purpose /ˈpɜːpəs/ *n* 1 [C] 目的 mùdì;意图〔圖〕yìtú. 2 [U] [正式用语]决心 juéxīn;意志 yìzhì. 3 [习语] **on purpose** 故意地 gùyìde;有意地 yǒuyìde. **purposeful** *adj* 坚〔堅〕定的 jiāndìngde;果断〔斷〕的 guǒduànde.

purr /pɜː(r)/ *v* [I] (猫)发〔發〕呼噜声〔聲〕fā hūlūshēng. **purr** *n* [C] 呼噜声 hūlūshēng.

purse[1] /pɜːs/ *n* [C] 1 钱〔錢〕包 qiánbāo;小钱袋 xiǎo qiándài. 2 (募集或捐赠的)一笔〔筆〕款 yìbǐkuǎn;一笔奖〔獎〕金 yìbǐ jiǎngjīn. 3 [美语]女用手提包 nǚyòng shǒutíbāo.

purse[2] /pɜːs/ *v* [T] 噘起(嘴唇) juēqǐ.

purser /ˈpɜːsə(r)/ *n* [C] (轮船上的)事务〔務〕长〔長〕shìwùzhǎng.

pursue /pəˈsjuː; *US* -ˈsuː/ *v* [T] [正式用语] 1 追赶〔趕〕zhuīgǎn;追捕 zhuībǔ. 2 进〔進〕行 jìnxíng;继〔繼〕续〔續〕jìxù: *~ one's studies* 深造. **pursuer** *n* [C].

pursuit /pəˈsjuːt; *US* -ˈsuːt/ *n* [正式用语] 1 [U] 追赶〔趕〕zhuīgǎn;追求 zhuīqiú;从〔從〕事 cóngshì. 2 [C, 常作 pl] 职〔職〕业〔業〕zhíyè;爱〔愛〕好 àihào.

purvey /pəˈveɪ/ *v* [T] [正式用语]供应〔應〕(食品等) gōngyìng;提供 tígōng. **purveyor** *n* [C].

pus /pʌs/ *n* [U] 脓〔膿〕nóng.

push[1] /pʊʃ/ *v* 1 [I, T] 推动〔動〕tuīdòng;推进〔進〕tuījìn: *~ a bike up the hill* 推自行车上山. *~ the plug in* 塞入塞子. 2 [T] [非正式用语]逼迫…做某事 bīpò…zuò mǒushì;催促 cuīcù. 3 [I, T] (*for*) 对〔對〕…施加压〔壓〕力以获〔獲〕得某物 duì…shījiā yālì yǐ huòdé mǒuwù: *~ sb for payment* 催逼某人付款. 4 [T] [非正式用语] 贩卖〔賣〕(毒品) fànmài. 5 [习语] **be pushed for sth** [非正式用语] 缺少 quēshǎo: *be ~ed for time* 缺少时间. 6 [短语动词] **push sb around** [非正式用语]摆〔擺〕布某人 bǎibù mǒurén. **push off** [非正式用语]走开〔開〕zǒukāi. **ˈpush-bike** *n* [C] [非正式用语]自行车 zìxíngchē;脚踏车 jiǎotàchē. **ˈpush-button** *adj* 用按钮操纵〔縱〕的 yòng ànniǔ cāozòng de. **ˈpush-chair** *n* [C] (折叠式)幼儿〔兒〕车 yòu'érchē. **pusher** *n* [C] [非正式用语]毒品贩子 dúpǐn fànzi.

push[2] /pʊʃ/ *n* [C, 常作 sing] 1 推 tuī;搡 sǎng. 2 奋〔奮〕力 fènlì;猛攻 měnggōng. 3 [习语] **give sb / get the push** [非正式用语]解雇〔僱〕某人 jiěgù mǒurén;被解雇 bèi jiěgù.

pussy /ˈpʊsɪ/ *n* [C] [*pl* -ies] (亦作 ˈ**pussy-cat**) (儿语)猫咪 māomī.

P

put /pʊt/ *v* [*pt*, *pp* ~, *pres part* ~ting] [T] 1 放 fàng; 放置 fàngzhì: *She ~ the book on the table*. 她把书放在桌子上.[喻] *They ~ the blame on me*. 他们责备我. 2 书〔書〕写〔寫〕shūxiě; 标〔標〕上 biāo shàng: ~ *his name on the form* 把他的名字写在表格上. 3 使处〔處〕于特定状〔狀〕态〔態〕shǐ chǔyú tèdìng zhuàngtài: ~ *sth right* 改正某事. 4 (a) (*to*) 提交 tíjiāo; 提出 tíchū: ~ *a proposal to a client* 向当事人提出建议. (b) 表达〔達〕biǎodá: ~ *sth politely* 有礼貌地表达某事. 5 [习语] **put one's cards on the table** ⇨ CARD. **put the clock back** ⇨ CLOCK. **put one's 'oar in** ⇨ OAR. **put sth right** ⇨ RIGHT[1]. **put sb / sth to 'rights** ⇨ RIGHT[3]. 6 [短语动词] **put sth a'bout** 传〔傳〕播 chuánbō; 散布(谣言等) sànbù. **put sth a'cross** (to sb) 沟〔溝〕通 gōutōng; 传达 chuándá. **put sth a'side** (a) (暂时)丢开〔開〕diūkāi; 放下 fàngxià: ~ *aside a book* 放下书. (b) 储存(钱) chǔcún. (c) 置之不理 zhì zhī bùlǐ; 忽视 hūshì: ~ *one's disagreements aside* 抛开自己的不同意见. **put sth at sth** 估计 gūjì: *I ~ the possible cost at £500*. 我估计可能值 500 英镑. **put sth a'way** 把…收起 bǎ… shōuqǐ; 放好 fànghǎo: ~ *the cup away in the cupboard* 把杯子收进柜橱里. **put sth 'back** (a) 把…放回原处 bǎ…fànghuí yuánchù: ~ *the book back on the shelf* 把书放回到书架上. (b) 倒拨〔撥〕(钟表的)指针 dàobō…zhǐzhēn. (c) 延误 yánwù; 拖延 tuōyán: ~ *the meeting back by one hour* 会议延误一小时. **put sth 'by** 储存…备〔備〕用 chǔcún…bèiyòng. **put sb down** (a) (公共汽车)让〔讓〕(乘客)下车 ràng…xiàchē. (b) [非正式用语] 贬低 biǎndī; 奚落 xīluò. **put sth down** (a) 放在…之上 fàngzài… zhī shàng. (b) 将〔將〕(飞机)降落 jiāng…jiàngluò; 着陆〔陸〕zhuólù. (c) 取缔 qǔdì; 镇压〔壓〕zhènyā: ~ *down a rebellion* 镇压叛乱. (d) 写下 xiěxià; 记下 jìxià. (e) 杀〔殺〕死(有病动物) shāsǐ. **put sth down to sth** 认〔認〕为〔爲〕某事系〔係〕由另一事引起 rènwéi mǒushì xì yóu lìngyíshì yǐnqǐ: *I ~ his failure down to laziness*. 我把他的失败归因于他的懒惰. **put sth forward** (a) 提出 tíchū; 建议〔議〕jiànyì: ~ *forward a new idea* 提出一新的构想. (b) 拨快(钟表)的指针 bōkuài… de zhǐzhēn. **put sth in** (a) 实〔實〕行 shíxíng; 做 zuò: ~ *in an hour's work* 做一小时工作. (b) 安装〔裝〕ānzhuāng; 设置 shèzhì: ~ *a new bath in* 安装新的澡盆. **put (sb / sth) in for sth** 参〔參〕加竞〔競〕赛 cānjiā jìngsài; 申请(工作等) shēnqǐng: ~ *a painting in for the competition* 把一幅画送去参赛. **put sb off** 推迟〔遲〕(同某人的)会〔會〕见 tuīchí huìjiàn. **put sb off (sth / sb)** (a) 打搅〔攪〕某人 dǎjiǎo mǒurén: *Don't ~ me off when I'm trying to concentrate*. 我正要集中注意力时, 别打搅我. (b) 使对…失去兴〔興〕趣 shǐ duì… shīqù xìngqù; 使反感 shǐ fǎngǎn. **put sth off** (a) 关〔關〕掉 guāndiào: ~ *the television off* 关掉电视机. (b) 推迟 tuīchí. **put sth 'on** (a) 穿上 chuānshàng: ~ *a coat on* 穿上外套. (b) 涂〔塗〕(化妆品等) tú. (c) 操作 cāozuò: ~ *on the television* 打开电视机. (d) 安排 ānpái; 提供 tígōng: ~ *on extra trains* 开加班火车. (e) 上演 shàngyǎn; 演出 yǎnchū: ~ *on a play* 安排一剧的演出. (f) 长胖 zhǎngpàng; 增加体〔體〕重 zēngjiā tǐzhòng: ~ *on a stone* (*in weight*) (体重)增加一㕧(的重量). **put sb out** (a) 使不安 shǐ bù'ān; 使恼〔惱〕怒 shǐ nǎonù. (b) 使不方便 shǐ bù fāngbiàn: *I hope my visit won't ~ you out*. 我希望我的拜访不致使你感到不便. **put sth out** (a) 熄灭〔滅〕xīmiè; 关掉 guāndiào: ~ *out the lights* 关灯. (b) 发〔發〕布 fābù; 广〔廣〕播 guǎngbō: ~ *out a warning* 发出警告. **put sth over** = PUT STH ACROSS. **put sb through** 为…接通电〔電〕话 wèi…jiētōng diànhuà. **put up sth** 进〔進〕行(抵抗等) jìnxíng: ~ *up a fight* 进行战斗. **put sb up** 提供食宿 tígōng shísù. **put sth up** (a) 举〔舉〕起 jǔqǐ; 抬〔擡〕起 táiqǐ: ~ *one's hand up* 举起手. (b) 建造 jiànzào; 搭建 dājiàn: ~ *a tent up* 支起帐篷. (c) 增加 zēngjiā: ~ *up the rent* 提高租金. (d) 提供(资金) tígōng. **put 'up** (at ...) 下榻(于…) xiàtà: ~ *up at a hotel* 下榻于一家旅馆. **put sb up to sth** 唆使…做坏〔壞〕事 suōshǐ…zuò huàishì. **put up with sb / sth** 容忍 róngrěn; 忍受 rěnshòu: ~ *up with bad behaviour* 容忍不良行为. **'put-down** *n* 贬低的话 biǎndī de huà.

putrefy /ˈpjuːtrɪfaɪ/ *v* [*pt*, *pp* -ied] [I] 腐烂〔爛〕fǔlàn; 腐败 fǔbài. **putrefaction** /ˌpjuːtrɪˈfækʃn/ *n* [U].

putrid /ˈpjuːtrɪd/ *adj* 腐烂〔爛〕的 fǔlànde; 腐败的 fǔbàide; 发〔發〕臭的 fāchòude.

putt /pʌt/ *v* [I, T] (高尔夫球)轻〔輕〕击〔擊〕(球) qīngjī.

putty /ˈpʌtɪ/ *n* [U] 油灰 yóuhuī; 腻子 nìzi.

puzzle /ˈpʌzl/ *n* [C] 1 难〔難〕题 nántí. 2 测验〔驗〕(智力、技巧等)的问题 cèyàn…de wèntí; 智力玩具 zhìlì wánjù: *a 'crossword ~* 纵横字谜. **puzzle** *v* 1 [T] 使迷惑 shǐ míhuò; 使为〔爲〕难 shǐ wéinán: *I'm ~d by his not replying to my letter*. 他不给我回信使我困惑不解. 2 [I] *over* 苦思 kǔsī. 3 [短语动词] **puzzle sth out** 苦思而解决 kǔsī ér jiějué.

PVC /ˌpiː viː ˈsiː/ *n* [U] 聚氯乙烯(一种塑料) jùlǜyǐxī.

pygmy (亦作 **pigmy**) /ˈpɪgmɪ/ *n* [C] [*pl*

-ies] 1 Pigmy（非洲等地的身体矮小的）俾格米人 Bǐgémǐrén. 2 侏儒 zhūrú; 矮人 ǎirén; 矮小的动〔動〕物 ǎixiǎo de dòngwù.

pyjamas /pəˈdʒɑːməz; *US* -ˈdʒæm-/ *n* [pl] 睡衣裤 shuìyīkù.

pylon /ˈpaɪlən; *US* -lɒn/ *n* [C] 电〔電〕缆〔纜〕塔 diànlǎntǎ.

pyramid /ˈpɪrəmɪd/ *n* [C] 1（古代埃及的）金字塔 jīnzìtǎ. 2 金字塔形之物 jīnzìtǎxíng zhī wù.

pyre /ˈpaɪə(r)/ *n* [C] 大堆可燃的木料 dàduī kěránde mùliào;（火葬用的）柴堆 cháiduī.

python /ˈpaɪθn; *US* -θɒn/ *n* [C] 蟒蛇 mǎngshé; 巨蛇 jùshé.

Q q

Q, q /kjuː/ *n* [C] [*pl* Q's, q's /kjuːz/] 英语的第十七个〔個〕字母 Yīngyǔde dìshíqīgè zìmǔ.

quack[1] /kwæk/ *v* [I], *n* [C]（鸭子）嘎嘎地叫 gāgāde jiào;（鸭子叫的）嘎嘎声〔聲〕gāgāshēng.

quack[2] /kwæk/ *n* [C] [非正式用语] 庸医〔醫〕yōngyī; 江湖医生 jiānghú yīshēng.

quad /kwɒd/ *n* [C] [非正式用语] 1 short for QUADRANGLE. 2 short for QUADRUPLET.

quadrangle /ˈkwɒdræŋgl/ *n* [C] 1 四边〔邊〕形 sìbiānxíng. 2（有建筑物围着的）方院 fāngyuàn.

quadruped /ˈkwɒdrʊped/ *n* [C] 四足动〔動〕物 sìzú dòngwù.

quadruple /ˈkwɒdrʊpl; *US* kwɒˈdruːpl/ *adj* 由四部分组成的 yóu sìbùfen zǔchéng de. **quadruple** *n* [C] 四倍 sìbèi. **quadruple** *v* [I, T] 使成四倍 shǐ chéng sìbèi; 以四乘（某数）yǐ sì chéng.

quadruplet /ˈkwɒdruːplet; *US* kwɒˈdruːp-/ *n* [C] 四胞胎中的一个〔個〕孩子 sìbāotāi zhōng de yígè háizi.

quagmire /ˈkwægmaɪə(r), 亦读 kwɒg-/ *n* [C] 沼泽〔澤〕zhǎozé; 泥潭 nítán.

quail[1] /kweɪl/ *n* [C] 鹑 chún; 鹌鹑 ānchún.

quail[2] /kweɪl/ *v* [I] [正式用语] 害怕 hàipà; 胆〔膽〕怯 dǎnqiè; 畏缩 wèisuō.

quaint /kweɪnt/ *adj* 古雅的 gǔyǎde; 奇特的 qítède. **quaintly** *adv*.

quake /kweɪk/ *v* [I] 震动〔動〕zhèndòng; 颤动 chàndòng.

qualification /ˌkwɒlɪfɪˈkeɪʃn/ *n* 1 [C] 资格 zīgé; 资历〔歷〕zīlì. 2 [U, C] 先决条〔條〕件 xiānjué tiáojiàn: *accept an offer with ~s* 有条件地接受报价. 3 [U] 取得资格 qǔdé zīgé.

qualify /ˈkwɒlɪfaɪ/ *v* [*pt*, *pp* -ied] 1 [I, T]（使）具有资格 jùyǒu zīgé;（使）合格 hégé;（使）合适〔適〕héshì: *She'll ~ as a doctor next year*. 她明年具备当医生的资格. 2 [T] 使不一般化 shǐ bú yìbānhuà; 使不极〔極〕端 shǐ bù jíduān. **qualified** *adj* 1 有资格的 yǒu zīgé de; 合格的 hégéde. 2 有限制的 yǒu xiànzhì de; 有保留的 yǒu bǎoliú de: *qualified approval* 有保留的同意.

qualitative /ˈkwɒlɪtətɪv; *US* -teɪt-/ *adj* 性质〔質〕的 xìngzhìde; 质量的 zhìliàngde.

quality /ˈkwɒlətɪ/ *n* [*pl* -ies] 1 [U, C] 品质〔質〕pǐnzhì. 2 [C] 特质 tèzhì; 特性 tèxìng: *Kindness is not one of her qualities*. 仁慈不是她的特点.

qualm /kwɑːm/ *n* [C] 怀〔懷〕疑 huáiyí; 疑虑〔慮〕yílǜ.

quandary /ˈkwɒndərɪ/ *n* [C] [*pl* -ies] 窘境 jiǒngjìng; 困惑 kùnhuò.

quantitative /ˈkwɒntɪtətɪv; *US* -teɪt/ *adj* 量的 liàngde; 数〔數〕量的 shùliàngde.

quantity /ˈkwɒntətɪ/ *n* [C, U] [*pl* -ies] 数〔數〕目 shùmù;（尤指巨大的）数量 shùliàng.

quantum /ˈkwɒntəm/ *n* [C] 量子 liàngzǐ. ˈ**quantum leap** *n* [C] 激增 jīzēng; 跃〔躍〕进〔進〕yuèjìn. ˈ**quantum theory** *n* [U] 量子理论〔論〕liàngzǐ lǐlùn.

quarantine /ˈkwɒrəntiːn; *US* ˈkwɔːr-/ [U]（防止传染病的）隔离〔離〕期 gélíqī. **quarantine** *v* [T] 将〔將〕…隔离 jiāng…gélí.

quarrel /ˈkwɒrəl; *US* ˈkwɔːrəl/ *n* [C] 1 争吵 zhēngchǎo; 吵架 chǎojià; 口角 kǒujiǎo. 2 抱怨的缘由 bàoyuànde yuányóu; 失和的原因 shīhéde yuányīn. **quarrel** *v* [-ll-; 美语 -l-] [I] 1 争吵 zhēngchǎo; 吵架 chǎojià; 口角 kǒujiǎo. 2 *with* 挑剔 tiāotì; 不同意 bù tóngyì. **quarrelsome** /-səm/ *adj* 爱〔愛〕争吵的 ài zhēngchǎo de.

quarry[1] /ˈkwɒrɪ; *US* ˈkwɔːrɪ/ *n* [C] 采〔採〕石场〔場〕cǎishíchǎng. **quarry** *v* [*pt*, *pp* -ied] [T] 从〔從〕采石场采得 cóng cǎishíchǎng cǎidé.

quarry[2] /ˈkwɒrɪ; *US* ˈkwɔːrɪ/ *n* [C, 常作 sing] [*pl* -ies] 猎〔獵〕物（鸟、兽）lièwù.

quart /kwɔːt/ *n* [C] 夸脱（液量单位，等于 2 品脱，或英制约 1.14 升）kuātuō.

quarter /ˈkwɔːtə(r)/ *n* 1 [C] 四分之一 sìfēn zhī yī. 2 [C] 一刻钟〔鐘〕（或 15 分钟）yíkèzhōng: *a ~ to four*; (*US*) *a ~ of four* 差一刻四点. *a ~ past six*; (*US*) *a ~ after six* 六点一刻. 3 [C] 季（度）jì; 三个〔個〕月 sāngèyuè. 4 [C]（城镇中的）区〔區〕qū; 地区 dìqū: *the business ~* 商业区. 5 [C]（提供帮助、消息等的）人士或团〔團〕体〔體〕rénshì huò tuántǐ. 6 **quarters** [pl] 营〔營〕房 yíngfáng; 住处〔處〕zhùchù: *married ~s* 已婚者的住所. **quarter** *v* [T] 1 将〔將〕…四等分 jiāng…sìděngfēn. 2 供给…住宿 gōngjǐ…zhùsù.

Q

ˌquarter ˈfinal *n* [C] 四分之一决赛 sì fēn zhī yī juésài. ˈquartermaster *n* [C] 军需官 jūnxūguān.

quarterly /ˈkwɔːtəlɪ/ *adj, adv* 季度的(地) jìdùde;按季度(的) àn jìdù. **quarterly** *n* [C] [*pl* -ies] 季刊 jìkān.

quartet /kwɔːˈtet/ *n* [C] 四重唱(曲) sìchóngchàng;四重奏(曲) sìchóngzòu.

quartz /kwɔːts/ *n* [U] 石英 shíyīng.

quash /kwɒʃ/ *v* [T] 废〔廢〕止 fèizhǐ;撤销 chèxiāo;宣布无〔無〕效 xuānbù wúxiào: ~ *a revolt/an appeal* 平息叛乱;撤销上诉.

quaver /ˈkweɪvə(r)/ *v* 1 [I] (声音)颤抖 chàndǒu. 2 [T] 用颤声〔聲〕唱 yòng chànshēng chàng;用颤声说 yòng chànshēng shuō. **quaver** *n* [C, 常作 sing] 颤音 chànyīn.

quay /kiː/ *n* [C] 码头〔頭〕mǎtóu.

queasy /ˈkwiːzɪ/ *adj* [-ier, -iest] (想)呕〔嘔〕吐的 ǒutùde;(感到)恶〔惡〕心的 ěxīnde.

queen /kwiːn/ *n* [C] 1 女王 nǚwáng. 2 王后 wánghòu. 3 (地位、相貌等)出众〔衆〕的女人 chūzhòng de nǚrén;出类〔類〕拔萃的女子 chū lèi bá cuì de nǚzǐ. 4 (国际象棋中的)后 hòu. 5 (纸牌中的)王后 wánghòu. 6 (蜜蜂、蚂蚁等的)后 hòu. queen ˈmother *n* [C] 太后 tàihòu.

queer /kwɪə(r)/ *adj* 1 奇怪的 qíguàide;不平常的 bù píngcháng de. 2 [俚,贬]同性恋〔戀〕的 tóngxìngliànde. 3 [旧,非正式用语]不舒服的 bù shūfu de. **queer** *n* [C] [俚,贬]男同性恋者 nán tóngxìngliànzhě.

quell /kwel/ *v* [T] 镇压〔壓〕zhènyā;平息 píngxī.

quench /kwentʃ/ *v* [T] 1 解(渴) jiě. 2 扑〔撲〕灭〔滅〕pūmiè;熄灭 xīmiè.

query /ˈkwɪərɪ/ *n* [C] [*pl* -ies] 问题 wèntí;疑问 yíwèn. **query** *v* [*pt, pp* -ied] [T] 1 对〔對〕…表示怀〔懷〕疑 duì…biǎoshì huáiyí. 2 问 wèn;询问 xúnwèn.

quest /kwest/ *n* [C] [正式用语](历时较久的)寻〔尋〕求 xúnqiú;寻找 xúnzhǎo.

question[1] /ˈkwestʃən/ *n* 1 [C] 问题 wèntí. 2 [C] 议〔議〕题 yìtí;需讨论〔論〕的问题 xū tǎolùn de wèntí. 3 [U] 疑问 yíwèn: *His honesty is beyond* ~. 他的诚实是无可怀疑的. 4 [习语] in ˈquestion 讨论中的 tǎolùn zhōng de. out of the ˈquestion 不可能的 bù kěnéng de. ˈquestion mark *n* [C] 问号〔號〕wènhào.

question[2] /ˈkwestʃən/ *v* [T] 1 问(某人)问题 wèn wèntí;询问 xúnwèn. 2 怀〔懷〕疑 huáiyí. **questionable** *adj* 成问题的 chéng wèntí de;可疑的 kěyíde.

questionnaire /ˌkwestʃəˈneə(r)/ *n* [C] 问题单 wèntídān;调查表 diàochábiǎo.

queue /kjuː/ *n* [C] (人或车辆等的)行列 hángliè,长〔長〕队〔隊〕chángduì. **queue** *v* [I] 排队 páiduì děnghòu.

quibble /ˈkwɪbl/ *v* [I] (为小事)争论〔論〕zhēnglùn. **quibble** *n* [C] 吹毛求疵 chuī máo qiú cī.

quiche /kiːʃ/ *n* [C] 蛋奶火腿蛋糕 dànnǎi huǒtuǐ dàngāo.

quick /kwɪk/ *adj* 1 快的 kuàide;迅速的 xùnsùde. 2 急躁的 jízàode;性急的 xìngjíde: *a* ~ *temper* 性情急躁. 3 聪〔聰〕敏的 cōngmǐnde;有才智的 yǒu cáizhì de: *He's* ~ *at* (*learning*) *languages*. 他敏于学习语言. 4 [习语] be quick off the mark ⇨ MARK[1]. quick on the uptake ⇨ UPTAKE. **quick** *adv* 快地 kuàide;迅速地 xùnsùde. **quick** *n* [sing] (指甲下的)嫩肉 nènròu. **quickly** *adv*. **quickness** *n* [U]. ˌquick-ˈwitted *adj* 聪明的 cōngmíngde;机〔機〕智的 jīzhìde.

quicken /ˈkwɪkən/ *v* [I, T] 加快 jiākuài;变〔變〕快 biànkuài.

quicksand /ˈkwɪksænd/ *n* [U, C] 流沙(区) liúshā.

quid /kwɪd/ *n* [C] [*pl* quid] [英国非正式用语]镑 bàng.

quiet /ˈkwaɪət/ *adj* 1 轻〔輕〕声〔聲〕的 qīngshēngde;安静的 ānjìngde. 2 不激动〔動〕的 bù jīdòng de;不烦恼〔惱〕的 bù fánnǎo de: *a* ~ *life* 平静的生活. 3 温和的 wēnhéde;文静的 wénjìngde. 4 (颜色)不鲜艳〔艷〕的 bù xiānyàn de;暗淡的 àndànde. **quiet** *n* 1 [U] 寂静 jìjìng;安静 ānjìng. 2 [习语] on the quiet 秘密地 mìmìde. **quieten** /-tn/ *v* [I, T] (使)安静 ānjìng;安静(或平静)下来 ānjìng xiàlái. **quietly** *adv*. **quietness** *n* [U].

quill /kwɪl/ *n* [C] 1 (a) 大羽毛 dà yǔmáo. (b) 羽毛笔〔筆〕yǔmáobǐ. 2 (豪猪的)刺 cì.

quilt /kwɪlt/ *n* [C] 被子 bèizi;被褥 bèirù. **quilted** *adj* 中间垫〔墊〕有软物的 zhōngjiān diàn yǒu ruǎnwù de.

quin /kwɪn/ (美语 quint /kwɪnt/) *n* [C] [非正式用语] short for QUINTUPLET.

quinine /kwɪˈniːn; *US* ˈkwaɪnaɪn/ *n* [U] 奎宁〔寧〕kuíníng;金鸡〔鷄〕纳霜 jīnjīnàshuāng.

quintet /kwɪnˈtet/ *n* [C] 五重唱(曲) wǔchóngchàng;五重奏(曲) wǔchóngzòu.

quintuplet /ˈkwɪntjuːplet; *US* kwɪnˈtuːplɪt/ *n* [C] 五胞胎中的一个〔個〕孩子 wǔbāotāi zhōng de yígè háizi.

quip /kwɪp/ *n* [C] 妙语 miàoyǔ;讽〔諷〕刺话 fěngcìhuà. **quip** *v* [-pp-] [I] 讥〔譏〕讽 jīfěng;说妙语 shuō miàoyǔ.

quirk /kwɜːk/ *n* [C] 1 古怪举〔舉〕动〔動〕gǔguài jǔdòng;怪癖 guàipǐ. 2 突发〔發〕事件 tūfā shìjiàn;偶然的事 ǒurándе shì.

quit /kwɪt/ *v* [-tt-; *pt, pp* quit, 或英国英语 ~ted] 1 [T] [非正式用语]停止(做) tíngzhǐ. 2

Q

[I, T] 离〔離〕开〔開〕líkāi；辞〔辭〕去 cíqù.

quite /kwaɪt/ *adv* **1** 达〔達〕到某种〔種〕程度 dádào mǒuzhǒng chéngdù；相当〔當〕xiāngdāng：～ *hot* 相当热. **2** 完全地 wánquánde；全部 quánbù：*She played* ～ *brilliantly!* 她演奏得确实很优美！**3**（用作表示同意）：*Q*～(*so*). 的确（如此）. **4**〔习语〕**quite a/an** 异〔異〕常的 yìchángde：*There's* ～ *a story about how they met.* 关于他们怎样相识有个非同寻常的故事.

quiver[1] /ˈkwɪvə(r)/ *v* [I, T] 颤动〔動〕chàndòng；抖动 dǒudòng. **quiver** *n* [C] 颤抖的动作 chàndǒude dòngzuò.

quiver[2] /ˈkwɪvə(r)/ *n* [C] 箭袋（或箭囊）jiàndài；箭筒 jiàntǒng.

quiz /kwɪz/ *n* [C] [*pl* **～zes**] 智力竞〔競〕赛 zhìlì jìngsài；答问比赛 dáwèn bǐsài. **quiz** *v* [**-zz-**] [T] 问…问题 wèn…wèntí；对〔對〕…测验〔驗〕duì…cèyàn.

quizzical /ˈkwɪzɪkl/ *adj* 戏〔戲〕弄的 xìnòngde；取笑的 qǔxiàode；揶揄的 yéyúde. **quizzically** /-klɪ/ *adv*.

quoit /kɔɪt; *US* kwɔɪt/ *n* **1** [C]（掷环套桩游戏中用的）铁环〔環〕（或绳圈等）tiěhuán. **2** **quoits** [用 sing v] 掷〔擲〕环套桩〔樁〕游戏〔戲〕zhìhuán tàozhuāng yóuxì.

quota /ˈkwəʊtə/ *n* [C] 配额 pèi'é；限额 xiàn'é.

quotation /kwəʊˈteɪʃn/ *n* **1** [C] 引文 yǐnwén；引语 yǐnyǔ. **2** [U] 引用 yǐnyòng；引证〔證〕yǐnzhèng. **3** [C] 估价〔價〕gūjià；报〔報〕价 bàojià. **quoˈtation marks** *n* [pl] 引号〔號〕（' ' 或 " "）yǐnhào.

quote /kwəʊt/ *v* **1** [I, T] 引用 yǐnyòng；引述 yǐnshù. **2** [T] 引证〔證〕yǐnzhèng. **3** [T] 报〔報〕…的价〔價〕bào…de jià；开〔開〕（价）kāi. **quote** *n* [非正式用语] **1** [C] short for QUOTATION 1. short for QUOTATION 3. **2** **quotes** [pl] short for QUOTATION MARKS (QUOTATION).

quotient /ˈkwəʊʃnt/ *n* [C] [数学] 商 shāng.

R r

R, r /ɑː(r)/ *n* [C] [*pl* **R's, r's** /ɑːz/] 英语的第十八个〔個〕字母 Yīngyǔ de dìshíbāgè zìmǔ.

rabbi /ˈræbaɪ/ *n* [C] 拉比（犹太教教士，犹太教法学导师）lābǐ.

rabbit /ˈræbɪt/ *n* [C] 兔 tù. **rabbit** *v* [I] *on* [非正式用语] 无〔無〕针对〔對〕性地长〔長〕谈 wú zhēnduìxìngde chángtán.

rabble /ˈræbl/ *n* [C] 乌〔烏〕合之众〔衆〕wū hé zhī zhòng. **ˈrabble-rousing** *adj* 煽动〔動〕性的 shāndòngxìngde.

rabid /ˈræbɪd/ *adj* **1** 患狂犬病的 huàn kuángquǎnbìng de. **2** [喻] 极〔極〕端的 jíduānde；疯〔瘋〕狂的 fēngkuángde：*a* ～ *Conservative* 偏激的英国保守党党员.

rabies /ˈreɪbiːz/ *n* [U] 狂犬病 kuángquǎnbìng.

race[1] /reɪs/ *n* [C] **1**（速度的）比赛 bǐsài，竞〔競〕赛 jìngsài. **2** 比赛 bǐsài；竞争 jìngzhēng：*the arms* ～ 军备竞赛. **race** *v* [I, T] **1** (*against*) 参〔參〕加速度竞赛 cānjiā sùdù jìngsài. **2**（使）疾走 jízǒu；（使）迅跑 xùnpǎo. **3** 参加赛马 cānjiā sàimǎ. **ˈracecourse** *n* [C] 赛马场〔場〕sàimǎchǎng；赛马跑道 sàimǎ pǎodào. **ˈracehorse** *n* [C] 赛马用的马 sàimǎ yòng de mǎ. **ˈrace-track** *n* [C] **1** 跑道 pǎodào. **2** [美语] 赛马场 sàimǎchǎng；（赛马）跑道 pǎodào.

race[2] /reɪs/ *n* **1** [C, U] 人种〔種〕rénzhǒng；种族 zhǒngzú. **2** [C]（动植物的）类〔類〕lèi；属〔屬〕shǔ；种 zhǒng；族 zú：*the human* ～ 人类. **3** [C] 民族 mínzú. **ˈrace relations** *n* [pl] 种族关〔關〕系〔係〕zhǒngzú guānxì.

racial /ˈreɪʃl/ *adj* 种〔種〕族的 zhǒngzúde；人种的 rénzhǒngde. **racialism**（亦作 **racism** /ˈreɪsɪzəm/）*n* [U] 种族偏见 zhǒngzú piānjiàn；种族主义〔義〕zhǒngzú zhǔyì. **racialist**（亦作 **racist** /ˈreɪsɪst/）*adj*, *n* [C]. **racially** *adv*.

rack[1] /ræk/ *n* [C] **1** 架子 jiàzi；挂〔掛〕物架 guàwùjià；搁物架 gēwùjià. **2**（火车、客机等坐位上方的）行李架 xínglǐjià.

rack[2] /ræk/ *v* **1** [T]（疾病等）使痛苦 shǐ tòngkǔ；折磨 zhémó. **2** [习语] **rack one's ˈbrains** 绞尽〔盡〕脑〔腦〕汁 jiǎo jìn nǎozhī；苦苦思索 kǔkǔ sīsuǒ.

rack[3] /ræk/ *n* [习语] **go to ˌrack and ˈruin** 毁灭〔滅〕huǐmiè；破坏〔壞〕pòhuài.

racket[1]（亦作 **racquet**）/ˈrækɪt/ *n* [C] **1**（网球、羽毛球等的）球拍 qiúpāi. **2** **rackets**（亦作 **racquets**）[用 sing v]（在四周有围墙的场地玩的）网〔網〕拍式墙〔牆〕球戏〔戲〕wǎngpāishì qiángqiúxì，墙网球戏 qiángwǎngqiúxì.

racket[2] /ˈrækɪt/ *n* [非正式用语] **1** [sing] 吵闹〔鬧〕chǎonào；喧嚷 xuānrǎng. **2** [C] 敲诈 qiāozhà；勒索 lèsuǒ. **racketeer** /ˌrækəˈtɪə(r)/ *n* [C] 敲诈勒索者 qiāozhà lèsuǒ zhě.

racy /ˈreɪsɪ/ *adj* [**-ier, -iest**] 生动〔動〕的 shēngdòngde；有趣的 yǒuqùde；不雅（有点下流）的 bùyǎde. **racily** *adv*. **raciness** *n* [U].

radar /ˈreɪdɑː(r)/ *n* [U] 雷达〔達〕léidá.

radiant /ˈreɪdɪənt/ *adj* **1** 光辉灿〔燦〕烂〔爛〕的 guānghuī cànlàn de；光芒四射的 guāngmáng sì shè de. **2**（人）容光焕发〔發〕的 róngguāng huànfā de；喜气〔氣〕洋洋的 xǐqì yángyáng de：

R

～ *beauty* 喜笑颜开的美人. **radiance** /-əns/ *n* [U]. **radiantly** *adv*.

radiate /ˈreɪdɪeɪt/ *v* [I, T] **1** 发〔發〕出(光或热) fāchū. **2** [喻]流露 liúlù; 显〔顯〕示 xiǎnshì: *She ～s confidence*. 她显示出信心.

radiation /ˌreɪdɪˈeɪʃn/ *n* [U] **1** 发〔發〕光 fāguāng; 放热〔熱〕 fàngrè; 辐射 fúshè. **2** 放射性 fàngshèxìng; 放射现象 fàngshè xiànxiàng.

radiator /ˈreɪdɪeɪtə(r)/ *n* [C] **1** 暖气〔氣〕装〔裝〕置 nuǎnqì zhuāngzhì; 散热〔熱〕器 sànrèqì. **2** (汽车等发动机的)冷却器 lěngquèqì.

radical /ˈrædɪkl/ *adj* **1** 根本的 gēnběnde; 基本的 jīběnde. **2** 完全的 wánquánde; 彻〔徹〕底的 chèdǐde. **3** 赞成彻底政治改革的 zànchéng chèdǐ zhèngzhì gǎigé de; 激进〔進〕的 jījìnde. **radical** *n* [C] 激进分子 jījìn fènzǐ. **radically** /-klɪ/ *adv*.

radii *pl* of RADIUS.

radio /ˈreɪdɪəʊ/ *n* [*pl* ～s] **1** [U] (a) 无〔無〕线〔綫〕电〔電〕传〔傳〕送 wúxiàndiàn chuánsòng. (b) 无线电广〔廣〕播 wúxiàndiàn guǎngbō. **2** [C] 收音机〔機〕 shōuyīnjī. **radio** *v* [I, T] 用无线电发〔發〕送讯息 yòng wúxiàndiàn fāsòng xùnxī; 发报〔報〕 fābào.

radioactive /ˌreɪdɪəʊˈæktɪv/ *adj* 放射性的 fàngshèxìngde; 放射性引起的 fàngshèxìng yǐnqǐ de. **radioactivity** /-ækˈtɪvətɪ/ *n* [U].

radiography /ˌreɪdɪˈɒgrəfɪ/ *n* [U] 射线〔綫〕照相(术) shèxiàn zhàoxiàng. **radiographer** /-fə(r)/ *n* [C] 射线摄〔攝〕影师〔師〕 shèxiàn shèyǐngshī.

radiology /ˌreɪdɪˈɒlədʒɪ/ *n* [U] 放射学〔學〕 fàngshèxué. **radiologist** *n* [C].

radish /ˈrædɪʃ/ *n* [C] (放在色拉中生吃的)小萝〔蘿〕卜〔蔔〕 xiǎoluóbo.

radium /ˈreɪdɪəm/ *n* [U] 镭 léi.

radius /ˈreɪdɪəs/ *n* [C] [*pl* **radii** /-dɪaɪ/] **1** 半径〔徑〕 bànjìng. **2** 半径范〔範〕围〔圍〕 bànjìng fànwéi: *within a two-mile ～ of the factory* 在工厂周围两英里以内.

raffia /ˈræfɪə/ *n* [U] 酒椰叶〔葉〕纤〔纖〕维 jiǔyēyè xiānwéi.

raffle /ˈræfl/ *n* [C] 对〔對〕奖〔獎〕售物 duìjiǎng shòuwù; 抽彩 chōucǎi. **raffle** *v* [T] 用对奖办〔辦〕法出售 yòng duìjiǎng bànfǎ chūshòu; 以抽彩中奖给(物) yǐ chōucǎi zhòngjiǎng gěi.

raft /rɑːft; *US* ræft/ *n* [C] 木排 mùpái; 木筏 mùfá; 筏子 fázi.

rafter /ˈrɑːftə(r); *US* ˈræf-/ *n* [C] 椽 chuán.

rag[1] /ræg/ *n* **1** [C] 破布 pòbù; 碎布 suìbù. **2** **rags** [pl] 破旧〔舊〕衣服 pòjiù yīfu. **3** [C] [非正式用语, 贬]报〔報〕纸 bàozhǐ.

rag[2] /ræg/ *n* [C] (学生为慈善募捐举行的)娱〔娛〕乐〔樂〕活动〔動〕 yúlè huódòng. **rag** *v* [-gg-] [T] [非正式用语]戏〔戲〕弄 xìnòng; 拿…取乐 ná…qǔlè.

rage /reɪdʒ/ *n* **1** [U, C] (一阵)狂怒 kuángnù; 盛怒 shèngnù. **2** [习语] (be) **all the ˈrage** [非正式用语]风〔風〕靡一时〔時〕的事物 fēngmǐ yìshí de shìwù; 时尚 shíshàng. **rage** *v* [I] **1** 大怒 dànù; 发〔發〕怒 fānù. **2** (风暴)狂吹 kuángchuī.

ragged /ˈrægɪd/ *adj* **1** (a) (衣服)破旧〔舊〕的 pòjiùde; 褴〔襤〕褛〔褸〕的 lánlǚde. (b) (人)衣衫褴褛的 yīshān lánlǚ de. **2** (外形)参差不齐〔齊〕的 cēncī bùqí de. **raggedly** *adv*.

ragtime /ˈrægtaɪm/ *n* [U] 雷格泰姆(20 世纪 20 年代流行的爵士音乐) léigétàimǔ.

raid /reɪd/ *n* [C] **1** 突击〔擊〕 tūjī; 突袭〔襲〕 tūxí. **2** (警察等)突然搜捕(或搜查) tūrán sōubǔ. **raid** *v* [T] (突然)袭击 xíjī; 突然搜捕 tūrán sōubǔ. **raider** *n* [C].

rail /reɪl/ *n* **1** [C] 横条〔條〕 héngtiáo; 横档〔檔〕 héngdàng; 扶手 fúshǒu. **2** [C] (挂东西用的)横杆 hénggān: *a towel ～* 挂毛巾的横杆. **3** [C, 尤作 pl] 铁〔鐵〕轨 tiěguǐ; 钢〔鋼〕轨 gāngguǐ. **4** [U] 铁路(交通, 运输) tiělù: *travel by ～* 乘火车旅行. **rail** *v* [短语动词] **rail sth in / off** 用栏〔欄〕杆围住 yòng lángān wéizhù; 用栏杆隔开〔開〕 yòng lángān gékāi. **railing** *n* [C, 尤作 pl]栏杆 lángān; 栅栏 zhàlan. **ˈrailroad** *n* [C] [美语]铁路 tiělù. **ˈrailway** *n* [C] **1** 铁路 tiělù; 铁道 tiědào. **2** 铁路系统(或部门) tiělù xìtǒng.

rain /reɪn/ *n* [U] 雨 yǔ; 雨水 yǔshuǐ. **rain** *v* **1** [I] (与 *it* 连用)下雨 xiàyǔ; 降雨 jiàngyǔ: *It ～ed all day*. 下了一整天雨. **2** [短语动词] **rain (sth) down** 大量流下(或落下) dàliàng liúxià. **rain sth off** [常作被动语态]因雨受阻 yīn yǔ shòuzǔ; 因雨中断〔斷〕(或延期、取消) yīn yǔ zhōngduàn. **rainbow** /ˈreɪnbəʊ/ *n* [C] 彩虹 cǎihóng. **ˈraincoat** *n* [C] 雨衣 yǔyī. **ˈrainfall** *n* [U] 降雨量 jiàngyǔliàng. **ˈrainforest** *n* [C] 雨林(热带多雨地区的密林) yǔlín.

rainy /ˈreɪnɪ/ *adj* [-ier, -iest] **1** 下雨的 xiàyǔde; 多雨的 duōyǔde. **2** [习语] **for a ˌrainy ˈday** 未雨绸缪 wèi yǔ chóumóu; 存钱〔錢〕以备〔備〕不时〔時〕之需 cúnqián yǐbèi bùshí zhī xū.

raise /reɪz/ *v* [T] **1** 举〔舉〕起 jǔqǐ; 使升高 shǐ shēnggāo. **2** (a) 增加(数量、容量等) zēngjiā: *～ sb's hopes* 唤起某人的希望. (b) 提高(声音) tígāo: *～ one's voice* 提高嗓门. **3** 使产〔產〕生 shǐ chǎnshēng; 使出现 shǐ chūxiàn: *～ doubts* 引起怀疑. **4** 使尽〔盡〕人皆知 shǐ jìn rén jiē zhī. **5** 使引起注意 shǐ yǐnqǐ zhùyì; 提出…讨论〔論〕 tíchū tǎolùn: *～ a new point* 提出新论点. **6** 召集 zhàojí; 集结 jíjié: *～ an army/money* 招募军队; 筹款. **7** (a) 种〔種〕植(作物) zhòngzhí; 饲养〔養〕(家畜) sìyǎng. (b) 养育(孩子) yǎngyù. **8** [习语] **raise ˈhell/the ˈroof** [非正式用语]大怒 dànù. **raise** *n* [C] [美语](工

R

资、薪金的)增加 zēngjiā.

raisin /ˈreɪzn/ *n* [C] 葡萄干〔乾〕pútáogān.

rake /reɪk/ *n* [C] (长柄的)耙子 pázi. **rake** *v* **1** [I,T] (用耙子)耙 pá. **2** [T] (用耙子)耙集 pájí;耙平 pápíng. **3** [短语动词] **rake sth in** [非正式用语]赚得(许多钱) zhuàndé: *She's really raking it in!* 她真赚了不少钱. **rake sth up** 重提(不愉快的往事) chóngtí;揭(疮疤) jiē. **ˈrake-off** *n* [C] [非正式用语](通常以不正当手段得到的)利润的分成 lìrùnde fēnchéng;回扣 huíkòu;佣金 yòngjīn.

rally /ˈrælɪ/ *n* [C] [*pl* **-ies**] **1** 群众〔衆〕集会〔會〕(或大会) qúnzhòng jíhuì. **2** 公路赛车(或公路汽车赛) gōnglù sàichē. **3** (网球等得分前的)对〔對〕打 duìdǎ. **rally** *v* [*pt*, *pp* **-ied**] [I,T] **1** 重新振作 chóngxīn zhènzuò. **2** (使)恢复〔復〕(健康等) huīfù. **3** [短语动词] **rally round** 前去帮〔幫〕助某人(或某事) qiánqù bāngzhù mǒurén.

ram /ræm/ *n* [C] **1** (未阉割的)公羊 gōngyáng. **2** = BATTERING-RAM (BATTER[1]). **ram** [-mm-] *v* [T] **1** 猛压〔壓〕měngyà;猛撞 měngzhuàng. **2** 猛推 měngtuī. **ˈram raid** *n* [C] 开〔開〕车〔車〕撞入商店抢〔搶〕劫 kāichē zhuàngrù shāngdiàn qiǎngjié. **ˈram-raider** *n* [C] 开车撞入商店抢劫者 kāichē zhuàngrù shāngdiàn qiǎngjiézhě.

ramble /ˈræmbl/ *n* [C] 漫步 mànbù. **ramble** *v* [I] **1** 漫步 mànbù;闲逛 xiánguàng. **2** [喻]漫谈 màntán;漫笔〔筆〕mànbǐ. **3** (植物)蔓生 mànshēng. **rambler** *n* [C]. **rambling** *adj* **1** (尤指建筑物)布局零乱〔亂〕的 bùjú língluàn de. **2** (讲话、文章)散漫芜〔蕪〕杂〔雜〕的 sǎnmàn wúzá de.

ramification /ˌræmɪfɪˈkeɪʃn/ *n* [C, 常作 pl] [正式用语] **1** 衍生结果 yǎnshēng jiéguǒ: *the ~s of the new system* 新体系的种种复杂后果. **2** 分支(或分枝) fēnzhī.

R

ramp /ræmp/ *n* [C] 斜坡 xiépō;坡道 pōdào;斜面 xiémiàn.

rampage /ræmˈpeɪdʒ/ *v* [I] 横冲〔衝〕直撞 héng chōng zhí zhuàng. **rampage** *n* [习语] **be/go on the ˈrampage** 狂暴的行为〔爲〕kuángbàode xíngwéi.

rampant /ˈræmpənt/ *adj* (疾病、罪恶)猖獗的 chāngjuéde, 不能控制的 bùnéng kòngzhì de.

rampart /ˈræmpɑːt/ *n* [C] (城堡周围堤状的)防御〔禦〕土墙〔牆〕fángyù tǔqiáng.

ramshackle /ˈræmʃækl/ *adj* (房屋或车辆)摇摇欲坠〔墜〕的 yáoyáo yùzhuì de;破烂〔爛〕不堪的 pòlàn bùkān de.

ran *pt* of RUN[1].

ranch /rɑːntʃ; *US* ræntʃ/ *n* [C] (美国)大牧场〔場〕dà mùchǎng;大牧牛场 dà mùniúchǎng. **rancher** *n* [C] 大牧场主(或经理) dà mùchǎngzhǔ.

rancid /ˈrænsɪd/ *adj* (含脂肪食物)腐臭的 fǔchòude;变〔變〕味的 biànwèide.

rancour (美语 -cor) /ˈræŋkə(r)/ *n* [U] [正式用语]积〔積〕怨 jīyuàn;深仇 shēnchóu. **rancorous** /-kərəs/ *adj*.

R & D /ɑːr ən ˈdiː/ *abbr* research and development 研发〔發〕yánfā;研究与〔與〕发展 yánjiū yǔ fāzhǎn.

random /ˈrændəm/ *adj* 随〔隨〕意的 suíyìde;胡乱〔亂〕的 húluànde;任意的 rènyìde. **random** *n* [习语] **at ˈrandom** 随便 suíbiàn;任意 rènyì. **randomly** *adv*.

randy /ˈrændɪ/ *adj* [**-ier**, **-iest**] [非正式用语,尤用于英国英语]性欲〔慾〕冲〔衝〕动〔動〕的 xìngyù chōngdòng de;好色的 hàosède.

rang *pt* of RING[1].

range[1] /reɪndʒ/ *n* **1** [C] 排 pái;行 háng;列 liè;脉 mài. **2** [C] 成套(或成系列)的东西 chéngtàode dōngxi;种〔種〕类〔類〕zhǒnglèi: *sell a wide ~ of books* 出售种类很多的书籍. **3** [C] (变化的)限度 xiàndù. **4** (a) [U] 视力或听〔聽〕力所达〔達〕到的距离〔離〕shìlì huò tīnglì suǒ dádào de jùlí. (b) [U, sing] (枪炮、导弹的)射程 shèchéng: *shot him at close ~* 在近距离向他射击. **5** [C] 射击〔擊〕场〔場〕shèjīchǎng;靶场 bǎchǎng.

range[2] /reɪndʒ/ *v* **1** [I] 在…之间变〔變〕化 zài…zhī jiān biànhuà: *Prices ~ from £70 to £100.* 售价从 70 英镑到 100 英镑不等. **2** [I] (*over*) [喻]包括 bāokuò;涉及 shèjí: *a talk ranging over many subjects* 涉及许多问题的谈话. **3** [T] [正式用语]使排成行 shǐ pái chéng háng.

ranger /ˈreɪndʒə(r)/ *n* [C] (担任巡逻的)护〔護〕林员 hùlínyuán.

rank[1] /ræŋk/ *n* **1** [C, U] 军阶〔階〕jūnjiē;军衔 jūnxián. **2** [C, U] 社会〔會〕地位 shèhuì dìwèi. **3** [C] 排 pái;行 háng;列 liè: *a ˈtaxi ~* 一列出租汽车. **4 the ranks** [pl] 士兵 shìbīng. **rank** *v* [I, T] (使)位居 wèijū: *~ among the world's best* 居于世界最优秀之列. **the ˌrank and ˈfile** *n* [sing] [用 sing 或 pl v] (某组织的)普通成员 pǔtōng chéngyuán.

rank[2] /ræŋk/ *adj* **1** (植物)茂密的 màomìde;生长过〔過〕盛的 shēngzhǎng guòshèng de. **2** 腐味的 fǔwèide;恶〔惡〕臭的 èchòude. **3** 完全的 wánquánde;不折不扣的 bùzhé búkòu de.

rankle /ˈræŋkl/ *v* [I] 引起怨恨 yǐnqǐ yuànhèn;痛苦不已 tòngkǔ bùyǐ.

ransack /ˈrænsæk; *US* rænˈsæk/ *v* [T] 彻〔徹〕底搜索 chèdǐ sōusuǒ;仔细搜查 zǐxì sōuchá.

ransom /ˈrænsəm/ *n* [C] 赎〔贖〕金 shújīn. **ransom** *v* [T] 赎出 shúchū;赎回 shúhuí;得赎金后〔後〕释〔釋〕放(某人) dé shújīn hòu shìfàng.

rant /rænt/ *v* [I] 大叫大嚷 dàjiào dàrǎng;大声[聲]地说 dàshēng de shuō.

rap /ræp/ *n* [C] **1** 敲击[擊](声) qiāojī;叩击(声) kòujī. **2** [习语] **take the rap for sth** [非正式用语](因代人受过而)受罚 shòufá. **rap** *v* [-pp-] [I, T] (轻而快地)敲击 qiāojī;急敲 jíqiāo.

rape /reɪp/ *v* [T] 强奸 qiángjiān. **rape** *n* [C, U] **1** 强奸 qiángjiān. **2** [喻]破坏[壞] pòhuài;损坏 sǔnhuài. **rapist** *n* [C].

rapid /ˈræpɪd/ *adj* 快的 kuàide;迅速的 xùnsùde. **rapidity** /rəˈpɪdətɪ/ *n* [U]. **rapidly** *adv*. **rapids** *n* [pl] 急流 jíliú;湍流 tuānliú.

rapport /ræˈpɔː(r); *US* -ˈpɔːrt/ *n* [U, sing] 融洽关[關]系[係] róngqià guānxì;和谐 héxié.

rapt /ræpt/ *adj* 着迷的 zháomíde;全神贯注的 quán shén guàn zhù de.

rapture /ˈræptʃə(r)/ *n* **1** [U] [正式用语]狂喜 kuángxǐ;极[極]高兴[興] jí gāoxìng. **2** [习语] **go into raptures about/over sth** 狂喜 kuángxǐ;欢[歡]喜若狂 huānxǐ ruò kuáng. **rapturous** *adj*: ~ *applause* 欢喜若狂的喝彩.

rare[1] /reə(r)/ *adj* [~r, ~st] 稀有的 xīyǒude;罕见的 hǎnjiànde. **rarely** *adv* 不常 bùcháng;难[難]得 nándé. **rareness** *n* [U].

rare[2] /reə(r)/ *adj* (肉)半熟的 bànshúde;煮得嫩的 zhǔ de nènde.

rarefied /ˈreərɪfaɪd/ *adj* **1** (空气)稀薄的 xībóde;缺氧的 quēyǎngde. **2** [喻]清高的 qīnggāode;精选[選]的 jīngxuǎnde.

raring /ˈreərɪŋ/ *adj* *to* 渴望的 kěwàngde.

rarity /ˈreərətɪ/ *n* [*pl* -ies] **1** [U] 稀有 xīyǒu;罕见 hǎnjiàn. **2** [C]珍品 zhēnpǐn;稀有的东西 xīyǒude dōngxi.

rascal /ˈrɑːskl; *US* ˈræskl/ *n* [C] **1** 小淘气[氣] xiǎo táoqì. **2** 不诚实[實]的人 bù chéngshí de rén;流氓 liúmáng;无[無]赖 wúlài.

rash[1] /ræʃ/ *adj* 鲁莽的 lǔmǎngde;轻[輕]率的 qīngshuàide. **rashly** *adv*. **rashness** *n* [U].

rash[2] /ræʃ/ *n* **1** [C] 疹子 zhěnzi. **2** [sing] [喻]爆发[發]一连串的事 bàofā yìliánchuànde shì: *a ~ of strikes* 一连串罢工.

rasher /ˈræʃə(r)/ *n* [C] 熏[燻]肉(或熏腿)片 xūnròupiàn.

rasp /rɑːsp; *US* ræsp/ *n* **1** [sing] 刺耳的锉磨声[聲] cì'ěrde cuò mó shēng. **2** [C] 粗锉刀 cūcuòdāo;木锉 mùcuò. **rasp** *v* [I, T] 用刺耳声说出 yòng cì'ěrshēng shuōchū;粗声粗气[氣]地说 cūshēng cūqì de shuō. **rasping** *adj*.

raspberry /ˈrɑːzbrɪ; *US* ˈræzberɪ/ *n* [C] [*pl* -ies] **1** [植物]悬[懸]钩子 xuángōuzǐ;覆盆子 fùpénzǐ. **2** [非正式用语](表示憎恶、嘲笑、不赞成等的)咂舌声[聲] zāshéshēng.

rat /ræt/ *n* [C] **1** 大鼠 dàshǔ. **2** [非正式用语] 不忠的人 bùzhōngde rén;变[變]节[節]小人 biànjié xiǎorén. **3** [习语] **the ˈrat race** 激烈的竞[競]争 jīliède jìngzhēng. **rat** *v* [-tt-] [I] (*on*) [非正式用语]泄露秘密 xièlòu mìmì;背叛 bèipàn. **ratty** *adj* [-ier, -iest] [英国非正式用语]暴躁的 bàozàode.

rate[1] /reɪt/ *n* [C] **1** 比率 bǐlǜ;率 lǜ: *a ~ of 3 miles per hour* 每小时3英里. *the ˈbirth ~* 出生率. **2** 价[價]格或质[質]量的量度 jiàgé huò zhìliàng de liángdù: *postage ~s* 邮资. *a first-~ ˈjob* 一等的工作. **3** 速度 sùdù. **4** **rates** [pl] (旧时,英国)不动[動]产[產]税 búdòngchǎnshuì. **5** [习语] **at ˈany rate** 无[無]论[論]如何 wúlùn rúhé. **at ˈthis/ˈthat rate** 照这[這](或那)种[種]情形 zhào zhèzhǒng qíngxíng;如果这样[樣](或那样)的话 rúguǒ zhèyàngde huà. **ˈratepayer** *n* [C] (旧时,英国持有不动产的)纳税人 nàshuìrén.

rate[2] /reɪt/ *v* [T] **1** 评价[價] píngjià;认[認]为[爲] rènwéi: *He is generally ~d as one of the best players*. 他被普遍地认为是最好的运动员之一. **2** 把…看成是 bǎ…kànchéng shì: *~ sb as a friend* 把某人看作朋友. **3** [非正式用语,尤用于美语]值得 zhídé.

rather /ˈrɑːðə(r); *US* ˈræ-/ *adv* **1** 在一定程度上 zài yídìng chéngdù shàng: *They were ~ surprised*. 他们有点吃惊. **2** [习语] **or rather** 更确[確]切地说 gèng quèqiède shuō: *last night, or ~ early this morning* 昨天夜里,说得更确切一点,是今天凌晨. **would rather ... (than)** 宁[寧]可 nìngkě;宁愿[願] nìngyuàn: *I'd ~ walk than go by bus*. 我宁愿走路,不愿坐公共汽车去.

ratify /ˈrætɪfaɪ/ *v* [*pt, pp* -ied] [T] 正式批准 zhèngshì pīzhǔn;(经签署)认[認]可 rènkě. **ratification** /ˌrætɪfɪˈkeɪʃn/ *n* [U].

rating /ˈreɪtɪŋ/ *n* **1** [C, U] 等级 děngjí;品级 pǐnjí. **2** [pl] (广播、电视的)收看(听)率 shōukànlǜ. **3** [尤用于英国英语](海军)士兵 shìbīng.

ratio /ˈreɪʃɪəʊ/ *n* [C] [*pl* ~s] 比 bǐ;比率 bǐlǜ: *The ~ of men to women was 3 to 1*. 男人和女人的比率是三比一.

ration /ˈræʃn/ *n* **1** [C] (食物的)定量 dìngliàng. **2** **rations** [pl] (日需)口粮 kǒuliáng. **ration** *v* [T] **1** 对[對]…实[實]行配给 duì…shíxíng pèijǐ. **2** 定量供应[應] dìngliàng gōngyìng.

rational /ˈræʃnəl/ *adj* **1** 有推理能力的 yǒu tuīlǐ nénglì de. **2** 理智的 lǐzhìde;明事理的 míngshìlǐde. **rationally** /-ʃnəlɪ/ *adv*.

rationale /ˌræʃəˈnɑːl; *US* -ˈnæl/ *n* [sing] 逻[邏]辑依据[據] luójí yījù;理论[論]基础[礎] lǐlùn jīchǔ;基本原理 jīběn yuánlǐ.

rationalize /ˈræʃnəlaɪz/ *v* **1** [I, T] 合理地说明 hélǐde shuōmíng;使合理 shǐ hélǐ. **2** [T]

R

(为提高效率、降低损耗而)改进〔進〕(体系、产业等) gǎijìn; 使合理化 shǐ hélǐhuà. **rationalization** /ˌræʃnəlaɪˈzeɪʃn; *US* -lɪˈz-/ *n* [C, U].

rattle /ˈrætl/ *v* **1** [I, T] (使)发〔發〕出连续〔續〕短促的尖利声〔聲〕 fāchū liánxù duǎncù de jiānlìshēng. **2** [T] [非正式用语]使…紧〔緊〕张〔張〕 shǐ…jǐnzhāng. **3** [短语动词] **rattle along, off, etc** 移动〔動〕时〔時〕发嘈杂〔雜〕声 yídòng shí fā cáozáshēng. **rattle sth off** (不假思索地)飞〔飛〕快说出 fēikuài shuōchū. **rattle** *n* [C] **1** 连续短促的尖利声 liánxù duǎncù de jiānlìshēng. **2** 嘎嘎作响〔響〕的玩具 gāgā zuò xiǎng de wánjù. ˈ**rattlesnake** *n* [C] 响尾蛇(美洲毒蛇) xiǎngwěishé.

ratty ⇨RAT.

raucous /ˈrɔːkəs/ *adj* 沙哑〔啞〕的 shāyǎde; 粗嘎的 cūgāde. **raucously** *adv*.

ravage /ˈrævɪdʒ/ *v* [T] 毁坏〔壞〕 huǐhuài; 严〔嚴〕重损毁 yánzhòng sǔnhuǐ. **the ravages** *n* [pl] 破坏的痕迹 pòhuàide hénjì; 灾〔災〕害 zāihài: *the ~s of time* 岁月的摧残.

rave /reɪv/ *v* [I] **1** 胡言乱〔亂〕语 húyán luànyǔ. **2** *about* [非正式用语]赞〔讚〕赏地说 zànshǎngde shuō. **rave** *adj* [非正式用语]赞扬〔揚〕的 zànyángde: *a ~ review* 极好的评论. **raving** *adj* 十足的 shízúde.

raven /ˈreɪvn/ *n* [C] 渡鸦(黑色,似乌鸦) dùyā. **raven** *adj* (毛发)乌〔烏〕亮的 wūliàngde.

ravenous /ˈrævənəs/ *adj* 极〔極〕饿的 jí'ède. **ravenously** *adv*.

ravine /rəˈviːn/ *n* [C] 深谷 shēngǔ; 峡〔峽〕谷 xiágǔ.

ravish /ˈrævɪʃ/ *v* [T] [正式用语][尤作被动语态]使狂喜 shǐ kuángxǐ; 使陶醉 shǐ táozuì; 使着迷 shǐ zháomí. **ravishing** *adj* 非常美丽〔麗〕的 fēicháng měilì de; 迷人的 mírénde.

R

raw /rɔː/ *adj* **1** 未煮过〔過〕的 wèi zhǔguò de; 生的 shēngde. **2** 未加工的 wèi jiāgōng de; 自然状〔狀〕态〔態〕的 zìrán zhuàngtài de: ~ *materials* 原料. **3** (人)未受训练〔練〕的 wèishòu xùnliàn de; 无〔無〕经〔經〕验〔驗〕的 wú jīngyàn de. **4** (皮肤)疼痛的 téngtòngde. **5** (天气)湿〔濕〕冷的 shīlěngde.

ray /reɪ/ *n* [C] **1** (光或热的)线〔綫〕 xiàn; 射线 shèxiàn. **2** [喻]一丝微光 yìsī wēiguāng: *a ~ of hope* 一线希望.

rayon /ˈreɪɒn/ *n* [U] 人造丝 rénzàosī.

raze (亦作 **rase**) /reɪz/ *v* [T] 摧毁 cuīhuǐ; 把…夷为〔爲〕平地 bǎ…yí wéi píngdì.

razor /ˈreɪzə(r)/ *n* [C] 剃刀 tìdāo; 刮胡〔鬍〕子刀 guā húzi dāo.

Rd *abbr* road.

re- /riː/ *prefix* 再 zài; 又 yòu; 重新 chóngxīn: *refill* 再装满(或充满). *reexamine* 再检查; 再询问.

reach /riːtʃ/ *v* **1** [T] 到达〔達〕 dàodá; 抵达 dǐdá: ~ *London* 到达伦敦. [喻] ~ *an agreement* 达成协议. **2** [I, T] 伸手触〔觸〕及 shēnshǒu chùjí; 拿到(某物) nádào: *He ~ed for his gun.* 他伸手去拿枪. *Can you ~ the book on the top shelf?* 你能够到架子顶上的那本书吗? **3** [I, T] 到(某处) dào: *Their land ~es (down to) the river.* 他们的土地延伸到河边. **4** [T] 与〔與〕…联〔聯〕系〔繫〕 yǔ…liánxì; 给…打电〔電〕话 gěi…dǎ diànhuà. **reach** *n* **1** [U] 伸手可及的距离〔離〕 shēnshǒu kějí de jùlí: *Medicines should be kept out of ~ of children.* 药品应该放在孩子够不着的地方. **2** [C 常作 pl]河段 héduàn.

react /rɪˈækt/ *v* [I] **1** (*to*) 作出反应〔應〕 zuòchū fǎnyìng; 反应 fǎnyìng. **2** *against* 反动〔動〕 fǎndòng; 反其道而行 fǎn qí dào ér xíng. **3** (*with*) [化学]起化学〔學〕反应(或作用) qǐ huàxué fǎnyìng.

reaction /rɪˈækʃn/ *n* **1** [C, U] 反应〔應〕 fǎnyìng. **2** [U] (政治上的)反对〔對〕改革 fǎnduì gǎigé; 反动〔動〕 fǎndòng. **3** [C] [化学]反应 fǎnyìng; 作用 zuòyòng. **reactionary** /-ʃənrɪ; *US* -ʃənerɪ/ *n* [C], *adj* [*pl* **-ies**] 反对改革(或进步)的(人) fǎnduì gǎigé de; 反动的(人) fǎndòngde.

reactor /rɪˈæktə(r)/ *n* [C] = NUCLEAR REACTOR (NUCLEAR).

read /riːd/ *v* [*pt*, *pp* **read** /red/] **1** [I, T] (a) 读〔讀〕 dú; 阅读 yuèdú: ~ *a book* 读书. (b) 朗读 lǎngdú. **2** [I] 有某些字样〔樣〕(或某种含义) yǒu mǒuxiē zìyàng: *The sign ~s 'No Entry'.* 牌子上写着"禁止入内". *Her reports always ~ well.* 她的报告读起来总是很不错. **3** [T] 理解 lǐjiě; 看懂 kàndǒng: ~ *sb's thoughts* 了解某人的思想. **4** [T] (度量仪器)指示 zhǐshì; 显〔顯〕示 xiǎnshì. **5** [T] 攻读 gōngdú; 学〔學〕习〔習〕 xuéxí. **6** [习语] ˌ**read between the ˈlines** 从字里〔裏〕行间领会〔會〕言外之意 cóng zìlǐ hángjiān lǐnghuì yán wài zhī yì. **readable** *adj* 易读的 yìdúde; (读起来)有趣味的 yǒu qùwèi de.

reader /ˈriːdə(r)/ *n* [C] **1** 读〔讀〕者 dúzhě. **2** 教科书〔書〕 jiàokēshū; 课本 kèběn; 读本 dúběn. **3** (英国大学的)高级讲〔講〕师〔師〕 gāojí jiǎngshī. **readership** *n* [sing] (报刊等的)读者人数〔數〕 dúzhě rénshù.

reading /ˈriːdɪŋ/ *n* **1** [U] (a) 阅读〔讀〕 yuèdú. (b) 读物 dúwù: *light ~* 轻松读物. **2** [C] (仪表等上的)读数〔數〕 dúshù; 度数 dùshù; 指示数 zhǐshìshù. **3** [C] 解释〔釋〕 jiěshì; 理解 lǐjiě: *My ~ of the situation is...* 我对形势的看法是…. **4** [C] (英国议会)(分别标志着议案提出、审议、表决等三个阶段的)三读之一 sān dú zhī yī.

ready /ˈredɪ/ *adj* [-ier, -iest] 1 (*for*/*to*) 准〔準〕备〔備〕好的 zhǔnbèi hǎo de: ~ *for action* 准备行动. ~ *to act* 准备行动. 2 愿〔願〕意的 yuànyìde. 3 *to* 即将〔將〕做某事 jíjiāng zuò mǒushì: *She looked ~ to collapse*. 她看样子快要垮下来. 4 快的 kuàide; 迅速的 xùnsùde: *a ~ answer* 脱口而出的回答. 5 容易得到的 róngyì dédào de. **readily** *adv* 1 毫不迟〔遲〕疑地 háo bù chíyí de. 2 容易地 róngyìde. **readiness** *n* [U]. **ready** *adv* 已经〔經〕yǐjīng: ~ *cooked* 已经做熟的. **ready** *n* [习语] **at the ˈready** 准备行动〔動〕zhǔnbèi xíngdòng; 随〔隨〕时〔時〕可用 suíshí kěyòng. **ˌready-ˈmade** *adj* 现成的 xiànchéngde.

real /rɪəl/ *adj* 1 真实〔實〕的 zhēnshíde; 实在的 shízàide. 2 真的 zhēnde; 真正的 zhēnzhèngde. **ˈreal estate** *n* [U] [尤用于美语, 法律]不动〔動〕产〔產〕búdòngchǎn.

realism /ˈrɪəlɪzəm/ *n* [U] 1 现实〔實〕xiànshí; 现实态〔態〕度(或行为等) xiànshí tàidù. 2 (文艺的)现实主义〔義〕xiànshí zhǔyì; 写〔寫〕实主义 xiěshí zhǔyì. **realist** *n* [C]. **realistic** /ˌrɪəˈlɪstɪk/ *adj*.

reality /rɪˈælətɪ/ *n* [*pl* -ies] 1 [U] 真实〔實〕zhēnshí; 实在 shízài. 2 [C] 真正看到或实际〔際〕经〔經〕历〔歷〕过〔過〕的事 zhēnzhèng kàndào huò shíjì jīnglì guò de shì: *the realities of war* 战争的实情. 3 [习语] **in reˈality** 事实上 shìshí shàng. **reality ˈtelevision** *n* [U], **reality TˈV** *n* [U] (娱乐性)纪实电〔電〕视 jìshí diànshì.

realize /ˈrɪəlaɪz/ *v* [T] 1 认〔認〕识〔識〕到 rènshi dào; 了解 liǎojiě. 2 [正式用语]实〔實〕现(计划等) shíxiàn. 3 [正式用语]卖〔賣〕得 màidé; 售得 shòudé. **realization** /ˌrɪəlaɪˈzeɪʃn; *US* -lɪˈz- / *n* [U].

really /ˈrɪəlɪ/ *adv* 1 事实〔實〕上 shìshí shàng; 实际〔際〕上 shíjì shàng. 2 非常 fēicháng. 3 (用于表示兴趣、惊讶等)当〔當〕真 dàngzhēn.

realm /relm/ *n* [C] 1 [正式用语]王国〔國〕wángguó. 2 [喻](活动或兴趣的)范〔範〕围〔圍〕fànwéi; 领域 lǐngyù.

reap /riːp/ *v* 1 [I, T] 收割 shōugē; 收获〔獲〕shōuhuò. 2 [T] [喻]获得 huòdé; 得到 dédào.

rear[1] /rɪə(r)/ *n* 1 **the rear** [sing] 后〔後〕部 hòubù; 后面 hòumiàn; 背后 bèihòu. 2 [习语] **ˌbring up the ˈrear** 殿后 diànhòu. **rear** *adj* 后部的 hòubùde; 后面的 hòumiànde; 背部的 bèibùde. **the ˈrearguard** *n* [C] 后卫〔衛〕部队〔隊〕hòuwèi bùduì.

rear[2] /rɪə(r)/ *v* 1 [T] (a) 养〔養〕育 yǎngyù; 抚〔撫〕养 fǔyǎng. (b) 饲养 sìyǎng. 2 [I] (*up*) (马等)用后〔後〕腿直立 yòng hòutuǐ zhílì. 3 [T] 抬起(头) táiqǐ.

reason[1] /ˈriːzn/ *n* 1 [C, U] 理由 lǐyóu; 原因 yuányīn. 2 [U] 理智 lǐzhì; 理性 lǐxìng; 推理力 tuīlǐlì; 判断〔斷〕力 pànduànlì. 3 [sing] 道理 dàolǐ; 情理 qínglǐ; 明智 míngzhì: *lose one's ~* 发疯. 4 [习语] **within reason** 理智的 lǐzhìde; 合理的 hélǐde.

reason[2] /ˈriːzn/ *v* 1 [I] 思考 sīkǎo; 推理 tuīlǐ. 2 [T] 推论〔論〕tuīlùn; 推断〔斷〕tuīduàn. 3 [短语动词] **reason with sb** 劝〔勸〕说 quànshuō; 说服 shuōfú. **reasoning** *n* [U] 推论 tuīlùn; 推理 tuīlǐ.

reasonable /ˈriːznəbl/ *adj* 1 公正的 gōngzhèngde; 合理的 hélǐde. 2 不太贵的 bú tàiguì de; 公道的 gōngdàode. **reasonably** *adv* 1 相当〔當〕地 xiāngdāngde. 2 合理地 hélǐde.

reassure /ˌriːəˈʃɔː(r); *US* -ˈʃʊər/ *v* [T] 使放心 shǐ fàngxīn; 使消除疑虑〔慮〕shǐ xiāochú yílǜ. **reassurance** *n* [U, C].

rebate /ˈriːbeɪt/ *n* [C] (作为减免或折扣的)部分退款 bùfèn tuìkuǎn; 折扣 zhékòu.

rebel /ˈrebl/ *n* [C] 1 反叛者 fǎnpànzhě; 造反者 zàofǎnzhě. 2 反抗者 fǎnkàngzhě. **rebel** /rɪˈbel/ *v* [-ll-] [I] 1 (*against*) 反抗(政府) fǎnkàng; 反叛 fǎnpàn. 2 反抗权〔權〕威 fǎnkàng quánwēi. **rebellion** /rɪˈbelɪən/ *n* [C, U] 反叛(行动) fǎnpàn. **rebellious** *adj*.

reboot /riːˈbuːt/ *v* [T] 重新启〔啓〕动〔動〕chóngxīn qǐdòng.

rebound /rɪˈbaʊnd/ *v* [I] 1 弹〔彈〕回 tánhuí; 反弹 fǎntán. 2 (*on*) 产〔產〕生事与〔與〕愿〔願〕违〔違〕的结果 chǎnshēng shì yǔ yuàn wéi de jiéguǒ. **rebound** /ˈriːbaʊnd/ *n* [习语] **on the ˈrebound** 在心灰意懒之余〔餘〕zài xīn huī yì lǎn zhī yú.

rebuff /rɪˈbʌf/ *n* [C] 断〔斷〕然拒绝 duànrán jùjué; 回绝 huíjué. **rebuff** *v* [T] 断然拒绝 duànrán jùjué; 回绝 huíjué.

rebuke /rɪˈbjuːk/ *v* [T] [正式用语]指责 zhǐzé; 非难〔難〕fēinàn: *He was ~d for being late*. 他因迟到受到指责. **rebuke** *n* [C, U].

recall /rɪˈkɔːl/ *v* [T] 1 回想起 huíxiǎng qǐ; 回忆〔憶〕起 huíyì qǐ; 记得 jìdé. 2 要求归〔歸〕还〔還〕yāoqiú guīhuán. **recall** /亦读 ˈriːkɔːl / *n* 1 [sing] 召回 zhàohuí; 唤回 huànhuí. 2 [U] 记忆力 jìyìlì.

recap /ˈriːkæp/ *v* [-pp-] [I, T] [非正式用语] short for RECAPITULATE.

recapitulate /ˌriːkəˈpɪtʃʊleɪt/ *v* [I, T] 扼要重述 èyào chóngshù; 概述 gàishù.

recede /rɪˈsiːd/ *v* [I] 1 后〔後〕退 hòutuì. 2 向后倾斜 xiànghòu qīngxié.

receipt /rɪˈsiːt/ *n* 1 [C] 收条〔條〕shōutiáo; 收据〔據〕shōujù. 2 **receipts** [pl] (营业)收到的款项 shōudàode kuǎnxiàng. 3 [U] [正式用语] 收到 shōudào.

receive /rɪˈsiːv/ *v* [T] 1 收到 shōudào; 接到

R

jiēdào. 2 经〔經〕受 jīngshòu; 遭受 zāoshòu: *~d severe injuries in the crash* 在撞车事故中受重伤. 3 接待 jiēdài; 款待 kuǎndài. 4 (无线电、电视)接收 jiēshōu. **receiver** *n* [C] 1 (电话)听〔聽〕筒 tīngtǒng. 2 收音机〔機〕shōuyīnjī; 电〔電〕视机 diànshìjī. 3 接受者 jiēshòuzhě; 收赃〔贓〕人 shōuzāngrén.

recent /ˈriːsnt/ *adj* 最近的 zuìjìnde; 近来的 jìnláide. **recently** *adv* 最近地 zuìjìnde; 近来地 jìnláide.

receptacle /rɪˈseptəkl/ *n* [C] [正式用语]容器 róngqì.

reception /rɪˈsepʃn/ *n* 1 [C] 招待会〔會〕zhāodàihuì; 宴会 yànhuì; 欢〔歡〕迎会 huānyínghuì. 2 [C] 欢迎 huānyíng; 接待 jiēdài: *be given a warm ~* 受到热情的欢迎. 3 [U](旅馆等的)接待处〔處〕jiēdàichù. 4 [U] (无线电、电视的)接收 jiēshōu; 接收质〔質〕量 jiēshōu zhìliàng. **receptionist** /-ʃənɪst/ *n* [C] (旅馆等的)接待员 jiēdàiyuán.

receptive /rɪˈseptɪv/ *adj* (对新思想等)善于接受的 shànyú jiēshòu de; 易接受的 yì jiēshòu de.

recess /rɪˈses; *US* ˈriːses/ *n* 1 [C, U] (工作等的)暂停 zàntíng; (法院的)休庭 xiūtíng; 休会〔會〕xiūhuì. 2 [C] 壁凹 bì'āo; 凹室 āoshì. 3 [C, 常作 pl] [喻]隐〔隱〕秘处〔處〕yǐnmìchù.

recession /rɪˈseʃn/ *n* 1 [C, U] (经济)衰退 shuāituì; 不景气〔氣〕bù jǐngqì. 2 [U] 后〔後〕退 hòutuì; 退回 tuìhuí; 撤回 chèhuí.

recharge /rɪˈtʃɑːdʒ/ *v* [T] 给…充电 gěi… chōngdiàn. [I] 充电 chōngdiàn. **reˈchargeable** *adj* 可充电的 kěchōngdiànde.

recipe /ˈresəpɪ/ *n* [C] 1 烹饪法 pēngrènfǎ; 食谱 shípǔ. 2 [喻]诀窍〔竅〕juéqiào; 方法 fāngfǎ: *a ~ for disaster* 应付灾难的诀窍.

recipient /rɪˈsɪpɪənt/ *n* [C] [正式用语]接受者 jiēshòuzhě.

reciprocal /rɪˈsɪprəkl/ *adj* 相互的 xiānghùde; 互惠的 hùhuìde: *~ trade agreements* 互惠贸易协定. **reciprocally** /-klɪ/ *adv*.

reciprocate /rɪˈsɪprəkeɪt/ *v* [I, T] [正式用语]互给 hùgěi; 互换 hùhuàn.

recital /rɪˈsaɪtl/ *n* [C] 独〔獨〕奏会〔會〕dúzòuhuì; 诗歌朗诵会 shīgē lǎngsònghuì; 音乐〔樂〕演奏会 yīnyuè yǎnzòuhuì.

recite /rɪˈsaɪt/ *v* [T] 1 背诵 bèisòng; 朗诵 lǎngsòng. 2 列举〔舉〕(名字、事实等) lièjǔ. **recitation** /ˌresɪˈteɪʃn/ *n* [C, U].

reckless /ˈreklɪs/ *adj* 鲁莽的 lǔmǎngde; 不顾〔顧〕后〔後〕果的 búgù hòuguǒ de. **recklessly** *adv*. **recklessness** *n* [U].

reckon /ˈrekən/ *v* [T] 1 [非正式用语]认〔認〕为〔為〕rènwéi; 以为 yǐwéi; 想 xiǎng: *I ~ we ought to go now*. 我想我们应当现在去. 2 估算 gūsuàn; 猜想 cāixiǎng. 3 计算 jìsuàn. 4 [短语动词] **reckon on sth** 依赖某事 yīlài mǒushì. **reckon with sb/sth** (a) 处〔處〕理 chǔlǐ; 对〔對〕待 duìdài. (b) 重视 zhòngshì: *a force to be ~ed with* 不可忽视的力量. **reckoning** *n* [U] 1 计算 jìsuàn; 估计 gūjì. 2 惩〔懲〕罚 chéngfá; 报〔報〕应〔應〕bàoyìng: *the day of ˈ~ing* 报应到来的日子.

reclaim /rɪˈkleɪm/ *v* [T] 1 要求归〔歸〕还〔還〕yāoqiú guīhuán. 2 开〔開〕垦〔墾〕kāikěn. **reclamation** /ˌrekləˈmeɪʃn/ *n* [U].

recline /rɪˈklaɪn/ *v* [I] [正式用语]斜倚 xiéyǐ; 靠 kào; 躺 tǎng.

recluse /rɪˈkluːs/ *n* [C] 隐〔隱〕士 yǐnshì.

recognize /ˈrekəgnaɪz/ *v* [T] 1 认〔認〕出 rènchū; 识〔識〕别 shíbié. 2 承认 chéngrèn; 认可 rènkě: *refuse to ~ a new government* 拒绝承认一新政府. 3 认识到 rènshi dào: *~ one's faults* 承认错误. 4 赏识 shǎngshí; 表彰 biǎozhāng. **recognition** /ˌrekəgˈnɪʃn/ *n* [U]. **recognizable** *adj*.

recoil /rɪˈkɔɪl/ *v* [I] 1 (因恐惧、厌恶等)畏缩 wèisuō; 退缩 tuìsuō. 2 (枪等)反冲〔衝〕fǎnchōng; 产〔產〕生后〔後〕坐力 chǎnshēng hòuzuòlì. **recoil** /ˈriːkɔɪl/ *n* [U, sing].

recollect /ˌrekəˈlekt/ *v* [I, T] 回忆〔憶〕huíyì; 想起 xiǎngqǐ; 记起 jìqǐ. **recollection** /-ˈlekʃn/ *n* 1 [C] 回忆起的事物 huíyì qǐ de shìwù; 往事 wǎngshì. 2 [U] 记忆力 jìyìlì; 回忆 huíyì.

recommend /ˌrekəˈmend/ *v* [T] 1 推荐〔薦〕tuījiàn; 荐举〔舉〕jiànjǔ; 称〔稱〕赞〔讚〕chēngzàn. 2 建议〔議〕jiànyì; 劝〔勸〕告 quàngào: *I ~ leaving / you leave early*. 我建议早点离开; 我劝你早点走. **recommendation** /-menˈdeɪʃn/ *n* [C, U].

recompense /ˈrekəmpens/ *v* [T] [正式用语]报〔報〕酬 bàochóu; 酬谢 chóuxiè; 回报 huíbào; 赔偿〔償〕péicháng. **recompense** *n* [sing, U] [正式用语]报酬 bàochóu; 赔偿 péicháng.

reconcile /ˈrekənsaɪl/ *v* [T] 1 使重新和好 shǐ chóngxīn héhǎo; 使和解 shǐ héjiě. 2 使一致 shǐ yízhì; 调和 tiáohé. 3 **~ oneself to** 使顺从〔從〕shǐ shùncóng; 使甘心(于) shǐ gānxīn. **reconciliation** /ˌrekənˌsɪlɪˈeɪʃn/ *n* [U, C].

reconnaissance /rɪˈkɒnɪsns/ *n* [C, U] 侦察 zhēnchá.

reconnoitre (美语 -ter) /ˌrekəˈnɔɪtə(r)/ *v* [I, T] 侦察(敌人的位置、地区等) zhēnchá.

record[1] /ˈrekɔːd; *US* ˈrekərd/ *n* [C] 1 记录〔錄〕jìlù; 记载 jìzǎi. 2 履历〔歷〕lǚlì. 3 最好的成绩 zuìhǎo de chéngjì: *a new world ~ in the 100 metres* 100 米新的世界记录. *~ profits* 创记录的利润. 4 唱片 chàngpiàn. 5

R

[习语] ˌoff the ˈrecord 非正式的 fēi zhèngshì de;不供发[發]表的 bú gōng fābiǎo de. on ˈrecord 记录在案的 jìlù zài'àn de;正式记录的 zhèngshì jìlù de. ˈrecord-player *n* [C] 唱机[機] chàngjī.

record[2] /rɪˈkɔːd/ *v* 1 [T] 记录[錄] jìlù;记载[載] jìzǎi. 2 [I,T] 录(音或图像) lù. 3 [T] (指仪器)显[顯]示 xiǎnshì;标[標]明 biāomíng.

recorder /rɪˈkɔːdə(r)/ *n* [C] 1 录[錄]音机[機] lùyīnjī;录像机 lùxiàngjī. 2 (八孔)直笛 zhídí. 3 (英国某些法院的)法官 fǎguān.

recording /rɪˈkɔːdɪŋ/ *n* [C] (声音、图像的)录[錄]制[製] lùzhì;录音 lùyīn;录像 lùxiàng.

recount /rɪˈkaʊnt/ *v* [T] [正式用语]详述 xiángshù;描述 miáoshù.

re-count /ˌriːˈkaʊnt/ *v* [T] 重新计算(尤指选票) chóngxīn jìsuàn;重数[數] chóngshǔ. **re-count** /ˈriːkaʊnt/ *n* [C] 重新计算 chóngxīn jìsuàn.

recoup /rɪˈkuːp/ *v* [T] 赔偿[償] péicháng;补[補]偿 bǔcháng;偿还[還] chánghuán.

recourse /rɪˈkɔːs/ *n* [习语] **have recourse to sth** [正式用语]求助于 qiúzhù yú;求援于 qiúyuán yú.

recover /rɪˈkʌvə(r)/ *v* 1 [I] (*from*) 恢复[復] huīfù;康复 kāngfù. 2 [T] 找回(遗失、被盗之物) zhǎohuí;重新得到 chóngxīn dédào. 3 [T] 重新控制(自己、自己的情绪等) chóngxīn kòngzhì. **recovery** *n* [U, sing].

recreation /ˌrekrɪˈeɪʃn/ *n* [C,U] 消遣 xiāoqiǎn;娱[娛]乐[樂] yúlè. **recreational** /ˌrekrɪˈeɪʃnl/ *adj* 娱乐的 yúlède. **recreational drug** (社交活动中偶尔使用的)娱乐用药[藥] yúlè yòngyào;娱乐性毒品 yúlèxìng dúpǐn.

recrimination /rɪˌkrɪmɪˈneɪʃn/ *n* [C,常用 pl v] 反责 fǎnzé;反诉 fǎnsù.

recruit /rɪˈkruːt/ *n* [C] 新兵 xīnbīng;新成员 xīn chéngyuán. **recruit** *v* [I,T] 吸收(新成员) xīshōu;征募(新兵) zhēngmù. **recruitment** *n* [U].

rectangle /ˈrektæŋgl/ *n* [C] 长[長]方形 chángfāngxíng;矩形 jǔxíng. **rectangular** /rekˈtæŋgjʊlə(r)/ *adj*.

rectify /ˈrektɪfaɪ/ *v* [*pt*, *pp* -ied] [T] 改正 gǎizhèng;纠正 jiūzhèng.

rector /ˈrektə(r)/ *n* [C] (英国教会的)教区[區]长[長] jiàoqūzhǎng. **rectory** /ˈrektərɪ/ *n* [C] [*pl* -ies] 教区长住所 jiàoqūzhǎng zhùsuǒ.

rectum /ˈrektəm/ *n* [C] [解剖]直肠[腸] zhícháng.

recuperate /rɪˈkuːpəreɪt/ *v* [I] (*from*) [正式用语]复[復]原 fùyuán;恢复(健康) huīfù. **recuperation** /rɪˌkuːpəˈreɪʃn/ *n* [U].

recur /rɪˈkɜː(r)/ *v* [-rr-] [I] 再发[發]生 zài fāshēng;重现 chóngxiàn. **recurrence** /rɪˈkʌrəns/ *n* [C,U] 重现 chóngxiàn. **recurrent** /rɪˈkʌrənt/ *adj*.

recycle /ˌriːˈsaɪkl/ *v* [T] 回收利用(废物等) huíshōu lìyòng. **reˈcycling bin** *n* [C] 垃圾回收箱 lājī huíshōu xiāng. **reˈcycling plant** *n* [C] 废[廢]品回收厂[廠] fèipǐn huíshōu chǎng.

red /red/ *adj* [~der, ~dest] 1 红的 hóngde;红色的 hóngsède. 2 (脸)通红的 tōnghóngde;涨[漲]红的 zhànghóngde. 3 (毛发)红褐色的 hónghèsède. 4 **Red** [非正式用语]共产[產]主义[義]的 gòngchǎn zhǔyì de. 5 [习语] **red ˈherring** 转[轉]移注意力的事 zhuǎnyí zhùyìlì de shì. ˌ**red ˈtape** 繁文缛节[節] fán wén rù jié. **red** *n* 1 [C,U] 红色 hóngsè. 2 [U] 红衣服 hóng yīfu: *dressed in* ~ 穿着红衣服. 3 **Red** [C] [非正式用语]共产主义者 gòngchǎn zhǔyì zhě. 4 [习语] **in the ˈred** 负债 fùzhài. ˈ**redhead** *n* [C] 红褐色头[頭]发[髮]的人 hónghèsè tóufa de rén. ˌ**red-ˈhot** *adj* 赤热[熱]的 chìrède;炽[熾]热的 chìrède.

redden /ˈredn/ *v* [I,T] (使)变[變]红 biàn hóng.

redeem /rɪˈdiːm/ *v* [T] 1 买[買]回 mǎihuí;赎[贖]回 shúhuí. 2 弥[彌]补[補] míbǔ;补救 bǔjiù. **redemption** /rɪˈdempʃn/ *n* [U].

redouble /ˌriːˈdʌbl/ *v* [T] 使再加倍 shǐ zàijiābèi;进[進]一步加强 jìnyíbù jiāqiáng;使变[變]得更大 shǐ biànde gèngdà: ~ *one's efforts* 加倍努力.

redress /rɪˈdres/ *v* [T] [正式用语]1 纠正 jiūzhèng;矫[矯]正 jiǎozhèng. 2 [习语] **redress the ˈbalance** 使恢复[復]均衡 shǐ huīfù jūnhéng;使重新相等 shǐ chóngxīn xiāngděng. **redress** *n* [U] [正式用语]纠正 jiūzhèng;矫正 jiǎozhèng.

reduce /rɪˈdjuːs; *US* -ˈduːs/ *v* [T] 1 减少 jiǎnshǎo;减小 jiǎnxiǎo. 2 (*to*) [常用被动语态]使处[處]于某种[種]状[狀]态[態] shǐ chǔyú mǒuzhǒng zhuàngtài: *He was ~d to tears.* 他流了泪. **reduction** /rɪˈdʌkʃn/ *n* 1 [C,U] 缩减 suōjiǎn;降低 jiàngdī;减少 jiǎnshǎo: ~*s in price* 降低价格. 2 [C] (图片、地图等的)缩图[圖] suōtú;缩版 suōbǎn.

redundant /rɪˈdʌndənt/ *adj* 1 被解雇[僱]的 bèi jiěgùde;失业[業]的 shīyède. 2 过[過]多的 guòduōde;过剩的 guòshèngde;多余[餘]的 duōyúde. **redundancy** /-dənsɪ/ *n* [C,U] [*pl* -ies].

reed /riːd/ *n* [C] 1 芦[蘆]苇[葦] lúwěi. 2 (乐器)簧片 huángpiàn.

reef /riːf/ *n* [C] 礁 jiāo;礁脉 jiāomài.

reek /riːk/ *n* [sing] 浓[濃]烈的臭味 nóngliède chòuwèi. **reek** *v* [I] (*of*) 发[發]出难[難]

闻气〔氣〕味 fāchū nánwén qìwèi.

reel[1] /riːl/ *n* [C] 1（电缆、棉纱等的）卷〔捲〕轴 juǎnzhóu；卷筒 juǎntǒng. 2（电影胶片）一盘〔盤〕yìpán；（电缆等的）一卷 yìjuǎn. **reel** *v* 1 [T] *in/out* 绕〔繞〕起 ràoqǐ；抽（或放）出 chōuchū. 2 [短语动词] **reel sth off** 一口气〔氣〕说出 yìkǒuqì shuōchū.

reel[2] /riːl/ *v* [I] 1 蹒跚 pánshān；摇晃 yáohuàng；摇摆〔擺〕yáobǎi. 2 [喻]（头脑）眩晕 xuànyùn；发〔發〕昏 fāhūn.

refectory /rɪˈfektrɪ/ *n* [C] [*pl* -ies]（学校等的）食堂 shítáng；餐厅〔廳〕cāntīng.

refer /rɪˈfɜː(r)/ *v* [-rr-] 1 [I] *to* (a) 说到 shuōdào；提到 tídào. (b) 涉及 shèjí；有关〔關〕yǒuguān. 2 [I] *to* 查看 chákàn；查阅 cháyuè. 3 [T] *to* 叫…求助于 jiào…qiúzhù yú.

referee /ˌrefəˈriː/ *n* [C] 1 [体育]裁判（员）cáipàn. 2 证〔證〕明人 zhèngmíngrén；介绍人 jièshàorén；推荐〔薦〕人 tuījiànrén.

reference /ˈrefərəns/ *n* 1 [C, U] 提到 tídào；说到 shuōdào；涉及 shèjí. 2 [C] 附注 fùzhù. 3 [C] 证〔證〕明文书〔書〕zhèngmíng wénshū；介绍（或推荐）信 jièshàoxìn. 4 [习语] **in/with reference to sth** [尤用于商业]关〔關〕于某事 guānyú mǒushì. ˈ**reference book** *n* [C] 工具书 gōngjùshū；参〔參〕考书 cānkǎoshū.

referendum /ˌrefəˈrendəm/ [*pl* -da /-də/ 或-dums] *n* [C] 全民投票 quánmín tóupiào；公民复〔復〕决（直接）投票 gōngmín fùjué tóupiào.

refine /rɪˈfaɪn/ *v* [T] 1 精制〔製〕jīngzhì；精炼〔煉〕jīngliàn；提纯 tíchún. 2 改良 gǎiliáng；改进〔進〕gǎijìn. **refined** *adj* 1 有教养〔養〕的 yǒu jiàoyǎng de；文雅的 wényǎde. 2 纯净的 chúnjìngde；精炼的 jīngliànde. **refinement** *n* 1 [U] 精炼 jīngliàn；精制 jīngzhì；提纯 tíchún. 2 [U] 文雅 wényǎ；有教养 yǒu jiàoyǎng. 3 [C] 改良 gǎiliáng；改进 gǎijìn. **refinery** *n* [C] [*pl* -ies] 精炼厂〔廠〕jīngliànchǎng.

R

reflate /ˌriːˈfleɪt/ *v* [I, T] 使（通货）再膨胀 shǐ zài péngzhàng. **reflation** /riːˈfleɪʃn/ *n* [U].

reflect /rɪˈflekt/ *v* 1 [T]（光、热、声等）反射 fǎnshè. 2 [T] [喻]表达〔達〕biǎodá；反映 fǎnyìng；显〔顯〕示 xiǎnshì：*The book faithfully ~s his ideas.* 这本书忠实地反映出他的主张. 3 [I] (*on*) 沉思 chénsī；深思 shēnsī. 4 [短语动词] **reflect on sb/sth** 深思 shēnsī；考虑〔慮〕kǎolǜ. **reflector** *n* [C] 反射器 fǎnshèqì；反射镜 fǎnshèjìng；反射物 fǎnshèwù.

reflection /rɪˈflekʃn/ *n* 1 [C]（镜中）映像 yìngxiàng. 2 [U] 反射光 fǎnshèguāng；反射热〔熱〕fǎnshèrè；回声〔聲〕huíshēng. 3 [C, U] 深思 shēnsī；考虑〔慮〕kǎolǜ：*on* ~ 再三考虑.

reflex /ˈriːfleks/ *n* [C]（亦作 ˈ**reflex action**）反射作用 fǎnshè zuòyòng.

reflexive /rɪˈfleksɪv/ *n* [C], *adj* [语法]反身的 fǎnshēnde：*a ~ verb* 反身动词. *In 'I cut myself', 'myself' is a ~ pronoun.* 在"*I cut myself*"句中，"*myself*"是反身代词.

reform /rɪˈfɔːm/ *v* [I, T] 改革 gǎigé；改良 gǎiliáng；改造 gǎizào. **reform** *n* [C, U] 改革 gǎigé；改良 gǎiliáng；改造 gǎizào. **reformer** *n* [C] 改革者 gǎigézhě；改良者 gǎiliángzhě；革新者 géxīnzhě.

re-form /ˌriː ˈfɔːm/ *v* [I, T] 重新形成 chóngxīn xíngchéng；重新组成 chóngxīn zǔchéng：*The army ~ed and attacked.* 军队重新编队后发起了进攻.

reformation /ˌrefəˈmeɪʃn/ *n* 1 [C, U] 改进〔進〕gǎijìn；改良 gǎiliáng；改造 gǎizào. 2 **the Reformation** [sing] 宗教改革（16 世纪欧洲改革天主教会的运动，产生了新教）zōngjiào gǎigé.

refract /rɪˈfrækt/ *v* [T] 使（光线）折射 shǐ zhéshè. **refraction** /-kʃn/ *n* [U].

refrain[1] /rɪˈfreɪn/ *v* [I] (*from*) [正式用语]抑制 yìzhì；克制 kèzhì.

refrain[2] /rɪˈfreɪn/ *n* [C]（歌曲的）叠〔疊〕句 diéjù；副歌（歌曲中重复演唱的部分）fùgē.

refresh /rɪˈfreʃ/ *v* [T] 1 使恢复〔復〕活力 shǐ huīfù huólì；使振作精神 shǐ zhènzuò jīngshen. 2 [习语]**refresh one's memory** 唤醒自己的记忆〔憶〕huànxǐng zìjǐ de jìyì. **re**ˈ**fresher course** *n* [C] 进〔進〕修课程 jìnxiū kèchéng. **refreshing** *adj* 1 提神的 tíshénde；使人振作的 shǐ rén zhènzuò de. 2 [喻]令人欣喜的 lìng rén xīnxǐ de；新奇的 xīnqíde. **refreshment** *n* 1 [正式用语]（精力的）恢复 huīfù；爽快 shuǎngkuài. 2 **refreshments** [pl] 茶点〔點〕chádiǎn；点心 diǎnxīn；饮料 yǐnliào.

refrigerate /rɪˈfrɪdʒəreɪt/ *v* [T] 冷冻 lěngdòng；冷藏 lěngcáng. **refrigeration** /rɪˌfrɪdʒəˈreɪʃn/ *n* [U]. **refrigerator** *n* [C] 冰箱 bīngxiāng.

refuel /ˌriːˈfjuːəl/ *v* [-ll-；美语 -l-] [I, T] 加燃料 jiā ránliào.

refuge /ˈrefjuːdʒ/ *n* [C, U] 避难〔難〕（所）bìnàn；庇护〔護〕（所）bìhù.

refugee /ˌrefjʊˈdʒiː/ *n* [C] 避难〔難〕者 bìnànzhě；难民 nànmín；流亡者 liúwángzhě.

refund /ˈriːfʌnd/ *n* [C] 退款 tuìkuǎn；偿〔償〕还〔還〕金额 chánghuán jīn'é. **refund** /rɪˈfʌnd/ *v* [T] 归〔歸〕还 guīhuán；偿还 chánghuán.

refusal /rɪˈfjuːzl/ *n* [C, U] 拒绝 jùjué.

refuse[1] /rɪˈfjuːz/ *v* [I, T] 拒绝 jùjué；回绝 huíjué：~ *permission* 不允许. ~ *to help* 不愿帮助.

refuse[2] /ˈrefjuːs/ *n* [U] 废〔廢〕物 fèiwù；垃圾 lājī.

regain /rɪˈgeɪn/ *v* [T] 恢复〔復〕huīfù;重回 chónghuí: ~ *one's strength* 恢复体力.

regal /ˈriːgl/ *adj* 国〔國〕王的 guówángde;王室的 wángshìde;豪华〔華〕的 háohuáde.

regalia /rɪˈgeɪlɪə/ *n* [U] 王权〔權〕的标〔標〕志(如王冠等) wángquánde biāozhì.

regard[1] /rɪˈgɑːd/ *v* [T] *as* 把…看作 bǎ…kànzuò;认〔認〕为〔爲〕rènwéi: *She is ~ed as the best teacher in the school*. 她被认为是学校里最好的教师. **regarding** (亦作 **as regards**) *prep* 关〔關〕于 guānyú.

regard[2] /rɪˈgɑːd/ *n* **1** [U] 注意 zhùyì;关〔關〕心 guānxīn: *with no ~ for safety* 不顾及安全. **2** [U] 尊重 zūnzhòng;敬重 jìngzhòng: *have a high ~ for sb* 极为尊敬某人. **3 regards** [pl] 致意 zhìyì;问候 wènhòu. **4** [习语] **in/with regard to sth** 关于 guānyú. **regardless (of)** *adv* 不顾〔顧〕búgù.

regatta /rɪˈgætə/ *n* [C] 划船比赛 huáchuán bǐsài;赛船会〔會〕sàichuánhuì.

regency /ˈriːʤənsɪ/ *n* [*pl* **-ies**] **1** [C] 摄〔攝〕政(期) shèzhèng. **2 the Regency** [sing] (英国)摄政时〔時〕期(1810—1820 年) shèzhèng shíqī.

regenerate /rɪˈʤenəreɪt/ *v* [I, T] (使在精神上)重生 chóngshēng;(使)新生 xīnshēng. **regeneration** /rɪˌʤenəˈreɪʃn/ *n* [U].

regent /ˈriːʤənt/ *n* [C] 摄〔攝〕政者 shèzhèngzhě.

reggae /ˈregeɪ/ *n* [U] 雷盖〔蓋〕音乐〔樂〕(西印度群岛的流行音乐) léigài yīnyuè;雷盖舞 léigàiwǔ.

regime /reɪˈʒiːm/ *n* [C] 政体〔體〕zhèngtǐ;政治制度 zhèngzhì zhìdù;政权〔權〕zhèngquán. **reˈgime change** *n* [U, C] 政权更替 zhèngquán gēngtì; 政府变〔變〕更 zhèngfǔ biàngēng.

regiment /ˈreʤɪmənt/ *n* [C] (军队)团〔團〕tuán. **regiment** *v* [T] 严〔嚴〕密地编组(或队) yánmì de biānzǔ. **regimental** /ˌreʤɪˈmentl/ *adj*.

region /ˈriːʤən/ *n* **1** [C] 地区〔區〕dìqū;地带〔帶〕dìdài. **2** [C] 行政区 xíngzhèngqū. **3** [习语] **in the region of sth** 大约 dàyuē;接近 jiējìn. **regional** *adj*.

register /ˈreʤɪstə(r)/ *n* [C] **1** 登记簿 dēngjìbù;注册簿 zhùcèbù;登记 dēngjì;注册 zhùcè. **2** (人声或乐器的)音区〔區〕yīnqū;声〔聲〕区 shēngqū. **register** *v* **1** [I] 登记(姓名) dēngjì. **2** [T] 注册 zhùcè;记录〔錄〕jìlù. **3** [I, T] (仪表等)指示 zhǐshì;显〔顯〕示 xiǎnshì. **4** [T] (面容)流露(情绪等) liúlù. **5** [T] 挂〔掛〕号〔號〕邮〔郵〕寄(信等) guàhào yóujì.

registrar /ˌreʤɪˈstrɑː(r)/ *n* [C] 登记员 dēngjìyuán;户籍员 hùjíyuán.

registration /ˌreʤɪˈstreɪʃn/ *n* [U] 登记 dēngjì;注册 zhùcè;挂〔掛〕号〔號〕guàhào. **regiˈstration number** *n* [C] (汽车)登记号码 dēngjì hàomǎ;牌照号码 páizhào hàomǎ.

registry office /ˈreʤɪstrɪ/ *n* [C] 户籍登记处〔處〕hùjí dēngjìchù.

regret[1] /rɪˈgret/ *v* [-tt-] [T] 因…懊悔 yīn…àohuǐ;因…遗憾 yīn…yíhàn;因…惋惜 yīn…wǎnxī: *Later, I ~ted my decision to leave*. 后来,我对决定离开感到遗憾. **regrettable** *adj* 使人悔恨的 shǐ rén huǐhèn de;令人遗憾的 lìng rén yíhàn de. **regrettably** *adv*.

regret[2] /rɪˈgret/ *n* [U, C] 懊悔 àohuǐ;遗憾 yíhàn. **regretful** *adj* 懊悔的 àohuǐde;遗憾的 yíhànde.

regular /ˈregjʊlə(r)/ *adj* **1** 定时〔時〕的 dìngshíde;定期的 dìngqīde; ~ *breathing* 均匀的呼吸. **2** 匀称〔稱〕的 yúnchènde;整齐〔齊〕的 zhěngqíde. **3** 经〔經〕常的 jīngchángde;正常的 zhèngchángde. **4** [语法](动词、名词等)按规则变〔變〕化的 àn guīzé biànhuà de. **5** (军队)正规的 zhèngguīde;常备〔備〕的 chángbèide: *a ~ soldier* 正规士兵. **regular** *n* [C] **1** 正规兵 zhèngguībīng;常备兵 chángbèibīng;职〔職〕业〔業〕军人 zhíyè jūnrén. **2** [非正式用语]常客 chángkè;老顾〔顧〕客 lǎo gùkè. **regularity** /ˌregjʊˈlærətɪ/ *n* [U]. **regularly** *adv* 定期地 dìngqīde;有规律地 yǒu guīlǜ de.

regulate /ˈregjʊleɪt/ *v* [T] **1** 控制 kòngzhì;管理 guǎnlǐ. **2** 调整 tiáozhěng;校准〔準〕jiàozhǔn.

regulation /ˌregjʊˈleɪʃn/ *n* **1** [C, 常作 pl] 规章 guīzhāng;规则 guīzé;法规 fǎguī;条〔條〕例 tiáolì. **2** [U] 控制 kòngzhì;管理 guǎnlǐ;校准〔準〕jiàozhǔn. **regulation** *adj* 规定的 guīdìngde;正规的 zhèngguīde: ~ *clothes* 规定的服装.

rehabilitate /ˌriːəˈbɪlɪteɪt/ *v* [T] 使(出狱者、病人)恢复正常生活 shǐ…huīfù zhèngcháng shēnghuó. **rehabilitation** /ˌriːəˌbɪlɪˈteɪʃn/ *n* [U].

rehearse /rɪˈhɜːs/ *v* [I, T] 排练〔練〕páiliàn;排演 páiyǎn. **rehearsal** *n* [C, U].

reign /reɪn/ *n* [C] 君主统治 jūnzhǔ tǒngzhì;(君主)统治时〔時〕期 tǒngzhì shíqī. **reign** *v* [I] **1** (君主等)统治 tǒngzhì. **2** [喻]支配 zhīpèi;盛行 shèngxíng: *Silence ~ed*. 万籁俱寂.

reimburse /ˌriːɪmˈbɜːs/ *v* [T] 偿〔償〕还〔還〕chánghuán;补〔補〕偿 bǔcháng. **reimbursement** *n* [C, U].

rein /reɪn/ *n* [C, 常作 pl] 缰绳〔繩〕jiāngshéng.

reincarnate /ˌriːˈɪnkɑːneɪt/ *v* [T] [常用被动语态]使转〔轉〕世化身 shǐ zhuǎnshì huàshēn. **reincarnation** /ˌriːɪnkɑːˈneɪʃn/ *n* [U, C].

R

reindeer /ˈreɪndɪə(r)/ *n* [C] [*pl* reindeer] 驯鹿 xùnlù.

reinforce /ˌriːɪnˈfɔːs/ *v* [T] 增援 zēngyuán; 加强 jiāqiáng. **reinforcement** *n* 1 [U] 增援 zēngyuán; 加强 jiāqiáng. 2 **reinforcements** [pl] 援军 yuánjūn; 增援部队[隊] zēngyuán bùduì.

reinstate /ˌriːɪnˈsteɪt/ *v* [T] 使复[復]原位 shǐ fù yuánwèi; 恢复原职[職] huīfù yuánzhí. **reinstatement** *n* [U].

reiterate /riːˈɪtəreɪt/ *v* [T] [正式用语]反复[復]做 fǎnfù zuò; 反复讲[講] fǎnfù jiǎng. **reiteration** /riːˌɪtəˈreɪʃn/ *n* [C, U].

reject /rɪˈdʒekt/ *v* [T] 1 拒绝 jùjué; 拒绝接受 jùjué jiēshòu. 2 抛弃[棄] pāoqì; 摈[擯]弃 bìnqì. **reject** /ˈriːdʒekt/ *n* [C] 被抛弃的东西 bèi pāoqìde dōngxi. **rejection** /rɪˈdʒekʃn/ *n* [U, C].

rejoice /rɪˈdʒɔɪs/ *v* [I] [正式用语]欣喜 xīnxǐ; 高兴[興] gāoxìng. **rejoicing** *n* [U] 欢[歡]喜 huānxǐ; 高兴 gāoxìng.

rejuvenate /rɪˈdʒuːvəneɪt/ *v* [T] 使变[變]年轻[輕] shǐ biàn niánqīng; 使恢复[復]青春活力 shǐ huīfù qīngchūn huólì. **rejuvenation** /rɪˌdʒuːvəˈneɪʃn/ *n* [U].

relapse /rɪˈlæps/ *v* [I] (疾病)复[復]发[發] fùfā; 重新陷入 chóngxīn xiànrù; 故态[態]复萌 gù tài fù méng. **relapse** *n* [C].

relate /rɪˈleɪt/ *v* 1 [I, T] (*to*) (使)有关[關]联[聯] yǒu guānlián. 2 [I] (*to*) 和睦相处[處] hémù xiāngchǔ. 3 [T] [正式用语]讲[講]述 jiǎngshù. **related** *adj* 有亲[親]戚关系[係]的 yǒu qīnqì guānxì de; 相关的 xiāngguānde.

relation /rɪˈleɪʃn/ *n* 1 [C] 亲[親]属[屬] qīnshǔ; 亲戚 qīnqì. 2 [U] 关[關]系[係] guānxì. 3 **relations** [pl] (国家、人民等之间的)关系 guānxì; 往来[來] wǎnglái. 4 [习语] **in relation to sth** [正式用语]涉及某事 shèjí mǒushì. **relationship** *n* [C] 1 关系 guānxì. 2 感情关系 gǎnqíng guānxì. 3 (与异性的)浪漫关系 làngmàn guānxì.

R

relative /ˈrelətɪv/ *adj* 1 比较的 bǐjiàode; 相对[對]的 xiāngduìde. 2 *to* [正式用语]有关[關]的 yǒuguānde; 相关的 xiāngguānde. **relative** *n* [C] 亲[親]属[屬] qīnshǔ; 亲戚 qīnqì. ˌ**relative** ˈ**clause** *n* [C] [语法]关系[係]从[從]句 guānxì cóngjù. **relatively** *adv* 适[適]度地 shìdùde; 相当[當]地 xiāngdāngde: ~*ly cheap food* 相当便宜的食品. ˌ**relative** ˈ**pronoun** *n* [C] [语法]关系代词(如在 *the woman who came* 这一短语中的 *who*) guānxì dàicí.

relax /rɪˈlæks/ *v* 1 [I, T] 使松[鬆]弛 shǐ sōngchí; 放松 fàngsōng; 变[變]得轻[輕]松 biànde qīngsōng. 2 [T] 使(规则等)放宽 shǐ fàngkuān. **relaxation** /ˌriːlækˈseɪʃn/ *n* 1 [U, C] 消遣 xiāoqiǎn; 娱乐[樂] yúlè. 2 [U] 松弛 sōngchí; 放松 fàngsōng. **relaxed** *adj* 松弛的 sōngchíde; 轻松的 qīngsōngde.

relay /ˈriːleɪ/ *n* 1 (a) [C, U] 接替人员 jiētì rényuán; 替班 tìbān. (b) ˈ**relay race** [C] (赛跑、游泳等)接力赛 jiēlìsài. 2 [C] 中继[繼]设备[備] zhōngjì shèbèi. **relay** /亦读 rɪˈleɪ/ *v* [*pt*, *pp* ~**ed**] [T] 中继转[轉]发[發] zhōngjì zhuǎnfā; 转播 zhuǎnbō.

release /rɪˈliːs/ *v* [T] 1 释[釋]放 shìfàng. 2 发[發]布(新闻等) fābù. 3 松[鬆]开[開] sōngkāi; 放开 fàngkāi: ~ *the brake* 松开闸. **release** *n* 1 [U, C] 释放 shìfàng; 发表 fābiǎo; 松开 sōngkāi. 2 [C] 发行(新影片等) fāxíng.

relegate /ˈrelɪgeɪt/ *v* [T] 使降低地位 shǐ jiàngdī dìwèi; 使降级 shǐ jiàngjí. **relegation** /ˌrelɪˈgeɪʃn/ *n* [U].

relent /rɪˈlent/ *v* [I] 变[變]温和 biàn wēnhé; 变宽容 biàn kuānróng. **relentless** *adj* 不间断[斷]的 bù jiànduàn de; 严[嚴]格的 yángéde.

relevant /ˈreləvənt/ *adj* 有关[關]的 yǒuguānde; 切题的 qiètíde. **relevance** /-vəns/ *n* [U]. **relevantly** *adv*.

reliable /rɪˈlaɪəbl/ *adj* 可靠的 kěkàode; 可信赖的 kě xìnlài de. **reliability** /rɪˌlaɪəˈbɪlətɪ/ *n* [U]. **reliably** *adv*.

reliant /rɪˈlaɪənt/ *adj on* 信赖的 xìnlàide; 依靠的 yīkàode. **reliance** /-əns/ *n* [U] 信赖 xìnlài; 依靠 yīkào.

relic /ˈrelɪk/ *n* [C] 1 遗物 yíwù; 遗迹 yíjì; 遗俗 yísú. 2 圣[聖]徒遗物 shèngtú yíwù; 圣物 shèngwù; 圣骨 shènggǔ.

relief[1] /rɪˈliːf/ *n* 1 [U, sing] (痛苦、忧虑等的)减轻[輕] jiǎnqīng, 解除 jiěchú: ~ *of suffering* 解除疼痛. 2 [U] 救济[濟] jiùjì; 解救 jiějiù. 3 [C] 换班人 huànbānrén; 接替人 jiētìrén; 轮[輪]班人 lúnbānrén.

relief[2] /rɪˈliːf/ *n* [U, C] 浮雕(法) fúdiāo. **reˈlief map** *n* [C] (用晕渲法、分层设色法或凸现法表示地面起伏的)地势[勢]图[圖] dìshìtú.

relieve /rɪˈliːv/ *v* [T] 1 减轻[輕] jiǎnqīng, 解除(痛苦、忧虑) jiěchú: *medicine to* ~ *the pain* 缓解疼痛的药. 2 接替 jiētì; 换班 huànbān. 3 调剂[劑] tiáojì. 4 [短语动词] **relieve sb of sth** [正式用语]解除(责任、工作) jiěchú: *He was* ~*d of his duties*. 他被免职. **relieved** *adj* 宽心的 kuānxīnde; 宽慰的 kuānwèide.

religion /rɪˈlɪdʒən/ *n* 1 [U] 宗教信仰 zōngjiào xìnyǎng. 2 [C] 宗教 zōngjiào.

religious /rɪˈlɪdʒəs/ *adj* 1 宗教的 zōngjiàode. 2 虔诚的 qiánchéngde; 笃信宗教的 dǔxìn zōngjiào de. **religiously** *adv* 有规律地 yǒu guīlǜ de.

relinquish /rɪˈlɪŋkwɪʃ/ *v* [T] [正式用语]放

弃〔棄〕fàngqì；让〔讓〕予 ràngyǔ：～ *one's duties* 放弃自己的职责.

relish /ˈrelɪʃ/ *v* [T] 享受 xiǎngshòu：*I don't ～ the idea of getting up so early.* 我不喜欢这么早起床的主意. **relish** *n* **1** [U] 滋味 zīwèi；美味 měiwèi. **2** 调味品 tiáowèipǐn；佐料 zuǒliào.

reluctant /rɪˈlʌktənt/ *adj* 不情愿〔願〕的 bù qíngyuàn de；勉强的 miǎnqiǎngde. **reluctance** /-təns/ *n* [U]. **reluctantly** *adv*.

rely /rɪˈlaɪ/ *v* [*pt*, *pp* -ied] [I] *on* 依靠 yīkào；依赖 yīlài；信任 xìnrèn.

remain /rɪˈmeɪn/ *v* **1** [常与形容词连用]保持不变〔變〕bǎochí búbiàn：～ *silent* 保持沉默. **2** [I] 剩下 shèngxià；剩余〔餘〕shèngyú；遗留 yíliú：*Not much ～ed of the house after the fire.* 火灾后,这所房子所剩无几. *She ～ed in the house after her friends had left.* 她的朋友走后,她仍留在屋里. **3** [I] 留待 liúdài；尚待 shàngdài：*There are only a couple of jobs ～ing now.* 现在只有两件工作有待完成. **remainder** /-də(r)/ *n* [sing, 亦作 sing 用 pl v] 剩余部分 shèngyú bùfen. **remains** *n* [pl] **1** 剩余物 shèngyúwù；残〔殘〕余 cányú. **2** [正式用语]遗体〔體〕yítǐ.

remand /rɪˈmɑːnd; *US* -ˈmænd/ *v* [T] 将〔將〕(被告、犯人)还〔還〕押候审〔審〕jiāng…huányā hòushěn. **remand** *n* [习语] **on remand** 还押中 huányā zhōng.

remark /rɪˈmɑːk/ *v* [I, T] (*on*) 谈论〔論〕tánlùn；评论 pínglùn：*They all ～ed on his youth.* 他们都谈到他的青年时期. **remark** *n* [C] 评论 pínglùn；评述 píngshù. **remarkable** *adj* 不平常的 bù píngcháng de；值得注意的 zhídé zhùyì de. **remarkably** *adv*.

remedial /rɪˈmiːdɪəl/ *adj* 治疗〔療〕的 zhìliáode；补〔補〕救的 bǔjiùde；矫〔矯〕正的 jiǎozhèngde.

remedy /ˈremədɪ/ *n* [C, U] [*pl* -ies] **1** 补〔補〕救 bǔjiù；纠正 jiūzhèng. **2** 治疗〔療〕zhìliáo. **remedy** *v* [*pt*, *pp* -ied] [T] 补救 bǔjiù；纠正 jiūzhèng；治疗 zhìliáo.

remember /rɪˈmembə(r)/ *v* **1** [I, T] 记得 jìdé；回忆〔憶〕起 huíyì qǐ. **2** [T] 给…钱〔錢〕gěi…qián；向…送礼〔禮〕xiàng…sònglǐ. **3** [短语动词] **remember sb to sb** 代某人向他人问候(或致意) dài mǒurén xiàng tārén wènhòu. **remembrance** /-brəns/ *n* [正式用语] **1** [U] 记忆 jìyì；回想 huíxiǎng. **2** [C] 纪念品 jìniànpǐn；纪念物 jìniànwù.

remind /rɪˈmaɪnd/ *v* [T] **1** 提醒 tíxǐng；使想起 shǐ xiǎngqǐ：*R～ me to buy some more milk, will you?* 提醒我再买些牛奶,好吗? **2** *of* 使产〔產〕生联〔聯〕想 shǐ chǎnshēng liánxiǎng：*He ～s me of his brother.* 他使我想起他的弟弟. **reminder** *n* [C] 催询(或催还、催缴)单〔單〕cuīxúndān.

reminisce /ˌremɪˈnɪs/ *v* [I] (*about*) 缅怀〔懷〕往事 miǎnhuái wǎngshì；回忆〔憶〕huíyì；话旧〔舊〕huàjiù. **reminiscences** *n* [pl] 经〔經〕验〔驗〕谈 jīngyàntán；回忆录〔錄〕huíyìlù. **reminiscent** *adj of* 缅怀往事的 miǎnhuái wǎngshì de；话旧的 huàjiùde；使人联〔聯〕想的 shǐ rén liánxiǎng de.

remission /rɪˈmɪʃn/ *n* **1** [U, C] 刑期减免 xíngqī jiǎnmiǎn；减刑 jiǎnxíng. **2** [U] 宽恕 kuānshù；赦免 shèmiǎn.

remit /rɪˈmɪt/ *v* [-tt-] [T] [正式用语] **1** 汇〔匯〕(款) huì；汇寄 huìjì. **2** 免除(费用、处罚) miǎnchú；取消 qǔxiāo. **remittance** *n* [C] 汇款额 huì kuǎn'é；汇款 huìkuǎn.

remnant /ˈremnənt/ *n* [C] 残〔殘〕余〔餘〕cányú；剩余 shèngyú.

remonstrate /ˈremənstreɪt; *US* rɪˈmɒnstreɪt/ *v* [I] (*with*) [正式用语]抗议〔議〕kàngyì；反对〔對〕fǎnduì：*～d with him about being late again* 对他再次迟到表示抗议.

remorse /rɪˈmɔːs/ *n* [U] 懊悔 àohuǐ；悔恨 huǐhèn；自责 zìzé. **remorseful** *adj*. **remorseless** *adj* **1** 无〔無〕情的 wúqíngde. **2** 无休止的 wú xiūzhǐ de.

remote /rɪˈməʊt/ *adj* [～r, ～st] **1** (*from*) 远〔遠〕离〔離〕的 yuǎnlíde. **2** (在时间或空间上)遥远的 yáoyuǎnde. **3** (*from*) 与〔與〕…无〔無〕关〔關〕的 yǔ…wúguānde. **4** (人)冷淡的 lěngdànde；漠不关心的 mò bù guānxīn de. **5** 微小的 wēixiǎode：*a ～ possibility* 微乎其微的可能性. **reˌmote conˈtrol** *n* [U] 遥控 yáokòng. **remotely** *adv* 轻〔輕〕微地 qīngwēide. **remoteness** *n* [U].

remove /rɪˈmuːv/ *v* [T] **1** 移开〔開〕yíkāi；挪走 nuózǒu. **2** 去掉 qùdiào；清除 qīngchú：～ *stains/doubts* 去除污迹；消除疑虑. **3** 把…免职〔職〕bǎ…miǎnzhí. **removal** *n* **1** [U] 移动〔動〕yídòng；去除 qùchú；免职 miǎnzhí. **2** [C] 搬迁〔遷〕bānqiān. **removed** *adj from* 有区〔區〕别的 yǒu qūbié de；不同的 bùtóngde. **remover** *n* [C, U]：*a ˈstain ～r* 去污剂.

remunerate /rɪˈmjuːnəreɪt/ *v* [T] [正式用语]报〔報〕酬 bàochóu；酬劳〔勞〕chóuláo. **remuneration** /rɪˌmjuːnəˈreɪʃn/ *n* [C, U]. **remunerative** /-ərətɪv; *US* -əreɪtɪv/ *adj* 有利的 yǒulìde；有报酬的 yǒu bàochóu de.

renaissance /rɪˈneɪsns; *US* ˈrenəsɑːns/ *n* **1 the Renaissance** [sing] (欧洲 14 至 16 世纪的)文艺〔藝〕复〔復〕兴〔興〕wényì fùxīng. **2** [C] 复兴 fùxīng.

renal /ˈriːnl/ *adj* [解剖]肾〔腎〕脏〔臟〕的 shènzàngde.

R

render /ˈrendə(r)/ *v* [T] [正式用语]1 致使 zhìshǐ;使成 shǐ chéng: *The shock ~ed him speechless.* 惊得他说不出话来.2 给予 jǐyǔ;回报[報] huíbào: *a payment for services ~ed* 服务的酬金.3 演出 yǎnchū;演奏 yǎnzòu. 4 翻译[譯] fānyì. **rendering** *n* [C] 表演 biǎoyǎn;演奏 yǎnzòu.

rendezvous /ˈrɒndɪvuː/ *n* [C] [*pl* **rendezvous** /-vuːz/] 1 约会[會] yuēhuì;会面 huìmiàn. 2 约会地 yuēhuìdì;聚会地 jùhuìdì. **rendezvous** *v* [I] (在指定地点)会合 huìhé;会面 huìmiàn.

rendition /renˈdɪʃn/ *n* [C] [正式用语]表演 biǎoyǎn;演奏 yǎnzòu.

renegade /ˈrenɪgeɪd/ *n* [C] 变[變]节[節]者 biànjiézhě;叛徒 pàntú;叛教者 pànjiàozhě.

renew /rɪˈnjuː; *US* -ˈnuː/ *v* [T] 1 重新开[開]始 chóngxīn kāishǐ: ~ *a friendship* 重修旧好.2 更新 gēngxīn. 3 注入新的力量 zhùrù xīnde lìliàng. 4 延期 yánqī;延长[長] yáncháng: ~ *a passport* 延长护照的期限. **renewal** *n* [C,U].

renounce /rɪˈnaʊns/ *v* [T] [正式用语]1 宣称[稱]与[與]…断[斷]绝关[關]系[係] xuānchēng yǔ … duànjué guānxi: ~ *one's faith* 背弃自己的信仰.2 声[聲]明放弃[棄] shēngmíng fàngqì.

renovate /ˈrenəveɪt/ *v* [T] 修复[復](旧建筑) xiūfù;整旧[舊]如新 zhěng jiù rú xīn. **renovation** /ˌrenəˈveɪʃn/ *n* [C,U].

renown /rɪˈnaʊn/ *n* [U] [正式用语]名望 míngwàng;声[聲]誉[譽] shēngyù. **renowned** *adj* 著名的 zhùmíngde.

rent[1] /rent/ *n* [U,C] 租金 zūjīn;租费 zūfèi. **rent** *v* [T] 1 租借 zūjiè;租用 zūyòng. 2 (*out*) 出租 chūzū. **rental** *n* [C] 租费 zūfèi.

rent[2] /rent/ *n* [C] (布、衣服等的)破洞 pòdòng;破裂处[處] pòlièchù.

renunciation /rɪˌnʌnsɪˈeɪʃn/ *n* [U] [正式用语]放弃[棄] fàngqì;拒绝承认[認] jùjué chéngrèn;宣布断[斷]绝关[關]系[係] xuānbù duànjué guānxì.

reorganize /ˌriːˈɔːgənaɪz/ *v* [I,T] 改组 gǎizǔ;改编 gǎibiān;整顿 zhěngdùn. **reorganization** /ˌriːˌɔːgənaɪˈzeɪʃn; *US* -nɪˈz-/ *n* [U, C].

Rep *abbr* [美语] Republican.

rep[1] /rep/ *n* [C] [非正式用语] short for REPRESENTATIVE 2.

rep[2] /rep/ *n* [U] [非正式用语] short for REPERTORY.

repair /rɪˈpeə(r)/ *v* [T] 修理 xiūlǐ;修补[補] xiūbǔ. **repair** *n* 1 [C,U] 修理 xiūlǐ;修补 xiūbǔ: *His car is under ~ at the moment.* 他的汽车此刻正在修理.2 [习语] in good/bad reˈpair 维修良好;维修不善.

reparation /ˌrepəˈreɪʃn/ *n* [C] [正式用语] 补[補]偿[償] bǔcháng;赔偿 péicháng.

repatriate /riːˈpætrɪeɪt; *US* -ˈpeɪt-/ *v* [T] 把…遣返回国[國] bǎ… qiǎnfǎn huíguó. **repatriation** /ˌriːpætrɪˈeɪʃn; *US* -ˌpeɪt-/ *n* [U].

repay /rɪˈpeɪ/ *v* [*pt, pp* **repaid** /rɪˈpeɪd/] [T] 1 付还[還](钱) fùhuán;偿[償]还 chánghuán. 2 报[報]答 bàodá;回报 huíbào: *How can I ~ your kindness?* 我怎样报答你的恩惠呢? **repayment** *n* [C,U].

repeal /rɪˈpiːl/ *v* [T] 废[廢]止(法令等) fèizhǐ;撤销 chèxiāo;取消 qǔxiāo. **repeal** *n* [U].

repeat /rɪˈpiːt/ *v* 1 [T] 重复[複] chóngfù;重说 chóngshuō;重做 chóngzuò. 2 ~ **oneself** 重复 chóngfù;重演 chóngyǎn. **repeat** *n* [C] 重复 chóngfù;重说 chóngshuō;重做 chóngzuò. **repeated** *adj* 重复的 chóngfùde;反复[復]的 fǎnfùde. **repeatedly** *adv*.

repel /rɪˈpel/ *v* [-ll-] [T] 1 击[擊]退 jītuì;驱[驅]逐 qūzhú. 2 使厌[厭]恶[惡] shǐ yànwù;使反感 shǐ fǎngǎn. **repellent** *adj* 令人厌恶的 lìng rén yànwù de;令人反感的 lìng rén fǎngǎn de. **repellent** *n* [C,U] 驱虫剂[劑] qūchóngjì.

repent /rɪˈpent/ *v* [I,T] (*of*) [正式用语]后[後]悔 hòuhuǐ;懊悔 àohuǐ. **repentance** *n* [U]. **repentant** *adj*.

repercussion /ˌriːpəˈkʌʃn/ *n* [C, 常作 pl] (深远的、间接的)反响[響] fǎnxiǎng;影响 yǐngxiǎng;后[後]果 hòuguǒ.

repertoire /ˈrepətwɑː(r)/ *n* [C] (艺术团体、演员、音乐家等可随时演出的)全部剧[劇]目 quánbù jùmù;全部节[節]目 quánbù jiémù.

repertory /ˈrepətrɪ; *US* -tɔːrɪ/ *n* [U] (同一剧团在同一剧院演出的)保留剧[劇]目轮[輪]演 bǎoliú jùmù lúnyǎn: *a ~ company* 保留剧目轮演剧团.

repetition /ˌrepɪˈtɪʃn/ *n* [C,U] 重复[複] chóngfù;重说 chóngshuō;重做 chóngzuò. **repetitive** /rɪˈpetətɪv/ *adj* 重复的 chóngfùde;反复[復]的 fǎnfùde. **repetitive ˈstrain injury** *n* [C, U] 重复性肌肉劳[勞]损症 chóngfùxìng jīròuláosǔn zhèng;办[辦]公室疼痛症 bàngōngshì téngtòngzhèng.

rephrase /ˌriːˈfreɪz/ *v* [T] 再措辞[辭] zài cuòcí;改变[變]措辞 gǎibiàn cuòcí.

replace /rɪˈpleɪs/ *v* [T] 1 放回 fànghuí. 2 代替 dàitì;取代 qǔdài. 3 替换 tìhuàn. **replacement** *n* 1 [U] 回归[歸]原位 huíguī yuánwèi;代替 dàitì. 2 [C] 替换 tìhuàn.

replay /ˌriːˈpleɪ/ *v* [T] 1 重赛 chóngsài. 2 重放(录音、录像) chóngfàng. **replay** /ˈriːpleɪ/ *n* [C] 重赛 chóngsài.

replenish /rɪˈplenɪʃ/ *v* [T] [正式用语]再装

R

〔裝〕满 zài zhuāngmǎn；补〔補〕充 bǔchōng.

replica /ˈreplɪkə/ *n* [C] 复〔複〕制〔製〕品 fùzhìpǐn.

reply /rɪˈplaɪ/ *v* [*pt, pp* -ied] [I, T] 回答 huídá；答复〔復〕dáfù. **reply** *n* [C] [*pl* -ies] 回答 huídá；答复 dáfù.

report[1] /rɪˈpɔːt/ *n* **1** [C] 报〔報〕告 bàogào；报道 bàodào. **2** [C] [英国英语]（学生的）成绩报告单〔單〕chéngjì bàogàodān. **3** [C, U] 传〔傳〕闻 chuánwén；谣言 yáoyán. **4** [C] [正式用语]爆炸声〔聲〕bàozhàshēng.

report[2] /rɪˈpɔːt/ *v* **1** [I, T] 报〔報〕道 bàodào. **2** [T] (*to*) 告发〔發〕gàofā；控告 kònggào. **3** [I] *to/for* 报到 bàodào. **reported speech** *n* [U] = INDIRECT SPEECH (INDIRECT). **reporter** *n* [C] 记者 jìzhě；新闻通讯员 xīnwén tōngxùnyuán.

repose /rɪˈpəʊz/ *v* [I] [正式用语]休息 xiūxi；躺 tǎng. **repose** *n* [U] [正式用语]休息 xiūxi.

reprehensible /ˌreprɪˈhensəbl/ *adj* [正式用语]应〔應〕受指责的 yīng shòu zhǐzé de.

represent /ˌreprɪˈzent/ *v* [T] **1** 代表（某人）dàibiǎo：~ *the Queen* 代表女王. **2**（在绘画、雕塑中）表现 biǎoxiàn. **3** 象征〔徵〕xiàngzhēng. **4** [T] 描绘〔繪〕miáohuì. **5** [正式用语]相当〔當〕于 xiāngdāng yú；是…的结果 shì…de jiēguǒ：*This figure ~s an increase of 10%*. 这个数字相当于增加 10%. **representation** /ˌreprɪzenˈteɪʃn/ *n* [U, C].

representative /ˌreprɪˈzentətɪv/ *n* [C] **1** 代表 dàibiǎo. **2** 代理商 dàilǐshāng；（公司派出的）推销员 tuīxiāoyuán. **representative** *adj* **1** 典型的 diǎnxíngde；有代表性的 yǒu dàibiǎoxìng de. **2** 代表制的 dàibiǎozhìde；代议〔議〕制的 dàiyìzhìde.

repress /rɪˈpres/ *v* [T] 抑制 yìzhì；控制 kòngzhì：~ *one's emotions/a nation* 抑制自己的情感；控制一个国家. **repression** /rɪˈpreʃn/ *n* [U]. **repressive** *adj* 严〔嚴〕厉〔厲〕的 yánlìde；残〔殘〕酷的 cánkùde.

reprieve /rɪˈpriːv/ *v* [T] 缓期执〔執〕行…的刑罚（尤指死刑）huǎnqī zhíxíng…de xíngfá. **reprieve** *n* [C] **1**（尤指死刑的）缓刑（令）huǎnxíng. **2** [喻]暂时〔時〕缓解 zànshí huǎnjiě.

reprimand /ˈreprɪmɑːnd; *US* -mænd/ *v* [T] 训斥 xùnchì；申斥 shēnchì；斥责 chìzé. **reprimand** *n* [C].

reprisal /rɪˈpraɪzl/ *n* [C, U] 报〔報〕复〔復〕bàofù；报复行动〔動〕bàofù xíngdòng.

reproach /rɪˈprəʊtʃ/ *v* [T] (*for*) 责备〔備〕zébèi；指责 zhǐzé. **reproach** *n* **1** [U] 责备 zébèi；指责 zhǐzé. **2** [C] 责备〔備〕的言词 zébèide yáncí. **3** [习语] **above/beyond reproach** 无〔無〕可指摘的 wú kě zhǐzhāi de.

reproduce /ˌriːprəˈdjuːs; *US* -ˈduːs/ *v* **1** [T] 复〔複〕制〔製〕fùzhì；翻版 fānbǎn. **2** [I, T] 繁殖 fánzhí；生殖 shēngzhí. **reproduction** /-ˈdʌkʃn/ *n* [C, U]. **reproductive** /-ˈdʌktɪv/ *adj* 繁殖的 fánzhíde；生殖的 shēngzhíde.

reproof /rɪˈpruːf/ *n* [C, U] [正式用语]责备〔備〕zébèi；指摘 zhǐzhāi. **reprove** /rɪˈpruːv/ *v* [T] [正式用语]责备 zébèi；指摘 zhǐzhāi.

reptile /ˈreptaɪl; *US* -tl/ *n* [C] 爬行动〔動〕物（如蜥蜴、蛇）páxíng dòngwù；爬虫 páchóng. **reptilian** /repˈtɪlɪən/ *adj*.

republic /rɪˈpʌblɪk/ *n* [C] 共和国〔國〕gònghéguó；共和政体〔體〕gònghé zhèngtǐ. **republican** *adj* 共和国的 gònghéguóde；共和政体的 gònghé zhèngtǐ de. **republican** *n* [C] **1** 拥〔擁〕护〔護〕共和政体者 yōnghù gònghé zhèngtǐ zhě. **2 Republican**（美国）共和党〔黨〕党员 Gònghédǎng dǎngyuán.

repudiate /rɪˈpjuːdɪeɪt/ *v* [T] [正式用语]拒绝接受 jùjué jiēshòu；与〔與〕…断〔斷〕绝往来 yǔ…duànjué wǎnglái. **repudiation** /rɪˌpjuːdɪˈeɪʃn/ *n* [U].

repugnant /rɪˈpʌgnənt/ *adj* [正式用语]令人厌〔厭〕恶〔惡〕的 lìng rén yànwù de；使人反感的 shǐ rén fǎngǎn de. **repugnance** /-nəns/ *n* [U].

repulse /rɪˈpʌls/ *v* [T] [正式用语]**1** 击〔擊〕退（敌人）jītuì. **2** [喻]拒绝接受 jùjué jiēshòu. **repulsion** /rɪˈpʌlʃn/ *n* [U] **1** 厌〔厭〕恶〔惡〕yànwù；反感 fǎngǎn. **2** [物理]排斥 páichì；斥力 chìlì. **repulsive** *adj* 令人厌恶的 lìng rén yànwù de；使人反感的 shǐ rén fǎngǎn de.

reputable /ˈrepjʊtəbl/ *adj* 声〔聲〕誉〔譽〕好的 shēngyù hǎo de；有声望的 yǒu shēngwàng de.

reputation /ˌrepjʊˈteɪʃn/ *n* [C, U] 名誉〔譽〕míngyù；名声〔聲〕míngshēng；名气〔氣〕míngqì.

repute /rɪˈpjuːt/ *n* [U] [正式用语] **1** 名誉〔譽〕míngyù；名声〔聲〕míngshēng. **2** 美名 měimíng；声望 shēngwàng：*a doctor of* ~ 名医. **reputed** *adj* 普遍认〔認〕为〔爲〕的 pǔbiàn rènwéi de. **reputedly** *adv*.

request /rɪˈkwest/ *n* **1** [C, U] 请求 qǐngqiú；要求 yāoqiú：*make a* ~ *for more money* 请求更多的资助. **2** [C] 要求的事物 yāoqiúde shìwù. **request** *v* [正式用语]请求 qǐngqiú；要求 yāoqiú.

require /rɪˈkwaɪə(r)/ *v* [T] **1** 需要 xūyào：*My car ~s some attention*. 我的汽车需要修理一下. **2** [正式用语][常用被动语态]命令 mìnglìng；要求 yāoqiú：*You are ~d to pay the fine*. 你被命令交罚款. **requirement** *n* [C] 需要的东西 xūyàode dōngxi.

requisite /ˈrekwɪzɪt/ *n* [C], *adj* [正式用语]必需品 bìxūpǐn；需要的 xūyàode；必要的 bìyàode.

rescue /ˈreskjuː/ *v* [T] 救援 jiùyuán；搭救

R

dājiù;营〔營〕救 yíngjiù. **rescue** *n* [C, U] 救援 jiùyuán;搭救 dājiù;营救 yíngjiù.

research /rɪˈsɜːtʃ; *US* ˈriːsɜːtʃ/ *n* [U, C] 研究 yánjiū;调查 diàochá. **research** /rɪˈsɜːtʃ/ *v* [I, T] 研究 yánjiū;调查 diàochá. **research and development** 研究与〔與〕发〔發〕展 yánjiū yǔ fāzhǎn;研发 yánfā. **researcher** *n* [C].

resemble /rɪˈzembl/ *v* [T] 像 xiàng;与〔與〕…相似 yǔ…xiāngsì. **resemblance** *n* [C, U] 相似 xiāngsì;相像 xiāngxiàng.

resent /rɪˈzent/ *v* [T] (因受伤害、委屈等)对〔對〕…感到愤恨(或怨恨、气愤) duì…gǎndào fènhèn: ～ *his success* 对他的成功心怀怨恨. **resentful** *adj*. **resentment** *n* [U, C].

reservation /ˌrezəˈveɪʃn/ *n* 1 [C, U] 保留条〔條〕件 bǎoliú tiáojiàn;保留意见 bǎoliú yìjiàn: *I have a few ～s about the plan*. 我对该计划有所保留. 2 [C] (坐位、房间等)预订 yùdìng. 3 [C] 居留地 jūliúdì.

reserve /rɪˈzɜːv/ *v* [T] 1 储备〔備〕chǔbèi;保留 bǎoliú. 2 预订 yùdìng: ～ *a seat on a train* 预订火车坐位. **reserve** *n* 1 [C] 储备 chǔbèi. 2 **reserves** [pl] 后〔後〕备部队〔隊〕hòubèi bùduì. 3 [C] 保留地 bǎoliúdì: *a* ˈ*nature* ～ 自然保护区. 4 [C] 预备(或替补)队员 yùbèi duìyuán. 5 [U] 拘谨 jūjǐn;寡言 guǎyán. 6 [习语] **in reˈserve** 储存 chǔcún;留以备用 liú yǐ bèiyòng. **reserved** *adj* 矜持的 jīnchíde;寡言的 guǎyánde.

reservoir /ˈrezəvwɑː(r)/ *n* [C] 水库 shuǐkù;蓄水池 xùshuǐchí.

reside /rɪˈzaɪd/ *v* [I] [正式用语] 1 居住 jūzhù;定居 dìngjū. 2 *in* 归〔歸〕于 guīyú;属〔屬〕于 shǔyú.

residence /ˈrezɪdəns/ *n* [正式用语] 1 [C] (尤指大的)住宅 zhùzhái;官邸 guāndǐ. 2 [U] 居住 jūzhù;定居 dìngjū. 3 [习语] **in** ˈ**residence** (官员等)驻在的 zhùzàide;住在任所的 zhù zài rènsuǒ de;住校的 zhùxiàode.

resident /ˈrezɪdənt/ *n* [C], *adj* 居民 jūmín;定居者 dìngjūzhě;定居的 dìngjūde;常驻的 chángzhùde. **residential** /ˌrezɪˈdenʃl/ *adj* 1 居住的 jūzhùde;住宅的 zhùzháide. 2 学〔學〕生寄宿的 xuéshēng jìsù de;(需)住宿在任所的 zhùsù zài rènsuǒ de.

residue /ˈrezɪdjuː; *US* -duː/ *n* [C] 残〔殘〕留物 cánliúwù;剩余〔餘〕物 shèngyúwù;残渣 cánzhā. **residual** /rɪˈzɪdjʊəl; *US* -dʒʊ- / *adj* 残留的 cánliúde;剩余的 shèngyúde.

resign /rɪˈzaɪn/ *v* 1 [I, T] 放弃〔棄〕fàngqì;辞〔辭〕去 cíqù. 2 [短语动词] **resign oneself to sth** 听〔聽〕任 tīngrèn;顺从〔從〕shùncóng. **resigned** *adj* 屈从的 qūcóngde;顺从的 shùncóngde.

resignation /ˌrezɪɡˈneɪʃn/ *n* 1 [C, U] 辞〔辭〕职〔職〕cízhí;放弃〔棄〕fàngqì. 2 [U] 屈从〔從〕qūcóng;顺从 shùncóng.

resilient /rɪˈzɪlɪənt/ *adj* 1 能复〔復〕原的 néng fùyuán de;弹〔彈〕回的 tánhuíde;有弹性的 yǒu tánxìng de. 2 [喻]能迅速恢复的 néng xùnsù huīfù de;有复原能力的 yǒu fùyuánnénglì de. **resilience** /-əns/ *n* [U].

resin /ˈrezɪn; *US* ˈrezn/ *n* [C, U] 1 树〔樹〕脂 shùzhī. 2 合成树脂 héchéng shùzhī.

resist /rɪˈzɪst/ *v* [T] 1 抵抗 dǐkàng;对〔對〕抗 duìkàng. 2 不受…的损害 búshòu…de sǔnhài;抗 kàng;耐 nài. 3 忍住 rěnzhù;顶住 dǐngzhù: ～ *temptation* 经得起诱惑. **resistance** *n* 1 [U, sing] (a) 抵抗 dǐkàng;对抗 duìkàng. (b) 抵抗力 dǐkànglì: *wind ～ance* 风的阻力. 2 **the resistance** [sing] [用 sing 或 pl v] (敌占区的)秘密抵抗组织〔織〕mìmì dǐkàng zǔzhī. **resistant** *adj* 抵抗的 dǐkàngde;抗拒的 kàngjùde;有阻力的 yǒu zǔlì de.

resistor /rɪˈzɪstə(r)/ *n* [C] 电〔電〕阻器 diànzǔqì.

resolute /ˈrezəluːt/ *adj* [正式用语]坚〔堅〕决的 jiānjuéde;坚定的 jiāndìngde. **resolutely** *adv*.

resolution /ˌrezəˈluːʃn/ *n* 1 [C] (会议的)正式决定 zhèngshì juédìng;决议〔議〕juéyì. 2 [C] 决定 juédìng;决心 juéxīn: *a New Year ～ to give up smoking* 新年伊始的戒烟决心. 3 [U] 坚〔堅〕决 jiānjué;坚定 jiāndìng. 4 [U] [正式用语]解决 jiějué;解答 jiědá.

resolve /rɪˈzɒlv/ *v* [T] [正式用语] 1 决定 juédìng;决心 juéxīn. 2 解决(疑问、问题等) jiějué. **resolve** *n* [C, U] 决心 juéxīn;决定 juédìng;坚〔堅〕决 jiānjué.

resonant /ˈrezənənt/ *adj* (声音)回声〔聲〕的 huíshēngde;回响〔響〕的 huíxiǎngde;洪亮的 hóngliàngde. **resonance** /-nəns/ *n* [U].

resort /rɪˈzɔːt/ *v* [I] *to* 求助 qiúzhù;凭〔憑〕借〔藉〕píngjiè;采〔採〕用 cǎiyòng. **resort** *n* [C] 度假胜〔勝〕地 dùjià shèngdì: *a* ˈ*seaside ～* 海滨度假胜地.

resound /rɪˈzaʊnd/ *v* [I] 1 (声音)回荡〔蕩〕huídàng;激起回响〔響〕jīqǐ huíxiǎng. 2 (*with*) (地方)引起回声〔聲〕yǐnqǐ huíshēng. **resounding** *adj* 1 响亮的 xiǎngliàngde;洪亮的 hóngliàngde: *～ing cheers* 响亮的欢呼声. 2 极〔極〕大的 jídàde: *a ～ing success* 重大的成功.

resource /rɪˈsɔːs, -ˈzɔːs; *US* ˈriːsɔːrs/ *n* [C, 常作 pl] 1 资源 zīyuán. 2 可给予帮〔幫〕助的东西 kě jǐyǔ bāngzhù de dōngxi. **resourceful** *adj* 善于随〔隨〕机〔機〕应〔應〕变〔變〕的 shànyú suí jī yìng biàn de;机敏的 jīmǐnde. **resourcefully** *adv*.

respect /rɪˈspekt/ *n* 1 [U] 尊敬 zūnjìng;敬重 jìngzhòng. 2 [U] 考虑〔慮〕kǎolǜ: *show ～ for her wishes* 重视她的愿望. 3 [C] 细节〔節〕

R

xìjié: *In some ~s, I agree with you*. 在某些方面,我同意你的意见.4 respects [pl] [正式用语]敬意 jìngyì; 问候 wènhòu. 5 [习语] **with respect to sth** [正式用语]关〔關〕于 guānyú; 涉及 shèjí. **respect** *v* [T] 尊敬 zūnjìng; 敬重 jìngzhòng; 考虑 kǎolǜ.

respectable /rɪˈspektəbl/ *adj* 1 值得尊敬的 zhídé zūnjìng de; 应〔應〕受敬重的 yīng shòu jìngzhòng de. 2 相当〔當〕数〔數〕量(或规模)的 xiāngdāng shùliàng de; 可观〔觀〕的 kěguānde: *a ~ income* 可观的收入. **respectability** /rɪˌspektəˈbɪlətɪ/ *n* [U]. **respectably** *adv*.

respectful /rɪˈspektfl/ *adj* 表示尊敬(或尊重)的 biǎoshì zūnjìng de; 恭敬的 gōngjìngde. **respectfully** *adv*.

respective /rɪˈspektɪv/ *adj* 各自的 gèzìde; 各个〔個〕的 gègède; 分别的 fēnbiéde. **respectively** *adv* 各自地 gèzìde; 各个地 gègède; 分别地 fēnbiéde.

respiration /ˌrespəˈreɪʃn/ *n* [U] [正式用语]呼吸 hūxī; 一次呼吸 yícì hūxī. **respiratory** /ˈrespɪrətrɪ, rɪˈspaɪərətrɪ; *US* -tɔːrɪ/ *adj* 呼吸的 hūxīde; 呼吸用的 hūxī yòng de.

respite /ˈrespaɪt, -pɪt/ *n* [U, sing] (不愉快的事)暂停 zàntíng, 暂时〔時〕缓解 zànshí huǎnjiě.

resplendent /rɪˈsplendənt/ *adj* [正式用语]灿〔燦〕烂〔爛〕的 cànlànde; 辉煌的 huīhuángde.

respond /rɪˈspɒnd/ *v* [I] (*to*) 1 回答 huídá. 2 作出反应〔應〕 zuòchū fǎnyìng; 响〔響〕应 xiǎngyìng. 3 有反应 yǒu fǎnyìng: *~ to treatment* 治疗生效.

response /rɪˈspɒns/ *n* 1 [C] 回答 huídá; 答复〔復〕 dáfù. 2 [C, U] 反应〔應〕 fǎnyìng; 响〔響〕应 xiǎngyìng.

responsibility /rɪˌspɒnsəˈbɪlətɪ/ *n* [*pl* -ies] 1 [U] 责任 zérèn; 负责 fùzé. 2 [C] 职〔職〕责 zhízé; 任务〔務〕 rènwù.

responsible /rɪˈspɒnsəbl/ *adj* 1 (*for*) 需负责任的 xū fù zérèn de; 承担〔擔〕责任的 chéngdān zérèn de: *~ for cleaning the car* 负责清洗汽车. 2 (*to*) 必须对〔對〕某人负责 bìxū duì mǒurén fùzé. 3 (*for*) 作为〔爲〕原由的 zuòwéi yuányóu de; 应〔應〕受责备〔備〕的 yīng shòu zébèi de: *Who's ~ for this mess?* 是谁弄得这么乱! 4 可靠的 kěkàode; 可信赖的 kě xìnlài de. 5 责任重大的 zérèn zhòngdà de. **responsibly** *adv*.

responsive /rɪˈspɒnsɪv/ *adj* 反应〔應〕灵〔靈〕敏的 fǎnyìng língmǐn de; 敏感的 mǐngǎnde.

rest[1] /rest/ *n* 1 [C, U] 休息 xiūxi; 睡眠 shuìmián. 2 [C] 支承物 zhīchéngwù; 支架 zhījià; 支座 zhīzuò: *an ˈarm-~* 扶手. 3 [C] [音乐]休止(符) xiūzhǐ. 4 [习语] **at ˈrest** (a) 静止 jìngzhǐ; 不动〔動〕 búdòng. (b) 安宁〔寧〕 ānníng.

restful *adj* 给人充分休息的 gěi rén chōngfèn xiūxi de; 令人有宁静感的 lìng rén yǒu níngjìnggǎn de. **restless** *adj* 运〔運〕动〔動〕不止的 yùndòng bùzhǐ de; 静不下来的 jìng bú xiàlái de; 不能安宁的 bùnéng ānníng de.

rest[2] /rest/ *v* 1 [I, T] (使)休息 xiūxi; (使)静止 jìngzhǐ. 2 [I, T] *on/against* 倚赖 yǐlài; 倚靠 yǐkào. 3 [I] *on* (目光)凝视 níngshì. 4 [习语] **rest assured** [正式用语]放心 fàngxīn. **rest on one's laurels** 自满 zìmǎn. 5 [短语动词] **rest on sth** 依靠 yīkào. **rest with sb** 责任全在于(某人) zérèn quán zàiyú.

rest[3] /rest/ *n* **the rest** 1 [sing] 剩余〔餘〕部分 shèngyú bùfen. 2 [pl] 其他人(或物) qítā rén.

restaurant /ˈrestrɒnt; *US* -tərənt/ *n* [C] 餐馆 cānguǎn; 饭店 fàndiàn.

restive /ˈrestɪv/ *adj* [正式用语]不受管束的 búshòu guǎnshù de; 不安宁〔寧〕的 bù ānníng de.

restoration /ˌrestəˈreɪʃn/ *n* 1 [U] 恢复〔復〕 huīfù; 复原 fùyuán. 2 **the Restoration** [sing] (1660 年英王查理二世的)王政复辟时〔時〕期 wángzhèng fùpì shíqī.

restorative /rɪˈstɔːrətɪv/ *adj* 恢复〔復〕健康(或体力)的 huīfù jiànkāng de. **restorative** *n* [C] 恢复健康(或体力)的食物(或药品) huīfù jiànkāng de shíwù.

restore /rɪˈstɔː(r)/ *v* [T] 1 [正式用语]归〔歸〕还〔還〕 guīhuán; 交还 jiāohuán. 2 使复〔復〕位 shǐ fùwèi; 使复职〔職〕 shǐ fùzhí. 3 重新采〔採〕用 chóngxīn cǎiyòng. 4 修复(建筑物、艺术品等) xiūfù; 整修 zhěngxiū. **restorer** *n* [C] (残损文物等的)修复者 xiūfùzhě.

restrain /rɪˈstreɪn/ *v* [T] 抑制 yìzhì; 遏制 èzhì. **restrained** *adj* 克制的 kèzhìde; 受约束的 shòu yuēshù de. **restraint** /rɪˈstreɪnt/ *n* 1 [C, U] 克制物 kèzhìwù; 起遏制作用的事物 qǐ èzhì zuòyòng de shìwù. 2 [U] 抑制 yìzhì; 遏制 èzhì.

restrict /rɪˈstrɪkt/ *v* [T] 限制 xiànzhì; 约束 yuēshù. **restriction** /rɪˈstrɪkʃn/ *n* [C, U]. **restrictive** *adj*.

result /rɪˈzʌlt/ *n* 1 [C, U] 结果 jiēguǒ; 效果 xiàoguǒ. 2 [C] 比赛结果 bǐsài jiēguǒ; 比分 bǐfēn; 成绩 chéngjì. 3 [C] (数学)答案 dá'àn; 答数〔數〕 dáshù. **result** *v* 1 [I] (*from*) 发〔發〕生 fāshēng; 产〔產〕生 chǎnshēng. 2 [短语动词] **result in sth** 结果是 jiēguǒ shì; 结果造成 jiēguǒ zàochéng. **resultant** *adj* [正式用语]因而发生的 yīn'ér fāshēng de; 作为〔爲〕结果的 zuòwéi jiēguǒ de.

resume /rɪˈzjuːm; *US* -ˈzuːm/ *v* 1 [I, T] 重新开〔開〕始 chóngxīn kāishǐ; 继〔繼〕续〔續〕 jìxù. 2 [T] [正式用语]重新得到 chóngxīn dédào; 重新占〔佔〕有 chóngxīn zhànyǒu: *~ one's seat*

R

重新坐下.

résumé /ˈrezjuːmeɪ; *US* ˌrezʊˈmeɪ/ *n* [C] 摘要 zhāiyào; 简历〔歷〕jiǎnlì.

resumption /rɪˈzʌmpʃn/ *n* [U, sing] [正式用语]重新开始 chóngxīn kāishǐ; 继〔繼〕续〔續〕jìxù.

resurrect /ˌrezəˈrekt/ *v* [T] 重新使用 chóngxīn shǐyòng; 使重新流行 shǐ chóngxīn liúxíng. **resurrection** /ˌrezəˈrekʃn/ *n* **1** [U] 重新起用 chóngxīn qǐyòng; 重新流行 chóngxīn liúxíng. **2 the Resurrection** [sing] (a) [宗教] 耶稣复〔復〕活 Yēsū fùhuó. (b) (最后审判日)全部死者的复活 quánbù sǐzhě de fùhuó.

resuscitate /rɪˈsʌsɪteɪt/ *v* [T] [正式用语] 使恢复〔復〕知觉〔覺〕shǐ huīfù zhījué; 使苏〔蘇〕醒 shǐ sūxǐng. **resuscitation** /rɪˌsʌsɪˈteɪʃn/ *n* [U].

retail /ˈriːteɪl/ *n* [U] 零售 língshòu; 零卖〔賣〕língmài. **retail** *adv* 以零售方式 yǐ língshòu fāngshì. **retail** *v* [I, T] 零售 língshòu; 零卖 língmài. **retailer** *n* [C] 零售商 língshòushāng.

retain /rɪˈteɪn/ *v* [T] [正式用语]**1** 保持 bǎochí; 保留 bǎoliú. **2** 付定金聘请(律师) fù dìngjīn pìnqǐng. **retainer** *n* [C] **1** 聘用定金 pìnyòng dìngjīn. **2** (为外出期间保留租房等而付的)定金 dìngjīn. **3** [古]仆〔僕〕人 púrén.

retaliate /rɪˈtælɪeɪt/ *v* [I] 报〔報〕复〔復〕bàofù; 以牙还〔還〕牙 yǐ yá huán yá. **retaliation** /rɪˌtælɪˈeɪʃn/ *n* [U].

retard /rɪˈtɑːd/ *v* [T] [正式用语]使放慢 shǐ fàngmàn; 使延迟〔遲〕shǐ yánchí. **retarded** *adj* 智力迟钝的 zhìlì chídùn de.

retch /retʃ/ *v* [I] 干〔乾〕呕〔嘔〕gān'ǒu.

retention /rɪˈtenʃn/ *n* [U] [正式用语]保持 bǎochí; 保留 bǎoliú.

retentive /rɪˈtentɪv/ *adj* 能记住的 néng jìzhù de; 记忆〔憶〕力强的 jìyìlì qiáng de.

reticent /ˈretɪsnt/ *adj* 沉默寡言的 chénmò guǎ yán de; 言不尽〔盡〕意的 yán bú jìn yì de. **reticence** /-sns/ *n* [U].

retina /ˈretɪnə; *US* ˈretənə/ *n* [C] [*pl* ~s 或 -ae /-niː/] 视网〔網〕膜 shìwǎngmó.

retinue /ˈretɪnjuː; *US* ˈretənuː/ *n* [C, 亦作 sing 用 pl v] (要人的)一批随〔隨〕员 yìpī suíyuán.

retire /rɪˈtaɪə(r)/ *v* **1** (a) [I] (*from*) 退休 tuìxiū; 退职〔職〕tuìzhí; 退役 tuìyì. (b) [T] 使…退休(或退职、退役) shǐ…tuìxiū. **2** [I] [正式用语]退下 tuìxià; 退出 tuìchū; 引退 yǐntuì. **3** [I] [正式用语]就寝〔寢〕jiùqǐn. **retired** *adj* 退休的 tuìxiūde; 退职的 tuìzhíde; 退役的 tuìyìde. **retirement** *n* [U]. **retiring** *adj* 离〔離〕群索居的 lí qún suǒ jū de; 过〔過〕隐〔隱〕居生活的 guò yǐnjū shēnghuó de.

retort /rɪˈtɔːt/ *v* [T] 反驳 fǎnbó; 回嘴说 huízuǐ shuō. **retort** *n* [C, U] 反驳 fǎnbó; 回嘴 huízuǐ.

retrace /riːˈtreɪs/ *v* [T] 折返 zhéfǎn; 沿(路线)重行 yán…chóngxíng: ~ *one's steps* 顺原路折回.

retract /rɪˈtrækt/ *v* [I, T] **1** 撤回 chèhuí; 收回(声明等) shōuhuí. **2** 缩回 suōhuí; 缩进〔進〕suōjìn: *A cat can ~ its claws.* 猫能缩回它的爪子. **retractable** *adj*. **retraction** /rɪˈtrækʃn/ *n* [C, U].

retread /ˈriːtred/ *n* [C] 翻新的轮〔輪〕胎 fānxīn de lúntāi.

retreat /rɪˈtriːt/ *v* [I] (尤指军队)退却 tuìquè, 后〔後〕退 hòutuì; 撤退 chètuì. **retreat** *n* [C, U] **1** 退却 tuìquè; 撤退 chètuì. **2** 隐〔隱〕退处〔處〕yǐntuìchù; 静居处 jìngjūchù.

retribution /ˌretrɪˈbjuːʃn/ *n* [U] [正式用语]应〔應〕得的惩〔懲〕罚 yīngdé de chéngfá; 报〔報〕应 bàoying.

retrieve /rɪˈtriːv/ *v* [T] [正式用语]**1** 重新得到 chóngxīn dédào; 取回 qǔhuí. **2** 纠正 jiūzhèng; 挽回 wǎnhuí. **retrieval** *n* [U] 再获〔獲〕得 zài huòdé; 取回 qǔhuí. **retriever** *n* [C] (经训练会衔回猎物的)猎〔獵〕犬 lièquǎn.

retrograde /ˈretrəgreɪd/ *adj* [正式用语]退化的 tuìhuàde; 恶〔惡〕化的 èhuàde; 衰退的 shuāituìde.

retrogression /ˌretrəˈgreʃn/ *n* [U] [正式用语]退化 tuìhuà; 衰退 shuāituì. **retrogressive** /-ˈgresɪv/ *adj*.

retrospect /ˈretrəspekt/ *n* [习语] **in retrospect** 回顾〔顧〕huígù; 追溯 zhuīsù. **retrospective** *adj* **1** 回顾的 huígùde; 追溯的 zhuīsùde. **2** (法律等)溯及既往的 sù jí jì wǎng de; 有追溯效力的 yǒu zhuīsù xiàolì de.

return[1] /rɪˈtɜːn/ *v* **1** [I] (a) 回 huí; 返回 fǎnhuí: ~ *home* 回家. (b) 恢复〔復〕原先的状〔狀〕态〔態〕huīfù yuánxiān de zhuàngtài. **2** [I] 归〔歸〕还〔還〕guīhuán; 送还 sònghuán; 退回 tuìhuí: ~ *damaged goods to the shop* 将破损货物退回商店. **3** [T] 选〔選〕出…为〔爲〕议〔議〕员 xuǎnchū…wéi yìyuán. **4** [T] 正式宣布 zhèngshì xuānbù: *The jury ~ed a verdict of guilty.* 陪审团宣布被告有罪的裁决.

return[2] /rɪˈtɜːn/ *n* **1** [C, U] 回来 huílái; 返回 fǎnhuí. **2** [C, 尤作 pl] 赢利 yínglì; 收益 shōuyì. **3** [C] 报〔報〕告 bàogào; 申报 shēnbào: *fill in one's tax ~* 填写税单. **4** [C] (亦作 **return ˈticket**) 来回票 láihuípiào; 往返票 wǎngfǎnpiào. **5** [习语] **in return (for sth)** 作为〔爲〕…的付款(或回报) zuòwéi…de fùkuǎn.

reunion /ˌriːˈjuːnɪən/ *n* **1** [C] 团〔團〕聚 tuánjù; 聚会〔會〕jùhuì. **2** [C, U] 重聚 chóngjù.

Rev (亦作 **Revd**) *abbr* Reverend.

rev /rev/ *v* [-vv-] [I, T] (*up*) (发动机)加快转〔轉〕速 jiākuài zhuànsù: ~ *the car (up)* 加快汽车速度.

reveal /rɪˈviːl/ *v* [T] 1 揭示 jiēshì;揭露 jiēlù: ~ *a secret* 泄露秘密. 2 展现 zhǎnxiàn;显〔顯〕示 xiǎnshì.

revel /ˈrevl/ *v* [-ll-;美语 -l-] [短语动词] **revel in sth** 陶醉 táozuì;沉迷 chénmí.

revelation /ˌrevəˈleɪʃn/ *n* 1 [U] 揭示 jiēshì;揭露 jiēlù. 2 [C] 被揭露的事 bèi jiēlùde shì.

revenge /rɪˈvendʒ/ *n* [U] 复〔復〕仇 fùchóu;报〔報〕复 bàofù. **revenge** *v* [T] ~ **oneself (on)** 报仇 bàochóu;报复 bàofù.

revenue /ˈrevənjuː; *US* -ənuː/ *n* [U,C] 收入 shōurù;(国家的)岁〔歲〕入 suìrù.

reverberate /rɪˈvɜːbəreɪt/ *v* [I] 发〔發〕出回声〔聲〕fāchū huíshēng;回响〔響〕huíxiǎng. **reverberation** /rɪˌvɜːbəˈreɪʃn/ *n* 1 [C,U] 回声 huíshēng;回响 huíxiǎng. 2 [C, 常作 *pl*] [喻]反响 fǎnxiǎng.

revere /rɪˈvɪə(r)/ *v* [T] [正式用语]崇敬 chóngjìng;尊敬 zūnjìng.

reverence /ˈrevərəns/ *n* [U] 崇敬 chóngjìng;尊敬 zūnjìng.

Reverend /ˈrevərənd/ *n* [C] 牧师〔師〕(或神父等)的尊称〔稱〕mùshide zūnchēng.

reverent /ˈrevərənt/ *adj* 恭敬的 gōngjìngde;虔敬的 qiánjìngde. **reverently** *adv*.

reversal /rɪˈvɜːsl/ *n* [C,U] 反向 fǎnxiàng;倒转〔轉〕dàozhuǎn;颠倒 diāndǎo.

reverse /rɪˈvɜːs/ *adj* 反向的 fǎnxiàngde;相反的 xiāngfǎnde. **reverse** *n* 1 **the reverse** [sing] 相反情况 xiāngfǎn qíngkuàng. 2 [U] (机动车)倒挡〔擋〕dàodǎng: *put the car into* ~ (*gear*) 汽车挂上倒挡. 3 [C] (钱币)反面 fǎnmiàn;背面 bèimiàn. **reverse** *v* 1 [T] 使反向 shǐ fǎnxiàng;使倒转〔轉〕shǐ dàozhuǎn. 2 [T] 使转化为〔爲〕自身的对〔對〕立面 shǐ zhuǎnhuà wéi zìshēn de duìlìmiàn: ~ *a decision* 取消一项决定. 3 [I,T] (使车辆)倒退行驶 dàotuì xíngshǐ. 4 [习语] **reverse the ˈcharges** 由接电〔電〕话一方付费 yóu jiē diànhuà yìfāng fùfèi.

revert /rɪˈvɜːt/ *v* [I] *to* 恢复〔復〕(原状) huīfù;归〔歸〕属〔屬〕于(原主)guīshǔ yú.

review /rɪˈvjuː/ *v* 1 [T] 再考虑〔慮〕zài kǎolǜ;再检〔檢〕查 zài jiǎnchá: ~ *the past* / *a decision* 回顾过去;复查一项决定. 2 [I,T] 评论〔論〕pínglùn. 3 [T] 检阅 jiǎnyuè. **review** *n* 1 [C,U] 再考虑 zài kǎolǜ;再检查 zài jiǎnchá. 2 [C] 评论文章 pínglùn wénzhāng;书〔書〕评 shūpíng;影评 yǐngpíng. 3 [C] 检阅 jiǎnyuè. **reviewer** *n* [C] 评论家 pínglùnjiā.

revise /rɪˈvaɪz/ *v* 1 [T] 修订 xiūdìng;校订 jiàodìng;订正 dìngzhèng. 2 [I,T] (*for*) 复〔復〕习〔習〕fùxí;温习 wēnxí. **revision** /rɪˈvɪʒn/ *n* 1 [C,U] 修订 xiūdìng;校订 jiàodìng;复习 fùxí. 2 [C] 修订本 xiūdìngběn;修订版 xiūdìngbǎn.

revitalize /riːˈvaɪtəlaɪz/ *v* [T] 使新生 shǐ xīnshēng;使恢复〔復〕生机〔機〕shǐ huīfù shēngjī.

revive /rɪˈvaɪv/ *v* [I,T] 1 使恢复〔復〕知觉〔覺〕shǐ huīfù zhījué. 2 重新使用 chóngxīn shǐyòng: ~ *old customs* 再兴旧风俗. **revival** *n* [C,U].

revoke /rɪˈvəʊk/ *v* [T] [正式用语]废〔廢〕除 fèichú;撤销 chèxiāo;取消 qǔxiāo.

revolt /rɪˈvəʊlt/ *v* 1 [I] (*against*) 反叛 fǎnpàn;叛乱〔亂〕pànluàn. 2 [T] 使厌〔厭〕恶〔惡〕shǐ yànwù;使反感 shǐ fǎngǎn. **revolt** *n* [C,U] 反叛 fǎnpàn;叛乱 pànluàn. **revolting** *adj* 令人作呕〔嘔〕的 lìng rén zuò'ǒu de;令人不愉快的 lìng rén bù yúkuài de.

revolution /ˌrevəˈluːʃn/ *n* 1 [C,U] 革命 gémìng. 2 [C] [喻](方法、情况的)彻〔徹〕底改变〔變〕chèdǐ gǎibiàn;大变革 dà biàngé: *the computer* ~ 计算机革命. 3 [C] 旋转〔轉〕一周 xuánzhuǎn yìzhōu. **revolutionary** *adj* 1 革命的 gémìngde. 2 大变革的 dà biàngé de: *a* ~*ary idea* 创新的思想. **revolutionary** *n* [C] [*pl* -ies] 革命者 gémìngzhě;革命活动〔動〕家 gémìng huódòngjiā. **revolutionize** /-ʃənaɪz/ *v* [T] 使发〔發〕生革命性剧〔劇〕变 shǐ fāshēng gémìngxìng jùbiàn.

revolve /rɪˈvɒlv/ *v* 1 [I] (*around*) 作圆周运〔運〕动〔動〕zuò yuánzhōu yùndòng;旋转〔轉〕xuánzhuǎn. 2 [短语动词] **revolve around sb/sth** 以某人(或某事)为〔爲〕中心 yǐ mǒurén wéi zhōngxīn: *The story* ~*s around the old man*. 故事以这位老人为主题.

revolver /rɪˈvɒlvə(r)/ *n* [C] 左轮〔輪〕手枪〔槍〕zuǒlún shǒuqiāng.

revue /rɪˈvjuː/ *n* [C] (由歌舞、滑稽短剧等组成的)时〔時〕事讽〔諷〕刺剧〔劇〕shíshì fěngcìjù.

revulsion /rɪˈvʌlʃn/ *n* [U, sing] 厌〔厭〕恶〔惡〕yànwù;憎恶 zèngwù.

reward /rɪˈwɔːd/ *n* [C,U] 报〔報〕答 bàodá;报偿〔償〕bàocháng;酬金 chóujīn;奖〔獎〕赏 jiǎngshǎng. **reward** *v* [T] 报答 bàodá;报偿 bàocháng;酬谢 chóuxiè;奖励〔勵〕jiǎnglì. **rewarding** *adj* 令人满意的 lìng rén mǎnyì de.

rewind /ˌriːˈwaɪnd/ *v* [*pt*, *pp* **rewound** /ˌriːˈwaʊnd/] [I,T] 倒回(影片、录音带等) dàohuí.

rhapsody /ˈræpsədɪ/ *n* [C] [*pl* -ies] 1 [音乐]狂想曲 kuángxiǎngqǔ. 2 狂喜 kuángxǐ.

rhetoric /ˈretərɪk/ *n* [U] 1 修辞〔辭〕学〔學〕xiūcíxué. 2 [贬]浮夸〔誇〕的言语 fúkuāde yányǔ;华〔華〕丽〔麗〕的辞藻 huálìde cízǎo. **rhetorical** /rɪˈtɒrɪkl; *US* -ˈtɔːr-/ *adj* 1 (疑问)修辞性(只求修辞效果,并不要求答复)的 xiūcíxìngde. 2 辞藻华丽的 cízǎo huálì de;夸张〔張〕的 kuāzhāng de.

rheumatism /ˈruːmətɪzəm/ *n* [U] 风〔風〕湿

R

〔濕〕病 fēngshībìng. **rheumatic** /ruːˈmætɪk/ *adj*, *n* [C].

rhino /ˈraɪnəʊ/ *n* [C] [*pl* ~s] [非正式用语] short for RHINOCEROS.

rhinoceros /raɪˈnɒsərəs/ *n* [C] 犀牛 xīniú.

rhododendron /ˌrəʊdəˈdendrən/ *n* [C] 杜鹃花 dùjuānhuā.

rhubarb /ˈruːbɑːb/ *n* [U] [植物]大黄 dàhuáng; 菜用大黄 càiyòng dàhuáng; (药用)大黄根 dàhuánggēn.

rhyme /raɪm/ *v* [I] 押韵〔韻〕yāyùn: '*Fall*' ~*s with* '*wall*'. fall 与 wall 押韵. **rhyme** *n* 1 [U] 押韵 yāyùn. 2 [C] 押韵词 yāyùncí; 同韵词 tóngyùncí. 3 [C] 押韵诗 yāyùnshī.

rhythm /ˈrɪðəm/ *n* 1 [C,U] 节〔節〕奏 jiézòu; 节律 jiélǜ. 2 [C] [喻](循环往复的)规则变〔變〕化 guīzé biànhuà: *the* ~ *of the tides* 潮汐的涨落. **rhythmic(al)** /ˈrɪðmɪk(l)/ *adj*.

rib /rɪb/ *n* [C] 1 (人的)肋骨 lèigǔ. 2 (织物的)凸起条〔條〕纹 tūqǐ tiáowén, 罗〔羅〕纹 luówén. **ribbed** *adj* (织物)有凸起条纹的 yǒu tūqǐ tiáowén de; 有罗纹的 yǒu luówén de.

ribbon /ˈrɪbən/ *n* [C,U] 缎带〔帶〕duàndài; 丝带 sīdài; 带子 dàizi.

rice /raɪs/ *n* [U] 稻 dào; 米 mǐ.

rich /rɪtʃ/ *adj* 1 富的 fùde; 富裕的 fùyùde. 2 昂贵的 ángguìde; 华〔華〕丽〔麗〕的 huálìde: ~ *clothes* 华丽的衣服. 3 *in* 盛产〔產〕的 shèngchǎnde; 丰〔豐〕富的 fēngfùde: *soil* ~ *in minerals* 矿物质多的土壤. 4 (食物)味浓〔濃〕的 wèinóngde; 油腻的 yóunìde. 5 (颜色)鲜艳〔艷〕的 xiānyànde; (声音)深沉的 shēnchénde. **rich** *n* 1 **the rich**[pl] 富人 fùrén. 2 **riches** [pl] 富有 fùyǒu; 财富 cáifù. **richly** *adv*. **richness** *n* [U].

rickety /ˈrɪkətɪ/ *adj* 摇晃的 yáohuàngde; 不牢靠的 bù láokào de.

rickshaw /ˈrɪkʃɔː/ *n* [C] 人力车 rénlìchē; 黄包车 huángbāochē.

ricochet /ˈrɪkəʃeɪ; *US* ˌrɪkəˈʃeɪ/ *v* [*pt*, *pp* -t- 或 -tt-] [I] (子弹击中物体表面后)弹〔彈〕起 tánqǐ; 跳飞〔飛〕tiàofēi; 弹跳 tántiào. **ricochet** *n* [C,U].

rid /rɪd/ *v* [-dd-; *pt*, *pp* **rid**] 1 [T] *of* [正式用语]使摆〔擺〕脱 shǐ bǎituō. 2 [习语] **get rid of sb/sth** 摆脱 bǎituō.

riddance /ˈrɪdns/ *n* [习语] **good riddance** (用以表达摆脱讨厌的人或事后的如释重负感): *He's finally gone. Good* ~! 他终于走了, 谢天谢地!

ridden *pp* of RIDE¹.

riddle¹ /ˈrɪdl/ *n* [C] 1 谜 mí; 谜语 míyǔ. 2 谜一般的人(或东西、状况)míyìbānde rén.

riddle² /ˈrɪdl/ *v* [T] *with* [尤作被动语态] 把…弄得满是窟窿 bǎ… nòngdé mǎn shì kūlóng: *a body* ~*d with bullets* 一身弹痕累累.

ride¹ /raɪd/ *v* [*pt* **rode** /rəʊd/, *pp* **ridden** /ˈrɪdn/] 1 [I,T] 骑(马、自行车等)qí. 2 [I] 乘坐 chéngzuò; 搭乘 dāchéng. 3 [T] 漂浮而行 piāofú ér xíng: *a ship riding the waves* 一艘乘风破浪的船. 4 [短语动词] **ride up** (衣服等)向上拱 xiàngshàng gǒng. **rider** *n* [C] 1 骑马(或自行车)的人 qímǎ de rén; 骑手 qíshǒu. 2 (文件等后面的)附文 fùwén, 附件 fùjiàn.

ride² /raɪd/ *n* [C] 1 乘骑 chéngqí; 乘坐 chéngzuò; 搭乘 dāchéng. 2 [习语] **take sb for a 'ride** [非正式用语]欺骗某人 qīpiàn mǒurén.

ridge /rɪdʒ/ *n* [C] 1 山脊 shānjǐ; 山脉〔脈〕shānmài. 2 脊 jǐ; 脊梁 jǐliang; 脊状〔狀〕物 jǐzhuàngwù.

ridicule /ˈrɪdɪkjuːl/ *n* [U] 嘲笑 cháoxiào; 嘲弄 cháonòng; 戏〔戲〕弄 xìnòng. **ridicule** *v* [T] 嘲笑 cháoxiào; 嘲弄 cháonòng.

ridiculous /rɪˈdɪkjʊləs/ *adj* 可笑的 kěxiàode; 荒谬的 huāngmiùde. **ridiculously** *adv*.

rife /raɪf/ *adj* (尤指不好的事)流行的 liúxíngde; 普遍的 pǔbiànde.

rifle¹ /ˈraɪfl/ *n* [C] 步枪〔槍〕bùqiāng; 来复〔復〕枪 láifùqiāng.

rifle² /ˈraɪfl/ *v* [T] 搜劫 sōujié; 劫掠 jiélüè.

rift /rɪft/ *n* [C] 1 裂缝 lièfèng; 裂口 lièkǒu. 2 [喻]裂痕 lièhén; 不和 bùhé.

rig¹ /rɪg/ *v* [-gg-] [T] 1 给(船只桅杆)装〔裝〕上帆和索具 gěi zhuāng shàng fān hé suǒjù. 2 [短语动词] **rig sb out** 为〔爲〕(某人)提供衣服(或装备等)wèi tígōng yīfu. **rig sth up** 临〔臨〕时〔時〕架起 línshí jiàqǐ. **rig** *n* [C] 1 船具(如帆、桅等)设备〔備〕chuánjù shèbèi. 2 (作某种用途的)设备 shèbèi; 装置 zhuāngzhì: *an* '*oil* ~ 油井钻探设备. **rigging** *n* [U] (船的)索具 suǒjù.

rig² /rɪg/ *v* [-gg-] [T] (用欺骗手段)操纵〔縱〕cāozòng; 控制 kòngzhì: ~ *an election* 操纵选举.

right¹ /raɪt/ *adj* 1 (行为)公正的 gōngzhèngde; 正当〔當〕的 zhèngdàngde. 2 正确〔確〕的 zhèngquède; 对〔對〕的 duìde: *the* ~ *answer* 正确答案. 3 最恰当的 zuì qiàdàng de; 最合适〔適〕的 zuì héshì de: *the* ~ *person for the job* 最适合做这工作的人. 4 健康的 jiànkāngde: *Do you feel all* ~? 你感觉好吗? *in one's* ~ *mind* 头脑正常. 5 [习语] **on the right 'track** ⇨TRACK. **put/set sth right** 纠正错误〔誤〕jiūzhèng cuòwù. **'right angle** *n* [C] 直角 zhíjiǎo; 90 度角 jiǔshídù jiǎo. **'right-angled** *adj*. **rightly** *adv* 公正地 gōngzhèngde; 正确〔確〕地 zhèngquède. **rightness** *n* [U].

right² /raɪt/ *adv* 1 精确〔確〕地 jīngquède:

R

Put it ~ in the middle. 把它放在正中间. 2 完全地 wánquánde: *Go ~ to the end of the road*. 一直走到这条路的尽头. 3 正确地 zhèngquède. 4 [习语] ˈright away 立刻 lìkè. right ˈnow 此刻 cǐkè.

right[3] /raɪt/ *n* 1 [U] 正确〔確〕zhèngquè; 公正 gōngzhèng; 正当〔當〕zhèngdàng. 2 [C, U] 权〔權〕利 quánlì; 正当要求 zhèngdàng yāoqiú: *You have no ~ to be here*. 你无权在这里. *basic political ~s* 基本政治权利. 3 [习语] be in the ˈright 有理 yǒulǐ; 正确 zhèngquè. by ˈrights 根据〔據〕正当权利 gēnjù zhèngdàng quánlì; 按理 ànlǐ. in one's own ˈright 凭〔憑〕本身的权利(或资格等) píng běnshēnde quánlì. put/set sb/sth to ˈrights 纠正 jiūzhèng; 使恢复〔復〕正常 shǐ huīfù zhèngcháng. ˌright of ˈway *n* 1 [U] (车辆的)先行权 xiānxíngquán. 2 [C] (在他人土地上通过的)通行权 tōngxíngquán.

right[4] /raɪt/ *v* [T] 改正 gǎizhèng; 纠正 jiūzhèng; 使恢复〔復〕正常 shǐ huīfù zhèngcháng: *~ a wrong* 改正错误. *The ship ~ed herself*. 船自行恢复平稳.

right[5] /raɪt/ *adj, adv* 右边〔邊〕的 yòubiānde; 右方的 yòufāngde; 往右 wǎngyòu; 向右 xiàngyòu. right *n* 1 [U] 右边 yòubiān; 右方 yòufāng. 2 the Right [sing] [用 sing 或 pl v] (政党、团体的)右翼 yòuyì; 右派 yòupài. ˈright-click *v* 右击〔擊〕yòujī: ~-click on the icon 右击该图〔圖〕标〔標〕. ~-click the mouse 右击鼠标键. ˈright-hand *adj* 右手的 yòushǒude; 右边的 yòubiānde; 右方的 yòufāngde. ˌright-ˈhanded *adj* (人)惯用右手的 guànyòng yòushǒu de. ˌright-hand ˈman *n* [C] 得力助手 délì zhùshǒu. the ˌright ˈwing *n* [sing] [用 sing 或 pl v] (政党等的)右翼 yòuyì. ˌright-ˈwing *adj*.

righteous /ˈraɪtʃəs/ *adj* 正直的 zhèngzhíde; 公正的 gōngzhèngde. righteously *adv*. righteousness *n* [U].

rightful /ˈraɪtfl/ *adj* 合法的 héfǎde; 正当〔當〕的 zhèngdàngde; 合理的 hélǐde: *the ~ owner* 合法所有人. rightfully *adv*.

rigid /ˈrɪdʒɪd/ *adj* 1 坚〔堅〕硬的 jiānyìngde; 不易弯〔彎〕的 bú yìwān de. 2 严〔嚴〕格的 yángéde; 不变〔變〕的 búbiànde. rigidity /rɪˈdʒɪdətɪ/ *n* [U]. rigidly *adv*.

rigorous /ˈrɪgərəs/ *adj* 1 精确〔確〕的 jīngquède; 严〔嚴〕密的 yánmìde. 2 严格的 yángéde; 严厉〔厲〕的 yánlìde. rigorously *adv*.

rigour (美语 -or) /ˈrɪgə(r)/ *n* [正式用语] 1 [U] 严〔嚴〕厉〔厲〕yánlì; 严格 yángé. 2 rigours [pl] 艰〔艱〕苦 jiānkǔ; 严酷 yánkù.

rim /rɪm/ *n* [C] (圆形物的)边〔邊〕biān; 边缘 biānyuán: *the ~ of a cup* 杯子的边缘. rim *v* [-mm-] [T] 成为〔爲〕…的边(缘) chéngwéi …de biān.

rind /raɪnd/ *n* [C, U] (水果的)硬皮 yìngpí; (干酪、腌肉的)外皮 wàipí.

ring[1] /rɪŋ/ *v* [*pt* rang /ræŋ/, *pp* rung /rʌŋ/] 1 [I, T] (钟、铃等)鸣 míng; 响〔響〕xiǎng; 发〔發〕出清脆响亮的声〔聲〕音 fāchū qīngcuì xiǎngliàng de shēngyīn. 2 [I, T] 打电〔電〕话 dǎ diànhuà. 3 [I] (*for*) 按铃 àn líng; 鸣铃 míng líng. 4 [I] (*with*) 响着(声音) xiǎngzhe. 5 [与 *adj* 连用] 产〔產〕生某种〔種〕效果 chǎnshēng mǒuzhǒng xiàoguǒ: *Her words rang true*. 她的话听起来很真实. 6 [习语] ring a ˈbell [非正式用语] 引起模糊回忆〔憶〕yǐnqǐ mōhu huíyì. 7 [短语动词] ring off [英国英语] 挂〔掛〕断〔斷〕电〔電〕话 guàduàn diànhuà. ring out 发出响亮清晰的声音 fāchū xiǎngliàng qīngxī de shēngyīn. ring sb up 给某人打电话 gěi mǒurén dǎ diànhuà. ring *n* 1 [C] 铃声 língshēng; 钟〔鐘〕声 zhōngshēng. 2 [sing] 特有的声音效果 tèyǒude shēngyīn xiàoguǒ; 语气〔氣〕yǔqì: *a ~ of truth* 听起来像是确有其事. 3 [C] [英国非正式用语] 电话 diànhuà. ˈringtone *n* [C] 手机〔機〕铃声 shǒujī língshēng: *polyphonic ~s* 和弦铃声.

ring[2] /rɪŋ/ *n* [C] 1 环〔環〕huán; 戒指 jièzhǐ. 2 环状〔狀〕物 huánzhuàngwù. 3 圆圈 yuánquān; 圆环 yuánhuán: *The children stood in a ~*. 孩子们站成一个圆圈. 4 集团〔團〕jítuán: *a ˈspy ~* 间谍网. 5 圆形表演场〔場〕yuánxíng biǎoyǎnchǎng: *a ˈcircus ~* 马戏团表演场. 6 拳击〔擊〕场 quánjīchǎng. ring *v* [*pt*, *pp* ~ed] [T] 1 围〔圍〕绕〔繞〕wéirào; 环绕 huánrào. 2 把…圈出 bǎ… quānchū; 绕…做圆形标〔標〕记 rào …zuò yuánxíng biāojì. ˈringleader *n* [C] (犯罪等的)头〔頭〕目 tóumù; 元凶〔兇〕yuánxiōng; 首恶〔惡〕shǒu'è. ˈring pull *n* [C] (易拉罐的)拉环 lāhuán. ˈring road *n* [C] 环城(或环形)公路 huánchéng gōnglù.

ringlet /ˈrɪŋlɪt/ *n* [C, 尤作 pl] (下垂的)长〔長〕卷〔捲〕发〔髮〕cháng juǎnfà.

rink /rɪŋk/ *n* [C] 溜冰场〔場〕liūbīngchǎng; 滑冰场 huábīngchǎng.

rinse /rɪns/ *v* [T] (用清水)冲洗 chōngxǐ; 漂洗 piǎoxǐ. rinse *n* 1 [C] 冲洗 chōngxǐ; 漂洗 piǎoxǐ. 2 [C, U] 染发〔髮〕液 rǎnfàyè.

riot /ˈraɪət/ *n* 1 [C] 暴乱〔亂〕bàoluàn; 骚动〔動〕sāodòng. 2 [sing] 鲜艳〔艷〕夺〔奪〕目 xiānyàn duómù: *a ~ of colour* 色彩缤纷. 3 [习语] run ˈriot ⇨RUN[1]. riot *v* [I] 参〔參〕加暴乱 cānjiā bàoluàn. rioter *n* [C]. riotous *adj* 闹〔鬧〕事的 nàoshìde; 无〔無〕秩序的 wú zhìxù de.

rip /rɪp/ *v* [-pp-] 1 [I, T] 撕破 sīpò; 拉开〔開〕lākāi. 2 [短语动词] rip sb off [俚] 欺诈(钱财) qīzhà. rip *n* [C] 裂缝 lièfèng; 裂口 lièkǒu.

R

ˈrip-cord *n* [C] (降落伞的)开伞[傘]索 kāisǎnsuǒ. ˈrip-off *n* [C] [俚]敲诈 qiāozhà; 偷窃[竊]tōuqiè.

ripe /raɪp/ *adj* [~r, ~st] 1 熟的 shúde; 成熟的 chéngshúde. 2 充分发[發]展的 chōngfèn fāzhǎn de. 3 *for* 时[時]机[機]成熟的 shíjī chéngshú de. **ripeness** *n* [U].

ripen /ˈraɪpən/ *v* [I,T] (使)成熟 chéngshú.

ripple /ˈrɪpl/ *n* [C] 1 涟漪 liányī; 微波 wēibō. 2 短促的轻[輕]笑声[聲]duǎncùde qīngxiàoshēng. **ripple** *v* [I,T] (使)起涟漪 qǐ liányī.

rise[1] /raɪz/ *v* [*pt* rose /rəʊz/, *pp* ~n /ˈrɪzn/] [I] 1 上升 shàngshēng. 2 [正式用语](a) 站起来 zhàn qǐlái. (b) 起床 qǐchuáng. 3 (太阳、月亮等)升起 shēngqǐ. 4 上涨[漲]shàngzhǎng. 5 渐高 jiàn gāo: *rising ground* 渐渐高起之地. 6 (风等)转[轉]强 zhuǎnqiáng: *The wind is rising*. 风势在增强. 7 地位(或级别、职位)升高 dìwèi shēnggāo. 8 [正式用语]反叛 fǎnpàn; 反抗 fǎnkàng. 9 (河流)发[發]源 fāyuán. 10 [习语] rise to the ocˈcasion 能应[應]付困难[難]néng yìngfù kùnnan. **rising** *n* [C] 武装[裝]叛乱[亂]wǔzhuāng pànluàn; 反叛 fǎnpàn.

rise[2] /raɪz/ *n* 1 [sing] 上升 shàngshēng; 升高 shēnggāo; 进[進]展 jìnzhǎn: *his ~ to power* 他上台掌权. 2 [C] 增加 zēngjiā. 3 [C] [英国英语](工资的)增加 zēngjiā. 4 [C] 小山 xiǎoshān. 5 [习语] give rise to sth 引起 yǐnqǐ; 导[導]致 dǎozhì.

risk /rɪsk/ *n* 1 [C,U] 危险[險]wēixiǎn; 风[風]险 fēngxiǎn. 2 [C] 保险对[對]象 bǎoxiǎn duìxiàng; 被保险的人(或物)bèi bǎoxiǎnde rén; 危险的根源 wēixiǎn de gēnyuán. 3 [习语] at one's own risk 自担[擔]风险 zì dān fēngxiǎn. at ˈrisk 处[處]境危险 chǔjìng wēixiǎn. run the risk of sth, take a ˈrisk 冒…的危险 mào…de wēixiǎn. **risk** *v* [T] 1 使冒危险 shǐ mào wēixiǎn. 2 冒…之险 mào…zhī xiǎn. 3 [习语] risk one's neck ⇨NECK. **risky** *adj* [-ier, -iest] 危险的 wēixiǎnde.

risotto /rɪˈzɒtəʊ/ *n* [C,U] [*pl* ~s] (用干酪、洋葱、肉等做成的)意大利汤[湯]饭 Yìdàlì tāngfàn.

rissole /ˈrɪsəʊl/ *n* [C] 炸肉(或鱼)饼 zháròubǐng; 炸肉(或鱼)丸 zháròuwán.

rite /raɪt/ *n* [C] (宗教)仪[儀]式 yíshì; 典礼[禮]diǎnlǐ.

ritual /ˈrɪtʃʊəl/ *n* [C,U] 1 (宗教)仪[儀]式 yíshì; 典礼[禮]diǎnlǐ. 2 (宗教仪式的)程序 chéngxù. **ritual** *adj* (宗教)仪式的 yíshìde; 依仪式而行的 yī yíshì ér xíng de.

rival /ˈraɪvl/ *n* [C] 竞[競]争者 jìngzhēngzhě; 对[對]手 duìshǒu. **rival** *v* [-ll-; 美语亦作-l-] [T] 与[與]…竞争 yǔ…jìngzhēng. **rivalry** *n* [C,U] [*pl* -ies] 竞争 jìngzhēng; 对抗 duìkàng.

river /ˈrɪvə(r)/ *n* [C] 江 jiāng; 河 hé.

rivet /ˈrɪvɪt/ *n* [C] 铆钉 mǎodīng. **rivet** *v* [T] 1 铆接 mǎojiē; 铆 mǎo. 2 [喻]吸引 xīyǐn; 吸引住…的注意力 xīyǐn zhù…de zhùyìlì. **riveting** *adj* 饶[饒]有兴[興]味的 ráo yǒu xìngwèi de.

road /rəʊd/ *n* 1 [C] 路 lù; 道路 dàolù; 公路 gōnglù. 2 [习语] the road to sth 实[實]现某事(或达到某目标)的途径[徑]shíxiàn mǒushì de tújìng: *on the ~ to success* 走向成功. ˈroad-block *n* [C] 路障 lùzhàng. ˈroad-hog *n* [C] 鲁莽而不顾[顧]他人的司机[機]lǔmǎng ér búgù tārén de sījī. ˈroad map *n* [C] 1 道路交通图[圖] dàolù jiāotōng tú. 2 路线图[圖]lùxiàntú, 行动计划 xíngdòng jìhuà. ˈroad rage *n* [U] 道路暴力 dàolù bàolì; 公路暴怒 gōnglù bàonù. ˈroad-works *n* [pl] 道路施工 dàolù shīgōng. ˈroadworthy *adj* (车辆)适[適]于在公路上行驶的 shìyú zài gōnglù shàng xíngshǐ de.

roam /rəʊm/ *v* [I,T] 漫步 mànbù; 漫游 mànyóu.

roar /rɔː(r)/ *n* [C] (狮等)吼叫声[聲]hǒujiàoshēng. **roar** *v* 1 (a) [I] 吼叫 hǒujiào; 咆哮 páoxiào. (b) [T] 大声叫喊 dàshēng jiàohǎn. 2 [I] 大笑 dàxiào. **roaring** *adj* [非正式用语]1 吼叫的 hǒujiàode; 喧闹[鬧]的 xuānnàode. 2 非常好的 fēicháng hǎo de: *do a ~ing trade* 生意兴隆. **roaring** *adv* 非常 fēicháng: *~ing drunk* 酩酊大醉.

roast /rəʊst/ *v* [I,T] 烤 kǎo; 烘 hōng. **roast** *adj* 烤(或烘)过[過]的 kǎoguòde. **roast** *n* [C] 烤肉 kǎoròu.

rob /rɒb/ *v* [-bb-] [T] 抢[搶]劫 qiǎngjié; 盗取 dàoqǔ. **robber** *n* [C] 强盗 qiángdào; 盗贼 dàozéi. **robbery** *n* [C,U] [*pl* -ies] 抢劫 qiǎngjié; 偷盗 tōudào.

robe /rəʊb/ *n* [C] 长[長]袍 cháng páo.

robin /ˈrɒbɪn/ *n* [C] 欧[歐]亚[亞]鸲 ōuyàqú; 旅鸫 lǚdōng.

robot /ˈrəʊbɒt/ *n* [C] 机[機]器人 jīqìrén.

robust /rəʊˈbʌst/ *adj* 强健的 qiángjiànde; 健康的 jiànkāngde. **robustly** *adv*. **robustness** *n* [U].

rock[1] /rɒk/ *n* 1 (a) [U] 岩[巖]yán; 岩层[層]yáncéng. (b) [C,U] 岩石 yánshí. 2 [C] 大石 dàshí. 3 [C] [英国英语]硬棒糖 yìngbàngtáng. 4 [习语] on the ˈrocks (a) (婚姻)濒于破裂 bīnyú pòliè. (b) (饮料)加冰块[塊]jiā bīngkuài. ˌrock-ˈbottom *n* [U] 最低点[點] zuìdīdiǎn. **rockery** *n* [C] [*pl* -ies] 岩石园[園]yánshíyuán; 假山庭园 jiǎshān tíngyuán.

rock[2] /rɒk/ *v* 1 [I,T] 轻[輕]轻摇动[動]qīngqīng yáodòng; 摇晃 yáohuàng. 2 [T] [喻]剧

R

〔劇〕烈震动 jùliè zhèndòng. 3 [习语] rock the 'boat 破坏〔壞〕平静的局面 pòhuài píngjìng de júmiàn. **rocker** *n* 1 [C](摇椅脚下的)弧形摇板 húxíng yáobǎn. 2 = ROCKING-CHAIR. 3 [习语] off one's rocker [俚]发〔發〕疯〔瘋〕fāfēng. 'rocking-chair *n* [C] 摇椅 yáoyǐ.

rock[3] (亦作 'rock music) /rɒk/ *n* [U] 摇滚〔滾〕乐〔樂〕yáogǔnyuè. ˌrock and 'roll (亦作 ˌrock 'n' 'roll) *n* [U] (初期的)摇滚乐 yáogǔnyuè.

rocket /'rɒkɪt/ *n* [C] 1 火箭 huǒjiàn. 2 烟火 yānhuǒ. **rocket** *v* [I] 迅速增加 xùnsù zēngjiā: *Prices are ~ing*. 物价在飞涨. 'rocket science *n* [U] 1 火箭学〔學〕huǒjiànxué. 2 [非正式用语] 高深的学问 gāoshēn de xuéwèn: *It's not rocket science*. 这并不是高深的学问。

rocky /'rɒkɪ/ [-ier, -iest] *adj* 1 岩〔巖〕石的 yánshíde; 多岩石的 duōyánshíde. 2 [非正式用语]不稳〔穩〕的 bùwěnde.

rod /rɒd/ *n* [C] 杆 gān; 竿 gān; 棒 bàng: *a 'fishing-~* 钓鱼竿.

rode *pt* of RIDE[1].

rodent /'rəʊdnt/ *n* [C] 啮〔嚙〕齿〔齒〕目动〔動〕物(如鼠、松鼠等)nièchǐmù dòngwù.

rodeo /rəʊ'deɪəʊ; US 'rəʊdɪəʊ/ *n* [C] [*pl* ~s] (美国)(牧人骑马并以缰绳套捕牛的)竞〔競〕技表演 jìngjì biǎoyǎn.

roe[1] /rəʊ/ *n* [U] 鱼卵 yúluǎn; 鱼子 yúzǐ.

roe[2] /rəʊ/ *n* [C] 狍 páo. 'roebuck *n* [C] 雄狍 xióngpáo.

rogue /rəʊg/ *n* [C] 流氓 liúmáng; 无〔無〕赖 wúlài; 恶〔惡〕棍 ègùn. **rogue 'state** *n* [C] 无〔無〕赖国〔國〕家 wúlài guójiā. **roguish** *adj* 调皮的 tiáopíde; 淘气〔氣〕的 táoqìde.

role (亦作 rôle) /rəʊl/ *n* [C] 1 角色 juésè. 2 作用 zuòyòng; 重要性 zhòngyàoxìng.

roll[1] /rəʊl/ *v* 1 [I,T] 滚〔滾〕动〔動〕gǔndòng. 2 [I] 转〔轉〕动 zhuàndòng; 旋转 xuánzhuǎn: *The clouds ~ed away*. 云散了. 3 [I,T] (使)摇摆〔擺〕yáobǎi; 摇晃 yáohuàng: *The ship was ~ing heavily*. 船摇晃得很厉害. 4 [T] (*up*) 把…卷〔捲〕成球形(或圆柱形) bǎ…juǎnchéng qiúxíng: *~ up a carpet* 把地毯卷起来. 5 [T] 碾平 niǎnpíng: *~ a lawn* 把草地碾平. 6 [I] 发〔發〕出低沉的声〔聲〕音 fāchū dīchénde shēngyīn: *The thunder ~ed in the distance*. 远处雷声隆隆. 7 [短语动词] roll in [非正式用语]大量涌来 dàliàng yǒng lái; 滚滚而来 gǔngǔn ér lái. roll up [非正式用语]到达〔達〕dàodá.

roll[2] /rəʊl/ *n* [C] 1 一卷 yìjuǎn; 卷状〔狀〕物 juǎnzhuàngwù: *a ~ of film* 一卷胶卷. 2 滚〔滾〕转〔轉〕gǔnzhuǎn; 摇晃 yáohuàng; 翻滚 fāngǔn. 3 小圆面〔麵〕包 xiǎo yuánmiànbāo. 4 名单〔單〕míngdān; 花名册 huāmíngcè. 5 隆隆声〔聲〕lónglóngshēng; 轰〔轟〕响〔響〕声 hōngxiǎngshēng: *the ~ of drums* 鼓声咚咚.

roller /'rəʊlə(r)/ *n* [C] 滚〔滾〕子 gǔnzi; 滚轴 gǔnzhóu; 滚筒 gǔntǒng. 'roller-skate *n* [C] 旱冰鞋 hànbīngxié; 轱辘鞋 gūlùxié. 'roller-skate *v* [I] 穿旱冰鞋滑行 chuān hànbīngxié huáxíng.

Rollerblade /'rəʊləbleɪd/ *n* [C] [专利]直排轮〔輪〕滑鞋 zhípái lúnhuáxié. **Rollerblade** *v* [I] 做直排轮滑 zuò zhípái lúnhuá.

rolling /'rəʊlɪŋ/ *adj* 1 起伏的 qǐfúde; 翻腾的 fānténgde: *~ hills / waves* 绵延起伏的山冈; 波浪起伏. 2 [习语] be 'rolling in it [非正式用语]有许多钱〔錢〕yǒu xǔduō qián. 'rolling-pin *n* [C] 擀面〔麵〕棍 gǎnmiàngùn.

Roman /'rəʊmən/ *n* [C], *adj* 古罗〔羅〕马人 gǔLuómǎrén; 古罗马的 gǔLuómǎde. ˌRoman 'Catholic *n* [C], *adj* 天主教徒 tiānzhǔjiàotú; 天主教的 tiānzhǔjiàode. ˌRoman 'Catholicism *n* [U]. ˌRoman 'numeral *n* [C] 罗马数〔數〕字(如 V, L, M, IV 等)Luómǎ shùzì.

romance /rəʊ'mæns/ *n* 1 [C,U] 风〔風〕流韵〔韻〕事 fēngliú yùnshì. 2 [C] 爱〔愛〕情故事 àiqíng gùshì; 冒险〔險〕故事 màoxiǎn gùshì. 3 [U] 浪漫性 làngmànxìng; 传〔傳〕奇性 chuánqíxìng.

romantic /rəʊ'mæntɪk/ *adj* 1 不切实〔實〕际〔際〕的 bú qiè shíjì de; 空想的 kōngxiǎngde. 2 多情的 duōqíngde. 3 有浪漫色彩的 yǒu làngmàn sècǎi de: *a ~ journey* 富于浪漫色彩的旅行. **romantic** *n* [C] 浪漫的人 làngmànde rén. **romantically** /-klɪ/ *adv*. **romanticism** /rəʊ'mæntɪsɪzəm/ *n* [U] 浪漫主义〔義〕làngmàn zhǔyì; 浪漫的情感(或态度等) làngmàn de qínggǎn. **romanticize** /rəʊ'mæntɪsaɪz/ *v* [I,T] 使浪漫化 shǐ làngmànhuà; 以浪漫方式行事(或说话) yǐ làngmàn fāngshì xíngshì.

romp /rɒmp/ *v* [I] (尤指儿童)玩耍 wánshuǎ; 嬉戏〔戲〕xīxì. **romp** *n* [C].

roof /ruːf/ *n* [C] 1 屋顶 wūdǐng; 车顶 chēdǐng. 2 顶 dǐng; 顶部 dǐngbù: *the ~ of the mouth* 上颌. **roof** *v* [I] 给…盖〔蓋〕上屋顶 gěi…gài shàng wūdǐng. **roofing** *n* [U] 屋面材料 wūmiàn cáiliào. 'roof-rack *n* [C] (机动车供装载行李等用的)车顶架 chēdǐngjià.

rook[1] /rʊk/ *n* [C] 秃鼻乌〔烏〕鸦 tūbí wūyā. **rookery** *n* [C] [*pl* -ies] 秃鼻乌鸦结巢处〔處〕tūbí wūyā jiécháochù.

rook[2] /rʊk/ *v* [T] [俚]敲诈(顾客)qiāozhà.

rook[3] /rʊk/ *n* [C] = CASTLE 2.

room /ruːm, rʊm/ *n* 1 [C] 室 shì; 房间 fángjiān. 2 [U] 空间 kōngjiān; 空位 kòngwèi: *Is there ~ for me in the car?* 汽车里还有我坐的空位吗? 3 [U] [喻]机〔機〕会〔會〕jīhuì; 范〔範〕围〔圍〕fànwéi: *~ for improvement* 改进的余地. **roomy** *adj* [-ier, -iest] 宽敞的

R

kuānchǎngde.

roost /ruːst/ *n* [C] 栖〔棲〕息处〔處〕qīxīchù. **roost** *v* [I] (鸟)栖息 qīxī.

rooster /ˈruːstə(r)/ *n* [C] [尤用于美语]公鸡〔鷄〕gōngjī.

root[1] /ruːt/ *n* **1** [C] 根 gēn. **2** **roots** [pl] (家族的)根 gēn. **3** [C] (头发、牙齿的)根 gēn. **4** [C] [喻]根源 gēnyuán; 根基 gēnjī: *Is money the ~ of all evil?* 金钱是万恶之源吗? **5** [C] [语法]词根 cígēn. **6** [习语] **take root** 建立 jiànlì; 确〔確〕立 quèlì.

root[2] /ruːt/ *v* **1** [I, T] (使)生根 shēnggēn. **2** [T] (使)站立不动〔動〕zhànlì búdòng: *~ed to the spot by fear* 吓得站在那里一动不动. **3** [T] [常用被动语态](思想等)牢固树〔樹〕立 láogù shùlì: *deeply ~ed feelings* 根深蒂固的感情. **4** [短语动词] **root sth out** 根除 gēnchú.

rope /rəʊp/ *n* **1** [C, U] 粗绳〔繩〕cū shéng; 索 suǒ. **2** [pl] (处理工作、问题等的)诀窍〔竅〕juéqiào: *show sb the ~s* 把诀窍教给某人. **rope** *v* [T] **1** 用绳系〔繫〕住 yòng shéng xìzhù. **2** [短语动词] **rope sb in to do sth** 说服某人参加 shuōfú mǒurén cānjiā. **rope sth off** 用绳子围〔圍〕起(或隔开) yòng shéngzi wéiqǐ. **ropy** (亦作 **ropey**) *adj* [-ier, -iest] [英国非正式用语]质〔質〕量差的 zhìliàng chà de; 蹩脚的 biéjiǎode.

rosary /ˈrəʊzərɪ/ *n* [C] [*pl* -ies] **1** (天主教徒念玫瑰经时用的)(一串)念珠 niànzhū. **2** 玫瑰经 méiguìjīng.

rose[1] *pt* of RISE[1].

rose[2] /rəʊz/ *n* **1** [C] 玫瑰 méiguì; 蔷〔薔〕薇 qiángwēi. **2** [U] 粉红色 fěnhóngsè; 玫瑰红 méiguihóng.

rosé /ˈrəʊzeɪ; *US* rəʊˈzeɪ/ *n* [U] 玫瑰红葡萄酒 méiguihóng pútáojiǔ.

rosette /rəʊˈzet/ *n* [C] 玫瑰花形物 méigui huāxíngwù; 玫瑰花形饰物 méigui huāxíng shìwù.

roster /ˈrɒstə(r)/ *n* [C] [尤用于美语]值勤人员表 zhíqín rényuán biǎo.

rostrum /ˈrɒstrəm/ *n* [C] [*pl* ~s 或 -tra /-trə/] 演讲〔講〕台 yǎnjiǎngtái; 讲坛〔壇〕jiǎngtán.

rosy /ˈrəʊzɪ/ *adj* [-ier, -iest] **1** 深粉红色的 shēnfěnhóngsède; 玫瑰红的 méiguihóngde. **2** [喻]有希望的 yǒu xīwàng de; 乐〔樂〕观〔觀〕的 lèguānde: *a ~ future* 美好的将来.

rot /rɒt/ *v* [-tt-] [I, T] (使)腐烂〔爛〕fǔlàn; 腐坏〔壞〕fǔhuài. **rot** *n* [U] **1** 腐烂 fǔlàn; 腐坏 fǔhuài. **2** [喻]情况逐渐变〔變〕坏 qíngkuàng zhújiàn biànhuài. **3** [旧, 非正式用语]胡说 húshuō.

rota /ˈrəʊtə/ *n* [C] [英国英语]勤务〔務〕轮〔輪〕值表 qínwù lúnzhíbiǎo.

rotary /ˈrəʊtərɪ/ *adj* 旋转〔轉〕的 xuánzhuǎnde; 转动〔動〕的 zhuǎndòngde.

rotate /rəʊˈteɪt; *US* ˈrəʊteɪt/ *v* [I, T] **1** (使)旋转〔轉〕xuánzhuǎn; (使)转动〔動〕zhuǎndòng. **2** (使)轮〔輪〕流 lúnliú; (使)循环〔環〕xúnhuán: *~ crops* 轮种庄稼. **rotation** /-ˈteɪʃn/ *n* **1** [U] 旋转 xuánzhuǎn; 转动 zhuǎndòng: *the rotation of the Earth* 地球的自转. **2** [C] (旋转的)一圈 yìquān.

rotor /ˈrəʊtə(r)/ *n* [C] (直升机的)旋翼 xuányì; (机器的)旋转〔轉〕部分 xuánzhuǎn bùfen.

rotten /ˈrɒtn/ *adj* **1** 腐烂〔爛〕的 fǔlànde; 变〔變〕质〔質〕的 biànzhìde. **2** [非正式用语]很坏〔壞〕的 hěnhuàide; 讨厌〔厭〕的 tǎoyànde.

rouge /ruːʒ/ *n* [U] 胭脂 yānzhi.

rough[1] /rʌf/ *adj* **1** (表面)不平的 bùpíngde; 粗糙的 cūcāode. **2** 粗鲁的 cūlǔde; 粗暴的 cūbàode; 粗野的 cūyěde. **3** 狂暴的 kuángbàode: *a ~ sea* 风浪大的海. **4** 不精确〔確〕的 bù jīngquè de; 粗略的 cūlüède: *a ~ guess/ sketch* 大致的猜想; 草图. **5** [习语] **ˈrough and ˌready** 将〔將〕就的 jiāngjiude. **rough** *adv* 简陋地 jiǎnlòude: *live / sleep ~* 餐风宿露; 随处栖身. **rough** *n* **1** [U] 粗糙的表面 cūcāode biǎomiàn. **2** [习语] **in ˈrough** 未完成 wèi wánchéng. **roughly** *adv* **1** 粗鲁地 cūlǔde; 粗暴地 cūbàode. **2** 大约 dàyuē; 大概 dàgài: *It will cost ~ly £100.* 它大约值 100 英镑. **roughness** *n* [U].

rough[2] /rʌf/ *v* **1** [习语] **ˈrough it** [非正式用语]过〔過〕不舒适〔適〕(或简陋)的生活 guò bù shūshì de shēnghuó. **2** [短语动词] **rough sb up** [非正式用语]施用暴力 shīyòng bàolì; 殴〔毆〕打 ōudǎ.

roughen /ˈrʌfn/ *v* [I, T] (使)变〔變〕粗糙 biàn cūcāo; (使)变毛糙 biàn máocāo.

roulette /ruːˈlet/ *n* [U] 轮〔輪〕盘〔盤〕赌 lúnpándǔ.

round[1] /raʊnd/ *adj* **1** 圆的 yuánde; 球形的 qiúxíngde; 环〔環〕形的 huánxíngde. **2** 来回的 láihuíde: *a ~ trip* 往返的旅行. **3** 用整数〔數〕表示的(如整十、整百等) yòng zhěngshù biǎoshì de. **roundly** *adv* 严〔嚴〕厉〔厲〕地 yánlìde. **roundness** *n* [U]. **ˌround-ˈshouldered** *adj* 弓背曲肩的 gōng bèi qū jiān de.

round[2] /raʊnd/ *adv* **1** 朝反方向 cháo fǎn fāngxiàng: *Turn your chair ~.* 把你的椅子转过来. **2** 循环〔環〕地 xúnhuánde: *The hands of a clock go ~.* 钟的指针周而复始地走动. **3** 成圆圈地 chéng yuánquān de: *A crowd gathered ~.* 一群人围了上来. *spin ~* 旋转. **4** 逐一 zhúyī: *Please pass these papers ~.* 请把这些文件分发给大家. **5** 迂回地 yūhuíde; 绕〔繞〕道地 ràodàode: *a long way ~* 绕远路. **6** 到某人家 dào mǒurén jiā:

Come ~ and see me. 请到我家来看看我.

round[3] /raʊnd/ *n* [C] 1 一连串的事件 yìliánchuànde shìjiàn: *the next ~ of talks* 下一轮会谈. 2 有规律的连续〔續〕的事情 yǒu guīlǜde liánxùde shìqing: *a postman's ~* 邮递员的投递路线. 3 (a) (比赛的)一轮〔輪〕yìlún, 一局 yìjú, 一场〔場〕yìchǎng, 一回合 yìhuíhé. (b) (高尔夫)一场 yìchǎng. (c) (拳击)一回合 yìhuíhé. 4 一份 yífèn. 5 面〔麵〕包片 miànbāopiàn. 6 (子弹的)一发〔發〕yìfā.

round[4] /raʊnd/ *prep* 1 环〔環〕绕〔繞〕huánrào; 围〔圍〕绕 wéirào: *The earth moves ~ the sun*. 地球绕着太阳转. 2 在…周围 zài…zhōuwéi: *a wall ~ the house* 房子周围的墙. 3 绕过〔過〕ràoguò: *walk ~ the corner* 步行绕过拐角. 4 在…各处〔處〕zài…gèchù; 向…各处 xiàng…gèchù: *look ~ the shop* 朝商店四下看. 5 在…附近 zài…fùjìn: *I've never seen him ~ here*. 我在这附近从未见过他.

round[5] /raʊnd/ *v* [T] 1 绕〔繞〕过〔過〕ràoguò; 环〔環〕绕而行 huánrào ér xíng: *~ a corner* 绕过拐角. 2 使成圆形 shǐ chéng yuánxíng. 3 [短语动词] **round sth off** 圆满完成 yuánmǎn wánchéng; 结束 jiéshù. **round sth up** (a) 集拢〔攏〕jílǒng: *~ up cattle* 把牛赶到一起. (b) 把(数字)调高为〔爲〕整数〔數〕bǎ… tiáogāo wéi zhěngshù.

roundabout /ˈraʊndəbaʊt/ *n* [C] 1 环〔環〕状〔狀〕交叉路(多条道路的交叉口, 车辆须绕行) huánzhuàng jiāochālù. 2 旋转〔轉〕木马 xuánzhuǎn mùmǎ. **roundabout** *adj* 绕道的 ràodàode; 间接的 jiànjiēde: *a ~ route* 绕远的路.

rounders /ˈraʊndəz/ *n* [用 sing v] (立柱代垒的)跑柱式棒球 pǎozhùshì bàngqiú.

rouse /raʊz/ *v* 1 [I, T] [正式用语]唤醒 huànxǐng; 弄醒 nòngxǐng. 2 [T] 使活跃〔躍〕shǐ huóyuè; 使产〔產〕生兴〔興〕趣 shǐ chǎnshēng xìngqù: *a rousing speech* 振奋人心的讲话.

rout /raʊt/ *v* [T] 彻〔徹〕底打败 chèdǐ dǎbài; 击〔擊〕溃 jīkuì. **rout** *n* [C] 大败 dàbài; 溃败 kuìbài.

route /ruːt; *US* raʊt/ *n* [C] 路 lù; 路线〔綫〕lùxiàn; 航线 hángxiàn. **route** *v* [T] 按某路线发〔發〕送 àn mǒu lùxiàn fāsòng.

routine /ruːˈtiːn/ *n* [C, U] 例行公事 lìxíng gōngshì; 惯例 guànlì; 常规 chángguī. **routine** *adj* 1 例行的 lìxíngde; 惯例的 guànlìde. 2 平淡的 píngdànde.

row[1] /rəʊ/ *n* [C] 1 一排 yìpái; 一行 yìháng; 一列 yíliè. 2 [习语] **in a row** 一个〔個〕接一个地 yígè jiē yígè de; 连续〔續〕地 liánxùde: *She's been to the cinema two evenings in a ~*. 她接连两个晚上去看电影了.

row[2] /rəʊ/ *v* [I, T] 划(船) huá. **row** *n* [C] 划船 huáchuán; 划船旅行 huáchuán lǚxíng. ˈ**rowing-boat** *n* [C] 划艇 huátǐng.

row[3] /raʊ/ *n* 1 [C] 吵架 chǎojià; 争吵 zhēngchǎo. 2 [U, sing] 喧闹〔鬧〕声〔聲〕xuānnàoshēng. **row** *v* [I] 大声争吵 dàshēng zhēngchǎo.

rowdy /ˈraʊdɪ/ *adj* [-ier, -iest] 吵闹〔鬧〕的 chǎonàode. **rowdy** *n* [C] [*pl* -ies] [旧, 贬] 大吵大闹的人 dàchǎo dànào de rén.

royal /ˈrɔɪəl/ *adj* 国〔國〕王的 guówángde; 女王的 nǚwángde; 王室的 wángshìde. **royal** *n* [C, 常作 pl] [非正式用语]王室成员 wángshì chéngyuán. ˌ**royal** ˈ**blue** *adj* 宝〔寶〕蓝〔藍〕bǎolán; 藏蓝 zànglán. **royalist** *n* [C] 保皇党〔黨〕成员 bǎohuángdǎng chéngyuán; 保皇主义〔義〕者 bǎohuángzhǔyìzhě. **royally** *adv* 盛大地 shèngdàde.

royalty /ˈrɔɪəltɪ/ *n* [*pl* -ies] 1 [U] 王族 wángzú; 王室成员 wángshì chéngyuán. 2 版税 bǎnshuì.

RSI /ɑːr es ˈaɪ/ *abbr* repetitive strain injury 重复〔複〕性肌肉劳〔勞〕损症 chóngfùxìng jīròu láosǔn zhèng; 办〔辦〕公室疼痛症 bàngōngshì téngtòngzhèng.

RSVP /ˌɑːr es viː ˈpiː/ *abbr* (on an invitation) please reply 请赐复〔復〕(请柬用语) qǐng cìfù.

rub /rʌb/ *v* [-bb-] 1 [I, T] 擦 cā; 磨 mó; 摩擦 mócā. 2 [T] 擦(净、干等) cā: *~ the surface dry* 把表面擦干. 3 [习语] **rub it in** [非正式用语]向某人提及令人不快的事 xiàng mǒurén tíjí lìng rén búkuài de shì. **rub sb up the wrong way** [非正式用语]惹恼〔惱〕某人 rě nǎo mǒurén. 4 [短语动词] **rub sb /sth down** (用毛巾)将〔將〕…擦干〔乾〕净 jiāng…cā gānjìng. **rub sth down** 磨光 móguāng; 磨平 mópíng. **rub sth in** 把(搽剂等)擦进〔進〕表层〔層〕bǎ…cājìn biǎocéng. **rub sth off** 擦掉 cādiào: *R~ the dirt off your trousers*. 把你裤子上的脏擦掉. **rub sth out** 用橡皮擦掉(铅笔痕迹) yòng xiàngpí cādiào. **rub** *n* [C] 擦 cā; 磨 mó; 摩擦 mócā.

rubber[1] /ˈrʌbə(r)/ *n* 1 [U] 橡胶〔膠〕xiàngjiāo. 2 [C] 橡皮(擦子) xiàngpí. ˌ**rubber** ˈ**band** *n* [C] 橡皮筋 xiàngpíjīn.

rubber[2] /ˈrʌbə(r)/ *n* [C] (桥牌的三局两胜的)比赛 bǐsài.

rubbish /ˈrʌbɪʃ/ *n* [U] 1 垃圾 lājī; 废〔廢〕物 fèiwù. 2 胡说 húshuō. **rubbishy** *adj* [非正式用语]无〔無〕价〔價〕值的 wú jiàzhí de.

rubble /ˈrʌbl/ *n* [U] 碎石 suìshí; 碎砖〔磚〕suìzhuān; 瓦砾〔礫〕wǎlì.

ruby /ˈruːbɪ/ *n* [C] [*pl* -ies] 红宝〔寶〕石 hóngbǎoshí.

rucksack /ˈrʌksæk/ *n* [C] (登山、旅行用的)背包 bēibāo.

rudder /ˈrʌdə(r)/ *n* [C] (船的)舵 duò;(飞机的)方向舵 fāngxiàngduò.

ruddy[1] /ˈrʌdɪ/ *adj* [-ier,-iest] 1 (脸色)红润的 hóngrùnde;气〔氣〕色好的 qìsè hǎo de. 2 红的 hóngde.

ruddy[2] /ˈrʌdɪ/ *adj*, *adv* [英俚](用以加强语气): *You're a ~ fool!* 你是个大傻瓜!

rude /ruːd/ *adj* [~r, ~st] 1 粗鲁的 cūlǔde;无〔無〕礼〔禮〕的 wúlǐde. 2 不得体〔體〕的 bù détǐ de;粗俗的 cūsúde. 3 令人不知所措的 lìng rén bù zhī suǒ cuò de;狂暴的 kuángbàode: *a ~ reminder* 使产生突然警觉之事. 4 [旧]粗制〔製〕的 cūzhìde. **rudely** *adv*. **rudeness** *n* [U].

rudiments /ˈruːdɪmənts/ *n* [pl] 初阶〔階〕chūjiē;入门 rùmén;基础〔礎〕jīchǔ. **rudimentary** /ruːdɪˈmentrɪ/ *adj* 1 初步的 chūbùde;基本的 jīběnde. 2 未发〔發〕展完全的 wèi fāzhǎn wánquán de.

ruffian /ˈrʌfɪən/ *n* [C] [旧]暴徒 bàotú;恶〔惡〕棍 ègùn.

ruffle /ˈrʌfl/ *v* [T] 1 把…弄皱〔皺〕bǎ…nòng zhòu;弄乱〔亂〕nòng luàn. 2 [喻]扰〔擾〕乱 rǎoluàn;打扰 dǎrǎo.

rug /rʌg/ *n* [C] 1 (铺于室内部分地面上的)小地毯 xiǎo dìtǎn. 2 毛毯 máotǎn.

rugby /ˈrʌgbɪ/ *n* [U] 橄榄〔欖〕球(运动)gǎnlǎnqiú.

rugged /ˈrʌgɪd/ *adj* 1 不平的 bùpíngde;多岩〔巖〕石的 duō yánshí de. 2 粗犷〔獷〕的 cūguǎngde;结实〔實〕的 jiēshide: *a ~ face* 健康的脸.

rugger /ˈrʌgə(r)/ *n* [U] [非正式用语,尤用于英国英语]橄榄〔欖〕球(运动)gǎnlǎnqiú.

ruin /ˈruːɪn/ *v* [T] 1 毁灭〔滅〕huǐmiè;毁坏〔壞〕huǐhuài. 2 使破产〔產〕shǐ pòchǎn. **ruin** *n* 1 [U] 毁灭 huǐmiè. 2 [C] 毁坏(建筑物等)huǐhuài: *The house is in ~s.* 那房子已成断壁残垣. 3 [U] 破产的原因 pòchǎnde yuányīn;败坏(或毁灭等)的原因 bàihuàide yuányīn: *Drink was his ~.* 他堕落是因为饮酒. **ruined** *adj* 毁坏了的 huǐhuàilede;破败的 pòbàide. **ruinous** *adj* 毁灭性的 huǐmièxìngde;破坏性的 pòhuàixìngde.

rule /ruːl/ *n* 1 [C] 规则 guīzé;规章 guīzhāng;条〔條〕例 tiáolì. 2 [C] 规律 guīlǜ;常规 chángguī. 3 [U] 管理 guǎnlǐ;统治 tǒngzhì: *under foreign ~* 在外国的统治下. 4 [习语] **as a ˈrule** 通常 tōngcháng. **rule of thumb** 粗略而实〔實〕用的估计方法 cūlüè ér shíyòng de gūjì fāngfǎ;根据〔據〕实际〔際〕经〔經〕验〔驗〕的作法 gēnjù shíjì jīngyàn de zuòfǎ. **rule** *v* 1 [I,T] 管理 guǎnlǐ;统治 tǒngzhì. 2 [I,T] 裁决 cáijué: *She ~d that the evidence could not be admitted.* 她裁定不能接受这个证据. *The judge ~d in his favour.* 法官的判决对他有利. 3 [T] 用尺画〔畫〕(线)yòng chǐ huà. 4 [习语] **rule the ˈroost** 当〔當〕家 dāngjiā;作主 zuòzhǔ;主宰 zhǔzǎi. 5 [短语动词] **rule sth out** 把…排除在外 bǎ…páichú zài wài;排除…的可能性 páichú…de kěnéngxìng. **ruler** *n* [C] 1 统治者 tǒngzhìzhě;管理者 guǎnlǐzhě. 2 尺 chǐ;直尺 zhíchǐ. **ruling** *n* [C] 裁决 cáijué;裁定 cáidìng.

rum /rʌm/ *n* [U] (甘蔗汁制的)朗姆酒 lángmǔjiǔ.

rumble /ˈrʌmbl/ *v* [T], *n* [C] 发〔發〕出持续〔續〕的低沉声〔聲〕fāchū chíxùde dīchénshēng;隆隆声 lónglóngshēng;辘辘声 lùlùshēng.

rummage /ˈrʌmɪʤ/ *v* [I] 翻找 fānzhǎo;搜寻〔尋〕sōuxún.

rumour (美语 -or) /ˈruːmə(r)/ *n* [C,U] 传〔傳〕闻 chuánwén;传说 chuánshuō;谣〔謠〕言 yáoyán. **rumoured** (美语 -ored) *adj* 传说的 chuánshuōde;谣传的 yáochuánde.

rump /rʌmp/ *n* 1 [C] (鸟的)尾梢 wěishāo;(兽的)臀部 túnbù. 2 ˌ**rump ˈsteak** [C,U] 后〔後〕腿部牛排 hòutuǐbù niúpái;臀部牛排 túnbù niúpái.

rumple /ˈrʌmpl/ *v* [T] 弄皱〔皺〕nòngzhòu;弄乱〔亂〕nòngluàn.

rumpus /ˈrʌmpəs/ *n* [sing] 喧闹〔鬧〕xuānnào;骚乱〔亂〕sāoluàn;吵闹 chǎonào.

run[1] /rʌn/ *v* [-nn-; *pt* **ran** /ræn/, *pp* **run**] 1 [I] 跑 pǎo;奔 bēn. 2 [T] 跑(一段距离)pǎo. 3 (a) [I] 跑步锻炼〔煉〕(或运动)pǎobù duànliàn. (b) [I,T] (参加)赛跑 sàipǎo. 4 [I,T] 快速行进〔進〕kuàisù xíngjìn: *The car ran down the hill.* 汽车驶下了山岗. 5 [I] 行驶 xíngshǐ: *The train ran past the signal.* 火车从信号旁驶过. 6 [I] (公共汽车)(沿规定路线)往来行驶 wǎnglái xíngshǐ. 7 [I] (道路)伸展 shēnzhǎn;延展 yánzhǎn: *The road ~s east.* 这条路向东伸展. 8 [T] 经〔經〕营〔營〕jīngyíng;管理 guǎnlǐ: *~ a hotel* 经营旅馆. 9 [I] 持续〔續〕chíxù: *The play ran for six months.* 这个剧连续演出了半年. 10 [I,T] (使某物)运〔運〕转〔轉〕yùnzhuǎn: *The heater ~s on electricity.* 加热器用电驱动. 11 [T] 通过〔過〕tōngguò: *~ a comb through one's hair* 用梳子拢头发. 12 [T] 运载 yùnzài: *I'll ~ you home.* 我用车送你回家. 13 [I] *for* [尤用于美语]竞〔競〕选〔選〕jìngxuǎn: *~ for president* 竞选总统. 14 [I,T] (使液体)流动〔動〕liúdòng: *a river that ~s into the sea* 一条入海的河流. 15 [I] (颜色)扩〔擴〕散 kuòsàn. 16 [常与形容词连用]变〔變〕成 biànchéng: *Supplies are ~ning low.* 供应品渐渐短缺. 17 [T] (报纸等)发〔發〕表 fābiǎo. 18 [T] 非法秘密地运(或携带)入某国〔國〕fēifǎ mìmì de yùn rù mǒuguó;走私 zǒusī: *~ drugs* 走私毒品. 19 [I] 有共同特征〔徵〕yǒu gòngtóng tèzhēng: *Red hair ~s*

R

in the family. 这一家人都是红头发. 20 [习语] **run amok** 横冲〔衝〕直撞 héng chōng zhí zhuàng. **run its course** ⇨COURSE[1]. **'run for it** 快跑躲避 kuàipǎo duǒbì. **run 'high** (情绪)激昂 jī'áng. **run 'riot / 'wild** 滋事 zīshì; 闹〔鬧〕事 nàoshì. **run the risk of** ⇨ RISK. **run to seed** ⇨SEED. **run short (of sth)** 快用完 kuài yòngwán; 缺少 quēshǎo. **run to waste** ⇨ WASTE[2]. 21 [短语动词] **run across sb** 偶然碰见 ǒurán pèngjiàn. **run after sb** (a) 追赶〔趕〕zhuīgǎn. (b) 追求(异性) zhuīqiú: *She's always ~ning after men*. 她总是在追求男人. **run a'long** 离〔離〕开〔開〕líkāi; 走开 zǒukāi. **run a'way (from sb/sth)** 跑开 pǎokāi; 逃走 táozǒu. **run a'way with one** (感情)完全控制自己 wánquán kòngzhì zìjǐ. **run away / off with sb** 私奔 sībēn; 离家出走 líjiā chūzǒu. **run (sth) down** (a) 耗尽〔盡〕能源 hàojìn néngyuán; 失去作用 shīqù zuòyòng. (b) 衰退 shuāituì; 逐渐失去作用 zhújiàn shīqù zuòyòng: *The company is being ~ down*. 这家公司越来越不景气. **run sb/sth down** (a) (车)把…撞倒(或撞伤等) bǎ…zhuàngdǎo. (b) 说…的坏〔壞〕话 shuō…de huàihuà. **run into sb/sth** (a) 偶然碰见 ǒurán pèngjiàn. (b) 遭遇(困难) zāoyù; (使)陷入(困境等) xiànrù. **run sth off** 印出 yìnchū; 复〔複〕印出 fùyìnchū. **run out** (协议等)失效 shīxiào; 过期 guòqī. **run out (of sth)** (a) 耗尽 hàojìn. (b) (供应品)用完 yòngwán. **run sb over** (车辆)(撞倒某人并)辗过 niǎnguò; 在…上驶过 zài…shàng shǐguò. **run through sth** (a) 排练〔練〕páiliàn. (b) 匆匆阅读 cōngcōng yuèdú; 匆匆检〔檢〕查 cōngcōng jiǎnchá. **run to sth** (a) 达〔達〕到(数量、数字等) dádào. (b) (钱)足够供…之用 zúgòu gòng…zhī yòng. **run sth up** (a) 升(旗) shēng. (b) 积〔積〕欠(账款、债务等) jīqiàn: ~ *up big debts* 积欠一大笔债. **run up against sth** 遇到(困难等) yùdào. **'runaway** *adj* 1 逃跑的 táopǎode; 逃避的 táobìde; 私奔的 sībēnde. 2 失去控制的 shīqù kòngzhì de. **'runaway** *n* [C] 逃跑者 táopǎozhě; 出逃者 chūtáozhě. **ˌrun-'down** *adj* 1 疲惫〔憊〕的 píbèide; 筋疲力尽的 jīn pí lì jìn de. 2 破损的 pòsǔnde; 失修的 shīxiūde. **'run-up** *n* [sing] (事件的)准〔準〕备〔備〕时〔時〕期 zhǔnbèi shíqī.

run[2] /rʌn/ *n* 1 [C] 跑 pǎo; 跑步 pǎobù; 奔跑 bēnpǎo. 2 [C] (乘汽车、火车等)旅行 lǚxíng. 3 [C] 持续〔續〕的演出 chíxùde yǎnchū. 4 [C] 时〔時〕期 shíqī; 一段时间 yíduàn shíjiān: *a ~ of bad luck* 一连串的不幸. 5 [sing] 一时对〔對〕某物的大量需求 yìshí duì mǒuwù de dàliàng xūqiú. 6 [C] (家畜的)饲养〔養〕场〔場〕sìyǎngchǎng. 7 [C] (板球、棒球所得的)分 fēn. 8 [习语] **on the 'run** 逃跑 táopǎo. **ˌrun-of-the-'mill** *adj* 一般的 yìbānde; 普通的 pǔtōngde.

rung[1] *pp* of RING[1].

rung[2] /rʌŋ/ *n* [C] 梯级 tījí; 梯子横档〔檔〕tīzǐ héngdàng.

runner /'rʌnə(r)/ *n* [C] 1 奔跑的人(或动物) bēnpǎode rén. 2 走私者 zǒusīzhě; 偷运〔運〕者 tōuyùnzhě: *a 'gun-~* 走私枪支的人. 3 (条状)滑行装〔裝〕置 huáxíng zhuāngzhì: *the ~s of a sledge* 雪橇的滑行板. **ˌrunner 'bean** *n* [C] 红花菜豆 hónghuā càidòu. **ˌrunner-'up** [*pl* **ˌrunners-'up**] *n* [C] (竞赛中的)第二名 dì'èrmíng, 亚〔亞〕军 yàjūn.

running /'rʌnɪŋ/ *n* [U] 1 跑 pǎo; 跑步 pǎobù; 赛跑 sàipǎo. 2 管理 guǎnlǐ; 操作 cāozuò. 3 [习语] **make the 'running** 定步调 dìng bùdiào; 做榜样〔樣〕zuò bǎngyàng. **running** *adj* 1 连续〔續〕的 liánxù- de: *a ~ battle* 持续的战斗. 2 接连 jiēlián: *win three times ~* 连胜三次. 3 (水)流动〔動〕的 liúdòngde.

runny /'rʌnɪ/ *adj* [-ier, -iest] [非正式用语] 1 水分过〔過〕多的 shuǐfèn guòduō de. 2 流泪〔淚〕的 liúlèide; 流涕的 liútìde.

runway /'rʌnweɪ/ *n* [C] (飞机的)跑道 pǎodào.

rupture /'rʌptʃə(r)/ *n* [C] 1 [正式用语](友好关系的)决裂 juéliè; 绝交 juéjiāo. 2 破裂 pòliè; 疝 shàn. **rupture** *v* [I, T] 1 [正式用语] 破裂 pòliè; 断〔斷〕绝 duànjué. 2 (使)发〔發〕疝气〔氣〕fā shànqì.

rural /'rʊərəl/ *adj* 乡〔鄉〕村的 xiāngcūnde; 在乡村的 zài xiāngcūn de.

ruse /ruːz/ *n* [C] 诡计 guǐjì; 计谋 jìmóu.

rush[1] /rʌʃ/ *v* 1 [I, T] 急速去(或来) jísù qù; 急速做 jísù zuò. 2 [T] (使某人)仓〔倉〕促行事 cāngcù xíngshì. 3 [T] 突然袭〔襲〕击〔擊〕tūrán xíjī. 4 [习语] **be rushed off one's feet** 使…疲于奔命 shǐ…pí yú bēn mìng. **rush** *n* 1 [C, U] 冲〔衝〕chōng; 奔 bēn; 急促的动〔動〕作 jícùde dòngzuò. 2 [sing] 急需 jíxū. 3 [sing, U] 繁忙的活动(时刻) fánmángde huódòng: *the Christmas ~* 圣诞节前的购物潮. **'rush-hour** *n* [C] (上下班时的)交通拥〔擁〕挤〔擠〕时〔時〕间 jiāotōng yōngjǐ shíjiān; (车辆)高峰时间 gāofēng shíjiān.

rush[2] /rʌʃ/ *n* [C] 灯〔燈〕心草 dēngxīncǎo.

rusk /rʌsk/ *n* [C] 面〔麵〕包干〔乾〕miànbāogān; 脆饼干 cuì bǐnggān.

Russia /'rʌʃə/ *n* [U] 俄国〔國〕Éguó.

Russian /'rʌʃən/ *adj* 俄国〔國〕的 Éguóde. **Russian** *n* 1 [C] 俄国人 Éguórén. 2 [U] 俄语 Éyǔ.

rust /rʌst/ *n* [U] 锈 xiù; 铁〔鐵〕锈 tiěxiù. **rust** *v* [I, T] (使)生锈 shēngxiù. **rusty** *adj* [-ier, -iest] 1 生锈的 shēngxiùde. 2 荒疏的 huāngshūde; 荒废〔廢〕的 huāngfèide: *His piano-playing is a bit ~y*. 他久未弹钢琴, 有点儿生疏了.

R

rustle /ˈrʌsl/ *v* 1 [I, T] (如风吹枯叶)沙沙作响〔響〕shāshā zuò xiǎng. 2 [T] [美语]偷盗(牛、马) tōudào. 3 [短语动词] **rustle sth up** 急速提供 jísù tígōng: ~ *up a meal* 急急忙忙弄出一顿饭. **rustle** *n* [C, U] 沙沙声〔聲〕shāshāshēng.

rut /rʌt/ *n* [C] 1 车辙 chēzhé. 2 陷入固定(而又乏味)的生活方式 xiànrù gùdìng de shēnghuó fāngshì: *be in a* ~ 墨守成规. **rutted** *adj* 有车辙的 yǒu chēzhé de.

ruthless /ˈruːθlɪs/ *adj* 残〔殘〕忍的 cánrěnde; 无〔無〕同情心的 wú tóngqíngxīn de. **ruthlessly** *adv*.

rye /raɪ/ *n* [U] 黑麦〔麥〕hēimài; 黑麦粒 hēimàilì; 黑麦威士忌酒 hēimài wēishìjìjiǔ.

S s

S, s /es/ *n* [C] [*pl* **S's, s's** /ˈesɪz/] 英语的第十九个〔個〕字母 Yīngyǔ de dìshíjiǔgè zìmǔ.

S *abbr* south(ern): *S Yorkshire* 约克郡南部

Sabbath /ˈsæbəθ/ *n* **the Sabbath** [sing] 安息日(犹太教为星期六,基督教为星期日) ānxīrì.

sabotage /ˈsæbətɑːʒ/ *n* [U] 蓄意破坏〔壞〕xùyì pòhuài; 阴〔陰〕谋破坏 yīnmóu pòhuài. **sabotage** *v* [T] 阴谋破坏(机器、计划等) yīnmóu pòhuài. **saboteur** /ˌsæbəˈtɜː(r)/ *n* [C] 阴谋(或蓄意)破坏者 yīnmóu pòhuàizhě.

sabre (美语 **saber**) /ˈseɪbə(r)/ *n* [C] 军刀 jūndāo; 马刀 mǎdāo.

saccharin /ˈsækərɪn/ *n* [U] 糖精 tángjīng.

sachet /ˈsæʃeɪ; *US* sæˈʃeɪ/ *n* [C] (塑料或纸的)小袋 xiǎodài.

sack[1] /sæk/ *n* [C] 粗布袋 cūbùdài; 麻袋 mádài; 大袋 dàdài. **ˈsackcloth** (亦作 **sacking**) *n* [U] 麻袋布 mádàibù; 粗麻布 cūmábù; 口袋布 kǒudàibù. **ˈsackful** *n* [C] 一袋的量 yídàide liàng.

sack[2] /sæk/ *v* [T] [非正式用语,尤用于英国英语]解雇〔僱〕jiěgù. **the sack** *n* [sing] 解雇 jiěgù: *give sb / get the* ~ 解雇某人;被解雇.

sack[3] /sæk/ *v* [T] (对占领的城市)洗劫 xǐjié; 劫掠 jiélüè.

sacrament /ˈsækrəmənt/ *n* [C] (宗教)圣〔聖〕礼〔禮〕shènglǐ; 圣事(如洗礼等) shèngshì. **sacramental** /ˌsækrəˈmentl/ *adj*.

sacred /ˈseɪkrɪd/ *adj* 1 神圣〔聖〕的 shénshèngde; 宗教的 zōngjiàode: *a* ~ *shrine* 圣地. 2 (*to*) 受崇敬的 shòu chóngjìng de: *In India the cow is a* ~ *animal*. 在印度牛是神圣的动物. 3 重大的 zhòngdàde; 庄〔莊〕严〔嚴〕的 zhuāngyánde: *a* ~ *promise / duty* 郑重的诺言;重大的责任.

sacrifice /ˈsækrɪfaɪs/ *n* 1 [U, C] (*to*) 献〔獻〕祭 xiànjì; 供奉 gòngfèng. 2 (a) [U] 牺〔犧〕牲 xīshēng. (b) [C] 供品 gòngpǐn; 祭品 jìpǐn: *make* ~*s* 作牺牲. **sacrifice** *v* (*to*) 1 [I, T] 献祭 xiànjì; 供奉 gòngfèng. 2 [T] 牺牲 xīshēng: ~ *a career to have a family* 为家庭牺牲事业. **sacrificial** /ˌsækrɪˈfɪʃl/ *adj*.

sacrilege /ˈsækrɪlɪdʒ/ *n* [C, 常用 sing, v] 亵〔褻〕渎〔瀆〕(圣物) xièdú; 渎圣〔聖〕(行为) dúshèng. **sacrilegious** /ˌsækrɪˈlɪdʒəs/ *adj*.

sad /sæd/ *adj* [~**der**, ~**dest**] 悲哀的 bēi'āide; 难〔難〕过〔過〕的 nánguòde; 伤〔傷〕心的 shāngxīnde: *a* ~ *person / song* 伤心的人;一首悲伤的歌曲. **sadden** *v* [I, T] (使)悲哀 bēi'āi; (使)难过 nánguò: ~*dened by his death* 因他的去世而悲伤. **sadly** *adv* 1 悲哀地 bēi'āide; 伤心地 shāngxīnde: *smile* ~*ly* 苦笑. 2 不幸地 búxìngde: *S*~*ly, we have no more money*. 我们可惜没有钱了. **sadness** *n* [U, C].

saddle /ˈsædl/ *n* [C] 1 马鞍 mǎ'ān; 鞍座 ānzuò; (自行车)车座 chēzuò. 2 鞍状〔狀〕山脊 ānzhuàng shānjǐ. 3 [习语] **in the ˈsaddle** (a) 骑着马 qí zhe mǎ. (b) [喻]处〔處〕于控制地位 chǔyú kòngzhì dìwèi. **saddle** *v* [T] 1 给(马)装〔裝〕鞍 gěi zhuāng'ān. 2 [短语动词] **saddle sb with sth** 使某人承担〔擔〕不愉快的任务〔務〕shǐ mǒurén chéngdān bù yúkuài de rènwù: ~*d with cleaning the car* 使承担讨厌的洗车任务. **ˈsaddle-bag** *n* [C] 马褡裢 mǎdālián; 鞍囊 ānnáng.

sadism /ˈseɪdɪzəm/ *n* [U] 施虐狂 shīnüèkuáng; 性施虐狂 xìngshīnüèkuáng. **ˈsadist** *n* [C] 施虐狂者 shīnüèkuángzhě; 性施虐狂者 xìngshīnüèkuángzhě. **sadistic** /səˈdɪstɪk/ *adj*.

sae /ˌes eɪ ˈiː/ *abbr* stamped addressed envelope 贴足邮〔郵〕票写〔寫〕明姓名地址的信封(供收信人回信时使用) tiēzú yóupiào xiěmíng xìngmíng dìzhǐ de xìnfēng.

safari /səˈfɑːrɪ/ *n* [C, U] (非洲的)游猎〔獵〕yóuliè: *on* ~ *in Kenya* 在肯尼亚游猎.

safe[1] /seɪf/ *adj* [~**r**, ~**st**] 1 (*from*) 安全的 ānquánde; 无〔無〕危险〔險〕的 wú wēixiǎn de: ~ *from attack* 免受攻击. 2 不会引起损害(或损失)的 búhuì yǐnqǐ sǔnhài de: *a* ~ *speed* 安全的速度. 3 平安的 píng'ānde: *The plane crashed but the pilot is* ~. 那架飞机失事了,但驾驶员安然无恙. 4 受保护〔護〕的 shòu bǎohù de. 5 小心的 xiǎoxīnde; 谨慎的 jǐnshènde: *a* ~ *driver* 谨慎的司机. 6 [习语] **(as) safe as ˈhouses** 非常安全 fēicháng ānquán. **for / in safe ˈkeeping** 妥善保管(或保护) tuǒshàn bǎoguǎn. **ˌsafe and ˈsound** 平安无事 píng'ān wúshì. **safe ˈhaven** *n* [C] 安全

区〔區〕域 ānquán qūyù；避难〔難〕所 bìnànsuǒ. safely *adv*. safeness *n* [U].

safe[2] /seɪf/ *n* [C] 保险〔險〕箱 bǎoxiǎnxiāng.

safeguard /ˈseɪfgɑːd/ *n* [C] (*against*) 安全设施 ānquán shèshī；保护〔護〕措施 bǎohù cuòshī. **safeguard** *v* [T] (*against*) 保护 bǎohù；保卫〔衛〕bǎowèi.

safety /ˈseɪftɪ/ *n* [U] 安全 ānquán；平安 píng'ān. ˈ**safety-belt** *n* [C] = SEAT-BELT (SEAT). ˈ**safety helmet** *n* [C] 安全帽 ānquánmào. ˈ**safety-pin** *n* [C] (安全)别针 biézhēn. ˈ**safety-valve** *n* [C] 1 安全阀 ānquánfá. 2 [喻]发〔發〕泄怒气〔氣〕的方式 fāxiè nùqì de fāngshì.

sag /sæg/ *v* [-gg-] [I] 1 (中间部分)下垂 xiàchuí；下弯〔彎〕xiàwān；下陷 xiàxiàn. 2 松〔鬆〕垂 sōng chuí.

saga /ˈsɑːgə/ *n* [C] 1 长〔長〕篇英雄故事 chángpiān yīngxióng gùshì；冒险〔險〕故事 màoxiǎn gùshì. 2 家世小说 jiāshì xiǎoshuō.

sage[1] /seɪdʒ/ *n* [C] [正式用语]贤〔賢〕哲 xiánzhé；智者 zhìzhě. **sage** *adj* 贤明的 xiánmíngde；智慧的 zhìhuìde.

sage[2] /seɪdʒ/ *n* [U] 鼠尾草(用作调味品) shǔwěicǎo.

said *pt*, *pp* of SAY.

sail[1] /seɪl/ *n* 1 [C,U] 帆 fān. 2 [sing] (乘船)航行 hángxíng：*go for a* ～ 乘船出游. 3 [C] (风车的)翼板 yìbǎn. 4 [习语] **set sail (from/to/for)** 启〔啟〕航 qǐháng.

sail[2] /seɪl/ *v* 1 [I] (乘船、机帆船等)航行 hángxíng. 2 [I] 启〔啟〕航 qǐháng. 3 [T] 航行于 hángxíng yú. 4 [I, T] 驾驶(船) jiàshǐ：*Can you* ～ (*a yacht*)? 你会驾驶(游艇)吗? 5 [短语动词] **sail through (sth)** 顺利地通过(考试等) shùnlìde tōngguò. **sailing** *n* [U] 帆船运〔運〕动〔動〕fānchuán yùndòng：*go* ～*ing* 坐帆船去. ˈ**sailing-boat** (亦作 ˈ**sailing-ship**) *n* [C] 帆船 fānchuán. **sailor** *n* [C] 水手 shuǐshǒu；海员 hǎiyuán.

saint /seɪnt, 或用于姓名前 sənt/ *n* [C] (基督教追封的)圣〔聖〕徒 shèngtú. **saintly** *adj* [-ier, -iest] 圣徒似的 shèngtúsìde；圣人似的 shèngrénsìde；神圣的 shénshèngde.

sake /seɪk/ *n* [习语] **for goodness', Heavens, etc sake** (用在命令、要求的词语之前或之后,表示恼怒等)：*For goodness'* ～ *hurry up!* 天哪,赶快! **for the sake of** 1 为〔爲〕了…的利益 wèile…de lìyì：*for the* ～ *of her children* 为了她孩子的利益. 2 为获〔獲〕得(或保持) wèi huòdé：*for the* ～ *of peace* 为了和平.

salad /ˈsæləd/ *n* [C, U] 1 色拉 sèlā；凉拌菜(如生菜、黄瓜、西红柿) liángbàncài. 2 有色拉的凉拌食品 yǒu sèlā de liángbànshípǐn：*a cheese* ～ 干酪色拉. ˈ**salad dressing** *n* [U] 色拉调味汁 sèlā tiáowèizhī.

salami /səˈlɑːmɪ/ *n* [U] 萨〔薩〕拉米香肠〔腸〕sālāmǐ xiāngcháng.

salary /ˈsælərɪ/ *n* [C] [*pl* -ies] (按周或按月计的)薪金 xīnjīn，薪水 xīnshuǐ. **salaried** *adj* 拿薪金的 ná xīnjīn de；领薪水的 lǐng xīnshuǐ de.

sale /seɪl/ *n* 1 [U,C] 卖〔賣〕mài；出售 chūshòu. 2 [C] 廉售 liánshòu；贱〔賤〕卖 jiànmài：*buy a dress in the* ～*s* 减价期间买了一件连衣裙. 3 [习语] **for sale** 待售 dàishòu. **on sale** 出售 chūshòu；上市 shàngshì. ˈ**sales ˌconference** *n* [C] 销售会〔會〕议〔議〕xiāoshòu huìyì. ˈ**salesman** *n* [C] [*pl* -men], ˈ**salesperson** [*pl* -people], ˈ**saleswoman** [*pl* -women] (女)售货员 shòuhuòyuán. ˈ**salesmanship** *n* [U] 推销术〔術〕tuīxiāoshù.

saline /ˈseɪlaɪn; *US* -liːn/ *adj* 咸〔鹹〕的 xiánde；含盐〔鹽〕的 hányánde.

saliva /səˈlaɪvə/ *n* [U] 口水 kǒushuǐ；唾液 tuòyè.

sallow /ˈsæləʊ/ *adj* (面色、气色)灰黄色的 huīhuángsède.

salmon /ˈsæmən/ *n* [*pl* salmon] 1 (a)[C] 鲑 guī；大马哈鱼 dàmǎhāyú. (b) [U] 鲑肉 guīròu. 2 [U]鲑肉色 guīròusè；橙红色 chénghóngsè.

salmonella /ˌsælməˈnelə/ *n* [U] 沙门氏菌 shāménshìjūn.

salon /ˈsælɒn; *US* səˈlɒn/ *n* [C] (美发、美容等营业性的)店 diàn,厅〔廳〕tīng,院 yuàn.

saloon /səˈluːn/ *n* [C] 1 (轮船、旅馆等)交谊室 jiāoyìshì；大厅〔廳〕dàtīng. 2[美语]酒吧间 jiǔbājiān. 3 (亦作 **saloon-car**)(供四、五人坐的)轿〔轎〕车 jiàochē. **saˈloon bar** = LOUNGE BAR (LOUNGE).

salt /sɔːlt/ *n* 1[U] 盐〔鹽〕yán；食盐 shíyán. 2 [C][化学]盐 yán. 3 [习语] **the salt of the ˈearth** 诚实〔實〕正派的人 chéngshí zhèngpài de rén. **take sth with a grain/pinch of salt** 对〔對〕…半信半疑 duì…bànxìn bànyí. **salt** *v* [T]加盐于(食物) jiā yán yú. ˈ**salt-cellar** *n* [C] 小盐瓶 xiǎo yánpíng. **salty** *adj* [-ier,-iest].

salute /səˈluːt/ *n* [C] 致敬 zhìjìng；敬礼〔禮〕jìnglǐ；行礼 xínglǐ. **salute** *v* [I,T] 1 向…致敬 xiàng…zhìjìng；致意 zhìyì. 2 赞〔讚〕扬〔揚〕zànyáng；颂扬 sòngyáng.

salvage /ˈsælvɪdʒ/ *n* [U] 1(火灾、洪水等的)财产〔產〕抢〔搶〕救 cáichǎn qiǎngjiù. 2 海上营〔營〕救 hǎi shàng yíngjiù. 3 可利用的废〔廢〕物 kě lìyòngde fèiwù；废物回收 fèiwù huíshōu. **salvage** *v* [T](从火灾、海难等中)抢救 qiǎngjiù.

salvation /sælˈveɪʃn/ *n* [U] 1[宗教]拯救

S

zhěngjiù;超度 chāodù. 2 救助者 jiùzhùzhě;解救方法(或途径) jiějiù fāngfǎ.

same /seɪm/ *adj* 1 the same 同一的 tóngyīde: *He's the ~ age as his wife*. 他同妻子同年. 2 同样〔樣〕的 tóngyàngde: *My car is the ~ as yours*. 我的汽车和你的一样. the same *pron* 1 同样的事物 tóngyàngde shìwù: *I bought a red dress and then she bought the ~*. 我买了一件红色连衣裙,之后她买了同样的. 2 [习语] all/just the same 仍然 réngrán;尽〔儘〕管如此 jǐnguǎn rúcǐ: *She's quite old, but very lively all the ~*. 她相当老了,但依然精力充沛. be all the same to ⇨ ALL[3]. same here 我也一样 wǒ yě yíyàng;我同意 wǒ tóngyì: '*I feel hot*.' '*S~ here*.' "我觉得热." "我也一样." the same *adv* 同样地 tóngyàngde: *The two words are pronounced the ~*. 这两个字发音相同. sameness *n* [U] 同一(性) tóngyī;相同(性) xiāngtóng;无〔無〕变〔變〕化 wú biànhuà.

sample /ˈsɑːmpl; *US* ˈsæmpl/ *n* [C] 样〔樣〕品 yàngpǐn;货样 huòyàng;样本 yàngběn: *wallpaper ~s* 壁纸样品. sample *v* [T] 抽样检〔檢〕验〔驗〕chōuyàng jiǎnyàn.

sanatorium /ˌsænəˈtɔːrɪəm/ *n* [*pl* ~s 或 -ria /-rɪə/] 疗〔療〕养〔養〕院 liáoyǎngyuàn.

sanctimonious /ˌsæŋktɪˈməʊnɪəs/ *adj* [贬]假装〔裝〕高尚(或正经)的 jiǎzhuāng gāoshàng de. sanctimoniously *adv*.

sanction /ˈsæŋkʃn/ *n* 1[U] 认〔認〕可 rènkě;批准 pīzhǔn. 2[C] 制裁 zhìcái;处〔處〕罚 chǔfá: *economic ~s* 经济制裁. sanction *v* [T] 认可 rènkě;批准 pīzhǔn;准许 zhǔnxǔ.

sanctity /ˈsæŋktətɪ/ *n* [U] 神圣〔聖〕shénshèng.

sanctuary /ˈsæŋktʃʊərɪ; *US* -ʊerɪ/ *n* [*pl* -ies] 1 [C] 圣〔聖〕地(如教堂、寺院等) shèngdì. 2 [C, U]庇护〔護〕所 bìhùsuǒ: *be offered ~* 受到庇护. 3 [C] 禁猎〔獵〕区〔區〕jìnlièqū;鸟兽〔獸〕保护区 niǎo shòu bǎohùqū.

sand /sænd/ *n* 1[U] 沙 shā. 2 [C, 常作 pl] 沙滩〔灘〕shātān;沙地 shādì. sand *v* [T] 1 用砂纸磨光 yòng shāzhǐ móguāng: *~ (down) the wood* 用砂纸磨光这块木料. 2 用沙覆盖〔蓋〕yòng shā fùgài. ˈsandbag *n* [C] 沙袋 shādài. ˈsand-castle *n* [C](儿童在海滨堆成的)沙堆模型城堡 shāduī móxíng chéngbǎo. ˈsand-dune = DUNE. ˈsandpaper *n*[C] 砂纸 shāzhǐ. ˈsandstone *n* [U] 沙岩 shāyán. sandy *adj* [-ier, -iest] 1 含沙的 hánshāde;覆盖着沙的 fùgàizhe shā de. 2 (头发)浅〔淺〕棕色的 qiǎn zōngsè de.

sandal /ˈsændl/ *n* [C] 凉鞋 liángxié.

sandwich /ˈsænwɪdʒ; *US* -wɪtʃ/ *n* [C] 三明治 sānmíngzhì;夹心面〔麵〕包片 jiāxīn miànbāopiàn: *a cheese ~* 乳酪三明治. sandwich *v* [T] 把…插入 bǎ…chārù;把…夹入 bǎ…jiārù;把…挤〔擠〕入 bǎ…jǐrù.

sane /seɪn/ *adj* [~r, ~st] 1 神志正常的 shénzhì zhèngcháng de;心智健全的 xīnzhì jiànquán de. 2 明智的 míngzhìde;理智的 lǐzhìde: *a ~ policy* 明智的政策. sanely *adv*.

sang *pt* of SING.

sanitary /ˈsænɪtrɪ; *US* -terɪ/ *adj* 1 清洁〔潔〕的 qīngjiéde;卫〔衛〕生的 wèishēngde: *~ conditions* 卫生条件. 2 保健的 bǎojiànde. ˈsanitary towel *n* [C] 卫生巾 wèishēngjīn.

sanitation /ˌsænɪˈteɪʃn/ *n* [U] 卫〔衛〕生系统 wèishēng xìtǒng;卫生设备〔備〕wèishēng shèbèi.

sanity /ˈsænətɪ/ *n* [U] 心智健康 xīnzhì jiànkāng;神志正常 shénzhì zhèngcháng.

sank *pt* of SINK[2].

sap[1] /sæp/ *v* [-pp-] [T] 使伤〔傷〕元气〔氣〕shǐ shāng yuánqì;消耗(精力等) xiāohào.

sap[2] /sæp/ *n* [U] 树〔樹〕液 shùyè. ˈsapling *n* [C] 幼树 yòushù.

sapphire /ˈsæfaɪə(r)/ *n* [C] 蓝〔藍〕宝〔寶〕石 lánbǎoshí. sapphire *adj* 蔚蓝色的 wèilánsède;宝石蓝色的 bǎoshílánsède.

sarcasm /ˈsɑːkæzəm/ *n* [U] 讽〔諷〕刺 fěngcì;挖苦 wākǔ;嘲笑 cháoxiào. sarˈcastic /sɑːˈkæstɪk/ *adj*. sarcastically /-klɪ/ *adv*.

sardine /sɑːˈdiːn/ *n* [C] 1 沙丁鱼 shādīngyú. 2 [习语] like sardines (像沙丁鱼般)拥〔擁〕挤〔擠〕yōngjǐ.

sari /ˈsɑːrɪ/ *n* [C] 莎丽〔麗〕(印度妇女用以裹身包头或裹身披肩的棉布或绸) shālì.

sarong /səˈrɒŋ; *US* -ˈrɔːŋ/ *n* [C] 莎龙〔龍〕(印尼人用以裹身的布,似裙) shālóng.

SAR /ˌes eiː ˈɑː(r)/ *abbr* Special Administrative Region 特别行政区〔區〕tèbié xíngzhèngqū.

SARS /sɑːz/ *abbr* severe acute respiratory syndrome 严〔嚴〕重急性呼吸综合征〔徵〕yánzhòng jíxìng hūxī zōnghézhēng;非典 fēidiǎn.

sash /sæʃ/ *n* [C] 腰带〔帶〕yāodài;饰带 shìdài;肩带 jiāndài.

sash-window /ˌsæʃ ˈwɪndəʊ/ *n* [C](上下)推拉窗 tuīlāchuāng.

sat *pt*, *pp* of SIT.

Satan /ˈseɪtn/ *n* 撒旦 Sādàn;魔鬼 móguǐ. Satanic /səˈtænɪk/ *adj*.

satchel /ˈsætʃəl/ *n* [C] 书〔書〕包 shūbāo;小背包 xiǎo bēibāo.

satellite /ˈsætəlaɪt/ *n* [C] 1 (a)卫〔衛〕星 wèixīng. (b)人造卫星 rénzào wèixīng. 2 [喻]卫星国〔國〕wèixīngguó. ˈsatellite channel *n* [C] 卫星电〔電〕视频道 wèixīng diànshì

S

píndào. **satellite television** *n* [U]卫星电〔電〕视 wèixīng diànshì.

satin /ˈsætɪn; *US* ˈsætn/ *n* [U] 缎子 duànzi.

satire /ˈsætaɪə(r)/ *n* **1**[U]讽〔諷〕刺 fěngcì. **2**[C] 讽刺作品 fěngcì zuòpǐn: *a* ~ *on snobbery* 描述势利小人的讽刺作品. **satirical** /səˈtɪrɪkl/ *adj*. **satirize** /ˈsætəraɪz/ *v* [T]讽刺 fěngcì.

satisfaction /ˌsætɪsˈfækʃn/ *n* **1** [U] 满意 mǎnyì; 满足 mǎnzú: *get* ~ *from one's work* 从自己的工作中得到满足. **2** [C] 使人满足的事 shǐ rén mǎnzú de shì; 乐〔樂〕事 lèshì; 快事 kuàishì. **3** [U]补〔補〕偿〔償〕bǔcháng; 道歉 dàoqiàn.

satisfactory /ˌsætɪsˈfæktərɪ/ *adj* 令人满意的 lìng rén mǎnyì de; 如意的 rúyìde; 可喜的 kěxǐde: ~ *progress* 可喜的进步. **satisfactorily** /-tərəlɪ/ *adv*.

satisfy /ˈsætɪsfaɪ/ *v* [*pt, pp* **-ied**] [T] **1** (使)满足 mǎnzú; (使)满意 mǎnyì: *enough food to* ~ *us* 有足够的食品满足我们的需要. **2** 满足(愿望、需要等) mǎnzú. **3** 向…提供证据〔據〕 xiàng…tígōng zhèngjù; 使…信服 shǐ…xìnfú: ~ *the police of my innocence* 向警方证实我的无辜. **satisfied** *adj* 满意的 mǎnyìde; 满足的 mǎnzúde.

saturate /ˈsætʃəreɪt/ *v* [T] **1** 浸透 jìntòu; 浸湿〔濕〕 jìnshī. **2** [常用被动语态]使充满 shǐ chōngmǎn. **saturated** *adj* **1** 极〔極〕湿的 jíshīde. **2** 饱和的 bǎohéde. **saturation** /sætʃəˈreɪʃn/ *n* [U].

Saturday /ˈsætədɪ/ *n* [U, C] 星期六 xīngqīliù.

sauce /sɔːs/ *n* **1** [C, U] 调味汁 tiáowèizhī; 酱〔醬〕 jiàng. **2** [U] [非正式用语]无〔無〕礼〔禮〕的话 wúlǐde huà. **saucy** *adj* [**-ier, -iest**] 无礼的 wúlǐde; 莽撞的 mǎngzhuàngde. **saucily** *adv*.

saucepan /ˈsɔːspən; *US* -pæn/ *n* [C] (有盖和长柄的)平底锅〔鍋〕 píngdǐguō.

saucer /ˈsɔːsə(r)/ *n* [C] 茶托 chátuō; 茶碟 chádié.

sauna /ˈsɔːnə, 亦读 ˈsaʊnə/ *n* [C]蒸汽浴 zhēngqìyù; 桑拿浴 sāngnáyù.

saunter /ˈsɔːntə(r)/ *v* [I] 漫步 mànbù; 闲逛 xiánguàng. **saunter** *n* [sing] 漫步 mànbù; 闲逛 xiánguàng.

sausage /ˈsɒsɪdʒ; *US* ˈsɔːs-/ *n* [C, U] 香肠〔腸〕 xiāngcháng; 腊〔臘〕肠 làcháng.

savage /ˈsævɪdʒ/ *adj* **1** 野蛮〔蠻〕的 yěmánde; 凶〔兇〕猛的 xiōngměngde: *a* ~ *animal* 凶猛的动物. **2** 残〔殘〕酷的 cánkùde; 恶〔惡〕毒的 èdúde: ~ *criticism* 粗暴的批评. **3**[蔑]未开〔開〕化的 wèi kāihuà de; 原始的 yuánshǐde. **savage** *n* [C][蔑]野蛮人 yěmánrén. **savage** *v* [T] 凶猛地攻击〔擊〕 xiōngměngde gōngjī: ~*d by a dog* 被狗咬. **savagely** *adv*. **savagery** *n* [U] 野蛮(或残暴)的行为〔爲〕 yěmánde xíngwéi.

save /seɪv/ *v* **1** [T] (*from*)援救 yuánjiù; 拯救 zhěngjiù; 保全 bǎoquán: ~ *sb's life* 救某人的命. **2** [I, T](*up, for*) 储存(钱)chǔcún; 积〔積〕攒 jīzǎn: ~ (*up*) *for a new car* 攒钱买新汽车. *S*~ *some cake for me!* 给我留些蛋糕! **3** (计算机)保存数据 bǎocún shùjù; 将〔將〕… 存盘〔盤〕 jiāng…cúnpán. **4** [T] 省去 shěngqù: *That will* ~ *you a lot of trouble*. 那将省去你许多麻烦. **5** [T](足球中)防止对〔對〕方得分 fángzhǐ duìfāng défēn. **6** [习语] **save (one's) face** 保全面子 bǎoquán miànzi. **save one's neck** ⇨NECK. **save** *n* [C] (足球中的)救球 jiùqiú. **saving** *n* **1** [C]节〔節〕省(或储存)的量 jiéshěngde liàng: *a saving of £5* 节省 5 英镑. **2 savings** [pl]储蓄金 chǔxùjīn; 存款 cúnkuǎn. ˈ**savings account** *n* [U] 储蓄账户 chǔxù zhànghù.

saviour (美语 **-or**) /ˈseɪvɪə(r)/ *n* [C] **1** 救助者 jiùzhùzhě; 挽救者 wǎnjiùzhě. **2 the Saviour** [宗教]救世主(耶稣基督) Jiùshìzhǔ.

savour (美语 **-or**) /ˈseɪvə(r)/ *n* [C, U] 滋味 zīwèi; 味道 wèidào; 风〔風〕味 fēngwèi. **savour** *v* [T] 品尝〔嘗〕 pǐncháng; 品味 pǐnwèi: ~ *the wine* 品酒. [喻] ~ *one's freedom* 享受自由.

savoury (美语 **-ory**) /ˈseɪvərɪ/ *adj* 咸〔鹹〕的 xiánde. **savoury** *n* [C] [*pl* **-ies**]咸味菜肴 xiánwèi càiyáo.

saw[1] *pt* of SEE.

saw[2] /sɔː/ *n* [C] 锯 jù. **saw** *v* [*pt* **~ed**, *pp* **~n** /sɔːn/ ; 美语 **~ed**] **1** [I, T]锯 jù; 锯成 jùchéng. **2** [I] 可被锯开〔開〕 kěbèi jùkāi: *Wood* ~*s easily*. 木材容易锯开. **3**[短语动词] **saw sth up** 将〔將〕…锯成块〔塊〕jiāng…jùchéng kuài. ˈ**sawdust** *n* [U] 锯末 jùmò. ˈ**sawmill** *n* [C]锯木厂〔廠〕 jùmùchǎng.

saxophone /ˈsæksəfəʊn/ *n* [C] [音乐]萨〔薩〕克斯管 sākèsīguǎn.

say /seɪ/ *v* [*pt, pp* **said** /sed/] [T] **1** 说 shuō; 讲〔講〕 jiǎng. **2** 表示(信息) biǎoshì: *It* ~*s here that she was killed*. 这里宣称, 她被杀害. **3** (用言语、手势等)表达〔達〕(思想、情感等) biǎodá: *What does this poem* ~ *to you?* 你以为这首诗意味着什么? **4** 表明(意见) biǎomíng. **5** 假定 jiǎdìng; 以为〔爲〕yǐwéi: *I'd* ~ *this can't be done*. 我以为此事完成不了. **6** [习语] **go without saying** 不用说 búyòng shuō. **you can say that again** [非正式用语]我同意 wǒ tóngyì. **that is to say** ⇨ THAT[1]. **say** *n* **1** [U, sing]决定权〔權〕 jué-

S

dìngquán: *a ~ in what happens* 有权决定做什么. 2 [习语] **have one's say** 表达意见 biǎodá yìjiàn. **saying** *n* [C] 格言 géyán; 谚语 yànyǔ.

scab /skæb/ *n* [C] 1 痂 jiā. 2 [非正式用语, 贬] 拒不参加罢〔罷〕工者 jù bù cānjiā bàgōng zhě.

scaffold /ˈskæfəʊld/ *n* [C] 1 脚手架 jiǎoshǒujià; 建筑〔築〕架 jiànzhùjià. 2 断〔斷〕头〔頭〕台 duàntóutái; 绞刑架 jiǎoxíngjià. **scaffolding** /ˈskæfəldɪŋ/ *n* [U] (建筑)脚手架 jiǎoshǒujià.

scald /skɔːld/ *v* [T] (被沸水、蒸汽)烫〔燙〕伤〔傷〕 tàngshāng. **scald** *n* [C] 烫伤 tàngshāng. **scalding** *adj* 滚〔滾〕烫的 gǔntàngde; 灼热〔熱〕的 zhuórède.

scale[1] /skeɪl/ *n* 1 [C] 鳞 lín; 鳞片 línpiàn. 2 [U] [英国英语] (水壶、水管等的)水锈 shuǐxiù; 水垢 shuǐgòu. **scale** *v* [T] 刮去…的鳞 guāqù… de lín. **scaly** *adj* [-ier, -iest].

scale[2] /skeɪl/ *n* 1 [C] 刻度 kèdù; 标〔標〕度 biāodù. 2 [C] 等级 děngjí; 级别 jíbié: *a salary ~* 薪金级别. 3 [C] 比例 bǐlì. 4 [C, U] 大小 dàxiǎo; 规模 guīmó; 范〔範〕围〔圍〕 fànwéi: *riots on a large ~* 大规模骚乱. 5 [C] [音乐] 音阶〔階〕 yīnjiē. **scale** *v* [短语动词] **scale sth up/down** 增加 zēngjiā; 缩减 suōjiǎn.

scale[3] /skeɪl/ *v* [T] 攀登(悬崖等) pāndēng.

scales /skeɪlz/ *n* [pl] 天平 tiānpíng; 磅秤 bàngchèng: *weigh oneself on the bathroom ~* 在浴室的磅秤上称体重.

scallop /ˈskɒləp/ *n* [C] 扇贝 shànbèi.

scalp /skælp/ *n* [C] (人的)头〔頭〕皮 tóupí. **scalp** *v* [T] 剥去…的头皮 bōqù…de tóupí.

scalpel /ˈskælpəl/ *n* [C] 解剖刀 jiěpōudāo; 手术〔術〕刀 shǒushùdāo.

scamper /ˈskæmpə(r)/ *v* [I] 跳跳蹦蹦 tiàotiàobèngbèng; 奔跑 bēnpǎo.

scampi /ˈskæmpɪ/ *n* [pl] 大虾〔蝦〕 dàxiā.

scan /skæn/ *v* [-nn-] 1 [T] 细看 xìkàn; 细察 xìchá: *~ the horizon* 细看地平线. 2 [T] 浏〔瀏〕览〔覽〕 liúlǎn: *~ the newspapers* 浏览报纸. 3 [T] [医] (用扫描器) 扫〔掃〕描检〔檢〕查 sǎomiáo jiǎnchá. 4 [I] (诗) 符合韵〔韻〕律 fúhé yùnlǜ. 5 [T] (计算机) 扫描 sǎomiáo. **scan** *n* [C] 扫描 sǎomiáo. **scanner** *n* [C] 扫描器 sǎomiáoqì.

scandal /ˈskændl/ *n* 1 [C, U] 公愤 gōngfèn; 引起公愤的举〔舉〕动〔動〕 yǐnqǐ gōngfèn de jǔdòng. 2 [U] 流言 liúyán; 诽谤 fěibàng. **scandalize** /-dəlaɪz/ *v* [T] 使震惊〔驚〕 shǐ zhènjīng; 使愤慨 shǐ fènkǎi. **scandalous** *adj*.

scant /skænt/ *adj* [正式用语] 不足的 bùzúde; 缺乏的 quēfáde. **scantily** *adv*. **scanty** *adj* [-ier, -iest] 不足的 bùzúde; 不够大的 búgòu dà de.

scapegoat /ˈskeɪpgəʊt/ *n* [C] 替罪羊 tìzuìyáng.

scar /skɑː(r)/ *n* [C] 1 伤〔傷〕疤 shāngbā; 伤痕 shānghén. 2 [喻] (精神上的) 创〔創〕伤 chuàngshāng. **scar** *v* [-rr-] [T] 给…留下伤痕 gěi… liúxià shānghén.

scarce /skeəs/ *adj* [~r, ~st] 缺乏的 quēfáde; 不足的 bùzúde; 供不应〔應〕求的 gōng bú yìng qiú de. **scarcely** *adv* 几〔幾〕乎不 jīhū bù; 仅〔僅〕仅 jǐnjǐn: *~ly enough food* 勉强够吃的食物. **scarcity** *n* [C, U] [*pl* -ies] 不足 bùzú; 缺乏 quēfá.

scare /skeə(r)/ *v* 1 [T] 使恐惧〔懼〕 shǐ kǒngjù; 使害怕 shǐ hàipà. 2 [I] 受惊〔驚〕吓〔嚇〕 shòu jīngxià: *He ~s easily.* 他容易受惊. **scare** *n* [C] 惊吓 jīngxià; 惊恐 jīngkǒng. **ˈscarecrow** *n* [C] 稻草人 dàocǎorén. **scary** /ˈskeərɪ/ *adj* [-ier, -iest] [非正式用语] 惊恐的 jīngkǒngde; 易受惊的 yì shòujīng de.

scarf /skɑːf/ *n* [C] [*pl* **scarves** /skɑːvz/ 或 ~s] 围〔圍〕巾 wéijīn; 头〔頭〕巾 tóujīn.

scarlet /ˈskɑːlət/ *n* [U], *adj* 鲜红色 xiānhóngsè; 鲜红的 xiānhóngde. ˌ**scarlet ˈfever** *n* [C] 猩红热〔熱〕 xīnghóngrè.

scathing /ˈskeɪðɪŋ/ *adj* 严〔嚴〕厉〔厲〕的 yánlìde; 刻薄的 kèbóde. **scathingly** *adv*.

scatter /ˈskætə(r)/ *v* 1 [I, T] (使)散开〔開〕 sànkāi. 2 [T] 撒 sǎ; 撒播 sǎbō: *~ seed* 播种. **ˈscatter-brain** *n* [C] 精神不集中的人 jīngshén bù jízhōng de rén; 健忘的人 jiànwàngde rén. **ˈscatter-brained** *adj*. **scattered** *adj* 分散的 fēnsànde; 稀疏的 xīshūde.

scavenge /ˈskævɪndʒ/ *v* [I, T] 1 (动物) 以(腐肉)为〔爲〕食 yǐ…wéi shí. 2 (在垃圾中) 搜寻〔尋〕食物 sōuxún shíwù. **scavenger** *n* [C] 食腐动〔動〕物 shí fǔ dòngwù; 拣〔揀〕破烂〔爛〕的人 jiǎn pòlàn de rén.

scenario /sɪˈnɑːrɪəʊ; *US* -ˈnær-/ *n* [C] [*pl* ~s] 1 剧〔劇〕本提纲〔綱〕 jùběn tígāng; 电〔電〕影(或戏剧等)脚本 diànyǐng jiǎoběn. 2 想像中的未来(一系列)事情 xiǎngxiàng zhōng de wèilái shìqing.

scene /siːn/ *n* [C] 1 (事件)发〔發〕生地点〔點〕 fāshēng dìdiǎn: *the ~ of the crime* 犯罪的现场. 2 (现实生活中的)事件 shìjiàn; 情景 qíngjǐng: *~s of horror during the fire* 火灾过程中可怕的情景. 3 吵闹〔鬧〕 chǎonào: *make a ~* 大吵大闹. 4 景色 jǐngsè; 景象 jǐngxiàng. 5 (戏剧等的)一场〔場〕 yìchǎng; 一个〔個〕情节〔節〕(或片断) yígè qíngjié. 6 (舞台)布景 bùjǐng. 7 [习语] **behind the scenes** (a) 在幕后〔後〕 zài mùhòu. (b) 秘密的 mìmìde. **on the scene** 在场 zàichǎng; 到场 dàochǎng. **scenery** *n* [U] 1 风〔風〕景 fēngjǐng; 景色 jǐngsè. 2 布景 bù-

S

jǐng. **scenic** /ˈsiːnɪk/ *adj* 风景优〔優〕美的 fēngjǐng yōuměi de.

scent /sent/ *n* 1 [C,U] 气〔氣〕味 qìwèi; 香味 xiāngwèi. 2[U][尤用于英国英语]香水 xiāngshuǐ. 3 [C](动物的)遗臭 yíxiù, 臭迹〔跡〕 xiùjì. 4[U](犬的)嗅觉〔覺〕 xiùjué. 5 [习语] **on the scent of sb/sth** 获〔獲〕得线〔綫〕索 huòdé xiànsuǒ;循臭迹追猎〔獵〕 xún xiùjì zhuī liè. **scent** *v* [T] 1 (a)嗅出 xiùchū;闻到 wéndào. (b)[喻]察觉 chájué;怀〔懷〕疑有 huáiyí yǒu: ~ *danger* 发觉危险. 2 使…有香味 shǐ…yǒu xiāngwèi: ~*ed paper* 有香味的纸.

sceptic (美语 sk-) /ˈskeptɪk/ *n* [C] 怀〔懷〕疑(论)者 huáiyízhě. **sceptical** *adj*. **scepticism** /ˈskeptɪsɪzəm/ *n* [U] 怀疑主义〔義〕 huáiyí zhǔyì; 怀疑态〔態〕度 huáiyí tàidù.

sceptre (美语 -er) /ˈseptə(r)/ *n* [C] (象征君主权位的)节〔節〕杖 jiézhàng, 王节 wángjié, 权〔權〕杖 quánzhàng.

schedule /ˈʃedjuːl; *US* ˈskedʒʊl/ *n* [C, U] 1 时〔時〕间表 shíjiānbiǎo; 计划〔劃〕表 jìhuàbiǎo: *production* ~*s* 生产进度表. *on*/*behind* ~ 按时间表;落后于计划(或预定时间). 2[美语] = TIMETABLE (TIME[1]). **schedule** *v* [T]将〔將〕…列入计划表(或进度表、时间表) jiāng…lièrù jìhuàbiǎo.

scheme /skiːm/ *n* [C] 1 组合 zǔhé;配合 pèihé: *a* ˈ*colour* ~ 色彩的调配. 2 计划〔劃〕 jìhuà: *a* ~ *for raising money* 筹款方案. 3 阴〔陰〕谋 yīnmóu; 诡计 guǐjì. **scheme** *v* [T] 搞阴谋 gǎo yīnmóu. **schemer** *n* [C] 搞阴谋者 gǎo yīnmóu zhě.

schizophrenia /ˌskɪtsəʊˈfriːnɪə/ *n* [U] 精神分裂症 jīngshénfēnlièzhèng. **schizophrenic** /-ˈfrenɪk/ *adj*, *n* 精神分裂症的 jīngshénfēnlièzhèngde; 精神分裂症患者 jīngshénfēnlièzhèng huànzhě.

scholar /ˈskɒlə(r)/ *n* [C] 1 学〔學〕者 xuézhě. 2 获〔獲〕奖〔獎〕学金(或津贴)的学生 huò jiǎngxuéjīn de xuéshēng. **scholarly** *adj*. **scholarship** *n* 1 [U] 学问 xuéwèn; 学识〔識〕 xuéshí. 2 [C]奖学金 jiǎngxuéjīn.

school[1] /skuːl/ *n* 1[C] 学〔學〕校 xuéxiào: *All children should go to* ~. 所有儿童都应当上学. *primary* / *secondary* ~ 小学;中学. *a driving* ~ 驾驶学校. 2[C] [美语]学院 xuéyuàn;大学 dàxué. 3 [U] (a) 上学 shàngxué: *Is she old enough for* ~? 她到了上学年龄吗? (b) 上课时〔時〕间 shàngkè shíjiān: *S*~ *starts at 9 am*. 上午九点上课. 4 **the school** [sing] 全校学生 quánxiào xuéshēng. 5 [C](大学的)院 yuàn; (大学的)系 xì: *medical* ~ 医学院. 6 [C] 学派 xuépài; 流派 liúpài: *the Dutch* ~ *of painting* 荷兰画派. **school** *v* [T] 训练〔練〕xùnliàn;控制 kòngzhì. **schooling** *n* [U] 教育 jiàoyù. **school-leaver** *n* [C] 中学毕〔畢〕业〔業〕生 zhōngxué bìyèshēng; 离〔離〕校生 líxiàoshēng; 辍学生 chuòxuéshēng. ˈ**schoolmaster**, ˈ**schoolmistress** *n* [C] (中小学)(女)教师〔師〕 jiàoshī.

school[2] /skuːl/ *n* [C] 鱼群 yúqún.

schooner /ˈskuːnə(r)/ *n* [C] 1 (两桅以上的)纵〔縱〕帆船 zòngfānchuán. 2 大玻璃杯 dà bōlíbēi.

science /ˈsaɪəns/ *n* 1 [U]科学〔學〕 kēxué; 科学研究 kēxué yánjiū. 2 [C, U]学科 xuékē; 某一门科学 mǒuyìmén kēxué. ˌ**science** ˈ**fiction** *n* [U] 科学幻想小说 kēxué huànxiǎng xiǎoshuō. **scientific** /ˌsaɪən-ˈtɪfɪk / *adj*. **scientifically** / -klɪ / *adv*. **scientist** / ˈsaɪəntɪst / *n* [C]科学家 kēxuéjiā.

scintillating /ˈsɪntɪleɪtɪŋ; *US* -təl-/ *adj* 焕发〔發〕才智的 huànfā cáizhì de.

scissors /ˈsɪzəz/ *n* [pl] 剪刀 jiǎndāo; 剪子 jiǎnzi: *a pair of* ~ 一把剪刀.

scoff /skɒf/ *v* [I] (*at*) 嘲笑 cháoxiào; 嘲弄 cháonòng.

scold /skəʊld/ *v* [I, T]叱责 chìzé; 责骂 zémà: ~ *a child for being naughty* 责备孩子淘气.

scone /skɒn; *US* skəʊn/ *n* [C]烤饼 kǎobǐng.

scoop /skuːp/ *n* [C] 1 勺〔杓〕sháo; 铲〔鏟〕子 chǎnzi. 2 抢〔搶〕先报〔報〕道的新闻 qiǎngxiān bàodào de xīnwén. **scoop** *v* [T] 1 用勺舀 yòng sháo yǎo; 用铲子铲 yòng chǎnzi chǎn. 2 [短语动词] **scoop sth out/up** 铲起 chǎnqǐ; 舀出 yǎochū.

scooter /ˈskuːtə(r)/ *n* [C] 1 (亦作 ˈ**motor-scooter**) 小型摩托车 xiǎoxíng mótuōchē. 2 (儿童游戏用的)踏板车 tàbǎnchē.

scope /skəʊp/ *n* 1 [U]机〔機〕会〔會〕 jīhuì: ~ *for improvement* 改进的机会. 2 [sing](处理、研究的)范〔範〕围〔圍〕fànwéi.

scorch /skɔːtʃ/ *v* 1 (a)[T]把…烧〔燒〕焦 bǎ…shāojiāo; 把…烤焦 bǎ…kǎojiāo. (b) [I] (表面)烧焦 shāojiāo; 烤焦 kǎojiāo. 2 [T] 使枯萎 shǐ kūwěi. **scorch** *n* [C] (布上的)焦痕 jiāohén.

S

score[1] /skɔː(r)/ *n* [C] 1 (比赛中的)得分 défēn; 比分 bǐfēn. 2 刻痕 kèhén; 抓痕 zhuāhén; 划〔劃〕痕 huáhén. 3 乐〔樂〕谱 yuèpǔ. 4[旧]二十 èrshí. 5 [习语] **on that score** 在那一点〔點〕上 zài nà yìdiǎn shàng. **pay/settle an old score** 算旧〔舊〕账 suàn jiùzhàng; 报〔報〕宿怨 bào sùyuàn.

score[2] /skɔː(r)/ *v* 1 [I, T](a)(在比赛中)记分 jìfēn. (b)(比赛中)得(分) dé. 2 [T] 在…上刻痕 zài…shàng kèhén; 在…上划〔劃〕痕 zài…shàng huáhén. 3 [I, T]获〔獲〕得(成功)huòdé. 4 [T] 编写〔寫〕(乐曲)biānxiě: ~*d for* *the piano* 为钢琴演奏编写的. **scorer** *n* 1（比赛中的）记分员 jìfēnyuán. 2 得分的运〔運〕动〔動〕员 défēnde yùndòngyuán.

scorn /skɔːn/ *n* [U] 轻〔輕〕蔑 qīngmiè; 鄙视 bǐshì. **scorn** *v* [T] 1 鄙视 bǐshì; 轻蔑 qīngmiè. 2 傲慢地拒绝 àomànde jùjué. **scornful** *adj*. **scornfully** *adv*.

scorpion /ˈskɔːpɪən/ *n* [C] 蝎子 xiēzi.

Scot /skɒt/ *n* [C] 苏〔蘇〕格兰〔蘭〕人 Sūgélánrén.

Scotch /skɒtʃ/ *n* [C,U] 苏〔蘇〕格兰〔蘭〕威士忌 Sūgélán wēishìjì.

scot-free /ˌskɒt ˈfriː/ *adj* 免受惩〔懲〕罚的 miǎnshòu chéngfá de: *escape* ～ 安然逃脱.

Scotland /ˈskɒtlənd/ *n* 苏〔蘇〕格兰〔蘭〕 Sūgélán.

Scots /skɒts/ *adj* 苏〔蘇〕格兰〔蘭〕的 Sūgélánde; 苏格兰人的 Sūgélánrénde; 苏格兰英语的 Sūgélán Yīngyǔ de.

Scottish /ˈskɒtɪʃ/ *adj* 苏〔蘇〕格兰〔蘭〕的 Sūgélánde; 苏格兰人的 Sūgélánrénde.

scoundrel /ˈskaʊndrəl/ *n* [C] 恶〔惡〕棍 ègùn; 无〔無〕赖 wúlài.

scour[1] /ˈskaʊə(r)/ *v* [T] 擦亮 cā liàng; 擦净 cājìng. **scour** *n* [sing] 擦 cā; 冲刷 chōngshuā. **scourer** *n* [C]（刷锅等用的）尼龙〔龍〕（或金属）网〔網〕垫〔墊〕 nílóng wǎngdiàn.

scour[2] /ˈskaʊə(r)/ *v* [T] 四处〔處〕搜索 sìchù sōusuǒ; 细查 xìchá: ～ *the area for the thief* 在该地区搜捕那个窃贼.

scourge /skɜːdʒ/ *n* [C] 苦难〔難〕的原因 kǔnàn de yuányīn: *the* ～ *of war* 战争造成的苦难.

scout /skaʊt/ *n* [C] 1 侦察员 zhēncháyuán; 侦察机〔機〕 zhēnchájī; 侦察舰〔艦〕 zhēnchájiàn. 2 **Scout** 童子军 tóngzǐjūn. 3 [短语动词] **scout about/around** 四处〔處〕寻〔尋〕找 sìchù xúnzhǎo.

scowl /skaʊl/ *n* [C] 怒容 nùróng. **scowl** *v* [I] (*at*) 怒视 nùshì.

scrabble /ˈskræbl/ *v* [短语动词] **scrabble about (for sth)** 摸索着寻〔尋〕找 mōsuǒzhe xúnzhǎo.

scraggy /ˈskrægɪ/ *adj* [-ier, -iest] [贬] 瘦的 shòude; 皮包骨的 pí bāo gǔ de.

scram /skræm/ *v* [-mm-] [I] [俚] 快走开〔開〕 kuài zǒu kāi.

scramble /ˈskræmbl/ *v* 1 [I] 爬 pá; 攀登 pāndēng. 2 [T] 炒(蛋) chǎo. 3 [T] 对〔對〕(电话通话)扰〔擾〕频 duì…rǎopín. 4 [短语动词] **scramble for sth** 争夺〔奪〕 zhēngduó; 竞〔競〕争 jìngzhēng: ～ *for the best seats* 抢最好的坐位. **scramble** *n* 1 [sing] 攀登 pāndēng; 爬行 páxíng. 2 [sing] 争夺 zhēngduó; 抢〔搶〕夺 qiǎngduó: *a* ～ *for seats* 抢坐位. 3 [C] 摩托车越野赛 mótuōchē yuèyěsài.

scrap[1] /skræp/ *n* 1 [C] 碎片 suìpiàn; 碎屑 suìxiè; 小块〔塊〕 xiǎokuài: *a* ～ *of paper* 一小片纸. [喻] ～*s of information* 零星的信息. 2 [U] 废〔廢〕料 fèiliào; 废物 fèiwù: ～ *metal* 废金属. **scrap** *v* [-pp-] [T] 抛弃〔棄〕 pāoqì; 废弃 fèiqì. ˈ**scrap-book** *n* [C] 剪贴簿 jiǎntiēbù; 剪报〔報〕资料簿 jiǎnbào zīliàobù. ˈ**scrap-heap** *n* [C] 1 废料堆 fèiliàoduī; 废物堆 fèiwùduī. 2 [习语] **on the scrap-heap** 不再需要的 búzài xūyào de. **scrappy** *adj* [-ier, -iest] 组织〔織〕不周密的 zǔzhī bù zhōumì de.

scrap[2] /skræp/ *n* [C] [非正式用语] 打架 dǎjià; 吵架 chǎojià. **scrap** *v* [-pp-] [I] 打架 dǎjià; 吵架 chǎojià.

scrape /skreɪp/ *v* 1 [T] (a) 擦净 cā jìng; 磨光 mó guāng; 刮削 guāxiāo. (b) (*from/off/away*) 除掉(泥、油漆等) chúdiào. 2 [T] 擦伤〔傷〕 cā shāng; 刮破 guā pò: ～ *one's arm on the wall* 在墙上擦伤了自己的手臂. 3 [I, T] 擦着某物 cā zhe mǒuwù: *The branch* ～*d against the side of the car*. 树枝擦着了汽车的一边. 4 [T] 刮成 guāchéng; 挖成 wāchéng: ～ (*out*) *a hole* 挖了一个洞. 5 [习语] **scrape (the bottom of) the ˈbarrel** 退而求其次 tuì ér qiú qícì; 勉强使用现有的物力(或人才) miǎnqiǎng shǐyòng xiànyǒu de wùlì. 6 [短语动词] **scrape sth together/up** (艰难地)积〔積〕攒(钱) jīzǎn; 凑集 còují: ～ *up enough to pay the gas bill* 凑够付煤气〔氣〕费的钱. **scrape** *n* [C] 1 刮擦声〔聲〕 guācāshēng. 2 擦伤 cāshāng; 擦痕 cāhén. 3 [非正式用语] 窘境 jiǒngjìng; 困境 kùnjìng.

scratch[1] /skrætʃ/ *v* 1 (a) [I,T] 划〔劃〕 huá; 抓 zhuā. (b) [T] 抓(或划)成(某状态) zhuāchéng. 2 [I,T] (为止痒而)搔(皮肤) sāo; 挠〔撓〕náo. 3 [习语] **scratch the surface** 触〔觸〕及表面 chù jí biǎomiàn; 处〔處〕理问题不彻〔徹〕底 chǔlǐ wèntí bú chèdǐ. 4 [短语动词] **scratch sth away, off, etc** 刮去某物 guāqù mǒuwù.

scratch[2] /skrætʃ/ *n* 1 [C] 抓(或划、刮)痕 zhuāhén; 抓(或划、刮)伤〔傷〕 zhuāshāng; 刮擦声〔聲〕 guācāshēng. 2 [sing] 挠〔撓〕 náo; 搔 sāo. 3 [习语] (**start sth**) **from ˈscratch** 从〔從〕头〔頭〕做起 cóng tóu zuòqǐ; 从零开〔開〕始 cóng líng kāishǐ. **up to scratch** 合格 hégé; 情况良好 qíngkuàng liánghǎo. ˈ**scratch card** *n* [C] 刮奖〔獎〕卡 guājiǎngkǎ. **scratchy** *adj* 1 使皮肤〔膚〕发〔發〕痒〔癢〕的 shǐ pífū fāyǎng de. 2 (唱片)发沙沙声的 fā shāshāshēng de.

scrawl /skrɔːl/ *v* [I,T] 1 潦草地写〔寫〕 liáocǎode xiě. 2 乱〔亂〕涂〔塗〕 luàntú; 乱画〔畫〕 luànhuà. **scrawl** *n* [C, sing] 潦草的笔〔筆〕迹 liáocǎode bǐjì.

scream /skriːm/ *v* 1 (a) [I] (因恐惧、痛苦、

愤怒等)尖声〔聲〕喊叫 jiānshēng hǎnjiào; 惊〔驚〕呼 jīnghū. (b)[T]喊出 hǎnchū. 2[I](风、机器等)发〔發〕出大而尖的声音 fāchū dà ér jiān de shēngyīn. 3[习语] **scream one's head off** ⇨HEAD[1]. **scream** *n* [C]尖叫声 jiānjiàoshēng;尖锐刺耳的声音 jiānruì cì'ěr de shēngyīn.

screech /skriːtʃ/ *v* 1 [I]发〔發〕出尖锐刺耳的声〔聲〕音 fāchū jiānruì cì'ěr de shēngyīn. 2 [T]尖叫 jiānjiào. 3 [I]痛苦(或愤怒)地尖叫 tòngkǔde jiānjiào. **screech** *n* [sing] 尖锐刺耳的声音 jiānruì cì'ěr de shēngyīn: *a ~ of brakes* 刹车的嘎吱声.

screen /skriːn/ *n* 1 [C] 屏 píng; 幕 mù; 帘〔簾〕lián; 帐〔帳〕zhàng; 隔板 gébǎn. 2 [C]掩蔽物 yǎnbìwù: *a ~ of trees around the house* 一道围绕着房子的树墙. 3 [C]银幕 yínmù. 4 [C]屏幕 píngmù. 5[sing] 电〔電〕影业〔業〕diànyǐngyè. 6 [C]纱门 shāmén;纱窗 shāchuāng. **screen** *v* [T] 1 遮蔽 zhēbì;掩护〔護〕yǎnhù. 2 检〔檢〕查 jiǎnchá;测试 cèshì;审〔審〕查 shěnchá. 3 放映 fàngyìng. **'screenplay** *n* [C] 电影剧〔劇〕本 diànyǐng jùběn. **'screensaver** *n* [C] 屏幕保护程序 píngmù bǎohù chéngxù. **'screenwash** *n* [U] (汽车)挡〔擋〕风〔風〕玻璃清洗液 dǎngfēng bōli qīngxǐyè.

screw /skruː/ *n* [C] 1 螺丝〔絲〕钉 luósīdīng; 螺丝 luósī;螺钉 luódīng. 2 拧〔擰〕nǐng;转〔轉〕动〔動〕zhuàndòng. 3 (船的)螺旋桨〔槳〕luóxuánjiǎng. 4 [英国⚠俚语]性交 xìngjiāo. 5 [习语] **have a screw loose** [英俚]神经〔經〕不太正常 shénjīng bútài zhèngcháng; 古怪 gǔguài. **screw** *v* 1 [T](用螺钉)拧紧〔緊〕nǐngjǐn. 2 [T]拧动 nǐngdòng; 拧紧 nǐngjǐn: *~ the lid on* 拧上盖. 3[I,T][英国⚠俚语]与〔與〕…性交 yǔ…xìngjiāo. 4 [短语动词] **screw sth up** (a) 扭曲(面孔) niǔqū: *~ed up her eyes in the bright sunshine* 在灿烂的阳光下眯起她的双眼. (b) 把(纸)揉成团〔團〕bǎ…róuchéng tuán. (c)[俚]弄糟 nòngzāo; 损坏〔壞〕sǔnhuài. **'screwdriver** *n* [C]改锥 gǎizhuī; 螺丝刀 luósīdāo; 螺丝起子 luósī qǐzi. **ˌscrewed-'up** *adj* [俚]弄糟的 nòngzāode; 搞乱〔亂〕的 gǎoluànde.

scribble /ˈskrɪbl/ *v* [I,T] 1 潦草书〔書〕写〔寫〕liáocǎo shūxiě: *~ (a note) on an envelope* 在信封上草草写上(附言). 2 乱〔亂〕涂〔塗〕luàntú;涂写 túxiě. **scribble** *n* 1 [U, sing] 潦草的笔〔筆〕迹 liáocǎode bǐjì. 2[C] 草草写成的东西 cǎocǎo xiěchéng de dōngxi.

scribe /skraɪb/ *n* [C] (印刷术发明前的)抄写〔寫〕员 chāoxiěyuán.

script /skrɪpt/ *n* 1 [C]剧〔劇〕本 jùběn; 脚本 jiǎoběn;讲〔講〕稿 jiǎnggǎo. 2 [U] 笔〔筆〕迹 bǐjì; 手迹 shǒujì. 3 [U] 文字体〔體〕系 wénzì tǐxì. **script** *v* [T] 为〔爲〕(电影等)写〔寫〕脚本 wèi…xiě jiǎoběn. **'script-writer** *n* [C] (电影、广播等的)撰稿人 zhuàngǎorén.

scripture /ˈskrɪptʃə(r)/ *n* 1 **Scripture** [U] (亦作 **the Scriptures**) [pl] 圣〔聖〕经〔經〕shèngjīng. 2 **scriptures** [pl] 经典 jīngdiǎn; 经文 jīngwén. **scriptural** *adj*.

scroll /skrəʊl/ *n* [C] 1 (a)(书写用的)卷轴 juǎnzhóu, 纸卷 zhǐjuǎn. (b) 在卷轴上写〔寫〕的古书〔書〕zài juǎnzhóu shàng xiě de gǔshū. 2 卷形物 juǎnxíngwù;卷形石雕饰物 juǎnxíng shídiāo shìwù. **scroll** *v*[I,T] (计算机荧屏上的资料)缓慢上下移动〔動〕huǎnmàn shàngxià yídòng; (计算机)显〔顯〕示(上下移动的)资料 xiǎnshì zīliào. **'scroll bar** *n* [C] 滚〔滾〕动条〔條〕gǔndòngtiáo.

scrounge /skraʊndʒ/ *v* [I,T][正式用语,常作贬]乞得 qǐdé;擅取 shànqǔ: *~ (£10) off a friend* 从朋友那里弄来10英镑. **scrounger** *n* [C].

scrub[1] /skrʌb/ *v* [-bb-] 1 [I,T]刷洗 shuāxǐ;擦洗 cāxǐ. 2 [T][非正式用语]取消 qǔxiāo. **scrub** *n* [sing] 刷洗 shuāxǐ; 擦洗 cāxǐ. **'scrubbing-brush** *n* [C] 硬刷子 yìngshuāzi.

scrub[2] /skrʌb/ *n* [U] 矮树〔樹〕丛〔叢〕ǎishùcóng;灌木丛 guànmùcóng.

scruff /skrʌf/ *n* [习语] **the scruff of the neck** 颈〔頸〕背 jǐngbèi.

scruffy /ˈskrʌfɪ/ *adj* [-ier, -iest] [非正式用语]肮〔骯〕脏〔髒〕的 āngzāngde;不整洁〔潔〕的 bù zhěngjié de;邋遢的 lātāde. **scruff** *n* [C] [非正式用语]邋遢的人 lātāde rén.

scruple /ˈskruːpl/ *n* [C, U] 顾〔顧〕忌 gùjì; 顾虑〔慮〕gùlǜ: *have no ~s about doing sth* 做…无所顾忌.

scrupulous /ˈskruːpjʊləs/ *adj* 1 一丝〔絲〕不苟的 yì sī bù gǒu de;细致的 xìzhìde. 2 诚实〔實〕的 chéngshíde. **scrupulously** *adv*.

scrutinize /ˈskruːtɪnaɪz/ *v* [T]仔细检〔檢〕查 zǐxì jiǎnchá; 彻〔徹〕底检查 chèdǐ jiǎnchá.

scrutiny /ˈskruːtɪnɪ/ *n* [*pl* -ies] [C, U] 细察 xìchá; 详查 xiángchá.

scuff /skʌf/ *v* 1[I,T]拖着(脚)走 tuōzhe zǒu. 2 [T]磨损 mósǔn.

scuffle /ˈskʌfl/ *v* [I] 扭打 niǔdǎ; 混战〔戰〕hùnzhàn. **scuffle** *n* [C].

sculpt = SCULPTURE.

sculptor /ˈskʌlptə(r)/ (*fem* **sculptress**) *n* [C]雕刻家 diāokèjiā; 雕塑家 diāosùjiā.

sculpture /ˈskʌlptʃə(r)/ *n* 1[U] 雕刻 diāokè; 雕塑 diāosù. 2[C, U] 雕刻品 diāokèpǐn; 雕塑品 diāosùpǐn. **sculpture** (亦作 **sculpt** /skʌlpt/) *v* [I, T]做(塑像、雕像) zuò; 雕刻 diāokè;雕塑 diāosù.

S

scum /skʌm/ *n* 1 [U]泡沫 pàomò；浮垢 fúgòu；浮渣 fúzhā. 2 [pl][喻,贬]渣滓 zhāzǐ；糟粕 zāopò.

scurry /ˈskʌrɪ/ *v* [*pt*, *pp* -ied] [I](小步)快跑 kuàipǎo；疾走 jízǒu.

scythe /saɪð/ *n* [U] 长〔長〕柄大镰刀 chángbǐng dàliándāo. **scythe** *v* [I,T] 用长柄大镰刀割(草等) yòng chángbǐng dàliándāo gē.

sea /siː/ *n* 1 **the sea** [U] 海 hǎi；海洋 hǎiyáng. 2(用于专有名词)海 hǎi；内海 nèihǎi. 3 [sing] 海浪 hǎilàng：*a heavy/calm* ～ 波涛汹涌的海面；风平浪静的海面. 4 [sing]大量 dàliàng；茫茫一片 mángmáng yípiàn：*a* ～ *of corn* 一大片庄稼. 5 [习语] **at sea** (a) 在海上 zài hǎishàng；在海上航行 zài hǎishàng hángxíng. (b)茫然 mángrán；不知所措 bù zhī suǒ cuò. **by sea** 由海路 yóu hǎilù；乘海船 chéng hǎichuán. **go to sea** 去当〔當〕水手 qù dāng shuǐshǒu. **put to sea** (离港)出航 chūháng；启〔啟〕航 qǐháng. ˈ**seaboard** *n* [C]海滨〔濱〕hǎibīn；沿海地区〔區〕yánhǎi dìqū；海岸 hǎi'àn. ˈ**seafaring** /-feərɪŋ/ *adj*, *n* [U] 航海(的) hánghǎi；航海业〔業〕hánghǎiyè；以航海为〔為〕业的 yǐ hánghǎi wéi yè de. ˈ**seafood** *n* [U] 海产〔產〕食品 hǎichǎn shípǐn；海味 hǎiwèi. ˈ**sea front** *n* [C,U] (城、镇的)滨海区 bīnhǎiqū. ˈ**seagoing** *adj* 适〔適〕于航海的 shì yú hánghǎi de；远〔遠〕洋航行的 yuǎnyáng hángxíng de. ˈ**seagull** *n* [C] = GULL. ˈ**seahorse** *n* [C] 海马 hǎimǎ. **sea-legs** *n* [pl] (航行时)在海船甲板上行走自如(或不晕)的能力 zài hǎichuán jiǎbǎn shàng xíngzǒu zìrú de nénglì. ˈ**sea-level** *n* [sing]海平面 hǎipíngmiàn. ˈ**sea-lion** *n* [C] 海狮〔獅〕hǎishī. ˈ**seaman** *n* [C] 水手 shuǐshǒu；海员 hǎiyuán；水兵 shuǐbīng. ˈ**seamanship** *n* [U] 航海技能 hánghǎi jìnéng；船舶驾驶术〔術〕chuánbó jiàshǐshù. ˈ**sea-shore** *n* [U]海岸 hǎi'àn；海滨 hǎibīn；海滩〔灘〕hǎitān. ˈ**seasick** *adj* 晕船的 yùnchuánde. ˈ**seaside** *n* [U] 海边〔邊〕hǎibiān；海滨(尤指度假胜地) hǎibīn. ˈ**seaward** *adj*, *adv* 朝海(的) cháo hǎi；向海(的) xiàng hǎi. ˈ**seaweed** *n* [U]海草 hǎicǎo；海藻 hǎizǎo. ˈ**seaworthy** *adj* (船)适于航海的 shì yú hánghǎi de.

seal[1] /siːl/ *n* [C] 海豹 hǎibào. ˈ**sealskin** *n* [U]海豹皮 hǎibàopí.

seal[2] /siːl/ *n* [C] 1 (a)封蜡〔蠟〕fēnglà；封铅 fēngqiān；火漆 huǒqī. (b) 印章 yìnzhāng；图〔圖〕章 túzhāng. 2 密封物 mìfēngwù；密封装〔裝〕置 mìfēng zhuāngzhì. 3 [习语] **seal of approval** 正式认〔認〕可 zhèngshì rènkě. **seal** *v* [T]1 在…上加封(或盖印) zài…shàng jiāfēng. 2 封住 fēngzhù. 3[正式用语]解决 jiějué；决定 juédìng：～ *a bargain* 成交. ～ *sb's fate* 决定某人的命运. 4 [短语动词] **seal sth off** 防止任何人进〔進〕入或离〔離〕开〔開〕(某地) fángzhǐ rènhérén jìnrù huò líkāi；封锁 fēngsuǒ：*Police* ～*ed off the building*. 警察把这座建筑物封锁起来.

seam /siːm/ *n* [C] 1 线〔綫〕缝 xiànfèng；接缝 jiēfèng. 2 层〔層〕céng；矿〔礦〕层 kuàngcéng.

seance /ˈseɪɑːns/ *n* [C] 降神会 jiàngshénhuì.

search /sɜːtʃ/ *v* [I,T] 搜寻〔尋〕sōuxún；搜索 sōusuǒ；搜查 sōuchá：～ (*her pockets*) *for money* 搜查(她的口袋看是否有)钱. **search** *n* [C] 1 搜寻 sōuxún；搜查 sōuchá. 2 [习语] **in search of** 寻找 xúnzhǎo. **searching** *adj* 1 (目光)锐利的 ruìlìde. 2(检查等)彻〔徹〕底的 chèdǐde. ˈ**search engine** *n* [C] (计算机网络)搜索引擎 sōusuǒ yǐnqíng. ˈ**searchlight** *n* [C] 探照灯〔燈〕tànzhàodēng. ˈ**search party** *n* [C] 搜索队〔隊〕sōusuǒduì. ˈ**search-warrant** *n* [C]搜查令 sōuchálìng；搜查证〔證〕sōucházhèng.

season /ˈsiːzn/ *n* [C] 1 季 jì；季节〔節〕jìjié. 2 时〔時〕节 shíjié：*the rainy* ～ 雨季. 3[习语] **in / out of season** (水果等)当〔當〕令的 dānglìngde；不当令的 bù dānglìng de. **season** *v* [T] 1 使适〔適〕用 shǐ shìyòng：～*ed wood* 干燥木材. [喻] *a* ～*ed politician* 有经验的政治家. 2 给(食物)调味 gěi…tiáowèi. **seasonable** /-əbl/ *adj* 1 (天气)合时的 héshíde. 2 (帮助等)及时的 jíshíde. **seasonal** *adj* 季节的 jìjiéde；季节性的 jìjiéxìngde：～*al trade* 季节性生意. **seasonally** *adv*. **seasoning** *n* [U] 调味品 tiáowèipǐn；作料 zuóliào. ˈ**season-ticket** *n* [C] 季票 jìpiào；月票 yuèpiào；长〔長〕期票 chángqīpiào.

seat /siːt/ *n* [C] 1 座 zuò；坐位 zuòwèi. 2(椅等的)座部 zuòbù. 3(车辆、音乐厅等的)坐位 zuòwèi：*There are no* ～*s left for the concert*. 音乐会没有剩余的坐位了. 4 臀部 túnbù：*the* ～ *of his trousers* 他的裤子臀部. 5 (活动等的)中心 zhōngxīn；所在地 suǒzàidì：*the* ～ *of government* 政府所在地. 6 (议会、委员会等的)席位 xíwèi. 7 [习语] **have/take a seat** 坐下 zuò xià. **seat** *v*[T]1[正式用语]使坐下 shǐ zuò xià；使就坐 shǐ jiùzuò：*please be* ～*ed* 请就坐. 2 有…的坐位 yǒu…de zuòwèi：*The cinema* ～*s 200*. 这个电影院设有 200 个坐位. ˈ**seat-belt** *n*[C](汽车、飞机的)安全带〔帶〕ānquándài. **seating** *n*[U] 坐位 zuòwèi.

secateurs /ˈsekətɜːz/ *n* [pl]修枝剪(刀) xiūzhījiǎn.

secede /sɪˈsiːd/ *v* [I] *from* (团体)脱离〔離〕tuōlí；退出 tuìchū. **secession** /sɪˈseʃn/ *n* [C,U] 脱离 tuōlí；退出 tuìchū.

secluded /sɪˈkluːdɪd/ *adj* 与〔與〕世隔绝的 yǔ shì géjué de；孤独〔獨〕的 gūdúde. **seclusion**

S

/sɪˈkluːʒn/ *n* [U] 隔绝 géjué;隐〔隱〕居 yǐnjū.

second[1] /ˈsekənd/ *adj* **1** 第二的 dì'èrde: *the ~ person to come* 要来的第二个人. **2** 附加的 fùjiāde;另一的 lìngyīde: *a ~ pair of shoes* 另一双鞋. **3** [习语] **second to none** 不亚〔亞〕于任何人(或事物)bú yà yú rènhérén: *As a writer, she's ~ to none.* 作为一位作家,她不亚于任何人. **second** *adv* 以第二位 yǐ dì'èrwèi: *come (in) ~ in a race* 赛跑获第二名. ˌ**second-ˈbest** *n*, *adj* 居第二位(的)jū dì'èrwèi; 次好(的) cìhǎo. ˌ**second-ˈclass** *adj*, *adv* 二级(的)èrjí; 乙等(的) yǐděng. ˌ**second-ˈhand** *adj* **1** 二手的 èrshǒude. **2** (新闻)得自他人的 dé zì tārén de. **secondly** *adv* 第二 dì'èr; 其次 qícì. ˌ**second ˈnature** *n* [U]第二天性 dì'èr tiānxìng; 习〔習〕性 xíxìng. ˌ**second-ˈrate** *adj* 二流的 èrliúde; 次等的 cìděngde. ˌ**second ˈthoughts** *n* [pl] 重新考虑〔慮〕chóngxīn kǎolǜ.

second[2] /ˈsekənd/ *n* **1 the second** [sing]第二名 dì'èrmíng; 第二位 dì'èrwèi: *the ~ to leave* 第二位离开的. **2** [C,常作 pl]次货 cìhuò; 等外品 děngwàipǐn. **3 seconds** [pl]第二道菜 dì'èrdào cài;第二份食物 dì'èrfèn shíwù. **4**(英国大学考试成绩的)第二等 dì'èrděng.

second[3] /ˈsekənd/ *n* [C] **1** 秒 miǎo. **2** [非正式用语]片刻 piànkè;瞬间 shùnjiān: *Wait a ~!* 稍等一会儿! ˈ**second hand** *n* [C]秒针 miǎozhēn.

second[4] /ˈsekənd/ *v* [T] (在辩论中)支持 zhīchí;赞同(提案等) zàntóng;附议〔議〕fùyì. **seconder** *n* 附议者 fùyìzhě.

second[5] /sɪˈkɒnd/ *v* [T] 调任 diàorèn; 调派 diàopài. **secondment** *n* [U].

secondary /ˈsekəndrɪ/ *adj* **1**(学校、教育)中等的 zhōngděngde. **2** 次要的 cìyàode: *of ~ interest* 没多少兴趣. **3** 继〔繼〕发〔發〕性的 jìfāxìngde: *a ~ infection* 继发性感染.

secrecy /ˈsiːkrəsɪ/ *n* [U] 保守秘密 bǎoshǒu mìmì; 秘密 mìmì.

secret /ˈsiːkrɪt/ *adj* **1** 秘密的 mìmìde; 保密的 bǎomìde: *~ information* 机密资料. **2** 未公开〔開〕承认〔認〕的 wèi gōngkāi chéngrèn de;秘而不宣的 mì ér bù xuān de: *a ~ admirer* 私下崇拜者. **3** 幽静的 yōujìngde; 人迹〔跡〕罕至的 rénjì hǎn zhì de. **secret** *n*[C]**1** 秘密 mìmì. **2** 秘诀 mìjué: *the ~ of her success* 她成功的秘诀. **3** 神秘 shénmì;奥秘 àomì: *the ~s of nature* 自然界的奥秘. **4** [习语]**in secret** 秘密地 mìmìde. ˌ**secret ˈagent** *n* [C] 特工人员 tègōng rényuán; 特务〔務〕tèwù. **secretly** *adv*. ˌ**secret ˈservice** *n* [C] 特务〔務〕机〔機〕构〔構〕tèwù jīgòu.

secretariat /ˌsekrəˈteərɪət/ *n*[C]秘书〔書〕处〔處〕mìshūchù;书记处 shūjìchù.

secretary /ˈsekrətrɪ; *US* -rəterɪ/ *n* [C] **1** 秘书〔書〕mìshū. **2** 干〔幹〕事 gànshi; 文书 wénshū. **secretarial** /ˌsekrəˈteərɪəl/ *adj*. **Secretary of State** *n* (a)[C](英国)大臣 dàchén. (b) [sing] (美国)国〔國〕务〔務〕卿 guówùqīng.

secrete /sɪˈkriːt/ *v* [T] **1** 分泌 fēnmì. **2** 隐〔隱〕藏 yǐncáng: *~ money in a drawer* 把钱藏在抽屉里. **secretion** /sɪˈkriːʃn/ *n* **1** [U]隐藏 yǐncáng. **2**[C]分泌 fēnmì.

secretive /ˈsiːkrətɪv/ *adj* 遮遮掩掩的 zhēzhē yǎnyǎn de; 守口如瓶的 shǒu kǒu rú píng de. **secretively** *adv*.

sect /sekt/ *n* [C] 派别 pàibié; 宗派 zōngpài. **sectarian** /sekˈteərɪən/ *adj* 派别的 pàibiéde; 宗派的 zōngpàide.

section /ˈsekʃn/ *n* [C] **1** 部分 bù fen. **2** 部门 bùmén;处〔處〕chù; 科 kē; 组 zǔ. **3** 断〔斷〕面 duànmiàn;剖面 pōumiàn;截面 jiémiàn. **sectional** *adj* **1** 组合的 zǔhéde;组装〔裝〕的 zǔzhuāngde. **2** 地区〔區〕的 dìqūde;地方性的 dìfāngxìngde.

sector /ˈsektə(r)/ *n* [C] **1**(工业等的)部门 bùmén: *the private / public ~* 私有部门;公有部门. **2** 战〔戰〕区〔區〕zhànqū;防区 fángqū.

secular /ˈsekjʊlə(r)/ *adj* 现世的 xiànshìde; 世俗的 shìsúde: *~ education* 世俗教育.

secure /sɪˈkjʊə(r)/ *adj* **1** 无〔無〕忧〔憂〕虑〔慮〕的 wú yōulǜ de; 无疑虑的 wú yílǜ de. **2** 确〔確〕定的 quèdìngde; 有把握的 yǒu bǎwò de: *a ~ job* 稳定的工作. **3** (*from/against*) 安全的 ānquánde. **4** 牢固的 láogùde;稳〔穩〕固的 wěngùde: *a ~ grip* 牢固的把手. **secure** *v*[T] **1** 系〔繫〕紧〔緊〕jìjǐn; 关〔關〕紧 guānjǐn;固定住 gùdìngzhù: *~ all the doors* 紧闭门户. **2** (*from/against*) 使安全 shǐ ānquán. **3**[正式用语]获〔獲〕得 huòdé: *~ a job* 找到工作. **securely** *adv*.

security /sɪˈkjʊərətɪ/ *n* [*pl* -ies] **1**[U] 安全 ānquán;平安 píng'ān. **2** [U](防攻击、刺探等的)安全措施 ānquán cuòshī: *tight ~ at the airport* 机场的严密保安措施. **3**[C, U]抵押品 dǐyāpǐn. **4** [C,常作 pl]证〔證〕券 zhèngquàn.

sedan /sɪˈdæn/ *n* [美语] = SALOON 3.

sedate /sɪˈdeɪt/ *adj* 安静的 ānjìngde; 严〔嚴〕肃〔肅〕的 yánsùde; 庄〔莊〕重的 zhuāngzhòngde. **sedately** *adv*.

sedation /sɪˈdeɪʃn/ *n* [U] 镇静作用 zhènjìng zuòyòng.

sedative /ˈsedətɪv/ *n* [C], *adj* 镇静药〔藥〕zhènjìngyào; 镇静的 zhènjìngde.

sedentary /ˈsedntrɪ; *US* -terɪ/ *adj* **1** (工作)坐着做的 zuòzhe zuò de. **2** (人)久坐的 jiǔzuòde.

S

sediment /ˈsedɪmənt/ *n* [U] 沉积〔積〕物 chénjīwù. **sedimentary** /-ˈmentrɪ/ *adj*.

seduce /sɪˈdjuːs/ *v* [T] 1 引诱 yǐnyòu; 勾引 gōuyǐn. 2 唆使 suōshǐ. **seduction** /sɪˈdʌkʃn/ *n* [C,U]. **seductive** /sɪˈdʌktɪv/ *adj* 吸引人的 xīyǐn rén de; 诱人的 yòurénde.

see[1] /siː/ *v* [*pt* saw /sɔː/ , *pp* ~n /siːn /] 1 [I][常与 can, could 连用]看 kàn; 看见 kànjiàn: *If you shut your eyes you can't* ~. 如果你闭上眼睛,你就看不见了. 2 [T][常与 can, could 连用]察觉〔覺〕 chájué; 看出 kànchū: *He couldn't* ~ *her in the crowd*. 他在人群中看不出她. 3 [T]观〔觀〕看(电影、电视节目等) guānkàn: *What did you* ~ *at the theatre last night?* 你昨天晚上在剧院看什么了? 4 [T][用于祈使句]参〔參〕看 cānkàn; 参见 cānjiàn: *S*~ *page 4*. 参看第 4 页. 5 [T]理解 lǐjiě; 明白 míngbai: *He didn't* ~ *the joke*. 他没听懂这个笑话. 6[T] 获〔獲〕悉 huòxī; 得知 dézhī: *I'll go and* ~ *if she's there*. 我要去弄清楚她是否在那儿. 7 [T]到…求医〔醫〕dào… qiúyī; 访问 fǎngwèn: ~ *a doctor* 去看医生. 8[T]遇见 yùjiàn: *I don't* ~ *her often now*. 目前我不常遇见她. 9[T] 保证〔證〕bǎozhèng; 检〔檢〕查 jiǎnchá: ~ *that the windows are shut* 务必把窗关好. 10[T]护〔護〕送 hùsòng: *Will you* ~ *him home?* 你送他回家吧! 11 [习语] **let me see** 让〔讓〕我想想看 ràng wǒ xiǎngxiǎng kàn. **(you) see** (你)明白 míngbai; (你)知道 zhīdào: *She couldn't come, (you) see, because she was ill*. 要知道,她不能来,因为她病了. **(not) see eye to ˈeye with sb** (不)完全一致 wánquán yízhì. ˌ**see for oneˈself** 亲〔親〕自去看 qīnzì qù kàn. **see how the ˈland lies** 了解情况 liáojiě qíngkuàng. ˌ**seeing is beˈlieving** 眼见为〔爲〕实〔實〕 yǎn jiàn wéi shí. **see the ˈlight** (a) 领悟 lǐngwù. (b) 皈依某宗教 guīyī mǒuzōngjiào. **see ˈred** 大怒 dànù. **see ˈsense** 明白事理 míngbai shìlǐ. **be ˈseeing things** 产〔產〕生幻觉 chǎnshēng huànjué. 12 [短语动词] **see about sth** 处〔處〕理(某事)chǔlǐ. **see sb about sth** 接受劝〔勸〕告 jiēshòu quàngào. **see sth in sb/sth** 觉得…有吸引力(或有意思) juédé… yǒu xīyǐnlì. **see sb off** 为…送行 wèi… sòngxíng. **see through sb/sth** 识〔識〕破 shípò. **see sth through** 把…进〔進〕行到底 bǎ… jìnxíng dàodǐ. **see to sth** 照看 zhàokàn; 关〔關〕照 guānzhào.

see[2] /siː/ *n*[C] [正式用语]主教的辖区〔區〕(或职位) zhǔjiào de xiáqū.

seed /siːd/ *n* 1 [C]种〔種〕子 zhǒngzi. 2 [U] (种植、喂鸟等的)种子 zhǒngzi. 3 [C,常作 pl]根源 gēnyuán: *the* ~*s of doubt* 不信任的根源. 4[C](尤指网球)种子选〔選〕手 zhǒngzi xuǎnshǒu. 5 [习语] **go to seed** (a) (植物)花谢结籽 huāxiè jiēzǐ. (b) (人)衰老 shuāilǎo; 不修边〔邊〕幅 bù xiū biānfú. **seed** *v* 1 [I](植物)结子 jiēzǐ. 2 [T]播种 bōzhòng. 3 [T](尤指网球,按得胜机会)安排(种子选手)的出场〔場〕次序 ānpái … de chūchǎng cìxù. **seedless** *adj* 无〔無〕子的 wúzǐde. **seedling** *n* [C] 幼苗 yòumiáo.

seedy /ˈsiːdɪ/ *adj* [-ier, -iest] 1 褴〔襤〕褛〔褸〕的 lánlǚde; 破旧〔舊〕的 pòjiùde. 2 [非正式用语]不舒服的 bù shūfu de: *feel* ~ 觉得不舒服. **seediness** *n* [U].

seek /siːk/ *v* [*pt*, *pp* sought /sɔːt/] [正式用语]1 [I, T]寻〔尋〕找 xúnzhǎo. 2 [T]请求 qǐngqiú: ~ *advice* 请教. 3 [T] [正式用语]设法 shèfǎ: ~ *to end the conflict* 试图结束冲突.

seem /siːm/ *v* [I] 好像 hǎoxiàng; 似乎 sìhū: *This book* ~*s interesting*. 这本书似乎有趣. **seeming** *adj* 表面上的 biǎomiànshàngde; 貌似的 màosìde: *her* ~*ing friendliness* 她表面上友好. **seemingly** *adv*.

seemly /ˈsiːmlɪ/ *adj* [-ier, -iest] (行为)恰当〔當〕的 qiàdàngde; 适〔適〕宜的 shìyíde; 得体〔體〕的 détǐde.

seen /siːn/ *pp* of SEE[1].

seep /siːp/ *v* [I] (液体)渗〔滲〕出 shènchū; 渗漏 shènlòu: *water* ~*ing through the cracks* 从裂缝渗出的水. **seepage** /-ɪdʒ/ *n* [U]渗出 shènchū; 渗漏 shènlòu.

seesaw /ˈsiːsɔː/ *n* 1 [C] 跷〔蹺〕跷板 qiāoqiāobǎn. 2 [sing]上下(或往复)的移动〔動〕shàngxià de yídòng. **seesaw** *v*[I] 上下(或来回)移动 shàngxià yídòng.

seethe /siːð/ *v* [I] 1 发〔發〕怒 fānù; 激动〔動〕 jīdòng: *seething (with rage) at his behaviour* 被他的行为(气得)火冒三丈. 2 (液体)起泡 qǐpào; 冒泡 màopào.

segment /ˈsegmənt/ *n*[C] 1 段 duàn; 节〔節〕 jié; 弓形 gōngxíng; 部分 bùfen. 2 (橙子、柠檬等的)瓣 bàn.

segregate /ˈsegrɪgeɪt/ *v* [T]使隔离〔離〕shǐ gélí; 对〔對〕…实〔實〕行种〔種〕族隔离 duì…shíxíng zhǒngzú gélí. **segregation** /ˌsegrɪˈgeɪʃn/ *n*[U].

seismic /ˈsaɪzmɪk/ *adj* 地震的 dìzhènde.

seize /siːz/ *v* 1 [T] 抓住 zhuāzhù; 捉住 zhuōzhù. 2 [I, T] 把握(时机等) bǎwò: ~*d (on) a chance to get revenge* 抓住机会报仇. 3[短语动词]**seize up** (机器)卡住 qiǎzhù.

seizure /ˈsiːʒə(r)/ *n* 1[C, U] 没收 mòshōu; 扣押 kòuyā. 2[C] (疾病的)发〔發〕作 fāzuò.

seldom /ˈseldəm/ *adv* 不常 bùcháng; 难〔難〕得 nándé.

select /sɪˈlekt/ *v* [T] 选〔選〕择〔擇〕 xuǎnzé; 挑选 tiāoxuǎn. **select** *adj* 1 精选的 jīngxuǎn-

S

de. 2 选择成员严〔嚴〕格的 xuǎnzé chéngyuán yángé de: *a ~ audience* 经过挑选的观众. **selection** /-kʃn/ *n* 1 [U]选择 xuǎnzé; 挑选 tiāoxuǎn. 2 [C]选中之物 xuǎn zhòng zhī wù; 供选择之物 gōng xuǎnzé zhī wù. **selective** *adj* 1 选择的 xuǎnzéde; 选择性的 xuǎnzéxìngde. 2 挑拣〔揀〕的 tiāojiǎnde.

self /self/ [*pl* **selves** /selvz/] *n* [C, U]本性 běnxìng; 本质〔質〕běnzhì; 自己 zìjǐ; 自我 zìwǒ.

self- /self-/ *prefix* 表示"自身的","由自身的","对〔對〕自身的" biǎoshì "zìshēnde", "yóu zìshēn de", "duì zìshēn de". ˌ**self-as'sured** *adj* 自信的 zìxìnde. ˌ**self-'catering** *adj* (假日、住宿等)自供伙食的 zì gōng huǒshí de. ˌ**self-'centred** *adj* 自我中心的 zìwǒ zhōngxīn de. ˌ**self-'confident** *adj* 自信的 zìxìnde. ˌ**self-'confidence** *n* [U]. ˌ**self-'conscious** *adj* (在他人面前)不自然的 bú zìrán de; 神经〔經〕过〔過〕敏的 shénjīng guòmǐn de. ˌ**self-'consciousness** *n* [U]. ˌ**self-con'tained** *adj* 1 不流露情感的 bù liúlù qínggǎn de; (人)不依赖他人的 bù yīlài tārén de. 2 (住所)有独〔獨〕立设施的 yǒu dúlì shèshī de; 门户独立的 ménhù dúlì de. ˌ**self-con'trol** *n* [U] 自我控制 zìwǒ kòngzhì; 自制 zìzhì. ˌ**self-de'fence** *n* [U] 自卫〔衛〕zìwèi. ˌ**self-em'ployed** *adj* 自己经营〔營〕的 zìjǐ jīngyíng de; 非受雇〔僱〕于人的 fēi shòugù yú rén de. ˌ**self-es'teem** *n*[U] 自尊 zìzūn; 自负 zìfù. ˌ**self-'evident** *adj* 不证〔證〕自明的 bú zhèng zì míng de. ˌ**self-'help** *n* [U] 自助 zìzhù; 自立 zìlì. ˌ**self-im'portant** *adj* [贬]自视过高的 zì shì guò gāo de. ˌ**self-im'portance** *n* [U] [贬]. ˌ**self-in'dulgent** *adj* [贬]放纵〔縱〕自己的 fàngzòng zìjǐ de. ˌ**self-in'dulgence** *n* [U]. ˌ**self-'interest** *n* [U] 私利 sīlì. ˌ**self-'pity** *n* [U][常作贬]自怜〔憐〕zìlián. ˌ**self-re'liant** *adj* 依靠自己的 yīkào zìjǐ de. ˌ**self-re'liance** *n* [U]. ˌ**self-re'spect** *n* [U] 自尊 zìzūn. ˌ**self-'righteous** *adj* 自以为〔爲〕是的 zì yǐwéi shì de. ˌ**self-'sacrifice** *n* [U] 自我牺〔犧〕牲 zìwǒ xīshēng. '**selfsame** *adj* 完全相同的 wánquán xiāngtóng de. ˌ**self-'satisfied** *adj* [贬]沾沾自喜的 zhānzhān zìxǐ de; 自鸣得意的 zì míng déyì de. ˌ**self-'service** *n* [U]自我服务〔務〕zìwǒ fúwù; 自助 zìzhù. '**self-suf'ficient** *adj* 自给自足的 zìjǐ zìzú de. ˌ**self-'willed** *adj* 任性的 rènxìngde; 固执〔執〕的 gùzhíde.

selfish /'selfɪʃ/ *adj* [贬]自私的 zìsīde; 利己的 lìjǐde. **selfishly** *adv*. **selfishness** *n* [U].

sell /sel/ *v* [*pt*, *pp* **sold** /səʊld/] 1 [I, T] 卖〔賣〕mài; 售 shòu; 销 xiāo. 2 [T] 经〔經〕售 jīngshòu; 经销 jīngxiāo: *Do you ~ needles?* 你卖针吗? 3 [I] 被售出 bèi shòu chū; 有销路 yǒu xiāolù; 有人买〔買〕yǒu rén mǎi: *Does this book ~ well?* 这种书销路好吗? 4[T]将〔將〕(某物)卖出 jiāng…màichū: *Scandals ~ newspapers*. 丑闻使报纸有了销路. 5 [T] 说服 shuōfú; 使接受 shǐ jiēshòu: *~ sb an idea* 说服某人接受某个主张. 6 [T] ~ **oneself** (a) 自我宣传〔傳〕zìwǒ xuānchuán; 推销自己 tuīxiāo zìjǐ. (b) (接受金钱等)出卖自己 chūmài zìjǐ. 7[习语] **sell sb/sth short** 认〔認〕识〔識〕不到…的真实〔實〕价〔價〕值 rènshi bú dào … de zhēnshí jiàzhí. **sell one's soul (to the devil)** (为名利)出卖灵〔靈〕魂 chūmài línghún. 8 [短语动词] **sell sth off** 甩卖 shuǎimài. **sell out** (a) 售完 shòuwán. (b) 背叛 bèipàn. **sell up** 出售(所有财物)chūshòu.

Sellotape /'seləʊteɪp/ *n* [U] [英国专利名] (透明的)胶〔膠〕带〔帶〕jiāodài: *mend a torn map with S~* 用胶带修补破损的地图.

selves *pl* of SELF.

semantics /sɪ'mæntɪks/ *n* [U] 语义〔義〕学〔學〕yǔyìxué.

semaphore /'seməfɔː(r)/ *n* [U] 旗语 qíyǔ. **semaphore** *v* [I, T]打旗语 dǎ qíyǔ; 用旗语发〔發〕出(信息) yòng qíyǔ fāchū.

semblance /'sembləns/ *n* [sing, U]外观〔觀〕wàiguān; 外表 wàibiǎo; 外貌 wàimào: *create a/some ~ of order* 造成表面上有秩序的样子.

semen /'siːmən/ *n* [U] 精液 jīngyè.

semi- /semɪ-/ *prefix* 表示"半","部分地" biǎoshì "bàn", "bùfende": *~-literate* 半文盲. '**semicircle** *n* [C] 半圆 bànyuán; 半圆形 bànyuánxíng. '**semicolon** *n* [C] 分号〔號〕(即";") fēnhào. '**semiconductor** *n* [C] 半导〔導〕体〔體〕bàndǎotǐ. ˌ**semi-de'tached** *adj* (住宅)半独〔獨〕立式的 bàndúlìshìde; (房子)与〔與〕另一房子共用一墙〔牆〕的 yǔ lìngyī fángzi gòngyòng yìqiáng de. ˌ**semi'final** *n*[C] 半决赛 bànjuésài.

seminar /'semɪnɑː(r)/ *n* [C] (专题)研讨会〔會〕yántǎohuì.

senate /'senɪt/ *n* [C, 亦作 sing 用 pl v]1 参〔參〕议〔議〕院 cānyìyuàn. 2 (某些大学的)理事会〔會〕lǐshìhuì, 评议会 píngyìhuì. **senator** (亦作 **Senator**) *n*[C]参议员 cānyìyuán.

send /send/ *v* [*pt*, *pp* **sent**] [T]1 寄 jì; 发〔發〕送 fāsòng: *~ a letter* 寄信. 2 使迅速移动〔動〕shǐ xùnsù yídòng: *The explosion sent them running*. 那次爆炸使他们四散奔逃. 3 使进〔進〕入(特定状态) shǐ jìnrù: *~ sb to sleep* 使某人入睡. 4 [习语] **send sb one's love** ⇨LOVE. 5 [短语动词] **send away for sth** 函购〔購〕hángòu; 函索 hánsuǒ. **send sb away** 解雇〔僱〕jiěgù. **send for sb/sth** 派人去叫 pài rén qù jiào; 派人去拿 pài rén qù ná.

S

send off for sth = SEND AWAY FOR STH. **send sth out** (a) 发出 fāchū; 放出 fàngchū; 射出 shèchū: *The sun ~s out light*. 太阳发出光. (b) 生出 shēngchū; 长〔長〕出 zhǎngchū: *plants that ~ out shoots* 长出芽的植物. **send sb/sth up** [非正式用语](用模仿的方式)取笑 qǔxiào. **'send-off** *n* [C]送行 sòngxíng; 送别 sòngbié.

senile /'si:naɪl/ *adj* 衰老的 shuāilǎode; 老年的 lǎoniánde. **senility** /sɪ'nɪlətɪ/ *n* [U].

senior /'si:nɪə(r)/ *adj* 1 (*to*)年长〔長〕的 niánzhǎngde; (地位等)较高的 jiàogāode. 2 Senior (父或母与子女同名时, 指年长者)长者 zhǎngzhě. **senior** *n* 1 [sing]较年长者 jiào niánzhǎng zhě: *He is three years her ~*. 他比她大三岁. 2 [C, 常作 pl]高年级学〔學〕生 gāoniánjí xuéshēng. **ˌsenior 'citizen** *n* [C] 老年人(指退休者) lǎoniánrén. **seniority** /ˌsi:nɪ'ɒrətɪ/ *n* [U]年长 niánzhǎng; 资深 zīshēn; 职〔職〕位高 zhíwèi gāo.

sensation /sen'seɪʃn/ *n* 1 [C, U]感觉〔覺〕gǎnjué; 感觉能力 gǎnjué nénglì. 2 [C, U]轰〔轟〕动〔動〕hōngdòng; 激动 jīdòng. **sensational** *adj* 1 轰动的 hōngdòngde; 令人兴〔興〕奋〔奮〕的 lìng rén xīngfèn de. 2 [非正式用语]绝妙的 juémiàode; 极〔極〕好的 jíhǎode.

sense /sens/ *n* 1 [C] 官能 guānnéng; 感官 gǎnguān. 2 [pl] 心智健全 xīnzhì jiànquán: *take leave of one's ~s* 发疯. 3 [sing]领悟 lǐngwù: *a ~ of humour* 幽默感. 4 [C]感觉〔覺〕gǎnjué: *a ~ of dread* 恐惧感. 5 [U]识〔識〕别(或判断)力 shíbiélì: *There's no ~ in doing that*. 做那件事没有道理. 6 [C](词等的)意义〔義〕yìyì. 7 [习语] **make sense** (a) 有意义 yǒu yìyì; 讲〔講〕得通 jiǎng dé tōng. (b) 是合情合理的 shì héqíng hélǐ de; 是明智的 shì míngzhì de. **make sense of sth** 理解 lǐjiě; 弄懂 nòngdǒng. **sense** *v* [T] 感觉到 gǎnjué dào; 意识到 yìshi dào: *~ danger* 意识到有危险.

senseless /'senslɪs/ *adj* 1 愚蠢的 yúchǔnde. 2 失去知觉〔覺〕的 shīqù zhījué de. **senselessly** *adv*. **senselessness** *n* [U].

S

sensibility /sensə'bɪlətɪ/ *n* [C, 常作 pl] 识〔識〕别力 shíbiélì; 敏感性 mǐngǎnxìng.

sensible /'sensəbl/ *adj* 1 识〔識〕别力强的 shíbiélì qiáng de; 合情理的 hé qínglǐ de; 切合实〔實〕际〔際〕的 qièhé shíjì de: *a ~ person/idea* 通情达理的人; 明智的主意. 2 ~ **of sth** [正式用语]觉〔覺〕察到 juéchá dào. **sensibly** *adv*.

sensitive /'sensətɪv/ *adj* 1 (*to*) 易受伤〔傷〕害的 yì shòu shānghài de; 易损坏〔壞〕的 yì sǔnhuài de; 敏感的 mǐngǎnde: *~ skin* 娇嫩的皮肤. *~ to light* 对光敏感. 2 易生气〔氣〕的 yì shēngqì de; 神经〔經〕质〔質〕的 shénjīngzhìde: *~ about his baldness* 对他自己秃头神经过敏. 3 [褒]有细腻感情的 yǒu xìnì gǎnqíng de; 理解的 lǐjiěde: *a ~ friend* 感情细腻的朋友. 4(仪器)灵〔靈〕敏的 língmǐnde. 5 需小心对待的 xū xiǎoxīn duìdài de: *a ~ issue* 需慎重对待的问题. **sensitivity** *n* [U]敏感性 mǐngǎnxìng.

sensitize /'sensɪtaɪz/ *v* [T] (*to*) 使敏感 shǐ mǐngǎn.

sensual /'senʃʊəl/ *adj* 1 感官享乐〔樂〕的 gǎnguān xiǎnglè de. 2 享受肉体〔體〕上快乐的(尤指性的) xiǎngshòu ròutǐshàng kuàilè de. **sensuality** /-'ælətɪ/ *n* [U]纵〔縱〕欲〔慾〕zòngyù.

sensuous /'senʃʊəs/ *adj* 刺激感官的 cìjī gǎnguān de; 给感官以快感的 gěi gǎnguān yǐ kuàigǎn de. **sensuously** *adv*. **sensuousness** *n* [U].

sent *pt*, *pp* of SEND.

sentence /'sentəns/ *n* 1 [C] [语法]句子 jùzi; 句 jù. 2 [C, U]判决 pànjué; 宣判 xuānpàn. **sentence** *v* [T] 判决 pànjué; 宣判 xuānpàn: *~ sb to death* 判某人死刑.

sentiment /'sentɪmənt/ *n* 1 [U, C, 常作 pl] 态〔態〕度 tàidù; 意见 yìjiàn. 2 [U][常作贬]脆弱的感情 cuìruòde gǎnqíng; 易激动〔動〕的感情 yì jīdòng de gǎnqíng. 3 **sentiments** [pl] 观〔觀〕点〔點〕guāndiǎn; 意见 yìjiàn.

sentimental /ˌsentɪ'mentl/ *adj* 1 情感的 qínggǎnde; 情绪的 qíngxùde. 2 [常作贬]感情脆弱的 gǎnqíng cuìruò de. **sentimentality** /-'tælətɪ/ *n* [U]情感过〔過〕于脆弱的特性 qínggǎn guòyú cuìruò de tèxìng. **sentimentally** *adv*.

sentry /'sentrɪ/ *n* [C] [*pl* -ies] 哨兵 shàobīng; 步哨 bùshào.

separate[1] /'seprət/ *adj* 1 不相连的 bù xiānglián de; 分开〔開〕的 fēnkāide: *~ rooms* 独用房间. 2 不同的 bùtóngde: *on three ~ occasions* 在三个不同场合. **separately** *adv*.

separate[2] /'sepəreɪt/ *v* 1 [I, T] (使)分离〔離〕fēnlí; (使)分开〔開〕fēnkāi. 2 [I](夫妻)分居 fēnjū. **separation** /-'reɪʃn/ *n* 1 [U] 分离 fēnlí; 分开 fēnkāi. 2[C] 分开的期间 fēnkāide qījiān. 3 [U, sing][法律](夫妇)分居 fēnjū.

September /sep'tembə(r)/ *n* [U, C] 九月 jiǔyuè.

septic /'septɪk/ *adj* 脓〔膿〕毒性的 nóngdúxìngde; 由病菌感染的 yóu bìngjūn gǎnrǎn de: *a ~ wound* 感染的伤口.

sepulchre (美语 **sepulcher**) /'seplkə(r)/ *n* [C][古](尤指在岩石中凿出的)坟墓 fénmù; 冢〔塚〕zhǒng.

sequel /'si:kwəl/ *n* [C] 1 后〔後〕续〔續〕hòuxù; 随〔隨〕之而来的事 suí zhī ér lái de shì. 2

续集 xùjí；续篇 xùpiān.

sequence /ˈsiːkwəns/ *n* [C, U] 一连串 yìliánchuàn；次序 cìxù；顺序 shùnxù.

sequin /ˈsiːkwɪn/ *n* [C] (衣服上作饰物用的)闪光装〔裝〕饰片 shǎnguāng zhuāngshìpiàn.

serene /sɪˈriːn/ *adj* 平静的 píngjìngde；宁〔寧〕静的 níngjìngde. **serenely** *adv*. **serenity** /sɪˈrenətɪ/ *n* [U].

sergeant /ˈsɑːdʒənt/ *n* [C] 1 中士 zhōngshì；军士 jūnshì. 2 巡佐 xúnzuǒ.

serial /ˈsɪərɪəl/ *n* [C]连载小说 liánzǎi xiǎoshuō；连本广〔廣〕播节〔節〕目 liánběn guǎngbō jiémù. **serial** *adj* 连续〔續〕的 liánxùde；连载的 liánzǎide；分次广播的 fēncì guǎngbō de. **serialize** /-aɪz/ *v* [T]连载 liánzǎi；连播 liánbō. ˈ**serial number** *n*[C] (纸币、支票等的)编号〔號〕biānhào.

series /ˈsɪəriːz/ *n* [C] [*pl* **series**] 连续〔續〕liánxù；接连 jiēlián；一系列 yíxìliè.

serious /ˈsɪərɪəs/ *adj* 1 严〔嚴〕肃〔肅〕的 yánsùde；庄〔莊〕重的 zhuāngzhòngde：*a* ～ *face* 严肃的面孔. 2 (书、音乐等)启〔啟〕发〔發〕思考的 qǐfā sīkǎo de. 3 严重的 yánzhòngde；危急的 wēijíde：*a* ～ *illness* 重病. 4 (*about*) 真诚的 zhēnchéngde；认〔認〕真的 rènzhēnde：*Are you* ～ *about this plan?* 这个计划你是认真对待吗? **seriously** *adv*. **seriousness** *n* [U].

sermon /ˈsɜːmən/ *n* [C] 讲〔講〕道 jiǎngdào；布道 bùdào.

serpent /ˈsɜːpənt/ *n* [C] [旧或诗]蛇 shé.

serrated /seˈreɪtɪd/ *adj* 有锯齿〔齒〕的 yǒu jùchǐ de.

serum /ˈsɪərəm/ [*pl* ～**s** 或 **sera** /ˈsɪərə/] *n* [C, U] 血清 xuèqīng.

servant /ˈsɜːvənt/ *n* [C] 仆〔僕〕人 púrén；佣〔傭〕人 yōngrén.

serve /sɜːv/ *v* 1 [I, T]为〔爲〕…工作 wèi…gōngzuò；当〔當〕仆〔僕〕人 dāng púrén. 2 [I, T] 供职〔職〕gòngzhí；服役 fúyì：～ *on a committee* 担任委员. 3 [I, T] (a)端上(饭菜)duān shàng. (b)(商店)接待(顾客)jiēdài. 4 [T]提供(服务) tígōng：*This bus* ～*s our area*. 这辆公共汽车为我们地区提供服务. 5[I](*for/as sth*) 适〔適〕合 shìhé：*This room* ～*s as a study*. 这个房间可作书房用. 6[T] 在狱中服刑 zài yùzhōng fúxíng：～ *a life sentence* 服无期徒刑. 7 [T][法律]送达〔達〕sòngdá. 8 [I, T] (网球等)发〔發〕(球) fā. 9 [习语] **serve sb right** 给某人应〔應〕得的惩〔懲〕罚 gěi mǒurén yīngdé de chéngfá. **serve** *n*[C](网球等的)发球 fāqiú. **server** *n* 1 (网球等的)发球人 fāqiúrén. 2 (计算机)服务〔務〕器 fúwùqì. **serving** *n* [C] (食物的)一份(或一客)yífèn.

service /ˈsɜːvɪs/ *n* 1[U]任职〔職〕rènzhí；服务〔務〕fúwù：*ten years'* ～ *in the army* 在军队服役十年. 2[U](车辆的)用处〔處〕yòngchù：*This car has given good* ～. 这辆汽车很好用. 3 [U](旅馆、餐馆等)接待顾〔顧〕客 jiēdài gùkè. 4[C]公用事业〔業〕的业务(或工作) gōngyòng shìyè de yèwù：*a* ˈ*bus* ～公共汽车营运. 5[C, 常作 pl]帮〔幫〕助 bāngzhù. 6[C] (政府的)部门 bùmén. 7 [C]军种〔種〕jūnzhǒng. 8 [C]礼〔禮〕拜仪〔儀〕式 lǐbài yíshì；宗教仪式 zōngjiào yíshì. 9 [C] 整套餐具 zhěngtào cānjù. 10[C, U](车辆、机器等的)维修 wéixiū. 11 [C](网球)发〔發〕球 fāqiú. 12[习语]**at your service** 随时〔時〕为〔爲〕你效劳〔勞〕suíshí wèi nǐ xiàoláo. **of service** 有用 yǒuyòng；有帮助 yǒu bāngzhù. **service** *v* [T] 维修(售出后的车辆等) wéixiū. **serviceable** *adj* 耐用的 nàiyòngde；有用的 yǒuyòngde. ˈ**service charge** *n*[C] 服务费 fúwùfèi；小费 xiǎofèi. ˈ**service industry** *n* [C] 服务业 fúwùyè. ˈ**serviceman** /-mən/ *n* [C] [*pl* **-men** /-mən/, *fem* ˈ**servicewoman** /-wʊmən/, *pl* **-women** /-wɪmɪn/] 军人 jūnrén. ˈ**service station** *n* [C] = PETROL STATION (PETROL).

serviette /ˌsɜːvɪˈet/ *n* = NAPKIN.

session /ˈseʃən/ *n* [C] 1(议会的)会〔會〕议〔議〕huìyì；(法庭的)开〔開〕庭 kāitíng. 2 学〔學〕年 xuénián；学期 xuéqī. 3 (从事某项活动的)一段时〔時〕间 yíduàn shíjiān：*a re*ˈ*cording* ～ 一场录音.

set[1] /set/ *n* 1[C]一套 yítào；一副 yífù；一组 yìzǔ. 2[C]收音机〔機〕shōuyīnjī；电〔電〕视机 diànshìjī. 3 [C, 亦作 sing 用 pl v](因志趣等相同而相互交往的)一群人 yìqúnrén. 4[C]布景 bùjǐng；场〔場〕景 chǎngjǐng. 5 [C](网球赛的)(一)盘〔盤〕pán. 6 [C]做(或卷)头〔頭〕发〔髮〕zuò tóufa.

set[2] /set/ *v* [-tt-; *pt*, *pp* **set**] 1 [T]放 fàng；置 zhì；摆〔擺〕放 bǎifàng：～ *a tray down on the table* 把托盘放在桌上. 2[T]使处〔處〕于某种〔種〕状〔狀〕态〔態〕shǐ chǔyú mǒuzhǒng zhuàngtài：～ *a prisoner free* 释放一犯人. 3[T]使开〔開〕始做 shǐ kāishǐ zuò：～ *sb thinking* 激发某人的思考. 4[T]指定 zhǐdìng；提出 tíchū：～ *an examination* 布置考试. 5 [T]调整好(使之可用) tiáozhěng hǎo：～ *the controls* 调整好控制装置. 6[T]在…上摆餐具(准备用餐)zài…shang bǎi cānjù. 7 [T]安排 ānpái；确〔確〕定 quèdìng：～ *a date for the wedding* 确定结婚的日期. 8[T]镶嵌 xiāngqiàn. 9 [I, T](使)变〔變〕硬 biànyìng；(使)凝固 nínggù：*The cement has* ～. 水泥已凝固. 10 [T]将〔將〕…接好(或复位)jiāng…jiēhǎo：～ *a broken bone* 使折骨复位. 11[T] (*to*)为〔爲〕(诗、歌)谱曲 wèi pǔqǔ；配乐〔樂〕pèiyuè. 12[I] (日、月)落 luò. 13[习语] **set an** ˈ**example** 树〔樹〕立榜样〔樣〕shùlì bǎngyàng. **set** ˈ**eyes on**

看见 kànjiàn. **set 'foot in** 进〔進〕入 jìnrù. **set 'light/'fire to sth, set sth on 'fire** 引火烧〔燒〕某物 yǐn huǒ shāo mǒuwù;使某物开始燃烧 shǐ mǒuwù kāishǐ ránshāo. **set one's 'heart on sth** 渴望 kěwàng. **set one's mind to sth** ⇨ MIND[1]. **set sth right** ⇨ RIGHT[1]. **set sb/sth to rights** ⇨ RIGHT[3]. **set sail** 启〔啟〕航 qǐháng. **set the 'scene** 描述实〔實〕况 miáoshù shíkuàng;叙述背景 xùshù bèijǐng. **set sb's 'teeth on edge** 使人难〔難〕受的 shǐ rén nánshòu de;恼〔惱〕人的 nǎorénde. 14 [短语动词] **set about sb** 攻击〔擊〕(或抨击) gōngjī. **set about sth** 开始 kāishǐ;着手 zhuóshǒu. **set sb back** [非正式用语]使花费 shǐ huāfèi. **set sb/sth back** 推迟〔遲〕tuīchí;耽搁 dānge;阻碍〔礙〕zǔ'ài. **set sth back (from)** 置于远〔遠〕处 zhì yú yuǎnchù. **set in** 开始(并可能持续) kāishǐ. **set off** 出发〔發〕chūfā;启程 qǐchéng. **set sth off** (a) 使爆炸 shǐ bàozhà. (b) 使开始 shǐ kāishǐ. (c)使有吸引力 shǐ yǒu xīyǐnlì: *This colour ~s off her eyes*. 这颜色把她的眼睛衬托得更漂亮了. **set on sb** 攻击 gōngjī. **set out** 出发 chūfā;启程 qǐchéng. **set out to do sth** (为某目的)开始做 kāishǐ zuò. **set sth out** (a) 安排 ānpái. (b) 陈述 chénshù;阐明 chǎnmíng: ~ *out one's ideas in an essay* 在短文中阐明自己的主张. **set 'to** 开始做 kāishǐ zuò. **set sth up** (a)摆〔擺〕放 bǎifàng;竖〔豎〕起 shùqǐ. (b) 创〔創〕立 chuànglì;开办〔辦〕kāibàn. **set (oneself) up as** (a)从〔從〕事(或经营)某种行业〔業〕cóngshì mǒuzhǒng hángyè. (b) 声称〔稱〕shēngchēng; 自称 zìchēng. **'set-back** *n*[C]妨碍发展的事物 fáng'ài fāzhǎn de shìwù. **'set-up** *n*[C] [非正式用语]组织〔織〕的结构〔構〕zǔzhīde jiégòu.

set[3] /set/ *adj* 1 [非正式用语]作好准〔準〕备〔備〕的 zuò hǎo zhǔnbèi de: ~ *to go* 准备好走. 2 (*on*)坚〔堅〕决的 jiānjuéde: *She's ~ on winning* 她决心获胜. 3 固定不变〔變〕的 gùdìng búbiàn de: *a ~ grin* 老是咧嘴笑. ~ *ideas about sth* 对某事的固定看法. 4 [习语] **set in one's ways** 积〔積〕习〔習〕难〔難〕改的 jīxí nángǎi de. **set book** *n*[C] 必修课本 bìxiū kèběn.

S

set-square /'set skweə(r)/ *n* [C] 三角板 sānjiǎobǎn.

settee /se'tiː/ *n* [C] = SOFA.

setter /'setə(r)/ *n* [C] 塞特种〔種〕猎〔獵〕犬 sàitèzhǒng lièquǎn.

setting /'setɪŋ/ *n* 1 [C]镶嵌 xiāngqiàn. 2 [C]环〔環〕境 huánjìng: *a rural ~* 乡村环境. 3[C](控制装置的)调节〔節〕tiáojié;位置的设定 wèizhìde shèdìng;挡〔擋〕dǎng. 4[sing](日、月等的)沉落 chénluò.

settle /'setl/ *v* 1 [I,T] 移民于(某地) yímín yú. 2 [I] 停歇 tíngxiē: *The bird ~d on a branch*. 那只鸟落在树枝上了. 3[I,T](使)舒适〔適〕shūshì: ~*d (back) in the chair* 舒舒服服地坐在椅子上. 4 [I,T] 支付 zhīfù;结算 jiésuàn. 5 [I,T](使)平静(或安静) píngjìng: ~ *sb's nerves* 使某人镇静下来. 6 [T]对〔對〕…达〔達〕成协〔協〕议〔議〕duì… dáchéng xiéyì;结束(争端)jiéshù;使和解 shǐ héjiě: ~ *an argument* 解决一争论. 7[I,T] (使)下沉 xiàchén;下降 xiàjiàng: *dust settling on the floor* 落在地上的灰尘. *The rain ~d the dust*. 雨水打落了灰尘. 8[短语动词] **settle down** 舒适地坐(或躺) shūshìde zuò. **settle (down) to sth** 全神贯注 quán shén guàn zhù;定下心来 dìng xià xīn lái. **settle for sth** 勉强认〔認〕可 miǎnqiǎng rènkě. **settle (sb) in** (帮助某人)在新居安顿下来 zài xīnjū āndùn xiàlái. **settle on sb/sth** 选〔選〕定 xuǎndìng;决定 juédìng. **settled** *adj* 不变〔變〕的 búbiànde: ~*d weather* 稳定的天气. **settler** *n*[C]移居者 yíjūzhě;移民 yímín.

settlement /'setlmənt/ *n* 1 [C,U] (纠纷、问题等)解决 jiějué;协〔協〕议〔議〕xiéyì;和解 héjiě. 2 [C]财产〔產〕(或金钱)的赠与〔與〕(或转让) cáichǎnde zèngyǔ. 3 [U,C]移民 yímín;殖民 zhímín.

seven /'sevn/ *pron*, *adj*, *n* [C] 七(的)qī. **seventh** /'sevnθ/ *pron*, *adj* 第七(的) dìqī. **seventh** *pron*, *n*[C] 七分之一 qīfēn zhī yī.

seventeen /ˌsevn'tiːn/ *pron*, *adj*, *n* [C] 十七(的) shíqī. **seventeenth** /ˌsevn'tiːnθ/ *pron*, *adj* 第十七(的) dìshíqī. **seventeenth** *pron*, *n*[C]十七分之一 shíqīfēn zhī yī.

seventy /'sevntɪ/ *pron*, *adj*, *n* [C] 七十(的) qīshí. **seventieth** /'sevntɪəθ/ *pron*, *adj* 第七十(的) dìqīshí. **seventieth** *pron*, *n* [C] 七十分之一 qīshífēn zhī yī.

sever /'sevə(r)/ *v* 1[T]切断〔斷〕qiēduàn;割断 gēduàn: ~ *a limb from the body* 割断一肢. 2 [T][喻]结束 jiéshù: ~ *relations with sb* 与某人断绝关系.

several /'sevrəl/ *adj*, *pron* 几〔幾〕个〔個〕(的) jǐgè; 数〔數〕个(的) shùgè.

severe /sɪ'vɪə(r)/ *adj* 1 严〔嚴〕格的 yángéde;严厉〔厲〕的 yánlìde: ~ *discipline* 严格的纪律. 2 恶〔惡〕劣的 èliède;猛烈的 měngliède;艰〔艱〕难〔難〕的 jiānnánde: *a ~ storm* 猛烈的风暴. **severely** *adv*. **severity** /sɪ'verətɪ/ *n* 1 [U]严格 yángé;严厉 yánlì. 2 **severities** [pl] 严厉的对〔對〕待 yánlìde duìdài;艰苦的经〔經〕历〔歷〕jiānkǔde jīnglì.

sew /səʊ/ *v* [*pt* ~**ed**, *pp* ~**n** /səʊn/] [I,T] 1 (用针线)缝 féng. 2 [短语动词]**sew sth up** (a)缝合 fénghé;缝补〔補〕féngbǔ. (b)[非正式用语]解决 jiějué.

sewage /'suːɪdʒ/ *n* [U] (下水道里的)污物

wūwù.

sewer /ˈsuːə(r)/ *n* [C] 下水道 xiàshuǐdào; 阴〔陰〕沟〔溝〕yīngōu; 污水管 wūshuǐguǎn.

sewn *pt* of SEW.

sex /seks/ *n* 1[U] 性 xìng; 性别 xìngbié. 2 [C]男人 nánrén; 女人 nǚrén. 3[U] 性交 xìngjiāo. **sexy** *adj* [-ier, -iest]性感的 xìnggǎnde. **sexily** *adv*. **sexiness** *n*[U].

sexism /ˈseksɪzəm/ *n*[U]性别偏见(尤指对女性)xìngbié piānjiàn. **sexist** *adj*, *n*[C].

sextant /ˈsekstənt/ *n* [C] 六分仪〔儀〕liùfēnyí.

sexton /ˈsekstən/ *n* [C] 教堂司事(管理教堂、敲钟、墓地等) jiàotáng sīshì.

sexual /ˈsekʃʊəl/ *adj* 性的 xìngde; 两性的 liǎngxìngde. **sexual intercourse** *n*[U] 性交 xìngjiāo. **sexuality** /-ˈæləti/ *n*[U]性别的特征〔徵〕(或特性) xìngbiéde tèzhēng; 性吸引 xìngxīyǐn; 性能力 xìngnénglì. **sexually** *adv*.

shabby /ˈʃæbɪ/ *adj* [-ier, -iest] 1 破旧〔舊〕的 pòjiùde; 衣衫褴〔襤〕褛〔褸〕的 yīshān lánlǚde. 2 (行为) 卑鄙的 bēibǐde; 不正当〔當〕的 bú zhèngdàng de. **shabbily** *adv*.

shack /ʃæk/ *n* [C] 简陋的木屋 jiǎnlòude mùwū; 棚屋 péngwū.

shackle /ˈʃækl/ *n* [C, 常作 pl] 1 镣铐 liàokào; 手铐 shǒukào; 脚镣 jiǎoliào. 2[喻]束缚 shùfù; 枷锁 jiāsuǒ. **shackle** *v*[T] 1 给…戴上镣铐 gěi…dàishàng liàokào. 2[喻]束缚 shùfù.

shade /ʃeɪd/ *n* 1[U] 荫〔蔭〕yīn; 阴〔陰〕凉处〔處〕yīnliángchù: *sit in the* ～ 坐在阴凉处. 2 [C]遮光物 zhēguāngwù: *a* ˈ*lamp-*～ 灯罩. 3 **shades** [pl] [非正式用语]墨镜 mòjìng. 4 [C]颜色 yánsè: *four* ～*s of blue* 四种深浅不同的蓝色. 5[C] 细微差别 xìwēi chābié: ～*s of meaning* 意义上的细微差别. 6 **a shade** [sing] 少量 shǎoliàng; 少许 shǎoxǔ: *a* ～ *warmer* 有点暖和. **shade** *v* 1 [T]为〔爲〕…挡〔擋〕光 wèi…dǎngguāng: ～ *one's eyes* 遮目. 2 [T]遮(光,灯等)zhē; 挡(光)dǎng. 3[T]绘〔繪〕(图画)的阴影 huì…de yīnyǐng. 4 [I](颜色)渐变〔變〕jiànbiàn: *green shading into blue* 由绿渐变为蓝.

shadow /ˈʃædəʊ/ *n* 1[C, U] 影子 yǐngzi; 阴〔陰〕影 yīnyǐng: *the* ～ *of the tree on the grass* 草地上的树影. 2[C]深色部分 shēnsè bùfen: ～*s under the eyes* 眼睛下面有黑圈. 3 [U](绘画的)暗部 ànbù. 4 **shadows** [pl]不完全的黑暗 bù wánquán de hēi'àn. 5[sing](某物的)痕迹 hénjì: *not a* ～ *of doubt* 毫无疑义. **shadow** *v* [T] 跟踪 gēnzōng; 盯…的梢 dīng…de shāo. **shadowy** *adj* 1 有影子的 yǒu yǐngzi de; 多阴凉的 duō yīnliáng de. 2 模糊的 móhude; 难〔難〕以捉摸的 nán yǐ zhuōmō de.

shady /ˈʃeɪdɪ/ *adj* [-ier, -iest] 1 背阴〔陰〕的 bèiyīnde; 遮阳〔陽〕的 zhēyángde. 2 [非正式用语]名声〔聲〕不好的 míngshēng bùhǎode; 靠不住的 kàobúzhùde: *a* ～ *character* 靠不住的人.

shaft /ʃɑːft; US ʃæft/ *n* [C] 1 箭杆〔桿〕jiàngǎn; 矛柄 máobǐng. 2(工具、斧子等的)柄 bǐng. 3 辕 yuán. 4 (矿井的)通道 tōngdào. 5 (机器的)轴 zhóu. 6 (光线等的)束 shù.

shaggy /ˈʃægɪ/ *adj* [-ier, -iest] 1(毛发)蓬乱〔亂〕的 péngluànde. 2 有粗浓〔濃〕毛发〔髮〕的 yǒu cūnóng máofà de.

shake[1] /ʃeɪk/ *v* [*pt* **shook** /ʃʊk/ , *pp* ～**n** /ˈʃeɪkən/] 1 [I, T] (使)摇动〔動〕yáodòng; 摆〔擺〕动 bǎidòng. 2 [I] 发〔發〕抖 fādǒu; 颤抖 chàndǒu. 3[T] 烦扰〔擾〕fánrǎo; 惊〔驚〕吓〔嚇〕jīngxià: *We were* ～*n by his death*. 他的逝世使我们震惊. 4 [习语] **shake hands** (**with sb**), **shake sb's hand** 握手(表示问候等) wòshǒu. **shake one's head** 摇头〔頭〕(表示否定、怀疑等) yáotóu. 5 [短语动词] **shake sb/sth off** 摆脱(某人或某事物)bǎituō. **shake sth up** 摇匀 yáoyún. ˈ**shake-up** *n*[C] 大改组 dà gǎizǔ; 大变〔變〕革 dà biàngé. **shakily** /-əlɪ/ *adv*. **shaky** *adj* [-ier, -iest] 1 (人)颤抖的 chàndǒude; 摇晃的 yáohuàngde. 2 不坚〔堅〕定的 bù jiāndìng de; 不稳〔穩〕定的 bù wěndìng de.

shake[2] /ʃeɪk/ *n* [C, 常作 sing]摇动〔動〕yáodòng; 震动 zhèndòng.

shale /ʃeɪl/ *n* [U] 页岩〔巖〕yèyán.

shall /ʃəl; 强式 ʃæl/ *modal v* [否定式 **shall not**, 缩略式 **shan't** /ʃɑːnt/, *pt* **should** / ʃʊd /, 否定式 **should not**, 缩略式 **shouldn't** /ˈʃʊdnt/] 1 (表示将来时): *We* ～/ *We'll arrive tomorrow*. 我们明天到达. 2 [正式用语](表示义务或决心): *You* ～ *have a new bike for your birthday, I promise*. 我许诺,你过生日会有一辆新的自行车. *You shan't beat me so easily next time*. 你下次不会那样容易地赢我了. 3 (表示提供意见或建议): *S*～ *I open the window?* 我可以开窗户吗? 4 (表示命令): *You* ˈ～ *go with her*. 你应当和她一起走.

shallot /ʃəˈlɒt/ *n* [C] 青葱 qīngcōng.

shallow /ˈʃæləʊ/ *adj* 1 浅〔淺〕的 qiǎnde: *a* ～ *river* 浅河. 2[贬]浅薄的 qiǎnbóde; 肤〔膚〕浅的 fūqiǎnde: *a* ～ *thinker* 肤浅的思想家. **shallowness** *n*[U]. **shallows** *n*[pl](河等的)浅水处〔處〕qiǎnshuǐchù; 浅滩〔灘〕qiǎntān.

sham /ʃæm/ *v* [-mm-] [I, T]假装〔裝〕jiǎzhuāng: ～ *illness* 装病. **sham** *n* 1 [C]假冒者 jiǎmàozhě; 赝品 yànpǐn. 2 [U] 假装 jiǎzhuāng. **sham** *adj* 假的 jiǎde; 假装的 jiǎzhuāngde: *a* ～ *fight* 模拟战.

S

shamble /ˈʃæmbl/ *v*[I] 蹒跚 pánshān；拖着脚走 tuōzhejiǎo zǒu. **shamble** *n* [sing]蹒跚 pánshān；拖着脚走的步态〔態〕tuōzhejiǎozǒu de bùtài.

shambles /ˈʃæmblz/ *n* [sing] 混乱〔亂〕hùnluàn；杂〔雜〕乱 záluàn.

shame /ʃeɪm/ *n* 1[U]羞耻 xiūchǐ；羞愧 xiūkuì：*feel ~ at having told a lie* 说谎后感到羞愧. 2[U]羞愧感 xiūkuìgǎn：*He has no ~*. 他不知羞耻. 3[U]耻辱 chǐrǔ：*bring ~ on one's family* 给某人的家庭带来耻辱. 4 [sing]遗憾的事 yíhànde shì：*It's / What a ~ you can't come*. 你不能来真是遗憾. 5 [习语] **put sb/sth to shame** 胜〔勝〕过〔過〕shèngguò；使相形见绌 shǐ xiāng xíng jiàn chù. **shame** *v*[T] 1 使感到羞耻 shǐ gǎndào xiūchǐ. 2 使蒙受羞辱 shǐ méngshòu xiūrǔ；使丢脸〔臉〕shǐ diūliǎn. 3 [短语动词] **shame sb into/out of doing sth** 使(某人)感到羞愧而做(不做)某事 shǐ gǎndào xiūkuì ér zuò mǒushì. **shamefaced** /ˌʃeɪmˈfeɪst/ *adj* 脸带〔帶〕愧色的 liǎn dài kuìsè de. **shameful** *adj* 可耻的 kěchǐde；丢脸的 diūliǎnde. **shamefully** /-əlɪ/ *adv*. **shameless** *adj* 无〔無〕耻的 wúchǐde；不知羞耻的 bùzhī xiūchǐ de.

shampoo /ʃæmˈpuː/ *n* 1[U, C] 洗发〔髮〕剂〔劑〕xǐfàjì；洗发液 xǐfàyè. 2[C]洗发 xǐfà. **shampoo** *v* [T]用洗发剂洗（头发）yòng xǐfàjì xǐ.

shamrock /ˈʃæmrɒk/ *n* [C, U]三叶草(一译白花酢浆草,爱尔兰的国花) sānyècǎo.

shandy /ˈʃændɪ/ *n* [C, U] 啤酒和柠〔檸〕檬汁混合的饮料 píjiǔ hé níngméngzhī hùnhé de yǐnliào.

shan't shall not. ⇨SHALL.

shanty town /ˈʃæntɪ taʊn/ *n*[C](城市的)棚户区〔區〕pénghùqū；贫民窟 pínmínkū.

shape /ʃeɪp/ *n* 1 [C, U] 形状〔狀〕xíngzhuàng；样〔樣〕子 yàngzi；外形 wàixíng：*a round ~* 圆形. 2[U][非正式用语]情况 qíngkuàng；状态〔態〕zhuàngtài：*She's in good ~*. 她的健康情况良好. 3[习语] **get/put sth into shape** 使有条〔條〕理 shǐ yǒu tiáolǐ. **take shape** 成形 chéngxíng. **shape** *v* 1[T] 使成形 shǐ chéngxíng：[喻] *~ sb's character* 塑造某人的性格. 2 [I] (*up*)进〔進〕展 jìnzhǎn：*Our plans are shaping up well*. 我们的计划进展顺利. **shapeless** *adj* 不定形的 bú dìngxíng de；无〔無〕形状的 wú xíngzhuàng de. **shapely** *adj* [-ier, -iest](尤指人的身材)匀称〔稱〕的 yúnchènde；形状美观〔觀〕的 xíngzhuàng měiguān de.

share /ʃeə(r)/ *n* 1 [C] 一份 yífèn；份儿〔兒〕fènr. 2[U, sing] (分担、得到等的)部分 bùfen：*your ~ of the blame* 你的一份过失. 3 [C] 股份 gǔfèn. **share** *v* 1 [T](*out*)均分 jūnfēn；分摊〔攤〕fēntān. 2[I, T] (*with*)共有 gòngyǒu；合用 héyòng：*~ a house with sb* 与某人合用一所房子. 3[I, T]分摊 fēntān；分享 fēnxiǎng：*~ (in) sb's joy* 分享某人的快乐. ˈ**shareholder** *n*[C]股东 gǔdōng. ˈ**share-out** *n* [sing]分摊 fēntān；分配 fēnpèi.

shark /ʃɑːk/ *n* [C] 1 鲨鱼 shāyú. 2 [非正式用语,贬]骗子 piànzi.

sharp /ʃɑːp/ *adj* 1 锋利的 fēnglìde；锐利的 ruìlìde：*a ~ knife* 锋利的刀. 2 轮〔輪〕廓清晰的 lúnkuò qīngxī de；明显〔顯〕的 míngxiǎnde：*a ~ outline* 清晰的轮廓. 3(弯、斜坡等)急转〔轉〕的 jízhuǎnde；陡峭的 dǒuqiàode. 4 突然的 tūránde：*a ~ rise/fall* 陡升;剧降. 5 (声音)刺耳的 cì'ěrde. 6(味道)刺鼻的 cìbíde；强烈的 qiángliède. 7 刺骨的 cìgǔde；剧〔劇〕烈的 jùliède：*a ~ wind / pain* 刺骨寒风;剧痛. 8 灵〔靈〕敏的 língmǐnde；机〔機〕警的 jījǐngde：*~ eyes* 灵敏的眼睛. 9 尖刻的 jiānkède；刻薄的 kèbóde：*~ words* 刻薄言词. 10[音乐](a)升半音的 shēng bànyīn de. (b)偏高的 piāngāode. 11[非正式用语]时〔時〕髦的 shímáode；漂亮的 piàoliàngde：*a ~ dresser* 穿着漂亮的人. **sharp** *n*[C][音乐]升半音 shēngbànyīn. **sharp** *adv* 1 准〔準〕时地 zhǔnshíde：*at seven (o'clock) ~* 7点正. 2 急剧地 jíjùde：*turn ~ left* 向左急转. 3[音乐]偏高 piāngāo. **sharpen** *v*[I, T](使)锋利 fēnglì；强烈 qiánglìè；陡峭 dǒuqiào；清晰 qīngxī. **sharpener** *n* 磨具 mójù；削具 xiāojù. **sharply** *adv*. **sharpness** *n* [U].

shatter /ˈʃætə(r)/ *v* 1 [I, T]粉碎 fěnsuì；砸碎 zásuì. 2 [T]使震惊〔驚〕shǐ zhènjīng：*~ed by the bad news* 因坏消息感到震惊. 3 [T] [非正式用语][常用被动语态]使筋疲力尽〔盡〕shǐ jīn pí lì jìn.

shave /ʃeɪv/ *v* 1 [I, T] (用剃刀)刮(胡须) guā. 2[T][非正式用语]掠过〔過〕lüèguò；擦过 cāguò. 3 [短语动词] **shave sth off (sth)** 削去 xiāoqù；刮掉 guādiào. **shave** *n* [C]剃 tì；刮 guā. **shaven** /ˈʃeɪvn/ *adj* 剃过的 tìguòde；刮过的 guāguòde. **shaver** *n*[C]电〔電〕动〔動〕剃刀 diàndòng tìdāo. **shavings** *n*[pl]刨花 bàohuā；薄木屑 bómùxiè.

shawl /ʃɔːl/ *n* [C] 披肩 pījiān；围〔圍〕巾 wéijīn.

she /ʃiː/ *pron* [用作动词的主语]她 tā；它 tā：*My sister says ~ is going*. 我的姐姐说她要走了.

sheaf /ʃiːf/ *n* [C] [*pl* **sheaves** /ʃiːvz/] 1(谷物收割后的)捆 kǔn；束 shù. 2(文件等的)束 shù，扎 zā.

shear /ʃɪə(r)/ *v* [*pt*, **~ed**, *pp* **shorn** /ʃɔːn/ 或 **~ed**] [T] 剪(羊)毛 jiǎn máo.

S

shears /ʃɪəz/ *n* [pl]大剪刀 dà jiǎndāo：*a pair of* ～ 一把大剪刀.

sheath /ʃiːθ/ *n* [C] [*pl* ～s /ʃiːðz/] 1 鞘 qiào；套 tào. 2 = CONDOM.

sheathe /ʃiːð/ *v* [T]把…插入鞘 bǎ…chārù qiào.

sheaves *pl* of SHEAF.

shed[1] /ʃed/ *n* [C] 棚 péng；货棚(或车棚等) huòpéng.

shed[2] /ʃed/ *v* [-dd-；*pt*, *pp* shed] [T]1 使脱落 shǐ tuōluò：*Flowers* ～ *their petals*. 花掉瓣. 2[正式用语]使流出 shǐ liúchū：～ *tears* 流泪. 3 去掉 qùdiào；除掉 chúdiào：～ *one's clothes* 脱掉衣服. 4 散发〔發〕sànfā：～ *light* 发出光.

she'd /ʃiːd/ 1 she had. ⇨ HAVE. 2 she would. ⇨ WILL[1], WOULD[1].

sheep /ʃiːp/ *n* [C] [*pl* sheep] 羊 yáng；绵羊 miányáng. ˈ**sheepdog** *n* [C] 牧羊犬 mùyángquǎn. ˈ**sheepskin** *n* [C, U]羊皮毯 yángpítǎn；羊皮袄〔襖〕yángpí'ǎo. **sheepish** *adj* 羞怯的 xiūqiède；局促不安的 júcù bù'ān de.

sheer /ʃɪə(r)/ *adj* 1 完全的 wánquánde；十足的 shízúde：～ *nonsense* 一派胡言. 2 (织物)极〔極〕薄的 jíbóde；透明的 tòumíngde. 3 陡峭的 dǒuqiàode；垂直的 chuízhíde：*a* ～ *drop* 垂直降落. **sheer** *adv* 陡峭地 dǒuqiàode；垂直地 chuízhíde.

sheet /ʃiːt/ *n* [C] 1 被单〔單〕bèidān；褥单 rùdān；床单 chuángdān. 2 薄板 bóbǎn；薄片 bópiàn：*a* ～ *of glass*/*paper* 一块玻璃；一张纸. 3 (水、冰等的)一片 yípiàn. ˈ**sheet music** *n*[U] (活页)乐〔樂〕谱 yuèpǔ.

sheikh (亦作 **sheik**) /ʃeɪk/ *n*[C] (阿拉伯)酋长〔長〕qiúzhǎng；首领 shǒulǐng.

shelf /ʃelf/ *n* [C] 1 架子 jiàzi；搁板 gēbǎn. 2 (悬崖上)突出的岩石 tūchūde yánshí.

shell /ʃel/ *n* [C] 1 壳〔殼〕(如蛋壳、果壳、贝壳等) qiào. 2 (尚未完工的房屋、船等的)框架 kuāngjià；骨架 gǔjià. 3 炮弹〔彈〕pàodàn. 4 [习语] **come out of one's shell** 不再羞怯(或缄默) búzài xiūqiè. **shell** *v* [T] 1 除去…的壳 chúqù…de qiào. 2 炮击〔擊〕pàojī. 3[短语动词] **shell out** [非正式用语]付(款) fù. ˈ**shellfish** *n*[C, U] [*pl* shellfish]有壳的水生动〔動〕物(如蟹、龙虾等) yǒuqiàode shuǐshēng dòngwù.

she'll /ʃiːl/ she will. ⇨ WILL[1].

shelter /ˈʃeltə(r)/ *n* 1[U] 掩蔽 yǎnbì；遮蔽 zhēbì；庇护〔護〕bìhù. 2[C] 躲避处〔處〕duǒbìchù；庇护所 bìhùsuǒ；避难〔難〕所 bìnànsuǒ. **shelter** *v* 1 [T]庇护 bìhù；为〔爲〕…提供避难所 wèi…tígòng bìnànsuǒ. 2 [I]躲避 duǒbì：～ *from the rain under the tree* 在树下避雨.

shelve[1] /ʃelv/ *v*[T] 1 把…放在架子(或搁板)上 bǎ…fàng zài jiàzi shàng. 2[喻]搁置(计划、问题等) gēzhì；缓议〔議〕huǎnyì.

shelve[2] /ʃelv/ *v* [I] (土地)逐渐倾斜 zhújiàn qīngxié.

shelves *pl* of SHELF.

shepherd /ˈʃepəd/ (*fem* **shepherdess** /ˌʃepəˈdes；*US* ˈʃepərdɪs/) *n* [C] 牧羊人 mùyángrén；羊倌 yángguān. **shepherd** *v* [T] 带〔帶〕领 dàilǐng；引导〔導〕yǐndǎo. **shepherd's pie** *n* [C, U] 肉馅土豆泥饼 ròuxiàn tǔdòuní bǐng.

sheriff /ˈʃerɪf/ *n*[C] (美国)县〔縣〕治安官 xiàn zhì'ānguān.

sherry /ˈʃerɪ/ *n* [U]雪利酒(西班牙、塞浦路斯等地所产黄色或褐色的葡萄酒) xuělìjiǔ.

shied *pt*, *pp* of SHY[2].

shield /ʃiːld/ *n* [C] 1 盾 dùn. 2 盾形徽章 dùnxíng huīzhāng. 3 (机器的)防护〔護〕装〔裝〕置 fánghù zhuāngzhì；护钣 hùbǎn. **shield** *v* [T]保护 bǎohù；庇护 bìhù.

shift[1] /ʃɪft/ *n* [C] 1(位置等的)改变〔變〕gǎibiàn；转〔轉〕变 zhuǎnbiàn. 2 轮〔輪〕班职〔職〕工 lúnbān zhígōng；班次工作时〔時〕间 bāncì gōngzuò shíjiān.

shift[2] /ʃɪft/ *v* 1 [I, T](使)改变〔變〕位置(或方向) gǎibiàn wèizhi. 2 [T][非正式用语]移开〔開〕yíkāi：～ *a stain* 去掉污迹.

shifty /ˈʃɪftɪ/ *adj* [-ier, -iest] 不可靠的 bù kěkào de；诡诈的 guǐzhàde.

shilling /ˈʃɪlɪŋ/ *n* [C] 先令(1971 年以前英国货币单位, 20 先令为 1 镑, 12 便士为 1 先令) xiānlìng.

shimmer /ˈʃɪmə(r)/ *v* [I] 发〔發〕微光 fā wēiguāng；闪光 shǎnguāng；闪烁〔爍〕shǎnshuò.

shin /ʃɪn/ *n* [C] 胫〔脛〕jìng；胫部 jìngbù. **shin** *v* [-nn-][短语动词] **shin up** (sth) 爬 pá；攀 pān.

shine /ʃaɪn/ *v* [*pt*, *pp* **shone** /ʃɒn/, 或用于下列第 3 义项时作 ～d] 1[I]照耀 zhàoyào；发〔發〕光 fāguāng；发亮 fāliàng. 2[I] (*in*/*at*) 出类〔類〕拔萃 chū lèi bá cuì：*She* ～*s in English*. 她的英语很出色. 3 [T][非正式用语]擦亮 cāliàng：～ *shoes* 把鞋擦亮. **shine** *n*[sing, U] 光亮 guāngliàng；光泽〔澤〕guāngzé：*Give your shoes a* ～. 把你的鞋擦一擦. **shiny** *adj* [-ier, -iest] 发亮的 fāliàngde；发光的 fāguāngde.

shingle /ˈʃɪŋgl/ *n* [U] (海滨)卵石 luǎnshí.

ship[1] /ʃɪp/ *n*[C] 1 海船 hǎichuán；(大)船 chuán；舰〔艦〕jiàn. 2[非正式用语]飞〔飛〕机〔機〕fēijī；飞艇 fēitǐng；宇宙飞船 yǔzhòu fēichuán. ˈ**shipmate** *n*[C] 同船船员(或旅客) tóngchuán chuányuán. ˈ**shipshape** *adj* 整齐〔齊〕的 zhěngqíde；井井有条〔條〕的 jǐngjǐng yǒu-

S

tiáo de. ˈ**shipwreck** *n* [C, U] 海难〔難〕hǎinàn; 船舶失事 chuánbó shīshì. ˈ**shipwreck** *v* [T] [常用被动语态] 使遭受海难 shǐ zāoshòu hǎinàn. ˈ**shipyard** *n* [C] 造船厂〔廠〕zàochuánchǎng.

ship[2] /ʃɪp/ *v* [-pp-] [T] (用船)运〔運〕yùn; 运送 yùnsòng. **shipment** *n* 1 [C] 装〔裝〕载的货物 zhuāngzàide huòwù. 2 [U] 装运 zhuāngyùn. **shipper** *n* [C] 托运人 tuōyùnrén; 发〔發〕货人 fāhuòrén. **shipping** *n* [U] (一国、一港口的)船舶 chuánbó; 船舶吨〔噸〕数〔數〕chuánbó dūnshù.

shirk /ʃɜːk/ *v* [I, T] 逃避(工作、责任等) táobì. **shirker** *n* [C].

shirt /ʃɜːt/ *n* [C] (男式)衬〔襯〕衫 chènshān.

shirty /ˈʃɜːtɪ/ *adj* [-ier, -iest] [非正式用语] 发〔發〕怒的 fānùde; 生气〔氣〕的 shēngqìde.

shit /ʃɪt/ *n* [⚠俚] 1 [U] 粪〔糞〕便 fènbiàn; 屎 shǐ. 2 [sing] 拉屎 lā shǐ. 3 [C] [贬] 讨厌〔厭〕的家伙 tǎoyànde jiāhuo. 4 [习语] **not give a shit (about sb/sth)** 毫不关〔關〕心 háo bù guānxīn. **shit** *v* [-tt-; *pt*, *pp* **shitted** 或 **shat** /ʃæt/] [⚠俚] 拉(屎) lā. **shit** *interj* [⚠俚] (用以表示恼怒). **shitty** *adj* [-ier, -iest] [⚠俚] 令人厌恶〔惡〕的 lìng rén yànwù de; 令人作呕〔嘔〕的 lìng rén zuò'ǒu de.

shiver /ˈʃɪvə(r)/ *v* [I] 颤抖 chàndǒu; 哆嗦 duōsuō. **shiver** *n* [C] 颤抖 chàndǒu; 哆嗦 duōsuō. **shivery** *adj*.

shoal[1] /ʃəʊl/ *n* [C] 鱼群 yúqún.

shoal[2] /ʃəʊl/ *n* [C] (海的)浅〔淺〕水处〔處〕qiǎnshuǐchù; 浅滩〔灘〕qiǎntān; 沙洲 shāzhōu.

shock /ʃɒk/ *n* 1 [C] 冲〔衝〕击〔擊〕chōngjī; 震动〔動〕zhèndòng. 2 [C] 电〔電〕震 diànzhèn; 电击 diànjī. 3 [U, C] 震惊〔驚〕zhènjīng; 惊愕 jīng'è. **shock** *v* [T] 使震惊(或惊愕、愤怒、恐惧等) shǐ zhènjīng. **shocking** *adj* 1 令人震惊的 lìng rén zhènjīng de: *~ing behaviour* 恶劣的行为. 2 [非正式用语] 极〔極〕坏〔壞〕的 jíhuàide; 糟糕的 zāogāode.

shod *pt*, *pp* of SHOE.

shoddy /ˈʃɒdɪ/ *adj* [-ier, -iest] 劣质〔質〕的 lièzhìde: *~ work* 次品.

shoe /ʃuː/ *n* [C] 1 鞋 xié. 2 [习语] **in sb's shoes** 处〔處〕于某人的地位(或处境) chǔyú mǒurénde dìwèi. **shoe** *v* [*pt*, *pp* **shod** /ʃɒd/] 给(马)钉蹄铁〔鐵〕gěi dīng títiě. ˈ**shoe-lace** *n* [C] 鞋带〔帶〕xiédài. ˈ**shoe-string** *n* [C] [习语] **on a shoestring** 以极〔極〕少的钱〔錢〕yǐ jíshǎode qián.

shone *pt*, *pp* of SHINE.

shoo /ʃuː/ *interj* 嘘! (驱赶鸟、猫、儿童时发出的声音) xū! **shoo** *v* [T] 用"嘘"声赶〔趕〕走 yòng "xū" shēng gǎnzǒu.

shook *pt* of SHAKE[1].

shoot[1] /ʃuːt/ *v* [*pt*, *pp* **shot** /ʃɒt/] 1 (a) [I, T] 开〔開〕(枪) kāi; 发〔發〕射(箭、子弹) fāshè. (b) [T] 击〔擊〕毙 jībì; 射伤〔傷〕shèshāng. 2 [I, T] 突然(或迅速)移动〔動〕tūrán yídòng: *Pain shot up his arm*. 他的手臂一阵剧痛. 3 [I, T] (为)拍照 pāizhào; 拍摄〔攝〕pāishè. 4 [I] (足球)射门 shèmén. 5 [I] (幼芽、枝、叶等)长〔長〕出 zhǎngchū; 发芽 fāyá. 6 [习语] **shoot one's mouth off** [非正式用语] 轻〔輕〕率地谈话 qīngshuàide tánhuà. ˈ**shooting-star** *n* [C] 流星 liúxīng.

shoot[2] /ʃuːt/ *n* [C] 1 芽 yá; 苗 miáo; 嫩枝 nènzhī. 2 狩猎〔獵〕shòuliè; 狩猎队〔隊〕shòulièduì.

shop /ʃɒp/ *n* [C] 1 [尤用于英国英语] 商店 shāngdiàn; 店铺 diànpù. 2 车间 chējiān; 工场〔場〕gōngchǎng; 作坊 zuōfang. 3 [习语] **talk shop** 谈论〔論〕自己的工作 tánlùn zìjǐde gōngzuò. **shop** *v* [-pp-] 1 [I] 去(商店)买〔買〕东西 qù mǎi dōngxi; 购〔購〕物 gòuwù: *~ for presents* 买礼物. 2 [T] [英俚] (向警方)告发〔發〕gàofā. 3 [短语动词] **shop around** 逐店选〔選〕购 zhú diàn xuǎngòu; 仔细寻〔尋〕找(物美价廉的商品) zǐxì xúnzhǎo. ˈ**shop assistant** *n* [C] 店员 diànyuán. ˌ**shop-ˈfloor** *n* [sing] (工厂的)生产〔產〕区〔區〕shēngchǎnqū; 工作场所 gōngzuò chǎngsuǒ. ˈ**shopkeeper** *n* [C] 店主 diànzhǔ; 零售商 língshòushāng. ˈ**shoplifter** *n* [C] 商店货物扒手 shāngdiàn huòwù páshǒu. ˈ**shoplifting** *n* [U]. ˌ**shop-ˈsteward** *n* [C] (同厂工人选出的)工会〔會〕管事 gōnghuì guǎnshì. **shopper** *n* [C]. **shopping** *n* [U] 1 买东西 mǎi dōngxi; 购物 gòuwù: *go ~ping* (去)买东西. 2 买到的东西 mǎidàode dōngxi.

shore[1] /ʃɔː(r)/ *n* [C] (海、湖等的)岸 àn; 滨〔濱〕bīn.

shore[2] /ʃɔː(r)/ *v* [短语动词] **shore sth up** (用支柱等)支撑 zhīchēng.

shorn *pp* of SHEAR.

short[1] /ʃɔːt/ *adj* 1 短的 duǎnde; 短暂〔暫〕的 duǎnzànde: *a ~ journey* 短途旅行. 2 矮的 ǎide. 3 短缺的 duǎnquēde; 不足的 bùzúde: *get ~ change* 被别人占了小便宜. 4 (*of*) (a) 不够的 búgòude: *~ of money* 缺钱. (b) 有一段距离〔離〕的 yǒu yíduàn jùlí de: *five miles ~ of our destination* 离我们的目的地有 5 英里路. 5 *on* [非正式用语] 缺少(某种特质)的 quēshǎode: *~ on tact* 不圆通. 6 (*with*) 说话尖刻的 shuōhuà jiānkè de: *I was a little ~ with her*. 我对她有点无礼. 7 [习语] **for short** 简称〔稱〕jiǎnchēng; 缩写〔寫〕suōxiě. **in short** 总〔總〕之 zǒngzhī; 简言之 jiǎn yán zhī. **in the short term** ⇨ TERM. **little / nothing short of** *n* 几〔幾〕乎 jīhū. **short cut** (a) 近路 jìnlù; 捷径〔徑〕jiéjìng. (b) 更快(或更有效)的方法 gèngkuàide fāngfǎ. ˈ**shortbread** *n* [U]

S

甜油酥饼 tián yóusūbǐng. ˌ**short-ˈchange** *v* [T] (故意)少找给钱〔錢〕shǎo zhǎogěi qián. ˌ**short ˈcircuit** *n* [C] [电]短路 duǎnlù. ˌ**short-ˈcircuit** *v* [I, T] (使)短路 duǎnlù. ˈ**shortcoming** *n* [C] [常作 pl] 缺点〔點〕quēdiǎn;短处〔處〕duǎnchù. ˈ**shortfall** *n* [C] 赤字 chìzì;亏〔虧〕空 kuīkong. ˈ**shorthand** *n* [U] 速记法 sùjìfǎ. ˌ**short-ˈhanded** *adj* 人手不足的 rénshǒu bùzú de. ˈ**short-list** *n* [C] (供最后挑选用的)候选〔選〕人名单〔單〕hòuxuǎnrén míngdān. ˈ**short-list** *v* [T]. **short-lived** *adj* 短命的 duǎnmìngde;短暂的 duǎnzànde. **shortness** *n* [U]. **short sight** *n* [U] 近视 jìnshì. ˌ**short-ˈsighted** *adj* (a) 近视的 jìnshìde. (b) [喻]目光短浅〔淺〕的 mùguāng duǎnqiǎn de;无〔無〕远〔遠〕见的 wú yuǎnjiàn de. ˌ**short-ˈtempered** *adj* 易怒的 yìnùde;脾气〔氣〕暴躁的 píqì bàozào de. ˌ**short-ˈterm** *adj* 短期的 duǎnqīde. ˌ**short ˈwave** *n* [U] 短波 duǎnbō.

short[2] /ʃɔːt/ *adv* 1 突然 tūrán: *stop* ~ 突然停止. 2 [习语] go short (of) 缺少 quēshǎo;欠缺 qiànquē. short of 除…外 chú…wài: *do anything* ~ *of murder* 除杀人外什么事都做.

short[3] /ʃɔːt/ *n* [C] 1 少量烈性酒精饮料 shǎoliàng lièxìng jiǔjīng yǐnliào. 2 (电影)短片 duǎnpiàn.

shortage /ˈʃɔːtɪdʒ/ *n* [C,U] 不足 bùzú;缺少 quēshǎo;短缺 duǎnquē.

shorten /ˈʃɔːtn/ *v* [I,T] 弄短 nòng duǎn;缩短 suōduǎn: ~ *a dress* 改短衣服.

shortly /ˈʃɔːtlɪ/ *adv* 1 立刻 lìkè;不久 bùjiǔ: *We are leaving* ~. 我们马上离开. 2 唐突地 tángtūde;无〔無〕礼〔禮〕地 wúlǐde: *speak* ~ *to sb* 不客气地和某人说话.

shot /ʃɒt/ *n* [C] 1 射击〔擊〕shèjī;开〔開〕枪〔槍〕kāiqiāng;射击声〔聲〕shèjīshēng. 2 击球 jīqiú;踢 tī: *a* ~ *at goal* 射门. 3 试图〔圖〕shìtú;设法 shèfǎ: *a* ~ *at solving the problem* 设法解决这个问题. 4 射手 shèshǒu;枪手 qiāngshǒu;炮手 pàoshǒu: *a poor* ~ 差劲的射手. 5 照相 zhàoxiàng;连续〔續〕镜头 liánxù jìngtóu. 6 [非正式用语](皮下)注射 zhùshè. 7 [习语] like a ˈshot 飞〔飛〕快地 fēikuàide. a shot in the ˈarm 起鼓舞(或振奋)作用的事 qǐ gǔwǔ zuòyòng de shì. a shot in the ˈdark 无〔無〕根据〔據〕的瞎猜 wú gēnjù de xiācāi. not by a long shot ⇨ LONG[1]. ˈ**shotgun** *n* [C] 猎〔獵〕枪 lièqiāng. ˈ**shot-put** *n* [sing] 推铅球 tuī qiānqiú.

should[1] /ʃəd; 强式 ʃʊd/ *modal v* [否定式 should not, 缩略式 shouldn't / ˈʃʊdnt /] 1 (用以表示义务): *You* ~ *leave now*. 你现在应该离开. 2 (用以表示推断): *We* ~ *arrive before dark*. 我们该在天黑前到达. 3 (用在某些形容词后接的 that 从句中): *We're sorry that you* ~ *have been given so much trouble*. 我们很抱歉给你添这么多麻烦. 4 (表示不太可能发生): *If she* ~ *come back, please tell me*. 要是她(竟然)回来,请告诉我. 5 [正式用语](表示目的): *He put flowers in the room so that it* ~ *look nice*. 他把花放在屋里,这样房间就好看. 6 (用以表示意见或劝告): *You* ~ *stop smoking*. 你应该戒烟. 7 (用作有礼貌的请求): *I* ~ *like to make a phone call, please*. 劳驾,我想打个电话. 8 (与疑问词连用,表示不感兴趣、不相信等): *How* ~ *I know?* 我怎么知道呢?

should[2] *pt* of SHALL.

shoulder /ˈʃəʊldə(r)/ *n* 1 [C] (a)肩 jiān;肩膀 jiānbǎng;肩胛 jiānjiǎ. (b) (衣服的)肩部 jiānbù. 2 **shoulders** [pl] 背的上部 bèide shàngbù;肩胛 jiānjiǎ. 3 [C] 肩状〔狀〕物 jiānzhuàngwù. 4 [习语] ˌshoulder to ˈshoulder (a) 肩并〔並〕肩 jiān bìng jiān. (b) 齐〔齊〕心协〔協〕力地 qíxīn xiélì de. **shoulder** *v* [T] 1 肩起 jiānqǐ;挑起 tiāoqǐ;担〔擔〕dān;扛 káng: [喻] ~ *the responsibility* 承担责任. 2 用肩顶 yòng jiān dǐng: ~*ed sb aside* 用肩膀把某人顶到一边. ˈ**shoulder-blade** *n* [C] 肩胛骨 jiānjiǎgǔ.

shouldn't /ˈʃʊdnt/ should not. ⇨ SHOULD[1].

shout /ʃaʊt/ *n* [C] 呼喊 hūhǎn;喊叫声〔聲〕hǎnjiàoshēng. **shout** *v* 1 [I,T] 呼喊 hūhǎn;喊叫 hǎnjiào;大声说 dàshēng shuō: *Don't* ~ *at me!* 别对我喊! ~ (*out*) *orders* 高声发出命令. 2 [短语动词] shout sb down 高声喝止(某人)说话 gāoshēng hèzhǐ shuōhuà. **shouting** *n* [U] 叫喊 jiàohǎn.

shove /ʃʌv/ *v* 1 [I,T] 猛推 měngtuī;挤〔擠〕jǐ;撞 zhuàng. 2 [短语动词] shove over /up [非正式用语]移动〔動〕(为腾出地方) yídòng: S~ over so I can sit down. 挤一挤让我能坐下. **shove** *n* [C] 猛推 měngtuī;挤 jǐ.

shovel /ˈʃʌvl/ *n* [C] 铲〔鏟〕chǎn;铁〔鐵〕锨 tiěxiān. **shovel** *v* [-ll-;美语 -l-] [T] (用铲子或铁锨)铲 chǎn.

show[1] /ʃəʊ/ *n* 1 [C] 演出 yǎnchū;表演 biǎoyǎn;节〔節〕目 jiémù. 2 [C] 展览〔覽〕zhǎnlǎn;展览会〔會〕zhǎnlǎnhuì. 3 [C,U] 外观〔觀〕wàiguān: *Her grief is all* ~. 她的悲痛全是做样子. 4 [U] 绝妙的(或给人以深刻印象的)展示 juémiàode zhǎnshì: *all the* ~ *of the circus* 马戏团的全部精彩演出. 5 [C, 常作 sing] [非正式用语]表现 biǎoxiàn: *put up a good* ~ 表现良好. 6 [习语] for ˈshow 为〔爲〕装〔裝〕门面 wèi zhuāng ménmiàn;为炫耀 wèi xuànyào: *She does it for* ~. 她为了炫耀而做. on ˈshow 在公开〔開〕展出 zài gōngkāi zhǎnchū. a

S

show of 'hands 举〔舉〕手表决 jǔ shǒu biǎojué. 'show business *n* [U] 演艺〔藝〕行业〔業〕yǎnyì hángyè. 'show-down *n* [C] 最后〔後〕的较量 zuìhòude jiàoliàng. 'show-jumping *n* [U] (赛马运动中的)超越障碍〔礙〕比赛 chāoyuè zhàng'ài bǐsài. showroom *n* [C] (商品)陈列室 chénlièshì; 展览室 zhǎnlǎnshì. showy *adj* [-ier, -iest] 引人注目的 yǐn rén zhùmù de; 夸〔誇〕示的 kuāshìde.

show² /ʃəʊ/ *v* [*pt* ~ed, *pp* ~n /ʃəʊn/] 1 [T] 使被看见 shǐ bèi kànjiàn; 出示 chūshì: ~ *your ticket at the gate* 在门口出示你的门票. 2 [I, T] 看得见 kàn de jiàn; 使显〔顯〕露 shǐxiǎnlù: *Black doesn't* ~ *the dirt*. 黑色不显脏. 3 [T] 给…指出 gěi…zhǐchū; 指示 zhǐshì: *S*~ *me which one you want*. 告诉我你要哪一个. 4 [T] 指引 zhǐyǐn; 引导〔導〕yǐndǎo: *S*~ *her in*. 领她进来. 5 [T] 表示 biǎoshì: *He* ~*ed me great kindness*. 他对我极为亲切. 6 [T] 证〔證〕明 zhèngmíng; 表明 biǎomíng: *She* ~*ed great courage*. 她表现得很有勇气. 7 [T] 说明 shuōmíng; 解释〔釋〕jiěshì: *She* ~*ed me how to do it*. 她告诉我如何做. 8 [习语] go to 'show 用以证明 yòng yǐ zhèngmíng. show one's 'face 露面 lòumiàn. show one's 'hand 表明意图〔圖〕biǎomíng yìtú. 9 [短语动词] show off 炫耀(自己的财富或能力等) xuànyào. show up (a) 显而易见 xiǎn ér yì jiàn: *The lines* ~*ed up in the light*. 轮廓在亮光下很醒目. (b) 来到 láidào; 出席 chūxí: *All the guests* ~*ed up*. 所有的客人都到了. showing *n* 1 [C] 陈列 chénliè; 展览〔覽〕zhǎnlǎn. 2 [sing] 表现 biǎoxiàn: *the company's poor* ~*ing* 公司经营状况不好. 'show-off *n* [C] 爱〔愛〕炫耀的人 ài xuànyào de rén.

shower /'ʃaʊə(r)/ *n* [C] 1 阵雨 zhènyǔ. 2 (a) 淋浴器 línyùqì. (b) 淋浴 línyù: *have a* ~ 洗淋浴. 3 大量涌到的事物 dàliàng yǒngdào de shìwù: *a* ~ *of stones* 一阵乱石. shower *v* 1 [I] 阵雨般降落 zhènyǔbān jiàngluò. 2 [T] (*with, on, upon*) (a) 使…落在(某人身上) shǐ…luòzài. (b) 大量地给予 dàliàngde jǐyǔ: ~ *sb with praise* 对某人大加赞扬. showery *adj* (天气)多阵雨的 duō zhènyǔ de.

shown *pt, pp* of SHOW².

shrank *pt* of SHRINK.

shrapnel /'ʃræpnəl/ *n* [U] 榴霰弹〔彈〕liúxiàndàn.

shred /ʃred/ *n* [C] 1 [尤作 pl] 碎片 suìpiàn; 细条〔條〕xìtiáo. 2 [喻] 最少量 zuì shǎoliàng: *not one* ~ *of proof* 没有一点证据. shred *v* [-dd-] [T] 撕碎 sī suì; 切碎 qiē suì.

shrewd /ʃruːd/ *adj* 有准〔準〕确〔確〕判断〔斷〕力(或常识)的 yǒu zhǔnquè pànduànlì de; 敏锐的 mǐnruìde; 精明的 jīngmíngde: *a* ~ *guess* 准确的猜测. shrewdly *adv*.

shriek /ʃriːk/ *v* 1 [I] 尖声〔聲〕叫喊 jiānshēng jiàohǎn. 2 [T] 尖声说出 jiānshēng shuōchū. shriek *n* [C] 尖叫声 jiānjiàoshēng.

shrill /ʃrɪl/ *adj* (声音)尖声〔聲〕的 jiānshēngde; 刺耳的 cì'ěrde. shrillness *n* [U].

shrimp /ʃrɪmp/ *n* [C] 小虾〔蝦〕xiǎoxiā.

shrine /ʃraɪn/ *n* [C] 1 圣〔聖〕陵 shènglíng; 圣骨匣 shènggǔxiá. 2 圣地 shèngdì; 神圣场〔場〕所 shénshèng chǎngsuǒ.

shrink /ʃrɪŋk/ *v* [*pt* shrank /ʃræŋk/, 或 shrunk /ʃrʌŋk/, *pp* shrunk] 1 [I, T] (使)收缩 shōusuō; 变〔變〕小 biàn xiǎo: *My shorts shrank in the wash*. 我的短裤洗后缩水了. 2 [短语动词] shrink (back / away) from sth / sb 退缩 tuìsuō; 畏缩 wèisuō. shrink from sth 不愿〔願〕做某事 búyuàn zuò mǒushì. shrinkage /-ɪdʒ/ *n* [U] 收缩过〔過〕程 shōusuō guòchéng; 收缩量 shōusuōliàng. shrunken /'ʃrʌŋkən/ *adj* 收缩的 shōusuōde.

shrivel /'ʃrɪvl/ *v* [-ll-; 美语 -l-] [I, T] (*up*) (使)枯萎 kūwěi; (使)萎缩 wěisuō; (使)皱〔皺〕缩 zhòusuō.

shroud /ʃraʊd/ *n* [C] 1 裹尸〔屍〕布 guǒshībù; 寿〔壽〕衣 shòuyī. 2 [喻] 遮蔽物 zhēbìwù; 覆盖〔蓋〕物 fùgàiwù: *a* ~ *of mist* 一层薄雾. shroud *v* [T] [常用被动语态] 覆盖 fùgài; 遮蔽 zhēbì: ~*ed in mystery* 笼罩在神秘中.

shrub /ʃrʌb/ *n* [C] 灌木 guànmù. shrubbery *n* [C, U] [*pl* -ies] 灌木丛〔叢〕guànmùcóng.

shrug /ʃrʌg/ *v* [-gg-] 1 [I, T] (表示怀疑等) 耸〔聳〕(肩) sǒng. 2 [短语动词] shrug sth off 对〔對〕(某事)不予理会〔會〕duì bù yǔ lǐhuì; 不屑一顾〔顧〕búxiè yí gù. shrug *n* [C] 耸肩 sǒngjiān.

shrunk *pt, pp* of SHRINK.

shrunken ⇨SHRINK.

shudder /'ʃʌdə(r)/ *v* [I] (人)发〔發〕抖 fādǒu; 战〔戰〕栗〔慄〕zhànlì. shudder *n* [C] 发抖 fādǒu; 战栗 zhànlì.

shuffle /'ʃʌfl/ *v* 1 [I] 拖着脚走 tuō zhe jiǎo zǒu. 2 [I, T] 不断〔斷〕改变〔變〕位置 búduàn gǎibiàn wèizhi; 坐立不安 zuò lì bù'ān. 3 [T] 洗(牌) xǐ. shuffle *n* 1 [sing] 拖着脚走 tuōzhe jiǎo zǒu. 2 [C] 改组 gǎizǔ.

shun /ʃʌn/ *v* [T] [-nn-] 避免 bìmiǎn.

shunt /ʃʌnt/ *v* 1 [I, T] 使(火车)转〔轉〕轨 shǐ zhuǎnguǐ. 2 [T] 把…转至另一地方 bǎ…zhuǎn zhì lìngyī dìfāng.

shush /ʃʊʃ/ *interj* 安静 ānjìng.

shut /ʃʌt/ *v* [-tt-; *pt, pp* ~] 1 (a) [T] 关〔關〕上 guānshàng; 关闭 guānbì. (b) [I] (门等) 关上 guānshàng: *The window won't* ~. 这窗户关不上. 2 [I, T] (使商店等)停止营

S

〔营〕业〔業〕tíngzhǐ yíngyè: *When does the baker's ~?* 面包房什么时候停止营业? 3 [T] 合拢〔攏〕hélǒng; 折〔摺〕拢 zhélǒng: *~ a book* 合上书. 4 [习语] **shut one's eyes to** 视而不见 shì ér bú jiàn. **shut up 'shop** 停业 tíngyè; 关张〔張〕guānzhāng. 5 [短语动词] **shut (sth) down** (使)停工 tínggōng; 关闭 guānbì. **shut sth off** 停止供应〔應〕(煤气、水等) tíngzhǐ gōngyìng. **shut sb / sth off** 使隔离〔離〕shǐ gélí. **shut (sth) up** (a) 关闭(房子的)全部门窗 guānbì quánbù mén chuāng. (b) 妥藏 tuǒcáng. **shut (sb) up** [非正式用语] (使)住口 zhùkǒu. **'shut-down** *n* [C] 停工 tínggōng; 停业 tíngyè; 关闭 guānbì.

shutter /ˈʃʌtə(r)/ *n* [C] 1 百叶〔葉〕窗 bǎiyèchuāng; 活动〔動〕的窗板 huódòngde chuāngbǎn. 2 (照相机的)快门 kuàimén. **shuttered** *adj* 百叶窗关〔關〕闭的 bǎiyèchuāng guānbì de.

shuttle /ˈʃʌtl/ *n* [C] 1 (定时往返两地的)班机〔機〕或公共汽车 bānjī huò gōnggòng qìchē. 2 (缝纫机的)摆〔擺〕梭 bǎisuō. **shuttle** *v* [I, T] (使)穿梭般来回移动〔動〕chuānsuōbān láihuí yídòng. **'shuttlecock** *n* [C] 羽毛球 yǔmáoqiú.

shy[1] /ʃaɪ/ *adj* 1 (人)害羞的 hàixiūde; 腼腆的 miǎntiǎnde. 2 (动物)易受惊〔驚〕的 yì shòujīng de; 胆〔膽〕怯的 dǎnqiède. **shyly** *adv*. **shyness** *n* [U].

shy[2] /ʃaɪ/ *v* [*pt*, *pp* **shied** /ʃaɪd/] 1 [I] (马)受惊〔驚〕shòujīng; 惊退 jīngtuì. 2 [短语动词] **shy away from sth** 避开〔開〕bìkāi; 回避 huíbì; 躲开 duǒkāi.

Siamese twins /ˌsaɪəmiːz ˈtwɪnz/ *n* [pl] 连体〔體〕双〔雙〕胞胎 liántǐ shuāngbāotāi.

sibilant /ˈsɪbɪlənt/ *adj*, *n* 发〔發〕咝〔嘶〕咝声〔聲〕的 fā sīsīshēng de; 咝咝声 sīsīshēng.

sibling /ˈsɪblɪŋ/ *n* [C] [正式用语]兄弟 xiōngdì; 姐妹 jiěmèi.

sick /sɪk/ *adj* 1 有病的 yǒubìngde; 患病的 huànbìngde: *care for ~ people in hospital* 照看住院的病人. 2 要呕〔嘔〕吐的 yào ǒutù de; 恶〔惡〕心的 ěxīnde: *feel ~* 觉得恶心. 3 *of* [非正式用语]厌〔厭〕倦的 yànjuànde; 腻烦的 nìfánde: *I'm ~ of his lies*. 我听够了他的谎言. 4 (*at / about*) [非正式用语]极〔極〕不愉快的 jí bù yúkuài de; 心烦意乱〔亂〕的 xīnfán yìluàn de: *We're ~ about losing*. 我们输了感到很懊丧. 5 [非正式用语]残〔殘〕酷的 cánkù de; 冒犯的 màofànde; 讨厌的 tǎoyànde: *~ jokes* 冒犯人的笑话. 6 [习语] **worried sick** 非常担〔擔〕心的 fēicháng dānxīn de. **the sick** *n* [pl] 病人 bìngrén; 患者 huànzhě. **'sick-leave** *n* [U] 病假 bìngjià.

sicken /ˈsɪkən/ *v* 1 [T] 使厌〔厭〕恶〔惡〕shǐ yànwù; 使恶心 shǐ ěxin: *Violence ~s him*. 暴力使他反感. 2 [I] (*for*) 生病 shēngbìng. **sickening** *adj* 令人厌恶的 lìng rén yànwù de.

sickle /ˈsɪkl/ *n* [C] 镰刀 liándāo.

sickly /ˈsɪklɪ/ *adj* [-ier, -iest] 1 多病的 duōbìngde. 2 不健康的 bú jiànkāng de; 病态〔態〕的 bìngtàide: *a ~ complexion* 病容. 3 令人作呕〔嘔〕的 lìng rén zuò'ǒu de; 令人厌〔厭〕恶〔惡〕的 lìng rén yànwù de: *a ~ atmosphere* 令人厌恶的气氛.

sickness /ˈsɪknɪs/ *n* 1 [C, U] 病 bìng; 疾病 jíbìng. 2 [U] 呕〔嘔〕吐 ǒutù; 作呕 zuò'ǒu.

side[1] /saɪd/ *n* [C] 1 面 miàn. 2 侧面 cèmiàn. 3 (纸等的)一面 yímiàn. 4 边〔邊〕缘 biānyuán; 边界 biānjiè: *the ~ of the bed* 床边. 5 (人体的)侧边 cèbiān; 胁〔脅〕xié: *a pain in one's ~* 胁痛. 6 面 miàn; 半边 bànbiān: *the sunny ~ of the street* 街道的向阳面. 7 (a) (竞赛等双方的)一方 yìfāng. (b) 一派(或一方)的观〔觀〕点〔點〕yípàide guāndiǎn. 8 方面 fāngmiàn: *study all ~s of a question* 研究一问题的各个方面. 9 [习语] **get on the right / wrong side of sb** 使某人愉快 shǐ mǒurén yúkuài; 使某人不愉快 shǐ mǒurén bù yúkuài. **on / from all 'sides** 在各方面 zài gè fāngmiàn; 从〔從〕各方面 cóng gè fāngmiàn. **on the 'big, 'small, etc side** 偏大 piāndà; 偏小 piānxiǎo. **put sth on/to one 'side** 暂缓处〔處〕理 zànhuǎn chǔlǐ; 搁置 gēzhì. **ˌside by 'side** 肩并〔竝〕肩地 jiān bìng jiān de. **take 'sides (with sb)** (在辩论中)支持某人 zhīchí mǒurén. **'sideboard** *n* [C] 餐具柜〔櫃〕cānjùguì. **'sideburns, 'sideboards** *n* [pl] 络腮胡〔鬍〕子 luòsāi húzi. **'side-effect** *n* [C] (药物等的)副作用 fùzuòyòng. **'sidelight** *n* [C] (机动车的)侧灯〔燈〕cèdēng; 边灯 biāndēng. **'sideline** *n* [C] (a) (足球等的)边线〔綫〕biānxiàn. (b) 副业〔業〕fùyè; 兼职〔職〕jiānzhí. **'sidelong** *adj* 横向的 héngxiàngde; 侧面的 cèmiànde: *a ~ glance* 斜视. **'side-road** *n* [C] 支线〔綫〕zhīxiàn; 叉路 chàlù; 小路 xiǎolù. **'side-step** *v* [-pp-] [I, T] (a) 横跨一步避开〔開〕héngkuà yíbù bìkāi. (b) [喻]回避(问题) huíbì. **'side-track** *v* [T] 转〔轉〕变〔變〕话题 zhuǎnbiàn huàtí. **'sidewalk** *n* [美语] ⇨PAVEMENT. **'sideways** *adv* 斜向一边 xié xiàng yìbiān; 斜着 xiézhe.

side[2] /saɪd/ *v* [短语动词] **side with** (在争论等中)支持(某人) zhīchí.

siding /ˈsaɪdɪŋ/ *n* [C] (铁路的)侧线〔綫〕cèxiàn; 旁轨 pángguǐ; 岔线 chàxiàn.

siege /siːdʒ/ *n* [C, U] 1 围〔圍〕困 wéikùn; 围城 wéichéng; 围攻 wéigōng. 2 [习语] **lay siege to** 包围 bāowéi; 围攻 wéigōng.

sieve /sɪv/ *n* [C] 筛〔篩〕(子) shāi; 滤〔濾〕器 lǜqì; 漏勺〔杓〕lòusháo. **sieve** *v* [T] 筛 shāi; 滤 lǜ.

S

sift /sɪft/ *v* 1 [T] 筛〔篩〕shāi;筛分 shāifēn;过〔過〕滤〔濾〕guòlǜ. 2 [I, T] [喻]详审〔審〕xiángshěn;细察 xìchá: ~ (*through*) *the evidence* 细查证据.

sigh /saɪ/ *v* 1 [I] 叹〔嘆〕气〔氣〕tànqì;叹息 tànxī. 2 [T] 叹息地表示 tànxīde biǎoshì. **sigh** *n* [C] 叹息 tànxī;叹息声〔聲〕tànxīshēng.

sight /saɪt/ *n* 1 [U] 视力 shìlì;视觉〔覺〕shìjué. 2 [U] 看 kàn;看见 kànjiàn: *our first ~ of land* 我们首次看到陆地. 3 [U] 视野 shìyě;视域 shìyù: *out of ~* 看不见. 4 (a) [C] 情景 qíngjǐng;景象 jǐngxiàng. (b) **sights** [pl] 名胜〔勝〕míngshèng;风〔風〕景 fēngjǐng: *the ~s of London* 伦敦的名胜. 5 [C] (枪等的)瞄准〔準〕器 miáozhǔnqì. 6 **a sight** [sing] [非正式用语] 滑稽可笑(或杂乱无章)的人(或物) huájī kěxiào de rén. 7 [习语] **at /on 'sight** 一见到某人(或某物)立即 yí jiàndào mǒurén lìjí. **in 'sight** (a) 看得见 kàndejiàn. (b) 在望 zàiwàng;在即 zàijí: *The end of the war is in ~.* 战争结束在望. **ˌsight for sore 'eyes** 乐〔樂〕于见到的物 lèyú jiàndào de wù. **sight** *v* [T] (尤指因接近)看见 kànjiàn. **sighted** *adj* 有视力的 yǒu shìlì de;看得见的 kàndéjiànde. **sighting** *n* [C] 被看见的人(或事物) bèi kànjiàn de rén;看见 kànjiàn. **'sightseeing** *n* [U] 观〔觀〕光 guānguāng;游览〔覽〕yóulǎn.

sign /saɪn/ *n* [C] 1 记号〔號〕jìhào;符号 fúhào. 2 牌子 páizi;招牌 zhāopai;指示牌 zhǐshìpái. 3 迹象 jìxiàng;痕迹 hénjì;征〔徵〕兆 zhēngzhào: *the ~s of suffering on her face* 她面部的痛苦表情. 4 (用手、头等的)示意动〔動〕作 shìyì dòngzuò;手势〔勢〕shǒushì. 5 [习语] **a ˌsign of the 'times** 某时〔時〕期的标〔標〕志〔誌〕mǒu shíqī de biāozhì. **sign** *v* 1 [I, T] 签〔簽〕(名) qiān;签字 qiānzì. 2 [短语动词] **sign sth away** 签字放弃〔棄〕(财产等) qiānzì fàngqì. **sign off** (a) (以签名)结束写〔寫〕信 jiéshù xiěxìn. (b) 宣布广〔廣〕播结束 xuānbù guǎngbō jiéshù. **sign on** 登记为〔爲〕失业〔業〕的(人) dēngjì wéi shīyè de. **sign (sb) on/up** 签约受雇〔僱〕qiānyuē shòugù. **'signpost** *n* [C] 路标 lùbiāo.

signal /ˈsɪgnəl/ *n* [C] 1 信号〔號〕xìnhào;暗号 ànhào;手势〔勢〕shǒushì: *A red light is a danger ~.* 红灯是危险的信号. 2 导〔導〕因 dǎoyīn;导火线〔綫〕dǎohuǒxiàn: *His speech was the ~ for applause.* 他的演讲赢得了掌声. 3 (铁路)信号机〔機〕xìnhàojī. 4 (无线电波的)信号 xìnhào. **signal** *v* [-ll-;美语 -l-] [I, T] (向…)发〔發〕信号 fā xìnhào;用信号联〔聯〕系〔繫〕yòng xìnhào liánxì. **'signal-box** *n* [C] (铁路上的)信号所 xìnhàosuǒ;信号房 xìnhàofáng.

signatory /ˈsɪgnətrɪ; *US* -tɔːrɪ/ *n* [C] [*pl* -ies] (协议、条约等)签〔簽〕约者 qiānyuēzhě;签约国〔國〕qiānyuēguó.

signature /ˈsɪgnətʃə(r)/ *n* [C] 签〔簽〕名 qiānmíng;签字 qiānzì;署名 shǔmíng. **'signature tune** *n* [C] 信号〔號〕曲 xìnhàoqǔ.

significance /sɪgˈnɪfɪkəns/ *n* [U] 意义〔義〕yìyì;重要性 zhòngyàoxìng. **significant** *adj* 1 有意义的 yǒu yìyì de;重要的 zhòngyàode. 2 意义深长〔長〕的 yìyì shēncháng de: *a ~ look* 意味深长的一瞥. **significantly** *adv*.

signify /ˈsɪgnɪfaɪ/ *v* [*pt*, *pp* -ied] 1 [T] (a) 表示…的意思 biǎoshì… de yìsi;意味 yìwèi. (b) 表示 biǎoshì;表明 biǎomíng. 2 [I] [正式用语]有重要性 yǒu zhòngyàoxìng;有关〔關〕系〔係〕yǒu guānxì.

silence /ˈsaɪləns/ *n* [U, C] 1 寂静 jìjìng;无〔無〕声〔聲〕wúshēng. 2 沉默 chénmò. 3 [习语] **in silence** 安静地 ānjìngde;无声地 wúshēngde. **silence** *v* [T] 使沉默 shǐ chénmò;使安静 shǐ ānjìng. **silencer** *n* [C] 消音器 xiāoyīnqì;消声器 xiāoshēngqì.

silent /ˈsaɪlənt/ *adj* 1 寂静的 jìjìngde;无〔無〕声〔聲〕的 wúshēngde. 2 沉默寡言的 chénmò guǎyán de;不作声的 bú zuòshēng de. 3 (字母)不发〔發〕音的 bù fāyīn de. **silently** *adv*.

silhouette /ˌsɪluːˈet/ *n* [C] 黑色轮〔輪〕廓(像) hēisè lúnkuò;侧影 cèyǐng;剪影 jiǎnyǐng. **silhouette** *v* [T] [常用被动语态]使现出轮廓(或影像) shǐ xiànchū lúnkuò: *trees ~d against the sky* 天空衬托出树的轮廓.

silicon /ˈsɪlɪkən/ *n* [U] 硅 guī. **silicon chip** *n* [C] 硅片 guīpiàn.

silk /sɪlk/ *n* [U] 丝〔絲〕sī;丝线〔綫〕sīxiàn. **silken** *adj* 柔软光滑的 róuruǎn guānghuá de;像丝一样〔樣〕光泽〔澤〕的 xiàng sī yíyàng guāngzé de. **'silkworm** *n* [C] 蚕〔蠶〕cán. **silky** *adj* [-ier, -iest] 柔软光滑的 róuruǎn guānghuá de;丝绸一样的 sīchóu yíyàng de.

sill /sɪl/ *n* [C] 窗台〔臺〕chuāngtái.

silly /ˈsɪlɪ/ *adj* [-ier, -iest] 傻〔儍〕的 shǎde;愚蠢的 yúchǔnde;愚昧的 yúmèide. **silliness** *n* [U].

silt /sɪlt/ *n* [U] 淤泥 yūní;淤沙 yūshā. **silt** *v* [短语动词] **silt (sth) up** 使淤塞 shǐ yūsè.

silver /ˈsɪlvə(r)/ *n* [U] 1 银 yín;白银 báiyín. 2 银器 yínqì;银币〔幣〕yínbì. 3 银白色 yínbáisè. **silver** *adj* 银的 yínde;像银的 xiàngyínde. **ˌsilver 'jubilee** *n* [C] (重大事件的)25周年纪念 èrshíwǔ zhōunián jìniàn. **ˌsilver 'medal** *n* [C] 银质〔質〕奖〔獎〕章 yínzhì jiǎngzhāng;银牌 yínpái. **ˌsilver-'plated** *adj* 镀银的 dùyínde. **'silversmith** *n* [C] 银匠 yínjiàng;银器商 yínqìshāng. **ˌsilver 'wedding** *n* [C] 银婚(结婚25周年纪念) yínhūn. **silvery** *adj* 似银的 sìyínde.

'SIM card /ˈsɪm kɑːd/ *n* [C] SIM 卡 SIM kǎ;手机〔機〕卡 shǒujīkǎ;智能卡 zhìnéngkǎ.

S

similar /ˈsɪmɪlə(r)/ *adj* 类〔類〕似的 lèisìde;相像的 xiāngxiàngde. **similarly** *adv*.

similarity /ˌsɪmɪˈlærətɪ/ *n* [*pl* -ies] **1** [U] 类〔類〕似 lèisì;相似 xiāngsì. **2** [C] 类似点〔點〕lèisìdiǎn;相似处〔處〕xiāngsìchù.

simile /ˈsɪmɪlɪ/ *n* [U,C] 明喻 míngyù (如 *as brave as a lion* 勇猛如狮).

simmer /ˈsɪmə(r)/ *v* **1** [I,T] 煨 wēi;炖 dùn. **2** [I] *with* 内心充满(难以控制的情感等) nèixīn chōngmǎn: *~ing with anger* 按捺着怒气. **3** [短语动词] **simmer down** 平静下来 píngjìng xiàlái;冷静下来 lěngjìng xiàlái.

simple /ˈsɪmpəl/ *adj* **1** 简单〔單〕的 jiǎndānde;简易的 jiǎnyìde: ~ *problem* 简单的问题. **2** 朴〔樸〕素的 pǔsùde;简朴的 jiǎnpǔde: ~ *food* 简单的食物. **3** 未充分发〔發〕展的 wèi chōngfèn fāzhǎn de: ~ *forms of life* 生物的初级形态. **4** 单一的 dānyīde. **5** 天真的 tiānzhēnde;率直的 shuàizhíde: *as ~ as a child* 像孩子一样天真. **6** 易受欺的 yì shòuqī de. **7** [非正式用语]头〔頭〕脑〔腦〕简单的 tóunǎo jiǎndān de. **simply** *adv* **1** 简单地 jiǎndānde;简易地 jiǎnyìde. **2** 绝对〔對〕地 juéduìde. **3** 只 zhǐ;仅〔僅〕jǐn: *She's simply here to help.* 她只是来这里帮忙.

simplicity /sɪmˈplɪsətɪ/ *n* [U] **1** 简单〔單〕jiǎndān;简易 jiǎnyì. **2** [习语] **be simplicity itˈself** 极〔極〕为〔爲〕容易 jí wéi róngyì.

simplify /ˈsɪmplɪfaɪ/ *v* [*pt*, *pp* -ied] [T] 简化 jiǎnhuà;使简易 shǐ jiǎnyì;使简明 shǐ jiǎnmíng. **simplification** /-fɪˈkeɪʃn/ *n* [C,U].

simulate /ˈsɪmjʊleɪt/ *v* [T] 假装〔裝〕jiǎzhuāng: ~ *interest* 假装有兴趣. **simuˈlation** *n* [C,U].

simultaneous /ˌsɪmlˈteɪnɪəs; *US* ˌsaɪm-/ *adj* 同时〔時〕发〔發〕生的 tóngshí fāshēng de;同时进〔進〕行的 tóngshí jìnxíng de;同步的 tóngbùde. **simultaneously** *adv*.

sin /sɪn/ *n* **1** [U] (违犯宗教戒律的)恶〔惡〕行 èxíng. **2** [C] (宗教、道德上的)罪 zuì;罪恶 zuì'è. **sin** *v* [-nn-] [I] 犯罪 fànzuì;犯过〔過〕错 fàn guòcuò. **sinful** /-fl/ *adj* 有过错的 yǒu guòcuò de;邪恶的 xié'ède.. **sinner** /ˈsɪnə(r)/ *n* [C].

since /sɪns/ *prep* [与完成时连用]从〔從〕…以后〔後〕cóng…yǐhòu;自…以来 zì…yǐlái: *I haven't seen him ~ Tuesday.* 自星期二以来我没有见到他. **since** *conj* **1** 自…以来 zì…yǐlái;从…以后 cóng…yǐhòu: *How long is it ~ you were here?* 你不在这里有多久了? **2** 因为〔爲〕yīnwèi: *S~ I have no money, I can't buy it.* 因为我没钱,不能买. **since** *adv* [与完成时连用]从那以后 cóng nà yǐhòu;此后 cǐhòu;后来 hòulái: *I met her last summer and haven't seen her ~.* 我去年夏天遇见她,此后再没有见到她.

sincere /sɪnˈsɪə(r)/ *adj* **1** (感情)真挚〔摯〕的 zhēnzhìde;真诚的 zhēnchéngde: ~ *friendship* 诚挚的友谊. **2** (人)诚实〔實〕的 chéngshíde;忠实的 zhōngshíde. **sincerely** *adv*. **sincerity** /sɪnˈserətɪ/ *n* [U].

sinew /ˈsɪnjuː/ *n* [C,U] 腱 jiàn;肌腱 jījiàn. **sinewy** *adj* 肌肉发〔發〕达〔達〕的 jīròu fādá de;坚〔堅〕韧〔韌〕的 jiānrènde.

sing /sɪŋ/ *v* [*pt* sang /sæŋ/, *pp* sung /sʌŋ/] **1** [I,T] 唱 chàng;歌唱 gēchàng. **2** [I] 发〔發〕嗡嗡声〔聲〕fā wēngwēngshēng;发鸣叫声 fā míngjiàoshēng. **singer** *n* [C]. **singing** *n* [U].

singe /sɪndʒ/ *v* [I,T] 烧〔燒〕焦 shāojiāo. **singe** *n* [C] (布等)轻〔輕〕微的烧焦 qīngwēide shāojiāo.

single /ˈsɪŋgl/ *adj* **1** 单〔單〕一的 dānyīde;单个〔個〕的 dāngède: *a ~ apple* 单独一个苹果. **2** 未婚的 wèihūnde;独〔獨〕身的 dúshēnde. **3** 单人的 dānrénde;一人用的 yìrén yòng de: *a ~ bed* 单人床. **4** [英国英语]单程的 dānchéngde. **single** *n* **1 singles** [U] 单打比赛 dāndǎ bǐsài. **2** [C] 单程票 dānchéngpiào. **3** [C] (一面只录一支乐曲的)单曲唱片 dānqǔ chàngpiàn. **single** *v* [短语动词] **single sb / sth out** 选〔選〕出 xuǎnchū;挑出 tiāochū;使突出 shǐ tūchū. ˌ**single ˈfile** *n* [C] 单行 dānháng;一路纵〔縱〕队〔隊〕yílù zòngduì. ˌ**single-ˈhanded** *adj*, *adv* 独自(的) dúzì;独立无〔無〕援(的) dúlì wúyuán. ˌ**single-ˈminded** *adj* 一心一意的 yìxīn yíyì de;专〔專〕一的 zhuānyīde. ˌ**single ˈparent** *n* [C] 单亲〔親〕dānqīn. **singly** /ˈsɪŋglɪ/ *adv* 个〔個〕别地 gèbiéde;一个一个地 yígè yígè de.

singsong /ˈsɪŋsɒŋ/ *n* **1** [C] 自娱歌唱会〔會〕zìyú gēchànghuì. **2** [sing] 有起伏节〔節〕奏的说话方式 yǒu qǐfú jiézòu de shuōhuà fāngshì.

singular /ˈsɪŋgjʊlə(r)/ *adj* **1** [语法]单〔單〕数〔數〕的 dānshùde: *a ~ verb* 单数动词. **2** [正式用语] (a) 突出的 tūchūde. (b) 异〔異〕常的 yìchángde;奇怪的 qíguàide. **singular** *n* [常作 sing] (词的)单数形式 dānshù xíngshì.

sinister /ˈsɪnɪstə(r)/ *adj* 不祥的 bùxiángde;凶〔兇〕兆的 xiōngzhàode;邪恶〔惡〕的 xié'ède: *a ~ place* 不祥之地.

sink[1] /sɪŋk/ *n* [C] (厨房内)洗涤〔滌〕槽 xǐdícáo.

sink[2] /sɪŋk/ *v* [*pt* sank /sæŋk/, *pp* sunk /sʌŋk/] **1** [I,T] 下沉 xiàchén;沉没 chénmò. **2** [I] (太阳等)下落 xiàluò;沉 chén. **3** [I,T] (使)变〔變〕低 biàn dī: *She sank to the ground.* 她倒在地上. **4** [I] 贬值 biǎnzhí;变弱 biàn ruò. **5** [T] 掘 jué;挖 wā: ~ *a well* 掘井. **6** [短语动词] **sink in / into** (a) (液体)渗

S

〔滲〕入 shènrù. (b) 被理解 bèi lǐjiě. **sink sth into sth** 投入(资金) tóurù.

sinuous /ˈsɪnjʊəs/ *adj* 弯〔彎〕曲的 wānqūde; 蜿蜒的 wānyánde.

sinus /ˈsaɪnəs/ *n* [C] 窦〔竇〕(颅骨中的孔穴) dòu.

sip /sɪp/ *v* [-pp-] [I, T] 小口地喝 xiǎokǒude hē; 抿 mǐn. **sip** *n* [C] 小口喝 xiǎokǒu hē; 抿 mǐn.

siphon /ˈsaɪfən/ *n* [C] 1 虹吸管 hóngxīguǎn. 2 虹吸瓶 hóngxīpíng. **siphon** *v* [短语动词] **siphon sth off / out** 用虹吸管抽出(液体) yòng hóngxīguǎn chōuchū. **siphon sth off** (非法地)抽取 chōuqǔ.

sir /sɜː(r)/ *n* (亦作 **Sir**) [sing] 1 [正式用语] 先生(对男子的礼貌称呼) xiānsheng. 2 爵士(用于爵士或准男爵的名字之前或姓名之前) juéshì.

sire /ˈsaɪə(r)/ *n* [C] 雄性种〔種〕兽〔獸〕 xióngxìng zhǒngshòu. **sire** *v* [T] (尤指种马) 繁殖 fánzhí.

siren /ˈsaɪərən/ *n* [C] 警报〔報〕器 jǐngbàoqì; 汽笛 qìdí.

sirloin /ˈsɜːlɔɪn/ *n* [C, U] 牛的上腰部肉 niúde shàngyāobù ròu; 牛里脊肉 niúlǐjǐròu.

sister /ˈsɪstə(r)/ *n* [C] 1 姐 jiě; 妹 mèi. 2 [英国英语] 护〔護〕士长〔長〕 hùshìzhǎng. 3 修女 xiūnǚ; 女教友 nǚ jiàoyǒu. 4 姐妹(为女权运动者所用) jiěmèi. **sisterly** *adj* 姐妹的 jiěmèide; 姐妹般的 jiěmèibānde.

sit /sɪt/ *v* [-tt-; *pt*, *pp* **sat** /sæt/] 1 (a) [I] 坐 zuò; 就坐 jiùzuò. (b) [I, T] (使)坐 zuò; (使)就坐 jiùzuò: ~ (*down*) *on the chair* 坐在椅子上. 2 [I] (国会、法庭等)开〔開〕会〔會〕 kāihuì; 开庭 kāitíng. 3 [I, T] (*for*) 参加(考试) cānjiā. 4 [I] (*for*) 摆〔擺〕好姿势〔勢〕(以便拍照、画像) bǎihǎo zīshì. 5 [习语] **sit on the ˈfence** 骑墙〔牆〕观〔觀〕望 qíqiáng guānwàng. ˌ**sit ˈtight** (a) 留在原处〔處〕 liú zài yuánchù. (b) 不采〔採〕取行动〔動〕 bù cǎiqǔ xíngdòng. 6 [短语动词] **sit around** 闲坐着 xián zuò zhe. **sit back** 歇息 xiēxi; 什么〔麼〕都不做 shénme dōu búzuò: ~ *back and watch television* 轻松地看电视. **sit in** 静坐示威 jìngzuò shìwēi. **sit in on sth** 列席(讨论会等) lièxí. **sit on** (a) 成为〔爲〕…的成员 chéngwéi…de chéngyuán. (b) 搁置 gēzhì. **sit up** 晚睡 wǎnshuì. **sit (sb) up** (使)坐起来 zuò qǐlái; 坐直 zuòzhí. ˈ**sit-in** *n* [C] 静坐示威 jìngzuò shìwēi.

site /saɪt/ *n* [C] 地点〔點〕 dìdiǎn; 现场〔場〕 xiànchǎng. **site** *v* [T] 设置 shèzhì.

sitting /ˈsɪtɪŋ/ *n* [C] 1 开〔開〕会〔會〕(或开庭)的期间 kāihuìde qījiān. 2 坐着被画〔畫〕像(或照相) zuòzhe bèi huàxiàng. 3 一批人就餐的时〔時〕间 yìpīrén jiùcān de shíjiān. 4 [习语] ˌ**sitting ˈduck** 容易击〔擊〕中的目标〔標〕 róngyì jīzhòng de mùbiāo. ˈ**sitting-room** *n* [C] 起居室 qǐjūshì; 会客室 huìkèshì.

situate /ˈsɪtjʊeɪt; *US* ˈsɪtʃʊeɪt/ *v* [T] [常用被动语态] 使位于 shǐ wèiyú: *a house ~d near the church* 靠近教堂的一所房子. **situated** *adj* (人)处〔處〕于某种境地的 chǔyú mǒuzhǒng jìngdì de: *I'm badly ~d at the moment*. 我此刻处境很坏.

situation /ˌsɪtʃʊˈeɪʃn/ *n* [C] 1 形势〔勢〕 xíngshì; 情况 qíngkuàng; 处〔處〕境 chǔjìng. 2 (城镇、建筑物等的)位置 wèizhi. 3 [正式用语] 有报〔報〕酬的工作 yǒu bàochóu de gōngzuò; 职〔職〕业〔業〕 zhíyè.

six /sɪks/ *pron, adj, n* [C] 1 六(的) liù. 2 [习语] **at sixes and sevens** [非正式用语] 乱〔亂〕七八糟 luànqībāzāo. **sixth** /sɪksθ/ *pron, adj* 第六(的) dìliù. **sixth** *pron, n* [C] 六分之一 liùfēn zhī yī.

sixteen /sɪkˈstiːn/ *pron, adj, n* [C] 十六(的) shíliù. **sixteenth** /sɪkˈstiːnθ/ *pron, adj* 第十六(的) dìshíliù. **sixteenth** *pron, n* [C] 十六分之一 shíliùfēn zhī yī.

sixty /ˈsɪkstɪ/ *pron, adj, n* [C] [*pl* **-ies**] 六十(的) liùshí. **sixtieth** /ˈsɪkstɪəθ/ *pron, adj* 第六十(的) dìliùshí. **sixtieth** *pron, n* [C] 六十分之一 liùshífēn zhī yī.

size /saɪz/ *n* 1 [U, C] 大小 dàxiǎo; 多少 duōshǎo. 2 [C] (服装等的)号〔號〕 hào; 尺码 chǐmǎ: ~ *five shoes* 五号鞋. **size** *v* 1 [T] 按大小(或多少)排列(或分类、编号) àn dàxiǎo páiliè. 2 [短语动词] **size sb / sth up** [非正式用语] 估计 gūjì; 判断〔斷〕 pànduàn. **sizeable** /-əbl/ *adj* 相当〔當〕大的 xiāngdāng dà de.

sizzle /ˈsɪzl/ *v* [I], *n* [C] [非正式用语] 发〔發〕咝〔噝〕咝声〔聲〕 fā sīsīshēng; 咝咝声 sīsīshēng.

skate /skeɪt/ *n* [C] 1 冰鞋 bīngxié. 2 旱冰鞋 hànbīngxié. 3 [习语] **get / put one's ˈskates on** [非正式用语] 赶〔趕〕快 gǎnkuài. **skate** *v* 1 [I] 滑冰 huábīng; 溜冰 liūbīng. 2 [习语] **be skating on thin ˈice** 履薄冰(或冒风险) lǚ bóbīng. 3 [短语动词] **skate over / round sth** 间接处〔處〕理 jiànjiē chǔlǐ. ˈ**skateboard** *n* [C] 滑板 huábǎn. **skater** *n* [C].

skeleton /ˈskelɪtn/ *n* [C] 1 骨骼 gǔgé; 骨架 gǔjià. 2 (建筑物的)骨架 gǔjià; 框架 kuāngjià. 3 纲〔綱〕要 gāngyào; 提要 tíyào. 4 最起码数〔數〕量的人员(或车辆等) zuìqǐmǎ shùliàng de rényuán: *a ~ staff* 一个人数最少的工作班子. 5 [习语] **skeleton in the ˈcupboard** 不可外扬〔揚〕的家丑〔醜〕 bùkě wàiyáng de jiāchǒu; 隐〔隱〕情 yǐnqíng. ˈ**skeleton key** *n* [C] 万〔萬〕能钥〔鑰〕匙 wànnéng yàoshi.

sketch /sketʃ/ *n* [C] 1 素描 sùmiáo; 速写〔寫〕 sùxiě. 2 简述 jiǎnshù; 概述 gàishù. 3 (喜剧性)短剧〔劇〕 duǎnjù. **sketch** *v* 1 [I, T] 画〔畫〕

S

速写 huà sùxiě;作素描 zuò sùmiáo. 2 [短语动词] sketch sth out 概述 gàishù; 草拟〔擬〕cǎonǐ. sketchy *adj* [-ier,-iest] 粗略的 cūlüède;概要的 gàiyàode.

skewer /ˈskjuːə(r)/ *n* [C] 串肉扦 chuànròuqiān;烤肉扦 kǎoròuqiān. skewer *v* [T] (用串肉扦)串起 chuànqǐ.

ski /skiː/ *n* [C] 滑雪板 huáxuěbǎn. ski *v* [*pt, pp* skied, *pres part* ~ing] [I] 滑雪 huáxuě: *go ~ing* 去滑雪. skier *n* [C].

skid /skɪd/ *n* [C] (车)打滑 dǎhuá;侧滑 cèhuá. skid *v* [-dd-] [I] (车等)滑向一侧 huá xiàng yícè;打滑 dǎhuá.

skies *pl* of SKY.

skilful (美语 skillful) /ˈskɪlfl/ *adj* 有技术〔術〕的 yǒu jìshù de;熟练〔練〕的 shúliànde: *a ~ player* 熟练的演奏者. skilfully *adv*.

skill /skɪl/ *n* [C, U] 技术〔術〕jìshù;技能 jìnéng;技艺〔藝〕jìyì. skilled *adj* 1 有技能的 yǒu jìnéng de;需要技术的 xūyào jìshù de;熟练〔練〕的 shúliànde. 2 有经〔經〕验〔驗〕的 yǒu jīngyàn de;训练过〔過〕的 xùnliànguòde: *~ed workers* 有经验的工人.

skim /skɪm/ *v* [-mm-] 1 [T] (从液体表面)撇去(浮物) piēqù. 2 [I,T] 掠过〔過〕lüèguò;擦过 cāguò. 3 [I,T] (*through*) 浏〔瀏〕览〔覽〕liúlǎn;略读〔讀〕lüèdú.

skin /skɪn/ *n* 1 [U] 皮 pí;皮肤〔膚〕pífū. 2 [C, U] (兽)皮 pí;毛皮 máopí;皮张〔張〕pízhāng. 3 [C,U] 果皮 guǒpí. 4 [C,U] (液体表面结成的)薄层〔層〕(如奶皮) bócéng. 5 [习语] by the ˌskin of one's ˈteeth 刚〔剛〕好 gānghǎo;勉强 miǎnqiǎng. get under sb's skin [非正式用语] (a) 使某人恼〔惱〕火 shǐ mǒurén nǎohuǒ. (b) 引起某人的关〔關〕注 yǐnqǐ mǒurénde guānzhù;吸引(某人) xīyǐn. be no skin off sb's nose [非正式用语]与〔與〕某人无〔無〕关 yǔ mǒurén wúguān. be skin and ˈbone(s) [非正式用语] 极〔極〕瘦 jíshòu. skin *v* [T] [-nn-] 剥去…的皮 bōqù…de pí. ˌskin-ˈdeep *adj* 肤浅〔淺〕的 fūqiǎnde;不持久的 bù chíjiǔ de. ˈskinflint *n* [C] 吝啬〔嗇〕鬼 lìnsèguǐ. ˈskinhead *n* [C] 留平头〔頭〕的青少年(尤指暴徒) liú píngtóude qīngshàonián. ˌskin-ˈtight *adj* (衣服)紧〔緊〕身的 jǐnshēnde. skinny *adj* [-ier,-iest] 极瘦的 jíshòude.

skint /skɪnt/ *adj* [英国非正式用语]无〔無〕钱〔錢〕的 wúqiánde;不名一文的 bù míng yì wén de.

skip[1] /skɪp/ *v* [-pp-] 1 [I] 轻〔輕〕快地跳 qīngkuàide tiào;蹦跳 bèngtiào. 2 [I] 跳绳〔繩〕tiàoshéng. 3 [I,T] 匆匆(或悄悄)离〔離〕开〔開〕cōngcōng líkāi: *~ the country* 匆匆离开这个国家. 4 [I] 匆匆(或随便)地由一地到另一地 cōngcōngde yóu yídì dào lìngyídì. 5 [T] 略过〔過〕lüèguò;漏过 lòuguò: *~ part of the book* 略过书中的一部分未看. 6 [T] 不参〔參〕加(会议等) bù cānjiā. skip *n* [C] 蹦跳 bèngtiào;跳绳 tiàoshéng;省略 shěnglüè.

skip[2] /skɪp/ *n* [C] 旧〔舊〕料桶 jiùliàotǒng.

skipper /ˈskɪpə(r)/ *n* [C] 船长〔長〕chuánzhǎng;队〔隊〕长 duìzhǎng. skipper *v* [I,T] 担〔擔〕任船长(或队长) dānrèn chuánzhǎng.

skirt /skɜːt/ *n* [C] 裙子 qúnzi. skirt *v* 1 [T] 在…的边〔邊〕缘 zài…de biānyuán;沿着…边缘走 yánzhe… biānyuán zǒu: *a wood ~ing the field* 在田野边上的树林. 2 [T] 避开〔開〕(话题等)bìkāi. ˈskirting-board *n* [U] 壁脚板 bìjiǎobǎn;踢脚板 tījiǎobǎn.

skittles /ˈskɪtlz/ *n* [U] 撞柱戏〔戲〕(沿球道以球击倒瓶状木柱的游戏) zhuàngzhùxì.

skulk /skʌlk/ *v* [I] 躲躲闪闪 duǒduǒ shǎnshǎn;鬼鬼祟祟 guǐguǐ suìsuì.

skull /skʌl/ *n* [C] 头〔頭〕骨 tóugǔ;颅〔顱〕骨 lúgǔ.

skunk /skʌŋk/ *n* [C] 臭鼬(北美产) chòuyòu.

sky /skaɪ/ *n* [U,C, 常作 sing] [*pl* skies /skaɪz/] 天 tiān;天空 tiānkōng. ˈskydiving *n* [U] 自由跳伞运〔運〕动〔動〕zìyóu tiàosǎn yùndòng. ˌsky-ˈhigh *adj* [非正式用语]极〔極〕高的 jígāode. ˈskylark *n* [C] 云〔雲〕雀 yúnquè. ˈskylight *n* [C] 天窗 tiānchuāng. ˈskyline *n* [C,常作 sing] (建筑物、山等在天空映衬下的)空中轮〔輪〕廓线〔綫〕kōngzhōng lúnkuòxiàn. ˈskyscraper *n* [C] 摩天楼〔樓〕mótiānlóu.

slab /slæb/ *n* [C] (石、木等的)厚板 hòubǎn.

slack[1] /slæk/ *adj* 1 不紧〔緊〕的 bùjǐnde;松〔鬆〕的 sōngde: *a ~ rope* 松弛的绳子. 2 懈怠的 xièdàide;疏忽的 shūhude. 3 不景气〔氣〕的 bùjǐngqìde;萧条〔條〕的 xiāotiáode: *Trade is ~.* 贸易不景气. slack *v* [I] 1 怠惰 dàiduò;偷懒 tōulǎn. 2 [短语动词] slack off / up 放松 fàngsōng;放慢 fàngmàn;减速 jiǎnsù. slackness *n* [U].

slack[2] /slæk/ the slack *n* [U] 1 (绳等的)松〔鬆〕弛部分 sōngchí bùfen. 2 [习语] take up the slack 拉紧〔緊〕绳〔繩〕子 lājǐn shéngzi.

slacken /ˈslækən/ *v* [I,T] 1 (使)松〔鬆〕弛 sōngchí. 2 (*off / up*) (使)放慢 fàngmàn;(使)迟〔遲〕缓 chíhuǎn.

slag /slæg/ *n* 1 [U] 矿〔礦〕渣 kuàngzhā;熔渣 róngzhā. 2 [C] [英贬,俚]荡〔蕩〕妇〔婦〕dàngfù. slag *v* [-gg-] [短语动词] slag sb off [英俚] 诋毁 dǐhuǐ;辱骂 rǔmà. ˈslag-heap *n* [C] 矿渣堆 kuàngzhāduī.

slam /slæm/ *v* [-mm-] 1 [I,T] 使劲〔勁〕关〔關〕shǐjìn guān;砰地关上 pēngde guānshàng. 2 [T] 猛击〔擊〕měngjī;使劲扔 shǐjìn rēng: *~ a book against the wall* 使劲把书朝墙扔过去. 3 [T] [非正式用语]批评 pīpíng. slam *n*

S

[C] 砰的一声〔聲〕pēngde yìshēng.

slander /ˈslɑːndə(r)/ *n* [U, C] 诽谤 fěibàng; 诋毁 dǐhuǐ. **slander** *v* [T] 诽谤 fěibàng; 中伤〔傷〕zhòngshāng. **slanderous** *adj*.

slang /slæŋ/ *n* [U] 俚语 lǐyǔ. **slang** *v* [T] 谩骂 mànmà.

slant /slɑːnt/ *v* 1 [I, T] (使)倾斜 qīngxié. 2 [T] [常作贬]有倾向地报〔報〕道 yǒu qīngxiàngde bàodào. **slant** *n* [C] 1 倾斜 qīngxié; 斜面 xiémiàn; 斜线〔綫〕xiéxiàn. 2 [非正式用语]观〔觀〕点〔點〕guāndiǎn; 看法 kànfǎ.

slap /slæp/ *v* [-pp-] [T] 1 掌击〔擊〕zhǎngjī; 掴〔摑〕guāi; 拍 pāi. 2 啪的一声〔聲〕放下 pāde yìshēng fàngxià: ~ *paint onto the wall* 劈里啪啦把颜料涂在墙上. **slap** *n* [C] 1 掌击 zhǎngjī; 掴 guāi; 拍 pāi. 2 [习语] a slap in the ˈface 侮辱 wǔrǔ. **slap** (亦作 ˌslap-ˈbang) *adv* [非正式用语]一直 yìzhí; 直接 zhíjiē: *The car ran ~ into the wall*. 汽车一直向前撞到墙上了.

slapdash /ˈslæpdæʃ/ *adj*, *adv* 草率的(地) cǎoshuàide; 马虎的(地) mǎhude.

slapstick /ˈslæpstɪk/ *n* [U] 打闹〔鬧〕剧〔劇〕dǎnàojù.

slap-up /ˈslæp ʌp/ *adj* [英国非正式用语](饭菜)第一流的 dìyīliúde.

slash /slæʃ/ *v* [T] 1 砍 kǎn; 砍击〔擊〕kǎnjī. 2 [非正式用语]大幅度削减 dàfúdù xuējiǎn: ~ *prices* 大减价. **slash** *n* [C] 1 砍 kǎn. 2 (长的)砍口 kǎnkǒu, 砍痕 kǎnhén.

slat /slæt/ *n* [C] 板条〔條〕bǎntiáo; 百叶〔葉〕板 bǎiyèbǎn.

slate /sleɪt/ *n* 1 [U] 板岩 bǎnyán; 页岩 yèyán. 2 [C] 石板瓦 shíbǎnwǎ. **slate** *v* [T] [非正式用语]严〔嚴〕厉〔厲〕批评 yánlì pīpíng.

slaughter /ˈslɔːtə(r)/ *n* [U] 1 屠宰 túzǎi; 宰杀〔殺〕zǎishā. 2 屠杀 túshā; 杀戮 shālù. **slaughter** *v* [T] 1 大量屠杀 dàliàng túshā. 2 [非正式用语]彻〔徹〕底打败 chèdǐ dǎbài. ˈ**slaughterhouse** *n* [C] 屠宰场〔場〕túzǎichǎng.

slave /sleɪv/ *n* [C] 1 奴隶〔隸〕núlì. 2 摆〔擺〕脱不了某种〔種〕习〔習〕惯的人 bǎituō bùliǎo mǒuzhǒng xíguàn de rén: *a ~ to drink* 酒鬼. **slave** *v* [I] 苦干〔幹〕kǔgàn; 刻苦工作 kèkǔ gōngzuò: ~ *away in the kitchen* 在厨房苦干. **slavery** *n* [U] 1 奴役 núyì; 奴隶身份 núlì shēnfen. 2 奴隶制 núlìzhì.

slaver /ˈslævə(r)/ *v* [I] (*over*) 1 流口水 liú kǒushuǐ; 垂涎 chuíxián. 2 [常作贬]渴望 kěwàng.

slavish /ˈsleɪvɪʃ/ *adj* [贬]无〔無〕独〔獨〕创〔創〕性的 wú dúchuàngxìng de: *a ~ copy* 毫无创意的摹写. **slavishly** *adv*.

slay /sleɪ/ *v* [*pt* **slew** /sluː/, *pp* **slain** /sleɪn/] [T] [正式用语或美语]残〔殘〕杀〔殺〕cánshā; 杀害 shāhài.

sledge /sledʒ/ (亦作 **sled** /sled/) *n* [C] 雪橇 xuěqiāo.

sledgehammer /ˈsledʒhæmə(r)/ *n* [C] 大锤 dà chuí.

sleek /sliːk/ *adj* 1 光滑而发〔發〕亮的 guānghuá ér fāliàng de: ~ *hair* 油亮的头发. 2 [常作贬]脑〔腦〕满肠〔腸〕肥的 nǎo mǎn cháng féi de.

sleep[1] /sliːp/ *n* 1 [U] 睡眠 shuìmián; 睡觉〔覺〕shuìjiào. 2 [sing] 睡眠时〔時〕间 shuìmián shíjiān. 3 [习语] ˌgo to ˈsleep 入睡 rùshuì. put to ˈsleep (a) 使(某人)入睡(尤指用麻醉剂) shǐ rùshuì. (b) 杀〔殺〕死(有病动物) shāsǐ. **sleepless** *adj* 失眠的 shīmiánde; 不眠的 bùmiánde.

sleep[2] /sliːp/ *v* [*pp*, *pt* **slept** /slept/] 1 [I] 睡 shuì; 睡眠 shuìmián; 睡着 shuìzháo. 2 [T] 为〔爲〕…提供床位 wèi…tígōng chuángwèi: *a flat that ~s six* 可睡六个人的一套房间. 3 [习语] sleep like a ˈlog/ˈtop [非正式用语]睡得很沉 shuì de hěn chén. sleep ˈtight [非正式用语][用于祈使句]睡个〔個〕好觉〔覺〕shuì gè hǎo jiào. 4 [短语动词] sleep around 与〔與〕多人发〔發〕生性关〔關〕系〔係〕yǔ duō rén fāshēng xìngguānxì. sleep in 睡懒觉 shuì lǎnjiào; 迟〔遲〕起 chí qǐ. sleep sth off 用睡眠消除(酒醉等) yòng shuìmián xiāochú. sleep on sth 把问题等留到第二天解决 bǎ wèntí děng liúdào dì'èrtiān jiějué. sleep through sth 未被(某事)吵醒 wèi bèi chǎoxǐng. sleep with sb 与某人发生性关系 yǔ mǒurén fāshēng xìngguānxì. **sleeper** *n* [C] 1 睡眠者 shuìmiánzhě. 2 [铁路]枕木 zhěnmù. 3 卧铺 wòpù. ˈ**sleeping-bag** *n* [C] 睡袋 shuìdài. ˈ**sleeping-car** *n* [C] 卧车 wòchē. ˈ**sleeping-pill** *n* [C] 安眠药〔藥〕丸 ānmián yàowán. **sleepy** *adj* [-ier, -iest] 1 想睡的 xiǎng shuì de; 瞌睡的 kēshuìde; 困乏的 kùnfáde. 2 (地方等)冷清的 lěngqīngde, 不热〔熱〕闹〔鬧〕的 bú rènào de: *a ~ little town* 宁静的小镇. **sleepily** *adv*.

sleet /sliːt/ *n* [U] 雨夹〔夾〕雪 yǔjiāxuě. **sleet** *v* [与 *it* 连用]下雨夹雪 xià yǔjiāxuě: *It's ~ing outside*. 外面下着雨夹雪.

sleeve /sliːv/ *n* [C] 1 袖子 xiùzi. 2 唱片套 chàngpiàntào. 3 [习语] have sth up one's sleeve 暗中已有打算、办〔辦〕法等 àn zhōng yǐ yǒu dǎsuàn、bànfǎ děng.

sleigh /sleɪ/ *n* [C] (尤指用马拉的)雪橇 xuěqiāo.

sleight /slaɪt/ *n* [习语] ˌsleight of ˈhand (变戏法等)手法熟练〔練〕shǒufǎ shúliàn.

slender /ˈslendə(r)/ *adj* 1 细长〔長〕的 xìchángde. 2 (人)苗条〔條〕的 miáotiáode, 纤〔纖〕弱的 xiānruòde. 3 微小的 wēixiǎode; 微薄的 wēibóde: *have a ~ chance* 机会极微小. **slenderness** *n* [U].

S

slept *pt*, *pp* of SLEEP².

slice /slaɪs/ *n* [C] 1 片 piàn;(尤指面包、肉)薄片 bópiàn. 2 [非正式用语]部分 bùfen: *take a ~ of the credit* 获得一份荣誉. 3 餐刀 cāndāo;菜刀 càidāo. 4 [习语] **a ˌslice of ˈlife** (小说中描述的)生活片段 shēnghuó piànduàn. **slice** *v* 1 [T] (*up*) 切片 qiēpiàn. 2 [I] *into* / *through* 切 qiē; 割 gē: *a knife slicing through butter* 切黄油的刀.

slick /slɪk/ *adj* 1 光滑的 guānghuáde;平滑的 pínghuáde. 2 圆滑而有效地完成的 yuánhuá ér yǒuxiàode wánchéng de. 3 [常贬](人)狡猾的 jiǎohuáde, 圆滑的 yuánhuáde.

slide¹ /slaɪd/ *n* 1 [sing] 滑 huá;滑动〔動〕huádòng. 2 [C] 滑道 huádào;滑坡 huápō;滑梯 huátī. 3 [C] 幻灯〔燈〕片 huàndēngpiàn. 4 [C] (显微镜的)承物玻璃片 chéng wù bōlipiàn.

slide² /slaɪd/ *v* [*pt*, *pp* **slid** /slɪd/] [I, T] 1 (使)滑动〔動〕huádòng. 2 (使)偷偷地行动 tōutōude xíngdòng. 3 [习语] **let sth ˈslide** 听〔聽〕其自然 tīng qí zìrán;放任其事 fàngrèn qí shì. **ˈslide-rule** *n* [C] 计算尺 jìsuànchǐ.

slight¹ /slaɪt/ *adj* 1 轻〔輕〕微的 qīngwēide;不重要的 bú zhòngyào de: *a ~ headache* 轻微的头痛. 2 细长〔長〕的 xìchángde;苗条〔條〕的 miáotiáode;纤〔纖〕弱的 xiānruòde;瘦小的 shòuxiǎode. 3 [习语] **not in the ˈslightest** 毫不 háo bù;一点〔點〕也不 yìdiǎn yě bù. **slightly** *adv* 1 稍微 shāowēi;略 lüè: *feel ~ly better* 觉得略为好些. 2 细长地 xìchángde: *a ~ly built boy* 身材瘦长的男孩. **slightness** *n* [U].

slight² /slaɪt/ *v* [T] 轻〔輕〕视 qīngshì;怠慢 dàimàn. **slight** *n* [C] 轻蔑 qīngmiè;怠慢 dàimàn. **slightingly** *adv*.

slim /slɪm/ *adj* [~mer, ~mest] 1 [褒]细长〔長〕的 xìchángde;苗条〔條〕的 miáotiáode. 2 微小的 wēixiǎode;稀少的 xīshǎode: *a ~ chance of success* 成功希望不大的机会. **slim** *v* [-mm-] [I] (用减食等办法)减轻〔輕〕体〔體〕重 jiǎnqīng tǐzhòng. **slimmer** *n* [C] 减肥者 jiǎnféizhě. **slimness** *n* [U].

slime /slaɪm/ *n* [U] 1 软泥 ruǎnní;黏土 niántǔ. 2 (蜗牛等的)黏液 niányè. **slimy** *adj* [-ier, -iest] 1 黏性的 niánxìngde;泥泞〔濘〕的 nínìngde. 2 [非正式用语]令人讨厌〔厭〕的 lìng rén tǎoyàn de; 谄媚的 chǎnmèide: *a slimy young man* 令人讨厌的年轻人.

sling /slɪŋ/ *n* [C] 吊索 diàosuǒ;吊带〔帶〕diàodài. **sling** *v* [*pt*, *pp* **slung** /slʌŋ/] [T] [非正式用语](用力)掷 zhì;抛 pāo: *We slung him out of the bar*. 我们把他扔出酒吧间.

slink /slɪŋk/ *v* [*pt*, *pp* **slunk** /slʌŋk/] [I] 溜走 liūzǒu;悄悄地走 qiāoqiāode zǒu.

slip¹ /slɪp/ *n* 1 [C] 滑 huá;溜 liū;失足 shīzú. 2 [C] 失误 shīwù;疏忽 shūhu;小错 xiǎocuò. 3 [C] 衬〔襯〕衣 chènyī;内衣 nèiyī. 4 = PILLOW-CASE (PILLOW). 5 [C] 纸条〔條〕zhǐtiáo. 6 [习语] **give sb the ˈslip** [非正式用语]摆〔擺〕脱(尾随者) bǎituō. **a ˈslip of a boy, girl, etc** 瘦削的男孩、女孩等 shòuxuēde nánhái、nǚhái děng.

slip² /slɪp/ *v* [-pp-] 1 [I] 滑倒 huádǎo;失足 shīzú: *He ~ped (over) in the mud*. 他在泥地里滑倒了. 2 [I, T] (使)溜走 liūzǒu;(使)悄悄地过〔過〕去 qiāoqiāode guòqù: *He ~ped the coin into his pocket*. 他把钱悄悄地塞进口袋. 3 [I] 滑落 huáluò;松〔鬆〕脱 sōngtuō: *The plate ~ped from my hand*. 盘子从我手中滑落. 4 [I, T] 匆忙地穿衣 cōngmángde chuānyī: ~ *on a coat* 匆匆穿上大衣. 5 [习语] **let sth slip** (a) 放走或错过(机会等) fàngzǒu huò cuòguò. (b) 无〔無〕意中泄漏(秘密等) wúyì zhōng xièlòu. **slip one's ˈmemory / ˈmind** (姓名,消息等)被遗忘 bèi yíwàng. 6 [短语动词] **slip up** [非正式用语]出错 chūcuò;失误 shīwù. **ˈslip-road** *n* [C] (连接高速公路的)岔道 chàdào. **ˈslip-stream** *n* [C] (飞机发动机的)尾流 wěiliú. **ˈslip-up** *n* [C] [非正式用语]出错 chūcuò;失误 shīwù.

slipper /ˈslɪpə(r)/ *n* [C] 拖鞋 tuōxié;便鞋 biànxié.

slippery /ˈslɪpərɪ/ *adj* [-ier, -iest] 1 (表面)光滑的 guānghuáde;易滑脱的 yì huátuō de. 2 [非正式用语](人)不老实〔實〕的 bù lǎoshi de, 不可靠的 bù kěkào de. 3 [非正式用语](问题)难〔難〕处〔處〕理的 nán chǔlǐ de, 棘手的 jíshǒude. 4 [习语] **the slippery ˈslope** [非正式用语]易导〔導〕致失败 yì dǎozhì shībài.

slipshod /ˈslɪpʃɒd/ *adj* 不认〔認〕真的 bú rènzhēnde;粗心的 cūxīnde.

slit /slɪt/ *n* [C] 狭长〔長〕的切口 xiáchángde qiēkǒu;裂缝 lièfèng. **slit** *v* [-tt-; *pt*, *pp* ~] [T] 切开〔開〕qiēkāi;撕裂 sīliè.

slither /ˈslɪðə(r)/ *v* [I] 不稳〔穩〕地滑动〔動〕bùwěnde huádòng.

sliver /ˈslɪvə(r)/ *n* [C] 薄片 bópiàn;碎片 suìpiàn: *a ~ of glass* 一片碎玻璃.

slob /slɒb/ *n* [C] [非正式用语][贬]肮〔骯〕脏〔髒〕、懒惰的人 āngzāng、lǎnduò de rén.

slog /slɒg/ *v* [-gg-] [I] [非正式用语] 1 辛苦工作 xīnkǔ gōngzuò: ~ (*away*) *at sth* 辛勤地工作. 2 艰〔艱〕难〔難〕地行走 jiānnánde xíngzǒu: ~ *up the hill* 艰难地爬山. **slog** *n* [sing, U] [非正式用语]苦活 kǔhuó;艰难的工作 jiānnánde gōngzuò.

slogan /ˈsləʊgən/ *n* [C] 标〔標〕语 biāoyǔ;口号〔號〕kǒuhào.

slop /slɒp/ *v* [-pp-] 1 [I] 溢出 yìchū;溅〔濺〕出 jiànchū. 2 [T] 使溢出 shǐ yìchū: *Don't ~*

the water all over the floor! 不要把水溅得满地都是! 3 [短语动词] **slop about / around** (指液体)晃荡[蕩](尤指在容器里) huàngdàng. **slop** *n* **slops** 脏[髒]水 zāngshuǐ; 污水 wūshuǐ.

slope /sləʊp/ *n* 1 [C, U] 斜线[綫] xiéxiàn; 斜度 xiédù. 2 [C] 倾斜面 qīngxiémiàn; 斜坡 xiépō. **slope** *v* 1 [I] 有斜度 yǒu xiédù. 2 [短语动词] **slope off** [英俚]走开[開] zǒukāi; 逃避工作 táobì gōngzuò.

sloppy /ˈslɒpɪ/ *adj* [-ier, -iest] 1 草率的 cǎoshuàide; 粗心的 cūxīnde: ~ *work* 粗心的工作. 2 [非正式用语]感情用事的 gǎnqíng yòng shì de; 伤[傷]感的 shānggǎnde: *a* ~ *love story* 伤心的爱情故事. 3 (衣服)肥大的 féidàde, 不合身的 bù héshēn de. 4 湿[濕]的 shīde; 不干[乾]净的 bù gānjìng de. **sloppily** *adv* 草率地 cǎoshuàide; 粗心地 cūxīnde; 伤感地 shānggǎnde. **sloppiness** *n* [U].

slosh /slɒʃ/ *v* 1 [I, T] (使)溅[濺] jiàn, 泼[潑] pō: ~ *water all over the floor* 把水溅了一地. 2 [T] [俚]打 dǎ. **sloshed** *adj* [俚]喝醉的 hēzuìde.

slot /slɒt/ *n* [C] 1 狭[狹]缝 xiáfèng: *put a coin in the* ~ 把一枚硬币投入孔中. 2 (用以安装某物的)沟[溝]槽 gōucáo. 3 [非正式用语] (在计划、程序单中的)适[適]当[當]位置 shìdàng wèizhi: ~*s for advertisements on television* 电视节目中插入广告的位置. **slot** *v* [-tt-] [T] 开[開]槽于 kāi cáo yú; 把…放入缝中 bǎ…fàngrù fèng zhōng.

sloth /sləʊθ/ *n* 1 [U] 懒惰 lǎnduò; 懒散 lǎnsǎn. 2 [C] (南美洲)树[樹]獭 shùtǎ. **slothful** *adj*.

slouch /slaʊtʃ/ *v* [I] 懒散地站、坐或行动[動] lǎnsǎnde zhàn、zuò huò xíngdòng. **slouch** *n* 1 [sing] 没精打采的姿态[態] méijīngdǎcǎide zītài; 懒洋洋地走动 lǎnyángyángde zǒudòng. 2 [习语] **be no slouch at sth** 善于做某事 shànyú zuò mǒushì.

slovenly /ˈslʌvnlɪ/ *adj* 不整洁[潔]的 bù zhěngjié de; 邋遢的 lātāde. **slovenliness** *n* [U].

slow[1] /sləʊ/ *adj* 1 慢的 mànde; 缓慢的 huǎnmànde: *a* ~ *vehicle* 行驶缓慢的车. 2 迟[遲]钝的 chídùnde; 笨的 bènde: *a* ~ *child* 迟钝的孩子. 3 不立即发[發]作的 bú lìjí fāzuò de. 4 乏味的 fáwèide; 不精彩的 bù jīngcǎi de: *a very* ~ *film* 极乏味的电影. 5 (钟表)走得慢的 zǒu de màn de. 6 [习语] **be slow off the mark** ⇨ MARK[1]. **slow on the uptake** ⇨ UPTAKE. ˈ**slow-coach** *n* [C] [非正式用语]慢性子的人 màn xìngzi de rén. **slowly** *adv*. **slowness** *n* [U].

slow[2] /sləʊ/ *adv* 1 缓慢地 huǎnmànde; 慢慢地 mànmànde: ~-*moving* 缓慢移动[動]的. 2 [习语] **go** ˈ**slow** (工人)怠工 dàigōng.

slow[3] /sləʊ/ *v* [I, T] (*down / up*) (使)慢下来 mànxiàlái. ˈ**slow-down** *n* [C] (生产活动等)放慢 fàng màn.

sludge /slʌdʒ/ *n* [U] 烂[爛]泥 lànní; 淤泥 yūní.

slug[1] /slʌg/ *n* [C] 蛞蝓 kuòyú.

slug[2] /slʌg/ *v* [-gg-] [T] [美语][非正式用语]用力打击[擊] yònglì dǎjī; 重击 zhòngjī.

slug[3] /slʌg/ *n* [C] [尤用于美语]枪[槍]弹[彈] qiāngdàn; 子弹 zǐdàn.

sluggish /ˈslʌgɪʃ/ *adj* 不活泼[潑]的 bù huópo de; 呆滞[滯]的 dāizhìde. **sluggishly** *adv*.

sluice /slu:s/ *n* [C] (亦作 ˈ**sluice-gate**) 水闸 shuǐzhá. **sluice** *v* [T] (用水)冲洗 chōngxǐ, 冲刷 chōngshuā.

slum /slʌm/ *n* [C] 陋巷 lòuxiàng; 贫民窟 pínmínkū. **slum** *v* [-mm-] [I] (亦作 **slum it**) 简陋地生活着 jiǎnlòude shēnghuózhe. **slummy** *adj*.

slumber /ˈslʌmbər/ *v* [I] [正式用语]安眠 ānmián. **slumber** *n* [U]. **slumbers** [pl] 睡眠 shuìmián.

slump /slʌmp/ *v* [I] 1 猛然落下 měngrán luòxià; 颓然倒下 tuírán dǎoxià. 2 (物价、贸易等)暴跌 bàodiē. **slump** *n* [C] (市面)不景气[氣] bù jǐngqì, 衰退 shuāituì.

slung *pt*, *pp* of SLING.

slur /slɜ:(r)/ *v* [-rr-] [T] 1 含糊不清地发[發]音 hánhu bùqīng de fāyīn; 模糊地写[寫] móhude xiě. 2 诋毁(某人的名誉) dǐhuǐ. **slur** *n* [C] 污辱 wūrǔ; 毁谤 huǐbàng: *a* ~ *on her name* 对她名声的污辱.

slush /slʌʃ/ *n* [U] 1 半融雪 bàn róng xuě; 雪泥 xuění. 2 [非正式用语][常贬]愚痴的伤[傷]感 yúchīde shānggǎn. ˈ**slush fund** *n* [C] 行贿钱[錢] xínghuìqián. **slushy** *adj* [-ier, -iest].

slut /slʌt/ *n* [C] [贬]不正经[經]的女人 bú zhèngjing de nǚrén; 荡[蕩]妇[婦] dàngfù. **sluttish** *adj*.

sly /slaɪ/ *adj* 狡猾的 jiǎohuáde; 狡诈的 jiǎozhàde; 偷偷摸摸的 tōutōumōmōde. **sly** *n* [习语] **on the** ˈ**sly** 秘密地 mìmìde. **slyly** *adv*. **slyness** *n* [U].

smack[1] /smæk/ *n* [C] 1 拍击[擊] pāijī; 拍击声 pāijīshēng. 2 [非正式用语](出声的)响[響]吻 xiǎngwěn. **smack** *v* [T] 1 (用掌)拍击 pāijī. 2 [习语] **smack one's lips** ⇨ LIP. **smack** *adv* 猛烈地 měngliède; 突然 tūrán: *run* ~ *into a wall* 猛然撞在墙上.

smack[2] /smæk/ *v* [短语动词] **smack of sth** 略带[帶]某种[種]味道 lüè dài mǒuzhǒng wèidào.

S

small /smɔːl/ *adj* 1 小的 xiǎode;少的 shǎode: *a ~ house* 小屋. 2 幼小的 yòuxiǎode: *~ children* 小孩子们. 3 小规模(经营)的 xiǎo guīmó de: *~ businesses* 小本经营. 4 不重要的 bú zhòngyào de;微不足道的 wēi bù zú dào de: *a ~ problem* 小问题. 5 [习语] feel ˈsmall 感到羞愧(或丢脸) gǎndào xiūkuì. a small ˈfortune 许多钱〔錢〕 xǔduō qián. the ˈsmall hours 半夜后三、四点〔點〕钟〔鐘〕 bànyè hòu sān、sì diǎnzhōng. small wonder ⇨ WONDER. **small** *n* [sing] (某物的)狭〔狹〕小部分 xiáxiǎo bùfen: *the ~ of the back* 腰背部. small ˈarms *n* [pl] 轻〔輕〕武器 qīng wǔqì. ˈsmallholding *n* [C] [英国英语]五十英亩〔畝〕以下的小片地 wǔshí yīngmǔ yǐxià de xiǎopiàndì. small-ˈminded *adj* 吝啬〔嗇〕自私的 lìnsè zìsī de;气〔氣〕量小的 qìliàng xiǎo de. smallness *n* [U]. ˈsmallpox *n* [U] 天花 tiānhuā. ˈsmall talk *n* [U] 闲聊 xiánliáo.

smart[1] /smɑːt/ *adj* 1 漂亮的 piàoliàngde;(衣着)整洁〔潔〕的 zhěngjiéde: *a ~ appearance / person* 漂亮的仪表(或人). 2 时〔時〕髦的 shímáode: *a ~ restaurant* 一家格调高雅的餐馆. 3 [尤用于美语]聪〔聰〕明的 cōngmingde;伶俐的 línglìde: *a ~ answer* 一个巧妙的回答. 4 轻〔輕〕快的 qīngkuàide;敏捷的 mǐnjiéde;剧〔劇〕烈的 jùliède;严〔嚴〕厉〔厲〕的 yánlìde: *a ~ pace* 轻快的脚步. *a ~ slap* 一记猛烈的耳光. **smarten** /ˈsmɑːtn/ *v* [短语动词] smarten (oneself / sb / sth) up 使(自己或某人、某物)更整洁 shǐ gèng zhěngjié. **smartly** *adv*. **smartness** *n* [U].

smart[2] /smɑːt/ *v* [I], *n* [U] (感觉)剧〔劇〕痛 jùtòng; 刺痛 cìtòng: *The smoke made my eyes ~.* 烟雾使我的眼睛刺痛.

smash /smæʃ/ *v* 1 [I,T] 打碎 dǎ suì;打破 dǎ pò: *~ a cup on the floor* 在地上摔碎一只杯子. 2 [I] *into, through, etc* 猛冲〔衝〕 měngchōng;撞入 zhuàngrù: *They ~ed into the wall.* 他们撞在墙上. 3 [T] 猛击〔擊〕 měngjī. 4 [T] [非正式用语]打败 dǎ bài; 击溃 jīkuì. **smash** *n* 1 [sing] 粉碎 fěnsuì;破碎声〔聲〕 pòsuìshēng. 2 [C] [网球]扣球 kòuqiú;杀〔殺〕球 shāqiú. 3 [C] (亦作 smash ˈhit) [非正式用语]极〔極〕为〔爲〕轰〔轟〕动〔動〕的戏〔戲〕剧〔劇〕、歌曲等 jí wéi hōngdòng de xìjù、gēqǔ děng. 4 = SMASH-UP. **smash** *adv* 碰撞地 pèngzhuàngde;破碎地 pòsuìde: *drive ~ into a wall* 驾车撞墙. **smashing** *adj* [英国非正式用语]极好的 jíhǎode. ˈsmash-up *n* [C] 撞车 zhuàngchē.

smattering /ˈsmætərɪŋ/ *n* [sing] *of* 肤〔膚〕浅〔淺〕的知识〔識〕 fūqiǎnde zhīshi;一知半解 yìzhībànjiě: *a ~ of French* 一知半解的法语.

smear /smɪə(r)/ *v* [T] 1 涂〔塗〕抹(油腻) túmǒ: *~ mud on the wall* 在墙上涂泥浆. 2 [喻]诽谤 fěibàng; 毁坏〔壞〕(名誉) huǐhuài. **smear** *n* [C] 1 污点〔點〕 wūdiǎn; 污迹〔跡〕 wūjì. 2 [喻]诽谤的话 fěibàngde huà. 3 (供显微镜检查疾病的)标〔標〕本 biāoběn.

smell[1] /smel/ *n* 1 [U] 嗅觉〔覺〕 xiùjué. 2 [C, U] 气〔氣〕味 qìwèi. 3 [C] 臭 chòu; 难〔難〕闻 nánwén: *What a ~!* 多么臭呀! 4 [C, 常作 sing] 嗅 xiù; 闻 wén: *Have a ~ of this.* 闻一下这个. **smelly** *adj* [-ier, -iest] [非正式用语]有臭味的 yǒu chòuwèi de.

smell[2] /smel/ *v* [*pt*, *pp* smelt /smelt/ 或 smelled] 1 [T] [常与 *can*, *could* 连用]嗅出 xiùchū;闻到 wéndào: *Can you ~ gas?* 你闻到煤气味了吗? 2 [I,T] 嗅 xiù; 闻 wén: *~ the flowers* 闻一闻这些花. 3 [I] 有嗅觉〔覺〕 yǒu xiùjué: *Can birds ~?* 鸟有嗅觉吗? 4 [I](a) (*of*) 发〔發〕出…气〔氣〕味 fāchū…qìwèi: *~ good / of soap* 闻起来很香(或有肥皂味). (b) 发出臭味 fāchū chòuwèi: *your feet ~* 你的脚发臭. 5 [习语] smell a ˈrat [非正式用语]注意某事不对〔對〕头〔頭〕 zhùyì mǒushì búduìtóu.

smile /smaɪl/ *n* [C] 微笑 wēixiào;笑容 xiàoróng. **smile** *v* [I] 微笑 wēixiào. **smilingly** *adv*.

smirk /smɜːk/ *v* [I] *n* [C] 傻〔傻〕笑 shǎxiào;得意的笑 déyìde xiào.

smithereens /ˌsmɪðəˈriːnz/ *n* [pl] [习语] smash, break, etc sth (in) to smithereens 将〔將〕某物捣、敲…成碎片 jiāng mǒuwù dǎo、qiāo…chéng suìpiàn.

smitten /ˈsmɪtən/ *adj* (*with*) 1 深受(某种感情)影响〔響〕的 shēn shòu yǐngxiǎng de. 2 突然喜爱〔愛〕(常指情爱) tūrán xǐ'ài: *I am rather ~ with her.* 我一下子爱上了她.

smock /smɒk/ *n* [C] 罩衫 zhàoshān;工作服 gōngzuòfú.

smog /smɒg/ *n* [U] 烟雾〔霧〕 yānwù.

smoke[1] /sməʊk/ *n* 1 [U] 烟 yān; 烟尘〔塵〕 yānchén. 2 [C] 吸烟 xī yān. 3 [习语] go up in ˈsmoke (a) 被烧〔燒〕光 bèi shāo guāng. (b) 以失败告终 yǐ shībài gàozhōng. ˈsmoke alarm *n* [C] 烟火报〔報〕警器 yānhuǒ bàojǐngqì;火灾〔災〕警报器 huǒzāi jǐngbàoqì;烟感报警器 yāngǎn bàojǐngqì. ˈsmoke-screen *n* [C] (a) 烟幕 yānmù. (b) [喻]障眼法 zhàngyǎnfǎ; 蒙〔矇〕骗人的话 mēngpiàn rén de huà. **smoky** *adj* [-ier, -iest].

smoke[2] /sməʊk/ *v* 1 [I] 冒烟 mào yān;起烟雾〔霧〕 qǐ yānwù. 2 [I,T] 抽烟 chōuyān;吸烟 xīyān. 3 [T] 熏制〔製〕(鱼,肉) xūnzhì. 4 [短语动词] smoke sb / sth out 熏走某人(或某物) xūn zǒu mǒurén. **smoker** *n* [C] 吸烟者 xī-

S

yānzhě. **smoking** *n* [C] 吸烟 xīyān; 抽烟 chōuyān.

smooth /smuːð/ *adj* 1 光滑的 guānghuáde; 平滑的 pínghuáde: ~ *skin* 光滑的皮肤. 2 平稳〔穩〕的 píngwěnde; 不摇晃的 bù yáohuàng de: *a* ~ *ride* 平稳的行驶. 3 (液体)调匀的 tiáoyúnde, 不结块〔塊〕的 bù jié kuài de. 4 无〔無〕困难〔難〕的 wú kùnnan de; 没问题的 méi wèntíde. 5 柔和的 róuhéde; 温和的 wēnhéde. 6 [常贬]奉承的 fèng chengde; 有礼〔禮〕貌的 yǒu lǐmào de. **smooth** *v* 1 [T] 使光滑 shǐ guānghuá; 把…弄平 bǎ…nòng píng; 使平稳 shǐ píngwěn; 使平静 shǐ píngjìng; 使缓和 shǐ huǎnhé. 2 [短语动词] **smooth sth over** 使(问题等)缓解 shǐ huǎnjiě. **smoothly** *adv*. **smoothness** *n* [U].

smother /ˈsmʌðə(r)/ *v* 1 [I, T] (使)窒息 zhìxī; 把…闷死 bǎ… mēnsǐ. 2 [T] (*in* / *with*) 覆盖〔蓋〕 fùgài: *a cake* ~*ed in cream* 涂有乳酪的饼. 3 [T] 闷住(火) mēnzhù; 闷熄 mēnxī: [喻] ~ *a yawn* 忍住哈欠.

smoulder (美语 **smol-**) /ˈsməʊldə(r)/ *v* [I] 文火闷烧〔燒〕 wénhuǒ mēnshāo: ~*ing ashes* 冒着烟的灰烬. [喻] *Hate* ~*ed within her*. 她心中积怨很久.

SMS /es em ˈes/ *abbr* short message (or messaging) service (手机)短信服务〔務〕 duǎnxìn fúwù.

smudge /smʌdʒ/ *n* [C] 污点〔點〕 wūdiǎn; 污迹〔跡〕 wūjì. **smudge** *v* 1 [T] 弄脏〔髒〕 nòng zāng; 涂〔塗〕污 tú wū. 2 [I] (墨水等)形成污迹 xíngchéng wūjì.

smug /smʌg/ *adj* [~**ger**, ~**gest**] 自满的 zìmǎnde; 沾沾自喜的 zhānzhān zìxǐ de. **smugly** *adv*. **smugness** *n* [U].

smuggle /ˈsmʌgl/ *v* [T] 私运〔運〕 sīyùn; 走私 zǒusī; 偷带〔帶〕(人或物) tōudài: ~ *drugs into the country* 私运毒品入境. ~ *a letter into prison* 把一封信偷偷地带进监狱. **smuggler** /ˈsmʌglə(r)/ *n* [C]. **smuggling** *n* [U].

smut /smʌt/ *n* 1 [C] 煤尘〔塵〕 méichén; 一片黑污 yípiàn hēiwū. 2 [U] 淫词 yíncí; 秽〔穢〕语 huìyǔ. **smutty** *adj*.

S

snack /snæk/ *n* [C] 小吃 xiǎochī; 快餐 kuàicān.

snag /snæg/ *n* [C] 1 意外的困难〔難〕 yìwàide kùnnan. 2 尖利或粗糙的突出物 jiānlì huò cūcāo de tūchūwù. **snag** *v* [-**gg**-] [T] (在尖利物上)钩住(或撕破) gōu zhù.

snail /sneɪl/ *n* [C] 蜗〔蝸〕牛 wōniú.

snake /sneɪk/ *n* [C] 1 蛇 shé. 2 [喻]阴〔陰〕险〔險〕的人 yīnxiǎnde rén. 3 [习语] **a ˌsnake in the ˈgrass** 伪〔僞〕装〔裝〕成朋友的敌〔敵〕人 wěizhuāng chéng péngyǒu de dírén. **snake** *v* [I] 蜿蜒前进〔進〕 wānyán qiánjìn; 蛇行 shéxíng.

snap /snæp/ *v* [-**pp**-] 1 [I, T] (使)发出断〔斷〕裂声〔聲〕或尖利声 fāchū duànlièshēng huò jiānlìshēng. 2 [I, T] 啪地一声关〔關〕上或打开〔開〕 pāde yìshēng guānshàng huò dǎkāi: ~ *shut* 啪地一声关上. 3 [I, T] 厉〔厲〕声说(话) lìshēng shuō: ~ *orders* 厉声地发布命令. 4 [I] (狗等)猛咬 měng yǎo: *The dog* ~*ped at her ankles*. 狗咬住她的脚踝. 5 [T] 拍照 pāizhào. 6 [习语] **snap one's ˈfingers** 打榧子(用食指或中指捻碰拇指发声) dǎ fěizi. **ˌsnap ˈout of it** [非正式用语]改变〔變〕情绪、习〔習〕惯等 gǎibiàn qíngxù、xíguàn děng. 7 [短语动词] **snap at sb** 厉声对〔對〕某人说话 lìshēng duì mǒurén shuōhuà. **snap at sth** 一下子咬住(某物) yíxiàzi yǎo zhù: [喻] ~ *at the chance to go on holiday* 抓住机会去度假. **snap sth up** 抢〔搶〕购〔購〕(某物) qiǎnggòu. **snap** *n* [C] 1 断裂、开关、厉声说话、拍照、突然咬住等(的声音) duànliè、kāi guān、lìshēng shuōhuà、pāizhào、tūrán yǎo zhù děng. 2 一阵天气〔氣〕(常指寒冷的) yízhèn tiānqì. 3 (亦作 **ˈsnapshot**) 快照 kuàizhào. **snap** *adj* 匆忙的 cōngmángde; 仓〔倉〕促的 cāngcùde: *a* ~ *decision* 仓促的决定. **snappy** *adj* [-**ier**, -**iest**] (a) 易怒的 yìnùde; 过〔過〕敏的 guòmǐnde. (b) 时〔時〕髦的 shímáode; 漂亮的 piàoliàngde. (c) 活泼〔潑〕的 huópode; 灵〔靈〕活的 línghuóde.

snare /sneə(r)/ *n* [C] 1 罗〔羅〕网〔網〕 luówǎng; 陷阱 xiànjǐng. 2 (使人上当的)圈套 quāntào. **snare** *v* [T] 诱捕 yòubǔ; 陷害 xiànhài.

snarl[1] /snɑːl/ *v* 1 [I] (狗等)嗥〔嘷〕叫 háojiào. 2 [I, T] (人)咆哮 páoxiào. **snarl** *n* [C] 嗥叫 háojiào; 咆哮 páoxiào.

snarl[2] /snɑːl/ *v* [非正式用语][短语动词] **snarl (sth) up** (使)缠〔纏〕结 chánjié; (使)混乱〔亂〕 hùnluàn: *The traffic was* ~*ed up*. 交通混乱. **ˈsnarl-up** *n* [C] [非正式用语]缠结 chánjié; (尤指交通)混乱 hùnluàn.

snatch /snætʃ/ *v* 1 [I, T] 抢〔搶〕 qiǎng; 夺〔奪〕取 duóqǔ: ~ *the child from her father* 从她的父亲手中抢走女孩. 2 [T] 迅速获〔獲〕得 xùnsù huòdé; 趁机〔機〕取得 chèn jī qǔdé: ~ *a kiss* 趁机一吻. **snatch** *n* 1 [sing] 抢 qiǎng; 夺 duó. 2 [C, 常作 pl] 片段 piànduàn; 短时 duǎnshí: ~*es of conversation* 谈话的片段.

sneak /sniːk/ *v* 1 [I] 偷偷地走 tōutōude zǒu; 偷偷摸摸地行动〔動〕 tōutōumōmōde xíngdòng: ~ *past sb* 偷偷地从某人身边经过. 2 [T] 偷取 tōu qǔ; 偷做 tōu zuò: ~ *money from the box* 从箱子中偷钱. 3 [I] 告状〔狀〕 gàozhuàng; 告密 gàomì. **sneak** *n* [C] 告密者 gàomìzhě. **sneakers** *n* [pl] [美语]胶〔膠〕底布鞋 jiāodǐ bùxié. **sneaking** *adj* (a) 偷偷摸摸的 tōutōumōmōde; 诡秘的 guǐmìde: *have a* ~*ing re-*

spect for sb 私下里尊敬某人.(b) 含糊的 hánhude;不明确〔確〕的 bù míngquè de: *a ~ing suspicion* 隐藏在心中的猜疑. **sneaky** *adj* [非正式用语][贬]鬼鬼祟祟的 guǐguǐsuìsuìde;偷偷摸摸的 tōutōumōmōde.

sneer /snɪə(r)/ *v* [I] (*at*) 嘲笑 cháoxiào;讥〔譏〕笑 jīxiào;说轻〔輕〕蔑话 shuō qīngmiè huà. **sneer** *n* [C] 嘲笑 cháoxiào;讥笑 jīxiào.

sneeze /sniːz/ *n* [C] 喷嚏 pēntì. **sneeze** *v* [I] **1** 打喷嚏 dǎ pēntì. **2** [习语] **not to be ˈsneezed at** [非正式用语]值得有的 zhíde yǒu de;不可轻〔輕〕视的 bùkě qīngshì de.

sniff /snɪf/ *v* **1** (a) [I] (有声音地)以鼻吸气〔氣〕yǐ bí xīqì. (b) [I, T] (*at*) 闻 wén;嗅 xiù;嗅出 xiù chū: ~ (*at*) *the roses* 闻玫瑰花的香味. **2** [短语动词] **sniff at sth** [常作被动语态]嗤之以鼻 chī zhī yǐ bí: *Her offer is not to be ~ed at*. 她的好意不可嗤之以鼻. **sniff sb out** 发〔發〕现某人 fāxiàn mǒurén. **sniff** *n* [C] 吸气声〔聲〕xīqìshēng;嗅 xiù.

snigger /ˈsnɪgə(r)/ *n* [C] 窃〔竊〕笑 qièxiào;暗笑 ànxiào. **snigger** *v* [I] (*at*) 窃笑 qièxiào;暗笑 ànxiào.

snip /snɪp/ *v* [-pp-] [I, T] 剪 jiǎn;剪去 jiǎnqù. **snip** *n* [C] **1** 剪 jiǎn. **2** [英国非正式用语]便宜货 piányihuò: *It's a ~ at only £10*. 只有十英镑,真便宜.

snipe /snaɪp/ *v* [I] **1** 伏击〔擊〕fújī;狙击 jūjī. **2** [喻]抨击 pēngjī. **sniper** *n* [C].

snippet /ˈsnɪpɪt/ *n* [C] (新闻、消息等)片段 piànduàn: ~ *of gossip* 闲谈的片断.

snivel /ˈsnɪvl/ *v* [-ll-;美语 -l-] [I] (伤心地)啼哭 tíkū;抽泣 chōuqì.

snob /snɒb/ *n* [C] 势〔勢〕利的人 shìlìde rén. **snobbery** *n* [C] 势利 shìlì. **snobbish** *adj*.

snog /snɒg/ *v* [-gg-] [I] [英国非正式用语]亲〔親〕吻拥〔擁〕抱 qīnwěn yōngbào.

snooker /ˈsnuːkə(r)/ *n* [U] 落袋台〔臺〕球 luò dài táiqiú. **snooker** *v* [T] 使(某人)处〔處〕于困境 shǐ chǔyú kùnjìng.

snoop /snuːp/ *v* [I] (*about* / *around*) 窥探 kuītàn;打听〔聽〕dǎting.

snooze /snuːz/ *v* [I] *n* [C] [非正式用语]小睡 xiǎoshuì;午睡 wǔshuì.

snore /snɔː(r)/ *v* [I] 打鼾 dǎhān. **snore** *n* [C] 鼾声〔聲〕hānshēng.

snorkel /ˈsnɔːkl/ *n* [C] (潜水用)通气〔氣〕管 tōngqìguǎn. **snorkel** *v* [-ll-;美语 -l-] [I] 戴通气管潜〔潛〕泳 dài tōngqìguǎn qiányǒng.

snort /snɔːt/ *v* **1** [I] 喷鼻息 pēn bíxī. **2** [I] (*at*) 发〔發〕哼声〔聲〕fā hēngshēng. **snort** *n* [C] 喷鼻息 pēn bíxī;鼻息声 bíxīshēng.

snout /snaʊt/ *n* [C] (动物的)口鼻部 kǒubíbù;(尤指)猪鼻 zhūbí.

snow[1] /snəʊ/ *n* [U] 雪 xuě;积〔積〕雪 jīxuě. ˈ**snowball** *n* [C] 雪球 xuěqiú. ˈ**snowball** *v* [I] (像滚雪球般)迅速增大(或增加) xùnsù zēngdà. ˈ**snowboard** *n* [C] 单〔單〕板滑雪板 dānbǎn huáxuěbǎn. **snowboard** *v* [I] 做单板滑雪 zuò dānbǎn huáxuě. ˈ**snowboarder** *n* [C] 单板滑雪者 dānbǎn huáxuězhě. ˈ**snowboarding** *n* [U] 单板滑雪 dānbǎn huáxuě. ˈ**snow-drift** *n* [C] (被风吹成的)雪堆 xuěduī. ˈ**snowdrop** *n* [C] [植物]雪莲 xuělián. ˈ**snowman** *n* [C] 雪人 xuěrén. ˈ**snow-plough** (美语 -**plow**) *n* [C] 扫〔掃〕雪机〔機〕sǎoxuějī. ˈ**snowstorm** *n* [C] 暴风〔風〕雪 bàofēngxuě.

snow[2] /snəʊ/ *v* **1** [I] [与 *it* 连用]下雪 xiàxuě;降雪 jiàngxuě: *It ~ed all day*. 下了一整天雪. **2** [短语动词] **snow sb in / up** [常用被动语态]被大雪困住(不能外出) bèi dàxuě kùnzhù. **snow sb under** [常用被动语态]被压〔壓〕倒 bèi yādǎo;被淹没 bèi yānmò. **snowy** *adj* [-**ier**, -**iest**].

snub /snʌb/ *v* [-bb-] [T] 冷落 lěngluò;怠慢 dàimàn. **snub** *n* [C] 冷落的言词或态〔態〕度 lěngluòde yáncí huò tàidù.

snub nose /ˈsnʌb nəʊz/ *n* [C] 狮〔獅〕子鼻 shīzibí. ˈ**snub-nosed** *adj*.

snuff[1] /snʌf/ *n* [U] 鼻烟 bíyān.

snuff[2] /snʌf/ *v* **1** [T] (*out*) 掐灭〔滅〕(蜡烛) qiāmiè. **2** [习语] ˈ**snuff it** [英国非正式用语]吹灯〔燈〕chuīdēng;死亡 sǐwáng. **3** [短语动词] **snuff sth out** 了结某事 liǎojié mǒushì.

snug /snʌg/ *adj* [-gg-] **1** 温暖的 wēnnuǎnde;舒适〔適〕的 shūshìde. **2** 紧〔緊〕贴的 jǐntiēde;紧身的 jǐnshēnde: *a ~ jacket* 紧身短上衣. **snugly** *adv*.

snuggle /ˈsnʌgl/ *v* [I] (*up* / *down*) 舒服地蜷伏 shūfude quánfú;挨紧〔緊〕āijǐn;偎依 wēiyī.

so[1] /səʊ/ *adv* **1** 这〔這〕么〔麼〕zhème;那么 nàme;到这种〔種〕程度 dào zhèzhǒng chéngdù: *not so big as I thought* 不像我想像的那么大. **2** 很 hěn;极〔極〕jí: *I'm so glad to see you*. 见到你我很高兴. **3** [习语] **so much for** ˈ**sb** / ˈ**sth** 关〔關〕于某人(或某事)要说的(或要做的)只有这些 guānyú mǒurén yào shuō de zhǐyǒu zhèxiē. ˌ**so much** ˈ**so that** 到这种程度,以致… dào zhèzhǒng chéngdù, yǐzhì….

so[2] /səʊ/ *adv* **1** 这〔這〕样〔樣〕zhèyàng;那样 nàyàng: *Kick the ball so*. 这样踢球. **2** (用以避免重复): '*Is he coming?*' '*I think so*.' "他来吗?""我想能来." **3**(用以表示同意): '*It's Friday today, not Thursday*.' '*So it is*.' "今天是星期五,不是星期四.""对的." **4** 也 yě: *You are young and so am I*. 你年轻,而我也是. **5**[习语] **and** ˈ**so on** 等等 děngděng. **so as to** 为〔為〕的是 wèi de shì;以便

S

yībiàn;使得 shǐdé: *He drove fast so as not to be late*. 他为了不迟到,把车开得很快. **so that** (a) 为的是 wèi de shì;以便 yǐbiàn;使得 shǐdé: *Hurry up and finish so that we can go home early*. 赶快结束,我们可以早点回家. (b)以致 yǐzhì;结果是 jiéguǒ shì: *Nothing was heard from her, so that people thought she was dead*. 没有听到她的任何消息,以致人们以为她死了. **so-and-so** /ˈsəʊ n səʊ/ *n* [C] [非正式用语] 1 某某人 mǒumǒurén. 2 讨厌〔厭〕的人 tǎoyànde rén: *That so-and-so lied to me*. 那个讨厌的人骗了我. **ˈso-called** *adj* 所谓的 suǒwèide: *Her so-called friends refused to help her*. 她的那些所谓的朋友拒绝帮助她.

so[3] /səʊ/ *conj* 1 所以 suǒyǐ;因而 yīn'ér: *He was hurt so I helped him*. 他受伤了,所以我帮助他. 2[非正式用语](表示目的): *I gave you a map so you wouldn't get lost*. 我给你一张地图,这样你就不会迷路了. 3(用以引出下文): *So she went and told the police*. 就这样,她去报告了警察. 4[习语] **so what**? [非正式用语]有什么〔麽〕了不起? yǒu shénme liǎobuqǐ? 那又怎么样〔樣〕nà yòu zěnmeyàng: '*She's lying about it*.' '*So what*?' "她对此事在说谎.""那又怎么样?"

soak /səʊk/ *v* 1 (a) [I] 浸 jìn;泡 pào. (b)使浸透 shǐ jìntòu;使吸收 shǐ xīshōu: ~ *the bread in milk* 把面包泡在牛奶里. 2 [T] (雨水等)淋湿〔濕〕lín shī;浇〔澆〕透 jiāo tòu: *The rain ~ed (through) his coat*. 雨把他的大衣淋透了. 3[短语动词] **soak sth up** 吸入(液体) xī rù: *Paper ~s up water*. 纸把水吸干〔乾〕了. **soak** *n* [C] 浸 jìn;泡 pào. **soaked, soaking** *adj* 湿透的 shītòude.

soap /səʊp/ *n* 1 [U] 肥皂 féizào. 2 [C] [非正式用语] = SOAP OPERA. **soap** *v* [T] 用肥皂(擦洗) yòng féizào. **ˈsoap opera** *n* [C, U] (电台或电视以角色的日常生活为题材的)连续〔續〕剧〔劇〕liánxùjù. **soapy** *adj* [-ier, -iest].

soar /sɔː(r)/ *v* [I] 1 (鸟)高飞〔飛〕gāofēi; 翱〔翺〕翔 áoxiáng. 2 [喻]高涨〔漲〕gāozhǎng;猛增 měngzēng: ~*ing prices* 飞涨的物价.

sob /sɒb/ *v* [-bb-] 1 [I] 呜〔嗚〕咽 wūyè;啜泣 chuòqì. 2 [短语动词] **sob sth out** 哭诉 kūsù. **sob** *n* [C] 哭泣 kūqì;哭泣声〔聲〕kūqìshēng. **ˈsob-story** *n* [C] [常贬] 伤〔傷〕感的故事 shānggǎnde gùshì.

sober /ˈsəʊbə(r)/ *adj* 1 未醉的 wèizuìde. 2 严〔嚴〕肃〔肅〕的 yánsùde;认〔認〕真的 rènzhēnde: *a ~ person* 严肃认真的人. **sober** *v* 1 [I, T](使)变〔變〕严肃 biàn yánsù. 2 [短语动词] **sober sb up** 使清醒 shǐ qīngxǐng. **soberly** *adv*.

soccer /ˈsɒkə(r)/ *n* [U] 英式足球 yīngshì zúqiú.

sociable /ˈsəʊʃəbl/ *adj* 友好的 yǒuhǎode;好交际〔際〕的 hào jiāojì de.

social /ˈsəʊʃl/ *adj* 1 社会〔會〕的 shèhuìde: ~ *customs* 社会习俗. 2 社会上的 shèhuì shàng de;社会地位的 shèhuì dìwèi de: *one's ~ equals* 与自己社会地位相同者. 3 社交的 shèjiāode;交际〔際〕的 jiāojìde: *a* ˈ~ *club* 联谊会. 4 (动物)群居的 qúnjūde. 5 [非正式用语]好交际的 hào jiāojì de;合群的 héqúnde. **ˌSocial and Liberal ˈDemocrats** *n* [pl] (英国)社会自由民主党〔黨〕Shèhuìzìyóumínzhǔdǎng. **ˌsocial ˈscience** *n* [C, U] 社会科学〔學〕shèhuì kēxué. **ˌsocial seˈcurity** *n* [U] 社会福利 shèhuì fúlì. **ˈsocial worker** *n* [C] 社会福利工作者 shèhuì fúlì gōngzuòzhě. **socially** *adv*.

socialism /ˈsəʊʃəlɪzəm/ *n* [U] 社会〔會〕主义〔義〕shèhuì zhǔyì. **socialist** *adj*, *n* [C].

socialize /ˈsəʊʃəlaɪz/ *v* [I] (与他人)往来 wǎnglái;交际〔際〕jiāojì.

society /səˈsaɪətɪ/ *n* [*pl* -ies] 1 [U] 社会〔會〕制度 shèhuì zhìdù. 2 [C, U] 社会 shèhuì. 3 [U] [正式用语]交往 jiāowǎng;陪同 péitóng: *in the ~ of her friends* 在她的朋友们的陪同下. 4 上流社会 shàngliú shèhuì;社交界 shèjiāojiè. 5 [C] (为某种共同兴趣组成的)团〔團〕体〔體〕tuántǐ,协〔協〕会 xiéhuì: *a drama ~* 戏剧社.

sociology /ˌsəʊsɪˈɒlədʒɪ/ *n* [U] 社会〔會〕学〔學〕shèhuìxué. **sociologist** *n* [C] 社会学家 shèhuìxuéjiā. **sociological** /-sɪəˈlɒdʒɪkl/ *adj*.

sock[1] /sɒk/ *n* [C] 短袜〔襪〕duǎn wà.

sock[2] /sɒk/ *n* [C] [非正式用语]拳打 quándǎ;殴〔毆〕打 ōudǎ. **sock** *v* [T] 拳打 quándǎ;殴打 ōudǎ.

socket /ˈsɒkɪt/ *n* [C] 孔 kǒng;穴 xué;插口 chākǒu;插座 chāzuò.

sod /sɒd/ *n* [C] 1[英国⚠俚语](用于咒骂)人 rén: *You rotten ~!* 你这个坏蛋! 2 困难〔難〕的事 kùnnande shì;麻烦的事 máfande shì.

soda /ˈsəʊdə/ *n* [U] 苏〔蘇〕打 sūdá;碳酸钠 tànsuānnà. **ˈsoda-water** *n* [U] 汽水 qìshuǐ.

sodden /ˈsɒdn/ *adj* 浸透了的 jìntòulede.

sodium /ˈsəʊdɪəm/ *n* [U] [化学]钠(Na) nà.

sofa /ˈsəʊfə/ *n* [C] 沙发〔發〕shāfā.

soft /sɒft/ *adj* 1 软的 ruǎnde;柔软的 róuruǎnde: *a ~ pillow* 柔软的枕头. 2 (表面)柔软的 róuruǎnde,光滑的 guānghuáde: ~ *skin* 光滑的皮肤. 3 (光线、色彩)柔和的 róuhéde. 4 (声调)轻〔輕〕柔的 qīngróude. 5 (轮廓、线条)不明显〔顯〕的 bù míngxiǎn de,模糊的 móhude. 6 (回答、语言)温和的 wēnhéde,文雅的 wényǎde. 7 轻松〔鬆〕的 qīngsōngde;容易的 róngyìde: *a ~ job* 轻松的工作. 8 (*on*) (过分)同

情的 tóngqíngde;(心肠)软的 ruǎnde: *Don't be too ~ on the class*. 在课堂上不要太软了. 9 [非正式用语][贬]软弱的 ruǎnruòde;缺乏勇气〔氣〕的 quēfá yǒngqì de;不果断〔斷〕的 bù guǒduàn de. 10 [非正式用语]傻〔傻〕的 shǎde;愚蠢的 yúchǔnde. 11 [习语] have a soft 'spot for 偏爱〔愛〕 piān'ài. ˌsoft-'boiled *adj* (蛋)煮得半熟的 zhǔ de bàn shú de. 'soft drink *n* [C] 无〔無〕酒精饮料 wú jiǔjīng yǐnliào. 'soft drug *n* [C] 软性毒品 ruǎnxìng dúpǐn. ˌsoft-'hearted *adj* 心肠〔腸〕软的 xīncháng ruǎn de. softly *adv*. softness *n* [U]. ˌsoft-'pedal *v* [-ll-; 美语 -l-] [I, T] [非正式用语]使(问题等)不严〔嚴〕重 shǐ bù yánzhòng. ˌsoft-'soap *v* [T] [非正式用语](向某人)灌米汤〔湯〕 guàn mǐtāng. 'software *n* [U] [计算机]软件 ruǎnjiàn.

soften /ˈsɒfn/ *v* 1 [I, T] (使)软化 ruǎnhuà;变〔變〕软弱 biàn ruǎnruò;使柔和 shǐ róuhé;使温和 shǐwēnhé. 2 [T] 使容易 shǐ róngyì;使轻〔輕〕松〔鬆〕 shǐ qīngsōng: *try to ~ the shock* 设法减弱冲击. 3 [短语动词] soften (sb) up [非正式用语]削弱(某人的)抗拒力 xuēruò kàngjùlì.

soggy /ˈsɒgɪ/ *adj* [-ier, -iest] 浸水的 jìnshuǐde;湿〔濕〕透的 shītòude.

soil /sɔɪl/ *n* [C, U] 泥土 nítǔ;土壤 tǔrǎng. soil *v* [I, T] 弄脏〔髒〕 nòng zāng;弄污 nòng wū.

sojourn /ˈsəʊdʒən; *US* səʊˈdʒɜːrn/ *n* [C] [正式用语](在某处)暂留 zàn liú,暂住 zàn zhù.

solace /ˈsɒlɪs/ *n* [C, U] [正式用语](给予)安慰(的事物) ānwèi.

solar /ˈsəʊlə(r)/ *adj* 太阳〔陽〕的 tàiyángde;日光的 rìguāngde: *~ power* 太阳能. the 'solar system *n* [常作 sing] 太阳系 tàiyángxì.

sold *pt, pp* of SELL.

solder /ˈsəʊldə(r)/ *n* [U] 焊料 hànliào. solder *v* [T] 焊接 hànjiē. 'soldering-iron *n* [C] 烙铁〔鐵〕 làotie.

soldier /ˈsəʊldʒə(r)/ *n* [C] 士兵 shìbīng;军人 jūnrén. soldier *v* [短语动词] ˌsoldier 'on 坚〔堅〕持下去 jiānchí xiàqù.

sole[1] /səʊl/ *n* [C, U] [*pl* sole, ~s] 鲽(鱼) dié;鳎(鱼) tǎ.

sole[2] /səʊl/ *n* [C] 脚底 jiǎodǐ;鞋底 xiédǐ;袜〔襪〕底 wàdǐ. sole *v* [T] (给鞋等)配底 pèi dǐ.

sole[3] /səʊl/ *adj* 1 单〔單〕独〔獨〕的 dāndúde;唯一的 wéiyīde: *the ~ owner* 唯一的所有者. 2 专〔專〕有的 zhuānyǒude;独用的 dúyòngde: *have ~ responsibility* 单独负责. solely /ˈsəʊlɪ/ *adv* 单独地 dāndúde;唯一地 wéiyīde;孤独地 gūdúde.

solemn /ˈsɒləm/ *adj* 1 庄〔莊〕严〔嚴〕的 zhuāngyánde;严肃〔肅〕的 yánsùde;隆重的 lóngzhòngde: *a ~ promise* 郑重的许诺. 2 表情严肃的 biǎoqíng yánsù de;一本正经〔經〕的 yì běn zhèngjing de: *a ~ face* 严肃的面孔. solemnly *adv*. solemnness *n* [U].

solemnity /səˈlemnətɪ/ *n* [*pl* -ies] [正式用语] [U] 庄〔莊〕严〔嚴〕 zhuāngyán;严肃〔肅〕 yánsù;隆重 lóngzhòng.

solicit /səˈlɪsɪt/ *v* 1 [I, T] (*for*) [正式用语]请求 qǐngqiú;恳〔懇〕求 kěnqiú;乞求 qǐqiú. 2 [I, T] (妓女)拉客 lākè.

solicitor /səˈlɪsɪtə(r)/ *n* [C] [英国英语](初级或事务)律师〔師〕 lǜshī.

solid /ˈsɒlɪd/ *adj* 1 固体〔體〕的 gùtǐde: *Water becomes ~ when it freezes*. 水结冰成为固体. 2 实〔實〕心的 shíxīnde. 3 坚〔堅〕固的 jiāngùde;牢固的 láogùde. 4 可靠的 kěkàode: *~ arguments* 有根据的论点. 5 纯质的 chúnzhìde;单〔單〕一的 dānyīde: *~ gold* 赤金. 6 一致的 yízhìde: *The workers were ~ on this issue*. 工人们在这件事上是一条心的. 7 连续〔續〕的 liánxùde: *sleep ten hours ~* 连续睡十个小时. 8 立体的 lìtǐde. solid *n* [C] 1 固体 gùtǐ. 2 立体 lìtǐ. solidly *adv*. solidity /səˈlɪdətɪ/ *n* [U].

solidarity /ˌsɒlɪˈdærətɪ/ *n* [U] 团〔團〕结一致 tuánjié yízhì.

solidify /səˈlɪdɪfaɪ/ *v* [*pt, pp* -ied] [I, T] (使)团〔團〕结 tuánjié;(使)坚〔堅〕固 jiāngù.

solitary /ˈsɒlɪtrɪ; *US* -terɪ/ *adj* 1 独〔獨〕居的 dújūde;孤独的 gūdúde. 2 唯一的 wéiyīde: *a ~ visitor* 唯一的客人. 3 荒凉的 huāngliángde;冷落的 lěngluòde.

solitude /ˈsɒlɪtjuːd; *US* -tuːd/ *n* [U] 孤独〔獨〕 gūdú;隐〔隱〕居 yǐnjū.

solo /ˈsəʊləʊ/ *n* [C] [*pl* ~s] 独〔獨〕奏曲 dúzòuqǔ;独唱曲 dúchàngqǔ: *a clarinet ~* 单簧管独奏曲. solo *adj, adv* 1 独自的(地) dúzìde: *a ~ flight* 单独飞行. 2 单〔單〕独表演的 dāndú biǎoyǎn de: *music for ~ flute* 横笛独奏音乐. soloist *n* 独唱者 dúchàngzhě;独奏者 dúzòuzhě.

solstice /ˈsɒlstɪs/ *n* [C] [天文]至点〔點〕 zhìdiǎn.

soluble /ˈsɒljʊbl/ *adj* 1 可溶解的 kě róngjiě de. 2 可解决的 kě jiějué de;可解答的 kě jiědá de. solubility *n* [U].

solution /səˈluːʃn/ *n* 1 (a) [C] 解答(问题) jiědá;解决(困难) jiějué. (b) [U] 解决的过〔過〕程或方法 jiějuéde guòchéng huò fāngfǎ. 2 (a) [U] 溶解 róngjiě. (b) [C, U] 溶液 róngyè.

solve /sɒlv/ *v* [T] 解答(问题等) jiědá;解释〔釋〕 jiěshì. solvable *adj*.

S

solvent /ˈsɒlvənt/ *adj* 能偿〔償〕还〔還〕的 néng chánghuán de. **solvent** *n* [C, U] 溶剂〔劑〕róngjì. **solvency** *n* [U] 偿付能力 chángfù nénglì.

sombre (美语 **somber**) /ˈsɒmbə(r)/ *adj* **1** 暗色的 ànsède; 昏暗的 hūn'ànde; 阴〔陰〕沉的 yīnchénde: ~ *colours* 暗色. **2** 忧〔憂〕郁〔鬱〕的 yōuyùde; 严〔嚴〕峻的 yánjùnde: *a ~ mood* 忧郁的心境. **sombrely** *adv*.

some[1] /sʌm, 弱式 səm/ *adj* **1** 一些 yìxiē; 若干 ruògān; 几〔幾〕个〔個〕jǐgè: *Have ~ milk.* 喝一点牛奶. ~ *children* 几个孩子. *S~ people have very bad manners.* 有些人的态度很不好. **2** 某一 mǒuyī: *She's living at ~ place in Surrey.* 她现在住在萨里郡的某地. **3** 大约 dàyuē; 大概 dàgài: ~ *twenty years ago* 大约在二十年以前. **4** 大量的 dàliàngde; 很大的 hěndàde: *for ~ time* 很久.

some[2] /sʌm/ *pron* **1** 一些 yìxiē; 若干 ruògān; 几〔幾〕个〔個〕jǐgè: *S~ of these books are quite useful.* 这些书中有几种是很有用的. **2** 部分 bùfen: *S~ of the guests didn't stay for long, but most did.* 一部分客人逗留时间不长,但大多数逗留了较长时间.

somebody /ˈsʌmbədɪ/ (亦作 **someone** /ˈsʌmwʌn/) *pron* **1** 某人 mǒurén; 有人 yǒurén: *There's ~ at the door.* 有人敲门. **2** 要人 yàorén; 大人物 dàrénwù: *She really thinks she's ~.* 她真以为自己是大人物.

somehow /ˈsʌmhaʊ/ *adv* **1** 以某种〔種〕方式 yǐ mǒuzhǒng fāngshì: *We'll get there ~.* 我们会设法到达那里的. **2** 由于某种(未知的)原因 yóuyú mǒuzhǒng yuányīn: *S~ I just don't think she'll come back.* 不知为什么,我确实不认为她会回来.

someone = SOMEBODY.

somersault /ˈsʌməsɔːlt/ *n* [C] 筋斗 jīndǒu. **somersault** *v* [I] 翻筋斗 fān jīndǒu.

something /ˈsʌmθɪŋ/ *pron* **1** 某物 mǒuwù; 某事 mǒushì: *I want ~ to eat.* 我要吃点东西. **2** 有意义〔義〕的事物 yǒu yìyì de shìwù: *I'm sure she knows ~ about this.* 我确信,她懂得这之中的门道. **3** [习语] **or something** [非正式用语]或诸如此类〔類〕的事物 huò zhū rú cǐ lèi de shìwù: *She caught flu or ~.* 她患了流感或别的什么病. ˌ**something like a** ˈ**sb/sth** (a) 类似某人(或某事物) lèisì mǒurén. (b) 近似于某人(或某事物) jìnsì yú mǒurén.

sometime /ˈsʌmtaɪm/ *adv* 在某一时〔時〕候 zài mǒuyī shíhòu: ~ *in May* 在五月份某个时候.

sometimes /ˈsʌmtaɪmz/ *adv* 有时〔時〕yǒushí: *I ~ receive letters from him.* 我有时收到他的来信.

somewhat /ˈsʌmwɒt; *US* -hwɒt/ *adv* 有点〔點〕儿〔兒〕yǒu diǎnr: *I was ~ surprised.* 我有点惊讶.

somewhere /ˈsʌmweə(r); *US* -hweər/ (美语 **someplace**) *adv* **1** 在某处〔處〕zài mǒuchù; 到某地 dào mǒudì: *It must be ~ near here.* 它一定在附近某处. **2** [习语] **get somewhere** ⇨ GET.

son /sʌn/ *n* **1** [C] 儿〔兒〕子 érzi. **2** (用作长者对年幼男子的称呼): *What's your name, ~?* 小伙子,你叫什么名字? ˈ**son-in-law** *n* [C] [*pl* ˈ**sons-in-law**] 女婿 nǚxù.

sonata /səˈnɑːtə/ *n* [C] [音乐]奏鸣曲 zòumíngqǔ.

song /sɒŋ/ *n* **1** [C] 歌曲 gēqǔ; 歌词 gēcí. **2** [U] 歌唱 gēchàng. **3** [习语] **for a** ˈ**song** [非正式用语]便宜地 piányide. **a song and** ˈ**dance** 小题大作 xiǎo tí dà zuò.

sonic /ˈsɒnɪk/ *adj* 声〔聲〕音的 shēngyīnde; 音速的 yīnsùde.

sonnet /ˈsɒnɪt/ *n* [C] 十四行诗 shísìhángshī.

soon /suːn/ *adv* **1** 不久 bùjiǔ; 即刻 jíkè: *We shall ~ be home.* 我们很快就要到家了. **2** 早 zǎo; 快 kuài: *How ~ can you be ready?* 你什么时候能准备好? **3** [习语] **as** ˈ**soon as** 一…就 yī…jiù; 立即 lìjí: *He left as ~ as he heard the news.* 他听到消息后立即离开. **no sooner . . . than** 一…就… yī…jiù …: *No ~er had she arrived than she had to leave again.* 她刚到就必须离开. **the** ˌ**sooner the** ˈ**better** 愈快愈好 yù kuài yù hǎo. **sooner. . . than** 宁〔寧〕可…(而不) nìngkě…; 宁愿〔願〕…(而不) nìngyuàn…: *I would ~er die than marry you.* 我宁死不愿同你结婚.

soot /sʊt/ *n* [U] 烟灰 yānhuī; 煤灰 méihuī. **sooty** *adj* [-ier, -iest] 被煤灰弄脏〔髒〕的 bèi méihuī nòng zāng de.

soothe /suːð/ *v* [T] **1** 使平静 shǐ píngjìng; 使镇定 shǐ zhèndìng. **2** 减轻〔輕〕(痛苦) jiǎnqīng. **soothing** *adj*.

sop /sɒp/ *n* [C] 安慰 ānwèi; 讨好 tǎohǎo.

sophisticated /səˈfɪstɪkeɪtɪd/ *adj* **1** 老练〔練〕的 lǎoliànde; 世故的 shìgùde; 有经〔經〕验〔驗〕的 yǒu jīngyàn de. **2** 复〔複〕杂〔雜〕的 fùzáde; 尖端的 jiānduānde: ~ *weapons* 尖端武器. **sophistication** /səˌfɪstɪˈkeɪʃn/ *n* [U].

soppy /ˈsɒpɪ/ *adj* [-ier, -iest] [非正式用语] 过〔過〕于伤〔傷〕感的 guòyú shānggǎn de.

soprano /səˈprɑːnəʊ/ *n* [C] [*pl* ~s] *adj* 女高音 nǚgāoyīn.

sorcerer /ˈsɔːsərə(r)/ (*fem* **sorceress** /-ɪs/) *n* [C] 男巫 nán wū; 男魔术〔術〕师〔師〕nán móshùshī. **sorcery** *n* [U] 巫术 wūshù.

sordid /ˈsɔːdɪd/ *adj* **1** (地方等)肮〔骯〕脏〔髒〕

S

的 āngzāngde，破烂〔爛〕的 pòlànde，邋遢的 lātāde. 2（人）卑鄙的 bēibǐde，下贱〔賤〕的 xiàjiànde. **sordidly** *adv*. **sordidness** *n* [U].

sore /sɔː(r)/ *adj* 1 疼痛的 téngtòngde；一碰就痛的 yípèng jiù tòng de. 2［正式用语］严〔嚴〕重的 yánzhòngde：*in ~ need* 在极度缺乏中. 3［尤作美国非正式用语］气〔氣〕恼〔惱〕的 qìnǎode；激怒的 jīnùde：*feel ~* 感觉恼火. 4［习语］**a ˌsore ˈpoint** 使人恼火（或惭愧）的话题 shǐ rén nǎohuǒ de huàtí. **stand/stick out like a sore ˈthumb** 十分显〔顯〕眼 shífēn xiǎnyǎn. **sore** *n* [C]（肌肤的）痛处〔處〕 tòngchù，伤〔傷〕处 shāngchù. **sorely** *adv* 极〔極〕 jí；非常 fēicháng：*~ly needed* 急需. **soreness** *n* [U].

sorrow /ˈsɒrəʊ/ *n* [C, U] 悲哀（的原因） bēi'āi；伤〔傷〕心事 shāngxīn shì.

sorry /ˈsɒrɪ/ *adj* 1 后〔後〕悔的 hòuhuǐde；难〔難〕过〔過〕的 nánguòde：*She was ~ for her past crimes*. 她为过去的罪行感到后悔. 2 同情的 tóngqíngde；怜〔憐〕悯的 liánmǐnde：*I do feel ~ for him*. 我的确同情他. 3 对〔對〕不起 duìbuqǐ；抱歉 bàoqiàn：*I'm ~, but I don't agree*. 我很抱歉，但我不能同意. 4 [-ier, -iest] 贫困的 pínkùnde；可怜的 kěliánde：*in a ~ state* 在贫困的状况之中. **sorry** *interj* 1（用于表示歉意）：*Sorry! Did I hurt you?* 对不起！我伤害你了吗？2（用于请求对方再说一遍）.

sort[1] /sɔːt/ *n* 1 [C] 种〔種〕类〔類〕 zhǒnglèi；类别 lèibié. 2［习语］**out of ˈsorts** 身体〔體〕不适〔適〕 shēntǐ búshì；脾气〔氣〕不好 píqi bùhǎo. **sort of** 有几〔幾〕分 yǒu jǐ fēn；有点〔點〕儿〔兒〕 yǒu diǎnr：*~ of pleased that it happened* 对那件事的发生多少有点欣慰.

sort[2] /sɔːt/ *v* 1 [T]（*out*）分类〔類〕 fēnlèi；拣〔揀〕选〔選〕 jiǎnxuǎn：*~ (out) the good and bad apples* 把好苹果和坏苹果分开. 2［短语动词］**sort sth out** (a) 整理 zhěnglǐ. (b) 解决 jiějué：*~ out a problem* 解决一个问题.

SOS /ˈes əʊ ˈes/ *n* [sing]（无线电）呼救信号〔號〕 hūjiù xìnhào.

so-so /ˌsəʊˈsəʊ/ *adj, adv*［非正式用语］平平 píngpíng；还〔還〕好 hái hǎo；不好不坏〔壞〕 bùhǎo búhuài：*'How are you feeling?' 'So-so.'* "你觉得怎么样？""还行."

soufflé /ˈsuːfleɪ; *US* suːˈfleɪ/ *n* [C, U] 蛋奶酥 dànnǎisū.

soul /səʊl/ *n* 1 [C] 灵〔靈〕魂 línghún. 2 [C, U] 精神 jīngshén；精力 jīnglì；热〔熱〕情 rèqíng：*put ~ into one's work* 全神贯注地工作. 3 [sing] 化身 huàshēn；典型 diǎnxíng：*the ~ of discretion* 谨慎的典型. 4 [C] 人 rén：*not a ~ to be seen* 一个人影也看不到. 5 = SOUL MUSIC (SOUL). **ˈsoul-destroying** *adj*（工作）单〔單〕调无〔無〕味的 dāndiào wúwèi de，无聊的 wúliáode. **soulful** *adj* 热情的 rèqíngde；深情的 shēnqíngde. **soulfully** *adv*. **soulless** *adj* 无情的 wúqíngde. **ˈsoul music** *n* [U] 灵乐〔樂〕（美国现代黑人通俗音乐） língyuè. **soul-searching** *n* [U] 反省 fǎnxǐng；反躬自问 fǎn gōng zì wèn.

sound[1] /saʊnd/ *adj* 1 健康的 jiànkāngde；健全的 jiànquánde：*a ~ body* 健康的身体. 2 细心的 xìxīnde；严〔嚴〕谨的 yánjǐnde：*a ~ worker* 一个细心的工人. 3 合理的 hélǐde；明智的 míngzhìde：*a ~ policy* 明智的政策. 4 彻〔徹〕底的 chèdǐde；充分的 chōngfènde：*be a ~ sleeper* 一个酣睡的人. **sound** *adv* 彻底地 chèdǐde；充分地 chōngfènde：*~ asleep* 熟睡的. **soundly** *adv* 彻底地 chèdǐde；充分地 chōngfènde；健全地 jiànquánde.

sound[2] /saʊnd/ *n* 1 [C, U] 声〔聲〕音 shēngyīn：*the ~ of drums* 鼓声. 2 [C] 印象 yìnxiàng；感觉〔覺〕 gǎnjué；语气〔氣〕 yǔqì；笔〔筆〕调 bǐdiào：*I don't like the ~ of him*. 我不喜欢他的语气. **ˈsound barrier** *n* [C] 声障 shēngzhàng；音障 yīnzhàng. **ˈsound effects** *n* [pl] 音响〔響〕效果 yīnxiǎng xiàoguǒ. **ˈsound-proof** *adj* 隔音的 géyīnde. **ˈsound-proof** *v* [T] 使（某物）隔音 shǐ géyīn. **ˈsound-track** *n* [C]（影片上的）声带〔帶〕 shēngdài.

sound[3] /saʊnd/ *v* 1 [I] 听〔聽〕起来（似乎） tīng qǐlái：*His story ~s genuine*. 他的故事听起来好像是真的. 2 [I, T]（使）发〔發〕声〔聲〕 fā shēng. 3 [T] 用声音发出（信号） yòng shēngyīn fāchū：*~ the alarm* 发布警报. 4 [T] 发…音 fā…yīn：*Don't sound the 'b' in 'dumb'*. "dumb"中的"b"不发音. 5［短语动词］**sound off**［非正式用语］大声吹嘘 dà shēng chuīxū.

sound[4] /saʊnd/ *v* 1 [I, T] 测（海等）深度 cè shēndù. 2［短语动词］**sound sb out (about/on sth)** 试探某人（对某事物）的意见 shìtàn mǒurén de yìjiàn.

soup /suːp/ *n* [U] 1 汤〔湯〕 tāng；羹 gēng. 2［习语］**in the ˈsoup**［非正式用语］处〔處〕于困难〔難〕中 chǔyú kùnnan zhōng；陷入困境 xiànrù kùnjìng.

sour /ˈsaʊə(r)/ *adj* 1 酸的 suān de；酸味的 suānwèide. 2 酸臭的 suānchòude；酸腐的 suānfǔde：*~ milk* 发酸了的奶. 3 脾气〔氣〕坏〔壞〕的 píqì huài de. 4［习语］**go/turn ˈsour** 变〔變〕得不愉快 biàn de bù yúkuài；变糟 biàn zāo. **sour** *v* [I, T]（使）变酸 biàn suān. **sourly** *adv*. **sourness** *n* [U].

source /sɔːs/ *n* [C] 源头〔頭〕 yuántóu；来源 láiyuán；出处〔處〕 chūchù：*the ~ of a river* 河流的源头. *the ~ of belief* 信念的来源.

south /saʊθ/ *n* [sing] 1 **the south** 南 nán；南

S

方 nánfāng. 2 the South (一国的)南部 nánbù, 南部地区〔區〕nánbù dìqū. **south** *adj* 1 南方的 nánfāngde;向南的 xiàngnánde. 2 (风)来自南方的 lái zì nánfāng de. **south** *adv* 向南 xiàng nán. ˌ**south-ˈeast** *n* [sing], *adj*, *adv* (位于,面向)东南(的) dōngnán. ˌ**south-ˈeastern** *adj*. **southerly** /ˈsʌðəlɪ/ *adj*, *adv* 1 向南 xiàng nán;在南方 zài nánfāng. 2 (风)来自南方的 lái zì nánfāng de. **southern** /ˈsʌðən/ *adj* (世界、国家等)南方的 nánfāngde, 南部的 nánbùde. **southerner** *n* [C] 南方人 nánfāng rén. **southward** /ˈsaʊðwəd/ *adj* 向南方的 xiàng nánfāng de. **southward(s)** *adv*. ˌ**south-ˈwest** *n* [sing], *adj*, *adv* (位于、面向)西南(的) xīnán. ˌ**south-ˈwestern** *adj*.

souvenir /ˌsuːvəˈnɪə(r)/ *n* [C] 纪念品 jìniànpǐn.

sovereign /ˈsɒvrɪn/ *n* [C] 国〔國〕王 guówáng;女王 nǚwáng. **sovereign** *adj* 1 (权力)最高的 zuìgāode, 无〔無〕上的 wúshàngde. 2 (国家、统治者)独〔獨〕立自主的 dúlì zìzhǔ de. **sovereignty** /ˈsɒvrəntɪ/ *n* [U] 君权〔權〕jūnquán;统治权 tǒngzhìquán;主权 zhǔquán.

Soviet /ˈsəʊvɪət/ *adj* (前)苏〔蘇〕联〔聯〕的 Sūliánde;苏联人的 Sūliánrénde.

sow[1] /saʊ/ *n* [C] 大母猪 dà mǔzhū.

sow[2] /səʊ/ *v* [*pt* ~ed, *pp* ~n /səʊn/ 或 ~ed] [T] 1 播种〔種〕bōzhòng. 2 传〔傳〕播 chuánbō;使产〔產〕生(感情等) shǐ chǎnshēng: ~ *discontent* 产生不满情绪.

soya bean /ˈsɔɪə biːn/ *n* [C] 大豆 dàdòu;黄豆 huángdòu.

spa /spɑː/ *n* [C] 矿〔礦〕泉(疗养地) kuàngquán.

space /speɪs/ *n* 1 [C, U] 空隙 kòngxì;间隔 jiàngé: *a narrow ~ between the chairs* 椅子间很小的空隙. 2 [C, U] 地方 dìfang;地位 dìwèi: *the wide open ~s* 开阔地. 3 [U] 空间 kōngjiān;余〔餘〕地 yúdì;未被占〔佔〕用之处〔處〕wèi bèi zhànyòng zhī chù: *There's not enough ~ here*. 这儿没有足够的余地了. 4 [U] (存在的)空间 kōngjiān: *stare into ~* 极目远眺. 5 [U] (亦作 ˌ**outer ˈspace**) 外层〔層〕空间 wàicéng kōngjiān;太空 tàikōng. 6 [C] 持续〔續〕时〔時〕间 chíxù shíjiān; 期间 qījiān: *within the ~ of a day* 一天之内. **space** *v* [T] (*out*) (均匀地)分隔开〔開〕fēngékāi. ˈ**space-age** *adj* 太空时代的 tàikōng shídài de. ˈ**spacecraft**, ˈ**spaceship** *n* [C] 宇宙飞〔飛〕船 yǔzhòu fēichuán; 航天器 hángtiānqì. ˈ**space exploration** *n* [U] 宇宙探索 yǔzhòu tànsuǒ. ˈ**space flight** *n* 1 [C] 航天飞行 hángtiān fēixíng. 2 [U] 宇宙旅行 yǔzhòu lǚxíng. ˈ**space programme** *n* [C] 航天计划〔劃〕hángtiān jìhuà. ˈ**space station** *n* [C] 航天站 hángtiānzhàn; 太空站 tàikōngzhàn. ˈ**spacesuit** *n* [C] 宇航服 yǔhángfú. ˈ**space travel** *n* [U] 宇宙旅行 yǔzhòu lǚxíng.

spacious /ˈspeɪʃəs/ *adj* 广〔廣〕阔的 guǎngkuòde;宽敞的 kuānchǎngde. **spaciousness** *n* [U].

spade /speɪd/ *n* [C] 1 铲〔鏟〕chǎn;铁〔鐵〕锹 tiěqiāo. 2 (纸牌)黑桃 hēitáo. ˈ**spadework** *n* [U] 艰〔艱〕苦的基础〔礎〕工作 jiānkǔde jīchǔ gōngzuò.

spaghetti /spəˈgetɪ/ *n* [U] 细圆面〔麵〕条〔條〕xì yuán miàntiáo.

Spain /speɪn/ *n* [U] 西班牙 Xībānyá.

span /spæn/ *n* [C] 1 跨度 kuàdù. 2 (时间的)自始至终 zì shǐ zhì zhōng: *the ~ of a person's life* 人的寿命. **span** *v* [-nn-] [T] 1 跨过〔過〕kuàguò;跨越 kuàyuè. 2 (时间)持续〔續〕chíxù;经〔經〕历〔歷〕jīnglì: *a life ~ning fifty years* 一生经历了五十个年头.

Spaniard /ˈspænjəd/ *n* [C] 西班牙人 Xībānyárén.

spaniel /ˈspænɪəl/ *n* [C] 一种〔種〕长〔長〕毛垂耳狗 yìzhǒng cháng máo chuí ěr gǒu.

Spanish /ˈspænɪʃ/ *adj* 西班牙的 Xībānyáde. **Spanish** *n* 1 [pl] the Spanish 西班牙人 Xībānyárén. 2 [U]西班牙语 Xībānyáyǔ.

spank /spæŋk/ *v* [T] 打(小孩)屁股 dǎ pìgu. **spank** *n* [C].

spanner /ˈspænə(r)/ (美语 **wrench**) *n* [C] 扳头〔頭〕bāntou;扳手 bānshou.

spar /spɑː(r)/ *v* [-rr-] [I] (*with*) 1 用拳轻〔輕〕击〔擊〕(练习拳击) yòng quán qīngjī. 2 斗〔鬥〕嘴 dòuzuǐ;争吵 zhēngchǎo.

spare[1] /speə(r)/ *adj* 1 (a) 剩余〔餘〕的 shèngyúde;多余的 duōyúde: *two ~ chairs* 两把多余的椅子. (b) (时间)空闲的 kòngxiánde. 2(人)瘦的 shòude. **spare** (亦作 ˌ**spare ˈpart**) *n* [C] 备〔備〕用部件 bèiyòng bùjiàn. **spare tyre** *n* [C] 备用轮〔輪〕胎 bèiyòng lúntāi.

spare[2] /speə(r)/ *v* [T] 1 抽出(时间) chōuchū;让〔讓〕给(金钱) rànggěi: *Can you ~ me a few minutes?* 你能给我几分钟时间吗? 2 节〔節〕约 jiéyuē;吝惜 lìnxī: *No expense was ~d*. 不惜花费大量金钱. 3 不伤〔傷〕害 bù shānghài;饶〔饒〕恕 ráoshù;赦免 shèmiǎn: *~ a prisoner's life* 饶犯人一命. 4[习语] **spare a ˈthought for** 考虑〔慮〕(下决心) kǎolǜ. **sparing** *adj* 节省的 jiéshěngde;不浪费的 bú làngfèi de. **sparingly** *adv*.

spark /spɑːk/ *n* [C] 1 火星 huǒxīng;火花 huǒhuā. 2 [常作 sing] [喻](事物的)迹〔跡〕象 jìxiàng: *not a ~ of decency in him* 他一点也不庄重. **spark** *v* 1 [I] 发〔發〕火花 fā huǒhuā;飞〔飛〕火星 fēi huǒxīng. 2[短语动词]

spark sth off 为〔爲〕…的直接原因 wéi… de zhíjiē yuányīn; 导〔導〕致 dǎozhì. ˈspark-plug (亦作 ˈsparking-plug) *n* [C] (内燃机的)火花塞 huǒhuāsāi.

sparkle /ˈspɑːkl/ *v* [I] 闪光 shǎnguāng; 闪耀 shǎnyào: [喻] *Her conversation ~d*. 她的谈话闪耀着才智. sparkle *n* [C, U] 闪光 shǎnguāng; 闪耀 shǎnyào: [喻] *a performance lacking in ~* 缺乏生气的表演. sparkling /ˈspɑːklɪŋ/ *adj*.

sparrow /ˈspærəʊ/ *n* [C] 麻雀 máquè.

sparse /spɑːs/ *adj* 稀少的 xīshǎode: *~ population* 人口稀少. sparsely *adv*. sparseness *n* [U].

spasm /ˈspæzəm/ *n* 1 [C, U]抽筋 chōujīn; 痉〔痙〕挛〔攣〕 jìngluán. 2 [C] 突然发〔發〕作 tūrán fāzuò. spasmodic /spæzˈmɒdɪk/ *adj* 1间歇的 jiànxiēde; 阵发性的 zhènfāxìngde. 2 痉挛引起的 jìngluán yǐnqǐ de. spasmodically *adv*.

spastic /ˈspæstɪk/ *n* [C], *adj* 痉〔痙〕挛〔攣〕的(人) jìngluánde; 患大脑〔腦〕麻痹的(人) huàn dànǎo mábì de.

spat *pt*, *pp* of SPIT².

spate /speɪt/ *n* [sing] 突然增多 tūrán zēngduō: *a ~ of robberies* 盗贼的突然增多.

spatial /ˈspeɪʃl/ *adj* 空间的 kōngjiānde; 关〔關〕于空间的 guānyú kōngjiān de. spatially *adv*.

spatter /ˈspætə(r)/ *v* [I, T] 溅〔濺〕 jiàn; 洒〔灑〕 sǎ; 泼〔潑〕 pō. spatter *n* [sing] 一阵洒落 yízhèn sǎluò; 阵雨 zhènyǔ.

spatula /ˈspætʃʊlə/ *n* [C] (涂敷用的)抹刀 mòdāo; 刮铲〔鏟〕 guā chǎn.

spawn /spɔːn/ *n* [U] (鱼、蛙等的)卵 luǎn, 子 zǐ. spawn *v* [I, T] 1(使鱼等)产〔產〕卵 chǎn luǎn. 2[喻]大量生产 dàliàng shēngchǎn.

speak /spiːk/ *v* [*pt* spoke /spəʊk/, *pp* spoken /ˈspəʊkən/] 1 [I] 说 shuō; 说话 shuōhuà: *I was ~ing to her about my plans*. 我正在和她讲我的打算. 2 [T] 能说(某种语言) néng shuō: *~ French* 能讲法语. 3 [I] 演说 yǎnshuō; 发〔發〕言 fāyán. 4 [T]说明 shuōmíng; 说出 shuōchū: *~ the truth* 说真话. 5 [I](不用言辞)表示意见 biǎoshì yìjiàn: *Actions ~ louder than words*. 行动胜于言辞. 6[习语] on ˈspeaking terms (与某人)熟识〔識〕到可以交谈的程度 shúshi dào kěyǐ jiāotán de chéngdù. speak one's ˈmind 公开〔開〕表达〔達〕观〔觀〕点〔點〕 gōngkāi biǎodá guāndiǎn. 7[短语动词] speak for sb (a) 陈述某人的意见 chénshù mǒurén de yìjiàn. (b) 为〔爲〕某人作证〔證〕 wèi mǒurén zuòzhèng. speak out 大胆〔膽〕明确〔確〕地说出意见 dàdǎn míngquè de shuōchū yìjiàn. speak up (a) 大点声〔聲〕说 dà diǎn shēng shuō. (b)说出 shuōchū.

speaker *n* [C] 1 发言者 fāyánzhě. 2 说某种〔種〕语言的人 shuō mǒuzhǒng yǔyán de rén: *a French ~er* 说法语的人. 3 short for LOUDSPEAKER.

spear /spɪə(r)/ *n* [C] 矛 máo; 枪〔槍〕 qiāng. spear *v* [T] (用矛)刺 cì. ˈspearhead *n* [C] 先头〔頭〕突击〔擊〕部队〔隊〕 xiāntóu tūjī bùduì; 先锋 xiānfēng. ˈspearhead *v* [T] 当〔當〕…的先锋 dāng…de xiānfēng.

spearmint /ˈspɪəmɪnt/ *n* [U] [植物]留兰〔蘭〕香 liúlánxiāng.

special /ˈspeʃl/ *adj* 1 特别的 tèbiéde; 特殊的 tèshūde. 2 专〔專〕门的 zhuānménde; 特设的 tèshède. 3 格外的 géwàide; 额外的 éwàide: *~ treatment* 额外的待遇. special *n* [C] 1 专列(车) zhuānliè; 特刊 tèkān; 号〔號〕外 hàowài: *a television ~ about the elections* 电视上关于选举的专题报道. 2[美国非正式用语] 大减价〔價〕 dà jiǎn jià; 特价 tèjià. Special Economic Zone *n* 经〔經〕济〔濟〕特区〔區〕 jīngjì tèqū. specialist *n* [C] 专家 zhuānjiā. specially *adv* 特别地 tèbiéde; 专门地 zhuānménde.

speciality /ˌspeʃɪˈælətɪ/ (美语尤作 specialty /ˈspeʃəltɪ/) *n* [C] 1 专〔專〕业〔業〕 zhuānyè; 特长 tècháng. 2 优〔優〕质〔質〕品 yōuzhìpǐn; 特产〔產〕 tèchǎn.

specialize /ˈspeʃəlaɪz/ *v* [I] (*in*) 成为专〔專〕家 chéngwéi zhuānjiā; 专门研究 zhuānmén yánjiū: *~ in modern history* 专攻近代史. specialization /-ˈzeɪʃn; *US* -lɪˈz-/ *n* [U].

species /ˈspiːʃiːz/ *n* [C] [*pl* species] (生物的)种〔種〕 zhǒng, 种类〔類〕 zhǒnglèi.

specific /spəˈsɪfɪk/ *adj* 1 具体〔體〕的 jùtǐde; 明确〔確〕的 míngquède: *~ instructions* 明确的指示. 2 特有的 tèyǒude; 特种的 tèzhǒngde; 特定的 tèdìngde: *for a ~ purpose* 为一个特定的目的. specifically /-klɪ/ *adv*.

specification /ˌspesɪfɪˈkeɪʃn/ *n* [C, 常作 pl] 规格 guīgé; 清单〔單〕 qīngdān; 说明书〔書〕 shuōmíngshū.

specify /ˈspesɪfaɪ/ *v* [*pt*, *pp* -ied] [T] 规定 guīdìng; 载明 zǎimíng; 详述 xiáng shù.

specimen /ˈspesɪmɪn/ *n* [C] 1 标〔標〕本 biāoběn; 样〔樣〕品 yàngpǐn; 样张〔張〕 yàngzhāng: *a ~ of her work* 她的工作质量的一个样品. 2 试样 shìyàng.

speck /spek/ *n* [C] 斑点〔點〕 bāndiǎn; 微粒 wēilì; 污点 wūdiǎn.

speckle /ˈspekl/ *n* [C](尤指皮毛上的)小斑点〔點〕 xiǎo bāndiǎn. speckled *adj*.

spectacle /ˈspektəkl/ *n* 1 [C]公开〔開〕展示 gōngkāi zhǎnshì; 场〔場〕面 chǎngmiàn. 2 [C] 景象 jǐngxiàng; 奇观〔觀〕 qíguān; 壮〔壯〕观 zhuàngguān. 3 [pl] [正式用语]眼镜 yǎnjìng.

spectacular /spekˈtækjʊlə(r)/ *adj* 壮〔壯〕

S

观〔觀〕的 zhuàngguānde；洋洋大观的 yángyáng dàguānde. **spectacularly** *adv*.

spectator /spekˈteɪtə(r)/ *n* [C] 观〔觀〕众〔衆〕guānzhòng；观看者 guānkànzhě.

spectrum /ˈspektrəm/ *n* [常作 sing] [*pl* **-tra** /-trə/] 1 光谱 guāngpǔ. 2[喻]系列 xìliè：*a* ～ *of opinions* 一系列的不同意见.

speculate /ˈspekjuleɪt/ *v* 1 [I,T]思考 sīkǎo；推测 tuīcè. 2 [I]投机〔機〕tóujī. **speculation** /-ˈleɪʃn/ *n* [C,U]. **speculative** *adj*.

sped /sped/ *pt*, *pp* of SPEED.

speech /spiːtʃ/ *n* 1 [U] 说话 shuōhuà；说话方式或能力 shuōhuà fāngshì huò nénglì. 2 [C] 演说 yǎnshuō；发〔發〕言 fāyán：*make a* ～ 发表演说. **speechless** *adj* 说不出话的 shuō bù chū huà de.

speed /spiːd/ *n* 1 [U]快 kuài；迅速 xùnsù：*move with great* ～ 行动很迅速. 2 [C,U]速度 sùdù：*a* ～ *of 10 kilometres an hour* 每小时 10 公里的速度.[习语] (**at**) **full speed** ⇨FULL. **speed** *v* [*pt*, *pp* **sped** /sped/, 第 2 义作 ～**ed**] 1 [I]迅速前进〔進〕xùnsù qiánjìn；快行 kuàixíng. 2 超速行驶 chāo sù xíngshǐ. 3[短语动词] **speed** (**sth**) **up** 加速 jiā sù；加快 jiā kuài：～ *up production* 加快生产. ˈ**speed camera** *n* [C] 车〔車〕速监〔監〕控摄〔攝〕像机〔機〕chēsù jiānkòng shèxiàngjī. ˈ**speed hump** *n* [C] 缓冲〔衝〕路拱 huǎnchōng lùgǒng；减速路脊 jiǎnsù lùjǐ. **speedometer** /spiːˈdɒmɪtə(r)/ *n* [C] 速度计 sùdùjì. ˈ**speedway** *n* [C,U] (摩托车)赛车跑道 sàichē pǎodào. **speedy** *adj* [-ier, -iest] 快的 kuàide；迅速的 xùnsùde.

spell[1] /spel/ *n* [C] 咒语 zhòuyǔ；符咒 fúzhòu：[喻] *under the* ～ *of a fascinating man* 被充满魅力的人迷住. ˈ**spell-bound** *adj* 被迷惑的 bèi míhuò de；入迷的 rùmíde.

spell[2] /spel/ *n* [C] 1 一段时〔時〕间 yíduàn shíjiān：*a* ～ *in prison* 在狱中服刑期间. 2(活动或工作的)一段时间 yíduàn shíjiān：*a* ～ *at the wheel* 开一段时间的车.

spell[3] /spel/ *v* [*pt*, *pp* **spelt** /spelt/ 或 **spelled** /speld/] 1 [I,T]用字母拼 yòng zìmǔ pīn；拼写〔寫〕pīnxiě. 2 [T](字母)拼成(词) pīnchéng：*C-A-T* ～*s cat*. C-A-T 拼成 cat. 3 [T] 招致 zhāozhì；带〔帶〕来 dàilái：*Does laziness always* ～ *failure?* 懒惰总是招致失败吗? 4[短语动词] **spell sth out** 讲清楚某事 jiǎng qīngchu mǒushì；说明 shuōmíng. ˈ**spellchecker** *n* [C] 拼写检〔檢〕查器 pīnxiě jiǎncháqì. **spelling** *n* 1 [U] (a) 拼写能力 pīnxiě nénglì. (b) 拼写 pīnxiě. 2 [C]拼法 pīnfǎ.

spend /spend/ *v* [*pt*, *pp* **spent** /spent/] 1 [I,T] (*on*) 用(钱) yòng；花费 huāfèi. 2 [T] 消磨(时间) xiāomó：～ *a week in hospital* 在医院中住了一星期. 3 [T] 花(时间等) huā：～ *one's energy cleaning the house* 花力气把房屋打扫干净. 4[习语] **spend a** ˈ**penny** [非正式用语][婉]去厕所 qù cèsuǒ. ˈ**spendthrift** *n* [C] 挥〔揮〕金如土者 huī jīn rú tǔ zhě. **spent** *adj* 衰竭的 shuāijiéde；耗尽〔盡〕的 hàojìnde；用过〔過〕的 yòngguòde.

sperm /spɜːm/ *n* [U] 精液 jīngyè；精子 jīngzǐ.

spew /spjuː/ *v* [I,T] (使)喷出 pēn chū；(使)射出 shè chū.

sphere /sfɪə(r)/ *n* [C] 1 球 qiú；球体〔體〕qiútǐ. 2(兴趣、活动、势力等的)范〔範〕围〔圍〕fànwéi，领域 lǐngyù. **spherical** /ˈsferɪkl/ *adj* 球形的 qiúxíngde.

spice /spaɪs/ *n* 1 [C,U] 香料 xiāngliào；调味品 tiáowèipǐn. 2 [U] [喻]趣味 qùwèi；风〔風〕味 fēngwèi：*add* ～ *to a story* 增添故事的兴味. **spice** *v* [T] 加香料于 jiā xiāngliào yú. **spicy** *adj* [-ier, -iest] 1 加香料的 jiā xiāngliào de；香的 xiāngde. 2[喻]有刺激性的 yǒu cìjīxìng de.

spick /spɪk/ *adj* [习语] ˌ**spick and** ˈ**span** 干〔乾〕净的 gānjìngde；整洁〔潔〕的 zhěngjiéde.

spider /ˈspaɪdə(r)/ *n* [C] 蜘蛛 zhīzhū. **spidery** *adj* (书法)笔〔筆〕划〔劃〕细长〔長〕的 bǐhuà xìcháng de.

spied /spaɪd/ *pt*, *pp* of SPY.

spike /spaɪk/ *n* [C] 1 尖端 jiānduān. 2(鞋底的)防滑钉 fánghuádīng. 3 穗 suì. **spike** *v* [T] 用尖物刺 yòng jiānwù cì. **spiky** *adj* [-ier, -iest].

spill /spɪl/ *v* [*pt*, *pp* **spilt** /spɪlt/ 或 ～**ed**] [I,T] 1(使)溢出 yìchū；(使)溅〔濺〕出 jiànchū. 2[习语] **spill the** ˈ**beans** [非正式用语]泄露秘密 xièlòu mìmì.

spin /spɪn/ *v* [-nn-; *pt* **spun** /spʌn/ 或 **span** /spæn/, *pp* **spun**] 1 [I,T] (使)快速旋转〔轉〕kuàisù xuánzhuǎn. 2 [I,T] 纺(纱,线) fǎng；纺绩 fǎngjī. 3 [T]编结 biānjié：*Spiders* ～ *webs*. 蜘蛛结网. 4 [T] [非正式用语][喻]编造(故事) biānzào. 5[短语动词] **spin sth out** 尽〔盡〕量使某物持续〔續〕jìnliàng shǐ mǒuwù chíxù；延长〔長〕yáncháng. **spin** *n* 1 [C,U] 旋转 xuánzhuǎn. 2 [C] 乘汽车兜一圈 chéng qìchē dōu yìquān. 3[习语] **in a** (**flat**) ˈ**spin** 惊〔驚〕慌失措 jīnghuāng shīcuò；晕头〔頭〕转向 yūn tóu zhuàn xiàng. ˌ**spin-**ˈ**drier** *n* [C] 旋转式脱水机〔機〕xuánzhuǎnshì tuōshuǐjī；甩干〔乾〕机 shuǎigānjī. ˈ**spin-off** *n* [C] 副产〔產〕品 fùchǎnpǐn.

spinach /ˈspɪnɪdʒ/ *n* [U] 菠菜 bōcài.

spinal /ˈspaɪnl/ *adj* [解剖]脊椎骨的 jǐzhuīgǔde.

spindle /ˈspɪndl/ *n* [C] 1 纺锤 fǎngchuí；锭子 dìngzi. 2 轴 zhóu. **spindly** /ˈspɪndlɪ/ *adj*

S

[-ier, -iest]细长〔長〕的 xìchángde.

spine /spaɪn/ *n* [C] 1 = BACKBONE (BACK[1]). 2(动植物的)针 zhēn, 刺 cì. 3 书〔書〕脊 shūjǐ. ˈ**spine-chilling** *adj* 令人毛骨悚然的 lìng rén máo gǔ sǒngrán de. **spineless** *adj* [贬]胆〔膽〕小的 dǎnxiǎode;无〔無〕骨气〔氣〕的 wú gǔqì de. **spiny** *adj* [-ier, -iest] 多刺的 duōcìde.

spinster /ˈspɪnstə(r)/ *n* [C] [有时贬]未婚女子 wèi hūn nǚzǐ;老处〔處〕女 lǎo chùnǚ.

spiral /ˈspaɪərəl/ *n* [C] 1 螺旋形 luóxuánxíng: *A snail's shell is a* ～. 蜗牛的壳是一个螺旋形. 2[常作 sing] 交替上升或下降 jiāotì shàngshēng huò xiàjiàng. **spiral** *adj* 螺旋形的 luóxuánxíngde. **spiral** *v* [-ll-; 美语 -l-] [I] 1 盘〔盤〕旋 pánxuán;螺旋形移动〔動〕luóxuánxíng yídòng. 2 增长〔長〕或减少 zēngzhǎng huò jiǎnshǎo.

spire /ˈspaɪə(r)/ *n* [C](尤指教堂的)塔尖 tǎjiān, 尖顶 jiāndǐng.

spirit /ˈspɪrɪt/ *n* 1 [C, U] 精神 jīngshén;心灵〔靈〕xīnlíng. 2[C] 灵魂 línghún;鬼怪 guǐguài. 3 [C]人 rén;人物 rénwù: *What a generous* ～! 多么慷慨的人啊! 4 [U]勇气〔氣〕yǒngqì;生气 shēngqì: *act with* ～ 勇敢的行为. 5 [sing] 态〔態〕度 tàidu: *It depends on the* ～ *in which it was done*. 那要看是抱什么态度干的. 6 [U] 精神实〔實〕质〔質〕jīngshén shízhì: *obey the* ～, *not the letter, of the law*. 服从法律的精神, 而不是它的字句. 7 **spirits** [pl] 情绪 qíngxù;心情 xīnqíng;兴〔興〕致 xìngzhì: *in high* ～*s* 兴高采烈. 8[C, 常作 pl] 烈酒 liè jiǔ. 9[习语] **in spirit** 在内心里〔裏〕zài nèixīn lǐ. **spirit** *v* [短语动词] **spirit sth/sb away/off** 迅速而神秘地带〔帶〕走 xùnsù ér shénmì de dàizǒu; 拐带 guǎidài. **spirited** *adj* 1 有勇气的 yǒu yǒngqì de;有生气的 yǒu shēngqì de. 2 有…情绪的 yǒu… qíngxù de;心情…的 xīnqíng… de: *high-/low-spirited* 高兴的;沮丧的.

spiritual /ˈspɪrɪtʃʊəl/ *adj* 1 精神的 jīngshénde;心灵〔靈〕的 xīnlíngde. 2 宗教的 zōngjiàode. **spiritual** *n* [C] 美国〔國〕黑人的圣〔聖〕歌 Měiguó hēirén de shènggē. **spiritually** *adv*.

spit[1] /spɪt/ *n* [C] 1 烤肉叉 kǎoròuchā. 2 伸入海中的狭〔狹〕长〔長〕陆〔陸〕地 shēnrù hǎizhōng de xiácháng lùdì;岬角 jiǎjiǎo.

spit[2] /spɪt/ *v* [-tt-; *pt*, *pp* **spat** /spæt/] 1 [I]吐(唾沫) tǔ. 2 [T] (*out*) (a) 吐出(某物) tǔchū. (b)(愤怒地)大声〔聲〕叫喊 dàshēng jiàohǎn: ～ (*out*) *a command* 厉声发布命令. 3 [I][与 *it* 连用](雨、雪)霏霏下降 fēifēi xiàjiàng. 4[习语] **be the spitting image of sb** ⇨ IMAGE. **spit** *n* [U] 唾液 tuòyè.

spite /spaɪt/ *n* [U] 1 恶〔惡〕意 è'yì;意欲造成痛苦 yìyù zàochéng tòngkǔ: *do sth out of* ～ 做某事是出于恶意. 2[习语] **in spite of** 不管 bùguǎn;不顾〔顧〕búgù: *They went out in* ～ *of the rain*. 尽管下雨, 他们还是出去了. **spite** *v* [T] 恶意对〔對〕待 è'yì duìdài;刁难〔難〕diāonàn. **spiteful** *adj*.

splash /splæʃ/ *v* 1 (a) [I] (水)溅〔濺〕jiàn;(水)滴 dī. (b) [T] 泼〔潑〕(水) pō: ～ *water on the floor* 在地板上泼水. 2 [T] 显〔顯〕示 xiǎnshì;鼓吹 gǔchuī: ～ *his name all over the newspapers* 在报纸上为他大力鼓吹. 3[短语动词] **splash out (on sth)** [非正式用语](在某事物上)大量花钱〔錢〕dàliàng huāqián. **splash** *n* [C] 溅 jiàn;飞〔飛〕溅声〔聲〕fēijiànshēng;溅污的斑点〔點〕jiànwū de bāndiǎn.

spleen /spli:n/ *n* [C] [解剖]脾 pí;脾脏〔臟〕pízàng.

splendid /ˈsplendɪd/ *adj* 1 壮〔壯〕丽〔麗〕的 zhuànglìde;辉煌的 huīhuángde: *a* ～ *view* 壮丽的景色. 2[非正式用语]极〔極〕好的 jíhǎode;令人满意的 lìng rén mǎnyì de: *a* ～ *performance* 极好的演出. **splendidly** *adv*.

splendour (美语 -dor) /ˈsplendə(r)/ *n* [U] 壮〔壯〕丽〔麗〕zhuànglì;光辉 guānghuī.

splice /splaɪs/ *v* [T] 绞接(绳头) jiǎojiē;拼接(木板等) pīnjiē.

splint /splɪnt/ *n* [C] (正骨用)夹〔夾〕板 jiābǎn.

splinter /ˈsplɪntə(r)/ *n* [C](木、玻璃等)碎片 suìpiàn. **splinter** *v* [I, T] (使)裂成碎片 liè chéng suìpiàn. **splinter group** *n* [C] (自原政党)分裂出来的派别 fēnliè chūlái de pàibié.

split /splɪt/ *v* [-tt-; *pt*, *pp* **split**] 1 [I, T] 劈开〔開〕pīkāi;(使)裂开 lièkāi. 2 [T]使分裂成派别 shǐ fēnliè chéng pàibié: *Arguments* ～ *the group*. 争吵使团体分裂. 3 [I, T] (*open*) (使)突然打开〔開〕tūrán dǎkāi: *The box* ～ (*open*). 箱子突然打开. 4 [T]分配 fēnpèi: ～ *the profits* 分配利润. 5 [I] [尤作美俚]离〔離〕开 líkāi: *Let's* ～! 我们走吧! 6 [习语] **split ˈhairs** 作细致的剖析 zuò xìzhìde pōuxī. **split one's ˈsides** 捧腹大笑 pěng fù dà xiào. 7[短语动词] **split up** 绝交 juéjiāo;离〔離〕婚 líhūn. **split** *n* 1 [C]裂开 lièkāi;裂缝 lièfèng. 2 [C]分开 fēnkāi;分化 fēnhuà. 3 [C] 分裂 fēnliè;分离 fēnlí. 4 **the splits** [pl] 劈叉 pǐchà. ˌ**split persoˈnality** *n* [C] 人格分裂症 réngé fēnliè zhèng. **split ˈsecond** *n* [C] 一刹那 yíchànà.

splutter /ˈsplʌtə(r)/ *v* 1 [I, T] (因激动等)急促地乱〔亂〕说 jícùde luànshuō. 2 [I]发〔發〕劈啪声 fā pīpāshēng;作爆裂声 zuò bàolièshēng: *The fire* ～*ed*. 这火劈劈啪啪地烧起来了. **splutter** *n* [C]劈啪声 pīpāshēng;爆裂声 bàolièshēng.

S

spoil /spɔɪl/ *v* [*pt*, *pp* ~t 或 ~ed] 1 [T]破坏〔壞〕pòhuài; 损害 sǔnhài: *Rain ~ed our holiday*. 下雨破坏了我们的假日. 2 [T] 宠〔寵〕坏 chǒng huài; 溺爱〔愛〕nì'ài. 3 [I](食物)变〔變〕坏 biàn huài, 腐败 fǔbài. **spoils** *n* [pl] [正式用语]赃〔贜〕物 zāngwù; (分得的)利益 lìyì. ˈ**spoil-sport** *n* [C] 扫〔掃〕兴〔興〕的人 sǎoxìngde rén.

spoke[1] /spəʊk/ *n* [C] 轮〔輪〕辐 lúnfú; 辐条〔條〕fútiáo.

spoke[2] *pt* of SPEAK.

spoken *pp* of SPEAK.

spokesman /ˈspəʊksmən/ [*pl* -**men** /-mən/] **spokesperson** [*pl* -**people**] **spokeswoman** [*pl* -**women**] *n* [C] 发〔發〕言人 fāyánrén.

sponge /spʌndʒ/ *n* 1 [C]海绵 hǎimián. 2 [C, U] 海绵状〔狀〕物 hǎimiánzhuàng wù. 3 = SPONGE-CAKE. **sponge** *v* 1 [T] 用海绵揩拭 yòng hǎimián kāishì. 2 [I] [非正式用语]白拿 bái ná; 揩油 kāiyóu: ~ *money off/from one's friends* 从朋友处讨钱. ˈ**sponge-cake** *n* [C, U] 松〔鬆〕糕 sōnggāo. **spongy** *adj* [-ier, -iest].

sponsor /ˈspɒnsə(r)/ *n* [C] 1 发〔發〕起人 fāqǐrén; 主办〔辦〕人 zhǔbànrén. 2 负责人 fùzérén; 担〔擔〕保人 dānbǎorén. **sponsor** *v* [T] 1 担保 dānbǎo; 倡议〔議〕chàngyì. 2 资助 zīzhù; 捐助 juānzhù. **sponsorship** *n* [U].

spontaneous /spɒnˈteɪnɪəs/ *adj* 自发〔發〕的 zìfāde; 自然产〔產〕生的 zìrán chǎnshēng de; 主动〔動〕的 zhǔdòngde: *a ~ offer of help* 主动提供帮助. **spontaneity** /ˌspɒntəˈneɪətɪ/ *n* [U]. **spontaneously** *adv*.

spoof /spuːf/ *n* [C] [非正式用语]滑稽的模仿 huájīde mófǎng.

spooky /ˈspuːkɪ/ *adj* [-ier, -iest] [非正式用语] 吓〔嚇〕人的 xiàrénde.

spool /spuːl/ *n* [C] 线〔綫〕轴 xiànzhóu; 卷轴 juǎnzhóu.

spoon /spuːn/ *n* [C] 匙 chí; 调羹 tiáogēng. **spoon** *v* [T] 用匙舀取 yòng chí yǎoqǔ. ˈ**spoon-feed** *v* [T] (对某人)作填鸭式灌输 zuò tiányāshì guànshū.

S

sporadic /spəˈrædɪk/ *adj* 偶尔〔爾〕发〔發〕生的 ǒu'ěr fāshēng de. **sporadically** /-klɪ/ *adv*.

spore /spɔː(r)/ *n* [C] [植物]孢子 bāozǐ.

sport /spɔːt/ *n* 1 [C, U]娱乐〔樂〕yúlè; 游戏〔戲〕yóuxì. 2 **sports** [pl] 运〔運〕动〔動〕会〔會〕yùndònghuì: *school ~s* 学校运动会. 3 [C] [非正式用语]公正的人 gōngzhèngde rén; 和善的人 héshànde rén. **sport** *v* [T] 炫耀 xuànyào; 夸〔誇〕示 kuāshì: ~ *a new beard* 炫耀新留的胡子. **sporting** *adj* 1 运动的 yùndòngde; 喜爱〔愛〕运动的 xǐ'ài yùndòng de. 2 公正的 gōngzhèngde. 3[习语] **a sporting ˈchance** 公平的机〔機〕会 gōngpíngde jīhuì. ˈ**sports car** *n* [C] 跑车 pǎochē; ˈ**sportsman**, ˈ**sportswoman** *n* [C] 运动员 yùndòngyuán. ˈ**sportsmanship** *n* [U] 运动道德 yùndòng dàodé; 体〔體〕育道德 tǐyù dàodé. **sporty** *adj* [-ier, -iest] 爱好或擅长〔長〕运动的 àihào huò shàncháng yùndòng de.

spot /spɒt/ *n* [C] 1 点〔點〕diǎn; 斑点 bāndiǎn. 2 污点 wūdiǎn; 污迹〔跡〕wūjì. 3(皮肤上的)红斑 hóngbān. 4 地点 dìdiǎn; 场〔場〕所 chǎngsuǒ: *the ~ where she died* 她死去的地方. 5[非正式用语]一点点 yìdiǎndiǎn; 少量 shǎoliàng: *a ~ of tea* 一小杯茶. 6[习语] **in a (tight) ˈspot** [非正式用语]在困难〔難〕的处〔處〕境中 zài kùnnande chǔjìng zhōng. **on the ˈspot** (a) 在场 zàichǎng. (b) 立即 lìjí; 当〔當〕场 dāngchǎng: *killed on the ~* 被当场杀死. **spot** *v* [-tt-] [T] 1[常用被动语态]使有斑点 shǐ yǒu bāndiǎn; 沾上污点 zhānshàng wūdiǎn. 2 认〔認〕出 rènchū; 发〔發〕现 fāxiàn. **spotted** *adj* 有斑点的 yǒu bāndiǎn de; 有污点的 yǒu wūdiǎn de. **spotless** *adj* 无〔無〕斑点的 wú bāndiǎn de; 纯洁〔潔〕的 chúnjiéde. **spotty** *adj* [-ier, -iest] (皮肤)有斑点的 yǒu bāndiǎn de.

spotlight /ˈspɒtlaɪt/ *n* [C] 聚光灯〔燈〕jùguāngdēng. **spotlight** *v* [T] 1 聚光照明 jùguāng zhàomíng. 2[喻]使显〔顯〕著 shǐ xiǎnzhù; 使注意 shǐ zhùyì: ~ *a problem* 注意一个问题.

spouse /spaʊs/ *n* [C] [正式用语][法律]配偶 pèi'ǒu.

spout /spaʊt/ *n* [C] 1 喷管 pēnguǎn; (水壶的)嘴 zuǐ: *a ~ on a teapot* 茶壶嘴. 2[习语] **up the ˈspout** [非正式用语]毁坏〔壞〕huǐhuài; 毁灭〔滅〕huǐmiè. **spout** *v* 1 [I, T](使液体)喷出 pēnchū, 喷射 pēnshè. 2 [T] [非正式用语]滔滔不绝地讲〔講〕tāotāo bùjué de jiǎng.

sprain /spreɪn/ *v* [T] 扭伤〔傷〕niǔshāng: ~ *an ankle* 扭伤了脚踝. **sprain** *n* [C] 扭伤 niǔshāng.

sprang *pt* of SPRING[2].

sprawl /sprɔːl/ *v* [I] 1 伸开〔開〕手足躺或坐 shēn kāi shǒu zú tǎng huò zuò. 2(植物)蔓生 mànshēng; (城市)无〔無〕计划〔劃〕地延伸 wú jìhuà de yánshēn. **sprawl** *n* [C, U] 伸开四肢的躺卧姿势〔勢〕shēn kāi sìzhī de tǎngwò zīshì; 蔓生 mànshēng; 无计划扩〔擴〕展 wú jìhuà kuòzhǎn: *urban ~* 城市无计划扩建.

spray[1] /spreɪ/ *n* [C] 小花枝 xiǎo huāzhī; 枝状〔狀〕饰物 zhīzhuàng shìwù.

spray[2] /spreɪ/ *n* 1 [U] 水花 shuǐhuā; 飞〔飛〕沫 fēimò; 浪花 lànghuā. 2 [C, U] 用作喷洒〔灑〕的液体〔體〕yòngzuò pēnsǎ de yètǐ. 3 [C] 喷雾

器 pēnwùqì. **spray** *v* **1** [T]向某物喷洒 xiàng mǒuwù pēnsǎ. **2** [I](液体)喷出 pēnchū.

spread /spred/ *v* [*pt*, *pp* **spread**] **1** [T]展开〔開〕zhǎnkāi;铺开 pūkāi: *The bird ~ its wings*. 鸟儿张开了翅膀. **2** [T]涂〔塗〕tú;敷 fū;抹 mǒ: *~ butter on bread* 在面包上抹黄油. **3** [I, T](使)传〔傳〕播 chuánbō;(使)散布 sànbù: *~ disease* 传染疾病. **4** [I]延长〔長〕yáncháng;展开 zhǎnkāi. **spread** *n* **1** [常作 sing] 范〔範〕围〔圍〕fànwéi;广〔廣〕度 guǎngdù. **2** [U] 传播 chuánbō;散布 sànbù: *the rapid ~ of the disease* 疾病的快速蔓延. **3** [C][非正式用语]丰〔豐〕盛的酒席 fēngshèngde jiǔxí;宴会〔會〕yànhuì. **4** [U, C]涂抹用的食物 túmǒ yòng de shíwù. ˈ**spread-eagle** *v* [T] 使手脚伸展着躺卧 shǐ shǒu jiǎo shēnzhǎnzhe tǎngwò. ˈ**spreadsheet** *n* [C] 空白表格 kòngbái biǎogé.

sprightly /ˈspraɪtlɪ/ *adj* [-ier, -iest] 活泼〔潑〕的 huópode;轻〔輕〕快的 qīngkuàide. **sprightliness** *n* [U].

spring[1] /sprɪŋ/ *n* **1** [C]泉 quán;源泉 yuánquán. **2** [C]弹〔彈〕簧 tánhuáng;发〔發〕条〔條〕fātiáo. **3** [C] 跳 tiào;跳跃〔躍〕tiàoyuè. **4** [U] 弹性 tánxìng;弹力 tánlì. **springy** *adj* [-ier, -iest].

spring[2] /sprɪŋ/ *v* [*pt* **sprang** /spræŋ/, *pp* **sprung** /sprʌŋ/] **1** [I] 跳跃〔躍〕tiàoyuè;突然移动〔動〕tūrán yídòng: *~ (up) from one's chair* 从椅子上一跃而起. *The door sprang open*. 那门突然打开. **2**[习语] **spring a** ˈ**leak** (船等)破裂漏水 pòliè lòu shuǐ. **3** [短语动词] **spring from sth** 来自某事物 lái zì mǒu shìwù;出身于 chūshēn yú. **spring sth on sb** (向某人)突然提出 tūrán tíchū: *She sprang the news on me*. 她突然告诉我那消息. **spring up** 迅速生长〔長〕或发〔發〕展 xùnsù shēngzhǎng huò fāzhǎn.

spring[3] /sprɪŋ/ *n* [C, U] 春天 chūntiān;春季 chūnjì. ˌ**spring-**ˈ**clean** *v* [T] 彻〔徹〕底打扫〔掃〕chèdǐ dǎsǎo. ˌ**spring-**ˈ**cleaning** *n* [U].

sprinkle /ˈsprɪŋkl/ *v* [T] 洒〔灑〕sǎ;散布 sànbù. **sprinkler** /-klə(r)/ *n* [C] 洒水器 sǎshuǐqì;喷水设备〔備〕pēn shuǐ shèbèi.

sprint /sprɪnt/ *v* [I] 全速奔跑 quánsù bēnpǎo;冲〔衝〕刺 chōngcì. **sprint** *n* [C] 快跑 kuàipǎo. **sprinter** *n* [C].

sprout /spraʊt/ *v* [I, T] 发〔發〕芽 fāyá;开〔開〕始生长〔長〕kāishǐ shēngzhǎng: [喻] *houses ~ing (up) on the edge of town* 在市区边缘出现的房屋群. **sprout** *n* [C] **1** 新芽 xīn yá;嫩枝 nèn zhī. **2** = BRUSSELS SPROUT.

sprung *pp* of SPRING[2].

spun *pp* of SPIN.

spur /spɜː(r)/ *n* [C] **1** 踢马〔馬〕刺 tīmǎcì. **2** [喻]刺激物 cìjīwù;鼓励〔勵〕品 gǔlìpǐn. **3**[习语] **on the spur of the moment** 一时〔時〕冲〔衝〕动〔動〕yìshí chōngdòng. **spur** *v* [-rr-] [T] (*on*) 鞭策 biāncè;激励 jīlì.

spurn /spɜːn/ *v* [T] 轻〔輕〕蔑地拒绝 qīngmiède jùjué;唾弃〔棄〕tuòqì.

spurt /spɜːt/ *v* **1** [I, T](使液体等)喷射 pēnshè;喷出 pēnchū. **2** [I]突然拼命努力 tūrán pīnmìng nǔlì;冲〔衝〕刺 chōngcì. **spurt** *n* [C] **1** 突然努力或加速 tūrán nǔlì huò jiāsù. **2** 突然喷射 tūrán pēnshè;爆发〔發〕bàofā.

sputter /ˈspʌtə(r)/ *v* [I] 连续〔續〕发〔發〕出喷溅〔濺〕唾沫声〔聲〕liánxù fāchū pēnjiàn tuòmò shēng.

spy /spaɪ/ *n* [C] [*pl* **-ies**] **1** 间谍 jiàndié;特务〔務〕tèwù. **2** 侦探 zhēntàn;密探 mìtàn. **spy** *v* [*pt*, *pp* **-ied**] **1** [I, T] (*on*)侦查 zhēnchá;暗中监〔監〕视 ànzhōng jiānshì. **2** [T][正式用语][謔]察看 chákàn;发〔發〕现 fāxiàn.

squabble /ˈskwɒbl/ *v* [I] *n* [C] 争吵 zhēngchǎo;口角 kǒujiǎo.

squad /skwɒd/ *n* [C, 亦作 sing 用 pl v] 小组 xiǎozǔ;班 bān: *a football ~* 足球队.

squadron /ˈskwɒdrən/ *n* [C, 亦作 sing 用 pl v] 骑兵中队〔隊〕qíbīng zhōngduì;(工兵、装甲兵等)连 lián;(海军)中队 zhōngduì;(空军)中队 zhōngduì.

squalid /ˈskwɒlɪd/ *adj* **1** 肮〔骯〕脏〔髒〕的 āngzāngde;邋遢的 lātāde. **2** 道德败坏〔壞〕的 dàodé bàihuài de;卑鄙的 bēibǐde. **squalidly** *adv*.

squall /skwɔːl/ *n* [C] **1** 大风〔風〕dàfēng;狂风 kuángfēng. **2** 高声〔聲〕叫喊 gāoshēng jiàohǎn;啼哭 tíkū. **squall** *v* [I] 高声叫喊 gāoshēng jiàohǎn;啼哭 tíkū.

squalor /ˈskwɒlə(r)/ *n* [U] 肮〔骯〕脏〔髒〕āngzāng;卑劣 bēiliè.

squander /ˈskwɒndə(r)/ *v* [T] (*on*) 浪费(时间、金钱) làngfèi.

square[1] /skweə(r)/ *adj* **1** 正方形的 zhèngfāngxíngde. **2** 成直角的 chéng zhíjiǎo de: *~ corners* 方角. **3** 平方的 píngfāngde: *six metres ~* 六平方米. **4** 诚实〔實〕的 chéngshíde;公正的 gōngzhèngde: *~ dealings* 公平交易. **5** 已付清的 yǐ fùqīng de;已结账〔賬〕的 yǐ jiézhàng de. **6** [习语] **a square meal** 一顿丰〔豐〕盛的饭菜 yídùn fēngshèngde fàncài. **be (all) square (with sb)** (a) (与对方)打成平局 dǎ chéng píngjú. (b) 不欠账 bú qiànzhàng. **square** *adv* 成直角地 chéng zhíjiǎo de. **squarely** *adv* **1** 成直角地 chéng zhíjiǎo de. **2** 面对〔對〕面地 miàn duì miàn de;直接地 zhíjiēde: *I looked her ~ly in the eye*. 我直瞪瞪地逼视她的眼睛. **3** 公正地 gōngzhèngde;诚实地 chéngshíde. **squareness** *n* [U]. **square root** *n* [C] 平方根 píngfānggēn: *The ~*

root of 4 is 2. 4的平方根是2.

square[2] /skweə(r)/ *n* [C] **1** 正方形 zhèngfāngxíng. **2** 正方形物 zhèngfāngxíng wù. **3** 广〔廣〕场〔場〕guǎngchǎng. **4** 平方 píngfāng. **5**[习语] **back to square one** 退还〔還〕到起点〔點〕tuìhuán dào qǐdiǎn.

square[3] /skweə(r)/ *v* **1** [T] 使成方形 shǐ chéng fāngxíng. **2** [T] 使成直角 shǐ chéng zhíjiǎo;使垂直 shǐ chuízhí. **3** [T]自乘 zìchéng. **4** [I,T] *with* [非正式用语](使)一致 yízhì;(使)相符 xiāngfú: ~ *the theory with the facts* 使理论与实际相符. **5** [T] [非正式用语]贿赂 huìlù;收买〔買〕shōumǎi. **6**[短语动词] **square sth off** 使成方形 shǐ chéng fāngxíng. **square up (with sb)** (向某人)付账 fùzhàng, 结算 jiésuàn.

squash[1] /skwɒʃ/ *v* **1** [T]压〔壓〕扁 yā biǎn;压平 yā píng. **2** [I,T]挤〔擠〕jǐ;挤进〔進〕jǐjìn: ~ *ten people into a car* 十个人挤进一辆汽车. **3** [T] 镇压(叛乱) zhènyā. **4** [T] 拒绝接受(建议) jùjué jiēshòu. **squash** *n* **1** [sing] 拥〔擁〕挤的人群 yōngjǐde rénqún. **2** [U,C]果子汁 guǒzizhī.

squash[2] /skwɒʃ/ *n* [U] (在围墙内用小网拍玩的)墙〔牆〕网〔網〕球戏〔戲〕qiángwǎngqiúxì.

squat /skwɒt/ *v* [-tt-] [I] **1** 蹲坐 dūnzuò. **2** 非法占〔佔〕用(空屋、土地) fēifǎ zhànyòng. **squat** *adj* 矮胖的 ǎipàngde. **squat** *n* [C] 非法占用的空屋、土地 fēifǎ zhànyòng de kōngwū、tǔdì. **squatter** *n* [C] 非法占用者 fēifǎ zhànyòngzhě.

squaw /skwɔː/ *n* [C] 北美印地安妇〔婦〕女 běiměi yìndì'ān fùnǚ.

squawk /skwɔːk/ *v* [I] **1**(尤指鸟类)发〔發〕出粗厉〔厲〕的叫声〔聲〕fāchū cūlìde jiàoshēng. **2**[非正式用语]大声诉苦或抗议〔議〕dà shēng sùkǔ huò kàngyì. **squawk** *n* [C].

squeak /skwiːk/ *v* [I,T] *n* [C] (作)短促刺耳的尖叫声〔聲〕duǎncù cì'ěrde jiānjiàoshēng. **squeaky** *adj* [-ier, -iest].

squeal /skwiːl/ *n* [C]长〔長〕声〔聲〕尖叫 chángshēng jiānjiào. **squeal** *v* [I] **1** 发〔發〕长而尖的叫声 fā cháng ér jiān de jiàoshēng. **2** [俚]告密 (尤指告发同谋者) gàomì.

squeamish /ˈskwiːmɪʃ/ *adj* **1** 易恶〔惡〕心的 yì ěxīn de;易呕〔嘔〕吐的 yì ǒutù de. **2** 易受惊〔驚〕的 yì shòujīng de;易生气〔氣〕的 yì shēngqì de. **squeamishly** *adv*. **squeamishness** *n* [U].

squeeze /skwiːz/ *v* **1** [T] 挤〔擠〕jǐ;榨 zhà: ~ *a sponge* 挤海绵. **2** [T] (*from* / *out of*)(从…中)榨取 zhàqǔ. **3** [I,T](指人)挤进〔進〕jǐjìn: ~ *into the back seat* 挤进后座. **4** [短语动词] **squeeze sth out of sb** 向某人榨取(情报等) xiàng mǒurén zhàqǔ. **squeeze** *n* **1** [C] 压〔壓〕榨 yāzhà;挤 jǐ. **2** [sing] 挤压 jǐyā;拥〔擁〕挤 yōngjǐ. **3** [C][非正式用语]财政困难〔難〕时〔時〕期 cáizhèng kùnnan shíqī.

squelch /skweltʃ/ *v* [I] 咯吱咯吱作响〔響〕gēzhī gēzhī zuò xiǎng. **squelch** *n* [C] 咯吱声〔聲〕gēzhīshēng.

squid /skwɪd/ *n* [C,U] 鱿鱼 yóuyú.

squint /skwɪnt/ *v* [I] **1** 斜着眼看 xiézhe yǎn kàn. **2** 眯着眼看 mīzhe yǎn kàn. **squint** *n* [sing] 斜视 xiéshì;斜视眼 xiéshìyǎn.

squirm /skwɜːm/ *v* [I] **1**(身子)扭动〔動〕niǔdòng. **2** 羞愧 xiūkuì;局〔侷〕促不安 júcù bù'ān. **squirm** *n* [C] 扭曲 niǔqū;扭动 niǔdòng.

squirrel /ˈskwɪrəl/ *n* [C] 松鼠 sōngshǔ.

squirt /skwɜːt/ *v* (a) [T] 使(液体、粉末)喷出 shǐ pēnchū. (b) [I] (液体、粉末)喷出 pēnchū. **squirt** *n* [C] 细的喷流 xìde pēnliú.

St *abbr* **1** saint. **2** street.

stab /stæb/ *v* [-bb-] **1** [I,T] (用刀、尖物)刺 cì;刺伤〔傷〕cìshāng. **2**[习语] **stab sb in the ˈback** 背叛(或中伤)某人 bèipàn mǒurén. **stab** *n* [C] **1** 刺 cì;戳 chuō. **2** 刺痛 cìtòng. **3** 企图〔圖〕qǐtú;尝〔嘗〕试 chángshì: *have a* ~ *at sth* 试做某事. **stabbing** *adj* 突然刺痛的 tūrán cìtòng de.

stable[1] /ˈsteɪbl/ *adj* [~r, ~st] 稳〔穩〕定的 wěndìngde; 坚〔堅〕固的 jiāngùde. **stability** /stəˈbɪlətɪ/ *n* [U]. **stabilize** /ˈsteɪbəlaɪz/ *v* [I,T] (使)稳定 wěndìng;(使)坚固 jiāngù. **stabilizer** *n* [C] 使稳定者 shǐ wěndìngzhě;稳定器 wěndìngqì.

stable[2] /ˈsteɪbl/ *n* [C] 厩 jiù;马〔馬〕棚 mǎpéng. **stable** *v* [T] 把(马)拴进〔進〕马厩 bǎ shuān jìn mǎjiù.

stack /stæk/ *n* [C] **1**(整齐的)一堆 yìduī: *a* ~ *of books* 一堆书. **2**(稻草等)堆 duī;垛 duò. **3** 高烟囱 gāo yāncōng;烟囱群 yāncōng qún. **4** **stacks of sth** [pl] [非正式用语]大量 dàliàng;一大堆 yí dà duī. **stack** *v* [T] 堆起 duīqǐ;堆放 duīfàng.

stadium /ˈsteɪdɪəm/ [*pl* ~s 或 -dia /-dɪə/] *n* [C] (有看台的)露天运〔運〕动〔動〕场〔場〕lùtiān yùndòngchǎng.

staff /stɑːf/ *n* **1** [C] 拐杖 guǎizhàng. **2** [C] (全体)工作人员 gōngzuò rényuán. **3** [U]当〔當〕权〔權〕人员 dāngquán rényuán;行政人员 xíngzhèng rényuán. **4** [C]参〔參〕谋人员 cānmóu rényuán. **staff** *v* [T] (为…)配备〔備〕工作人员 pèibèi gōngzuò rényuán.

stag /stæg/ *n* [C] 牡鹿 mǔlù.

stage /steɪdʒ/ *n* **1** [C]舞台 wǔtái. **2** **the stage** [sing] 演员的职〔職〕业〔業〕yǎnyuánde zhíyè;舞台生涯 wǔtái shēngyá. **3** [常作 sing] [喻]出事地点〔點〕chūshì dìdiǎn. **4**(进展的)时〔時〕期 shíqī, 阶〔階〕段 jiēduàn: *at an early* ~ *in her life* 在她一生的早期. **5**(行程中)两

S

站间的距离〔離〕liǎng zhàn jiān de jùlí. 6[习语] be/ go on the 'stage 当〔當〕(或成为)演员 dāng yǎnyuán. **stage** *v* [T] 上演 shàngyǎn. **'stage-coach** *n* [C] 公共马车 gōnggòng mǎchē. **ˌstage-'manager** *n* [C] 舞台监〔監〕督 wǔtái jiāndū.

stagger /'stægə(r)/ *v* 1 [I](行走)摇晃 yáohuàng;蹒跚 pánshān. 2 [T](新闻等)使震惊〔驚〕shǐ zhènjīng. 3 [T] 使(某事)错开〔開〕shǐ cuòkāi. **stagger** *n* [sing] 摇晃 yáohuàng;蹒跚 pánshān.

stagnant /'stægnənt/ *adj* 1 (水)不流动〔動〕的 bù liúdòng de, 污浊〔濁〕的 wūzhuóde. 2[喻] 不发〔發〕展的 bù fāzhǎn de;不景气〔氣〕的 bù jǐngqì de.

stagnate /stæg'neɪt/ *v* [I] 1 迟〔遲〕钝 chídùn;不活泼〔潑〕bù huópo. 2 不流动〔動〕bù liúdòng;成为死水 chéngwéi sǐshuǐ. **stagnation** /-ʃn/ *n* [U].

staid /steɪd/ *adj* 沉着的 chénzhuóde;严〔嚴〕肃〔肅〕的 yánsùde. **staidly** *adv*. **staidness** *n* [U].

stain /steɪn/ *v* 1 (a) [T] 沾污 zhānwū;污染 wūrǎn. (b) [I] 被沾污 bèi zhānwū;被污染 bèi wūrǎn. 2 [T]给(木材、织物等)着色 gěi zhuósè, 染色 rǎnsè. **stain** *n* 1[U] 染料 rǎnliào;着色剂〔劑〕zhuósèjì. 2 [C] 污点〔點〕wūdiǎn;沾污处〔處〕zhānwūchù. 3 [C]玷污(某人)名声〔聲〕的事物 diànwū míngshēng de shìwù. **stained 'glass** *n* [U] 彩色玻璃 cǎisè bōlí. **stainless** *adj* (尤指钢)不锈的 búxiùde.

stair /steə(r)/ *n* 1 **stairs** [pl] 楼〔樓〕梯 lóutī: *a flight of ~s* 一段楼梯. 2 [C] 梯级 tījí: *sitting on the bottom ~* 坐在楼梯的最下面一级上. **'staircase, 'stairway** *n* [C] (建筑物内的)楼梯 lóutī.

stake /steɪk/ *n* 1 [C]木桩〔樁〕mùzhuāng. 2 [C,常作 pl] 赌注 dǔzhù;赌金 dǔjīn. 3 [C] 投资 tóuzī: *I have a ~ in the company's success.* 我在这家公司有投资以期获利. 4[习语] **at stake** 冒风〔風〕险〔險〕mào fēngxiǎn. **stake** *v* [T] 1 用桩撑住 yòng zhuāng chēngzhù. 2 用(金钱等)打赌 yòng dǎdǔ. 3 [习语] **stake a claim** 声〔聲〕称〔稱〕(对某物)有所有权〔權〕shēngchēng yǒu suǒyǒuquán. 4 [短语动词] **stake sth out** [尤用于美语][非正式用语](尤指警方)持续〔續〕监〔監〕视(某处) chíxù jiānshì.

stale /steɪl/ *adj* 1(食品)不新鲜的 bù xīnxiān de. 2 陈旧〔舊〕的 chénjiùde;乏味的 fáwèide. 3 (运动员等)因过〔過〕劳〔勞〕而表现不佳的 yīn guò láo ér biǎoxiàn bù jiā de. **staleness** *n* [U].

stalemate /'steɪlmeɪt/ *n* [C, U] 1 (国际象棋)王棋受困 wángqí shòu kùn. 2 僵局 jiāngjú;对〔對〕峙 duìzhì.

stalk[1] /stɔːk/ *n* [C] 茎〔莖〕jīng;花梗 huāgěng;叶〔葉〕柄 yèbǐng.

stalk[2] /stɔːk/ *v* 1 [I] 高视阔步 gāo shì kuò bù;大踏步走 dà tàbù zǒu. 2 [T] 偷偷走近(野兽等) tōutōu zǒu jìn: ~ *deer* 潜近鹿群. **stalker** *n* [C] 潜〔潛〕随〔隨〕猎〔獵〕物者 qián suí lièwù zhě.

stall /stɔːl/ *n* [C] 1 (畜舍内的)分隔栏〔欄〕fēngélán. 2 售货摊〔攤〕shòuhuòtān. 3 **stalls** [pl] (戏院正厅)前排坐位 qiánpái zuòwèi. **stall** *v* 1 [I, T] (使汽车等)发〔發〕生故障 fāshēng gùzhàng. 2 [I, T] (使飞机)失速而无〔無〕法控制 shī sù ér wúfǎ kòngzhì. 3 [I]拖延(时间) tuōyán.

stallion /'stælɪən/ *n* [C] 雄马(尤指种马) xióngmǎ.

stamina /'stæmɪnə/ *n* [U] 持久力 chíjiǔlì;耐力 nàilì.

stammer /'stæmə(r)/ *v* 1 [I]口吃 kǒuchī;结结巴巴地说 jiējiēbābāde shuō. 2 [T] (*out*) 结结巴巴地说出(某事) jiējiēbābāde shuōchū: ~ (*out*) *an apology* 结结巴巴地说声道歉. **stammer** *n* [sing] 口吃 kǒuchī;结巴 jiēbā.

stamp[1] /stæmp/ *n* [C] 1 邮〔郵〕票 yóupiào;印花 yìnhuā. 2 图〔圖〕章 túzhāng;印 yìn. 3 印记 yìnjì;图记 tújì;标〔標〕记 biāojì. 4 顿足 dùn zú;跺脚 duò jiǎo. **'stamp album** *n* [C] 集邮簿 jíyóu bù.

stamp[2] /stæmp/ *v* 1 [I, T] (用脚)踩踏 cǎità. 2 [T] *A on B*; *B with A* 印(图案、日期等)于 yìn yú. 3 [T]贴邮〔郵〕票于 tiē yóupiào yú. 4 (*on*) [T] 给予印象 jǐyǔ yìnxiàng: ~ *one's personality on sth* 在某事中留下个人性格的痕迹. 5[短语动词] **stamp sth out** 消灭〔滅〕xiāomiè;镇压〔壓〕zhènyā.

stampede /stæm'piːd/ *n* [C] 惊〔驚〕跑 jīngpǎo;奔窜〔竄〕bēncuàn. **stampede** *v* [I, T] (使)惊跑 jīngpǎo;(使)溃散 kuìsàn.

stance /stæns/ *n* [C] 1 (高尔夫球等)(准备)击〔擊〕球的姿势〔勢〕jī qiú de zīshì. 2 态〔態〕度 tàidu;观〔觀〕点〔點〕guāndiǎn: *her ~ on nuclear arms* 她对核武器的立场.

stand[1] /stænd/ *n* 1 [sing] 停止 tíngzhǐ;停顿 tíngdùn: *come to a ~* 停下来. 2 [C] 架 jià;台〔臺〕tái: *a music ~* 乐谱架. 3 [C] 售货摊〔攤〕shòuhuòtān;陈列架 chénlièjià. 4 [C] 看台 kàntái. 5 [C]抵抗 (时期) dǐkàng: *make a ~* 准备抵抗. 6[美语] = WITNESS-BOX (WITNESS) (法庭中的)证〔證〕人席 zhèngrénxí. **standpoint** *n* [C] 立场〔場〕lìchǎng;观〔觀〕点〔點〕guāndiǎn.

stand[2] /stænd/ *v* [*pt*, *pp* **stood** /stʊd/] 1 [I] 站 zhàn;立 lì. 2 [I]高度为〔爲〕gāodù wéi: *She ~s five foot six*. 她身高五英尺六英寸. 3 [T] 使直立 shǐ zhílì;竖〔豎〕起 shùqǐ: ~ *the ladder against the wall* 把梯子靠

S

墙竖立. 4 [I] 位于 wèiyú; 在某处〔處〕zài mǒuchù. 5 [I] 坚〔堅〕持 jiānchí; 维持原状〔狀〕wéichí yuánzhuàng: *My decision ~s*. 我的决心不变. 6 [T] 为…付账〔賬〕wèi…fùzhàng: *~ sb a meal* 请某人吃一顿饭. 7 [I] (*for*) 作…的候选〔選〕人 zuò…de hòuxuǎnrén: *~ for parliament* 当议会议员候选人. 8 [习语] **stand a chance** 有机〔機〕会〔會〕(成功等) yǒu jīhuì. **stand firm / fast** 坚〔堅〕定不移 jiāndìng bù yí. **stand one's ground** ⇨ GROUND[1]. **stand on one's own (two) feet** 独〔獨〕立自主 dúlì zìzhǔ. **stand out like a sore thumb** ⇨ SORE. **stand to reason** 明显〔顯〕合理 míngxiǎn hélǐ; 按照常情 ànzhào chángqíng. 9 [短语动词] **stand by** (a) 袖手旁观〔觀〕xiù shǒu páng guān. (b) 准〔準〕备〔備〕行动〔動〕zhǔnbèi xíngdòng. **stand by sb** 支持某人 zhīchí mǒurén. **stand by sth** 信守(诺言等) xìn shǒu. **stand down** 退职〔職〕tuìzhí; 退出 tuìchū. **stand for sth** (a) 代表 dàibiǎo: *PO ~s for Post Office*. PO 代表 Post Office. (b) [非正式用语] 容忍 róngrěn; 允许 yǔnxǔ: *She doesn't ~ for disobedience*. 她不容许对她不服从. **stand in (for sb)** 代替(某人) dàitì. **stand out** (a) 明显 míngxiǎn; 突出 tūchū. (b) 继〔繼〕续〔續〕抵抗 jìxù dǐkàng: *~* **out against the enemy** 坚持抵抗敌人. **stand sb up** [非正式用语] 不遵守(同某人的)约定 bù zūnshǒu yuēdìng. **stand up for sb/sth** 支持某人(或某事) zhīchí mǒurén. **stand up to sb** 对〔對〕抗某人 duìkàng mǒurén. **stand up to sth** (物料) 经〔經〕用 jīng yòng; 耐久 nài jiǔ. **stand-by** *n* (a) [U] 待命 dàimìng; 准备(状态) zhǔnbèi. (b) [C] 后〔後〕备人员 hòubèi rényuán; 备用物 bèiyòngwù. **stand-in** *n* [C] 替身 tìshēn; 代替者 dàitìzhě. **stand-offish** *adj* 冷淡的 lěngdànde; 不友好的 bù yǒuhǎo de.

standard /ˈstændəd/ *n* [C] 1 标〔標〕准〔準〕biāozhǔn; 规格 guīgé. 2 水平 shuǐpíng; 水准 shuǐzhǔn: *the ~ of her school work* 她的学业水平. 3 旗 qí; 旗帜〔幟〕qízhì. **standard** *adj* 正常的 zhèngchángde; 普通的 pǔtōngde: *~ sizes of paper* 纸的普通尺寸. **standardize** / US -daɪz/ *v* [T] 使标〔標〕准〔準〕化 shǐ biāozhǔnhuà; 使合规格 shǐ hé guīgé. ˈ**standard lamp** *n* [C] 落地灯〔燈〕luòdìdēng. **standard of ˈliving** *n* [C] 生活水平 shēnghuó shuǐpíng.

standing /ˈstændɪŋ/ *n* [U] 1 身份 shēnfen; 地位 dìwèi; 名望 míngwàng. 2 持续〔續〕时〔時〕间 chíxù shíjiān: *debts of long ~* 长期欠债. **standing** *adj* 永存的 yǒngcúnde; 常备〔備〕的 chángbèide: *a ~ army* 常备军.

stank *pt* of STINK.

stanza /ˈstænzə/ *n* [C] (诗的)节〔節〕jié.

staple[1] /ˈsteɪpl/ *n* [C] 骑马钉 qímǎdīng; 钉书〔書〕钉 dìngshūdīng. **staple** *v* [T] 用骑马钉钉住 yòng qímǎdīng dìngzhù. **stapler** *n* [C] 钉书机〔機〕dìngshūjī.

staple[2] /ˈsteɪpl/ *n* [C] 主要产〔產〕品 zhǔyào chǎnpǐn; 名产 míngchǎn. **staple** *adj* 主要的 zhǔyàode: *Their ~ diet is rice*. 他们的主食是米饭.

star /stɑː(r)/ *n* [C] 1 星 xīng. 2 星状〔狀〕物 xīngzhuàngwù; 星号〔號〕xīnghào. 3 (演员等) 明星 míngxīng. 4 [星相] 命星 mìngxīng: *born under a lucky ~* 生来福星高照. **star** *v* [-rr-] (a) [I] 当〔當〕(电影等的) 主角 dāng zhǔjué. (b) [T] (电影等)使(某人)担任主角 shǐ dānrèn zhǔjué. ˌ**Stars and ˈStripes** *n* 星条〔條〕旗 xīngtiáoqí; 美国〔國〕国〔國〕旗 Měiguó guóqí. ˈ**stardom** / ˈstɑːdəm/ *n* [U] 明星的身份、地位 míngxīngde shēnfen、dìwèi. ˈ**starfish** *n* [C] [动物] 海星 hǎixīng. **starry** *adj*.

starboard /ˈstɑːbɔːd/ *n* [U] (船、飞机的) 右舷 yòuxián.

starch /stɑːtʃ/ *n* [U] 1 淀〔澱〕粉 diànfěn. 2 (浆棉布用的) 浆〔漿〕粉 jiāngfěn. **starch** *v* [T] 给(衣服)上浆 gěi shàng jiāng. **starchy** *adj* [-ier, -iest].

stare /steə(r)/ *v* [I] (*at*) 凝视 níngshì; 盯着看 dīngzhe kàn. **stare** *n* [C] 凝视 níngshì; 盯 dīng.

stark /stɑːk/ *adj* 1 荒凉的 huāngliángde: *a ~ landscape* 一片荒凉的景色. 2 显〔顯〕而易见的 xiǎn ér yì jiàn de; 鲜明的 xiānmíngde: *in ~ contrast* 成鲜明的对比. **stark** *adv* 完全地 wánquánde: *~ naked* 赤裸的.

starling /ˈstɑːlɪŋ/ *n* [C] 欧〔歐〕椋鸟 ōuliángniǎo; 燕八哥 yànbāgē.

starry ⇨ STAR.

start[1] /stɑːt/ *n* 1 [C, 常作 sing] 出发〔發〕chūfā; 起点〔點〕qǐdiǎn; 开〔開〕端 kāiduān. 2 **the start** [sing] 起跑线〔綫〕qǐpǎoxiàn. 3 [U, C] 优〔優〕先起跑的时〔時〕间或距离〔離〕yōuxiān qǐpǎo de shíjiān huò jùlí.

start[2] /stɑːt/ *v* 1 [I] (*out*) 出发〔發〕chūfā; 动〔動〕身 dòngshēn. 2 [I, T] 开〔開〕始 kāishǐ; 着手 zhuóshǒu. 3 [I, T] (*up*) 开动〔動〕(机器等) kāidòng; 发动 fādòng: *The car won't ~*. 这辆汽车发动不起来. 4 [T] 创〔創〕办〔辦〕chuàngbàn; 发起 fāqǐ: *~ a business* 创办一项事业. 5 [习语] **start the ball rolling** ⇨ BALL[1]. [短语动词] **start off** 开始活动 kāishǐ huódòng. **start (sb) off (on sth)** (使某人) 开始(进行某事) kāishǐ. **start out (to do sth)** [非正式用语] 着手(进行某事) zhuóshǒu. **starter** *n* [C] 1 起动装〔裝〕置 qǐdòng zhuāngzhì; 启〔啟〕动器 qǐdòngqì. 2 第一道菜 dìyídào cài. 3 起跑发令员 qǐpǎo fālìngyuán. 4 [习语]

for ˈstarters 首先 shǒuxiān.

startle /ˈstɑːtl/ *v* [T] 使大吃一惊〔驚〕shǐ dà chī yì jīng.

starve /stɑːv/ *v* 1 [I,T] (使)挨饿 āi'è; (使)饿死 è sǐ. 2 [I] [非正式用语] 觉〔覺〕得饥〔饑〕饿 juéde jī'è: *I'm starving*. 我饿了. 3 [T] [常作被动语态] (使某人)缺乏 quēfá; 渴望 kěwàng: *children ~d of love* 渴望被人疼爱的孩子们. starvation /-ˈveɪʃn/ *n* [U].

state[1] /steɪt/ *n* 1 [C] 状〔狀〕态〔態〕zhuàngtài; 状况 zhuàngkuàng; 情形 qíngxíng: *a poor ~ of health* 健康不佳. 2 (亦作 State) [C] 国〔國〕家 guójiā; 领土 lǐngtǔ. 3 (亦作 State) [C] 州 zhōu; 邦 bāng: *Ohio is a ~ in America*. 俄亥俄是美国的一个州. state ˈline *n* [C] (美国)州界线〔綫〕zhōujièxiàn. 4 (尤作 the State) [U] 政府 zhèngfǔ. 5 [U] 仪〔儀〕式 yíshì; 礼〔禮〕仪 lǐyí: *buried in ~* 以隆重的礼仪安葬. state *adj* 1 政府的 zhèngfǔde; 国家的 guójiāde. 2 礼仪的 lǐyíde; 礼节〔節〕性的 lǐjiéxìngde. stately *adj* [-ier, -iest] 庄〔莊〕严〔嚴〕的 zhuāngyánde; 威严的 wēiyánde; 高贵的 gāoguìde.

state[2] /steɪt/ *v* [T] 陈述 chénshù; 说明 shuōmíng. statement *n* [C] 1 陈述 chénshù; 声〔聲〕明 shēngmíng; 声明书〔書〕shēngmíngshū. 2 财务〔務〕报〔報〕表 cáiwù bàobiǎo: *a bank ~* 银行结单.

statesman /ˈsteɪtsmən/ *n* [C] [*pl* -men] 政治家 zhèngzhìjiā. ˈstatesmanship *n* [U] 政治家的才能(和智慧) zhèngzhìjiāde cáinéng.

static /ˈstætɪk/ *adj* 静止的 jìngzhǐde; 固定的 gùdìngde. static *n* [U] 1 天电〔電〕干扰〔擾〕tiāndiàn gānrǎo. 2 (亦作 ˌstatic elecˈtricity) 静电 jìngdiàn.

station /ˈsteɪʃn/ *n* [C] 1 所 suǒ; 台〔臺〕tái; 站 zhàn: *a ˈbus ~* 公共汽车站. 2 火车站 huǒchēzhàn. 3 广〔廣〕播公司 guǎngbō gōngsī. station *v* [T] 驻扎〔紮〕(部队)于(某处) zhùzhā yú; 置(某人)于(某地) zhì yú. ˈstation-wagon *n* [C] [美语] = ESTATE CAR (ESTATE).

stationary /ˈsteɪʃənrɪ/ *adj* 不移动〔動〕的 bù yídòng de; 固定的 gùdìngde: *~ traffic* 交通堵塞.

stationer /ˈsteɪʃnə(r)/ *n* [C] 文具商 wénjùshāng. stationery /ˈsteɪʃənrɪ; *US* -nerɪ/ *n* [U] 文具 wénjù.

statistics /stəˈtɪstɪks/ *n* 1 [pl] 统计 tǒngjì; 统计数〔數〕字 tǒngjì shùzì. 2 [U] 统计学〔學〕tǒngjìxué. statistical /-kl/ *adj*. statistically /-klɪ/ *adv*. statistician /ˌstætɪˈstɪʃn/ *n* [C] 统计学家 tǒngjìxuéjiā; 统计员 tǒngjìyuán.

statue /ˈstætʃuː/ *n* [C] 雕像 diāoxiàng; 塑像 sùxiàng; 铸〔鑄〕像 zhùxiàng. statuette /ˌstætʃʊˈet/ *n* [C] 小雕像 xiǎo diāoxiàng; 小塑像 xiǎo sùxiàng.

stature /ˈstætʃə(r)/ *n* [U] 1 身材 shēncái; 身高 shēngāo. 2 [喻] (凭才能、成就而获得的)名望 míngwàng.

status /ˈsteɪtəs/ *n* [U] 身份 shēnfen; 地位 dìwèi. ˈstatus symbol *n* [C] 表示地位高的东西 biǎoshì dìwèi gāo de dōngxi. status quo /ˈsteɪtəs kwəʊ/ *n* [C] 现状〔狀〕xiànzhuàng.

statute /ˈstætʃuːt/ *n* [C] 法令 fǎlìng; 法规 fǎguī. statutory /-trɪ; *US* -tɔːrɪ/ *adj* 法定的 fǎdìngde; 依法的 yīfǎde.

staunch /stɔːntʃ/ *adj* 忠诚的 zhōngchéngde; 坚〔堅〕定的 jiāndìngde. staunchly *adv*.

stave /steɪv/ *v* [*pt*, *pp* ~d 或 stove /stəʊv/] [短语动词] stave sth in 击〔擊〕穿 jīchuān; 凿〔鑿〕孔于 záo kǒng yú. stave sth off [*pt*, *pp* ~d] 避开〔開〕(某事物) bìkāi; 延缓 yánhuǎn.

stay /steɪ/ *v* 1 [I] 停留 tíngliú; 保持 bǎochí: *~ at home* 呆在家里. *~ sober* 保持清醒. 2 [I] 暂住 zàn zhù; 逗留 dòuliú: *~ at a hotel* 住旅馆. 3 [T] 停止 tíngzhǐ; 推迟〔遲〕tuīchí: *~ the progress of the disease* 防止疾病恶化. 4 [习语] stay clear of sb/sth ⇨ CLEAR[1]. stay put 留在原处〔處〕liú zài yuánchù; 固定不动〔動〕gùdìng búdòng. 5 [短语动词] stay up 不睡觉〔覺〕bú shuìjiào. stay *n* [C] 1 停留时〔時〕间 tíngliú shíjiān; 逗留期 dòuliúqī: *a long ~ in hospital* 长期住医院. 2 [法律] 延期 yánqī; 缓期 huǎnqī: *a ~ of execution* 缓期执行. ˈstaying-power *n* [U] = STAMINA.

steadfast /ˈstedfɑːst; *US* -fæst/ *adj* 固定的 gùdìngde; 不变〔變〕的 búbiànde; 不动〔動〕摇的 bú dòngyáo de. steadfastly *adv*.

steady /ˈstedɪ/ *adj* [-ier, -iest] 1 坚〔堅〕固的 jiāngùde; 牢靠的 láokàode: *hold the ladder ~* 把梯子扶好. 2 稳〔穩〕定的 wěndìngde; 平稳的 píngwěnde: *a ~ speed* 平稳的速度. 3 可靠的 kěkàode; 扎〔紮〕实〔實〕的 zhāshide: *a ~ worker* 可靠的工作者. 4 不变〔變〕的 búbiànde: *a ~ purpose* 不变的目标. steady *adv* 平稳地 píngwěnde. steady *v* [-ied] [I, T] (使)稳定 wěndìng; (使)坚固 jiāngù. steadily *adv* 稳定地 wěndìngde.

steak /steɪk/ *n* [C, U] 肉片 ròupiàn; 鱼片 yúpiàn; 牛(猪)排 niúpái.

steal /stiːl/ *v* [*pt* stole /stəʊl/, *pp* stolen /ˈstəʊlən/] 1 [I, T] (*from*) 偷 tōu; 窃〔竊〕取 qièqǔ. 2 [T] 偷袭〔襲〕tōuxí; 巧取 qiǎoqǔ: *~ a kiss* 偷吻. 3 [I] 偷偷地行动〔動〕tōutōude xíngdòng. 4 [习语] steal the show 抢〔搶〕出风〔風〕头〔頭〕qiǎng chū fēngtou.

S

stealth /stelθ/ *n* [U] 秘密行动〔動〕mìmì xíngdòng. **stealthy** *adj* [-ier, -iest].

steam /stiːm/ *n* [U] 1 蒸汽 zhēngqì. 2 蒸汽压〔壓〕力 zhēngqì yālì. 3 [习语] **run out of steam** 筋疲力尽〔盡〕jīn pí lì jìn. **steam** *v* 1 [I] 放出蒸汽 fàng chū zhēngqì. 2 [I]用蒸汽开〔開〕动 yòng zhēngqì kāidòng. 3 [T] 蒸煮 zhēngzhǔ. 4[短语动词] **steam (sth) up** (使)蒙上水汽 méng shàng shuǐqì;(使)有蒸汽 yǒu zhēngqì. **'steam-engine** *n* [C] 蒸汽机〔機〕zhēngqìjī. **steamer** *n* [C] 1 汽船 qìchuán;轮〔輪〕船 lúnchuán. 2 蒸锅〔鍋〕zhēngguō. **'steamroller** *n* [C] 蒸汽压〔壓〕路机 zhēngqì yālùjī. **steamy** *adj*.

steel /stiːl/ *n* [U] 钢〔鋼〕gāng. **steel** *v* [T] 使(自己)硬着心肠〔腸〕shǐ yìngzhe xīncháng: ~ *oneself* (*against a cry for help*) 硬着心肠(不去救人).

steep[1] /stiːp/ *adj* 1 陡峭的 dǒuqiàode. 2[非正式用语] 过〔過〕高的 guògāode;过分的 guòfènde: ~ *prices* 不合理的高价. **steeply** *adv*. **steepness** *n* [U].

steep[2] /stiːp/ *v* 1 [I, T]浸 jìn;泡 pào. 2[短语动词] **steep (sb/ oneself) in sth** (使)精通某事物 jīngtōng mǒu shìwù.

steeple /'stiːpl/ *n* [C] (教堂的)尖顶 jiāndǐng. **'steeplechase** *n* [C] 障碍〔礙〕赛跑或赛马 zhàng'ài sàipǎo huò sàimǎ. **'steeplejack** *n* [C] 烟囱或尖塔等的修理工人 yāncōng huò jiāntǎ děng de xiūlǐ gōngrén.

steer /stɪə(r)/ *v* [I, T] 1 驾驶 (车,船等) jiàshǐ. 2 [习语] **steer clear of sb/sth** ⇨ CLEAR[1]. **'steering-wheel** *n* [C] 方向盘〔盤〕fāngxiàngpán.

stem[1] /stem/ *n* [C] (a) 茎〔莖〕jīng. (b) (高酒杯等的)脚 jiǎo. **stem** *v* [-mm-] [短语动词] **stem from sth** 起源于 qǐyuán yú. **'stem cell** *n* [C] 干〔幹〕细胞 gànxìbāo.

stem[2] /stem/ *v* [T] [-mm-] 堵塞 dǔsāi;挡〔擋〕住 dǎngzhù.

stench /stentʃ/ *n* [C] 恶〔惡〕臭 èchòu.

stencil /'stensl/ *n* [C] 1 模版 móbǎn;型版 xíngbǎn. 2 用模版印的图〔圖〕文 yòng móbǎn yìn de tú wén. **stencil** *v* [-ll-; 美语 -l-] [I, T] (用)模版印刷 móbǎn yìnshuā.

step[1] /step/ *n* [C] 1 (a) (脚)步 bù. (b) 步幅 bùfú. 2 步态〔態〕bùtài;脚步声〔聲〕jiǎobùshēng: *heard her ~ on the stair* 听见她在楼梯上的脚步声. 3(某过程的)一步 yí bù: *take ~s to help her* 采取步骤帮助她. 4 台阶〔階〕táijiē;梯级 tījí. 5 **steps** [pl] 折〔摺〕梯 zhétī. 6[习语] **in/out of step (with)** (a) (与他人)脚步取齐〔齊〕(或不齐) jiǎobù qǔ qí. (b) (与他人)步调一致(或不一致) bùdiào yízhì. **mind / watch one's 'step** 谨慎 jǐnshèn;小心 xiǎoxīn. **ˌstep by 'step** 逐步地 zhúbùde. **'step-ladder** *n* [C] 折梯 zhétī.

step[2] /step/ *v* [-pp-] [I] 1 走 zǒu;步行 bùxíng. 2 *in, out, up, etc* (向某方向)走动〔動〕zǒudòng. 3 [习语] **'step on it** [非正式用语]快走 kuài zǒu;赶〔趕〕快 gǎnkuài. **ˌstep out of 'line** 出格 chūgé;越轨 yuèguǐ. 4[短语动词] **step aside, step down** 让〔讓〕位 ràngwèi;辞〔辭〕职〔職〕cízhí. **step in** 插手 chāshǒu;干预 gānyù. **step sth up** 增加 zēngjiā;促进〔進〕cùjìn. **'stepping-stone** *n* [C] 1 (过河的)垫〔墊〕脚石 diànjiǎoshí. 2 [喻](通向成功的)阶〔階〕段 jiēduàn;进身之阶 jìn shēn zhī jiē.

step- /step-/ *prefix* [表示"继"、"后"]: '~*-daughter* 前妻或前夫所生女儿.

stereo /'sterɪəʊ/ *adj* 立体〔體〕声〔聲〕的 lìtǐshēngde. **stereo** *n* 1 [U] 立体声 lìtǐshēng: *in* ~ 立体声的. 2 [C] 立体声音响〔響〕器材 lìtǐshēng yīnxiǎng qìcái.

stereotype /'sterɪətaɪp/ *n* [C] 固定的形式 gùdìngde xíngshì;老一套 lǎoyítào.

sterile /'steraɪl; *US* 'sterəl/ *adj* 1 不结果实〔實〕的 bù jiē guǒshí de;不育的 búyùde. 2 (土地)贫瘠的 pínjíde;不毛的 bùmáode. 3 [喻]无〔無〕结果的 wú jiéguǒ de: *a ~ argument* 无结果的辩论. 4 无菌的 wújūnde. **sterility** /stəˈrɪlətɪ/ *n* [U]. **sterilize** /'sterəlaɪz/ *v* [T] 使不结果实 shǐ bù jiē guǒshí;使绝育 shǐ juéyù;杀〔殺〕菌 shā jūn.

sterling /'stɜːlɪŋ/ *n* [U] 英国〔國〕货币〔幣〕Yīngguó huòbì. **sterling** *adj* [正式用语]优〔優〕秀的 yōuxiùde;纯正的 chúnzhèngde.

stern[1] /stɜːn/ *adj* 严〔嚴〕厉〔厲〕的 yánlìde;严格的 yángéde. **sternly** *adv*.

stern[2] /stɜːn/ *n* [C] 船尾 chuánwěi.

steroid /'sterɔɪd, 'stɪərɔɪd/ *n* [C] [生化]类〔類〕固醇 lèigùchún.

stethoscope /'steθəskəʊp/ *n* [C] 听〔聽〕诊器 tīngzhěnqì.

stew /stjuː/ *v* [T] 炖〔燉〕dùn;煨 wēi;焖〔燜〕mèn. **stew** *n* 1 [C, U] 炖肉 dùn ròu. 2[习语] **in a stew** [非正式用语]着急 zháojí;烦恼〔惱〕fánnǎo.

steward /'stjʊəd; *US* 'stuːəd/ *n* [C] 1 (亦作 **stewardess** /ˌstjʊə'des; *US* ˌstuːə'des/) (船、飞机的)乘务〔務〕员 chéngwùyuán,服务员 fúwùyuán. 2(赛马、舞会等的)干〔幹〕事 gànshi,组织〔織〕者 zǔzhīzhě.

stick[1] /stɪk/ *n* [C] 1 枝条〔條〕zhītiáo;枯枝 kūzhī. 2 木棍 mùgùn: *a 'walking-~* 手杖. 3 (细圆的)条状〔狀〕物(如粉笔等) tiáozhuàngwù. 4 [习语] **give sb 'stick** [非正式用语] 严〔嚴〕责某人 yán zé mǒurén.

stick[2] /stɪk/ *v* [*pt*, *pp* **stuck** /stʌk/] 1 [I, T] *in, into, through, etc* 刺穿 cì chuān;插入 chā rù: ~ *the knife into the cheese* 把刀插入干酪. 2 [I, T] (使)粘住 zhānzhù; 粘贴 zhāntiē. 3 [T] [非正式用语]放置 fàngzhì;插在 chā zài: *S~ it in the bag*. 把它放进口袋里. 4 [I] 卡住 qiǎzhù; 陷住 xiànzhù: *The key stuck in the lock*. 钥匙在锁中卡住了. 5 [T] [非正式用语]忍受 rěnshòu;容忍 róngrěn: *I can't ~ it*. 我不能容忍. 6[习语] **stick one's neck out** 冒险〔險〕 màoxiǎn. **stick one's nose into sth** ⇨ NOSE[1]. **stick one's oar in** ⇨ OAR. **stick out like a sore thumb** ⇨ SORE. **stick to one's guns** [非正式用语]坚〔堅〕持立场〔場〕 jiānchí lìchǎng. **stuck in a groove** ⇨ GROOVE. 7[短语动词] **stick around** [非正式用语]在附近(逗留或等候) zài fùjìn. **stick at sth** 坚持做某事 jiānchí zuò mǒushì. **stick by sb** 继〔繼〕续〔續〕支持某人 jìxù zhīchí mǒurén. **stick sth out** (使)伸出 shēnchū; (使)突出 tūchū: ~ *one's tongue out* 伸出舌头. **stick it / sth out** [非正式用语]坚持到底 jiānchí dàodǐ. **stick to sb / sth** 忠于(朋友、理想等) zhōng yú. **stick up** 竖〔豎〕起 shùqǐ;向上突出 xiàngshàng tūchū. **stick up for sb/ sth** 维护〔護〕 wéihù; 支持 zhīchí. **sticker** *n* [C] (背面)有黏胶〔膠〕的标〔標〕签〔簽〕 yǒu niánjiāo de biāoqiān. **'sticking-plaster** *n* [C, U] = PLASTER 3. **'stick-in-the-mud** *n* [C] [非正式用语]反对〔對〕变〔變〕革的人 fǎnduì biàngé de rén. **sticky** *adj* [-ier, -iest] 1 黏性的 niánxìngde. 2[非正式用语]困难〔難〕的 kùnnande: *a ~ situation* 艰难的处境.

stiff /stɪf/ *adj* 1 坚〔堅〕硬的 jiānyìngde;不易弯〔彎〕曲的 bú yì wānqū de: ~ *cardboard* 坚硬的纸板. 2 难〔難〕于移动〔動〕的 nán yú yídòng de;难搅〔攪〕拌的 nán jiǎobàn de: *a ~ paste* 黏稠的浆糊. 3 难的 nánde;费劲〔勁〕的 fèijìnde: *a ~ climb* 艰难的攀登. 4 冷淡的 lěngdànde; 生硬的 shēngyìngde. 5 强烈的 qiángliède;猛烈的 měngliède: *a ~ breeze* 强劲的风. 6[习语] **a stiff upper lip** 沉着的 chénzhuóde;坚强的 jiānqiángde. **stiff** *adv* [非正式用语]极〔極〕度地 jídùde;非常 fēicháng: *bored ~* 厌烦极了. **stiffly** *adv*. **stiffness** *n* [U].

stiffen /ˈstɪfn/ *v* [I, T] (使)变〔變〕硬 biàn yìng;(使)变僵硬 biàn jiāngyìng.

stifle /ˈstaɪfl/ *v* 1 [I, T] (使)窒息 zhìxī;闷死 mēnsǐ. 2 [T]抑制 yìzhì;镇压〔壓〕 zhènyā: ~ *a yawn* 忍住呵欠.

stigma /ˈstɪgmə/ *n* [C, U] 耻辱 chǐrǔ;污点〔點〕 wūdiǎn.

stile /staɪl/ *n* [C] (供人越过篱或墙的)踏级 tàjí;台阶〔階〕 táijiē.

still[1] /stɪl/ *adj* 1 不动〔動〕的 búdòngde;静止的 jìngzhǐde;无〔無〕声〔聲〕的 wúshēngde. 2 (饮料)不起泡的 bù qǐ pào de. **still** *v* [T] 使平静 shǐ píngjìng;止住 zhǐzhù. **'stillborn** *adj* 1 (婴儿)死产〔產〕的 sǐchǎnde. 2 [喻](思想、计划等)不成功的 bù chénggōng de, 流产的 liúchǎnde.

still[2] /stɪl/ *adv* 1 还〔還〕 hái;仍旧〔舊〕 réngjiù: *He is ~ busy*. 他还很忙. 2 还要 háiyào;更 gèng: *Tom is tall, but Mary is taller ~*. 汤姆很高,而玛丽更高. 3 (虽然…)还是 háishì: *It's raining. Still, we must go shopping*. 外面正下着雨,然而我们必须出去买东西.

still[3] /stɪl/ *n* [C] 蒸馏器 zhēngliúqì.

stilt /stɪlt/ *n* [C] 高跷〔蹺〕 gāoqiāo.

stilted /ˈstɪltɪd/ *adj* (言谈,举止等)生硬的 shēngyìngde, 不自然的 bú zìrán de.

stimulant /ˈstɪmjʊlənt/ *n* [C] 兴〔興〕奋〔奮〕剂〔劑〕 xīngfènjì.

stimulate /ˈstɪmjʊleɪt/ *v* [T] 1 刺激 cìjī;促进〔進〕 cùjìn: ~ *interest* 激发兴趣. 2 鼓励〔勵〕发〔發〕展 gǔlì fāzhǎn. **stimulating** *adj*. **stimulation** /stɪmjʊˈleɪʃn/ *n* [U].

stimulus /ˈstɪmjʊləs/ *n* [C] [*pl* -li /-laɪ/] 刺激物 cìjīwù; 鼓励〔勵〕 gǔlì: *a ~ to hard work* 对勤奋工作的鼓励.

sting[1] /stɪŋ/ *n* [C] 1 (昆虫的)刺 cì; 螫针 shìzhēn. 2 螫伤〔傷〕处〔處〕 shìshāng chù. 3 刺痛 cìtòng;刺伤〔傷〕 cìshāng.

sting[2] /stɪŋ/ *v* [*pt*, *pp* stung /stʌŋ /] [I, T] 1 刺 cì;螫 shì. 2 (突然)感到刺痛 gǎn dào cìtòng: [喻] *a ~ing attack* 尖锐的抨击.

stingy /ˈstɪndʒɪ/ *adj* [-ier, -iest] [非正式用语]吝啬〔嗇〕的 lìnsède;小气〔氣〕的 xiǎoqìde. **stingily** /-əlɪ/ *adv*. **stinginess** *n* [U].

stink /stɪŋk/ *v* [*pt* stank /stæŋk / 或 stunk / stʌŋk /, *pp* stunk] [I] 1 发〔發〕恶〔惡〕臭 fā èchòu. 2[非正式用语]很糟糕 hěn zāogāo; 很不正当〔當〕 hěn bú zhèngdàng. 3 [短语动词] **stink sth out** 充满臭气〔氣〕 chōngmǎn chòuqì. **stink** *n* 1 [C] 臭气 chòuqì;臭味 chòuwèi. 2 [sing] [俚]麻烦 máfan;忙乱〔亂〕 mángluàn.

stint /stɪnt/ *v* [I, T] **stint on sth; stint sb (of sth)** 限制 xiànzhì;节〔節〕制 jiézhì. **stint** *n*[C] (工作)定额 dìng'é.

stipulate /ˈstɪpjʊleɪt/ *v* [T] 规定 guīdìng; 约定 yuēdìng. **stipulation** /-ˈleɪʃn/ *n* [U].

stir /stɜː(r)/ *v* [-rr-] 1 [T] 搅〔攪〕拌 jiǎobàn. 2 [I, T] (使)移动〔動〕 yídòng. 3 [T] (*up*) 激起 jīqǐ; 鼓动 gǔdòng: *speakers ~ring up the crowd* 鼓动群众的演说者. 4 [I] [俚]搬弄是非 bānnòng shìfēi. **stir** *n* [sing] 骚动 sāodòng;激动 jīdòng. **stirring** *adj* 激动的 jīdòngde;鼓舞人心的 gǔwǔ rénxīn de.

stirrup /ˈstɪrəp/ *n* [C] 马镫 mǎdèng.

S

stitch /stɪtʃ/ *n* 1 [C] (a)(缝纫或缝合的)一针 yì zhēn. (b) (编织的)一针 yì zhēn, 一钩 yì gōu. 2 [C] 缝线〔綫〕féngxiàn;针脚 zhēnjiǎo. 3 [sing] (胁部)突然剧〔劇〕痛 tūrán jùtòng. 4 [习语] **not have a ˈstitch on / not be wearing a ˈstitch** 赤身裸体〔體〕chìshēn luǒtǐ. **in ˈstitches** [非正式用语]大笑不止 dà xiào bùzhǐ. **stitch** *v* [I, T] 缝 féng;缝合 fénghé.

stoat /stəʊt/ *n* [C] 鼬 yòu.

stock[1] /stɒk/ *n* 1 [C, U] 存货 cúnhuò;现货 xiànhuò. 2 [C, U]供给 gōngjǐ;储备〔備〕chǔbèi. 3 [U] = LIVESTOCK. 4 [C, 常用 pl v] 股本 gǔběn;公债 gōngzhài. 5 [U] 汤〔湯〕料 tāngliào;高汤 gāotāng. 6[习语] **in / out of stock** 有(或无)存货 yǒu cúnhuò. **take stock of sth** 检〔檢〕查 jiǎnchá;估量 gūliang. **stock** *adj* 陈腐的 chénfǔde;老一套的 lǎoyítàode: *a ~ phrase* 老一套的话语. **ˈstockbroker** *n* [C] 证〔證〕券经〔經〕纪人 zhèngquàn jīngjìrén. **ˈstock exchange** *n* [C] 证券交易所 zhèngquàn jiāoyìsuǒ. **ˈstock-market** *n* [C] 证券市场〔場〕zhèngquàn shìchǎng. **ˈstockpile** *v* [T] 贮〔貯〕存物资 zhùcún wùzī;囤积〔積〕túnjī. **ˈstockpile** *n* [C]. **ˌstock-ˈstill** *adv* 静止地 jìngzhǐde;不动〔動〕地 búdòngde. **ˈstocktaking** *n* [U] 盘〔盤〕点〔點〕存货 pándiǎn cúnhuò.

stock[2] /stɒk/ *v* [T] 1 供应〔應〕gōngyìng;备〔備〕货 bèihuò. 2[短语动词] **stock up (on sth)** 储备(某物) chǔbèi.

stockade /stɒˈkeɪd/ *n* [C] 栅栏〔欄〕zhàlan.

stockings /ˈstɒkɪŋz/ *n* [pl] (长统)袜〔襪〕wà.

stocky /ˈstɒkɪ/ *adj* [-ier, -iest] 矮胖的 ǎipàngde;粗壮〔壯〕的 cūzhuàngde. **stockily** *adv*.

stodge /stɒdʒ/ *n* [U][俚]干〔乾〕硬而难〔難〕消化的食物 gān yìng ér nán xiāohuà de shíwù. **stodgy** *adj* [-ier, -iest] 1 干硬的 gānyìngde;不好消化的 bùhǎo xiāohuà de. 2 迟〔遲〕钝的 chídùnde.

stoic /ˈstəʊɪk/ *n* [C] 禁欲〔慾〕主义〔義〕者 jìnyù zhǔyì zhě. **stoical** *adj*. **stoically** /-klɪ/ *adv*. **stoicism** /ˈstəʊɪsɪzəm/ *n* [U] 禁欲主义 jìnyù zhǔyì.

stoke /stəʊk/ *v* [短语动词] **stoke (sth) up** 给(锅炉等)添燃料 gěitiān ránliào. **stoker** *n* [C].

stole[1] /stəʊl/ *n* [C] 披肩 pījiān;圣〔聖〕带〔帶〕shèngdài.

stole[2] *pt* of STEAL.

stolen *pp* of STEAL.

stomach /ˈstʌmək/ *n* 1 [C] 胃 wèi. 2 [C] 腹部 fùbù;肚子 dùzi. 3 [U] 希望 xīwàng;渴求 kěqiú: *have no ~ for an argument* 不想争论. **stomach** *v* [T] 容忍 róngrěn;忍受 rěnshòu.

stone /stəʊn/ *n* 1 [U] 石头〔頭〕shítou. 2 [C] 石块〔塊〕shíkuài. 3 [C] 宝〔寶〕石 bǎoshí. 4 [C] (果)核 hé. 5 [C] [*pl* **stone**] 呖(英国重量单位,等于 14 磅或 6.35 公斤) shí. 6 [C] (身体中的)结石 jiéshí. 7 [习语] **a stone's throw** 短距离〔離〕duǎn jùlí. **stone** *v* [T] 1 向…扔石头 xiàng…rēng shítou. 2 去…的核 qù…de hé. **the ˈStone Age** *n* [sing] 石器时〔時〕代 shíqì shídài. **stoned** *adj* [非正式用语] 1 烂〔爛〕醉的 lànzuìde. 2 在毒品刺激下的 zài dúpǐn cìjī xià de. **ˌstone-ˈdeaf** *adj* 完全聋〔聾〕的 wánquán lóng de.

stony /ˈstəʊnɪ/ *adj* [-ier, -iest] 1 多石的 duōshíde: *a ~ path* 碎石小径. 2 冷酷无〔無〕情的 lěngkù wúqíng de. **stonily** /-əlɪ/ *adv*.

stood *pt, pp* of STAND[2].

stool /stuːl/ *n* [C] (小)凳子 dèngzi.

stoop /stuːp/ *v* 1 [I] 弯〔彎〕腰 wān yāo;俯身 fǔ shēn. 2 [短语动词] **stoop to sth** 屈从〔從〕qūcóng;堕〔墮〕落 duòluò. **stoop** *n* [sing] 弯腰 wān yāo;曲身 qū shēn.

stop[1] /stɒp/ *n* [C] 1 停止 tíngzhǐ;中止 zhōngzhǐ: *came to a ~* 停了下来. 2 车站 chēzhàn. 3 = FULL STOP. 4[习语] **put a stop to sth** 使停止 shǐ tíngzhǐ;制止 zhìzhǐ.

stop[2] /stɒp/ *v* [-pp-] 1 [T] 使停止 shǐ tíngzhǐ;停住 tíngzhù. 2 [T] 阻碍〔礙〕zǔ'ài;防止 fángzhǐ: *~ her (from) leaving* 不让她离开. 3 [I] 终止(活动、工作) zhōngzhǐ: *The engine ~ped.* 引擎停了. 4 [I]中止 zhōngzhǐ;暂停 zàntíng: *Where does the bus ~?* 公共汽车停在哪儿? 5 [T] 拒绝给予(应给之物) jùjué jǐyǔ;拒付 jùfù: *~ a cheque* 止付支票. 6 [I] [非正式用语]停留 tíngliú;逗留 dòuliú. 7 [短语动词] **stop off** 中途稍作停留 zhōngtú shāo zuò tíngliú. **stop over** 中途停留(和过夜) zhōngtú tíngliú. **ˈstopcock** *n* [C] 阀门 fámén;水龙〔龍〕头〔頭〕shuǐlóngtóu. **ˈstopgap** *n* [C] 临〔臨〕时〔時〕替代者 línshí tìdàizhě. **ˈstopover** *n* [C] 中途停留 zhōngtú tíngliú. **stoppage** /-pɪdʒ/ *n* [C] 停工 tínggōng. **stopper** *n* [C] 堵塞物 dǔsèwù;栓 shuān. **ˈstop-press** *n* [C] (报纸开印后临时加插的)最后消息 zuìhòu xiāoxi.

storage /ˈstɔːrɪdʒ/ *n* [U] 仓〔倉〕库 cāngkù;货栈〔棧〕huòzhàn.

store /stɔːr/ *n* [C] 1 贮〔貯〕藏 zhùcáng;库存量 kùcúnliàng. 2 仓〔倉〕库 cāngkù;栈〔棧〕房 zhànfáng. 3 百货商店 bǎihuò shāngdiàn. 4[习语] **in store** (a) 准〔準〕备〔備〕着 zhǔnbèizhe. (b) 必将〔將〕发〔發〕生 bìjiāng fāshēng: *What's in ~ for us today?* 今天会发生什么事? **set great / not much store by** 非常

重视(或不太重视) fēicháng zhòngshì. **store** *v* [T] 1 (*up*) 储备 chǔbèi;贮藏 zhùcáng. 2 存(家具等)入仓库 cúnrù cāngkù.

storey /ˈstɔːrɪ/ *n* [C] (房屋的)一层〔層〕 yìcéng.

stork /stɔːk/ *n* [C] 鹳 guàn.

storm /stɔːm/ *n* [C] 1 风〔風〕暴 fēngbào;暴风雨 bàofēngyǔ. 2(感情上的)激动〔動〕 jīdòng,暴发〔發〕 bàofā: *a* ~ *of anger* 一阵暴怒. 3 [习语] **take by storm** 攻占〔佔〕gōngzhàn;强夺〔奪〕 qiángduó. **storm** *v* 1 [T] 攻占 gōngzhàn;袭〔襲〕取 xíqǔ. 2 [I]暴怒 bàonù;咆哮 páoxiào. **stormy** *adj* [-ier, -iest].

story[1] /ˈstɔːrɪ/ *n* [C] [*pl* -ies] 1 历〔歷〕史 lìshǐ;故事 gùshì;传〔傳〕奇 chuánqí. 2 新闻报〔報〕道 xīnwén bàodào. 3[非正式用语]谎言 huǎngyán;假话 jiǎhuà.

story[2] [美语] = STOREY.

stout /staʊt/ *adj* 1 粗壮〔壯〕的 cūzhuàngde;结实〔實〕的 jiēshide. 2(人)微胖的 wēipàngde. 3[正式用语]坚〔堅〕定的 jiāndìngde;勇敢的 yǒnggǎnde. **stout** *n* [U] 烈性黑啤酒 lièxìng hēi píjiǔ. **stoutly** *adv*.

stove /stəʊv/ *n* [C] 火炉〔爐〕 huǒlú.

stow /stəʊ/ *v* [T] (*away*) (细心)收藏 shōucáng. **ˈstowaway** *n* [C] (无票)偷乘者 tōuchéngzhě.

straddle /ˈstrædl/ *v* [T] 叉开〔開〕腿坐或站立于 chǎkāi tuǐ zuò huò zhànlì yú.

straight[1] /streɪt/ *adj* 1 直的 zhíde;笔〔筆〕直的 bǐzhíde: *a* ~ *line* 直线. 2 水平的 shuǐpíngde. 3 整齐〔齊〕的 zhěngqíde;有条〔條〕理的 yǒutiáolǐ de. 4 正直的 zhèngzhíde;坦率的 tǎnshuài de. 5(酒等)不搀〔攙〕水的 bù chān shuǐ de. 6 [俚]异〔異〕性恋〔戀〕的 yìxìngliànde. 7[习语] **keep a straight face** 板起面孔 bǎnqǐ miànkǒng. **straightness** *n* [U].

straight[2] /streɪt/ *adv* 1 直 zhí;成直线〔綫〕地 chéng zhíxiàn de: *walk* ~ 一直走. 2 一直地 yìzhíde;直接地 zhíjiēde: *Come* ~ *home*. 直接回家. 3 坦诚地 tǎnchéngde;直截了当〔當〕地 zhíjié-liǎodàng de: *Tell her* ~ *what you think*. 把你的想法直截了当地告诉她. 4[习语] **go ˈstraight** 改邪归〔歸〕正 gǎi xié guī zhèng. **straight aˈway** *adv* 立刻 lìkè;马上 mǎshàng.

straight[3] /streɪt/ *n* [C] (尤指跑道的)直线〔綫〕部分 zhíxiàn bùfen.

straighten /ˈstreɪtn/ *v* [I, T] (使)变〔變〕直 biàn zhí;(使)变平整 biàn píngzhěng.

straightforward /streɪtˈfɔːwəd/ *adj* 1 正直的 zhèngzhíde;坦率的 tǎnshuàide;老实〔實〕的 lǎoshide. 2 易懂的 yìdǒngde;易做的 yìzuòde. **straightforwardly** *adv*.

strain[1] /streɪn/ *n* 1 [C, U](拉)紧〔緊〕 jǐn;紧张〔張〕 jǐnzhāng;拉力 lālì: *put* ~ *on a rope* 把绳子拉紧. 2 (a) [C, U] (对耐力、忍受力等的)考验〔驗〕 kǎoyàn: *a* ~ *on our relations* 对我们关系的一个考验. (b) [U] (因有压力而产生的)痛苦 tòngkǔ;烦恼〔惱〕 fánnǎo. 3 [C, U] 劳〔勞〕损 láosǔn;过〔過〕分劳累 guòfèn láolèi.

strain[2] /streɪn/ *v* 1 [I, T] 竭力 jiélì;全力以赴 quán lì yǐ fù: ~ (*every muscle*) *to move it* 用足力气去搬动它. 2 [T] 扭伤〔傷〕 niǔshāng. 3 [T]过〔過〕滤〔濾〕 guòlǜ. 4 [T] 竭力使(某物)超过极〔極〕限 jiélì shǐ chāoguò jíxiàn: ~ *one's authority* 滥用权力. **strained** *adj* 勉强的 miǎnqiǎngde;不自然的 bú zìrán de. **strainer** *n* [C] 过滤器 guòlǜqì.

strain[3] /streɪn/ *n* [C] (昆虫、病毒等的)系 xì;品种〔種〕 pǐnzhǒng.

strait /streɪt/ *n* 1 [C] 海峡〔峽〕 hǎixiá. 2 **straits** [pl] 困难〔難〕 kùnnan;窘迫 jiǒngpò: *in terrible* ~*s* 在极度困难中.

strait-jacket /ˈstreɪtdʒækɪt/ *n* [C] (给精神病患者等用的)约束衣 yuēshùyī.

strait-laced /ˌstreɪtˈleɪst/ *adj* 拘谨的 jūjǐnde;严〔嚴〕谨的 yánjǐnde.

strand /strænd/ *n* [C] 1 (线、绳等的)(一)股 gǔ. 2[喻](故事等的)发〔發〕展线〔綫〕索 fāzhǎn xiànsuǒ.

stranded /ˈstrændɪd/ *adj* 陷于困境的 xiànyú kùnjìng de.

strange /streɪndʒ/ *adj* 1 陌生的 mòshēngde. 2 不寻〔尋〕常的 bù xúncháng de;奇异〔異〕的 qíyìde: *What* ~ *ideas you have!* 你的想法真特别! **strangely** *adv*. **strangeness** *n* [U]. **stranger** *n* [C] 1 陌生人 mòshēngrén. 2 外地人 wàidìrén;异〔異〕乡〔鄉〕人 yìxiāngrén.

strangle /ˈstræŋgl/ *v* [T] 勒死 lēisǐ;绞死 jiǎosǐ. **ˈstranglehold** *n* [C, 常作 sing] 紧〔緊〕扼 jǐn è;束缚 shùfù: *They have a* ~*hold on the economy*. 他们有力地控制着经济. **strangler** *n* [C].

strap /stræp/ *n* [C] 带〔帶〕 dài;皮带 pídài. **strap** *v* [-pp-] [T]用带束住 yòng dài shùzhù;捆〔綑〕扎〔紮〕 kǔnzā. **strapping** *adj* (人)高大的 gāodàde,强壮〔壯〕的 qiángzhuàngde.

strata *pl* of STRATUM.

strategic /stræˈtiːdʒɪk/ *adj* 1 战〔戰〕略的 zhànlüède;策略的 cèlüède. 2 有战略意义〔義〕的 yǒu zhànlüè yìyì de. **strategically** /-klɪ/ *adv*.

strategy /ˈstrætədʒɪ/ *n* 1 [C]对〔對〕策 duìcè;措施 cuòshī. 2 [U] 策略 cèlüè;战〔戰〕略 zhànlüè;计谋 jìmóu. **strategist** *n* [C] 战略家 zhànlüèjiā.

stratosphere /ˈstrætəsfɪə(r)/ *n* [sing] 平流层〔層〕 píngliúcéng;同温层 tóngwēncéng.

stratum /ˈstrɑːtəm/ *n* [C] [*pl* -ta /-tə/]

S

1 地层〔層〕dìcéng；岩层 yáncéng. 2(社会)阶〔階〕层 jiēcéng.

straw /strɔː/ *n* 1 [U] 稻草 dàocǎo；麦〔麥〕秆〔稈〕màigǎn. 2 [C](一根)稻草 dàocǎo. 3 [C] (喝汽水等用的)吸管 xīguǎn. 4[习语] **the last / final straw** (使人终于不胜负荷的)最后〔後〕的量 zuìhòude liàng.

strawberry /ˈstrɔːbrɪ; *US* -berɪ/ *n* [C] [*pl* -ies] 草莓 cǎoméi.

stray /streɪ/ *v* [I] 走离〔離〕zǒulí；迷路 mílù. **stray** *n* [C] 迷失的动〔動〕物(或人) míshīde dòngwù. **stray** *adj* 1 走失的 zǒushīde：*a ~ dog* 一只走失的狗. 2 孤立的 gūlìde；孤单〔單〕的 gūdānde.

streak /striːk/ *n* [C] 1 条〔條〕纹 tiáowén；线〔綫〕条 xiàntiáo. 2(性格上不好的)特征〔徵〕tèzhēng：*a ~ of cruelty* 残忍的性格. 3 短时〔時〕间 duǎn shíjiān；一阵子 yízhènzi：*a ~ of good luck* 一阵好运气. **streak** *v* 1 [T] 在…上加条纹 zài…shàng jiā tiáowén. 2 [I]飞〔飛〕跑 fēipǎo. **streaky** *adj* [-ier, -iest]有条纹的 yǒu tiáowén de.

stream /striːm/ *n* [C] 1 小河 xiǎohé；溪流 xīliú. 2 人流 rénliú；水流 shuǐliú；一连串 yìliánchuàn：*a ~ of abuse* 不断的辱骂. 3 学〔學〕生智力水平的分组 xuéshēng zhìlì shuǐpíng de fēnzǔ. 4[习语] **with / against the stream** 顺应〔應〕(或反对)潮流 shùnyìng cháoliú. **stream** *v* [I] 1 流 liú；流出 liúchū. 2 (在风中)飘〔飄〕扬〔揚〕piāoyáng：*with her long hair ~ing* 飘动着她的长发. **streamer** *n* [C] 狭〔狹〕长〔長〕的纸条〔條〕xiáchángde zhǐtiáo. **ˈstreamline** *v* [T] 1 使成流线〔綫〕型 shǐ chéng liúxiànxíng. 2 使效率更高 shǐ xiàolǜ gènggāo. **ˈstreamlined** *adj*.

street /striːt/ *n* [C] 1 街道 jiēdào. 2[习语] **ˈstreets ahead of** [非正式用语]前面很远〔遠〕qiánmiàn hěnyuǎn. **up one's street** [非正式用语]在自己的兴〔興〕趣等范〔範〕围〔圍〕内 zài zìjǐ de xìngqù děng fànwéi nèi. **ˈstreetcar** *n* [C] [美语] = TRAM.

strength /streŋθ/ *n* 1 [U]力 lì；力量 lìliang. 2 [C] 长〔長〕处〔處〕chángchu；强点〔點〕qiángdiǎn：*Her intelligence is one of her ~s.* 她的才智是她的一个长处. 3 [U] 人力 rénlì；实〔實〕力 shílì：*The army is below ~.* 这支军队不足额定兵员. 4[习语] **on the strength of** 根据〔據〕(某事物) gēnjù；由于 yóuyú：*buy it on the ~ of his advice* 由于他的劝告而买它. **strengthen** *v* [I, T] (使)强化 qiánghuà；加强 jiāqiáng.

strenuous /ˈstrenjʊəs/ *adj* 费劲〔勁〕的 fèijìnde；用力的 yònglìde. **strenuously** *adv*. **strenuousness** *n* [U].

stress /stres/ *n* 1 (a) [U](精神上的)紧〔緊〕张 jǐnzhāng，压〔壓〕力 yālì. (b) [C]造成压力的事物 zào chéng yālì de shìwù. 2 [U]强调 qiángdiào；重视 zhòngshì：*put ~ on the need to improve* 强调改进的需要. 3 [C, U] 重读〔讀〕zhòngdú；重音 zhòngyīn. **stress** *v* [T] 着重 zhuózhòng；强调 qiángdiào.

stretch /stretʃ/ *v* 1 [T] 伸展 shēnzhǎn；扩〔擴〕大 kuòdà；拉长〔長〕lācháng. 2 [I] (能)延伸 yánshēn；(能)拉长 lācháng. 3 [I, T] 伸长(或伸出)四肢等 shēncháng sìzhī děng. 4 [I] 延伸 yánshēn；连绵 liánmián：*fields ~ing for miles* 连绵数英里的田野. 5 [T]滥〔濫〕用(权力) lànyòng. 6[习语] **stretch one's legs** 去散步 qù sànbù. 7[短语动词] **stretch (oneself) out** 躺着舒展身体〔體〕tǎngzhe shūzhǎn shēntǐ. **stretch** *n* 1 [C] 拉长 lācháng；伸展 shēnzhǎn. 2 [U] 伸展的能力 shēnzhǎnde nénglì；弹〔彈〕性 tánxìng. 3 [C] 一片连绵(土地) yípiàn liánmián；一段持续〔續〕(时间) yíduàn chíxù：*ten hours at a ~* 持续十个小时. **stretchy** *adj* [-ier, -iest].

stretcher /ˈstretʃə(r)/ *n* [C] 担〔擔〕架 dānjià.

stricken /ˈstrɪkən/ *adj* (*by* / *with*) 受害的 shòuhàide；受灾〔災〕的 shòuzāide：*~ with terror* 受恐怖折磨的.

strict /strɪkt/ *adj* 1 严〔嚴〕格的 yángéde；严厉〔厲〕的 yánlìde. 2 (a) 明确〔確〕的 míngquède；确切的 quèqiède：*the ~ sense of a word* 词的确切含义. (b)完全的 wánquánde；绝对〔對〕的 juéduìde：*in ~ secrecy* 绝对保密. **strictly** *adv*. **strictness** *n* [U].

stride /straɪd/ *v* [*pt* **strode** /strəʊd/, *pp* 罕用 **stridden** /ˈstrɪdn/] 1 [I]大踏步走 dà tàbù zǒu. 2[短语动词] **stride over / across sth** 一步跨过〔過〕某物 yí bù kuàguò mǒuwù. **stride** *n* [C] 1 大步 dà bù；阔步 kuòbù. 2[习语] **take sth in one's stride** 轻〔輕〕易地做某事 qīngyìde zuò mǒushì.

strident /ˈstraɪdənt/ *adj* (声音)粗厉〔厲〕的 cūlìde, 刺耳的 cì'ěrde：*~ protests* 尖厉的抗议声.

strife /straɪf/ *n* [U] 争吵 zhēngchǎo；冲〔衝〕突 chōngtū.

strike[1] /straɪk/ *v* [*pt*, *pp* **struck** /strʌk/] 1 [T]打击〔擊〕dǎjī. 2 [T] 攻击 gōngjī. 3 [T] 擦出(火) cāchū；打出 dǎchū：*~ a match* 擦火柴. 4 [T]发〔發〕现 fāxiàn；找到(金矿等) zhǎodào. 5 [I, T] (钟等)敲 qiāo；(使)响〔響〕xiǎng：*The clock struck (four).* 钟敲了(四下). 6 [I] 罢〔罷〕工 bàgōng. 7 [T]给…以印象 gěi…yǐ yìnxiàng：*She ~s me as a clever girl.* 她给我的印象是一个聪明的女孩子. 8 [T]完成 wánchéng；达〔達〕成 dáchéng：*~ a bargain* 成交. 9 [T] (用冲压法)铸〔鑄〕造 zhùzào：*~ a medal* 铸制纪念

章. 10 [T] 使(某人)突然成为〔爲〕 shǐ tūrán chéng wéi: *struck dumb* 突然说不出话来. 11[习语] **strike camp** 拔营〔營〕 bá yíng. **strike a ˈchord with sb** 打动〔動〕某人(的心) dǎdòng mǒurén. **strike it rich** 突然致富 tūrán zhìfù. 12 [短语动词] **strike sth off (sth)** 将〔將〕某物除去(或取消) jiāng mǒuwù chúqù. **strike out** (a) (用力)打击 dǎjī. (b) 创〔創〕新(路线) chuàngxīn. **strike up** 开〔開〕始 kāishǐ.

strike[2] /straɪk/ *n* [C] 1 罢〔罷〕工 bàgōng. 2 (油田等的)发〔發〕现 fāxiàn. 3[习语] **be (out) on ˈstrike** 进〔進〕行罢工 jìnxíng bàgōng.

striking /ˈstraɪkɪŋ/ *adj* 显〔顯〕著的 xiǎnzhùde; 引人注目的 yǐn rén zhùmù de.

string[1] /strɪŋ/ *n* 1 [C, U] 细绳〔繩〕 xìshéng; 带〔帶〕子 dàizi. 2 [C] (乐器的)弦 xián. 3 **the strings** [pl] 弦乐器演奏者 xiányuèqì yǎnzòuzhě. 4 [C] (串在线上的)一串 yíchuàn: *a ~ of beads* 一串珠子. 5 [C] 一连串(事物) yìliánchuàn: *a ~ of accidents* 一连串的事故. 6[习语] **with no ˈstrings (attached)** [非正式用语](帮助等)无〔無〕附加条〔條〕件 wú fùjiā tiáojiàn. **stringy** *adj* [-ier, -iest] 像线〔綫〕的 xiàngxiànde.

string[2] /strɪŋ/ *v* [*pt*, *pp* **strung** /strʌŋ/] [T] 1 装〔裝〕弦于(提琴、球拍等) zhuāng xián yú. 2(用线)穿 chuān, 串起 chuànqǐ. 3 (*up*) (用线、绳)缚, 扎〔紮〕或吊起 fù, zā huò diàoqǐ. 4 [短语动词] **string along (with sb)** (暂与某人)作伴 zuòbàn; 跟随〔隨〕(某人) gēnsuí. **string sb along** 误导〔導〕某人 wùdǎo mǒurén. **string (sb/sth) out** (使某人、某物)有间隔地成行展开〔開〕 yǒu jiàngé de chéngháng zhǎnkāi. **strung up** *adj* 神经〔經〕紧〔緊〕张〔張〕的 shénjīng jǐnzhāng de.

stringent /ˈstrɪndʒənt/ *adj* (指规则等)严〔嚴〕格的 yángéde. **stringently** *adv*.

strip /strɪp/ *v* [-pp-] 1 [I, T] 剥去 bōqù; 脱去 tuōqù; 除去 chúqù. 2 [T] *of* 剥夺〔奪〕(某人的财产等) bōduó: *~ sb of his liberty* 剥夺某人的自由. 3 [T] (*down*) 拆卸(机器等) chāixiè. **strip** *n* 狭〔狹〕长〔長〕的一片(材料、土地等) xiáchángde yípiàn. ˈ**strip cartoon** = COMIC STRIP (COMIC). **stripper** *n* [C] 脱衣舞表演者 tuōyīwǔ biǎoyǎnzhě. ˈ**strip-tease** *n* [C, U] 脱衣舞 tuōyīwǔ.

stripe /straɪp/ *n* [C] 1 条〔條〕纹 tiáowén. 2 (军队的)阶〔階〕级臂章(通常为 V 字形) jiējí bìzhāng. **striped** *adj* 有条纹的 yǒu tiáowén de. **stripy** *adj*.

strive /straɪv/ *v* [*pt* **strove** /strəʊv/, *pp* **striven** /ˈstrɪvn/] [I][正式用语] 1 努力 nǔlì; 奋〔奮〕斗〔鬥〕 fèndòu: *~ to succeed* 力争获得成功. 2 争斗 zhēngdòu.

strode *pt* of STRIDE.

stroke[1] /strəʊk/ *n* [C] 1(一)击〔擊〕 jī; 打击 dǎjī. 2(划船、游泳等的)一划 yìhuá. 3 (网球, 板球等的)击球动〔動〕作 jīqiú dòngzuò. 4(写字的)一笔〔筆〕 yìbǐ, 一画〔畫〕 yíhuà. 5(钟的)鸣〔鳴〕声〔聲〕 míngshēng. 6 中风〔風〕 zhòngfēng. 7 *of* 一件(幸事或不幸等) yíjiàn. 8[习语] **at a ˈstroke** 一下子 yíxiàzi.

stroke[2] /strəʊk/ *v* [T] (用手)抚〔撫〕摸 fǔmō. **stroke** *n* [常作 sing] 抚摸 fǔmō.

stroll /strəʊl/ *n* [C] 散步 sànbù; 溜达〔達〕 liūda. **stroll** *v* [I] 散步 sànbù; 溜达 liūda. **stroller** *n* [C] 1 散步者 sànbùzhě; 闲逛者 xiánguàngzhě. 2[美语]婴儿〔兒〕车 yīng'érchē.

strong /strɒŋ; *US* strɔːŋ/ *adj* [~**er** /-ŋgə(r)/, ~**est** /-ŋgɪst/] 1 (a) 强壮〔壯〕的 qiángzhuàngde; 强有力的 qiángyǒulìde. (b) 坚〔堅〕固的 jiāngùde; 强大的 qiángdàde. 2 坚定的 jiāndìngde; 不动〔動〕摇的 bú dòngyáo de: *a ~ will* 坚强的意志. 3 (a)(感官效果)强烈的 qiángliède: *a ~ smell* 一股强烈的气味. (b)(口味)浓〔濃〕厚的 nónghòude: *~ coffee* 浓咖啡. 4(酒)酒精含量高的 jiǔjīng hánliàng gāo de, 烈性的 lièxìngde. 5(人数等)达〔達〕到…的 dádào…de: *an army 2000 ~* 两千大军. 6[习语] **going ˈstrong** 仍然精力充沛 réngrán jīnglì chōngpèi; 有力继〔繼〕续〔續〕(运动等) yǒu lì jìxù. **strong on sth** 擅长〔長〕做某事 shàncháng zuò mǒushì. ˈ**stronghold** *n* [C] 1 堡垒〔壘〕 bǎolěi; 要塞 yàosài. 2[喻]据〔據〕点〔點〕 jùdiǎn; 根据地 gēnjùdì. **strongly** *adv*.

strove *pt* of STRIVE.

struck *pt*, *pp* of STRIKE[1].

structural /ˈstrʌktʃərəl/ *adj* 结构〔構〕的 jiégòude; 构造的 gòuzàode. **structurally** *adv*.

structure /ˈstrʌktʃə(r)/ *n* 1 [C, U] 构〔構〕造 gòuzào; 结构 jiégòu; 组织〔織〕 zǔzhī. 2 [C] 构造物 gòuzàowù; 建筑〔築〕物 jiànzhùwù. **structure** *v* [T] 计划〔劃〕 jìhuà; 组织 zǔzhī.

struggle /ˈstrʌgl/ *v* [I] 1 (a) 争斗〔鬥〕 zhēngdòu; 搏斗 bódòu. (b)挣扎 zhēngzhá: *~ to get free* 挣扎着要逃脱. 2 努力 nǔlì; 奋〔奮〕斗 fèndòu: *~ to earn a living* 努力谋生. **struggle** *n* 1 [C] 争斗 zhēngdòu; 搏斗 bódòu. 2[常作 sing] 努力 nǔlì; 奋斗 fèndòu.

strum /strʌm/ *v* [I, T] (*on*) 乱〔亂〕弹〔彈〕(琴等) luàntán.

strung *pt*, *pp* of STRING[2].

strut[1] /strʌt/ *n* [C] (构架的)支柱 zhīzhù; 撑杆 chēnggān.

strut[2] /strʌt/ *v* [-tt-] [I] 大摇大摆〔擺〕地走 dàyáo dàbǎi de zǒu; 高视阔步 gāoshì kuòbù.

stub /stʌb/ *n* [C] 1 (铅笔)头〔頭〕 tóu; (烟)蒂 dì. 2(支票)存根 cúngēn. **stub** *v* [-bb-] 1[T] 绊(脚) bàn; 碰 pèng. 2 [短语动词] **stub sth**

S

out 捻熄(尤指香烟) niǎnxī.

stubble /ˈstʌbl/ *n* [U] 1 茬 chá; 残〔殘〕株 cán zhū. 2 短髭 duǎn zī. **stubbly** /ˈstʌblɪ/ *adj*.

stubborn /ˈstʌbən/ *adj* 1 顽固的 wángùde; 坚〔堅〕定的 jiāndìngde. 2 难〔難〕移动〔動〕的 nán yídòng de; 难治的 nánzhìde: *a ~ cough* 难治好的咳嗽. **stubbornly** *adv*. **stubbornness** *n* [U].

stubby /ˈstʌbɪ/ *adj* [-ier, -iest] 短粗的 duǎncūde; 矮胖的 ǎipàngde.

stuck[1] *pt*, *pp* of STICK[2].

stuck[2] /stʌk/ *adj* 1 不能动〔動〕的 bùnéng dòng de; 不能继〔繼〕续〔續〕(做某事)的 bùnéng jìxù de. 2 *with* [非正式用语]不要(某人、某物)在一起 búyào zài yìqǐ: *~ with sb all day* 不要和某人整天在一起. 3 [习语] **get stuck in (to sth)** [非正式用语]积〔積〕极〔極〕地开〔開〕始(做某事) jījíde kāishǐ.

stud[1] /stʌd/ *n* [C] 1 (衬衫)领扣 lǐngkòu. 2 鞋钉 xiédīng. **stud** *v* [-dd-] [T] [常用被动语态]装〔裝〕饰 zhuāngshì; 点〔點〕缀 diǎnzhuì.

stud[2] /stʌd/ *n* [C] 1 养〔養〕马〔馬〕场〔場〕yǎng mǎ chǎng; 种〔種〕马场 zhǒngmǎ chǎng. 2 [非正式用语 ⚠](尤指性欲旺盛的)小伙子 xiǎohuǒzi.

student /ˈstjuːdnt; *US* ˈstuː-/ *n* [C] 1 [英国英语]大学〔學〕生 dàxuésheng. 2 中、小学生 zhōng、xiǎo xuésheng; 学者 xuézhě; 研究者 yánjiūzhě. **student ˈloan** *n* [C] 学生贷款 xuéshēng dàikuǎn; 助学贷款 zhùxué dàikuǎn.

studio /ˈstjuːdɪəʊ; *US* ˈstuː-/ *n* [C] [*pl* ~s] 1(画家、摄影者的)工作室 gōngzuòshì. 2 (电影)摄影棚 shèyǐngpéng; 播音室 bōyīnshì; (电视)播送室 bōsòngshì.

studious /ˈstjuːdɪəs; *US* ˈstuː-/ *adj* 1 好学〔學〕的 hàoxuéde; 用功的 yònggōngde. 2 仔细的 zǐxìde; 用心的 yòngxīnde. **studiously** *adv*.

study[1] /ˈstʌdɪ/ *n* [*pl* -ies] 1 [U] (亦作 studies [pl]) 学〔學〕习〔習〕 xuéxí; 研究 yánjiū. 2 [C] 研究项目 yánjiū xiàngmù: *a ~ of the country's problems* 国家问题的研究. 3 研究成果(如著作等) yánjiū chéngguǒ. 4 [C] 书〔書〕房 shūfáng. 5 [C] (a) 习作 xízuò; 试作 shìzuò. (b) 练〔練〕习曲 liànxíqǔ.

study[2] /ˈstʌdɪ/ *v* [*pt*, *pp* -ied] 1 [I, T] 学〔學〕 xué; 学习〔習〕 xuéxí. 2 [T] 细看 xì kàn; 细想 xì xiǎng.

stuff[1] /stʌf/ *n* [U] 1 原料 yuánliào; 材料 cáiliào; 资料 zīliào. 2 东西 dōngxi; 物品 wùpǐn: *Put your ~ in your room*. 把你的东西放在你的房间里. 3 [习语] **do one's ˈstuff** 一显〔顯〕身手 yì xiǎn shēnshǒu.

stuff[2] /stʌf/ *v* 1 [T] 把…装〔裝〕满 bǎ…zhuāngmǎn; 塞进〔進〕 sāijìn. 2 [I] 把馅塞入(待烹煮的鸡、鸭等肚中) bǎ xiàn sāirù. 3 [T] 剥制〔製〕(标本) bōzhì. 4 [I, T] [非正式用语]吃饱 chī bǎo. 5 [习语] **get ˈstuffed** [英国非正式用语](表示愤怒、鄙视等). **stuffing** *n* [U] 1 (垫子等的) 填料 tiánliào; 填充剂〔劑〕 tiánchōngjì. 2 (待烹煮的鸡、鸭肚中的)填料 tiánliào.

stuffy /ˈstʌfɪ/ *adj* [-ier, -iest] 1 通风〔風〕不良的 tōngfēng bù liáng de; 闷热〔熱〕的 mēnrède. 2 [非正式用语](人)古板的 gǔbǎnde; 拘谨的 jūjǐnde. **stuffiness** *n* [U].

stumble /ˈstʌmbl/ *v* [I] 1 绊跌 bàndiē; (几乎)绊倒 bàndǎo. 2 (说话)出错 chū cuò. 3 [短语动词] **stumble across / on / upon sth** 意外地发〔發〕现(某事物) yìwàide fāxiàn. **stumble** *n* [C] 绊跌 bàndiē; 出错 chūcuò. **ˈstumbling-block** *n* [C] 障碍〔礙〕物 zhàng'àiwù; 绊脚石 bànjiǎoshí.

stump /stʌmp/ *n* [C] 1 树〔樹〕桩〔樁〕 shùzhuāng. 2 残〔殘〕余〔餘〕部分 cányú bùfen. 3 [板球]三柱门的柱 sānzhùménde zhù. **stump** *v* 1 [I] 笨重地行走 bènzhòngde xíngzǒu. 2 [T] [非正式用语]难〔難〕住 nánzhù; 使为〔為〕难 shǐ wéinán. **stumpy** *adj* [-ier, -iest] 短粗的 duǎncūde.

stun /stʌn/ *v* [-nn-] [T] 1 把…打晕 bǎ…dǎyūn. 2 (a)使震惊〔驚〕 shǐ zhènjīng; 使不知所措 shǐ bù zhī suǒ cuò. (b)给(某人)以好印象 gěi yǐ hǎo yìnxiàng. **stunning** *adj* [非正式用语] 漂亮的 piàoliangde; 极〔極〕好的 jíhǎode.

stung *pt*, *pp* of STING[2].

stunk *pp* of STINK.

stunt[1] /stʌnt/ *n* [C] 1 惊〔驚〕人之举〔舉〕 jīng rén zhī jǔ. 2 特技表演 tèjì biǎoyǎn. **ˈstunt man, ˈstunt woman** *n* [C] (拍危险镜头时)当〔當〕演员替身的特技演员 dāng yǎnyuán tìshēn de tèjì yǎnyuán.

stunt[2] /stʌnt/ *v* [T] 阻碍〔礙〕…的发〔發〕育成长〔長〕 zǔ'ài…de fāyù chéngzhǎng.

stupendous /stjuːˈpendəs; *US* stuː-/ *adj* 巨大的 jùdàde; 惊〔驚〕人的 jīngrénde; 极〔極〕好的 jíhǎode. **stupendously** *adv*.

stupid /ˈstjuːpɪd; *US* ˈstuː-/ *adj* 笨的 bènde; 愚蠢的 yúchǔnde. **stupidity** /-ˈpɪdətɪ/ *n* [C, U]. **stupidly** *adv*.

stupor /ˈstjuːpə(r); *US* ˈstuː-/ *n* [C, U] 昏迷 hūnmí; 不省人事 bù xǐng rénshì.

sturdy /ˈstɜːdɪ/ *adj* [-ier, -iest] 强健的 qiángjiànde; 坚〔堅〕实〔實〕的 jiānshíde. **sturdily** /-əlɪ/ *adv*.

stutter /ˈstʌtə(r)/ *v* [I, T] *n* = STAMMER.

sty[1] /staɪ/ *n* [C] [*pl* -ies] = PIGSTY (PIG).

sty[2] (亦作 **stye**) /staɪ/ *n* [C] [*pl* **sties** 或 **styes**] 睑〔瞼〕腺炎 jiǎnxiànyán; 麦〔麥〕粒肿〔腫〕 màilìzhǒng.

S

style /staɪl/ *n* 1 [C, U] 风〔風〕格 fēnggé；作风 zuòfēng；风度 fēngdù；文体〔體〕 wéntǐ. 2 [U] 优〔優〕越性 yōuyuèxìng；优势〔勢〕 yōushì. 3 [C, U]（衣服等的）最新式样〔樣〕 zuì xīn shìyàng；时〔時〕式 shíshì. 4 [C]型式 xíngshì；设计样式 shèjì yàngshì. 5 [习语]（**not /more**）**sb's style**（非或较合乎）某人所好 mǒurén suǒ hào：*Big cars are not my* ～. 我不喜爱大汽车. **style** *v* [T] 设计（成某种式样） shèjì. **stylish** *adj* 时髦的 shímáode；漂亮的 piàoliangde. **stylist** *n* [C]（服装等）设计师〔師〕 shèjìshī. **stylistic** /-ˈlɪstɪk/ *adj* 文体（上）的 wéntǐde. **stylize** *v* [T] 按千篇一律的风格处〔處〕理 àn qiānpiānyīlǜde fēnggé chǔlǐ.

stylus /ˈstaɪləs/ *n* [C]（唱机的）唱针 chàngzhēn.

suave /swɑːv/ *adj* [有时贬]温和的 wēnhéde；文雅的 wényǎde.

sub /sʌb/ *n* [C] [非正式用语] 1 short for SUBMARINE. 2 代替者（尤指替补球员） dàitìzhě.

subconscious /ˌsʌbˈkɒnʃəs/ *adj* 潜〔潛〕意识〔識〕的 qiányìshíde. **the subconscious** *n* [sing] 潜意识 qiányìshí. **subconsciously** *adv*.

subcontinent /ˌsʌbˈkɒntɪnənt/ *n* [C] 次大陆〔陸〕 cìdàlù.

subdirectory /ˈsʌbdaɪˌrektərɪ/ *n* [C]（计算机中的）子目录〔錄〕 zǐmùlù.

subdivide /ˌsʌbdɪˈvaɪd/ *v* [I, T]（把…）再分 zài fēn；细分 xì fēn. **subdivision** /-dɪˈvɪʒn/ *n* [C, U].

subdue /səbˈdjuː; *US* -ˈduː/ *v* [T] 1 使屈服 shǐ qūfú；征服 zhēngfú. 2 使柔和 shǐ róuhé；使安静 shǐ ānjìng：*～d lighting* 柔和的灯光.

subject[1] /ˈsʌbdʒɪkt/ *n* [C] 1 题目 tímù；主题 zhǔtí：*the ～ of the book* 那本书的主题. 2 学〔學〕科 xuékē；科目 kēmù. 3[语法]主语 zhǔyǔ. 4 国〔國〕民 guómín；臣民 chénmín.

subject[2] /sʌbˈdʒekt/ *v* [T] 1 征服 zhēngfú；使服从〔從〕 shǐ fúcóng. 2 *to* 使经〔經〕历〔歷〕 shǐ jīnglì；使遭受 shǐ zāoshòu：*～ sb to criticism* 使某人受批评. **subjection** /-ʃn/ *n* [U].

subject[3] /ˈsʌbdʒɪkt/ *adj* (*to*) 1 隶〔隸〕属〔屬〕的 lìshǔde；受支配的 shòu zhīpèi de：*～ to the law* 受法律约束. 2 在…条〔條〕件下 zài … tiáojiàn xià；依照 yīzhào：*～ to confirmation* 须经过批准. 3 常有的 chángyǒude；常遭受的 cháng zāoshòu de：*～ to frequent colds* 经常患感冒.

subjective /səbˈdʒektɪv/ *adj* 1 主观〔觀〕的 zhǔguānde；受个〔個〕人感情影响〔響〕的 shòu gèrén gǎnqíng yǐngxiǎng de. 2 [哲学]内心的 nèixīnde；想像的 xiǎngxiàngde. **subjectively** *adv*. **subjectivity** /ˌsəbdʒekˈtɪvətɪ/ *n* [U].

sublet /ˌsʌbˈlet/ *v* [-tt-; *pt*; *pp* **sublet**] [I, T]（将房屋）转〔轉〕租（给他人） zhuǎn zū.

sublime /səˈblaɪm/ *adj* 最大的 zuìdàde；伟〔偉〕大的 wěidàde；至高无〔無〕上的 zhì gāo wú shàng de. **sublimely** *adv*.

submarine /ˌsʌbməˈriːn; *US* ˈsʌbməriːn/ *n* [C] 潜〔潛〕水艇 qiánshuǐtǐng.

submerge /səbˈmɜːdʒ/ *v* 1 [I, T]放于水下 fàng yú shuǐxià；进〔進〕入水中 jìnrù shuǐzhōng. 2 [T] 使淹没 shǐ yānmò；使沉没 shǐ chénmò. **submersion** /səbˈmɜːʃn/ *n* [U] 浸没 jìnmò；淹没 yānmò；潜〔潛〕入水中 qiánrù shuǐzhōng.

submission /səbˈmɪʃən/ *n* 1 [U]投降 tóuxiáng；归〔歸〕顺 guīshùn. 2 [U, C]建议〔議〕 jiànyì；意见 yìjiàn.

submissive /səbˈmɪsɪv/ *adj* 服从〔從〕的 fúcóngde；顺从的 shùncóngde. **submissively** *adv*. **submissiveness** *n* [U].

submit /səbˈmɪt/ *v* [-tt-] 1 [I] (*to*) 服从〔從〕 fúcóng；屈服 qūfú. 2 [T]提议〔議〕 tíyì；提出声〔聲〕辩 tíchū shēngbiàn.

subordinate /səˈbɔːdɪnət; *US* -dənət/ *adj* 1 下级的 xiàjíde；从〔從〕属〔屬〕的 cóngshǔde. 2 次要的 cìyàode. **subordinate** *n* [C]部下 bùxià；下级职〔職〕员 xiàjí zhíyuán. **subordinate** /səˈbɔːdɪneɪt/ *v* [T] (*to*) 把…列为〔為〕下级 bǎ…lièwéi xiàjí；使在次要地位 shǐ zài cìyào dìwèi.

subscribe /səbˈskraɪb/ *v* 1 [I, T] 认〔認〕捐（款项） rènjuān；捐助 juānzhù. 2 [I] (*to*) 订阅（杂志、报纸等） dìngyuè. 3[短语动词] **subscribe to sth** 同意 tóngyì；赞成 zànchéng. **subscriber** *n* [C]. **subscription** /səbˈskrɪpʃn/ *n* 1 [U] 捐助 juānzhù；订阅 dìngyuè；签〔簽〕署 qiānshǔ. 2 [C] 捐款 juānkuǎn；预订费 yùdìngfèi；会〔會〕费 huìfèi.

subsequent /ˈsʌbsɪkwənt/ *adj* (*to*) 后〔後〕来的 hòuláide；随〔隨〕后的 suíhòude. **subsequently** *adv* 接着 jiēzhe；然后 ránhòu.

subservient /səbˈsɜːvɪənt/ *adj* 奉承的 fèngchéngde；谄媚的 chǎnmèide. **subservience** /-əns/ *n* [U]. **subserviently** *adv*.

subside /səbˈsaɪd/ *v* [I] 1（洪水）退落 tuìluò. 2（土地、建筑物）下沉 xiàchén. 3 平息 píngxī；平静 píngjìng. **subsidence** /səbˈsaɪdns, ˈsʌbsɪdns/ *n* [C, U] 降落 jiàngluò；下沉 xiàchén；平息 píngxī.

subsidiary /səbˈsɪdɪərɪ; *US* -dɪerɪ/ *adj* 辅〔輔〕助的 fǔzhùde；补〔補〕充的 bǔchōngde；次要的 cìyàode；附属〔屬〕的 fùshǔde：*a ～ role* 配角. **subsidiary** *n* [C] [*pl* **-ies**]子公司 zǐgōngsī；附属机〔機〕构〔構〕 fùshǔ jīgòu.

subsidy /ˈsʌbsədɪ/ *n* [C] [*pl* **-ies**] 补〔補〕助金 bǔzhùjīn；津贴费 jīntiēfèi. **subsidize** /ˈsʌbsɪdaɪz/ *v* [T] 给予补助（或津贴） jǐyǔ bǔ-

S

zhù.

subsist /səbˈsɪst/ *v* [I] 维持生活 wéichí shēnghuó;活下去 huó xià qù. **subsistence** *n* [U] 生活 shēnghuó;生计 shēngjì.

substance /ˈsʌbstəns/ *n* 1 [C,U]物质〔質〕wùzhì. 2 [U] 实〔實〕质 shízhì;本质 běnzhì;要义〔義〕yàoyì. 3 [U]重要性 zhòngyàoxìng;重大意义 zhòngdà yìyì: *a speech with little* ~ 无大意义的演说.

substantial /səbˈstænʃl/ *adj* 1 巨大的 jùdàde: *a* ~ *amount* 一笔大数目. 2 坚〔堅〕固的 jiāngùde;结实〔實〕的 jiēshide. **substantially** *adv* 1 大量地 dàliàngde. 2 基本上 jīběnshang;大体〔體〕上 dàtǐshang.

substantiate /səbˈstænʃɪeɪt/ *v* [T] 证〔證〕实〔實〕zhèngshí;证明 zhèngmíng.

substitute /ˈsʌbstɪtjuːt/ *n* [C] 代替人 dàitìrén;代用品 dàiyòngpǐn. **substitute** *v* [I,T] (*for*) 代替 dàitì;作代替者 zuò dàitìzhě. **substitution** /ˌsʌbstɪˈtjuːʃn/ *n* [C,U].

subsume /səbˈsjuːm; *US* -suːm/ *v* [T] [正式用语]包括 bāokuò;纳入 nàrù.

subterfuge /ˈsʌbtəfjuːdʒ/ *n* [C,U] 诡计 guǐjì;花招 huāzhāo.

subterranean /ˌsʌbtəˈreɪnɪən/ *adj* = UNDERGROUND 1.

subtitle /ˈsʌbtaɪtl/ *n* [C] 1(书籍的)副标〔標〕题 fù biāotí. 2[常作 sing] (印在外国影片下方的)译〔譯〕文字幕 yìwén zìmù.

subtle /ˈsʌtl/ *adj* 1 微妙的 wēimiàode;难〔難〕以捉摸的 nán yǐ zhuōmō de: *a* ~ *difference* 细微的不同. 2 精明的 jīngmíngde;巧妙的 qiǎomiàode: *a* ~ *plan* 一个巧妙的方法. 3 敏锐的 mǐnruìde;灵〔靈〕敏的 língmǐnde. **subtlety** *n* [U,C] [*pl* -ies]. **subtly** /ˈsʌtlɪ/ *adv*.

subtract /səbˈtrækt/ *v* [T] (*from*) 减去 jiǎnqù;扣除 kòuchú. **subtraction** /-ʃn/ *n* [C,U].

suburb /ˈsʌbɜːb/ *n* [C]市郊 shìjiāo;郊区〔區〕jiāoqū. **suburban** /səˈbɜːbən/ *adj*. **suburbia** /səˈbɜːbɪə/ *n* [U] 郊区(居民的生活) jiāoqū.

subvert /sʌbˈvɜːt/ *v* [T] 颠覆(政府) diānfù. **subversion** /-ʃn/ *n* [U]. **subversive** *adj* 颠覆性的 diānfùxìngde.

subway /ˈsʌbweɪ/ *n* [C] 1 地道 dìdào. 2[美语]地铁〔鐵〕dìtiě.

succeed /səkˈsiːd/ *v* 1 [I] (*in*)成功 chénggōng;完成 wánchéng: ~ *in winning the race* 这次赛跑获得胜利. 2 [T] 继〔繼〕续〔續〕jìxù;继任 jìrèn: ~ *sb as president* 继某人之后担任总统. 3 [I](*to*) 继承 jìchéng.

success /səkˈses/ *n* 1 [U] 成功 chénggōng;成就 chéngjiù;发〔發〕迹〔跡〕fājì. 2 [C] 取得成功的人或事 qǔdé chénggōng de rén huò shì. **successful** *adj*. **successfully** *adv*.

succession /səkˈseʃn/ *n* 1 [U] 连续〔續〕liánxù;继〔繼〕续 jìxù. 2 [C] 一连串 yìliánchuàn. 3 [习语] in sucˈcession 一个〔個〕接一个(的) yígè jiē yígè;连续地 liánxùde. **successive** *adj* 连续的 liánxùde;接连的 jiēliánde. **successor** *n* [C] 继承人 jìchéngrén;接班人 jiēbānrén;后〔後〕继者 hòujìzhě.

succinct /səkˈsɪŋkt/ *adj* 简明的 jiǎnmíngde. **succinctly** *adv*. **succinctness** *n* [U].

succulent /ˈsʌkjʊlənt/ *adj* 1 多汁的 duōzhīde;美味的 měiwèide. 2(植物)肉质〔質〕的 ròuzhìde.

succumb /səˈkʌm/ *v* [I] (*to*) [正式用语]屈服 qūfú;屈从〔從〕qūcóng;不再抵抗(诱惑、疾病等) bú zài dǐkàng.

such /sʌtʃ/ *adj* 1 那样〔樣〕的 nàyàngde;这〔這〕种〔種〕的 zhèzhǒngde: ~ *countries as France* 像法国那样的国家. 2 (a)这样大的 zhèyàng dà de: *Don't be in* ~ *a hurry*. 不要这样匆忙. (b) 达〔達〕到某种〔種〕程度的 dádào mǒu zhǒng chéngdù de: ~ *a boring speech* 如此枯燥无味的演讲. **such** *pron* 1 某一类〔類〕mǒu yí lèi;这(个) zhè;那(个) nà;这些 zhèxiē;那些 nàxiē: *S*~ *were her words*. 那些正是她的话. *His behaviour was* ~ *that everyone disliked him*. 他的行为就是这样,因而每个人都不喜欢他. 2[习语] as such 按照通常意义 ànzhào tōngcháng yìyì;照此 zhào cǐ. **such as** 例如 lìrú. ˈ**such-and-such** *pron, adj* 某种(事物) mǒu zhǒng. **suchlike** /ˈsʌtʃlaɪk/ *pron, adj* 同类的(事物) tónglèide.

suck /sʌk/ *v* 1 [I,T] 吸 xī;啜 chuò. 2 [T] 含(在嘴里) hán;舔 tiǎn. 3 [T]卷〔捲〕入 juǎnrù;吸入 xīrù: *The current* ~*ed her under the water*. 洪流把她卷入水中. 4 [T] (泵等)抽出 chōu chū. **suck** *n* [C] 吸 xī;啜 chuò;舔 tiǎn. **sucker** *n* [C] 1 (动物的)吸盘〔盤〕xīpán. 2 凹面(橡胶)吸盘 āomiàn xīpán. 3[非正式用语]易受骗者 yì shòupiàn zhě. 4 *for* 喜爱〔愛〕(某人、某事物)的人 xǐ'ài de rén: *a* ~*er for old films* 喜爱旧影片的人.

suckle /ˈsʌkl/ *v* [T] 哺乳 bǔrǔ;喂奶 wèi nǎi.

suction /ˈsʌkʃn/ *n* [U] 吸 xī;吸住 xīzhù.

sudden /ˈsʌdn/ *adj* 突然的 tūránde;急速的 jísùde. **suddenly** *adv*. **suddenness** *n* [U].

suds /sʌdz/ *n* [pl] 肥皂泡沫 féizào pàomò.

sue /sjuː; *US* suː/ *v* [I,T] 控诉 kòngsù;控告 kònggào.

suede /sweɪd/ *n* [U] 绒面革 róngmiàngé.

suet /ˈsuːɪt, *Brit* 亦读 ˈsjuːɪt/ *n* [U] 板油 bǎnyóu.

suffer /ˈsʌfə(r)/ *v* 1 [I] (*from* / *with*)

S

受苦 shòu kǔ;受害 shòu hài;吃苦头〔頭〕chīkǔtóu. 2 [T] 遭受 zāoshòu;蒙受 méngshòu;经〔經〕历〔歷〕jīnglì. 3 [T]忍受 rěnshòu;忍耐 rěnnài:～ *fools* 容忍傻瓜. 4 [I] 变〔變〕坏〔壞〕biàn huài;变差 biàn chà. **suffering** *n* [U] (亦作 **sufferings**) [pl] 痛苦 tòngkǔ;不幸 búxìng.

suffice /sə'faɪs/ *v* [I] [正式用语]能满足 néng mǎnzú.

sufficient /sə'fɪʃnt/ *adj* 足够的 zúgòude;充分的 chōngfènde. **sufficiency** /-nsɪ/ *n* [sing] 充足 chōngzú;足量 zú liàng. **sufficiently** *adv*.

suffix /'sʌfɪks/ *n* [C] 后〔後〕缀 hòuzhuì;词尾 cíwěi.

suffocate /'sʌfəkeɪt/ *v* [I,T] 1 (使)窒息 zhìxī;(使)呼吸困难〔難〕hūxī kùnnan. 2(把…)闷死 mēnsǐ. **suffocation** /ˌsʌfə'keɪʃn/ *n* [U].

sugar /'ʃʊgə(r)/ *n* [U] 糖 táng. **sugar** *v* [T] 加糖于 jiā táng yú;使甜 shǐ tián. **'sugar-cane** *n* [U] 甘蔗 gānzhe. **sugary** *adj* 1 甜的 tiánde. 2 甜情蜜意的 tiánqíng mìyì de.

suggest /sə'dʒest; *US* səg'dʒ-/ *v* [T] 1 提议〔議〕tíyì;建议 jiànjì. 2 启〔啟〕发〔發〕qǐfā;提醒 tíxǐng;暗示 ànshì. **suggestion** /-tʃn/ *n* 1 [U] 建议 jiànyì;提议 tíyì;启发 qǐfā;暗示 ànshì. 2 [C] (所提)意见、计划〔劃〕等 yìjiàn、jìhuà děng. **suggestive** *adj* 提醒的 tíxǐngde;暗示的 ànshìde. **suggestively** *adv*.

suicide /'su:ɪsaɪd, *Brit* 亦读 'sju:ɪ-/ *n* 1 [C,U]自杀〔殺〕zìshā: *commit* ～ 自杀. 2 [C]自杀者 zìshāzhě. 3 [U] [喻]自取灭〔滅〕亡 zì qǔ mièwáng. **suicidal** *adj* 1(可能导致)自杀的 zìshāde. 2(想要)自杀的 zìshāde.

suit[1] /su:t, *Brit* 亦读 sju:t/ *n* [C] 1 一套衣服 yítào yīfu. 2 (为某活动穿的)套装〔裝〕tàozhuāng. 3 一组同花纸牌 yìzǔ tónghuā zhǐpái. **'suitcase** *n* [C] (旅行用)衣箱 yīxiāng.

suit[2] /su:t, *Brit* 亦读 sju:t/ *v* 1 [I,T] (使)合适〔適〕héshì;(对某人)方便 fāngbiàn. 2 [T] (尤指衣服等)合适 héshì,配(身) pèi. 3 [非正式用语] ～ **oneself** 自便 zìbiàn;自主 zìzhǔ. **suitable** / -əbl / *adj* 适当〔當〕的 shìdàngde;适宜的 shìyíde. **suitably** *adv*. **suitability** *n* [U]. **suited** *adj* 适合的 shìhéde;适当的 shìdàngde.

suite /swi:t/ *n* [C] 1 一套家具 yítào jiājù. 2 一套房间 yítào fángjiān. 3 [音乐]组曲 zǔqǔ.

sulk /sʌlk/ *v* [I] 生闷气〔氣〕shēng mènqì. **sulky** *adj* [-ier,-iest].

sullen /'sʌlən/ *adj* 生气〔氣〕的 shēngqìde;闷闷不乐〔樂〕的 mènmèn bú lè de. **sullenly** *adv*. **sullenness** *n* [U].

sulphur (美语 **sulfur**) /'sʌlfə(r)/ *n* [U] [化学]硫(S) liú. **sulphuric** /sʌl'fjʊərɪk/ *adj*.

sultan /'sʌltən/ *n* [C] 苏〔蘇〕丹(某些伊斯兰国家统治者) sūdān.

sultana /sʌl'tɑ:nə/ *n* [C] 无〔無〕核小葡萄 wú hé xiǎo pútáo.

sultry /'sʌltrɪ/ *adj* [-ier, -iest] 1(天气)闷热〔熱〕的 mēnrède. 2(女人)性感的 xìnggǎnde;迷人的 mírénde.

sum /sʌm/ *n* [C] 1 算术〔術〕suànshù. 2 金额 jīn'é;款项 kuǎnxiàng. 3 总〔總〕数〔數〕zǒngshù;[数学]和 hé. **sum** *v* [-mm-] [短语动词] **sum (sth) up** 合计 héjì;总结 zǒngjié. **sum sb/sth up** 形成对〔對〕…的意见 xíngchéng duì …de yìjiàn.

summary /'sʌmərɪ/ *n* [C] [*pl* -ies] 总〔總〕结 zǒngjié;概括 gàikuò;摘要 zhāiyào. **summary** *adj* 1 即时〔時〕的 jíshíde;速决的 sùjuéde: *a* ～ *execution* 立即处决. 2 概括的 gàikuòde;扼要的 èyàode. **summarize** /-raɪz/ *v* [T] 总结 zǒngjié;摘要 zhāiyào.

summer /'sʌmə(r)/ *n* [C,U] 夏季 xiàjì. ˌ**Summer 'Palace** *n* 颐和园(園) Yíhéyuán. **summery** *adj* 如夏季的 rú xiàjì de;适〔適〕合夏季的 shìhé xiàjì de.

summit /'sʌmɪt/ *n* [C] 1 顶点〔點〕dǐngdiǎn. 2 最高级会〔會〕谈 zuìgāojí huìtán.

summon /'sʌmən/ *v* [T] 1 召唤 zhàohuàn;传〔傳〕唤 chuánhuàn. 2 (*up*) 鼓起 gǔqǐ;发〔發〕挥 fāhuī: ～ (*up*) *all one's courage* 鼓足勇气.

summons /'sʌmənz/ *n* [C] (法庭)传〔傳〕票 chuánpiào. **summons** *v* [T]把传票送达〔達〕(某人) bǎ chuánpiào sòngdá.

sun /sʌn/ *n* 1 **the sun** [sing] 太阳〔陽〕tàiyáng. 2(亦作 **the sun**) [sing,U] 阳光 yángguāng;日光 rìguāng. 3 [C] (尤指有卫星的)恒星 héngxīng. 4[习语] **under the 'sun** 在世界上(任何地方) zài shìjiè shàng. **sun** *v* [-nn-] ～ **oneself** 晒〔曬〕太阳 shài tàiyáng. **'sunbathe** *v* [I] 沐日光浴 mù rìguāngyù. **'sunbeam** *n* [C] (一道)日光 rìguāng. **'sunburn** *n* [U] 日炙 rìzhì;晒黑 shàihēi. **sunburnt** *adj* 晒伤〔傷〕的 shàishāngde;晒黑的 shàihēide. **'sun-glasses** *n* [pl]太阳眼镜 tàiyáng yǎnjìng. **'sunlight** *n* [U] 日光 rìguāng. **sunny** *adj* [-ier,-iest] 1 阳光充足的 yángguāng chōngzú de. 2 愉快的 yúkuàide;高兴〔興〕的 gāoxìngde. **'sunrise** *n* [U]日出 rìchū;黎明 límíng. **'sunset** *n* 1 [U] 黄昏 huánghūn;日落 rìluò. 2 [C] 落日 luòrì,夕阳〔陽〕xīyáng. **'sunshade** *n* [C] 遮阳伞〔傘〕zhēyángsǎn. **'sunshine** *n* [U] 阳光 yángguāng;日光 rìguāng. **'sunstroke** *n* [U] 中暑 zhòngshǔ;日射病 rìshèbìng. **'suntan** *n* [C] (皮肤的)晒黑 shàihēi.

Sunday /'sʌndɪ/ *n* [U,C] 星期日 xīngqīrì.

sundry /ˈsʌndrɪ/ *adj* 各种〔種〕的 gèzhǒngde;不同的 bùtóngde. **sundries** *n* [pl] 杂〔雜〕物 záwù.

sung *pp* of SING.

sunk *pt*, *pp* of SINK².

sunken /ˈsʌŋkən/ *adj* **1** 沉没海底的 chénmò hǎidǐ de. **2**(面颊等)凹陷的 āoxiànde. **3** 低于周围〔圍〕平面的 dī yú zhōuwéi píngmiàn de.

super /ˈsuːpə(r), ˈsjuː-/ *adj* [非正式用语] 特级的 tèjíde;极〔極〕好的 jíhǎode.

superb /suːˈpɜːb, ˈsjuː-/ *adj* 杰〔傑〕出的 jiéchūde; 头〔頭〕等的 tóuděngde. **superbly** *adv*.

superconductor /ˈsuːpəkənˌdʌktə(r)/ *n* [C] 超导〔導〕体〔體〕chāodǎotǐ.

superficial /ˌsuːpəˈfɪʃl, ˌsjuː-/ *adj* **1** 表面的 biǎomiànde;表皮的 biǎopíde. **2** 肤〔膚〕浅〔淺〕的 fūqiǎnde;浅薄的 qiǎnbóde: *a ~ knowledge* 一知半解. **superficiality** /ˌsuːpəˌfɪʃɪˈælətɪ/ *n* [U]. **superficially** *adv*.

superfluous /suːˈpɜːfluəs, sjuː-/ *adj* 过〔過〕剩的 guòshèngde;多余〔餘〕的 duōyúde;不必要的 bú bìyào de. **superfluously** *adv*.

superhuman /ˌsuːpəˈhjuːmən, sjuː-/ *adj* (力气、身材等)超过〔過〕常人的 chāoguò chángrén de;超人的 chāorénde.

superimpose /ˌsuːpərɪmˈpəuz, ˌsjuː-/ *v* [T] (*on*) 把…放在另一物之上 bǎ…fàngzài lìng yí wù zhī shàng.

superintend /ˌsuːpərɪnˈtend, ˌsjuː-/ *v* [I, T] 监〔監〕督 jiāndū; 指挥(工作等) zhǐhuī. **superintendent** *n* [C] **1** 监督人 jiāndūrén;指挥者 zhǐhuīzhě. **2** 警察长〔長〕jǐngcházhǎng.

superior /suːˈpɪərɪə(r), sjuː-/ *adj* **1** 优〔優〕越的 yōuyuède; 优良的 yōuliángde; 较高的 jiàogāode. **2** [贬] 有优越感的 yǒu yōuyuègǎn de. **superior** *n* [C] 上级 shàngjí;长〔長〕官 zhǎngguān. **superiority** /suːpɪərɪˈɒrətɪ; *US* -ˈɔːr- / *n* [U].

superlative /suːˈpɜːlətɪv, sjuː-/ *adj* **1** 最高的 zuìgāode;无〔無〕上的 wúshàngde. **2** [语法] 最高级的 zuìgāojíde. **superlative** *n* [C] 最高级 zuìgāojí.

supermarket /ˈsuːpəmɑːkɪt, ˈsjuː-/ *n* [C] 超级市场〔場〕chāojí shìchǎng; 自选〔選〕商场 zìxuǎn shāngchǎng.

supernatural /ˌsuːpəˈnætʃrəl, sjuː-/ *adj* 超自然的 chāo zìrán de;神奇的 shénqíde;不可思议〔議〕的 bùkě sīyì de.

superpower /ˈsuːpəpauə(r), ˈsjuː- / *n* [C] 超级大国〔國〕chāojí dàguó.

supersede /ˌsuːpəˈsiːd/ *v* [T] 代替 dàitì;接替 jiētì.

supersonic /ˌsuːpəˈsɒnɪk, ˌsjuː-/ *adj* 超声〔聲〕的 chāoshēngde;超音速的 chāoyīnsùde.

superstar /ˈsuːpəstɑː(r)/ *n* [C] (娱乐界的) 超级明星 chāojí míngxīng.

superstition /ˌsuːpəˈstɪʃn, ˌsjuː-/ *n* [C, U] 迷信 míxìn; 迷信行为〔爲〕míxìn xíngwéi. **superstitious** *adj*.

supervise /ˈsuːpəvaɪz, ˈsjuː-/ *v* [I, T] 监〔監〕督 jiāndū;管理 guǎnlǐ;指导〔導〕zhǐdǎo. **supervision** /ˌsuːpəˈvɪʒn/ *n* [U] 监督 jiāndū;管理 guǎnlǐ;指导 zhǐdǎo. **supervisor** *n* [C] 监督人 jiāndūrén;管理员 guǎnlǐyuán;指导者 zhǐdǎozhě.

supper /ˈsʌpə(r)/ *n* [C, U] 晚餐 wǎncān.

supple /ˈsʌpl/ *adj* 易弯曲的 yì wānqū de;柔软的 róuruǎnde. **suppleness** *n* [U].

supplement /ˈsʌplɪmənt/ *n* [C] **1** 增补〔補〕zēngbǔ;补遗 bǔyí. **2** (报刊的)增刊 zēngkān. **supplement** *v* [T] (*with*) 补充 bǔchōng;增补 zēngbǔ. **supplementary** /-ˈmentrɪ; *US* -terɪ/ *adj* 补充的 bǔchōngde;附加的 fùjiāde.

supply /səˈplaɪ/ *v* [*pt*, *pp* -**ied**] [T] **1** 供给 gōngjǐ;供应〔應〕gōngyìng: *~ gas to a house* 向住宅供应煤气. *~ sb with food* 供给某人食物. **2** 满足(需要) mǎnzú. **supply** *n* [*pl* -**ies**] **1** [U] 供给 gōngjǐ;供应 gōngyìng. **2** [C, 尤作 pl] 供应品 gōngyìngpǐn;贮〔貯〕备〔備〕zhùbèi: *food supplies* 食物贮备. **supplier** *n* [C] 供应者 gōngyìngzhě;供应厂〔廠〕商 gōngyìng chǎngshāng.

support /səˈpɔːt/ *v* [T] **1** 支撑 zhīchēng;支持 zhīchí. **2** 供养〔養〕gōngyǎng;维持 wéichí: *~ a family* 养家. **3** 拥〔擁〕护〔護〕yōnghù;赞助 zànzhù;鼓励〔勵〕gǔlì: *~ a political party* 拥护某一政党. **4** (为某队等)捧场〔場〕pěngchǎng. **5** 支持(或肯定)(某一理论等) zhīchí. **support** *n* **1** [U] 支持 zhīchí;支撑 zhīchēng;供养 gōngyǎng;拥护 yōnghù;赞助 zànzhù. **2** [C] 支撑物 zhīchēngwù;支持者 zhīchízhě;供养者 gōngyǎngzhě;赞助人 zànzhùrén. **3** [U] (政党、球队等的)支持者 zhīchízhě;拥护者 yōnghùzhě. **supporter** *n* [C]. **supportive** *adj* 支持的 zhīchíde;赞助的 zànzhùde;鼓励〔勵〕的 gǔlìde.

suppose /səˈpəuz/ *v* [T] **1** 假定 jiǎdìng;认〔認〕定 rèndìng: *Let us ~ (that) the news is true*. 让我们假定这消息是正确的. **2** 猜测 cāicè;想像 xiǎngxiàng: *Do you ~ he's gone?* 你猜他已经走了吗? **3** [习语] **be supposed to** (a) 被期望 bèi qīwàng;应〔應〕该 yīnggāi. (b) [非正式用语][用于否定]被允许 bèi yǔnxǔ;获〔獲〕准 huò zhǔn: *You're not ~d to leave early*. 你不许早走. **supposedly** /-ɪdlɪ/ *adv* (根据)推测 tuīcè;猜想 cāixiǎng;大概 dàgài;恐怕 kǒngpà. **supposing** *conj* 假使 jiǎshǐ;倘若 tǎngruò.

supposition /ˌsʌpəˈzɪʃn/ *n* **1** [U] 假定 jiǎdìng;想像 xiǎngxiàng. **2** [C] 猜测 cāicè;假定

(的事物) jiǎdìng.

suppress /səˈpres/ *v* [T] **1** 制止 zhìzhǐ;镇压〔壓〕zhènyā;平定 píngdìng: ～ *a revolt* 镇压叛乱. **2** 抑制 yìzhì;隐〔隱〕瞒 yǐnmán;防止 fángzhǐ: ～ *the truth* 隐瞒真相. **suppression** /-ʃn/ *n* [U].

supreme /suːˈpriːm, sjuː-, sə-/ *adj* **1** 最高的 zuìgāode;至上的 zhìshàngde. **2** 最大的 zuìdàde;最重要的 zuì zhòngyào de. **supremacy** /suːˈpreməsɪ/ *n* [U]. **supremely** *adv*.

surcharge /ˈsɜːtʃɑːdʒ/ *n* [C] 额外费 éwàifèi.

sure /ʃɔː(r); *US* ʃʊər/ *adj* **1** 无〔無〕疑的 wúyíde;一定的 yídìngde;确〔確〕信的 quèxìnde: *I think he's coming but I'm not quite* ～. 我想他会来的,但我还不十分肯定. **2** 可靠的 kěkàode;稳〔穩〕妥的 wěntuǒde: *a* ～ *cure for colds* 治感冒的良药. **3** *to* 肯定的 kěndìngde;一定会〔會〕(做某事)的 yídìng huì de: *He's* ～ *to be late*. 他肯定要迟到. **4** [习语] **be sure to** 务〔務〕必 wùbì. **make sure** (**of sth** / **that...**) (a) 查明 chámíng;核实〔實〕héshí. (b) 保证〔證〕出现 bǎozhèng chūxiàn. **sure** *adv* **1** [非正式用语][尤用于美语]当〔當〕然 dāngrán;的确 díquè: *It* ～ *is cold!* 天气的确冷! **2** [习语] ˌ**sure eˈnough** 果然 guǒrán: *I said he would be late and* ～ *enough, he was*. 我说过他要迟到,果然不错,他迟到了. **surely** *adv* **1** 当然 dāngrán. **2** (表示希望、确信无疑等): *Surely not!* 决不!

surety /ˈʃʊərətɪ/ *n* [*pl* **-ies**] [C, U] **1** 担〔擔〕保品 dānbǎopǐn. **2** 保证〔證〕人 bǎozhèngrén.

surf /sɜːf/ *n* [U] 拍岸浪 pāi àn làng. **surf** *v* 作网〔網〕上冲浪 zuò wǎngshàng chōnglàng. ˈ**surfboard** *n* [C] 冲〔衝〕浪板 chōnglàngbǎn. **surfing** *n* [U] 冲浪(运动) chōnglàng.

surface /ˈsɜːfɪs/ *n* **1** [C] 面 miàn;表面 biǎomiàn. **2** [sing] 水面 shuǐmiàn;液面 yèmiàn. **3** [sing] [喻]外表 wàibiǎo;外观〔觀〕wàiguān: *She was angry, in spite of her calm* ～. 尽管她外表平静,实际上她动怒了. **surface** *adj*. **surface** *v* **1** [T] 进〔進〕行表面处〔處〕理 jìnxíng biǎomiàn chǔlǐ;使成平面 shǐ chéng píngmiàn: ～ *the roads* 铺路面. **2** [I] 浮出水面 fúchū shuǐmiàn: [喻] *not* ～ *until noon* 一直睡到中午才起床. ˈ**surface mail** *n* [U] 普通邮〔郵〕件(非航空邮件) pǔtōng yóujiàn.

surfeit /ˈsɜːfɪt/ *n* [sing] 过〔過〕量 guòliàng;过度 guòdù;(尤指)饮食过量 yǐnshí guòliàng.

surge /sɜːdʒ/ *v* [I] **1** 波动〔動〕bōdòng;汹〔洶〕涌 xiōngyǒng. **2** (心潮)起伏 qǐfú;(一阵)激动 jīdòng. **surge** *n* [C] **1** 波浪起伏 bōlàng qǐ fú;汹涌 xiōngyǒng;澎湃 péngpài. **2** 急剧〔劇〕上升 jíjù shàng shēng.

surgeon /ˈsɜːdʒən/ *n* [C] 外科医〔醫〕生 wàikē yīshēng.

surgery /ˈsɜːdʒərɪ/ *n* [*pl* **-ies**] **1** [U] 外科 wàikē;外科手术〔術〕wàikē shǒushù. **2** [C] 手术室 shǒushùshì.

surgical /ˈsɜːdʒɪkl/ *adj* 外科的 wàikēde;外科手术〔術〕的 wàikē shǒushù de. **surgically** /-klɪ/ *adv*.

surly /ˈsɜːlɪ/ *adj* [**-ier, -iest**] 粗暴的 cūbàode;不友好的 bù yǒuhǎo de. **surliness** *n* [U].

surmount /səˈmaʊnt/ *v* **1** [T] 克服(困难) kèfú;战〔戰〕胜〔勝〕zhànshèng. **2** [习语] **be surmounted by** [正式用语]在…顶上有 zài… dǐngshang yǒu;装〔裝〕在…顶上 zhuāngzài… dǐngshang: *a church* ～*ed by a tower* 有尖塔的教堂.

surname /ˈsɜːneɪm/ *n* [C] 姓 xìng.

surpass /səˈpɑːs/ *v* [T] [正式用语]超越 chāoyuè;胜〔勝〕过〔過〕shèngguò.

surplus /ˈsɜːpləs/ *n* [C] 余〔餘〕款 yúkuǎn;盈余 yíngyú;剩余(物资) shèngyú;过〔過〕剩 guòshèng.

surprise /səˈpraɪz/ *n* [U, C] **1** 惊〔驚〕奇 jīngqí;使人惊奇的事物 shǐ rén jīngqí de shìwù. **2** [习语] **take sb by surprise** 出其不意地使某人… chū qí bú yì de shǐ mǒurén…. **surprise** *v* [T] **1** 使(某人)吃惊 shǐ chījīng. **2** 意外地发〔發〕现 yìwàide fāxiàn;撞见 zhuàngjiàn: ～ *a burglar* 撞见一个窃贼. **surprised** *adj* 惊奇的 jīngqíde;吃惊的 chījīngde. **surprising** *adj*. **surprisingly** *adv*.

surrender /səˈrendə(r)/ *v* **1** [I, T] (*oneself*) (*to*) 停止抵抗 tíngzhǐ dǐkàng;投降 tóuxiáng;自首 zìshǒu. **2** [T] 放弃〔棄〕fàngqì;交出 jiāochū. **3** [短语动词] **surrender (oneself) to** 听〔聽〕任…摆〔擺〕布〔佈〕tīngrèn…bǎibù;陷于… xiànyú…. **surrender** *n* [U, C] 屈服 qūfú;投降 tóuxiáng;放弃 fàngqì.

surround /səˈraʊnd/ *v* [T] 包围〔圍〕bāowéi;围绕〔繞〕wéirào. **surround** *n* [C] 围绕物 wéiràowù;花边〔邊〕huābiān. **surrounding** *adj*. **surroundings** *n* [pl] 周围的事物 zhōuwéide shìwù;环〔環〕境 huánjìng.

surveillance /sɜːˈveɪləns/ *n* [U] 监〔監〕视 jiānshì;监督 jiāndū: *under* ～ 置于监视之下.

survey /səˈveɪ/ *v* [T] **1** 环〔環〕视 huánshì;眺望 tiàowàng;全面观〔觀〕察 quánmiàn guānchá. **2** 测量(土地) cèliáng;勘定 kāndìng. **3** 检〔檢〕查 jiǎnchá;调查 diàochá. **survey** /ˈsɜːveɪ/ *n* [C] **1** 概观〔觀〕gàiguān;(全面)考察 kǎochá. **2** 测量(制图或记录) cèliáng. **3** (房屋等的)检〔檢〕查 jiǎnchá, 查勘 chákān. **surveyor** /səˈveɪə(r)/ *n* [C] 测量员 cèliángyuán;勘测员 kāncèyuán.

survival /səˈvaɪvl/ *n* **1** [U] 生存 shēngcún;幸存 xìngcún;残〔殘〕存 cáncún. **2** [C] 幸存者

xìngcúnzhě；残存物 cáncúnwù.

survive /sə'vaɪv/ *v* [I, T] 活下来 huóxiàlái；残〔殘〕存 cáncún；比…活得长〔長〕bǐ…huóde cháng：*She ~d her husband*. 她比她的丈夫活得长. **survivor** *n* [C] 幸存者 xìngcúnzhě；逃生者 táoshēngzhě.

susceptible /sə'septəbl/ *adj* **1** *to* 易受感动〔動〕的 yì shòu gǎndòng de；易被感染的 yì bèi gǎnrǎn de：~ *to cold* 容易感冒. **2** 易受影响〔響〕的 yì shòu yǐngxiǎng de；敏感的 mǐngǎnde. **susceptibility** /səˌseptə'bɪlətɪ/ *n* [U].

suspect /sə'spekt/ *v* [T] **1** 疑有 yíyǒu；觉〔覺〕得 juéde；猜想 cāixiǎng：*We ~ that he's dead*. 我们猜想他死了. **2** 觉得可疑 juéde kěyí；怀〔懷〕疑 huáiyí：~ *the truth of her statement* 怀疑她的说明的真实性. **3** *of* 怀疑某人(有罪) huáiyí mǒurén：~ *sb of lying* 怀疑某人在说谎. **suspect** /'sʌspekt/ *n* [C] 嫌疑犯 xiányífàn；可疑分子 kěyí fènzǐ. **suspect** /'sʌspekt/ *adj* 可疑的 kěyíde；靠不住的 kàobuzhù de.

suspend /sə'spend/ *v* [T] **1** (*from*) 吊 diào；悬〔懸〕挂〔掛〕xuánguà：~ *a lamp from the ceiling* 天花板上吊着一盏灯. **2** 推迟〔遲〕tuīchí；中止 zhōngzhǐ；暂停 zàntíng：~ *judgement* 缓期宣判. **3** (*from*) 暂令停职〔職〕等 zàn lìng tíngzhí děng：*They ~ed two boys from school*. 他们暂令两个孩子停学.

suspenders /sə'spendəz/ *n* [pl] **1** [英国英语] 吊袜〔襪〕带〔帶〕diàowàdài. **2** [美语] = BRACE 3.

suspense /sə'spens/ *n* [U] (对可能发生的事的) 担〔擔〕心 dānxīn, 紧〔緊〕张〔張〕感 jǐnzhānggǎn.

suspension /sə'spenʃn/ *n* [U] **1** 悬〔懸〕挂〔掛〕xuánguà；悬浮 xuánfú. **2** (车辆的)减震装〔裝〕置 jiǎnzhènzhuāngzhì. **su'spension bridge** *n* [C] 吊桥〔橋〕diàoqiáo.

suspicion /sə'spɪʃn/ *n* **1** (a) [U] 怀〔懷〕疑 huáiyí；疑心 yíxīn；嫌疑 xiányí：*arrested on ~ of murder* 因杀人嫌疑而被捕. (b) [C] 疑心 yíxīn；猜疑 cāiyí. **2** [sing] 一点〔點〕儿〔兒〕yìdiǎnr：*a ~ of sadness* 一丝悲伤. **suspicious** *adj* 可疑的 kěyíde；疑心的 yíxīnde. **suspiciously** *adv*.

sustain /sə'steɪn/ *v* [T] **1** [正式用语] 支撑 zhīchēng, 承受住 chéngshòu zhù. **2** 维持(生命或存在) wéichí. **3** 蒙受 méngshòu；遭受 zāoshòu：~ *an injury* 受伤. **sustainable de'velopment** *n* [U] 可持续〔續〕发〔發〕展 kě chíxù fāzhǎn.

sustenance /'sʌstɪnəns/ *n* [U] [正式用语] 食物 shíwù；营〔營〕养〔養〕yíngyǎng.

swab /swɒb/ *n* [C] (医用)棉花球 miánhuāqiú；药〔藥〕签〔籤〕yàoqiān. **swab** *v* [-bb-] [T] (用棉花球)擦洗(伤口等) cāxǐ.

swagger /'swægə(r)/ *v* [I] 昂首阔步 ángshǒu kuòbù；摆〔擺〕架子 bǎijiàzi. **swagger** *n* [sing] 昂首阔步 ángshǒu kuòbù；摆架子 bǎijiàzi.

swallow[1] /'swɒləʊ/ *n* [C] 燕子 yànzi.

swallow[2] /'swɒləʊ/ *v* **1** [I, T] 吞下 tūnxià；咽〔嚥〕下 yànxià. **2** [T] (*up*) 吞没 tūnmò；用尽〔盡〕yòng jìn：*earnings ~ed up by bills* 被欠账耗尽的收入. **3** [T] [非正式用语] 忍受(侮辱) rěnshòu. **4** [T] [非正式用语] 轻〔輕〕信 qīngxìn：*I'm not ~ing that story!* 我不相信那件事! **5** [T] 不流露(感情) bù liúlù. **swallow** *n* [C] 咽 yàn；吞 tūn；吞咽的量 tūn yàn de liàng.

swam *pt* of SWIM.

swamp /swɒmp/ *n* [C, U] 沼泽〔澤〕地 zhǎozédì. **swamp** *v* [T] **1** 使淹没 shǐ yānmò. **2** [喻]使应〔應〕接不暇 shǐ yīngjiē bù xiá；使不知所措 shǐ bù zhī suǒ cuò：*~ed with requests* 请求多得应接不暇. **swampy** *adj* [-ier, -iest] (多)沼泽的 zhǎozéde.

swan /swɒn/ *n* [C] 天鹅 tiān'é. **swan** *v* [-nn-] [I] *around* / *off* 闲荡〔蕩〕xiándàng；游逛 yóuguàng. **'swan-song** *n* [C] 诗人, 音乐〔樂〕家的最后〔後〕作品 shīrén、yīnyuèjiā de zuìhòu zuòpǐn.

swap (亦作 **swop**) /swɒp/ *v* [-pp-] [I, T] (*with*) [非正式用语]交换 jiāohuàn；代替 dàitì：~ *seats with sb* 与别人交换坐位. **swap** *n* [C] 交换 jiāohuàn；交换物 jiāohuànwù.

swarm /swɔːm/ *n* [C] (昆虫等)一大群 yí dà qún. **swarm** *v* [I] **1** 大群地移动〔動〕dà qún de yídòng：*a crowd ~ing through the gate* 拥过大门的人群. **2** [短语动词] **swarm with sb/sth** 到处〔處〕挤〔擠〕满人(或物) dàochù jǐ mǎn rén：*beaches ~ing with people* 到处挤满人的海滩.

swat /swɒt/ *v* [-tt-] [T] 重拍 zhòngpāi；拍死 pāi sǐ.

sway /sweɪ/ *v* **1** [I, T] (使)摇摆〔擺〕yáobǎi；(使)摆动〔動〕bǎidòng. **2** [T] 支配 zhīpèi；影响〔響〕yǐngxiǎng. **sway** *n* [U] **1** 摇摆 yáobǎi；摇动 yáodòng. **2** [正式用语]统治 tǒngzhì；支配 zhīpèi；影响 yǐngxiǎng.

swear /sweə(r)/ *v* [*pt* **swore** /swɔː(r)/, *pp* **sworn** /swɔːn/] **1** [I] (*at*) 发〔發〕誓 fāshì；诅咒 zǔzhòu. **2** [T] 强调 qiángdiào；郑〔鄭〕重地说 zhèngzhòngde shuō；认〔認〕真地说 rènzhēnde shuō：~ *to tell the truth* 保证说真话. **3** [I, T] (使)宣誓 xuānshì. **4** [短语动词] **swear by sth** 使用并〔並〕深信 shǐyòng bìng shēnxìn. **swear sb in** 使某人宣誓就职〔職〕shǐ mǒurén xuānshì jiùzhí. **'swear-word** *n* [C] 骂人的话 mà rén de huà.

S

sweat /swet/ *n* 1 [U] 汗 hàn. 2 a sweat [sing] 出汗 chū hàn; 一身汗 yìshēn hàn. 3 [U] [非正式用语]艰〔艱〕苦的工作 jiānkǔde gōngzuò. **sweat** *v* [I] 1 出汗 chū hàn. 2 焦虑〔慮〕jiāolǜ; 焦急 jiāojí. 3 [习语] **sweat ˈblood** [非正式用语] (a) 拼命工作 pīn mìng gōngzuò. (b) 着急 zháojí; 担〔擔〕心 dānxīn. **ˈsweat-shirt** *n* [C] (长袖)棉毛衫 miánmáoshān. **sweaty** *adj* [-ier, -iest] 汗湿〔濕〕透的 hàn shītòu de.

sweater /ˈswetə(r)/ *n* [C] 毛线〔綫〕衫 máoxiànshān; 紧〔緊〕身套衫 jǐn shēn tàoshān.

swede /swiːd/ *n* [C, U] [植物]瑞典芜〔蕪〕菁 Ruìdiǎn wújīng.

sweep[1] /swiːp/ *v* [*pt*, *pp* **swept** /swept/] 1 [I, T] 扫〔掃〕sǎo; 扫除 sǎochú: ~ *the floor* 扫地. 2 [T] 带〔帶〕走 dàizǒu; 席卷〔捲〕xíjuǎn: *The sea swept him along.* 海浪把他卷走了. 3 [I, T] 掠过〔過〕lüèguò; 扫过 sǎoguò: *A huge wave swept (over) the deck.* 大浪掠过甲板. 4 [I] 威仪〔儀〕地走动〔動〕wēiyíde zǒudòng. 5 [I] 连绵 liánmián; 延伸 yánshēn: *The coast ~s northwards.* 海岸向北方延伸. 6 [习语] **sweep sb off his/her feet** 使某人倾心(或激动) shǐ mǒurén qīngxīn. **sweep sth under the carpet** 掩盖〔蓋〕某事 yǎngài mǒushì. **sweeper** *n* [C] 清洁〔潔〕工 qīngjiégōng; 扫除者 sǎochúzhě. **sweeping** *adj* 1 广〔廣〕泛的 guǎngfànde; 深远〔遠〕的 shēnyuǎnde: ~ *changes* 彻底的改革. 2 (过于)笼〔籠〕统的 lǒngtǒngde; 概括的 gàikuòde: *a ~ statement* 概括的陈述.

sweep[2] /swiːp/ *n* 1 [C] 扫〔掃〕sǎo; 扫除 sǎochú. 2 [C] 扫动〔動〕sǎodòng; 挥动 huīdòng. 3 [sing, U] [喻]范〔範〕围〔圍〕fànwéi; 空间 kōngjiān: *the broad ~ of a novel* 一部小说的丰富的内容. 4 [C] (道路、河流的)弯〔彎〕曲处〔處〕wānqūchù. 5 = CHIMNEY-SWEEP (CHIMNEY).

sweet /swiːt/ *adj* 1 甜的 tiánde; 甜味的 tiánwèide. 2 讨人喜欢〔歡〕的 tǎo rén xǐhuande; 漂亮的 piàoliangde: *a ~ face* 讨人喜欢的脸庞. 3 可爱〔愛〕的 kě'àide; 可亲〔親〕的 kěqīnde: *a ~ little boy* 可爱的小男孩. 4 新鲜的 xīnxiānde; 纯净的 chúnjìngde: *the ~ smell of the countryside* 乡村的清新空气. 5 香的 xiāngde; 芬芳的 fēnfāngde: *Don't the roses smell ~!* 多么香的玫瑰花! 6 [习语] **a sweet ˈtooth** 爱吃甜食 ài chī tiánshí. **sweet** *n* [C] 1 糖果 tángguǒ. 2 甜食 tiánshí. **ˈsweet corn** *n* [U] 甜玉米 tián yùmǐ. **sweeten** *v* [I, T] (使)变〔變〕甜 biàn tián; 变得可爱 biàn de kě'ài. **sweetener** *n* [C] (调味用)甜料 tiánliào. **ˈsweetheart** *n* [C] [旧]情人 qíngrén. **sweetly** *adv*. **sweetness** *n* [U]. **ˈsweet-talk** *v* [T] (*into*) 用好话劝〔勸〕说… yòng hǎohuà quànshuō….

swell /swel/ *v* [*pt* **swelled** /sweld/, *pp* **swollen** /ˈswəʊlən/ 或 **swelled**] [I, T] 1 (使)膨胀 péngzhàng; (使)增大 zēngdà: *a swollen ankle* 肿大的脚踝. 2 (使)隆起 lóngqǐ; (使)鼓起 gǔqǐ. **swell** *n* [U, sing] (海上的)浪涛〔濤〕làngtāo. **swelling** *n* [C] 身上的肿〔腫〕处〔處〕shēnshàngde zhǒngchù.

swelter /ˈsweltə(r)/ *v* [I] 酷热〔熱〕kùrè.

swept *pt*, *pp* of SWEEP[1].

swerve /swɜːv/ *v* [I] (使)突然转〔轉〕向 tūrán zhuǎnxiàng: *The car ~d to avoid her.* 汽车突然转向以躲开她. **swerve** *n* [C] 转向 zhuǎnxiàng.

swift[1] /swɪft/ *adj* 快的 kuàide; 迅速的 xùnsùde: *a ~ reply* 敏捷的回答. **swiftly** *adv*. **swiftness** *n* [U].

swift[2] /swɪft/ *n* [C] 雨燕 yǔyàn.

swig /swɪɡ/ *v* [-gg-] [T] [非正式用语](大口地)喝 hē; 痛饮 tòngyǐn.

swill /swɪl/ *v* [T] 1 冲洗 chōngxǐ; 冲刷 chōngshuā. 2 [非正式用语]大口地喝 dà kǒu de hē; 痛饮 tòngyǐn: ~ *tea* 大口地喝茶. **swill** *n* [U] 泔脚 gānjiǎo; 猪饲料 zhū sìliào.

swim /swɪm/ *v* [*pt* **swam** /swæm/, *pp* **swum** /swʌm/, **-mm-**] 1 [I] 游泳 yóuyǒng; 游水 yóushuǐ. 2 [T] 游过〔過〕yóuguò: ~ *the English Channel* 游过英吉利海峡. 3 [I] (*in/with*) 浸 jìn; 泡 pào; (用水)覆盖〔蓋〕fùgài. 4 [I] 摇晃 yáohuàng; 眼花 yǎnhuā; 眩晕 xuànyùn: *His head swam.* 他头晕. **swim** *n* [C] 1 游泳 yóuyǒng; 游水 yóushuǐ: *go for a ~* 去游泳. 2 [习语] **in/out of the swim** 了〔瞭〕解(或不了解)当〔當〕前的事 liǎojiě dāngqiánde shì. **swimmer** *n* [C] 游泳者 yóuyǒngzhě. **ˈswimming-bath**, **ˈswimming-pool** *n* [C] 游泳池 yóuyǒngchí. **ˈswimming-costume**, **ˈswim-suit** *n* [C] (女)游泳衣 yóuyǒngyī. **ˈswimming-trunks** *n* [pl] (男)游泳裤 yóuyǒngkù.

swindle /ˈswɪndl/ *v* [T] 诈取 zhàqǔ; 骗取 piànqǔ. **swindle** *n* [C] 诈骗 zhàpiàn; 骗局 piànjú. **swindler** *n* [C] 诈骗犯 zhàpiànfàn; 骗子 piànzi.

swing /swɪŋ/ *v* [*pt*, *pp* **swung** /swʌŋ/] [I, T] 1 (使)摆〔擺〕动〔動〕bǎidòng; (使)摇摆 yáobǎi: ~ *one's arms* 摆动双臂. 2 (使)旋转〔轉〕xuánzhuǎn; (使)转向 zhuǎnxiàng: ~ *round the corner* 在街角处拐弯. 3 (使)改变〔變〕观〔觀〕点〔點〕gǎibiàn guāndiǎn: *a speech that ~s the voters* 改变选民观点的一篇演说. 4 [习语] **swing into ˈaction** 迅速采〔採〕取行动 xùnsù cǎiqǔ xíngdòng. **swing** *n* 1 [C] 摆动

bǎidòng;摇摆 yáobǎi. 2 [U, sing] (强烈)节〔節〕奏感 jiézòugǎn. 3 [C] 改变观点 gǎibiàn guāndiǎn. 4 [C] 秋〔鞦〕千〔韆〕qiūqiān. 5 [习语] **go with a 'swing** 活跃〔躍〕而精彩 huóyuè ér jīngcǎi. **ˌswings and 'roundabouts** [非正式用语][尤用于英国英语]有得有失(的事) yǒu dé yǒu shī. **'swing state** *n* [C] (美国大选中)起决定性作用的州 qǐ juédìngxìng zuòyòng de zhōu.

swingeing /ˈswɪndʒɪŋ/ *adj* [尤用于英国英语]大量的 dàliàngde;沉重的 chénzhòngde.

swipe /swaɪp/ *v* [T] [俚] 1 猛击〔擊〕měngjī. 2 偷 tōu. **swipe** *n* [C] 猛击 měngjī. **'swipe card** *n* [C] 通行卡 tōngxíngkǎ; 磁卡 cíkǎ.

swirl /swɜːl/ *v* [I,T] (使)打旋 dǎxuán;(使)旋动〔動〕xuándòng: *dust ~ing about the room* 在房间里打着旋的尘土. **swirl** *n* [C] 旋动 xuándòng;涡〔渦〕旋 wōxuán.

swish /swɪʃ/ *v* [I,T] 嗖地挥动〔動〕sōude huīdòng;(使)作窸窣声〔聲〕zuò xīsūshēng. **swish** *n* [sing] 嗖嗖声 sōusōushēng;窸窣声 xīsūshēng;沙沙声 shāshāshēng. **swish** *adj* [非正式用语]时〔時〕髦的 shímáode;昂贵的 ángguìde.

switch /swɪtʃ/ *n* [C] 1 (电路)开〔開〕关〔關〕kāiguān;电〔電〕闸 diànzhá: *a 'light-~* 电灯开关. 2 转〔轉〕变〔變〕zhuǎnbiàn;转换 zhuǎnhuàn. **switch** *v* 1 [I,T] (使)转变 zhuǎnbiàn;(使)改换 gǎihuàn: *~ to using gas* 改为使用煤气. 2 [I,T] (使)交换位置 jiāohuàn wèizhi: *~ the two batteries (round)* 对换两组电池. 3 [短语动词] **switch sth on/off** (用开关)接通(或切断)(电路等) jiē tōng. **'switchboard** *n* [C] (电话)交换台 jiāohuàntái;配电盘〔盤〕pèidiànpán.

swivel /ˈswɪvl/ *v* [-ll-; 美语 -l-] [I,T] (使)旋转〔轉〕xuánzhuǎn: *~ (round) in one's chair* 在转椅中转过身来.

swollen *pp* of SWELL.

swoop /swuːp/ *v* [I] (飞下)猛扑〔撲〕měngpū;猝然攻击〔擊〕cùrán gōngjī: [喻] *Police ~ed (on the house) at dawn.* 警察于拂晓时(对那所房子)进行了突然搜查. **swoop** *n* [C] 1 猛扑 měngpū. 2 突然袭击 tūrán xíjī.

swop = SWAP.

sword /sɔːd/ *n* [C] 剑〔劍〕jiàn; 刀 dāo. **'swordfish** *n* [C] 剑鱼 jiànyú;旗鱼 qíyú.

swore *pt* of SWEAR.

sworn[1] *pp* of SWEAR.

sworn[2] /swɔːn/ *adj* 极〔極〕度的 jídùde;极深的 jíshēnde: *~ friends/enemies* 知己的朋友;不共戴天的敌人.

swum *pp* of SWIM.

swung *pt, pp* of SWING.

syllable /ˈsɪləbl/ *n* [C] 音节〔節〕yīnjié: *'Table' has two ~s.* "table"一词有两个音节. **syllabic** /sɪˈlæbɪk/ *adj*.

syllabus /ˈsɪləbəs/ *n* [C] 教学〔學〕大纲〔綱〕jiàoxué dàgāng;(学习)提纲 tígāng.

symbol /ˈsɪmbl/ *n* [C] 符号〔號〕fúhào;记号 jìhào;象征〔徵〕xiàngzhēng: *The dove is a ~ of peace.* 鸽子是和平的象征. **symbolic** /sɪmˈbɒlɪk/ *adj* (使用)符号的 fúhàode;象征(性)的 xiàngzhēngde. **symbolically** *adv*. **symbolism** /ˈsɪmbəlɪzəm/ *n* [U] 符号(的使用) fúhào;象征(手法) xiàngzhēng. **symbolize** /ˈsɪmbəlaɪz/ *v* [T] 作(某事物的)符号 zuò fúhào;象征(某事物) xiàngzhēng.

symmetry /ˈsɪmətrɪ/ *n* [U] 1 对〔對〕称〔稱〕duìchèn. 2 匀称 yúnchèn. **symmetric** /sɪˈmetrɪk/ (亦作 **symmetrical** /-ɪkl/) *adj*.

sympathetic /ˌsɪmpəˈθetɪk/ *adj* 1 同情的 tóngqíngde;有同情心的 yǒu tóngqíngxīn de: *~ looks* 表示同情的样子. 2 (人)可爱〔愛〕的 kě'àide,讨人喜欢〔歡〕的 tǎo rén xǐhuan de. **sympathetically** /-klɪ/ *adv*.

sympathize /ˈsɪmpəθaɪz/ *v* [I] (*with*) 同情 tóngqíng;表示同情 biǎoshì tóngqíng. **sympathizer** *n* [C] 支持者 zhīchízhě;同情者 tóngqíngzhě.

sympathy /ˈsɪmpəθɪ/ *n* [*pl* -ies] 1 [U] 同情 tóngqíng;怜〔憐〕悯 liánmǐn;慰问 wèiwèn. 2 **sympathies** [pl] 同感 tónggǎn;赞同 zàntóng;同意 tóngyì.

symphony /ˈsɪmfənɪ/ *n* [C] [*pl* -ies] 交响〔響〕乐〔樂〕曲 jiāoxiǎngyuèqǔ.

symptom /ˈsɪmptəm/ *n* [C] 1 症状〔狀〕zhèngzhuàng;症候 zhènghòu. 2 (常指坏事的)征〔徵〕兆 zhēngzhào: *~s of discontent* 不满的征兆. **symptomatic** /-ˈmætɪk/ *adj* 症状的 zhèngzhuàngde;征兆的 zhēngzhàode.

synagogue /ˈsɪnəgɒg/ *n* [C] 犹〔猶〕太教堂 Yóutài jiàotáng.

synchronize /ˈsɪŋkrənaɪz/ *v* [I,T] (使)同时〔時〕发〔發〕生 tóngshí fāshēng;(使)同步 tóngbù: *~ watches* 把表校准一下.

syndicate /ˈsɪndəkət/ *n* [C] [经济]辛迪加 xīndíjiā;企业〔業〕联〔聯〕合组织 qǐyè liánhé zǔzhī. **syndicate** /ˈsɪndɪkeɪt/ *v* [T] 通过〔過〕报〔報〕业辛迪加(在多家报纸上)发〔發〕表(文章等) tōngguò bàoyè xīndíjiā fābiǎo.

syndrome /ˈsɪndrəum/ *n* [C] [医药]综合征〔徵〕zōnghézhēng.

synonym /ˈsɪnənɪm/ *n* 同义〔義〕词 tóngyìcí. **synonymous** /sɪˈnɒnɪməs/ *adj*.

synopsis /sɪˈnɒpsɪs/ *n* [C] [*pl* -opses /-siːz/] (书、剧本的)提要 tíyào.

syntax /ˈsɪntæks/ *n* [U] 造句(法) zàojù. **syntactic** /sɪnˈtæktɪk/ *adj* 句法的 jùfǎde.

synthesis /ˈsɪnθəsɪs/ *n* [U,C] [*pl* -theses

/-siːz/] 综合 zōnghé;合成(法) héchéng;合成物 héchéngwù. **synthetic** /sɪnˈθetɪk/ *adj* (人工)合成的 héchéngde: ~ *fabric* 人造织物. **synthesize** /ˈsɪnθəsaɪz/ *v* [T] 用合成法制〔製〕造 yòng héchéngfǎ zhìzào. **synthetically** /-klɪ/ *adv*.

syphilis /ˈsɪfɪlɪs/ *n* [U] 梅毒 méidú.

syphon = SIPHON.

syringe /sɪˈrɪndʒ/ *n* [C] 注射器 zhùshèqì. **syringe** *v* [T] (用注射器等)注射 zhùshè, 冲洗 chōngxǐ.

syrup /ˈsɪrəp/ *n* [U] 糖浆〔漿〕tángjiāng.

system /ˈsɪstəm/ *n* 1 [C] 系统 xìtǒng. 2 [C] 体〔體〕制 tǐzhì; 体系 tǐxì: *a* ~ *of government* 政体. 3 [U] 制度 zhìdù;秩序 zhìxù;规律 guīlǜ. **systematic** /-ˈmætɪk/ *adj* 有系统的 yǒu xìtǒng de;有秩序的 yǒu zhìxù de;有规律的 yǒu guīlǜ de. **systematically** /-klɪ/ *adv*.

T t

T, t /tiː/ *n* [C] [*pl* **T's, t's** /tiːz/] 英语的第二十个〔個〕字母 Yīngyǔde dì'èrshíge zìmǔ. ˈ**T-shirt** *n* [C] T 恤衫 Ti xùshān.

ta /tɑː/ *interj* [英国非正式用语]谢谢 xièxie.

tab /tæb/ *n* [C] 垂片 chuípiàn;小条〔條〕xiǎotiáo.

tabby /ˈtæbɪ/ *n* [C] [*pl* -ies] (亦作 ˈ**tabby-cat**) 花猫 huāmāo.

table /ˈteɪbl/ *n* [C] 1 桌子 zhuōzi. 2 目录〔錄〕mùlù;一览〔覽〕表 yìlǎnbiǎo;项目表 xiàngmùbiǎo. **table** *v* [T]把(…)列入议〔議〕程 bǎ lièrù yìchéng;提出(讨论) tíchū. ˈ**table-cloth** *n* [C] 桌布 zhuōbù. ˈ**table dancer** *n* [C] 桌上艳〔艷〕舞女郎 zhuōshàng yànwǔ nǚláng. ˈ**table dancing** *n* [U] 桌上艳舞 zhuōshàng yànwǔ. ˈ**tablespoon** 大汤〔湯〕匙 dà tāngchí. ˈ**tablespoonful** *n* [C] 一大汤匙的量 yí dà tāngchí de liàng. ˈ**table tennis** *n* [U] 乒乓球 pīngpāngqiú.

tablet /ˈtæblɪt/ *n* [C] 1 药〔藥〕片 yàopiàn. 2 (肥皂)块〔塊〕kuài. 3 碑 bēi;牌匾 páibiǎn.

tabloid /ˈtæblɔɪd/ *n* [C] 小报〔報〕xiǎobào.

taboo /təˈbuː; *US* tæˈbuː/ *n* [C, U] [*pl* ~s] 禁忌 jìnjì. **taboo** *adj* 禁忌的 jìnjìde;禁止的 jìnzhǐde.

tabulate /ˈtæbjʊleɪt/ *v* [T] 把…列成表 bǎ …liè chéng biǎo.

tacit /ˈtæsɪt/ *adj* 心照不宣的 xīnzhào bùxuān de: ~ *agreement* 默契. **tacitly** *adv*.

tack /tæk/ *n* 1 [C] 平头〔頭〕钉 píngtóudīng. 2 [U, sing] [喻]方针 fāngzhēn;政策 zhèngcè: *change* ~ 改变方针. 3 [C] 粗缝 cū féng. **tack** *v* [T] (用粗针脚)缝 féng.

tackle /ˈtækl/ *v* 1 [T] 处〔處〕理 chǔlǐ;解决 jiějué;对〔對〕付 duìfu. 2 [T] (*about*) 坦白地(向某人)谈(某事) tǎnbáide tán. 3 [I,T] [橄榄球]擒抱(对方带球球员) qínbào. 4 [T] 抓住 zhuāzhù. **tackle** *n* 1 [C] [橄榄球]擒抱 qínbào. 2 [U] 用具 yòngjù;装〔裝〕备〔備〕zhuāngbèi. 3 [U] 滑车 huáchē;复〔複〕滑车 fùhuáchē.

tacky /ˈtækɪ/ *adj* [非正式用语]俗气〔氣〕的 súqide;邋遢的 lātāde: ~ *jewellery* 俗气的首饰.

tact /tækt/ *n* [U] 老练〔練〕lǎoliàn;机〔機〕智 jīzhì;得体〔體〕détǐ. **tactful** *adj* 老练的 lǎoliànde;机智的 jīzhìde;得体的 détǐde. **tactfully** *adv*. **tactless** *adj*. **tactlessly** *adv*.

tactic /ˈtæktɪk/ *n* 1 [C, 常作 pl] 手段 shǒuduàn;策略 cèlüè. 2 **tactics** [亦作 sing 用 pl v] 战〔戰〕术〔術〕zhànshù. **tactical** *adj* 战术上的 zhànshùshangde;策略上的 cèlüèshangde: *a* ~*al move* 有谋略的一招. **tactician** /tækˈtɪʃn/ *n* [C] 战术家 zhànshùjiā.

tadpole /ˈtædpəʊl/ *n* [C] 蝌蚪 kēdǒu.

tag /tæg/ *n* 1 [C] 标〔標〕签〔簽〕biāoqiān. 2 [U] (儿童)捉人游戏〔戲〕zhuō rén yóuxì. **tag** *v* [-gg-] 1 [T] 贴标签 tiē biāoqiān. 2 [短语动词] **tag along/after/behind** 紧〔緊〕跟 jǐngēn;尾随〔隨〕wěisuí.

tail /teɪl/ *n* [C] 1 尾巴 wěiba. 2 尾状〔狀〕物 wěizhuàngwù;尾部 wěibù: *the* ~ *of an aircraft* 飞机的尾部. 3 [非正式用语](盯梢的)特务〔務〕tèwù;暗探 àntàn. 4 **tails** [pl] 钱〔錢〕币〔幣〕的背面 qiánbìde bèimiàn. **tail** *v* 1 [T] 跟踪(某人) gēnzōng. 2 [短语动词] **tail off/away** 变〔變〕少 biàn shǎo;缩小 suōxiǎo;变弱 biàn ruò. ˈ**tailback** *n* [C] (车辆因受阻而排成的)长〔長〕队〔隊〕cháng duì. **tailless** *adj*. ˈ**tail-light** *n* [C] (车辆的)尾灯〔燈〕wěidēng. ˈ**tail wind** *n* [C] 顺风〔風〕shùnfēng.

tailor /ˈteɪlə(r)/ *n* [C] 裁缝 cáifeng;成衣匠 chéngyījiàng. **tailor** *v* [T] 1 裁制〔製〕(衣服) cáizhì: *a well-~ed suit* 裁制得好的一套衣服. 2 适〔適〕应〔應〕(特定目的) shìyìng. ˌ**tailor-ˈmade** *adj* 1 定制的 dìngzhìde;特制的 tèzhìde. 2 [喻]合适的 héshìde: *She is* ~-*made for the job*. 她干这个工作完全合适.

taint /teɪnt/ *v* [T] 使感染 shǐ gǎnrǎn;使腐败 shǐ fǔbài. **taint** *n* [sing] 感染的迹〔跡〕象 gǎnrǎnde jìxiàng;腐败的痕迹 fǔbàide hénjì.

take[1] /teɪk/ *v* [*pt* **took** /tʊk/, *pp* ~n /ˈteɪkən/] 1 [T] 拿 ná;取 qǔ;握 wò;抱 bào: ~ *her hand* 握住她的手. *She took him in her arms*. 她拥抱他. 2 [T] 携〔攜〕带〔帶〕xiédài;带领 dàilǐng;陪伴 péibàn: *T*~ *an umbrella with you*. 带着你的伞. *She took a friend home*. 她把一位朋友带回家. 3

[T] 擅自取走 shànzì qǔzǒu；错拿 cuònά；偷去 tōuqù：*Who has ~n my bicycle?* 谁骑走了我的自行车？**4** [T] 拿去 nάqù；得到 dédào：*This line is ~n from a poem by Keats.* 这行诗选自济慈的一篇诗作。**5** [T] 占〔佔〕有 zhànyǒu：~ *a town* (*in war*) (战争中)占领一座城镇. *He took first prize.* 他夺得头奖. **6** [T] 接受 jiēshòu；收到 shōudào：~ *advice* 接受劝告. ~ *the blame* 受到责备. *Will you ~ £450 for the car?* 你这辆车卖450英镑行吗？**7** [T] 按时〔時〕收到(尤指所订报刊) ànshí shōudào：*He ~s The Times.* 他订阅《泰晤士报》. **8** [T] 吃 chī；喝 hē：*Do you ~ sugar in your tea?* 你在茶里放糖吗？**9** [T] 容纳得下 róngnà de xià：*The car ~s five people.* 这辆车容得下五个人. **10** [T] 能忍受 néng rěnshòu：*He can't ~ being criticized.* 他受不了批评. **11** [T] 对〔對〕待 duìdài；应〔應〕付 yìngfù：*She took her mother's death very badly.* 她对她母亲之死万分悲痛. **12** [T] 感觉〔覺〕gǎnjué；感受 gǎnshòu：~ *pleasure in being cruel* 在残酷无情中取乐. **13** [T] 以为〔爲〕yǐwéi；认〔認〕为 rènwéi：*What do you ~ this to be?* 你以为这是什么？**14** [T] 需要 xūyào；要求 yāoqiú：*The work took four hours.* 这工作需要4个小时. **15** [T] 穿用 chuānyòng：*What size shoes do you ~?* 你穿几号鞋？**16** [T] 参加(考试) cānjiā：~ *a driving test* 参加驾驶执照考试. **17** [T] 记录〔錄〕jìlù；写〔寫〕下 xiěxià：~ *notes* 做笔记. ~ *the names of the volunteers* 记下志愿人员的姓名. **18** [T] 拍摄〔攝〕(照片) pāishè. **19** [T] 测量 cèliáng：*The doctor took my temperature.* 医生测量我的体温. **20** [T] 负责 fùzé；指导〔導〕zhǐdǎo：~ *a class, course, etc* 主持一个班级、讲座等. **21** [I] 产〔產〕生预期效果 chǎnshēng yùqī xiàoguǒ：*The smallpox injection did not ~.* 那种天花预防注射没有效果. **22** [T] 使用 shǐyòng；采〔採〕取 cǎiqǔ；搭乘 dāchéng：~ *a bus into town* 搭乘公共汽车进城. ~ *the first road on the left* 在第一个路口向左拐. **23** [T] (与名词连用表示进行某动作)：~ *a bath / walk / holiday* 洗澡(或散步、度假). **24** [习语] **take its course** ⇨ COURSE[1]. **take heart** ⇨ HEART. **25** [短语动词] **take sb aback** 使某人震惊〔驚〕shǐ mǒurén zhènjīng. **take after sb** (长相、性格)像(其父母) xiàng. **take sth apart** (将机器等)拆开〔開〕chāikāi. **take sth away** (a) 减去 jiǎnqù：*T~ 5 from 10, and that leaves 5.* 10减去5，余5. (b) (饭菜)外卖〔賣〕wàimài，带走 dàizǒu. (c) 使消失 shǐ xiāoshī：*a pill to ~ the pain away* 使疼痛消失的一粒药丸. **take sb/sth away** 移开 yíkāi；除掉 chúdiào. **take sb/sth back** (a) 承认说错了话 chéngrèn shuō cuò le huà. (b) 同意退货(或接回某人) tóngyì tuì huò：*This shop only ~s goods back if you have your receipt.* 如果你有发票，这家商店才同意退货. **take sb back** (**to sth**) 使回想起(某事) shǐ huíxiǎng qǐ. **take sth down** (a) 记下某事 jìxià mǒushì. (b) 拆除 chāichú. **take sb in** 欺骗 qīpiàn：*Don't be ~n in by him.* 不要被他欺骗了. **take sth in** (a) (为赚钱)在家做工作 zài jiā zuò gōngzuò：~ *in washing* 在家替人洗衣服. (b) (将衣服)改瘦 gǎi shòu. (c) 包括 bāokuò：*The trip took in several cities.* 这次旅行包括几个城市. (d) 理解 lǐjiě；注意 zhùyì：*I couldn't ~ in everything she said.* 我不能理解她所说的每一件事. **take 'off** (a) (飞机)起飞〔飛〕qǐfēi. (b) (计划等)很快成功 hěn kuài chénggōng. **take sb off** [非正式用语]模仿 mófǎng：*She's good at taking off her teachers.* 她善于模仿她的教师们. **take sth off** (**sth**) (a) 脱下 tuōxià；除去 chúqù：~ *off one's hat* 脱帽. (b) 取消(火车班次等) qǔxiāo. (c) 扣除 kòuchú；减去 jiǎnqù：~ *50p off* (*the price*) 减价50便士. (d) 休假 xiūjià；休息 xiūxī：~ *a week off to go on holiday* 休息一星期去度假. **take on sth** 呈现(某种性质、样子) chéngxiàn. **take sth on** 决定做(某事) juédìng zuò. **take sb on** (a) 接受(某人)作为对手 jiēshòu zuòwéi duìshǒu. (b) 雇〔僱〕用(某人) gùyòng. **take sb/sth on** (车辆、飞机等)许可搭乘(或装载) xǔkě dāchéng. **take sb out** 陪伴某人出门 péibàn mǒurén chū mén：~ *her out to dinner* 陪伴她去参加宴会. **take sth out** (a) 切除(身体的一部分) qiēchú：~ *out a tooth* 拔去一颗牙. (b) 获〔獲〕得(官方文件) huòdé：~ *out a licence* 领到许可证. **take it out of sb** [非正式用语]使某人疲乏 shǐ mǒurén pífá：*That run really took it out of me.* 那次跑得我筋疲力尽. **take it/sth out on sb** [非正式用语]向某人出气〔氣〕xiàng mǒurén chūqì. **take over** (**from sb**) 接手 jiēshǒu；接任 jiērèn. **take sth 'over** 控制 kòngzhì；管理 guǎnlǐ：~ *over another business* 再管理一个企业. **take to sth** (a) 开〔開〕始做某种活动(或工作) kāishǐ zuò mǒuzhǒng huódòng：*took to cycling ten miles a day* 开始每天骑十英里的自行车. (b) 躲避 duǒbì；逃入 táorù：~ *to the woods to avoid capture* 逃进森林以免被捕. **take to sb/sth** 开始喜欢〔歡〕kāishǐ xǐhuan. **take sth up** (a) 拿起 náqǐ；举〔舉〕起 jǔqǐ：*took up a knife* 拿起一把刀. (b) 改短(衣服等) gǎi duǎn. (c) 开始做(某活动) kāishǐ zuò：*took up cycling, chess* 开始骑车、下棋. (d) 继〔繼〕续〔續〕做(未完成的事) jìxù zuò. (e) 占〔佔〕用(时间或空间) zhànyòng：*This table ~s up half the room.* 这张桌子占了半间屋

T

子. (f) 接受(一个建议) jiēshòu. **take up with sb** 开始与〔與〕某人交往(或友好) kāishǐ yǔ mǒurén jiāowǎng. **take sth up with sb** (口头或书面)向某人谈及某事 xiàng mǒurén tánjí mǒushì. **take sth upon oneself** 承担〔擔〕chéngdān; 担任 dānrèn. **be taken with sb/sth** 对某人(或某事)有兴〔興〕趣(或吸引力) duì mǒurén yǒu xìngqù. **ˈtake-away** *n* [C] (a) (食品)外卖的餐馆 wàimài de cānguǎn. (b) 在外卖餐馆买〔買〕的饭菜 zài wàimài cānguǎn mǎi de fàncài: *go for a ~-away* 去外卖餐馆买吃的. **ˈtake-off** *n* [C] (飞机)起飞 qǐfēi. **ˈtake-over** *n* (对某企业的)接收 jiēshōu.

take[2] /teɪk/ *n* [C] (一次拍摄的连续)镜头〔頭〕jìngtóu.

taker /ˈteɪkə(r)/ *n* [C] 收取者 shōuqǔzhě; 接受者 jiēshòuzhě.

takings /ˈteɪkɪŋz/ *n* [pl] 收入 shōurù; 进〔進〕款 jìnkuǎn.

talcum powder /ˈtælkəm/ *n* [U] 爽身粉 shuǎngshēnfěn.

tale /teɪl/ *n* [C] **1** 故事 gùshi: *~s of adventure* 冒险故事. **2** 报〔報〕告 bàogào; 记述 jìshù. **3** 谣言 yáoyán; 流言蜚语 liúyán-fēiyǔ.

talent /ˈtælənt/ *n* [C, U] 天才 tiāncái; 才能 cáinéng: *have a ~ for music* 有音乐天才. **talented** *adj* 有才能的 yǒu cáinéng de; 有才干〔幹〕的 yǒu cáigàn de.

talk[1] /tɔːk/ *v* **1** [I] 说话 shuōhuà; 谈话 tánhuà: *He was ~ing to a friend.* 他正在和一个朋友谈话. **2** [I] 有讲话能力 yǒu jiǎnghuà nénglì: *Can the baby ~ yet?* 这婴孩会讲话了吗? **3** [T] 讨论〔論〕tǎolùn; 谈论 tánlùn: *We ~ed politics all evening.* 我们整个晚上在谈论政治. **4** [I] 闲聊 xiánliáo; 漫谈 màntán. **5** [I] 招供 zhāogòng: *Has the prisoner ~ed yet?* 犯人已招供了吗? **6** [短语动词] **talk down to sb** 高人一等地对〔對〕某人讲话 gāo rén yìděng de duì mǒurén jiǎnghuà. **talk sb into/out of doing sth** 说服某人做(或不做)某事 shuōfú mǒurén zuò mǒushì. **talk sth over** 商量 shāngliáng; 讨论 tǎolùn. **talkative** /ˈtɔːkətɪv/ *adj* 健谈的 jiàntánde; 多嘴的 duōzuǐde. **talker** *n* [C]. **ˈtalking-point** *n* [C] 讨论的题目 tǎolùnde tímù. **ˈtalking-to** *n* [sing] 责备〔備〕zébèi; 斥责 chìzé.

talk[2] /tɔːk/ *n* **1** [C, U] 交谈 jiāotán; 谈话 tánhuà. **2** [U] 闲话 xiánhuà; 谣言 yáoyán. **3** [C] (非正式的)发〔發〕言 fāyán. **4 talks** [pl] (正式)讨论〔論〕tǎolùn. **ˈtalk show** *n* [C] 脱口秀 tuōkǒuxiù; (电视)访谈节〔節〕目 fǎngtán jiémù.

tall /tɔːl/ *adj* **1** (身材)高的 gāode. **2** 有某种〔種〕高度的 yǒu mǒuzhǒng gāodù de: *Tom is six feet ~.* 汤姆身高六英尺. **3** [习语] **a tall ˈorder** 难〔難〕完成的任务〔務〕nán wánchéng de rènwù; 苛求 kēqiú. **a tall ˈstory** 难以相信的故事 nán yǐ xiāngxìn de gùshi.

tally /ˈtælɪ/ *n* [C] [*pl* **-ies**] 计算 jìsuàn; 计分 jìfēn. **tally** *v* [*pt*, *pp* **-ied**] [I] 符合 fúhé; 吻合 wěnhé.

talon /ˈtælən/ *n* [C] (猛禽的)爪 zhuǎ.

tambourine /ˌtæmbəˈriːn/ *n* [C] 铃鼓 línggǔ.

tame /teɪm/ *adj* [~r, ~st] **1** 驯服了的 xùnfúlede: *a ~ monkey* 驯服的猴子. **2** (人)顺从〔從〕的 shùncóngde, 听〔聽〕话的 tīnghuàde: *Her husband is a ~ little man.* 她的丈夫是一个温顺的小个子. **3** 沉闷的 chénmènde; 平淡的 píngdànde; 乏味的 fáwèide: *The film has a rather ~ ending.* 那电影的结局相当平淡无味. **tame** *v* [T] 驯服 xùnfú; 使顺从 shǐ shùncóng: *~ a lion* 驯狮. **tamely** *adv*. **tameness** *n* [U]. **tamer** *n* [C] 驯兽〔獸〕者 xùnshòuzhě: *a lion-~r* 驯狮者.

tamper /ˈtæmpə(r)/ *v* [I] *with* 干预 gānyù; 乱〔亂〕弄 luàn nòng.

tampon /ˈtæmpɒn/ *n* [C] 月经〔經〕棉栓 yuèjīng miánshuān.

tan /tæn/ *n* **1** [C] 晒〔曬〕黑的肤〔膚〕色 shàihēide fūsè. **2** [U] 黄褐色 huánghèsè. **tan** *v* [-nn-] **1** [T] 鞣(革) róu; 硝(皮) xiāo. **2** [I, T] (使皮肤)晒成棕褐色 shài chéng zōnghèsè. **3** [习语] **tan sb's hide** [非正式用语]痛打某人 tòngdǎ mǒurén.

tandem /ˈtændəm/ *n* **1** [C] 前后〔後〕双〔雙〕座自行车〔車〕qián hòu shuāngzuò zìxíngchē. **2** [习语] **in ˈtandem** 并〔竝〕肩(工作) bìngjiān; 共同(经营) gòngtóng.

tandoori /tænˈdʊərɪ/ *n* [C, U] 唐杜里(在泥炉中烹制的印度食品) tángdùlǐ.

tang /tæŋ/ *n* [C, 常作 sing] 强烈的气〔氣〕味 qiángliède qìwèi.

tangent /ˈtændʒənt/ *n* **1** [C] 切线〔綫〕qiēxiàn; [数学]正切 zhèngqiē. **2** [习语] **go off at a ˈtangent** 思想行动〔動〕等突然改变〔變〕sīxiǎng xíngdòng děng tūrán gǎibiàn.

tangerine /ˌtændʒəˈriːn; *US* ˈtændʒəriːn/ *n* [C] 红橘 hóngjú; 小蜜橘 xiǎo mìjú.

tangible /ˈtændʒəbl/ *adj* **1** [正式用语]可触〔觸〕知的 kě chùzhī de. **2** 明确〔確〕的 míngquède; 确实〔實〕的 quèshíde: *~ proof* 明确的证据. **tangibly** *adv*.

tangle /ˈtæŋgl/ *n* **1** [C] (线、头发等的)缠〔纏〕结 chánjié. **2** [sing] 混乱〔亂〕hùnluàn: *in a ~* 在混乱状态中. **tangle** *v* **1** [I, T] (使)缠结 chánjié; (使)混乱 hùnluàn: *~d hair* 乱蓬蓬的头发. **2** [I] *with* (与人)争吵 zhēngchǎo.

tango /ˈtæŋgəʊ/ *n* [C] [*pl* ~s] 探戈舞(曲) tàngēwǔ.

tank /tæŋk/ *n* [C] **1** (盛液体或气体的)大容器 dà róngqì. **2** 坦克 tǎnkè.

T

tankard /ˈtæŋkəd/ *n* [C] 大酒杯 dà jiǔbēi.

tanker /ˈtæŋkə(r)/ *n* [C] 油轮〔輪〕yóulún; 罐车 guànchē.

tantalize /ˈtæntəlaɪz/ *v* [T] (引起兴趣而不给予满足的)逗弄 dòunòng; 使干〔乾〕着急 shǐ gānzháojí.

tantamount /ˈtæntəmaunt/ *adj to* (与某事物)效果相同 xiàoguǒ xiāngtóng.

tantrum /ˈtæntrəm/ *n* [C] (尤指小孩)发〔發〕脾气〔氣〕fā píqì.

tap[1] /tæp/ *n* 1 [C] (液体或气体管道的)龙〔龍〕头〔頭〕lóngtóu. 2 [习语] **on tap** 现成的 xiànchéngde; 就在手头的 jiù zài shǒutóu de. **tap** *v* [-pp-] [T] 1 使(从龙头中)流出 shǐ liúchū; 汲取(树液) jíqǔ. 2 开发〔發〕kāifā; 获〔獲〕取 huòqǔ: ~ *a country's resources* 开发国家资源. 3 窃〔竊〕听〔聽〕(电话) qiètīng.

tap[2] /tæp/ *v* [I, T] *n* [C] 轻〔輕〕打 qīng dǎ; 轻拍 qīng pāi: ~ *sb on the shoulder* 轻拍某人的肩膀. ˈ**tap-dancing** *n* [U] 踢踏舞 tītàwǔ.

tape /teɪp/ *n* 1 (a) [C, U] 狭〔狹〕带〔帶〕xiá dài; 带尺 dàichǐ. (b) [C] (赛跑)终点〔點〕线〔綫〕zhōngdiǎnxiàn. 2 [U, C] = MAGNETIC TAPE (MAGNET). **tape** *v* [T] 1 用带子捆扎〔紮〕yòng dàizi kǔnzā. 2 用磁带录〔錄〕音 yòng cídài lùyīn. 3 [习语] **have sb/sth taped** [非正式用语][尤用于英国英语](彻底)了解某事物 liáojiě mǒu shìwù. ˈ**tape-measure** *n* [C] 卷〔捲〕尺 juǎnchǐ; 带尺 dàichǐ. ˈ**tape-recorder** *n* [C] 磁带录音机 cídài lùyīnjī.

taper[1] /ˈteɪpə(r)/ *v* 1 [I, T] (使)逐渐变〔變〕细 zhújiàn biàn xì; 变尖 biàn jiān. 2 [I] *off* 变少 biàn shǎo; 逐渐终止 zhújiàn zhōngzhǐ.

taper[2] /ˈteɪpə(r)/ *n* [C] 细蜡〔蠟〕烛〔燭〕xì làzhú.

tapestry /ˈtæpəstrɪ/ *n* [C, U] [*pl* **-ies**] 花毯 huā tǎn; 挂〔掛〕毯 guàtǎn.

tar /tɑː(r)/ *n* [U] 焦油 jiāoyóu; 沥〔瀝〕青 lìqīng. **tar** *v* [-rr-] 1 [T] 涂〔塗〕焦油 tú jiāoyóu; 铺沥青 pū lìqīng. 2 [习语] **tarred with the same ˈbrush** 是一路货色 shì yílù huòsè; 是一丘之貉 shì yì qiū zhī hé.

tarantula /təˈræntjulə; *US* -tʃələ/ *n* [C] 一种毒蜘蛛 yìzhǒng dú zhīzhū.

target /ˈtɑːgɪt/ *n* 1 [C] 靶 bǎ; 目标〔標〕mùbiāo. 2 [C] (被批评的)对〔對〕象 duìxiàng. 3 [C, U] (生产等的)指标 zhǐbiāo, 目标 mùbiāo: *achieve a sales* ~ 完成销售指标. **target** *v* [T] 瞄准〔準〕miáozhǔn.

tariff /ˈtærɪf/ *n* [C] 1 关〔關〕税率 guānshuìlǜ. 2 (旅馆等的)价〔價〕目表 jiàmùbiǎo.

Tarmac /ˈtɑːmæk/ *n* [U] 1 (*P*)(铺路面的)碎石和沥〔瀝〕青的混合材料 suìshí hé lìqīng de hùnhé cáiliào. 2 **tarmac** 沥青碎石路面 lìqīng suìshí lùmiàn.

tarnish /ˈtɑːnɪʃ/ *v* 1 [I, T] (尤指金属表面)(使)失去光泽〔澤〕shīqù guāngzé: *Brass* ~*es easily*. 铜器容易失去光泽. 2 [T] 玷污(名誉) diànwū.

tarpaulin /tɑːˈpɔːlɪn/ *n* [C, U] 防水帆布 fángshuǐ fānbù; 油布 yóubù.

tart[1] /tɑːt/ *n* [C] 果馅饼 guǒ xiànbǐng.

tart[2] /tɑːt/ *adj* 1 酸的 suānde; 辛辣的 xīnlàde. 2 [喻]刻薄的 kèbóde; 尖刻的 jiānkède: *a* ~ *reply* 尖刻的回答. **tartly** *adv*. **tartness** *n* [U].

tart[3] /tɑːt/ *n* [C] [俚, 贬](举止)轻〔輕〕佻的女子 qīngtiāode nǚzǐ. **tart** *v* [短语动词] **tart sb/sth up** [非正式用语][贬]把…打扮得俗气〔氣〕bǎ…dǎbàn de súqì.

tartan /ˈtɑːtn/ *n* [U, C] 花格图〔圖〕案 huāgé tú'àn; (尤指)苏〔蘇〕格兰〔蘭〕格子呢 Sūgélán gézini.

tartar /ˈtɑːtə(r)/ *n* [U] 牙垢 yágòu.

task /tɑːsk; *US* tæsk/ *n* 1 [C] (尤指困难的)任务〔務〕rènwu, 工作 gōngzuò. 2 [习语] **take sb to task** 指责(或批评)某人 zhǐzé mǒurén. ˈ**task force** *n* [C] 特遣部队〔隊〕tèqiǎn bùduì. ˈ**taskmaster** (*fem* ˈ**taskmistress**) *n* [C] 监〔監〕工 jiāngōng.

tassel /ˈtæsl/ *n* [C] (旗、帽等上的)缨 yīng; 流苏〔蘇〕liúsū.

taste[1] /teɪst/ *n* 1 [U] 味觉〔覺〕wèijué. 2 [sing] 味道 wèidào; 滋味 zīwèi: *Sugar has a sweet* ~. 糖有甜味. 3 [sing] 一口 yìkǒu; 一点〔點〕儿〔兒〕yìdiǎnr. 4 [U] 鉴〔鑒〕赏力 jiànshǎnglì; 审〔審〕美力 shěnměilì: *Your choice of colours shows good* ~. 你对颜色的选择很有眼光. 5 [C, U] 爱〔愛〕好 àihào; 嗜好 shìhào. 6 [习语] **in good/bad taste** (举止)适〔適〕当〔當〕(或失当) shìdàng. **a taste of one's own medicine** ⇨ MEDICINE. **tasteful** *adj* 有鉴赏力的 yǒu jiànshǎnglì de; 有判断〔斷〕力的 yǒu pànduànlì de. **tastefully** *adv*. **tasteless** *adj* 1 (食物)无〔無〕味的 wúwèide. 2 无鉴赏力的 wú jiànshǎnglì de; 无判断力的 wú pànduànlì de. **tastelessly** *adv*. **tasty** *adj* [-ier, -iest] 美味的 měiwèide; 可口的 kěkǒude.

taste[2] /teɪst/ *v* 1 [T] 品尝〔嘗〕(出) pǐncháng; 辨(味) biàn. 2 [I] (*of*) 有…味道 yǒu …wèidào: ~ *bitter* / *sweet* 有苦(或甜)味. 3 [T] 试…的味道 shì…de wèidào: *She* ~*d the soup*. 她尝尝汤的味道. 4 [T] [喻]体〔體〕验〔驗〕tǐyàn; 感受 gǎnshòu: ~ *freedom* / *success* 尝到自由(或成功)的甜头.

tatters /ˈtætəz/ *n* [pl] [习语] **in tatters** (a) (衣物)破旧〔舊〕的 pòjiùde. (b) [喻]毁坏〔壞〕的 huǐhuàide. **tattered** *adj* 破烂〔爛〕的 pòlànde; 褴〔襤〕褛〔褸〕的 lánlǚde.

tattoo[1] /təˈtuː; *US* tæˈtuː/ *v* [T] (在皮肤上)刺(花纹) cì. **tattoo** *n* [C] [*pl* ~**s**] 文身

wénshēn.

tattoo[2] /tə'tuː; *US* tæ'tuː/ *n* [C] [*pl* ～s] (配有军乐的)归〔歸〕营〔營〕游行 guī yíng yóuxíng.

taught *pt*, *pp* of TEACH.

taunt /tɔːnt/ *v* [T] 辱骂 rǔmà; 侮辱 wǔrǔ. **taunt** *n* [C] 辱骂 rǔmà; 侮辱 wǔrǔ.

taut /tɔːt/ *adj* (绳索等)拉紧〔緊〕的 lājǐnde; (神经)紧张〔張〕的 jǐnzhāngde. **tautly** *adv*. **tautness** *n* [U].

tautology /tɔː'tɒlədʒɪ/ *n* [C, U] [*pl* -ies] 同义〔義〕反复〔復〕tóngyì fǎnfù; 赘述 zhuìshù. **tautological** /ˌtɔːtə'lɒdʒɪkl/ *adj*.

tavern /'tævən/ *n* [C] [旧]酒店 jiǔdiàn; 小旅馆 xiǎo lǚguǎn.

tawny /'tɔːnɪ/ *adj* 黄褐色的 huánghèsède; 茶色的 chásède.

tax /tæks/ *n* [C, U] 税 shuì; 税收 shuìshōu. **tax** *v* [T] **1** 对〔對〕…征税 duì … zhēng shuì. **2** 要求(某人)纳税 yāoqiú nàshuì. **3** 使负重担 shǐ fù zhòngdàn; 使受压〔壓〕力 shǐ shòu yālì: ～ *sb's patience* 考验某人的耐心. **taxable** *adj* 可征〔徵〕税的 kě zhēngshuì de: ～*able income* 应课税的收入. **taxation** /tæk'seɪʃn/ *n* [U] 征税 zhēngshuì; 税制 shuìzhì; 税项 shuìxiàng. **'tax avoidance** *n* [U] 避税 bìshuì. **'tax evasion** *n* [U] 逃税 táoshuì. **ˌtax-'free** *adj* 免税的 miǎnshuìde. **'taxpayer** *n* [C] 纳税人 nàshuìrén. **'tax return** *n* [C] 个〔個〕人所得税申报〔報〕表 gèrén suǒdéshuì shēnbàobiǎo.

taxi /'tæksɪ/ *n* [C] (亦作 **'taxi-cab**) 出租汽车 chūzū qìchē; 计程车 jìchéngchē. **taxi** *v* [I] (飞机)滑行 huáxíng. **'taxi rank** *n* [C] 出租汽车停车处〔處〕chūzū qìchē tíngchēchù.

tea /tiː/ *n* **1** (a) [U] 茶叶〔葉〕cháyè. (b) [C, U] 茶 chá. **2** [C, U] 代茶(用其他植物沏成的饮料) dài chá: *mint* ～ 薄荷茶. **3** [C, U] (a) (午后)茶点〔點〕chádiǎn. (b) (傍晚)简便小吃 jiǎnbiàn xiǎochī. **'tea-bag** *n* [C] 小包茶叶 xiǎo bāo cháyè; 袋茶 dàichá. **'tea-caddy** /-kædɪ/ [*pl* -dies] *n* [C] 茶叶罐 cháyèguàn. **'tea-chest** *n* [C] 茶叶箱 cháyèxiāng. **'teacup** *n* [C] 茶杯 chábēi. **'teapot** *n* [C] 茶壶〔壺〕cháhú. **'tea-service** (亦作 **'tea-set**) *n* [C] 一套茶具 yítào chájù. **'teaspoon** *n* [C] 茶匙 cháchí. **'teaspoonful** *n* [C] 一茶匙的量 yì cháchí de liàng. **'tea-strainer** *n* [C] 滤〔濾〕茶器 lǜcháqì. **'tea-time** *n* [U] (下午)吃茶点时〔時〕间 chī chádiǎn shíjiān. **'tea-towel** (亦作 **'tea-cloth**) 擦茶具的抹布 cā chájù de mābù.

teach /tiːtʃ/ *v* [*pt*, *pp* **taught** /tɔːt/] [I, T] 教(某人) jiāo; 讲〔講〕授 jiǎngshòu: *He taught them art*. 他教他们美术. ～ *a child (how) to swim* 教一个孩子游泳. **teacher** *n* [C] (尤指中小学)教师〔師〕jiàoshī. **teaching** *n* **1** [U] 教学〔學〕工作 jiàoxué gōngzuò: *earn a living by* ～*ing* 以教书为生. **2** [C, 常作 pl] 教义〔義〕jiàoyì: *the* ～*ings of Jesus* 耶稣的教导.

teak /tiːk/ *n* [U] 柚木 yòumù.

team /tiːm/ *n* [C, 亦作 sing, 与 pl v 连用] **1** (一)队〔隊〕duì; (一)组 zǔ: *a football* ～ 足球队. **2** 工作小组 gōngzuò xiǎozǔ: *a* ～ *of surgeons* 外科医师小组. **team** *v* [I] *up (with)* (与某人)合作 hézuò. **ˌteam 'spirit** *n* [U] 集体〔體〕(或协作)精神 jítǐ jīngshén. **'team-work** *n* [U] 团〔團〕队合作 tuánduì hézuò; 有组织〔織〕的合作 yǒu zǔzhīde hézuò.

tear[1] /tɪə(r)/ *n* **1** [C, 常作 pl] 眼泪〔淚〕yǎnlèi. **2** [习语] **in 'tears** 哭泣 kūqì. **'tear-drop** *n* [C] 泪珠 lèizhū. **tearful** *adj* 哭泣的 kūqìde; 要哭的 yào kū de; 含泪的 hánlèide. **tearfully** *adv*. **'tear-gas** *n* [U] 催泪毒气〔氣〕cuīlèi dúqì. **tear-jerker** *n* [C] [非正式用语]催人泪下的故事 cuī rén lèi xià de gùshì.

tear[2] /teə(r)/ *v* [*pt* **tore** /tɔː(r)/, *pp* **torn** /tɔːn/] **1** [T] 撕开〔開〕sīkāi; 撕裂 sīliè; 戳破 chuōpò: ～ *a sheet of paper* 撕破一张纸. **2** [T] 拉掉 lādiào; 撕去 sīqù: ～ *a page out of a book* 撕下一页书. **3** [I] (被)撕破 sīpò; (易)撕碎 sīsuì: *This cloth* ～*s easily*. 这种布料容易被撕破. **4** [I] 飞〔飛〕跑 fēipǎo; 狂奔 kuángbēn; 冲〔衝〕chōng: *We tore home*. 我们飞奔回家. **5** [T] 破坏〔壞〕…的安宁〔寧〕pòhuài…de ānníng; 扰〔擾〕乱〔亂〕rǎoluàn: *a country torn by civil war* 内战不宁的国家. **6** [习语] **be torn between A and B** (两者之间)作痛苦的抉择〔擇〕zuò tòngkǔde juézé. **7** [短语动词] **tear sth down** 弄倒(或拆除)(建筑物) nòng dǎo. **tear sth up** 撕破(一张纸) sīpò. **tear** *n* [C] 撕破处〔處〕sīpòchù; 裂口 lièkǒu. **'tearaway** *n* [C] 鲁莽的青年 lǔmǎngde qīngnián.

tease /tiːz/ *v* [I, T] 取笑 qǔxiào; 嘲笑 cháoxiào; 戏〔戲〕弄 xìnòng. **tease** *n* [C] (爱)嘲弄别人的人 cháonòng biérén de rén. **teaser** *n* [C] [非正式用语]难〔難〕题 nántí.

teat /tiːt/ *n* [C] **1** 乳头〔頭〕rǔtóu; 奶头 nǎitóu. **2** 橡胶〔膠〕奶嘴 xiàngjiāo nǎizuǐ.

tech /tek/ *n* [C] [非正式用语] short for TECHNICAL COLLEGE (TECHNICAL).

technical /'teknɪkl/ *adj* **1** 技术〔術〕的 jìshùde; 应〔應〕用科学〔學〕的 yìngyòng kēxué de. **2** 专〔專〕科的 zhuānkēde: *the* ～ *terms of physics* 物理专业术语. **3** 工艺〔藝〕的 gōngyìde; 技巧的 jìqiǎode. **4** 按严〔嚴〕格法律意义〔義〕的 àn yángé fǎlǜ yìyì de. **'technical college** (英国)技术学院 jìshù xuéyuàn. **technical-**

T

ity /ˌteknɪˈkælətɪ/ *n* [C] [*pl* -ies] 不重要的(专业)细节〔節〕bú zhòngyào de xìjié. **technically** /-klɪ/ *adv*.

technician /tekˈnɪʃn/ *n* [C] 技术〔術〕人员 jìshù rényuán; 技师〔師〕jìshī.

technique /tekˈniːk/ *n* **1** [C] 技术〔術〕jìshù; 技巧 jìqiǎo; 方法 fāngfǎ. **2** [U] 技能 jìnéng.

technocrat /ˈteknəkræt/ *n* [C] [常贬]专〔專〕家治国〔國〕(或管理企业) zhuānjiā zhìguó; 技术〔術〕专〔專〕家官员(或经理) jìshù zhuānjiā guānyuán.

technology /tekˈnɒlədʒɪ/ *n* [U] 工艺〔藝〕学〔學〕gōngyìxué. **technological** /ˌteknəˈlɒdʒɪkl/ *adj*. **technologist** *n* [C] 技术〔術〕(或工艺)专〔專〕家 jìshù zhuānjiā.

teddy bear /ˈtedɪ beə(r)/ *n* [C] 玩具熊 wánjùxióng.

tedious /ˈtiːdɪəs/ *adj* 沉闷的 chénmènde; 乏味的 fáwèide; 厌〔厭〕烦的 yànfánde: *a* ~ *lecture* 冗长乏味的演说. ~ *work* 令人厌烦的工作. **tediously** *adv*.

tee /tiː/ *n* [C] **1** [高尔夫球]发〔發〕球处〔處〕fāqiúchù. **2** 球座(高尔夫球发球小台) qiúzuò. **tee** *v* [短语动词] **tee off** (自球座)发球 fāqiú. **tee (sth) up** (将球)放在球座上(准备发球) fàng zài qiúzuòshàng.

teem[1] /tiːm/ *v* [I] *with* 大量出现 dàliàng chūxiàn; 涌现 yǒngxiàn: *The river was ~ing with fish*. 河中出现了很多鱼.

teem[2] /tiːm/ *v* [I] [与 *it* 连用] (大雨)倾盆而下 qīngpén ér xià.

teenage /ˈtiːneɪdʒ/ *adj* (十几岁)青少年的 qīngshàoniánde: ~ *fashions* 青少年流行款式.

teenager /ˈtiːneɪdʒə(r)/ *n* [C] (十几岁的)男女青少年 nán nǚ qīngshàonián.

teens /tiːns/ *n* [pl] 十三至十九岁之间 shísān zhì shíjiǔ suì zhī jiān: *girls in their* ~ 少女们.

teeter /ˈtiːtə(r)/ *v* [I] 摇摇欲坠〔墜〕yáoyáo yù zhuì; 步履不稳〔穩〕地行走 bùlǚ bùwěn de xíngzǒu.

teeth /tiːθ/ *pl* of TOOTH.

teethe /tiːð/ *v* [I] 出乳牙 chū rǔyá. **ˈteething troubles** *n* [pl] 事情开〔開〕始时〔時〕遇到的麻烦 shìqing kāishǐ shí yùdào de máfan; 开头〔頭〕难〔難〕kāitóunán.

teetotal /tiːˈtəʊtl; *US* ˈtiːtəʊtl/ *adj* 戒酒的 jièjiǔde; 反对〔對〕饮酒的 fǎnduì yǐn jiǔ de. **teetotaller** *n* [C].

telecommunications /ˌtelɪkəˌmjuːnɪˈkeɪʃnz/ *n* [pl] 电〔電〕信 diànxìn.

telecommute /ˈtelɪkəˌmjuːt/ *v* [I] 电〔電〕子通勤 diànzǐ tōngqín; 远〔遠〕程办〔辦〕公 yuǎnchéng bàngōng. **ˈtelecommuter** *n* [C] 电子通勤者 diànzǐ tōngqínzhě; 远程办公者 yuǎnchéng bàngōngzhě. **ˈtelecommuting** *n* [U] 电子通勤 diànzǐ tōngqín; 远程办公 yuǎnchéng bàngōng.

telecottage /ˈtelɪˌkɒtɪdʒ/ *n* [C] (尤指农村地区供大家使用的)计算机〔機〕房 jìsuànjīfáng.

telegram /ˈtelɪgræm/ *n* [C] 电〔電〕报〔報〕diànbào; 电信 diànxìn.

telegraph /ˈtelɪgrɑːf; *US* -græf/ *n* [U] (打)电〔電〕报〔報〕diànbào; (通)电信 diànxìn. **telegraph** *v* [I, T] 打电报 dǎ diànbào. **telegraphic** /ˌtelɪˈgræfɪk/ *adj*.

telepathy /tɪˈlepəθɪ/ *n* [U] 心灵〔靈〕感应〔應〕xīnlíng gǎnyìng. **telepathic** /ˌtelɪˈpæθɪk/ *adj*.

telephone /ˈtelɪfəʊn/ *n* [C, U] 电〔電〕话 diànhuà; 电话机〔機〕diànhuàjī. **telephone** *v* [I, T] 打电话 dǎ diànhuà; 通电话 tōng diànhuà. **ˈtelephone-box** (亦作 **ˈtelephone booth**) *n* [C] (公用)电话间 diànhuàjiān. **ˈtelephone directory** *n* [C] 电话簿 diànhuàbù. **ˈtelephone exchange** *n* [C] 电话交换机 diànhuà jiāohuànjī. **ˈtelephone number** *n* [C] 电话号〔號〕码 diànhuà hàomǎ.

telephonist /tɪˈlefənɪst/ *n* [C] 电〔電〕话接线〔綫〕员 diànhuà jiēxiànyuán.

telephoto lens /ˌtelɪˈfəʊtəʊ lenz/ *n* [C] 摄〔攝〕远〔遠〕镜头〔頭〕shè yuǎn jìngtóu.

telescope /ˈtelɪskəʊp/ *n* [C] 望远〔遠〕镜 wàngyuǎnjìng. **telescope** *v* [I, T] (使)嵌进〔進〕qiàn jìn; (使)套入 tào rù: *When the trains collided, the first two carriages (were) ~d*. 火车相撞时，前二节车厢撞挤在一起了. **telescopic** /ˌtelɪˈskɒpɪk/ *adj*.

teleshopping /ˈtelɪˌʃɒpɪŋ/ *n* [U] 远〔遠〕程购〔購〕物 yuǎnchéng gòuwù; 电〔電〕视商店 diànshì shāngdiàn.

teletext /ˈtelɪtekst/ *n* [U] 电〔電〕视电报〔報〕diànshì diànbào; 电视文字广〔廣〕播 diànshì wénzì guǎngbō.

television /ˈtelɪvɪʒn/ *n* **1** [U] 电〔電〕视 diànshì. **2** [C] (亦作 **ˈtelevision set**) 电视机〔機〕diànshìjī. **televise** /ˈtelɪvaɪz/ *v* [T] 电视播送 diànshì bōsòng. **ˈtelevision screen** *n* [C] 电视屏 diànshìpíng.

telework /ˈtelɪwɜːk/ *v* [I] 电〔電〕子通勤 diànzǐ tōngqín; 远〔遠〕程办〔辦〕公 yuǎnchéng bàngōng. **ˈteleworker** *n* [C] 电子通勤者 diànzǐ tōngqínzhě; 远程办公者 yuǎnchéng bàngōngzhě. **ˈteleworking** *n* [U] 电子通勤 diànzǐ tōngqín; 远程办公 yuǎnchéng bàngōng.

telex /ˈteleks/ *n* **1** [U] 用户电〔電〕报〔報〕yònghù diànbào; 电传〔傳〕系统 diànchuán xìtǒng. **2** [C] 用户电报收发〔發〕的消息 yònghù

T

diànbào shōu fā de xiāoxī; 电传 diànchuán. **telex** *v* [T] 以电传发出(信息) yǐ diànchuán fāchū.

tell /tel/ *v* [*pt*, *pp* **told** /təʊld/] **1** [T] 告诉 gàosù; 告知 gàozhī: *I told her my name*. 我把我的名字告诉她. **2** [T] 吩咐 fēnfù; 劝〔勸〕告 quàngào: *I told them to go*. 我叫他们走开. **3** [I, T] 肯定 kěndìng; 断〔斷〕定 duàndìng: *How can you ~ which key to use?* 你怎么能断定用哪一个钥匙? **4** [T] (向某人)提供情况 tígōng qíngkuàng. **5** [I] (*on*) (对某人)产〔產〕生(不愉快)效果 chǎnshēng xiàoguǒ: *All this hard work is ~ing on him*. 这些繁重的工作他吃不消了. **6** [I] [非正式用语]泄露(秘密) xièlòu: *You promised not to ~*. 你保证过不泄密. **7** [习语] **all told** 总〔總〕共 zǒnggòng. **I 'told you so** [非正式用语]如我所言 rú wǒ suǒyán. **tell 'tales (about sb)** 揭人之短 jiē rén zhī duǎn. **tell the 'time** (看钟表)说出时〔時〕刻 shuōchū shíkè. **8** [短语动词] **tell A and B apart** 辨别(两者之差别) biànbié. **tell sb off** 斥责某人 chìzé mǒurén. **tell on sb** [非正式用语]揭发〔發〕某人 jiēfā mǒurén: *John told on his sister*. 约翰告他姐姐的状. **teller** *n* [C] **1** (银行)出纳员 chūnàyuán. **2** (选票)点〔點〕票员 diǎnpiàoyuán. **telling** *adj* 有效的 yǒuxiàode; 有力的 yǒulìde: *a ~ing argument* 有力的论据.

tell-tale /'telteɪl/ *n* [C] 搬弄是非者 bānnòng shìfēi zhě; 谈论〔論〕别人私事者 tánlùn biérén sīshì zhě. **tell-tale** *adj* 暴露内情的 bàolù nèiqíng de: *a ~ blush* 暴露隐情的脸红.

telly /'telɪ/ *n* [C, U] [*pl* **-ies**] [非正式用语] short for TELEVISION.

temerity /tɪ'merətɪ/ *n* [U] [正式用语]鲁莽 lǔmǎng; 冒失 màoshi.

temp /temp/ *n* [C] [非正式用语]临〔臨〕时〔時〕雇〔僱〕员 línshí gùyuán.

temper /'tempə(r)/ *n* **1** [C] 心情 xīnqíng; 情绪 qíngxù: *in a good/bad ~* 心情好(或不佳)的. **2** [sing, U] 怒气〔氣〕nùqì; 脾气 píqì: *in a ~* 在发脾气. **3** [习语] **keep/lose one's temper** 忍住(或发)脾气 rěnzhù píqi. **temper** *v* [T] 使缓和 shǐ huǎnhé; 减轻〔輕〕jiǎnqīng; 调和 tiáohé: *justice ~ed with mercy* 恩威兼施. **-tempered** /-tempəd/ (用以构成复合形容词)有某种〔種〕性情脾气的 yǒu mǒuzhǒng xìngqíng píqi de: *a ˌbad-'tempered man* 脾气不好的人.

temperament /'temprəmənt/ *n* [U, C] 性情 xìngqíng; 气〔氣〕质〔質〕qìzhì. **temperamental** /temprə'mentl / *adj* **1** 神经〔經〕质的 shénjīngzhìde; 情绪波动〔動〕的 qíngxù bōdòng de: *Children are often ~al*. 孩子们往往是情绪不稳定的. **2** 气质的 qìzhìde; 性格的 xìnggéde. **temperamentally** /-telɪ/ *adv*.

temperate /'tempərət/ *adj* **1** 有节〔節〕制的 yǒu jiézhì de; 不过〔過〕分的 bú guòfèn de. **2** (气候)温和的 wēnhéde.

temperature /'temprətʃə(r); *US* 'tempərtʃʊər/ *n* **1** [C, U] 温度 wēndù. **2** [习语] **have a 'temperature** 发〔發〕烧〔燒〕fāshāo.

tempest /'tempɪst/ *n* [C] [正式用语]暴风〔風〕雨 bàofēngyǔ. **tempestuous** /tem'pestʃʊəs/ *adj* 有暴风雨的 yǒu bàofēngyǔ de; 剧〔劇〕烈的 jùliède: [喻] *a tempestuous love-affair* 一场引起轩然大波的风流韵事.

temple[1] /'templ/ *n* [C] 神殿 shéndiàn; 庙〔廟〕宇 miàoyǔ; 寺院 sìyuàn.

temple[2] /'templ/ *n* [C] [解剖]太阳〔陽〕穴 tàiyángxué.

tempo /'tempəʊ/ *n* [C] [*pl* **~s**; 于第 2 义作 **tempi** /'tempi:/] **1** (行动、活动的)速度 sùdù: *the ~ of city life* 城市生活的节拍. **2** [音乐]速度 sùdù; 拍子 pāizi.

temporal /'tempərəl/ *adj* [正式用语] **1** 暂〔暫〕时〔時〕的 zànshíde; 时间上的 shíjiānshàngde. **2** 世俗的 shìsúde; 现世的 xiànshìde.

temporary /'temprərɪ; *US* -pərərɪ/ *adj* 暂〔暫〕时〔時〕的 zànshíde; 临〔臨〕时的 línshíde. **temporarily** /'temprərəlɪ; *US* ˌtempə'rerəlɪ/ *adv*.

tempt /tempt/ *v* [T] **1** 引诱(某人干坏事) yǐnyòu; 勾引 gōuyǐn: *Nothing could ~ her to tell lies*. 没有什么东西能诱使她说谎. **2** 吸引 xīyǐn; 诱导〔導〕yòudǎo.

temptation /temp'teɪʃn/ *n* **1** [U] 引诱 yǐnyòu; 勾引 gōuyǐn. **2** [C] 有迷惑力(或吸引力)之物 yǒu míhuòlì zhī wù. **tempting** *adj* 吸引人的 xīyǐnrénde: *a ~ing offer* 吸引人的提议.

ten /ten/ *pron*, *adj*, *n* [C] 十(的) shí. **tenth** *pron*, *adj* 第十(的) dìshí; 第十个〔個〕dìshígè. **tenth** *pron*, *n* [C] 十分之一 shífēn zhī yī.

tenable /'tenəbl/ *adj* **1** 可防守的 kě fángshǒu de; 守得住的 shǒudézhùde. **2** (职位)可保持的 kě bǎochí de, 可维持的 kě wéichí de.

tenacious /tɪ'neɪʃəs/ *adj* 抓紧〔緊〕的 zhuājǐnde; 顽强的 wánqiángde. **tenacity** /tɪ'næsətɪ/ *n* [U].

tenant /'tenənt/ *n* [C] 房客 fángkè; 佃户 diànhù. **tenancy** /-ənsɪ/ *n* [*pl* **-ies**] **1** [U] 租赁 zūlìn; 租佃 zūdiàn. **2** [C] 租期 zūqī.

tend[1] /tend/ *v* [I] *to* 倾向 qīngxiàng; 趋〔趨〕向于 qūxiàng yú: *He ~s to make too many mistakes*. 他常常错误百出.

tend[2] /tend/ *v* [T] [正式用语]照管 zhàoguǎn; 照料 zhàoliào: *shepherds ~ing their flocks* 照管羊群的牧羊人.

tendency /ˈtendənsɪ/ *n* [C] [*pl* -ies] **1** 趋〔趨〕向 qūxiàng；趋势〔勢〕qūshì：*a ～ to get fat* 发胖的趋势. **2**（事物运动或变化的）趋向 qūxiàng，倾向性 qīngxiàngxìng：*an increasing ～ for parents to help at school*. 越来越多的父母去学校帮助小孩儿念书.

tender[1] /ˈtendə(r)/ *adj* **1** 温和的 wēnhéde；亲〔親〕切的 qīnqiède. **2** 触〔觸〕痛的 chùtòngde；敏感的 mǐngǎnde. **3** 脆弱的 cuìruòde；易损坏〔壞〕的 yì sǔnhuài de. **4**（肉）嫩的 nènde. **tenderly** *adv*. **tenderness** *n* [U].

tender[2] /ˈtendə(r)/ *v* **1** [T] [正式用语]提供 tígōng；提出 tíchū：*He ～ed his resignation*. 他提出辞呈. **2** [I] (*for*) 投标〔標〕tóubiāo：～ *for the construction of a new motorway* 投标承建一条新的高速公路. **tender** *n* [C] 投标 tóubiāo.

tendon /ˈtendɒn/ *n* [C] 筋 jīn；腱 jiàn.

tenement /ˈtenəmənt/ *n* [C]（几家合住的）经〔經〕济〔濟〕公寓 jīngjì gōngyù.

tenet /ˈtenɪt/ *n* [C] [正式用语]原则 yuánzé；教义〔義〕jiàoyì；信条〔條〕xìntiáo.

tenner /ˈtenə(r)/ *n* [C] [英国非正式用语]十英镑(纸币) shí yīngbàng.

tennis /ˈtenɪs/ *n* [U] 网〔網〕球 wǎngqiú. ˈ**tennis court** *n* [C] 网球场〔場〕wǎngqiúchǎng.

tenor /ˈtenə(r)/ *n* [C] **1** (a) [音乐]男高音 nángāoyīn；男高音歌手 nángāoyīn gēshǒu；男高音乐〔樂〕曲 nángāoyīn yuèqǔ. (b) 次中音乐器 cì zhōngyīn yuèqì：*a ～ saxophone* 次中音萨克斯管. **2** [正式用语]大意 dàyì；要旨 yàozhǐ.

tenpin bowling /ˌtenpɪn ˈbəʊlɪŋ/ *n* [U]（十柱）保龄〔齡〕球 bǎolíngqiú.

tense[1] /tens/ *adj* [～r, ～st] **1** 拉紧〔緊〕的 lājǐnde. **2**（神经）紧张〔張〕的 jǐnzhāngde. **tense** *v* [I, T]（使）拉紧 lā jǐn；（使）紧张 jǐnzhāng：*He ～d his muscles*. 他紧绷着肌肉. **tensely** *adv*.

tense[2] /tens/ *n* [C] [语法]时〔時〕态〔態〕shítài：*the present / past / future ～* 现在(或过去、将来)时.

tension /ˈtenʃn/ *n* **1** [U] 拉紧〔緊〕lā jǐn；[物理]张〔張〕力 zhānglì；拉力 lālì：*the ～ of the rope* 这条绳索的拉力. **2** [U]（情绪、神经等的）紧张 jǐnzhāng；激动〔動〕jīdòng. **3** [U, C, 常作 pl] 紧张(局势) jǐnzhāng；不安(状态) bù'ān：*political ～(s)* 政治紧张的局势. **4** [U] 电〔電〕压〔壓〕diànyā：*high-～ cables* 高压电缆.

tent /tent/ *n* [C] 帐〔帳〕篷 zhàngpeng.

tentacle /ˈtentəkl/ *n* [C]（动物的）触〔觸〕角 chùjiǎo；触须〔鬚〕chùxū；触手 chùshǒu.

tentative /ˈtentətɪv/ *adj* 试验〔驗〕性的 shìyànxìngde；暂时的 zànshíde：*make a ～ offer* 提出试探性报价. **tentatively** *adv*.

tenterhooks /ˈtentəhʊks/ *n* [习语] (**be**) **on** ˈ**tenterhooks** 忧〔憂〕虑〔慮〕不安 yōulǜ bù'ān.

tenth ⇨ TEN.

tenuous /ˈtenjʊəs/ *adj* 单〔單〕薄的 dānbóde；纤〔纖〕细的 xiānxìde；细微的 xìwēide：*a ～ relationship* 微不足道的关系.

tepid /ˈtepɪd/ *adj* 温热〔熱〕的 wēnrède.

term /tɜːm/ *n* **1** [C] 期 qī；期间 qījiān；限期 xiànqī：*the president's ～ of office* 总统的任期. **2** [C] 学〔學〕期 xuéqī：*end-of-～ exams* 期终考试. **3** [C]（有专门意义的）词 cí；术〔術〕语 shùyǔ：*technical ～* 专业术语. **4 terms** [pl] (a)（协议的）条〔條〕件 tiáojiàn. (b)（买卖双方协定的）价〔價〕钱〔錢〕jiàqián. **5 terms** [pl] 说法 shuōfa；措辞〔辭〕cuòcí：*I'll explain this in general ～s first*. 我将首先对此作总的说明. **6** [习语] **be on good, friendly, bad** ˈ**terms with** (与某人)关〔關〕系〔係〕良好(或友善、恶劣) guānxì liánghǎo. **come to terms with sth** 终于接受 zhōngyú jiēshòu. **in the** ˈ**long/**ˈ**short term** 长〔長〕(或短)期 chángqī. **in terms of sth** 关于… guānyú…；以…观〔觀〕点〔點〕yǐ…guāndiǎn：*in ～s of economics* 从经济原则来看. **term** *v* [T] 将(某人、某物)称〔稱〕为〔爲〕… jiāng chēngwéi ….

terminal /ˈtɜːmɪnl/ *adj*（致死疾病）晚期的 wǎnqīde，末期的 mòqīde. **terminal** *n* [C] **1**（民用）航空集散站 hángkōng jísànzhàn. **2**（计算机的）终端 zhōngduān. **terminally** /-nəlɪ/ *adv*.

terminate /ˈtɜːmɪneɪt/ *v* [I, T] 终止 zhōngzhǐ；结束 jiéshù. **termination** /ˌtɜːmɪˈneɪʃn/ *n* [U, C] 终止 zhōngzhǐ；终点〔點〕zhōngdiǎn；结束 jiéshù；结局 jiéjú：*the termination of a contract* 合约的终止.

terminology /ˌtɜːmɪˈnɒlədʒɪ/ *n* [U, C] [*pl* -ies] 术〔術〕语 shùyǔ；专〔專〕业〔業〕名词 zhuānyè míngcí.

terminus /ˈtɜːmɪnəs/ *n* [C] [*pl* -ni /-naɪ/ 或 ～es]（铁路、公路、公共汽车的）终点〔點〕(站) zhōngdiǎn.

termite /ˈtɜːmaɪt/ *n* [C] 白蚁〔蟻〕báiyǐ.

terrace /ˈterəs/ *n* [C] **1** 一排房屋 yìpái fángwū. **2**（房侧的）铺砌地面 pūqì dìmiàn. **3** 梯田 tītián. **4**（梯级宽的露天）台阶〔階〕táijiē. **terrace** *v* [T] 使成阶梯 shǐ chéng jiētī；开〔開〕成梯田 kāi chéng tītián：*～d houses* 梯级状的成排房屋.

terrain /teˈreɪn, ˈtereɪn/ *n* [C, U] 地面 dìmiàn；地形 dìxíng；地带〔帶〕dìdài：*hilly ～* 丘陵地带.

terrestrial /təˈrestrɪəl/ *adj* **1** 陆〔陸〕地(上)的 lùdìde；陆生的 lùshēngde. **2** 地球(上)的 dìqiúde.

T

terrible /ˈterəbl/ *adj* 1 可怕的 kěpàde;骇人的 hàirénde;令人极〔極〕不舒服的 lìng rén jí bù shūfu de: *a ~ war / accident* 可怕的战争(或意外事件). 2 难〔難〕以忍受的 nán yǐ rěnshòu de;极端的 jíduānde: *~ toothache* 难以忍受的牙痛. 3 [非正式用语]极坏〔壞〕的 jíhuàide;很糟的 hěnzāode. *What ~ food!* 伙食多么糟糕啊! **terribly** *adv* [非正式用语]很 hěn;非常 fēicháng: *~ busy* 非常忙.

terrier /ˈterɪə(r)/ *n* [C] 㹴(一种小狗) gēng.

terrific /təˈrɪfɪk/ *adj* [非正式用语] 1 很大的 hěndàde;极〔極〕端的 jíduānde: *a ~ storm* 狂风暴雨. 2 极好的 jíhǎode;了不起的 liǎobùqǐde. **terrifically** /-klɪ/ *adv* 极度地 jídùde;非常 fēicháng.

terrify /ˈterɪfaɪ/ *v* [*pt*, *pp* -ied] [T] 使恐怖 shǐ kǒngbù;恐吓〔嚇〕kǒnghè: *I'm terrified of dogs.* 我怕狗.

territorial /ˌterəˈtɔːrɪəl/ *adj* 领土的 lǐngtǔde;领地的 lǐngdìde.

territory /ˈterətrɪ; *US* -tɔːrɪ/ *n* [C, U] [*pl* -ies] 1 领土 lǐngtǔ;版图〔圖〕bǎntú: *Spanish ~* 西班牙的领土. 2 (人、动物占领的)领地 lǐngdì. 3 (某人负责的)地区〔區〕(或范围) dìqū.

terror /ˈterə(r)/ *n* (a) [U] 恐怖 kǒngbù;惊〔驚〕骇 jīnghài. (b) [C] 引起恐怖的事物 yǐnqǐ kǒngbù de shìwù. **terrorism** /-rɪzəm/ *n* [U] 恐怖主义〔義〕kǒngbù zhǔyì. **terrorist** *adj*, *n* [C]. **terrorize** *v* [T] 充满恐怖 chōngmǎn kǒngbù;使恐惧〔懼〕shǐ kǒngjù;恐吓〔嚇〕kǒnghè.

terse /tɜːs/ *adj* (说话、文笔等)精练〔練〕的 jīngliànde;简明的 jiǎnmíngde. **tersely** *adv*. **terseness** *n* [U].

test /test/ *n* [C] 1 (对人,事物的)试验〔驗〕shìyàn;测验 cèyàn: *a ˈdriving ~* 驾驶考试. *a ˈblood ~* 验血. 2 (对知识或能力的)考查 kǎochá,测试 cèshì. **test** *v* [T] 测验 cèyàn;试验 shìyàn;检〔檢〕验 jiǎnyàn. ˈ**test match** *n* [C] (板球、橄榄球等的)国〔國〕际〔際〕比赛 guójì bǐsài. ˈ**test-tube** *n* [C] 试管 shìguǎn.

testament /ˈtestəmənt/ *n* [C] [正式用语] 1 (*to*) 确〔確〕实〔實〕的证〔證〕明 quèshí de zhèngmíng. 2 **Testament** [基督教](两部)圣〔聖〕经〔經〕(之一) shèngjīng: *the New T~* 《新约全书》.

testicle /ˈtestɪkl/ *n* [C] 睾丸 gāowán.

testify /ˈtestɪfaɪ/ *v* [*pt*, *pp* -ied] [I, T] 1 证〔證〕明 zhèngmíng;证实〔實〕zhèngshí;声〔聲〕明 shēngmíng. 2 (*to*) [正式用语]成为〔爲〕…的证据〔據〕chéngwéi…de zhèngjù.

testimonial /ˌtestɪˈməʊnɪəl/ *n* [C] 1 (能力、资格、品德等的)证〔證〕明书〔書〕zhèngmíngshū. 2 奖〔獎〕品 jiǎngpǐn;奖状〔狀〕jiǎngzhuàng.

testimony /ˈtestɪmənɪ; *US* -məʊnɪ/ *n* [U, C] [*pl* -ies] 证〔證〕据〔據〕zhèngjù;证言 zhèngyán.

tetanus /ˈtetənəs/ *n* [U] 破伤〔傷〕风〔風〕pòshāngfēng.

tether /ˈteðə(r)/ *n* [C] (拴牲口的)系〔繫〕绳〔繩〕xìshéng;系链 xìliàn. **tether** *v* [T] (用绳、链)拴 shuān.

text /tekst/ *n* 1 [U] 正文 zhèngwén;本文 běnwén. 2 [C] 原文 yuánwén. 3 [C] (指定要学的)书〔書〕shū;必读〔讀〕书 bìdú shū. 4 [C] (《圣经》中的)经〔經〕文 jīngwén,经句 jīngjù. **text** *v* [T] 发〔發〕送文字信息给 fāsòng wénzì xìnxī gěi. [I] 发送文字信息 fāsòng wénzì xìnxī. ˈ**textbook** *n* [C] 教科书 jiàokēshū. ˈ**text message** *n* [C] 文字信息 wénzì xìnxī. ˈ**text messaging** *n* [U] 文字信息发送 wénzì xìnxī fāsòng. **textual** /ˈtekstʃʊəl/ *adj* [正式用语]正文的 zhèngwénde;原文的 yuánwénde;在正文中的 zài zhèngwén zhōng de;在教科书内的 zài jiàokēshū nèi de.

textile /ˈtekstaɪl/ *n* [C, 常作 pl] 纺织〔織〕品 fǎngzhīpǐn.

texture /ˈtekstʃə(r)/ *n* [C, U] (织物的)质〔質〕地 zhìdì, 外观〔觀〕wàiguān.

than /ðən, 罕强式 ðæn/ *conj*, *prep* 1 比 bǐ: *Sylvia is taller ~ me.* 西尔维亚比我高. 2 (用于 *more* 或 *less* 后表示时间、距离等的比较关系): *It cost more ~ £100.* 这个东西值100多英镑. *It's less ~ a mile to the station.* 离车站不到一英里.

thank /θæŋk/ *v* 1 [T] 道谢 dàoxiè;感谢 gǎnxiè. 2 [习语] ˌno, ˈ**thank you** 不了,谢谢你 bùle, xièxie nǐ. ˈ**thank you** 谢谢你 xièxie nǐ. **thankful** *adj* 感谢的 gǎnxiède;感激的 gǎnjīde. **thankfully** *adv*. **thankless** *adj* 不感谢的 bù gǎnxiè de: *a ~less task* 吃力不讨好的工作. **thanks** *n* [pl] 1 谢意 xièyì;谢忱 xièchén. 2 [习语] **thanks to sb/sth** 由于 yóuyú;因为〔爲〕yīnwéi;幸亏〔虧〕xìngkuī. **thanks** *interj* [非正式用语]谢谢你 xièxie nǐ. ˈ**thanksgiving** *n* [C, U] 1 感恩 gǎn'ēn;感恩祈祷〔禱〕gǎn'ēn qídǎo. 2 **Thanksgiving (Day)** (美国、加拿大的)感恩节〔節〕Gǎn'ēnjié.

that[1] /ðæt/ *adj*, *pron* [*pl* **those** /ðəʊz/] 1 那 nà;那个〔個〕nàge: *Look at ~ man standing there.* 瞧站在那儿的那个男人. *Those are nice hats.* 那些是精美的帽子. 2 [习语] **that is (to say)** 就是说 jiùshì shuō;即 jí. **that** *adv* 如此 rúcǐ;那样〔樣〕nàyàng: *The film wasn't ~ bad.* 这电影并不那么差劲.

that[2] /ðət, 罕强式 ðæt/ *conj* [引导各种从句]: *She said ~ she would come.* 她说她要来.

T

that[3] /ðət, 罕强式 ðæt/ *relative pron* 1 [在从句中作动词的主语]: *You're the only person ~ can help me.* 你是唯一能帮助我的人. 2 [在从句中作动词的宾语, 但常被省略]: *The pen ~ you gave me is a nice one.* 你给我的那支笔是一支好笔.

thatch /θætʃ/ *n* [C, U] 茅屋顶 máowūdǐng. **thatch** *v* [T] 用茅草盖〔蓋〕(屋顶) yòng máocǎo gài.

thaw /θɔː/ *v* 1 [I, T] (冰、雪等)(使)融化 rónghuà. 2 [T] 使化成水 shǐ huàchéng shuǐ; 使软化 shǐ ruǎnhuà: *~ frozen food* 化开冰冻的食物. 3 [I] [喻](人、行为等)变〔變〕得友善 biàndé yǒushàn, 缓和 huǎnhé. **thaw** *n* [C, 常作 sing] (天气)解冻 jiědòng.

the /ðə, ðɪ 强式 ðiː/ *definite article* 1 (指特定的事物): *T~ sky was blue.* 天空是蓝色的. *Please close ~ window.* 请关窗. 2 (指一类中的所有人或物): *T~ dog is a popular pet.* 狗是一种流行的宠物. 3 (表示某集团或国籍): *~ rich* 富有者. *~ French* 法国人. 4 (用于地理名称前): *~ Mediterranean* 地中海. *~ Atlantic (Ocean)* 大西洋. 5 (用于乐器前): *play ~ piano* 弹钢琴. 6 (用于计量单位前): 每一… měi yī…: *paid by ~ hour* 以每小时计酬. 7 (用于形容词, 副词最高级前): *~ best day of your life* 你一生中最美好的一天. **the** *adv* (用于比较关系)愈 yù, 越 yuè: *T~ more I read, ~ less I understand.* 我越看越不懂.

theatre (美语 **theater**) /ˈθɪətə(r)/ *n* 1 [C] 戏〔戲〕院 xìyuàn; 剧〔劇〕场〔場〕 jùchǎng. 2 **the theatre** [sing] 剧本的写〔寫〕作和演出 jùběn de xiězuò hé yǎnchū. 3 [C] 讲〔講〕堂 jiǎngtáng; 会〔會〕场 huìchǎng. 4 [C] = OPERATING-THEATRE (OPERATE). ˈ**theatre-goer** *n* [C] 戏迷 xìmí. **theatrical** /θɪˈætrɪkl/ *adj* 1 戏院的 xìyuànde; 剧场的 jùchǎngde. 2 做作的 zuòzuòde; 不自然的 bú zìrán de.

theft /θeft/ *n* [C, U] 偷盗 tōudào.

their /ðeə(r)/ *adj* 他们的 tāmende; 她们的 tāmende; 它们的 tā mende: *They have lost ~ dog.* 他们的狗丢失了. **theirs** /ðeəz/ *pron* 他们的(东西) tāmende; 她们的(东西) tāmende: *That dog is ~, not ours.* 那只狗是他们的, 不是我们的.

them /ðəm; 强式 ðem/ *pron* 1 (用作动词或介词的宾语): *Give ~ to me.* 把它们给我. *Did you eat all of ~?* 你是否都吃光了? 2 [非正式用语] (用以代替 *him* 或 *her*): *If someone comes in, ask ~ to wait.* 如果有人来, 请他等一会儿.

theme /θiːm/ *n* [C] 1 题目 tímù; 主题 zhǔtí. 2 [音乐]主题 zhǔtí; 主旋律 zhǔ xuánlǜ. ˈ**theme park** *n* [C] (有专题娱乐活动的)专〔專〕题乐〔樂〕园〔園〕 zhuāntí lèyuán. ˈ**theme song** *n* [C] 主题歌 zhǔtígē.

themselves /ðəmˈselvz/ *pron* 1 [反身]他们自己 tāmen zìjǐ; 她们自己 tāmen zìjǐ; 它们本身 tāmen běnshēn: *They ˈhurt ~.* 他们伤害了自己. 2 (用于加强语气): *They ~ have often made that mistake.* 他们自己也常犯那个错误. 3 [习语] (**all**) **by themˈselves** (a) 独〔獨〕自地 dúzìde; 单〔單〕独地 dāndúde. (b) 独力地 dúlìde; 无〔無〕助地 wúzhùde.

then /ðen/ *adv* 1 当〔當〕时〔時〕 dāngshí; 届时 jièshí: *I was still unmarried ~.* 那时我还未结婚. 2 然后〔後〕 ránhòu; 接着 jiēzhe; 于是 yúshì: *We stayed in Rome and ~ in Naples.* 我们先住在罗马, 后来住在那不勒斯. 3 那么〔麽〕 nàme; 因此 yīncǐ: '*It isn't here.*' '*T~ it must be in the car.*' "它不在这儿." "那么, 它一定在汽车里." 4 而且 érqiě; 还〔還〕有 háiyǒu: *There's the soup to heat, ~ there's the bread to butter.* 汤要加热, 还有面包要涂黄油.

thence /ðens/ *adv* [古][正式用语] 从〔從〕那里〔裏〕 cóng nàlǐ.

theology /θɪˈɒlədʒɪ/ *n* [U] 神学〔學〕 shénxué. **theologian** /ˌθɪəˈləʊdʒən/ *n* [C]. **theological** /ˌθɪəˈlɒdʒɪkl/ *adj*.

theorem /ˈθɪərəm/ *n* [C] [数学]命题 mìngtí; 定理 dìnglǐ.

theory /ˈθɪərɪ/ *n* [*pl* -ies] 1 [C] 学〔學〕说 xuéshuō; 论〔論〕 lùn: *Darwin's ~ of evolution* 达尔文的进化论. 2 [U] (与实践相对的)理论 lǐlùn, 道理 dàolǐ. **theoretical** /ˌθɪəˈretɪkl/ *adj*.

therapeutic /ˌθerəˈpjuːtɪk/ *adj* 治疗〔療〕的 zhìliáode; 疗法的 liáofǎde.

therapy /ˈθerəpɪ/ *n* [U] 治疗〔療〕 zhìliáo; 疗法 liáofǎ. **therapist** *n* [C].

there[1] /ðeə(r)/ *adv* 1 在那里〔裏〕 zài nàlǐ; 往那里 wǎng nàlǐ: *We'll soon be ~.* 不久我们就去那里. 2 在那点〔點〕上 zài nàdiǎn shang; 在那个〔個〕方面 zài nàge fāngmiàn: *Don't stop ~!* 别在那儿停! 3 (用以引起注意): *T~'s the bell for lunch.* 午饭铃响了. 4 [习语] ˌ**there and ˈthen** 当〔當〕场〔場〕 dāngchǎng; 当时〔時〕 dāngshí. **there** *interj* 1 (用以表示胜利、沮丧、鼓励等): *T~! You've woken the baby!* 看! 你把孩子吵醒了. 2 (用以安慰幼儿): *T~, ~! You'll soon feel better.* 好啦, 好啦! 你呆一会儿就好了.

there[2] /ðə(r); 强式 ðeə(r)/ *adv* (用作动词, 尤其是 *be* 的主语): *T~'s a man at the door.* 门口有人.

thereabouts /ˈðeərəbaʊts/ *adv* 在那附近 zài nà fùjìn; 左右 zuǒyòu; 前后〔後〕 qiánhòu; 大约 dàyuē.

T

thereafter /ˌðeərˈɑːftə(r); *US* -ˈæf-/ *adv* [正式用语]此后〔後〕cǐhòu; 其后 qí hòu.

thereby /ˌðeəˈbaɪ/ *adv* [正式用语] 借〔藉〕以 jièyǐ; 从〔從〕而 cóng'ér; 由此 yóucǐ.

therefore /ˈðeəfɔː(r)/ *adv* 所以 suǒyǐ; 因此 yīncǐ.

thereupon /ˌðeərəˈpɒn/ *adv* [正式用语]于是 yúshì; 因而 yīn'ér.

thermal /ˈθɜːml/ *adj* **1** 热〔熱〕的 rède; 热量的 rèliàngde. **2** (衣物)保暖的 bǎonuǎnde; 防寒的 fánghánde.

thermometer /θəˈmɒmɪtə(r)/ *n* [C] 温度计 wēndùjì; 寒暑表 hánshǔbiǎo.

Thermos (亦作 ˈ**Thermos flask**) /ˈθɜːməs/ *n* [C] (*P*)保暖瓶 bǎonuǎnpíng; 热〔熱〕水瓶 rèshuǐpíng.

thermostat /ˈθɜːməstæt/ *n* [C] 恒温器 héngwēnqì.

thesaurus /θɪˈsɔːrəs/ *n* [C] [*pl* ~**es** 或 -**ri** /-raɪ/] 类〔類〕属〔屬〕词典 lèishǔ cídiǎn.

these ⇨THIS.

thesis /ˈθiːsɪs/ *n* [C] [*pl* **theses** /ˈθiːsiːz/] **1** 论〔論〕文 lùnwén. **2** 学〔學〕位论文 xuéwèi lùnwén.

they /ðeɪ/ *pron* [主格] **1** 他们 tāmen; 她们 tāmen; 它们 tāmen. **2** 人们 rénmen: *T~ say we're going to have a hot summer*. 人家说今年夏天将很热. **3** [非正式用语](用以代替 *he* 或 *she*): *If anyone comes late, ~'ll have to wait*. 谁要是迟到,他就得等着.

they'd /ðeɪd/ **1** they had ⇨HAVE. **2** they would ⇨WILL[1], WOULD[1].

they'll /ðeɪl/ they will ⇨WILL[1].

they're /ðeə(r)/ they are ⇨BE.

they've /ðeɪv/ they have ⇨HAVE.

thick /θɪk/ *adj* **1** 厚的 hòude; 粗的 cūde: *a ~ slice of bread* 厚厚的一片面包. *a wall 2 feet ~* 两英尺厚的墙. **2** 密的 mìde; 密集的 mìjíde; 茂密的 màomìde: *~ hair* 浓密的头发. *a ~ forest* 茂密的森林. **3** (液体)浓〔濃〕的 nóngde; 稠的 chóude; 半固体〔體〕的 bàn gùtǐde. **4** 阴〔陰〕霾的 yīnmáide; 不清明的 bù qīngmíng de: *a ~ fog* 浓雾. **5** [非正式用语] 愚笨的 yúbènde; 迟〔遲〕钝的 chídùnde. **thick** *adv* **1** 厚厚地 hòuhòude; 浓〔濃〕浓地 nóngnóngde: *spread the butter too ~* 黄油涂得太厚了. **2** [习语] ˌ**thick and** ˈ**fast** 又快又多 yòu kuài yòu duō. **thick** *n* [习语] **in the thick of sth** 某事物最活跃〔躍〕的部分 mǒu shìwù zuì huóyuè de bùfen. **through** ˌ**thick and** ˈ**thin** 在艰〔艱〕险〔險〕的情况下 zài jiānxiǎn de qíngkuàng xià. **thicken** *v* [I, T] (使)变〔變〕厚 biàn hòu; (使)变浓 biàn nóng: *~en the soup* 使肉汁变浓. **thickly** *adv*. **thickness** *n* **1** [U] 厚 hòu; 厚度 hòudù; 浓 nóng; 浓度 nóngdù: *4 centimetres in ~ness* 四厘米厚. **2** [C] (一)层〔層〕céng. ˌ**thick**ˈ**set** *adj* (身体)矮胖的 ǎipàngde, 结实〔實〕的 jiēshíde. ˌ**thick**-ˈ**skinned** *adj* 脸〔臉〕皮厚的 liǎnpí hòu de; 感觉〔覺〕迟〔遲〕钝的 gǎnjué chídùn de.

thicket /ˈθɪkɪt/ *n* [C] 灌木丛〔叢〕guànmùcóng.

thief /θiːf/ *n* [C] [*pl* **thieves** /θiːvz/] 贼 zéi. **thieve** /θiːv/ *v* [I, T] 偷窃〔竊〕tōuqiè; 做贼 zuò zéi.

thigh /θaɪ/ *n* [C] 大腿 dàtuǐ; 股 gǔ.

thimble /ˈθɪmbl/ *n* [C] 顶针箍 dǐngzhēngū.

thin /θɪn/ *adj* [~**ner**, ~**nest**] **1** 薄的 bóde; 细的 xìde. **2** 瘦的 shòude. **3** (液体)稀薄的 xībóde, 淡的 dànde: *~ soup* 淡汤. **4** 稀疏的 xīshūde: *~ hair* 稀疏的头发. *The audience is rather ~ tonight*. 今晚听众很少. **5** 显〔顯〕而易见的 xiǎn ér yì jiàn de; 透明的 tòumíngde: *a ~ mist* 薄雾. **6** 弱的 ruòde; 无〔無〕力的 wúlìde: *a ~ excuse* 勉强的借口. **7** [习语] **the thin end of the** ˈ**wedge** 可引起严〔嚴〕重后〔後〕果的小事 kě yǐnqǐ yánzhòng hòuguǒ de xiǎoshì. **thin** *adv* 薄 bó; 稀 xī; 细 xì; 疏 shū: *cut the bread too ~* 面包切得太薄了. **thin** *v* [-**nn**-] [I, T] (使)变〔變〕薄 biàn bó; (使)变稀 biàn xī; (使)变淡 biàn dàn; (使)变细 biàn xì; (使)变瘦 biàn shòu. **thinly** *adv*. **thinness** *n* [U].

thing /θɪŋ/ *n* **1** [C] 物 wù; 事物 shìwù; 东西 dōngxi: *What is that ~ on the table?* 桌子上的东西是什么? **2 things** [pl] **(a)** (个人的)用品 yòngpǐn, 用具 yòngjù, 所有物 suǒyǒuwù: *Bring your swimming ~s*. 带上你的游泳用品. **(b)** 情况 qíngkuàng; 景况 jǐngkuàng; 形势〔勢〕xíngshì: *How are ~s?* 景况如何? **3** [C] 任务〔務〕rènwù; 工作 gōngzuò; 做法 zuòfǎ. **4** [C] 题目 tímù; 主题 zhǔtí: *There's another ~ I want to ask you about*. 我还有一件事要问你. **5** [C] (用以指人或动物)东西 dōngxi; 家伙 jiāhuo: *She's a sweet little ~*. 她是个可爱的小家伙. **6 the thing** [sing] **(a)** 最适〔適〕合的东西 zuì shìhé de dōngxi: *A holiday will be just the ~ for you*. 休假将对你正合适. **(b)** 时〔時〕髦的式样〔樣〕shímáode shìyàng; 风〔風〕行的型式 fēngxíngde xíngshì. **7** [习语] **for** ˈ**one thing** 首先 shǒuxiān; 一则 yìzé. **have a thing about sb / sth** [非正式用语]感到厌〔厭〕恶〔惡〕gǎndào yànwù. **the** ˌ**thing** ˈ**is** 要考虑〔慮〕的问题是 yào kǎolǜ de wèntí shì.

think /θɪŋk/ *v* [*pt*, *pp* **thought** /θɔːt/] **1** [I] 想 xiǎng; 思索 sīsuǒ; 考虑〔慮〕kǎolǜ. **2** [T] 认〔認〕为〔為〕rènwéi; 以为 yǐwéi: *Do you ~ it's going to rain?* 你以为天会下雨吗? **3** [T] 想像 xiǎngxiàng: *I can't ~ why* *he came*. 我想像不出他来干什么. 4 [T] 打算 dǎsuàn; 想要 xiǎng yào: *I ~ I'll go for a swim*. 我打算去游泳. 5 [习语] **think a'loud** 自言自语 zìyán zìyǔ; 说出(自己的)想法 shuō chū xiǎngfǎ. **think better of (doing) sth** 经〔經〕考虑后决定不做某事 jīng kǎolǜ hòu juédìng búzuò mǒushì. **think highly, a lot, a little, etc of sb / sth** 评价〔價〕高(或不高等) píngjià gāo: *I don't ~ much of our new teacher*. 我认为我们的新老师不怎么样. **think nothing of sth** 认为(做某事)很平常(或轻松) rènwéi hěn píngcháng. 6 [短语动词] **think about sth** 考虑 kǎolǜ; 盘〔盤〕算 pánsuàn. **think of sth** (a) 考虑 kǎolǜ; 思考 sīkǎo. (b) 考虑(可能的方案) kǎolǜ: *We're ~ing of going to Venice*. 我们正考虑去威尼斯. (c) 想像 xiǎngxiàng; 想一想 xiǎng yì xiǎng: *Just ~ of the cost!* 想一想那费用吧! (d) 想起 xiǎngqǐ: *I can't ~ of her name*. 我记不起她的名字了. **think sth out / through** 仔细思考 zǐxì sīkǎo; 全面考虑 quánmiàn kǎolǜ. **think sth over** 慎重考虑 shènzhòng kǎolǜ. **think sth up** 想出 xiǎngchū; 设计出 shèjìchū. **think** *n* [sing] [非正式用语]想 xiǎng; 想法 xiǎngfǎ.

thinker /ˈθɪŋkə(r)/ *n* [C] 思想家 sīxiǎngjiā: *a great ~* 一位伟大的思想家.

thinking /ˈθɪŋkɪŋ/ *n* [U] 思想 sīxiǎng; 想法 xiǎngfǎ. **thinking** *adj* 思想的 sīxiǎngde; 有思想的 yǒu sīxiǎng de.

third /θɜːd/ *pron, adj* 第三(的) dìsān. **third** *pron, n* [C] 三分之一 sānfēn zhī yī. **the ˌthird deˈgree** *n* [sing] 疲劳〔勞〕讯问 píláo xùnwèn; 逼供 bīgòng. **thirdly** *adv*. **ˌthird ˈparty** *n* [C] 第三者 dìsānzhě: *ˌ~-party inˈsurance* 第三者责任保险. **the ˌthird ˈperson** *n* [sing] [语法]第三人称〔稱〕 dìsān rénchēng. **ˌthird-ˈrate** *adj* 三等的 sānděngde; 下等的 xiàděngde. **the ˌThird ˈWorld** *n* [sing] 第三世界 dìsān shìjiè.

thirst /θɜːst/ *n* 1 [U, sing] 渴 kě; 口渴 kǒukě. 2 [sing] [喻]渴望 kěwàng; 热望 rèwàng: *a ~ for knowledge* 求知欲. **thirst** *v* [短语动词] **thirst for sth** 渴望 kěwàng; 热望 rèwàng: *~ for revenge* 渴望复仇. **thirsty** *adj* [-ier, -iest] 渴的 kěde; 使人口渴的 shǐ rén kǒukě de; 渴望的 kěwàng de.

thirteen /ˌθɜːˈtiːn / *pron, adj, n* [C] 十三(的) shísān. **thirteenth** /ˌθɜːˈtiːnθ/ *pron, adj* 第十三(的) dìshísān. **thirteenth** *pron, n* [C] 十三分之一 shísānfēn zhī yī.

thirty /ˈθɜːtɪ/ *pron, adj, n* [C] [*pl* -ies] 三十(的) sānshí. **thirtieth** /ˈθɜːtɪəθ / *pron, adj* 第三十(的) dìsānshí. **thirtieth** *pron, n* [C] 三十分之一 sānshífēn zhī yī.

this /ðɪs/ *adj, pron* [*pl* **these** /ðiːz /] 1 这〔這〕 zhè; 这个〔個〕 zhège: *Look at ~ box*. 看这个盒子. 2 [非正式用语] 某 mǒu; 某个 mǒuge: *Then ~ man came in*. 接着,有人进来了. **this** *adv* 如此 rúcǐ; 这样地 zhèyàngde: *It was about ~ high*. 它大约有这么高.

thistle /ˈθɪsl/ *n* [C] [植物]蓟 jì.

thong /θɒŋ; *US* θɔːŋ/ *n* [C] 皮条〔條〕 pítiáo; 皮鞭 píbiān.

thorn /θɔːn/ *n* 1 (a) [C] 刺 cì; 棘 jí. (b) [C, U] 荆棘 jīngjí. 2 [习语] **a thorn in one's flesh / side** 经〔經〕常使人烦恼〔惱〕的人(或事物) jīngcháng shǐ rén fánnǎo de rén. **thorny** *adj* [-ier, -iest] 1 有刺的 yǒucìde; 多刺的 duōcìde. 2 [喻] 棘手的 jíshǒude; 多困难〔難〕的 duō kùnnan de: *a ~y problem* 棘手的问题.

thorough /ˈθʌrə; *US* ˈθʌrəʊ/ *adj* 1 彻〔徹〕底的 chèdǐde; 完善的 wánshànde; 详尽〔盡〕的 xiángjìnde. 2 (办事)周到的 zhōudàode, 全面的 quánmiànde, 仔细的 zǐxìde. **ˈthorough-going** *adj* 彻底的 chèdǐde; 十足的 shízúde: *a ˌ~going reˈvision* 彻底修订. **thoroughly** *adv*. **thoroughness** *n* [U].

thoroughbred /ˈθʌrəbred/ *n* [C], *adj* (犬、马等)良种〔種〕(的) liángzhǒng; 纯种(的) chúnzhǒng.

thoroughfare /ˈθʌrəfeə(r)/ *n* [C] [正式用语]大街 dàjiē; 通道 tōngdào.

those *pl* of THAT[1].

though /ðəʊ/ *conj* 1 虽〔雖〕然 suīrán; 尽〔儘〕管 jǐnguǎn: *They bought the car, even ~ they couldn't really afford it*. 他们买汽车,尽管他们不可能真正买得起它. 2 可是 kěshì; 然而 rán'ér; 不过〔過〕 búguò: *It's possible, ~ unlikely*. 这是可能的,然而是靠不住的. **though** *adv* 可是 kěshì; 然而 rán'ér: *I expect you're right—I'll ask him, ~*. 我希望你是对的——然而我还要问问他.

thought[1] *pt, pp* of THINK.

thought[2] /θɔːt/ *n* 1 [C] 想法 xiǎngfǎ; 意见 yìjiàn. 2 [U] 思想 sīxiǎng; 思维能力 sīwéi nénglì. 3 [U] 思潮 sīcháo; 思想 sīxiǎng: *modern scientific ~* 现代科学思想. 4 [U, C] 关〔關〕心 guānxīn; 顾〔顧〕虑〔慮〕 gùlǜ; 挂〔掛〕念 guàniàn. 5 [习语] **second ˈthoughts** 改变〔變〕想法 gǎibiàn xiǎngfǎ. **thoughtful** *adj* 1 深思的 shēnsīde; 思考的 sīkǎode. 2 关心的 guānxīnde; 体〔體〕贴的 tǐtiēde. **thoughtfully** *adv*. **thoughtless** 不关心别人的 bù guānxīn biérén de; 自私的 zìsīde. **thoughtlessly** *adv*.

thousand /ˈθaʊznd/ *pron, adj, n* [C] 1 千 qiān. 2 (亦作 **thousands** [pl]) [非正式用语] 许许多多 xǔxǔ duōduō; 无〔無〕数〔數〕 wúshù:

T

A ~ thanks. 多谢. thousandth /ˈθaʊznθ/ *pron, adj* 第一千(的) dìyìqiān. thousandth *pron, n* [C] 千分之一 qiānfēn zhī yī.

thrash /θræʃ/ *v* 1 [T] (用鞭、棍等)痛打 tòngdǎ. 2 [T] 打败 dǎbài; 胜〔勝〕过〔過〕 shèngguò. 3 [I] 猛烈地移动〔動〕 měngliède yídòng; 颠簸 diānbǒ: *He ~ed about in the water*. 他用力打着水游泳. 4 [短语动词] thrash sth out 研讨并〔並〕解决(问题) yántǎo bìng jiějué. thrashing *n* [C] 1 殴〔毆〕打 ōudǎ; 痛打 tòngdǎ. 2 失败 shībài; 大败 dàbài.

thread /θred/ *n* 1 [C, U] (一段)线〔綫〕 xiàn. 2 [C] [喻]思路 sīlù; 线索 xiànsuǒ. 3 [C] 螺纹 luówén. thread *v* [T] 1 穿线于 chuān xiàn yú; 将〔將〕线穿过〔過〕 jiāng xiàn chuān guò. 2 把(珍珠等)穿成一串 bǎ chuān chéng yīchuàn. 3 把(影片、磁带等)装〔裝〕进〔進〕(机器) bǎ zhuāng jìn. 4 [习语] thread one's way through (sth) (小心地)挤〔擠〕过 jǐguò. ˈthreadbare /-beə(r)/ *adj* (衣服等)穿旧〔舊〕的 chuānjiùde.

threat /θret/ *n* 1 [C, U] 恐吓〔嚇〕 kǒnghè; 威胁〔脅〕 wēixié. 2 [C] 造成威胁的人或事物 zàochéng wēixié de rén huò shìwù: *He is a ~ to society*. 他是一个有害社会的危险分子. 3 [C, 常作 sing] 坏〔壞〕兆头〔頭〕 huài zhàotou; 不祥之兆 bùxiáng zhī zhào.

threaten /ˈθretn/ *v* 1 [T] 恐吓〔嚇〕 kǒnghè; 威胁〔脅〕 wēixié; 要挟〔挾〕 yāoxié: *They ~ed to kill all the passengers*. 他们要挟要杀掉全部乘客. 2 [I, T] 预示 yùshì: *Black clouds ~ rain*. 乌云预示要下雨. 3 [I] (坏事)似将〔將〕发〔發〕生 sì jiāng fāshēng, 可能来临〔臨〕 kěnéng láilín: *Danger ~ed*. 随时有危险发生. 4 [T] 对〔對〕…造成威胁 duì… zàochéng wēixié. threatening *adj*. threateningly *adv*.

three /θriː/ *pron, adj, n* [C] 三(的) sān. ˌthree-diˈmensional *adj* 三维的 sānwéide; 三度的 sāndùde.

thresh /θreʃ/ *v* [T] 打(麦、谷等) dǎ.

threshold /ˈθreʃhəʊld/ *n* [C] [正式用语] 1 门槛〔檻〕 ménkǎn. 2 [喻]开〔開〕始 kāishǐ; 开端 kāiduān; 入门 rùmén: *on the ~ of a new career* 在新事业的开端.

threw *pt* of THROW.

thrift /θrɪft/ *n* [U] (金钱的)节〔節〕约 jiéyuē. thrifty *adj* [-ier, -iest].

thrill /θrɪl/ *n* [C] (a) (一阵)激动〔動〕 jīdòng. (b) 刺激性 cìjīxìng; 震颤感 zhènchàngǎn. thrill *v* [T] 使激动 shǐ jīdòng; 使兴〔興〕奋〔奮〕 shǐ xīngfèn. thriller *n* [C] 富于刺激性的小说、戏〔戲〕剧〔劇〕或电〔電〕影 fù yú cìjīxìng de xiǎoshuō、xìjù huò diànyǐng.

thrive /θraɪv/ *v* [*pt* thrived 或 throve /θrəʊv/, *pp* thrived 或 thriven /ˈθrɪvn/] [I] 繁荣〔榮〕 fánróng; 兴〔興〕旺 xīngwàng; 茁壮〔壯〕成长〔長〕 zhuózhuàng chéngzhǎng: *a thriving business* 生意兴隆的买卖.

throat /θrəʊt/ *n* [C] 1 咽喉 yānhóu. 2 颈〔頸〕前部 jǐng qiánbù.

throb /θrɒb/ *v* [-bb-] [I] (心脏、脉搏等)跳动〔動〕 tiàodòng, 悸动 jìdòng. throb *n* [C].

throes /θrəʊz/ *n* [习语] in the throes of sth 为〔爲〕某事而忙碌 wèi mǒushì ér mánglù.

thrombosis /θrɒmˈbəʊsɪs/ [*pl* -ses /-siːz/] *n* [C, U] 血栓(形成) xuèshuān.

throne /θrəʊn/ *n* 1 [C] (国王、女王的)宝〔寶〕座 bǎozuò, 御座 yùzuò. 2 the throne [sing] 王位 wángwèi; 王权〔權〕 wángquán.

throng /θrɒŋ; *US* θrɔːŋ/ *n* [C] [正式用语]人群 rénqún; 群众〔衆〕 qúnzhòng. throng *v* [I, T] 群集 qúnjí; 拥〔擁〕挤〔擠〕 yōngjǐ.

throttle /ˈθrɒtl/ *v* [T] 掐死 qiāsǐ; 勒死 lēisǐ. throttle *n* [C] (发动机的)节流阀 jiéliúfá.

through /θruː/ *prep* 1 穿过〔過〕 chuānguò; 通过 tōngguò: *The train went ~ the tunnel*. 火车通过隧道. *The River Thames flows ~ London*. 泰晤士河流经伦敦. 2 从〔從〕头〔頭〕到尾 cóngtóu dàowěi; 自始至终 zì shǐ zhì zhōng: *She won't live ~ the night*. 她活不过今天夜里了. 3 [美语] 一直到(并包括) yìzhí dào; 直至 zhízhì: *Monday ~ Thursday* 从星期一到星期四. 4 由于 yóuyú; 因为〔爲〕 yīnwéi; 经〔經〕由 jīngyóu: *arrange insurance ~ a bank* 经由一家银行安排保险. *The accident happened ~ lack of care*. 这个意外事件的发生是由于不小心. 5 越过(障碍) yuèguò: *smuggle drugs ~ customs* 偷运毒品过海关. through *adv* 1 穿过 chuānguò; 通过 tōngguò: *It's very crowded in here—can you get ~?* 这里很挤——你能过得去吗? 2 自始至终 zì shǐ zhì zhōng; 从头到尾 cóngtóu dàowěi. 3 通过障碍〔礙〕 tōngguò zhàng'ài: *The ambulance drove straight ~*. 救护车直闯过去. 4 [英国英语] 接通电〔電〕话 jiētōng diànhuà: *I tried to ring you but I couldn't get ~*. 我给你打过电话,但没有打通. 5 [习语] ˌthrough and ˈthrough 彻〔徹〕头彻尾地 chètóu chèwěi de. 6 [短语动词] be through (with sb / sth) 已结束(友谊等) yǐ jiéshù: *Keith and I are ~*. 基思和我已不来往了. through *adj* 直通的 zhítōngde; 直达〔達〕的 zhídáde: *a ~ train* 直达列车.

throughout /θruːˈaʊt/ *prep, adv* 1 各方面 gèfāngmiàn; 到处〔處〕 dàochù: *They're sold ~ the world*. 它们在全世界到处有售. 2 始终 shǐzhōng: *I watched the film and cried ~*. 我看那部电影时从头到尾哭个不停.

T

throw /θrəʊ/ *v* [*pl* threw /θruː/, *pp* ~n /θrəʊn/] 1 [I, T] 抛 pāo; 掷〔擲〕zhì; 投 tóu; 扔 rēng. 2 [T] 用力移动〔動〕(身体的某部分) yònglì yídòng: ~ *up one's hands in horror* 惊吓得举起双手. 3 [T] on / off 匆匆穿上(或脱下) cōngcōng chuānshang. 4 [T] 摔倒 shuāidǎo; 摔下 shuāixià: *The horse threw him*. 这马把他摔下来. 5 [T] [喻]投向 tóuxiàng: *She threw me an angry look*. 她对我怒目而视. *The trees threw long shadows on the grass*. 树在草地上投下长长的影子. 6 [T] (在陶钧上)制〔製〕作(陶坯) zhìzuò. 7 [T] [非正式用语]惊〔驚〕扰〔擾〕jīngrǎo; 使不安 shǐ bù'ān: *The interruptions threw him*. 诸多干扰使他心烦意乱. 8 [T] 使处〔處〕于某种〔種〕状〔狀〕态〔態〕shǐ chǔyú mǒuzhǒng zhuàngtài: *Hundreds were ~n out of work*. 数以百计的人失去了工作. 9 [T] 按动(开关) àndòng. 10 [T] 举〔舉〕行(聚会) jǔxíng. 11 [习语] throw cold water on sth ⇨ COLD[1]. throw a fit ⇨ FIT[3]. throw sb in at the deep end [非正式用语]强人所难〔難〕qiǎng rén suǒ nán. throw in the sponge / towel 认〔認〕输 rènshū. throw light on sth ⇨ LIGHT[1]. throw one's weight about 专〔專〕权〔權〕zhuānquán; 仗势〔勢〕欺人 zhàngshì qī rén. 12 [短语动词] throw sth away (a) 丢弃〔棄〕(某物) diūqì; 处理掉 chǔlǐdiào. (b) 浪费掉(机会) làngfèidiào. throw sth in 额外加赠 éwài jiāzèng. throw oneself into sth 积〔積〕极〔極〕地做(某事) jījíde zuò. throw sb / sth off 摆〔擺〕脱 bǎituō; 甩掉 shuǎidiào. throw oneself on sb / sth [正式用语] 依赖 yīlài; 听〔聽〕从〔從〕tīngcóng: ~ *oneself on the mercy of others* 恳求别人的宽恕. throw sb out 赶〔趕〕走(某人) gǎnzǒu. throw sth out 拒绝 jùjué; 否决 fǒujué. throw sth together 匆匆拼凑成 cōngcōng pīncòu chéng. throw up 呕〔嘔〕吐 ǒutù. throw sth up (a) 辞〔辭〕去(职业) cíqù. (b) 引起注意 yǐnqǐ zhùyì. throw *n* [C] 1 投 tóu; 掷 zhì; 抛 pāo; 扔 rēng. 2 投掷的距离〔離〕tóuzhìde jùlí. thrower *n* [C].

thru [美语] = THROUGH.

thrush /θrʌʃ/ *n* [C] 画〔畫〕眉鸟 huàméiniǎo.

thrust /θrʌst/ *v* [*pt*, *pp* thrust] [I, T] 猛推 měng tuī; 冲〔衝〕chōng; 刺 cì; 戳 chuō. thrust *n* 1 [C] 猛推 měng tuī; 冲 chōng; 刺 cì; 戳 chuō. 2 [U] (机器的)推力 tuīlì. 3 [U] [喻]要旨 yàozhǐ; 要点〔點〕yàodiǎn.

thud /θʌd/ *n* [C] 重击〔擊〕(软物)声〔聲〕zhòngjīshēng. thud *v* [-dd-] [I] 砰地落下(或打击) pēngde luòxià.

thug /θʌg/ *n* [C] 暴徒 bàotú; 恶〔惡〕棍 ègùn.

thumb /θʌm/ *n* [C] 1 大拇指 dàmǔzhǐ. 2 [习语] thumbs ˈup / ˈdown 肯定(或否定) kěndìng. under sb's ˈthumb 在某人的控制下 zài mǒurén de kòngzhì xià. thumb *v* 1 [I, T] (*through*) 以拇指翻动〔動〕(书页) yǐ mǔzhǐ fāndòng. 2 [习语] thumb a ˈlift (向过路车辆竖起拇指表示)要求免费搭车 yāoqiú miǎnfèi dāchē. ˈthumb-nail *n* [C] 拇指甲 mǔzhǐjiǎ. ˈthumb-nail *adj* 文字简洁〔潔〕的 wénzì jiǎnjié de: *a ~-nail sketch* 简略的描述. ˈthumbtack *n* [C] [美语]图〔圖〕钉 túdīng.

thump /θʌmp/ *v* 1 [I, T] 重击〔擊〕zhòngjī; 拳击 quánjī. 2 [I] 剧〔劇〕烈跳动〔動〕jùliè tiàodòng: *His heart ~ed with excitement*. 他兴奋得心头怦怦直跳. thump *n* [C] 重击声〔聲〕zhòngjīshēng; 砰然声 pēngránshēng.

thunder /ˈθʌndə(r)/ *n* [U] (a) 雷 léi; 雷声〔聲〕léishēng. (b) (似雷的)轰〔轟〕隆声 hōnglōngshēng: *the ~ of guns* 大炮的隆隆声. thunder *v* 1 [I] [与 *it* 连用]打雷 dǎléi: *It's been ~ing all night*. 夜间一直在打雷. 2 [I] 发〔發〕出雷鸣般的隆隆声 fāchū léimíngbānde lónglóngshēng. 3 [T] 大声说 dà shēng shuō. ˈthunder-bolt *n* [C] 1 雷电〔電〕交加 léidiàn jiāojiā. 2 [喻]意外的可怕事件. yìwàide kěpà shìjiàn; 晴天霹雳〔靂〕qíngtiān pīlì. ˈthunderclap *n* [C] 雷响〔響〕léixiǎng; 霹雳 pīlì. thunderous *adj* 雷声似的 léishēng shì de: *~ous applause* 雷鸣般的掌声. ˈthunderstorm *n* [C] 雷暴 léibào.

Thursday /ˈθɜːzdɪ/ *n* [U, C] 星期四 xīngqīsì.

thus /ðʌs/ *adv* [正式用语] 1 如此 rúcǐ. 2 因而 yīnér; 因此 yīncǐ; 所以 suǒyǐ.

thwart /θwɔːt/ *v* [T] [正式用语]阻挠〔撓〕zǔnáo; 阻止 zǔzhǐ.

thyme /taɪm/ *n* [U] [植物]百里香 bǎilǐxiāng.

thyroid /ˈθaɪrɔɪd/ thyroid ˈgland *n* [C] 甲状〔狀〕腺 jiǎzhuàngxiàn.

tiara /tɪˈɑːrə/ *n* [C] 妇〔婦〕女的冠状〔狀〕头〔頭〕饰 fùnǚde guānzhuàng tóushì.

tic /tɪk/ *n* [C] (尤指面肌)抽搐 chōuchù.

tick[1] /tɪk/ *n* [C] 1 (钟表等的)滴答声〔聲〕dīdāshēng. 2 [非正式用语]一刹那 yíchànà; 片刻 piànkè: *I'll be with you in a ~*. 我一会儿就来陪你. 3 (核对账目等用的)记号〔號〕(或对号,常用✓) jìhào. tick *v* 1 [I] (钟表等)滴答作响〔響〕dīdā zuòxiǎng. 2 [T] (*off*) 标〔標〕以(✓)记号 biāo yǐ jìhào. 3 [习语] what makes sb ˈtick [非正式用语]某人行为〔爲〕的动〔動〕机〔機〕(是什么) mǒurén xíngwéi de dòngjī. 4 [短语动词] tick sb off [非正式用语] 责备〔備〕zébèi; 斥责 chìzé. tick over 照常进〔進〕行 zhàocháng jìnxíng.

tick[2] /tɪk/ *n* [C] [动物]扁虱〔蝨〕biǎnshī.

ticket /ˈtɪkɪt/ *n* [C] 1 票 piào; 车票 chē-

T

piào; 入场〔場〕券 rùchǎngquàn. 2 (货物上的)标〔標〕签〔簽〕 biāoqiān. 3 (给违反交通规则者的)传〔傳〕票 chuánpiào.

tickle /ˈtɪkl/ *v* 1 [T] 搔痒〔癢〕 sāoyǎng. 2 [I, T] (使)觉〔覺〕得痒 juédé yǎng. 3 [T] 逗乐〔樂〕 dòulè; 使高兴〔興〕 shǐ gāoxìng. **tickle** *n* [C] 痒 yǎng; 搔痒 sāoyǎng. **ticklish** *adj* 1 怕痒的 pàyǎngde. 2 [非正式用语](问题)需小心处〔處〕理的 xū xiǎoxīn chǔlǐ de; 棘手的 jíshǒude.

tidal /ˈtaɪdl/ *adj* 潮汐的 cháoxīde; 有潮的 yǒucháode. ˈ**tidal** ˌ**power** *n* [U] 潮汐能 cháoxīnéng. ˈ**tidal wave** *n* [C] 海浪 hǎilàng; 海啸〔嘯〕 hǎixiào.

tide /taɪd/ *n* 1 (a) [C, U] 潮汐 cháoxī. (b) [C] 潮水 cháoshuǐ: *Beware of strong ~s.* 提防汹涌的潮水. 2 [C, 常作 sing] 潮流 cháoliú; 趋〔趨〕势〔勢〕 qūshì. **tide** *v* [短语动词] **tide sb over (sth)** 帮〔幫〕助某人渡过〔過〕(难关) bāngzhù mǒurén dùguò. ˈ**tide-mark** *n* [C] (沙滩上的)高潮痕 gāocháohén.

tidings /ˈtaɪdɪŋz/ *n* [pl] [古或谑]消息 xiāoxī; 音信 yīnxìn: *glad ~* 好消息.

tidy /ˈtaɪdɪ/ *adj* [-ier, -iest] 1 整洁〔潔〕的 zhěngjiéde: *a ~ room / girl* 整洁的房间(或女孩). 2 [非正式用语]相当〔當〕大的 xiāngdāng dà de: *a ~ sum of money* 相当大的一笔钱. **tidily** *adv*. **tidiness** *n* [U]. **tidy** *v* [*pt, pp* -ied] [I, T] (使)整洁 zhěngjié: *~ (up) the room* 整理房间.

tie[1] /taɪ/ *v* [*pres part* **tying** /ˈtaɪɪŋ/] 1 [T] (用带、绳等)捆扎〔紮〕 kǔnzhā; 系〔繫〕 jì; 结 jié: *A label was ~d to the handle.* 把手上系着一个标签. *~ (up) a parcel* 捆扎一个包裹. 2 [T] 把(带子等)打结 bǎ dǎjié: *~ one's shoe-laces* 系鞋带. 3 [I] 打结 dǎjié; 结起 jiéqǐ: *Does this dress ~ in front?* 这衣服是在前面打结的吗? 4 [I, T] 打成平局 dǎ chéng píngjú: *The two teams ~d.* 两队打成平局. 5 [短语动词] **tie sb down** 约束某人 yuēshù mǒurén. **tie in (with sth)** 一致 yízhì; 有联〔聯〕系〔係〕 yǒu liánxì. **tie sb up** (a) 捆绑某人 kǔnbǎng mǒurén. (b) [非正式用语][常用被动语态]使某人很忙 shǐ mǒurén hěn máng: *I'm ~d up now; can you come back later?* 我现在正忙,你能不能晚一点回来? **tie sth up** 占〔佔〕用资金等(以致不能移作他用) zhànyòng zījīn děng.

tie[2] /taɪ/ *n* [C] 1 领带〔帶〕 lǐngdài. 2 (结扎用的)带子 dàizi; 绳〔繩〕子 shéngzi. 3 [喻]关〔關〕系〔係〕 guānxì; 联〔聯〕系 liánxì: *family ~s* 家庭关系. 4 束缚 shùfù; 牵〔牽〕累 qiānlěi. 5 (比赛中)不分胜〔勝〕负 bùfēn shèng fù, 平局 píngjú. ˈ**tie-breaker** *n* [C] 平局决胜制 píngjú juéshèngzhì.

tier /tɪə(r)/ *n* [C] 一排(坐位) yìpái.

tiff /tɪf/ *n* [C] 小口角 xiǎo kǒujiǎo.

tiger /ˈtaɪgə(r)/ *n* [C] 1 虎 hǔ. 2 (*also* **tiger eˈconomy**) 小龙〔龍〕经〔經〕济〔濟〕 xiǎolóng jīngjì. **tigress** /ˈtaɪgrɪs/ *n* [C] 母虎 mǔhǔ.

tight /taɪt/ *adj* 1 紧〔緊〕的 jǐnde; 牢固的 láogùde: *a ~ knot* 死结. 2 (a) 紧密的 jǐnmìde: *These shoes are too ~.* 这双鞋太紧了. (b) 密封的 mìfēngde: ˈ*air ~* 不透气的. ˈ*water ~* 不漏水的. 3 拉紧的 lājǐnde; 绷紧的 bēngjǐnde: *a ~ belt* 绷紧的腰带. 4 密集的 mìjíde: [喻] *a ~ schedule* 紧凑的日程安排. 5 [非正式用语](钱)难〔難〕得到的 nán dédào de. 6 [俚]喝醉的 hēzuìde. 7 [非正式用语]小气〔氣〕的 xiǎoqìde; 吝啬〔嗇〕的 lìnsède. 8 [习语] **in a tight corner / spot** 处〔處〕于困境 chǔyú kùnjìng. **tight** *adv* 紧紧地 jǐnjǐnde; 牢牢地 láoláode: *The bags are packed ~.* 这包扎得很紧. **tighten** *v* [I, T] (使)变〔變〕紧 biàn jǐn: *~ (up) the screws* 拧紧螺钉. ˌ**tight-ˈfisted** *adj* [非正式用语]吝啬的 lìnsède; 小气的 xiǎoqìde. **tightly** *adv*. **tightness** *n* [U]. ˈ**tightrope** *n* [C] 绷紧的钢〔鋼〕索(杂技表演用) bēngjǐnde gāngsuǒ. **tights** *n* [pl] 裤袜〔襪〕 kùwà.

tile /taɪl/ *n* [C] 1 瓦 wǎ; 瓦片 wǎpiàn. 2 [习语] **on the ˈtiles** [非正式用语](在外)寻〔尋〕欢〔歡〕作乐〔樂〕 xúnhuān zuòlè; 花天酒地 huā tiān jiǔ dì. **tiled** *adj*.

till[1] =UNTIL.

till[2] /tɪl/ *n* [C] (账台中)放钱〔錢〕的抽屉〔屜〕 fàng qián de chōuti.

till[3] /tɪl/ *v* [T] 耕种〔種〕 gēngzhòng.

tiller /ˈtɪlə(r)/ *n* [C] 舵柄 duòbǐng.

tilt /tɪlt/ *v* [I, T] (使)倾斜 qīngxié. **tilt** *n* [C] 1 倾斜 qīngxié; 斜坡 xiépō. 2 [习语] **(at) full tilt** ⇨FULL.

timber /ˈtɪmbə(r)/ *n* 1 [U] (a) 木材 mùcái; 木料 mùliào. (b) 用材林 yòng cái lín. 2 [C] 栋木 dòngmù; 大梁 dàliáng. **timbered** *adj*.

time[1] /taɪm/ *n* 1 [U] 时〔時〕间 shíjiān: *The world exists in space and ~.* 世界存在于空间和时间中. 2 [U] 一段时间 yíduàn shíjiān: *Is there ~ for another cup of tea?* 有没有再喝一杯茶的时间? 3 [U] 钟〔鐘〕点〔點〕 zhōngdiǎn: *The ~ is 2 o'clock.* 时间是两点钟. 4 [U, C] (作某事所费的)时间 shíjiān: *The winner's ~ was 11 seconds.* 获胜者所用时间是 11 秒. 5 [U] (做某事的)时候 shíhòu, 时刻 shíkè: *It's ˈlunch-~.* 是午餐的时候了. *It's ~ for us to go now.* 现在是我们该走的时候了. 6 [C] 次数〔數〕 cìshù; 回 huí: *He failed the exam three ~s.* 他三次考试不及格. 7 [C, 常作 pl] 时代 shídài; 时期

T

shíqī: *in prehistoric* ~*s* 在史前时期. 8 [U] [音乐]拍子 pāizi; 节〔節〕拍 jiépāi: *beat* ~ 打拍子. 9 [习语] ahead of one's ˈtime 思想超越时代(的人) sīxiǎng chāoyuè shídài. all the ˈtime 始终 shǐzhōng; 一直 yìzhí. at ˈall times 经〔經〕常 jīngcháng; 随〔隨〕时 suíshí. at ˈone time 从〔從〕前 cóngqián; 一度 yídù. at a ˈtime 每次 měicì; 依次 yīcì. at ˈtimes 有时 yǒushí. behind the ˈtimes 旧〔舊〕式的 jiùshìde; 过〔過〕时的 guòshíde; 落伍的 luòwǔde. do ˈtime [俚]服徒刑 fú túxíng. for the time ˈbeing 暂时 zànshí. from ˌtime to ˈtime 有时 yǒushí; 不时 bùshí; 偶尔〔爾〕ǒu'ěr. have no time for sb / sth 不喜欢〔歡〕某人(或某事物) bù xǐhuan mǒurén. have the ˌtime of one's ˈlife [非正式用语] 异〔異〕常高兴〔興〕(或兴奋) yìcháng gāoxìng. in ˈtime 总〔總〕有一天 zǒng yǒu yìtiān; 最后〔後〕 zuìhòu. on ˈtime 准〔準〕时 zhǔnshí; 按时 ànshí. take one's ˈtime 不着急 bù zháojí. ˌtime after ˈtime, ˌtime and (time) aˈgain 反复〔復〕地 fǎnfùde; 多次 duōcì. ˈtime bomb *n* [C] 定时炸弹〔彈〕 dìngshí zhàdàn. ˈtime-limit *n* [C] 期限 qīxiàn. times *prep* 乘以 chéng yǐ: *5* ~*s 2 is 10*. 5 乘以 2 等于 10. times *n* [pl] (用以表示倍数): *This book is three* ~*s as long as that one*. 这本书的篇幅是那本的三倍. ˈtime-scale *n* [C] (事件发生的)一段时间 yíduàn shíjiān. ˈtimeshare *n* 1 [U] 分时享用度假住房方式 fēnshí xiǎngyòng dùjià zhùfáng fāngshì. 2 [C] 分时享用的度假住房 fēnshí xiǎngyòng de dùjià zhùfáng. ˈtime-sharing *n* [U] 1 [计算机] (两个以上)用户同时操作(的方法) yònghù tóngshí cāozuò. 2 轮〔輪〕流使用度假住房 lúnliú shǐyòng dùjià zhùfáng. ˈtime-signal *n* [C] 报〔報〕时信号〔號〕 bàoshí xìnhào. ˈtime-switch *n* [C] 定时开〔開〕关〔關〕 dìngshí kāiguān. ˈtimetable *n* [C] 1 时刻表 shíkèbiǎo. 2 课程表 kèchéngbiǎo.

time[2] /taɪm/ *v* [T] 1 安排…的时间 ānpái … de shíjiān; 为〔爲〕…选〔選〕择〔擇〕时机〔機〕 wèi … xuǎnzé shíjī: *She* ~*d her journey so that she arrived early*. 她适当安排旅程的时间,因而及早到达了. 2 计算…的时间 jìsuàn … de shíjiān. timer *n* [C] 记时员 jìshíyuán; 记时器 jìshíqì. timing *n* [U] 时机〔機〕的选〔選〕择〔擇〕 shíjīde xuǎnzé.

timely /ˈtaɪmlɪ/ *adj* [-ier, -iest] 及时〔時〕的 jíshíde; 适〔適〕时的 shìshíde.

timid /ˈtɪmɪd/ *adj* 胆〔膽〕怯的 dǎnqiède. timidity /tɪˈmɪdətɪ/ *n* [U]. timidly *adv*.

tin /tɪn/ *n* 1 [U] 锡 xī. 2 [C] [英国英语]罐头〔頭〕 guàntou; 听〔聽〕 tīng: *a* ~ *of beans* 一听蚕豆. tin *v* [-nn-] [T] 装〔裝〕…罐头 zhuāng … guàntou: ~*ned peaches* 罐头桃子. tin ˈfoil *n* [U] (包装用)锡纸 xīzhǐ. tinny *adj* [-ier, -iest] 1 锡的 xīde. 2 (声音)细弱无〔無〕力的 xìruò wúlì de. ˈtin-opener *n* [C] [英国英语]开〔開〕罐头刀 kāi guàntou dāo.

tinge /tɪndʒ/ *v* [T] (*with*) 1 (较淡地)着色于 zhuó sè yú, 染 rǎn. 2 [喻]使略受影响〔響〕 shǐ lüè shòu yǐngxiǎng: *admiration* ~*d with envy* 略含妒意的赞美. tinge *n* [C, 常作 sing] (淡淡的)色彩 sècǎi; (些微的)痕迹〔跡〕 hénjì: *a* ~ *of sadness in her voice* 她的声音中略带悲伤.

tingle /ˈtɪŋgl/ *v* [I] 感到刺痛 gǎn dào cìtòng: [喻] ~ *with excitement* 感到兴奋. tingle *n* [C, 常作 sing] 刺痛感 cìtònggǎn.

tinker /ˈtɪŋkə(r)/ *v* [I] (*with*) 随〔隨〕便地做 suíbiànde zuò; (以外行方式)瞎忙 xiāmáng.

tinkle /ˈtɪŋkl/ *v* [I] 发〔發〕丁当〔當〕声〔聲〕 fā dīngdāngshēng. tinkle *n* [C] 1 丁当声 dīngdāngshēng; 丁丁声 dīngdīngshēng. 2 [英国非正式用语] 电〔電〕话通话 diànhuà tōnghuà.

tinsel /ˈtɪnsl/ *n* [U] (装饰用的)闪光金属〔屬〕片(或丝) shǎnguāng jīnshǔpiàn.

tint /tɪnt/ *n* [C] 颜色的浓〔濃〕淡 yánsède nóng dàn; 色度 sèdù; (尤指)浅〔淺〕色 qiǎnsè. tint *v* [T] 着色于 zhuósè yú; 给…染色 gěi… rǎnsè.

tiny /ˈtaɪnɪ/ *adj* [-ier, -iest] 极〔極〕小的 jíxiǎode.

tip[1] /tɪp/ *n* [C] 1 尖端 jiānduān; 末端 mòduān: *the* ~*s of one's fingers* 手指尖. 2 附加在顶端的小物件 fùjiā zài dǐngduān de xiǎo wùjiàn: *a stick with a rubber* ~ 带橡皮头的手杖. 3 [习语] on the tip of one's ˈtongue 即将〔將〕想起(某事) jíjiāng xiǎngqǐ; (某事)就在嘴边〔邊〕 jiù zài zuǐbiān. the tip of the ˈiceberg 大问题的小迹〔跡〕象 dà wèntí de xiǎo jìxiàng. tip *v* [-pp-] [T] 装〔裝〕上尖头〔頭〕(或附加物) zhuāngshàng jiāntóu: ~*ped cigarettes* 过滤嘴香烟. ˈtiptoe *n* [习语] on ˈtiptoe 踮着脚尖 diànzhe jiǎojiān: *stand on* ~*toe to see over sb's head* 踮着脚隔着别人的头观看. *walk on* ~*toe so as not to be heard* 踮着脚走以免被人听见. ˈtiptoe *v* [I] (踮着脚)悄悄地走 qiāoqiāode zǒu: *She* ~*toed out*. 她悄悄地走出去. ˌtipˈtop *adj* [非正式用语]第一流的 dìyīliúde.

tip[2] /tɪp/ *v* [-pp-] 1 [I, T] (a) (使)倾斜 qīngxié. (b) (*over*) (使)翻倒 fāndǎo; (使)倾覆 qīngfù. 2 [T] [尤用于英国英语] 倾泻〔瀉〕 qīngxiè; 倒 dào. tip *n* [C] 1 倒垃圾处〔處〕 dào lājī chù. 2 [非正式用语]脏〔髒〕地方 zāng dìfang.

tip[3] /tɪp/ *n* [C] 1 (给服务员等的)小费 xiǎofèi. 2 劝〔勸〕告 quàngào; 提示 tíshì. tip *v* [-pp-] 1 [I, T] 给…小费 gěi…xiǎofèi: ~ *the waiter* 给侍者小费. 2 [短语动词] tip sb off [非正式用语]告诫某人 gàojiè mǒurén; 提示某

T

人 tíshì mǒurén. 'tip-off *n* [C] 提示 tíshì；告诫 gàojiè.

tipple /'tɪpl/ *n* [C] [非正式用语]烈酒 lièjiǔ.

tipsy /'tɪpsɪ/ *adj* [-ier, -iest] [非正式用语] 微醉的 wēizuìde.

tire[1] /'taɪə(r)/ *v* [I,T] (使)疲劳〔勞〕píláo；(使)疲倦 píjuàn: *The long walk ~d them (out).* 走这趟远路把他们累坏了. **tired** *adj* 1 疲劳的 píláode；累的 lèide. 2 *of* 厌〔厭〕烦的 yànfánde: *I'm ~d of watching television.* 我对看电视感到厌烦了. **tiredness** *n* [U]. **tireless** *adj* 不易疲倦的 búyì píjuàn de；不累的 búlèide. **tiresome** *adj* 令人厌倦的 lìng rén yànjuànde；讨厌的 tǎoyànde.

tire[2] [美语] = TYRE.

tissue /'tɪʃuː/ *n* 1 [U,C] [生理]组织〔織〕zǔzhī: *nerve ~* 神经组织. 2 [U] (亦作 '**tissue-paper**) 薄纸 bó zhǐ；棉纸 mián zhǐ. 3 [C] (用作手帕的)纸巾 zhǐjīn. 4 [C] [喻]一套 yítào；一连串 yìliánchuàn: *a ~ of lies* 一连串的谎话.

tit[1] /tɪt/ *n* [C] 山雀 shānquè.

tit[2] /tɪt/ *n* [习语] ˌ**tit for** '**tat** /tæt/ 针锋相对〔對〕zhēn fēng xiāng duì；以牙还〔還〕牙 yǐ yá huán yá.

tit[3] /tɪt/ *n* [C] [⚠俚] (女子的)乳房 rǔfáng，奶头〔頭〕nǎitóu.

titbit /'tɪtbɪt/ *n* [C] 1 (少量而美味的)食品 shípǐn. 2 珍闻 zhēnwén；趣闻 qùwén.

titillate /'tɪtɪleɪt/ *v* [T] 刺激(某人)(尤指性欲) cìjī.

title /'taɪtl/ *n* 1 [C] 标〔標〕题 biāotí；题目 tímù. 2 [C] 称〔稱〕号〔號〕chēnghào；头〔頭〕衔 tóuxián. 3 [C] [运动]冠军 guànjūn. 4 [U, C] [法律]权〔權〕利 quánlì；所有权 suǒyǒuquán. **titled** *adj* 有贵族头衔的 yǒu guìzú tóuxián de: *a ~d lady* 命妇(如女公爵). '**title-deed** *n* [C] (财产)所有权契据〔據〕suǒyǒuquán qìjù. '**title-role** *n* [C] 剧〔劇〕名角色 jùmíng juésè.

titter /'tɪtə(r)/ *v* [I] 窃〔竊〕笑 qièxiào；傻〔傻〕笑 shǎxiào. **titter** *n* [C].

TNT /ˌtiː en 'tiː/ *n* [U] 褐色炸药〔藥〕hèsè zhàyào.

to[1] /tə, tʊ 或 tuː；强式 tuː/ *prep* 1 向 xiàng；对〔對〕duì；往 wǎng: *walk to the shops* 走着去商店. 2 至…状〔狀〕态〔態〕zhì… zhuàngtài；趋〔趨〕向 qūxiàng: *rise to power* 上台掌权. 3 达〔達〕dá；到 dào: *The dress reaches to her ankles.* 她的连衣裙垂至脚踝. 4 直到(并包括) zhídào: *from Monday to Friday* 从星期一到星期五. 5 (时间)在…之前 zài … zhī qián: *It's ten to three.* 两点五十(分钟). 6 (引导间接宾语): *I gave it to Peter.* 我把它给彼得了. 7 属〔屬〕于 shǔyú: *the key to the door* 开门的钥匙. 8 (表示比较): *I prefer walking to climbing.* 我喜欢步行，不愿爬山. *We won by 6 goals to 3.* 我们以 6 比 3 获胜.

to[2] /tə, tʊ 或 tuː；强式 tuː/ [构成动词不定式] 1 (用作动词的宾语): *He wants to go.* 他要去. 2 (表示目的、效果、结局): *They came (in order) to help me.* 他们来(为了要)帮助我. 3 (用来代替动词不定式以避免重复): '*Will you come?*' '*I hope to.*' "你来不来?""我希望来."

to[3] /tuː/ *adv* 1 (门)关〔關〕上 guānshang: *Push the door to.* 把门关上. 2 [习语] ˌ**to and** '**fro** 来回地 láihuíde；往复〔復〕地 wǎngfùde.

toad /təʊd/ *n* [C] [动物]蟾蜍 chánchú.

toadstool /'təʊdstuːl/ *n* [C] 真菌 zhēnjūn；蕈 xùn；(尤指)毒蕈 dúxùn.

toast[1] /təʊst/ *n* [U] 烤面〔麵〕包 kǎo miànbāo. **toast** *v* 1 [I, T] 烤(面包等) kǎo. 2 [T] 烤火 kǎohuǒ. **toaster** *n* [C] (电)烤面包器 kǎo miànbāo qì.

toast[2] /təʊst/ *v* [T] 为〔爲〕…祝酒 wèi … zhùjiǔ: *~ the bride and bridegroom* 举杯祝贺新郎新娘. **toast** *n* [C] 祝酒 zhùjiǔ；受敬酒的人 shòu jìngjiǔ de rén: *propose / drink a ~* 祝酒(或干杯).

tobacco /tə'bækəʊ/ *n* [U] 烟草 yāncǎo；烟叶〔葉〕yānyè. **tobacconist** /tə'bækənɪst/ *n* [C] 烟草商 yāncǎoshāng；香烟店 xiāngyāndiàn.

toboggan /tə'bɒgən/ *n* [C] 平底雪橇 píngdǐ xuěqiāo. **toboggan** *v* [I] 坐雪橇滑行 zuò xuěqiāo huáxíng.

today /tə'deɪ/ *adv, n* [U] 1 (在)今天 jīntiān. 2 现在 xiànzài；当〔當〕代 dāngdài: *the young people of ~* 现在的年轻人.

toddle /'tɒdl/ *v* [I] (尤指小孩的)蹒跚行走 pánshān xíngzǒu. **toddler** *n* [C] 学〔學〕走的小孩 xué zǒu de xiǎohái.

to-do /tə'duː/ *n* [C, 常作 sing] [*pl* ~s] [非正式用语]纷扰〔擾〕fēnrǎo；喧闹 xuānnào.

toe /təʊ/ *n* [C] 1 (a) 脚趾 jiǎozhǐ. (b) (鞋，袜的)足尖部 zújiānbù. 2 [习语] **on one's** '**toes** 准〔準〕备〔備〕行动〔動〕的 zhǔnbèi xíngdòng de. **toe** *v* [习语] **toe the** '**line** 听〔聽〕从〔從〕命令 tīngcóng mìnglìng. '**toe-nail** *n* [C] 趾甲 zhǐjiǎ.

toffee /'tɒfɪ；*US* 'tɔːfɪ/ *n* [C, U] 乳脂糖 rǔzhītáng；太妃糖 tàifēitáng.

together /tə'geðə(r)/ *adv* 1 共同 gòngtóng；一起 yìqǐ: *They went for a walk ~.* 他们一起出去散步. 2 (结合)在一起 zài yìqǐ；集拢〔攏〕地 jílǒngde: *Tie the ends ~.* 把末端绑在一起. 3 同时〔時〕tóngshí: *All his troubles happened ~.* 他所有的麻烦事同时来了. 4 一致 yízhì；协〔協〕调 xiétiáo. 5 [习语]

get it to'gether [俚](使某事物)有组织[織] yǒu zǔzhī, 受控制 shòu kòngzhì. **together with** 和 hé; 加之 jiāzhī; 连同 liántóng. **togetherness** *n* [U] 友爱[愛] yǒu'ài.

toil /tɔɪl/ *v* [I] (*away*) [正式用语]辛劳[勞]地工作 xīnláode gōngzuò; 艰[艱]难[難]地行动[動] jiānnánde xíngdòng. **toil** *n* [U] [正式用语] *n* 苦工 kǔgōng; 难事 nánshì.

toilet /'tɔɪlɪt/ *n* [C] 盥洗室 guànxǐshì. **'toilet-paper** *n* [U] 卫[衛]生纸 wèishēng zhǐ. **toiletries** *n* [pl] 卫生用品 wèishēng yòngpǐn; 化妆[妝]品 huàzhuāngpǐn. **'toilet-roll** *n* [C] 卫生卷纸 wèishēng juǎnzhǐ.

token /'təʊkən/ *n* [C] **1** 标[標]志 biāozhì; 记号[號] jìhào; 象征[徵] xiàngzhēng: *a* ~ *of my affection* 我的深情的象征. **2** (金属的)代币[幣] dàibì; 专[專]用币 zhuānyòngbì. **3** 礼[禮]券 lǐquàn: *a book* ~ 书券. **token** *adj* 象征性的 xiàngzhēngxìngde; 装[裝]样[樣]子的 zhuāngyàngzide: ~ *one-day strikes* 象征性的一天罢工.

told *pt, pp* of TELL.

tolerate /'tɒləreɪt/ *v* [T] **1** 容忍 róngrěn; 宽恕 kuānshù: *I won't* ~ *such behaviour.* 我不能容忍这种行为. **2** 忍受 rěnshòu: ~ *heat / noise* 忍受炎热(或吵闹). **tolerable** /-rəbl/ *adj* 可忍受的 kě rěnshòu de; 可容许的 kě róngxǔ de; 尚好的 shànghǎode. **tolerably** *adv* 尚好 shànghǎo; 相当[當]地 xiāngdāngde. **tolerance** /-rəns/ *n* [U] 容忍 róngrěn; 忍受 rěnshòu; 宽恕 kuānshù: *religious / racial tolerance* 宗教(或种族)上的宽恕. **tolerant** /-rənt/ *adj* 容忍的 róngrěnde; 忍受的 rěnshòude; 宽恕的 kuānshùde. **toleration** /ˌtɒlə'reɪʃn/ *n* [U] 容忍 róngrěn; 忍受 rěnshòu; 宽恕 kuānshù.

toll[1] /təʊl/ *n* [C] **1** (道路、桥梁等的)通行费 tōngxíngfèi. **2** 损失 sǔnshī; 代价[價] dàijià: *the death-* ~ *in the earthquake* 地震的死亡人数.

toll[2] /təʊl/ *v* [I, T] (缓慢而有规律地)敲钟[鐘] qiāo zhōng. **toll** *n* [sing] 钟声[聲] zhōngshēng.

tomato /tə'mɑːtəʊ; *US* -meɪ-/ *n* [C] [*pl* ~**es**] 西红柿 xīhóngshì.

tomb /tuːm/ *n* [C] 坟墓 fénmù. **'tombstone** *n* [C] 墓碑 mùbēi.

tomboy /'tɒmbɔɪ/ *n* [C] (男孩似的)顽皮姑娘 wánpí gūniang.

tom-cat /'tɒm kæt/ *n* [C] 雄猫 xióngmāo.

tomorrow /tə'mɒrəʊ/ *adv, n* [U] **1** (在)明天 míngtiān. **2** 不久的将[將]来 bùjiǔde jiānglái.

ton /tʌn/ *n* **1** [C] (重量单位)吨(英吨 =2240 磅, 美吨=2000 磅) dūn. **2 tons** [pl] [非正式用语]大量 dàliàng; 沉重 chénzhòng: ~*s of money* 许多钱.

tone[1] /təʊn/ *n* **1** [C] 声[聲]音 shēngyīn; (尤指)音质[質] yīnzhì; 音调 yīndiào: *the sweet* ~*(s) of a piano* 钢琴的悦耳的声音. **2** [C] (打电话时听到的)信号[號] xìnhào: *the engaged* ~ (电话)占线信号. **3** [sing] 特性 tèxìng; 格调 gédiào: *the serious* ~ *of the article* 这篇文章的严肃格调. **4** [C] 色调 sèdiào; 明暗度 míng'àndù. **5** [C] [音乐]全音程 quán yīnchéng. ˌ**tone-'deaf** *adj* 不能分辨音调的 bùnéng fēnbiàn yīndiào de.

tone[2] /təʊn/ *v* **1** [T] (给…)定调子 dìng diàozi. **2** [短语动词] **tone (sth) down** (使)减轻[輕] jiǎnqīng; (使)缓和 huǎnhé. **tone in (with sth)** (颜色)调和 tiáohé. **tone (sth) up** (使)提高 tígāo; (使)加强 jiāqiáng: *Exercise* ~*s up the body.* 运动能使身体结实.

tongs /tɒŋz/ *n* [pl] 钳 qián; 夹[夾]子 jiāzi.

tongue /tʌŋ/ *n* **1** [C] (a) 舌头[頭] shétou. (b) [喻]讲[講]话的方式(或态度) jiǎnghuàde fāngshì: *He has a sharp* ~. 他说话尖刻. **2** [C] [正式用语]语言 yǔyán. **3** [C, U] (牛等的)口条[條] kǒutiáo. **4** [C] 舌状[狀]物(如鞋舌) shézhuàngwù. **5** [习语] **with one's tongue in one's 'cheek** 毫无[無]诚意地说话 háo wú chéngyì de shuōhuà. **'tongue-tied** *adj* 张[張]口结舌的 zhāngkǒu jiéshé de. **'tongue-twister** *n* [C] 拗口令 àokǒulìng.

tonic /'tɒnɪk/ *n* **1** [C, U] 滋补[補]品 zībǔpǐn; 补药[藥] bǔyào. **2** [C] 使人感到健康快乐[樂]的事物 shǐ rén gǎndào jiànkāng kuàilè de shìwù. **3** [C, U] = tonic water. **'tonic water** *n* [C, U] 奎宁[寧]水(一种以奎宁调味的饮料) kuíníngshuǐ.

tonight /tə'naɪt/ *adv, n* [U] (在)今晚 jīnwǎn.

tonnage /'tʌnɪdʒ/ *n* [U, C] (船的)吨位 dūnwèi.

tonne /tʌn/ *n* [C] (公制)吨(=1 000公斤) dūn.

tonsil /'tɒnsɪl/ *n* [C] 扁桃体[體] biǎntáotǐ; 扁桃腺 biǎntáoxiàn. **tonsillitis** /ˌtɒnsɪ'laɪtɪs/ *n* [U] 扁桃体炎 biǎntáotǐ yán.

too /tuː/ *adv* **1** 也 yě; 又 yòu; 还[還] hái: *She plays the guitar and sings* ~. 她会弹吉他,也会唱歌. **2** 太 tài; 过[過]分 guòfèn: *You're driving* ~ *fast!* 你(开车)开得太快了! **3** [习语] **all/only too** 很 hěn; 非常 fēicháng: *only* ~ *pleased to help* 非常愿意帮助.

took *pt* of TAKE[1].

tool /tuːl/ *n* [C] 工具 gōngjù; 用具 yòngjù. **'toolbar** *n* [C] (计算机)工具条[條] gōngjùtiáo.

T

toot /tuːt/ *n* [C] (号角发出的)短鸣声〔聲〕duǎnmíngshēng. **toot** *v* [I, T] (使)发〔發〕嘟嘟声 fā dūdūshēng.

tooth /tuːθ/ *n* [*pl* **teeth** /tiːθ/] **1** [C] 牙齿〔齒〕yáchǐ. **2** [C] (梳、锯、耙等的)齿 chǐ. **3** **teeth** [pl] [非正式用语]有效的力量 yǒuxiàode lìliàng: *The present law must be given more teeth.* 必须使现行法律发挥更大的威力. **4** [习语] **get one's teeth into sth** [非正式用语]专〔專〕心处〔處〕理某事 zhuānxīn chǔlǐ mǒushì. **in the teeth of sth** 不顾〔顧〕某事 búgù mǒushì. ˈ**toothache** *n* [U] 牙痛 yátòng. ˈ**tooth-brush** *n* [C] 牙刷 yáshuā. **toothed** /tuːθt/ *adj* 有齿的 yǒuchǐde. **toothless** *adj*. ˈ**toothpaste** *n* [U] 牙膏 yágāo. ˈ**toothpick** *n* [C] 牙签〔簽〕yáqiān.

top[1] /tɒp/ *n* **1** [C] 顶部 dǐngbù; 顶端 dǐngduān: *at the ~ of the hill* 在山顶. **2** [C] (物的)上面 shàngmiàn; 上边〔邊〕shàngbiān: *the ~ of the table* 桌面. **3** [sing] 最高地位 zuìgāo dìwèi; 首位 shǒuwèi. **4** [C] 罩子 zhàozi; 套子 tàozi: *a pen ~* 笔帽 bǐmào. **5** [C] (尤指女用)上衣 shàngyī. **6** [习语] **at the top of one's ˈvoice** 以最大嗓音 yǐ zuìdà sǎngyīn. **from ˌtop to ˈbottom** 从〔從〕头〔頭〕到底 cóngtóu dàodǐ; 全部地 quánbùde. **get on top of sb** [非正式用语] (工作)使人吃不消 shǐ rén chībùxiāo. **on top of sth** (a) 熟练〔練〕掌握 shúliàn zhǎngwò; 善于控制 shànyú kòngzhì. (b) 加在…上面 jiā zài … shàngmiàn. **on ˌtop of the ˈworld** 非常高兴〔興〕fēicháng gāoxìng: *He feels on ~ of the world today.* 他今天觉得非常高兴. **ˌover the ˈtop** [尤用于英国非正式用语]过〔過〕火 guòhuǒ; 过头 guòtóu. **top ˈbrass** [俚]高级官员 gāojí guānyuán; 高级管理人员 gāojí guǎnlǐ rényuán. **top ˈdog** [俚]主要人物(或团体) zhǔyào rénwù. **top** *adj* (地位、级别或程度)最高的 zuìgāode: *a room on the ~ floor* 位于顶层的房间. *at ~ speed* 以最快速度. **ˌtop ˈhat** *n* [C] 大礼〔禮〕帽 dà lǐmào. **ˌtop-ˈheavy** *adj* 头重脚轻〔輕〕的 tóu zhòng jiǎo qīng de. **topless** *adj* (妇女)袒胸的 tǎnxiōngde. ˈ**topmost** *adj* 最高的 zuìgāode. **ˌtop ˈsecret** *adj* 绝密的 juémìde. ˈ**topsoil** *n* [U] 表土层〔層〕biǎotǔcéng.

top[2] /tɒp/ *v* [-pp-] [T] **1** 给…加顶 gěi…jiā dǐng; 盖〔蓋〕gài: *a cake ~ped with icing* 敷糖霜的饼. **2** 超过〔過〕chāoguò; 胜〔勝〕过 shèngguò; 高于 gāo yú: *Exports have ~ped £100 million.* 出口额已经超过一亿镑. **3** 获〔獲〕第一名 huò dìyīmíng. **4** [短语动词] **top (sth) up** 装〔裝〕满(未满的容器) zhuāng mǎn: *~ up with petrol* 加满汽油. *~ up a drink* 斟满酒. ˈ**top-up card** *n* [C] (即付即打式手机的)电〔電〕话卡 diànhuàkǎ; 充值卡 chōngzhíkǎ.

top[3] /tɒp/ *n* [C] 陀螺 tuóluó.

topic /ˈtɒpɪk/ *n* [C] 论〔論〕题 lùntí; 话题 huàtí. **topical** *adj* (与)当〔當〕前有关〔關〕的 dāngqián yǒuguān de: *~al issues* 时事.

topple /ˈtɒpl/ *v* [I, T] (使)倒塌 dǎotā; 推翻 tuīfān: [喻] *The crisis ~d the government.* 危机使政府垮台.

torch /tɔːtʃ/ *n* [C] **1** [英国英语]手电〔電〕筒 shǒudiàntǒng. **2** 火把 huǒbǎ; 火炬 huǒjù. ˈ**torchlight** *n* [U] 手电筒的(或火炬的)光 shǒudiàntǒng de guāng: *a ~light procession* 火炬游行.

tore *pt* of TEAR[2].

torment /ˈtɔːment/ *n* (a) [U] 剧〔劇〕烈痛苦 jùliè tòngkǔ; 折磨 zhémó. (b) [C] 烦恼〔惱〕的原因 fánnǎo de yuányīn. **torment** /tɔːˈment/ *v* [T] **1** 使受剧烈痛苦 shǐ shòu jùliè tòngkǔ; 折磨 zhémó. **2** 烦扰〔擾〕fánrǎo; 使苦恼〔惱〕shǐ kǔnǎo. **tormentor** /tɔːˈmentə(r)/ *n* [C].

torn *pp* of TEAR[2].

tornado /tɔːˈneɪdəʊ/ *n* [C] [*pl* **~es**] 飓风 jùfēng; 龙〔龍〕卷〔捲〕风 lóngjuǎnfēng.

torpedo /tɔːˈpiːdəʊ/ *n* [C] [*pl* **~es**] 鱼雷 yúléi. **torpedo** *v* [T] 用鱼雷袭〔襲〕击〔擊〕yòng yúléi xíjī.

torrent /ˈtɒrənt; *US* ˈtɔːr-/ *n* [C] **1** 激流 jīliú; 洪流 hóngliú. **2** [喻]爆发〔發〕bàofā; 迸发 bèngfā: *a ~ of abuse* 连续不断的谩骂. **torrential** /təˈrenʃl/ *adj* 激流的 jīliúde; 激流似的 jīliú shì de: *~ial rain* 暴雨.

torso /ˈtɔːsəʊ/ *n* [C] [*pl* **~s**] (人体的)躯〔軀〕干〔幹〕qūgàn.

tortoise /ˈtɔːtəs/ *n* [C] 乌〔烏〕龟〔龜〕wūguī. ˈ**tortoiseshell** *n* [U] 玳瑁壳〔殼〕dàimàoké.

tortuous /ˈtɔːtʃʊəs/ *adj* **1** 弯〔彎〕弯曲曲的 wānwānqūqūde; 曲折的 qūzhéde. **2** 含混不清的 hánhùn bùqīng de; 拐弯抹角的 guǎiwān mòjiǎo de.

torture /ˈtɔːtʃə(r)/ *v* [T] 拷打 kǎodǎ; 折磨 zhémó; 使受剧〔劇〕烈痛苦 shǐ shòu jùliè tòngkǔ. **torture** *n* **1** [U] 拷打 kǎodǎ; 折磨 zhémó; 严〔嚴〕刑 yánxíng. **2** [C, U] 剧烈痛苦 jùliè tòngkǔ. **torturer** *n* [C].

Tory /ˈtɔːrɪ/ *n* [C] [*pl* **-ies**] *adj* (英国)保守党〔黨〕员 Bǎoshǒudǎngyuán.

toss /tɒs; *US* tɔːs/ *v* **1** [T] 扔 rēng; 抛 pāo; 掷〔擲〕zhì. **2** [T] 猛然扭(头) měngrán niǔ. **3** [I, T] (使)摇摆〔擺〕yáobǎi; (使)动〔動〕荡〔蕩〕dòngdàng: *I kept ~ing and turning all night.* 我整夜在床上翻来覆去. **4** [T] 轻〔輕〕拌 qīng bàn; 轻搅〔攪〕qīng jiǎo: *~ a salad* 搅拌色拉. **5** [I, T] 掷(硬币)作决定 zhì zuò juédìng:

Let's ~ to see who goes first. 让我们掷硬币决定谁第一个走. **toss** *n* [C] 扔 rēng; 抛 pāo; 掷 zhì; 摇摆 yáobǎi: *with a ~ of her head* 把她的头一扬. **'toss-up** *n* [sing] 机[機]会[會]相等 jīhuì xiāngděng.

tot[1] /tɒt/ *n* [C] **1** 小孩 xiǎoháir. **2** 一小杯(酒) yì xiǎo bēi.

tot[2] /tɒt/ *v* [-tt-] [短语动词] **tot sth up** [非正式用语]合计 héjì; 总[總]计 zǒngjì.

total /ˈtəʊtl/ *n* **1** [C] 总[總]数[數] zǒngshù; 全体[體] quántǐ; 合计 héjì. **2** [习语] **in ˈtotal** 总共 zǒnggòng. **total** *adj* 全部的 quánbùde; 完全的 wánquánde. **total** *v* [-ll-; 美语亦作 -l-] [T] **1** 计算…的总和 jìsuàn…de zǒnghé. **2** 总数达[達] zǒngshù dá: *The number of visitors ~led 15 000*. 参观者总共一万五千人. **totality** /təʊˈtæləti/ *n* [U] [正式用语]全体 quántǐ; 总数 zǒngshù. **totally** *adv* 完全地 wánquánde; 全部地 quánbùde: *~ly blind* 全盲的.

totalitarian /ˌtəʊtælɪˈteərɪən/ *adj* 极[極]权[權]主义[義]的 jíquán zhǔyì de.

totter /ˈtɒtə(r)/ *v* [I] **1** 蹒跚 pánshān; 踉跄[蹌] liàngqiàng. **2** 摇摇欲坠[墜] yáoyáo yù zhuì.

touch[1] /tʌtʃ/ *v* **1** [I, T] (用手)轻[輕]摸 qīngmō, 轻碰 qīngpèng: *The dish is hot—don't ~ (it)!* 这盘子烫极了——别摸! **2** [I, T] 接触[觸] jiēchù; 碰到 pèngdào: *The two wires ~ed*. 那两条电线搭在一起了. **3** [T] 吃 chī; 喝 hē: *He hasn't ~ed any food for two days*. 他两天没有吃东西了. **4** [T] [常用被动语态]使感动[動] shǐ gǎndòng; 使悲哀 shǐ bēi'āi: *We were greatly ~ed by your thoughtfulness*. 对你的关心我们深受感动. **5** [T] 比得上 bǐdéshàng; 及得上 jídéshàng: *No one can ~ him as an actor*. 作为一个演员, 没有人能及得上他. **6** [习语] **touch wood** 摸摸木头[頭](以避免灾祸) mōmō mùtou. **7** [短语动词] **touch down** (飞机)着陆[陸] zhuólù. **touch sth off** 触[觸]发[發](或引起)某事 chùfā mǒushì. **touch on/upon sth** (简要地)论[論]及(或谈到) lùnjí. **touch sth up** 稍作修改(以改进) shāo zuò xiūgǎi. **'touch-down** *n* [C] (飞机)降落 jiàngluò. **touched** *adj* **1** 感谢的 gǎnxiède. **2** 轻微疯[瘋]癫的 qīngwēi fēngdiān de. **touching** *adj* 引起同情的 yǐn qǐ tóngqíng de; 使人伤[傷]感的 shǐ rén shānggǎn de.

touch[2] /tʌtʃ/ *n* **1** [C, 常作 sing] 触[觸] chù; 接触 jiēchù. **2** [U] (官能)触觉[覺] chùjué. **3** [sing] 触摸时[時]的感觉 chùmō shí de gǎnjué: *The material has a velvety ~*. 这料子摸起来有天鹅绒的感觉. **4** [C] 细节 xìjié; 细微之处[處] xìwēi zhī chù: *put the finishing ~es to the project* 给这个计划作最后加工. **5** [sing] 少许 shǎoxǔ; 微量 wēiliàng: *a ~ of frost in the air* 空气中略有寒意. **6** [sing] 作风[風] zuòfēng; 手法 shǒufǎ: *Her work shows that professional ~*. 她的作品显露出专业技巧. **7** [U] [足球]边[邊]线[綫]以外区[區]域 biānxiàn yǐwài qūyù: *The ball is in ~*. 球出了边线. **8** [习语] **in/out of 'touch (with sb)** 有(或无)联[聯]系[係] yǒu liánxì. **ˌtouch-and-'go** *adj* 无[無]把握的 wú bǎwò de; 有风险[險]的 yǒu fēngxiǎn de. **'touch screen** *n* [C] 触摸屏 chùmōpíng.

touchy /ˈtʌtʃɪ/ *adj* [-ier, -iest] 易怒的 yìnùde; 暴躁的 bàozàode.

tough /tʌf/ *adj* **1** 坚[堅]韧[韌]的 jiānrènde; 不易切开[開]或打破的 búyì qiēkāi huò dǎpò de. **2** (肉)咬不动[動]的 yǎo bú dòng de. **3** 能耐劳[勞]的 néng nàiláo de; 坚强的 jiānqiángde. **4** 困难[難]的 kùnnande: *a ~ problem* 棘手的问题. **5** 强硬的 qiángyìngde; 严[嚴]厉[厲]的 yánlìde: *~ laws to deal with terrorism* 对待恐怖主义的严厉的法律. **6** 不幸的 búxìngde: *~ luck* 恶运. **toughen** /ˈtʌfn/ *v* [I, T] (使)变[變]坚强 biàn jiānqiáng; (使)变强硬 biàn qiángyìng. **toughness** *n* [U].

toupee /ˈtuːpeɪ; *US* tuːˈpeɪ/ *n* [C] 假发[髮] jiǎfà.

tour /tʊə(r)/ *n* [C] **1** 旅游 lǚyóu: *a round-the-world ~* 环球旅行. **2** 参观[觀] cānguān: *a ~ of the palace* 参观宫殿. **tour** *v* [I, T] 参观 cānguān; 旅游 lǚyóu. **tourism** /ˈtʊərɪzəm/ *n* [U] 旅游业[業] lǚyóuyè. **tourist** *n* [C] 旅游者 lǚyóuzhě; 观光客 guānguāngkè.

tournament /ˈtɔːnəmənt; *US* ˈtɜːrn-/ *n* [C] 比赛 bǐsài; 联[聯]赛 liánsài: *a ˈchess ~* 象棋比赛.

tourniquet /ˈtʊənɪkeɪ; *US* ˈtɜːrnɪkət/ *n* [C] [医学]止血带[帶] zhǐxuèdài; 压[壓]脉器 yāmàiqì.

tout /taʊt/ *v* **1** [I, T] 招徕(生意) zhāolái; 兜售 dōushòu. **2** [T] [英国英语]卖[賣]黑市票 mài hēishìpiào. **tout** *n* [C] 推销员 tuīxiāoyuán; 兜售者 dōushòuzhě.

tow /təʊ/ *v* [T] (用绳索)拖 tuō, 拉 lā. **tow** *n* **1** [C] 拖 tuō; 拉 lā. **2** [习语] **in tow** [非正式用语]在一起 zài yìqǐ; 跟随[隨] gēnsuí. **on tow** 被拖(或拉) bèi tuō. **'tow-path** *n* [C] 纤[縴]路 qiànlù.

towards /təˈwɔːdz; *US* tɔːrdz/ (亦作 **toward** /təˈwɔːd; *US* tɔːrd/) *prep* **1** 向 xiàng; 对[對] duì; 朝 cháo: *walk ~ the door* 向门口走去. **2** 趋[趨]于达[達]成 qū yú dáchéng: *steps ~ unity* 走向统一的步骤. **3** 关[關]于 guānyú; 对于 duìyú: *friendly ~ tourists* 对游客热情. **4** (时间)接近 jiējìn, 将[將]近 jiāngjìn: *~ the end of the 19th cen-*

T

tury 将近 19 世纪末. 5 为〔爲〕了 wèile.

towel /ˈtaʊəl/ *n* [C] 毛巾 máojīn; 手巾 shǒujīn. **towelling** (美语-l-) *n* [U] 毛巾布 máojīnbù.

tower /ˈtaʊə(r)/ *n* [C] 1 塔 tǎ; 塔状〔狀〕建筑〔築〕 tǎzhuàng jiànzhù. 2 [习语] **a ˌtower of ˈstrength** 可依靠的人 kě yīkào de rén; 靠山 kàoshān. **tower** *v* [I] *above/over* 远〔遠〕高于 yuǎn gāo yú. **ˈtower block** *n* [C] [英国英语] (高层)公寓(或办公)大楼〔樓〕 gōngyù dàlóu. **towering** *adj* 极〔極〕高的 jígāode; 极大的 jídàde.

town /taʊn/ *n* 1 (a) [C] 市镇 shìzhèn; 城镇 chéngzhèn. (b) [C, 亦作 sing 用 pl v] 城镇居民 chéngzhèn jūmín. 2 [U] 市区〔區〕 shìqū; 商业〔業〕中心区 shāngyè zhōngxīnqū. 3 [U] (一地区的)主要城镇 zhǔyào chéngzhèn. 4 [U] 城市 chéngshì; 都市 dūshì: ~ *life* 城市生活. 5 [习语] **go to ˈtown** [非正式用语]以极〔極〕大的精力(或热情)去做 yǐ jídà de jīnglì qù zuò. **(out) on the ˈtown** (夜间)去城里寻〔尋〕欢〔歡〕作乐〔樂〕 qù chénglǐ xúnhuān zuòlè. **ˌtown ˈclerk** *n* [C] 城镇书〔書〕记(掌管案卷) chéngzhèn shūjì. **ˌtown ˈcouncil** *n* [C] 镇政会〔會〕 zhènzhènghuì. **ˌtown ˈhall** *n* [C] 镇公所 zhèngōngsuǒ; 市政厅〔廳〕 shìzhèngtīng. **township** /ˈtaʊnʃɪp/ *n* [C] (南非)黑人居住的镇(或郊区) hēirén jūzhù de zhèn.

toxic /ˈtɒksɪk/ *adj* [正式用语]有毒的 yǒudúde.

toy /tɔɪ/ *n* [C] 玩具 wánjù. **toy** *v* [短语动词] **toy with sth** (a)不很认〔認〕真地考虑〔慮〕 bù hěn rènzhēn de kǎolǜ. (b) 心不在焉地摆〔擺〕弄 xīn bú zài yān de bǎinòng: ~ *with a pencil* 摆弄一支铅笔.

trace /treɪs/ *v* [T] 1 追踪 zhuīzōng; 跟踪 gēnzōng; 查找 cházhǎo: *I cannot* ~ *the letter*. 我查不到那封信. 2 描述 miáoshù; 找出(某事的)根源 zhǎochū gēnyuán. 3 (用透明纸)复〔複〕制〔製〕 fùzhì. **trace** *n* 1 [C,U] 痕迹 hénjì; 足迹 zújì: ~*s of an ancient civilization* 古代文明的遗迹. *disappear without* ~ 消失得无影无踪. 2 [C] 微量 wēiliàng; 少量 shǎoliàng: ~*s of poison in his blood* 他血液中的少量毒素. **tracing** *n* [C] (图画等的)复制品 fùzhìpǐn; 摹绘〔繪〕图〔圖〕 móhuìtú. **ˈtracing-paper** *n* [U] 透明描图纸 tòumíng miáotúzhǐ.

track /træk/ *n* [C] 1 路 lù; 小径〔徑〕 xiǎojìng. 2 车辙 chēzhé; 行踪 xíngzōng; 踪迹 zōngjì; 足迹 zújì. 3 (火车)轨道 guǐdào. 4 跑道 pǎodào. 5 一段录〔錄〕音 yíduàn lùyīn. 6 [习语] **hot on sb's tracks** ⇨HOT. **in one's ˈtracks** [非正式用语]当〔當〕场〔場〕 dāngchǎng; 突然 tūrán: *stop him in his* ~*s* 让他当场下不来台. **keep/lose track of sb/sth** 保持(或失去)对〔對〕…的联〔聯〕系〔係〕 bǎochí duì…de liánxì. **make ˈtracks** 离〔離〕去 líqù. **on the right/wrong ˈtrack** 想法对(或错) xiǎngfǎ duì. **track** *v* 1 [T] 追踪 zhuīzōng. 2 [短语动词] **track sb/sth down** 追踪而发〔發〕现 zhuīzōng ér fāxiàn. **tracker** *n* [C]. **ˈtrack record** *n* [C] 过〔過〕去的成就 guòqùde chéngjiù. **ˈtrack suit** *n* [C] (训练时穿的)运〔運〕动〔動〕外套 yùndòng wàitào.

tract[1] /trækt/ *n* [C] 1 一片土地 yípiàn tǔdì; 地带〔帶〕 dìdài. 2 [解剖]道 dào; 束 shù; 系统 xìtǒng: *the respiratory* ~ 呼吸系统.

tract[2] /trækt/ *n* [C] (宗教或政治内容的)小册子 xiǎocèzi.

traction-engine /ˈtrækʃn ˌendʒɪn/ *n* [C] 牵〔牽〕引车 qiānyǐnchē.

tractor /ˈtræktə(r)/ *n* [C] 拖拉机〔機〕 tuōlājī.

trade[1] /treɪd/ *n* 1 (a) [U] 贸易 màoyì; 商业〔業〕 shāngyè. (b) [C] 行业 hángyè: *She's in the book* ~. 她做书籍生意. 2 [U,C] 职〔職〕业 zhíyè; 手艺〔藝〕 shǒuyì: *He's a carpenter by* ~. 他做木匠. **ˈtrade mark** *n* [C] 商标〔標〕 shāngbiāo. **ˈtrade name** *n* [C] 商品名称〔稱〕 shāngpǐn míngchēng. **ˈtradesman** *n* [C] 店主 diànzhǔ; 商人 shāngrén. **ˈtrade talks** *n* [*pl*] 贸易谈判 màoyì tánpàn; 贸易对〔對〕话 màoyì duìhuà. **ˌtrade ˈunion** *n* [C] 工会〔會〕 gōnghuì. **ˌtrade-ˈunionist** *n* [C] 工会会员 gōnghuì huìyuán.

trade[2] /treɪd/ *v* 1 [I] 从〔從〕事贸易 cóngshì màoyì; 做买〔買〕卖〔賣〕 zuò mǎimài. 2 [T] (*for*) 交换 jiāohuàn; 交易 jiāoyì. 3 [短语动词] **trade sth in** (用旧物折价)贴换新物 tiēhuàn xīn wù. **trade on sth** (利用某事)谋取私利 móuqǔ sīlì. **trader** *n* [C].

tradition /trəˈdɪʃn/ *n* (a) [C] 传〔傳〕统的信仰(或习惯等) chuántǒngde xìnyǎng. (b) [U] 传统 chuántǒng. **traditional** /-ʃənl/ *adj*. **traditionally** *adv*.

traffic /ˈtræfɪk/ *n* [U] 1 交通 jiāotōng; 通行 tōngxíng; 往来 wǎnglái. 2 (船只、飞机的)航行 hángxíng. 3 运〔運〕输业〔業〕务〔務〕 yùnshū yèwù. 4 (非法)交易 jiāoyì. **traffic** *v* [-ck-] [I] (*in*) 做生意 zuò shēngyì; (尤指非法的)买〔買〕卖〔賣〕 mǎimài. **trafficker** *n* [C]. **ˈtraffic cone** *n* [C] 路锥〔錐〕 lùzhuī; 锥〔錐〕形路标〔標〕 zhuīxíng lùbiāo. **ˈtraffic island** *n* [C] (交通)安全岛 ānquándǎo. **ˈtraffic jam** *n* [C] 交通阻塞 jiāotōng zǔsè. **ˈtraffic-light** *n* [C, 常作 pl] 交通管理灯〔燈〕 jiāotōng guǎnlǐ dēng; 红绿灯 hónglǜdēng. **ˈtraffic warden** *n* [C] 停车场管理员 tíngchēchǎng guǎnlǐyuán.

tragedy /ˈtrædʒədɪ/ *n* [*pl* -ies] 1 [C,U] 悲惨事件 bēicǎn shìjiàn; 惨案 cǎn'àn. 2 (a) [C] (一出)悲剧〔劇〕 bēijù. (b) [U] 悲剧(戏剧的一种类型) bēijù.

T

tragic /ˈtrædʒɪk/ *adj* **1** 悲惨的 bēicǎnde；悲痛的 bēitòngde：*a ～ accident* 悲惨的事故．**2** 悲剧〔劇〕的 bēijùde. **tragically** /-klɪ/ *adv*.

trail /treɪl/ *n* [C] **1** 痕迹〔跡〕hénjì. 足迹 zújì. **2**（荒野中的）小径〔徑〕xiǎojìng. **trail** *v* **1** [I, T]（使）拖在后〔後〕面 tuō zài hòumiàn. **2** [I] 缓慢地走（尤指跟在后面）huǎnmànde zǒu. **3** [I]（在比赛中）失利 shīlì. **4** [I]（植物）蔓延 mànyán. **5** [T] 追踪 zhuīzōng；尾随〔隨〕wěisuí. **6** [习语] **hot on sb's trail** ⇨HOT. **trailer** *n* [C] **1** 拖车 tuōchē；挂〔掛〕车 guàchē. **2**（电影的）预告片 yùgàopiàn.

train[1] /treɪn/ *n* [C] **1** 列车 lièchē；火车 huǒchē. **2** 一系列 yíxìliè；一连串 yìliánchuàn：*a ～ of thought* 一系列的想法．**3** 拖地的长〔長〕衣裙 tuō dì de cháng yīqún. **4**（人、动物等的）队〔隊〕列 duìliè.

train[2] /treɪn/ *v* **1** [I, T] 训练〔練〕xùnliàn；培养〔養〕péiyǎng：*～ a football team* 训练一足球队．**2** [T] 瞄准〔準〕miáozhǔn：*～ a gun on the enemy* 把枪口瞄准敌人．**3** [T] 使（植物）沿着一定方向生长〔長〕shǐ yánzhe yídìng fāngxiàng shēngzhǎng：*～ roses up a wall* 使蔷薇爬上墙生长．**trainee** /treɪˈniː/ *n* [C] 受训者 shòuxùnzhě. **trainer** *n* [C] **1** 教练员 jiàoliànyuán；驯兽〔獸〕人 xùnshòurén. **2** [常作 pl] 运〔運〕动〔動〕鞋 yùndòngxié. **training** *n* [U] 训练 xùnliàn；锻炼〔煉〕duànliàn.

traipse /treɪps/ *v* [I] [非正式用语] 疲惫〔憊〕地走 píbèide zǒu.

trait /treɪt, treɪ/ *n* [C] 特性 tèxìng；品质 pǐnzhì.

traitor /ˈtreɪtə(r)/ *n* [C] 叛徒 pàntú；卖〔賣〕国〔國〕贼 màiguózéi.

tram /træm/ *n* [C] 有轨电〔電〕车 yǒuguǐ diànchē.

tramp /træmp/ *v* **1** [I] 用沉重的脚步走 yòng chénzhòng de jiǎobù zǒu. **2** [I, T] 徒步远〔遠〕行 túbù yuǎn xíng：*～ over the hills* 徒步翻越山冈〔岡〕. **tramp** *n* [C] **1** 流浪者 liúlàngzhě. **2** 长〔長〕途步行 chángtú bùxíng.

trample /ˈtræmpl/ *v* **1** [I, T] (*on*) 踩坏〔壞〕cǎi huài；践〔踐〕踏 jiàntà. **2** [I] *on* 蔑视 mièshì；粗暴地对〔對〕待 cūbàode duìdài.

trampoline /ˈtræmpəliːn/ *n* [C]（杂技表演用的）蹦床〔牀〕bèngchuáng.

trance /trɑːns; *US* træns/ *n* [C] 恍惚 huǎnghū；失神 shīshén.

tranquil /ˈtræŋkwɪl/ *adj* [正式用语] 平静的 píngjìngde；安宁〔寧〕的 ānníngde. **tranquillity**（美语亦作-l-）/træŋˈkwɪlətɪ/ *n* [U] 平静 píngjìng；安宁 ānníng. **tranquillize**（美语亦作-l-）*v* [T] 使安静（尤指用药物）shǐ ānjìng. **tranquillizer** *n* [C]（美语亦作-l-）镇静剂〔劑〕zhènjìngjì. **tranquilly** *adv*.

transact /trænˈzækt/ *v* [T] [正式用语] 办〔辦〕理 bànlǐ；处〔處〕理 chǔlǐ；执〔執〕行 zhíxíng. **transaction** /-ˈzækʃn/ *n* **1** [U] 办理 bànlǐ；处理 chǔlǐ. **2** [C] 事务〔務〕shìwù；事项 shìxiàng；交易 jiāoyì. **3 transactions** [pl]（学术团体的）会〔會〕议〔議〕记录〔錄〕huìyì jìlù，会报〔報〕huìbào.

transatlantic /ˌtrænzətˈlæntɪk/ *adj* 大西洋彼岸的 Dàxīyáng bǐ'àn de；横渡大西洋的 héngdù Dàxīyáng de.

transcend /trænˈsend/ *v* [T] [正式用语] 超出 chāochū；超过〔過〕chāoguò：*～ human knowledge* 超出人类的知识．

transcontinental /ˌtrænzˌkɒntɪˈnentl/ *adj* 横贯大陆〔陸〕的 héngguàn dàlù de.

transcribe /trænˈskraɪb/ *v* [T] **1** 抄写〔寫〕chāoxiě；照抄 zhàochāo. **2** 改写成（特定形式）gǎixiě chéng：*～d in phonetic symbols* 用音标标出．**3** 改编（乐曲）gǎibiān. **transcript** /ˈtrænskrɪpt/ *n* [C] 抄本 chāoběn；副本 fùběn. **transcription** /-ˈskrɪpʃn/ *n* [U, C].

transfer[1] /trænsˈfɜː(r)/ *v* [-rr-] **1** [I, T] 转〔轉〕移 zhuǎnyí；调动〔動〕diàodòng：*He was ～red to the sales department.* 他调到销售部去了．**2** [T] 让〔讓〕渡（财产等）ràngdù；转让 zhuǎnràng. **transferable** *adj* 可转让的 kě zhuǎnràng de；可让渡的 kě ràngdù de：*This ticket is not ～able.* 此票不得转让．

transfer[2] /ˈtrænsfɜː(r)/ *n* **1** [C, U] 转〔轉〕移 zhuǎnyí；传〔傳〕递〔遞〕chuándì；调动〔動〕diàodòng；过〔過〕户 guòhù. **2** [C] 可移印的图〔圖〕案 kě yíyìn de tú'àn. ˈ**transfer lounge** *n* [C] 转机〔機〕室 zhuǎnjīshì.

transfix /trænsˈfɪks/ *v* [T] [正式用语][常用被动语态]（使受惊恐而）不能动〔動〕弹〔彈〕（或思想、说话）bùnéng dòngtan.

transform /trænsˈfɔːm/ *v* [T] 改变〔變〕（形状、性质等）gǎibiàn. **transformation** /ˌtrænsfəˈmeɪʃn/ *n* [C, U]. **transformer** *n* [C] 变〔變〕压〔壓〕器 biànyāqì.

transfusion /trænsˈfjuːʒn/ *n* [C, U] 输血 shūxuè.

transgress /trænzˈgres/ *v* [I, T] [正式用语] 超越（限度）chāoyuè；违〔違〕反（法律、规则等）wéifǎn. **transgression** /-ˈgreʃn/ *n* [C, U].

transient /ˈtrænzɪənt; *US* ˈtrænʃnt/ *adj* 短暂的 duǎnzànde；片刻的 piànkède.

transistor /trænˈzɪstə(r), -ˈsɪst-/ *n* [C] **1** 晶体〔體〕管 jīngtǐguǎn. **2** 晶体管收音机〔機〕jīngtǐguǎn shōuyīnjī. **transistorized** /-təraɪzd/ *adj* 装〔裝〕有晶体管的 zhuāng yǒu jīngtǐguǎn de.

transit /ˈtrænzɪt, -sɪt/ *n* [U] 运〔運〕输 yùnshū；搬运 bānyùn：*goods damaged in ～* 运

输中损坏的货物.

transition /træn'zɪʃn/ *n* [C, U] 转〔轉〕变〔變〕zhuǎnbiàn; 过〔過〕渡 guòdù. **transitional** /-ʃənl/ *adj*.

transitive /'trænsətɪv/ *adj* [语法]及物的 jíwùde.

transitory /'trænsɪtrɪ; *US* -tɔ:rɪ/ *adj* 短暂的 duǎnzànde; 片刻的 piànkède.

translate /trænz'leɪt/ *v* 1 [I, T] 翻译〔譯〕fānyì: ~ (*the book*) *from French into Russian* (将此书)从法文翻译成俄文. 2 [T] (*into*) 解释〔釋〕jiěshì; 说明 shuōmíng: ~ *ideas into practice* 把那种设想表现在实际行动中. **translation** /-'leɪʃn/ *n* [C, U]. **translator** *n* [C].

translucent /trænz'lu:sənt/ *adj* 半透明的 bàn tòumíng de.

transmission /trænz'mɪʃn/ *n* 1 [U] 传〔傳〕送 chuánsòng. 2 [C] (电视、无线电的)播送 bōsòng. 3 [C] (汽车的)传动〔動〕系统 chuándòng xìtǒng.

transmit /trænz'mɪt/ *v* [-tt-] [T] 1(用无线电)传〔傳〕播 chuánbō, 传送 chuánsòng. 2 传递〔遞〕chuándì; 传达〔達〕chuándá. **transmitter** *n* [C] (无线电)发〔發〕射机〔機〕fāshèjī, 发报〔報〕机 fābàojī.

transparent /træns'pærənt/ *adj* 1 透明的 tòumíngde: *Glass is* ~. 玻璃是透明的. 2 易懂的 yìdǒngde; 显〔顯〕而易见的 xiǎn ér yì jiàn de. **transparency** /-rənsɪ/ *n* [*pl* -ies] 1 [U] 透明 tòumíng; 透明性 tòumíngxìng. 2 [C] 幻灯〔燈〕片 huàndēngpiān; 透明正片 tòumíng zhèngpiàn. **transparently** *adv*.

transplant /træns'plɑ:nt; *US* -'plænt/ *v* 1 [T] 移植 yízhí; 移种〔種〕yízhòng. 2 [T] 人工移植(器官、皮肤等) réngōng yízhí. 3 [I, T] [喻]迁〔遷〕移 qiānyí. **transplant** /'trænsplɑ:nt; *US* -plænt / *n* [C] (器官、皮肤等的)人工移植 réngōng yízhí: *a heart* ~ 心脏移植.

transport /træn'spɔ:t/ *v* [T] 运〔運〕输 yùnshū; 搬运 bānyùn. **transport** /'trænspɔ:t/ *n* [U] 1 (美语亦作 **transportation** /ˌtrænspɔ:'teɪʃn/) 运输(系统) yùnshū. 2 运输工具 yùnshū gōngjù. **transporter** *n* [C] (大型)运输车 yùnshūchē.

transpose /træn'spəʊz/ *v* [T] 1 使互换位置 shǐ hùhuàn wèizhì. 2 [音乐]使变〔變〕调 shǐ biàndiào. **transposition** /ˌtrænspə'zɪʃn/ *n* [C, U].

transvestite /trænz'vestaɪt/ *n* [C] 有异〔異〕性打扮癖的人 yǒu yìxìng dǎbànpǐ de rén.

trap /træp/ *n* [C] 1 (捕兽的)陷阱 xiànjǐng, 捕捉机〔機〕bǔzhuōjī. 2 [喻](陷人的)圈套 quāntào, 诡计 guǐjì. 3 轻〔輕〕便双〔雙〕轮〔輪〕马车 qīngbiàn shuānglún mǎchē. 4 [俚]嘴 zuǐ. **trap** *v* [-pp-] [T] 1 使陷入困境 shǐ xiànrù kùnjìng. 2 诱捕 yòubǔ; 使堕〔墮〕入圈套 shǐ duòrù quāntào. 3 施诡计于 shī guǐjì yú; 欺骗 qīpiàn. **'trapdoor** *n* [C] 地板活门 dìbǎn huómén; 天窗 tiānchuāng. **trapper** *n* [C] (设陷阱)捕兽〔獸〕者 bǔshòuzhě.

trapeze /trə'pi:z; *US* træ-/ *n* [C] (杂技表演用)吊架 diàojià.

trash /træʃ/ *n* [U] 1[非正式用语](材料、作品等)废〔廢〕物 fèiwù, 糟粕 zāopò. 2 [美语]垃圾 lājī. **'trashcan** *n* [C] [美语]垃圾桶 lājītǒng. **trashy** *adj* [-ier, -iest] [非正式用语]毫无〔無〕价〔價〕值的 háowú jiàzhí de.

trauma /'trɔ:mə; *US* 'traʊmə/ *n* 1 [U] 精神创〔創〕伤〔傷〕jīngshén chuāngshāng. 2 [C] [非正式用语]痛苦 tòngkǔ; 不幸 búxìng. **traumatic** /trɔ:'mætɪk; *US* traʊ-/ *adj*.

travel /'trævl/ *v* [-ll-; 美语 -l-] 1 [I, T] 旅游 lǚyóu. 2 [T] 旅行(或走过)(一段距离) lǚxíng. 3 [I] 移动〔動〕yídòng; 走 zǒu: *Light* ~*s faster than sound*. 光比声音快. **travel** *n* 1 [U] 旅行 lǚxíng; 旅游 lǚyóu: *space* ~ 太空旅行. 2 **travels** [pl] (尤指)出国〔國〕旅游 chū guó lǚyóu. **'travel agent** *n* [C] 旅行代理人 lǚxíng dàilǐrén. **travelled** [美语-l-] *adj* 富于旅行经〔經〕验〔驗〕的 fù yú lǚxíng jīngyàn de: *a well-~ writer* 见多识广的作家. **traveller** [美语 -l-] *n* [C] 1 旅行者 lǚxíngzhě; 旅客 lǚkè. 2 旅行推销员 lǚxíng tuīxiāoyuán. **'traveller's cheque** *n* [C] 旅行支票 lǚxíng zhīpiào.

traverse /trə'vɜ:s/ *v* [T] [正式用语]横越 héngyuè; 穿过〔過〕chuānguò.

travesty /'trævəstɪ/ *n* [C] [*pl* -ies] 歪曲的模仿 wāiqūde mófǎng: *a* ~ *of justice* 对正义的歪曲.

trawl /trɔ:l/ *v* [I, T] 拖网〔網〕捕鱼 tuōwǎng bǔ yú. **trawler** *n* [C] 拖网渔船 tuōwǎng yúchuán.

tray /treɪ/ *n* [C] 碟 dié; 盘〔盤〕pán; 托盘 tuōpán.

treacherous /'tretʃərəs/ *adj* 1 背信弃〔棄〕义〔義〕的 bèi xìn qì yì de; 不忠实〔實〕的 bù zhōngshí de. 2 危险〔險〕的 wēixiǎnde: ~ *tides* 危险的潮头. **treacherously** *adv*. **treachery** /-tʃərɪ/ *n* [U, C] [*pl* -ies].

treacle /'tri:kl/ *n* [U] 糖浆〔漿〕tángjiāng. **treacly** *adj*.

tread /tred/ *v* [*pt* **trod** /trɒd/, *pp* **trodden** /'trɒdn/] 1 [I] 走 zǒu; 踏 tà; 踩 cǎi. 2 [T] 践〔踐〕踏 jiàntà; 踩碎 cǎisuì. 3 [T] 踏成 tàchéng; 踩出(一条小路) cǎichū. 4 [习语] **ˌtread on sb's 'toes** [非正式用语]冒犯(或得罪)某人 màofàn mǒurén. **ˌtread 'water** 踩水 cǎishuǐ. **tread** *n* 1 [sing] 步法 bùfǎ; 脚步声〔聲〕jiǎo-

T

bùshēng. 2 [C, U] (轮胎的)胎面 tāimiàn. 3 [C] (台阶的)踏面 tàmiàn.

treason /ˈtriːzn/ *n* [U] 叛逆 pànnì; 谋反 móufǎn. **treasonable** /-zənəbl/ *adj* 叛逆的 pànnìde; 叛国〔國〕的 pànguóde.

treasure /ˈtreʒə(r)/ *n* 1 [U] 金银财宝〔寶〕 jīn yín cáibǎo; 财富 cáifù. 2 [C] 被珍爱〔愛〕的人或物 bèi zhēn'ài de rén huò wù. **treasure** *v* [T] 珍重 zhēnzhòng; 重视 zhòngshì. **treasurer** *n* [C] 会〔會〕计 kuàijì; 出纳 chūnà; 掌管财务〔務〕的人 zhǎngguǎn cáiwù de rén. ˈ**treasure trove** /trəʊv/ *n* [U] (发现的)无〔無〕主财宝〔寶〕 wú zhǔ cáibǎo.

treasury /ˈtreʒərɪ/ *n* **the Treasury** [sing] [用 sing 或 pl v] (英国)财政部 cáizhèngbù.

treat /triːt/ *v* [T] 1 对〔對〕待 duìdài: *They ~ their children badly.* 他们对待子女很不好. 2 当〔當〕作 dàngzuò; 看作 kànzuò: *~ it as a joke* 把它当作笑话. 3 治疗〔療〕 zhìliáo: *~ a patient* 给病人治病. 4 处〔處〕理 chǔlǐ: *~ crops with insecticide* 用杀虫剂处理作物. 5 宴请 yànqǐng; 款待 kuǎndài. **treat** *n* [C] 1 乐〔樂〕事 lèshì. 2 请客 qǐngkè; 款待 kuǎndài.

treatise /ˈtriːtɪz, -tɪs/ *n* [C] (专题)论〔論〕文 lùnwén.

treatment /ˈtriːtmənt/ *n* [C, U] 对〔對〕待 duìdài; 待遇 dàiyù; 处〔處〕理 chǔlǐ; 治疗〔療〕 zhìliáo: *medical ~* 治疗.

treaty /ˈtriːtɪ/ *n* [C] [*pl* -ies] 条〔條〕约 tiáoyuē; 协〔協〕定 xiédìng: *a* ˈ*peace ~* 和平条约.

treble[1] /ˈtrebl/ *adj*, *n* [C] 三倍(的) sān bèi; 三重(的) sān chóng: *He earns ~ my salary.* 他挣的薪水是我的三倍. **treble** *v* [I, T] (使)成三倍 chéng sān bèi; (使)增加二倍 zēngjiā èr bèi.

treble[2] /ˈtrebl/ *n* [C] [音乐]最高音部 zuìgāo yīnbù. **treble** *adj* 高音的 gāoyīnde; 声〔聲〕调高的 shēngdiào gāo de: *a ~ recorder* 高音竖笛.

tree /triː/ *n* [C] 树〔樹〕 shù; 乔〔喬〕木 qiáomù. **treeless** *adj* 无〔無〕树木的 wú shùmù de.

trek /trek/ *v* [-kk-] [I] *n* [C] 长〔長〕途跋涉 chángtú báshè.

trellis /ˈtrelɪs/ *n* [C] (葡萄等的)架 jià, 棚 péng.

tremble /ˈtrembl/ *v* [I] 1 发〔發〕抖 fādǒu; 哆嗦 duōsuō. 2 轻〔輕〕轻摇晃(或颤动) qīngqīng yáohuàng: *The leaves ~d in the breeze.* 树叶在微风中摇晃. 3 焦虑〔慮〕 jiāolǜ; 担〔擔〕忧〔憂〕 dānyōu: *She ~d at having to make a decision.* 她为必须作出决定而不安. **tremble** *n* [C] 发抖 fādǒu; 震颤 zhènchàn: *a ~ in her voice* 她的声音有点发抖.

tremendous /trɪˈmendəs/ *adj* 1 极〔極〕大的 jídàde; 巨大的 jùdàde: *a ~ explosion* 巨大的爆炸. 2 [非正式用语]非常的 fēichángde; 极好的 jíhǎode. **tremendously** *adv*.

tremor /ˈtremə(r)/ *n* [C] 发〔發〕抖 fādǒu; 震动〔動〕 zhèndòng: ˈ*earth ~s* 地面的震动.

trench /trentʃ/ *n* [C] 地沟〔溝〕 dìgōu; 战〔戰〕壕 zhànháo.

trend /trend/ *n* [C] 倾向 qīngxiàng; 趋〔趨〕势〔勢〕 qūshì: *the ~ towards smaller families* 家庭小型化的趋势. ˈ**trend-setter** *n* [C] 时〔時〕髦款式带〔帶〕头〔頭〕者 shímáo kuǎnshì dàitóuzhě. **trendy** *adj* [-ier, -iest] [非正式用语]时髦的 shímáode.

trespass /ˈtrespəs/ *v* [I] (*on*) 非法侵入(私地) fēifǎ qīnrù. **trespass** *n* [U, C] 非法入侵 fēifǎ rùqīn. **trespasser** *n* [C].

trestle /ˈtresl/ *n* [C] 支架 zhījià; 搁凳 gēdèng. ˌ**trestle-**ˈ**table** *n* [C] 用支架支撑的桌子 yòng zhījià zhīchēng de zhuōzi.

trial /ˈtraɪəl/ *n* 1 [C, U] 审〔審〕问 shěnwèn; 审讯 shěnxùn. 2 [C, U] 试验〔驗〕 shìyàn; 测试 cèshì; 试用 shìyòng. 3 [C] 讨厌〔厭〕的人(或物) tǎoyànde rén. 4 [习语] **on** ˈ**trial** (a) 受审 shòushěn. (b) 在测试中 zài cèshì zhōng. ˌ**trial and** ˈ**error** 反复〔復〕试验(以找出错误) fǎnfù shìyàn. ˌ**trial** ˈ**run** *n* [C] 初步测试 chūbù cèshì.

triangle /ˈtraɪæŋgl/ *n* [C] 三角形 sānjiǎoxíng. **triangular** /traɪˈæŋgjʊlə(r)/ *adj*.

tribe /traɪb/ *n* [C] 部落 bùluò; 宗族 zōngzú. **tribal** *adj*. ˈ**tribesman** *n* [C] 部落中的(男性)成员 bùluò zhōng de chéngyuán.

tribunal /traɪˈbjuːnl/ *n* [C] 审〔審〕判员 shěnpànyuán; 法官 fǎguān; 法庭 fǎtíng.

tributary /ˈtrɪbjʊtrɪ; *US* -terɪ/ *n* [C] [*pl* -ies] 支流 zhīliú.

tribute /ˈtrɪbjuːt/ *n* [C, U] 贡献〔獻〕 gòngxiàn; 贡品 gòngpǐn; 赞〔讚〕扬〔揚〕 zànyáng: *pay ~ to her courage* 赞扬她的勇气.

trick /trɪk/ *n* [C] 1 戏〔戲〕法 xìfǎ; 把戏 bǎxì: *conjuring ~s* 变戏法. 2 诡计 guǐjì; 骗术〔術〕 piànshù: *play a ~ on sb* 对某人施诡计. 3 窍〔竅〕门 qiàomén; 技巧 jìqiǎo. 4 一圈(牌) yìquān. 5 [习语] **do the** ˈ**trick** [非正式用语]起作用 qǐ zuòyòng; 奏效 zòuxiào. **trick** *v* [T] 欺骗 qīpiàn; 哄骗 hǒngpiàn: *He was ~ed into giving away all his money.* 他被骗去他所有的钱. **trickery** *n* [U] 欺骗 qīpiàn; 诡计 guǐjì. **tricky** *adj* [-ier, -iest] 1 困难〔難〕的 kùnnande; 复〔復〕杂〔雜〕的 fùzáde: *a ~y position* 需慎重对待的处境. 2 (指人)狡猾的 jiǎohuáde; 奸诈的 jiānzhàde.

trickle /ˈtrɪkl/ *v* [I] 滴流 dīliú; 细流 xìliú: *Tears ~d down her cheek.* 眼泪从她的脸上滴下来. **trickle** *n* [C] 滴流 dīliú; 细流 xìliú:

~ *of blood* 血滴.

tricycle /ˈtraɪsɪkl/ *n* [C] 三轮〔輪〕车 sānlúnchē.

tried *pt, pp* of TRY¹.

trifle /ˈtraɪfl/ *n* 1 [C] 小事 xiǎo shì; 无〔無〕价〔價〕值的东西 wú jiàzhí de dōngxi. 2 [C, U] 甜食 tiánshí; 糕点〔點〕gāodiǎn. 3 [习语] **a trifle** [正式用语]稍微 shāowēi; 有一点儿〔兒〕yǒu yìdiǎnr: *They felt a ~ sad*. 他们觉得有点伤心. **trifle** *v* [I] *with* 轻〔輕〕视 qīngshì; 随〔隨〕便(对待) suíbiàn. **trifling** *adj* 不重要的 bú zhòngyào de; 微不足道的 wēi bù zú dào de.

trigger /ˈtrɪgə(r)/ *n* [C] (尤指枪的)扳机〔機〕bānjī. **trigger** *v* [T] (*off*) 引起 yǐnqǐ; 激发〔發〕jīfā.

trill /trɪl/ *n* [C] 1 颤抖声〔聲〕chàndǒushēng; (鸟的)啭〔囀〕鸣 zhuànmíng. 2 [音乐]颤音 chànyīn. **trill** *v* [I, T] 用颤音唱或奏 yòng chànyīn chàng huò zòu.

trilogy /ˈtrɪlədʒɪ/ *n* [C] [*pl* -ies] (戏剧、小说等的)三部曲 sānbùqǔ.

trim /trɪm/ *adj* [~mer, ~mest] [褒] 1 整洁〔潔〕的 zhěngjiéde; 整齐〔齊〕的 zhěngqíde. 2 修长〔長〕的 xiūchángde; 苗条〔條〕的 miáotiáode. **trim** *v* [-mm-] [T] 1 使整洁 shǐ zhěngjié; 修剪 xiūjiǎn. 2 装〔裝〕饰 zhuāngshì. **trim** *n* 1 [C, 常作 sing] 修剪 xiūjiǎn. 2 [习语] **in (good) trim** 在最佳状〔狀〕态〔態〕中 zài zuì jiā zhuàngtài zhōng. **trimming** *n* [C, 常作 pl] (a) 装饰物 zhuāngshìwù. (b) 通常伴随〔隨〕(或附加)物 tōngcháng bànsuí wù: *roast beef with all the ~mings* 烤牛肉及各种配料.

Trinity /ˈtrɪnətɪ/ *n* **the Trinity** [基督教](圣父、圣子、圣灵)三位一体〔體〕sānwèi yìtǐ.

trinket /ˈtrɪŋkɪt/ *n* [C] 小件饰物 xiǎo jiàn shìwù.

trio /ˈtriːəʊ/ *n* [C] [*pl* ~s] 1 三个〔個〕一组 sāngè yìzǔ; 三位一体〔體〕sānwèi yìtǐ. 2 [音乐] 三重奏 sānchóngzòu; 三人合唱 sānrén héchàng.

trip /trɪp/ *v* [-pp-] 1 [I] (*over/up*) (被…) 绊倒 bàndǎo. 2 [T] (a) (*up*) 使失足 shǐ shīzú; 使摔倒 shǐ shuāidǎo. (b) 使犯错误 shǐ fàn cuòwù. 3 [I] 轻〔輕〕快地走动〔動〕qīngkuàide zǒudòng. **trip** *n* [C] 1 (短途)旅行 lǚxíng; 远〔遠〕足 yuǎnzú. 2 [俚](吸毒者的)幻觉〔覺〕体〔體〕验〔驗〕huànjué tǐyàn. 3 绊倒 bàndǎo; 失足 shīzú. **tripper** *n* [C] 短途旅游者 duǎntú lǚyóuzhě.

tripe /traɪp/ *n* [U] 1(食用)牛肚 niúdǔ. 2 [俚] 废〔廢〕话 fèihuà.

triple /ˈtrɪpl/ *adj* 三部分合成的 sānbùfèn héchéng de; 三方的 sānfāngde. **triple** *v* [I, T] (使)增至三倍 zēng zhì sānbèi.

triplet /ˈtrɪplɪt/ *n* [C] 三胞胎(中的一个) sānbāotāi.

triplicate /ˈtrɪplɪkət/ *n* [习语] **in ˈtriplicate** 一式三份(其中一份为正本) yíshì sānfèn.

tripod /ˈtraɪpɒd/ *n* [C] 三脚架 sānjiǎojià.

trite /traɪt/ *adj* (言论等)平凡的 píngfánde; 陈腐的 chénfǔde.

triumph /ˈtraɪʌmf/ *n* (a) [C] 巨大的成就 jùdàde chéngjiù. (b) [U] 成功(或胜利)的喜悦 chénggōngde xǐyuè. **triumph** *v* [I] (*over*) 获〔獲〕得胜〔勝〕利(或成功) huòdé shènglì; 击〔擊〕败(对方) jībài. **triumphal** /traɪˈʌmfl/ *adj* 胜利的 shènglìde; 成功的 chénggōngde. **triumphant** /traɪˈʌmfnt/ *adj* 庆祝胜利的 qìngzhù shènglì de. **triumphantly** *adv*.

triva /ˈtrɪvɪə/ *n* [pl] 琐碎的事物 suǒsuìde shìwù.

trivial /ˈtrɪvɪəl/ *adj* 不重要的 bú zhòngyào de; 琐碎的 suǒsuìde. **triviality** /ˌtrɪvɪˈælətɪ/ *n* [C, U] [*pl* -ies]. **trivialize** *v* [T] 使显〔顯〕得不重要 shǐ xiǎnde bú zhòngyào.

trod *pt* of TREAD.

trodden *pp* of TREAD.

trolley /ˈtrɒlɪ/ *n* [C] 1 手推车 shǒutuīchē. 2 (用以送食物的)小台〔檯〕车 xiǎo táichē.

trombone /trɒmˈbəʊn/ *n* [C] [音乐]长〔長〕号〔號〕chánghào. **trombonist** *n* [C].

troop /truːp/ *n* 1 **troops** [pl] 军队〔隊〕jūnduì; 部队 bùduì. 2 [C] 一群(人或动物) yìqún. **troop** *v* [I] 成群结队而行 chéngqún jiéduì ér xíng. **trooper** *n* [C] 装〔裝〕甲兵 zhuāngjiǎbīng; 骑兵 qíbīng.

trophy /ˈtrəʊfɪ/ *n* [C] [*pl* -ies] 1 奖〔獎〕品 jiǎngpǐn. 2 (胜利)纪念品 jìniànpǐn.

tropic /ˈtrɒpɪk/ *n* 1 (a) [C, 常作 sing] [天文]回归〔歸〕线〔綫〕huíguīxiàn. (b) **the tropics** [pl] 热〔熱〕带〔帶〕rèdài. 2 [习语] **tropic of Cancer** /ˈkænsə(r)/ 北回归〔歸〕线〔綫〕(北纬 23°27′) běi huíguīxiàn. **tropic of Capricorn** /ˈkæprɪkɔːn/ 南回归线(南纬 23°27′) nán huíguīxiàn. **tropical** *adj* 热带〔帶〕(地区)的 rèdàide.

trot /trɒt/ *v* [-tt-] 1 [I] (马)小跑 xiǎopǎo. 2 [I] (人)快步走 kuàibù zǒu. 3 [短语动词] **trot sth out** [非正式用语][贬](重复而乏味地)说出 shuōchū: ~ *out the same old excuses* 重复提那老一套借口. **trot** *n* 1 [sing] 小跑 xiǎopǎo; 快步走 kuàibù zǒu. 2 [习语] **on the ˈtrot** [非正式用语]一个〔個〕接一个地 yígè jiē yígède; 不断〔斷〕地 búduànde.

trouble /ˈtrʌbl/ *n* 1 [C, U] 烦恼〔惱〕fánnǎo; 忧〔憂〕虑〔慮〕yōulǜ; 困难〔難〕kùnnan: *You shouldn't have any ~ finding the house*. 你不必为找房子而伤脑筋. 2 [U] 不便 búbiàn; 麻烦 máfan: *I don't want to be any ~ to you*. 我不想打扰你. 3 [C, U] 纠纷 jiū-

T

fēn；动〔動〕乱〔亂〕dòngluàn：*the ~s in Northern Ireland* 北爱尔兰的动乱.4 [U] 疾病 jíbìng：*have back ~* 有背脊骨病.5 [U] (机器的)故障 gùzhàng：*engine ~* 发动机出毛病.6 [习语] ˌget into ˈtrouble (a) 陷入困境 xiànrù kùnjìng. (b) 招致责罚 zhāozhì zéfá. **get sb into ˈtrouble** [非正式用语]使(未婚女子)怀〔懷〕孕 shǐ huáiyùn. **take the ˈtrouble to do sth** 不怕麻烦尽〔盡〕力做(某事) búpà máfan jìnlì zuò. **trouble** *v* 1 [T] 使烦恼 shǐ fánnǎo；使忧虑 shǐ yōulǜ；使苦恼 shǐ kǔnǎo. 2 [T] [正式用语](用于请求)打扰〔擾〕dǎrǎo；烦劳〔勞〕fánláo：*I'm sorry to ~ you, but could you tell me the way to the station?* 对不起烦劳你了，你能告诉我去车站的路吗？3 [I] [正式用语]费心 fèixīn；费劲〔勁〕fèijìn；麻烦(自己) máfan. **troubled** *adj* 为〔爲〕难的 wéinánde；担〔擔〕心的 dānxīnde. **ˈtroublemaker** *n* [C] 常惹麻烦的人 cháng rě máfan de rén. **troublesome** *adj* 造成烦恼的 zàochéng fánnǎo de；讨厌〔厭〕的 tǎoyànde.

trough /trɒf; *US* trɔːf/ *n* [C] 1 饲料槽 sìliàocáo；水槽 shuǐcáo. 2 [物理]波谷 bōgǔ. 3 [气象]低压〔壓〕槽 dīyācáo.

troupe /truːp/ *n* [C, 亦作 sing 用 pl v] 剧〔劇〕团〔團〕jùtuán；戏〔戲〕班 xìbān.

trousers /ˈtraʊzəz/ *n* [pl] 裤子 kùzi；长〔長〕裤 chángkù：*a pair of ~* 一条裤子.

trout /traʊt/ *n* [C] [*pl* trout] 鳟鱼 zūnyú.

trowel /ˈtraʊəl/ *n* [C] 1 抹泥刀 mònídāo. 2 泥铲〔鏟〕子 níchǎnzi.

truant /ˈtruːənt/ *n* [C] 逃学〔學〕者 táoxuézhě；旷〔曠〕课者 kuàngkèzhě：*play ~* 逃学. **truancy** /-ənsɪ/ *n* [U].

truce /truːs/ *n* [C] 休战〔戰〕xiūzhàn.

truck[1] /trʌk/ *n* [C] 1 [英国英语][铁路]敞篷货车 chǎngpéng huòchē. 2 [尤用于美语]货车 huòchē；卡车 kǎchē.

truck[2] /trʌk/ *n* [习语] **have no truck with sb** [正式用语]不与〔與〕打交道 bù yǔ dǎ jiāodào.

trudge /trʌdʒ/ *v* [I] 步履艰〔艱〕难〔難〕地走 bùlǚ jiānnán de zǒu. **trudge** *n* [C, 常作 sing] 长〔長〕途跋涉 chángtú báshè.

true /truː/ *adj* [~r, ~st] 1 符合事实〔實〕的 fúhé shìshí de；真实〔實〕的 zhēnshíde. 2 真的 zhēnde；确〔確〕实的 quèshíde：*my ~ feelings for you* 我对你的真实感情. 3 忠实的 zhōngshíde；忠诚的 zhōngchéngde：*a ~ friend* 忠实的朋友. 4 准〔準〕确〔確〕的 zhǔnquède；确切的 quèqiède：*a ~ copy* 准确的副本. 5 [习语] **come ˈtrue** (指希望、梦)成为〔爲〕事实 chéng wéi shìshí. **true to sth** 符合事实 fúhé shìshí：*~ to life* 符合现实. **true** *n* [习语] **out of ˈtrue** 位置不正 wèizhì búzhèng：*The door is out of ~.* 这扇门位置不正.

truly /ˈtruːlɪ/ *adv* 1 真正地 zhēnzhèngde；确〔確〕实〔實〕地 quèshíde：*a ~ brave action* 真正勇敢的行为. 2 忠诚地 zhōngchéngde；忠实地 zhōngshíde；诚恳〔懇〕地 chéngkěnde：*feel ~ grateful* 诚挚地感谢. 3 真实地 zhēnshíde；如实地 rúshíde.

trump /trʌmp/ *n* 1 [C] 王牌 wángpái. 2 [习语] ˌturn/ˌcome up ˈtrumps [非正式用语]意外的帮〔幫〕助(或慷慨) yìwàide bāngzhù. **trump** *v* [T] 1 出王牌吃掉(一牌) chū wángpái chīdiào. 2 [短语动词] **trump sth up** [常用被动语态]编造(罪名) biānzào：*~ed-up charges* 捏造的罪名. **ˈtrump-card** *n* [C] [喻]最有效的手段 zuì yǒuxiàode shǒuduàn.

trumpet /ˈtrʌmpɪt/ *n* [C] 喇叭 lǎba. **trumpet** *v* 1 [I, T] 大声〔聲〕宣告 dàshēng xuāngào. 2 [I] (象)吼叫 hǒujiào. **trumpeter** *n* [C] 吹喇叭的人 chuī lǎba de rén；号〔號〕兵 hàobīng.

truncate /trʌŋˈkeɪt; *US* ˈtrʌnkeɪt/ *v* [T] 截短 jié duǎn.

truncheon /ˈtrʌntʃən/ *n* [C] 短粗的棍棒 duǎncūde gùnbàng；警棍 jǐnggùn.

trundle /ˈtrʌndl/ *v* [I, T] (使)沉重地滚〔滾〕动〔動〕(或移动) chénzhòngde gǔndòng.

trunk /trʌŋk/ *n* 1 [C] 树〔樹〕干〔幹〕shùgàn. 2 [C] 大衣箱 dà yīxiāng. 3 [C] 象鼻 xiàngbí. 4 [C, 常作 sing] 躯〔軀〕干 qūgàn. 5 **trunks** [pl] 男游泳裤 nán yóuyǒngkù. 6 [C] [美语](汽车后部的)行李箱 xínglǐxiāng. **ˈtrunkcall** *n* [C] [英国英语][旧]长〔長〕途电〔電〕话 chángtú diànhuà. **ˈtrunk-road** *n* [C] 公路干线〔綫〕gōnglù gànxiàn.

truss /trʌs/ *v* [T] 1 捆牢 kǔn láo；扎〔紮〕紧〔緊〕zā jǐn. 2 (烹烤前)把(鸡等)扎好 bǎ zāhǎo. **truss** *n* [C] 1 (疝气)托带〔帶〕tuōdài. 2 (屋顶、桥梁等的)桁架 héngjià.

trust[1] /trʌst/ *n* 1 [U] 信任 xìnrèn；信赖 xìnlài. 2 [U] 责任 zérèn；职〔職〕责 zhízé. 3 [C] 托管财产〔產〕tuōguǎn cáichǎn：*money kept in a ~* 受托管的钱. 4 [习语] **take sth on trust** 不经〔經〕证〔證〕明(而相信) bù jīng zhèngmíng. **trusting** *adj* 信任的 xìnrènde；不疑的 bùyíde. **trustingly** *adv*. **trustworthy** *adj* 可信赖的 kě xìnlài de；可靠的 kěkàode. **trusty** *adj* [-ier, -iest] [古或谑]可靠的 kěkàode；可信任的 kě xìnrèn de.

trust[2] /trʌst/ *v* [T] 1 信任 xìnrèn；相信 xiāngxìn：*You can ~ me.* 你可以相信我. 2 依靠 yīkào；信得过〔過〕xìn dé guò：*You can't ~ young children with matches.* 你不能把火柴交给小孩子. 3 [正式用语]希望 xīwàng：*I ~ you are well.* 我希望你身体好.

trustee /trʌˈstiː/ *n* [C] 受托管者 shòu tuōguǎn zhě.

truth /truːθ/ *n* [*pl* ~s /truːðz/] 1 [U] 真实〔實〕zhēnshí; 真实性 zhēnshíxìng: *There's no ~ in what he says.* 他所说的毫不真实. 2 [U] 事实 shìshí; 真相 zhēnxiàng: *tell the ~* 说真话. 3 [C] 真理 zhēnlǐ; 真义〔義〕zhēnyì: *scientific ~s* 科学的真理. **truthful** *adj* 1 (人)诚实的 chéngshíde, 说真话的 shuō zhēnhuà de. 2 (叙述)真实的 zhēnshíde, 如实的 rúshíde. **truthfully** *adv*. **truthfulness** *n* [U].

try[1] /traɪ/ *v* [*pt*, *pp* tried] 1 [I] 试做 shì zuò; 尝〔嘗〕试 chángshì: *He tried to escape.* 他试图逃跑. 2 [T] 试验〔驗〕shìyàn; 试用 shìyòng: *Have you tried this new soap?* 你试用过这种新型肥皂吗? 3 [T] 审〔審〕问 shěnwèn; 审判 shěnpàn: *He was tried for murder.* 他以杀人受审. 4 [T] 使忍受极〔極〕度劳〔勞〕累(或艰难困苦) shǐ rěnshòu jídù láolèi; 考验〔驗〕kǎoyàn: *You're ~ing my patience!* 你在考验我的耐心! 5 [习语] **try one's hand at sth** 试行 shìxíng; 做起来看 zuòqǐlái kàn. 6 [短语动词] **try sth on** (a) 试穿(衣服等) shì chuān. (b) [非正式用语]试探(某事可否被容忍) shìtàn: *Stop ~ing it on!* 别耍花招! **try sth out** 试用(某物) shìyòng. **tried** *adj* 经〔經〕证〔證〕明有效的 jīng zhèngmíng yǒuxiào de. **trying** *adj* 难〔難〕对〔對〕付的 nán duìfù de; 使人厌〔厭〕烦的 shǐ rén yànfán de.

try[2] /traɪ/ *n* [C] [*pl* -ies] 1 尝〔嘗〕试 chángshì; 试图〔圖〕shìtú. 2 (橄榄球赛中)在对〔對〕方球门线〔綫〕后〔後〕面带〔帶〕球触〔觸〕地 zài duìfāng qiúménxiàn hòumiàn dài qiú chù dì.

tsar /zɑː(r)/ *n* [C] (1917 年前俄国)沙皇 shāhuáng. **tsarina** /zɑːˈriːnə/ *n* [C] (旧俄)女皇(或皇后) nǚhuáng.

T-shirt ⇨T, t.

tsunami /tsuːˈnɑːmɪ/ *n* (*pl* ~ *or* ~*s*)海啸〔嘯〕.

tub /tʌb/ *n* [C] 1 桶 tǒng; 盆 pén. 2 浴缸 yùgāng; 洗澡 xǐzǎo.

tuba /ˈtjuːbə; *US* ˈtuːbə/ *n* [C] [音乐]大号〔號〕dàhào.

tubby /ˈtʌbɪ/ *adj* [-ier, -iest] [非正式用语]矮胖的 ǎipàngde; 肥圆的 féiyuánde.

tube /tjuːb; *US* tuːb/ *n* 1 [C] 管 guǎn; 管道 guǎndào. 2 [C] (金属或塑料)软管 ruǎnguǎn. 3 **the tube** [U, sing] (伦敦)地下铁〔鐵〕道 dìxià tiědào. 4 [C] [解剖]管 guǎn. **tubing** *n* [U] 管形材料 guǎnxíng cáiliào. **tubular** /ˈtjuːbjʊlə(r); *US* ˈtuː-/ *adj* 管状〔狀〕的 guǎnzhuàngde.

tuber /ˈtjuːbə(r); *US* ˈtuː-/ *n* [C] [植物]块〔塊〕茎〔莖〕kuàijīng.

tuberculosis /tjuːˌbɜːkjʊˈləʊsɪs; *US* tuː-/ *n* [U] (尤指肺)结核(病) jiéhé.

TUC /ˌtiː juː ˈsiː/ *n* **the TUC** [sing] (= Trades Union Congress) 英国〔國〕职〔職〕工大会〔會〕Yīngguó zhígōng dàhuì.

tuck /tʌk/ *v* 1 [T] 打褶裥 dǎ zhějiǎn; 缩拢〔攏〕suōlǒng; 塞置于 sāizhì yú. *He ~ed his shirt into his trousers.* 他把衬衣下摆塞进裤子里. 2 [T] (舒适地)裹住(某人、某物) guǒzhù. 3 [短语动词] **tuck in** [非正式用语]尽〔盡〕情地吃 jìnqíngde chī; 大吃 dà chī. **tuck sb up** 盖〔蓋〕好被子 gài hǎo bèizi. **tuck** *n* 1 [C] (衣服的)褶裥 zhějiǎn. 2 [U] [英国非正式用语](尤指小孩爱吃的)食品 shípǐn.

Tuesday /ˈtjuːzdɪ; *US* ˈtuː-/ *n* [U, C]星期二 xīngqī'èr.

tuft /tʌft/ *n* [C] (羽毛、草等)一束 yíshù, 一簇 yícù.

tug /tʌg/ *v* [-gg-] [I, T] (*at*) 用力拉 yòng lì lā. **tug** *n* [C] 1 猛拉 měng lā; 拖拉 tuōlā 2 (亦作 ˈ**tugboat**) 拖船 tuōchuán.

tuition /tjuːˈɪʃn; *US* tuː-/ *n* [U] [正式用语] 教学〔學〕jiàoxué; 学费 xuéfèi: *have private ~* 请私人教学.

tulip /ˈtjuːlɪp; *US* ˈtuː-/ *n* [C] [植物]郁金香 yùjīnxiāng.

tumble /ˈtʌmbl/ *v* 1 [I, T] (使)跌倒 diēdǎo; (使)跌落 diēluò. 2 [I] 打滚 dǎ gǔn; 乱〔亂〕动〔動〕luàn dòng. 3 [短语动词] **tumble down** 倒塌 dǎotā; 垮掉 kuǎdiào. **tumble to sth** [非正式用语]了解 liǎojiě; 看穿 kànchuān. **tumble** *n* [C, 常作 sing] 坠〔墜〕落 zhuìluò; 倒塌 dǎotā. ˈ**tumbledown** *adj* 倒塌的 dǎotāde; 残〔殘〕破的 cánpòde. ˈ**tumble-drier** *n* [C] 滚筒式干〔乾〕衣机〔機〕gǔntǒngshì gānyījī.

tumbler /ˈtʌmblə(r)/ *n* [C] 平底无〔無〕把酒杯 píngdǐ wú bà jiǔbēi.

tummy /ˈtʌmɪ/ *n* [C] [*pl* -ies] [非正式用语]胃 wèi; 肚子 dùzi.

tumour (美语 -or) /ˈtjuːmə(r); *US* ˈtuː-/ *n* [C] 肿〔腫〕瘤 zhǒngliú.

tumult /ˈtjuːmʌlt; *US* ˈtuː-/ *n* [U, sing] [正式用语] 1 吵闹〔鬧〕chǎonào; 喧哗〔嘩〕xuānhuá. 2 混乱〔亂〕hùnluàn; 骚乱 sāoluàn. **tumultuous** /tjuːˈmʌltʃʊəs; *US* tuː-/ *adj* [正式用语]吵闹的 chǎonàode; 喧哗的 xuānhuáde.

tuna /ˈtjuːnə/ *n* [C, U] [*pl* **tuna** 或~s] 金枪〔槍〕鱼 jīnqiāngyú.

tune /tjuːn; *US* tuːn/ *n* 1 [C] 曲调 qǔdiào; 明显〔顯〕的旋律 míngxiǎnde xuánlǜ. 2 [习语] ˌ**in**/ˌ**out of** ˈ**tune** (a) 调子正确〔確〕(或不正确) diàozi zhèngquè. (b) [喻]协〔協〕调(或不协调) xiétiáo; 和谐(或不和谐) héxié. **to the** ˈ**tune of sth** [非正式用语]达〔達〕到…数〔數〕量 dádào…shùliàng: *fined to the ~ of £1,000.* 罚款达1 000镑. **tune** *v* [T] 1 (为乐器)调音 tiáo yīn. 2 调整(机器) tiáozhěng. 3 [短语动词] **tune in (to sth)** (收音机)调谐 tiáoxié; 收听

T

〔聽〕 shōutīng. **tuneful** *adj* (曲调)悦耳的 yuè'ěrde. **tunefully** *adv*. **tuner** *n* [C] 调音师〔師〕 tiáoyīnshī. **'tuning-fork** *n* [C] 音叉 yīnchā.

tunic /'tju:nɪk; *US* 'tu:-/ *n* [C] **1**(警察、士兵的)紧〔緊〕身上衣 jǐn shēn shàngyī. **2** (系带的)宽大外衣 kuāndà wàiyī.

tunnel /'tʌnl/ *n* [C] 隧道 suìdào; 地道 dìdào. **tunnel** *v* [-ll-; 美语 -l-] [I, T] 掘地道 jué dìdào.

turban /'tɜ:bən/ *n* [C] (某些亚洲国家)男用头〔頭〕巾 nányòng tóujīn.

turbine /'tɜ:baɪn/ *n* [C] 涡〔渦〕轮〔輪〕机〔機〕 wōlúnjī; 透平 tòupíng.

turbulent /'tɜ:bjʊlənt/ *adj* 混乱〔亂〕的 hùnluànde; 狂暴的 kuángbàode; 骚〔騷〕乱的 sāoluànde: ～ *passions* 狂热的情感. ～ *waves* 汹涌的波涛. **turbulence** /-ləns/ *n* [U].

tureen /tə'ri:n, tjʊ'ri:n/ *n* [C] (盛汤的)大盖〔蓋〕碗 dà gàiwǎn.

turf /tɜ:f/ *n* [*pl* ～s 或 **turves**] **1**(a) [U] 草地 cǎodì; 草皮 cǎopí. (b) [C] 草皮块〔塊〕 cǎopíkuài. **2 the turf** [sing] 赛马 sàimǎ. **turf** *v* [T] **1** 铺草皮于 pū cǎopí yú. **2** [短语动词] **turf sb/sth out** [英国非正式用语]赶〔趕〕走(某人) gǎn zǒu; 扔掉(某物) rēngdiào.

turkey /'tɜ:kɪ/ *n* (a) [C] 火鸡〔鷄〕 huǒjī. (b) [U] 火鸡肉 huǒjīròu.

turmoil /'tɜ:mɔɪl/ *n* [C, 常作 sing, U] 骚动〔動〕 sāodòng; 混乱〔亂〕 hùnluàn.

turn[1] /tɜ:n/ *v* **1** [I, T] (使)旋转〔轉〕 xuánzhuǎn; (使)转动〔動〕 zhuàndòng: *The earth ～s round the sun*. 地球绕着太阳转. ～ *a key in a lock* 转动钥匙开锁. **2** [I, T] (使)翻转 fānzhuǎn; (使)转过〔過〕来 zhuǎnguòlái: *She ～ed to look at me*. 她转过身来看着我. **3** [I, T] (使)转向 zhuǎnxiàng; (使)转弯〔彎〕 zhuǎnwān: *T～ left by the church*. 在教堂旁边左转弯. **4** [I, T] (使)绕〔繞〕过 ràoguò: *The car ～ed the corner*. 那辆汽车在街角处拐弯了. **5** [常与 *adj* 连用](使)变〔變〕成 biànchéng; (使)成为〔爲〕 chéngwéi: *The milk has ～ed sour*. 牛奶变酸了. *She's just ～ed 50*. 她正好五十岁. **6** [I, T] (*from*) *to*/*into* (使)转化 zhuǎnhuà: *Caterpillars ～ into butterflies*. 毛虫蜕化为蝴蝶. **7** [T] 指向 zhǐxiàng; 瞄准〔準〕 miáozhǔn: ～ *one's attention to the question of money* 考虑钱的问题. **8** [习语] **not turn a 'hair** 不畏惧〔懼〕 bú wèijù; 不惊〔驚〕慌 bù jīnghuāng. **turn one's back on sb/sth** 拒绝(帮助) jùjué; 不顾〔顧〕 búgù. **turn a blind 'eye to sth** 故意忽视 gùyì hūshì. **turn the clock back** ⇨CLOCK. **turn a deaf 'ear to sth** 不听〔聽〕 bù tīng; 对〔對〕…充耳不闻 duì…chōng ěr bù wén. **turned 'out** 打扮 dǎbàn: *be elegantly ～ed out* 打扮得很讲究. **turn one's hand to sth** 着手 zhuóshǒu; 开〔開〕始学〔學〕习〔習〕 kāishǐ xuéxí. **turn over a new 'leaf** 改过〔過〕自新 gǎiguò zìxīn. **turn the 'tables on sb** 扭转形势〔勢〕 niǔzhuǎn xíngshì. **turn 'tail** 逃跑 táopǎo. **turn up one's 'nose at sb/sth** [非正式用语]看不起 kàn bu qǐ; 嗤之以鼻 chī zhī yǐ bí. **turn up trumps** ⇨TRUMP. **9** [短语动词] **turn (sb) against sb** (使)不友好 bù yǒuhǎo; (使)采〔採〕取敌〔敵〕对态〔態〕度 cǎiqǔ díduì tàidù. **turn sb away** 不准进〔進〕入 bùzhǔn jìnrù; 拒不帮助 jù bù bāngzhù. **turn (sb) back** (使)往回走 wǎng huí zǒu. **turn sb/sth down** 拒绝 jùjué. **turn sth down** (调节炉具、收音机等)使热〔熱〕度(或音量)降低 shǐ rèdù jiàngdī. **turn 'in** [非正式用语]去睡觉〔覺〕 qù shuìjiào. **turn sb in** [非正式用语]告发〔發〕 gàofā; 告密 gàomì. **turn sb 'off** [非正式用语]使厌〔厭〕烦(或厌恶) shǐ yànfán. **turn sth off** 关〔關〕掉(水流等) guāndiào: ～ *off the tap* 关上水龙头. **turn on sb** 袭〔襲〕击〔擊〕 xíjī. **turn sb 'on** [非正式用语]使生快感 shǐ shēng kuàigǎn. **turn sth on** 打开(水流等) dǎkāi: ～ *on the radio* 打开收音机. **turn 'out** (a) (以某方式)发生 fāshēng; 证〔證〕明为 zhèngmíng wéi: *Everything ～ed out well*. (结果)一切顺利. (b) 在场〔場〕 zàichǎng. **turn sth out** (a) 关掉 guāndiào; 熄灭〔滅〕 xīmiè. (b) 出空 chū kōng: ～ *out the cupboards* 把柜橱出空. (c) 生产〔產〕 shēngchǎn; 培养〔養〕 péiyǎng. **turn sb out (of sth)** 赶〔趕〕走 gǎn zǒu. **turn sth over** (a) 仔细考虑〔慮〕 zǐxì kǎolǜ. (b) 营〔營〕业〔業〕额达〔達〕… yíngyè'é dá…. **turn sth/sb over to sb** 移交 yíjiāo; 交给 jiāogěi: *The thief was ～ed over to the police*. 那贼已被送交警察. **turn to sb** 寻〔尋〕求帮助 xúnqiú bāngzhù. **turn up** 到达 dàodá. **turn (sth) up** 发掘出 fājuéchū; (使)暴露 bàolù: *The book you've lost will probably ～ up somewhere*. 你遗失的那本书大概会在什么地方找到的. **turn sth up** (调节炉具、收音机等)使热度(或音量)升高 shǐ rèdù shēnggāo. **'turn-off** *n* [C] 支路 zhīlù; 岔道 chàdào. **'turn-out** *n* [C, 常作 sing] 出席(或参与)的人数〔數〕 chūxíde rénshù. **'turnover** *n* [sing] 营业额 yíngyè'é: *Their annual ～over is £10 million*. 他们一年的营业额为一千万镑. **'turn-up** *n* [C] **1** [常作 pl] (裤脚的)卷〔捲〕边〔邊〕 juǎn biān. **2** [非正式用语]意外的事 yìwàide shì: *a ～-up for the book* (意想不到的)突发事件.

turn[2] /tɜ:n/ *n* [C] **1** 转〔轉〕动〔動〕 zhuàndòng; 旋转 xuánzhuǎn. **2** 转弯〔彎〕 zhuǎnwān; 转向 zhuǎnxiàng. **3** 变〔變〕化 biànhuà; 转折 zhuǎnzhé: *Business has taken a ～ for the worse*. 生意越来越不好做了. **4** 机〔機〕会〔會〕 jīhuì; 轮〔輪〕值 lúnzhí: *It's your ～ to* *choose*. 轮到你挑选了. 5 (新年或世纪的)开〔開〕始 kāishǐ. 6 (戏院的)短节〔節〕目 duǎn jiémù. 7 生病 shēngbìng. 8 惊〔驚〕吓〔嚇〕jīngxià. 9 [习语] at every ˈturn 处〔處〕处 chùchù; 每次 měi cì. done to a ˈturn (食物)火候适当〔當〕huǒhòu shìdàng. in ˈturn 依次 yīcì; 轮〔輪〕流 lúnliú. ˌout of ˈturn 不合时〔時〕宜 bù hé shíyí. take (it in) ˈturns to do sth 轮流去做 lúnliú qù zuò: *The children took it in ~s to play on the swing*. 孩子们轮流打秋千.

turning /ˈtɜːnɪŋ/ *n* [C] (路的)转弯〔彎〕处〔處〕zhuǎnwānchù. ˈturning-point *n* [C] 转折点〔點〕zhuǎnzhédiǎn; 转机〔機〕zhuǎnjī.

turnip /ˈtɜːnɪp/ *n* [C, U] 萝〔蘿〕卜〔蔔〕luóbo.

turnpike /ˈtɜːnpaɪk/ *n* [C] [美语](收费)高速公路 gāosù gōnglù.

turnstile /ˈtɜːnstaɪl/ *n* [C] (十字形)转〔轉〕门 zhuànmén.

turntable /ˈtɜːnteɪbl/ *n* [C] (唱机的)转盘〔盤〕zhuànpán.

turpentine /ˈtɜːpəntaɪn/ *n* [U] 松节〔節〕油 sōngjiéyóu.

turquoise /ˈtɜːkwɔɪz/ *adj* 绿蓝〔藍〕色的 lǜlánsède. turquoise *n* [C, U] 绿松石 lǜsōngshí.

turret /ˈtʌrɪt/ *n* [C] 1 角楼〔樓〕jiǎolóu; 小塔 xiǎotǎ. 2 [C] 炮塔 pàotǎ.

turtle /ˈtɜːtl/ *n* [C] 海龟〔龜〕hǎiguī.

tusk /tʌsk/ *n* [C] (象、野猪等的)獠牙 liáoyá.

tussle /ˈtʌsl/ *v* [I] *n* [C] 扭打 niǔdǎ; 争斗〔鬥〕zhēngdòu.

tut /tʌt/ (亦作 ˌtut-ˈtut) *interj* (表示不耐烦)嘘 xū! 啧 zé!

tutor /ˈtjuːtə(r); *US* ˈtuː-/ *n* [C] 1 私人教师〔師〕sīrén jiàoshī; 家庭教师 jiātíng jiàoshī. 2 [英国英语](大学)导〔導〕师 dǎoshī. tutor *v* [I, T] (个别地)教学〔學〕jiàoxué; 当〔當〕…的导师 dāng…de dǎoshī. tutorial /tjuːˈtɔːrɪəl; *US* tuː-/ *n* [C] (教师的)指导期 zhǐdǎo qī. tutorial *adj* 家庭教师的 jiātíng jiàoshī de; (大学)导师的 dǎoshīde.

tuxedo /tʌkˈsiːdəʊ/ *n* [C] [*pl* ~s] [美语](男用)晚礼〔禮〕服 wǎn lǐfú.

TV /ˌtiː ˈviː/ *n* [C, U] 电〔電〕视 diànshì.

twaddle /ˈtwɒdl/ *n* [U] [非正式用语]无〔無〕聊的话 wúliáode huà; 废〔廢〕话 fèihuà.

twang /twæŋ/ *n* [C] 1 拨〔撥〕弦声〔聲〕bōxiánshēng. 2 鼻声 bíshēng; 鼻音 bíyīn. twang *v* [I, T] (使)发〔發〕拨弦声 fā bōxiánshēng.

tweak /twiːk/ *v* [T] 拧〔擰〕níng; 扭 niǔ; 捏 niē: ~ *a child's nose* 捏小孩儿的鼻子. tweak *n* [sing].

tweed /twiːd/ *n* 1 [U] 花呢 huāní. 2 tweeds [pl] (一套)花呢衣服 huāní yīfu.

tweet /twiːt/ *v* [I] *n* [C] [非正式用语](小鸟的)啁啾声〔聲〕zhōujiūshēng.

tweezers /ˈtwiːzəz/ *n* [pl] 镊〔鑷〕子 nièzi.

twelve /twelv/ *pron, adj, n* [C] 十二(的) shíèr. twelfth /twelfθ/ *pron, adj* 第十二(的) dìshí'èr. twelfth *pron, n* [C] 十二分之一 shí'èrfēn zhī yī.

twenty /ˈtwentɪ/ *pron, adj, n* [C] [*pl* -ies] 二十(的) èrshí. twentieth /ˈtwentɪəθ/ *pron, adj* 第二十(的) dì'èrshí. twentieth *pron, n* [C] 二十分之一 èrshífēn zhī yī. twenty-four/seven, twenty-four seven, 24/7 *adv* 全天营〔營〕业〔業〕quántiān yíngyè; 无〔無〕休息日 wú xiūxirì. He's on duty ~. 他全年无休二十四小时当值.

twice /twaɪs/ *adv* 两次 liǎngcì; 两倍 liǎngbèi. *I've read this book ~*. 这本书我已看过两遍了. *Your room is ~ as big as mine*. 你的房间比我的大一倍.

twiddle /ˈtwɪdl/ *v* [I, T] 抚〔撫〕弄 fǔnòng; 把玩 bǎwán.

twig[1] /twɪg/ *n* [C] 细枝 xìzhī; 嫩枝 nènzhī.

twig[2] /twɪg/ *v* [-gg-] [I, T] [英国非正式用语]懂得 dǒngdé; 了解 liǎojiě.

twilight /ˈtwaɪlaɪt/ *n* [U] 黄昏 huánghūn.

twill /twɪl/ *n* [U] 斜纹布 xiéwénbù.

twin /twɪn/ *n* [C] 孪〔孿〕生儿〔兒〕之一 luánshēng'ér zhī yī. twin *adj* 完全相像的 wánquán xiāngxiàng de: ~ *beds* 两张相同的单人床.

twine /twaɪn/ *n* [U] 多股线〔綫〕duō gǔ xiàn; 细绳〔繩〕xì shéng. twine *v* [I, T] 卷〔捲〕绕〔繞〕juǎnrào.

twinge /twɪndʒ/ *n* [C] (一阵)剧〔劇〕痛 jùtòng; 刺痛 cìtòng: [喻] *a ~ of guilt* 一阵内疚.

twinkle /ˈtwɪŋkl/ *v* [I] 1 闪烁〔爍〕shǎnshuò; 闪耀 shǎnyào: *stars twinkling in the sky* 天上闪烁着的星星. 2 (眼睛)闪闪发〔發〕光 shǎnshǎn fā guāng. twinkle *n* [sing]: *a ~ in her eyes* 她眼中的闪光.

twirl /twɜːl/ *v* 1 [I, T] (使)快速旋转〔轉〕kuàisù xuánzhuǎn. 2 [T] 扭转 niǔzhuǎn; 卷〔捲〕曲 juǎnqū; 捻弄 niǎnnòng. twirl *n* [C] 旋转 xuánzhuǎn.

twist /twɪst/ *v* 1 [T] 缠〔纏〕绕〔繞〕chánrào; 盘〔盤〕绕 pánrào: ~ *string round one's fingers* 把绳子缠绕在手指上. 2 [I, T] 转〔轉〕动〔動〕zhuǎndòng; 旋转 xuánzhuǎn: *She ~ed (her head) round*. 她扭过头去. 3 [I, T] (使)扭曲 niǔqū; 挤〔擠〕压〔壓〕jǐyā: *The car was a pile of ~ed metal*. 那辆汽车已经成了一堆压缩的废铁了. 4 [T] 扭伤 niǔshāng. 5 [T] 转动 zhuǎndòng; 拧〔擰〕开〔開〕nǐngkāi: ~ *the lid off the jar* 拧开瓶盖. 6 [I] (道路、河流)曲折 qūzhé, 盘旋 pánxuán. 7 [T] 曲解 qūjiě: ~ *sb's words* 曲解

T

某人的话. 8 [习语] ˌtwist sb's ˈarm [非正式用语]说服 shuōfú; 强迫 qiángpò. **twist sb round one's little ˈfinger** [非正式用语]任意摆〔擺〕布(某人) rènyì bǎibù. **twist** *n* [C] 1 搓 cuō; 转 zhuǎn; 扭 niǔ; 拧 nǐng. 2 扭曲状〔狀〕 niǔqūzhuàng. 3 转变〔變〕 zhuǎnbiàn; 发〔發〕展 fāzhǎn: *by a strange ~ of fate* 命运的奇异转变.

twit /twɪt/ *n* [C] [英国非正式用语]傻〔傻〕瓜 shǎguā.

twitch /twɪtʃ/ *n* [C] (肌肉的)抽搐 chōuchù. **twitch** *v* 1 [I] 抽搐 chōuchù. 2 [I, T] (突然的)拉动〔動〕 lādòng; 急扯 jíchě.

twitter /ˈtwɪtə(r)/ *v* [I] 1 (鸟)吱吱地叫 zhīzhīde jiào. 2 (人)因兴〔興〕奋〔奮〕而快速地说 yīn xīngfèn ér kuàisùde shuō. **twitter** *n* [sing].

two /tuː/ *pron, adj, n* [C] [*pl* ~s] 1 二 èr; 两 liǎng. 2 [习语] **put ˌtwo and ˌtwo toˈgether** 推测(真相) tuīcè. **ˌtwo-ˈfaced** *adj* 两面派的 liǎngmiànpàide. **ˈtwofold** *adj, adv* (a) 两部分的 liǎngbùfènde. (b) 两倍(的) liǎngbèi. **ˌtwo-ˈway** *adj* (道路)双〔雙〕向的 shuāngxiàngde.

tycoon /taɪˈkuːn/ *n* [C] [非正式用语]实〔實〕业〔業〕界巨头〔頭〕 shíyèjiè jùtóu.

tying ⇨TIE¹.

type /taɪp/ *n* 1 [C] 类〔類〕型 lèixíng; 种〔種〕类 zhǒnglèi: *many different ~s of computers* 各式各样的计算机. 2 [U] [印刷]活字 huózì; 铅字 qiānzì: *italic ~* 斜体字. **type** *v* [I, T] (用打字机或文字处理机)打印 dǎyìn. **type-cast** /ˈtaɪpkɑːst / *v* [*pt, pp* **type-cast**] [T] [尤用被动语态]让〔讓〕(演员)担〔擔〕任擅长〔長〕的角色 ràng dānrèn shàncháng de juésè. **ˈtypescript** *n* [C] (打印的)文件 wénjiàn. **ˈtypewriter** *n* [C] 打字机〔機〕 dǎzìjī. **typing** *n* [U] 打字(技术) dǎzì. **typist** *n* [C] 打字员 dǎzìyuán.

typhoid /ˈtaɪfɔɪd/ *n* [U] 伤〔傷〕寒 shānghán.

typhoon /taɪˈfuːn/ *n* [C] 台风〔風〕 táifēng.

typhus /ˈtaɪfəs/ *n* [U] 斑疹伤〔傷〕寒 bānzhěn shānghán.

typical /ˈtɪpɪkl/ *adj* 典型的 diǎnxíngde; 代表性的 dàibiǎoxìngde: *a ~ British home* 典型的英国式住房. **typically** /-klɪ/ *adv*.

typify /ˈtɪpɪfaɪ/ *v* [*pt, pp* **-ied**] [T] 作…的模范〔範〕 zuò…de mófàn.

typist ⇨TYPE.

tyrannical /tɪˈrænɪkl/ *adj* 暴君的 bàojūnde; 专〔專〕制的 zhuānzhìde.

tyrannize /ˈtɪrənaɪz/ *v* [I, T] (*over*) (对…)施暴政 shī bàozhèng; 暴虐统治 bàonüè tǒngzhì.

tyranny /ˈtɪrənɪ/ *n* [U] 暴虐 bàonüè; 暴行 bàoxíng; 残〔殘〕暴 cánbào.

tyrant /ˈtaɪərənt/ *n* [C] 暴君 bàojūn.

tyre /taɪə(r)/ *n* [C] 轮〔輪〕胎 lúntāi.

U u

U, u /juː/ *n* [C] [*pl* **U's, u's** /juːz/] 英语的第二十一个〔個〕字母 Yīngyǔde dì'èrshíyīgè zìmǔ. **U-turn** *n* [C] 1 (车辆)掉头〔頭〕 diàotóu; 向后〔後〕转〔轉〕 xiànghòuzhuǎn. 2 [非正式用语](彻底)改变看法 gǎibiàn kànfǎ.

ubiquitous /juːˈbɪkwɪtəs/ *adj* [正式用语](似乎)普遍存在的 pǔbiàn cúnzài de.

udder /ˈʌdə(r)/ *n* [C] (牛、羊的)乳房 rǔfáng.

UFO /juː ef ˈəʊ 或 juːfəʊ/ *n* [C] [*pl* ~s] (= unidentified flying object) 不明飞〔飛〕行物 bùmíng fēixíngwù; 飞碟 fēidié.

ugh /发类似 ɜː 的音/ *interj* (用以表示厌恶或恐惧)啊! ā; 喔唷! wōyō: *Ugh! What a horrible smell!* 喔唷! 多么难闻的气味!

ugly /ˈʌglɪ/ *adj* [-ier, -iest] 1 丑〔醜〕陋的 chǒulòude; 难〔難〕看的 nánkànde. 2 险〔險〕恶〔惡〕的 xiǎn'ède: *an ~ situation* 险恶的局势. **ugliness** *n* [U].

UK /juːˈkeɪ/ *abbr* **the UK** (= the United Kingdom) 联〔聯〕合王国〔國〕 Liánhé Wángguó.

ulcer /ˈʌlsə(r)/ *n* [C] 溃疡〔瘍〕 kuìyáng. **ulcerate** *v* [I, T] (使)生溃疡 shēng kuìyáng. **ulcerous** *adj*.

ulterior /ʌlˈtɪərɪə(r)/ *adj* 隐〔隱〕秘的 yǐnmìde; 别有用心的 bié yǒu yòngxīn de: *an ~ motive* 不可告人的目的.

ultimate /ˈʌltɪmət/ *adj* 最后〔後〕的 zuìhòude; 最远〔遠〕的 zuìyuǎnde. **ultimately** *adv* 最后 zuìhòu.

ultimatum /ˌʌltɪˈmeɪtəm/ *n* [C] [*pl* ~s 或 **-ta** /-tə/] 最后〔後〕通牒 zuìhòu tōngdié; 哀的美敦书〔書〕 āidìměidūnshū.

ultraviolet /ˌʌltrəˈvaɪələt/ *adj* 紫外线〔綫〕的 zǐwàixiànde.

umbilical cord /ʌmˈbɪlɪkl/ *n* [C] 脐〔臍〕带〔帶〕 qídài.

umbrella /ʌmˈbrelə/ *n* [C] 1 雨伞〔傘〕 yǔsǎn. 2 [喻]保护〔護〕伞 bǎohùsǎn.

umpire /ˈʌmpaɪə(r)/ *n* [C] 仲裁人 zhòngcáirén; 裁判员 cáipànyuán. **umpire** *v* [I, T] 裁判 cáipàn.

umpteen /ˈʌmptiːn/ *pron* [非正式用语]许多 xǔduō; 无〔無〕数〔數〕 wúshù: *read ~ books on the subject* 看过无数本关于这个学科的书.

umpteenth /ˈʌmptiːnθ/ *pron*: *for the ~th time* 无数次.

UN /juː ˈen/ *abbr* the UN (= The United Nations) 联〔聯〕合国〔國〕Liánhéguó.

unable /ʌnˈeɪbl/ *adj* 不能的 bùnéngde; 不会〔會〕的 búhuìde.

unaccountable /ˌʌnəˈkaʊntəbl/ *adj* [正式用语]无〔無〕法解释〔釋〕的 wúfǎ jiěshì de. **unaccountably** *adv*.

unaccustomed /ˌʌnəˈkʌstəmd/ *adj* **1** *to* 不习〔習〕惯的 bù xíguàn de: ~ *to speaking in public* 不习惯于在大庭广众中说话. **2** 不平常的 bù píngcháng de; 奇怪的 qíguàide.

unanimous /juːˈnænɪməs/ *adj* 一致同意的 yízhì tóngyì de: *a ~ decision* 全体一致同意的决定. **unanimity** /ˌjuːnəˈnɪmətɪ/ *n* [U].

unanswerable /ˌʌnˈɑːnsərəbl; *US* ˌʌnˈæn-/ *adj* 无〔無〕可辩驳的 wú kě biànbó de.

unarmed /ˌʌnˈɑːmd/ *adj* 非武装〔裝〕的 fēi wǔzhuāng de.

unassuming /ˌʌnəˈsjuːmɪŋ; *US* -ˈsuː-/ *adj* 不摆〔擺〕架子的 bù bǎi jiàzi de; 谦逊〔遜〕的 qiānxùnde.

unattached /ˌʌnəˈtætʃt/ *adj* **1** 无〔無〕关〔關〕系〔係〕的 wú guānxì de; 独〔獨〕立的 dúlìde. **2** 未婚的 wèihūnde; 无固定伴侣的 wú gùdìng bànlǚ de.

unattended /ˌʌnəˈtendɪd/ *adj* 没人照顾〔顧〕的 méirén zhàogù de; 无〔無〕伴的 wúbànde: *Never leave a baby ~.* 不要把婴孩留下无人照顾.

unavoidable /ˌʌnəˈvɔɪdəbl/ *adj* 不可避免的 bùkě bìmiǎn de.

unaware /ˌʌnəˈweə(r)/ *adj* (*of*) 不知道的 bù zhīdào de; 没察觉〔覺〕到的 méi chájuédào de. **unawares** /-ˈweəz/ *adv* 意外地 yìwàide; 突然 tūrán: *catch / take sb ~s* 把某人吓一跳.

unbalanced /ˌʌnˈbælənst/ *adj* (神经)不正常的 bú zhèngcháng de; (精神)错乱〔亂〕的 cuòluànde.

unbearable /ʌnˈbeərəbl/ *adj* 忍受不了的 rěnshòu bù liǎo de. **unbearably** *adv*.

unbeatable /ˌʌnˈbiːtəbl/ *adj* 不可战〔戰〕胜〔勝〕的 bùkě zhànshèng de: ~ *value for money* 金钱万能.

unbelievable /ˌʌnbɪˈliːvəbl/ *adj* 不可信的 bùkě xìn de; 惊〔驚〕人的 jīngrénde. **unbelievably** *adv*.

unborn /ˌʌnˈbɔːn/ *adj* 未诞生的 wèi dànshēng de.

unbroken /ˌʌnˈbrəʊkən/ *adj* 不中断〔斷〕的 bù zhōngduàn de; (纪录等)未被打破的 wèi bèi dǎpò de: *ten hours of ~ sleep* 连续十小时的睡眠.

unbutton /ˌʌnˈbʌtn/ *v* [T] 解开〔開〕…的钮扣 jiěkāi…de niǔkòu.

uncalled-for /ʌnˈkɔːld fɔː(r)/ *adj* 没有理由的 méiyǒu lǐyóu de; 不必要的 bú bìyào de; 不应〔應〕当〔當〕的 bù yīngdāng de.

uncanny /ʌnˈkænɪ/ *adj* [-ier, -iest] 不自然的 bú zìrán de; 神秘的 shénmìde.

unceremonious /ˌʌnˌserɪˈməʊnɪəs/ *adj* **1** 非正式的 fēi zhèngshì de; 随〔隨〕便的 suíbiànde. **2** 粗鲁的 cūlǔde; 无〔無〕礼〔禮〕的 wúlǐde. **unceremoniously** *adv*.

uncertain /ʌnˈsɜːtn/ *adj* **1** 不明确〔確〕的 bù míngquè de; 无〔無〕把握的 wú bǎwò de: *be ~ about what to do* 对要做什么事拿不定主意. **2** 靠不住的 kàobúzhùde; 易变〔變〕的 yìbiànde: ~ *weather* 变化莫测的天气. **uncertainly** *adv*. **uncertainty** *n* [C, U] [*pl* -ies].

uncharitable /ˌʌnˈtʃærɪtəbl/ *adj* 严〔嚴〕厉〔厲〕的 yánlìde; 无〔無〕情的 wúqíngde.

unchecked /ˌʌnˈtʃekt/ *adj* 未被制止的 wèi bèi zhìzhǐ de.

uncivilized /ˌʌnˈsɪvəlaɪzd/ *adj* 野蛮〔蠻〕的 yěmánde; 未开〔開〕化的 wèi kāihuà de; 不文明的 bù wénmíng de.

uncle /ˈʌŋkl/ *n* [C] 伯父 bófù; 叔父 shūfù; 舅父 jiùfù; 姑丈 gūzhàng; 姨夫 yífu.

uncomfortable /ʌnˈkʌmftəbl; *US* -fərt-/ *adj* **1** 不舒服的 bù shūfu de. **2** 不自然的 bú zìrán de; 不安的 bù'ānde. **uncomfortably** *adv*.

uncommon /ʌnˈkɒmən/ *adj* 不普通的 bù pǔtōng de; 不平常的 bù píngcháng de. **uncommonly** *adv* [正式用语] 显〔顯〕著地 xiǎnzhùde; 极〔極〕端地 jíduānde.

uncompromising /ʌnˈkɒmprəmaɪzɪŋ/ *adj* 不妥协〔協〕的 bù tuǒxié de; 坚〔堅〕定的 jiāndìngde.

unconcerned /ˌʌnkənˈsɜːnd/ *adj* 不感兴〔興〕趣的 bù gǎn xìngqù de; 漠不关〔關〕心的 mò bù guānxīn de.

unconditional /ˌʌnkənˈdɪʃənl/ *adj* 绝对〔對〕的 juéduìde; 无〔無〕条〔條〕件的 wú tiáojiàn de: ~ *surrender* 无条件投降.

unconscious /ʌnˈkɒnʃəs/ *adj* 无〔無〕意识〔識〕的 wú yìshí de; 不知道的 bù zhīdào de; 失去知觉〔覺〕的 shīqù zhījué de: *knocked ~* 被打昏过去. ~ *of danger* 不知道有危险. **unconsciously** *adv*.

uncountable /ʌnˈkaʊntəbl/ *adj* 不可数〔數〕的 bùkě shǔ de: *'Butter' is an ~ noun*. "butter"一词是不可数名词.

uncouth /ʌnˈkuːθ/ *adj* (人、动作等)粗野的 cūyěde; 笨拙的 bènzhuōde.

uncover /ʌnˈkʌvə(r)/ *v* [T] **1** 移去…的覆

盖〔蓋〕物 yíqù⋯de fùgàiwù. 2 揭露 jiēlù; 宣布 xuānbù.

undaunted /ʌnˈdɔːntɪd/ *adj* [正式用语]无〔無〕畏的 wúwèide; 大胆〔膽〕的 dàdǎnde.

undecided /ˌʌndɪˈsaɪdɪd/ *adj* 未定的 wèidìngde; 未决的 wèijuéde.

undeniable /ˌʌndɪˈnaɪəbl/ *adj* 确〔確〕实〔實〕的 quèshíde; 不能否认〔認〕的 bùnéng fǒurèn de. **undeniably** *adv*.

under /ˈʌndə(r)/ *prep* 1 在⋯之下 zài⋯zhī xià; (位置)低于 dī yú. 2 被⋯遮蔽着 bèi⋯zhēbìzhe: *Most of the iceberg is* ~ *the water*. 冰山的大部分在水面以下. 3 少于 shǎo yú: ~ *£50* 少于五十英镑. 4 在⋯情况下 zài⋯qíngkuàng xià; 在⋯影响〔響〕下 zài⋯yǐngxiǎng xià: ~ *construction* 在建造中. ~ *these circumstances* 在这些情况下. 5 在⋯统治(或管理)下 zài⋯tǒngzhì xià: *Britain* ~ *Thatcher* 在撒切尔治下的英国. 6 根据〔據〕gēnjù: ~ *the terms of the contract* 根据合同规定. 7 使用(某名称) shǐyòng: *She wrote* ~ *the name of George Eliot*. 她用乔治·埃利奥特的名字写作. **under** *adv* 在下面 zài xiàmian; (尤指)在水下 zài shuǐ xià.

under- *prefix* 1 在⋯下面 zài⋯ xiàmiàn: *~current* 潜流. 2 不足 bùzú: *~ripe* 欠收.

underarm /ˈʌndərɑːm/ *adj*, *adv* [运动]低手式的(地)(投球时手低于肩) dī shǒushì de.

undercarriage /ˈʌndəkærɪdʒ/ *n* [C] (飞机的)起落架 qǐluòjià.

undercharge /ˌʌndəˈtʃɑːdʒ/ *v* [I, T] 少讨⋯的价〔價〕钱〔錢〕shǎo tǎo ⋯de jiàqián.

underclothes /ˈʌndəkləʊðz/ *n* [pl] = UNDERWEAR.

undercover /ˌʌndəˈkʌvə(r)/ *adj* 秘密的 mìmìde; 暗中进〔進〕行的 ànzhōng jìnxíng de.

undercurrent /ˈʌndəkʌrənt/ *n* [U] 1 潜流 qiánliú. 2 [喻](思想、情绪的)暗流 ànliú: *an* ~ *of bitterness* 一股悲痛的暗流.

undercut /ˌʌndəˈkʌt/ *v* [-tt-; *pt*, *pp* undercut] [T] 削低(商品)价〔價〕格 xuēdī jiàgé.

underdeveloped /ˌʌndədɪˈveləpt/ *adj* (国家)不太发〔發〕达〔達〕的 bútài fādá de, 未充分开〔開〕发的 wèi chōngfèn kāifā de.

underdog /ˈʌndədɒg; *US* -dɔːg/ *n* [C] 竞〔競〕争中处〔處〕于劣势〔勢〕者 jìngzhēngzhōng chǔyú lièshì zhě.

underdone /ˌʌndəˈdʌn/ *adj* (尤指肉)不太熟的 bú tài shú de.

underestimate /ˌʌndərˈestɪmeɪt/ *v* [T] 低估 dīgū; 看轻〔輕〕kànqīng: ~ *the enemy's strength* 低估敌人的力量.

underfed /ˌʌndəˈfed/ *adj* 吃得太少的 chīde tài shǎo de.

underfoot /ˌʌndəˈfʊt/ *adv* 在脚下 zài jiǎoxià: *The grass was wet* ~. 脚下的草地是湿的.

undergo /ˌʌndəˈgəʊ/ *v* [*pt* -went /-ˈwent/, *pp* -gone /-ˈgɒn; *US* -ˈgɔːn/] [T] 经〔經〕历〔歷〕jīnglì; 遭受 zāoshòu.

undergraduate /ˌʌndəˈgrædʒʊət/ *n* [C] 大学〔學〕肄业〔業〕生 dàxué yìyèshēng.

underground /ˈʌndəgraʊnd/ *adj* 1 地下的 dìxiàde; 在地下的 zài dìxià de. 2 [喻]秘密的 mìmìde; 隐〔隱〕蔽的 yǐnbìde. **the underground** *n* [sing] 1 地下铁〔鐵〕道 dìxià tiědào. 2 秘密政治活动〔動〕mìmì zhèngzhì huódòng. **underground** /ˌʌndəˈgraʊnd/ *adv* 在地下 zài dìxià. ˌ**underground eˈconomy** *n* [C] 地下经济〔濟〕dìxià jīngjì.

undergrowth /ˈʌndəgrəʊθ/ *n* [U] (生在大树下的)下层〔層〕林丛〔叢〕xiàcéng líncóng.

underhand /ˌʌndəˈhænd/ *adj* 暗中(或秘密)进〔進〕行的 ànzhōng jìnxíng de; 诡诈的 guǐzhàde.

underlie /ˌʌndəˈlaɪ/ *v* [*pt* -lay /-ˈleɪ/, *pp* -lain /-ˈleɪn/, *pres p* lying] [T] 位于⋯之下 wèiyú⋯ zhī xià; 作为〔爲〕⋯的基础〔礎〕zuòwéi⋯de jīchǔ.

underline /ˌʌndəˈlaɪn/ *v* [T] 1 划〔劃〕线〔綫〕于⋯之下 huá xiàn yú⋯ zhī xià. 2 [喻]强调 qiángdiào; 使突出 shǐ tūchū.

undermanned /ˌʌndəˈmænd/ *adj* 人员不足的 rényuán bùzú de.

undermine /ˌʌndəˈmaɪn/ *v* [T] 1 (逐渐)削弱 xuēruò; (暗中)破坏〔壞〕pòhuài: *Repeated failure ~d his confidence*. 屡遭失败削弱了他的信心. 2 在⋯下挖坑道 zài⋯xià wā kēngdào.

underneath /ˌʌndəˈniːθ/ *prep*, *adv* 在(⋯)下面 zài xiàmiàn; 在(⋯)底下 zài dǐxià.

underpants /ˈʌndəpænts/ *n* [pl] (男用)衬裤 chènkù.

underpass /ˈʌndəpɑːs; *US* -pæs/ *n* [C] 地下通道 dìxià tōngdào.

underprivileged /ˌʌndəˈprɪvəlɪdʒd/ *adj* 被剥夺〔奪〕基本社会〔會〕权〔權〕利的 bèi bōduó jīběn shèhuì quánlì de.

underrate /ˌʌndəˈreɪt/ *v* [T] 低估 dīgū; 过〔過〕低评价〔價〕guò dī píngjià.

underside /ˈʌndəsaɪd/ *n* [C] 下侧 xiàcè; 下部表面 xiàbù biǎomiàn.

undersigned /ˌʌndəˈsaɪnd/ *n* **the undersigned** [C] [*pl* **the undersigned**] [正式用语](在文件末尾的)签〔簽〕名人 qiānmíng rén: *We, the* ~ ... 我们,本文件之签名人声明⋯.

understand /ˌʌndəˈstænd/ *v* [*pt*, *pp* -stood /-ˈstʊd/] 1 [I, T] 懂得 dǒngdé; 了

U

解 liáojiě: *She can ~ French perfectly.* 法语她完全懂得. *I don't ~ what the problem is.* 我不了解这个问题是什么. 2 [I, T] 理解 lǐjiě; 谅解 liàngjiě: *No one ~s me.* 没有人理解我. 3 [T] [正式用语]获〔獲〕悉 huòxī; 听〔聽〕说 tīngshuō: *I ~ that you wish to leave.* 我听说你要离去. 4 [习语] ˌ**make oneself under'stood** 把(自己的)意思表达〔達〕清楚 bǎ yìsī biǎodá qīngchǔ. **understandable** *adj* 能懂的 néngdǒngde; 可理解的 kě lǐjiě de. **understandably** *adv*. **understanding** *n* 1 [U] 智力 zhìlì; 理解力 lǐjiělì. 2 [U] 体〔體〕谅 tǐliàng; 谅解 liàngjiě. 3 [C] 协〔協〕议〔議〕xiéyì. **understanding** *adj* 体谅的 tǐliàngde; 理解的 lǐjiě de.

understate /ˌʌndəˈsteɪt/ *v* [T] 没有充分地陈述 méiyǒu chōngfènde chénshù: *~ the extent of the problem* 没有充分表达问题的范围. **understatement** /ˈʌndəsteɪtmənt/ *n* [C, U].

understudy /ˈʌndəstʌdɪ/ *n* [C] [*pl* -ies] 候补〔補〕人员 hòubǔ rényuán; (尤指)预备〔備〕演员 yùbèi yǎnyuán.

undertake /ˌʌndəˈteɪk/ *v* [*pt* -took /-ˈtʊk/, *pp* ~n /-ˈteɪkən/] [T] [正式用语] 1 承担〔擔〕chéngdān; 负起责任 fùqǐ zérèn. 2 *to* 同意 tóngyì; 答应〔應〕dāying. **undertaking** *n* [C] 1 任务〔務〕rènwu; 事业〔業〕shìyè. 2 [正式用语]答应 dāying; 许诺 xǔnuò.

undertaker /ˈʌndəteɪkə(r)/ *n* [C] 承办〔辦〕殡〔殯〕葬者 chéngbàn bìnzàng zhě.

undertone /ˈʌndətəʊn/ *n* [C] 1 低声〔聲〕dī shēng; 低调 dī diào: *speak in ~s* 低声说话. 2 潜〔潛〕在的意义〔義〕(或感情) qiánzàide yìyì.

undervalue /ˌʌndəˈvæljuː/ *v* [T] 低估…的价〔價〕值 dī gū…de jiàzhí.

underwater /ˌʌndəˈwɔːtə(r)/ *adj, adv* 在水面下(的) zài shuǐmiànxià.

underwear /ˈʌndəweə(r)/ *n* [U] 内衣 nèiyī.

underworld /ˈʌndəˈwɜːld/ *n* **the underworld** [sing] 1 下流社会〔會〕xiàliú shèhuì; 黑社会 hēi shèhuì. 2 [神话]阴〔陰〕间 yīnjiān; 地府 dìfǔ.

underwrite /ˌʌndəˈraɪt/ *v* [*pt* -wrote /-ˈrəʊt/, *pp* -written /-ˈrɪtn/] [T] 给…保险〔險〕gěi…bǎoxiǎn; 同意赔款(尤指海上保险) tóngyì péikuǎn.

undesirable /ˌʌndɪˈzaɪərəbl/ *adj* 可能招致损害的 kěnéng zhāozhì sǔnhài de; 不合需要的 bù hé xūyào de. **undesirable** *n* [C] 不受欢〔歡〕迎的人 bú shòu huānyíng de rén.

undeveloped /ˌʌndɪˈveləpt/ *adj* 不发〔發〕达〔達〕的 bù fādá de; 未开〔開〕发的 wèi kāifā de.

undies /ˈʌndɪz/ *n* [pl] [非正式用语](女用)内衣 nèiyī.

undo /ʌnˈduː/ *v* [*pt* -did /-ˈdɪd/, *pp* -done /-ˈdʌn/] [T] 1 解开〔開〕jiěkāi; 使松〔鬆〕开 shǐ sōngkāi. 2 使无〔無〕效 shǐ wúxiào; 废〔廢〕弃〔棄〕fèiqì: *He undid all my good work.* 他毁掉了我所有的成绩. **undoing** *n* [sing] [正式用语]造成(某人)失败的原因 zàochéng shībài de yuányīn.

undoubted /ʌnˈdaʊtɪd/ *adj* 无〔無〕疑的 wúyíde; 肯定的 kěndìngde; 真正的 zhēnzhèngde. **undoubtedly** *adv*.

undress /ˌʌnˈdres/ *v* 1 [I] 脱衣服 tuō yīfu; 宽衣 kuān yī. 2 [T] 脱去…的衣服 tuōqù…de yīfu. **undressed** *adj* 不穿衣服的 bù chuān yīfu de.

undue /ˌʌnˈdjuː; *US* -ˈduː/ *adj* [正式用语] 过〔過〕分的 guòfènde; 过度的 guòdùde: *with ˌ~ ˈhaste* 过分匆忙地. **unduly** *adv*.

undulate /ˈʌndjʊleɪt/ *v* [I] 波动〔動〕bōdòng; 起伏 qǐfú: *The road ~s through the hills.* 这条路从山间蜿蜒而过.

undying /ʌnˈdaɪɪŋ/ *adj* [正式用语]不朽的 bùxiǔde; 永恒的 yǒnghéngde: *~ love* 永恒的爱情.

unearth /ʌnˈɜːθ/ *v* [T] 1 发〔發〕掘 fājué. 2 发现 fāxiàn: *~ the truth* 发现真理.

unearthly /ʌnˈɜːθlɪ/ *adj* 1 神秘的 shénmìde; 鬼怪的 guǐguàide. 2 [非正式用语]不合理的 bù hélǐ de; 荒谬的 huāngmiùde: *at this ~ hour* 在这不方便的时刻.

uneasy /ʌnˈiːzɪ/ *adj* [-ier, -iest] (身,心)不舒畅的 bù shūchàng de; 不自在的 bú zìzài de; 不安的 bù'ānde. **uneasily** *adv*. **uneasiness** *n* [U].

uneconomic /ˌʌnˌiːkəˈnɒmɪk, ˌʌnˌek-/ *adj* 不经〔經〕济〔濟〕的 bù jīngjì de.

unemployed /ˌʌnɪmˈplɔɪd/ *adj* 失业〔業〕的 shīyède. **the unemployed** *n* [pl] 失业者 shīyèzhě. **unemployment** /-ˈplɔɪmənt/ *n* [U].

unequal /ˌʌnˈiːkwəl/ *adj* 1 不同的 bùtóngde; 不相等的 bù xiāngděng de. 2 不平等的 bù píngděng de. 3 *to* [正式用语]不胜〔勝〕任的 bú shèngrèn de; 不够坚〔堅〕强的 búgòu jiānqiáng de. **unequally** *adv*.

unequivocal /ˌʌnɪˈkwɪvəkl/ *adj* [正式用语]含义〔義〕清楚(或明确)的 hányì qīngchu de. **unequivocally** *adv*.

uneven /ˌʌnˈiːvn/ *adj* 1 不平坦的 bù píngtǎn de; 不均匀的 bù jūnyún de. 2 (质量)有差异〔異〕的 yǒu chāyì de; 不一致的 bù yízhì de.

unexpected /ˌʌnɪkˈspektɪd/ *adj* 未料到的 wèi liàodào de; 意外的 yìwàide. **unexpectedly** *adv*.

unfailing /ʌnˈfeɪlɪŋ/ *adj* [褒]永恒的 yǒng-

U

héngde；不断〔斷〕的 búduànde.

unfair /ˌʌnˈfeə(r)/ *adj* 不公正的 bù gōngzhèng de；不公平的 bù gōngpíng de：～ *remarks / competition* 不公平的评论(或竞争). **unfairly** *adv*.

unfaithful /ˌʌnˈfeɪθfl/ *adj* 不忠实〔實〕的 bù zhōngshí de；(尤指对丈夫或妻子)不贞洁〔潔〕的 bù zhēnjié de.

unfamiliar /ˌʌnfəˈmɪlɪə(r)/ *adj* **1** 陌生的 mòshēngde；生疏的 shēngshūde. **2** *with* 不熟悉的 bù shúxī de；外行的 wàihángde：*I'm ～ with this type of computer*. 我对这种计算机不熟悉.

unfasten /ʌnˈfɑːsn；US ʌnˈfæsn/ *v* [T] 解开〔開〕jiěkāi；打开 dǎkāi.

unfinished /ʌnˈfɪnɪʃt/ *adj* 未完成的 wèi wánchéng de：～ *business* 未完成的日常工作.

unfit /ˌʌnˈfɪt/ *adj* 不合适〔適〕的 bù héshì de；不适当〔當〕的 bú shìdàng de.

unfold /ʌnˈfəʊld/ *v* **1** [T] 展开〔開〕zhǎnkāi；打开 dǎkāi. **2** [I, T] [喻](使)显〔顯〕露 xiǎnlù；表明 biǎomíng：*as the story ～ed* 正如事件经过所表明的.

unforeseen /ˌʌnfɔːˈsiːn/ *adj* 意料之外的 yìliào zhī wài de.

unforgettable /ˌʌnfəˈgetəbl/ *adj* 难〔難〕忘的 nánwàngde.

unfortunate /ʌnˈfɔːtʃənət/ *adj* **1** 不幸的 búxìngde. **2** 令人遗憾的 lìng rén yíhàn de：*an ～ remark* 令人遗憾的话. **unfortunately** *adv*.

unfounded /ˌʌnˈfaʊndɪd/ *adj* 无〔無〕根据〔據〕的 wú gēnjù de.

unfriendly /ˌʌnˈfrendlɪ/ *adj* [-ier, -iest] 不友好的 bù yǒuhǎo de.

unfurl /ˌʌnˈfɜːl/ *v* [I, T] 展开〔開〕zhǎnkāi；打开 dǎkāi.

unfurnished /ʌnˈfɜːnɪʃt/ *adj* 无〔無〕家具设备〔備〕的 wú jiājù shèbèi de.

ungainly /ʌnˈgeɪnlɪ/ *adj* 笨拙的 bènzhuōde；难〔難〕看的 nánkànde.

ungodly /ˌʌnˈgɒdlɪ/ *adj* **1** 不敬神的 bú jìng shén de. **2** [非正式用语]不合理的 bù hélǐ de；不讲〔講〕道理的 bù jiǎng dàolǐ de：*at this ～ hour* 在这不合适的时刻.

ungrateful /ʌnˈgreɪtfl/ *adj* 不领情的 bù lǐngqíng de.

U

unguarded /ˌʌnˈgɑːdɪd/ *adj* (尤指说话)不留神的 bù liúshén de；粗心的 cūxīnde.

unhappy /ʌnˈhæpɪ/ *adj* [-ier, -iest] 不快乐〔樂〕的 bú kuàilè de. **unhappily** *adv*. **unhappiness** *n* [U].

unhealthy /ʌnˈhelθɪ/ *adj* [-ier, -iest] **1** 不健康的 bú jiànkāng de. **2** 有损健康的 yǒu sǔn jiànkāng de.

unheard-of /ʌnˈhɜːd ɒv/ *adj* 前所未闻的 qián suǒ wèi wén de；空前的 kōngqiánde.

unicorn /ˈjuːnɪkɔːn/ *n* [C] [神话]似马的独〔獨〕角兽〔獸〕sì mǎ de dújiǎoshòu.

unidentified /ˌʌnaɪˈdentɪfaɪd/ *adj* 不能识〔識〕别的 bùnéng shíbié de；未查明的 wèi chámíng de.

uniform /ˈjuːnɪfɔːm/ *n* [C, U] 制服 zhìfú. **uniform** *adj* 不变〔變〕的 búbiànde；一律的 yílǜde. **uniformed** *adj*：*～ed police officers* 穿制服的警官. **uniformity** /ˌjuːnɪˈfɔːmətɪ/ *n* [U].

unify /ˈjuːnɪfaɪ/ *v* [*pt, pp* -ied] [T] 统一 tǒngyī；使一致 shǐ yízhì. **unification** /ˌjuːnɪfɪˈkeɪʃn/ *n* [U].

unilateral /ˌjuːnɪˈlætrəl/ *adj* 单〔單〕方面的 dānfāngmiànde；片面的 piànmiànde：～ *disarmament* 单方面裁军.

union /ˈjuːnɪən/ *n* **1** [C] (a) = TRADE UNION (TRADE[1]). (b) 协〔協〕会〔會〕xiéhuì；联〔聯〕合会 liánhéhuì. **2** [C] 联邦 liánbāng；联盟 liánméng. **3** [U] [正式用语]联合 liánhé；合并〔併〕hébìng. **the ˌUnion ˈJack** *n* [sing] 联合王国〔國〕国旗 Liánhé Wángguó guóqí.

unique /juːˈniːk/ *adj* **1** 唯一的 wéiyīde；独〔獨〕一无〔無〕二的 dú yī wú èr de. **2** *to* 仅〔僅〕与〔與〕…有关〔關〕的 jǐn yǔ…yǒuguān de：*problems ～ to blind people* 盲人遇到的特殊问题. **3** [非正式用语]不寻〔尋〕常的 bù xúncháng de；独特的 dútède：*a ～ singing voice* 难得的好歌喉. **uniquely** *adv*.

unisex /ˈjuːnɪseks/ *adj* 男女皆宜的 nán nǚ jiē yí de.

unison /ˈjuːnɪsn, -zn/ *n* [习语] **in unison** (a) 齐〔齊〕唱 qíchàng；齐奏 qízòu. (b) [喻]一致 yízhì；调和 tiáohé.

unit /ˈjuːnɪt/ *n* [C] **1** 单〔單〕位(指构成整体的人、物、团体等) dānwèi. **2** (组织的)单位 dānwèi：*the university research ～* 大学研究小组. **3** (机器的)部件 bùjiàn：*the central processing ～ of a computer* 计算机的中央处理部件. **4** (计量)单位 dānwèi：*The metre is a ～ of length*. 米是长度单位.

unite /juːˈnaɪt/ *v* [I, T] (使)联〔聯〕合 liánhé；(使)合并〔併〕hébìng；(使)团〔團〕结 tuánjié. **the UˌnitedˈKingdom** *n* [sing] (大不列颠及北爱尔兰)联合王国〔國〕Liánhé Wángguó. **the UˌnitedˈNations** *n* [sing] 联合国 Liánhéguó. **the United ˈStates** *n* [sing] (亦作 **the United States of America**) 美国 Měiguó.

unity /ˈjuːnətɪ/ *n* [U] 联〔聯〕合 liánhé；统一 tǒngyī；协〔協〕调 xiétiáo；一致 yízhì.

universal /ˌjuːnɪˈvɜːsl/ *adj* 普遍的 pǔbiànde；全体〔體〕的 quántǐde. **universally** *adv*.

universe /ˈjuːnɪvɜːs/ *n* **the universe** [sing]

宇宙 yǔzhòu.

university /ˌjuːnɪˈvɜːsətɪ/ *n* [C] [*pl* -ies] (a) 大学〔學〕dàxué. (b) 大学人员(师生员工等) dàxué rényuán.

unkempt /ˌʌnˈkempt/ *adj* 不整洁〔潔〕的 bù zhěngjié de: ~ *hair* 蓬乱的头发.

unkind /ˌʌnˈkaɪnd/ *adj* 不和善的 bù héshàn de; 不客气〔氣〕的 bú kèqì de; 刻薄的 kèbóde.

unknown /ˌʌnˈnəʊn/ *adj* 不知道的 bù zhīdào de; 未知的 wèizhīde.

unleaded /ʌnˈledɪd/ *adj* 无〔無〕铅的 wúqiānde.

unleash /ʌnˈliːʃ/ *v* [T] [正式用语]解开〔開〕…的束缚 jiěkāi…de shùfù; 释〔釋〕放(能量) shìfàng.

unless /ənˈles/ *conj* 除非 chúfēi; 如果不 rúguǒ bù: *You will fail* ~ *you work harder*. 你如果不更加努力工作,你将失败.

unlike /ʌnˈlaɪk/ *adj*, *prep* 不相同的 bù xiāngtóng de; 和…不同 hé…bùtóng.

unlikely /ʌnˈlaɪklɪ/ *adj* (a) 未必(是真)的 wèibìde; 不大可能(发生)的 bú dà kěnéng de: *He's* ~ *to get better*. 他不大可能好起来了. (b) 不一定有希望的 bù yīdìng yǒu xīwàng de: *an* ~ *candidate for the job* 希望不大的求职申请人.

unload /ˌʌnˈləʊd/ *v* 1 [I, T] (从…)卸下货物 xièxià huòwù. 2 [T] (*on* / *on to*) 把不想要的…交给(他人) bǎ bù xiǎng yào de…jiāo gěi; 摆〔擺〕脱… bǎituō.

unlock /ˌʌnˈlɒk/ *v* [T] 开〔開〕…的锁 kāi…de suǒ.

unlucky /ʌnˈlʌkɪ/ *adj* 不幸的 búxìngde; 倒霉的 dǎoméide.

unmanned /ˌʌnˈmænd/ *adj* (尤指宇宙飞船) 无〔無〕人驾驶的 wú rén jiàshǐ de.

unmask /ˌʌnˈmɑːsk; *US* -ˈmæsk/ *v* [T] 撕下…的假面具 sīxià…de jiǎmiànjù; 揭露 jiēlù.

unmentionable /ʌnˈmenʃənəbl/ *adj* 说不出口的 shuō bù chū kǒu de.

unmistakable /ˌʌnmɪˈsteɪkəbl/ *adj* 不会〔會〕错的 búhuì cuò de; 不会被怀〔懷〕疑的 búhuì bèi huáiyí de. **unmistakably** *adv*.

unmitigated /ʌnˈmɪtɪgeɪtɪd/ *adj* [正式用语](坏人、坏事)一无〔無〕是处〔處〕的 yì wú shì chù de: *an* ~ *disaster* 十足的灾难.

unmoved /ˌʌnˈmuːvd/ *adj* 无〔無〕动〔動〕于衷的 wú dòng yú zhōng de; 冷淡的 lěngdànde: ~ *by her tears* 没有被她的眼泪打动.

unnatural /ʌnˈnætʃrəl/ *adj* 1 不自然的 bú zìrán de; 不正常的 bù zhèngcháng de: ~ *silence* 不正常的寂静. 2 不合情理的 bùhé qínglǐ de; 反常的 fǎnchángde: ~ *behavior* 反常的行为.

unnecessary /ʌnˈnesəsrɪ; *US* -səserɪ/ *adj* 不必要的 bú bìyào de; 不需要的 bù xūyào de. **unnecessarily** *adv*.

unnerve /ˌʌnˈnɜːv/ *v* [T] 使丧〔喪〕失勇气〔氣〕shǐ sàngshī yǒngqì; 使失去信心 shǐ shīqù xìnxīn.

unnoticed /ˌʌnˈnəʊtɪst/ *adj* 未被注意的 wèi bèi zhùyì de; 被忽视的 bèi hūshì de.

unobtrusive /ˌʌnəbˈtruːsɪv/ *adj* [正式用语]不引人注意的 bù yǐn rén zhùyì de.

unofficial /ˌʌnəˈfɪʃl/ *adj* 非官方的 fēi guānfāng de.

unpalatable /ʌnˈpælətəbl/ *adj* [正式用语] 1 不好吃的 bù hǎochī de; 味道不好的 wèidào bùhǎo de. 2 [喻]难〔難〕于接受的 nán yú jiēshòu de; 无〔無〕法认〔認〕同的 wú fǎ rèntóng de: *his* ~ *views* 他的使人不以为然的见解.

unpleasant /ʌnˈpleznt/ *adj* 1 (使人)不愉快的 bù yúkuài de; 讨厌〔厭〕的 tǎoyànde: *an* ~ *smell* 讨厌的气味. 2 很不友好的 hěn bù yǒuhǎo de. **unpleasantness** *n* [U].

unprecedented /ʌnˈpresɪdentɪd/ *adj* 前所未有的 qián suǒ wèi yǒu de; 空前的 kōngqiánde.

unpredictable /ˌʌnprɪˈdɪktəbl/ *adj* (人、行为)难〔難〕以预知的 nán yǐ yù zhī de: *I never know how she will react, she's so* ~. 我不知道她会如何反应,她这个人反复无常.

unprintable /ʌnˈprɪntəbl/ *adj* (文章等)不宜印出的 bù yí yìnchū de.

unqualified /ʌnˈkwɒlɪfaɪd/ *adj* 1 不合格的 bù hégé de; 无〔無〕资格的 wú zīgé de: ~ *to teach* 不能胜任教学工作. 2 无限制的 wú xiànzhì de; 无条〔條〕件的 wú tiáojiàn de: *an* ~ *disaster* 彻底的失败.

unquestionable /ʌnˈkwestʃənəbl/ *adj* 毫无〔無〕疑问的 háowú yíwèn de; 确〔確〕实〔實〕的 quèshíde. **unquestionably** *adv*.

unravel /ʌnˈrævl/ *v* [-ll-; 美语 -l-] 1 [I, T] 拆散(线团等) chāisǎn. 2 [T] [喻]解决 jiějué; 阐明 chǎnmíng: ~ *a mystery* 阐明一件神秘的事.

unreal /ˌʌnˈrɪəl/ *adj* 虚构〔構〕的 xūgòude; 不真实〔實〕的 bù zhēnshí de. **unreality** /ˌʌnrɪˈælətɪ/ *n* [U].

unreasonable /ʌnˈriːzənəbl/ *adj* 不合理的 bù hélǐ de; 不讲〔講〕道理的 bù jiǎng dàolǐ de.

unremitting /ˌʌnrɪˈmɪtɪŋ/ *adj* 不放松〔鬆〕的 bú fàngsōng de; 不停止的 bù tíngzhǐ de.

unrest /ˌʌnˈrest/ *n* [U] 不安 bù'ān; (社会)动〔動〕乱〔亂〕dòngluàn: *political* ~ 政治动乱.

unrivalled (美语 -l-) /ʌnˈraɪvld/ *adj* 无〔無〕对〔對〕手的 wú duìshǒu de; 无双〔雙〕的 wúshuāngde.

unroll /ˌʌnˈrəʊl/ *v* [I, T] (由卷曲状态)展开〔開〕zhǎnkāi.

unruffled /ˌʌnˈrʌfld/ *adj* 平静的 píngjìngde; 不混乱[亂]的 bú hùnluàn de.
unruly /ʌnˈruːlɪ/ *adj* 难[難]控制的 nán kòngzhì de; 不守规矩的 bù shǒu guīju de.
unsavoury (美语 -vory) /ˌʌnˈseɪvərɪ/ *adj* 不好的 bùhǎode; 令人厌[厭]恶[惡]的 lìng rén yànwù de.
unscathed /ˌʌnˈskeɪðd/ *adj* 未受伤[傷]害的 wèi shòu shānghài de.
unscrupulous /ʌnˈskruːpjʊləs/ *adj* 无[無]耻的 wúchǐde; 不讲[講]道德的 bù jiǎng dàodé de.
unseat /ˌʌnˈsiːt/ *v* [T] **1** 使落马 shǐ luòmǎ. **2** 使退位 shǐ tuìwèi; 罢[罷]免 bàmiǎn.
unseemly /ʌnˈsiːmlɪ/ *adj* [正式用语]不适[適]当[當]的 bú shìdàng de; 不适宜的 bú shìyí de: ~ *behaviour* 不适当的行为.
unsettle /ˌʌnˈsetl/ *v* [T] 使不安定 shǐ bù āndìng; 扰[擾]乱[亂] rǎoluàn: ~*d weather* 不稳定的天气.
unsightly /ʌnˈsaɪtlɪ/ *adj* 难[難]看的 nánkànde.
unsound /ˌʌnˈsaʊnd/ *adj* **1** 不健全的 bú jiànquán de; 不健康的 bú jiànkāng de; 虚弱的 xūruòde. **2** [习语] **of** ˌ**unsound** ˈ**mind** [法律]精神错乱[亂]的 jīngshén cuòluàn de.
unspeakable /ʌnˈspiːkəbl/ *adj* 说不出的 shuō bùchū de; 无[無]法形容的(坏事) wúfǎ xíngróng de: ~ *sadness* 无法形容的悲哀.
unstuck /ˌʌnˈstʌk/ *adj* **1** 未粘住的 wèi zhānzhù de; 松[鬆]开[開]的 sōngkāide. **2** [习语] ˌ**come unˈstuck** [非正式用语]失败 shībài.
unswerving /ʌnˈswɜːvɪŋ/ *adj* 不改变[變]的 bù gǎibiàn de; 坚[堅]定的 jiāndìngde: ~ *loyalty* 始终不渝的忠诚.
unthinkable /ˌʌnˈθɪŋkəbl/ *adj* 不必考虑[慮]的 búbì kǎolǜ de; 不能想像(或接受)的 bùnéng xiǎngxiàng de.
untidy /ʌnˈtaɪdɪ/ *adj* [-ier, -iest] 不整洁[潔]的 bù zhěngjié de.
untie /ʌnˈtaɪ/ *v* [*pt*, *pp* ~d, *pres p* untying] [T] 解开[開](绳结等) jiěkāi.
until /ənˈtɪl/ (亦作 **till** /tɪl/) *prep*, *conj* 直到…时[時](为止) zhídào…shí: *Wait* ~ *the rain stops*. 等到雨停了再说吧.
untold /ˌʌnˈtəʊld/ *adj* [正式用语]无[無]数[數]的 wúshùde; 数不清的 shǔ bù qīng de.
untoward /ˌʌntəˈwɔːd; *US* ʌnˈtɔːd/ *adj* [正式用语]不幸的 búxìngde; (造成)困难[難]的 kùnnande.
unused[1] /ˌʌnˈjuːzd/ *adj* 未用过[過]的 wèi yòngguò de; 新的 xīnde.
unused[2] /ˌʌnˈjuːst/ *adj* *to* 不习[習]惯的 bù xíguàn de; 不熟悉的 bù shúxī de.
unusual /ʌnˈjuːʒl/ *adj* 不平常的 bù píngcháng de; 奇怪的 qíguàide. **unusually** *adv*.
unveil /ˌʌnˈveɪl/ *v* [T] **1** 除去(…的)面纱或幕布等 chúqù miànshā huò mùbù děng. **2** 揭露 jiēlù.
unwarranted /ʌnˈwɒrəntɪd/ *adj* [正式用语]未经[經]证[證]实[實]的 wèi jīng zhèngshí de; 不正当[當]的 bú zhèngdàng de.
unwieldy /ʌnˈwiːldɪ/ *adj* 难[難]操纵[縱]的 nán cāozòng de; 笨重的 bènzhòngde.
unwind /ˌʌnˈwaɪnd/ *v* [*pt*, *pp* -wound /-ˈwaʊnd/] **1** [I, T] 解开[開](毛线团等) jiěkāi. **2** [I] [非正式用语]放松[鬆] fàngsōng.
unwitting /ʌnˈwɪtɪŋ/ *adj* [正式用语]无[無]意的 wúyìde; 不知道的 bù zhīdào de. **unwittingly** *adv*.
unwrap /ʌnˈræp/ *v* [-pp-] [T] 打开[開] dǎkāi; 解开 jiěkāi.
up /ʌp/ *adv* **1** 趋[趨]于较高处[處] qū yú jiàogāochù: *Lift your head up*. 把头抬起来. **2** 处于直立姿势[勢] chǔyú zhílì zīshì: *stand up* 站起来. **3** 起床 qǐchuáng: *Is Anne up yet?* 安妮起床了吗? **4** 往重要的地方 wǎng zhòngyàode dìfang: *go up to London* 上伦敦去. **5** (*to*) 靠近 kàojìn: *He came up* (*to me*) *and asked the time*. 他走到我跟前问什么时间. **6** (表示增加): *Profits are up again*. 利润又增加了. **7** 完全地 wánquánde; 彻[徹]底地 chèdǐde: *The stream has dried up*. 溪水已干涸了. **8** 成碎片 chéng suìpiàn: *tear the paper up* 把纸撕碎. **9** [非正式用语]发[發]生 fāshēng: *What's up?* 出什么事了? **10** [习语] **up against sth** 面对[對](困难、问题) miànduì. ˌ**up and ˈdown** (a) 前前后[後]后 qiánqián hòuhòu; 往返地 wǎngfǎnde: *walk up and down* 走来走去. (b) 起伏 qǐfú: *The boat bobbed up and down in the water*. 那小船在水中上下颠簸. **up for sth** (a) (因某项过失)受审[審] shòushěn. (b) 正被考虑[慮] zhèng bèi kǎolǜ; 提供 tígōng. **up to sb** 某人的职[職]责 mǒurén de zhízé. **up to sth** (a) 作为[爲]最大数[數]量 zuòwéi zuìdà shùliàng; 多达[達] duō dá: *My car takes up to four people*. 我的汽车最多能坐四个人. (b) 直到 zhídào: *up to now* 直到现在. (c) 能胜[勝]任 néng shèngrèn: *I don't feel up to going to work*. 我不舒服,不能上班. **up** *prep* **1** 向(或在)高处 xiàng gāochù: *go up the stairs* 上楼梯. **2** 沿着 yánzhe: *There's another telephone-box up the road*. 沿路还有一个电话亭. **up** *adj* **1** 向上的 xiàngshàngde; 上行的 shàngxíngde: *the up escalator* 上行的自动扶梯. **2** 在整修的 zài zhěngxiū de: *The road is up*. 路面在整修中. **up** *v* [-pp-] [T] [非正式用语]增加 zēngjiā. ˌ**up-and-ˈcoming** *adj* (人)可能成功的 kěnéng chénggōng de. ˌ**ups and ˈdowns** *n*

U

[pl] 盛衰 shèngshuāi；沉浮 chénfú.

upbringing /ˈʌpbrɪŋɪŋ/ *n* [U] 抚〔撫〕育 fǔyù；教养〔養〕jiàoyǎng.

update /ˌʌpˈdeɪt/ *v* [T] 使现代化 shǐ xiàndàihuà；更新 gēngxīn.

upheaval /ʌpˈhiːvl/ *n* [C, U] 急剧〔劇〕变〔變〕动〔動〕jíjù biàndòng.

uphill /ˌʌpˈhɪl/ *adv* 往上坡 wǎng shàngpō. **uphill** *adj* 艰〔艱〕难〔難〕的 jiānnánde：*an ～ task* 艰难的任务.

uphold /ˌʌpˈhəʊld/ *v* [*pt*, *pp* -held /-held/] [T] 1 支持 zhīchí；赞成 zànchéng：*～ the law* 维护法律. 2 确〔確〕认〔認〕(决议等) quèrèn.

upholster /ˌʌpˈhəʊlstə(r)/ *v* [T] 为〔爲〕(沙发、椅子等)装〔裝〕上垫〔墊〕子、弹〔彈〕簧、套子等 wèi zhuāngshàng diànzi、tánhuáng、tàozi děng. **upholsterer** *n* [C]. **upholstery** *n* [U] 家具装饰材料 jiājù zhuāngshì cáiliào.

upkeep /ˈʌpkiːp/ *n* [U] 保养〔養〕(费) bǎoyǎng；维修(费) wéixiū：*the ～ of a house* 房屋的维修费.

upland /ˈʌplənd/ *n* [C, 尤作 pl] 高地 gāodì.

up-market /ˈʌp ˌmɑːkɪt/ *adj* [非正式用语] 高级的 gāojíde；高档〔檔〕的 gāodàngde：*an ～ restaurant* 高级饭店.

upon /əˈpɒn/ *prep* [正式用语] ＝ON[2] 1, 2, 6, 11, 12, 14.

upper /ˈʌpə(r)/ *adj* 1 在上面的 zài shàngmiàn de：*the ～ lip* 上唇. 2 [习语] the upper ˈhand 有利地位 yǒulì dìwèi；控制 kòngzhì：*gain the ～ hand* 占上风. **upper** *n* [C] 鞋帮〔幫〕xiébāng. **the ˌupper ˈclass** *n* [C] 上流社会〔會〕shàngliú shèhuì. **ˌupper-ˈclass** *adj*. **ˈuppermost** *adj*, *adv* (位置、地位)最高(的) zuìgāo，最重要(的) zuì zhòngyào：*thoughts ～most in his mind* 他心中最主要的想法.

upright /ˈʌpraɪt/ *adj* 1 垂直的 chuízhíde；直立的 zhílìde. 2 正直的 zhèngzhíde. **upright** *n* [C] 立柱 lìzhù.

uprising /ˈʌpraɪzɪŋ/ *n* [C] 起义〔義〕qǐyì；暴动〔動〕bàodòng.

uproar /ˈʌprɔː(r)/ *n* [U, 常作 sing] 吵闹〔鬧〕chǎonào；骚动〔動〕sāodòng. **uproarious** /ʌpˈrɔːrɪəs/ *adj* 吵闹的 chǎonàode；骚动的 sāodòngde.

uproot /ˌʌpˈruːt/ *v* [T] 1 连根拔起 lián gēn báqǐ. 2 [喻]迫使(自己等)离〔離〕开〔開〕家乡〔鄉〕pòshǐ líkāi jiāxiāng.

upset /ˌʌpˈset/ *v* [-tt-; *pt*, *pp* upset] [T] 1 使不安 shǐ bù'ān；使烦恼〔惱〕shǐ fánnǎo：*be ～ by the bad news* 被坏消息弄得心神不宁. 2 使感觉〔覺〕不舒服 shǐ gǎnjué bù shūfu：*Milk ～s her stomach*. 她喝牛奶感到不舒服. 3 打乱〔亂〕dǎluàn；扰〔擾〕乱 rǎoluàn：*～ one's plans* 打乱计划. 4 打翻 dǎfān；弄翻 nòngfān：*～ a glass of water* 打翻一杯水. **upset** /ˈʌpset/ *n* 1 [U, C] 翻倒 fāndǎo；扰乱 rǎoluàn；不安 bù'ān. 2 [C] 不舒服 bù shūfu：*a stomach ～* 肠胃不适.

upshot /ˈʌpʃɒt/ *n* the upshot [sing] (*of*) 结果 jiéguǒ；结局 jiéjú.

upside-down /ˌʌpsaɪd ˈdaʊn/ *adj*, *adv* 1 颠倒(的) diāndǎo. 2 [喻]混乱〔亂〕(的) hùnluàn：*Burglars had turned the house ～*. 窃贼把屋子翻得乱七八糟.

upstage /ˌʌpˈsteɪdʒ/ *v* [T] 将〔將〕(对某人的注意力)引向自己 jiāng yǐn xiàng zìjǐ.

upstairs /ˌʌpˈsteəz/ *adv*, *adj* 往楼〔樓〕上(的) wǎng lóushàng；在楼上(的) zài lóushàng.

upstanding /ˌʌpˈstændɪŋ/ *adj* [正式用语] 1 强健的 qiángjiànde. 2 诚实〔實〕的 chéngshíde；正派的 zhèngpàide.

upstart /ˈʌpstɑːt/ *n* [C] [贬]新贵 xīnguì；暴发〔發〕户 bàofāhù.

upstream /ˌʌpˈstriːm/ *adv* 在上游 zài shàngyóu；向上游 xiàng shàngyóu.

uptake /ˈʌpteɪk/ [习语] ˌquick / ˌslow on the ˈuptake 理解力强(或弱)的 lǐjiělì qiáng de.

uptight /ˌʌpˈtaɪt/ *adj* [非正式用语]神经〔經〕紧〔緊〕张〔張〕的 shénjīng jǐnzhāng de.

up-to-date /ˌʌp tə ˈdeɪt/ *adj* 1 现代的 xiàndàide；时〔時〕新的 shíxīnde：*～ equipment* 新式装备. 2 (包含)最新信息的 zuìxīn xìnxī de：*an ～ report* 最新报告.

upward /ˈʌpwəd/ *adj* 向上的 xiàngshàngde；上升的 shàngshēngde. **upwards** (亦作 **upward**) *adv* 向上地 xiàngshàngde；上升地 shàngshēngde.

uranium /jʊˈreɪnɪəm/ *n* [U] [化学]铀 yóu.

urban /ˈɜːbən/ *adj* 城市的 chéngshìde；都市的 dūshìde.

urchin /ˈɜːtʃɪn/ *n* [C] 街头〔頭〕流浪儿〔兒〕jiētóu liúlàng'ér.

urge /ɜːdʒ/ *v* [T] 1 催促 cuīcù；力劝〔勸〕lìquàn：*They ～d her to come back soon*. 他们催促她立刻回来. 2 (竭力)推荐〔薦〕tuījiàn；力陈 lìchén：*～ caution* 特别提出要小心谨慎. 3 驱〔驅〕赶〔趕〕qūgǎn；驱策 qūcè. **urge** *n* [C] 强烈的欲〔慾〕望 qiángliède yùwàng：*a sudden ～ to run away* 突然想逃跑.

urgent /ˈɜːdʒənt/ *adj* 紧〔緊〕急的 jǐnjíde；急迫的 jípòde. **urgency** /ˈɜːdʒənsɪ/ *n* [U]. **urgently** *adv*.

urine /ˈjʊərɪn/ *n* [U] 尿 niào. **urinate** *v* [I] 排尿 páiniào；小便 xiǎobiàn.

urn /ɜːn/ *n* [C] 1 骨灰瓮 gǔhuīwèng. 2 (金属)大茶壶〔壺〕dà cháhú.

US /ˌjuː ˈes/ *abbr* the US ＝ the United

States (of America): *a US citizen* 美国公民.

us /əs, 强式: ʌs/ *pron* [*we* 的宾格]我们 wǒmen.

USA /ˌjuː es ˈeɪ/ *abbr* **the USA** = the United States of America 美利坚〔堅〕合众〔衆〕国〔國〕Měilìjiān Hézhòngguó: *visit the USA* 访问美国.

usage /ˈjuːsɪdʒ; *US* ˈjuːzɪdʒ/ *n* **1** [U, C] [语言]惯用法 guànyòngfǎ: *a guide to modern English* ~ 现代英语惯用法手册. **2** [U] 用法 yòngfǎ.

use[1] /juːz/ *v* [*pt, pp* ~**d** /juːzd/] [T] **1** 用 yòng; 使用 shǐyòng; 应〔應〕用 yìngyòng: ~ *a pen to write* 用钢笔写字. **2** 消耗 xiāohào; 用尽〔盡〕yòngjìn: *The car ~d 20 litres of petrol for the journey*. 汽车在路上消耗了二十公升汽油. **3** 利用(某人) lìyòng. **4** [短语动词] **use sth up** 用尽 yòngjìn. **usable** *adj*. **used** *adj* 用旧〔舊〕了的 yòng jiù le de: ~*d cars* 旧汽车. **user** *n* [C] 使用者 shǐyòngzhě; 用户 yònghù.

use[2] /juːs/ *n* **1** [U, sing] 用 yòng; 使用 shǐyòng; 运〔運〕用 yùnyòng. **2** [C, U] 用途 yòngtú; 用处〔處〕yòngchù: *a tool with many ~s* 有多种用途的工具. **3** [U] (a) 使用的能力 shǐyòngde nénglì: *lose the ~ of one's legs* 失去双腿的功能. (b) 使用权〔權〕shǐyòngquán: *You can have the ~ of my car*. 你可以使用我的汽车. **4** [U] 价〔價〕值 jiàzhí; 效用 xiàoyòng: *It's no ~ worrying about it*. 为它着急是没有用的. **5** [习语] **ˌcome into / ˌgo out of ˈuse** 开〔開〕始(或停止)被使用 kāishǐ bèi shǐyòng. **in ˈuse** 正在使用 zhèngzài shǐyòng. **make use of sth** 使用 shǐyòng; 利用 lìyòng. **of use** 有用的 yǒuyòngde. **useful** /ˈjuːsfl/ *adj* 实〔實〕用的 shíyòngde; 适〔適〕用的 shìyòngde; 有帮〔幫〕助的 yǒu bāngzhù de. **usefully** *adv*. **usefulness** *n* [U]. **useless** *adj* **1** 无〔無〕用的 wúyòngde; 无益的 wúyìde. **2** [非正式用语]做不好的 zuò bù hǎo de; 差劲〔勁〕的 chàjìnde. **uselessly** *adv*. **username** *n* [C] 用户名 yònghùmíng.

used /juːst/ *adj* **to** (对某事物)已熟悉 yǐ shúxī, 已习〔習〕惯 yǐ xíguàn: *You will soon be / get ~ to the weather*. 你不久将会习惯于这种天气的.

used to /ˈjuːs tə; 元音前及末尾读作 ˈjuːs tuː/ *modal v* (表示过去的习惯或状况): *I ~ play football when I was a boy*. 我小时候常常踢足球.

usher /ˈʌʃə(r)/ *n* [C] (戏院,公共场所等的)引座员 yǐnzuòyuán. **usher** *v* [T] **1** 引导〔導〕yǐndǎo; 带〔帶〕领 dàilǐng. **2** [短语动词] **usher sth in** [正式用语]开〔開〕创〔創〕kāichuàng; 开始(或引进) kāishǐ. **usherette** /ˌʌʃəˈret/ *n* [C] 女引座员 nǚ yǐnzuòyuán.

USSR /ˌjuː es es ˈɑː(r)/ *abbr* **the USSR** = the Union of Soviet Socialist Republics (前)苏〔蘇〕维埃社会〔會〕主义〔義〕共和国〔國〕联〔聯〕盟 Sūwéi'āi Shèhuìzhǔyì Gònghéguó Liánméng.

usual /ˈjuːʒl/ *adj* 通常的 tōngchángde; 平常的 píngchángde; 惯常的 guànchángde: *We'll meet at the ~ place*. 我们将在老地方碰头. **usually** /ˈjuːʒəlɪ/ *adv* 通常地 tōngcháng de; 惯常地 guàncháng de.

usurp /juːˈzɜːp/ *v* [T] [正式用语]篡夺〔奪〕cuànduó; 侵占〔佔〕qīnzhàn. **usurper** *n* [C].

utensil /juːˈtensl/ *n* [C] [正式用语]器皿(尤指家庭用具) qìmǐn.

uterus /ˈjuːtərəs/ *n* [C] [解剖] = WOMB.

utility /juːˈtɪlətɪ/ *n* [*pl* -**ies**] **1** [U] 有用 yǒuyòng; 实〔實〕用 shíyòng. **2** [C] 公用事业〔業〕gōngyòng shìyè.

utilize /ˈjuːtəlaɪz/ *v* [T] [正式用语]利用 lìyòng. **utilization** /ˌjuːtəlaɪˈzeɪʃn/ *n* [U].

utmost /ˈʌtməʊst/ *adj* 最远〔遠〕的 zuìyuǎnde; 最大的 zuìdàde; 极〔極〕度的 jídùde: *of the ~ importance* 极重要的. **utmost** *n* [sing] 极端 jíduān; 最大限度 zuìdà xiàndù: *I shall do my ~*. 我将尽最大努力.

utter[1] /ˈʌtə(r)/ *adj* 完全的 wánquánde; 十足的 shízúde: ~ *darkness* 漆黑. **utterly** *adv*.

utter[2] /ˈʌtə(r)/ *v* [T] 用口发〔發〕出(声音) yòng kǒu fāchū; 说(话) shuō. **utterance** /ˈʌtərəns/ *n* [C] [正式用语]话 huà; 言词 yáncí.

U-turn ⇨ U, u.

V v

V, v /viː/ *n* [C] [*pl* **V's, v's** /viːz/] **1** 英语的第二十二个〔個〕字母 Yīngyǔde dì'èrshí'èrgè zìmǔ. **2** 罗〔羅〕马数〔數〕字五(V) Luómǎ shùzì wǔ.

v *abbr* **1** versus. **2** volt(s). **3** very.

vacancy /ˈveɪkənsɪ/ *n* [C] [*pl* -**ies**] **1** 空职〔職〕kòngzhí; 空缺 kòngquē. **2** 空房 kòngfáng; 空余〔餘〕住处〔處〕kòngyú zhùchù.

vacant /ˈveɪkənt/ *adj* **1** 空的 kōngde; 未被占〔佔〕用的 wèi bèi zhànyòng de. **2** (头脑)空虚的 kōngxūde; 无思想的 wú sīxiǎng de: *a ~ expression* 茫然的表情.

vacate /vəˈkeɪt, veɪˈkeɪt/ *v* [T] [正式用语]使空出 shǐ kòngchū; 搬出 bānchū.

vacation /vəˈkeɪʃn; *US* veɪ-/ *n* [C] **1** (大

学)假期 jiàqī. 2 [尤用于美语]休假 xiūjià.

vaccinate /ˈvæksɪneɪt/ *v* [T] 给(某人)接种〔種〕疫苗 gěi jiēzhòng yìmiáo. **vaccination** /ˌvæksɪˈneɪʃn/ *n* [C, U].

vaccine /ˈvæksiːn; *US* vækˈsiːn/ *n* [C, U] 疫苗 yìmiáo.

vacuum /ˈvækjuəm/ *n* [C] [*pl* ~s 或科技用语作 **vacua** /-juə/] 真空 zhēnkōng: [喻] *a ~ in his life since his wife died* 自从他妻子去世后,他的生活很空虚. **vacuum** *v* [I, T] 用真空吸尘〔塵〕器清扫〔掃〕yòng zhēnkōng xīchénqì qīngsǎo. ˈ**vacuum cleaner** *n* [C] 真空吸尘器 zhēnkōng xīchénqì. ˈ**vacuum flask** *n* [C] 保温瓶 bǎowēnpíng.

vagabond /ˈvægəbɒnd/ *n* [C] [旧]流浪者 liúlàngzhě.

vagina /vəˈdʒaɪnə/ *n* [C] [解剖]阴〔陰〕道 yīndào.

vagrant /ˈveɪgrənt/ *n* [C] [正式用语][法律]流浪者 liúlàngzhě; 无〔無〕业〔業〕游民 wú yè yóumín. **vagrancy** /-rənsɪ/ *n* [U].

vague /veɪg/ *adj* [~r, ~st] 1 模糊的 móhude; 不清楚的 bù qīngchu de. 2 暧〔曖〕昧的 àimèide; 不明确〔確〕的 bù míngquè de. **vaguely** *adv*. **vagueness** *n* [U].

vain /veɪn/ *adj* 1 自负的 zìfùde; 自视过〔過〕高的 zì shì guògāo de. 2 徒劳〔勞〕的 túláode; 无〔無〕效果的 wú xiàoguǒ de: *a ~ attempt* 徒劳的尝试. 3 [习语] **in** ˈ**vain** 徒劳 túláo; 徒然 túrán. **vainly** *adv*.

vale /veɪl/ *n* [C] [诗或地名]山谷 shāngǔ.

valentine /ˈvæləntaɪn/ *n* [C] (在二月十四日圣瓦伦丁节所祝贺的)情人 qíngrén.

valet /ˈvæleɪ, ˈvælɪt/ *n* [C] 男仆〔僕〕nánpú.

valiant /ˈvælɪənt/ *adj* 勇敢的 yǒnggǎnde; 英勇的 yīngyǒngde. **valiantly** *adv*.

valid /ˈvælɪd/ *adj* 1 (法律上)有效的 yǒuxiàode: *The ticket is ~ until 1st May.* 乘车券可用到五月一日为止. 2 有根据〔據〕的 yǒu gēnjù de; 正当〔當〕的 zhèngdàngde. **validate** *v* [T] [正式用语]使有效 shǐ yǒuxiào; 证〔證〕实〔實〕zhèngshí. **validity** /vəˈlɪdətɪ/ *n* [U].

valley /ˈvælɪ/ *n* [C] 溪谷 xīgǔ; 山谷 shāngǔ.

valour (美语 -or) /ˈvælə(r)/ *n* [U] [修辞] 英勇 yīngyǒng; 勇敢 yǒnggǎn.

valuable /ˈvæljuəbl/ *adj* 1 贵重的 guìzhòngde; 值钱〔錢〕的 zhíqiánde. 2 有用的 yǒuyòngde; 很有价〔價〕值的 hěn yǒu jiàzhí de: *~ advice* 宝贵的劝告. **valuables** *n* [pl] 贵重物品 guìzhòng wùpǐn.

valuation /ˌvæljuˈeɪʃn/ *n* 1 [U] 估价〔價〕gūjià. 2 [C] 评定的价值 píngdìngde jiàzhí.

value /ˈvæljuː/ *n* 1 (a) [C, U] 价〔價〕值 jiàzhí. (b) [U] 值(与价格相比而言) zhí: *This large packet is good ~ at 99p.* 这一大包只卖九十九便士,很合算. 2 [U] 实〔實〕用性 shíyòngxìng; 重要性 zhòngyàoxìng: *the ~ of regular exercise* 经常练习的好处. 3 **values** [pl] 准〔準〕则 zhǔnzé; 标〔標〕准 biāozhǔn: *high moral ~s* 崇高的道德准则. **value** *v* [T] 1 (给某物)估价 gūjià; 定价 dìngjià. 2 重视 zhòngshì; 尊重 zūnzhòng: *I ~ my secretary.* 我尊重我的秘书. ˌ**value** ˈ**added tax** *n* [U] 增值税 zēngzhíshuì. **valueless** *adj* 无〔無〕价值的 wú jiàzhí de. **valuer** *n* [C] 估价者 gūjiàzhě.

valve /vælv/ *n* [C] (a) 阀 fá; 活门 huómén. (b) (心、血管的)瓣膜 bànmó.

vampire /ˈvæmpaɪə(r)/ *n* [C] 吸血鬼 xīxuèguǐ.

van /væn/ *n* [C] 大篷货车 dàpéng huòchē.

vandal /ˈvændl/ *n* [C] 故意破坏〔壞〕(他人)财物者 gùyì pòhuài cáiwù zhě. **vandalism** /-dəlɪzəm/ *n* [U] 故意破坏财物的行为〔爲〕gùyì pòhuài cáiwù de xíngwéi. **vandalize** /-dəlaɪz/ *v* [T] 恣意破坏(财物等) zìyì pòhuài.

vanguard /ˈvængɑːd/ *n* **the vanguard** [sing] 1 先头〔頭〕部队〔隊〕xiāntóu bùduì. 2 [喻](运动或学术研究的)先驱〔驅〕者 xiānqūzhě.

vanilla /vəˈnɪlə/ *n* [U] 香草香精 xiāngcǎo xiāngjīng.

vanish /ˈvænɪʃ/ *v* [I] 1 突然消失 tūrán xiāoshī. 2 不复〔復〕存在 bú fù cúnzài: *Her hopes of finding a new job have ~ed.* 她找新工作的希望已经落空.

vanity /ˈvænətɪ/ *n* [U] 1 自大 zìdà; 虚荣〔榮〕心 xūróngxīn. 2 [正式用语]无〔無〕价〔價〕值 wú jiàzhí: *the ~ of pleasure* 寻欢作乐的空虚性.

vanquish /ˈvæŋkwɪʃ/ *v* [T] [正式用语]征服 zhēngfú; 击〔擊〕败 jībài.

vaporize /ˈveɪpəraɪz/ *v* [I, T] (使)汽化 qìhuà.

vapour (美语 -or) /ˈveɪpə(r)/ *n* [U] 蒸气〔氣〕zhēngqì: ˈ*water ~* 水蒸气.

variable /ˈveərɪəbl/ *adj* 变〔變〕化的 biànhuàde; 可变的 kěbiànde. **variable** *n* [C] 可变物 kěbiànwù; 变量 biànliàng. **variably** *adv*.

variant /ˈveərɪənt/ *adj*, *n* [C] 不同(的) bùtóng; 变〔變〕异〔異〕(的) biànyì: *~ spellings of a word* 一个词的不同拼法.

variation /ˌveərɪˈeɪʃn/ *n* 1 [C, U] 变〔變〕化 biànhuà; 改变 gǎibiàn: *~(s) in temperature* 温度的变化. 2 [C] [音乐]变奏 biànzòu; 变奏曲 biànzòuqǔ.

varicose vein /ˈværɪkəus veɪn/ *n* [C, 常作

pl] 静脉〔脈〕曲张〔張〕 jìngmài qūzhāng.

varied /ˈveərɪd/ *adj* 1 各种〔種〕各样〔樣〕的 gèzhǒng gèyàng de. 2 多变〔變〕化的 duō biànhuà de; 多样的 duōyàngde.

variety /vəˈraɪətɪ/ *n* [*pl* -ies] 1 [U] 多样〔樣〕化 duōyànghuà: *a life full of* ~ 多样化的生活. 2 [sing] 若干不同的事物 ruògān bùtóng de shìwù; 种〔種〕种 zhǒngzhǒng: *a wide* ~ *of interests* 兴趣的广泛性. 3 [C] 变〔變〕种 biànzhǒng; 变体〔體〕 biàntǐ: *rare varieties of birds* 鸟类的稀有品种. 4 [U] (音乐、舞蹈、杂耍等的)联〔聯〕合演出 liánhé yǎnchū: *a* ~ *act* 一幕杂耍表演.

varifocal /ˌverɪˈfəʊkl/ *adj* 变〔變〕焦的 biànjiāo de: These glasses have ~ lenses. 这些眼镜带有变焦镜片. **varifocals** *n* [*pl*] 变〔變〕焦眼镜 biànjiāo yǎnjìng.

various /ˈveərɪəs/ *adj* 1 不同的 bùtóngde; 各式各样〔樣〕的 gèshì gèyàng de: *This dress comes in* ~ *colours*. 这种衣服有各式各样的颜色. 2 不止一个〔個〕的 bùzhǐ yígè de: *at* ~ *times* 多次. **variously** *adv*.

varnish /ˈvɑːnɪʃ/ *n* [C,U] 清漆 qīngqī. **varnish** *v* [T] 给…涂〔塗〕清漆 gěi…tú qīngqī.

vary /ˈveərɪ/ *v* [*pt*, *pp* -ied] 1 [I] (大小、数量等)呈现不同 chéngxiàn bùtóng: *Car prices* ~ *greatly*. 汽车的售价差异很大. 2 [I, T] (使)变〔變〕化 biànhuà; (使)改变 gǎibiàn: ~ *one's route* 改变路线.

vase /vɑːz; *US* veɪs, veɪz/ *n* [C] 花瓶 huāpíng.

vast /vɑːst; *US* væst/ *adj* 巨大的 jùdàde; 广〔廣〕大的 guǎngdàde: *a* ~ *desert* 大沙漠. **vastly** *adv*: ~*ly improved* 很大改进的. **vastness** *n* [U].

VAT /ˌviː eɪ ˈtiː, 亦读作 væt/ *abbr* value added tax 增值税 zēngzhíshuì.

vat /væt/ *n* [C] 大桶 dàtǒng; 大缸 dàgāng.

vault[1] /vɔːlt/ *n* [C] 1 保险〔險〕库 bǎoxiǎnkù. 2 地下室 dìxiàshì; (尤指)地下墓室 dìxià mùshì. 3 拱顶 gǒngdǐng.

vault[2] /vɔːlt/ *v* [I, T] (*over*) (以手撑物)跳跃〔躍〕 tiàoyuè: ~ (*over*) *a wall* 跳过围墙. **vault** *n* [C] (撑物)跳跃 tiàoyuè. **vaulter** *n* [C] (撑物)跳跃者 tiàoyuèzhě: *a* ˈ*pole-* ~*er* 撑竿跳运动员.

VDU /ˌviː diː ˈjuː/ *abbr* visual display unit [计算机]视频显〔顯〕示器 shìpín xiǎnshìqì.

veal /viːl/ *n* [U] (食用)小牛肉 xiǎo niúròu.

veer /vɪə(r)/ *v* [I] 改变〔變〕方向 gǎibiàn fāngxiàng.

vegetable /ˈvedʒtəbl/ *n* [C] 植物 zhíwù; (尤指)蔬菜 shūcài. **vegetable** *adj* 植物的 zhíwùde; 蔬菜的 shūcàide: ~ *oils* 植物油.

vegetarian /ˌvedʒɪˈteərɪən/ *n* [C] 吃素的人 chī sù de rén.

vegetate /ˈvedʒɪteɪt/ *v* [I] [喻]过〔過〕枯燥单〔單〕调的生活 guò kūzào dāndiào de shēnghuó.

vegetation /ˌvedʒɪˈteɪʃn/ *n* [U] 植被 zhíbèi.

vehement /ˈviːəmənt/ *adj* (感情)强烈的 qiángliède; 热〔熱〕情的 rèqíngde. **vehemence** /-məns/ *n* [U]. **vehemently** *adv*.

vehicle /ˈvɪəkl; *US* ˈviːɪkl/ *n* [C] 1 车辆〔輛〕 chēliàng. 2 [正式用语](传递思想等的)工具 gōngjù.

veil /veɪl/ *n* 1 [C] 面纱 miànshā. 2 [sing] [正式用语]掩饰物 yǎnshìwù; 遮盖〔蓋〕物 zhēgàiwù: *a* ~ *of mist* 一层雾. **veil** *v* [T] 1 给…带〔帶〕面纱 gěi…dài miànshā. 2 [喻]掩饰 yǎnshì; 遮盖 zhēgài; 隐〔隱〕蔽 yǐnbì.

vein /veɪn/ *n* 1 [C] 静脉〔脈〕 jìngmài. 2 [C] 叶〔葉〕脉 yèmài; 翅脉 chìmài. 3 [C] 矿〔礦〕脉 kuàngmài: *a* ~ *of gold* 黄金矿脉. 4 [sing] 方式 fāngshì; 风〔風〕格 fēnggé: *in a comic* ~ 喜剧的风格.

velocity /vɪˈlɒsətɪ/ *n* [U, C] [*pl* -ies] [正式用语][物理]速度 sùdù.

velvet /ˈvelvɪt/ *n* [U] 丝绒 sīróng; 天鹅绒 tiān'éróng. **velvety** *adj* (天鹅绒般)柔软光滑的 róuruǎn guānghuá de.

vendetta /venˈdetə/ *n* [C] 家族仇杀〔殺〕 jiāzú chóushā.

vending-machine /ˈvendɪŋ məˌʃiːn/ *n* [C] (投币式)自动〔動〕售货机〔機〕 zìdòng shòuhuòjī.

vendor /ˈvendə(r)/ *n* [C] 1 摊〔攤〕贩 tānfàn. 2 [法律](房地产的)卖〔賣〕方 màifāng.

veneer /vəˈnɪə(r)/ *n* 1 [C,U] (镶饰表面用的)贴面板 tiēmiànbǎn. 2 [sing] [喻](掩盖真情的)外表 wàibiǎo, 虚饰 xūshì. **veneer** *v* [T] 给…贴面板 gěi…tiē miànbǎn.

venerable /ˈvenərəbl/ *adj* [正式用语](因年老等而)值得尊敬的 zhídé zūnjìng de.

venerate /ˈvenəreɪt/ *v* [T] [正式用语]崇敬 chóngjìng; 崇拜 chóngbài. **veneration** /ˌvenəˈreɪʃn/ *n* [U].

venereal disease /vəˌnɪərɪəl dɪˈziːz/ *n* [C,U] 性病 xìngbìng.

vengeance /ˈvendʒəns/ *n* 1 [U] 报〔報〕仇 bàochóu. 2 [习语] **with a** ˈ**vengeance** [非正式用语]极〔極〕端地 jíduānde; 过〔過〕分地 guòfènde; 彻〔徹〕底地 chèdǐde.

vengeful /ˈvendʒfl/ *adj* [正式用语]有复〔復〕仇心的 yǒu fùchóuxīn de; 图〔圖〕谋报〔報〕复的 túmóu bàofù de.

venison /ˈvenɪzn, -ɪsn/ *n* [U] 鹿肉 lùròu.

venom /ˈvenəm/ *n* [U] 1 (毒蛇的)毒液 dúyè. 2 [喻]恶〔惡〕意 èyì; 怨恨 yuànhèn. **venomous** *adj*: *a* ~*ous snake* 毒蛇. *a* ~*ous*

V

glance 恶狠狠的一瞥.

vent /vent/ *n* 1 [C] (气、水等的)出口 chūkǒu. 2 [习语] **give 'vent to sth** (任意地)表达〔達〕biǎodá; 发〔發〕泄 fāxiè; 吐露 tǔlù: *give ~ to one's feelings* 抒发自己的感情. **vent** *v* [T] (*on*) 发泄(感情) fāxiè. *He ~ed his anger on his brother*. 他拿他的弟弟出气.

ventilate /ˈventɪleɪt; *US* -təleɪt/ *v* [T] 使空气流通 shǐ kōngqì liútōng.

ventilation /ˌventɪˈleɪʃn; *US* -təˈl-/ *n* [U]. **ventilator** *n* [C] 通风〔風〕设备〔備〕tōngfēng shèbèi.

ventriloquist /venˈtrɪləkwɪst/ *n* [C] 口技 kǒujì.

venture /ˈventʃə(r)/ *n* [C] 冒险〔險〕màoxiǎn; 冒险事业〔業〕màoxiǎn shìyè: *a ˈbusiness ~* 商业投机. **venture** *v* [正式用语] 1 [I] 冒险 màoxiǎn; (敢于)遭受危险或损失 zāoshòu wēixiǎn huò sǔnshī. 2 [T] 敢于(说话) gǎnyú.

venue /ˈvenjuː/ *n* [C] 会〔會〕场〔場〕huìchǎng; 聚集地 jùjídì: *a ~ for the football match* 足球场.

veranda (亦作 **verandah**) /vəˈrændə/ *n* [C] 走廊 zǒuláng; 阳〔陽〕台〔臺〕yángtái.

verb /vɜːb/ *n* [C] [语法]动〔動〕词 dòngcí.

verbal /ˈvɜːbl/ *adj* 1 言语的 yányǔde; 字句的 zìjùde. 2 口头〔頭〕的 kǒutóude. 3 [语法]动〔動〕词的 dòngcíde. **verbally** /ˈvɜːbəlɪ/ *adv* 口头上 kǒutóushang. **verbal 'noun** *n* [C] [语法]动名词(如在 *Swimming is a good form of exercise*. 这个句子中, swimming 一词是动名词.) dòngmíngcí.

verbose /vɜːˈbəʊs/ *adj* [正式用语]噜苏〔蘇〕的 lūsūde; 冗长〔長〕的 rǒngchángde. **verbosity** /vɜːˈbɒsətɪ/ *n* [U].

verdict /ˈvɜːdɪkt/ *n* [C] 1 (陪审团的)裁决 cáijué: *a ~ of guilty / not guilty* 判决有罪(或无罪). 2 定论〔論〕dìnglùn; 意见 yìjiàn.

verge /vɜːdʒ/ *n* [C] 1 边〔邊〕缘 biānyuán; 边界 biānjiè. 2 [习语] **on the 'verge of sth** 接近于 jiējìn yú; 濒于 bīnyú: *on the ~ of war* 处于战争的边缘. **verge** *v* [短语动词] **verge on sth** 极〔極〕接近于 jí jiējìn yú.

verify /ˈverɪfaɪ/ *v* [*pt*, *pp* -ied] [T] 证〔證〕实〔實〕zhèngshí; 查对〔對〕cháduì; 核实 héshí. **verifiable** *adj*. **verification** /ˌverɪfɪˈkeɪʃn/ *n* [U].

veritable /ˈverɪtəbl/ *adj* [正式用语][谑]名副其实〔實〕的 míng fù qí shí de; 确〔確〕实的 quèshíde: *a ~ liar* 十足的说谎者.

vermin /ˈvɜːmɪn/ *n* [U] [常用 pl v] 1 害兽〔獸〕hàishòu; 害虫 hàichóng. 2 [喻]害人虫 hàirénchóng; 歹徒 dǎitú.

vernacular /vəˈnækjʊlə(r)/ *adj*, *n* [C] (用)本国〔國〕语(的) běnguóyǔ; (用)方言(的) fāngyán.

versatile /ˈvɜːsətaɪl; *US* -tl/ *adj* 多才多艺〔藝〕的 duō cái duō yì de. **versatility** /ˌvɜːsəˈtɪlətɪ/ *n* [U].

verse /vɜːs/ *n* 1 [U] 诗 shī; 诗体〔體〕shītǐ; 韵〔韻〕文 yùnwén. 2 [C] 诗节〔節〕shījié. 3 [C] (《圣经》的)(一)节 jié.

versed /vɜːst/ *adj in* [正式用语]精通的 jīngtōngde; 熟练〔練〕的 shúliànde.

version /ˈvɜːʃn; *US* -ʒn/ *n* [C] 1 类〔類〕型 lèixíng; 形式 xíngshì: *the film ~ of the play* 由那个话剧改拍的电影. 2 描述 miáoshù; 说法 shuōfǎ: *There were three ~s of what happened*. 关于所发生的事有三种说法.

versus /ˈvɜːsəs/ *prep* (诉讼、比赛中)对〔對〕duì: *England ~ Brazil* 英国对巴西.

vertebra /ˈvɜːtɪbrə/ *n* [C] [*pl* -brae /-briː/] [解剖]脊椎骨 jǐzhuīgǔ. **vertebrate** /ˈvɜːtɪbreɪt/ *n* [C], *adj* 脊椎动〔動〕物 jǐzhuī dòngwù; 有脊椎的 yǒu jǐzhuī de.

vertical /ˈvɜːtɪkl/ *adj* 垂直的 chuízhíde. **vertical** *n* [sing] 垂直线〔綫〕(或位置) chuízhíxiàn. **vertically** /-klɪ/ *adv*.

vertigo /ˈvɜːtɪgəʊ/ *n* [U] 眩晕 xuànyùn; (尤指高处俯视性)头〔頭〕晕 tóuyūn.

very[1] /ˈverɪ/ *adv* 1 很 hěn; 甚 shèn; 颇 pō: *~ little / quickly* 很小(或快). 2 最 zuì; 极〔極〕其 jíqí: *the ~ best quality* 最好的质量. 3 [习语] **very likely** ⇨LIKELY.

very[2] /ˈverɪ/ *adj* 1 实〔實〕在的 shízàide; 正是的 zhēngshìde: *This is the ~ book I want!* 这正是我想要的书! 2 极〔極〕端的 jíduānde: *at the ~ end* 最终. 3 (用以加强语气): *The ~ thought of it upsets me*. 正是想到此事使我心中不安.

vessel /ˈvesl/ *n* [C] [正式用语] 1 船 chuán; 舰〔艦〕jiàn. 2 容器 róngqì; 器皿 qìmǐn.

vest[1] /vest/ *n* [C] 1 [英国英语]汗衫 hànshān. 2 [美语](西服的)背心 bèixīn.

vest[2] /vest/ *v* 1 [T] *in*, *with* [正式用语] [常用被动语态]授予 shòuyǔ; 给予 jǐyǔ: *the authority ~ed in her* 赋于她的权力. *~ sb with authority* 授权给某人. 2 [习语] **have a vested interest in sth** (对某事物)保有既得利益 bǎo yǒu jìdé lìyì.

vestige /ˈvestɪdʒ/ *n* [C] [正式用语]痕迹〔跡〕hénjì; 遗迹 yíjì: *not a ~ of truth in the report* 这个报告一点也不真实.

vet[1] /vet/ *n* [C] [非正式用语] short for VETERINARY SURGEON (VETERINARY).

vet[2] /vet/ *v* [-tt-] [T] 检〔檢〕查 jiǎnchá; 审〔審〕查 shěnchá.

veteran /ˈvetərən/ *n* [C] 老练〔練〕者 lǎoliànzhě; 老手 lǎoshǒu; 老兵 lǎobīng. ˌ**veteran** ˈ**car** *n* [C] (1916年以前尤指1905年以前制造的)老式汽车 lǎoshì qìchē.

veterinary /ˈvetrɪnrɪ; *US* ˈvetərɪnerɪ/ *adj* 兽〔獸〕医〔醫〕的 shòuyīde. ˌ**veterinary** ˈ**surgeon** *n* [C] [正式用语]兽医 shòuyī.

veto /ˈviːtəʊ/ *n* [*pl* ~**es**] (a) [C, U] 否决权〔權〕fǒujuéquán. (b) [C] 否决(或禁止)的声〔聲〕明 fǒujuéde shēngmíng. **veto** *v* [T] 否决 fǒujué; 禁止 jìnzhǐ: ~ *a proposal* 否决一项提案.

vex /veks/ *v* [T] [正式用语]使烦恼〔惱〕shǐ fánnǎo; 使苦恼 shǐ kǔnǎo. **vexation** /vekˈseɪʃn/ *n* [C, U]. **vexed** *adj* (问题)引起争论〔論〕的 yǐnqǐ zhēnglùn de.

via /ˈvaɪə/ *prep* 经〔經〕过〔過〕jīngguò; 经由 jīngyóu.

viable /ˈvaɪəbl/ *adj* (尤指计划,事业)可行的 kěxíngde; 能成功的 néng chénggōng de. **viability** /ˌvaɪəˈbɪlətɪ/ *n* [U].

viaduct /ˈvaɪədʌkt/ *n* [C] 高架桥〔橋〕gāojiàqiáo.

vibrate /vaɪˈbreɪt; *US* ˈvaɪbreɪt/ *v* [I, T] (使)摆〔擺〕动〔動〕bǎidòng; (使)摇动 yáodòng: *The house ~s whenever a heavy lorry passes*. 当重型卡车经过时,那房屋就会晃. **vibration** /-ˈbreɪʃn/ *n* [C, U].

vicar /ˈvɪkə(r)/ *n* [C] 教区〔區〕牧师〔師〕jiàoqū mùshī. **vicarage** /ˈvɪkərɪdʒ/ *n* [C] 教区牧师的住宅 jiàoqū mùshī de zhùzhái.

vice[1] /vaɪs/ *n* **1** [C, U] 罪恶〔惡〕zuì'è; 不道德行为〔爲〕bú dàodé xíngwéi. **2** [C] [非正式用语][谑]缺点〔點〕quēdiǎn; 坏习〔習〕惯 huài xíguàn: *Chocolate is one of his ~s*. 他有个小毛病,就是爱吃巧克力.

vice[2] /vaɪs/ *n* [C] 老虎钳 lǎohǔqián.

vice- /vaɪs-/ *prefix* 副的 fùde; 次的 cìde: ~-*president* 副总统.

vice versa /ˌvaɪsə ˈvɜːsə/ *adv* 反过〔過〕来(也是一样) fǎnguòlái: *We gossip about them and ~*. 我们议论他们,反过来,他们也同样议论我们.

vicinity /vɪˈsɪnətɪ/ *n* [习语] **in the** ˈ**vicinity (of sth)** (在)邻〔鄰〕近 línjìn; (在)附近 fùjìn.

vicious /ˈvɪʃəs/ *adj* **1** 有恶〔惡〕意的 yǒu èyì de; 邪恶的 xié'ède; 堕落的 duòluòde. **2** [习语] **a vicious** ˈ**circle** 恶性循环〔環〕èxìng xúnhuán. **viciously** *adv*.

V

victim /ˈvɪktɪm/ *n* [C] 受害者 shòuhàizhě; 牺牲者 xīshēngzhě: ~*s of the flood* 水灾的受害者. **victimize** *v* [T] (不正当地)使受害 shǐ shòuhài; 欺侮 qīwǔ. **victimization** /ˌvɪktɪmaɪˈzeɪʃn; *US* -mɪˈz-/ *n* [U].

victor /ˈvɪktə(r)/ *n* [C] [正式用语]胜〔勝〕利者 shènglìzhě; 战〔戰〕胜者 zhànshèngzhě.

victory /ˈvɪktərɪ/ *n* [C, U] [*pl* -**ies**] 胜〔勝〕利 shènglì; 战〔戰〕胜 zhànshèng. **victorious** /vɪkˈtɔːrɪəs/ *adj* 胜利的 shènglìde; 战胜的 zhànshèngde.

video /ˈvɪdɪəʊ/ *n* [*pl* ~**s**] **1** [U, C] 电〔電〕视录〔錄〕像 diànshì lùxiàng. **2** [C] 录像机〔機〕lùxiàngjī. **video** *v* [T] 录制〔製〕(电视节目). lùzhì. ˈ**video conference** *n* [C] 视频会〔會〕议〔議〕shìpín huìyì; 电视会议 diànshì huìyì. **video-on-de**ˈ**mand** *n* [U] 视频点〔點〕播 shìpín diǎnbō. ˈ**video player** *n* [C] 放像机 fàngxiàngjī; 视频播放器 shìpín bōfàngqì. ˈ**video recorder** (亦作 ˌ**video ca**ˈ**ssette recorder**) *n* [C] 录像机 lùxiàngjī. ˈ**videotape** *n* [U, C] 录像带〔帶〕lùxiàngdài.

vie /vaɪ/ *v* [*pres part* **vying** /ˈvaɪɪŋ/] [I] *with* (与某人)争夺〔奪〕zhēngduó.

view[1] /vjuː/ *n* **1** [U] 看 kàn; 观〔觀〕察 guānchá; 视力 shìlì; 视野 shìyě: *The lake came into ~*. 看见那个湖了. *in full ~ of the crowd* 在大家都能看得见的地方. **2** [C] 看见的东西 kànjiànde dōngxi: *a magnificent ~ from the top of the mountain* 从山顶上看到的壮丽景色. **3** [C] (个人的)意见 yìjiàn, 观〔觀〕点〔點〕guāndiǎn: *In my ~, nurses deserve better pay*. 我的看法是,护士应得更高的工资. **4** [习语] **in view of sth** 考虑〔慮〕到 kǎolǜ dào; 鉴〔鑒〕于 jiànyú: *In ~ of the weather, we will cancel the outing*. 因天气关系,我们要取消这次郊游. **on** ˈ**view** 展览〔覽〕着 zhǎnlǎnzhe; 陈列着 chénlièzhe. **with a view to doing sth** 打算做某事 dǎsuàn zuò mǒushì. ˈ**viewfinder** *n* [C] (照相机的)取景器 qǔjǐngqì. ˈ**viewpoint** *n* [C] 观点 guāndiǎn ⇨ POINT[1].

view[2] /vjuː/ *v* [正式用语] **1** [T] 考虑〔慮〕kǎolǜ: ~ *the problem with some concern* 以焦急的心情考虑这个问题. **2** [I] 察看 chákàn; 注视 zhùshì; 检〔檢〕查 jiǎnchá. **3** [I, T] 看(电视) kàn. **viewer** *n* [C] 电〔電〕视观众〔衆〕diànshì guānzhòng.

vigil /ˈvɪdʒɪl/ *n* [C] 值夜 zhíyè; 守夜 shǒuyè.

vigilant /ˈvɪdʒɪlənt/ *adj* [正式用语]警戒的 jǐngjiède; 警惕的 jǐngtìde. **vigilance** /-ləns/ *n* [U]. **vigilantly** *adv*.

vigour (美语 -**or**) /ˈvɪgə(r)/ *n* [U] 力量 lìliàng; 体〔體〕力 tǐlì; 活力 huólì; 精力 jīnglì. **vigorous** *adj* 强有力的 qiáng yǒulì de; 精力充沛的 jīnglì chōngpèi de. **vigorously** *adv*.

vile /vaɪl/ *adj* [~**r**, ~**st**] **1** 卑鄙的 bēibǐde; 讨厌〔厭〕的 tǎoyànde. **2** [非正式用语]极〔極〕坏〔壞〕的 jíhuàide; 恶〔惡〕劣的 èliède: ~ *weather* 恶劣的天气. **vilely** /ˈvaɪllɪ/ *adv*.

villa /ˈvɪlə/ *n* [C] 别墅 biéshù: *rent a ~*

in Spain 在西班牙租一幢别墅.

village /ˈvɪlɪdʒ/ *n* [C] 乡〔鄉〕村 xiāngcūn; 村庄〔莊〕cūnzhuāng. **villager** *n* [C] 村民 cūnmín.

villain /ˈvɪlən/ *n* [C] **1** [英俚]罪犯 zuìfàn. **2** 坏〔壞〕人 huàirén; 恶〔惡〕棍 ègùn. **3** [习语] **the 'villain of the piece** [尤谑]惹祸〔禍〕的人 rěhuòde rén; 为〔爲〕害之物 wéihài zhī wù.

vindicate /ˈvɪndɪkeɪt/ *v* [T] [正式用语] **1** 澄清…的责难〔難〕(或嫌疑) chéngqīng…de zénán; 为〔爲〕…辩白 wèi…biànbái. **2** 证〔證〕明…属〔屬〕实〔實〕(或正当、有效) zhèngmíng…shǔshí. **vindication** /ˌvɪndɪˈkeɪʃn/ *n* [C, U].

vindictive /vɪnˈdɪktɪv/ *adj* 有报〔報〕复〔復〕心的 yǒu bàofùxīn de. **vindictively** *adv*. **vindictiveness** *n* [U].

vine /vaɪn/ *n* [C] 藤本植物 téngběn zhíwù; 葡萄(藤) pútáo. **vineyard** /ˈvɪnjəd/ *n* [C] 葡萄园〔園〕pútáoyuán.

vinegar /ˈvɪnɪgə(r)/ *n* [U] 醋 cù. **vinegary** *adj*.

vintage /ˈvɪntɪdʒ/ *n* [C] 某一年所产〔產〕的葡萄 mǒuyìnián suǒchǎn de pútáo; (该年葡萄所酿的)葡萄酒 pútáojiǔ. **vintage** *adj* **1** 古老而品质〔質〕优〔優〕良的 gǔlǎo ér pǐnzhì yōuliáng de. **2** (汽车)(1917 年到 1930 年制造的)老牌的 lǎopáide.

vinyl /ˈvaɪnl/ *n* [U] [化学]乙烯基(塑料) yǐxījī.

viola /vɪˈəʊlə/ *n* [C] 中提琴 zhōng tíqín.

violate /ˈvaɪəleɪt/ *v* [T] **1** 违〔違〕犯(誓言、条约等) wéifàn. **2** 亵〔褻〕渎〔瀆〕(圣地) xièdú. **3** [喻]侵犯 qīnfàn; 冒犯 màofàn. **violation** /ˌvaɪəˈleɪʃn/ *n* [U, C].

violent /ˈvaɪələnt/ *adj* **1** 猛烈的 měngliède; 凶〔兇〕暴的 xiōngbàode: *a ~ attack* 猛攻. **2** (感情)强烈的 qiángliède; 由强烈感情引起的 yóu qiángliè gǎnqíng yǐnqǐ de: *a ~ argument* 激烈的争吵. **3** 厉〔厲〕害的 lìhàide; 极〔極〕度的 jídùde: *a ~ thunder* 迅雷. **violence** /-ləns/ *n* [U] **1** 暴行 bàoxíng. **2** 猛烈 měngliè; 暴力 bàolì. **violently** *adv*.

violet /ˈvaɪələt/ *n* **1** [C] 紫罗〔羅〕兰〔蘭〕zǐluólán. **2** [U] 紫罗兰色 zǐluólánsè; 紫色 zǐsè.

violin /ˌvaɪəˈlɪn/ *n* [C] 小提琴 xiǎo tíqín. **violinist** *n* [C] 小提琴手 xiǎo tíqínshǒu.

VIP /ˌviː aɪ ˈpiː/ *abbr*, *n* [C] very important person 要人 yàorén.

viper /ˈvaɪpə(r)/ *n* [C] 蝰蛇 kuíshé; 毒蛇 dúshé.

viral ⇨ VIRUS.

virgin /ˈvɜːdʒɪn/ *n* [C] 处〔處〕女 chǔnǚ. **virgin** *adj* **1** 处女的 chǔnǚde; 童贞的 tóngzhēnde; 纯洁〔潔〕的 chúnjiéde: *~ snow* 洁白的雪. **2** 未开〔開〕发〔發〕的 wèi kāifā de; 原始的 yuánshǐde: *~ soil* 处女地. **virginity** /vəˈdʒɪnətɪ/ *n* [U] 处女身份 chǔnǚshēnfen; 童贞 tóngzhēn; 纯洁 chúnjié.

virile /ˈvɪraɪl; *US* ˈvɪrəl/ *adj* 强有力的 qiáng yǒulì de; 有男子气概的 yǒu nánzǐ qìgài de; 雄纠纠的 xióngjiūjiūde; 有男性生殖力的 yǒu nánxìng shēngzhílì de. **virility** /vəˈrɪlətɪ/ *n* [U].

virtual /ˈvɜːtʃʊəl/ *adj* 实〔實〕际〔際〕上的 shíjìshàngde; 事实上的 shìshíshàngde: *The deputy manager is the ~ head of the business*. 副经理是企业的实际负责人. **virtually** /ˈvɜːtʃʊəlɪ/ *adv* 在各重要方面 zài gè zhòngyào fāngmiàn; 几〔幾〕乎 jīhū. **virtual re'ality** *n* [U] 虚拟〔擬〕现实〔實〕xūnǐ xiànshí.

virtue /ˈvɜːtʃuː/ *n* **1** [U] 美德 měidé; 善良 shànliáng. **2** [C] 良好的性格 liánghǎode xìnggé: *Patience is a ~*. 耐心是一种良好的性格. **3** [C, U] 长〔長〕处〔處〕chángchù; 优〔優〕点〔點〕yōudiǎn: *The great ~ of the plan is its cheapness*. 这个方案的一大优点是省钱. **4** [习语] **by virture of sth** [正式用语]由于 yóuyú; 因为〔爲〕yīnwéi. **virtuous** *adj* 有道德的 yǒu dàodé de; 善良的 shànliángde.

virus /ˈvaɪrəs/ *n* [C] (a) 病毒 bìng dú. (b) [非正式用语]病毒性疾病 bìngdúxìng jíbìng. (c) (计算机)病毒 bìngdú. **viral** /ˈvaɪrəl/ *adj* (似)病毒的 bìngdúde; 病毒引起的 bìngdú yǐnqǐ de: *a viral infection* 病毒性感染. **'virus protection** *n* [U] (计算机)病毒防护〔護〕bìngdú fánghù.

visa /ˈviːzə/ *n* [C] 签〔簽〕证〔證〕qiānzhèng.

viscount /ˈvaɪkaʊnt/ *n* [C] 子爵 zǐjué. **viscountess** *n* [C] **1** 子爵夫人 zǐjué fūren. **2** 女子爵 nǚ zǐjué.

vise [美语] ⇨ VICE[2].

visible /ˈvɪzəbl/ *adj* 看得见的 kàndejiànde; 可见的 kějiànde. **visibility** /ˌvɪzəˈbɪlətɪ/ *n* [U] 能见度 néngjiàndù. **visibly** *adv* 明显〔顯〕地 míngxiǎnde.

vision /ˈvɪʒn/ *n* **1** [U] 视力 shìlì; 视觉〔覺〕shìjué. **2** [U] 洞察力 dòngchálì; 想像力 xiǎngxiànglì: *problems caused by lack of ~* 由于缺乏眼力而造成的问题. **3** [C] 幻想 huànxiǎng; 想像 xiǎngxiàng; 想像的东西 xiǎngxiàngde dōngxi: *~s of great wealth* 发财的梦想.

visionary /ˈvɪʒənrɪ; *US* -ʒənerɪ/ *adj* **1** 有远〔遠〕见的 yǒu yuǎnjiàn de; 有洞察力的 yǒu dòngchálì de. **2** 空想的 kōngxiǎngde; 不切实〔實〕际〔際〕的 bú qiè shíjì de. **visionary** *n* [C] [*pl* **-ies**] 有远见(或智慧)的人 yǒu yuǎnjiàn de rén.

V

visit /ˈvɪzɪt/ *v* 1 [I, T] 访问 fǎngwèn; 参观〔觀〕cānguān; 游览〔覽〕yóulǎn: ~ *a friend*/ *Rome* 访问朋友(或罗马). 2 [T] 视察 shìchá; 巡视 xúnshì. 3 [I] *with* [美语]去某人处〔處〕(尤指聊天) qù mǒuréchù. **visit** *n* [C] 访问 fǎngwèn; 参观 cānguān; 游览 yóulǎn; 视察 shìchá: *pay a* ~ *to a friend* 访问朋友. **visitor** *n* [C] 访问者 fǎngwènzhě; 宾〔賓〕客 bīnkè; 观光客 guānguāngkè; 视察者 shìcházhě.

visor /ˈvaɪzə(r)/ *n* [C] (头盔的)面甲 miànjiǎ, 面罩 miànzhào.

vista /ˈvɪstə/ *n* [C] [正式用语] 1 远〔遠〕景 yuǎnjǐng. 2 [喻](对往事)一连串的追忆〔憶〕yìliánchuànde zhuīyì; (对前景)一系列的展望 yíxìliède zhǎnwàng: *scientific discoveries that open up a new* ~ *of the future* 开创新的远景的科学发现.

visual /ˈvɪʒuəl/ *adj* 看的 kànde; 看得见的 kàndejiànde; 用于看的 yòng yú kàn de. ˌ**visual** ˈ**aid** *n* [C] 直观〔觀〕教具 zhíguān jiàojù. ˌ**visual disˈplay unit** *n* [C] 荧〔熒〕光数〔數〕字显〔顯〕示器 yíngguāng shùzì xiǎnshìqì. **visualize** *v* [T] 使形象化 shǐ xíngxiànghuà. **visually** *adv*.

vital /ˈvaɪtl/ *adj* 1 极〔極〕端重要的 jíduān zhòngyào de; 必不可少的 bì bùkě shǎo de: *a* ~ *part of the machine* 这机器的极其重要的部件. 2 精力充沛的 jīnglì chōngpèi de; 有活力的 yǒu huólì de. 3 生命的 shēngmìngde; 与〔與〕生命有关〔關〕的 yǔ shēngmìng yǒuguān de. **vitality** /vaɪˈtælətɪ/ *n* [U] 生命力 shēngmìnglì; 活力 huólì; 生气〔氣〕shēngqì. **vitally** /-təlɪ/ *adv*. ˌ**vital staˈtistics** *n* [pl] [非正式用语]妇〔婦〕女三围〔圍〕尺寸(胸围,腰围,臀围) fùnǚ sān wéi chǐcùn.

vitamin /ˈvɪtəmɪn; *US* ˈvaɪt-/ *n* [C] 维生素 wéishēngsù.

vitriolic /ˌvɪtrɪˈɒlɪk/ *adj* [正式用语]敌〔敵〕意的 díyìde; 恶〔惡〕意的 èyìde.

vivacious /vɪˈveɪʃəs/ *adj* 活泼〔潑〕的 huópode; 有生气〔氣〕的 yǒu shēngqì de. **vivaciously** *adv*. **vivacity** /vɪˈvæsətɪ/ *n* [U].

vivid /ˈvɪvɪd/ *adj* 1 (色彩、光线等)鲜艳〔艷〕的 xiānyànde; 强烈的 qiángliède. 2 清晰的 qīngxīde; 生动〔動〕的 shēngdòngde: *a* ~ *description* 生动的描述. **vividly** *adv*.

vivisection /ˌvɪvɪˈsekʃn/ *n* [U] 活体〔體〕解剖 huótǐ jiěpōu.

vixen /ˈvɪksn/ *n* [C] 雌狐 cí hú.

vocabulary /vəˈkæbjʊlərɪ; *US* -lerɪ/ [*pl* -ies] *n* 1 [C] 词汇〔彙〕cíhuì; 总〔總〕词汇量 zǒng cíhuìliàng. 2 [C, U] (某人、某行业所用的)词汇 cíhuì; 语汇 yǔhuì: *the* ~ *of a three-year-old* 三岁孩子的词汇. 3 [C] 词汇表 cíhuìbiǎo.

vocal /ˈvəʊkl/ *adj* 1 声〔聲〕音的 shēngyīnde; 有声的 yǒushēngde; 发〔發〕音的 fāyīnde. 2 直言不讳〔諱〕的 zhíyán búhuì de. **vocal** *n* [C, 常作 pl] (流行歌曲的)歌唱 gēchàng. ˌ**vocal** ˈ**cords** *n* [pl] 声带〔帶〕shēngdài. **vocalist** /-kəlɪst/ *n* [C] 歌手 gēshǒu; 歌唱家 gēchàngjiā. **vocally** /-kəlɪ/ *adv*.

vocation /vəʊˈkeɪʃn/ *n* [C, U] 1 天职〔職〕tiānzhí; 使命 shǐmìng: *She thinks nursing is her* ~. 她认为护理工作是她的天职. 2 [正式用语]行业〔業〕hángyè; 职业 zhíyè. **vocational** /-ʃənl/ *adj* 职业的 zhíyède; 业务〔務〕的 yèwùde: ~*al training* 专业训练.

vociferous /vəˈsɪfərəs/ *adj* 呼喊的 hūhǎnde; 大叫的 dàjiàode: *a* ~ *group of demonstrators* 一批喧闹的示威者. **vociferously** *adv*.

vodka /ˈvɒdkə/ *n* [U] 伏特加(酒) fútèjiā.

vogue /vəʊg/ *n* [C, U] 流行式 liúxíngshì; 时〔時〕髦 shímáo: *a new* ~ *for low-heeled shoes* 新近流行低后跟鞋.

voice /vɔɪs/ *n* 1 (a) [C] 说话声〔聲〕shuōhuàshēng; 嗓音 sǎngyīn: *recognize sb's* ~ 认出某人的声音. (b) [U] 发〔發〕音能力 fāyīn nénglì: *He's lost his* ~. 他嗓子哑了. 2 [U, sing] 发言权〔權〕fāyánquán: *They should be allowed a* ~ *in deciding their future*. 他们应被允许有决定他们的未来的发言权. **voice** *v* [T] 用言语表达〔達〕(感情等) yòng yányǔ biǎodá. ˈ**voicemail** *n* 1 [U] 语音邮〔郵〕件 yǔyīn yóujiàn. 2 [C] 语音信息 yǔyīn xìnxī.

void /vɔɪd/ *n* [C, 常作 sing] 空间 kōngjiān; 空位 kōngwèi. **void** *adj* [正式用语] 1 空的 kōngde; 空虚的 kōngxūde. 2 *of* 没有的 méiyǒude; 缺乏的 quēfáde. 3 无〔無〕价〔價〕值的 wú jiàzhí de. **void** *v* [T] [法律]使无效 shǐ wúxiào.

volatile /ˈvɒlətaɪl; *US* -tl/ *adj* (情绪、行为)反复〔復〕无〔無〕常的 fǎnfù wúcháng de.

vol au vent /ˈvɒləvɑːŋ/ *n* [C] (用鱼、肉等作馅的)酥皮合子 sūpí hézi.

volcano /vɒlˈkeɪnəʊ/ *n* [C] [*pl* ~**es**] 火山 huǒshān. **volcanic** /-ˈkænɪk/ *adj*.

volition /vəˈlɪʃn; *US* vəʊ-/ *n* [习语] **of one's own volition** [正式用语]自愿地 zìyuànde.

volley /ˈvɒlɪ/ *n* [C] 1 (箭,子弹等)齐〔齊〕射 qíshè. 2 [网球、足球等](球落地前的)截击〔擊〕jiéjī. **volley** *v* 1 [I] (枪炮)齐发 qífā. 2 [I, T] (在球落地前)截击 jiéjī. ˈ**volleyball** *n* [U] 排球(赛) páiqiú.

volt /vəʊlt/ *n* [C] 伏特(电压单位) fútè.

V

voltage *n* [U, C]电〔電〕压〔壓〕diànyā; 伏特数〔數〕fútè shù.

voluble /ˈvɒljʊbl/ *adj* [正式用语]爱〔愛〕说话的 ài shuōhuà de; 喋喋不休的 dié dié bùxiū de. **volubly** *adv*.

volume /ˈvɒljuːm; *US* -jəm/ *n* **1** [C] (一)册 cè; (一)卷 juàn. **2** [U, C] 容积〔積〕róngjī; 体〔體〕积 tǐjī. **3** [U] 总〔總〕数 zǒngshù: *The ~ of exports fell last month*. 上月的出口数量大减. **4** [U] 音量(控制) yīnliàng; 响〔響〕度 xiǎngdù.

voluminous /vəˈluːmɪnəs/ *adj* [正式用语] **1** (衣服)用料多的 yòng liào duō de; 肥大的 féidàde; 宽松〔鬆〕的 kuānsōngde: *the ~ folds of a blanket* 毯子的宽阔褶层. **2** (文字)大量的 dàliàngde; 长〔長〕篇的 chángpiānde.

voluntary /ˈvɒləntrɪ; *US* -ˈterɪ/ *adj* **1** 自愿〔願〕的 zìyuànde; 主动〔動〕的 zhǔdòngde: *Attendance is ~*. 出席是自愿的. **2** 义〔義〕务〔務〕的 yìwùde; 无〔無〕偿〔償〕的 wúchángde: *a ~ organization* 义务性的组织. **voluntarily** /-trəlɪ; *US* ˌvɒlənˈterəlɪ/ *adv*.

volunteer /ˌvɒlənˈtɪə(r)/ *n* [C] **1** 自愿〔願〕参加者 zìyuàn cānjiāzhě. **2** 志愿军 zhìyuànjūn. **volunteer** *v* **1** [I, T] 自愿做(某事) zìyuàn zuò. **2** [I] *for* 志愿参军 zhìyuàn cānjūn.

voluptuous /vəˈlʌptʃʊəs/ *adj* **1**[正式用语] (妇女)体〔體〕态〔態〕丰〔豐〕满的 tǐtài fēngmǎn de. **2** (给人以)感官享受的 gǎnguān xiǎngshòu de. **voluptuously** *adv*.

vomit /ˈvɒmɪt/ *v* [I, T] 呕〔嘔〕吐 ǒutù. **vomit** *n* [U] 呕吐物 ǒutù wù.

vote /vəʊt/ *n* **1** [C] 表决 biǎojué. **2 the vote** [sing] 选〔選〕票数〔數〕xuǎnpiàoshù; 得票数 dépiàoshù: *the Labour ~* 工党的得票数. **3 the vote** [sing] 选举〔舉〕权〔權〕xuǎnjǔquán. **vote** *v* **1** [I, T] (正式)表明观〔觀〕点〔點〕biǎomíng guāndiǎn: *~ for / against sb* 投票赞成(或反对)某人. *~ on the suggestion* 对那个提议的表决. **2** [T] 表决通过〔過〕(某项拨款) biǎojué tōngguò. **voter** *n* [C].

vouch /vaʊtʃ/ *v* [I] *for* (为某人及其行为)担〔擔〕保 dānbǎo; 保证〔證〕bǎozhèng.

voucher /ˈvaʊtʃə(r)/ *n* [C] 凭〔憑〕单〔單〕píngdān; 代金券 dàijīnquàn.

vow /vaʊ/ *n* [C] 誓约 shìyuē; 许愿〔願〕xǔyuàn. **vow** *v* [T] 起誓要… qǐshì yào…; 许愿要 xǔyuàn yào.

vowel /ˈvaʊəl/ *n* [C] (a) 元音 yuányīn. (b) 元音字母 yuányīn zìmǔ.

voyage /ˈvɔɪɪdʒ/ *n* [C] 航海 hánghǎi; 航行 hángxíng. **voyage** *v* [I] [正式用语]航海 hánghǎi; 航行 hángxíng. **voyager** *n* [C].

vs *abbr* versus.

vulgar /ˈvʌlgə(r)/ *adj* **1** 粗俗的 cūsúde; 粗陋的 cūlòude; 粗鄙的 cūbǐde. **2** 趣味不高的 qùwèi bùgāo de; 通俗的 tōngsúde; 庸俗的 yōngsúde. **vulgarity** /vʌlˈgærətɪ/ *n* [U].

vulnerable /ˈvʌlnərəbl/ *adj* **1** 易受攻击〔擊〕的 yì shòu gōngjī de. **2** 脆弱的 cuìruòde; 敏感的 mǐngǎnde. **vulnerability** /ˌvʌlnərəˈbɪlətɪ/ *n* [U].

vulture /ˈvʌltʃə(r)/ *n* [C] **1** 秃鹫 tūjiù. **2** [喻]贪婪而残〔殘〕酷的人 tānlán ér cánkù de rén.

vying ⇨ VIE.

W w

W, w /ˈdʌbljuː/ *n* [C] [*pl* **W's, w's** /ˈdʌbljuːz/] 英语的第二十三个〔個〕字母 Yīngyǔde dì'èrshísāngè zìmǔ.

W *abbr* **1** west(ern): *W Yorkshire* 西约克郡 **2** watt(s).

wad /wɒd/ *n* [C] **1** (纸、钞票等)一卷〔捲〕yìjuǎn; 一沓 yìdá. **2** (一块)软物 ruǎnwù; (软质)填料 tiánliào: *a ~ of cotton wool* 一团棉花.

waddle /ˈwɒdəl/ *v* [I] (如鸭子般)蹒跚而行 pánshān ér xíng. **waddle** *n* [sing].

wade /weɪd/ *v* **1** [I] 跋涉 báshè; 蹚(水) tāng. **2** [短语动词] **wade into sth** 抨击〔擊〕pēngjī; 猛烈攻击(某事物) měngliè gōngjī. **wade through sth** 费力地阅读〔讀〕fèilìde yuèdú. **wading-bird** (亦作 **wader**) *n* [C] 涉禽 shèqín.

wafer /ˈweɪfə(r)/ *n* [C] 薄脆饼 bócuìbǐng.

waffle[1] /ˈwɒfl/ *v* [I] [英国非正式用语]唠〔嘮〕叨 láodao; 胡扯 húchě. **waffle** *n* [U].

waffle[2] /ˈwɒfl/ *n* [C] 蛋奶小脆饼 dàn nǎi xiǎocuìbǐng; 威化饼干〔乾〕wēihuà bǐnggān.

waft /wɒft; *US* wæft/ *v* [I, T] (使)飘〔飄〕荡〔蕩〕piāodàng: *The scent ~ed into the room*. 香气飘进屋子里来了. **waft** *n* [C].

wag /wæg/ *v* [-gg-] [I, T] (使)摇摆〔擺〕yáobǎi; (使)摇动〔動〕yáodòng: *The dog ~ged its tail*. 狗摇动尾巴. **wag** *n* [C].

wage[1] /weɪdʒ/ *n* [C] [常作 pl](按周或月计算的)工资 gōngzī: *fight for higher ~s* 为更高的工资而斗争. *a ~ increase* 增加工资.

wage[2] /weɪdʒ/ *v* [T] (*against / on*) 从〔從〕事(战争等) cóngshì: *~ a war on poverty* 对贫穷宣战.

wager /ˈweɪdʒə(r)/ *n* [C], *v* [I, T] [旧] [正式用语] = BET.

waggle /ˈwægl/ *v* [I, T] (来回或上下)小幅度摆〔擺〕动〔動〕xiǎo fúdù bǎidòng.

W

wagon (英语亦作 waggon) /ˈwæɡən/ *n* [C] 1 (四轮)运〔運〕货车 yùnhuòchē. 2 (铁路)货车 huòchē.

wail /weɪl/ *v* (a) [I, T] (大声)哀号〔號〕āiháo; 恸〔慟〕哭 tòngkū: *a ~ing child* 哭叫的孩子. (b) [I] 尖啸〔嘯〕jiānxiào; 呼啸 hūxiào. **wail** *n* [C] 恸哭 tòngkū; 呼啸 hūxiào.

waist /weɪst/ *n* [C] 1 腰 yāo. 2 中间细的部分 zhōngjiān xìde bùfen. **waistcoat** /ˈweɪstkəʊt; *US* ˈweskət/ *n* [C] 背心 bèixīn; 马甲 mǎjiǎ. ˈ**waistline** *n* [C] 腰围〔圍〕yāowéi.

wait[1] /weɪt/ *v* 1 [I] 等 děng; 期待 qīdài: *We had to ~ an hour for the train*. 我们得等一个小时的火车. *I'm ~ing to see the manager*. 我正等着见经理. *I can't ~ to tell her!* 我等不及了,急于要告诉她! 2 [T] 准〔準〕备〔備〕好 zhǔnbèi hǎo: *He is ~ing his opportunity*. 他正在等待着机会. 3 [I] 暂缓处〔處〕理 zànhuǎn chǔlǐ; 推迟〔遲〕tuīchí: *The matter isn't urgent; it can ~*. 这件事不急,可以暂缓处理. 4 [习语] ˌ**wait and** ˈ**see** 等着瞧 děngzhe qiáo. **wait on sb hand and** ˈ**foot** 无〔無〕微不至地照顾〔顧〕wú wēi bú zhì de zhàogù. 5 [短语动词] **wait on sb** (进餐时)伺候某人 cìhòu mǒurén. **wait up (for sb)** (为等候某人)不睡觉〔覺〕bú shuìjiào. **waiter** (*fem* **waitress** /ˈweɪtrɪs/) *n* [C] (饭店)服务〔務〕员 fúwùyuán. ˈ**waiting-list** *n* [C] 等候者名单 děnghòuzhě míngdān. ˈ**waiting-room** *n* [C] 候车室 hòuchēshì; 候诊室 hòuzhěnshì.

wait[2] /weɪt/ *n* [C, 常作 sing] 等候 děnghòu; 等待 děngdài; 等候的时〔時〕间 děnghòude shíjiān: *We had a long ~ for the bus*. 我们等公共汽车等了很久.

waive /weɪv/ *v* [T] [正式用语]不坚〔堅〕持 bù jiānchí; 放弃〔棄〕fàngqì: *~ a fee* 放弃服务费.

wake[1] /weɪk/ *v* [*pt* **woke** /wəʊk/, *pp* **woken** /ˈwəʊkən/] 1 [I, T] (*up*) (使)醒来 xǐnglái: *What time did you ~ up?* 你是什么时候醒的? 2 [习语] **one's** ˈ**waking hours** 醒着的时〔時〕候 xǐnzhede shíhou. 3 [短语动词] **wake up to sth** 认〔認〕识〔識〕到 rènshí dào.

wake[2] /weɪk/ *n* [C] 1 (船的)尾波 wěibō; 航迹〔跡〕hángjì. 2 [习语] **in the** ˈ**wake of sth** 随〔隨〕着…之后〔後〕suízhe…zhī hòu.

waken /ˈweɪkən/ *v* [I, T] [正式用语] = WAKE[1].

Wales /weɪlz/ *n* 威尔〔爾〕士 Wēiěrshì.

walk[1] /wɔːk/ *v* 1 [I] 走 zǒu; 步行 bùxíng. 2 [T] 与〔與〕(某人)同行(至某处) yǔ tóngxíng: *I'll ~ you home*. 我陪你走回家去. 3 [T] (牵着狗)散步 sànbù. 4 [短语动词] **walk away/off with sth** [非正式用语] (a) 轻〔輕〕易取胜〔勝〕qīngyì qǔshèng. (b) 偷走某物 tōu zǒu mǒuwù. **walk into sth** [非正式用语] (a) (因不慎)落入圈套 luòrù quāntào: *~ into a trap* 落入陷阱. (b) 轻易获〔獲〕得(一份工作) qīngyì huòdé. **walk out** [非正式用语]罢〔罷〕工 bàgōng. **walk out (of sth)** 愤而退席 fèn ér tuìxí. **walk out on sb** [非正式用语]遗弃〔棄〕某人 yíqì mǒurén. **walk over sb** [非正式用语]虐待某人 nüèdài mǒurén. ˈ**walk-about** *n* [C] (要人)在群众〔衆〕中散步 zài qúnzhòng zhōng sànbù. **walker** *n* [C]. ˈ**walking-stick** *n* [C] 手杖 shǒuzhàng. ˈ**Walkman** *n* [C] [*pl* ~s] [专利](随身)小型放音机〔機〕xiǎoxíng fàngyīnjī. ˌ**walk-**ˈ**on** *adj* 无〔無〕台词的角色的 wú táicí de juésè de. ˈ**walk-out** *n* [C] 突然的罢工 tūránde bàgōng. ˈ**walk-over** *n* [C] 轻易取得的胜利 qīngyì qǔdé de shènglì.

walk[2] /wɔːk/ *n* 1 [C] 走 zǒu; 步行 bùxíng: *My house is a five-minute ~ from the shops*. 从商店到我家要走五分钟. 2 [sing] 走步的姿态〔態〕zǒubùde zītài; 步法 bùfǎ: *a slow ~* 慢步走. 3 [C] 行走的道路 xíngzǒude dàolù; 人行道 rénxíngdào; 散步场〔場〕所 sànbù chǎngsuǒ. 4 [习语] **a walk of** ˈ**life** 职〔職〕业〔業〕zhíyè; 行业 hángyè.

walkie-talkie /ˌwɔːkɪ ˈtɔːkɪ/ *n* [C] [非正式用语]步话机〔機〕bùhuàjī.

wall /wɔːl/ *n* [C] 1 围〔圍〕墙〔牆〕wéiqiáng. 2 墙壁 qiángbì. 3 [喻]似墙之物 sì qiáng zhī wù: *a ~ of fire* 一道火墙. *the abdominal ~* 腹壁. 4 [习语] **go to the** ˈ**wall** (尤指经济)失败 shībài; 破产〔產〕pòchǎn. **up the** ˈ**wall** [非正式用语]大怒 dà nù; 发〔發〕狂 fā kuáng: *That noise is driving me up the ~!* 那种噪声快把我逼疯了! **wall** *v* 1 [T] 用墙围住 yòng qiáng wéizhu. 2 [短语动词] **wall sth in/off** 用墙围住(或隔开) yòng qiáng wéizhu. **wall sth up** 用墙(或砖)堵住 yòng qiáng dǔzhu. ˈ**wallflower** *n* [C] 墙头〔頭〕花 qiángtóuhuā. ˈ**wallpaper** *n* [U] 糊壁纸 húbìzhǐ. ˈ**wallpaper** *v* [T] (用糊壁纸)糊(墙) hú. ˌ**wall-to-**ˈ**wall** *adj* (室内地面覆盖物)覆盖〔蓋〕全部地面的 fùgài quánbù dìmiàn de.

wallet /ˈwɒlɪt/ *n* [C] 皮夹〔夾〕子 píjiāzi; 钱〔錢〕包 qiánbāo.

wallop /ˈwɒləp/ *v* [T] [非正式用语]猛击〔擊〕měngjī; 痛打 tòngdǎ.

wallow /ˈwɒləʊ/ *v* [I] (*in*) 1 (在泥水中)打滚 dǎ gǔn. 2 [喻]沉迷于 chénmí yú: *~ in luxury* 沉迷于享乐之中. *~ in self-pity* 溺于自怜.

Wall Street /ˈwɔːl striːt/ *n* [U] (纽约)华〔華〕尔〔爾〕街 Huá'ěrjiē.

wally /ˈwɒlɪ/ *n* [C] [*pl* -ies] [英国非正式用

语]傻〔傻〕瓜 shǎguā.

walnut /ˈwɔːlnʌt/ *n* (a) [C] 胡桃 hútáo; 胡桃树〔樹〕 hútáoshù. (b) [U] 胡桃木 hútáomù.

walrus /ˈwɔːlrəs/ *n* [C] 海象 hǎixiàng.

waltz /wɔːls; *US* wɔːlts/ *n* [C] 华〔華〕尔〔爾〕兹舞 huá'ěrzī wǔ; 圆舞曲 yuánwǔqǔ. **waltz** *v* [I] 跳华尔兹舞 tiào huá'ěrzī wǔ.

wand /wɒnd/ *n* [C] 魔杖 mózhàng.

wander /ˈwɒndə(r)/ *v* **1** [I, T] 漫游 mànyóu; 徘徊 páihuái: ~ *round the town* 在小镇上闲逛. ~ *the streets* 在街上溜达. **2** [I] (思想)离〔離〕开〔開〕正题 líkāi zhèngtí. **wanderer** *n* [C]. **wanderings** *n* [pl] 漫游(旅行) mànyóu.

wane /weɪn/ *v* [I] **1** (月亮)变〔變〕小 biàn xiǎo, 亏〔虧〕 kuī. **2** 衰退 shuāituì; 减弱 jiǎnruò. **wane** *n* [习语] **on the wane** 减弱 jiǎnruò; 衰退 shuāituì.

wangle /ˈwæŋgl/ *v* [T] [非正式用语]使用诡计获〔獲〕得 shǐyòng guǐjì huòdé: ~ *an extra week's holiday* 不正当地取得一星期的额外假期.

want[1] /wɒnt; *US* wɔːnt/ *v* [T] **1** 要 yào; 想要 xiǎng yào: *They* ~ *a new car*. 他们想要一辆新汽车. *I* ~ *to go home*. 我想回家. **2** 需要 xūyào; 要求 yāoqiú: *The grass* ~*s cutting*. 这草地需要修剪了. **3** *to* 应〔應〕该 yīnggāi: *You* ~ *to be more careful*. 你应该更小心些. **4** [正式用语]缺乏 quēfá. **5** 搜查 sōuchá; 寻〔尋〕找 xúnzhǎo: *He is* ~*ed by the police*. 警方在通缉他. **6** [习语] **be found wanting** 不可靠 bù kěkào; 能力不够 nénglì búgòu. **7** [短语动词] **want for** 因缺乏而受苦 yīn quēfá ér shòu kǔ: *They* ~ *for nothing*. 他们什么也不缺.

want[2] /wɒnt; *US* wɔːnt/ *n* **1** [C, 常作 pl] 需要的东西 xūyàode dōngxi. **2** [sing] [U] [正式用语] 缺乏 quēfá; 缺少 quēshǎo: *die from/for* ~ *of water* 因缺水而死.

WAP /wæp/ *abbr* wireless application protocol 无〔無〕线〔綫〕应〔應〕用协〔協〕议〔議〕 wúxiàn yìngyòng xiéyì. ˈ**WAP phone** *n* [C] WAP 手机〔機〕 WAP shǒujī; 上网〔網〕手机 shàngwǎng shǒujī; 网络行动〔動〕电〔電〕话 wǎngluò xíngdòng diànhuà.

war /wɔː(r)/ *n* [C, U] **1** 战〔戰〕争 zhànzhēng; 战争时〔時〕期 zhànzhēng shíqī: *the First World W*~ 第一次世界大战. *at* ~ 处于战争状态. **2** [喻]冲〔衝〕突 chōngtū; 斗〔鬥〕争 dòuzhēng; 竞〔競〕争 jìngzhēng: *a trade* ~ 贸易战. *the* ~ *on drugs* 打击贩毒的斗争. **3** [习语] **have been in the ˈwars** [非正式用语]受过〔過〕创〔創〕伤〔傷〕 shòuguò chuāngshāng. **warfare** /ˈwɔːfeə(r)/ *n* [U] 战争 zhànzhēng; 交战 jiāozhàn. ˈ**war game** *n* [C] 作战演习〔習〕 zuòzhàn yǎnxí. ˈ**warhead** *n* [C] 导〔導〕弹〔彈〕头〔頭〕 dǎodàntóu. ˈ**warring** *adj* 敌〔敵〕对〔對〕的 díduìde; 相互斗争的 xiānghù dòuzhēng de: ~*ring tribes* 敌对的部落. ˈ**warlike** *adj* **1** 准〔準〕备〔備〕作战的 zhǔnbèi zuòzhàn de. **2** 好战的 hàozhànde; 侵略的 qīnlüède. ˈ**warpath** *n* [习语] **on the ˈwarpath** [非正式用语]准备作战(或争吵) zhǔnbèi zuòzhàn. ˈ**warship** *n* [C] 军舰〔艦〕 jūnjiàn. ˈ**wartime** *n* [U] 战时〔時〕 zhànshí.

warble /ˈwɔːbl/ *v* [I, T] (尤指鸟)叫出柔和的颤音 jiào chū róuhéde chànyīn. **warbler** *n* [C] 鸣禽 míngqín.

ward /wɔːd/ *n* [C] **1** 病房 bìngfáng. **2** 行政区〔區〕划〔劃〕 xíngzhèng qūhuà. **3** 受监〔監〕护〔護〕者 shòu jiānhùzhě. **ward** *v* [短语动词] **ward sth off** 避开〔開〕 bìkāi; 防止 fángzhǐ.

warden /ˈwɔːdn/ *n* [C] 管理员 guǎnlǐyuán; 监〔監〕护〔護〕人 jiānhùrén: *the* ~ *of a youth hostel* 青年招待所的管理人.

warder /ˈwɔːdə(r)/ *n* [C] (*fem* **wardress** /ˈwɔːdrɪs/) [英国英语]狱吏 yùlì; 看守 kānshǒu.

wardrobe /ˈwɔːdrəʊb/ *n* [C] **1** 衣柜〔櫃〕 yīguì; 衣橱 yīchú. **2** [常作 sing] (个人的)全部衣服 quánbù yīfu. **3** (剧场的)戏〔戲〕装〔裝〕 xìzhuāng; 行头〔頭〕 xíngtou.

ware /weə(r)/ *n* **1**[U] 器皿 qìmǐn; 制〔製〕造品 zhìzàopǐn: ˈ*silver* ~ 银器. **2 wares** [pl] [旧]商品 shāngpǐn; 货物 huòwù. ˈ**warehouse** *n* [C] 仓〔倉〕库〔庫〕 cāngkù; 货栈〔棧〕 huòzhàn.

warm /wɔːm/ *adj* **1** 温和的 wēnhéde; 温暖的 wēnnuǎnde: ~ *water* 温水. **2** 保暖的 bǎonuǎnde: *a* ~ *jumper* 保暖的紧身套衫. **3** 热〔熱〕心的 rèxīnde; 同情的 tóngqíngde: *a* ~ *welcome* 热烈的欢迎. **4** 暖色的 nuǎnsède. **warm** *v* **1** [I, T] (使)变〔變〕暖 biàn nuǎn. **2** [短语动词] **warm to sb/sth** (a) 喜欢〔歡〕上某人 xǐhuanshang mǒurén. (b) (对某事物)更有兴〔興〕趣 gèng yǒu xìngqù. **warm up** (比赛前的)热身练〔練〕习〔習〕 rèshēn liànxí. **warm (sth) up** (使某事物)更活跃〔躍〕 gèng huóyuè. ˌ**warm-ˈblooded** *adj* (动物)温血的 wēnxuède. ˌ**warm-ˈhearted** *adj* 热情的 rèqíngde; 富于同情心的 fùyú tóngqíngxīn de. **warmly** *adv*. **warmth** *n* [U] 温暖 wēnnuǎn; 温和 wēnhé.

warn /wɔːn/ *v* [T] 警告 jǐnggào; 告诫 gàojiè: *I* ~*ed her that it would cost a lot*. 我提醒过她,那东西很贵. *They were* ~*ed not to climb the mountain in bad weather*. 他们被警告过,天气不好时不要去爬那座山. **warning** *n* [C, U] 警告 jǐnggào; 提醒 tíxǐng: *He didn't listen to my* ~*ing*. 他不

听我的告诫. **warning** *adj* 警告的 jǐnggàode; 告诫的 gàojiède: *~ing signals* 示警的信号. ˈ**warning ˌtriangle** *n* [C] 三角警示标[標]志[誌] sānjiǎo jǐngshì biāozhì.

warp /wɔːp/ *v* **1** [I, T] (使)翘[翹]起 qiàoqǐ; (使)变[變]弯[彎] biàn wān. **2** [T] [喻]使有偏见 shǐ yǒu piānjiàn; 使作不公正判断[斷] shǐ zuò bùgōngzhèng pànduàn; 歪曲(事实等) wāiqū: *a ~ed mind* 反常的心态. **warp** *n* [C, 常作 sing] 弯曲 wānqū; 偏见 piānjiàn; 反常 fǎncháng.

warrant /ˈwɒrənt; *US* ˈwɔːr-/ *n* [C] 授权[權]证[證] shòuquánzhèng; 委任状[狀] wěirènzhuàng: *a ~ for his arrest* 可逮捕他的逮捕证. **warrant** *v* [T] [正式用语]证明为[爲]正当[當] zhèngmíng wéi zhèngdàng; 辩明为有理 biànmíng wéi yǒulǐ. **warranty** *n* [U, C] [*pl* -ies] (书面)担[擔]保 dānbǎo; 保证书[書] bǎozhèng shū.

warren /ˈwɒrən; *US* ˈwɔːrən/ *n* [C] **1** 养[養]兔场[場] yǎngtùchǎng. **2** [喻]拥[擁]挤[擠]的(或易迷路的)地区[區]或房屋 yōngjǐde dìqū huò fángwū.

warrior /ˈwɒrɪə(r); *US* ˈwɔːr-/ *n* [C] [正式用语](尤指旧时的)战[戰]士 zhànshì.

wart /wɔːt/ *n* [C] 疣 yóu; 瘊子 hóuzi.

wary /ˈweərɪ/ *adj* [-ier, -iest] 谨慎的 jǐnshènde; 小心的 xiǎoxīnde. **warily** *adv*.

was ⇨ BE.

wash[1] /wɒʃ/ *v* **1** [T] 洗 xǐ; 洗涤[滌] xǐdí: *~ one's hands/clothes* 洗手(或衣服). **2** [I] 洗澡 xǐzǎo: *I had to ~ and dress in a hurry*. 我得匆匆洗个澡,穿好衣服. **3** [I] (指布料)洗后[後]不褪色(或不缩水) xǐ hòu bú tuìshǎi: *Does this sweater ~ well?* 这件套头毛衣耐洗吗? **4** [I, T] (水)冲走 chōngzǒu; 卷[捲]去 juǎnqù: *Pieces of the wrecked boat were ~ed to the shore*. 遇难船只的残骸碎物已冲到岸上去了. **5** [I] [非正式用语]被接受(或相信) bèi jiēshòu: *That argument/excuse just won't ~*. 这种论点(或借口)使人无法接受. **6** [习语] **wash one's hands of sth** 洗手不干[幹] xǐshǒu búgàn; 不再负责 bú zài fùzé. **7** [短语动词] **wash sth away** (水)将[將]某物冲掉(或冲至别处) jiāng mǒuwù chōngdiào. **wash sth down** (a) 冲洗 chōngxǐ. (b) (用水将食物)吞下 tūnxià. **wash sth out** (a) 将某物(及其内部)洗净 jiāng mǒuwù xǐ jìng. (b) (比赛因雨而)被取消 bèi qǔxiāo. **wash (sth) up** 刷洗餐具 shuāxǐ cānjù. **washable** *adj* 耐洗的 nàixǐde. ˈ**wash-basin** *n* [C] 脸[臉]盆 liǎnpén. ˌ**washed ˈout** *adj* **1** 洗后褪色的 xǐ hòu tuìshǎi de. **2** (人的面色)苍[蒼]白怠倦的 cāngbái dàijuàn de. ˌ**washing-ˈup** *n* [U] (餐后)刷洗餐具 shuāxǐ cānjù. **washing-ˈup liquid** *n* [U] (洗餐具的)洗涤液 xǐdíyè. ˈ**wash-out** *n* [C] [非正式用语]完全失败 wánquán shībài. ˈ**washroom** *n* [C] [美语]盥洗室 guànxǐshì.

wash[2] /wɒʃ/ *n* **1** [C, 常作 sing] 洗 xǐ; 洗涤[滌] xǐdí: *give the car a good ~* 把汽车好好冲洗一下. **2** the wash [sing] (即将)洗涤的衣服 xǐdíde yīfu. **3** [sing] (因行船)搅[攪]动[動]的水 jiǎodòngde shuǐ.

washer /ˈwɒʃə(r); *US* ˈwɔː-/ *n* [C] **1** [机械]垫[墊]圈 diànquān. **2** [非正式用语]洗衣机[機] xǐyījī; 洗涤[滌]机 xǐdíjī.

washing /ˈwɒʃɪŋ; *US* ˈwɔː-/ *n* [U] **1** (要)洗的衣服 xǐde yīfu. **2** 洗 xǐ; 洗涤[滌] xǐdí. ˈ**washing-machine** *n* [C] 洗衣机[機] xǐyījī. ˈ**washing-powder** *n* [U] 洗衣粉 xǐyīfěn.

wasn't /ˈwɒznt; *US* ˈwʌznt/ (= was not) ⇨ BE.

wasp /wɒsp/ *n* [C] [动物]黄蜂 huángfēng.

wastage /ˈweɪstɪdʒ/ *n* [U] **1** 消耗量 xiāohàoliàng; 损耗量 sǔnhàoliàng. **2** 损耗 sǔnhào; 缩减 suōjiǎn: *natural ~* 自然减员.

waste[1] /weɪst/ *v* [T] **1** 浪费 làngfèi; 滥[濫]用 lànyòng. **2** 未充分利用 wèi chōngfèn lìyòng: *~ an opportunity* 错过机会. **3** [正式用语]使消瘦 shǐ xiāoshòu.

waste[2] /weɪst/ *n* **1** [U, sing] 浪费 làngfèi; 消耗 xiāohào: *a ~ of time* 浪费时间. **2** [U] 废[廢]物 fèiwù; 废料 fèiliào: *industrial ~* 工业废料. **3** [U, C, 常作 pl] 荒地 huāngdì; 原野 yuányě: *the ~s of the Sahara* 撒哈拉大沙漠. **4** [习语] **go/run to waste** 被浪费 bèi làngfèi. **waste** *adj* **1** (土地)无[無]法利用的 wúfǎ lìyòng de; 荒芜[蕪]的 huāngwúde: *~ ground* 荒地. **2** 无用的 wúyòngde; 废弃[棄]的 fèiqìde: *~ paper* 废纸. **wasteful** *adj* 造成浪费的 zàochéng làngfèi de: *~ful processes* 造成浪费的程序. **wastefully** *adv*. ˌ**waste-ˈpaper basket** *n* [C] 废纸篓[簍] fèizhǐlǒu.

watch[1] /wɒtʃ/ *v* **1** [I, T] 看 kàn; 注视 zhùshì. **2** [T] [非正式用语]小心 xiǎoxīn; 当[當]心 dāngxīn: *~ one's language/manners* 注意自己的语言(或态度). **3** [习语] **watch one's step** ⇨ STEP[1]. **4** [短语动词] **watch ˈout** 警戒 jǐngjiè; 提防 dīfang. **watch over sb/sth** 保护[護] bǎohù; 守卫[衛] shǒuwèi; 留心 liúxīn. **watcher** *n* [C].

watch[2] /wɒtʃ/ *n* **1** [C] 手表[錶] shǒubiǎo. **2** [sing, U] 看 kàn; 注意 zhùyì; 监[監]视 jiānshì: *keep (a) close ~ on her* 密切监视她. **3** [sing] 看守人 kānshǒurén. **4** [C] (船上)值班时[時]间 zhíbān shíjiān. ˈ**watch-dog** *n* [C] **1** 看门[門]狗 kānméngǒu. **2** [喻]监察人 jiāncharén. **watchful** *adj* 密切注意的 mìqiè zhùyì de. ˈ**watchman** /-mən/ *n* [C] [*pl*

-men /-mən/] 警卫[衛]员 jǐngwèiyuán; 守夜者 shǒuyèzhě. ˈ**watchword** *n* [C] 标[標]语 biāoyǔ; 口号[號] kǒuhào.

water[1] /ˈwɔːtə(r)/ *n* 1 (a) [U] 水 shuǐ. (b) [U] 自来水 zìláishuǐ. (c) [sing] 大片的水(江、湖等) dàpiànde shuǐ: *He fell in the ~ and drowned.* 他落水淹死了. (d) [sing] 水面 shuǐmiàn: *swim under ~* 潜水. 2 **waters** [pl] (a) (江、湖等的)水域 shuǐyù. (b) 领海 lǐnghǎi: *in British ~s* 在英国领海内. 3 [习语] **under ˈwater** 被水淹没 bèi shuǐ yānmò. ˈ**water-cannon** *n* [C] 水炮 shuǐpào. ˈ**water-closet** *n* [C] [旧]厕所 cèsuǒ. ˈ**water-colour** (美语 -color) *n* (a) **water-colours** [pl] 水彩颜料 shuǐcǎi yánliào. (b) [C] 水彩画[畫] shuǐcǎihuà. ˈ**watercress** *n* [U] 水田芥 shuǐtiánjiè. ˈ**waterfall** *n* [C] 瀑布 pùbù. ˈ**waterfront** *n* [C, 常作 sing] 滨[濱]水区[區] bīnshuǐqū. ˈ**water-hole** *n* [C] 水坑 shuǐkēng. **waterlogged** /-lɒgd; *US* -lɔːgd/ *adj* 1 (土地)水浸的 shuǐjìn de. 2 (船)浸满水的 jìn mǎn shuǐ de. ˈ**watermark** *n* [C] 水印 shuǐyìn. ˈ**water-melon** *n* [C] 西瓜 xīguā. ˈ**water-mill** *n* [C] 水力磨坊 shuǐlì mòfáng. ˈ**waterproof** *n* [C], *adj* 雨衣 yǔyī; 防水的 fángshuǐde. ˈ**waterproof** *v* [T] 使防水 shǐ fángshuǐ. ˈ**watershed** *n* [C] 1 分水岭[嶺] fēnshuǐlǐng. 2 [喻](事情发展的)转[轉]折点[點] zhuǎnzhédiǎn. ˈ**waterside** *n* [sing] 河边[邊](或湖畔、海滨) hébiān. ˈ**water-ski** *v* [I] (由艇拖曳)滑水 huáshuǐ. ˈ**water-skiing** *n* [U]. ˈ**water-table** *n* [C] 地下水位 dìxià shuǐwèi. ˈ**watertight** *adj* 1 不漏水的 bú lòu shuǐ de. 2 [喻]无[無]懈可击[擊]的 wú xiè kě jī de. ˈ**waterway** *n* [C] 水路 shuǐlù; 航道 hángdào. ˈ**waterworks** *n* [亦作 sing, 用 pl v] 1 自来水厂[廠] zìláishuǐ chǎng. 2 [习语] **turn on the ˈwaterworks** [非正式用语][贬]掉眼泪[淚] diào yǎnlèi.

water[2] /ˈwɔːtə(r)/ *v* 1 [T] 给…浇[澆]水 gěi…jiāoshuǐ; 灌溉 guàngài: *~ the lawn* 在草地上洒水. 2 [T] 给(动物)水喝 gěi shuǐ hē. 3 [I] 流泪[淚] liú lèi; 淌口水 tǎng kǒushuǐ. 4 [短语动词] **water sth down** (a) 搀[攙]水 chānshuǐ; 冲淡 chōngdàn. (b) [喻]减弱 jiǎnruò; 打折扣 dǎ zhékòu: *~ down a speech* 把讲话改得缓和些. ˈ**watering-can** *n* [C] 洒[灑]水壶[壺] sǎshuǐhú.

watery /ˈwɔːtərɪ/ *adj* 1 含水过[過]多的 hán shuǐ guò duō de. 2 (颜色)淡的 dànde.

watt /wɒt/ *n* [C] 瓦特(电功率单位) wǎtè.

wave /weɪv/ *v* 1 [I, T] 挥手 huī shǒu; 招手 zhāo shǒu. 2 [T] 向…挥手示意(向某方向移动) xiàng… huī shǒu shìyì: *The guard ~d us on.* 警卫员挥手让我们继续前进. 3 [T] 摇动[動] yáodòng; 摆[擺]动 bǎidòng: *~ a flag* 摇动一面旗. 4 [I] (往复或上下)摆动 bǎidòng: *branches waving in the wind* 随风摆动的树枝. 5 [短语动词] **wave sth aside** 对[對]…置之不理 duì…zhì zhī bùlǐ; 对…不屑一顾[顧] duì…búxiè yígù. **wave** *n* [C] 1 大浪头[頭](尤指海浪) dà làngtou; 波涛[濤] bōtāo. 2 波动 bōdòng; 挥动 huīdòng: *with a ~ of his hand* 挥动他的手. 3 波纹 bōwén; 鬈曲 quánqū: *the ~s in her hair* 她头发上的波纹. 4 (突然)高涨[漲] gāozhǎng; 高潮 gāocháo: *a ~ of panic* 惊恐的高潮. 5 (热、光等的)波 bō: *radio ~s* 无线电波. ˈ**wavelength** *n* [C] 1 波长[長] bōcháng. 2 波段 bōduàn. ˈ**wave power** *n* [U] 波力 bōlì; 波能 bōnéng. **wavy** *adj* [-ier, -iest] 成波浪形的 chéng bōlàng xíng de; 有波纹的 yǒu bōwén de: *a wavy line* 波状线. *wavy hair* 鬈发.

waver /ˈweɪvə(r)/ *v* [I] 1 减弱 jiǎnruò; 动[動]摇 dòngyáo. 2 犹[猶]豫不决 yóuyù bùjué. 3 摇曳 yáoyè; 摇晃 yáohuàng.

wax[1] /wæks/ *n* [U] 蜡[蠟] là; 蜂蜡 fēnglà. **wax** *v* [T] 给…上蜡 gěi…shànglà: *~ the floor* 在地板上打蜡.

wax[2] /wæks/ *v* [I] 1 (月亮)渐圆 jiàn yuán. 2 [修辞](逐渐)变[變]成 biànchéng: *~ eloquent* (逐渐)畅谈起来.

way[1] /weɪ/ *n* 1 [C] 方法 fāngfǎ; 方式 fāngshì: *the best ~ to help people* 助人的最佳方法. 2 [sing] 作风[風] zuòfēng; 态[態]度 tàidu: *the rude ~ in which he spoke to us* 他对我们说话的粗野态度. 3 [C] 方面 fāngmiàn; (某)点[點] diǎn: *In some ~s, I agree with you.* 在某些方面我同意你. 4 **ways** [pl] 习[習]惯 xíguàn: *She is not going to change her ~s.* 她不想改变她的习惯. 5 [C] 路 lù; 道路 dàolù. 6 [C] 路线[綫] lùxiàn; 路途 lùtú: *ask sb the ~ to the airport* 问人家去飞机场走哪条路. 7 [sing] 方向 fāngxiàng: *He went the other ~.* 他向另一方向走去. 8 [sing] 距离[離] jùlí: *It's a long ~ to London.* 离伦敦很远. 9 [sing] [用于动词之后]开[開]动[動] kāidòng; 进[進]行 jìnxíng: *He made his ~ home.* 他回家了. 10 [习语] **by the ˈway** 顺便说(一句) shùnbiàn shuō; 附带[帶]说说 fùdài shuōshuō. **by way of sth** [正式用语]当[當]作 dāngzuò; 作为[爲] zuòwéi: *say something by ~ of introduction* 说几句作为开场白. **get/have one's (own) ˈway** 为所欲为 wéi suǒ yù wéi. **give ˈway** 断[斷]裂 duànliè; 倒塌 dǎotā. **give way to sb/sth** (a) 让[讓]…在先 ràng…zài xiān. (b) 被…代替 bèi…dàitì: *Sorrow gave ~* **to smiles.** 悲伤过后出现了微

W

笑. (c) 让步 ràngbù: *give* ~ *to their demands* 对他们的要求让步. **go out of one's way (to do sth)** 特地(去做某事) tèdì; 不怕麻烦(去做某事) búpà máfan. **go one's own 'way** 独〔獨〕断〔斷〕独行 dú duàn dú xíng. **make 'way (for sb/sth)** (为…)让路 rànglù. **ˌno 'way** [非正式用语]决不 juébù. **on one's 'way** 在路上 zài lùshang. **ˌout of the 'way** (a) 完成的 wánchéngde. (b) 偏远〔遠〕的 piānyuǎnde. (c) 不普通的 bù pǔtōng de. **out of/in the 'way** 不妨碍〔礙〕(或妨碍) bù fáng'ài; 不阻拦〔攔〕(或阻拦) bù zǔlán. **under 'way** 在进行中 zài jìnxíng zhōng. **way of 'life** 生活方式 shēnghuó fāngshì.

way[2] /weɪ/ *adv* [非正式用语]很远〔遠〕 hěn yuǎn: *She finished the race* ~ *ahead of the others*. 她第一个跑到终点,远远领先于其他选手. **ˌway-'out** *adj* [非正式用语]不寻〔尋〕常的 bù xúncháng de; 奇怪的 qíguàide.

waylay /ˌweɪ'leɪ/ *v* [*pt*, *pp* -laid /-'leɪd/] [T] 伏击〔擊〕 fújī; 拦〔攔〕路抢〔搶〕劫 lánlù qiǎngjié; 拦住(别人)问讯 lánzhù wènxùn.

wayward /'weɪwəd/ *adj* 任性的 rènxìngde; 倔强的 juéjiàngde: *a* ~ *child* 任性的孩子.

WC /ˌdʌbljuː 'siː/ *abbr* (= water-closet) 厕所 cèsuǒ.

we /wiː/ *pron* [主格]我们 wǒmen: *We are all going to visit him*. 我们都去看望他.

weak /wiːk/ *adj* 1 虚弱的 xūruòde; 脆弱的 cuìruòde; 无〔無〕力的 wúlìde: *still* ~ *after his illness* 他病后仍很虚弱. 2 不牢的 bùláode; 软弱的 ruǎnruòde: *a* ~ *joint* 不牢固的接合. *a* ~ *team* 弱队. 3 懦弱的 nuòruòde; 易受影响〔響〕的 yì shòu yǐngxiǎng de: *a* ~ *leader* 缺乏权威的领袖. 4 无说服力的 wú shuōfúlì de: *a* ~ *argument* 无力的论据. 5 不易察觉〔覺〕的 búyì chájué de; 微弱的 wēiruòde: ~ *sound/light* 微弱的声音(或光线). 6 差的 chàde; 不行的 bùxíngde: ~ *at mathematics* 数学成绩差. 7 稀薄的 xībóde: ~ *tea* 淡茶. **weaken** *v* [I, T] (使)变〔變〕弱 biàn ruò. **ˌweak-'kneed** *adj* [喻]易屈服的 yì qūfú de; 不坚〔堅〕定的 bù jiāndìng de. **weakling** /'wiːklɪŋ/ *n* [C] [贬]软弱的人 ruǎnruòde rén. **weakly** *adv*. **weakness** *n* 1 [U] 虚弱 xūruò; 脆弱 cuìruò. 2 [C] 弱点〔點〕 ruòdiǎn; 缺点 quēdiǎn: *We all have our little* ~*nesses*. 我们都有些小缺点. 3 [C] 嗜好 shìhào: *a* ~*ness for cream cakes* 特别喜欢吃奶油蛋糕.

wealth /welθ/ *n* 1 [U] 财富 cáifù; 财产〔產〕 cáichǎn. 2 [sing] [正式用语]丰〔豐〕富 fēngfù; 大量 dàliàng: *a book with a* ~ *of illustrations* 有大量插图的书. **wealthy** *adj* [-ier, -iest] 富的 fùde; 丰富的 fēngfùde.

wean /wiːn/ *v* 1 [T] 使断〔斷〕奶 shǐ duànnǎi. 2 [短语动词] **wean sb from sth** 使戒掉 shǐ jièdiào.

weapon /'wepən/ *n* 1 [C] 武器 wǔqì. 2 [习语] **weapon of mass destruction** 大规模杀〔殺〕伤〔傷〕性武器 dàguīmó shāshāngxìng wǔqì. **weaponry** *n* [U] 武器(总称) wǔqì.

wear[1] /weə(r)/ *v* [*pt* **wore** /wɔː(r)/, *pp* **worn** /wɔːn/] 1 [T] 穿 chuān; 戴 dài: ~ *a dress* 穿一身连衣裙. 2 [T] (脸上)带〔帶〕着 dàizhe, 显〔顯〕出 xiǎnchū: ~ *a smile* 带着微笑. 3 [I, T] (使)磨损 mósǔn; 用旧〔舊〕 yòng jiù: *The carpets are starting to* ~. 地毯渐渐磨坏了. 4 [I] 耐用 nàiyòng; 耐久 nàijiǔ: *These shoes have worn well*. 这些鞋耐穿. 5 [T] [非正式用语]同意 tóngyì; 容忍 róngrěn. 6 [短语动词] **wear (sth) away** 用薄 yòng bó; 用坏〔壞〕 yòng huài. **wear (sth) down** (使)逐渐变〔變〕小(或变薄等) zhújiàn biàn xiǎo. **wear sb down** 使衰弱 shǐ shuāiruò. **wear off** 逐渐消失 zhújiàn xiāoshī. **wear on** (时间)过〔過〕去 guòqù; 消磨(时间) xiāomó. **wear (sth) out** (使)不能再用 bùnéng zài yòng; (把…)用坏 yòng huài. **wear sb out** 使某人筋疲力尽〔盡〕 shǐ mǒurén jīn pí lì jìn.

wear[2] /weə(r)/ *n* [U] 1 穿 chuān;戴 dài: *a dress for evening* ~. 晚礼服. 2 (穿戴的)衣物 yīwù; 服装〔裝〕 fúzhuāng: '*mens*~ 男装. 3 用坏〔壞〕 yòng huài; 损耗 sǔnhào: *The carpet is showing signs of* ~. 这条地毯看来已经磨损了. 4 耐用性 nàiyòngxìng: *There's a lot of* ~ *in these shoes yet*. 这些鞋还可以穿一阵. 5 [习语] **ˌwear and 'tear** 用坏 yòng huài; 磨损 mósǔn.

weary /'wɪərɪ/ *adj* [-ier, -iest] 疲倦的 píjuànde; 困〔睏〕乏的 kùnfáde. **wearily** *adv*. **weariness** *n* [U]. **weary** *v* [*pt*, *pp* -ied] [I, T] (*of*) (使)疲乏 pífá; (使)厌〔厭〕烦 yànfán.

weasel /'wiːzl/ *n* [C] [动物]黄鼬 huángyòu.

weather[1] /'weðə(r)/ *n* 1 [U] 天气〔氣〕 tiānqì; 气象 qìxiàng. 2 [习语] **under the 'weather** [非正式用语]不舒服 bù shūfu. **'weather-beaten** *adj* 饱经〔經〕风〔風〕霜的 bǎojīng fēngshuāng de. **'weather forecast** *n* [C] 天气预报〔報〕 tiānqì yùbào. **'weatherman** *n* [C] [*pl* -men /-men/] [非正式用语]天气预报员 tiānqì yùbàoyuán. **'weatherproof** *adj* 不受气候影响〔響〕的 bú shòu qìhòu yǐngxiǎng de. **'weather-vane** *n* [C] 风向标〔標〕 fēngxiàngbiāo.

weather[2] /'weðə(r)/ *v* 1 [I, T] (因风吹雨打而使)变〔變〕形 biànxíng, 变色 biànsè. 2 [T] (平安)渡过〔過〕 dùguò; 经〔經〕受住 jīngshòuzhù: ~ *a storm/crisis* 经受住暴风雨(或危机).

weave /wiːv/ *v* [*pt* **wove** /wəʊv/ 或于第 4

义作 ~d, *pp* woven /ˈwəʊvn/ 或于第 4 义作 ~d] 1 [I, T] 编 biān; 织〔織〕zhī. 2 [T] 把…编成(花环、花圈等) bǎ…biānchéng: ~ *flowers into a wreath* 把花编制成一个花圈. 3 [T] [喻]编造(故事) biānzào. 4 [I, T] (使)迂回〔迴〕行进〔進〕 yūhuí xíngjìn: ~ *through the traffic* 在车辆中迂回穿行. **weave** *n* [C] 编织法 biānzhīfǎ; 编织的式样〔樣〕 biānzhīde shìyàng. **weaver** *n* [C].

web /web/ *n* [C] 1 (蜘蛛等的)网〔網〕wǎng. 2 [喻]一套 yítào; 一堆 yìduī. 3 蹼 pǔ. 4 the Web 万〔萬〕维网 Wànwéiwǎng. **webbed** *adj* 有蹼的 yǒupǔde. ˈ**webcam** *n* [C] 网络摄〔攝〕像机〔機〕 wǎngluò shèxiàngjī. **webmaster** *n* [C] 网站管理员 wǎngzhàn guǎnlǐyuán; 网站维护〔護〕者 wǎngzhàn wéihùzhě. ˈ**web page** *n* [C] 网页 wǎngyè. ˈ**web site** *n* [C] 网站 wǎngzhàn.

wed /wed/ *v* [*pt*, *pp* ~ded 或 wed] [I, T] [旧](使)结婚 jiéhūn.

we'd /wiːd/ 1 (= we had) ⇨ HAVE. 2 (= we would) ⇨ WILL[1], WOULD[1].

wedding /ˈwedɪŋ/ *n* [C] 婚礼〔禮〕 hūnlǐ. ˈ**wedding-ring** 结婚戒指 jiéhūn jièzhi.

wedge /wedʒ/ *n* [C] 1 楔子 xiēzi. 2 楔形物 xiēxíngwù: *a ~ of cake* 一角蛋糕. **wedge** *v* [T] 把…楔住 bǎ…xiēzhù: ~ *the door open* 把开着的门楔住.

wedlock /ˈwedlɒk/ *n* [U] [旧]婚姻 hūnyīn.

Wednesday /ˈwenzdɪ/ *n* [U, C] 星期三 xīngqīsān.

wee /wiː/ *adj* [苏格兰语]小的 xiǎode.

weed /wiːd/ *n* [C] 1 杂〔雜〕草 zácǎo. 2 [非正式用语]瘦弱的人 shòuruòde rén. **weed** *v* 1 [I, T] 除草 chú cǎo. 2 [短语动词] **weed sth/sb out** 除去 chúqù; 淘汰 táotài: ~ *out the lazy students* 清除懒惰的学生. **weedy** *adj* [-ier, -iest] 1 杂草丛〔叢〕生的 zácǎo cóngshēng de. 2 [非正式用语]瘦弱的 shòuruòde.

week /wiːk/ *n* [C] 1 星期 xīngqī; 周 zhōu. 2 一星期的工作日 yìxīngqīde gōngzuòrì: *a 35-hour* ~ 35 小时的工作周. 3 [习语] ˌ**week after** ˈ**week**; **week in**, **week** ˈ**out** 每个〔個〕星期(都) měi gè xīngqī. ˈ**weekday** *n* [C] 周日(一周中除星期六和星期日以外的任何一天) zhōurì. ˌ**week**ˈ**end** *n* [C] 周末(星期六和星期日) zhōumò. **weekly** *adj*, *adv* 每周一次(的) měizhōu yícì. **weekly** *n* [C] [*pl* -ies] 周报〔報〕 zhōubào; 周刊 zhōukān.

weep /wiːp/ *v* [*pt*, *pp* wept /wept/] [I, T] [正式用语]哭泣 kūqì. **weeping** *adj* (树)有垂枝的 yǒu chuízhī de.

weigh /weɪ/ *v* [T] 1 称〔稱〕…的重量 chēng…de zhòngliàng: *She ~ed herself on the scales*. 她在体重器上称体重. 2 重(若干) zhòng: ~ *10 kilograms* 重十公斤. 3 (*up*) 权〔權〕衡 quánhéng; 斟酌 zhēnzhuó. 4(仔细)对〔對〕比 duìbǐ: ~ *one plan against another* 对比一个计划与另一个计划的优劣. 5[习语] **weigh** ˈ**anchor** 起锚 qǐmáo; 起航 qǐháng. 6 [短语动词] **weigh sb down** (a) 使负重 shǐ fùzhòng. (b) 使忧〔憂〕虑〔慮〕 shǐ yōulǜ; 使沮丧〔喪〕 shǐ jǔsàng. **weigh in** (**with sth**) [非正式用语](在讨论中)提出(重要意见) tíchū. **weigh on sb** 使担〔擔〕心 shǐ dānxīn; 使担忧 shǐ dānyōu. **weigh sth out** 称出 chēngchū; 量出 liángchū.

weight /weɪt/ *n* 1 [U] 重 zhòng; 重量 zhòngliàng: *My ~ is 70 kilograms*. 我的体重是 70 公斤. 2 [C]砝码 fǎmǎ; 秤砣 chèngtuó: *a 100-gram* ~ 100 克的砝码. 3 [C] 重物 zhòngwù. 4 [C, U]重量单〔單〕位 zhòngliàng dānwèi. 5 [U]重要性 zhòngyàoxìng; 影响〔響〕力 yǐngxiǎnglì: *opinions that carry* ~ 有重大影响的意见. 6 [sing] 思想负担〔擔〕 sīxiǎng fùdān; 难〔難〕题 nántí: *feel a great ~ of responsibility* 觉得责任很重. 7 [习语] **be / take a weight off one's mind** ⇨ MIND[1]. ˌ**over** / ˌ**under** ˈ**weight** 过〔過〕重(或份量不足) guòzhòng. **put on / lose** ˈ**weight** 体〔體〕重增加(或减轻) tǐzhòng zēngjiā. **weight** *v* [T]1 (*down*) 使负重 shǐ fùzhòng. 2[常用被动语态]使偏向… shǐ piānxiàng…; 偏袒 piāntǎn: *The law is ~ed towards rich people*. 这法律是偏袒有钱人的. **weightless** *adj* 失重的 shīzhòngde. ˈ**weight-lifting** *n* [U] 举〔舉〕重 jǔzhòng. ˈ**weight-lifter** *n* [C]. **weighty** *adj* [-ier, -iest] 1 重的 zhòngde. 2 [喻]重要的 zhòngyàode; 重大的 zhòngdàde.

weir /wɪə(r)/ *n* [C] 堰 yàn; 鱼梁〔樑〕yúliáng.

weird /wɪəd/ *adj* 1 超自然的 chāo zìrán de; 怪诞的 guàidànde: ~ *shrieks* 怪诞的尖叫. 2 [非正式用语]离〔離〕奇的 líqíde; 古怪的 gǔguàide; 不寻〔尋〕常的 bù xúncháng de. **weirdly** *adv*. **weirdness** *n* [U].

welcome /ˈwelkəm/ *v* [T] 1 欢〔歡〕迎 huānyíng; 迎接 yíngjiē. 2 (对接受某事物)感到高兴〔興〕 gǎn dào gāoxìng: *The decision has been ~d by everyone*. 这个决定使大家很高兴. **welcome** *interj* (对客人说)"欢迎!" "huānyíng!": *W~ home!* 欢迎你回家! **welcome** *n* [C] 欢迎 huānyíng; 接待 jiēdài. **welcome** *adj* 1 受欢迎的 shòu huānyíng de; 令人愉快的 lìng rén yúkuài de: *a ~ change* 可喜的变化. 2 *to* 欣然允许的 xīnrán yǔnxǔ de: *You're ~ to use my car*. 欢迎你借用我的汽车. 3 [习语] **You're** ˈ**welcome** (用作回答对方感谢的话)不用谢 búyòng xiè; 别客气〔氣〕 bié kèqì.

weld /weld/ *v* [T] 焊接 hànjiē. **weld** *n* [C]

焊接 hànjiē. **welder** *n* [C]焊工 hàngōng.

welfare /ˈwelfeə(r)/ *n* [U] 健康 jiànkāng; 幸福 xìngfú; 福利 fúlì. **the ˌWelfare ˈState** *n* [sing] 福利国〔國〕家 fúlì guójiā.

well[1] /wel/ *interj* (表示惊讶,犹豫,同意等): *W～, . . . I don't know about that*. 啊,我不知道这事. *W～, ～, so you've come at last!* 好了,好了,你终于来了!

well[2] /wel/ *adj* [**better** /ˈbetə(r)/, **best** /best/] **1** 健康的 jiànkāngde: *feel/get ～* 感到(或恢复)健康. **2** 满意的 mǎnyìde; 良好的 liánghǎode: *All is not ～ at home*. 家里不是样样都好. **3** 恰当〔當〕的 qiàdàngde; 适〔適〕宜的 shìyíde; 可取的 kěqǔde: *It would be ～ to start early*. 早一点动身为好.

well[3] /wel/ *adv* [**better** /ˈbetə(r)/, **best** / best /] **1** 好 hǎo; 对〔對〕duì; 令人满意地 lìng rén mǎnyì de: *The children behaved ～*. 孩子们很乖. **2** 完全地 wánquánde; 彻〔徹〕底地 chèdǐde: *Shake the mixture ～*. 把这个混合物充分摇匀. **3** 有理由地 yǒu lǐyóu de; 合理地 hélǐde: *You may ～ be right*. 你当然是对的. **4** 到相当〔當〕的程度 dào xiāngdāngde chéngdù: *drive at ～ over the speed limit* 开车的速度大大超过了速度限制. **5**[习语] **as well** (**as sb / sth**) (除…外) 还〔還〕hái, 也 yě; 此外 cǐwài. **do ˈwell** 成功 chénggōng; 进〔進〕展 jìnzhǎn. **do well to do sth** 做得好(或聪明) zuòde hǎo. **leave/let well aˈlone** 维持原状〔狀〕wéichí yuánzhuàng. **may / might** (**just**) **as well do sth** 还〔還〕是做… 为〔爲〕好 háishì zuò…wéi hǎo. **ˌvery ˈwell** (常在不愿意的情况下表示同意或服从). **ˌwell and ˈtruly** 完全地 wánquánde. **well done** (表示赞扬或祝贺)做得好的 zuòde hǎo de; (受到)祝贺的 zhùhède. **well in** (**with sb**) (与某人)友好 yǒuhǎo. **well ˈoff** 幸运〔運〕的 xìngyùnde; 富裕的 fùyùde. **ˌwell ˈout of sth** 幸好未(受损失等) xìnghǎo wèi. **ˌwell-adˈvised** *adj* 有见识〔識〕的 yǒu jiànshí de; 审〔審〕慎的 shěnshènde. **ˈwell-being** *n* [U] 幸福 xìngfú; 健康 jiànkāng. **ˌwell-ˈbred** *adj* 有礼〔禮〕貌的 yǒu lǐmào de; 有教养〔養〕的 yǒu jiàoyǎng de. **ˌwell-conˈnected** *adj* (与有钱、有势的人)有亲〔親〕友关〔關〕系〔係〕的 yǒu qīnyǒu guānxì de. **ˌwell -ˈdone** *adj* (食物、肉)熟透的 shútòude. **ˌwell-ˈearned** *adj* 值得的 zhídéde; 应〔應〕得的 yīngdéde. **ˌwell -ˈheeled** *adj* [非正式用语]有钱〔錢〕的 yǒuqiánde. **ˌwell-inˈformed** *adj* 有见识的 yǒu jiànshi de. **ˌwell-inˈtentioned** *adj* 善意的 shànyìde. **ˌwell-ˈknown** *adj* 著名的 zhùmíngde. **ˌwell-ˈmeaning** *adj* = WELL-INTENTIONED. **well-nigh** / ˈwelnaɪ / *adv* [正式用语]几〔幾〕乎 jīhū. **ˌwell-ˈread** *adj* 读〔讀〕书〔書〕多的 dúshū duō de; 博学〔學〕的 bóxuéde. **ˌwell-ˈspoken** *adj* 善于词令的 shànyú cílìng de. **ˌwell-ˈtimed** *adj* 正合时〔時〕宜的 zhènghé shíyí de; 准〔準〕时的 zhǔnshíde. **ˌwell-to-ˈdo** *adj* 富有的 fùyǒude. **ˈwell-wisher** *n* [C] 希望(别人成功, 快乐)的人 xīwàngde rén; 表示良好祝愿〔願〕的人 biǎoshì liánghǎo zhùyuàn de rén.

well[4] /wel/ *n* [C] **1** 井 jǐng. **2** 楼〔樓〕梯井 lóutījǐng. **well** *v* [I] (*up*) 涌出 yǒngchū; 流出 liúchū: *Tears ～ed up in his eyes*. 眼泪从他的眼眶中涌出.

we'll /wiːl/ **1** (= we shall) ⇨ SHALL. **2** (= we will) ⇨ WILL[1].

wellington (亦作 **ˌwellington ˈboot**) /ˈwelɪŋtən/ *n* [C] 惠灵〔靈〕顿长〔長〕统靴 Huìlíngdùn chángtǒngxuē.

welter /ˈweltə(r)/ *n* [sing] 混杂〔雜〕hùnzá; 混乱〔亂〕hùnluàn: *a ～ of details* 许多细节混在一起.

wend /wend/ *v* [习语] **wend one's way** [古或谑](慢)走 zǒu.

went *pt* of GO[1].

wept *pt*, *pp* of WEEP.

were ⇨ BE.

we're /wɪə(r)/ (= we are) ⇨ BE.

weren't /wɜːnt/ (= were not) ⇨ BE.

werewolf /ˈwɪəwʊlf/ *n* [C] [*pl* **-wolves** /-wʊlvz/] [神话] 狼人 lángrén.

west /west/ *n* [sing] **1 the west** 西 xī; 西部 xībù; 西方 xīfāng. **2 the West** (a) 西方国〔國〕家(西欧和美国) xīfāng guójiā. (b) (国家的)西部 xībù. **west** *adj* **1** 在西方的 zài xīfāng de; 向西的 xiàng xī de. **2**(风)来自西方的 lái zì xīfāng de. **west** *adv* 向西方 xiàng xīfāng. **ˈwestbound** /ˈwestbaʊnd/ *adj* 西行的 xī xíng de. **westerly** *adj*, *adv* **1** 在西方(的) zài xīfāng; 向西(的) xiàngxī. **2**(风)来自西方(的) lái zì xīfāng. **westward** /ˈwestwəd / *adj* 向西 xiàng xī. **westward(s)** *adv*.

western /ˈwestən/ *adj* 西的 xīde; 西方的 xīfāngde; 西部的 xībùde; 在西方的 zài xīfāng de. **western** *n* [C] (美国的)西部电〔電〕影或小说 xībù diànyǐng huò xiǎoshuō. **westerner** *n* [C] 西方人 xīfāngrén; (尤指)美国西部人 Měiguó xībùrén. **westernize** *v* [T] 使西洋化 shǐ xīyánghuà; 使欧〔歐〕化 shǐ ōuhuà.

wet /wet/ *adj* [**～ter**, **～test**] **1** 湿〔濕〕的 shīde; 潮的 cháode: *～ clothes / roads* 湿的衣服(或马路). **2** 下雨的 xiàyǔde; 多雨的 duōyǔde: *～ weather* 雨天. **3** 尚未干〔乾〕的(或凝固的) shàng wèi gān de. **4**[非正式用语][贬]无〔無〕目的的 wú mùdì de; 弱的 ruòde. **5** [习语] **a ˌwet ˈblanket** [非正式用语]扫〔掃〕兴〔興〕的人 sǎoxìng de rén. **ˌwet ˈthrough** 湿透

W

shītòu. **wet** *n* 1 the wet [sing] 雨天 yǔtiān. 2 [C] [英国非正式用语]稳〔穩〕健的政治家 wěnjiànde zhèngzhìjiā. **wet** *v* [-tt-; *pt*, *pp* **wet** 或 **~ted**] [T] 弄湿 nòng shī. **ˈwet suit** *n* [C] (保暖的)潜〔潛〕水服 qiánshuǐfú.

we've /wiːv/ (= we have) ⇨ HAVE.

whack /wæk; *US* hwæk/ *v* [T] 重击〔擊〕zhòngjī; 用力打 yòng lì dǎ. **whack** *n* [C] 1 重击(声) zhòngjī. 2 [非正式用语]一份 yífèn. **whacked** *adj* [非正式用语]筋疲力尽〔盡〕的 jīn pí lì jìn de. **whacking** *n* [C] [旧][非正式用语]殴〔毆〕打 ōudǎ. **whacking** *adj* [非正式用语]特大的 tèdàde; 极〔極〕大的 jídàde.

whale /weɪl; *US* hweɪl/ *n* 1 [C][动物] 鲸 jīng. 2[习语] **have a ˈwhale of a time** [非正式用语] 玩得极〔極〕愉快 wánde jí yúkuài. **whaler** *n* [C] 1 捕鲸船 bǔjīngchuán. 2 捕鲸者 bǔjīngzhě. **whaling** *n* [U] 捕鲸 bǔ jīng.

wharf /wɔːf; *US* hwɔːrf / *n* [C] [*pl* **~s** 或 **wharves** /wɔːvz; *US* hwɔːrvz/] 码头〔頭〕mǎtóu.

what /wɒt; *US* hwɒt/ *adj*, *pron* 1(表示疑问)什么〔麽〕shénme; 哪些 nǎxiē: *W~ time is it?* 现在是什么时候? *W~ are you reading?* 你在看什么书? 2 什么东西 shénme dōngxi: *Tell me ~ happened next*. 告诉我后来发生了什么事. 3(表示惊讶,感叹)多么 duōme; 何等 héděng: *W~ a good idea!* 多么好的主意! 4 [习语] **what about . . . ?** ⇨ ABOUT[1]. **what for** 为〔爲〕什么(目的) wèishénme: *W~ is this tool used for?* 这工具是作什么用的? *W~ did you do that for?* 你做那事是为了什么? **what if** 如果…将〔將〕会〔會〕怎样〔樣〕rúguǒ… jiāng huì zěnyàng. **what's more** 而且 érqiě; 更重要的 gèng zhòngyào de. **what's ˈwhat** 什么东西有用(或重要) shénme dōngxi yǒuyòng. **what with sth** (用以列举各种原因)由于… yóuyú….

whatever /wɒtˈevə(r); *US* hwɒt-/ *adj*, *pron* 1 任何(事物) rènhé; 每样〔樣〕(事物) měiyàng: *You can eat ~ you like*. 你愿意吃什么,就吃什么. 2 不论〔論〕什么〔麽〕búlùn shénme; 不管什么 bùguǎn shénme: *Keep calm, ~ happens*. 不论出什么事都要保持镇静. 3 (表示惊讶)什么 shénme: *W~ do you mean?* 你究竟是什么意思? **whatever, whatsoever** *adv* (用于加强语气)(究竟是)什么 shénme: *no doubt ~* 毫无〔無〕疑问.

wheat /wiːt; *US* hwiːt/ *n* [U] 小麦〔麥〕xiǎomài.

wheedle /ˈwiːdl; *US* ˈhwiːdl/ *v* [I, T] [贬] (用奉承手法等)获〔獲〕得 huòdé: *She ~d the money out of her brother*. 她用花言巧语从她哥哥那里弄到这笔钱.

wheel /wiːl; *US* hwiːl/ *n* [C] 1 轮〔輪〕lún; 车轮 chēlún. 2 = STEERING-WHEEL (STEER). 3[习语] **at / behind the ˈwheel** (a) 驾驶 jiàshǐ. (b) [喻]控制 kòngzhì. **wheel** *v* 1 [T]推(或拉)动〔動〕(车) tuīdòng. 2 [I] 旋转〔轉〕运〔運〕动 xuánzhuǎn yùndòng. 3 [习语] ˌ**wheel and ˈdeal** [非正式用语][尤用于美语](用精明的,常指欺骗的方法)讨价〔價〕还〔還〕价 tǎojià huánjià. **ˈwheelbarrow** *n* [C] 手推车 shǒutuīchē. **ˈwheelchair** *n* [C] 轮椅 lúnyǐ. **-wheeled** [构成复合形容词]: *a three-wheeled vehicle* 三轮车.

wheeze /wiːz; *US* hwiːz/ *v* [I] 喘气〔氣〕chuǎnqì; 喘息 chuǎnxī. **wheeze** *n* [C] 喘息声〔聲〕chuǎnxīshēng. **wheezy** *adj* [-ier, -iest].

whelk /welk; *US* hwelk/ *n* [C] [动物]峨螺 éluó.

when /wen; *US* hwen/ *adv* 1 在什么〔麽〕时〔時〕候(或场合) zài shénme shíhòu: *W~ did you come?* 你是什么时候来的? 2 在那时 zài nàshí; 其时 qíshí: *Sunday is the day ~ few people work*. 星期日是很少有人工作的日子. *Her last visit to the town was in May, ~ she saw the new hospital*. 她上次访问这个城镇是在五月份,那时她参观了那所新医院. **when** *conj* 1 当〔當〕…时 dāng… shí; 在…时候 zài… shíhòu: *It was raining ~ we arrived*. 我们到达时正下着雨. 2 考虑〔慮〕到 kǎolǜdào; 既然 jìrán: *Why buy a new car ~ your present one runs well?* 既然你现在的汽车还好使,为什么买新车?

whence /wens; *US* hwens/ *adv* [古][正式用语]从〔從〕那里〔裏〕cóng nàlǐ.

whenever /wenˈevə(r); *US* hwen-/ *conj* 1 在任何时〔時〕候 zài rènhé shíhòu; 无〔無〕论〔論〕何时 wúlùn héshí: *I'll discuss it ~ you like*. 我要同你商量那件事,随便你什么时候都行. 2 每当〔當〕měi dāng; 每逢 měi féng: *I go ~ I can*. 我有空就去. **whenever** *adv* (用于疑问中表示惊讶)(究竟在)什么时候(或场合) shénme shíhóu.

where /weə(r); *US* hweə(r)/ *adv* 1 在哪里 zài nǎlǐ; 在何方 zài héfāng; 往哪里 wǎng nǎlǐ: *W~ does he live?* 他住在哪儿? 2(用于表示地点的词语之后)在那(地方) zài nà; 到那(地方) dào nà: *the place ~ you last saw it* 你上次看到它的地方. *one of the few countries ~ people drive on the left* 少数靠左行驶的国家之一. *He then went to London, ~ he stayed for three days*. 他后来去伦敦,在那里呆了三天. **where** *conj* (在)…的地方…de dìfang: *Put it ~ we can all see it*. 把它放在我们都看得见的地方. **ˈwhereabouts** *adv* 在什么地方 zài shénme dìfang; 靠近哪里 kàojìn nǎlǐ: *W~abouts*

W

did you find it? 你在哪儿找到它的? **whereabouts** *n* [C, 用 sing 或 pl v] 所在 suǒzài; 下落 xiàluò: *Her ~abouts is / are unknown*. 她的下落不明. **where'as** *conj* 然而 rán'er; 反之 fǎnzhī: *He gets to work late every day ~as she is always early*. 他每天很晚才工作,然而她经常很早. **where'by** *adv* [正式用语]靠那个[個] kào nàge; 借以 jièyǐ: *He thought of a plan ~by he might escape*. 他考虑一个可以逃跑的办法. **whereu'pon** *conj* [正式用语]在这以后[後] zài zhè yǐhòu; 于是 yúshì.

wherever /ˌweər'eve(r); *US* ˌhweər-/ *conj* **1** 无[無]论[論]在哪里 wúlùn zài nǎlǐ; 在任何地方 zài rènhé dìfang: *I'll find him, ~ he is*. 不管他在哪儿我都要把他找到. **2** 到处[處] dàochù; 各处 gèchù: *Crowds of people queue to see her ~ she goes*. 她所到之处都有人排队等着看她. **wherever** *adv* (表示惊讶)(究竟)在哪儿[兒] zài nǎr.

wherewithal /'weəwɪðɔːl; *US* 'hweər-/ *n* **the wherewithal** [sing] [正式用语]必要的钱[錢]财 bìyàode qiáncái: *Does he have the ~ to buy a car?* 他有必要的钱去买汽车吗?

whet /wet; *US* hwet/ *v* [-tt-] [习语] **whet sb's appetite for sth** 促进[進]某人的胃口(或欲望) cùjìn mǒurénde wèikǒu.

whether /'weðə(r); *US* 'hweðər/ *conj* 是否 shìfǒu: *I don't know ~ to accept or refuse*. 我不知道接受好呢,还是拒绝好.

which /wɪtʃ; *US* hwɪtʃ/ **1** *adj, pron* 哪一个[個] nǎyígè; 哪一些 nǎyìxiē: *W~ way shall we go —up the hill or along the road?* 我们走哪一条路——上山还是沿这条路走? **2** *pron* (指前面提到的事物): *This is the car ~ she drove*. 这就是她驾驶的那辆汽车. *His best film, ~ won many awards, was about Gandhi*. 他的最佳影片,就是荣获许多奖的那一部,是关于甘地的. **3** *pron* [正式用语](指前文的内容): *He said he had lost the key, ~ was untrue*. 他说他遗失了钥匙,那是瞎说.

whichever /wɪtʃ'evə(r); *US* hwɪtʃ-/ *adj, pron* **1** 随[隨]便哪一个 suíbiàn nǎyígè; …中的一个… zhōng de yígè: *Take ~ hat you like best*. 你最喜欢哪一顶帽子,随便挑吧. **2** 不论[論]哪一个(或一些) búlùn nǎyígè: *W~ way you travel, it is expensive*. 你不论采取什么方式旅行,都是很费钱的. **whichever** *adj, pron* (表示惊讶) (究竟)哪个[個](或哪些) nǎge.

whiff /wɪf; *US* hwɪf/ *n* [C] **1** (轻微的)气[氣]味 qìwèi. **2** [喻]少量 shǎoliàng; 一点[點]儿[兒] yì diǎnr.

while /waɪl; *US* hwaɪl/ *conj* **1** 当[當]…的时[時]候 dāng…de shíhòu: *She fell asleep ~ watching television*. 她在看电视的时候睡着了. **2**(表示对比或相反): *She likes tea, ~ I prefer coffee*. 她爱喝茶,而我喜欢咖啡. **3** [正式用语]虽[雖]然 suīrán: *W~ I want to help, I do not think I can*. 虽然我要去帮助,但我觉得我帮不了. **while** *n* [sing] (一段)时间 shíjiān: *for a long ~* 很长一段时间. **while** *v* [短语动词] **while sth away** (悠闲地)消磨(时间) xiāomó.

whilst /waɪlst; *US* hwaɪlst/ *conj* = WHILE.

whim /wɪm; *US* hwɪm/ *n* [C, U] 一时[時]的兴[興]致 yìshíde xìngzhì; 突然的念头[頭] tūránde niàntou.

whimper /'wɪmpə(r); *US* 'hwɪ-/ *v* [I] 呜[嗚]咽 wūyè; 啜泣 chuòqì. **whimper** *n* [C].

whimsical /'wɪmzɪkl; *US* 'hwɪ-/ *adj* 异[異]想天开[開]的 yìxiǎng tiānkāi de; 闹着玩儿[兒]的 nàozhe wánr de.

whine /waɪn; *US* hwaɪn/ *n* [C] 哀鸣声[聲] āimíngshēng; 呜[嗚]呜声 wūwūshēng. **whine** *v* [I] **1** 发[發]哀鸣声 fā āimíngshēng; 作呜呜声 zuò wūwūshēng: *The dog was whining to come in*. 那条狗呜呜地叫着要进来. **2** 抱怨 bàoyuàn; 哀诉 āisù: *a child that never stops whining* 不断抱怨的孩子.

whinny /'wɪnɪ; *US* 'hwɪ-/ *n* [C] [*pl* -ies] 马嘶 mǎsī. **whinny** *v* [*pt, pp* -ied] [I]马嘶声[聲] mǎsīshēng.

whip[1] /wɪp; *US* hwɪp/ *n* **1** [C]鞭子 biānzi. **2** [C](政党的组织秘书)发[發]给本党议[議]员(要求参加辩论或选举)的命令 fāgěi běndǎng yìyuán de mìnglìng. **3** [C, U] (用蛋奶搅打成的)甜食 tiánshí.

whip[2] /wɪp; *US* hwɪp/ *v* [-pp-] **1** [T] 鞭笞 biānchī; 抽打 chōudǎ. **2** [I, T] 快速(或突然)移动[動] kuàisù yídòng: *He ~ped out a knife*. 他突然抽出一把刀来. **3** [T] 搅[攪]打(蛋、奶油等) jiǎodǎ. **4** [短语动词] **whip sth up** 激发[發](民众的强烈感情) jīfā; 唤起 huànqǐ. **whipping** *n* [C, U] 鞭打 biāndǎ. **'whip-round** *n* [C][英国非正式用语]募捐 mùjuān.

whirl /wɜːl; *US* hw-/ *v* **1** [I, T] (使)旋转[轉] xuánzhuǎn. **2** [I] 眩晕 xuànyūn; (头脑)混乱[亂]不清 hùnluàn bùqīng: *Her mind was ~ing*. 她的头脑混乱不清. **whirl** *n* [sing] **1** 旋转 xuánzhuǎn. **2** (一系列)快速活动[動] kuàisù huódòng. **3** 混乱 hùnluàn. **4** [习语] **give sth a 'whirl** [非正式用语]试试某事物 shìshì mǒu shìwù. **'whirlpool** *n* [C] 旋涡[渦] xuánwō. **'whirlwind** *n* [C] 旋风[風] xuànfēng: [喻] *a ~wind romance* 仓促间的风流韵事.

W

whirr (美语尤作 **whir**) /wɜː(r); *US* hw-/ *n* [C, 常作 sing] *n* 呼呼声〔聲〕hūhūshēng; 飕〔颼〕飕声 sōusōushēng. **whirr** (美语尤作 **whir**) *v* [I] 发〔發〕呼呼声 fā hūhūshēng; 作飕飕声 zuò sōusōushēng.

whisk /wɪsk; *US* hw-/ *v* [T] **1** (很快地)掸〔撣〕扫〔掃〕dǎnsǎo, 挥动〔動〕huīdòng, 带〔帶〕走 dàizǒu: *They ~ed him off to prison.* 他们突然把他带进监牢. **2** 搅〔攪〕打(鸡蛋等) jiǎodǎ. **whisk** *n* [C] 打蛋器 dǎdànqì.

whisker /ˈwɪskə(r); *US* ˈhwɪ-/ *n* **1** [C](猫等的)须〔鬚〕xū. **2 whiskers** [pl] 连鬓〔鬢〕胡〔鬍〕子 lián bìn húzi.

whisky (美语或爱尔兰语作 **whiskey**) /ˈwɪskɪ; *US* ˈhwɪ-/ *n* [U, C] [*pl* **-ies**] 威士忌酒 wēishìjì jiǔ.

whisper /ˈwɪspə(r); *US* hwɪ-/ *v* **1** [I, T] (a) 耳语 ěryǔ; 低声〔聲〕说话 dīshēng shuōhuà. (b) 私下说话 sīxià shuōhuà; 秘密传〔傳〕闻 mìmì chuánwén. **2** [I](树叶)沙沙地响〔響〕shāshāde xiǎng; (风)发〔發〕飒〔颯〕飒声 fā sàsàshēng. **whisper** *n* [C] 低声 dīshēng; (树叶、风等的)沙沙声 shāshāshēng; 耳语 ěryǔ.

whist /wɪst; *US* hwɪst/ *n* [U]惠斯特(一种纸牌游戏) Huìsītè.

whistle /ˈwɪsl; *US* ˈhwɪ-/ *n* [C] **1** 口哨声〔聲〕kǒushàoshēng; 汽笛声 qìdíshēng; 哨子声 shàozishēng; (鸟的)啭〔囀〕鸣声 zhuànmíngshēng: [喻] *the ~ of the wind through the trees* 穿过树林的风的呼啸声. **2** 哨子 shàozi; 汽笛 qìdí. **whistle** *v* **1** (a) [I] 吹口哨 chuī kǒushào; 吹哨子 chuī shàozi; 发〔發〕汽笛声 fā qìdíshēng. (b) [T] 用口哨吹出(曲调) yòng kǒushào chuīchū. **2** 发啸〔嘯〕声行进〔進〕fā xiàoshēng xíngjìn: *The bullets ~d past us.* 子弹飕飕地从我们身边飞过.

white /waɪt; *US* hwaɪt/ *adj* [~r, ~st] **1** 白的 báide; 白色的 báisède; 雪白的 xuěbáide. **2** 白种〔種〕人的 báizhǒngrénde. **3**(脸色)苍〔蒼〕白的 cāngbáide. **4**(咖啡)加牛奶(或奶油)的 jiā niúnǎi de. **5** [习语] **a white elephant** 无〔無〕用(而昂贵)的财物 wúyòngde cáiwù. **a white lie** (无恶意的)小谎言 xiǎo huǎngyán. **white** *n* **1** [U] 白色 báisè. **2** [C] 白种人 báizhǒngrén. **3** [C, U] 蛋白 dànbái; 蛋清 dànqīng. **4** [C]眼白 yǎnbái. ˌ**white-ˈcollar** *adj* (工作者)白领的(不使用体力的) báilǐngde. **the ˈWhite House** *n* [sing] 白宫(美国总统府) Báigōng. **whiten** *v* [I, T] (使)变〔變〕白 biàn bái; (使)更白 gèng bái. **whiteness** *n* [U]. ˌ**White ˈPaper** *n* [C]白皮书〔書〕báipíshū. ˈ**whitewash** *n* **1** [U] 石灰水(刷白用) shíhuīshuǐ. **2** [C, U] [喻]粉饰 fěnshì; 掩饰 yǎnshì. ˈ**whitewash** *v* [T] **1** 粉刷(墙壁等) fěnshuā. **2** [喻]掩盖〔蓋〕(错误) yǎngài.

Whitsun /ˈwɪtsn; *US* ˈhwɪ-/ *n* [U, C] 圣〔聖〕灵〔靈〕降临〔臨〕节〔節〕(复活节后第七个星期日及其前后几天) Shènglíng Jiànglínjié.

whittle /ˈwɪtl; *US* ˈhwɪ-/ *v* **1** [I, T] 切 qiē; 削 xuē. **2**[短语动词] **whittle sth down / away** 将〔將〕某物削薄(或削减) jiāng mǒuwù xuē bó: *The value of our savings is being slowly ~d down by inflation.* 我们的积蓄被通货膨胀蚕食了.

whiz /wɪz; *US* hwɪz/ *v* [**-zz-**] [I] [非正式用语] **1** 高速移动〔動〕gāo sù yídòng. **2** 作飕〔颼〕飕声〔聲〕zuò sōusōushēng.

whizz-kid /ˈwɪzkɪd; *US* ˈhwɪz-/ *n* [C] [非正式用语]迅速获〔獲〕得成功的人 xùnsù huòdé chénggōng de rén.

who /huː/ *pron* **1** (用作主语)谁 shéi: *W~ is the woman in the black hat?* 那个戴黑帽子的女人是谁? **2**[非正式用语](用作宾语, 可用 *whom* 代替) 谁 shéi: *W~ are you phoning?* 你给谁打电话? *W~ do you want to speak to?* 你要跟谁说话? **3** 那个〔個〕人 nàge rén; 其人 qírén: *The people ~ called yesterday want to buy the house.* 昨天打电话来的人想买这所房子. *My husband, ~ has been ill, hopes to see you soon.* 我的丈夫病了,他希望很快见到你.

whoever /huːˈevə(r)/ *pron* **1**…的那个〔個〕人…de nàge rén: *W~ says that is a liar.* 说那个话的人是在撒谎. *You must speak to ~ is the head of the department.* 你必须和部门的领导去说. **2** 无〔無〕论〔論〕谁 wúlùn shéi; 任何人 rènhérén: *W~ rings, I don't want to speak to them.* 无论谁来电话,我都不愿意接. **whoever** *pron* [表示惊讶] (究竟是)谁 shéi.

whole /həʊl/ *adj* **1** 完全的 wánquánde; 全部的 quánbùde; 整个〔個〕的 zhěnggède: *He told us the ~ story.* 他给我们讲全部的经历. **2** 未受伤〔傷〕的 wèi shòushāng de; 未损坏〔壞〕的 wèi sǔnhuài de: *She swallowed the sweet ~.* 她把糖囫囵吞下去了. **3** [习语] **go the whole hog** [非正式用语]完全地(或彻底地)做 wánquánde zuò. **whole** *n* **1 the whole** [sing] *of* 某事物的全部 mǒu shìwù de quánbù. **2** [C] 整体〔體〕zhěngtǐ; 全体 quántǐ. **3** [习语] **on the whole** 总〔總〕的来看 zǒngde lái kàn. ˌ**whole-ˈhearted** *adj* 全心全意的 quánxīn quányì de. ˌ**whole-ˈheartedly** *adv*. ˈ**wholemeal** *n* [U]全麦〔麥〕面〔麵〕粉 quánmài miànfěn. ˌ**whole ˈnumber** *n* [C] 整数〔數〕zhěngshù. **wholly** /ˈhəʊlɪ/ *adv* 完全地 wánquánde; 全部地 quánbùde: *I'm not wholly convinced.* 我不完全相信.

wholesale /ˈhəʊlseɪl/ *n* [U] 批发〔發〕pīfā. **wholesale** *adj*, *adv* **1** 批发的 pīfāde. **2** 大批地 dàpīde; 大规模的(地) dà guīmó de: *the*

~ *slaughter of animals* 大规模捕杀动物. **wholesaler** *n* [C] 批发商 pīfāshāng.

wholesome /ˈhəʊlsəm/ *adj* 1(食物)有益于健康的 yǒuyì yú jiànkāng de. 2[褒](道德上)有益的 yǒuyìde.

whom /huːm/ *pron* [正式用语] 1(用作宾语)谁 shéi: *W~ did she invite?* 她邀请谁了? 2(用作宾语,以引出修饰人的从句): *The person to ~ this letter is addressed died two years ago*. 这封信的收信人两年前就去世了.

whoop /huːp, wuːp; *US* hwuːp/ *n* [C] 1 大叫 dà jiào; 高呼 gāo hū. 2 咳嗽和哮喘声〔聲〕 késòu hé xiàochuǎnshēng. **whoop** *v* [I] 发〔發〕叫喊声 fā jiàohǎnshēng; 高呼 gāo hū. ˈ**whooping cough** *n* [U] 百日咳 bǎirìké.

whore /hɔː(r)/ *n* [C] [旧或贬]妓女 jìnǚ.

whose /huːz/ 1 *pron, adj* 谁的 shéide: *W~ (house) is that?* 那是谁的(房子)? 2 *pron* (指前面提到的人)那个〔個〕的 nàgede: *the children ~ mother is a doctor* 母亲是医生的那些孩子.

why /waɪ; *US* hwaɪ/ *adv* 1 为〔爲〕什么〔麼〕 wèishénme: *W~ are you late?* 你为什么迟到? 2 为了哪个〔個〕(原因) wèile nǎge: *Nobody understands ~ she left him*. 没有人知道她离开他的原因. 3 [习语] **why not** (用以提出建议或表示同意): *W~ not go now?* 现在就去好不好?

wick /wɪk/ *n* 1 [C] 烛〔燭〕芯 zhúxīn; 灯〔燈〕芯 dēngxīn. 2[习语] **get on sb's wick** [英国非正式用语]招惹某人 zhāorě mǒurén.

wicked /ˈwɪkɪd/ *adj* 1 不道德的 bú dàodé de; 邪恶〔惡〕的 xié'ède. 2 意欲伤〔傷〕害的 yì yù shānghài de. 3 恶作剧〔劇〕的 èzuòjùde; 淘气〔氣〕的 táoqìde: *a ~ grin* 顽皮的笑. **wickedly** *adv*. **wickedness** *n* [U].

wicker /ˈwɪkə(r)/ *n* [U] 编制〔製〕的柳条〔條〕(或藤条) biānzhìde liǔtiáo. ˈ**wickerwork** (用枝条编制的)编制品 biānzhìpǐn.

wicket /ˈwɪkɪt/ *n* [C] (a) [板球]三柱门 sānzhùmén. (b) 三柱门之间的场〔場〕地 sānzhùmén zhī jiān de chǎngdì.

wide /waɪd/ *adj* [~r, ~st] 1 宽广〔廣〕的 kuānguǎngde; 宽阔的 kuānkuòde: *a ~ river* 宽阔的河流. 2 有…宽度的 yǒu…kuāndùde: *12 metres ~* 12米宽. 3 广泛的 guǎngfànde; 广大的 guǎngdàde: *a ~ range of interests* 广泛的兴趣. 4 远〔遠〕离〔離〕目标〔標〕的 yuǎnlí mùbiāo de. 5 [习语] **give sb a wide berth** 避开〔開〕某人 bìkāi mǒurén. **wide of the ˈmark** 离目的很远的 lí mùdì hěn yuǎn de. **wide** *adv* 充分地 chōngfènde; 完全地 wánquánde: *He was ~ awake*. 他很精神,毫无睡意. ~ *open* 完全打开. ˌ**wide-ˈeyed** *adj* 目瞪口呆的 mù dèng kǒu dāi de. **widely** *adv* 1 达〔達〕到大的程度 dádào dàde chéngdù: *Prices vary ~ly from shop to shop*. 商店和商店之间的价格有很大不同. 2 遍布 biànbù; 广泛地 guǎngfànde: *travel ~ly* 到处游历. 3 被大家…地 bèi dàjiā…de: *It is ~ly known that...* 大家都知道…. **widen** *v* [I, T] (使)变〔變〕宽 biàn kuān; 加宽 jiā kuān; 扩〔擴〕大 kuòdà. ˈ**widescreen television** *n* 1 [C] 宽荧〔熒〕屏电〔電〕视机〔機〕 kuānyíngpíng diànshìjī. 2 [U] 宽荧屏电视 kuānyíngpíng diànshì. ˈ**widespread** *adj* 扩展的 kuòzhǎnde; 普及的 pǔjíde.

widow /ˈwɪdəʊ/ *n* [C] 寡妇〔婦〕 guǎfu. **widow** *v* [T] [常用被动语态]使丧〔喪〕偶 shǐ sàng'ǒu. **widower** *n* [C] 鳏夫 guānfū.

width /wɪdθ, wɪtθ/ *n* [U,C] 宽度 kuāndù.

wield /wiːld/ *v* [T] 使用 shǐyòng: ~ *an axe* 挥动斧头. ~ *power* 行使权力.

wife /waɪf/ *n* [C] [*pl* **wives** /waɪvz/] 妻 qī.

wi-fi, Wi-Fi /ˈwaɪfaɪ/ *n* [U] 无〔無〕线上网〔網〕协〔協〕议〔議〕 wúxiàn shàngwǎng xiéyì: The hotel had no ~. 这家酒店不能无线上网.

wig /wɪg/ *n* [C] 假发〔髮〕 jiǎfà.

wiggle /ˈwɪgl/ *v* [I, T] (使)摆〔擺〕动〔動〕 bǎidòng; 扭动 niǔdòng: *The baby was wiggling its toes*. 那婴儿正在扭动脚趾头. **wiggle** *n* [C].

wigwam /ˈwɪgwæm; *US* -waːm/ *n* [C] (旧时北美印地安人使用的)棚屋 péngwū.

wild /waɪld/ *adj* 1(a)(动物)未驯服的 wèi xùnfú de; 野的 yěde. (b) (植物)野生的 yěshēngde; 非栽培的 fēi zāipéi de. 2(人)未开〔開〕化的 wèi kāihuà de; 野蛮〔蠻〕的 yěmánde. 3(土地)荒芜〔蕪〕的 huāngwúde; 无〔無〕人居住的 wú rén jūzhù de. 4 暴风〔風〕雨的 bàofēngyǔde: ~ *weather* 暴风雨天气. 5 激动〔動〕的 jīdòngde; 狂热〔熱〕的 kuángrède. 6 轻〔輕〕率的 qīngshuàide; 鲁莽的 lǔmǎngde: *a ~ guess* 乱猜. 7 *about* [非正式用语]极〔極〕热爱〔愛〕的(或热心的) jí rè'ài de. 8[习语] **run ˈwild** ⇨ RUN¹. **wild** *n* 1 **the wild** [sing] 自然状〔狀〕态〔態〕(或环境) zìrán zhuàngtài. 2 **the wilds** [pl] 荒地 huāngdì; 人烟稀少地区〔區〕 rényān xīshǎo dìqū. ˌ**wildcat** ˈ**strike** *n* [C] (未经工会允许的)突然罢〔罷〕工 tūrán bàgōng. ˌ**wild-ˈgoose chase** *n* [C] [非正式用语]毫无希望的追寻〔尋〕 háowú xīwàng de zhuīxún. ˈ**wildlife** *n* [U] 野生动物 yěshēng dòngwù. **wildly** *adv* 1 野蛮地 yěmánde. 2 [非正式用语]极 jí; 非常 fēicháng. **wildness** *n* [U].

wilderness /ˈwɪldənɪs/ *n* [C, 常作 sing] 1 荒地 huāngdì. 2 [习语] **in the ˈwilderness** 不再处〔處〕于重要的(或有影响的)地位 bú zài chǔyú zhòngyào de dìwèi.

wiles /waɪlz/ *n* [pl] 诡计 guǐjì.

wilful (美语亦作 willful) /ˈwɪlfl/ *adj* 1 (坏事)故意做的 gùyì zuò de. 2 (人)任性的 rènxìngde, 固执〔執〕的 gùzhíde. **wilfully** *adv*.

will[1] /wɪl/ *modal v* [缩略式 'll /l/; 否定式 will not, 缩略式 won't /wəʊnt/; *pt* would /wəd/ 强读 /wʊd/, 缩略式 'd /d/, 否定式 would not, 缩略式 wouldn't /wʊdnt/] 1 (表示将来)将〔將〕要 jiāngyào: *He ~ / He'll be here tomorrow*. 他明天将在这儿. 2 (表示可能性)可能 kěnéng; 该是 gāishì: *That ~ be the postman at the door*. 这准是邮递员来了. 3 (表示愿意或意图)愿〔願〕yuàn; 要 yào: *We ~ not obey you*. 我们不愿意听从你. 4 (表示请求或邀请): *W~ you come this way please?* 你请这边来好吗? 5 (用于发出命令或指示): *You ~ carry out my instructions!* 你要执行我的指示! 6(用于叙述真理): *Oil ~ float on water*. 油浮在水面上. 7 (用于叙述习惯): *She would sit there, hour after hour, doing nothing*. 她往往坐在那里老半天,什么事也不干. 8 (表示执意要做的事): *He ˈ~ smoke between courses at dinner*. 他偏偏要在吃饭的时候抽烟.

will[2] /wɪl/ *v* [T] 1 用意志力使 yòng yìzhìlì shǐ. 2 [正式用语] (在遗嘱中规定)遗赠(财产)与〔與〕(某人) yízèng yǔ.

will[3] /wɪl/ *n* 1 [U, sing]意志 yìzhì. 2 [U, sing] (亦作 ˈ**will-power** [U]) 自我控制 zìwǒ kòngzhì; 自制力 zìzhìlì: *He has a strong / weak ~*. 他的意志坚强(或薄弱). 3 [U, C] 决心 juéxīn: *the ~ to live* 求生的决心. 4 [U] 愿〔願〕望 yuànwàng; 旨意 zhǐyì: *the ~ of God* 上帝的旨意. 5 [C] 遗嘱〔囑〕yízhǔ. 6 [习语] **at will** 随〔隨〕意 suíyì; 任意 rènyì.

willing /ˈwɪlɪŋ/ *adj* 1 (*to*) 愿〔願〕意的 yuànyìde; 乐〔樂〕意的 lèyìde: *~ to learn* 愿意学习. 2 心甘情愿的 xīngān qíngyuàn de: *a ~ helper* 自愿的帮助者. **willingly** *adv*. **willingness** *n* [U].

willow (亦作 ˈ**willow-tree**) /ˈwɪləʊ/ *n* [C] 柳 liǔ; 柳树〔樹〕liǔshù.

wilt /wɪlt/ *v* [I] 1 (植物)枯萎 kūwěi; 蔫 niān. 2 [喻](人)又累又乏 yòu lèi yòu fá.

wily /ˈwaɪlɪ/ *adj* [-ier, -iest] 狡猾的 jiǎohuáde.

wimp /wɪmp/ *n* [C][非正式用语] [贬]懦弱的人(尤指男人) nuòruòde rén.

win /wɪn/ [-nn-; *pt*, *pp* **won** /wʌn/] *v* 1 [I, T] 获〔獲〕胜〔勝〕huòshèng; 取得成功 qǔdé chénggōng. 2 [T] 赢得 yíngdé; 获得 huòdé. 3 [T] 取得 qǔdé: *try to ~ support for one's ideas* 争取对自己意见的支持. 4[习语] **win (sth) ˌhands ˈdown** 轻〔輕〕而易举〔舉〕地取得 qīng ér yì jǔ de qǔdé. 5 [短语动词] **win sb over / round** 获得支持(尤指通过劝说) huòdé zhīchí. **win** *n* [C] 成功 chénggōng; 胜利 shènglì. **winner** *n* [C]. **winning** *adj* 1 胜利的 shènglìde. 2 吸引人的 xīyǐn rén de; 动〔動〕人的 dòngrénde: *a ~ning smile* 动人的微笑. **winnings** *n* [pl] 赢得的钱〔錢〕yíng dé de qián.

wince /wɪns/ *v* [I] (因疼痛、悲伤等而)皱〔皺〕眉蹙眼 zhòuméi cùyǎn. **wince** *n* [C] 皱眉蹙眼(的表情) zhòuméi cùyǎn.

winch /wɪntʃ/ *n* [C] 绞车 jiǎochē. **winch** *v* [T] 用绞车拉动〔動〕yòng jiǎochē lādòng.

wind[1] /wɪnd/ *n* 1 [C,U] 风〔風〕fēng. 2 [U] (尤指运动时的)呼吸 hūxī. 3 [U](胃肠中的)气〔氣〕qì. 4[习语] **get wind of sth** [非正式用语]听〔聽〕到(某事的)风声〔聲〕(或秘密) tīngdào fēngshēng. **put the wind up sb** [非正式用语] 使某人害怕 shǐ mǒurén hàipà. **wind** *v* [T] 使气急 shǐ qìjí; 使喘息 shǐ chuǎnxī. ˈ**windfall** *n* [C] 1 风吹落的果实〔實〕fēng chuīluò de guǒshí. 2[喻]意外的收获〔獲〕yìwàide shōuhuò; 横财 héngcái. ˈ**wind farm** *n* [C] 风力发〔發〕电〔電〕场〔場〕fēnglì fādiànchǎng. ˈ**wind instrument** *n* [C] 吹奏乐〔樂〕器 chuīzòu yuèqì. ˈ**windmill** *n* [C] 风车 fēngchē. ˈ**windpipe** *n* [C] [解剖]气管 qìguǎn. ˈ**wind power** *n* [U] 风〔風〕力 fēnglì; 风〔風〕能 fēngnéng. ˈ**windscreen** (美语 ˈ**windshield**) *n* [C] 挡〔擋〕风玻璃 dǎng fēng bōli. ˈ**windscreen wiper** *n* [C] (挡风玻璃上的)刮水器 guāshuǐqì. ˈ**windsurfing** *n* [U] 帆板运〔運〕动〔動〕fānbǎn yùndòng. ˈ**windsurfer** *n* [C]. ˈ**windswept** *adj* (a) 受强风吹的 shòu qiángfēng chuī de. (b) (人的头发等)被风刮得不整齐〔齊〕的 bèi fēng guāde bù zhěngqí de. **windy** *adj* [-ier, -iest] 多风的 duōfēngde: *a ~y day* 刮风的一天.

wind[2] /waɪnd/ *v* [*pt*, *pp* **wound** /waʊnd/] 1 [I, T] (使)迂回〔迴〕前进〔進〕yūhuí qiánjìn: *The river ~s (its way) through the countryside*. 这条河蜿蜒地流过乡村地区. 2 [T]将〔將〕…缠绕〔繞〕(在轴上) jiāng…chánrào. 3 [T] (*up*) 上(钟,表的)发〔發〕条〔條〕shàng fātiáo. 4 [短语动词] **wind sth back, down, forward, etc** (摇动把手)使某物移动〔動〕shǐ mǒuwù yídòng: *~ a window down* 将玻璃窗摇下. **wind down** (a) (钟表等)慢下来后〔後〕停止 mànxiàlái hòu tíngzhǐ. (b) [非正式用语](人)(紧张后)放松〔鬆〕fàngsōng. **wind (sth) down** (停职前)减少工作 jiǎnshǎo gōngzuò. **wind up** [非正式用语] 安顿(下来) āndùn: *We eventually wound up in a little cottage by the sea*. 我们终于在海滨的一所小屋子里住下来. **wind (sth) up** 结束 jiéshù. **wind sb up** [非正式用语]使某人激动 shǐ mǒurén jīdòng.

window /ˈwɪndəʊ/ *n* [C] 窗 chuāng; 窗口 chuāngkǒu. ˈ**window-box** *n* [C] 窗槛〔檻〕花箱 chuāngkǎn huāxiāng. ˈ**window-dressing** *n* [U] 橱窗布置 chúchuāng bùzhì. ˈ**window-pane** *n* [C] 窗玻璃 chuāngbōli. ˈ**window-shopping** *n* [U] 浏〔瀏〕览〔覽〕橱窗 liúlǎn chúchuāng. ˈ**window-sill** *n* [C] 窗台 chuāngtái.

wine /waɪn/ *n* [C,U] 葡萄酒 pútaojiǔ; 果子酒 guǒzijiǔ. **wine** *v* [习语] ˌ**wine and** ˈ**dine** (用)酒宴招待(或被招待) jiǔyàn zhāodài.

wing /wɪŋ/ *n* 1 [C] 翼 yì; 翅膀 chìbǎng. 2 [C](飞行器的)机〔機〕翼 jīyì. 3 [C] 侧厅〔廳〕cètīng; 耳房 ěrfáng: *add a new* ~ *to a hospital* 给一家医院加盖一座新的侧楼. 4 [C] (汽车的)翼子板 yìzibǎn. 5 [C, 常作 sing] (政党中的)派别 pàibié: *the left / right* ~ (某政党的)左(或右)翼. 6 [C] (足球等场地的)边〔邊〕侧 biān cè. 7 **the wings** [pl] (舞台上观众看不到的)两侧 liǎng cè. 8 [习语] **take sb under one's** ˈ**wing** 置某人于自己的保护〔護〕下 zhì mǒurén yú zìjǐde bǎohù xià. **wing** *v* 1 [I,T] 飞〔飛〕行 fēixíng. 2 [T] 打伤〔傷〕(鸟翼) dǎ shāng. ˈ**winged** *adj* 有翅膀的 yǒu chìbǎng de. **winger** *n* [C] (足球等的)边锋队〔隊〕员 biānfēng duìyuán. ˈ**wing-span** *n* [C] 翼展 yìzhǎn.

wink /wɪŋk/ *v* [I] 1 (*at*) 眨一只〔隻〕眼 zhǎ yìzhī yǎn; 使眼色 shǐ yǎnsè. 2(星光等)闪耀 shǎnyào; 闪烁〔爍〕shǎnshuò. **wink** *n* 1 [C] 眨眼 zhǎyǎn; 眨眼示意 zhǎyǎn shìyì. 2 [sing] 打盹 dǎdǔn: *I didn't sleep a* ~. 我没有打过盹. 3 [习语] **have forty** ˈ**winks** [非正式用语]小睡 xiǎo shuì; 打盹 dǎdǔn.

winkle /ˈwɪŋkl/ *n* [C] (食用)海螺 hǎiluó.

winner, winning ⇨ WIN.

winter /ˈwɪntə(r)/ *n* [U,C] 冬季 dōngjì. **winter** *v* [I] [正式用语]过〔過〕冬 guò dōng; 越冬 yuè dōng. ˌ**winter** ˈ**sports** *n* [pl] 冬季运〔運〕动〔動〕dōngjì yùndòng. **wintry** /ˈwɪntrɪ/ *adj*.

wipe /waɪp/ *v* [T] 1 擦 cā; 揩 kāi; 抹 mǒ: ~ *the dishes with a cloth* 用抹布把碟子擦干. ~ *the writing off the blackboard* 把黑板上的字抹去. 2 [短语动词] **wipe sth out** (a) 彻〔徹〕底摧毁 chèdǐ cuīhuǐ: *war* ~*d out whole villages*. 战争摧毁了整座整座的村庄. (b) 取消(欠款) qǔxiāo; 还〔還〕清(债务) huánqīng. **wipe sth up** 擦净 cājìng: ~ *up the milk you spilt* 把你洒的牛奶擦干净. **wipe** *n* [C] 擦 cā; 揩 kāi; 抹 mǒ.

wire /ˈwaɪə(r)/ *n* 1 [C,U] 金属〔屬〕线〔綫〕jīnshǔxiàn. 2 [C] [非正式用语][尤用于美语]电〔電〕报〔報〕diànbào. **wire** *v* [T] 1 用金属线捆绑 yòng jīnshǔxiàn kǔnbǎng. 2 给…安装〔裝〕电线 gěi…ānzhuāng diànxiàn. 3[美语]发〔發〕电报给 fā diànbào gěi. **wiring** *n* [U] 供电系统 gōngdiàn xìtǒng. **wiry** *adj* 1 (硬而韧)似金属丝的 sì jīnshǔsī de. 2 (人)瘦而结实〔實〕的人 shòu ér jiēshi de rén.

wireless /ˈwaɪəlɪs/ *n* [C] [旧]无〔無〕线〔綫〕电〔電〕wúxiàndiàn. **wireless** *adj* 无(无)线的 wúxiànde.

wisdom /ˈwɪzdəm/ *n* [U] 1 智慧 zhìhuì; 才智 cáizhì. 2[正式用语]明智的思想、言论〔論〕等 míngzhìde sīxiǎng、yánlùn děng. ˈ**wisdom-tooth** *n* [C] 智牙 zhìyá.

wise /waɪz/ *adj* [~r, ~st] 1 有知识〔識〕的 yǒu zhīshide; 聪〔聰〕明的 cōngmíngde; 明智的 míngzhìde. 2 [习语] **none the** ˈ**wiser** (和以前一样)不明白 bù míngbai. **wisely** *adv*.

wish /wɪʃ/ *v* 1 [T] *to* [正式用语]想要 xiǎng yào: *He* ~*es to be alone*. 他要一人独处. 2 [T] 要(不大可能的事)实〔實〕现 yào shíxiàn: *I* ~ (*that*) *I could be an astronaut*. 但愿我能成为一名宇航员. 3 [T]祝愿〔願〕zhùyuàn: ~ *sb good luck / happy birthday* 祝某人走运(或生日快乐). 4 [I] (*for*) 默默盼祷〔禱〕mòmò pàndǎo: *Blow out the candles and* ~! 吹灭(生日蛋糕上的)蜡烛,默默盼祷! **wish** *n* 1 [C]愿望 yuànwàng; 希望 xīwàng: *I have no* ~ *to interfere, but...* 我本不愿意打扰,但…. 2 [C] 希望(得到)的事物 xīwàngde shìwù. 3 **wishes** [pl] 祝福 zhùfú: *My father sends his best* ~*es*. 我的父亲表示他的祝福. ˌ**wishful** ˈ**thinking** *n* [U] 仅〔僅〕基于愿望的想法 jǐn jīyú yuànwàng de xiǎngfǎ.

wishy-washy /ˈwɪʃɪwɒʃɪ; *US* -wɔːʃɪ/ *adj* [非正式用语]弱的 ruòde; 浅〔淺〕的 qiǎnde; 淡的 dànde.

wisp /wɪsp/ *n* [C] 小捆 xiǎokǔn; 小把 xiǎobǎ; 小束 xiǎoshù: *a* ~ *of hair* 一绺头发. *a* ~ *of smoke* 一缕青烟. **wispy** *adj*.

wistful /ˈwɪstfl/ *adj* 发〔發〕愁的 fāchóude; 渴望的(尤指过去的或不可能的事物) kěwàngde. **wistfully** /-fəlɪ/ *adv*.

wit /wɪt/ *n* 1 (a) [U] 机〔機〕智而幽默的能力 jīzhì ér yōumò de nénglì. (b) [C] 机智而幽默的人 jīzhì ér yōumò de rén. 2(亦作 **wits**) [U, pl] 智慧 zhìhuì; 智力 zhìlì. 3 [习语] **at one's wits'** ˈ**end** 不知所措 bù zhī suǒ cuò. **have / keep one's** ˈ**wits about one** 时〔時〕刻警惕 shíkè jǐngtì; 随〔隨〕机应〔應〕变〔變〕suí jī yìng biàn. **scare, frighten, etc sb out of his / her** ˈ**wits** 惊〔驚〕吓〔嚇〕某人 jīngxià mǒurén. **witticism** /ˈwɪtɪsɪzəm/ *n* [C] 妙语 miàoyǔ; 打趣话 dǎqùhuà. **witty** *adj* [-ier,-iest] 幽默的 yōumòde; 诙谐的 huīxiéde. **wittily** *adv*.

witch /wɪtʃ/ *n* [C] 女巫 nǚwū; 巫婆 wūpó. ˈ**witchcraft** *n* [U] 巫术〔術〕wūshù; 魔法

W

mófǎ. ˈwitch-doctor *n* [C] 巫医〔醫〕wūyī. ˈwitch-hunt *n* [C] 政治迫害 zhèngzhì pòhài.

with /wɪð, wɪθ/ *prep* **1** (a) 和…(在一起) hé…: *live ~ one's parents* 和父母在一起生活. *discuss it ~ an expert* 和专家一起研究. (b) 由…照看 yóu…zhàokàn: *leave a child ~ a baby-sitter* 把孩子交给一位临时保姆照看. **2** 具有 jùyǒu; 带〔帶〕着 dàizhe: *a coat ~ two pockets* 有两个口袋的大衣. *a girl ~ blue eyes* 蓝眼睛的女孩子. **3** (a) (表示使用的工具或方法)用 yòng; 以 yǐ: *cut it ~ a knife* 用刀把它切开. (b) (表示使用的材料): *Fill the bottle ~ water*. 把这个瓶子灌满水. **4** 支持 zhīchí; 拥〔擁〕护〔護〕yōnghù: *The managers are ~ us*. 经理们都支持我们. **5** (表示反对,对立)对〔對〕… duì…; 与〔與〕… yǔ…: *argue ~ Rosie* 与罗西争辩. **6** 因为〔爲〕yīnwèi; 由于 yóuyú: *tremble ~ fear* 怕得发抖. **7** (表示方式、方法): *look at one's daughter ~ pride* 自豪地看着女儿. **8** (表示同一方向): *sail ~ the wind* 顺风驶船. **9** 对于 duìyú; 关〔關〕于 guānyú: *be patient ~ them* 对他们有耐心. **10** 随〔隨〕着 suízhe: *Skill comes ~ experience*. 熟能生巧. **11** 尽〔儘〕管 jǐnguǎn; 虽〔雖〕然 suīrán: *W~ all her faults, we still like her*. 尽管她有许多缺点,我们仍然喜欢她. **12** [习语] **be ˈwith sb** [非正式用语]明白某人说的话 míngbái mǒurén shuōde huà: *I'm not really ~ you, I'm afraid, so could you explain it again?* 我真的不懂你的话,很抱歉,你能再解释一下吗? **ˈwith it** [旧][俚] (a) 时〔時〕髦的 shímáode. (b) 消息灵〔靈〕通的 xiāoxi língtōng de; 敏感的 mǐngǎnde.

withdraw /wɪðˈdrɔː, 亦读 wɪθˈd-/ *v* [*pt* **-drew** /-ˈdruː/, *pp* **~n** /-ˈdrɔːn/] **1** [T] 取走 qǔzǒu; 拿开〔開〕ná kāi: *~ money from one's bank account* 从银行账户取款. **2** [I, T] [正式用语](使)退出 tuìchū; (使)撤走 chèzǒu: *~ troops from the battle* 从战斗中撤退部队. **3** [I, T] (使)不参加 bù cānjiā: *~ from an argument* 不参加争辩. **4** [T] 撤销(诺言、言论等) chèxiāo: *If I don't have a reply by tonight I shall ~ my offer*. 如果今晚以前不给我一个答复,我将撤回我提出的条件. **withdrawal** /-ˈdrɔːəl/ *n* [C, U] 收回 shōuhuí; 取回 qǔhuí; 撤走 chèzǒu; 撤销 chèxiāo. **withdrawal symptoms** *n* [pl] (断绝毒品供应所呈的)脱瘾〔癮〕症状〔狀〕tuō yǐn zhèngzhuàng. **withdrawn** *adj* (人)内向的 nèixiàngde; 孤独〔獨〕的 gūdúde.

wither /ˈwɪðə(r)/ *v* [I, T] (使)枯萎 kūwěi; (使)凋〔彫〕谢 diāoxiè: *The hot summer had ~ed the grass*. 炎热的盛夏已使草枯萎了. [喻] *Their hopes ~ed*. 他们的希望破灭了. **withering** *adj* (使人)羞惭的 xiūcánde: *a ~ing look* 使人难堪的一瞥.

withhold /wɪðˈhəʊld, 亦读作 wɪθˈh-/ *v* [*pt, pp* **-held** /-ˈheld/] [T] [正式用语]拒绝给予 jùjué jǐyú: *~ permission* 拒不准许.

within /wɪˈðɪn/ *prep* 在…里面 zài…lǐmiàn; 不超出 bù chāochū: *~ the city walls* 在城墙以内. *~ seven days* 不超过七天. **within** *adv* [正式用语]在内部 zài nèibù: *I could feel the anger rising ~*. 我感到怒火在心中燃烧.

without /wɪðˈaʊt/ *prep* **1** 没有 méiyǒu: *You can't buy things ~ money*. 你没有钱就买不了东西. **2** [与 *-ing* 形式连用]不 bù: *He can't speak German ~ making mistakes*. 他每说德语必有错误.

withstand /wɪðˈstænd, 亦读作 wɪθˈs-/ *v* [*pt, pp* **-stood** /-ˈstʊd/] [T] [正式用语]抵住 dǐzhù; 承受住 chéngshòuzhù; 反抗 fǎnkàng: *~ an attack* 禁得住攻击. *~ hard weather* 承受住恶劣天气.

witness /ˈwɪtnɪs/ *n* [C] **1** 目击〔擊〕者 mùjīzhě; 见证〔證〕人 jiànzhèngrén. **2** [法律]证人 zhèngrén. **3** 连署人 liánshǔrén. **4** [正式用语]证明 zhèngmíng; 证据〔據〕zhèngjù; 见证 jiànzhèng. **witness** *v* [T] **1** 亲〔親〕见 qīnjiàn; 目击 mùjī: *~ an accident* 亲眼看见一次意外事件. **2** 作…的证人 zuò…de zhèngrén; 作…的连署人 zuò…de liánshǔrén. **ˈwitness-box** *n* [C] 证人席 zhèngrénxí.

witticism, witty ⇨ WIT.

wives *pl* of WIFE.

wizard /ˈwɪzəd/ *n* [C] **1** 男巫 nánwū; 术〔術〕士 shùshì. **2** 奇才 qícái: *a financial ~* 理财能手.

wizened /ˈwɪznd/ *adj* (皮肤)干〔乾〕瘪〔癟〕的 gānbiěde.

wobble /ˈwɒbl/ *v* [I, T] (使)摇摆 yáobǎi; (使)晃动〔動〕huàngdòng. **wobbly** *adj* [非正式用语]摇摆〔擺〕的 yáobǎide; 不稳〔穩〕的 bùwěnde: *a wobbly chair* 摇晃不稳的椅子.

woe /wəʊ/ *n* [旧][正式用语] **1** [U] 悲哀 bēi'āi; 悲痛 bēitòng. **2 woes** [pl] 麻烦事 máfánshì; 不幸的事 búxìng de shì. **woeful** *adj* [正式用语] **1** 悲哀的 bēi'āide; 伤〔傷〕心的 shāngxīnde. **2** 糟糕的 zāogāode.

wok /wɒk/ *n* [C] (中国式)锅〔鍋〕guō.

woke *pt* of WAKE[1].

woken *pp* of WAKE[1].

wolf /wʊlf/ *n* [C] [*pl* **wolves** /wʊlvz/] 狼 láng. **wolf** *v* [T] (*down*) [非正式用语]狼吞虎咽〔嚥〕láng tūn hǔ yàn.

woman /ˈwʊmən/ *n* [*pl* **women** /ˈwɪmɪn/] **1** [C] 成年女子 chéngnián nǚzǐ; 妇〔婦〕女 fùnǚ. **2** [U] 女性 nǚxìng; 女人 nǚrén. **3 the**

W

woman [sing] 女性的特点〔點〕nǚxìngde tèdiǎn; 女人气〔氣〕质〔質〕nǚrén qìzhì. **womanhood** *n* [U] 女子的状〔狀〕态〔態〕和特性 nǚzǐde zhuàngtài hé tèxìng. **womanizer** *n* [C] 与〔與〕许多女子交往的男子(尤指有性关系) yú xǔduō nǚzǐ jiāowǎng de nánzǐ. **'womankind** *n* [U] [正式用语]女子(总称) nǚzǐ. **womanly** *adj* 像女子的 xiàng nǚzǐ de; 女性的 nǚxìngde. **Women's Libe'ration** *n* [U] 妇女解放 fùnǚ jiěfàng. **women's rights** *n* [pl] 妇女权〔權〕益 fùnǚ quányì; 女权 nǚquán.

womb /wuːm/ *n* [C] 子宫 zǐgōng.

won *pt, pp* of WIN.

wonder /ˈwʌndə(r)/ *v* **1** [I, T] 好奇 hàoqí; 自问 zìwèn: *I ~ who she is*. 我纳闷她究竟是谁. **2** [I] 请问 qǐng wèn: *I ~ if you could come earlier*. 请问您是否能早一点来? **3** [I] (*at*)[正式用语]惊〔驚〕奇 jīngqí; 惊叹〔嘆〕jīngtàn: *I ~ that you weren't killed*. 你竟未遇难, 令人称奇. **wonder** *n* **1** (a) [U] 惊奇 jīngqí; 惊叹 jīngtàn. (b) [C] 令人惊奇的事物 lìng rén jīngqí de shìwù: *the ~s of modern medicine* 现代医学的奇迹. *a ~ drug* 特效药. **2**[习语] **do/work wonders** 有(意想不到的)效果 yǒu xiàoguǒ. **it's a wonder that...** 令人惊奇的是… lìng rén jīngqí de shì…: *It's a ~ that they weren't all killed*. 令人惊奇的是他们竟然没有全都遇难. **no/little/small wonder** 这并不(或不太)出奇 zhè bìngbù chūqí. **wonderful** *adj* 极〔極〕好的 jíhǎode; 惊人的 jīngrénde; 奇妙的 qímiàode. **wonderfully** *adv*.

wonky /ˈwɒŋkɪ/ *adj* [英国非正式用语]不稳〔穩〕的 bùwěnde; 弱的 ruòde.

won't /wəʊnt/ (= will not) ⇨WILL[1].

woo /wuː/ *v* [T] **1** 寻〔尋〕求…的支持 xúnqiú …de zhīchí: *~ voters* 拉选票. **2**[旧]向(女子)求婚 xiàng qiúhūn.

wood /wʊd/ *n* **1** [U] 木头〔頭〕mùtou; 木材 mùcái. **2** [C, 尤作 pl] 树〔樹〕林 shùlín. **3**[习语] **ˌout of the 'wood(s)** [非正式用语]脱离〔離〕困境 tuōlí kùnjìng. **wooded** *adj* 多树木的 duō shùmù de. **wooden** *adj* **1** 木制〔製〕的 mùzhìde. **2**(举止)僵硬的 jiāngyìngde, 笨拙的 bènzhuōde. **'woodland** /-lənd/ *n* [U] 森林地区〔區〕sēnlín dìqū. **'woodpecker** *n* [C]啄木鸟 zhuómùniǎo. **'woodwind** /-wɪnd/ *n* [sing] [用 sing 或 pl v] 木管乐〔樂〕器 mùguǎn yuèqì. **'woodwork** *n* [U] **1**(建筑物的)木结构〔構〕部分 mùjiégòu bùfen. **2** 木工活 mùgōnghuó. **'woodworm** *n* [U, C] 蛀木虫(钻的孔洞) zhùmùchóng. **woody** *adj* [-ier, -iest] **1** 长〔長〕满树木的 zhǎngmǎn shùmù de: *a ~y hillside* 树木茂盛的山坡. **2**(似)木头的 mùtoude.

woof /wʊf/ *interj, n* [C] [非正式用语]狗的低吠声〔聲〕gǒude dī fèi shēng; 模仿狗叫的声音 mófǎng gǒujiào de shēngyīn.

wool /wʊl/ *n* [U] (a) 羊毛 yángmáo; (其他)动〔動〕物的毛 dòngwùde máo. (b) 毛线〔綫〕máoxiàn; 毛织〔織〕品 máozhīpǐn. **woollen** (美语-l-) *adj* 毛纺的 máofǎngde; 羊毛制〔製〕的 yángmáo zhì de. **wollens** (美语-l-) *n* [pl] 毛织服装〔裝〕máozhī fúzhuāng. **woolly** (美语亦作 -l-) *adj* [-ier, -iest] **1** 羊毛制的 yángmáo zhì de; 羊毛状的 yángmáozhuàngde. **2** (人、思想)糊涂〔塗〕的 hútude; 混乱〔亂〕的 hùnluànde. **woolly** *n* [C] [*pl* -ies] [非正式用语]毛线衣 máoxiànyī.

word /wɜːd/ *n* **1** [C] 词 cí; 单〔單〕词 dāncí. **2** [C] 话 huà; 言词 yáncí: *Don't say a ~ about it*. 对那事什么也别说. **3** [C] 谈话 tánhuà: *have a ~ / a few ~s with sb* 与某人谈话. **4** [U] 消息 xiāoxi; 音讯 yīnxùn: *Please send me ~ of your arrival*. 请你把到达的消息告诉我. **5** [sing] 诺言 nuòyán; 保证〔證〕bǎozhèng: *I give you my ~ that I will come back*. 我向你保证, 我是要回来的. **6** (常作 the word) [sing] 命令 mìnglìng; 口令 kǒulìng: *The officer gave the ~ to fire*. 军官下令开火. **7**[习语] **by ˌword of 'mouth** 口头〔頭〕地 kǒutóude. **have 'words with sb** 和人争吵 hé rén zhēngchǎo. **in 'other words** 换句话说 huàn jù huà shuō. **in a 'word** 简言之 jiǎn yán zhī. **not in so many 'words** 并没有说明白 bìng méiyǒu shuō míngbai. **take sb's 'word for it** 相信某人的话 xiāngxìn mǒurén de huà. **too funny, stupid, etc for 'words** [非正式用语]极〔極〕为〔爲〕可笑、愚蠢等 jíwéi kě xiào、yúchǔn děng. **ˌword for 'word** 逐字地(翻译) zhúzìde. **word** *v* [T] 以言词表达〔達〕yǐ yáncí biǎodá. **wording** *n* [sing] 措辞〔辭〕cuòcí. **ˌword-'perfect** *adj* 能背诵的 néng bèisòng de. **'word processor** *n* [C] 文字处〔處〕理机〔機〕wénzì chǔlǐjī. **wordy** *adj* [-ier, -iest] 多言的 duōyánde; 唠〔嘮〕叨的 láodaode.

wore *pt* of WEAR[1].

work[1] /wɜːk/ *n* **1** [U] 职〔職〕业〔業〕zhíyè; 业务〔務〕yèwù: *He's been looking for ~ for a year*. 他找工作已找了一年了. **2** [U] 劳〔勞〕动〔動〕láodòng; 工作 gōngzuò: *Do you like hard ~?* 你喜欢繁重的劳动吗? **3** [U] 待做的事 dài zuò de shì; 作业 zuòyè: *I've plenty of ~ to do*. 我有许多事要做. **4** [U] 制〔製〕作品 zhìzuò pǐn; 工艺〔藝〕品 gōngyìpǐn; 成品 chéngpǐn: *the ~ of young sculptors* 年轻雕刻家的作品. **5** [C] 著作 zhùzuò; 作品 zuòpǐn: *the ~s of Shakespeare* 莎士比亚的著作. **6 works** [用 sing 或 pl v] 工厂〔廠〕gōngchǎng: *a 'gas~* 煤气厂. **7 works** [pl]

建筑〔築〕(或维修)工程 jiànzhù gōngchéng: ˈ*road-* ~*s* 道路施工. 8 **the works** [pl](机器的)活动部件 huódòng bùjiàn. 9 [习语] **at ˈwork** (a) 在工作的地方 zài gōngzuò de dìfang. (b) 在运〔運〕转〔轉〕zài yùnzhuǎn; 在起作用 zài qǐ zuòyòng: *new technology at* ~ 在起作用的新技术. **set to ˈwork** 着手工作 zhuóshǒu gōngzuò. **have one's ˈwork cut out** 有困难〔難〕的事要做 yǒu kùnnan de shì yào zuò. **in ˈwork / out of ˈwork** 有(或没有)工作 yǒu gōngzuò. **ˈworkbench** *n* [C] 工作台 gōngzuòtái. **ˈworkbook** *n* [C] 作业本 zuòyèběn. **ˈworkforce** *n* [C, 亦作 sing 用 pl v] (全厂的)劳动力 láodònglì. **ˈworkload** *n* [C] 工作量 gōngzuòliàng. **ˈworkman** *n* [C] (男)劳工 láogōng. **ˈworkmanlike** *adj* 工作熟练〔練〕的 gōngzuò shúliàn de. **ˈworkmanship** *n* [U] 手艺 shǒuyì; 技艺 jìyì. **ˌwork of ˈart** *n* [C] 精致〔緻〕的工艺品 jīngzhìde gōngyìpǐn. **ˈworkshop** *n* [C] 1 车间 chējiān; 工场〔場〕gōngchǎng. 2 研讨会〔會〕yántǎohuì; 讲〔講〕习〔習〕班 jiǎngxíbān. **ˈwork-shy** *adj* 不愿〔願〕工作的 bú yuàn gōngzuò de; 懒惰的 lǎnduòde. **ˈworktop** *n* [C] (厨房的)工作面 gōngzuòmiàn.

work[2] /wɜːk/ *v* 1 [I] 工作 gōngzuò; 劳〔勞〕动〔動〕láodòng; 做 zuò: *I've been* ~*ing hard all day*. 我辛苦地工作了一整天. 2 [I] 运〔運〕转〔轉〕yùnzhuǎn; 活动 huódòng; 起作用 qǐ zuòyòng: *The lift is not* ~*ing*. 电梯失灵了. 3 [I] 有预期的效果(或作用) yǒu yùqīde xiàoguǒ: *Will your plan* ~*?* 你的想法会有效吗? 4 [T] 使工作 shǐ gōngzuò; 开〔開〕动 kāidòng. 5 [T] 管理 guǎnlǐ; 经〔經〕营〔營〕jīngyíng: ~ *a mine* 经营一个矿山. 6 [T] 耕(地) gēng. 7 [I] (*against*/*for*) 努力反对〔對〕(或促成)(某事物) nǔlì fǎnduì: *a politician who* ~*s for peace* 为争取和平而努力的政治家. 8 [T] (用压,锤打等方法)制〔製〕作(或定形) zhìzuò: ~ *clay*/*dough* 揉捏黏土(或面团). 9 [I, T] (使)移动到(新的位置) yídòng dào: ~ *one's way through a boring book* 从头到尾阅读一本枯燥无味的书. 10 [习语] **work loose** ⇨LOOSE. **work to ˈrule** 怠工(故意刻板地按规章办事以降低效率) dàigōng. **work wonders** ⇨WONDER. 11 [短语动词] **work sth off** (通过努力)除去 chúqù; (做工)偿〔償〕清(债务) chángqīng: *He* ~*ed off his anger by digging the garden*. 他用在园中掘土的办法来发泄愤怒. **work out** (a) (按某种方式)发〔發〕展 fāzhǎn, 结果 jiéguǒ: *The situation* ~*ed out well*. 形势发展结果良好. (b) (体育)锻炼〔煉〕duànliàn. **work out at sth** 等于 děngyú: *The total* ~*s out at £180*. 总数为 180 英镑. **work sb out** [非正式用语]了〔瞭〕解某人 liǎojiě mǒurén. **work sth out** (a) 计算出 jìsuànchū: ~ *out the new price* 算出新的价格. (b) 解决 jiějué; 解答 jiědá: ~ *out a problem* 解决一个问题. (c) 设计出 shèjìchū: ~ *out a new scheme* 设计出新的方法. **work sb/oneself up** 使某人(或自己)激动起来 shǐ mǒurén jīdòng qǐlái: *He gets very* ~*ed up about criticism*. 他对批评意见非常激动. **work sth up** 逐步发展(或增加) zhúbù fāzhǎn: ~ *up business* 逐步发展生意. *I can't* ~ *up much energy to go out*. 我不可能有更多的精力去参加社交活动了. **work up to sth** 逐步进〔進〕展到… zhúbù jìnzhǎn dào…: *The music* ~*ed up to a lively finish*. 乐曲在结束时达到了高潮. **worker** *n* [C] 工作者 gōngzuòzhě. **ˈwork-out** *n* [C] 体〔體〕育锻炼〔煉〕(期间) tǐyù duànliàn. **ˌwork-to-ˈrule** *n* [C] (故意刻板地按规章办事以降低效率的)怠工 dàigōng.

workable /ˈwɜːkəbl/ *adj* 可操作的 kě cāozuò de; 可运〔運〕转〔轉〕的 kě yùnzhuǎn de; 可使用的 kě shǐyòng de: *a* ~ *plan* 行得通的计划.

workaholic /ˌwɜːkəˈhɒlɪk/ *n* [C] [非正式用语]工作迷 gōngzuòmí.

working /ˈwɜːkɪŋ/ *adj* 1 做工作的 zuò gōngzuò de: *the* ~ *population* 劳动力. 2 工作上的 gōngzuòshàng de; 为〔爲〕工作的 wèi gōngzuò de: ~ *hours*/*clothes* 工作时间(或工作服). 3 有基础〔礎〕的 yǒu jīchǔ de: *a* ~ *knowledge of Russian* 可以对付工作的俄语水平. 4[习语] **in ˈworking order** 能正常操作的 néng zhèngcháng cāozuò de. **working** *n* 1 **workings** [pl] (机器,组织等的)工作过〔過〕程(或方式) gōngzuò guòchéng. 2[C] 矿〔礦〕坑 kuàngkēng; 采〔採〕石场〔場〕cǎishíchǎng. **the ˌworking ˈclass** *n* [C] 工人阶〔階〕级 gōngrén jiējí. **ˌworking-ˈclass** *adj*. **ˈworking-party** *n* [C] 工作组(受委任调查并作出报告的小组) gōngzuòzǔ.

world /wɜːld/ *n* 1 **the world** [sing] (a) 地球 dìqiú; 世界 shìjiè. (b) 地球上的某部分 dìqiúshàngde mǒu bùfen; …世界 …shìjiè: *the French-speaking* ~ 说法语的地区. 2 [C] 行星 xíngxīng; 天体〔體〕tiāntǐ: *life on other* ~*s* 其他星球上的生命. 3 [C] 生存的时〔時〕间(或状况) shēngcún de shíjiān: *this* ~ *and the next* 今世和来世. 4 **the world** [sing] (a) 世事 shìshì; 世情 shìqíng: *a man*/*woman of the* ~ 世故深的男人(或女人). (b) 每个〔個〕人 měigèrén: *I don't want the whole* ~ *to know about it*. 我不要每个人都知道这件事. 5 [C] …界 …jiè; 范围〔圍〕fànwéi: *the insect* ~ 昆虫世界. *the* ~ *of sport* 体育界. 6[习语] **how, why, where, etc in the world**(用以加强语气)到底 dàodǐ:

How in the ~ did you manage to do it? 你到底是怎样办理这件事的? ˌout of this ˈworld [非正式用语]好得不得了 hǎode bùdéliǎo. a/the ˈworld of difference/good, etc [非正式用语]极〔極〕大的差别(或好处)等 jídàde chābié děng: *My holiday did me a ~ of good.* 我的度假对我大有好处. ˌworld-ˈclass *adj* 世界上一流的 shìjièshang yīliúde. ˌworld-ˈfamous *adj* 世界闻名的 shìjiè wénmíng de. worldly *adj* 1 物质〔質〕的(非精神的) wùzhìde. 2 生活经〔經〕验〔驗〕丰〔豐〕富的 shēnghuó jīngyàn fēngfù de. worldliness *n* [U]. ˌworld ˈpower *n* [C] 世界强国〔國〕 shìjiè qiángguó. World Trade Organisation *n* 世界贸易组织〔織〕 Shìjiè Màoyì Zǔzhī; 世贸组织 Shìmào Zǔzhī. ˌworld ˈwar *n* [C] 世界大战〔戰〕 shìjiè dàzhàn. ˌworld-ˈwide *adj, adv* 遍及全世界的(地) biànjí quánshìjiè de. World Wide ˈWeb *n* [U] 万〔萬〕维网〔網〕 Wànwéiwǎng.

worm /wɜːm/ *n* [C] 1 (a) 蠕虫 rúchóng. (b) 昆虫的幼虫 kūnchóng de yòuchóng: ˈ*wood* ~ 蛀木虫. 2 [非正式用语][贬]懦弱的人 nuòruòde rén; 可怜〔憐〕虫 kěliánchóng. worm *v* [I, T] (使)蠕动〔動〕 rúdòng; (使)缓慢地移动 huǎnmànde yídòng: *He ~ed his way through the narrow tunnel.* 他缓慢地钻过狭窄的隧道.

worn[1] *pp* of WEAR[1].

worn[2] /wɔːn/ *adj* 损坏〔壞〕的 sǔnhuàide; 破烂〔爛〕的 pòlànde. ˌworn-ˈout *adj* 1 (破旧得)不能再用的 bùnéng zài yòng de. 2 筋疲力尽〔盡〕的 jīn pí lì jìn de.

worry /ˈwʌrɪ/ *v* [*pt, pp* -ied] 1 [I] (*about*) 担〔擔〕心 dānxīn; 发〔發〕愁 fāchóu: *I'm worried about my son.* 我担心我的儿子. 2 [T] 使担心 shǐ dānxīn; 使发愁 shǐ fāchóu. 3 [T] (用口)咬住 yǎozhù; 撕咬 sīyǎo: *The dog was ~ing a rat.* 那条狗撕咬着一只老鼠. worried *adj* 担心的 dānxīnde; 烦恼〔惱〕的 fánnǎode. worry *n* [*pl* -ies] 1 [U] 担心 dānxīn; 烦恼 fánnǎo. 2 [C] 令人担忧〔憂〕的事物 lìng rén dānyōu de shìwù. worrying *adj* 忧心忡忡的 yōuxīn chōngchōng de; 令人担忧的 lìng rén dānyōu de.

worse /wɜːs/ *adj* [BAD 的比较级] 1 更坏〔壞〕的 gènghuàide; 更差的 gèngchàde; 更恶〔惡〕劣的 gèng èliè de: *Her work is bad, but his is ~.* 她的工作不好,但他更差. 2 健康恶化 jiànkāng èhuà: *She got ~ in the night.* 晚上她的病情恶化了. 3 [习语] be none the ˈworse (for sth) 未受伤〔傷〕害 wèi shòu shānghài. the ˌworse for ˈwear 破旧〔舊〕的 pòjiùde; 损坏的 sǔnhuàide; 疲倦的 píjuànde. worse *adv* 1 更坏 gènghuài; 更糟 gèngzāo: *She cooks badly, but I cook ~.* 她饭菜做得不好,而我更差. 2 (比以前)更严〔嚴〕重 gèng yánzhòng: *It's raining ~ than ever.* 雨下得更大了. 3 [习语] ˌworse ˈoff 更穷〔窮〕 gèng qióng; 更不愉快 gèng bu yúkuài; 更不健康 gèng bu jiànkāng. worse *n* [U] 更坏的东西 gèng huài de dōngxi. worsen *v* [I, T] (使)更坏 gèng huài; (使)恶化 èhuà.

worship /ˈwɜːʃɪp/ *n* [U] 1 (对上帝或神的)崇拜 chóngbài. 2 (对某人或某事物的)敬仰 jìngyǎng, 热〔熱〕爱〔愛〕 rè'ài. worship *v* [-pp-; 美语 -p-] [I, T] 崇拜 chóngbài; 尊敬 zūnjìng. worshipper (美语 -p-) *n* [C].

worst /wɜːst/ *adj* [BAD 的最高级] 最坏〔壞〕的 zuìhuàide; 最差的 zuìchàde; 最恶〔惡〕劣的 zuì èliè de: *the ~ storm for years* 几年来最厉害的暴风雨. worst *adv* 最坏地 zuìhuàide. worst *n* 1 the worst [sing] 最坏的部分 zuìhuàide bùfen; 最坏者 zuìhuàizhě. 2 [习语] at (the) ˈworst 最坏的情况 zuìhuàide qíngkuàng. if the ˌworst comes to the ˈworst 若最坏的事发〔發〕生 ruò zuìhuàide shì fāshēng.

worth /wɜːθ/ *adj* 1 值…的 zhí… de; 相当〔當〕于…价〔價〕值的 xiāngdāng yú…jiàzhí de: *a car ~ £5000* 一辆值五千英镑的汽车. 2 值得…的 zhíde…de: *The book is ~ reading.* 这本书值得一读. 3 [习语] for ˌall one is ˈworth [非正式用语]竭尽〔盡〕全力 jié jìnquánlì; 拼命 pīnmìng. ˈworth it 很值得 hěn zhídé. ˌworth sb's ˈwhile 对〔對〕某人有好处〔處〕 duì mǒurén yǒu hǎochù. worth *n* [U] 1 值…金额的量 zhí…jīn'é de liàng: *a pound's ~ of apples* 值一英镑的苹果. 2 价值 jiàzhí. worthless *adj* 1 无〔無〕价值的 wú jiàzhíde. 2 (人)品质〔質〕坏〔壞〕的 pǐnzhì huài de. worthˈwhile *adj* 值得(花时间、金钱、精力)的 zhídéde; 合算的 hésuànde.

worthy /ˈwɜːðɪ/ *adj* [-ier, -iest] 1 (*of*) 值得的 zhídéde: ~ *of blame* 应受责备. 2 值得尊敬的 zhídé zūnjìng de.

would[1] /wəd; 强式 wʊd/ *modal v* [缩略式 'd /d/, 否定式 would not, 缩略式 wouldn't /ˈwʊdnt/] 1 (a) (表示一件设想事情的结果): *If he shaved his beard off, he ~ look much younger.* 他如果把胡子刮去,就显得年轻多了. (b) (用以提出客气的请求): *W~ you open a window, please?* 请您开一扇窗,好吗? 2 (用以提出一个意见): *I ~ think the film will last about 90 minutes.* 我想这电影大约需要 90 分钟左右. 3 (用以提出建议或邀请): *W~ you like a sandwich?* 您想吃三明治吗? 4 (用以表达合意的做法): *I'd love a cup of coffee.* 我倒想喝一杯咖啡. ˈwould-be *adj* 希望成为…的 xīwàng

W

chéngwéi… de: *a ~-be artist* 即将成为艺术家的人.

would[2] *pt* of WILL[1].

wouldn't 1 would not ⇨ WILL[1]. 2 would not ⇨ WOULD[1].

wound[1] /wuːnd/ *n* [C] 伤〔傷〕shāng; 伤口 shāngkǒu: *a bullet ~* 枪伤. **wound** *v* [T] 1 使受伤 shǐ shòushāng; 伤害 shānghài. 2 伤害(某人的感情等) shānghài.

wound[2] *pt, pp* of WIND[2].

wove *pt* of WEAVE.

woven *pp* of WEAVE.

wow /waʊ/ *interj* [非正式用语](用以表示惊奇或钦佩)嚄! huō!

wrangle /ˈræŋgl/ *v* [I] *n* [C] 争吵 zhēngchǎo; 口角 kǒujiǎo.

wrap /ræp/ *v* [-pp-] [T] 1 缠〔纏〕绕〔繞〕chánrào; 包 bāo; 裹 guǒ: *~ (up) a parcel* 捆好一个包裹. *W~ a cloth round your leg.* 把你的腿用布缠起来. 2 [习语] **be wrapped up in sb/sth** [非正式用语]被隐〔隱〕藏于…之中 bèi yǐncáng yú…zhī zhōng. 3[短语动词] **wrap (sb/oneself) up** 给…穿上暖和的衣服 gěi…chuānshàng nuǎnhuo de yīfu. **wrap sth up** [非正式用语]完成(任务) wánchéng; 签〔簽〕订(协议) qiāndìng. **wrap** *n* [C]外套 wàitào; 罩件(如围巾、披风等) zhàojiàn. **wrapper** *n* [C] 包装〔裝〕纸 bāozhuāngzhǐ. **wrapping** *n* [C, U] 包装材料 bāozhuāng cáiliào.

wrath /rɒθ; *US* ræθ/ *n* [U] [正式用语][旧] 怒火 nùhuǒ; 暴怒 bàonù.

wreak /riːk/ *v* [T] [正式用语]使遭受打击〔擊〕shǐ zāoshòu dǎjī.

wreath /riːθ/ *n* [C] [*pl* ~s /riːðz/] 花圈 huāquān; 花环〔環〕huāhuán.

wreathe /riːð/ *v* [T](*in/with*) [正式用语][常用被动语态]覆盖〔蓋〕fùgài; 包围〔圍〕bāowéi: *hills ~d in mist* 隐藏在雾中的群山.

wreck /rek/ *n* [C] 1 破坏〔壞〕pòhuài; (尤指船只等)失事 shīshì. 2 失事的船只等 shīshìde chuánzhī děng. 3 [非正式用语]健康极〔極〕度受损的人 jiànkāng jídù shòusǔnde rén. **wreck** *v* [T] 破坏 pòhuài; 使失事 shǐ shīshì: *The train had been ~ed by vandals.* 那列火车已被坏人破坏了. [喻] *The weather ~ed all our plans.* 天气恶劣, 我们的计划全毁了. **wreckage** *n* [U] (被毁物的)残〔殘〕骸 cánhái.

wren /ren/ *n* [C] [动物]鹪鹩 jiāoliáo.

wrench /rentʃ/ *v* [T] 1 猛扭 měng niǔ; 猛拉 měng lā: *~ a door open* 用力把门拉开. 2 扭伤〔傷〕(足踝等) niǔshāng. **wrench** *n* 1 [C] 猛扭 měng niǔ; 猛拉 měng lā. 2 [C] [美语]扳手 bānshǒu. 3 [sing] (离别时的)一阵悲痛 yízhèn bēitòng.

wrestle /ˈresl/ *v* [I] 1 (*with*) 摔跤 shuāijiāo; 角力 jiǎolì. 2 *with* (为对付某事物而)斗〔鬥〕争 dòuzhēng; 努力 nǔlì. **wrestler** *n* [C] 摔跤运〔運〕动〔動〕员 shuāijiāo yùndòngyuán.

wretch /retʃ/ *n* [C] 不幸的人 búxìngde rén; 可怜〔憐〕的人 kěliánde rén.

wretched /ˈretʃɪd/ *adj* 1 极〔極〕不愉快的 jí bù yú kuài de: *His stomach-ache made him feel ~.* 他胃痛得十分难受. 2 使人苦恼〔惱〕的 shǐ rén kǔnǎo de; 令人难〔難〕受的 lìng rén nánshòu de. 3[非正式用语]恶〔惡〕劣的 èliède; 该死的 gāisǐde: *That ~ dog!* 那只该死的狗! **wretchedly** *adv.* **wretchedness** *n* [U].

wriggle /ˈrɪgl/ *v* 1 [I, T] 蠕动〔動〕rúdòng; 扭动 niǔdòng; 蜿蜒而行 wānyán ér xíng: *Stop wriggling and sit still!* 不要扭来扭去, 坐着别动! 2[短语动词] **wriggle out of doing sth** [非正式用语]避免做(讨厌的工作) bìmiǎn zuò. **wriggle** *n*[C].

wring /rɪŋ/ *v* [*pt, pp* **wrung** /rʌŋ/] [T] 1(*out*) 拧〔擰〕níng; 绞出(液体) jiǎochū. 2 [喻]费力(从某人处)榨出(金钱等) fèilì zhàchū. 3 拧(鸟的脖子) níng. 4[习语] ˌ**wring one's** ˈ**hands** 扭(或搓)手(表示悲痛等) niǔ shǒu. ˌ**wringing** ˈ**wet** 湿〔濕〕得可拧出水来的 shīde kě níngchū shuǐ lái de. **wringer** *n* [C] 甩干〔乾〕机〔機〕shuǎigānjī.

wrinkle /ˈrɪŋkl/ *n* [C, 常作 pl] (皮肤的)皱〔皺〕纹 zhòuwén. **wrinkle** *v* [I, T] (使)起皱纹 qǐ zhòuwén. **wrinkly** *adj.*

wrist /rɪst/ *n* [C] 腕 wàn; 腕关〔關〕节〔節〕wànguānjié. ˈ**wrist-watch** *n* [C]手表〔錶〕shǒubiǎo.

writ /rɪt/ *n* [C] (法院的)令状〔狀〕lìngzhuàng.

write /raɪt/ *v* [*pt* **wrote** /rəʊt/, *pp* **written** /ˈrɪtn/] 1 [I, T] 书〔書〕写〔寫〕shūxiě; 写字 xiě zì. 2 [T] 写出 xiěchū; 填写 tiánxiě: *~ a report/book* 写出一份报告(或一本书). 3 [I, T] 写信并寄出 xiě xìn bìng jìchū: *She promised to ~ to me every week.* 她答应每星期给我写信. 4 [T] 填写(文件, 表格) tiánxiě: *~ a cheque* 开出支票. 5 [习语] **be written all over sb's** ˈ**face** 形之于色 xíng zhī yú sè; 脸〔臉〕上流露出 liǎnshàng liúlù chū. 6 [短语动词] **write sth down** 写下 xiěxià; 记下 jìxià. **write off/away(to sb/sth)** 给…写信订购〔購〕(或讯问等) gěi…xiě xìn dìnggòu. **write sb/sth off** (a) 认〔認〕为〔爲〕…无〔無〕用(或失败) rènwéi…wúyòng. (b) 严〔嚴〕重损坏〔壞〕yánzhòng sǔnhuài; 报〔報〕废〔廢〕bàofèi. (c) 勾销(债务) gōuxiāo; 注销 zhùxiāo. **write sth out** 全部写出 quánbù xiěchū. **write sth up** 详细写出 xiángxì xiěchū. ˈ**write-off** *n* [C] 严重损毁(不值得修理)的车辆 yánzhòng sǔnhuǐ de chēliàng. ˈ**write-up** *n* [C] (事件

的)记录〔錄〕 jìlù；报道 bàodào.

writer /ˈraɪtə(r)/ *n* [C] 1 书〔書〕写〔寫〕人 shūxiěrén. 2 作家 zuòjiā；作者 zuòzhě.

writhe /raɪð/ *v* [I] (因痛苦而)翻滚 fāngǔn；折腾 zhēteng.

writing /ˈraɪtɪŋ/ *n* 1 [U] 书〔書〕写〔寫〕 shūxiě；文件 wénjiàn. 2 [U]字迹〔跡〕 zìjì；笔〔筆〕迹 bǐjì. 3 **writings**[pl] (某作家的)作品 zuòpǐn；著作 zhùzuò. ˈ**writing-paper** *n* [U] 信纸 xìnzhǐ.

written *pp* of WRITE.

wrong /rɒŋ; *US* rɔːŋ/ *adj* 1 不道德的 bú dàodé de；不正当〔當〕的 bú zhèngdàng de；非法的 fēifǎde：*It is ~ to steal.* 偷窃是不道德的. 2 错误的 cuòwùde；不正确〔確〕的 bú zhèngquè de：*a ~ answer* 错误的答案. *prove that sb is ~* 证实某人是错误的. 3 不适〔適〕合的 bú shìhé de；并非最合意的 bìngfēi zuì héyì de：*catch the ~ train* 搭错了火车. 4 有故障的 yǒu gùzhàng de；有毛病的 yǒu máobìng de：*What's ~ with the engine?* 发动机出什么故障了? **wrong** *adv* 1 错误地 cuòwùde：*You've spelt my name ~.* 你把我的名字拼错了. 2[习语] **go ˈwrong** (a) 犯错误 fàn cuòwù. (b) (机器)出故障 chū gùzhàng. (c) 结果不好 jiéguǒ bùhǎo；失败 shībài. **wrong** *n* 1 [U] 罪恶〔惡〕 zuì'è；坏〔壞〕事 huàishì：*know the difference between right and ~* 懂得是与非. 2 [C][正式用语] 非正义〔義〕的行为〔爲〕 fēi zhèngyì de xíngwéi；不公正的事 bù gōngzhèng de shì. 3[习语] **in the ˈwrong** 对〔對〕错误负责 duì cuòwù fùzé；有罪 yǒu zuì. **on the wrong ˈtrack** ⇨ TRACK. **wrong** *v* [T] 对…不公正 duì…bù gōngzhèng；冤屈 yuānqū. ˈ**wrongdoer** *n* [C] 做坏事的人 zuò huàishì de rén. ˈ**wrongdoing** *n* [U]. **wrongful** *adj* 不公正的 bù gōngzhèng de；不公平的 bùgōngpíng de；不正当〔當〕的 búzhèngdàng de；非法的 fēifǎde：*~ful dismissal (from a job)* 非法解雇. **wrongfully** *adv*. **wrongly** *adv*.

wrote *pt* of WRITE.

wrought iron /ˌrɔːt ˈaɪən/ *n* [U] 熟(或锻)铁〔鐵〕 shútiě.

wrung *pt*, *pp* of WRING.

wry /raɪ/ *adj* 1 嘲笑的 cháoxiàode；揶揄的 yéyúde：*a ~ smile* 嘲弄的微笑. 2 扭歪的 niǔwāide；歪斜的 wāixiéde：*a ~ face* 鬼脸. **wryly** *adv*.

WTO /ˌdʌbljuː tiː ˈəʊ/ *abbr* World Trade Organisation 世贸组织〔織〕Shìmào Zǔzhī；世界贸易组织 Shìjiè Màoyì Zǔzhī.

WWW /ˌdʌbljuː dʌbljuː ˈdʌbljuː/ *abbr* World Wide Web 万〔萬〕维网〔網〕 Wànwéiwǎng.

Y

X x

X, x /eks/ *n* [C] [*pl* **X's, x's** /ˈeksɪz/] 1 英语的第二十四个〔個〕字母 Yīngyǔde dì'èrshísìge zìmǔ. 2 罗〔羅〕马数〔數〕字十 (X) Luómǎ shùzì shí. 3[数学]第一个未知数 dìyīgè wèizhīshù.

xenophobia /ˌzenəˈfəʊbɪə/ *n* [U] 对〔對〕外国人(或事物)的憎恨或畏惧〔懼〕 duì wàiguórén de zēnghèn huò wèijù.

Xerox /ˈzɪərɒks/ *n* [C] [专利] (a) 复〔複〕印机〔機〕 fùyìnjī. (b) 影印件 yǐngyìnjiàn. **xerox** *v* [T] 影印 yǐngyìn；复印 fùyìn.

Xmas /ˈkrɪsməs, ˈeksməs/ *n* [U, C] [非正式用语]圣〔聖〕诞节〔節〕 Shèngdànjié.

X-ray /ˈeks reɪ/ *n* [C] (a) X射线〔綫〕 X shèxiàn；X光 X guāng. (b) X光照片 X guāng zhàopiàn：*a chest ~* 胸部X光照片. **X-ray** *v* [T] 用X光检〔檢〕查(或治疗) yòng X guāng jiǎnchá.

xylophone /ˈzaɪləfəʊn/ *n* [C] [音乐]木琴 mùqín.

Y y

Y, y /waɪ/ *n* [C] [*pl* **Y's, y's** /waɪz/] 英语的第二十五个〔個〕字母 Yīngyǔde dì'èrshíwǔgè zìmǔ. **Y-fronts** *n* [pl] [英国专利]男用内裤 nán yòng nèikù.

yacht /jɒt/ *n* [C] 1(竞赛用)小帆船 xiǎo fānchuán；快艇 kuàitǐng. 2 游艇 yóutǐng. **yachting** *n* [U] 驾驶快艇的技术〔術〕jiàshǐ kuàitǐng de jìshù.

yam /jæm/ *n* [C] 山药〔藥〕 shānyào；薯蓣属〔屬〕植物 shǔyùshǔ zhíwù.

Yank /jæŋk/ *n* [C] [英国非正式用语][贬]美国〔國〕佬 Měiguólǎo.

yank /jæŋk/ *v* [I, T] 突然猛拉 tūrán měnglā.

yap /jæp/ *v* [-pp-] [I]1(狗)狂吠 kuángfèi. 2 [非正式用语]吵嚷 chǎorǎng；瞎扯 xiāchě.

yard[1] /jɑːd/ *n* [C] 码(=3英尺, 0.914米) mǎ. ˈ**yardstick** *n* [C] [喻]衡量的标〔標〕准〔準〕 héngliángde biāozhǔn.

yard[2] /jɑːd/ *n* [C] 1 院子 yuànzi. 2 场〔場〕地 chǎngdì：*a ˈship-~* 船坞.

yarn /jɑːn/ *n* 1 [U] 纱线〔綫〕 shāxiàn. 2 [C] [非正式用语]故事 gùshì；奇谈 qítán.

yawn /jɔːn/ *v* [I] 1 打哈欠 dǎ hāqian. 2 张〔張〕开〔開〕 zhāngkāi；裂开 lièkāi：*a ~ing gap* 敞开的裂口. **yawn** *n* [C]打哈欠 dǎ hāqian.

yd *abbr* [*pl* ~s] = yard[1] 码 mǎ.

yeah /jeə/ *interj* [非正式用语]是! shì!

year /jɪə(r)，亦读 jɜː(r)/ *n* [C] **1**(太阳)年 nián. **2**(历)年 nián. **3** 一年 yìnián: *the financial / school* ~ 财政(或学习)年度. **4**[习语] ˌ**all (the) year ˈround** 一年到头〔頭〕yìnián dàotóu. **year ˈin, year ˌout; year after ˈyear** 年复〔復〕一年地 nián fù yì nián de; 年年 nián nián. **yearly** *adj, adv* 每年 měinián; 一年一次的(地) yìnián yícì de.

yearn /jɜːn/ *v* [I] *for; to* 想念 xiǎngniàn; 渴望 kěwàng: *He ~ed for his home*. 他想家了. **yearning** *n* [C, U] 怀〔懷〕念 huáiniàn; 渴望 kěwàng.

yeast /jiːst/ *n* [C, U] 酵母 jiàomǔ.

yell /jel/ *v* [I, T] 叫喊 jiàohǎn; 叫嚷 jiàorǎng. **yell** *n* [C] 大喊 dàhǎn; 大叫 dàjiào.

yellow /ˈjeləʊ/ *adj* **1**(颜色)黄的 huáng de. **2**[非正式用语][贬]胆〔膽〕怯的 dǎnqiède; 卑鄙的 bēibǐde. **yellow** *v* [I, T] (使)变〔變〕黄色 biàn huángsè: *The papers had ~ed with age*. 纸张因年久而发黄. **yellowish** *adj* 淡黄色的 dàn huángsè de. ˌ**yellow ˈpages** *n* [sing 或 pl v] (电话簿中的)黄页 huángyè.

yelp /jelp/ *v* [I], *n* [C] (因痛苦,愤怒等)叫喊 jiàohǎn.

yen[1] /jen/ *n* [C] [*pl* **yen**] 圆(日本货币单位) yuán.

yen[2] /jen/ *n* [常作 sing] [非正式用语]渴望 kěwàng; 热〔熱〕望 rèwàng: *a ~ to visit India* 想去印度观光.

yes /jes/ *interj* 是 shì; 是的 shìde: *Y~, I'll come with you*. 是的,我愿意跟你们在一起. **yes** *n* [C] (表示同意,肯定,接受等的答复)是 shì; 赞成 zànchéng.

yesterday /ˈjestədɪ, -deɪ/ *adv, n* [U] **1** (在)昨天 zuótiān. **2** 不久以前 bùjiǔ yǐqián.

yet /jet/ *adv* **1** 到此时〔時〕dào cǐshí; 到那时 dào nàshí: *They haven't come ~*. 他们至今尚未来过. **2** 不久的将〔將〕来 bùjiǔde jiānglái; 早晚 zǎowǎn: *She may surprise us all ~*. 她总有一天会使我们吃惊的. **3** 更 gèng; 更加 gèngjiā: *~ another government report* 另一个政府工作报告. **4** 还〔還〕hái; 尚 shàng; 仍然 réngrán: *I have ~ to meet him*. 我还没有见到他. **5**[习语] **as ˈyet** 到目前为〔為〕止 dào mùqián wéizhǐ; 到当〔當〕时为止 dào dāngshí wéizhǐ. **yet** *conj* 然而 rán'ér; 可是 kěshì: *a clever ~ simple idea* 一个聪明的然而是简单的主意.

yew (亦作 ˈ**yew-tree**) /juː/ *n* [C] [植物]紫杉 zǐshān.

Y-fronts ⇨Y, y.

yield /jiːld/ *v* **1** [T] 产〔產〕生 chǎnshēng; 生长〔長〕出 shēngzhǎngchū: *The tax increase would ~ £10 million a year*. 增税将每年提供一千万英镑. **2** [I] (*to*) [正式用语]屈服 qūfú; 让〔讓〕步 ràngbù: *~ to temptation* 禁不住诱惑. **3** [T] [正式用语]放弃〔棄〕对〔對〕…的控制 fàngqì duì…de kòngzhì. **yield** *n* [C] 产量 chǎnliàng; 收获〔獲〕量 shōuhuòliàng: *a ~ of three tonnes of wheat per hectare* 每公顷小麦产量三吨. **yielding** *adj* **1** 易弯〔彎〕曲的 yì wānqū de. **2**[喻]顺从〔從〕的 shùncóngde; 不固执〔執〕的 bú gùzhí de.

yippee /ˈjɪpiː/ *interj* [非正式用语](用以表示愉快或兴奋)好啊! hǎo'a!

yodel /ˈjəʊdl/ *v* [-ll-; 美语 -l-] [I, T] 用真假嗓音交替而唱 yòng zhēn jiǎ sǎngyīn jiāotì ér chàng.

yoga /ˈjəʊgə/ *n* [U] 瑜伽(古代印度哲学的一派) yújiā.

yoghurt /ˈjɒgət; *US* ˈjəʊgərt/ *n* [U, C] 酸乳酪 suān rǔlào.

yoke /jəʊk/ *n* **1** [C] 牛轭 niú'è. **2** [sing] [正式用语][喻]束缚 shùfù; 羁绊 jībàn; 奴役 núyì: *free from the ~ of slavery* 从奴隶制的枷锁下解放出来.

yokel /ˈjəʊkl/ *n* [C] [谑或贬] 乡〔鄉〕下佬 xiāngxiàlǎo.

yolk /jəʊk/ *n* [C, U] 蛋黄 dànhuáng.

yonder /ˈjɒndə(r)/ *adj, adv* [古]那边〔邊〕的 nàbiānde; 远〔遠〕处〔處〕的 yuǎnchùde; 在那边 zài nàbiān; 在远处 zài yuǎnchù.

you /juː/ *pron* **1** 你 nǐ; 你们〔們〕nǐmen. **2**[非正式用语]任何人 rènhé rén: *It's easier to cycle with the wind behind ~*. 顺着风骑车省力.

you'd /juːd/ **1** you had ⇨HAVE. **2** you would⇨WILL[1], WOULD[1].

you'll /juːl/ you will ⇨WILL[1].

young /jʌŋ/ *adj* [~**er** /-ŋgə(r)/, ~**est** /-ŋgɪst/] 年轻〔輕〕的 niánqīngde; 幼小的 yòuxiǎode; 初期的 chūqīde: *a ~ woman/nation* 年轻的妇女(或国家). **young** *n* [pl] **1** (鸟兽的)仔 zǎi; 雏〔雛〕chú. **2 the young** 年轻人 niánqīngrén; 青年们 qīngniánmen. **youngish** *adj* 相当〔當〕年轻的 xiāngdāng niánqīngde. **youngster** /-stə(r)/ *n* [C]年轻人 niánqīngrén;孩子 háizi.

your /jɔː(r); *US* jʊər/ *adj* 你的 nǐde; 你们〔們〕的 nǐmende: *How old are ~ children?* 你的孩子们多大了? **yours** /jɔːz; *US* jʊərz/ *pron* **1** 你的 nǐde; 你们的 nǐmende: *Is that book ~s?* 那本书是你的吗? **2**(常作 **yours**)(用于书信的结尾): *Y~s faithfully / sincerely/ truly* (相当于中文书信结尾的"谨上")你的忠实的….

you're /jʊə(r), 亦读 jɔː(r)/ you are ⇨BE.

Y

yourself /jɔːˈself; *US* jʊərˈself/ *pron* [*pl* **-selves** /-ˈselvz/] 1(反身)你自己 nǐ zìjǐ: *Have you hurt* ~? 你弄伤(自己)了吗? 2 (用以加强语气)你亲〔親〕自 nǐ qīnzì; 你本人 nǐ běnrén: *You told me so* ~. 你亲自对我说的. 3[习语] (**all**) **by yourˈself/yourˈselves** (a) 单〔單〕独〔獨〕dāndú; 独自 dúzì. (b) 全靠自己 quán kào zìjǐ; 独力 dúlì.

youth /juːθ/ *n* [*pl* ~s /juːðz/] 1 [U]青春 qīngchūn; 青年时〔時〕期 qīngnián shíqī: *in my* ~ 我年轻的时候. 2 [C] 青年 qīngnián; 少年 shàonián. 3 (亦作 **the youth**) [亦作 sing, 用 pl v] 青年人(总称) qīngniánrén. **youthful** *adj* 年轻〔輕〕的 niánqīngde; 似年轻的 sì niánqīng de. ˈ**youth hostel** *n* [C] 青年招待所 qīngnián zhāodàisuǒ.

you've /juːv/ you have ⇨HAVE.

yuck /jʌk/ *interj* [非正式用语](用以表示厌恶、反感等)啐! cuì!

yule /juːl/ *n* [U] [古]圣〔聖〕诞节〔節〕Shèngdànjié.

yuppie /ˈjʌpɪ/ *n* [C] [非正式用语]雅皮士(年轻有为的专业人士) yǎpíshì.

yurt /jɜːt/ *n* [C] 蒙古包 měnggǔbāo; 毡〔氈〕房 zhānfáng.

Z z

Z, z /zed; *US* ziː/ *n* [C] [*pl* **Z's, z's** /zeds; *US* ziːz/] 英语的第二十六个〔個〕字母 Yīngyǔde dì'èrshíliùgè zìmǔ.

zany /ˈzeɪnɪ/ *adj* [**-ier, -iest**] [非正式用语]滑稽的 huájīde; 傻〔傻〕的 shǎde.

zap /zæp/ *v* [T] 消灭〔滅〕xiāomiè; 消除 xiāochú; 擦除 cāchú. ˈ**zapper** *n* [C] 1 [非正式用语] (电视等的)遥控器 yáokòngqì. 2 [美语] 灭〔滅〕虫〔蟲〕器 mièchóngqì.

zeal /ziːl/ *n* [U] [正式用语]热〔熱〕心 rèxīn; 热情 rèqíng. **zealous** /ˈzeləs/ *adj* 热心的 rèxīnde; 热情的 rèqíngde.

zealot /ˈzelət/ *n* [C] [有时贬](尤指宗教, 政治上的)狂热〔熱〕者 kuángrèzhě.

zebra /ˈzebrə, ˈziːbrə/ *n* [C] [动物]斑马 bānmǎ. ˌ**zebra** ˈ**crossing** *n* [C] 人行横道线〔綫〕rén xíng héngdàoxiàn.

zenith /ˈzenɪθ/ *n* [C] (名誉、幸运等的)顶峰 dǐngfēng.

zero /ˈzɪərəʊ/ *pron, adj, n* [C] [*pl* ~s]1 零 líng. 2 最低点〔點〕zuìdīdiǎn; 无〔無〕wú. 3 (刻度上的)零位 língwèi: *The temperature was ten degrees below* ~. 温度为零下 10 度. **zero** *v* [短语动词] **zero in on sth** 瞄准〔準〕miáozhǔn. ˈ**zero-hour** *n* [U] (尤指军事行动)开〔開〕始时〔時〕刻 kāishǐ shíkè.

zest /zest/ *n* 1 [U, sing] (a) (极大的)兴〔興〕趣 xìngqù; 乐〔樂〕趣 lèqù; 热〔熱〕情 rèqíng. (b) 所增加的兴趣(或魅力)(的性质) suǒ zēngjiā de xìngqù. 2 [U] 橙子(或柠檬)的外皮 chéngzide wàipí.

zigzag /ˈzɪgzæg/ *n* [C] 之字形(线条、道路等) zhīzìxíng; 锯齿〔齒〕形物 jùchǐxíng wù. **zigzag** *v* [**-gg-**] [I] 曲折地前进〔進〕qūzhéde qiánjìn: *The path* ~*s up the cliff*. 这条小径曲曲折折地向峭壁延伸.

zinc /zɪŋk/ *n* [U] [化学]锌 (Zn) xīn.

zip (亦作 **zip-fastener**) /zɪp/ *n* [C] 拉链 lāliàn; 拉锁 lāsuǒ. **zip** *v* [**-pp-**] [T] 用拉链拉开〔開〕或扣上 yòng lāliàn lākāi huò kòushàng. **Zip code** *n* [C] [美语]邮〔郵〕政编码 yóuzhèng biānmǎ. **zipper** *n* [C] [尤用于美语] = zip.

zither /ˈzɪðə(r)/ *n* [C] 齐〔齊〕特儿〔兒〕琴 qítèr qín.

zodiac /ˈzəʊdɪæk/ *n* **the zodiac** [sing] [天文]黄道带〔帶〕huángdàodài.

zombie /ˈzɒmbɪ/ *n* [C] [非正式用语]麻木不仁(或不动脑筋)的人 mámù bùrén de rén.

zone /zəʊn/ *n* [C] (有某特点或用途的)区〔區〕域(或范围) qūyù: *a time* ~ 时区. *a nuclear-free* ~ 无核区.

zoo /zuː/ *n* [C] [*pl* ~s] 动〔動〕物园〔園〕dòngwùyuán.

zoology /zəʊˈɒlədʒɪ/ *n* [U] 动〔動〕物学〔學〕dòngwùxué. **zoological** /ˌzəʊəˈlɒdʒɪkl/ *adj*. **zoologist** *n* [C] 动物学家 dòngwùxuéjiā.

zoom /zuːm/ *v* [I] 1(嗡嗡或隆隆地)疾行 jíxíng. 2 [喻] [非正式用语]猛涨〔漲〕měngzhǎng; 急升 jíshēng. 3[短语动词] **zoom in/out**(镜头)移近(或移远)目标〔標〕yíjìn mùbiāo. ˈ**zoom lens** *n* [C] 可变〔變〕焦距镜头〔頭〕kěbiàn jiāojù jìngtóu.

zucchini /zʊˈkiːnɪ/ *n* [C] [*pl* **zucchini** 或 ~s] [尤用于美语]小胡瓜 xiǎo húguā.

汉 英 词 典

Chinese-English Dictionary

用 法 说 明
GUIDE TO THE USE OF THE DICTIONARY

一、条目 ENTRIES

1. 本词典所收单字(打头字)条目按汉语拼音字母次序排列。同音同调的单字按起笔丶(点)一(横)丨(直)丿(撇)乛(折,包括亅乚𠃍𡿨等笔形)的顺序排列。 Single-character entries are arranged in alphabetical order of pinyin romanization (i. e. hanyu pinyin). Characters identical in romanization and tone are arranged according to their first stroke, in the following order: 丶 dot, 一 horizontal, 丨 vertical, 丿 left-falling and 乛 turning stroke (including 亅乚𠃍𡿨).

2. 多字条目按第一个字分别列于单字条目之下。各多字条目亦按汉语拼音字母次序排列。 Multiple-character entries are grouped by their first character and listed under the corresponding single-character entries in alphabetical order of pinyin romanization (i. e. hanyu pinyin).

3. 简化汉字除"讠""门""纟""贝""见""钅""饣""车""马""鱼""页""风""齿""鸟"等常用偏旁构成的字外,在圆括号(　)内注明繁体字。单字条目中,如果只是某一义项需标繁体字,则在该义项号码后用黑体标出。 Simplified characters are followed by their orthodox version in round brackets (　), except those formed by common simplified radicals like "讠""门""纟""贝""见""钅""饣""车""马""鱼""页""风""齿""鸟" etc. In a single-character entry, if the orthodox version of the character only exists in one of the meanings, it is printed in bold type following the number of the corresponding meaning.

二、注音 PHONETIC NOTATION

1. 汉语拼音的声调符号(ˉ阴平,ˊ阳平,ˇ上声,ˋ去声)标在音节的主要母音上。轻声不标符号。 Symbols of tones (ˉ first tone or *yinping* , ˊ second tone or *yangping* , ˇ third tone or *shangsheng* , ˋ fourth tone or *qusheng*) are given above the main vowel of Chinese syllables. This does not apply to a light tone.

2. 儿化音在词的基本读音后加"r"。 Showing a nonsyllabic "r" as a suffix means you should add an "r" sound to the preceding syllable.

3. 单字另有其他不同读音时，在该条目最后（另起一行）注明"see also..."。 A single-character with more than one pronunciation will have a note (starting another line) "see also..." at the end of that entry.

三、释义 MEANINGS

1. 单字和复词条目（除结构形式和成语词组外）尽可能注明语法词类，词类略语套以圆括号（ ）。 Parts of speech and abbreviations are given for single and multiple-character entries (except structural patterns and idioms) whenever possible.

2. 不同词类，除少数可以合并释义者外，用罗马数字分开，并分项进行释义。 Headwords with different parts of speech are translated separately, divided by Roman numerals, except for some cases which can be combined in one meaning.

3. 条目一般用英语对应词释义。有些条目注有语法特征、使用范围等的说明，以方括号[ ]表示。 Entries are usually translated by their English equivalents. In some entries, grammatical information, subject fields, etc. are also given. They appear in square brackets [ ].

4. 修辞略语套以尖括号〈 〉。 Abbreviations of rhetorical devices are given in angle brackets〈 〉.

5. 汉语特有名词（无英语对应词）用汉语拼音（不加调号）对译，并用斜体字表示。 Special Chinese nouns with no English equivalents are rendered in Chinese pinyin (with no tonal symbols) and shown in italics.

四、检字法 INDEXING SYSTEM

本词典正文前有部首检字表。检字方法：①根据字的部首在表（一）内查到该部首的号码；②在表（二）内按部首号码和字的笔画（字的笔画数不含其部首）查到该字的汉语拼音。 This dictionary provides an indexing system at the beginning of the Chinese-English section on pages 4 to 5. Searching method: ① identify the radical and note the number located next to it; ② use this number to find the radical and its derivatives (according to the number of strokes) in the table on pages 5 to 33. This will give you the pinyin romanization (i.e. hanyu pinyin) and direct you to the correct entry.

略 语 表
ABBREVIATIONS

(名)名词 noun
(形)形容词 adjective
(介)介词 preposition
(代)代词 pronoun
(量)量词 measure word
(连)连词 conjunction
(动)动词 verb
(副)副词 adverb
(数)数词 numeral
(叹)叹词 interjection
(象)象声词 onomatopoeia
(助)助词 particle

〈口〉口语 colloquial
〈旧〉旧时用语 archaic
〈套〉套语 polite formula
〈书〉书面语 literary
〈贬〉贬义 derogatory
〈简〉简称 abbreviation
〈婉〉婉辞 euphemism
〈敬〉敬辞 polite expression
〈谦〉谦辞 humble expression

部首检字表
RADICAL INDEX

(一) 部首目录

部首左边的号码表示部首的次序

123 矢
124 禾
125 白
126 瓜
127 鸟(鳥)
128 用
氺（见水）
129 矛
聿（见肀）
艮（见艮）
130 疋(⺪)
131 皮
母（见毋）

六　画

132 衣
133 羊(⺶ ⺷)
134 米
135 耒
136 老
137 耳
138 臣
139 西(覀)
140 页(頁)
141 虍
142 虫
143 缶
144 舌
145 竹(⺮)
146 臼
147 自
148 血
149 舟
150 羽
聿（见肀）
151 艮(艮)
152 糸(糹 见纟)

七　画

153 辛
154 言(訁 见讠)
155 麦(麥)
156 走
157 赤
158 豆
車（见车）
159 酉
160 辰
161 豕
162 卤(鹵)
163 里
貝（见贝）
見（见见）
164 足(⻊)
165 豸
166 谷
167 釆
168 身
169 角

八　画

170 青
171 其
172 雨(⻗)
173 齿(齒)
飠（见饣）

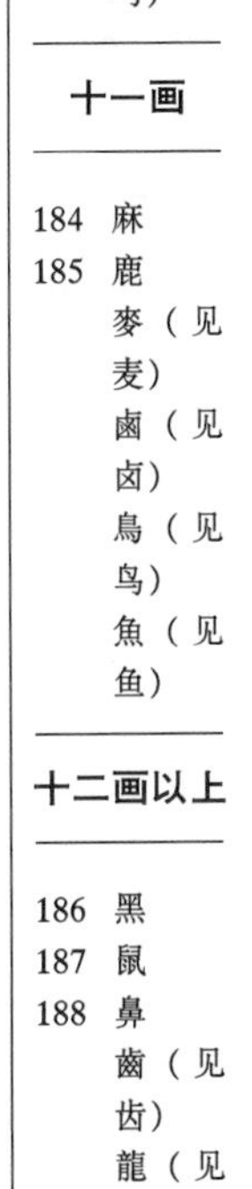

174 金（釒 见钅）
175 隹
176 鱼(魚)
門（见门）

九　画

177 音
178 革
頁（见页）
179 骨
180 食（飠 见饣）
181 鬼
風（见风）
韋（见韦）

十　画

182 鬥
183 髟
馬（见马）

十一画

184 麻
185 鹿
麥（见麦）
鹵（见卤）
鳥（见鸟）
魚（见鱼）

十二画以上

186 黑
187 鼠
188 鼻
齒（见齿）
龍（见龙）

(二) 检字表

(1) 丶部

义 yì
丫 yā
丸 wán
之 zhī
为 wéi; wèi
头 tóu; tou
主 zhǔ
半 bàn
州 zhōu
农 nóng
良 liáng
举 jǔ
叛 pàn

(2) 一部

一 yī

一至二画

七 qī
丁 dīng
三 sān
干 gān; gàn
于 yú
下 xià; xia
上 shàng; shang
丈 zhàng
万 wàn
与 yǔ; yù
才 cái

三画

丰 fēng
天 tiān
夫 fū
开 kāi
井 jǐng
无 wú
专 zhuān
丐 gài
五 wǔ
不 bù
丑 chǒu
屯 tún
互 hù
牙 yá

四画

平 píng
击 jī
未 wèi
末 mò
正 zhēng; zhèng
甘 gān
世 shì
且 qiě
可 kě; kè
丙 bǐng
册 cè
东 dōng
丝 sī

五画

夹 gā; jiā; jiá
亚 yà
再 zài
吏 lì
百 bǎi
而 ér
丞 chéng

六画

来 lái
严 yán
巫 wū
丽 lì
甫 fǔ
更 gēng; gèng

十五画以上

(齋) zhāi
(褻) xiè
襄 xiāng
赢 yíng

(7) 冫部

一至五画

习 xí
冲 chōng; chòng
次 cì
决 jué
冰 bīng
冻 dòng
况 kuàng
冷 lěng
冶 yě

六至八画

冽 liè
净 jìng
凉 liáng; liàng
凌 líng
(凍) dòng
凄 qī
准 zhǔn
凋 diāo

九画以上

凑 còu
减 jiǎn
凛 lǐn
凝 níng

(8) 冖部

冗 rǒng
写 xiě
军 jūn
罕 hǎn
冠 guān; guàn
冢 zhǒng
冥 míng
冤 yuān

(9) 讠(言)部

二画

计 jì
订 dìng
讣 fù
认 rèn
讥 jī

三画

讨 tǎo
让 ràng
讯 xùn
讪 shàn
议 yì
讫 qì
训 xùn
记 jì

四画

访 fǎng
讲 jiǎng
讳 huì
讴 ōu
论 lùn
讼 sòng
许 xǔ
讹 é
讽 fěng
设 shè
诀 jué

五画

评 píng
证 zhèng
诃 hē
诅 zǔ
识 shí
诊 zhěn
诈 zhà
诉 sù
诋 dǐ
译 yì
词 cí
诏 zhào

六画

诧 chà
该 gāi
详 xiáng
诨 hún
诓 kuāng
试 shì
诗 shī
诘 jié
(誇) kuā
诙 huī
诚 chéng
诠 quán
诛 zhū
话 huà
诞 dàn
诟 gòu
诡 guǐ
询 xún
诣 yì

七画

说 shuì; shuō
诫 jiè
诬 wū
语 yǔ
误 wù
诱 yòu
诲 huì
诳 kuáng
诵 sòng
(認) rèn

八画

谊 yì
谅 liàng
谆 zhūn
谈 tán
请 qǐng
诸 zhū
诺 nuò
读 dú
诽 fěi
课 kè
(論) lùn
谁 shéi
谀 yú
调 diào; tiáo
谄 chǎn

九画

谛 dì
谙 ān
谚 yàn
谜 mí
谎 huǎng
谋 móu
谍 dié
谏 jiàn
谐 xié
谒 yè
谓 wèi
谗 chán
(諱) huì

十画

谤 bàng
谦 qiān
(講) jiǎng
谟 mó
谣 yáo
谢 xiè

十一画

谪 zhé
谨 jǐn
(謳) ōu
谩 màn
谬 miù

十二画

(識) shí
谰 lán
谱 pǔ
(證) zhèng
谲 jué
(譏) jī

十三至十四画

(議) yì
(護) hù
谴 qiǎn
(譯) yì

十五画以上

(讀) dú
(讓) ràng
(讒) chán

(10) 二部

二 èr
干 gān; gàn
于 yú
亏 kuī
五 wǔ
开 kāi
井 jǐng
专 zhuān
元 yuán
无 wú
云 yún
些 xiē

(11) 十部

十 shí

二至六画

支 zhī
卉 huì
古 gǔ
考 kǎo
毕 bì
华 huá
协 xié
克 kè
卒 zú
丧 sāng; sàng
卓 zhuó
直 zhí
卑 bēi
阜 fù
卖 mài
(協) xié

七至十画

南 nán
真 zhēn
(喪) sāng; sàng
啬 sè
乾 qián
(乾) gān
博 bó

十一画以上

(準) zhǔn
(幹) gàn
(嗇) sè
斡 wò
兢 jīng
翰 hàn

矗 chù

(12) 厂部

厂 chǎng

二至六画

厅 tīng
仄 zè
历 lì
厄 è
厉 lì
压 yā; yà
厌 yàn
励 lì
厕 cè

七至十画

厘 lí
厚 hòu
原 yuán
厢 xiāng
厩 jiù
厥 jué
厨 chú
厦 shà
雁 yàn

十一画以上

斯 sī
(厲) lì
(廠) chǎng
(厭) yàn
(勵) lì
(曆) lì
(歷) lì
赝 yàn
(壓) yā; yà

(13) 匚部

二至五画

区 qū
匹 pǐ
巨 jù
匠 jiàng
医 yī

六画以上

匿 nì
匪 fěi
匾 biǎn
匮 kuì
(區) qū
(匯) huì
颐 yí

(14) 卜(⺊)部

卜 bǔ

二至四画

卡 kǎ; qiǎ
占 zhàn
外 wài
贞 zhēn

五画以上

卦 guà
卧 wò
卓 zhuó
桌 zhuō

(15) 刂部

二至四画

刈 yì
刊 kān
刑 xíng
列 liè
划 huá; huà
刚 gāng
则 zé
创 chuāng; chuàng
刎 wěn

五画

判 pàn
别 bié; biè
利 lì
删 shān
刨 bào; páo

六画

剂 jì
刻 kè
刺 cì
到 dào
刽 guì
刹 chà; shā
制 zhì
刮 guā
剁 duò
刷 shuā; shuà

七画

前 qián
剃 tì
荆 jīng
削 xiāo; xuē
剐 guǎ
剑 jiàn

八画

剜 wān
剖 pōu
(剛) gāng
剔 tī
(剮) guǎ
剥 bāo; bō
剧 jù

九至十一画

副 fù
割 gē
(創) chuāng; chuàng
剩 shèng
剽 piāo
剿 jiǎo

十二画以上

(劃) huá; huà
(劇) jù
(劍) jiàn
(劊) guì
(劑) jì

(16) 冂部

冈 gāng
冉 rǎn
同 tóng
网 wǎng
肉 ròu
罔 wǎng
周 zhōu

(17) 八(丷)部

八 bā

二至五画

公 gōng
分 fēn; fèn
兰 lán
半 bàn
只 zhī; zhǐ
兴 xīng; xìng
关 guān
并 bìng
共 gòng
兑 duì
兵 bīng
弟 dì

六至八画

卷 juǎn; juàn
(並) bìng
具 jù
单 dān
典 diǎn
养 yǎng
前 qián
酋 qiú
首 shǒu
真 zhēn
益 yì
兼 jiān

九至十五画

黄 huáng
兽 shòu
普 pǔ
奠 diàn
曾 céng; zēng
(義) yì
(與) yǔ; yù
(養) yǎng
舆 yú
(興) xīng; xìng

(18) 人(入)部

人 rén
入 rù

一至三画

个 gè
今 jīn
从 cóng
介 jiè
以 yǐ
仓 cāng
令 lǐng; lìng
丛 cóng

四至五画

伞 sǎn
全 quán
会 huì; kuài
合 hé
企 qǐ
众 zhòng
含 hán
余 yú
巫 wū
(夾) gā; jiā; jiá

六至九画

舍 shě; shè
命 mìng
(倉) cāng
拿 ná
龛 kān
盒 hé

十画以上

禽 qín
舒 shū
(傘) sǎn
(會) huì; kuài
(舖) pù
(龕) kān

(19) 亻部

一至二画

亿 yì
仁 rén
什 shén; shí
仆 pú
仇 chóu

仍 réng
化 huā;huà
仅 jǐn

三画

们 men
仕 shì
仗 zhàng
付 fù
代 dài
仙 xiān
仪 yí
仟 qiān
他 tā
仔 zǐ

四画

仿 fǎng
伉 kàng
伙 huǒ
伪 wěi
传 chuán;zhuàn
伟 wěi
休 xiū
伎 jì
伍 wǔ
伏 fú
优 yōu
伐 fá
仲 zhòng
价 jià;jie
伦 lún
份 fèn
件 jiàn
任 rèn
伤 shāng
仰 yǎng
似 shì;sì
伊 yī

五画

位 wèi
住 zhù
伴 bàn
估 gū
体 tǐ
何 hé
(佔) zhàn
但 dàn
伸 shēn
佃 diàn
伶 líng
作 zuō;zuò
伯 bó
佣 yōng;yòng
低 dī
你 nǐ
伺 cì;sì
佛 fó

六画

佼 jiǎo
依 yī
佯 yáng
(併) bìng
侠 xiá
佳 jiā
侍 shì
佶 jí
佬 lǎo
供 gōng;gòng
使 shǐ
佰 bǎi
例 lì
侄 zhí
侥 jiǎo
侦 zhēn
侣 lǚ
侃 kǎn
侧 cè
侩 kuài
侏 zhū
侨 qiáo
侈 chǐ
佩 pèi

七画

信 xìn
俨 yǎn
俪 lì
便 biàn;pián
俩 liǎ
(俠) xiá
俏 qiào
修 xiū
俚 lǐ
保 bǎo
促 cù
俘 fú
俭 jiǎn
俗 sú
侮 wǔ
(係) xì
俑 yǒng
俊 jùn
俟 sì
侵 qīn
侯 hóu

八画

倌 guān
倍 bèi
俯 fǔ
(倣) fǎng
倦 juàn
俸 fèng
债 zhài
借 jiè
值 zhí
(倆) liǎ
倚 yǐ
俺 ǎn
倒 dǎo;dào
倾 qīng
倘 tǎng
(條) tiáo
俱 jù
倡 chàng
(個) gè
候 hòu
(倫) lún
俾 bǐ
健 jiàn
倔 jué;juè

九画

停 tíng
偏 piān
做 zuò
偃 yǎn
偕 xié
偿 cháng
偶 ǒu
偎 wēi
偷 tōu
傀 kuǐ
假 jiǎ;jià
(偉) wěi

十画

傧 bīn
傍 bàng
储 chǔ
傲 ào
(備) bèi
(傑) jié

十一画

(傭) yōng;yòng
(僅) jǐn
(傳) chuán;zhuàn
催 cuī
(傷) shāng
傻 shǎ
像 xiàng

十二画

僧 sēng
(僱) gù
(僥) jiǎo
儆 jǐng
僚 liáo
(僕) pú
(僞) wěi
(僑) qiáo

十三画以上

(億) yì
(儀) yí
僵 jiāng
(價) jià;jie
(儘) jǐn
(儍) shǎ
(儉) jiǎn
(儈) kuài
僻 pì
(儐) bīn
儒 rú
(優) yōu
(償) cháng
(儷) lì
(儼) yǎn

(20) 勹部

一至四画

勺 sháo
匀 yún
勿 wù
勾 gōu;gòu
句 jù
匆 cōng
包 bāo
旬 xún

五画以上

匍 pú
(芻) chú
够 gòu

(21) 儿部

儿 ér
元 yuán
允 yǔn
兄 xiōng
充 chōng
光 guāng
兑 duì
先 xiān
克 kè
(兒) ér
党 dǎng
兜 dōu
兢 jīng

(22) 几(𠘨)部

几 jī;jǐ
凡 fán
凤 fèng
夙 sù
凫 fú
壳 ké;qiào
秃 tū
凯 kǎi
凭 píng
(殼) ké;qiào
(凱) kǎi
(鳳) fèng
凳 dèng

(23) 厶部

允 yǔn

(33)
忄(小)部

一至三画

(37)
门(門)部

门 mén
(門) mén

一至五画

闩 shuān
闪 shǎn
闭 bì
问 wèn
闯 chuǎng
闷 mēn; mèn
闰 rùn
(開) kāi
闲 xián
间 jiān; jiàn
(閒) xián
闹 nào
闸 zhá

六至七画

阂 hé
闺 guī
闻 wén
阀 fá
阁 gé
阅 yuè
阄 jiū

八画以上

阐 chǎn
阉 yān
阎 yán
阔 kuò
阑 lán
阙 què
(關) guān
(闡) chǎn
(鬮) jiū

(38)
辶(辶)部

二至三画

边 biān; bian
辽 liáo
迂 yū
达 dá
迈 mài
过 guò; guo
迅 xùn
迁 qiān
迄 qì
巡 xún

四至五画

这 zhè
进 jìn
远 yuǎn
运 yùn
违 wéi
还 hái; huán
连 lián
近 jìn
返 fǎn
迎 yíng
迟 chí
述 shù
迥 jiǒng
迭 dié
迫 pǎi; pò
迢 tiáo

六画

迹 jì
送 sòng
迸 bèng
迷 mí
逆 nì
逃 táo
选 xuǎn
适 shì
追 zhuī
退 tuì
逊 xùn

七画

(這) zhè
递 dì
逗 dòu
逋 bū
速 sù
逐 zhú
逝 shì
逍 xiāo
逞 chěng
途 tú
造 zào
透 tòu
逢 féng
逛 guàng
通 tōng; tòng

八至十画

逻 luó
(過) guò
逶 wēi
(進) jìn
逸 yì
逮 dǎi; dài
道 dào
遂 suì
(運) yùn
遍 biàn
(達) dá
逼 bī
遇 yù
遏 è
遗 yí
逾 yú
遁 dùn
遐 xiá
(違) wéi
遨 áo
(遠) yuǎn
遣 qiǎn
遥 yáo
(遞) dì
(遜) xùn

十一画以上

(適) shì
遮 zhē
遭 zāo
遛 liù
遴 lín
遵 zūn
(邁) mài
(遷) qiān
(遼) liáo
(遲) chí
(選) xuǎn
遽 jù
(還) hái; huán
邀 yāo
避 bì
邈 miǎo
(邊) biān
邋 lā
(邏) luó

(39)
工部

工 gōng
左 zuǒ
巧 qiǎo
功 gōng
式 shì
巩 gǒng
贡 gòng
巫 wū
攻 gōng
汞 gǒng
差 chā; chà; chāi
项 xiàng

(40)
土部

土 tǔ

二至三画

去 qù
圣 shèng
在 zài
寺 sì
至 zhì
尘 chén
地 de; dì
场 cháng; chǎng

四画

坟 fén
坊 fáng
坑 kēng
坛 tán
社 shè
坏 huài
址 zhǐ
坚 jiān
坝 bà
坐 zuò
坂 bǎn
坍 tān
均 jūn
坎 kǎn
坞 wù
块 kuài
坠 zhuì

五至六画

垃 lā
幸 xìng
坪 píng
坯 pī
垄 lǒng
坦 tǎn
坤 kūn
坡 pō
型 xíng
垮 kuǎ
城 chéng
垫 diàn
垢 gòu
垛 duǒ; duò
垒 lěi
垠 yín
垦 kěn

七至九画

埂 gěng
埋 mái; mán
埃 āi
培 péi
(執) zhí
堵 dǔ
域 yù
基 jī
(堅) jiān
堑 qiàn
堂 táng
堆 duī
埠 bù
堕 duò
(報) bào
堪 kān
塔 tǎ
堤 dī
(場) cháng; chǎng
堡 bǎo
(塊) kuài

十至十二画

(塗) tú
塞 sāi; sài
塘 táng

塑 sù
墓 mù
填 tián
塌 tā
(塢) wù
境 jìng
(塵) chén
墙 qiáng
(墊) diàn
墟 xū
墅 shù
(墜) zhuì
(墮) duò
墩 dūn
增 zēng
(墳) fén
墨 mò

十三画以上

(壇) tán
壅 yōng
(墻) qiáng
(墾) kěn
壁 bì
壕 háo
壑 hè
(壘) lěi
(壟) lǒng
(壞) huài
疆 jiāng
壤 rǎng
(壩) bà

(41) 士部

士 shì

三至四画

壮 zhuàng
志 zhì
吉 jí
壳 ké; qiào
声 shēng
(壯) zhuàng

七画以上

壶 hú
壹 yī
喜 xǐ
(壺) hú
鼓 gǔ
(臺) tái
嘉 jiā
(壽) shòu
(賣) mài

(42) 艹部

一至四画

艺 yì
艾 ài
节 jiē; jié
芒 máng
芝 zhī
芋 yù
芳 fāng
芦 lú
劳 láo
芙 fú
芜 wú
芸 yún
苇 wěi
芽 yá
芬 fēn
苍 cāng
花 huā
芹 qín
芥 jiè
芭 bā
苏 sū

五画

范 fàn
苹 píng
茉 mò
苦 kǔ
苛 kē
若 ruò
茂 mào
苗 miáo
英 yīng
茁 zhuó
苟 gǒu
苞 bāo
茎 jīng
苔 tái
茅 máo
茄 jiā; qié

六画

茫 máng
荡 dàng
荒 huāng
荧 yíng
荣 róng
荤 hūn
荆 jīng
茸 róng
茬 chá
荐 jiàn
草 cǎo
茧 jiǎn
茵 yīn
茴 huí
荟 huì
茶 chá
荏 rěn
荫 yīn; yìn
荔 lì
药 yào

七画

(華) huá
荸 bí
莽 mǎng
莲 lián
(莖) jīng
莫 mò
莴 wō
莠 yǒu
莓 méi
莅 lì
荷 hé; hè
获 huò
(莊) zhuāng

八画

萍 píng
菠 bō
菩 pú
萤 yíng
营 yíng
萦 yíng
菁 jīng
菱 líng
著 zhù
黄 huáng
菲 fěi
萌 méng
萝 luó
菌 jūn; jùn
(萵) wō
菜 cài
萎 wěi
菊 jú
萧 xiāo
菇 gū

九画

落 là; luò
蒂 dì
(韮) jiǔ
(葉) yè
葬 zàng
募 mù
(萬) wàn
董 dǒng
葆 bǎo
葡 pú
葱 cōng
葵 kuí
(葦) wěi

十画

(蒞) lì
蓑 suō
蓄 xù
蒙 mēng; méng; Měng
蒜 suàn
(蓋) gài
蓝 lán
墓 mù
幕 mù
蓦 mò
(夢) mèng
(蒼) cāng
蓖 bì
蓬 péng
蓓 bèi
(蔭) yīn; yìn
蒸 zhēng

十一画

蔗 zhè
蔽 bì
蔼 ǎi
蔷 qiáng
暮 mù
摹 mó
慕 mù
蔓 màn
蔑 miè
蔚 wèi

十二画

(蕩) dàng
蕊 ruǐ
(蕪) wú
蕉 jiāo
蔬 shū
蕴 yùn

十三画

薄 báo; bó
薪 xīn
(薦) jiàn
薮 sǒu
蕾 lěi
(薑) jiāng
(薔) qiáng
(蘋) píng
薯 shǔ
(薈) huì
(獲) huò
(蕭) xiāo

十四至十五画

(藍) lán
藏 cáng; zàng
藐 miǎo
(舊) jiù
藕 ǒu
(藝) yì
(藪) sǒu
(繭) jiǎn
(藥) yào
藤 téng

十六画以上

藻 zǎo
蘑 mó
(蘆) lú
孽 niè
(蘇) sū
(蘭) lán
(蘿) luó
蘸 zhàn

(43) 大部

大 dà; dài

一至五画

太 tài
央 yāng
夯 hāng
夹 gā;jiā;jiá
夸 kuā
夺 duó
尖 jiān
夷 yí
(夾) gā;jiā;jiá
奉 fèng
奈 nài
奔 bēn;bèn
奇 jī;qí
奄 yǎn
奋 fèn

六画

奖 jiǎng
奕 yì
美 měi
牵 qiān
契 qì

七至九画

套 tào
奚 xī
奢 shē
爽 shuǎng
奠 diàn
奥 ào

十一画以上

(奪) duó
(獎) jiǎng
(奮) fèn

(44)
廾(在下)部

卉 huì
弁 biàn
异 yì
弃 qì
弄 nòng
弊 bì

(45)
尢部

尤 yóu
尴 gān
(尷) gān

(46)
寸部

寸 cùn

二至六画

对 duì
寺 sì
寻 xún
导 dǎo
寿 shòu
将 jiāng;jiàng
封 fēng
耐 nài

七画以上

辱 rǔ
射 shè
(專) zhuān
尊 zūn
(尋) xún
(對) duì
(導) dǎo

(47)
弋部

式 shì
贰 èr

(48)
扌部

扎 zā;zhā
打 dá;dǎ
扑 pū
扒 bā;pá
扔 rēng
扩 kuò
扪 mén
扛 káng
扣 kòu
托 tuō
执 zhí
扫 sǎo;sào
扬 yáng

四画

抖 dǒu
抗 kàng
护 hù
扶 fú
抚 fǔ
技 jì
抠 kōu
扰 rǎo
扼 è
拒 jù
找 zhǎo
批 pī
扯 chě
抄 chāo
扮 bàn
抢 qiǎng
折 zhē;zhé;shé
抓 zhuā
扳 bān
投 tóu
抑 yì
抛 pāo
拟 nǐ
抒 shū
抉 jué
扭 niǔ
把 bǎ;bà
报 bào

五画

拧 níng;nǐng
拉 lā;lá
拦 lán
拌 bàn
抨 pēng
抹 mā;mǒ;mò
拓 tà;tuò
拔 bá
拢 lǒng
拣 jiǎn
拈 niān
担 dān;dàn
押 yā
抽 chōu
拐 guǎi
拙 zhuō
拎 līn
拖 tuō
拍 pāi
拆 chāi
拥 yōng
抵 dǐ
拘 jū
抱 bào
择 zé;zhái
抬 tái
抿 mǐn
拂 fú
披 pī
招 zhāo
拨 bō
拗 ào;niù
拇 mǔ

六画

挖 wā
按 àn
挤 jǐ
拼 pīn
挥 huī
挟 xié
拭 shì
挂 guà
持 chí
拮 jié
拷 kǎo
拱 gǒng
挞 tà
挎 kuà
挠 náo
挡 dǎng
拽 zhuài
拴 shuān
拾 shí
挑 tiāo;tiǎo
挺 tǐng
括 kuò
指 zhǐ
挣 zhēng;zhèng
挪 nuó
拯 zhěng

七画

捞 lāo
捕 bǔ
捂 wǔ
(挾) xié
振 zhèn
捎 shāo
捍 hàn
捏 niē
捉 zhuō
捆 kǔn
捐 juān
损 sǔn
捌 bā
捋 lǚ
捡 jiǎn
挫 cuò
捣 dǎo
换 huàn
挽 wǎn
捅 tǒng
挨 āi;ái

八画

(捲) juǎn
控 kòng
接 jiē
掠 lüè
掂 diān
掷 zhì
掸 dǎn
掮 qián
探 tàn
捧 pěng
(掛) guà
措 cuò
描 miáo
捺 nà
掩 yǎn
捷 jié
排 pái
掉 diào
掳 lǔ
授 shòu
(採) cǎi
捻 niǎn
(捨) shě
捶 chuí
推 tuī
掀 xiān
掬 jū
掏 tāo
掐 qiā
掇 duō
(掃) sǎo;sào
据 jù
掘 jué

九画

揽 jiǎo
搁 gē
搓 cuō
搂 lōu;lǒu
揍 zòu
搽 chá
搭 dā
(揀) jiǎn
揠 yà
揩 kāi
揽 lǎn
提 dī;tí
(揚) yáng
揭 jiē
揣 chuāi;
chuǎi
援 yuán
揪 jiū
插 chā
(揑) niē
搜 sōu
搀 chān
搔 sāo
揆 kuí
揉 róu
握 wò

十画

摈 bìn
搞 gǎo
搪 táng
摄 shè
摸 mō
(搧) shān
搏 bó
摁 èn
摆 bǎi
摇 yáo
(搶) qiǎng
携 xié
搬 bān
摊 tān

十一画

摘 zhāi
摔 shuāi
撇 piē;piě
(摳) kōu
(摟) lōu;lǒu
撂 liào
(摺) zhé
摧 cuī

十二画

撤 chè
(撈) lāo
撵 niǎn
(撻) tà
(撓) náo
撕 sī
撒 sā;sǎ
撩 liāo;liáo
撅 juē
撑 chēng
(撲) pū
撮 zuǒ
(撣) dǎn
擒 qín
播 bō
撬 qiào
(撫) fǔ
(撥) bō
撰 zhuàn

十三画

擅 shàn
(擁) yōng
擂 léi;
lèi
擀 gǎn
撼 hàn
(擋) dǎng
(據) jù
(擄) lǔ
操 cāo
(擇) zé;zhái
(撿) jiǎn
(擔) dān;
dàn

十四画

(擰) níng;
nǐng
(擯) bìn
擦 cā
(擠) jǐ
(擴) kuò
(擲) zhì
(擡) tái
擤 xǐng
(擬) nǐ

十五至十七画

(擾) rǎo
(擺) bǎi
(攏) lǒng
攒 zǎn
(攙) chān
(攔) lán

十八画以上

(攝) shè
(攤) tān
攥 zuàn
攫 jué
(攪) jiǎo
(攬) lǎn

(49)
小(⺌)部

小 xiǎo

一至四画

少 shǎo;
shào
尔 ěr
尘 chén
尖 jiān
光 guāng
劣 liè
当 dāng;
dàng
肖 xiào

五至八画

尚 shàng
尝 cháng
省 shěng;
xǐng
党 dǎng
堂 táng
常 cháng
雀 què

九至十画

掌 zhǎng
辉 huī
(當) dāng;
dàng
(嘗) cháng
(黨) dǎng
耀 yào

(50)
口部

口 kǒu

二画

叶 yè
古 gǔ
右 yòu
叮 dīng
可 kě;kè
号 háo;hào
占 zhān;
zhàn
只 zhī;zhǐ
史 shǐ
兄 xiōng
叱 chì
句 jù
叽 jī
叹 tàn
台 tái
司 sī
叼 diāo
叫 jiào
叩 kòu
召 zhào
另 lìng

三画

问 wèn
吁 xū;yù
吓 hè;xià
吐 tǔ;tù
吉 jí
吊 diào
合 hé
吃 chī
向 xiàng
后 hòu
名 míng
各 gè
吸 xī
吗 má;mǎ;
ma

四画

吝 lìn
吨 dūn
吭 háng;
kēng
呈 chéng
吞 tūn
呓 yì
呆 dāi
吱 zī
吾 wú
吠 fèi
呕 ǒu
否 fǒu
呃 è
呀 yā
吵 chǎo
呗 bei
员 yuán
呐 nà
吟 yín
吩 fēn
呛 qiāng;
qiàng
告 gào
听 tīng
吹 chuī
吻 wěn
呜 wū
吮 shǔn
君 jūn
吧 bā;ba
吼 hǒu

五画

味 wèi
哎 āi
咕 gū
呵 hē
呸 pēi
咀 jǔ
呻 shēn
呷 xiā
咒 zhòu
咄 duō
呼 hū
知 zhī
咋 zǎ
和 hé;hè
huó
呱 gū;guā
咎 jiù
鸣 míng
咆 páo

帚 zhǒu
录 lù
彗 huì
(尋) xún
(彙) huì
(歸) guī

(61) 尸部

尸 shī

一至四画

尺 chǐ
尼 ní
尽 jǐn;jìn
层 céng
屁 pì
尾 wěi
局 jú
尿 niào

五至六画

居 jū
届 jiè
屈 qū
昼 zhòu
屏 bǐng;píng
屎 shǐ
(屍) shī
屋 wū

七画

展 zhǎn
屑 xiè
屐 jī

八画以上

屠 tú
屡 lǚ
犀 xī
属 shǔ;zhǔ
孱 chán
(屢) lǚ
(層) céng
履 lǚ
(屬) shǔ;zhǔ

(62) 己(巳)部

己 jǐ
已 yǐ
巴 bā
包 bāo
异 yì
导 dǎo
岂 qǐ
忌 jì
巷 hàng;xiàng

(63) 弓部

弓 gōng

一至五画

引 yǐn
弘 hóng
弛 chí
张 zhāng
弦 xián
弧 hú
弥 mí
弩 nǔ

六至九画

弯 wān
弭 mǐ
弱 ruò
弹 dàn;tán
(張) zhāng
粥 zhōu
弼 bì
强 jiàng;qiáng;qiǎng
(發) fā

十一画以上

(彆) biè
(彈) dàn;tán
(彌) mí
疆 jiāng
(彎) wān

(64) 屮部

(芻) chú

(65) 女部

女 nǚ

二至三画

奶 nǎi
奴 nú
妆 zhuāng
妄 wàng
奸 jiān
如 rú
妇 fù
妃 fēi
她 tā
好 hǎo;hào
妈 mā

四画

妨 fáng
妒 dù
妍 yán
妩 wǔ
妓 jì
妪 yù
妣 bǐ
妙 miào
妥 tuǒ
妊 rèn
妖 yāo
姊 zǐ
妞 niū
(妝) zhuāng

五画

妾 qiè
妹 mèi
姑 gū
妻 qī
姐 jiě
姓 xìng
委 wěi
姗 shān
始 shǐ

六画

姹 chà
姣 jiāo
姿 zī
姜 jiāng
姘 pīn
娄 lóu
娃 wá
姥 lǎo
要 yāo;yào
威 wēi
耍 shuǎ
姨 yí
姻 yīn
娇 jiāo
(姙) rèn

七画

娴 xián
娘 niáng
娱 yú
娟 juān
娥 é
娩 miǎn
娓 wěi
婀 ē

八画

婆 pó
婶 shěn
婉 wǎn
婵 chán
婊 biǎo
娶 qǔ
娼 chāng
(婁) lóu
婴 yīng
婢 bì
婚 hūn
(婦) fù

九至十画

媒 méi
媪 ǎo
嫂 sǎo
婿 xù
媚 mèi
嫁 jià
嫉 jí
嫌 xián
媾 gòu
媳 xí
媲 pì

十一画以上

嫩 nèn
嫡 dí
(嫗) yù
嫖 piáo
嫦 cháng
(嬋) chán
嬉 xī
(嫵) wǔ
(嬌) jiāo
(嬸) shěn
孀 shuāng

(66) 幺部

乡 xiāng
幻 huàn
幼 yòu
幽 yōu
(幾) jī;jǐ

(67) 子(孑)部

子 zǐ;zi
孑 jié

一至四画

孔 kǒng
孕 yùn
存 cún
孙 sūn
孝 xiào
孜 zī

五画以上

学 xué
享 xiǎng
孟 mèng
孤 gū
孢 bāo
孪 luán
孩 hái
(孫) sūn
孰 shú
(學) xué
(孿) luán

(68) 纟(糸)部

一至三画

纠 jiū
红 hóng

纤 xiān
约 yuē
纨 wán
级 jí
纪 jì

四画

纹 wén
纺 fǎng
纬 wěi
纯 chún
纱 shā
纲 gāng
纳 nà
纵 zòng
纶 lún
纷 fēn
纸 zhǐ
纽 niǔ

五画

绊 bàn
线 xiàn
练 liàn
组 zǔ
绅 shēn
细 xì
织 zhī
绌 chù
终 zhōng
绉 zhòu
经 jīng;jìng

六画

绞 jiǎo
统 tǒng
绑 bǎng
绒 róng
结 jiē;jié
绕 rào
绘 huì
给 gěi;jǐ
绗 háng
绛 jiàng
络 luò
绚 xuàn
绝 jué
(絲) sī

七画

继 jì
(經) jīng;
jìng
绢 juàn
绥 suí
绣 xiù

八画

综 zōng
绽 zhàn
绩 jì
绪 xù
续 xù
绫 líng
(綫) xiàn
绯 fēi
绰 chuò
(網) wǎng
(綱) gāng
绳 shéng
(綸) lún
维 wéi
绵 mián
绷 bēng;
běng;
bèng
绸 chóu
缀 zhuì
绿 lǜ

九画

缔 dì
缕 lǚ
编 biān
(練) liàn
缄 jiān
缅 miǎn
缆 lǎn
缉 jī
缓 huǎn
缎 duàn
(緯) wěi
缘 yuán

十至十一画

缟 gǎo
缤 bīn
缠 chán
缢 yì
缜 zhěn
缚 fù
(緻) zhì
缝 féng;
fèng
(縐) zhòu
缩 suō
缥 piāo
(縷) lǚ
缨 yīng
(總) zǒng
(縱) zòng
缫 sāo

十二画

(織) zhī
缮 shàn
(繞) rào
缭 liáo
(繩) shéng

十三画以上

缰 jiāng
(繪) huì
缴 jiǎo
(繽) bīn
(繼) jì
(纏) chán
(續) xù
(變) biàn
(纖) xiān
(纔) cái
(纜) lǎn

(69) 马(馬)部

马 mǎ
(馬) mǎ

二至四画

驭 yù
闯 chuǎng
驮 tuó
驯 xùn
驰 chí
驴 lǘ
驱 qū
驳 bó

五画

驼 tuó
驻 zhù
驶 shǐ
驷 sì
驸 fù
驹 jū
驿 yì
驾 jià

六至八画

骇 hài
骂 mà
骄 jiāo
骆 luò
骋 chěng
验 yàn
骏 jùn
骑 qí

九画以上

骗 piàn
骚 sāo
骛 wù
腾 téng
(驅) qū
骡 luó
(驚) jīng
(驕) jiāo
(驛) yì
(驗) yàn
骤 zhòu
骥 jì
(驢) lǘ

(70) 巛部

(災) zāi
巢 cháo

(71) 灬部

四至七画

杰 jié
点 diǎn
羔 gāo
烈 liè
热 rè
(烏) wū
烹 pēng
焉 yān

八至九画

煮 zhǔ
(爲) wéi;
wèi
(無) wú
焦 jiāo
然 rán
煎 jiān
蒸 zhēng
照 zhào
煞 shā;shà

十画以上

熬 áo
熙 xī
熏 xūn
熊 xióng
熟 shú
(熱) rè
熹 xī
燕 yàn

(72) 斗部

斗 dǒu;dòu
料 liào
斜 xié
斟 zhēn
斡 wò

(73) 文部

文 wén
齐 qí
吝 lìn
斋 zhāi
虔 qián
紊 wěn
斑 bān

(74) 方部

方 fāng
房 fáng
(於) yú
放 fàng
施 shī
旁 páng
旅 lǚ
旌 jīng
族 zú
旋 xuán;
xuàn
旗 qí

(75) 火部

- 火 huǒ

一至三画

- 灭 miè
- 灰 huī
- 灯 dēng
- 灾 zāi
- 灶 zào
- 灿 càn
- 灼 zhuó
- 灵 líng
- (災) zāi

四画

- 炕 kàng
- 炎 yán
- 炉 lú
- 炬 jù
- 炖 dùn
- 炒 chǎo
- 炙 zhì
- 炊 chuī

五画

- 炫 xuàn
- 烂 làn
- 荧 yíng
- 炳 bǐng
- 炼 liàn
- 炽 chì
- 炭 tàn
- 炯 jiǒng
- 炸 zhá; zhà
- 炮 bāo; páo; pào
- 烁 shuò

六至七画

- 烫 tàng
- 烤 kǎo
- 耿 gěng
- 烘 hōng
- 烦 fán
- 烧 shāo
- 烛 zhú
- 烟 yān
- 烩 huì
- 烙 lào
- 烬 jìn
- 焖 mèn
- 焊 hàn
- 烽 fēng
- 焕 huàn

八至十画

- 焙 bèi
- 焚 fén
- 焰 yàn
- 煸 biān
- 煤 méi
- (煉) liàn
- 煨 wēi
- 煅 duàn
- 煌 huáng
- 熔 róng
- (熒) yíng
- (榮) róng
- 煽 shān
- 熄 xī
- 熘 liū

十一至十二画

- 熨 yùn
- (燙) tàng
- (熾) chì
- 燧 suì
- (營) yíng
- (燒) shāo
- 燎 liáo
- 燃 rán
- (燈) dēng

十三画以上

- (燦) càn
- 燥 zào
- (燭) zhú
- (燴) huì
- (燼) jìn
- 爆 bào
- (爍) shuò
- (爐) lú
- (爛) làn

(76) 心部

- 心 xīn

一至三画

- 必 bì
- 忘 wàng
- 闷 mèn
- 志 zhì
- 忐 tǎn
- 忌 jì
- 忍 rěn

四至五画

- 态 tài
- 忠 zhōng
- 怂 sǒng
- 念 niàn
- 忿 fèn
- 忽 hū
- 总 zǒng
- 毖 bì
- 思 sī
- 怎 zěn
- 怨 yuàn
- 急 jí
- 怠 dài
- 怒 nù

六画

- 恋 liàn
- 恣 zì
- 恙 yàng
- 恐 kǒng
- 恶 ě;è; wù
- 虑 lǜ
- 恩 ēn
- 息 xī
- 恳 kěn
- 恕 shù

七至八画

- 悬 xuán
- 患 huàn
- 悉 xī
- 悠 yōu
- 您 nín
- (惡) ě;è; wù
- 惹 rě
- 惠 huì
- 惑 huò
- 悲 bēi
- 惩 chéng
- 惫 bèi

九画

- 意 yì
- 慈 cí
- 想 xiǎng
- 感 gǎn
- 愚 yú
- (愛) ài
- 愈 yù
- 愁 chóu

十至十一画

- 愿 yuàn
- (態) tài
- (慶) qìng
- 憋 biē
- 慧 huì
- (憂) yōu
- (慮) lǜ
- (慫) sǒng
- 憨 hān
- 慰 wèi

十二画以上

- (憲) xiàn
- (憑) píng
- (憊) bèi
- (應) yīng; yìng
- (懇) kěn
- (懲) chéng
- (懸) xuán
- (戀) liàn

(77) 户部

- 户 hù

一至四画

- 启 qǐ
- 房 fáng
- 戾 lì
- 肩 jiān
- 所 suǒ

五画以上

- 扁 biǎn
- 扇 shān; shàn
- 扈 hù
- 扉 fēi
- 雇 gù

(78) 礻(示)部

一至四画

- 礼 lǐ
- 社 shè
- 视 shì
- 祈 qí

五至七画

- 祛 qū
- 祖 zǔ
- 神 shén
- 祝 zhù
- 祠 cí
- 祥 xiáng
- 祷 dǎo
- 祸 huò

八画以上

- 禅 chán; shàn
- (禍) huò
- 禄 lù
- 福 fú
- (禪) chán; shàn
- (禮) lǐ
- (禱) dǎo

(79) 王部

- 王 wáng

一至四画

- 主 zhǔ
- 玉 yù
- 全 quán
- 弄 lòng; nòng
- 玖 jiǔ
- 玛 mǎ
- 玩 wán
- 环 huán
- 现 xiàn
- 玫 méi

(槳) jiǎng

十二画

(樹) shù
橱 chú
(樸) pǔ
橇 qiāo
(橋) qiáo
樵 qiáo
橹 lǔ
橙 chéng
橘 jú
(機) jī

十三至十四画

檀 tán
(隸) lì
(檔) dàng
(檢) jiǎn
(檸) níng
(櫃) guì
(檻) kǎn

十五画以上

(櫟) lì
(權) quán
(欄) lán
(鬱) yù

(82) 犬部

犬 quǎn
状 zhuàng
戾 lì
(狀) zhuàng
哭 kū
臭 chòu;xiù
献 xiàn
(獸) shòu
(獻) xiàn

(83) 歹部

歹 dǎi

二至五画

列 liè
死 sǐ
夙 sù
歼 jiān
残 cán
殃 yāng
殆 dài

六画以上

毙 bì
殊 shū
殉 xùn
殓 liàn
殚 dān
殖 zhí
(殘) cán
殡 bìn
(殫) dān
(斃) bì
(殮) liàn
(殯) bìn
(殲) jiān

(84) 车(車)部

车 chē;jū

一至四画

轧 yà;zhá
军 jūn
轨 guǐ
轩 xuān
转 zhuǎn;zhuàn
轮 lún
斩 zhǎn
软 ruǎn
轰 hōng

五至七画

轱 gū
轶 yì
轴 zhóu
轻 qīng
较 jiào
载 zǎi;zài
轿 jiào
辅 fǔ
辆 liàng
(輕) qīng

八至九画

辈 bèi
(輛) liàng
辉 huī
(輪) lún
辍 chuò
辐 fú
辑 jí
输 shū

十画以上

辖 xiá
舆 yú
辗 zhǎn
辘 lù
(轉) zhuǎn;zhuàn
辙 zhé
(轎) jiào
(轟) hōng

(85) 戈部

戈 gē

一至三画

划 huá;huà
戎 róng
戍 shù
成 chéng
戏 xì
戒 jiè
我 wǒ

四至八画

或 huò
哉 zāi
战 zhàn
咸 xián
威 wēi
栽 zāi
载 zǎi
戚 qī
裁 cái
(幾) jǐ

九画以上

戡 kān
截 jié
戮 lù
(戰) zhàn
戴 dài
(戲) xì
戳 chuō

(86) 比部

比 bǐ
毕 bì
毖 bì
毙 bì
皆 jiē

(87) 瓦部

瓦 wǎ;wà

三至九画

瓮 wèng
瓷 cí
瓶 píng
甄 zhēn
(甕) wèng

(88) 止部

止 zhǐ
正 zhēng;zhèng
此 cǐ
步 bù
武 wǔ
歧 qí
肯 kěn
歪 wāi
耻 chǐ
(歲) suì
(歷) lì
(歸) guī

(89) 攴部

敲 qiāo

(90) 日部

日 rì

一至三画

旦 dàn
旧 jiù
早 zǎo
旬 xún
旭 xù
旷 kuàng
时 shí
旱 hàn

四画

旺 wàng
昙 tán
昔 xī
杳 yǎo
昆 kūn
昌 chāng
明 míng
昏 hūn
易 yì
昂 áng

五画

春 chūn
昧 mèi
是 shì
显 xiǎn
映 yìng
星 xīng
昨 zuó
昵 nì
昭 zhāo

六至七画

晕 yūn;yùn
晖 huī
(時) shí
晋 jìn
晒 shài
(晉) jìn
晓 xiǎo
晃 huǎng;huàng
晌 shǎng
匙 chí
晤 wù
晨 chén
晦 huì
晚 wǎn
(晝) zhòu

八画

晾 liàng
普 pǔ
景 jǐng
晴 qíng
暑 shǔ

晰 xī
量 liáng; liàng
暂 zàn
晶 jīng
智 zhì

九至十一画

暗 àn
暖 nuǎn
暇 xiá
暮 mù
暧 ài
暴 bào

十二画以上

(曇) tán
(曉) xiǎo
(曆) lì
曚 méng
曙 shǔ
(曖) ài
(曠) kuàng
曝 bào; pù
曦 xī
(曬) shài

(91)
日(⺜)部

曰 yuē

二至八画

曲 qǔ
旨 zhǐ
曳 yè
者 zhě
沓 dá; tà
冒 mào
(書) shū
冕 miǎn
曾 céng
替 tì
最 zuì
(嘗) cháng

(92)
贝(貝)部

贝 bèi
(貝) bèi

二至四画

贞 zhēn
则 zé
负 fù
贡 gòng
财 cái
员 yuán
贮 zhù
账 zhàng
责 zé
贤 xián
败 bài
贪 tān
贬 biǎn
贫 pín
货 huò
质 zhì
贩 fàn
购 gòu
贯 guàn

五画

(貯) zhù
贰 èr
贱 jiàn
贲 bì
贴 tiē
贵 guì
(買) mǎi
贷 dài
贸 mào
贻 yí
费 fèi
贺 hè

六至七画

赃 zāng
资 zī
贼 zéi
贾 gǔ
贿 huì
赁 lìn
(賓) bīn
(實) shí
赈 zhèn
赊 shē

八画

赔 péi
(賬) zhàng
赋 fù
(賣) mài
赌 dǔ
赎 shú
(賢) xián
(賤) jiàn
赏 shǎng
赐 cì
(質) zhì

九画以上

赖 lài
赛 sài
赚 zhuàn
赘 zhuì
(購) gòu
赠 zèng
赞 zàn
赡 shàn
(贓) zāng
(贖) shú

(93)
见(見)部

见 jiàn
(見) jiàn

二至七画

观 guān
视 shì
现 xiàn
规 guī
觅 mì
觉 jiào; jué
览 lǎn
觊 jì
舰 jiàn

八画以上

靓 liàng
(親) qīn
(覬) jì
觐 jìn
觑 qù
(覺) jiào; jué
(覽) lǎn
(觀) guān

(94)
父部

父 fù
爷 yé
斧 fǔ
爸 bà
釜 fǔ
爹 diē
(爺) yé

(95)
牛(牜⺧)部

牛 niú

二至四画

牢 láo
牡 mǔ
告 gào
牦 máo
牧 mù
物 wù

五至七画

牯 gǔ
牵 qiān
牲 shēng
特 tè
牺 xī
(牽) qiān
犁 lí

八画以上

犄 jī
犊 dú
犀 xī
犒 kào
靠 kào
犟 jiàng
(犢) dú
(犧) xī

(96)
手部

手 shǒu

四至八画

承 chéng
拜 bài
挛 luán
拳 quán
挈 qiè
挚 zhì
拿 ná
掌 zhǎng
掰 bāi
掣 chè

九画以上

摩 mó
(摯) zhì
擎 qíng
(擊) jī
擘 bò
攀 pān
(攣) luán

(97)
毛部

毛 máo
尾 wěi
毡 zhān
毫 háo
毯 tǎn
毽 jiàn
麾 huī
氅 chǎng
(氈) zhān

(98)
气部

气 qì
氢 qīng
氨 ān
氧 yǎng
(氣) qì
(氫) qīng
氮 dàn

(99)
攵部

二至五画

收 shōu
攻 gōng
改 gǎi
孜 zī
放 fàng
败 bài
政 zhèng
故 gù

六至七画

效 xiào
致 zhì
敌 dí
敝 bì
(啟) qǐ

盐 yán
监 jiān
盎 àng

六画

盗 dào
盖 gài
盔 kuī
盛 chéng; shèng
蛊 gǔ
盒 hé
盘 pán

八画以上

(盞) zhǎn
盟 méng
(監) jiān
(盡) jìn
(盤) pán
盥 guàn
(蠱) gǔ
(鹽) yán

(122) 钅(金)部

一至三画

针 zhēn
钉 dīng; dìng
钓 diào
钗 chāi

四画

钙 gài
钝 dùn
钞 chāo
钟 zhōng
钠 nà
钢 gāng
钧 jūn
钥 yào; yuè
钦 qīn
钩 gōu
钨 wū
钮 niǔ

五画

钱 qián
钳 qián
钵 bō
钹 bó
钻 zuān; zuàn
钾 jiǎ
铃 líng
铁 tiě
铅 qiān
铆 mǎo

六画

铵 ǎn
铲 chǎn
铰 jiǎo
铐 kào
铛 dāng
铝 lǚ
铜 tóng
铠 kǎi
铣 xǐ
铤 tǐng
铧 huá
铭 míng
银 yín

七画

锌 xīn
锐 ruì
锒 láng
铸 zhù
铺 pū; pù
链 liàn
销 xiāo
锁 suǒ
铿 kēng
锄 chú
锅 guō
锉 cuò
锈 xiù
锋 fēng

八画

锭 dìng
鎯 láng
(錶) biǎo
错 cuò
锚 máo
锛 bēn
(錢) qián
(鋼) gāng
锡 xī
锣 luó
(鍋) guō
锤 chuí
锥 zhuī
锦 jǐn
锨 xiān
键 jiàn
(録) lù
锯 jù
锰 měng

九至十画

锵 qiāng
镀 dù
镁 měi
镂 lòu
锲 qiè
锹 qiāo
(鍾) zhōng
锻 duàn
镑 bàng
镐 gǎo
镇 zhèn
(鏵) huá
(鎧) kǎi
镍 niè
(鎢) wū
镌 juān

十一至十二画

镜 jìng
(鏇) xuàn
(鏟) chǎn
(鏗) kēng
镖 biāo
镗 táng
(鏤) lòu
(鏘) qiāng
(鐘) zhōng
镣 liào

十三画

镰 lián
(鐵) tiě
(鐺) dāng
镯 zhuó

十四画以上

(鑄) zhù
镳 biāo
镶 xiāng
(鑰) yào; yuè
(鑼) luó
(鑽) zuān; zuàn

(123) 矢部

矢 shǐ
矣 yǐ
知 zhī
矩 jǔ
矫 jiǎo
短 duǎn
矮 ǎi
(矯) jiǎo

(124) 禾部

禾 hé

二至三画

利 lì
秃 tū
秀 xiù
私 sī
秆 gǎn
和 hé; hè; huó
秉 bǐng
委 wěi
季 jì

四画

科 kē
秋 qiū
秕 bǐ
秒 miǎo
香 xiāng
种 zhǒng; zhòng

五画

秘 mì; bì
秤 chèng
秣 mò
乘 chéng
租 zū
秧 yāng
积 jī
秩 zhì
称 chèn; chēng

六至七画

秸 jiē
秽 huì
移 yí
税 shuì
稍 shāo
(稈) gǎn
程 chéng
稀 xī
黍 shǔ

八画

稚 zhì
稗 bài
稠 chóu
颓 tuí
颖 yǐng

九至十一画

(稭) jiē
(稱) chèn; chēng
(種) zhǒng; zhòng
稳 wěn
稼 jià
稿 gǎo
稷 jì
(穀) gǔ
稽 jī
稻 dào
黎 lí
(積) jī
穆 mù

十二画以上

穗 suì
黏 nián
(穢) huì
馥 fù
(穩) wěn

(125) 白部

白 bái

一至三画

百 bǎi
皂 zào
帛 bó

的 de;dí

四画以上

皇 huáng
皆 jiē
泉 quán
皎 jiǎo
皑 ái
皓 hào
魄 pò
(皚) ái

(126)
瓜部

瓜 guā
瓢 piáo
瓣 bàn
瓤 ráng

(127)
鸟(鳥)部

鸟 niǎo
(鳥) niǎo

二至四画

(鳧) fú
鸡 jī
鸣 míng
(鳳) fèng
鸥 ōu
鸦 yā
鸩 zhèn

五画

鸵 tuó
鸭 yā
鸳 yuān

六至八画

鸿 hóng
鸾 luán
鸽 gē
鹄 gǔ;hú
鹅 é
鹊 què
鹏 péng
鹌 ān

九画以上

鹤 hè
(鷄) jī
(鷗) ōu
鹦 yīng
鹫 jiù
鹬 yù
鹰 yīng
鹳 guàn
(鸞) luán

(128)
用部

用 yòng
甩 shuǎi
甫 fǔ
甭 béng

(129)
矛部

矛 máo
柔 róu
矜 jīn
(務) wù

(130)
疋(⻊)部

蛋 dàn
疏 shū
楚 chǔ
疑 yí

(131)
皮部

皮 pí
皱 zhòu
颇 pō
皴 cūn
(皺) zhòu

(132)
衣部

衣 yī

二至六画

表 biǎo
衰 shuāi
衷 zhōng
袅 niǎo
袭 xí
袋 dài
装 zhuāng
裁 cái
裂 liè
亵 xiè

七画以上

裘 qiú
(裏) lǐ
裔 yì
(裝) zhuāng
裹 guǒ
(製) zhì
褒 bāo
(褻) xiè
襄 xiāng
(襲) xí

(133)
羊(⺶⺷)部

羊 yáng

一至四画

养 yǎng
差 chā;chà;chāi
美 měi
姜 jiāng
羔 gāo
恙 yàng
羞 xiū

五画以上

着 zhāo;zháo;zhe;zhuó
盖 gài
羚 líng
羡 xiàn
善 shàn
翔 xiáng
(義) yì
群 qún
(養) yǎng
羹 gēng

(134)
米部

米 mǐ

二至四画

类 lèi
娄 lóu
屎 shǐ
籽 zǐ
料 liào
粉 fěn

五至八画

粒 lì
粘 zhān
粗 cū
粪 fèn
粟 sù
粥 zhōu
粱 liáng
粮 liáng
粳 jīng
粹 cuì
精 jīng
粼 lín

九画以上

糊 hū;hú;hù
糖 táng
糕 gāo
糙 cāo
糜 mí
糠 kāng
糟 zāo
(糞) fèn
(糧) liáng
糯 nuò
(糴) dí

(135)
耒部

耕 gēng
耘 yún
耗 hào
耙 bà;pá

(136)
老部

老 lǎo
考 kǎo

(137)
耳部

耳 ěr

二至四画

取 qǔ
耶 yē
闻 wén
耷 dā
耿 gěng
耽 dān
耻 chǐ
耸 sǒng

五至七画

聋 lóng
职 zhí
聆 líng
聊 liáo
联 lián
聒 guō
(聖) shèng
聘 pìn

八画以上

聚 jù
聪 cōng
(聲) shēng
(聰) cōng
(聳) sǒng
(聯) lián
(職) zhí
(聾) lóng
(聽) tīng

(138)
臣部

臣 chén
卧 wò
(臨) lín

(139)
西(覀)部

西 xī
要 yāo;yào
栗 lì
票 piào

粟 sù
覆 fù
(羈) jī

(140)
页(頁)部

页 yè
(頁) yè

二至三画

顶 dǐng
顷 qǐng
项 xiàng
顺 shùn
须 xū

四至五画

烦 fán
顽 wán
顾 gù
顿 dùn
颂 sòng
颁 bān
预 yù
硕 shuò
颅 lú
领 lǐng
颈 jǐng
颇 pō

六至八画

颊 jiá
颌 hé
颐 yí
(頭) tóu
(頰) jiá
频 pín
(頸) jǐng
颓 tuí
颖 yǐng
颗 kē

九至十画

额 é
颜 yán
题 tí
颚 è
(類) lèi
颠 diān
(願) yuàn

十一画以上

(顧) gù
嚣 xiāo
颤 chàn; zhàn
(顯) xiǎn
(顱) lú
颧 quán

(141)
虍部

二至五画

虎 hǔ
虏 lǔ
虐 nüè
虔 qián
虑 lǜ
虚 xū
(處) chǔ; chù
彪 biāo

六画以上

虞 yú
(號) háo; hào
(虜) lǔ
(慮) lǜ
(膚) fū
(戲) xì
(虧) kuī

(142)
虫部

虫 chóng

一至四画

虱 shī
虻 méng
虾 xiā
虹 hóng
虽 suī
蚁 yǐ
蚤 zǎo
蚂 mǎ
蚊 wén
蚌 bàng
蚕 cán
蚝 háo

五画

蛇 shé
蛀 zhù
蛆 qū
蛊 gǔ
蚱 zhà
蚯 qiū
蛋 dàn

六至七画

蛮 mán
蛙 wā
蛰 zhé
蛔 huí
蛐 qū
蛤 gé; há
蛛 zhū
蜕 tuì
蜗 wō
蛾 é
蜂 fēng

八画

蜜 mì
蜿 wān
蜷 quán
蝉 chán
蜻 qīng
蜡 là
蜚 fēi
蝇 yíng
(蝸) wō
蜘 zhī

九画

蝙 biān
蝶 dié
蝴 hú
蝠 fú
(蝨) shī
蝎 xiē
蝮 fù
蝗 huáng
(蝦) xiā

十至十一画

螃 páng
(螢) yíng
蟒 mǎng
融 róng
螟 míng
(蟄) zhé
螳 táng
螺 luó

十二画以上

(蟲) chóng
(蠅) yíng
(蟬) chán
(蟻) yǐ
蟾 chán
蟹 xiè
蠕 rú
(蠔) háo
蠢 chǔn
蠡 lí
(蠟) là
(蠱) gǔ
(蠶) cán
(蠻) mán

(143)
缶部

缸 gāng
缺 quē
罂 yīng
罐 guàn
(罎) tán

(144)
舌部

舌 shé
乱 luàn
舍 shě; shè
甜 tián
舒 shū
辞 cí
舔 tiǎn

(145)
竹(⺮)部

竹 zhú

二至四画

竿 gān
笃 dǔ
笔 bǐ
笑 xiào
笋 sǔn

五画

笠 lì
笺 jiān
笨 bèn
笼 lóng; lǒng
笛 dí
符 fú
笞 chī
第 dì
笤 tiáo

六画

筐 kuāng
等 děng
筑 zhù
策 cè
筚 bì
筛 shāi
筒 tǒng
答 dā; dá
筏 fá
(筍) sǔn
筵 yán
筋 jīn
(筆) bǐ

七画

筷 kuài
简 jiǎn
筹 chóu
签 qiān
(節) jiē; jié

八画

箔 bó
管 guǎn
箍 gū
(箋) jiān
算 suàn
箩 luó

九画

篓 lǒu
箭 jiàn
篇 piān
箱 xiāng
(範) fàn
箴 zhēn

十画

篱 lí
篙 gāo
篝 gōu
(築) zhù
篮 lán
篡 cuàn
(篳) bì
(篩) shāi
篦 bì
篷 péng

十一至十二画

簇 cù
簧 huáng
(簍) lǒu
篾 miè
簪 zān

十三至十四画

簿 bù
(簾) lián
簸 bǒ;bò
籁 lài
(簽) ·qiān
籍 jí
(籌) chóu
(籃) lán

十五画以上

(籠) lóng;lǒng
(籤) qiān
(籬) lí
(籮) luó
(籲) yù

(146)
臼部

臼 jiù
(兒) ér
舂 chōng
(與) yǔ;yù
舅 jiù
(舉) jǔ
(舊) jiù

(147)
自部

自 zì
息 xī
臭 chòu;xiù

(148)
血部

血 xiě;xuè
衅 xìn
(衆) zhòng

(149)
舟部

舟 zhōu

三至四画

舢 shān
舫 fǎng
航 háng
舰 jiàn
舱 cāng
般 bān

五画以上

舵 duò
舷 xián
舸 gě
盘 pán
舶 bó
船 chuán
艇 tǐng
艘 sōu
(盤) pán
(艙) cāng
(艦) jiàn

(150)
羽部

羽 yǔ

三至六画

扇 shàn
翅 chì
翁 wēng
翎 líng
(習) xí
翔 xiáng
翘 qiáo;qiào

八画以上

翠 cuì
翩 piān
翰 hàn
翱 áo
翼 yì
(翹) qiáo;qiào
翻 fān

(151)
艮(艮)部

良 liáng
艰 jiān
即 jí
垦 kěn
恳 kěn
既 jì
暨 jì
(艱) jiān

(152)
糸部

一至五画

系 jì;xì
紊 wěn
素 sù
索 suǒ
紧 jǐn
(紮) zā;zhā
累 léi;lěi;lèi

六画以上

紫 zǐ
絮 xù
(緊) jǐn
(縈) yíng
(縣) xiàn
繁 fán
(繫) jì;xì
(纍) léi

(153)
辛部

辛 xīn
辜 gū
辞 cí
辟 bì;pì
辣 là
辨 biàn
辩 biàn
(辦) bàn
辫 biàn
(辭) cí
瓣 bàn
(辮) biàn
(辯) biàn

(154)
言部

言 yán
(這) zhè
誉 yù
誊 téng
誓 shì
警 jǐng
(譽) yù
譬 pì

(155)
麦(麥)部

麦 mài
(麥) mài
麸 fū
(麩) fū
(麵) miàn

(156)
走部

走 zǒu
赴 fù
赳 jiū
赶 gǎn
起 qǐ
越 yuè
趁 chèn
趋 qū
超 chāo
(趕) gǎn
趣 qù
趟 tàng
(趨) qū

(157)
赤部

赤 chì
赦 shè
赫 hè
赭 zhě

(158)
豆部

豆 dòu
豇 jiāng
(豈) qǐ
壹 yī
短 duǎn
登 dēng
豌 wān
(頭) tóu
(豐) fēng
(豔) yàn

(159)
酉部

二至四画

酋 qiú
酒 jiǔ
酌 zhuó
配 pèi
酝 yùn
酗 xù

五至七画

酣 hān
酥 sū
酱 jiàng
酬 chóu
酩 míng
酪 lào
酿 niàng
酵 jiào
酷 kù
酶 méi
酸 suān

八至九画

醇 chún
醉 zuì
醋 cù
醒 xǐng
(醜) chǒu

十一画以上

(醫) yī
(醬) jiàng

鱼 yú
(魚) yú

四至六画

鲁 lǔ
鲍 bào
鲜 xiān
鲑 guī
鲨 shā
鲢 lián
鲤 lǐ
鲫 jì

八画以上

鲸 jīng
鳄 è
鳊 biān
鳏 guān
鳍 qí
鳖 biē
鳔 biào
鳞 lín
(鱷) è

(177) 音部

音 yīn
章 zhāng
竟 jìng
韵 yùn
(韻) yùn
(響) xiǎng

(178) 革部

革 gé

二至八画

勒 lè;lēi
靴 xuē
靶 bǎ
鞍 ān
鞋 xié
(鞏) gǒng
鞘 qiào;shāo
鞠 jū

九画以上

鞭 biān

(179) 骨部

骨 gǔ

三至八画

(骯) āng
骷 kū
骸 hái

九画以上

(髒) zāng
髓 suǐ
(體) tǐ

(180) 食部

食 shí
餐 cān

(181) 鬼部

鬼 guǐ
魁 kuí
魅 mèi
魂 hún
魄 pò
魔 mó

(182) 鬥部

(鬥) dòu
(鬧) nào

(183) 髟部

(髮) fà
髻 jì
髭 zī
鬃 zōng
鬈 quán
(鬆) sōng
鬓 bìn
(鬍) hú
(鬢) bìn
(鬚) xū

(184) 麻部

麻 má
(麽) me
麾 huī
摩 mó
磨 mó;mò
縻 mí
靡 mí;mǐ
魔 mó

(185) 鹿部

鹿 lù
(塵) chén
麓 lù
(麗) lì
鏖 áo
麝 shè

(186) 黑部

黑 hēi
墨 mò
默 mò
黔 qián
(點) diǎn
黜 chù
黝 yǒu
黩 dú
(黨) dǎng
黯 àn
(黷) dú

(187) 鼠部

鼠 shǔ

(188) 鼻部

鼻 bí
鼾 hān

A a

阿 ā [used before a pet name, a surname or a title of family and other relationships]: ～大 the eldest. ～哥 elder brother. ～婆 granny
see also ē

阿飞(飛) āfēi (名) hoodlum; hooligan; street rowdy

阿訇 āhōng (名) ahung; imam

阿拉伯 Ālābó (名) Arab; Arabian; Arabic: ～人 Arab. ～半岛 the Arabian Peninsula; Arabia. ～国家 Arab countries. ～数字 Arabic numerals. ～语 Arabic

阿门(門) āmén (动) amen

阿司匹林 āsīpǐlín (名) aspirin

阿姨 āyí (名) **1** term of address for any woman of one's mother's generation; auntie **2** nursemaid **3** nanny; babysitter

啊 ā (叹) [a cry of surprise or amazement]: ～！这地方多美哇！Oh, what a beautiful place!

腌 ā
see also yān

腌臜 āzā (形) filthy; dirty

啊 á (叹) [pressing for an answer or asking for something to be repeated]: ～？你说什么？Pardon?

啊 ǎ (叹) [expressing surprise]: ～，你怎么啦？Gosh, what's the matter with you?

啊 à (叹) [expressing sudden realization]: ～，原来是你！Ah, so it's you.

啊 a (助) **1** [used at the end of a sentence to convey a feeling of admiration or an undertone of warning]: 多好的天气～！What a fine day! 你可要小心～！Do be careful! 这是真的～？Is this really true? **2** [used before a pause in order to attract attention]: 你～，这样下去可不行！Look! You can't go on like this. **3** [used after each item of a series of things]: 桃～，梨～，苹果～，我们都有. We have all sorts of fruit — peaches, pears, apples.

哀 āi (名) **1** grief, sorrow: 喜怒～乐 joy, anger, grief and happiness **2** mourning: 志～ express one's mourning for the deceased **3** pity: ～怜 have pity on sb.

哀悼 āidào (动) mourn or grieve for the deceased; lament over sb.'s death: 向死者家属表示深切的～ express one's heartfelt condolences to the family of the deceased

哀告 āigào (动) beg piteously; implore; supplicate

哀号(號) āiháo (动) cry with sorrow; wail

哀鸣 āimíng (动) whine; wail

哀求 āiqiú (动) entreat; implore: 苦苦～ beg piteously

哀伤(傷) āishāng (形) grieved; saddened

哀思 āisī (名) sad memories (of the deceased); grief: 寄托～ give expression to one's grief

哀叹(嘆) āitàn (动) sigh sorrowfully (for)

哀痛 āitòng (名) grief; deep sorrow

哀乐(樂) āiyuè (名) funeral music; dirge

哎 āi (叹) [showing surprise or discontent]: ～！是老王啊！Why, it's Old Wang! ～，你怎么不早跟我说呢？But why didn't you tell me sooner?

哎呀 āiyā (叹) [expressing surprise]: ～！我的笔丢了.Oh, dear! I've lost my pen. ～，这瓜真甜哪！Ah, this melon is really sweet!

埃 āi (名) **1** dust **2** angstrom (Å)

挨 āi (动) **1** get close to; be next or near to: ～着我坐 sit by my side. 那两座房子紧～着. The two houses are next to each other. 我六十～边了. I'm getting on for sixty. **2** in sequence; by turns: ～家～户 from door to door. ～个儿 one by one. ～次 one after another. 还没～到你呢. It isn't your turn yet.
see also ái

唉 āi (叹) [a verbal response to inquiry]: ～，来啦！Yes, I'm coming.
see also ài

唉声(聲)叹(嘆)气(氣) āishēng-tànqì sigh in despair

癌 ái (名) cancer; carcinoma: ～转移 metastasis. ～扩散 carcinomatous infiltration. 致～物质 cancinogenic substance

癌细胞 áixìbāo (名) cancer cell

癌症 áizhèng (名) cancer

A

皑(皚) ái (形) 〈书〉 pure white (snow or frost)

皑皑 ái'ái (形) pure white: 白雪～ an expanse of snow

挨 ái (动) **1** suffer; endure: ～饿 suffer from hunger; go hungry. ～骂 get a scolding. ～打 take a beating; be spanked. ～批评 be criticized sharply **2** drag out: ～日子 drag out a miserable existence **3** delay; stall: ～时间 play for time

see also āi

挨斗(鬥) áidòu (动) be denounced (at a public meeting)

挨整 áizhěng (动) be the target of criticism or attack

霭 ǎi (名) 〈书〉 mist; haze: 暮～ evening haze

蔼 ǎi (形) friendly; amiable: 和～可亲 kindly; amiable; affable

嗳(噯) ǎi (叹) [expressing disagreement]: ～,别客气了. Come on. Don't be too polite. ～,你搞混啦. No, no, you got it all mixed up. ～,不是这种茶. No, it's not this kind of tea.

see also ài

矮 ǎi (形) **1** short (of stature) **2** low: 一堵～墙 a low wall. 他在大学里～我一级. He was one class my junior at college.

矮墩墩 ǎidūndūn (形) dumpy; stumpy

矮小 ǎixiǎo (形) undersized (of stature or house): 身材～ short and of slight build

矮子 ǎizi (名) a short person; dwarf; pygmy

隘 ài I (形) narrow: 狭～ narrow; narrow-minded II (名) pass: 要～ a strategic pass. 关～ (mountain) pass

艾 ài (名) **1** Chinese mugwort: ～绒 moxa **2** 〈书〉 end; stop: 方兴未～ be just unfolding

艾滋病 àizībìng (名) AIDS (Acquired Immune Deficiency Syndrome)

碍(礙) ài (动) hinder; obstruct; be in the way of: 有～健康 be harmful (or detrimental) to health. ～于情面 for fear of hurting sb.'s sensibilities

碍口 àikǒu (形) too embarrassing to bring up

碍事 àishì (动) stand in the way: 这个大箱子太～了. This big trunk stands just in the way.

碍手碍脚 àishǒu-àijiǎo be in the way; be a hindrance

唉 ài (叹) **1** [a sigh of sadness or regret]: ～,太晚了! Oh, It's too late! **2** sound of sighing

see also āi

爱(愛) ài (动) **1** love: ～祖国 love one's country. 母～ maternal love **2** like; be fond of: ～看电影 like watching movies **3** be apt to; be in the habit of: ～发脾气 be apt to lose one's temper

爱…不… ài…bù…[used before reduplicated verbs meaning "do as you like"]:爱信不信 believe it or not. 他爱去不去. He can go or not, for all I care.

爱不释(釋)手 ài bù shìshǒu so delighted with sth. that one can scarcely take one's eyes off it

爱称(稱) àichēng (名) term of endearment; pet or affectionate name

爱戴 àidài (动) love and esteem: 受到人民的～ enjoy the love and esteem of the people

爱抚(撫) àifǔ (动) show tender care for; caress

爱国(國) àiguó (动) love one's country; be patriotic: ～者 patriot. ～主义 patriotism

爱好 àihào I (动) love; like; be keen on: ～和平 be peace-loving. ～运动 be keen on sports. 足球～者 football fan II (名) interest; hobby: 种花是我的～. Gardening is my hobby.

爱护(護) àihù (动) cherish; treasure; protect: ～公物 take good care of public property

爱恋(戀) àiliàn (动) fall in love with

爱面子 ài miànzi be intent on saving face

爱莫能助 ài mò néng zhù willing and yet unable to help; be willing to lend a hand but unable to do so

爱慕 àimù (动) adore; admire fondly

爱情 àiqíng (名) love (between man and woman)

爱人 àiren (名) **1** spouse; husband or wife **2** sweetheart

爱惜 àixī (动) treasure; cherish: ～时间 not waste one's time

爱心 àixīn (名) love; loving heart

爱憎 ài-zēng (名) love and hate: ～分明 be clear whom to love and whom to hate

嗳(噯) ài (叹) [ejaculation showing regret or annoyance]: ～,早知如此,我就不去了. Oh! Had I known what it would be like, I wouldn't have gone there at all.
see also ǎi

暧(曖) ài (形)〈书〉(of daylight) dim

暧昧 àimèi (形) 1 ambiguous; equivocal: 在这个问题上,他的态度～. He takes an ambiguous stand on this matter. 2 shady; dubious: 关系～. Their relationship is dubious.

安 ān I (动) 1 put sb. in a suitable position 2 install; fix; fit: ～电话 have a telephone installed 3 harbour (an intention): ～坏心 harbour evil intentions II (形) 1 peaceful; quiet; tranquil; calm: 心神不～ feel worried (about sth.) 2 tranquillize; stabilize: 使他～下心来 calm him down; set his mind at ease 3 be content or satisfied: ～于现状 be content with the status quo; take the world as one finds it III (名) safety: 转危为～ turn danger into safety; be out of danger

安 ān (副)〈书〉[interrogative word] 1 where; what: 其故～在? What is the cause? 2 how: ～能若无其事? How can you behave as if nothing has happened?

安瓿 ānbù (名) ampoule

安插 ānchā (动) place in a certain position; assign a job to sb.; plant: ～亲信 plant one's supporters in key positions

安定 āndìng I (形) stable; settled: 那里局势不～. The situation there is not stable. II (动) stabilize; maintain: ～人心 reassure the public

安顿 āndùn (动) help settle in; find a place for; arrange properly for

安放 ānfàng (动) lay; place with: 烈士墓前～着花圈. Wreaths were laid at the martyr's tomb.

安分 ānfèn (形) honest and dutiful: ～守己 law-abiding and well-behaved

安抚(撫) ānfǔ (动) console; reassure

安好 ānhǎo (形) safe and sound; well: 全家～,请勿挂念. You may rest assured that everyone in the family is fine.

安家 ānjiā (动) settle in; make one's home in a place

安检(檢) ānjiǎn (名) security check

安静 ānjìng (形) quiet; peaceful: 病人需要～. The patient needs peace and quiet. 保持～. Keep quiet!

安居乐(樂)业(業) ānjū-lèyè live in peace and work contentedly

安康 ānkāng (名) good health

安乐(樂) ānlè (名) peace and comfort: ～窝 cosy nest. ～椅 easy chair ～死 mercy killing; euthanasia

安眠 ānmián (动) sleep peacefully: ～药 sleeping pill (or tablet); soporific

安宁(寧) ānníng (形) 1 peaceful; tranquil: 保持心情～ maintain the peace of mind 2 calm; composed; free from worry

安排 ānpái (动) arrange; plan; fix up: 为游客～旅行日程 arrange itineraries for the tourists

安培 ānpéi (名) ampere: ～计 ammeter; amperemeter. ～小时 ampere-hour

安全 ānquán (形、名) safe; secure: ～到达 arrive safe and sound. 交通～ traffic safety. ～带 safety belt (or strap); seat belt. ～岛 safety (or pedestrian) island. ～阀 safety valve. ～帽 safety helmet. ～门 emergency exit. ～梯 fire escape. ～灯 safety lamp

安全理事会(會) Ānquán Lǐshìhuì (名) The (U.N.) Security Council

安全套 ānquántào (名) condom

安然 ānrán (形) 1 safely: ～无事 safe and sound; without a slight hitch 2 peacefully; at rest: 只有把真相告诉他,他心里才会～. You can only set his mind at rest by telling him the whole truth.

安身 ānshēn (动) take shelter: 无处～ have nowhere to live; have no roof over one's head

安神 ānshén (动) calm (or soothe) the nerves

安生 ānshēng (形) 1 peaceful; free from worry 2 quiet; still: 这孩子一会儿也不～. The child simply won't keep quiet.

安适(適) ānshì (形) quiet and comfortable: ～的生活 a life of ease and comfort

安危 ān-wēi (名) safety and danger; safety: 不顾个人～ despite the danger to oneself

安慰 ānwèi (动) 1 comfort; console 2 reassuring: ～奖 consolation prize

安稳 ānwěn (形) safe and steady

安息 ānxī (动) 1 rest; go to sleep 2 rest in peace: 烈士们,～吧! May our martyrs rest in peace!

安闲(閒) ānxián (形) carefree; leisurely

安详 ānxiáng (形) calm; composed; placid: 举止～ behave with quiet dignity
安歇 ānxiē (动) 1 go to bed; retire for the night 2 take a rest
安心 ānxīn (动) feel at ease; set one's mind at rest: ～工作 work single-mindedly
安逸 ānyì (形) carefree and comfortable: 生活～ live in comfort
安营(營) ānyíng (动) set up a camp; camp out
安葬 ānzàng (动) bury (the dead)
安之若素 ān zhī ruò sù be imperturbable
安置 ānzhì (动) find a place for; help settle down; arrange for: ～新来的学生 find accommodation for the new student
安装(裝) ānzhuāng (动) install: ～电话 have a telephone installed

鞍 ān (名) saddle

鞍马(馬) ānmǎ (名) 1 pommelled horse; side horse 2 saddle and horse
鞍子 ānzi (名) saddle

氨 ān (名) ammonia

谙 ān (动)〈书〉 know well: 不～水性 be no swimmer

谙熟 ānshú (动) be familiar; be versed: ～唐诗 be well versed in Tang poetry

庵 ān (名) 1 hut 2 nunnery; Buddhist convent

鹌 ān

鹌鹑 ānchún (名) quail

俺 ǎn (代) I; we [referring only to the speakers themselves]: ～爹 my father. ～村 our village

铵 ǎn (名) ammonium

案 àn (名) 1 case; law case: 破～ clear up a criminal case 2 record; file: 有～可查 be on record (or file) 3 a plan submitted for consideration; proposal: 提～ proposal; motion. 决议草～ a draft resolution

案板 ànbǎn (名) kneading or chopping board
案件 ànjiàn (名) law case; case: 行凶抢劫～ a case of robbery with violence
案卷 ànjuàn (名) records; files; archives
案例 ànlì (名) case: ～摘要 digest of a case. ～研究 case study
案情 ànqíng (名) details of a case; case: 了解～ make a thorough investigation of the case
案头(頭) àntóu (名) desk; on one's desk: ～日历 desk calendar
案子 ànzi (名) 1〈口〉case; law case 2 long table; counter: 肉～ meat counter

按 àn I (动) 1 press; push down: ～电钮 press (or push) a button 2 hold sth. back; shelve 3 restrain; control: ～不住心头怒火 be unable to restrain (or control) one's temper 4 in accordance with; in the light of; on the basis of: ～我说的办. Do as I told you. 5 check; refer to II (名) note: 编者～ editor's note

按兵不动(動) àn bīng bù dòng hold the troops in readiness for combat; bide one's time; take no action
按部就班 ànbù-jiùbān observe the proper order of doing things; act according to the usual procedure
按揭 ànjiē (名) mortgage: ～购房 take out a mortgage to buy a house
按劳(勞)分配 àn láo fēnpèi distribution according to work
按理 ànlǐ (副) according to reason; normally: ～说他不应该管她的事. He is not supposed to interfere in her affairs.
按脉(脈) ànmài (动) feel (or take) the pulse
按摩 ànmó (动) massage: ～器 massager
按捺 ànnà (动) restrain; contain: ～不住激动的心情 be unable to contain one's excitement
按钮 ànniǔ (名) push button
按期 ànqī (副) on schedule; on time: ～出发 start on time
按时(時) ànshí (副) on time; on schedule: ～到达 arrive on time
按说 ànshuō (副) in the ordinary course of events; normally: ～这时候该下雪了. Normally it should be snowing by now (or this time of the year).
按需分配 àn xū fēnpèi distribution according to need
按语 ànyǔ (名) note; comment
按照 ànzhào (介) according to; in accordance with; in the light of; on the basis of: ～预定计划完成任务 fulfil the task on schedule

黯 àn (形) dim; gloomy

黯淡 àndàn see "暗淡" àndàn
黯然 ànrán (形)〈书〉 1 dim; faint: ～失色

pale into insignificance 2 in low spirits; sadly: ~泪下 shed tears sadly

暗 àn (形) 1 dark; dim; dull: 天色渐~. It's getting dark. 2 hidden; secret: 明人不做~事. One who is aboveboard does nothing on the sly. 3 hazy: 情况若明若~. The situation is a little murky.

暗暗 àn'àn (副) secretly; inwardly; to oneself: 他觉得有人~跟踪. He felt he was being tailed.

暗藏 àncáng (动) hide; conceal: ~的敌人 a hidden enemy

暗娼 ànchāng (名) unlicensed prostitute

暗淡 àndàn (形) dim; faint; dismal; gloomy: 前途~ a gloomy future. 灯光~ The light is dim.

暗地里(裏) àndìli (副) secretly; on the sly

暗害 ànhài (动) 1 murder; incriminate 2 stab in the back

暗号(號) ànhào (名) secret signal (or sign)

暗盒 ànhé (名) magazine; cassette

暗箭 ànjiàn (名) a stab in the back: ~难防. It is hard to guard against snipers.

暗礁 ànjiāo (名) submerged reef (or rock)

暗杀(殺) ànshā (动、名) assassinate; assassination

暗示 ànshì (动) drop a hint; hint: 他用眼睛~我,让我走开. The look on his face suggested that I was in the way.

暗室 ànshì (名) darkroom

暗算 ànsuàn (动) plot against; entrap

暗锁 ànsuǒ (名) built-in lock

暗滩(灘) àntān (名) hidden shoal

暗探 àntàn (名) detective; secret agent

暗无(無)天日 àn wú tiānrì dark days; total absence of justice

暗箱 ànxiāng (名) camera bellows; camera obscura

暗笑 ànxiào (动) laugh in one's sleeve; snigger

暗语 ànyǔ (名) code word

暗中 ànzhōng (副) 1 in the dark: ~摸索 grope in the dark 2 in secret; surreptitiously: ~操纵 pull strings from behind the scenes

暗自 ànzì (副) inwardly; secretly; to oneself: ~盘算 secretly calculate. ~思量 turn sth. over in one's mind

岸 àn (名) bank; shore; coast: 江~ a river bank. 海~ coast; seashore. 上~ go ashore

岸然 ànrán (形) in a solemn manner: 道貌~ look dignified

肮(骯) āng

肮脏(髒) āngzāng (形) dirty; filthy; foul: ~的勾当 dirty deal; foul play

昂 áng I (动) hold (one's head) high II (形) high; soaring: 雄赳赳,气~~ fearless and militant

昂贵 ángguì (形) very expensive; costly

昂然 ángrán (形) upright and fearless

昂首阔步 ángshǒu-kuòbù stride forward

昂扬(揚) ángyáng (形) high-spirited: 斗志~ have high morale

盎 àng (名) an ancient vessel with a big belly and a small mouth

盎然 àngrán (形) abundant; full; overflowing: 春意~. Spring is in the air.

凹 āo (形) concave; hollow; sunken; dented: ~凸不平 rugged

凹透镜 āotòujìng (名) concave lens

凹陷 āoxiàn (形) hollow; sunken; depressed: 双颊~ sunken (or hollow) cheeks

鏖 áo (动)〈书〉engage in fierce battle

鏖战(戰) áozhàn (动)〈书〉fight hard; engage in fierce battle

熬 áo (动) 1 boil; stew: ~粥 cook gruel. ~药 decoct medicinal herbs 2 endure (pain or hardships): ~白了头 suffer so much that one's hair has turned grey prematurely

熬煎 áojiān (名) suffering; torture: 受尽~ be subjected to all kinds of suffering

熬夜 áoyè (动) stay up late; burn the midnight oil

遨 áo (动) stroll; saunter

遨游 áoyóu (动) roam; wander

嗷 áo

嗷嗷 áo'áo (象): 疼得~叫 scream with pain

翱 áo (动)〈书〉take wing

翱翔 áoxiáng (动) hover; soar: 雄鹰在空中~. Eagles hover in the sky.

袄(襖) ǎo (名) a short Chinese-style coat or jacket: 皮~ a fur coat. 棉~ a cotton-padded jacket

媪 ǎo (名)〈书〉old woman

傲 ào I (形) proud; haughty II (动) refuse to yield to; brave; defy

傲岸 ào'àn (形)〈书〉supercilious; haughty: ～不群 proud and aloof
傲骨 àogǔ (名) lofty and unyielding character
傲慢 àomàn (形) arrogant; haughty: 态度～ be arrogant; put on airs
傲气(氣) àoqì (名) air of arrogance; haughtiness: ～十足 extremely haughty or arrogant
傲然 àorán (副) loftily; unyieldingly
傲视 àoshì (动) turn up one's nose at; scorn; treat with disdain

奥 ào (形) profound; abstruse; difficult to understand
奥林匹克运(運)动(動)会(會) Àolínpǐkè Yùndònghuì (名) Olympic Games; Olympiad
奥秘 àomì (名) profound mystery
奥妙 àomiào (形) profound; subtle; secret

澳 ào (名) an inlet of the sea; bay
澳门(門) Àomén (名) Macao

懊 ào (形) 1 regretful; remorseful 2 annoyed; vexed
懊悔 àohuǐ (动) regret; repent: 我～捅了这么大的娄子. I regret having made such a blunder.
懊恼(惱) àonǎo (形) annoyed; vexed; upset: 他心里很～. He was quite upset.
懊丧(喪) àosàng (形) dejected; depressed

拗 ào
see also niù
拗口 àokǒu (形) hard to pronounce; awkward-sounding: ～话 tongue-twister

B b

捌 bā (数) eight [used for the simpler, though normal, form 八 on cheques, etc. to avoid mistakes or alterations]

八 bā (数) eight
八宝(寶) bābǎo (名) eight treasures (choice ingredients of certain special dishes): ～饭 eight-treasure rice pudding
八成 bāchéng I (名) eighty percent: ～新 eighty percent new; practically new. 事情有了～啦. We stand a fair chance of success. II (副) most probably; most likely: ～他不来了. Most likely he won't come at all.
八方 bāfāng (名) all quarters; all around: 四面～ in all directions; from all quarters
八股 bāgǔ (名) 1 eight-legged style (a literary style prescribed for the imperial civil service examinations during Ming and Qing Dynasties) 2 stereotyped writing
八卦 bāguà (名) the Eight Trigrams (eight combinations of three lines—all solid, all broken or a combination of solid and broken lines—joined in pairs to form 64 hexagrams, formerly used in divination)
八路军 Bālùjūn (名) the Eighth Route Army (led by the Chinese Communist Party during the War of Resistance Against Japan)
八面玲珑(瓏) bāmiàn línglóng be slick (in social intercourse); try to please everybody or offend nobody
八仙 Bāxiān (名) the Eight Immortals (in the legend): ～过海, 各显神通 like the Eight Immortals soaring over the ocean, each showing his or her special skill
八仙桌 bāxiānzhuō (名) a big square table for eight people
八月 bāyuè (名) 1 August 2 the eighth month of the lunar year: ～节 the Mid-Autumn Festival (15th day of the 8th lunar month)
八字 bāzì (名) character 八: ～还没见一撇儿. Nothing tangible is in sight yet.

扒 bā (动) 1 hold on to: ～墙头儿 hold on to the top of the wall 2 dig up; rake; pull down: ～房 pull down the house 3 push aside: ～开芦苇 push aside the reeds 4 strip off; take off: 他把鞋袜一～, 光着脚蹚水. Taking off his shoes and socks, he waded across barefoot.
see also pá
扒拉 bāla (动) touch lightly: 把钟摆～一下 set the pendulum swinging

巴 bā (动) 1 hope earnestly; look forward to: 朝～夜望 be waiting anxiously day and night 2 cling to; stick to: 爬山虎～在墙上. The ivy climbs over the wall. 粥～锅了. The porridge has stuck to the pot. 3 be close to; be next to: 前不～村, 后不着店 with neither villages ahead nor inns behind — stranded in an out-of-the-way place

巴不得 bābude 〈口〉 be only too glad (to do sth.); eagerly look forward to; earnestly wish: 他～立刻开始工作. He is only too glad to get down to work at once.

巴结 bājie I (动) fawn on; curry favour with: ～某人 try to win sb's favour II (形) hard-working: 他工作很～. He is very hard-working.

巴士 bāshì (名) bus

巴望 bāwàng (动) look forward to; earnestly hope

巴眨 bāzha (动) blink; wink

巴掌 bāzhang (名) palm; hand: 打他一～ slap him on the cheek

疤 bā (名) scar

疤痕 bāhén (名) scar

芭 bā

芭蕉 bājiāo (名) *bajiao*; banana

芭蕾舞 bālěiwǔ (名) ballet

吧 bā I (象): ～的一声, 把树枝折断了. The branch broke with a snap. II (动)〈口〉 draw on (one's pipe, etc.)

see also ba

吧台(臺) bātái (名) bar

拔 bá (动) **1** pull out; winkle out: ～草 pull up weeds. ～牙 pull out (or extract) a tooth **2** suck out (usually something poisonous) **3** choose; select (usually people of talent): 选～ select (from candidates) **4** lift; raise: ～起嗓子 raise one's voice **5** stand out; surpass: 出类～萃 be outstanding **6** capture; seize: 连～敌人五个据点 capture five enemy strongholds in succession **7** cool in water: 把西瓜放在冰水里～一～ cool a watermelon in ice water

拔除 báchú (动) wipe out; remove: ～障碍 remove an obstacle

拔河 báhé (名) tug-of-war

拔火罐儿(兒) báhuǒguànr (名) cupping

拔尖儿(兒) bájiānr I (形)〈口〉 tiptop; top-notch: 他们种的花生是～的. The peanuts they grow are top-notch. II (动) push oneself to the front

拔苗助长(長) bá miáo zhù zhǎng try to help the saplings grow by pulling them upward—spoil things by excessive enthusiasm

拔腿 bátuǐ (动) step forward: ～就跑 dash off

跋 bá I (动) trudge over mountains: ～山涉水 travel across mountains and rivers II (名) postscript

跋扈 báhù (形) domineering; bossy

跋涉 báshè (动) trudge; trek: 长途～ trudge over a long distance; trek; make a long arduous journey

靶 bǎ (名) target: 打～ shooting (or target) practice

靶场(場) bǎchǎng (名) shooting range; range

靶心 bǎxīn (名) centre of a target; bull's-eye

靶子 bǎzi (名) target

把 bǎ I (动) **1** hold; grasp; grip: 他紧紧地～住我的手. He held my hand tightly. **2** hold (a baby while it relieves itself) **3** control; monopolize; dominate: 不要什么都～着不放手. Do not keep such a tight control on things. **4** guard; watch: ～门 guard a gate II (名) **1** handle (of a pushcart, etc.): 自行车～ the handlebar of a bicycle **2** bundle; bunch: 草～ a bundle of hay III (量) **1** [for an instrument with a handle]: 一～刀 a knife. 一～茶壶 a teapot. 一～椅子 a chair. **2** [for a handful of sth.]: 一～米 a handful of rice. 一～花 a bunch of flowers **3** [used with certain abstract nouns]: 有一～年纪 be getting on in years. 有～力气 be quite strong. 加～劲 make a special effort; put on a spurt **4** [used to indicate an offer to lend sb. a hand]: 拉他一～ give (or lend) him a hand **5** about; or so: 个～月 about a month; a month or so. 百～人 some hundred people IV (介) [The usage of 把 often causes inversion with the object placed before the verb]: 请～门带上. Shut the door, please. ～水搅浑 muddy the water; create confusion. 这一趟可～他累坏了. That trip really tired him out.

see also bà

把柄 bǎbǐng (名) handle: 给人抓住～ give sb. a handle

把持 bǎchí (动) control; dominate; monopolize: ～机构内一切重要位置 occupy all the key positions in the institution

把舵 bǎduò (动) hold the rudder; take the helm; steer

把风(風) bǎfēng (动) stand guard; keep watch

把关(關) bǎguān (动) 1 guard a pass 2 check on: 层层～ make checks at all levels. 把好质量关 make a careful check of the quality (of goods)

把酒 bǎjiǔ (动) 1 raise one's wine cup 2 fill a wine cup for sb.: ～言欢 converse cheerfully over a glass of wine

把势 bǎshi (名)〈口〉1 *wushu* (武术): 练～ practise *wushu* (martial arts) 2 person skilled in a trade: 车～ carter 3 skill

把手 bǎshou (名) handle; grip; knob

把守 bǎshǒu (动) guard: 分兵～各个关口 divide up one's forces to guard the passes

把头(頭) bǎtóu (名) labour contractor; gangmaster

把稳(穩) bǎwěn (形) trustworthy; dependable: 办事～ be a conscientious worker

把握 bǎwò I (动) hold; grasp: ～时机 seize the opportunity II (名) assurance; certainty: 有成功的～. Success is as good as assured.

把戏(戲) bǎxì (名) 1 acrobatics; jugglery 2 trick: 耍鬼～ play tricks

把兄弟 bǎxiōngdì (名) sworn brothers

霸 bà I (名) 1 chief of feudal princes; overlord 2 tyrant; despot; bully: 恶～ local tyrant (or despot) 3 hegemonist power II (动) dominate; lord it over; tyrannize over: 各～一方 each lording it over his own sphere of influence

霸道 bàdào I (名) (feudal) rule by force II (形) savage; high-handed: 横行～ ride rough-shod over

霸道 bàdao (形) (of liquor, medicine, etc.) strong; potent

霸权(權) bàquán (名) hegemony; supremacy: ～主义 hegemonism

霸王 bàwáng (名) 1 overlord; despot 2 Hegemon King (a title assumed by Xiang Yu 项羽 232—202 B.C.)

霸占(佔) bàzhàn (动) forcibly occupy; illegally take possession of: ～别国领土 forcibly occupy the territory of another country

坝(壩) bà (名) 1 dam 2 dyke; embankment 3 sandbar 4 flatland; plain

罢(罷) bà (动) 1 stop; cease: 作～ let the matter drop. 欲～不能 cannot but carry on 2 dismiss: ～职 remove from office; dismiss 3 finish: 吃～晚饭 after finishing supper

罢黜 bàchù (动)〈书〉1 dismiss from office 2 ban; reject

罢工 bàgōng (名) strike; go on strike

罢官 bàguān (动) dismiss from office

罢课 bàkè (名) students' strike

罢了 bàle (助) [used at the end of a statement to indicate something not worth mentioning]: 这有什么,我不过做了我应该做的事～. I have only done what I ought to. That's all.

罢了 bàliǎo (动) [used to indicate reluctance or displeasure on the part of the speaker]: 他不愿来也就～. Well, if he doesn't want to come, it can't be helped.

罢免 bàmiǎn (动) recall: ～权 right of recall; recall

罢市 bàshì (名) shopkeepers' strike

罢手 bàshǒu (动) give up; stop: 不试验成功,决不～. We will go on with the experiment until we succeed.

罢休 bàxiū (动) give up; let the matter drop [often used in a negative sentence]: 不达目的,决不～. We'll keep on trying until we reach our goal.

耙 bà I (名) harrow II (动) draw a harrow over (a field); harrow
see also pá

把 bà (名) 1 grip; handle: 茶壶～儿 the handle of a teapot. 枪～儿 rifle butt 2 stem (of a leaf, flower or fruit)
see also bǎ

把子 bàzi (名) handle: 刀～the handle of a knife

爸 bà (名) pa; dad; father

爸爸 bàba (名) papa; dad; father

吧 ba (助) 1 [used at the end of a sentence to indicate suggestion, request or command]: 帮帮他～. Let's give him a hand. 2 [used at the end of a sentence to indicate agreement or approval]: 好～,我答应你了. OK, I promise. 3 [used at the end of a sentence to indicate doubt or conjecture]: 他今天大概不来了～? He is not likely to come today, is he? 4 [used to indicate a pause suggesting a dilemma]: 走～,不好,不走～,也不好. It's no good if we go; if we don't, it's no good either.
see also bā

掰 bāi (动) break off with the fingers and thumb: 把饼～成两半 break the cake in two

白 bái I (形) 1 snowwhite: 一件～府绸衬衫 a white poplin shirt 2 clear; made clear: 真相大～. The whole truth is out. 3 pure; plain; blank: ～开水 plain boiled water. ～卷 a blank paper II (副) 1 in vain; to no effect: ～跑一趟 make a fruitless trip. ～费力气 It's a waste of effort. 2 free of charge; gratis: ～送 be given gratis (or as a gift). ～送我都不要. I wouldn't have it as a gift. III (名) 1 White (as a symbol of reaction): ～军 the White army 2 spoken part in opera, etc.: 独～ soliloquy; monologue. 对～ dialogue IV (动) state; explain: 自～ confessions

白白 báibái (副) in vain; for nothing; to no purpose: 时间就这么～地过了. Time slipped by with nothing achieved.

白班儿(兒) báibānr (名)〈口〉day shift

白璧微瑕 báibì wēi xiá a spot in white jade—a slight blemish or small failing in a person's character; a minor defect in anything that would otherwise be perfect

白布 báibù (名) plain white cloth; calico

白菜 báicài (名) Chinese cabbage

白痴(癡) báichī (名) 1 idiocy 2 idiot

白炽(熾) báichì (名) white heat; incandescence: ～灯 incandescent lamp

白搭 báidā〈口〉no use; no good: 和他争辩也是～. It's no use arguing with him.

白带(帶) báidài (名) leucorrhoea; whites

白丁 báidīng (名) a person of no academic or official titles; commoner

白费 báifèi (动) waste: ～唇舌 waste one's breath. ～心思 bother one's head for nothing

白宫 Bái Gōng (名) the White House

白骨 báigǔ (名) white bones (of the dead); bleached bones

白果 báiguǒ (名) ginkgo; gingko

白鹤 báihè (名) white crane

白喉 báihóu (名) diphtheria

白话 báihuà (名) unrealizable wish or unfounded argument: 空口说～ make empty promises

白话 báihuà (名) the written form of modern Chinese (putonghua): ～诗 free verse written in the vernacular

白桦(樺) báihuà (名) white birch

白金 báijīn (名) platinum

白净 báijìng (形) (of skin) fair and clear

白酒 báijiǔ (名) spirit usu. distilled from sorghum or maize; white spirit

白领 báilǐng (名) white-collar

白茫茫 báimángmáng (形) (of cloud, mist, snow, flood water, etc.) a vast expanse of whiteness: 在辽阔的田野上铺了一层雪, ～的一眼望不到尽头. The fields covered with snow became a vast expanse of whiteness stretching to infinity.

白米 báimǐ (名) (polished) rice: ～饭 (cooked) rice

白面(麵) báimiàn (名) wheat flour; fine flour

白面书生 báimiàn shūshēng (名) a young handsome scholar

白描 báimiáo (名) 1 line drawing in the traditional ink and brush style 2 simple, straightforward style of writing

白沫 báimò (名) frothy saliva; foam: 口吐～ foam at the mouth. ～飞溅 speck while talking

白内障 báinèizhàng (名) cataract

白皮书 báipíshū white paper

白热(熱) báirè (名) white heat; incandescence

白热(熱)化 báirèhuà (形) white-hot: 争论达到了～的程度 The debate became white-hot.

白人 báirén (名) white man or woman

白刃 báirèn (名) naked sword: ～战 bayonet charge; hand-to-hand combat

白日做梦(夢) báirì zuòmèng daydream; indulge in wishful thinking: 这是～. This is daydreaming.

白色 báisè I (形) white (colour) II (名) White (as a symbol of reaction): ～恐怖 the white terror

白色污染 báisè wūrǎn (名) "white pollution"; plastic/non-biodegradable litter

白手起家 báishǒu qǐjiā start from scratch

白薯 báishǔ (名) sweet potato

白糖 báitáng (名) (refined) white sugar

白天 báitiān (名) daytime; day

白条(條) báitiáo (名) a promissory note with little binding force

白铁(鐵) báitiě (名) galvanized iron

白头(頭) báitóu (名) hoary head; old age

白头(頭)偕老 báitóu xiélǎo live in conjugal bliss to a ripe old age

白血病 báixuèbìng (名) leukaemia

白血球 báixuèqiú (名) white blood cell

B

白眼 báiyǎn (名) contemptuous look: 遭人～ be treated with disdain

白杨(楊) báiyáng (名) white poplar

白银 báiyín (名) silver

白纸黑字 báizhǐ-hēizì (written) in black and white

白昼(晝) báizhòu (名) daytime

白字 báizì (名) wrongly written or mispronounced character; wrong word; malapropism: ～连篇 full of malapropisms

百 bǎi (数) 1 hundred 2 numerous; all kinds of: ～花盛开. A hundred flowers are in full bloom.

百般 bǎibān (副) in a hundred and one ways; in every possible way; by every means: ～抵赖 try by every means imaginable to deny

百倍 bǎibèi (形) a hundredfold; a hundred times

百尺竿头(頭),更进(進)一步 bǎichǐ gāntóu, gèng jìn yī bù forge further ahead; make still further progress

百发(發)百中 bǎifā-bǎizhòng (as in archery and shooting) every shot hits the target

百废(廢)俱兴(興) bǎi fèi jù xīng get all neglected projects started at once

百分比 bǎifēnbǐ (名) percentage: 按～计算 in terms of percentage

百分之百 bǎifēn zhī bǎi a hundred per cent; absolutely: 有～的把握 be a hundred per cent sure; be absolutely certain

百感交集 bǎi gǎn jiāojí all sorts of feelings well up in one's heart

百花齐(齊)放,百家争鸣 bǎihuā qífàng, bǎijiā zhēngmíng let a hundred flowers blossom and a hundred schools of thought contend

百货 bǎihuò (名) general merchandise: 日用～ articles of daily use; basic commodities. ～商店 department store; general store

百科全书(書) bǎikē quánshū (名) encyclopaedia

百孔千疮(瘡) bǎikǒng-qiānchuāng be riddled with holes; afflicted with social ills; be seriously damaged

百炼(煉)成钢(鋼) bǎi liàn chéng gāng be tempered into steel; be tempered into a person of iron will

百年 bǎinián (名) 1 a hundred years; a very long period 2 lifetime: ～之后〈婉〉 when sb. has passed away; after sb.'s death

百年大计 bǎinián dàjì (名) a project of vital and lasting importance; an undertaking of great moment and long-range significance

百思不解 bǎi sī bù jiě remain puzzled despite much thought

百万(萬) bǎiwàn (数) million: ～富翁 millionaire

百闻不如一见(見) bǎi wén bùrú yī jiàn it is better to see once than hear a hundred times; seeing is believing

百无(無)聊赖 bǎi wú liáolài languish in boredom; overcome with boredom

百姓 bǎixìng (名) common people

百叶(葉)窗 bǎiyèchuāng (名) shutter; blind; jalousie

百依百顺 bǎiyī-bǎishùn docile and obedient; all obedience

百战(戰)百胜(勝) bǎizhàn-bǎishèng fight a hundred battles, win a hundred victories; invincible

百折不挠(撓) bǎi zhé bù náo not flinch despite repeated reverses; be undaunted by repeated setbacks; be indomitable

佰 bǎi (数) hundred [used for the simpler, though normal, form 百 on cheques, etc. to avoid mistakes or alterations]

柏 bǎi (名) cypress

柏树(樹) bǎishù (名) cypress

柏油 bǎiyóu (名) pitch; tar; asphalt

摆(擺) bǎi I (动) 1 put; place; arrange: 把东西～好 put the things in order. ～事实,讲道理 present the facts and reason things out 2 put on; assume: ～架子 put on airs 3 sway; wave: 他向我直～手. He kept waving his hand at me. II (名) pendulum

摆布 bǎibu (动) order about; manipulate: 任人～ allow others to lord it over oneself

摆动(動) bǎidòng (动) swing; sway

摆渡 bǎidù 1 (名) ferry; ferryboat 2 (动) ferry across (a river)

摆阔 bǎikuò (动) parade one's wealth; be ostentatious and extravagant

摆弄 bǎinòng (动) 1 move back and forth; fiddle with: 不要～那架打字机了. Don't fiddle with the typewriter. 2 twist

(someone) round one's little finger
摆平 bǎipíng (动) be fair to; be impartial to
摆谱儿(兒) bǎipǔr (动) keep up appearances; act ostentatiously
摆设 bǎishè (动) furnish and decorate (a room): 屋里～得很美观. The room is beautifully furnished.
摆设 bǎishe (名) furnishings
摆脱 bǎituō (动) get rid of (restraint, difficulty, or any other undesirable state of things): ～困境 extricate oneself from an awkward predicament. ～羁绊 to shake off the yoke. ～旧的传统 break away from the old tradition

败 bài (动) 1 be defeated in battle or beaten in a contest: ～下阵来 lose a battle. 主队以二比三～于客队. The home team lost to the visitors 2 to 3. 2 defeat (enemy): 大～侵略军 inflict a severe defeat on the aggressor troops 3 fail: 不能以成～论英雄. Success or failure is no measure of a person's ability. 4 spoil: 成事不足,～事有余 be unable to accomplish anything but quite capable of spoiling the whole show 5 counteract: ～毒 counteract a toxin 6 decay; wither: 枯枝～叶 dead twigs and withered leaves
败北 bàiběi (动)〈书〉suffer defeat; be defeated
败笔(筆) bàibǐ (名) 1 a faulty stroke in calligraphy or painting 2 a faulty expression in writing
败坏(壞) bàihuài (动) ruin; undermine: ～某人的名誉 blacken sb.'s good name; damage sb.'s reputation. 道德～ degenerate; be depraved
败火 bàihuǒ (动) relieve inflammation or internal heat
败家子 bàijiāzǐ (名) spendthrift; wastrel; prodigal
败类(類) bàilèi (名) scum of a community; degenerate; renegade: 民族～ scum of a nation
败露 bàilù (动) (of a plot, etc.) be discovered or exposed: 阴谋终于～. The conspiracy was eventually uncovered.
败落 bàiluò (动) be on the decline: 家道～. The family lived in reduced circumstances.
败退 bàituì (动) retreat in defeat
败胃 bàiwèi (动) spoil one's appetite
败兴(興) bàixìng (形) in low spirits: 他乘兴而来,～而归. He came in ebullient good spirits but went back very much disappointed.
败仗 bàizhàng (名) lost battle; defeat
败阵 bàizhèn (动) be defeated on the battlefield: ～而逃 lose the field and take to flight
败子 bàizǐ (名) spendthrift, wastrel: ～回头了. The prodigal has returned.

拜 bài I (动) 1 make a courtesy call: 回～ pay a return call 2 form ceremoniously a certain relationship with sb.: ～他为师 respectfully offer oneself as sb.'s disciple; ceremoniously acknowledge sb. as one's master II〈敬〉[used before a verb]: ～读大作 respectfully peruse your work
拜把子 bài bǎzi (动) become sworn brothers
拜倒 bàidǎo (动) prostrate oneself; fall on one's knees; grovel: ～在某人脚下 grovel (or lie prostrate) at the feet of sb.
拜访 bàifǎng (动) pay a visit; pay a call on: 正式～ official visit
拜会(會) bàihuì (动) pay an official call; call on
拜见(見) bàijiàn (动) 1 pay a formal visit; call to pay respects 2 meet one's senior or superior
拜年 bàinián (动) pay a New Year call
拜堂 bàitáng (动) (of bride and groom) perform the marriage ceremony
拜托 bàituō (动)〈敬〉request sb. to do sth.: ～您捎个信儿给他. Would you kindly take a message to him?
拜谒 bàiyè (动) 1 pay a formal visit; call to pay respects 2 pay homage (at a monument, mausoleum, etc.)

稗 bài I (名) barnyard grass II (形)〈书〉insignificant; unofficial
稗官野史 bàiguān-yěshǐ unofficial histories
稗子 bàizi (名) barnyard grass; barnyard millet

斑 bān I (名) spot; speck; speckle: 油～ oil stains. 雀～ speckles II (形) spotted; striped
斑白 bānbái (形) grizzled; greying: 两鬓～ greying at the temples; with greying temples
斑驳 bānbó (形)〈书〉mottled; motley: ～陆离 variegated
斑点(點) bāndiǎn (名) spot; stain
斑斓 bānlán (形) gorgeous; bright-

B

coloured; multicoloured: 五彩～ a blaze of multifarious colours

斑马(馬) bānmǎ (名) zebra

斑纹 bānwén (名) stripe; streak

癍 bān (名) abnormal pigmentary deposits on the skin; flecks

班 bān I (名) **1** class; team: 学习～ study class. 作业～ work team **2** shift; duty: 日夜三～倒 work round the clock in three shifts **3** squad II (量) **1** [for a group of people]: 这～青年人真了不起. They're a fine bunch of young people. **2** [used to indicate the number of runs in transportation]: 搭下一～汽车进城 take the next bus to town III (形) regularly-run; regular; scheduled: ～车 regular bus service

班车(車) bānchē (名) regular bus (service)

班次 bāncì (名) **1** order of classes or grades at school: 她～比我高. She was in a higher class than me. **2** number of runs of flights: 增加货车～ increase the number of runs of freight trains

班底 bāndǐ (名) **1** ordinary members of a theatrical troupe **2** core members of an organization

班房 bānfáng (名)〈口〉 jail: 坐～ be (put) in jail

班机(機) bānjī (名) airliner; regular air service: 京广～ scheduled flights between Beijing and Guangzhou

班门(門)弄斧 Bān mén nòng fǔ show off one's skill with the axe before Lu Ban (the ancient master carpenter); show off one's scanty knowledge in the presence of an expert

班长(長) bānzhǎng (名) **1** class monitor **2** squad leader **3** (work) team leader

班主任 bānzhǔrèn (名) grade adviser; a teacher in charge of a class

班子 bānzi (名) **1** (old use) theatrical troupe **2** group; team: 领导～ a leading body (or group). 生产～ a production team

扳 bān (动) pull; turn: ～倒 pull down. ～着指头算 count on one's fingers

扳机(機) bānjī (名) trigger

扳手 bānshou (名) **1** spanner; wrench **2** lever (on a machine)

扳子 bānzi (名) spanner; wrench

颁 bān (动)promulgate; issue

颁布 bānbù (动) promulgate; issue; publish: ～法令 promulgate a decree

颁发(發) bānfā (动) **1** issue; promulgate: ～命令 issue an order (or directive) **2** award: ～奖章 award a medal (or a certificate of commendation)

颁行 bānxíng (动、名) promulgate; promulgation

般 bān (名)kind; way; like: 百～ in a hundred ways. 暴风雨～的掌声 thunderous applause

般配 bānpèi (形) well matched; well suited

瘢 bān (名) scar

瘢痕 bānhén (名) scar

搬 bān (动) **1** take away; move; remove: 把东西～走 take the junk away **2** move (house): 他早就～走了. He moved away long ago. **3** apply indiscriminately: 生～硬套 copy mechanically and apply indiscriminately

搬家 bānjiā (动) move (house)

搬弄 bānnòng (动) **1** move sth. about; fiddle with: ～枪栓 fiddle with the rifle bolt **2** show off; display: ～学问 show off one's erudition **3** instigate; incite: ～是非 sow the seeds of dissension

搬运(運) bānyùn (动) carry; transport: ～货物 transport goods. ～工人 (of railway station, airport, etc.) porter; docker

坂 bǎn (名)〈书〉 slope

板 bǎn I (名) **1** board; plank; plate: 切菜～ chopping block. 钢～ steel plate **2** shutter: 上～儿 put up the shutters **3** clappers **4** an accented beat in traditional Chinese music; time; measure II (形) **1** hard: 地～了,不好锄. The ground is too hard to hoe. **2** stiff; unnatural: 他们都那样活泼,显得我太～了. I looked a bit stiff while they were so lively. III (动) look serious: 他～着脸不说话. He put on a grave expression, saying nothing.

板凳 bǎndèng (名) wooden bench or stool

板胡 bǎnhú (名) a bowed stringed instrument with a thin wooden soundboard

板结 bǎnjié (动) harden: ～的土壤 hardened and impervious soil

板栗 bǎnlì (名) Chinese chestnut

板刷 bǎnshuā (名)scrubbing brush

板牙 bǎnyá (名) **1** front tooth; incisor **2** molar

板眼 bǎnyǎn (名) **1** measure in traditional

Chinese music 2 orderliness：他说话有板有眼. He is always concise in whatever he says.

板滞(滯) bǎnzhì (形) stiff; dull

板子 bǎnzi (名) 1 board; plank 2 bamboo or birch for corporal punishment

版 bǎn (名) 1 printing plate (or block)：铜～ copperplate. 制～ plate making 2 edition：初～ first edition. 绝～ out of print 3 page (of a newspaper)：头～新闻 front-page news

版本 bǎnběn (名) edition

版次 bǎncì (名) the order in which a book is printed; impression

版画(畫) bǎnhuà (名) etching

版面 bǎnmiàn (名) 1 space of a whole page 2 layout (or make-up) of a printed sheet：～设计 layout

版权(權) bǎnquán (名) copyright：～所有 all rights reserved

版式 bǎnshì (名) format：以新的～重版 re-issued in a new format

版税 bǎnshuì (名) royalty (on books)

版图(圖) bǎntú (名) domain; territory：～辽阔 be vast in territory

瓣 bàn I (名) 1 petal 2 segment or section (of a tangerine, etc.); clove (of garlic) 3 valve; lamella：三尖～ tricuspid valve. 鳃～ gill lamella II (量) [as applied to a petal, a leaf or a fragment of fruit]：把苹果切成四～儿 cut the apple in four

瓣膜 bànmó (名) valve

半 bàn (形) 1 half; semi-：～小时 half an hour. 一个～月 one and a half months. ～机械化 semi-mechanized 2 in the middle; halfway：～山腰 halfway up a hill 3 very little; the least bit：一星～点 a wee bit 4 partly; about half：房门～开着. The door was half open.

半…半… bàn…bàn… [used before two corresponding words to indicate that two opposing ideas exist simultaneously]：半推半就 yield with a show of reluctance. 半心半意 half-hearted. 半信半疑 half-believing, half-doubting. 半吞半吐 ambiguous. 半明半暗 murky

半辈子 bànbèizi (名) the first or second half of one's lifetime; half one's lifetime

半边(邊) bànbiān (形) half of sth.; one side of sth.：～天 half of the sky

半成品 bànchéngpǐn (名) semi-manufactured goods; semi-finished articles or products

半导(導)体(體) bàndǎotǐ (名) semiconductor：～集成电路 semiconductor integrated circuit ～收音机 transistor radio

半岛 bàndǎo (名) peninsula

半点(點) bàndiǎn (形) the least bit：没有～私心 be completely unselfish

半封建 bànfēngjiàn (形) semifeudal

半工半读(讀) bàngōng-bàndú part work, part study：出国～ go abroad on a work-study programme

半截 bànjié (名) half (a section) of sth.：他话只说了～儿. He stopped short when he had scarcely finished what he had to say.

半斤八两(兩) bànjīn-bāliǎng six of one and half a dozen of the other; tweedledum and tweedledee

半径(徑) bànjìng (名) radius

半决赛 bànjuésài (名) (of sports) semi-finals

半空中 bànkōngzhōng in mid air; in the air

半路 bànlù (名) halfway; on the way：走到～天就黑了. It was already dark when we had scarcely got halfway.

半路出家 bànlù chūjiā switch to a new profession or a new field of study late in life

半票 bànpiào (名) half-price ticket; half fare

半瓶醋 bànpíngcù (名) a person who has just a little learning; smatterer

半旗 bànqí (名) half-mast：下～ fly a flag at half-mast

半球 bànqiú (名) hemisphere：东～ the Eastern hemisphere. 北～ the Northern hemisphere

半晌 bànshǎng (名) quite a while：他想了～才想起来. It was quite some time before he recalled it.

半身不遂 bànshēn bùsuí paralysis of one side of the body; hemiplegia

半数(數) bànshù (名) half the number; half：～以上 more than half

半天 bàntiān (名) 1 half of the day：前～ morning. 后～ afternoon 2 a long time; quite a while：等了～他才来. We waited and waited till he came.

半途而废(廢) bàntú ér fèi give up halfway

半夜 bànyè (名) midnight; in the middle of the night：会议一直开到～. The meeting lasted until midnight.

半夜三更 bànyè-sāngēng in the depth of

night; late at night
半圆 bànyuán (名) semicircle
半殖民地 bànzhímíndì (名) semicolony: ～半封建社会 semicolonial, semi-feudal society
拌 bàn (动) mix: 小葱～豆腐 bean curd and scallion salad 给牲口～饲料 mix fodder for animals
拌种(種) bànzhǒng (名) seed dressing
拌嘴 bànzuǐ (动) bicker; squabble; quarrel
伴 bàn I (名) companion; partner: 旅～ fellow-traveller. 作～ keep sb. company II (动) accompany
伴唱 bànchàng (名) vocal accompaniment
伴侣 bànlǚ (名) companion; mate; partner: 结为终身～ become lifelong partners; become man and wife
伴随(隨) bànsuí (动) accompany; follow
伴奏 bànzòu (动) accompany (with musical instruments): 钢琴～ piano accompaniment
绊 bàn (动) (cause to) stumble; trip: ～手～脚 be in the way. ～了一跤 trip over sth.
绊脚石 bànjiǎoshí (名) stumbling block; obstacle
扮 bàn (动) 1 play the part of; disguise oneself as: 他在戏里～一位老渔翁. In the opera he plays the part of an old fisherman. 2 put on (an expression): ～鬼脸 make grimaces; make faces
扮相 bànxiàng (名) the make-up of an actor or actress
扮演 bànyǎn (动) play the part of; act
办(辦) bàn (动) 1 handle; manage; attend to: 怎么～? What is to be done? 2 set up; run: 村里新～了一所中学. A new middle school has been set up in the village. 3 purchase; get sth. ready: ～酒席 prepare a feast; give a banquet 4 punish (by law); bring to book: 严～ punish severely
办案 bàn'àn (动) handle a case
办报(報) bànbào (动) run a newspaper
办法 bànfǎ (名) way; means; measure; ways and means: 她有～解决这个问题. She is capable of tackling the problem.
办公 bàngōng (动) attend to one's routine duties; handle official business: ～厅 general office
办理 bànlǐ (动) handle; conduct; transact: ～手续 go through the formalities (or procedure). 这些事情你可以斟酌～. You may handle these matters at your own discretion.
办事 bànshì (动) handle affairs; work: ～认真 work conscientiously
办学(學) bànxué (动) run a school
邦 bāng (名) nation; state; country: 邻～ a neighbouring country; neighbour state
邦交 bāngjiāo (名) relations between two countries; diplomatic relations: 建立(断绝, 恢复)～ establish (sever, resume) diplomatic relations
梆 bāng (名) watchman's bamboo or wooden clapper
梆子 bāngzi (名) 1 watchman's clapper 2 wooden clappers with bars of unequal length
帮(幫) bāng I (动) help; assist: 互～互学 learn from and help each other. ～他一点忙 help him out II (名) 1 outer leaf (of cabbage, etc.) 2 gang; band; clique: 匪～ bandit gang III (量) [often said of a group of people]: 他带来了一～小朋友. He brought with him a group of children.
帮办(辦) bāngbàn I (动) assist in managing: ～军务 assist in handling military affairs II (名) deputy: 副国务卿～ Deputy Under Secretary (of the U.S. Department of State)
帮倒忙 bāng dàománg (动) do sb. a disservice
帮工 bānggōng I (动) lend a hand with farmwork II (名) farmhand; farm labourer
帮会(會) bānghuì (名) secret society; underworld gang
帮忙 bāngmáng (动) help; give (or lend) a hand; do a favour
帮派 bāngpài (名) faction: ～斗争 factional strife
帮腔 bāngqiāng (动) chime in with similar ideas
帮手 bāngshou (名) assistant
帮闲(閒) bāngxián (动) serve the rich and powerful by literary hack work, etc.: ～文人 literary hack
帮凶 bāngxiōng (名) accomplice; accessory
帮助 bāngzhù (动) help; assist: 互相～ mutual aid

榜 bǎng (名) 1 a list of names posted up: 光荣～ honour roll. 发～ publish the list of successful candidates 2 notice; proclamation

榜样 bǎngyàng (名) good example; model: 为别人作出～ set a good example to the others

膀 bǎng (名) 1 shoulder: ～阔腰圆 broad-shouldered and solidly-built; of a powerful build 2 wing (of a bird)
see also páng

膀臂 bǎngbì (名) 1 upper arm 2 reliable assistant; right-hand man

膀子 bǎngzi (名) 1 upper arm; arm: 光着～ naked to the waist 2 wing: 鸭～ duck wings

绑 bǎng (动) tie up; truss up

绑架 bǎngjià (动) kidnap

绑票 bǎngpiào (动) kidnap sb. and hold him to ransom

绑腿 bǎngtuǐ (名) leg wrappings

谤 bàng (动) slander; defame; vilify

磅 bàng I (名) 1 pound 2 scales: 搁在～上称一称 put sth. on the scale II (动) weigh: ～体重 weigh oneself on the scales
see also páng

磅秤 bàngchèng (名) platform scale; platform balance

镑 bàng (名) pound sterling

傍 bàng (动) draw near; be close to: 依山～水 situated at the foot of a hill with a stream nearby

傍大款 bàng dàkuǎn be supported by a wealthy man (usually of a woman, often implying a sexual relationship)

傍晚 bàngwǎn (名) toward evening; at nightfall; at dusk

棒 bàng I (名) stick; club; cudgel: 垒球～ softball bat II (形)〈口〉strong, good, excellent: ～小伙子 a strong young fellow. 功课～ do well in one's studies

棒槌 bàngchui (名) wooden club (used to beat clothes in washing)

棒球 bàngqiú (名) baseball

棒子 bàngzi (名) 1 stick; club; cudgel 2 maize; corn 3 ear of maize (or corn); corncob: ～面 cornmeal

蚌 bàng (名) freshwater mussel; clam

褒 bāo (动) praise; honour; commend

褒贬 bāo-biǎn (动) pass judgement on; appraise: ～人物 pass judgement on personages. 不加～ make neither commendatory nor censorious remarks; neither praise nor censure

褒贬 bāobian (动) criticize; condemn: 别在背地里～人. Don't speak ill of anybody behind their back.

褒义(義) bāoyì (名) commendatory: ～词 commendatory term

包 bāo I (动) 1 wrap: 把东西～起来 wrap things up (with a piece of paper or cloth or something else). ～饺子 make *jiaozi* (dumplings) 2 surround; encircle; envelop: 火苗～住了这座建筑物. The building was enveloped in flames. 3 include; contain: 无所不～ all-inclusive; all-embracing 4 undertake to fulfil the assignment 5 assure; guarantee: ～你满意. You'll like it, I assure you. 6 hire; charter: ～一只船 hire (or charter) a boat. ～机 a chartered plane II (名) 1 bundle; package; pack; packet; parcel: 邮～ parcel 2 bag: 书～ satchel; school bag 3 (量) [for packages, bundles, etc.]: 一～香烟 a packet (or pack) of cigarettes. 一～棉纱 a bale of cotton yarn

包办(辦) bāobàn (动) 1 take sole charge of 2 do things or make decisions without consulting others: ～婚姻 arranged marriage

包庇 bāobì (动) shield; harbour; cover up: ～坏人坏事 shield evildoers and cover up their evil deeds

包藏 bāocáng (动) contain; harbour; conceal: ～祸心 harbour evil intentions

包场(場) bāochǎng (动) book all or most of the seats in the theatre or cinema; make a block booking

包抄 bāochāo (动) outflank; envelop: 分三路～过去 outflank the enemy in three directions

包车(車) bāochē (名) 1 chartered bus or car 2 private vehicle 3 rickshaw

包二奶 bāo èrnǎi keep a mistress

包袱 bāofu (名) 1 cloth-wrapper 2 a bundle

wrapped in cloth **3** load; weight; burden: 我的思想～丢掉了. It's a load (or weight) off my mind.

包干(乾) bāogān (动) undertake to do a job until it is completed: 分片～ assign a task to an individual or group to be completed within a time limit

包工 bāogōng I (动) undertake to perform work within a time limit and according to specifications; contract for a job II (名) job contract: ～制 job contract system

包工头 bāogōngtóu head of a contracted job

包谷(穀) bāogǔ (名) maize; corn

包裹 bāoguǒ I (动) wrap up; bind up II (名) bundle; package; parcel: 邮政～ postal parcel. ～单 parcel form

包含 bāohán (动) contain; embody; imply: 这句话～好几层意思. This statement has several implications.

包涵 bāohan (动)〈套〉 excuse; forgive: 我英文讲得不好,请多多～. Excuse (me for) my poor English.

包机(機) bāojī (名) chartered plane

包括 bāokuò (动) include; consist of; comprise; incorporate: ～我在内,大家都有责任. All of us, including myself, are to blame.

包揽(攬) bāolǎn (动) monopolize all work to serve private ends: ～词讼 engage in pettifoggery

包罗(羅) bāoluó (动) cover (usually a wide range); embrace (usually many or all aspects)

包罗(羅)万(萬)象 bāoluó wànxiàng embrace a wide spectrum of ideas, subjects, etc.: ～,美不胜收 contain everything that's fine and fascinating

包容 bāoróng I(形) tolerant; magnanimous II(动) contain; hold

包围(圍) bāowéi (动) surround; encircle

包厢 bāoxiāng (名) box at the theatre, opera house, etc.

包销 bāoxiāo (动) have exclusive selling rights

包扎(紮) bāozā (动) wrap up; bind up; pack: ～伤口 bind up (or dress) a wound

包装 bāozhuāng (动、名) pack; package: ～车间 packing department. ～箱 packing box (or case)

包子 bāozi (名) steamed stuffed bun

炮 bāo (动) **1** quick-fry; sauté: ～羊肉 quick-fried mutton **2** dry by heat see also páo; pào

苞 bāo (名) bud; unopened flower: 含～待放 be in bud

龅 bāo

龅牙 bāoyá (名) bucktooth

胞 bāo I (名) afterbirth II (形) born of the same parents: ～兄弟 full brothers

孢 bāo

孢子 bāozǐ (名) spore

剥 bāo (动) shell; peel; skin: ～花生 shell peanuts. ～洋葱 skin an onion. ～桔子 peel a tangerine see also bō

雹 báo (～子)(名) hail; hailstone

薄 báo (形) **1** thin; flimsy: ～纸 thin paper **2** weak; light: ～酒 a light wine **3** coldly; shabbily: 待他不～ treat him quite generously **4** infertile: ～田 infertile land see also bó

薄板 báobǎn (名) sheet metal; sheet: 不锈钢～ stainless sheet steel

宝(寶) bǎo I (名) treasure: 粮食是～中之～. Grain is the treasure of treasures. II (形) precious; treasured: ～刀 a treasured sword III〈敬〉[said of a friend's family, etc. in old days]: ～眷 your good wife and children; your family

宝贝(貝) bǎobèi (名) **1** treasured object; treasure **2** darling; baby **3** a person with fantastic or absurd ideas: 这人真是个～! What a crank he is!

宝贵 bǎoguì I (形) valuable; precious: ～意见 valuable suggestion II (动) value; treasure; set store by: 这是极可～的经验. This is a very valuable (or rewarding) experience.

宝剑(劍) bǎojiàn (名) a double-edged sword

宝库(庫) bǎokù (名) treasure-house

宝石 bǎoshí (名) precious stone; gem

宝塔 bǎotǎ (名) pagoda

宝物 bǎowù (名) treasure

宝藏 bǎozàng (名) precious (mineral) deposits: 发掘地下～ tap mineral resources

宝座 bǎozuò (名) throne

保 bǎo I (动) 1 protect; defend; safeguard: ～家卫国 protect our homes and defend our country; safeguard our homeland 2 keep; maintain; preserve: ～温 keep (sth.) warm or hot 3 guarantee; ensure: ～质～量 ensure both quality and quantity 4 go bail for sb.: ～外就医 be bailed out for medical treatment II (名) guarantor: 作～ stand guarantor (or surety) for sb.

保安 bǎo'ān (动) 1 ensure public security; maintain law and order 2 ensure safety (for workers engaged in production)

保镖 bǎobiāo (名) bodyguard

保不住 bǎobuzhù (副) most likely; more likely than not: ～会下雨. Most probably it's going to rain.

保藏 bǎocáng (动) keep in store; preserve (sth.) from damage or loss

保持 bǎochí (动) keep; maintain: ～安静 keep quiet. ～冷静的头脑 keep a cool head; keep cool. 跟群众～密切联系 keep close to the masses. ～中立 remain neutral; maintain neutrality. ～警惕 maintain vigilance; be on the alert

保存 bǎocún (动) preserve; conserve; keep: ～优良传统 preserve the fine traditions. ～得很完整 be well preserved; be kept intact

保单(單) bǎodān (名) guarantee slip

保管 bǎoguǎn I (动) take care of: ～图书 take care of library books II (副) certainly; surely: 他～不知道. He certainly doesn't know.

保护(護) bǎohù (动) protect; safeguard: ～国家财产 protect state property. ～人民的利益 safeguard the people's interests. ～关税 protective tariff. ～国 protectorate. ～贸易主义 protectionism. ～人 guardian

保皇党(黨) bǎohuángdǎng (名) royalists

保驾 bǎojià (动) [showing a sense of humour] escort the Emperor: 放心吧,我给你～. Don't worry. I'll escort you.

保健 bǎojiàn (名) health protection; health care: 妇幼～ maternal and child hygiene; mother and child care. ～食品 health food. ～操 keep-fit exercise

保洁 bǎojié (名) cleaning service

保龄球 bǎolíngqiú (名) bowling; bowling ball

保留 bǎoliú (动) 1 retain: 仍然～他年轻时的工作作风 still retain the work style of his youthful days 2 hold (or keep) back; reserve: ～以后再答复的权利 reserve the right to reply at a later date. 持～意见 have reservations. ～剧目 repertory; repertoire. ～条款 reservation clause

保密 bǎomì (动) maintain secrecy; keep sth. secret: 这事绝对～. This is strictly confidential.

保姆 bǎomǔ (名) 1 (children's) nurse or domestic help 2 child-care worker

保全 bǎoquán (动) 1 save from damage; preserve: ～面子 save face 2 maintain; keep in good repair

保墒 bǎoshāng (名) preservation of soil moisture

保释(釋) bǎoshì (动) release on bail; bail: 准予(不准)～ accept (refuse) bail

保守 bǎoshǒu I (动) guard; keep: ～国家机密 guard state secrets II (形) conservative: ～思想 conservative ideas (or thinking)

保税区(區) bǎo shuìqū (名) bonded area

保送 bǎosòng (动) recommend sb. for admission to school, etc.

保卫(衛) bǎowèi (动) defend; safeguard: ～祖国 defend one's country

保温 bǎowēn (动) keep warm; heat preservation: ～层 insulating layer. ～杯 thermos mug

保鲜 bǎoxiān (动) keep fresh (of fruit, vegetables, etc.); preserve freshness

保险(險) bǎoxiǎn I (名) insurance: 人寿(海损)～ life (maritime) insurance. ～公司 insurance company II (形) 1 safe: 这样做可不～. It wouldn't be safe to pursue such a course. 2 be bound to: 他明天～会来. He is sure to come tomorrow.

保险(險)刀 bǎoxiǎndāo (名) safety razor

保险(險)丝 bǎoxiǎnsī (名) fuse; fuse-wire

保修 bǎoxiū (名) guarantee to keep sth. in good repair: ～一年 a year's guarantee

保养(養) bǎoyǎng (动) 1 take good care of (or conserve) one's health: 他～得好. He is well preserved. 2 maintain; keep in good repair: 机器～ maintenance (or upkeep) of machinery

保佑 bǎoyòu (动) bless and protect

保育 bǎoyù (名) child care; child welfare: ～员 child-care worker; nurse

保障 bǎozhàng (动) ensure; guarantee; safeguard: ～人民言论自由 guarantee freedom of speech for the people. ～国家安全 assure national security

保证 bǎozhèng I (动) pledge; guarantee; assure; ensure: ~完成任务 pledge (or guarantee) to fulfil the task. ~履行 pledge to fulfil (obligation, etc.) II (名) guarantee: 成功的~ a guarantee of success

保证人 bǎozhèngrén (名) 1 guarantor 2 bail

保值 bǎozhí (动) guarantee the value: ~期 value-guarantee period

保重 bǎozhòng (动) take care of oneself: 多多~. Take good care of yourself.

堡 bǎo (名) fort; fortress

堡垒(壘) bǎolěi (名) fort; fortress; stronghold; blockhouse

葆 bǎo 〈书〉 I (名) luxuriant growth II (动) preserve; retain: 永~青春 keep alive at all times one's youthful fervour

饱 bǎo I (形) 1 have eaten one's fill; be full: 我~了. I am full. 2 full; plump: 谷粒很~. The grains are quite plump. II (副) fully; to the full: ~尝旧日的辛酸 taste to the full the bitter hardships of the old days. ~经优患 suffer untold tribulations III (动) satisfy: 一~眼福 enjoy to the full watching a show, match, performance, etc.

饱餐 bǎocān (动) eat to one's heart's content: ~一顿 have a big meal; eat and drink one's fill

饱嗝儿(兒) bǎogér (名) hiccup; belch: 打~ give a belch; hiccup; have a belch

饱和 bǎohé (名) saturation

饱经(經)风(風)霜 bǎo jīng fēngshuāng having had one's fill of hardships and difficulties

饱满(滿) bǎomǎn (形) full; plump: 颗粒~的小麦 plump-eared wheat. 精神~ vigorous; energetic

饱学(學) bǎoxué (形) learned; erudite; scholarly: ~之士 a learned scholar; a man of great erudition

报(報) bào I (动) 1 announce; declare 2 reply; respond; requite: ~以热烈的掌声 respond with warm applause. 以怨~德 requite kindness with ingratitude; return evil for good II (名) 1 newspaper 2 periodical; journal: 画~ pictorial. 周~ weekly. 学~ college journal 3 bulletin; report: 喜~ report of success, a happy event, etc.; glad tidings; good news 4 telegram; cable: 发~机 transmitter

报案 bào'àn (动) report to the police an act violating the law or endangering social security

报表 bàobiǎo (名) forms for reporting to the higher organizations

报仇 bàochóu (动) avenge; revenge: ~雪恨 avenge a gross injustice

报酬 bàochou (名) reward; remuneration; pay: 不计~ not think in terms of remuneration

报答 bàodá (动) repay; requite: ~老师的关怀 repay the teacher for all his kindness

报到 bàodào (动) report for work; check in; register: 向大会秘书处~ check in at the secretariat of the congress

报道 bàodào I (动) report (news); cover: ~会议情况 cover the conference II (名) news reporting; story: 他们写了一篇关于小麦丰收的~. They wrote an article describing the bumper harvest of wheat.

报恩 bào'ēn (动) pay a debt of gratitude; repay a person for his kindness

报废(廢) bàofèi (动) discard any article or equipment which is no longer useful; scrap

报复(復) bàofù (动) make reprisal; retaliate: 图谋~ nurse thoughts of revenge; contemplate retaliation

报告 bàogào I (动) report; make known: 向上级~ report to the higher authorities II (名) report; speech; lecture: 总结~ summing-up report. ~文学 reportage

报关(關) bàoguān (动) apply to customs to comply with import or export regulations

报国(國) bàoguó (动) dedicate one's life to the cause of the country

报户口 bào hùkǒu (动) apply for a residence permit; report at the police station

报价(價) bàojià (名) quoted price

报捷 bàojié (动) report a success; announce a victory

报界 bàojiè (名) the press; journalistic circles; the journalists

报警 bàojǐng (动) 1 report (an imminent danger) to the police 2 give an alarm

报刊 bàokān (名) newspapers and periodicals; the press

报考 bàokǎo (动) enter (oneself) for the examination

报名 bàomíng (动) enter one's name; sign up: ~参加百米赛跑 sign up to participate in the 100-metre dash

报幕 bàomù (动) announce the items on a (theatrical) programme: ～员 announcer

报社 bàoshè (名) newspaper office

报失 bàoshī (动) report lost property to the authorities

报时(時) bàoshí (动) give the correct time (particularly referring to the correct time given by the radio station or telephone bureau to all inquirers)

报摊(攤) bàotān (名) news-stand; news agent's; news stall

报务(務)员 bàowùyuán (名) telegraph operator; radio operator

报喜 bàoxǐ (动) report a success worthy of celebration

报销 bàoxiāo (动) 1 ask for reimbursement 2〈口〉write off; wipe out

报晓(曉) bàoxiǎo (动) (of a cock, bell, etc.) herald the break of day; be a harbinger of dawn

报效 bàoxiào (动) render service to repay sb.'s kindness

报信 bàoxìn (动) pass on a message to (sb.)

报应(應) bàoyìng (名) retribution; judgment (on sb.)

报章 bàozhāng (名) newspapers: ～杂志 newspapers and magazines

报纸 bàozhǐ (名) 1 newspaper 2 newsprint

暴 bào (形) 1 sudden and violent: ～饮～食 eat and drink immoderately 2 cruel; savage: 残～ atrocious 3 short-tempered; hot-tempered: 脾气～ have a hot temper

暴病 bàobìng (名) a sudden serious illness: 得～ suddenly fall gravely ill

暴跌 bàodiē (动) steep fall (in price); slump

暴动(動) bàodòng (名) insurrection; rebellion

暴发(發) bàofā (动) 1 break out: 山洪～. Torrents of water swept down the mountain. 2 suddenly become wealthy and powerful: ～户 upstart

暴风(風) bàofēng (名) 1 storm wind 2 storm (force 11 wind)

暴风(風)雨 bàofēngyǔ (名) rainstorm; storm; tempest: ～般的掌声 thunderous applause

暴风(風)骤雨 bàofēng-zhòuyǔ (名) violent storm; hurricane; tempest

暴光 bàoguāng (名) exposure

暴君 bàojūn (名) tyrant; despot

暴力 bàolì (名) violence; force; brute force

暴利 bàolì (名) huge ill-gotten gains: 牟取～ reap staggering (or colossal) profits

暴戾 bàolì (形)〈书〉ruthless and tyrannical; cruel and ferocious

暴烈 bàoliè (形) violent; fierce: 性情～ have a fiery temper

暴露 bàolù (动) expose; reveal; lay bare: ～身份 reveal one's identity. ～无遗 be thoroughly exposed

暴乱(亂) bàoluàn (名) rebellion; revolt: 平定～ suppress (or put down, quell) a rebellion

暴民 bàomín (名) mob

暴虐 bàonüè (形) ruthless; tyrannical: ～无道 reign tyrannically and defy all ethical principles

暴殄天物 bàotiǎn tiānwù wilfully destroy Mother Nature's belongings—recklessly waste what is given to us by nature

暴跳如雷 bàotiào rú léi stamp with fury; fly into a rage

暴徒 bàotú (名) ruffian; thug; hooligan

暴行 bàoxíng (名) outrage; atrocity

暴雨 bàoyǔ (名) torrential rain; rainstorm

暴躁 bàozào (形) irascible; irritable: 性情～ easily get into a violent temper

暴涨(漲) bàozhǎng (动) (of floods, prices, etc.) rise suddenly or sharply

暴政 bàozhèng (名) tyranny; despotic rule

暴卒 bàozú (动) die suddenly

爆 bào (动) 1 explode; burst: 车胎～了. The tyre's burst. 2 quick-fry; quick-boil: ～羊肉 quick-fried mutton

爆炒 bàochǎo (动) 1 quick-fry 2 promote feverishly

爆发(發) bàofā (动) erupt; burst out; break out: 火山～. The volcano erupted. 战争～. War broke out.

爆料 bàoliào (动) unveil; expose, esp. as a news story

爆冷门(門) bào lěngmén produce an unexpected winner; a dark horse bobs up

爆满 bàomǎn (形) fully packed

爆破 bàopò (动) blow up; demolish; dynamite; blast

爆炸 bàozhà (动) explode; blow up; detonate

爆竹 bàozhú (名) firecracker: 放～ let off firecrackers

曝 bào

B

see also pù

曝光 bàoguāng (名) exposure

豹 bào (名) leopard; panther

抱 bào I (动) 1 hold or carry in one's arms; embrace; hug 2 have one's first child or grandchild 3 adopt (a child) 4 hang together: ~成团 gang up 5 cherish; harbour: 不~幻想 cherish no illusions 6 hatch (eggs); brood II (量) [indicating quantity of material as being held by both arms]: 一~草 an armful of hay

抱病 bàobìng (动) be ill; be in poor health: 长期~ have been ill for a long time

抱不平 bào bùpíng feel indignant at the injustice suffered by another: 打~ put up a fight against an injustice on sb.'s behalf

抱残(殘)守缺 bàocán-shǒuquē stick to old-fashioned ideas and refuse to change; be a stick-in-the-mud

抱负 bàofù (名) aspiration; ambition: 很有~ have high aspirations; be very ambitious

抱恨 bàohèn (动) be weighed down with a deep sense of regret: ~终天 be subject to lifelong remorse

抱歉 bàoqiàn (动) be sorry; regret: 到迟了, 很~. I'm sorry, I'm late.

抱头(頭)鼠窜(竄) bàotóu shǔcuàn cover one's head with both hands and run away like a coward; flee helter-skelter

抱头(頭)痛哭 bàotóu tòngkū weep in each other's arms; cry on each other's shoulder

抱团(團)儿(兒) bàotuánr gang up; hang together

抱怨 bàoyuàn (动)complain; grumble

抱罪 bàozuì (动) have a guilty conscience; be conscience-stricken

刨 bào I (动) plane sth. down; plane: ~木板 plane a board II (名) plane; planer; planing machine

see also páo

刨床(牀) bàochuáng (名) planer; planing machine

刨子 bàozi (名) plane

鲍 bào

鲍鱼(魚) bàoyú (名) 1 abalone 2 〈书〉 salted fish

杯 bēi (名) 1 cup: 茶~ teacup. 一~茶 a cup of tea. 一~水 a glass of water 2 (prize)cup; trophy: 银~ silver cup

杯弓蛇影 bēigōng-shéyǐng mistake the reflection of a bow in the wine cup for a snake—be too panicky and often get unnecessarily scared

杯水车(車)薪 bēishuǐ-chēxīn try to put out a burning cartload of wood with a cup of water—make a ridiculously inadequate effort to save a grave situation

杯子 bēizi (名) cup; glass

悲 bēi (形) sad; sorrowful; melancholy: ~不自胜 be overwhelmed with grief. 慈~ compassionate; merciful

悲哀 bēi'āi (形) grieved; sorrowful

悲惨(慘) bēicǎn (形) miserable; tragic: ~景象 a tragic scene or spectacle

悲悼 bēidào (动) mourn; grieve over sb.'s death

悲愤 bēifèn (名) grief and indignation

悲歌 bēigē I (名) 1 sad melody; stirring strains 2 elegy; dirge II (动) sing with solemn fervour

悲观(觀) bēiguān (形) pessimistic: ~情绪 pessimism

悲欢(歡)离(離)合 bēi-huān-lí-hé the meetings and partings, the joys and sorrows—generally referring to varied and often bitter experiences of life

悲剧(劇) bēijù (名) tragedy

悲凉 bēiliáng (形) sad and dreary; desolate; forlorn

悲泣 bēiqì (动) weep with grief

悲伤(傷) bēishāng (形) sad; miserable

悲叹(嘆) bēitàn (动) bemoan; lament

悲天悯人 bēitiān-mǐnrén feel both grieved and indignant at the depravity of human society and the suffering of the masses

悲痛 bēitòng (名) grief; sorrow: 感到深切的~ be deeply grieved; be overcome with sorrow

悲喜交集 bēi-xǐ jiāojí have mixed feelings; feel grief and joy intermingled

悲壮(壯) bēizhuàng (形)solemn and stirring

背 bēi (动) 1 carry on one's back 2 bear; shoulder: 这个责任我还~得起. I presume I am up to this job.

see also bèi

背包 bēibāo (名) 1 knapsack; rucksack; field pack 2 blanket roll

背包袱 bēi bāofu (动) have a weight (or load) on one's mind

背负 bēifù (动) bear; carry on one's back; have on one's shoulder

*背黑锅(鍋) bēi hēiguō (动)〈口〉take the blame for the fault of others; be made a scapegoat

背债 bēizhài (动) be in debt; be saddled with debts

卑 bēi (形) 1 low: 地势～湿. The terrain is low-lying and damp. 2 inferior: ～不足道 too inferior to be worth mentioning 3 〈书〉 modest; humble: ～辞厚礼 send a humble message along with expensive gifts

卑鄙 bēibǐ (形) base; ammoral; despicable: ～无耻 devoid of any sense of shame; shameless. ～龌龊 base and vile

卑躬屈节(節) bēigōng-qūjié be spineless and servile; bow and scrape

卑贱(賤) bēijiàn (形) 1 low, humble: 出身～ be of humble station or origin (in the old society) 2 mean and low

卑劣 bēiliè (形) base; mean; despicable: ～行径 base conduct. ～手法 a mean (or despicable) trick

卑怯 bēiqiè (形) weak-kneed; abject: ～行为 abject behaviour

卑微 bēiwēi (形) petty and low; mean

卑污 bēiwū (形) depraved

卑下 bēixià (形) base; low

碑 bēi (名) an upright stone tablet; stele: 人民英雄纪念～ the Monument to the People's Heroes. 墓～ tombstone

碑帖 bēitiè (名) a rubbing from a stone inscription (usu. as a model for calligraphy)

碑文 bēiwén (名) an inscription on a tablet

碑志 bēizhì (名) a record of events inscribed on a tablet

北 běi I (名) north: ～风 a north wind. 城～ north of the city. 华～ north China. ～屋 a room with a southern exposure II (动)〈书〉 be defeated: 连战皆～ be defeated in one battle after another

北半球 běibànqiú (名) the Northern Hemisphere

北冰洋 Běibīngyáng (名) the Arctic (Ocean)

北斗星 běidǒuxīng (名) the Big Dipper; the Plough

北方 běifāng (名) 1 north 2 the northern part of the country, esp. the area north of the Yellow River; the North: ～话 northern dialect. ～人 Northerner

北国(國) běiguó (名)〈书〉 the northern part of the country; the North

北极(極) běijí (名) 1 the North Pole; the Arctic Pole 2 the north magnetic pole

北京 Běijīng (名) Beijing (Peking)

北京人 Běijīngrén (名) Peking man (Sinanthropus pekinensis)

北美洲 Běi Měizhōu (名) North America

北纬(緯) běiwěi (名) north (or northern) latitude

北温带(帶) běiwēndài (名) the north temperate zone

焙 bèi (动) bake over a slow fire: ～干 dry over a fire. ～制 cure sth. by drying it over a fire

焙烧(燒) bèishāo (动) roast; bake

倍 bèi I (量) times: -fold: 四～ four times; fourfold. 二的五～是十. Five times two is ten. 增长了五～ increase by 500%; register a 500% increase; be six times as much. 产量成～增长. Output has doubled and redoubled. II (形) double; twice as much: 事半功～ get twice the result with half the effort

倍数(數) bèishù (名) multiple

蓓 bèi

蓓蕾 bèilěi (名) bud

悖 bèi 〈书〉 be contrary to; go against: ～理 contrary to reason. 并行不～ be parallel and not contrary to each other; not be mutually exclusive; can be carried out simultaneously without affecting each other

悖谬 bèimiù (形)〈书〉 absurd; preposterous

悖入悖出 bèirù-bèichū ill-gotten, ill-spent; easy come, easy go

辈 bèi (名) 1 people of similar interests; people of one kind or another: 无能之～ mediocre people 2 generation: 他比我长(小)一～. He's one generation my senior (junior). 他俩同～. They belong to the same generation. 3 lifetime: 后半～儿 the latter part of one's life

辈出 bèichū (动) come forth in large numbers: 人才～ Large numbers of talented people are coming to the fore.

辈分 bèifen (名) seniority in the family or clan; position in the family hierarchy

B

背 bèi I (名) 1 the back of the body; the back of an object 2 at the back: ~山面海 with hills behind and the sea in front II (动) 1 hide sth. from view; do sth. behind sb.'s back: 没有什么~人的事 have nothing to hide from anyone 2 recite from memory; learn by heart (or by rote): ~台词 recite the words of an actor's part; speak one's lines 3 act contrary to; violate; break: ~约 break one's promise; go back on one's word III (形) 1 out-of-the-way: ~街 back street; side street 2 hard of hearing 3〈口〉unlucky
see also bēi

背道而驰 bèi dào ér chí run in opposite directions; run counter to; be diametrically opposed to

背地里(裏) bèidìli (副) behind sb.'s back; in private; on the sly

背风(風) bèifēng (形) out of the wind; on the lee side; leeward

背光 bèiguāng (动) be shaded from the sun; be sheltered from direct light

背后(後) bèihòu (名) 1 behind; at the back; in the rear: 门~ behind the door. 房子~ at the back of the house 2 behind sb.'s back: 有话当面说,不要~乱说. Speak openly when you've got anything to say, but don't gossip behind anybody's back.

背井离(離)乡(鄉) bèijǐng-líxiāng leave one's native place to earn a livelihood elsewhere (esp. against one's will)

背景 bèijǐng (名) background; backdrop: 历史~ historical background (or setting)

背静 bèijing (形) quiet and secluded

背靠背 bèikàobèi 1 back to back 2 examine or criticize sb. without his knowledge

背离(離) bèilí (动) deviate from; depart from: ~原意 deviate from one's original intentions

背面 bèimiàn (名) the reverse side of an object: 信封的~ the back of an envelope

背叛 bèipàn (动) betray; forsake

背弃(棄) bèiqì (动) abandon; desert; renounce: ~自己的诺言 go back on one's word

背时(時) bèishí (形) 1 behind the times 2 ill-fated; unfortunate

背书(書) bèishū I (动) recite a book from memory II (名) endorsement (on a cheque); signature or seal on the back of a cheque

背水一战(戰) bèi shuǐ yī zhàn fight with one's back to the river — fight to win or die in the attempt

背诵 bèisòng (动) recite from memory

背心 bèixīn (名) a sleeveless garment: 汗~ vest; singlet. 毛~ sleeveless woollen sweater

背信弃(棄)义(義) bèixìn-qìyì break faith with sb.; be perfidious: ~的行为 a breach of faith; an act of perfidy

背阴(陰) bèiyīn (形) (a spot) entirely shaded from the sun

背影 bèiyǐng (名) a view of sb.'s back; a figure viewed from behind

背约 bèiyuē (动) break an agreement; go back on one's word; fail to keep one's promise

褙 bèi (动) stick one piece of cloth or paper on top of another

贝(貝) bèi (名) 1 shellfish 2 cowrie

贝壳(殼) bèiké (名) shell

贝类(類) bèilèi (名) shellfish; molluscs

备(備) bèi I (动) 1 be equipped with; have: 德才兼~ have both political integrity and professional knowledge 2 prepare; get ready: ~而不用 get things ready not for immediate use, but for future occasions 3 provide (or prepare) against; take precautions against: 以~万一 prepare against all eventualities II (名) equipment: 军~ military equipment; armaments III (副) fully; in every possible way: ~受欢迎 be given a rousing welcome

备案 bèi'àn (动) report to the higher organization a case to be put on record (or on file) for future reference

备查 bèichá (动) for future reference

备耕 bèigēng (动) get things ready for ploughing and sowing

备荒 bèihuāng (动) prepare against natural disasters

备件 bèijiàn (名) spare parts

备考 bèikǎo (名) appendices or notes supplied for reference

备课 bèikè (动) (of a teacher or student) prepare lessons

备料 bèiliào (动) 1 get the raw materials ready 2 prepare feed (for livestock)

备忘录(録) bèiwànglù (名) 1 memorandum;

aide-memoire 2 memorandum book

备用 bèiyòng (动) reserve; spare: ~轮胎 a spare tyre

备战(戰) bèizhàn (动) 1 prepare for war: 扩军~ arms expansion and war preparations 2 be prepared against war

备至 bèizhì (副) to the utmost; in every possible way: 关怀~ show sb. every consideration

备注 bèizhù (名) remarks (a column reserved for additional information in a form)

惫(憊) bèi (形) exhausted; fatigued

被 bèi I (名) quilt: 棉~ cotton-wadded quilt II(介)[introducing the agent in a passive sentence]: 他~蛇咬伤. He was bitten by a snake. III (助)[used before a notional verb to indicate that the subject is the receiver]: ~捕 be arrested; be under arrest. ~选为主席 be elected chairman

被剥削阶(階)级 bèibōxuējiējí (名) the exploited class

被单(單) bèidān (名) (bed) sheet

被动(動) bèidòng (形) passive: 陷于~地位 land oneself in a passive position. ~语态 passive voice

被服 bèifú (名) bedding and clothing (esp. for army use)

被告 bèigào (名) defendant; the accused

被害人 bèihàirén (名) the injured party; the victim

被里(裏) bèilǐ (名) the underside of a quilt

被面 bèimiàn (名) the facing of a quilt

被迫 bèipò (动) be compelled; be forced; be constrained: ~作出这个决定 be compelled to make this decision

被褥 bèirù (名) bedding; bedclothes

被套 bèitào (名) 1 bedding bag 2 (bag-shaped) quilt cover 3 cotton wadding for a quilt

被选(選)举(舉)权(權) bèi-xuǎnjǔquán (名) the right to be elected

被压(壓)迫民族 bèiyāpò mínzú (名) oppressed nation

被子 bèizi (名) quilt

呗 bei (助) 1[indicating that the idea is simple and easy to understand]: 你不会骑车就学~. You can't ride a bike? Well, learn to. 2 [indicating agreement with reluctance]: 你一定要去, 就去~. Well, go if you insist.

贲 bēn

贲门(門) bēnmén (名) cardia

奔 bēn (动) 1 run quickly: ~驰 gallop; run about 2 hurry: ~走 dash around (on business) 3 flee: 东~西窜 flee helter-skelter

see also bèn

奔波 bēnbō (动) rush about; hurry back and forth

奔驰 bēnchí (动) run fast; speed: 火车~而过. The train sped past.

奔放 bēnfàng (形) bold and unrestrained; untrammelled; uninhibited: 热情~ brimming over with deep emotion

奔赴 bēnfù (动) rush to (a place); hurry to

奔流 bēnliú I (动) flow at great speed; pour: ~入海 empty into the sea. 铁水~ molten iron comes pouring out II (名) racing current; running stream

奔忙 bēnmáng (动) be dashing about all day

奔命 bēnmìng (动) dash around on business: 疲于~ be run off one's feet

奔跑 bēnpǎo (动) run

奔丧(喪) bēnsāng (动) hasten home for the funeral of a parent

奔逃 bēntáo (动) flee; run away: 四散~ flee in all directions; flee helter-skelter; stampede

奔腾 bēnténg (动) 1 gallop: 犹如万马~ like ten thousand galloping horses 2 surge forward; roll on in waves

奔泻(瀉) bēnxiè (动) (of torrents) rush down; pour down

奔走 bēnzǒu (动) rush about; be busy running about: ~呼号 campaigning for (a cause); crusading for. ~相告 run around telling people the news; lose no time in passing on the news

锛 bēn I (名)(~子) adze II (动) cut with an adze

本 běn I (名) 1 the root or stem of a plant 2 foundation; basis; origin: 舍~逐末 attend to trifles and neglect essentials 3 capital; principal: 还~付息 pay back the capital (or principal) plus interest 4 book: 账~儿 account book. 日记~ diary. 照相~ photograph album 5 edition; version: 普及~ popular edition II (形) 1 original: ~意 original idea; real intention. 我~想不去. Originally I didn't mean to go. 2 one's own: ~厂 this factory 3 this; current; present: ~

周(月) this week (month); the current week (month) III (介) according to; based on IV (量) [for books, albums, etc.]: 两~书 two books

本草 běncǎo (名) a book on Chinese (herbal) medicine: 《~纲目》 *Compendium of Materia Medica*

本初子午线(綫) běnchū zǐwǔxiàn (名) the first meridian; the prime meridian

本地 běndì (名) this locality: ~口音 local accent

本分 běnfèn I (名) one's duty: 尽~ do one's duty (or part) II (形) contented with one's lot

本国(國) běnguó (名) homeland; one's own country: ~资源 national resources

本行 běnháng (名) one's line; one's own profession

本家 běnjiā (名) a member of the same clan; a distant relative with the same family name

本届 běnjiè (形) current; this year's: ~毕业生 this year's graduates

本金 běnjīn (名) capital; principal

本科 běnkē (名) undergraduate course; regular college course: ~学生 undergraduate

本来(來) běnlái I (形) original: ~的面貌 true features II (副) 1 originally; at first: ~他身体不好,现在很结实了. Originally he was in poor health but he is quite strong now. 2 it goes without saying; of course: ~就该快办. Of course we should act promptly.

本领 běnlǐng (名) skill; ability; capability: ~高强 of superb skill

本命年 běnmìngnián (名) every 12th year after the year of one's birth

本末 běn-mò (名) 1 the whole course of an event from beginning to end; ins and outs: 详述~ recount the whole story in detail 2 the fundamental and the incidental: ~倒置 take the branch for the root; put the incidental before the fundamental

本能 běnnéng (名) instinct

本钱(錢) běnqián (名) capital

本人 běnrén (名) 1 oneself; in person: 这事还是由他~来谈吧. He had better bring up the matter himself. 2 I (me, myself)

本色 běnsè (名) 1 true (or inherent) qualities; distinctive character: 军人的~ inherent qualities of a soldier 2 natural colour: ~棉毛衫 a sweater of natural colour

本身 běnshēn (名) itself: 这幅画~并没有什么价值. The painting itself is of very little value.

本事 běnshì (名) source material; original story: 《莎氏乐府~》 *Tales from Shakespeare*

本事 běnshi (名) ability

本题 běntí (名) the subject under discussion; the point at issue: 这一段文章与~无关,应该删去. This paragraph should be crossed out as it is irrelevant to the point at issue.

本土 běntǔ (名) one's native place

本位 běnwèi (名) 1 standard: 金~ gold standard 2 one's own department or unit: ~主义 departmental selfishness

本文 běnwén (名) 1 this essay, article, the present paper, etc. 2 the main body of a book; the original (or source) text

本性 běnxìng (名) a person's character; innate quality; nature; inherent quality: ~难移. It is difficult to alter one's character.

本义(義) běnyì (名) original meaning; literal sense

本意 běnyì (名) original idea; real intention: 他的~是好的. He meant well.

本着 běnzhe (介) in line with; in the light of; in conformity with

本质(質) běnzhì (名) essence; true nature

本子 běnzi (名) book; notebook: 笔记~ notebook

本族语 běnzúyǔ (名) native language; mother tongue

畚 běn (动) scoop up with a dustpan

畚箕 běnjī (名) 1 a bamboo or wicker scoop 2 dustpan

奔 bèn (动) 1 go straight towards; head for: 直~办公室 head straight for the office 2 〈口〉 approach: 他是~六十的人了. He's getting on for sixty.
see also bēn

奔命 bènmìng 〈口〉 be in a desperate hurry

奔头(頭)儿(兒) bèntour (名) 〈口〉 prospect

笨 bèn (形) 1 slow; stupid; thick: 愚~ stupid; slow-witted 2 clumsy; awkward: 他这人~手~脚. He is clumsy. 3 cumbersome; unwieldy: 家具

太～，搬起来很不方便. The furniture is too cumbersome to move.

笨蛋 bèndàn (名) fool; idiot

笨口拙舌 bènkǒu-zhuōshé slow and awkward in speech; inarticulate

笨鸟(鳥)先飞(飛) bèn niǎo xiān fēi a slow bird should make an early start

笨重 bènzhòng (形) heavy; cumbersome: ～的体力劳动 heavy manual labour

笨拙 bènzhuō (形) clumsy; awkward; stupid: 动作～ clumsy (or awkward) in movement. ～的伎俩 stupid tricks

崩 bēng (动) **1** collapse: 山～ landslide; landslip **2** burst: 这次会谈已经谈～了. The talks have broken down. **3** hit by bursting: 爆竹～了他的手. The firecracker went off in his hand. **4** 〈口〉 execute by shooting; shoot **5** (of an emperor) die

崩溃 bēngkuì (动) collapse; break down; crumble

崩裂 bēngliè (动) burst (or break) apart; crack: 炸药轰隆一声，山石～. Boom! The dynamite sent the rocks flying.

崩塌 bēngtā (动) collapse; crumble

崩陷 bēngxiàn (动) fall in; cave in

嘣 bēng (象) [the sound of sth. throbbing or bursting]: 我心里兴奋得～～直跳. My heart is throbbing with excitement.

绷 bēng I (动) **1** stretch tight or straight: 把绳子～直了. The rope is stretched taut. **2** spring; bounce: 弹簧～飞了. The spring jumped out. II (名) baste; tack; pin

see also běng; bèng

绷带 bēngdài (名) bandage

绷子 bēngzi (名) embroidery frame; hoop; tambour

甭 béng (动) don't; needn't: ～再说了. Don't say any more. ～管他. Leave him alone.

绷 běng (动)〈口〉 **1** ～着脸 pull a long face **2** strain oneself: ～住劲 strain all one's muscular strength

see also bēng; bèng

迸 bèng (动) spout; spurt; burst forth: 火星乱～. The sparks are flying all around. 沉默了半天，他才～出几句话来. He kept quiet for a little while before he blurted out a few words.

迸发(發) bèngfā (动) burst forth; burst out: 笑声从四面八方～出来. There was an outburst of laughter from all sides.

迸裂 bèngliè (动) split; burst (open)

迸流 bèngliú (动) gush; pour; spurt

泵 bèng (名) pump: 离心～ centrifugal pump

蹦 bèng (动) leap; jump; spring: 他不用使劲一～就过了沟. He leaped over the ditch without effort.

蹦迪 bèngdí (动) disco dancing

蹦极(極) bèngjí (名) bungee jumping

绷 bèng (动) **1** split open; crack: ～了一条缝儿. There is a crack in it. **2** (副)〈口〉 [used before such adjectives as "hard", "straight", "bright", etc. to indicate superior degree] very: ～硬 very hard; extremely stiff

see also bēng; běng

逼 bī (动) **1** force; compel; drive: ～得她走投无路. She was driven into a corner. **2** press for; extort: ～租 press for payment of rent **3** press on towards; press up to; close in on: 直～城下 press up to the city wall

逼宫 bīgōng (动) (of ministers, etc.) force the king or emperor to abdicate

逼供 bīgòng (动) extort a confession (usually by torture)

逼近 bījìn (动) press on towards; close in on; approach; draw near: 天色～黄昏. It is approaching dusk.

逼迫 bīpò (动) force; compel; pressurize

逼人 bīrén (形) pressing; threatening: 形势～. The situation spurs us on.

逼上梁山 bī shàng Liángshān be driven to join the Liangshan Marsh rebels; be driven to revolt; be forced to make a desperate move

逼债 bīzhài (动) press for payment of debts; dun

逼真 bīzhēn (形) **1** lifelike; true to life: 这幅画画得十分～. This is really a lifelike picture. **2** distinctly; clearly: 听得～ hear distinctly

荸 bí

荸荠(薺) bíqí (名) water chestnut (Eleocharis tuberosa)

鼻 bí (名) nose

鼻儿(兒) bír (名) **1** a hole in an article, utensil, etc. large enough for sth. to pass; eye: 针～ the eye of a needle. 门～ bolt staple **2** 〈口〉 whistle

鼻孔 bíkǒng (名) nostril

鼻梁 bíliáng (名) bridge of the nose

鼻腔 bíqiāng (名) nasal cavity

鼻青脸(臉)肿(腫) bíqīng-liǎnzhǒng a bloody nose and a swollen face; badly battered: 打得～ be beaten black and blue

鼻塞 bísè (动) have a stuffy nose

鼻涕 bítì (名) nasal mucus; snivel: 流～ have a running nose

鼻息 bíxī (名) breath: 仰人～ be totally dependent on sb. and allow oneself to be dictated to

鼻烟壶(壺) bíyānhú (名) snuff bottle

鼻炎 bíyán(名) rhinitis

鼻音 bíyīn (名) nasal sound: 说话带～ speak with a twang

鼻子 bízi(名) nose: 鹰钩～ aquiline nose. 牵着～走 lead a person by the nose

鼻祖 bízǔ (名) the earliest ancestor; originator (of a tradition, school of thought, etc.)

鄙 bǐ I (形) 1 low; mean; vulgar: 卑～ mean; despicable II (代)〈谦〉 my: ～意 in my poor (or humble) opinion III (动)〈书〉 despise; disdain; scorn: 可～ despicable

鄙薄 bǐbó I (动) despise; scorn II (形) uncouth

鄙吝 bǐlìn (形)〈书〉 1 coarse 2 stingy; miserly; mean

鄙陋 bǐlòu (形) superficial; shallow: ～无知 shallow and ignorant; superficial and ill-informed; illiterate

鄙弃(棄) bǐqì (动) disdain; loathe: ～这种庸俗作风 disdain such philistine practices

鄙人 bǐrén (代)〈谦〉 your humble servant

鄙视 bǐshì (动) despise; disdain; hold in contempt

鄙俗 bǐsú (形) coarse; philistine

笔(筆) bǐ I (名) 1 pen: 圆珠～ ball-point pen. 钢～ pen. 自来水～ fountain pen. 毛～ writing brush 2 technique of writing, calligraphy or drawing: 文～ style of writing 3 stroke; touch: 这个字的第一～ the first stroke of the character. 你给他写信时,替我带一～. Give him my best regards when you write to him. II (量) [amount (of money)]: 一～钱 a sum of money; a fund

笔触(觸) bǐchù (名) brush stroke in Chinese painting and calligraphy; style of writing: 简练的～ simple skilful strokes; a terse style

笔底下 bǐdǐxia (名) ability to write: ～不错 write well. ～来得快 write with ease (or facility)

笔调 bǐdiào (名) (of writing) tone; style: 讽刺的～ (in) a satirical style

笔法 bǐfǎ (名) technique of writing, calligraphy or drawing

笔锋 bǐfēng (名) 1 the tip of a writing brush 2 vigour of style in writing; stroke; touch

笔杆(桿) bǐgǎn (名) 1 the shaft of a pen or writing brush; penholder 2 pen: 耍～〈口〉 wield the pen. ～子 a facile writer; one who writes well

笔画(畫) bǐhuà (名) strokes of a Chinese character

笔迹 bǐjì (名) a person's handwriting; hand

笔记 bǐjì I (动) take down (in writing) II (名) 1 notes: 记～ take notes. ～本 notebook 2 literary genre consisting mainly of random notes: ～小说 literary sketches

笔记本电(電)脑(腦) bǐjìběn diànnǎo (名) notebook computer; laptop computer

笔力 bǐlì (名) vigour of strokes in calligraphy or drawing; vigour of style in literary composition: ～雄健 powerful strokes; vigorous style

笔立 bǐlì (动) stand erect; stand upright

笔录(錄) bǐlù I (动) put down (in writing); take down II (名) notes; record

笔名 bǐmíng (名) pen name; pseudonym

笔墨 bǐmò (名) pen and ink; words; writing: 我们的感受不是用～可以形容的. Words can not describe how I felt. 操～生涯 earn a living by the pen

笔试 bǐshì (名) written examination

笔顺 bǐshùn (名) order of strokes observed in calligraphy

笔挺 bǐtǐng (形) 1 (standing) very straight; bolt upright 2 well-pressed; trim: 衣服～ immaculately dressed

笔头(頭) bǐtóu I (名) 1 nib; pen point 2 ability to write; writing skill II (形) written; in written form: ～练习 written exercises

笔误 bǐwù (名) a slip of the pen

笔心 bǐxīn (名) 1 pencil lead 2 refill (for a pen)

笔译(譯) bǐyì (名) written translation

笔者 bǐzhě (名) [often referring to the

author himself] the author; the present writer

笔直 bǐzhí (形) perfectly straight; bolt upright: ～的马路 straight avenue. 身子挺得～ stand straight; sit bolt upright

匕 bǐ (名) an ancient type of spoon

匕首 bǐshǒu (名) dagger

比 bǐ I (动) 1 compare; emulate: ～得上 compare favourably with. 我哪能～得了您. How can I compare with you? ～先进 emulate the advanced 2 as... as; compare to: 坚～金石 as solid as a rock 3 make a gesture: 连说带～ gesticulate 4 copy; model after: ～着旧衣裁新衣 pattern a new garment on an old one II (介) 1 [indicating difference in manner or degree by comparison]: 他～我学得好. He's learned more than me. 2 [indicating difference in quantity]: 这一带水稻产量～小麦高两倍. The output of rice is three times that of wheat in this area. 3 [indicating the different scores won by two contestants or contesting teams]: 甲队以二～一胜乙队. Team A beat team B (by a score of) two to one. 现在几～几? What's the score?

比比 bǐbǐ (副) 1 frequently; many times 2 everywhere: ～皆是 can be found everywhere; be legion

比方 bǐfang I (动) likened to: 他的品德只宜用松柏来～. His integrity can only be compared to the pine and cypress. II (名) analogy; instance: 打～ draw an analogy. 拿盖房子作～ take for instance the building of a house

比分 bǐfēn (名) score: 场上～是三比二. The score is three to two.

比画(畫) bǐhua (动) gesture; gesticulate: 他～着讲. He managed to make himself understood by gesticulating.

比价(價) bǐjià (名) price relations; parity; rate of exchange: 工农业产品～ the price parities between industrial and agricultural products

比较 bǐjiào I (动) compare; contrast: ～级 comparative degree. ～文学 comparative literature. 有～才能鉴别. Only by comparing can we distinguish. II (介) [to indicate difference in manner or degree]: 煤产量～去年有显著的增长. Coal output shows a marked increase as compared with last year. III (副) fairly; comparatively; relatively; quite; rather: 我～爱看电影. Relatively speaking, I like films. 这篇文章写得～好. This article is comparatively well-written.

比例 bǐlì (名) 1 ratio; proportion: 3 与 4 的～等于 9 与 12 的～. The ratio of three to four is nine to twelve. 按～地协调发展 a proportionate and coordinated growth 2 scale: 按～绘制 be drawn to scale

比例尺 bǐlìchǐ (名) 1 scale: 这张地图的～是四十万分之一. The scale of the map is 1∶400,000. 2 architect's scale; engineer's scale

比邻(鄰) bǐlín I (名) neighbour; next-door neighbour II (形) near; next to: 跟我们～的国家 the neighbour states of our country

比率 bǐlǜ (名) ratio; rate

比美 bǐměi (动) compare favourably with

比拟(擬) bǐnǐ I (动) compare: 无可～ be incomparable. 难以～ be hardly comparable II (名) analogy; metaphor; comparison: 这种～是不恰当的. It is inappropriate to draw such a parallel.

比热(熱) bǐrè (名) specific heat

比如 bǐrú (连) for example; for instance; such as

比赛 bǐsài (名) match; competition: 足球～ football match. 象棋～ chess tournament. 演说～ speech (oratorial) contest. ～项目 event

比试 bǐshi (动) 1 have a competition 2 make gestures

比翼 bǐyì (动) fly wing to wing: ～齐飞 fly side by side. ～鸟 a pair of lovebirds—a devoted couple

比喻 bǐyù (名) metaphor; analogy; figure of speech: 打个～ by way of analogy. 这只是一个～的说法. This is only a metaphor.

比照 bǐzhào (动) 1 copy; model on 2 contrast

比值 bǐzhí (名) specific value; ratio: 8∶4 的～(比率)为 2∶1. The ratio of 8 to 4 is 2 to 1.

比重 bǐzhòng (名) 1 proportion: 工业在整个国民经济中的～ the proportion of industry in the national economy as a whole 2 specific gravity

秕 bǐ (形) (of grain) not plump; blighted

秕糠 bǐkāng (名) 1 chaff 2 worthless stuff
秕子 bǐzi (名) blighted grain
妣 bǐ (名)〈书〉one's deceased mother
彼 bǐ (代) 1 that; those; the other; another: ～时 at that time. 由此及～ proceed from one to the other 2 the other party: 知己知～ know one's opponent as well as oneself
彼岸 bǐ'àn (名) the other shore; Faramita
彼此 bǐcǐ (代) 1 each other; one another 2〈套〉[often said twice to show that both sides are in the same position]: 您辛苦啦! ——～～! You have been working very hard! — So have you!
愎 bì (形) wilful; obstinate; perverse: 刚～ self-willed
闭 bì (动) 1 shut; close: ～上眼 close one's eyes. ～口不谈 refuse to say anything about; remain silent. ～嘴! Hold your tongue! (Shut up!) 2 stop up; obstruct: ～住气 hold one's breath
闭关(關)自守 bìguān zì shǒu close the country to international intercourse
闭路电(電)视 bìlù diànshì (名) closed-circuit television; closed circuit
闭门(門)羹 bìméngēng [often used in phr.]: 飨以～ slam the door in sb.'s face. 吃～ be denied admittance
闭门(門)思过(過) bì mén sī guò shut oneself up and ponder over one's mistakes
闭门(門)造车(車) bì mén zào chē make a cart behind closed doors; divorce oneself from reality and act blindly
闭幕 bìmù (动) 1 the curtain falls 2 close; conclude: 会议已胜利～. The conference has come to a successful close. ～词 closing address (or speech). ～式 closing ceremony
闭塞 bìsè I (动) stop up; block: 管道～. The pipes were blocked. II (形) 1 hard to get to; out-of-the-way; inaccessible: 以前这一带交通～. In the past this district was rather inaccessible. 2 ill-informed
闭音节(節) bìyīnjié (名) closed syllable
敝 bì I (形)〈书〉shabby; worn-out; ragged: ～衣 ragged clothing; shabby(or worn-out) clothes II (代)〈谦〉my; our; this: ～处 my place
敝俗 bìsú (名) corrupt customs; bad habits
敝帚自珍 bìzhǒu zì zhēn cherish sth. of one's own for sentimental reasons

蔽 bì (动) cover; shelter; hide: 掩～ screen; cover. 隐～ conceal; take cover. 浮云～日. Floating clouds hid the sun.
弊 bì (名) 1 fraud; abuse; malpractice: 舞～ practise fraud; engage in corrupt practices 2 disadvantage; harm: 有利有～. There are both advantages and disadvantages.
弊案 bì'àn (名) scandal involving a politician
弊病 bìbìng (名) drawback; disadvantage
弊端 bìduān (名) abuse; corrupt practice
必 bì I (副) certainly; surely; necessarily: ～不可少 absolutely necessary; indispensable II (动) must; have to; be bound to: 事～躬亲 attend to everything personally
必定 bìdìng (副) certainly; surely: 他～会来. He is sure to come. 我以前～见过你. Surely I have met you before.
必恭必敬 bìgōng-bìjìng reverent and respectful; extremely deferential
必然 bìrán I (形) inevitable; certain: ～结果 inevitable outcome. ～趋势 inexorable trend II (名) necessity: ～规律 inexorable law. ～性 necessity; inevitability; certainty
必修课 bìxiūkè (名) a required (or obligatory) course
必须 bìxū (动) must; have to: ～向大家讲明. It must be made clear to all. ～有耐心. It is imperative to have patience.
必需 bìxū (形) necessary; indispensable: 空气是生活所～的. Air is indispensable to life. 日用～品 daily necessities
必要 bìyào (形) requisite; necessary; indispensable: 为一个企业提供～的资金 provide the capital needed for an enterprise. 没有～再讨论了. There's no need to discuss it any more. ～劳动 necessary labour. ～前提 prerequisite; precondition. ～条件 essential condition; prerequisite. ～性 necessity
毖 bì caution: 惩前～后 learn from past mistakes to avoid future ones
秘 bì
see also mì
秘鲁 Bìlǔ (名) Peru
碧 bì I (名)〈书〉emerald II (形) bluish green; blue: ～海 the blue sea. ～空 a clear blue sky; an azure sky. ～草

green grass

碧绿 bìlǜ (形) dark green

碧血 bìxuè (名) blood shed in a just cause

碧玉 bìyù (名) jasper

庇 bì (动) shelter; protect; shield

庇护(護) bìhù (动) shelter; shield; take under one's wing: ～权 right of asylum. ～所 asylum; sanctuary

庇荫(蔭) bìyìn (动) 1 (of a tree, etc.) give shade 2 shield

毕(畢) bì I (动) finish; accomplish; conclude: 阅～请放回原处. Please replace after reading. II (副)〈书〉 fully; altogether; completely: 原形～露 show one's true colours

毕竟 bìjìng (副) after all; all in all; in the final analysis

毕生 bìshēng (名) all one's life; lifetime

毕肖 bìxiào (形)〈书〉 resemble closely; be the very image of: 画得神情～ paint a lifelike portrait of sb.

毕业(業) bìyè (动) graduate; finish school: ～生 graduate. ～论文 graduation thesis. ～典礼 graduation ceremony; commencement

哔(嗶) bì

哔叽(嘰) bìjī (名) serge

筚(篳) bì (名) a bamboo or wicker fence

筚路蓝(藍)缕(縷) bìlù-lánlǚ〈书〉 drive a cart in ragged clothes to break fresh ground—endure great hardships in pioneer work

毙(斃) bì (动) 1 die; get killed 2〈口〉 execute; shoot

毙命 bìmìng (动) meet a violent death; get killed

陛 bì (名)〈书〉 a flight of steps leading to a palace hall

陛下 bìxià (名) [a title for addressing or speaking of a king or queen] Your Majesty; His or Her Majesty

痹 bì (名) pain or numbness in the joints and muscles; rheumatism

裨 bì (名)〈书〉 benefit; advantage: 无～于事. It won't help matters.

裨益 bìyì (名)〈书〉 benefit; advantage; profit: 大有～ be of great benefit

婢 bì (名) slave girl; servant girl

婢女 bìnǚ (名) slave girl; servant girl

币(幣) bì (名) money; currency: 硬～ hard currency. 银～ silver coin. 纸～ paper money; bank-notes

币值 bìzhí (名) currency value: ～稳定. The currency is stable.

蓖 bì

蓖麻 bìmá (名) castor-oil plant

篦 bì (动) comb: ～头 comb one's hair

篦子 bìzi (名) a bamboo comb with fine teeth on both sides

辟 bì I (名)〈书〉 monarch; sovereign: 复～ restore a monarchy; restoration II (动)〈书〉 ward off

see also pì

辟邪 bìxié (动) exorcise evil spirits

避 bì (动) 1 avoid; evade; shun: ～风头 lie low. ～而不谈 evade the question; avoid the subject. ～风雨 seek shelter from wind and rain. 不～艰险 defy hardships and dangers 2 prevent; keep away; repel: ～孕 contraception

避风(風)港 bìfēnggǎng (名) haven

避雷针 bìléizhēn (名) lightning rod

避免 bìmiǎn (动) avoid; refrain from; avert: ～主观地看问题 avoid looking at problems subjectively

避难(難) bìnàn (动) take refuge; seek asylum: ～所 refuge; sanctuary; asylum; haven

避暑 bìshǔ (动) be away from a hot place in the summer; spend a holiday at a summer resort

避嫌 bìxián (动) avoid doing anything that may cause misunderstanding; avoid arousing suspicion

避重就轻(輕) bì zhòng jiù qīng 1 evade major tasks and choose minor ones 2 avoid major issues while dwelling on irrelevant details

璧 bì (名) an ancient piece of jade, round, flat and with a hole in its centre

璧还(還) bìhuán (动)〈敬〉 return sth. to its owner or decline a gift

壁 bì (名) 1 wall: 容器～ the wall of a container 2 cliff: 峭～ a precipitous cliff; precipice

壁橱 bìchú (名) a built-in wardrobe or cupboard; closet

壁虎 bìhǔ (名) house lizard; gecko

B

壁画(畫) bìhuà (名) mural painting; fresco

壁垒(壘) bìlěi (名) rampart; camp: ~分明. There is a clear line of demarcation between the two schools of thought. ~森严 closely guarded; strongly fortified; sharply divided

壁立 bìlì (形) (of cliffs, etc.) stand like a wall; rise steeply

壁炉(爐) bìlú (名) fireplace

壁球 bìqiú (名) squash

壁毯 bìtǎn (名) wall tapestry

壁纸 bìzhǐ (名) wallpaper

臂 bì (名) 1 arm: 左~ the left arm. 助一~之力 give sb. a hand 2 upper arm

臂膀 bìbǎng (名) arm

臂章 bìzhāng (名) 1 armband; armlet 2 shoulder emblem

弼 bì (动)〈书〉 assist

煸 biān (动) stir-fry before stewing

蝙 biān

蝙蝠 biānfú (名) bat

鳊 biān

鳊鱼(魚) biānyú (名) bream

编 biān I (动) 1 weave; plait: ~竹筐 plait bamboo baskets 2 organize; arrange 3 edit; compile: ~词典 edit or compile a dictionary 4 write; compose: ~剧本 write plays 5 fabricate; invent; make up; cook up: 瞎~ sheer fabrication II (名) part of a book; book; volume

编导(導) biāndǎo I (动) write and direct (a play, film, etc.) II (名) playwright-director; choreographer-director; scenarist-director

编队(隊) biānduì I (动) form into columns; organize into teams II (名) formation (of ships or aircraft): ~飞行 formation flight (or flying)

编号(號) biānhào I (动) number II (名) serial number

编辑 biānjí I (动) edit; compile II (名) editor; compiler: 总~ editor-in-chief; chief editor. ~部 editorial department

编剧(劇) biānjù I (动) write a play, scenario, etc. II (名) playwright; screenwriter; scenarist

编码 biānmǎ (动) coding

编目 biānmù I (动) make a catalogue; catalogue II (名) catalogue; list

编年史 biānniánshǐ (名) annals; chronicle

编排 biānpái (动) arrange; lay out: 文字和图片的~ the layout of pictures and articles

编审(審) biānshěn I (动) read and edit II (名) senior editor

编外 biānwài (of personnel) not on the permanent staff

编写(寫) biānxiě (动) 1 compile: ~教科书 compile a textbook 2 write; compose: ~剧本 write plays

编译(譯) biānyì (动) translate and edit

编造 biānzào (动) 1 compile; draw up; work out: ~预算 draw up a budget 2 fabricate; invent: ~谎言 fabricate lies. ~情节 invent a story 3 create out of the imagination: 古代人民~的神话 myths invented by the ancients

编者 biānzhě (名) editor; compiler: ~按 editor's note; editorial note

编织(織) biānzhī (动) weave; knit; plait: ~毛衣 knit a sweater

编制 biānzhì I (动) 1 weave; plait; braid: ~竹器 plait bamboo articles 2 work out; draw up: ~生产计划 work out a production plan. ~教学大纲 draw up a syllabus II (名) authorized strength; establishment: 部队~ establishment (for army units). 缩小~ reduce the staff

编纂 biānzuǎn (动) compile: ~词典 compile (or edit) a dictionary

鞭 biān I (名) 1 whip; lash 2 an iron staff (used as a weapon in ancient China) 3 sth. resembling a whip: 教~ (teacher's) pointer 4 a string of small firecrackers II (动) flog; whip; lash: ~马 whip a horse

鞭策 biāncè (动) spur on; urge on; encourage: 这是对我们的~. This is an encouragement to us.

鞭长(長)莫及 biān cháng mò jí beyond the reach of one's power; too far away to be helpful

鞭笞 biānchī (动)〈书〉 flog; lash

鞭打 biāndǎ (动) whip; lash; flog; thrash

鞭炮 biānpào (名) 1 firecrackers 2 a string of small firecrackers

鞭辟入里(裏) biān pì rù lǐ penetrating; incisive; in-depth

鞭挞(撻) biāntà (动)〈书〉 lash; castigate

鞭子 biānzi (名) whip

边(邊) biān (名) 1 side: 海~ seaside. 河~ riverside 2 border(as an ornament): 花~儿 lace border 3 frontier; border: 守卫~疆 guard the border 4 limit; bound: 无~无际 boundless 5 close by (an object): 站在窗~ stand by the window

边(邊) bian [suffix of a noun of locality]: 这~here. 东~ in the east. 左~ on the left. 前~ in front. 里~ inside

边…边… biān … biān … [used before two verbs respectively to indicate simultaneous actions]: 边干边学 train on the job

边陲 biānchuí (名)〈书〉border area; frontier

边防 biānfáng (名) guarding the border: ~部队 frontier guards

边关(關) biānguān (名) frontier pass: 镇守~ guard a frontier pass; hold a frontier command

边际(際) biānjì (名) limit; bound; boundary: 汪洋大海,漫无~. a boundless sea; a vast expanse of water. 不着~ wide of the mark

边疆 biānjiāng (名) border; borderland; frontier; frontier region

边界 biānjiè (名) boundary; border: 划定~ delimit boundaries. 越过~cross a boundary; cross the border. ~事件 border incident. ~线 boundary line. ~争端 boundary dispute

边境 biānjìng (名) border; frontier: 封锁~ close the frontiers; seal off the borders

边卡 biānqiǎ (名) border checkpoint or post

边区(區) biānqū (名) border area (or region)

边塞 biānsài (名) frontier fortress

边线(綫) biānxiàn (名) 1 sideline 2 (in baseball) foul line

边沿 biānyán (名) border; frontier: ~地带 borders; areas near the frontier

边缘 biānyuán (名) 1 edge; fringe; verge; brink 2 marginal; borderline: ~科学 frontier science

边缘化 biānyuánhuà (动) decentre; marginalize

边远(遠) biānyuǎn (形) remote; outlying: ~地区 remote region

边寨 biānzhài (名) borderland village

扁 biǎn (形) flat: 一只~盒子 a flat box. 纸箱子压~了. The cardboard box was crushed.

扁担 biǎndan (名) carrying pole; shoulder pole

扁豆 biǎndòu (名) hyacinth bean

扁桃腺 biǎntáoxiàn (名) tonsil: ~炎 tonsillitis; inflammation of the tonsils

扁圆 biǎnyuán (形) oblate

褊 biǎn (形)〈书〉narrow; cramped

褊急 biǎnjí (形)〈书〉narrow-minded and short-tempered

褊狭(狹) biǎnxiá (形)〈书〉narrow: 气量~ narrow-minded

匾 biǎn (名) 1 a horizontal board inscribed with words of praise (occasionally a silk banner embroidered for the same purpose): 绣金~ embroidering a silk banner in letters of gold 2 a big round shallow basket

匾额 biǎn'é (名) a horizontal inscribed board

贬 biǎn (动) 1 demote 2 reduce; devalue: ~价出售 sell at a reduced price 3 censure; condemn

贬斥 biǎnchì 1 (动)〈书〉demote 2 denounce

贬黜 biǎnchù (动) demote

贬低 biǎndī (动) deliberately underestimate; play down

贬义(義) biǎnyì (名) derogatory sense: ~词 derogatory term

贬谪 biǎnzhé (动) banish from the court

贬值 biǎnzhí (动)(of currency) devalue; devaluate; depreciate

辨 biàn (动) differentiate; distinguish; discriminate: 明~是非 discriminate between right and wrong. 不~真伪 fail to distinguish between truth and falsehood

辨别 biànbié (动) differentiate; distinguish; discriminate: ~真伪 distinguish the true from the false. ~方向 take one's bearings

辨认(認) biànrèn (动) identify; recognize: ~面貌 recognize one's face

辨析 biànxī (动) differentiate and analyse; discriminate

辩(辯) biàn (动) argue; dispute; debate: 我同她争~过好几次. I've argued with her many times.

辩白 biànbái (动) try to justify oneself

辩驳 biànbó (动) dispute; refute

辩才 biàncái (名)〈书〉eloquence; oratory

辩护(護) biànhù (动) 1 speak in defence of; try to justify or defend: ~士 apologist.

B

不要替他～了. Don't try to defend him. 2 plead; defend: 为被告人～plead for the accused. ～权 right to defence. ～人 defender; counsel

辩解 biànjiě (动) make excuses

辩论(論) biànlùn (动) argue; debate: ～会 a debate

辩证(證) biànzhèng (形) dialectical: ～的统一 dialectical unity. 事物发展的～规律 the dialectical law of the development of things. ～法 dialectics. ～逻辑 dialectical logic

辩证(證)法 biànzhèngfǎ (名) dialectics: 唯物～ materialist dialectics. ～的世界观 the dialectical world outlook

辩证(證)唯物主义(義) biànzhèng wéwùzhǔyì (名) dialectical materialism: ～观点 a dialectical materialist point of view. ～者 dialectical materialist

辫(辮) biàn (名) plait; braid; pigtail: 梳小～儿 wear pigtails. 蒜～ a braid of garlic

辫子 biànzi (名) 1 plait; braid; pigtail: 梳～ wear one's hair in braids. 把问题梳梳～ sort out the problems 2 a mistake or shortcoming that may be exploited by an opponent; handle: 别让他抓住咱们的～. Don't give him a handle against us.

忭 biàn (形)〈书〉glad; happy

变(變) biàn I (动) 1 change; become different: 情况～了. The situation has changed. 2 transform; change; turn: ～农业国为工业国 turn an agricultural country into an industrial power II (名) an unexpected turn of events: 事～incident

变本加厉(厲) biàn běn jiā lì worsen; be further intensified

变电(電)站 biàndiànzhàn (名) (transformer) substation

变动(動) biàndòng (名) change; alteration: 人事～ change of personnel. 国际形势发生了很大的～. The world situation has undergone great change.

变法 biànfǎ (名) political reform

变革 biàngé (动、名) transform; change: 社会～ social change

变更 biàngēng (动) change; alter; modify: ～作息时间 alter the daily timetable.

变故 biàngù (名) an unforeseen event; catastrophe

变卦 biànguà (动) suddenly change one's mind; go back on one's word

变化 biànhuà (名、动) change; vary: 化学～ chemical change. 他的战术～多端. His tactics are varied.

变幻 biànhuàn (动) change irregularly; fluctuate: ～莫测 changeable; unpredictable. 风云～ fast-changing situation

变换 biànhuàn (动) vary; alternate: ～手法 vary one's tactics

变节(節) biànjié (动) betray one's country or party: ～分子 traitor; renegade

变脸(臉) biànliǎn (动) suddenly turn hostile

变量 biànliàng (名) variable

变乱(亂) biànluàn (名) turmoil; social upheaval

变卖(賣) biànmài (动) sell off (one's property)

变迁(遷) biànqiān (名) changes; vicissitudes: 人事～ personnel changes

变色 biànsè (动) 1 change colour 2 discolour 3 show signs of displeasure or anger

变色龙(龍) biànsèlóng (名) chameleon

变态(態) biàntài I (名) metamorphosis II (形) abnormal; anomalous; perversive: ～心理 abnormal psychology. ～反应 allergy

变天 biàntiān (名) 1 change of weather 2 euphemism for restoration of reactionary rule

变通 biàntōng (动) make changes according to specific conditions

变戏(戲)法 biàn xìfǎ perform conjuring tricks; conjure; juggle

变现 biànxiàn (动) liquidate; realize

变相 biànxiàng (形) in disguised form; covert: ～贪污 a disguised form of corruption

变心 biànxīn (动) cease to be faithful

变形 biànxíng (动) be out of shape; warp: 这箱子压得～了. The box has been crushed out of shape. 这些木板已经～了. These boards have warped.

变压(壓)器 biànyāqì (名) transformer

变样(樣) biànyàng (动) change in shape or appearance

变异(異) biànyì (名) variation

变质(質) biànzhì (动) go bad; be intrinsically changed for the worse: 这肉～了. The meat has gone bad. 蜕化～ become degenerate

变种(種) biànzhǒng (名) 1 mutation; variety 2 variety; variant

遍 biàn I (形) all over; everywhere II (动) spread all over: 我们的朋友~天下. We have friends all over the world. III (量) [indicating the process of an action from beginning to end]: 这本书我从头到尾看过两~. I've read the book twice from cover to cover. 请再说一~. Please say it again.

遍布 biànbù (动) be found everywhere; spread all over

遍地 biàndì (名) everywhere; all over: ~都是 be found everywhere. ~开花 (of good things) spring up all over the place

遍及 biànjí (动) extend (or spread) all over

遍体鳞伤(傷) biàntǐ línshāng be covered all over with cuts and bruises

便 biàn I (形) 1 convenient; handy: 顾客称~. Customers find this very convenient. 2 if it is considered proper: 悉听尊~ please yourself; act at one's own discretion 3 informal; plain; ordinary: ~装 ordinary (or everyday) clothes II (名) piss or shit; urine or excrement: 粪~ excrement; night soil III (副) then: 如果她这次还不来, 她~没有什么借口了. If she doesn't appear this time, then she won't have any excuse. IV (连) [showing possible concession]: 只要依靠群众, ~是最大的困难, 也能克服. So long as we can rely on the masses, we can overcome any difficulty, however great it may be.

see also pián

便池 biànchí (名) urinal

便当(當) biàndang (形) simple; easy: 这个房间收拾起来很~. It's no trouble tidying up the room.

便道 biàndào (名) 1 shortcut: 抄~走 take a shortcut 2 pavement; sidewalk: 行人走~. Pedestrians walk on the pavement.

便饭 biànfàn (名) a homely meal; potluck

便服 biànfú (名) 1 everyday clothes; informal dress 2 civilian clothes

便函 biànhán (名) an informal letter sent by an organization

便壶(壺) biànhú (名) urinal; chamber pot

便笺(箋) biànjiān (名) notepaper; memo; memo pad

便捷 biànjié (形) quick and convenient

便览(覽) biànlǎn (名) brief guide: 旅游~ tourist guide

便利 biànlì (形) 1 convenient; easy: 交通~ have convenient communications; be conveniently located 2 render services to: 日夜商店~群众. A shop that is open round the clock saves the customers a lot of trouble.

便秘 biànmì (名) constipation

便民 biànmín (动) for the convenience of the people: ~措施 convenient service for the people

便盆 biànpén (名) bedpan

便桥(橋) biànqiáo (名) a makeshift bridge

便条(條) biàntiáo (名) 1 a brief note 2 notepaper

便鞋 biànxié (名) slippers

便血 biànxiě (名) having (or passing) blood in one's stool

便宴 biànyàn (名) informal dinner: 设~招待 give a dinner for sb.

便衣 biànyī (名) 1 civilian clothes; plain clothes: ~公安人员 plainclothes public security personnel; public security personnel in plain clothes 2 plainclothesman

便宜行事 biànyí xíng shì act at one's discretion; act as one sees fit

便于(於) biànyú (动) be easy to; be convenient for: ~计算 easy to calculate; easily calculable

便中 biànzhōng (副) at one's convenience: ~请告知. Please let me know at your convenience.

弁 biàn (名) 1 a man's cap used in ancient times 2 a low-ranking officer in old China

弁言 biànyán (名)〈书〉foreword; preface

镳 biāo (名) 1〈书〉bit (of a bridle): 分道扬~ part company each pursuing his own course 2 see "镖" biāo

标(標) biāo (名) 1 mark; sign: 商~ trade mark. 路~ road sign 2 put a mark, tag or label on; label: 商品都~了价格. Every article has a price tag on it. 3 prize; award; championship 4 outward sign; symptom: 治~不如治本 would rather seek a permanent cure than temporary relief 5 tender; bid: 招~ invite tenders

标榜 biāobǎng (动) 1 brag about; parade: ~学术自由 brag about academic freedom 2 boost; praise excessively: 互相~ boost each other

标本 biāoběn (名) specimen; sample: 昆虫~ insect specimen

B

标兵 biāobīng (名) 1 parade guards (usu. spaced out along parade routes) 2 example; pacesetter: 树立～ set a good example

标尺 biāochǐ (名) 1 surveyor's rod; staff 2 staff gauge 3 rear sight

标底 biāodǐ (名) estimate a lower limit on bids; pre-tender

标点(點) biāodiǎn I (名) punctuation: ～符号 punctuation mark II (动) punctuate

标定 biāodìng (动) demarcate: ～边界线 demarcate a boundary by setting up boundary markers (done jointly by the two parties concerned)

标号(號) biāohào (名) grade: 钢材的～ the grade of steel

标记 biāojì (名) sign; mark; symbol

标价(價) biāojià I (动) mark a price II (名) marked price

标明 biāomíng (动) mark; indicate

标签(簽) biāoqiān (名) label; tag: 贴上～ stick on a label. 价目～ price tag

标枪(槍) biāoqiāng (名) javelin

标题 biāotí (名) title; heading; headline; caption: 通栏大字～ banner headline; banner

标新立异(異) biāoxīn-lìyì try to be deliberately unconventional; put forward novel ideas just to show one is different from the ordinary run

标语 biāoyǔ (名) slogan; poster

标志 biāozhì I (名) sign; mark; symbol: 兴旺发达的～ a sign of prosperity II (动) indicate; mark; symbolize: ～着时代的开始 mark the beginning of a new era

标致 biāozhi (形)(usu. of women) pretty

标准(準) biāozhǔn (名) standard; criterion: 合乎～ up to standard. 实践是真理的唯一～. Practice is the sole criterion of truth. ～时 standard time. ～音 standard pronunciation

镖 biāo (名) a dartlike weapon

镖局 biāojú (名) a professional establishment which provides armed escorts or security guards

膘 biāo (名) fat (of an animal): 长～ get fat; put on flesh

飙 biāo (名) violent wind; whirlwind

飙车 biāochē (动) speed

彪 biāo (名)〈书〉young tiger

彪炳 biāobǐng (动)〈书〉shine: ～千古 shine through the ages

彪悍 biāohàn (形) valiant; intrepid; doughty

彪形大汉(漢) biāoxíng dàhàn burly chap; hefty fellow

表 biǎo I (名) 1 surface; outside; external: 由～及里 proceed from the outside to the inside 2 model; example 3 table; form; list: 时间～ timetable; schedule; form. 申请～ application form 4 meter; gauge: 温度～ thermometer 5 (錶) watch: 手～(wrist) watch 6 the relationship between the children or grandchildren of a brother and a sister or of sisters: ～兄 cousin (see "姑表" gūbiǎo; "姨表" yíbiǎo) 7 memorial to an emperor II (动) show; express: 深～同情 show deep sympathy. 聊～微意 so as to express one's appreciation; as a token of one's gratitude

表白 biǎobái (动) vindicate; show: ～诚意 show one's sincerity

表册 biǎocè (名) statistical forms; book of tables or forms: 公文报告～ documents, written reports and statistical forms

表达(達) biǎodá (动) express (thoughts and feelings)

表带(帶) biǎodài (名) watchband; watch strap

表格 biǎogé (名) form; table: 空白～ a blank form. 填写～ fill in a form

表功 biǎogōng (动) 1 brag about one's deeds 2 praise; commend

表决 biǎojué (动) decide by vote; vote: 付～ put to the vote; take a vote. ～权 right to vote; vote

表里(裏)如一 biǎo lǐ rú yī behave exactly in the same way as one thinks one ought to; think and act in one and the same way

表露 biǎolù (动) show; reveal: 他并没有～出焦急的心情. He didn't reveal his anxiety.

表蒙子 biǎoméngzi (名) watch glass; crystal

表面 biǎomiàn (名) surface; face; outside; appearance: 地球的～ the surface of the earth. ～价值 face value

表面化 biǎomiànhuà (动) come to the surface; surface: 矛盾～了. The contradiction has surfaced.

表明 biǎomíng (动) make known; make clear; state clearly; indicate: ～立场

state one's position. ～决心 declare one's determination

表皮 biǎopí (名) 1 surface 2 epidermis; cuticle

表亲(親) biǎoqīn (名) 1 cousin 2 cousinship

表情 biǎoqíng I (动) express one's feelings II (名) expression: 面部～ facial expression

表示 biǎoshì (动) show; express; indicate: ～关切 show concern. ～热烈欢迎 extend a warm welcome

表述 biǎoshù (动) state; explain: ～清楚 be articulate

表率 biǎoshuài (名) example; model: 老师要做学生的～. The teacher should set a good example to his pupils.

表态(態) biǎotài (动) make known one's position

表现 biǎoxiàn I (名) expression; manifestation: 反对机会主义的各种～ oppose opportunism in all its manifestations II (动) 1 show; display; manifest: ～出极大的勇敢和智慧 display great courage and wisdom 2 show off: 好～ like to show off

表演 biǎoyǎn I (动) perform act; play: ～节目 give a performance; put on a show II (名) performance; exhibition: 杂技～ acrobatic performance

表扬(揚) biǎoyáng (动) praise; commend: ～信 commendatory letter

表语 biǎoyǔ (名) predicative

表彰 biǎozhāng (动) cite (in dispatches); commend

裱

biǎo (动) mount (a picture, a painting, etc.)

裱褙 biǎobèi (动) mount (a picture)

裱糊 biǎohú (动) paper (a wall, ceiling, etc.)

婊

biǎo

婊子 biǎozi (名) prostitute; bitch

鳔

biào (名) 1 swim bladder; air bladder 2 fish glue

瘪(癟)

biē

see also biě

瘪三 biēsān (名) a wretched-looking tramp who lives by begging or stealing

憋

biē (动) 1 suppress; hold back; restrain: ～不住 be unable to hold oneself back. ～着一肚子火 bottle up one's anger. ～着一肚子气 have pent-up grievances 2 suffocate; feel oppressed: 屋里太闷, ～得人透不过气来. The room is so stuffy that one cannot breathe freely.

鳖

biē (名) soft-shelled turtle

蹩

bié (动) sprain (one's ankle or wrist)

蹩脚 biéjiǎo (形) inferior; shoddy: ～货 shoddy work

别

bié I (名) difference; distinction: 天渊之～ a world of difference. 性～ sex II (动) 1 leave: 告～ take leave (of). 久～重逢 meet again after a long separation 2 differentiate; distinguish: ～其真伪 determine whether it's true or false 3 fasten with a pin or clip: 把表格～在一起 pin (or clip) the forms together 4 stick in: 腰里～着手枪 with a pistol stuck in one's belt III (形) other; another: ～处 another place; elsewhere IV (副) 1 don't: ～忘了. Don't forget ～忙! No hurry. Take your time. 2 [used with 是 to express difference]: 他怎么还没来, ～是病了吧? Why hasn't he come yet? I hope he's not ill.

see also biè

别出心裁 bié chū xīncái start something unique; deliberately adopt a different approach

别动(動)队(隊) (名) biédòngduì special detachment; secret agent squad

别号(號) biéhào (名) alias

别具匠心 bié jù jiàngxīn show ingenuity; have originality

别具一格 bié jù yī gé have a unique (or distinctive) style

别开(開)生面 bié kāi shēngmiàn develop a new style; break fresh ground

别离(離) biélí (动) leave; depart

别名 biémíng (名) alternative name

别人 biéren (名) other people; others; people: ～想法不同. Other people think differently.

别墅 biéshù (名) villa

别有用心 bié yǒu yòngxīn have ulterior motives; have an axe to grind

别针 biézhēn (名) 1 safety pin; pin 2 brooch

别致 biézhì (形) novel; delightful: 这座房子的建筑结构非常～. The architecture of the house is uniquely delightful.

别字 biézì (名) incorrectly written or mispronounced character; malapropism

B

瘪(癟) biě (形) shrivelled; shrunken; deflated: 车胎~了. The tyre is flat.
see also biē

别(彆) biè
see also bié

别扭 bièniu (形) 1 awkward; clumsy; difficult: 这个人脾气真~. He is temperamentally unpredictable. 2 cannot see eye to eye: 闹~ be at odds. 两个人素来有些别别扭扭的. The two of them are often at loggerheads with each other.

濒 bīn (动) 1 be close to (the sea, a river, etc.); border on: 东~大海 overlook the sea on the east 2 be on the point of: ~死 on the verge of death; dying

濒临(臨) bīnlín (动) be close to; border on; be on the verge of: 这个国家~太平洋. The country is on the pacific coast.

濒危 bīnwēi (动) 1 be in imminent danger: ~珍稀动物 rare animals on the brink of extinction 2 be critically ill: ~病人 dying patient

濒于(於) bīnyú (动) be on the brink of: ~破产 teeter on the edge of bankruptcy

宾(賓) bīn (名) guest: 贵~ distinguished guest; guest of honour

宾馆 bīnguǎn (名) guesthouse

宾客 bīnkè (名) guests; visitors

宾语 bīnyǔ (名) object: 直接~ direct object. 间接~ indirect object

宾至如归(歸) bīn zhì rú guī (of a hotel or guesthouse) where guests feel at home; a home (away) from home

滨(濱) bīn I (名) bank; brink; shore: 海~ beech; seashore II (动) be close to (the sea, a river, etc.): ~海 by the sea; coastal

傧(儐) bīn

傧相 bīnxiàng (名) attendant of the bride or bridegroom at a wedding: 男~ best man. 女~ bridesmaid

缤(繽) bīn

缤纷 bīnfēn (形)〈书〉in riotous profusion: 五彩~ multicoloured. 落英~ a profusion of falling petals

彬 bīn

彬彬有礼(禮) bīnbīn yǒu lǐ courteous; urbane

鬓(鬢) bìn (名) temples; hair on the temples

鬓发(髮) bìnfà (名) hair on the temples: ~灰白 greying at the temples

殡(殯) bìn (动) carry a coffin to the burial place (or a crematory)

殡仪(儀)馆 bìnyíguǎn (名) funeral parlour (or home)

殡葬 bìnzàng (名) funeral and interment

摈(擯) bìn (动)〈书〉discard; get rid of: ~弃不用 reject

摈斥 bìnchì (动) reject: ~异己 dismiss those who hold different opinions

摈弃(棄) bìnqì (动) abandon; discard: ~陋习 cast away undesirable customs

冰 bīng I (名) ice II (动) cool in the ice; ice: 把那瓶汽水~上. Have that bottle of lemonade iced.

冰雹 bīngbáo (名) hail

冰场(場) bīngchǎng (名) skating (or ice) rink

冰川 bīngchuān (名) glacier

冰刀 bīngdāo (名) (ice) skates

冰点(點) bīngdiǎn (名) freezing point

冰雕 bīngdiāo (名) ice carving; ice sculpture

冰冻(凍) bīngdòng (动) freeze: ~三尺,非一日之寒. The fact that the water has frozen up cannot be attributed to the coldness of one single day—the trouble is deep-rooted.

冰毒 bīngdú (名) ice (illegal drug)

冰棍儿(兒) bīnggùnr (名) ice-lolly; popsicle; ice-sucker; frozen sucker

冰窖 bīngjiào (名) ice cell

冰冷 bīnglěng (形) ice-cold

冰淇淋 bīngqílín (名) ice cream

冰球 bīngqiú (名) 1 ice hockey 2 puck

冰山 bīngshān (名) iceberg

冰释(釋) bīngshì (动)〈书〉(of misgivings, misunderstandings, etc.) disappear or vanish without a trace

冰霜 bīngshuāng (名) 1 symbol of moral integrity 2 symbol of gravity: 冷若~ look frosty

冰糖 bīngtáng (名) rock sugar

冰天雪地 bīngtiān-xuědì a world of frozen ice and drifting snow; a mass of ice and snow

冰箱 bīngxiāng (名) icebox; refrigerator;

freezer

冰鞋 bīngxié (名) skating boots; skates

冰镇 bīngzhèn (形) iced: ～西瓜 iced watermelon

兵 bīng (名) 1 soldier: 当～ enlist in the army, navy or air force. 新～ recruit 2 weapon 3 army; troops 4 military strategy: 纸上谈～ be an armchair strategist

兵变(變) bīngbiàn (名) mutiny

兵不厌(厭)诈 bīng bù yàn zhà nothing is too deceitful in war; all's fair in war

兵法 bīngfǎ (名) art of war; military strategy and tactics

兵工厂(廠) bīnggōngchǎng (名) munitions (or ordnance) factory

兵贵神速 bīng guì shénsù speed is a factor of incalculable value in war; lightning speed is the essence of the art of war

兵荒马(馬)乱(亂) bīnghuāng-mǎluàn the chaos of war; the turbulence of war

兵祸(禍) bīnghuò (名) disaster of war

兵家 bīngjiā (名) military strategist in ancient China; (in wartime) military commander: ～必争之地 a strategic stronghold

兵力 bīnglì (名) military strength

兵马(馬) bīngmǎ (名) military forces

兵马(馬)俑 (名) bīngmǎyǒng terracotta soldiers; clay figures of warriors

兵器 bīngqì (名) arms; weapons; weaponry

兵强马(馬)壮(壯) bīngqiáng-mǎzhuàng a well-trained and well-equipped army

兵权(權) bīngquán (名) military power; military leadership

兵士 bīngshì (名) ordinary soldier

兵团(團) bīngtuán (名) a large military unit consisting of several armies or divisions; corps: 主力～ main force

兵役 bīngyì (名) military service: 服～ serve in the armed force. ～制 conscription

兵营(營) bīngyíng (名) military camp; barracks

兵站 bīngzhàn (名) military depot

兵种(種) bīngzhǒng (名) arm of the services

禀 bǐng (动) 1 report (to one's superior); petition 2 receive; be endowed with

禀承 bǐngchéng see "秉承" bǐngchéng

禀赋 bǐngfù (名) natural endowment; gift: ～聪明 gifted or talented

禀告 bǐnggào (动) report (to one's superior)

禀性 bǐngxìng (名) natural disposition

饼 bǐng (名) 1 cake: 月～ moon cake. 烙～ pancake 2 shaped like a cake: 铁～ discus

饼干(乾) bǐnggān (名) biscuit; cracker

屏 bǐng (动) 1 hold (one's breath) 2 reject; abandon

see also píng

屏弃(棄) bǐngqì (动) discard; throw away

屏息 bǐngxī (动) hold one's breath: 听众～静听. The audience listened intently with bated breath.

丙 bǐng (名) 1 the third of the ten Heavenly Stems 2 third: ～等 the third grade; grade C

炳 bǐng (形)〈书〉bright; splendid; remarkable

柄 bǐng (名) 1 handle: 刀～ the handle of a knife 2 stem (of a flower, leaf or fruit)

秉 bǐng (动)〈书〉1 grasp; hold: ～烛 hold a candle 2 control; preside over: ～政 hold political power

秉承 bǐngchéng (动)〈书〉act on (sb.'s advice or instructions)

秉公 bǐnggōng (副) justly; impartially

秉正 bǐngzhèng (形) fair-minded; upright

病 bìng I (动) be taken ill: 她昨天病了. She fell ill yesterday. II (名) 1 disease; ailment: 心脏～ heart trouble; heart disease. 流行～ epidemic disease 2 fault; defect: 语～ faulty expression

病变(變) bìngbiàn (名) pathological changes

病虫(蟲)害 bìng-chónghài (名) plant diseases and insect pests

病床(牀) bìngchuáng (名) 1 hospital bed 2 sickbed

病毒 bìngdú (名) virus

病房 bìngfáng (名) ward (of a hospital); sickroom: 隔离～ isolation ward. 内科～ medical ward

病根 bìnggēn (名) 1 an old complaint 2 the root cause of a trouble

病故 bìnggù (动) die of illness

病号(號) bìnghào (名) sick person; patient: 他是个老～. He is a valetudinarian.

病假 bìngjià (名) sick leave: 请～ ask for sick leave

病菌 bìngjūn (名) pathogenic bacteria; germs

病理 bìnglǐ (名) pathology

病历(歷) bìnglì (名) medical record; case history

病例 bìnglì (名) case (of illness)
病情 bìngqíng (名) state of an illness; patient's condition
病人 bìngrén (名) patient; invalid
病入膏肓 bìng rù gāohuāng the disease is beyond cure
病态(態) bìngtài (名) morbid (or abnormal) state: ～心理 morbid psychology (or mentality)
病危 bìngwēi (动) be critically ill
病因 bìngyīn (名) cause of disease; pathogeny
病愈 bìngyù (动) recover (from an illness)
病院 bìngyuàn (名) a specialized hospital: 精神～ mental hospital. 传染～ isolation hospital
病灶 bìngzào (名) focus (of a disease)

并(併、並) bìng I (动) combine; merge; incorporate II (副) **1** simultaneously; side by side **2** (not) at all [used before a negative for emphasis]: 这件毛衣～不便宜. This sweater is not at all cheap. III (连) and

并存 bìngcún (动) exist side by side; coexist
并轨 bìngguǐ (动) integrate
并购 bìnggòu (名) mergers and acquisitions (M&A); buyout; take over
并驾齐(齊)驱(驅) bìngjià-qíqū run neck and neck; keep pace with sb.
并肩 bìngjiān (副) shoulder to shoulder; side by side: ～作战 fight shoulder to shoulder
并立 bìnglì (动) exist side by side; be on a par
并列 bìngliè (动) stand side by side: ～句 compound sentence
并排 bìngpái (副) side by side; abreast
并且 bìngqiě (连) and; besides; moreover; furthermore
并吞 bìngtūn (动) swallow up; annex: ～别国领土 annex part or the whole of another country's territory
并行不悖 bìngxíng bù bèi not be mutually exclusive
并重 bìngzhòng (动) lay equal stress on; pay equal attention to

拨(撥) bō I (动) **1** turn, move with finger, stick etc.; stir; poke: ～船 row a boat. ～电话号码 dial a telephone number **2** set aside; assign; allocate: ～出一大笔款子供基本建设用 appropriate a large sum for capital construction II (量) group; batch: 已经去了两～人了. Two groups of people have been sent there.

拨款 bōkuǎn I (动) allocate funds II (名) appropriation: 军事～ military appropriations
拨乱(亂)反正 bō luàn fǎn zhèng bring order out of chaos; set things to rights
拨弄 bōnong (动) **1** fiddle with: ～火盆里的木炭 poke the charcoal in the brazier. ～琴弦 pluck the strings of a fiddle **2** stir up: ～是非 stir up trouble; make trouble **3** manipulate

播 bō (动) **1** sow **2** broadcast

播放 bōfàng (动) broadcast
播送 bōsòng (动) broadcast; transmit; beam: ～新闻 broadcast news
播音 bōyīn (动) transmit; broadcast: ～室 broadcasting studio. ～员 announcer
播种(種) bōzhǒng (动) sow seeds: ～机 seeder; planter

钵 bō (名) **1** earthen bowl **2** alms bowl (of a Buddhist monk)

波 bō (名) **1** wave; ripples: 微～ microwave **2** an unexpected turn of events: 风～ disturbance; scene

波长(長) bōcháng (名) wavelength
波动(動) bōdòng I (动) fluctuate; be unstable: 物价～ price fluctuation II (名) wave motion
波段 bōduàn (名) wave band
波及 bōjí (动) spread to; engulf; affect: 经济危机～整个西方世界. The economic crisis affected the entire Western world.
波澜 bōlán (名) great waves; billows: ～起伏 with one climax following another. ～壮阔 surging forward with great momentum
波浪 bōlàng (名) wave
波涛(濤) bōtāo (名) great waves; billows: ～汹涌 roaring waves
波纹 bōwén (名) **1** ripple **2** corrugation
波折 bōzhé (名) twists and turns; setback

菠 bō

菠菜 bōcài (名) spinach
菠萝(蘿) bōluó (名) pineapple

玻 bō

玻璃 bōli (名) glass: 雕花～ cut glass; crystal. ～杯 glass. ～板 glass plate. ～钢 glass fibre reinforced plastic. 教堂里的彩色～ stained glass. 有机～ organic glass;

plastic

剥 bō

see also bāo

剥夺(奪) bōduó (动) deprive; expropriate; strip: ～政治权利 deprive sb. of political rights. ～权力 divest sb. of his power

剥离(離) bōlí (动) (of tissue, skin, covering, etc.) come off; peel off

剥落 bōluò (动) peel off: 墙上的石灰已～了. The plaster on the walls has peeled off.

剥削 bōxuē I (动) exploit II (名) exploitation: ～阶级 exploiting class. ～者 exploiter

脖 bó (名) neck

脖子 bózi (名) neck: 骑在某人的～上 lord it over sb.

勃 bó (形) suddenly

勃勃 bóbó (形) thriving; vigorous; exuberant: 生气～ full of vigor. 兴致～ in high spirits. 野心～ full of ambition

勃发(發) bófā (动) 1 thrive; prosper 2 break out: 战争～. War broke out.

勃然 bórán (副) agitatedly; excitedly: ～变色 show signs of displeasure; show a sudden change of countenance. ～大怒 fly into a rage; flare up; raise the roof

博 bó I (形) rich; abundant; plentiful: 地大物～ vast territory and rich natural resources II (动) win; gain: 聊～一笑 just for your amusement

博爱(愛) bó'ài (名) fraternity; brotherhood; universal love

博彩 bócǎi (名) gambling industry; lottery

博导(導) bódǎo (名) Ph. D. supervisor

博得 bódé (动) win; gain: ～同情 enlist one's sympathy. ～赞扬 win praise. ～好评 have a favourable reception; be well received

博古通今 bógǔ-tōngjīn have an extensive knowledge of the past and present; erudite and well-informed

博客 bókè (名) blog

博览(覽) bólǎn (动) read extensively: ～群书 well-read

博览(覽)会(會) bólǎnhuì (名) (international) fair; trade fair

博取 bóqǔ (动) gain; try to court: ～欢心 curry favour. ～信任 try to win sb.'s confidence

博士 bóshì (名) 1 doctor: ～学位 doctorate 2 court academician (in feudal China)

博闻强记 bówén-qiángjì have wide knowledge and a retentive memory

博物 bówù (名) natural science: ～学家 naturalist

博物馆 bówùguǎn (名) museum: 历史～ the Museum of History

博学(學) bóxué (形) learned; erudite: ～之士 learned scholar; a walking dictionary. ～多才 learned and versatile

薄 bó I (形) 1 slight; meagre; small: ～酬 small reward 2 ungenerous; unkind; mean: ～待 treat frivolously II (动) 1 despise; belittle: 鄙～ despise; scorn 2 〈书〉 approach; near: 日～西山 like the setting sun over the western hills; in one's declining years

see also báo

薄饼 bóbǐng (名) thin pancake

薄脆 bócuì (名) cracker

薄礼 bólǐ (名) my small (or unworthy) gift

薄利 bólì (名) small profits

薄命 bómìng (形) (usu. of women) born under an unlucky star; ill-fated

薄膜 bómó (名) 1 membrane 2 film: 塑料～ plastic film

薄暮 bómù (名)〈书〉 dusk; twilight

薄情 bóqíng (形) inconstant in love; fickle

薄弱 bóruò (形) weak; frail: ～环节 a weak link. 意志～ weak-willed

薄雾(霧) bówù (名) mist; haze

搏 bó I (动) 1 wrestle; fight; combat; struggle: 肉～ hand-to-hand fight (or combat) 2 pounce on II (名) beat; throb: 脉～ pulse

搏动(動) bódòng (动) beat rhythmically; throb

搏斗(鬥) bódòu (动) wrestle; fight; struggle: 与风浪～ battle with the tempestuous waves

膊 bó (名) arm: 赤～ naked to the waist

钹 bó (名) cymbals

泊 bó (动) anchor a ship; be at anchor; moor: 停～ lie at anchor. 飘～ drift along

see also pō

泊船 bóchuán (动) moor a boat

泊位 bówèi (名) berth: 深水～ deep-water berth

箔 bó (名) 1 screen (of reeds, sorghum stalks, etc.): 苇～ reed screen 2 bamboo tray for raising silkworms **3** foil; tinsel: 金～ gold foil (or leaf) **4** paper tinsel (burnt as paper currency for the dead)

帛 bó (名)〈书〉silks: 布～ silk and satin. ～画 painting on silk. ～书 (ancient) characters inscribed on silk; book copied on silk

伯 bó (名) **1** father's elder brother; uncle **2** the eldest of brothers **3** earl; count

伯父 bófù (名) father's elder brother; uncle

伯爵 bójué (名) earl; count: ～夫人 countess

伯母 bómǔ (名) aunt; wife of father's elder brother

舶 bó (名) seagoing vessel of considerable size: 船～ ship. ～来品 imported goods

驳 bó I (动) refute; contradict: 反～ retort. 辩～ repel by argument II (形)〈书〉of different colours: 斑～ particoloured; variegated

驳斥 bóchì (动) refute; denounce

驳船 bóchuán (名) barge; lighter

驳倒 bódǎo (动) demolish sb.'s argument; succeed in refuting

驳回 bóhuí (动) reject; turn down; overrule

驳面子 bó miànzi not spare sb.'s sensibilities

驳运(運) bóyùn (动) transport by lighter; lighter; barge

跛 bǒ (形) lame: ～了一只脚 lame in one leg; crippled

跛子 bǒzi (名) lame person; cripple

簸 bǒ (动) winnow with a fan; fan: ～谷 winnow away the chaff

see also bò

簸扬(揚) bǒyáng (动) winnow

簸 bò

see also bǒ

簸箕 bòji (名) **1** dustpan **2** winnowing fan **3** loop (of a fingerprint)

擘 bò (名)〈书〉thumb: 巨～ an authority in a certain field

擘画(畫) bòhuà (动)〈书〉plan; arrange: 机构新立,一切均待～. We have to do a lot of planning as this is a new organization.

逋 bū (动)〈书〉flee: ～逃 flee; abscond

捕 bǔ (动) catch; seize; arrest: ～鱼 catch fish. 被～ be arrested; be under arrest

捕风(風)捉影 bǔfēng-zhuōyǐng speak or act on hearsay evidence; make groundless charges

捕获(獲) bǔhuò (动) catch; capture; seize: 当场～ be caught red-handed. ～量 catch (of fish etc.)

捕捞(撈) bǔlāo (动) fish for (aquatic animals and plants); catch

捕猎 bǔliè (动) hunt

捕食 bǔshí (动) catch and feed on; prey on

捕捉 bǔzhuō (动) catch; seize: ～害虫 catch harmful insects. ～逃犯 capture an escapee

哺 bǔ I (动) feed (a baby); nurse II (名)〈书〉the food in one's mouth

哺乳 bǔrǔ (动) breastfeed: ～动物 mammal. ～室 nursing room

哺育 bǔyù (动) **1** feed: ～雏鸟 (of mother birds) feed young birds **2** nurture; foster; bring up

卜 bǔ I (名) divination; fortune-telling: ～卦 divine by the Eight Trigrams II (动) **1**〈书〉foretell; predict: 胜败可～. Victory or defeat can be predicted. 前途未～. It is hard to foretell sb.'s future. **2**〈书〉select; choose: ～居 make one's home

补(補) bǔ I (动) **1** mend; patch; repair: ～袜子 darn socks. ～车胎 fix a tyre **2** fill; supply; make up for: 弥～损失 retrieve a loss **3** nourish: ～品 tonics II (名)〈书〉benefit; use; help: 不无小～. not be without some advantage; be of some help. 无～于事 won't help

补白 bǔbái (名) filler (in a newspaper or magazine)

补偿(償) bǔcháng (动) compensate; make up: ～某人所受的损失 make compensation for sb.'s loss. ～差额 make up a deficiency. ～贸易 compensation trade

补充 bǔchōng I (动) replenish; supplement; complement; add: ～人力 replenish manpower. ～库存 replenish the stock. ～两点意见 have two more points. 互相～ complement each other; be mutually complementary II (形) additional; complementary; supplementary: ～读物 supplementary reading material. ～规定 additional regulations.

～说明 additional remarks
补丁 bǔdìng (动) patch: 打～ put (or sew) a patch on; patch up worn-out clothes
补发(發) bǔfā (动) supply again (sth. lost, etc.); reissue; issue or distribute behind schedule: ～增加的工资 pay increased wages retroactively. 通知～. Notice will be forwarded subsequently.
补花 bǔhuā (名) appliqué
补给 bǔjǐ (动) supply: ～品 supplies
补救 bǔjiù (动) remedy: ～办法 corrective measures; remedy. 无可～ be past (or beyond) remedy; irremediable; irreparable
补考 bǔkǎo (动) retake an examination
补课 bǔkè (动) give tutorials to students who have missed classes; private tutoring; touch up sth. not done properly
补品 bǔpǐn (名) tonic; restoratives
补缺 bǔquē (动) **1** fill a vacancy **2** supply a deficiency
补税 bǔshuì (动) **1** pay a tax one has evaded **2** pay an overdue tax
补贴 bǔtiē (名) subsidy; allowance: 粮食～ grain subsidy. 生活～ living allowances. 地区～ weighting (allowance)
补习(習) bǔxí (动) take lessons after school or work
补选(選) bǔxuǎn (动) by-election: ～人民代表 hold a by-election for a people's deputy
补血 bǔxuè (动) enrich the blood: 猪肝能～. Pork liver is a blood-builder.
补养(養) bǔyǎng (动) take a tonic or nourishing food to build up one's health
补药(藥) bǔyào (名) tonic
补遗 bǔyí (名) addendum
补益 bǔyì (名)〈书〉benefit; help: 有所～ be of some help (or benefit)
补语 bǔyǔ (名) complement
补助 bǔzhù (名) subsidy; allowance: ～金 grant-in-aid; subsidy
补缀 bǔzhuì (动) mend (clothes); patch: 缝连～ mend and darn
补足 bǔzú (动) bring up to full strength; make up a deficiency

部 bù I (名) **1** part; section: 分为三～ divide into three parts (or sections). 南～ the southern part **2** unit; ministry; department; board: 外交～ the Ministry of Foreign Affairs. 编辑～ editorial board (or office) **3** headquarters: 团～ regimental headquarters **4** 〈书〉command: 所～ troops under one's command II (量): 一～电影 a film. 一～好作品 a fine work of literature
部队(隊) bùduì (名) **1** army; armed forces **2** troops; force; unit
部分 bùfen (名) part; section; share: 脸的上半～ the upper part of the face. 居民中的大～人 a large section of the inhabitants. 一本分为三～的小说 a novel in three parts
部件 bùjiàn (名) parts; components; assembly
部落 bùluò (名) tribe: ～社会 tribal society
部门(門) bùmén (名) department; branch: 政府各～ various departments of the government. 有关～ the departments concerned
部首 bùshǒu (名) radicals by which characters are arranged in traditional Chinese dictionaries
部属(屬) bùshǔ (形) affiliated to a ministry: ～机构 organizations affiliated to the ministry
部署 bùshǔ (动) dispose; deploy: ～兵力 deploy troops for battle. 战略～ a strategic plan; strategic deployment
部位 bùwèi (名) position; place; location
部下 bùxià (名) **1** troops under one's command **2** subordinate
部长(長) bùzhǎng (名) minister; head of a department: 外交部～ Minister of Foreign Affairs. ～会议 Council of Ministers. ～助理 assistant minister

埠 bù (名) **1** wharf; pier **2** port: 本～ this port. 外～ other ports. 商～ a commercial (or trading) port

不 bù (副) **1** [used to form a negative]: ～严重 not serious. ～正确 incorrect. ～合法 illegal. ～可能 impossible. ～小心 careless. 拿～动 too heavy to carry. 睡～好 not sleep well **2** [used as a negative answer]: 他知道吧? ——～, 他不知道. He knows, doesn't he? —No, he doesn't. **3** [used at the end of a sentence to form a question]: 你明儿来～? Are you coming tomorrow? **4** [inserted in reiterative locutions, usually preceded by 什么, to indicate indifference]: 什么难学～难学, 我一定学会. No matter how hard it is, I'll learn how to do it. **5** [used together with 就 to indicate a choice]: 他这会儿～是在车间就是在实验室. He's either in the workshop or in the laboratory.

不安 bù'ān (形) **1** turbulent; unstable: 动荡～ unstable and unsettling **2** uneasy; disturbed; worried: 坐立～ restless. 听了这消息我心里很～. I was rather disturbed by the news.

不白之冤 bù bái zhī yuān gross injustice

不败之地 bù bài zhī dì invincible position: 立于～ be in an invincible position

不备(備) bùbèi (形) unprepared; off guard: 乘其～ catch sb. off guard

不必 bùbì (副) need not; not have to: ～紧张. Take it easy. There is nothing to be nervous about.

不便 bùbiàn (形) **1** inconvenient; inappropriate; unsuitable: 交通～ poor transport facilities. 如果对你没有什么～的话,我想提早办. I'd like to make it earlier, if that's not inconvenient to you. **2** 〈口〉 short of cash: 手头～ be short of cash; be hard up

不…不… bù…bù… **1** [used to make an emphatic negative form of two words identical or similar in meaning]: 不骄不躁 not conceited or rash; free from arrogance and rashness. 不慌不忙 unhurried; calm; leisurely. 不知不觉 unawares **2** [used with two words of opposite meanings to indicate an intermediate state]: 不大不小 neither too big nor too small; just right. 不冷不热 neither cold nor hot. 不死不活 neither dead nor alive; half-dead **3** [the first 不 is the condition of the second 不]: 不见不散. We won't leave until we meet.

不测 bùcè (名) accident; mishap; contingency: 以防～ be prepared for any eventuality. 险遭～ have a narrow escape

不成 bùchéng I (动) won't do; not going to succeed: 盲目按照他的指令办事,那是～的. To follow his instructions blindly won't lead you anywhere. II (助) [used at the end of a tag question]: 难道就这样算了～? How can we let it go at that?

不成文法 bùchéngwénfǎ unwritten law

不逞之徒 bùchěng zhī tú desperado

不齿(齒) bùchǐ (动) 〈书〉 despise: ～于人类 held in contempt by all

不耻下问 bù chǐ xià wèn not feel ashamed to solicit advice from one's inferiors; modest enough to consult one's subordinates

不出所料 bù chū suǒ liào as expected; within one's expectations

不辞(辭)而别 bù cí ér bié leave without saying good-bye; take French leave

不辞(辭)辛苦 bù cí xīnkǔ make nothing of hardships; stint no effort

不错 bùcuò (形) **1** correct; right: 一点儿～ perfectly correct; quite right **2** [to indicate what has been said is right]: ～,他明天来这儿. Yes, he will come tomorrow. **3** 〈口〉 not bad; pretty good: 他的中文挺～. His Chinese is not bad.

不打自招 bù dǎ zì zhāo confess without being pressed; make a confession without duress

不大 bùdà (副) **1** not very; not too: ～自然 not very natural. ～清楚 not too clear **2** not often: 他最近～来. He has made himself scarce recently.

不但 bùdàn (连) not only: 我～听到过,而且看见过. I not only heard about it, but actually saw it.

不当(當) bùdàng (形) unsuitable; improper; inappropriate: 处理～ not be handled properly. 措词～ wrong choice of words; inappropriately worded

不倒翁 bùdǎowēng (名) tumbler; "survivor"

不道德 bùdàodé (形) immoral

不得 bùdé (动) must not; may not; not be allowed: ～在剧场抽烟. Smoking is not allowed in the theatre.

不得 bùdé [used after a verb indicating that such an action cannot or should not be taken]: 去～ must not go. 马虎～ mustn't (or can't afford to) be careless

不得不 bùdé bù (副) have no choice (or option) but to; cannot but; have to: 时间不早了,我～走了. It's getting late. I'm afraid I have to leave now.

不得了 bùdéliǎo I (形) desperately serious; disastrous: 没有什么～的事. There's nothing seriously wrong. II [used after 得 as a complement] extremely; exceedingly: 高兴得～ be extremely happy; be wild with joy III (叹) Good heavens!

不得人心 bù dé rénxīn not enjoy popular support; be unpopular

不得要领 bù dé yàolǐng fail to grasp the essence; miss the main points; unable to get the hang of sth.

不得已 bùdéyǐ act against one's will; have no alternative but to; can not help but:

～而求其次 have to choose the second best; have to give up one's first choice. 实在～，他只好走着去火车站. He had no alternative but to walk to the railway station.

不等 bùděng (形) vary; differ: 长短～ vary in length. 大小～ differ (or vary) in size

不迭 bùdié (副) [used only after a verb to indicate haste] **1** cannot afford to: 后悔～ look back with regret, but it's too late **2** incessantly: 叫苦～ complain endlessly

不定 bùdìng I (副) not sure: 他一天～来多少次. He comes I don't know how many times a day. II (形) indefinite: ～冠词 indefinite article. ～式 infinitive

不动(動)产(產) bùdòngchǎn (名) real estate; immovable property; immovables

不动(動)声(聲)色 bù dòng shēngsè maintain one's composure; not betray one's feelings

不冻(凍)港 bùdònggǎng (名) ice-free port; open port

不端 bùduān (形) improper; dishonourable: 品行～ dishonourable behaviour; immoral conduct

不断(斷) bùduàn (副) unceasing; uninterrupted; continuous; constant: 在医院时，～有人来看他. While he was in hospital, people kept on coming to see him.

不对(對) bùduì (形) **1** incorrect; wrong: 这样做～. It's wrong to act like that. **2** [indicating what has been said is wrong]: ～，我可没那么说. No, I didn't say so actually.

不…而… bù…ér… [indicate a result without a direct cause or condition]: 不谋而合 agree without prior consultation

不二法门(門) bù èr fǎmén the only correct approach; the only proper course to take

不乏 bùfá (动) there is no lack of: ～先例. There is no lack of precedents. ～其人. Such people are not rare.

不法 bùfǎ (形) lawless; illegal; unlawful: ～之徒 a lawless person. ～行为 unlawful practice; an illegal act

不凡 bùfán (形) out of the ordinary; out of the common run: 自命～ consider oneself a person of no ordinary talent; have an unduly high opinion of oneself

不妨 bùfáng (副) there is no harm in; might as well: ～一试. There is no harm in trying. 你～先同他联系一下. You might as well contact him first.

不费吹灰之力 bù fèi chuī huī zhī lì with the slightest effort; effortlessly

不分青红皂白 bù fēn qīng-hóng-zào-bái indiscriminately

不分胜(勝)负 bù fēn shèng-fù tie; draw; come out even

不服 bù fú (动) refuse to obey (or comply): ～输 refuse to take defeat lying down. ～主席的裁决 refuse to accept the chairman's ruling

不服水土 bù fú shuǐtǔ (of a stranger) not accustomed to the climate or the particular type of food of a new place

不符 bùfú (动) not agree (or tally, square) with; not conform to; be inconsistent with: 言行～. One's deeds do not match one's words. 与事实～ be inconsistent (or at variance) with the facts

不干(乾)不净 bùgān-bùjìng unclean; filthy: 嘴里～ be foulmouthed

不甘 bùgān (动) unreconciled to; not resigned to; unwilling: ～落后 unwilling to lag behind. ～寂寞 unwilling to remain obscure; fond of the limelight

不甘心 bù gānxīn not reconciled to; not resigned to

不敢当(當) bùgǎndāng 〈谦〉 [a polite expression in reply to a compliment] I wish I could deserve your compliment; you flatter me

不恭 bùgōng (形) disrespectful

不共戴天 bù gòng dài tiān will not live under the same sky (with one's enemy)— absolutely irreconcilable: ～的敌人 sworn enemy

不苟 bùgǒu (形) not lax; not casual; careful; conscientious: 工作一丝～ work most conscientiously ～言笑 sober; sedate; taciturn

不够 bùgòu (形) not enough; insufficient; inadequate: 我们的教室～. We don't have enough classrooms. 分析～深入 The analysis lacks depth. *or* This is not quite an in-depth analysis.

不顾(顧) bùgù (动) in spite of; regardless of: ～后果 regardless of the consequences. ～自身安危 never think of one's own safety

不关(關) bùguān (动) have nothing to do with; do not concern: 这～你的事! It's none of your business!

不管 bùguǎn (动) no matter (what, how, etc.); regardless of: ～结果如何 whatever the results. ～怎样 in any case; anyway

不轨 bùguǐ (名) acting against the law or discipline: 图谋～ contemplate conspiratorial activities

不过(過) bùguò I (副) 1 [used after an adjective to form the superlative degree]: 那就再好～了! It could not be better! *or* That would be superb. 2 only; merely; no more than: 这本字典不过 10 美元. This dictionary costs no more than ten dollars. II (连) but; however; only: 病人精神还不错, ～胃口不大好. The patient feels pretty well, but he hasn't much of an appetite.

不含糊 bù hánhu 〈口〉 1 unambiguous; unequivocal; explicit: 以毫～的语言作出回答 answer in unequivocal terms; answer explicitly 2 not ordinary; really good: 他这活儿做得真～. He's really done a good job.

不寒而栗(慄) bù hán ér lì tremble with fear; make one's blood run cold

不好惹 bù hǎorě not to be trifled with; not to be pushed around; to stand no nonsense

不好意思 bù hǎoyìsi 1 feel bashful; be ill at ease 2 find it embarrassing (to do sth.): ～再提要求 hesitate to make another request

不合 bùhé (动) not conform to; unsuitable for; be out of keeping with: ～规定 in disagreement with the rules. ～标准 not up to the (required) standard; below the mark. 脾气～ be temperamentally incompatible. ～时宜 behind the times; unseasonable; out of step with modern life

不和 bùhé (动) 1 be at loggerheads; be at odds 2 discord: 制造～ sow discord

不怀(懷)好意 bù huái hǎoyì harbour evil designs; harbour malicious intentions; be up to no good

不欢(歡)而散 bùhuān ér sàn part in displeasure or anger; (of a meeting, etc.) break up in discord

不会(會) bùhuì (动) 1 be unlikely; will not (act, happen, etc.): 她～不知道. It's not likely that she doesn't know. 2 have not learned to; be unable to: 他～开车. He cannot drive a car. 3 [used to show displeasure]: 你就～打个电话问一问? Couldn't you have phoned up and asked?

不讳(諱) bùhuì 〈书〉 without concealing anything: 供认～ candidly confess; make a clean breast of something. 直言～ speak bluntly; be outspoken

不羁 bùjī (形) 〈书〉 unconventional

不及 bùjí (动) 1 not as good as; inferior to: 这本书～那本书有趣. This book is not as interesting as that one. 2 find it too late: 躲避～ be too late to dodge; could not avoid getting into trouble

不即不离(離) bùjí-bùlí be neither too intimate nor too distant; keep sb. at a respectful distance

不计其数(數) bù jì qí shù countless; innumerable

不济(濟) bùjì (形) not in full strength; not good: 精力～了 not as energetic as before 她眼力～了. Her eyesight is failing.

不假思索 bù jiǎ sīsuǒ without thinking; without hesitation; readily (also "不加思索")

不见(見)得 bù jiànde not necessarily; not likely: ～合逻辑 not necessarily logical. 他今晚～会来. It seems unlikely that he will come tonight.

不结盟 bùjiéméng non-alignment: ～国家 non-aligned countries. ～政策 policy of non-alignment

不解 bùjiě I (动) not understand: 迷惑～ be puzzled II (形) indissoluble: ～之缘 an indissoluble bond

不禁 bùjīn (副) can't help (doing sth.); can't refrain from: 他难过得～哭了起来. He felt so sad that he couldn't help crying.

不仅(僅) bùjǐn I (副) not the only one: 这～是我一个人的主张. I'm not the only one who holds this view. II (连) not only: ～如此 not only that; nor is this all; moreover

不景气(氣) bù jǐngqì 1 depression; recession; slump 2 depressing state

不胫(脛)而走 bù jìng ér zǒu get round fast; spread far and wide

不久 bùjiǔ (名) 1 soon; before long: 我们～就要毕业了. We'll soon graduate from this school. 2 not long after; soon after: 种完树～就下了一场雨. It rained soon after we had planted the trees.

不咎既往 bù jiù jìwǎng not censure sb. for his past misdeeds; let bygones be bygones

不拘 bùjū I (动) not stick to; not confine oneself to: ～小节 not bother about trivialities; not be punctilious. 字数～ No limit is set on the length (for an article). II (连) whatever: ～什么工作我都愿意接受. I'm ready to accept whatever job comes along.

不倦 bùjuàn (形) tireless; untiring; indefatigable: 诲人～ be tireless in teaching; teach with tireless zeal

不堪 bùkān I (动) cannot bear; cannot stand: ～设想 dreadful to contemplate. ～入耳 unpleasant to the ear; disgusting II (助) utterly; extremely: 疲惫～ extremely tired; exhausted. 狼狈～ be embarrassed beyond endurance

不亢不卑 bùkàng-bùbēi neither overbearing nor servile; be neither humble nor disrespectful

不可 bùkě (动) 1 cannot; should not; must not: 两者～偏废. Neither can be neglected. ～剥夺的权利 an inalienable right 2 [used together with 非 to indicate what one is set to do]: 这部电影太精彩了,我非看～. The film is extremely good; I just cannot miss it.

不可救药(藥) bùkě jiù yào incorrigible; beyond cure; hopeless; past praying for

不可开(開)交 bùkě kāijiāo [used only after 得 as its complement to indicate what one cannot free oneself from]: 忙得～ be up to one's eyes in work; be awfully (or terribly) busy

不可磨灭(滅) bùkě mómiè indelible: ～的印象 indelible (everlasting) impressions

不可胜(勝)数(數) bùkě shèngshǔ countless; numerable

不可收拾 bùkě shōushi irremediable; unmanageable; out of hand

不可思议(議) bùkě sīyì inconceivable; unimaginable

不可同日而语 bùkě tóngrì ér yǔ cannot be mentioned in the same breath

不可一世 bùkě yīshì consider oneself second to none in the world

不可逾越 bùkě yúyuè impassable; insurmountable; insuperable: ～的鸿沟 an impassable chasm. ～的障碍 an insurmountable (or insuperable) barrier

不可知论(論) bùkězhīlùn (名) agnosticism

不可终日 bùkě zhōng rì be unable to carry on even for a single day; be in a desperate situation: 惶惶～ be very worried; full of anxiety

不可捉摸 bùkě zhuōmō elusive; unpredictable; difficult to ascertain: ～的想法 intangible ideas. 情况～. The situation is hard to size up.

不客气(氣) bù kèqi I (形) impolite; rude; blunt: 说句～的话 to put it bluntly II 〈套〉(in reply to one's thanks) you're welcome; don't mention it; not at all III 〈套〉[used to express gratitude for sb.'s offer] please don't bother; I'll help myself

不快 bùkuài (形) 1 be unhappy; be displeased; be in low spirits 2 be indisposed; feel under the weather

不愧 bùkuì (动) be worthy of; deserve to be called; prove oneself to be: 他～为英雄. He has proved himself to be a hero.

不劳(勞)而获(獲) bù láo ér huò reap without sowing; live off the labour of others

不理 bùlǐ (动) refuse to acknowledge; pay no attention to; take no notice of; ignore

不力 bùlì (形) not do one's best; ineffective: 办事～ prove incompetent in one's work. 领导～ not exercise effective leadership

不利 bùlì (形) 1 unfavourable; disadvantageous; harmful; detrimental: ～条件 unfavourable conditions 2 unsuccessful: 首战～ lose the first battle

不良 bùliáng (形) bad; harmful; unhealthy: ～倾向 unhealthy trends. ～影响 harmful (or adverse) effects. 存心～ harbour evil intentions

不了了之 bùliǎo liǎo zhī let the matter take its own course; end up without any tangible results

不料 bùliào (副) unexpectedly; to one's surprise

不灵(靈) bùlíng (形) not work; be ineffective: 这架收音机～了. The radio doesn't work. 老太太耳朵有点～了. The old lady is hard of hearing.

不露声(聲)色 bù lù shēngsè not show one's feelings, intentions, etc.

不伦(倫)不类(類) bùlún-bùlèi neither fish nor fowl; nondescript: ～的比喻 an incongruous metaphor; a far-fetched analogy

不论(論) bùlùn (连) no matter (what, who, how, etc.); whether... or...; regardless of: ～性别年龄 regardless (or irrespective) of sex and age

不落窠臼 bù luò kējiù not follow the beaten track; have an original style

不满(滿) bùmǎn (形) resentful; discontented; dissatisfied: 心怀～ nurse a grievance

不忙 bùmáng (动) there's no hurry; take one's time: 你～就走. No need to leave in such a hurry.

不毛之地 bù máo zhī dì barren land; desert

不免 bùmiǎn (副) unavoidable: 忙中～有错. We tend to make mistakes when we do things in a hurry.

不妙 bùmiào (形) (of a turn of events) not too encouraging; far from good; anything but reassuring

不明 bùmíng (形) not clear; unknown: 失踪的士兵至今下落～. We don't know yet the whereabouts of the missing soldiers. ～飞行物 unidentified flying object (UFO)

不谋而合 bù móu ér hé agree without prior consultation; happen to hold identical views: 我们的意见～. Our views happened to coincide.

不偏不倚 bùpiān-bùyǐ evenhanded; impartial; unbiased

不平 bùpíng I (名) injustice; unfairness; wrong; grievance II (形) indignant; resentful: 愤愤～ very indignant; deeply resentful

不平等条(條)约 bùpíngděng tiáoyuē (名) unequal treaty

不平衡 bùpínghéng disequilibrium: 工农业发展～ the disequilibrium between the development of industry and agriculture

不期而遇 bù qī ér yù meet by chance; have a chance encounter

不起眼儿(兒) bù qǐyǎnr not noticeable; not attractive

不巧 bùqiǎo (副) unfortunately

不切实(實)际(際) bùqiè shíjì unrealistic; unpractical; impracticable: ～的设想 an impracticable idea; an unrealistic notion

不求甚解 bù qiú shèn jiě seek no perfect understanding; be content with imperfect understanding

不屈 bùqū (动) never give in; never yield

不屈不挠(撓) bùqū-bùnáo unyielding; indomitable

不然 bùrán I (动) not so: 其实～. Actually this is not so. II [used at the beginning of a sentence to indicate disagreement] no: ～,事情没有那么简单. No, it's not as simple as that. III (连) or else; otherwise; if not: 你得更用功一点,～考试就会不及格. You ought to work a bit harder, or you'll fail in the exams.

不仁 bùrén (形) **1** not benevolent; heartless **2** benumbed: 麻木～ apathetic

不忍 bùrěn (动) cannot bear to: 母亲～再听他对她的孩子的严厉训斥. The mother couldn't bear to hear him speak so harshly of her child any more.

不日 bùrì (副)〈书〉within the next few days; in a few days

不如 bùrú (动) not as good as; inferior to: 我画图～他. I can't draw as well as he does.

不三不四 bùsān-bùsì **1** dubious; shady: ～的人 a person of dubious (or shady) character **2** neither one thing nor the other; neither fish nor fowl: 说些～的话 make frivolous remarks

不善 bùshàn I (形) bad; ill: 来意～ come with evil intentions. 处理～ not handle properly; mishandle II (动) not good at: ～管理 not good at managing things. ～辞令 not eloquent, not good at speeches

不胜(勝) bùshèng (副) **1** [inserted between two duplicate verbs to indicate that one is unable to do anything]: 防～防 be open to attack from any quarters **2** very; extremely: ～感激 be very grateful; appreciate it very much

不胜(勝)枚举(舉) bùshèng méi jǔ too numerous to enumerate

不失时(時)机(機) bù shī shíjī let slip no opportunity; lose no time; make hay while the sun shines

不时(時) bùshí (副) from time to time

不识(識)时(時)务(務) bù shí shíwù **1** show no understanding of the times **2** not be sensible **3** fail to make use of available chances

不识(識)抬举(舉) bù shí táiju fail to appreciate sb.'s kindness

不是 bùshi (名) fault; blame: 这就是你的～了. It's your fault.

不适(適) bùshì (形) unwell; indisposed: 略感～ be feeling a bit out of sorts

不死心 bù sǐxīn unwilling to give up; unresigned

不速之客 bù sù zhī kè uninvited (or unexpected) guest

不通 bùtōng (形) 1 be obstructed; be blocked up; be impassable: 水池堵塞～了. The sink is blocked. 此路～. No Through Road. 电话～. The line's dead. 行～ won't work; won't do 2 not make sense; be illogical; be ungrammatical: 文章写得～. The article is full of grammar and other errors.

不同 bùtóng (形) different from; as distinct from

不同凡响(響) bùtóng fánxiǎng outstanding; out of the ordinary

不痛不痒(癢) bùtòng-bùyǎng not in-depth; superficial; perfunctory: ～的批评 superficial criticism

不图(圖) bùtú (动) not seek; not strive for: ～名利 not hanker after fame or gain

不妥 bùtuǒ (形) improper; inappropriate: 措词～ inappropriate wording. 处理～ an improper way of handling the matter

不外 bùwài (动) not beyond the scope of; nothing other than: 周末,他们～是看部电影、逛逛公园. At weekends they do nothing but go to the pictures or take a stroll in the park.

不闻不问 bùwén-bùwèn be indifferent to sth.

不问 bùwèn (动) 1 pay no attention to; disregard; ignore: ～宗教信仰 irrespective of religious belief 2 let go unpunished; let off

不务(務)正业(業) bù wù zhèngyè 1 not engage in honest work 2 ignore one's proper occupation; not attend to one's proper duties

不惜 bùxī (动) 1 stint no effort; not spare: ～工本 spare neither effort nor money 2 not scruple (to do sth.)

不相干 bù xiānggān be irrelevant; have nothing to do with: ～的话 irrelevant remarks. 这事跟你们～. It has nothing to do with you.

不相上下 bù xiāng shàng-xià equally matched; roughly the same: 水平～ be nearly identical in quality (level)

不详 bùxiáng (形) 〈书〉 1 not in detail 2 not quite clear: 他的家庭背景情况～. Little is known about his family background.

不祥 bùxiáng (形) ominous; inauspicious: ～之兆 an ill omen

不像话 bù xiànghuà 1 unreasonable: 要你们自己掏钱喝酒就～了. It would be unreasonable to have drinks on you. 2 shocking; outrageous: 这种行为真～. Such behaviour is downright shocking.

不像样(樣) bù xiàngyàng 1 unpresentable: 这件大衣太～. This overcoat is hardly presentable. 2 beyond recognition: 破得～ worn to shreds

不肖 bùxiào (形) 〈书〉 unworthy: ～子孙 unworthy descendants

不屑 bùxiè (动) disdain to do sth.; not consider sth. worth doing: ～一顾 scorn to take a look

不懈 bùxiè (动) untiring; unremitting; indefatigable: 坚持～ persevere unremittingly

不兴(興) bùxīng (动) 1 out of fashion; outmoded 2 impermissible; not allowed: ～这样做. That's not allowed.

不行 bùxíng (形) 1 won't do; be out of the question 2 be no good; won't work: 这个计划～. This plan just won't work.

不省人事 bù xǐng rénshì fall into a state of unconsciousness; be in a coma

不幸 bùxìng I (名) misfortune; adversity: 遭～ meet with a misfortune II (形) 1 unfortunate; sad: ～的遭遇 unfortunate experience 2 unfortunately: 他的话～而言中. His remarks have unfortunately proved correct.

不休 bùxiū (动) [used as adverbial modifier] endlessly; ceaselessly: 争论～ argue endlessly; keep on arguing

不修边(邊)幅 bù xiū biānfú untidy; be untidy in dress

不朽 bùxiǔ (动) immortal: ～的著作 an immortal masterpiece. 人民英雄永垂～! Eternal glory to the people's heroes!

不许 bùxǔ (动) not allow; must not: ～抽烟. No smoking. ～动! Don't move!

不学(學)无(無)术(術) bùxué-wúshù have neither learning nor skill; be ignorant and incompetent; lack neither knowledge nor ability

不言而喻 bù yán ér yù it goes without saying; it is self-evident

不要 bùyào (副) don't: ～那样傲慢. Don't be so arrogant.

不要紧(緊) bù yàojǐn it doesn't matter; never mind; it's not serious

不要脸(臉) bù yàoliǎn have no sense of shame; shameless: 真 ~! What a nerve!

不一 bùyī (形) vary; differ: 色彩~ vary in colour. 大小~ differ in size

不宜 bùyí (形) unsuitable; inadvisable: ~操之过急. It's no use trying to get everything done overnight.

不遗余(餘)力 bù yí yúlì spare no effort; do one's utmost

不已 bùyǐ (动) endlessly; incessantly: 赞叹~ praise repeatedly

不以为(爲)然 bù yǐ wéi rán show disapproval of sth.

不义(義)之财 bùyì zhī cái ill-gotten gains

不翼而飞(飛) bù yì ér fēi disappear mysteriously; melt into thin air; vanish

不用 bùyòng (副) need not: ~惊慌. You needn't panic. *or* There is no need to panic.

不由得 bùyóude cannot help; cannot but

不由自主 bù yóu zìzhǔ can't help; unrestrainedly: ~地流下眼泪 couldn't refrain from tears

不约而同 bù yuē ér tóng agree with one another without prior consultation

不在 bù zài (动) not be in; be out: 他~,我能帮你做什么呢? He is not in at the moment. What can I do for you?

不在乎 bù zàihu not mind; not care: 满~ couldn't care less

不在意 bù zàiyì 1 pay no attention to; take no notice of; not mind 2 negligent; careless

不择(擇)手段 bù zé shǒuduàn by fair means or foul; by hook or by crook; unscrupulously

不怎么(麽) bù zěnme not very; not particularly: 他~能干. He is not particularly capable.

不折不扣 bùzhé-bùkòu 1 to the letter: ~地贯彻政策 carry out the policy to the letter 2 out-and-out

不争气(氣) bù zhēngqì fail to live up to expectations; be disappointing: 这孩子太~! The child is hopelessly disappointing!

不正之风(風) bù zhèng zhī fēng malpractice; unhealthy tendency

不知不觉(覺) bùzhī-bùjué unconsciously; unwittingly; without being aware of it

不知死活 bù zhī sǐ-huó act recklessly

不知所措 bù zhī suǒ cuò be at a loss; be at one's wits' end

不知所云 bù zhī suǒ yún not know what sb. is talking about or what one has said

不值 bùzhí (动) not worth: ~一文 not worth a penny; worthless. ~一提 not worth mentioning

不只 bùzhǐ (连) not only; not merely

不至于(於) bùzhìyú not as far as; unlikely: 他学习是不好,可也~不及格啊. He certainly is not one of the best students, but not so bad as to fail.

不治之症 bùzhì zhī zhèng incurable disease

不置可否 bù zhì kě-fǒu decline to comment; neither confirm nor deny; be noncommittal; hedge: 他对此问题采取~的态度. He refused to say yes or no on this matter.

不中意 bù zhòngyì not to one's liking

不中用 bù zhōngyòng unfit for anything; no good; useless: 这把刀~,去换一把吧. This knife is no good. Go and fetch another one. 你这~的东西! You are good-for-nothing!

不准 bùzhǔn (动) not allow; forbid; prohibit: 此处~吸烟 Smoking is not allowed here. *or* No Smoking!

不着边际(際) bù zhuó biānjì not to the point; wide of the mark; entirely irrelevant

不足 bùzú I (形) not enough; insufficient; inadequate: 给养~ be short of supplies. 资金~ lack funds. 人手~ be understaffed II (动) 1 not worth: ~道 not be worth mentioning; of no consequence. ~为奇 not at all surprising; nothing out of the common; nothing to speak of 2 cannot; should not: ~为训 not to be taken as an established rule; not to be regarded as an example to be followed

布 bù I (名) cloth: ~鞋 cloth shoes. 花~ cotton prints II (动) 1 declare; announce; publish; proclaim: 公~于众 make known to the public; be made public 2 spread; disseminate: 控制疾病传~ check the spread of disease. 小水电站遍~全国 Small hydropower stations can be found all over the country. 3 dispose; arrange; deploy: 在楼前~上岗哨 deploy sentinels in front of the building

布帛 bùbó (名) cloth and silk; cotton and silk fabrics

布道 bùdào (动) preach

布防 bùfáng (动) send soldiers to guard a place

布告 bùgào (名) notice; bulletin; proclamation: 张贴～ put up a notice. ～栏 notice board; bulletin board

布谷(穀)鸟(鳥) bùgǔniǎo (名) cuckoo

布景 bùjǐng (名) 1 composition (of a painting) 2 setting; scenery

布局 bùjú (名) 1 overall arrangement; layout; distribution: 新市区的～ layout of a new urban district 2 composition (of a picture, piece of writing, etc.)

布雷 bùléi (动) lay mines; mine: 在港口～ mine a harbour

布匹 bùpǐ (名) cloth; piece goods

布施 bùshī I (动)〈书〉give alms II (名) donation

布置 bùzhì (动) 1 fix up; arrange; decorate: ～房间 arrange a room 2 assign; make arrangements for; give instructions about: ～工作 assign work; give instructions about an assignment

怖 bù (动) fear; be afraid of: 恐～ terror; horror. 可～ horrible; frightful

簿 bù (名) book: 练习～ exercise book. 账～ account book. 登记～ register

簿记 bùjì (名) bookkeeping

簿子 bùzi (名) notebook; book

步 bù I (名) 1 step; pace: 邮局离这儿只有几～路. The post office is only a few steps away. 快～走 walk at a quick pace 2 stage; step: 撤军工作分两～进行. The troops will be pulled out in two stages. 3 condition; situation; state: 事情怎么发展到这一～? How did things get into such a mess? II (动) walk; go on foot: 散～ take a walk

步兵 bùbīng (名) 1 infantry; foot 2 infantryman; foot soldier

步调 bùdiào (名) pace; step: ～一致 keep in step. 统一～ synchronize their (our, your) steps

步伐 bùfá (名) step; pace: 加快～ quicken one's pace. 跟上时代的～ keep abreast of the times

步履维艰(艱) bùlǚ wéi jiān〈书〉have difficulty moving about; plod along

步枪(槍) bùqiāng (名) rifle

步人后(後)尘(塵) bù rén hòuchén follow in other people's footsteps

步行 bùxíng (动) go on foot; walk

步骤 bùzhòu (名) step; move; measure: 这是改善我们工作的具体～. This is a practical move to improve our work. 采取适当的～ take proper steps

C c

擦 cā (动) 1 put (or spread) on: 在脸上～油 put (or smooth) some cream on the face. ～药 apply medical lotion to a wound 2 rub: ～火柴 strike a match. 手上～破一点皮 just a scratch on the hand 3 clean; wipe: ～桌子 wipe the table. ～地板 mop (or scrub) the floor. ～皮鞋 polish shoes 4 pass lightly over or touch lightly against: ～肩而过 brush past sb. 燕子～水飞过 swallows skimming the water 5 scrape into shreds

擦边(邊)球 cābiānqiú (名) edge ball: 打～ circumvent the law by doing sth. quasi-legal

嚓 cā (象) screech: 汽车～的一声停住了. The car screeched to a stop.

猜 cāi (动) guess; speculate: 你～谁来了? Guess who's here.

猜测 cāicè (动) guess; conjecture: 那不过是～. That's only guesswork.

猜忌 cāijì (动) be suspicious and resentful

猜谜儿(兒) cāimèir (动) guess a riddle

猜拳 cāiquán (名) a finger-guessing game

猜想 cāixiǎng (动) suppose; guess

猜疑 cāiyí (动) suspect

裁 cái (动) 1 cut (paper, cloth, etc.): ～纸 cut paper. ～衣服 cut out a new garment 2 cut down; reduce: ～员 reduce (or dismiss) the staff 3 judge; decide 4 check; sanction: 经济制～ economic sanction

裁定 cáidìng (名) ruling

裁缝 cáifeng (名) tailor; dressmaker

裁减 cáijiǎn (动) cut down; reduce: ～人员 cut down the staff of an organization. ～军费 reduction of military expenditure

裁剪 cáijiǎn (动) cut out: ～衣服 cut out garments

裁决 cáijué I (动) rule: 依法～ adjudicate according to law II (名) ruling; verdict

裁军 cáijūn (名) disarmament

裁判 cáipàn (名) 1 judgment 2 referee

才 cái (名) 1 ability; talent; gift: 文～ literary talent. 人～ a person of talent 2 people of a certain type: 蠢～ fool. 奴～ flunkey

C

才(纔) cái (副) 1 [used before a verb to indicate that sth. has just happened or is rather late by general standards]: 我～喂了孩子. I've just fed the baby. 他四十岁～结婚. He got married (as late as) when he was forty. 你怎么～来? Why are you so late? 2 [used in the main clause of a complex sentence to indicate that the condition stated in the subordinate clause is a prerequisite]: 等客人都走了,她～坐下来休息. She sat down for a rest only after all the guests had left. 只有用功,～能通过考试. One must work hard if one wishes to pass the exam. 3 [used before a phrase to indicate that the number is small] only: 她～五岁. She is only five years old. 怎么～三本书? How come there are only three books? 4 [used for emphasis]: 你不知道～怪呢? It would be strange if you didn't know! 我～不去呢! I am (certainly) not going!

才干(幹) cáigàn (名) ability; competence

才华(華) cáihuá (名) (literary or artistic) talent: 一位很有～的演员 a gifted actor

才能 cáinéng (名) ability; talent

才气(氣) cáiqì (名) literary talent: ～横溢 highly gifted

才疏学(學)浅(淺) cáishū-xuéqiǎn 〈谦〉 have little talent and less learning; be an indifferent scholar

才学(學) cáixué (名) talent and learning; scholarship

才智 cáizhì (名) ability and intelligence

才子 cáizǐ (名) gifted scholar: ～佳人 gifted scholars and beautiful ladies (in Chinese romances)

材 cái (名) material: 木～ timber. 教～ teaching material

材料 cáiliào (名) material; data: 建筑～ building material. 原～ raw material

财 cái (名) wealth

财宝(寶) cáibǎo (名) money and valuables

财产(產) cáichǎn (名) property: 公共～ public property

财富 cáifù (名) wealth: 精神～ spiritual wealth. 物质～ material wealth

财经(經) cáijīng (名) finance and economics

财迷 cáimí (名) miser; money-grubber

财团(團) cáituán (名) financial group: 国际～ consortium

财务(務) cáiwù (名) financial affairs

财物 cáiwù (名) property; belongings: 个人～ personal effects

财源 cáiyuán (名) financial resources: 广开～ explore all financial resources

财政 cáizhèng (名) (public) finance: ～收支平衡 balance of revenue and expenditure. ～赤字 financial deficits. ～年度 financial (or fiscal) year

财主 cáizhu (名) rich man; moneybags

采(採) cǎi (动) 1 pick; pluck; gather: ～花 pick flowers. ～药 cull medicinal herbs 2 mine; extract: ～煤 mine coal

采伐 cǎifá (动) cut down (trees); fell

采访 cǎifǎng (动) (of a reporter) gather material; cover: ～新闻 cover news. ～一位名作家 interview a famous writer

采购(購) cǎigòu (动) purchase: ～员 purchasing agent

采集 cǎijí (动) gather; collect: ～标本 collect specimens

采矿(礦) cǎikuàng (名) mining: 露天～ opencut (or opencast) mining

采煤 cǎiméi (名) coal mining

采纳 cǎinà (动) accept; adopt

采取 cǎiqǔ (动) adopt; take: ～紧急措施 take emergency measures

采撷 cǎixié (动) 〈书〉 1 pick; pluck 2 gather

采样(樣) cǎiyàng (名) sampling

采用 cǎiyòng (动) employ; adopt; use: ～新技术 adopt new techniques

采油 cǎiyóu (名) oil extraction

采摘 cǎizhāi (动) pluck; pick

睬 cǎi (动) pay attention to; take notice of: 别～他. Take no notice of him.

踩 cǎi (动) step on; tread; trample

彩 cǎi (名) 1 colour: 五～缤纷 colourful 2 coloured silk: 张灯结～ decorate with lanterns and coloured ribbons 3 applause; cheer: 喝～ acclaim; cheer 4 variety; splendour: 丰富多～ rich and varied 5 prize: 中～ win a prize (in a lottery, etc.)

彩虹 cǎihóng (名) rainbow

彩礼(禮) cǎilǐ (名) betrothal gifts (from the man's to his fiancée's family)

彩民 cǎimín (名) lottery player

彩排 cǎipái (名) dress rehearsal

彩票 cǎipiào (名) lottery ticket

彩色 cǎisè (名) multicolour; colour: ～电视

colour television. ～胶片 colour film

菜 cài (名) 1 vegetable: 蔬～ vegetable. 咸～ pickles 2 dish; course: 荤～ meat dish. 素～ vegetable dish. 一道～ a course

菜单(單) càidān (名) menu

菜刀 càidāo (名) kitchen knife

菜花 càihuā (名) cauliflower

菜市场(場) càishìchǎng (名) food market

菜肴 càiyáo (名) cooked food (usu. meat dishes)

菜油 càiyóu (名) rape oil

菜园(園) càiyuán (名) vegetable garden; vegetable farm

菜籽 càizǐ (名) 1 vegetable seeds 2 rapeseed

餐 cān I (名) food; meal: 中～ Chinese food. 西～ Western food. 快～ fast food. 一顿美～ a delicious meal. 午～ lunch. 野～ picnic II (动) eat: 聚～ have a Dutch treat

餐车(車) cānchē (名) dining car

餐巾 cānjīn (名) napkin

餐具 cānjù (名) tableware; cutlery

餐厅(廳) cāntīng (名) 1 dining room 2 restaurant

餐饮 cānyǐn (名) food and drink: ～业 catering industry

参(參) cān (动) 1 join; take part in: ～军 join the army; enlist. ～战 enter war 2 refer; consult: ～阅 consult; read for reference

see also cēn; shēn

参观(觀) cānguān (动) visit (place, exhibition, etc.): ～游览 visit places of interest; go sightseeing

参加 cānjiā (动) join; attend; take part in: ～示威游行 join the demonstration. ～会议 attend a meeting. ～会谈 take part in talks

参见(見) cānjiàn (动) 1 see also; cf.: ～第九章. See also Chapter 9. 2 pay one's respects to (a superior, etc.)

参看 cānkàn (动) 1 see also; cf.: ～下面注释 see note below 2 consult; read sth. for reference

参考 cānkǎo (动) consult; refer to: 仅供～ for reference only. ～书 reference book

参谋 cānmóu (名) 1 staff officer: ～长 chief of staff 2 adviser

参议(議)员 cānyìyuán (名) senator

参与(與) cānyù (动) participate in: ～各项活动 take part in various activities

参赞 cānzàn (名) counsellor: 商务～ commercial counsellor. 文化～ cultural counsellor

参照 cānzhào (动) consult; refer to

参酌 cānzhuó (动) consider (a matter) in the light of actual conditions

惭 cán (形) feel ashamed: 大言不～ brag brazenly

惭愧 cánkuì (形) feel ashamed or abashed

蚕(蠶) cán (名) silkworm

蚕茧(繭) cánjiǎn (名) silkworm cocoon

蚕食 cánshí (动) nibble (at another country's territory)

蚕丝(絲) cánsī (名) natural silk; silk

残(殘) cán (形) 1 incomplete; deficient: ～品 sub-standard goods 2 remnant; remaining: ～兵败将 remnants of a routed army. ～冬 the last days of winter 3 maimed; crippled 4 savage: 凶～ cruel

残暴 cánbào (形) brutal; cruel and ferocious

残存 cáncún (形) remnant; remaining; surviving

残废(廢) cánfèi I (形) crippled; maimed II (名) a maimed person; cripple

残羹剩饭 cángēng-shèngfàn remains of a meal; leftovers

残骸 cánhái (名) remains; wreckage: 敌机～ the wreckage of an enemy plane

残害 cánhài (动) cruelly injure or kill

残疾 cánjí (名) deformity: ～人 a disabled (or handicapped) person

残局 cánjú (名) 1 the final phase of a chess game 2 the situation resulting from the failure of an undertaking: 收拾～ clear up the mess

残酷 cánkù (形) cruel; brutal; ruthless

残缺 cánquē (形) incomplete; fragmentary: 这套茶具～不全. This tea set is incomplete.

残忍 cánrěn (形) cruel; ruthless

残杀(殺) cánshā (动) slaughter; massacre: 自相～ mutual slaughter

残余(餘) cányú (名) remnants; survivals: 封建～ survivals of feudalism

残渣余(餘)孽 cánzhā-yúniè dregs of society; old diehards

残障 cánzhàng (名) disability: 导致～的疾病 a disabling disease ～者 a disabled person

惨(慘) cǎn (形) 1 miserable; pitiful; tragic: ～不忍睹 too

horrible to look at. ～遭不幸 die a tragic death **2** cruel; savage: ～无人道 brutal; inhuman **3** to a serious degree; disastrously: 输得很～ suffer a devastating defeat in a match

惨案 cǎn'àn (名) tragic incident; massacre

惨白 cǎnbái (形) pale: 脸色～ look ghostly pale

惨败 cǎnbài (名) crushing defeat

惨淡 cǎndàn (形) gloomy; dismal; bleak: 月光～ dim moonlight. ～经营 take great pains in one's difficult enterprise

惨烈 cǎnliè (形) tragic; traumatic; devastating

惨痛 cǎntòng (形) grievous; bitter; painful: ～的教训 a bitter lesson

惨重 cǎnzhòng (形) heavy; disastrous: 损失～ suffer heavy losses. 伤亡～ suffer heavy casualties

惨状(狀) cǎnzhuàng (名) miserable condition; pitiful sight

灿(燦) càn

灿烂(爛) cànlàn (形) bright; magnificent; splendid: ～的阳光 brilliant sunshine. ～的未来 bright future

璨 càn (名) gem; precious stone

仓(倉) cāng (名) storehouse; warehouse: 粮～ granary

仓促 cāngcù (形) hurriedly; hastily: 时间～ time is pressing. 走得～ leave in a hurry

仓皇 cānghuáng (形) in panic; in a hurry: ～失措 be panic-stricken. ～逃窜 flee in panic

仓库 cāngkù (名) warehouse; storehouse: 清理～ take stock

沧(滄) cāng (形) (of the sea) dark blue

沧海 cānghǎi (名) the blue sea; the sea

沧海一粟 cānghǎi yī sù a drop in the ocean

沧桑 cāngsāng (名) the changes of the world: 饱经～ have experienced many vicissitudes of life

苍(蒼) cāng (形) **1** dark green or blue: ～松 green pines. ～天 the blue sky **2** grey; ashy: ～白 pale

苍翠 cāngcuì (形) dark green; verdant: ～的山峦 green mountains

苍劲(勁) cāngjìng (形) **1** old and strong **2** (of calligraphy or painting) vigorous; bold

苍老 cānglǎo (形) (of look) old; aged

苍凉 cāngliáng (形) desolate; bleak

苍茫 cāngmáng (形) **1** vast; boundless: ～大地 vast land **2** indistinct; hazy: 暮色～ gathering dusk

苍蝇(蠅) cāngying (名) fly: ～拍子 fly-swatter

舱(艙) cāng (名) cabin: 客～ (passenger) cabin. 货～ hold

藏 cáng (动) **1** hide; conceal **2** store; lay by

see also zàng

藏匿 cángnì (动) conceal; hide

藏身 cángshēn (动) hide oneself; lie low: ～之处 shelter

藏书(書) cángshū (名) a collection of books

藏拙 cángzhuō (动) hide one's inadequacy by keeping quiet

糙 cāo (形) rough; coarse: ～米 brown rice; unpolished rice. 粗～ rough; slipshod

操 cāo I (动) **1** hold; grasp **2** act; do; operate: ～之过急 act with undue haste; be overhasty **3** speak (a language or dialect): ～本地口音 speak with a local accent II (名) drill; exercise

操办(辦) cāobàn (动) manage affairs

操场(場) cāochǎng (名) playground; sports ground

操持 cāochí (动) manage: ～家务 manage household affairs

操劳(勞) cāoláo (动) work hard: ～过度 overwork oneself

操练(練) cāoliàn (动) drill; practise

操心 cāoxīn (动) concern; worry about; take pains: 没少～ put one's heart and soul into sth. 操碎了心 lavish enormous pains

操行 cāoxíng (名) (of a student) moral conduct

操纵(縱) cāozòng (动) **1** operate; control 无线电～ radio control **2** manipulate: 幕后～ manipulate from behind the scenes; pull strings. ～市场 rig the market

操作 cāozuò (动) operate (a machine)

槽 cáo (名) **1** trough; manger **2** groove; slot

嘈 cáo (形) noisy

嘈杂(雜) cáozá (形) noisy: 人声～ a hubbub of voices

草 cǎo I (名) grass; straw II (形) careless; rough; hasty III (动) draft: 起～文件 draft a document

草案 cǎo'àn (名) draft (of a plan, law, etc.): 决议～ a draft
草包 cǎobāo (名) 1 straw bag 2 blockhead; good-for-nothing
草草 cǎocǎo (副) hastily; carelessly: ～了事 hurry through the work. ～收场 wind up the affair in great haste
草地 cǎodì (名) grassland; meadow; lawn
草稿 cǎogǎo (名) manuscript; draft
草根 cǎogēn (名) grass-root
草菅人命 cǎojiān rénmìng treat human life as if it were not worth a straw; treat human life like dirt
草料 cǎoliào (名) forage; fodder
草莽 cǎomǎng (名) uncultivated land; wilderness: ～英雄 greenwood hero
草帽 cǎomào (名) straw hat
草莓 cǎoméi (名) strawberry
草木皆兵 cǎo mù jiē bīng be panic-stricken; feel exceedingly nervous
草皮 cǎopí (名) sod; turf
草坪 cǎopíng (名) lawn
草签(簽) cǎoqiān (动) initial: ～协议 initial an agreement
草书(書) cǎoshū (名) rapid, cursive style of writing
草率 cǎoshuài (形) careless; rash: ～从事 take hasty action; act rashly or carelessly
草图(圖) cǎotú (名) sketch; draft
草席 cǎoxí (名) straw mat
草鞋 cǎoxié (名) straw sandals
草药(藥) cǎoyào (名) medicinal herbs; herbal medicine
草原 cǎoyuán (名) steppe; grasslands; prairie

测 cè (动) 1 survey; measure 2 predict: 变化莫～ unpredictable; constantly changing
测定 cèdìng (动) survey and determine
测绘(繪) cèhuì (动) survey and draw
测量 cèliáng (动) survey; measure
测评 cèpíng (动) assess; examine
测验(驗) cèyàn (动、名) test

恻 cè (形) sorrowful: 凄～ sad; grieved: ～隐 compassion; pity

厕 cè (名) lavatory; toilet; W.C.: 公～ public lavatory. 男～ men's (room, toilet). 女～ women's (room, toilet)
厕所 cèsuǒ (名) lavatory; toilet; W.C.

侧 cè I (名) side; flank: 两～ on both sides II (动) lean; incline
侧记 cèjì (名) sidelights
侧面 cèmiàn (名) side; profile: ～像 profile
侧重 cèzhòng (动) lay emphasis on; stress

策 cè (名) plan; scheme; strategy: 献～ present a strategy
策动(動) cèdòng (动) instigate; stir up; engineer: 阴谋～政变 plot a coup d'état
策划(劃) cèhuà (动) 1 plan; plot: ～阴谋 hatch a plot. 幕后～ scheme behind the scenes 2 design: ～一个晚会 design a party. 这个电视节目的总～ the chief designer of the TV programme
策略 cèlüè I (名) tactics II (形) tactful
策源地 cèyuándì (名) source; place of origin: 战争～ a source of war

册 cè I (名) volume: 这套书共四～. This book is in four volumes. II (量) copy: 一千～ 1,000 copies (of a book)

参(參) cēn
see also cān; shēn
参差 cēncī (形) uneven; not uniform

曾 céng (副) once; formerly; sometime ago: 他～教过我英文. He once taught me English.
see also zēng
曾几(幾)何时(時) céng jǐ hé shí 〈书〉 before long; not long after
曾经(經) céngjīng (副) once; formerly: 他们～是好友,现在不是了. They were good friends but are no longer so now.
曾经(經)沧(滄)海 céng jīng cānghǎi have much experience of life; have seen the world

层(層) céng (名) 1 layer; stratum: 一～油漆 a coat of paint 2 storey; floor: 五～大楼 a five-storey building. 二～楼 the first floor (in American English: the second floor)
层层 céngcéng (副) layer upon layer: ～把关 check at each level
层出不穷(窮) céng chū bù qióng emerge in an endless stream; come thick and fast
层次 céngcì (名) 1 arrangement of ideas, colours etc.: 这篇文章～分明. The essay is well organized. 2 administrative or education levels: 这些人～不高. These people are not very well educated.
层峦(巒)叠(疊)嶂 céngluán dié-zhàng peaks rising one upon another
层面 céngmiàn (名) level; dimension

蹭 cèng (动) 1 rub; scrape: 他摔倒时把膝盖～破了. He scraped his knee when he slipped and fell. 2 be smeared with: 小心～油漆 Mind the fresh paint; wet paint **3** dillydally; loiter: 磨～ dawdle; dillydally

差 chā (名) **1** difference; discrepancy; dissimilarity: 时～ time difference **2** mistake: 偏～ deviation
see also chà; chāi

差别 chābié (名) difference; disparity: 年龄～ disparity in age

差错 chācuò (名) **1** mistake; error; slip **2** mishap; accident: 万一这孩子出了～怎么办? What if anything should happen to the child?

差额 chā'é (名) balance; difference; margin: ～选举 multi-candidate election. 补足～ make up the balance (or difference)

差价(價) chājià (名) price difference: 地区～ regional price differences. 季节～ seasonal variations in price

差距 chājù (名) gap; disparity; difference: 他说的跟做的有很大的～. There is a big gap between what he says and what he does.

差强人意 chā qiáng rényì not too disappointing; passable

差异(異) chāyì (名) difference; divergence; discrepancy: 这两个地区气候～很大. These two regions differ greatly in climate.

喳 chā

喳喳 chāchā (象) whispering sound; whisper: 她在他耳边～两句. She whispered a few words in his ear.

插 chā (动) **1** stick in; insert; thrust: ～花瓶 put flowers in a vase **2** interpolate; insert: ～入几句话 put in a few additional words

插翅难(難)飞(飛) chā chì nán fēi can hardly escape even if one grew a pair of wings; be unable to escape even if given wings

插话 chāhuà (动) chip in

插曲 chāqǔ (名) **1** interlude **2** songs in a film or play **3** episode

插入 chārù (动) **1** insert **2** plug in

插手 chāshǒu (动) **1** take part: 这事他们自己能对付,用不着我～. I don't have to join in since they can manage it by themselves. **2** have a hand in; poke one's nose into; meddle in

插图(圖) chātú (名) illustration; plate

插销 chāxiāo (名) **1** bolt (for a door, window, etc.) **2** plug

插秧 chāyāng (动) transplant rice seedlings

插嘴 chāzuǐ (动) interrupt; chip in: 插不上嘴 cannot get a word in edgeways

插座 chāzuò (名) socket

叉 chā I (名) **1** fork: 干草～ hayfork; pitchfork **2** cross: 在每个错字上打个～ put a cross on each wrongly spelt word II (动) work with a fork; fork: ～鱼 spear fish
see also chǎ

杈 chā (名) wooden fork; hayfork; pitchfork
see also chà

茬 chá (名) **1** stubble: 麦～ wheat stubble **2** crop; batch: 二～韭菜 the second crop of Chinese chives

茶 chá (名) **1** tea: 沏～ make tea. 浓(淡)～ strong (weak) tea. 红(绿)～ black (green) tea **2** certain kinds of drink or liquid food: 杏仁～ almond paste

茶杯 chábēi (名) teacup

茶房 cháfáng (名) waiter; steward

茶馆 cháguǎn (名) teahouse

茶壶(壺) cháhú (名) teapot

茶话会(會) cháhuàhuì (名) tea party

茶几 chájī (名) tea table; teapoy

茶具 chájù (名) tea set

茶叶(葉) cháyè (名) tea; tea leaves

茶余(餘)饭后(後) cháyú-fànhòu over a cup of tea or after a meal: 作为～谈笑的题材 as a topic for after-dinner chit-chat

搽 chá (动) put on or rub into the skin; apply: ～雪花膏 put on vanishing cream. ～药 apply ointment, lotion, etc.

查 chá (动) **1** check; examine; inspect: ～谣言 chase down a rumour. ～血 have a blood test **2** look into; investigate; find out **3** look up; consult: ～字典 look up a word in the dictionary. ～档案 look into the archives

查办(辦) chábàn (动) investigate and deal with accordingly: 撤职～ dismiss a person from office and prosecute him

查抄 cháchāo (动) make an inventory of a criminal's possessions and confiscate them

查点(點) chádiǎn (动) check the number or amount of; make an inventory of

查对(對) cháduì (动) check; verify: ~材料 check the data. ~原文 check the version against the original
查访 cháfǎng (动) go around and make inquiries; investigate
查封 cháfēng (动) seal up; close down
查获(獲) cháhuò (动) hunt down and seize; ferret out; track down
查禁 chájìn (动) ban; prohibit
查究 chájiū (动) investigate and ascertain (cause, responsibility, etc.): ~责任 find out who should be held responsible for what has happened
查看 chákàn (动) look over; inspect; examine: ~账目 examine the accounts
查明 chámíng (动) prove through investigation; find out; ascertain: 事实真相已经~. The truth of the matter has been established through investigation.
查票 chápiào (动) check tickets
查询 cháxún (动) inquire about: ~地址 inquire sb.'s address
查夜 cháyè (动) be on night patrol
查阅 cháyuè (动) consult; look up: ~技术资料 consult technical data; look up technical literature
查账(賬) cházhàng (动) check (or audit, examine) accounts
查证 cházhèng (动) investigate and verify; check: ~属实 have been verified

楂 chá (名) short, bristly hair or beard; stubble

碴 chá (动) be cut (by broken glass, china, etc.)

碴儿(兒) chár (名) 1 broken pieces; fragments: 冰~ small pieces of ice. 玻璃~ fragments of glass 2 the cause of a quarrel; quarrel: 找~打架 pick a quarrel (with sb.)

察 chá (动) examine; look into; scrutinize; observe: ~其言, 观其行 examine his words and watch his deeds; check what he says against what he does

察觉(覺) chájué (动) become aware of; discover; perceive
察看 chákàn (动) inspect; look carefully at; observe: ~地形 survey the terrain
察言观(觀)色 cháyán-guānsè try to read sb.'s thoughts from his words and facial expression; weigh up sb.'s words and watch the expression on his face

叉 chǎ (动) part in the shape of a fork: ~腿站着 stand with one's legs apart
see also chā

诧 chà (动) be surprised

诧异(異) chàyì (动) be surprised; be astonished

姹 chà (形)〈书〉beautiful

姹紫嫣红 chàzǐ-yānhóng deep purples and bright reds; a riot of brilliant purple and tender crimson

差 chà I 1 (动) differ from; fall short of: ~得远 a far cry 2 be short of: ~5分两点 five (minutes) to two. ~两个人 two people short. 我还~你多少钱? How much more do I owe you? II (形) 1〈口〉wrong: 这你可说~了. You're wrong there. 2 not up to standard; poor: 质量不算太~. The quality is not too bad.
see also chā; chāi

差不多 chàbùduō (形) 1 almost; nearly: 他走了~两年了. It's nearly two years since he left. 2 about the same; similar: 她俩~大. They are about the same age. 3 just about right (or enough); not far off; not bad 4 almost used up: 鸡蛋吃得~了. There aren't many eggs left.
差点(點)儿(兒) chàdiǎnr I (形) not good enough; not quite up to the mark II (副) almost; nearly; on the verge of: 她~摔倒. She very nearly fell.
差劲(勁) chàjìn (形) no good; disappointing: 这活干得太~. This work was too poorly done.

刹 chà (名) Buddhist temple
see also shā

刹那 chànà (名) instant: 一~ in an instant; in a flash; in the twinkling of an eye

岔 chà I (名) branch; fork: 三~路口 a fork in the road; a junction of three roads II (动) turn off

岔开(開) chàkāi (动) 1 branch off: 公路在这儿~了. The highway branches here. 2 diverge to (another topic); change (the subject of conversation) 3 stagger: 把我们的休假日~ stagger our days off
岔子 chàzi (名) accident; trouble: 机器出了什么~? What's wrong with the

machine?

杈 chà (名) branch (of a tree)
see also chā

衩 chà (名) vent (or slit) in the sides of a garment

C

差 chāi I (动) send on an errand; dispatch: ～人去送封信 send a letter by messenger. 出～ be away on business trip II (名) errand; job: 兼～ hold more than one job concurrently; moonlight
see also chā; chà

差旅费 chāilǚfèi (名) travel allowances (for a business trip)

差遣 chāiqiǎn (动) send sb. on an errand or mission; dispatch; assign: 你可～别人去干. You can assign somebody else to do the job.

差使 chāishi (名) official post; billet; commission

差事 chāishi (名) errand; assignment

差役 chāiyì (名) 1 corvée 2 runner or bailiff in a feudal *yamen*

拆 chāi (动) 1 take apart; tear open: ～信 open a letter. ～机器 disassemble a machine; take a machine apart 2 pull down; demolish: ～房子 pull down a house

拆除 chāichú (动) demolish; dismantle; remove: ～军事基地 dismantle military bases

拆穿 chāichuān (动) expose; reveal; unmask: ～骗局 expose a fraud

拆毁 chāihuǐ (动) demolish; destroy

拆伙 chāihuǒ (动) dissolve a partnership; part company

拆借 chāijiè (名) short-term loan

拆开(開) chāikāi (动) take apart; open; separate

拆散 chāisǎn (动) break (a set)

拆散 chāisàn (动) break up (a marriage, family, etc.)

拆台(臺) chāitái (动) let sb. down; cut the ground from under sb.'s feet; pull away a prop

拆线(綫) chāixiàn (动) take out stitches

拆卸 chāixiè (动) dismantle; disassemble; dismount

钗 chāi (名) hairpin (formerly worn by women for adornment)

柴 chái (名) firewood

柴草 cháicǎo (名) firewood; faggot

柴米油盐(鹽) chái-mǐ-yóu-yán fuel, rice, oil and salt — basic daily necessities

柴油 cháiyóu (名) diesel oil: ～机车 diesel locomotive. ～机 diesel engine

豺 chái (名) jackal

豺狼 cháiláng (名) jackals and wolves — cruel and evil people

搀(攙) chān (动) 1 support or help sb. ～着病人进屋 help the patient by the arm into the room 2 mix; blend: 往沙子里～石灰 mix lime into sand

搀扶 chānfú (动) support sb. with one's hand

搀和 chānhuo (动) mix

搀假 chānjiǎ (动) adulterate

搀杂(雜) chānzá (动) mix; mingle

缠(纏) chán (动) 1 twine; wind: ～线球 wind yarn into a ball 2 tangle; tie up; pester: ～住不放 stick to one like a burr. 我女儿～住我给她讲故事. My daughter has been pestering me to tell her a story.

缠绵 chánmián (形) 1 (of illness or feelings) lingering 2 touching; moving

缠绕(繞) chánrào (动) 1 twine; bind; wind 2 worry; harass

禅(禪) chán (名) 1 deep meditation; dhyana: 坐～ sit in meditation 2 Buddhist: ～堂 meditation room
see also shàn

婵(嬋) chán

婵娟 chánjuān 〈书〉 I (形) lovely [used in ancient writings to describe women] II (名) the moon

蝉(蟬) chán (名) cicada

蝉联(聯) chánlián (动) continue to hold a post or title

蟾 chán

蟾蜍 chánchú (名)〈书〉 1 toad 2 the moon

谗(讒) chán (动) slander; backbite

谗言 chányán (名) slanderous report; calumny; false charge

馋(饞) chán (形) greedy; gluttonous: 嘴～ fond of good food; greedy

馋涎欲滴 chánxián yù dī start drooling

馋嘴 chánzuǐ (形) gluttonous

孱 chán (形) frail; weak

孱弱 chánruò (形) frail; delicate (in health)

潺 chán

潺潺 chánchán (象) murmur; babble; purl: ～流水 a murmuring stream

产(産) chǎn I (动) 1 give birth to: ～卵 lay eggs 2 produce; yield: ～棉区 cotton-producing area II (名) 1 product; produce: 土特～ local speciality 2 property; estate: 房地～ real estate. 家～ family possessions

产地 chǎndì (名) place of production

产妇(婦) chǎnfù (名) lying-in woman

产科 chǎnkē (名) 1 obstetrical (or maternity) department 2 obstetrics: ～医生 obstetrician

产量 chǎnliàng (名) output; yield: 煤～ output of coal

产卵 chǎnluǎn (动) (of birds) lay eggs; (of fish) spawn

产品 chǎnpǐn (名) product; produce: 农～ farm produce. 畜～ livestock product

产权(權) chǎnquán (名) property right: ～归属 property ownership. ～转移 transfer of property right

产生 chǎnshēng (动) 1 produce; engender; bring about; give rise to: ～好的结果 yield good results. ～坏的影响 exert a bad influence 2 emerge; come into being: 问题～了. Problems have emerged.

产物 chǎnwù (名) outcome; result

产销 chǎn-xiāo (名) production and marketing

产业(業) chǎnyè (名) 1 estate; property 2 industrial: ～革命 the Industrial Revolution

产值 chǎnzhí (名) output value

铲(鏟) chǎn I (名) shovel: 锅～ slice II (动) shovel: ～煤 shovel coal. 把地～平 scrape the ground even; level the ground with a shovel or spade

铲除 chǎnchú (动) root out; eradicate

铲子 chǎnzi (名) shovel

阐(闡) chǎn (动) explain; interpret

阐明 chǎnmíng (动) expound; clarify: ～观点 clarify one's views

阐释(釋) chǎnshì (动) explain; expound; interpret

阐述 chǎnshù (动) expound; elaborate; set forth: 各方～了自己对这一问题的立场. Each side set forth its position on this question.

谄 chǎn (动) flatter; fawn on; toady

谄媚 chǎnmèi (动) flatter; fawn on; toady

谄谀 chǎnyú (动) flatter

颤 chàn (动) quiver; tremble; vibrate: 他激动得说话声音都发～了. His voice quivered with emotion.
see also zhàn

颤动(動) chàndòng (动) vibrate; quiver: 树叶在微风中～. The leaves quivered in the breeze.

颤抖 chàndǒu (动) shake; tremble; quiver; shiver: 冻得全身～ shiver all over with cold

颤音 chànyīn (名) trill; shake

忏(懺) chàn (动) repent

忏悔 chànhuǐ (动) 1 repent 2 confess (one's sins)

昌 chāng (形) prosperous; flourishing

昌盛 chāngshèng (形) prosperous: 把中国建设成为一个繁荣～的社会主义国家 Build China into a prosperous socialist country.

猖 chāng

猖獗 chāngjué (形) rampant; unbridled; run wild

猖狂 chāngkuáng (形) outrageous; furious: ～反扑 counterattack with unbridled fury

娼 chāng (名) prostitute

娼妇(婦) chāngfù (名) bitch; whore

娼妓 chāngjì (名) prostitute; streetwalker

尝(嘗) cháng I (动) taste; experience: 艰苦备～ endure all hardships II (副) ever: 未～晤面 have never met before

尝试 chángshì (动) attempt; try

尝新 chángxīn (动) have a taste of what is just in season

偿(償) cháng (动) repay; compensate: 补～损失 compensate for the loss

偿还(還) chánghuán (动) pay back: ～债务 pay one's debts

偿命 chángmìng (动) pay with one's life (for a murder)

偿清 chángqīng (动) clear off: ~债务 clear off all one's debts

裳 cháng (名) skirt (worn in ancient China)

常 cháng I (形) 1 ordinary; common; normal: 人情之~ normal in human relationships. 反~ unusual; abnormal. 习以为~ be used (or accustomed) to sth. 2 invariable: 四季~青 evergreen II (副) frequently; often: 这里你~来吗? Do you often come here?

常常 chángcháng (副) frequently; often; usually; generally: ~得到老师表扬 be often praised by the teacher

常规 chángguī (名) convention; routine; common practice: ~武器 conventional weapons

常会(會) chánghuì (名) regular meeting (or session)

常见(見) chángjiàn (形) common: 不~ unusual. ~病 common disease

常客 chángkè (名) frequent guest or visitor

常年 chángnián (名) 1 all the year round; for a very long period of time 2 year in year out

常青 chángqīng (形) evergreen

常情 chángqíng (名) common sense; normal practice: 人之~ natural human feelings. 按照~,他会准时回来的. Under normal circumstances he would be back in time.

常任 chángrèn (形) permanent; standing: 安理会~理事国 permanent member of the Security Council

常设 chángshè (形) standing; permanent: ~机构 standing body; permanent organization

常识(識) chángshí (名) 1 general knowledge 2 common sense

常态(態) chángtài (名) normality; normal state of affairs: 恢复~ come back to normal

常务(務) chángwù (形) day-to-day business; routine: ~委员会 standing committee

常言 chángyán (名) saying; aphorism

常驻 chángzhù (形) resident; permanent: ~记者 resident correspondent. ~联合国代表 permanent representative to the United Nations

嫦 cháng

嫦娥 cháng'é (名) the goddess of the moon

长(長) cháng I (形) long: ~袍 long gown; robe. ~跑 long-distance running. ~篇大论 make a lengthy speech; write a lengthy article II (名) 1 length: 全~ the overall length 2 strong point; forte: 取~补短 overcome one's shortcomings by learning from others' strong points see also zhǎng

长城 Chángchéng (名) the Great Wall

长处(處) chángchù (名) good qualities; strong points

长度 chángdù (名) length

长短 chángduǎn (名) 1 length: 这两条裙子~差不多. The two skirts are about the same length. 这件上衣~对他不合适. The jacket doesn't fit him. 2 merits and demerits; strong and weak points: 议论别人~ gossip about sb. 3 accident; mishap

长方形 chángfāngxíng (名) rectangle

长工 chánggōng (名) hired farmhand

长江 Chángjiāng (名) the Changjiang (Yangtze) River

长颈(頸)鹿 chángjǐnglù (名) giraffe

长久 chángjiǔ (形) lasting; permanent: ~之计 long-term planning; lasting solution

长空 chángkōng (名) vast sky

长裤 chángkù (名) trousers; pants; slacks

长眠 chángmián (动) 〈婉〉 demise; death

长年 chángnián (名) all the year round

长期 chángqī (形) over a long period of time; long-term: ~共存,互相监督 long-term co-existence and mutual supervision

长衫 chángshān (名) gown; long gown

长寿(壽) chángshòu (名) long life; longevity: 祝您健康~. I wish you good health and a long life.

长叹(嘆) chángtàn (动) heave a deep sigh

长途 chángtú (名) long-distance: ~旅行 make a long journey. ~电话 long-distance (or trunk) call. ~汽车 long-distance bus; coach

长线(綫) chángxiàn (名) 1 long-term; long-range 2 over-supply; over-production

长项 chángxiàng (名) strong point; sth. one is good at

长远(遠) chángyuǎn (形) long-term; long-range: ~利益 long-term interests. ~规

划 long-term (or long-range) plan

长征 chángzhēng (名) 1 expedition; long march 2 the Long March

长治久安 chángzhì jiǔ'ān lasting political stability

长足 chángzú (形) rapid; speedy: ～的进步 rapid progress

场(場) cháng I (名) 1 level open ground (usually used for threshing grains) 2 fair; market place II (量) [said of something which has happened]: 一～大雨 a heavy fall of rain

see also chǎng

肠(腸) cháng (名) intestines

肠断(斷) chángduàn (形) broken-hearted

场(場) chǎng I (名) 1 site; spot: 会～ conference hall. 战～ battlefield. 篮球～ basketball court 2 farm: 农～ farm. 养鸡～ chicken farm 3 stage: 登～ come on the stage; appear on the scene 4 (of drama) scene: 第二幕第一～ Act II, Scene 1 5 field: 电(磁)～ electric (magnetic) field II (量) [for sports and recreation]: 一～电影 a film show. 一～球赛 a ball game

see also cháng

场地 chǎngdì (名) place; site

场合 chǎnghé (名) occasion: 在某种～ on certain occasions

场面 chǎngmiàn (名) 1 scene (in drama, fiction, etc.); event; occasion 2 appearance; front; façade

场所 chǎngsuǒ (名) place (for certain activities): 公共～ a public place

厂(廠) chǎng (名) factory; mill; plant; works: 汽车～ car factory. 机床～ machine tool plant. 钢铁～ iron and steel works. 造船～ shipyard. 炼油～ oil refinery

厂房 chǎngfáng (名) 1 factory building 2 workshop

厂家 chǎngjiā (名) factory; manufacturer

厂矿(礦) chǎng-kuàng (名) factories and mines

厂商 chǎngshāng (名) firm: 承包～ contractor

厂长(長) chǎngzhǎng (名) director of a factory

敞 chǎng I (动) open; uncover: ～着门 leave the door open II (形) spacious: 宽～ spacious; roomy

敞开(開) chǎngkāi (动) open wide: 大门～着. The gate was wide open. ～供应 unlimited supply. ～思想 speak one's mind

氅 chǎng (名) cloak: 大～ overcoat

唱 chàng (动) 1 sing: ～歌 sing a song 2 call; cry: 鸡～三遍. The cock has crowed for the third time.

唱段 chàngduàn (名) aria: 京剧～ an aria from a Beijing opera

唱高调 chàng gāodiào use high-sounding words

唱机(機) chàngjī (名) gramophone; record player

唱片 chàngpiàn (名) record; disc: 放～ play a gramophone record. 灌～ cut a disc

唱腔 chàngqiāng (名) music for voices in a Chinese opera

唱戏(戲) chàngxì (动)〈口〉act in an opera

倡 chàng (动) initiate; advocate

倡导(導) chàngdǎo (动) initiate; propose

倡议(議) chàngyì (动) recommend; propose: ～书 written proposal; proposal

怅(悵) chàng (形) disappointed; sorry: 走访不遇为～. Sorry not to have found you at home.

怅然 chàngrán (形) disappointed; upset: ～而返 come away disappointed

怅惘 chàngwǎng (形) depressed; dispirited

畅(暢) chàng (形) 1 smooth; unimpeded: ～通无阻 proceed without hindrance. 流～ fluent 2 free; uninhibited: ～饮 drink one's fill. ～谈 talk animatedly

畅快 chàngkuài (形) happy; carefree

畅所欲言 chàng suǒ yù yán speak one's mind freely

畅通 chàngtōng (形) unblocked; unimpeded

畅想 chàngxiǎng (动) give full play to one's imagination

畅销 chàngxiāo (动) sell well; sell like hot cakes: 中国丝绸～国外. Chinese silk fabrics sell well on foreign markets. ～书 best-seller

畅叙 chàngxù (动) chat cheerfully: ～旧日友情 relive an old friendship

畅游 chàngyóu (动) enjoy a good swim or a sightseeing trip

抄 chāo (动) 1 copy; transcribe: ～稿件 make a fair copy of the

manuscript 2 plagiarize 3 search and confiscate 4 go by a more direct way: ～近路 take a shortcut 5 fold (one's arms): ～着手站在一边 stand by with folded arms

抄本 chāoběn (名) hand-copied book; transcript

抄获(獲) chāohuò (动) search and seize; ferret out

抄件 chāojiàn (名) duplicate; copy; carbon copy or copies [usually in abbreviated form c. c.]

抄袭(襲) chāoxí (动) 1 plagiarize 2 follow other people's example regardless objective condition 3 attack the enemy by making a detour

抄写(寫) chāoxiě (动) make a clear copy; transcribe

钞 chāo (名) bank note; paper money: 现～ cash

钞票 chāopiào (名) bank note

超 chāo I (动) exceed; surpass; overtake II [used as prefix]: ultra-; super-; extra-: ～自然的 supernatural

超产(産) chāochǎn (动) overfulfil a production target

超车(車) chāochē (动) overtake other vehicles (in violation of traffic regulations)

超出 chāochū (动) overstep; go beyond; exceed: ～范围 go beyond the scope (or bounds)

超导(導) chāodǎo (名) superconduction

超短波 chāoduǎnbō (名) ultrashort wave

超短裙 chāoduǎnqún (名) miniskirt

超额 chāo'é (动) overfulfil the quota: ～利润 superprofit

超过(過) chāoguò (动) outstrip; surpass; exceed

超级 chāojí (形) super: ～大国 superpower. ～市场 supermarket

超假 chāojià (动) overstay one's leave

超龄 chāolíng over-age

超群 chāoqún (形) outstanding; superb

超然 chāorán (形) aloof; neutral

超生 chāoshēng (动) exceed the birth control quota

超声(聲)波 chāoshēngbō (名) supersonic (wave)

超市 chāoshì (名) supermarket

超速 chāosù I (动) exceed the speed limit II (名) hyper-velocity

超脱 chāotuō I (形) unbiased; unconventional II (动) stand aloof: 要～一些 be detached from sth. ～现实 dissociate oneself from one's social environment

超音速 chāoyīnsù (名) supersonic speed

超越 chāoyuè (动) surmount; transcend; surpass: ～职权范围 overstep one's authority

超载 chāozài (动) overload

超支 chāozhī (动) overspend

超重 chāozhòng (动) overweight: ～行李 excess luggage

朝 cháo I (名) 1 dynasty: 唐～ the Tang Dynasty. 改～换代 dynastic changes 2 court: ～臣 court official II (介) facing; towards: 这门～外开. This door opens outwards. 这是～南的房子. This house has a southern exposure. see also zhāo

朝拜 cháobài (动) pay respects to (a sovereign); pay religious homage to; worship

朝代 cháodài (名) dynasty

朝贡 cháogòng (动) pay tribute (to an imperial court)

朝圣(聖) cháoshèng (名) pilgrimage; hadj

朝廷 cháotíng (名) royal (or imperial) court

潮 cháo I (名) 1 tide: 涨(落)～了. The tide is in (on the ebb). 2 upsurge: 学～ student movement II (形) damp; moist: 受～ get damp

潮流 cháoliú (名) 1 tide 2 trend: 历史～ historical trend. 赶～ follow the trend

潮湿(濕) cháoshī (形) moist; damp

潮水 cháoshuǐ (名) tidewater

潮汐 cháoxī (名) morning and evening tides; tide

嘲 cháo (动) ridicule; mock: 冷～热讽 sarcastic remarks

嘲讽 cháofěng (动) sneer at; taunt

嘲弄 cháonòng (动) mock; poke fun at

嘲笑 cháoxiào (动) laugh at; ridicule

巢 cháo (名) nest: 鸟～ bird's nest. 匪～ nest (or den) of robbers; bandits' lair

巢穴 cháoxué (名) lair; den; nest; hideout

炒 chǎo (动) 1 stir-fry; fry: 蛋～饭 fried rice with eggs. ～鸡蛋 scrambled eggs 2 heat sth. up; sensationalize: 经过媒介～作 be heated up by the media

炒股 chǎogǔ (动) buy and sell stocks; speculate in stocks

炒鱿鱼(魚) chǎoyóuyú sack; fire: 被～ get the sack. 炒了老板的鱿鱼 resign

炒作 chǎozuò (动) sensationalize; spin: 媒体～ media spin

吵 chǎo (动) 1 make a noise 2 disturb 3 quarrel; wrangle; squabble: 为一些小事～嘴 bickering over small matters

吵架 chǎojià (动) quarrel; have a row

吵闹 chǎonào (动) 1 wrangle; kick up a row 2 make a lot of noise

吵嘴 chǎozuǐ (动) quarrel; bicker

车(車) chē I (名) 1 vehicle: ～水马龙 heavy traffic 2 wheeled machine or instrument: 纺～ spinning wheel. 水～ waterwheel 3 machine II (动) 1 lathe; turn 2 lift water by waterwheel
see also jū

车床(牀) chēchuáng (名) lathe

车次 chēcì (名) train number

车费 chēfèi (名) fare

车工 chēgōng (名) turner; lathe operator

车轱辘 chēgūlu (名)〈口〉wheel (of a vehicle)

车行 chēháng (名) car dealer

车祸(禍) chēhuò (名) traffic (or road) accident

车间 chējiān (名) workshop; shop

车库 chēkù (名) garage

车辆(輛) chēliàng (名) vehicle; car

车轮(輪) chēlún (名) wheel (of a vehicle)

车皮 chēpí (名) railway carriage or wagon

车票 chēpiào (名) train or bus ticket; ticket

车速 chēsù (名) speed of a motor vehicle

车胎 chētāi (名) tyre

车厢 chēxiāng (名) railway carriage; railroad car

车站 chēzhàn (名) station; stop

扯 chě (动) 1 pull: ～后腿 hold sb. back (from action); be a drag on sb. 2 tear: 把信～得粉碎 tear a letter to pieces 3 chat; gossip: ～家常 chat about everyday domestic details. 别～远了. Don't wander from the subject.

扯淡 chědàn (动) talk nonsense

扯谎 chěhuǎng (动) tell a lie; lie

扯皮 chěpí (动) dispute over trifles; wrangle

澈 chè (形) (of water) clear; limpid: 清～ crystal clear

撤 chè (动) 1 remove; take away: 把盘子、碗～了 clear away the dishes 2 withdraw: ～退 retreat. ～回 withdraw

撤兵 chèbīng (动) withdraw or pull back troops

撤除 chèchú (动) dismantle: ～军事设施 dismantle military installations

撤换 chèhuàn (动) dismiss and replace

撤回 chèhuí (动) recall; withdraw: ～大使 recall an ambassador. ～声明 retract a statement

撤离(離) chèlí (动) withdraw from; evacuate; leave

撤退 chètuì (动) withdraw; pull out; retreat

撤销 chèxiāo (动) cancel; revoke: ～其职务 dismiss a person from his post. ～处分 rescind a penalty

撤职(職) chèzhí (动) dismiss or discharge sb. from his post; remove sb. from office

彻(徹) chè (形) thorough; penetrating: 透～的了解 perfect understanding

彻底 chèdǐ (形) thorough; thoroughgoing

彻骨 chègǔ (形) to the bone: 寒风～. The bitter wind chills one to the bone.

彻头(頭)彻尾 chètóu-chèwěi out and out: 那是～的谎言. That's a lie, pure and simple.

彻夜 chèyè (名) all through the night: ～不眠 lie awake all night

掣 chè (动) 1 pull; tug 2 draw

嗔 chēn(动) be angry; be displeased; be annoyed

嗔怪 chēnguài (动) blame; disapprove of

嗔怒 chēnnù (动) get angry; be angered

瞋 chēn (动)〈书〉stare angrily; glare: ～目而视 stare at sb. angrily

沉 chén I (动) 1 sink: 星～月落. The stars have become indistinct and the moon is down. 2 be calm; concentrate 3 lower: 把脸一～ pull a long face II (形) 1 deep; profound: 睡得很～ be sound asleep. ～醉 dead drunk; be intoxicated 2 heavy

沉沉 chénchén (形) deep: 暮气～ lifeless; apathetic

沉甸甸 chéndiāndiān (形) heavy

沉淀(澱) chéndiàn (动、名) sediment; precipitate: 溶液里有～. There is some sediment in the solution.

沉积(積) chénjī (动) deposit; precipitate

沉寂 chénjì (形) 1 quiet; still: 四面一片～. All is still. 2 (of news) entirely blocked: 消息～. There is absolutely no news.

沉浸 chénjìn (动) immerse; steep: ～在幸福的回忆中 be immersed in happy memories

沉静 chénjìng (形) 1 quiet; calm: ～下来 grow quiet and still 2 (of one's character, mood or appearance) calm; peaceful; placid

沉闷 chénmèn (形) 1 (of weather, atmosphere, etc.) oppressive 2 depressed; in low spirits: 心情～ feel depressed 3 (of one's character) dull

沉湎 chénmiǎn (动)〈书〉 wallow in; abandon oneself to

沉没 chénmò (动) sink

沉默 chénmò (形) 1 reticent; uncommunicative: ～寡言的人 a person of few words 2 silent: 保持～ keep silent

沉溺 chénnì (动) indulge in: ～于享乐 indulge in pleasure

沉睡 chénshuì (动) be fast asleep

沉思 chénsī (动) be lost in thought; ponder; contemplate

沉痛 chéntòng (形) 1 deeply grieved: ～的哀悼 profound condolences 2 bitter: ～的教训 bitter lesson

沉稳 chénwěn (形) steady; sedate; staid

沉吟 chényín (动) hesitate and mutter to oneself; be unable to make up one's mind and think aloud

沉冤 chényuān (名) gross injustice; unrighted wrong: ～莫白 suffered grievous wrongs

沉重 chénzhòng (形) heavy: ～的打击 a heavy blow. 心情～ with a heavy heart

沉住气(氣) chénzhùqì keep calm; keep one's head; be steady

沉着 chénzhuó (形) cool-headed; composed; calm; steady: 勇敢～ brave and steady

沉醉 chénzuì (动) become intoxicated

忱 chén (名)〈书〉 sincere feeling: 热～ zeal; warmheartedness

辰 chén (名) 1 celestial bodies: 星～ stars 2 time; day; occasion: 诞～ birthday

辰时(時) chénshí (名) the period of the day from 7 a.m. to 9 a.m.

晨 chén (名) morning: 清～ dawn; early morning. ～光熹微 first faint rays of the morning sun

晨星 chénxīng (名) stars at dawn: 寥若～ as few as stars in the morning sky

臣 chén (名) official under a feudal ruler; subject; minister

臣服 chénfú (动) submit oneself to the rule of; acknowledge allegiance to

臣民 chénmín (名) subjects (of a feudal ruler)

尘(塵) chén (名) 1 dust; dirt: 一～不染 spotless 2 this human world

尘埃 chén'āi (名) dust: 放射性～ radioactive dust

尘土 chéntǔ (名) dust

尘嚣 chénxiāo (名) hubbub; uproar

陈(陳) chén I (动) 1 put on display 2 state; explain II (形) old; stale: ～酒 aged wine. ～醋 mature vinegar

陈兵 chénbīng (动) mass (station) troops: ～百万 deploy a million troops

陈词滥(濫)调 chéncí-làndiào hackneyed phrase; platitude; cliché: 满口～ mouth the bromide

陈腐 chénfǔ (形) stale; antiquated: ～观念 outworn concept

陈规 chénguī (名) outmoded conventions: 打破～ abolish outmoded conventions

陈货 chénhuò (名) old stock; shopworn goods

陈迹 chénjì (名) a thing of the past; relic

陈旧(舊) chénjiù (形) out-of-date; outmoded; obsolete; old-fashioned

陈列 chénliè (动) display; exhibit: ～馆 exhibition hall. ～品 exhibit

陈设 chénshè (名) furnishings: 房间里的～朴素大方. The room was furnished simply and in good taste.

陈述 chénshù (动) state: ～自己的意见 state one's views; make one's suggestions. ～句 declarative sentence

衬(襯) chèn I (动) 1 line; place sth. underneath: ～上一层纸 put a piece of paper underneath 2 serve as a contrast: 绿叶～红花 red flowers set off by the green leaves II (名) lining; liner: 丝～里 silk-lining

衬裤 chènkù (名) underpants

衬里(裏) chènlǐ (名) lining

衬裙 chènqún (名) underskirt; slip

衬衫 chènshān (名) shirt

衬托 chèntuō (动) set off; serve as a foil to

衬衣 chènyī (名) underclothes; shirt

趁 chèn (介) 1 take advantage of; avail oneself of: ～这个机会讲几句话

take this opportunity to say a few words. ～火打劫 loot a burning house; fish in troubled waters **2** while: ～热打铁 strike while the iron's hot

趁机(機) chènjī (副) take advantage of the occasion; seize the chance

趁早 chènzǎo (副) as early as possible; before it is too late

称(稱) chèn (动) fit; match; suit: 领带跟上衣很相～. The tie matches the jacket.
see also chēng

称心 chènxīn (动) to one's liking; just as one wishes: 这事办得大家都～如意. This matter was settled to the satisfaction of all parties.

称职(職) chènzhí (动) be competent; fill a post with credit

撑 chēng (动) **1** support; prop up: ～起帐篷 put up a tent **2** maintain; keep up: 累了就休息一下,别硬～着. Take a rest when you are tired. Don't stick it out. **3** punt with a pole: ～船 pole a boat **4** open: ～伞 unfold an umbrella **5** overfill: 我吃得～着了. I'm too full.

撑腰 chēngyāo (动) support; back up

瞠 chēng (动)〈书〉stare: ～目结舌 wild-eyed and tongue-tied; dumbfounded

称(稱) chēng I (动) **1** call: 我们都～他王大叔. We all call him uncle Wang. **2** weigh; scale **3** acclaim; praise II (名) name: 四川有天府之国之～. Sichuan is known as the heavenly land of plenty. 俗～ popular name
see also chèn

称霸 chēngbà (动) seek hegemony; dominate

称道 chēngdào (动) speak approvingly of

称得起 chēngdeqǐ be worthy of the name of: 万里长城真～为天下奇观. The Great Wall really deserves to be called a world wonder.

称号(號) chēnghào (名) title; designation

称呼 chēnghu I (动) call; address: 我该怎么～她? How should I address her? II (名) form of address

称快 chēngkuài (动) express one's gratification: 拍手～ clap one's hands to show one's desire is gratified

称颂 chēngsòng (动) praise; extol; eulogize

称王称霸 chēngwáng-chēngbà lord it over; ride roughshod over; domineer

称羡 chēngxiàn (动) express one's admiration; envy

称雄 chēngxióng (动) rule over a region like a sovereign

称赞(讚) chēngzàn (动) praise; acclaim; commend

成 chéng I (动) **1** become; turn into: 积水～河. Water accumulated turns into a river. **2** accomplish; succeed: 事情没有搞～. The task remains unfulfilled. **3** reach to a considerable numbers or amounts: ～千上万的人 tens of thousands of people. ～倍 (increase) by several times. ～群 in groups; in large numbers. ～批 in batches; one group after another **4** all right; OK: ～! 就这么办吧. OK. Go ahead. 你不去可不～. No, you must go. II (名) achievement; result: 坐享其～ sit idle and enjoy the fruits of others' labour III (形) **1** fully developed; fully grown: ～人 adult **2** established; ready-made: ～衣 ready-made clothes. 既～事实 established fact; fait accompli IV (量) one tenth: 增产两～ a 20% increase in output. 这件衣服有九～新. This jacket is 90 percent new.

成败 chéng-bài (名) success or failure: ～在此一举. Success or failure hinges on this final move.

成本 chéngběn (名) cost: 生产～ production cost. ～核算 cost accounting

成材 chéngcái (动) **1** grow into useful timber **2** become a useful person

成分 chéngfèn (名) **1** composition; component part; ingredient: 化学～ chemical composition **2** one's class status or family background

成风(風) chéngfēng (动) become a common practice; prevail: 蔚然～ become the order of the day

成功 chénggōng I (动) succeed II (形) successful

成规 chéngguī (名) established practice; set rules; conventions: 墨守～ stick to conventions

成果 chéngguǒ (名) positive result; accomplishment

成绩 chéngjì (名) achievement; success: 学习～ school record

成家 chéngjiā (动) **1** (of a man) get married: ～立业 get married and start one's career **2** become expert

成见(見) chéngjiàn (名) preconceived idea;

C

prejudice

成交 chéngjiāo (动) strike a bargain; conclude a transaction; clinch a deal: ～额 volume of business

成就 chéngjiù (名) achievement; accomplishment; attainment; success

成立 chénglì (动) 1 set up; found; establish: 中华人民共和国～ the founding of the People's Republic of China 2 be tenable; hold water: 这个论点不能～. That argument is untenable.

成名 chéngmíng (动) become famous: ～成家 establish one's reputation as an authority

成年 chéngnián I (动) grow up; come of age II (副) year after year

成品 chéngpǐn (名) end (or finished) product

成气(氣)候 chéng qìhou make good: 成不了气候 will not get anywhere

成器 chéngqì (动) grow up to be a useful person

成亲(親) chéngqīn (动) get married

成全 chéngquán (动) help sb. to achieve his aim

成色 chéngsè (名) 1 the percentage of gold or silver in a coin, etc. 2 quality

成熟 chéngshú (动、形) ripe; mature: 庄稼～了. The crops are ripe. 他思想还不～. He is still immature.

成套 chéngtào (名) whole (or complete) set: ～设备 complete sets of equipment

成为(爲) chéngwéi (动) become; turn into: ～海军基地 become a naval base

成问题 chéng wèntí be a problem; be open to doubt

成效 chéngxiào (名) effect; result: 显著的～ marked success

成心 chéngxīn (副) on purpose; intentionally; deliberately: 他这是～气我. It was his intention to make me angry.

成性 chéngxìng by nature

成药(藥) chéngyào (名) patent medicine

成衣 chéngyī (名) ready-made clothes

成语 chéngyǔ (名) idiom; proverb; set phrase

成员 chéngyuán (名) member: ～国 member state

成灾(災) chéngzāi (动) cause disaster: 暴雨～. The heavy rainstorm caused serious damage.

成长(長) chéngzhǎng (动) grow up

诚 chéng I (形) sincere; honest II (副)〈书〉really; indeed

诚恳(懇) chéngkěn (形) sincere: ～听取意见 listen to criticisms with an open mind

诚实(實) chéngshí (形) honest

诚心诚意 chéngxīn chéngyì sincerity; good faith

诚信 chéngxìn (形) honesty and trust; faith: ～危机 crisis of trust and good faith

诚挚(摯) chéngzhì (形) sincere; cordial: ～友好的气氛 a sincere and friendly atmosphere

城 chéng (名) 1 city 2 city wall; wall: 长～ the Great Wall 3 town: ～乡差别 the difference between town and country

城堡 chéngbǎo (名) castle

城池 chéngchí (名) city wall and moat; city

城防 chéngfáng (名) the defence of a city: ～部队 city garrison

城关(關) chéngguān (名) the area just outside a city gate

城郭 chéngguō (名) city walls; city

城郊 chéngjiāo (名) outskirts of a town

城楼(樓) chénglóu (名) a tower over a city gate; gate tower

城门(門) chéngmén (名) city gate

城墙(墻) chéngqiáng (名) city wall

城区(區) chéngqū (名) the city proper: ～和郊区 the city proper and the suburbs

城市 chéngshì (名) town; city

城镇 chéngzhèn (名) cities and towns

盛 chéng (动) 1 ladle; dish out: ～饭 fill a bowl with rice 2 hold; contain: 罐子太小, ～不下这么多奶. The jar is too small to hold this much milk.
see also shèng

盛器 chéngqì (名) vessel; receptacle

呈 chéng (动) 1 appear; assume (form, colour, etc.): 叶～椭圆形. The leaf is oval in shape. 2 submit; present

呈报(報) chéngbào (动) submit a report

呈递(遞) chéngdì (动) present; submit: ～国书 present credentials

呈文 chéngwén (名) document submitted to a superior; memorial; petition

呈现 chéngxiàn (动) present (a certain appearance); appear; emerge: 我国各条战线～着一片大好形势. A good situation prevails on all fronts in our country.

程 chéng (名) 1 rule; regulation: 章～ rules; constitution 2 order; procedure: 议～ agenda 3 journey: 启～ set out on a journey 4 distance: 路～ distance of travel. 射～ range

程度 chéngdù (名) level; degree; extent: 技术～ technical level. 在一定～上 to a greater or lesser extent. 在不同～上 in varying degrees

程控 chéngkòng (名) pre-programmed automatic control: ～电话 program-control telephone

程序 chéngxù (名) 1 order; procedure; course: 法律～ legal procedure. 符合～ be in order 2 programme

乘 chéng (动) 1 ride: ～公共汽车 go by bus. ～火车(飞机、船)旅行 travel by train (plane, boat) 2 take advantage of 3 multiply: 五～三等于十五. Five times three is fifteen. *or* 5 multiplied by 3 is 15.

乘法 chéngfǎ (名) multiplication

乘风(風)破浪 chéngfēng-pòlàng brave the wind and the waves

乘机(機) chéngjī (副) seize the opportunity: ～反攻 seize the opportunity to counterattack

乘客 chéngkè (名) passenger

乘凉 chéngliáng (动) enjoy the cool

乘人之危 chéng rén zhī wēi take advantage of the precarious position of others

乘胜(勝) chéngshèng (副) exploit a victory: ～前进 advance on the crest of a victory

乘务(務)员 chéngwùyuán (名) attendant on a train

乘兴(興) chéngxìng (副) spurred on by momentary enthusiasm

乘虚 chéngxū (副) take advantage of a weak point; act when sb. is off guard

惩(懲) chéng (动) punish; penalize

惩办(辦) chéngbàn (动) punish: ～罪犯 punish criminals

惩罚(罰) chéngfá (动) punish; penalize

惩前毖后(後) chéngqián-bìhòu learn from past mistakes to avoid future ones

惩治 chéngzhì (动) punish: ～腐败 combat corruption

澄 chéng (形) clear; transparent

澄清 chéngqīng I (形) clear; transparent II (动) clear up; clarify: ～事实 clarify certain facts

see also dèng

橙 chéng (名) 1 orange 2 orange colour: ～黄 orange (colour)

承 chéng (动) 1 bear; hold; carry 2 undertake; contract (to do a job): ～做各式家具 undertake to make all kinds of furniture 3 〈套〉 be indebted: ～您过奖. You flatter me.

承办(辦) chéngbàn (动) undertake

承包 chéngbāo (动) contract: ～商 contractor

承担(擔) chéngdān (动) assume; undertake: ～义务 fulfil an obligation. ～一切费用 bear the cost

承蒙 chéngméng 〈套〉 be indebted to; be granted a favour

承诺 chéngnuò (动) promise to undertake

承认(認) chéngrèn (动) 1 admit; acknowledge; recognize: ～错误 acknowledge one's mistake 2 give diplomatic recognition; recognize

承受 chéngshòu (动) bear; sustain; withstand; endure: ～极大的痛苦 endure great pain. ～种种考验 undergo every kind of test. ～力 endurance

承袭(襲) chéngxí (动) 1 adopt; follow (a tradition, etc.) 2 inherit (a peerage, etc.)

丞 chéng (名) assistant officer (in ancient China)

丞相 chéngxiàng (名) prime minister (in ancient China)

逞 chěng (动) 1 show off; flaunt: ～英雄 play the hero. ～威风 flaunt one's power 2 carry out; succeed in an evil design: 得～ succeed in one's schemes 3 indulge, give free rein to: ～性子 be wilful

逞能 chěngnéng (动) show off one's skill; parade one's ability

逞凶 chěngxiōng (动) act violently

骋 chěng (动)〈书〉 gallop: 驰～文坛 play a major part in the literary world

骋怀(懷) chěnghuái (动)〈书〉 give free rein to one's thoughts and feelings

秤 chèng (名) steelyard; scale

痴(癡) chī (形) 1 silly; idiotic: ～人说梦 a tale told by an idiot. 白～ idiot 2 crazy about: 书～

bookworm

痴呆 chīdāi (形) dull-witted; stupid

痴情 chīqíng (名) passionate but often unrequited love

痴心 chīxīn (名) infatuation: ～妄想 wishful thinking; daydream

吃 chī (动) 1 eat; take: ～药 take medicine 2 eat at: ～馆子 eat at a restaurant 3 live on: 靠山～山 those living on a mountain live off the mountain 4 wipe out: 又～掉敌军一个团 annihilate another enemy regiment. ～一个子儿 take a piece (in chess) 5 exhaust; be a strain 6 absorb; soak up: 这种纸不～墨. This kind of paper does not absorb ink. 7 suffer; incur

吃不开(開) chībùkāi be unpopular: 不懂英文的人在这个公司是～的. This company has no use for people who don't know English.

吃不消 chībuxiāo be unable to stand (exertion, fatigue, etc.): 怕他的身体～. We are afraid he won't be able to stand the strain. 全天工作她恐怕～. A full-time job may be too much for her.

吃穿 chī-chuān (名) food and clothing: ～不愁 not have to worry about food and clothing

吃醋 chīcù (动) be jealous (usu. about rivalry in love)

吃得开(開) chīdekāi be popular; be much sought after

吃得消 chīdexiāo be able to stand (exertion, fatigue, etc.)

吃饭 chīfàn (动) 1 eat; have a meal: ～了吗? Have you had your meal? 2 make a living: 靠捕鱼～ make a living by fishing

吃官司 chī guānsi get into trouble with the law; be put behind the bar

吃喝玩乐(樂) chī-hē-wán-lè eat, drink and be merry; idle away one's time in pleasureseeking

吃回扣 chī huíkòu get commission (illegally)

吃紧(緊) chījǐn (形) (of political, military, financial situation) tense; critical

吃惊(驚) chījīng be startled; be shocked; be amazed; be taken aback: 大吃一惊 greatly surprised

吃苦 chīkǔ (动) bear hardships: ～耐劳 endure hardships and be capable of hard work

吃苦头(頭) chī kǔtou suffer: 蛮干是要～的. If you act rashly you are bound to suffer.

吃亏(虧) chīkuī (动) 1 stand to lose; get the worst of it: 跟他作生意你是要～的. You will stand to lose if you do business with him. 2 at a disadvantage

吃老本 chī lǎoběn live off one's past gains; rest on one's laurels

吃力 chīlì (形) strenuous; difficult: ～不讨好的差使 a thankless but demanding job

吃奶 chīnǎi (动) suck the breast: ～的孩子 sucking child; suckling

吃素 chīsù (动) avoid eating meat and fish; be a vegetarian

吃闲(閒)饭 chī xiánfàn lead an idle life; be a loafer or sponger

吃香 chīxiāng (形)〈口〉be very popular; be much sought after; be in vogue

吃一堑,长一智 chī yī qiàn, zhǎng yī zhì a fall into the pit, a gain in your wit

笞 chī (动)〈书〉beat with a stick, cane, etc.: 鞭～ flog; whip

嗤 chī (动) sneer: ～笑 laugh at; sneer at. ～之以鼻 snort; give an impatient snort

迟(遲) chí (形) 1 late: 他来～了. He's late. 2 slow; tardy

迟迟 chíchí (形) slow; tardy: ～不决 hesitate for a long time without making a decision

迟到 chídào (动) be late: 他上班从不～. He is never late for work.

迟钝 chídùn (形) slow-witted

迟缓 chíhuǎn (形) slow; sluggish: 进展～ make slow progress

迟暮 chímù (名) dusk; twilight

迟疑 chíyí (动) hesitate: 毫不～ without hesitation

迟早 chízǎo (副) sooner or later; early or late

持 chí (动) 1 hold; grasp: ～枪 hold a gun 2 keep; maintain: ～中立态度 maintain a neutral attitude 3 support; keep; maintain: 维～ maintain 4 manage; run: 主～ be in charge of. 操～ manage; handle 5 oppose: 相～不下 be locked in stalemate

持家 chíjiā (动) run one's home: 勤俭～ be thrifty in running one's home

持久 chíjiǔ (形) lasting; enduring: ～和平 lasting peace. ～战 protracted war

持平 chípíng (动) keep a balance

持续(續) chíxù (动) continue; sustain: 产量

～稳定上升 a steady increase in output

持有 chíyǒu（动）hold：～外交护照 hold a diplomatic passport. ～不同意见 hold differing views

持之以恒 chí zhī yǐ héng persevere

持重 chízhòng（形）prudent；cautious；discreet：老成～ experienced and prudent

匙 chí（名）spoon：汤～ soup spoon

踟 chí

踟蹰 chíchú（动）hesitate；waver

池 chí（名）1 pool；pond：游泳～ swimming pool. 养鱼～ fish pond 2 an enclosed space with raised sides：舞～ dance floor. 乐～ orchestra pit

池塘 chítáng（名）pond；pool

弛 chí（动）〈书〉relax；slacken：一张一～ tension alternating with relaxation

弛缓 chíhuǎn（动）relax；calm down

驰 chí（动）1 speed；gallop 2 spread：～名 well known

驰骋 chíchěng（动）〈书〉gallop

驰名 chímíng（动）become well known；be famous：～中外 enjoy a high reputation both at home and abroad

耻 chǐ（名）shame；disgrace；humiliation：不知～ have no sense of shame. 引以为～ regard sth. as a disgrace

耻辱 chǐrǔ（名）shame；disgrace；humiliation

耻笑 chǐxiào（动）sneer at；ridicule

齿（齒）chǐ（名）1 tooth 2 a tooth-like part of anything

齿冷 chǐlěng（动）〈书〉laugh scornfully：令人～ inspire cold disdain

齿轮（輪）chǐlún（名）gear wheel；gear

侈 chǐ（形）〈书〉extravagant；wasteful：～谈 talk glibly about. 奢～ luxurious；extravagant

褫 chǐ（动）〈书〉strip；deprive

褫夺（奪）chǐduó（动）strip；deprive：～公权 deprive sb. of civil rights

尺 chǐ I（量）*chi*，a unit of length（1/3 of a metre）II（名）ruler

尺寸 chǐcùn（名）size；measurement；dimensions：量～ take sb.'s measurements

尺度 chǐdù（名）yardstick；criterion

炽（熾）chì（形）flaming；ablaze：～烈 raging；scorching. ～热 red-hot；sweltering

赤 chì（形）1 red：面红耳～ be red in the face；be flushed 2 loyal；sincere：～胆忠心 utter devotion；wholehearted dedication 3 bare：～足 barefoot

赤膊 chìbó（形）stripped to the waist；barebacked：～上阵 throw away all disguise；come out into the open

赤潮 chìcháo（名）red tide

赤诚 chìchéng（形）absolutely sincere

赤道 chìdào（名）the equator

赤金 chìjīn（名）pure gold

赤裸裸 chìluǒluǒ（形）1 stark naked 2 undisguised；naked

赤贫 chìpín（形）utterly destitute；in grinding poverty

赤子 chìzǐ（名）1 newborn baby：～之心 utter innocence；sincere love 2 the people

赤字 chìzì（名）deficit

翅 chì（名）wing：～膀 wing. 鱼～ shark's fins

叱 chì（动）rebuke：怒～ rebuke angrily. ～骂 curse；scold roundly

斥 chì（动）shout；scold；denounce：痛～ vehemently denounce；shout at (sb.) angrily

斥责 chìzé（动）rebuke；denounce

饬 chì（动）〈书〉1 put in order；readjust：整～ put in order；strengthen (discipline, etc.) 2 order：严～ issue strict orders

充 chōng I（形）ample；full；sufficient II（动）1 pose as；pass sth. off as：～好人 pretend to be kind-hearted 2 serve as；act as：～向导 serve as a guide 3 fill；charge：～电 charge (a battery)

充斥 chōngchì（动）flood；be full of：外国商品～市场. The market was glutted with goods from abroad.

充当（當）chōngdāng（动）act as；serve as；play the part of

充电（電）chōngdiàn（动）recharge：～电池 rechargable battery

充耳不闻 chōng ěr bù wén turn a deaf ear to

充分 chōngfèn（形）full；ample；abundant：有～的信心 be full of confidence. ～证据 ample evidence

充公 chōnggōng（动）confiscate

充饥（饑）chōngjī（动）allay (or appease) one's hunger

充满（滿）chōngmǎn（动）fill；be filled with

充沛 chōngpèi（形）plentiful；abundant；

C

full of: 精力～ vigorous; energetic
充任 chōngrèn (动) fill the post of; hold the position of: 聘请他～顾问 ask him to be our adviser
充塞 chōngsè (动) fill (up); cram
充实(實) chōngshí I (形) substantial; rich: 内容～ substantial in content II (动) substantiate; enrich: ～领导班子 strengthen the leadership
充数(數) chōngshù (动) merely make up the number: 滥竽～ be hardly qualified for the job
充血 chōngxuè (名) congestion; hyperaemia
充裕 chōngyù (形) abundant; plentiful: 时间～ have ample (or plenty of) time
充值 chōngzhí (动) recharge with money: ～卡 rechargeable card
充足 chōngzú (形) adequate; ample; sufficient; abundant: 证据～ have ample evidence. 阳光～ full of sunshine; sunny

春 chōng (动) pound; pestle: ～米 husk rice with mortar and pestle

冲 chōng I (动) **1** pour boiling water on: ～茶 make tea **2** rinse; flush; wash away: ～厕所 flush the toilet **3** (衝) charge; rush; dash: ～锋陷阵 charge forward **4** (衝) clash; collide: ～突 conflict **5** develop: ～胶卷 develop a piece of film II (名)(衝) important hub
see also chòng
冲冲 chōngchōng (形) excitedly: 怒气～ in a towering rage
冲刺 chōngcì (动) spurt; sprint
冲淡 chōngdàn (动) dilute; water down; weaken; play down: ～戏剧效果 weaken the dramatic effect
冲动(動) chōngdòng I (名) impulse: 出于一时～ act on impulse II (动) get excited; be impetuous: 别～. Don't get excited.
冲击(擊) chōngjī I (动) lash; pound: 海浪～着岩石. The waves lashed at the rocks. II (名) impact
冲积(積) chōngjī (名) alluviation
冲剂(劑) chōngjì (名) (of medicine) mixture to be taken with boiling water, wine, etc.
冲垮 chōngkuǎ (动) wash away; shatter
冲浪 chōnglàng (动) surf: ～板 surfboard. ～运动 surfing
冲破 chōngpò (动) break through; breach
冲散 chōngsàn (动) break up; scatter; disperse
冲杀(殺) chōngshā (动) charge forward; rush ahead
冲刷 chōngshuā (动) erode; wash away
冲天 chōngtiān (形) towering; soaring: 干劲～ with boundless enthusiasm. 怒气～ in a towering rage
冲突 chōngtū (动) conflict; clash: 武装～ an armed conflict
冲撞 chōngzhuàng (动) **1** collide; bump; ram **2** offend

憧 chōng

憧憧 chōngchōng (形) flickering; moving: 人影～ people's shadows moving back and forth
憧憬 chōngjǐng (动) long for; visualize: ～着光明的未来 visualize a bright future

忡 chōng

忡忡 chōngchōng (形) grieved: 忧心～ very worried; full of anxiety

虫(蟲) chóng (名) insect; worm: ～害 insect pest

崇 chóng I (形) high; lofty II (动) esteem; worship
崇拜 chóngbài (动) worship; adore: 英雄～ hero worship
崇高 chónggāo (形) lofty; high: ～的理想 a lofty ideal. ～的威望 high prestige
崇敬 chóngjìng (动) respect; revere: 受到人民的～ be held in high esteem by the people

重 chóng I (副) over again: 老调～弹 harp on the same old tune. ～访英伦 revisit England II (动) repeat III (量) layer: 万～山 ranges of hills. 双～领导 dual leadership
see also zhòng
重版 chóngbǎn (动) reprint
重唱 chóngchàng (名) a piece of music for two or more performers: 二～ duet
重重 chóngchóng (形) layer upon layer: 困难～ endless difficulties. 顾虑～ full of misgivings
重蹈覆辙 chóng dǎo fùzhé follow the track of the overturned cart; follow the same old road to ruin
重叠(疊) chóngdié (动) overlap: 精简～的行政机构 streamline the administrative structure
重返 chóngfǎn (动) return
重逢 chóngféng (动) meet again: 旧友～ meeting of old friends (after a long separation)
重复(複) chóngfù (动) repeat; duplicate

重婚 chónghūn (名) bigamy
重申 chóngshēn (动) reaffirm; reiterate; restate: ~我们的立场 reaffirm our stand
重围(圍) chóngwéi (名) tight encirclement by the enemy
重温旧(舊)梦(夢) chóng wēn jiù-mèng revive an old dream; recall or relive an old experience
重新 chóngxīn (副) again; anew; afresh: ~开始 start afresh. ~考虑 reconsider
重演 chóngyǎn (动) 1 repeat a performance or put on an old play 2 recur: 历史~ history repeating itself
重洋 chóngyáng (名) the seas and oceans: 远涉~ travel across the oceans
重整旗鼓 chóng zhěng qígǔ rally one's forces (after a defeat)
重奏 chóngzòu (名) ensemble: 四~ quartet

宠(寵) chǒng (动) spoil; dote on: 得~ be in sb.'s good graces. 失~ fall from grace. 这孩子给~坏了. The child is spoiled.
宠爱(愛) chǒng'ài (动) make a pet of sb.; dote on
宠儿(兒) chǒng'ér (名) pet; favourite
宠物 chǒngwù (名) pet
宠信 chǒngxìn (动) favour and trust unduly (a subordinate)

冲(衝) chòng I (形)〈口〉 with force; dynamically; vigorously: 他干活真~. He works with vim and vigour. 烟味真~. The tobacco smells strong. II (介) facing; towards: 窗户~南开. The window faces south. 那话不是~你说的. That remark wasn't directed at you.
see also chōng

抽 chōu (动) 1 take out (from in between): 从书架上~出一本书 take a book from the shelf 2 sprout; bud: 小麦~穗了. The wheat is coming into ear. 小树~出了嫩芽. The saplings are budding. 3 draw: ~水 draw water (from the well, etc.) 4 shrink: 这种布一洗就~. Washing shrinks this kind of cloth. 5 lash; whip; thrash
抽搐 chōuchù (动) twitch
抽打 chōudǎ (动) lash; whip; thrash
抽调 chōudiào (动) transfer
抽风(風) chōufēng (动) 1 pump air: ~机 air pump 2 have convulsions; go into convulsions 3 go crazy
抽奖 chōujiǎng (名) lucky draw; sweepstake
抽筋 chōujīn (动) cramp: 腿~ have a cramp in the leg
抽空 chōukòng (动) manage to find time
抽泣 chōuqì (动) sob
抽签(籤) chōuqiān (动) draw (or cast) lots
抽纱 chōushā (名) drawnwork
抽身 chōushēn (动) get away (from one's work)
抽屉 chōuti (名) drawer
抽象 chōuxiàng (形) abstract: ~的概念 an abstract concept
抽烟 chōuyān (动) smoke (a cigarette or a pipe)

畴(疇) chóu (名)〈书〉 1 kind; division: 范~ category 2 farmland

踌(躊) chóu

踌躇 chóuchú (动) hesitate; shilly-shally: ~不前 mark time; hesitate to make a move
踌躇满(滿)志 chóuchú mǎn zhì be enormously proud of one's success; have smug complacency

筹(籌) chóu (动) prepare; plan: 统~ overall planning. ~款 raise money (or funds). ~办 make preparations; make arrangements
筹备(備) chóubèi (动) prepare; arrange
筹措 chóucuò (动) raise (money): ~旅费 raise money for travelling expenses
筹划(劃) chóuhuà (动) plan to do sth.: 这里正在~建设一座水力发电站. We are planning to build a hydroelectric station here.
筹集 chóují (动) raise (money): ~基金 raise funds
筹建 chóujiàn (动) prepare to construct or establish sth.
筹码 chóumǎ (名) chip; counter: 作为这场政治交易的~ used as bargaining counters in the political deal

酬 chóu I (名) reward; payment: 稿~ payment for an article or book written II (动) fulfil; realize: 壮志未~ with one's ambitions unfulfilled
酬报(報) chóubào (名) reward; remuneration
酬宾(賓) chóubīn (名) bargain sales
酬金 chóujīn (名) monetary reward; remuneration
酬劳(勞) chóuláo (名) recompense; reward
酬谢 chóuxiè (动) present sb. with a gift as

a reward or as a token of one's appreciation

愁 chóu (动) worry; be anxious

愁肠(腸) chóucháng (名) pent-up feelings of sadness: ~百结 feel melancholy deep down in one's heart

愁眉 chóuméi (名) knitted brows; worried look: ~不展 knit one's brows. ~苦脸 look worried and miserable; have a worried look; pull a long face

愁闷 chóumèn (形) feel gloomy; be depressed

愁容 chóuróng (名) worried look

愁绪 chóuxù (名)〈书〉pensive melancholy

仇 chóu (名) 1 hatred; enmity; animosity 2 enemy; foe: 亲痛~快 sadden one's own folk and gladden one's enemies

仇敌(敵) chóudí (名) foe; enemy

仇恨 chóuhèn (名) hatred; hostility

仇人 chóurén (名) personal enemy

仇视 chóushì (动) look upon with hatred; be hostile to

惆 chóu

惆怅(悵) chóuchàng (形) melancholy; depressed

稠 chóu (形) 1 thick: 粥太~了. The porridge is too thick. 2 dense

稠密 chóumì (形) dense: 人烟~ densely populated

绸 chóu (名) silk fabric; silk

绸缎 chóuduàn (名) silk and satin

瞅 chǒu (动) glimpse; glance: 我朝周围瞧了一下, 一眼~见她. I looked around and glimpsed her.

丑(醜) chǒu (形) 1 ugly 2 disgraceful; shameful; scandalous: 出~ make a fool of oneself

丑八怪 chǒubāguài (名)〈口〉a very ugly person

丑恶(惡) chǒu'è (形) ugly; hideous; despicable: ~嘴脸 ugly features

丑化 chǒuhuà (动) uglify; vilify

丑角 chǒujué (名) clown; buffoon

丑陋 chǒulòu (形) ugly

丑态(態) chǒutài (名) ugly (or ludicrous) performance; disgusting manner: ~百出 act like a buffoon

丑闻 chǒuwén (名) scandal

臭 chòu (形) 1 smelly; stinking; foul: ~鸡蛋 a rotten egg 2 disgusting: 摆~架子 put on lousy airs
see also xiù

臭虫(蟲) chòuchóng (名) bedbug

臭骂 chòumà (动) curse angrily: 挨了一顿~ get a dressing down

臭名昭著 chòumíng zhāozhù notorious; infamous

臭气(氣) chòuqì (名) bad smell; stink

臭味相投 chòuwèi xiāngtóu birds of a feather flock together; people of the same ilk like each other

臭氧洞 chòuyǎngdòng (名) hole in the ozone layer

初 chū I (名) beginning II (形) 1 early: ~冬 early winter 2 first (in order): ~雪 first snow. ~三 the third day of a lunar month 3 for the first time: ~露锋芒 display one's talent for the first time 4 elementary; rudimentary: ~中 junior middle school 5 original: ~衷 original intention

初版 chūbǎn (名) first edition

初步 chūbù (形) initial; preliminary; tentative: ~意见 tentative opinion (proposal)

初出茅庐(廬) chū chū máolú at the beginning of one's career; young and inexperienced: ~的作家 fledgling writer

初次 chūcì (名) the first time: ~见面 see sb. for the first time

初等 chūděng (形) elementary; primary: ~教育 primary education

初稿 chūgǎo (名) first draft; draft

初级 chūjí (形) elementary; primary: ~产品 primary products

初交 chūjiāo (名) new acquaintance

初恋(戀) chūliàn (名) first love

初露头(頭)角 chū lù tóujiǎo just begin to show talent: ~的作家 a budding writer

初期 chūqī (名) initial stage; early days: 革命~ in the early days of the revolution

初生之犊(犢) chū shēng zhī dú newborn calf: ~不畏虎. Newborn calves do not fear tigers — young people are fearless.

初试 chūshì (名) preliminary examination

初旬 chūxún (名) in the first ten days of a month

初诊 chūzhěn (名) first consultation

出 chū I (动) 1 go or come out: ~太阳了. The sun's come out. ~国 go abroad. ～狱 be released from prison **2** issue; put forth: ～主意 offer advice. ～通知 put up a notice. ～证明 issue a certificate **3** produce: 这个厂～的汽车 the cars made by this factory. ～新书 publish new books **4** arise; happen; occur: ～事故 There was an accident. ～问题 go wrong **5** exceed; go beyond: 不～三年 within three years. 怎么多～三个人? How come there are three more people? **6** vent; put forth: ～气 vent one's spleen. ～疹子 have measles II (**齣**) (量) a dramatic piece: 一～戏 an opera; a play

出 chū **1** [used after a verb to indicate outward movement or completed action]: 拿～证件 produce one's papers. 选～新主席 elect a new chairman. 我说不～口. I find it too embarrassing to mention it. 他答不～这道题. He can't answer this question. **2** [indicating identification]: 我看不～他有多大年纪. I can't tell how old he is. 你能听～这是谁的声音? Can you identify this voice?

出版 chūbǎn (动) publish: ～社 publishing house. ～物 publication

出殡(殯) chūbìn (动) hold a funeral procession

出兵 chūbīng (动) dispatch troops (to a place)

出岔子 chū chàzi run into trouble; go wrong

出差 chūchāi (动) be on a business trip

出产(産) chūchǎn (动) produce; manufacture

出场(場) chūchǎng (动) **1** come on the stage; appear on the scene **2** enter the arena

出车(車) chūchē (动) dispatch a vehicle

出丑(醜) chūchǒu (动) make a fool of oneself; cut a sorry figure

出处(處) chūchù (名) source (of a quotation or allusion)

出错 chūcuò (动) make mistakes

出动(動) chūdòng (动) **1** go into action: 全校～扫雪. The whole school turned out to sweep the snow. **2** send out; dispatch: ～军舰 dispatch warships. ～警察驱散示威队伍. The police were called out to break up the demonstration.

出尔(爾)反尔 chū ěr fǎn ěr go back on one's word; contradict oneself

出发(發) chūfā (动) **1** set out; start off: 我们 6 点～. We'll set out at six. **2** start from; proceed from: 从长远利益～ from the long-range view

出风(風)头(頭) chū fēngtóu seek the limelight

出轨 chūguǐ (动) **1** be derailed **2** overstep the bounds: ～行为 an act deviating from normal practice

出海 chūhǎi (动) put to sea

出汗 chūhàn (动) perspire; sweat: 出一身汗 sweat all over

出乎意料 chūhū yìliào unexpectedly: 他的去世太～了. His death was really too sudden and unexpected.

出活 chūhuó (动) be efficient

出击(擊) chūjī (动) launch an attack

出家 chūjiā (动) become a Buddhist monk or nun

出嫁 chūjià (动) (of a woman) get married

出界 chūjiè (动) out of bounds; outside

出借 chūjiè (动) lend; loan

出境 chūjìng (动) leave the country: ～签证 exit visa. 驱逐～ deport. ～许可证 exit permit

出局 chūjú (动) be eliminated; be put out of the running

出口 chūkǒu I (动) **1** speak; utter **2** export II (名) exit

出来(來) chūlái (动) come out; emerge: 月亮～了. The moon has come out.

出来(來) chūlái [used after a verb to indicate outward movement or completed action]: 他从屋里走～. He came out of the room. 论文写～了. The thesis is completed.

出类(類)拔萃 chūlèi-bácuì preeminent; outstanding: ～的人物 an outstanding figure

出力 chūlì (动) contribute one's strength; exert oneself

出笼(籠) chūlóng (动) **1** come out of the steamer of cooking **2** 〈贬〉 come forth; appear; come out into the open

出路 chūlù (名) way out; outlet

出马(馬) chūmǎ (动) go into action; take the field: 亲自～ take up the matter oneself; take personal charge of the matter

出卖(賣) chūmài (动) **1** offer for sale; sell **2** betray; sell out

出毛病 chū máobìng go wrong; be out of order

出面 chūmiàn (动) act in one's own capacity or on sb.'s behalf: 这事得你亲自～. You'll have to take up the matter personally. ～调停 act as a mediator

出名 chūmíng (动) become famous or well known

出没 chūmò (动) appear and disappear; haunt: ～无常 appear or disappear unpredictably

出谋划(劃)策 chūmóu-huàcè give counsel; mastermind: 在幕后～ mastermind a scheme from behind the scenes

出纳 chūnà (名) cashier; the work of a cashier

出品 chūpǐn I (动) produce; manufacture; make II (名) product

出其不意 chū qí bù yì take sb. by surprise

出奇 chūqí (形) extraordinary; exceptional [usu. used as an adverbial adjunct or a complement]: 今天真是～地热. It's unusually hot today.

出奇制胜(勝) chū qí zhì shèng win by a surprise attack

出气(氣) chūqì (动) give vent to one's spleen

出勤 chūqín (动) **1** turn out for work: 全体～ full attendance **2** be out on duty

出去 chūqù (动) go out; get out: ～走走 go out for a walk

出去 chūqù (动) [used after a verb to indicate outward movement]: 把烟放～. Let out the smoke. 侵略者被赶～了. The invaders were driven off.

出让(讓) chūràng (动) sell (one's own things): 自行车减价～ sell one's bicycle at a reduced price

出人头(頭)地 chū rén tóu dì stand out among one's fellows

出任 chūrèn (动)〈书〉 take up the post of

出入 chūrù I (动) come in and go out: ～证 pass (identifying a staff member, etc.) II (名) discrepancy; divergence: 他说的和事实有～. What he says does not square with the facts.

出色 chūsè (形) outstanding; remarkable; splendid

出身 chūshēn (名) **1** family background **2** one's previous occupation

出神 chūshén (动) be lost in thought; be spellbound: 想得～ be in a trance

出生 chūshēng (动) be born: ～地 birthplace. ～证 birth certificate

出生入死 chūshēng-rùsǐ go through fire and water; brave countless dangers

出师(師) chūshī (动) **1** finish one's apprenticeship **2** dispatch troops to fight; send out an army

出使 chūshǐ (动) serve as an envoy abroad; be sent on a diplomatic mission

出示 chūshì (动) show; produce: ～证件 produce one's papers

出事 chūshì (动) have an accident: 出了什么事? What's wrong?

出售 chūshòu (动) offer for sale; sell

出台(臺) chūtái (动) make a public appearance: 最近将～房改新方案. A new plan for the housing reform will be announced soon.

出庭 chūtíng (动) appear in court: ～作证 appear in court as a witness

出头(頭) chūtóu I (动) **1** raise one's head; free oneself (from misery) **2** appear in public; come to the fore II [used after a round number] a little over; odd: 他刚四十～. He's just a little over forty.

出头(頭)露面 chūtóu-lùmiàn make a public appearance; be in the limelight

出土 chūtǔ (动) be unearthed; be excavated: ～文物 unearthed historical relics

出席 chūxí (动) attend; be present (at a meeting, banquet, etc.)

出息 chūxi (名) (of a person) promise: 有～ promising. 没～ good-for-nothing

出现 chūxiàn (动) appear; emerge: ～了一个新问题. A new problem has arisen.

出洋相 chū yángxiàng (动) lay oneself to ridicule; make a spectacle of oneself

出游 chūyóu (动) go on a (sightseeing) tour

出于(於) chūyú (动) start from: ～自愿 of one's own accord

出院 chūyuàn (动) leave hospital; be discharged from hospital after recovery

出诊 chūzhěn (动) (of a doctor) make a house call

出征 chūzhēng (动) go on an expedition

出众(衆) chūzhòng (形) outstanding: 人才～ a talented person; a person of outstanding talent

出租 chūzū (动) hire out; rent out; lease out: ～汽车 taxicab; taxi

厨 chú (名) kitchen

厨房 chúfáng (名) kitchen: ～用具 kitchen ware; cooking utensils

厨师(師) chúshī (名) cook; chef

橱 chú (名) cabinet; closet: 壁～ built-in cabinet. 衣～ wardrobe. 书～

bookcase. 碗～ cupboard

橱窗 chúchuāng (名) show window; showcase; shopwindow

橱柜(櫃) chúguì (名) cupboard

除 chú I (动) 1 get rid of; do away with; remove 2 divide: 五～十得二. 10 divided by 5 is 2. II (介) 1 except: ～此而外 with the exception of this 2 besides

除草 chúcǎo (动) weed: ～机 weeder. ～剂 weed killer; herbicide

除法 chúfǎ (名) division

除非 chúfēi (连) [often used in conjunction with 才, 否则, 不然, etc. to indicate that what follows is a necessary condition]: only if; unless: ～动手术, 否则她就没救了. She will die unless she has an operation. ～你亲自去请他, 不然他是不会来的. Only when you go and ask him personally will he come.

除根 chúgēn (动) 1 dig up the roots; root out 2 cure once and for all

除了 chúle (介) except: ～她, 谁也不会唱这支歌. No one can sing this song except her. 她～接电话以外, 还要打字. Besides answering phone calls, she does some typing.

除外 chúwài (动) be excepted; not including: 博物馆每天开放, 星期一～. The museum is open every day except Monday.

除夕 chúxī (名) New Year's Eve

锄 chú I (名) hoe II (动) 1 work with a hoe; hoe: ～草 weed with a hoe 2 uproot; eliminate; wipe out: ～奸 eliminate traitors

锄头(頭) chútou (名) hoe

刍(芻) chú (名)〈书〉hay; fodder: 反～ ruminate; chew the cud

刍议(議) chúyì (名)〈谦〉a modest proposal

雏(雛) chú (名) 1 young (bird) 2 nestling; fledgling

雏形 chúxíng (名) microcosm; embryonic form

储 chǔ (动) store up: 冬～白菜 cabbages stored for the winter

储备(備) chǔbèi I (动) store; reserve; put by II (名) reserve: 黄金～ gold reserve. 外汇～ foreign exchange reserve

储藏 chǔcáng I (动) keep; preserve: 鲜果～ preservation (or storage) of fresh fruit. ～室 storeroom II (名) deposit: 丰富的石油～ abundant oil deposits

储存 chǔcún (动) store; put away: ～余粮 store up surplus grain. ～核武器 stockpile nuclear weapons

储量 chǔliàng (名) reserves

储蓄 chǔxù (动、名) save; deposit: ～所 savings bank. 活期(定期)～ current (deposit) account

楚 chǔ I (形) clear; neat: 一清二～ perfectly clear. 衣冠～～ immaculately dressed II (名)〈书〉suffering: 苦～ distress; suffering

础(礎) chǔ (名) plinth: ～石 the stone base of a column; plinth. 基～ foundation; base

处(處) chǔ (动) 1 get along (with sb.): ～得来 be on good terms; get along well 2 deal with; handle: ～事 handle affairs; manage matters 3 be in a certain position: ～于困难地位 be in a difficult position. 设身～地 put oneself in another's position.

see also chù

处罚(罰) chǔfá (动) punish; penalize

处方 chǔfāng (名) prescription; recipe

处方药(藥) chǔfāngyào (名) prescription medicine

处分 chǔfèn (名) disciplinary action; punishment: 警告～ disciplinary warning. 免予～ exempt sb. from punishment. 行政～ administrative disciplinary measure

处境 chǔjìng (名) (usu.) unfavourable situation; plight: ～尴尬 be in an embarrassing situation. ～危险 be in a dangerous (or precarious) situation; be in peril

处决 chǔjué (动) execute: 依法～ execute in accordance with the law; implement a death sentence

处理 chǔlǐ (动) 1 handle; attend to; dispose of: ～国家大事 attend to state affairs. ～废物 waste disposal 2 treat by a special process: 热～ heat treatment 3 sell at a reduced price: ～价格 reduced price; bargain price. ～品 goods sold at reduced or sale prices

处女 chǔnǚ (名) virgin: ～地 virgin soil

处世 chǔshì (动) conduct oneself in social life

处死 chǔsǐ (动) put to death; execute

处心积(積)虑(慮) chǔxīn-jīlǜ deliberately scheme or plan (sth. evil)

C

处于(於) chǔyú (动) be in a certain condition (state): ～优势 be in a favourable condition

处置 chǔzhì (动) deal with; handle: ～得宜 handle matters with propriety

畜 chù (名) domestic animal; livestock
see also xù

畜生 chùsheng (名) 1 domestic animal 2 beast; dirty swine

怵 chù (动) fear: ～场 feel apprehensive

矗 chù (动)〈书〉stand tall and upright: ～立 tower over

处(處) chù (名) 1 place: 住～ dwelling place; apartment. 停车～ parking lot; car park. 长～ strong point. 共同之～ common feature. 心灵深～ in the recesses of the heart. 几～人家 several homesteads 2 department; office: 秘书～ secretariat. 总务～ general affairs department
see also chǔ

处处 chùchù (副) everywhere; in all respects

黜 chù (动)〈书〉remove sb. from office; dismiss: 罢～ dismiss (a government official)

绌 chù (形)〈书〉inadequate; insufficient: 相形见～ prove inferior by comparison; be outshone

触(觸) chù (动) 1 touch: ～觉 sense of touch 2 move: ～景生情 The sight strikes a chord in one's heart.

触电(電) chùdiàn (动) get an electric shock: 小心～! Danger! Electricity!

触动(動) chùdòng (动) 1 touch; move slightly 2 stir up sb.'s feelings

触发(發) chùfā (动) touch off; trigger

触犯 chùfàn (动) offend; violate: 我什么地方～了你? What have I done to offend you? ～法律 violate (or break) the law

触角 chùjiǎo (名) feeler; antenna

触摸屏 chùmōpíng (名) touch screen

触目惊(驚)心 chùmù-jīngxīn startling; shocking

触怒 chùnù (动) make angry; enrage

揣 chuāi (动) keep sth. in one's clothes: 把孩子～在怀里 hold a baby in arms
see also chuǎi

揣 chuǎi (动)〈书〉estimate; conjecture: ～测 guess. ～摩 try to figure out
see also chuāi

踹 chuài (动) kick: 一脚把门～开 kick the door open

穿 chuān (动) 1 wear; put on: ～上大衣 put on your coat. 她～绿裙子. She is in a green skirt. 2 pierce through; penetrate: 看～ see through 3 pass through; cross: ～过马路 cross a street

穿帮(幫) chuānbāng (动) give away (the show); let the cat out of the bag; reveal unintentionally

穿插 chuānchā I (动) 1 do alternately 2 insert II (名) episode; interlude

穿戴 chuāndài (名) what one wears: ～整齐 be neatly dressed

穿孔 chuānkǒng I (动) bore (or punch) a hole II (名) perforation

穿梭 chuānsuō (动) shuttle back and forth: ～外交 shuttle diplomacy

穿越 chuānyuè (动) pass through; cut across

穿凿(鑿) chuānzáo (动) give a far-fetched (or strained) interpretation; read too much into sth.: ～附会 give strained interpretations and draw far-fetched analogies

穿针引线(綫) chuānzhēn-yǐnxiàn act as a go-between

穿着 chuānzhuó (名) dress; what one wears

川 chuān (名) 1 river: 山～ mountains and rivers 2 plain; lowland area

川流不息 chuān liú bù xī flow past in an endless stream; come in a never-ending stream

椽 chuán (名) rafter

传(傳) chuán (动) 1 pass; pass on 2 spread: 消息很快～开了. The news runs apace. 3 hand down: 祖～秘方 a secret recipe handed down from the ancestors 4 summon: ～证人 summon a witness 5 transmit; conduct: ～热 transmit heat 6 infect; catch 7 convey; express: ～神 bring out the true meaning
see also zhuàn

传播 chuánbō (动) propagate; disseminate; popularize: ～先进技术 popularize an advanced technique

传布 chuánbù (动) disseminate; spread

传抄 chuánchāo (动) copy privately
传达(達) chuándá (动) pass on; relay: ~信息 relay a message. ~会议精神 transmit the spirit of the meeting. ~室 reception office
传单(單) chuándān (名) leaflet; handbill
传导(導) chuándǎo (动、名) conduct; conduction
传递(遞) chuándì (动) transmit; deliver; transfer: ~信息 transmit messages
传呼 chuánhū (动) (of a public telephone custodian) notify sb. of a phone call; page: ~电话 neighbourhood telephone service
传家宝(寶) chuánjiābǎo (名) family heirloom; a cherished tradition
传教 chuánjiào (动) teach and spread the Christian religion abroad; do missionary work: ~士 missionary
传媒 chuánméi (名) media: 大众~ mass media ~界 media circles
传票 chuánpiào (名) (court) summons; subpoena
传奇 chuánqí (名) 1 legend: ~式的英雄 legendary hero 2 romances of the Tang and Song dynasties (618 – 1279) 3 poetic dramas of the Ming and Qing dynasties (1368 – 1911)
传染 chuánrǎn (动) infect; be contagious: ~病 infectious (or contagious) disease
传神 chuánshén (形) vivid; lifelike: ~之笔 a fine vivid touch (in writing or painting)
传声(聲)筒 chuánshēngtǒng (名) 1 megaphone mouthpiece 2 parrot
传授 chuánshòu (动) pass on (knowledge, skill, etc.); impart
传输 chuánshū (动) transmission
传说 chuánshuō I (动) rumour has it; people say II (名) lore; legend: 民间~ folklore
传诵 chuánsòng (动) circulated; be widely read
传统 chuántǒng (名) tradition; conventions: ~观念 traditional ideas
传闻 chuánwén (名) hearsay; rumour: ~失实. The rumour proves unfounded.
传销 chuánxiāo (名) network marketing; tiercing
传扬(揚) chuányáng (动) spread: 他的声名~四方. His reputation spread far and wide.
传阅 chuányuè (动) pass round or circulate
传真 chuánzhēn (名) facsimile; fax: 发~ send a fax; fax. ~机 fax machine

船 chuán (名) boat; ship: 上~ board a ship; go on board; embark. 下~ disembark. ~上交货 free on board
船舶 chuánbó (名) shipping
船舱(艙) chuáncāng (名) cabin
船坞(塢) chuánwù (名) dock; shipyard: 浮~ floating dock
船员 chuányuán (名) (ship's) crew
船长(長) chuánzhǎng (名) captain; skipper
船只(隻) chuánzhī (名) ship; vessel

喘 chuǎn (动) breathe with difficulty; pant: 哮~ asthma
喘气(氣) chuǎnqì (动) 1 pant; gasp: 喘不过气来 be out of breath 2 take a breather; have a break: 喘口气儿再干. Let's take a breather before we go on.
喘息 chuǎnxī (动) 1 pant; gasp for breath 2 breathing spell

舛 chuǎn (名)〈书〉error; mishap: 命途多~ suffer many a setback during one's life. ~误 error; mishap

串 chuàn I (动) 1 string together: 把鱼~起来 string the fish together 2 get things mixed up: 电话~线. The lines have crossed. 3 go from place to place; run about: ~亲戚 go around visiting one's relatives II (量)string; cluster: 一~珠子 a string of beads. 一~钥匙 a bunch of keys. 一~葡萄 a cluster of grapes
串联(聯) chuànlián I (动) make contact II (名) series connection: ~电阻 series resistance
串通 chuàntōng (动) gang up; collaborate; collude: ~一气 act in collusion

窗 chuāng (名) window: 玻璃~ glass window. ~明几净. The window is bright and the desk clean.
窗户 chuānghu (名) opening in a wall for letting in air and light; window
窗口 chuāngkǒu (名) 1 the place near a window 2 wicket; window (for tickets, etc.)
窗帘(簾) chuānglián (名) (window) curtain
窗台(臺) chuāngtái (名) window-sill

疮(瘡) chuāng (名) sore; running sore: ~疤 scar

创(創) chuāng (名) wound: ~伤 a damaged place in the body; wound; trauma. ~痕 scar
see also chuàng

C

幢 chuáng (名) a stone pillar inscribed with Buddha's name or Buddhist scripture
see also zhuàng

幢幢 chuángchuáng (形)〈书〉 flickering; swinging from side to side: 人影～ shadows of people moving about

床(牀) chuáng I (名) bed: 单人～ single bed. 双人～ double bed. 折叠～ folding bed. 马上上～睡觉去 get straight into bed II (量): 一～被子 one quilt

床单(單) chuángdān (名) sheet

床铺(舖) chuángpù (名) bed

闯 chuǎng (动) rush; force one's way in or out: 横冲直～ dash around madly; jostle and elbow one's way. ～出一条新路子 break a new path; blaze a trail

闯祸(禍) chuǎnghuò (动) get into trouble or cause disaster

闯将(將) chuǎngjiàng (名) bold general; pathbreaker

闯劲(勁) chuǎngjìn (名) heroic effort; pioneering spirit

怆(愴) chuàng (形)〈书〉 very sad: ～然泪下 shed tears in sadness

创(創) chuàng (动) initiate; achieve (sth. for the first time): ～办 set up. ～记录 set a record
see also chuāng

创见(見) chuàngjiàn (名) originality; original idea

创建 chuàngjiàn (动) found; establish: ～新的机构 found a new organization

创举(舉) chuàngjǔ (名) pioneering work; something that has never been undertaken

创立 chuànglì (动) found; originate

创始 chuàngshǐ (动) originate; initiate: ～人 founder; founder member; founding father

创收 chuàngshōu (动) generate profits; earn extra money

创新 chuàngxīn (动) discard old ideas and bring forth new ones; blaze new trails

创业(業) chuàngyè (动) start an undertaking; do pioneering work: 有～精神 have the spirit of a pathbreaker

创意 chuàngyì I (动) create new ideas II (名) new ideas: 颇有～ be highly original in concept; be innovative

创造 chuàngzào (动) create; produce: ～新记录 make a record. ～奇迹 create miracles; work wonders. ～力 creative power. ～性 creativeness; creativity

创作 chuàngzuò I (动) create (write literary works): ～经验 creative experience II (名) literary and artistic creation

炊 chuī (动) cook: ～具 cooking utensils. ～事 cooking; kitchen work. ～烟 smoke from a kitchen chimney

吹 chuī (动) 1 blow; exhale: 把蜡烛～灭 blow out the candle. ～哨 whistle. ～一口气 breathe out. 雨打风～ weather beaten. ～起床号 sound the reveille 2 play (wind instruments): ～笛子 play the flute 3〈口〉 brag; boast: 自～自擂 blow one's own trumpet. ～得天花乱坠 give an extravagant account of. ～～拍拍 flatter and toady 4〈口〉 break off; break up; fall through: 她跟她的男朋友～了. She has broken with her boy friend. 原来的计划告～了. The original plan has fallen through.

吹打 chuīdǎ (动) perform with wind and percussion instruments

吹风(風) chuīfēng (动) 1 get in a draught 2 dry (hair, etc.) with a blower: ～器 hair dryer 3 diliberately let out inside information in an informal way: 给大家吹吹风 give people a briefing (usually matters of some importance)

吹拂 chuīfú (动) (of breeze) gently pass; flicker away

吹鼓手 chuīgǔshǒu (名) trumpeter; eulogist

吹灰之力 chuī huī zhī lì with the least effort: 不费～ be as easy as blowing off dust; require little effort

吹毛求疵 chuī máo qiú cī find fault; split hairs; nitpick

吹牛 chuīniú (动) boast; brag: ～拍马 boast and flatter

吹捧 chuīpěng (动) flatter; lavish praise on: 互相～ flatter each other; engage in mutual flattery so as to boost each other's importance

吹嘘 chuīxū (动) brag; lavish praise on oneself or others: 自我～ self-praise

吹奏 chuīzòu (动) play any musical instrument

槌 chuí (名) mallet; beetle: 碾～ pestle. 鼓～儿 drumstick

垂 chuí (动) 1 hang down; droop; let fall: ～柳 drooping willow. ～泪

shed tears 2〈书〉approaching：～老 getting on in years

垂钓 chuídiào（动）fish with a hook and line; go angling

垂暮 chuímù（名）dusk; before sundown：～之年 evening of life

垂青 chuíqīng（动）〈书〉look upon sb. with special favour

垂手可得 chuí shǒu kě dé extremely easy to obtain

垂死 chuísǐ（形）moribund; dying：～挣扎 put up a last-ditch struggle

垂头(頭)丧(喪)气(氣) chuítóu-sàngqì crestfallen; dejected; depressed

垂危 chuíwēi（动）be critically ill; be at one's last gasp

垂涎 chuíxián（动）covet; slaver：～三尺 drool with envy

垂直 chuízhí（形）vertical

捶 chuí（动）bang; pound：～背 pound sb.'s back (as in massage). ～胸顿足 beat one's breast and stamp one's feet (in deep sorrow, etc.); be mad with grief

锤 chuí（名）hammer

锤炼(煉) chuíliàn（动）1 temper 2 polish

春 chūn（名）1 spring：～风 spring breeze. ～意 savour of springtime 2 life; vitality：妙手回～. Expert medical knowledge brings the dying back to life. 3 love; lust; stirrings of love

春播 chūnbō（名）spring sowing

春耕 chūngēng（名）spring ploughing

春光 chūnguāng（名）scenes of spring：～明媚 the enchanting beauty of springtime

春季 chūnjì（名）the spring season; spring

春节(節) Chūnjié（名）the Spring Festival

春秋 chūnqiū（名）1 spring and autumn; year 2 age：～正富 in the prime of youth

春色 chūnsè（名）spring scenery：～满园 a garden permeated with the charms of springtime

春天 chūntiān（名）spring; springtime

春意盎然 chūnyì àngrán spring is in the air

淳 chún（形）〈书〉pure; honest：～厚 kind and honest. ～朴 simple-hearted and honest

醇 chún I（名）〈书〉mellow wine; good wine II（形）pure; mellow; rich：酒味～. The wine is mellow.

唇 chún（名）lip：上（下）～ upper (lower) lip

唇膏 chúngāo（名）lipstick

唇枪(槍)舌剑(劍) chúnqiāng-shéjiàn cross verbal swords; argue heatedly

唇舌 chúnshé（名）argument：费一番～ take a lot of explaining or arguing. 白费～ a waste of breath

纯 chún（形）1 pure; unmixed：～毛 pure wool 2 pure and simple：～系无稽之谈. It's nonsense, pure and simple. 3 accomplished：工夫不～. The skill is far from accomplished.

纯粹 chúncuì（形）1 pure; unadulterated 2 simply; purely：这～是为目前打算. This is purely meant to serve the present purposes.

纯洁(潔) chúnjié（形）pure; unselfish and honest：心地～ pure in thought

纯净 chúnjìng（形）pure; clean

纯利 chúnlì（名）net profit

纯朴(樸) chúnpǔ（形）simple; unsophisticated：～敦厚 simple and honest

纯熟 chúnshú（形）skilful; well versed：技术～ highly skilled

纯真 chúnzhēn（形）pure; sincere：～无邪 pure and innocent

纯正 chúnzhèng（形）pure; unadulterated：酒味～. The wine has a pure taste. 动机～ have no selfish motives

纯种(種) chúnzhǒng（名）purebred：～牛 purebred cattle

蠢 chǔn（形）stupid; foolish：～笨 clumsy; awkward. ～货 idiot; fool

蠢动(動) chǔndòng（动）1 wriggle 2 create disturbances

戳 chuō（动）jab; poke; thrust：在纸上～个洞 poke a hole in the paper

戳穿 chuōchuān（动）1 puncture 2 lay bare; expose：～谎言 give the lie to sth.

戳子 chuōzi（名）〈口〉stamp; seal

辍 chuò（动）〈书〉stop; cease：～学 discontinue one's studies

啜 chuò（动）sob：～泣 sob

绰 chuò（形）〈书〉ample; spacious：～～有余 more than enough

绰号(號) chuòhào（名）nickname

疵 cī（名）flaw; defect：～点 flaw; fault

呲 cī〈口〉give a tongue-lashing：挨了一顿～儿 get a good talking-to

瓷 cí（名）porcelain; china：～器 porcelain; chinaware. ～砖 ceramic tile; glazed tile

慈 cí (形) kind; loving

慈爱(愛) cí'ài (名) kindly affection

慈悲 cíbēi (名) mercy; benevolence; pity: 发～ have pity; be merciful

慈母 címǔ (名) loving mother

慈善 císhàn (形) charitable; benevolent; philanthropic: ～事业 charities

慈祥 cíxiáng (形) kind: ～的面容 a kind face

磁 cí (名) **1** magnetism: ～铁 magnet. ～场 magnetic field **2** porcelain; china

磁带(帶) cídài (名) tape: ～录音机 tape recorder

磁化 cíhuà (名) magnetization: ～水 magnetized water

磁卡 cíkǎ (名) magnetic card

磁盘(盤) cípán (名) (magnetic) disk

磁悬浮列车 cíxuánfú lièchē (名) maglev train

雌 cí (形) female

雌雄 cí-xióng (名) male and female: 决一～ have a showdown (to see which side will emerge victorious)

辞(辭) cí I (名) **1** diction; phraseology: 修～ rhetoric **2** a form of classical Chinese II (动) **1** take leave **2** decline **3** dismiss; resign **4** shirk: 不～劳苦 spare no effort

辞别 cíbié (动) bid farewell to; say goodbye to

辞呈 cíchéng (名) (written) resignation: 提出～ submit (or hand in) one's resignation

辞典 cídiǎn (名) dictionary; lexicon

辞令 cílìng (名) language appropriate to the occasion: 外交～ diplomatic language. 善于～ good at speech; eloquent

辞让(讓) círàng (动) politely decline

辞退 cítuì (动) dismiss; discharge

辞谢 cíxiè (动) decline with thanks

辞行 cíxíng (动) say goodbye to friends or relatives before setting out on a journey

辞藻 cízǎo (名) flowery language; rhetoric

辞职(職) cízhí (动) resign

词 cí (名) **1** word; term: 同义～ synonym. 反义～ antonym. 技术～ technical term **2** speech; statement: 开幕～ opening speech. 台～ lines (of an opera or play) **3** classical poetry conforming to a definite pattern: 宋～ such poems of the Song Dynasty

词典 cídiǎn (名) dictionary; lexicon

词法 cífǎ (名) morphology

词汇(彙) cíhuì (名) vocabulary

词句 cíjù (名) words and phrases; expressions

词类(類) cílèi (名) part of speech

词序 cíxù (名) word order

词义(義) cíyì (名) the meaning of a word

词源 cíyuán (名) etymology

词藻 cízǎo (名) rhetoric

词缀 cízhuì (名) affix

词组 cízǔ (名) word group; phrase

祠 cí (名) ancestral temple: ～堂 ancestral hall

此 cǐ (代) this: ～处 this place; here. ～人 this man. ～等 this kind. ～辈 such people

此后(後) cǐhòu (连) after this; hereafter

此刻 cǐkè (名) at this moment; now

此路不通 cǐ lù bù tōng **1** No Through Road (road sign) **2** blind alley

此起彼伏 cǐqǐ-bǐfú rise and fall alternately; recur

此时(時) cǐshí (名) right now: ～此刻 at this very moment. ～此地 here and now

此外 cǐwài (连) besides; moreover; in addition

此致 cǐzhì (动) greetings written at the end of a letter addressed to somebody by name

次 cì I (名) order; sequence: 依～ one by one in due order. 车～ train number. 五～列车 train No. 5 II (形) **1** second; next: ～日 next day **2** second-rate; inferior: ～品 goods of poor quality; defective goods III(量): 三～ three times. 首～ first time

次大陆(陸) cìdàlù (名) subcontinent

次贷 cìdài (名) subprime: ～危机 subprime mortgage crisis

次等 cìděng (形) second-class; inferior

次品 cìpǐn (名) substandard products; defective goods

次数(數) cìshù (名) number of times; frequency: ～不多 not very often

次序 cìxù (名) order; sequence

次要 cìyào (形) less important; secondary; minor

刺 cì I (名) thorn; splinter: 鱼～ small bone of a fish. 手上扎了个～ get a thorn (or splinter) in one's hand. 她说话带～. There was a ring of sarcasm in her words. II (动) **1** prick; stab **2** assassinate: 被～ be assassinated **3** irritate; criticize: 讽～ satirize

刺刀 cìdāo (名) bayonet

刺耳 cì'ěr (形) ear-piercing; unpleasant to the ear: ～的话 harsh words

刺骨 cìgǔ (形) piercing to the bones; biting

刺激 cìjī (动) 1 stimulate: 物质～ material incentive 2 upset; irritate

刺客 cìkè (名) assassin

刺杀(殺) cìshā I (动) assassinate II (名) bayonet charge

刺探 cìtàn (动) make secret inquiries; pry; spy: ～军情 gather military intelligence

刺猬 cìwèi (名) hedgehog

刺绣 cìxiù (名) embroidery

刺眼 cìyǎn (形) dazzling; offending to the eye: 亮得～ dazzlingly bright. 打扮得～ be loudly dressed

赐

cì I (动) grant II (名) gift: 赏～ grant (or bestow) a reward. 请即～复. Be so kind as to give me a prompt reply.

伺

cì

see also sì

伺候 cìhou (动) wait on; serve: 难～ hard to please; fastidious

聪(聰)

cōng

聪慧 cōnghuì (形) bright; intelligent

聪明 cōngmíng (形) intelligent; bright; clever: ～能干 bright and capable

聪颖 cōngyǐng (形) intelligent; bright

匆

cōng hurriedly; hastily: 来去～～ pay sb. a flying visit; make hurried visits

匆促 cōngcù (形) hastily; in a hurry: 时间～ be pressed for time

匆忙 cōngmáng (形) hastily; in a hurry: 走得很～ leave in a hurry

葱

cōng (名) onion; scallion: 大～ green Chinese onion. 小～ spring onion. 洋～ onion

葱翠 cōngcuì (形) fresh green

葱花 cōnghuā (名) chopped spring onion

葱绿 cōnglǜ (形) pale yellowish green

淙

cóng

淙淙 cóngcóng (象) gurgling: 流水～ a gurgling stream

从(從)

cóng I (介) [used to indicate the starting point] from; pass by: ～现在起 from now on. 河水～桥下流过. The river flows by under the bridge. 火车～这个隧道通过. The train passes through this tunnel. ～东到西 from east to west. ～昏迷中醒过来 regain consciousness (from a coma). ～理论上讲 theoretically speaking II (副) [equivalent to 从来 when used before a negative word] ever: 我～没去过意大利. I've never been to Italy. III (动) 1 follow; obey; adopt: ～命 comply with sb.'s wish. ～宽处理 treat leniently 2 join: ～军 join the army; enlist IV (名) 1 follower; attendant: 随～ attendant 2 secondary; accessary: 主～ the primary and the secondary

从此 cóngcǐ (连) from now on; since then; henceforth

从…到… cóng…dào… from. . . to . . . : 从早到晚 from morning till night. 从古到今 from ancient times to the present. 从头到尾 from beginning to end. 从上到下 from top to bottom; from the higher levels to grass roots

从而 cóng'ér (连) thus; thereby

从犯 cóngfàn (名) accessory

从简 cóngjiǎn (动) conform to the principle of simplicity

从句 cóngjù (名) subordinate clause

从来(來) cónglái (副) always; all along: 他～没提过这事. He's never mentioned this before.

从略 cónglüè (动) be omitted: 此处引文～. The quotation is omitted here.

从前 cóngqián (名) before; in the past; formerly: 他～不是这样. He wasn't like this before.

从容 cóngróng (形) 1 calm; unhurried: ～不迫 remain cool-headed and steady 2 plentiful: 时间很～. There's still plenty of time.

从事 cóngshì (动) 1 go in for; be engaged in: ～科研工作 be engaged in scientific research. ～文学创作 take up writing as a profession; be engaged in literary work. ～技术革新 work on technical innovations 2 deal with: 慎重～ act cautiously; steer a cautious course

从属(屬) cóngshǔ (动) be subordinate to: ～地位 subordinate status

从速 cóngsù (副) as soon as possible; without delay: ～处理 attend to the matter as soon as possible

从头(頭) cóngtóu (副) from the beginning

从小 cóngxiǎo (副) from childhood: 他～就

喜欢画画. He's loved painting ever since he was a child.

从业(業) cóngyè (动) obtain employment: ～人员 the employed

从中 cóngzhōng (副) out of; from among; therefrom: ～渔利 profit from. ～吸取教训 draw a lesson from it

C

从(叢) cóng (名) 1 clump; thicket: 树～ bush; shrubbery 2 a group of people or things

丛林 cónglín (名) jungle; forest

丛生 cóngshēng (动) grow thickly: 荆棘～ be overgrown with brambles

丛书(書) cóngshū (名) a series of books; collection: 自学～ selfstudy series

凑 còu (动) 1 put (or gather) together; pool: ～在一起 crowd together. ～钱 raise a fund 2 happen by chance; take advantage of: 正～上是个星期天. It happened to be a Sunday. 3 move close to

凑合 còuhe I (动) 1 gather together 2 make do: 有什么就～着用什么吧. Let's make do with what we have. II (形) passable: 他的英文还～. His English is not too bad.

凑巧 còuqiǎo (形) luckily; by coincidence; as luck would have it

凑趣儿(兒) còuqùr (动) show a similar interest (just to please sb.)

凑热(熱)闹 còu rènào 1 join in the fun 2 add trouble to: 他们够忙的了,别再去～了. They're busy enough as it is. Leave them alone.

凑数(數) còushù (动) make up the number or amount

粗 cū I (形) 1 thick: ～绳 a thick rope 2 coarse; crude; rough: ～砂纸 coarse sandpaper. ～盐 crude salt. 活干得很～. The work is crudely done. 3 husky; hoarse (of sb.'s voice): ～声～气 with a gruff voice 4 careless; negligent: ～疏 be careless. ～心大意 be negligent 5 rude; coarse; unrefined: ～人 a blunt man. ～里～气 rough 6 roughly: ～具规模 roughly put sth. into shape

粗暴 cūbào (形) rude; rough; brutal

粗笨 cūbèn (形) clumsy; unwieldy

粗糙 cūcāo (形) rough; coarse; crude: 皮肤～ rough skin. 做工～ crudely made; of poor workmanship

粗茶淡饭 cūchá-dànfàn homely meal

粗放 cūfàng (形) 1 free and easy 2 extensive: ～型发展 extensive growth

粗犷(獷) cūguǎng (形) 1 rugged; straightforward and uninhibited 2 rough; boorish

粗话 cūhuà (名) coarse language

粗活 cūhuó (名) heavy manual labour; unskilled work

粗粮(糧) cūliáng (名) coarse food grain (e.g. maize, sorghum, millet, etc. as distinct from wheat and rice)

粗劣 cūliè (形) of poor quality

粗陋 cūlòu (形) coarse and crude

粗鲁 cūlǔ (形) rude; boorish

粗略 cūlüè (形) rough; sketchy: ～的了解 some rough ideas about sth.

粗浅(淺) cūqiǎn (形) superficial; shallow

粗疏 cūshū (形) careless; inattentive

粗率 cūshuài (形) rough and careless; ill-considered: ～的决定 an ill-considered decision

粗俗 cūsú (形) coarse; unrefined

粗心 cūxīn (形) careless; thoughtless: ～大意 negligent; careless; inadvertent

粗野 cūyě (形) rude; boorish

粗枝大叶(葉) cūzhī-dàyè crude and careless; sloppy; slapdash

粗制(製)滥(濫)造 cūzhì-lànzào manufacture in a crude and slipshod way

粗壮(壯) cūzhuàng (形) 1 sturdy; brawny; strong: 身材～ be sturdily built 2 (of voice) deep and resonant

猝 cù (形)〈书〉sudden; abrupt; unexpected

猝然 cùrán (副) suddenly; abruptly; unexpectedly

簇 cù I (量) cluster; bunch: 一～鲜花 a bunch of flowers II (动) form a cluster; pile up: 花团锦～ rich multi-coloured decorations

簇新 cùxīn (形) brand new

簇拥(擁) cùyōng (动) cluster round (sb.)

醋 cù (名) 1 vinegar 2 jealousy (as in love affairs): 吃～ feel jealous. ～意 (feeling of) jealousy

促 cù I (动) promote; urge II (形) hurried; urgent: 呼吸短～ pant; be short of breath

促成 cùchéng (动) help to bring about; facilitate

促进(進) cùjìn (动) promote; accelerate: ～贸易 promote trade

促使 cùshǐ (动) impel; spur; encourage

促销 cùxiāo (动) have a sales promotion: 打

~战 launch a sales campaign
促膝谈心 cù xī tánxīn sit side by side and talk intimately; have a heart-to-heart talk
蹿(躥) cuān (动) leap up
窜(竄) cuàn (动) flee; scurry: 东逃西~ flee in all directions. 鼠~ scurry like rats
窜犯 cuànfàn (动) raid: ~边境的匪徒 the bandits that invaded the border area
窜扰(擾) cuànrǎo (动) harass: ~活动 harassment
窜逃 cuàntáo (动) flee in disorder; scurry off
篡 cuàn (动) usurp: ~权 usurp power. ~位 usurp the throne
篡夺(奪) cuànduó (动) usurp; seize
篡改 cuàngǎi (动) tamper with; falsify: ~历史 distort history
摧 cuī (动) destroy: ~折 break; snap: 无坚不~ all-conquering
摧残(殘) cuīcán (动) wreck; destroy; devastate: ~身体 ruin one's health
摧毁 cuīhuǐ (动) shatter; smash; destroy
摧枯拉朽 cuīkū-lāxiǔ (as easy as) crushing dry undergrowth and smashing rotten wood
催 cuī (动) hurry; urge; press; speed up: ~办 press sb. to expedite some business matter
催促 cuīcù (动) urge; press; hasten
催眠 cuīmián (动) lull (to sleep); hypnotize; mesmerize: ~曲 lullaby
催命 cuīmìng (动) persistently urge; press hard
璀 cuǐ
璀璨 cuǐcàn (形)〈书〉bright: ~夺目 dazzling
淬 cuì (动) temper by dipping in water, oil, etc.; quench: ~火 quench
淬砺(礪) cuìlì (动)〈书〉temper oneself through severe trials
瘁 cuì〈书〉overworked; tired: 心力交~ be physically and mentally tired from overwork
粹 cuì I (形) pure II (名) essence; the best: 精~ essence
啐 cuì (动) spit: ~他一口 spit at him
翠 cuì (形) emerald green; green
翠绿 cuìlǜ (形) emerald green; jade green
脆 cuì (形) 1 fragile; brittle: 这纸太~. This kind of paper is too fragile. 2 crisp: ~梨 crisp pear 3 (of voice) clear: 嗓音~ a crisp voice
脆弱 cuìruò (形) (of health or feelings) fragile; frail; weak : 感情~ emotionally fragile
村 cūn (名) village: ~庄 village; hamlet
村口 cūnkǒu (名) entrance to a village
村镇 cūnzhèn (名) villages and small towns
皴 cūn (动) (of skin) chapped (from the cold); cracked: 孩子的手~了. The child's hands were chapped from the cold.
存 cún (动) 1 exist; live; survive 2 store; keep; preserve: ~粮过冬 store up grain for the winter 3 place sth. for safe keeping; deposit: 把钱~在银行里 put money in a bank. ~自行车 park one's bicycle. ~行李 check one's luggage 4 cherish; harbour: 不~幻想 harbour no illusions
存车(車)处(處) cúnchēchù (名) parking lot (for bicycles)
存储 cúnchǔ (名) storage; memory: ~容量 memory capacity. ~器 memory (of a computer)
存档(檔) cúndàng (动) keep in the archives; file
存放 cúnfàng (动) leave in sb.'s care
存根 cúngēn (名) counterfoil; stub: 支票~ cheque stub
存户 cúnhù (名) depositor
存活 cúnhuó (动) survive: ~率 rate of survival
存货 cúnhuò (名) goods in stock: 减价出清~ a clearance sale
存款 cúnkuǎn (名) deposit; bank savings: 活期~ current account. 定期~ deposit or savings account
存盘(盤) cúnpán (动) save (a document to a computer disk)
存亡 cún-wáng (动) live or die; survive or perish: 生死~的战斗 a life-and-death struggle
存心 cúnxīn (副) intentionally; deliberately; on purpose: 我不是~这么做的. I didn't do it on purpose.
存疑 cúnyí (动) leave a question open

存在 cúnzài (动) exist: ～这种可能性. There is the possibility. *or* It is possible.

存折 cúnzhé (名) deposit book; bankbook

忖 cǔn (动) turn sth. over in one's mind: ～度 ponder; speculate

D

寸 cùn I (量) *cun*, a unit of length (= 1/30 metre) II (形) little; small: ～进 a little progress. 得～进尺 be insatiable

寸步 cùnbù (名) a tiny step; a single step: ～难行 unable to move a single step. ～不离 follow sb. closely; keep close to sb. ～不让 refuse to yield

磋 cuō (动) consult

磋商 cuōshāng (动) consult: 我们将与有关部门～后决定. We'll make a decision after consultation with the departments concerned.

搓 cuō (动) rub with the hands

搓板 cuōbǎn (名) washboard

蹉 cuō

蹉跎 cuōtuó (动) waste time: ～岁月 idle away one's time

撮 cuō I (动) scoop up II (量) pinch: 一～盐 a pinch of salt. 一小～匪徒 a handful of bandits

撮合 cuōhé (动) make a match; act as go-between

撮弄 cuōnòng (动) 1 make fun of; play a trick on; tease 2 abet; instigate; incite

措 cuò (动) arrange; manage; handle: ～置得当 be handled properly. 惊慌失～ be seized with panic. 不知所～ be at a loss what to do; be at one's wit's end

措辞(辭) cuòcí (名) wording; diction: ～不当 inappropriate wording. ～强硬 strongly worded

措施 cuòshī (名) measure; suitable action: 采取重大～ adopt an important measure

措手不及 cuò shǒu bù jí be caught unprepared: 打他个～ make a surprise attack on them

措置 cuòzhì (动) handle; manage; arrange: ～得当 be handled properly

错 cuò I (名) mistake; error; fault: 她没～,别怪她. It's not her fault, don't blame her. II (形) 1 wrong; mistaken; erroneous: ～字 wrong character. 你弄～了. You've got it wrong. 东西拿～了 take sth. by mistake 2 interlocked and jagged: 犬牙交～ jigsaw-like; interlocking. ～综复杂 intricate; complex III (动) 1 alternate; stagger: 把他们的假期～开. Stagger their holidays. 2 grind; rub: ～牙 grind one's teeth

错爱(愛) cuò'ài (动) 〈谦〉 undeserved kindness

错车(車) cuòchē (动) (of vehicle) give the right of way: 互相～ make way for each other

错怪 cuòguài (动) blame sb. wrongly

错过(過) cuòguò (动) miss; let slip: ～机会 miss an opportunity

错觉(覺) cuòjué (名) illusion; misconception: 这样会给人造成～. This will give people a false impression.

错乱(亂) cuòluàn (形) in disorder: 精神～ insane

错落 cuòluò (形) strewn at random: ～有致 in picturesque disorder. ～不齐 scattered here and there

错失 cuòshī (动) miss; let slip: ～良机 let slip a golden opportunity

错位 cuòwèi (动) malposition; misplace; dislocate

错误 cuòwù I (名) mistake; error: 犯～ make a mistake; commit an error. ～百出 full of mistakes II (形) wrong; mistaken; erroneous: ～的结论 wrong conclusion

错综复(複)杂(雜) cuòzōng-fùzá intricate; complex

挫 cuò (动) 1 frustrate; defeat 2 subdue; lower: ～其锋芒 blunt the edge of one's advance. ～敌人的锐气 deflate the enemy's arrogance

挫败 cuòbài (动) frustrate; thwart; defeat

挫伤(傷) cuòshāng I (名) bruise II (动) discourage

挫折 cuòzhé (名) setback; reverse: 遭受～ suffer setbacks

锉 cuò I (名) file: ～刀 file II (动) make smooth with a file; file

D d

搭 dā (动) 1 put up; build: ～桥 put up a bridge. ～帐篷 pitch a tent 2 hang over; put over 3 come into contact; join: 他们已经～上了关系. They have established contact. **4** add; chip in: 我现在只能～上二三十元钱. I can only afford to put in some twenty or thirty *yuan* at the moment. **5** carry: 请你把我这台电视机～回家吧. Please help carry this TV set home (in your car). **6** take (a ship, plane, etc.); travel (or go) by: ～火车去上海 go to Shanghai by train. ～长途汽车 travel by coach. 你～我的车吧. Let me give you a lift in my car.

搭车 dāchē (动) **1** go by bus, car, etc. **2** take the opportunity by following suit: ～效应 chain reaction

搭档(檔) dādàng I (动) cooperate; team up II (名) partner: 老～ old partner

搭话 dāhuà (动) strike up a conversation; get a word in

搭伙 dāhuǒ (动) **1** join as one the party going somewhere **2** eat regularly in (a mess, etc.)

搭救 dājiù (动) rescue; go to one's rescue

搭配 dāpèi I (动) arrange (in pairs or group); combine II (名) collocation

搭腔 dāqiāng (动) answer; respond: 我提醒他约会时间,但他没有～. I reminded him of the appointment, but he didn't make any response.

搭桥(橋) dāqiáo (动) **1** put up a bridge **2** be a matchmaker; serve as a bridge

搭讪 dāshàn (动) strike up a conversation with sb.; make some humorous remarks to save face

搭手 dāshǒu (动) give a hand; help

答 dā

see also dá

答理 dāli (动) [often used in a negative sentence] respond; acknowledge sb.'s greeting, etc.: 他甚至不～我. He didn't even return my greeting.

答应(應) dāying (动) **1** answer; reply; respond: 我敲了几下门,但没人～. I knocked at the door several times, but there was no answer. **2** promise; agree: 他～帮我的忙. He promised to help me.

耷 dā (形) 〈书〉 big-eared

耷拉 dāla (动) droop; hang down: 他～着肩膀. His shoulders drooped.

达(達) dá (动) **1** reach; attain: 我们不～目的决不罢休. We will never give up until we achieve our goal. 总数已～三千. The total figure has reached 3,000. **2** express; convey; communicate: 下～命令 give orders. 词不～意. Words fail to convey one's ideas. 通情～理 be understanding and reasonable **3** extend: 铁路四通八～. The railways extend in all directions.

达标(標) dábiāo (动) reach a set standard

达成 dáchéng (动) reach; conclude: ～一项协议 reach an agreement. ～交易 strike a bargain

达旦 dádàn (动) until dawn

达到 dádào (动) achieve; attain; reach: ～目的 achieve (or attain) the goal. ～要求 meet the requirements. ～高潮 come to a climax

达观(觀) dáguān (形) taking things philosophically

达官贵人 dáguān-guìrén high-ranking officials; dignitaries

达意 dáyì (动) have successfully conveyed (or expressed) one's ideas

打 dá (量) dozen: 一～袜子 a dozen socks. 论～出售 sell by the dozen

see also dǎ

答 dá (动) **1** answer; reply; respond: ～非所问 make an irrelevant reply **2** return (a visit, etc.); reciprocate: ～礼 return a salute

see also dā

答案 dá'àn (名) answer; solution; 问题的～ solution to the problem. 练习～ key to an exercise

答辩(辯) dábiàn (动) reply (to a charge, query or an argument): ～会 oral examination for M.A. or Ph.D. candidates, etc.

答复(復) dáfù (动) reply (formally)

答谢 dáxiè (动) extend appreciation (for sb.'s kindness or hospitality): ～宴会 a return banquet

答疑 dáyí (动) answer questions

沓 dá (量) pile (of paper; etc.); pad: 一～报纸 a pile of newspapers. 一～信纸 a pad of letter paper

see also tà

打 dǎ I (动) **1** strike; hit; beat: ～稻子 thresh rice **2** break; smash. 碗～了. The bowl is broken. **3** fight; attack: ～仗 fight a battle. ～游击 fight as a guerrilla **4** construct; build: ～坝 con-

struct a dam. ～基础 lay a foundation **5** make (in a smithy); forge: ～首饰 make jewellery. ～刀 forge a knife **6** knit; weave: ～草鞋 plait straw sandals. ～毛衣 knit a sweater **7** make a mark on; draw: ～手印 put one's fingerprint (on a document). ～印 mimeograph. ～问号 put a question mark. ～格子 draw squares (on paper etc.) **8** tie up: ～行李 pack one's luggage; pack up **9** spray; spread: ～农药 spray insecticide. 在地板上～蜡 wax the floor **10** dig; bore: ～井 dig (or sink) a well **11** raise; hoist: ～伞 hold (or put) up an umbrella. ～起精神来 raise one's spirits **12** send; dispatch: ～电报 send a telegram. ～电话 make a phone call. ～信号 give a signal. ～枪 fire a gun **13** remove; get rid of: ～旁杈 prune the side branches **14** draw; fetch: ～开水 fetch boiled water. 从井里～水 draw water from a well **15** collect; reap: ～柴 gather firewood. ～了一千斤粮食 get in 1,000 *jin* of grain **16** buy: ～油 buy oil. ～饭 buy food and take it out from a canteen **17** catch; hunt: ～鱼 catch fish. ～鸟 shoot a bird **18** work out; draw: ～草稿 draw a draft **19** do; engage in: ～短工 work as a seasonal labourer. ～夜班 be on the night shift **20** play: ～篮球 play basketball. ～太极拳 do *taiji* (shadow boxing). ～扑克 play cards **21** [indicate certain body movements]: ～哆嗦 shiver. ～手势 make a gesture. ～喷嚏 sneeze **22** adopt; use: ～个比方 draw an analogy **23** estimate; reckon: 成本～二百块钱 estimate the cost at 200 *yuan* II (介) from; since: 你～哪儿来? Where did you come from? ～那以后 since then

see also dá

打靶 dǎbǎ (名) target (or shooting) practice

打败 dǎbài (动) **1** defeat; beat **2** suffer a defeat; be defeated

打扮 dǎbàn (动) dress up; make up; deck out

打包 dǎbāo (动) **1** bale; pack **2** (in a restaurant) have a doggie bag

打抱不平 dǎ bàobùpíng interfere on behalf of the injured party

打草惊(驚)蛇 dǎ cǎo jīng shé act rashly and alert the enemy: 不要～. Let sleeping dogs lie.

打岔 dǎchà (动) interrupt; cut in: 别～吧! 我还没说完呢. Don't interrupt me, please! I haven't finished yet.

打场(場) dǎcháng (动) thresh grain

打成一片 dǎchéng yīpiàn become one with; identify oneself with

打倒 dǎdǎo (动) overthrow; down with

打得火热(熱) dǎde huǒrè be very thick with each other

打的 dǎdí (动) take a taxi

打动(動) dǎdòng (动) move; touch: 这番话～了他的心. He was moved by these words.

打赌 dǎdǔ (动) bet; wager: 我敢～, 他明天准来. I bet he'll come tomorrow.

打断(斷) dǎduàn (动) **1** break **2** interrupt: ～思路 interrupt sb.'s train of thought. ～别人的话 cut sb. short

打盹儿(兒) dǎdǔnr doze off; take a nap

打发(發) dǎfa (动) **1** send; dispatch: 赶快～人去请医生. Send for a doctor at once. **2** dismiss; send away: 他把孩子们～走了. He sent the children away. **3** while away (one's time)

打翻 dǎfān (动) overturn; capsize: 一个大浪把小船～了. A huge wave capsized the boat.

打工 dǎgōng (动) work for others; be employed: 业余时间打打工 pick up a part-time job after work. ～仔 manual worker

打躬作揖 dǎgōng-zuòyī bow and scrape

打官腔 dǎ guānqiāng speak in bureaucratic jargon

打官司 dǎ guānsi go to law

打哈欠 dǎ hāqian yawn

打鼾 dǎhān (动) snore

打火 dǎhuǒ (动) strike sparks from a flint: ～机 lighter

打击(擊) dǎjī I (动) hit; strike; attack II (名) blow; attack

打架 dǎjià (动) engage in a brawl; come to blows; fight

打假 dǎjiǎ (动) crack down on counterfeit goods

打交道 dǎ jiāodao have dealings with; come into contact with: 那个人容易～. That chap is easy to get along with.

打搅(攪) dǎjiǎo (动) disturb; trouble: 请别～. Please do not disturb.

打劫 dǎjié (动) rob; plunder; loot: 趁火～ loot a burning house

打卡 dǎkǎ (动) punch a card

打开(開) dǎkāi (动) 1 open; unfold: ~窗户 open the window. 把盖子~ take off the lid. ~天窗说亮话 frankly speaking 2 turn on; switch on: ~收音机(电灯) turn on the radio (light)

打瞌睡 dǎ kēshuì doze off; nod

打捞(撈) dǎlāo (动) get out of the water; salvage: ~沉船 salvage a sunken ship

打雷 dǎléi (动) thunder

打量 dǎliang (动) measure with the eye; size up: 上下~ look sb. up and down

打猎(獵) dǎliè (动) go hunting

打乱(亂) dǎluàn (动) throw into confusion; upset: ~计划 disrupt a plan; upset a scheme

打落水狗 dǎ luòshuǐgǒu completely crush a defeated enemy

打马虎眼 dǎ mǎhuyǎn pretend to be ignorant of sth. (in order to gloss it over); act dumb

打埋伏 dǎ máifu 1 lie in ambush; set an ambush; ambush 2 hold sth. back for one's own use

打破 dǎpò (动) break; smash: ~僵局 break a deadlock. ~记录 break a record. ~沙锅问到底 insist on getting to the bottom of the matter

打气(氣) dǎqì (动) 1 inflate; pump up: 给车胎~ inflate (or pump up) a tyre. ~筒 tyre pump 2 bolster up (or boost) the morale; encourage

打趣 dǎqù (动) tease; make fun of

打拳 dǎquán (动) do shadowboxing

打扰(擾) dǎrǎo (动) disturb

打扫(掃) dǎsǎo (动) clean; sweep: ~房间 clean a room

打手 dǎshǒu (名) hired roughneck (or thug); hatchet man

打算 dǎsuàn I (动) plan; intend II (名) plan; intention

打碎 dǎsuì (动) break into pieces; smash: 花瓶~了. The vase is smashed to pieces.

打胎 dǎtāi (动) have an (induced) abortion

打铁(鐵) dǎtiě (动) forge iron: 趁热~ strike while the iron's hot

打听(聽) dǎting (动) ask about; inquire about: 你可以去附近派出所~一下. You can make inquiries at the police station nearby.

打通 dǎtōng (动) get through; open up: 湖底~一条甬道. A passage was tunnelled under the lake. ~思想 talk sb. round

打退堂鼓 dǎ tuìtánggǔ beat a retreat; back out

打消 dǎxiāo (动) give up; dispel: 她~了出国的念头. She gave up the idea of going abroad.

打印 dǎyìn (动) mimeograph

打油诗 dǎyóushī (名) doggerel; ragged verse

打鱼(魚) dǎyú (动) fish: 以~为生 fish for a living

打杂(雜)儿(兒) dǎzár (动) do odds and ends

打战(戰) dǎzhàn (动) shiver; tremble; shudder: 她吓得浑身~. She trembled with fear.

打仗 dǎzhàng (动) fight a battle; go to war

打招呼 dǎ zhāohu 1 greet sb. (by word or gesture) 2 notify; inform; give sb. a tip

打折扣 dǎ zhékòu 1 sell at a discount; give a discount 2 fall short of a requirement or promise

打针 dǎzhēn (动) give or receive an injection

打主意 dǎ zhǔyi 1 think of a plan: 打定主意 make up one's mind 2 try to obtain; seek: 他正在打你的主意,要你帮忙呢. He is thinking of enlisting your help.

打字 dǎzì (动) typewrite; type: ~机 typewriter. ~员 typist

打坐 dǎzuò (动) (of a Buddhist or Taoist monk) sit in meditation

大 dà I (形) 1 big; large; great: ~房间 a large room. ~问题 a big problem. ~团结 great unity 2 heavy; strong: ~风~雨 heavy rain and strong wind 3 loud: 声音太~ too loud 4 of age: 你的孩子多~了? How old is your child? 5 eldest: ~哥 eldest brother. 老~ the eldest among the brothers and sisters 6 main; major; general: ~路 main road. ~手术 major operation 7 of size: 你穿多~的鞋? What size shoes do you wear? 8 [used to give force to a time word or expression]: ~白天 in broad daylight. ~清早 early in the morning II (副) 1 greatly; fully; in a big way; on a large scale: ~笑 laugh heartily. ~哭 cry bitterly. ~闹一场 make a big scene 2 [used after 不 to indicate low degree or frequency]: 她不~会说英语. She doesn't speak much English. 我不~出门. I sel-

dom go out.
see also dài

大白 dàbái (动) come out; become known: 真相～ The truth has been brought to light.

大白菜 dàbáicài (名) Chinese cabbage

D

大半 dàbàn I (名) more than half; most: 来客中～是妇女. Most of the guests were women. II (副) very likely; most probably

大本 dàběn (名) 4-year university undergraduate program leading to a BA degree

大本营(營) dàběnyíng (名) base camp; headquarters

大便 dàbiàn (名) bowel movement; shit: ～不通 (suffer from) constipation

大伯 dàbó (名) father's elder brother; uncle

大部 dàbù (名) greater part

大材小用 dàcái xiǎo yòng waste one's talent on a petty job

大臣 dàchén (名) minister (of a monarchy)

大吃大喝 dàchī dàhē eat and drink to one's heart's content; have extravagantly lavish meals

大吹大擂 dàchuī-dàléi make a great fanfare; make a big noise

大慈大悲 dàcí-dàbēi infinitely merciful

大打出手 dà dǎ chūshǒu strike violently; attack brutally

大大 dàdà (副) greatly; enormously: 生产效率～提高. Productivity has risen greatly.

大…大… dà…dà… [placed before related nouns, verbs or adjectives as an intensifier]: 大红大绿 loud colours. 大吵大闹 make a scene; set up a terrific racket. 大吃大喝 eat and drink immoderately. 大鱼大肉 plenty of meat and fish

大大咧咧 dàdàliēliē (of a person) careless; casual

大胆(膽) dàdǎn (形) bold; daring; audacious

大刀阔斧 dàdāo-kuòfǔ boldly and resolutely; drastically

大道 dàdào (名) 1 broad road 2 the way to a bright future

大抵 dàdǐ (副) generally speaking; in the main

大地 dàdì (名) the earth: ～回春. Spring returns to the earth.

大典 dàdiǎn (名) grand ceremony

大动(動)脉(脈) dàdòngmài (名) main artery

大豆 dàdòu (名) soybean

大都 dàdū (副) for the most part; mostly

大度 dàdù (形)〈书〉magnanimous: ～宽容 magnanimous and tolerant

大队(隊) dàduì (名) 1 a military unit corresponding to the battalion or regiment 2 a large body of: ～人马 large contingent of troops

大多 dàduō (副) for the most part; mostly

大多数(數) dàduōshù (名) great majority; vast majority; the bulk

大而化之 dà ér huà zhī carelessly; sloppily

大发(發)雷霆 dà fā léitíng fly into a violent rage

大凡 dàfán (副) generally; in most cases

大方 dàfang (形) natural and poised; unaffected: 举止～ behave with grace and ease. 这衣服款式很～. The style of this dress is in good taste.

大放厥词 dàfàng jué cí spout a stream of empty rhetoric; be full of sound and fury

大粪(糞) dàfèn (名) human excrement; night soil

大腹便便 dàfù piánpián pot-bellied; big-bellied

大概 dàgài I (形) general; rough; approximate: 一个～印象 a general impression. ～数字 an approximate figure II (副) probably: 他～病了. He is probably ill. III (名) general idea: 我只记了个～. I have only some rough idea.

大纲(綱) dàgāng (名) general outline

大哥大 dàgēdà (名) cellular phone; cellphone; mobile phone

大公无(無)私 dàgōng-wúsī selfless; unselfish

大功 dàgōng (名) great merit; extraordinary service: 立了～ have performed exceptionally meritorious services. ～告成 be crowned with success

大观(觀) dàguān (名) grand sight: 洋洋～ spectacular; grandiose; imposing

大规模 dàguīmó large-scale; extensive; massive: ～生产 mass production. ～植树 plant trees on a large scale

大锅(鍋)饭 dàguōfàn (名) food prepared in a big pot: 吃～ with everybody eating from the same big pot

大海捞(撈)针 dàhǎi lāo zhēn look for a needle in a haystack

大好 dàhǎo (形) very good: ～时机 golden opportunity

大合唱 dàhéchàng (名) cantata; chorus

大亨 dàhēng (名) magnate

大红 dàhóng (形) bright red; scarlet

大话 dàhuà (名) big talk; boast: 说～ talk big; brag

大伙儿(兒) dàhuǒr (代) we all; all of us

大计 dàjì (名) a programme of lasting importance: 百年～ a matter of fundamental importance for generations to come

大家 dàjiā I (代) all; everybody II (名) great master; authority: 书法～ a great master of calligraphy

大街 dàjiē (名) main street; avenue; street: 逛～ have a look round in the business centre; go window-shopping

大惊(驚)小怪 dàjīng-xiǎoguài make a fuss over: 有什么值得～的? What's all the fuss about?

大局 dàjú (名) **1** overall public interest: 顾全～ take the interests of the whole into account **2** overall situation: ～已定. There is no doubt about the overall situation.

大快人心 dà kuài rénxīn gratify the popular feeling; to the immense satisfaction of the masses

大款 dàkuǎn (名) tycoon; moneybags

大理石 dàlǐshí (名) marble

大力 dàlì (副) vigorously; energetically: ～提倡 make strenuous efforts to promote

大量 dàliàng (形) **1** a large number; a great quantity: ～情报 a vast amount of information. ～财富 enormous wealth. ～事实 a host of facts **2** generous; magnanimous: 宽宏～ magnanimous; large-minded

大楼(樓) dàlóu (名) large building: 居民～ apartment house; block of flats

大陆(陸) dàlù (名) continent; mainland: ～架 continental shelf

大略 dàlüè (副) generally; roughly

大麻 dàmá (名) **1** hemp **2** marijuana

大米 dàmǐ (名) rice

大名鼎鼎 dàmíng dǐngdǐng famous; well-known; celebrated

大模大样(様) dàmú-dàyàng in an ostentatious manner; with a swagger

大拇指 dàmǔzhǐ (名) thumb

大难(難) dànàn (名) disaster; catastrophe

大脑(腦) dànǎo (名) cerebrum

大逆不道 dà nì bú dào high treason and heresy; worst offence

大年 dànián (名) **1** good year; bumper year; (of fruit trees) on-year **2** lunar year

大牌 dàpái (名) big name: ～歌星 big-name singer

大批 dàpī (形) large quantities or number: ～工厂 a large number of factories. ～金钱 a large sum (or amount) of money

大气(氣) dàqì (名) **1** atmosphere; air: ～层 atmospheric layer. ～污染 air pollution **2** heavy breathing: 跑得直喘～ breathe heavily from running

大权(權) dàquán (名) power over major issues; authority: ～独揽 concentrate power in one man's hands

大人 dàren (名) **1** adult; grown-up **2** 〈旧〉 Your Excellency

大人物 dàrénwù (名) big shot; dignitary

大扫(掃)除 dàsǎochú (名) thorough clean-up

大厦 dàshà (名) large building

大赦 dàshè (名) amnesty; general pardon

大声(聲)疾呼 dàshēng jíhū utter fervent words of warning (usually against danger)

大失所望 dà shī suǒ wàng greatly disappointed

大师(師) dàshī (名) great master: 国画～ a great master of traditional Chinese painting

大师(師)傅 dàshifu (名) cook; chef

大使 dàshǐ (名) ambassador: ～馆 embassy

大事 dàshì I (名) major event; important matter: 头等～ a matter of vital importance II (副) in a big way: ～渲染 grossly embellish; exaggerate

大势(勢) dàshì (名) general trend of events: ～所趋 the trend of the times. ～已去. The game is up. *or* The situation is hopeless.

大手大脚 dàshǒu-dàjiǎo wasteful; extravagant

大肆 dàsì (副) without restraint; wantonly: ～宣扬 propagate unrestrainedly. ～吹嘘 boast

大…特… dà…tè… [each placed before the same verb or adjective as an intensifier]: 大错特错 be grievously mistaken. 大书特书 write volumes about

大提琴 dàtíqín (名) violoncello; cello

大体(體) dàtǐ I (副) on the whole; by and large; roughly: ～相同 more or less the same II (名) general interest; funda-

mental principle: 识～,顾大局 keep both the cardinal principles and the overall situation in mind
大庭广(廣)众(衆) dàtíng-guǎng-zhòng a big crowd in a big courtyard; in public; openly before everybody

D

大同小异(異) dàtóng-xiǎoyì similar in major principles but different on minor points
大腕 dàwàn (名) star; master-hand: ～歌星 pop star. ～人物 celebrity
大王 dàwáng (名) king; magnate
大显(顯)身手 dà xiǎn shēnshǒu display all one's skill or ability
大显(顯)神通 dà xiǎn shéntōng give full play to one's power or remarkable skill
大相径(徑)庭 dà xiāng jìng tíng 〈书〉 be widely divergent; seriously contradict each other
大小 dàxiǎo (名) **1** size: 这鞋我穿上～正合适. These shoes are just my size. **2** big or small: ～五个图书馆 five libraries of varying sizes **3** degree of seniority: 说话没个～ speak bluntly to elderly people **4** adults and children: 全家～五口. There are five people in the family altogether.
大写(寫) dàxiě (名) **1** the capital form of a Chinese numeral **2** capitalization: ～字母 capital letter
大兴(興) dàxīng (动) go in for sth. in a big way: ～土木 launch massive construction projects
大型 dàxíng (形) large; large-scale: ～企业 large enterprise
大熊猫 dàxióngmāo (名) giant panda
大修 dàxiū (名) overhaul; heavy repair
大选(選) dàxuǎn (名) general election
大学(學) dàxué (名) university; college: ～生 university (or college) student
大言不惭 dàyán bù cán brag unblushingly
大业(業) dàyè (名) great cause; great undertaking
大衣 dàyī (名) overcoat; topcoat
大义(義)凛然 dàyì lǐnrán be awe-inspiring in defence of a just cause
大义(義)灭(滅)亲(親) dàyì miè qīn punish one's relatives severely according to law in order to uphold justice
大意 dàyì (名) general idea; main points; gist
大意 dàyi (形) careless: 粗心～ be negligent
大有文章 dà yǒu wénzhāng there's sth. intricate behind all this apparent simplicity
大有作为(爲) dà yǒu zuòwéi there is plenty of room for one to display one's talents
大约 dàyuē (副) approximately; about: 这部电影～要演两小时. This film will last about two hours.
大张(張)旗鼓 dà zhāng qí-gǔ give wide publicity to sth.; in a big way
大丈夫 dàzhàngfu (名) true man; real man; man
大志 dàzhì (名) lofty aim: 胸怀～ have a great ambition
大致 dàzhì (副) generally; roughly; approximately; more or less
大智若愚 dàzhì ruò yú a man of great wisdom often looks like a dullard
大众(衆) dàzhòng (名) the masses; the people: ～化 popular; in a popular style. ～歌曲 popular songs for the masses
大专 dàzhuān (名) 3-year diploma program; junior college
大自然 dàzìrán (名) nature; Mother Nature
大宗 dàzōng (形) **1** a large amount **2** staple

呆 dāi I (形) **1** slow-witted; dull: ～子 idiot. ～滞 dull; slow-moving. ～头～脑 dull-looking **2** blank; wooden: 吓得发～ be stupefied. ～若木鸡 struck dumb as a wooden chicken; be dumbstruck; transfixed (with fear or amazement) II (动) stay: ～在家里 stay at home
呆板 dāibǎn (形) rigid; inflexible; stereotyped
呆账(賬) dāizhàng (名) bad debt

待 dāi (动) 〈口〉 stay: 他在那里～了三天. He stayed there for three days.
see also dài

歹 dǎi (形) bad; evil; vicious: 为非作～ do evil
歹徒 dǎitú (名) ruffian; evildoer

逮 dǎi (动) capture; catch: 猫～老鼠. Cats catch mice.
see also dài

戴 dài (动) **1** put on; wear: ～上帽子 put on one's hat. ～眼镜 wear glasses **2** respect; honour: 爱～ love and respect
戴罪立功 dàizuì lìgōng atone for one's crimes by doing good deeds

带(帶) dài I (名) **1** belt; girdle; ribbon; band; tape: 皮～ leather belt. 丝～ silk ribbon. 录音～ recording tape. 鞋～ shoelaces **2** tyre: 自行车～ bicycle tyre **3** zone; area; belt:

热～ tropical zone. 这一～ in these areas II (动) 1 take; bring; carry: ～上雨衣. Take your raincoat along. 我能～孩子来吗? Can I bring my children with me? 我没～钱. I haven't any money on me. 2 [suggesting doing sth. at an opportune moment]: 上街时请给～点茶叶来. When you go out, please get me some tea. 3 bear; have; with: 一件～帽的雨衣 a raincoat with a hood. 他面～笑容看着我. He looked at me with a smile. 这梨～点酸味. This pear tastes a bit sour. 4 lead; head: ～队 lead a group of people. ～兵 be in command of troops 5 look after; bring up; raise: ～孩子 look after children. 他是他奶奶～大的. He was brought up by his grandmother.

带劲(勁) dàijìn (形) 1 in high spirits; energetic; forceful 2 interesting; exciting; wonderful: 这场足球赛真～. This football match is terrifically exciting.

带领 dàilǐng (动) lead; guide

带路 dàilù (动) lead the way; act as a guide

带头(頭) dàitóu (动) take the lead; take the initiative; set an example: 起～作用 play a leading role

带孝 dàixiào (动) wear mourning for a parent; be in mourning

带子 dàizi (名) belt; girdle; ribbon; band; tape

大 dài

see also dà

大夫 dàifu (名) doctor; physician

代 dài

I (动) take the place of; act for (or on behalf of) others: 我～他去. I'll go in his stead. ～课 take over a class for an absent teacher. 请～我向他问好. Please give him my regards. ～主任 acting director II (名) 1 historical period: 古～ ancient times. 汉～ the Han Dynasty 2 generation: 元宵节在中国～～相传. The Lantern Festival has been observed in China from generation to generation.

代办(辦) dàibàn I (动) do or act for others: 这件事请你～吧. Could you do this for me? II (名) chargé d'affaires: 临时～ chargé d'affaires ad interim

代表 dàibiǎo I (名) representative; deputy; delegate: ～团 delegation; mission. ～大会 congress II (动) represent; stand for: ～时代精神 embody the spirit of the era. 他～学校热烈欢迎我们. He gave us a warm welcome on behalf of their school. ～人物 representative figure

代词 dàicí (名) pronoun

代沟 dàigōu (名) generation gap

代号(號) dàihào (名) code name

代价(價) dàijià (名) price; cost: 不惜任何～ at any cost; at all costs

代劳(勞) dàiláo (动) do sth. for sb.; take trouble on sb.'s behalf: 这事请你～一下. Will you do this for me, please?

代理 dàilǐ (动) 1 act on sb.'s behalf; act for: ～厂长 acting manager of a factory 2 act as agent (or proxy, procurator)

代理人 dàilǐrén (名) agent; deputy; proxy

代数 dàishù (名) algebra

代替 dàitì (动) replace; substitute (for); take the place of

代销 dàixiāo (动) be commissioned to sell sth.

代谢 dàixiè (动) 1 supersession 2 metabolize

代言人 dàiyánrén (名) spokesman; mouthpiece

代用品 dàiyòngpǐn (名) substitute

袋 dài

I (名) bag; sack: 麻～ sack. 外交信～ diplomatic pouch. 邮～ mailbag. 工具～ tool kit II (量): 一～面粉 a sack of flour

袋装(裝) dàizhuāng (形) in bags: ～奶粉 milk powder in bags

贷 dài

(动) 1 borrow or lend: ～方 credit side. ～款 provide a loan; loan; credit 2 shift (responsibility); shirk: 责无旁～ be duty-bound

待 dài

(动) 1 treat; deal with: 平等～人 treat people as one's equals. ～人接物 the way one gets along with people 2 wait for; await: 等～时机 wait for an opportunity to take action; bide one's time. 有～改进 remain to be improved 3 going to; about to: 她到飞机场时,飞机正～起飞. The plane was about to take off when she arrived at the airport.

see also dāi

待岗(崗) dàigǎng (动) be waiting for a job

待命 dàimìng (动) await orders

待续(續) dàixù (动) to be continued

待业(業) dàiyè (动) be unemployed; wait for employment

待遇 dàiyù (名) 1 treatment: 最惠国～ most-favoured-nation treatment 2 pay;

wages; salary: ～优厚 excellent pay and conditions

怠 dài (形) idle; slack

怠惰 dàiduò (形) idle; lazy; indolent

怠工 dàigōng (动) slow down; go slow: 消极～ go slow

怠慢 dàimàn (动) 1 cold-shoulder; slight: 受到～ suffer slights. 不要～了客人. See that none of the guests are neglected. 2 〈套〉[used as an apology for not having properly entertained a visitor]: ～了! I'm afraid I have been a poor host.

殆 dài I (形)〈书〉dangerous: 危～ in great danger II (副) nearly; almost: 敌人伤亡～尽. The enemy were practically wiped out.

逮 dài (动)〈书〉reach: 力有未～ beyond one's reach
see also dǎi

逮捕 dàibǔ (动) arrest; take into custody: ～证 arrest warrant

单(單) dān I (形) 1 one; single: ～人床 single bed. ～行道 single track. ～亲家庭 one-parent family. ～人独马 single-handed 2 odd: ～日 odd days. ～数 odd number II (副) 1 separately; alone: 这几张照片要～放着. Keep these photos in a separate place. 2 only; solely; alone: ～凭热情还不够 Enthusiasm alone isn't enough III (名) 1 sheet: 床～ bed sheet 2 bill; list: 名～ name list. 菜～ menu. 账～ bill

单边(邊) dānbiān (形) unilateral

单薄 dānbó (形) 1 (of clothing) thin: 穿得～ be thinly dressed 2 thin and weak; frail 3 poor; flimsy: 论据～ a feeble argument. 内容～ thin in content

单纯 dānchún (形) 1 simple; pure: 思想～ simple-minded 2 alone; merely; purely: 别～追求数量. Don't strive for quantity alone.

单词 dāncí (名) word

单打 dāndǎ (名) singles: 男子(女子)～ men's (women's) singles

单刀直入 dāndāo zhí rù come straight to the point

单调 dāndiào (形) monotonous; dull; drab: 声音～ in a monotonous tone. 色彩～ dull colouring

单独(獨) dāndú (副) alone; by oneself; on one's own: 她～住一套房子. She has a flat to herself. 我要和他～谈一谈. I want to have a talk with him alone.

单据(據) dānjù (名) bill; receipt; voucher

单人房 dānrénfáng (名) single-bed room

单身 dānshēn (形) single; unmarried: ～汉 bachelor. ～宿舍 quarters for single men or women

单位 dānwèi (名) 1 unit of measurement: 长度～ a unit of length 2 unit of an organization: 行政～ administrative unit. 基层～ grass-roots unit. 你在哪个～工作? Where do you work?

单相思 dānxiāngsī unrequited love

单行本 dānxíngběn (名) offprint; separate edition

单一 dānyī (形) single; unitary: ～种植 monoculture. 训练方式～. The training methods are simplistic.

单元 dānyuán (名) unit: 二号楼五～ Entrance No. 5, Building 2

单子 dānzi (名) 1 list: 开个～ make out a list 2 bed sheet

单字 dānzì (名) individual character; separate word

殚(殫) dān (动)〈书〉exhaust: ～精竭虑 rack one's brains

耽 dān

耽搁 dānge (动) 1 stop over; stay: 我在去纽约途中,要在旧金山～一两天. I'll stop over in San Francisco for a day or two on my way to New York. 2 delay: 这项调查不能～. This investigation must not be delayed.

耽误 dānwù (动) hinder; hold up; spoil sth. because of delay: ～功夫 waste time. 别把病～了. Seek medical advice in time.

担(擔) dān (动) 1 carry on a shoulder pole: ～水 carry water 2 take on; undertake: ～风险 take (or run) risks. 承～全部责任 take on full responsibility
see also dàn

担保 dānbǎo (动) assure; guarantee: 出口信贷～ export credit guarantees. ～人 guarantor; guarantee

担当(當) dāndāng (动) take on; undertake; assume: 我情愿～这个责任. I am willing and ready to shoulder the responsibility.

担负 dānfù (动) bear; shoulder; take on: ～一项任务 take on a task. ～费用 bear the expenses

担纲(綱) dāngāng (动) play a major role (in a project)

担架 dānjià (名) stretcher; litter

担惊(驚)受怕 dānjīng-shòupà be stricken with anxiety and fear

担任 dānrèn (动) hold the post of; take charge of: ～领导职务 assume a leading position. ～会议主席 take the chair

担心 dānxīn (动) worry; feel anxious: ～她的健康 worry about her health

丹 dān (形) red

丹青 dānqīng (名)〈书〉painting: ～妙笔 superb artistry (in painting)

丹田 dāntián (名) the pubic region: ～之气 deep breath controlled by the diaphragm

丹心 dānxīn (名) a loyal heart; loyalty

掸(撣) dǎn (动) brush lightly; whisk: ～掉身上的雪花 brush the snow off one's coat

掸子 dǎnzi (名) duster: 鸡毛～ feather duster

胆(膽) dǎn (名) 1 gall bladder 2 courage; guts; bravery: 壮～ fortify sb.'s spirit 3 inner container: 热水瓶～ the glass liner of a thermos flask

胆大 dǎndà (形) bold; audacious: ～包天 extremely daring; foolhardy. ～妄为 reckless and defiant

胆敢 dǎngǎn (动) dare; venture; have the courage to: ～一试 dare to try

胆固醇 dǎngùchún (名) cholesterol

胆寒 dǎnhán (动) be terrified; be struck with terror

胆量 dǎnliàng (名) courage; guts: 很有～ have a lot of guts

胆略 dǎnlüè (名) courage and resourcefulness: ～过人 be exceptionally courageous and resourceful

胆囊 dǎnnáng (名) gall bladder

胆怯 dǎnqiè (形) timid; shy

胆小 dǎnxiǎo (形) chicken-hearted; timid; cowardly: ～鬼 coward

胆战(戰)心惊(驚) dǎnzhàn-xīnjīng tremble with fear

胆子 dǎnzi (名) courage; nerve: 好大的～! What a nerve!

惮(憚) dàn (动)〈书〉fear; dread

弹(彈) dàn (名) 1 ball; pellet 2 bullet; bomb: ～坑 shell crater. ～药 ammunition. ～头 warhead see also tán

弹道 dàndào (名) trajectory: ～导弹 ballistic missile. ～火箭 ballistic rocket

弹弓 dàngōng (名) catapult; slingshot

弹头(頭) dàntóu (名) warhead; bullet; projectile nose

弹丸 dànwán (名) 1 pellet; bullet 2 a small bit of land: ～之地 a tiny little place

弹药(藥) dànyào (名) ammunition: ～库 ammunition depot (or storehouse)

弹子 dànzi (名) 1 a pellet shot from a slingshot 2 marble: 打～ play marbles 3 billiards

淡 dàn (形) 1 thin; light: 天高云～. The sky is high; the clouds are pale. ～绿 light (or pale) green 2 tasteless; weak: ～茶 weak tea. ～而无味 tasteless 3 indifferent; apathetic: 冷～ cold; distant 4 slack; dull: 生意清～. Business is slack. 5 meaningless; trivial: 扯～ talk nonsense

淡泊 dànbó (形) not seek fame and wealth

淡薄 dànbó (形) 1 thin; light 2 (of feelings, interest, etc.) flag: 他对象棋的兴趣逐渐～了. His interest in chess has begun to flag. 3 (of impression) faint; dim; hazy: 他童年的印象已经～了. His childhood memories have grown dim.

淡季 dànjì (名) off-season

淡漠 dànmò (形) 1 indifferent; apathetic 2 faint; dim; hazy

淡然 dànrán (形) indifferent; cool

淡水 dànshuǐ (名) fresh water

淡雅 dànyǎ (形) simple and in good taste

啖 dàn (动)〈书〉1 eat 2 feed 3 entice; lure

氮 dàn (名) nitrogen (N): ～肥 nitrogenous fertilizer

诞 dàn I (名) 1 birth 2 birthday II (形) absurd; fantastic: 荒～ fantastic

诞辰 dànchén (名) birthday

诞生 dànshēng (动) be born; come into being; emerge

旦 dàn (名) 1〈书〉dawn; daybreak: 元～ New Year's Day 2 the female character type in traditional Chinese

opera, etc.
旦夕 dànxī (名)〈书〉in a short while: 危在～ in imminent danger
担(擔) dàn I (量) *dan*, a unit of weight (50 kilograms) II (名) a carrying pole and the loads on it; load; burden
see also dān
担子 dànzi (名) load; burden; task: 他的工作～重. His workload is heavy.
但 dàn (连) but; yet; nevertheless
但是 dànshì (连) but; yet; still; nevertheless
但书(書) dànshū (名) proviso
但愿(願) dànyuàn (动) if only; I wish: ～他能及时赶到. If only he could arrive in time! ～如此. I wish it were true!
蛋 dàn (名) **1** egg **2** an egg-shaped thing: 泥～儿 mud ball
蛋白 dànbái (名) egg white
蛋白质(質) dànbáizhì (名) protein
蛋糕 dàngāo (名) cake
蛋黄 dànhuáng (名) yolk
当(當) dāng I (动) **1** work as; serve as: 他想～教员. He wants to be a teacher. **2** bear; accept; deserve: 敢做敢～ be ready to act boldly and take full responsibility for it **3** manage; be in charge of: ～家 run the household **4** should; ought to **5** equal: 实力相～ nearly equal in strength II (介) **1** in sb.'s presence; to sb.'s face: ～着大家谈一谈. Let's hear what you have to say. **2** just at (a certain time or place): 当…的时候 [used at the beginning of a sentence as an adverbial adjunct] when...; at the time...
see also dàng
当班 dāngbān (动) be on a shift
当兵 dāngbīng (动) get into uniform; join the army
当场(場) dāngchǎng (副) on the spot; then and there: ～抓住 catch red-handed
当初 dāngchū (名) originally; in the beginning; in the first place: ～这儿是一片沙漠. This area was a desert in the past. 记得～怎么对你讲的? Remember what I told you, eh?
当代 dāngdài (名) the present age: ～文学 contemporary literature
当道 dāngdào I (名) the middle of the road: 别在～站着. Don't stand in the way. II (动) be in power; hold sway
当地 dāngdì (名) in the locality; local: ～人 local people. ～时间 local time
当红 dānghóng (形) in vogue: ～明星 a popular star
当机(機)立断(斷) dāng jī lì duàn make a prompt and timely decision
当即 dāngjí (副) at once; right away
当家作主 dāngjiā zuòzhǔ be master in one's own house
当今 dāngjīn (名) now; at present; nowadays: ～之世 in the world of today
当局 dāngjú (名) the authorities: 政府～ the government authorities
当空 dāngkōng (动) high above in the sky: 皓月～. A bright moon is hanging high up in the sky.
当面 dāngmiàn (副) to sb.'s face; in sb.'s presence: ～撒谎 tell a barefaced lie; speak with one's tongue in one's cheek
当年 dāngnián (名) **1** in those years (or days) **2** the prime of life: 他正～. He is in his prime.
see also dàngnián
当前 dāngqián I (名) present; current: ～的国际形势 the current (or present) international situation II (动) be faced with: 大敌～ be confronted by a formidable enemy
当权(權) dāngquán (动) be in power
当然 dāngrán (形) of course; without doubt: 朋友有困难, ～要帮助. It goes without saying that we should help a friend in difficulty. ～同盟军 natural ally. 理所～. That is just as it should be. *or* This is a matter of course.
当仁不让(讓) dāng rén bù ràng be ready to tackle anything one is capable of; decline no responsibility that one thinks one ought to bear
当时(時) dāngshí (名) then; at that time
当事人 dāngshìrén (名) **1** (to a lawsuit) party; litigant; client **2** person concerned; interested party
当头(頭) dāngtóu (动) right overhead: 烈日～照 The sun is shining overhead. ～一棒 a head-on blow
当务(務)之急 dāng wù zhī jí a burning issue of the moment; a top priority
当心 dāngxīn (动) look out; take care; be careful: ～, 汽车来了. Look out! There is a car coming. ～路滑. Watch your steps. The road is slippery. ～危险

Look out!
当选(選) dāngxuǎn (动) be elected
当政 dāngzhèng (动) be in power
当之无(無)愧 dāng zhī wú kuì be worthy of; fully deserve
当众(衆) dāngzhòng (副) in the presence of all; in public

裆(襠) dāng (名) crotch (of trousers)

铛(鐺) dāng (象) clank; clang

挡(擋) dǎng I (动) 1 block; keep off: ~道 block the road; get in the way. ~雨 keep off the rain 2 cover: ~亮 cover the light II (名) gear: 高速(低速)~ top (bottom) gear
挡驾 dǎngjià (动) turn away a visitor with some excuse; decline to see a guest
挡箭牌 dǎngjiànpái (名) 1 shield 2 excuse; pretext

党(黨) dǎng (名) 1 political party: 入~ join the party 2 gang; clique; faction: 死~ sworn follower
党报(報) dǎngbào (名) 1 party newspaper 2 the Party organ
党风(風) dǎngfēng (名) a party's work style; party members' conduct
党纲(綱) dǎnggāng (名) party programme
党籍 dǎngjí (名) party membership: 开除~ expel from the party
党纪 dǎngjì (名) party discipline
党派 dǎngpài (名) political parties and groups
党徒 dǎngtú (名) 1 member of a reactionary political party 2 henchmen
党委 dǎngwěi (名) Party committee
党性 dǎngxìng (名) Party spirit
党羽 dǎngyǔ (名) adherents; henchmen
党员 dǎngyuán (名) party member

当(當) dàng I (动) 1 treat as; regard as; take for: 她把他~作自己的亲生儿子. She treats him as her own son. 2 equal to: 他一个人能~两个人用. He can do the work of two persons. 3 think: 我~你不知道. I thought you didn't know. 4 pawn: ~衣服 pawn one's clothes II (形) proper; right: 用词不~ not properly worded; inappropriate wording; wrong choice of words
see also dāng
当年 dàngnián (名) the same year; that very year
当铺(舖) dàngpù (名) pawnshop
当日 dàngrì (名) the same day; that very day: ~有效 valid for the date of issue only
当时(時) dàngshí (副) right away; at once; immediately: 听到这消息,她~就昏了过去. She fainted the moment she heard the news.
当天 dàngtiān (名) the same day; that very day
当真 dàngzhēn I (动) take seriously: 我只是开个玩笑,何必~呢? I was only joking. Why take it so seriously? II (副) really: 她说想要买一架钢琴,后来~买了. She said she wanted to buy a piano, and she did. III (形) true: 这话~? Is it really true?

荡(蕩) dàng I (动) 1 swing; sway: ~秋千 play on a swing. ~桨 pull on the oars 2 loaf: 游~ loaf about 3 clear away; sweep off: ~涤 cleanse; wash away. 扫~ mopping up II (形) of loose morals: 放~ dissolute; dissipated. 淫~ lustful; lascivious III (名) shallow lake; marsh: 芦苇~ a reed marsh
荡漾 dàngyàng (动) ripple; undulate

档(檔) dàng (名) 1 files; archives: 查~ consult the files 2 grade: 高~商品 high-grade goods 3 crosspiece (of a table, etc.)
档案 dàng'àn (名) files; archives; record: ~管理员 archivist

刀 dāo (名) 1 knife; sword: ~子 pocket knife 2 sth. shaped like a knife: 冰~ ice skates
刀叉 dāo-chā (名) knife and fork
刀口 dāokǒu (名) 1 the edge of a knife 2 the crucial point 3 cut; incision
刀片 dāopiàn (名) razor blade
刀枪(槍) dāo-qiāng (名) sword and spear; weapons
刀鞘 dāoqiào (名) sheath; scabbard
刀刃 dāorèn (名) the edge of a knife
刀山火海 dāoshān-huǒhǎi fire and water: 为了正义事业~也敢闯 would go through fire and water for the cause of justice

祷(禱) dǎo (动) pray: ~告 pray; say one's prayers

蹈 dǎo (动) 1 〈书〉 tread; step: 赴汤~火 go through fire and water; defy all difficulties and dangers. 循规~矩 observe rules docilely; conform to convention 2 skip: 舞~ dance

倒 dǎo (动) 1 fall; topple: 墙~了. The wall has fallen down. 摔~ fall over. 风把树刮~了. The gale uprooted the tree. 2 collapse; be overthrown; close down: ~台 fall from power. 那家工厂~了. That factory has gone bankrupt. 3 change; exchange: ~车 change trains or buses. ~班 work in shifts
see also dào

倒闭 dǎobì (动) close down; go bankrupt: 银行~ bankruptcy of a bank

倒戈 dǎogē (动) turn one's coat; transfer one's allegiance

倒卖(賣) dǎomài (动) resell at a profit; scalp

倒霉 dǎoméi (动) have bad luck; get into trouble

倒手 dǎoshǒu (动) change hands (in order to sell sth.)

倒塌 dǎotā (动) collapse; topple down

倒胃口 dǎowèikou spoil one's appetite

倒爷(爺) dǎoyé (名) profiteer

岛(島) dǎo (名) island: ~国 island country. ~屿 islands

捣(搗) dǎo (动) pound with a pestle, etc.; beat; smash

捣蛋 dǎodàn (动) make trouble: 调皮~ be mischievous

捣鬼 dǎoguǐ (动) play underhand tricks

捣毁 dǎohuǐ (动) smash up; destroy

捣乱(亂) dǎoluàn (动) make trouble; create a disturbance

导(導) dǎo (动) 1 lead; guide; divert 2 transmit; conduct: ~电 electric conduction

导弹(彈) dǎodàn (名) guided missile

导航 dǎoháng (名) navigation

导火线(綫) dǎohuǒxiàn (名) 1 (blasting) fuse 2 an apparently insignificant incident leading to a big conflict: 战争的~ an incident that touches off a war

导师(師) dǎoshī (名) 1 tutor; teacher; supervisor 2 guide of a great cause; teacher

导体(體) dǎotǐ (名) conductor: 非~ non-conductor. 超~ superconductor

导言 dǎoyán (名) introduction; introductory remarks; foreword

导演 dǎoyǎn I (动) direct (a film, play, etc.) II (名) director

导游 dǎoyóu I (名) tourist guide II (动) guide a tour: ~图 tourist map

导致 dǎozhì (动) lead to; result in; bring about; cause: 恶劣的卫生条件常常~许多疾病. Bad sanitary conditions always breed diseases of various kinds.

盗 dào I (动) steal; rob II (名) thief; robber: ~贼 robbers; bandits

盗版 dàobǎn (名) illegal copy; pirate copy; piracy

盗匪 dàofěi (名) bandits; robbers

盗汗 dàohàn (名) night sweat

盗猎 dàoliè (名) illegal hunting; poaching

盗窃(竊) dàoqiè (动) steal: ~犯 thief; burglar

盗用 dàoyòng (动) usurp: ~公款 embezzle public funds

悼 dào (动) mourn; grieve: 哀~死者 mourn for the deceased

悼词 dàocí (名) memorial speech; funeral oration: 致~ deliver a funeral oration

悼念 dàoniàn (动) mourn; grieve over: 沉痛~ mourn with deep grief

道 dào I (名) 1 road; way; path: 山间小~ a mountain path. 河~ the course of a river 2 line: 划一条红~ draw a red line. 斜~ a slanting line 3 way; method: 养生之~ the way to keep fit. 头头是~ closely reasoned and well argued 4 doctrine; principle 5 Taoism; Taoist: ~士 a Taoist priest II (动) 1 say; speak; talk: 说长~短 idly chatter; gossip: 能说会~ have a glib tongue. 常言~ as the saying goes 2 think; suppose III (量) 1 [for anything in the form of a line]: 一~缝儿 a crack 2 [for doors, walls, etc.]: 两~门 two successive doors. 三~防线 three lines of defence 3 [for orders or questions]: 一~命令 an order. 四~数学题 four maths questions 4 course of dish: 五~菜的正餐 a five-course dinner

道德 dàodé (名) morals; morality: ~败坏 degenerate

道观(觀) dàoguàn (名) Taoist temple

道贺 dàohè (动) congratulate

道家 Dàojiā (名) Taoist school

道教 Dàojiào (名) Taoism

道具 dàojù (名) stage properties; props

道理 dàoli (名) 1 principle; truth 2 reason;

sense; argument: 讲～ appeal to reason

道路 dàolù (名) road; way; path: 为两国首脑会谈铺平～ pave the way for summit talks between the two countries

道貌岸然 dàomào ànrán pose as a person of high morals; look dignified

道歉 dàoqiàn (动) apologize

道听(聽)途说 dàotīng-túshuō hearsay; rumour; gossip

道谢 dàoxiè (动) express one's gratitude; thank

道义(義) dàoyì (名) morality and justice: ～上的支持 moral support

到 dào I (动) 1 arrive; reach: 火车3点钟～. The train arrives at three o'clock. 2 go to; leave for: ～南方去 go to the south. ～我家来 come to (or drop in at) my home. 他～过欧洲. He has been to Europe. II (形) thoughtful; considerate: 不～之处请原谅. Please excuse me if I have not been thoughtful enough. III [used after a verb as a complement to indicate success]: 买～ have bought sth. 找～ find sth. 办得～ can be done. 说～做～ be as good as one's word. 想不～你来了. I didn't expect you would come. IV (介) up until; up to: 从星期一～星期五 from Monday to Friday. ～目前为止 up to the present; so far

到场(場) dàochǎng (动) be present; show up; turn up

到处(處) dàochù (副) at all places; everywhere: 烟头不要～乱扔. Don't drop cigarette ends about.

到达(達) dàodá (动) arrive; get to; reach

到底 dàodǐ (动) to the end; to the finish: 打～ fight to the finish

到底 dàodǐ (副) 1 at last; finally; in the end: 可他～还是没去. But he still didn't go in the end. 2 after all; in the final analysis: 他～还是个孩子. After all, he's only a child. 3 [used in an interrogative sentence to indicate an attempt to get to the bottom of the matter]: 你～是什么意思? What on earth do you mean? 你～去不去? Are you going or not?

到点(點) dàodiǎn it's time to do sth.; time is up

到来(來) dàolái (名) arrival; advent

到期 dàoqī (动) become due; expire: 这本杂志今天～. The magazine is due for return today. 签证下月～. The visa expires next month.

到任 dàorèn (动) take office; arrive at one's post

到手 dàoshǒu (动) in one's hands; in one's possession

到头(頭)来(來) dàotóulái (副) in the end; finally

到位 dàowèi (动) be in position: 工作很～ do a perfect job. 措施～ take substantial measures. 资金～了. The capital is in place.

倒 dào I (动) 1 turn upside down; move backward; reverse; invert: 把瓶子～过来 turn the bottle upside down. ～车 back a car. ～装词序 inverted order 2 pour; tip; dump: ～一杯茶 pour a cup of tea. ～垃圾桶 empty the dustbin II (副) 1 [indicating an opposite effect. cf. 反而]: 我明白你是想帮忙,但这一来事情～更麻烦了. I know you meant to help but you've made the matter even more complicated. 我看他～还不错. As I see it, he is rather a nice chap. 别看他八十多了,身体～很结实. Though he is over eighty, he's as sound as a bell. 2 [indicating that while one admits the merits of sth. he points out a drawback]: 那本小说～是有意思,可太长了. That novel is fairly interesting but too long. 他～没说他不喜欢她. He didn't say (straight away) that he didn't like her. 说起来～容易,做起来难啊! It's easier said than done. 3 [indicating impatience]: 你～是去呀,还是不去? Are you going or are you not?
see also dǎo

倒彩 dàocǎi (名) booing; hooting: 喝～ make catcalls

倒打一耙 dào dǎ yī pá make unfounded countercharges; recriminate

倒计时(時) dàojìshí (动) countdown: 我们申奥进入～. Our bid to host the Olympic Games has entered the countdown stage.

倒立 dàolì (动) stand upside down

倒数(數) dàoshǔ (动) count backwards: ～第三行 the third line from the bottom. ～第二行 the last line but one

倒退 dàotuì (动) go backwards

倒行逆施 dàoxíng-nìshī 1 go against the historical trend; push a reactionary policy; try to put the clock back 2 perverse acts

D

倒叙 dàoxù (动) flashback
倒影 dàoyǐng (名) inverted image; reflection in water
倒置 dàozhì (动) place upside down: 本末～ put the unimportant before the important. 小心轻放,请勿～! Handle with care! This side up!
稻 dào (名) rice; paddy: ～草 rice straw. ～田 paddy field
得 dé (动) 1 get; gain; obtain: ～病 fall ill. 取～经验 gain experience. 二三～六 Twice three is six. ～分 score 2 be finished; be ready: 饭～了 Dinner is ready.
see also de; děi
得不偿(償)失 dé bù cháng shī the loss outweighs the gain
得逞 déchěng (动) have one's way; succeed (in doing evil)
得宠(寵) déchǒng (动) find favour with sb.; be in sb.'s good graces
得寸进(進)尺 dé cùn jìn chǐ give him an inch and he'll take a mile; reach for a yard after getting an inch
得当(當) dédàng (形) proper; suitable; fitting: 安排～ be properly arranged. 措词～ aptly worded
得到 dédào (动) get; obtain; gain; receive
得法 défǎ (形) do sth. in the proper way; have the knack (of doing sth.): 学习不～ fail to learn in the proper way
得过(過)且过 dé guò qiě guò muddle along; drift along; get by however one can
得力 délì (形) capable; competent: ～助手 capable assistant; right-hand man. 办事～ get things done promptly
得人心 dé rénxīn (动) have the support of the people; be popular
得胜(勝) déshèng (动) win victory: ～归来 return in triumph (or with flying colours)
得失 dé-shī (名) gain and loss; advantages and disadvantages: 个人～ personal gain or loss. 各有～ each has its advantages and disadvantages
得势(勢) déshì (动) get the upper hand; be in power
得体(體) détǐ (形) (of words or behaviour) proper; appropriate: 讲话～ speak in appropriate terms
得天独(獨)厚 dé tiān dú hòu abound in gifts of nature
得心应(應)手 déxīn-yìngshǒu handle with ease; be in one's element
得宜 déyí (形) proper; appropriate; suitable: 处置～ handle properly
得益 déyì (动) benefit; profit
得意 déyì (形) complacent: ～扬扬 be immensely proud of oneself. ～忘形 allow one's achievements to turn one's head; get dizzy with success
得志 dézhì (动) achieve one's ambition: 少年～ have a successful career at an early age
得罪 dézuì (动) offend
德 dé (名) 1 virtue; morals: 品～ moral character. ～才兼备 have both ability and moral integrity; be both capable and noble-minded 2 heart; mind: 同心同～ be of one heart and one mind 3 kindness; favour: 以怨报～ return evil for good
德高望重 dégāo-wàngzhòng be held in high esteem for one's moral integrity or intellectual achievement; be of whole character and high prestige
德行 déxíng (名) moral integrity; moral conduct
德育 déyù (名) moral education
地 de (助) [used after an adjective, a noun or a phrase to form an adverbial adjunct before the verb]: 狐狸偷偷～跑进果园. The fox sneaked into the orchard. 他喝醉酒似～叫嚷. He shouted as if he were drunk.
see also dì
的 de (助) I used after an adjectival 1 [as an attribute used after a noun]: 花～颜色 the colour of the flower 2 [used after a verb as an attribute]: 讨论～问题 matter for discussion 3 [used after an adjective]: 聪明～孩子 clever child [when the adjective is preceded by an intensifier or when it is in a reduplicated form, 的 is obligatory; as in 很高～山 very high mountains. 大大～眼睛 very big eyes] 4 [used after a pronoun]: 我～爸爸 my father 5 [used after a numeral]: 出一身～汗 sweat all over. 两天～时间 two days' time [when a numeral is combined with an ordinary classifier rather than a noun classifier, 的 is usually not to be used, as in 三个孩子 three children or 四匹马 four horses] 6 [used after a phrase, 的 is obligatory in this case]: 我对这个问题～看法 my views

on this issue. 我刚听到～消息 the news I heard just now II other situations in which 的 is used 1 [used between the subject noun and the verb, functioning similarly as "of"]: 谣言～传播很惊人. The spread of the rumour is shocking. 2 [used between a verb and its object for emphatic purposes]: 他写～书. It was he who wrote the book. 她是去年买～这条裙子. It was last year that she bought this skirt. 3 [used between a personal pronoun and a noun to indicate one's role or the fact that one is the recipient of the action]: 今天的会谁～主席? Who is the chairman of today's meeting? 这部电影是我姐姐～主角. My sister plays the lead in this film. 开她～玩笑 play a joke on her 4 [used after words belonging to the same parts of speech with a function similar to that of "and so on" or "etc."]: 我不喜欢花儿草儿～! I don't like flowers, grass and things like that! 她尽说吃啊穿啊～. She talks about nothing but food and clothing, etc. 5 [attached to a verb, a noun, a pronoun or an adjective as a nominalizer]: 卖书～ the bookseller

see also dí

得 de (助) 1 [used between a verb or an adjective and its complement to indicate result, possibility or degree]: 走～快 walk fast. 唱～好 sing well. 办～到 it can be done. 拿～动 can carry it. 雪下～大. It snowed heavily. 病～厉害 be very ill. 好～很 very good. 冷～打哆嗦 shiver with cold 2 [used after certain verbs to indicate possibility]: 这种蘑菇吃～. This kind of mushroom is edible. 衬衣太短,穿不～了. The shirt is too short for me now. 这话可说不～. We (You) mustn't say things like that.

see also dé; děi

得 děi (动) 1 need: 写这篇文章至少～一个月. It will take at least a month to complete this article. 2 must; have to: 我～走了. I must go now. 我～事先告诉他. I have to tell him in advance. 3 will be sure to: 要不快走,你就～迟到了. Hurry up or you'll be late.

see also dé; de

灯(燈) dēng (名) lamp; light: 煤油～ kerosene lamp. 电～ electric light

灯光 dēngguāng (名) 1 lamplight 2 (stage) lighting: 舞台～ stage lights. ～球场 floodlit court, field, etc.

灯会(會) dēnghuì (名) lantern festival

灯火 dēnghuǒ (名) lights: ～辉煌 brilliantly illuminated. ～管制 blackout

灯笼(籠) dēnglong (名) lantern

灯谜 dēngmí (名) riddles written on lanterns; lantern riddles

灯泡 dēngpào (名) light bulb

灯塔 dēngtǎ (名) lighthouse; beacon

灯罩 dēngzhào (名) lampshade

登 dēng (动) 1 ascend; mount; scale (a height): ～山 mountaineering. ～上讲台 mount the platform. ～上峰顶 reach the summit 2 publish; record; enter: ～广告 advertise (in a newspaper). ～消息 publish news (in a newspaper)

登报(報) dēngbào (动) publish in the newspaper

登场(場) dēngchǎng (动) come on stage

登峰造极(極) dēngfēng-zàojí (of skill, learning, etc.) reach the peak of perfection; reach the pinnacle of scholastic attainment

登机(機) dēngjī (动) board a plane

登基 dēngjī (动) be enthroned

登记 dēngjì (动) register; enter one's name: 结婚～ marriage registration. 在旅馆～住宿 check in at a hotel

登陆(陸) dēnglù (动) land; disembark (from a ship)

登台(臺) dēngtái (动) come on stage; mount a platform: ～表演 put on a show

登载 dēngzǎi (动) carry (in newspapers or magazines)

等 děng I (名) grade; class; rank: 一～奖 first prize. 头～票 first class ticket. 一～品 top quality goods II (形) equal: 长短相～ be equal in length III (动) wait; await: ～车 wait for a bus. ～上级批准 await approval by the higher authorities IV (代) 1 [used after a personal pronoun or a noun to indicate plural number]: 老李～三人 Lao Li and two others. 我～五人 the five of us 2 and so on; etc.: 梨、苹果、葡萄～ pears, apples, grapes and so on 3 [used to end an enumeration]: 北京、上海、广州～大城市 big cities such as Beijing, Shanghai, and Guangzhou

D

等待 děngdài (动) wait; await: ～时机 bide one's time

等到 děngdào (连) by the time; when

等等 děngděng and so on; and so on and so forth; etc.

等号(號) děnghào (名) equality sign

等候 děnghòu (动) wait; await; expect: ～命令 wait for instructions; await orders

等级 děngjí (名) 1 grade; rank 2 order and degree; social stratum: ～制度 hierarchy. ～观念 the concept of (social) status

等价(價) děngjià of equal value: ～交换 exchange at equal value

等量齐(齊)观(觀) děngliàng-qíguān equate; put on a par

等同 děngtóng (动) equate; treat as equivalent

等外 děngwài (形) substandard: ～品 substandard product

等闲(閒) děngxián (形) ordinary; unimportant: ～视之 treat lightly

等于(於) děngyú (动) 1 be equal to; be equivalent to: 三加二～五. Three plus two is five. 2 be the same as; amount to; be tantamount to

澄 dèng (动) (of liquid) settle: ～清 become clear; clarify
see also chéng

瞪 dèng (动) open one's eyes wide; stare; glare: 我～了他一眼. I gave him a stare. 干～眼 look on helplessly

凳 dèng (名) stool; bench: 方～ square stool. 长～ bench

滴 dī I (动) drip: 他脸上的汗水直往下～. Sweat kept dripping from his face. ～眼药 put drops in one's eyes II (量) drop: 一～眼泪 a teardrop

滴答 dīdā (象) tick; tick-tack: 钟摆～～的响声 the tick-tack of the clock

滴答 dīda (动) drip: 屋顶～着水. The roof is dripping water.

滴水穿石 dī shuǐ chuān shí little strokes fell big oaks; constant dripping wears away stone

堤 dī (名) dyke; embankment: ～岸 embankment. ～坝 dykes and dam. ～防 dyke

提 dī
see also tí

提防 dīfang (动) guard against; take precautions against

低 dī I (形) low: ～地 low land. ～潮 low tide; low ebb. ～声 in a low voice II (动) let droop; hang down: ～头 lower one's head

低保 dībǎo (名) government subsidy provided to low-income families

低沉 dīchén (形) 1 overcast: ～的天空 an overcast sky 2 (of voice) low and deep 3 low-spirited; downcast

低调 dīdiào (名) 1 low-tone 2 low-key; low profile

低估 dīgū (动) underestimate; underrate

低谷 dīgǔ (名) at a low ebb; in the doldrums

低级 dījí (形) 1 elementary; rudimentary; lower 2 vulgar; low: ～趣味 vulgar taste

低廉 dīlián (形) (of price) cheap; reasonable

低劣 dīliè (形) inferior; low-grade

低落 dīluò (形) low; downcast: 情绪～ be depressed; in sagging spirits

低迷 dīmí (形) stagnant: 经济持续～. The economy remains in the doldrums.

低三下四 dīsān-xiàsì humble; servile

低洼(窪) dīwā (形) (of land) low-lying

低下 dīxià (形) (of status) low; lowly; humble

涤(滌) dí (动) wash; cleanse

涤荡(蕩) dídàng (动) wash away; clean up

涤纶(綸) dílún (名) polyester fibre

嘀 dí

嘀咕 dígu (动) 1 talk in whispers; talk in a low voice 2 have misgivings about sth.: 我心里一直～这件事. It's been on my mind all the while.

嫡 dí (形) of lineal descent; closely related

嫡亲(親) díqīn (名) blood relations

嫡系 díxì (名) direct line of descent: ～部队 troops under one's direct control

笛 dí (名) 1 (～子) flute 2 whistle: 汽～ siren

敌(敵) dí I (名) enemy; foe: 劲～ a formidable enemy. ～机 an enemy plane II (动) fight; resist; withstand: 寡不～众 be outnumbered

敌对(對) díduì (形) hostile; antagonistic: ～情绪 a hostile attitude

敌情 díqíng (名) the enemy's situation

敌视 díshì (动) be hostile (or antagonistic) to

敌手 díshǒu (名) rival; opponent

敌特 dítè (名) enemy agent

敌意 díyì (名) hostility; animosity

的 dí

see also de

的确 díquè (副) indeed; really: 这本书～很好. This book is really good.

的确良 díquèliáng (名) dacron

的士 díshì (名) taxi

籴(糴) dí (动) buy in (grain)

底 dǐ (名) 1 bottom; base: 海～ sea bed 2 end (of a year or month): 年～ the end of a year 3 the heart of a matter; ins and outs: 刨根问～ get to the bottom of the matter 4 a copy or duplicate kept as a record: 留个～儿 keep a copy on file 5 background: 蓝～白花 white flowers on a blue background 6 end: 干到～ carry sth. through to the end

底层(層) dǐcéng (名) 1 (英) ground floor; (美) first floor 2 bottom; the lowest rung of the ladder: 在社会的最～ at the bottom of society

底稿 dǐgǎo (名) draft; manuscript

底牌 dǐpái (名) cards in one's hand; hand: 亮～ show one's hand

底片 dǐpiàn (名) negative; photographic plate

底细 dǐxì (名) ins and outs; exact details

底下 dǐxia (名) 1 under; below; beneath: 床～ under the bed 2 next; later; afterwards: 我们～再谈吧. We can discuss it later.

底线(綫) dǐxiàn (名) bottom line; baseline

底蕴 dǐyùn (名) 1 inside information 2 inner strength

底子 dǐzi (名) 1 bottom; base: 鞋～ the sole of a shoe 2 foundation: 他的英语语法～好. He has a good grounding in English grammar. 3 rough draft or sketch: 画画儿得先打个～. Make a rough sketch before you draw. 4 master copy 5 remnant: 货～ remnants of stock

诋 dǐ (动) 〈书〉 slander; defame

诋毁 dǐhuǐ (动) slander; vilify

抵 dǐ (动) 1 support; sustain: 重盖前先用东西把这片墙～住. Prop something against the wall before it is rebuilt. 2 resist; withstand 3 compensate for; make good: ～命 a life for a life 4 mortgage: 用房屋作～ mortgage a house 5 be equal to 6 〈书〉 arrive; reach: 六日～京 arrive in Beijing on the 6th

抵偿(償) dǐcháng (动) compensate

抵触(觸) dǐchù (动) conflict; contradict: 与法律相～ go against the law. ～情绪 resentment; feeling of antagonism

抵达(達) dǐdá (动) arrive; reach

抵挡(擋) dǐdǎng (动) keep out; ward off; check; withstand: ～风沙 keep out wind and dust

抵抗 dǐkàng (动) resist; stand up to: 奋起～ put up a stubborn resistance

抵赖 dǐlài (动) deny: 不容～ undeniable

抵消 dǐxiāo (动) offset; cancel out; balance: ～药物的作用 counteract the effect of a medicine

抵押 dǐyā (动) mortgage: ～品 security; pledge

抵御(禦) dǐyù (动) resist; withstand: ～自然灾害 withstand natural calamities

抵制 dǐzhì (动) resist; boycott

抵罪 dǐzuì (动) be punished for a crime

邸 dǐ (名) the residence of a high official: 官～ official residence

帝 dì (名) 1 the Supreme Being: 上～ God 2 emperor: 称～ proclaim oneself emperor

帝国(國) dìguó (名) empire: 罗马～ the Roman Empire

帝国(國)主义(義) dìguózhǔyì (名) imperialism

帝王 dìwáng (名) emperor; monarch

帝制 dìzhì (名) monarchy

谛 dì (形) 〈书〉 carefully; attentively: ～听 listen attentively. ～视 examine closely; scrutinize

蒂 dì (名) the base of a fruit: 根深～固 deep-rooted; inveterate

缔 dì

缔交 dìjiāo (动) 1 make friends with 2 establish diplomatic relations

缔结 dìjié (动) conclude: ～条约 conclude a treaty

缔约 dìyuē (动) conclude (or sign) a treaty: ～国 signatory to a treaty. ～双方 both contracting parties

缔造 dìzào (动) found; create (a party, state, or school of thought)

弟 dì (名) younger brother: ~~ younger brother. ~兄 brothers. ~子 disciple; pupil; follower

第 dì [prefix for ordinal numbers]: ~三世界 the Third World

第一 dìyī (形) first; primary; foremost: 获得~名 come out first in the competition with a championship

第一线(綫) dìyīxiàn (名) forefront; front line: 战斗在~ be in the forefront of the fighting; be in the van of the struggle

递(遞) dì I (动) hand over; pass; give: 把书~给我. Give me the book. ~眼色 wink at sb. II (副) successively; in sequential order: ~增(减) increase (decrease) by degrees

递交 dìjiāo (动) present; submit: ~国书 (of an ambassador) present one's credentials

递送 dìsòng (动) send; deliver

递增 dìzēng (动) increase progressively

地 dì (名) **1** the earth **2** land; soil: 高~ highland. 盐碱~ saline and alkaline land (or soil) **3** field: 麦~ wheat field **4** ground; floor: 水泥~ cement floor **5** place; locality **6** position; situation: 立于不败之~ entrench oneself in an invincible position **7** background **8** distance: 十里~ a distance of ten *li*

see also de

地板 dìbǎn (名) (wooden) floor

地步 dìbù (名) **1** condition; situation; plight (usu. unfavourable) **2** extent: 兴奋到不能入睡的~ be too excited to fall asleep

地大物博 dìdà-wùbó vast in territory and rich in resources

地带(帶) dìdài (名) region; zone: 危险~ a danger zone

地道 dìdào (名) tunnel

地道 dìdao (形) **1** pure; genuine: ~的中国花茶 genuine Chinese jasmine tea **2** 〈口〉 up to standard; fine: 这活干得真~. They have done an excellent job of work.

地点(點) dìdiǎn (名) place; site

地段 dìduàn (名) a section of an area

地方 dìfāng (名) locality (as distinct from the central administration): ~政府 local government

地方 dìfang (名) **1** place: 你住什么~? Where do you live? **2** space; room: 这张桌子太占~. That desk takes up too much space. **3** part; respect: 他也有对的~. He is also partly right.

地基 dìjī (名) **1** ground **2** foundation

地窖 dìjiào (名) cellar

地界 dìjiè (名) the boundary of a piece of land

地雷 dìléi (名) land mine

地理 dìlǐ (名) geography

地面 dìmiàn (名) the earth's surface; ground

地盘(盤) dìpán (名) territory under one's control; domain

地皮 dìpí (名) land for building

地痞 dìpǐ (名) local ruffian

地平线(綫) dìpíngxiàn (名) horizon

地壳(殼) dìqiào (名) the earth's crust

地勤 dìqín (名) ground service

地球 dìqiú (名) the earth; the globe: ~卫星 earth satellite. ~物理学 geophysics. ~仪 (terrestrial) globe

地球村 dìqiúcūn (名) global village

地区(區) dìqū (名) area; district; region: 森林~ forest area. ~冲突 regional conflict

地权(權) dìquán (名) land ownership

地热(熱) dìrè (名) terrestrial heat: ~能源 geothermal energy resources

地上 dìshang (名) on the ground: 从~拣起 pick up from the ground

地势(勢) dìshì (名) physical features of a place; relief

地摊(攤) dìtān (名) street vendor's stand (with goods spread out on the ground)

地毯 dìtǎn (名) carpet; rug

地铁 dìtiě (名) subway; underground; metro

地图(圖) dìtú (名) map

地位 dìwèi (名) position; status: 政治~ political position. 国际~ international status. 平等~ on an equal footing

地峡(峽) dìxiá (名) isthmus

地下 dìxià (名) underground: ~宫殿 underground palace. ~核试验 underground nuclear test. ~室 basement; cellar. ~铁道 underground railway; tube; subway. ~工作 underground work

地心 dìxīn (名) the earth's core: ~引力 terrestrial gravity; gravity

地形 dìxíng (名) topography; terrain

地狱(獄) dìyù (名) hell; inferno: 打入十八层~ be cast into outer darkness

地域 dìyù (名) region; district ~政治 geopolitics

地震 dìzhèn (名) earthquake; seism: ~预报

seismic forecast

地址 dìzhǐ (名) address

地质(質) dìzhì (名) geology

地主 dìzhǔ (名) landlord: 恶霸～ despotic landlord

地租 dìzū (名) land rent

颠 diān I (动) totter; tumble; fall II (名) top; summit

颠簸 diānbǒ (动) jolt; bump; toss: 船在海上～着. The boat was tossed about in the sea.

颠倒 diāndǎo (动) 1 put upside down; reverse; invert: 画挂～了. The picture is upside down. 把次序～就行了. Reverse the order, and it will be all right. 2 be confused: 神魂～ be in a trance; be infatuated

颠倒黑白 diāndǎo hēi-bái confound black and white; confuse right and wrong

颠覆 diānfù (动) overturn; subvert: ～活动 subversive activities

颠来(來)倒去 diānlái-dǎoqù over and over: ～没个完 keep harping on sth.

颠沛流离(離) diānpèi-liúlí go tramping; drift from place to place

颠扑(撲)不破 diānpū bù pò irrefutable; indisputable: ～的真理 irrefutable truth

颠三倒四 diānsān-dǎosì disorganized; incoherent; disorderly

癫 diān (形) insane; mentally deranged: ～痫 epilepsy

巅 diān (名) mountain peak; summit

掂 diān (动) weigh in the hand: ～～这有多重. Weigh this in your hand.

掂量 diānliàng (动) 1 weigh in the hand 2 think over; weigh up: 你～着办. Just do as you think fit.

踮 diǎn (动) tiptoe

点(點) diǎn I (名) 1 drop: 雨～ raindrops 2 dot; spot; speck: 污～ stain 3 point: 沸～ boiling point. 优～ strong point. 一～五 one point five (1.5) 4 aspect; feature: 特～ characteristic feature II (动) 1 put a dot 2 touch on briefly: ～一下就行了 have only to touch on it briefly 3 drip: ～眼药 put drops in the eyes 4 check; check to see that the number is correct 5 select; choose: ～菜 order dishes (in a restaurant) 6 hint; point out: 一～他就明白了. He quickly took the hint. 7 light; kindle: ～灯 light a lamp III (量) 1 a little; some: 吃一～东西 have something to eat. 她好～了. She is a bit better now. 2 [used to indicate time]: 五～钟 five o'clock. 几～了? What time is it now? 到～了! It's time. 误～ behind time; late

点拨(撥) diǎnbo (动) show how to do sth.; coach by giving the essence of sth.

点播 diǎnbō (动) request a programme to be broadcast or televised

点菜 diǎncài (动) order dishes from a menu

点滴 diǎndī (名) 1 a bit 2 intravenous drip

点火 diǎnhuǒ (动) 1 light a fire 2 stir up trouble

点击(擊) diǎnjī (动) click

点名 diǎnmíng (动) 1 call the roll 2 mention sb. specifically: 他～要你去. He mentioned you as the person he specifically wanted.

点破 diǎnpò (动) show up sth. (particularly a secret) in a few words

点燃 diǎnrán (动) light; kindle

点头(頭) diǎntóu (动) nod (as a sign of greeting, approval, etc.): 他～了. He nodded agreement (approval).

点头(頭)哈腰 diǎntóu-hāyāo (动) bow and scrape

点心 diǎnxin (名) light refreshments

点缀 diǎnzhuì (动) embellish; adorn

点子 diǎnzi (名) 1 drop; speck 2 beat: 鼓～ drumbeat 3 key point: 他这话说到～上了. He has come to the point. 4 idea: 他～多. He's full of ideas. 鬼～ tricks

典 diǎn I (名) 1 standard work: 词～ dictionary. 引经据～ quote from classics; quote great masters 2 allusion; literary quotation 3 ceremony: 盛～ a grand ceremony II (动) mortgage

典当(當) diǎndàng (动) mortgage; pawn

典范(範) diǎnfàn (名) model; paragon

典故 diǎngù (名) allusion

典籍 diǎnjí (名) ancient books and records

典礼(禮) diǎnlǐ (名) ceremony; celebration

典型 diǎnxíng I (名) typical case; model II (形) typical; representative: ～人物 a typical character

典雅 diǎnyǎ (形) (of diction, etc.) refined; elegant

碘 diǎn (名) iodine (I): ～酒 tincture of iodine

淀 diàn I (澱) (动) settle; precipitate II (名) shallow lake

淀粉 diànfěn (名) starch

靛 diàn (名) indigo: ～青 indigo-blue

奠 diàn (动) 1 establish; settle 2 make offerings to the spirits of the dead

奠定 diàndìng (动) establish; settle: ～基础 lay the groundwork

奠基 diànjī (动) lay a foundation

垫(墊) diàn I (名) pad; cushion; mat: 椅～ chair cushion. 鞋～ insole. 床～ mattress II (动) 1 put sth. under sth. else to raise it or make it level; pad 2 pay for sb. and expect to be repaid later: 我先给你～上吧. Let me pay it for you now (you can pay me back later).

垫肩 diànjiān (名) shoulder pad

垫平 diànpíng (动) level up: 把路～ level a road

垫子 diànzi (名) mat; pad; cushion

店 diàn (名) 1 shop; store 2 inn: 住～ stop at an inn

店铺(舖) diànpù (名) shop; store

店员 diànyuán (名) shop assistant; salesman: 女～ saleswoman

惦 diàn (动) continue to think about

惦记 diànjì (动) keep thinking about

惦念 diànniàn (动) be anxious about; worry about

玷 diàn (名) a flaw in a piece of jade

玷辱 diànrǔ (动) bring disgrace on

玷污 diànwū (动) stain; sully: ～某人的名誉 sully sb.'s reputation

电(電) diàn I (名) electricity II (动) give or get an electric shock

电报(報) diànbào (名) telegram; cable: ～挂号 cable address

电表 diànbiǎo (名) 1 ammeter or voltmeter 2 kilowatt-hour meter

电冰箱 diànbīngxiāng (名) refrigerator; fridge

电波 diànbō (名) electric wave

电场(場) diànchǎng (名) electric field

电唱机(機) diànchàngjī (名) gramophone; record player

电车(車) diànchē (名) trolley-bus

电池 diànchí (名) battery

电传(傳) diànchuán (名) telex: ～机 teleprinter

电磁 diàncí (名) electromagnetism

电灯(燈) diàndēng (名) electric light

电动(動) diàndòng (形) power-driven

电镀 diàndù (名) electroplating

电工 diàngōng (名) electrician

电焊 diànhàn (名) electric welding

电话 diànhuà (名) telephone: 长途～ long distance call. 打～ make a phone call. ～簿 telephone directory. ～分机 extension

电话卡 diànhuàkǎ (名) phone card

电汇(匯) diànhuì (名) remittance by telegram

电机(機) diànjī (名) generator; electric motor

电极(極) diànjí (名) electrode

电缆(纜) diànlǎn (名) electric cable

电力 diànlì (名) electric power; power

电疗(療) diànliáo (名) electrotherapy

电铃 diànlíng (名) electric bell

电流 diànliú (名) electric current

电炉(爐) diànlú (名) 1 electric stove; hot plate 2 electric furnace

电路 diànlù (名) circuit: 集成～ integrated circuit

电码 diànmǎ (名) (telegraphic) code

电脑(腦) diànnǎo (名) computer

电钮 diànniǔ (名) push button: 按～ press a button

电气(氣) diànqì (名) electric: ～机车 electric locomotive. ～化 electrification

电器 diànqì (名) electrical equipment (or appliance)

电容 diànróng (名) electric capacity; capacitance: ～器 capacitor

电扇 diànshàn (名) electric fan

电视 diànshì (名) television; TV: ～发射机 television transmitter. ～屏幕 television screen. ～塔 television tower. ～台 television station. ～转播 television relay. ～转播卫星 television transmission satellite

电台(臺) diàntái (名) 1 transmitter-receiver; transceiver 2 radio station

电梯 diàntī (名) lift; elevator

电筒 diàntǒng (名) (electric) torch; flashlight

电网(網) diànwǎng (名) electrified wire netting

电文 diànwén (名) text (of a telegram)

电线(綫) diànxiàn (名) (electric) wire

电信 diànxìn (名) telecommunications

电讯 diànxùn (名) 1 (telegraphic) dispatch 2 telecommunication
电压(壓) diànyā (名) voltage
电唁 diànyàn (动) send a telegram of condolence
电影 diànyǐng (名) film; movie: ~院 cinema. ~制片厂 (film) studio
电源 diànyuán (名) power source; mains: 接上~ connect with the mains
电子 diànzǐ (名) electron: ~管 electron tube; valve. ~计算机 computer
电子商务(務) diànzǐ shāngwù e-commerce
电子信箱 diànzǐ xìnxiāng email box
电子邮件 diànzǐ yóujiàn email; electronic message
电阻 diànzǔ (名) resistance

佃 diàn (动) rent land (from a landlord)
佃户 diànhù (名) tenant (farmer)
佃农(農) diànnóng (名) tenant farmer
佃租 diànzū (名) land rent

殿 diàn (名) hall; palace: 佛~ Buddhist temple
殿下 diànxià (名) Your Highness; His or Her Highness

貂 diāo (名) marten

凋 diāo (动) wither; languish; decay
凋零 diāolíng (动) wither; fall into decay
凋谢 diāoxiè (动) (of trees or flowers) wither or fall

碉 diāo
碉堡 diāobǎo (名) pillbox

雕 diāo I (动) carve; engrave: 浮~ relief. ~梁画栋 with rich interior decorations II (名) vulture
雕虫(蟲)小技 diāo chóng xiǎojì trifling skill
雕花 diāohuā (名) carving: ~家具 carved furniture. ~玻璃 cut glass
雕刻 diāokè (动) carve; engrave: 玉石~ jade carving
雕塑 diāosù (名) sculpture
雕像 diāoxiàng (名) statue: 大理石~ marble statue. 半身~ bust
雕琢 diāozhuó (动) chisel and carve

刁 diāo (形) tricky; artful; sly
刁悍 diāohàn (形) cunning and fierce
刁滑 diāohuá (形) sly
刁难(難) diāonàn (动) make things difficult for sb.: 百般~ try by all means to create difficulties for sb.

叼 diāo (动) hold in the mouth

调 diào I (动) 1 transfer; shift: ~任 be transferred to another post. ~军队 move troops 2 allocate: ~来一批新货 a batch of new goods was allocated to us II (名) 1 accent: 东北~儿 Northeast accent 2 melody; tune 3 tone; tune: 升~ rising tone (or tune). 降~ falling tone (or tune)
see also tiáo
调兵遣将(將) diàobīng-qiǎnjiàng dispatch officers and men
调拨(撥) diàobō (动) allocate; allot
调查 diàochá (动) investigate; survey: 农村~ rural survey
调动(動) diàodòng (动) 1 transfer; shift: ~工作 transfer sb. to another post 2 move (troops) 3 bring into play; mobilize: ~一切积极因素 bring every positive factor into play
调度 diàodù (动) 1 dispatch (trains, buses, etc.) 2 manage; control: 生产~ production management. ~室 control room. ~员 controller
调换 diàohuàn (动) exchange; change; swop
调回 diàohuí (动) recall (troops, etc.)
调集 diàojí (动) assemble; muster: ~兵力 concentrate large forces
调配 diàopèi (动) allocate; deploy
调遣 diàoqiǎn (动) dispatch; assign: ~军队 dispatch troops
调研 diàoyán (名) investigation and research
调子 diàozi (名) 1 tune; melody 2 tone (of speech); note: 定~ set the tone

掉 diào (动) 1 fall; drop: 扣子~了. The button has come off. ~眼泪 shed tears 2 lose; be missing: 这段~了几个字. A few words are missing from this paragraph. 我的提包~了. I've lost my handbag. 3 fall behind: 他~在后面了. He is lagging behind. 4 exchange: ~座位 change seats 5 turn: 把车头~过来 turn the car round 6 [used as a complement after certain verbs]: 扔~ throw away. 擦~ wipe off
掉队(隊) diàoduì (动) drop out; fall behind
掉价(價) diàojià (动) fall in price; devalue
掉色 diàoshǎi (动) lose colour; fade
掉头(頭) diàotóu (动) turn round; turn

about

掉以轻(輕)心 diào yǐ qīngxīn dismiss sth. as of no consequence; treat sth. lightly

掉转(轉) diàozhuǎn (动) turn round: ~身子 turn round

D

吊 diào (动) 1 hang; suspend 2 lift up or let down with a rope 3 condole; mourn; send one's condolences to 4 revoke; withdraw: ~销 revoke (a licence, etc.)

吊车(車) diàochē (名) crane

吊灯(燈) diàodēng (名) pendent lamp

吊环(環) diàohuán (名) rings

吊桥(橋) diàoqiáo (名) suspension bridge

吊死 diàosǐ (动) be hanged by the neck; hang oneself

吊唁 diàoyàn (动) offer one's condolences: ~函电 messages of condolence

钓 diào (动)angle; fish with hook and bait

钓饵 diào'ěr (名) bait

钓竿 diàogān (名) fishing rod

钓钩 diàogōu (名) fishhook

钓具 diàojù (名) fishing tackle

钓鱼(魚) diàoyú (动) angle; go fishing

钓鱼(魚)台(臺) diàoyútái (名)Angler's Terrace (name of the state guest house)

跌 diē (动) 1 fall; tumble: 他~了一跤. He tripped and fell down. 2 drop; fall: 物价下~. Prices have dropped.

跌倒 diēdǎo (动) fall; tumble

跌跌撞撞 diēdiēzhuàngzhuàng stagger along; dodder

跌跤 diējiāo (动) 1 trip (or stumble) and fall; fall 2 make a mistake; meet with a setback

跌落 diēluò (动) fall; drop

爹 diē (名) 〈口〉 dad; daddy: ~娘 father and mother; mum and dad. ~~ dad.

谍 dié (名) 1 espionage: ~报 intelligence 2 spy: 间~ spy. 从事间~活动 engaged in espionage activities

碟 dié (名) small dish: ~子 small dish

喋 dié

喋喋不休 diédié bù xiū rattle away; talk endlessly

喋血 diéxuè 〈书〉 bloodshed

蝶 dié (名) butterfly: 蝴~ butterfly. ~泳 butterfly stroke

牒 dié (名) official document or note: 最后通~ ultimatum

迭 dié I (动) alternate; change: 更~ alternate II (副) repeatedly: ~起 happen repeatedly

叠(疊) dié (动) 1 pile up; overlap: 重~ overlap 2 fold: 把信~好 fold a letter

叠字 diézì (名) reduplication

丁 dīng (名) 1 man: 壮~ able-bodied man. 园~ gardener 2 members of a family; population 3 fourth 4 small cubes of meat or vegetable; cubes: 辣子肉~ diced pork with chilli

丁当(當) dīngdāng (象) tinkle; jingle

丁冬 dīngdōng (象) dingdong

丁香 dīngxiāng (名) 1 lilac 2 clove

丁字 dīngzì (形) T-shaped

疔 dīng (名) malignant boil

叮 dīng (动) 1 sting; bite: 一个虫子~了我一下. An insect stung me. 2 ask again; make sure: 我又~了他一句. I asked him again.

叮当(當) dīngdāng see "丁当" dīngdāng

叮咛(嚀) dīngníng (动) exhort; urge

叮嘱(囑) dīngzhǔ (动) warn repeatedly; exhort

盯 dīng (动) gaze at; stare at; fix one's eyes on: 大家的眼睛都~住了靶心. All eyes were fixed on the bull's-eye.

盯梢 dīngshāo (动) tail sb.; shadow sb.

钉 dīng I (名) nail; tack II (动) 1 follow closely; tail 2 urge; press: 你要经常~着他一点,免得他忘了. You'll have to remind him from time to time lest he should forget.

see also dìng

钉梢 dīngshāo (动) shadow sb.; tail sb.

钉子 dīngzi (名) 1 nail 2 snag: 碰~ meet with a flat refusal

顶 dǐng I (名) top; peak; summit: 山~ mountaintop. 屋~ roof II (动) 1 carry on the head 2 retort: ~撞 contradict sb. 3 go against; brave: ~风 brave the wind 4 push from below; prop up: 嫩芽把土~起来了. The sprouts have pushed through the earth. 5 take the place of; substitute; replace: ~别人的名字 assume sb. else's name 6 equal; be equivalent to III (量) [for sth. with a top]: 一~帽子 a hat. 一~帐子 a

mosquito net IV (副) very; most: ～有用 most useful. 那个～小的盆 that smallest pot
顶点(點) dǐngdiǎn (名) summit pinnacle; end
顶端 dǐngduān (名) top; peak; apex
顶多 dǐngduō (副) at (the) most; at best
顶峰 dǐngfēng (名) peak; summit; pinnacle
顶好 dǐnghǎo (形) very good
顶级 dǐngjí (形) top: ～专家 a top specialist
顶尖 dǐngjiān (名) tip; top: ～人物 outstanding person; the cream of the people
顶梁柱 dǐngliángzhù (名) pillar; backbone
顶事 dǐngshì (形) be useful; serve the purpose: 多穿件毛线衣也还～. It does serve the purpose to put on another woollen sweater.
顶替 dǐngtì (动) take sb.'s place; replace: 冒名～ pass oneself off as somebody else with an assumed name
顶天立地 dǐngtiān-lìdì of gigantic stature; of indomitable spirit
顶头(頭)上司 dǐngtóu shàngsi one's immediate superior
顶用 dǐngyòng (形) be of use (or help); serve the purpose: 孩子太小, 不～. The child is too young to help.
顶住 dǐngzhù (动) withstand; stand up to: ～巨大的外部压力 withstand tremendous outside pressure
顶嘴 dǐngzuǐ (动) talk back
鼎 dǐng (名) an ancient cooking vessel; tripod
鼎鼎大名 dǐngdǐng dàmíng of high reputation; celebrated; famous
鼎沸 dǐngfèi (形) noisy and confused: 人声～ confused and loud noises
定 dìng I (动) 1 decide; fix; set: ～计划 draw up a plan. ～时间 fix a time 2 calm down: 心神不～ be absent-minded; be perturbed II (副)〈书〉surely; certainly; definitely
定案 dìng'àn I (动) make a verdict; decide on a plan II (名) verdict; final decision
定调子 dìng diàozi set the tone for sth.
定额 dìng'é (名) quota; norm: 生产～ production quota
定岗(崗) dìnggǎng (动) fix the number of posts and staff (in the workplace)
定稿 dìnggǎo I (动) finalize a manuscript II (名) final version; final text
定价(價) dìngjià I (动) fix a price II (名) fixed price; price
定见(見) dìngjiàn (名) definite opinion
定金 dìngjīn (名) deposit
定睛 dìngjīng (动) fix one's eyes upon; gaze at: ～细看 scrutinize
定居 dìngjū (动) settle down: ～点 settlement
定局 dìngjú I (名) foregone conclusion II (动) settle finally: 事情还没～. The matter isn't settled yet.
定理 dìnglǐ (名) theorem: 基本～ fundamental theorem
定量 dìngliàng (名) ration; fixed quantity: ～供应 rationing
定律 dìnglǜ (名) law: 万有引力～ the law of universal gravitation
定论(論) dìnglùn (名) final conclusion: 这个问题还没有～. It remains an open question.
定期 dìngqī I (形) regular; at regular intervals; periodical: ～检查 regular check-ups. ～刊物 periodical publication II (动) fix (or set) a date
定然 dìngrán (副) certainly; definitely
定神 dìngshén (动) 1 collect oneself; pull oneself together 2 concentrate one's attention
定时(時)炸弹(彈) dìngshí zhàdàn time bomb
定位 dìngwèi (动) position (oneself)
定型 dìngxíng (动) finalize the design; become fixed
定性 dìngxìng (动) determine the nature of sth.: ～分析 qualitative analysis
定义(義) dìngyì (名) definition: 下～ give a definition; define
定语 dìngyǔ (名) attribute: ～从句 attributive clause
定罪 dìngzuì (动) declare sb. guilty
定做 dìngzuò (动) have sth. made to order (or measure): ～的衣服 tailor-made clothes
碇 dìng (名) a heavy stone used as an anchor; killick
锭 dìng (名) 1 ingot-shaped tablet 2 spindle
订 dìng (动) 1 conclude; draw up: ～条约 conclude a treaty. ～合同 enter into a contract. ～日期 fix a date. ～生产指标 set a production target 2 subscribe to; book; order: ～报纸 subscribe to a newspaper. ～票 book a ticket. ～一桌酒席 order a dinner 3 make correc-

D

tions; revise: 修～ revise **4** staple together

订单(單) dìngdān (名) order (for goods); order form

订购(購) dìnggòu (动) order (goods)

订户 dìnghù (名) subscriber

订婚 dìnghūn (动) be engaged (or betrothed)

订货 dìnghuò (动) order goods

订立 dìnglì (动) conclude (a treaty, agreement, etc.)

订阅 dìngyuè (动) subscribe to (a newspaper, periodical, etc.)

订正 dìngzhèng (动) make corrections

钉 dìng (动) **1** nail: ～钉子 drive in a nail **2** sew on: ～扣子 sew a button on

see also dīng

丢 diū (动) **1** lose; be missing: 我的笔～了. I've lost my pen. **2** throw; cast; toss: ～个石头到水里 throw a stone into the water **3** put (or lay) aside; dismiss (from one's mind): 只有一件事～不开. There is only one thing I cannot easily dismiss from my mind.

丢掉 diūdiào (动) **1** lose **2** throw away; discard; get rid of: ～官僚主义习气 get rid of bureaucracy

丢脸(臉) diūliǎn (动) lose face; be disgraced: 你这样做真～! You ought to be ashamed of what you did!

丢面子 diū miànzi lose face

丢弃(棄) diūqì (动) abandon; discard

丢三落四 diūsān-làsì be always forgetting things

丢失 diūshī (动) lose; let slip; miss

东(東) dōng (名) **1** east: ～郊 eastern suburbs **2** master; owner: 房～ landlord **3** host: 做～ stand treat; play the host

东半球 dōngbànqiú (名) the Eastern Hemisphere

东道 dōngdào (名) host: ～国 host country. ～主 host

东方 dōngfāng (名) **1** the east **2** the East; the Orient

东家 dōngjiā (名) master; boss

东经(經) dōngjīng (名) east longitude

东拉西扯 dōnglā-xīchě drag in irrelevant matters; talk at random; ramble

东拼西凑 dōngpīn-xīcòu scrape together; knock together: 那篇文章是～的. That article is a hodge-podge.

东山再起 dōngshān zài qǐ stage a comeback

东西 dōng-xī (名) east and west; from east to west

东西 dōngxi (名) **1** thing: 我没买什么～. I didn't buy anything. **2** [expressing a feeling of affection or hatred for a person or animal] thing; creature: 这小～真可爱. What a sweet little thing! 真不是～! What a despicable creature!

东…西… dōng…xī… here...there: 东张西望 look around. 东奔西跑 dash around. 东一句,西一句 talk incoherently

冬 dōng (名) winter: ～季 (or ～天) winter

冬眠 dōngmián (名) winter sleep; hibernation

董 dǒng

董事 dǒngshì (名) director; trustee: ～会 board of directors (or trustees). ～长 chairman of the board

懂 dǒng (动) understand; know: 我不～你谈的什么. I don't understand what you are driving at. ～法文 know French. ～礼貌 have good manners

懂行 dǒngháng (形) know the business; know the ropes

懂事 dǒngshì (形) sensible; perceptive: ～的孩子 a sensible child

动(動) dòng (动) **1** move; stir: 别～! Don't move! **2** act; get moving: 群众普遍地～起来了. The masses all got moving. **3** use: ～脑筋 use one's head **4** change; alter: 改～ change **5** touch (one's heart); arouse: ～感情 be carried away by emotion; get worked up

动不动 dòngbudòng (副) easily; frequently: ～就发脾气 be apt to lose one's temper; be liable to flare up at any moment

动产(產) dòngchǎn (名) movable property

动词 dòngcí (名) verb

动荡(蕩) dòngdàng (名) turbulence; upheaval; unrest

动画(畫)片 dònghuàpiàn (名) animated cartoon; cartoon

动机(機) dòngjī (名) motive; intention: ～好,效果不一定好. The result may not be necessarily satisfactory, though you act with the best of intentions.

动静 dòngjing (名) sound of people speaking or moving about: 屋子里一点～也没有. Nobody is stirring in the house.

动力 dònglì (名) 1 power 2 driving force; motivation; impetus

动乱(亂) dòngluàn (名) turmoil; disturbance; upheaval: 十年～时期 the decade of turmoil. 社会～ social upheaval

动脉(脈) dòngmài (名) artery

动漫 dòngmàn (名) anime and manga; cartoons

动气(氣) dòngqì (动)〈口〉 take offence; get angry

动情 dòngqíng (动) 1 feel excited 2 fall in love

动人 dòngrén (形) moving; touching: ～的情景 a moving scene

动身 dòngshēn (动) set out on a journey; leave

动手 dòngshǒu (动) 1 touch: 请勿～! Please don't touch! ～动脚 get fresh with sb. 2 start work; get to work: 大家一齐～! Everybody get to work! 3 raise a hand to strike; hit out: 谁先动的手? Who struck the first blow?

动手术(術) dòngshǒushù (动) 1 perform an operation; operate on sb. 2 undergo an operation; be operated on

动态(態) dòngtài (名) tendency; trends; developments: 科技新～ recent developments in science and technology

动听(聽) dòngtīng (形) interesting or pleasant to the ear

动武 dòngwǔ (动) use force; start a fight; come to blows

动物 dòngwù (名) animal: ～园 zoo. ～学 zoology. ～志 fauna

动向 dòngxiàng (名) trend; tendency: 密切注意敌人～. Keep a close watch on the enemy's movements.

动心 dòngxīn (动) be attracted by; one's desire, interest or enthusiasm is aroused

动摇 dòngyáo (动) move; shake; waver: ～分子 wavering element. ～军心 shake the morale

动议(議) dòngyì (名) motion: 紧急～ an urgent motion

动用 dòngyòng (动) employ; draw on (resources, funds, etc.): ～库存 draw on stock

动员 dòngyuán (动) mobilize; arouse

动辄 dòngzhé (副)〈书〉 easily; at every turn

动真格儿(兒) dòngzhēngér take real action; take strong action

动作 dòngzuò (名) movement; action: ～敏捷(缓慢) quick (slow) in one's movements

动作片 dòngzuòpiàn (名) action movie

冻(凍) dòng I (动) 1 freeze: ～肉 frozen meat 2 feel very cold: 我～坏了. I'm freezing. 手～了. One's hands numbed with cold. II (名) jelly: 肉～儿 jellied meat

冻冰 dòngbīng (动) freeze: 河上～了. The river is frozen.

冻僵 dòngjiāng (形) frozen stiff; numb with cold

冻结 dòngjié (动) freeze: 工资～ wage freeze. ～的资产 frozen assets

栋(棟) dòng (量): 一～楼房 a building

栋梁 dòngliáng (名) 1 ridge-pole and beam 2 pillar of the state

洞 dòng (名) hole; cavity; cave

洞察 dòngchá (动) see through clearly; have an insight into: ～力 insight; discernment

洞若观(觀)火 dòng ruò guān huǒ see something as clearly as a blazing fire

洞悉 dòngxī (动) know clearly; understand thoroughly

洞穴 dòngxué (名) cave; cavern

恫 dòng

恫吓(嚇) dònghè (动) threaten; intimidate

都 dōu (副) 1 all; both: 这些我～喜欢. I like them all. 我俩～想去. Both of us want to go. 2 all [referring to causes]: ～是你多嘴,看她生气了. Look, she is annoyed. It's all because of your unsolicited remarks. 3 already: ～八点了,你怎么还不走? It's already eight o'clock, why are you still here? 我～十八岁了,别把我当小孩子. Don't treat me like a child. I'm already eighteen. 4 even: 这种事连小孩～知道. Even a child knows all this. 我中学～没上过. I didn't even go to middle school.
see also dū

兜 dōu I (名) pocket; bag: 网～儿 string bag II (动) 1 wrapped up in a piece of cloth, etc.: 用手绢～着一些葡萄 carry some grapes wrapped up in a handkerchief 2 move round: 我们开车在城里～了一圈. We went for a drive around in town. 说话别～圈子. Come straight to the point. Don't beat about the bush.

兜风(風) dōufēng (动) go for a drive

兜揽(攬) dōulǎn (动) canvass; solicit: ～生意 solicit business

兜售 dōushòu (动) peddle; hawk

D

斗 dǒu I (量) *dou*, measurement of capacity (10 litres) II (名) an object shaped like a cup or dipper: 烟～ (tobacco) pipe. 漏～ funnel

see also dòu

斗胆 dǒudǎn (动) 〈谦〉 make bold; venture: 我～说一句,这件事您做错了. May I venture to say that you were wrong here.

斗笠 dǒulì (名) bamboo hat

斗篷 dǒupeng (名) cape; cloak

斗室 dǒushì (名) 〈书〉 a small room

抖 dǒu (动) 1 shake: ～掉雨衣上的雪. Shake the snow off one's raincoat. 2 tremble; shiver; quiver: 浑身直～ tremble all over. 冷得发～ shiver with cold 3 rouse; stir up: ～起精神 pluck up one's spirits 4 get on in the world: 他现在～起来了. His star is rising.

抖动(動) dǒudòng (动) shake; tremble; vibrate

抖擞(擻) dǒusǒu (动) enliven; rouse: 精神～ full of energy; full of vim and vigour

陡 dǒu I (形) steep; precipitous: ～坡 abrupt slope. 悬崖～壁 precipice; cliff II (副) suddenly; abruptly: 天气～变. The weather changed suddenly.

陡峻 dǒujùn (形) high and precipitous

陡峭 dǒuqiào (形) precipitous

斗(鬥) dòu (动) 1 fight; struggle against: 与风浪搏～ battle with the winds and waves 2 contest with; contend with: ～智 duel of wits. 我～不过你. I'm not your match. 3 (of cocks, crickets, etc.) fight: ～鸡 cockfighting

see also dǒu

斗争 dòuzhēng I (动) 1 struggle; fight; combat 2 strive for; fight for II (名) struggle

斗志 dòuzhì (名) fighting will; morale: ～昂扬 have high morale

豆 dòu (名) bean: 咖啡～ coffee beans. 蚕～ broad beans. 豌～ peas. ～角 French beans

豆腐 dòufu (名) bean curd

豆制(製)品 dòuzhìpǐn (名) bean products

痘 dòu (名) smallpox

痘苗 dòumiáo (名) (bovine) vaccine

逗 dòu I (动) 1 play with; tease; tantalize: ～孩子玩 tantalize a child 2 attract; charm; amuse: ～人发笑 set people laughing. 这小女孩很～人喜欢. She's a charming little girl. 3 stay; stop II (形) funny: 这话真～! What a funny remark!

逗号(號) dòuhào (名) comma (,)

逗留 dòuliú (动) stay; stop: 中途在东京～两小时 stop over at Tokyo for two hours

逗趣儿(兒) dòuqùr (动) set people laughing; amuse

都 dū (名) 1 capital 2 big city: 通～大邑 big cities

see also dōu

都城 dūchéng (名) capital

都会(會) dūhuì (名) chief city; capital city

都市 dūshì (名) big city; metropolis

嘟 dū I (象) honk: 汽车喇叭～～响. The car tooted. II (动) pout: ～起了嘴 pout

嘟囔 dūnang (动) mutter to oneself; mumble

督 dū (动) superintend and direct

督察 dūchá (动) superintend; supervise

督促 dūcù (动) supervise sb. and urge him to go ahead

毒 dú I (名) 1 poison; toxin: 病～ virus. 服～自杀 commit suicide by taking poison 2 narcotics: 吸～ take drugs II (形) 1 poisonous; noxious 2 malicious; cruel; fierce: 这人心肠真～! What a cruel man! ～打 give sb. a good beating III (动) kill with poison

毒草 dúcǎo (名) 1 poisonous weeds 2 harmful speech, writing, etc.

毒害 dúhài (动) poison (sb.'s mind)

毒计 dújì (名) ruthless scheme; deadly plot

毒辣 dúlà (形) vicious; murderous

毒品 dúpǐn (名) drugs

毒气(氣) dúqì (名) poison gas

毒蛇 dúshé (名) poisonous snake; viper

毒手 dúshǒu (名) murderous scheme: 下～ lay murderous hands on sb.; prepare a treacherous trap for sb.

毒素 dúsù (名) poison; toxin

毒枭(梟) dúxiāo (名) drug pusher; drug smuggler

毒药(藥) dúyào (名) poison; toxicant

渎(瀆) dú (动) 〈书〉 show disrespect or contempt:

亵～ blaspheme

读职(職) dúzhí (名) malfeasance; dereliction of duty

读(讀) dú (动) 1 read; read aloud: 你～过这本书吗? Have you read this book? 请你～给我听. Could you read it (aloud) for me, please? 2 go to school or college: 他～完大学后就在这里开始工作. He started to work here after finishing college.

读本 dúběn (名) textbook; reader

读书(書) dúshū (动) 1 read; study 2 attend school: ～人 an intellectual

读数(數) dúshù (名) reading: 标度～ scale reading

读物 dúwù (名) reading material: 通俗～ popular literature

读音 dúyīn (名) pronunciation

读者 dúzhě (名) reader: ～来信 readers' letters; letters to the editor

黩(黷) dú (动) 1 blacken; defile 2 act wantonly

黩武 dúwǔ (动) militaristic; warlike; bellicose: 穷兵～ engage in unjust military ventures

犊(犢) dú (名) calf

牍(牘) dú (名) 1 wooden tablets or slips for writing (in ancient times) 2 documents; archives; correspondence

独(獨) dú (形) 1 only; sole: ～(生)子 only son 2 alone: ～往～来 seldom go anywhere in company

独霸 dúbà (动) dominate exclusively; monopolize

独白 dúbái (名) soliloquy; monologue

独裁 dúcái (名) dictatorship; autocratic rule: ～者 autocrat; dictator. ～政治 autocracy

独唱 dúchàng (名) (vocal) solo

独出心裁 dú chū xīncái show originality; be original

独创(創) dúchuàng (名) original creation: ～一格 create a style all one's own. ～性 originality

独当(當)一面 dú dāng yī miàn be capable of handling affairs of a whole department

独到 dúdào (形) original: ～之处 originality

独断(斷)独行 dúduàn-dúxíng act autocratically

独夫 dúfū (名) autocrat: ～民贼 autocrat and traitor to the people

独家 dújiā (形) exclusive: ～新闻 exclusive news. ～经销 exclusive rights for sales. ～代理 sole agent

独角戏(戲) dújiǎoxì (名) monodrama; one-man show

独揽(攬) dúlǎn (动) arrogate; monopolize: ～大权 arrogate all powers to oneself

独立 dúlì I (动) stand alone II (名) independence III (形) independent; on one's own: ～思考 think independently

独苗 dúmiáo (名) only son and heir

独幕剧(劇) dúmùjù (名) one-act play

独木桥(橋) dúmùqiáo (名) single-plank bridge; difficult path

独身 dúshēn I (名) live apart from one's family II (动) unmarried; single; celibate

独生子女 dúshēng zǐnǚ only child

独树(樹)一帜(幟) dú shù yī zhì start a separate school of thought

独特 dútè (形) unique; distinctive: ～的风格 a unique style

独一无(無)二 dúyī-wú'èr unique; unparalleled; unmatched

独占(佔) dúzhàn (动) enjoy exclusively; monopolize

独资 dúzī (名) exclusive investment

独自 dúzì (副) alone; by oneself

独奏 dúzòu (名) (instrumental) solo: 钢琴～ piano solo

堵 dǔ I (动) 1 stop up; block up: 路～住了. The road is blocked. 2 feel suffocated; oppressed; stifled II (量): 一～墙 a wall

堵塞 dǔsè (动) stop up; block up: 交通～ traffic jam

堵嘴 dǔzuǐ (动) silence sb.

睹 dǔ (动) see: 目～ witness. 目～者 eyewitness. 熟视无～ turn a blind eye to

赌 dǔ (动) 1 gamble: ～本 money to gamble with; resources for risky ventures. ～场 gambling den. ～棍 gambler 2 bet: 打～ make a bet; bet

赌博 dǔbó (名) gambling

赌气(氣) dǔqì (动) feel wronged or frustrated and act rashly: ～走了 dash off in a fit of pique

赌钱(錢) dǔqián (动) (for money) gamble; play

赌咒 dǔzhòu (动) take an oath; swear

赌注 dǔzhù (名) stake

D

笃 dǔ (形) 1 sincere; earnest: ～志 tenacious of purpose 2 (of an illness) serious; critical: 病～ be terminally ill

笃信 dǔxìn (动) sincerely believe in; be a loyal adherent of

肚 dǔ (～子) (名) tripe

see also dù

度 dù I (名) 1 degree: 长～ length. 温～ temperature. 硬～ hardness. 湿～ humidity 2 limit; extent; degree: 劳累过～ overwork oneself 3 tolerance; magnanimity: 大～ be magnanimous 4 consideration: 把生死置之～外 give no thought to personal safety II (动) spend; pass: 欢～佳节 joyously celebrate a festival. ～假 spend one's holidays III (量) 1 occasion; time: 再～ once more. 一年一～ once a year 2 [a unit or measurement for angles, temperature, etc.] degree: 90～的角 an angle of 90 degrees. 摄氏 100～100℃. 3 kilowatt-hour: 一～电 one kilowatt-hour

see also duó

度假村 dùjiàcūn (名) holiday village; holiday resort

度量 dùliàng (名) tolerance; magnanimity: ～大 broad-minded. ～小 narrow-minded

度量衡 dùliànghéng (名) length, capacity and weight; weights and measures

度日 dùrì (动) do for a living: ～如年 the miserable days drag on like years

度数(數) dùshu (名) number of degrees; reading

渡 dù I (动) 1 cross (a river, the sea, etc.): ～江 cross a river 2 tide over; pull through: ～过难关 tide over a difficulty II (名) ferry

渡船 dùchuán (名) ferryboat; ferry

渡口 dùkǒu (名) ferry

渡轮(輪) dùlún (名) ferry steamer; ferry boat

镀 dù (动) plate: 电～ galvanizing. ～金 gold-plating; gilding. ～银 silver-plating; silvering

杜 dù (动) prevent; eradicate: 以～流弊 so as to put an end to any abuse or malpractice

杜绝 dùjué (动) stop; prevent; put an end to: ～贪污和浪费 prevent corruption and waste

杜撰 dùzhuàn (动) fabricate; make up

肚 dù (名) belly

see also dǔ

肚皮 dùpí (名) belly

肚脐(臍) dùqí (名) navel; belly button

妒 dù (动) be jealous (or envious) of; envy

妒忌 dùjì (动) be jealous (or envious) of; envy

端 duān I (名) 1 end; extremity: 笔～ the tip of a writing brush 2 beginning: 开～ beginning 3 reason; cause: 无～ without reason; unwarranted II (形) upright; proper: ～庄 dignified; sedate. 品行不～ misbehaviour III (动) hold sth. level with both hands; carry: ～托盘 carry a tray. ～饭菜 bring food in

端量 duānliang (动) look sb. up and down

端倪 duānní (名) clue; inkling: 略有～ have some clues

端午节(節) duānwǔjié (名) the Dragon Boat Festival (the 5th day of the 5th lunar month)

端详 duānxiáng I (名) details II (形) dignified and serene: 举止～ behave with dignity

端详 duānxiang (动) scrutinize; look sb. up and down

端正 duānzhèng I (形) 1 upright; regular: 五官～ have regular features. 坐得～ sit straight in one's seat 2 proper; correct: 品行～ correct in behaviour; respectable II (动) rectify; correct: ～态度 make sure one's attitude is correct

短 duǎn I (形) short; brief: ～裤 shorts. ～评 brief comment II (动) 1 lack; be short of: 只～两个人. Only two people are absent. 2 owe: 你还～我三元钱. You still owe me three *Yuan*. III (名) weak point; fault: 揭人的～儿 pick on sb.'s weakness. 说长道～ gossip

短兵相接 duǎnbīng xiāng jiē fight at close quarters

短波 duǎnbō (名) short wave

短处(處) duǎnchù (名) shortcoming; weakness; fault

短促 duǎncù (形) very brief; short: 时间～ pressed for time. 呼吸～ short of breath

短工 duǎngōng (名) casual labourer; seasonal labourer: 打～ be a casual labourer; find a seasonal job

短见(見) duǎnjiàn (名) 1 short-sighted view

2 suicide: 寻～ attempt suicide; commit suicide
短路 duǎnlù (名) short circuit
短命 duǎnmìng (形) die young; short-lived
短跑 duǎnpǎo (名) dash; sprint
短篇小说 duǎnpiān xiǎoshuō (名) short story
短期 duǎnqī (名) short-term; short period: ～贷款 short-term loan
短浅(淺) duǎnqiǎn (形) narrow and shallow: 目光～ short-sighted. 见识～ badly informed and superficial
短缺 duǎnquē (名) shortage; deficiency
短信 duǎnxìn (名) cell-phone message; text message; SMS; GSM
短小 duǎnxiǎo (形) short and small: 身材～ of small stature
短小精悍 duǎnxiǎo jīnghàn short but well-built; short and pithy
短语 duǎnyǔ (名) phrase
短暂 duǎnzàn (形) of short duration; brief: 生命是～的. Life is short.

断(斷) duàn I (动) 1 break; snap; cut: 绳子～了. The rope snapped. 桥～了. The bridge is broken. ～电 cut off electricity. 联系中～ lose contact (with) 2 judge; decide: 当机立～ make a prompt decision II (副) 〈书〉[used only in negative sentences] absolutely; decidedly: ～无此理 absolutely absurd; the height of absurdity
断肠(腸) duàncháng (形) heart-broken; broken-hearted
断炊 duànchuī (动) run out of food and fuel; can't keep the pot boiling
断定 duàndìng (动) form a judgment; conclude
断断续(續)续 duànduànxùxù intermittently: 他～在这里住了五年. He has lived here off and on for five years.
断根 duàngēn (动) (of an illness) be completely cured
断后(後) duànhòu (动) 1 cover the retreat 2 have no progeny
断交 duànjiāo (动) 1 break off a friendship 2 sever diplomatic relations
断句 duànjù (动) punctuate
断绝 duànjué (动) break off; cut off; sever: ～关系 break off all relationship. ～交通 cut off all communications
断奶 duànnǎi (动) wean
断气(氣) duànqì (动) breathe one's last; die
断然 duànrán I (形) resolute; drastic: 采取～措施 take drastic measures II (副) absolutely
断送 duànsòng (动) forfeit (one's life, future, etc.); ruin
断线(綫) duànxiàn I (名) a string being broken II (动) disconnect; break off; sever
断言 duànyán (动) assert
断章取义(義) duàn zhāng qǔ yì quote sb.'s words out of context; distort a statement, etc.

段 duàn (量) section; part: 一～路 certain distance. 一～话 a passage from a speech. 一～时间 a period of time
段落 duànluò (名) 1 paragraph 2 phase; stage

煅 duàn (动) forge: ～铁 forge iron

锻 duàn (动) forge
锻工 duàngōng (名) 1 forging 2 forger
锻炼(煉) duànliàn (动) 1 take physical exercise 2 temper; steel; toughen
锻造 duànzào (名) forging; smithing

缎 duàn (名) satin

堆 duī I (动) pile; stack: 粮食～满仓. The granary was piled high with grain. II (名) heap; pile; stack: 土～ mound. 草～ haystack III (量) heap; pile; crowd: 一～人 a crowd of people
堆放 duīfàng (动) heap; stack
堆积(積) duījī (动) pile up; heap up
堆砌 duīqì (动) 1 pile up (hewn rocks, etc.) 2 write in florid language

兑 duì (动) exchange; convert
兑换 duìhuàn (动) exchange; convert: ～率 rate of exchange. ～处 money changer
兑现 duìxiàn (动) 1 cash (a cheque, etc.) 2 realize; fulfil

对(對) duì I (动) 1 treat; against: 她～我很好. She treats me well. ～付 cope with. 反～ be against 2 face: ～着镜子看 look at oneself in the mirror. 把枪口～准敌人 aim one's gun at the enemy. ～坐 sit face to face 3 compare; check: 校～ proofread 4 adjust: ～表 adjust (or set) the watch. ～距离 (of a camera) adjust the distance 5 bring two things into contact; fit one into the other: ～暗号 exchange code words. ～火儿 (of smoking) Give me a light, please. **6** mix; add: 牛奶里～水了. The milk has been adulterated with water. **7** answer; reply **8** suit; agree: ～口味儿 suit one's taste II (形) correct; right: 你说得～. What you said is correct. 是他的不～. It's his fault. III (量) pair; couple: 一～花瓶 a pair of vases. 一～夫妇 a married couple IV (介): 她～我说的. She said this to me. 我～他笑. I smiled at him. 这是我～她的看法. This is my opinion of her. ～某事的态度 (one's) attitude towards sth.

对白 duìbái (名) dialogue (in a novel, film or play)

对半 duìbàn (副) half-and-half; fifty-fifty

对比 duìbǐ (动) contrast; compare: 形成鲜明的～ form a sharp contrast

对簿公堂 duìbù gōngtáng be interrogated in court

对不起 duìbuqǐ **1** 〈套〉 I'm sorry; excuse me; pardon me; I beg your pardon **2** let sb. down; be unfair to sb.

对策 duìcè (名) countermeasure

对称(稱) duìchèn (名) symmetry

对答 duìdá (动) answer; reply: ～如流 answer fluently

对待 duìdài (动) treat; approach; handle

对得起 duìdeqǐ be worthy of; not let sb. down; treat sb. fairly (also as "对得住")

对等 duìděng (名) reciprocity; equity: 在～的基础上 on a reciprocal basis

对方 duìfāng (名) opposite side; the other party

对付 duìfu (动) **1** deal with; cope with; tackle: ～敌人 deal with the enemy **2** make do; get by: 这把伞还可以～着用. The umbrella is still serviceable.

对过(過) duìguò (名) opposite; across the way: 学校～的那个商店 the shop across the school

对号(號) duìhào (动) check the number: ～入座 sit in the right seat

对话 duìhuà (名) dialogue

对讲(講)机(機) duìjiǎngjī (名) walkie-talkie

对劲(勁) duìjìn (形) **1** be to one's liking; suit one: 这支毛笔写起字来不～. This writing brush is not easy to handle when you use it. 他俩很～. The two of them are getting along well. **2** normal; right: 他今天有些不～. He is not quite himself today.

对开(開) duìkāi I (动) **1** (of trains, buses or ships) run from opposite directions **2** divide into two halves; go fifty-fifty II (名) folio

对抗 duìkàng I (名) confrontation II (动) resist; oppose

对口 duìkǒu (动) fit in with one's training or speciality: 工作～ a job one is trained for

对立 duìlì (名) antagonism; antithesis; opposition: ～面 opposites. ～统一 unity of opposites

对联(聯) duìlián (名) antithetical couplet (written on scrolls, etc.)

对门(門) duìmén (名) the house opposite

对面 duìmiàn I (名) **1** opposite: 加油站在学校～. The petrol station is opposite the school. **2** right in front: 一辆车从～开过来. A car is coming towards us. II (副) face to face

对牛弹(彈)琴 duì niú tánqín play the lute to a cow; talk over sb.'s head; address the wrong audience

对手 duìshǒu (名) **1** opponent; adversary **2** match; equal: 他不是你的～. He's no match for you.

对台(臺)戏(戲) duìtáixì (名) rival performance or show: 唱～ put on a rival show

对头(頭) duìtóu (形) **1** correct; on the right track **2** normal; right: 你的脸色不～. You're not looking well.

对头(頭) duìtou (名) **1** enemy: 死～ sworn enemy **2** opponent; adversary

对外 duìwài (形) external; foreign: ～贸易 foreign trade. ～开放 opening to the outside world

对虾(蝦) duìxiā (名) prawn

对象 duìxiàng (名) **1** target; object: 研究～ objective of a research project **2** boy or girl friend

对应(應) duìyìng (形) corresponding

对于(於) duìyú (介)大家～这个问题的看法是一致的. Their views on this problem are identical. ～我来说,这没什么关系. As far as I am concerned, it doesn't matter.

对照 duìzhào (动) compare; collate: ～检查 make self-criticism. 把新本与旧本～一下. Collate the new copy with the old one.

对症下药(藥) duì zhèng xià yào decide on measures to solve problems according to specific circumstances

对质(質) duìzhì (名) confrontation (in court)

对峙 duìzhì (动) confront each other: 武装～

military confrontation

队(隊) duì (名) 1 team; group: 篮球～ basketball team. 军乐～ military band. 游击～ guerrilla forces 2 a row (or line) of people: 排成两～ fall into two lines

队伍 duìwu (名) 1 troops 2 ranks; contingent: 游行～ procession; parade

队形 duìxíng (名) formation: ～飞行 formation flying. 战斗～ in battle formation

队长(長) duìzhǎng (名) group leader; team leader

敦 dūn (形) honest; sincere: ～请 cordially invite; earnestly request

敦促 dūncù (动) urge; press

敦厚 dūnhòu (形) honest and sincere

敦实(實) dūnshi (形) sturdy: 这人长得很～. He has a powerful build, though short in stature.

墩 dūn (名) block: 土～ mound. 菜～(子) chopping board. 树～ stump. 桥～ pier (of a bridge)

墩布 dūnbù (名) mop

吨(噸) dūn (量) ton (t.)

吨位 dūnwèi (名) tonnage

蹲 dūn (动) 1 squat 2 stay: ～在家里 stay at home

蹲点(點) dūndiǎn (动) (of cadres) stay at a selected grass-roots unit to help improve the work and gain firsthand experience

盹 dǔn (动) doze: 打～儿 doze off; get a wink of sleep

炖 dùn (动) 1 stew: ～牛肉 stewed beef 2 warm sth.: ～酒 warm (up) wine

顿 dùn I (动) 1 pause 2 arrange; settle: 安～ arrange for; settle in 3 stamp: ～脚 stamp one's foot II (名) pause III (量): 三～饭 three meals. 挨了一～骂 get a scolding IV (副) suddenly: 茅塞～开 be suddenly enlightened

顿挫 dùncuò (名) pause and transition in rhythm or melody: 抑扬～ modulation in tone

顿号(號) dùnhào (名) a slight-pause mark used to set off items in a series (、)

顿时(時) dùnshí (副) immediately; at once

囤 dùn (名) a grain bin

see also tún

钝 dùn (形) 1 blunt; dull: ～刀 a blunt knife 2 stupid: 迟～ dull-witted; slow

盾 dùn (名) shield: ～牌 shield

遁 dùn (动) escape; flee; fly

遁词 dùncí (名) subterfuge; quibble

咄 duō

咄咄逼人 duōduō bī rén aggressive; overbearing

咄咄怪事 duōduō guàishì inconceivable absurdity

多 duō I (形) 1 many; much; more: 很～人 many people. 这菜油太～. The dish is too rich. 更～的帮助 more help 2 odd; over; more than: 五十～岁 over fifty years old. 一个～月 more than a month. 三十～年 thirty-odd years 3 much more; far more: 病人今天好～了. The patient is much better today. 这部电影比那部要有意思～了. Compared with that film, this one is far more interesting. 这样做就容易～了. It is much easier to do it this way. 4 too many; too much; excessive: ～了十张票. There are ten tickets too many. 我在那里～住了几天. I stayed there a few days longer. II (副) [indicating degree or extent]: 这孩子～大了? How old is this child? 他要在这里呆～久? How long is he going to stay here? 我倒想看看她有～能干! I'd like to see how capable she is!

多半 duōbàn (副) 1 the greater part; most; mostly: 他们之中～是大学生. Most of them are students. 2 probably; most likely: 瞧! 这天～要下雨. Look at the sky. It's most likely going to rain.

多边(邊) duōbiān (形) multilateral: ～会谈 multilateral talks. ～贸易 multilateral trade

多才多艺(藝) duōcái-duōyì versatile: ～的人 a resourceful person

多愁善感 duōchóu-shàngǎn sentimental

多此一举(舉) duō cǐ yī jǔ make an unnecessary move: 何必～? Why take the trouble to do that?

多次 duōcì (副) many times; repeatedly

多多益善 duōduō yì shàn the more the better

多发病 duōfābìng (名) frequently occurring illness; recurrent disease

多方 duōfāng (副) in many ways; in every way: ～设法 try every possible means

多功能 duōgōngnéng (形) multifunctional; multi-purpose

D

多寡 duō-guǎ (名) number; amount: ～不等 vary in amount or number

多极(極) duōjí (形) multipolar: ～化 multipolarization

多亏(虧) duōkuī (动) thanks to; luckily [indicating that owing to some favourable condition, a misfortune is avoided]: 这孩子没受伤, ～了你的帮助. Thanks to your help, the child is unhurt.

多么(麽) duōme (副) [used in an exclamatory or a compound sentence indicating high degree] how; what; however: ～美的地方! What a beautiful place! 他跑得～快啊! How fast he runs! 不管天气～冷, 他都坚持户外锻炼. However cold it was, he never stopped taking outdoor exercises.

多媒体(體) duōméitǐ (名) multimedia

多面手 duōmiànshǒu (名) a versatile person

多谋善断(斷) duōmóu-shànduàn resourceful and decisive

多情 duōqíng (形) susceptible

多少 duōshǎo (副) somewhat; more or less; to some extent: 他讲的～有点道理. There's something in what he says. 他～有点不高兴. He's not entirely happy about it.

多少 duōshao (代) 1 how many; how much: 有～人来参加晚会? How many people are coming to the party? 他干了～了? How much has he done? 2 [used to indicate an uncertain quantity]: 我说过～遍了,叫你别去那儿! Didn't I tell you not to go there! 他懂～! How much does he know!

多事 duōshì (形) 1 meddlesome: 怪我～. I shouldn't have meddled in this. 2 eventful

多数(數) duōshù (名) majority; most: 绝大～ an overwhelming majority. ～票 majority vote

多谢 duōxiè (动) 〈套〉 many thanks; thanks a lot

多心 duōxīn (形) oversensitive

多样(樣) duōyàng (形) diversified; varied; manifold: ～化 diversity

多余(餘) duōyú (形) 1 extra; surplus: 有～的一份. There is an extra copy. ～农产品 surplus farm products 2 unnecessary; superfluous: 你这话是～的. What you said is unnecessary.

多元论(論) duōyuánlùn (名) pluralism

多云(雲) duōyún (形) cloudy

多种(種)经(經)营(營) duōzhǒng jīngyíng diversified economy

多嘴 duōzuǐ (动) speak out of turn: ～多舌 gossipy; long-tongued. 别～! Shut up!

哆 duō

哆嗦 duōsuo (动) tremble; shiver: 气得直～ tremble with rage. 冷得打～ shiver with cold

掇 duō (动) pick up: 拾～ tidy up

度 duó (动) 〈书〉 surmise; estimate

see also dù

踱 duó (动) pace; stroll: ～来～去 pace to and fro; pace up and down

夺(奪) duó (动) 1 take by force; seize: ～权 seize power 2 strive for; win: ～高产 strive for high yields. ～金牌 (try) to win a gold medal 3 force one's way: ～门而出 force one's way out. 她的眼泪～眶而出. Tears welled out from her eyes.

夺目 duómù (动) dazzle the eyes: 光彩～ dazzling; brilliant

夺取 duóqǔ (动) capture; seize; wrest

朵 duǒ (量): 一～花 a flower. 一～云 a cloud

垛 duǒ (名) 1 buttress 2 battlements

see also duò

躲 duǒ (动) avoid; hide; dodge: 你怎么老～着他? Why do you always try to avoid him? ～雨 take shelter from the rain

躲避 duǒbì (动) 1 hide (of person or animal) 2 avoid; dodge; evade: ～开人群 keep away from the crowd

躲藏 duǒcáng (动) hide (or conceal) oneself; go into hiding

躲闪 duǒshǎn (动) dodge; evade: 躲躲闪闪 be evasive; equivocate

惰 duò (形) lazy; indolent: 懒～ lazy

惰性 duòxìng (名) inertia

堕(墮) duò (动) fall; sink

堕落 duòluò (动) (of mind; behaviour) be corrupted; degenerate

堕胎 duòtāi (动) have an abortion

舵 duò (名) rudder; helm

舵手 duòshǒu (名) steersman; helmsman

垛 duò I (动) pile up neatly; stack: 把木头～起来 pile up the logs II (名) pile; stack: 麦～ a stack of wheat

see also duǒ

剁 duò (动) chop; cut: ～肉馅 chop up (or mince) meat

跺 duò (动) stamp (one's foot)

E e

阿 ē (动) cater for

see also ā

阿弥(彌)陀佛 Ēmítuófó Amitabha; may Buddha preserve us; merciful Buddha

阿谀奉承 ēyú fèngcheng fawn on; flatter

婀 ē

婀娜 ēnuó (形) (of a woman's bearing) graceful

额 é (名) 1 forehead 2 quota; a fixed number or amount: 超～ above quota. 贸易～ volume of trade

额定 édìng (形) specified (number or amount): ～人数 the maximum number of persons allowed. ～工资 regular pay

额度 édù (名) quota; specified amount: 信贷～ credit line

额头(頭) étóu (名) forehead

额外 éwài (形) extra; additional: ～开支 extra expenses. ～负担 additional burden

峨 é (形) 〈书〉 high: 巍～ towering; lofty

鹅 é (名) goose

鹅卵石 éluǎnshí (名) cobblestone; cobble

鹅毛 émáo (名) goose feather: ～大雪 snow in big flakes

娥 é (名) pretty young woman: 宫～ palace maid

娥眉 éméi (名) 1 delicate eyebrows 2 beautiful woman

蛾 é (名) moth

讹 é I (动) extort; blackmail II (名) error: 以～传～ pass on a wrong message from one person to another; relay a wrong message

讹传(傳) échuán (名) unfounded rumour

讹诈 ézhà (动) blackmail: 核～ nuclear blackmail. ～钱财 extort money under false pretences

恶(惡) ě

see also è; wù

恶心 ěxin I (动) feel sick; feel nauseated II (形) disgusting; revolting

恶(惡) è I (名) evil; vice; wickedness: 无～不作 stop at no evil II (形) 1 vicious; fierce; ferocious: 一场～战 a fierce battle. ～狼 a ferocious wolf 2 evil; wicked: ～人 evildoer

see also ě; wù

恶霸 èbà (名) local tyrant (or despot)

恶臭 èchòu (名) foul smell; stench

恶毒 èdú (形) vicious; malicious; venomous: ～攻击 make vicious attacks against. 手段～ vicious means

恶感 ègǎn (名) ill feeling; malice; resentment

恶搞 ègǎo I (动) spread mischievous stories II (名) evil-doing; parody

恶贯满(滿)盈 è guàn mǎnyíng be guilty of too many crimes to escape punishment

恶棍 ègùn (名) ruffian; scoundrel; bully

恶果 èguǒ (名) evil consequence; disastrous effect

恶狠狠 èhěnhěn (形) fierce; ferocious

恶化 èhuà (动) worsen; deteriorate: 病情～了. The patient's condition has worsened. 形势不断～. The situation has steadily deteriorated.

恶劣 èliè (形) bad; evil; disgusting: 品质～ be morally corrupt. ～手段 despicable means. ～气候 inclement climate

恶魔 èmó (名) demon; devil

恶习(習) èxí (名) bad habit

恶性 èxìng (形) malignant; pernicious: ～循环 vicious circle. ～肿瘤 malignant tumour

恶言 èyán (名) abusive language

恶意 èyì (名) evil (or ill) intentions; malice

恶运(運) èyùn (名) bad luck

恶兆 èzhào (名) ill (or bad) omen

恶作剧(劇) èzuòjù (名) practical joke; mischief

噩 è (形) shocking; upsetting

噩耗 èhào (名) sad news (of someone's death)

噩梦(夢) èmèng (名) nightmare

厄 è (名) 〈书〉 1 disaster; adversity 2 strategic point: 险～ a strategic pass

厄运(運) èyùn (名) misfortune

扼 è (动) 1 clutch; grip 2 guard; control

扼杀(殺) èshā (动) strangle; smother

扼守 èshǒu (动) hold (a strategic point); guard

扼要 èyào (形) concise; to the point: 简明～ brief and precise

呃 è

呃逆 ènì (名) hiccup

遏 è (动) check; hold back: 怒不可～ cannot restrain one's anger; be fired with indignation; be in a towering rage

遏止 èzhǐ (动) check; hold back

遏制 èzhì (动) restrain; contain; keep within limits

愕 è (形) stunned; astounded

愕然 èrán (形) stunned; astounded

颚 è (名) 1 jaw: 上(下)～ upper (lower) jaw 2 palate

腭 è (名) palate: 硬(软)～ hard (soft) palate

鳄(鱷) è (名) crocodile; alligator

鳄鱼(魚) èyú (名) crocodile; alligator: ～的眼泪 crocodile tears

饿 è I (形) hungry: 挨～ go hungry II (动) starve: ～死 starve to death

欸(誒) ē or ēi (叹) [used to attract attention]: ～,你快来! Hey! Come over here. ～,你说什么? Eh? What did you say?
see also é;ě;è

欸(誒) é or éi (叹) [used to express surprise]: ～,怎么停电了! Why, the electricity is off!
see also ē;ě;è

欸(誒) ě or ěi (叹) [used to express disapproval]: ～,可不能这样说哇. I'm afraid you can't talk like that.
see also ē;é;è

欸(誒) è or èi (叹) [used to indicate response or agreement]: ～, 来 了! Yes, I'm coming. ～,我就给他送去. All right, I'll send it over to him immediately.
see also ē;é;ě

恩 ēn (名) 1 kindness; favour; grace: 报～ repay a person for his kindness 2 matrimonial happiness

恩爱(愛) ēn'ài (名) conjugal love

恩赐 ēncì I (动) bestow (favours, charity, etc.) II (名) favour; charity

恩德 ēndé (名) favour; kindness; grace

恩典 ēndiǎn (名) favour; grace

恩惠 ēnhuì (名) favour; kindness; grace

恩将(將)仇报(報) ēn jiāng chóu bào return evil for good

恩情 ēnqíng (名) great kindness

恩人 ēnrén (名) benefactor

恩怨 ēn-yuàn (名) feelings of gratitude or resentment: 不计较个人～ never let personal feelings of gratitude or resentment interfere with matters

摁 èn (动) press (with the hand or finger): ～电钮 press (or push) a button

摁钉儿(兒) èndīngr (名)〈口〉 drawing pin

摁扣儿(兒) ènkòur (名)〈口〉 snap fastener

而 ér (连) 1 express coordination: 美丽～善良 beautiful and kind-hearted. 朴素～大方 simple and with good taste 2 [similar to "but" or "yet"]: 华～不实 flashy without substance. 这颜色艳～不俗. This colour is bright but not garish. 3 [connect cause and effect; aim and means or action]: 因病～辞职 resign on health grounds. 为找工作～奔跑 hunting for a job. 匆匆～来 come in a hurry 4 [indicate change from one state to another]: 由远～近 approach from afar. 由上～下 from top to bottom

而后(後) érhòu (副) after that; then

而今 érjīn (名) now; at the present time

而且 érqiě (连) and also; moreover; in addition: 他不但很懂画,～自己画得也不错. He knows a lot about painting, and he paints well himself. 不仅下了雪,～下得很大. It not only snowed but also snowed heavily.

而已 éryǐ (助) that is all; nothing more: 不过开个玩笑～. It's only a joke.

儿(兒) ér I (名) 1 son 2 child: 小～ little child 3 youngster; youth II [retroflex ending]: 小猫～ kitten

儿歌 érgē (名) nursery rhymes; children's song

儿化 érhuà (名) [a phonetic phenomenon — the retroflex ending "r"]: 猫儿 (māor) cat. 花儿 (huār) flower. 他火儿了. He got angry.

儿科 érkē (名) paediatrics: ～医生 paediatrician

儿女 ér-nǚ (名) sons and daughters; youth: ～情长 be immersed in love

儿孙(孫) ér-sūn (名) children and grandchildren; descendants

儿童 értóng (名) children

儿媳妇(婦)儿 érxífur (名) daughter-in-law

儿戏(戲) érxì (名) trifling matter: 这可不是～. It's no trifling matter.

儿子 érzi (名) son

耳 ěr I (名) ear II (形) on both sides; flanking; side: ～房 side rooms

耳背 ěrbèi (形) hard of hearing

耳边(邊)风(風) ěrbiānfēng (名) sth. goes in at one ear and out at the other: 把某事当作～ turn a deaf ear to sth.

耳聪(聰)目明 ěrcōng-mùmíng clear-headed and clear-sighted

耳朵 ěrduo (名) ear: ～尖 have sharp ears. ～软 credulous; easily influenced

耳光 ěrguāng (名) a slap on the ear

耳环(環) ěrhuán (名) earrings

耳机(機) ěrjī (名) earphone

耳鸣 ěrmíng (名) tinnitus; ringing in the ear

耳目 ěrmù (名) ears and eyes: ～一新 find everything fresh and new. ～闭塞 ill-informed. ～众多 have many people serving as one's eyes and ears; have many spies

耳熟 ěrshú (形) familiar to the ear

耳闻 ěrwén (动) hear of (or about): ～目睹 what one sees and hears

耳语 ěryǔ (动) whisper

饵 ěr (名) bait

尔(爾) ěr (代)〈书〉 **1** you **2** that

尔后(後) ěrhòu (名)〈书〉 thereafter; subsequently

尔虞我诈 ěryú-wǒzhà mutual deception; each trying to cheat and outwit the other

二 èr I (数) two: ～十 twenty. ～两茶叶 two *liang* of tea. ～楼(英) first floor; (美) second floor II (形) different: ～心 disloyalty; half-heartedness

二百五 èrbǎiwǔ (名)〈口〉 a stupid person

二重唱 èrchóngchàng (名) (vocal) duet

二重性 èrchóngxìng (名) dual character; duality

二等 èrděng (形) second-class; second-rate

二胡 èrhú (名) *erhu*; a two-stringed bowed instrument

二话 èrhuà (名) demur; objection: ～不说 without demur

二流子 èrliúzi (名) loafer; idler; hooligan

二奶 èrnǎi (名) kept woman; second wife; mistress

二月 èryuè (名) February

贰 èr (数) two [used for the numeral 二 on cheques, banknotes, etc. to avoid mistakes or alterations]

F

F f

发(發) fā I (动) **1** send out; issue; dispatch; distribute: ～电报 send a telegram (or cable). ～通知 issue a notice. ～炮 fire a cannon. ～工资 pay wages **2** utter: ～言 take the floor. ～议论 comment on sth. **3** come into existence; occur: 旧病复～ have another attack of one's old illness. ～了大水. A flood occurred. **4** become; get into a certain state: ～红 turn red. ～臭 become smelly (or off). ～潮 get damp. ～胖 become fat. ～酸 turn sour. ～面 let the dough rise **5** feel: 腿～麻 have pins and needles in one's leg. ～怒 get angry. ～痒 itch II (量) [for ammunition]: 两～炮弹 two shells
see also fà

发榜 fābǎng (动) publish a list of successful candidates

发报(報) fābào (动) transmit messages by radio: ～机 telegraph transmitter

发表 fābiǎo (动) publish; issue: ～文章 publish an article. ～声明 issue (or make) a statement. ～意见 state one's views. ～演说 make a speech

发布 fābù (动) issue; release: ～命令 issue orders. ～新闻 release news

发财 fācái (动) get rich; make a good deal of money

发愁 fāchóu (动) worry; be anxious

发出 fāchū (动) **1** send out; issue: ～稿 send a manuscript to the press. ～命令

give an order 2 give off: ～香味 give off a fragrant smell
发怵 fāchù (动) feel timid; grow apprehensive: 这件事我有点～. I'm a little nervous about it.
发达(達) fādá (形) developed; flourishing: ～国家 developed country
发呆 fādāi (动) stare blankly
发电(電) fādiàn (动) generate electricity: ～站 power station. ～厂 power plant; power station. ～机 generator
发动(動) fādòng (动) 1 start; launch: ～战争 launch a war. ～机器 start a machine. ～机 engine; motor 2 arouse; mobilize: ～群众 arouse (or mobilize) the masses
发抖 fādǒu (动) shiver; shake; tremble: 冷得～ shiver with cold. 气得～ shake with anger
发放 fāfàng (动) grant; provide: ～贷款 grant a loan
发奋(奮) fāfèn (动) 1 make a determined effort 2 work energetically
发愤 fāfèn (动) make a determined effort: ～图强 make a determined effort to help revitalize the nation
发疯 fāfēng (动) go mad; lose one's senses; be out of one's mind
发福 fāfú (动) put on weight; grow stout
发光 fāguāng (动) give out light; shine; be luminous
发汗 fāhàn (动) induce perspiration (as by drugs): ～药 sudorific; diaphoretic
发号(號)施令 fāhào-shīlìng issue orders; order people about
发话 fāhuà (动) give orders or instructions
发慌 fāhuāng (动) feel nervous; get flustered
发挥 fāhuī (动) 1 give play to; bring into play: ～群众的积极性 bring the initiative of the masses into full play. ～专长 give full play to sb.'s professional knowledge or skill. 他今天～得很好. He performed well today. 2 develop (an idea, a theme, etc.); elaborate: 借题～ seize on a minor incident to make an issue of it
发昏 fāhūn (动) feel dizzy; lose one's head; become confused
发火 fāhuǒ (动) get angry; flare up; lose one's temper
发迹 fājì (动) (of a poor man) gain fame and wealth
发家 fājiā (动) build up a family fortune
发奖(獎) fājiǎng (动) award prizes
发酵 fājiào (动) ferment
发觉(覺) fājué (动) find; realize; discover
发掘 fājué (动) excavate; unearth; explore: ～古墓 excavate an ancient tomb. ～潜力 explore the latent potential of sb. or sth.
发狂 fākuáng (动) go mad; go crazy
发困 fākùn (动) feel drowsy; feel sleepy
发愣 fālèng (动) 〈口〉 be in a daze
发亮 fāliàng (动) shine
发霉 fāméi (动) go mouldy
发面(麵) fāmiàn I (动) leaven dough II (名) leavened dough
发明 fāmíng (动、名) invent; invention: 印刷术是中国首先～的. Printing was first invented by the Chinese. ～家 inventor
发胖 fāpàng (动) put on weight; get fat
发脾气(氣) fā píqi (动) lose one's temper; fly into a rage
发票 fāpiào (名) invoice; bill; receipt: 开～ make out a bill; write a receipt
发起 fāqǐ (动) 1 initiate; sponsor: ～人 sponsor; initiator 2 start; launch: ～进攻 launch an attack
发情 fāqíng (名) oestrus: ～期 heat period; oestrus; breeding season
发球 fāqiú (动) serve a ball: 换～! Change service!
发人深省 fā rén shēn xǐng thought provoking; provide food for thought
发烧(燒) fāshāo (动) run a fever; have a temperature
发烧(燒)友 fāshāoyǒu (名) fan; fancier: 音响～ hi-fi enthusiast
发射 fāshè (动) launch; project; discharge; fire: ～宇宙飞船 launch a spaceship
发生 fāshēng (动) happen; occur; take place
发誓 fāshì (动) take an oath; vow; pledge
发售 fāshòu (动) sell; put on sale
发条(條) fātiáo (名) clockwork spring
发问 fāwèn (动) ask or raise a question
发现 fāxiàn (动) find; discover
发泄 fāxiè (动) give vent to; vent: ～怨气 give vent to one's grievances
发信 fāxìn (动) post a letter: ～人 addresser
发行 fāxíng (动) (of currency, books, etc.) issue; publish; distribute: ～纸币 issue paper money. ～书刊 publish books and magazines. ～影片 release a film

发芽 fāyá (动) sprout
发言人 fāyánrén (名) spokesman: 政府~ government spokesman
发炎 fāyán (动、名) inflammation: 伤口~了. The wound has become inflamed.
发扬(揚) fāyáng (动) (of spirit, tradition, etc.) develop; foster; carry on
发音 fāyīn (名) pronunciation: ~器官 vocal organs
发育 fāyù (名) growth; development: ~健全 physically well developed
发源 fāyuán (动) originate: ~地 place of origin; source
发展 fāzhǎn (动) **1** develop; expand; grow: ~大好形势. The situation, which is very good as it is, calls for further expansion. **2** recruit: ~新党员 recruit new Party members
发展中国(國)家 fāzhǎnzhōng guójiā (名) developing country
发作 fāzuò (动) **1** break out; show effect: 酒性~. The effect of the liquor is being felt. **2** flare up: 歇斯底里大~ have a bad fit of hysterics
罚(罸) fá (动) punish; penalize: 赏~分明 be fair in the administration of the law; be fair in passing critical judgment
罚单 fádān (名) fine ticket
罚款 fákuǎn (动) fine
罚球 fáqiú (名) penalty shot (in basketball); penalty kick (in football)
乏 fá I (动) lack: ~味 tasteless; dull II (形) tired; weary: 走~了 feel dog-tired from a long walk
伐 fá (动) **1** fell; cut down: ~木 felling; lumbering **2** strike; attack: 征~ send a punitive expedition
阀 fá (名) **1** a powerful person or family: 军~ warlord. 财~ financial magnate **2** valve: ~门 valve. 安全~ safety valve
筏 fá (名) raft: 橡皮~ rubber raft
法 fǎ (名) **1** law: 守~ observe the law; be law-abiding. 违~ break the law **2** method; way: 作~ way of doing. 教学~ teaching method; pedagogical methodology
法案 fǎ'àn (名) proposed law; bill
法办(辦) fǎbàn (动) deal with according to law; punish by law; bring to justice
法宝(寶) fǎbǎo (名) a magic weapon
法场(場) fǎchǎng (名) execution ground
法典 fǎdiǎn (名) code; statute book
法定 fǎdìng (形) legal; statutory: ~汇率 official rate (of exchange); pegged rate of exchange. ~年龄 legal age. ~期限 legal time limit. ~人数 quorum
法官 fǎguān (名) judge; justice
法规 fǎguī (名) laws and regulations; rules
法纪 fǎjì (名) law and discipline: 目无~ act in complete disregard of law and discipline
法警 fǎjǐng (名) bailiff
法郎 fǎláng (名) franc (currency)
法理 fǎlǐ (名) legal principle; theory of law: ~学 jurisprudence
法令 fǎlìng (名) laws and decrees; decree
法律 fǎlǜ (名) law: ~保护 legal protection. ~承认 de jure recognition. ~根据 legal basis. ~规定 legal provisions. ~手续 legal procedure. ~效力 legal effect. ~制裁 legal sanction. ~顾问 legal adviser
法盲 fǎmáng (名) a person ignorant of the law
法人 fǎrén (名) legal person
法师(師) fǎshī (名) Master (a title of respect for a Buddhist or Taoist priest)
法事 fǎshì (名) religious rituals (or services)
法术(術) fǎshù (名) magic touch
法庭 fǎtíng (名) court
法网(網) fǎwǎng (名) the web of justice; the arm of the law
法西斯 fǎxīsī (名) fascist: ~主义 fascism
法学(學) fǎxué (名) the science of law: ~家 jurist
法医(醫) fǎyī (名) coroner; forensic medical examiner
法院 fǎyuàn (名) court of justice; law court; court: 最高~ the Supreme Court
法则 fǎzé (名) rule; law: 自然~ law of nature
法制 fǎzhì (名) legal system; legal institutions
法治 fǎzhì (动) rule by law
法子 fǎzi (名) way; method
砝 fǎ
砝码 fǎmǎ (名) weight [used on a scale]
珐 fà
珐琅 fàláng (名) enamel: ~质 enamel
发(髮) fà (名) hair: 理~ haircut

see also fā
发型 fàxíng (名) hair style
发指 fàzhǐ (动) boil with anger: 令人～ make one's hair bristle with anger

帆 fān (名) sail
帆布 fānbù (名) canvas
帆船 fānchuán (名) sailing boat; junk

番 fān (量) **1** kind: 别有一～风味 have an altogether different flavour **2** [for actions which take time or effort]: 下了一～功夫 put in a lot of effort. 三～五次 time and again
番号(號) fānhào (名) designation of a military unit
番茄 fānqié (名) tomato: ～酱 tomato ketchup. ～汁 tomato juice
番薯 fānshǔ (名) sweet potato

幡 fān (名) long narrow flag; streamer

翻 fān (动) **1** turn (over, up, upside down, etc.): ～车了. The car turned over. 船～了. The ship capsized. 把领子向上～ turn the collar up. ～到第二十页 turn to p. 20 **2** cross; get over: ～墙 climb over a wall. ～山越岭 cross over mountain after mountain **3** rummage; search: ～箱倒柜 rummage through chests and cupboards **4** translate: 把书～成中文 translate the book into Chinese **5** increase twofold; double: 粮食产量～了一番. The grain output is doubled. ～两番 be quadrupled **6** 〈口〉 fall out; break up: 他们闹～了. They quarrelled and split up. *or* They fell out.
翻案 fān'àn (动) reverse a verdict
翻版 fānbǎn (名) reprint; reproduction
翻地 fāndì (动) plough
翻斗 fāndǒu (名) tipping bucket; skip bucket
翻跟头(頭) fān gēntou turn a somersault
翻滚 fāngǔn (动) roll; tumble: 波浪～. The waves rolled furiously.
翻悔 fānhuǐ (动) back out (of a commitment, promise, etc.); fail to make good one's promise
翻来(來)覆去 fānlái-fùqù **1** toss from side to side: 他～睡不着. He tossed and turned in bed, unable to sleep. **2** again and again; repeatedly: ～地想一件事 mull over a problem
翻脸(臉) fānliǎn (动) fall out; suddenly turn hostile: ～不认人 turn against a friend. 两人吵～了脸. The two of them fell out.
翻然 fānrán (副) (change) quickly and completely: ～悔悟 wake up to one's error
翻身 fānshēn (动) **1** turn over (one's body) **2** free oneself; be liberated: ～农奴 emancipated serfs
翻腾 fānténg (动) **1** seethe; rise; surge: 波浪～ seething waves **2** rummage
翻天覆地 fāntiān-fùdì earth-shaking: ～的变化 an earth-shaking change
翻胃 fānwèi (名) gastric disorder
翻新 fānxīn (动) renovate; make over: 工厂～ the renovation of the factory
翻修 fānxiū (动) rebuild: ～马路 repair the roads
翻译(譯) fānyì I (动) translate; interpret: ～电码 decode; decipher. ～片 dubbed film II (名) translator; interpreter
翻印 fānyìn (动) reprint; reproduce
翻阅 fānyuè (动) browse; leaf through

烦 fán I (形) **1** vexed; irritated; annoyed: 心～ feel vexed. 真～人! How annoying! **2** tired of: 厌～ be fed up with II (动) trouble: ～你帮我寄一封信. Could I ask you to post a letter for me?
烦劳(勞) fánláo (动) trouble sb.; bother
烦闷 fánmèn (形) unhappy; be worried; depressed
烦恼(惱) fánnǎo (形) worried; vexed: 自寻～ worry oneself for nothing
烦扰(擾) fánrǎo (动) **1** bother; disturb **2** feel disturbed
烦琐 fánsuǒ (形) over-elaborate; loaded down with trivial details: ～的手续 over-elaborate procedure; tedious formalities
烦琐哲学(學) fánsuǒ zhéxué **1** scholasticism **2** 〈口〉 over-elaboration
烦躁 fánzào (形) irritable; agitated

繁 fán (形) numerous; manifold: ～星满天 a starry sky. 头绪纷～ have too many things to attend to
繁花 fánhuā (名) flowers in full bloom; full-blown flowers
繁华(華) fánhuá (形) flourishing; bustling; busy: ～的街道 busy street
繁忙 fánmáng (形) busy: 工作～ be very busy with one's work
繁茂 fánmào (形) lush: 草木～ a lush growth of trees and grass
繁荣(榮) fánróng (形) flourishing; prosperous; booming: 经济～ a prosperous

economy. ～昌盛 thriving and prosperous

繁冗 fánrǒng (形) lengthy and tedious

繁缛 fánrù (形) over-elaborate

繁盛 fánshèng (形) thriving; flourishing; prosperous

繁琐 fánsuǒ (形) see "烦琐" fánsuǒ

繁体(體)字 fántǐzì (名) the original complex form of a simplified Chinese character

繁杂(雜) fánzá (形) numerous and diverse; miscellaneous: ～的日常事务 daily chores of all sorts; trivialities of everyday life

繁殖 fánzhí (动) breed; reproduce: ～力 reproductive capacity; fertility. ～率 breeding rate

繁重 fánzhòng (形) heavy; strenuous: ～的工作 strenuous work. ～的任务 arduous task

凡 fán I (形) commonplace; ordinary: 非～ extraordinary II (名) this mortal world; the earth: 天仙下～ a celestial beauty come down to earth III (副) every; any; all

凡人 fánrén (名) 1 ordinary person 2 mortal

凡士林 fánshìlín (名) vaseline

凡事 fánshì (名) everything

凡是 fánshì (副) every; any; all: ～去过北京的人都说北京很美. Those who have been to Beijing all say it's beautiful.

凡庸 fányōng (形) commonplace; ordinary

矾 fán (名) vitriol; alum

反 fǎn I (动) 1 turn over: 易如～掌 as easy as turning one's hand over. ～败为胜 turn defeat into victory 2 oppose; be against: ～法西斯 anti-fascist. ～问 ask in retort II (形) in an opposite direction; inside out: 大衣穿～了 wear one's coat inside out III (副) on the contrary; instead

反霸 fǎnbà (动) anti-hegemonist

反比例 fǎnbǐlì (名) inverse proportion

反驳 fǎnbó (动) refute; retort; rebut

反差 fǎnchā (名) contrast: ～太大 very sharp contrast

反常 fǎncháng (形) unusual; abnormal

反冲(衝) fǎnchōng (动) recoil; kick

反刍(芻) fǎnchú (动) ruminate; chew the cud: ～动物 ruminant

反串 fǎnchuàn (动) perform occasionally in an art form which is not the usual field of the actor or the actress

反帝 fǎndì (动) anti-imperialist

反动(動) fǎndòng (形) reactionary

反对(對) fǎnduì (动) oppose; be against; fight; combat: ～殖民统治的斗争 fight against colonial rule. ～不正之风 combat unhealthy trends. ～意见 objection (to a decision, resolution, etc.). ～党 opposition party; the Opposition. ～派 opposition faction. ～票 negative vote; dissenting vote

反而 fǎn'ér (副) instead; on the contrary

反封建 fǎn fēngjiàn anti-feudal

反腐 fǎnfǔ I (动) combat corruption II (名) anti-corruption

反复(復) fǎnfù I (副) repeatedly; again and again; over and over again II (形) changeable; fickle: ～无常 capricious; changeable III (名) relapse; reversal: 他的病最近有～. He relapsed into his old illness recently.

反感 fǎngǎn (形) be averse to; repugnant; disgusted with (sb. or sth.)

反革命 fǎngémìng (名) counter-revolutionary

反攻 fǎngōng (动) counter-attack: ～倒算 counter-attack to settle old scores; retaliate

反光 fǎnguāng (名) reflection of light: ～镜 (or 板) reflector

反过(過)来(來) fǎnguolai conversely; the other way round: ～也是一样. It's the same the other way round.

反话 fǎnhuà (名) irony

反悔 fǎnhuǐ (动) go back on one's word (or promise)

反击(擊) fǎnjī (动) strike back; counter-attack: 自卫～ counter-attack in self-defence

反间 fǎnjiàn (动) sow distrust or dissension among one's enemies (by spreading rumours, etc.)

反抗 fǎnkàng (动) resist; revolt: ～精神 rebellious spirit

反恐 fǎnkǒng I (动) fight terrorism II (名) anti-terrorism

反馈 fǎnkuì (名) feedback

反面 fǎnmiàn (名) 1 back; reverse side; wrong side 2 negative side: ～角色 negative role; villain. ～的教训 a lesson learnt from negative experience 3 opposite; the other side of the matter

反目 fǎnmù (动) fall out; have a falling-out

反叛 fǎnpàn (动) revolt; rebel

反扑(撲) fǎnpū (动) attack in retaliation
反倾销 fǎn qīngxiāo anti-dumping
反射 fǎnshè I (动) reflect: 月亮~到水里. The moon is reflected in the water. ~板 (of traffic) reflector II (名) reflection; reflex: 条件~ conditioned reflex
反手 fǎnshǒu backhand: ~抽球 backhand drive
反思 fǎnsī (动) reflect; rethink
反贪 fǎntān I (动) fight against corruption II (名) anti-corruption
反弹 fǎntán (动) rebound; bounce back; backlash
反问 fǎnwèn I (动) ask (a question) in reply II (名) rhetorical question
反响(響) fǎnxiǎng (名) repercussion
反省 fǎnxǐng (动) introspect; exercise self-examination
反咬 fǎnyǎo (动) invent a charge against sb.: ~一口 make a false countercharge
反义(義)词 fǎnyìcí (名) antonym
反应(應) fǎnyìng I (名) reaction: 化学~ chemical reaction. ~堆 reactor. 连锁~ chain reaction. 阳性(阴性)~ positive (negative) reaction II (动) react; respond
反映 fǎnyìng (动) 1 reflect; mirror; portray; depict 2 report; make known: 向上级~ report to the higher level
反正 fǎnzhèng (副) anyway; anyhow; in any case: 不管你怎么说, ~我不会同意. Whatever you say, I won't agree to it.
反证 fǎnzhèng I (名) disproof; counter-evidence II (动) give counter-evidence
反之 fǎnzhī (连) otherwise; conversely; on the contrary
反作用 fǎnzuòyòng (名) counteraction; reaction

返 fǎn (动) return: ~回 return; go back. 一去不复~ be gone forever
返潮 fǎncháo (动) get damp
返程 fǎnchéng (名) return trip
返工 fǎngōng (动) do a poorly done job over again
返航 fǎnháng (动) make a return voyage (or flight)
返老还(還)童 fǎnlǎo-huántóng recover one's youthful vigour; feel rejuvenated
返青 fǎnqīng (动) (of winter crops or transplanted seedlings) turn green

泛 fàn (动) 1 〈书〉 float: ~舟西湖 go boating on the West Lake 2 be suffused with; spread: 脸上~出红晕 bring a blush into one's cheeks. 广~ extensive; wide 3 flood; inundate
泛泛 fànfàn (形) general; not penetrating: ~而谈 talk in general terms. ~之交 casual acquaintance
泛滥(濫) fànlàn (动) 1 be in flood; overflow: 河水~. The river was in flood. 2 spread unchecked: ~成灾 run rampant; run wild
泛指 fànzhǐ (动) make a general reference; be used in a general sense

范(範) fàn (名) 1 model; example; pattern: 典~ example. 示~ demonstrate 2 limits
范畴(疇) fànchóu (名) category
范例 fànlì (名) example; model
范围(圍) fànwéi (名) scope; limits; range

梵 fàn
梵文 fànwén (名) Sanskrit

贩 fàn I (动) peddle; buy for resale: ~毒 traffic in narcotics II (名) dealer; pedlar: 小~ pedlar; vendor
贩卖(賣) fànmài (动) peddle; traffic; sell: ~军火 traffic in arms. ~人口 human traffic
贩运(運) fànyùn (动) transport goods for sale; traffic
贩子 fànzi (名) dealer; monger: 战争~ warmonger. 马~ horse dealer

饭 fàn (名) cooked rice; meal: 米~ (cooked) rice
饭菜 fàncài (名) food
饭店 fàndiàn (名) 1 hotel 2 restaurant
饭馆 fànguǎn (名) restaurant
饭盒 fànhé (名) lunch-box
饭局 fànjú (名) dinner invitation; dinner appointment
饭量 fànliàng (名) appetite; an amount of food eaten at one time
饭厅(廳) fàntīng (名) dining room; dining hall
饭桶 fàntǒng (名) 1 rice bucket 2 big eater 3 good-for-nothing (person)
饭碗 fànwǎn (名) 1 rice bowl 2 job; means of livelihood: 丢~ lose one's job

犯 fàn I (动) 1 violate; offend (against law, etc.) 2 attack; invade 3 have an attack of (an old illness): 他的心脏病又~了. He had another heart attack. 4 commit (a mistake, crime, etc.): ~错误 make a mistake II (名) criminal:

杀人～ murderer. 战～ war criminal
犯病 fànbìng (动) have an attack of one's old illness; fall ill again
犯不着 fànbuzháo 〈口〉 not worthwhile
犯愁 fànchóu (动) worry; be anxious
犯得着 fàndezháo worthwhile [usu. in rhetorical question]: 为这点小事～生气吗? Is it worthwhile getting angry over such a trifling matter?
犯法 fànfǎ (动) violate (or break) the law
犯规 fànguī (名) foul
犯人 fànrén (名) convict; prisoner
犯罪 fànzuì (动) commit a crime (or an offence): ～分子 offender; criminal
方 fāng I (形) square: ～桌 square table II (名) 1 direction: 东～ the east. 前～ the front. 四面八～ in all directions. 远～ a faraway place 2 side; party: 双～ both sides (or parties) 3 method; way: 想～设法 try every means possible. 千～百计 in a hundred and one ways; by every conceivable means. 领导有～ exercise good leadership 4 prescription: 处～ prescription III (副) just: 年～二十 be just twenty years old. ～兴未艾 be in the ascendant; be in full swing IV (量) 1 [for square objects]: 一～砚台 one ink-stone 2 (short for 平方 or 立方): 一～土 a cubic metre of earth
方案 fāng'àn (名) plan; scheme; programme: 提出初步～ put forward a preliminary plan
方便 fāngbiàn I (形) 1 convenient: 在你～的时候 (do this) at your convenience 2 proper: 在这儿谈私事不大～. It's not proper to talk about private matters here. II (动)〈婉〉1 go to the lavatory: 你要不要～一下? Do you want to use the lavatory? 2 have money to spare: 手头不～ have little money to spare
方便面(麵) fāngbiànmiàn (名) instant noodles
方才 fāngcái (名) just now: 她～还在这儿. She was here just a moment ago.
方程 fāngchéng (名) equation: ～式 equation
方法 fāngfǎ (名) method; way; means
方格 fānggé (名) check
方面 fāngmiàn (名) aspect; respect; side: 在这～ in this respect. 问题的不同～ different aspects of a matter
方式 fāngshì (名) way; fashion; pattern: 生活～ way of life; lifestyle. 斗争～ form of struggle. 领导～ style of leadership
方位 fāngwèi (名) position; direction
方向 fāngxiàng (名) direction; orientation: ～盘 steering wheel. ～舵 rudder
方言 fāngyán (名) dialect
方圆 fāngyuán (名) 1 neighbourhood 2 circumference
方针 fāngzhēn (名) guiding principle; policy
方子 fāngzi (名) prescription: 开～ write out a prescription
芳 fāng I (形) fragrant; sweet-smelling: ～草 fragrant grass II (名) good name or reputation; virtue: 流～百世 leave a good name to posterity
芳香 fāngxiāng (形) fragrant: ～剂 aromatic
芳心 fāngxīn (名) the heart of a young woman
房 fáng (名) 1 house: 平～ bungalow. 楼～ a building of two or more storeys 2 room: 书～ study. 客～ guest room. 病～ ward
房产(產) fángchǎn (名) house property
房地产(產) fángdìchǎn (名) real estate: ～开发 property development
房车 fángchē (名) caravan; trailer; touring car
房顶 fángdǐng (名) roof
房东(東) fángdōng (名) landlord or landlady
房间 fángjiān (名) room: 一套～ an apartment; a flat; a suite
房客 fángkè (名) tenant (of a room or house); lodger
房奴 fángnú (名) mortgage slave
房事 fángshì (名) sexual intercourse (between a married couple)
房屋 fángwū (名) houses; buildings
房檐 fángyán (名) eaves
房子 fángzi (名) 1 house; building 2 room
房租 fángzū (名) rent (for a house, flat, etc.)
坊 fáng workshop; mill: 作～ workshop. 油～ small oil mill
防 fáng I (动) guard against; prevent: 预～ prevent sth. from happening; take precautions. ～患未然 take preventive measures. ～微杜渐 nip an evil in the bud. 以～万一 be prepared for all eventualities II (名) defence: 国～ national defence. 堤～ dyke; embankment
防暴警察 fángbào jǐngchá riot squad; riot police
防备(備) fángbèi (动) guard against; take precautions against
防不胜(勝)防 fáng bùshèng fáng impossible

F

to put up an all-round effective defence
防潮 fángcháo (形) dampproof
防尘(塵) fángchén (形) dustproof
防磁 fángcí (形) antimagnetic
防弹(彈) fángdàn (形) bulletproof; shellproof
防盗 fángdào (动) guard against theft; take precautions against burglars
防冻(凍) fángdòng (动) prevent frostbite
防毒 fángdú (名) gas defence: ~面具 gas mask
防范(範) fángfàn (动) be on guard; keep a lookout
防风(風)林 fángfēnglín (名) windbreak; shelterbelt
防腐 fángfǔ (形) antiseptic; anticorrosive
防洪 fánghóng (动) prevent or control flood
防护(護) fánghù (动) protect; shelter
防火 fánghuǒ I (动) prevent fire II (形) fireproof
防火墙(牆) fánghuǒqiáng (名) fire wall
防空 fángkōng (名) air defence; antiaircraft: ~壕 air-raid dugout. ~警报 air-raid warning. ~洞 air-raid shelter
防涝(澇) fánglào (动) prevent waterlogging
防晒 fángshài (名) sunblock; sunscreen; SPF
防身 fángshēn (动) defend oneself against violence: ~术 self-defence skills
防守 fángshǒu (动) defend; guard
防暑 fángshǔ (名) heatstroke (or sunstroke) prevention
防水 fángshuǐ (形) waterproof
防伪(偽) fángwěi (动) fake-proof; antifake
防卫(衛) fángwèi (动) defend
防务(務) fángwù (名) defence
防线(綫) fángxiàn (名) defence line
防锈 fángxiù (形) antirust
防汛 fángxùn (名) flood prevention or control
防疫 fángyì (名) epidemic prevention: ~针 inoculation
防御(禦) fángyù (名) defence
防震 fángzhèn I (动) take precautions against earthquakes II (形) shockproof
防止 fángzhǐ (动) prevent; guard against; avoid
防治 fángzhì (动) prevent and cure (illness)

妨 fáng (动) hinder; hamper; impede; obstruct
妨碍(礙) fáng'ài (动) hinder; hamper; impede; obstruct
妨害 fánghài (动) impair; jeopardize; be harmful to

访 fǎng (动) visit; call on: ~友 call on a friend. 回~ a return visit. 互~ exchange visits
访问 fǎngwèn (动) **1** visit; call on **2** interview. 采~ (of a reporter) gather material; cover; interview

仿(倣) fǎng (动) **1** imitate; copy **2** resemble; be like: 相~ be similar
仿佛 fǎngfú (动) **1** seem; as if **2** be more or less the same; be alike
仿生学(學) fǎngshēngxué (名) bionics
仿效 fǎngxiào (动) imitate; follow suit
仿造 fǎngzào (动) copy; be modelled on
仿照 fǎngzhào (动) imitate; copy; follow
仿真 fǎngzhēn (动) simulate; emulate: ~技术 simulation technology. ~器 emulator. ~生态圈 artificial ecosphere
仿制(製) fǎngzhì (动) copy; be modelled on: ~品 imitation

舫 fǎng (名) boat: 画~ a gaily-painted pleasure-boat

纺 fǎng (动) spin
纺车(車) fǎngchē (名) spinning wheel
纺锤 fǎngchuí (名) spindle
纺纱 fǎngshā (名) spinning: ~工人 spinner. ~机 spinning machine
纺织(織) fǎngzhī (名) spinning and weaving: ~厂 textile mill. ~品 textile; fabric

放 fàng (动) **1** put; place: 把杯子~在桌子上 put the glass on the table. 菜里少~点盐. Don't put too much salt in the dish. ~回原处 put it where it belongs **2** let go; set free; release: 释~ set free. 把水~掉 let the water out. ~开他! Let go of him! **3** let oneself go; give way to: ~开嗓子唱 try to sing loudest. ~声痛哭 cry unrestrainedly **4** give off: ~光 shine **5** shoot: ~枪 fire a gun **6** let off: ~鞭炮 let off firecrakers **7** blossom; open: 百花齐~ a hundred flowers blossom **8** put out to pasture: ~牛 graze cattle. ~鸭 tend ducks. ~羊娃 shepherd **9** lay aside: 这事不急,先~一~再说. This matter is not urgent. Let's put it aside for the moment. **10** expand; make larger or longer: 把裙子~长二英寸 let the skirt out two inches at the edge

11 readjust to a certain extent: 声音～轻些! Lower your voice! 速度～慢点儿 slow down a bit 12 show; play (film, radio, etc.) ～电影 show a film. ～录音 play a tape recorder

放出 fàngchū (动) give out; let out; emit

放大 fàngdà (动) enlarge; magnify; amplify: ～镜 magnifying glass. ～照片 have a photograph enlarged; blow up

放荡(蕩) fàngdàng (形) 1 dissipated; dissolute 2 unconventional: ～不羁 unconventional and unrestrained

放电(電) fàngdiàn (名) (electric) discharge

放风(風) fàngfēng (动) 1 let in fresh air 2 let prisoners out for exercise or to relieve themselves 3 leak information; spread rumours

放工 fànggōng (动) (of workers) knock off

放过(過) fàngguò (动) let off; let slip: 不要～这个好机会. Don't let slip this good opportunity.

放火 fànghuǒ (动) set fire to; commit arson

放假 fàngjià (动) have a holiday or vacation; have a day off

放空炮 fàng kōngpào talk big; make empty promises; indulge in idle boasting

放宽 fàngkuān (动) relax rules or restrictions: ～期限 extend a time limit. ～条件 modify the terms

放牧 fàngmù (动) herd; graze

放屁 fàngpì I (动) break wind; fart II (名) bullshit; crap

放弃(棄) fàngqì (动) abandon; give up; renounce: ～权利 relinquish one's right

放晴 fàngqíng (动) (of weather) clear up

放任 fàngrèn I (动) let pass unchecked: ～自流 let things drift (or slide) II (名) laissez-faire

放哨 fàngshào (动) stand sentry

放射 fàngshè (动) radiate: ～疗法 radiotherapy. ～性 radioactivity

放生 fàngshēng (动) set captive animals free

放手 fàngshǒu (动) 1 let go; release one's hold 2 have a free hand: 你～干吧. Just go ahead boldly with your work.

放肆 fàngsì (形) audacious; unbridled; wanton: 胆敢如此～! How dare you take such liberties!

放松(鬆) fàngsōng (动) relax; slacken; loosen: ～警惕性 relax one's vigilance

放心 fàngxīn (动) feel relieved; set one's mind at rest; be at ease: ～不下 feel anxious

放行 fàngxíng (动) let sb. or sth. pass

放学(學) fàngxué (动) school is over (for the day)

放眼 fàngyǎn (动) take a broad view; look afar: ～世界 have the whole world in mind

放映 fàngyìng (动) show; project: ～机 (film) projector

放债 fàngzhài (动) lend money for interest

放置 fàngzhì (动) put; place: ～不用 lay up; lay aside

放逐 fàngzhú (动) send into exile; exile

放纵(縱) fàngzòng (动) 1 give free rein to 2 indulge

非 fēi I (名) wrong; evildoing: 混淆是～ confuse right and wrong. 为～作歹 do evil II (形) un-, non-, etc.: ～正义 unjust. ～正式 informal III (动) not; no: 答～所问 give an irrelevant answer IV (副) insist on; simply must: 我～要你去. I insist on your going. 这工作今天～得完成. This work simply must be done today.

非…不… fēi…bù… possible only if...: 非工作人员不得入内 for staff members only. 他非你不见. He will see nobody but you. 该票非特许不得转让. This ticket is not transferable unless with special permission.

非…不可 fēi…bùkě [an emphatic expression] must; have to; will inevitably: 我非要试试不可. I simply must have a try. 你不听我的话非倒霉不可. If you don't listen to me, you are bound to run into trouble.

非常 fēicháng I (形) extraordinary; unusual: ～时期 unusual times. ～措施 emergency measures II (副) very; extremely; highly: ～抱歉 awfully (or terribly) sorry. ～必要 highly necessary. ～精彩 simply marvellous

非但 fēidàn (连) not only

非得 fēiděi (动) must; have got to: 你～亲自去一趟. You have to go in person.

非法 fēifǎ (形) illegal; unlawful: ～活动 unlawful (or illegal) activities. ～收入 illicit income

非凡 fēifán (形) outstanding; extraordinary; uncommon: ～的人物 an outstanding person

非金属(屬) fēijīnshǔ non-metal

非礼(禮) fēilǐ (形) 〈书〉 rude

非难(難) fēinàn (动) blame; censure; re-

F

proach

非人 fēirén (形) inhuman: ~待遇 inhuman treatment

非同凡响(響) fēi tóng fánxiǎng unique; extraordinary

非同小可 fēi tóng xiǎokě no small matter

非议(議) fēiyì (动) reproach; censure: 无可~ beyond (or above) reproach

非正式 fēizhèngshì (形) unofficial; informal

非洲 Fēizhōu (名) Africa

F

扉 fēi (名) door leaf

扉页(頁) fēiyè (名) title page

蜚 fēi

蜚声(聲) fēishēng (动)〈书〉 make a name; become famous: ~文坛 become famous in the literary world

绯 fēi (形) red

绯红 fēihóng (形) bright red; crimson: 脸羞得~ blush with shame

飞(飛) fēi (动) 1 fly; hover; flutter 2 swiftly: ~奔 dash. ~驰 speed along

飞船 fēichuán (名) airship

飞地 fēidì (名) enclave

飞碟 fēidié (名) flying saucer; UFO

飞蛾投火 fēi'é tóu huǒ seek one's own destruction like a moth darting toward a fire

飞黄腾达(達) fēihuáng téngdá become a rising star in the political world

飞机(機) fēijī (名) aircraft; aeroplane; plane: 直升~ helicopter. ~场 airport. ~库 hangar

飞溅(濺) fēijiàn (动) splash: 浪花~到岩石上. The waves splashed on the rocks.

飞快 fēikuài (形) 1 very fast; at lightning speed: ~前进 march ahead at full speed 2 extremely sharp: 这把刀~. This knife is razor-sharp.

飞轮(輪) fēilún (名) 1 flywheel 2 free wheel (of a bicycle)

飞毛腿 fēimáotuǐ (名) fleet-footed runner

飞盘(盤) fēipán (名) frisbee (disk)

飞禽 fēiqín (名) birds: ~走兽 birds and beasts; fauna

飞逝 fēishì (动) (of time) slip by; elapse; fly

飞舞 fēiwǔ (动) dance in the air; flutter: 雪花~. Snowflakes are dancing in the wind.

飞翔 fēixiáng (动) circle in the air; hover

飞行 fēixíng (名) flight; flying

飞檐 fēiyán (名) upturned eaves (on Chinese buildings)

飞扬(揚) fēiyáng (动) fly upward; rise: 尘土~. Clouds of dust are rising. 歌声~. The sound of singing is floating in the air.

飞扬(揚)跋扈 fēiyáng-báhù arrogant and domineering

飞跃(躍) fēiyuè (动) leap: ~发展 develop by leaps and bounds

飞涨(漲) fēizhǎng (动) (of prices, etc.) soar; shoot up: 物价~. Prices are spiralling.

妃 fēi (名) 1 imperial concubine 2 the wife of a prince

妃子 fēizi (名) imperial concubine

腓 féi (名) calf (of the leg): ~骨 fibula

肥 féi I (形) 1 fat: ~猪 a fat pig. ~肉 fat meat; fat 2 (of land; soil) fertile; rich 3 loose; wide: 裤腿太~了. The trousers are too fat in the leg (or too baggy). II (名) fertilizer; manure: 化~ chemical fertilizer. 绿~ green manure

肥厚 féihòu (形) plump; fleshy

肥力 féilì (名) fertility (of soil)

肥料 féiliào (名) fertilizer; manure: 有机~ organic fertilizer

肥胖 féipàng (形) fat: ~病 obesity

肥缺 féiquē (名) lucrative post

肥硕 féishuò (形) big and fleshy

肥田 féitián (动) enrich the soil

肥沃 féiwò (形) fertile; rich

肥皂 féizào (名) soap: 洗脸~ toilet soap

肥皂剧(劇) féizàojù (名) soap opera

肥壮(壯) féizhuàng (形) stout and strong

诽 fěi (动) slander: ~谤 slander

菲 fěi

菲薄 fěibó I (形) humble: ~的礼物 a small gift II (动) belittle; despise: 不宜妄自~. You should not go so far as to depreciate your real ability or achievement.

匪 fěi I (名) bandit; robber II (副)〈书〉 not: 获益~浅 reap no little benefit

匪帮(幫) fěibāng (名) bandit gang

匪巢 fěicháo (名) bandits' lair

匪军 fěijūn (名) bandit troops

匪徒 fěitú (名) gangster; bandit

吠 fèi (动) (of a dog) bark

废(廢) fèi I (动) give up; abolish: 半途而～ give up halfway. ～寝忘食 (so absorbed in a book as to) forget to eat and sleep II (形) waste; useless; disused: ～物处理 waste disposal

废除 fèichú (动) abolish; abrogate (law, treaty, rule, etc.)

废黜 fèichù (动) dethrone; depose

废话 fèihuà (名) superfluous words; nonsense: ～连篇 pages and pages of nonsense

废料 fèiliào (名) waste material

废品 fèipǐn (名) 1 reject 2 scrap; waste: ～回收 waste recovery. ～加工 recycle waste material

废弃(棄) fèiqì (动) discard; abandon; cast aside: ～陈规旧习 discard outdated regulations and customs

废人 fèirén (名) 1 disabled person 2 good-for-nothing

废水 fèishuǐ (名) waste water: ～处理 waste water treatment

废铁(鐵) fèitiě (名) scrap iron

废物 fèiwù (名) 1 waste material; trash 2 good-for-nothing

废墟 fèixū (名) ruins

废止 fèizhǐ (动) abolish; put an end to

废纸 fèizhǐ (名) waste paper

废置 fèizhì (动) put aside as useless

肺 fèi (名) lungs: ～癌 lung cancer. ～病 pulmonary disease; tuberculosis (TB)

肺腑 fèifǔ (名) the bottom of one's heart: 出自～ from the depths of one's heart

肺活量 fèihuóliàng (名) vital capacity

肺结核 fèijiéhé (名) tuberculosis (TB)

肺炎 fèiyán (名) pneumonia

痱 fèi

痱子 fèizi (名) prickly heat: ～粉 prickly-heat powder

沸 fèi (动) boil

沸点(點) fèidiǎn (名) boiling point

沸腾 fèiténg (动) 1 boil 2 seethe with excitement: 热血～ brim with excitement

费 fèi I (动) cost; spend; consume (too much money, time, energy, etc.): ～尽心机 rack one's brains in scheming; leave no stone unturned to do sth. II (名) fee; charge; dues; expenses: 学～ tuition fees; tuition. 会～ membership dues. 生活～ living expense. 房租～ rent. 车～ fare III (形) consuming too much; wasteful: 用电热器太～电. An electric heater consumes too much electricity.

费工 fèigōng (动) take a lot of work; require a lot of labour

费工夫 fèi gōngfu (动) take time and energy

费解 fèijiě (形) hard to understand; obscure; unintelligible

费劲(勁) fèijìn (形) energy-consuming; strenuous

费力 fèilì (动) require great effort; be strenuous: ～不讨好 do a hard but thankless job

费钱(錢) fèiqián (形) costly; expensive

费神 fèishén (动)〈套〉may I trouble you (to do sth.)

费事 fèishì (动) give or take a lot of trouble

费心 fèixīn (动) take the trouble: 她为组织这次晚会费了不少心. She took a lot of trouble to organize this party.

费用 fèiyòng (名) cost; expenses; expenditure: 生产～ production cost. 生活～ cost of living; living expenses

分 fēn I (动) 1 divide; separate; part: 剧～三场演出. This play is divided into three scenes. ～而治之 divide and rule. 难舍难～ be reluctant to part with each other 2 distribute; allot; assign: 我～到了一个新任务. I was assigned a new task. 3 distinguish; tell one from another: 不～青红皂白 make no distinction between black and white (right and wrong). 我总是～不清他和他的弟弟. I can never tell him from his brother. II (名) 1 branch (of an organization): ～公司 a branch company 2 fraction: 四～之三 three-fourths. 二～之一 half 3 point; mark: 甲队又得了两～! Team A scores another two points! III (量) 1 (of time or degree) minute (= 1/60 of an hour or degree) 2 (of money) *fen* (=1/100 of a *yuan*) 3 (of weight) *fen* (=1/2 gram) 4 (of area) *fen* (= 66.666 sq. metres) 5 (of length) *fen* (=1/3 centimetre)
see also fèn

分包 fēnbāo (动) subcontract

分贝(貝) fēnbèi (名) decibel (db)

分崩离(離)析 fēnbēng-líxī disintegrate; fall

F

to pieces; come apart

分辨 fēnbiàn (动) distinguish; differentiate: ～真假善恶 distinguish truth from falsehood and good from evil

分辩(辯) fēnbiàn (动) defend oneself (against a charge); offer an explanation: 不容～ refuse to hear any explanation

分别 fēnbié I (动) 1 part; say goodbye to each other 2 distinguish; differentiate II (副) 1 differently: ～对待 treat differently 2 respectively; separately: 两案～处理. The two cases will be dealt with separately.

分布 fēnbù (动) distribute; spread; scatter

分寸 fēncùn (名) sense of propriety: 他措词很有～. He chose his words very carefully. 在公共场合讲话,有时不易掌握～. On public occasions, it is sometimes difficult to know what is proper to say and what is not.

分担(擔) fēndān (动) share responsibility for

分道扬(揚)镳 fēndào yángbiāo part company, each going his own way

分等 fēnděng (动) grade; classify

分发(發) fēnfā (动) distribute; hand out; issue

分赴 fēnfù (动) leave for (different destinations)

分割 fēngē (动) cut apart; separate; carve up

分隔 fēngé (动) separate; partition off

分工 fēngōng (名) division of labour: 有～也有协作. There is division of work as well as coordination of effort.

分号(號) fēnhào (名) 1 semicolon 2 branch (of a firm, etc.)

分红 fēnhóng (动) share out extra profits

分洪 fēnhóng (名) flood diversion

分化 fēnhuà (动) become divided; break up; split up: 贫富两极～ polarization of rich and poor. ～瓦解 disintegrate

分会(會) fēnhuì (名) branch society, association, etc.; subcommittee

分机(機) fēnjī (名) (telephone) extension: ～号码 extension number

分家 fēnjiā (动) divide up family property among children

分解 fēnjiě (动) resolve; decompose; break down

分界线(綫) fēnjièxiàn (名) demarcation line; boundary

分居 fēnjū (动、名) (usu. of a married couple) separate; separation

分开(開) fēnkāi (动) separate; part

分类(類) fēnlèi (动) classify

分离(離) fēnlí (动) separate: 理论不可与实践～. Theory cannot be separated from practice.

分裂 fēnliè (动) split; break up

分流 fēnliú (动) divert; branch off; shunt: 人员～ reposition redundant personnel

分米 fēnmǐ (名) decimetre (dm)

分泌 fēnmì (动) secrete

分娩 fēnmiǎn (名) childbirth

分明 fēnmíng I (形) clearly distinguished; distinct: 事情的是非必须～. The rights and wrongs of the case are to be distinguished. II (副) clearly; plainly; evidently

分派 fēnpài (动) assign (to different persons)

分配 fēnpèi (动) allocate; assign; distribute: 给新来的人～工作 assign jobs to newcomers

分批 fēnpī (副) in batches; in groups

分期 fēnqī (副) by stages: ～付款 payment by instalments

分歧 fēnqí (名) dispute; difference; divergence: 他们的意见有～. Their views are divergent. 制造～ sow dissension

分清 fēnqīng (动) distinguish; draw a clear line between

分散 fēnsàn (动) disperse; scatter; decentralize: ～注意力 divert attention. ～精力 diffuse one's energies

分身 fēnshēn (动) spare time to attend to sth. else

分手 fēnshǒu (动) part company; say goodbye

分数(數) fēnshù (名) 1 fraction 2 mark; grade

分水岭(嶺) fēnshuǐlǐng (名) watershed; line of demarcation

分摊(攤) fēntān (动) share: ～费用 share the expenses

分庭抗礼(禮) fēntíng-kànglǐ stand up to sb. as an equal

分头(頭) fēntóu (副) separately; severally

分文 fēnwén (名) a single penny

分析 fēnxī (动) analyse: 深入～ make an in-depth analysis

分享 fēnxiǎng（动）share（joy，rights，etc.）：～胜利的喜悦 share the joys of success

分晓（曉）fēnxiǎo（名）outcome；solution：此事还未见～. The outcome of the matter is still uncertain.

分心 fēnxīn（动）1 divert one's attention 2 claim attention：这件事您多～了. This would claim a good deal of your attention.

分野 fēnyě（名）dividing line：两种学派的～ the dividing line between the two schools of thought

分忧（憂）fēnyōu（动）share sb.'s worries；help solve difficult problems

分赃（贜）fēnzāng（动）divide the spoils；share the booty（or loot）

分支 fēnzhī（名）branch of any organization or main part

分子 fēnzǐ（名）1 numerator of a fraction 2 molecule

分组 fēnzǔ（动）divide into groups

芬 fēn（名）sweet smell；fragrance

芬芳 fēnfāng（形）fragrant；sweet

吩 fēn

吩咐 fēnfu（动）tell；bid；order；instruct

纷 fēn（形）numerous；confused：大雪～飞. The snow is falling thick and fast.

纷繁 fēnfán（形）numerous and complicated：头绪～ too many loose ends to tidy up

纷纷 fēnfēn（形）1 one after another；in succession：他们～要求发言. They all clamoured to take the floor. 2 numerous and confused：落叶～. The leaves are falling in profusion.

纷乱（亂）fēnluàn（形）numerous and disorderly：～的说话声 hullabaloo

纷扰（擾）fēnrǎo（名）confusion；turmoil

纷纭 fēnyún（形）diverse and confused：众说～，莫衷一是. There is no general agreement as opinions differ widely.

纷至沓来（來）fēnzhì-tàlái come thick and fast；keep pouring in

坟（墳）fén（名）grave；tomb

坟地 féndì（名）graveyard；cemetery

坟墓 fénmù（名）grave；tomb

焚 fén（动）burn：～香 burn incense. 忧心如～. Anxiety gnaws one's heart.

焚膏继（繼）晷 fén gāo jì guǐ burn the midnight oil

焚化 fénhuà（动）burn；cremate

焚毁 fénhuǐ（动）destroy by fire；burn down

焚烧（燒）fénshāo（动）burn

粉 fěn I（名）1 powder：磨成～ grind into powder；pulverize. 花～ the pollen of flowers. 奶～ powdered milk. 面～ flour. 香～ face powder 2 vermicelli（made from bean or sweet potato starch）II（形）1 whitewashed：～墙 whitewashed wall 2 pink：～色 pink colour

粉笔（筆）fěnbǐ（名）chalk

粉墨登场（場）fěnmò dēngchǎng make oneself up and go on stage；embark on a political venture

粉身碎骨 fěnshēn-suìgǔ（of human body）be smashed to pieces；be crushed to a pulp

粉饰 fěnshì（动）gloss over；whitewash

粉刷 fěnshuā（动）whitewash

粉丝 fěnsī（名）fan

粉碎 fěnsuì（动）1 smash；shatter；crush：～军事进攻 shatter an offensive 2 broken to pieces

粉条（條）fěntiáo（名）vermicelli noodles

粪（糞）fèn（名）excrement；dung；droppings

粪便 fènbiàn（名）excrement and urine；night soil；stool

粪肥 fènféi（名）manure；dung

粪土 fèntǔ（名）dung and dirt；muck：视如～ look upon as dirt；be considered worthless

愤 fèn（名）anger；indignation：公～ public indignation

愤愤不平 fènfèn bùpíng feel indignant

愤恨 fènhèn（动）indignantly resent；detest

愤激 fènjī（形）excited and indignant；roused

愤慨 fènkǎi（名）righteous indignation

愤懑 fènmèn（动）go into a huff；be resentful

愤怒 fènnù（名）indignation；anger；wrath

愤世嫉俗 fènshì-jísú detest the unjust practices of human society；detest the ways of the world；be cynical

奋（奮）fèn（动）exert oneself；act vigorously：振～ rouse oneself. ～不顾身 charge forward regardless of personal safety

奋斗(鬥) fèndòu (动) fight to achieve a goal; struggle; strive: 艰苦～ work arduously

奋发(發) fènfā (动) rouse oneself; exert oneself: ～图强 work hard for the prosperity of one's country; go all out to make the country strong

奋力 fènlì (动) do all one can; spare no effort

奋起 fènqǐ (动) rise vigorously: ～反抗 rise up in resistance

奋勇 fènyǒng (动) summon up one's courage: ～前进 advance bravely; forge ahead courageously

奋战(戰) fènzhàn (动) fight bravely: ～到底 fight to the bitter end

分 fèn (名) 1 component: 水～ moisture content 2 what is within the scope of one's rights or obligations: 本～ one's duty. 过～ excessive; going too far; overdone

see also fēn

分量 fènliang (名) weight: 他这话说得很有～. What he has just said is no casual comment.

分内 fènnèi (名) one's duty; duty-bound: 照顾她姨妈是她～的事. It's her duty to look after her aunt.

分外 fènwài I(名) outside the scope of one's duty II(副) particularly; especially: ～激动 very excited. ～美丽 extremely beautiful

分子 fènzǐ (名) member; element: 积极～ activist. 知识～ intellectual

忿 fèn see "愤" fèn

份 fèn I (名) share; portion: 股～ stock; share II (量): 一～礼品 a gift. 一～报纸 a copy of a newspaper. 一～《中国日报》a copy of *China Daily*

份额 fèn'é (名) share; portion

份子 fènzi (名) one's share of expenses for a joint undertaking: 凑～ club together to get someone a present.

丰(豐) fēng (形) 1 plentiful: ～衣足食 have ample food and clothing 2 great: ～功伟绩 great achievements; magnificent contributions

丰碑 fēngbēi (名) monument

丰产(產) fēngchǎn (名) high yield; bumper crop

丰富 fēngfù I (形) rich; abundant; plentiful: 资源～ rich in natural resources. ～多彩 rich and varied II (动) enrich: ～精神生活 enrich one's spiritual life

丰厚 fēnghòu (形) rich and generous: ～的礼品 generous gifts. 收入～ have a handsome income

丰满(滿) fēngmǎn (形) 1 full and round; well-developed; full-grown: 体形～ a well-shaped body. 羽毛～ full-fledged 2 plentiful

丰茂 fēngmào (形) lush; luxuriant: 水草～ lush pasture

丰年 fēngnián (名) bumper harvest year; good year

丰沛 fēngpèi (形) plentiful: 雨水～ have plenty of rain

丰盛 fēngshèng (形) rich; sumptuous: ～的酒席 a sumptuous dinner

丰收 fēngshōu (名) bumper harvest: ～在望 A good harvest is in sight.

丰硕 fēngshuò (形) plentiful and enormous: ～的成果 rich harvest; great success

丰腴 fēngyú (形) 1 full and round; buxom and fair; plump 2 rich and fertile 3 sumptuous

丰裕 fēngyù (形) in plenty: 生活～ live in plenty; be comfortably off

封 fēng I(动) 1 seal: 把信～好 seal a letter. 大雪～山. Heavy snow has sealed off the mountain passes. 2 confer (a title, territory, etc.) upon: ～官许愿 offer high posts and make lavish promises II (量): 三～信 three letters. 一～饼干 a pack of biscuits

封闭 fēngbì (动) 1 seal up: 用蜡～瓶口 seal a bottle with wax 2 close down: 一家出版社被～了. One publishing house was closed down.

封存 fēngcún (动) seal up for safekeeping

封底 fēngdǐ (名) (of a book) back cover

封顶 fēngdǐng (动) impose a ceiling on: ～工资 salary cap; cap on salaries

封官许愿(願) fēngguān xǔyuàn promise high posts and other favours

封建 fēngjiàn (形) feudal: ～主义 feudalism

封口 fēngkǒu (动) 1 seal: 信～了吗? Is the letter sealed? 2 heal: 腿上的伤已经～了. The leg wound has healed. 3 speak with a tone of finality: 不～ open-ended

封面 fēngmiàn (名) (of a book) front cover

封杀(殺) fēngshā (动) ban: 遭到～ be

banned; be disqualified

封锁 fēngsuǒ (动) blockade; block; seal off: 消息~ news blockade. ~边境 close the border. 经济~ economic blockade

封条(條) fēngtiáo (名) a strip of paper bearing an official seal and the date for the sealing of doors, drawers, etc.

烽 fēng (名) beacon

烽火 fēnghuǒ (名) 1 a signal fire used to give the border alarm in ancient China; beacon: ~台 beacon tower 2 flames of war: ~连天 raging flames of war

烽烟 fēngyān (名) beacon-fire

蜂 fēng (名) bee; wasp: 蜜~ honeybee

蜂房 fēngfáng (名) any of the six-sided wax cells in a honeycomb

蜂蜜 fēngmì (名) honey

蜂王精 fēngwángjīng (名) royal jelly

蜂窝(窩) fēngwō (名) honeycomb

蜂窝(窩)式移动(動)电(電)话 fēngwōshì yídòng diànhuà cellular phone

蜂拥(擁) fēngyōng (动) swarm; flock: ~而至 come in swarms

峰 fēng (名) 1 peak; summit: 山~ mountain peak 2 hump: 驼~ camel's hump

峰会 fēnghuì (名) summit; summit conference

峰峦(巒) fēngluán (名) ridges and peaks

锋 fēng (名) 1 the cutting edge of a knife or a sword 2 van: 先~ vanguard

锋利 fēnglì (形) 1 (of knives, etc.) sharp; keen 2 (of style) incisive

锋芒 fēngmáng (名) 1 sharp edge of a sword; spearhead 2 outward show of one's talent and dynamism: ~毕露 make a display of one's talent; show off one's ability

风(風) fēng (名) 1 wind; draft: ~雨无阻 regardless of the weather. ~平浪静 the wind has subsided and the waves have calmed down; calm and peaceful 2 style; practice; custom: 不正之~ unhealthy trend. 文~ style of writing 3 scene; view: ~景 scenery; landscape 4 news; information: 走~ leak news. 闻~而动 act without delay upon hearing the news

风暴 fēngbào (名) windstorm; storm

风波 fēngbō (名) disturbance

风采 fēngcǎi (名) charisma

风潮 fēngcháo (名) agitation; political unrest

风车(車) fēngchē (名) windmill

风尘(塵) fēngchén (名) travel fatigue: ~仆仆 endure the hardships of a long journey; be travel-worn

风传(傳) fēngchuán (名) hearsay; rumour

风吹草动(動) fēngchuī-cǎodòng slight disturbance

风度 fēngdù (名) elegant manners: 有~ behave with grace and ease. ~翩翩 have an elegant and graceful carriage

风范 fēngfàn (名) way; style: 大家~ integrity of scholarship. 领袖~ great leadership

风干(乾) fēnggān (动) air-dry

风格 fēnggé (名) style: 独特~ unique style

风光 fēngguāng (名) scene; view; sight: 大好~ a wonderful sight

风寒 fēnghán (名) chill; cold

风和日暖 fēnghé-rìnuǎn warm and sunny weather

风华(華) fēnghuá (名) charisma and talent: ~正茂 in the flower of youth

风化 fēnghuà (名) morals; decency: 有伤~ be offensive to general standards of behaviour

风化 fēnghuà (动) weather; wear away: ~的岩石 rocks weathered by wind

风景 fēngjǐng (名) scenery; landscape: ~如画 picturesque. ~区 scenic spot. ~优美 scenic beauty

风景线(綫) fēngjǐngxiàn (名) landscape; scene: 一道亮丽的~ an attractive scene

风镜 fēngjìng (名) goggles

风口 fēngkǒu (名) draught: 站在~ stand in the draught

风浪 fēnglàng (名) stormy waves

风雷 fēngléi (名) wind and thunder

风力 fēnglì (名) wind force; wind power

风凉话 fēngliánghuà (名) sarcastic remarks: 说~ make critical comments from the sidelines

风流 fēngliú (形) 1 talented and meritorious: ~人物 legendary figures; truly great men 2 gifted and unconventional 3 romantic

风马(馬)牛不相及 fēng mǎ niú bù xiāng jí have nothing to do with each other; be totally unrelated

风帽 fēngmào (名) hood

风貌 fēngmào (名) characteristic style and features

F

风靡一时(時) fēngmǐ yīshí fashionable for a time; à la mode
风起云(雲)涌 fēngqǐ-yúnyǒng surging and fast-changing
风气(氣) fēngqì (名) general mood; common practice; atmosphere: 社会～ social morals
风琴 fēngqín (名) organ (musical instrument)
风情 fēngqíng (名) flirtatious expressions: 卖弄～ coquettish
风趣 fēngqù (名) humour; wit: 一句很有～的话 a witty remark
风骚 fēngsāo I (名)〈书〉literary excellence II (形) coquettish
风沙 fēngshā (名) dust storm
风扇 fēngshàn (名) electric fan
风尚 fēngshàng (名) prevailing custom or practice
风声(聲) fēngshēng (名) news; rumour: 听到～ get wind of sth. ～很紧. The situation is tense. 走漏～ leak information
风湿(濕) fēngshī (名) rheumatism
风势 fēngshì (名) the force of the wind: ～越来越大. The wind is blowing harder and harder.
风霜 fēngshuāng (名) hardships experienced in life or on a journey: 饱经～ weather-beaten
风水 fēngshuǐ (名) geomantic omen: ～先生 geomancer
风俗 fēngsú (名) social customs: ～画 genre painting; genre
风头(頭) fēngtou (名) 1 a straw in the wind: 避避～ lie low before the dust has settled 2 public attention: 想出～ seek publicity
风土 fēngtǔ (名) natural conditions and social customs of a place: ～人情 local conditions and customs
风调雨顺 fēngtiáo-yǔshùn favourable weather (for the crops)
风味 fēngwèi (名) distinctive flavour; local colour: 地方～ local flavour. ～菜 local delicacies; typical local dishes
风闻 fēngwén (动) learn through hearsay; get wind of
风险(險) fēngxiǎn (名) risk: 冒～ run risks
风险投资 fēngxiǎn tóuzī risk investment; venture capital
风箱 fēngxiāng (名) bellows
风向 fēngxiàng (名) wind direction: 看～ see which way the wind blows
风行 fēngxíng (动) be in fashion; become prevalent: ～一时 be popular for a while
风雅 fēngyǎ (形) polite; refined: 举止～ have refined social manners
风言风语 fēngyán-fēngyǔ gossip; groundless talk
风衣 fēngyī (名) windcheater; windbreaker
风雨 fēngyǔ (名) trials and hardships: ～飘摇 unstable; tottering. ～同舟 stand together through thick and thin
风云(雲) fēngyún (名) fast-changing situation: ～变幻 a changeable situation. ～人物 influential man; man of the hour
风韵(韻) fēngyùn (名) (of a woman) graceful bearing; charm
风筝 fēngzheng (名) kite: 放～ fly a kite
风烛(燭)残(殘)年 fēngzhú cánnián aging and ailing like a candle guttering in the wind
风姿 fēngzī (名) graceful bearing; charisma

疯

fēng (形) mad; insane; crazy
疯癫 fēngdiān (形) insane; mad
疯狗 fēnggǒu (名) mad dog
疯狂 fēngkuáng (形) wild, crazy, frenzied: ～反扑 a desperate counterattack
疯牛病 fēngniúbìng mad cow disease; bovine spongiform encephalopathy (BSE)
疯人院 fēngrényuàn (名) madhouse; lunatic asylum
疯子 fēngzi (名) lunatic; madman

枫

fēng (名) maple

逢

féng (动) come across; meet; chance upon: 每～佳节 on every festive occasion. 久别重～ meet again after a long separation. ～场作戏 join in the fun on occasion
逢集 féngjí (名) market day
逢年过(過)节(節) féng nián guò jié on New Year's Day or other festivals
逢凶化吉 féng xiōng huà jí turn danger into safety

缝

féng (动) sew; stitch: ～扣子 sew on a button. ～被子 stitch a quilt
see also fèng
缝补(補) féngbǔ (动) sew and mend
缝合 fénghé (动) sew up(a wound); suture
缝纫 féngrèn (名) sewing; tailoring: ～机 sewing machine

讽 fěng (动) mock; satirize: 冷嘲热～ sarcasm
讽刺 fěngcì (动) satirize; mock
讽喻 fěngyù (名) parable; allegory
奉 fèng (动) 1 present or receive with respect: ～上年历一本 send with respect a calendar. ～上级指示 be instructed by higher authorities 2 esteem; revere: ～为典范 look upon as a model. 信～基督教 believe in Christianity. 侍～ attend to or look after sb. with respect
奉承 fèngcheng (动) flatter; fawn upon; toady: ～话 flattery
奉告 fènggào (动) have the honour to inform: 无可～. No comment.
奉公守法 fènggōng-shǒufǎ be law-abiding
奉还(還) fènghuán (动) return sth. with thanks
奉命 fèngmìng (动) receive orders or instructions
奉陪 fèngpéi (动)〈敬〉keep sb. company: 恕不～. Sorry not to be able to keep you company.
奉劝(勸) fèngquàn (动)〈敬〉give advice to sb.; advise
奉若神明 fèng ruò shénmíng worship sb. or sth.; make a fetish of sth.
奉送 fèngsòng (动)〈敬〉offer as a gift
奉献(獻) fèngxiàn (动) offer as a tribute; present with all respect
奉行 fèngxíng (动) pursue (a policy, etc.)
奉养 fèngyǎng (动) support and wait upon (one's parents, etc.)
奉召 fèngzhào (动) be summoned
俸 fèng (名) pay; salary: 薪～ an official's salary
凤(鳳) fèng (名) phoenix: ～凰 phoenix
缝 fèng (名) seam; crack; slit: 无～钢管 seamless steel tube. 裤～ crease. ～隙 chink; crack
see also féng
佛 fó (名) 1 Buddha 2 Buddhism 3 statue of Buddha
佛教 Fójiào (名) Buddhism: ～徒 Buddhist
佛经(經) fójīng (名) Buddhist Scripture
佛龛(龕) fókān (名) niche for a statue of Buddha
佛门(門) fómén (名) Buddhism: ～弟子 followers of Buddhism; Buddhists
佛堂 fótáng (名) family hall for worshipping Buddha
佛像 fóxiàng (名) statue (or image) of Buddha
佛学(學) fóxué (名) Buddhism
佛爷(爺) fóye (名) Buddha
否 fǒu (动) 1 deny; negate: ～认 deny 2 no: 是～ whether or not
否定 fǒudìng (动) negate; deny
否决 fǒujué (动) vote against; veto: 提案被～了. The motion was voted down. ～权 veto power; veto
否则 fǒuzé (连) otherwise; if not; or else: 咱们现在就干，～就晚了. Let's get down to work at once, otherwise it'll be too late.
夫 fū (名) 1 husband 2 man: 匹～ ordinary man. 船～ boatman. 农～ farmer; peasant
夫妇(婦) fū-fù (名) husband and wife: 新婚～ newly married couple; newlyweds
夫妻 fū-qī (名) man and wife
夫人 fūren (名) Mrs.; Madame; Lady: 某某～ Madame So-and-so. 大使及其～ the ambassador and his wife
夫子 fūzǐ (名) a Confucian scholar
麸(麩) fū (名): ～皮 (wheat) bran. ～子 (wheat) bran
肤(膚) fū (名) skin
肤皮潦草 fūpí liáocǎo cursory; casual; perfunctory
肤浅(淺) fūqiǎn (形) skin-deep; superficial; shallow
肤色 fūsè (名) colour of skin; complexion
敷 fū (动) 1 apply (powder, ointment, etc.): 外～ for external application 2 be sufficient for: 入不～出 unable to make both ends meet
敷衍 fūyǎn (动) be perfunctory: ～了事 do sth. perfunctorily; muddle through one's work. ～塞责 perform one's duty in a perfunctory manner
孵 fū (动) hatch; incubate: ～小鸡 hatch chickens
孵化 fūhuà (动) hatch; incubate: 人工～ artificial incubation
孵卵 fūluǎn (动) hatch; brood; incubate
芙 fú
芙蓉 fúróng (名) 1 cottonrose hibiscus 2 lotus
扶 fú (动) 1 support with the hand: ～着盲人过马路 help the blind man across the road by taking his arm. ～着梯子! Hold the ladder! ～某人站起来 as-

sist sb. to his feet **2** help; relieve: 救死~伤 heal the wounded and rescue the dying

扶病 fúbìng (副) in spite of illness: ~出席 turn up in spite of illness

扶持 fúchí (动) help; support

扶老携幼 fúlǎo-xiéyòu helping the old and the young by the hand (on a journey)

扶贫 fúpín (名) aid-the-poor programme

扶手 fúshou (名) **1** rail; banisters **2** armrest: ~椅 armchair

扶梯 fútī (名) staircase

扶养(養) fúyǎng (动) bring up; foster: ~成人 bring up (a child)

扶植 fúzhí (动) foster; prop up: ~傀儡政权 prop up a puppet regime

扶助 fúzhù (动) help; assist; support: ~病残 help the sick and the disabled

福 fú (名) good fortune; blessing; happiness

福利 fúlì (名) welfare; well-being: ~国家 welfare state. 群众~ the well-being of the masses

福气(氣) fúqi (名) happy lot; good fortune

福星 fúxīng (名) lucky star

福音 fúyīn (名) **1** Gospel **2** glad tidings

辐 fú (名) spoke: 轮~ spoke of a wheel

辐射 fúshè (名) radiation

幅 fú I (名) width of cloth; size of a painting, photographs, etc. II (量) [for cloth, painting, etc.]: 一~画 a picture; a painting

幅度 fúdù (名) range; scope; extent: 大~增长 increase by a big margin

幅员 fúyuán (名) the size of a country: ~广大 vast in territory

蝠 fú (名) bat

浮 fú I (动) **1** float: ~萍 floating duckweed **2** swim **3** exceed: 人~于事 have an excessive number of staff; be overstaffed II (形) **1** on the surface: ~土 dust on the surface **2** superficial; flighty; frivolous: 她这个人有点~. She is a bit flighty.

浮标(標) fúbiāo (名) buoy

浮财 fúcái (名) movable property

浮沉 fúchén (动) now sink, now emerge; drift along: 与世~ swim with the tide

浮雕 fúdiāo (名) relief (sculpture)

浮动(動) fúdòng (动) **1** float; drift **2** be unsteady; fluctuate: ~工资 floating wages. ~汇率 floating exchange rate

浮华(華) fúhuá (形) showy; flashy; ostentatious

浮夸(誇) fúkuā (形) boastful; untruthful: 他这人作风~. He is given to boasting.

浮力 fúlì (名) buoyancy

浮桥(橋) fúqiáo (名) pontoon (or floating) bridge

浮现 fúxiàn (动) appear in one's mind: 往事~在我眼前. My mind flashed back to scenes of the past.

浮想 fúxiǎng (名) **1** thoughts flashing across one's mind **2** recollections

浮躁 fúzào (形) impetuous; impulsive

浮肿(腫) fúzhǒng (名) dropsy; oedema

俘 fú I (动) capture; take prisoner II (名) prisoner of war; captive

俘虏(虜) fúlǔ I (动) capture; take prisoner II (名) captive; prisoner of war (P.O.W.)

伏 fú I (动) **1** bend over **2** lie with one's face downward **3** subside; go down: 此起彼~ rise and fall; be rising everywhere **4** hide: 昼~夜出 hide by day and come out at night. 埋~ lie in ambush II (名) hot season; dog days

伏笔(筆) fúbǐ (名) a remark suggestive of later developments in a story, etc.

伏兵 fúbīng (名) troops in ambush

伏击(擊) fújī (动) ambush: 遭到~ fall into an ambush

伏特 fútè (名) volt

伏天 fútiān (名) hot summer days; dog days

伏帖 fútiē (形) **1** comfortable **2** (of a person) docile; obedient; submissive

符 fú I (名) symbol: 音~ musical notes II (动) tally with; square with: 与事实不~ not square with the facts

符号(號) fúhào (名) **1** symbol; mark; sign: 标点~ punctuation mark **2** insignia

符合 fúhé (动) accord with; conform to; be in line with: ~要求 accord with the demands. ~实际情况 tally with the actual situation

符咒 fúzhòu (名) Taoist magic figures or incantations

凫(鳧) fú (名) wild duck

服 fú I(名) clothes: 制~ uniform. 军~ army uniform. 工作~ work clothes II(动) 1 take (medicine): 日~三次,每次两片. To be taken three times a day, two (tablets) each time. 2 serve: ~兵役 serve in the army (navy, airforce, etc.). ~刑 serve a sentence 3 be convinced; obey 4 convince: 以理~人 convince by reasoning 5 be accustomed to: 水土不~ not accustomed to the climate
see also fù

服从(從) fúcóng (动) obey; be subordinated to: ~命令 obey orders. 少数~多数. The minority should submit to the majority.

服毒 fúdú (动) take poison

服气(氣) fúqì (动) be convinced: 他是错的,但很难叫他~. He is wrong, but it is difficult to convince him.

服丧(喪) fúsāng (动) be in mourning (for the death of a kinsman, etc.)

服侍 fúshi (动) wait upon; attend: ~病人 attend the sick

服饰 fúshì (名) dress and personal adornment

服输 fúshū (动) admit (or acknowledge) defeat

服帖 fútiē (形) 1 obedient; submissive 2 proper; well handled: 事情都弄得服服帖帖. Everything has been done properly.

服务(務) fúwù (动) give service to; serve: ~很周到. The service is very good. ~行业 service trades. ~员 attendant. ~台 service desk (or counter); information and reception desk

服务(務)器 fúwùqì (名) server

服药(藥) fúyào (动) take medicine

服役 fúyì (动) be on active service; enlist (in the armed forces)

服装(裝) fúzhuāng (名) dress; garment; costume: 民族~ national costume

服罪 fúzuì (动) plead guilty

拂 fú (动) 1 touch: 春风~面. The spring breeze touched my cheeks. 2 whisk; flick

拂拭 fúshì (动) whisk or wipe off

拂晓(曉) fúxiǎo (名) dawn; daybreak

府 fǔ (名) 1 government office: 首~ capital 2 official residence; mansion: 总统~ presidential palace 3 〈敬〉 your home: 贵~ your home 4 prefecture

府上 fǔshang (名)〈敬〉 your home; your family: ~在哪里? Where is your home?

腐 fǔ I (形) rotten; stale; corroded: 流水不~. Running water is never stale. II (名) bean curd

腐败 fǔbài (形) 1 rotten; decayed 2 corrupt

腐化 fǔhuà (形) corrupt; degenerate; depraved: 贪污~ corrupt and degenerate

腐烂(爛) fǔlàn (形) 1 decomposed 2 corrupt; rotten: 极端~ rotten to the core

腐蚀 fǔshí (动) corrupt; corrode: ~剂 corrosive

腐朽 fǔxiǔ (形) rotten; decayed; decadent

腐殖质(質) fǔzhízhì (名) humus

俯 fǔ (动) bend; lower; bow: ~冲 (of a bird or an aeroplane) dive

俯瞰 fǔkàn (动) look down at; overlook

俯拾即是 fǔ shí jí shì be easily found anywhere; be very common

俯视 fǔshì (动) look down at; overlook

俯首帖耳 fǔshǒu-tiē'ěr be obedient; be submissive; be servile

抚(撫) fǔ (动) 1 stroke 2 comfort; console: 安~ appease; pacify 3 nurture; foster: ~养 bring up; foster; raise

抚爱(愛) fǔ'ài (动) caress; fondle

抚摩 fǔmó (动) stroke

抚弄 fǔnòng (动) stroke; fondle

抚慰 fǔwèi (动) comfort; console; soothe

抚恤 fǔxù (动) comfort and compensate the family of a person who was hurt at work and/or died as a consequence: ~金 pension or compensation

抚育 fǔyù (动) foster; nurture; tend: ~子女 bring up children

甫 fǔ (副)〈书〉 just; only: 年~二十 have just reached the age of twenty

辅 fǔ (动) assist; complement; supplement: 相~相成 complement each other; be complementary (to each other)

辅导(導) fǔdǎo (动) coach; give tutorials to: ~员 assistant; instructor

辅音 fǔyīn (名) consonant

辅助 fǔzhù I (动) assist II(形) supplementary; subsidiary: ~教材 supplementary reading material. ~机构 auxiliary body

辅佐 fǔzuǒ (动) assist a ruler in governing a country

F

脯 fǔ (名) 1 preserved fruit: 梨～ preserved pears 2 dried meat

斧 fǔ (名)(～子) axe

斧头(頭) fǔtou (名) axe; hatchet

釜 fǔ (名) cauldron: ～底抽薪 take a drastic measure to deal with an emergency. ～底游鱼 a person whose fate is as good as sealed

父 fù (名) 1 father: ～亲 father 2 male relative: 伯～ father's elder brother; uncle. 祖～ grandfather

父老 fùlǎo (名) elders (of a country or district)

父母 fù-mǔ (名) father and mother; parents

父系 fùxì (名) paternal line

缚 fù (动) tie up: 束～ tie; bind up

富 fù (形) rich; wealthy; abundant

富贵 fùguì (名) wealth and rank: 荣华～ wealth and honours

富豪 fùháo (名) rich and powerful people

富丽(麗)堂皇 fùlì tánghuáng splendid; magnificent

富农(農) fùnóng (名) rich peasant

富强 fùqiáng (形) prosperous and powerful

富饶(饒) fùráo (形) richly endowed; abundant: ～的土地 a land of plenty

富庶 fùshù (形) rich and populous

富态(態) fùtai (形) portly; stout

富翁 fùwēng (名) rich man; moneybags

富有 fùyǒu I (形) rich; wealthy II (动) be rich in; be full of: ～生命力 be full of vitality

富余(餘) fùyu (动) have enough and to spare

富裕 fùyù (形) well-to-do; prosperous; well off: ～农户 well-to-do farmers

富足 fùzú (形) rich; plentiful; abundant

副 fù I (形) 1 deputy; assistant; vice-: ～主任 deputy director: ～经理 assistant manager. ～主席 vice-chairman. ～教授 associate professor 2 auxiliary; subsidiary; secondary: ～品 substandard goods II (量) 1 pair; set: 一～眼镜 a pair of glasses. 两～手套 two pairs of gloves 2 [for facial expressions]: 一～笑脸 a smiling face. 一～庄严的面孔 a dignified appearance

副本 fùběn (名) duplicate; transcript; copy

副产(產)品 fùchǎnpǐn (名) by-product

副词 fùcí (名) adverb

副官 fùguān (名) adjutant; aide-de-camp

副刊 fùkān (名) supplement: 文学～ literary supplement

副食 fùshí (名) non-staple food (including meat, vegetables, etc.): ～商店 grocer's; grocery

副手 fùshǒu (名) assistant

副题 fùtí (名) subtitle

副业(業) fùyè (名) sideline; side occupation

副作用 fùzuòyòng (名) (of medicine) side effect; by-effect

讣 fù (名) obituary

讣告 fùgào (名) obituary notice

赴 fù (动) go to; attend: ～宴 attend a banquet

赴任 fùrèn (动) go to one's post; leave for an assignment

赴汤(湯)蹈火 fùtāng dǎohuǒ go through fire and water

赋 fù I (名) tax II (动) 1 bestow on; endow with: ～予 bestow; endow. 秉～ natural endowments 2 compose (a poem): ～诗一首 compose a poem

赋税 fùshuì (名) taxes; levy

赋闲(閒) fùxián (形) (of an official, etc.) be unemployed

复(複、復) fù I (动) 1 turn around; turn back; repeat: 反～无常 capricious. ～写 duplicate. 旧病～发 have a relapse 2 answer: 电～ cable reply 3 recover; resume: 康～ (of health) recover. 收～国土 recover one's motherland. 官～原职 restored to one's official post 4 revenge: 报～ retaliate. ～仇 revenge II (副) again: 周而～始 go round and begin again. 一去不～返 leave never to return; gone for ever

复辟 fùbì (动) restore a dethroned monarch; stage a comeback

复查 fùchá (动) check; re-examine

复出 fùchū (动) make a comeback; resurface

复发(發) fùfā (动) have a relapse; recur: 旧病～ have a relapse (of an old illness)

复工 fùgōng (动) return to work (after a strike or lay-off)

复古 fùgǔ (动) restore ancient ways

复合 fùhé (形) compound; complex: ～词 compound word

复核 fùhé (动) check; re-examine
复会(會) fùhuì (动) resume a session
复活 fùhuó I (动) bring back to life; revive II (名) Resurrection: ～节 Easter
复旧(舊) fùjiù (动) restore (or revive) old ways; return to the past
复刊 fùkān (动) resume publication
复述 fùshù (动) repeat; retell
复数(數) fùshù (名) plural number
复苏(蘇) fùsū (动) come back to life (or consciousness)
复习(習) fùxí (动) review; revise: 总～ general revision (of one's lessons)
复写(寫) fùxiě (动) make carbon copies; duplicate
复信 fùxìn I (动) write a letter in reply II (名) letter in reply; reply
复兴(興) fùxīng (动) revive: 文艺～ the Renaissance
复姓 fùxìng (名) two-character surname
复印 fùyìn (动) photocopy; duplicate; xerox
复员 fùyuán (动) demobilize: ～军人 demobilized soldier; ex-serviceman
复原 fùyuán (动) recover from an illness; be restored to health
复杂(雜) fùzá (形) complicated; complex
复制(製) fùzhì (动) duplicate; reproduce; copy: ～品 replica; reproduction

覆 fù (动) 1 cover 2 overturn: 前车之～,后车之鉴. The upset of the cart ahead is a warning to the cart behind.
覆盖(蓋) fùgài (动) cover: 积雪～着地面. The ground is covered with a layer of snow.
覆没 fùmò (动) 1 〈书〉 capsize and sink 2 (of troops) be annihilated: 敌人全军～. The enemy troops were entirely wiped out.
覆灭(滅) fùmiè (动) be destroyed; collapse completely
覆水难(難)收 fù shuǐ nán shōu it is no use crying over spilt milk
覆亡 fùwáng (名) fall (of a nation)
覆辙 fùzhé (名) the track of an overturned cart: 重蹈～ follow the same disastrous course

蝮 fù
蝮蛇 fùshé (名) Pallas pit viper

馥 fù (名)〈书〉 fragrance
馥郁 fùyù (形)〈书〉 (of fragrance) strong; rich

腹 fù (名) belly; abdomen; stomach
腹背受敌(敵) fù-bèi shòu dí be attacked front and rear
腹地 fùdì (名) hinterland
腹稿 fùgǎo (名) a draft worked out in one's mind
腹腔 fùqiāng (名) abdominal cavity
腹痛 fùtòng (名) abdominal pain
腹泻(瀉) fùxiè (名) diarrhoea

付 fù (动) 1 pay: ～账 pay a bill. ～税 pay taxes. ～息 pay interest. 分期～款 pay in instalments 2 hand (or turn) over to: ～印 send to the press. 托～ entrust. ～之一炬 commit to the flames. ～诸实施 put into practice
付出 fùchū (动) pay out; expend: ～代价 pay a price. ～辛勤的劳动 put in a lot of hard work
付诸东(東)流 fù zhū dōng liú (of efforts) have proven futile; have been wasted

附 fù (动) 1 add; attach; enclose: 依～ be sb.'s protégé; sponge on sb. ～笔 add a postscript. ～寄一张照片 enclose a photo 2 get close to; be near: ～耳交谈 talk in whispers
附带(帶) fùdài I (副) in passing; incidentally: ～说一下 mention in passing; by the way II (动) attach: 不～条件 with no conditions (or strings) attached
附和 fùhè (动) echo; parrot: ～别人的意见 parrot other people's views
附加 fùjiā I (动) add; attach II(形) additional; attached; appended: ～值 added value. ～值税 value-added tax; VAT. ～条款 additional article; memorandum clause
附件 fùjiàn (名) 1 appendix; annex 2 (of a machine) accessory; attachment
附近 fùjìn (名) nearby; neighbouring; in the vicinity: ～的城镇 neighbouring towns. 住在～ live nearby. 就在公园～ (It is) in the vicinity of the park.
附录(録) fùlù (名) appendix
附上 fùshàng (动) enclose herewith: 随信～商品目录一份. A catalogue of commodities is enclosed herewith.
附设 fùshè (动) have as an attached institution: 这个学院～一所中学. There is a middle school attached to the institute.
附属(屬) fùshǔ (形) affiliated; attached: 医学院～医院 a hospital attached to a medical college. ～机构 affiliated organization

F

附言 fùyán (名) postscript (P. S.)
附议(議) fùyì (动) second a motion
附庸 fùyōng (名) a vassal kingdom; dependency
附注 fùzhù (名) notes appended to a book; annotations
附着 fùzhuó (动) adhere; stick to: ～力 adhesive force; adhesion

驸 fù

驸马(馬) fùmǎ (名) emperor's son-in-law

阜 fù I (名)〈书〉mound II (形) abundant: 物～民丰 products abound and the people live in plenty

服 fù (量) (for Chinese medicine) dose: 一～药 a dose of medicine
see also fú

负 fù I (动) 1 carry on the back or shoulder; bear: 肩～重任 shoulder heavy responsibilities. 如释重～ feel a heavy load off one's mind; feel greatly relieved 2 owe: ～债 be in debt 3 fail in one's duty or obligation; betray: ～约 break a promise. 忘恩～义 be ungrateful 4 lose (a battle, game, etc.); be defeated: 不分胜～ end in a draw; break even 5 suffer: ～伤 be wounded; be injured 6 rely on: ～险固守 put up a stubborn defence by relying on one's strategic position II (形) minus; negative: ～一点五 minus one point five (－1.5). ～号 negative sign

负担(擔) fùdān I (动) bear (a burden); shoulder: ～旅费 bear travel expenses II (名) burden; load: 思想～ mental burden. 家庭～ family burden
负号(號) fùhào (名) negative sign
负荷 fùhè (名) load
负极(極) fùjí (名) negative pole
负疚 fùjiù (动) feel guilty
负累 fùlěi (名) burden; load: 家庭～ family burden
负数(數) fùshù (名) negative number
负心 fùxīn (形) ungrateful (esp. in love); heartless
负隅顽抗 fùyú wánkàng (of an enemy) put up a stubborn resistance
负责 fùzé I(动) be responsible for; be in charge of: 这里谁～? Who is in charge here? 我～校对. I'll be responsible for proof-reading. 一切后果将由你～. You will be held responsible for all the consequences. ～人 person in charge II (形) responsible; conscientious: 对工作很～ be very conscientious in one's work
负重 fùzhòng (动) carry a heavy load or task
负罪 fùzuì (动) bear the blame

妇(婦) fù (名) 1 woman: ～幼 (or 孺) women and children 2 married woman: 少～ young married woman 3 wife: 夫～ husband (or man) and wife

妇产(產)科 fùchǎnkē (名) (department of) gynaecology and obstetrics
妇科 fùkē (名) (department of) gynaecology: ～医生 gynaecologist
妇女 fùnǚ (名) woman
妇人 fùrén (名) married woman

G g

夹(夾) gā
see also jiā; jiá

夹肢窝(窩) gāzhīwō (名) armpit

嘎 gā

嘎巴 gābā (象) crack; snap
嘎嘎 gāgā (象) quack

咖 gā
see also kā

咖喱 gālí (名) curry: ～牛肉 beef curry

该 gāi I (动) 1 should; ought to: 他早～到了. He should have arrived. 这人～受惩罚. This chap ought to be punished. 2 be one's turn to do sth.: ～你了. It's your turn now. 下一个～谁发言? Who's the next speaker? 3 owe: 我～你多少钱? How much do I owe you? II (代) this; that; it; the abovementioned: 这是本地最大的医院, ～医院有七百张病床. This is the biggest hospital in the locality. It has 700 beds. III (副) [used for emphasis]: 你瞧, 这么晚了, 妈妈又～唠叨了! Look! It's late. Mother will grumble again. 要是我能跟你一块去, 那～多好哇! How nice it would be if I could go with you!

该死 gāisǐ (形)〈口〉[used to express anger]: 你这～的笨蛋! You damn fool! ～的天气! What wretched weather! ～! 我忘带钥匙了. Damn it! I've forgotten my key.

改 gǎi (动) 1 change; transform: 把卧室～成起居室 convert a bedroom

into a sitting room. 河流～道. The river changed its course. ～朝换代 dynastic changes 2 alter; correct: ～裙子 alter a skirt. ～缺点 overcome one's shortcomings. ～作业 correct (or go over) students' homework (or papers)

改编 gǎibiān (动) 1 adapt; rewrite: 这部电影是由一本小说～的. This film is adapted from a novel. 2 (of troops) reorganize

改变(變) gǎibiàn (动) change; alter; transform: ～主意 change one's mind

改道 gǎidào (动) 1 change one's route 2 (of a river) change its course

改掉 gǎidiào (动) give up; drop: ～坏习惯 give up bad habits

改动(動) gǎidòng (动) change; modify: 这篇文章我只～了一些词句. I've only made a few changes in the wording of this article.

改革 gǎigé (动、名) reform: 土地～ land reform. 文字～ reform of a writing system

改观(觀) gǎiguān (动) take on a new look; change in appearance

改过(過) gǎiguò (动) correct one's errors: ～自新 mend one's ways; turn over a new leaf

改行 gǎiháng (动) change one's profession (or occupation)

改换 gǎihuàn (动) change; replace

改嫁 gǎijià (动) (of a woman) remarry

改进(進) gǎijìn (动) improve; make better: ～企业管理 improve business management

改口 gǎikǒu (动) correct oneself (in conversation); change one's tone

改良 gǎiliáng (动) improve; ameliorate; reform: ～主义 reformism

改期 gǎiqī (动) change the date: 会议～举行. The meeting has been postponed.

改日 gǎirì (副) another day; some other day

改善 gǎishàn (动) improve; better: ～生活条件 improve living conditions

改头(頭)换面 gǎitóu-huànmiàn change the appearance but not the substance; dish up in a new form

改弦更张(張) gǎixián-gēngzhāng start afresh

改邪归(歸)正 gǎixié-guīzhèng turn over a new leaf

改写(寫) gǎixiě (动) rewrite; adapt

改选(選) gǎixuǎn (动) re-elect

改造 gǎizào (动) transform; reform; remould: ～自然 transform nature

改正 gǎizhèng (动) correct; amend; put right: ～错误 correct one's mistakes

改组 gǎizǔ (动) reorganize; reshuffle: ～内阁 reshuffle the cabinet

盖(蓋)

gài I (名) lid; cover: 茶壶～ teapot lid II (动) 1 cover: 遮～ cover up. ～章 put the chop (a seal) on 2 overwhelm: 欢呼声～过了他的叫声. Cheers drowned his shouting. 3 build: ～医院 build a hospital. ～楼房 put up a building

盖棺论(論)定 gài guān lùn dìng only when a person is dead can final judgment be passed on him

盖世 gàishì (形) unparalleled: ～无双 peerless

盖章 gàizhāng (动) affix one's seal; seal; stamp

盖子 gàizi (名) lid; cover: 揭～ take the lid off

丐

gài (名) beggar: 乞～ beggar

钙

gài (名) calcium (Ca)

概

gài I (形) general; approximate: 梗～ outline II (副) without exception; categorically: ～不追究 no action will be taken (against sb. for his past offences). 商品售出, ～不退换. Articles sold may not be returned.

概况 gàikuàng (名) general situation; brief account of sth.

概括 gàikuò (动) summarize; generalize: ～地说 generally speaking; briefly

概率 gàilǜ (名) probability

概略 gàilüè (名) outline; summary: 这只是故事的～. This is only a synopsis.

概论(論) gàilùn (名) outline

概念 gàiniàn (名) concept; notion; idea

概算 gàisuàn (名) budgetary estimate

概要 gàiyào (名) essentials; outline

干

gān I (名) shield II(动) 1 offend: ～犯 encroach upon 2 concern: 这不～你的事. It is none of your business.

干(乾)

gān I (形) 1 dry; dried: ～毛巾 dry towel. ～果 dried fruits 2 empty: 酒瓶～了. The wine bottle is empty. 外强中～ outwardly strong but inwardly weak 3 relatives not linked by blood: ～爹 father by affection. ～儿子 adopted son II(副) with no result; in vain: ～打雷不下雨 all thunder and no rain. 我～等了

G

他半天. I wasted a lot of time waiting for him (and he didn't turn up). ～着急 be worried but unable to do anything
see also gàn

干巴 gānba (形) dried up; shrivelled; wizened: 树叶都晒～了. The leaves have dried up under the sun. ～的皮肤 wizened skin

干巴巴 gānbābā (形) 1 dried up; wizened 2 dull and dry: 文章写得～的. The article is dull.

干杯 gānbēi (动) drink a toast; cheers

干瘪(癟) gānbiě (形) shrivelled; wizened

干草 gāncǎo (名) hay: ～垛 haystack

干脆 gāncuì I (形) frank and straightforward: 他这人很～. He is frank and straightforward. 回答～点! Give me a simple, clear-cut answer! II (副) simply; just: 他～一直保持沉默. He simply kept silent all the time. 你～亲自跟他谈谈吧. You'd better talk to him yourself.

干电(電)池 gāndiànchí (名) dry battery

干戈 gāngē (名) weapons: 动～ take up arms; go to war

干旱 gānhàn (形) (of weather or soil) arid; dry

干涸 gānhé (动) (of a river) dry up; run dry

干净 gānjìng (形) 1 clean: ～利落 neat and tidy 2 completely; totally: 把责任推了个～ absolutely refuse to accept any responsibility

干渴 gānkě (形) very thirsty; parched

干枯 gānkū (形) dried-up; withered: 地上落满了～的树叶. The ground is covered with withered fallen leaves.

干酪 gānlào (名) cheese

干粮(糧) gānliáng (名) dry ready food

干扰(擾) gānrǎo (动) disturb; interfere; obstruct

干涉 gānshè I (动) interfere; intervene; meddle: 互不～内政 noninterference in each other's internal affairs II (名) relation: 二者了无～. The two of them have nothing to do with each other.

干瘦 gānshòu (形) skinny; bony

干洗 gānxǐ (动、名) dry-clean; dry cleaning

干预 gānyù (动) intervene; meddle

干燥 gānzào (形) dry; arid: ～剂 drier; desiccating agent. 沙漠地方气候很～. The climate is very dry in the desert area.

杆 gān (名) pole; post: 旗～ flagstaff; flagpole
see also gǎn

竿 gān (名) pole; rod: 竹～ bamboo pole. 钓鱼～ fishing rod

肝 gān (名) liver: ～癌 liver cancer. ～炎 hepatitis

肝胆(膽) gāndǎn (名) 1 open-heartedness; sincerity: ～相照,荣辱与共 treating each other with all sincerity and sharing weal or woe 2 heroic spirit

肝功能 gāngōngnéng (名) liver function

肝火 gānhuǒ (名) irscibility; spleen: 动～ vent one's spleen; get worked up. ～旺 hot-tempered; irascible

肝脏(臟) gānzàng (名) liver

甘 gān I (形) sweet; pleasant: ～泉 sweet spring water II (副) willingly; of one's own accord

甘拜下风(風) gān bài xiàfēng candidly acknowledge one's inferiority; willingly yield to sb.'s superior knowledge or skill

甘苦 gānkǔ (名) 1 joys and sorrows: 同甘共苦 share the joys and sorrows 2 hardships and difficulties experienced in work

甘露 gānlù (名) sweet dew; superior drink

甘美 gānměi (形) (of water) sweet and refreshing

甘薯 gānshǔ (名) sweet potato

甘心 gānxīn (动) 1 be willing to 2 be content with

甘休 gānxiū (动) be willing to give up; take it lying down

甘油 gānyóu (名) glycerine

甘愿(願) gānyuàn (副) willingly

甘蔗 gānzhe (名) sugar cane

泔 gān

泔水 gānshuǐ (名) swill; slops

柑 gān (名) mandarin orange

柑橘 gānjú (名) oranges and tangerines

尴(尷) gān

尴尬 gāngà (形) awkward; embarrassed: 处境～ be in an awkward position

赶(趕) gǎn (动) 1 catch up with: ～上世界先进水平 catch up with the advanced in the world 2 hurry; rush: ～路 hurry on one's way. 我们必须～回去. We must hurry back. ～任务 rush through one's job **3** take; catch: ～头班车 catch the first bus **4** drive: 把牛～上山 drive the cattle up the hill. ～大车 drive a cart. 把敌人～走 drive the enemy away **5** happen to: 他～巧在家. He happened to be at home. 今天正～上是母亲的生日. Today happens to be mother's birthday.

赶集 gǎnjí (动) go to the local market (or village fair)

赶紧(緊) gǎnjǐn (副) lose no time; hasten

赶快 gǎnkuài (副) hasten; at once; quickly: 时间不早了,我们～走吧. It's getting late. Let's leave at once.

赶忙 gǎnmáng (副) hurry; make haste: 他～道歉. He hastened to apologize.

赶巧 gǎnqiǎo (副) happen to; it so happened that

赶时(時)髦 gǎn shímáo follow the fashion

杆(桿) gǎn I (名) the shaft or arm of sth.: 秤～ the arm of a steelyard. 钢笔～儿 penholder. 枪～ the barrel of a rifle II (量) [for sth. with a shaft]: 一～秤 a steelyard. 一～枪 a rifle

see also gān

秆(稈) gǎn (名) stalk: 麦～ wheat stalk. 高粱～ sorghum stalk

擀 gǎn (动) roll (dough): ～面杖 rolling pin. ～面条 make noodles

感 gǎn I (动) **1** feel; sense: 深～力不从心. I feel keenly that my ability falls short of my wishes. **2** move; touch: 深有所～ be deeply moved II (名) sense; feeling: 责任～ sense of responsibility. 自卑～ inferiority complex

感触(觸) gǎnchù (名) thoughts and feelings aroused by what one sees or hears

感到 gǎndào (动) feel: 我～有些冷. I feel a bit chilly.

感动(動) gǎndòng (动) move; touch: ～得流下眼泪 be moved to tears

感恩 gǎn'ēn (动) feel grateful; be thankful

感官 gǎnguān (名) sense organs

感光 gǎnguāng (名) sensitization

感化 gǎnhuà (动) reform a misguided person through persuasion, etc.; send an erring person for corrective training

感激 gǎnjī (动) feel grateful; be thankful; feel indebted: 不胜～ be deeply grateful

感觉(覺) gǎnjué I (名) feeling; sense; perception; sensation II (动) feel; sense; perceive

感慨 gǎnkǎi (动) sigh with deep feeling

感冒 gǎnmào (名) cold; flu: 患～ catch cold; have a touch of flu

感情 gǎnqíng (名) **1** feelings; emotion; sentiment: 动～ be carried away by one's emotions. ～用事 act impetuously. 伤～ hurt sb.'s feelings **2** affection; love

感染 gǎnrǎn (动) **1** infect: 细菌～ bacterial infection **2** influence; affect: 艺术～力 artistic appeal

感受 gǎnshòu I (动) catch (disease): ～风寒 catch a chill II (名) understanding; impression: ～很深 be deeply impressed

感叹(嘆) gǎntàn (动) sigh over sth. that strikes a chord: ～词 interjection. ～号 exclamation mark

感想 gǎnxiǎng (名) reflections; thoughts; impressions

感谢 gǎnxiè (动) thank; be grateful: 衷心的～ heartfelt thanks

感性 gǎnxìng (形) (of knowledge) perceptual

感应(應) gǎnyìng (名) **1** response; reaction; interaction **2** induction: 电磁～ electromagnetic induction

感召 gǎnzhào (动) move and inspire

敢 gǎn I (动) dare: 我～说他要试一试. I dare say he'd like to have a try. II (形) bold; daring: 果～ courageous and resolute

敢于(於) gǎnyú (动) dare to; have the courage to: 他～同不健康的现象作斗争. He has the courage to combat unhealthy trends.

橄 gǎn

橄榄(欖) gǎnlǎn (名) olive: ～球 rugby

干(幹) gàn I (名) **1** trunk; main part: 树～ tree trunk; trunk. 骨～ backbone **2** 〈简〉(干部) cadre: 高～ senior cadre (or official) II(动) do; work: ～活儿 work; do manual labour. 你想～什么? What do you want to do?

see also gān

干部 gànbù (名) cadre: 各级领导～ leading cadres at all levels

干掉 gàndiào (动)〈口〉kill; get rid of

干将(將) gànjiàng (名) capable person; go-getter

干劲(勁) gànjìn (名) vigour; drive; enthusiasm: ～冲天 with soaring enthusiasm.

～十足 be full of vigour
干练(練) gànliàn (形) capable and experienced
干吗 gànmá 〈口〉 **1** why; why on earth: ～这么大惊小怪? Why all this fuss? **2** what to do: 你明天打算～? What are you going to do tomorrow?
干事 gànshi (名) person in charge of a particular kind of work
干细胞 gànxìbāo (名) stem cell
干线(綫) gànxiàn (名) main line: 交通～ main lines of communication

G

缸 gāng (名) big jar or crock: 水～ water vat. 金鱼～ goldfish bowl
缸子 gāngzi (名) mug; bowl
肛 gāng (名) anus
肛门(門) gāngmén (名) anus
冈(岡) gāng (名) ridge (of a hill)
刚(剛) gāng I (副) **1** just; exactly: 这件雨衣我穿上～好. This raincoat fits me perfectly. 大小～合适 just the right size **2** just; only a short while ago: 电影～开始. The film has just started. 他～～还在这儿. He was here only a moment ago. 我～来的时候觉得有些孤独. I felt a bit lonely when I first came here. **3** just; only at this moment: 我～想给他打电话,他就来了. He came just as I was about to call him. 他～要走. He is just about to leave. 我～进屋就下雨了. I had hardly come into the room when it began to rain. **4** just; no more than: ～够 just (or barely) enough. 这条裙子～过膝. The skirt comes just below my knees. II (形) firm; strong; hard: 柔中有～. Strength is hidden under an appearance of gentleness.
刚愎自用 gāngbì zìyòng self-willed; opinionated
刚才 gāngcái (名) just now; a moment ago: ～你说什么来着? What did you say just now?
刚刚 gānggāng (副) just; only; exactly
刚好 gānghǎo (副) **1** just; exactly: 时间～. The time is just about right. **2** it so happened that: 我俩～在同一个班里. We happened to be in the same class.
刚健 gāngjiàn (形) (of character, style, bearing, etc.) vigorous; forceful; bold; robust
刚劲(勁) gāngjìng (形) (of handwriting) forceful and vigorous
刚…就… gāng…jiù… as soon as; no sooner than; immediately: 他刚搬进来就又想搬出去. No sooner had he moved in than he wanted to move out again.
刚强 gāngqiáng (形) (of character, will) firm; staunch; unyielding
刚巧 gāngqiǎo (副) happen; it so happened that
刚毅 gāngyì (形) resolute and steadfast
刚正 gāngzhèng (形) staunch and upright
刚直 gāngzhí (形) outspoken and upright
钢(鋼) gāng (名) steel: 炼～ steel-making. 不锈～ stainless steel
钢笔(筆) gāngbǐ (名) fountain pen
钢材 gāngcái (名) steel products
钢管 gāngguǎn (名) steel tube: 无缝～ seamless steel tube
钢筋 gāngjīn (名) reinforcing bar: ～混凝土 reinforced concrete
钢精锅(鍋) gāngjīngguō (名) aluminium pan
钢盔 gāngkuī (名) steel helmet
钢琴 gāngqín (名) piano: 弹～ play the piano
钢丝(絲) gāngsī (名) steel wire: 走～ high-wire walking (acrobatics). ～床 spring bed
钢铁(鐵) gāngtiě (名) iron and steel; steel
纲(綱) gāng (名) **1** the headrope of a fishing net **2** key link; guiding principle **3** class: 哺乳动物～ the class of mammals
纲领 gānglǐng (名) guiding principle; programme
纲目 gāngmù (名) detailed outline
纲要 gāngyào (名) outline; essentials
港 gǎng (名) port; harbour
港口 gǎngkǒu (名) port; harbour
港湾(灣) gǎngwān (名) bay; harbour
港务(務)局 gǎngwùjú (名) port office
岗(崗) gǎng (名) **1** hillock; mound **2** sentry; post: 站～ stand sentry
岗楼(樓) gǎnglóu (名) watchtower
岗哨 gǎngshào (名) sentry post; sentry
岗位 gǎngwèi (名) post: 坚守～ stand fast at one's post
杠 gàng (名) **1** thick stick; bar: 单～ horizontal bar. 双～ parallel bars **2** thick line drawn as a mark

杠杆(桿) gànggǎn (名) lever

高 gāo (形) 1 tall; high: ~个子男人 a tall man. 这堵墙有三米~. This wall is three metres high. ~喊 shout at the top of one's voice 2 advanced; superior: ~等教育 higher education. ~中 senior high school. ~水平 advanced level. ~见 wise idea

高矮 gāo'ǎi (名) height

高昂 gāo'áng (形) 1 high; elated 2 dear; expensive; costly

高傲 gāo'ào (形) supercilious; arrogant; haughty

高不可攀 gāo bùkě pān too high to reach; unattainable

高产(產) gāochǎn (名) high yield

高超 gāochāo (形) superb; excellent: 技艺~ superb skill

高潮 gāocháo (名) 1 high tide 2 upsurge; climax: 全剧的~ the climax of a play

高大 gāodà (形) tall and big

高档(檔) gāodàng (形) of top grade quality: ~商品 expensive goods

高等 gāoděng (形) higher: ~学院 institution of higher learning

高低 gāodī (名) 1 height: 估不出山崖的~ have no idea how high the cliff is. 声调的~ the pitch of a voice 2 difference in degree: 难分~ hard to tell which is better 3 sense of propriety; appropriateness: 不知~ have no sense of propriety

高地 gāodì (名) highland

高调 gāodiào (名) high-sounding words: 唱~ mouth high-sounding words

高度 gāodù I (名) altitude; height: 飞行~ flying altitude II (形) highly; to a high degree: ~赞扬 speak highly of. ~重视 attach great importance to

高峰 gāofēng (名) peak; summit; height: ~时间 peak (or rush) hours

高高在上 gāogāo zài shàng stand high above the masses; hold oneself aloof from the masses

高阁 gāogé (名) 1 mansion 2 shelf: 束之~ be shelved

高贵 gāoguì (形) 1 noble; high: ~品质 noble quality 2 privileged

高呼 gāohū (动) shout loudly: 振臂~ raise one's arm and shout at the top of one's voice

高级 gāojí (形) 1 senior; high-ranking; high-level: ~官员 high-ranking official 2 high-grade; high-quality: ~化妆品 de luxe cosmetics

高价(價) gāojià (名) high price

高架路 gāojiàlù (名) overpass; overhead way; elevated road

高峻 gāojùn (形) high and steep

高亢 gāokàng (形) loud and sonorous; resounding

高考 gāokǎo (名) college entrance examination

高科技 gāokējì high technology; hi-tech; state-of-the-art technology

高空 gāokōng (名) high altitude; upper air: ~作业 work high above the ground

高利贷 gāolìdài (名) usury

高粱 gāoliang (名) sorghum

高龄 gāolíng (名) advanced in years

高楼(樓)大厦 gāolóu-dàshà huge buildings

高炉(爐) gāolú (名) blast furnace

高论(論) gāolùn (名)〈敬〉brilliant remarks

高帽子 gāomàozi (名) 1 tall paper hat (worn as a sign of humiliation) 2 flattery

高妙 gāomiào (形) ingenious; masterly: 手艺~ superb craftsmanship

高明 gāomíng I (形) wise; brilliant: 见解~ brilliant ideas II (名) wise or skilful person: 另请~. Find a better qualified person (for the job).

高攀 gāopān (动) make friends or forge ties of kinship with someone of a higher social position: 不敢~. I dare not aspire to the honour.

高频 gāopín (名) high frequency

高强 gāoqiáng (形) excel in; be skilled in: 武艺~ excel in martial arts

高跷(蹺) gāoqiāo (名) stilts: 踩~ walk on stilts

高尚 gāoshàng (形) noble; lofty

高烧(燒) gāoshāo (名) high fever: 发~ have (or run) a high fever

高射炮 gāoshèpào (名) anti-aircraft gun (or artillery)

高深 gāoshēn (形) advanced; profound

高视阔步 gāoshì-kuòbù stalk; strut; prance

高手 gāoshǒu (名) master-hand; ace: 象棋~ an ace at chess

高寿(壽) gāoshòu (名) 1 longevity: 祝你~ wish you a long life 2〈敬〉your venerable age

高耸(聳) gāosǒng (动) stand tall and erect; tower: ~入云 tower into the clouds

高速 gāosù (名) high speed: ~前进 advance

G

at high speed. ～公路 motorway; expressway; freeway

高谈阔论(論) gāotán-kuòlùn indulge in lengthy and empty talk

高危 gāowēi (形) high-risk; highly vulnerable: 艾滋病～人群 AIDS-prone group

高温 gāowēn (名) high temperature

高新技术(術) gāo-xīn jìshu high and new technology; sophisticated technology

高兴(興) gāoxìng (形) glad; happy; pleased; cheerful

G

高血压(壓) gāoxuèyā (名) hypertension; high blood pressure

高压(壓) gāoyā (名) 1 high pressure 2 high voltage 3 high-handed: ～政策 high-handed policy

高雅 gāoyǎ (形) elegant; refined

高原 gāoyuán (名) highland; plateau

高瞻远(遠)瞩(矚) gāozhān-yuǎnzhǔ stand high and see far; show great foresight

高涨(漲) gāozhǎng (动) rise; upsurge

高招 gāozhāo (名) wise move

高枕无(無)忧(憂) gāo zhěn wú yōu sit back and relax; sleep soundly without any worries

高姿态(態) gāozītài (名) lofty stance (showing oneself capable of tolerance and generosity)

膏 gāo (名) 1 cream; ointment; paste: 牙～ toothpaste 2 fat

膏药(藥) gāoyao (名) plaster: 贴～ apply a plaster to

篙 gāo (名) punt-pole

羔 gāo (名) lamb

羔羊 gāoyáng (名) lamb; kid

糕 gāo (名) cake; pudding: 蛋～ cake

糕点(點) gāodiǎn (名) cake; pastry

睾 gāo

睾丸 gāowán (名) testis; testicle

搞 gǎo (动) 1 do; make: ～工作 do work. ～生产 engage in production. 你在这儿～什么名堂? What are you up to here? ～几个菜 prepare a few dishes. ～阴谋诡计 go in for intrigue and conspiracy. ～一个图书馆 set up a library 2 get hold of: ～几个人来帮助搬家 get some people to help move house. 你能～两张歌剧票吗? Can you get me two tickets for the opera?

搞定 gǎodìng (动) fix; settle; wangle: 货源已经～. The supply is secured.

搞对(對)象 gǎo duìxiàng date; go steady

搞鬼 gǎoguǐ (动) play tricks; be up to some mischief

搞好 gǎohǎo (动) do a good job of; do well

搞活 gǎohuó (动) enliven; vitalize; invigorate

搞笑 gǎoxiào (动) amuse; make fun

镐 gǎo (名) pick; pickaxe

稿 gǎo (名) 1 draft; sketch: 初～ first draft. 这不过是个初～. This is only a first draft. 2 manuscript; original text: 定～ finalize a text

稿费 gǎofèi (名) payment for an article or book written

稿件 gǎojiàn (名) manuscript; contribution

缟 gǎo (名) thin white silk

缟素 gǎosù (名) mourning dress

告 gào (动) 1 tell; inform; notify: 电～ inform by telegraph; cable 2 accuse; sue: 到法院去～某人 sue sb. for sth. 3 ask for; request 4 announce; declare: 宣～ declare; proclaim. 自～奋勇 volunteer to do sth. 大功～成. The task is at last accomplished.

告别 gàobié (动) take leave of; say goodbye to: ～家乡 bid farewell to one's home town. 向遗体～ pay one's last respects to the deceased

告辞(辭) gàocí (动) take leave of one's host; bid farewell

告发(發) gàofā (动) inform against (sb. to the police); accuse sb. (of an offence)

告急 gàojí (动) report the emergency to the higher level

告假 gàojià (动) ask for leave

告捷 gàojié (动) 1 win victory: 初战～ win the first battle 2 report a victory

告诫 gàojiè (动) warn; exhort

告密 gàomì (动) inform against sb.

告示 gàoshi (名) official notice; bulletin

告诉 gàosù (动) tell; let know: 请你～他,今天晚上七点钟开会. Please tell him that the meeting is fixed for seven o'clock this evening.

告知 gàozhī (动) inform; notify

告终 gàozhōng (动) come to an end; end up: 以失败～ end in failure

告状(狀) gàozhuàng (动) 1 bring a lawsuit against sb. 2 lodge a complaint against sb. (with his superior)

割 gē (动) cut: ~草 cut grass; mow. ~草机 (lawn) mower

割爱(愛) gē'ài (动) give up what one treasures

割断(斷) gēduàn (动) cut off; sever

割据(據) gējù (动) set up a separatist regime by force of arms: 封建~ feudal separatist rule

割裂 gēliè (动) (of abstract matters) cut apart; separate; isolate: 不要把这两个问题~开来. Don't separate these two issues.

割让(讓) gēràng (动) cede: ~领土 cession of territory

哥 gē (名) (elder) brother

哥儿(兒) gēr (名) brothers; boys: 你们~几个? How many boys are there altogether in your family?

哥儿(兒)们 gērmen (名)〈口〉1 brothers 2 buddies; pals

哥哥 gēge (名) (elder) brother

歌 gē I (名) song II (动) sing

歌唱 gēchàng (动) sing (usu. in praise): ~家 singer; vocalist

歌功颂德 gēgōng-sòngdé eulogize; sing the praises of sb.

歌喉 gēhóu (名) singing voice: 婉转的~ a beautiful voice

歌剧(劇) gējù (名) opera

歌曲 gēqǔ (名) song

歌手 gēshǒu (名) singer; vocalist

歌颂 gēsòng (动) sing the praises of; extol; eulogize

歌坛(壇) gētán (名) the circle of singers

歌厅(廳) gētīng (名) karaoke parlour; singing club

歌舞 gēwǔ (名) song and dance: ~升平 put on a façade of peace and prosperity

歌谣 gēyáo (名) ballad; folk song

歌咏 gēyǒng (名) singing

戈 gē (名) dagger-axe (an ancient weapon)

疙 gē

疙瘩 gēda (名) 1 pimple; lump; knot 2 misunderstanding; misgivings: 解开他心上的~ dispel his misgivings

鸽 gē (名) pigeon; dove: 信~ carrier pigeon

咯 gē (象)

咯咯 gēgē (象) chuckle; titter

咯吱 gēzhī (象) creak

see also kǎ

胳 gē

胳臂 gēbei (名) arm

胳膊 gēbo (名) arm: ~肘儿 elbow

搁 gē (动) 1 put 2 put aside; shelve: 这件事得~一~再办. We'll have to put the matter aside for the time being.

G

搁浅(淺) gēqiǎn (动) be stranded: 船~了. The ship got stranded.

搁置 gēzhì (动) lay aside; shelve

革 gé I (名) leather; hide: ~制品 leather goods. 制~厂 tannery II (动)expel;dismiss

革除 géchú (动) 1 get rid of; abolish: ~陈规陋习 abolish outmoded regulations and practices 2 dismiss; remove from office

革命 gémìng I (名) revolution II (动) make revolution: ~家 revolutionary

革新 géxīn (动、名) innovate;innovation: 技术~ technological innovation

革职(職) gézhí (动) remove from office; dismiss; sack

嗝 gé (名) 1 belch 2 hiccup

膈 gé (名) diaphragm

膈膜 gémó (名) diaphragm

隔 gé (动) 1 separate; partition: 把一间屋~成两间 partition a room into two 2 at a distance from; at an interval of: 相~甚远 be very far away from each other. 你~些时候再来吧. Come again some other time. ~一天一次 once every other day

隔岸观(觀)火 gé àn guān huǒ watch a fire from the other side of the river; look on unconcerned at troubles elsewhere

隔壁 gébì (名) next door: 住在~ live next door. ~邻居 nextdoor neighbour

隔断(斷) géduàn (动) cut off; separate

隔阂 géhé (名) estrangement; misunderstanding: 语言~ language barrier

隔绝 géjué (动) completely cut off; isolated: 和外界~ be cut off from the outside world

隔离(離) gélí (动) keep apart; isolate:

种族～ racial segregation; apartheid. ～病房 isolation ward

隔膜 gémó (名) lack of mutual understanding

隔墙(牆)有耳 gé qiáng yǒu ěr walls have ears; beware of eavesdroppers

隔音 géyīn (名) sound insulation: ～室 soundproof room

蛤 gé (名) clam

see also há

蛤蜊 gélí (名) clam

阁 gé (名) 1 pavilion 2 cabinet: 组～ form a cabinet

阁楼(樓) gélóu (名) attic; loft; garret

阁下 géxià (名)〈敬〉Your Excellency; His or Her Excellency

格 gé (名) 1 line: 横～纸 ruled paper. 打～ draw lines on the paper 2 squares; check: ～子窗帘布 checked curtain 3 shelf: 这书架有三～. This bookcase has three shelves. 每服一小～. Dose: one measure each time. 4 standard; pattern; style: 合～ up to standard. 别具一～ have a style of its own 5 case: 主～ the nominative case. 宾～ the objective case

格调 gédiào (名) (literary or artistic) style

格斗(鬥) gédòu (名) grapple; fight

格格不入 gégé bù rù be incompatible with; be like a square peg in a round hole

格局 géjú (名) pattern; set-up; structure: 新的世界～ the new structure of the world. 这篇文章写得很乱,简直不成个～. This essay is badly organized; it hardly holds together.

格律 gélǜ (名) set rules for tonal patterns and rhyme scheme in classical Chinese verse and poetic drama

格式 géshì (名) form; pattern: 公文～ various forms in documentary language

格外 géwài (副) especially; exceptionally: 你要～小心. You can't be too careful. 今年冬天～冷. This winter is exceptionally cold.

格言 géyán (名) maxim; motto

格子 gézi (名) check: ～布 checked fabric

舸 gě (名) barge

个(個) gè (量) 1 [the measure word most extensively used esp. before nouns which do not have special measure words of their own]: 一～人 one person. 两～桃 two peaches. 三～星期 three weeks. 四～问题 four problems 2 [used between a verb and its object]: 洗～澡 have a bath. 理～发 have a haircut 3 [used before a numeral to indicate approximation]: 有～二十分钟就够了. About twenty minutes would be enough. 4 [used between a verb and its complement]: 他说～不停. He talked on and on. 明天我们要玩～痛快. We'll have a wonderful time tomorrow.

个案 gè'àn (名) individual case

个别 gèbié (形) 1 individual: ～辅导 individual tutorial. 跟学生～谈话 have private talks with individual students 2 very few; rare: 那是～情况. That was an isolated case. 这只是～人的事. This matter is of concern to a couple of people only.

个儿(兒) gèr (名) 1 size; height; stature 2 persons or things taken singly: 挨～握手问好 shake hands with and greet them one by one

个个 gègè (名) each; every one; all: 你的孩子～都很聪明. All your children are very bright.

个例 gèlì (名) accidental case; exceptional case

个人 gèrén (名) 1 individual: ～私事 private affairs. ～项目 individual events. ～主义 selfishness; individualism. ～崇拜 personality cult 2 oneself: 在我～看来 in my opinion

个体(體) gètǐ (名) individual: ～经济 individual economy

个性 gèxìng (名) individual character; individuality; personality

个子 gèzi (名) height; stature; build

各 gè (代) each; every: "～位先生,女士" "Ladies and gentlemen". ～国 each country. ～奔前程 each follows his own career. ～持己见 each sticks to his own view. ～行其是 each goes his own way. ～得其所 each is properly provided for; each has a role to play

各个(個) gègè I (代) each; every; one by one: ～方面 every aspect II (副) separately: ～击破 destroy one by one

各…各… gè…gè… 1 each . . . his own . . . : 各走各的路 each goes his own way 2 all kinds of: 各行各业 all walks of life. 各式

各样 of various kinds
各行各业(業)gèháng gèyè all walks of life; all trades and professions
各级 gèjí (名) different levels: ～领导机关 leading bodies at all levels
各界 gèjiè (名) all circles: ～人士 personalities of various circles
各色 gèsè (形) of all kinds; of every description: ～货物 goods of all kinds
各位 gèwèi (代) **1** everybody (a term of address): ～请注意. Attention please, everybody. **2** every: ～代表 fellow delegates
各有千秋 gè yǒu qiānqiū each has his merits (or strong points); each has something to recommend him
各自 gèzì (代) each; respective: 既要～努力,也要彼此帮助. This calls for both individual effort and mutual help.
各自为(爲)政 gèzì wéi zhèng each acts wilfully regardless of overall interest

给 gěi I (动) **1** give: 他～我三本书. He gave me three books. 把孩子～我. Give me the child. **2** let; allow: ～我看看. Let me have a look. 我～你看一件东西. Let me show you something. II (介) **1** [used immediately after a verb to indicate the handing over of certain things] give: 把大衣交～他. Give him the coat. 把钥匙留～我. Leave the key with me. 请把杯子递～我. Please pass me the glass. **2** [introducing the object of one's service] for; to: 她～孩子们唱了一支歌. She sang a song for the children. 我～你讲个故事吧. Let me tell you a story. 他～她送去一束花. He sent her a bunch of flowers. **3** [as a passive indicator, as 被]: 我的钱包～人偷走了. I had my wallet stolen. 报纸～风吹走了. The newspaper was blown away by the wind. III (助) [used before the main verb of the sentence, often concurrently with 叫, or 让 or 把 for emphasis]: 我差点把这事～忘了. I almost forgot this altogether.
see also jǐ
给以 gěiyǐ (动) [followed by a direct object, usually an abstract noun] give; grant: 模范工作者应该～适当奖励. Model workers should be duly awarded.

根 gēn I (名) **1** root: 扎～ take root. 连～拔 pull up by the root **2** root; foot; base: 舌～ the root of the tongue. 城～ the foot of a city wall **3** cause; origin; source; root: 祸～ the root of trouble. 刨～问底 get to the root of a matter II (量) [for long and thin objects]: 一～火柴 a match. 两～筷子 a pair of chopsticks
根本 gēnběn I (形) basic; fundamental; essential: ～利益 fundamental interest. ～原因 root cause. ～原则 cardinal principle II(名) foundation; base: 应从～上考虑解决问题的方法. We must seek a permanent solution to the problem. III(副) **1** [often used in the negative] at all; simply: 你～就不明白. You don't understand it at all. 这事我～不知道. I have absolutely no idea about this matter. **2** radically; thoroughly: ～改变这种状况 thoroughly change the situation
根除 gēnchú (动) root out; eradicate; completely do away with
根底 gēndǐ (名) **1** foundation: 他的英文～很好. He has a good grounding in English. **2** cause; root: 追问～ inquire into the cause of the matter
根基 gēnjī (名) foundation; basis: 打好～ lay a solid foundation
根据(據) gēnjù I (动) on the basis of; according to: 这部电影是～一个真实故事写成的. This film is based on a true story. ～具体情况 in the light of specific conditions II(名) basis; grounds: 这话有～吗? Is this statement based on facts? 毫无～ utterly groundless
根绝 gēnjué (动) eradicate; exterminate
根深蒂固 gēnshēn-dìgù deep-rooted: ～的偏见 deep-rooted prejudice
根由 gēnyóu (名) cause; origin
根源 gēnyuán (名) source; origin; root: 历史～ historical roots
根治 gēnzhì (动) effect a permanent cure

跟 gēn I (动) follow: 他后面～着一群人. He was followed by a crowd. II (名) heel: 鞋后～ the heel of a shoe III (介) **1** [denoting the same function as that of 和,同] with: 我～他一样高. He and I are of the same height. 我～你一起去. I'll go with you. **2** to; towards [as 向,对]: 这事你最好～他谈. You'd better discuss this with him. 别～我过不去! Don't be difficult with me!
跟班 gēnbān (动) join a regular shift or class
跟斗 gēndou (名) **1** fall: 跌了一个～ have a fall **2** somersault: 翻～ do a somersault

G

跟风(風) gēnfēng (动) follow a trend blindly; jump on the bandwagon

跟前 gēnqián (名) in front of; near: 到我~来! Come closer!

跟随(隨) gēnsuí (动) follow: 孩子~父亲出去了. The boy has gone out with his father.

跟踪(蹤) gēnzōng (动) tail; follow closely: ~追击 be in hot pursuit

羹 gēng (名) a thick soup: 鸡蛋~ egg custard

羹匙 gēngchí (名) soup spoon; tablespoon

耕 gēng (动) plough; till: 春~ spring ploughing. 精~细作 intensive and careful cultivation

耕畜 gēngchù (名) farm animal

耕地 gēngdì I (名) arable land II (动)plough

耕耘 gēngyún (动) ploughing and weeding; cultivate: 着意~, 自有收获. Set your mind on ploughing, and you will reap a good harvest.

耕种(種) gēngzhòng (动) till; cultivate

耕作 gēngzuò (名) cultivation; farming

更 gēng I (动) change; replace: ~新 update; refresh II (名) one of the five two-hour periods into which the night was formerly divided: 打~ beat the watches. 三~半夜 in the dead of night
see also gèng

更迭 gēngdié (动) alternate; change: 内阁~ a change of cabinet

更动(動) gēngdòng (动) change; alter: 人事~ personnel change

更番 gēngfān (副) alternately; by turns

更改 gēnggǎi (动) change; alter: 在细节安排上有一点~. There is a little change about the details of the arrangement.

更换 gēnghuàn (动) change; replace: ~衣裳 change one's clothes

更替 gēngtì (动) replace; substitute

更新 gēngxīn (动) replace; renew; update: 设备~ equipment renewal. ~技术 update technology

更衣 gēngyī (动) change one's clothes: ~室 changing room; locker room

更正 gēngzhèng I (动) make corrections (of errors in statements or newspaper articles) II(名)corrigenda

耿 gěng (形) dedicated; honest and just

耿耿 gěnggěng (形) 1 devoted; dedicated: 忠心~ loyal; dedicated 2 have sth. on one's mind; be troubled: ~于怀 take sth. to heart

耿直 gěngzhí (形) honest and frank; upright: 秉性~ be upright by nature

埂 gěng (名) 1 a low bank of earth between fields [also as "田埂"] 2 an earth dyke (or embankment)

梗 gěng I (名) (of plants) stalk; stem II (动) 1 straighten; straighten up one's neck 2 obstruct; block: 从中作~ make it difficult for sb. to go ahead with sth.

梗概 gěnggài (名) outline; gist; highlight

梗塞 gěngsè (动) clog; block; obstruct: 交通~ traffic jam. 心肌~ myocardial infarction

梗阻 gěngzǔ (动) block; hamper: 肠~ intestinal obstruction

哽 gěng (动) choke (with emotion); feel a lump in one's throat: ~咽 choke with sobs

更 gèng (副) even; more; still more; further: 这本书比那本书~有趣. This book is even more interesting than that one. ~重要的是… What is more important.... ~大的成功 still greater success
see also gēng

更加 gèngjiā (副) more; still more; even more: 天色渐亮, 晨星~稀少了. At daybreak, the stars were becoming even more sparse.

工 gōng (名) 1 worker; workman; the working class: 熟练~ skilled worker. 矿~ miner 2 work; labour: 上~去 go to work. 这事很费~. It requires a lot of hard work. 3 (construction) project: 动~ begin a project. 竣~ complete a project 4 industry: 化~ chemical industry 5 person-day: 这项工程需要几个~? How many man-days will it take to complete this project?

工本 gōngběn (名) cost (of production): 不惜~ spare no expense

工笔(筆) gōngbǐ (名) a type of traditional Chinese painting characterized by fine brushwork and close attention to detail

工厂(廠) gōngchǎng (名) factory; mill; plant; works

工场(場) gōngchǎng (名) workshop

工程 gōngchéng (名) engineering; project: 土木~ civil engineering. 水利~ water conservancy project. ~师 engineer

工地 gōngdì (名) building or construction

site
工段 gōngduàn (名) 1 a section of a construction project 2 workshop section
工夫 gōngfu (名) 1 time: 五天的～ five days' time. 有～再来吧. Come again when you have time. 2 effort; work; labour: 花了好大～ put in a lot of work 3 workmanship; skill; art: 练～ (of actors, athletes, etc.) practise. 这画～真到家. This painting shows superb skill.
工会(會) gōnghuì (名) trade union
工件 gōngjiàn (名) workpiece
工匠 gōngjiàng (名) craftsman; artisan
工具 gōngjù (名) tool; instrument: 生产～ implements of production. 运输～means of transport. ～书 reference book; dictionary
工力 gōnglì (名) skill; craftsmanship: ～深厚 remarkable craftsmanship
工龄 gōnglíng (名) length of service; standing
工钱(錢) gōngqian (名) 1 payment for odd jobs 2 〈口〉wages; pay
工人 gōngrén (名) worker; workman: ～阶级 the working class
工伤(傷) gōngshāng (名) injury incurred during work
工商界 gōng-shāngjiè (名) industrial and commercial circles; business circles
工商业(業) gōng-shāngyè (名) industry and commerce
工时(時) gōngshí (名) man-hour
工事 gōngshì (名) defence works
工头(頭) gōngtóu (名) foreman
工效 gōngxiào (名) work efficiency
工薪阶(階)层(層) gōngxīn jiēcéng wage or salary earners
工薪族 gōngxīnzú (名) salaried persons; wage earners
工休日 gōngxiūrì (名) day off; holiday
工业(業) gōngyè (名) industry: 轻(重)～ light (heavy) industry. ～革命 the Industrial Revolution. ～化 industrialization
工艺(藝) gōngyì (名) technology; craft: 手～handicraft. ～美术 arts and crafts
工于(於)心计 gōngyú xīnjì adept at scheming; very calculating
工整 gōngzhěng (形) careful and neat: 他字写得～极了. He has very neat handwriting.
工资 gōngzī (名) wages; salary: ～表 payroll; pay sheet. ～级别 wage scale
工作 gōngzuò I (名) work; job: ～服 work clothes. ～证 employee's card II (动) work: ～早餐 working breakfast. ～语言 working language. ～日 working day
工作者 gōngzuòzhě (名) people who do a particular type of job: 文艺～ literary and art workers; writers and artists. 医务～ a medical worker
攻 gōng (动) 1 attack; take the offensive: ～城 lay siege to a city. ～下敌人的桥头堡 capture the enemy bridgehead 2 study; specialize in: 他是专～地质学的. He specializes in geology.
攻打 gōngdǎ (动) attack; assault
攻读(讀) gōngdú (动) study; make a study of: 他正～博士学位. He is trying for a Ph. D.
攻关(關) gōngguān (动) tackle a key problem; storm a strategic pass
攻击(擊) gōngjī (动) 1 attack; assault: 发起总～ launch a general offensive 2 slander; vilify
攻坚(堅) gōngjiān (动) assault fortified positions
攻克 gōngkè (动) overcome; capture
攻势(勢) gōngshì (名) offensive: 采取～ take the offensive. 冬季～ winter offensive
攻陷 gōngxiàn (动) storm; capture: ～一个城市 capture a city
攻心 gōngxīn (动) launch a psychological attack
功 gōng (名) 1 meritorious deeds; merit; achievement: 记一大～ be cited for one's outstanding service 2 skill (of dancers, gymnasts, etc.): 练～ practise one's skill
功败垂成 gōng bài chuí chéng suffer defeat on the verge of success
功臣 gōngchén (名) a person who has rendered outstanding service to his country
功德 gōngdé (名) meritorious and beneficent deeds
功底 gōngdǐ (名) grounding in basic skills: 扎实的～ solid grounding
功夫 gōngfu (名) see "工夫"gōngfu
功绩 gōngjì (名) merits and achievements; contribution
功课 gōngkè (名) schoolwork; homework
功亏(虧)一篑 gōng kuī yī kuì fall short of one's goal for want of a final effort
功劳(勞) gōngláo (名) credit; contribution (to a cause)
功利 gōnglì (名) utility; material gain: ～主

义 utilitarianism

功名 gōngmíng (名) scholarly honour or official rank (in feudal times)

功能 gōngnéng (名) function: ～性障碍 functional disorder

功效 gōngxiào (名) efficacy; effect

功勋(勳) gōngxūn (名) meritorious service

功业(業) gōngyè (名) exploits; achievements

供 gōng (动) supply; provide: ～水 water supply. ～电 power supply. ～不上 be in short supply. ～不应求 supply falls short of demand
see also gòng

供给 gōngjǐ (动) supply; provide; furnish

供求 gōng-qiú (名) supply and demand: ～平衡 balance between supply and demand

供销 gōng-xiāo (动) supply and market: ～(合作)社 supply and marketing cooperative

供养(養) gōngyǎng (动) support; provide for (one's parents or elders)

供应(應) gōngyìng (名) supply: 市场～ market supplies

恭 gōng (形) respectful; reverent: ～贺 congratulate. ～候光临 request the pleasure of one's company

恭敬 gōngjìng (形) respectful

恭顺 gōngshùn (形) respectful and submissive

恭维 gōngwei (动) flatter; compliment: ～话 flattery; compliments

恭喜 gōngxǐ (名)〈套〉congratulations

公 gōng I (名) official business: 办～ do office or administrative work. 非～莫入 no admittance except on business II (形) 1 public; state-owned: ～私合营 joint state-private ownership 2 fair; just: 办事不～ unjust in handling affairs 3 metric: ～制 metric system 4 male (animal): ～鸡 cock; rooster. ～鸭 drake. ～牛 bull III (动) make public: ～之于世 make known to the public; be made public

公安 gōng'ān (名) public security: ～局 public security bureau. ～人员 public security officer

公报(報) gōngbào (名) communiqué; bulletin: 联合～ joint communiqué. 新闻～ press communiqué

公布 gōngbù (动) make public; announce: ～法令 promulgate a decree

公差 gōngchāi (名) official duty: 出～ go on official business

公尺 gōngchǐ (名) metre (m)

公道 gōngdào I (名) justice: 主持～ uphold justice II (形) fair; impartial

公德 gōngdé (名) public morality

公敌(敵) gōngdí (名) public enemy

公断(斷) gōngduàn (名) 1 arbitration 2 impartial verdict

公费 gōngfèi (形) at public (or state) expense: ～医疗 free medical care (services)

公分 gōngfēn (名) 1 centimetre (cm) 2 gram (g)

公愤 gōngfèn (名) public indignation

公干(幹) gōnggàn (名) business: 有何～? What important business brings you here?

公告 gōnggào (名) announcement; proclamation

公公 gōnggong (名) 1 husband's father; father-in-law 2 grandpa (used to address any elderly man)

公共 gōnggòng (形) public; common; communal: ～财产 public property. ～厕所 public conveniences. ～卫生 public health (or hygiene). ～汽车 bus

公海 gōnghǎi (名) high seas

公害 gōnghài (名) environmental pollution

公函 gōnghán (名) official letter

公家 gōngjiā (名) the state; the public: ～的财产 public property

公斤 gōngjīn (名) kilogram (kg)

公爵 gōngjué (名) duke

公开(開) gōngkāi I (形) open; overt; public: ～露面 make public appearances. ～的秘密 an open secret. ～信 open letter II (动) make public: ～化 come out into the open

公款 gōngkuǎn (名) public fund

公里 gōnglǐ (名) kilometre (km)

公理 gōnglǐ (名) 1 universally accepted truth 2 axiom

公历(曆) gōnglì (名) the Gregorian calendar

公立 gōnglì (形) established and maintained by the government: ～学校 state-run school

公粮(糧) gōngliáng (名) agricultural tax paid in grain

公路 gōnglù (名) highway: 高速～ motorway

公论(論) gōnglùn (名) public opinion

公民 gōngmín (名) citizen: ～权 civil rights. ～投票 referendum; plebiscite

公民社会 gōngmín shèhuì civil society

公墓 gōngmù (名) cemetery

公平 gōngpíng (形) fair; just; impartial; equitable: ～合理 fair and reasonable. ～交易 fair deal

公婆 gōng-pó (名) husband's father and mother

公仆(僕) gōngpú (名) public servant

公顷 gōngqǐng (名) hectare (ha)

公然 gōngrán (副) openly; brazenly

公认(認) gōngrèn (动) generally recognize; universally acknowledge

公社 gōngshè (名) commune: 原始～ primitive commune. 人民公社 people's commune

公审(審) gōngshěn (名) public (or open) trial

公示 gōngshì (动) 1 make a public announcement 2 opportunity for public comment

公式 gōngshì (名) formula

公式化 gōngshìhuà I (名) formulism (in art and literature) II (形) stereotyped

公事 gōngshì (名) public affairs; official business: ～公办 business is business

公司 gōngsī (名) company; firm; corporation

公诉 gōngsù (名) public prosecution: ～人 public prosecutor

公文 gōngwén (名) official document

公务(務) gōngwù (名) official duty: ～员 civil servant; government employee

公物 gōngwù (名) public property

公休 gōngxiū (名) official holiday

公演 gōngyǎn (动) perform in public

公益 gōngyì (名) public welfare

公用 gōngyòng (形) for public use; communal: ～电话 public telephone

公有 gōngyǒu (形) publicly-owned: ～制 public ownership

公寓 gōngyù (名) apartment house; block of flats

公元 gōngyuán (名) A. D.; the Christian era: ～前 B. C.

公园(園) gōngyuán (名) park

公约 gōngyuē (名) 1 pact; convention: 北大西洋～ the North Atlantic Treaty 2 joint pledge

公允 gōngyǔn (形) fair and proper: 持论～ be just and fair in passing judgment

公债 gōngzhài (名) government bonds; treasury bonds

公章 gōngzhāng (名) official seal

公正 gōngzhèng (形) just; fair; impartial

公证 gōngzhèng (名) notarization: ～人 notary public; notary

公职(職) gōngzhí (名) public employment

公众(衆) gōngzhòng (名) the public

公主 gōngzhǔ (名) princess

公子 gōngzǐ (名) son of a feudal prince or high official: 花花～ playboy. ～哥儿 dandy

弓 gōng I (名) bow: ～箭 bow and arrow. ～弦 bowstring II (动) bend; arch: ～着腿坐着 sit with one's legs crossed

弓子 gōngzi (名) 1 bow (of a stringed instrument) 2 anything bow-shaped

躬 gōng I (动) bow II (副)〈书〉personally: ～逢其盛 be present on the grand occasion

宫 gōng (名) palace: 皇～ imperial palace. 少年～ children's palace. 工人文化～ the Workers' Cultural Palace

宫殿 gōngdiàn (名) palace

宫廷 gōngtíng (名) 1 palace 2 royal or imperial court

巩(鞏) gǒng

巩固 gǒnggù I (动) [often used in figurative sense] consolidate; strengthen; solidify II (形) firm; solid; stable

汞 gǒng (名) mercury (Hg)

拱 gǒng I (动) 1 join hands: ～手 make an obeisance by joining hands with one's forearms slightly raised 2 hunch; arch: 猫～了～腰. The cat arched its back. 3 push without using one's shoulder 4 (of pigs, etc.) dig earth with the snout 5 sprout up through the earth II (名) arch

拱门(門) gǒngmén (名) arched door; arch

拱桥(橋) gǒngqiáo (名) arch bridge

贡 gòng (名) tribute: 进～ pay tribute (to an imperial court)

贡品 gòngpǐn (名) articles of tribute

贡献(獻) gòngxiàn I (动) contribute; dedicate; devote II (名) contribution

共 gòng I (动) share: 同甘苦, ～患难 share weal and woe II (形) common; general: ～性 common characteristic III(副)1 together 2 in all; altogether: 一~四十人 altogether forty people

共产(産)党(黨) gòngchǎndǎng (名) the Communist Party

共产(産)主义(義) gòngchǎnzhǔyì (名) communism

共处(處) gòngchǔ (动、名) coexist; coexistence: 和平~peaceful coexistence

共存 gòngcún (动) coexist

共和 gònghé (名) republic: ~国 republic

共计 gòngjì (动) amount to; add up to; total

共鸣 gòngmíng (名) 1 resonance 2 sympathetic response: 引起~ strike a responsive chord

共青团(團) gòngqīngtuán (名)〈简〉(共产主义青年团) the Communist Youth League

共识(識) gòngshí (名) common understanding; concensus

共事 gòngshì (动) work together

共同 gòngtóng I (形) common: ~关心的问题 matter of common concern. ~点 common ground II (副) together; jointly: ~努力 make joint efforts

共同体(體) gòngtóngtǐ (名) community: 欧洲经济~ the European Economic Community

共享 gòngxiǎng (动) enjoy together; share

供 gòng (动) 1 lay (offerings) 2 confess; own up: 口~ oral confession see also gōng

供词 gòngcí (名) confession; deposition

供奉 gòngfèng (动) enshrine and worship

供认(認) gòngrèn (动) confess: ~不讳 candidly confess

供职(職) gòngzhí (动) hold office

篝 gōu

篝火 gōuhuǒ (名) bonfire; campfire

勾 gōu (动) 1 tick: 把你想去的地方~出来. Tick (off) the places you are interested in. 2 cancel; cross out; strike out [usu. followed by 掉,销,去,etc.]: 把他的名字~掉. Cross out his name. 把旧账一笔~销. Write off all the debts at one stroke. 3 draw; delineate: ~出轮廓 draw an outline of sth. 4 evoke; call to mind: 这游戏~起了我对童年的回忆. This game reminds me of my childhood. see also gòu

勾搭 gōuda (动) 1 engage jointly in wrongdoing: 他跟贼~上了. He ganged up with some thieves. 2 seduce

勾画(畫) gōuhuà (动) sketch out

勾结 gōujié (动) collude with; conspire with

勾通 gōutōng (动) work hand in glove with

勾销 gōuxiāo (动) liquidate; strike out; write off at one stroke

勾引 gōuyǐn (动) tempt; seduce; lure

沟(溝) gōu (名) 1 ditch; trench; channel 2 groove; rut; furrow

沟壑 gōuhè (名) gully; ravine

沟渠 gōuqú (名) irrigation canals

沟通 gōutōng (动) link up; connect

钩 gōu I (名) 1 hook: 钓鱼~ fish-hook. 挂衣~clothes-hook 2 tick (as a check mark) II (动) 1 catch hold of with a hook: 她的裙边给钉子~住了. The edge of her skirt caught on a nail. 2 crochet: ~花边 crochet lace

钩心斗(鬥)角 gōuxīn-dòujiǎo intrigue against each other

钩针 gōuzhēn (名) crochet hook; ~编织品 crochet

苟 gǒu (形) careless; negligent: 一丝不~ be scrupulous about every detail

苟安 gǒu'ān (动) seek transient peace

苟活 gǒuhuó (动) survive in humiliation

苟且 gǒuqiě (动) drift along; muddle along: ~偷安 seek transient peace by hook or by crook

苟全 gǒuquán (动) preserve one's humble existence at all costs

苟同 gǒutóng (动) [used in negative sentences] readily agree: 未敢~ beg to differ

苟延残(殘)喘 gǒuyán-cánchuǎn be on one's last leg; be at one's last gasp

狗 gǒu (名) dog

狗胆(膽)包天 gǒudǎn bāo tiān monstrously audacious

狗急跳墙(墻) gǒu jí tiào qiáng a cornered beast will bite indiscriminately or do something desperate; when a person is driven into a corner, he is capable of anything

狗皮膏药(藥) gǒupí gāoyao quack medicine

狗屁 gǒupì (名) bullshit; nonsense: ~不通 unreadable rubbish

狗腿子 gǒutuǐzi (名)〈口〉lackey; henchman

狗尾续(續)貂 gǒuwěi xù diāo a wretched sequel to a fine work

狗血喷头(頭) gǒuxuè pēn tóu pour invective upon sb.'s head: 骂得～ let loose a stream of savage invective against sb.

狗仗人势(勢) gǒu zhàng rén shì be a bully who has the backing of a powerful person

媾 gòu 〈书〉 **1** wed: 婚～ marriage **2** reach agreement: ～和 make peace **3** coition: 交～ copulate

诟 gòu I (名)〈书〉 shame; humiliation II (动) revile; talk abusively

诟病 gòubìng (动)〈书〉 denounce; castigate: 为世～ become an object of universal condemnation

诟骂 gòumà (动) curse; abuse

垢 gòu I (名) **1** dirt; filth: 油～grease; stain **2** 〈书〉disgrace; humiliation: 含～忍辱 endure contempt and insults II (形) dirty; filthy

够 gòu I (形) enough; sufficient; adequate: 她昨晚没睡～. She didn't have enough sleep last night. 这些钱交学费～了吗? Is this money enough for the tuition fee? 我真受～了! I've really had enough of it! II (动) reach; be up to (a certain standard, etc.): 你能～着那棵树吗? Can you reach that tree? III (副) rather; really; quite: 这房子可真～大的. This house is really big. 他今天～累的了. He is rather tired today.

够格 gòugé (动) be qualified; be up to standard

够呛(嗆) gòuqiàng (形) hard to bear; terrible: 忙得～be terribly busy. 疼得～ unbearably painful. 这个人真～! This man is just impossible!

够味儿(兒) gòuwèir 〈口〉 just the right flavour; quite satisfactory

勾 gòu

see also gōu

勾当(當) gòudàng (名) (dirty) deal

构(構) gòu (动) form; compose; construct: ～词 form a word. 虚～ fabrication

构成 gòuchéng (动) form; constitute; make up: ～威胁 pose (or constitute) a threat. 这台机器是由三个主要部分～的. This machine is made up of three major parts.

构件 gòujiàn (名) component part

构思 gòusī (动) (of writers or artists) work out the plot of a story or the composition of a painting

构想 gòuxiǎng (名) idea; concept; conception

构造 gòuzào (名) structure: 人体～ the structure of the human body

购(購) gòu (动) buy; purchase

购买(買) gòumǎi (动) purchase; buy: ～力 purchasing power

购物 gòuwù (动) go shopping; purchase: ～中心 shopping centre

购销 gòu-xiāo (名) purchase and sale

购置 gòuzhì (动) purchase

沽 gū

沽名钓誉(譽) gūmíng-diàoyù angle for fame and compliments; crave popular acclaim

辜 gū (名) guilt; crime: 无～ not guilty; innocent. 死有余～. Death could not atone for all his crimes.

辜负 gūfù (动) fail to live up to; disappoint; let down; be unworthy of

轱 gū

轱辘 gūlu (名) wheel

咕 gū (象) (of hens, etc.) cluck

咕咚 gūdōng (象) splash; plump: ～一声掉进水里 fall into the water with a splash

咕嘟 gūdu (象) gurgle

咕噜 gūlū (象) **1** rumble; gurgle; roll **2** murmur; whisper

咕哝(噥) gūnong (动) mutter; grumble: 他在～些什么? What is he muttering about?

估 gū (动) estimate; appraise; reckon: 低～ underestimate

估计 gūjì (动) estimate; appraise; reckon: ～形势 make an appraisal of the situation. 我们必须～到这种可能性. We must take this possibility into consideration. 我～他会接受这项工作. I reckon he will accept this job.

估价(價) gūjià I (动) evaluate; appraise II (名) estimated price

估量 gūliáng (动) appraise; assess: 不可～的损失 an incalculable loss

姑 gū I (名) **1** aunt (father's sister) **2** sister-in-law (husband's sister) **3** nun: 尼～ Buddhist nun. 道～ Taoist nun II (副) tentatively; for the time being

姑娘 gūniang (名) girl

G

姑且 gūqiě (副) tentatively; for the time being: 此事～不谈. We will leave the matter aside for the time being.
姑嫂 gū-sǎo (名) sisters-in-law
姑妄言之 gū wàng yán zhī these are random remarks
姑息 gūxī (动) appease; indulge: ～养奸 to condone evil is to foster its growth
菇 gū (名) mushroom
箍 gū I (名) hoop; band II (动) bind round; hoop
呱 gū
see also guā
呱呱 gūgū 〈书〉 the cry of a baby
孤 gū (形) lonely; isolated; solitary: ～岛 an isolated island
孤傲 gū'ào (形) aloof and arrogant
孤单(單) gūdān (形) 1 alone: ～一人 all alone; a lone soul 2 lonely; friendless
孤独(獨) gūdú (形) lonely; solitary: 过着～的生活 live in solitude
孤儿(兒) gū'ér (名) orphan
孤芳自赏 gūfāng zì shǎng indulge in self-admiration; be narcissistic
孤寂 gūjì (形) lonely
孤家寡人 gūjiā-guǎrén a person alienated from the masses
孤苦伶仃 gūkǔ-língdīng lonely and helpless
孤立 gūlì I (形) isolated: 处于～地位 find oneself in an isolated position II (动) isolate: ～敌人 isolate the enemy
孤零零 gūlínglíng (形) all alone; lone
孤陋寡闻 gūlòu-guǎwén (形) superficial and ill-informed
孤僻 gūpì (形) unsociable and eccentric
孤掌难(難)鸣 gūzhǎng nán míng it's difficult to succeed without support
孤注一掷(擲) gūzhù yī zhì risk everything on one attempt; put all one's eggs in one basket
鼓 gǔ I (名) drum: 打～ beat a drum. ～点 drumbeats II (动) 1 rouse; agitate: ～起勇气 pluck up one's courage 2 blow with bellows, etc.: ～风 work a bellows
鼓吹 gǔchuī (动) advocate; preach; play up
鼓动(動) gǔdòng (动) agitate; arouse; instigate
鼓励(勵) gǔlì (动) encourage; urge
鼓舞 gǔwǔ (动) inspire; hearten: 形势很～人心. The situation is most inspiring. ～士气 boost the morale of the soldiers
鼓噪 gǔzào (动) make an uproar; clamour
鼓掌 gǔzhǎng (动) clap one's hands; applaud: ～通过 approve by acclamation
古 gǔ (形) ancient: ～时候 in ancient times. ～画 ancient painting. ～籍 antiquarian books
古板 gǔbǎn (形) conservative and obdurate
古代 gǔdài (名) ancient times; antiquity: ～文化 ancient civilization
古典 gǔdiǎn (形) classical
古董 gǔdǒng (名) antique: ～商 antiquarian
古怪 gǔguài (形) odd; eccentric: 脾气～ eccentric character. 样子～ queer-looking
古话 gǔhuà (名) old saying
古迹 gǔjì (名) historic site; place of historic interest
古籍 gǔjí (名) ancient books: ～商人 an antiquarian bookseller
古老 gǔlǎo (形) ancient; age-old
古人 gǔrén (名) the ancients; our forefathers
古色古香 gǔsè-gǔxiāng antique; quaint
古玩 gǔwán (名) antiques; curios: ～铺 a curiosity shop
古往今来(來) gǔwǎng-jīnlái from ancient times to the present age; from time immemorial
古文 gǔwén (名) 1 classical Chinese 2 ancient Chinese prose
古物 gǔwù (名) historical relics
古稀 gǔxī (名) seventy years of age: 年近～ approaching seventy
古雅 gǔyǎ (形) quaint
牯 gǔ (名) bull: ～牛 bull
贾 gǔ (名) merchant
蛊(蠱) gǔ (名) legendary venomous insect
蛊惑人心 gǔhuò rénxīn excite popular feelings; resort to demagogy
骨 gǔ (名) 1 bone 2 character; spirit: 傲～ lofty and unyielding character
骨干(幹) gǔgàn (名) backbone; mainstay
骨骼 gǔgé (名) skeleton
骨灰 gǔhuī (名) ashes (of a dead body): ～盒 cinerary casket
骨架 gǔjià (名) skeleton; framework: 小说的～ the framework of the novel
骨科 gǔkē (名) department of orthopaedics
骨牌 gǔpái (名) dominoes
骨气(氣) gǔqì (名) moral integrity

骨肉 gǔròu (名) flesh and blood; kindred: 亲生~ one's own flesh and blood. ~兄弟 blood brothers
骨髓 gǔsuǐ (名) marrow
骨头(頭) gǔtou (名) bone: 懒~ lazybones. 软~ a spineless creature; be chicken-hearted. ~架子 skeleton
骨折 gǔzhé (名) fracture
骨子里(裏) gǔzilǐ 〈口〉 in one's bones; in one's heart

谷 gǔ (名) 1 valley; gorge: 深~ a deep valley 2 (穀) cereal; grain 3 (穀) millet
谷仓(倉) gǔcāng (名) granary; barn
谷草 gǔcǎo (名) straw
谷歌 gǔgē (名) google
谷物 gǔwù (名) cereal; grain
谷子 gǔzi (名) 1 millet 2 unhusked rice

鹄 gǔ (名)〈书〉 target (in archery): 中~ hit the target
see also hú
鹄的 gǔdì (名) 1 target 2 aim

股 gǔ I (名) 1 thigh 2 (of an organization) section II(量) 1 [for strand-like things]: 一~泉水 stream of spring water. 三~毛线 three-ply wool 2 [for smell, air, energy, etc.]: 一~香味儿 a whiff of delicious smell. 一~烟 a puff of smoke. 一~劲儿 a burst of energy 3 group: 一~敌人 a group of enemy soldiers
股本 gǔběn (名) capital stock
股东(東) gǔdōng (名) shareholder; stockholder
股份 gǔfèn (名) share; stock
股金 gǔjīn (名) money paid for shares (in a partnership or cooperative)
股民 gǔmín (名) shareholder; stock buyer
股票 gǔpiào (名) share; stock: ~交易所 stock exchange. ~经纪人 stockbroker; stockjobber
股市 gǔshì (名) stock exchange
股息 gǔxī (名) dividend

汩 gǔ
汩汩 gǔgǔ (象) gurgle: ~流水 gurgling water

雇(僱) gù (动) hire; employ
雇工 gùgōng (名) hired labourer
雇农(農) gùnóng (名) hired farmhand
雇佣(傭) gùyōng (动) employ; hire: ~军 mercenary army. ~劳动 wage labour
雇员 gùyuán (名) employee
雇主 gùzhǔ (名) employer

顾(顧) gù (动) 1 turn round and look at: 环~四周 look around 2 attend to: 只~自己 think only in terms of one's own interest. 兼~give consideration to both sides. 不~个人安危 with no thought for personal safety. ~全大局 take the whole situation into consideration. 这么多事你~得过来吗? Can you manage so many things by yourself?
顾此失彼 gùcǐ-shībǐ cannot attend to one thing without losing sight of the other
顾及 gùjí (动) take into account; give consideration to
顾忌 gùjì (名) scruple; misgivings: 毫无~ be unscrupulous; have no scruples
顾客 gùkè (名) customer; client
顾虑(慮) gùlǜ (名) worry; misgivings; apprehension: ~重重 be full of misgivings
顾名思义(義) gù míng sī yì as the term or title suggests
顾盼 gùpàn (动) look around
顾全 gùquán (动) show consideration for: ~大局 take the overall interests into account
顾问 gùwèn (名) adviser; consultant
顾主 gùzhǔ (名) customer; client; patron

故 gù I (名) 1 reason; cause: 无~缺席 be absent without reason. 不知何~ not know why 2 incident: 事~ accident 3 friend; acquaintance: 非亲非~ neither relative nor friend II (副) on purpose: ~弄玄虚 deliberately complicate a simple issue; purposely make a mystery of simple things. ~作惊讶 put on a show of surprise. 明知~犯 wilfully violate (a law or rule) III (形) old; former: 依然如~ the same as before IV (动) die: 病~ die of illness V (连) therefore
故步自封 gù bù zì fēng be contented with the existing state of affairs and refuse to forge ahead
故都 gùdū (名) ancient capital
故宫 gùgōng (名) the Imperial Palace: ~博物院 the Palace Museum
故技 gùjì (名) stock trick: ~重演 play the same old trick
故交 gùjiāo (名) old friend
故居 gùjū (名) former residence
故弄玄虚 gù nòng xuánxū purposely make a

mystery of simple things; deliberately mystify things
故人 gùrén (名) old friend
故事 gùshi (名) 1 story; tale: 民间～ folk tale 2 plot: ～情节 the plot of a story
故土 gùtǔ (名) native land
故乡(鄉) gùxiāng (名) native place; hometown
故意 gùyì (副) purposely; intentionally; deliberately: 他～这么做的. He did it on purpose. 我不是～要刺伤你. I didn't mean to hurt your feelings. ～刁难 deliberately make things difficult for sb.
故障 gùzhàng (名) trouble; something wrong (with a machine): 机器出了～. The machine has broken down.

固 gù (形) 1 firm; solid: 加～ strengthen; reinforce 2 firmly; resolutely: ～辞 resolutely refuse; firmly decline
固定 gùdìng I (动) fix; regularize: 把业余学习～下来 set a regular time for spare-time study II (形) fixed; regular: 没有～的想法 have no fixed idea. ～职业 a permanent job. ～资产 fixed assets
固然 gùrán (副) [used to acknowledge a fact in order to make a contrary statement which is the speaker's real purpose] no doubt; it is true: 她的嗓子～不错,但是她不会唱. True, she has a good voice but she doesn't know how to sing.
固守 gùshǒu (动) 1 defend tenaciously 2 stick to
固体(體) gùtǐ (名) solid: ～燃料 solid fuel
固有 gùyǒu (形) intrinsic; inherent; innate: ～属性 intrinsic properties
固执(執) gùzhí I (形) stubborn; obstinate II (动) persist in: ～己见 stick stubbornly to one's own opinion

痼 gù
痼疾 gùjí (名) chronic illness

梏 gù (名) wooden handcuffs: 桎～ fetters; shackles

瓜 guā (名) melon; gourd: 西～ watermelon. 南～ pumpkins. 黄～ cucumber
瓜分 guāfēn (动) carve up: ～别国领土 carve up the territory of another country
瓜葛 guāgé (名) connection; involvement
瓜熟蒂落 guāshú-dìluò things will be easily settled once conditions are ripe
瓜子 guāzǐ (名) melon seeds

呱 guā
see also gū
呱呱 guāguā (象) (of ducks) quack; (of frogs) croak; (of crows) caw
呱呱叫 guāguājiào (形)〈口〉very good indeed; first-rate

刮 guā (动) 1 scrape: ～鱼鳞 scale a fish. ～胡子 shave 2 blow: ～大风了. It's blowing hard.
刮脸(臉) guāliǎn (动) shave (the face): ～刀 razor
刮目相看 guāmù xiāng kàn look at sb. with new eyes; treat sb. with increased respect

寡 guǎ (形) 1 few; scant: 沉默～言 reticent; uncommunicative. ～不敌众 be hopelessly outnumbered 2 tasteless: 索然～味 dull and monotonous. 清汤～水 watery and insipid 3 widowed: 守～ live in widowhood. ～妇 widow
寡廉鲜耻 guǎlián-xiǎnchǐ lost to shame; shameless
寡人 guǎrén (代) I, the sovereign; we [used by a royal person in proclamations instead of I]
寡头(頭) guǎtóu (名) oligarch: 金融～ financial oligarchy

剐(剮) guǎ (动) cut to pieces: 千刀万～ be hacked to pieces

褂 guà (名) gown: 大～儿 long gown. ～子 short gown

挂(掛) guà I (动) 1 hang; put up; suspend: 墙上～着一幅画. A picture is hanging on the wall. 一轮明月当空～着. A bright moon hung in the sky. 2 get caught: 钉子把裙子～住了. Her skirt got caught on a nail. 3 call; ring up: 我要给他～电话. I'll phone him up. 4 hang up (the receiver): 他把电话～上了. He's hung up. 5 be concerned about: 别把这事～在心上. Don't worry about it. 6 register (at a hospital): ～外科 register for surgery II (量) [for things in strings]: 一～拖车 a trailer. 几～鞭炮 several strings of firecrackers
挂彩 guàcǎi (动) 1 be wounded in battle 2 decorate for festive occasions
挂齿(齒) guàchǐ (动) mention: 这点小事,何足～. Such a trifling matter is not worth mentioning.
挂钩 guàgōu (动) 1 couple (two railway

coaches) 2 get in touch with; establish contact with

挂号(號) guàhào (动) 1 register (at a hospital) 2 send by registered mail: ～信 registered letter

挂面(麵) guàmiàn (名) fine dried noodles; vermicelli

挂名 guàmíng (形) nominal; only in name

挂念 guàniàn (动) worry about; miss: 十分～ miss sb. very much

挂牌 guàpái (动) hang out one's shingle or license: ～牙医 licensed dentist

挂失 guàshī (动) report the loss of sth.

挂帅(帥) guàshuài (动) take command

挂毯 guàtǎn (名) tapestry

挂羊头(頭),卖(賣)狗肉 guà yángtóu, mài gǒuròu engage in dishonest business by putting up a façade of honesty

卦 guà (名) divinatory symbols: 占～ divination

乖 guāi (形) 1 (of a child) well-behaved; obedient: 真是个～孩子. There's a dear. 2 clever

乖戾 guāilì (形) disagreeable; unreasonable; perverse

乖谬 guāimiù (形) absurd; aberrant

乖僻 guāipì (形) eccentric; odd

乖巧 guāiqiǎo (形) 1 clever 2 cute; lovely

拐 guǎi (动) 1 turn: 往左～ turn to the left. ～进一条胡同 turn into an alley 2 limp: 一～一～地走 limp along; hobble along 3 abduct; kidnap

拐点 guǎidiǎn (名) inflection point; flex point

拐棍 guǎigùn (名) walking stick

拐角 guǎijiǎo (名) (at a street) corner; turning

拐骗 guǎipiàn (动) 1 abduct 2 swindle: ～钱财 swindle money (out of sb.)

拐弯(彎) guǎiwān (动) 1 turn a corner; turn 2 turn round; pursue a new course

拐弯(彎)抹角 guǎiwān-mòjiǎo talk in a roundabout way; beat about the bush

拐杖 guǎizhàng (名) walking stick

怪 guài I (形) strange; odd; queer; unusual; peculiar II (动) blame: 这不能～他,只～我没交代清楚. This is not his fault. I am to blame for not having made the whole thing clear to him. III (名) monster; demon; evil being: 鬼～ demons; ghosts IV (副) quite; rather: 这箱子～沉的. The suitcase is rather heavy.

怪不得 guàibude no wonder; so that's why: 原来她父母都是钢琴家,～她弹得这么好! So her parents are both pianists! No wonder she plays the piano so well.

怪诞 guàidàn (形) strange; weird

怪话 guàihuà (名) cynical remark; complaint: 说～ make cynical remarks

怪模怪样(樣) guàimú-guàiyàng odd; bizarre; grotesque

怪僻 guàipì (形) (of a person or his behaviour) eccentric

怪胎 guàitāi (名) teratism; monster

怪物 guàiwu (名) 1 monster 2 an eccentric person

怪异(異) guàiyì (形) strange; unusual

怪罪 guàizuì (动) blame (sb.)

官 guān (名) 1 government official; officer: 外交～ diplomat. ～兵 officers and men 2 organ: 感～ sense organ

官场(場) guānchǎng (名) officialdom; official circles

官邸 guāndǐ (名) official residence

官方 guānfāng (形) official: ～消息 official sources

官话 guānhuà (名) 1 mandarin 2 bureaucratic jargon

官架子 guānjiàzi (名) the airs of an official: 摆～ put on bureaucratic airs

官吏 guānlì (名) government officials (in feudal society)

官僚 guānliáo (名) bureaucrat; government official

官僚主义(義) guānliáozhǔyì (名) bureaucracy: ～作风 bureaucratic style of work; bureaucratic way of doing things

官能 guānnéng (名) (organic) function; sense: 视、听、嗅、味、触这五种～ the five senses of sight, hearing, smell, taste and touch

官腔 guānqiāng (名) official jargon: 打～ speak in bureaucratic jargon

官司 guānsi (名) lawsuit: 打～ go to law against sb; sue sb.

官衔 guānxián (名) official title

官瘾(癮) guānyǐn (名) strong desire for public office; love for an official post

官员 guānyuán (名) official

官职(職) guānzhí (名) government post; official position

棺 guān (名) coffin: ～材 coffin

倌 guān (名) 1 herdsman: 羊～儿 shepherd. 马～儿 groom 2 a hired hand in certain service trades: 堂～儿 waiter

关(關) guān I (动) 1 shut; close: ～窗户 shut the window 2 turn off: ～电灯 turn off the light 3 lock up: ～进监狱 put in prison 4 close down: 昨天又有两家工厂～了. Two more factories closed down yesterday. 5 concern; involve: 这事与你无～. It's none of your business. 事～大局 The matter is of concern to the overall situation. II (名) 1 pass; check 2 barrier; critical juncture: 技术难～ a technical difficulty 3 customs house

关闭 guānbì (动) 1 close; shut 2 (of a shop or factory) close down; shut down

关怀(懷) guānhuái (动) pay serious attention to; be concerned about

关键 guānjiàn (名) key; crux: 问题的～ the crux of the matter. ～时刻 at the critical moment

关节(節) guānjié (名) joint: ～炎 arthritis

关口 guānkǒu (名) 1 strategic pass 2 juncture

关联(聯) guānlián (动) be related; be connected: 国家的外交政策和经济政策是相互～的. The foreign and economic policies of a country are interrelated.

关门(門) guānmén (动) 1 close; shut: 随手～ shut the door after you. 商店几点～? When does the shop close? 2 refuse to accept or tolerate different views

关卡 guānqiǎ (名) checkpoint

关切 guānqiè (动) be deeply concerned

关税 guānshuì (名) customs duty; tariff: 保护～ protective tariff. 特惠～ preferential tariff. ～壁垒 tariff barrier. ～豁免 exemption from customs duties

关头(頭) guāntóu (名) juncture; moment: 紧要～ a critical moment or juncture

关系(係) guānxì I (名) 1 relation; relationship: 外交～ diplomatic relations. 夫妻～ relations between husband and wife. 他俩的～不好. They are not on good terms with each other. *or* They don't get along. 2 ties; connections: 社会～ one's social connections 3 bearing: 没～. It doesn't matter. ～不大. It doesn't make much difference. 4 [indicating cause or condition]: 由于时间～, 就谈到这里吧. Since time is limited, I'll leave it at that. II (动) concern; affect; involve: 这是个原则问题, ～到我们所有的人. This is a matter of principle which concerns all of us.

关心 guānxīn (动) be concerned about; concern oneself with; pay great attention to: 我们应当～青年一代的思想教育. We should pay great attention to the moral education of the younger generation.

关押 guānyā (动) put in prison; take into custody

关于(於) guānyú (介) about; on; with regard to; concerning: 一本～中国的书 a book about China. ～你的要求, 我们准备在会上讨论一下. As for your request, we have decided to discuss it at the meeting.

关照 guānzhào (动) 1 look after; keep an eye on: 我走后请你多～我的孩子. While I'm away, will you please keep an eye on my children? 2 notify by word of mouth; tell: 你～他们一声, 我一会儿就回来. Please bring them the message that I'll be back soon.

关注 guānzhù (动) pay close attention to: 承蒙～, 深以为感. I am very grateful for the trouble you have taken on my behalf.

鳏 guān (形) wifeless; widowered

鳏夫 guānfū (名) bachelor or widower

冠 guān (名) hat; crest; crown: 衣～整齐 be neatly dressed. 树～ the crown of a tree. 鸡～ cock's comb; crest

see also guàn

冠冕堂皇 guānmiǎn tánghuáng high-sounding

冠心病 guānxīnbìng (名) coronary heart disease

观(觀) guān I (动) look at; watch; observe II (名) 1 sight; view: 奇～ wonderful sight; wonder. 改～ change in appearance 2 conception of the nature of things; way of looking at things: 世界～ world outlook

观测 guāncè (动) observe and survey: ～气象 make weather observations

观察 guānchá (动) observe; examine: ～地形 survey the terrain; topographical survey. ～家(员) observer. ～所 observation post

观点(點) guāndiǎn (名) viewpoint; standpoint

观感 guāngǎn (名) impressions of a visit

观光 guānguāng (动) be on a sightseeing trip

观看 guānkàn (动) watch; view: ～动静 watch what is happening. ～一场比赛 watch a game

观礼(禮) guānlǐ (动) attend a celebration or ceremony

观摩 guānmó (动) view and learn from each other's work; watch and emulate

观念 guānniàn (名) idea; concept

观赏 guānshǎng (动) watch and enjoy: ～艺术 the visual arts

观望 guānwàng (动) 1 look around 2 wait and see

观象台(臺) guānxiàngtái (名) observatory

观音 guānyīn (名) Guanyin; the Goddess of Mercy

观众(衆) guānzhòng (名) audience; spectator; viewer

管 guǎn I (名) tube; pipe: 血～ blood vessel. 电子～ electron tube. 水～ water pipe. 单簧～ clarinet II (量) [for tube-shaped things]: 一～牙膏 a tube of toothpaste III (动) 1 be in charge of; run; be responsible for: ～家 run the house. 他是～实验室的. He is in charge of the laboratory. 2 control; take care of: 这些孩子得～～了. These children must be taken in hand. 这件事你来～. Will you take care of this matter? 3 mind; attend to; bother about: 别～他. Leave him alone. 我才不～呢! I can't be bothered. 别～人家怎么说. Never mind what other people say. IV (介) [in conjunction with 叫]: 他们～我叫小胖子. They call me "little fatty".

管保 guǎnbǎo (动) guarantee; assure: 这外套～很合适. I can assure you that this jacket will fit you perfectly.

管道 guǎndào (名) pipeline

管家 guǎnjiā (名) 1 housekeeper 2 butler

管教 guǎnjiào (动) take sb. in hand; subject sb. to discipline

管理 guǎnlǐ (动) manage; administer; run: ～部门 administrative office. 企业～ business management

管事 guǎnshì (动) 1 be in charge: 这里谁～? Who's in charge here? 2 be effective; be of use: 这药很～儿. This medicine is very effective. 问他不～. It's no use asking him.

管束 guǎnshù (动) restrain; control: 严加～ keep sb. under strict control

管辖 guǎnxiá (动) have control over: 在～范围之内 come within the jurisdiction of. ～权 jurisdiction

管弦乐(樂) guǎnxiányuè (名) orchestral music: ～队 orchestra

管乐(樂)器 guǎnyuèqì (名) wind instrument

管制 guǎnzhì (动) 1 control: ～灯火 enforce a blackout 2 put sb. under surveillance

管子 guǎnzi (名) tube; pipe

馆 guǎn (名) house; hall; shop: 旅～ hotel. 宾～ guesthouse. 理发～ barbershop. 茶～ teahouse. 饭～ restaurant. 照相～ photo studio. 博物～ museum. 展览～ exhibition hall. 美术～ art gallery. 体育～ gymnasium. 图书～ library

馆子 guǎnzi (名) restaurant: 下～ eat at a restaurant; dine out

冠 guàn

see also guān

冠军 guànjūn (名) champion

灌 guàn (动) 1 irrigate: 引水～田 irrigate the fields 2 fill; pour: 暖瓶都～满了. The thermos flasks have all been filled. ～醉 get sb. drunk

灌唱片 guàn chàngpiàn make a gramophone record

灌溉 guàngài (动) irrigate: ～面积 irrigated area. ～渠 irrigation canal

灌木 guànmù (名) bush; shrub

灌输 guànshū (动) instil into; imbue with

灌注 guànzhù (动) pour into; fill

罐 guàn (名) jar; canister; tin: 一～茶叶 a canister of tea. 一～纸烟 a tin of cigarettes. 水～ water pitcher

罐头(頭) guàntou (名) tin; can: ～食品 tinned (or canned) food

鹳 guàn (名) stork

盥 guàn (动)〈书〉 wash

盥洗 guànxǐ (动) wash one's hands and face: ～室 washroom. ～用具 toilet articles

贯 guàn (动) 1 pass through: 学～古今 combine classical training with modern scholarship 2 follow in a continuous line: 鱼～而入 enter one after another

贯彻(徹) guànchè (动) carry through (or out); implement: ～一项决议 put a decision into effect

贯穿 guànchuān (动) run through
贯通 guàntōng (动) 1 have a perfect understanding of: 豁然～ feel suddenly enlightened 2 link up: 这条铁路已全线～. The whole railway line has been joined up.
贯注 guànzhù (动) concentrate on: 全神～ be wholly absorbed

惯 guàn I (形) be used to; be in the habit of: 我过不～这里的生活. I'm not used to the life here. II (动) spoil; indulge: 别把孩子～坏了. Don't spoil the child.

惯犯 guànfàn (名) habitual offender
惯技 guànjì (名) old trick
惯例 guànlì (名) usual practice; convention: 国际～ international practice
惯性 guànxìng (名) inertia
惯用 guànyòng (形) habitual; customary: ～伎俩 customary tactics; old tricks

光 guāng I (名) 1 light; ray: 月～ moonlight. 太阳～ sunshine. 爱克斯～ X ray 2 brightness; lustre: 这只银盘闪闪发～. This silver plate has a fine lustre. 两眼无～ dull eyed 3 glory; honour: 为祖国争～ win honour for one's country 4 scenery: 春～明媚 the savoury scene of springtime. 观～ on a sightseeing trip II (形) 1 smooth; glossy; polished 2 bare; naked: ～脚 barefoot 3 used up: 钱用～了. I've spent all my money. III (副) solely; only; merely; alone: ～有好的意愿还不够. Good intention alone is not enough.

光笔(筆) guāngbǐ (名) light pen
光标(標) guāngbiāo (名) cursor
光彩 guāngcǎi (名) splendour; brilliance; radiance: ～夺目 dazzlingly brilliant
光复(復) guāngfù (动) recover (lost territory, etc.)
光杆(桿)儿(兒) guānggǎnr (名) 1 a bare stalk 2 a man without a following
光顾(顧) guānggù (动) patronize
光怪陆(陸)离(離) guāngguài-lùlí bizarre and gaudy
光棍 guānggùn (名) unmarried man; bachelor
光滑 guānghuá (形) smooth; glossy; sleek
光辉 guānghuī (名) radiance; brilliance; glory: 太阳的～ the brilliance of the sun
光洁(潔) guāngjié (形) polished and spotless
光景 guāngjǐng (名) 1 circumstances 2 scene: 我童年时代的～在脑海里闪过. Scenes of my childhood flashed through my mind. 3 about; around: 他父亲有60岁～. His father is about 60 years old.
光亮 guāngliàng (形) bright; shiny
光临(臨) guānglín 〈敬〉 gracious presence (of a guest, etc.): 敬请～. Your presence is cordially requested.
光溜溜 guāngliūliū (形) 1 smooth; slippery: ～的地板 well polished floor 2 bare; naked: 孩子们脱得～的在河里洗澡. The children are bathing naked in the river.
光芒 guāngmáng (名) rays of light; radiance
光明 guāngmíng I (名) light: 从黑暗走向～ go through darkness to the light II (形) 1 bright; promising: ～的前途 bright future 2 openhearted: ～磊落 open and aboveboard
光盘(盤) guāngpán (名) optical disk: 音乐～ CD. 视频～ VCD
光谱 guāngpǔ (名) spectrum
光驱(驅) guāngqū (名) disk drive
光圈 guāngquān (名) diaphragm; aperture; stop
光荣(榮) guāngróng (名) glory; honour; credit: ～称号 a title of honour. ～传统 a glorious tradition
光润 guāngrùn (形) (of skin) smooth
光头(頭) guāngtóu (名) 1 shaven head 2 bald head
光秃秃 guāngtūtū (形) bald; bare; barren
光纤(纖) guāngxiān (名) optical fibre
光线(綫) guāngxiàn (名) light; ray: ～不好 poor light
光耀 guāngyào I (名) brilliant light II (形) glorious; honourable
光阴(陰) guāngyīn (名) time: ～似箭. Time flies.
光泽(澤) guāngzé (名) lustre; gloss; sheen
光照 guāngzhào (名) illumination
光宗耀祖 guāngzōng-yàozǔ bring honour to one's ancestors

广(廣) guǎng I (形) broad; vast; extensive: 见多识～ have wide experience and extensive knowledge. 消息流传很～. The news has spread far and wide. II (动) broaden; spread

广播 guǎngbō (动) broadcast: ～电台 broadcasting station. 实况～ live broadcast. ～员 radio announcer
广博 guǎngbó (形) (of one's knowledge)

extensive; wide
广场(場) guǎngchǎng (名) public square
广大 guǎngdà (形) 1 vast; wide; extensive: 幅员~ vast in territory 2 numerous: ~群众 the broad masses of the people
广度 guǎngdù (名) scope; range: ~和深度 scope and depth
广泛 guǎngfàn (形) extensive; wide-ranging; widespread: ~的兴趣 a wide range of interest. ~地征求意见 solicit opinions from all quarters
广柑 guǎnggān (名) orange
广告 guǎnggào (名) advertisement: 做~ advertise. ~画 poster. ~牌 billboard. 电视~ TV commercial. ~宣传 promotion
广阔 guǎngkuò (形) vast; wide; broad: ~的田野 a vast stretch of country. ~的前景 broad prospects
广袤 guǎngmào (名)〈书〉 length and breadth of land
广义(義) guǎngyì (名) broad sense: ~地说 in a broad sense; broadly speaking
犷(獷) guǎng (形) rustic; shaggy and uncouth: ~悍 tough and intrepid
逛 guàng (动) stroll; roam: ~商店 go window-shopping. ~大街 stroll around the streets
逛荡(蕩) guàngdang (动) loaf about
规 guī I (名) rule; regulation: 校~ school regulations II (动) 1 plan; map out: ~划 plan 2 admonish; advise: ~劝 admonish
规程 guīchéng (名) rules; regulations: 操作~ rules of operation
规定 guīdìng I (动) 1 stipulate: 宪法~男女平等. The Constitution stipulates that men and women are equal. 2 fix; set: 在~的时间内 within the fixed time. ~的指标 a set quota II (名) rule; stipulation
规范(範) guīfàn (名) standard; norm: 合乎~ conform to the standard
规格 guīgé (名) specifications; standards: 统一的~ unified standards. 不合~ not be up to standard
规划(劃) guīhuà (名) plan; programme: 长远~ long-term planning. 全面~ comprehensive programme
规矩 guīju I (名) rule; established practice: 按老~办事 do things according to the old custom II (形) well-behaved; well-disciplined: ~点! Behave yourself!
规律 guīlǜ (名) law; regular pattern: 客观~ objective law
规模 guīmó (名) scale; scope; dimensions: ~宏大 broad in scale
规劝(勸) guīquàn (动) admonish; advise
规则 guīzé I (名) rule; regulation: 交通~ traffic regulations II (形) regular
规章 guīzhāng (名) rule; regulation: ~制度 rules and regulations
闺 guī (名) boudoir
闺房 guīfáng (名) boudoir
闺女 guīnü (名) 1 girl; maiden 2〈口〉 daughter
硅 guī (名) silicon (Si)
硅谷 guīgǔ (名) silicon valley
鲑 guī (名) salmon
归(歸) guī I (动) 1 go back to; return: ~国华侨 returned overseas Chinese. ~期 date of return. 无家可~ be homeless 2 converge; come together: 条条大河~大海. All rivers lead to the sea. 这几本书应~为一类. These books ought to be put under one category. 3 turn over to; put under sb.'s care: ~国家所有 be turned over to the state. 这事应~你管. This matter comes within your jurisdiction. II [used between reduplicated verbs] despite: 吵架~吵架,可他俩还是很相爱. They love each other despite their frequent quarrels.
归案 guī'àn (动) bring to justice: 捉拿~ arrest and bring to justice
归并(併) guībìng (动) incorporate into; merge into
归档(檔) guīdàng (动) place on file; file away; file
归根结底 guīgēn-jiédǐ in the final analysis: ~,人民的意志是不可抗拒的. In the final analysis the will of the people is irresistible.
归功 guīgōng (动) [usu. used with 于] give the credit to; attribute the success to: 我们的一切成就都~于正确的政策. We owe all our success to correct policy.
归还(還) guīhuán (动) give back; return: 你要按时把书~给图书馆. You must return this book to the library on time.
归结 guījié (动) sum up; put in a nutshell: 问题虽很复杂,~起来不外三个方面. The

G

questions, though very complicated, may be summed up as coming under three categories.
归咎 guījiù (动) lay the blame on; blame: 不能把一切错误都～于他. We can't put all the blame on him alone.
归拢(攏) guīlǒng (动) put together
归纳 guīnà (动) sum up; conclude: ～大意 sum up the main ideas. ～法 inductive method; induction
归侨(僑) guīqiáo (名) returned overseas Chinese
归属(屬) guīshǔ (动) belong to
归顺 guīshùn (动) pledge allegiance
归宿 guīsù (名) a place where a person really belongs; natural end: 人生的～ the end of life's journey
归天 guītiān (动) die; pass away
归向 guīxiàng (动) turn towards: 人心～ the trend of the popular feelings
归心似箭 guīxīn sì jiàn be anxious to return
归于(於) guīyú (动) belong to; be attributed to: 光荣～英雄的人民. Glory goes to the heroic people. 经过磋商,大家的意见已经～一致了. We reached an agreement after consultation.
归罪 guīzuì (动) lay the blame on

瑰 guī (形) marvellous

瑰宝(寶) guībǎo (名) rarity; treasure
瑰丽(麗) guīlì (形) extremely beautiful; magnificent

龟(龜) guī (名) tortoise; turtle

see also jūn
龟缩 guīsuō (动) withdraw into passive defence; hole up

鬼 guǐ (名) 1 devil; ghost; spirit 2 [a term of abuse]: 懒～ lazybones. 胆小～ coward. 酒～ drunkard 3 sinister plot; dirty trick: 心里有～ have something on one's conscience II (形) 1 stealthy; surreptitious: ～头～脑 stealthy; sneaky 2 damnable: ～地方 a lousy place 3 〈口〉 clever; quick: 这孩子真～. What a clever child!
鬼把戏(戲) guǐbǎxì (名) dirty trick: 玩弄～ play a dirty trick
鬼点(點)子 guǐdiǎnzi (名) wicked idea
鬼怪 guǐguài (名) ghosts and monsters; forces of evil
鬼鬼祟祟 guǐguǐsuìsuì sneaking; stealthy; furtive
鬼话 guǐhuà (名) damned lie
鬼魂 guǐhún (名) ghost; spirit; apparition
鬼混 guǐhùn (动) fool around
鬼脸(臉) guǐliǎn (名) wry face; grimace: 做～ make faces; make grimaces
鬼神 guǐshén (名) ghosts and supernatural beings
鬼胎 guǐtāi (名) ulterior motive; sinister design: 心怀～ harbour evil intentions
鬼头(頭)鬼脑(腦) guǐtóu guǐnǎo thievish; furtive; stealthy
鬼蜮 guǐyù (名) demon: ～伎俩 evil tactics

轨 guǐ (名) 1 rail; track: 单(双)～ single (double) track. 出～ be derailed 2 order; regularity: 常～ normal practice. 走上正～ get on to the right path. 越～ overstep the bounds of propriety
轨道 guǐdào (名) 1 track 2 orbit: 卫星～ the orbit of a satellite 3 course: 生产已走上～. Production has come to normal.
轨迹 guǐjì (名) 1 locus 2 orbit

诡 guǐ (形) deceitful; tricky

诡辩(辯) guǐbiàn (名) sophistry; quibbling
诡称(稱) guǐchēng (动) falsely allege; pretend
诡计 guǐjì (名) trick; cunning scheme: ～多端 be very crafty; be full of tricks
诡谲 guǐjué (形)〈书〉 fantastic
诡秘 guǐmì (形) mysterious; secretive: 行踪～ mysterious in one's movements
诡诈 guǐzhà (形) crafty; cunning; treacherous

桂 guì (名) 1 cassia-bark tree 2 laurel 3 sweet-scented osmanthus
桂冠 guìguān (名) laurel
桂花 guìhuā (名) sweet-scented osmanthus
桂圆 guìyuán (名) longan: ～肉 dried longan pulp

柜(櫃) guì (名) cupboard; cabinet: 书～ bookcase. 五斗～ chest of drawers
柜台(臺) guìtái (名) sales counter: 站～ serve behind the counter

贵 guì (形) 1 expensive; costly; dear: 这地方东西很～. Things are expensive here. 2 precious; valuable: 人～有自知之明. Self-knowledge is wisdom. 3 noble; honoured: ～客 guest of honour 4 〈敬〉 your: ～国 your country. ～姓? May I ask your name?
贵宾(賓) guìbīn (名) distinguished guest: ～室 VIP's room

贵重 guìzhòng (形) valuable; precious: ～物品 valuables
贵族 guìzú (名) noble; aristocrat; aristocracy
跪 guì (动) kneel
跪拜 guìbài (动) worship on bended knees
跪倒 guìdǎo (动) go down on one's knees
刽(劊) guì (动) cut off; chop off
刽子手 guìzishǒu (名) **1** executioner **2** slaughterer
滚 gǔn (动) **1** roll: 球～进洞里. The ball rolled into the hole. 眼泪顺着脸颊～下来. Tears were rolling down her cheeks. **2** [a term of abuse]: ～出去! Get out of here! ～开! Get away! **3** boil: 水～了. The water is boiling.
滚蛋 gǔndàn (动) beat it; scram; get lost
滚动(動) gǔndòng (动) roll; trundle
滚瓜烂(爛)熟 gǔnguā lànshú (recite, etc.) fluently
滚滚 gǔngǔn (形) rolling; surging: 大江～东去. The Great River surges eastward in billowing waves.
滚烫(燙) gǔntàng (形) boiling hot; scalding hot
滚梯 gǔntī (名) escalator
滚圆 gǔnyuán (形) round as a ball
滚珠 gǔnzhū (名) ball: ～轴承 ball-bearing
棍 gùn (名) **1** rod; stick **2** scoundrel: 恶～ ruffian; rascal. 赌～ gambler
棍棒 gùnbàng (名) club; cudgel; stick
棍子 gùnzi (名) rod; stick
郭 guō (名) the outer wall of a city
聒 guō (形) noisy: ～噪 noisy; clamorous
锅(鍋) guō (名) pot; pan; cooker: 炒菜～ frying pan
锅巴 guōbā (名) rice crust
锅炉(爐) guōlú (名) boiler
国(國) guó (名) country; state; nation: 全～各地 all over the country. 收归～有 be nationalized
国策 guócè (名) national policy
国产(產) guóchǎn (形) made in one's own country
国耻 guóchǐ (名) national humiliation
国都 guódū (名) national capital
国度 guódù (名) state; nation
国法 guófǎ (名) national law
国防 guófáng (名) national defence
国歌 guógē (名) national anthem
国格 guógé (名) national prestige; national dignity
国画(畫) guóhuà (名) traditional Chinese painting
国徽 guóhuī (名) national emblem
国会(會) guóhuì (名) parliament; (美) Congress; (日) the Diet
国货 guóhuò (名) goods produced in one's own country
国籍 guójí (名) nationality: 双重～ dual nationality
国计民生 guójì-mínshēng the national economy and the people's livelihood
国际(際) guójì (名) international: ～地位 international status. ～形势 the international (or world) situation. ～影响 international repercussions
国际(際)法 guójìfǎ (名) international law
国际(際)歌 Guójìgē (名) *The Internationale*
国际(際)主义(義) guójìzhǔyì (名) internationalism
国家 guójiā (名) country; state; nation
国教 guójiào (名) state religion
国界 guójiè (名) national boundaries
国境 guójìng (名) territory; border: ～线 boundary line
国君 guójūn (名) monarch
国库 guókù (名) national treasury: ～券 treasury bonds
国立 guólì (形) state-run: ～大学 state university
国民 guómín (形) national: ～收入 national income. ～生产总值 gross national product (GNP)
国难(難) guónàn (名) national calamity
国内 guónèi (名) internal; domestic: ～战争 civil war. ～市场 domestic (or home) market. ～贸易 domestic trade
国旗 guóqí (名) national flag
国企 guóqǐ (名) state-owned enterprise
国情 guóqíng (名) national conditions: (美国的)～咨文 State of the Union Message
国庆(慶) guóqìng (名) National Day (celebrations)
国事 guóshì (名) state affairs: ～访问 state visit
国书(書) guóshū (名) (diplomatic) credentials
国体(體) guótǐ (名) **1** state system **2** national prestige
国土 guótǔ (名) national territory; land: 神

G

圣的～ our sacred land

国外 guówài (名) external; overseas; abroad: ～市场 overseas (or foreign) market. 去～ go abroad

国王 guówáng (名) king

国务(務)院 guówùyuàn (名) 1 the State Council 2(美) the State Department

国宴 guóyàn (名) state banquet

国营(營) guóyíng (形) state-operated; state-run: ～经济 state-owned economy. ～农场 state farm. ～企业 state enterprise

国有 guóyǒu (动) state-owned: ～企业 state-owned enterprise. ～化 nationalization. 收归～ bring sth. under state control; nationalize

国葬 guózàng (名) state funeral

国债 guózhài (名) national debt; the internal and external debts of a nation

果 guǒ I (名) 1 fruit: 开花结～ blossom and bear fruit. 水～ fruit. 干～ dried fruit 2 result; consequence: 自食其～ reap what one has sown. 恶～ a disastrous result II (形) resolute; determined III (副) really; as expected: ～不出所料 just as one expected

果断(斷) guǒduàn (形) resolute; decisive: 采取～措施 take decisive measures

果脯 guǒfǔ (名) preserved fruit; candied fruit

果敢 guǒgǎn (形) courageous and resolute

果酱(醬) guǒjiàng (名) jam

果木 guǒmù (名) fruit tree

果品 guǒpǐn (名) fruit

果然 guǒrán (副) really; as expected; sure enough: ～是他. It was him as expected. 眼见为实，这回我去西湖，发现～不错. Seeing is believing. I visited the West Lake this time and found it really worth seeing.

果仁儿(兒) guǒrénr (名) kernel

果实(實) guǒshí (名) fruit; gains: ～累累 fruit growing in close clusters

果树(樹) guǒshù (名) fruit tree

果园(園) guǒyuán (名) orchard

果真 guǒzhēn (副) really; truly

果子 guǒzi (名) fruit: ～露 (or 汁) fruit syrup

裹 guǒ (动) wrap; bind: 用毛巾把孩子～起来 wrap the baby in a towel

裹足不前 guǒ zú bù qián hesitate to move forward; mark time

过(過) guò I (动) 1 pass; cross: ～河 cross a river. ～马路 cross the road. 从这条街上～ pass through this street. 我～两天再来. I'll come again in a couple of days. 2 make sth. go through a process: 我们来把这些练习再～一遍. Let's go over these exercises once again. 先～秤 weigh (it) first. ～数 count (them) 3 spend (life, time): 假期～得怎么样? How did you spend your holiday? ～生日 celebrate one's birthday. ～日子 live one's life. 我妈妈跟我们～. My mother lives with us. 4 exceed; go beyond: 日产～万吨. The output per day is over 10,000 tons. 水深～膝. The water is more than knee-deep. II [used after a verb as a complement] 1 past; through; over: 跳～篱笆墙 jump over a fence. 闪电划～天空. Lightning flashed across the sky. 走～树林 walk past the wood 2 turn; over: 翻～这一页. turn this page over. 转～身 turn round 3 better than: 我说不～她. I can't outargue her. 谁也跑不～他. No one can run as fast as he can. III (名) error; fault: 功～ merits and faults. 记～ record one's demerits. 改～ correct one's mistakes

过场(場) guòchǎng (名) 1 (of drama) interlude 2 (of Chinese operas) cross the stage 3 [used with 走]: 走～ do sth. as a mere formality

过程 guòchéng (名) process; course

过错 guòcuò (名) fault; mistake: 这不是你的～. That's not your fault.

过道 guòdào (名) corridor

过得去 guòdequ 1 be able to get through 2 so-so; passable; not too bad: 他的字写的还～. His handwriting is not too bad. 他们之间的关系～. They are on fairly good terms, as it is. 3 feel at ease: 我心里怎么能～呢? How can I feel at ease?

过度 guòdù (形) excessive; undue; over-: 饮酒～ drink immoderately. ～疲劳 be overworked; be dog-tired

过渡 guòdù (名) transition

过分 guòfèn (形) excessive; undue; going too far: ～的要求 excessive demands. ～着重 put undue emphasis on

过关(關) guòguān (动) pass a barrier; pass a test; reach a standard: 蒙混～ get by under false pretences. 这项新产品的质量还没～. The quality of this new product is not yet up to standard.

过河拆桥(橋) guòhé chāiqiáo pull down the bridge after crossing the river—cold-shoulder a person who has helped one get over a difficulty; be ungrateful

过后(後) guòhòu (名) afterwards; later

过户 guòhù (动) transfer ownership

过活 guòhuó (动) make a living; live

过火 guòhuǒ (形) carry things too far; overdo: 你玩笑开得太～了. This is going beyond a joke.

过激 guòjī (形) too drastic; extremist: ～言论 extremist opinions

过继(繼) guòjì (动) adopt a young relative

过奖(獎) guòjiǎng (动) overpraise; pay undeserved compliments to: 您～了. You flatter me.

过节(節) guòjié (动) celebrate a festival

过境 guòjìng (动) pass through the territory of a country; be in transit: ～签证 transit visa

过来(來) guòlái (动) [used after a verb and often preceded by 得 or 不 to show sufficiency of time; ability or quantity]: 图书馆里好书太多,简直看不～. There are too many good books in the library for me to read. 你一个人忙得～吗? Can you manage by yourself?

过来(來) guòlái (动) come over; come up: 请～! Will you come over here please?

过来(來) guòlái (动) **1** [used after a verb to indicate moving towards the speaker]: 一个老头正朝我走～. An old man is coming towards me. 把那本书拿～. Bring me that book. **2** [used after a verb to indicate turning around towards the speaker]: 他转过身来对我说话. He turned round and spoke to me. 把那一页翻～. Turn that page back. **3** [used after a verb to indicate returning to the normal state]: 她从昏迷中醒～了. She came to. *or* She regained her consciousness.

过量 guòliàng (形) excessive; over: 饮酒～ drink beyond sensible limits

过虑(慮) guòlǜ (动) be overanxious

过滤(濾) guòlǜ (动) filter; infiltrate: ～器 filter. ～嘴 filter tip (of a cigarette)

过敏 guòmǐn I (名) allergy II (动) be allergic: 她对烟味～. She is allergic to smoke.

过目 guòmù (动) look over (for check or approval)这是名单,请您～. Here's the list for you to go over.

过年 guònián (动) celebrate (or spend) the New Year

过期 guòqī (动) expire; be overdue: ～作废 invalid after the specified date. 合同明年～. The contract expires next year. ～杂志 back number of a magazine. 你从图书馆借来的书,早就～了. The books you borrowed from the library have long been overdue for return.

过谦 guòqiān (动) be too modest: 你～了. You are being too modest.

过去 guòqù (名) past; former; previous: 请不要再提～了. Let us forget about the past. ～的事就算了吧. Let bygones be bygones. 这个地方～很穷. This place was poverty-stricken in the past. 她比～活泼多了. She is much more lively than she used to be.

过去 guòqù (动) go over; pass by: 他刚从这儿～. He has just passed by. 我～看看. I'll go over and see how it is.

过去 guòqù (动) **1** [used after a verb to indicate moving away from the speaker]: 把球给他扔～. Toss him the ball. 她向海滩跑～. She ran towards the beach. **2** [used after a verb to indicate turning the side away from the speaker]: 她转过身去,望着大海. She turned back and looked at the sea. 把这一页翻～. Turn this page over. **3** [used after a verb to indicate loss of consciousness]: 她晕～了. She has fainted. **4** through: 这儿人太多,我挤不～. It's too crowded here, I can't get through. 大家都知道他,他骗不～. People know him too well to be kidded.

过人 guòrén (形) surpass; excel: 才华～ be outstanding in talent. ～的记忆力 remarkable memory

过日子 guòrìzi live; get along: 勤俭～ live a frugal life

过甚 guòshèn (动) exaggerate: ～其词 overstate the case

过剩 guòshèng (动) excess; surplus: 生产～ overproduction

过失 guòshī (名) fault; error; slip

过时(時) guòshí (形) out-of-date; outmoded; out of fashion: 这是～的说法. This is a dated expression.

过头(頭) guòtóu (形) go beyond the limit; overdo: 他的话说～了. He has gone too far in his statement. 聪明～ be too clever by half

G

过问 guòwèn (动) take an interest in; concern oneself with; bother about: 亲自～ look into a matter personally

过夜 guòyè (动) spend the night; stay overnight; put up for the night

过意不去 guòyì bùqù feel sorry; feel apologetic: 这事给你添了不少麻烦,真～. I'm very sorry to have put you to so much trouble.

过瘾(癮) guòyǐn (形) satisfy a craving; enjoy oneself to the full; do sth. to one's heart's content: 今天晚上玩得真～. I had an absolutely wonderful time tonight.

过硬 guòyìng (形) have a perfect mastery of sth.; be truly proficient in sth.: 他的技术还不～. His technique (or skill) is still far from perfect.

过于(於) guòyú (副) too; unduly; excessively: ～劳累 overtired. ～谨慎 be overcautious

过(過) guo (助) 1 [expressing the completion of action]: 我吃～午饭就去. I'll go right after lunch. 房间已经打扫～. The room has been cleaned. 2 [indicating completion of action as an experience]: 我读～这本书. I have read this book. 你去～伦敦吗? Have you been to London? 他以前当～兵. He was once a soldier. 她从来没生～病. She has never been ill. 天气从来没有这么冷～. It has never been so cold.

过磅 guòbàng (动) weigh (on the scales)

过不去 guòbuqù 1 cannot get through: 路太窄,车子～. The road is too narrow for the car to get through. 2 find fault with; be hard on: 别老是跟我～. Don't always try to find fault with me. 3 feel apologetic: 叫你等了这半天,我心里真～. I'm awfully sorry to have kept you waiting so long. 面子上～ feel ashamed or disgraced

H h

哈 hā I (动) breathe out (with the mouth open) II (象): ～～大笑 laugh heartily; roar with laughter III (叹) [expressing complacency or satisfaction]: ～～,我猜着了. Aha, I've got (or guessed) it. ～～,这回可输给我了. Aha, you've lost to me for once.

哈欠 hāqian (名) yawn: 打～ give a yawn

哈腰 hāyāo (动)〈口〉1 bend one's back; stoop 2 bow: 点头～ bow and scrape

蛤 há

see also gé

蛤蟆 háma (名) 1 frog 2 toad

嗨 hāi

嗨哟 hāiyō (叹) heave ho; yo-heave-ho; yo-ho

咳 hāi (叹) [expressing regret or surprise]: ～,我怎么这样糊涂! Dammit! How stupid I was!

see also ké

骸 hái (名) 1 bones of the body; skeleton 2 body: 形～ the human body. 遗～ (dead) body; corpse; remains

骸骨 háigǔ (名) human bones; skeleton

孩 hái (名) child: 小女～儿 a little girl

孩提 háití (名)〈书〉early childhood

孩子 háizi (名) 1 child: 男～ boy. 女～ girl 2 son or daughter; children: 她有两个～. She has two children.

孩子气(氣) háiziqì (形) childish: 他越来越～了. He is getting more childish than ever.

还(還) hái (副) 1 still; yet: ～有一些具体细节要安排. Some details have yet to be worked out. 2 even more; still more: 今天比昨天～冷. It's even colder today than yesterday. 3 also; too; in addition: 他们参观了这所学校,～参观了工厂和医院. They visited some factories, hospitals as well as the school. 4 rather; fairly: 屋子收拾的倒～干净. The room is kept quite clean and tidy. 5 even: 你跑那么快～赶不上他,何况我呢? If a good runner like you can't catch up with him, how can I? 6 [used for emphasis]: 那～用说! That goes without saying. 7 [indicating that sth. quite unexpected has happened]: 他～真有办法. He really is resourceful.

see also huán

还是 háishì I (副) 1 still; nevertheless; all the same: 尽管下雨,运动会～照常进行. The sports meet went on as planned despite the rain. 2 had better: 你～戒烟吧,吸烟对身体不好. You had better quit smoking. It's harmful to your health. II (连) or: 你是去加拿大,~去美国? Are you going to Canada or the United States? III [indicating that sth. unexpected has happened]: 我没想到这事儿~真难办. I didn't realize that the matter was so difficult to handle.

海 hǎi I (名) 1 sea or big lake 2 a great number of people or things coming together: 人~ a sea of people; crowds of people. 林~ a vast stretch of forest II (形) extra large; of great capacity

海岸 hǎi'àn (名) seacoast; coast; seashore: ~线 coastline

海拔 hǎibá (名) height above sea level; elevation: ~四千米 4,000 metres above sea level; with an elevation of 4,000 metres

海报(報) hǎibào (名) playbill; poster

海滨(濱) hǎibīn (名) seashore; seaside: ~胜地 seaside resort

海产(產) hǎichǎn (名) marine products

海带(帶) hǎidài (名) seaweed; kelp

海岛 hǎidǎo (名) island

海盗 hǎidào (名) pirate; sea rover: ~船 pirate ship. ~行为 piracy

海底 hǎidǐ (名) the bottom of the sea; seabed; sea floor: ~捞月 engage in an impossibly difficult undertaking; a forlorn hope. ~捞针 look for a needle in a haystack. ~油田 offshore oilfield. ~资源 seabed resources; submarine resources. ~电缆 submarine cable

海港 hǎigǎng (名) seaport; harbour: ~设备 harbour installations

海关(關) hǎiguān (名) customs house; customs: ~人员 customs officer. ~手续 customs formalities

海归 hǎiguī (名) people returning to their country after finishing their overseas education; overseas educated

海疆 hǎijiāng (名) coastal areas and territorial seas

海角 hǎijiǎo (名) cape; promontory: 天涯~ the four corners of the earth; (to) the end of the earth

海军 hǎijūn (名) navy: ~基地 naval base

海口 hǎikǒu (名) 1 seaport 2 [often used in conjunction with 夸]: 夸~ make a wild boast

海枯石烂(爛) hǎikū-shílàn (even if) the seas run dry and the rocks crumble

海阔天空 hǎikuò-tiānkōng as boundless as the sea and sky; unrestrained and far-ranging: ~地聊个没完 chat about everything under heaven with great gusto

海量 hǎiliàng (名) 1 〈敬〉 magnanimity 2 huge capacity for alcoholic drinks

海轮(輪) hǎilún (名) seagoing (or ocean-going) vessel

海米 hǎimǐ (名) dried shrimps

海绵 hǎimián (名) 1 sponge 2 foam rubber

海内 hǎinèi (名) within the four seas; throughout the country

海鸥(鷗) hǎi'ōu (名) seagull

海上 hǎishàng (名) at sea; on the sea: ~作业 operation on the sea. ~运输 maritime transportation

海参(參) hǎishēn (名) sea slug; sea cucumber; trepang

海市蜃楼(樓) hǎishì shènlóu mirage

海誓山盟 hǎishì-shānméng (make) swear an oath of eternal fidelity; vow eternal love

海滩(灘) hǎitān (名) seashore; beach

海豚 hǎitún (名) dolphin

海外 hǎiwài (名) overseas; abroad: ~华侨 overseas Chinese

海湾(灣) hǎiwān (名) bay; gulf

海味 hǎiwèi (名) choice seafood

海峡(峽) hǎixiá (名) strait; channel: 台湾~ the Taiwan Straits

海鲜 hǎixiān (名) seafood

海啸(嘯) hǎixiào (名) tsunami; tidal wave

海燕 hǎiyàn (名) petrel

海洋 hǎiyáng (名) seas and oceans; ocean: ~性气候 maritime (or marine) climate. ~资源 marine resources

海域 hǎiyù (名) sea area; maritime space

海员 hǎiyuán (名) seaman; sailor: ~俱乐部 seamen's club

海运(運) hǎiyùn (名) sea transportation; ocean shipping

海蜇 hǎizhé (名) jellyfish

害 hài I (名) evil; harm; calamity: 灾~ calamity; disaster. 两~相权取其轻 of the two evils choose the lesser II (形) harmful; destructive; injurious: ~鸟 harmful bird III (动) 1 do harm to; impair; cause trouble to: ~人不浅 do people great harm 2 kill; murder: 遇~ be murdered or assassinated 3 contract (an illness); suffer from: ~了一场大病 fall gravely ill 4 feel: ~羞 feel ashamed

害病 hàibìng (动) fall ill

害虫(蟲) hàichóng (名) injurious insect; pest

害处(處) hàichù (名) harm: ~多,好处少 do more harm than good

H

害怕 hàipà (动) fear; be afraid; be scared: 他们什么也不～. They have nothing to fear.

害群之马(馬) hài qún zhī mǎ one who brings disgrace on or constitutes a danger to his group; a rotten apple in the barrel

害臊 hàisào (形)〈口〉 feel ashamed; be bashful

害羞 hàixiū (形) be bashful; be shy: 她有些～. She was a bit shy.

骇 hài (动) be astonished; be shocked

骇人听(聽)闻 hài rén tīngwén shocking; appalling

骇异(異) hàiyì (形) be shocked; be astonished

H

鼾 hān (动) snore: ～声 snore

憨 hān (形) 1 foolish; silly: ～痴 idiotic 2 naive; honest

憨厚 hānhòu (形) honest and good-natured

憨直 hānzhí (形) frank and straightforward

酣 hān (形) (drink, etc.) to one's heart's content: ～饮 drink one's fill. ～歌 lusty singing

酣畅(暢) hānchàng (形) grow merry on wine; be sound asleep

酣睡 hānshuì (动) sleep soundly; be fast asleep

寒 hán (形) 1 cold: ～风刺骨. The cold wind cut one to the marrow. 他受了点～. He caught a chill. 2 afraid; fearful: 胆～ be terrified 3 poor; needy: 贫～ impoverished

寒潮 háncháo (名) cold wave

寒带(帶) hándài (名) frigid zone

寒噤 hánjìn (动) tremble (with cold or fear): 使人打～ send shivers down one's spine

寒冷 hánlěng (形) cold; icy

寒流 hánliú (名) cold current

寒舍 hánshè (名)〈谦〉 my humble home

寒暑表 hánshǔbiǎo (名) thermometer

寒酸 hánsuān (形) (of a poor intellectual in the old days) humble and shabby; unmannerly and acerbic

寒微 hánwēi (形)〈书〉 of low station: 出身～ of humble origin

寒心 hánxīn (形) bitterly disappointed

寒暄 hánxuān (动) exchange greetings

寒意 hányì (名) a nip (or chill) in the air

寒战(戰) hánzhàn (名) (also "寒颤") shiver

含 hán (动) 1 keep in the mouth: ～一口水 hold some water in the mouth. 2 contain: ～着眼泪 fill with tears 3 nurse; suggest: ～恨 nurse grievances. 她脸上～怒. Her expression suggested anger.

含苞 hánbāo (动)〈书〉 be budding: ～待放 be in bud

含垢忍辱 hángòu-rěnrǔ endure contempt and insults

含糊 hánhu (形) 1 ambiguous; vague: ～不清 equivocal. ～其词 talk evasively 2 careless; perfunctory: 这事一点儿也不能～. This matter should be handled with great care.

含混 hánhùn (形) equivocal; evasive: 言词～,令人费解. The wording is too ambiguous to be readily intelligible.

含金量 hánjīnliàng (名) gold content: ～很高的品牌 a very worthy brand

含沙射影 hán shā shè yǐng attack sb. by innuendo; make insinuating remarks

含笑 hánxiào (动) have a smile on one's face: ～点头 nod with a smile

含辛茹苦 hánxīn-rúkǔ suffer hardships and privations

含蓄 hánxù I (动) contain; embody II (形) 1 implicit; veiled: ～的批评 veiled criticism 2 reserved

含义(義) hányì (名) meaning; implication: 这句话的～不是很清楚. The implication of this remark is far from explicit.

含冤 hányuān (动) suffer a gross injustice

函 hán (名) letter: 公～ official letter. 复～ a reply

函购(購) hángòu (动) purchase by mail; mail order: ～部 mail-order department

函件 hánjiàn (名) letters; correspondence

函授 hánshòu (动) teach by correspondence; give a correspondence course: ～学校 correspondence school

涵 hán I (动) contain II (名) culvert: 桥～ bridges and culverts

涵洞 hándòng (名) culvert

涵盖(蓋) hángài (动) include; cover: ～面很广 cover a wide range of areas

涵养(養) hányǎng (名) ability to control oneself; self-restraint: 他很有～. He never allows himself to be provoked.

罕 hǎn (形) rarely; seldom: ～见 rare. ～闻 seldom heard of. 人迹～至 show little trace of human habitation

喊 hǎn (动) 1 shout; cry out; yell: ~口号 shout slogans. 贼~捉贼 thief shouting "Stop thief!" 2 call (a person): 请~他一声. Give him a yell, please.

喊叫 hǎnjiào (动) shout; cry out

汗 hàn (名) sweat; perspiration: 出~ sweat; perspire. ~流浃背 streaming with sweat; soaked with sweat

汗马(馬)功劳(勞) hàn mǎ gōngláo 1 distinctions won on the battlefield; war exploits 2 one's notable achievements in any discipline or project or any kind of constructive work

汗毛 hànmáo (名) fine hair on the human body

汗衫 hànshān (名) undershirt; T-shirt

汗水 hànshuǐ (名) sweat

汗颜 hànyán 〈书〉 blush with shame

旱 hàn (名) 1 dry spell; drought: 抗~ combat drought. 久~逢甘雨. A soothing rain falls on the parched earth. 2 dryland: ~稻 dry rice 3 on land: ~路 overland route (as opposed to waterway)

旱冰场(場) hàn bīngchǎng (名) roller-skating rink

旱季 hànjì (名) dry season

旱情 hànqíng (名) drought; damage caused by a drought

旱灾(災) hànzāi (名) drought

悍 hàn (形) 1 brave; bold: 一员~将 a brave general 2 intrepid; ferocious: 凶~ fierce and intrepid; ferocious

悍然 hànrán (副) outrageously; brazenly; flagrantly; without any scruples: ~入侵 outrageously invade

焊 hàn (动) weld; solder: 气~ gas welding

焊接 hànjiē (名) welding; soldering

捍 hàn (动) defend; guard

捍卫(衛) hànwèi (动) defend; guard; protect: ~国家主权 uphold state sovereignty. ~民族利益 protect national interests

汉(漢) hàn (名) 1 the Han nationality 2 Chinese (language) 3 man: 好~ true man; hero

汉奸 hànjiān (名) traitor (to China): ~卖国贼 traitor and collaborator; quisling

汉人 Hànrén (名) the Hans; the Han people

汉学(學) Hànxué (名) 1 the Han school of classical philology 2 Sinology: ~家 Sinologist

汉语 hànyǔ (名) Chinese (language): ~拼音字母 the Chinese phonetic alphabet

汉字 Hànzì (名) Chinese character: 简化~ simplified Chinese characters

汉族 Hànzú (名) the Han nationality, China's main nationality

翰 hàn(名)〈书〉 writing brush: 挥~ write (a poem, a letter, etc. with a brush)

翰墨 hànmò (名)〈书〉 brush and ink—writing, painting, or calligraphy

瀚 hàn (形)〈书〉 vast: 浩~ vast; immense

憾 hàn (名) regret: 引以为~ consider it a matter for regret

撼 hàn (动) shake: 摇~ shake violently. 震~天地 shake the world

夯 hāng I (名) rammer; tamper II (动) ram; tamp; pound

吭 háng (名) throat: 引~高歌 sing lustily
see also kēng

航 háng I (名) boat; ship II (动) navigate (by water or air): ~线 air or shipping line; route. 夜~ night navigation. 首~ maiden voyage or flight

航班 hángbān (名) scheduled flight; flight number

航标(標) hángbiāo (名) navigation mark; buoy

航程 hángchéng (名) voyage; passage; distance travelled

航道 hángdào (名) channel; waterway; course: 主~ the main channel

航海 hánghǎi (名) navigation: ~日志 logbook; log

航空 hángkōng (名) aviation: 民用~ civil aviation. ~公司 airline company; airways. ~货运 airfreight. ~母舰 aircraft carrier. ~协定 air transport agreement. ~信 airmail letter; air letter; airmail

航路 hánglù (名) air or sea route: ~标志 route markings

航天 hángtiān (名) spaceflight: ~飞机 space shuttle. ~通信 space communication (SPACECOM). ~站 spaceport

航向 hángxiàng (名) course (of a ship or plane): 改变~ change course

航行 hángxíng (动) 1 navigate by water; sail: 内河~ inland navigation 2 navigate by air; fly: 空中~ aerial navigation

H

航运(運) hángyùn (名) shipping: ～公司 shipping company

行 háng I (名) 1 line; row: 排成两～ fall into two lines. 一路上杨柳成～. The roads are lined with willows. 2 trade; profession; line of business: 各～各业 all trades and professions; all walks of life. 改～ change one's profession; switch to a new profession 3 business firm: 银～ bank II (动) (of brothers and sisters) list according to seniority: 你～几? ——我～三. Where do you come among your brothers and sisters? — I'm the third. III (量) [for anything forming a line]: 一～树 a row of trees. 四～诗句 four lines of verse
see also xíng

H

行道 hángdào (名) trade; profession
行话 hánghuà (名) professional jargon; cant
行家 hángjia (名) expert; specialist
行列 hángliè (名) ranks: 参加革命～ join the ranks of the revolution
行情 hángqíng (名) quotations (on the market); prices: ～表 quotations list
行市 hángshi (名) quotations (on the market); prices
行业(業) hángyè (名) trade; profession; industry: 服务～ service trades

绗 háng (动) sew with long stitches: ～被子 sew on the quilt cover with long stitches

巷 hàng
see also xiàng
巷道 hàngdào (名) tunnel

豪 háo I (名) a person of outstanding talent: 文～ a literary giant II (形) 1 forthright; unrestrained: ～气 undaunted spirit 2 despotic; bullying: 土～ local despot. 巧取～夺 take away by force or fraud
豪放 háofàng (形) uninhibited: ～不羁 unconventional and uninhibited
豪富 háofù I (形) powerful and wealthy II (名) powerful and wealthy people
豪华(華) háohuá (形) luxurious; sumptuous: ～的饭店 a luxury hotel. ～版 a de luxe edition
豪杰(傑) háojié (名) person of outstanding talent; hero
豪举(舉) háojǔ (名) 1 a bold move 2 a munificent act
豪迈(邁) háomài (形) bold; heroic: ～的气概 heroic spirit
豪门(門) háomén (名) rich and powerful family; wealthy and influential clan
豪气(氣) háoqì (名) heroism; heroic spirit
豪强 háoqiáng I (形) despotic; tyrannical II (名) despot; bully
豪情 háoqíng (名) lofty sentiments: ～壮志 lofty sentiments and aspirations
豪爽 háoshuǎng (形) outspoken and straightforward
豪兴(興) háoxìng (名) ebullient high spirits; exhilaration; keen interest
豪言壮(壯)语 háoyán-zhuàngyǔ brave words; proud remarks
豪宅 háozhái (名) luxury house

壕 háo (名) 1 moat 2 trench: 掘～ dig trenches; dig in. 防空～ air-raid dugout
壕沟(溝) háogōu (名) 1 trench 2 ditch

嚎 háo (动) howl; wail
嚎啕 háotáo (动) cry loudly; wail

毫 háo I (名) 1 fine long hair: 羊～笔 a writing brush made of goat's hair 2 writing brush 3 milli-: ～米 millimetre. ～升 millilitre II (副) [used in the negative] in the least; at all: ～不犹豫 without the slightest hesitation. ～无诚意 without the least sincerity. ～无二致 without any noticeable difference
毫厘 háolí (名) the least bit; an iota: ～不差 without the slightest error; perfectly accurate
毫毛 háomáo (名) [often used figuratively] soft hair on the body: 不准你动他一根～. You are not allowed to do the least harm to him.

蚝(蠔) háo (名) oyster: ～油 oyster sauce

号(號) háo (动) 1 howl; roar: 北风怒～. A north wind is howling. 2 wail; cry piteously
see also hào
号啕 háotáo (动) cry loudly: ～大哭 wail bitterly

嗥(嘷) háo (动) (of a jackal or wolf) howl

好 hǎo I (形) 1 good; fine; nice: ～天气 nice weather. ～脾气 good-natured. 这本小说很～. This is an excellent novel. 这话说得太～了. This is a very apt remark. 你还是别答应～. You'd better make no promise. 2 be in good health; get well: 他身体一直很～. He's been in good health. 他的病～了. He's recovered from his illness. **3** friendly; kind: ～朋友 good friend **4** [as a polite formula]: 你～! Hello! ～睡! Good night! **5** [used after a verb to indicate the completion of an action]: 计划定～了. The plan's been drawn up. 坐～吧, 要开会了. Please be seated. The meeting is going to begin. **6** [indicating praise, approval or dissatisfaction]: ～, 就这么办. OK, it's settled. ～了, 不要再说了. All right, let's leave it at that. II (副) **1** [used before a verb to indicate that sth. is easy]: 这问题～解决. The problem can be easily solved. 那篇文章～懂. That essay is easy to read. **2** [used before 多, 久, 长, etc.] a good many: ～久 quite long. 他学了～几年英语. He's been learning English for quite a few years. **3** [used before certain adjectives to indicate high degree]: ～深的一条河! What a deep river! 街上～热闹! What a busy street! 你这个人～糊涂! You are such a fool! 前些日子我～忙了一阵. I was quite busy some time ago. **4** [used to introduce a purpose]: 你留个电话, 有事我～跟你联系. Give me your telephone number so that I can contact you when necessary. 别忘了带伞, 下雨～用. Don't forget to take your umbrella in case it rains. III (名) **1** [indicating acclamation]: 观众连声叫～. The audience broke into loud cheers. **2** [indicating a greeting]: 向你的父母问～. Give my love to your parents. 你去见着他, 别忘了给我捎个～儿. Don't forget to convey my regards, when you see him.

see also hào

好办(辦) hǎobàn (形) easy to do: 这事～. That's easy.

好比 hǎobǐ (动) can be compared to; like: 军民关系～鱼和水的关系. The people are to the army what water is to fish.

好吃 hǎochī (形) nice; delicious

好处(處) hǎochù (名) **1** benefit; advantage: 对我们都有～ be of benefit to us all. 这对你们有～. It will do you good. **2** gain; profit: 没有人会从中得到～. Nobody will profit from it.

好歹 hǎodǎi I (名) **1** what's good and what's bad: 不知～ unable to appreciate a favour **2** most unfortunate happening [usually referring to sb.'s death]: 万一她有个～, 这可怎么办? What if something should happen to her? II (副) in any case; whatever: 她要是在这里, ～也能拿个主意. If she were here, she would give us a word of advice in any case.

好多 hǎoduō (形)〈口〉 a good many; a good deal; a lot of

好感 hǎogǎn (名) good impression: 对他有～ have a soft spot for him

好汉(漢) hǎohàn (名) brave man; true man; hero

好好儿(兒) hǎohāor (副) **1** in a proper way; when every thing is in order: ～地照顾他 take good care of him **2** to one's heart's content; to the best of one's ability: 咱们～聊一聊. Let's have a good chat.

好话 hǎohuà (名) **1** a good word: 给他说句～ put in a good word for him **2** word of praise: 爱听～ be fond of praise

好家伙 hǎojiāhuo my goodness; good heavens: ～, 这真贵呀! My goodness, it's really expensive.

好看 hǎokàn (形) **1** fine; nice **2** interesting: 这本小说很～. This novel is very interesting. **3** honoured; proud: 儿子得了金牌, 我的脸上也～. I'm proud of my son who has won a gold medal. **4** in an embarrassing situation: 让我上台表演, 这不是要我～吗? You're putting me on the spot if you want me to perform on the stage.

好评 hǎopíng (名) favourable comment; high opinion: 这部小说博得读者的～. This novel was well received by the reading public.

好容易 hǎoróngyì (副) not without great difficulty: 他们～才找到我这儿. They had no small difficulty finding my place. (also as "好不容易")

好商量 hǎoshāngliang can be settled through discussion

好使 hǎoshǐ (形) be convenient to use; work well: 这台机器～. This machine works well.

好事多磨 hǎoshì duō mó the road to happiness is strewn with setbacks

好似 hǎosì (动) seem; be like: ～秋风扫落叶 like the autumn wind scuttling fallen leaves

好听(聽) hǎotīng (形) pleasing to the ear: ～的话 fine words. 这支歌～. This is a

H

very pleasant song.

好玩儿(兒) hǎowánr (形) interesting; amusing

好像 hǎoxiàng (动) seem; be like: ～要下雨. It looks like rain. 到这儿就～到了自己家一样. You'll feel as if you were at home while here. 他今天～不怎么舒服. It seems that he is not quite himself today.

好笑 hǎoxiào (形) laughable; funny; ridiculous: 这有什么～的? What's so funny?

好心 hǎoxīn (名) good intention: 一片～ with the best of intentions

好意 hǎoyì (名) good intention; kindness: 谢谢您的～. Thank you for your kindness. 不怀～ harbour ulterior motives

好意思 hǎoyìsi have the cheek: 亏他～说出这种话来! He had even the cheek to say such things!

好转(轉) hǎozhuǎn (动) turn for the better; improve: 形势～. The situation took a favourable turn.

耗 hào I (动) 1 consume; cost: ～费时间的工作 a time-consuming job 2 waste time; dawdle: 别～着了, 快走吧. Stop dawdling and get going. II (名) bad news: 噩～ the passing away (of a friend or a relative or someone we love and respect)

耗费 hàofèi (动) consume; expend: ～人力物力 spend both manpower and material resources. 他们在这项工程上～了大量金钱. They spent a great amount of money on the project.

耗竭 hàojié (动) exhaust; use up: 资源～ be drained of natural resources

耗子 hàozi (名) rat: ～药 ratsbane

号(號) hào (名) 1 name: 国～ the name of a dynasty. 绰～ nickname 2 alias; assumed name; alternative name 3 business house: 银～ banking house. 分～ branch (of a firm, etc.) 4 mark; sign; signal: 问～ question mark. 击掌为～ clap as a signal 5 number: 五～楼 Building No. 5. 编～ serial number 6 size: 大(中、小)～ large (medium, small) size: 你要几～的鞋? What size shoe would you like? 7 date: 今天几～? ——十三～. What date is it today? — The 13th. 8 order: 发～施令 issue orders 9 any brass wind instrument: 军～ bugle. 小～ trumpet 10 anything used as a horn: 螺～ conch-shell trumpet; conch 11 bugle call; any call made on a bugle: 熄灯～ the lights-out. 吹起床～ sound the reveille

see also háo

号称(稱) hàochēng (动) 1 be known as: 四川～天府之国. Sichuan is known as a land of plenty. 2 claim to be: 敌人的这个师～一万二千人. The enemy division claimed to be twelve thousand strong.

号角 hàojiǎo (名) 1 bugle; horn 2 bugle call

号令 hàolìng (动) command; order: ～三军 issue orders to the three armed services

号码 hàomǎ (名) number: 电话～ telephone number

号外 hàowài (名) extra (of a newspaper)

号召 hàozhào (名) call; appeal

浩 hào (形) great; vast; grand

浩大 hàodà (形) very great; huge; vast: 工程～. It's a project of great magnitude.

浩荡(蕩) hàodàng (形) vast and mighty: ～的长江 the mighty Changjiang (Yangtse) River

浩瀚 hàohàn (形) vast; immense: ～的沙漠 a vast expanse of desert

浩劫 hàojié (名) disaster; calamity; catastrophe

浩气(氣) hàoqì (名) noble spirit: ～长存. Imperishable is the noble spirit.

浩如烟海 hào rú yānhǎi (of data, etc.) vast in scope like the boundless sea

皓 hào (形) 1 white: ～首 hoary head 2 bright; luminous: ～月当空. A bright moon hung in the sky.

好 hào (动) 1 like; love; be fond of: ～学 eager to learn. ～管闲事 be meddlesome or nosy 2 be liable to: ～伤风 easily catch cold. ～发脾气 apt to lose one's temper

see also hǎo

好吃懒做 hàochī-lǎnzuò be fond of food but averse to work

好大喜功 hàodà-xǐgōng have a passion for the grandiose; crave for grandeur and success

好高骛远(遠) hàogāo-wùyuǎn aim too high

好客 hàokè (形) be hospitable

好奇 hàoqí (形) be curious: ～心 curiosity

好强 hàoqiáng (形) eager to put one's best foot forward

好色 hàosè (动) be driven by lust: ～之徒

lecher; libertine; womanizer

好胜(勝) hàoshèng (形) eager to excel in everything

好事 hàoshì (形) meddlesome: ～之徒 busybody; mischief-maker

好恶(惡) hào-wù (名) likes and dislikes

好逸恶(惡)劳(勞) hàoyì-wùláo love ease and comfort but hate to work

好战(戰) hàozhàn (形) warlike: ～分子 hawkish elements; warmongers

诃 hē (动) scold

呵 hē (动) 1 breathe out (with the mouth open): ～一口气 breathe out; exhale 2 scold: ～责 scold sb. severely; give sb. a dressing down

呵斥 hēchì (动) berate; excoriate

呵呵 hēhē (象) guffaw: ～大笑 laugh heartily; roar with laughter; guffaw

呵护 hēhù (动) care; take care; look after

嗬 hē (叹) [expressing astonishment] ah; oh: ～, 真了不得! Oh, it's really terrific!

喝 hē (动) 1 drink: ～茶 drink tea. ～酒 drink wine 2 drink alcoholic liquor: 爱～ like drinking. ～醉了 be drunk

see also hè

涸 hé (动)〈书〉dry up

核 hé I (名) 1 pit; stone: 桃～ peach-pit; peach-stone. 无～水果 stoneless fruit 2 nucleus: 原子～ atomic nucleus II (动) examine; check: ～准 approve; ratify

see also hú

核查 héchá (动) check; examine and verify

核弹(彈)头(頭) hédàntóu (名) nuclear warhead

核电(電)站 hédiànzhàn (名) nuclear power station

核定 hédìng (动) check and ratify; appraise and decide

核对(對) héduì (动) check: ～数字 check figures. ～事实 check the facts

核讹诈 hé'ézhà (名) nuclear blackmail

核计 héjì (动) assess; calculate

核能 hénéng (名) nuclear energy

核实(實) héshí (动) verify; check: ～的产量 verified output

核算 hésuàn (名) business accounting: 成本～ cost accounting

核桃 hétao (名) walnut

核武器 héwǔqì (名) nuclear weapon

核心 héxīn (名) nucleus; core; kernel; the heart of the matter: ～力量 force at the core. ～人物 key person; key figure

劾 hé (动) expose sb.'s misdeeds or crimes: 弹～ impeach

河 hé (名) river

河岸 hé'àn (名) river bank

河床(牀) héchuáng (名) riverbed

河谷 hégǔ (名) river valley

河流 héliú (名) rivers: ～沉积 fluvial (or fluviatile) deposit

河渠 héqú (名) rivers and canals; waterways

河山 héshān (名) rivers and mountains; land; territory: 锦绣～ the beautiful land of one's country

河套 hétào (名) the bend of a river

河豚 hétún (名) globefish; balloonfish; puffer

河网(網) héwǎng (名) a network of waterways

何 hé〈书〉1 [denoting interrogation]: ～人 who. ～时 what time; when. ～处 what place; where 2 [often used in rhetorical questions]: 谈～容易 Could it be that easy? 有～不可? What's wrong with it?

何必 hébì (副) there is no need; why: 既然不会下雨, ～带伞. Why take the umbrella with you if it is not going to rain?

何不 hébù (副) why not: 既然有事, ～早说? Since you have a previous engagement, why didn't you say so?

何尝(嘗) hécháng (副) [used in a negative sentence, often in the form of a question]: 我～不想去, 只是没工夫罢了. Not that I have no inclination to go; I just haven't got the time.

何等 héděng I (形) what kind: 你知道他是～人物? Have you any idea what sort of person he is? II (副) [used in an exclamatory sentence to indicate sth. extraordinary]: 这是～巧妙的技术! What superb skill!

何妨 héfáng (副) why not; might as well: ～试试? Why not have a try?

何苦 hékǔ (副) why bother; is it worth the trouble: 你～在这些小事上伤脑筋? Why bother about such trifles?

何况 hékuàng (连) much less; let alone: 他

在生人面前都不习惯讲话，～要到大庭广众之中. He is not used to talking with a stranger, let alone before a big audience.

何其 héqí（副）[indicating disagreement] how; what: ～糊涂! How silly!

何去何从(從) héqù-hécóng what course to follow: ～，速作抉择. You must quickly decide for yourselves what course to take.

何如 hérú（代）how about: 请试验一下～? You'll try it out first, won't you?

何谓 héwèi（动）〈书〉what is meant by: ～幸福? What does happiness mean?

何许 héxǔ（代）〈书〉where; what kind of: 他是～人? Where is he from? *or* What sort of person is he?

H

何以 héyǐ〈书〉I（动）how: ～教我? How would you advise me? II（代）why: ～变卦? Why all this sudden change?

何在 hézài（动）where: 理由～? For what reason?

何止 hézhǐ（副）far more than: 例子～这些. These are merely a few instances.

荷 hé（名）lotus

see also hè

荷包 hébāo（名）1 small bag (for carrying money and odds and ends); pouch 2 pocket (in a garment)

荷包蛋 hébāodàn（名）1 poached eggs 2 fried eggs

荷尔蒙 hé'ěrméng（名）hormone

荷花 héhuā（名）lotus

合 hé（动）1 close; shut: 把书～上 close a book. 她听到这个消息笑得～不拢嘴来. She grinned from ear to ear at the good news. 2 join; combine; ～力 make a joint effort 3 suit; agree: 正～我意. That exactly falls in with what I have in mind. 4 be equal to; add up to: 一公顷～十五市亩. A hectare is equal to 15 *mu*.

合办(辦) hébàn（动）jointly run

合璧 hébì（动）(of two different things) combine harmoniously; match well

合并(併) hébìng（动）combine: 这三个提议可以合并以便讨论. These three proposals can be combined to facilitate discussion.

合唱 héchàng（名）chorus: ～团 chorus

合成 héchéng（动）compose; compound: 由重要原料～ be compounded of important raw materials. ～洗涤剂 synthetic detergent. ～纤维 synthetic fibre

合法 héfǎ（形）legal; lawful; legitimate; rightful: ～地位 legal status. ～手段 legitimate means

合格 hégé（形）qualified; up to standard: ～的教师 a qualified teacher. 质量检查～ quality checked

合乎 héhū（动）conform with (or to); correspond to; accord with; tally with: ～规律 conform to the laws. ～要求 measure up to the requirement

合伙 héhuǒ（动）form a partnership: ～经营 go in for a joint venture. ～人 partner

合计 héjì（动）amount to; add up to; total

合计 héji（动）1 think over; figure out: 他一天到晚心里老～这件事. He thought the matter over and over all day. 2 consult: 大家～～这个问题该怎么处理. Let's put our heads together and decide how the problem is to be tackled.

合金 héjīn（名）alloy: ～钢 alloy steel

合理 hélǐ（形）rational; reasonable; equitable: ～使用 rational utilization. 他说的话很～. What he says is very reasonable.

合理化 hélǐhuà（动、名）rationalize; rationalization: ～建议 rationalization proposal

合力 hélì（动）make a concerted effort

合龙(龍) hélóng（动）1 closure (of a dam, dyke, etc.) 2 join the two sections of a bridge, etc.

合谋 hémóu I（动）conspire; plot together II（名）conspiracy

合拍 hépāi（动）in time; in step; in harmony: 与时代～ in step with the times

合情合理 héqíng hélǐ fair and reasonable

合群 héqún（形）get on well with others; sociable

合身 héshēn（形）fit: 这件上衣很～. This jacket fits well.

合适(適) héshì（形）suitable; appropriate; becoming; right: 这个字用在这里不～. This is not the proper word to use here.

合算 hésuàn（形）paying; worthwhile

合同 hétóng（名）contract: 签订～ sign a contract. 撕毁～ tear up a contract. ～工 contract worker

合意 héyì（动）suit; be to one's liking (or taste)

合营(營) héyíng（动）jointly operate; cooperatively manage

合影 héyǐng I (名) group photo (or picture) II (动) have a group photo taken: ~留念 have a group photo taken to mark the occasion

合资 hézī (动) pool capital; enter into partnership: ~企业 joint venture

合奏 hézòu (名) instrumental ensemble

合作 hézuò (动) cooperate; collaborate; work together: 互相~ cooperate with each other. ~经济 cooperative economy; cooperative sector of the economy. ~社 cooperative; co-op

颌 hé (名)〈书〉jaw: 上(下)~ the upper (lower) jaw

盒 hé (名) box; case: 一~火柴 a box of matches. 铅笔~ pencil case; pencil box

禾 hé (名) standing grain (esp. rice)

禾苗 hémiáo (名) seedlings of cereal crops

和 hé I (形) **1** gentle; mild; kind **2** harmonious; on good terms: ~睦相处 be on friendly terms II (名) **1** peace: 讲~ make peace **2** sum: 两数之~ the sum of the two numbers III (动) draw; tie: 那盘棋~了. The game of chess ended in a draw. IV (介) [denoting relations, comparison, etc.]: ~这件事没有关系 have nothing to do with the matter. 他~我一样高. He's as tall as I. V (连) and: 你~我 you and I
see also hè; huó

和蔼 hé'ǎi (形) kindly; good-natured: ~可亲 amiable

和畅(暢) héchàng (形) (of a wind) gentle: 春风~. The spring wind is gentle and caressing.

和风(風) héfēng (名) soft breeze: ~细雨 like a gentle breeze and light rain—in a gentle and mild way

和好 héhǎo (动) become reconciled: ~如初 be on good terms as ever; restore good relations

和缓 héhuǎn I (形) gentle; mild: 语气~ speak in mild terms II (动) ease up; relax: ~一下气氛 relax the tense atmosphere

和解 héjiě (动) become reconciled

和局 héjú (名) drawn game; draw; tie

和睦 hémù (形) harmonious; amicable: 保持~关系 maintain amicable relations

和暖 hénuǎn (形) pleasantly warm; genial: 天气~. The weather is getting warm.

和盘(盤)托出 hé pán tuōchū reveal the whole truth; make a clean breast of sth.

和平 hépíng I (名) peace: 保卫世界~ safeguard world peace. ~共处 peaceful coexistence. ~演变 peaceful evolution II (形) mild: 中药药性~. Chinese herbal medicine is mild.

和气(氣) héqì I (形) gentle; kind; polite; good-natured II (名) harmonious relationship: 别为小事伤了~. Don't let this trifling matter affect our good relationship.

和善 héshàn (形) kind and gentle; amiable

和尚 héshàng (名) Buddhist monk

和声(聲) héshēng (名) harmony

和事老 héshìlǎo (名) peacemaker

和谈 hétán (名) peace talks

和谐 héxié (形) harmonious

和煦 héxù (形) pleasantly warm; genial

和颜悦色 héyán-yuèsè be kindly and genial

和约 héyuē (名) peace treaty

和衷共济(濟) hézhōng-gòngjì work with a concerted effort; act in concert with each other

鹤 hè (名) crane

鹤发(髮)童颜 hèfà-tóngyán white-haired but healthy-looking; hale and hearty

鹤立鸡(鷄)群 hè lì jīqún stand out most conspicuously among his peers

赫 hè I (形) conspicuous; grand: 显~ distinguished and influential; illustrious II (量) hertz: 千~ kilohertz. 兆~ megahertz

赫赫 hèhè (形) illustrious; very impressive: ~有名的人物 a person of great renown

赫然 hèrán (形) **1** impressively; awesomely **2** terribly (angry): ~而怒 get into a furious temper; fly into a rage

荷 hè I (动)〈书〉carry on one's shoulder or back II (名) burden; responsibility: 肩负重~ shoulder heavy responsibilities III [often used in letter writing] be granted a favour: 感~ feel grateful
see also hé

壑 hè (名) gully; big pool: 千山万~ an interminable range of mountains and valleys

吓(嚇) hè I (动) threaten; intimidate II (叹) [ex-

pressing annoyance]：～，怎么能这样呢？ My goodness, how could it be like that?
see also xià

褐 hè I (名) coarse cloth or clothing II (形) brown

褐煤 hèméi (名) brown coal lignite

喝 hè (动) shout loudly; yell：大～一声 give a loud shout
see also hē

喝彩 hècǎi (动) acclaim; cheer：齐声～ cheer in chorus

喝倒彩 hè dàocǎi make catcalls

和 hè (动) 1 join in the singing 2 compose a poem in reply to a friend, using the same rhyme sequence
see also hé; huó

H

贺 hè (动) congratulate：～词 speech (or message) of congratulation; congratulations; greetings. ～电 message of congratulation; congratulatory telegram. ～信 letter of congratulation

贺卡 hèkǎ (名) greeting card：生日～ birthday card. 新年～ New Year's card

贺年 hènián (动) extend New Year greetings：～片 New Year card

贺岁(歲)片 hèsuìpiàn (名) New Year's film

贺喜 hèxǐ (动) congratulate sb. on a happy occasion (e. g. a wedding, the birth of a child, etc.)

黑 hēi (形) 1 black：～板 blackboard 2 dark：天～了. It's getting dark. ～马 dark horse 3 secret; shady：～交易 shady deal 4 wicked; sinister：～心 evil-minded

黑暗 hēi'àn (形) dark：～的角落里 in a dark corner. 在～的旧社会 in the dark old society. ～时期 Dark Ages (in Europe)

黑白 hēi-bái (名) black and white; right and wrong：混淆～ confound black and white; confuse right and wrong

黑帮(幫) hēibāng (名) reactionary gang; sinister gang; cabal

黑话 hēihuà (名) (bandits') argot; (thieves') cant

黑金 hēijīn (名) black money

黑客 hēikè (名) hacker

黑名单(單) hēimíngdān (名) blacklist

黑幕 hēimù (名) inside story of a plot：揭穿～ expose a sinister plot

黑屏 hēipíng (名) black screen

黑人 hēirén (名) 1 Black people; Afro-American 2 a person who has no residence card

黑色幽默 hēisè yōumò black humour

黑哨 hēishào (名) "black whistle" (incorrect decision made by corrupt referee)

黑社会(會) hēishèhuì (名) the underworld

黑市 hēishì (名) black market

黑手党(黨) hēishǒudǎng (名) Mafia

黑匣子 hēixiázi (名) black box

黑箱操作 hēixiāng cāozuò "black case work"; dubious practices

黑压(壓)压 hēiyāyā (形) a dense or dark mass of：广场上～地站满了人. Masses of people crowded the square.

黑夜 hēiyè (名) night

黑油油 hēiyōuyōu (形) jet black; shiny black：～的头发 shiny black hair

嘿 hēi (叹) hey：～！快走吧！Hey, hurry up! ～，下雪了！Why, it's snowing!

痕 hén (名) mark; trace：刀～ a scar left by a knife-cut. 泪～ tear stains

痕迹 hénjì (名) mark; trace; vestige：旧日的～几乎完全消失了. The vestiges of bygone days have almost entirely disappeared.

很 hěn (副) very; quite; awfully：～高兴 very happy. ～满意 feel very pleased. ～有价值 be of great value

狠 hěn I (形) 1 ruthless; relentless：凶～ ferocious and ruthless 2 firm; resolute：～～的批评 severe criticism II (动) suppress (one's feelings); harden (the heart)：我～着心把泪止住. I made a terrific effort to refrain from tears.

狠毒 hěndú (形) vicious; venomous

狠心 hěnxīn I (形) cruel-hearted; heartless; merciless II (动) make a determined effort

恨 hèn (动) 1 hate：～之入骨 feel bitter hatred for sb. ～铁不成钢 be unusually strict with sb. and anxious to see him make instant progress 2 regret：遗～ eternal regret

亨 hēng (形) smooth

亨通 hēngtōng (形) smooth and prosperous：万事～. One is blessed with good fortune in everything. *or* Everything goes well.

哼 hēng (动) 1 groan; moan：痛得直～～ groan with pain 2 hum; croon:

～着曲子 hum a tune
see also hng

恒 héng I（形）1 permanent；lasting：永～ eternal；everlasting 2 usual；common；constant：～言 common saying II（名）perseverance：持之以～ go on with perseverance

恒温 héngwēn（名）constant temperature

恒心 héngxīn（名）perseverance；constancy：她这人有志气，有～. She is ambitious and tenacious of purpose.

恒星 héngxīng（名）(fixed) star

横 héng（形）1 horizontal；transverse：～梁 horizontal beam. 纵～ vertical and horizontal 2 across；sideways：～写 write words sideways. 一队飞机～过我们的头顶. A squadron of planes flew past overhead. 3 move crosswise；traverse：这条铁路～贯五省. The railway traverses five provinces. 4 unrestrainedly；turbulently：老泪～流. Tears streamed down one's old cheeks. 5 violently；fiercely；flagrantly：～加阻挠 wilfully obstruct. ～冲直撞 dash around madly；run amok
see also hèng

横跨 héngkuà（动）stretch over or across

横切 héngqiē（动）crosscut

横扫(掃) héngsǎo（动）sweep across；sweep away

横生 héngshēng（动）1 grow wild：荆棘～ be overgrown with brambles 2 be overflowing with；be full of：妙趣～ brim with wit and humour

横竖(豎) héngshù（副）〈口〉in any case；anyway

横行 héngxíng（动）run wild；run amok：～一时 run wild for a time. ～霸道 ride roughshod (over)

横征暴敛(斂) héngzhēng-bàoliǎn extort excessive taxes and levies

衡 héng I（名）weighing apparatus II（动）weigh；measure；judge：～情度理 judging by common sense

衡量 héngliáng（动）weigh；measure；judge：～得失 weigh the pros and cons

衡器 héngqì（名）weighing apparatus

横 hèng（形）1 harsh and unreasonable；perverse：～话 harsh and unreasonable words 2 unexpected：～祸 unexpected calamity
see also héng

横财 hèngcái（名）ill-gotten wealth (or gains)：发～ get rich by foul means

横蛮(蠻) hèngmán（形）rude and unreasonable

横死 hèngsǐ（动）die a violent death

哼 hng（叹）[expressing dissatisfaction or doubt] humph：～，你信他的! Humph! you believe him?
see also hēng

烘 hōng（动）1 dry or warm by the fire：把湿衣服～干 dry the wet clothes by the fire 2 set off：～托 set off by contrast

烘焙 hōngbèi（动）cure (tea or tobacco leaves)

烘烤 hōngkǎo（动）toast；bake

烘托 hōngtuō（动）1 (in Chinese painting) add shading in ink around an object to make it stand out 2 set off by contrast；throw into sharp relief

烘箱 hōngxiāng（名）oven

哄 hōng（象）roars of laughter
see also hǒng；hòng

哄传(傳) hōngchuán（动）(of rumours) circulate widely

哄动(動) hōngdòng（动）cause a sensation；make a stir

哄抢(搶) hōngqiǎng（动）make a scramble for (public property, goods, etc.)

哄抬(擡) hōngtái（动）drive up (prices)

哄堂大笑 hōngtáng dàxiào set the whole room roaring with laughter；explode into loud laughter

轰(轟) hōng I（象）bang；boom：～的一声，震得山鸣谷应. The hills resounded with a bang. II（动）1 rumble；bombard；explode：万炮齐～ cannonade 2 shoo away；drive off：～下台 oust sb. from office；hoot sb. off the stage

轰动(動) hōngdòng（动）cause a sensation；make a stir：～全国 cause a nationwide sensation. 全场～ make a stir in the audience

轰轰烈烈 hōnghōnglièliè on a grand and spectacular scale；vigorous；dynamic

轰击(擊) hōngjī（动）shell；bombard：～敌人阵地 shell enemy positions

轰隆 hōnglōng（象）rumble；roll

轰鸣 hōngmíng（动）thunder；roar：马达～. Motors roared.

轰炸 hōngzhà（动）bomb：～机 bomber

H

鸿 hóng I（名）1 swan；wild goose 2〈书〉letter：远方来～ a letter from afar II（形）great；grand：～图 grand plan；grand design

鸿沟（溝）hónggōu（名）wide gap；chasm：不可逾越的～ an unbridgeable gap；an impassable chasm

鸿雁 hóngyàn（名）wild goose

虹 hóng（名）rainbow

红 hóng I（形）1 red：～铅笔 red pencil 2 revolutionary；red 3 popular；successful：～极一时 enjoy great popularity for a time II（名）1 red cloth worn as a sign of festivity, etc. 2 bonus；dividend

红白喜事 hóngbái xǐshì（名）weddings and funerals

红包 hóngbāo（名）a red paper envelope containing money as a gift；bonus

红茶 hóngchá（名）black tea

红尘（塵）hóngchén（名）human society：看破～ see through the vanity of human life

红光满（滿）面 hóngguāng mǎnmiàn glowing with health；in the pink of health

红军 Hóngjūn（名）the Red Army

红利 hónglì（名）bonus；extra dividend

红领巾 hónglǐngjīn（名）1 red scarf（worn by Young Pioneers）2 Young Pioneer

红绿灯（燈）hónglǜdēng（名）traffic light；traffic signal

红木 hóngmù（名）mahogany

红娘 hóngniáng（名）matchmaker；go-between

红旗 hóngqí（名）red flag or banner：工业战线上一面～ a pace-setter on the industrial front

红人 hóngrén（名）favourite follower（of a person in power）；a rising star

红润 hóngrùn（形）ruddy；rosy：脸色～ ruddy complexion；rosy cheeks

红烧（燒）hóngshāo（动）braise in soy sauce：～肉 pork braised in brown sauce

红十字会（會）Hóngshízìhuì（名）the Red Cross

红薯 hóngshǔ（名）sweet potato

红外线（綫）hóngwàixiàn（名）infrared ray

红血球 hóngxuèqiú（名）red blood cell

红眼 hóngyǎn（动）1 become infuriated；see red 2 be envious；be jealous of

红药（藥）水 hóngyàoshuǐ（名）mercurochrome

红晕 hóngyùn（名）blush；flush：脸上泛出～ one's face blushing scarlet

红肿（腫）hóngzhǒng（形）red and swollen

洪 hóng I（形）big；vast：～涛 turbulent waves II（名）flood：防～ control or prevent flood

洪峰 hóngfēng（名）flood peak；peak water level

洪亮 hóngliàng（形）loud and clear；sonorous：～的回声 loud reverberations

洪流 hóngliú（名）mighty torrent；powerful current

洪水 hóngshuǐ（名）flood；flood water

宏 hóng（形）great；grand；magnificent

宏大 hóngdà（形）grand；great：规模～ on a great scale；vast in scope

宏观（觀）hóngguān（形）1 macroscopic 2 macro：～经济学 macroeconomics

宏论（論）hónglùn（名）esteemed opinion

宏图（圖）hóngtú（名）great plan；grand prospect：展～ hold out a promising prospect

宏伟（偉）hóngwěi（形）magnificent；grand：～建筑 magnificent building

宏愿（願）hóngyuàn（名）great aspirations；noble ambition

宏旨 hóngzhǐ（名）main theme；cardinal principle：无关～ not a matter of cardinal principle

弘 hóng I（形）great；grand；magnificent II（动）enlarge；expand

弘大 hóngdà（形）grand

弘扬（揚）hóngyáng（动）carry forward；develop；enhance

泓 hóng I（形）（of water）deep II（量）：一～秋水 an expanse of autumn water

哄 hǒng（动）1 fool；humbug：你这是～我. You're kidding me. 2 coax；humour：她很会～孩子. She knows how to coax children to do one thing or another.

see also hōng；hòng

哄骗 hǒngpiàn（动）cheat；coax；humbug；hoodwink

哄 hòng（动）make an uproar：一～而散 scatter in an uproar

see also hōng；hǒng

侯 hóu（名）1 marquis：～爵 marquis 2 a nobleman or a high official

瘊 hóu（名）wart：～子 wart

喉 hóu (名) larynx; throat

喉咙(嚨) hóulóng (名) throat: ～痛 have a sore throat

喉舌 hóushé (名) mouthpiece: 我们的报纸是人民的～. Our newspaper represents the voice of the people.

猴 hóu (名) monkey: ～子 monkey

吼 hǒu (动) 1 roar; howl: 狮子～ the roar of a lion 2 (of wind, siren, etc.) howl; whistle; thunder: 风浪的～声 the roar of the wind and waves

厚 hòu I (形) 1 thick: ～棉衣 a heavy padded coat 2 deep; profound: 深情～谊 great kindness and cordiality 3 kind; magnanimous: 忠～ honest and kind-hearted 4 large; generous: ～利 substantial gains. ～酬 handsome reward 5 rich or strong in flavour II (动) favour; stress: ～此薄彼 be prejudiced in favour of one and against the other

厚爱(愛) hòu'ài (名) 1 adoration 2 your kindness

厚薄 hòubó (名) thickness

厚道 hòudào (形) kind and sincere

厚度 hòudù (名) thickness

厚礼(禮) hòulǐ (名) generous gift

厚脸(臉)皮 hòuliǎnpí thick-skinned; brazen; shameless: 厚着脸皮说 have the cheek to say

厚望 hòuwàng (名) great expectations: 不负～ live up to sb.'s expectations; not let sb. down

厚颜 hòuyán (形) impudent; brazen: ～无耻 shameless

厚意 hòuyì (名) good will; kindness: 多谢你的～. Thank you for your kindness.

候 hòu I (动) 1 wait; await: 请稍～一会儿. Please wait a moment. 2 inquire after: 致～ send one's regards II (名) 1 time; season: 时～ time 2 condition; state: 症～ symptom

候补(補) hòubǔ (名) a candidate (for a vacancy); an alternate member

候车(車)室 hòuchēshì (名) waiting room (in a railway or bus station)

候鸟(鳥) hòuniǎo (名) migratory bird; migrant

候选(選)人 hòuxuǎnrén (名) candidate: 提出～ nominate candidates

候诊 hòuzhěn (动) wait for one's turn to see the doctor: ～室 waiting room (in a hospital)

后 hòu (名) empress; queen

后(後) hòu (名) 1 behind; at the back: 屋～ behind (or at the back of) a house. ～排 back row 2 after; afterwards; later: 不久以～ soon afterwards; before long 3 (名) offspring: 无～ without male offspring; without issue

后备(備) hòubèi (名) reserve: 留有～ keep sth. in reserve. ～基金 reserve fund. ～军 reserve forces

后辈 hòubèi (名) 1 younger generation 2 posterity

后尘(塵) hòuchén 〈书〉 (literally) dust kicked up by someone walking in front: 步人～ follow in sb.'s footsteps

后代 hòudài (名) 1 later periods (in history) 2 later generations; descendants

后盾 hòudùn (名) backing; support: 坚强的～ powerful backing

后方 hòufāng (名) rear: ～勤务 rear service; logistics (service)

后跟 hòugēn (名) heel (of a shoe or sock)

后顾(顧) hòugù (动) 1 give attention to what is left back at home: 无暇～ cannot attend to what is left behind. ～之忧 trouble back at home 2 look back: ～与前瞻 sum up the past and plan for the future

后果 hòuguǒ (名) consequence; aftermath: 承担～ be responsible for the consequences

后患 hòuhuàn (名) future trouble: ～无穷 a source of endless trouble

后悔 hòuhuǐ (动) regret; repent: ～莫及 repent bitterly; no use crying over spilt milk

后继(繼) hòujì (动) succeed; carry on: ～无人 with nobody to carry on the work

后劲(勁) hòujìn (名) 1 after-effect: 这酒～大. This kind of liquor has a strong delayed effect. 2 reserve strength; stamina

后进(進) hòujìn (名) 1 laggard 2 junior member of a profession

后来(來) hòulái (名) afterwards; later

后来(來)居上 hòu lái jū shàng those who come later on the scene often surpass their predecessors

后路 hòulù (名) 1 communication lines to the rear; route of retreat: 切断敌人的～

cut off the enemy's route of retreat 2 room for manoeuvre

后妈 hòumā（名）stepmother

后门(門) hòumén（名）1 back door (or gate)：大院的～ the back gate of a compound 2 "back-door" dealings

后面 hòumian（名）1 at the back; in the rear; behind 2 later

后起 hòuqǐ（形）(of people of talent) of the younger generation：～之秀 a promising young person

后勤 hòuqín（名）rear service; logistics：～部 rear-service department; logistics department (or command). ～基地 logistics base; rear supply base. ～支援 logistic support

后人 hòurén（名）1 future generations 2 posterity; descendants

后生可畏 hòushēng kě wèi the younger generation deserves respect

后世 hòushì（名）1 later ages 2 later generations

后事 hòushì（名）1 [often seen in novels or narratives in chronological order] later developments 2 funeral affairs：料理～ make arrangements for a funeral

后台(臺) hòutái（名）1 backstage：～老板 backstage boss; behind-the-scenes backer 2 backstage supporter; behind-the-scenes backer：～很硬 have very strong backing

后天 hòutiān I（名）day after tomorrow II（形）postnatal; acquired

后头(頭) hòutou（名）at the back; in the rear; behind

后退 hòutuì（动）draw back; fall back; retreat

后卫(衛) hòuwèi（名）1 rearguard 2 (in football) full back：左～ left back. 右～ right back 3 (in basketball) guard

后遗症 hòuyízhèng（名）sequelae

后裔 hòuyì（名）descendant; offspring

后者 hòuzhě（名）the latter

后缀 hòuzhuì（名）suffix

糊 hū（动）plaster：用灰把墙缝～上 plaster up cracks in the wall. ～一层泥 spread a layer of mud

see also hú; hù

乎 hū I（助）〈书〉[expressing doubt or conjecture]：有朋自远方来，不亦乐～？ Is it not delightful to have friends coming from afar? II [verbal suffix]：出～意料 exceed one's expectations; come to one as a surprise. 超～寻常 be out of the ordinary run III [suffix of adjective or adverb]：确～重要 very important indeed; of unmistakable importance. 迥～不同 entirely different

呼 hū I（动）1 breathe out; exhale 2 shout; cry out：～口号 shout slogans 3 call：～之即来 call one's name, and one will instantly appear; be at one's beck and call II（象）：北风～～地吹. A north wind is shrieking.

呼风(風)唤雨 hūfēng-huànyǔ summon wind and rain—exercise magic power

呼喊 hūhǎn（动）call out; shout

呼号(號) hūháo（动）wail; cry out in distress：奔走～ go about campaigning for a cause

呼号(號) hūhào（名）1 call sign; call letters 2 catchword (of an organization)

呼唤 hūhuàn（动）call; shout to：远处有人在～我们. Somebody is calling us in the distance.

呼机(機) hūjī（名）pager

呼叫 hūjiào（动）1 call out; shout 2 call：～信号 calling signal

呼救 hūjiù（动）call for help

呼噜 hūlu〈口〉snore：打～ snore

呼声(聲) hūshēng（名）cry; voice：群众的～ the popular demand. 世界舆论的～ world opinion

呼吸 hūxī（动）breathe; respire：出去～新鲜空气 go out for a breath of fresh air. ～困难 breathe with difficulty. 口对口～ mouth-to-mouth respiration. 人工～ artificial respiration. 他的～迟缓而困难. His breathing is laboured.

呼啸(嘯) hūxiào（动）whistle; scream：歹徒～而遁. The hooligans broke up amidst loud shouts and screams.

呼应(應) hūyìng（动）echo; work in concert with：遥相～ echo each other from afar

呼吁(籲) hūyù（动）appeal; call on：～援助灾区难民 appeal for assistance to refugees from affected areas

忽 hū I（动）neglect; overlook; ignore II（副）suddenly：～发奇想 have a brainwave

忽地 hūdì（副）suddenly; all of a sudden

忽而 hū'ér（副）now... now... [often used before similar constructive verbs or adjectives]：～说～笑 talk and laugh by turns

忽略 hūlüè（动）neglect; overlook; lose

sight of: 错误虽小,但不可~. The mistake may be small, but it should not be overlooked.

忽然 hūrán (副) suddenly; all of a sudden

忽闪 hūshan (动) (of the eyes) flash; sparkle

忽视 hūshì (动) ignore; overlook; neglect

壶(壺) hú (名) **1** kettle; pot: 水~ kettle. 茶~ teapot. 油~ oil can **2** bottle; flask: 暖~ thermos bottle (or flask)

胡 hú I (名) **1** non-Han nationalities living in the north and west in ancient times **2** (鬍) moustache; beard; whiskers II (副) recklessly; outrageously: ~闹 act outrageously

胡扯 húchě (动) talk nonsense; chatter idly

胡话 húhuà (名) ravings; wild talk

胡搅(攪) hújiǎo (动) **1** pester sb.; annoy sb. with unreasonable demands **2** buttonhole sb. and argue one's case most unreasonably and incoherently: ~蛮缠 pester sb. endlessly

胡来(來) húlái (动) **1** mess things up **2** run wild; invite trouble

胡乱(亂) húluàn (副) carelessly; casually; at random: ~写了几行 scribble a few lines. ~猜测 make wild guesses

胡闹 húnào (动) act wilfully and make a scene

胡琴 húqín (名) *huqin*, two-stringed bowed instrument

胡说 húshuō I (动) talk nonsense; drivel II (名) nonsense: ~八道 sheer nonsense; rubbish

胡思乱(亂)想 húsī-luànxiǎng give free rein to fancy

胡同 hútòng (名) lane; alley; *hutong*

胡须(鬚) húxū (名) beard, moustache or whiskers

胡言乱(亂)语 húyán-luànyǔ talk nonsense; rave

胡诌(謅) húzhōu (名) tall story; fabrication

胡子 húzi (名) beard, moustache or whiskers

胡作非为(爲) húzuò-fēiwéi act in defiance of the law or public opinion; act wantonly

湖 hú (名) lake

湖滨(濱) húbīn (名) lakeside

湖泊 húpō (名) lakes

糊 hú I (名) paste II (动) stick with paste; paste: ~窗户 paste a sheet of paper over a lattice window. ~墙 paper a wall
see also hū; hù

糊口 húkǒu (动) keep body and soul together; eke out a living by doing odd jobs

糊涂(塗) hútu (形) muddle-headed; confused; bewildered: ~思想 muddled thinking. 一时~ in a moment of aberration

蝴 hú

蝴蝶 húdié (名) butterfly

猢 hú

猢狲(猻) húsūn (名) a kind of monkey; macaque: 树倒~散. When a person falls from power, his followers scatter.

核 hú
see also hé

核儿(兒) húr (名)〈口〉**1** stone; pit; core: 杏~ apricot stone. 梨~ pear core **2** sth. resembling a fruit stone: 煤~ partly burnt coals or briquets

囫 hú

囫囵(圇) húlún (形) whole: ~吞下 swallow sth. whole. ~吞枣 accept book knowledge without real understanding or analysis

鹄 hú (名) swan
see also gǔ

鹄候 húhòu (动)〈书〉await respectfully; expect: ~回音 I am looking forward to an early reply from you

鹄望 húwàng (动) eagerly look forward to

狐 hú (名) fox

狐臭 húchòu (名) body odour; bromhidrosis

狐假虎威 hú jiǎ hǔ wēi act outrageously on the strength of one's powerful connections

狐狸 húli (名) fox: 露出~尾巴 show a person's evil intentions; show the cloven hoof

狐媚 húmèi (动) bewitch by cajolery; entice by flattery

狐群狗党(黨) húqún-gǒudǎng a pack of rogues; a gang of scoundrels

狐疑 húyí (名) doubt; suspicion: 满腹～ be full of misgivings; be very suspicious

弧 hú (名) arc

弧光 húguāng (名) arc light; arc: ～灯 arc lamp; arc light

弧形 húxíng (名) arc; curve

浒 hǔ (名) waterside

虎 hǔ I (名) tiger II (形) brave; vigorous: ～～有生气 be full of vigour

虎口 hǔkǒu (名) tiger's mouth—jaws of death: ～余生 escape from the clutches of the enemy

虎视眈眈 hǔ shì dāndān (动) glare like a tiger eyeing its prey; look with covetous eyes

虎头(頭)蛇尾 hǔtóu-shéwěi a fine start and poor finish

虎穴 hǔxué (名) tiger's den

琥 hǔ

琥珀 hǔpò (名) amber

唬 hǔ (动)〈口〉bluff: 你别～人. Quit bluffing.

糊 hù (名) paste: 辣椒～ chilli paste. 玉米～ (cornmeal mush)

see also hū; hú

糊弄 hùnong (动) kid; deceive; hoodwink: 你别～我. Don't kid me.

户 hù (名) 1 door: 门～ door 2 household; family: 全村有好几百～. There are several hundred households in the village. 3 (bank) account: 存～ (bank) depositor

户籍 hùjì (名) 1 census register; household register 2 registered permanent residence

户口 hùkǒu (名) 1 number of households and total population 2 registered permanent residence: 迁～ report to the local authorities for change of domicile. 报～ register or apply for permanent residence. ～普查 census. ～登记本 household registration book

户头(頭) hùtóu (名) (bank) account: 开～ open an account

户型 hùxíng (名) type of apartment

户主 hùzhǔ (名) head of a household

护(護) hù (动) 1 protect; guard; shield: ～航 escort; convoy 2 shield from censure: ～短 speak in defence of what is wrong

护短 hùduǎn (动) shield a shortcoming or fault; attempt to justify one's mistakes

护肤 hùfū I (动) take care of one's skin; look after one's skin II (名) skin care: ～用品 skincare products. ～液 body lotion. ～水 soothing toner

护理 hùlǐ (动) nurse; tend: ～伤病员 nurse the sick and the wounded

护士 hùshi (名) (hospital) nurse

护送 hùsòng (动) escort; convoy

护养(養) hùyǎng (动) 1 cultivate; nurse; rear: ～秧苗 cultivate seedlings; nurse young plants 2 maintain: ～公路 maintain a highway

护照 hùzhào (名) passport: 外交～ diplomatic passport. 公务～ service passport

扈 hù (名)〈书〉retinue: ～从 retinue; retainer

怙 hù (动)〈书〉rely on

怙恶(惡)不悛 hù è bù quān persist in an iniquitous course and refuse to mend

互 hù (副) mutual; each other: ～通有无 exchange of needed goods. ～不干涉 mutual non-interference. ～不侵犯 mutual non-aggression

互动(動) hùdòng I (动) interact II (名) interaction

互访 hùfǎng (动) exchange visits

互换 hùhuàn (动) exchange

互惠 hùhuì (形) mutually beneficial; reciprocal: 平等～ equality and mutual benefit

互利 hùlì (形) mutually beneficial; of mutual benefit

互联网(網) hùlián wǎng (名) internet

互相 hùxiāng (副) mutual; mutually: ～排斥 be mutually exclusive. ～尊重 mutual respect. ～支持 mutual support. ～勾结 work in collusion

互助 hùzhù (动) help each other: ～合作 mutual aid and cooperation

化 huā (动) spend; expend: ～钱不少 spend a good deal of money; cost a lot of money

see also huà

花 huā I (名) 1 flower; blossom; bloom: ～盆 flower pot. 献～ floral tribute 2 anything resembling a flower: 火～ spark. 雪～ snowflakes 3 fireworks: 放～ a show of fireworks 4 pattern; design: 白地蓝～ blue patterns on a white surface 5 wound: 挂～ get wounded in battle II (形) 1 multicoloured; coloured; variegated 2 (of eyes) blurred; dim III (动) spend; expend: ～了不少钱 spend a lot of money. 很～时间 take a lot of time; be time-consuming

花白 huābái (形) (of hair)grey; grizzled: 头发～ with greying hair; grey-haired

花瓣 huābàn (名) petal

花边(邊) huābiān (名) 1 decorative border; floral border 2 lace 3 fancy borders in printing

花茶 huāchá (名) scented tea: 茉莉～ jasmine tea

花朵 huāduǒ (名) flower

花费 huāfèi (动) spend: ～心血 go to great pains

花费 huāfei (名) expenditure; expenses

花粉 huāfěn (名) pollen: ～过敏 hay fever

花岗(崗)岩 huāgāngyán (名) granite

花好月圆 huāhǎo-yuèyuán (as a congratulatory message for wedding in old days) the flowers are in bloom, and the moon is full — perfect conjugal felicity

花花公子 huāhuā gōngzǐ dandy; coxcomb; fop; playboy

花花绿绿 huāhuālǜlǜ brightly coloured

花花世界 huāhuā shìjiè worldly temptations; vanity fair

花环(環) huāhuán (名) garland

花卉 huāhuì (名) 1 flowers and plants 2 traditional Chinese painting of flowers and plants

花甲 huājiǎ (名) a cycle of sixty years: 年逾～ over sixty years old

花剑(劍) huājiàn (名) foil: ～运动员 foil fencer; foilsman

花镜 huājìng (名) presbyopic glasses

花篮(籃) huālán (名) a basket of flowers

花名册 huāmíngcè (名) register (of names); membership roster; muster roll

花木 huāmù (名) flowers and trees (in parks or gardens)

花鸟(鳥) huāniǎo (名) traditional Chinese painting of flowers and birds: ～画 flower-and-bird painting

花瓶 huāpíng (名) vase

花圃 huāpǔ (名) flower nursery

花腔 huāqiāng (名) 1 florid ornamentation in Chinese opera singing; coloratura: ～女高音 coloratura soprano; coloratura 2 crafty talk: 耍～ talk craftily

花圈 huāquān (名) wreath: 献～ lay a wreath

花色 huāsè (名) 1 design and colour 2 (of merchandise) variety of designs, sizes, colours, etc.: ～繁多 a great variety of designs and colours

花哨 huāshao (形) 1 garish; gaudy 2 no lack of variety

花生 huāshēng (名) peanut; groundnut

花束 huāshù (名) a bunch of flowers; bouquet

花天酒地 huātiān-jiǔdì wine, women and song; a dissipated life

花团(團)锦簇 huātuán-jǐncù rich multi-coloured decorations

花纹 huāwén (名) decorative pattern; figure

花消 huāxiao (名) cost; expense

花心 huāxīn (形) lecherous: ～男人 a lecherous man

花絮 huāxù (名) titbits (of news); sidelights

花言巧语 huāyán-qiǎoyǔ fine and pleasant words

花样(樣) huāyàng (名) 1 kind; variety 2 trick: 玩～ play tricks. ～滑冰 figure skating

花园(園) huāyuán (名) flower garden; garden

花招 huāzhāo (名) 1 apparently skilful movement in *wushu* (武术); flourish 2 trick; game: 玩弄～ play tricks

花枝招展 huāzhī zhāozhǎn (of women) be gaudily dressed

花子 huāzi (名) beggar

哗(嘩) huā (象): 铁门～的一声关上了. The iron gate was shut with a clang. 流水～～地响. The water was gurgling.
see also huá

哗啦 huālā (象): ～一声墙倒了. The wall fell with a crash.

划(劃) huá (动) 1 paddle; row: ～船 paddle (or row) a boat; go boating 2 scratch; cut: ～火柴 strike a match. 手上～了一个口子 get a scratch on one's hand; cut one's hand 3 be to one's profit; pay: 老实一点总～得来. It pays to be honest.
see also huà

划拳 huáquán (动) play finger-guessing game in a drinking-bout

划算 huásuàn (动) 1 calculate; weigh: ～来,～去 weigh the pros and cons 2 be to one's profit; pay

H

滑 huá I (形) **1** slippery; smooth: 又圆又～的小石子 smooth, round pebbles. 路面有雪～得很. The road is slippery with snow. **2** cunning; crafty; as slippery as an eel II (动) slip; slide

滑板 huábǎn (名) **1** skateboard **2** slide

滑冰 huábīng (名) skate; ice skating; skating: ～场 skating rink

滑稽 huájī (形) funny; farcical; comical

滑溜 huáliu (形)〈口〉smooth: 缎子被面摸着挺～. The satin quilt cover feels soft and smooth.

滑轮(輪) huálún (名) pulley; block

滑腻 huánì (形) (of the skin) soft; velvety; creamy

H

滑坡 huápō (名) **1** landslide; landslip **2** decline; retrogression

滑润 huárùn (形) smooth; well-lubricated

滑头(頭) huátóu I (名) slippery fellow; sly old fox II (形) foxy; sly; slick

滑翔 huáxiáng (动) glide: ～机 glider; sailplane

滑行 huáxíng (动) slide; coast: 飞机在跑道上～. The plane taxied along the runway.

滑雪 huáxuě (名) skiing: ～板 skis

华(華) huá I (形) **1** brilliant; magnificent; splendid **2** prosperous; flourishing: 繁～ flourishing; thriving **3** flashy; extravagant: 奢～ extravagant; luxurious **4** grizzled; grey: ～发 grey hair II (名) **1** best part; cream: 精～ the cream; the essence **2** China: 来～正式访问 come to China on an official visit

华而不实(實) huá ér bù shí showy and superficial

华贵 huáguì (形) luxurious; sumptuous; costly

华丽(麗) huálì (形) magnificent; resplendent; gorgeous: 服饰～ gaudily dressed. ～的词藻 florid language; ornate style

华侨(僑) huáqiáo (名) overseas Chinese

华夏 huáxià (名) an ancient name for China

华裔 huáyì (名) a person of Chinese descent

华语 huáyǔ (名) Chinese (language)

哗(嘩) huá noise; clamour: 寂静无～ silent and still; very quiet
see also huā

哗变(變) huábiàn (动) mutiny

哗然 huárán (形) in an uproar; in commotion: 舆论～. There was a public clamour.

哗众(衆)取宠(寵) huá zhòng qǔ chǒng win transient popularity with claptrap; play to the gallery

话 huà I (名) word; remark: 说几句～ say a few words; make a few remarks II (动) talk about; speak about: ～家常 engage in chitchat

话别 huàbié (动) talk with a friend on the eve of his departure; say goodbye; bid farewell

话柄 huàbǐng (名) subject for ridicule

话锋 huàfēng (名) course of conversation: 把～一转 switch to another topic

话剧(劇) huàjù (名) modern drama; stage play

话题 huàtí (名) theme of conversation

话筒 huàtǒng (名) **1** microphone **2** telephone transmitter **3** megaphone

话务(務)员 huàwùyuán (名) telephone operator

话音 huàyīn (名) **1** one's voice in speech **2** tone; implication

话语权 huàyǔquán the right to speak; voice: 争夺～ fight to have one's voice heard

画(畫) huà I (动) draw; paint: ～画 draw a picture. ～一张草图 make a sketch II (名) drawing; painting; picture: 年～ New Year picture. 油～ oil painting III (形) be decorated with paintings or pictures: ～栋雕梁 painted pillars and carved beams (of a magnificent building)

画报(報) huàbào (名) illustrated magazine or newspaper; pictorial

画饼充饥(饑) huà bǐng chōngjī draw cakes to stay hunger—to comfort oneself with imaginations

画册 huàcè (名) album

画家 huàjiā (名) painter; artist

画卷 huàjuàn (名) picture scroll

画廊 huàláng (名) **1** painted corridor **2** (picture) gallery

画龙(龍)点(點)睛 huà lóng diǎn jīng put the finishing touches to a piece of writing

画面 huàmiàn (名) **1** general appearance of a picture; tableau **2** frame

画蛇添足 huà shé tiān zú draw a snake and add feet to it—spoil the show by doing sth. quite superfluous

画室 huàshì (名) an artist's studio

画图(圖) huàtú I (动) draw designs, maps, etc. II (名) picture

画像 huàxiàng I (动) draw a portrait; portray II (名) portrait; portrayal: 巨幅～ huge portrait. 自～ self-portrait

画展 huàzhǎn (名) art exhibition; exhibition of paintings

划(劃) huà I (动) 1 delimit; differentiate: ～界 delimit a boundary 2 appropriate; assign: ～款 appropriate a sum of money 3 plan: ～策 plan; scheme II (名) stroke (of a Chinese character)
see also huá

划拨(撥) huàbō (动) transfer; appropriate

划分 huàfēn (动) 1 divide: ～成小组 divide into groups 2 differentiate: ～两种不同类型的错误 differentiate the two different types of error

划清 huàqīng (动) draw a clear line of demarcation; make a clear distinction

划时(時)代 huàshídài (形) epoch-making: 具有～的意义 have epoch-making significance

划一 huàyī (形) standardized; uniform

化 huà I (动) 1 change; turn; transform: ～险为夷 turn danger into safety. ～害为利 turn harm into good; turn a disadvantage into an advantage 2 melt; dissolve: 用水～开 dissolve in water 3 digest; get rid of: ～痰 reduce phlegm 4 burn up: 火～ cremate II [added to an adjective or noun to form a verb]-ize;-ify: 机械～ mechanize. 工业～ industrialize. 现代～ modernize. 知识～和专业～ become more educated and more competent
see also huā

化肥 huàféi (名) chemical fertilizer

化工厂(廠) huàgōngchǎng (名) chemical plant

化合 huàhé (名) chemical combination: ～物 chemical compound

化名 huàmíng (名) an assumed name; pseudonym

化脓(膿) huànóng (动) fester; suppurate: 伤口～了. The wound is festering.

化身 huàshēn (名) incarnation; embodiment: 正义的～ the embodiment of justice

化石 huàshí (名) fossil

化为乌(烏)有 huà wéi wūyǒu vanish completely; come to naught

化纤(纖) huàxiān (名) chemical fibre

化学(學) huàxué (名) chemistry: 应用～ applied chemistry. 理论～ theoretical chemistry. ～成分 chemical composition. ～反应 chemical reaction

化验(驗) huàyàn (名) chemical examination; laboratory test: ～单 laboratory test report. ～室 laboratory

化妆(妝) huàzhuāng (动) put on make-up; make up: ～品 cosmetics

化装(裝) huàzhuāng (动) 1 (of actors) make up 2 disguise oneself: ～舞会 masquerade

怀(懷) huái I (名) 1 bosom: 她把孩子搂在～里. She held the child in her arms. 2 mind: 襟～坦白 frank and straightforward II (动) 1 keep in mind; cherish: 少～大志 begin to cherish lofty aspirations in his youth. 不～好意 harbour evil intentions 2 think of; yearn for: ～友 think about a friend 3 conceive (a child): ～了孩子 be expecting a baby

怀抱 huáibào (名) bosom: 回到祖国的～ return to one's homeland

怀鬼胎 huái guǐtāi have evil intentions; harbour sinister plans

怀恨 huáihèn (动) harbour a grudge; bear ill will; nurse grievances

怀旧(舊) huáijiù (动) miss old times or old friends

怀念 huáiniàn (动) cherish the memory of: ～故乡 think of one's hometown with nostalgic longing

怀疑 huáiyí (动、名) doubt; suspect: 引起～ arouse suspicion. 我～他今天来不了. I have a hunch that he won't be able to come today.

怀孕 huáiyùn (动) be pregnant; conceived: ～期 period of pregnancy

槐 huái (名) Chinese scholartree; locust tree

踝 huái (名) ankle: ～骨 ankle-bone

坏(壞) huài I (形) 1 bad: 不～ not bad. ～人～事 evildoers and evil deeds 2 badly; awfully; very: 吓～了 be badly scared. 累～了 be dog-tired. 渴～了 be parched II (动) go bad; spoil; ruin: 鱼～了. The fish has gone bad. III (名) evil idea; dirty trick: 使～ play a dirty trick

坏处(處) huàichu (名) harm; disadvantage: 这对你没有～. It won't do you any harm.

H

坏蛋 huàidàn (名)〈口〉bad egg; scoundrel; bastard

坏话 huàihuà (名) malicious remarks; unpleasant words; vicious talk: 讲别人～ speak ill of others

坏事 huàishì I (名) bad thing; evil deed II (动) ruin sth.; make things worse: 急躁只能～. Impetuosity will only make things worse.

坏心眼儿(兒) huàixīnyǎnr (名) evil intention; ill will

坏账 huàizhàng (名) bad debts; uncollectible debts; bad account

欢(歡) huān (形) 1 joyfully; merrily: ～呼 shout joyfully; cheer. ～唱 sing merrily. ～声雷动 There was a burst of thunderous applause. 2 cheerfully; with a vengeance; in full swing: 雨下得正～. The rain is coming down with a vengeance.

欢畅(暢) huānchàng (形) have a wonderful time; thoroughly enjoy oneself

欢度 huāndù (动) spend (an occasion) joyfully: ～佳节 celebrate a festival with jubilation

欢聚 huānjù (动) happily gather: ～一堂 be gathered here

欢快 huānkuài (形) cheerful; light; lively: ～的乐曲 light music; a lively melody

欢乐(樂) huānlè (形) happy and gay; merry: ～的心情 (in) a merry mood

欢庆(慶) huānqìng (动) celebrate with jubilation

欢送 huānsòng (动) send off (usually referring to a collective affair): ～会 farewell party; send-off meeting

欢腾 huānténg (动) rejoice; be overjoyed

欢天喜地 huāntiān-xǐdì wild with joy; overjoyed: ～迎新年 greet the New Year with boundless joy

欢喜 huānxǐ I (形) joyful; happy; delighted: 满心～ be over-joyed II (动) like; be fond of; delight in: 她～弹钢琴. She likes to play the piano.

欢心 huānxīn (名) favour; liking; love: 博取～ curry someone's favour

欢欣 huānxīn (形) joyous; elated: ～鼓舞 feel greatly encouraged; be elated

欢迎 huānyíng (动) welcome; greet: ～贵宾 welcome distinguished guests. 这部小说深受读者～. This novel is well received. ～词 welcoming speech; address of welcome

还(還) huán (动) 1 go (or come) back: ～家 return home 2 give back; return; repay: 到期要～的书 a book due for return. ～债 repay a debt. ～嘴 talk back; retort 3 give or do sth. in return: ～礼 send a present in return; return a salute
see also hái

还本 huánběn (动) repay the principal (or capital): ～付息 repay capital with interest

还击(擊) huánjī (动) fight back; return fire; counter-attack: 自卫～ fight back in self-defence

还价(價) huánjià (动) make a counter-offer; make a counter-bid: 讨价～ bargain; haggle

还清 huánqīng (动) pay off: ～债务 pay off one's debts

还手 huánshǒu (动) strike back

还俗 huánsú (动) (of Buddhist monks and nuns or Taoist priests) resume secular life

还原 huányuán (动) (of things) be restored to the original state or shape

环(環) huán I (名) 1 ring; hoop: 光～ halo. 耳～ earring 2 link: 最薄弱的一～ the weakest link II (动) surround; encircle; hem in: 四面～山 be surrounded on all sides by mountains

环抱 huánbào (动) surround; encircle; hem in

环保 huánbǎo I (名) environmental protection. II (形) environmentally friendly

环顾(顧) huángù (动)〈书〉look about (or round); look all round

环节(節) huánjié (名) 1 link: 主要～ a key link 2 segment

环境 huánjìng (名) environment; surroundings; circumstances: 换换～ go elsewhere for a change ～污染 pollution (of the environment)

环球 huánqiú (名) 1 round the world: ～旅行 transglobe expedition; a round-the-world tour 2 the earth; the whole world

环绕(繞) huánrào (动) surround; encircle; revolve around: 地球～太阳旋转. The earth revolves round the sun.

环视 huánshì (动) look around

环行 huánxíng (动) going in a ring: ～一周

make a circuit. ～公路 ring road; belt highway

缓 huǎn I (形) slow; unhurried: ～流 flow slowly. ～步 walk in a leisurely way; walk at a relaxed pace II (动) 1 delay; postpone; put off: ～兵之计 play stalling tactics 2 recuperate; revive; come to: 过了好一阵他才～过来. It was a long time before he came to.

缓冲(衝) huǎnchōng (动) buffer; cushion: ～地带 buffer zone. ～国 buffer state

缓和 huǎnhé I (动) 1 relax; ease up; mitigate; alleviate: ～紧张局势 relax the tension 2 calm down II (名) détente

缓急 huǎnjí (名) greater or lesser urgency: 分别轻重～加以处理 handle matters in the order of importance and urgency

缓慢 huǎnmàn (形) slow: 行动～ slow to act. 进展～ make slow progress; proceed at a snail's pace

缓期 huǎnqī (动) postpone a deadline; suspend: ～付款 delay (or defer) payment

缓刑 huǎnxíng (名) reprieve; probation

浣 huàn (动)〈书〉wash: ～衣 wash clothes

宦 huàn (名) 1 official 2 eunuch

宦官 huànguān (名) eunuch

宦海 huànhǎi (名) officialdom; official circles: ～升沉 political ups and downs

宦途 huàntú (名) career as a government official

患 huàn I (名) 1 trouble; peril; disaster: 防～于未然 take preventive measures; provide against a rainy day 2 anxiety; worry: 何～之有. There's no cause for anxiety. II (动) contract; suffer from: ～病 suffer from an illness; fall ill; be ill

患得患失 huàndé-huànshī worry about personal loss; be swayed by considerations of gain or loss

患难(難) huànnàn (名) trials and tribulations; adversity; trouble: ～之交 a friend in need; a rough-weather friend. ～与共 go through thick and thin together; share weal and woe

患者 huànzhě (名) patient; sufferer

涣 huàn (动) melt; vanish

涣然 huànrán (形) melt away; disappear; vanish

涣散 huànsàn (形、动) lax; slack: 纪律～ be lax in discipline. ～斗志 sap sb.'s morale; demoralize

焕 huàn (形) shining; glowing

焕发(發) huànfā (动) shine; glow; irradiate: 精神～ be full of vim and vigour

焕然一新 huànrán yī xīn take on an entirely new look

换 huàn (动) 1 exchange; barter; trade: ～货 exchange goods; barter 2 change: ～衣服 change one's clothes. ～车 change buses (trains)

换班 huànbān (动) 1 change shifts 2 relieve a person on duty

换季 huànjì (动) change garments for a new season

换取 huànqǔ (动) give sth. in exchange for; get in return

换算 huànsuàn (名) conversion: ～表 conversion table

换汤(湯)不换药(藥) huàn tāng bù huàn yào offer the same old stuff but with a different label

换文 huànwén (名) exchange of notes (or letters)

唤 huàn (动) call out: 呼～ call; shout

唤起 huànqǐ (动) 1 arouse: ～民众 arouse the masses of the people 2 call; attract: ～人们的注意 attract people's attention

唤醒 huànxǐng (动) wake up; awaken

幻 huàn I (形) unreal; imaginary; illusory: 虚～ unreal; illusory; imaginary II (动) undergo a surprising change: 变～莫测 change unpredictably

幻灯(燈) huàndēng (名) slide show: 放～ show slides. ～机 slide projector

幻境 huànjìng (名) dreamland; fairyland

幻觉(覺) huànjué (名) illusion; hallucination

幻灭(滅) huànmiè (动) melt into thin air

幻术(術) huànshù (名) magic; conjuring art

幻想 huànxiǎng (名) illusion; figment of one's imagination: 不抱～ have no illusions

幻象 huànxiàng (名) optical illusion; phantom; phantasm

荒 huāng I (形) 1 waste: 地～了. The land lies uncultivated. 2 desolate; barren: ～岛 desert (or uninhabited) island. ～山 barren hill II (动) neglect;

be out of practice: 别把学业～了. Don't neglect your studies. III (名) 1 wasteland; uncultivated land: 垦～ open up (or reclaim) wasteland 2 shortage; scarcity: 房～ housing shortage. 3 famine; crop failure: 储粮备～ store up grain against famine

荒诞 huāngdàn (形) preposterous; absurd; ludicrous: ～的想法 a crazy idea

荒地 huāngdì (名) wasteland; uncultivated (or undeveloped) land

荒废(廢) huāngfèi (动) 1 (of land) be left uncultivated; lie waste 2 waste: ～时间 waste time 3 (of studies, lessons, etc.) neglect; be out of practice

荒凉 huāngliáng (形) bleak and desolate; wild: 一片～ a scene of desolation

荒谬 huāngmiù (形) absurd; preposterous: ～的论点 a preposterous proposition

荒漠 huāngmò (名) desert; wilderness

荒年 huāngnián (名) famine (or lean) year

荒僻 huāngpì (形) desolate and out-of-the-way

荒疏 huāngshū (形) rusty: 他的古典文学有点～了. He is a bit rusty on classical literature.

荒唐 huāngtáng (形) absurd; fantastic; preposterous: ～可笑 ridiculous; absurd

荒芜(蕪) huāngwú (形) lie waste; overgrown with weeds

荒淫 huāngyín (形) debauched: ～无耻 dissipated and unashamed; given to debauchery

荒原 huāngyuán (名) wasteland; wilderness

慌 huāng (形) nervous; scared: 不要～! Don't panic! ～了神 be scared out of one's wits. ～了手脚 be scared and not know what to do; be flustered

慌乱(亂) huāngluàn (形) flurried; in a hurry

慌忙 huāngmáng (形) in a great rush; in a flurry; hurriedly

慌张(張) huāngzhāng (形) flurried; flustered; confused: 神色～ be in a fluster

黄 huáng I (形) yellow; sallow II (名) short for the Yellow River: 治～ harness the Yellow River

黄道吉日 huángdào jírì propitious (or auspicious) date; lucky day

黄澄澄 huángdēngdēng (形) golden: ～的麦穗儿 golden ears of wheat

黄豆 huángdòu (名) soya bean; soybean

黄瓜 huángguā (名) cucumber

黄花鱼(魚) huánghuāyú (名) yellow croaker

黄昏 huánghūn (名) dusk

黄金 huángjīn (名) gold: ～储备 gold reserve. ～时代 golden age

黄酒 huángjiǔ (名) yellow rice wine

黄粱美梦(夢) huángliáng měimèng pipe dream; a fool's paradise

黄牛 huángniú (名) ox

黄泉 huángquán (名) the world of the dead; the underworld

黄色 huángsè I (名) yellow II (形) decadent; obscene; pornographic: ～电影 pornographic movie; sex film

黄铜 huángtóng (名) brass

黄土 huángtǔ (名) loess: ～高原 loess plateau

黄油 huángyóu (名) 1 butter 2 lubricating grease (or oil)

黄种(種) huángzhǒng (名) the yellow race

磺 huáng (名) sulphur

磺胺 huáng'àn (名) sulphanilamide (SN)

簧 huáng (名) 1 reed: ～乐器 reed instrument 2 spring: 弹～秤 spring balance

皇 huáng (名) emperor; sovereign: 女～ empress

皇帝 huángdì (名) emperor

皇宫 huánggōng (名) (imperial) palace

皇后 huánghòu (名) empress

皇室 huángshì (名) imperial family (or house)

皇太子 huángtàizǐ (名) crown prince

惶 huáng fear; anxiety: ～悚 sudden fear; fright

惶惶 huánghuáng (形) alarmed: ～不可终日 get scared and fidgety all day; be on tenterhooks

惶惑 huánghuò (形) perplexed

惶恐 huángkǒng (形) terrified; frightened

煌 huáng (形) bright; brilliant: 明星～～. The stars are bright.

蝗 huáng (名) locust: ～灾 plague of locusts

蝗虫(蟲) huángchóng (名) locust

谎 huǎng (名) lie; falsehood

谎话 huǎnghuà (名) lie; falsehood: 说～ tell a lie; lie

谎言 huǎngyán (名) lie; falsehood

恍 huǎng (形) 1 suddenly 2 [used in combination with 如,若] seem; as if: ～如梦境 (all this happened) as if in a dream

恍惚 huǎnghū (形) 1 in a trance; absent-minded: 精神～ be absent-minded **2** dimly; faintly; seemingly: ～记得 have a hazy notion

恍然大悟 huǎngrán dàwù suddenly realize; suddenly see the light

晃 huǎng (动) **1** shine bright **2** flash past

see also huàng

幌 huǎng

幌子 huǎngzi (名) **1** shop sign; signboard **2** pretence; pretext; façade

晃 huàng (动) sway; rock

see also huǎng

晃荡(蕩) huàngdàng (动) rock; shake; sway: 小船在水里直～. The small boat rocked to and fro on the water.

晃动(動) huàngdòng (动) rock; sway: 别～桌子. Don't wobble the desk.

晃悠 huàngyou (动) shake from side to side; hobble; stagger: 他晃晃悠悠往前走. He was hobbling along.

麾 huī I (名) standard of a commander [used in ancient times] II (动) despatch: ～军前进 order an army to push ahead

挥 huī (动) **1** wave; wield: ～手 wave one's hand. **2** wipe off: ～泪 wipe one's eyes **3** despatch (an army) **4** scatter; disperse: ～金如土 squander money; play ducks and drakes with money

挥动(動) huīdòng (动) brandish; wave: ～大棒 brandish a big stick. ～拳头 shake one's fist

挥发(發) huīfā (动) volatilize

挥霍 huīhuò (动) spend freely; squander: ～无度 spend one's money recklessly

挥手 huīshǒu (动) wave one's hand; wave: ～告别 wave farewell; wave goodbye to sb.

挥舞 huīwǔ (动) wave; wield; brandish: ～花束表示欢迎 wave bouquets in welcome

辉 huī I (名) brightness; splendour II (动) shine

辉煌 huīhuáng (形) brilliant; splendid; glorious: 灯火～ brilliantly illuminated; ablaze with lights

辉映 huīyìng (动) shine; reflect: 灯光月色,交相～. The lanterns and the moon vied with each other for radiance.

晖 huī (名) sunshine; sunlight

灰 huī I (名) **1** ash: 炉～ ashes from a stove **2** dust: 积了厚厚的一层～ accumulate a thick layer of dust **3** lime; (lime) mortar: ～墙 plastered wall II (形) **1** grey: ～马 a grey horse **2** discouraged: 心～意懒 disillusioned

灰暗 huī'àn (形) murky grey; gloomy: ～的天空 a gloomy (or overcast) sky

灰白 huībái (形) greyish white; ashen; pale: 脸色～ look pale

灰尘(塵) huīchén (名) dust; dirt: 掸掉桌上的～ dust the table

灰浆(漿) huījiāng (名) mortar

灰烬(燼) huījìn (名) ashes: 化为～ be reduced to ashes

灰溜溜 huīliūliū (形) gloomy; dejected; crestfallen: 他看起来有点～的样子. He looked a little depressed.

灰蒙蒙 huīmēngmēng (形) dusky; gloomy; misty

灰色 huīsè (形) **1** grey; ashy **2** pessimistic; gloomy

灰色收入 huīsè shōurù grey income

灰心 huīxīn (动) lose heart; be discouraged; be disappointed

恢 huī (形) extensive; vast

恢复(復) huīfù (动) **1** resume; renew: ～邦交 resume diplomatic relations. ～青春 regain youthful vigour **2** recover; regain: ～健康 recover one's health **3** restore; reinstate; rehabilitate: ～名誉 (of a person's reputation) rehabilitate. ～秩序 restore order. ～期 convalescence

恢恢 huīhuī (形) 〈书〉 extensive; vast: 天网～. Justice has long arms.

诙 huī

诙谐 huīxié (形) humorous; jocular

徽 huī (名) emblem; badge; insignia: 国～ national emblem. 校～ school badge. 帽～ cap insignia

徽号(號) huīhào (名) title of honour

徽章 huīzhāng (名) badge; insignia

回 huí I (动) **1** return; go back: ～家 return home. ～乡 return to one's hometown. 放～原处 put back where it was **2** turn round: ～过身来 turn round **3** answer; reply: ～信 send one a reply; write back II (量) **1** chapter: 这部小说共一百二十～. This novel contains 120

H

chapters. **2** [used to indicate frequency of action]: 来过一～ have been here once

回报(報) huíbào (动) **1** report back **2** repay; requite; reciprocate: ～他的盛情 repay him for his hospitality or kindness **3** retaliate; pay sb. in his own coin

回报率 huíbàolǜ (名) rate of return; return

回避 huíbì (动) evade; dodge; avoid (meeting sb.): ～要害问题 evade the crucial issue

回潮 huícháo (动) **1** (of dried things) get damp again **2** resurgence; reversion

回春 huíchūn (动) **1** (of spring) return: 大地～. Spring returns to the earth. **2** bring back to life: ～灵药 a miraculous cure; a wonderful remedy

回答 huídá (动) answer; reply

回荡(蕩) huídàng (动) resound; reverberate

回访 huífǎng (动) pay a return call

回放 huífàng (动) playback; replay

回复(復) huífù (动) reply (to a letter)

回顾(顧) huígù (动) look back; review: ～过去 look back on the past

回归(歸)线(綫) huíguīxiàn (名) the Tropic of Capricorn or Cancer

回合 huíhé (名) round; bout: 第一个～的胜利 a first-round victory

回话 huíhuà (名) reply; answer

回击(擊) huíjī (动) fight back; return fire; counter-attack

回见(見) huíjiàn (动)〈套〉 see you later (or again); cheerio

回教 Huíjiào (名) Islam

回敬 huíjìng (动) return a compliment; do or give sth. in return

回绝 huíjué (动) decline; refuse: 一口～ flatly refuse

回扣 huíkòu (名) sales commission

回来(來) huílai (动) return; come back; be back: 他就～. He'll be back in a minute.

回流 huíliú (动) flowback: 资金～ turnover of funds

回笼(籠) huílóng (动) **1** steam again **2** withdraw surplus money from circulation

回落 huíluò (动) fall after a rise: 物价已有～. The price has gone down.

回民 Huímín (名) the Huis; the Hui people

回去 huíqù (动) return; go back; be back

回去 huíqù [used after a verb to indicate returning to where sth. came from]: 请把这封信给他退～. Please return the letter to him.

回升 huíshēng (动) rise again (after a fall); pick up: 贸易～. Trade is picking up again. 气温～. The temperature has gone up again.

回声(聲) huíshēng (名) echo

回收 huíshōu (动) collect; recycle

回首 huíshǒu (动) **1** turn one's head; turn round **2** 〈书〉 look back upon; recollect

回溯 huísù (动) recall; look back upon: ～过去,瞻望未来 recall the past and look ahead

回头(頭) huítóu I (动) **1** turn one's head; turn round **2** repent: 浪子～ return of the prodigal son. 现在～还不算晚. It's not too late to repent. ～是岸. Repentance is salvation. II (副)〈口〉 later: ～再谈. We'll discuss it later. ～见! See you later! Bye now!

回味 huíwèi I (名) aftertaste II (动) call sth. to mind and ponder over it: ～他刚看过的电影 ponder over what he saw in the film

回响(響) huíxiǎng (动) reverberate; echo; resound: 歌声在山谷中激起了～. The valley echoed with the sound of singing.

回想 huíxiǎng (动) think back; recollect; recall

回心转(轉)意 huíxīn-zhuǎnyì come around to the correct way of thinking

回信 huíxìn I (动) write in reply; write back: 望早日～. I look forward to hearing from you soon. II (名) **1** a reply **2** a verbal message in reply; reply

回旋 huíxuán (动) **1** circle round: 飞机在上空～. The aeroplane is circling overhead. **2** manoeuvre: 还有～余地. There is still room for manoeuvre.

回忆(憶) huíyì (动) call to mind; recollect; recall: ～录 reminiscences; memoirs; recollections

回音 huíyīn (名) **1** echo **2** reply: 立候～ await an early reply

回执(執) huízhí (名) a short note acknowledging receipt of sth.; receipt

洄

huí 〈书〉 (of water) whirl

洄游 huíyóu (名) migration of fish

茴

huí

茴香 huíxiāng (名) fennel: ～油 fennel oil

蛔 huí

蛔虫(蟲) huíchóng (名) roundworm

悔 huǐ (动) regret; repent: ～不当初 regret not having pursued a different course. ～改 repent and mend one's ways

悔过(過) huǐguò (动) repent one's error; be repentant: ～自新 repent and turn over a new leaf

悔恨 huǐhèn (动) deeply regret; be filled with remorse

悔悟 huǐwù (动) realize one's error and bitterly regret it

悔罪 huǐzuì (动) show penitence

毁 huǐ (动) **1** destroy; ruin; damage **2** burn up: 焚～ destroy by fire; burn down **3** defame; slander: 诋～ vilify; slander

毁谤 huǐbàng (动) slander; malign; calumniate

毁坏(壞) huǐhuài (动) destroy; damage: ～庄稼 damage the crops

毁灭(滅) huǐmiè (动) destroy; exterminate; wipe out

毁损 huǐsǔn (动) damage; impair

毁誉(譽) huǐ-yù (名) praise or blame; praise or censure: 不计～ regardless of praise or censure

毁约 huǐyuē (动) break one's promise; scrap a contract or treaty

汇(匯、彙) huì I (动) **1** converge: 百川所～ where a hundred streams converge **2** gather together: ～印成书 collect relevant articles and have them published in book form **3** remit: ～款 remit money. 电～ telegraphic transfer II (名) things collected; assemblage; collection: 词～ vocabulary; lexical items

汇报(報) huìbào (动) report; give an account of: ～工作 report to sb. on one's work

汇编 huìbiān (名) compilation; collection; corpus: 资料～工作 compilation of reference material. 文件～ a collection of documents

汇合 huìhé (动) converge; join; flow together: 这两条河在什么地方～? Where do the two rivers converge?

汇集 huìjí (动) **1** collect; compile: ～材料 collect all relevant data **2** come together; converge; assemble

汇款 huìkuǎn I (动) remit money; make a remittance II (名) remittance: 收到一笔～ receive a remittance. ～单 money order

汇率 huìlǜ (名) exchange rate: 固定～ fixed (exchange) rate. 浮动～ floating (exchange) rate

汇票 huìpiào (名) draft; bill of exchange; money order: 银行～ bank draft. 邮政～ postal money order

汇总(總) huìzǒng (动) gather; collect; pool: 把材料～上报 submit the collected data to the leadership

讳(諱) huì I (动) avoid as taboo: ～莫如深 refuse to breathe a word about the matter. 隐～ cover up. 直言不～ speak bluntly; call a spade a spade II (名) forbidden word; taboo

讳疾忌医(醫) huìjí-jìyī seek no medical advice lest one should be known as a victim of disease—conceal one's fault for fear of criticism

讳言 huìyán (动) dare not or decline to speak up: 毫不～ make no bones about telling the truth

彗 huì (名) 〈书〉 broom

彗星 huìxīng (名) comet

慧 huì (形) intelligent; bright: 智～ wisdom; intelligence

慧眼 huìyǎn (名) **1** a mind which perceives both past and future **2** mental discernment (or perception); insight

卉 huì (名) (various kinds of) grass: 奇花异～ rare flowers and plants

惠 huì (名) favour; kindness; benefit: 受～ receive kindness (or favour); be favoured. 互～ mutual benefit

惠存 huìcún (动) 〈敬〉 please keep (this photograph, book, etc. as a souvenir); presented to so-and-so

秽(穢) huì (形) **1** dirty: 污～ filthy. ～土 dirt; refuse **2** ugly; abominable: ～行 abominable behaviour; immoral conduct

贿 huì (名) bribe: 受～ accept (or take) bribes

贿赂 huìlù (名) **1** bribe **2** bribery

会(會) huì I (动) 1 get together; assemble: 下午在校门口～齐. We'll assemble at the school gate this afternoon. 2 meet; see: 上星期你～着他没有? Did you meet him last week? 3 can; be able to: ～使筷子 can use chopsticks. ～英语 know English 4 be likely to; be sure to: 他不～不来. He is sure to come. 5 be good at; be skilful in: 能说～道 have a smooth tongue; have the gift of the gab; be a glib talker 我不太～下棋. I am not very good at chess. II (名) 1 meeting; gathering; party; get-together; conference: 欢迎～ welcoming party. 年～ annual meeting (or convention) 2 association; society; union: 帮～ secret society. 工～ trade union. ～址 the site of an association or society 3 chief city; capital: 都～ city; metropolis. 省～ provincial capital 4 moment; an opportune moment: 机～ opportunity.

see also kuài

会餐 huìcān (动) dine together among friends or colleagues; have a dinner party (usually sponsored by an organization)

会场(場) huìchǎng (名) meeting-place; conference (or assembly) hall

会费 huìfèi (名) membership dues

会合 huìhé (动) join forces; meet; converge; assemble

会话 huìhuà (名) conversation (as in a language course)

会见(見) huìjiàn (动) meet with

会客 huìkè (动) receive a visitor (or guest): ～时间 visiting hours. ～室 reception room

会儿(兒) huìr (名)〈口〉moment: 一～ little while. 等～. Wait a moment. 我去一～就回来. I won't be long.

会面 huìmiàn (动) meet; come together

会商 huìshāng (动) hold a conference or consultation

会师(師) huìshī (动) join forces

会水 huìshuǐ (动) know how to swim: 他不～. He is no swimmer.

会谈 huìtán (名) talks: 双边～ bilateral talks. 最高级～ summit meeting. ～纪要 minutes of talks; summary of a conversation

会堂 huìtáng (名) assembly hall; hall: 人民大～ the Great Hall of the People

会同 huìtóng (动) (handle an affair) jointly: ～有关部门办理 handle the matter jointly with other organizations concerned

会晤 huìwù (动) meet: 两国外长定期～. The foreign ministers of the two countries meet regularly.

会心 huìxīn (形) understanding; knowing: ～的微笑 a knowing smile

会演 huìyǎn (名) joint performance (by a number of theatrical troupes, etc.): 文艺～ theatrical festival

会议(議) huìyì (名) meeting; conference: 全体～ plenary session

会员 huìyuán (名) member: 正式～ full (or full-fledged) member. ～人数 membership. ～国 member state (or nation). ～证 membership card. ～资格 the status of a member; membership; credentials

会展 huìzhǎn (名) exhibition; convention

会诊 huìzhěn (名) consultation of doctors; (group) consultation

烩(燴) huì (动) 1 braise: ～虾仁 braised shrimp meat 2 cook (rice or shredded pancakes) with meat, vegetables and water

荟(薈) huì (名)〈书〉luxuriant growth (of plants)

荟萃 huìcuì (动) (of distinguished people) gather together; assemble: 人才～ a galaxy of talent

绘(繪) huì (动) paint; draw

绘画(畫) huìhuà (名) drawing; painting

绘声(聲)绘色 huìshēng-huìsè vivid; lively: ～的描述 a vivid description

绘制(製) huìzhì (动) draw (a design, plan or blueprint, etc.)

诲 huì (动) teach; instruct: ～人不倦 teach with tireless zeal. ～淫～盗 propagate sex and violence

晦 huì (形) dark; obscure; gloomy

晦气(氣) huìqì (形) unlucky: 自认～ be resigned to one's bad luck

晦涩 huìsè (形) hard to understand; obscure: ～的语言 obscure language (in poetry, drama, etc.)

荤 hūn (名) meat or fish: ～菜 meat dishes. ～油 lard. 她不吃～. She's a vegetarian.

昏 hūn I (名) dusk: 晨～ at dawn and dusk II (形) 1 dark; dim 2 confused; muddled: 利令智～ be blinded by lust for gain III (动) lose consciousness;

faint：～倒 fall down in a faint; fall unconscious
昏暗 hūn'àn（形）dim; dusky：～的灯光 a dim light
昏沉 hūnchén（形）1 murky：暮色～ dusk falls after sunset 2 dazed; befuddled：头脑～ feel in a daze
昏花 hūnhuā（形）blurred; dim-sighted：老眼～ dim-sighted from old age
昏黄 hūnhuáng（形）yellow; faint; dim：月色～ faint moonlight. ～的灯光 a dim light
昏厥 hūnjué（动）faint; swoon：～过去 fall into a coma; faint away
昏聩 hūnkuì（形）decrepit and muddle-headed
昏乱(亂) hūnluàn（形）dazed and confused; befuddled
昏迷 hūnmí（名）stupor; coma：处于～状态 be in a state of unconsciousness; be in a coma. ～不醒 remain unconscious
昏睡 hūnshuì（名）a deep slumber; lethargy
昏死 hūnsǐ（动）faint; fall into a coma
昏天黑地 hūntiān-hēidì 1 pitch-dark 2 dizzy：我觉得～. I suddenly felt everything went black. 3 decadent：～的生活 a dissipated life
昏眩 hūnxuàn（形）dizzy; giddy
昏庸 hūnyōng（形）fatuous; muddle-headed; imbecile; stupid
婚 hūn I（动）wed; marry II（名）marriage; wedding
婚礼(禮) hūnlǐ（名）wedding ceremony; wedding
婚配 hūnpèi（动）marry：他们尚未～. They are not married yet.
婚事 hūnshì（名）marriage; wedding
婚外情 hūnwàiqíng（名）extramarital affair; affair：他有过一段～. He once had an affair.
婚姻 hūnyīn（名）marriage; matrimony：～自由 freedom of marriage. 美满的～ a happy marriage; conjugal felicity. ～法 marriage law. ～介绍所 marriage brokering centre; match-making centre
婚约 hūnyuē（名）marriage contract; engagement：解除～ break off one's engagement
浑 hún（形）1 muddy; turbid：～水 muddy water 2 foolish; stupid 3 simple and natural; unsophisticated 4 whole; all over
浑蛋 húndàn（名）blackguard; wretch; scoundrel; bastard; skunk
浑厚 húnhòu（形）1 simple and honest 2 (of writing, painting, etc.) simple and vigorous; (of handwriting) bold and vigorous
浑浑噩噩 húnhún'è'è ignorant; muddle-headed
浑朴(樸) húnpǔ（形）simple and natural; unsophisticated
浑然一体(體) húnrán yī tǐ an integral entity
浑身 húnshēn（名）from head to foot; all over：吓得～发抖 tremble all over with fear. ～湿透 be wet through. ～是劲 bursting with energy
浑水摸鱼(魚) húnshuǐ mō yú fish in troubled waters
浑浊(濁) húnzhuó（形）muddy; turbid
魂 hún（名）1 soul 2 mood; spirit：神～不定 feel distracted 3 the lofty spirit of a nation
魂不附体(體) hún bù fù tǐ be scared out of one's wits
魂魄 húnpò（名）soul
馄 hún
馄饨 húntun（名）wonton; dumpling soup
混 hùn（动）1 mix; confuse：～为一谈 lump together; confuse one thing with another. 不要搞～了. Don't mix them up. 2 pass for; pass off as：鱼目～珠 pass off the sham as genuine 3 muddle along; drift along：～日子 drift along aimlessly; idle away one's time 4 get along with sb.：同他们～得很熟 get familiar with them
混纺 hùnfǎng（名）blending：～织物 blend fabric
混合 hùnhé（动）mix; blend; mingle：～物 mixture. ～双打 mixed doubles
混乱(亂) hùnluàn（名）confusion; chaos：陷于～ be thrown into confusion
混凝土 hùnníngtǔ（名）concrete：～结构 concrete structure
混同 hùntóng（动）confuse; mix up
混淆 hùnxiáo（动）obscure; blur; confuse; mix up：～黑白 mix up black and white. ～视听 mislead the public; confuse public opinion
混血儿(兒) hùnxuè'ér（名）half-breed; a person whose parents are of different races
混杂(雜) hùnzá（动）mix; mingle：鱼龙～ good and bad people get mixed up

混账(賬) hùnzhàng (名) scoundrel; bastard; son of a bitch: ～话 impudent remark

混浊(濁) hùnzhuó (形) muddy; turbid: ～的空气 foul (or stale) air

诨 hùn (名) joke; jest: 打～ make gags

诨名 hùnmíng (名) nickname

豁 huō (动) 1 slit; break; crack: ～了一个口子 make an opening 2 give up; sacrifice: ～出去了 be ready to pay any price
see also huò

活 huó I (动) live: ～到老,学到老. One is never too old to learn. II (形) 1 alive; living: 在他～着的时候 during his lifetime. ～捉 capture alive. ～字典 a walking dictionary 2 vivid; lively: 脑子很～ be resourceful 3 movable; moving: ～水 flowing water 4 exactly; simply: ～像 look exactly like III (名) 1 work: 针线～儿 needlework. 庄稼～ farm work 2 product: 这批～儿做得好. This batch of products is well made.

活宝(寶) huóbǎo (名) a bit of a clown; a funny fellow; a rare crank

活动(動) huódòng 1 (动) move about; exercise: 出去～～. Go out and stretch your limbs. 2 shaky; unsteady; loose: 这个螺丝～了. This screw is loose. 3 movable; mobile; flexible: ～房屋 mobile home 4 use personal influence or irregular means: 替他～～ put in a word for him; use one's influence on his behalf II (名) activity; manoeuvre: 户外～ outdoor activities. 政治～ political activities. ～余地 room for manoeuvre

活该 huógāi (动) 〈口〉 serve sb. right

活计 huójì (名) 1 handicraft work; manual labour 2 handiwork; work

活力 huólì (名) vigour; vitality; energy: 充满青春的～ brim with youthful vigour

活灵(靈)活现 huólíng-huóxiàn vivid; lifelike

活路 huólù (名) 1 means of subsistence; way out 2 workable method

活命 huómìng (动) 1 earn a bare living; scrape along; eke out an existence 2 〈书〉 save sb.'s life

活泼(潑) huópo (形) lively; vivacious; vivid: 天真～的孩子. lively children. 文字～ written in a lively style

活期 huóqī (形) current: ～储蓄 current deposit; demand deposit

活受罪 huóshòuzuì 〈口〉 have a hell of a life

活像 huóxiàng (动) look exactly like; be the spit and image of; be an exact replica of: 他长得～他父亲. He is the very spit (or image) of his father.

活血 huóxuè (动) invigorate the circulation of blood

活页 huóyè (名) loose-leaf: ～笔记本 loose-leaf notebook

活跃(躍) huóyuè I (形) brisk; active; dynamic: 市场～. Business is brisk. II (动) enliven; animate; invigorate: ～气氛 enliven the atmosphere

和 huó (动) mix (powder) with water, etc.: ～点儿灰泥 prepare some plaster. ～面 knead dough
see also hé; hè

火 huǒ I (名) 1 fire: 生～ make a fire 2 firearms; ammunition: 交～ exchange fire 3 anger; temper: 心头～起 flare up II (形) 1 fiery; flaming 2 urgent; pressing: ～急 extremely urgent

火把 huǒbǎ (名) torch

火爆 huǒbào (形) vigorous; exuberant; full of excitement: 生意～. Business is brisk. ～新闻 sensational news

火并(併) huǒbìng (动) open fight between factions

火柴 huǒchái (名) match: ～盒 matchbox

火车(車) huǒchē (名) train: ～票 railway ticket. ～站 railway station. ～头 (railway) engine; locomotive. ～时刻表 railway timetable; train schedule

火红 huǒhóng (形) red as fire; fiery; flaming: ～的太阳 a flaming sun

火候 huǒhou (名) 1 duration and degree of heating 2 level of attainment 3 a crucial moment

火花 huǒhuā (名) spark: ～四溅 sparks flying off in all directions

火化 huǒhuà (名) cremation

火急 huǒjí (形) urgent; pressing: 十万～ most urgent

火箭 huǒjiàn (名) rocket: 发射～ launch a rocket

火警 huǒjǐng (名) fire alarm

火炬 huǒjù (名) torch: ～赛跑 torch race

火坑 huǒkēng (名) abyss of suffering: 跳出～ escape from the living hell

火辣辣 huǒlàlà (形) burning: ～的太阳 a scorching sun. 脸上觉得～的 feel one's cheeks burning (as with shame)

火力 huǒlì (名) firepower; fire

火炉(爐) huǒlú (名) (heating) stove

火苗 huǒmiáo (名) tongues of flame; flames

火气(氣) huǒqì (名) **1** internal heat **2** anger; fiery temper

火器 huǒqì (名) firearms

火上加油 huǒshàng jiā yóu pour oil on the flames

火烧(燒)眉毛 huǒ shāo méimao extremely urgent: ~的事 a matter of the utmost urgency

火石 huǒshí (名) flint

火速 huǒsù (副) at top speed; post-haste

火腿 huǒtuǐ (名) ham

火险(險) huǒxiǎn (名) fire insurance

火线(綫) huǒxiàn (名) battle (or firing, front) line

火星 huǒxīng (名) **1** spark: ~迸发 a shower of sparks **2** Mars

火性 huǒxìng (名)〈口〉bad temper; hot temper

火焰 huǒyàn (名) flame: ~喷射器 flamethrower

火药(藥) huǒyào (名) gunpowder: ~库 powder magazine. ~桶 powder keg

火灾(災) huǒzāi (名) fire (as a disaster); conflagration

火葬 huǒzàng (名) cremation: ~场 crematorium; crematory

火中取栗 huǒzhōng qǔ lì pull sb.'s chestnuts out of the fire

火种(種) huǒzhǒng (名) kindling material; kindling; tinder

火烛(燭) huǒzhú (名) anything that may cause a fire: 小心~! Beware of fires!

伙 huǒ I (名) **1** mess; board; meals: 包~ get or supply meals at a fixed rate; board **2** partner; mate **3** partnership; company: 合~ enter into partnership II (量): 一~强盗 a band of robbers

伙伴 huǒbàn (名) partner; companion

伙房 huǒfáng (名) kitchen (in a school, factory, etc.)

伙计 huǒji (名) **1** partner **2**〈口〉fellow; mate: ~, 上哪儿去? Where are you going, man? **3** salesman; salesclerk; shop assistant

伙食 huǒshí (名) mess; food; board; meals: 管理~ handle messing arrangements. ~补助 food allowance.

伙同 huǒtóng (动) be in league with; act in collusion with

夥 huǒ (形)〈书〉much; a great deal; many; numerous: 获益甚~ have derived much benefit

豁 huò I (形) clear; open; open-minded; generous: ~达大度 large-minded II (动) exempt; remit
see also huō

豁亮 huòliàng (形) **1** roomy and bright **2** sonorous; resonant

豁免 huòmiǎn (动) exempt; remit: 外交~ diplomatic immunity

豁然贯通 huòrán guàntōng feel suddenly enlightened

豁然开(開)朗 huòrán kāilǎng suddenly see the light; be enlightened all of a sudden

祸(禍) huò I (名) misfortune; disaster; calamity: 车~ traffic accident II (动) bring disaster upon; ruin

祸不单(單)行 huò bù dān xíng misfortunes never come singly

祸端 huòduān (名)〈书〉the source of the disaster; the cause of the trouble

祸根 huògēn (名) the root of the trouble

祸国(國)殃民 huòguó-yāngmín bring calamity to the country and the people

祸害 huòhai I (名) disaster; curse; scourge II (动) damage; destroy

祸患 huòhuàn (名) disaster; calamity

祸首 huòshǒu (名) arch-criminal; main culprit

祸胎 huòtāi (名) the root of the trouble; the cause of the disaster

祸心 huòxīn (名) evil intent: 包藏~ harbour malicious intentions

霍 huò (副) suddenly; quickly

霍乱(亂) huòluàn (名) cholera

霍然 huòrán I (副) suddenly; quickly: 手电筒~一亮. Suddenly somebody flashed an electric torch. II (动)〈书〉(of an ailment) be quickly restored to health

获(獲) huò (动) **1** capture; catch: 捕~ capture **2** obtain; win; reap: ~利 make a profit; reap profits. **3** get in; harvest: 收~ get in

获得 huòdé (动) gain; obtain; acquire; win; achieve: ~独立 win independence. ~宝贵经验 gain valuable experience

获奖(獎) huòjiǎng (动) win a prize

获救 huòjiù (动) be rescued

获取 huòqǔ (动) obtain; gain; procure: ~

暴利 reap staggering profits

获胜(勝) huòshèng (动) win victory; be victorious; triumph

获悉 huòxī (动)〈书〉learn (of an event)

或 huò I (副) perhaps; maybe; probably: 代表团明晨～可到达. The delegation will probably arrive tomorrow morning. II (连) or; either... or...: 你～他必须参加这个会. Either you or he must attend the meeting. ～多～少卷了进去 more or less involved in the affair

或许 huòxǔ (副) perhaps; maybe: ～她已经改变了主意. Maybe she has changed her mind.

或者 huòzhě I (副) perhaps; maybe: 快点走, ～还赶得上末班车. Hurry up, and we may catch the last bus. II (连) or; either ...or...: 请把这个口信转达给李先生～他的夫人. Please pass on this oral message to Mr. or Mrs. Li.

惑 huò (动) 1 be puzzled; be bewildered: 大～不解 be greatly puzzled 2 delude; mislead: 造谣～众 create rumours to misguide the public

货 huò (名) 1 goods; commodity: 送～ delivery of goods. ～畅其流 ensure the smooth flow of commodities 2 money: 通～ currency 3 blockhead: 蠢～ blockhead; idiot

货币(幣) huòbì (名) money; currency: 周转～ vehicle currency. 自由兑换～ convertible currency. ～危机 monetary crisis. ～贬值 currency devaluation; currency depreciation

货舱(艙) huòcāng (名) (cargo) hold; cargo bay (of a plane)

货车(車) huòchē (名) 1 goods train; freight train 2 goods van (or wagon); freight car (or wagon) 3 lorry; truck

货船 huòchuán (名) freighter; cargo ship; cargo vessel: 定期～ cargo liner

货单(單) huòdān (名) manifest; waybill; shipping list

货款 huòkuǎn (名) money for buying or selling goods; payment for goods

货色 huòsè (名) 1 goods: ～齐全. We offer goods of every specification. 2 junk; trash; rubbish

货物 huòwù (名) goods; commodity; merchandise

货样(樣) huòyàng (名) sample goods; sample

货源 huòyuán (名) source of goods; supply of goods: ～充足 an ample supply of goods

货运(運) huòyùn (名) freight transport: ～单 waybill. ～费 shipping cost; freight charges

货栈(棧) huòzhàn (名) warehouse

货真价(價)实(實) huòzhēn-jiàshí 1 the goods are genuine and the price is fair 2 through and through; out-and-out; dyed-in-the-wool: ～的好战分子 out-and-out hawkish elements

J j

激 jī I (动) 1 surge; dash: 海水冲击礁石, ～起高高的浪花. The waves broke against the rocks, sending up a fountain of spray. 2 arouse; stimulate; excite: ～于义愤 aroused by a sense of justice or by righteous indignation II (形) sharp; fierce; violent: ～流 strong currents. ～战 fierce fighting

激昂 jī'áng (形) impassioned: ～慷慨 speak fervour and with indignation

激荡(蕩) jīdàng (动) agitate; surge; rage: 海水～的声音 the sound of surging waves

激动(動) jīdòng (动) excite; stir: ～人心的场面 a stirring scene. ～得流下眼泪 be moved to tears

激发(發) jīfā (动) arouse; stimulate; set off: ～群众的积极性 arouse popular enthusiasm

激愤 jīfèn (形) be roused to anger; indignant

激光 jīguāng (名) laser: ～束 laser beam

激光唱片 jīguāng chàngpiàn CD; compact disc

激化 jīhuà (动) sharpen; intensify; become acute: 矛盾进一步～. The contradictions intensified further.

激活 jīhuó (动) activate

激将(將)法 jījiàngfǎ (名) the tactics of prodding sb. into action

激进(進) jījìn (形) radical: ～派 radicals

激励(勵) jīlì (动) encourage; impel; urge: ～将士 give a pep talk to officers and men. ～士气 boost morale

激烈 jīliè (形) (of action and argument) intense; sharp; fierce; acute: 大家争论得很～. We (They) all argued heatedly.
激怒 jīnù (动) enrage; infuriate; exasperate
激切 jīqiè (形)〈书〉blunt and vehement: 言辞～ in blunt and vehement terms
激情 jīqíng (名) strong emotion; enthusiasm: 他充满欢乐的～. He is bursting with joy.
激素 jīsù (名) hormone
激增 jīzēng (动) increase sharply; soar; shoot up: 价格～. Prices are rocketing.

跻(躋) jī (动)〈书〉ascend; mount: 使国家的科学～于世界先进之列 raise the level of the country's science to the advanced level of the world

积(積) jī I (动) amass; store up; accumulate: ～少成多. Many a little makes a mickle. II (形) long-standing; long-pending; age-old: ～案 a long-pending case. ～弊 age-old malpractice
积淀(澱) jīdiàn (名) accumulation; accretion: 历史～ historical accretion
积极(極) jījí (形) 1 positive: ～因素 positive factor. ～作用 positive role 2 active; energetic; vigorous: ～分子 activist. ～性 zeal; initiative; enthusiasm
积聚 jījù (动) gather; accumulate; build up: ～财富 accumulate wealth. ～力量 build up strength
积劳(勞)成疾 jī láo chéng jí break down under the strain of long years of strenuous work; fall ill from prolonged overwork
积累 jīlěi (动、名) accumulate; accumulation: ～经验 accumulate experience
积木 jīmù (名) toy bricks
积习(習) jīxí (名) old habit; long-standing practice: ～难改. It is very difficult to change one's old habit.
积蓄 jīxù (名) savings
积压(壓) jīyā (动) keep long in stock; overstock
积怨 jīyuàn (名) bottled-up rancour; piled-up grievances
积攒 jīzǎn (动)〈口〉save (or collect) bit by bit: ～肥料 collect farmyard manure
积重难(難)返 jī zhòng nán fǎn unhealthy old customs die hard

击(擊) jī (动) 1 beat; hit; strike: ～鼓 beat a drum 2 attack; assault: 声东～西 make a feint to the east and attack in the west
击败 jībài (动) defeat; beat; vanquish
击毙(斃) jībì (动) shoot dead; kill
击毁 jīhuǐ (动) smash; wreck; destroy
击剑(劍) jījiàn (名) fencing
击溃 jīkuì (动) rout; annihilate; crush
击落 jīluò (动) shoot down; bring down; down: ～敌机七架 bring down seven enemy planes
击破 jīpò (动) break up; destroy; rout
击中 jīzhòng (动) hit: ～目标 hit the target. ～要害 hit the nail on the head; strike home

基 jī I (名) 1 base; foundation: 路～ roadbed; bed. 奠～ lay a foundation 2 radical; base; group II (形) basic; key; primary; cardinal
基本 jīběn (形) 1 basic; fundamental: ～要求 basic requirements. ～原则 fundamental principles. ～知识 rudimentary knowledge 2 main; essential: ～条件 principal conditions. ～词汇 basic vocabulary; basic word-stock. ～工资 basic wage (or salary). ～建设 capital construction
基层(層) jīcéng (名) basic level; primary level; grass-roots unit
基础(礎) jīchǔ (名) foundation; base; basis: 打～ lay a foundation. 物质～ material base. ～工业 basic industries. ～教育 elementary education. ～科学 basic science. ～课 basic courses (of a college curriculum). ～设施 infrastructure (such as energy and transport)
基地 jīdì (名) base: 军事～ military base. 工业～ industrial base. 原料～ source of raw materials
基点(點) jīdiǎn (名) basic point; starting point; centre
基调 jīdiào (名) 1 fundamental key; main key 2 keynote: 他讲话的～是团结. The keynote of his speech was unity.
基督 Jīdū (名) Christ: ～教 Christianity; the Christian religion. ～徒 Christian
基金 jījīn (名) fund: ～会 foundation
基石 jīshí (名) foundation stone; cornerstone
基数(數) jīshù (名) 1 cardinal number 2 base: 以 1965 年的产量为～ taking the output of 1965 as the base
基因 jīyīn (名) gene
基于(於) jīyú (介) according to; in view

J

of: ～以上理由我不赞成他的意见. For reasons mentioned above, I do not agree with him.

奇 jī (形) odd (number): ～数 odd number
see also qí

畸 jī (形) 1 lopsided; unbalanced 2 irregular; abnormal

畸形 jīxíng I (名) deformity; malformation II (形) lopsided; unbalanced; abnormal: ～发展 lopsided development. ～现象 abnormal phenomenon

犄 jī

犄角 jījiǎo (名) corner: 屋子～ a corner of the room

犄角 jījiao (名) horn: 牛～ ox horn

羁(羈) jī 〈书〉 I (名) bridle; headstall: 无～之马 a horse without a bridle II (动) 1 restrict; restrain: 放荡不～ lead a Bohemian life 2 stay; stop over; detain

羁绊 jībàn (名)〈书〉 trammels; fetters; yoke

羁押 jīyā (动)〈书〉 detain; take into custody

稽 jī (动) 1 check; examine; investigate: 无～之谈 a tall tale 2 stay; stop over

稽核 jīhé (动) check; examine: ～账目 audit accounts

稽留 jīliú (动)〈书〉 delay; detain: 因事～ be detained by business

几 jī I (名) a small table: 茶～儿 tea table; teapoy II (幾)(副) nearly; almost; practically: 到会者～三千人. Nearly 3,000 people attended the meeting.
see also jǐ

几乎 jīhū (副) nearly; almost; practically: 我～忘了. I very nearly forgot all about it. 他～一夜没睡. He lay awake practically the whole night.

讥(譏) jī (动) laugh at; ridicule

讥讽 jīfěng (动) satirize; hold sb. up to ridicule

讥诮 jīqiào (动)〈书〉 sneer at; make gibes about; speak ironically about

讥笑 jīxiào (动) ridicule; sneer at

机(機) jī I (名) 1 machine; engine: 缝纫～ sewing machine. ～床 machine tool. 影印～ photocopier 2 aircraft; aeroplane; plane: 客～ passenger plane. 运输～ transport plane 3 crucial point; pivot; key link: 转～ a turning point 4 chance; occasion; opportunity: 趁～ take advantage of the occasion; seize the opportunity (or chance). 随～应变 act according to circumstances II (形) 1 organic: 有～体 organism. 无～化学 inorganic chemistry 2 flexible; quick-witted: ～智 clever; resourceful

机场(場) jīchǎng (名) airport; airfield; aerodrome

机车(車) jīchē (名) locomotive; engine: 内燃(电力、蒸汽)～ diesel (electric, steam) locomotive

机动(動) jīdòng (形) 1 power-driven; motorized: ～车 motor-driven (or motor) vehicle 2 flexible; expedient; mobile: ～处置 deal with sth. flexibly. ～性 mobility; flexibility 3 in reserve; for emergency use: ～力量 reserve force. ～费 reserve fund

机构(構) jīgòu (名) 1 mechanism: 传动～ transmission mechanism 2 organization; set-up: 政府～ government organization. 精简～ simplify (or streamline) the administrative structure

机关(關) jīguān (名) 1 mechanism; gear: 起动～ starting gear 2 office; organ; body: 领导～ leading bodies. ～报 official newspaper. ～干部 government functionary; office worker 3 intrigue; ruse: ～算尽 use up all one's tricks. 识破～ see through a ruse

机会(會) jīhuì (名) chance; opportunity: 千载一时的好～ a rare opportunity in a lifetime

机会(會)主义(義) jīhuìzhǔyì (名) opportunism

机警 jījǐng (形) alert; sharp-witted; vigilant

机灵(靈) jīling (形) clever; smart; quick-minded

机密 jīmì I (形) secret; classified; confidential: ～文件 classified papers; confidential documents II (名) secret: 严守国家～ strictly guard state secrets

机敏 jīmǐn (形) alert and resourceful

机能 jīnéng (名) function

机器 jīqì (名) machine; machinery; apparatus: 安装新～ install new machinery. 国家～ state apparatus (or machine). ～

人 robot. ～油 lubricating oil; lubricant

机械 jīxiè I (名) machinery; machine; mechanism: ～故障 mechanical failure (or breakdown). ～工程学 mechanical engineering II (形) mechanical; inflexible; rigid: ～地照搬别人的经验 apply other people's experience mechanically

机械化 jīxièhuà (动、名) mechanize; mechanization: 农业～ mechanization of agriculture; mechanization of farm work. ～部队 mechanized force (or troops, unit)

机要 jīyào (形) confidential: ～工作 confidential work. ～秘书 confidential secretary

机宜 jīyí (名) guiding principles; guidelines: 面授～ brief sb. on how to act under certain circumstances; give confidential instructions in person

机遇 jīyù (名) good fortune; opportunity

机缘 jīyuán (名) good luck; opportunity: ～凑巧 as luck would have it; by chance; by a concatenation of lucky events

机制 jīzhì (名) mechanism: 运行～ operating mechanism

机智 jīzhì (形) quick-witted; resourceful

机组 jīzǔ (名) 1 unit; set: 发电～ generating unit (or set) 2 aircrew; flight crew

叽(嘰) jī (象): 小鸟～～叫. Little birds chirp.

叽咕 jīgu (动) talk in a low voice; whisper; mutter: 他们俩叽叽咕咕不知谈了多久. The two of them have been talking in whispers for God knows how long.

叽叽喳喳 jījizhāzhā (象) (of birds) chirp; twitter

肌 jī (名) muscle; flesh

肌肤(膚) jīfū (名) (human) skin

肌腱 jījiàn (名) tendon

肌理 jīlǐ (名)〈书〉skin texture: ～细腻 fine-textured skin

肌肉 jīròu (名) muscle: ～发达 muscular

肌体(體) jītǐ (名) human body; organism

饥(饑) jī I (形) hungry; starving; II (名) famine; crop failure: ～民 famine victims

饥不择(擇)食 jī bù zé shí a hungry person is not choosy about his food

饥肠(腸) jīcháng (名)〈书〉empty stomach

饥饿 jī'è (名) hunger; starvation

饥寒交迫 jī-hán jiāopò suffer hunger and cold; live in hunger and cold; be poverty-stricken

饥荒 jīhuang I (名) famine; crop failure II (形)〈口〉be hard up

鸡(鷄) jī (名) chicken: 公～ cock; rooster. 母～ hen. 雏～ chick; chicken. ～窝 roost; henhouse

鸡蛋 jīdàn (名) (hen's) egg: ～糕 (sponge) cake

鸡飞(飛)蛋打 jīfēi-dàndǎ suffer a loss both ways

鸡肋 jīlèi (名)〈书〉things of little value which one is not particularly keen on but reluctant to throw away

鸡毛蒜皮 jīmáo-suànpí trivialities

鸡犬不宁(寧) jī-quǎn bù níng there is a scene of general turmoil—everybody is disturbed one way or the other

鸡尾酒 jīwěijiǔ (名) cocktail: ～会 cocktail party

缉 jī (动) seize; arrest

缉毒 jīdú (动) investigate drug smuggling; capture drug smugglers; combat narcotics: ～队 narcotics squad. ～犬 drug-detection dog; sniffer dog

缉拿 jīná (动) seize; arrest; apprehend: ～凶手 apprehend the murderer

缉私 jīsī (动) seize smugglers or smuggled goods; suppress smuggling: ～人员 anti-contraband personnel

疾 jí I (名) 1 disease; sickness; illness: 眼～ eye trouble 2 suffering; pain; difficulty: ～苦 sufferings; hardships II (动) hate; abhor: ～恶如仇 hate evils and evildoers like sworn enemies III (形) fast; quick: ～驰而过 gallop off; speed past

疾病 jíbìng (名) disease; illness: 治～ treatment of disease

疾风(風)劲(勁)草 jífēng jìngcǎo sturdy grass withstands strong winds; misfortune is a test for a person's character

嫉 jí (动) 1 be jealous; be envious 2 hate

嫉妒 jídù (动) be jealous of; envy

嫉恨 jíhèn (动) envy and hate; hate out of jealousy

瘠 jí (形)〈书〉1 lean; thin and weak 2 barren; poor; lean: ～土 poor soil; barren land

瘠薄 jíbó (形) (of land) barren; unpro-

J

ductive

吉 jí (形) lucky; auspicious; propitious: 万事大~. All is well. *or* Everything is fine.

吉卜赛人 jíbǔsàirén (名) Gypsy

吉利 jílì (形) lucky; auspicious; propitious

吉庆(慶) jíqìng (形) auspicious; propitious; happy

吉他 jítā (名) guitar

吉祥 jíxiáng (形) lucky; auspicious; propitious

吉凶 jí-xiōng (名) good or ill luck; fate

吉兆 jízhào (名) good omen; propitious sign

佶 jí (形) 〈书〉 robust and sturdy

佶屈聱牙 jíqū áoyá difficult to articulate: ~之词 tongue twister

籍 jí (名) 1 book; record: 古~ ancient books 2 native place; home town; birthplace: 祖~ one's ancestral birthplace 3 membership: 国~ nationality; citizenship. 党~ party affiliation

籍贯 jíguàn (名) the place of one's birth or origin

棘 jí (名) 1 sour jujube 2 thorn bushes; brambles

棘手 jíshǒu (形) thorny; difficult to handle; knotty: ~的问题 a thorny problem; a hard nut to crack

楫 jí 〈书〉 oar: 舟~ boat

辑 jí I (动) collect; compile; edit: 编~ edit; compile II (名) part; volume; division

辑录(録) jílù (动) compile

集 jí I (动) gather; assemble: ~各家之长 incorporate the strong points of various schools. 惊喜交~ astonishment mingled with joy II (名) 1 fair; market: 赶~ go to market 2 collection; anthology: 诗~ a collection of poems. 影~ an album of pictures 3 volume; part: 这部影片分上、下两~, 今晚放映. The film which is in two parts will be shown tonight.

集成电(電)路 jíchéng diànlù integrated circuit

集合 jíhé (动) gather; assemble; muster; call together: ~地点 assembly place. 我们在校门口~. We shall assemble at the school gate.

集会(會) jíhuì (名) assembly; rally; gathering; meeting: ~自由 freedom of assembly. 群众~ mass rally

集结 jíjié (动) mass; concentrate; build up: 军队~待命. Troops are assembling to await orders.

集锦 jíjǐn (名) a collection of choice specimens: 花鸟画~ outstanding examples of flower-and-bird paintings

集权(權) jíquán (名) centralization of state power; concentration of power

集散地 jísàndì (名) collecting and distributing centre; distributing centre

集市 jíshì (名) (country) fair; market

集思广(廣)益 jísī-guǎngyì let us pool our ideas; let us put our heads together

集体(體) jítǐ (名) collective: ~创作 collective effort. ~领导 collective leadership. ~化 collectivization. ~农场 collective farm. ~安全 collective security. ~舞 group dancing

集团(團) jítuán (名) group; clique; circle; bloc: 统治~ the ruling clique; the ruling circle. 军事~ a military bloc. ~政治 bloc politics. ~公司 corporation group; conglomerate

集训 jíxùn (动) bring people together for training

集腋成裘 jí yè chéng qiú many a little makes a mickle; pool small resources to help accomplish a big project

集邮(郵) jíyóu (名) stamp collecting; philately: ~簿 stamp-album

集约 jíyuē (形) intensive: ~型发展 intensive development. 技术~企业 technology-intensive enterprise

集中 jízhōng (动) concentrate; centralize; focus; amass; put together: ~精力 concentrate one's efforts. ~大量财富 amass vast material resources. ~管理 centralized management. ~营 concentration camp

集装(裝)箱 jízhuāngxiāng (名) container: ~船 container ship. ~海港 container port. ~运输 container shipment

集资 jízī (动) raise funds; pool resources

及 jí I (动) reach; come up to; attain: 力所能~ what is in one's power II (连) [connecting nouns and noun phrases, the coordinate 及 is preceded by a noun or nouns of greater importance] and: 词典~其他参考书 dictionaries and other reference books

及格 jígé (动) pass a test, examination,

etc.; pass; be up to the standard

及时(時) jíshí (形) **1** timely; in good time: ～的忠告 timely advice **2** promptly; without delay: 有问题就～解决. Problems, if any, should be solved without delay.

及早 jízǎo (副) at an early date; as soon as possible; before it is too late: 有病要～治. It is necessary to see a doctor at once when you are ill.

汲 jí (动) draw (water): 从井里～水 draw water from a well

汲汲 jíjí (形)〈书〉anxious; avid: ～于名利 avid for fame and wealth

汲取 jíqǔ (动) draw; derive: ～营养 derive nourishment from. 从中～教训 draw a lesson from it

极(極) jí I (名) **1** the utmost point; extreme: 无所不用其～ go to any lengths. 荒谬之～ be the height of absurdity. ～而言之 talk in extreme terms **2** pole: 北(南)～ the North (South) Pole II (副) extremely; exceedingly: ～为重要 of the utmost importance. 冷～了 extremely cold

极点(點) jídiǎn (名) the limit; the extreme: 我们忍耐到了～. Our tolerance has reached its limit.

极度 jídù (形) extreme; exceeding: ～困难 exceedingly difficult. ～兴奋 be elated

极端 jíduān (形) extreme; exceeding: ～仇视 show extreme hatred for. ～腐败 rotten to the core. ～左倾分子 extreme left elements; ultra-leftists

极乐(樂)世界 jílè shìjiè (名) (in Buddhism) Sukhavati; Pure Land; Western Paradise

极力 jílì (副) do one's utmost; spare no effort: ～劝阻 try very hard to dissuade sb. from doing sth. ～否认 deny vehemently

极目 jímù (副) look as far as the eye can see: ～远眺 gaze far into the distance

极其 jíqí (副) most; extremely; exceedingly: ～深刻 extremely profound. ～艰巨 exceptionally arduous

极权(權)主义(義) jíquánzhǔyì (名) totalitarianism

极盛 jíshèng (名) heyday; zenith; acme: ～时期 golden age; prime

极限 jíxiàn (名) the maximum; the limit

极刑 jíxíng (名) capital punishment; the death penalty

岌 jí (形)〈书〉(of a mountain) lofty; towering

岌岌 jíjí (形)〈书〉precarious: ～可危 be in imminent danger; be placed in jeopardy

级 jí (名) **1** level; rank; grade: 高～ higher level. 部长～会谈 talks at ministerial level. 七～地震 an earthquake of magnitude 7 (on the Richter scale) **2** grade: 同～不同班 of the same grade but not of the same class **3** step: 石～ stone steps

级别 jíbié (名) rank; level; grade; scale: 工资～ wage scale; grade on the wage scale

急 jí I (动) **1** be impatient; be anxious: ～着要到前线去 be impatient to leave for the front **2** worry: 火车快开了,他还不来,实在～人. It is really exasperating that he has not turned up when the train is about to leave. **3** be irritated; be annoyed; be nettled: 没说上几句话他就～了. After a few words he was already getting quite worked up. **4** be eager to help: ～公好义 be zealous for the common weal; ready to stand up for justice II (形) **1** fast; rapid; violent: 水流很～. The current is swift. *or* It's a strong current. ～风暴雨 violent storm; tempest; hurricane **2** urgent; pressing: ～电 urgent telegram. 他走得很～. He left in a hurry. 告～ appeal for emergency help

急病 jíbìng (名) acute disease

急促 jícù (形) **1** hurried; rapid: ～的脚步声 hurried footsteps. 呼吸～ be panting **2** (of time) short; pressing: 时间很～,要速作决定. Time presses, and we must make a quick decision.

急功近利 jígōng jìnlì eager for instant success and quick profit

急件 jíjiàn (名) urgent document or dispatch

急救 jíjiù (名) first aid; emergency treatment: ～药箱 first-aid kit. ～站 first-aid station

急剧(劇) jíjù (形) rapid; sharp; sudden: ～的变化 drastic change. ～转折 abrupt turn. ～上升 steep rise. ～下降 sudden drop

急遽 jíjù (形) rapid; sharp; sudden

急流 jíliú (名) **1** torrent; rapid stream; rapids **2** jet stream; jet flow

急流勇退 jíliú yǒngtuì make a resolute decision to retire at the height of one's career

急忙 jímáng (形) in a hurry; in haste; hurriedly; hastily: 他穿上大衣,~赶去车站. He put on his overcoat and hurried to the station.

急难(難) jínàn I (名)〈书〉misfortune; time of trouble; grave danger II (动) be anxious to help (those in grave danger)

急迫 jípò (形) urgent; pressing; imperative: 最~的任务 the most pressing task. 形势~ critical juncture

急起直追 jíqǐ-zhízhuī hurry and catch up with; do one's utmost to overtake

急切 jíqiè (形) 1 eager; impatient: ~地盼望 eagerly look forward to; wait impatiently for 2 in a hurry; in haste

急速 jísù (副) very fast; at high speed; rapidly: ~行驶 drive at high speed. 情况~变化. The situation changed fast.

急性子 jíxìngzi I (形) of impatient disposition; quick-tempered II (名) an impetuous person

急需 jíxū I (动) be badly in need of: 提供~的资金 provide much-needed funds II (名) urgent need: 以应~ so as to meet an urgent need

急于(於) jíyú (动) be eager to; be anxious to; be impatient to: ~回去 anxious to go back. ~求成 overanxious for quick results; impatient for success

急躁 jízào (形) 1 irritable; irascible 2 impetuous; rash; impatient: 防止~情绪 guard against impetuosity

急诊 jízhěn (名) emergency call; emergency treatment: ~病人 emergency case. ~室 emergency ward

急中生智 jízhōng shēng zhì suddenly hit upon a way out at the last minute; show resourcefulness in an emergency

急转(轉)直下 jízhuǎn-zhíxià (of situation, plot of a play, etc.) develop rapidly and smoothly after taking a sudden turn

即

jí I (动) 1 approach; reach; be near: 可望而不可~ be within sight but inaccessible 2 assume; undertake: ~位 ascend the throne; assume office 3 be; mean; namely: 此陌生人~约翰逊教授. This stranger is no other than professor Johnson. II (副) promptly; at once: 闻过~改 correct one's mistake as soon as it is pointed out

即便 jíbiàn (连) even; even if; even though: ~你当头儿,也不该摆架子. You shouldn't put on airs even if you were in charge.

即将(將) jíjiāng (副) be about to; be on the point of: 理想~实现. The ideal is about to come true. 春节~来临. The Spring Festival is just around the corner.

即景生情 jíjǐng shēng qíng the scene touches a responsive chord in one's heart

即刻 jíkè (副) at once; immediately; instantly

即日 jírì (名)〈书〉1 this or that very day: ~生效 come into effect this very day 2 within the coming few days

即时(時) jíshí (副) immediately; forthwith: ~交货 prompt delivery. ~付款 immediate payment

即使 jíshǐ (连) even; even if; even though

即席 jíxí〈书〉I (形) impromptu; extemporaneous: ~讲话 speak impromptu; make an impromptu (or extemporaneous) speech II (动) take one's seat (at a dinner table, etc.)

即兴(興) jíxìng (形) impromptu; extemporaneous: ~之作 an improvisation.

亟

jí (副)〈书〉urgently; anxiously; earnestly: ~盼 earnestly hope. ~待解决 demand prompt solution

脊

jǐ (名) 1 spine; backbone 2 ridge: 山~ the ridge of a hill or mountain. 屋~ the ridge of a roof

脊背 jǐbèi (名) back (of a human being or any other vertebrate)

脊梁 jǐliang (名) back (of the human body): ~骨 backbone; spine

脊椎 jǐzhuī (名) vertebra: ~动物 vertebrate. ~骨 vertebra; spine

济(濟) jǐ

see also jì

济济 jǐjǐ (形) (of people) many; numerous: 人才~ an abundance of talented people; a galaxy of talent

挤(擠)

jǐ (动) 1 squeeze; press: ~牙膏 squeeze toothpaste out of a tube. ~牛奶 milk the cow 2 jostle; push against: ~进去 force (or elbow, shoulder, push) one's way in; squeeze in. 把他们的产品~出世界市场 edge their products out of world market. 人多~不进去. There are so many people there that it is impossible to squeeze in. 3 crowd; pack; cram: ～做一团 pressed close together; packed like sardines. 礼堂已经～满了. The assembly hall is filled to capacity.

挤眉弄眼 jǐméi-nòngyǎn make eyes; wink

几(幾) jǐ (数) 1 how many: ～点钟了? What's the time? 你能在这里住～天? How many days can you stay here? 2 a few; several; some: 说～句话 say a few words. ～十 tens; dozens; scores. 十～岁的孩子 teenager. 二十～个人 twenty odd people. 所剩无～. There is not much left.
see also jī

几分 jǐfēn (形) a bit; somewhat; rather: 她说的有～道理. There is a grain of truth in what she said. ～怀疑 be somewhat suspicious. 有～醉意 be a bit tipsy

几何 jǐhé I (代)〈书〉 how much; how many: 不知尚有～ have yet to know how much is left II (名) geometry: ～图形 geometric figure

几何学(學) jǐhéxué (名) geometry: 解析～ analytic geometry. 立体～ solid geometry. 平面～ plane geometry

几时(時) jǐshí (代) what time; when: 你们～回来? What time will you come back?

几许 jǐxǔ (代)〈书〉 how much; how many: 不知～. No one can tell how much.

己 jǐ (名) oneself; one's own; personal: 舍～为公 make personal sacrifices for the public good. 引为～任 consider oneself duty-bound to; regard as one's duty. 请各抒～见. Everybody is requested to air his own views.

己方 jǐfāng (名) one's own side

给 jǐ I (动) supply; provide: 自～自足 self-sufficiency II (形) ample; well provided for: 家～户足. Every household is comfortably off.
see also gěi

给养(養) jǐyǎng (名) provisions; victuals: ～充足 be abundantly provisioned

给予 jǐyǔ (动)〈书〉 give; render: ～支持 offer support. ～同情 show sympathy

寂 jì (形) 1 quiet; still; silent: 万籁俱～. All is quiet and still. 2 lonely; lonesome; solitary: 枯～ lonely and bored stiff

寂静 jìjìng (形) quiet; still; silent: 在～的深夜里 in the still of the night

寂寞 jìmò (形) lonely; lonesome: 感到～ feel lonely

寂然 jìrán (形)〈书〉 silent; still

济(濟) jì (动) 1 cross a river: 同舟共～ make a concerted effort to tide over the difficulty 2 save: 缓不～急 slow action cannot save a critical situation 3 be of help; benefit: 无～于事 not help matters; be of no benefit
see also jǐ

剂(劑) jì I (名) a pharmaceutical or other chemical preparation: 针～ injection. 片～ tablet. 干燥～ drying agent; desiccant. 防腐～ preservative; antiseptic II (量): 一～中药 a dose of Chinese herbal medicine

剂量 jìliàng (名) dosage; dose

计 jì I (动) count; compute; calculate; estimate: 不～其数 countless; innumerable II (名) 1 meter; gauge: 雨量～ rain gauge 2 idea; stratagem; plan: 中～ fall into a trap. 长远之～ from a long-term point of view. ～上心来 a new idea flashed across one's mind; strike out a plan

计策 jìcè (名) stratagem; plan

计划(劃) jìhuà I (名) plan; project; programme: 可行的～ a feasible (or workable) plan. 五年～ five-year plan. ～经济 planned economy. 指导性～ guidance plan. 指令性～ mandatory plan. ～外项目 projects outside the plan. ～生产 planned production. ～生育 family planning; birth control II (动) map out; plan: 我们～周末去纽约. We plan to go to New York at the weekend.

计件 jìjiàn (动) reckon by the piece: ～工资 piece-rate wage. ～工作 piecework

计较 jìjiào (动) 1 haggle over; fuss about: 斤斤～ be too calculating; weigh and balance at every turn. 从不～个人名利 give no thought to personal fame and gain 2 argue; dispute: 我不同你～,等你气平了再说. I won't argue with you until you have calmed down. 3 think over; plan

计量 jìliàng (动) measure; calculate; estimate: 不可～ inestimable

计谋 jìmóu (名) scheme; stratagem

计算 jìsuàn I (动) count; compute; calculate: ～产值 calculate the output value. ～尺 slide rule II (名) consideration; planning: 做事不能没个～. We shouldn't do anything without a plan.

计算机(機) jìsuànjī (名) computer: ～程序设

计 computer programming. ～存储器 computer storage. ～软件 computer software. ～硬件 computer hardware

计算器 jìsuànqì (名) calculator

计议(議) jìyì (动) deliberate; talk over; consult: 从长～ take one's time in coming to a decision

迹 jì (名) 1 mark; trace: 足～ footprint. 血～ bloodstain 2 remains; ruins; vestige: 古～ relics of historical interest

迹象 jìxiàng (名) sign; indication: 有～表明情况将进一步改善. There are indications that the situation will further improve.

绩 jì (名) achievement; accomplishment; merit: 战～ military achievement (or exploits). 功～ merits and achievements; contributions

髻 jì (名) hair worn in a bun or coil

技 jì (名) skill; ability; trick: ～巧 technique. 有一～之长 be good at one branch of knowledge or type of skill

技工 jìgōng (名) 1 skilled worker 2 mechanic; technician

技能 jìnéng (名) technical ability; occupational skills; mastery of a skill or technique: 生产～ skill in production

技师(師) jìshī (名) technician

技术(術) jìshù (名) technology; skill; technique: ～水平 technical competence. ～转让 technology transfer. ～鉴定 technical appraisal. ～革新 technological innovation; technical innovation. ～工人 skilled worker. ～力量 technical force; technical personnel. ～员 technician. ～知识 technological know-how; technical knowledge. ～资料 technical data; technological data. ～开发中心 centres for technological development. ～标准 technical norms

技艺(藝) jìyì (名) skill; artistry: ～精湛 highly skilled; masterly

伎 jì (名) 1 ruse; trick: 故～重演 be up to one's old tricks again; play the same old trick 2 a singsong girl in ancient China

伎俩(倆) jìliǎng (名) trick; intrigue; manoeuvre

妓 jì (名) prostitute: ～女 prostitute. ～院 brothel; whorehouse

寄 jì (动) 1 send; post; mail: ～信 post a letter; mail a letter. ～包裹 send a parcel by post 2 entrust; deposit; place: ～希望于青年 place hopes on the youth 3 depend on: ～食 live with a relative or friend for want of financial support

寄存 jìcún (动) deposit; leave with; check: 把大衣～在衣帽间 check one's overcoat at the cloakroom. 行李～处 left-luggage office; checkroom

寄放 jìfàng (动) leave with; leave in the care of: 我要外出一段时间,这些书可以～在你那里吗? I'll be away for some time. May I leave these books with you?

寄父 jìfù (名) foster father

寄卖(賣) jìmài (动) consign for sale on commission; put on sale in a second-hand shop: ～商店 commission shop

寄人篱(籬)下 jì rén lí xià have to depend on sb. for a living

寄生 jìshēng (名) parasitism: ～生活 parasitic life

寄生虫(蟲) jìshēngchóng (名) parasite

寄宿 jìsù (动) 1 lodge: 我暂时～在朋友家里. I am staying at a friend's house for the time being. 2 (of students) board: ～生 resident student; boarder. ～学校 boarding school; residential college

寄托 jìtuō (动) 1 send to the care of sb.; leave with sb.: 把孩子～在邻居家里 entrust one's child to the care of a neighbour 2 place (hope, etc.) on: 作者把自己的思想感情～在剧中主人翁身上. The author projects his own thoughts and feelings into the personality of the hero of his play.

寄养(養) jìyǎng (动) entrust one's child to the care of sb.

寄予 jìyǔ (动) 1 place (hope, etc.) on: 国家对青年一代～很大的希望. The state places great hopes on the younger generation. 2 show; express: ～深切的同情 be extremely sympathetic to

骥 jì (名)〈书〉a thoroughbred horse

觊(覬) jì (动)〈书〉attempt; hope

觊觎 jìyú (动)〈书〉cast greedy eyes on; covet

稷 jì (名) 1 millet 2 the god of grains worshipped by ancient emperors: 社～ the country

季 jì (名) 1 season: 一年四～ all the year round. 雨～ rainy season; monsoon. 旱～ dry season. 2 the end of an epoch: 清～ the end of the Qing dynasty 3 the last month of a season: ～春 the last month of spring

季度 jìdù (名) quarter (of a year): ～报告 a quarterly report

季风(風) jìfēng (名) monsoon: ～气候 monsoon climate

季节(節) jìjié (名) season: ～性 seasonal. ～工 seasonal worker. 旅游～ tourist season. 收获～ harvest time

季刊 jìkān (名) quarterly

悸 jì (动)〈书〉(of the heart) throb with fear: 心有余～ shake with lingering fear; shudder at the thought of

祭 jì (动) 1 hold a memorial ceremony for 2 offer a sacrifice to: ～天 offer a sacrifice to Heaven; worship Heaven

祭奠 jìdiàn (动) hold a memorial ceremony for

祭品 jìpǐn (名) sacrificial offerings; oblation

祭祀 jìsì (动) (of old customs) offer sacrifices to gods or ancestors

祭文 jìwén (名) funeral oration; elegiac address

祭祖 jìzǔ (动) offer sacrifices to one's ancestors

际(際) jì (名) 1 border; boundary; edge: 天～ horizon. 无边无～ boundless 2 between; among; inter-: 星～旅行 space travel. 国～ international 3 inside: 脑～ in one's head (or mind) 4 occasion; time: 临别之～ at parting 5 one's lot: 遭～ unfavourable turns in life; misfortune

鲫 jì (名) crucian carp

系(繫) jì (动) tie; fasten; do up; button up: ～安全带 fasten one's seat belt. 把衣服扣子～上 button up a jacket. ～着领带 wear ties
see also xì

系泊 jìbó (动) moor (a boat)

既 jì I (副) already: ～成事实 fait accompli; accomplished fact. ～得利益 vested interests II (连) 1 since; as; now that: ～来之,则安之. Since you are here, you may as well stay on and enjoy yourself. 2 [often used together with such adverbs as 且,又,也] both... and; as well as: 这本书～有趣,又有教育意义. This book is both interesting and instructive.

既然 jìrán (连) since; as; now that: ～如此 such being the case; under these circumstances

既往不咎 jìwǎng bù jiù let bygones be bygones; forgive sb.'s past misdeeds

暨 jì 〈书〉 1 and 2 up to; till: ～今 up till now

记 jì I (动) 1 remember; bear in mind: ～不清 cannot recall exactly. 我们要牢牢～住这点. We must bear this firmly in mind. 2 write (or jot, take) down; record: ～在笔记本上 write it down in a notebook. ～下这些号码 jot down these numbers II (名) 1 notes; record: 游～ travel notes. 大事～ a chronicle of events 2 mark; sign: 暗～儿 secret mark 3 birthmark: 他左边眉毛上方有块～. There is a birthmark just above his left eyebrow. III (量): 一～耳光 a slap in the face

记得 jìde (动) remember: 过了这些年,我都记不得他的名字了. After so many years, I don't quite remember his name.

记分 jìfēn (动) 1 keep the score; record the points (in a game) 2 register a student's marks 3 record work points: ～册 (teacher's) markbook. ～牌 scoreboard

记功 jìgōng (动) cite sb. for meritorious service; record a merit

记过(過) jìguò (动) record a demerit

记号(號) jìhao (名) mark; sign: 做个～ make a sign; mark out

记恨 jìhèn (动) bear grudges

记录(録) jìlù I (动) take notes; keep the minutes; record: 教授堂上讲的我都～下来了. I took careful notes of the professor's lecture. II (名) 1 minutes; notes; record: 会议～ the minutes of a meeting. 会谈～ a transcript of talks. 逐字～ verbatim record. ～本 minute book. ～片 documentary film; documentary 2 note-taker: 这次讨论请你做～好吗? Would you take notes at the discussion? 3 record: 创～ set a record; chalk up a record. 打破～ break a record

记述 jìshù (动) record and narrate

记性 jìxing (名) memory: ～好 have a good (retentive) memory. ～坏 have a poor memory

记叙 jìxù (动) narrate: ～文 narration; narrative

J

记忆(憶) jìyì (动) remember; recall: 就我～所及 to the best of my memory. ～力 the faculty of memory; memory
记忆(憶)犹(猶)新 jìyì yóu xīn still remain fresh in one's memory (mind)
记载 jìzǎi I (动) put down in writing; record II(名) record; account
记账(賬) jìzhàng (动) 1 keep accounts 2 charge to an account
记者 jìzhě (名) reporter; correspondent; newsman; journalist: 新闻～ newspaper reporter; newsman. 特派～ special correspondent. ～招待会 press conference

忌 jì I (动) 1 be jealous of: 猜～ suspicious and jealous 2 avoid; shun; abstain from: ～生冷 avoid eating any raw or cold food 3 quit; give up: ～酒 give up alcohol; abstain from drinking. ～烟 quit (give up) smoking II (名) fear; dread; scruple: 横行无～ ride roughshod; act without scruples
忌辰 jìchén (名) the anniversary of the death of a parent, ancestor, or anyone else held in esteem
忌惮(憚) jìdàn (动)〈书〉 dread; fear: 肆无～ act wildly in defiance of law and public opinion; be unscrupulous
忌妒 jìdu (动) be jealous of; envy: 出于～ out of jealousy
忌讳(諱) jìhuì I (名) taboo: 犯～ violate (or break) a taboo II (动) 1 avoid as taboo: 他～人家叫他的外号. He resents being called by his nickname. 2 avoid as harmful; abstain from: 在学习上，最～的是有始无终. In study the worst danger is give up halfway.
忌口 jìkǒu (动) abstain from certain food (as when one is ill); be on a diet

纪 jì (名) 1 discipline: 军～ military discipline. 党～国法 party discipline and the law of the land. 违法乱～ break the law and violate discipline 2 record: ～事 chronicle 3 age; epoch: 中世～ the Middle Ages
纪律 jìlǜ (名) discipline: 遵守～ observe discipline. 劳动～ labour discipline; labour regulations. 违反～ breach of discipline. ～松弛 lax discipline. 给予～处分 take disciplinary measures against sb.
纪念 jìniàn I (动) commemorate; mark: ～大会 commemoration meeting. ～国际儿童节 observe International Children's Day II (名) 1 souvenir; keepsake; memento: 这张照片给你作个～吧. Keep this photo as a souvenir. 2 commemoration day; anniversary: 一百周年～ centenary. ～册 autograph book; autograph album. ～品 souvenir; keepsake; memento. ～日 commemoration day. ～章 souvenir badge. ～碑 monument; memorial tablet. ～馆 memorial hall. ～堂 memorial hall
纪实(實) jìshí (名) record of actual events: ～文学 reportage literature
纪行 jìxíng (名) travel notes: 西伯利亚～ Siberian travel notes
纪要 jìyào (名) summary of minutes; summary: 会谈～ summary of conversations (or talks)
纪元 jìyuán (名) 1 the beginning of an era (e.g. an emperor's reign) 2 epoch; era: 世界历史的新～ a new era in world history

继(繼) jì I (动) continue; succeed; follow: 前赴后～ advance wave upon wave II (副) then; afterwards: 他初感头晕，～又呕吐. Feeling dizzy, he began to vomit.
继承 jìchéng (动) inherit; carry on: ～财产 inherit property. ～权 right of inheritance
继承人 jìchéngrén (名) heir; successor; inheritor: 直系～ lineal successor. 法定～ heir at law; legal heir
继而 jì'ér (副) then; afterwards
继父 jìfù (名) stepfather
继母 jìmǔ (名) stepmother
继任 jìrèn (动) take over sb's job: ～首相 succeed sb. as prime minister
继往开(開)来(來) jìwǎng-kāilái carry forward the cause of the older generation and break new ground
继位 jìwèi (动) succeed to the throne
继续(續) jìxù (动) continue; go on: ～学习 continue with his studies. ～执政 continue in office; remain in power. ～有效 remain in force; be still valid. ～教育 continuing education. 战斗～到第二天凌晨. The fighting went on till the small hours of the next morning.

家 jiā I (名) 1 family; household: 他～一共有四口人. There are four people in his family. ～事 family matters; domestic affairs 2 home: 回～ go (come) home 3 a person or family engaged in a certain profession: 行～ professional;

J

expert **4** a specialist in a certain field: 科学～ scientist. 画～ painter **5** a school of thought; school: 百～争鸣. A hundred schools of thought contend. II 〈谦〉[used to address one's senior in age]: ～父 my father. ～兄 my elder brother III (形) domestic; tamed: ～畜 domestic animal; livestock IV (量) [used to count the number of families and enterprises]: 两～饭馆 two restaurants. 一～电影院 a cinema. 两～人家 two families

家产(產) jiāchǎn (名) family property

家常 jiācháng (名) domestic trivia: ～话 small talk; chitchat

家常便饭 jiācháng biànfàn **1** potluck; homely meal **2** common occurrence

家丑(醜) jiāchǒu (名) family scandal; the skeleton in the cupboard (or closet): ～不可外扬. Don't wash your dirty linen in public.

家传(傳) jiāchuán (形) handed down from the older generations of the family: ～秘方 a secret recipe handed down from the ancestors

家畜 jiāchù (名) domestic animal; livestock

家当(當) jiādàng (名)〈口〉 family belongings; property

家底 jiādǐ (名) family property or savings: ～薄 without substantial resources

家伙 jiāhuo (名)〈口〉 **1** tool; utensil; weapon **2** fellow; guy: 小～ little chap; kid

家教 jiājiào (名) **1** family education; upbringing: ～很严 be very strict with one's children **2** private tutor (usu. referring to a college student serving as sb.'s tutor)

家境 jiājìng (名) domestic financial situation; family circumstances: ～困难 live in straitened family circumstances

家具 jiājù (名) furniture: 一套～ a set of furniture

家眷 jiājuàn (名) **1** wife and children; one's family **2** wife **3** dependants

家谱 jiāpǔ (名) family tree; genealogical tree; genealogy

家禽 jiāqín (名) domestic fowl; poultry

家书(書) jiāshū (名) **1** a letter home **2** a letter from home

家属(屬) jiāshǔ (名) family members; (family) dependants

家庭 jiātíng (名) family; household: ～背景 family background. ～成员 family members. ～出身 family origin. ～负担 family responsibilities. ～妇女 housewife. ～副业 household sideline production. ～收入 family income. ～作业 homework. ～教师 private tutor. 大～ extended family. 核心～ nuclear family. ～破裂 the breakup of a marriage

家务(務) jiāwù (名) household duties: ～劳动 housework; household chores

家乡(鄉) jiāxiāng (名) hometown; native place

家小 jiāxiǎo (名)〈口〉 wife and children

家信 jiāxìn (名) a letter to or from one's family

家业(業) jiāyè (名) family property

家用 jiāyòng (名) family expenses; housekeeping money

家喻户晓(曉) jiāyù-hùxiǎo widely known; known to all: 斯诺这个名字在中国已～. The name Snow is a household word in China.

家园(園) jiāyuán (名) home; homeland: 重建～ rebuild one's homeland; rebuild one's village or town. 重返～ return to one's homeland

家长(長) jiāzhǎng (名) **1** the head of a family; patriarch **2** the parent or guardian of a child

家政 jiāzhèng (名) housekeeping; homemaking; domestic economy: ～服务公司 household service company. ～服务员 housekeeper

家族 jiāzú (名) clan; family

夹(夾)

jiā I (动) **1** press from both sides; place in between: 把枫叶～在书里. Put the maple leaves between the pages. 用筷子～菜 pick up food with chopsticks. 他被汽车门～住了. He was caught in the door of a bus. **2** mix; mingle; intersperse: ～在人群里 be in the midst of a crowd. ～心巧克力 filled chocolate II (名) clip, clamp, folder, etc.: 纸～ paper clip. 发～ hairpin. 衣～ clothes peg

see also gā; jiá

夹带(帶) jiādài (动) carry secretly; smuggle: 邮寄包裹不能～信件. Don't put a letter in anything you send by parcel post.

夹缝 jiāfèng (名) crack; crevice

夹攻 jiāgōng (动) attack from both sides; converging attack; pincer attack: 受到两面～ be under a pincer attack; be

J

under attack from both sides
夹杂(雜) jiāzá (动) be mixed up with; be mingled with
夹子 jiāzi (名) 1 clip; tongs: 弹簧～ spring clip 2 folder; wallet: 文件～ folder; binder. 皮～ wallet; pocketbook

佳 jiā (形) good; fine; beautiful: ～景 fine landscape; beautiful view. 成绩甚～ achieve very good results. ～节 happy festive occasion; festival. ～宾 a welcome guest. ～肴 delicacies
佳话 jiāhuà (名) an anecdote or good deed on everybody's lips; a much-told tale
佳境 jiājìng (名)〈书〉state of ecstasy
佳期 jiāqī (名) wedding (or nuptial) day
佳人 jiārén (名)〈书〉beautiful woman; beauty
佳音 jiāyīn (名) welcome news; glad tidings; favourable reply

J

加 jiā (动) 1 add; plus: 二～三等于五. Two and three makes five. 2 increase; augment: 要求～工资 demand a raise in one's pay 3 put in; add; append: 汤里～点盐 put some salt in the soup. ～大压力 increase the pressure. ～注解 add explanatory notes to 4 [used to indicate the taking of a certain action]: 大～赞扬 praise highly; lavish praise on. 不～考虑 give no consideration to
加班 jiābān (动) work overtime; work an extra shift: ～费 overtime emolument
加倍 jiābèi (动) double; redouble: ～努力 redouble one's efforts. 产量可以在五年内～. The output will double in five years.
加法 jiāfǎ (名) addition
加工 jiāgōng (动、名) 1 process: 食品～ food processing. 这篇文章需要～. This article needs touching up a little bit. 2 machining; working: 冷～ cold working. 机～ machining. ～厂 processing factory
加害 jiāhài (动) injure; do harm to; incriminate
加紧(緊) jiājǐn (动) step up; speed up; intensify: ～生产 step up production
加剧(劇) jiājù (动) aggravate; intensify; exacerbate: ～紧张局势 aggravate tension
加快 jiākuài (动) quicken; accelerate; pick up speed: ～步子 quicken one's pace
加盟 jiāméng (动) become a member of an alliance or union; join
加冕 jiāmiǎn (名) coronation
加强 jiāqiáng (动) strengthen; enhance; augment; reinforce: ～纪律 strengthen discipline. ～控制 tighten one's control. ～兵力 reinforce the army
加入 jiārù (动) 1 add; mix; put in 2 join; accede to: ～联合国 join the United Nations
加深 jiāshēn (动) deepen: ～理解 get a better grasp of sth. ～印象 make a deeper impression on sb.
加速 jiāsù (动) quicken; speed up; accelerate; expedite: ～发展工业 speed up the development of industry. ～植物的生长 hasten the growth of plants
加以 jiāyǐ I (动) [used to indicate how to deal with the matter previously mentioned]: 原计划须～小小修改. It is necessary to make some minor changes in the original plan. II (连) in addition; moreover: 天气太冷, ～孩子也病了, 今天我就不来了. I won't come today. It's too cold, and what's more, my child is ill.
加油 jiāyóu (动) 1 oil; lubricate: 这台机器该～了. This machine needs oiling. 2 refuel: 空中～ in flight (or air) refuelling. ～站 filling (or petrol, gas) station 3 make an extra effort: ～干 work with added vigour
加重 jiāzhòng (动) 1 make or become heavier; increase the weight of: ～工作量 add to one's workload 2 make or become more serious; aggravate: 病情～了. The patient's condition worsened.

痂 jiā (名) scab; crust: 结～ form a scab; crust

嘉 jiā 1 good; fine: ～宾 honoured guest; welcome guest 2 praise; commend: 他的精神可～. The spirit he has shown is worthy of praise.
嘉奖(奬) jiājiǎng (动) bestow praise, honour or reward
嘉许 jiāxǔ (动)〈书〉praise; approve

茄 jiā

see also qié
茄克 jiākè (名) jacket

枷 jiā (名) cangue

枷锁 jiāsuǒ (名) yoke; chains; shackles; fetters: 摆脱～ throw off the yoke

夹(夾) jiá (形) double-layered; lined: ～袄 lined jacket
see also gā; jiā

颊(頰) jiá（名）cheek：两～红润 rosy cheeks

甲 jiǎ（名）1 the first of the ten Heavenly Stems 2 first：～级 first rate; Class A. 桂林山水～天下. The landscape of Guilin is the finest under heaven. 3［used as a substitute］～方和乙方 the first party and the second party 4 shell; carapace：龟～ tortoise shell 5 nail：手指～ fingernail 6 armour：装～车 armoured car

甲板 jiǎbǎn（名）deck

甲骨文 jiǎgǔwén（名）inscriptions on oracle bones of the Shang Dynasty（c. 16th — 11th century B. C.）

甲壳(殼) jiǎqiào（名）crust：～动物 crustacean

甲鱼(魚) jiǎyú（名）soft-shelled turtle

岬 jiǎ（名）1 cape; promontory 2 a narrow passage between mountains：～角 cape; promontory

钾 jiǎ（名）potassium (K)

钾肥 jiǎféi（名）potash fertilizer

假 jiǎ I（形）false; fake; sham; phoney; artificial：～肢 artificial limb II（动）borrow; loan：久～不归 keep a borrowed article for a long time with no thought of returning it III（连）if; suppose：～令 in case

see also jià

假扮 jiǎbàn（动）disguise oneself as

假充 jiǎchōng（动）pretend to be; pose as：～内行 pass for a professional

假定 jiǎdìng I（动）suppose; assume; grant; presume：～他明天起程，后天就可以到达上海. Suppose he sets out tomorrow, he will be in Shanghai the following day. II（名）hypothesis

假发(髮) jiǎfà（名）wig

假公济(濟)私 jiǎ gōng jì sī seek personal gain at public expense

假话 jiǎhuà（名）lie; falsehood：说～ tell lies

假借 jiǎjiè（动）make use of：～外力 make use of outside forces. ～名义 under the guise of; in the name of; under false pretences

假冒 jiǎmào（动）pass oneself off as; palm off (a fake as genuine)：谨防～ Beware of imitations. ～商品 counterfeit goods; imitations

假面具 jiǎmiànjù（名）mask; false front

假仁假义(義) jiǎrén-jiǎyì hypocrisy; sham kindness

假如 jiǎrú（连）if; supposing; in case：～天下雨，我就不来了. If it rains, I won't come.

假若 jiǎruò（连）if; supposing; in case

假山 jiǎshān（名）miniature hills; rockery

假设 jiǎshè I（动）suppose; assume; grant; presume II（名）hypothesis：科学～ a scientific hypothesis

假使 jiǎshǐ（连）if; in case; in the event that：～他同意，那就很好. If he agrees, well and good.

假释 jiǎshì（动）release on parole（or on probation）

假手 jiǎshǒu（动）do evil through another person：～于人 make use of sb. to achieve one's malicious purpose

假说 jiǎshuō（名）hypothesis

假托 jiǎtuō（动）1 make a pretext 2 under sb. else's name 3 by means of; through the medium of

假想 jiǎxiǎng I（名）imagination; hypothesis; supposition II（形）imaginary; hypothetical; fictitious：～敌 imaginary enemy

假象 jiǎxiàng（名）false appearance; false impression; false front

假惺惺 jiǎxīngxīng（形）hypocritically; unctuously

假牙 jiǎyá（名）false tooth; denture

假意 jiǎyì I（名）unction; insincerity; hypocrisy II（副）deliberately; affectedly; insincerely：他～笑着问，刚来的这位是谁呢？He smirked, asking "who is the person who just came in?"

假造 jiǎzào（动）1 forge; counterfeit：～证件 forge a certificate 2 invent; fabricate：～理由 cook up an excuse

假肢 jiǎzhī（名）artificial limb; prosthetic limb

假装(裝) jiǎzhuāng（动）pretend; feign; simulate; make believe：～不知道 pretend to know nothing; feign ignorance

稼 jià 1 sow (grain)：耕～ ploughing and sowing; farm work. ～穑 sowing and reaping; farming; farm work 2 cereals; crops：庄～ crops

嫁 jià（动）1（of a woman）marry 2 shift; transfer：～祸于人 lay the blame on sb. else; shift the trouble on to sb.

嫁接 jiàjiē（动）graft

嫁娶 jiàqǔ (名) marriage

嫁妆(妝) jiàzhuang (名) dowry; trousseau

价(價) jià (名) 1 price: 要～ the asking price. 市～ market price. 议～ negotiated price 2 value: 等～交换 exchange of equal values. 估～ estimate the value of; evaluate 3 valence: 氢是一～的元素. Hydrogen is a one-valence element.
see also jie

价格 jiàgé (名) price: 批发(零售)～ wholesale (retail) price. ～补贴 price subsidies from the state

价目 jiàmù (名) marked price; price: ～表 price list

价钱(錢) jiàqian (名) price: 讲～ bargain. ～公道 a fair (or reasonable) price

J

价值 jiàzhí (名) 1 value: 使用～ use value. ～规律 law of value. ～观念 value system; values. 剩余～ surplus value 2 worth; value: ～二百万元的援助 two million *yuan* worth of aid. 毫无～ worthless

价值连城 jià zhí liánchéng invaluable; priceless

假 jià (名) holiday; vacation: 请～ ask for leave. 寒～ winter vacation. 病～ sick leave. 学术～ sabbatical leave
see also jiǎ

假期 jiàqī (名) 1 vacation 2 period of leave

假日 jiàrì (名) holiday; day off

架 jià I (名) frame; rack; shelf; stand: 窗～ window frame. 行李～ luggage-rack. 衣～ clothes hanger. 书～ bookshelves II (动) 1 put up; erect: ～桥 put up (or build) a bridge. ～起接收天线 set up a receiving antenna 2 fend off; ward off; withstand 3 support; prop; help: ～着拐走 walk on crutches 4 kidnap; take sb. away forcibly 5 fight; quarrel: 劝～ try to part quarrelling parties III (量): 一～电视机 a TV set

架空 jiàkōng I (形) impracticable; unpractical II (动) make sb. a mere figurehead

架设 jiàshè (动) erect; put up (above ground or water level, as on stilts or posts): ～帐篷 erect a tent. ～输电线路 erect power transmission lines

架势(勢) jiàshi (名)〈口〉posture; stance; manner: 摆出一副盛气凌人的～ assume a domineering posture

架子 jiàzi (名) 1 frame; stand; rack; shelf: 脸盆～ washstand 2 framework; skeleton; outline: 写文章搭个～ make an outline for an essay 3 airs; haughty manner: 摆～ put on airs 4 posture; stance

驾 jià (动) 1 harness; draw (a cart, etc.) 2 drive (a vehicle); pilot (a plane); sail (a boat)

驾轻(輕)就熟 jiàqīng-jiùshú drive a light carriage on a familiar road; have no difficulty handling familiar matters

驾驶 jiàshǐ (动) drive (a vehicle); pilot (a ship or plane): ～盘 steering wheel. ～室 driver's cab. ～员 driver; pilot. ～执照 driving (or driver's) licence

驾驭 jiàyù (动) 1 drive (a cart, horse, etc.): 这匹马不好～. This horse is difficult to control. 2 control; master: ～形势 take the situation in hand

驾照 jiàzhào (名) driving license

煎 jiān (动) 1 fry in shallow oil: ～鱼 fried fish 2 simmer in water; decoct: ～药 decoct medicinal herbs

煎熬 jiān'áo (动) suffer; torture; torment

兼 jiān (形) 1 double; twice: ～旬 twenty days 2 simultaneously; concurrently: ～管 be concurrently in charge of; also look after. ～而有之 have both (merits and defects; advantages and disadvantages) at the same time. 身～数职 hold several posts simultaneously

兼备(備) jiānbèi (动) have both qualities; be in possession of both: 德才～ have both political integrity and ability

兼并(併) jiānbìng (动) annex (territory, property, etc.)

兼程 jiānchéng (动) travel at double speed: 日夜～ travel day and night

兼顾(顧) jiāngù (动) give consideration to (or take account of) two or more things; consider the needs of both parties: 统筹～ make overall plans and take all factors into consideration

兼任 jiānrèn I (动) hold a concurrent job II (形) part-time: ～教师 part-time teacher

兼容 jiānróng (形) compatible

兼收并(並)蓄 jiānshōu-bìngxù incorporate into something factors of diverse nature

兼职(職) jiānzhí I (动) moonlight; hold two or more posts concurrently: ～过多 hold too many posts at the same time II (名) concurrent post; moonlighting

间 jiān I [indicating a connection or relationship]: 劳资之～ between labour and capital II [indicating time or space within the given limits]: 世～ (in) the world. 田～ (in) the fields. 晚～ (in the) evening; (at) night III(名) room: 洗澡～ bathroom. 衣帽～ cloakroom IV (量): 一～卧室 a bedroom
see also jiàn

间不容发(髮) jiān bù róng fà be in imminent danger

肩 jiān I (名) shoulder: 并～战斗 fight shoulder to shoulder II (动) take on; undertake; shoulder; bear: 身～重任 shoulder heavy responsibilities

肩膀 jiānbǎng (名) shoulder

肩负 jiānfù (动) take on; undertake; shoulder; bear: ～伟大任务 undertake a great task

肩章 jiānzhāng (名) 1 shoulder ornament 2 epaulet

笺(箋) jiān (名)〈书〉 1 writing paper: 信～ letter paper 2 letter 3 annotation; commentary

笺注 jiānzhù (名)〈书〉 notes and commentary on ancient texts

歼(殲) jiān (动) annihilate; exterminate; wipe out

歼灭(滅) jiānmiè (动) annihilate; wipe out; destroy: ～敌军 wipe out enemy troops. ～战 war or battle of annihilation

缄 jiān (动) seal; close: ～封 seal a letter

缄口 jiānkǒu (动)〈书〉 hold one's tongue

缄默 jiānmò (动) keep silent; be reticent. 保持～ remain silent

缄札 jiānzhá (名) a letter

监(監) jiān I (动) supervise; inspect; watch II (名) prison; jail

监测 jiāncè (动) monitor

监察 jiānchá (动) supervise; control: ～制度 supervisory system

监督 jiāndū I (动) supervise; superintend; control: 国际～ international control. ～权 authority to supervise II (名) supervisor

监工 jiāngōng I (动) supervise work; oversee II (名) overseer; supervisor

监护(護) jiānhù (名) guardianship: ～人 guardian

监禁 jiānjìn (动) take into custody; imprison; put in jail (or prison)

监牢 jiānláo (名) prison; jail

监理 jiānlǐ (动) supervise; inspect and manage

监视 jiānshì (动) keep watch on; keep an eye on: 严密～ keep a close watch. ～敌人的行动 keep watch on the movements of the enemy

监守 jiānshǒu (动) have custody of; guard; take care of

监听(聽) jiāntīng (动) monitor

监狱(獄) jiānyù (名) prison; jail

坚(堅) jiān I (形) 1 hard; solid; firm; strong: ～冰 solid ice; hard ice. ～果 hard nut 2 firmly; steadfastly; resolutely: ～信 firmly believe. ～不吐实 refuse to tell the truth II (名) a heavily fortified point; fortification; stronghold: 攻～ storm strongholds

坚壁清野 jiānbì-qīngyě strengthen defence works, evacuate non-combatants, hide provisions and livestock, and clear away all surrounding trees and cabins

坚不可摧 jiān bùkěcuī indestructible; impregnable

坚持 jiānchí (动) persist in; persevere in; uphold; insist on; stick to; adhere to: ～原则 adhere (or stick) to principle. ～己见 hold on to one's own views. ～到底 stick it out; carry through firmly to the end. ～不懈 persevere

坚定 jiāndìng (形) firm; staunch; steadfast: ～不移 firm and unshakable; unswerving. ～的立场 a firm stand

坚固 jiāngù (形) firm; solid; sturdy; strong: ～耐用 strong and durable

坚决 jiānjué (形) firm; resolute; determined: ～支持 firmly support; stand firmly by. ～反对 resolutely oppose

坚苦卓绝 jiānkǔ zhuójué showing the utmost fortitude

坚强 jiānqiáng I (形) strong; firm; staunch: 意志～ strong-willed. ～不屈 staunch and unyielding II (动) strengthen

坚忍 jiānrěn (形) steadfast and persevering (in face of difficulties)

坚韧(韌) jiānrèn (形) firm and tenacious

坚如磐石 jiān rú pánshí as firm as a rock; rock-firm

坚实(實) jiānshí (形) solid; substantial: ～的基础 a solid foundation

坚守 jiānshǒu (动) stick to; hold fast to: ～

岗位 stand fast at one's post

坚挺 jiāntǐng (形) strong: 人民币～. The RMB is strong.

坚毅 jiānyì (形) firm and persistent; tenacious of purpose

坚硬 jiānyìng (形) hard; solid

坚贞 jiānzhēn (形) faithful; constant: ～不屈 remain loyal and unyielding

尖 jiān I (名) 1 point; tip; top: 针～ the point of a needle or pin; pinpoint. 指～ fingertip. 塔～ the pointed top of a tower 2 the best of its kind; the pick of the bunch; the cream of the crop: 拔～儿的 top-notch II (形) 1 pointed; tapering: ～下巴 a pointed chin. 削～铅笔 sharpen a pencil 2 shrill; sharp: ～叫 scream. 耳朵～ have sharp ears. 鼻子～ have an acute sense of smell. ～嗓子 shrill voice

尖兵 jiānbīng (名) 1 (military) a point 2 trailblazer; pathbreaker; pioneer; vanguard

尖端 jiānduān I (名) pointed end; acme; the highest point; peak: 科学的～ the pinnacle of science II (形) most advanced; sophisticated: ～科学 most advanced branches of science; frontiers of science. ～武器 sophisticated weapons

尖刻 jiānkè (形) acrimonious; caustic; biting: 说话～ speak with sarcasm; make caustic remarks

尖利 jiānlì (形) 1 sharp; keen; cutting: ～的钢刀 a sharp knife 2 shrill; piercing: ～的叫声 a shrill cry

尖锐 jiānruì (形) 1 sharp-pointed 2 penetrating; incisive; sharp: 看问题很～ make a penetrating analysis of problems 3 shrill; piercing: ～的哨声 the shrill sound of a whistle 4 intense; acute; sharp: ～的对立 be directly opposed to each other. ～的斗争 acute struggle

尖酸 jiānsuān (形) acrid; acrimonious; tart: ～刻薄 acerbic and bitterly sarcastic

尖子 jiānzi (名) the best of the kind; the cream

艰(艱) jiān (形) difficult; hard

艰巨 jiānjù (形) arduous; extremely difficult: ～的任务 a difficult task. 付出～的劳动 make tremendous efforts

艰苦 jiānkǔ (形) arduous; difficult; hard; tough: ～的年代 hard times. ～朴素 hard work and plain living

艰难(難) jiānnán (形) difficult; hard: 步履～ walk with difficulty; plod along; dodder

艰涩(澀) jiānsè (形) involved and abstruse; intricate and obscure: 文词～ involved and abstruse writing

艰深 jiānshēn (形) difficult to understand; abstruse

艰险(險) jiānxiǎn (名) hardships and dangers: 不避～ brave hardships and dangers

艰辛 jiānxīn (名) hardships: 历尽～ experience all kinds of hardships

奸 jiān I (形) 1 wicked; evil; treacherous: ～计 an evil plot 2 self-seeking and wily II (名) 1 traitor: 内～ a secret enemy agent within one's ranks; hidden traitor. 汉～ traitor to the Chinese nation; traitor 2 illicit sexual relations: 通～ have illicit sexual relations; commit adultery

奸猾 jiānhuá (形) treacherous; crafty; deceitful

奸佞 jiānnìng 〈书〉 I (形) crafty and fawning II (名) crafty sycophant

奸商 jiānshāng (名) unscrupulous merchant; profiteer

奸污 jiānwū (动) rape or seduce

奸细 jiānxi (名) spy; enemy agent

奸险(險) jiānxiǎn (形) wicked and crafty; treacherous; malicious

奸邪 jiānxié 〈书〉 I (形) crafty and evil; treacherous II (名) a crafty evil person

奸淫 jiānyín I (名) illicit sexual relations; adultery II (动) rape or seduce: ～烧杀 rape and loot; rape and plunder

奸诈 jiānzhà (形) fraudulent; crafty; treacherous

简 jiǎn I (形) simple; simplified; brief: ～而言之 in brief; in short; to put it in a nutshell II (名) 1 bamboo slips [used as a kind of paper in ancient times] 2 letter: 书～ letters; correspondence III (动) 〈书〉 select; choose: ～拔 select and promote

简报(報) jiǎnbào (名) bulletin; brief report: 会议～ conference bulletin; brief reports on conference proceedings. 新闻～ news bulletin

简编 jiǎnbiān (名) [often used in books' titles] short course; concise book

简便 jiǎnbiàn (形) simple and convenient; handy: ～的方法 a simple and convenient method; a handy way. 烹调～ easy to cook. 手续～ simple procedures

简称(稱) jiǎnchēng I (名) the abbreviated form of a name; abbreviation II (动) be called sth. for short

简单(單) jiǎndān (形) 1 simple; uncomplicated: ～明了 brief and to the point; simple and clear; concise and explicit. 解释～明了. Explanations are simple but clear. 2 rough and plain; casual: ～粗暴 rough and rude. 头脑～ simple-minded

简短 jiǎnduǎn (形) brief: 他的文章～有力. His article was brief and forceful.

简化 jiǎnhuà (动) simplify: ～工序 simplify working processes. ～手续 reduce the formalities

简化汉(漢)字 jiǎnhuà hànzì 1 simplify Chinese characters (i. e. reduce the number of strokes and eliminate complicated variants) 2 simplified Chinese characters

简洁(潔) jiǎnjié (形) succinct; terse; pithy: ～生动的语言 terse and lively language. 文笔～ written concisely

简历(歷) jiǎnlì (名) biographical notes; résumé; curriculum vitae (cv)

简练(練) jiǎnliàn (形) terse; succinct; pithy

简陋 jiǎnlòu (形) simple and crude: 设备～ simple and crude equipment; crudely appointed

简略 jiǎnlüè (形) simple (in content); brief; sketchy: 他提供的材料过于～. The information he gave is too brief.

简明 jiǎnmíng (形) simple and clear, concise: ～扼要 brief and to the point. ～新闻 news in brief

简朴(樸) jiǎnpǔ (形) simple and unadorned; plain: 生活～ a simple lifestyle; plain living

简写(寫) jiǎnxiě (动) 1 write a Chinese character in simplified form 2 simplify a book for beginners: ～本 simplified edition

简讯 jiǎnxùn (名) news in brief

简要 jiǎnyào (形) concise and to the point; brief: ～的介绍 a brief discription; briefing

简易 jiǎnyì (形) 1 simple and easy: ～的办法 a simple and easy method 2 simply constructed; simply equipped; unsophisticated: ～读物 easy reading

简章 jiǎnzhāng (名) general regulations; notice

简直 jiǎnzhí (副) simply; at all: 这一队轿车, 一辆跟着一辆, ～没个完. The procession of cars, one following another, was simply endless.

剪 jiǎn I (名) scissors; shears; clippers II (动) 1 cut (with scissors); clip; trim: ～发 have a haircut. ～羊毛 shear a sheep 2 wipe out; exterminate: ～除 wipe out; annihilate; remove

剪报(報) jiǎnbào (名) newspaper clipping

剪裁 jiǎncái (动) 1 cut out (a garment); tailor 2 cut out unwanted material (from a piece of writing)

剪彩 jiǎncǎi (动) cut the ribbon at an opening ceremony

剪刀 jiǎndāo (名) scissors; shears: ～差 price scissors

剪辑 jiǎnjí (名) 1 film editing 2 selected photos, recordings, etc. after editing

剪票 jiǎnpiào (动) punch a ticket

剪影 jiǎnyǐng (名) 1 paper-cut silhouette 2 outline; sketch

剪纸 jiǎnzhǐ (名) paper-cut

茧(繭) jiǎn (名) 1 cocoon: 蚕～ silkworm cocoon. ～绸 pongee 2 callus: 老～ thick callus

柬 jiǎn (名) card; note; letter: 请～ invitation card

拣(揀) jiǎn (动) 1 choose; select; pick out: ～最重要的说. Pick out the most important things you have got to say. 2 see "捡" jiǎn

拣选(選) jiǎnxuǎn (动) select; choose

减 jiǎn (动) 1 subtract; deduct: 五～二得三. Five minus two is three. *or* Two from five is three. 2 reduce; decrease; cut: ～半 reduce by half. ～价 reduce prices; at a reduced rate. ～产 decrease (or drop) in output. ～速 slow down

减法 jiǎnfǎ (名) subtraction

减肥 jiǎnféi (动) reduce weight; slim: ～操 slimming exercise. ～食品 diet food

减免 jiǎnmiǎn (动) 1 mitigate or annul (a punishment) 2 reduce or remit (taxation, etc.)

减排 jiǎnpái (名) pollutant discharge reduction; carbon emission reduction: 汽车尾气～ reduction of car exhaust. 二氧化碳～ CO2 emission reduction

减轻(輕) jiǎnqīng (动) lighten; ease; allevi-

ate; mitigate: ～工作 cut down on one's workload. ～痛苦 alleviate pain
减弱 jiǎnruò (动) weaken; abate
减色 jiǎnsè (动) lose lustre; become less attractive; detract from the merit of
减少 jiǎnshǎo (动) reduce; decrease; lessen; cut down: ～开支 cut down expenditure; retrench expenses
减退 jiǎntuì (动) drop; go down: 视力(记忆力)～. One's eyesight (memory) is failing.
减刑 jiǎnxíng (动) reduce a penalty; mitigate a sentence
减压 jiǎnyā (动) reduce pressure; decompress; reduce stress
减灾 jiǎnzāi (动) disaster relief
碱 jiǎn (名) 1 alkali 2 soda: 纯～ soda (ash). ～地 alkaline land
检(檢) jiǎn (动) 1 check up; inspect; examine: ～定 examine and determine 2 restrain oneself; be careful in one's conduct: 行为不～ depart from correct conduct; improper conduct; misdemeanour
检查 jiǎnchá I (动) check; inspect; examine: ～工作 check up on work. ～质量 check the quality. ～身体 have a physical examination; have a medical check-up II (名) 1 check; examination: 新闻～ press censorship. ～哨 checkpost. ～站 checkpoint; checkpost; inspection station 2 self-criticism: 做～ criticize oneself
检察 jiǎnchá (名) procuratorial work: ～官 public procurator (or prosecutor)
检点(點) jiǎndiǎn (动) 1 examine; check: ～行李 check the luggage 2 be cautious (about what one says or does): 言行有失～ be careless about one's words and acts; be indiscreet in one's speech and conduct
检举(舉) jiǎnjǔ (动) report (an offence) to the authorities; inform against (an offender): ～信 letters of accusation
检索 jiǎnsuǒ (动) look up; refer to: 信息～系统 information retrieval system
检讨 jiǎntǎo (名) self-criticism: 做～ make a self-criticism
检修 jiǎnxiū (动) examine and repair; overhaul: ～汽车 overhaul a car
检验(驗) jiǎnyàn (动) test; examine; inspect: 商品～ commodity inspection
检疫 jiǎnyì (动) quarantine
检阅 jiǎnyuè (动) review (troops, etc.); inspect: ～仪仗队 review a guard of honour
捡(撿) jiǎn (动) pick up; collect; gather: ～破烂 collect waste
睑(瞼) jiǎn: 眼～ eyelid
俭(儉) jiǎn (形) thrifty; frugal
俭朴(樸) jiǎnpǔ (形) thrifty and simple; economical: 生活～ lead a thrifty and simple life. 衣着～ dress simply
俭省 jiǎnshěng (形) economical; thrifty: ～过日子 live a frugal life
渐 jiàn (副) gradually; by degrees: 天气～冷. It is getting cold.
渐变(變) jiànbiàn (名) gradual change
渐渐 jiànjiàn (副) gradually; by degrees; little by little
渐进(進) jiànjìn (动) advance gradually; progress step by step: 循序～ advance by stages
间 jiàn I (名) space in between; opening: 团结无～ closely united II (动) 1 separate: ～隔 be separated from. 黑白相～ chequered with black and white 2 sow discord
see also jiān
间谍 jiàndié (名) spy: ～活动 espionage
间断(斷) jiànduàn (动) be disconnected; be interrupted: 从不～ without interruption
间隔 jiàngé (名) interval; intermission: 幼苗～匀整. The seedlings are evenly spaced.
间或 jiànhuò (副) occasionally; now and then; sometimes; once in a while: 大家聚精会神地听着, ～有人笑一两声. Everybody listened intently; once or twice somebody broke into a laugh.
间接 jiànjiē (形) indirect; second-hand: ～经验 indirect experience. ～选举 indirect election
间隙 jiànxì (名) interval; gap; space
间歇 jiànxiē (名) intermittence; intermission
谏 jiàn (动)〈书〉 remonstrate with (one's superior or friend); expostulate with; admonish: ～止 admonish against sth.; advise sb. to refrain from

doing sth.

践(踐) jiàn (动) 1 trample; tread 2 act on; carry out: ~诺 keep one's promise (or word)

践踏 jiàntà (动) tread on; trample underfoot: ~别国主权 trample on the sovereignty of other countries

践约 jiànyuē (动) keep a promise; keep an appointment

贱(賤) jiàn (形) 1 low-priced; inexpensive; cheap: ~卖 cheap sale 2 lowly; humble: 贫~ poor and lowly 3 mean; base; despicable: 下~ shameless; base

溅(濺) jiàn (动) splash; spatter: ~落 splash down

饯(餞) jiàn (动) give a farewell dinner: 为人~行 give a farewell dinner for sb.

荐(薦) jiàn (动) recommend: ~举 recommend sb. for a post. 毛遂自~ volunteer one's services

鉴(鑒) jiàn I (名) 1 ancient bronze mirror 2 warning; object lesson: 引以为~ take warning from it II (动) 1 reflect; mirror: 水清可~. The water is so clear that it shines like a mirror. 2 inspect; scrutinize; examine: 请~核. Please check.

鉴别 jiànbié (动) distinguish; differentiate; judge: 有比较才能~. Only by comparing can one distinguish. ~真假 judge whether it is sham or genuine; distinguish between the false and the true

鉴定 jiàndìng I (名) appraisal (of a person's strong and weak points): 工作~ an evaluation of one's work II (动) appraise; identify; authenticate; determine: ~文物年代 determine the date of a cultural relic

鉴戒 jiànjiè (名) warning; object lesson

鉴赏 jiànshǎng (动) appreciate: ~能力 ability to appreciate (painting, music, etc.); connoisseurship

鉴于(於) jiànyú (介) in view of; seeing that: ~上述原因 for the abovementioned reasons

见(見) jiàn I (动) 1 see; catch sight of: 所~所闻 what one sees and hears. ~义勇为 never hesitate to fight for justice 2 meet with; be exposed to: 冰~热就化. Ice melts with heat. 3 show evidence of; appear to be: ~诸行动 be translated into action. 病已~轻. The patient's condition has improved. 4 refer to; see; vide: ~第36页 see page 36 5 meet; call on; see: 你~到他了没有? Did you meet him? II (名) view; opinion: 依我之~ in my opinion; to my mind. 真知灼~ profound understanding and penetrating insight

见长(長) jiàncháng (动) be good at; be expert in

见得 jiàndé (动) [only used in negative statements or questions] seem; appear: 怎么~他来不了? Why do you think he won't come?

见地 jiàndì (名) insight; judgment: 很有~ have keen insight; show sound judgment

见风(風)使舵 jiàn fēng shǐ duò trim one's sails; act as the occasion dictates

见怪 jiànguài (动) mind; take offence: 事情没给您办好,请不要~. I hope you will forgive me for not having fulfilled my mission.

见鬼 jiànguǐ (动) 1 fantastic; preposterous; absurd: 这真是~,他怎么一转眼就不见了. That's fantastic. He's vanished in the twinkling of an eye. 2 go to hell: 让他~去吧! To hell with him!

见好 jiànhǎo (动) (of a patient's condition) get better; mend: 她的病~了. She's mending.

见机(機) jiànjī (动) as befits the occasion; according to circumstances: ~行事 do as one thinks fit

见解 jiànjiě (名) view; opinion; understanding: 相同~ identical views. 个人~ personal opinion

见利忘义(義) jiàn lì wàng yì forget what is right at the sight of profit

见面 jiànmiàn (动) meet; see: 他们多年没有~了. They haven't seen each other for years. *or* It's many years since they parted.

见仁见智 jiànrén-jiànzhì different people have different views even about the same question

见识(識) jiànshi (名) experience; general knowledge: 长~ enrich one's knowledge; broaden one's horizons

见世面 jiàn shìmiàn see the world; enrich one's experience

见外 jiànwài (动) regard sb. as an outsider:

J

你对我这样客气,倒有点~了. You stand so much on ceremony that you make me feel like a stranger.

见闻 jiànwén (名) what one sees and hears; knowledge; information: 增长~ add to one's knowledge and experience. ~广 well-informed

见习(習) jiànxí (动) learn on the job; be on probation: ~技术员 technician on probation. ~医生 intern

见效 jiànxiào (动) become effective; produce the desired result: 我们的一切努力均未~. All our efforts proved fruitless.

见笑 jiànxiào (动) laugh at (me or us): 我手拙,您可别~. Now don't laugh at me for my clumsiness.

J

见异(異)思迁(遷) jiàn yì sī qiān be inconstant or irresolute: 他这个人~. He changes his mind every time he sees something different.

见证 jiànzhèng (名) witness; testimony: ~人 eyewitness; witness

舰(艦) jiàn (名) warship; naval vessel: ~队 fleet; naval force

舰艇 jiàntǐng (名) naval ships and boats; naval vessels

剑(劍) jiàn (名) sword; sabre: ~柄 the handle of a sword; hilt. ~鞘 scabbard

剑拔弩张(張) jiànbá-nǔzhāng be at daggers drawn; sabre-rattling

箭 jiàn (名) arrow: ~在弦上,不得不发. The arrow is on the bowstring, and there is no turning back.

箭步 jiànbù (名) a sudden big stride forward

件 jiàn I (量) [indicating those things which can be counted]: 一~衬衫 a shirt. 两~事情 two things. 三~行李 three pieces of luggage II (名) letter; correspondence; paper; document: 信~ letters; mail. 来~ a communication, document, etc. received. 密~ confidential (or classified) documents; secret papers

建 jiàn (动) 1 build; construct; erect: ~电站 build a power station. 重~家园 rebuild one's homeland 2 establish; set up; found: ~都 make (a place) the capital. ~党 found a party 3 propose; advocate: ~议 make a suggestion

建材 jiàncái (名) building materials; construction materials

建交 jiànjiāo (动) establish diplomatic relations

建立 jiànlì (动) build; establish; set up; found: ~友谊 forge ties of friendship; make friends with. ~统一战线 form a united front. ~信心 build up one's confidence

建设 jiànshè (动) build; construct 社会主义~ socialist construction

建设性 jiànshèxìng (形) constructive: ~的意见 constructive suggestions

建树(樹) jiànshù 〈书〉 I (动) make a contribution; contribute II (名) contribution; achievements: 他在这方面颇有~. He has made great achievements in this field.

建议(議) jiànyì I (动) propose; suggest; recommend: 他们~休会. They propose that the meeting be adjourned. II (名) proposal; suggestion; recommendation: 有益的~ constructive suggestions. 合理化~ rationalization proposal

建造 jiànzào (动) build; construct; make: ~船只 shipbuilding

建制 jiànzhì (名) organizational system: 部队~ the organizational system of the army

建筑(築) jiànzhù I (动) build; construct; erect: ~地下铁道 build a subway (or an underground railway) II (名) 1 building; structure; edifice: 古老的~ an ancient building. 宏伟的~ a magnificent structure. ~材料 building materials. ~工地 construction site 2 architecture: ~师 architect

键 jiàn (名) key: 琴~ a piano key

键盘(盤) jiànpán (名) keyboard; fingerboard

毽 jiàn (名) shuttlecock

毽子 jiànzi (名) shuttlecock: 踢~ kick the shuttlecock (as a game)

健 jiàn I (形) healthy; strong II (动) 1 strengthen; toughen; invigorate: ~胃 be good for the stomach 2 be strong in; be good at: ~谈 be good at casual conversation; be a magnificent conversationalist

健步 jiànbù (动) walk with vigorous strides: ~如飞 walk fast and with springy steps

健儿(兒) jiàn'ér (名) 1 valiant fighter 2 good athlete: 乒坛~ skilful ping-pong players

健将(將) jiànjiàng (名) master sportsman; top-notch player: 运动～ master sportsman

健康 jiànkāng I (名) health; physique: ～状况 state of health; physical condition II (形) healthy; sound: 身体～ be in good health. 祝你～! I wish you good health. 情况基本上是～的. The situation is basically sound.

健美 jiànměi (形) strong and handsome; vigorous and graceful: ～运动 bodybuilding

健全 jiànquán I (形) sound; perfect: 体魄～ sound in body and mind. 组织～ organizationally perfect II (动) strengthen; amplify; perfect: ～规章制度 make necessary amendments to the rules and regulations

健身 jiànshēn (动) keep fit: ～运动 keep-fit exercises. ～房 gym. ～器材 gym equipment

健忘 jiànwàng (形) forgetful; having a failing memory: ～症 amnesia

健在 jiànzài (动)〈书〉(of a person of advanced age) be still living and in good health; be still going strong

健壮(壯) jiànzhuàng (形) healthy and strong; robust

腱 jiàn (名) tendon

腱鞘 jiànqiào (名) tendon sheath

将(將) jiāng I (动) 1 do sth.; handle (a matter): 慎重～事 handle a matter with care 2 (in chess)check 3 put sb. on the spot 4 incite sb. to action; challenge; prod: 他做事稳重,你～他也没用. It's no use trying to prod him, he is so steady and calm. II (介) 1 with; by means of; by: ～功折罪 make amends for one's crime by good deeds 2 [after 将 comes the object to be followed by *vt*. to form inversion]: ～革命进行到底. Carry the revolution through to the end. III (副) be going to; be about to; will; shall: 明晨～有霜冻. Frost is expected tomorrow morning. 必～以失败告终 be certain to end in failure IV [indicating contradiction]: ～信～疑 half believing; half doubting V [used in between the verb and the complement of direction]: 传～出去 (of news, etc.) spread abroad

see also jiàng

将计就计 jiāng jì jiù jì turn the opponent's stratagem to one's own advantage

将近 jiāngjìn (动) be close to; nearly; almost: ～一百人 close to a hundred people. ～完成 nearing completion. 他～四十岁了. He is close on forty.

将就 jiāngjiu (动) make do with; make the best of; put up with: 衣服稍微小了点,你～着穿吧. This coat is a bit too tight, but perhaps you could make do with it.

将军 jiāngjūn I (名) general II (动) check; challenge: 他在会上将了我一军. He put me on the spot at the meeting.

将来(來) jiānglái (名) future: 在不远的～ in the not too distant future

将息 jiāngxī (动) rest; recuperate

将要 jiāngyào (副) be going to; will; shall: 会议～在大厅举行. The meeting will be held in the main hall.

浆(漿) jiāng I (名) thick liquid: 糖～ syrup. 纸～ pulp. ～果 berry II (动) starch: ～衣服 starch clothes. ～洗 wash and starch

see also jiàng

江 jiāng (名) 1 river 2 the Changjiang (Yangtze) River: ～南 south of the lower reaches of the Changjiang River

江河日下 jiāng-hé rì xià deteriorate with each passing day; go from bad to worse

江湖 jiānghú (名) 1 rivers and lakes 2 all corners of the country: 流落～ drift about

江湖 jiānghú (名) 1 itinerant entertainers, quacks, etc. 2 trade of such people: ～骗子 swindler; charlatan. ～医生 quack; mountebank

江山 jiāngshān (名) 1 rivers and mountains; land; landscape: ～如画 a picturesque landscape; beautiful scenery. ～易改,本性难移. It's easy to change rivers and mountains but hard to alter a person's nature. *or* A fox may grow grey, but never good. 2 country; state power

豇 jiāng

豇豆 jiāngdòu (名) cowpea

僵 jiāng (形) 1 stiff; numb: 他的手足都冻～了. His limbs became stiff with cold. 2 deadlocked: 事情搞～了. Things have come to a deadlock.

僵持 jiāngchí (动) (of both parties) refuse to budge; reach a deadlock: 双方～好久.

J

For quite some time, neither party was willing to compromise. 谈判陷入～状态. The negotiations have bogged down in a stalemate.

僵化 jiānghuà (动) become rigid; inflexible; ossify: 思想～ a rigid (or ossified) way of thinking

僵局 jiāngjú (名) deadlock; impasse; stalemate: 打破～ break a deadlock. 谈判陷入～. The negotiations have reached an impasse.

僵尸(屍) jiāngshī (名) corpse

僵死 jiāngsǐ (形) stiff and dead; ossified

僵硬 jiāngyìng (形) **1** stiff: 觉得四肢～ feel stiff in the limbs **2** rigid; inflexible: ～的态度 a stiff manner; rigid attitude

J

疆

jiāng (名) boundary; border

疆场(場) jiāngchǎng (名) battlefield

疆界 jiāngjiè (名) boundary; border

疆土 jiāngtǔ (名) territory

疆域 jiāngyù (名) territory; domain

缰

jiāng (名) reins; halter: ～绳 reins; halter

姜(薑)

jiāng (名) ginger: ～汁酒 ginger ale

桨(槳)

jiǎng (名) oar

奖(獎)

jiǎng I (动) encourage; praise; reward: ～许 praise; give encouragement to. 有功者～. Anyone who has distinguished himself by his performance will be rewarded. ～勤罚懒 reward the diligent and punish the lazy II (名) award; prize; reward: 发～ give awards; give prizes. 得～ win a prize

奖杯 jiǎngbēi (名) cup (as a prize)

奖惩 jiǎng-chéng (名) rewards and punishments: ～制度 system of rewards and penalties

奖金 jiǎngjīn (名) money award; bonus; premium

奖励(勵) jiǎnglì (动、名) encourage and reward; award; reward: 物质～ material reward. ～发明 give awards to innovators or inventors as an encouragement; encourage innovations. ～制度 bonus system

奖牌 jiǎngpái (名) medal

奖品 jiǎngpǐn (名) prize; award; trophy

奖券 jiǎngquàn (名) lottery ticket

奖赏 jiǎngshǎng (动) award; reward

奖学(學)金 jiǎng xué jīn (名) scholarship

奖章 jiǎngzhāng (名) medal; decoration

奖状(狀) jiǎngzhuàng (名) certificate of merit; citation

讲(講)

jiǎng (动) **1** speak; say; tell: ～故事 tell stories. ～几句话 say a few words. ～几点意见 make a few remarks **2** explain; make clear; interpret: ～明立场 state one's stand in explicit (or unequivocal) terms. 这个字有几个～法. This word is capable of several interpretations. **3** bargain; negotiate: ～价钱 bargain over the price; negotiate the terms **4** stress; pay attention to; be particular about: ～质量 stress quality; be quality conscious

讲稿 jiǎnggǎo (名) the draft or text of a speech; lecture notes

讲和 jiǎnghé (动) make peace; settle a dispute

讲话 jiǎnghuà I (动) speak; talk; address: 他在会上讲了话. He addressed the meeting. II (名) **1** speech; talk: 鼓舞人心的～ an inspiring speech **2** [often used in a book title] guide; introduction: 《政治经济学～》 *A Guide to Political Economy*

讲解 jiǎngjiě (动) explain: ～要点 expound the essential points

讲究 jiǎngjiu I (动) be particular about; pay attention to; stress; strive for: ～效率 strive for efficiency II (形) exquisite; tasteful: 这家旅馆布置得很～. This hotel is beautifully furnished. III (名) careful study: 这篇社论大有～. The leading article needs careful study.

讲课 jiǎngkè (动) teach; lecture

讲理 jiǎnglǐ (动) **1** argue things out **2** be reasonable: 蛮不～ be utterly unreasonable; be impervious to reason

讲明 jiǎngmíng (动) explain; make clear; state explicitly

讲情 jiǎngqíng (动) intercede; plead for sb.

讲师(師) jiǎngshī (名) lecturer

讲授 jiǎngshòu (动) lecture; instruct; teach

讲述 jiǎngshù (动) tell about; give an account of; narrate; relate

讲台(臺) jiǎngtái (名) lecture platform; rostrum; podium

讲坛(壇) jiǎngtán (名) **1** platform; rostrum **2** forum

讲学(學) jiǎngxué (动) give lectures (on an academic subject): 应邀来我校～ come on

invitation to give lectures at our college
讲演 jiǎngyǎn (名) lecture; speech
讲义(義) jiǎngyì (名) (mimeographed or xeroxed) teaching materials
讲座 jiǎngzuò (名) a course of lectures; series of lectures
酱(醬) jiàng I (名) 1 a thick sauce made from soya beans, flour, etc. 2 sauce; paste; jam: 芝麻～ sesame jam. 番茄～ tomato sauce II (形) cooked or pickled in soy sauce: ～肉 pork cooked in soy sauce; braised pork seasoned with soy sauce
酱菜 jiàngcài (名) vegetables pickled in soy sauce; pickles
酱油 jiàngyóu (名) soy sauce; soy
酱园(園) jiàngyuán (名) a shop making and selling sauce, pickles, etc.; sauce and pickle shop
将(將) jiàng (名) 1 general 2 commander-in-chief, the chief piece in Chinese chess
see also jiāng
将官 jiàngguān (名)〈口〉high-ranking military officer; general
将领 jiànglǐng (名) high-ranking military officer; general
将士 jiàngshì (名)〈书〉officers and men; commanders and fighters
浆(漿) jiàng
see also jiāng
浆糊 jiànghu (名) paste
匠 jiàng (名) craftsman; artisan: 能工巧～ skilled craftsmen. 铁～ blacksmith. 鞋～ shoemaker. 石～ stonemason. 木～ carpenter
匠人 jiàngrén (名) artisan; craftsman
匠心 jiàngxīn (名)〈书〉ingenuity; craftsmanship: 独具～ show distinctive ingenuity; show great originality
降 jiàng (动) fall; drop; lower: ～雨 a fall of rain; rainfall. ～价 cut prices. 许多消费品价格已经～了. The prices of many consumer goods have dropped.
see also xiáng
降低 jiàngdī (动) reduce; cut down; drop; lower: ～生产成本 reduce production costs
降格 jiànggé (动)〈书〉lower one's standard or status: ～以求 have to be content with a second best
降级 jiàngjí (动) demote
降临(臨) jiànglín (动) befall; arrive; come: 夜色～. Darkness (or night) fell.
降落 jiàngluò (动) descend; land: 飞机的～ the landing of aircraft. 强迫～ forced landing. ～伞 parachute
降水 jiàngshuǐ (名) precipitation: 人工～ artificial precipitation. ～量 precipitation
降温 jiàngwēn (动、名) 1 lower the temperature (as in a workshop): ～设备 cooling system 2 drop in temperature
降雨 jiàngyǔ (名) rainfall
绛 jiàng (形) deep red; crimson
绛紫 jiàngzǐ (形) dark reddish purple
强 jiàng (形) stubborn; unyielding: 倔～ stubborn; obstinate
see also qiáng; qiǎng
强嘴 jiàngzuǐ (动) reply defiantly; answer back; talk back
犟 jiàng (形) obstinate; stubborn; self-willed
浇(澆) jiāo (动) 1 pour liquid on; sprinkle water on: 大雨～得他全身都湿透了. He was soaked. 2 irrigate; water: ～花 water flowers. ～地 irrigate the fields
浇灌 jiāoguàn (动) 1 water; irrigate 2 pour: ～混凝土 pour concrete
浇铸(鑄) jiāozhù (名) casting; pouring: ～机 casting machine
交 jiāo I (动) 1 hand in; give up; turn over; deliver: ～还 give back; return. ～税 pay tax. ～作业 hand in one's homework 2 (of places or periods of time) meet; join: ～界 have a common boundary 3 reach (a certain hour or season): ～冬以后 since winter set in 4 cross; intersect: 圆周内两直径必相～. Any two diameters of a circle intersect each other. 5 associate with: ～朋友 make friends 6 have sexual intercourse; mate; breed: 杂～ crossbreed II (名) 1 friend; acquaintance; friendship; relationship: 点头之～ a nodding acquaintance. 建～ establish diplomatic relations 2 business transaction; deal; bargain: 成～ strike a bargain; conclude a transaction; clinch a deal III (形) 1 mutual; reciprocal; each other 2 both; together; simultaneous: 饥寒～迫 be plagued by hunger and cold
交班 jiāobān (动) hand over to the next

J

shift; hand over one's official duties

交叉 jiāochā (动) 1 intersect; cross; criss-cross: ~路口 an intersection 2 overlap: 他们的意见有点~. Their views overlap.

交差 jiāochāi (动) report to one's immediate superior when his mission has been duly accomplished

交错 jiāocuò I (动) interlock; criss-cross II (形) staggered

交代 jiāodài (动) 1 hand over: ~工作 hand over work to one's successor; brief one's successor on his work 2 explain; make clear; brief; tell: ~任务 brief sb. on his task 3 account for: 这次你又怎么~? What excuse can you offer this time? 4 confess: ~罪行 confess a crime (also as "交待")

交底 jiāodǐ (动) explain what the matter really is; give the bottom line

交锋 jiāofēng (动) cross swords; engage in a battle or contest

交付 jiāofù (动) 1 pay: ~佣金 pay commission 2 hand over; deliver; consign: ~表决 put to the vote. ~使用 be made available to the users

交割 jiāogē (动) complete a business transaction

交公 jiāogōng (动) hand over to the collective or the state

交互 jiāohù (副) 1 each other; mutually 2 alternately; in turn: 两种策略~使用 use the two tactics alternately

交换 jiāohuàn (动) exchange; swop: ~意见 exchange views; compare notes. ~房子 exchange homes. 实物~ barter. ~留学生 exchange students between two countries

交火 jiāohuǒ (动) exchange fire; engage in fight

交货 jiāohuò (名) delivery: 即期~ prompt delivery. 分批~ partial delivery. ~港 port of delivery. ~期 date of delivery

交集 jiāojí (动) (of different feelings) be mixed; occur simultaneously: 悲喜~ have mixed feelings of grief and joy

交际(際) jiāojì (名) social intercourse; communication: 语言是人们的~工具. Language is the means by which people communicate with each other. 他不善于~. He is not sociable. ~场合 social occasion

交加 jiāojiā (动)〈书〉(of two things) occur simultaneously: 风雨~. Wind and rain raged. 悲喜~. Grief mingled with joy.

交接 jiāojiē (动) 1 join; connect 2 hand over and take over: ~班 relief of a shift. ~手续(仪式) handing over procedure (ceremony) 新老干部的~ the smooth succession of younger cadres to old ones. 政权的顺利~ smooth transfer of government

交界 jiāojiè (动) (of two or more places) have a common boundary: 三省~的地方 a place where three provinces meet; the juncture of three provinces

交卷 jiāojuàn (动) 1 hand in an examination paper 2 fulfil one's task; carry out an assignment

交口称(稱)誉(譽) jiāokǒu chēngyù unanimously praise; sing sb.'s praises: 群众~ be held in high esteem by the public

交流 jiāoliú I (动) exchange; interflow; interchange: ~经验 exchange experiences; draw on each other's experience. 文化~ cultural exchange II (形) alternating: ~电 alternating current

交纳 jiāonà (动) pay (to the state or an organization); hand in: ~会费 pay membership dues

交配 jiāopèi (名) mating; copulation: ~期 mating season

交情 jiāoqing (名) friendship; friendly relations; acquaintanceship: 讲~ do things for the sake of friendship

交融 jiāoróng (动) blend; mingle: 水乳~ be in perfect harmony

交涉 jiāoshè (动) negotiate; make representations: 办~ carry on negotiations with; take up a matter with. 口头~ verbal representations

交谈 jiāotán (动) converse; chat; have chitchat

交替 jiāotì (动) 1 supersede; replace: 新旧~. The new takes the place of the old. 2 do sth. alternately; take turns: ~使用 use alternately

交通 jiāotōng (名) traffic; communications: ~规则 traffic regulations. ~工具 means of transport. 公路~ highway traffic. ~事故 traffic (or road) accident. ~阻塞 traffic jam (or block)

交头(頭)接耳 jiāotóu-jiē'ěr speak in each other's ears; whisper to each other

交往 jiāowǎng (动) associate with; make contact with: ~甚密 have intimate association with

交尾 jiāowěi (名) mating; pairing; coupling

交响(響)乐(樂) jiāoxiǎngyuè (名) symphony; symphonic music: ~队 symphony orchestra; philharmonic orchestra

交心 jiāoxīn (动) open one's heart to; lay one's heart bare

交易 jiāoyì (名) business; deal; trade; transaction: 现款~ cash transaction. 商品~会 trade fair; commodities fair. 政治~ a political deal. 做~ make a deal. 达成~ close or seal a deal. ~额 volume of trade

交易所 jiāoyìsuǒ (名) exchange: 证券~ stock exchange

交谊 jiāoyì (名)〈书〉friendship; friendly relations

交游 jiāoyóu (动)〈书〉make friends: ~甚广 have a wide circle of acquaintances

交战(戰) jiāozhàn (动) be at war; wage war: ~状态 state of war. ~双方 the two belligerent parties

交账(賬) jiāozhàng (动) 1 hand over the accounts 2 account for

交织(織) jiāozhī (动) interweave; intertwine; mingle

胶(膠) jiāo I (名) 1 glue; gum 2 rubber II (动) stick with glue; glue III (形) gluey; sticky; gummy

胶版 jiāobǎn (名) offset plate: ~印刷 offset printing

胶布 jiāobù (名) 1 rubberized fabric 2 adhesive tape

胶卷(捲) jiāojuǎn (名) roll film; film

胶囊 jiāonáng (名) capsule

胶片 jiāopiàn (名) film: 缩微~ microfiche

胶水 jiāoshuǐ (名) mucilage; glue

胶鞋 jiāoxié (名) rubber overshoes; galoshes

胶印 jiāoyìn (名) offset printing; offset lithography; offset: ~机 offset press; offset (printing) machine

胶着 jiāozhuó (形) deadlocked; stalemated: ~状态 deadlock; stalemate; impasse

郊 jiāo (名) suburbs; outskirts: 京~ the suburbs of Beijing

郊区(區) jiāoqū (名) suburban district; suburbs; outskirts

郊外 jiāowài (名) the countryside around a city; outskirts

郊游 jiāoyóu (名) outing; excursion

姣 jiāo (形)〈书〉handsome; beautiful-looking

教 jiāo (动) teach; instruct: ~书 teach school; teach. 他~我们开车. He taught us how to drive a car.
see also jiào

椒 jiāo (名) any of several hot spice plants: 辣~ chilli; red pepper. 胡~ pepper

娇(嬌) jiāo I (形) 1 tender; lovely; charming 2 fragile; frail; delicate 3 squeamish; finicky II (动) pamper; spoil: 别把孩子~坏了. Don't spoil the child.

娇滴滴 jiāodīdī (形) affectedly sweet; delicate and fragile

娇惯 jiāoguàn (动) pamper; coddle; spoil: ~孩子 pamper a child

娇媚 jiāomèi (形) 1 coquettish 2 sweet and charming

娇嫩 jiāonèn (形) 1 tender and lovely 2 fragile; delicate: ~的身子 delicate health

娇气(氣) jiāoqi (形) pampered; spoiled

娇生惯养(養) jiāoshēng-guànyǎng spoilt by indulgent parents

骄(驕) jiāo (形) proud; arrogant; conceited: ~必败. Pride goes before a fall.

骄傲 jiāo'ào I (形) arrogant; conceited: ~自大 swollen with pride; conceited and arrogant II (动) be proud; take pride in: 为…感到~ take pride in III (名) pride: 民族的~ the pride of the nation

骄横 jiāohèng (形) arrogant and imperious; extremely overbearing

骄矜 jiāojīn (形)〈书〉self-important; proud; haughty

骄奢淫逸 jiāoshē-yínyì live a life of luxury and indulge in pleasure; wallow in luxury and pleasure; be extravagant and dissipated

焦 jiāo I (形) 1 burnt; scorched; charred 2 worried; anxious: 心~ anxious; worried II (名) coke: 炼~ coking

焦点(點) jiāodiǎn (名) 1 focal point; focus 2 central issue; point at issue: 争论的~ the point at issue

焦急 jiāojí (形) anxious and restless; worried: ~万分 full of anxiety

焦虑(慮) jiāolǜ (形) anxious; worried; apprehensive

焦炭 jiāotàn (名) coke: 沥青~ pitch coke

焦头(頭)烂(爛)额 jiāotóu-làn'é badly battered; in a terrible fix; in a very awkward situation

焦躁 jiāozào (形) restless with anxiety; impatient; fretful

焦灼 jiāozhuó (形)〈书〉deeply worried; very anxious

蕉 jiāo (名) any of several broadleaf plants: 香~ banana.

礁 jiāo (名) reef: ~石 reef; rock. 触~ strike a reef; run up on a rock

嚼 jiáo (动) masticate; chew; munch: 别在背后~舌. Don't gossip behind one's back.

see also jué

铰 jiǎo (动)〈口〉1 cut with scissors: ~成两半 cut in two; cut into halves; cut in half 2 bore with a reamer; ream: ~孔 ream a hole

铰链 jiǎoliàn (名) hinge: ~接合 hinge joint

佼 jiǎo (形)〈书〉handsome; beautiful

佼佼 jiǎojiǎo (形)〈书〉above average; outstanding

皎 jiǎo (形) clear and bright: ~月 a bright moon

皎皎 jiǎojiǎo (形) very clear and bright; glistening white

皎洁(潔) jiǎojié (形) (of moonlight) bright and clear

狡 jiǎo (形) crafty; foxy; cunning: ~计 crafty trick; ruse

狡辩(辯) jiǎobiàn (动) quibble; resort to sophistry

狡猾 jiǎohuá (形) sly; crafty; cunning; tricky

狡赖 jiǎolài (动) deny (by resorting to sophistry)

狡兔三窟 jiǎotù sān kū it is a poor mouse that has only one hole

狡黠 jiǎoxiá (形)〈书〉sly; crafty; cunning

狡诈 jiǎozhà (形) deceitful; crafty; cunning

饺 jiǎo (名) dumpling: 蒸~ steamed dumplings

饺子 jiǎozi (名) dumpling (with meat and vegetable stuffing); *jiaozi*; ravioli

绞 jiǎo I (动) 1 twist; wring; entangle: 把衣服~干 wring out wet clothes. ~尽脑汁 rack one's brains; cudgel one's brains 2 hang by the neck: ~架 gallows. ~索 (the gangman's) noose II (量) skein; hank: 一~毛线 a skein of woollen yarn

绞车(車) jiǎochē (名) winch; windlass

绞杀(殺) jiǎoshā (动) strangle

绞痛 jiǎotòng (名) angina: 肚子~ abdominal angina; colic. 心~ angina pectoris

绞刑 jiǎoxíng (名) death by hanging: 上~ be hanged by the neck

搅(攪) jiǎo (动) 1 stir; mix: 把粥~一~ give the porridge a stir 2 disturb; annoy: 别打~她. Don't disturb her.

搅拌 jiǎobàn (动) stir; mix: ~机 mixer

搅动(動) jiǎodòng (动) mix; stir

搅和 jiǎohuo (动) 1 mix; blend; mingle: 别把这两件事~在一起. Don't mix up the two different matters. 2 mess up; spoil

搅浑 jiǎohún (动) stir and make muddy: 把水~ muddy the waters; deliberately create confusion

搅混 jiǎohun (动)〈口〉mix; blend; mingle

搅乱(亂) jiǎoluàn (动) confuse; throw into disorder

搅扰(擾) jiǎorǎo (动) disturb; annoy; cause trouble

矫(矯) jiǎo I (动) rectify; straighten out; adjust; correct II (形) strong; brave: ~若游龙 as powerful as a flying dragon

矫健 jiǎojiàn (形) robust; full of vim and vigour: ~的步伐 vigorous strides

矫揉造作 jiǎoróu zàozuò affected; pretentious

矫枉过(過)正 jiǎo wǎng guò zhèng go beyond the proper limits in correcting an error

矫正 jiǎozhèng (动) correct; put right; rectify: ~发音 correct sb.'s pronunciation mistakes. ~偏差 correct a deviation. ~错误 correct an error

侥(僥) jiǎo

侥幸 jiǎoxìng (形) lucky; by luck; by a fluke: ~取胜 win by sheer good luck

缴 jiǎo (动) 1 pay; hand over; hand in: ~房租 pay house rent. ~税 pay taxes. 上~ turn over (or in) to the state 2 capture: ~获三架机枪 capture three machine guns

缴获(獲) jiǎohuò (动) capture; seize

缴械 jiǎoxiè (动) 1 disarm 2 lay down one's arms

脚 jiǎo (名) 1 foot: 赤～ barefoot 2 base; foot: 山～ the foot of a hill

脚本 jiǎoběn (名) script; scenario: 电影～ film script

脚步 jiǎobù (名) step; pace: 加快～ quicken one's pace

脚跟 jiǎogēn (名) heel: 站稳～ stand firm; gain a firm footing (in society)

脚力 jiǎolì (名) strength of one's legs

脚镣 jiǎoliào (名) fetters; shackles

脚手架 jiǎoshǒujià (名) scaffold

脚踏两(兩)只(隻)船 jiǎo tà liǎng zhī chuán sit on the fence

脚踏实(實)地 jiǎo tà shídì earnest and down-to-earth; conscientious and practical: ～工作 work in a down-to-earth manner

脚印 jiǎoyìn (名) footprint

脚趾 jiǎozhǐ (名) toe

脚注 jiǎozhù (名) footnote

角 jiǎo (名) 1 horn: 牛～ ox horn. 鹿～ antler 2 bugle; horn: 号～ bugle 3 sth. in the shape of a horn: 菱～ water caltrop 4 corner: 拐～ corner 5 angle: 锐(钝)～ acute (obtuse) angle. 直～ right angle
see also jué

角度 jiǎodù (名) 1 degree of an angle 2 point of view; angle: 如果光从自己的～来看问题,意见就难免不一致. If everybody looks at the question from the angle of his own interest, opinions are bound to differ.

角落 jiǎoluò (名) 1 corner: 在房间～里 in a corner of the room 2 remote place: 在祖国每一～里 in the remote parts of the country

角膜 jiǎomó (名) cornea

剿 jiǎo (动) send armed forces to suppress; put down: ～匪 suppress bandits

窖 jiào (名) cellar or pit for storing things: 菜～ vegetable cellar

觉(覺) jiào (名) sleep: 睡一～ catch up on some sleep. 午～ afternoon nap
see also jué

校 jiào (动) 1 check; proof-read; collate: ～长条样 read galley proofs 2 compare
see also xiào

校对(對) jiàoduì I (动) 1 proof-read; proof 2 check against the original; calibrate II (名) proofreader

校样 jiàoyàng (名) proof sheet; proof

校阅 jiàoyuè (动) read and revise

校正 jiàozhèng (动) proof-read and correct; rectify: ～错字 correct misprints

校准(準) jiàozhǔn (名) calibration: 方位～ bearing calibration

较 jiào I (动) compare: 工作～前更为努力 work even harder than before II (副) comparatively; relatively; fairly; quite; rather: ～好 fairly good; quite good III (形) clear: 彰明～著 conspicuous

较量 jiàoliàng (动) 1 have a contest; have a trial of strength 2 carefully consider

教 jiào I (动) teach; instruct: 因材施～ teach according to ability. 请～ ask for advice; consult II (名) religion: 信～ believe in a religion; be religious. 基督～ Christianity
see also jiāo

教案 jiào'àn (名) teaching notes

教材 jiàocái (名) teaching material

教程 jiàochéng (名) 1 course of study 2 (published) lectures

教导(導) jiàodǎo I (动) instruct; teach; give guidance II (名) teaching; guidance

教皇 jiàohuáng (名) the Pope; the Pontiff

教会(會) jiàohuì (名) (the Christian) church: ～学校 missionary school

教诲 jiàohuì (名)〈书〉teaching; instruction: 谆谆～ earnest guidance

教科书(書) jiàokēshū (名) text-book

教练(練) jiàoliàn I (动) train; drill; coach II (名) coach; instructor: 足球～ football coach. ～员 coach; instructor; trainer

教师(師) jiàoshī (名) teacher

教士 jiàoshì (名) priest; clergyman; Christian missionary

教室 jiàoshì (名) classroom; schoolroom

教授 jiàoshòu I (名) professor: 副～ associate professor. 客座～ visiting professor; guest professor II (动) instruct; teach: ～历史 lecture on history

教唆 jiàosuō (动) instigate; abet; incite; put sb. up to sth.: ～犯 abettor

教堂 jiàotáng (名) church; cathedral

教条(條) jiàotiáo (名) dogma; doctrine; creed; tenet: ～主义 dogmatism; doctrinairism

教徒 jiàotú (名) follower of a religion

教务(務) jiàowù (名) educational administration: ～长 Dean of Studies. ～处 Dean's Office

教学(學) jiàoxué (名) **1** impart knowledge to students: ～相长. Teaching helps the teacher as well as the students. **2** teaching and studying: ～大纲 teaching programme; syllabus. ～方针 principles of teaching

教训 jiàoxun I (名) lesson; moral: 吸取～ draw a lesson (or moral) from sth.; take warning from sth. II (动) chide; teach sb. a lesson; give sb. a dressing down; lecture sb. (for wrongdoing, etc.)

教养(養) jiàoyǎng I (动) educate and train (the younger generation) II (名) moral education; culture breeding: 有～的 cultured

教育 jiàoyù I (名) education: ～部 Ministry of Education II (动) teach; educate; inculcate: 我们从中得到很大～. We've learnt a great deal from this.

教员 jiàoyuán (名) teacher; instructor: 汉语～ a teacher of Chinese

酵 jiào: 发～ ferment; leaven

酵母 jiàomǔ (名) yeast

叫 jiào I (动) **1** cry; shout: 大～一声 give a loud cry; shout; cry out loudly. 狗～ bark; yap **2** call; greet: 有人～你. Somebody is calling you. **3** hire; order: ～个出租汽车 hail a taxi **4** name; call: 人们～他汤姆大叔. People call him Uncle Tom. 你～什么名字? What's your name? **5** ask; advise: ～他进来吗? Shall I ask him (to come) in? 医生～他戒烟. The doctor advised him to give up smoking. II (介) [used to introduce a passive construction]: ～你猜对了. You've guessed right.

叫板 jiàobǎn (动) challenge: 向强手～ challenge the strong rival

叫喊 jiàohǎn (动) shout; yell; howl

叫花子 jiàohuāzi (名) 〈口〉 beggar

叫唤 jiàohuan (动) cry out; call out: 疼得直～ scream with pain

叫苦 jiàokǔ (动) complain; moan and groan: ～不迭 pour out a stream of grievances; complain endlessly

叫卖(賣) jiàomài (动) cry one's wares; peddle: 沿街～ hawk one's wares in the streets

叫屈 jiàoqū (动) complain of being wronged

叫嚷 jiàorǎng (动) shout; howl; clamour

叫嚣 jiàoxiāo (动) clamour; raise a hue and cry: 战争～ clamour for war. 大肆～ raise a terrific hue and cry

叫座 jiàozuò (动) attract a large audience: 这戏很～. This play appeals to the audience.

叫做 jiàozuò (动) be called; be known as: 这种装置～呼吸分析器. This apparatus is called breathalyser.

轿(轎) jiào (名) (～子) sedan (chair)

轿车(車) jiàochē (名) bus or car: 大～ bus; coach. 小～ car; limousine; sedan

秸(稭) jiē (名) stalks left after threshing; straw: 麦～ wheat straw

秸秆(稈) jiēgǎn (名) straw

结 jiē (动) bear (fruit); form (seed): 开花～果 blossom and bear fruit

see also jié

结巴 jiēba I (动) stammer; stutter II (名) stammerer; stutterer

结实(實) jiēshí (动) bear fruit; fructify

结实(實) jiēshi (形) **1** solid; sturdy; durable: 这张桌子很～. This is a very solid table. 绑～点. Tie it fast. **2** strong; sturdy; tough: 他长得很～. He is of strong build.

接 jiē (动) **1** come into contact with; come close to: ～近 approach; draw near **2** connect; join; put together: 请～上去! Carry on, please! 请～286 分机. Put me through to Extension 286, please. **3** catch; take hold of: ～球 catch a ball **4** receive: ～到一封信 receive a letter. ～电话 answer the phone **5** meet; welcome: 到飞机场～一个代表团 meet a delegation at the airport

接班 jiēbān (动) take one's turn on duty; take over from; succeed; carry on: 谁接你的班? Who will take over from you? ～人 successor

接触(觸) jiēchù I (动) come into contact with; get in touch with: 代表团～了各界人士. The delegation met with people from all circles. II (名) contact: ～不良 loose (or poor) contact. 保持～ maintain contact; keep in touch. 脱离～ disengage

接待 jiēdài (动) receive; admit: ～外宾 receive foreign visitors. 受到亲切～ be accorded a cordial reception. ～室 reception room. ～单位 host organization

接二连(連)三 jiē'èr-liánsān one after another; in quick succession: 他～收到朋友来信. Letters come from his friends one after another. 捷报～地传来. Reports of the victory came in quick succession. *or* Tidings of victory poured in thick and fast.

接风(風) jiēfēng (动) give a dinner for a visitor from afar

接管 jiēguǎn (动) take over

接轨 jiēguǐ (动) integrate:与国际～ integrate into the international community; adopt the international practice

接济(濟) jiējì (动) give financial or another form of assistance to

接见(見) jiējiàn (动) meet with sb.; grant an interview to

接近 jiējìn (动) be close to; near; approach: ～国际水平 approach the international level. 该项工程～完成. The project is nearing completion. 这个人不容易～. That man is rather difficult to approach.

接力 jiēlì (名) relay: ～赛跑 relay race; relay

接连 jiēlián (副) on end; in a row; in succession: ～好几天 for days on end. ～三小时 for three hours at a stretch

接纳 jiēnà (动) admit (into an organization): ～新会员 admit new members

接洽 jiēqià (动) take up a matter with; arrange (business, etc.) with; consult with: 同有关部门～ take up a matter with the department concerned. 他来～工作. He's here on business.

接壤 jiērǎng (动) border on; be contiguous to; be bounded by: ～地区 contiguous areas

接生 jiēshēng (动) deliver a child; practise midwifery

接收 jiēshōu (动) **1** receive: ～无线电信号 receive radio signals **2** take over (property, etc.); expropriate: ～这一家饭店 take over this hotel **3** admit: ～新会员 recruit new members

接受 jiēshòu (动) accept: ～邀请 accept an invitation. ～意见 take sb.'s advice ～考验 face up to a test

接替 jiētì (动) take over; replace

接通 jiētōng (动) put through: 电话～了吗? Have you got through?

接头(頭) jiētóu (动) contact; get in touch with; meet: 我找谁～? Who shall I get in touch with? ～地点 contact point; rendezvous

接吻 jiēwěn (动) kiss

接应(應) jiēyìng (动) **1** come to sb.'s aid (or assistance) **2** supply: 水泥一时～不上. Cement was in short supply at the time.

接踵 jiēzhǒng (动)〈书〉follow on sb.'s heels; in the wake of: 来访者～而至. Visitors came one after another.

接种(種) jiēzhòng (动) inoculate; have an inoculation

接着 jiēzhe (动) **1** catch: 你～我从树上扔下的苹果好吗? You catch the apples I throw down from the tree, won't you? **2** follow; carry on: 一个～一个 one after another. 请～讲下去. Please go on.

揭 jiē (动) **1** tear off; take off: 把墙上那张布告～下来. Take down that notice from the wall. **2** uncover; lift (the lid, etc.): ～盖子 take the lid off sth.; bring sth. into the open **3** expose; show up; bring to light: ～老底 expose sb.'s past failings. ～人疮疤 touch sb's sore spot; touch sb. on the raw **4**〈书〉raise; hoist: ～竿而起 raise a bamboo pole to serve as a standard of revolt

揭穿 jiēchuān (动) expose; show up: ～谎言 expose a lie. ～阴谋 lay bare an evil plot. 他的假面具被～了. His mask has been torn off.

揭底 jiēdǐ (动) reveal the inside story

揭短 jiēduǎn (动) disclose sb.'s faults

揭发(發) jiēfā (动) expose; unmask; bring to light

揭开(開) jiēkāi (动) uncover; reveal; open: ～宇宙的奥秘 uncover the mystery of the universe

揭露 jiēlù (动) expose; uncover; bring to light: ～丑闻 reveal or publish a scandal. ～其真面目 expose sb.'s true features. ～矛盾 bring the contradictions to light

揭密 jiēmì (动) unveil; disclose; expose

揭幕 jiēmù (动) unveil (a monument, etc.): ～式 unveiling ceremony

揭示 jiēshì (动) **1** announce; promulgate **2** reveal; bring to light

J

揭晓(曉) jiēxiǎo (动) announce; make known; publish: 选举结果已经～. The result of the election has been announced.

皆 jiē (副)〈书〉all; each and every: 人人～知. It is known to all.

皆大欢(歡)喜 jiē dà huānxǐ to the satisfaction of all

阶(階) jiē (名) steps; stairs: 台～ a flight of steps

阶层(層) jiēcéng (名) (social) stratum: 社会～ social stratum

阶段 jiēduàn (名) stage; phase: 过渡～ transitional stage (or period). 第一～的工程已经完成. The first phase of the project has been completed.

J

阶级 jiējí (名) (social) class: ～斗争 class struggle. ～分析 class analysis. ～矛盾 class contradictions

阶梯 jiētī (名) a flight of stairs; ladder; stepping stone

阶下囚 jiēxiàqiú (名) prisoner; captive

街 jiē (名) street: 上～买东西 go shopping downtown

街道 jiēdào (名) 1 street 2 what concerns the neighbourhood: ～办事处 subdistrict office. ～委员会 neighbourhood committee

街坊 jiēfang (名)〈口〉neighbours

街谈巷议(議) jiētán-xiàngyì street gossip; the talk of the town

街头(頭) jiētóu (名) street corner; street: 流落～ tramp the streets; drift along homeless in a city

节(節) jiē

see also jié

节骨眼 jiēguyǎn (名) critical juncture

疖(癤) jiē (名)(～子) 1 furuncle; boil 2 knot (in wood)

洁(潔) jié (形) clean: 整～ clean and tidy; clean and neat

洁白 jiébái (形) spotlessly white; pure

洁净 jiéjìng (形) clean; spotless

洁具 jiéjù (名) sanitary ware; toilet ware

洁身自好 jié shēn zì hào 1 preserve one's moral integrity 2 mind one's own business in order to keep out of trouble

诘 jié (动)〈书〉closely question; interrogate: ～问 closely question; interrogate; crossexamine

拮 jié

拮据 jiéjū (形) in straitened circumstances; short of money; hard up

结 jié I (动) 1 tie; knit; knot; weave: ～网 weave a net 2 congeal; form; forge; cement: ～痂 form a scab; scab 3 settle; conclude: ～账 settle accounts II (名) knot: 打～ tie a knot

see also jiē

结案 jié'àn (动) wind up a case

结拜 jiébài (动) become sworn brothers or sisters

结伴 jiébàn (动) go with: ～而行 go or travel in a group

结冰 jiébīng (动) freeze; ice up

结彩 jiécǎi (动) adorn (or decorate) with festoons: 张灯～ decorate with lanterns and festoons

结成 jiéchéng (动) form: ～同盟 form an alliance; become allies. ～一伙 gang up; band together

结党(黨)营(營)私 jiédǎng-yíngsī form a clique to gain private ends; gang up for selfish purposes

结构(構) jiégòu (名) structure; composition; construction: 经济～ economic structure. 文章～ organization of an essay. 消费～ consumption pattern. 技术～ technological makeup. ～严密 well organized. 钢筋混凝土～ reinforced concrete structure

结果 jiéguǒ I (名) result; outcome: 必然～ inevitable result. 刻苦学习的～ the result of painstaking hard work II (动) kill; finish off

结合 jiéhé (动) 1 combine; unite; integrate; link: 劳逸～ combine work with rest 2 be united in wedlock

结婚 jiéhūn (动) marry; get married: ～登记 marriage registration. ～证书 marriage certificate

结交 jiéjiāo (动) make friends with; associate with

结晶 jiéjīng I (动) crystallize II (名) 1 crystal 2 crystallization: 智慧的～ a crystallization of wisdom. 劳动的～ the fruit of labour

结局 jiéjú (名) final result; outcome; ending: 悲惨的～ a tragic ending

结论(論) jiélùn (名) 1 conclusion (of a syllogism) 2 conclusion; verdict: 得出～

draw (or come to, reach) a conclusion

结盟 jiéméng (动) form an alliance; ally; align: 不～政策 non-alignment policy

结亲(親) jiéqīn (动) 1 〈口〉 marry; get married 2 (of two families) become related by marriage

结社 jiéshè (动) form an association: ～自由 freedom of association

结识(識) jiéshí (动) get acquainted with sb.; make the acquaintance of sb.

结束 jiéshù (动) end; finish; conclude; wind up; close: ～讲话 wind up a speech. 会议下午5时～. The meeting lasted till 5 p.m. ～语 concluding remarks

结算 jiésuàn (动) settle accounts; close an account

结尾 jiéwěi (名) ending; winding-up stage

结业(業) jiéyè (动) complete a course; wind up one's studies; finish school

结余(餘) jiéyú (名) cash surplus; surplus; balance

结怨 jiéyuàn (动) provoke hatred

结账(賬) jiézhàng (动) settle (or square) accounts; balance books

截 jié I (动) 1 cut; sever: ～成两段 cut in two 2 stop; check; stem: ～流 dam a river. ～球 intercept a pass 3 by (a specified time); up to: ～至八月底 up to the end of August II (量) section; chunk; length: 一～儿木头 a log

截长(長)补(補)短 jié cháng bǔ duǎn draw on the strong points to offset the weaknesses: 我们要彼此～. We must give full play to our abilities to make up for our shortcomings.

截断(斷) jiéduàn (动) 1 cut off; block: ～敌人的退路 cut off the enemy's retreat 2 cut short; interrupt

截获(獲) jiéhuò (动) intercept and capture

截然 jiérán (副) sharply; completely: ～不同 poles apart; completely different. ～相反 diametrically opposite

截止 jiézhǐ (动) end; close: ～日期 closing date. 报名已经～了. Registration has closed.

劫 jié I (动) 〈书〉 1 rob; hold up; plunder; raid: 抢～ loot 2 coerce; compel II (名) calamity; disaster; misfortune: 浩～ a great calamity. ～后余生 be a survivor of a disaster

劫持 jiéchí (动) kidnap; hold under duress; hijack: ～飞机 hijack an aeroplane

劫机(機)者 jiéjīzhě (名) hijacker

劫掠 jiélüè (动) plunder; loot

劫狱(獄) jiéyù (动) break into a jail to rescue a prisoner

节(節) jié I (名) 1 joint; node; knot: 竹～ bamboo joint. 骨～ joint (of bones) 2 division; part: 音～ syllable 3 festival; red-letter day; holiday: 过～ celebrate (or observe) a festival. 春～ the Spring Festival. 国庆～ National Day 4 item: 细～ details 5 integrity: 气～ moral or political integrity II (动) 1 abridge: ～译 abridged translation 2 economize; save: ～煤 economize on coal III (量) section; length: 一～铁管 a length of iron pipe. 八～车厢 eight railway coaches

see also jiē

节俭(儉) jiéjiǎn (形、名) thrifty; frugal: 提倡～ encourage frugality

节节 jiéjié (副) successively: ～胜利 go from victory to victory. ～败退 keep on retreating

节流 jiéliú (动) reduce expenditure

节录(録) jiélù I (动) extract II (名) excerpt

节目 jiémù (名) programme; item (on a programme); number: 晚会的～ programme for the evening party: ～单 programme; playbill

节拍 jiépāi (名) metre; musical rhythm

节日 jiérì (名) festival; red-letter day; holiday: ～气氛 festive atmosphere

节省 jiéshěng (动) economize; save; use sparingly; cut down on: ～时间 save time. ～行政开支 cut down on government expenditure

节食 jiéshí (动) be on a diet

节外生枝 jiéwài shēng zhī raise unexpected side issues

节衣缩食 jiéyī-suōshí economize on food and clothing; live frugally

节余(餘) jiéyú (名) surplus (as a result of economizing)

节育 jiéyù (名) birth control

节约 jiéyuē (动) practise economy; economize; save: ～能源 conserve energy

节制 jiézhì I (动) control; regulate; check; be moderate in: ～饮食 eat and drink moderately II (名) temperance; abstinence

节奏 jiézòu (名) musical rhythm: ～明快 lively rhythm

捷 jié I (名) victory; triumph: 大～ a great victory. 报～ announce a victory II (形) prompt; nimble; quick: 敏～ quick; nimble; agile

捷报(報) jiébào (名) news of victory or success: ～频传. News of victory keeps pouring in.

捷径(徑) jiéjìng (名) short cut: 走～ take a short cut

捷足先登 jiézú xiān dēng the race is to the swiftest; the early bird catches the worm

睫 jié (名) eyelash; lash: ～毛 eyelash; lash

竭 jié (动) exhaust; use up

竭诚 jiéchéng (副) wholeheartedly; with all one's heart; in all sincerity

竭尽(盡) jiéjìn (动) use up; exhaust: ～全力 spare no effort; do one's utmost; do all one can

竭力 jiélì (副) do one's utmost; strain every nerve: ～支持 give all-out support. ～反对 vigorously oppose

竭泽(澤)而渔 jié zé ér yú drain the pond to get all the fish; kill the goose that lays the golden eggs

杰(傑) jié I (形) outstanding; prominent II (名) outstanding person; hero

杰出 jiéchū (形) outstanding; remarkable; prominent: ～贡献 a brilliant contribution

杰作 jiézuò (名) masterpiece

孑 jié (形)〈书〉lonely; all alone

孑然 jiérán (形)〈书〉solitary; lonely; alone: ～一身 live all alone in this wide human world

解 jiě (动) 1 separate; divide: 溶～ dissolve. 难～难分 be too deeply involved (in an affair) 2 untie; undo: ～鞋带 undo shoelaces. ～扣儿 unbutton 3 allay; dispel; dismiss: ～毒 detoxicate. ～乏 relieve fatigue; refresh 4 explain; interpret; solve: 注～ annotate. ～题 solve a problem 5 understand; comprehend: 费～ hard to understand. 百思不～ fail to understand even after pondering a hundred times. 令人不～ puzzling; incomprehensible 6 relieve oneself: 小～ go to the lavatory (to urinate)
see also jiè

解嘲 jiěcháo (动) try to cover up or gloss over sth. when ridiculed

解除 jiěchú (动) remove; relieve; get rid of: ～职务 remove sb. from his post; relieve sb. of his office. ～合同 terminate a contract. ～武装 disarm. ～禁令 lift a ban. ～婚约 dissolve an engagement

解答 jiědá (动) answer; explain: ～疑难问题 answer difficult questions

解冻(凍) jiědòng (动) 1 thaw; unfreeze: ～季节 thawing season 2 unfreeze (funds, assets, etc.)

解读(讀) jiědú (动) decode; interpret; analyse

解放 jiěfàng (动、名) liberate; emancipate: 妇女～ the emancipation of women. 民族～运动 national liberation movement

解雇(僱) jiěgù (动) dismiss; fire; sack

解恨 jiěhèn (动) vent one's bottled-up spleen

解禁 jiějìn (动) lift a ban

解救 jiějiù (动) rescue (from the jaws of danger); save; deliver

解决 jiějué (动) 1 solve; resolve; settle: ～纠纷 settle a dispute. ～困难 overcome a difficulty 2 dispose of; finish off: 把敌人完全～了. We have wiped out all the enemy troops.

解开(開) jiěkāi (动) untie; undo: ～上衣 unbutton one's jacket. ～这个谜 unveil the mystery

解渴 jiěkě (动) quench one's thirst

解闷 jiěmèn (动) divert oneself from boredom

解密 jiěmì (动) decrypt; decipher

解聘 jiěpìn (动) dismiss (an employee)

解剖 jiěpōu (动) dissect: 尸体～ autopsy; postmortem examination. ～学 anatomy

解气(氣) jiěqì (动) work off one's steam

解散 jiěsàn (动) 1 dismiss: ～队伍 dismiss; disband 2 dissolve; disband: ～组织 disband an organization. ～议会 dissolve a parliament

解释(釋) jiěshì (动) explain; expound; interpret: ～法律 interpret laws. 这事你怎么～? How do you account for this?

解手 jiěshǒu (动) relieve oneself; go to the toilet (or lavatory)

解说 jiěshuō (动) explain orally; comment

解体(體) jiětǐ (动) disintegrate; fall apart: 社会的～ the disintegration of society

解脱 jiětuō (动) free (or extricate) oneself:

使政府从危机中～出来 extricate the government from a crisis

解围(圍) jiěwéi (动) 1 force the enemy to raise a siege; rescue troops from enemy encirclement 2 help sb. out of a predicament; save sb. from an embarrassing situation

解职(職) jiězhí (动) dismiss from office; discharge; relieve sb. of his post

姐 jiě (名) 1 elder sister; sister 2 general term for young women

姐夫 jiěfu (名) elder sister's husband; brother-in-law

姐姐 jiějie (名) elder sister; sister

戒 jiè I (动) 1 guard against: 力～骄傲 strictly guard against conceit 2 exhort; admonish; warn: 引以为～ take warning from sth. 3 give up; drop; stop: ～烟 give up smoking. ～酒 stop drinking II (名) 1 Buddhist monastic discipline: 受～ attain the full status of a monk or nun 2 (finger) ring: 钻～ diamond ring

戒备(備) jièbèi (动) guard; take precautions; be on the alert: ～森严 be heavily guarded

戒除 jièchú (动) give up; drop; stop: ～恶习 get rid of a bad habit

戒毒 jièdú (动) give up drugs; abstain from drugs: ～所 drug rehibilitation centre

戒律 jièlǜ (名) religious discipline; commandment

戒心 jièxīn (名) vigilance; wariness: 对某人怀有～ be wary of sb.'s tricks or evil intentions

戒严(嚴) jièyán (动、名) enforce martial law; impose a curfew; cordon off an area to prevent criminals from getting away: 宣布～ proclaim martial law

戒指 jièzhi (名) (finger) ring

诫 jiè (动) warn; admonish: 告～ give warning; admonish

介 jiè (动) 1 be situated between; lie between: 这座山～于两县之间. The mountain lies between two counties. 2 take seriously; take to heart; mind: 不～意 not mind

介词 jiècí (名) preposition

介人 jièrù (动) intervene; interpose; get involved

介绍 jièshào (动) 1 introduce; present: 让我～一下,这就是王先生. Allow me to introduce Mr. Wang. ～对象 find sb. a boy or girl friend 2 recommend: 我给你～一本书. I'll recommend you a book. ～人 sponsor. ～信 recommendation; reference 3 let know; brief: ～情况 brief sb. on the situation. ～经验 pass on experience

疥 jiè (名) scabies

芥 jiè (名) mustard

芥末 jièmo (名) mustard

界 jiè (名) 1 boundary: 国～ the boundary of a country 2 scope; extent: 眼～ field of vision; mental horizons 3 circles: 新闻～ press circles. 各～人士 people from all walks of life 4 primary division; kingdom: 动(植、矿)物～ the animal (vegetable, mineral) kingdom

界面 jièmiàn (名) interface

界石 jièshí (名) boundary stone or tablet

界线(綫) jièxiàn (名) 1 boundary line 2 dividing line; bounds

界限 jièxiàn (名) 1 demarcation line; dividing line; limits; bounds: 划清～ draw a distinction 2 limit; end

借 jiè (动) 1 borrow: 跟人～书 borrow books from sb. 2 lend: ～书给他 lend the book to him 3 make use of; take advantage of (an opportunity, etc.) 4 use as a pretext: ～酒浇愁 take to drinking to drown one's sorrows

借贷 jièdài (动) borrow or lend money

借刀杀(殺)人 jiè dāo shā rén make use of another person to get rid of an adversary

借端 jièduān (动) use as a pretext: ～生事 make trouble on a pretext

借故 jiègù (副) find an excuse for

借光 jièguāng 〈套〉 excuse me

借鉴(鑒) jièjiàn (动) use for reference; benefit by another person's experience; draw on the experience of: ～外国的经验 use the experience of other countries for reference

借据 jièjù (名) receipt for a loan; IOU

借口 jièkǒu I (动) use as an excuse (or pretext) II (名) excuse; pretext: 制造～ invent an excuse

借款 jièkuǎn I (动) borrow or lend money; ask for or offer a loan II (名) loan

借题发(發)挥 jiè tí fāhuī seize on an incident to exaggerate or distort matters;

J

seize upon an incident to make a fuss

借问 jièwèn (动)〈敬〉may I ask

借助 jièzhù (动) have the aid of; draw support from: ~外资 with the help of foreign capital

解 jiè

解送 jièsòng (动) send under guard

see also jiě

届 jiè I (动) fall due: ~期 when the day comes; on the appointed date II (量) [used before a regular meeting or each year's graduates]: 本~联大 the present session of the U. N. General Assembly. 本~毕业生 this year's graduates

J

届满(滿) jièmǎn (动) at the expiration of one's term of office: 任期~. The term of office has expired.

届时(時) jièshí (副) when the time comes; at the appointed time; on the occasion

价(價) jie (助) [used after an adverb for emphasis]: 震天~响 make a terrific noise

see also jià

津 jīn (名) 1 ferry crossing; ford: ~渡 a ferry crossing 2 saliva

津津乐(樂)道 jīnjīn lè dào relate with gusto; talk about with great relish

津津有味 jīnjīn yǒu wèi with relish; with gusto; with keen pleasure: 听得~ listen with absorbing interest

津贴 jīntiē (名) subsidy; allowance: 岗位~ subsidies appropriate to particular jobs

津液 jīnyè (名) 1 body fluid 2 saliva

禁 jīn (动) contain (or restrain) oneself: 不~流下眼泪 can't hold back one's tears. ~不住 can't help doing sth.

see also jìn

禁受 jīnshòu (动) bear; stand; endure

襟 jīn (名) 1 front of a garment 2 brothers-in-law whose wives are sisters

襟怀(懷) jīnhuái (名)〈书〉bosom; (breadth of) mind: ~坦白 open and above-board; frank-hearted

巾 jīn (名) a piece of cloth (as used for a towel, scarf, kerchief, etc.): 手~ (face) towel. 围~ scarf. 餐~ napkin

巾帼(幗) jīnguó (名) woman: ~英雄 heroine

今 jīn (名) 1 modern; present-day: ~人 contemporaries; people of our era 2 today: ~明两天 today and tomorrow. ~晚 tonight; this evening 3 this (year): ~冬 this (coming) winter 4 now; the present: 至~ to date; until now; up to now. 从~以后 from now on; henceforth

今后(後) jīnhòu (名) from now on; in the days to come; henceforth; hereafter; in future: ~的十年内 in the next decade; in the coming ten years

今年 jīnnián (名) this year

今日 jīnrì (名) 1 today 2 present; now: ~中国 China today

今生 jīnshēng (名) this life

今世 jīnshì (名) 1 this life 2 this age; the contemporary age

今天 jīntiān (名) 1 today: 一年前的~ a year ago today 2 the present; now

今朝 jīnzhāo (名)〈书〉today; the present; now

今昔 jīn-xī (名) the present and the past; today and yesterday

矜 jīn (形) 1 self-important; conceited: 骄~之气 overweening pride; an air of self-importance 2 restrained; reserved

矜持 jīnchí (形) restrained; reserved: 举止~ have a reserved manner; look self-conscious

金 jīn I (名) 1 metals: 合~ alloy. 五~店 hardware store 2 money: 现~ cash; ready money 3 ancient metal percussion instruments: ~鼓齐鸣. All the gongs and drums are beating. 4 gold (Au): ~币 gold coin. ~条 gold bar II (形) golden: ~婚 golden wedding

金碧辉煌 jīnbì-huīhuáng (of a building, etc.) dazzlingly splendid and magnificent

金蝉(蟬)脱壳(殼) jīnchán tuō qiào slip out of a predicament like a cicada sloughing its skin; escape by cunning manoeuvring

金城汤(湯)池 jīnchéng-tāngchí impregnable fortified city

金额 jīn'é (名) amount (or sum) of money

金刚(剛)石 jīngāngshí (名) diamond

金黄 jīnhuáng (形) golden yellow

金科玉律 jīnkē-yùlǜ golden rule

金钱(錢) jīnqián (名) money

金融 jīnróng (名) finance; banking: ~寡头 financial oligarch (or magnate). ~市场

money market

金属(屬) jīnshǔ (名) metal: 黑色～ ferrous metal. 有色～ non-ferrous metal

金玉 jīnyù (名)〈书〉[often used metaphorically] precious; magnificent: ～良言 wise counsel

金字塔 jīnzìtǎ (名) pyramid

金字招牌 jīnzì zhāopái 1 (of a business firm) of good repute 2 distinguished title

筋 jīn (名) 1 muscle 2 tendon; sinew 3 anything resembling a tendon or vein: 叶～ ribs of a leaf. 钢～ reinforcing steel; steel reinforcement

筋斗 jīndǒu (名) 1 somersault: 翻～ turn a somersault 2 fall; tumble: 摔了个～ trip over sth. and fall

筋骨 jīngǔ (名) bones and muscles — physique

筋疲力尽(盡) jīnpí-lìjìn exhausted; worn out; dog-tired

斤 jīn (量) *jin*, Chinese unit of weight (= 1/2 kilogram)

斤斤计较 jīnjīn jìjiào worry about petty gain or loss; bother about trifling matters

斤两(兩) jīnliǎng (名) weight: 他的话有～. His words carry weight.

谨 jǐn (形) 1 careful; cautious; scrupulous: ～小慎微 overcautious particularly in small matters. ～守规则 strictly adhere to the rules. ～言慎行 be cautious in whatever one says or does 2 solemnly; sincerely: ～致谢意. Please accept my sincere thanks.

谨防 jǐnfáng (动) guard against; beware of

谨慎 jǐnshèn (形) prudent; careful; cautious; circumspect: 谦虚～ modest and prudent

紧(緊) jǐn (形) 1 tight; taut; close: 把绳子拉～ pull the rope taut. 把螺丝拧～ drive the screw tight. 这件上衣前身太～. This jacket is a bit too tight in the front. 放学后～接着有足球比赛. There will be a football match right after school. 2 urgent; pressing; tense: 风刮得～. It's blowing hard. 3 strict; stringent: 管得～ exercise strict control over; be strict with 4 hard up; short of money: 手头～ be short of money; be hard up. ～缺商品 commodities in short supply

紧凑 jǐncòu (形) compact; terse; well-knit: 这篇文章很～. The article is well organized.

紧急 jǐnjí (形) urgent; pressing; critical: 情况～. The situation is critical. ～措施 emergency measures. ～会议 emergency meeting. ～着陆 emergency landing

紧紧 jǐnjǐn (副) closely; tightly; firmly

紧密 jǐnmì (形) close together; inseparable: ～合作 close cooperation. ～联系 close contact

紧迫 jǐnpò (形) pressing; urgent; imminent: 时间～ be pressed for time. 任务～. The task is urgent.

紧俏 jǐnqiào (形) in great demand but short supply

紧缩 jǐnsuō (动) reduce; retrench; tighten: 开支～ cut down expenses. ～编制 reduce staff. ～措施 austerity measures

紧要 jǐnyào (形) critical; crucial; vital: ～关头 critical moment (or juncture); crucial moment. 无关～ of no consequence; of no importance

紧张(張) jǐnzhāng (形) 1 nervous; in a flurry: 神情～ look nervous. 慢慢来,别～. Take it easy. Don't be so nervous. 2 tense; intense; strained: ～局势 a tense situation. 关系～ strained relations 3 in short supply; tight: 人力～ inadequate manpower

锦 jǐn I (名) brocade II (形) bright and beautiful: 前程似～ splendid prospects; glorious future

锦标(標) jǐnbiāo (名) prize; trophy; title: ～赛 championship contest; championships

锦缎 jǐnduàn (名) brocade

锦上添花 jǐnshàng tiān huā make what is already good still better

锦绣 jǐnxiù (形) beautiful; splendid: ～山河 a land of charm and beauty

仅(僅) jǐn (副) only; merely; barely: ～次于 second only to. ～供参考 for your reference only. ～存一人. There was only one survivor.

仅仅 jǐnjǐn (副) only; merely; barely: 这～是问题的一面. This is only one side of the picture.

尽(儘) jǐn I (动) 1 within the limits of: ～着三天把事情办妥. Get the work done properly within three days. 2 give priority to: 先～老年人和小孩儿上车. Let the old people and children get on the bus first. II (副) 1 to the greatest extent: ～早 as soon as

possible; at the earliest possible date 2 [used before a word indicating direction, to denote "most"] at the furthest end of: ～北边 the northernmost end, etc.
see also jìn

尽管 jǐnguǎn I (副) feel free to; not hesitate to: 有什么建议～提. Please feel free to make suggestions. 你～说吧. Say all that you have got to say. II (连) though; even though; in spite of; despite: ～有几个国家反对, 决议还是通过了. The resolution was passed in spite of opposition from a number of countries.

尽可能 jǐnkěnéng (副) as far as possible; to the best of one's ability: ～多邀请些人. Invite as many guests as possible.

尽快 jǐnkuài (副) as quickly (or soon, early) as possible: 请～答复. Please reply at your earliest convenience.

尽量 jǐnliàng (副) to the best of one's ability; as far as possible: 把你亲眼看见的～反映给大家. Tell everybody what you saw as far as possible.

进(進) jìn I (动) 1 advance; move forward; move ahead: 不～则退. Make headway, or you'll fall behind. 2 enter; come or go into: ～教室 enter the classroom. ～大学 enter college 3 receive: ～款 income 4 eat; drink; take: 共～晚餐 have supper together 5 submit; present: ～言 offer advice; make a suggestion 6 [used after a verb] into; in: 走～车间 walk into the workshop. 把钉子钉～墙壁 drive the nail into the wall II (名) any of the several rows of houses within an old-style residential compound

进逼 jìnbī (动) (of an army) close in on; advance on; press on towards: 步步～ tighten the encirclement

进步 jìnbù I (动) advance; progress; improve: 你～很快. You are making rapid progress. II (形) (politically) progressive: 思想～ have progressive ideas. ～人士 progressive personages

进程 jìnchéng (名) course; process; progress: 历史～ the course of history

进出口 jìn-chūkǒu (名) import and export

进度 jìndù (名) 1 rate of progress (or advance): 加快～ quicken the pace (or tempo) 2 planned speed; schedule: 按照～完成这项工程. This project is to be completed according to plan. ～表 progress chart

进发(發) jìnfā (动) set out; start: 游行者向华盛顿～. The marchers started for Washington.

进犯 jìnfàn (动) intrude into; invade: 打退～的敌人 beat back the invading enemy

进攻 jìngōng (动) attack; assault: 发起～ launch an attack. 猛烈的～ massive offensive

进化 jìnhuà (名) evolution: ～论 the theory of evolution

进货 jìnhuò (动) lay in a stock; replenish one's stock

进军 jìnjūn (动) (of an army) march; advance

进口 jìnkǒu I (动) 1 call at a port: ～港 port of entry 2 import: ～商 importer. ～许可证 import license II (名) entrance

进来(來) jìnlái I (动) come (or get) in; enter: 让他～. Show him in. II [used after a verb, meaning going or coming in]: 她哼着小调走～. She came in humming a tune.

进取 jìnqǔ (动) keep forging ahead; be enterprising: ～心 enterprising spirit; initiative

进去 jìnqù I (动) go in; enter: 你～看看. Go in and have a look. II [used after a verb to express the idea of coming or going in]: 把桌子搬～ move the table in

进入 jìnrù (动) enter; get into: ～阵地 get into position. ～决赛阶段 enter the finals. ～角色 get into the picture

进退 jìn-tuì (动) advance or retreat: ～自如. There is ample room for manoeuvre. ～维谷 caught in a dilemma

进行 jìnxíng (动) 1 be in progress; be under way; go on: 学习～得怎么样? How are you getting on with your studies? 2 carry on; carry out; conduct: ～讨论 hold discussions. ～实地调查 make on-the-spot investigations. ～科学实验 engage in scientific experiment. ～核试验 conduct a nuclear test. ～侵略 commit aggression. ～表决 put to the vote. ～英勇斗争 wage a heroic struggle 3 be on the march; march; advance: ～曲 march

进修 jìnxiū (动) take a refresher course: 在职～ in-service training; on-the-job training. ～班 extramural class; higher training class

J

进一步 jìnyībù (形) go a step further; further: ～发展友好关系 further develop the friendly relations. 对中国历史有～了解 have a better understanding of the history of China. ～扩大开放 extend the scope of opening up

进展 jìnzhǎn (动) make progress; make headway: ～顺利 making good progress. 谈判毫无～. The talks have made no headway.

进驻 jìnzhù (动) (of troops) enter and garrison (a town, city, etc.)

晋(晉) jìn (动) **1** enter; advance **2** promote: 加官～爵 be promoted to a higher post

晋级 jìnjí (动) rise in rank; be promoted

晋升 jìnshēng (动) promote to a higher office

觐 jìn: ～见 present oneself before (a monarch). 朝～ go on a pilgrimage

禁 jìn I (动) **1** prohibit; forbid; ban: 严～烟火 Smoking and lighting fires strictly forbidden (or prohibited). ～酒 prohibition of alcoholism **2** imprison; detain: 监～ imprison. 软～ put under house arrest II (名) **1** what is forbidden by law or custom: 违～品 contraband (goods) **2** forbidden area: 宫～ the imperial palace
see also jīn

禁闭 jìnbì (名、动) confinement (as a punishment); be kept in detention

禁地 jìndì (名) forbidden ground; restricted area: 这是～. This is out of bounds.

禁毒 jìndú (动) drug control; prohibition on drugs

禁锢 jìngù (动) **1** debar from holding office (in feudal times) **2** keep in custody; imprison; put in jail **3** confine

禁忌 jìnjì I (动) avoid; abstain from (hot or rich food) II (名) taboo

禁区(區) jìnqū (名) **1** forbidden zone; restricted zone: 空中～ restricted airspace **2** (wildlife or plant) preserve; reserve; natural park **3** (football) penalty area

禁运(運) jìnyùn (动) embargo: 实行～ place an embargo. ～品 contraband

禁止 jìnzhǐ (动) prohibit; ban; forbid: ～入内 No admittance. ～停车 No parking. ～通行 No thoroughfare. *or* Closed to traffic. ～招贴 post no bills

噤 jìn (动) **1** keep silent **2** shiver: 寒～ shiver

噤若寒蝉(蟬) jìn ruò hánchán dare not air one's views out of fear

近 jìn (形) **1** near; close: 离圣诞节很～了. Christmas is drawing near. 附～的邮局 the post office near by. ～在咫尺 be close at hand. ～年来 in recent years. ～在眼前 right before one's eyes **2** approaching: 年～六十 getting on for sixty **3** intimate; closely related: 亲～ on intimate terms **4** easy to understand: 浅～ simple and easy to understand

近代 jìndài (名) modern times: ～史 modern history

近海 jìnhǎi (名) coastal waters; inshore; offshore: ～渔业 inshore fishing. ～钻探 offshore drilling

近乎 jìnhu (动) be close to; be little short of: ～荒谬的论点 an argument bordering on absurdity

近郊 jìnjiāo (名) outskirts of a city; suburbs

近况 jìnkuàng (名) recent developments; present condition: 不知你～如何? How are things with you?

近来(來) jìnlái (名) recently; of late; lately

近邻(鄰) jìnlín (名) near neighbour

近旁 jìnpáng (名) nearby; near: 大楼～ near the building

近期 jìnqī (名) in the near future

近日 jìnrì (名) **1** recently; in the past few days **2** within the next few days

近视 jìnshì (名) myopia; nearsightedness; shortsightedness

近视眼 jìnshiyǎn (名) myopia; nearsightedness; shortsightedness: 他是～. He is shortsighted (or nearsighted).

近水楼(樓)台(臺) jìn shuǐ lóutái the advantage of being in a favourable position

近似 jìnsì (动) approximate; be similar: ～值 approximate value

近义词 jìnyìcí (名) near synonym

劲(勁) jìn (名) **1** strength; energy: 用～ put forth strength. 她仿佛有使不完的～. She seems to have inexhaustible energy. **2** vigour; spirit; drive; zeal: 鼓～ boost one's morale **3** air; manner; expression: 瞧他那高兴～儿. See how pleased he is. **4** interest; relish; gusto: 下棋没～, 咱们去游泳吧. Playing chess is no fun; let's go swimming.
see also jìng

J

劲头(頭) jìntóu (名) 1 strength; energy 2 vigour; spirit; drive; zeal: 工作有～ be full of drive in one's work

浸 jìn (动) soak; steep: 把衬衣在温水中浸两分钟. Soak the shirts in lukewarm water for two minutes.

浸泡 jìnpào (动) soak

浸染 jìnrǎn (动) be contaminated; be addicted

浸润 jìnrùn (动) soak; infiltrate: 雨水～着的田野 rain-soaked fields.

浸透 jìntòu (动) soak; saturate; steep; infuse: 汗水～了他的衬衣. His shirt was soaked with sweat.

浸渍 jìnzì (动) soak; ret; macerate: 亚麻～ flax retting. ～剂 soaker

J

尽(盡) jìn I (形) 1 exhausted; finished: 取之不～ inexhaustible. 无穷无～ endless; boundless 2 to the utmost; to the limit: 用～力气 exert oneself to the utmost II (动) 1 use up; exhaust: 一言难～. The story can't be told in a few words. 2 try one's best; put to the best use: ～最大努力 do one's best; exert one's utmost effort III (副) all; exhaustive: 不可～信 not to be believed word for word; to be taken with a grain of salt. ～人皆知 be known to all
see also jǐn

尽力 jìnlì (动) do all one can; try one's best: ～而为 do one's best; do everything in one's power. 我们将～援助你们. We'll render you all possible assistance.

尽量 jìnliàng (副) (drink or eat) to the full

尽情 jìnqíng (副) to one's heart's content: ～欢笑 cheer and laugh heartily

尽头(頭) jìntóu (名) end; limit: 学问是没有～的. Learning is without limit.

尽兴(興) jìnxìng (动) to one's heart's content; enjoy oneself to the full

尽职(職) jìnzhí (动) do one's duty; faithfully carry out one's duties: 他工作一向很～. He has always been a devoted worker.

烬(燼) jìn (名) cinder: 灰～ ashes; cinders

京 jīng (名) 1 the capital of a country 2〈简〉(北京) Beijing

京城 jīngchéng (名) the capital of a country

京都 jīngdū (名) the capital of a country

京剧(劇) jīngjù (名) Beijing opera (also as "京戏")

惊(驚) jīng (动) 1 start; be frightened: 恶梦把她～醒了. She woke up from a nightmare with a start. ～呆了 be dumbfounded. 大吃一～ be taken aback 2 surprise; startle; alarm: 令人震～的消息 startling news 3 shy: 听到喊声,马～了. The horse shied at the loud noise.

惊诧 jīngchà (形)〈书〉 surprised; amazed; astonished

惊动(動) jīngdòng (动) alarm; alert; bother; disturb: 别为这么点儿小事～他. Don't bother him about such a trifling matter.

惊愕 jīng'è (形)〈书〉 stunned; stupefied; terror-stricken

惊弓之鸟(鳥) jīng gōng zhī niǎo a bird once wounded by an arrow starts at the mere twang of a bowstring; a panic-stricken person

惊骇 jīnghài (形)〈书〉 frightened; panic

惊慌 jīnghuāng (形) alarmed scared; panic-stricken: ～失措 frightened out of one's wits. 不必～. Don't panic.

惊魂未定 jīnghún wèi dìng still feel nervous from a bad shock; still badly shaken

惊恐 jīngkǒng (形) alarmed and panicky; terrified; panic-stricken; seized with terror: ～万状 be terrified beyond description

惊奇 jīngqí (形) surprised; amazed

惊扰(擾) jīngrǎo (动) alarm; agitate: 自相～ raise a false alarm

惊人 jīngrén (形) astonishing; amazing; alarming: ～的毅力 amazing willpower

惊悚片 jīngsǒngpiàn (名) thriller

惊叹(嘆) jīngtàn (动) wonder at; marvel at; exclaim (with admiration): ～号 exclamation mark(!)

惊涛(濤)骇浪 jīngtāo-hàilàng 1 raging waves; stormy sea 2 a sea of troubles

惊天动(動)地 jīngtiān-dòngdì earth-shaking; world-shaking: ～的胜利 earth-shaking victory

惊悉 jīngxī (动) be shocked to learn

惊喜 jīngxǐ (动、名) be pleasantly surprised; a pleasant surprise

惊吓(嚇) jīngxià (动) frighten; scare: 这孩子受了～. The child had a shock.

惊险(險) jīngxiǎn (形) breathtaking; thrilling: ～的表演 breathtaking performance. ～的场面 thrilling scene. ～小说 thriller

惊心动(動)魄 jīngxīn-dòngpò soul-stirring
惊醒 jīngxǐng (动) 1 wake up with a start 2 rouse suddenly from sleep; awaken
惊讶 jīngyà (形) surprised; amazed; astonished; astounded
惊疑 jīngyí (形) surprised and bewildered; apprehensive and perplexed
惊异(異) jīngyì (形) surprised; amazed; astonished; astounded
惊蛰(蟄) jīngzhé (名) the Waking of Insects (3rd solar term)

鲸 jīng (名) whale

鲸鱼(魚) jīngyú (名) whale

旌 jīng (名) an ancient type of banner hoisted on a featherdecked mast

旌旗 jīngqí (名) banners and flags: ~迎风招展. Flags fluttered in the wind.

粳 jīng

粳稻 jīngdào (名) round-grained nonglutinous rice; japonica rice
粳米 jīngmǐ (名) polished round-grained nonglutinous rice

精 jīng I (形) 1 refined; picked; choice: ~盐 purified salt. ~制糖 refined sugar. ~白米 polished white rice 2 perfect; excellent 3 meticulous; fine; precise: 这花瓶的工艺很~. This vase is an exquisite work of art. 4 smart; bright; clever and capable 5 skilled; conversant; proficient: ~于绘画 skilled in painting II (名) 1 energy; spirit: 聚~会神 focus one's attention; be all intent 2 essence; extract: 酒~ alcohol 3 sperm; semen; seed: 受~ fertilization 4 goblin; spirit; demon: 害人~ ogre; mischief-maker

精兵简政 jīngbīng-jiǎnzhèng trim staff and simplify administration; streamline the administration
精彩 jīngcǎi (形) brilliant; splendid; wonderful: ~的杂技表演 a wonderful acrobatic performance
精诚 jīngchéng (名)〈书〉absolute sincerity; good faith: ~所至, 金石为开. Absolute sincerity can move a heart of stone.
精萃 jīngcuì (名) cream; pick
精打细算 jīngdǎ-xìsuàn careful calculation and strict budgeting; practise economy by meticulous calculation
精读(讀) jīngdú I (动) read in depth II (名) intensive reading
精干(幹) jīnggàn (形) 1 (of a body of troops, etc.) small in number but well-trained; crack 2 keen-witted and capable
精耕细作 jīnggēng-xìzuò intensive and meticulous farming; intensive cultivation
精光 jīngguāng (形) having nothing left or on
精悍 jīnghàn (形) capable and vigorous
精华(華) jīnghuá (名) cream; essence; quintessence
精简 jīngjiǎn (动) retrench; simplify; cut; reduce: ~机构 simplify (or streamline) the administrative structure. ~会议 cut meetings to a minimum
精力 jīnglì (名) energy; vigour; stamina: ~充沛 very energetic; full of vigour. 集中~解决主要问题 solve the main problems with concentrated effort
精练(練) jīngliàn (形) concise; succinct; terse: 语言~ succinct and precise language
精炼(煉) jīngliàn (动) refine; purify
精良 jīngliáng (形) excellent; superior; of the best quality
精灵(靈) jīngling I (名) spirit; demon II (形) (of a child) clever; smart; intelligent
精美 jīngměi (形) exquisite; elegant: ~的刺绣 exquisite embroidery
精密 jīngmì (形) precise; accurate: ~仪器 precision instrument
精明 jīngmíng (形) astute; shrewd; sagacious: ~的政治家 an astute statesman. ~强干 intelligent and capable; able and efficient
精疲力竭 jīngpí-lìjié exhausted; dog-tired; tired out; spent
精辟 jīngpì (形) penetrating; incisive: ~的论述 a brilliant exposition
精品 jīngpǐn (名) fine works; quality goods
精巧 jīngqiǎo (形) exquisite; ingenious: ~的牙雕 exquisite ivory carving
精确(確) jīngquè (形) accurate; exact; precise: ~的统计 accurate statistics
精锐 jīngruì (形) crack; picked: ~部队 crack troops; picked troops
精深 jīngshēn (形) profound: 博大~ characterized by extensive knowledge and profound scholarship
精神 jīngshén (名) 1 spirit; mind; con-

J

sciousness: 国际主义～the spirit of internationalism. ～面貌 mental outlook. ～鼓励 moral encouragement. ～文明 ethical or spiritual values. ～生活 cultural life 2 essence; gist; spirit: 文件的主要～the gist of the document

精神 jīngshen I (名) vigour; vitality; drive: ～饱满 full of vigour (or vitality); energetic. 没有～listless; languid II (形) lively; spirited; vigorous

精神病 jīngshénbìng (名) mental illness; mental disorder; psychosis

精算 jīngsuàn (动) actuary: ～师 actuarist

精髓 jīngsuǐ (名) marrow; pith; quintessence

精通 jīngtōng (动) be proficient in; well-versed in; have a good command of; master: ～业务 be professionally proficient. ～英语 have a good command of English

精细 jīngxì (形) meticulous; fine; careful: 手工十分～ show fine workmanship

精心 jīngxīn (副) meticulously; painstakingly; elaborately: ～护理 nurse with loving care

精选 jīngxuǎn (动) carefully chosen; select

精益求精 jīng yì qiú jīng constantly improve one's skill; keep improving: 对技术～ constantly improve one's skill

精英 jīngyīng (名) essence; cream; elite

精湛 jīngzhàn (形) consummate; exquisite: 工艺～exquisite workmanship; perfect craftsmanship

精制(製) jīngzhì (动) make with extra care; refine

精致(緻) jīngzhì (形) fine; exquisite; delicate

精装(裝) jīngzhuāng (形) (of books) clothbound; hardback; hardcover: ～本 de luxe edition

菁 jīng

菁华(華) jīnghuá (名) essence; cream; quintessence

睛 jīng (名) eyeball: 目不转～地看着 fix one's eye on; gaze fixedly at

荆 jīng (名) chaste tree; vitex

荆棘 jīngjí (名) thistles and thorns; brambles: ～丛生 be overgrown with brambles

荆条(條) jīngtiáo (名) twigs of the chaste tree (used for weaving baskets, etc.)

兢 jīng

兢兢业(業)业 jīngjīngyèyè (act) with caution and with a will

晶 jīng (形) brilliant; glittering: 水～ crystal. 亮～～ shining; glistening. ～莹 sparkling and transparent

晶体(體) jīngtǐ (名) crystal

晶体(體)管 jīngtǐguǎn (名) transistor: 硅～ silicon transistor. ～收音机 transistor radio

茎(莖) jīng (名) stem (of a plant); stalk

经(經) jīng I (名) 1 warp (of textile) 2 longitude: 东～30度 30 degrees E longitude 3 scripture; classics: 佛～ Buddhist scripture. 圣～ the Holy Bible II (动) 1 pass through; undergo: 途～巴黎 pass through Paris. ～卡拉奇回国 return home via Karachi 2 manage; deal in: ～商 go into business 3 stand; endure: ～得起时间的考验 can stand the test of time III (介) after; as a result of: ～他一说,我才明白. I didn't understand until he elaborated on the question.

see also jìng

经常 jīngcháng I (形) day-to-day; everyday; daily: ～工作 routine work; day-to-day work II(副)frequently; constantly; regularly; often: 大家最好～交换意见. We'd better regularly exchange views among ourselves. 他～帮助他人. He never fails to help others.

经典 jīngdiǎn I (名) 1 classics 2 scriptures: 佛教～ Buddhist scriptures II (形) classical: 马列主义～著作 Marxist-Leninist classics; classical works of Marxism-Leninism

经度 jīngdù (名) longitude

经费 jīngfèi (名) funds; outlay: 行政～ administrative expenditure

经管 jīngguǎn (动) be in charge of: ～财务 be in charge of financial affairs

经过(過) jīngguò I (动) 1 pass; go through; undergo: 这汽车～展览馆吗? Does this bus pass the Exhibition Hall? 2 as a result of; after; through: ～充分讨论,大家取得了一致意见. Agreement was reached after full-scale discussion. II (名) process; course: 事件的全部～ the whole course of the incident; what actually happened from start to finish

经纪 jīngjì I (动) manage (a business) II (名) manager; broker

经济(濟) jīngjì I (名) 1 economy: 国民～ national economy. 市场～ market economy. 计划～ planned economy. 国营～ the state sector of the economy. ～地位 economic status; economic position. ～基础 economic base; economic basis. ～法规 economic statutes. ～实体 economic entity. ～危机 economic crisis. ～学 economics. ～学家 economist. ～援助 economic aid. ～效益 economic results. ～特区 special economic zones. ～杠杆 economic lever 2 of industrial or economic value: ～作物 industrial crops; cash crops 3 financial condition; income: ～宽裕 well-off; well-to-do II (形) economical; thrifty: ～实惠 economical and practical

经久 jīngjiǔ (形) 1 prolonged: ～不息的掌声 prolonged applause 2 durable: ～耐用 durable

经理 jīnglǐ I (动) handle; manage II (名) manager; director

经历(歷) jīnglì I (动) go through; undergo; experience: 工业正～着一场伟大的革命. Industry is undergoing a great revolution. II (名) experience: 他这人～多,见识广. He's a man of wide knowledge and experience.

经手 jīngshǒu (动) handle; deal with: 这件事是他～的. He's the one who handled this matter. ～人 a transactor

经受 jīngshòu (动) undergo; experience; withstand; stand; weather: ～时间的考验 stand the test of time

经纬(緯)度 jīngwěidù (名) latitude and longitude

经销 jīngxiāo (动) sell on commission: ～处 agency

经心 jīngxīn (形) careful; conscientious: 漫不～ careless; casual; negligent; absent-minded

经验(驗) jīngyàn (名) experience: 交流～ exchange experience. ～丰富 have rich experience; be very experienced

经营(營) jīngyíng (动) manage; run; engage in: 发展多种～ promote a diversified economy. 苦心～ work with painstaking effort

经由 jīngyóu (动) via; by way of: ～东京去纽约 be bound for New York via Tokyo

经传(傳) jīngzhuàn (名) classical works; classics: 名不见～ not be a well-known personality; a mere nobody

井 jǐng (名) 1 well: 打～ sink a well; drill a well. ～底之蛙 a person with limited outlook or a narrow view of the world 2 sth. in the shape of a well: 矿～ pit; mine. 油～ oil well

井架 jǐngjià (名) derrick

井井有条(條) jǐngjǐng yǒu tiáo in perfect order; shipshape; methodical: ～地工作 work methodically

井然 jǐngrán (形) 〈书〉 orderly; neat and tidy; well arranged; methodical: 秩序～ in good order

阱 jǐng (名) trap; pitfall; pit

警 jǐng I (形) alert; vigilant: ～醒 be a light sleeper. ～觉 watchful; vigilant II (动) warn; alarm: ～告 warn. ～钟 alarm clock III (名) 1 alarm: 火～ fire alarm 2 〈简〉(警察) police: ～亭 police box

警报(報) jǐngbào (名) alarm; warning; alert: 拉～ sound the alarm (or siren)

警备(備) jǐngbèi (动) guard; garrison: ～区 garrison command. ～司令部 garrison headquarters

警察 jǐngchá (名) police; policeman: 交通～ traffic policeman

警告 jǐnggào I (动) warn; caution; admonish: 提出严重～ issue a serious warning II (名) warning (as a disciplinary measure): 给予～处分 give sb. a disciplinary warning

警戒 jǐngjiè (动) 1 warn; admonish 2 be on the alert against; guard against; keep a close watch on: 采取～措施 take precautionary measures. ～线 cordon; security line

警句 jǐngjù (名) aphorism; epigram

警觉(覺) jǐngjué (名) vigilance; alertness

警犬 jǐngquǎn (名) police dog

警示 jǐngshì (名) warning; caution

警惕 jǐngtì I (动) be on guard against; watch out for; be vigilant II (名) vigilance: 提高～ heighten one's vigilance

警卫(衛) jǐngwèi I (动) guard: ～员 bodyguard II (名) (security) guard

警衔(銜) jǐngxián (名) rank (of police officer)

儆 jǐng (动) warn; admonish: 惩一～百 punish one to warn a hundred

景 jǐng (名) 1 view; scenery; scene: 西湖十～ the ten (tourist) attractions of the West Lake 2 situation; condition: 远～规划 long-term planning 3 scenery (of a play or film): 换～ change of scenery **4** scene (of a play): 第三幕第一～ Act III, scene I

景点(點) jǐngdiǎn (名) scenic spot; site of tourist attraction

景观 jǐngguān (名) landscape

景况 jǐngkuàng (名) state of affairs; circumstances: 她家的～日益见好. Her family is becoming much better-off every day.

景气(氣) jǐngqì (名) prosperity; boom: 不～ depression; slump

景色 jǐngsè (名) scenery; view; scene; landscape: 日出的时候～特别美丽. The view is wonderful at sunrise.

景泰蓝(藍) jǐngtàilán (名) cloisonné enamel

景物 jǐngwù (名) scenery: ～宜人. The landscape is delightful.

景象 jǐngxiàng (名) scene; sight; picture

景仰 jǐngyǎng (动) respect and admire; hold in high esteem

景致 jǐngzhì (名) view; scenery; scene: 窗口望出去～真美. You get a wonderful view from the window.

颈(頸)

jǐng (名) neck

颈项 jǐngxiàng (名) neck

颈椎 jǐngzhuī (名) cervical vertebra

竟

jìng I (动) finish; complete: 未～之业 unaccomplished cause; unfinished task II(副) **1** in the end; eventually: 有志者事～成. Where there's a will there's a way. **2** unexpectedly; actually: 谁知他～答应了. Who would have expected that he eventually agreed to it. **3** go so far as to; go to the length of; have the impudence (or effrontery) to

竟敢 jìnggǎn (动) have the audacity; have the impertinence; dare: 他～如此说话. He had the audacity to talk like that.

竟然 jìngrán (副) **1** unexpectedly; to one's surprise; actually: 这样宏伟的建筑,～只用十个月就完成了. It is amazing that it took merely ten months to complete such a magnificent building. **2** go so far as to; go to the length of; have the impudence (or effrontery) to

境

jìng (名) **1** border; boundary: 国～ national boundary. 入～签证 entry visa. 越～ cross the border illegally **2** place; area; territory: 敌～ enemy territory **3** condition; situation; circumstances: 困～ difficult position; predicament. 处于逆～ be in adverse circumstances

境地 jìngdì (名) condition; circumstances: 陷入孤立的～ land oneself in utter isolation

境界 jìngjiè (名) **1** boundary **2** extent reached; plane attained; state; realm: 理想～ ideal state; ideal

境况 jìngkuàng (名) circumstances; financial situation: ～不佳 one's financial prospects are not very bright

境遇 jìngyù (名) circumstances; one's lot: 极困难的～ extremely adverse circumstances

镜

jìng (名) **1** looking glass; mirror: 哈哈～ distorting mirror **2** lens; glass: 放大～ magnifying glass; magnifier. 墨～ sunglasses

镜头(頭) jìngtóu (名) **1** camera lens: 远摄～ telephoto lens; tele-lens. 广角～ wide-angle lens. 变焦～ zoom lens **2** shot; scene: 特写～ close-up. 抢～ seek limelight

竞(競)

jìng (动) compete; contest; vie

竞标(標) jìngbiāo (动) competitive bidding

竞技 jìngjì (名) sports; athletics: ～场 arena

竞赛 jìngsài (名) contest; competition; emulation; race: 体育～ athletic contest (or competition). 军备～ arms race

竞选(選) jìngxuǎn (动) enter into an election contest; campaign for (office); run for: ～总统 run for the presidency

竞争 jìngzhēng (动) compete: 自由～ free competition. ～优势 competitive edge. 有～性 be competitive. 市场～ competition for market

净

jìng I (形) **1** clean: ～水 clean water. 擦～ wipe sth. clean **2** net: ～收入 net income. ～重 net weight. ～利 net profit **3** completely: 用～ use up II (副) only; merely; nothing but: 这几天～下雨. It has been raining for the past few days.

净化 jìnghuà (动) purify: 水的～ purification of water

净手 jìngshǒu (动) wash one's hands; relieve oneself

净值 jìngzhí (名) net worth; net value: 出口～ net export value. 进口～ net import value

静

jìng (形) still; quiet; calm: 风平浪～ calm and tranquil. 请～一～.

Please be quiet.

静电(電) jìngdiàn (名) static electricity: 有~ be electrostatic

静观(觀) jìngguān (动) watch quietly

静脉(脈) jìngmài (名) vein

静默 jìngmò (动) mourn in silence; observe silence: ~致哀 stand in silent tribute to the memory of the deceased

静悄悄 jìngqiāoqiāo (形) very quiet and still

静态(態) jìngtài (名) static state

静养(養) jìngyǎng (动) rest quietly to recuperate; convalesce

静止 jìngzhǐ (动) be static; be motionless; be at a standstill

静坐 jìngzuò (动) 1 sit quietly: ~示威 sit-in (demonstration) 2 sit still as a form of breathing exercise (somewhat like yoga)

靖 jìng 1 peace; tranquillity 2 pacify: ~乱 put down a rebellion

敬 jìng (动) 1 respect: 尊~ respect; esteem; honour. 致~ pay one's respects; salute. ~请光临 request the honour of your presence 2 offer politely: ~茶 serve tea

敬爱(愛) jìng'ài (动) respect and love: ~的领袖 respected and beloved leader

敬而远(遠)之 jìng ér yuǎn zhī keep someone at a respectful distance

敬酒 jìngjiǔ (动) propose a toast; toast

敬礼(禮) jìnglǐ (动) 1 salute; give a salute 2 extend one's greetings 3 〈敬〉[often used at the end of a letter]: 此致~ with best regards

敬佩 jìngpèi (动) esteem; admire; think highly of

敬仰 jìngyǎng (动) revere; venerate; have the greatest admiration for: 深受人民的爱戴和~ enjoy the deep love and reverence of the people

敬业 jìngyè (动) be dedicated to one's job: ~精神 professional dedication; professional ethics. 爱岗~ love one's job and be devoted to work

敬意 jìngyì (名) respect; tribute: 以表~as a token of esteem. 表示衷心的~ extend one's heartfelt respects; pay sincere tribute

敬重 jìngzhòng (动) deeply respect; revere; honour

痉(痙) jìng

痉挛(攣) jìngluán (名) convulsion; spasm

径(徑) jìng I (名) 1 footpath; path; track 2 way; means: 捷~ an easy way; short cut 3 diameter: 半~ radius II (副) directly; straightaway

径庭 jìngtíng (形)〈书〉very unlike: 大相~ diametrically opposed; widely divergent

径自 jìngzì (副) without leave; without consulting anyone: 没等散会,他~走了. He left abruptly before the meeting was over.

胫(脛) jìng (名) shin: ~骨 shin bone; tibia

劲(勁) jìng (形) strong; powerful; sturdy: ~敌 formidable adversary; strong opponent. ~旅 strong contingent; crack troops

see also jìn

经(經) jìng (名) warping (textile)

see also jīng

窘 jiǒng (形) 1 in straitened circumstances; hard up: 他一度生活很~. He was rather hard up for a time. 2 awkward; embarrassed; ill at ease

窘境 jiǒngjìng (名) awkward situation; predicament; plight

窘迫 jiǒngpò (形) 1 poverty-stricken; very poor: 生活~ live in reduced circumstances 2 hard pressed; embarrassed; in a predicament: 处境~ find oneself in a predicament

炯 jiǒng (形) bright; shining

炯炯 jiǒngjiǒng (形)〈书〉(of eyes) bright; shining: 他目光~有神. He has a pair of bright piercing eyes.

迥 jiǒng (形)〈书〉widely different

迥然 jiǒngrán (副) far apart; widely different: ~不同 poles apart; not in the least alike

阄(鬮) jiū (名) lot: 抓~儿 draw lots

揪 jiū (动) hold tight; seize: ~着绳子往上爬 climb up by pulling hard at a rope

揪辫(辮)子 jiū biànzi seize sb.'s pigtail—seize upon sb.'s mistake or shortcoming as a ground for attack

究 jiū (动) study carefully; go into; investigate: 深~ make a thorough investigation into the matter; get to the bottom of a matter. ～其根源 trace sth. to its origin

究竟 jiūjìng I (名) outcome; what actually happened: 大家都想知道个～. Everybody wants to know what actually happened. II (副) 1 [used in an interrogative sentence to make further inquiries] actually; exactly: 你～想说什么? What on earth do you want to say? 2 after all; in the end: 他～经验丰富,说的话有道理. After all, he is very experienced and talks reasonably.

赳 jiū

赳赳 jiūjiū (形) valiant; gallant: 雄～ valiant; gallant

纠 jiū

jiū (动) 1 entangle: ～缠 get entangled (or bogged down) 2 gather together: ～合一伙流氓 band together a bunch of hoodlums 3 correct; rectify: ～错 correct (or rectify) a mistake

纠察 jiūchá I (动) maintain order at a public gathering II (名) picket: ～线 picket line

纠缠(纏) jiūchán (动) 1 get entangled; be in a tangle: 中止在枝节问题上～不休 stop endless quibbling over side issues 2 nag; worry; pester: 他忙着呢,别～他了. He's busy. Don't keep nagging at him.

纠纷 jiūfēn (名) dispute; issue: 种族～ racial dispute. 国家间的～ disputes between countries

纠风(風) jiūfēng (动) rectify unhealthy tendencies

纠葛 jiūgé (名) entanglement; dispute

纠集 jiūjí (动) get together; muster; gang up: ～一批流氓 gather together a bunch of hooligans

纠正 jiūzhèng (动) correct; put right; redress: ～错误 correct a mistake; redress an error. ～不正之风 check unhealthy tendencies

酒 jiǔ

jiǔ (名) alcoholic drink; wine; liquor; spirits

酒吧 jiǔbā (名) bar; bar room; pub

酒菜 jiǔcài (名) food and drink; food to go with wine or liquor

酒厂(廠) jiǔchǎng (名) brewery; winery; distillery

酒店 jiǔdiàn (名) wine shop; public house

酒馆 jiǔguǎn (名) bar; pub

酒鬼 jiǔguǐ (名) drunkard

酒会(會) jiǔhuì (名) cocktail party; reception

酒家 jiǔjiā (名) wine shop; restaurant

酒精 jiǔjīng (名) ethyl alcohol; alcohol

酒量 jiǔliàng (名) capacity for liquor: 他～很大. He's a heavy drinker. *or* He drinks like a fish.

酒囊饭袋 jiǔnáng-fàndài a good-for-nothing

酒肉朋友 jiǔròu péngyǒu fair-weather friends

酒窝(窩) jiǔwō (名) dimple

酒席 jiǔxí (名) feast

韭(韮)

jiǔ: ～菜 fragrant-flowered garlic; (Chinese) chives. 青～ young chives; chive seedlings

九

jiǔ (数) 1 nine: ～中 No. 9 Middle School 2 each of the nine nine-day periods beginning from the day after the Winter Solstice: 三～ the third nine-day period after the Winter Solstice; the coldest days of winter 3 many; numerous: ～曲桥 a zigzag bridge

九九归(歸)一 jiǔ jiǔ guī yī when all is said and done; in the last analysis; after all: ～,还是他的话对. What he says is after all right.

九牛二虎之力 jiǔ niú èr hǔ zhī lì tremendous effort: 我们费了～才把事情办妥. It was only after great effort that we brought the matter to a successful conclusion.

九牛一毛 jiǔ niú yī máo a drop in the ocean

九泉 jiǔquán (名)〈书〉grave; the nether world: ～之下 in the nether regions; after death

九死一生 jiǔ sǐ yī shēng a narrow escape from death; a close shave

九霄云(雲)外 jiǔxiāo yúnwài far, far away; beyond the highest heavens: 把个人安危抛到～ in total disregard of personal safety

九月 jiǔyuè (名) 1 September 2 the ninth month of the lunar year; the ninth moon

九州 jiǔzhōu (名) a poetic name for China

久

jiǔ (形) 1 for a long time; long: 很～以前 long ago. ～别重逢 meet again after a long separation 2 of a specified duration: 你在北京住了有多～? How long have you been living in Beijing?

久而久之 jiǔ ér jiǔ zhī in the course of time; as time passes

久久 jiǔjiǔ (副) for a long, long time: 他心情激动,～不能成寐. He got so excited that he lay awake for a long time.

久违(違) jiǔwéi 〈套〉 haven't seen you for ages: ～了. 这几年你上哪儿去啦? Long time no see. Where have you been all these years?

久仰 jiǔyǎng 〈套〉 I'm very pleased to meet you

久远(遠) jiǔyuǎn (形) far back; ages ago; remote: 年代～ of the remote past; time-honoured

玖 jiǔ (数) nine [the complicated form of 九, used on cheques, etc., to avoid alteration]

就 jiù I (动) **1** get near to; move towards: ～着烛光用餐 dine by candlelight **2** undertake; engage in; enter upon: ～学 go to school. ～席 take one's seat **3** accomplish 功成业～ (of a person's career) be crowned with success **4** accommodate oneself to; suit; fit: 只好～我们现在手头有的东西做了. We'll have to make do with what we've got at present. **5** go with: 炒鸡蛋～饭 have some scrambled eggs to go with the rice II (介) with regard to; concerning; on: ～我所知 so far as I know III (副) **1** at once; right away: 我这～来. I'll be coming right away. 晚饭一会儿～得. Dinner will be ready in a minute. **2** as early as; already: 他 1936 年～成了电影明星了. He became a film star as early as 1936. **3** as soon as; right after: 他卸下行李～上床睡了. He went to bed as soon as he had unpacked the luggage. **4** [connecting two clauses, the first being the premise of the second]: 只要努力,～能掌握外语. So long as you work hard, you will be able to master a foreign language. **5** [inserted in two identical words or phrases, indicating that one is conceding sth.]: 丢了～丢了吧,以后小心点. If it's lost, it's lost. Just be more careful from now on. **6** [indicating all along, from the start]: 我本来～不懂法语. I never said I knew French. **7** only; merely; just: ～他一人知道事情的真相. He alone knows the whole truth of the matter. 我～要几张纸. I just want a few sheets of paper. **8** exactly; precisely: 他～住在这儿. This is where he lives. IV (连) even if: 你～不说,我也会知道. I'll find out even if you don't breathe a word.

就便 jiùbiàn (副) at sb.'s convenience; while you're at it: ～也替我在旅馆定个房间. While you're about it, make a reservation at the hotel for me too.

就此 jiùcǐ (副) at this point; here and now; thus: 会议～结束. The meeting was thus brought to an end.

就地 jiùdì (副) on the spot: ～解决问题 settle the problem on the spot

就地取材 jiùdì qǔcái draw on local resources

就范(範) jiùfàn (动) submit; give in

就近 jiùjìn (副) (do or get sth.) at a nearby place; in the neighbourhood; without having to go far

就寝(寢) jiùqǐn (动) 〈书〉 retire for the night; go to bed

就任 jiùrèn (动) take up one's post; take office

就事论(論)事 jiù shì lùn shì consider a matter as it stands: 不能～. Never consider a matter in isolation or out of context.

就是 jiùshì I (副) quite right; exactly; precisely: ～嘛,天气预报～这么说的. Precisely. That's just what the weatherman said. II (连) [same as "即使" jíshǐ] even if; even: ～他请我,我也不去. I won't go even if he asks me to. III (助) [placed at the end of a sentence often with 了, indicating it is positive]: 放心吧,我照办～了. Don't worry. I will do just as you say.

就手 jiùshǒu see "就便" jiùbiàn

就算 jiùsuàn (连)〈口〉 even if; granted that: ～你考试考得不错,也不应该骄傲吧. Granted you have done well in the exam, still there is no reason to be cocky.

就位 jiùwèi (动) take one's place; take one's seat

就绪 jiùxù (动) (of preparations) be completed: 一切都已～. Everything is in order.

就要 jiùyào (副) be about to; be going to; be on the point of: 火车～开了. The train is about to start. 飞机过两分钟～起飞了. The plane takes off in two minutes.

就业(業) jiùyè (动) obtain employment; take up an occupation; get a job: 充分～ full employment

就医(醫) jiùyī (动) seek medical advice; go to a doctor

就义(義) jiùyì (动) lay down one's life for a just cause; die a martyr: 英勇～ die a hero's death

就职(職) jiùzhí (动) assume office: 宣誓～ take the oath of office; be sworn in. ～演说 inaugural speech

鹫 jiù (名) vulture

厩 jiù (名) stable; cattle-shed; pen: ～肥 barnyard manure

救 jiù (动) 1 rescue; save; salvage: 营～ come to one's rescue. 溺水的孩子被～了. The drowning child was saved. 2 help; relieve; succour: 生产自～ make a living with one's own hands after a natural disaster

J

救国(國) jiùguó (动) save the nation

救护(護) jiùhù (动) relieve a sick or injured person; give first-aid: ～车 ambulance. ～站 first-aid station

救火 jiùhuǒ (动) fight fires; put out fires: ～车 fire engine. ～队 fire brigade. ～队员 fireman; firefighter

救急 jiùjí (动) help sb. to cope with an emergency; help meet an urgent need

救济(濟) jiùjì (动) relieve; succour: ～金 relief fund. ～灾区人民 provide relief to the people in a disaster area

救命 jiùmìng (动) save sb.'s life: ～! Help! ～恩人 saviour

救生 jiùshēng (形) life-saving: ～带 lifebelt. ～圈 lifebuoy. ～设备 lifesaving appliance; life-preserver

救死扶伤(傷) jiùsǐ-fúshāng heal the wounded and rescue the dying

救星 jiùxīng (名) liberator; emancipator

救援 jiùyuán (动) rescue; come to sb.'s help

救治 jiùzhì (动) bring a patient out of danger; treat and cure

旧(舊) jiù I (形) 1 past; old-fashioned; old: ～传统 the old tradition. ～事重提 bring up the old problem again 2 used; worn; old: ～书 used (or second-hand) books 3 former; onetime: ～居 former residence. ～地重游 revisit a place one has been to II (名) old friendship; old friend: 故～ old acquaintances

旧恶(惡) jiù'è (名) old grievance; old wrong: 不念～ forgive and forget

旧货 jiùhuò (名) secondhand goods; junk: ～店 second-hand shop; junk shop. ～市场 flea market

旧交 jiùjiāo (名) old acquaintance

旧历(曆) jiùlì (名) the old Chinese calendar; the lunar calendar

旧事 jiùshì (名) a past event; an old matter

旧址 jiùzhǐ (名) site (of a former organization, building, etc.): 这是我们学校的～. This is where our school used to be.

臼 jiù (名) 1 mortar: 石～ stone mortar 2 any mortar-shaped thing 3 joint (of bones): 脱～ dislocation (of joints)

臼齿(齒) jiùchǐ (名) molar

舅 jiù (名) 1 uncle (mother's brother) 2 wife's brother; brother-in-law 3 〈书〉husband's father

舅父 jiùfù (名) mother's brother; uncle

舅母 jiùmǔ (名) aunt (wife of mother's brother)

疚 jiù (名)〈书〉remorse: 感到内～ have a guilty conscience (about)

柩 jiù (名) a coffin with a corpse in it

柩车(車) jiùchē (名) hearse

咎 jiù I (名) fault; blame: 归～于人 shift the blame on to sb. else II (动) censure; punish; blame: 既往不～ let bygones be bygones

咎由自取 jiù yóu zì qǔ have only oneself to blame

车(車) jū (名) chariot, one of the pieces in Chinese chess

see also chē

疽 jū (名) subcutaneous ulcer; deep-rooted ulcer

狙 jū

狙击(擊) jūjī (动) snipe: ～手 sniper

鞠 jū

鞠躬 jūgōng (动) bow: ～致谢 bow one's thanks. ～尽瘁 exert oneself to the utmost to accomplish a task

掬 jū (动) hold with both hands: 笑容可～ smile broadly

拘 jū I (动) 1 arrest; detain 2 restrain; restrict; limit; constrain: 无～无束 unrestrained; free and easy II (形) inflexible: ～泥 rigidly adhere to (formalities, etc.); overscrupulous

拘捕 jūbǔ (动) arrest

拘谨 jūjǐn (形) overcautious; reserved: 跟别

人在一起时,他有些～. He was rather reserved in company.

拘留 jūliú (动) detain; be taken into custody:～所 house of detention; lockup

拘票 jūpiào (名) arrest warrant; warrant

拘束 jūshù I (动) restrain; restrict II (形) constrained; awkward; ill at ease:不要～. Make yourself at home.

驹 jū (名) **1** colt **2** foal:怀～ be in (or with) foal

居 jū (动) **1** reside; dwell; live:侨～国外 reside abroad. 分～两地 (of man and wife) live at different places **2** be (in a certain position); occupy (a place):～首位 occupy first place; rank first. 身～要职 hold an important post **3** claim; assert: 以学者自～claim to be a scholar **4** store up; lay by: 囤积～奇 hoarding and profiteering

居安思危 jū ān sī wēi think of danger in times of peace; be vigilant in peacetime

居多 jūduō (动) be in the majority:他所写的文章,关于文艺理论方面的～. Most of his essays deal with the theory of literature and art.

居高临(臨)下 jū gāo lín xià occupy a commanding position (or height)

居功 jūgōng (动) claim credit for oneself:～自傲 become arrogant because of one's achievements

居间 jūjiān (副) (mediate) between two parties: ～调停 mediate between two parties; act as mediator

居留 jūliú (动) reside: 长期～ permanent residence. ～权 right of residence. ～证 residence permit

居民 jūmín (名) resident; inhabitant: ～点 residential area

居然 jūrán (副) **1** unexpectedly; to one's surprise: 他～做出这种事来. Who would have thought he could do such a thing? **2** go so far as to; have the impudence (or effrontery) to:～当面撒谎 go so far as to tell a bare-faced lie

居室 jūshì (名) room: 二～ a two-room flat

居心 jūxīn (动) harbour (evil) intentions; be bent on:～不良 be up to no good. 他们～何在? What are they up to?

居中 jūzhōng I (副) see "居间" jūjiān II (动) be placed in the middle: 小标题～. Centre the subheading. ～是一幅山水画. Placed in the middle is a landscape painting.

居住 jūzhù (动) live; reside; dwell: ～条件 housing conditions. ～面积 living space

菊 jú (名) chrysanthemum: ～花 chrysanthemum

桔 jú see "橘" jú

橘 jú (名) tangerine

橘汁 júzhī (名) orange juice

橘子 júzi (名) tangerine

局 jú I (名) **1** chessboard **2** situation; stage of affairs: 时～ the current situation. 全～ the overall situation; the situation as a whole **3** ruse; trap: 骗～ fraud; trap; swindle **4** limit **5** office; bureau; department: 邮～ post office. 电话～ telephone exchange **6** shop: 书～ publishing house II (量) [for chess, table tennis, etc.]: 第一～比赛 the first game of a match

局部 júbù (名) part (as opposed to the whole): ～地区 some areas; parts of an area. ～麻醉 local anaesthesia. ～战争 local war; partial war

局促 júcù (形) **1** (of place) narrow; cramped **2** (of time) short **3** feel or show constraint: ～不安 ill at ease

局面 júmiàn (名) aspect; phase; situation: 打开～ open up a new vista; make a breakthrough; bring about a new situation

局内人 júnèirén (名) a person in the know; insider

局势(勢) júshì (名) situation: 国际～ the international situation. 紧张～ tense situation; tension

局外人 júwàirén (名) outsider

局限 júxiàn (动) be limited; confine: ～性 limitations. 我希望讲演者不要～于一个方面. I hope the speaker would not confine himself to one single aspect.

局长(長) júzhǎng (名) director (of a bureau)

举(舉) jǔ I (动) **1** lift; raise; hold up: ～杯 raise one's glass (to propose a toast) **2** start: ～义 rise in revolt **3** elect; choose: 公～他当代表 choose him as representative **4** cite; enumerate: ～例 cite as an example. ～不胜～ too many to enumerate II (形) whole; entire: ～国欢腾. The whole na-

J

tion is jubilant. ~世闻名 be known all over the world; enjoy a worldwide reputation III (名) act; deed
举办(辦) jǔbàn (动) conduct; hold; run
举报 jǔbào (动) report an offence: ~专线 corruption hotline. ~信箱 mailbox for complaints. ~人 informant; informer
举措 jǔcuò (名) move; act
举动(動) jǔdòng (名) move; act; conduct
举例 jǔlì (动) give an example: ~说明 to illustrate
举目 jǔmù (动)〈书〉 raise the eyes; look: ~远眺 look into the distance. ~无亲 live alone far away from one's family; be a stranger in a strange land
举棋不定 jǔ qí bù dìng hesitate about (or over) what move to make; be unable to make up one's mind; indecisive; shilly-shally
举世 jǔshì (名) throughout the world; universally: ~皆知 known to all. ~公认 universally acknowledged. ~无双 unrivalled; matchless
举手 jǔshǒu (动) raise (or put up) one's hand or hands: ~表决 vote by a show of hands
举行 jǔxíng (动) hold (a meeting, ceremony, etc.): ~会谈 hold talks. ~罢工 stage a strike
举一反三 jǔ yī fǎn sān infer from what is already known
举证 jǔzhèng (动) provide proof
举止 jǔzhǐ (名) bearing; manner; air: ~庄重 carry oneself with dignity
举重 jǔzhòng (名) weightlifting
举足轻(輕)重 jǔ zú qīng-zhòng hold the balance; play a decisive role: 处于~的地位 occupy a pivotal position

矩 jǔ (名) 1 carpenter's square; square 2 rules; regulations: 循规蹈~ to observe all rules and regulations; law-abiding
矩形 jǔxíng (名) rectangle

沮 jǔ (动) 1 〈书〉stop; prevent: ~其成行 stop sb. from going 2 turn gloomy; turn glum
沮丧(喪) jǔsàng (形) dejected; depressed; dispirited; discouraged: 敌人士气~. The enemy's morale is low.

龃 jǔ
龃龉 jǔyǔ (名)〈书〉 bickering; disagreement

咀 jǔ
咀嚼 jǔjué (动) 1 chew 2 mull over; ruminate; chew the cud

聚 jù (动) assemble; gather; get together: 大家~在一起庆祝一下. Let's get together and celebrate it.
聚宝(寶)盆 jùbǎopén treasure bowl—a place rich in natural resources; bonanza
聚变(變) jùbiàn (名) fusion: 核~nuclear fusion. 受控~controlled fusion
聚餐 jùcān (动) dine together (usu. on festive occasions); have a dinner party
聚合 jùhé I (动) get together II (名) polymerization: 定向 ~ stereoregular (or stereotactic) polymerization
聚会(會) jùhuì I (动) get together; meet: 老朋友~在一起总令人追忆往事. The meeting of old friends is always an occasion for reminiscences. II (名) get-together
聚集 jùjí (动) gather; assemble; collect: ~力量 accumulate strength
聚焦 jùjiāo (动) focus
聚精会(會)神 jùjīng-huìshén concentrate one's attention; with attention: ~地听 listen with great attention
聚居 jùjū (动) inhabit a region (as an ethnic group); live together
聚敛(斂) jùliǎn (动) amass wealth by heavy taxation; amass illegally
聚首 jùshǒu (动)〈书〉 gather; meet
聚众(衆) jùzhòng (动) assemble a crowd; gather a mob: ~闹事 gather a mob to make trouble

巨 jù (形) huge; tremendous; gigantic: ~款 a huge sum of money. ~变 tremendous changes
巨擘 jùbò (名) an authority in a certain field
巨大 jùdà (形) huge; tremendous; enormous; gigantic; immense: ~的胜利 a tremendous victory. ~的力量 tremendous force; immense strength. ~的工程 a giant project
巨额 jù'é (名) a huge sum: ~利润 enormous profits. ~赤字 huge financial deficits
巨人 jùrén (名) giant; colossus: 文学界~ literary giant
巨头(頭) jùtóu (名) magnate; tycoon: 金融~ financial magnate
巨细 jù-xì (名) big and small: 事无~ all matters, big and small
巨著 jùzhù (名) monumental work

炬 jù (名) 1 torch 2 fire: 付之一~ be burnt down; be committed to the flames

拒 jù (动) 1 resist; repel: ~敌 resist the enemy; keep the enemy at bay 2 refuse; reject: ~不投降 refuse to surrender

拒捕 jùbǔ (动) resist arrest

拒付 jùfù (动) refuse payment; dishonour (a cheque)

拒绝 jùjué (动) 1 refuse: ~参加 refuse to participate 2 reject; turn down; decline: ~无理要求 turn down (or reject) unreasonable demands. ~诱惑 resist the temptation

距 jù I (名) distance: 行~ the distance between rows of plants II (动) be apart (or away) from; be at a distance from: 两地相~十里. The two places are 10 *li* apart. ~今已有十年. That was ten years ago.

距离(離) jùlí I (名) 1 distance: 飞行的~有200英里. The plane covered a distance of 200 miles. 2 discrepancy: 双方的观点有很大的~. There is a great discrepancy between the views of both sides. II (动) be apart (or away) from; be at a distance from: ~车站15里 15 *li* from the station

遽 jù (副) hurriedly; hastily: ~下结论 jump to a conclusion; draw a hasty conclusion

遽然 jùrán (副)〈书〉suddenly; abruptly: ~变色 suddenly change colour (as one gets angry or annoyed)

具 jù I (名) utensil; tool; implement: 农~ farm tool (or implement); agricultural implement II (量)〈书〉: 一~座钟 a desk clock III (动) possess; have: 初~规模 begin to take shape

具备(備) jùbèi (动) possess; have; be provided with: ~入学条件 be qualified for admission to a school

具名 jùmíng (动) sign; put one's name to a document, etc.; affix one's signature

具体(體) jùtǐ (形) concrete; specific; particular (as opposed to abstract): 对于~情况作~的分析 make a concrete analysis of concrete conditions. 会未能取得~成果. No tangible results have been achieved at the conference. ~日期未定. No exact date has been fixed.

具体(體)而微 jù tǐ ér wēi small but complete; comprehensive; miniature

具文 jùwén (名) mere formality; dead letter: 一纸~ a mere scrap of paper

具有 jùyǒu (动) possess; have; be provided with: ~伟大的历史意义 have great historical significance

惧(懼) jù (动) fear; dread: ~内 henpecked. ~怕 fear; dread. 毫无所~ fearless

俱 jù (副) all; completely: 一应~全 complete with everything. 面面~到 considerate in all respects

俱乐(樂)部 jùlèbù (名) club

飓 jù

飓风(風) jùfēng (名) hurricane

句 jù I (名) sentence II (量): 两~诗 two lines of verse. 在这个问题上,我说不了几~. I can only say a few words on this matter.

句号(號) jùhào (名) full stop; full point; period (。)(.)

句子 jùzi (名) sentence: ~结构 sentence structure

据(據) jù I (动) occupy; seize: ~为己有 take sth. illegally for one's own use; appropriate II (介) 1 rely on; depend on: ~险固守 fall back on a natural barrier to put up a resistance 2 according to; on the grounds of: ~我所知 as far as I know. ~条例 according to the regulations. ~理力争 argue vigorously on justifiable grounds III (名) evidence; certificate: 查无实~. Investigation reveals no evidence (against the suspect).

据称(稱) jùchēng (动) it is said; allegedly

据点(點) jùdiǎn (名) strongpoint; fortified point; stronghold

据守 jùshǒu (动) guard; be entrenched in: 掘壕~ dig in; entrench oneself

据说 jùshuō (动) it is said; they say: ~他不久要出国了. They say he is going abroad soon.

据悉 jùxī (动) it is reported

剧(劇) jù I (名) theatrical work; drama; play; opera: 独幕~ one-act play. 电视~ TV play II (形) acute; severe; intense: ~痛 a severe pain. ~变 a drastic change. 人口~增 a drastic expansion of population

剧本 jùběn (名) 1 drama; play 2 script; (film) scenario; (Beijing opera, opera, etc.) libretto

剧场(場) jùchǎng (名) theatre

剧烈 jùliè (形) violent; acute; severe; fierce: ~运动 strenuous exercise. ~的社会变动 radical social changes. ~的战斗 a fierce fighting

剧目 jùmù (名) a list of plays or operas: 保留~ repertoire

剧情 jùqíng (名) the story (or plot) of a play or opera: ~简介 synopsis

剧团(團) jùtuán (名) theatrical company; opera troupe; troupe

剧作家 jùzuòjiā (名) playwright; dramatist

锯 jù I (名) saw: 手~ handsaw. 圆~ circular saw II (动) cut with a saw; saw: ~木头 saw wood

圈 juān (动) 1 shut in a pen; pen in: 把羊群~起来 herd the sheep into the pens 2 〈口〉 lock up; put in jail
see also juàn; quān

涓 juān (名)〈书〉 a tiny stream

捐 juān I (动) 1 relinquish; abandon 2 contribute; donate; subscribe: ~钱 donate money; 募~ solicit contributions; appeal for donations II (名) tax: 上~ pay a tax

捐弃(棄) juānqì (动)〈书〉 relinquish; abandon: ~前嫌 forget past grievances; let bygones be bygones

捐躯(軀) juānqū (动) go to one's death; lay down one's life

捐税 juānshuì (名) taxes and levies

捐献 juānxiàn (动) contribute (to an organization); donate; present: 他把全部藏书~给图书馆. He presented to the library his whole collection of books.

捐赠 juānzèng (动) contribute (as a gift); donate; present

捐助 juānzhù (动) offer (financial or material assistance); contribute; donate

娟 juān (形)〈书〉 beautiful; graceful

娟秀 juānxiù (形)〈书〉 beautiful; graceful: 字迹~ beautiful handwriting; a graceful hand

镌 juān (动) engrave

镌刻 juānkè (动)〈书〉 engrave

卷(捲) juǎn I (动) 1 roll up: ~起袖子 roll up one's sleeves 2 sweep off; carry along: 一个大浪把那条小渔船~走了. A huge wave swept the fishing boat away. II (名) cylindrical mass of sth.; roll: 铺盖~儿 bedding roll III (量) roll; spool; reel: 一~软片 a roll of film. 一~棉纸 a roll of tissue (or toilet paper)
see also juàn

卷入 juǎnrù (动) be drawn into; be involved in: ~一场冲突 be drawn into a conflict

卷逃 juǎntáo (动) disappear with valuables

卷土重来(來) juǎn tǔ chóng lái stage a come-back

卷烟 juǎnyān(名) 1 cigarette 2 cigar

眷 juàn

眷恋(戀) juànliàn (动) be sentimentally attached to (a person or place)

眷念 juànniàn (动) think fondly of; feel nostalgic about

眷属(屬) juànshǔ (名) family dependants

卷 juàn I (名) 1 book 2 examination paper: 交~ hand in one's examination paper 3 file; dossier: 查~ look through the files II (量) volume: 该书共分上、下两~. This book consists of two volumes. 该图书馆藏书十万~. This library has a collection of 100,000 volumes.
see also juǎn

卷子 juànzi (名) examination paper: 看~ grade papers

卷宗 juànzōng (名) 1 folder 2 file; dossier

圈 juàn (名) pen; fold; sty: 羊~ sheepfold 猪~ pigsty. ~肥 barnyard manure
see also juān; quān

倦 juàn (形) weary; tired: 面有~容 look tired. 孜孜不~ tirelessly; diligently

绢 juàn (名) thin, tough silk

隽 juàn

隽永 juànyǒng (形)〈书〉 meaningful

撅 juē (动) 1 stick up; pout: ~着尾巴 sticking up the tail. ~嘴 purse (up) one's lips 2 〈口〉 break (sth. long and narrow); snap: 把拐杖~成两段 break the stick in two

觉(覺) jué I (动) 1 feel: 身上~着冷 feel cold 2 wake (up); awake: 如梦初~ feel as if waking from a dream 3 become aware; become awakened II (名) sense: 触~ sense of touch
see also jiào

觉察 juéchá（动）detect; become aware of; perceive: 他～到机器出了毛病了. He sensed that something was wrong with the machine.

觉得 juéde（动）1 feel: 一点儿也不～苦恼 not feel upset at all 2 think; feel: 我～不必事事都告诉他. I don't think we have to tell him everything. 你～这部电影怎么样? What do you think of the film?

觉悟 juéwù I（名）consciousness; awareness; understanding: 政治～ political consciousness (or understanding). 阶级～ class consciousness II（动）come to understand; become aware of; become politically awakened: ～了的人民 an awakened people

觉醒 juéxǐng（动）awaken

厥 jué（动）faint; lose consciousness; fall into a coma: 昏～ fall down in a faint

蹶 jué（动）1 fall 2 suffer a setback: 一～不振 never recover from a setback; curl up after a fall

攫 jué（动）seize; grab: ～为己有 seize possession of; appropriate

攫取 juéqǔ（动）seize; grab; take by force: ～暴利 rake in exorbitant profits

爵 jué（名）1 the rank of nobility; peerage: 封～ confer a title (of nobility) upon 2 an ancient wine vessel with three legs and a loop handle

爵士 juéshì（名）knight; Sir

爵士乐(樂) juéshìyuè（名）jazz; jazz music

爵位 juéwèi（名）the rank (or title) of nobility

嚼 jué（动）masticate; chew

see also jiáo

角 jué I（名）1 role; part; character: 主～ leading (or principal) role; main character 2 type of role (in traditional Chinese drama): 旦～ female role. 丑～ clown 3 actor or actress: 名～ a famous actor or actress II（动）contend; wrestle: 口～ quarrel

see also jiǎo

角斗(鬥) juédòu（动）wrestle: ～场 wrestling ring

角力 juélì（动）have a trial of strength; wrestle

角色 juésè（名）1 role; part: 扮演了不光彩的～ play a contemptible role 2 type of role (in traditional Chinese drama)

角逐 juézhú（动）contend; enter into rivalry

谲 jué（动）cheat; swindle: ～诈 cunning; craft

决 jué I（动）1 decide; determine: 犹豫不～ hesitate; be in two minds; be unable to reach a decision. ～一雌雄 fight it out 2 execute a person: 枪～ execute by shooting 3 (of a dyke, etc.) be breached; burst II（副）[before a negative word] definitely; certainly; under any circumstances: ～不妥协 will under no circumstances come to terms. ～不退缩 will never yield an inch from this stand

决策 juécè I（动）make policy; make a strategic decision: ～者 policy-maker. II（名）policy decision; decision of strategic importance: 作出重大～ take a major policy decision

决定 juédìng I（动）decide; resolve; make up one's mind II（名）decision; resolution: 通过一项～ pass a resolution. ～性的时刻 a crucial point (or moment)

决断(斷) juéduàn I（动）make a decision II（名）resolve; decisiveness; resolution

决计 juéjì I（动）have decided; have made up one's mind: 我～明天就走. I have decided to leave tomorrow. II（副）definitely; certainly: 那样办～没错儿. We definitely can't go wrong that way.

决裂 juéliè（动）break with; rupture: 谈判～. The negotiations broke down.

决然 juérán（副）〈书〉1 resolutely; determinedly 2 definitely; unquestionably; undoubtedly: 道听途说的～不能算作很准确的消息. Hearsay definitely can't be regarded as accurate information.

决赛 juésài（名）finals: 半～ semi-finals

决胜(勝) juéshèng（动）decide the issue of the battle

决死 juésǐ（形）life-and-death: ～的斗争 a life-and-death struggle; a last-ditch fight

决算 juésuàn（名）final accounts; final accounting of revenue and expenditure: 国家～ final state accounts

决心 juéxīn（名）determination; resolution: 新年的～ New Year's resolutions. 下定～ make up one's mind. ～书 written pledge

决议(議) juéyì（名）resolution: ～草案 draft resolution. 通过～ adopt or pass a resolution. 执行～ implement a resolution

决意 juéyì (动) have one's mind made up; be determined; be resolved

决战(戰) juézhàn (名) decisive battle; decisive engagement

诀 jué I (名) 1 rhymed formula 2 knack; tricks of the trade: 秘～ a special skill; secret of success II (动) bid farewell; part: 永～ part never to meet again; part for ever. ～别 bid farewell; part

诀窍(竅) juéqiào (名) knack; tricks of the trade; key to success

抉 jué (动)〈书〉pick out; single out

抉择(擇) juézé (动)〈书〉choose; select: 作出～ make one's choice

掘 jué (动) dig: ～井 dig (or sink) a well. 发～ excavate (historic relics, etc.)

崛 jué〈书〉rise abruptly

崛起 juéqǐ (动) 1 (of a mountain, etc.) rise abruptly; suddenly appear on the horizon 2 rise (as a political force)

倔 jué

see also juè

倔强 juéjiàng (形) stubborn; unbending

绝 jué I (动) 1 cut off; sever: ～交 sever any relations with 2 be exhausted; be used up: 弹尽粮～ completely run out of ammunition and provisions II (形) 1 desperate; hopeless: ～境 hopeless situation; impasse. ～症 incurable disease 2 unique; superb; matchless: ～技 unique skill 3 leaving no leeway; making no allowance; uncompromising: 不要把话说～. Don't say anything that leaves no room for compromise. III (副) 1 extremely; most: ～好的机会 the best possible opportunity 2 [used before a negative word] absolutely; in the least; by any means; on any account: ～无此意 have absolutely no such intentions. ～非偶然 by no means accidental

绝版 juébǎn (动) be out of print

绝笔(筆) juébǐ (名) verse or essay written before the writer's death; painting completed before the artist's death

绝壁 juébì (名) precipice; cliff

绝代 juédài (形)〈书〉unique among one's contemporaries; peerless: 才华～ unrivalled talent

绝倒 juédǎo (动)〈书〉split one's sides with laughter; roar with laughter: 令人～ sidesplitting

绝顶 juédǐng I (副) extremely; utterly: ～聪明 extremely intelligent II (名) the top of a mountain peak

绝对(對) juéduì (形) 1 absolute: ～多数 overwhelming majority. ～服从 absolute obedience. ～化 in absolute terms 2 absolutely; perfectly; definitely: ～可靠 absolutely reliable

绝后(後) juéhòu (动) 1 without issue; heirless 2 never to be seen again: 此事空前～. It has never happened before nor is it likely to happen again.

绝迹 juéjì (动) disappear; vanish; be completely wiped out; extinct: 天花病在很多国家都已～. Smallpox has been stamped out in most countries.

绝句 juéjù (名) *jueju*, a poem of four lines, each containing five or seven characters, with a strict tonal pattern and rhyme scheme

绝口 juékǒu (动) 1 [used only after the negative word 不] stop talking: 赞不～ give unstinted praise; praise profusely. 骂不～ heap endless abuse upon 2 keep one's mouth shut: ～不提 never say a single word about; avoid mentioning

绝路 juélù (名) road to ruin; blind alley; a dead end; impasse: 自寻～ bring ruin upon oneself

绝伦(倫) juélún (形) unsurpassed; unequalled; peerless; matchless: 精美～ exquisite beyond compare; superb. 荒谬～ utterly absurd; utterly preposterous

绝密 juémì (形) top-secret; most confidential

绝妙 juémiào (形) extremely clever; ingenious; extremely wonderful; perfect: ～的一招 a very wise move; a masterstroke. ～的讽刺 perfect irony

绝情 juéqíng (形) heartless; cruel

绝然 juérán (副) completely; absolutely

绝色 juésè (形) exceedingly beautiful; of unrivalled beauty

绝食 juéshí (动) fast; go on a hunger strike

绝望 juéwàng (动) give up all hope; despair: ～的挣扎 desperate struggle

绝无(無)仅(僅)有 juéwú-jǐnyǒu the only one of its kind; unique

绝缘 juéyuán (名) insulation: ～体

insulator. ～线 covered wire. ～材料 insulating material; insulant

绝招 juézhāo（名）1 unique skill 2 unexpected tricky move (as a last resort)

绝种(種) juézhǒng（动）(said of animals) become extinct

倔 juè（形）gruff; surly: 这老头儿脾气～. That old man has a gruff manner.

see also jué

军(軍) jūn（名）1 armed forces; army; troops: 参～ join the army 2 army (as a military unit): 全歼敌人一个～ wipe out an enemy army

军备(備) jūnbèi（名）armament; arms: 扩充～ engage in arms expansion. ～竞赛 armament (or arms) race. ～控制 arms control

军队(隊) jūnduì（名）armed forces; army; troops

军阀 jūnfá（名）warlord

军法 jūnfǎ（名）military criminal code; military law: ～从事 punish by military law. ～审判 court-martial

军费 jūnfèi（名）military expenditure

军服 jūnfú（名）military uniform; uniform: ～呢 army coating

军工 jūngōng（名）1 war industry 2 military project

军官 jūnguān（名）officer

军火 jūnhuǒ（名）munitions; arms and ammunition: ～工业 munitions industry; armament industry. ～库 arsenal. ～商 munitions merchant; arms dealer; merchant of death

军机(機) jūnjī（名）1 military plan: 贻误～ frustrate or fail to carry out a military plan 2 military secret: 泄漏～ leak a military secret

军纪 jūnjì（名）military discipline

军舰(艦) jūnjiàn（名）warship; naval vessel

军旗 jūnqí（名）army flag; colours; ensign: ～礼 colours salute

军情 jūnqíng（名）military (or war) situation: 刺探～ spy on the military movements; collect military information

军区(區) jūnqū（名）military region; (military) area command

军人 jūnrén（名）soldier; serviceman; member of the army

军师(師) jūnshī（名）1 strategist in ancient China 2 adviser

军事 jūnshì（名）military affairs: ～大国 major military power. ～基地 military base. ～科学 military science. ～素质 military qualities; fighting capability. ～演习 military manoeuvre. ～学院 military academy

军属(屬) jūnshǔ（名）soldier's dependants; soldier's family

军衔 jūnxián（名）military rank

军械 jūnxiè（名）ordnance; armament: ～处 ordnance department. ～库 ordnance depot; arms depot; armoury

军心 jūnxīn（名）soldiers' morale: 大振～ boost the morale of the troops

军需 jūnxū（名）1 military supplies: ～库 military supply depot. ～品 military supplies; military stores 2 quartermaster

军医(醫) jūnyī（名）medical officer; military surgeon

军营(營) jūnyíng（名）military camp; barracks

军长(長) jūnzhǎng（名）army commander

军种(種) jūnzhǒng（名）(armed) services

军装(裝) jūnzhuāng（名）military (or army) uniform; uniform

均 jūn I（形）equal; even: 财富分配不～ uneven distribution of wealth II（副）without exception; all: 所有国家～派代表出席了会议. All countries were represented at the meeting.

均等 jūnděng（形）equal; impartial; fair

均分 jūnfēn（动）divide equally; share out equally

均衡 jūnhéng（形）balanced; proportionate; harmonious; even: 国民经济～地发展. The national economy has developed harmoniously.

均势(勢) jūnshì（名）balance of power; equilibrium of forces; equilibrium: 核～ nuclear parity

均匀 jūnyún（形）even; well distributed: 今年的雨水很～. Rainfall has been fairly well distributed this year.

钧 jūn 1 an ancient unit of weight (equal to 30 *jin*) 2〈敬〉you; your: ～座 Your Excellency

菌 jūn（名）1 fungus 2 bacterium

see also jùn

龟(龜) jūn

see also guī

龟裂 jūnliè（动）1 (of parched earth) be full of cracks 2 (of skin) chap

J

君 jūn (名) 1 monarch; sovereign; supreme ruler 2 gentleman; Mr.: 诸~ gentlemen. 张~ Mr. Zhang

君权(權) jūnquán (名) monarchical power

君主 jūnzhǔ (名) monarch; sovereign: ~国 monarchical state; monarchy. ~立宪 constitutional monarchy. ~制 monarchy. ~专制 autocratic monarchy; absolute monarchy

君子 jūnzǐ (名) a man of noble character; gentleman: 伪~ hypocrite. 正人~ a man of moral integrity. ~协定 gentlemen's agreement

菌 jùn (名) mushroom

see also jūn

浚(濬) jùn (动) dredge: ~渠 dredge a canal

竣 jùn (动) complete; finish: 告~ have been completed. ~工 (of a project) be completed

峻 jùn (形) 1 (of mountains) high: 高山~岭 high mountains and steep cliffs 2 harsh; severe; stern: 严刑~法 harsh law and severe punishment

峻峭 jùnqiào (形) high and steep

俊 jùn (形) 1 handsome: 这孩子长得挺~的. The child is quite handsome. 2 a person of outstanding talent

俊杰(傑) jùnjié (名) a person of outstanding talent; hero

俊美 jùnměi (形) pretty; handsome

俊俏 jùnqiào (形) pretty and charming

俊秀 jùnxiù (形) pretty; of delicate beauty

骏 jùn

骏马(馬) jùnmǎ (名) fine horse; steed

K k

喀 kā (象) noise made in coughing or vomiting

喀嚓 kāchā (象) crack; snap: ~一声树枝断了. The branch broke with a crack.

咖 kā

see also gā

咖啡 kāfēi (名) coffee: ~馆 café. 速溶~ instant coffee. ~因 caffeine

卡 kǎ〈简〉1 (卡路里) calorie 2 (卡片) card

see also qiǎ

卡车(車) kǎchē (名) lorry; truck

卡片 kǎpiàn (名) card: ~目录 card catalogue. ~索引 card index

卡通 kǎtōng (名) 1 caricature; cartoon 2 animated cartoon

咯 kǎ (动) cough up: ~痰 cough up phlegm. ~血 spit blood

see also gē

开(開) kāi (动) 1 open: ~门 open the door 2 make an opening; open up; reclaim: ~运河 dig a canal. ~荒 reclaim land 3 open out; come loose: 桃树~花了. The peach trees are blossoming. 4 lift (a ban, restriction, etc.): ~禁 lift a ban 5 start; operate: ~拖拉机 drive a tractor. ~飞机 fly (or pilot) an airplane. ~电视机 turn on the TV 6 (of troops, etc.) set out; move: 军队正~往前线. The troops are leaving for the front. 7 set up; run: ~工厂 set up a factory 8 begin; start: 九月~学 school begins in September. ~演 The curtain rises. 9 hold (a meeting, exhibition, etc.): ~运动会 hold an athletic meet 10 make a list of; write out: ~方子 write a prescription. ~一个户头 open an account 11 pay (wages, fares, etc.): ~销 spending 12 boil: 水~了. The water is boiling. 13 [used after a verb to indicate expansion or development]: 消息传~了. The news has spread far and wide. 这支歌流行~了. The song has become very popular.

开(開) kāi 1 [used after a verb to indicate separation]: 躲~ get out of the way. 把门推~ push the door open 2 [used after a verb to indicate capacity]: 这间屋子小,人太多了坐不~. The room is too small to hold too many people.

开拔 kāibá (动) (of troops) move; set out

开办(辦) kāibàn (动) open; set up; start: ~训练班 run a training course

开本 kāiběn (名) format; book size: 十六~ 16 mo. 三十二~ 32 mo

开采(採) kāicǎi (动) mine; extract; exploit: ~煤炭 mine coal. ~石油 recover petroleum

开场(場) kāichǎng (动) begin: 戏已经~了. The play has already begun. ~白 opening remarks; prologue

开车(車) kāichē (动) 1 drive or start a car,

train, etc. 2 set a machine in motion; get it going

开诚布公 kāichéng-bùgōng come straight to the point and speak frankly

开除 kāichú (动) expel; discharge: ~学籍 expel from school

开创(創) kāichuàng (动) start; initiate: ~新时代 usher in a new era. ~新局面 create a new situation

开刀 kāidāo (动) 1〈口〉perform or have a surgical operation; operate or be operated on: 给病人~ operate on a patient 2 make sb. the first target of attack

开导(導) kāidǎo (动) convince sb. by patient analysis; help sort out sb.'s ideas

开动(動) kāidòng (动) start; set in motion: ~机器 start a machine. ~脑筋 use one's brains

开端 kāiduān (名) beginning; start: 良好的~ a good beginning

开发(發) kāifā (动) develop; open up; exploit: ~海底石油 exploit offshore petroleum resources. ~荒地 reclaim wasteland. ~新产品 develop a new product. ~商 developer. ~智力 tap intellectual resources

开放 kāifàng (动) 1 come into bloom: 百花~. A hundred flowers are in blossom. 2 be open to traffic or public use 3 be open (to the public): ~政策 the policy of opening to the outside world. 沿海~城市 coastal cities opening to foreigners

开赴 kāifù (动) leave for; be bound for: ~前线 be sent to the front

开工 kāigōng (动) 1 (of a factory, etc.) go into operation: ~不足 operate under capacity 2 (of work on a construction project, etc.) start

开关(關) kāiguān (名) switch

开国(國) kāiguó (动) found a state: ~大典 founding ceremony (of a state). ~元勋 founding father

开航 kāiháng (动) 1 become open for navigation 2 set sail

开户 kāihù (动) open an account

开花 kāihuā (动) blossom; bloom; flower: ~结果 blossom and bear fruit — yield positive results

开化 kāihuà (动) become civilized

开会(會) kāihuì (动) hold or attend a meeting

开火 kāihuǒ (动) open fire: ~!〈口令〉Fire!

开戒 kāijiè (动) break an abstinence (from smoking, drinking, etc.)

开局 kāijú (名) beginning: 良好的~ a good beginning

开卷 kāijuàn (动) open a book; read: ~考试 open-book examination

开垦(墾) kāikěn (动) open up (or reclaim) wasteland; bring under cultivation

开口 kāikǒu (动) 1 open one's mouth; start to talk: 难以~ difficult to bring up the matter 2 put the first edge on a knife

开阔 kāikuò I (形) 1 open; wide: ~的广场 an open square 2 tolerant: 心胸~ broad-minded; unbiased II (动) widen: ~眼界 broaden one's experience (or horizons)

开朗 kāilǎng (形) open and clear: 豁然~ suddenly see the light; feel illuminated

开绿灯(燈) kāi lǜdēng give the green light; give the go-ahead

开门(門)见(見)山 kāimén jiàn-shān come straight to the point

开明 kāimíng (形) enlightened: ~人士 enlightened personages

开幕 kāimù (动) 1 the curtain rises 2 open; inaugurate: ~词 opening speech (or address). ~式 opening ceremony

开盘 kāipán I (动) give an opening quotation; take a position II (名) opening price

开辟 kāipì (动) open up; start: ~航线 open an air or sea route. ~财源 tap new financial resources; explore new sources of revenue. ~新的途径 blaze a trail

开启 kāiqǐ (动) 1 unseal; unlock 2 start; open up

开枪(槍) kāiqiāng (动) open fire; shoot

开腔 kāiqiāng (动) begin to speak; open one's mouth: 他半天不~. For a long while he kept his mouth shut.

开窍(竅) kāiqiào (动) begin to know things; have one's ideas straightened out

开设 kāishè (动) 1 open (a shop, factory, etc.) 2 offer (a course in college, etc.)

开始 kāishǐ I (动) begin; start: ~生效 take effect; come into effect (or force) II (名) initial stage; beginning; outset

开释(釋) kāishì (动) release (a prisoner)

开水 kāishuǐ (名) 1 boiling water 2 boiled water

开庭 kāitíng (动) open court session; call the court to order

开通 kāitong (形) open-minded; liberal

开头(頭) kāitóu (名) beginning; start: 你从

K

一～就错了. You've been wrong from the very start.

开脱 kāituō (动) absolve; exonerate: ～罪责 absolve sb. from guilt or blame. 替某人～ plead for sb.

开拓 kāituò (动) open up: ～精神 enterprising spirit

开外 kāiwài (助) over; above: 他看起来有四十～. He looks a little over forty.

开玩笑 kāi wánxiào 1 crack a joke; joke; make fun of: 我是跟你～的. I was only joking. 2 treat sth. as insignificant: 这可不是～的事. This is no joking matter.

开往 kāiwǎng (动) (of a train, ship, etc.) leave for; be bound for: ～广州的特快 the Guangzhou express

开胃 kāiwèi (动) whet (or stimulate) the appetite

开小差 kāi xiǎochāi 1 (of a soldier) desert 2 be absent-minded: 用心听讲,思想就不会～. If you listen carefully, your attention won't wander.

K

开销 kāixiao (名) expenses: 日常的～ daily expenses; running expenses

开心 kāixīn (动) 1 feel happy; rejoice 2 amuse oneself at sb.'s expense; make fun of sb.: 别拿他～了. Don't crack jokes at his expense.

开业(業) kāiyè (动) 1 (of a shop, etc.) start business 2 (of a lawyer, doctor, etc.) start practice

开源节(節)流 kāiyuán jiéliú increase income and reduce expenditure

开展 kāizhǎn I (动) develop; launch; unfold: ～批评和自我批评 carry out criticism and self-criticism. ～经济协作 develop economic cooperation II (形) open-minded; politically progressive

开张(張) kāizhāng (动) 1 begin doing business 2 make the first transaction of a day's business

开支 kāizhī I(动) pay (expenses); defray II (名) expenses; expenditure; spending: 节省～ cut down expenses. 军费～ military spending

开宗明义(義) kāizōng-míngyì make clear the purpose and main theme from the very beginning

揩 kāi (动) wipe: ～泪 wipe away one's tears. 把桌子～干净 wipe the table clean. ～油 get petty advantages at the expense of other people or the state; scrounge

慨 kǎi (形) 1 indignant 2 deeply touched: 感～ sigh with emotion

慨然 kǎirán (副) 1 with deep feeling: ～长叹 sigh like a furnace; sigh with a feeling of regret 2 generously: ～相赠 give sth. of value to sb. as a gift

楷 kǎi (名) 1 model; pattern 2 (in Chinese calligraphy) regular script: 小～ regular script in small characters. 大～ regular script in big characters

楷模 kǎimó (名) model; pattern

楷书(書) kǎishū (名) (in Chinese calligraphy) regular script

铠(鎧) kǎi

铠甲 kǎijiǎ (a suit of) armour

凯(凱) kǎi I (名) triumphant strains II (形) triumphant; victorious

凯歌 kǎigē (名) a song of triumph; paean

凯旋 kǎixuán (动) return in triumph: ～而归 return in victory

刊 kān I (名) periodical; publication: 报～ newspapers and magazines. 半月～ biweekly II (动) 1 print; publish 2 delete or correct: ～误 correct misprint

刊登 kāndēng (动) publish in a newspaper or magazine; carry

刊物 kānwù (名) publication: 定期～ periodical (publication)

刊载 kānzǎi (动) publish (in a newspaper or magazine); carry

堪 kān (动) 1 may; can: ～当重任 be capable of holding a position of great responsibility 2 bear; endure: 不～设想 be dreadful to contemplate

勘 kān (动) 1 read and correct the text of; collate 2 investigate; survey

勘测 kāncè (动) survey

勘察 kānchá (名) 1 reconnaissance 2 prospecting

勘探 kāntàn (动) explore; prospect

勘误 kānwù (动) correct errors in printing: ～表 errata; corrigenda

龛(龕) kān (名) niche; shrine: 佛～ Buddhist altar

看 kān (动) 1 look after; take care of; tend: ～门 watch the gate; be in charge of the opening and closing of a gate. ～孩子 look after children; baby sitting 2 keep under surveillance: ～住那坏蛋,别让他跑了! Keep an eye on that rascal. Don't let him sneak away.

see also kàn

看管 kānguǎn (动) 1 look after; attend to: ～行李 look after the luggage 2 guard; watch: ～俘虏 guard the captives

看护(護) kānhù I (动) nurse: ～病人 nurse the sick II (名) hospital nurse

看家 kānjiā (动) look after the house; mind the house

看家本领 kānjiāběnlǐng one's special skill

看守 kānshǒu I (动) watch; guard: ～犯人 guard prisoners. ～所 lockup for prisoners awaiting trial; detention house II (名) turnkey; warder

看守内阁 kānshǒunèigé caretaker cabinet

看押 kānyā (动) take into custody; detain

槛(檻) kǎn (名) threshold

侃 kǎn

侃大山 kǎndàshān 〈口〉 chat idly

侃侃而谈 kǎnkǎn ér tán speak with fervour and assurance

坎 kǎn (名) bank; ridge: 田～儿 a raised path through fields

坎肩儿(兒) kǎnjiānr (名) sleeveless jacket; cape

坎坷 kǎnkě (形) 1 bumpy; rough: ～不平的路 a rugged road 2 〈书〉 full of frustrations: ～不平的一生 a life full of setbacks and misfortunes

砍 kǎn (动) cut; chop; hack: 把树枝～下来 cut (or lop) off a branch. ～柴 cut firewood. 把树～倒 fell a tree

砍伐 kǎnfá (动) fell (trees)

瞰 kàn (动) look down from a height; overlook: 鸟～ get a bird's-eye view

看 kàn (动) 1 see; look at; watch: ～电影 see a film; go to the cinema. ～电视 watch TV. ～球赛 watch a ball game 2 read: ～报 read a newspaper. ～书 read (a book); do some reading 3 think; consider: 你对他怎么～? What do you think of him? 4 look upon: regard: 把人民的利益～得高于一切 put the interests of the people above all else 5 treat (a patient or an illness): 大夫把她的肺炎～好了. The doctor has cured her of pneumonia. 6 look after; take care of 7 call on; visit; see: ～朋友 call on a friend. ～医生 go and see a doctor 8 depend on: 明天是否去长城,完全得～天气了. Whether we'll make a trip to the Great Wall tomorrow wholly depends on the weather. 9 [used after a verb in reduplicated form indicating "let sb. try"]: 试试～ have a try. 尝尝～. Just taste this. 让我想想～. Let me think it over.

see also kān

看扁 kànbiǎn (动) underestimate sb.

看病 kànbìng (动) 1 (of a doctor) attend to a patient 2 (of a patient) see a doctor

看不惯 kànbuguàn cannot bear the sight of; frown upon: 这种浪费现象我们～. We hate to see such waste. 我～这个女人. I can't stand the sight of the woman.

看不起 kànbuqǐ look down upon; scorn; despise

看成 kànchéng (动) look upon as; regard as: 你把我～什么人了? What do you take me for?

看出 kànchū (动) make out; see: ～问题的所在 see where the shoe pinches

看穿 kànchuān (动) see through: ～他的诡计 see through sb.'s trick

看待 kàndài (动) look upon; regard; treat

看到 kàndào (动) see; catch sight of

看得起 kàndeqǐ have a good opinion of; think highly of

看法 kànfǎ (名) a way of looking at things; view

看惯 kànguàn (动) be accustomed to the sight of: 这种事我已经～了. I've already got used to this kind of things.

看好 kànhǎo (动) have good prospects: 市场～ the market is smiling

看见(見) kànjiàn (动) catch sight of; see

看来(來) kànlái (动) it seems (or appears); it looks as if: ～好像要下雨. It looks like rain. ～他并不喜欢这样的电影. Evidently he doesn't like this kind of film.

看破 kànpò (动) see through: ～红尘 be disillusioned with this human world

看齐(齊) kànqí (动) 1 dress: 向右(左)～! Dress right (left), dress! 2 keep up with; emulate: 向先进工作者～ emulate the advanced workers

看轻(輕) kànqīng (动) underestimate; make light of: 谁也不应～自己的力量. Nobody should underestimate his own strength.

看透 kàntòu (动) 1 understand thoroughly 2 see through

看望 kànwàng (动) call on; visit; see: ～老同学 call on an old schoolmate

看着办(辦) kànzhebàn do as one sees it fit

K

看中 kànzhòng (动) take a fancy to; settle on: 这些布你～了哪块? Which piece of cloth is to your liking?

看重 kànzhòng (动) regard as important; value; set store by: ～传统友谊 set store by the ties of traditional friendship

康 kāng (形) healthy

康复(復) kāngfù (动) restore to health; recover: 祝您早日～. Hope you'll soon be well again.

康乐(樂) kānglè (名) peace and happiness

康庄(莊)大道 kāngzhuāng dàdào broad road

慷 kāng

慷慨 kāngkǎi (形) 1 vehement; fervent: ～激昂 impassioned; vehement. ～陈词 speak very vehemently 2 generous; liberal: ～援助 generous assistance. ～解囊 help sb. generously with money

慷慨就义(義) kāngkǎi jiùyì die a hero's death; meet one's death like a hero

糠 kāng (名) chaff; bran; husk

扛 káng (动) carry on the shoulder; shoulder: ～枪 shoulder a gun. ～着麻袋 carry a sack on the shoulder. ～长活 work as a farm labourer

亢 kàng (形) overbearing; haughty: 不～不卑 behave modestly but without undue self-effacement

炕 kàng I (名) *kang* (a big hollow bed made of brick and heated by fire in the winter, usually seen in Northeast and North China) II (动) bake or dry by the heat of a fire: 把湿衣服摊在炕上～干 spread the wet clothes on a heated *kang* to dry

抗 kàng (动) 1 resist; combat; fight: ～灾 fight natural calamities. ～震 shockproof. ～敌 resist the enemy. ～热 heat-resistant 2 refuse; defy: ～捐～税 refuse to pay levies and taxes 3 contend with; be a match for: 分庭～礼 stand up to sb. as an equal

抗辩(辯) kàngbiàn I (动) reject charges and plead not guilty II (名) counterplea

抗旱 kànghàn (动) fight (or combat) a drought

抗衡 kànghéng (动) contend with sb. as an equal

抗洪 kànghóng (动) fight (or combat) a flood

抗击(擊) kàngjī (动) resist; beat back: ～侵略者 resist the aggressors

抗拒 kàngjù (动) resist; defy

抗菌素 kàngjūnsù (名) antibiotic

抗日战(戰)争 Kàng Rì Zhànzhēng the War of Resistance Against Japan

抗体(體) kàngtǐ (名) antibody

抗议(議) kàngyì (动) protest: 提出～ lodge a protest. ～集会 protest rally. ～照会 note of protest

伉 kàng

伉俪(儷) kànglì (名)〈书〉 married couple; husband and wife

考 kǎo (动) 1 give or take an examination, test or quiz: 我～～你. Let me test you. ～上大学 pass the entrance examination of a university 2 check; inspect 3 study; investigate; verify: 待～ remain to be verified

考查 kǎochá (动) examine; check: ～学生成绩 check students' work

考察 kǎochá (动) 1 inspect; make an on-the-spot investigation: 出国～ go abroad on a study tour: ～组 study group 2 observe and study

考古 kǎogǔ I (动) engage in archaeological studies II (名) archaeology: ～学 archaeology. ～学家 archaeologist

考核 kǎohé (动) examine; check; assess (sb.'s proficiency): ～制度 examination system

考究 kǎojiu I (动) 1 observe and study; investigate 2 be fastidious about; be particular about: 穿衣服不必过于～. One need not be too particular about dress. II (形) fine: 装潢～ finely bound

考据(據) kǎojù (名) textual criticism; textual research

考虑(慮) kǎolǜ (动) think over; consider: 积极～ give a favourable consideration. 让我～一下. Let me think it over.

考勤 kǎoqín (动) check upon work attendance: ～簿 attendance record

考生 kǎoshēng (名) candidate for an entrance examination; examinee

考试 kǎoshì (名) examination; test

考研 kǎoyán (动) take a qualifying exam for graduate studies

考验(驗) kǎoyàn (名) test; trial: 经受了严峻的～ have stood a severe test

考证 kǎozhèng (名) textual criticism; textual research

K

烤 kǎo (动) bake; roast; toast: ～鸭 roast duck. ～馒头 toasted steamed bun. 把湿衣裳～干 dry wet clothes by a fire. 我们围炉～火. All of us sat around a brazier to warm ourselves.

烤炉(爐) kǎolú (名) oven

拷 kǎo (动) flog; beat; torture

拷贝(貝) kǎobèi (名) copy

拷打 kǎodǎ (动) flog; beat; torture: 严刑～ subject sb. to torture

拷问 kǎowèn (动) torture sb. during interrogation; interrogate with torture

铐 kào I (名) handcuffs II (动) put handcuffs on; handcuff: 把犯人～起来 handcuff the criminal

靠 kào (动) 1 lean against; lean on: 她把头～在他的肩上. She leaned her head on his shoulder. 2 keep to; get near; come up to: 我们的车～近机场了. Our car is approaching the airport. 3 near; by: 他～窗坐着. He is sitting by the window. 4 depend on; rely on: 他家里～他维持生活. His family depended on him for support. 5 trust: 可～ reliable; trustworthy

靠岸 kào'àn (动) pull in to shore; draw alongside

靠边(邊) kàobiān (动) keep to the side: ～! ～! Out of the way, please! ～儿站 stand aside; step aside; get out of the way

靠不住 kàobuzhù unreliable; undependable; untrustworthy: 这人～. This chap is not to be trusted. 这消息～. This information is unreliable.

靠得住 kàodezhù reliable; dependable; trustworthy

靠拢(攏) kàolǒng (动) draw close; close up: 向前～! Close ranks!

靠山 kàoshān (名) backer; patron: 他有强有力的～. He has strong backing.

犒 kào (动) reward with food and drink: ～赏 reward a victorious army, etc. with food and drink

磕 kē (动) 1 knock (against sth. hard): 摔了一跤, 脸上～破了皮 fall and get a scratch on the face 2 knock sth. out of a vessel, container, etc.

磕碰 kēpèng (动) 1 knock against; collide with; bump against 2 clash; squabble

磕头(頭) kētóu (动) kowtow

瞌 kē

瞌睡 kēshuì (形) sleepy; drowsy: 打～ doze off; nod; have a nap

苛 kē (形) severe; exacting: ～待 treat harshly. ～政 tyranny

苛捐杂(雜)税 kējuān-záshuì exorbitant taxes and levies

苛刻 kēkè (形) harsh: ～的条件 harsh terms

苛求 kēqiú (动) make excessive demands; be hypercritical

窠 kē (名) nest; burrow

窠臼 kējiù (名) (of literary or artistic work) stereotype: 不落～ show originality

棵 kē (量): 一～树 a tree. 一～大白菜 a (head of) Chinese cabbage

颗 kē (量): 一～珠子 a pearl. 一～黄豆 a soya bean

颗粒 kēlì (名) 1 anything small and roundish (as a bean, pearl, etc.); pellet 2 grain: ～归仓 every grain to the granary

科 kē I (名) 1 a branch of academic or vocational study: 文～ the liberal arts. 理～ the natural sciences. 产～ department of obstetrics 2 a division or subdivision of an administrative unit; section: 财务～ finance section. 总务～ services section 3 family: 猫～动物 animals of the cat family II (动) pass a sentence: ～以罚金 impose a fine on sb.; fine

科班 kēbān (名) regular professional training: ～出身 be a professional by training

科幻 kēhuàn (名) science fiction

科技 kējì (名) science and technology: ～大学 polytechnic university. ～界 scientific and technological circles. ～术语 scientific and technical terminology

科教片 kējiàopiàn (名) popular science film; educational film

科教兴(興)国(國) kējiào xīngguó rejuvenate the nation through the advancement of science and education

科举(舉) kējǔ (名) imperial examinations

科目 kēmù (名) subject (in a curriculum); course; branch of study

科室 kēshì (名) administrative or technical offices: ～人员 office staff (or personnel)

科学(學) kēxué (名) science; scientific knowledge: ～家 scientist. ～普及读物 popular science books; popular science.

～实验 scientific experiment

科学(學)院 kēxuéyuàn (名) academy of sciences: 中国～ the Chinese Academy of Sciences

科研 kēyán (名) scientific research: ～机构 scientific research institution. ～人员 scientific research personnel. ～攻关 tackle key scientific research projects

科长(長) kēzhǎng (名) section chief

咳 ké (动) cough: ～嗽糖 cough drops

see also hāi

壳(殼) ké (名) shell: 鸡蛋～ eggshell. 核桃～ walnut shell

see also qiào

渴 kě I (形) thirsty: 解～ quench one's thirst. 我都快～死了. I'm literally parched. II (副) yearningly: ～念 yearn for

渴望 kěwàng (动) thirst for; long for; yearn for; hanker after

K

可 kě I (动) 1 approve: 不置～否 decline to comment; be non-committal 2 can; may: ～兑换 convertible. 阅览室的书籍不～携出室外. The books in this reading room are not to be taken out. 3 need (doing); be worth (doing): ～读性 readability. 城里没有多少地方～看的. There isn't much worth seeing in the city. II (副) 1 [used to emphasize the tone of the speaker]: ～别忘了. Mind you don't forget it. 你～来了! So you're here at last! 2 [used to emphasize the tone of an interrogative sentence]: 你～曾跟他谈过这个问题? Did you ever bring up the question with him?

see also kè

可爱(愛) kě'ài (形) lovable; lovely: ～的祖国 my beloved country. 多～的孩子! How cute the child is!

可悲 kěbēi (形) sad; lamentable

可鄙 kěbǐ (形) contemptible; despicable; mean: 行为～ act contemptibly

可变(變) kěbiàn (形) variable

可持续(續)发(發)展 kěchíxù fāzhǎn (名) sustainable development

可耻 kěchǐ (形) shameful; disgraceful; ignominious

可歌可泣 kěgē-kěqì move one to song and tears: ～的英雄事迹 moving heroic deeds

可耕地 kěgēngdì (名) arable land; cultivable land

可观(觀) kěguān (形) considerable; impressive; sizable: 数目～ a considerable figure

可贵 kěguì (形) valuable; praiseworthy; commendable: ～的品质 fine qualities. ～的贡献 valuable contribution

可恨 kěhèn (形) hateful; detestable; abominable

可见(見) kějiàn (连) it is thus clear (or evident, obvious) that: 只有几个学生通过了考试, ～考题是很难的. Only a few students passed the exam, so you can see that the paper must have been extremely stiff.

可敬 kějìng (形) worthy of respect; respected

可靠 kěkào (形) reliable; dependable; trustworthy: ～消息 reliable information. ～后方 a secure rear area

可可 kěkě (名) cocoa

可口 kěkǒu (形) good to eat; nice; tasty; palatable: 这汤很～. This soup is very delicious.

可怜(憐) kělián I (形) 1 pitiful; pitiable; poor: ～虫 pitiful creature; wretch. 一副～相 a pitiable look 2 meagre; wretched; miserable; pitiful: 他的英语知识贫乏得～. His knowledge of English is far from adequate. II (动) have pity on; pity: 没人～他. Nobody feels sorry for him.

可能 kěnéng I (形) possible; probable: 这是完全～的. It's entirely possible. II (副) probably; maybe: 他～会改变主意. He may change his mind. III (名) possibility: 他没有当选为总统的～. There is no likelihood of his being elected to the presidency.

可怕 kěpà (形) fearful; frightful; terrible; terrifying: 真～! How dreadful! 干吧! 没什么～的. Go ahead! There's nothing to be afraid of.

可欺 kěqī (形) easily cowed or bullied

可气(氣) kěqì (形) annoying; exasperating

可巧 kěqiǎo (副) as luck would have it; by a happy coincidence

可亲(親) kěqīn (形) amiable; affable; genial

可取 kěqǔ (形) desirable: 你亲自去拜访他一下是十分～的. It is highly desirable that you go and see him in person.

可是 kěshì (连) but; yet; however: 这房间虽小, ～很安静. The room is small but very quiet.

可塑性 kěsùxìng (名) plasticity
可谓 kěwèi (动) one may well say; it may be said; it may be called: 这机会～千载难逢. This may be the chance of a lifetime.
可恶(惡) kěwù (形) hateful; abominable; detestable
可惜 kěxī (形) it's a pity; it's too bad: ～我不在场. What a pity I wasn't there.
可喜 kěxǐ (形) gratifying; heartening: ～的成就 gratifying achievements
可笑 kěxiào (形) laughable; ridiculous; ludicrous; funny: 简直～! It's simply ridiculous!
可行 kěxíng (形) advisable; feasible: ～性研究 feasibility study. 是否～, 请斟酌. Please consider if this idea is feasible.
可疑 kěyí (形) suspicious; dubious; questionable: 形迹～ look suspicious; be fishy
可以 kěyǐ I (动) can; may: 你～走了. You may go now. II (形)〈口〉1 passable; pretty good; not bad: 她的英语还～. Her English is not too bad. 2 awful: 他今天忙得真～. He's as busy as a bee today.
刻 kè I (动) carve; engrave; cut: ～字 engrave words (on stone, blocks). 木～ woodcut II (量) a quarter (of an hour): 五点一～ a quarter past five III (名) moment: 此～ at the moment IV (形) 1 cutting; penetrating: 尖～acrimonious; biting; sarcastic 2 in the highest degree: 深～ penetrating; profound
刻板 kèbǎn (形) mechanical; stiff; inflexible: ～地照抄 copy mechanically
刻本 kèběn (名) block-printed edition: 宋～ a Song Dynasty block-printed edition
刻薄 kèbó (形) unkind; harsh; mean: 说话～ speak unkindly; make caustic remarks. 待人～ treat people meanly
刻不容缓 kè bùróng huǎn brook no delay; demand immediate attention; be very urgent
刻毒 kèdú (形) venomous; cruel; spiteful: ～的语言 venomed remarks
刻骨 kègǔ (形) deeply ingrained; deep-rooted: ～仇恨 deep-seated hatred. ～铭心 remember with gratitude to the end of one's life
刻画(畫) kèhuà (动) depict; portray
刻苦 kèkǔ (形) 1 assiduous; hardworking; painstaking: ～耐劳 endure hardships without complaining 2 simple and frugal: 生活～ lead a simple and frugal life
嗑 kè (动) crack sth. between the teeth: ～瓜子儿 crack melon seeds
克 kè I (动) 1 restrain: ～制 exercise restraint 2 overcome; subdue; capture (a city, etc.): ～敌制胜 defeat the enemy and win victory 3 set a time limit: ～期完工 set a date for completing the work II (名) gram (g)
克服 kèfú (动) 1 surmount; overcome; conquer: ～困难 overcome a difficulty. ～官僚主义 get rid of red tape 2〈口〉put up with (inconveniences, etc.)
克己奉公 kèjǐ-fènggōng be wholeheartedly devoted to public duty; work selflessly for the public interest
克隆 kèlóng (动) clone: ～羊 a cloned sheep
克制 kèzhì (动) restrain; exercise restraint: ～感情 control one's temper
可 kè
see also kě
可汗 kèhán (名) khan
课 kè I (名) 1 subject; course: 主～ the main subject. 必修～ required courses 2 class: 上～ go to class. 上午有四节～. There are four classes in the morning. 讲(听)～ give (attend) a lecture 3 lesson: 第一～ Lesson One II (动) levy: ～以重税 levy heavy taxes
课本 kèběn (名) textbook
课程 kèchéng (名) course; curriculum: ～表 school timetable
课堂 kètáng (名) classroom; schoolroom: ～教学 classroom instruction (or teaching). ～讨论 classroom discussion
课题 kètí (名) 1 a question for study or discussion 2 problem; task: 提出新的～ pose a new problem
课外 kèwài (形) extracurricular; outside class; after school: ～作业 homework. ～阅读 additional reading
课文 kèwén (名) text
客 kè (名) 1 visitor; guest 2 traveller; passenger: ～机 passenger plane; airliner 3 customer: 房～ boarder; lodger 4 live in a strange place; be a stranger: 作～他乡 live in a strange land 5 a person engaged in some particular pursuit: 政～ politician. 刺～ assassin
客车(車) kèchē (名) 1 passenger train 2

bus; coach

客串 kèchuàn (动) be a guest actor or player: 她在他的电视节目中出场～. She made a guest appearance on his TV show.

客店 kèdiàn (名) inn

客队(隊) kèduì (名) visiting team

客房 kèfáng (名) guest room

客观(觀) kèguān (形) objective: ～规律 objective law. ～世界 objective world

客户 kèhù (名) customer

客满(滿) kèmǎn (形) (of theatre tickets, etc.) sold out; full house

客气(氣) kèqi (形) 1 polite; courteous: 他待人很～. He is very polite to people. 别～. Please don't stand on ceremony. *or* Make yourself at home. *or* Please don't bother. 2 modest: 您太～了. You are being too modest.

客人 kèrén (名) 1 visitor; guest 2 guest (at a hotel, etc.)

客套 kètào (名) polite formula

K

客厅(廳) kètīng (名) drawing room; parlour

客运(運) kèyùn (名) passenger transport; passenger traffic

客栈(棧) kèzhàn (名) inn

恪 kè 〈书〉 scrupulously and respectfully

恪守 kèshǒu (动) strictly abide by (a treaty, promise, etc.): ～诺言 honour one's commitment

肯 kěn (动) 1 agree; consent 2 be willing to; be ready to: ～干 be willing to do hard work. ～帮人忙 be ready to help others

肯定 kěndìng I (动) 1 affirm; confirm; approve; regard as positive: ～成绩 affirm the achievements. ～事实 confirm a fact 2 be definite; be sure: 去不去,我们还不能～. We are not sure yet whether we'll go or not. *or* We have yet to decide whether to go or not. II (形) positive; affirmative: ～的判断 a positive assessment. ～的答复 an affirmative answer

啃 kěn (动) 1 gnaw; nibble: 2 take great pains with one's studies: ～书本 read with great difficulty but with little understanding; make laborious efforts to read

啃老族 kěnlǎozú (名) NEET; boomerang kid; dropout

恳(懇) kěn I (形) earnestly; sincerely: ～谈 talk earnestly II (动) request; beseech; entreat: 敬～光临 request your gracious presence

恳切 kěnqiè (形) earnest; sincere: 言词～ speak in an earnest tone. ～希望 sincerely hope

恳求 kěnqiú (动) implore; entreat; beseech: ～某人办件事 beg sb. to do sth.

垦(墾) kěn (动) cultivate (land); reclaim (wasteland): ～荒 reclaim wasteland; bring wasteland under cultivation; open up virgin soil

坑 kēng I (名) 1 hole; pit; hollow: 泥～ mud puddle. 水～ puddle. 粪～ manure pit. 一个萝卜一个～ one radish, one hole — each has his own assignment and there is nobody to spare 2 tunnel; pit: 矿～ pit II (动) 1 bury alive 2 entrap; cheat: ～人 cheat people

坑道 kēngdào (名) 1 gallery 2 tunnel

坑害 kēnghài (动) lead into a trap; entrap

吭 kēng (动) utter a sound or a word: 一声不～ without saying a word

see also háng

吭声(聲) kēngshēng (动) utter a sound or word

铿(鏗) kēng (象) clang; clatter

铿锵(鏘) kēngqiāng (形) ring; clang: 这首诗读起来音调～. This poem is both majestic and sonorous.

空 kōng I (形) empty; hollow; void: ～屋子 an empty room. ～想 idle dream. 街上～无一人. The street is as good as deserted. II (名) sky; air: 晴～ a clear sky III (副) for nothing: ～跑一趟 make a fruitless trip

see also kòng

空洞 kōngdòng I (名) cavity: 牙齿的～ a tooth cavity II (形) empty; hollow: ～无物 lacking in substance; devoid of content. ～的许诺 hollow promise

空泛 kōngfàn (形) vague and general; not specific: ～的议论 vague and general remarks; generalities

空话 kōnghuà (名) empty talk; idle talk

空幻 kōnghuàn (形) visionary; illusory

空间 kōngjiān (名) space: 外层～ outer space. ～技术 space technology. ～科学 space science

空降 kōngjiàng (动) land troops by parachutes ～兵 airborne force; parachute landing force

空军 kōngjūn (名) air force: ～基地 air base

空口无(無)凭(憑) kōngkǒu wú píng a mere spoken statement is no guarantee

空旷(曠) kōngkuàng (形) open; spacious: ~的原野 an expanse of open country; champaign

空气(氣) kōngqì (名) 1 air: 新鲜~ fresh air. ~冷却 air-cooling. ~调节器 air conditioner. ~污染 air pollution 2 atmosphere: ~紧张 a tense atmosphere

空前 kōngqián (形) unprecedented; as never before: 盛况~ an unprecedentedly grand occasion

空前绝后(後) kōngqián-juéhòu unique; unprecedented and impossibly difficult to recur

空手道 kōngshǒudào (名) karate

空调 kōngtiáo (名) 1 air-conditioning 2 air-conditioner

空头(頭) kōngtóu I (名) (on the stock exchange) bear; shortseller II (形) nominal; phony: ~政治家 armchair politician

空头(頭)支票 kōngtóu zhīpiào 1 bad cheque 2 empty promise; lip service

空投 kōngtóu (动) airdrop; paradrop

空文 kōngwén (名) ineffective law, rule, etc.: 一纸~ a mere scrap of paper

空袭(襲) kōngxí (动) make an air raid; launch an air attack

空想 kōngxiǎng (名) idle dream; fantasy; utopia

空心 kōngxīn I (形) hollow: ~树 a tree hollow inside II (动) become hollow: 萝卜~了. The turnip has gone spongy.

空虚 kōngxū (形) hollow; void: 生活~ have no aim in life. 敌人后方~. The enemy rear is weakly defended.

空运(運) kōngyùn (动) transport by aircraft; airlift: ~救灾物资 airlift relief supplies (to a stricken area)

空战(戰) kōngzhàn (名) air battle; aerial combat

空中 kōngzhōng (名) in the sky; in the air; aerial; overhead: ~加油 air refuelling; inflight refuelling. ~掩护 air umbrella; air cover. ~劫持 hijacking

空中楼(樓)阁 kōngzhōng lóugé castles in the air

空中小姐 kōngzhōng xiǎojiě (名) air hostess

恐 kǒng (动) fear; dread: 惊~ be alarmed

恐怖 kǒngbù (名) terror: 白色~ white terror. ~分子 terrorist

恐吓(嚇) kǒnghè (动) threaten; intimidate: ~信 blackmailing letter; threatening letter

恐慌 kǒnghuāng (形) panic: ~万状 panic-stricken

恐惧(懼) kǒngjù (动) fear; dread: ~不安 be in fear and anxiety

恐怕 kǒngpà (副) 1 I'm afraid: 今晚~他不会来了. I'm afraid he won't come tonight. 2 perhaps; I think: 他走了~有十天了. It's ten days now, I think, since he left. ~你是对的. Perhaps you are right.

孔 kǒng I (名) hole; opening; aperture: 钥匙~ keyhole. 通气~ ventilator II (量): 一~土窑 a cave-dwelling

孔道 kǒngdào (名) a narrow passage providing the only means of access to a certain place

孔雀 kǒngquè (名) peacock

孔隙 kǒngxì (名) small opening; hole

孔穴 kǒngxué (名) hole; cavity

空 kòng I (动) leave empty or blank: 每段开头要~两格. Leave two blank spaces at the beginning of each paragraph. II (形) unoccupied; vacant: ~座 a vacant seat III (名) 1 empty space: 屋里一点~都没有了. There isn't any space left in the room. 2 free time; spare time: 有~到我这儿来. Come over when you have time.
see also kōng

空白 kòngbái (名) blank space: 填补核物理学理论上的~ fill the gaps in the theory of nuclear physics. ~表格 blank form

空缺 kòngquē (名) vacant position; vacancy

空隙 kòngxì (名) space; gap; interval

空暇 kòngxiá (名) free time; spare time; leisure

空闲(閒) kòngxián I (动) be free: 等你~的时候,咱俩去看场电影. Let's go and see a film when you're free. II (名) free time; spare time; leisure

空子 kòngzi (名) 1 gap; opening 2 chance; opportunity: 严防坏人钻~ take strict precautions against giving evildoers an opening

控 kòng (动) 1 accuse; charge: 指~ accuse 2 control; dominate: 遥~ remote control; telecontrol

控告 kònggào (动) charge; accuse; complain: ~某人犯罪 accuse sb. of a crime

控股公司 kònggǔ gōngsī (名) holding company

控诉 kòngsù (动) accuse; denounce: ~殖民主义的罪恶 condemn the evils of colonialism

控制 kòngzhì (动) control; dominate; command: ~局面 have (or take) the situation in hand. ~局势 keep the situation under control. ~感情 control one's temper

抠(摳) kōu I (动) 1 dig or dig out with a finger or sth. pointed; scratch: ~洞 scratch a hole 2 carve; cut: 在镜框边上~点花儿 carve a design on a picture frame 3 delve into; study meticulously: 死~字眼儿 be overscrupulous about the use of language; deliberately find fault with the wording II (形) stingy; miserly: ~门儿 stingy; miserly

口 kǒu I (名) 1 mouth 2 opening; entrance; mouth: 河~ the mouth of a river. 入~ entrance. 瓶~ the mouth of a bottle 3 cut; hole: 伤~ wound; cut. 衣服撕破了个~ tear a hole in one's jacket 4 the edge of a knife: 刀~ the edge of a knife II (量): 一~井 a well

口岸 kǒu'àn (名) port: 通商~ trading port. 入境~ port of entry. 离境~ port of departure

口碑 kǒubēi (名) reputation; word of mouth: ~太烂 have a bad reputation. 依靠~来推动销售 promote sales by word of mouth

口才 kǒucái (名) eloquence: 他很有~. He is very eloquent.

口吃 kǒuchī (动) stutter; stammer: 他一激动就~. He stammers when he gets excited.

口齿(齒) kǒuchǐ (名) 1 enunciation: ~清楚 clear enunciation 2 ability to speak: ~伶俐 speak fluently

口袋 kǒudai (名) pocket; bag; sack: 面~ flour sack. 塑料~ plastic bag

口服 kǒufú (动) 1 profess to be convinced: 心服~ be sincerely convinced 2 take orally: 不得~ not to be taken orally

口福 kǒufú (名) gourmet's luck; the luck to eat delicacies

口供 kǒugòng (名) confession; testimony; a statement made by the accused under examination

口号(號) kǒuhào (名) slogan; watchword

口红 kǒuhóng (名) lipstick

口角 kǒujué (名) quarrel; bicker: 发生了~ have a quarrel

口径(徑) kǒujìng (名) 1 bore; calibre: 小~步枪 small-bore rifle 2 requirements; specifications; line of action: 统一~ agree on a story; have the same story. 说话~一致 speak along the same line. 不合~ fail to meet the requirements

口诀 kǒujué (名) a pithy formula (often in rhyme)

口渴 kǒukě (形) thirsty

口令 kǒulìng (名) 1 word of command 2 password; watchword; countersign

口蜜腹剑(劍) kǒumì-fùjiàn honey-mouthed and dagger-hearted; hypocritical and malignant; play a double game

口气(氣) kǒuqì (名) 1 tone; note: 严肃的~ a serious tone. ~强硬的声明 a strongly worded statement 2 manner of speaking: 他的~真不小. He talked big. 3 what is actually meant; implication: 听他的~, 他并不反对我们的建议. Judging by the way he spoke, he was not really against our proposal.

口腔 kǒuqiāng (名) oral cavity: ~卫生 oral hygiene. ~医院 stomatological hospital

口琴 kǒuqín (名) mouth organ; harmonica

口若悬(懸)河 kǒu ruò xuán hé let loose a flood of eloquence; be eloquent

口舌 kǒushé (名) 1 quarrel; dispute 2 talking round: 不必费~了. You might as well save your breath.

口实(實) kǒushí (名) a cause for gossip

口是心非 kǒushì-xīnfēi say yes and mean no; say one thing and mean another

口授 kǒushòu (动) 1 teach orally; give oral instruction 2 dictate

口述 kǒushù (动) give an oral account

口水 kǒushuǐ (名) saliva: 流~ slobber

口头(頭) kǒutóu (形) oral: ~通知 notify orally. ~汇报 verbal report. ~上赞成, 实际上反对 agree in words but oppose in deeds. ~表决 voice vote; vote by "yes" and "no". ~抗议 verbal protest. ~声明 oral statement

口头(頭)禅(禪) kǒutóuchán (名) pet phrase

口味 kǒuwèi (名) 1 a person's taste: 合~ suit one's taste. 各人~不同. Tastes differ. 2 the flavour or taste of food

口信 kǒuxìn (名) verbal message

口译(譯) kǒuyì (名) oral interpretation

口音 kǒuyīn (名) 1 voice 2 accent: 说话带~ speak with an accent

口语 kǒuyǔ (名) spoken language

口罩 kǒuzhào (名) surgical mask (worn over nose and mouth); mouth mask

寇 kòu I (名) bandit; invader; enemy: 敌～ the (invading) enemy II (动) invade: 入～ invade (a country)

叩 kòu (动) 1 knock: ～门 knock at a door 2 ～头 kowtow

扣 kòu (动) 1 button; buckle: 把衣服～上 button (up) one's coat. ～扣子 do up the buttons 2 detain; take into custody; arrest: 把罪犯～起来. Keep the criminal in custody. 3 deduct: ～工资 deduct a part of sb.'s pay 4 hit: ～球 smash the ball

扣除 kòuchú (动) deduct: ～物价因素 allow for price changes

扣留 kòuliú (动) detain; arrest; hold in custody: ～驾驶执照 suspend a driving licence

扣帽子 kòumàozi put a (political) label on sb.

扣人心弦 kòu rén xīnxián exciting; thrilling; soul-stirring: 一场～的比赛 an exciting match

扣压(壓) kòuyā (动) withhold; suppress

扣押 kòuyā (动) 1 detain; hold in custody 2 distrain

扣子 kòuzi (名) 1 knot 2 button

窟 kū (名) 1 hole; cave: 石～ cave; grotto 2 den: 匪～ a robbers' den. 赌～ a gambling-den

窟窿 kūlong (名) 1 hole; cavity: 耗子～ rat-hole 2 deficit; debt: 补～ make up a deficit

枯 kū (形) 1 (of a plant, etc.) withered: ～草 withered grass. ～叶 dead leaves 2 (of a well, river, etc.) dried up: 河水～了. The river has run dry.

枯肠(腸) kūcháng (名)〈书〉impoverished mind: 搜索～ rack one's brains (for ideas or expressions)

枯槁 kūgǎo (形) 1 withered 2 haggard: 形容～ look haggard

枯黄 kūhuáng (形) withered and yellow: 树叶～了. The leaves have turned yellow.

枯竭 kūjié (形) dried up; exhausted: 水源～. The source has dried up. 资金～. The capital has been exhausted.

枯木逢春 kūmù féng chūn (of an ill-starred elderly person) get a new lease of life

枯萎 kūwěi (形) withered

枯燥 kūzào (形) dull and dry; uninteresting: ～无味 dry as dust

骷 kū

骷髅(髏) kūlóu (名) 1 human skeleton 2 human skull; death's head

哭 kū (动) cry; weep; sob: 放声大～ cry loudly. 痛～ cry bitterly; cry one's eyes out. ～笑不得 not know whether to laugh or to cry

哭泣 kūqì (动) cry; weep; sob

哭穷(窮) kūqióng (动) go about telling people how hard up one is, which is not usually the case

哭诉 kūsù (动) complain tearfully

苦 kǔ I (形) bitter: ～药 bitter medicine II (名) hardship; suffering; pain: ～中作乐 find joy in hardship III (动) 1 cause sb. suffering; give sb. a hard time: 这事可～了他了. This matter really gave him a hard time. 2 suffer from; be troubled by: ～旱 suffer from drought IV (副) painstakingly; doing one's utmost: 勤学～练 study and train hard. ～干 work hard

苦差 kǔchāi (名) hard and unprofitable job; thankless job

苦楚 kǔchǔ (名) suffering; misery; distress

苦处(處) kǔchu (名) suffering; hardship; difficulty

苦工 kǔgōng (名) hard (manual) work; hard labour

苦功 kǔgōng (名) painstaking effort

苦海 kǔhǎi (名) sea of bitterness; abyss of misery: 脱离～ get out of the abyss of misery

苦口 kǔkǒu (动) 1 (admonish) in earnest: ～相劝 earnestly advise (or exhort). ～婆心 admonish sb. earnestly 2 bitter to the taste: 这些话都是～良药. The advice may be unpalatable, but it will do you good.

苦闷 kǔmèn (形) depressed; dejected; feeling low

苦难(難) kǔnàn (名) suffering; misery; distress: ～岁月 hard times

苦恼(惱) kǔnǎo (形) vexed; worried

苦涩(澀) kǔsè (形) 1 bitter and astringent 2 pained; agonized; anguished

苦思 kǔsī (动) think hard; cudgel one's brains: ～冥想 think long and hard

苦头(頭) kǔtou (名) suffering: 他吃尽了～. He endured untold sufferings. 你现在不改,今后迟早要吃～. If you don't correct it now, sooner or later you'll have to pay for it.

苦笑 kǔxiào (名) forced smile; wry smile

苦心 kǔxīn (名) trouble taken; pains: 煞费～ take great pains

苦战(戰) kǔzhàn (动) fight a bitter battle; struggle hard

苦衷 kǔzhōng (名) difficulties that one is reluctant to bring to the notice of others: 难言的～ feelings of pain or embarrassment which are hard to describe

库 kù (名) warehouse; storehouse: ～房 storeroom. 军火～ arsenal. 汽车～ garage

库藏 kùcáng (动) have in storage: 这个图书馆～图书三十万册. There are 300,000 books in the library.

库存 kùcún (名) stock; reserve: 有大量～ have a large stock of goods. 商品～ commodity inventories. ～现金 cash holding

K

裤 kù (名) trousers; pants: 短～ shorts. 牛仔～ jeans

裤衩 kùchǎ (名) pants; underpants

酷 kù (形) 1 cruel; oppressive: ～吏 a cruel (feudal) official 2 very; extremely: ～寒 severe cold. ～好 be very fond of 3 cool

酷爱(愛) kù'ài (动) ardently love

酷刑 kùxíng (名) cruel (or savage) torture

夸(誇) kuā (动) 1 exaggerate; overstate; boast: ～口 boast; brag 2 praise: 老师～她字写得漂亮. The teacher praised her for her beautiful handwriting.

夸大 kuādà (动) exaggerate; overstate; magnify: ～困难 exaggerate the difficulties. ～其词 make an overstatement; overstate the case

夸奖(獎) kuājiǎng (动) praise; commend: 这部新电影受到大家的～. The new film has received high praise from everyone.

夸口 kuākǒu (动) boast; brag; talk big

夸夸其谈 kuākuā qí tán indulge in verbiage; glib and empty

夸耀 kuāyào (动) brag about; show off; flaunt: 他喜欢～自己的学识. He loves showing off his knowledge.

夸张(張) kuāzhāng I (动) exaggerate; overstate: 艺术～ artistic exaggeration II (名) hyperbole

垮 kuǎ (动) collapse; fall; break down: 这座老房子快～了. This old building is falling to pieces. 他的身体累～了. His health broke down from overwork.

垮台(臺) kuǎtái (动) collapse; fall from power

挎 kuà (动) 1 carry on the arm: ～着个篮子 with a basket on one's arm. ～着胳膊走 walk arm in arm 2 carry sth. over one's shoulder or at one's side: ～着照相机 have a camera slung over one's shoulder

挎包 kuàbāo (名) satchel

跨 kuà (动) 1 step; stride: ～进屋子 step into the room 2 bestride; straddle: ～上战马 mount (or bestride) a warhorse 3 cut across; go beyond: ～年度 over the year-end. ～学科 interdisciplinary. ～国公司 transnational corporation; multinational

跨度 kuàdù (名) span

跨越 kuàyuè (动) stride across; leap over; cut across: ～障碍 surmount an obstacle

胯 kuà (名) hip: ～骨 hipbone; innominate bone

会(會) kuài

see also huì

会计 kuàijì (名) 1 accounting 2 bookkeeper; accountant: ～年度 financial (or fiscal) year

侩(儈) kuài (名) middleman: 市～ sordid merchant

脍(膾) kuài (名)〈书〉 meat chopped into small pieces; minced meat

脍炙人口 kuàizhì rénkǒu (of a piece of good writing, etc.) win popular acclaim; enjoy great popularity

块(塊) kuài I (名) piece; lump; cube; chunk: 石～ blocks of stone. 冰～ ice cubes II (量) 1 [for a slice or chunk of sth.]: 三～巧克力 three chocolate bars. 一～面包 a piece of bread. 两～肥皂 two cakes of soap 2〈口〉*yuan*, the basic unit of money in China: 三～钱 three *yuan*

快 kuài I (形) 1 fast; quick; rapid: ～速阅读 fast (or speed) reading. 进步很～ rapid progress 2 quick-witted; ingenious 3 sharp: ～刀 a sharp knife 4 straightforward: 心直口～ straightforward and outspoken 5 pleased; happy; gratified: 心中不～ feel bad II

(动) hurry up; make haste: ～上车吧! Hurry up and get on the bus! ～, 我们已经迟到了. Quick, we are late already. III (副) soon; before long: 他～回来了. He'll be back soon. 电影～开演了. The film is about to begin.

快餐 kuàicān (名) quick meal; fast food; snack: ～部 snack counter

快车(車) kuàichē (名) express train or bus: 特别～ special express

快递(遞) kuàidì (动) express delivery: ～件 an express mail

快活 kuàihuo (形) happy; merry; cheerful

快件 kuàijiàn (名) express mail

快乐(樂) kuàilè (形) happy; joyful; cheerful

快速 kuàisù (形) fast; quick; high-speed: ～电子计算机 high-speed computer

快慰 kuàiwèi (形) reassured and happy; extremely pleased

快意 kuàiyì (形) pleased; satisfied; comfortable

快嘴 kuàizuǐ (名) one who has a loose mouth

筷 kuài (名) (～子) chopsticks: 碗～ bowls and chopsticks. 一双～子 a pair of chopsticks

宽 kuān I (形) 1 wide; broad: ～银幕 wide screen. ～肩膀 broad-shouldered 2 generous; lenient: 从～处理 treat with leniency II (名) width; breadth: 这张桌子两米～, 三米长. The table is three metres long and two metres wide. III (动) 1 relax; relieve: 把心～下来. Don't worry. 2 extend: 限期能再～几天吗? Can the deadline be extended a few more days? *or* Can you give me a few days grace?

宽敞 kuānchang (形) spacious; roomy; commodious: ～的厅堂 a spacious hall

宽畅(暢) kuānchàng (形) free from worry; happy

宽大 kuāndà (形) 1 spacious; roomy: ～的客厅 a spacious drawing room 2 lenient; magnanimous: ～处理 lenient treatment. ～为怀 be magnanimous or lenient (with an offender)

宽带(帶) kuāndài (名) broadband

宽待 kuāndài (动) treat with leniency; be lenient in dealing with

宽度 kuāndù (名) width; breadth: 领海～ the extent of the territorial sea

宽广(廣) kuānguǎng (形) broad; extensive; vast: ～的广场 a broad square. 心胸～ broad-minded

宽宏大量 kuānhóng-dàliàng large-minded; magnanimous

宽厚 kuānhòu (形) 1 broadminded 2 kind and sincere: 待人～ treat people with kindness and sincerity

宽旷(曠) kuānkuàng (形) extensive; vast: ～的草原 a vast stretch of grasslands

宽阔 kuānkuò (形) broad; wide: ～的林阴道 a broad (or wide) avenue

宽容 kuānróng (形) tolerant; lenient

宽恕 kuānshù (动) forgive; pardon: 请求～ ask for forgiveness

宽松(鬆) kuānsōng (形) 1 loose and comfortable 2 not crowded 3 not stringent; free from worry; easy

宽慰 kuānwèi (动) comfort; console: ～她几句. Say something to comfort her.

宽心 kuānxīn (形) feel relieved: 说几句～话 say a few reassuring words

宽裕 kuānyù (形) well-to-do; comfortably off; ample: 生活～ be comfortably off. 时间很～. There's plenty of time yet.

款 kuǎn (名) 1 section of an article in a legal document, etc.; paragraph 2 a sum of money; fund: 拨～ allocate a sum of money for a specific purpose. 汇～ remit money 3 the name of sender or recipient inscribed on a painting or a piece of calligraphy presented as a gift: 上～ the name of the recipient. 下～ the name of the painter or calligrapher

款待 kuǎndài (动) treat cordially; entertain: ～客人 entertain guests. 盛情～ hospitality

款式 kuǎnshì (名) pattern; style; design

款项 kuǎnxiàng (名) a sum of money; fund

款子 kuǎnzi (名) a sum of money

诓 kuāng (动) deceive; hoax: ～骗 deceive; hoax; dupe. 我哪能～你? How could I deceive you?

哐 kuāng (象) crash; bang: ～的一声, 脸盆掉在地上了. The basin fell with a crash.

哐啷 kuānglāng (象) crash: ～一声把门关上 bang the door shut

筐 kuāng (名) (～子) basket: 一～苹果 a basket of apples

狂 kuáng (形) 1 mad; crazy: 发～ go mad. ～人 lunatic; maniac 2 violent: ～风 strong fast wind 3 wild: 欣喜

K

若～ be wild (or beside oneself) with joy **4** arrogant; overbearing

狂飙 kuángbiāo (名) hurricane

狂欢(歡) kuánghuān (名) revelry; carnival; public merrymaking

狂热(熱) kuángrè (形) fanatical: ～的信徒 a fanatical follower; fanatic. ～的民族沙文主义 fanatical national chauvinism

狂人 kuángrén (名) madman; maniac

狂妄 kuángwàng (形) wildly arrogant; presumptuous: ～自大 arrogant and conceited. ～的野心 a wild ambition

狂言 kuángyán (名) ravings; wild language

诳 kuáng

诳语 kuángyǔ (名) lies; falsehood

矿(礦) kuàng (名) **1** ore (or mineral) deposit: 报～ report where deposits are found **2** ore: 铁～ iron ore **3** mine: 煤～ coal mine; colliery

K

矿藏 kuàngcáng (名) mineral resources: ～丰富 be rich in mineral resources. ～储量 (ore) reserves

矿产(產) kuàngchǎn (名) mineral products; minerals

矿床(牀) kuàngchuáng (名) mineral (or ore) deposit; deposit

矿工 kuànggōng (名) miner

矿井 kuàngjǐng (名) mine; pit

矿泉 kuàngquán (名) mineral spring: ～水 mineral water

矿山 kuàngshān (名) mine

矿石 kuàngshí (名) ore

矿物 kuàngwù (名) mineral: ～界 mineral kingdom. ～学 mineralogy

旷(曠) kuàng(形) **1** vast; spacious: 地～人稀 a vast territory with a sparse population **2** free from worries and petty ideas: 心～神怡 in a cheerful frame of mind

旷达(達) kuàngdá (形) broad-minded; big-hearted

旷工 kuànggōng (动) deliberately stay away from work

旷古 kuànggǔ (形) from time immemorial

旷课 kuàngkè (动) skip school; play truant

旷日持久 kuàngrì-chíjiǔ long-drawn-out; protracted; prolonged: ～的战争 long-drawn-out war

旷野 kuàngyě (名) wilderness

框 kuàng I (名) frame; case; circle: 镜～ picture frame. 窗～ window frame; window case. 眼镜～ frames (of spectacles) II (动) draw a frame round: 用红线把标题～起来 frame the heading in red

框架 kuàngjià (名) frame

框框 kuàngkuang (名) **1** frame; circle **2** restriction; convention; set pattern: 打破旧～ break outmoded conventions

眶 kuàng (名) the socket of the eye: 热泪盈～ one's eyes filling with tears

况 kuàng I (名) condition; situation: 近～如何? How have you been recently? II (动) compare: 以古～今 draw parallels from history III (连)〈书〉moreover; besides

况且 kuàngqiě (连) moreover; besides

窥 kuī (动) peep; spy

窥测 kuīcè (动) spy out: ～时机 bide one's time

窥见(見) kuījiàn (动) get (or catch) a glimpse of; detect

窥视 kuīshì (动) peep at; spy on

窥伺 kuīsì (动) lie in wait for; be on watch for

窥探 kuītàn (动) spy upon; pry into: ～军事秘密 pry into military secrets

亏(虧) kuī I (名) loss: 盈～ profit and loss. 转～为盈 turn loss into gain II (动) **1** lose; be deficient: 理～ be in the wrong **2** treat unfairly: 你放心吧, ～不了你. Don't worry, we won't let you down. **3** thanks to: ～他及时叫醒了我. Luckily, he woke me up in time. **4** [often said with a touch of irony]: ～他说得出口! And he had the nerve to say so!

亏本 kuīběn (动) lose money in business; lose one's capital: ～生意 a losing proposition

亏待 kuīdài (动) treat unfairly; treat shabbily

亏空 kuīkong I (动) be in debt II (名) debt; deficit: 弥补～ meet (or make up) a deficit; make up (for) a loss

亏蚀 kuīshí I (名) eclipse of the sun or moon II (动) lose (money) in business

亏损 kuīsǔn (名) **1** loss; deficit: 企业～ loss incurred in an enterprise **2** general debility

亏心 kuīxīn (动) have a guilty conscience: ～事 a wrong deed that troubles (or weighs on) one's conscience

盔 kuī (名) helmet

盔甲 kuījiǎ (名) a suit of armour

岿(巋) kuī

岿然 kuīrán (形) towering; lofty

魁 kuí I (名) chief; head: 罪～ chief criminal; arch-criminal II (形) of stalwart build

魁首 kuíshǒu (名) a person who is outstanding in his time: 文章～ the best writer of the day

魁伟(偉) kuíwěi (形) big and tall

魁梧 kuíwú (形) big and tall; stalwart

葵 kuí (名) certain herbaceous plants with big flowers: 向日～ sunflower. 锦～ high mallow

葵花 kuíhuā (名) sunflower: ～子 sunflower seeds

葵扇 kuíshàn (名) palm-leaf fan

揆 kuí 〈书〉 I (动) conjecture; consider; estimate: ～度 observe and estimate; conjecture. ～情度理 considering the circumstances and judging by common sense II (名) principle; standard

睽 kuí

睽睽 kuíkuí (形) stare; gaze: 众目～之下 in the public eye

傀 kuǐ

傀儡 kuǐlěi (名) puppet: ～戏 puppet show; puppet play. ～政府 puppet government; puppet regime

愧 kuì (形) ashamed; conscience-stricken: 问心无～ have a clear conscience. 于心有～ have a guilty conscience

愧恨 kuìhèn (形) ashamed and remorseful; remorseful: ～交集 overcome with shame and remorse

愧色 kuìsè (名) a look of shame: 面有～ look ashamed. 毫无～ look unashamed

溃 kuì (动) 1 (of a dyke or dam) burst: ～堤 burst the dyke 2 break through (an encirclement): ～围南奔 break through the encirclement and head south 3 be routed: ～不成军 be utterly routed; flee helter-skelter 4 fester; ulcerate

溃败 kuìbài (动) be defeated; be routed

溃决 kuìjué (动) (of a dyke or dam) burst

溃烂(爛) kuìlàn (动) fester; ulcerate

溃逃 kuìtáo (动) escape in disorder; flee helter-skelter

溃退 kuìtuì (动) beat a precipitate retreat

溃疡(瘍) kuìyáng (名) ulcer: 胃～ gastric ulcer

愦 kuì (形) muddle-headed: 昏～ muddle-headed

匮 kuì (形)〈书〉 deficient: ～乏 short (of supplies); deficient

馈 kuì (动) make a present of: ～赠 present (a gift); make a present of sth.

坤 kūn (形) female; feminine: ～表 woman's watch

昆 kūn (名)〈书〉 1 elder brother 2 offspring: 后～ descendants; offspring

昆虫(蟲) kūnchóng (名) insect: ～学 entomology; insectology. ～学家 entomologist

昆仲 kūn-zhòng (名) elder and younger brothers; brothers

捆 kǔn I (动) tie; bind; bundle up: ～行李 tie up one's baggage. ～谷草 bundle up millet stalks. 把他～起来 tie him up II (量) bundle: 一～柴火 a bundle of firewood

捆绑 kǔnbǎng (动) truss up; bind; tie up

捆扎(紮) kǔnzā (动) tie up; bundle up

困 kùn I (动) 1 be stranded; be hard pressed: 为病所～ be afflicted with illness 2 surround; pin down: 把敌人～在山谷里 pin the enemy down in the valley II (形) 1 tired: ～乏 tired; fatigued 2 sleepy: 你～了就睡吧. Go to bed if you feel sleepy.

困惫(憊) kùnbèi (形) very tired

困顿 kùndùn (形) 1 tired out; exhausted 2 in financial straits

困惑 kùnhuò (形) perplexed; puzzled: ～不解 feel bewildered

困境 kùnjìng (名) difficult position; predicament; straits: 陷于～ fall into dire straits; find oneself in a tight corner; be caught in a dilemma. 摆脱～ extricate oneself from a difficult position

困窘 kùnjiǒng (形) in straitened circumstances

困倦 kùnjuàn (形) sleepy

困苦 kùnkǔ (形) poverty-stricken; (live) in

privation：艰难～ difficulties and hardships

困难(難) kùnnan (名) 1 difficulty： 克服～ surmount difficulties. ～重重 be beset with difficulties 2 financial difficulties; straitened circumstances：生活～ live in straitened circumstances

困兽(獸)犹(猶)斗(鬥) kùnshòu yóu dòu cornered animals will still fight; beasts at bay will fight back

廓 kuò I (形) wide; extensive; boundless II (名) exterior features：轮～ outline

廓清 kuòqīng (动) sweep away; clean up; liquidate

扩(擴) kuò (动) expand; enlarge; extend

扩充 kuòchōng (动) expand; strengthen; augment：～军备 arms (or armaments) expension. ～设备 augment the equipment

L

扩大 kuòdà (动) enlarge; expand; extend：～范围 extend the limits. ～眼界 widen one's outlook; broaden one's horizons. ～耕地面积 expand the area under cultivation. ～会议 enlarged meeting (or session, conference)

扩散 kuòsàn (动) spread; diffuse：核～ nuclear proliferation

扩音器 kuòyīnqì (名) 1 megaphone 2 audio amplifier

扩展 kuòzhǎn (动) expand; spread; extend; develop

扩张(張) kuòzhāng (动) expand; enlarge; extend; spread：对外～ expansionism; foreign aggrandizement. 领土～ territorial expansion

阔 kuò (形) 1 wide; broad; vast 2 wealthy; rich：摆～ flaunt one's wealth

阔别 kuòbié (动) separate for a long time：～多年的朋友 long-separated friends

阔步 kuòbù (动) take big strides：～前进 advance with giant strides

阔绰 kuòchuò (形) living in luxury and extravagance：生活～ lead an extravagant life; spend lavishly

阔气(氣) kuòqi (形) extravagant; lavish; luxurious：摆～ parade one's wealth

括 kuò (动) 1 draw together (muscles, etc.); contract 2 include

括号(號) kuòhào (名) brackets ([ ], ( ), 〈 〉)

L l

垃 lā

垃圾 lājī (名) rubbish; garbage; refuse; disposal：～箱 dustbin; garbage can. ～堆 rubbish heap

拉 lā (动) 1 pull; draw; tug; drag：使劲～，我来推. Pull hard while I push. ～上窗帘 draw the curtains 2 transport by vehicle; haul：～货 haul goods 3 move (troops to a place)：把二连～到河那边去 move Company Two to the other side of the river 4 play (certain musical instruments)：～小提琴(手风琴) play the violin (accordion) 5 drag out; draw out; space out：～长声音说话 drawl. ～开距离 leave distances in between 6 give (or lend) a hand; help：他有困难，要～他一把. We must help him out. 7 drag in; implicate：自己做的事，为什么要～上别人？Why drag in others when it was all your own doing? 8 try to establish; claim：～关系 try to establish some sort of relationship (with sb. usually for sordid purposes) 9 〈口〉 empty the bowels： ～肚子 suffer from diarrhoea; have loose bowels 10 chat：～家常 have a chat
see also lá

拉扯 lāche (动)〈口〉 1 drag; pull 2 take great pains to bring up (a child) 3 implicate; drag in 4 chat

拉关(關)系(係) lā guānxi try to establish a relationship with sb.; cotton up to

拉后(後)腿 lā hòutuǐ hold sb. back; be a drag on sb.

拉锯 lājù (动) work a two-handed saw：～战 seesaw battle

拉拉队(隊) lālā duì (名) cheering squad

拉拢(攏) lālǒng (动) draw sb. over to one's side (in factional strife)

拉屎 lāshǐ (动)〈口〉 empty the bowels; shit

拉锁儿(兒) lāsuǒr (名) zip fastener; zipper

拉杂(雜) lāzá (形) rambling; jumbled; ill-organized：这篇文章写得太～. This article is badly organized.

邋 lā (形)〈口〉 slovenly; sloppy：～遢 slovenly; sloppy; tatty

拉 lá (动) slash; slit; cut; make a gash in: ~玻璃 cut the glass. 手上~了一个口子 cut one's hand; get a cut in the hand
see also lā

喇 lǎ

喇叭 lǎba (名) 1 brass-wind instruments in general or any of these instruments 2 loudspeaker: ~筒 megaphone

喇叭裤 lǎbakù (名) flared trousers; bell-bottoms

喇嘛 lǎma (名) lama: ~教 Lamaism. ~庙 lamasery

落 là (动) 1 leave out; be missing: 这里~了两个字. Two words are missing here. 2 leave behind; forget to bring: 对不起, 我把信用卡~在家里了. Sorry, I left my credit card at home. 3 lag (or fall, drop) behind: ~下很远 fall (or be left) far behind
see also luò

蜡(蠟) là (名) 1 wax 2 candle: 点上一支~. Light a candle. 3 polish: 地板~ floor wax; floor polish

蜡版 làbǎn (名) mimeograph stencil (already cut)

蜡笔(筆) làbǐ (名) wax crayon

蜡纸 làzhǐ (名) 1 wax paper 2 stencil paper; stencil: 刻~ cut a stencil

蜡烛(燭) làzhú (名) (wax) candle

腊(臘) là

腊肠(腸) làcháng (名) sausage

腊月 làyuè (名) the twelfth month of the lunar year; the twelfth moon

辣 là I (形) 1 peppery; hot 2 vicious; ruthless: 心毒手~ vicious and ruthless; wicked and cruel II (动) (of smell or taste) burn; bite; sting: ~得舌头发麻. The hot taste burns the tongue.

辣酱(醬) làjiàng (名) chilli sauce

辣椒 làjiāo (名) hot pepper; chilli: ~粉 chilli powder. ~油 chilli oil

辣手 làshǒu I (名) ruthless method II (形) 1 vicious; ruthless 2 thorny; knotty: 这件事真~. That's really a thorny problem.

啦 la (助) [the representation of the combined sounds "le" and "a", denoting exclamation, interrogation, etc.]: 他真来~! He has turned up, indeed! 这回我可亲眼看见她~! This time I've actually seen her with my own eyes.

来(來) lái I (动) 1 come; arrive: 跟我~! Come along with me. 他们还没有~. They haven't come yet. 2 crop up; take place: 问题~了. Problems have cropped up. 3 [replacing a verb]: 你歇歇, 让我~吧. You take a rest. Let me do it. ~一盘棋. Let's have a game of chess. 再~一个! Encore! 4 [used with 得 or 不 to indicate possibility]: 他们俩很合得~. The two of them are getting along very well. 5 [used before a verb to indicate that one is about to do sth.]: 大家~想办法. Let's put our heads together. 6 [used after a verb or verbal phrase to indicate what one has come for]: 我们贺喜~了. We have come to offer our congratulations. 7 [used before a verb to indicate the purpose of such an action]: 我们将开个会~交流经验. We'll hold a meeting to exchange experiences. 8 [used after a verb as a complement to indicate moving forward in the direction of the speaker]: 过~! Come over here! 各个方面都传~了振奋人心的消息. Encouraging news poured in from all quarters. 9 [used after a verb to indicate the result]: 一觉醒~ wake up after a sound sleep II (助) 1 ever since: 十多天~ for the last ten days and more. 两千年~ over the past 2,000 years 2 [used after numerals 十,百,千, etc., to indicate approximate number] about; over: 二十~个 around twenty. 五十~岁 over fifty (years old) 3 [used after numerals 一,二,三, to enumerate reasons]: 一~…, 二~… in the first place..., in the second place...

来宾(賓) láibīn (名) guest; visitor: 表演节目, 招待~ give performances to entertain the guests

来不及 láibují there's not enough time (to do sth.); it's too late (to do sth.): ~细谈了. There's no time for me to go into detail.

来到 láidào (动) arrive; come: 雨季~了. The rainy season has set in. 春天终于~了. Spring is here at long last.

来得及 láidejí there's still time; be able to do sth. in time; be able to make it: 电影三点开始, 你现在走还~. The film starts at three. You can still make it if you go now.

L

来回 láihuí I（名）a round trip; a return trip: ～有多远? How far is it there and back? ～票 return ticket; round-trip ticket II（副）back and forth; to and fro: 在走廊里～走动 pace up and down the corridor

来劲(勁) láijìn（动）full of enthusiasm; in high spirits

来历(歷) láilì（名）origin; source; antecedents; background; past history: 查明～ trace sth. to its source; ascertain a person's antecedents. ～不明的人 a person of dubious background or of questionable antecedents. 这张油画可有一段不平凡的～. This oil painting has an unusual history. ～不明的飞机 unidentified aircraft

来临(臨) láilín（动）arrive; come; approach

来龙(龍)去脉(脈) láilóng-qùmài origin and development; the entire process: 事情的～ the whole story from beginning to end

来路 láilù（名）origin; antecedents: ～不明 unidentified; of dubious background

来日方长(長) láirì fāng cháng there will be ample time

来势(勢) láishì（名）the momentum which sth. of tremendous power or significance gains as it approachs; oncoming force

来头(頭) láitou（名）1 connections; backing: ～不小 have plenty of backing from influential quarters 2 the motive behind (sb.'s words, etc.)

来往 láiwǎng I（名）dealings; contact: 我跟他从来没有任何～. I've never had any contact with him. II（动）1 have dealings with; make contact with: 我们俩不大～. The two of us have seen very little of each other. 2 come and go

来由 láiyóu（名）reason; cause

来源 láiyuán I（名）source; origin: 经济～ source of income II（动）originate; stem from: 知识～于实践. Knowledge stems from practice.

来之不易 lái zhī bù yì it has not come easily; hard-earned; hard-won

赖

lài（动）1 rely on; depend on: 完成任务，有～于大家的努力. The success of the work depends on everyone's efforts. 2 hang on in a place; drag out one's stay in a place: ～着不走 overstay one's visit 3 deny one's error or responsibility; go back on one's word: ～是～不掉的. It's no use trying to get away with it. 4 blame sb. wrongly; put the blame on sb. else: 自己做错了，不能～别人. You should not blame others for what is your own fault. 5〈口〉blame: 这事全～我. I'm entirely to blame for that.

赖皮 làipí（形）〈口〉rascally; shameless; unreasonable: 要～ act shamelessly; have no sense of shame

赖账(賬) làizhàng（动）1 repudiate a debt 2 go back on one's word

癞

lài（名）1 leprosy 2 scabies

癞皮狗 làipígǒu（名）1 mangy dog 2 loathsome creature

癞子 làizi（名）a person suffering from scabby head

籁

lài（名）1 an ancient musical pipe 2 sound; noise: 万～俱寂. It was all quiet and still.

阑

lán I（形）late: 夜～人静 in the stillness of the night II（名）railing; balustrade

阑干 lángān（形）crisscross: 星斗～. The sky is dotted with stars.

阑尾 lánwěi（名）appendix: ～炎 appendicitis

澜

lán（名）billows: 波～ huge waves. 推波助～ add fuel to the fire; aggravate an already complicated situation.

谰

lán（动）calumniate; slander

谰言 lányán（名）calumny; slander: 无耻～ a shameless slander

兰(蘭)

lán（名）orchid

兰花 lánhuā（名）orchid

栏(欄)

lán（名）1 fence; railing; balustrade; hurdle: 跨～赛跑 hurdle race; the hurdles 2 pen; shed: 牛～ cowshed. 羊～ sheep-pen 3 column: 布告～ bulletin board; notice board. 广告～ classified ads

栏(欄)杆 lángān（名）railing; banisters; balustrade

栏目 lánmù（名）a column (in a newspaper); a programme (on TV)

拦(攔)

lán（动）bar; block; hold back: ～住去路

block the way. 他刚要提问,就被老师～住了. He was trying to ask when the teacher cut him short.

拦河坝(壩) lánhébà (名) a dam across a river; dam

拦截 lánjié (动) intercept: ～增援的敌人 intercept enemy reinforcements

拦路 lánlù (动) block the way: ～抢劫 waylay; hold up; mug

拦路虎 lánlùhǔ (名) obstacle; stumbling block

拦腰 lányāo (副) by the waist; round the middle: 大坝把河水～截断. The dam cut the river in the middle.

拦阻 lánzǔ (动) block; hold back; obstruct

褴(襤) lán

褴褛(褸) lánlǚ (形) ragged; shabby: 衣衫～ shabbily dressed; dressed in rags

蓝(藍) lán I (形) blue II (名) indigo plant

蓝本 lánběn (名) 1 the source material on which later work is based; chief source 2 original version (of a literary work)

蓝领 lánlǐng (名) blue-collar

蓝图(圖) lántú (名) blueprint

篮(籃) lán (名)(～子) basket

篮球 lánqiú (名) basketball: ～场 basketball court. ～队 basketball team

岚 lán (名) haze; vapour; mist

懒 lǎn (形) 1 lazy; indolent; slothful 2 sluggish; drowsy: 身上发～ feel drowsy

懒得 lǎnde (动) not feel like (doing sth.); not be in the mood to; be disinclined to: 我～出去. I have no inclination to go out. *or* I don't feel like going out.

懒惰 lǎnduò (形) lazy

懒汉(漢) lǎnhàn (名) sluggard; idler; lazybones

懒散 lǎnsǎn (形) sluggish; negligent; slack: 学习～ careless about one's studies

懒洋洋 lǎnyángyáng (形) sluggish; listless

览(覽) lǎn (动) 1 look at; see; view: 游～ go sightseeing; tour 2 read: 博～ read extensively. 浏～ glance over; skim through (or over); browse through

揽(攬) lǎn (动) 1 pull sb. into one's arms; take into one's arms: 母亲把孩子～在怀里. The mother carried the child in her arms. 2 fasten with a rope, etc.: 用绳子～上 put a rope around sth. 3 take on; take upon oneself; canvass: ～活儿 take on work. 他把责任都～到自己身上. He took all the responsibility on himself. 4 grasp; monopolize: 包～ monopolize; undertake the whole thing. ～权 arrogate power to oneself

缆(纜) lǎn (名) 1 hawser; mooring rope; cable: 解～ cast off; set sail 2 thick rope; cable: 电～ power cable; cable

缆车(車) lǎnchē (名) cable car: ～铁道 cable railway

滥(濫) làn I (动) overflow; flood II (形) excessive; indiscriminate: ～施轰炸 indiscriminate bombing; wanton bombing

滥调 làndiào (名) hackneyed tune; worn-out theme: 陈词～ overused expressions; tired old bromides; clichés

滥用 lànyòng (动) abuse; misuse: use indiscriminately: ～职权 abuse one's power

滥竽充数(數) lànyú chōng shù be a layman who passes himself off as an expert; be an incompetent person or a person unequal to his task

烂(爛) làn I (形) 1 sodden; mashed; pappy: 牛肉烧得太～了. The beef is overdone. 2 worn out: 衣服穿～了. The clothes are worn out. ～衣服 worn-out clothes 3 messy: 一本～账 messy accounts. ～摊子 an awful mess II (动) rot; fester: 伤口～了. The wound is festering.

烂漫 lànmàn (形) 1 bright-coloured; brilliant: 山花～ bright mountain flowers in full bloom 2 unaffected: 天真～ naive; innocent

烂泥 lànní (名) mud; slush: ～塘 a muddy pond

烂熟 lànshú (形) 1 thoroughly cooked 2 know sth. thoroughly: 台词背得～ learn one's lines thoroughly

烂尾楼 lànwěilóu (名) unfinished building; half-finished building

烂醉 lànzuì (形) dead drunk: ～如泥 be dead drunk; be as drunk as a lord

郎 láng (名) 1 an ancient official title 2 [referring to certain kinds of people]: 令～ your son. 新～ bridegroom. 货～ street vendor 3 [pet address by woman to her husband or lover] my darling

郎中 lángzhōng (名) a physician trained in herbal medicine

廊 láng (名) porch; corridor; veranda: 回~ winding corridor. 长~ The Long Corridor (in the Summer Palace, Beijing). 画~ picture gallery

廊檐 lángyán (名) the eaves of a veranda

锒 láng

锒头(頭) lángtou (名) hammer

锒 láng

锒铛(鐺) lángdāng I (名) iron chains: ~入狱 be chained and thrown into prison II (象) clank; clang

狼 láng (名) wolf

狼狈 lángbèi (形) in a difficult position; in a tight corner: ~不堪 in an extremely awkward position. ~逃窜 flee in panic

狼狈为(爲)奸 lángbèi wéi jiān act in collusion (or cahoots) with each other; work hand in glove with; band together

狼藉 lángjí (形)〈书〉 in disorder; scattered about in a mess: 杯盘~ wine cups and dishes lying about in a mess. 声名~ notorious; in disrepute; discredited

狼吞虎咽 lángtūn-hǔyàn gobble up; wolf down; devour ravenously

狼心狗肺 lángxīn-gǒufèi 1 cruel and unscrupulous; brutal and cold-blooded 2 ungrateful

狼烟四起 lángyān sìqǐ smoke signals rising on all sides

狼子野心 lángzǐ yěxīn wolfish nature; vicious ambition

朗 lǎng (形) 1 light; bright: 天~气清 The sky is clear and bright. 2 loud and clear

朗读(讀) lǎngdú (动) read aloud; read loudly and clearly

朗朗 lǎnglǎng I (象) the sound of reading aloud II (形) bright; light

朗诵 lǎngsòng (动) read aloud with expression; recite; declaim

浪 làng I (名) wave; billow; breaker: 海~ waves of the sea. 声~ sound wave II (形) unrestrained; dissolute: 放~ dissolute; dissipated

浪潮 làngcháo (名) tide; wave: 罢工~ a wave of strikes

浪荡(蕩) làngdàng I (动) loiter about; loaf about II (形) dissolute; dissipated

浪费 làngfèi (动) waste; squander: ~资源 squander resources

浪花 lànghuā (名) spray; spindrift

浪迹 làngjì (动) roam (or wander) about: ~天涯 rove all over the world

浪漫 làngmàn (形) 1 rakish; sluttish 2 romantic

浪头(頭) làngtou (名)〈口〉 1 wave 2 trend: 赶~ follow the trend (or the fashion)

浪子 làngzǐ (名) prodigal; loafer; wastrel: ~回头. The prodigal has returned.

捞(撈) lāo (动) 1 drag for; dredge up; fish for; scoop up from the water: ~水草 dredge up water plants. ~鱼 net fish; catch fish 2 get by improper means; gain: 趁机~一把 seek personal gains out of a messy situation; fish in troubled waters

捞稻草 lāo dàocǎo try to take advantage of sth.; make capital of sth.

捞取 lāoqǔ (动) fish for; gain: ~政治资本 fish for political capital; seek political advantage

捞油水 lāo yóushui get a squeeze

牢 láo I (名) 1〈书〉 pen; fold: 豕~ pigpen 2 sacrifice: 太~ sacrificial ox 3 prison; jail: 坐~ be in prison; serve time II (形) firm; fast; durable: ~不可破 unbreakable; indestructible

牢房 láofáng (名) prison cell

牢固 láogù (形) firm; secure: ~的根基 solid foundations

牢记 láojì (动) keep firmly in mind; remember well: 我将永远~你的教诲. I will always bear your instructions in mind.

牢靠 láokào (形) 1 firm; strong; sturdy: 这堵墙不太~. This wall is not strong enough. 2 dependable; reliable: 办事~ dependable (or reliable) in handling affairs

牢笼(籠) láolóng (名) 1 cage; bonds 2 trap; snare: 陷入~ fall into a trap; be entrapped

牢骚 láosāo (名) discontent; grievance; complaint: 大发~ give vent to peevish complaints

劳(勞) láo I (名) 1 work; labour: ~绩 fruits of hard work. 多~多得 more pay for more work **2** fatigue; toil: 积～成疾 break down or fall ill from overwork **3** meritorious deed; service: 汗马之～ distinction won in battle; war exploits II (动) **1** put sb. to the trouble of: ～你帮个忙. Could you give me a hand? **2** express one's appreciation (to the performer of a task); reward: ～军 bring greetings and gifts to army units

劳保 láobǎo (名)〈简〉(劳动保险) labour insurance

劳动(動) láodòng (动) **1** work; labour: 不～者不得食. He who does not work, neither shall he eat. **2** do physical labour; do manual labour: ～保护 labour protection. ～模范 model worker. ～强度 labour intensity. ～生产率 labour productivity

劳动(動)力 láodònglì (名) **1** workforce; labour: ～不足 short of manpower; short-handed **2** capacity for physical labour: 丧失～ lose one's ability to work; be disabled **3** able-bodied person

劳顿 láodùn (形)〈书〉fatigued; wearied: 旅途～ fatigued by a long journey; travel-worn

劳改 láogǎi (名) reform through labour

劳驾 láojià (动)〈套〉[polite formula used when one requests people to make way, etc.] excuse me; may I trouble you: ～替我带个信儿. Would you mind taking a message for me?

劳苦 láokǔ (名) toil; hard work: 不辞～ spare no pains. ～大众 toiling masses; labouring people

劳累 láolèi (形) tired; run-down; overworked

劳力 láolì (名) labour; labour force: 合理安排～ rational allocation of labour

劳民伤(傷)财 láomín-shāngcái exhaust the people and drain the treasury

劳神 láoshén (动) be a tax on one's mind; trouble; bother

劳务(務) láowù (名) labour service: ～费 service charge. ～输出 export of labour services. ～人员 contract workers

劳逸结合 láo-yì jiéhé strike a proper balance between work and rest

劳资 láo-zī (名) labour and capital: ～关系 industrial relations. ～纠纷 labour dispute

痨(癆) láo (名) consumptive disease; tuberculosis; consumption: 肺～ pulmonary tuberculosis. ～病 tuberculosis; TB

老 lǎo I (形) **1** old; aged: ～农 old farmer. 活到～,学到～. You will never cease to learn as long as you live. **2** of long standing; old: ～朋友 an old friend. ～战士 a veteran fighter. ～习惯 old habits **3** outdated: ～式 old-fashioned; outmoded; outdated **4** tough; overgrown: 肉太～. The meat is too tough. 菠菜～了. The spinach is overgrown. II (副) **1** for a long time: ～没见你啊. I haven't seen you for ages. **2** always (doing sth.): ～惦记着这件事. He couldn't get his mind off the matter. **3** very: ～早 very early. ～远 far away III (名) old people: 敬～ respect for the aged IV [prefix placed before surnames, ordinal numbers among brothers and sisters, certain animals and plants]: ～王 Lao Wang. ～二 the second child or brother. ～玉米 maize

老百姓 lǎobǎixìng (名)〈口〉common people; ordinary people; civilians

老板 lǎobǎn (名) boss; shopkeeper; proprietor

老伴儿(兒) lǎobànr (名)〈口〉(of an old married couple) husband or wife: 我的～ my old man or woman

老本 lǎoběn (名) principal; capital: 把～输光 lose one's last stakes

老成 lǎochéng (形) experienced; steady: 少年～ young but steady; old head on young shoulders. ～持重 experienced and prudent

老大 lǎodà I (形)〈书〉old II (名) **1** eldest child (in a family) **2** master of a sailing vessel III (副) greatly; very: 心中～不高兴 feel very displeased

老大难(難) lǎodànán (名) long-standing difficult problem; old thorny problem

老大娘 lǎodàniáng (名) [often used to address a stranger senior in age] aunty; granny

老大爷(爺) lǎodàye (名) [often used to address a stranger senior in age] uncle; grandpa

老弟 lǎodì (名) [a familiar form of address to a man much younger than oneself] young man; young fellow; my boy

老调 lǎodiào (名) hackneyed theme; plati-

L

tude: ～重弹 play the same old tune
老干(幹)部 lǎogànbù (名) veteran cadre
老公 lǎogōng (名) husband
老汉(漢) lǎohàn (名) old man
老好人 lǎohǎorén (名) a person who is good-natured but indifferent to matters of principle; one who avoids giving offence to anybody
老狐狸 lǎohúli (名) 1 old fox 2 crafty scoundrel
老虎 lǎohǔ (名) tiger
老虎机(機) lǎohǔjī (名) slot machine (for gambling)
老化 lǎohuà (名) ageing
老话 lǎohuà (名) 1 old saying; saying; adage 2 remarks about the old days
老奸巨猾 lǎojiān-jùhuá a crafty old scoundrel; a wily old fox
老练(練) lǎoliàn (形) seasoned; experienced: 她办事很～. She is experienced and does a good job of work.

L

老龄 lǎolíng (名) ageing: ～问题 the problem of ageing
老路 lǎolù (名) old road; beaten track
老马(馬)识(識)途 lǎomǎ shí tú an old hand is always a good guide
老迈(邁) lǎomài (形) aged; senile
老年 lǎonián (名) old age: ～人 old people; the aged. ～医学 gerontology
老婆 lǎopo (名)〈口〉wife
老气(氣)横秋 lǎoqì héngqiū 1 arrogant on account of one's seniority 2 apathetic
老前辈 lǎoqiánbèi (名) senior person in one's profession
老人家 lǎorenjia (名) 1 a respectful form of address for an old person: 您～今年多大年纪了? How old are you, granddad (grandma)? 2 parent: 你们～今年快七十岁了吧? Your parents are getting on for seventy, aren't they?
老生常谈 lǎoshēng chángtán shopworn phrases; platitudes
老师(師) lǎoshī (名) teacher
老师(師)傅 lǎoshīfu (名) master craftsman; experienced worker
老实(實) lǎoshi (形) 1 honest; frank: 忠诚～ loyal and honest. ～说,我很不赞成这个意见. Honestly, I don't like the idea at all. 2 well-behaved; good: 这孩子可～了. The child is really well behaved. ～巴交 soft-spoken and timid 3 simpleminded; naive; easily taken in
老手 lǎoshǒu (名) old hand; veteran: 开车的～ an old hand in driving; a good driver
老鼠 lǎoshǔ (名) mouse; rat
老太太 lǎo tàitai (名) old lady; venerable Madam
老态(態)龙(龍)钟(鍾) lǎotài lóngzhōng senile; decrepit
老头(頭)儿(兒) lǎotóur (名) old man; old chap
老外 lǎowài (名) foreigner
老顽固 lǎowángu (名) old stick-in-the-mud; diehard; old fogey
老乡(鄉) lǎoxiāng (名) fellow-townsman; fellow-villager
老小 lǎo-xiǎo (名) old people and children; one's family dependants: 一家～ the whole family
老羞成怒 lǎo xiū chéng nù be shamed into anger
老朽 lǎoxiǔ (形) decrepit and behind the times
老爷(爺) lǎoye (名) 1 master; bureaucrat; overlord: 做官当～ act as "overlord". ～作风 bureaucratic style of work 2 (maternal) grandfather; grandpa
老鹰 lǎoyīng (名) eagle; hawk
老于(於)世故 lǎoyú shìgù experienced in the ways of society; worldly-wise
老丈人 lǎozhàngren (名) father-in-law
老账(賬) lǎozhàng (名) old debts; longstanding debts: 翻～ bring up old scores
老子 lǎozi (名) 1 father 2 I, your father (said in anger to show disrespect for sb.)

佬 lǎo (名) man; guy; fellow: 阔～ a rich guy

姥 lǎo

姥姥 lǎolao (名) (maternal) grandmother; grandma

涝(澇) lào (名) waterlogging: 防～ prevent waterlogging. 排～ drain waterlogged fields

烙 lào (动) 1 iron: ～衣服 iron clothes 2 bake in a pan: ～两张饼 bake a couple of cakes
烙饼 làobǐng (名) a kind of pancake
烙印 làoyìn (名) brand: 带有不少封建思想的～ bear the stamp of feudal ideology

酪 lào (名) 1 junket 2 thick fruit juice; fruit jelly

乐(樂) lè I (形) happy; cheerful; joyful: ～不可

支 be overjoyed II (动) **1** be glad to; find pleasure in; enjoy: ～此不疲 always enjoy it **2** laugh; be amused: 你～什么呀? What are you laughing at? *or* What's the joke? III (名) joy: 助人为～ find pleasure in helping others
see also yuè

乐得 lèdé (动) readily take the opportunity to; be only too glad to: 既然如此,我们～先听听别人的意见. In that case, we'll be only too glad to hear what they have to say first.

乐观(觀) lèguān (形) optimistic; hopeful; sanguine: ～的看法 an optimistic view. 对前途很～ be optimistic about the future. ～主义 optimism. ～主义者 optimist

乐极(極)生悲 lè jí shēng bēi extreme joy begets sorrow

乐趣 lèqù (名) delight; pleasure; joy: 生活的～ joys of life; spices of life

乐天 lètiān (形) carefree; happy-go-lucky: ～派 optimist

乐意 lèyì I (动) be willing to; be ready to: ～帮忙 be willing and ready to help II (形) pleased; happy: 他看来有点不～. He looked somewhat displeased.

乐园(園) lèyuán (名) paradise: 人间～ paradise on earth. 儿童～ children's playground

乐滋滋 lèzīzī (形)〈口〉contented; pleased: 他听了别人夸奖他心里总是～的. He is always highly pleased to hear people praise him.

勒

lè (动) **1** stop: ～马 rein in **2** force; coerce: ～交 force sb. to hand sth. over **3**〈书〉carve; engrave: ～碑 carve on a stone tablet
see also lēi

勒逼 lèbī (动) force; coerce

勒令 lèlìng (动) compel (by legal authority); order

勒索 lèsuǒ (动) extort; blackmail: ～钱财 extort money from sb.

了

le (助) **1** [used after a verb or adjective to indicate completion of work or change]: 我们提前完成～任务. We have completed the task ahead of schedule. 水位已降低～两米. The water level has fallen by two metres. **2** [modal particle placed at the end of a sentence to indicate a change]: 他们现在是外交部的干部～. They are officials at the Foreign Ministry now. **3** [used at the end of a sentence to show a past event]: 上星期天,他带孩子上动物园～. Last Sunday, he took his children to the zoo. **4** [used at the end of an imperative sentence to indicate advice]: 别说话～! Stop talking! 走～, 走～! Hurry up and let's go!
see also liǎo

勒

lēi (动) tie or strap sth. tight
see also lè

雷

léi (名) **1** thunder **2** mine: 布～ lay mines. 扫～ sweep mines

雷达(達) léidá (名) radar

雷电(電) léidiàn (名) thunder and lightning

雷动(動) léidòng (形) thunderous: 掌声～ thunderous applause

雷管 léiguǎn (名) detonator; detonating cap; blasting cap; primer

雷厉(厲)风(風)行 léilì-fēngxíng act vigorously and speedily

雷声(聲) léishēng (名) thunderclap; thunder: ～隆隆 the rumble (or roll) of thunder. ～大,雨点小 loud thunder but small raindrops; much has been said but little is accomplished

雷霆 léitíng (名) **1** thunderclap; thunderbolt **2** tremendous power; wrath: 大发～ fly into a rage. ～万钧 as powerful as a thunderbolt

雷同 léitóng (形) **1** echoing other people's ideas **2** (of writing a speech) duplicate; identical

雷雨 léiyǔ (名) thunderstorm

擂

léi (动) hit; beat: ～了一拳 give sb. a punch
see also lèi

累(纍)

léi
see also lěi, lèi

累累 léiléi (形) clusters of; heaps of: 果实～ heavily laden with fruit

累赘 léizhui I (形) **1** burdensome; cumbersome **2** wordy; verbose II (名) encumbrance; burden; nuisance

蕾

lěi (名) flower bud; bud

蕾铃 lěilíng (名) cotton buds and bolls

磊

lěi

磊落 lěiluò (形) open and upright: 光明～ open and above-board

L

累 lěi I (动) 1 pile up; accumulate: 日积月～ accumulate gradually 2 involve: 连～ involve; implicate; get sb. into trouble II (形) continuous; repeated ～戒不改 refuse to mend one's ways despite repeated warnings. 长篇～牍 voluminous
see also léi; lèi

累积(積) lěijī (动) accumulate

累及 lěijí (动) implicate; involve: ～无辜 involve innocent people

累计 lěijì I (动) add up II (名) accumulative total; grand total

累进(進) lěijìn (名) progression: ～税 progressive tax; progressive taxation

累累 lěilěi I (副) again and again; many times II (形) innumerable; countless: 罪行～ have committed numerous crimes

累卵 lěiluǎn (名) a stack of eggs — liable to collapse any moment; precarious: 危如～ in an extremely precarious situation

L

垒(壘) lěi I (动) build by piling up bricks, stones, earth, etc.: ～一道墙 build a wall II (名) rampart

泪(淚) lèi (名) tear; teardrop

泪痕 lèihén (名) tear stains

泪水 lèishuǐ (名) tear; teardrop

泪珠 lèizhū (名) teardrop

类(類) lèi I (名) kind; type; class; category: 同～ be of a kind; belong to the same category. 物以～聚. Birds of a feather flock together. II (动) resemble; be similar to: 画虎不成反～犬 try to draw a tiger and end up with the likeness of a dog

类比 lèibǐ (名) analogy: 对两件事进行～ draw an analogy between the two things

类别 lèibié (名) classification; category: 文件的～ classification of documents

类人猿 lèirényuán (名) anthropoid (ape)

类似 lèisì (形) similar; analogous: 经历相～ of similar background

类推 lèituī (动) reason by analogy: 其余～. The rest can be deduced similarly.

类型 lèixíng (名) type

擂 lèi
see also léi

擂台(臺) lèitái (名) ring (for martial contests); arena: 摆～ give an open challenge; throw down the gauntlet. 打～ take up the challenge; pick up the gauntlet

累 lèi I (形) tired; fatigued; weary: ～极了 tired out; worn out; exhausted II (动) 1 tire; strain; wear out 2 work hard; toil: 你～了一天, 该休息了. You should have a break, as you have been working all day.
see also léi; lěi

肋 lèi (名) 1 rib: ～骨 rib 2 costal region: 两～ both sides of the chest

肋膜 lèimó (名) pleura: ～炎 pleurisy

棱 léng (名) 1 arris; edge: 桌子～儿 edges of a table 2 corrugation; ridge: 瓦～ ridges of a tiled roof

棱角 léngjiǎo (名) 1 edges 2 sharp-wittedness

冷 lěng (形) 1 cold: ～天 the cold season; cold days. 你～不～? Are you cold? 2 cold in manner 3 unfrequented; deserted; out-of-the-way 4 strange; rare: ～僻的词 rare or unfamiliar word

冷冰冰 lěngbīngbīng (形) ice-cold; icy; frosty: ～的态度 frosty manner

冷不防 lěngbufáng unexpectedly; suddenly

冷餐会(會) lěngcānhuì (名) buffet reception

冷藏 lěngcáng (动) refrigerate; keep in cold storage: ～库 cold storage; freezer. ～箱 refrigerator; fridge

冷场(場) lěngchǎng (名) 1 awkward situation on the stage resulting from an actor entering late or forgetting his lines 2 awkward silence at a meeting

冷嘲热(熱)讽 lěngcháo-rèfěng characterized by biting irony and sarcasm; jeering and sneering

冷淡 lěngdàn I (形) 1 cheerless; desolate 2 cold; indifferent: 反应～ a cold response II (动) treat coldly; cold-shoulder; slight

冷冻(凍) lěngdòng (动) freeze: ～机 freezer

冷汗 lěnghàn (名) cold sweat: 出～ be in a cold sweat; break out in a cold sweat

冷荤 lěnghūn (名) cold meat; cold buffet

冷箭 lěngjiàn (名) sniper's shot; a stab in the back: 放～ make a sneak attack

冷静 lěngjìng (形) sober; calm: 头脑～ sober-minded; level-headed; cool-headed. 保持～ keep calm and composed

冷酷 lěngkù (形) unfeeling; hard-hearted: ～无情 ruthless; merciless; cold-blooded

冷落 lěngluò I (形) unfrequented; desolate

II (动) treat coldly; cold-shoulder; leave out in the cold: ～某人 leave sb. out in the cold

冷门(門) lěngmén (名) 1 a profession, trade or branch of learning that receives little attention: 过去这门学科是个～. This discipline used to attract very little notice in the past. 2 an unexpected winner; dark horse: 那次比赛出了个～. The contest produced an unexpected winner.

冷漠 lěngmò (形) cold and detached; unconcerned; indifferent

冷暖 lěngnuǎn (名) changes in temperature: 注意～ be careful about changes of weather; take care of oneself. 关心群众的～ be concerned with the well-being of the masses

冷盘(盤) lěngpán (名) cold dish; hors d'oeuvres

冷僻 lěngpì (形) 1 deserted; out-of-the-way 2 rare; unfamiliar: ～的字眼 rarely used words

冷枪(槍) lěngqiāng (名) sniper's shot

冷清 lěngqīng (形) cold and cheerless; desolate; lonely; deserted

冷却 lěngquè (动) cool off: ～系统 cooling system

冷水 lěngshuǐ (名) 1 cold water: 泼～ pour cold water on; dampen sb.'s enthusiasm. ～浴 cold bath 2 unboiled water

冷飕飕 lěngsōusōu (形) chilly; chilling

冷笑 lěngxiào (动) sneer; laugh scornfully

冷言冷语 lěngyán-lěngyǔ sarcastic or ironical remarks

冷眼 lěngyǎn (名) 1 cool detachment: ～旁观 look on with a cold eye 2 cold shoulder: ～相待 give the cold shoulder to sb.

冷饮 lěngyǐn (名) cold drinks

冷遇 lěngyù (名) cold reception; cold shoulder: 遭到～ be given the cold shoulder; be left out in the cold

冷战(戰) lěngzhàn (名) cold war

冷战(戰) lěngzhan (动) 〈口〉 shiver: 打～ shiver with cold

愣

lèng (动) look distracted; be stupefied: 发～ stare blankly; look distracted. 听到这消息他～住了. He was struck dumb by the news.

离(離)

lí (动) 1 leave; part from; be away from: 她～家已经多年了. She's been away from home for many years. 2 off; away; from: 学校～火车站不远. The school is not far from the railway station. 3 without; independent of: 人～了空气就无法生存. Men cannot live without air. 发展工业～不了资金. Industry cannot develop without funds.

离别 líbié (动) part (for a long period); leave; bid farewell: 我～故乡已经两年了. It's two years since I left my home town.

离婚 líhūn (动) divorce

离间 líjiàn (动) sow discord; drive a wedge between; set one party against another

离境 líjìng (动) leave a country or place: ～签证 exit visa. ～许可证 exit permit

离奇 líqí (形) odd; fantastic; bizarre: ～的故事 a fantastic story. ～的地方 a bizarre place

离任 lírèn (动) leave one's post: ～回国 leave one's post for home. 即将～的总统 the outgoing president

离散 lísàn (动) be separated from one another

离题 lítí (动) digress from the subject; stray from the point: 发言不要～. Please do not digress from the subject.

离休 líxiū (动) retire on full pay

离职(職) lízhí (动) 1 leave one's job temporarily for specific purposes 2 leave office; quit a job: ～金 severance pay

篱(籬)

lí (名) hedge; fence: 竹～茅舍 thatched cottage with bamboo fence

篱笆 líba (名) bamboo or twig fence

厘

lí I (量) 1 *li*, a unit of length (= 1/3 millimetre) 2 *li*, a unit of weight (= 0.05 grams) 3 *li*, a unit of area (= 0.666 square metres 4 *li*, one thousandth of a *yuan* 5 *li*, a unit of monthly interest rate (= 0.1%): 月利率二～七 a monthly interest of 0.27% 6 *li*, a unit of annual interest rate (= 1%): 年利率三～ an annual interest of 3% II (名) a fraction; the least: 分～不差 without the slightest error; just right

厘米 límǐ (量) centimetre

罹

lí (动) suffer from; meet with: ～病 fall ill

罹难(難) línàn (动) 〈书〉 1 die in a disaster or an accident 2 be murdered

梨

lí (名) pear.

犁 lí I (名) plough II (动) work with a plough; plough: 地已～了两遍. The fields have been ploughed twice.

黎 lí (名)〈书〉multitude; host: ～庶 the multitude

黎民 límín (名)〈书〉the common people; the multitude

黎明 límíng (名) dawn; daybreak

蠡 lí (名)〈书〉**1** calabash shell serving as a dipper; dipper **2** seashell

蠡测 lícè (动)〈书〉make a superficial estimate of

礼(禮) lǐ (名) **1** ceremony; rite: 婚～ wedding ceremony. 丧～ funeral **2** courtesy; etiquette; manners: 行～ (give a) salute. 彬彬有～ refined and polite **3** gift; present: 送～ give a present; send a gift

礼拜 lǐbài (名) **1** religious service: 做～ go to church; attend a religious service. ～堂 church **2**〈口〉week: 下～ next week **3**〈口〉day of the week: 今天～几? What day is it today? **4**〈口〉Sunday: 今儿个～. Today is Sunday. ～天 Sunday

礼宾(賓) lǐbīn (名) protocol; official etiquette: ～顺序 protocol order; protocol precedence. ～规则 protocol rules

礼宾(賓)司 Lǐbīnsī (名) the Protocol Department

礼服 lǐfú (名) ceremonial robe or dress; full dress; formal dress

礼花 lǐhuā (名) fireworks display

礼教 lǐjiào (名) the Confucian or feudal ethical code

礼节(節) lǐjié (名) courtesy; etiquette; protocol; ceremony: ～性拜访 a courtesy call

礼貌 lǐmào (名) courtesy; manners: 有～ courteous; polite. 没～ have no manners

礼炮 lǐpào (名) salvo; (gun) salute

礼品 lǐpǐn (名) gift; present: ～部 gift and souvenir department or counter (of a shop)

礼让(讓) lǐràng (动) give precedence to sb. out of courtesy or thoughtfulness

礼尚往来(來) lǐ shàng wǎng-lái **1** courtesy demands reciprocity **2** treat a man the way he treats you; pay a man back in his own coin

礼堂 lǐtáng (名) assembly hall; auditorium

礼物 lǐwù (名) gift; present

礼仪(儀) lǐyí (名) etiquette; rite; protocol

礼遇 lǐyù (名) courteous reception or treatment: 受到隆重的～ be given red-carpet treatment

李 lǐ (名) (～子) plum

里 lǐ I (名) **1** neighbourhood: 邻～ people of the neighbourhood **2**〈书〉home town; native place: 返～ return to one's home town II (量) *li*, a Chinese unit of length (＝1/2 kilometre)

里(裏) lǐ (名) **1** lining: 衣～儿 the lining of a garment **2** inside: ～间 inner room

里边(邊) lǐbian (名) inside; in; within: 这件事～有问题. There is something wrong with the matter.

里程 lǐchéng (名) **1** distance of a journey **2** course of development; course

里程碑 lǐchéngbēi (名) milestone: 历史的～ a milestone in history

里脊 lǐji (名) tenderloin

里弄 lǐlòng (名) lanes and alleys; neighbourhood

里手 lǐshǒu (名) old hand; expert

里头(頭) lǐtou (名) inside; interior

里应(應)外合 lǐ yìng wài hé strike from both within and without

里子 lǐzi (名) lining

里(裏) li **1** in; inside: 屋～ in the room **2** [used after 这,那,哪 to indicate direction of place]: 这～ here. 那～ there

理 lǐ I (名) **1** texture; grain (in wood, skin, etc.): 纹～ texture; grain **2** reason; logic; truth: 合～ reasonable **3** natural science, esp. physics: ～工科 science and engineering II (动) **1** manage; run: 当家～事 run the household; manage domestic affairs **2** put in order; tidy up: ～发 have a haircut. ～一～书籍 put the books in order **3** [often used in negative sentences] pay attention to; acknowledge: 置之不～ dismiss sth. as of no consequence

理财 lǐcái (动) manage financial matters

理睬 lǐcǎi (动) [often used in negative sentences] pay attention to; show interest in: 不予～ turn a deaf ear to; pay no heed to; ignore

理会(會) lǐhuì (动) **1** understand; comprehend **2** [often used in negative sentences] take notice of; pay attention to: 大家说了半天,他也没有～. He didn't

L

seem to pay any attention while people kept talking to him all the time.

理解 lǐjiě（动）understand; comprehend：我们能～你们的困难. We understand your difficulty. ～力 comprehension

理科 lǐkē（名）**1** science faculty **2** natural sciences

理亏(虧) lǐkuī（动）be in the wrong

理疗(療) lǐliáo（名）physiotherapy

理论(論) lǐlùn（名）theory：～与实践 theory and practice. 在～上 in theory; theoretically

理念 lǐniàn（名）notion; concept; principle

理赔 lǐpéi（动）settle claims：保险～ settle insurance claims

理屈词穷(窮) lǐqū-cíqióng defeated in argument and so unable to defend oneself any longer; unable to advance any further arguments

理事 lǐshì（名）member of a council; director：常任～国 permanent member state of a council. ～会 council; board of directors

理顺 lǐshùn（动）straighten out; bring into better balance：～各方面的关系 straighten out relations between various sectors

理所当(當)然 lǐ suǒ dāngrán as a matter of course; naturally

理想 lǐxiǎng（名）ideal; dream：～主义者 idealist. 最～的方案 the most ideal plan. 她实现了当演员的～. Her dream of becoming an actress finally came true.

理性 lǐxìng（名）reason：失去～ lose one's reason

理由 lǐyóu（名）reason; ground; argument：～充足 fully justifiable. 毫无～ not justified. 他的抱怨完全没有～. His complaint is totally groundless. 我们有充分的～相信他. We have every reason to believe him.

理直气(氣)壮(壯) lǐzhí-qìzhuàng with perfect assurance：～地谈话 speak freely with great confidence

理智 lǐzhì（名）reason; intellect：丧失～ lose one's senses

俚

lǐ（形）vulgar

俚俗 lǐsú（形）coarse; unrefined; uncultured

俚语 lǐyǔ（名）slang

鲤

lǐ（名）carp

立

lì I（动）**1** stand：起～ stand up **2** erect; set up：～碑 erect a monument **3** found; establish; set up：～国 found a state. ～合同 sign a contract. ～业 establish a business **4** exist; live：自～ be on one's feet; live on one's own II（形）upright; erect; vertical III（副）immediately; instantaneously：～见功效 produce immediate results

立案 lì'àn（动）**1** register; put on record **2** place a case on file for investigation and prosecution

立场(場) lìchǎng（名）position; stand; standpoint：得有个～ must take a stand. ～坚定 be steadfast in one's stand; take a firm position

立法 lìfǎ（动）legislate; make laws：～机关 legislative body; legislature. ～权 legislative power

立方 lìfāng I（名）**1** cube：三的～ the cube of 3; 3^3 **2**〈简〉(立方体) cube II（量）cubic metre; stere：一～土 one cubic metre of earth

立竿见(見)影 lì gān jiàn yǐng get instant results

立功 lìgōng（动）render meritorious service; win honour; make contributions：～奖状 certificate of merit

立即 lìjí（副）immediately; at once：～行动 take immediate action. ～答复 give a prompt reply

立交桥(橋) lìjiāoqiáo（名）overpass; flyover; motorway interchange

立刻 lìkè（副）immediately; at once; right away：～出发 set off at once

立论(論) lìlùn I（动）set forth one's views; present one's arguments II（名）argument; position

立体(體) lìtǐ（形）**1** three-dimensional; stereoscopic：～感 three-dimensional effect. ～交叉桥 overpass; flyover. ～声 stereophony; stereo **2** (in geometry) solid：～几何 solid geometry

立宪(憲) lìxiàn（名）constitutionalism：君主～ constitutional monarchy. ～政体 constitutional government; constitutionalism

立意 lìyì I（动）be determined; make up one's mind II（名）conception; approach：这部电影～新颖. This film is fresh in its approach.

立正 lìzhèng（动）stand at attention：～! Attention!

L

立志 lìzhì (动) resolve; be determined: ～改革 be determined to carry out reforms

立足 lìzú (动) 1 have a foothold somewhere: 获得～之地 gain a footing 2 base oneself upon: ～于自立更生 be based on self-reliance

立足点(點) lìzúdiǎn (名) 1 foothold; footing 2 standpoint; stand

粒 lì I (名) grain; granule; pellet: 砂～ grains of sand II (量) [for grain-like things] 一～米 a grain of rice. 三～子弹 three bullets. 每次服五～ 5 pills each time

粒子 lìzǐ (名) particle: 带电～ charged particle. 高能～ energetic particle

莅(蒞) lì (动)〈书〉arrive; be present: ～会 be present at a meeting

莅临(臨) lìlín (动)〈书〉arrive; be present: 敬请～ request the honour of your presence

笠 lì (名) a large bamboo or straw hat with a conical crown and broad brim

戾 lì I (名) crime; sin: 罪～ guilt, crime II (形) perverse; unreasonable: 乖～ cantankerous; perverse

唳 lì〈书〉cry (of a crane)

丽(麗) lì (形) beautiful: 风和日～ the weather is glorious; a beautiful day with a gentle breeze blowing

俪(儷) lì (名) pair; couple: 伉～ husband and wife; married couple

栗 lì (名)(～子) chestnut

栗(慄) lì (动) tremble; shudder: 不寒而～ tremble with fear

吏 lì (名) official; mandarin: 贪官污～ corrupt officials

厉(厲) lì (形) 1 strict; rigorous: ～禁 strictly prohibit 2 stern; severe: ～声 in a stern voice

厉兵秣马(馬) lìbīng-mòmǎ make ready for battle; maintain combat readiness

厉行 lìxíng (动) strictly enforce; rigorously enforce; make great efforts to carry out: ～节约 practise strict economy

砺(礪) lì〈书〉I (名) whetstone II (动) whet; sharpen

励(勵) lì (动) encourage: 奖～ reward; award. 勉～ encourage

励精图(圖)治 lì jīng tú zhì (usu. of a feudal ruler) make vigorous efforts to achieve prosperity

励志 lìzhì (动) pursue a goal with determination

利 lì I (形) 1 sharp: ～刃 a sharp sword or blade. ～爪 sharp claws 2 favourable: 有～的形势 favourable situation II (名) 1 advantage; benefit: 有～有弊. There are both advantages and disadvantages. 2 profit; interest: 连本带～ both principal and interest. ～改税 replace profit delivery with tax payments III (动) do good to; benefit: ～己～人 benefit other people as well as oneself

利弊 lì-bì (名) advantages and disadvantages; gains and losses: 权衡～ weigh the pros and cons

利害 lì-hài (名) advantages and disadvantages; gains and losses: 不计～ regardless of gains or losses. ～冲突 conflict of interest. 有～关系的一方 an interested party. 晓以～ make someone see where the advantages and disadvantages lie

利害 lìhai (形) terrible; formidable: 今年冬天冷得～. It's been terribly cold this winter. 这着棋十分～. That's a very cunning move.

利令智昏 lì lìng zhì hūn be fuddled by the desire for gain; be blinded by lust for gain

利率 lìlǜ (名) rate of interest; interest rate

利落 lìluo (形) 1 agile; nimble; dexterous: 动作～ agile 2 neat; orderly 3 settled; finished: 事情已经办～了. The matter is all settled.

利润 lìrùn (名) profit: ～留成 retain part of the profits; keep a portion of the profits

利息 lìxī (名) interest

利益 lìyì (名) interest; benefit; profit: 国家～ national interest. 个人～ personal interest. 受～的驱使 be driven by interest

利用 lìyòng (动) 1 use; utilize; make use of: ～工业废料 make use of industrial wastes 2 take advantage of; exploit: ～职权 abuse one's power. ～率 utilization ratio. ～系数 utilization coefficient

利诱 lìyòu (动) lure by promise of gain

利欲熏心 lìyù xūn xīn be obsessed with the desire of gain

痢 lì (名) dysentery

痢疾 lìji (名) dysentery：细菌性～ bacillary dysentery

例 lì I (名) 1 example; instance：举～ give an example; cite an instance. 举～说明 illustrate 2 precedent：援～ quote (or follow) a precedent. 破～ make an exception 3 case; instance 4 rule; regulation：旧～ an old rule. 不在此～ That is an exception. II (形) regular; routine

例会(會) lìhuì (名) regular meeting

例假 lìjià (名) 1 official holiday; legal holiday 2 menstrual period; period

例句 lìjù (名) illustrative sentence; model sentence; example

例如 lìrú (动) for instance; for example (e.g.); such as

例外 lìwài (名) exception：毫无～ without exception

例行公事 lìxíng gōngshì 1 routine; routine business 2 mere formality

例证 lìzhèng (名) illustration; example; case in point

例子 lìzi (名) example; case; instance

栎(櫟) lì (名) oak

砾(礫) lì (名) gravel; shingle：～石 gravel

隶(隸) lì I (动) be subordinate to; be under II (名) a person in servitude：奴～ slave

隶属(屬) lìshǔ (动) be subordinate to; be under the jurisdiction or command of; be affiliated to

力 lì I (名) 1 power; strength; ability：人～ manpower. 物～ material resources. 兵～ military strength. 能～ ability; capability. ～所能及 in one's power 2 force：磁～ magnetic force. 离心～ centrifugal force 3 physical strength：～不能支 unable to stand the strain any longer II (副) do all one can; make every effort：～戒 strictly avoid; do everything possible to avoid. ～图 try hard to; strive to

力不从(從)心 lì bù cóng xīn a case of ability falling short of one's wishes; unable to do as much as one would like to

力量 lìliang (名) 1 physical strength 2 power; force; strength：国防～ defence capability. 知识就是～. Knowledge is power.

力气(氣) lìqi (名) physical strength; effort：他很有～. He is a man of great strength.

力求 lìqiú (动) do one's best to; strive to

力学(學) lìxué (名) mechanics：航空～ aeromechanics. 波动～ wave mechanics

历(歷) lì I (动) go through undergo; experience：～尽艰辛 have gone through all kinds of hardships II (形) all previous (occasions, sessions, etc.) III (副) covering all; one by one：～试诸方，均无成效 have tried all recipes, but to no avail IV (名) (曆) calendar：阴(阳)～ lunar (solar) calendar

历程 lìchéng (名) course：回忆走过的～ recall the course one has traversed

历次 lìcì (名) all previous (occasions, etc.)

历代 lìdài (名) past dynasties

历法 lìfǎ (名) calendar

历届 lìjiè (名) all previous (sessions, governments, etc.)：～大会 all previous conferences

历来(來) lìlái (名) always; all through the ages：～主张 have consistently held. ～如此. This has always been the case.

历历在目 lìlì zài mù come clearly into view; remain fresh in one's memory

历年 lìnián (名) over the years：～的积蓄 savings over the years

历时(時) lìshí (动) last (a period of time)：～两个月的调查 the investigation which lasted two months.

历史 lìshǐ (名) history; past records：～清白 have a clean record. ～文物 historical relics. ～遗产 legacy of history; historical heritage. ～潮流 historical trend. ～人物 historical figure. 有～意义 have historical significance. ～性的大事 a historic event. 创～最高水平 hit an all-time high

历史唯物主义(義) lìshǐ wéiwù-zhǔyì historical materialism

历史唯心主义(義) lìshǐ wéixīn-zhǔyì historical idealism

历书(書) lìshū (名) almanac

沥(瀝) lì

沥青 lìqīng (名) pitch; tar; bitumen

荔 lì

荔枝 lìzhī (名) litchi

俩(倆) liǎ 〈口〉 1 two: 咱～ we two; the two of us 2 some; several: 就这么～人? Just these few people?

帘(簾) lián (名) 1 curtain: 窗～ window curtain 2 〈旧〉 flag as shop sign: 酒～ wine shop sign

廉 lián (形) 1 honest 2 cheap, inexpensive: 价～物美 (of goods in a shop) cheap but good

廉耻 liánchǐ (名) sense of shame

廉价(價) liánjià (形) low-priced; cheap: ～出售 sell at a low price

廉洁(潔) liánjié (形) honest: ～奉公 be upright and honest in performing official duties

廉政 liánzhèng (名) honest and clean government

镰 lián (名) sickle: ～刀 sickle

L

怜(憐) lián (动) pity; sympathize with: 同病相～. Fellow sufferers sympathize with each other.

怜悯 liánmǐn (动) pity; take pity on

怜惜 liánxī (动) have pity on

联(聯) lián I (动) unite; join; relate: ～产责任制 output-related responsibility system II (名) antithetical couplet: 春～ Spring Festival couplet

联邦 liánbāng (名) federation; commonwealth: ～共和国 federal republic. ～调查局 the (U. S.) Federal Bureau of Investigation (FBI). 英～ the British Commonwealth of Nations

联播 liánbō (名) radio hook-up: 新闻～ news hook-up

联大 Liándà (名) 〈简〉 (联合国大会) the United Nations General Assembly

联防 liánfáng (名) joint defence

联合 liánhé I (动) unite; ally II (名) alliance; union III (形) joint; combined: ～政府 coalition government. ～声明 joint communiqué. ～收割机 combine harvester. ～举办 jointly organize or sponsor. ～承包工程 joint contract projects

联合国(國) Liánhéguó (名) the United Nations (U. N.): ～安全理事会 the United Nations Security Council. ～大会 the United Nations General Assembly. ～秘书处 the United Nations Secretariat. ～宪章 the United Nations Charter

联合会(會) liánhéhuì (名) federation; union: 妇女～ women's federation. 学生～ students' union

联欢(歡) liánhuān (动) have a get-together (or a party)

联结 liánjié (动) join; connect; tie

联络 liánluò I (动) get in touch with II (名) contact; liaison: ～处 liaison office

联盟 liánméng (名) alliance; league; coalition: 工农～ worker-peasant alliance

联名 liánmíng (形) jointly signed: ～上书 submit a joint letter

联赛 liánsài (名) league matches: 足球～ league football matches

联网 liánwǎng (名) connected network; links

联系(係) liánxì I (动) contact; get in touch with; link: 请你去跟他～. Will you please contact him? 理论～实际 apply theory to reality II (名) contact; tie; connection: 保持～ keep in contact with; be in touch

联想 liánxiǎng (动) associate sth. with (in the mind)

联运(運) liányùn (名) through transport: ～票 through ticket

连 lián I (动) link; join; connect: 血肉相～ be bound together like one's own flesh and blood. 这几句话～不起来. These sentences are disconnected. II (名) (of army) company III (副) in succession: ～年丰收 reap rich harvests for many years running. ～唱了十支歌 sing ten songs one after another IV (介) 1 even: 这事～我妈都不知道, 别说我了! Even my mother is in the dark about it, to say nothing of me! 我～想都没有想过. I didn't even give it a thought. 2 including: 这个办公室～我共有十人. There are ten people in this office including me. 这本字典～邮费共十元. This dictionary is 10 *yuan*, postage included.

连词 liáncí (名) conjunction

连…带(帶)… lián…dài… 1 [indicating two nearly simultaneous actions] and; while: 连蹦带跳 hopping and skipping; vivacious 2 as well as; and: 我们村连老带小共100人左右. There are altogether some 100 people in our village, including the old people and children.

连贯 liánguàn I (动) link up; connect II

(形) coherent; consistent: 文章写得很不～. This article is badly organized. ～性 coherence; continuity

连环(環) liánhuán (名) chain of rings: ～画 picture-story book

连接 liánjiē (动) join; link

连襟 liánjīn (名) husbands of sisters

连累 liánlěi (动) get sb. into trouble: 受～ be implicated

连忙 liánmáng (副) promptly; at once: 他～道歉. He hastened to apologize.

连绵 liánmián (形) continuous; unbroken; uninterrupted: 雨雪～. It has been raining and snowing for days on end.

连年 liánnián (名) in successive or consecutive years; for years running

连篇 liánpiān (形) throughout a piece of writing: 白字～ full of malapropisms (or wrongly written words)

连任 liánrèn (动) be reappointed or re-elected consecutively: ～两届总统 be elected president for two consecutive terms

连日 liánrì (名) for days on end

连锁 liánsuǒ (名) linkage; chain: ～店 chain store. ～反应 chain reaction

连天 liántiān (形) 1 reaching (or scraping) the sky: 湖水～. The water and the sky seem to meet. 2 incessantly: 叫苦～ incessantly complain

连同 liántóng (介) together with; including

连续(續) liánxù (副) continuously; successively; in a row: ～下了五天雨. It rained for five days running. 事故～发生. Accidents occurred one after another.

连续(續)剧 liánxùjù (名) serial drama; serial: 电视～ TV serial; soap opera on TV

连夜 liányè (副) the same night; that very night: 他～赶回了家. He rushed back home that very night.

连衣裙 liányīqún (名) a woman's dress

连载 liánzǎi (动) publish in serial form

连长(長) liánzhǎng (名) company commander

涟 lián (名) ripples

涟漪 liányī (名) ripples

莲 lián (名) lotus

莲花 liánhuā (名) lotus flower; lotus

莲蓬 liánpeng (名) seedpod of the lotus

莲子 liánzǐ (名) lotus seed

鲢 lián (名) silver carp

敛(斂) liǎn (动) 1 hold back; restrain: ～容 assume a serious expression 2 collect: 横征暴～ extort heavy taxes and levies

脸(臉) liǎn (名) face: 笑～ a smiling face. 丢～ lose face. 不要～ shameless. 没～见人 too ashamed to face anyone. 居然有～说这种话 have the cheek to say such things

脸蛋儿(兒) liǎndànr (名) (usu. children's) cheeks; face: 粉红色的小～多可爱! What lovely little rosy cheeks!

脸红 liǎnhóng (动) 1 blush with shame; blush 2 flush with anger

脸颊(頰) liǎnjiá (名) cheeks; face

脸面 liǎnmiàn (名) 1 face 2 self-respect; sb.'s feelings; face: 看在我的～上 for my sake. 不顾～ have no thought for one's dignity. 丢了～ have lost face

脸盘(盤)儿(兒) liǎnpánr (名) face

脸皮 liǎnpí (名) face; cheek: 厚～ thick-skinned; shameless. ～薄 thin-skinned; sensitive

脸谱 liǎnpǔ (名) types of facial make-up in Beijing operas

脸色 liǎnsè (名) 1 look; complexion: ～苍白 look pale 2 facial expression: ～严厉 look stern. 看他的～我就知道他很高兴. I can see from the expression on his face that he is pleased.

脸型 liǎnxíng (名) the shape of one's face; facial features: 圆～ a full (or round) face

恋(戀) liàn (动) love; feel attached to: 初～ first love. ～家 reluctant to be away from home

恋爱(愛) liàn'ài (动) love; be in love

恋恋不舍(捨) liànliàn bù shě be reluctant to part with

炼(煉) liàn (动) smelt; refine

炼钢(鋼) liàngāng (名) steel-making

炼乳 liànrǔ (名) condensed milk

炼铁(鐵) liàntiě (名) iron-smelting

炼油 liànyóu (名) oil refining

练(練) liàn I (动) practise; train; drill: ～嗓子 practise singing II (形) experienced: 老～ experienced and assured

练兵 liànbīng (名) troop training: ～场 drill ground

L

练达(達) liàndá (形) experienced and worldly-wise

练功 liàngōng (动) do exercises in gymnastics, wushu, acrobatics, etc; practise one's skill

练习(習) liànxí I (动) practise II (名) exercise: 做～ do exercises. ～簿 exercise-book

殓(殮) liàn (动) put a body into a coffin

链 liàn (名) chain: 表～ watch chain

链接 liànjiē I (动) be linked to II (名) links

链条(條) liàntiáo (名) chain

链子 liànzi (名) chain

粱 liáng (名) fine millet; fine grain

梁 liáng (名) beam: 横～ cross beam. 桥～ bridge. 山～ mountain ridge

梁上君子 liángshàng jūnzǐ burglar; thief

凉 liáng I (名) coolness; cold: 着～ catch cold II (形) **1** cool; cold: ～风 cool breeze. ～菜 cold dish **2** discouraged; disappointed: 他一听这消息心就～了. He felt bitterly disappointed at the news.
  see also liàng

凉快 liángkuài I (形) nice and cool II (动) cool oneself; cool off

凉爽 liángshuǎng (形) nice and cool; pleasantly cool

凉台(臺) liángtái (名) balcony; veranda

凉亭 liángtíng (名) pavilion; summer house

凉席 liángxí (名) summer sleeping mat

凉鞋 liángxié (名) sandals

良 liáng (形) good; fine

良辰美景 liángchén-měijǐng a fine day and an enchanting scene

良好 liánghǎo (形) good: 动机～ good intentions. ～的气氛 favourable atmosphere. ～的基础 a sound foundation

良机(機) liángjī (名) good opportunity: 坐失～. Let slip a golden opportunity.

良师(師)益友 liángshī-yìyǒu good teacher and helpful friend

良心 liángxīn (名) conscience: 说句～话 to be fair. 没～ heartless; ungrateful. ～不安 have a guilty conscience

良药(藥)苦口 liángyào kǔ kǒu good medicine tastes bitter but it helps

良莠不齐(齊) liáng-yǒu bù qí the good and the bad are intermingled

良种(種) liángzhǒng (名) fine seeds or breed; improved seed strains

粮(糧) liáng (名) grain

粮仓(倉) liángcāng (名) granary; barn

粮草 liángcǎo (名) army provisions

粮荒 liánghuāng (名) food shortage; grain shortage

粮库 liángkù (名) grain depot

粮食 liángshi (名) grain; cereals; food

量 liáng (动) measure: ～身材 take sb.'s measurements
  see also liàng

量具 liángjù (名) measuring tool: ～刃具厂 measuring-and cutting-tools plant

两(兩) liǎng I (数) **1** two: ～间房子 two rooms. ～党制 bipartisan system. ～百 two hundred **2** both (sides): ～相情愿 both parties are willing **3** a few; some: 我过～天再来. I'll come again in a couple of days. 让我讲～句. Let me say a few words. II (量) *liang*, Chinese traditional unit of weight, equivalent to 0.05 kilo: 二～茶叶 two *liang* of tea

两败俱伤(傷) liǎng bài jù shāng both sides suffer; end in defeat for both sides

两边(邊) liǎngbiān (名) both sides: ～讨好 try to please both sides

两便 liǎngbiàn (形) be convenient to both sides

两回事 liǎng huí shì two different matters (also as 两码事)

两极(極) liǎngjí (名) the two poles of the earth: ～分化 polarization

两口子 liǎngkǒuzi (名) husband and wife; couple

两面 liǎngmiàn (名) both sides; both aspects: ～派 double-dealer. ～三刀 double-dealing

两难(難) liǎngnán (形) be unable to decide between two unpleasant choices: 进退～ be in a dilemma

两栖(棲) liǎngqī (形) amphibious: ～登陆 amphibious landing

两全其美 liǎng quán qí měi act in such a way as to satisfy the two contending parties or resolve the contradiction confronting a person: 无法～ find it hard to please either party

两手 liǎngshǒu (名) dual tactics: 作～准备 prepare oneself for both eventualities

两性 liǎngxìng (名) both sexes: ～关系 sexual relations

两袖清风(風) liǎngxiù qīngfēng (of an official) remain uncorrupted

两翼 liǎngyì (名) both wings; both flanks

两用 liǎngyòng (形) dual-purpose

靓 liàng (形) beautiful

靓丽(麗) liànglì (形) beautiful

凉 liàng (动) let sth. cool off: 让茶泡一会儿,~一下再喝. Let the tea brew and cool a little before you drink it.
see also liáng

谅 liàng (动) 1 forgive; understand: 互~互让 mutual understanding and mutual accommodation 2 presume; suppose: ~他也不敢. I don't think he dare.

谅解 liàngjiě (动) understand; make allowance for: 互相~ mutual understanding. 达成~ reach an understanding

晾 liàng (动) dry in the air; dry in the sun: 她把衣服~在绳子上. She hung the washing on the line. ~干 dry by airing

亮 liàng I (形) 1 light; bright; shiny: 天~了. Day is breaking. 把皮鞋擦~ polish the shoes. 这里真~. It's very bright in here. 2 loud and clear: 他的嗓子洪~. He has a rich resonant voice. 3 enlightened; clear: 你这一说,我心里头~了. Your remarks are most enlightening. II (动) 1 light: 灯~了. The light is on. 2 reveal; show: ~底 disclose one's real intention. ~思想 reveal (or lay bare) one's thoughts

亮底 liàngdǐ (动) reveal the whole story; put one's cards on the table

亮点(點) liàngdiǎn (名) shining spot

亮度 liàngdù (名) brightness

亮光 liàngguāng (名) light: 一道~ a shaft of light

亮晶晶 liàngjīngjīng (形) sparkling; glittering; glistening: ~的星星 bright stars. ~的露珠 glistening dewdrops

亮丽 liànglì (形) beautiful; wonderful; brilliant

亮色 liàngsè (名) 1 bright colour 2 attraction; eye-catching quality

亮堂 liàngtang (形) 1 light; bright 2 clear; enlightened: 我心里~多了. I feel very much enlightened.

亮堂堂 liàngtāngtāng (形) brightly lit; brilliant

亮相 liàngxiàng (动) 1 strike a pose (on the stage) 2 declare one's position; state one's views

亮铮铮 liàngzhēngzhēng (形) shining; gleaming

踉 liàng

踉跄(蹌) liàngqiàng (动) stagger: ~而行 stagger along

辆(輛) liàng (量) (for vehicles): 一~卡车 a lorry. 两~轿车 two cars

量 liàng I (动) measure; estimate: ~才录用 assign people jobs commensurate with their abilities II (名) 1 quantity; amount 2 capacity: 酒~ capacity for drinking. 他饭~大. He's a big eater.
see also liáng

量变(變) liàngbiàn (名) quantitative change

量词 liàngcí (名) classifier; measure word

量力 liànglì (动) make an accurate estimate of one's own strength or ability: 自不~ overrate one's ability. ~而行 act according to one's ability

量体(體)裁衣 liàng tǐ cái yī cut the garment according to the figure; act according to actual circumstances

量子 liàngzǐ (名) quantum

撩 liāo (动) 1 raise; lift up: ~起帘子 raise the curtain 2 sprinkle (water)
see also liáo

聊 liáo I (动) chat: 闲~ have a casual conversation. 我想找你~~. I'd like to have a chat with you. II (副) merely; just: ~表谢意 just to show my appreciation

聊天儿(兒) liáotiānr (动)〈口〉chat

潦 liáo

潦草 liáocǎo (形) 1 (of handwriting) careless; illegible: 字迹~. The handwriting is nothing but a scribble. 2 sloppy: 工作~ work in a slipshod way

潦倒 liáodǎo (形) be down and out

燎 liáo (动) burn

燎原 liáoyuán (动) set the prairie ablaze

撩 liáo (动) 1 tease; tantalize 2 provoke; stir up
see also liāo

撩拨(撥) liáobō (动) 1 tease; banter 2 incite; provoke

嘹 liáo

L

嘹亮 liáoliàng (形) loud and clear; resonant

僚 liáo (名) official: 官～ official; bureaucrat. 同～ colleague

缭 liáo

缭乱(亂) liáoluàn (形) confused: 心绪～ in a confused state of mind. 眼花～ be dazzled

缭绕(繞) liáorào (动) float in the air: 炊烟～ smoke curling up from kitchen chimneys

寥 liáo (形) 1 few; scanty: ～～可数 limited in number 2 silent; deserted: 寂～ deserted and lonely

寥廓 liáokuò (形) boundless; vast: ～的天空 the vast sky

疗(療) liáo (动) treat; cure: 治～ give medical treatment to a patient

疗程 liáochéng (名) course of treatment

疗法 liáofǎ (名) therapy: 针灸～ acupuncture therapy

疗效 liáoxiào (名) curative effect

疗养(養) liáoyǎng (动) recuperate; convalesce: ～院 sanatorium

辽(遼) liáo (形) distant; faraway

辽阔 liáokuò (形) vast; extensive; boundless: ～的土地 vast territory

了 liǎo I (动) 1 (瞭) know; understand: 明～ understand 2 end; solve: 没完没～ endless II [used after a verb as a complement to 得 or 不 to indicate possibility]: 办得～ can manage it. 受不～ cannot stand it
see also le

了不得 liǎobude (形) 1 terrific; extraordinary: 气得～ fly into a rage. 高兴得～ extremely happy. 这有什么～? What's so unusual about this? 2 terrible; awful: 可～啦,小孩到处找不到. Good God! The child is nowhere to be found.

了不起 liǎobuqǐ (形) amazing; terrific: 一个～的人 a great man. ～的成就 an amazing achievement. 自以为～ be conceited; swell with pride

了得 liǎode (形) [used at the end of a sentence with 还 to indicate that the situation is serious]: 哎呀! 这还～! Dear me! This is awful.

了结 liǎojié (动) finish; settle; put an end to

了解 liǎojiě I (动) 1 know; understand: 我很～他. I know him well. 他不～情况. He doesn't understand the situation. ～中东近来发展状况 keep abreast of the recent development in the Middle East 2 find out; inquire: 你能去～一下这个问题吗? Will you go and find out about this matter? II (名) knowledge; understanding: 促进双方之间的～ promote mutual understanding

了然 liǎorán (动) understand; be clear: 一目～ be clear at a glance

了如指掌 liǎorú zhǐ zhǎng know sth. like the back of one's hand

了事 liǎoshì (动) dispose of a matter; get sth. over: 草草～ hurry through things. 敷衍～ get things done perfunctorily

料 liào I (动) expect; predict; anticipate: ～事如神 predict things like a prophet. 不出所～ as was expected II (名) 1 material; stuff: 原～ raw material. 燃～ fuel. 他不是当医生的～. He hasn't got the makings of a doctor. 2 (grain) feed: 多给牲口加点～. Put more grain in the fodder.

料到 liàodào (动) foresee; expect: 没～他会来. We didn't expect him to come.

料酒 liàojiǔ (名) cooking wine

料理 liàolǐ (动) arrange; manage; take care of: ～家务 manage household affairs

料想 liàoxiǎng (动) expect; presume

料子 liàozi (名) material for making clothes (usu. wool)

撂 liào (动) 〈口〉 put down; leave behind: ～挑子 throw up one's job

瞭 liào

瞭望 liàowàng (动) watch; look into the distance from a height: ～台 watch tower

镣 liào (名) shackles

镣铐 liàokào (名) handcuffs; shackles; leg irons; chains

咧 liě

咧嘴 liězuǐ (动) grin: 他咧着嘴笑. He grinned. 疼得直～ grin with pain

列 liè I (动) 1 line up: ～队欢迎 line up to welcome sb. 2 arrange; list: ～清单 make an inventory. ～入议程 place sth. on the agenda. ～表 make a list; arrange (figures in tables) II (名) row; file; rank: 站在斗争的最前～ stand in the forefront of the struggle III (量) [for things in a row]: 一～火车 a train

列车(車) lièchē (名) train: 特快～ express train. 直达～ through train. ～时刻表 train schedule

列岛 lièdǎo (名) a chain of islands; archipelago

列举(舉) lièjǔ (动) enumerate; list: ～大量事实 cite numerous facts

列宁(寧)主义(義) Lièníngzhǔyì (名) Leninism

列强 lièqiáng (名) big powers

列席 lièxí (动) attend (a meeting) as a non-voting delegate

列传(傳) lièzhuàn (名) biographies

烈 liè (形) 1 strong; violent; intense: ～酒 spirit; a strong drink. ～火 raging flames 2 upright; staunch: 刚～ upright and unyielding 3 sacrificing oneself for a just cause: 壮～牺牲 die a heroic death

烈日 lièrì (名) burning (or scorching) sun

烈士 lièshì (名) martyr

烈属(屬) lièshǔ (名) family of a martyr

烈性 lièxìng (形) 1 (of temper) fierce; violent 2 (of alcohol) strong

烈性子 lièxìngzi (名) fiery disposition; spitfire

洌 liè (形) cold: 凛～ piercingly cold

裂 liè (动) split; break: 木板～(开)了. The plank cracked. 分～ split; break up

裂变(變) lièbiàn (名) fission: 核～ nuclear fission

裂缝 lièfèng (名) crack; rift; fissure

裂痕 lièhén (名) slight crack; rift

裂开(開) lièkāi (动) split open; rend

裂口 lièkǒu (名) crack; split

裂纹 lièwén (名) slight crackle

劣 liè (形) bad; inferior; of low quality

劣等 lièděng (形) poor; quality of low-grade

劣根性 liègēnxìng (名) deep-rooted bad habits

劣迹 lièjì (名) misdeed; evildoing

劣势(勢) lièshì (名) inferior position: 处于～ be in an inferior position

猎(獵) liè (动) hunt: ～狗 hunting dog; hound. ～户 (or ～人) hunter

猎奇 lièqí (动) hunt for novelty; seek novelty

猎枪(槍) lièqiāng (名) hunting rifle

猎取 lièqǔ (动) 1 hunt: ～野兽 hunt wild animals 2 pursue; seek; hunt for: ～个人名利 pursue personal fame and gain

猎头(頭) liètóu (名) head-hunter: ～公司 head-hunting company

拎 līn (动) carry; lift: ～着桶 carry a bucket (by hand)

遴 lín

遴选(選) línxuǎn (动)〈书〉select sb. for a post; select; choose

磷 lín (名) phosphorus (P)

磷肥 línféi (名) phosphate fertilizer

磷火 línhuǒ (名) phosphorescent light

嶙 lín

嶙峋 línxún (形) 1 (of rocks, cliffs, etc.) jagged; rugged: 怪石～ jagged rocks of grotesque shapes 2 (of a person) bony; thin: 瘦骨～ all skin and bones

鳞 lín (名) (of fish) scale: 遍体～伤 be covered with bruises or injuries (like the scale of a fish)

鳞次栉(櫛)比 líncì-zhìbǐ (of buildings) row upon row of

鳞甲 línjiǎ (名) scale and shell

粼 lín

粼粼 línlín (形) (of water) clear; crystalline: ～碧波 ripples of a clear, blue lake

林 lín (名) 1 woods; grove; forest: 竹～ bamboo grove. ～场 forestry centre; tree farm 2 circles: 艺～ art circles 3 forestry

林带(帶) líndài (名) forest belt

林立 línlì (动) stand in great numbers (like trees in a forest)

林业(業) línyè (名) forestry

林阴(陰)道 línyīndào (名) avenue; boulevard

淋 lín (动) pour; drench: 日晒雨～ weather-beaten. ～湿了 get wet in the rain; be soaked

淋巴 línbā (名) lymph

淋漓 línlí (形) 1 dripping wet: 大汗～ dripping with sweat. 鲜血～ dripping with blood 2 (of writing or speech) free from inhibition: 痛快～ impassioned. ～尽致 vividly and incisively; thoroughly

L

淋浴 línyù (名) shower bath; shower

霖 lín (名) continuous heavy rain: 甘～ good soaking rain; timely rain

琳 lín (名) beautiful jade

琳琅满(滿)目 línláng mǎnmù a collection of fine and exquisite things; a feast for the eyes

临(臨) lín (动) 1 face; overlook: 居高～下 occupy a commanding position. ～街的窗户 a window overlooking the street. 如～大敌 as if facing a formidable enemy 2 arrive; befall: 希亲～指导. We hope you will come personally to give guidance. 3 be about to; just before; on the point of: ～睡 before going to bed. ～行 before departure

临别 línbié (动) at parting; just before departure

临床(牀) línchuáng (形) clinical: ～经验 clinical experience

临机(機) línjī (动)〈书〉as the occasion requires: ～应变 make changes as the situation demands

临近 línjìn (动) be close to: ～黎明 close on daybreak. 考试～了. The examination session is drawing near.

临摹 línmó (动) copy (a model of calligraphy or painting)

临时(時) línshí (形) 1 at the time when sth. happens: ～通知 a short notice. ～改动 a last-minute change 2 temporary; provisional: ～政府 provisional government. ～措施 temporary measure. ～代办 chargé d'affaires ad interim. ～工 odd-job man; temporary worker

临头(頭) líntóu (动) befall; happen: 大祸～. Disaster is imminent.

临危 línwēi (动) 1 be dying (from illness) 2 facing death or deadly peril: ～不惧 betray no fear in the hour of danger

临阵磨枪(槍) línzhèn mó qiāng start to prepare only at the last moment

临阵脱逃 línzhèn tuōtáo sneak away at a critical juncture

临终 línzhōng (动) immediately before one's death: ～遗言 deathbed testament

邻(鄰) lín I (名) neighbour: 近～ a close neighbour II (形) neighbouring: ～县 a neighbouring county. ～座 an adjacent seat

邻邦 línbāng (名) neighbouring country

邻接 línjiē (动) border on; be next to

邻近 línjìn I (形) near; close to; adjacent to II (名) vicinity

邻居 línjū (名) neighbour: 隔壁～ a next-door neighbour

邻里 línlǐ (名) neighbourhood; neighbours

凛 lǐn (形) 1 strict; stern; severe 2 afraid; apprehensive

凛冽 lǐnliè (形) biting cold

凛凛 lǐnlǐn (形) 1 cold: 寒风～ a piercing wind 2 stern; awe-inspiring: 威风～ dignified and awe-inspiring

凛然 lǐnrán (形) stern; awe-inspiring. 正气～ show awe-inspiring righteousness

吝 lìn (形) stingy; mean

吝啬(嗇) lìnsè (形) stingy; miserly; mean: ～鬼 miser; niggard; skinflint

吝惜 lìnxī (动) stint: 不～自己的力量 spare no effort

赁 lìn (动) rent; hire: 房屋出～ house to let. 租～公司 a leasing company

凌 líng (动) 1 insult: 欺～ bully. 盛气～人 overbearing 2 approach: ～晨 before dawn 3 rise high; tower aloft

凌驾 língjià (动) override; place oneself above: ～一切 override all other considerations; of overriding importance

凌空 língkōng (动) be high up in the air

凌厉(厲) línglì (形) quick and forceful: 攻势～ make a swift and fierce attack

凌乱(亂) língluàn (形) in disorder; in a mess: ～不堪 in an awful mess

凌辱 língrǔ (动) insult; humiliate

凌霄 língxiāo (动) reach up to heaven

凌云(雲)壮(壯)志 língyún zhuàngzhì (cherish) soaring aspirations

菱 líng (名) water caltrop (also as "菱角")

陵 líng (名) 1 hill; mound 2 tomb; mausoleum: 十三～ the tombs of 13 Ming emperors; the Ming Tombs

陵墓 língmù (名) mausoleum; tomb

陵园(園) língyuán (名) cemetery

绫 líng (名) a thin silk fabric: ～罗绸缎 silks and satins

羚 líng (名) (～羊) antelope

零 líng I (数) 1 zero sign (0); nought: 五～六号 No. 506 (number five-o-six). 三块～五分 three *yuan* and five *fen* 2 nought; zero; nil: 一减一等于～. One minus one leaves nought (or zero).

3 zero (on a thermometer): 摄氏～下十度 10 degrees below zero centigrade; minus ten degrees centigrade II (名) odd; with a little extra: 年纪六十有～ a little more than sixty years old III (形) 1 fractional 2 withered: 凋～ (of flowers) fallen and scattered about

零工 línggōng (名) 1 odd job; short-term hired labour 2 odd-job man; casual labourer

零件 língjiàn (名) spare parts; spares

零乱(亂) língluàn (形) same as "凌乱" língluàn

零落 língluò (形) 1 withered and fallen: 草木～. The grass and trees are all withered. 2 decayed: 凄凉～的景象 a scene of utter desolation 3 scattered; sporadic: ～的枪声 sporadic shooting

零钱(錢) língqián (名) 1 small change; change 2 pocket money

零敲碎打 língqiāo-suìdǎ do sth. bit by bit, off and on; adopt a piecemeal approach

零散 língsǎn (形) scattered: 桌子上～地放着几本书. There are several books lying scattered on the desk.

零食 língshí (名) between-meal nibbles; snacks

零售 língshòu (动) retail; sell retail: ～店 retail shop; retail store. ～价格 retail price

零碎 língsuì I (形) scrappy; fragmentary; piecemeal: ～活儿 odd jobs II (名) odds and ends; oddments; bits and pieces

零头(頭) língtóu (名) 1 money in low-value coins or notes; change 2 remnant (of cloth): 一块～布 a remnant

零星 língxīng (形) 1 fragmentary; odd; piecemeal: ～材料 fragmentary material 2 scattered; sporadic: ～小雨 occasional drizzles; scattered shower

零用 língyòng I (动) (of money) be earmarked for small incidental expenses II (名) pocket money

玲 líng

玲珑(瓏) línglóng (动) 1 (of things) ingeniously and delicately wrought; exquisite: 小巧～ fine and delicate 2 (of women) nimble

玲珑(瓏)剔透 línglóng tītòu (形) exquisitely carved; beautifully wrought: ～的玉雕 exquisitely wrought jade carvings

聆 líng

(动)〈书〉 listen; hear: ～教 hear your instructions

聆听(聽) língtīng (动) listen (respectfully)

龄 líng

(名) 1 age; years: 年～ age. 学～儿童 schoolage children 2 length of time; duration: 工～ length of service; years of service

囹 líng

囹圄 língyǔ (名)〈书〉 jail; prison: 身陷～ be behind prison bars; be thrown into prison

铃 líng

(名) 1 bell: 门～ doorbell 2 anything in the shape of a bell: 哑～ dumb-bell. 棉～ cotton boll

伶 líng

(名)〈旧〉 actor or actress

伶仃 língdīng (形) left alone without help; lonely: 孤苦～ alone and uncared for

伶俐 línglì (形) clever; bright; quick-witted

翎 líng

(名) plume; tail feather; quill: 孔雀～ peacock plumes; peacock feathers

灵(靈) líng

I (形) 1 quick; clever; sharp: 耳朵很～ have sharp ears 2 efficacious; effective: ～药 an effective remedy. 这法子很～. This method works. II (名) 1 spirit; intelligence: 心～ the mind; the soul 2 fairy; sprite; elf: ～怪 elf; goblin 3 remains of the deceased; bier: 守～ stand as guards at the bier; keep vigil beside the bier

灵便 língbian (形) 1 nimble; agile: 他手脚还～. He is still agile. 2 easy to handle; handy

灵丹妙药(藥) língdān-miàoyào miraculous cure; panacea

灵感 línggǎn (名) inspiration

灵魂 línghún (名) soul; spirit: ～深处 in the recesses of one's mind; in the depth of one's soul

灵活 línghuó (形) 1 nimble; agile; quick: 脑筋～ be quick-witted; have a supple mind. 手脚～ dexterous and quick in action 2 flexible; elastic

灵机(機) língjī (名) sudden inspiration; brainwave: 她～一动,想出了一个好办法. She had a brainwave and found a good solution.

灵柩 língjiù (名) a coffin containing a corpse; bier

灵敏 língmǐn (形) sensitive; keen; agile; acute: 这架仪器～度很高. This instrument is highly sensitive.

L

灵巧 língqiǎo (形) dexterous; nimble; clever; ingenious: 心思～ clever and resourceful

灵通 língtōng (形) having quick access to information; well-informed: 消息～人士 well-informed sources

灵性 língxìng (名) intelligence

灵验(驗) língyàn (形) 1 efficacious; effective 2 (of a prediction, etc.) accurate; right: 他的预言果然～. His prediction had proved correct.

令 lǐng (量) ream (of paper)

see also lìng

领 lǐng I (名) 1 neck: 引～而望 eagerly look forward to 2 collar; neckband 3 outline; main point: 要～ main points; essentials II (量): 一～席 a mat III (动) 1 lead; usher: ～兵打仗 lead troops into battle 2 receive; draw; get: ～奖 receive a prize (or an award). ～养老金 draw one's pension 3 understand; comprehend; grasp

领班 lǐngbān (名) gaffer; foreman

领带(帶) lǐngdài (名) necktie; tie

领导(導) lǐngdǎo I (动) lead; exercise leadership II (名) leadership; leader

领地 lǐngdì (名) 1 manor (of a feudal lord) 2 territory

领队(隊) lǐngduì (名) leader of a group

领港 lǐnggǎng I (动) pilot a ship into or out of a harbour; pilot II (名) (harbour) pilot

领海 lǐnghǎi (名) territorial waters; territorial sea: ～范围 extent of territorial waters. ～宽度 breadth of the territorial sea

领航 lǐngháng I (动) navigate; pilot II (名) navigator; pilot

领会(會) lǐnghuì (动) understand; comprehend; grasp: 我还没有～你的意思. I still don't see your point.

领教 lǐngjiào (动) 1 〈套〉[used to indicate approval or appreciation] thanks; much obliged: 您说得很对, ～～! You're quite right there. I'm much obliged to you. 2 ask advice: 有点儿小事向您～. I've a problem, which may not be terribly important, but I would like to ask your advice.

领结 lǐngjié (名) bow tie

领空 lǐngkōng (名) territorial sky (or air); territorial air space

领口 lǐngkǒu (名) 1 collarband; neckband 2 the place where the two ends of a collar meet

领略 lǐnglüè (动) have a taste of; realize; appreciate

领情 lǐngqíng (动) feel grateful to sb.; appreciate the kindness: 你们的好意,我十分～. I very much appreciate your kindness.

领取 lǐngqǔ (动) receive; draw; get: ～身份证 get one's ID card

领事 lǐngshì (名) consul: 总～ consul general. 副～ vice-consul. ～馆 consulate

领水 lǐngshuǐ (名) 1 inland waters 2 territorial waters

领土 lǐngtǔ (名) territory: 保卫国家的～完整 safeguard a country's territorial integrity. ～扩张 territorial expansion; territorial aggrandizement. ～要求 territorial claim

领悟 lǐngwù (动) comprehend; grasp: ～能力 perceptibility

领先 lǐngxiān (动) be in the lead; lead: 客队～五分. The visiting team led by five points. 他们首批～登上了山顶. They were among the first to reach the hill top.

领袖 lǐngxiù (名) leader

领养(養) lǐngyǎng (动) adopt (a child)

领域 lǐngyù (名) 1 territory; domain 2 field; sphere; realm: 文学～ the realm of literature

领章 lǐngzhāng (名) collar badge; collar insignia

岭(嶺) lǐng (名) 1 mountain range 2 mountain; ridge: 翻山越～ cross over mountain after mountain. 崇山峻～ high mountain ridges

另 lìng (形、副) another; separately; on another occasion: ～有任命 have another appointment. ～一回事 another matter. ～议 discuss the matter on some other occasion. ～寄 post separately; post under separate cover

另类(類) lìnglèi (形) alternative: ～作家 unconventional writer. ～治疗法 alternative treatment

另起炉(爐)灶(竈) lìng qǐ lúzào make a fresh start; start all over again

另外 lìngwài (副) in addition

另眼相看 lìng yǎn xiāng kàn treat sb. with special respect

令 lìng I (名) 1 command; order; decree: 下～ issue an order. 法～ laws and decrees 2 season: 当～ in season. 夏

～时间 summer time **3** an ancient official title：县～ county magistrate **4** drinking game II (形) **1** 〈书〉 good; excellent：～名 good name; reputation **2** 〈敬〉 your：～尊 your father. ～堂 your mother. ～爱 your daughter. ～郎 your son III (动) make; cause：～人鼓舞 heartening; inspiring; encouraging. ～人深思 make one ponder long and deeply

see also lǐng

令箭 lìngjiàn (名) an arrow-shaped token of authority used in the army in ancient China

令行禁止 lìng xíng jìn zhǐ strict enforcement of orders and prohibitions; every order is executed without fail

溜 liū I (动) **1** slide; glide：从山坡上～下来 slide down a slope **2** sneak off; slip away：～掉 sneak off; slip away II (形) smooth：滑～ slippery

see also liù

溜冰 liūbīng (名) skating：～场 skating rink

溜达(達) liūda (动)〈口〉 stroll; saunter; go for a walk (or stroll)

溜须(鬚)拍马(馬) liūxū-pāimǎ 〈口〉 fawn on; toady to; shamelessly flatter

溜之大吉 liū zhī dàjí sneak away

熘 liū (动) sauté (with thick gravy); quick-fry：～鱼片 fish slices sauté

浏(瀏) liú 〈书〉 **1** (of water) clear; limpid **2** (of wind) swift

浏览(覽) liúlǎn (动) glance over; skim through; browse through：～各种报刊 browse among newspapers and magazines

流 liú I (动) **1** flow：江水东～. The river flows east. ～汗 sweat. ～泪 shed tears **2** move from place to place; drift; wander **3** spread：～传甚广 spread far and wide **4** change for the worse; degenerate：～于形式 be reduced to a mere formality **5** banish; send into exile II (名) **1** stream of water：河～ river. 逆～而上 sail against the current **2** sth. resembling a stream of water; current：气～ air current. 电～ electric current **3** class; rate; grade：三教九～ people of different types, schools and persuasions

流弊 liúbì (名) corrupt practices; abuses

流产(產) liúchǎn I (动) **1** have an abortion; have a miscarriage **2** miscarry; fall through：他的计划～了. His plan fell flat. II (名) abortion; miscarriage：人工～ induced abortion

流畅(暢) liúchàng (形) easy and smooth：文笔～ write with ease and grace

流传(傳) liúchuán (动) spread; circulate; hand down：古代～下来的寓言 fables handed down from ancient times

流窜(竄) liúcuàn (动) (of bandits, enemy troops etc.) flee hither and thither

流弹(彈) liúdàn (名) stray bullet

流荡(蕩) liúdàng (动) roam about; rove

流动(動) liúdòng I (动) flow：～资金 circulating fund. ～人口 floating (or mobile) population. 人材～ talent flow. 溪水缓缓地～. The brook flowed sluggishly. II (形) going from place to place; on the move; mobile：～货车 shop-on-wheels. ～电影放映队 mobile film projection team

流毒 liúdú I (动) exert a pernicious (or baneful) influence：～甚广 exert a widespread pernicious influence II (名) pernicious influence; baneful influence

流放 liúfàng (动) **1** banish; send into exile **2** float (logs) downstream

流寇 liúkòu (名) **1** roving bandits **2** roving rebel bands

流浪 liúlàng (动) roam about; lead a vagrant life：～街头 roam the streets. ～汉 tramp; vagrant

流离(離)失所 liúlí shī suǒ drift about aimlessly; wander about homeless

流利 liúlì (形) fluent; smooth：她说一口～的英语. She speaks fluent English.

流连忘返 liúlián wàng fǎn be so enchanted by the scenery as to forget to return

流量 liúliàng (名) rate of flow; flow; discharge：河道～ discharge of a river

流露 liúlù (动) reveal; betray; show unintentionally：真情的～ a revelation of one's true feelings

流落 liúluò (动) wander about destitute：～他乡 wander destitute far from home

流氓 liúmáng (名) **1** rogue; hoodlum; hooligan; gangster **2** immoral (indecent) behaviour; hooliganism：耍～ behave like a hoodlum

流派 liúpài (名) school; sect：学术～ schools of thought

流失 liúshī (动) run off; be washed away：水土～ soil erosion. 人材～ talent drain

流逝 liúshì (动) (of time) pass; elapse：时光～ time passes

流水 liúshuǐ (名) running water：～线 assembly line. ～作业 assembly line method; conveyer system

流速 liúsù (名) 1 velocity of flow 2 current velocity

流体(體) liútǐ (名) fluid: ～力学 hydromechanics; fluid mechanics

流通 liútōng (动) circulate: 空气～ ventilation

流亡 liúwáng (动) be forced to leave one's native land; go into exile: ～政府 government-in-exile

流线(綫)型 liúxiànxíng (名) streamline: ～汽车 streamlined car

流行 liúxíng (形) prevalent; popular; fashionable; in vogue

流行病 liúxíngbìng (名) epidemic disease: ～学 epidemiology

流血 liúxuè (动) bleed; shed blood

流言 liúyán (名) rumour; gossip: ～蜚语 rumours and slanders

流域 liúyù (名) valley; river basin; drainage area: 黄河～ the Yellow River valley (or basin)

琉 liú

琉璃 liúlí (名) coloured glaze: ～塔 glazed pagoda. ～瓦 glazed tile

硫 liú (名) sulphur (S)

硫化 liúhuà (名) vulcanization: ～物 sulphide

硫磺 liúhuáng (名) sulphur

硫酸 liúsuān (名) sulphuric acid

留 liú (动) 1 remain; stay: 你可以继续～任. You can stay on. 2 detain 3 reserve; keep; save: ～座位 reserve a seat for sb. 4 let grow; grow; wear: ～胡子 grow a beard 5 accept; take: 把礼物～下 accept a present 6 leave: 他把书都～在我这里了. He left all the books with me. ～言簿 visitors' book

留步 liúbù (动)〈套〉don't bother to see me out; don't bother to see me any further

留存 liúcún (动) 1 preserve; keep: 此稿～ keep this copy on file 2 remain; be extant

留后(後)路 liúhòulù keep a way open for retreat; leave a way out

留话 liúhuà (动) leave a message; leave word

留级 liújí (动) (of pupils, etc.) fail to go up to the next grade; repeat the year's work

留恋(戀) liúliàn (动) 1 be reluctant to part (from sb. or with sth.); have a sentimental attachment for 2 recall with nostalgia

留难(難) liúnàn (动) make things difficult for sb.; make it too hot for sb.

留念 liúniàn (动) accept or keep as a souvenir

留情 liúqíng (动) show mercy: 手下～ be lenient

留神 liúshén (动) on the alert; take care: 过马路要～. Be careful when you cross the street.

留声(聲)机(機) liúshēngjī (名) gramophone; phonograph

留守 liúshǒu (动) stay behind to take care of things

留宿 liúsù (动) 1 put up a guest for the night 2 stay overnight; put up for the night

留心 liúxīn (动) be attentive: ～听讲 listen attentively to a lecture

留学(學) liúxué (动) study abroad: ～生 student studying abroad; returned student. 自费～生 self-supporting student. 公费～生 government-sponsored student

留言 liúyán (动) leave one's comments; leave a message

留意 liúyì (动) be careful: 这两个字有细微差别,必须～. There are subtle distinctions between these two words. You have got to be careful.

留影 liúyǐng (动) have a picture taken as a memento

瘤 liú (名)(～子) tumour: 毒～ malignant tumour. 良性～ benign tumour

榴 liú (名) pomegranate

榴弹(彈) liúdàn (名) high-explosive shell: ～炮 howitzer

柳 liǔ (名) willow

柳条(條) liǔtiáo (名) willow twig; wicker: ～筐 wicker basket

柳絮 liǔxù (名) (willow) catkin

六 liù (数) six

六亲(親) liùqīn (名) the six relations (father, mother, elder brothers, younger brothers, wife, children); one's kin: ～不认 refuse to have anything to do with all one's relatives and friends

六神无(無)主 liù shén wú zhǔ in a trance

六月 liùyuè (名) 1 June 2 the sixth month of the lunar year

溜 liù (名) 1 swift current 2 rainwater from the roof 3 roof gutter 4 row: 一~平房 a row of one-storeyed houses 5 surroundings; neighbourhood: 这~儿果木树很多. There are plenty of fruit trees round here.
see also liū

遛 liù (动) saunter; stroll: ~大街 go window-shopping. ~马 walk a horse. ~弯儿 take a walk; go for a stroll

陆(陸) liù (数) six [used for the numeral 六 on cheques, etc. to avoid mistakes or alterations]
see also lù

龙(龍) lóng (名) 1 dragon 2 dragon as imperial symbol: ~袍 imperial robe 3 a huge extinct reptile: 恐~ dinosaur

龙飞(飛)凤(鳳)舞 lóngfēi-fèngwǔ 1 characteristic of a winding magnificent mountain range 2 lively flourishes in calligraphy

龙卷风(風) lóngjuǎnfēng (名) tornado

龙套 lóngtào (名) actor playing a supporting role; utility man: 跑~ carry a spear in the supporting role; be "a supporting role" actor

龙王 lóngwáng (名) the Dragon King (the God of Rain in Chinese mythology)

龙虾(蝦) lóngxiā (名) lobster

龙眼 lóngyǎn (名) longan

龙争虎斗(鬥) lóngzhēng-hǔdòu a fierce struggle between two evenly-matched opponents

龙钟(鍾) lóngzhōng (形)〈书〉decrepit; senile: 老态~ senile; aged and doddering

龙舟 lóngzhōu (名) dragon boat: ~竞渡 dragon-boat regatta; dragon-boat race

聋(聾) lóng (形) deaf; hard of hearing

聋哑(啞) lóngyǎ (形) deaf and dumb; deaf-mute. ~人 deaf-mute

聋子 lóngzi (名) a deaf person

砻(礱) lóng I (名) rice huller II (动) hull (rice)

笼(籠) lóng (名) 1 cage; coop: 鸟~ birdcage. 鸡~ chicken coop 2 basket; container 3 (food) steamer: 蒸~ food steamer
see also lǒng

笼屉 lóngtì (名) bamboo or wooden utensil for steaming food; food steamer

隆 lóng I (形) 1 grand 2 prosperous; thriving 3 intense; deep: ~冬 the depth of winter. ~情厚谊 profound sentiments of friendship II (动) bulge

隆隆 lónglóng (象) rumble: 雷声(炮声)~ the rumble of thunder (gunfire)

隆重 lóngzhòng (形) grand; solemn; ceremonious: ~的典礼 a grand ceremony. ~接待 red-carpet reception

垄(壟) lǒng (名) 1 ridge (in a field) 2 raised path between fields

垄断(斷) lǒngduàn (动) control; monopolize: ~集团 monopoly group. ~价格 monopoly price. ~资本 monopoly capital. ~市场 monopolize the market

拢(攏) lǒng (动) 1 approach; reach: ~岸 come alongside the shore 2 add up; sum up (accounts) 3 hold (or gather) together 4 comb (hair)

拢子 lǒngzi (名) a fine-toothed comb

笼(籠) lǒng I (动) envelop; cover: 烟~雾罩 be enveloped in mist II (名) a large box or chest; trunk
see also lóng

笼络 lǒngluò (动) win people over by unfair means: ~人心 try to win popular support by hook or by crook

笼统 lǒngtǒng (形) general; vague: 他的话说得很~. He spoke in general terms.

笼罩 lǒngzhào (动) envelop; shroud: 湖面上晨雾~. The lake is enveloped in morning mist.

弄 lòng (名) lane; alley; alleyway
see also nòng

弄堂 lòngtáng (名) lane; alley; alleyway

搂(摟) lōu (动) 1 gather up; rake together: ~柴火 rake up twigs, dead leaves, etc. (for fuel) 2 hold up; tuck up: ~起袖子 roll up one's sleeves 3 extort: ~钱 extort money
see also lǒu

娄(婁) lóu

娄子 lóuzi (名) trouble; blunder: 捅~ make a blunder; get into trouble

L

楼(樓) lóu (名) **1** a storeyed building: 办公～ office building **2** storey; floor: 一～(英) ground floor; (美) first floor. 二～(英) first floor; (美) second floor **3** superstructure: 城～ city-gate tower

楼花 lóuhuā (名) apartments sold before they are built

楼盘(盤) lóupán (名) building

楼上 lóushàng (名) upstairs

楼市 lóushì (名) property market

楼梯 lóutī (名) stairs; staircase

楼下 lóuxià (名) downstairs

搂(摟) lǒu (动) hold in one's arms; hug; embrace

see also lōu

搂抱 lǒubào (动) hug; embrace

篓(簍) lǒu (名)(～子) basket: 字纸～ wastepaper basket

漏 lòu I (动) **1** leak: 水壶～了. The kettle leaks. **2** divulge; leak: 走～消息 leak information **3** be missing; leave out: 这一行～了两个字. Two words are missing from the line. II (名) water clock; hour glass: ～尽更残. The night is waning.

漏洞 lòudòng (名) **1** leak **2** flaw; hole; loophole: 他的话里有许多～. His argument is full of loopholes.

漏斗 lòudǒu (名) funnel

漏税 lòushuì (动) evade payment of a tax; evade taxation

漏网(網) lòuwǎng (动) (of criminal, enemies, etc.) escape unpunished

漏嘴 lòuzuǐ (动) let slip a remark; make a slip of the tongue

镂(鏤) lòu (动) engrave; carve

镂空 lòukōng (动) hollow out: ～的象牙球 hollowed-out ivory ball

露 lòu (动)〈口〉reveal; show: ～一手 show off

see also lù

露富 lòufù (动) have one's wealth revealed

露脸(臉) lòuliǎn (动) **1** appear on public occasions **2** enjoy the limelight

露马(馬)脚 lòu mǎjiǎo give oneself away; let the cat out of the bag

露面 lòumiàn (动) make public appearances; appear in public

露头(頭) lòutóu (动) appear; emerge: 太阳还没有～,我们就起来了. We got up before sunrise.

露馅儿(兒) lòuxiànr (动) give the game away; spill the beans; let the cat out of the bag

露一手 lòu yīshǒu show off one's skills

陋 lòu (形) **1** plain; ugly: 丑～ ugly **2** humble; mean: ～室 a cramped flat. ～巷 a mean alley **3** vulgar; corrupt; undesirable: ～习 corrupt customs; bad habits. ～规 objectionable practices **4** (of knowledge) scanty; limited: 孤～寡闻 ignorant and ill-informed

庐(廬) lú (名) hut; cottage

庐山真面 Lúshān zhēnmiàn the truth about a person or a matter

庐舍 lúshè (名)〈书〉house; farmhouse

炉(爐) lú I (名) stove; furnace: 围～烤火 sit round a fire to get warm. 煤气～ gas stove II (量) heat: 一～钢 a heat of steel

炉火纯青 lúhuǒ chúnqīng high degree of perfection

炉灶(竈) lúzào (名) kitchen range; cooking range: 另起～ make a fresh start

芦(蘆) lú

芦苇(葦) lúwěi (名) reed: ～荡 reed marshes

颅(顱) lú (名) cranium; skull

颅骨 lúgǔ (名) skull

卤(鹵) lǔ I (名) **1** bittern **2** thick gravy used as a sauce for noodles, etc.: 打～面 noodles served with thick gravy II (动) stew (whole chicken or duck, large cuts of meat, etc.) in soy sauce: ～鸡 pot-stewed chicken

虏(虜) lǔ I (动) take prisoner II (名) captive; prisoner of war

虏获(獲) lǔhuò I (动) capture II (名) captives and captured arms

掳(擄) lǔ (动) carry off; plunder

掳掠 lǔlüè (动) pillage; loot: 奸淫～ rape and loot

鲁 lǔ (形) **1** stupid; dull **2** rash; rough; rude

鲁钝 lǔdùn (形) dull-witted; obtuse; stupid

鲁莽 lǔmǎng (形) crude and rash; rash: ～行事 act rashly

橹 lǔ (名) scull; sweep

鹿 lù (名) deer: 公～ stag; buck. 母～ doe. 小～ fawn

鹿角 lùjiǎo (名) **1** deerhorn; antler **2** abatis

鹿茸 lùróng (名) pilose antler (of a young stag)

鹿死谁手 lù sǐ shuí shǒu who will win the prize or gain supremacy: ～, 尚难逆料. It's still hard to tell who will emerge the victor.

麓 lù (名)〈书〉 the foot of a hill or mountain

辘 lù

辘辘 lùlù (象) rumble: 车轮的～声 the rumbling of cart wheels. 饥肠～ so hungry that one's stomach rumbles; feel famished

路 lù (名) **1** road; path; way: 大～ broad road; highway. 小～ path; trail. ～灯 street lamp **2** journey; distance: 走很远的～ walk a long distance; make a long journey **3** way; means: 生～ means of livelihood **4** sequence; line; logic: 思～ train of thought **5** route: 七～公共汽车 No. 7 bus **6** sort; grade; class: 头～货 top-notch goods. 一～货 the same sort; birds of a feather

路标(標) lùbiāo (名) road sign; route sign

路不拾遗 lù bù shí yí no one picks up anything on the road and claims it as his own

路程 lùchéng (名) distance travelled; journey: 三天～ a three days' journey

路费 lùfèi (名) travelling expenses

路径(徑) lùjìng (名) **1** route; way: ～不熟 not know one's way around **2** method; ways and means

路途 lùtú (名) **1** road; path **2** way; journey: ～遥远 a long way to go; far away

路线(綫) lùxiàn (名) **1** route; itinerary: 旅行的～ the route of a journey. 参观～图 visitors' itinerary **2** line: 政治～ political line

路子 lùzi (名) way; approach: ～不对等于白费劲儿. A wrong approach is a waste of effort. 我们的路子走对了. We are on the right track.

露 lù I (名) **1** dew **2** beverage distilled from flowers, fruit or leaves; syrup: 果子～ fruit syrup II (动) show; reveal; betray: 不～声色 not betray one's feelings or intentions. ～出原形 reveal one's true colours
see also lòu

露骨 lùgǔ (形) thinly veiled; undisguised; naked: ～干涉 flagrantly interfere. 你说得这样～, 他不会不懂. You spoke in such undisguised terms that he could not miss the point.

露酒 lùjiǔ (名) alcoholic drink mixed with fruit juice

露水 lùshui (名) dew

露宿 lùsù (动) sleep in the open

露天 lùtiān in the open (air); outdoors: ～剧场 open-air theatre. ～煤矿 opencast coal mine

露头(頭)角 lù tóujiǎo (of a young person) begin to show ability or talent

露营(營) lùyíng (动) camp (out); encamp; bivouac

露珠 lùzhū (名) dewdrop

戮 lù (动) **1** kill; slay: 杀～ slaughter **2** 〈书〉 unite; join: ～力 join hands. ～力同心 unite in a concerted effort; make concerted efforts

录(錄) lù I (动) **1** record; write down; copy: 抄～ copy down. 记～在案 put on record **2** employ; hire: ～用 employ; take sb. on the staff **3** tape-record: 报告已经～下来了. The speech has been tape-recorded. II (名) record; register; collection: 回忆～ memoirs; reminiscences

录供 lùgòng (动) take down a confession or testimony during an interrogation

录取 lùqǔ (动) enrol; recruit; admit: 他已被～. He has been admitted to college or recruited by a factory, etc.

录入 lùrù (动) type in; input: 电脑～员 a computer keyboarder

录像 lùxiàng (名) videotape; video: ～机 video recorder

录音 lùyīn (名) sound recording: 磁带～ tape recording. 放～ play back the recording. ～带 magnetic tape; tape. ～机 (tape) recorder

录用 lùyòng (动) employ

禄 lù (名) official's salary in feudal China; emolument: 高官厚～ high position and handsome emolument

碌 lù (形) **1** commonplace; mediocre **2** busy

碌碌 lùlù (形) **1** mediocre; commonplace:

~无能 incompetent 2 busy with miscellaneous work：忙忙~ busy going about one's routine

陆(陸) lù（名）land：水~交通 land and water communications
see also liù

陆地 lùdì（名）dry land；land

陆军 lùjūn（名）ground force；land force；army

陆路 lùlù（名）land route：走~ travel by land．~交通 overland communication；land communication

陆续(續) lùxù（副）one after another；in succession：来宾~地到了．The visitors have arrived one after another．

陆战(戰)队(隊) lùzhànduì（名）marine corps；marines

驴(驢) lǘ（名）donkey；ass

旅 lǚ I（动）travel；stay away from home II（名）1 brigade 2 troops；force：劲~ a powerful army；a crack force

旅伴 lǚbàn（名）travelling companion；fellow traveller

旅程 lǚchéng（名）route；itinerary

旅费 lǚfèi（名）travel expenses

旅馆 lǚguǎn（名）hotel

旅居 lǚjū（动）reside abroad：~海外 reside abroad

旅客 lǚkè（名）hotel guest；traveller；passenger

旅途 lǚtú（名）journey；trip：~见闻 notes on a journey；traveller's notes

旅行 lǚxíng（动）travel；journey；tour：~社 travel service．~团 touring party．~指南 guidebook．~支票 traveller's cheque

旅游 lǚyóu（动）tour：~业 tourist industry；tourism．~鞋 sneakers

旅长(長) lǚzhǎng（名）brigade commander

屡(屢) lǚ（副）repeatedly；time and again：~战~胜 score one victory after another．~见不鲜 common occurrences；nothing new

屡次 lǚcì（副）time and again；repeatedly：~打破全国纪录 repeatedly break the record

缕(縷) lǚ I（名）thread：千丝万~的联系 connected in a thousand and one ways II（量）wisp；strand：一~烟 a wisp of smoke．一~麻 a strand of hemp III（副）detailed；in detail：~陈 state in detail［used in addressing one's superior］

捋 lǚ（动）smooth out with the fingers；stroke：~胡子 stroke one's beard

铝 lǚ（名）aluminium（Al）

侣 lǚ（名）companion；associate：伴~ companion；partner

履 lǚ I（名）1 shoe：革~ leather shoes 2 footstep II（动）1 carry out；honour；fulfil：~约 honour an agreement；keep an appointment 2 tread on；walk on：~险如夷 go over a dangerous pass as if walking on level ground

履带(帶) lǚdài（名）caterpillar tread；track：~式拖拉机 caterpillar（or crawler）tractor

履历(歷) lǚlì（名）personal details（of education and work experience）；curriculum vitae；résumé

履行 lǚxíng（动）perform；fulfil；carry out：~职责 do one's duty．~诺言 keep one's promise；fulfil（or carry out）one's promise

率 lǜ（名）rate；proportion；ratio：人口增长~ the rate of population growth．废品~ the rate（or proportion）of rejects
see also shuài

虑(慮) lǜ I（动）consider；ponder；think over：深谋远~ be deeply thoughtful and far-seeing；think deeply and plan carefully II（名）concern；anxiety；worry：疑~ misgivings

滤(濾) lǜ（动）strain；filter：过~ filter．~嘴香烟 filter-tip cigarettes．~纸 filter paper

律 lǜ I（名）law；statute；rule II（动）restrain；keep under control：严以~己 be strict with oneself；exercise strict self-discipline

律师(師) lǜshī（名）lawyer；（英）barrister；（英）solicitor；（美）attorney

律诗 lǜshī（名）*lüshi*，a poem of eight lines，each containing five or seven characters，with a strict tonal pattern and rhyme scheme

绿 lǜ（形）green：~叶 green leaves．~油油的秧苗 green and lush seedlings

绿茶 lǜchá（名）green tea

绿灯(燈) lǜdēng（名）1 green light 2 permission to go ahead with some project；

green light：开～ give the green light to

绿肥 lǜféi（名）green manure

绿化 lǜhuà（动）make (a place) green by planting trees, flowers, etc.; afforest：植树造林，～祖国. Plant trees everywhere to make the country green.

绿卡 lǜkǎ（名）green card; permanent resident status

绿色 lǜsè（名）green colour：～食品 green food; health food

绿洲 lǜzhōu（名）oasis

峦（巒）luán（名）〈书〉1 low but steep and pointed hill 2 mountains in a range

挛（攣）luán contraction：拘～ contraction. 痉～ spasm; convulsions

鸾（鸞）luán（名）a mythical bird like the phoenix

孪（孿）luán（名）twin

孪生 luánshēng（名）twin：～姐妹 twin sisters

卵 luǎn（名）ovum; egg; spawn

卵巢 luǎncháo（名）ovary

卵翼 luǎnyì（动）cover with wings as in brooding; shield：～之下 under the wing of

乱（亂）luàn I（形）1 in disorder; in a confusion：屋里很～. The room is in a mess. 2 confused (state of mind)：我心里很～. My mind is in a confused state. II（名）disorder; upheaval; chaos; riot; unrest; turmoil：十年内～ a decade of turmoil. 叛～ armed rebellion; mutiny III（动）confuse; mix up; jumble：扰～ create confusion; disturb

乱弹（彈）琴 luàntánqín（动）〈口〉act or talk like a fool; talk nonsense

乱哄哄 luànhōnghōng（形）in noisy disorder; in a hubbub; tumultuous; in an uproar

乱离（離）luànlí（动）be torn apart by war; be rendered homeless by war

乱伦（倫）luànlún（动）commit incest

乱码 luànmǎ（名）messy code; confused code; illegible characters

乱蓬蓬 luànpēngpēng（形）dishevelled; tangled; unkempt：～的头发 dishevelled (tangled) hair

乱七八糟 luànqībāzāo at sixes and sevens; in a mess; in terrible disorder

乱说 luànshuō（动）talk foolishly or irresponsibly; talk nonsense

乱套 luàntào（动）muddle things up; turn things upside down

乱糟糟 luànzāozāo（形）1 chaotic; messy 2 confused; perturbed

乱真 luànzhēn（动）(of fakes) look genuine：以假～ pass off a fake as genuine

乱子 luànzi（名）disturbance; chaos; trouble

掠 lüè（动）1 plunder; pillage; sack 2 sweep past; brush past; graze; skim over：海鸥～过浪面 seagulls skimming the waves

掠夺（奪）lüèduó（动）plunder; rob; pillage：～成性 be predatory by nature

掠美 lüèměi（动）claim credit due to others

略 lüè I（形）brief; sketchy：简～ sketchy; simple. ～述大意 give a brief account II（副）slightly; a little; somewhat：～有所闻 know a little about the matter. ～胜一筹 slightly better; a notch above sb. III（名）1 summary; brief account; outline：史～ outline history. 事～ a short biographical account 2 strategy; plan; scheme：策～ tactics. 雄才大～ (a person of) great talent and bold vision IV（动）1 omit; delete; leave out：从～ be omitted 2 capture; seize

略略 lüèlüè（副）slightly; briefly：他行前～说了几句. He spoke just a few words before he left.

略图（圖）lüètú（名）sketch map; sketch

略微 lüèwēi（副）slightly; a little; somewhat：～有点感冒 have a slight cold; have a touch of flu

略语 lüèyǔ（名）abbreviation; shortening

沦（淪）lún（动）1 sink：沉～ sink into depravity, etc. 2 fall; be reduced to

沦落 lúnluò（动）fall low; be reduced to poverty：～街头 be driven on to the streets

沦丧（喪）lúnsàng（动）be lost; be ruined：道德～ decay of morals

沦亡 lúnwáng（动）(of a country) be conquered (or subjugated)

沦陷 lúnxiàn（动）(of territory, etc.) be occupied by the enemy; fall into enemy hands：～区 enemy-occupied area

轮（輪）lún I（名）1 wheel：齿～ gear wheel 2 sth. resembling a wheel; disc; ring：光～ halo. 年～ annual ring 3 steamboat; steamer：江

L

~ river steamer II (动) take turns: ~值 on duty by turns. 下一个就~到你了. It will be your turn next. III (量) 1 [for the sun, the moon, etc.]: 一~红日 a red sun. 一~明月 a bright moon 2 round: 新的一~会谈 a new round of talks

轮班 lúnbān (动) in shifts; in relays; in rotation

轮船 lúnchuán (名) steamer; steamship; steamboat

轮番 lúnfān (副) take turns: ~去做 do the work by turns

轮换 lúnhuàn (动) rotate; take turns

轮廓 lúnkuò (名) outline; contour; rough sketch

轮流 lúnliú (副) take turns; do sth. in turn: 他俩~值夜班. They work on night shifts in turn.

轮胎 lúntāi (名) tyre

轮子 lúnzi (名) wheel

轮作 lúnzuò (名) crop rotation

伦(倫) lún (名) 1 human relationships, esp. as conceived by feudal ethics 2 logic; order 3 peer; match: 英勇绝~ peerless; matchless

伦比 lúnbǐ (动) rival; equal: 无与~ unrivalled; unequalled; peerless

伦次 lúncì (名) coherence; logical sequence: 语无~ speak incoherently

伦理 lúnlǐ (名) ethics; moral principles

纶(綸) lún (名) 1 black silk ribbon 2 fishing line 3 synthetic fibre

论(論) lùn I (名) 1 view; opinion; statement: 高~ your brilliant views; your wise counsel. 舆~ public opinion. 社~ editorial 2 dissertation; essay 3 theory: 进化~ the theory of evolution. 唯物~ materialism II (动) 1 discuss; talk about; discourse: 讨~ discuss 2 mention; regard; consider: 相提并~ mention in the same breath; place on a par 3 decide on; determine: ~罪 mete out punishments

论处(處) lùnchǔ (动) decide on sb.'s punishment; punish

论点(點) lùndiǎn (名) argument; thesis: 这篇文章~突出,条理分明. The essay is well organized, giving prominence to all the main points of argument.

论调 lùndiào (名)〈贬〉view; argument: 这种~很容易迷惑人. Such views are apt to mislead people.

论断(斷) lùnduàn (名) inference; judgment; thesis: 作出~ draw an inference

论据(據) lùnjù (名) grounds of argument; argument

论理 lùnlǐ 1 normally; as things should be: ~她早该回家了. Normally, she should have gone home. 2 logic: 合乎~ be logical; stand to reason

论述 lùnshù (动) discuss; expound

论坛(壇) lùntán (名) forum; tribune

论题 lùntí (名) proposition

论文 lùnwén (名) thesis; dissertation; treatise; paper: 学术~ an academic thesis (or paper). 科学~ a scientific treatise

论战(戰) lùnzhàn (名) polemic; debate

论证 lùnzhèng I (名) demonstration; proof II (动) expound and prove

论著 lùnzhù (名) treatise; work; book

论资排辈 lùnzī-páibèi arrange in order of seniority

啰(囉) luō

啰嗦 luōsuō (形) 1 long-winded; wordy: 他说话太~. He's far too long-winded. 2 complicated; troublesome: 这些手续真~. All these formalities are much too complicated.

螺 luó (名) 1 spiral shell; snail: 田~ field snail 2 whorl (in fingerprint)

螺钿 luódiàn (名) mother-of-pearl inlay: ~漆盘 lacquer tray inlaid with mother-of-pearl

螺钉 luódīng (名) screw: 木~ wood screw

螺母 luómǔ (名) (screw) nut

螺丝(絲) luósī (名)〈口〉screw: ~刀 screwdriver

螺纹 luówén (名) 1 whorl (in fingerprint) 2 thread (of a screw)

螺旋 luóxuán (名) 1 spiral; helix: ~式发展 spiral development; developing in spirals. ~线 helical line; spiral. ~桨 (screw) propeller 2 screw

骡 luó (名)(~子) mule

罗(羅) luó I (动) 1 catch birds with a net: 门可~雀 visitors are extremely few 2 collect; gather together 3 display; spread out: ~列 set out; marshal II (名) 1 sieve; sift 2 a kind of silk gauze: ~扇 silk gauze fan 3 a net for catching birds

罗列 luólìe (动) 1 spread out; set out 2

enumerate：～事实 enumerate the facts

罗盘(盤) luópán (名) compass

罗网(網) luówǎng (名) net; trap：自投～ walk right into the trap

罗织(織) luózhī (动) frame up：～罪名 cook up charges

罗致 luózhì (动) enlist the services of; secure sb. in one's employment; collect; gather together：～人材 enlist the services of talented people

逻(邏) luó (动) patrol：巡～ patrol

逻辑 luóji (名) logic：合乎～ be logical

萝(蘿) luó (名) trailing plants：藤～ Chinese wistaria

萝卜(蔔) luóbo (名) radish

箩(籮) luó (名) a square-bottomed bamboo basket

箩筐 luókuāng (名) a large bamboo or wicker basket

锣(鑼) luó (名) gong：～鼓喧天 a deafening sound of gongs and drums

瘰 luǒ

瘰疬(癧) luǒlì (名) scrofula

裸 luǒ (形) bare; naked; exposed：赤～～ stark-naked; undisguised

裸露 luǒlù (形) uncovered; exposed

裸体(體) luǒtǐ (形) naked; nude

裸线(綫) luǒxiàn (名) bare wire

落 luò I (动) 1 fall; drop：花～ flowers fall 2 go down; set：太阳～山了. The sun has set. 3 lower：把帘子～下来 lower the blinds 4 decline; come down; sink：衰～ decline; go downhill 5 lag behind; fall behind：名～孙山 fail in a competitive exam 6 leave behind; stay behind：不～痕迹 leave no trace; disappear without a trace 7 get：～空 come to nothing II (名) 1 whereabouts：下～ whereabouts 2 settlement：村～ a small village; hamlet
see also là

落泊 luòbó (形) be in dire straits; be down and out (also as "落魄")

落成 luòchéng (名) completion (of a building, etc.)：～典礼 inauguration ceremony (for a building, etc.)

落得 luòdé (动) be landed in; end up in (in a disgraceful state)：～关进监狱 be landed (or end up) in prison

落地 luòdì (动) (of babies) be born：呱呱～ be born into the world with a cry. ～灯 floor lamp; standard lamp

落发(髮) luòfà (动) be tonsured (to become a Buddhist monk or nun)

落后(後) luòhòu I (动) fall behind; lag behind：不甘～ hate to be outshone; be unwilling to lag behind II (形) backward：～地区 backward areas; less developed areas

落户 luòhù (动) settle：在边远地区～ settle in a remote border area

落脚 luòjiǎo (动) stay (for a time); stop over; put up：找个地方～ find a place to stay. 在客店～ put up at an inn

落井下石 luò jǐng xià shí hit a person when he's down

落空 luòkōng (动) come to nothing; fail; fall through：两头～ fall between two stools. 希望～ be disappointed

落款 luòkuǎn (动) write the names of the sender and the recipient on a painting, gift or letter; inscribe (a gift, etc.)

落落大方 luòluò dàfāng natural and graceful

落落寡合 luòluò guǎ hé standoffish; aloof

落实(實) luòshí I (形) practicable; workable：生产计划要订得～. Production plans must be practicable. II (动) 1 fix (or decide) in advance; ascertain; make sure：交货时间还没有最后～. The date of delivery hasn't been fixed yet. 2 carry out; fulfil; implement; put into effect：～措施 implement measures

落水狗 luòshuǐgǒu (名) a cur fallen into the water：痛打～ be merciless with evildoers when they are in disgrace

落汤(湯)鸡(鷄) luòtāngjī like a drowned rat; soaked through

落套 luòtào (动) conform to a conventional pattern

落拓 luòtuò (形) 1 〈书〉 be in reduced circumstances and feel bitterly disappointed 2 untrammelled by convention：～不羁 unconventional and uninhibited

落网(網) luòwǎng (动) (of a criminal) be caught; be captured; be brought to justice

落伍 luòwǔ (动) fall behind the ranks; drop behind; drop out

落选(選) luòxuǎn (动) not be elected; lose an election

骆 luò (名) a white horse with a black mane, mentioned in ancient Chi-

L

nese books
骆驼 luòtuo (名) camel
络 luò I (名) sth. resembling a net: 橘～ tangerine pith. 丝瓜～ loofah II (动) 1 hold sth. in place with a net: 她头上～着一个发网. She kept her hair in place with a net. 2 twine; wind: ～纱 winding yarn; spooling
络腮胡(鬍)子 luòsāihúzi (名) whiskers; full beard
络绎(繹)不绝 luòyì bù jué in an endless stream: 参观展览会的人～. A continuous stream of visitors came to the exhibition.

M m

抹 mā (动) wipe: ～桌子 wipe a table clean
see also mǒ; mò
抹布 mābù (名) a piece of rag to clear things with
妈 mā (名) 1 mummy; mum; mother 2 a form of address for a married woman one generation one's senior: 姑～ (paternal) aunt. 姨～ (maternal) aunt
妈妈 māma (名) mama; mum; mummy; mother
麻 má I (名) hemp; flax; jute II (形) 1 coarse; pitted; spotty: ～子(脸) a pock-marked face. 镜子上怎么有这么多～点儿? How come the mirror is so spotty? 2 numb; tingle: 腿发～ have pins and needles in one's legs. 舌头发～ one's tongue is tingling
麻痹 mábì I (名) paralysis: 小儿～ infantile paralysis II (动) benumb; lull: ～人们的斗志 lull (or blunt) people's fighting will III (形) lacking in vigilance: ～大意 be careless; be off guard
麻布 mábù (名) 1 gunny cloth; sackcloth 2 linen
麻袋 mádài (名) sack; gunny-bag
麻烦 máfan I (形) troublesome; inconvenient: 这事恐怕太～了. It's too much trouble, I'm afraid. 自找～ ask for trouble II (动) trouble; bother; put sb. to trouble: 我懒得～. I can't be bothered. ～你了. Thank you for the trouble you've taken on my behalf.
麻将(將) májiàng (名) mahjong
麻利 máli (形) quick and neat; dexterous; deft: 手脚～ quick and neat (with work)
麻木 mámù (形) numb: ～不仁 apathetic; insensitive
麻雀 máquè (名) sparrow
麻绳(繩) máshéng (名) rope made of hemp, flax, etc.
麻药(藥) máyào (名) anaesthetic
麻疹 mázhěn (名) measles
麻子 mázi (名) 1 pockmarks 2 a person with a pock-marked face
麻醉 mázuì I (名) anaesthesia; narcosis: 针刺～ acupuncture anaesthesia. ～剂 anaesthetic; narcotic. ～品 narcotic; drug. ～师 anaesthetist II (动) anaesthetize; poison
吗 má (代) what: 你在这儿干～? What are you doing here?
see also mǎ; ma
马(馬) mǎ (名) horse: 母～ mare. 种～ stallion; stud. 小～ pony. 中途换～ change (swop) horses in midstream
马鞍 mǎ'ān (名) saddle
马鞭 mǎbiān (名) horsewhip
马不停蹄 mǎ bù tíng tí hurry (to a place); nonstop
马车(車) mǎchē (名) (horse-drawn) carriage or cart
马达(達) mǎdá (名) motor
马大哈 mǎdàhā (名) a careless person; scatterbrain
马灯(燈) mǎdēng (名) barn lantern
马夫 mǎfū (名) groom
马褂 mǎguà (名) mandarin jacket
马后(後)炮 mǎhòupào (名) belated effort (action or advice): 他这个人一贯爱放～. He always comes up with belated advice. *or* He is always wise after the event.
马虎 mǎhū (形) careless; casual: ～了事 get sth. done in a slapdash (or sloppy) manner. 这孩子聪明倒聪明,就是太～. This child is clever for sure, but he is a bit too careless.
马甲 mǎjiǎ (名) a sleeveless garment
马脚 mǎjiǎo (名) sth. that gives the game away: 露～ show the cloven hoof; give oneself away; let the cat out of the bag
马厩 mǎjiù (名) stable
马克思主义(義) Mǎkèsīzhǔyì (名) Marxism
马裤 mǎkù (名) riding breeches
马拉松 mǎlāsōng (名) marathon

马力 mǎlì (名) horsepower (h. p.): 开足～ at full speed
马铃薯 mǎlíngshǔ (名) potato
马路 mǎlù (名) road; street; avenue
马马虎虎 mǎmǎhūhū (形) 1 careless; casual 2 passable; not so bad; so-so: 他的英文怎么样? ——～,不至于迷路. Does he speak good English? — Just so-so. But he won't get lost. 这本书有意思吗? ——～,反正不值得买. How about this book? — Not so bad, but not worth buying.
马前卒 mǎqiánzú (名) pawn; cat's-paw
马赛克 mǎsàikè (名) mosaic
马上 mǎshàng (副) at once; straight away; right away; immediately: 告诉他等一等, 我～就回来. Tell him to wait. I'll be right back. 我们必须～出发. We must set off at once. 演出～就要开始了. The performance will begin at any moment.
马桶 mǎtǒng (名) 1 nightstool 2 toilet
马戏(戲) mǎxì (名) circus: ～团 circus troupe
马掌 mǎzhǎng (名) horseshoe

玛 mǎ

玛瑙 mǎnǎo (名) agate

码 mǎ I (量) 1 yard (yd.) 2 [indicating things of the same kind]: 两～事 two entirely different matters II (名) a sign or thing indicating number: 页～ page number. 价～ marked price. 筹～ counter; chip
码头(頭) mǎtou (名) wharf; dock; pier

吗 mǎ

see also má; ma
吗啡 mǎfēi (名) morphine

蚂 mǎ

蚂蟥 mǎhuáng (名) leech
蚂蚁(蟻) mǎyǐ (名) ant

骂 mà (动) scold; curse; swear: ～人 swear (at people). ～人话 abusive language; swear word
骂街 màjiē (动) shout abuses in the street
骂骂咧咧 màmàliēliē be foul-mouthed

嘛 ma (助) 1 [used at the end of a sentence to show what precedes it is obvious]: 这样做就是不对～! Of course it was acting improperly! 孩子总是孩子～! Children are children! 2 [used within a sentence to mark a pause]: 你～,就不用亲自去了. As for you, I don't think you have to go in person.

吗 ma (助) [used at the end of a declarative sentence to transform it into a question]: 你找我～? Are you looking for me? 他们那儿有野生动物～? Do they have wild life there? 吃完饭散散步好～? Shall we take a walk after dinner?

see also má; mǎ

埋 mái (动) bury

see also mán
埋藏 máicáng (动) lie hidden in the earth
埋伏 máifu (动、名) 1 ambush: 设下～ lay an ambush. 中～ fall into an ambush 2 hide; lie in wait
埋名 máimíng (动) conceal one's identity; live incognito
埋没 máimò (动) 1 neglect; stifle: ～人材 fail to do justice to talent 2 cover up; bury
埋头(頭) máitóu (动) immerse oneself in; be engrossed in: ～苦干 quietly immerse oneself in hard work. ～读书 bury oneself in books
埋葬 máizàng (动) bury

买(買) mǎi (动) buy; purchase: ～东西 buy things; go shopping. ～得起 can afford. ～不起 cannot afford
买办(辦) mǎibàn (名) comprador
买单 mǎidān (动) pay the bill
买断(斷) mǎiduàn (动) buy the ownership of sth.
买方 mǎifāng (名) the buying party; buyer
买好 mǎihǎo (动) try to win sb.'s favour; play up to
买卖(賣) mǎimai (名) buying and selling; business; trade: 做成一笔～ make a deal. ～兴隆. The business is brisk. ～人 businessman; trader; merchant. 买空卖空 speculate (in stocks, etc.)
买通 mǎitōng (动) bribe; buy over; buy off
买账(賬) mǎizhàng (动) acknowledge the superiority or seniority of; show respect for: 谁也不买他的账. No one gives a damn what he says.
买主 mǎizhǔ (名) buyer; customer

麦(麥) mài (名) wheat: ～苗 wheat seedling. ～茬 wheat stubble
麦片 màipiàn (名) oatmeal: ～粥 oatmeal porridge

M

麦收 màishōu (名) wheat harvest

麦穗 màisuì (名) ear of wheat; wheat head

卖(賣) mài (动) 1 sell: ~不出去 not sell well 2 betray: ~友求荣 betray one's friend in pursuit of power and wealth 3 make an effort: ~劲儿 exert oneself; spare or stint no effort

卖唱 màichàng (动) make a living by singing

卖点(點) màidiǎn (名) selling point

卖方 màifāng (名) the selling party; seller

卖乖 màiguāi (动) show off one's cleverness

卖国(國) màiguó (动) betray one's country: ~条约 traitorous treaty. ~行为 treasonable act. ~贼 traitor (to one's country)

卖力 màilì (动) exert all one's strength; spare no effort

卖命 màimìng (动) do a killing job for somebody or some clique

卖弄 màinong (动) show off: ~学问 show off one's erudition

卖俏 màiqiào (动) coquette; flirt

卖身 màishēn (动) sell oneself: ~契 an indenture by which one sells oneself. ~投靠 sell one's soul in exchange for personal gain

卖艺(藝) màiyì (动) make a living as a performer

卖淫 màiyín (名) prostitution

卖座 màizuò (动) attract large audiences: 这个电影可~啦. This film is a box-office smash.

迈(邁) mài I (动) step; stride: ~过门槛 step over the threshold II (形) advanced in years: 年~ aged

迈步 màibù (动) take a step; step forward: 迈出第一步 make the first step

迈进(進) màijìn (动) stride forward; advance with big strides

脉(脈) mài (名) 1 arteries and veins: 血~ blood veins. 叶~ veins in a leaf 2 pulse: 号~ feel sb.'s pulse
see also mò

脉搏 màibó (名) pulse

脉冲(衝) màichōng (名) pulse

脉络 màiluò (名) train of thought; sequence of ideas: ~分明 well organized

蛮(蠻) mán I (形) rough; unreasoning: 野~ savage. ~不讲理 cannot be brought to reason II (副) quite; pretty: 他俩的关系~不错. They are on pretty good terms.

蛮干(幹) mángàn (动) act rashly: 那纯粹是~. That's downright foolhardy.

蛮横 mánhèng (形) rude and unreasonable: 这些要求~无理. The demands are (or go) beyond all reason.

蛮劲(勁) mánjìn (名) sheer animal strength

埋 mán
see also mái

埋怨 mányuàn (动) complain; grumble; blame: 她这个人老爱~. She is always complaining. 别互相~了! Stop blaming each other!

瞒(瞞) mán (动) hide the truth from: 不~你说 to tell you the truth. 他~着我做出了决定. He made the decision without my prior knowledge or consent.

瞒哄 mánhǒng (动) deceive; pull the wool over sb.'s eyes

瞒天过(過)海 mán tiān guò hǎi practise deception

馒 mán

馒头(頭) mántou (名) steamed bun; steamed bread

满(滿) mǎn I (形) 1 full; filled; packed: ~天 all over the sky. ~眼 have one's eyes filled with; meet the eye on every side. ~心 have one's heart filled with. 瓶子~了. The bottle is full (of liquid). 大厅里坐~了人. The hall was packed with people. ~山松树. The hill was covered with pine trees. 他~身大汗. He is sweating all over. 2 content; satisfied: 自~ conceited; complacent II (副) completely; entirely: ~不在乎 not seem to care in the least. 这屋子已经~舒服的了. This room is perfectly comfortable as it is. III (动) reach the limit; expire: 假期~了. The vacation is over. 她明天就~三岁了. She will be three years old tomorrow.

满城风(風)雨 mǎn chéng fēngyǔ (become) the talk of the town: 闹得~ cause a scandal

满额 mǎn'é (动) fulfil the (enrolment, etc.) quota

满分 mǎnfēn (名) full marks

满腹 mǎnfù have one's mind filled with: ~

M

牢骚 full of grievances; full of grumbles. ～狐疑 filled with suspicion; full of misgivings

满怀(懷) mǎnhuái I (动) be imbued with: ～信心 be full of confidence II (名) bosom: 撞了个～ bump right into sb.

满口 mǎnkǒu (副) (speak) profusely; glibly: ～答应 readily agree

满面 mǎnmiàn (名) have one's face covered with: ～笑容 beam; be all smiles. ～红光 glow with health. ～春风 be radiant with happiness; beam with pleasure

满目 mǎnmù come into view: ～荒凉. The site was a scene of desolation.

满腔 mǎnqiāng (名) have one's bosom filled with: ～热情 full of enthusiasm. ～悲愤 full of grief and indignation

满堂红 mǎntánghóng (名) all-round victory

满意 mǎnyì (形) satisfied; pleased: 他对他新的工作很～. He is pleased with his new job.

满月 mǎnyuè I (名) full moon II (动) a baby's completion of its first month of life: 孩子明天就～了. The baby will be a month old tomorrow.

满载 mǎnzài (动) loaded to capacity; fully loaded; laden with: ～而归 return with fruitful results

满足 mǎnzú (动) 1 feel content; feel satisfied: ～现状 be content with things as they are 2 satisfy; meet: ～要求 meet the demands of. ～需要 meet the needs of. ～愿望 satisfy one's desire. ～已有成就 rest on one's laurels

满座 mǎnzuò (动) have a capacity audience; have a full house

漫 màn I (动) overflow; brim over: 池塘的水～出来了. The pool overflowed its banks. II (形) 1 free; casual: ～步 stroll; roam. ～不经心 careless; casual; negligent. ～无目标 aimless; at random 2 all over the place: ～无边际 boundless; rambling. ～山遍野 all over the countryside and plains. ～天大雪 big flakes of snow drifting across the sky

漫笔(筆) mànbǐ (名) random thoughts (or notes); informal essay

漫长(長) màncháng (形) very long; endless: ～的岁月 long years. ～的道路 a long way to go

漫画(畫) mànhuà (名) caricature; cartoon

漫骂 mànmà (动) fling abuse at sb.

漫漫 mànmàn (形) very long; boundless

漫谈 màntán (动) have an informal discussion

漫天 màntiān (形) 1 all over the sky: ～大雾 a dense fog covering the sky 2 boundless; limitless: ～大谎 a monstrous lie

漫溢 mànyì (动) overflow; flood; brim over

漫游 mànyóu (动) go on a pleasure trip; roam; wander

慢 màn I (形) slow: ～车 slow train. 反应～ have a slow reaction. 我的表～了. My watch loses. 钟～了 10 分钟. The clock is ten minutes slow. II (副) slowly: ～～说 speak slowly III (动) 1 slow down: ～点儿! Slow down a bit! 2 postpone; defer: 这事先～点儿告诉她. Don't tell her about it yet.

慢慢 mànmàn (副) slowly; gradually: ～来. Take your time; Don't be in a rush. 他～就会懂得的. He'll understand it sooner or later.

慢腾腾 màntēngtēng (形) unhurriedly; sluggishly: 这样～地走,什么时候才能走到呢? When will you ever get there if you walk in such a leisurely manner?

慢条(條)斯理 màntiáo-sīlǐ leisurely; unhurriedly; imperturbably

慢性 mànxìng (形) 1 chronic: ～病 chronic disease 2 slow (in taking effect): ～毒药 slow poison

慢悠悠 mànyōuyōu (形) unhurriedly; leisurely

谩 màn (形) disrespectful; rude

谩骂 mànmà (动) hurl (or fling) abuses; vilify

蔓 màn

蔓生植物 mànshēng zhíwù (名) trailing plant

蔓延 mànyán (动) spread; extend: 疾病～得很快. The disease spread very fast.

幔 màn (名) curtain; screen: ～帐 curtain; canopy

忙 máng I (形) busy; fully occupied: 大～人 a busy man. ～死了 be terribly busy. 他一个人～不过来. He can't manage all this by himself. 他正～着写文章. He is busy writing an article. II (动) hurry; hasten: ～什么,再坐会儿吧. There is no tearing hurry. Stay a bit longer.

忙碌 mánglù (形) busy; bustling about

忙乱(亂) mángluàn (动) act hurriedly in a

M

messy situation

芒 máng (名) awn; beard

芒刺在背 mángcì zài bèi feel prickled down one's back—feel nervous and uneasy

芒果 mángguǒ (名) mango

茫 máng

茫茫 mángmáng (形) a boundless expanse of; vast: ～大海 a vast sea. ～草原 boundless grasslands

茫然 mángrán (形) ignorant; in the dark; at a loss: 感到～ feel completely in the dark. ～不知所措 be at a loss what to do; be at sea. 显出～的神情 look perplexed; have a confounded look

盲 máng (形) blind

盲肠(腸) mángcháng (名) caecum

盲从(從) mángcóng (动) follow blindly

盲点(點) mángdiǎn (名) blind spot

盲动(動) mángdòng (动) act blindly; act rashly

盲流 mángliú (名) unemployed migrant; vagabond

盲目 mángmù (形) blind: ～崇拜 blind faith. ～乐观 unrealistic optimism. ～性 blindness

盲区(區) mángqū (名) blind zone

盲人 mángrén (名) blind person: ～摸象 like the blind men trying to size up the elephant—take a part for the whole

盲文 mángwén (名) braille

莽 mǎng

莽苍(蒼) mǎngcāng (形) (of scenery) blurred; misty: 烟雨～ blurred with mist and rain

莽莽 mǎngmǎng (形) 1 luxuriant; rank 2 (of fields, plains, etc.) vast; boundless

莽原 mǎngyuán (名) wilderness overgrown with grass

莽撞 mǎngzhuàng (形) reckless; impetuous; rash: ～的小伙子 a rude fellow

蟒 mǎng (名) boa; python

蟒蛇 mǎngshé (名) boa; python

猫 māo (名) cat: 小～ kitten. ～叫 mewing; purring

猫步 māobù (名) (modelling) catwalk: 走～ do the catwalk

猫腻 māonì (名) something fishy; unfair conduct in a game

猫头(頭)鹰 māotóuyīng (名) owl

毛 máo I (名) 1 hair; feather; down: 羽～ feather 2 wool: 纯(全)～ pure wool 3 mildew: 长～了 become mildewed II (形) 1 semi-finished: ～坯 semi-finished product 2 little; small: ～孩子 a small child; a mere child 3 careless; crude; rash: ～头～脑 rash; impetuous 4 panicky; scared; flurried: 这下可把他吓～了. He's scared stiff. III (量): *mao*, one-tenth of a *yuan*

毛笔(筆) máobǐ (名) writing brush

毛病 máobìng (名) 1 trouble; breakdown: 汽车出～了. Something is wrong with the car. 2 illness: 他胃有～. He has stomach trouble. 3 defect; fault; shortcoming

毛糙 máocao (形) crude; coarse; careless: 做工～. The work is crude

毛虫(蟲) máochóng (名) caterpillar

毛发(髮) máofà (名) hair (on the human body and head)

毛骨悚然 máogǔ sǒngrán with one's hair standing on end—absolutely horrified: 令人～ send cold shivers down one's spine; make one's blood run cold and one's flesh creep

毛巾 máojīn (名) towel

毛孔 máokǒng (名) pore

毛料 máoliào (名) woollen fabric

毛驴(驢) máolǘ (名) donkey

毛毛雨 máomáoyǔ (名) drizzle

毛皮 máopí (名) fur

毛茸茸 máorōngrōng (形) hairy; downy

毛手毛脚 máoshǒu-máojiǎo carelessly (in handling things): 这孩子～地把碗给打了. The child clumsily broke the bowl.

毛遂自荐(薦) Máo Suì zì jiàn volunteer one's services; offer oneself for the job

毛毯 máotǎn (名) woollen blanket

毛细血管 máoxì xuèguǎn (名) blood capillary

毛线(綫) máoxiàn (名) knitting wool

毛衣 máoyī (名) woollen sweater

毛躁 máozao (形) 1 short-tempered; irritable 2 rash and careless

毛泽(澤)东(東)思想 Máo Zédōng Sīxiǎng (名) Mao Zedong Thought

毛毡(氈) máozhān (名) felt

毛织(織)品 máozhīpǐn (名) 1 wool fabric; woollens 2 woollen knitwear

毛重 máozhòng (名) gross weight

M

牦 máo

牦牛 máoniú (名) yak

锚 máo (名) anchor: 抛~ cast anchor; drop anchor. 起~ weigh anchor. ~地 anchorage

矛 máo (名) spear

矛盾 máodùn I (名) contradiction: ~百出 teem with contradictions II (动) contradict: 自相~ contradict oneself; be inconsistent. 互相~ contradict each other

矛头(頭) máotóu (名) spearhead: ~指向坏人坏事. The attack is spearheaded against evildoers and evil deeds.

茅 máo

茅草 máocǎo (名) cogongrass: ~棚 thatched hut (or shack)

茅房 máofáng (名)〈口〉latrine

茅坑 máokēng (名)〈口〉latrine pit

茅塞顿开(開) máo sè dùn kāi suddenly see the light; be suddenly enlightened

茅舍 máoshè (名)〈书〉thatched cottage

茅屋 máowū (名) thatched cottage

铆 mǎo (动) rivet

铆钉 mǎodīng (名) rivet

茂 mào (形) 1 luxuriant; lush; profuse: 根深叶~ have deep roots and exuberant foliage 2 rich and splendid

茂密 màomì (形) (of plants) dense; thick: ~的森林 a dense forest

茂盛 màoshèng (形) luxuriant; thriving; flourishing

冒 mào I (动) 1 emit; give off; send out (or up, forth): 浑身~汗 sweat all over. ~气 be steaming. 烟囱正在~烟. The chimney is belching smoke. 2 risk; brave: ~风险 run risks. ~着生命危险 at the risk of one's own life. ~雪 brave the snow II (副) 1 boldly; rashly: ~猜一下 make a bold guess 2 falsely (claim, etc.): ~称 falsely claim. ~领养老金 claim (or obtain) pension under false pretences

冒充 màochōng (动) pretend to be; pass oneself off as: ~内行 pretend to be an expert; pose as an expert

冒犯 màofàn (动) offend; affront: 他的话~了她. His words offended her.

冒号(號) màohào (名) colon (:)

冒火 màohuǒ (动) be enraged; flare up

冒尖儿(兒) màojiānr (动) be outstanding: 他在班里~. He is top-notch in his class.

冒进(進) màojìn (动) advance rashly

冒昧 màomèi (形) make bold; venture; take the liberty of: 恕我~提出一个问题. Forgive me for taking the liberty to ask a question. ~陈辞 venture an opinion

冒名 màomíng (动) assume another's name: ~顶替 pretend to be somebody by assuming his name

冒牌 màopái (动) a counterfeit of a well-known trade mark; imitation; fake: ~货 imitation; fake. ~医生 a quack doctor

冒失 màoshi (形) rash; abrupt: 说话~ speak rashly. ~鬼 harum-scarum

冒头(頭) màotóu (动) (of ideas; tendencies) begin to crop up

冒险(險) màoxiǎn (动) take a risk; take chances: ~家 adventurer. ~政策 adventurist policy

帽 mào (名) hat; cap: 草~ straw hat. 军~ army cap. 安全~ safety helmet. 笔~儿 the cap of a pen. 螺钉~ screw cap

帽子 màozi (名) 1 hat; cap; headgear 2 label; tag; brand: 乱扣~ indiscriminately label people as

貌 mào (名) looks; appearance: 美~ good looks. 新~ new look. 人不可~相. Never judge people by their appearance.

貌合神离(離) màohé-shénlí (of two people) be apparently in harmony but essentially at variance

貌似 màosì (动) seem (or appear) to be: ~公正 appear to be impartial

贸 mào (名) trade: 外~ foreign trade

贸然 màorán (副) rashly; hastily; without careful consideration: ~下结论 draw a hasty conclusion; jump to a conclusion

贸易 màoyì (名) trade: 对外~ foreign trade. 国内~ domestic trade. ~差额 balance of trade. ~额 volume of trade; turnover. ~逆差 unfavourable balance of trade. ~顺差 favourable balance of trade

么(麼) me [suffix]: 什~ what. 多~ how. 怎~ why; how. 这~ such; so; in this way

M

没 méi see “没有” méiyǒu
see also mò
没关(關)系(係) méi guānxi it doesn't matter; it's nothing; that's all right; never mind
没精打采 méijīng-dǎcǎi listless; in low spirits
没脸(臉) méiliǎn be ashamed; feel embarrassed: ～见人 be too embarrassed to face anyone
没…没… méi…méi… 1 [each used before a synonym to emphasize negation]: 没完没了 endless. 没羞没臊 shameless 2 [each used before an antonym to in-dicate failure to distinguish things]: 没轻没重 tactless. 没大没小 impolite (to an elder); impudent
没趣 méiqù (形) feel neglected; feel snubbed: 没有人理他,他觉得～,只好走了. Feeling that he was out in the cold, he slunk off. 自讨～ ask for a snub
没什(甚)么(麼) méi shénme 1 as “没关系” méi guānxi 2 don't mention it; it's a pleasure; you're welcome
没事 méishì (动) 1 be free; have nothing to do 2 it doesn't matter; never mind
没事找事 méishì zhǎoshì 1 ask for trouble 2 be fault-finding
没戏(戲) méixì (形) hopeless: 他追她,～. He has no hope of winning her heart.
没羞 méixiū (形) unabashed
没意思 méi yìsi 1 uninteresting; boring 2 bored: 觉得～ feel bored
没有 méiyǒu I (动) 1 [used to negate 有] not have; be without: ～钱 have no money. ～人在家. There is no one at home. 鱼～水就活不了. The fish can't live without water. 2 not so... as: 事情～你说的那么容易. Things are not as easy as you said. 3 less than: ～两个星期他就走了. He left in less than two weeks. 后来～几天她就死了. She died only a few days later. II (副) 1 [used to form the negation of a completed action]: 我昨天～去. I didn't go yesterday. 商店还～关门. The shop hasn't closed yet. 2 [used to form the negation of a past experience]: 他～去过巴黎. He has never been to Paris.

煤 méi (名) coal: 原～ raw coal
煤矿(礦) méikuàng (名) coal mine; colliery: ～工人 coal miner
煤气(氣) méiqì (名) gas: ～灯 gas lamp. ～炉 gas stove
煤球 méiqiú (名) (egg-shaped) briquet
煤炭 méitàn (名) coal: ～工业 coal industry
煤田 méitián (名) coalfield
煤油 méiyóu (名) kerosene: ～灯 kerosene lamp. ～炉 kerosene stove

媒 méi (名) 1 matchmaker; go-between: 做～ act as a matchmaker 2 intermediary
媒介 méijiè (名) medium; vehicle: 传染疾病的～ vehicle of disease. 新闻～ news media
媒婆 méipó (名) professional female matchmaker
媒人 méirén (名) matchmaker; go-between
媒体 méitǐ (名) media; medium

玫 méi
玫瑰 méiguì (名) rose

枚 méi (量) [for small objects]: 一～纪念章 a badge. 两～古币 two ancient coins

霉 méi (名) mould; mildew: 发～ go mouldy; mildew
霉菌 méijūn (名) mould
霉烂(爛) méilàn (动) become mildewed; go rotten

莓 méi (名) certain kinds of berries: 草～ strawberry

梅 méi (名) plum
梅毒 méidú (名) syphilis
梅花 méihuā (名) plum blossom

酶 méi (名) enzyme; ferment: 消化～ digestive ferment

眉 méi (名) eyebrow
眉飞(飛)色舞 méifēi-sèwǔ highly exultant; enraptured (usu. of a person speaking)
眉开(開)眼笑 méikāi-yǎnxiào beam with joy; be wreathed in smiles
眉来(來)眼去 méilái-yǎnqù make eyes at each other; flirt with each other
眉毛 méimao (名) eyebrow; brow
眉目 méimù (名) 1 features; looks: ～清秀 have delicate features 2 logic; sequence of ideas: 这篇文章～清楚. The article is well organized.
眉目 méimu (名) prospect of a solution; sign of a positive outcome: 我们的计划已经有点～了. We are getting somewhere with our plan.

眉批 méipī (名) notes made at the top of a page

眉梢 méishāo (名) the tip of the brow: 喜上～ look very happy

眉头(頭) méitóu (名) brows: 皱～ knit the brows; frown

眉宇 méiyǔ (名) forehead

美 měi (形) 1 pretty; beautiful 2 very satisfactory; good: ～酒 good wine. 物～价廉 good and inexpensive. 日子过得挺～ live a happy life

美不胜(勝)收 měi búshèng shōu more beautiful things than one can take in

美差 měichāi (名) cushy job

美称(稱) měichēng (名) laudatory title; good name

美德 měidé (名) virtue; moral excellence

美发店 měifàdiàn (名) hair salon; hairdresser's

美感 měigǎn (名) sense of beauty; aesthetic feeling

美工 měigōng (名) 1 art designing 2 art designer

美观(觀) měiguān (形) beautiful; artistic; pleasing to the eye: ～大方 simple and artistic

美好 měihǎo (形) (of abstract things) happy; bright: ～的将来 bright future. ～的日子 happy days

美化 měihuà (动) beautify; embellish: ～环境 beautify the environment

美景 měijǐng (名) beautiful scenery (or landscape)

美丽(麗) měilì (形) beautiful

美满(滿) měimǎn (形) happy; perfectly satisfactory: ～的婚姻 a happy marriage

美梦(夢) měimèng (名) fond dream

美妙 měimiào (形) splendid; wonderful; beautiful: ～的音乐 splendid music. ～的诗句 beautiful verse

美名 měimíng (名) good name; good reputation: ～天下扬. Good name spreads far and wide.

美容 měiróng I (动) improve one's looks; receive treatment to increase one's beauty II (名) beauty treatment: ～院 beauty parlour. ～手术 plastic surgery; cosmetic surgery

美食 měishí (名) good food; table delicacies: ～家 gourmet

美术(術) měishù (名) fine arts: 工艺～ arts and crafts. ～馆 art gallery. ～家 artist. ～片 (of film) cartoons. ～字 artistic calligraphy; art lettering

美味 měiwèi (名) delicious food; delicacy

美学(學) měixué (名) aesthetics

美言 měiyán (动) put in a good word for sb.

美中不足 měi zhōng bù zú a flaw in something which might otherwise be perfect; a fly in the ointment

美滋滋 měizīzī (形) extremely pleased with oneself

镁 měi (名) magnesium (Mg)

镁光 měiguāng (名) magnesium light

每 měi I (代) every; each: ～天 every day. ～周一次 once every week. ～小时六十公里 sixty kilometres per hour II (副) every time; whenever

每当(當) měidāng (连) whenever; every time: ～下雨,他都要背痛. His back aches whenever it rains.

每况愈下 měi kuàng yù xià steadily deteriorate; go from bad to worse

寐 mèi (动)〈书〉sleep: 梦～以求 long (or yearn) for sth. day and night

昧 mèi I (动) hide; conceal: 拾金不～ not pocket the money one happens to pick up II (形) be ignorant of: 愚～无知 ignorant or illiterate

昧心 mèixīn (do evil) against one's conscience

魅 mèi (名) evil spirit; demon

魅力 mèilì (名) glamour; enchantment; fascination: 艺术～ artistic charm. 领导人的～ the charisma of a leader. 她很有～. She is very attractive.

妹 mèi (名) younger sister; sister (also as "妹妹")

媚 mèi I (动) flatter; fawn on; toady to; curry favour with II (形) charming; fascinating; enchanting: 春光明～ the spring scenery exudes radiance and charm

媚骨 mèigǔ (名) obsequiousness

媚外 mèiwài (动) fawn on foreign powers

闷 mēn I (形) 1 stuffy; close: 屋里人太多,空气太～. It's really stuffy with so many people in the room. 2 (of a sound) muffled: 说话～声～气的 speak in a muffled voice II (动) cover tightly: ～一会儿, 茶味就出来了. Let the tea brew for a while and the flavour will come

out. 把事儿～在心里 bottle unpleasant things up; brood over unpleasant things
see also mèn

闷气(氣) mēnqì (形) stuffy; close

闷热(熱) mēnrè (形) hot and stuffy; stifling hot

闷头(頭)儿(兒) mēntóur (副) quietly; silently: ～干 work quietly; plod away silently

门(門) mén I (名) 1 door; gate; entrance: 前(后)～ front (back) door. 登～拜访 pay a call on sb. at his home 2 valve; switch: 气～ air valve. 电～ switch 3 way to do sth.; knack: 我新到,对这儿的事还不摸～. I'm new here. I don't know anything yet. 这件事有～了. The matter looks hopeful. 4 family: 豪～ wealthy and influential family 5 (religious) sect; school (of thought): 佛～ Buddhism 6 phylum II (量): 一～大炮 a cannon. 两～功课 two subjects (courses)

门当(當)户对(對) méndāng-hùduì be well-matched in social status (for marriage)

门道 méndào (名) 1 way to do sth. 2 social connections; contacts

门第 méndì (名) family status

门房 ménfáng (名) 1 porter's lodge 2 gate-keeper; doorman

门户 ménhù (名) 1 door; gate 2 gateway; important passageway 3 faction; sect: ～之见 sectarian bias

门禁 ménjìn (名) guarded entrance: ～森严 with the entrances heavily guarded

门警 ménjǐng (名) police guard at an entrance

门槛(檻) ménkǎn (名) threshold

门客 ménkè (名) retainer

门口 ménkǒu (名) entrance; doorway

门框 ménkuàng (名) door frame

门帘(簾) ménlián (名) door curtain

门铃 ménlíng (名) doorbell

门路 ménlù (名) 1 social connections to be made use of; pull: 找～ seek help through one's social connections 2 knack; way: 摸到一点～ begin to know the ropes

门面 ménmiàn (名) 1 the façade of a shop; shop front 2 appearance; façade: 装点～ keep up appearances; do some window dressing. ～话 formal meaningless remarks; lip service

门牌 ménpái (名) house number; house plate

门票 ménpiào (名) entrance ticket: 不收～ admission free

门市 ménshì (名) retail sales: ～部 retail department; sales department

门厅(廳) méntīng (名) entrance hall; portico

门庭若市 mén-tíng ruò shì The house is often crowded with visitors

门徒 méntú (名) disciple; follower

门外汉(漢) ménwàihàn (名) layman

门卫(衛) ménwèi (名) entrance guard

门牙 ményá (名) front tooth

门诊 ménzhěn (名) outpatient service (in a hospital): ～病人 outpatient; clinic patient. ～部 clinic; outpatient department

扪 mén (动) lay one's hand on

扪心自问 ménxīn zìwèn examine one's conscience

闷 mèn (形) 1 bored; depressed; in low spirits: 心里～得慌 feel bored stiff 2 tightly closed; sealed
see also mēn

闷棍 mèngùn (名) staggering blow (with a cudgel)

闷葫芦(蘆) mènhúlu (名) enigma; puzzle: 别人都知道了,只有他还装在～里. Everyone else knows about it, but he is still in the dark.

闷雷 mènléi (名) muffled thunder

闷闷不乐(樂) mènmèn bú lè depressed; unhappy

闷气(氣) mènqì (名) the sulks: 生～ be sulky

焖 mèn (名) braise: ～牛肉 braised beef. ～饭 cook rice over a slow fire

们 men 1 [used after a personal pronoun or a noun to show plural number]: 我～ we. 你～ you. 孩子～ the children. 人～ people 2 [们 is not used when the pronoun or noun is preceded by a numeral or an intensifier: 三个教师 three teachers. 很多姑娘 many girls]

蒙 mēng I (动) 1 cheat; deceive: 你在～我吧? You're kidding me! 2 make a random guess: 你～对了. You've made a lucky guess! II (形) unconscious; senseless: 给打～了 be knocked senseless; be stunned by a blow
see also méng; Měng

蒙蒙亮 mēngmēngliàng first glimmer of

M

dawn; daybreak：天刚～ at daybreak

蒙骗 mēngpiàn（动）deceive; hoodwink; delude

蒙头(頭)转(轉)向 mēngtóu zhuànxiàng lose one's bearings; one's brain is in a whirl; utterly confused

虻 méng（名）horsefly; gadfly：牛～ gadfly

氓 méng（名）the common people

蒙 méng I（动）1 cover：～住眼睛 be blindfolded. ～头睡大觉 tuck oneself in and sleep like a log 2 thanks to：承～指教，太感谢了. Thank you very much for your advice. ～你夸奖 thank you for your compliment II（名）ignorance：启～ enlighten

see also mēng; Měng

蒙蔽 méngbì（动）deceive; hoodwink; pull the wool over sb.'s eyes：广大人民群众是不会永远受～的. Not all the people can be fooled all the time.

蒙混 ménghùn（动）muddle through：～过关 get by under false pretences

蒙昧 méngmèi（形）1 uncivilized; uncultured; illiterate 2 ignorant; unenlightened

蒙蒙 méngméng（形）drizzly; misty：细雨～ a fine rain. 烟雾～ misty

蒙受 méngshòu（动）suffer; sustain：～损失 sustain a loss. ～耻辱 suffer humiliation

蒙在鼓里(裏) méng zài gǔlǐ be kept in the dark

曚 méng（名）dim daylight

朦 méng

曚眬(矓) ménglóng（形）drowsy; half asleep：睡眼～ eyes heavy with sleep; drowsy

朦 méng

朦胧(朧) ménglóng（形）dim; hazy; obscure：～的景色 misty view

萌 méng（动）sprout; bud; germinate

萌发(發) méngfā（动）sprout; shoot：树木～了新叶. Leaves are beginning to sprout from trees.

萌芽 méngyá I（动）sprout; shoot; bud II（名）rudiments：消灭于～状态 nip in the bud

盟 méng（名）1 alliance：结～ form an alliance. ～兄 sworn brothers 2 league

盟国(國) méngguó（名）allied country; ally

盟军 méngjūn（名）allied forces

盟友 méngyǒu（名）ally

盟约 méngyuē（名）treaty of alliance

懵 měng（形）muddled

懵懂 měngdǒng（形）muddled; ignorant

蒙 Měng the Mongol nationality

see also mēng; méng

蒙古 Měnggǔ（名）Mongolia：～人 Mongolian. ～语 Mongol (language)

蒙古包 měnggǔbāo（名）yurt

蒙古族 Měnggǔzú（名）the Mongol (Mongolian) nationality

锰 měng（名）manganese (Mn)：～结核 manganese nodule. ～钢 manganese steel

猛 měng（形）1 fierce; violent; vigorous：～虎 a fierce tiger. ～干 work vigorously. 产量～增 a sharp increase in output. 用力过～ use too much strength; overexert oneself 2 suddenly; abruptly：～一转身 turn around sharply

猛劲(勁)儿(兒) měngjìnr（名）great vigour：工作有股子～ work with vim and vigour

猛进(進) měngjìn（动）push ahead vigorously：突飞～ advance by leaps and bounds

猛烈 měngliè（形）vigorous; fierce; violent：发动～的进攻 launch a vigorous offensive. ～的炮火 heavy shellfire

猛禽 měngqín（名）bird of prey

猛然 měngrán（副）suddenly; abruptly：～想起一件事 remember sth. in a flash. ～一拉 pull with a jerk

猛士 měngshì（名）a brave fighter

猛兽(獸) měngshòu（名）beast of prey

猛醒 měngxǐng（动）suddenly realize (or wake up) (also as "猛省")

梦(夢) mèng（名）dream：做～ dream. 白日～ daydream

梦话 mènghuà（名）1 words uttered in one's sleep：说～ talk in one's sleep 2 nonsense; raving

梦幻 mènghuàn（名）dream; illusion

梦见(見) mèngjiàn（动）see in a dream; dream about：昨晚她～自己上大学了. She dreamt about going to university last night.

M

梦境 mèngjìng (名) dreamland; dreamlike world: 如入～ feel as if one were in a dream

梦寐 mèngmèi (名) dream; sleep: ～难忘 be unable to forget sth. even in one's dreams. ～以求 long for sth. day and night

梦乡(鄉) mèngxiāng (名) dreamland: 进入～ fall asleep

梦想 mèngxiǎng I (动) hope in vain; have a fond dream of: 他从未～过会搞得这么好. Little did he dream of doing so well. II (名) fond dream

梦呓(囈) mèngyì (名) (as "梦话" mènghuà) talking in one's sleep; somniloquy

梦游症 mèngyóuzhèng (名) sleep-walking; somnambulism

孟 mèng

孟浪 mènglàng (形) rash; impetuous; impulsive: 不可～行事. Don't act on the spur of the moment.

咪 mī

咪咪 mīmī (象) mew; miaow

M

眯 mī (动) 1 narrow (one's eyes): ～着眼瞧 squint at 2 take a nap: ～一会儿 take a short nap; have forty winks
see also mí

眯缝 mīfeng (动) narrow

靡 mí (形) waste: 奢～ wasteful; extravagant. ～费 waste; spend extravagantly
see also mǐ

糜 mí I (名) gruel II (形) 1 rotten 2 wasteful; extravagant

糜烂(爛) mílàn (形) rotten; dissipated; debauched: 生活～ lead a dissipated life

迷 mí I (动) 1 be confused; be lost: ～路了. get lost. ～失方向 lose one's bearings 2 be fascinated by: 她被他～住了. She is crazy about him. 看书入～了 be absorbed in reading 景色～人 fascinating scenery. 财～心窍 be obsessed by lust for wealth II (名) fan; enthusiast: 足球～ a football fan. 官～ a person who craves power

迷彩 mícǎi (名) camouflage colour

迷宫 mígōng (名) maze; labyrinth

迷糊 míhu (形) 1 (of vision) dim: 看～了 be dazzled by (multicolours; patterns, etc.) 2 dazed; muddled: 睡～了 dazed with sleep. 他这个人有点～. He's somewhat muddle-headed.

迷魂汤(湯) míhúntāng (名) magic potion: 灌～ flatter sb. lavishly

迷魂阵(陣) míhúnzhèn (名) a confusing scheme; maze; trap: 摆～ lay out a bewildering scheme

迷惑 míhuò (动) puzzle; confuse; perplex; baffle: 感到～不解 feel puzzled; feel perplexed. ～敌人 confuse the enemy

迷恋(戀) míliàn (动) indulge in; be infatuated with

迷茫 mímáng (形) 1 vast and hazy: 大雪纷飞, 原野一片～. The vast plain was blurred by the swirling flakes of snow. 2 confused; perplexed; dazed: 神情～ look confused

迷失 míshī (动) lose (one's way, etc.): ～方向 lose one's bearings; get lost

迷途 mítú (名) wrong path: 误入～ go astray

迷惘 míwǎng (形) perplexed; at a loss

迷雾(霧) míwù (名) 1 dense fog 2 foggy situation that misleads people

迷信 míxìn (名) 1 superstition: ～思想 superstitious ideas 2 blind faith; blind worship: 破除～ do away with blind faith

谜 mí (名) 1 riddle: 猜～ guess a riddle 2 enigma; mystery; puzzle

谜底 mídǐ (名) answer to a riddle

谜语 míyǔ (名) riddle; conundrum

眯 mí (动) (of dust, etc.) get into one's eye: 我～了眼了. Something has got into my eyes.
see also mī

弥(彌) mí 1 full; overflowing: ～漫 fill (the air, etc.) 2 cover; fill: ～缝 try to gloss over or remedy a fault 3 more: 欲盖～彰 try to cover up a fault only to make it more glaring

弥补(補) míbǔ (动) make up; remedy; make good: ～损失 make up for (or make good) a loss. ～缺陷 remedy a defect

弥合 míhé (动) close; bridge: ～裂痕 close a rift

弥漫 mímàn (动) fill the air; spread all over the place: 硝烟～. The fumes of gunpowder filled the air.

弥天大谎 mítiān dàhuǎng outrageous lie

靡 mǐ

see also mí

靡靡之音 mǐmǐzhīyīn decadent music; cheap sentimental song

米 mǐ I（名）1 rice 2 shelled or husked seed：花生～ peanut seed II（量）metre

米饭 mǐfàn（名）cooked rice

米粉 mǐfěn（名）1 ground rice 2 rice-flour noodles

米黄 mǐhuáng（形）cream-coloured

弭 mǐ（动）put down；get rid of；remove：～患 remove the source of trouble

泌 mì：分～ secrete

泌尿科 mìniàokē（名）urological department

秘 mì（形）secret：～史 inside story

see also bì

秘方 mìfāng（名）secret recipe：祖传～ a secret family recipe

秘诀 mìjué（名）secret formula；secret

秘密 mìmì I（形）secret；confidential：～活动 clandestine activities. ～文件 confidential document II（名）secret：保守～ keep（sth.）secret. 泄露～ disclose a secret

秘书(書) mìshū（名）secretary：私人～ private secretary. 机要～ confidential secretary. ～处 secretariat. ～长 secretary-general

蜜 mì（名）honey

蜜蜂 mìfēng（名）honeybee；bee

蜜饯(餞) mìjiàn（名）preserved fruit

蜜月 mìyuè（名）honeymoon

密 mì（形）1 dense；close；thick：～林 dense (or thick) forest. ～不透风 airtight 2 close；intimate：～友 close friend 3 meticulous：周～ carefully considered；meticulous 4 secret：绝～ top secret；strictly confidential. ～电 cipher telegram

密布 mìbù（动）densely covered：阴云～. Dark clouds cover the sky.

密度 mìdù（名）density；thickness：人口～ population density

密封 mìfēng（动）1 seal up：～的文件 sealed documents 2 seal airtight：～的容器 hermetically sealed chamber

密集 mìjí（形）dense；concentrated；crowded together：人口～ densely populated. 枪声～ heavy gunfire

密件 mìjiàn（名）confidential paper or letter；classified document

密码 mìmǎ（名）cipher；secret code

密密麻麻 mìmìmámá（形）close and numerous；thickly dotted：天上的星星～. The sky is thickly studded with stars.

密谋 mìmóu（动）conspire；plot；scheme

密切 mìqiè（形）1 close；intimate：～配合 act in close coordination with. ～相关 be closely related 2 carefully；closely：～注视 watch closely；follow with the greatest attention

密使 mìshǐ（名）secret envoy；secret emissary

密谈 mìtán（名）secret talk

密探 mìtàn（名）secret agent；spy

密植 mìzhí（名）close planting

觅 mì（动）look for；seek：～食（usu. for birds or animals) look for food

眠 mián（名）1 sleep：不～之夜 a sleepless night 2 dormancy：冬～ hibernation

棉 mián（名）cotton：～纺织品 cotton textiles. ～衣（裤）cotton-padded clothes（trousers）

棉袄(襖) mián'ǎo（名）cotton-padded jacket

棉被 miánbèi（名）a quilt with cotton wadding

棉布 miánbù（名）cotton cloth；cotton

棉纺 miánfǎng（名）cotton spinning：～厂 cotton mill

棉花 miánhua（名）cotton：～签（cotton）swab

棉毛衫 miánmáoshān（名）cotton（interlock）jersey

棉纱 miánshā（名）cotton yarn

棉田 miántián（名）cotton field

棉线(綫) miánxiàn（名）cotton thread；cotton

棉絮 miánxù（名）a cotton wadding（for a quilt）

棉籽 miánzǐ（名）cottonseed

绵 mián（形）1 soft 2 continuous

绵亘 miángèn（动）（of mountains, etc.）stretch in an unbroken chain

绵绵 miánmián（形）continuous, unbroken：春雨～. The spring rain never ceases to fall.

绵延 miányán（动）（usu. of mountain ranges) be continuous；stretch long and unbroken

绵羊 miányáng (名) sheep

腼 miǎn

腼腆 miǎntiǎn (形) shy; bashful: 这个人有些～. He is a little shy.

缅 miǎn (形) remote; far back

缅怀(懷) miǎnhuái (动) cherish the memory of; recall: ～往事 recall past events. ～战争中牺牲的战士们. We cherish the memory of the fallen heroes in the war.

免 miǎn (动) 1 excuse (or free) sb. from sth.; exempt: ～试 be excused from an examination. ～去手续 dispense with the formalities. ～学费 waive tuition 2 remove from office; dismiss: 任～(事项) appointments and removals 3 avoid; avert; escape: 再检查一遍以～出错. Check it once more to avoid possible mistakes. 4 not allowed: 闲人～进 No admittance except on business.

免不了 miǎnbùliǎo unavoidable: 管这么大的工厂, 困难是～的. In running such a big factory there are bound to be difficulties.

M

免除 miǎnchú (动) 1 avoid; prevent 2 excuse; exempt; relieve: ～债务 remit a debt

免得 miǎndé (连) so as not to; so as to avoid: 穿上大衣, ～感冒. Put on your overcoat so that you won't catch cold. 我再说明一下自己的观点, ～引起误解. To avoid any misunderstanding, let me clearly reiterate my position. 你回来时给我买几张邮票, ～我自己又跑一趟. Buy me some stamps on your way back to save me a trip.

免费 miǎnfèi (动) free of charge; free: ～医疗 free medical care. ～入场 admission free

免冠 miǎnguān (形) without a hat on; bareheaded: 半身～正面相片 a half-length, bareheaded, full-faced photo

免票 miǎnpiào I (名) free pass; free ticket II (动) free of charge

免税 miǎnshuì (动) 1 duty-free; tax-free: ～商店 duty-free shop 2 exempt from taxation

免疫 miǎnyì (名) immunity (from disease)

免职(職) miǎnzhí (动) remove sb. from office

免罪 miǎnzuì (动) exempt from punishment

冕 miǎn (名) crown: 加～(礼) coronation

勉 miǎn (动) 1 encourage; urge: 互～ encourage one another. 自～ spur oneself on 2 try to do what is almost beyond one's power or act against one's will

勉励(勵) miǎnlì (动) encourage; urge

勉强 miǎnqiǎng I (形) 1 do one's best despite difficulty or lack of experience: 弄不了就别～弄了. Leave it if you can't manage. Don't overexert yourself. 2 reluctantly; grudgingly: ～同意 reluctantly agree. ～笑了笑 force a smile 3 inadequate; unconvincing; far-fetched: 这个理由很～. This is a lame excuse. 4 barely enough: ～的多数 a bare majority. ～维持生活 eke out a bare living; scrape along. ～够用 earn just enough to get by II (动) force sb. to do sth. 要是他不愿意去, 就不要～他了. Don't force him to go if he doesn't want to.

娩 miǎn (名) childbirth: 分～ childbirth; delivery

面 miàn I (名) 1 face: ～对～ face to face. ～带笑容 have a smile on one's face 2 surface; top; cover: 水～ the surface of the water 3 side; aspect: 四～进攻 attack from all sides 4 [used to form a noun of locality]: 上～ above. 下～ under. 里～ inside. 外～ outside. 前～ in the front. 后～ at the back. 左～ the left side. 北～ the northern side 5 scale; range: 知识～ the scope of one's knowledge. 受灾～ (disaster) afflicted area 6 (麵)wheat flour; flour: 白～ wheat flour. 玉米～ corn flour 7 powder: 胡椒～ ground pepper. 辣椒～ chilli powder II (副) personally; directly: ～告 tell sb. in person III (量) [for flat and smooth objects]: 一～镜子 a mirror. 两～旗帜 two flags

面包 miànbāo (名) bread: ～房 bakery

面额 miàn'é (名) denomination: 各种～的纸币 banknotes of different denominations

面粉 miànfěn (名) wheat flour; flour

面红耳赤 miànhóng-ěrchì flush red: 他们争得～. They argued till their faces turned red with excitement (or anger).

面糊 miànhú (名) paste

面黄肌瘦 miànhuáng-jīshòu lean and haggard; pale and thin

面积(積) miànjī (名) area：总～ the total area. 棉花种植～ the acreage under cotton. 展览会～为三千平方米. The exhibition covers a floor space of 3,000 square metres.

面颊(頰) miànjiá (名) cheek

面具 miànjù (名) mask：防毒～ gas mask

面孔 miànkǒng (名) face：板起～ put on a stern expression

面料 miànliào (名) (textile) material

面临(臨) miànlín (动) be faced with; be confronted with; be up against：～一场严重的危机 be faced with a serious crisis

面貌 miànmào (名) 1 face; features 2 (of things) appearance; look; aspect：精神～ mental outlook. ～一新 take on a new look (or aspect)

面面俱到 miànmiàn jù dào attend to each and every aspect of a matter

面面相觑 miànmiàn xiāng qù gaze at each other in blank dismay; exchange uneasy glances

面目 miànmù (名) 1 face; features; visage：～清秀 delicate features. ～可憎 repulsive appearance 2 (of things) appearance; look：～全非 be changed or distorted beyond recognition. ～一新 take on an entirely new look

面庞(龐) miànpáng (名) contours of the face; face：圆胖的～ a plump, round face

面洽 miànqià (动) discuss in person：详情请与来人～. As to details, you can work them out with the bearer of the note.

面前 miànqián (名) in front of; in the face of; before

面容 miànróng (名) facial features; face：～消瘦 look wan

面色 miànsè (名) complexion：～红润 have ruddy cheeks. ～苍白 look pale

面纱 miànshā (名) veil

面生 miànshēng (形) look unfamiliar

面试 miànshì (名) interview：进行～ hold an interview. ～没通过 fail an interview

面熟 miànshú (形) look familiar：他看着～，就是想不起来是谁. He looks familiar but I simply can't remember his name.

面谈 miàntán (动) speak to sb. face to face; talk in person

面条(條) miàntiáo (名) noodles

面团(團) miàntuán (名) dough

面向 miànxiàng (动) turn one's face to; turn in the direction of; face：科技～经济建设. Science and technology are geared to economic development.

面谢 miànxiè (动) thank sb. in person

面罩 miànzhào (名) face guard

面子 miànzi (名) 1 outer part; outside：大衣的～ the outside of an overcoat 2 reputation; face; self-respect：爱～ be anxious to save one's face. 丢～ lose face. 给～ take care not to offend one's susceptibilities

苗 miáo (名) 1 sprout; seedling：麦～儿 wheat seedling 2 sth. resembling a young plant：火～儿 flame 3 the young of some animals：鱼～ fish fry

苗圃 miáopǔ (名) nursery (of young plants)

苗条(條) miáotiao (形) (of a woman) slender; slim

苗头(頭) miáotou (名) symptom of a trend; a straw in the wind：不良倾向的～ symptoms of unhealthy tendencies. ～不对 Things are not going the right way.

描 miáo (动) 1 trace; copy：～图样 trace a design 2 touch up; retouch：～眉 pencil one's eyebrows

描画(畫) miáohuà (动) draw; paint; depict; describe：风景之美难以用语言来～. The beauty of the scenery beggars description.

描绘(繪) miáohuì (动) depict; describe; portray：这部小说生动地～了农村发生的巨大变化. The novel vividly depicts the great changes that have taken place in the countryside.

描述 miáoshù (动) describe

描写(寫) miáoxiě (动) describe; depict; portray

瞄 miáo (动) aim

瞄准(準) miáozhǔn (动) take aim：～靶心 aim at the bull's-eye

秒 miǎo (量) second (= 1/60 of a minute)

秒表 miǎobiǎo (名) stopwatch

渺 miǎo (形) 1 distant and indistinct; vague：烟波浩～ (of lake, etc.) vast and misty. ～无人迹 remote and uninhabited 2 tiny; insignificant：～不足道 insignificant; negligible; of no consequence

渺茫 miǎománg (形) remote; vague; uncertain：音信～ haven't heard from sb. for ages. 前途～. The future is full of uncertainties.

渺无(無)音信 miǎo wú yīnxìn there has been no news whatsoever about sb. ; nothing has been heard since

渺小 miǎoxiǎo (形) tiny; negligible; insignificant (of abstract matters)

邈 miǎo (形)〈书〉far away; remote

藐 miǎo

藐视 miǎoshì (动) despise; look down upon; belittle

藐小 miǎoxiǎo (形) tiny; negligible; insignificant; paltry

庙(廟) miào (名) temple: ～会 temple fair

庙宇 miàoyǔ (名) temple

妙 miào (形) 1 wonderful; excellent; fine: 这主意真～. This idea is really great. 绝～的讽刺 a supreme irony 2 ingenious; clever; subtle: 莫名其～ incomprehensible. ～计 wise move; brilliant idea

妙龄 miàolíng (名) youthfulness (of a girl): 正当～ be in the bloom of youth

妙趣横生 miàoqù héngshēng full of wit and humour; brim over with interest

M

妙手回春 miàoshǒu huí chūn (of a doctor) ingeniously bring the dying back to life

妙语 miàoyǔ (名) witty remark: ～惊人 wisecracks that really tickle. ～连珠 a stream of witticisms

灭(滅) miè (动) 1 (of a light, fire, etc.) go out: 灯～了. The lights went out. 2 extinguish; put out: ～火 put out a fire 3 destroy; wipe out; exterminate: ～鼠 kill rats

灭顶 mièdǐng (动) be drowned; be swamped

灭迹 mièjì (动) destroy the evidence (of one's evildoing)

灭绝 mièjué (动) become extinct: 一些珍奇动物现已面临～的危险. Some rare animals are in danger of becoming extinct.

灭绝人性 mièjué rénxìng inhuman; savage

灭口 mièkǒu (动) (of a criminal) kill a witness or accomplice to prevent leakage of information

灭亡 mièwáng (动) perish; die out; be doomed: 自取～ court destruction

蔑 miè (动) 1 slight; disdain: 轻～ disdain 2 smear: 诬～ slander; vilify

蔑视 mièshì (动) despise; scorn; show contempt for

篾 miè (名) 1 thin bamboo strip 2 the rind of reed or sorghum

民 mín (名) 1 the people: ～众 the masses. ～歌 folk song. 军～ the military and civilians. ～以食为天. Food is a basic need of man. 2 a member of a nationality: 藏～ a Tibetan 3 a person of a certain occupation: 农～ peasant. 渔～ fisherman. 牧～ herdsman

民办(辦) mínbàn (形) run by the community: ～小学 community primary school

民兵 mínbīng (名) militia; militiaman; militiawoman

民不聊生 mín bù liáo shēng the people have no means of livelihood

民调 míndiào (名) opinion poll

民法 mínfǎ (名) civil law

民愤 mínfèn (名) public indignation

民工 míngōng (名) 1 a labourer working on a public project 2 a manual worker or an odd-job man from a rural area

民航 mínháng (名) civil aviation: 中国～总局 CAAC (General Administration of Civil Aviation of China)

民间 mínjiān (形) 1 of the common people; popular; folk: ～传说 folk legend; folklore. ～故事 folktale; folk story. ～艺术 folk art 2 non-governmental; people-to-people: ～团体 non-governmental organizations (NGOs)

民警 mínjǐng (名) people's police; people's policeman

民情 mínqíng (名) 1 popular customs 2 public feeling

民权(權) mínquán (名) civil rights

民生 mínshēng (名) the people's livelihood: 国计～ the national economy and the people's livelihood

民事 mínshì (名) relating to civil law; civil: ～案件 civil case. ～纠纷 civil litigation. ～诉讼 civil action (or process, lawsuit)

民俗 mínsú (名) folk custom; folkways: ～学 folklore

民心 mínxīn (名) popular feelings; common aspirations of the people: 深得～ enjoy the ardent support of the people

民谣 mínyáo (名) folk rhyme

民意 mínyì (名) the will of the people: ～测验 public opinion poll; poll

民营 mínyíng (形) privately owned and operated: ～企业 private enterprise

民用 mínyòng (形) for civil use; civil: ～航空 civil aviation

民乐(樂) mínyuè (名) music, for traditional instruments

民运(運) mínyùn (名) 1 civil transport 2 the army's propaganda and organizational work among the civilians during the revolutionary wars led by the Chinese Communist Party 3 mass movement; mass campaign

民政 mínzhèng (名) civil administration

民众(衆) mínzhòng (名) the masses; the common people

民主 mínzhǔ I (名) democracy II (形) democratic: 作风～ a democratic working style. ～人士 democratic personages. ～协商 democratic consultation

民主党(黨)派 mínzhǔ dǎngpài democratic parties

民主集中制 mínzhǔ-jízhōngzhì democratic centralism

民族 mínzú (名) nation; nationality: 中华～ the Chinese nation. 少数～ ethnic group; minority nationality. ～败类 scum of a nation. ～利己主义 national egoism. ～英雄 national hero. ～主义 nationalism. ～自决 national self-determination. ～自治 autonomy of minority nationalities

悯 mǐn (动) pity: 怜～ commiserate; pity

敏 mǐn (形) quick; nimble; agile

敏感 mǐngǎn (形) sensitive; susceptible: 对天气变化很～ be very susceptible to changes in weather. 对尘埃很～ allergic to dust

敏捷 mǐnjié (形) quick; nimble; agile: 动作～ quick or agile in movement

敏锐 mǐnruì (形) sharp; acute; keen: 目光～ have sharp eyes. 嗅觉～ have a keen sense of smell

泯 mǐn (动) vanish; die out: ～灭 die out; disappear; vanish

抿 mǐn (动) 1 smooth (hair, etc.) with a wet brush 2 close lightly; tuck: ～着嘴笑 smile with slightly closed lips 3 sip: ～一口酒 take a sip of the wine

冥 míng (形) 1 dark; obscure: 幽～ dark hell; the nether world 2 deep; profound: ～思 be deep in thought 3 dull; stupid: ～顽 thickheaded; stupid 4 of the nether world

冥思苦想 míngsī-kǔxiǎng think long and hard; rack (or cudgel) one's brains

冥顽 míngwán (形)〈书〉 thick-headed; stupid: ～不灵 impenetrably thickheaded

瞑 míng

瞑目 míngmù (动) die with eyes closed; die without regret: 死不～ die with regret

螟 míng (名) snout moth's larva

螟虫(蟲) míngchóng (名) snout moth's larva

明 míng I (形) 1 bright; brilliant: ～月 a bright moon. 灯火通～ be brightly lit 2 clear; distinct: 方向不～. The orientation is not clear. 指～出路 point the way out 3 open; overt; explicit: ～枪暗箭 both overt and covert attacks. ～说了吧 frankly speaking 4 sharp-eyed; clear-sighted: 眼～手快 quick of eye and deft of hand 5 next: ～天 tomorrow. ～年 next year II (名) sight: 双目失～ go blind in both eyes III (动) know; understand: 不～真相 not know the facts; be ignorant of the actual situation

明暗 míng-àn (名) light and shade

明白 míngbai I (形) 1 clear; obvious; plain: 问题讲得很～. The problem is clearly expounded. 2 frank; explicit; unequivocal: 不明不白的关系 equivocal relationship. 你还是跟他讲～了好. It would be best to let him know everything about it. 3 sensible; reasonable: ～人 a sensible person II (动) understand; realize; know: 你～我的意思吗? Do you see what I mean? ～事理 have good sense. 我～了. Oh, I see.

明摆(擺)着 míngbǎizhe obvious; clear; plain: 一个～的问题 an obvious problem

明辨是非 míng biàn shì-fēi make a clear distinction between right and wrong

明察秋毫 míng chá qiūháo (usu. of officials) be sharp-minded enough to perceive the minutest detail; have an extremely discerning eye

明畅(暢) míngchàng (形) lucid and smooth

明澈 míngchè (形) bright and limpid; crystal clear: ～的眼睛 bright and limpid eyes. 湖水～如镜. The lake is as bright and clear as a mirror.

明兜 míngdōu (名) patch pocket

明晃晃 mínghuǎnghuǎng (形) shining; gleaming: ～的刺刀 gleaming bayonets

明火执(執)仗 mínghuǒ-zhízhàng do evil

openly; a daring robbery

明净 míngjìng (形) bright and clean: 橱窗~ a bright and clean shop window

明快 míngkuài (形) 1 lucid and lively; sprightly: ~的笔调 a lucid and lively style. ~的节奏 sprightly rhythm 2 straightforward: ~的性格 (of a person) a forthright character

明朗 mínglǎng (形) 1 bright and clear: ~的天空 a clear sky 2 clear; obvious: 事情的性质逐渐~了. The nature of the case is being brought to light. 态度~ take a clear-cut stand 3 forthright; bright and cheerful; breezy: ~的性格 an open and forthright character. 这些作品都具有~的风格. All these works are written in a vivid, broadly cheerful style.

明亮 míngliàng (形) 1 bright; well-lit: 灯光~ be brightly lit 2 bright; shining: ~的眼睛 bright eyes. 星光~. The stars are shining. 3 become clear: 我心里~多了. I'm much clearer on the matter now.

明了(瞭) míngliǎo I (动) understand; be clear about: ~实际情况 have a clear understanding of the actual situation II (形) clear; plain: 简单~ simple and clear

明媚 míngmèi (形) bright and beautiful: 春光~. The spring days are bright and charming.

明明 míngmíng (副) obviously; undoubtedly: 别骗我了,你~是这个意思嘛. Don't you think you can fool me. This is obviously what you mean.

明目张(張)胆(膽) míngmùzhāng-dǎn brazenly; flagrantly; without caring about any onlookers

明确(確) míngquè I (形) clear and definite; unequivocal: ~的立场 a clear-cut stand. ~的答复 a definite answer. 分工~ clear divison of labour II (动) make clear; make definite: ~当前的任务 be clear about (our) present tasks

明人不做暗事 míngrén bù zuò ànshì an horest man does nothing unhand; a good person doesn't do bad things

明日 míngrì (名) 1 tomorrow 2 the near future

明睿 míngruì (形) wise and farsighted

明升暗降 míngshēng-ànjiàng a promotion in appearance but a demotion in fact: 使某人~ kick sb. upstairs

明说 míngshuō (动) speak frankly; speak openly: 我对你~了吧. I'll be frank with you. 他虽没~,心里却有想法. He didn't say anything definitely, although he had ideas of his own. 这事不便~. We'd better not talk about it so clearly.

明文 míngwén (名) (of laws, regulations, etc.) proclaimed in writing: ~规定 stipulate in explicit terms; clearly stipulated in writing

明晰 míngxī (形) clear; distinct: 雾散了,远处的村庄越来越~了. As the mist thinned, the village in the distance became more and more distinct.

明显(顯) míngxiǎn (形) clear; obvious: ~的进步 marked progress. 很~ evidently

明信片 míngxìnpiàn (名) postcard

明星 míngxīng (名) star: 电影~ film star; movie star

明眼人 míngyǎnrén (名) a person of good sense

明哲保身 míng zhé bǎo shēn be worldly wise and play safe in all activities

明争暗斗(鬥) míngzhēng-àndòu both open strife and veiled rivalry; factional strife, both overt and covert

明证 míngzhèng (名) clear proof; evidence

明知故犯 míngzhī-gùfàn commit an offence with the full knowledge of its implications; do sth. which one knows is wrong

明知故问 míngzhī-gùwèn ask while knowing the answer; ask a question as if one does not know the answer

明智 míngzhì (形) sensible: 他这样决定是~的. It was wise of him to make such a decision.

鸣 míng (动) 1 (of birds, animals or insects) cry; utter a cry: 鸟~ the chirp of a bird. 鸡~ the crow of a cock 2 ring; sound: 耳~ ringing in the ears 3 express; voice; air: 自~得意 be smug; sing one's own praises. ~笛 blow a whistle. ~礼炮 21 响 fire a salute of 21 guns

鸣不平 míng bùpíng complain of unfairness; cry out against injustice

鸣冤叫屈 míngyuān-jiàoqū complain and call for redress; voice grievances

名 míng I (名) 1 name: 你叫什么~字? What's your name? 给孩子起个~儿 name a baby. 以…为~ in the name of ...; under the pretext of ... 2 fame;

M

reputation: 不为～，不为利 seek neither fame nor wealth II (形) well-known; famous; celebrated: ～电影演员 a film star. ～画 a famous painting III (量) [for persons]: 两百～代表 two hundred delegates. 第一～ come in first; win first place

名不副实(實) míng bù fù shí the name falls short of the reality; be more in name than in reality

名不虚传(傳) míng bù xūchuán enjoy a well-deserved reputation; live up to one's reputation

名册 míngcè (名) register; roll

名产(產) míngchǎn (名) famous product

名称(稱) míngchēng (名) name (of a thing or organization)

名词 míngcí (名) 1 noun 2 term: 技术～ technical term

名次 míngcì (名) position in a name list; place in a competition: 按比赛成绩排列～ arrange the names of contestants in the order of their results

名存实(實)亡 míngcún-shíwáng exist only in name; be only an empty title

名单(單) míngdān (名) name list: 候选人～ list of candidates

名额 míng'é (名) the number of people assigned or allowed: 代表～ the number of deputies to be elected or sent. 招生～ the number of students to be enrolled; enrolment. ～有限 the number of people allowed is limited

名分 míngfèn (名) a person's status

名副其实(實) míng fù qí shí the name matches the reality; be sth. in reality as well as in name; be worthy of the name (also as "名符其实")

名贵 míngguì (形) famous and precious; rare: ～药材 rare medicinal herbs. 这只花瓶十分～. This vase is priceless.

名利 mínglì (名) fame and gain: ～双收 gain both fame and wealth

名列前茅 míng liè qiánmáo be among the best of the successful candidates; come out at the top

名流 míngliú (名) distinguished personages; celebrities: 社会～ noted public figures

名门(門) míngmén (名) an old and well-known family; a distinguished family; an illustrious family

名目 míngmù (名) names of things; items: ～繁多 a multitude of items; names of every description. 巧立～ invent all imaginable terms (as pretexts for exorbitant taxes or to pay an expense account)

名牌 míngpái (名) 1 famous brand: ～香烟 a famous brand of cigarettes. ～优质产品 brand name and quality goods 2 nameplate; name tag

名片 míngpiàn (名) visiting card; calling card

名气(氣) míngqì (名)〈口〉 reputation; fame; name: 很有点～ enjoy a considerable reputation; be quite well-known

名人 míngrén (名) famous person

名声(聲) míngshēng (名) reputation; repute; renown: ～很坏 be notorious. 享有好～ enjoy a good reputation. ～在外 be quite well known

名胜(勝) míngshèng (名) well-known scenic spot: ～古迹 scenic spots and historical sites

名堂 míngtang (名) 1 variety; item: 这个剧团虽小，～可真不少. Small as it is, this troupe has an amazingly large repertoire. 鬼～ dirty trick. 你在搞什么～? What are you up to? 2 result; achievement: 他决心要搞出点～来. He is determined to achieve something. 这样谈下去，恐怕谈不出什么～. I'm afraid it will get us nowhere if we go on like this. 3 what lies behind sth.; reason: 他突然离开伦敦，这里面一定有～. There must be something behind his sudden departure from London.

名望 míngwàng (名) fame and prestige: 有～的大夫 a famous doctor

名下 míngxià (名) under sb.'s name: 这笔账记在我～吧. Charge these expenses to my account. ～无虚 one's reputation is justified

名义(義) míngyì (名) 1 name: 我以总统的～ in my capacity as president. 代表学院并以个人的～ on behalf of the college and in my own name 2 nominal; in name: 他只不过～上是我们的经理. He is nothing but our nominal manager.

名誉(譽) míngyù I (名) fame; reputation: ～扫地 be discredited; one's reputation was permanently damaged II (形) honorary: ～主席 honorary chairman

名正言顺 míngzhèng-yánshùn perfectly justifiable

名著 míngzhù (名) masterpiece: 文学～ a literary masterpiece

名字 míngzi (名) name

名作 míngzuò (名) masterpiece

铭 míng I (名) inscription: 座右～ motto II (动) engrave: ～诸肺腑 be engraved in one's memory

铭记 míngjì (动) engrave on one's mind; always remember

铭刻 míngkè (动) inscribe; engrave on one's mind

铭心 míngxīn (形) be engraved on one's heart—be remembered with gratitude

酩 míng

酩酊大醉 míngdǐng dàzuì be dead drunk

命 mìng (名) 1 life: 救～! Help! 逃～ run for one's life. ～在旦夕 be on one's last legs 2 lot; fate; destiny: 苦～ hard lot; cruel fate. ～该如此 Fate would have it so. 3 order; command: 待～ await orders. ～题 set the question; set the paper

命定 mìngdìng (形) determined by fate; predestined

命根子 mìnggēnzi (名) life-blood; one's very life

M

命令 mìnglìng (名) order; command: 下～ issue an order. 服从～ obey orders. ～句 imperative sentence

命脉(脈) mìngmài (名) lifeline; lifeblood: 水利是农业的～. Irrigation is the lifeblood of agriculture.

命名 mìngmíng (动) give a name to (e.g. a building): 伦敦的大本钟是以本杰明·霍尔～的. Big Ben in London is named after Sir Benjamin Hall.

命题 mìngtí I (动) assign a topic; set a question II (名) proposition

命运(運) mìngyùn (名) destiny; fate; lot: 掌握自己的～ take one's destiny in one's own hand. ～捉弄人. Fate always teases people.

命中 mìngzhòng (动) hit the target; score a hit: 她第一枪就～靶心. Her first shot hit the bull's-eye.

谬 miù (形) wrong; false: ～见 a wrong view. 大～不然 be entirely wrong or grossly mistaken

谬论(論) miùlùn (名) fallacy; false (or absurd) theory

谬误 miùwù (名) falsehood; error; mistake: ～百出 full of mistakes; teem with errors

摸 mō (动) 1 feel; stroke; touch: 这衣料～着很软. This material feels soft. 不要～那个按钮. Don't touch that button. 2 feel for; grope for; fumble: ～着上楼 grope one's way upstairs. 从手提包里～出一支笔 fish out a pen from her handbag 3 try to find out; feel out; sound out: ～清情况 try to find out how things stand. ～不着头脑 unable to make head or tail of sth. ～透他的脾气 get to know him (or his temperament) well

摸底 mōdǐ (动) know (or find out) the real situation: 下基层去～ go down to the grass roots units to find out about the real situation. 我想摸他的底. I am thinking of sounding him out.

摸门(門)儿(兒) mōménr learn the ropes; get the hang of sth.: 这机器看起来不好掌握,可是过几个星期你就能摸着门儿了. This machine looks difficult to handle at first, but you'll get the hang of it after a few weeks.

摸索 mōsuǒ (动) 1 grope; feel about; fumble: 他们～着走下黑暗的甬道. They felt their way down the dark passage. 2 try to find out: ～熊猫的生活规律 try to find out the habits of the panda

摸透 mōtòu (动) get to know sb. or sth. very well: ～某人的脾气 get to know sb. inside out

磨 mó (动) 1 rub: ～墨 rub an ink stick against an ink stone. 这只鞋～脚. My shoe's rubbing. 你大衣的胳膊肘上～了一个洞. You've rubbed a hole in the elbow of your coat. 手上～了一个泡. His hand was blistered from the rubbing. 轮胎～平了. The tyre is badly worn (out). 2 sharpen; polish; grind: ～刀 sharpen a knife. ～成粉末 grind sth. into powder. ～大理石 polish marble 3 dawdle; while away (time): ～时间 kill time. 快走吧,别～时间了. Stop dawdling and get going. 4 wear down; torment: 多跟她～一～她就会答应的. She will agree if you keep on at her. 这病真～人! What a torment this illness is!

see also mò

磨蹭 móceng (动) move slowly; dawdle: 别～了! Stop dawdling!

磨床(牀) móchuáng (名) grinding machine; grinder

磨刀不误砍柴工 mó dāo bù wù kǎncháigōng sharpening the axe won't interfere with

the cutting of firewood
磨刀霍霍 mó dāo huòhuò sharpening one's sword; sabre-rattling
磨合 móhé (动) mesh; work to fit together suitably; rub along together
磨炼(煉) móliàn (动) temper oneself; steel oneself
磨灭(滅) mómiè (动) wear away; efface; obliterate: 不可～的功勋 ineffaceable achievements. 留下不可～的印象 leave an indelible impression
磨砂灯(燈)泡 móshā dēngpào frosted bulb
磨损 mósǔn (动) wear and tear
磨洋工 mó yánggōng loaf on the job; dawdle along

蘑 mó (名) mushroom

蘑菇 mógu I (名) mushroom II (动) 1 worry; pester; keep on at: 你别跟她～了. Don't pester her. 2 dawdle; dilly-dally: 已经晚了,你还在这里～! It's late already. Why are you still dawdling around here!

摩 mó (动) 1 rub; scrape; touch: ～天大楼 skyscraper 2 mull over; study: 揣～ try to fathom
摩擦 mócā I (动) rub II (名) 1 friction: ～生电. Friction generates electricity. 2 clash: 与某人发生～ have a brush with sb.
摩登 módēng (形) modern; fashionable
摩肩接踵 mójiān-jiēzhǒng jostle each other in a crowd
摩拳擦掌 móquán-cāzhǎng be eager for a fight; yearn for the fray
摩托 mótuō (名) motor: ～车 motorcycle

魔 mó I (名) evil spirit; demon; monster: 着了～似的 like one possessed; under a charm II (形) magic; mystic: ～力 magic power
魔怪 móguài (名) demons and monsters
魔鬼 móguǐ (名) devil; demon; monster
魔力 mólì (名) magic power; magic; charm
魔术(術) móshù (名) magic; conjuring: ～师 magician; conjurer
魔王 mówáng (名) 1 Prince of the Devils 2 tyrant; despot; fiend
魔掌 mózhǎng (名) evil hands; devil's clutches
魔爪 mózhǎo (名) devil's claws; tentacles

谟 mó (名) 〈书〉 plan: 宏～ a grand plan; a great project

模 mó I (名) 1 pattern; standard: 楷～ model; paragon 2 imitate 3 〈简〉(模范) model: 劳～ model worker II (动) imitate
see also mú
模范(範) mófàn (名) model; fine example: 劳动～ model worker. ～事迹 exemplary deeds
模仿(倣) mófǎng (动) imitate; copy; mimic
模糊 móhu I (形) blurred; indistinct; dim; vague: 字迹～了. The writing is faded. ～的印象 a vague idea of sth. II (动) obscure; confuse; mix up: ～两者的界限 blur the line of distinction of the two
模棱两可 móléng liǎngkě equivocal; ambiguous; ready to accept either course: ～的态度 an equivocal attitude
模拟(擬) mónǐ (动) imitate; simulate: ～测验 mock exam. ～飞行 simulated flight
模式 móshì (名) mode; model: 管理～ mode of management. 给我们提供了一个新的～ Provide us with a new model
模特儿(兒) mótèr (名) model
模型 móxíng (名) 1 model: 船的～ a model of a ship; a model ship 2 mould; matrix; pattern

摹 mó (动) copy; trace: 临～ copy a model of calligraphy or painting
摹本 móběn (名) facsimile; copy
摹拟(擬) mónǐ (动) imitate; simulate

膜 mó (名) 1 membrane: 细胞～ cell membrane 2 film; thin coating: 塑料薄～ plastic film
膜拜 móbài (动) worship: 顶礼～ prostrate oneself in worship; pay homage to

馍 mó (名) steamed bun; steamed bread

抹 mǒ (动) 1 apply; smear; put on: ～点雪花膏 put on a little vanishing cream. 面包上～点黄油 spread some butter on a piece of bread. ～药膏 apply ointment 2 wipe; erase: ～眼泪 wipe one's eyes. ～掉这几个字. Cross out these few words.
see also mā; mò
抹黑 mǒhēi (动) blacken sb.'s name; throw mud at; discredit
抹杀(殺) mǒshā (动) blot out; obliterate: ～事实 deny the facts. ～成绩 negate the achievements. 一笔～ write off at one stroke

磨 mò I (名) mill; millstones: 推～ use a handmill. 电～ electric mill II

(动) grind; mill: ～豆腐 grind soya beans to make bean curd
see also mó

磨坊 mòfáng (名) mill (also as "磨房")

磨盘(盤) mòpán (名) millstones

末 mò (名) 1 tip; end 2 end; last stage: ～班车 the last bus. 周～ weekend. 明～ the end of the Ming Dynasty 3 non-essentials; minor details: 本～倒置 put the cart before the horse 4 powder; dust: 茶叶～儿 powdered tea; tea dust. 锯～ sawdust. 肉～ minced meat

末班车(車) mòbānchē (名) 1 last bus 2 last chance or turn

末代 mòdài (名) the last reign of a dynasty: ～皇帝 the last emperor (of a dynasty)

末了 mòliǎo (名) last; finally; in the end: 但～他还是去了. But he left eventually.

末路 mòlù (名) impasse; doom: 穷途～ have come to a dead end

末年 mònián (名) last years of a dynasty or reign

末期 mòqī (名) final phase; last stage: 五十年代～ in the late fifties. 第二次世界大战～ the last stage of the Second World War

末日 mòrì (名) 1 doomsday; Day of Judgment; Judgment Day: ～审判 Last Judgment 2 end; doom: 封建王朝的～ the end of a feudal dynasty

末梢 mòshāo (名) tip; end: ～神经 nerve ending

末尾 mòwěi (名) end: 书～ at the end of a book

末叶(葉) mòyè (名) last years of a century

沫 mò (名) foam; froth: 啤酒～ froth on beer. 肥皂～ lather

茉 mò

茉莉 mòlì (名) jasmine: ～花茶 jasmine tea

抹 mò (动) daub; plaster: ～墙 plaster a wall. ～灰 plastering
see also mā; mǒ

抹不开(開) mòbukāi feel embarrassed: 怕他脸上～ afraid of embarrassing him

秣 mò I (名) fodder II (动) feed animals

秣马(馬)厉(厲)兵 mòmǎ-lìbīng feed the horses and sharpen the weapons—prepare for battle

莫 mò (副) not: 非公～入 No admittance except on business. 请～见怪. Please don't take it to heart. ～管闲事 mind your own business

莫不 mòbù (副) there's no one who doesn't or isn't: 众人～为之感动. There was no one who was unmoved.

莫测高深 mòcè gāoshēn enigmatic; unfathomable; too profound to be understood

莫大 mòdà (形) greatest; utmost: ～的幸福 the greatest happiness. 感到～的光荣 feel greatly honoured. ～的侮辱 a gross insult

莫非 mòfēi (副) can it be possible that: 这人～就是我当年的同学? Could this man be my old school friend?

莫名其妙 mò míng qí miào be unable to make head or tail of sth.; be baffled: 你这些话真叫我～. It puzzles me that you should have made such remarks. 她～地哭了起来. Quite unexpectedly, she burst out crying. (also as "莫明其妙")

莫逆 mònì (形) very friendly; intimate: ～之交 bosom friends; be on the best of terms

莫须有 mòxūyǒu (形) groundless; fabricated: ～的罪名 a fabricated (or unwarranted) charge

漠 mò I (名) desert: 沙～ desert II (形) indifferent; unconcerned: 冷～ cold and indifferent

漠不关(關)心 mò bù guānxīn indifferent; apathetic

漠漠 mòmò (形) 1 misty; foggy 2 vast and lonely: ～荒原 a vast expanse of wasteland

漠然 mòrán (形) indifferent; apathetic: ～置之 look on the problem with unconcern; treat the matter with complete indifference

漠视 mòshì (动) ignore; overlook; treat with indifference: ～群众的利益是根本不允许的. It is absolutely impermissible to ignore the interest of the masses.

寞 mò (形) lonely; solitary: 寂～ lonely; loneliness

陌 mò (名) a footpath between fields

陌路 mòlù (名)〈书〉stranger: 视同～ be treated like a stranger

陌生 mòshēng (形) strange; unfamiliar: ～人 stranger

蓦 mò (副) suddenly: ～地 suddenly; unexpectedly; all of a sudden. ～然

M

suddenly

墨 mò I (名) ink; ink stick: 研～ rub an ink stick on an inkstone. 油～ printing ink II (形) black; dark: ～绿 dark green. 一个～黑的夜晚 one pitch-dark night

墨迹 mòjì (名) 1 ink marks: ～未干 before the ink is dry 2 sb.'s writing or painting: 这是鲁迅的～. This is Lu Xun's calligraphy.

墨镜 mòjìng (名) sunglasses

墨守成规 mò shǒu chéngguī stick to convention; stay in a rut

墨水 mòshuǐ (名) 1 ink 2 book learning: 他肚子里还有点～. He's a bit of a scholar.

墨汁 mòzhī (名) prepared Chinese ink

默 mò I (形) silent: ～不作声 keep silent II (动) write from memory: ～生字 write the new words from memory

默哀 mò'āi (动) stand in silent tribute: ～三分钟 observe three minutes' silence

默默 mòmò (副) quietly; silently: ～无言 remain speechless; not uttering a word. ～无闻 unknown to the public; without attracting public attention. ～相视 gaze at each other in silence

默契 mòqì (名) tacit agreement (or understanding): 达成～ reach a tacit agreement

默然 mòrán (形) silent; speechless: ～无语 fall silent

默认(認) mòrèn (动) tacitly approve; acquiesce in

默写(寫) mòxiě (动) write from memory

默许 mòxǔ (动) tacitly consent to

脉(脈) mò

see also mài

脉脉 mòmò (形) affectionately: 温情～ full of tender affection

没 mò (动) 1 sink; submerge: 轮船沉～了. The ship sank into the sea. 潜水艇～入水中. The submarine submerged. 2 rise beyond; overflow: 雪深～膝. The snow was knee-deep. 3 disappear; hide: 出～ often appear

see also méi

没齿(齒)不忘 mò chǐ bù wàng will never forget to the end of one's days; remember for the rest of one's life (also as "没世不忘")

没落 mòluò (动) decline; wane: ～贵族 declining aristocrat

没收 mòshōu (动) confiscate; expropriate

哞 mōu (象) [deep sound made by cattle] moo; low

谋 móu (动) 1 plan; scheme: 预～ plan beforehand; premeditate. 足智多～ wise and full of stratagems; resourceful 2 consult: 不～而合 agree without prior consultation 3 work for; seek: ～求和平 seek peace. 不～私利 not work for personal gains

谋财害命 móucái-hàimìng (动) murder sb. for his money

谋反 móufǎn (动) conspire against the state; plot a rebellion

谋害 móuhài (动) plot to murder

谋划(劃) móuhuà (动) plan and contrive

谋面 móumiàn (动) meet each other or be acquainted with sb.: 我与此人素未～. I've never met him so far.

谋求 móuqiú (动) seek; strive for: ～两国关系正常化 seek normalization of relations between the two countries. ～解决办法 try to find a solution

谋取 móuqǔ (动) try to gain; seek

谋杀(殺) móushā (动) murder

谋生 móushēng (动) seek a livelihood; make a living: ～的手段 a means of life

谋士 móushì (名) adviser; counsellor

谋事 móushì (动) 1 plan matters: ～在人,成事在天 man proposes, God disposes; Man must try though his success depends upon the will of Heaven 2 look for a job

牟 móu (动) try to gain; seek; obtain: ～取 seek; obtain. ～利 seek profit

眸 móu (名) pupil (of the eye); eye: 明～皓齿 have bright eyes and white teeth

眸子 móuzi (名) pupil (of the eye); eye

某 mǒu (代) certain; some: ～人 a certain person. ～日 at a certain date. 在～种程度上 to some (or a certain) extent. 在～种意义上 in a sense

某某 mǒumǒu (代) so-and-so: ～大夫 Dr. so-and-so; a certain doctor. ～学校 a certain school

模 mú (名) mould; matrix; pattern

see also mó

模具 mújù (名) mould; matrix; pattern

模样(樣) múyàng (名) 1 appearance; look: 她是什么～? What did she look like? 这孩子的～像他妈妈. The child takes after his mother. **2** (of time and age only) approximately; about: 那男的四十来岁～. The man was probably in his early forties.

模子 múzi (名) mould; pattern: 一个～里铸出来的 made out of the same mould; as like as two peas

亩(畝)

mǔ (量) *mu*, a unit of area (= 0.667 hectares): ～产量 per *mu* yield

牡

mǔ (形) male: ～牛 bull

牡丹 mǔdan (名) tree peony; peony

牡蛎(蠣) mǔlì (名) oyster

母

mǔ I (名) **1** mother **2** one's female elders: 祖～ grandmother. 伯～ aunt II (形) female (animal): ～鸡 hen. ～狗 bitch. ～牛 cow. ～马 mare

母爱(愛) mǔ'ài (名) maternal love

母公司 mǔgōngsī (名) parent company

母机(機) mǔjī (名) **1** machine tool **2** mother aircraft; launching aircraft

母老虎 mǔlǎohǔ (名) **1** tigress **2** vixen; shrew; termagant

母亲(親) mǔqīn (名) mother

M 母系 mǔxì (名) **1** maternal side: ～亲属 maternal relatives **2** matriarchal

母校 mǔxiào (名) one's old school; Alma Mater

母性 mǔxìng (名) maternal instinct

母语 mǔyǔ (名) mother tongue

拇

mǔ

拇指 mǔzhǐ (名) **1** thumb **2** big toe

墓

mù (名) grave; tomb; mausoleum

墓碑 mùbēi (名) tombstone; gravestone

墓地 mùdì (名) graveyard; cemetery

墓志 mùzhì (名) inscription on the memorial tablet within a tomb

暮

mù I (名) dusk; evening: 薄～ dusk II (形) towards the end; late: ～春 late spring

暮霭 mù'ǎi (名) evening haze

暮年 mùnián (名) old age; evening of life

暮气(氣) mùqì (名) lethargy; apathy: ～沉沉 lifeless; apathetic

暮色 mùsè (名) dusk; twilight: ～苍茫 gathering dusk; widening shades of dusk; lengthening shadows of dusk

幕

mù (名) **1** curtain; screen: ～启. The curtain rises. ～落. The curtain falls. 夜～ the veil of night **2** act: 第一～ the first act; Act 1

幕布 mùbù (名) (theatre) curtain; (cinema) screen

幕后(後) mùhòu (名) backstage; behind the scenes: ～策划 backstage manoeuvring. 退居～ retire backstage. ～操纵 pull strings from behind the scenes. ～交易 behind the scenes deal; backstage deal

幕间休息 mùjiān xiūxi interval; intermission

幕僚 mùliáo (名) **1** aides and staff **2** assistant to a ranking official or general in old China

募

mù (动) raise; collect; enlist: ～款 collect contributions. ～兵 recruit soldiers

募集 mùjí (动) raise; collect: ～资金 raise a fund

募捐 mùjuān (动) raise funds; solicit donations

慕

mù (动) admire; yearn for: 爱～ love; adore. 仰～ admire; worship. ～名而来 come to see a person on account of his established reputation

木

mù I (名) **1** tree: 草～ grass and trees. 伐～fell trees. 见木不见林 can't see the wood for the trees **2** wood: 桃花心～ mahogany. ～箱 wooden box II (形) numb; wooden: 两脚都冻～了. Both feet were numb with cold. ～头～脑 wooden-headed; dull-witted

木板 mùbǎn (名) plank; board: ～床 plank bed

木材 mùcái (名) timber; lumber: ～厂 timber mill

木柴 mùchái (名) firewood

木耳 mù'ěr (名) an edible fungus

木筏 mùfá (名) raft

木工 mùgōng (名) **1** woodwork; carpentry **2** woodworker; carpenter

木匠 mùjiang (名) carpenter

木刻 mùkè (名) woodcut; xylography

木料 mùliào (名) timber; lumber

木马(馬) mùmǎ (名) **1** vaulting horse **2** (children's) hobby-horse; rocking horse

木乃伊 mùnǎiyi (名) mummy

木偶 mù'ǒu (名) wooden figure; puppet: ～剧 puppet show

木排 mùpái (名) raft

木片 mùpiàn (名) wood chip

木器 mùqì (名) wooden furniture

木然 mùrán (形) stupefied

木炭 mùtàn (名) charcoal: ～画 charcoal

drawing
木头(頭) mùtóu (名) wood; log; timber
木星 mùxīng (名) Jupiter
木已成舟 mù yǐ chéng zhōu the wood is already made into a boat—what is done cannot be undone; it is a fait accompli
沐 mù (动) wash one's hair
沐浴 mùyù (动) bathe; be bathed in
目 mù (名) 1 eye: 双~失明 go blind in both eyes. 历历在~ all appears distinct in one's mind 2 item: 细~ inventory. 书~ book list
目标(標) mùbiāo (名) 1 target; objective: 命中~hit the target. 攻击~ target of attack 2 goal; aim; objective: 他不能把~定得那么高. He cannot set his sights very high.
目不识(識)丁 mù bù shí dīng be totally illiterate
目不暇接 mù bù xiá jiē the eye cannot take it all in; there are too many things for the eye to take in (also as "目不暇给")
目不转(轉)睛 mù bù zhuǎn jīng look fixedly; gaze intently
目次 mùcì (名) table of contents; contents
目瞪口呆 mùdèng-kǒudāi stunned; stupefied; dumbstruck: 吓得~ be struck dumb with fear; be so scared as to stand gaping
目的 mùdì (名) purpose; aim; goal; objective; end: 最终~ ultimate aim. 达到~的手段 a means to an end. 不可告人的~ ulterior motives. ~地 destination
目睹 mùdǔ (动) see with one's own eyes; witness
目光 mùguāng (名) sight; vision; view: ~远大 far-sighted. ~短浅 short-sighted
目击(擊) mùjī (动) see with one's own eyes; witness: ~者 witness. ~者所谈的经过 an eyewitness account
目空一切 mù kōng yīqiè look down upon everyone; be supercilious
目录(録) mùlù (名) catalogue; list: 图书~ library catalogue. 展品~ a catalogue of exhibits
目前 mùqián (名) at present; at the moment: ~形势 the present situation. 到~为止 up till the present moment; up till now; so far
目送 mùsòng (动) watch sb. go (when seeing sb. off)
目无(無)法纪 mù wú fǎjì disregard law and discipline
目眩 mùxuàn (形) dizzy; dazzled
目中无(無)人 mùzhōng wú rén consider nobody worth his notice; be supercilious
睦 mù (形) peaceful; harmonious
睦邻(鄰) mùlín (动) be on friendly terms with one's country's neighbours: ~政策 good-neighbour policy
牧 mù (动) herd; tend: ~马 herd horses. ~羊 tend sheep
牧草 mùcǎo (名) graze; pasture
牧场(場) mùchǎng (名) grazing land; pasture
牧歌 mùgē (名) pastoral song
牧民 mùmín (名) herdsman
牧区(區) mùqū (名) pastoral area
牧师(師) mùshi (名) pastor; minister; clergyman
牧童 mùtóng (名) shepherd; buffalo boy
牧业(業) mùyè (名) animal husbandry
穆 mù (形) solemn; reverent: 肃~ solemn
穆斯林 mùsīlín (名) Moslem; Muslim

N

N n

拿 ná I (动) 1 hold: 她手里~着一把伞. She has an umbrella in her hand. 把这支枪~着! Hold this gun! 2 take; bring: ~去 take it away. ~来 bring it here 3 seize; capture: ~下敌人的一个据点 capture an enemy stronghold 4 deliberately make things difficult: ~某人一把 put sb. in a difficult position. 他想~我一手. He wanted to make things difficult for me. II (介) 1 with: ~热水洗 wash (it) in hot water. ~事实证明 prove with facts 2 [introducing the object to be followed by a verbal phrase]: 我简直~这孩子没办法. This child is just impossible; I simply can't do anything with him. 他们总是~他开玩笑. They are always making fun of him. 她~我当孩子看. She treats me as a child.
拿不出去 nábuchūqù not be presentable: 我这笔赖字~. My poor handwriting is not presentable. (also as "拿不出手")
拿不起来(來) nábuqǐlái cannot manage: 这

种工作他～. He cannot manage this kind of work.

拿得起,放得下 nádeqǐ, fàngdexià can take it up or put it down—be adaptable to circumstances

拿得稳(穩) nádewěn (动) be sure of: 这事儿我～. I'm sure of this. (also as "拿得准").

拿定主意 ná dìng zhǔyi make up one's mind: 对这件事我还没～. I haven't made up my mind on this matter.

拿架子 ná jiàzi (动) put on airs

拿腔拿调 náqiāng-nádiào speak in an affected tone of voice

拿手 náshǒu (形) good at; adept; expert: 炸虾是我的～菜. Fried prawns is my speciality. ～好戏 a game or trick one is good at

拿着鸡(鷄)毛当(當)令箭 názhe jīmáo dàng lìngjiàn take a chicken feather for a warrant to issue orders—treat one's superior's casual remark as an order and make a big fuss about it

拿主意 ná zhǔyi decide; make up one's mind: 你自己～吧. You'd better make your own decision. 我的主意拿定了. My mind is made up. 拿不定主意 be wavering

N

哪 nǎ I (代) 1 which; what: 你想借～本书? Which book do you want to borrow? 他是～国人? What country is he from? 你最喜欢～种颜色? What is your favourite colour? 你～天有时间? When (or which day) are you free? 2 any: 你借～本书都可以. You can borrow any book you like. 这两种颜色我～种都不喜欢. I like neither of the colours. ～天都行. Any day will do. II (副) [used in a rhetorical question]: ～有你这样对待老人的? How could you treat old people like this? 没有他的帮助你～能有今天? How could you possibly be what you are today without his help?

see also na; něi

哪个(個) nǎge (代) 1 which; which one: ～公司? Which company? 你要～? Which one do you want? 2 who: ～? Who is it?

哪里(裏) nǎli I (代) where; wherever: 你在～住? Where do you live? 在～工作都一样. It doesn't make any difference where I work. ～有压迫,～就有反抗. Where there is oppression, there is resistance. II [used to form a rhetorical question]: 我～知道他已经走了? How could I know he had left already? 他～会说汉语,不过认识几个字罢了. He doesn't really speak Chinese. He only knows a few characters. 你的帮助太大了.——～～. You have given us a lot of help.—It is nothing.

哪能 nǎnéng [used in rhetorical questions to express negation] how can; how could: 我～去这种地方呢? How could I go to such a place? 你可别骗我.——～呢? Don't you fool me! —How could I?

哪怕 nǎpà (连) even; even if; even though; no matter how: ～下再大的雨我也得去. I'll have to go even if it rains cats and dogs.

哪儿(兒) nǎr 〈口〉 as "哪里" nǎli

哪些 nǎxiē (代) [used before a noun in plural number] which; who; what: ～是你的? Which ones are yours? ～人去参加晚会了? Who went to the party? 你买了～东西? What have you bought?

哪样(樣) nǎyàng (代) what kind (also as "哪种"): 你要～颜色的? What colour do you prefer? 你说的是～的餐巾? What kind of napkin do you mean?

捺 nà I (动) press down; restrain: ～着性子 control one's temper II (名) right-falling stroke (in Chinese characters)

呐 nà

呐喊 nàhǎn (动) shout loudly; cry out; cheer

钠 nà (名) sodium (Na)

纳 nà (动) 1 receive; accept; admit: 采～ adopt 2 pay; offer: 交～公粮 pay taxes in grain 3 sew in close stitches: ～鞋底子 stitch soles (of cloth shoes)

纳粹 Nàcuì (名) Nazi: ～分子 Nazi. ～主义 Nazism

纳贿 nàhuì (动) 1 take bribes 2 offer bribes

纳闷儿(兒) nàmènr 〈口〉 feel puzzled; be perplexed; wonder

纳米 nàmǐ (名) nanometer; NM; millimicron: ～技术 nanotechnology

纳入 nàrù (动) bring (or channel) into: ～正轨 bring sth. on to the right course. ～国家计划 incorporate sth. into the state plan

纳税 nàshuì (动) pay taxes

纳税人 nàshuìrén (名) tax payer

那 nà I (代) that: ～是谁? Who is that (man)? ～是可以理解的. That is understandable. II (连) then; in that case: ～你自己呢? What about yourself then? ～我就一个人去了. In that case I'll go alone.

那个(個) nàge I (代) that: ～问题 that problem II 〈口〉[used before a verb or an adjective to indicate a certain degree of exaggeration]: 看他～得意劲儿. Look how complacent he is! III 〈口〉[used to avoid a blunt or direct statement]: 你刚才跟他讲话的样子也太～了. The way you talked to him was a little too —how shall I put it? Well, you know what I mean.

那里(裏) nàli (代) that place; there: ～气候怎么样? What's the weather like there?

那么(麼) nàme I (代) 1 like that; in that way: 他不该～说. He shouldn't have said that. ～做会伤她的感情的. It would hurt her feelings if you did so. 我哥哥没有～高. My brother is not that tall. ～点儿 so little; so few: ～些 so much; so many 2 [used before a number to stress approximation] about; or so: 再有～二十来分钟就够了. Another twenty minutes or so will probably be enough. II (连) then; in that case: 既然电影不好看, ～我们回家吧. Since this film is no good, let's go home then.

那儿(兒) nàr (代) 〈口〉 1 see "那里" nàli 2 [used after 打, 从, 由] that time; then: 打～起, 她就用心念书了. She's been studying hard since then.

那时(時) nàshí (代) at that time; then; in those days

那些 nàxiē (代) those

那样(樣) nàyàng (代) like that; such; so; of that kind: 他不像你～仔细. He's not so careful as you are. 没你说的～好 not as good as you said. ～做不行. It won't do to act the way you did. 我不懂她会急成～. I don't know why she's so worried about it.

那阵儿(兒) nàzhènr during that period (of time); then: ～, 天天下雨. There was an unbroken spell of wet weather during that time. (also as "那阵子")

哪 na (助) [equivalent to 啊]: 加油干～! Speed up! Come on!
see also nǎ; něi

乃 nǎi I (动)〈书〉 be: 失败～成功之母. Failure is the mother of success. II (副) then; so: 因山势高峻, ～在山腰休息片刻. As the slope was steep, so we took a breather halfway up the hill.

乃至 nǎizhì (连) and even: 他的学术成就引起了全中国～全世界人民的敬佩. His academic achievement has aroused admiration in China and even throughout the world.

奶 nǎi I (名) 1 breasts 2 milk II (动) breastfeed: ～孩子 breastfeed (or suckle) a baby

奶粉 nǎifěn (名) powdered milk

奶酪 nǎilào (名) cheese

奶妈 nǎimā (名) wet nurse

奶奶 nǎinai (名) (paternal) grandmother

奶牛 nǎiniú (名) milk cow; milch cow

奶油 nǎiyóu (名) cream

奈 nài

奈何 nàihé (动) 1 to no avail: 无可～ absolutely helpless 2 do sth. to a person: 他就是不答应, 你又奈他何! If he flatly refused, what could you do about it?

耐 nài (动) be able to bear; endure: ～穿 can stand hard wear; be durable. 吃苦～劳 work hard despite hardships. 这种料子很～洗. This material washes well. 她再也～不住性子了. She could not hold back her anger any longer.

耐烦 nàifán (形) patient: 不～ impatient

耐寒 nàihán (形) cold-resistant

耐旱 nàihàn (形) drought-enduring: ～植物 drought-enduring plant

耐火 nàihuǒ (形) fire-resistant; refractory

耐久 nàijiǔ (形) durable

耐力 nàilì (名) endurance; stamina

耐磨 nàimó (形) wear-resisting; wearproof

耐人寻(尋)味 nài rén xúnwèi afford food for thought

耐心 nàixīn (形) patient: ～说服 try patiently to persuade

耐性 nàixìng (名) patience; endurance

耐用 nàiyòng (形) durable: ～品 durable goods; durables

南 nán (名) south: 华北～部 the southern part of north China. ～屋 a room with a northern exposure

南半球 nánbànqiú (名) the Southern Hemisphere

南北 nán-běi (名) 1 north and south: ～对话 North-South dialogue 2 from north to south: 大江～ both sides of the Yangtse River

南方 nánfāng (名) 1 south 2 the southern part of the country: ～话 southern

N

dialect. ～人 southerner

南瓜 nánguā (名) pumpkin

南国(國) nánguó (名) the southern part of the country: ～风光 southern scenery

南极(極) nánjí (名) the South Pole; the Antarctic

南美洲 Nán Měizhōu South America

南腔北调 nánqiāng-běidiào (名) (speak with) a mixed accent

南亚(亞) Nán Yà (名) South Asia: ～次大陆 the South Asian subcontinent

南辕北辙 nányuán-běizhé act in a way that defeats one's purpose; move in the opposite direction

喃 nán

喃喃 nánnán (动) mutter; murmur; mumble: ～自语 mutter to oneself

男

nán (名) man; male: ～主人公 (in a play) the hero. ～演员 actor. ～学生 boy student

男扮女装(裝) nán bàn nǚzhuāng a man disguised as a woman

男盗女娼 nándào-nǚchāng behave like thieves and whores; be out-and-out scoundrels

男低音 nándīyīn (名) bass

男儿(兒) nán'ér (名) man: 好～ a fine man

男方 nánfāng (名) the bridegroom's or husband's side

男高音 nángāoyīn (名) tenor

男孩儿(兒) nánháir (名) boy

男女关(關)系(係) nán-nǚ guānxi relations between the two sexes: 不正当的～ illicit sexual relations

男朋友 nánpéngyou (名) boyfriend

男人 nánrén (名) man; husband

男生 nánshēng (名) man student; boy student

男声(聲) nánshēng (名) male voice: ～合唱 men's chorus; male chorus

男性 nánxìng (名) the male sex

男子 nánzǐ (名) man; male: ～单(双)打 men's singles (doubles). ～团体赛 men's team event

男子汉(漢) nánzǐhàn (名) man: 不像个～ not manly; not man enough

难(難)

nán I (形) **1** hard; difficult: ～写 difficult to write. ～忘 unforgettable. ～逃法网 cannot escape punishment **2** bad; unpleasant: ～吃 taste bad. ～听 unpleasant to the ear II(动) put sb. into a difficult position: 这可把我～住了! It put me on the spot!

see also nàn

难保 nánbǎo (动) one cannot say for sure: 今天～不下雨. You can't say for sure that it won't rain today.

难产(産) nánchǎn (名) (of childbirth) difficult labour; dystocia

难处(處) nánchǔ (动) hard to get along with: 他一点儿也不～. He is not difficult to get along with at all.

难处(處) nánchu (名) difficulty; trouble: 他有他的～. He has his own difficulties.

难道 nándào (副) [make an emphatic rhetorical question]: ～太阳会从西边出来吗? Could the sun rise from the west? ～你不是就喜欢那玩意儿吗? Don't you just love that?

难得 nándé (形) **1** hard to come by; rare: 机会～ a rare chance **2** seldom; rarely: 这样的大雨是很～遇到的. Such torrential rains have scarcely occurred.

难怪 nánguài I (连) no wonder: 外面下雪了, ～这么冷. No wonder it's so cold. It's snowing. II (动) be understandable; be pardonable: 他刚来, 搞错了也～. He can hardly be blamed for the mistake since he is new here.

难关(關) nánguān (名) difficulty; crisis: 渡过～ get over a crisis. 攻克技术～ break down a technical barrier. ～重重 a bundle of difficulties

难过(過) nánguò I (动) have a hard time: 日子真～ lead a miserable life II (形) **1** not feel well: 我今天肚子有点～. I have stomach trouble today. **2** feel sad; be grieved: 她接到母亲去世的消息, 非常～. She was deeply grieved to learn of her mother's death.

难解难分 nánjiě-nánfēn be locked together (in a struggle); be inextricably involved (in a dispute)

难堪 nánkān (形) embarrassed: 使某人～ embarrass sb. 处于～的地位 be in an embarrassing situation

难看 nánkàn (形) **1** ugly **2** unhealthy; pale: 你的脸色这么～, 不是病了吧? You don't look well. Are you ill? 他吃了一惊, 脸色变得很～. He was stunned and his face took on a ghastly expression. **3** embarrassing; shameful: 通不过考试就太～了. It would be awful not to be able to pass the exam.

难免 nánmiǎn (形) hard to avoid; unavoidable

难能可贵 nán néng kě guì accomplish something difficult and so deserve praise; estimable; commendable

难色 nánsè (名) a show of reluctance or embarrassment

难舍(捨)难分 nánshě-nánfēn loath to part from each other

难受 nánshòu (形) **1** feel unwell; feel uncomfortable: 毛衣太小, 穿着～. The sweater is too tight and it's so uncomfortable on me. **2** feel unhappy; feel bad: 他心里很～. He felt ill and wretched.

难说 nánshuō (动) it's hard to say; you never can tell

难题 nántí (名) baffling problem; a hard nut to crack: 出～ set difficult questions

难听(聽) nántīng (形) **1** unpleasant to hear **2** offensive; coarse: 你怎么老是骂人, 多～! Don't be so foul-mouthed. It's disgusting! **3** scandalous: 这事情说出去多～. The story will cause a scandal once it gets out.

难为(爲)情 nánwéiqíng shy; embarrassed: 当着这么多人唱歌, 真有点～. It's embarrassing to sing in front of so many people.

难以 nányǐ (副) difficult to: ～想像 unimaginable. ～置信 incredible. ～形容 beyond description. ～捉摸 unfathomable. ～出口 too embarrassed to say it. ～逆料 be difficult to predict

难(難)

nàn I (名) calamity; disaster: 逃～ flee from danger. 多灾多～ be dogged by misfortunes II (动) blame: 非～ blame; reproach

see also nán

难民 nànmín (名) refugee: ～营 refugee camp

难兄难弟 nànxiōng-nàndì fellow sufferers; two of a kind

难友 nànyǒu (名) fellow sufferer

囊

náng (名) bag; sack; pocket: 胶～ capsule. 胆～ gall bladder

囊空如洗 náng kōng rú xǐ with empty pockets; penniless; not having a penny to bless oneself with; broke

囊括 nángkuò (动) embrace; include

囊肿(腫) nángzhǒng (名) cyst; benign tumour

挠(撓)

náo (动) **1** scratch: ～痒痒 scratch an itch **2** hinder: 阻～ obstruct **3** yield; flinch: 不屈不～ indomitable; unyielding

挠头(頭) náotóu (形) difficult to tackle: ～的事 a knotty problem

恼(惱)

nǎo (动) be angry; be annoyed: 把某人惹～了 annoy sb. 烦～ vexed; worried

恼恨 nǎohèn (动) be irritated and full of grievances

恼火 nǎohuǒ (形) annoyed; irritated; vexed

恼怒 nǎonù (形) angry; indignant; furious

恼羞成怒 nǎo-xiū chéng nù be shamed into anger

脑(腦)

nǎo (名) brain

脑袋 nǎodai (名) head

脑海 nǎohǎi (名) brain; mind: 深深地印入～ be engraved on one's mind

脑筋 nǎojīn (名) **1** brains; mind; head: 动～ use one's brains (or head) **2** way of thinking; ideas

脑力劳(勞)动(動) nǎolì láodòng mental work: ～者 mental worker; brain worker

脑满(滿)肠(腸)肥 nǎomǎn-chángféi idle rich

脑死亡 nǎosǐwáng brain death

脑汁 nǎozhī (名) brains: 绞尽～ rack (or cudgel) one's brains

脑子 nǎozi (名) **1** the brain **2** brains; mind; head: 没～ have no brains

闹

nào I (形) noisy: 这儿太～, 咱们到别处去吧! It's too noisy here. Let's go somewhere else. II (动) **1** make a loud noise; create a disturbance: 叫孩子们别～了. Tell the children to stop making so much noise. 大～一场 create a tremendous uproar; make a big scene **2** give vent to (one's anger, resentment, etc.): ～脾气 vent one's spleen; be in a tantrum. ～矛盾 (of two people) fall out **3** suffer from: ～水灾 suffer from a flood. ～肚子 have loose bowels (or diarrhoea) **4** do; make; undertake: ～罢工 go on strike. 把问题～清楚 straighten things out. 原来是～了一个误会. It turned out to be a misunderstanding.

闹别扭 nào bièniu be at loggerheads with sb.

闹病 nàobìng (动) fall ill; be ill

闹不清 nàobuqīng cannot tell; be unclear about: 我～这信是谁写的. I'm not clear who wrote this letter.

闹翻 nàofān (动) fall out with sb.

闹鬼 nàoguǐ (动) be haunted
闹哄哄 nàohōnghōng (形) clamorous; noisy
闹剧(劇) nàojù (名) farce
闹情绪 nào qíngxù be disgruntled; fall into a mood
闹市 nàoshì (名) busy streets; downtown area
闹事 nàoshì (动) make trouble; create a disturbance
闹笑话 nào xiàohuà make a fool of oneself; make a stupid mistake
闹意见(見) nào yìjiàn be divided in opinion and engage in bickerings
闹灾(災) nàozāi (动) be hit by a calamity
闹着玩儿(兒) nàozhe wánr joke: 你别当真,我是跟你~的. Don't take it so seriously. I was only joking.
闹中取静 nào zhōng qǔ jìng seek peace and quiet in noisy surroundings
闹钟(鐘) nàozhōng (名) alarm clock

呢 ne (助) **1** [used at the end of an interrogative sentence]: 怎么办~? What is to be done? 她什么时候来~? When will she be coming? 我喜欢他,你~? I like him. What about you? (or and you?) 我的大衣~? Where is my coat? **2** [used at the end of a statement to give emphasis]: 还远着~! It is still far away! 写一本好书得用好几年的时间~! It would take several years to write a good book! 我才不去~! I for one wouldn't go! 昨晚来了十个人~! As many as ten people were around last night! 经理正在开会~. The manager is at a meeting. **3** [used to make a pause within a sentence] see also ní

哪 něi (代) which; what
see also nǎ; na

馁 něi (形) disheartened; dispirited: 气~ lose heart; be disheartened

内 nèi I (名) inside; inner part or side: 入~ go inside; enter. 请勿入~ No admittance. 共八人,夫人包括在~. Altogether eight, wives included. II [used after a noun to indicate place, time, scope or limits] within; in; inside: 校~ in the school. 室~ indoor. 最近几天~ in a few days. 市~交通 urban traffic III [used before a noun or verb in forming a compound word] inner; internal

内宾(賓) nèibīn (名) Chinese guest (as distinguished from "外宾" foreign guest)
内部 nèibù (名) inside; internal; interior: 国家~事务 domestic affairs of a country. ~刊物 restricted publication
内存 nèicún (名) memory
内当(當)家 nèidāngjiā (名) **1** wife **2** wife of one's master, employer or landlord
内地 nèidì (名) inland; hinterland: ~城市 inland city
内分泌 nèifēnmì (名) endocrine; internal secretion
内服 nèifú (动) (of medicine) to be taken orally
内阁 nèigé (名) cabinet: 影子~ shadow cabinet. ~大臣 cabinet minister
内功 nèigōng (名) inner strength; quiet strength
内涵 nèihán (名) connotation
内行 nèiháng (名、形) expert; adept: 她在针灸方面很~. She is an expert at acupuncture. 充~ pose as an expert
内河 nèihé (名) inland river (or waterway)
内讧 nèihòng (名) internal conflict; internal strife
内奸 nèijiān (名) hidden traitor
内疚 nèijiù (名) guilty conscience: 感到~ feel guilty
内科 nèikē (名) (department of) internal medicine: ~医生 physician
内陆(陸) nèilù (名) inland; interior: ~国 landlocked country
内乱(亂) nèiluàn (名) civil strife; internal disorder
内幕 nèimù (名) inside story; dealings behind the scenes: ~交易 backdoor dealing
内勤 nèiqín (名) **1** office staff **2** internal or office work (as distinguished from work carried on mainly outside the office)
内情 nèiqíng (名) inside information; the inside story
内燃机(機) nèiránjī (名) internal-combustion engine
内容 nèiróng (名) content: ~丰富 have substantial content. ~提要 synopsis; résumé
内务(務) nèiwù (名) internal affairs
内线(綫) nèixiàn (名) **1** planted agent **2** inside (telephone) connections
内详 nèixiáng (动) name and address of sender enclosed
内向 nèixiàng (形) introvert
内销 nèixiāo (动) sell on the domestic mar-

ket

内心 nèixīn (名) heart; innermost being: 发自～深处 from the bottom of one's heart

内需 nèixū (名) domestic market demand: 拉动～ stimulate domestic market demand

内衣 nèiyī (名) underclothes

内因 nèiyīn (名) internal cause; intrinsic cause

内忧(憂)外患 nèiyōu-wàihuàn domestic trouble and foreign invasion

内在 nèizài (形) intrinsic; inherent; internal: ～规律 inherent law. ～因素 internal factor

内脏(臟) nèizàng (名) internal organs

内债 nèizhài (名) domestic debt

内战(戰) nèizhàn (名) civil war

内政 nèizhèng (名) internal (or domestic, home) affairs: 互不干涉～ non-interference in each other's internal affairs

嫩 nèn (形) 1 tender; delicate: ～芽 tender shoot 2 light: ～绿 pale green 3 inexperienced; unskilled

能 néng I (动) can; be able to: 你明天～去吗? Can you go tomorrow? 他不～不那样做. He had to do it the way he did. II (名) 1 ability; capability; skill: 无～ incompetent. 一专多～ good at many things and expert in one 2 energy: 原子～ atomic energy. 太阳～ solar energy

能干(幹) nénggàn (形) able; capable; competent

能够 nénggòu (动) can; be able to; be capable of

能耗 nénghào (名) energy consumption

能力 nénglì (名) ability; capability: ～强 have great ability; be very capable

能量 néngliàng (名) energy

能耐 néngnai (名)〈口〉ability; skill: 这人没什么～. He is good for nothing.

能…能… néng … néng … be able to do both. . . and . . . : 能屈能伸 be adaptable to circumstances. 能上能下 be ready to accept a higher position or a lower one. 能文能武 equally good in either civilian or military affairs; able to do both mental and manual work

能人 néngrén (名) able person

能手 néngshǒu (名) expert; a dab hand

能说会(會)道 néngshuō-huìdào have a glib tongue

能源 néngyuán (名) energy source: ～危机 energy crisis. 节约～ energy conservation

能者多劳(勞) néngzhě duōláo able people should do more work; the abler a man is, the busier he gets

嗯 ńg or ń (叹)[used for having words repeated when not heard]: ～,你说什么? What? what did you say?
see also ňg; ǹg

嗯 ňg or ň (叹) [used to indicate surprise]: ～,怎么又不见了? Hey! It's gone again. ～! 你怎么还没去? What! You haven't started yet?
see also ńg; ǹg

嗯 ǹg or ǹ (叹) [indicating response]: 他～了一声,就走了. He merely mumbled "H'm", and went away.
see also ńg; ňg

霓 ní (名) secondary rainbow

霓虹灯(燈) níhóngdēng (名) neon light

尼 ní (名) Buddhist nun

尼姑 nígū (名) Buddhist nun

尼龙(龍) nílóng (名) nylon

泥 ní (名) 1 mud; mire 2 mashed vegetable or fruit: 枣～ date paste. 土豆～ mashed potato
see also nì

泥巴 níbā (名) mud; mire

泥浆(漿) níjiāng (名) slurry; mud

泥坑 níkēng (名) mud pit; morass; quagmire

泥泞(濘) nínìng (形) muddy; miry: ～的道路 a muddy road

泥菩萨(薩) nípúsà (名) clay idol: ～过河,自身难保 like a clay idol fording a river—hardly able to save oneself (let alone anyone else)

泥鳅 níqiū (名) loach; eel

泥人 nírén (名) clay figurine: 彩塑～ painted clay figurine

泥沙 níshā (名) silt

泥石流 níshíliú (名) mud-rock flow

泥水匠 níshuǐjiàng (名) bricklayer; tiler; plasterer (also as "泥瓦匠")

泥塘 nítáng (名) mire; bog; morass

泥土 nítǔ (名) 1 earth; soil 2 clay

呢 ní (名) woollen cloth
see also ne

呢喃 nínán (形) twittering (of swallows)

呢绒 nírōng (名) wool fabric
呢子 nízi (名) woollen cloth

拟(擬) nǐ (动) 1 draw up; draft: ～稿 make a draft. ～一个计划草案 draft a plan 2 intend; plan: ～于月底回家 plan to come home by the end of the month
拟订 nǐdìng (动) draw up; draft; work out: ～具体办法 work out specific measures (also as "拟定")
拟人 nǐrén (名) personification
拟议(議) nǐyì (名) proposal; recommendation

你 nǐ (代) 1 you [second person singular]: ～喜欢吗? Do you like it? ～的父母 your parents. ～方 your side; you. ～校 your school 2 you; one; anyone: 他的才学叫～不得不佩服. You cannot but admire him for his talent and learning.
你好 nǐhǎo [used as a greeting] how do you do; how are you; hello
你们 nǐmen (代) you [second person plural]
你死我活 nǐsǐ-wǒhuó life-and-death; mortal: ～的斗争 a life-and-death struggle
你追我赶(趕) nǐzhuī-wǒgǎn try to outdo the other; vie with one another

N

溺 nì (动) 1 drown: ～死 be drowned 2 be addicted to; indulge
溺爱(愛) nì'ài (动) spoil (a child); be excessively fond of

逆 nì (动) go against; counter: ～时代潮流而动 go against the trend of the times. ～风 contrary wind
逆差 nìchā (名) deficit; unfavourable balance: 国际收支～ adverse balance of international payments. 贸易～ trade deficit
逆耳 nì'ěr (形) unpleasant to the ear: 忠言～. Good advice often sounds unpleasant.
逆风(風) nìfēng 1 against the wind: ～航行 sail against the wind 2 contrary wind
逆光 nìguāng (名) backlighting
逆境 nìjìng (名) adverse circumstances; adversity
逆来(來)顺受 nì lái shùn shòu submit to adversity meekly; be resigned to fate; to take insults philosophically; to take the rough with the smooth
逆流 nìliú 1 adverse current; countercurrent 2 against the current: ～而上 to move against the tide
逆水 nìshuǐ against the current: ～行舟 sailing against the current
逆行 nìxíng (动) (of vehicles) go in a direction not allowed by traffic regulations
逆转(轉) nìzhuǎn (动) take a turn for the worse; worsen

匿 nì (动) hide; conceal: 隐～ go into hiding; conceal one's identity
匿迹 nìjì (动) go into hiding; stay incognito: 销声～ lie low
匿名 nìmíng (形) anonymous: ～信 anonymous letter

腻 nì (形) 1 (of food) greasy; oily: 这烤鸭太油～. This roast duck is too rich for me. 汤有点儿～. The soup is a bit too oily. 2 be bored; be tired of: ～得慌 bored stiff 3 meticulous: 细～ meticulous care
腻烦 nìfan I (形) be bored; be fed up II (动) loathe; hate: 我真～他. I'm really fed up with him.
腻人 nìrén 1 be boring or tedious 2 (of food that is too greasy or sweet) make one sick
腻味 nìwei I (形) be bored; be fed up: 这部电影真叫人～. This film is really boring. II (动) hate; loathe: 我最～肥肉. I hate fatty pork.

泥 nì (动) cover or daub with plaster, putty, etc.
see also ní
泥子 nìzi (名) putty

昵 nì (形) close; intimate: 亲～ very intimate

拈 niān (动) pick up (with the thumb and one or two fingers): 信手～来 pick up at random. ～轻怕重 pick easy jobs and shirk hard ones

黏 nián (形) sticky; glutinous: ～米 glutinous rice
黏合 niánhé (动) bind; adhere: ～剂 binder; adhesive
黏结 niánjié (动) cohere: ～力 cohesion; cohesive force. ～性 cohesiveness
黏性 niánxìng (名) stickiness; viscidity; viscosity
黏液 niányè (名) mucus

年 nián (名) 1 year: 去～ last year. 明～ next year. ～复一～ year after year; year in year out. 近～来 in recent years 2 annual; yearly: ～计划 annual plan. ～产量 annual output; annual yield 3 age: ～过半百 over fifty (years old). ～事已高 advanced in age. 童～ childhood 4

New Year; New Year's Day; Spring Festival: 拜～ pay a New Year call
年表 niánbiǎo (名) chronological table
年成 niáncheng (名) the year's harvest: 好～ a good harvest. ～不好 a lean year
年初 niánchū (名) the beginning of a year
年代 niándài (名) **1** age; years; time: 战争～ in the war years **2** a decade (of a century): 八十～ the eighties
年底 niándǐ (名) the end of a year
年度 nián dù (名) year: 财政～financial year; fiscal year. ～预算 annual budget
年富力强 niánfù-lìqiáng in the prime of life; in one's prime
年糕 niángāo (名) New Year cake (made of glutinous rice flour)
年关(關) niánguān (名) the end of the year (formerly the time for settling accounts)
年号(號) niánhào (名) the title of an emperor's reign
年华(華) niánhuá (名) time; years: 虚度～ idle away one's time
年画(畫) niánhuà (名) New Year pictures
年货 niánhuò (名) special purchases for the New Year: 办～ do New Year shopping
年级 niánjí (名) grade (in school): 小学六～ the 6th form (or grade). 大学三～学生 3rd year (university) student
年纪 niánjì (名) age: 你父亲多大～了? How old is your father? 上了～ old; advanced in years; getting on in years. ～轻 young
年鉴(鑑) niánjiàn (名) yearbook; almanac
年景 niánjǐng (名) the year's harvest
年历(曆) niánlì (名) a year calendar
年龄 niánlíng (名) age: 退休～ retirement age
年轮(輪) niánlún (名) (of trees) annual ring; growth ring
年迈(邁) niánmài (形) old; aged: ～力衰 old and infirm; senile
年轻(輕) niánqīng (形) young: ～人 young people. ～力壮 young and vigorous. ～一代 the younger generation
年岁(歲) niánsuì (名) age
年头(頭) niántóu (名) **1** year: 他去世已经三个～了. It's three years since his death. **2** years; long time: 这顶帽子可有～了. This hat has lasted me many years. **3** days; times: 那～ in those days **4** harvest: 今年～真好. This year's harvest is very good indeed.
年限 niánxiàn (名) fixed number of years: 攻读学位的最低～ the minimum length of time required by a degree course. 工具使用～ the service life of a tool
年夜 niányè (名) the lunar New Year's Eve: ～饭 family reunion dinner on the lunar New Year's Eve
年幼 niányòu (形) young; under age: ～无知 young and ignorant
年月 niányuè (名) days; years
年长(長) niánzhǎng (形) older in age; senior
年终 niánzhōng (名) the end of the year; year-end: ～结账 year-end settlement of accounts

捻 niǎn I (动) twist with one's fingers: ～线 twist thread II (名) sth. made by twisting: 纸～儿 a paper spill
捻子 niǎnzi (名) **1** spill **2** wick

撵 niǎn (动) drive away; oust; expel: 把人～出去 drive sb. away

碾 niǎn (动) crush; grind: ～碎 be ground to powder
碾子 niǎnzi (名) roller: 石～ stone roller

念 niàn I (动) **1** think of; miss: 想～ miss sb. 十分挂～miss sb. very much **2** study; be a pupil: ～书 go to school. 他～中学了. He is in middle school now. ～历史 study history **3** read aloud: ～信 read a letter (aloud) II (名) idea; thought: 私心杂～ selfish considerations
念叨 niàndao (动) be always talking about; harp on: 你在～什么? What are you muttering about?
念经(經) niànjīng (动) chant scriptures
念旧(舊) niànjiù (动) keep old friendships in mind; remember old friends
念念不忘 niànniàn bù wàng (动) always keep in mind
念头(頭) niàntou (名) thought; idea; intention

娘 niáng (名) **1** mother; ma; mum: 爹～ father and mother **2** a form of address for an elderly married woman: 老大～ grandma **3** a young woman: 新～ bride
娘家 niángjia (名) a married woman's parents' home
娘娘 niángniáng (名) **1** empress or imperial concubine of the first rank: 正宫～ emperor's wife; empress **2** goddess: ～庙 a temple dedicated to the worship of a goddess
娘胎 niángtāi (名) mother's womb: 出了～ be born. 从～带来的记 a birthmark

N

酿(釀) niàng (动) 1 make by fermentation: ～酒 make wine. ～啤酒 brew beer. ～酒业 winemaking industry; brewery 2 make (honey): 蜜蜂～蜜. Bees make honey. 3 lead to; result in: ～祸 lead to disaster

酿成 niàngchéng (动) (of disasters) lead to; bring on; breed

酿造 niàngzào (动) make (wine, vinegar, etc.) by fermentation

袅 niǎo (形) slender and delicate: ～娜 slender and graceful

袅袅 niǎoniǎo (形) 1 curling upwards: 炊烟～. Smoke is spiralling upward from kitchen chimneys. 2 waving in the wind 3 lingering: 余音～. The residue of the sound still remains in the ears of the hearers.

鸟(鳥) niǎo (名) bird

鸟瞰 niǎokàn (动) get a bird's-eye view: ～全城 get a bird's-eye view of the city

尿 niào I (名) urine II (动) urinate; make (or pass) water

尿布 niàobù (名) diaper; nappy

尿检 niàojiǎn (名) urine test; urinalysis

N

捏(揑) niē (动) 1 hold between the fingers; pinch: ～住这支笔. Hold the pen. 2 mould with thumb and fingers; mould: ～泥人儿 mould clay figurines. ～饺子 make dumplings

捏合 niēhé (动) mediate; act as go-between

捏一把汗 niē yī bǎ hàn sweat with anxiety or fear

捏造 niēzào (动) fabricate; concoct: ～事实 invent a story; make up a story

蹑(躡) niè

蹑手蹑脚 nièshǒu-nièjiǎo walk on tiptoe

孽 niè (名) sin; evil: 作～ do evil. 妖～ evildoer; monster

镍 niè (名) nickel (Ni)

您 nín (代)〈敬〉 you

宁(寧) níng (形) peaceful; tranquil

see also nìng

宁静 níngjìng (形) peaceful; tranquil; quiet: ～的夜晚 a tranquil night. 心里不～ feel disturbed

柠(檸) níng

柠檬 níngméng (名) lemon

拧(擰) níng (动) 1 twist; wring: 把毛巾～干 wring out a wet towel 2 pinch; tweak: ～了他一把 give him a pinch

see also nǐng

狞(獰) níng (形) ferocious; hideous

狞笑 níngxiào (动) grin hideously

凝 níng (动) 1 congeal; curdle; coagulate 2 concentrate one's attention

凝固 nínggù (动) solidify: ～点 solidifying point

凝结 níngjié (动) condense; coagulate; congeal: 池面上～了一层冰. There is a thin layer of ice over the pond.

凝聚 níngjù (动) condense: 这部名著～着他毕生的心血. This masterpiece is an embodiment of his painstaking lifelong effort. ～力 cohesive force; cohesion

凝神 níngshén (副) with fixed attention: ～思索 think over the matter with concentrated attention

凝视 níngshì (动) gaze fixedly; stare

凝思 níngsī (动) be lost in thought

凝滞(滯) níngzhì (形) stagnate; sluggish: ～的目光 dull, staring eyes

拧(擰) nǐng I (动) twist; screw: ～开瓶盖 screw (or twist) the cap off a bottle. ～紧螺丝 tighten up a screw II (形) 1 wrong; mistaken: 你把意思搞～了. You've misinterpreted the meaning. 2 be at cross purposes: 两个人越说越～. The more they talked, the more they disagreed.

see also níng

宁(寧) nìng (连) rather

see also níng

宁可 nìngkě (连) would rather; better: 我～自己干. I'd rather do it myself. ～站着死, 绝不跪着生 would rather die on one's feet than live on one's knees

宁肯 nìngkěn (连) would rather; better

宁缺毋滥(濫) nìng quē wú làn rather go without than have something shoddy; better fewer but better

宁死不屈 nìng sǐ bù qū rather die than surrender; prefer death to dishonour

宁愿(願) nìngyuàn see "宁可" nìngkě

妞 niū (名)〈口〉 girl

牛 niú (名) ox: 母~ cow. 公~ bull. 小~ calf
牛痘 niúdòu (名) smallpox pustule; vaccine pustule: 种~ give or get smallpox vaccination
牛犊(犢) niúdú (名) calf
牛角尖 niújiǎojiān (名) an insignificant or insoluble problem: 钻~ take unnecessary pains to study an insoluble problem; split hairs
牛劲(勁) niújìn (名) 1 great strength; tremendous effort 2 stubbornness; obstinacy; tenacity
牛马(馬) niúmǎ (名) beasts of burden
牛毛 niúmáo (名) ox hair: 多如~ countless; innumerable
牛奶 niúnǎi (名) milk
牛排 niúpái (名) beefsteak
牛棚 niúpéng (名) cowshed
牛皮 niúpí (名) 1 ox-hide 2 boasting; bragging: 吹~ talk big; brag
牛脾气(氣) niúpíqi (名) stubbornness; obstinacy
牛皮纸 niúpízhǐ (名) brown paper
牛气(氣) niúqi (形) arrogant; overbearing
牛肉 niúròu (名) beef
牛市 niúshì bull market

忸 niǔ

忸怩 niǔní (形) unnaturally shy: ~作态 behave coyly; be affectedly shy

扭 niǔ (动) 1 turn round: 她~过身去哭了起来. She turned away and wept. 他~过头来瞪着她. He turned around and stared at her. 把收音机~大声点儿! Turn the radio a bit louder! 2 twist; wrench: 把铁丝~断 twist and break a wire 3 sprain: ~了腰 sprain one's back 4 grapple (or wrestle) with: 两人~在一起. They were wrestling with each other. 5 (of body movement) sway from side to side; swing: 她走路一~一~的. She walks with a swaying gait.
扭打 niǔdǎ (动) wrestle; grapple
扭亏(虧)为(爲)盈 niǔ kuī wéi yíng turn losses into profits; turn an unfavourable balance into a favourable one
扭捏(揑) niǔnie (形) affectedly shy
扭伤(傷) niǔshāng (动) sprain; wrench: 脚~了 have sprained one's ankle
扭秧歌 niǔ yāngge dance the yangko
扭转(轉) niǔzhuǎn (动) 1 turn round: ~身子 (of a person) turn round 2 turn back; reverse: ~局势 reverse a situation; turn the tables. ~乾坤 bring about a radical change in the situation; reverse the course of events

钮 niǔ (名) button; knob: 按~ push a button. 电~ switch; button. ~扣 (on a garment) button

纽 niǔ (名) 1 button 2 bond; tie
纽带(帶) niǔdài (名) link; tie; bond: 友谊的~ ties of friendship

拗 niù (形) stubborn; obstinate; difficult: 一个脾气很~的老头 a very stubborn old man
see also ào
拗不过(過) niùbuguò unable to make sb. change his mind

农(農) nóng (名) 1 farming; agriculture: 务~ go in for agriculture. ~产品 agricultural products; farm produce 2 peasant; farmer: 棉~ cotton grower. 贫下中~ poor and lower-middle peasants
农场(場) nóngchǎng (名) farm: 国营~ state farm
农村 nóngcūn (名) rural area; countryside: ~集市 village fair
农夫 nóngfū (名) farmer
农户 nónghù (名) peasant household
农会(會) nónghuì (名) peasant association
农活 nónghuó (名) farm work
农具 nóngjù (名) farm tools
农历(曆) nónglì (名) the traditional Chinese calendar; the lunar calendar
农忙 nóngmáng (名) busy farming season
农贸市场(場) nóngmào shìchǎng a market of farm produce (in urban areas)
农民 nóngmín (名) peasant; peasantry
农奴 nóngnú (名) serf: ~主 serf owner
农时(時) nóngshí (名) farming season: 不违~ do farm work in the right season
农田 nóngtián (名) farmland; cultivated land: ~基本建设 capital construction on farmland. ~水利 irrigation and water conservancy
农闲(閒) nóngxián (名) slack farming season
农药(藥) nóngyào (名) farm chemical; pesticide
农业(業) nóngyè (名) agriculture; farming: ~人口 agricultural population. ~革命 green revolution

农艺(藝)师(師) nóngyìshī (名) agronomist

农作物 nóngzuòwù (名) crops

浓(濃) nóng (形) 1 thick; dense; concentrated: ~茶 strong tea. ~烟 dense smoke. ~眉 heavy (thick) eyebrows 2 (of degree or extent) great; rich: 兴趣很~ take great delight in sth.

浓度 nóngdù (名) density; concentration

浓厚 nónghòu (形) 1 dense; thick 2 (of atmosphere; colour, interest, etc.) strong

浓密 nóngmì (形) dense; thick: ~的枝叶 thick foliage

浓缩 nóngsuō (动) concentrate; enrich: ~牛奶 condensed milk. ~铀 enriched uranium

浓郁 nóngyù (形) (of fragrance) strong; rich: 玫瑰花发出~的香味. The roses give off a rich perfume.

浓妆(妝) nóngzhuāng (名) heavy make-up and gaudy dress: ~艳抹 rich attired and heavily made up

脓(膿) nóng (名) pus

脓包 nóngbāo (名) 1 pustule 2 worthless fellow; good-for-nothing

脓疮(瘡) nóngchuāng (名) running sore

脓肿(腫) nóngzhǒng (名) abscess

弄 nòng (动) 1 do; make; handle; manage; get: 你在这儿~什么? What are you up to here? 你把我~糊涂了. You've made me confused. 这么大个工厂, 你~得了吗? Can you manage such a big factory? 菜~咸了. You've put too much salt in the dish. 把问题~清楚 get the problems sorted out; set sb. straight about sth. 2 play with; meddle with: 小孩子爱~沙土. Children like to play with sand. 别老~那把伞了! Stop meddling with that umbrella! 3 get; fetch: 去~点吃的来. Go and get something to eat.
see also lòng

弄错 nòngcuò (动) make a mistake; misunderstand: 你~了. You've got it wrong. *or* You are mistaken.

弄好 nònghǎo (动) 1 do well: 把事情~ do a good job. 弄不好, 她会生气的. Otherwise, she'll get angry. 2 finish doing sth.: 计划~了没有? Is the plan ready?

弄坏(壞) nònghuài (动) ruin or spoil sth.: 把事情~ spoil the show

弄僵 nòngjiāng (动) bring to a deadlock; end in deadlock

弄巧成拙 nòng qiǎo chéng zhuō one is only making a fool of oneself by trying to be clever

弄清 nòngqīng (动) make clear; clarify; understand fully: ~问题所在 find where the problem lies. ~事实 set the facts straight. ~是非 distinguish right from wrong

弄权(權) nòngquán (动) maintain power by playing politics

弄虚作假 nòngxū-zuòjiǎ practise fraud; resort to deception

弄糟 nòngzāo (动) spoil sth.; make a mess of things

奴 nú (名) slave

奴才 núcai (名) flunkey; lackey: ~相 servile behaviour; servility

奴化 núhuà (动) enslave: ~政策 policy of enslavement

奴隶(隸) núlì (名) slave: ~主 slave owner

奴仆(僕) núpú (名) servant; flunkey

奴性 núxìng (名) servility; slavishness

奴颜婢膝 núyán-bìxī (形) subservient; servile

奴役 núyì (动) enslave; keep in bondage

弩 nǔ (名) crossbow

努 nǔ

努力 nǔlì (动) try hard; make great efforts; exert oneself: ~工作 work hard. 尽最大~ do one's utmost; do the best one can

努嘴 nǔzuǐ (动) pout one's lips as a signal

怒 nù (形) anger; in a rage; furious: 发~ get angry; fly into a rage. ~不可遏 boil with rage. ~不敢言 feel indignant but dare not to speak out

怒潮 nùcháo (名) raging tide

怒冲冲 nùchōngchōng (形) in a towering temper; furious

怒发(髮)冲(衝)冠 nùfà chōng guān bristle with anger

怒号(號) nùháo (动) howl; roar: 狂风~. The wind is howling.

怒吼 nùhǒu (动) roar; howl

怒火 nùhuǒ (名) flames of fury; fury: 满腔~ be filled with fury. ~中烧 to burn with anger; be boiling with rage

怒气(氣) nùqì (名) anger; rage; fury: ~冲天 be in a towering rage; give way to unbridled fury. ~未消 be still nursing

with one's anger
怒涛(濤) nùtāo (名) angry waves
女 nǚ (名) 1 woman; female: ～工 woman worker. ～职员 female staff (member). ～售货员 saleswoman. ～演员 actress. ～英雄 heroine. ～流 the female sex 2 daughter; girl: 子～ sons and daughters; children
女大十八变(變) nǚ dà shíbā biàn there is no telling what a girl will look like when she grows up
女儿(兒) nǚ'ér (名) daughter; girl
女服务(務)员 nǚfúwùyuán (名) waitress; air hostess; stewardess
女高音 nǚgāoyīn (名) soprano
女红 nǚgōng (名) needlework
女孩儿(兒) nǚháir (名) girl
女皇 nǚhuáng (名) empress
女郎 nǚláng (名) young woman; maiden; girl
女朋友 nǚpéngyou (名) girl friend
女气(氣) nǚqi (形) effeminate
女强人 nǚqiángrén (名) a strong woman; a woman of exceptional ability
女权(權) nǚquán (名) women's rights
女人 nǚrén (名) woman; womenfolk
女人 nǚren (名)〈口〉wife
女色 nǚsè (名) woman's charms: 好～ be fond of women; be a womanizer
女神 nǚshén (名) goddess
女生 nǚshēng (名) woman student; school girl
女士 nǚshì (名) [polite form of address for women]: ～们… Ladies...
女王 nǚwáng (名) queen
女性 nǚxìng (名) the female sex
女婿 nǚxu (名) son-in-law
女主人 nǚzhǔren (名) hostess
女子 nǚzǐ (名) woman; female: ～单(双)打 women's singles (doubles). ～团体赛 women's team event
暖 nuǎn I (形) warm: 风和日～. The wind is gentle and the weather warm. II (动) warm up: 靠近火边来～～身子. Come near the fire and warm yourself.
暖房 nuǎnfáng (名) greenhouse; hothouse
暖壶(壺) nuǎnhú (名) thermos flask; thermos bottle
暖和 nuǎnhuo (形) warm; nice and warm
暖流 nuǎnliú (名) warm current
暖瓶 nuǎnpíng see "暖壶" nuǎnhú
暖气(氣) nuǎnqì (名) central heating: ～管 radiator
暖色 nuǎnsè (名) warm colour
暖洋洋 nuǎnyángyáng (形) warm
疟(瘧) nüè (名) malaria
see also yào
疟疾 nüèji (名) malaria; ague
虐 nüè (形) cruel; tyrannical
虐待 nüèdài (动) maltreat; ill-treat
虐杀(殺) nüèshā (动) kill sb. by maltreatment
虐政 nüèzhèng (名) tyrannical government; tyranny
挪 nuó (动) move; shift
挪动(動) nuódòng (动) move; shift
挪用 nuóyòng (动) 1 divert (funds) 2 embezzle: ～公款 misappropriation (or embezzlement) of public funds
懦 nuò (形) faint-hearted; weak-kneed
懦夫 nuòfū (名) coward
懦弱 nuòruò (形) cowardly; weak
糯 nuò
糯米 nuòmǐ (名) glutinous rice
诺 nuò (名) 1 promise: 许～ promise 2 yes: 唯唯～～的人 a yes-man
诺言 nuòyán (名) promise: 履行～ fulfil one's promise; keep one's word

O o

噢 ō (叹) [indicating sudden realization]: ～, 原来是你! Oh, so it's you!
噢唷 ōyō (叹) [indicating surprise or a feeling of pain]: ～, 这么大的苹果! Oh, what a big apple! ～, 好烫! Ouch, it's terribly hot!
哦 ó (叹) [indicating doubt]: ～! 会有这样的事? What! How could there be such things? *or* Really?
哦 ò (叹) [indicating understanding or realization]: ～, 我懂了. Oh! I see. ～, 我想起来了. Ah, I've got it.
讴(謳) ōu I (动) sing II (名) folk songs
讴歌 ōugē (动) sing the praises of

鸥(鷗) ōu (名) gull: 海~ seagull

欧(歐) Ōu 〈简〉(欧洲) Europe

欧亚(亞)大陆(陸) Ōu-Yà dàlù Eurasia

欧元 Ōu'yuán (名) the euro

欧洲 Ōuzhōu (名) Europe: ~共同体 the European Economic Community (E. E. C.). ~货币 Euro-currency

殴(毆) ōu (动) beat up; hit: 斗~ fight with fists

殴打 ōudǎ (动) beat up; hit: 互相~ come to blows; exchange blows

藕 ǒu (名) lotus root

藕断(斷)丝(絲)连 ǒuduàn-sīlián (of lovers) separated but still in each other's thought

藕粉 ǒufěn (名) lotus root starch

偶 ǒu I (名) 1 image; idol: 木~ puppet 2 mate; spouse: 配~ spouse II (形) even (number); in pairs III (副) by chance; by accident; occasionally: ~遇 meet by chance; run across

偶尔(爾) ǒu'ěr (副) once in a long while; occasionally: 他只是~来玩儿. He drops in only occasionally.

P

偶合 ǒuhé (名) coincidence: 我们在这一点上见解一致完全是~,事先并没有商量过. It was a mere coincidence that we held identical views on this point, for we had no prior consultation.

偶然 ǒurán (形) accidental; fortuitous; chance: ~现象 accidental phenomena. 她~听到了这个消息. She learnt the news by chance.

偶数(數) ǒushù (名) even number

偶像 ǒuxiàng (名) image; idol: ~崇拜 idolatry. ~化 idolize

呕(嘔) ǒu (动) vomit; throw up: 发~ be sick. 令人作~ make one sick; nauseating; revolting

呕吐 ǒutù (动) vomit; throw up

呕心沥(瀝)血 ǒuxīn-lìxuè work one's heart out

沤(漚) òu (动) soak; steep

沤肥 òuféi (动) make compost by waterlogging

怄(慪) òu (动) 1 irritate; annoy 2 be irritated

怄气(氣) òuqì (动) be annoyed and sulky: 怄了一肚子气 have a bellyful of repressed grievances

P p

啪 pā (象) bang

啪嚓 pāchā (象) a sudden loud noise as made by sth. falling to the ground and breaking apart

啪嗒 pādā (象) [quick, light sound as made by footsteps, typewriters, etc.] clatter; patter

趴 pā (动) 1 lie on one's stomach; lie prone 2 bend over: ~在桌子上画图 bend over the desk, drawing pictures

扒 pá (动) 1 rake up 2 stew; braise: ~羊肉 stewed mutton

see also bā

扒手 páshǒu (名) pickpocket

耙 pá I (名) rake: 木~ wooden rake II (动) rake; harrow: ~地 rake the soil level

see also bà

爬 pá (动) 1 crawl; creep 2 climb; scramble: ~山 climb a mountain

爬虫(蟲) páchóng (名) reptile

爬格子 pá gézi crawl over squared or lined paper — write (esp. in order to make a living)

爬行 páxíng (动) crawl; creep: ~动物 reptile. ~通货膨胀 creeping inflation

怕 pà I (动) 1 fear; dread; be afraid of 2 cannot stand; will be affected by: 这种材料不~水. This kind of material is waterproof. 3 feel anxious about; feel concerned for or about: 女孩子大都~胖. Most girls are afraid of being overweight. II (副) I suppose; perhaps: 他~来不了吧. I'm afraid he won't be able to come. 这趟~要用十天吧. This trip will take about ten days, I should think. ~要下雨了,你最好呆在家里. It looks like rain, so better stay at home.

怕老婆 pà lǎopo be henpecked

怕人 pàrén I (动) dread to meet people; be shy II (形) frightening; terrifying; horrible: 屋子里黑得~. It's frighteningly dark inside the room.

怕事 pàshì (动) be afraid of getting involved

怕是 pàshì 〈口〉 I guess; I suppose; maybe; perhaps: 你~病了吧? You're ill, aren't you?

怕死 pàsǐ (动) fear death：～鬼 coward

怕羞 pàxiū (形) coy; shy; bashful

帕 pà (名) handkerchief

拍 pāi I (动) 1 clap; pat; beat：～球 bounce a ball. ～巴掌 clap one's hands. ～掉身上的土 whisk the dust off one's clothes. ～～他的肩膀 pat him on the shoulder 2 take (a picture)：～照 take a picture. ～电影 shoot (or make) a film 3 send (a telegram, etc.)：～电报 send a telegram 4 flatter; fawn on：吹牛～马 ready to boast and flatter II (名) 1 bat; racket：乒乓球～ table-tennis bat. 网球～ tennis racket 2 (of music) beat; time：一小节三～ three beats in a bar

拍板 pāibǎn (动) 1 rap the gavel：～成交 strike a bargain; clinch a deal 2 have the final say：这事得由经理亲自～. The manager has the final say in this matter.

拍马(馬)屁 pāi mǎpì 〈口〉flatter; fawn on

拍卖(賣) pāimài (动) auction

拍摄(攝) pāishè (动) take a picture; shoot

拍手 pāishǒu (动) clap one's hands; applaud：～叫好 clap and shout "bravo!". ～称快 clap and cheer; applaud (to express joy as the triumph of justice)

拍照 pāizhào (动) take a picture; have a picture taken

拍纸簿 pāizhǐbù (名) (writing) pad

拍子 pāizi (名) 1 bat; racket 2 beat; time：打～ beat the time

排 pái I (动) 1 line up; arrange in order：～队 queue up; stand in a line. ～座位 make a seating arrangement 2 drain; discharge：～废水 discharge waste water 3 rehearse：～戏 rehearse a play II (名) 1 row; line：前(后)～ front (back) row 2 platoon 3 raft：木～ timber raft III (量) row：两～树 two rows of trees

排版 páibǎn (动) set type

排比 páibǐ (名) parallelism

排查 páichá (名) troubleshooting; screening

排场(場) páichang (名) a show of extravagance; grand style

排斥 páichì (动) repel; exclude; reject：～异己 discriminate against those who do not belong to the same inner circle

排除 páichú (动) get rid of; remove; eliminate：～障碍 remove an obstacle. ～故障 fix a breakdown. ～一种可能性 rule out a possibility. ～疑虑 preclude all doubts. ～外来干扰 remove outside interference

排毒 páidú (名) eliminate toxicant; excrete toxins

排队(隊) páiduì (动) line up; queue up：～买票 line up for tickets. ～上车 queue up for a bus

排骨 páigǔ (名) spare-ribs

排行 páiháng (动) (of brothers and sisters) list according to seniority among brothers and sisters：他～第三. He's the third child of the family.

排行榜 páihángbǎng (名) list of candidates in order of merits or demerits

排挤(擠) páijǐ (动) squeeze out (people)：互相～ each trying to squeeze the other out

排解 páijiě (动) mediate; reconcile：～纠纷 mediate a dispute

排涝(澇) páilào (动) drain flooded fields

排练(練) páiliàn (动) rehearse：～节目 have a rehearsal

排列 páiliè (动) put in order; rank：按字母顺序～ arrange in alphabetical order

排球 páiqiú (名) volleyball

排山倒海 páishān-dǎohǎi overwhelming

排外 páiwài 1 exclusive 2 anti-foreign：盲目～ blind opposition to everything foreign. ～主义 xenophobia

排污 páiwū (动) emit pollutants：～系统 pollutant emission system

排泄 páixiè (动) 1 excrete 2 drain

排演 páiyǎn (动) rehearse

徘 pái

徘徊 páihuái (动) 1 pace up and down 2 hesitate; waver

牌 pái (名) 1 plate; tablet：门～ doorplate. 车～ number plate (on a vehicle). 招～ shop sign; signboard 2 trade mark; brand：名～货 goods of a well-known brand 3 cards, dominoes, etc.：扑克～ playing cards. 桥～ bridge

牌坊 páifāng (名) memorial archway (or gateway)

牌价(價) páijià (名) 1 list price 2 market quotation

牌照 páizhào (名) licence plate; licence tag

牌子 páizi (名) 1 plate; sign 2 brand; trademark：老～ old brand; well-known brand

P

迫 pǎi

see also pò

迫击(擊)炮 pǎijīpào (名) mortar

派 pài I (动) send; dispatch: ～人去了解情况 send people to gather information. ～代表团出席大会 send a delegation to the conference. ～军队 dispatch troops. ～你一个工作 set you a task II (名) 1 group; school; faction: 学～ school of thought. 党～ political party. 反对～ opposition party. 右～ rightist 2 style; matter; air: 气～ bearing III (量) 1 [for factions]: 两～意见 two different views 2 [for scene, situation, language etc., preceded by 一]: 形势一～大好. The situation is excellent. 一～欣欣向荣的景象 a prosperous scene. 一～胡言 a pack of nonsense

派别 pàibié (名) group; school; faction: ～斗争 factional strife

派出所 pàichūsuǒ (名) local police station; police substation

派对 pàiduì (名) party

派遣 pàiqiǎn (动) send; dispatch: ～代表团 send a delegation

派生 pàishēng (动) derive from

派头(頭) pàitóu (名) style; manner: 他～真不小! He certainly puts on quite a show!

派系 pàixì (名) factions

派用场(場) pài yòngchǎng put to use; turn to account: 这东西将来也许好派用场. It may come in handy some day.

攀 pān (动) 1 climb; clamber: 高不可～ too high to reach; unattainable 2 seek connections in high places

攀比 pānbǐ (动) cite the cases of others in support of one's own claim

攀登 pāndēng (动) climb; clamber; scale: ～科学技术新高峰 scale new heights in science and technology

攀高枝儿(兒) pān gāozhīr make friends or claim ties of kinship with someone of a higher social position

攀亲(親) pānqīn (动) claim kinship

攀升 pānshēng (动) climb: 大幅～ a sharp increase. 一路～ have been on the rise all the time

攀谈 pāntán (动) engage in small talk; engage in chitchat

攀岩 pānyán (名) rock climbing

攀折 pānzhé (动) break off (twigs, etc.): 请勿～花木. Please don't pick the flowers or break off the branches.

蹒 pán

蹒跚 pánshān (动) limp; hobble

盘(盤) pán I (名) tray; plate; dish: 银～ silver plate. 茶～ tea tray. 磨～ millstone. 棋～ chessboard II (动) 1 coil; wind: 蛇～成一团. The snake coiled up. ～山小路 a winding mountain path 2 check; examine: ～根究底 try to get to the bottom of a matter 3 take inventory: ～点 take stock III (量) [for things wound flat or for things shaped like a plate]: 两～磁带 two spools (or reels) of tape. 三～菜 three dishes. 一～棋 a game of chess

盘剥 pánbō (动) exploit by means of usury

盘查 pánchá (动) interrogate and examine

盘缠 pánchan (名) travelling expenses

盘根错节(節) pángēn-cuòjié deep-rooted; too complicated to cope with

盘踞 pánjù (动) illegally or forcibly occupy: ～在山里的土匪 bandits entrenched in the mountain

盘儿(兒)菜 pánrcài (名) ready-to-cook dish of meat, vegetables, etc. (sold at the food market)

盘算 pánsuàn (动) calculate; plan

盘腿 pántuǐ (动) cross one's legs

盘问 pánwèn (动) cross-examine; interrogate

盘旋 pánxuán (动) spiral; circle: 顺着山路～而上 wind one's way up the mountain path. 飞机在上空～. The aircraft circled in the sky.

盘子 pánzi (名) tray; plate; dish

磐 pán

磐石 pánshí (名) huge rock: 坚如～ as solid as a rock

判 pàn (动) 1 judge; decide: ～卷子 mark examination papers. ～案 decide a case 2 sentence; condemn: ～了死刑 be sentenced to death

判别 pànbié (动) differentiate; distinguish: ～真假 distinguish the true from the false

判处(處) pànchǔ (动) sentence; condemn: ～三年徒刑 be sentenced to three years' imprisonment

判定 pàndìng (动) judge; decide; determine

判断(斷) pànduàn I (动) judge; decide; determine: ～是非 judge (decide) what is right and what is wrong. ～力 the ability

P

to judge correctly; judgment II (名) judgment

判决 pànjué (动) reach a verdict; pass judgment: ～有罪(无罪) pronounce sb. guilty (not guilty)

判明 pànmíng (动) distinguish; ascertain: ～真相 ascertain the facts

判若两(兩)人 pàn ruò liǎng rén have become quite a different person; no longer be one's old self

判罪 pànzuì (动) declare guilty; convict

畔 pàn (名) side; bank: 河～ river bank. 湖～ the shore of a lake

叛 pàn (动) betray: ～国 be guilty of high treason

叛变(變) pànbiàn (动) defect; turn traitor: ～投敌 go over to the enemy

叛乱(亂) pànluàn I (动) rebel II (名) insurrection; rebellion: 煽动～ incite people to rise in rebellion. ～政府 insurgent government

叛逆 pànnì I (动) rebel against II (名) rebel: 封建礼教的～ a rebel against feudal ethics

叛逃 pàntáo (动) desert and flee one's country; defect: ～者 defector; deserter

叛徒 pàntú (名) traitor; renegade

盼 pàn (动) 1 hope for; long for; expect: ～自由 long for freedom. ～着你早日归来 look forward to your early return 2 look; look round

盼头(頭) pàntou (名) good prospects: 这事有～了. The matter stands a fair chance of success.

盼望 pànwàng (动) hope for; long for; look forward to: ～和平统一 long for peaceful reunification

滂 pāng

滂沱 pāngtuó (形) torrential: 大雨～. It's raining very heavily.

旁 páng I (名) 1 side: 路～ roadside 2 lateral radical of a Chinese character II (形) other; else: ～人 other people

旁边(邊) pángbiān (名) side: 坐在桌子～ sit at the table

旁观(觀) pángguān (动) look on: 袖手～ look on with folded arms. ～者 onlooker. ～者清, 当局者迷. The spectators see the game better than the players.

旁敲侧击(擊) pángqiāo-cèjī attack by innuendo; beat about the bush

旁若无(無)人 páng ruò wú rén look self-assured or supercilious

旁听(聽) pángtīng (动) be a visitor at a meeting; visit or sit in on a class: ～席 visitors' seats; public gallery

旁证 pángzhèng (名) circumstantial evidence; collateral evidence

磅 páng

see also bàng

磅礴 pángbó (形) boundless; majestic

螃 páng

螃蟹 pángxiè (名) crab

膀 páng

see also bǎng

膀胱 pángguāng (名) bladder

彷 páng

彷徨 pánghuáng (动) walk back and forth without knowing where to go; hesitate

庞(龐) páng

庞大 pángdà (形) huge; enormous; colossal: 开支～ colossal expenditure

庞然大物 pángrán dàwù colossus; huge monster

庞杂(雜) pángzá (形) unwieldy and complex: 机构～ unwieldy administrative structure

胖 pàng (形) fat; stout; plump: ～子 a plump person. 长～了 put on weight

抛 pāo (动) 1 throw; toss; fling: ～球 throw (or toss) a ball. ～出一个假声明 dish out (or trot out) a phoney statement 2 leave behind: 被～在后面 be left far behind

抛光 pāoguāng (名) polishing; buffing

抛锚 pāomáo (动) 1 cast anchor 2 (of vehicles) break down: 汽车中途～了. The car broke down on the way.

抛弃(棄) pāoqì (动) desert; forsake; discard: ～朋友 discard one's old friends. 被丈夫～了的女人 a woman forsaken by her husband

抛售 pāoshòu (动) sell (goods, shares, etc.) in large quantities

抛头(頭)露面 pāotóu-lùmiàn 〈贬〉 appear in public

抛砖(磚)引玉 pāozhuān-yǐnyù volunteer to

P

give an opinion so that others may follow suit

炮 páo (动) prepare Chinese medicine by roasting it in a pan
see also bāo; pào

炮制(製) páozhì (动) 1 prepare Chinese medicine, as by roasting, baking, simmering, etc. 2 concoct; cook up: 如法～ act after the same fashion; follow suit

袍 páo (名) robe; gown: 皮～子 fur robe

咆 páo

咆哮 páoxiào (动) roar: ～如雷 roar with rage

刨 páo (动) 1 dig; excavate: ～坑儿 dig a pit. ～地 dig the ground. ～土豆 dig (up) potatoes 2 deduct; exclude; minus
see also bào

刨根儿(兒) páogēnr get to the root of the matter

跑 pǎo I (动) 1 run: ～得快 run fast. 长～ long-distance running. ～百米 run the 100-metre dash 2 run away; escape; flee: 他～了. He's vanished. 车胎～气了. The tyre is flat. 3 walk: ～了二十里路 have walked twenty *li* 4 run about doing sth.; run errands: ～龙套 carry a spear in the supporting role. ～买卖 be a travelling salesman. 我～了几个图书馆才借到这本书. I had to run around to several libraries to get this book. II [used as a complement of a verb] away: 吓～ frighten away. 给刮～了 be blown off

跑步 pǎobù (动) run

跑道 pǎodào (名) runway; track

跑买(買)卖(賣) pǎo mǎimai be a commercial traveller

跑腿儿(兒) pǎotuǐr run errands; do legwork

泡 pào I (名) 1 bubble: 肥皂～ soap bubbles. 冒～儿 bubble up; rise in bubbles 2 sth. shaped like a bubble: 手上起～ get blisters on one's palm. 电灯～ electric light bulb II (动) steep; soak

泡吧 pàobā (动) kill time in a bar; hit the bars; go bar hopping

泡病号(號) pào bìnghào shun work on pretence of illness

泡菜 pàocài (名) pickled vegetables; pickles

泡茶 pàochá (动) make tea

泡蘑菇 pào mógu 1 play for time; play stalling tactics 2 importune; pester

泡沫 pàomò (名) foam; froth

泡妞 pàoniū (动) chase after girls; pick up hot chicks

泡汤(湯) pàotāng (动) 1 fall flat; fall through 2 dawdle; dilly-dally

泡影 pàoyǐng (名) visionary hope; bubble: 化为～ vanish like soap bubbles; melt into thin air

疱 pào (名) blister; bleb

炮 pào (名) 1 cannon; artillery piece 2 firecracker
see also bāo; páo

炮兵 pàobīng (名) artillery

炮弹(彈) pàodàn (名) (artillery) shell

炮灰 pàohuī (名) cannon fodder

炮火 pàohuǒ (名) gunfire; artillery fire

炮击(擊) pàojī (动) bombard

炮舰(艦) pàojiàn (名) gunboat: ～政策 gunboat policy

炮筒 pàotǒng (名) barrel (of a gun)

呸 pēi (叹) pah; bah; pooh: ～! 胡说八道! Bah! That's sheer nonsense!

胚 pēi (名) embryo

胚胎 pēitāi (名) embryo

培 péi (动) 1 bank up with earth: ～土 earth up 2 cultivate; foster: ～训人员 train personnel

培养(養) péiyǎng (动) nurture; foster: ～技术人才 train technical personnel. ～好习惯 develop good habits

培育 péiyù (动) cultivate; foster; breed: ～小麦新品种 breed new varieties of wheat

培植 péizhí (动) cultivate

赔 péi (动) 1 compensate; pay for: 如果东西损坏,你得～. If any article is damaged, you'll have to pay for it. 2 stand a loss: ～钱 lose money in business

赔本 péiběn (动) run a business at a loss

赔不是 péi bùshi apologize

赔偿(償) péicháng (动) compensate; pay for: ～损失 compensate for a loss; make good a loss. 照价～ compensate according to the cost. 战争～ war reparations

赔款 péikuǎn (名) indemnity; reparations

赔礼(禮) péilǐ (动) apologize: ～道歉 make an apology to sb. for sth.

赔钱(錢) péiqián (动) 1 sustain economic

losses; lose money in business: ～的买卖 a business run at a loss 2 pay for a loss; pay damages
赔笑 péixiào (动) smile apologetically or obsequiously
赔罪 péizuì (动) apologize
陪 péi (动) accompany; keep sb. company: ～客人到飞机场 accompany a visitor to the airport. ～病人 look after a patient
陪伴 péibàn (动) keep sb. company
陪衬(襯) péichèn I (动) serve as a contrast; set off II (名) foil
陪读 péidú (动) 1 accompany a spouse studying away from home, usu. overseas 2 (of parents) accompany young students studying away from home
陪嫁 péijià (名) dowry
陪审(審) péishěn (动) serve on a jury: ～团 jury. ～员 juror; juryman
陪同 péitóng (动) accompany: ～前往参观 accompany sb. on a visit. ～团团长 chairman of a reception committee; head of a hosting team
沛 pèi (形) abundant: 精力充～ be full of energy; full of vim and vigour
配 pèi I (名) spouse; wife: 原～ first wife II (动) 1 join in marriage: 婚～ marry 2 mate (animals): ～马 mate horses 3 compound; mix: ～颜色 mix colours. ～药 make up a prescription 4 match: 颜色不～. The colours don't match. 5 deserve; be worthy of; be qualified: 她不～当翻译. She has more to learn before she can be an interpreter. 6 distribute according to plan; allocate
配备(備) pèibèi I (动) 1 allocate; provide; equip: 给他～必要的参考书. Provide him with necessary reference books. 这些舰艇～有大口径炮. These ships are fitted with large-calibre guns. 2 deploy: ～兵力 deploy troops II (名) outfit; equipment: 现代化的～ modern equipment
配额 pèi'é (名) quota: 出口～ export quota
配方 pèifāng I (动) make up a prescription II (名) prescription; formula
配合 pèihé (动) coordinate; cooperate: 我们必须在工作中密切～. We must coordinate our efforts in work. ～行动 take concerted action
配给 pèijǐ (动) ration
配件 pèijiàn (名) accessory, fittings (of a machine, etc.)
配角 pèijué (名) supporting role; minor role
配偶 pèi'ǒu (名) spouse: 外交官及其～ diplomats and their spouses
配套 pèitào (动) form a complete set: 成龙～ assemble the parts to form a complete set. ～器材 necessary accessories
配音 pèiyīn (动) dub (a film)
配乐(樂) pèiyuè (动) dub in background music
配制(製) pèizhì (动) compound; make up: ～药剂 compound medicines
配种(種) pèizhǒng (动) breed; practise artificial insemination
佩 pèi (动) 1 wear (at the waist, etc.): ～刀 wear a sword 2 admire
佩带(帶) pèidài (动) wear: ～徽章 wear a badge
佩服 pèifu (动) admire: 我～他这个人既聪明而又刻苦. I admire him for his intelligence and industry.
喷 pēn (动) 1 spurt; spout; gush: 水从破水管里直往外～. Water spurted from the broken pipe. 2 spray; sprinkle: ～漆 spray paint. ～水车 water-spraying truck. ～雾器 sprayer; atomiser
see also pèn
喷薄 pēnbó (形) burst forth (of sun): 一轮红日～欲出. The sun is blazing through the morning mist.
喷饭 pēnfàn (动) laugh so hard as to spew one's food; split one's sides with laughter: 令人～ screamingly funny
喷壶(壺) pēnhú (名) watering can
喷气(氣) pēnqì jet-propelled: ～式飞机 jet aircraft; jet. ～客机 jet airliner. 大型～飞机 jumbo jet
喷泉 pēnquán (名) fountain
喷洒(灑) pēnsǎ (动) spray; sprinkle
喷射 pēnshè (动) spurt; jet
喷嚏 pēntì (名) sneeze: 打～ sneeze
盆 pén (名) basin; tub; pot: 脸～ washbasin. 澡～ bathtub. 花～ flowerpot
盆地 péndì (名) basin
盆景 pénjǐng (名) potted landscape
喷 pèn
see also pēn
喷香 pènxiāng (形) fragrant; delicious
烹 pēng (动) boil; cook

P

烹饪 pēngrèn (名) cooking; culinary art: ～法 cookery; cuisine. 擅长～ be good at cooking

烹调 pēngtiáo (名) cooking; cuisine: 中国式～ Chinese cuisine

怦 pēng (象) [describing heartbeat] pit-a-pat: 他的心～～直跳. His heart is beating fast.

砰 pēng (象) [indicating a sudden loud noise caused by knocking or a heavy fall]: 门～的一声关上了. The door shut with a bang. *or* The door slammed shut.

抨 pēng

抨击(擊) pēngjī (动) attack (in speech or writing); lash out at

澎 péng (动) splash; spatter

澎湃 péngpài (动) surge: 波涛～. Waves surge forward. 热情～的诗篇 a poem overflowing with emotion

膨 péng

膨胀(脹) péngzhàng (动) expand; swell; inflate: 金属受了热就会～. Metals expand when heated. 通货～ inflation. ～系数 coefficient of expansion

蓬 péng I (动) fluffy; dishevelled: ～着头 with dishevelled hair II (量) [for lush flowers, plants, etc.]: 一～竹子 a clump of bamboo

蓬勃 péngbó (形) vigorous; flourishing; full of vitality: ～发展的经济形势 flourishing economic situation

蓬松(鬆) péngsōng (形) fluffy; puffy: ～的头发 fluffy hair

蓬头(頭)垢面 péngtóu-gòumiàn with a dirty face and dishevelled hair; unkempt

篷 péng (名) covering or awning on a car, boat, etc.

朋 péng (名) friend: 高～满座. Present on the occasion (or at the banquet, party, etc.) were all guests of distinction.

朋比为奸 péngbǐwéijiān to conspire together for evil ends; to work hand in glove

朋党(黨) péngdǎng (名) clique; cabal

朋友 péngyou (名) friend: 男(女)～ boy (girl) friend

棚 péng (名) shed: 凉～ awning. 牲口～ livestock shed. 车～ bicycle shed or park

鹏 péng (名) roc

鹏程万(萬)里 péngchéng wànlǐ have an exceedingly bright future

捧 pěng (动) 1 hold in both hands: ～着盘子 hold a dish in both hands 2 extol; flatter: ～场 uncritical flattery. 为某人吹～ sing the praises of sb.

捧腹大笑 pěngfù dàxiào roar with laughter; burst out laughing; laugh one's head off

碰 pèng (动) 1 touch; bump: 别～那只花瓶! Don't touch that vase! 猫把奶瓶～翻了. The cat knocked the milk bottle over. 2 meet; run into: 在街上～到一个朋友 run into a friend in the street. ～到困难 run up against difficulties. 3 take one's chance: ～运气 try one's luck

碰杯 pèngbēi (动) clink glasses; exchange toasts

碰壁 pèngbì (动) run up against a stone wall; be rebuffed. 到处～ run into snags everywhere

碰钉子 pèng dīngzi meet with a rebuff

碰见(見) pèngjiàn (动) meet unexpectedly; run into

碰巧 pèngqiǎo (副) by chance; by coincidence: 我～也在那里. I happened to be there too.

碰头(頭) pèngtóu (动) meet and discuss; put (our, your, their) heads: ～会 brief meeting; briefing

坯 pī (名) base; semi-finished product; blank

批 pī I (动) 1 make written comments on (a report, etc.): ～文件 write instructions on a document 2 criticize: 挨～ be criticized II (量) batch; lot; group: 新到的一～货物 a new lot of goods. ～量生产 batch production. 分两～走 go (or leave) in two groups

批驳 pībó (动) refute; rebut; criticize

批发(發) pīfā (动) 1 wholesale: ～价 wholesale price 2 (of an official document) be authorized for dispatch

批改 pīgǎi (动) go over; correct: ～作业 correct students' papers

批判 pīpàn (动) criticize; repudiate

批评 pīpíng I (动) criticize II (名) criticism: 受到严厉的～ come in for harsh criticism

批示 pīshì (名) written instructions or comments on a report

批语 pīyǔ (名) written remarks; comment

批阅 pīyuè (动) read (official papers) and

P

make comments

批注 pīzhù (动) annotate; be furnished with notes and commentary

批准 pīzhǔn (动) approve; endorse; sanction: ~条约 ratify a treaty. ~某人的请求 grant one's request. ~书 instrument of ratification

披 pī (动) 1 drape over one's shoulders: ~着斗篷 have a cape hanging from one's shoulders 2 split open; crack: 这根竹竿~了. The bamboo pole has split.

披风(風) pīfēng (名) cloak

披肩 pījiān (名) cape

披荆斩棘 pījīng-zhǎnjí cleave a path through the jungle

披露 pīlù (动) 1 publish; announce 2 reveal; disclose: 要求不~姓名 ask not to be identified; speak on condition of anonymity

披星戴月 pīxīng-dàiyuè travel night and day

霹 pī

霹雳(靂) pīlì (名) thunderbolt: 晴天~ a bolt from the blue

霹雳(靂)舞 pīlìwǔ (名) break-dancing

劈 pī (动) 1 split; chop; cleave: ~木柴 chop wood 2 right against (one's face, etc.)

劈头(頭) pītóu (副) 1 straight on the head; right in the face: ~一拳 hit sb. right on the head 2 (say) at the very start: 他进来~就问:"试验成功了没有?" The moment he entered he asked: "Is the experiment successful yet?"

琵 pí

琵琶 pípá (名) a plucked string instrument with a fretted fingerboard

毗 pí (动) adjoin; be adjacent to: ~连 border on. ~连国 contiguous state. ~连空间 contiguous space

啤 pí

啤酒 píjiǔ (名) beer

脾 pí (名) spleen

脾气(氣) píqi (名) 1 temperament; disposition: ~很好 be good-natured; have a good temper 2 bad temper: 发~ lose one's temper; flare up

皮 pí I (名) 1 skin: 香蕉~ banana skin. 树~ bark. 土豆~ potato peel 2 leather; hide: ~靴 leather boots. ~大衣 fur coat 3 cover; wrapper: 书~儿 dust jacket 4 a broad, flat piece (of some thin material); sheet: 塑料~的 plastic-coated II (形) 1 become soft and soggy: 花生~了. The peanuts have gone soggy. 2 naughty: 这孩子真~! What a naughty child! 3 thick-skinned; impervious (to criticism): 他老挨批评,都~了. He is always in for criticism so he no longer cares.

皮包 píbāo (名) bag; briefcase

皮包公司 píbāo gōngsī a fly-by-night company

皮包骨 pí bāo gǔ (形) skinny: 瘦得~ be all skin and bone

皮草 pícǎo (名) leather and fur

皮尺 píchǐ (名) tape-measure; tape

皮带(帶) pídài (名) leather belt

皮肤(膚) pífū (名) skin

皮革 pígé (名) leather; hide

皮货 píhuò (名) fur; pelt

皮毛 pímáo (名) 1 fur 2 superficial knowledge: 略知~ have only a rudimentary knowledge (of a subject)

皮棉 pímián (名) ginned cotton

皮球 píqiú (名) rubber ball; ball

皮实(實) píshi (形) sturdy; durable

皮箱 píxiāng (名) leather suitcase

皮笑肉不笑 pí xiào ròu bù xiào put on a false smile; smile hypocritically

皮鞋 píxié (名) leather shoes: ~油 shoe polish

疲 pí (形) tired; weary: 精~力尽 exhausted; tired out; dog-tired

疲惫(憊) píbèi (形) tired out; exhausted

疲乏 pífá (形) worn-out; tired

疲倦 píjuàn (形) tired; fatigued

疲劳(勞) píláo (形) exhausted; weary

疲软 píruǎn I (形) fatigued and weak II (动) weaken; slump: 目前美元在外汇市场上~. U.S. dollar is weakening on foreign exchanges.

疲塌 píta (形) slack; sluggish; negligent: 工作~ be slack in doing one's work

疲于(於)奔命 píyú bēnmìng be kept constantly on the run; be weighed down with work

痞 pǐ (名) ruffian; riff-raff: 地~ local ruffian

匹 pǐ I (动) be equal to; be a match for II (量) 1 [for horses, etc.]: 三~马 three horses 2 [for cloth]: 一~布 a

P

bolt of cloth

匹敌(敵) pǐdí (动) be equal to; be well matched: 无与～ peerless

匹夫 pǐfū (名) ordinary man: 国家兴亡,～有责. Every man has a share of responsibility for the fate of his country.

匹配 pǐpèi (动) mate; marry

癖 pǐ (名) addiction; weakness for: 嗜酒成～ be addicted to drinking

癖好 pǐhào (名) favourite hobby; fondness for: 我对书法有特别～. I have a special liking for calligraphy.

劈 pǐ (动) 1 divide; split: 把毛线～成三股 split the wool (thread) into three strands 2 break off; strip off: ～白菜帮子 peel the outer leaves off cabbages 3 injure one's legs or fingers by opening them too wide

劈柴 pǐchai (名) firewood

屁 pì (名) wind (from bowels): 放～ break wind; fart

屁股 pìgu (名) 1 buttocks; bottom: 他拍拍～走了. He walks away leaving things in a mess. 2 end; butt: 香烟～ cigarette butt

媲 pì

媲美 pìměi (动) compare favourably with; rival

辟 pì I (动) 1 open up 2 refute; repudiate: ～谣 refute a rumour; deny a rumour II (形) penetrating: 精～ profound; incisive
see also bì

譬 pì (名) example; analogy

譬如 pìrú for example

僻 pì (形) 1 out-of-the-way; secluded: ～巷 side lane. ～静之处 a secluded place 2 eccentric: 怪～ eccentric

篇 piān I (名) 1 a piece of writing 2 sheet (of paper, etc.): 歌～儿 song sheet II (量) [for paper, article, etc.]: 三～纸 three sheets of paper. 一～文章 a piece of writing; an essay

篇幅 piānfu (名) 1 length (of a piece of writing) 2 space (on a printed page): 由于～有限 because of limited space. 报纸用大量～报道了这件事. The press gave the incident wide coverage.

篇章 piānzhāng (名) writings: ～结构 structure of a literary composition. 历史的新～ a new chapter in history

偏 piān I (形) inclined to one side; slant; leaning: 南～西 south by west. 中～右 (take a position) right of centre II (动) move to one side: 太阳～西了. The sun is to the west. 往左～一点儿! Move a bit to the left! III (副) deliberately; contrary to what is expected: 你为什么～要派他出国呢? Why on earth should you send him abroad? 医生劝他不要抽烟, 他～要抽. The doctor advised him to give up smoking, but he simply wouldn't listen.

偏爱(愛) piān'ài (动) have partiality for sth.; have a soft spot for sb.

偏差 piānchā (名) deviation; error

偏方 piānfāng (名) folk prescription

偏废(廢) piānfèi (动) attach undue importance to one thing to the neglect of the other: 二者不可～. Neither should be overemphasized at the expense of the other.

偏激 piānjī (形) going to extremes: 意见～ hold extreme views

偏见(見) piānjiàn (名) prejudice; bias: 对某人有～ be prejudiced against sb.

偏离(離) piānlí (动) deviate; diverge: ～正宗 constitute a departure from the orthodox school

偏旁 piānpáng (名) radical (of Chinese characters)

偏僻 piānpì (形) remote; out-of-the-way: ～的山村 a remote mountain village

偏偏 piānpiān (副) 1 deliberately: 她～不承认. She just wouldn't admit it. 2 contrary to what is expected: 事态的发展～同他的愿望相反. Things have turned out differently contrary to his expectations. 3 [used to single out an exception, often with displeasure]: 干吗～选他? Why choose him, of all people?

偏巧 piānqiǎo (副) it so happened that; as luck would have it

偏食 piānshí (名) 1 partial eclipse: 日～ partial solar eclipse 2 partiality for a limited variety of food; a one-sided diet

偏袒 piāntǎn (动) be partial to; take sides with: 她总是～自己的孩子. She always takes sides with her own child.

偏听(聽)偏信 piāntīng-piānxìn heed and trust only one side; listen only to one side; be biased

偏向 piānxiàng I (名) erroneous tendency; deviation II (动) be partial to

偏心 piānxīn (形) partial: 他对谁都不～. He is not partial to anybody.
偏远(遠) piānyuǎn (形) remote; faraway: ～地区 remote districts
偏重 piānzhòng (动) lay particular stress on

翩 piān

翩翩 piānpiān (形) 1 (of dancing) lightly: ～起舞 dance gracefully 2 elegant: ～少年 a suave young man

片 piān

片子 piānzi (名) 1 a roll of film 2 film; movie 3 gramophone record; disc
see also piàn

便 pián

see also biàn
便宜 piányi I (形) cheap; inexpensive: ～货 a bargain; goods sold at bargain prices II (名) small advantages; petty gains: 贪小～ covet small advantages

片 piàn I (名) 1 a flat; thin piece: 皂～ soap flakes. 雪～ snowflakes. 肉～ sliced pork. 眼镜～ lens 2 incomplete; fragmentary: ～言 a few words II (量) 1 [for things in slices]: 一～面包 a slice of bread. 两～药 two tablets 2 [said of an expanse of land or water]: 一～汪洋 a vast expanse of water 3 [for scenery, weather, language, mood, etc.]: 一～欢腾 a scene of jubilation. 一～漆黑 a pall of darkness. 一～繁荣景象 a glowing picture of prosperity
see also piān
片段 piànduàn (名) part; passage; fragment: 文章的～ extracts from an article. 生活的～ an episode of sb.'s life
片剂(劑) piànjì (名) tablet
片刻 piànkè (名) an instant; a moment; a short while
片面 piànmiàn (形) 1 unilateral: ～废止 unilateral repudiation 2 one-sided: ～观点 a one-sided view. ～地看问题 look at problems one-sidedly

骗 piàn (动) 1 deceive; fool; hoodwink: ～人 deceive people. 受～ be taken in; be deceived. 你～我. You're kidding me. 2 cheat; swindle
骗局 piànjú (名) fraud; swindle; hoax: 政治～ a political swindle; 揭穿～ expose a fraud
骗取 piànqǔ (动) gain sth. by cheating: ～信任 win sb.'s confidence by false pretences. ～钱财 cheat sb. out of money or property. ～选票 wangle votes
骗术(術) piànshù (名) deceitful trick; sleight of hand
骗子 piànzi (名) swindler

漂 piāo (动) float; drift: 天上～着云彩. Clouds are floating in the sky. 小船顺流～去. The boat glided down the stream. ～洋过海 sail across the ocean
see also piǎo; piào
漂泊 piāobó (动) lead a wandering life; drift: ～异乡 drift aimlessly in a strange land
漂浮 piāofú I (动) float II (形) (of style of work) superficial; showy
漂流 piāoliú (动) 1 drift about 2 see "漂泊" piāobó

剽 piāo I (动) rob II (形) nimble; swift
剽悍 piāohàn (形) agile and brave; quick and fierce
剽窃(竊) piāoqiè (动) plagiarize; lift

飘 piāo (动) float (in the air); flutter: 红旗～～. Red flags are fluttering. 窗外～着雪花. Outside the window, snow flakes are whirling.
飘带(帶) piāodài (名) streamer; ribbon
飘荡(蕩) piāodàng (动) flutter; drift; wave
飘零 piāolíng (动) 1 (of flowers) fade and fall 2 (of people) wander; drift; be homeless
飘飘然 piāopiāorán (形) feel satisfied; walk on air
飘扬(揚) piāoyáng (动) flutter; wave: 红旗迎风～. The red flag is fluttering in the wind.
飘摇 piāoyáo (动) sway; shake: 风雨～ tottering; teetering on the edge of collapse

缥 piāo

缥缈 piāomiǎo (形) hazy; dimly discernible: 虚无～ visionary; illusory

瓢 piáo (名) gourd ladle

瓢泼(潑)大雨 piáopō dàyǔ heavy rain; downpour

嫖 piáo (动) go whoring

嫖客 piáokè (名) brothel-goer; whoremonger

漂 piǎo (动) 1 bleach 2 rinse

P

see also piāo; piào

漂白 piǎobái (动) bleach

瞟 piǎo (动) glance sideways at: ~了他一眼 look askance at him

票 piào (名) 1 ticket: 公共汽车~ bus ticket. 门~ admission ticket 2 ballot: 投~ cast a ballot; vote. ~箱 ballot box 3 banknote; bill: 零~儿 notes of small denominations; change

票额 piào'é (名) face value

票房 piàofáng (名) booking office; box office: ~价值 box-office receipts; box-office takings

票价(價) piàojià (名) the price of a ticket; admission fee

票据(據) piàojù (名) bill; note

票友 piàoyǒu (名) amateur performer (of Beijing opera, etc.)

漂 piào

see also piāo; piǎo

漂亮 piàoliang (形) 1 handsome; good-looking; pretty: ~的小伙子 a handsome young man. ~的小姑娘 a pretty little girl. ~的花园 a beautiful garden. 打扮得漂漂亮亮的 be smartly dressed 2 brilliant; splendid: 说一口~的汉语 speak excellent Chinese. 射门射得真~! A beautiful shot! ~话 fine words; high-sounding words

撇 piē (动) 1 cast aside; throw overboard; neglect: ~开 leave aside; bypass. ~开次要问题 leave aside questions of minor importance. ~弃 abandon; desert 2 skim: ~油 skim off the grease. ~沫儿 skim off the scum

see also piě

瞥 piē (动) shoot a glance at: 妻子~了他一眼. His wife darted a look at him. 一~ (get) a glimpse of sth.

撇 piě I (动) throw; fling; cast II (名) left-falling stroke (in Chinese characters) III (量) [for sth. in the shape of a stroke]: 两~胡子 a pair of moustaches

see also piē

撇嘴 piězuǐ (动) curl one's lip (in contempt, disbelief or disappointment); twitch one's mouth

拼 pīn (动) 1 put together; piece together: ~积木 play toy bricks. 把两块布~在一起 put two pieces of cloth together side by side 2 be ready to risk one's life (in fighting, work, etc.): ~到底 fight to the bitter end. 我跟你~了. I'll fight it out with you.

拼搏 pīnbó (动) struggle hard; exert oneself to the utmost; go all out: ~精神 the spirit of hard struggle

拼凑 pīncòu (动) piece together; patch

拼命 pīnmìng I (动) risk one's life; be reckless II (副) with all one's might; desperately: ~干 work despite fatigue. ~奔跑 run like crazy

拼盘(盤) pīnpán (名) assorted cold dishes; hors d'oeuvres

拼死 pīnsǐ (动) risk one's life; defy death

拼写(寫) pīnxiě (动) spell

拼音 pīnyīn (动) 1 combine sounds into syllables 2 phoneticize: ~文字 alphabetic (system of) writing. ~字母 phonetic alphabet

姘 pīn have illicit relations with: ~头 lover; kept mistress

频 pín I (副) frequently; repeatedly: ~~点头 nod repeatedly II (名) frequency

频道 píndào (名) TV channel: 调到三~ turn to Channel 3

频繁 pínfán (形) frequently; often: 来往~ have frequent contacts with

频率 pínlǜ (名) frequency: ~范围 frequency range

频频 pínpín (副) again and again; repeatedly: ~招手 wave one's hand again and again. ~举杯 propose repeated toasts

贫 pín (形) 1 poor; impoverished: 一~如洗 be destitute. ~油国 oil-poor country 2 garrulous; loquacious: 她的嘴真~. She is a real chatterbox.

贫乏 pínfá (形) poor; short; lacking: 语言~ flat, monotonous language. 知识~ be lacking in knowledge

贫寒 pínhán (形) poor; poverty-stricken: 家境~ come from an impoverished family

贫瘠 pínjí (形) (of land) barren; infertile: 土壤~ poor soil

贫苦 pínkǔ (形) poor

贫困 pínkùn (形) poor: 生活~ live in poverty. ~线 poverty line. ~地区 poverty-stricken area

贫民 pínmín (名) poor people; pauper: 城市~ the urban poor. ~窟 slum

贫穷(窮) pínqióng (形) poor; needy: ~落后 poor and backward

贫血 pínxuè (名) anaemia

P

品 pǐn I (名) 1 article; product: 工业~ industrial products. 农产~ farm produce 2 grade; rank: 上~ top grade 3 character; quality: 人~ moral quality; character. ~学兼优 (of a student) superior both morally and intellectually II (动) taste sth. with discrimination; savour: ~茶 sample tea. ~味儿 savour the flavour

品尝(嘗) pǐncháng (动) taste; sample

品德 pǐndé (名) moral character

品格 pǐngé (名) moral character

品貌 pǐnmào (名) looks; appearance

品名 pǐnmíng (名) the name of a commodity

品牌 pǐnpái (名) brand: ~产品 brand goods. 创~ establish a brand

品评 pǐnpíng (动) judge; comment on

品头(頭)论(論)足 pǐntóu-lùnzú find fault; be overcritical

品位 pǐnwèi (名) taste: 这些画~都很高. These paintings are all of high taste. 这人~太低. This man has truly dreadful taste.

品行 pǐnxíng (名) conduct; behaviour: ~端正 well-behaved

品性 pǐnxìng (名) moral conduct

品质(質) pǐnzhì (名) 1 (of a person) character; quality: 道德~ moral character 2 quality (of commodities, etc.): ~优良 of fine quality

品种(種) pǐnzhǒng (名) 1 breed; variety: 小麦的优良~ improved strain of wheat 2 variety; assortment: 货物~齐全 have a good assortment of goods. 花色~ the variety of colours and designs

聘 pìn (动) 1 invite; engage; employ: ~专家 hire an expert 2 betroth: ~礼 betrothal gift

聘请 pìnqǐng (动) invite; hire

聘书(書) pìnshū (名) letter of appointment; contract

乒 pīng I (象): ~的一声枪响 the crack of a rifle or pistol II (名) table tennis; ping-pong: ~坛 table tennis circles

乒乓 pīngpāng I (象) rattle II (名) table tennis; ping-pong

瓶 píng (名) bottle; jar; vase: 牛奶~ a milk bottle. 热水~ thermos flask. 花~ flower vase

瓶颈(頸) píngjǐng (名) bottleneck

屏 píng (名) screen

see also bǐng

屏风(風) píngfēng (名) screen

屏幕 píngmù (名) screen (on a TV or computer monitor): 电视~ telescreen; screen

屏障 píngzhàng (名) protective screen: 天然~ natural defence for sth.

平 píng I (形) 1 flat; level; even; smooth: ~川 flat land; plain. 路面不~ the road is rugged. ~躺 lie flat. 把褶子烫~ iron out the wrinkles (on a dress, etc.) 2 on the same level; in a draw: 双方打成十五~. The two teams tied at 15-15. 这场足球最后踢~了. The football game ended in a draw. 3 equal; fair; impartial: 持~之论 unbiased view 4 calm; peaceful; quiet: 海上风~浪静. The sea was calm. 心~气和 even-tempered; unruffled 5 average; common: ~日 on ordinary days. 学习成绩~~ have average school results II (动) 1 level: 把地~一~ level the ground 2 calm; pacify: ~民愤 alleviate popular indignation. 气~了. feel pacified 3 put down; suppress: ~叛 put down a rebellion 4 equal: ~世界纪录 equal a world record

平安 píng'ān (形) safe and sound: ~到达 arrive safe and sound. ~无事. All is well. 一路~! Have a good trip! *or* Bon voyage!

平白 píngbái (形) for no reason whatsoever: ~无故 for no apparent reason

平辈 píngbèi (名) of the same generation

平常 píngcháng I (形) ordinary; commonplace: 不~ unusual; rare II(名) usually: 他~不怎么说话. Usually, he talks little. ~我坐地铁上班. I go to work by tube as a rule. 这种蝴蝶~看不到. This kind of butterfly is rarely to be seen.

平淡 píngdàn (形) flat; insipid; dull: ~无味 insipid

平等 píngděng (名) equality: ~待遇 equal treatment. 男女~ equality between man and woman. ~互利 equality and mutual benefit. ~协商 consultation on the basis of equality. ~权利 equal rights

平定 píngdìng (动) 1 calm down: 局势逐渐~下来. The situation gradually came back to normal. 2 suppress; put down: ~叛乱 put down a rebellion

平凡 píngfán (形) ordinary; common: 过着~的生活 live an ordinary life

平反 píngfǎn (动) redress (a mishandled

P

case); rehabilitate

平方 píngfāng (名) square: ～米 square metre

平房 píngfáng (名) one-storey house; bungalow

平分 píngfēn (动) divide equally: ～秋色 (of two parties) have equal shares (of honour, power, glory, etc.)

平和 pínghé (形) gentle; mild; moderate; placid: 性情～ be of gentle disposition

平衡 pínghéng (名) balance; equilibrium: 收支～ balance between income and expenditure. 失去～ lose one's balance. ～木 balance beam

平滑 pínghuá (形) level and smooth

平缓 pínghuǎn (形) gently; mild; gentle: 语调～ a mild tone. 地势～. The terrain slopes gently.

平价(價) píngjià I (动) stabilize prices II (名) 1 stabilized (or normalized, moderate) prices 2 par; parity

平静 píngjìng (形) calm; quiet; tranquil: ～的海面 a calm sea. ～的山村 a quiet mountain village

平局 píngjú (名) (of sports) draw; tie: 比赛最后打成～. The game ended in a draw.

P

平均 píngjūn (形) average: ～收入 average income. ～每年增长百分之五 increase by an average of 5% a year. ～主义 equalitarianism; egalitarianism. ～寿命 average lifespan. ～汇率 mid-point rate. ～利润 average profit

平列 píngliè (动) place side by side; place on a par with each other

平炉(爐) pínglú (名) open-hearth furnace

平面 píngmiàn (名) plane

平民 píngmín (名) the common people

平平 píngpíng (形) average; mediocre

平铺直叙 píngpū-zhíxù speak or write in a dull, flat way

平起平坐 píngqǐ-píngzuò sit as equals at the same table; be on an equal footing

平权 píngquán (名) equal rights; equity; parity: ～法案 affirmative action law

平生 píngshēng (名) all one's life; one's whole life: ～的愿望 one's lifelong aspiration

平时(時) píngshí (名) 1 in normal times 2 in peacetime

平手 píngshǒu (名) draw: 两队打了个～. The two teams drew.

平素 píngsù (名) usually

平台(臺) píngtái (名) platform: 信息交换～ information exchange interface. 这次会议为双方的互动建立了一个～. The meeting has established a basis for interaction between the two sides.

平坦 píngtǎn (形) (of land, etc.) level; even; smooth: 生活的道路并不～. The road of life is by no means smooth.

平稳(穩) píngwěn (形) smooth and steady: 汽车开得很～. The car ran very smoothly. 物价～. Prices are stable.

平息 píngxī (动) 1 calm down; subside: 一阵大风暴～了. The storm has subsided. *or* The trouble has blown over. 2 put down (a rebellion, etc.); suppress

平心而论(論) píngxīn ér lùn in all fairness; to give sb. his due

平信 píngxìn (名) 1 ordinary mail 2 surface mail

平行 píngxíng (形) 1 of equal rank; on an equal footing; parallel: ～组织 organizations of equal rank; parallel organizations 2 parallel; simultaneous: ～作业 parallel operations 3 parallel: ～线 parallel lines

平易近人 píngyì jìn rén modest and unassuming; folksy

平庸 píngyōng (形) mediocre; commonplace: 才能～ of mediocre calibre

平原 píngyuán (名) plain; flat lands

平整 píngzhěng I (形) neat; smooth II (动) level

平装(裝) píngzhuāng (名) paperback: ～本 paperback edition

评 píng (动) 1 comment; criticize; review: 短～ brief commentary. 书～ book review 2 judge; appraise: ～分 give marks; grade papers

评比 píngbǐ (动) compare and assess

评定 píngdìng (动) judge; evaluate; assess

评分 píngfēn (动) give a mark; mark (students' papers, etc.); score

评功 pínggōng (动) appraise sb.'s merits

评估 pínggū (动) assess: 资产～ property assessment

评价(價) píngjià (动) appraise; evaluate: ～历史人物 appraise historical figures. 高度～ set a high value on; speak highly of; set great store by

评理 pínglǐ (动) 1 decide which side is right 2 reason things out

评论(論) pínglùn I (动) comment on: ～家 critic; reviewer. ～员 commentator. 专栏～员 columnist II (名) comment; commentary

评判 píngpàn (动) pass judgment on

评选(選) píngxuǎn (动) choose through public appraisal

评议(議) píngyì (动) appraise sth. through discussion

评语 píngyǔ (名) comment; remark

评注 píngzhù (名) notes and commentary

坪 píng (名) level ground: 草～ lawn. 停车～ car park; parking lot

苹(蘋) píng

苹果 píngguǒ (名) apple

萍 píng (名) duckweed

萍水相逢 píng-shuǐ xiāng féng (of strangers) meet by chance; chance encounter

凭(憑) píng I (动) **1** rely on; be based on: ～良心办事 act in accordance with the dictates of one's conscience. ～票入场 admission by ticket only. 打仗不能只～勇敢. One can't rely on physical courage alone in battle. **2** lean on; lean against: ～栏远眺 lean on a railing and gaze into the distance II (名) evidence; proof: 真～实据 iron-clad evidence. 口说无～. Verbal statements are retractable. III (连) no matter (what, how, etc.): ～你跑多快，我也赶得上. I'll catch up with you no matter how fast you run.

凭借(藉) píngjiè (动) rely on; by means of: 人类的思维是～语言来进行的. Man thinks in words.

凭据(據) píngjù (名) evidence; proof

凭空 píngkōng (副) without foundation; groundless: ～捏造 a sheer fabrication

凭证 píngzhèng (名) proof; evidence

泊 pō (名) pool; lake

see also bó

坡 pō (名) slope: 山～ hillside. 陡～ a steep slope. 平～ a slight (or gentle, gradual) slope

坡度 pōdù (名) slope; gradient: 六十度～ a slope of 60 degrees

颇 pō (副) quite; rather; considerably: 影响～大 have considerable influence. 他说的～有道理. He does talk sense.

泼(潑) pō I (动) sprinkle; splash; spill: 往地上～点水. Sprinkle some water on the ground. ～水节 Water-Sprinkling Festival II (形) rude and unreasonable; shrewish: 撒～ act nastily and refuse to be placated

泼妇(婦) pōfù (名) shrew; vixen

泼辣 pōla (形) **1** shrewish **2** pungent; forceful: 文章写得很～. The essay is written in a pungent style. **3** bold and vigorous: 大胆～ bold and vigorous

泼冷水 pō lěngshuǐ (动) pour cold water on; dampen the enthusiasm; discourage

婆 pó (名) **1** old woman **2** husband's mother; mother-in-law: ～家 husband's family

婆婆 pópo (名) **1** husband's mother; mother-in-law **2** grandmother

婆婆妈妈 pópomāmā **1** dodder and chat like an old woman **2** emotionally fragile

婆娑 pósuō (形) whirling; dancing: 杨柳～. The willow branches swayed in the breeze.

破 pò I (形) **1** broken; damaged; torn; worn-out: 杯子～了. The glass is broken. ～衣服 worn-out clothes. ～房子 a tumbledown house **2** of poor quality: ～嗓子 a poor voice. 这支～笔! This lousy pen! II (动) **1** break; split; cleave; cut: ～成两半 break (or split) into two. ～浪前进 plough through the waves **2** get rid of; do away with; abolish: ～除旧的习惯 abolish the outmoded practice. ～记录 break a record **3** defeat: 大～敌军 deal a crushing blow at the enemy **4** find out the truth about; lay bare: 看～ see through. ～案 clear a criminal case

破败 pòbài (形) ruined; dilapidated

破产(產) pòchǎn (动) **1** go bankrupt: 公司～了. The company has gone broke. 宣布～ declare bankruptcy **2** fall through: 阴谋～了. The plot has fallen through.

破费 pòfèi (动)〈套〉spend money; go to some expense: 你为什么这么～呢? Why should you go to such expense?

破釜沉舟 pòfǔ-chénzhōu be determined to fight to the bitter end; go to any length (to achieve one's goal)

破格 pògé (动) break a rule; make an exception: ～提升 break a rule to promote sb. ～接待 break protocol to honour sb.

破坏(壞) pòhuài (动) destroy; wreck; undermine; sabotage: ～分子 saboteur. ～力 destructive power. ～性 destructiveness. ～关系 undermine rela-

P

tions. ～名誉 damage sb.'s reputation. ～协定 violate an agreement. ～生产 sabotage production

破获(獲) pòhuò (动) solve a criminal case: ～一个间谍网 uncover a spy ring

破镜重圆 pòjìng chóng yuán reunion of husband and wife after a rupture or separation

破口大骂 pòkǒu dàmà let loose a stream of savage invective

破烂(爛) pòlàn I (形) tattered; ragged; worn-out II (名) junk; scrap; waste: 捡～ collect waste

破例 pòlì (动) break a rule; make an exception

破裂 pòliè (动) break; split; crack: 谈判～了. The negotiations broke down. 外交关系～ severance (break-off) of diplomatic relations

破落 pòluò (动) decline (in wealth and position): ～贵族家庭 an impoverished aristocratic family

破门(門)而入 pò mén ér rù force open the door

破灭(滅) pòmiè (动) (of hopes; illusions) vanish; evaporate; be shattered or dashed to pieces: 幻想～ be disillusioned. 希望～ shattered hopes

P

破碎 pòsuì (形) tattered; broken

破天荒 pòtiānhuāng for the first time; unprecedentedly

破晓(曉) pòxiǎo (动) dawn: 天色～ day breaks

破绽 pòzhàn (名) flaw; weak point: ～百出 be riddled with holes

破折号(號) pòzhéhào (名) dash (—)

迫 pò I (动) 1 compel; force; press: 被～离开家乡 be compelled to leave one's hometown. 为饥寒所～ be driven to desperation by cold and hunger. ～降 forced landing 2 approach; go near: ～近 get close to II (形) urgent; pressing: 从容不～ calm and unhurried

see also pǎi

迫不得已 pòbùdéyǐ have no alternative but (to do sth.); be compelled to do sth. against one's will

迫不及待 pò bù jí dài too impatient to wait

迫害 pòhài (动) persecute: 政治～ political persecution

迫近 pòjìn (动) approach; draw near

迫切 pòqiè (形) urgent; pressing: ～的需要 an urgent need. ～的心情 eager desire

迫使 pòshǐ (动) force; compel: ～议案在国会通过 force the bill through the Congress. ～进行自卫 compel sb. to defend himself

迫在眉睫 pò zài méijié extremely urgent; imminent

魄 pò (名) 1 soul: 魂飞～散 (be frightened) out of one's wits 2 vigour; spirit: 气～ boldness of vision

魄力 pòli (名) daring and resolution; boldness: 工作有～ be bold and resolute in one's work

剖 pōu (动) 1 cut; dissect: ～腹 Caesarean section. ～腹自杀 hara-kiri 2 analyse; examine: ～明事理 make an in-depth analysis

剖腹产(產) pōufùchǎn (名) Caesarean birth

剖面 pōumiàn (名) section: 横～ cross section. 纵～ longitudinal section

剖析 pōuxī (动) analyse; dissect: 这篇文章～事理十分透彻. This essay gives a very penetrating analysis of the general trend of things.

扑(撲) pū (动) 1 dedicate all one's energies to a cause: 一心～在工作上 devote oneself heart and soul to one's work 2 rush at: 香气～鼻. A fragrant scent assails my nostrils. 3 flap: 鸟儿～打着翅膀. The bird flapped its wings. 4 bend over

扑哧 pūchī (象) titter; snigger

扑粉 pūfěn (名) face powder

扑克 pūkè (名) 1 playing cards: 打～ play cards 2 poker

扑空 pūkōng (动) come away empty-handed: 昨天我去找他, 扑了个空. Yesterday I went to see him, but unfortunately he was not in.

扑面 pūmiàn (动) blow on one's face: 春风～. The spring wind caressed our faces.

扑灭(滅) pūmiè (动) stamp out; put out; extinguish: ～火灾 put out a fire

扑腾 pūtēng (象) thump; thud

扑腾 pūteng (动) move up and down: 他的心里直～. His heart was beating fast.

扑通 pūtōng (象) flop; thump; splash; pit-a-pat: ～一声跳进水里 plunge into the water with a splash

仆 pū (动) fall forward: 前～后继 one stepping into the breach as another falls

铺 pū (动) 1 spread; extend; unfold: ～桌布 spread a tablecloth 2 pave;

lay: ～铁轨 lay a railway track. ～平道路 pave the way for
see also pù

铺盖(蓋) pūgài (名) bedding: ～卷儿 bedding roll; luggage roll

铺设 pūshè (动) lay; build: ～输油管 lay oil pipes

铺天盖(蓋)地 pūtiān-gàidì blot out the sky and the earth

铺张(張) pūzhāng (形) extravagant: ～浪费 extravagance and waste

菩 pú

菩萨(薩) púsà (名) 1 Bodhisattva 2 Buddhist idol: ～心肠 kind-hearted and merciful

匍 pú

匍匐 púfú (动) crawl; creep: ～前进 crawl forward

葡 pú

葡萄 pútáo (名) grape

仆(僕) pú (名) servant

仆从(從) púcóng (名) footman; flunkey; henchman

仆人 púrén (名) (domestic) servant

普 pǔ (形) general; universal: ～天下 all over the world

普遍 pǔbiàn (形) universal; general: ～现象 universal phenomenon. ～规律 universal law. ～裁军 general disarmament. ～真理 universal truth

普查 pǔchá (名) general investigation (or survey): 人口～ census

普及 pǔjí (动) popularize; disseminate; spread

普通 pǔtōng (形) ordinary; common; average: ～一兵 an ordinary soldier; a rank-and-filer. ～话 Putonghua; common speech (of the Chinese language); standard Chinese pronunciation. ～护照 ordinary passport

普选(選) pǔxuǎn (名) general election

谱 pǔ I (名) 1 table; chart: 家～ family tree; genealogy. 食～ cookbook 2 manual; guide: 棋～ chess manual 3 music score: 乐～ music score 4 sth. to count on; a fair amount of confidence: 心里没个～儿 have no definite plan yet II (动) compose; set to music: ～曲 set a song to music

谱写(寫) pǔxiě (动) compose (music)

朴(樸) pǔ (形) simple; plain

朴实(實) pǔshí (形) 1 simple; plain: ～无华 simple and unadorned 2 sincere and honest

朴素 pǔsù (形) simple; plain: 衣着～ simply dressed. 生活～ plain living

圃 pǔ (名) garden: 苗～ seed plot; (seedling) nursery

铺(舖) pù (名) 1 shop; store 2 plank bed
see also pū

铺位 pùwèi (名) (on a train, ship, etc.) bunk; berth

瀑 pù (名) waterfall

瀑布 pùbù (名) waterfall

曝 pù (动) expose to the sun
see also bào

Q q

期 qī I (名) 1 a period of time; phase; stage: 假～ vacation. 学～ school term. 革命初～ the initial stage of the revolution 2 scheduled time: 到～ fall due. 限～ time limit (or deadline) II (量) [for issues of papers, stages of a project, etc.]: 第一～工程 the first phase of the project. 最近的一～《时代》周刊 the latest issue of *Time* III (动) expect: 不～而遇 meet by chance; meet unexpectedly

期待 qīdài (动) hope; expect; look forward to: ～着胜利的时刻 look forward to the day of victory. ～早日答复 look forward to an early reply

期房 qīfáng (名) forward delivery housing

期货 qīhuò (名) futures: ～价格 forward price. ～合同 forward contract; futures contract. ～市场 futures market

期间 qījiān (名) time; period; course: 春节～ during the Spring Festival

期刊 qīkān (名) periodical

期望 qīwàng I (动) hope; expect; count on II (名) expectation: 不辜负祖国的～ live up to the expectations of one's mother land

期望值 qīwàngzhí (名) expectations: ～过高

unrealistic expectations

期限 qīxiàn (名) allotted time; time limit; deadline: 有效～ term of validity. 规定～ a target date

欺 qī (动) 1 deceive; cheat: ～人之谈 deceitful words; deceptive talk 2 bully: ～人 bully people; play the bully

欺负 qīfu (动) bully; treat sb. high-handedly

欺凌 qīlíng (动) bully and humiliate

欺骗 qīpiàn (动) deceive; cheat; dupe; swindle

欺软怕硬 qīruǎn-pàyìng bully the weak and fear the strong

欺上瞒(瞞)下 qīshàng-mánxià deceive one's superiors and delude (or dupe) one's subordinates

欺生 qīshēng (动) 1 bully or cheat strangers 2 (of horses, mules, etc.) be ungovernable by strangers

欺侮 qīwǔ (动) bully; humiliate

欺压(壓) qīyā (动) bully and oppress

欺诈 qīzhà (动) cheat; swindle

栖(棲) qī (动) 1 (of birds) perch 2 dwell; stay

栖身 qīshēn (动) stay; seek shelter

栖息 qīxī (动) (of birds) perch; rest

漆 qī I (名) lacquer; paint: ～器 lacquerware II (动) varnish; lacquer; paint

漆黑 qīhēi (形) pitch-dark: ～一团 pitch-dark; be entirely ignorant of

戚 qī (名) 1 relative: 亲朋～友 relatives and friends 2 sorrow; sadness: 休～相关 share joys and sorrows

七 qī (数) seven

七…八… qī…bā… [inserted in between two nouns or verbs to indicate a disorderly state of affairs]: 七零八落 scattered here and there; in disorder. 七拼八凑 piece together; knock together. 七上八下 be agitated; be perturbed. 七嘴八舌 with everybody trying to get a word in

七绝 qījué (名) a four-line poem with seven characters to a line

七律 qīlǜ (名) an eight-line poem with seven characters to a line

七月 qīyuè (名) July

柒 qī (数) seven [used for the numeral 七 on cheques, etc., to avoid mistakes or alterations]

沏 qī (动) infuse: ～茶 infuse tea; make tea

妻 qī (名) wife

妻离(離)子散 qīlí-zǐsàn have a broken home, with one's wife and children drifting apart

凄 qī (形) 1 (of wind and rain) chilly; cold 2 (悽) sad; wretched: ～楚 miserable 3 bleak and desolate: ～清 lonely and sad

凄惨(慘) qīcǎn (形) wretched; miserable; tragic

凄厉(厲) qīlì (形) (of a sound) sad and shrill: ～的叫声 a shrill cry

凄凉 qīliáng (形) dreary; miserable

凄切 qīqiè (形) (usually of a sound) plaintive; mournful

蹊 qī

蹊跷(蹺) qīqiāo (形) odd; queer; fishy

齐(齊) qí I (形) 1 neat; even; in good order: 整～ neat and tidy. 草剪得很～. The grass is evenly mown. 高矮不～ not of uniform height 2 all ready; complete: 人都到～了. Everyone is here. 东西都准备～了. Everything is ready. 3 similar; alike: 人心～ all people work with one mind II (动) reach the height of: 水～腰深. The water is waist-deep. III (副) together; simultaneously: 大家～动手. Everyone lent a hand. ～声欢呼 cheer in unison

齐备(備) qíbèi (形) all ready: 万事～. Everything is ready.

齐全 qíquán (形) (of stock, etc.) complete: 货物～ have a satisfactory variety of goods

齐心 qíxīn (形) be of one mind (or heart): ～协力 work as one; make concerted efforts; work in concert

齐奏 qízòu (动) play (instruments) in unison

脐(臍) qí (名) navel; umbilicus: ～带 umbilical cord

鳍 qí (名) fin

其 qí (代) 1 [used within a sentence to refer to sb. or sth. mentioned earlier] he; she; it; they: 听～自然 let things take their natural course. 使～更加美丽 make it more beautiful 2 his; her; its; their: 使人各尽～能 make everybody do his best 3 that; such：确有～事. That is certainly a fact. 正当～时 just at that moment. 如闻～声 as if we heard him speak

其次 qícì (名)next; secondly; then：首先要重视内容，～还要注意文风. Pay attention first of all to the content, and then the style. 质量是主要的，数量还在～. Quality is primary while quantity is of secondary importance.

其实(實) qíshí (副) actually; in fact; as a matter of fact

其他 qítā (代) other; else：还有～事吗? Anything else? ～人就不用去了. Others needn't go.

其余(餘) qíyú (代) the rest; the remainder：～的人跟我来. The others come with me. ～的都是妇女. All the rest are women.

其中 qízhōng (名) among whom; among which：这所学校有 800 名学生，～30％是外国人. This school has 800 students, and 30 percent of them are foreigners. 有十个人获奖，她就是～一个. Ten people won prizes and she was one of them.

旗 qí (名) flag; banner：国～ national flag

旗杆 qígān (名) flagpole

旗号(號) qíhào (名)〈贬〉 banner; flag

旗舰(艦) qíjiàn (名) flagship

旗开(開)得胜(勝) qí kāi déshèng win the first battle; win speedy success

旗手 qíshǒu (名) standard-bearer

旗语 qíyǔ (名) semaphore; flag signal

旗帜(幟) qízhì (名) 1 banner; flag 2 stand：～鲜明 have a clear-cut stand

棋 qí (名) chess game：下一盘～ have a game of chess. 象～ Chinese chess. ～盘 chessboard. ～子 piece (in a board game); chessman

棋逢对(對)手 qí féng duìshǒu be well matched in a contest

歧 qí I (名) fork; branch II (形) divergent; different：～义 different interpretations

歧路 qílù (名) branch road; forked road

歧视 qíshì (动) discriminate against：种族～ racial discrimination. ～性法律 discriminatory law. ～待遇 discriminatory treatment

歧途 qítú (名) wrong path：被引入～ be led astray

奇 qí (形) 1 strange; queer; rare; unusual：～耻大辱 a most painful humiliation 2 unexpected; surprising：～袭 surprise attack

see also jī

奇兵 qíbīng (名) an ingenious military move

奇才 qícái (名) a rare talent; genius

奇怪 qíguài (形) strange; odd; surprising：真～，他今天不来. It's strange that he should be absent today.

奇观(觀) qíguān (名) marvellous spectacle; wonder

奇迹 qíjì (名) miracle; wonder：创造～ work wonders; perform miracles. 历史～ a marvel of history; a miracle in history

奇景 qíjǐng (名) wonderful view

奇妙 qímiào (形) marvellous; wonderful; intriguing

奇谈 qítán (名) strange tale; absurd argument

奇特 qítè (形) peculiar; queer; singular

奇闻 qíwén (名) intriguing story

奇形怪状(狀) qíxíng-guàizhuàng grotesque in shape or appearance

奇异(異) qíyì (形) 1 fantastic; bizarre 2 curious：他用～的眼光望着过路的人. He looked at the passers-by with curious eyes.

奇遇 qíyù (名) 1 fortuitous meeting 2 adventure

奇装(裝)异(異)服 qízhuāng-yìfú bizarre dress; outlandish clothes

崎 qí

崎岖(嶇) qíqū (形) rugged：～不平 rugged

骑 qí (动) ride (esp. on animal or bicycle)：～马 ride a horse; be on horseback. ～车 go by bicycle. ～在人民头上称王称霸 ride roughshod over the people

骑兵 qíbīng (名) cavalry

骑虎难(難)下 qí hǔ nán xià difficult to extricate oneself from a most embarrassing or dangerous situation

骑墙 qíqiáng (动) sit on the fence：～观望 sit on the fence and adopt a wait-and-see attitude

畦 qí (名) rectangular pieces of land in a field

祈 qí (动) pray

祈祷(禱) qídǎo (动) pray; say one's prayers

Q

祈求 qíqiú (动) earnestly hope; pray for

启(啟) qǐ (动) 1 awaken: ~蒙 enlighten; enlightenment. ~蒙老师 teacher who introduces one to a certain field of study 2 start; initiate 3 open: 幕~. The curtain rises.

启程 qǐchéng (动) set out; start on a journey

启齿(齒) qǐchǐ (动) open one's mouth; start to talk about sth.: 难以~ find it difficult to bring the matter up

启动(動) qǐdòng (动) start up; activate

启发(發) qǐfā (动) arouse; inspire; enlighten: 他们的经验对我们很有~. Their experience has served as a great source of inspiration for us. ~式 (of teaching method) heuristic method

启示 qǐshì (名) enlightening guidance; illuminating remarks

启事 qǐshì (名) notice; announcement

企 qǐ

企求 qǐqiú (动) seek for; hanker after: 从不~个人名利 never seek personal fame or wealth

企图(圖) qǐtú I (动) try; attempt; contrive II (名) attempt; scheme: 蓄意~ a deliberate attempt

企业(業) qǐyè (名) enterprise; business: ~家 entrepreneur. ~管理 business management. ~素质 business performance. 私人~ private enterprise

乞 qǐ (动) beg

乞丐 qǐgài (名) beggar

乞怜(憐) qǐlián (动) beg for pity

乞求 qǐqiú (动) beg (for); supplicate: ~宽恕 beg (for) forgiveness

乞讨 qǐtǎo (动) go begging

起 qǐ I (动) 1 rise; get up: 早晨6点~床 get up at six in the morning. 早睡早~ early to bed and early to rise 2 rise; grow: ~风了. the wind is rising. ~疑心 become suspicious. ~义 rise up (against) 3 appear: 手上~泡 get blisters on one's hand. 脸上~皱纹 get wrinkles on one's face 4 begin; start: 从那时~ since then. 从明天~ starting from tomorrow 5 remove; extract: ~钉子 draw out a nail. ~瓶塞 open a bottle 6 draft: ~草文件 draft a doc ument. ~草稿子 make a draft 7 build; set up: 白手~家 start (an enterprise) from scratch II (量) 1 case: 两~罪案 two criminal cases 2 batch; group: 已经有三~人参观过这里了. Three groups of visitors have been here.

起 qǐ 1 [used as a complement after a verb indicating upward movement or beginning of an action]: 提~箱子匆匆往外走 lift the suitcase and hurry off. 拿~武器 take up arms. 唱~歌, 跳~舞 start singing and dancing. 他也抽~烟了! He too has started smoking! 引~注意 draw people's attention 2 [used after a verb together with 得 or 不 as meaning "can afford" or "cannot afford"]: 买得~ can afford to buy. 买不~ cannot afford to buy. 经得~考验 can stand the test. 负不~责任 cannot take the responsibility

起笔(筆) qǐbǐ (名) the first stroke of a Chinese character

起步 qǐbù (动) start; move: 这项工程尚属~阶段. This project is still in its initial stages.

起草 qǐcǎo (动) draft; draw up: ~文件 draw up a document. ~讲话稿 draft a speech

起程 qǐchéng (动) start on a journey: 明日~ set out tomorrow

起初 qǐchū (名) at first; at the beginning

起床(牀) qǐchuáng (动) get up (from bed)

起点(點) qǐdiǎn (名) starting point

起动(動) qǐdòng (动) (of a train, machine, etc.) start: 火车刚~. The train is leaving.

起飞(飛) qǐfēi (动) (of aircraft) take off: 经济~ economic take-off

起伏 qǐfú (动) (of waves, mountain ranges, etc.) rise and fall

起哄 qǐhòng (动) 1 make trouble; create disturbance 2 (of a crowd of people) jeer; boo and hoot

起价(價) qǐjià (名) starting price

起劲(勁) qǐjìn (形) vigorously; energetically: 干得很~ work with great enthusiasm

起居 qǐjū (名) daily life: ~室 sitting room

起来(來) qǐlai (动) get up; rise; arouse: 他~得太晚. He got up too late. 你~, 让老太太坐下. Please stand up and give the seat to the old lady. 群众~了. The masses have been aroused.

起来(來) qǐlai (动) [used as a complement after a verb] 1 [indicating upward movement]: 把旗举~ raise the flag **2** [indicating beginning and continuation of an action]: 天气冷~了. It's getting cold. 哭~了 burst out crying **3** [indicating completion of an action or fulfilment of a purpose]: 哦, 我想~了! Now I've got it! 包~ wrap sth. up **4** [indicating impressions]: 听~满有道理. It sounds quite reasonable. 看~还可以. It looks all right. 这支笔写~很滑溜. This pen writes smoothly.

起立 qǐlì (动) stand up; rise to one's feet

起码 qǐmǎ (形) minimum; rudimentary; elementary: ~的要求 minimum requirements. ~的知识 elementary knowledge

起毛 qǐmáo (动) (of woollen cloth) pill: 这种料子爱~. This material pills easily.

起锚 qǐmáo (动) weigh anchor; set sail

起色 qǐsè (名) improvement: 他工作很有~. His work shows signs of improvement. 他的病有了~. He has begun to pick up.

起身 qǐshēn (动) get up; rise to one's feet

起誓 qǐshì (动) take an oath; swear

起诉 qǐsù (动) bring a suit against sb.; sue: ~人 suitor; prosecutor. ~书 indictment; bill of complaint

起头(頭) qǐtóu I (名) beginning; in the beginning; at first: 这事从~就错了. It was a mistake from the very start. ~我不懂. I was at a loss at first. II (动) start; begin: 先从这儿~. Let's start from here.

起先 qǐxiān (名) at first; in the beginning

起义(義) qǐyì I (动) revolt; rise up II (名) uprising

起因 qǐyīn (名) cause; origin: 事故的~ the cause of the accident

起用 qǐyòng (动) reinstate (an official who has retired or been dismissed); rehabilitate

起源 qǐyuán I (名) origin: 生命的~ the origin of life II (动) originate; stem from: 一切知识均~于劳动. All knowledge originates from labour.

起运(運) qǐyùn (动) start shipment

起重机(機) qǐzhòngjī (名) hoist; crane

起皱(皺) qǐzhòu (动) wrinkle; crease; crumple: 这种料子不~. This material won't crease.

岂(豈)

qǐ (副) [as 难道, used in written language, usu. before a negative word to form a rhetorical question]: ~非白日做梦? Isn't that daydreaming? ~非咄咄怪事? It's preposterous, isn't it?

岂敢 qǐgǎn (动) 〈套〉 you flatter me; I don't deserve your compliment.

岂有此理 qǐ yǒu cǐ lǐ preposterous; outrageous: 真是~! This is really outrageous!

泣

qì (动) weep; sob: ~不成声 choke with tears

弃(棄)

qì (动) abandon; discard: ~之可惜. It would be a pity to throw it away.

弃权(權) qìquán I (动) abstain from voting II (名) abstention

弃置 qìzhì (动) put aside; discard: ~不用 be discarded; lie idle

契

qì (名) contract; agreement: 地~ land deed. 默~ tacit agreement

契合 qìhé (动) agree with; tally with

契约 qìyuē (名) contract; deed; charter: 签订~ sign a contract

砌

qì I (动) build by laying bricks or stones: ~墙 build a wall II (名) step: 雕栏玉~ carved balustrades and marble steps

器

qì (名) **1** utensil; ware: 漆~ lacquerware. 瓷~ chinaware; porcelain. 玉~ jade article. 乐~ musical instrument **2** organ: 生殖~ private parts; genitals

器材 qìcái (名) equipment; material: 照相~ photographic equipment

器官 qìguān (名) physical organ: 消化~ digestive organs. 发音~ organs of speech. 呼吸~ respiratory apparatus

器件 qìjiàn (名) parts of an apparatus: 电子~ electronic device

器具 qìjù (名) utensil; appliance: 日用~ household utensils

器量 qìliàng (名) tolerance: ~小 narrow-minded; petty

器皿 qìmǐn (名) containers esp. for use in the house

器械 qìxiè (名) apparatus; appliance; instrument: 医疗~ medical appliances. 体育~ sports apparatus. 光学~ optical instrument

器乐(樂) qìyuè (名) instrumental music

器重 qìzhòng (动) think highly of (someone at a lower level)

气(氣)

qì I (名) **1** air; fresh air: 大~层 the atmosphere. 空~ air. 打开窗户透透~. Open the window to let in some fresh air. **2** gas: 煤~ gas. 毒

Q

～ poisonous gas **3** breath：喘粗～ pant. 上～不接下～ be out of breath **4** smell：香～sweet smell；fragrance. 臭～ foul smell **5** airs；manner：官～ bureaucratic airs **6** spirit；morale：朝～蓬勃 full of vigour. 泄～ be discouraged；be dampened. 士～ morale II（动）**1** make angry；enrage：我故意～他一下. I was deliberately trying to make him angry. **2** get angry；be enraged：～得直哆嗦 tremble with rage **3** bully；insult：受～ be bullied or maltreated

气冲冲 qìchōngchōng（形）furious；enraged

气喘 qìchuǎn I（动）gasp for breath；be out of breath：～嘘嘘 II（名）asthma：阵发性～ spasmodic asthma

气垫(墊) qìdiàn（名）air cushion：～船 hovercraft；cushioncraft

气度 qìdù（名）boldness of vision and large-mindedness

气短 qìduǎn（形）**1** be short of breath **2** discouraged；disheartened

气氛 qìfēn（名）atmosphere：亲切友好的～ cordial and friendly atmosphere

气愤 qìfèn（形）indignant；furious

气概 qìgài（名）lofty；spirit：英雄～ heroic spirit

气缸 qìgāng（名）air cylinder；cylinder

气功 qìgōng（名）*qigong*，a system of deep breathing exercises

气管 qìguǎn（名）windpipe；trachea：～炎 tracheitis

气候 qìhòu（名）**1** climate：海洋性～ oceanic climate **2** situation：政治～ political climate. 这人成不了～. That man won't get anywhere.

气呼呼 qìhūhū（形）in a huff；panting with rage：～地离去 go off in a huff

气话 qìhuà（名）words said in a fit of rage：他说的是～. He just said it to vent his anger.

气急败坏(壞) qìjí bàihuài be utterly discomfited and exasperated

气节(節) qìjié（名）moral；integrity：民族～ patriotic moral courage

气绝 qìjué（动）stop breathing —die：～身亡 draw one's last breath

气浪 qìlàng（名）blast (of an explosion)

气力 qìlì（名）physical strength；effort：使出全身～ exert all one's strength

气量 qìliàng（名）tolerance：～大 large-minded；magnanimous. ～小 narrow-minded

气流 qìliú（名）**1** air current **2** (in phonetics) breath

气恼(惱) qìnǎo（形）get angry

气馁 qìněi（形）(feel) discouraged (or down-hearted)

气派 qìpài（名）imposing manner；dignified air：那幢大楼好～. That building is really imposing.

气泡 qìpào（名）air bubble；bubble

气魄 qìpò（名）daring；boldness of vision；imposing manner

气球 qìqiú（名）balloon

气色 qìsè（名）complexion；colour：～很好 look very well

气势(勢) qìshì（名）great force of imposing posture：～磅礴 of tremendous force；of great momentum

气势(勢)汹(洶)汹 qìshì xiōngxiōng fierce；overbearing

气死人 qìsǐrén driving one crazy；infuriating；exasperating

气体(體) qìtǐ（名）gas

气头(頭)上 qìtóushang in a fit of anger；in a temper：他正在～，连妈妈的话都听不进去. He's in a temper right now, and won't even listen to his mother.

气味 qìwèi（名）**1** smell；odour：～难闻. The smell is awful. **2**〈贬〉smack；taste：～相投 be birds of a feather

气温 qìwēn（名）air temperature

气息 qìxī（名）**1** breath：～奄奄 at one's last gasp **2** scent：春花的～ the scent of spring flowers

气象 qìxiàng（名）atmospheric phenomena：～预报 weather forecast

气象万(萬)千 qìxiàng wànqiān a scene majestic in all its variety

气压(壓) qìyā（名）atmospheric pressure

气焰 qìyàn（名）overbearing pride；arrogance：～万丈 be enormously haughty

气质(質) qìzhì（名）**1** temperament；disposition **2** qualities；makings

讫

qì settled；completed：收～ received in full

迄

qì up to；till：～今 up to now；to this day；so far

汽

qì（名）steam；vapour

汽车(車) qìchē（名）automobile；car：～队 motorcade；fleet of cars. ～库 garage. ～旅店 motel

汽船 qìchuán（名）steamship；steamer

汽笛 qìdí（名）steam whistle；siren：鸣～

sound a siren

汽水 qìshuǐ (名) soda water; lemonade

汽艇 qìtǐng (名) motor boat

汽油 qìyóu (名) petrol; gasoline; gas

掐 qiā (动) 1 pinch; nip: ～花 nip off a flower 2 clutch: ～死 strangle. ～脖子 seize sb. by the throat

掐断(斷) qiāduàn (动) nip off; cut off: ～水源 cut off the water supply

卡 qiǎ I (动) 1 wedge; get stuck: 鱼刺～在他的喉咙里. A fish-bone sticks in his throat. 2 block; check: 他及时～住了这笔钱. He withheld the money in good time. ～住敌人的退路 block the enemy's retreat II (名) 1 clip; fastener: 发～ (also as "～子") hairpin 2 checkpoint: 关～ checkpoint

see also kǎ

洽 qià I (形) be in harmony: 融～ be on good terms II (动) consult; arrange with: ～商 contact sb. and discuss

恰 qià I (形) appropriate; proper II (副) just; exactly

恰当(當) qiàdàng (形) proper; suitable; fitting; appropriate: 用词～ proper choice of words. 这个问题处理得不～. The problem was not properly handled.

恰好 qiàhǎo (副) just right; as luck would have it: 当时我～在场. It happened that I was on the spot.

恰恰 qiàqià (副) just; exactly; precisely: ～相反 just the opposite. ～12点钟 twelve o'clock sharp

恰巧 qiàqiǎo (副) by chance; fortunately: ～他也不想去. Fortunately he didn't want to go either.

恰如其分 qià rú qí fèn apt; appropriate; just right: ～的结论 an appropriate conclusion

谦 qiān (形) modest: ～和 modest and amiable

谦恭 qiāngōng (形) modest and courteous

谦让(讓) qiānràng (动) modestly decline: 不要～了. Don't decline. You can be too modest.

谦虚 qiānxū (形) modest; self-effacing: 她是非常～的人. She is a very modest and unassuming sort of person.

谦逊(遜) qiānxùn (形) modest and unassuming

牵(牽) qiān (动) lead along; pull; drag: 手～手 hand in hand

牵肠(腸)挂(掛)肚 qiāncháng-guàdù feel deep anxiety

牵扯 qiānchě (动) involve; drag in: 这件事～到他. He is involved in the matter.

牵动(動) qiāndòng (动) affect; influence: ～全局 affect the entire situation

牵挂(掛) qiānguà (动) worry; be concerned about: 没有～ free from care. 不要～家里. Don't worry about us at home.

牵累 qiānlěi (动) 1 tie down: 受家务～ be tied down by household chores 2 implicate: 你犯错误不要～别人. Don't involve other people in your mistakes.

牵连 qiānlián (动) implicate; involve: ～他人 involve others in trouble

牵强 qiānqiǎng (形) far-fetched or forced: ～附会 make a far-fetched interpretation

牵涉 qiānshè (动) involve; drag in: 他的发言～到很多人. He made unpleasant references to many people in his speech.

牵头(頭) qiántóu (动) take the lead; lead off; be the first to do sth.: 谁来～? Who will lead off?

牵线(綫) qiānxiàn (动) 1 pull strings 2 act as go-between

牵引 qiānyǐn (动) pull; draw; tow: ～力 pulling force

牵制 qiānzhì (动) pin down; tie up: ～行动 containing action. ～敌人 pin down the enemy

签(簽) qiān I (动) sign; autograph: ～字 sign (one's name) II(名)1 label; sticker: 标～ label. 书～ book-marker 2 (籤) bamboo slips used for divination, gambling or contest purposes: 抽～ draw lots 3 a slender pointed piece of bamboo or wood: 牙～ toothpick

签单 qiāndān (动) 1 sign for payment 2 pay the bill

签到 qiāndào (动) sign in to show one's presence at a meeting or in office: ～处 sign-in desk

签订 qiāndìng (动) conclude and sign (an agreement etc.): ～条约 sign a treaty. ～合同 sign a contract

签发(發) qiānfā (动) sign and issue (a document, certificate, etc.)

签名 qiānmíng (动) sign one's name; autograph: 作者亲笔～的书 an autographed book

签收 qiānshōu (动) sign after receiving sth.

签署 qiānshǔ (动) sign: ～协定 sign an agreement. ～意见 write comments and sign one's name (on a document)

Q

签证 qiānzhèng (名) visa: 入(出)境~ entry (exit) visa. 过境~ transit visa. ~处 visa office. ~费 visa fee. ~申请表 visa application form

签字 qiānzì (动) sign; affix one's signature: ~国 signatory state; signatory

铅 qiān (名) lead (Pb)

铅笔(筆) qiānbǐ (名) pencil

铅球 qiānqiú (名) shot: 推~ shot-put

铅字 qiānzì (名) (printing) type; letter

千 qiān (数) 1 thousand: 两~ two thousand. 成~上万 thousands of. ~百万 millions 2 a great number of: ~方百计 in a thousand and one ways

千变(變)万(萬)化 qiānbiàn-wànhuà ever-changing

千差万(萬)别 qiānchā-wànbié differ in a thousand and one ways

千锤百炼(煉) qiānchuí-bǎiliàn 1 thoroughly steeled or tempered: 在长期斗争中~ be tempered in protracted struggles 2 (of literary works) be polished meticulously

千方百计 qiānfāng-bǎijì by every possible means; do everything possible

千古 qiāngǔ (名) through the ages; for all time: 为~罪人 stand condemned through the ages. ~遗恨 eternal regret

千金 qiānjīn (名) 1 a thousand pieces of gold; a lot of money: ~难买 not to be bought with money. 一掷~ spend lavishly 2 daughter

千军万(萬)马(馬) qiānjūn wàn mǎ a powerful and well-equipped army

千钧一发(髮) qiān jūn yī fà in imminent peril: ~的时刻 at this critical juncture

千里之行始于(於)足下 qiānlǐ zhī xíng shǐ yú zú xià one sets out on a long journey by taking the first step—great success is an accumulation of smaller successes

千篇一律 qiān piān yī lǜ stereotyped

千秋 qiānqiū (名) 1 a thousand years; centuries: ~万代 throughout the ages; for generations to come 2 〈敬〉 birthday (other than one's own)

千丝(絲)万(萬)缕(縷) qiānsī-wànlǚ a thousand and one links: 有着~的联系 be bound together by countless ties

千瓦 qiānwǎ (名) kilowatt

千万(萬) qiānwàn I (数) ten million; millions upon millions II (副) [used of exhortation or a friendly warning]: ~要小心! Do be careful! 你~别听他的. You must under no circumstances believe what he says.

千辛万(萬)苦 qiānxīn-wànkǔ untold hardships: 历尽~ undergo innumerable hardships

千言万(萬)语 qiānyán-wànyǔ thousands of words: ~无法表达我对你们的心情. I cannot convey my feelings in words.

千载一时(時) qiān zǎi yī shí extremely rare: ~的机会 a golden opportunity; the chance of a lifetime

迁(遷) qiān (动) 1 move: ~往他处 move to another place. ~出 emigration. ~入 immigration 2 change: 时过境~. The situation has changed with the passage of time.

迁户口 qiān hùkǒu report to the local authorities for change of domicile; change one's residence registration

迁就 qiānjiù (动) accommodate oneself to: 坚持原则, 不能~. Stick to principle and refuse to give in. *or* Do not compromise on matters of principle.

迁居 qiānjū (动) move house

迁移 qiānyí (动) move; migrate

仟 qiān (数) thousand [used for the numeral 千 on cheques, etc., to avoid mistakes or alterations]

阡 qiān (名) 〈书〉 a footpath between fields, running north and south

潜(濳) qián (动) hide

潜藏 qiáncáng (动) hide; go into hiding

潜伏 qiánfú (动) hide; conceal; lie low: ~的敌人 hidden enemy. ~危机 a latent crisis. ~的疾病 an insidious disease. ~期 incubation period

潜规则 qiánguīzé (名) hidden rules; implicit rules

潜力 qiánlì (名) latent capacity; potential; potentiality: 有很大~ have great potentialities. 挖掘~ tap potentials

潜能 qiánnéng (名) potential

潜入 qiánrù (动) 1 slip into; sneak into; steal in 2 dive; submerge

潜水 qiánshuǐ (动) go under water; dive: ~员 diver; frogman. ~艇 submarine

潜逃 qiántáo (动) abscond: 携公款~ abscond with public funds

潜心 qiánxīn (副) with great concentration

潜行 qiánxíng (动) 1 move under water 2 move stealthily

潜移默化 qiányí-mòhuà (of sb.'s character, thinking, etc.) change imperceptibly

潜意识(識) qiányìshí (名) the subconscious; subconsciousness

潜在 qiánzài (形) latent; potential: ～力量 latent power. ～危险 potential danger

前 qián I (名) 1 front: ～厅 front hall. 门～ in front of the gate 2 forward; ahead: 向～看 look forward; look ahead 3 ago; before: 三天～ three days ago. 午饭～ before lunch II (形) 1 preceding: ～一阶段 the preceding stage. 战～ pre-war 2 former: ～总统 ex-president 3 first; front: ～三名 the first three places (in a competition). ～几行 the preceding lines III (动) go forward; go ahead: 勇往直～ go bravely forward

前辈 qiánbèi (名) older generation

前车(車)之鉴(鑒) qiánchē zhī jiàn warning taken from the overturned cart ahead; lessons drawn from others' mistakes

前程 qiánchéng (名) future; prospect; career: 远大～ a bright future. ～黯淡 have bleak prospects

前额 qián'é (名) forehead

前方 qiánfāng (名) front; ahead; the front lines

前锋 qiánfēng (名) 1 vanguard 2 forward

前赴后(後)继(繼) qiánfù-hòujì advance wave upon wave

前功尽(盡)弃(棄) qiángōng jìn qì all that has been achieved has come to nothing; lose all the results of previous efforts; all labour lost

前后(後) qián-hòu (名) 1 in front and behind: ～左右 on all sides; all around 2 from beginning to end; altogether: 写这本书～用了我一年的时间. It took me one year to write this book. 她～去过那儿三次. She's been there three times altogether. 3 about; around (a certain time): 国庆节～ around National Day

前进(進) qiánjìn (动) go forward; advance

前景 qiánjǐng (名) prospect; perspective: 美好的～ bright prospects. 开辟美丽的～ open up a beautiful vista

前例 qiánlì (名) precedent: 史无～ unprecedented

前列 qiánliè (名) front row; forefront; van: 站在斗争的～ stand in the forefront of the struggle

前门(門) qiánmén (名) front door; front gate

前面 qiánmian (名) 1 in front; ahead: 看! ～有个林子. Look! there is a wood ahead. 2 above; preceding: ～提到的问题 the problems mentioned above. ～那一页 the preceding page

前年 qiánnián (名) the year before last

前仆后(後)继(繼) qiánpū-hòujì (of martyrs) no sooner has one fallen than another steps into the breach

前前后(後)后 qiánqiánhòuhòu 1 the whole story; the ins and outs 2 from beginning to the end (in time)

前驱(驅) qiánqū (名) forerunner; pioneer

前人 qiánrén (名) forefathers; predecessors: ～栽树,后人乘凉 one generation plants the trees in whose shade another generation rests—profiting by the labour of one's forefathers; sweating for the benefit of future generations

前任 qiánrèn (名) predecessor: 他的～ his predecessor. ～总统 ex-president. ～秘书长 former secretary-general

前哨 qiánshào (名) outpost; advance guard

前身 qiánshēn (名) predecessor: 这所大学的～是一个研究中心. This university grew out of a research centre.

前台(臺) qiántái (名) 1 proscenium 2 (on) the stage

前提 qiántí (名) premise; prerequisite; precondition

前天 qiántiān (名) the day before yesterday

前途 qiántú (名) future; prospect: ～无量 have boundless prospects; have unlimited possibilities

前夕 qiánxī (名) eve: 圣诞节～ Christmas eve. 胜利的～ on the eve of the victory

前嫌 qiánxián (名) previous ill will; old grudge: ～尽释 to have agreed to bury the hatchet

前线(綫) qiánxiàn (名) front; frontline: ～国家 frontline country

前言 qiányán (名) preface; foreword; introduction

前沿 qiányán (名) forward position: ～防御 frontier defence

前夜 qiányè (名) eve

前因后(後)果 qiányīn-hòuguǒ cause and effect: 他知道这件事的～. He knows the story from beginning to end.

前瞻 qiánzhān (动) look ahead: 一份富有～性的计划 a forward-looking plan

前兆 qiánzhào (名) omen; forewarning: 地

震的～ warning signs (or indications) of an earthquake
前者 qiánzhě (名) the former
前缀 qiánzhuì (名) prefix
前奏 qiánzòu (名) prelude
乾 qián
乾坤 qiánkūn (名) heaven and earth; the universe: 扭转～ bring about a radical change in the existing state of affairs
掮 qián (动) carry on the shoulder
掮客 qiánkè (名) broker: 政治～ political broker
虔 qián (形) sincere
虔诚 qiánchéng (形) pious; devout: ～的佛教徒 devout Buddhist
黔 qián
黔驴(驢)技穷(窮) Qián lǘ jì qióng the proverbial donkey has exhausted its tricks; be at one's wit's end
钱(錢) qián I (名) money: 挣～ make money. ～包 purse; wallet. 这个多少～? How much is this? II (量) *qian*, a unit of weight (= 5 grams)
钱币(幣) qiánbì (名) coin
钱财 qiáncái (名) money; wealth
钳 qián I (名) pincers; pliers; forceps: 老虎～ pincer pliers. 火～ fire (or coal) tongs. II (动) grip; clamp
钳工 qiángōng (名) fitter
钳制 qiánzhì (动) hold tight; clamp down on
浅(淺) qiǎn (形) 1 shallow: ～海 shallow sea. ～滩 shoal 2 simple; easy: 这些读物内容～. These reading materials are quite easy. 3 superficial: 认识很～ superficial understanding. 交情很～ not on familiar terms 4 (of colour) light: ～蓝 light blue. ～黄 pale yellow
浅薄 qiǎnbó (形) shallow; superficial
浅见(見) qiǎnjiàn (名) superficial view: 依我～ in my humble opinion
浅陋 qiǎnlòu (形) (of knowledge) meagre; mean
浅显(顯) qiǎnxiǎn (形) plain; easy to read and understand: ～的道理 a plain truth
浅易 qiǎnyì (形) simple and easy: ～读物 easy readings
遣 qiǎn (动) 1 send; dispatch: 派～ dispatch. 调兵～将 deploy forces 2 dispel; expel: ～闷 dispel boredom
遣返 qiǎnfǎn (动) repatriate: ～战俘 repatriate prisoners of war
遣散 qiǎnsàn (动) disband; send away
遣送 qiǎnsòng (动) send back; repatriate: ～出境 deport; send out of the country
谴 qiǎn
谴责 qiǎnzé (动) condemn; denounce
歉 qiàn (名) 1 apology: 道～ offer (or make) an apology; apologize 2 crop failure
歉收 qiànshōu (动) have a poor harvest
歉意 qiànyì (名) apology; regret: 表示～ offer an apology. 谨致～ please accept my apologies. 深表～ express one's deep regret
堑 qiàn (名) moat; chasm: 天～ natural chasm. ～壕 trench; entrenchment
欠 qiàn (动) 1 owe: ～债 owe a debt 2 short of; lacking: ～妥 not entirely proper. 身体～佳 not in very good health 3 raise slightly (a part of the body): 她～身去摸床边的灯开关. She rose slightly to feel for the bedside switch. 4 yawn: 呵～ yawn
欠缺 qiànquē I (动) be deficient in; be short of: 经验还～ lacking in experience II (名) shortcoming; deficiency
欠条(條) qiàntiáo (名) a bill signed in acknowledgement of debt; IOU
嵌 qiàn (动) inlay; embed: 镶～着玉石的托盘 a tray inlaid with jade
锵(鏘) qiāng (象) clang; gong
枪(槍) qiāng (名) gun; rifle: 手～ pistol; revolver. 机～ machine gun
枪毙(斃) qiāngbì (动) execute by shooting; have one shot
枪弹(彈) qiāngdàn (名) bullet; cartridge
枪法 qiāngfǎ (名) marksmanship
枪杆(桿)子 qiānggǎnzi (名) the barrel of a gun; gun; arms
枪决 qiāngjué (动) execute by shooting
枪林弹(彈)雨 qiānglín-dànyǔ a hail of bullets; scene of heavy fighting
枪杀(殺) qiāngshā (动) kill by shooting; shoot dead
枪声(聲) qiāngshēng (名) shot; crack
枪手 qiāngshǒu (名) marksman; gunner

Q

枪膛 qiāngtáng (名) bore (of a gun)

呛(嗆) qiāng (动) choke; (of food or drink) go down the wrong way: 我~了一口. It went down the wrong way.

see also qiàng

腔 qiāng (名) **1** cavity: 口~ the oral cavity. 满~热血 full of patriotic enthusiasm **2** tune; pitch: 高~ high-pitched tune; falsetto **3** accent: 南~北调 a mixed accent. 学生~ schoolboy talk **4** speech: 答~ answer

腔调 qiāngdiào (名) **1** tune: 他俩唱的是一个~. The two of them sing the same tune. **2** accent; intonation: 她谈话带北方~. She speaks with a northern accent.

墙(牆) qiáng (名) wall: ~壁 wall. ~报 wall newspaper

蔷(薔) qiáng

蔷薇 qiángwēi (名) rose

强 qiáng (形) **1** strong; powerful: 富~ rich and prosperous. 工作能力~ capable. 风力不~. The wind is not strong. **2** better: 生活一年比一年~. Life is getting better each year. **3** a bit more than: 三分之一~ slightly more than one third

see also jiàng; qiǎng

强暴 qiángbào I (形) violent; brutal II (名) violence; brutality: 不畏~ defy brute force

强大 qiángdà (形) powerful: 阵容~的代表团 strong delegation; high-powered delegation

强盗 qiángdào (名) robber; bandit

强调 qiángdiào (动) stress; emphasize

强度 qiángdù (名) intensity: 劳动~ labour intensity. 钢的~ the strength of the steel

强国(國) qiángguó (名) powerful nation; power

强化 qiánghuà (动) strengthen; intensify; consolidate

强加 qiángjiā (动) impose; force: ~于人 impose (one's views, etc.) on others

强奸 qiángjiān (动) rape; violate: ~民意 defile public opinion

强劲(勁) qiángjìng (形) powerful; forceful: ~的东风 a strong east wind

强烈 qiángliè (形) strong; intense; violent: ~的愿望 a strong desire. ~反对 strong objection. ~谴责 vehemently condemn; vigorously denounce

强迫症 qiángpòzhèng (名) obsessive compulsive disorder (OCD); obsession; compulsion

强权(權) qiángquán (名) power; might: ~政治 power politics

强盛 qiángshèng (形) (of a country) powerful and prosperous

强势(勢) qiángshì (名) going strong; great force

强心剂(劑) qiángxīnjì (名) cardiac stimulant; cardiotonic

强行 qiángxíng (动) by force: ~闯入 force one's way in

强硬 qiángyìng (形) strong; unyielding; formidable: ~路线 hard line

强制 qiángzhì (动) force; compel (by political or economic means): ~措施 compulsory measure. ~机关 institution of coercion

强壮(壯) qiángzhuàng (形) strong; sturdy; robust

抢(搶) qiǎng (动) **1** snatch; grab: 她从我手里把信~了过去. She snatched the letter from me. **2** rob; loot **3** vie for; scramble for: ~球 scramble for the ball **4** rush: ~时间 seize the hour; race against time. ~先 try to be the first to do sth.; anticipate; forestall

抢白 qiǎngbái (动) tell off; dress down; rebuff

抢答 qiǎngdá (动) race to be the first to answer a question

抢夺(奪) qiǎngduó (动) grab; seize

抢饭碗 qiǎng fànwǎn fight for a job; snatch sb. else's job

抢购(購) qiǎnggòu (动) rush to purchase

抢劫 qiǎngjié (动) rob; loot; plunder

抢镜头(頭) qiǎng jìngtóu **1** (of a cameraman) fight for a vantage point from which to take a news picture **2** steal the show; be fond of being in the limelight

抢救 qiǎngjiù (动) rescue: ~稀有动物 rescue rare animals. ~病人 give emergency treatment to a patient

抢收 qiǎngshōu (动) get the harvest in quickly

抢手 qiǎngshǒu (形) (of goods) in great demand

抢险(險) qiǎngxiǎn (动) speedily carry out rescue work

抢眼 qiǎngyǎn (形) eye-catching; arresting

抢注 qiǎngzhù (动) preregister; back order: 域名~ cybersquatting

强 qiǎng (动) make an effort; strive: ～作笑脸 force a smile
see also jiàng; qiáng

强词夺(奪)理 qiǎngcí-duólǐ resort to sophistry

强迫 qiǎngpò (动) force; compel; coerce

强求 qiǎngqiú (动) impose; forcibly demand: 写文章可以有各种风格,不必～一律. No uniformity should be imposed since styles of writing vary.

襁 qiǎng

襁褓 qiǎngbǎo (名) swaddling clothes: ～中 be in one's infancy

呛(嗆) qiàng (动) irritate (respiratory organs): 什么味儿这么～鼻子? What smell is it which irritates the nose so much?
see also qiāng

跄(蹌) qiàng

跄踉 qiàngliàng (动) stagger

敲 qiāo (动) knock; beat; strike: ～锣打鼓 beat gongs and drums. ～警钟 sound the tocsin

敲打 qiāoda (动) beat; tap

敲诈 qiāozhà (动) blackmail; extort; racketeer: ～钱财 extort money

敲竹杠 qiāo zhúgàng (动) overcharge sb. or extort money from him by taking advantage of his weakness or ignorance

Q

悄 qiāo

悄悄 qiāoqiāo (副) quietly; stealthily: 他～地走了. He left quietly.

橇 qiāo (名) sledge; sled; sleigh

跷(蹺) qiāo I (动) lift up (a leg); hold up (a finger): ～着腿坐着 sit with one's legs crossed II (名) stilts

锹 qiāo (名) spade

翘(翹) qiáo (动) 1 raise (one's head) ～首 raise one's head (and look ahead) 2 become warped
see also qiào

乔(喬) qiáo

乔木 qiáomù (名) arbor; tall tree

乔迁(遷) qiáoqiān (动) move to a new place

乔装(裝)打扮 qiáozhuāng dǎbàn disguise oneself; masquerade

侨(僑) qiáo I (动) live abroad II (名) a person living abroad: 华～ overseas Chinese. 外～ foreign nationals; aliens

侨胞 qiáobāo (名) countrymen (or nationals) residing abroad; overseas compatriots

侨汇(匯) qiáohuì (名) overseas remittance

侨居 qiáojū (动) reside abroad: ～国 country of residence

侨眷 qiáojuàn (名) relatives of nationals living abroad

侨民 qiáomín (名) a national residing abroad

侨务(務) qiáowù (名) affairs concerning nationals living abroad

侨乡(鄉) qiáoxiāng (名) village or town inhabited by relatives of overseas Chinese and returned overseas Chinese

桥(橋) qiáo (名) bridge

桥墩 qiáodūn (名) (bridge) pier; abutment

桥梁 qiáoliáng (名) bridge

桥牌 qiáopái (名) bridge (a card game): 打～ play bridge

桥头(頭) qiáotóu (名) either end of a bridge

憔 qiáo

憔悴 qiáocuì (形) haggard; withered

樵 qiáo (名) firewood: ～夫 woodman

瞧 qiáo (动) look; see: 等着～吧. Wait and see. 你～着办吧. You can do as you see fit.

瞧不起 qiáobuqǐ look down upon; hold in contempt

瞧得起 qiáodeqǐ think much (or highly) of sb.

巧 qiǎo (形) 1 skilful; clever; ingenious: ～匠 a skilled workman 2 cunning; deceitful; artful: 花言～语 honeyed words; deceitful talk 3 coincidental; fortuitous; by a happy chance: 真～! What a coincidence! 真不～! 他今天又不在家. Unfortunately, he is out again today.

巧夺(奪)天工 qiǎo duó tiāngōng wonderful workmanship; superb craftsmanship

巧合 qiǎohé (名) coincidence

巧立名目 qiǎo lì míngmù invent various names of items; concoct various pretexts

巧妙 qiǎomiào (形) (of methods, skills,

etc.) ingenious; clever
巧遇 qiǎoyù (动) encounter by chance
窍(竅) qiào (名) a key to sth.: 诀～ knack; trick of a trade
窍门(門) qiàomén (名) key (to a problem); knack: 找～ try to find something that lends itself readily to the solution of a problem
壳(殼) qiào (名) shell; hard surface
see also ké
撬 qiào (动) prise; pry: 把箱子盖～开 prise the top off a box
翘(翹) qiào (动) stick up; rise on one end; tilt
see also qiáo
翘辫(辮)子 qiào biànzi kick the bucket
翘尾巴 qiào wěiba be cocky
鞘 qiào (名) sheath; scabbard
see also shāo
峭 qiào (形) high and steep: 陡～ precipitous
峭壁 qiàobì (名) cliff; precipice
俏 qiào (形) pretty; smart; cute: 打扮得真～ wear the cutest dress
俏丽(麗) qiàolì (形) pretty
俏皮 qiàopi (形) (of manners or speeches) lively or amusing; witty
俏皮话 qiàopihuà (名) 1 witty remark 2 sarcastic remark
切 qiē (动) cut; slice: ～菜 cut vegetables
see also qiè
切除 qiēchú (动) amputate
切磋 qiēcuō (动) exchange experience; compare notes
切断(斷) qiēduàn (动) cut off: ～电源 cut off the electricity supply. ～交通 sever communication lines
切片 qiēpiàn (名) section: ～检查 cut sections (of organic tissues) for microscopic examination
切入 qiērù (动) penetrate into: ～点 point of contact
切削 qiēxiāo (动) cut: 金属～ metal cutting
茄 qié (名) eggplant; aubergine
see also jiā
茄子 qiézi (名) eggplant; aubergine
且 qiě I (副) 1 for the time being: 你～等一下. Will you please wait a little while? 2 not to mention; let alone: ～不说你, 连他最好的朋友的话他都不听. He would not listen even to his best friend, not to mention you. 3 for a long time: 这菜～煮呢. This dish takes a long time to cook. II (连) both... and...: 既高～大 both tall and big-boned
且慢 qiěmàn (动) wait a moment; not leave so soon: ～, 我还有个问题要问你. Wait a minute, I have one more question to ask.
妾 qiè (名) concubine
锲 qiè (动)〈书〉 carve; engrave
锲而不舍(捨) qiè ér bù shě work with perseverance
挈 qiè (动) 1 take along: ～眷 take one's family along 2 take up: 提纲～领 keep the key points; put it in a nutshell
怯 qiè (形) timid; cowardly; nervous
怯场(場) qièchǎng (动) have stage fright
怯懦 qiènuò (形) timid; cowardly
怯弱 qièruò (形) timid and weak-willed
惬 qiè (形)〈书〉 satisfied
惬意 qièyì (形) pleased; satisfied
切 qiè I (动) correspond to; fit: 他说话不～实际. What he says is unrealistic. II (形) eager; anxious: 回家心～ be anxious to return home. 学习心～ eager to study III (副) be sure to: ～不可麻痹大意. Be sure to guard against carelessness.
see also qiē
切合 qièhé (动) suit; fit in with: 作计划要～实际. Plans should be drawn up in the light of realities.
切换 qiēhuàn (动) cut-over; switch-over
切身 qièshēn (形) 1 of immediate concern to oneself: ～利益 one's immediate or vital interests 2 personal: ～体会 personal understanding
切实(實) qièshí (形) 1 practical; realistic; feasible: ～有效的办法 practical and effective measures. ～可行的计划 a feasible plan 2 conscientiously; earnestly: ～改正错误 correct one's mistakes in real earnest. ～履行 implement in real earnest
切题 qiètí (形) keep to the point

窃(竊) qiè I (动) steal: 盗～ steal II (副) secretly; surreptitiously; furtively: ～笑 laugh up one's sleeve. ～听 eavesdrop; bug

窃取 qièqǔ (动) steal; usurp; grab: ～要职 occupy a key post by foul means. ～情报 steal secret information

窃贼 qièzéi (名) thief; burglar

亲(親) qīn I (形) 1 related by blood: ～姐妹 blood sisters. 2 intimate: ～热 on intimate terms II (名) 1 parent: 母～ mother. 双～ parents. 2 relative: 近～ close relative 3 marriage: 定～ betrothal III (动) kiss see also qìng

亲爱(愛) qīn'ài (形) dear; beloved

亲笔(筆) qīnbǐ I (副) in one's own handwriting II (名) one's own handwriting

亲骨肉 qīngǔròu (名) one's own flesh and blood (i. e. parents and children, brothers and sisters)

亲近 qīnjìn I (形) close; intimate: 他们俩很～. The two of them are on very intimate terms. II (动) be friends with: 他对人冷嘲热讽, 谁都不愿～他. He is so sarcastic that no one wants to be friends with him.

亲眷 qīnjuàn (名) one's relatives

亲口 qīnkǒu (副) (say sth.) personally: 这是他～告诉我的. He told me this himself.

亲密 qīnmì (形) close; intimate: ～无间 be close associates

亲昵 qīnnì (形) very intimate: ～的称呼 an affectionate form of address

亲戚 qīnqi (名) relative

亲切 qīnqiè (形) cordial; warm: 回到离别多年的故乡, 感到一切格外～. On returning to my hometown after years of absence, I felt I was in specially congenial company.

亲热(熱) qīnrè (形) warm and affectionate

亲人 qīnrén (名) 1 kinsfolk or spouse 2 beloved ones

亲善 qīnshàn (形) close and friendly

亲身 qīnshēn (形) personal; firsthand: ～经历 personal experience

亲生 qīnshēng (形) one's own (children, parents): ～儿女 one's own children)

亲事 qīnshi (名) marriage

亲手 qīnshǒu (副) with one's own hands; personally; oneself

亲属(屬) qīnshǔ (名) relatives

亲王 qīnwáng (名) prince

亲信 qīnxìn (名) trusted follower

亲眼 qīnyǎn (副) with one's own eyes: 这是我～看见的. I saw it with my own eyes.

亲友 qīnyǒu (名) relatives and friends; kith and kin

亲子鉴(鑒)定 qīnzǐ jiàndìng (名) confirmation of (disputed) paternity

亲自 qīnzì (副) personally; in person: ～看看 see for oneself. ～动手 do the job oneself. ～拜访 make a personal call. ～过问 look into the matter personally

亲嘴 qīnzuǐ (动) kiss

钦 qīn

钦差大臣 qīnchāi dàchén imperial envoy; emissary from the top organization

钦佩 qīnpèi (动) admire; esteem: 深感～ have great admiration for

侵 qīn (动) invade; intrude into

侵犯 qīnfàn (动) intrude; encroach upon; violate: ～一国主权 violate a country's sovereignty. ～人权 infringe upon human rights

侵略 qīnlüè (动、名) invade; aggression: ～者 aggressor. ～战争 war of aggression. 文化～ cultural aggression

侵扰(擾) qīnrǎo (动) invade and harass: ～边境 harass a country's frontiers; make border raids

侵入 qīnrù (动) invade; intrude into: ～领海 intrude into a country's territorial waters

侵蚀 qīnshí (动) corrode; erode: 风雨～的屋顶 the weather-beaten roof. ～作用 corrosive action

侵吞 qīntūn (动) 1 swallow up; annex: ～别国领土 annex another country's territory 2 embezzle; misappropriate: ～公款 embezzle public funds

侵袭(襲) qīnxí (动) invade and attack: 受到台风～的地区 areas hit by the typhoon

侵占(佔) qīnzhàn (动) invade and occupy; seize: ～别国领土 invade and occupy another country's territory. 被～的领土 occupied land

勤 qín I (形) 1 hard-working; diligent; industrious: ～学苦练 study diligently and train hard 2 frequently; regularly: 他来得最～. He comes very often. II (名) (office, school, etc.) attendance: 值～ be on duty. 考～ check on work attendance

勤奋(奮) qínfèn (形) diligent; hard-working

勤工俭(儉)学(學) qíngōng-jiǎnxué part-work and part-study

勤俭(儉) qínjiǎn (形) hard-working and thrifty: ～建国 build up the country through thrift and hard work

勤恳(懇) qínkěn (形) diligent and conscientious: 工作～ work earnestly and conscientiously

勤快 qínkuai (形) hard-working and fond of physical labour

勤劳(勞) qínláo (形) diligent; industrious: ～致富 get rich through diligent labour

勤勉 qínmiǎn (形) diligent; assiduous

勤务(務) qínwù (名) duty; service: ～兵 orderly

勤杂(雜)工 qínzágōng (名) odd-job man; handyman

芹 qín

芹菜 qíncài (名) celery

禽 qín (名) birds: 家～ domestic fowls; poultry

禽兽(獸) qínshòu (名) birds and beasts: 衣冠～ a beast of a man; a human beast

擒 qín (动) capture; catch; seize

噙 qín (动) hold in the mouth or the eyes: ～着眼泪 eyes filled with tears

琴 qín (名) 1 a general name for stringed instruments: 胡～ fiddle. 竖～ harp. 小提～ violin 2 piano: 钢～ piano

琴键 qínjiàn (名) key (on a musical instrument)

琴弦 qínxián (名) string (of a musical instrument)

寝(寢) qǐn (动) get into bed; sleep: 废～忘食 forget to eat and sleep. 就～ go to bed

寝食 qǐn-shí (名) sleeping and eating

寝室 qǐnshì (名) bedroom; dormitory

沁 qìn (动) ooze; seep: 额上～出了汗珠. Beads of sweat stood on his forehead.

青 qīng (形) 1 blue or green: ～天 blue sky 2 black: ～布 black cloth 3 young (people): ～工 young workers

青菜 qīngcài (名) green vegetables

青出于(於)蓝(藍) qīng chūyú lán the pupil often surpasses the master

青春 qīngchūn (名) youth: 充满～活力 be bursting with youthful vigour. ～期 puberty

青翠 qīngcuì (形) fresh and green

青光眼 qīngguāngyǎn (名) glaucoma

青花瓷 qīnghuācí (名) blue and white porcelain

青黄不接 qīng-huáng bù jiē temporary shortage

青睐(睞) qīnglài (名) favour; good graces: 受到某人的～ be in sb.'s good graces

青梅竹马(馬) qīngméi-zhúmǎ a man and a woman who had an innocent affection for each other in childhood

青年 qīngnián (名) youth; young people

青涩 qīngsè (形) green; young and inexperienced; immature

青少年 qīng-shàonián (名) teenagers: ～犯罪 juvenile delinquency

青天 qīngtiān (名) blue sky: ～霹雳 a bolt from the blue

青铜 qīngtóng (名) bronze: ～器 bronze ware. ～时代 the Bronze Age

青蛙 qīngwā (名) frog

清 qīng I (形) 1 clean; clear; pure: 溪水～澈. The water of the steam is crystal clear. 2 distinct; clarified: 说不～ hard to explain. 数不～ countless 3 quiet: 享～福 live in quiet comfort II (动) settle; clear up: ～账 settle the account

清白 qīngbái (形) pure; clean; unsullied: 历史～ be of unsullied antecedents

清仓(倉) qīngcāng (动) 1 make an inventory of a warehouse 2 sell all one's holdings

清查 qīngchá (动) check

清偿(償) qīngcháng (动) pay off; clear off: ～债务 pay off (or clear off) debts. ～能力 liquidity

清晨 qīngchén (名) early morning

清除 qīngchú (动) clear away; get rid of; eliminate: ～垃圾 clear away rubbish. ～官僚主义的恶习 get rid of the bureaucratic practices

清楚 qīngchu I (形) clear; distinct: 他说话不～. He doesn't speak distinctly. II (动) be clear about; understand: 这件事我不太～. I don't know much about the matter.

清脆 qīngcuì (形) (of voice) clear and melodious

清单(單) qīngdān (名) detailed list; inventory

Q

清淡 qīngdàn (形) **1** light; delicate: ~的食物 light food **2** dull; slack: 生意~. Business is slack.

清点(點) qīngdiǎn (动) check; make an inventory: ~货物 take stock

清风(風) qīngfēng (名) cool breeze

清高 qīnggāo (形) noble-minded and unwilling to swim with the tide

清官 qīngguān (名) honest and upright official

清规戒律 qīngguī jièlǜ taboos and prohibitions; rigorous regulations

清洁(潔) qīngjié (形) clean: 整齐~ clean and tidy

清净 qīngjìng (形) peace and quiet: 图~ seek peace and quiet

清静 qīngjìng (形) quiet: ~的地方 a quiet place

清冷 qīnglěng (形) chilly: ~的秋夜 a chilly autumn night

清理 qīnglǐ (动) put in order: ~账目 check up on the accounts. ~文件 sort out the documents

清凉 qīngliáng (形) cool and refreshing: ~饮料 cold drinks

清明 qīngmíng I (名) Pure Brightness; a day around April 5th or 6th when one pays respects to a dead person at his or her tomb II (形) clear and bright: 月色~. The moonlight is bright.

清贫 qīngpín (形) poor or in straitened circumstances

清爽 qīngshuǎng (形) **1** fresh and cool: 雨后空气特别~. The air after rain is especially cool and refreshing. **2** relieved; relaxed: 心里~了 feel relieved

清算 qīngsuàn (动) **1** clear accounts **2** settle accounts; liquidate; expose and criticize

清晰 qīngxī (形) distinct; clear: 发音~ clear articulation

清洗 qīngxǐ (动) **1** rinse; wash **2** purge; comb out (undesirable elements)

清闲(閒) qīngxián I (形) at leisure II (名) quiet leisure: 享~ enjoy a quiet life

清香 qīngxiāng (名) delicate fragrance; faint scent (of flowers)

清醒 qīngxǐng I (形) clear-headed; sane: 头脑~ clear-headed II (动) regain consciousness: 病人已经~过来了. The patient has come to.

清秀 qīngxiù (形) delicate and pretty: 面目~ of fine, delicate features

清样(樣) qīngyàng (名) proof: 长条~ galley proof

清一色 qīngyīsè (形) all of the same colour; uniform; homogeneous

清早 qīngzǎo (名) early in the morning; early morning

清真 qīngzhēn (形) Islamic; Muslim: ~寺 mosque

蜻 qīng

蜻蜓 qīngtíng (名) dragonfly

蜻蜓点(點)水 qīngtíng diǎn shuǐ touch on sth. lightly

倾(傾) qīng (动) **1** incline; lean: 左~ leftist (deviation) **2** pour out; empty: ~囊相助 give all possible financial assistance **3** collapse

倾巢出动(動) qīngcháo chūdòng 〈贬〉 turn out in full force

倾倒 qīngdǎo (动) **1** topple and fall; topple over **2** greatly admire

倾倒 qīngdào (动) empty; pour out: ~垃圾 dump rubbish

倾覆 qīngfù (动) overturn; topple; overthrow

倾家荡(蕩)产(產) qīngjiā-dàngchǎn go bankrupt or broke

倾慕 qīngmù (动) adore

倾盆大雨 qīngpén dàyǔ heavy downpour; rain cats and dogs

倾诉 qīngsù (动) say everything (that is on one's mind)

倾听(聽) qīngtīng (动) listen attentively to: ~民众的呼声 listen attentively to what the masses have to say

倾向 qīngxiàng I (名) trend; tendency II (动) prefer: 我~于同意他的意见. I tend (or am inclined) to agree with him.

倾销 qīngxiāo (动) dump (goods)

倾斜 qīngxié (动) tilt; incline; slope; slant

倾泻(瀉) qīngxiè (动) pour; come down in torrents

倾心 qīngxīn (动) admire; fall in love with: 一见~ fall in love at first sight

倾注 qīngzhù (动) pour: 把全部心血~到工作中去 throw oneself into one's work heart and soul

轻(輕) qīng I (形) **1** light (in weight): 像羽毛一样~ as light as a feather **2** small in degree: 年纪很~ be very young. 伤势不~ be seriously wounded **3** light; easy: ~罚 light punishment. 工作很~. It's an easy job. **4** gently; softly: ~声点! Be quiet! II (动)

belittle; make light of: 文人相～ scholars often scorn one another. ～敌 underestimate enemy strength; underestimate one's adversary

轻便 qīngbiàn (形) light; portable

轻而易举(舉) qīng ér yì jǔ easy to accomplish

轻浮 qīngfú (形) frivolous; flighty: 举止～ behave frivolously

轻工业(業) qīnggōngyè (名) light industry

轻举(舉)妄动(動) qīngjǔ-wàngdòng act rashly; take reckless action

轻快 qīngkuài (形) 1 brisk; spry: 迈着～的步伐 walk at a brisk pace 2 light-hearted: ～的曲调 lively tune

轻描淡写(寫) qīngmiáo-dànxiě touch on lightly; mention casually

轻蔑 qīngmiè (形) scornful; contemptuous

轻飘飘 qīngpiāopiāo (形) light as a feather; buoyant: 想到自己的成功,她脚底下～的. Drunk with success, she felt as if treading on air.

轻巧 qīngqiǎo (形) 1 simple and easy: 你说得倒～. You talk as if it were that simple. 2 deft; dexterous: 动作～ act with agility and grace

轻柔 qīngróu (形) soft; gentle: 柳枝～ pliable willow twigs. ～的声音 a gentle voice

轻纱 qīngshā (名) fine gauze

轻生 qīngshēng (动) commit suicide

轻视 qīngshì (动) look down on; despise; underestimate

轻手轻脚 qīngshǒu-qīngjiǎo gently; softly: 护士进出都～的,怕惊醒病人. The nurse tiptoed in and out so as not to wake the patient.

轻率 qīngshuài (形) rash; hasty; indiscreet: ～的态度 reckless attitude. ～从事 act rashly

轻松 qīngsōng (形) relaxed: ～愉快 thoroughly relaxed

轻佻 qīngtiāo (形) frivolous; skittish

轻微 qīngwēi (形) light; slight; trifling: ～的损害 slight damage

轻信 qīngxìn (动) be credulous; readily believe

轻型 qīngxíng (形) light-duty; light: ～载重汽车 light-duty truck

轻易 qīngyì (副) 1 easily: 成功不是～就能取得的. Success doesn't come easily. 2 lightly; rashly: 他从不～发表意见. He never expresses an opinion on the spur of the moment.

轻音乐(樂) qīngyīnyuè (名) light music

轻盈 qīngyíng (形) slim and graceful; lithe; lissom

轻重 qīng-zhòng (名) 1 weight: ～不一 different in weight 2 degree of seriousness; relative importance: 无足～ of no consequence 3 propriety: 此人说话有时不知～. The chap doesn't know how to talk properly under certain circumstances.

轻装(裝) qīngzhuāng (名) with light packs (or equipment): ～就道 travel light

氢(氫)

qīng (名) hydrogen (H): ～弹 H-bomb

情

qíng (名) 1 feelings; affection; sentiment: 爱～ love. 热～ enthusiasm 2 favour; kindness: 求～ plead with sb. 3 situation; condition: 病～ patient's condition

情报(報) qíngbào (名) information; intelligence: 刺探～ pry for information. ～机关 intelligence agency

情不自禁 qíng bù zì jìn cannot help (doing sth.): ～地叫了起来 can't help crying out

情操 qíngcāo (名) moral integrity; noble mind

情场(場) qíngchǎng (名) the arena of love; the tournaments of love: ～得意 be lucky in love. ～老手 womanizer

情敌(敵) qíngdí (名) rival in a love triangle

情调 qíngdiào (名) sentiment; emotional appeal

情分 qíngfen (名) mutual affection natural to various types of human relationship

情感 qínggǎn (名) feelings; emotion

情歌 qínggē (名) love song

情节(節) qíngjié (名) 1 (of story, play, etc.) plot: 故事～曲折. The story has a complicated plot. 2 circumstances: ～严重的案子 a serious case

情景 qíngjǐng (名) scene; sight; circumstances: 感人的～ a moving sight

情况 qíngkuàng (名) situation; condition; state of affairs: 生产～ production situation. 在这种～下 under these circumstances. 那要看～而定. That depends. *or* It all depends.

情理 qínglǐ (名) reason; sense: 合乎～ be reasonable; stand to reason. 不近～ unreasonable; irrational

情侣 qínglǚ (名) sweethearts; lovers

情面 qíngmian (名) feelings; sensibilities:

留～ spare sb.'s sensibilities

情趣 qíngqù (名) 1 disposition and taste: 他们二人～相投. The two of them find each other congenial. 2 good taste; appeal: 这首诗很有～. This poem is a model of good taste.

情人 qíngrén (名) sweetheart; lover

情商 qíngshāng (名) emotional quotient; EQ

情书(書) qíngshū (名) love letter

情同手足 qíng tóng shǒuzú like brothers; with brotherly love for each other

情投意合 qíngtóu-yìhé find so much in common with one another; see eye to eye in everything

情形 qíngxing (名) condition

情绪 qíngxù (名) 1 mood; spirit; morale: ～很低 be in low spirits 2 moodiness; the sulks: 闹～ be in a fit of depression

情义(義) qíngyì (名) friendship; comradeship

情谊 qíngyì (名) friendly feelings; affection: 兄弟～ fraternal affection

情意 qíngyì (名) love; affection; goodwill

情有可原 qíng yǒu kě yuán excusable; pardonable

情愿(願) qíngyuàn I (动) be willing to: 两相～ by mutual consent II (副) would rather; prefer: 她～死也不肯受屈辱. She would prefer death to dishonour.

Q

晴 qíng (形) fine; clear: 天转～了. It's clearing up.

晴空 qíngkōng (名) clear sky; cloudless sky: ～万里 a clear and boundless sky

晴朗 qínglǎng (形) fine; sunny

晴天 qíngtiān (名) fine day; sunny day

晴天霹雳(靂) qíngtiān pīlì a bolt from the blue

擎 qíng (动) hold up; lift up

请 qǐng (动) 1 request; ask: ～人帮忙 ask for help. ～医生 send for a doctor 2 〈敬〉 please: ～坐. Sit down, please.

请安 qǐng'ān (动) pay respects to sb.; wish sb. good health

请便 qǐngbiàn (动) do as you wish; please yourself: 你要是想现在去,那就～吧. Well, if you wish to leave now, go ahead.

请假 qǐngjià (动) ask for leave: 请一天假 ask for one day's leave. 她请病假回家了. She's gone home on sick leave.

请柬 qǐngjiǎn (名) invitation card

请教 qǐngjiào (动) ask for advice; consult: 这件事你得去～专家. You must consult an expert on such a matter. 虚心向别人～. Learn modestly from others.

请客 qǐngkè (动) stand treat; entertain guests; give a dinner party; play the host

请求 qǐngqiú (动) ask; request: ～宽恕 ask for forgiveness

请示 qǐngshì (动) ask for instructions: 向上级～ ask one's seniors for instructions

请帖 qǐngtiě (名) invitation card: 发～ send out invitations

请问 qǐngwèn (动) may I ask...: ～现在几点钟了? Excuse me, could you tell me what time it is now?

请勿 qǐngwù (动) please don't: ～吸烟 No smoking. ～践踏草地. Keep off the lawn.

请愿(願) qǐngyuàn (动) present a petition; petition: ～书 petition

请战(戰) qǐngzhàn (动) ask for a battle assignment: ～书 a written request for a battle assignment

请罪 qǐngzuì (动) confess one's fault; apologize

顷 qǐng I (量) unit of area (＝6.6667 hectares): 碧波万～ a boundless expanse of blue water II (名) 〈书〉 a little while: 少～ after a while. ～刻 in an instant; instantly

亲(親) qìng

see also qīn

亲家 qìngjia (名) families related by marriage

庆(慶) qìng (动) celebrate; congratulate: ～丰收 celebrate a bumper harvest. 国～ National Day

庆典 qìngdiǎn (名) celebration: 大～ grand celebrations

庆贺 qìnghè (动) congratulate; celebrate

庆幸 qìngxìng (动) rejoice: 她为自己还活着感到～. She considers herself fortunate to have survived the accident.

庆祝 qìngzhù (动) celebrate: ～胜利 celebrate the victory

穹 qióng (名) 1 vault; dome 2 the sky: 苍～ the heavens

穷(窮) qióng I (形) 1 poor; poverty-stricken 2 exhausted; pushed to the limit: 山～水尽 at the end of one's tether; in desperate straits **3** extremely; exceedingly: ～奢极欲 indulge in extravagance and luxury. ～忙 be up to one's ears in work II (名) limit; end: 无～无尽 endless; inexhaustible

穷光蛋 qióngguāngdàn (名) pauper; poor wretch

穷极(極)无(無)聊 qióngjí wúliáo **1** utterly bored **2** absolutely senseless

穷尽(盡) qióngjìn (名) limit; end: 人类的知识是没有～的. Human knowledge is without end.

穷开(開)心 qióngkāixīn **1** enjoy oneself despite poverty **2** seek joy amidst sorrow; try to enjoy oneself despite one's suffering

穷苦 qióngkǔ (形) poverty-stricken; impoverished

穷困 qióngkùn (形) poverty-stricken; destitute

穷日子 qióngrìzi (名) days of poverty; straitened circumstances

穷山恶(惡)水 qióngshān-èshuǐ barren mountains and unruly rivers; barren hills and untamed rivers

穷酸 qióngsuān (形) (of a scholar) miserably poor and pedantic

穷途末路 qióngtú-mòlù be in an impasse; have come to a dead end

穷乡(鄉)僻壤 qióngxiāng-pìrǎng a remote backward place in the countryside

穷凶极(極)恶(惡) qióngxiōngjí'è extremely vicious; utterly atrocious

琼(瓊) qióng (名) fine jade

秋 qiū (名) **1** autumn: 深～ late autumn **2** harvest time: 麦～ time for the wheat harvest **3** year: 千～万代 for thousands of years

秋波 qiūbō (名) the bright and clear eyes of a beautiful woman: 送～ (of a woman) cast amorous glances; make eyes; ogle

秋毫 qiūháo (名) sth. too small to be easily discernible: 明察～ be so sharp-eyed as to be able to detect the smallest flaws

秋季 qiūjì (名) the autumn season

秋千 qiūqiān (名) swing: 打～ have a swing

秋色 qiūsè (名) autumn scenery

秋收 qiūshōu (名) autumn harvest

丘 qiū (名) mound; hillock: 沙～ a sand dune. 坟～ grave

丘陵 qiūlíng (名) hills: ～地带 hilly land

蚯 qiū

蚯蚓 qiūyǐn (名) earthworm

酋 qiú (名) chief of a tribe; chieftain: 匪～ bandit chief

酋长(長) qiúzhǎng (名) chief of a tribe; sheik(h); emir

求 qiú (动) **1** beg; entreat; request: ～你帮个忙. May I ask you a favour? ～教 seek counsel. ～见 request an audience; ask for an interview **2** seek; strive for: 不～个人名利 seek neither personal fame nor gain **3** demand: 供不应～. Supply falls short of demand.

求爱(愛) qiú'ài (动) court; woo

求和 qiúhé (动) sue for peace

求婚 qiúhūn (动) propose

求见(見) qiújiàn (动) ask to see; request an interview; beg for an audience

求救 qiújiù (动) ask for immediate rescue when in distress; send an S. O. S.; cry for help

求情 qiúqíng (动) plead; beg for leniency: 向他～ plead with him

求全 qiúquán (动) **1** demand perfection: ～责备 nitpick; find fault and demand perfection **2** try to round sth. off: 委曲～ stoop to compromise

求饶(饒) qiúráo (动) beg for mercy

求生 qiúshēng (动) seek survival

求同存异(異) qiú tóng cún yì seek common ground while reserving differences: 求大同,存小异 seek common ground on major issues while reserving differences on minor ones

求学(學) qiúxué (动) pursue one's studies

求援 qiúyuán (动) ask for help; request reinforcements

求之不得 qiú zhī bù dé most welcome: 一个～的好机会 a golden opportunity

求知 qiúzhī (动) seek knowledge

求职 qiúzhí (动) apply for a job; seek employment: ～信 application letter

裘 qiú (名) fur coat

球 qiú (名) **1** ball: 篮～ basketball. 网～ tennis **2** the globe; the earth: 东半～ the Eastern Hemisphere **3** anything shaped like a ball: 雪～ snowball

球门(門) qiúmén (名) goal

球迷 qiúmí (名) (ball game) fan: 足球～ football fan

球拍 qiúpāi (名) **1** (tennis, badminton, etc.) racket **2** (ping-pong) bat

球赛 qiúsài (名) ball game; match

球网(網) qiúwǎng (名) net (for ball games)
球鞋 qiúxié (名) gym shoes; tennis shoes; sneakers
球艺(藝) qiúyì (名) ball game skills
球员(員) qiúyuán (名) player (of basketball; football, etc.)
囚 qiú I (动) imprison II (名) prisoner; captive
囚犯 qiúfàn (名) prisoner; convict
囚禁 qiújìn (动) imprison; put in jail
泅 qiú (动) swim: ～渡 swim across
趋(趨) qū (动) 1 tend towards; tend to become: 大势所～ irresistible general trend 2 hasten; hurry along: ～前 hasten forward
趋势(勢) qūshì (名) trend; tendency: 他的病有好转的～. His condition is turning for the better.
趋同 qūtóng (动) converge
趋向 qūxiàng I (名) trend; tendency II (动) tend to; incline to: 问题～明朗. The problem is being cleared up.
祛 qū (动) dispel; drive away: ～暑 drive away summer heat
祛除 qūchú (动) dispel; get rid of; drive out: ～疑虑 dispel one's misgivings. ～邪气 eliminate unhealthy trends
区(區) qū I (名) 1 area; district; region: 山～ mountain area. 风景～ scenic spot 2 an administrative division: 自治～ autonomous region II (动) distinguish
区别 qūbié I (动) distinguish: ～好坏 distinguish between good and bad II (名) difference: 这两种意见没有什么大的～. There isn't much difference between these two views.
区区 qūqū (形) trivial; trifling: ～小事,何足挂齿. Such a trifling matter is hardly worth mentioning.
区域 qūyù (名) area; district; region
躯(軀) qū (名) the human body: 为国捐～ lay down one's life for one's country
躯干(幹) qūgàn (名) truck; torso
躯壳(殼) qūqiào (名) the body (as opposed to the soul)
躯体(體) qūtǐ (名) body
驱(驅) qū (动) 1 drive (a horse, car, etc.): ～车前往 drive (in a vehicle) to a place 2 expel; disperse: ～出国境 deport 3 run quickly: 长～直入 drive straight ahead without hindrance
驱除 qūchú (动) drive away; get rid of
驱散 qūsàn (动) disperse; dispel; break up: ～人群 disperse a crowd. 阳光～了薄雾. The sun dispelled the mist.
驱使 qūshǐ (动) 1 order about 2 prompt; urge: 为良心所～ follow the dictates of one's own conscience
驱逐 qūzhú (动) drive out; expel; banish: ～出境 deport; expel. ～舰 destroyer
蛆 qū (名) maggot
曲 qū I (形) 1 bent; crooked: ～径通幽 a winding path leading to a secluded spot 2 wrong; unjustifiable: 是非～直 the rights and wrongs of a matter II (名) bend (of a river, etc.)
see also qǔ
曲解 qūjiě (动) twist; distort; misinterpret
曲里(裏)拐弯(彎) qūliguǎiwān zigzag
曲线(綫) qūxiàn (名) curve
曲折 qūzhé I (形) 1 winding: 小径～通过树林. The path winds through the woods. 2 not straight or smooth; tortuous: 生活的道路是～的. Life is full of twists and turns. II (名) complications: 你不知道这件事的～. You don't know the complications involved in this matter.
曲直 qū-zhí (名) right and wrong
蛐 qū
蛐蛐儿(兒) qūqur (名) cricket
屈 qū I (动) 1 bend; crook: ～膝 bend one's knees 2 subdue; submit; yield to: 宁死不～ would rather die than yield. 不～不挠 indomitable; dauntless; unyielding 3 be in the wrong: 理～词穷 unable to advance any tenable argument in defence of one's case II (名) wrong; injustice: 受～ be wronged
屈才 qūcái (动) be assigned a job unworthy of one's talents
屈从(從) qūcóng (动) submit to; yield to (sb.): ～外界压力 yield (succumb) to pressure from outside
屈打成招 qū dǎ chéng zhāo confess oneself guilty under torture
屈服 qūfú (动) submit; yield; bow to: ～于社会的压力 yield to social pressure
屈辱 qūrǔ (名) humiliation; disgrace
屈膝 qūxī (动) go down on one's knees: ～求饶 beg for mercy

屈指可数(數) qūzhǐ kě shǔ can be counted on one's fingers; very few

渠 qú (名) ditch; canal; channel: 灌溉～ irrigation canal

渠道 qúdào (名) 1 irrigation ditch 2 medium of communication; channel: 通过外交～ through diplomatic channels

取 qǔ (动) 1 take; get; fetch: ～款 draw money (from one's account). ～证 take evidence 2 aim at; seek: 自～灭亡 court destruction; dig one's own grave 3 adopt; choose: 录～ enrol; admit

取材 qǔcái (动) draw materials: 就地～ make use of local materials

取长(長)补(補)短 qǔcháng-bǔduǎn learn from others' strong points to offset one's weaknesses

取代 qǔdài (动) replace; substitute: 我们必须找人～他. We must find somebody to replace him. 进口～战略 import-substituting strategy

取道 qǔdào (动) by way of; via

取得 qǔdé (动) get; gain; obtain: ～进步 make progress. ～成功 achieve success. ～领导同意 obtain the approval of the leaders. ～一致 reach agreement

取缔 qǔdì (动) ban; outlaw

取经(經) qǔjīng (动) 1 go on a pilgrimage to India for Buddhist scriptures 2 learn from the experience of others

取决 qǔjué (动) depend on; be decided by: 你能否通过考试将～于你个人的努力. Whether or not you will pass the exam depends on your own effort.

取乐(樂) qǔlè (动) seek pleasure; find amusement: 饮酒～ drink and make merry

取名 qǔmíng (动) give a name to or be named

取闹 qǔnào (动) 1 kick up a row; make trouble: 无理～ be deliberately provocative 2 amuse oneself at sb.'s expense; make fun of

取巧 qǔqiǎo (动) resort to trickery: 投机～ seek personal gain through shady transactions

取舍(捨) qǔ-shě (动) accept or reject: 你得自己决定～. You have to make your own choice.

取向 qǔxiàng (名) orientation: 价值～ moral values; value system

取消 qǔxiāo (动) cancel; abolish: ～一次会议 cancel (or call off) a meeting. ～合同 cancel a contract. ～禁令 lift a ban. ～债务 debt cancellation

取笑 qǔxiào (动) make fun of; ridicule

娶 qǔ (动) marry (a woman); take to wife: ～亲 (of a man) get married

曲 qǔ (名) 1 music: 作～ compose music 2 song; tune; melody: 唱一支～子 sing a song

see also qū

曲调 qǔdiào (名) tune; melody

曲艺(藝) qǔyì (名) folk art forms including ballad-singing, storytelling, comic dialogues, etc.

趣 qù (名) interest; delight: 有～ interesting; amusing; delightful

趣事 qùshì (名) interesting things; fun

趣味 qùwèi (名) 1 interest; delight: 很有～ of great interest 2 taste; liking: 低级～ vulgar taste

去 qù I (动) 1 go; leave: ～乡下 go to the countryside. 他下周～巴黎. He will leave for Paris next week. 我没有～过她家. I've never been to her home. ～电话 give sb. a ring 2 remove; get rid of: ～皮 remove the skin; peel. ～掉精神负担 get the load off one's mind II (形) the one before this: ～年 last year. ～冬 last winter III 1 [used after a verb to indicate an action taking place at some distance from the speaker]: 进～ go in 2 [used before a verb to indicate that an action is to take place]: 我～考虑考虑. Let me think it over. 他自己～作主好啦! Let him decide it for himself. 我们～想想办法. We'll try to find a way out. 3 [used after a V-O construction to indicate why sb. is away]: 她买东西～了. She has gone shopping. 4 [used between a verbal phrase (or a prep. construction) and a verb (or a verbal phrase) to indicate that the former is the means while the latter is the end]: 用冷静的头脑～分析问题 analyze the problem with a cool head

去病 qùbìng (动) prevent or cure disease

去处(處) qùchù (名) 1 place to go; whereabouts 2 place; site: 一个幽静的～ a beautiful quiet place

去火 qùhuǒ reduce internal heat; relieve inflammation or fever

去世 qùshì (动) (of grown-up people) die; pass away

去向 qùxiàng (名) the direction in which sb. has gone: 不知～ be nowhere to be found

觑 qù (动) look; gaze: 面面相～ gaze at each other in astonishment or despair

圈 quān I (名) circle; ring: 飞机在空中转了两～. The airplane circled twice in the air. II (动) 1 enclose; encircle: 用篱笆把菜园～起来 enclose the vegetable garden with a fence 2 mark with a circle: ～阅文件 circle one's name on a document to show that one has read it; tick off decisions. 请把那个错字～了. Please cross out the wrong word.
 see also juān; juàn

圈定 quāndìng (动) draw a circle to show approval or selection

圈套 quāntào (名) trap: 落入～ fall or walk into a trap; play into sb.'s hands

圈子 quānzi (名) circle; ring: 站成一个～ stand in a circle. 说话不要绕～. Don't beat about the bush. 搞小～ form a clique

拳 quán (名) 1 fist 2 boxing: 打～ practise shadow boxing

拳打脚踢 quándǎ-jiǎotī cuff and kick; beat up

拳击(擊) quánjī (名) boxing; pugilism: ～台 boxing ring

Q

鬈 quán (形) curly; wavy: ～发 curly hair

鬈曲 quánqū (形) crimpy; crinkly; curly

蜷 quán (动) curl up; huddle up

蜷伏 quánfú (动) huddle up

蜷曲 quánqū (动) curl; coil; twist

颧 quán (名) cheekbone

颧骨 quángǔ (名) cheekbone

权(權) quán I (名) 1 right: 公民～ civil right. 优先～ priority. 选举和被选举～ the right to vote and stand for election. 没有发言～ have no say in the matter 2 power; authority: 立法～ legislative power. 当～ in power. 越～ overstep one's authority. 受～ be authorized (to do sth.) 3 advantageous position: 主动～ initiative. 霸～ hegemony II (动) weigh: ～衡轻重 weigh the pros and cons

权贵 quánguì (名) influential officials; bigwigs

权衡 quánhéng (动) weigh; balance: ～利弊 weigh the advantages and disadvantages

权力 quánlì (名) power; authority: 国家～机关 organ of state power. 行使～ invoke the authority. ～下放 delegate powers

权利 quánlì (名) right: 受教育的～ the right to education. 政治～ political rights

权且 quánqiě (副) for the time being: ～不用管它. Let's leave it at that.

权势(勢) quánshì (名) power and influence

权术(術) quánshù (名) political trickery: 玩弄～ play politics

权威 quánwēi (名) authority: 学术～ academic authority. ～人士 an authoritative person

权限 quánxiàn (名) limits of authority

权宜 quányí (形) expedient: ～之计 expediency

权益 quányì (名) rights and interests: 民族经济～ national economic rights and interests

全 quán I (形) 1 whole; entire: ～世界 the whole world. ～国 all over the country. ～称 full name. 昨天～天 all day yesterday 2 complete: 货物很～ have a great variety of goods. ～套书 a complete set of books. 设备齐～ be fully equipped. 东西准备～了吗? Is everything ready? 3 perfect; intact: 十～十美 be perfect in every way II (副) completely; entirely: ～错了. It's all wrong. 衣服～湿了 be wet through

全部 quánbù (名) all; whole; complete; total: 事情的～真相 the whole truth of the matter. ～开支 the total expenditure

全才 quáncái (名) a versatile person

全场(場) quánchǎng (名) 1 the whole audience; all those present 2 (sports) full-court; all-court

全称(稱) quánchēng (名) full name

全会(會) quánhuì (名) plenary session; plenum

全集 quánjí (名) complete or collected works

全家福 quánjiāfú (名) 1 a photograph of the whole family 2 hotchpotch (as a dish)

全局 quánjú (名) overall situation: ～观点 overall point of view. ～性问题 a matter of overall importance

全力 quánlì (名) with all one's strength: ～以赴 go all out; spare no effort

全貌 quánmào (名) overall picture

全面 quánmiàn (名、形) overall; all-round; comprehensive: ～崩溃 total collapse. ～性 totality. 照顾～ take into account the overall situation

全民 quánmín (名) the whole people: ～所有制 ownership by the whole people

全能 quánnéng (名) all-round: ～冠军 all-round champion

全年 quánnián (名) annual; yearly: ～收入 annual income

全盘(盤) quánpán (形) overall; comprehensive: ～考虑 give overall consideration to

全球 quánqiú (名) the whole world: ～战略 global strategy

全权(權) quánquán (名) full powers; plenary powers: 特命～大使 ambassador plenipotentiary and extraordinary. ～代表 plenipotentiary

全神贯注 quánshén guànzhù be absorbed in; be preoccupied with: ～地听着 listen with absorbing interest

全盛 quánshèng (形) flourishing; in full bloom; in the heyday: ～时代 golden age

全速 quánsù (名) full speed: ～前进 advance at full speed

全体(體) quántǐ (名) all; entire: ～起立热烈鼓掌 standing ovation. ～工作人员 the whole staff. ～辞职 resign en bloc. ～出席 full attendance. ～会议 plenary session

全心全意 quánxīn-quányì wholeheartedly; heart and soul: ～地为人民服务. Serve the people wholeheartedly.

全职 quánzhí (形) full-time: ～工作 a full-time job. ～太太 a full-time house-wife

痊 quán

痊愈 quányù (动) fully recover from an illness

诠 quán

诠释(釋) quánshì (动) annotate; make explanatory notes

泉 quán (名) spring: 温～ hot spring. 喷～ fountain

泉水 quánshuǐ (名) spring water; spring

犬 quǎn (名) dog: 猎～ hunting dog; hound. 警～ police dog

犬牙交错 quǎnyá jiāocuò jigsaw-like

券 quàn (名) ticket, coupon: 入场～ admission ticket. 国库～ treasury bond

劝(勸) quàn (动) advise; urge: ～他戒烟 advise him to give up smoking. ～他休息 urge him to take a rest

劝导(導) quàndǎo (动) advise; exhort

劝告 quàngào (动) warn; urge; exhort

劝解 quànjiě (动) 1 try to make sb. stop worrying; pacify 2 mediate

劝酒 quànjiǔ (动) urge sb. to drink (at a banquet)

劝说 quànshuō (动) try to persuade

劝阻 quànzǔ (动) dissuade sb. from doing sth.

缺 quē (动) be short of; lack: ～人 be short of personnel. 这本书～了两页. There are two pages missing from this book. 这里～新鲜水果. Fresh fruit is scarce here. ～乏信心 be lacking in confidence

缺德 quēdé (形) mean; wicked: 做～事 do sth. mean. 他这样做可真～. It's wicked of him to act like that.

缺点(點) quēdiǎn (名) shortcoming; weakness; defect

缺乏 quēfá (动) lack; be short of: ～经验 lack experience. ～自知之明 overrate one's ability

缺货 quēhuò be in short supply; be out of stock

缺斤短两(兩) quējīn-duǎnliǎng give short weight

缺口 quēkǒu (名) breach; gap: 碗边儿上碰了个～儿. The bowl has a broken edge.

缺勤 quēqín (动) be absent from work

缺少 quēshǎo (动) lack; be short of: ～雨水 lack adequate rainfall

缺失 quēshī (名) loss; lack

缺席 quēxí (动) be absent from a meeting, etc.: ～审判 trial by default

缺陷 quēxiàn (名) defect; drawback; flaw

缺心眼儿(兒) quē xīnyǎnr 1 simple-minded; scatter-brained 2 dull-witted; mentally deficient; retarded

瘸 qué (动)〈口〉be lame; limp: ～子 a lame person; cripple

阙 què (名) 1 watchtower on either side of a palace gate 2 imperial palace

却 què I (副) but; yet; however: 她很同情他，～又不知说什么好. She was

Q

full of sympathy for him, yet she didn't know what to say. II (动) 1 step back: 退～ retreat 2 decline; refuse: 推～ decline 3 [used after certain verbs to indicate the completion of an action]: 冷～ cool off. 了～一个心愿 fulfil a wish

却步 quèbù (动) step back: 不要因为困难而～. Don't flinch from difficulties.

鹊 què (名) magpie

雀 què (名) sparrow

雀斑 quèbān (名) freckle

雀跃(躍) quèyuè (动) jump for joy

确(確) què I (形) true; authentic; reliable: 正～ correct II (副) firmly; definitely: ～乎 really

确保 quèbǎo (动) ensure; guarantee: ～安全 guarantee the safety

确定 quèdìng (动) fix; determine; decide on

确立 quèlì (动) establish

确切 quèqiè (形) definite; exact; precise: 用词～ use words with precision

确认(認) quèrèn (动) affirm; acknowledge: 谨～ have the honour to confirm

确实(實) quèshí I (形) true; certain; reliable: ～性 reliability II (副) really; indeed

确信 quèxìn (动) be deeply convinced

确凿(鑿) quèzáo (形) based on truth; reliable: ～的证据 conclusive evidence. ～的事实 irrefutable facts

确诊 quèzhěn (动) make a definite diagnosis

群 qún I (名) crowd; group: 人～ crowd. 羊～ a flock of sheep II (量) group; herd; flock: 一～人 a crowd of people. 一～牛 a herd of cattle. 一～蜜蜂 a swarm of bees

群策群力 qúncè-qúnlì pool everyone's ideas and make concerted efforts

群岛(島) qúndǎo (名) archipelago

群氓 qúnméng (名) mob

群情 qúnqíng (名) public sentiment; feelings of the masses: ～鼎沸. Popular feeling ran high.

群众(衆) qúnzhòng (名) the masses: ～路线 the mass line. ～运动 mass movement; mass campaign

裙 qún (名) skirt: 围～ apron

裙带(帶) qúndài (名) connected through one's female relatives: 通过～关系 through petticoat influence

裙子 qúnzi (名) skirt

R r

然 rán I (形) 1 right; correct: 不以为～ fail to give one's blessing to 2 like that: 不～ or else; otherwise. 当～ of course II (连) but; however; nevertheless: 此事虽小，～亦不可忽视. This is a matter of no great importance, but it should by no means be ignored. III [suffix of certain adverbs and adjectives indicating the state of affairs]: 忽～ suddenly; all of a sudden. 显～ obviously. 欣～ happily

然而 rán'ér (连) yet; but; however

然后(後) ránhòu (副) then; after that; afterwards

燃 rán (动) burn; light: ～灯 light a lamp. ～香 burn incense

燃料 ránliào (名) fuel

燃眉之急 rán méi zhī jí a matter of great urgency

燃烧(燒) ránshāo (动、名) 1 burn: ～弹 incendiary bomb 2 combustion

燃脂 ránzhī I (动) burn fat II (名) fat burning

染 rǎn (动) 1 dye: 把头发～黑 have one's hair dyed black 2 catch (a disease); acquire (a bad habit, etc.); contaminate: 感～风寒 catch a cold. 污～ pollution. 一尘不～ not soiled by a speck of dust; spotless

染料 rǎnliào (名) dyestuff; dye: 活性～ reactive dye

染指 rǎnzhǐ (动) take a share of sth. one is not entitled to; have a finger in every pie

冉 rǎn 〈书〉 slowly

冉冉 rǎnrǎn (副) slowly; gradually

嚷 rāng

see also rǎng

嚷嚷 rāngrang (动) 1 shout; yell 2 make widely known

瓤 ráng (名) pulp; flesh; pith: 西瓜～ the pulp (or flesh) of a watermelon

R

壤 rǎng (名) 1 soil: 沃～ fertile soil; rich soil 2 earth: 天～ heaven and earth 3 area: 穷乡僻～ a remote and hardly accessible village

嚷 rǎng (动) shout; yell; make an uproar: 别～了! Stop yelling. *or* Don't make such a noise.
see also rāng

让(讓) ràng I (动) 1 give way; give in; give up: ～步 make concessions. 请～一～. Excuse me. 他比你小,要～着他点儿. You should humour him a little bit since he is younger. 2 let sb. have sth. at a fair price: 如果你急需,我可以把我的新车～给你. I can let you have my new car (at cost price) if you need one badly. 3 invite; offer: ～座 offer one's seat to sb. 把大家～进屋里. Ask all of them to come in. 4 let; allow: ～我想想. Let me think it over. 妈妈不～他去. Mother won't let him go. 对不起,～你久等了. Sorry to have kept you waiting. II (介) [used in a passive sentence to introduce the agent]: 她的脸～蜜蜂叮了. She was stung on the cheek by a bee.

让步 ràngbù (动) make a concession; give in; give way: 作出必要的～ make necessary concessions

让开(開) ràngkāi (动) get out of the way; step aside; make way

让路 rànglù (动) make way for sb. or sth.

让位 ràngwèi (动) 1 resign sovereign authority; abdicate 2 offer one's seat to sb.; step aside to make way for sb. else

让座 ràngzuò (动) 1 offer (or give up) one's seat to sb. 2 invite guests to be seated

饶(饒) ráo I (动) have mercy on; forgive: 求～ beg for mercy. 这回～了我吧! Let me off this time, please! II (形) rich; plentiful: ～有风趣 full of wit and humour

饶命 ráomìng (动) spare sb.'s life

饶舌 ráoshé (形) garrulous

饶恕 ráoshù (动) forgive; pardon

扰(擾) rǎo (动) disturb; harass

扰乱(亂) rǎoluàn (动) create confusion; disturb: ～治安 create social disturbances

扰民 rǎomín (动) disturb residents

绕(繞) rào (动) 1 wind; coil: ～线圈 wind wire into a coil 2 move round; circle: 老鹰在空中～着圈儿飞. The eagle is flying around in the sky. 3 bypass; go round: ～过暗礁 bypass hidden reefs

绕道 ràodào (动) make a detour

绕口令 ràokǒulìng (名) tongue-twister

绕圈子 rào quānzi circle; go round and round

绕弯(彎)子 rào wānzi beat about the bush

绕嘴 ràozuǐ (形) (of a sentence, etc.) be difficult to articulate: ～字 tongue-twister

惹 rě (动) 1 invite or ask for (sth. undesirable): ～麻烦 ask for trouble. ～是非 stir up trouble 2 offend; provoke: 我～不起他. I cannot afford to offend him. 他可不是好～的. He's not a man to be trifled with. 3 attract; cause: ～人注意 attract attention. 不要～人讨厌. Don't make a nuisance of yourself.

惹祸(禍) rěhuò (动) court disaster

惹事 rěshì (动) stir up trouble

惹是生非 rěshì-shēngfēi create trouble

热(熱) rè I (形) 1 hot: 屋里太～. It's too hot in the room. ～腾腾 steaming hot 2 ardent; warmed: ～情 warm-hearted. ～爱 ardent love II (名) 1 heat: 摩擦生～. Friction generates heat. 2 fever: 发～ run a fever 3 rush; craze: 淘金～ gold rush. 排球～ volleyball craze III (动) heat (up): 把菜～一下 heat up the dish

热忱 rèchén (名) zeal; enthusiasm and devotion: 满腔～ full of enthusiasm

热诚 rèchéng (形) warm and sincere: ～的爱戴 ardent love and devotion

热带(帶) rèdài (名) the tropics: ～病学 tropical medicine. ～植物 tropical plants. ～雨林 rainforest

热点 rèdiǎn (名) hotspot; hot issue

热乎乎 rèhūhū (形) warm

热火朝天 rèhuǒ cháotiān bustling with activity; in full swing: 生产～. Production is in full swing.

热辣辣 rèlālā (形) burning hot; scorching: 他觉得脸上～的. He felt his cheeks burning.

热浪 rèlàng (名) heatwave

热泪(淚) rèlèi (名) hot tears; tears of joy, sorrow or gratitude: ～盈眶 one's eyes brimming with tears

热恋(戀) rèliàn (动) fall head over heels in love

热量 rèliàng (名) quantity of heat

热烈 rèliè (形) warm; enthusiastic; ardent: ～的欢迎 warm welcome

热卖(賣) rèmài (动) sell like hot cakes: ～商品 very popular goods

热门(門) rèmén (名) in great demand; popular: ～货 goods which are in great demand. ～话题 a subject of great topical interest; a topical subject

热闹 rènào I (形) lively; bustling with noise and excitement: 交易会很～. The fair was bustling with activity. II (名) fun: 让我们看看～. Let's watch the fun. III (动) liven up; have a jolly time: ～一番 have fun; have a jolly time

热气(氣) rèqì (名) steam; heat: ～腾腾 most enthusiastic

热钱 rèqián (名) hot money

热切 rèqiè (形) fervent; earnest: ～的愿望 earnest wish

热情 rèqíng I (名) enthusiasm; zeal; warmth: 对工作充满～ be full of enthusiasm for one's work II (形) warm; enthusiastic; fervent: ～的支持 enthusiastic support

热水袋 rèshuǐdài (名) hot-water bottle (or bag)

热线 rèxiàn (名) hotline

R

热心 rèxīn (形) warm-hearted; enthusiastic: ～肠 warm-heartedness; a warm-hearted (or sympathetic) and helpful person

热血 rèxuè (名) spirit of devotion to a righteous cause: ～沸腾 actuated by righteous indignation

热中 rèzhōng (动) 1 hanker after; crave 2 be fond of; be keen on

人 rén (名) 1 human being; man; person; people: 男～ man. 女～ woman. 大～ adult. 中国～ Chinese 2 a person engaged in a particular activity: 军～ soldier. 工～ worker. 客～ guest. 主～ host. 领导～ leader. 监护～ guardian 3 people; other people: 助～为乐 consider it a pleasure to be of service to others 4 personality; character: 为～老实忠厚 honest and sincere by nature 5 everybody; each: ～所共知 as is known to all

人才 réncái (名) 1 a talented person; talent; qualified (trained) personnel: ～出众 have outstanding ability. ～济济 a galaxy of talent. ～外流 brain drain 2 handsome appearance: 一表～ be rather good-looking

人称(稱) rénchēng (名) person: 第一～ the first person. ～代词 personal pronoun

人道 réndào I (名) humanity; human sympathy II (形) human; humane: 不～ inhuman. ～主义 humanitarianism

人丁 réndīng (名) population; number of people in a family: ～兴旺 have a growing family; have a flourishing population

人定胜(勝)天 rén dìng shèng tiān man can conquer nature

人格 réngé (名) 1 personality; character; moral quality: ～高尚 be a person of noble character or moral integrity. 法律～ legal personality. 双重～ dual personality 2 human dignity

人工 réngōng I (形) man-made; artificial: ～呼吸 artificial respiration. ～流产 induced abortion. ～降雨 artificial rainfall II (名) 1 manual work; work done by hand 2 manpower: 修这座水库需要多少～? How many man-days will be needed to build this reservoir?

人和 rénhé (名) popular support: 天时、地利、～ favorable climatic, geographical and human conditions

人寰 rénhuán (名)〈书〉human world; the world

人迹 rénjì (名) vestiges of human presence; traces of human inhabitation

人际(際)关(關)系(係) rénjì guānxì (名) interpersonal relationships

人家 rénjiā (名) 1 household: 三户～ three households 2 family: 殷实～ a well-to-do family

人家 rénjia (代) 1 [used to refer to people other than oneself] other people: 别管～怎么说 take no notice of what other people might say. 东西总是～的好. The grass is always greener on the other side of the hill. 2 [used to refer to a certain person or people]: 我想我应该去,这个晚会是～专门为我举办的. I think I ought to go since they have arranged this party especially for me. 你把东西快给～送回去吧! You had better send it back to him! 3 [used to refer to the speaker himself]: ～等你等了半天了. I've been waiting for you all this while.

人间 rénjiān (名) the human world; man's world; the world: ～奇迹 a man-made miracle. ～地狱 a hell on earth. ～天堂 heaven on earth

人均 rénjūn (动) per capita

人口 rénkǒu (名) **1** population: ～普查 census. ～爆炸 population explosion **2** number of people in a family: 家里～不多 only a few people in one's family

人来(來)疯 rénláifēng (of a child) show off his liveliness before visitors

人类(類) rénlèi (名) mankind; humanity: ～征服自然的斗争 man's struggle to conquer nature. ～学 anthropology. ～起源 origin of mankind

人力 rénlì (名) manpower; labour power: ～资源 human resources

人马(馬) rénmǎ (名) **1** forces; troops **2** staff; set-up

人们 rénmen (名) people; men: ～都说他不错. People all speak well of him.

人民 rénmín (名) the people: ～币 *Renminbi* (RMB), currency of the People's Republic of China

人命 rénmìng (名) human life: ～关天的大事 a matter of life and death

人品 rénpǐn (名) moral character: ～很好 be a person of good moral character

人气(氣) rénqì (名) popularity: ～急升 quickly become popular; 聚敛～ make sth. attractive and popular

人情 rénqíng (名) **1** human feelings; sympathy; sensibilities: 不近～ unreasonable; contrary to the ways of the world **2** favour: 做个～ do sb. a favour **3** human relationship: ～世故 worldly wisdom. ～之常 natural and normal practice in human relationship

人权(權) rénquán (名) human rights

人群 rénqún (名) crowd

人人 rénrén (名) everybody; everyone

人山人海 rénshān-rénhǎi huge crowds of people

人蛇 rénshé (名) illegal immigrant

人身 rénshēn (名) human body; person: ～攻击 personal attack. ～安全 personal safety. ～伤害 personal injury

人参(參) rénshēn (名) ginseng

人生 rénshēng (名) life: ～观 outlook on life. ～哲学 philosophy of life

人生地不熟 rén shēng dì bù shú be unfamiliar with the place and the people; be a stranger in a strange place

人士 rénshì (名) personage; public figure: 消息灵通～ well-informed sources. 知名～ well-known public figures; celebrities. 文化界～ cultural circles

人世 rénshì (名) this world; the world: ～沧桑 vicissitudes of life

人事 rénshì (名) **1** occurrences in human life **2** personnel matters: ～部门 personnel department. ～调动 transfer of personnel **3** consciousness of the outside world: 不省～ lose consciousness **4** ways of the world: 不懂～ unacquainted with the ways of the world **5** anything that a person is capable of: 尽～ do what is humanly possible in time of adversity

人手 rénshǒu (名) manpower; hand: ～不够 short of hands

人寿(壽)保险(險) rénshòu bǎoxiǎn life insurance

人体炸弹 réntǐ zhàdàn suicide bomb

人为(爲) rénwéi I (形) artificial: ～的障碍 an artificial barrier II (名) human effort: 事在～. Everything depends upon human effort.

人文 rénwén (名) humanity: ～学科 humanities; liberal arts. ～主义 humanism. ～景观 places of cultural interest

人物 rénwù (名) **1** figure; personage: 历史～ a historical figure. 大～ a dignitary. 小～ a nobody; a nonentity **2** character (in a literary work): 典型～ typical character. ～塑造 characterization

人心 rénxīn (名) popular feeling; the will of the people: 得～ enjoy popular support. 振奋～ boost popular morale. 大快～ most gratifying to the popular masses. 收买～ curry favour with the public. 深入～ strike root in the hearts of the people

人行道 rénxíngdào (名) pavement; sidewalk

人行横道 rénxíng héngdào (名) pedestrian crossing; zebra crossing

人性 rénxìng (名) human nature; humanity

人选(選) rénxuǎn (名) candidate; person properly chosen (for a job)

人烟 rényān (名) inhabitants: ～稀少(稠密) be sparsely (densely) populated

人影 rényǐng (名) **1** the shadow of a human figure **2** the trace of a person's presence; figure: 她看见一个～在黑暗中消失了. She caught sight of a figure disappearing into the darkness. 我等了半天,连个～也不见. I waited and waited but not a single soul turned up.

人员 rényuán (名) personnel; staff

人缘 rényuán (名) relations with people; popularity: ~好 on good terms with everybody

人造 rénzào (形) man-made; artificial: ~纤维 artificial fibre. ~革 imitation leather. ~橡胶 synthetic rubber. ~黄油 margarine. ~卫星 man-made satellite

人证 rénzhèng (名) testimony of a witness

人之常情 rén zhī chángqíng the way of the world; the normal practice in human relationships

人质(質) rénzhì (名) hostage: 作~ be held as a hostage; take sb. hostage

人种(種) rénzhǒng (名) ethnic group; race: ~学 ethnology

仁 rén I (形) benevolent II (名) 1 benevolence: ~至义尽 have done everything possible in terms of traditional ethical code 2 kernel: 核桃~ walnut meat

仁爱(愛) rén'ài (名) kind-heartedness

仁慈 réncí (名) benevolence; mercy

仁义(義)道德 rényì-dàodé virtue and morality

仁者见(見)仁,智者见智 rénzhě jiàn rén, zhìzhě jiàn zhì different people have different views; opinions differ

荏 rěn

荏苒 rěnrǎn 〈书〉 (of time) pass quickly or imperceptibly

忍 rěn (动) 1 endure; tolerate; put up with: ~着点儿,别为了一点儿小事发火. Be patient. Don't lose your temper over trivial matters. 2 be hard-hearted enough to; have the heart to: 残~ cruel; ruthless

忍不住 rěnbuzhù unable to bear; cannot help (doing sth.): ~笑了起来 can't help laughing

忍耐 rěnnài (动) exercise patience; restrain oneself

忍气(氣)吞声(聲) rěnqì-tūnshēng endure humiliation in silence

忍让(讓) rěnràng (动) be forbearing and conciliatory

忍辱负重 rěn rǔ fù zhòng submit to humiliation for the sake of an important mission that one feels obliged to fulfil

忍受 rěnshòu (动) bear; endure: ~艰难困苦 endure hardships

忍痛 rěntòng (副) very reluctantly

忍无(無)可忍 rěn wú kě rěn be provoked beyond endurance

忍心 rěnxīn (动) have the heart to; be hardhearted enough to: 我不~看着她受苦. I don't have the heart to watch her writhing with pain.

认(認) rèn (动) 1 recognize; identify: 你变多了,我都~不出你了! You've changed so much that I could hardly recognize you! 他的字真难~. His scrawl is hardly legible. 2 admit; recognize: ~输 admit defeat. 否~ deny

认出 rènchū (动) recognize; make out; identify

认错 rèncuò (动) admit one's mistake

认得 rènde (动) know; recognize: 这人你~吗? Do you know this man? 我已经认不得他了. I could no longer recognize him.

认定 rèndìng (动) be deeply convinced; set one's mind on

认购(購) rèngòu (动) offer to buy; subscribe: ~公债 subscribe for (government) bonds

认可 rènkě (动) approve: 点头~ nod approval

认领 rènlǐng (动) claim (lost property)

认清 rènqīng (动) see clearly: ~当前形势 acquaint oneself with the current situation

认生 rènshēng (动) (of a child) be shy with strangers

认识(識) rènshi I (动) 1 know; recognize: 我听说过他,但我不~他. I know of him, but I don't know him. 2 understand: ~自己的错误 realize one's error II (名) understanding; knowledge; cognition: 感性(理性)~ perceptual (rational) knowledge. ~水平 level of understanding

认输 rènshū (动) admit defeat; throw in the towel; give up

认同 rèntóng (动) identify with

认为(爲) rènwéi (动) think; consider: 我~你这样做不对. I don't think it's right to act the way you do.

认账(賬) rènzhàng (动) admit what one has said or done

认真 rènzhēn I (形) conscientious; earnest; serious: 工作~ be conscientious in one's work II (动) take seriously; take to heart: 别对这件事~. Don't take the matter seriously.

认证 rènzhèng I (动) legalize; attest; authenticate II (名) attestation; authentication

认罪 rènzuì (动) plead guilty

任 rèn I (动) 1 appoint: 公司新～的经理 the newly appointed manager of the company 2 assume a post; take up a job: ～教 be a teacher 3 let; allow: 有很多优质衣料～你挑选. There is a beautiful collection of dress materials for you to choose from. II (名) official post; office: 上～ assume office. 离～ leave office. ～内 during one's term (or tenure) of office. 前～ one's predecessor III (量) [for official terms]: 做过两～大使 have twice been ambassador

任何 rènhé (代) any; whatever: 没有～希望. There isn't any hope. 他没有～理由不去. He has no reason whatsoever not to go.

任劳(勞)任怨 rènláo-rènyuàn work hard regardless of unfair criticism or unjustifiable complaints

任免 rèn-miǎn (动) appoint and dismiss: ～事项 appointments and removals

任命 rènmìng (动) appoint: ～他为会议主席 appoint him chairman of the meeting. ～状 letter of appointment; commission

任凭(憑) rènpíng I (介) at one's convenience; at one's discretion: 这件事～他去作主吧. I'll leave the matter to his discretion. II (连) no matter (how, what, etc.): ～我怎么努力,他总是不满意. No matter how hard I tried, it just wouldn't please him.

任期 rènqī (名) term of office; tenure of office: 每届总统～四年. The president is elected for a term of four years.

任人唯贤(賢) rèn rén wéi xián appoint people on their merits; meritocracy

任务(務) rènwu (名) task; mission; assignment

任性 rènxìng (形) wilful; self-willed

任意 rènyì (副) wantonly; wilfully: ～行动 unrestricted action. ～畅谈 talk freely. ～涨价 arbitrarily raise prices; jack up the price

任职(職) rènzhí (动) hold a post; be in office: 在政府部门～ work (or hold a post) in a government institution

任重道远(遠) rènzhòng-dàoyuǎn the burden is heavy and the road is long—shoulder heavy responsibilities

妊(姙) rèn (动) be pregnant

妊娠 rènshēn (名) gestation; pregnancy

刃 rèn (名) 1 the edge of a knife, sword, etc.; blade: 刀～ knife blade. 那把刀卷～了. The edge of that knife is turned. 2 sword; knife: 利～ sharp sword. 白～战 bayonet fighting

刃具 rènjù (名) cutting tool

韧(靭) rèn (形) pliable but strong; tenacious

韧带(帶) rèndài (名) ligament

韧性 rènxìng (名) toughness; tenacity

扔 rēng (动) 1 throw; toss; cast: ～手榴弹 throw a hand-grenade 2 throw away; cast aside: 把它～了吧. Throw it away. 请不要乱～果皮、纸屑. Please do not litter. 他早把这事～在脑后了. He's completely forgotten about it.

仍 réng (副) still; yet: 他的病势～不见好. He is not any better. ～须努力 must continue to work hard

仍旧(舊) réngjiù (副) as before; still; yet: 莎士比亚的故居保存得～和当年一样. Shakespeare's cottage is kept as it was in his lifetime. 他～是老样子. He still looks the same.

仍然 réngrán (副) still; yet

日 rì (名) 1 sun: ～出 sunrise. ～落 sunset 2 daytime: ～～夜夜 day and night 3 day: 多～不见. Haven't seen you for ages. 我们改～再谈. Let's talk about it some other day (or time). 4 daily; every day: ～趋强壮 grow stronger with each passing day. 产量～增. Output is going up every day.

日报(報) rìbào (名) daily paper: 《人民日报》 *Renmin Ribao* (*the People's Daily*)

日常 rìcháng (形) day-to-day; everyday: ～工作 daily work; routine duties. ～生活 everyday life. ～事务 routine business

日场(場) rìchǎng (名) matinée

日程 rìchéng (名) programme; schedule: 访问～ itinerary of a visit. 工作～ work schedule; programme of work. 会议～ agenda

日光 rìguāng (名) sunlight: ～浴 sun-bath

日光灯(燈) rìguāngdēng (名) fluorescent lamp

日积(積)月累 rìjī-yuèlěi accumulate over a long period

日记 rìjì (名) diary: 记～ keep a diary

R

日渐 rìjiàn (副) with each passing day; day by day

日久 rìjiǔ with the passing of time: ～天长 in (the) course of time; with the passage of time. ～见人心 It takes time to know a person well.

日历(曆) rìlì (名) calendar

日暮途穷(窮) rìmù-túqióng come to a dead end

日期 rìqī (名) date: 出发的～ departure date. 信的～是哪一天? When is the letter dated?

日新月异(異) rìxīn-yuèyì change with each passing day; make rapid progress

日以继(繼)夜 rì yǐ jì yè night and day; round the clock

日益 rìyì (副) increasingly; day by day: 起到～重要的作用 play an increasingly important role. ～改进 improve day by day

日用 rìyòng (形) of everyday use: ～必需品 daily necessities. ～品 basic commodities

日照 rìzhào (名) sunshine

日子 rìzi (名) 1 day; date: 定～ fix a date 2 time (counted by days): 他离家有些～了. He's been away from home for some time. 这些～她有些不舒服. She hasn't been feeling well recently. 3 life; livelihood: 幸福的～ happy days. 最近我的～不好过. I have a hard time these days.

容 róng I (动) 1 hold; contain: 我觉得很窘,真有点儿无地自～. I felt so embarrassed that I did not know what to do with myself. 2 tolerate: 宽～ be tolerant. 大量～人 magnanimous 3 allow; permit: 不～怀疑 without doubt. 此事不～迟延. This matter admits of no delay. II (名) looks; appearance: 笑～ a smiling face

容光焕发(發) róngguāng huànfā glowing with health; have a radiant face

容积(積) róngjī (名) volume

容量 róngliàng (名) capacity

容貌 róngmào (名) appearance; looks

容纳 róngnà (动) hold; have a capacity of: 这个球场可以～十万人. The stadium can hold 100,000 people.

容器 róngqì (名) vessel; container

容情 róngqíng (动) [usu. used in a negative sentence] show mercy

容人 róngrén (动) regard people with kindly tolerance; be tolerant towards others

容忍 róngrěn (动) tolerate; put up with: 我们不能～这种态度. We can't tolerate this attitude.

容身 róngshēn (动) shelter oneself; make a living: 无～之地 have nowhere to rest

容许 róngxǔ (动) permit; allow: 局势的恶化不～我们再等待了. Faced with the worsening situation, we can't afford to wait any longer.

容易 róngyì (形) 1 easy: 写简化字比繁体字～得多. Simplified characters are much easier than complicated forms. 2 likely: 这屋顶雨天～漏. The roof is apt to leak when it rains.

溶 róng (动) dissolve: ～液 solution

溶化 rónghuà (动) dissolve

溶剂(劑) róngjì (名) solvent

溶解 róngjiě (动) dissolve: ～度 solubility

熔 róng (动) melt

熔点(點) róngdiǎn (名) melting (or fusing) point

熔化 rónghuà (动) melt

熔岩(巖) róngyán (名) lava

戎 róng (名)〈书〉army; military affairs: ～马生涯 army life

绒 róng (名) 1 fine hair; down: 鸭～ eiderdown. 羽～衣 down-padded anorak 2 cloth with a soft nap: 天鹅～ velvet. 灯芯～ corduroy. 法兰～ flannel

绒毛 róngmáo (名) fine hair; down; villus

绒线(綫) róngxiàn (名) 1 floss for embroidery 2 knitting wool: ～衫 woollen sweater

绒衣 róngyī (名) sweat shirt

荣(榮) róng I (名) honour; glory II (形) 1 honourable; glorious: ～获第一名 win first prize 2 prosperous; flourishing: 欣欣向～ flourishing; thriving

荣华(華)富贵 rónghuá-fùguì glory, splendour, wealth and rank

荣获(獲) rónghuò (动) get or win sth. as an honour

荣辱 róng-rǔ (名) honour or disgrace: ～与共 (of friends) share honour or disgrace, weal or woe

荣幸 róngxìng (形) honoured: 感到～ feel honoured

荣耀 róngyào (名) honour; glory

荣誉(譽) róngyù (名) honour; credit: 为祖国争～ win honour for one's country. 爱护公司的～ cherish the good name of the company

茸 róng I (形) fine and soft; downy II (名) young pilose antler

融 róng (动) **1** melt; thaw **2** blend; fuse: 水乳交～ blend as well as milk and water; be in perfect harmony

融合 rónghé (动) fuse; merge: 铜与锡的～ the fusion of copper and tin

融化 rónghuà (动) melt; thaw: 冰雪开始～. The snow and ice are beginning to thaw.

融会(會)贯通 rónghuì guàntōng gain thorough understanding through comprehensive study of the subject

融解 róngjiě (动) melt; become liquid

融洽 róngqià (形) harmonious: 关系～ be on friendly terms. 气氛～ harmonious atmosphere

融通 róngtōng (动) circulate: ～资金 circulate funds

融资 róngzī (动) financing

冗 rǒng (形) superfluous; redundant: ～词赘句 redundant words and expressions

冗长(長) rǒngcháng (形) lengthy; longwinded: ～的讲演 a lengthy speech

冗员 rǒngyuán (名) redundant personnel

冗杂(雜) rǒngzá (形) (of affairs) miscellaneous; multifarious; complicated

柔 róu (形) **1** soft; flexible: ～嫩 supple and tender **2** gentle; mild: 温～ gentle and tender. ～中有刚 firm but gentle; an iron hand in a velvet glove

柔道 róudào (名) judo

柔和 róuhé (形) soft; gentle; mild: 光线～ soft light. 颜色～ a soft colour. ～的声音 a gentle voice

柔情 róuqíng (名) tender feelings; tenderness: ～蜜意 tender affection

柔软 róuruǎn (形) soft; lithe: ～的动作 lithe movements

柔弱 róuruò (形) weak; delicate: 身体～ in delicate health; weak; frail

揉 róu (动) rub: ～眼睛 rub one's eyes. ～面 knead dough

揉搓 róucuo (动) rub; knead

蹂 róu

蹂躏 róulìn (动) trample on; ravage: ～人权 trample on human rights

肉 ròu (名) **1** meat; flesh: 瘦～ lean meat. 猪～ pork. 牛～ beef. 羊～ mutton **2** pulp; flesh (of fruit): 果～ pulp of fruit

肉搏 ròubó (动) fight hand-to-hand: ～战 hand-to-hand combat; bayonet fighting

肉麻 ròumá (形) nauseating; sickening; disgusting

肉末 ròumò (名) minced meat

肉松(鬆) ròusōng (名) dried fluffy meat

肉体(體) ròutǐ (名) the human body; flesh

肉眼 ròuyǎn (名) naked eye: ～看不到 be invisible to the naked eye

肉欲 ròuyù (名) carnal desire

蠕 rú (动) wriggle; squirm

蠕动(動) rúdòng (动) wriggle; squirm

儒 rú (名) **1** Confucianism; Confucianist **2** scholar; learned man

儒家 rújiā (名) the Confucian school

如 rú I (动) **1** be like or similar to; as if: 了～指掌 know sth. like the back of one's hand **2** be as good as [used in negative sentences only]: 我不～他. I cannot compare with him. **3** in accordance with; as: ～期偿还 return sth. in due time II (连) if: ～不同意,请告诉我. If you don't agree, please let me know.

如常 rúcháng (动) as usual: 早起～ get up early as usual

如出一辙 rú chū yī zhé be exactly the same

如此 rúcǐ (代) so; such; in this way: ～勇敢 so courageous. 事已～,后悔也是枉然. As it is, regret won't help matters.

如法炮制(製) rú fǎ páozhì follow the prescribed rules; follow a set pattern

R

如故 rúgù (动) **1** as before: 依然～ remain the same as before **2** like old friends: 一见～ feel like old friends at the first meeting

如果 rúguǒ (连) if; in case; in the event of: ～你钱不够,我可以借些给你. If you are short of money, I can lend you some. ～我是你,我就接受邀请. If I were you, I would accept the invitation.

如何 rúhé (代) how; what: 你觉得这本小说～? How do you like this novel? 他不知～是好. He didn't know what to do.

如虎添翼 rú hǔ tiān yì like adding wings to a tiger; be further strengthened

如火如荼 rúhuǒ-rútú like a raging fire: 争取民族独立的斗争～,迅猛发展. The struggle for national independence spread like wildfire.

如饥(饑)似渴 rújī-sìkě voraciously; eagerly

如胶(膠)似漆 rújiāo-sìqī be deeply attached to each other

如今 rújīn (名) now; nowadays: ～人们对业余生活有更迫切的愿望. People nowadays have a stronger desire for spare-time activities.

如狼似虎 rúláng-sìhǔ as ferocious as wolves and tigers; like beasts of prey

如临(臨)大敌(敵) rú lín dàdí as if faced with a formidable foe

如梦(夢)初醒 rú mèng chū xǐng as if awakening from a dream

如期 rúqī (副) as scheduled: ～完成 fulfilled on schedule

如实(實) rúshí (副) strictly according to the facts: ～汇报情况 report exactly as things stand

如释(釋)重负 rú shì zhòngfù as if relieved of a heavy load

如数(數) rúshù (副) exactly the number or amount: ～偿还 pay back in full

如数(數)家珍 rú shǔ jiāzhēn as if enumerating one's family treasures; show thorough familiarity with a subject

如同 rútóng (动) like; as: 灯火通明,～白昼 be brilliantly lit as if it were daytime

如下 rúxià (动) as follows: 全文～. The full text follows.

如意 rúyì (形) as one wishes: 称心～ ideal; after one's own heart. ～算盘 wishful thinking

如鱼(魚)得水 rú yú dé shuǐ feel just like fish in water; be in congenial company or do congenial work

如愿(願) rúyuàn (动) achieve one's goal: ～以偿 have one's wish fulfilled; achieve (or obtain) what one wishes

如坐针毡(氈) rú zuò zhēnzhān be on pins and needles; be on tenterhooks

汝 rǔ (代)〈书〉you

辱 rǔ I (名) disgrace; dishonour: 羞～ humiliation; terrible disgrace II (动) bring disgrace (or humiliation) to; insult

辱骂 rǔmà (动) abuse; call sb. names

辱没 rǔmò (动) bring disgrace to; be unworthy of

乳 rǔ (名) 1 breast 2 milk: 炼～ condensed milk 3 newborn (animal); sucking: ～牛 milk cow

乳白 rǔbái (形) milk white; cream colour: ～玻璃 opal glass

乳房 rǔfáng (名) 1 breast 2 (of a cow, goat, etc.) udder

乳酪 rǔlào (名) cheese

乳名 rǔmíng (名) child's pet name

乳母 rǔmǔ (名) wet nurse

乳牛 rǔniú (名) dairy cattle; milch cow

乳头(頭) rǔtóu (名) nipple; teat

乳臭未干(乾) rǔxiù wèi gān be young and inexperienced; be wet behind the ears

乳汁 rǔzhī (名) milk

褥 rù (名) mattress

褥单(單) rùdān (名) bed sheet

褥子 rùzi (名) cotton padded mattress

入 rù I (动) 1 enter: ～境 enter a country. ～场券 admission ticket. 列～议程 put on the agenda 2 join; become a member of: ～党 join the party II (名) income: ～不敷出 income falling short of expenditure; unable to make ends meet

入超 rùchāo (名) unfavourable balance of trade; import surplus

入耳 rù'ěr (形) pleasant to the ear: 不堪～ (of language) offensive to the ear

入股 rùgǔ (动) buy a share; become a shareholder

入伙 rùhuǒ (动) join a gang; join in a partnership

入境 rùjìng (动) enter a country: ～签证 entry visa

入口 rùkǒu I (动) enter the mouth II (名) entrance: 剧院～处 entrance to a theatre

入库 rùkù (动) be put in storage; be laid up

入殓(殮) rùliàn (动) encoffin

入门(門) rùmén (动) cross the threshold; learn the rudiments of a subject

入迷 rùmí (形) be fascinated; be enchanted; be completely absorbed

入侵 rùqīn (动) invade; intrude

入神 rùshén (形) 1 be entranced: 听得～ listen spellbound 2 superb; marvellous: 这幅画画得真是～. This painting is really a masterpiece.

入时(時) rùshí (形) fashionable; à la mode

入手 rùshǒu (动) start with; take as the point of departure: 不知从何～ not know where to start

入睡 rùshuì (动) go to sleep; fall asleep

入土 rùtǔ (动) be buried; be interred: 快～了 have one foot in the grave

入围 rùwéi (动) qualify for: ～赛 qualifying match (or contest). 已～ become a

qualifier
入伍 rùwǔ (动) enlist; join the army
入席 rùxí (动) take one's seat at a banquet, ceremony, etc.
入学(學) rùxué (动) **1** start school: ～年龄 school age **2** enter a school: ～考试 entrance examination
入狱(獄) rùyù (动) be put in prison; be thrown into jail

软 ruǎn (形) **1** soft; flexible: 绸子摸起来很～. Silk feels soft. **2** soft; mild; gentle: 别对他太～. Don't be too soft with him. **3** weak; feeble: 两腿发～. One's legs feel weak. **4** easily moved or influenced: 心～ tender-hearted. 手～ be soft-hearted in handling matters
软钉子 ruǎndīngzi (名) a soft nail—a mild (or tactful) refusal or refutation
软膏 ruǎngāo (名) ointment; paste
软骨头(頭) ruǎngǔtou (名) a spineless person; a coward
软化 ruǎnhuà (动) soften; win over by soft tactics
软和 ruǎnhuo (形)〈口〉soft: ～的大衣 a soft coat
软件 ruǎnjiàn (名) (of computers) software
软禁 ruǎnjìn (动) put sb. under house arrest
软绵绵 ruǎnmiánmián (形) **1** soft: 这支歌～的. This song is too sentimental. **2** weak: 她病好了,但身体仍然～的. She's recovered but still weak.
软木 ruǎnmù (名) cork: ～塞 cork (as a stopper)
软驱(驅) ruǎnqū (名) floppy disk drive
软弱 ruǎnruò (形) weak; feeble; flabby: ～无能 weak and incompetent. ～可欺 be weak and easy to bully
软席 ruǎnxí (名) soft seat or berth (on a train)
软硬兼施 ruǎn-yìng jiān shī use both hard and soft tactics
软着陆(陸) ruǎnzhuólù soft landing

蕊 ruǐ (名) stamen or pistil: 雄～ stamen. 雌～ pistil

瑞 ruì (形) auspicious; lucky
瑞雪 ruìxuě (名) timely snow

锐 ruì **1** sharp; keen: 尖～ sharp; keen. ～意改革 be keen on reforms **2** vigour; fighting spirit: 养精蓄～ conserve strength and energy
锐不可当(當) ruì bùkě dāng be irresistible
锐角 ruìjiǎo (名) acute angle
锐利 ruìlì (形) sharp; keen: ～的匕首 a sharp dagger. 目光～ sharp-eyed. ～的笔锋 a sharp pen; a vigorous style
锐敏 ruìmǐn (形) sensitive; keen: ～的嗅觉 a keen sense of smell
锐气(氣) ruìqì (名) dash; drive: 挫敌～ deflate the enemy's arrogance

闰 rùn
闰年 rùnnián (名) leap year
闰月 rùnyuè (名) leap month

润 rùn I (形) moist; sleek: 湿～ moist. 嗓音圆～ a sweet mellow voice II (动) **1** moisten; lubricate **2** embellish; touch up III (名) profit; benefit: 利～ profit
润肤 rùnfū (动) moisturise the skin: ～露 body lotion; skin softener
润滑 rùnhuá (动) lubricate: ～油 lubricating oil; lubrication oil
润色 rùnsè (动) polish (a piece of writing, etc.); touch up

若 ruò I (动) like; seem; as if: ～有所思 seem lost in thought. ～隐～现 appear dimly visible II (连) if: 他～能来,我们一定热烈欢迎. If he could come, we would give him a warm welcome.
若非 ruòfēi (连) if not: ～他提醒,我早就把它忘得一干二净了. I might have forgotten all about the matter if he had not reminded me of it.
若干 ruògān (数) a certain number: ～年 a number of years. ～次 several times
若是 ruòshì (连) if
若无(無)其事 ruò wú qí shì act as if nothing had happened; keep perfectly calm

弱 ruò (形) **1** weak; feeble: 年老体～ feeble from old age. 由～变强 go from weakness to strength **2** inferior: 她能力～. She is not very capable. **3** a little less than: 五分之一～ a little less than one fifth
弱不禁风(風) ruò bù jīn fēng be in extremely delicate health; look very fragile
弱点(點) ruòdiǎn (名) weakness; weak point
弱化 ruòhuà (动) weaken: ～形式 weak form
弱肉强食 ruòròu-qiángshí the law of the jungle
弱势(勢) ruòshì (形) disadvantage; going weak: 处于～ be in a disadvantageous position. ～群体 the disadvantaged
弱项 ruòxiàng (名) weak point; vulnerabi-

lity
弱小 ruòxiǎo (形) small and weak: ～民族 small and weak nations
弱智 ruòzhì (形) mentally deficient; retarded: ～儿童 a retarded child

S s

撒 sā (动) 1 let go; cast: ～网 cast a net. 把手～开 let go one's hold 2 throw off all restraint; let oneself go: ～泼 swearing and crying hysterically
see also sǎ
撒谎 sāhuǎng (动)〈口〉tell a lie; lie
撒娇(嬌) sājiāo (动) act like a pampered child
撒尿 sāniào (动)〈口〉piss; pee
撒气(氣) sāqì (动) 1 (of a ball, tyre, etc.) leak; go soft; be flat: 汽车的后带～了. The back tyre of the car is flat. 2 vent one's anger or ill temper
撒手 sāshǒu (动) let go: ～不管 wash one's hands of the business
撒腿 sātuǐ (动) start (running): ～就跑 make off at once; take to one's heels
撒野 sāyě (动) behave rudely

洒(灑) sǎ (动) sprinkle; spray; spill; shed: ～除草剂 spray herbicide. 别把牛奶～了. Don't spill the milk.
洒泪(淚) sǎlèi (动) shed tears
洒脱 sǎtuō (形) free and easy

撒 sǎ (动) 1 scatter; sprinkle; spread: ～化肥 spread fertilizer. ～种子 sow seeds 2 spill; drop
see also sā
撒播 sǎbō (动) broadcast sowing: ～机 broadcast seeder

飒 sà
飒飒 sàsà (象) sough; rustle: 秋风～ the soughing autumn wind

塞 sāi I (动) fill in; squeeze in; stuff: 手提包不太满,还可以再～几本书. There is still room in the bag, so we can squeeze a few more books in. 水管～住了. The waterpipe is blocked. II (名) stopper: 瓶～ a bottle cork
see also sài
塞子 sāizi (名) stopper; cork; plug; spigot

腮 sāi (名) cheek
腮红 sāihóng (名) blusher; blush
腮帮(幫)子 sāibāngzi (名)〈口〉cheek

塞 sài (名) strategic stronghold
see also sāi
塞外 Sàiwài (名) beyond (or north of) the Great Wall

赛 sài I (名) match; game; competition; contest: 篮球～ basketball match. 田径～ track and field events II (动) compare favourably with; surpass; overtake
赛车(車) sàichē (名) 1 cycle racing; motorcycle race; automobile race 2 racing bicycle
赛过(過) sàiguò (动) overtake; surpass; exceed
赛马(馬) sàimǎ (名) horse race
赛跑 sàipǎo (名) race: 长距离～ long-distance race. 一百米～ 100-metre dash. 越野～ cross-country race
赛事 sàishì (名) sports event; match; game

三 sān (数) 1 three: ～方面会谈 tripartite talks 2 more than two; several; many: ～灾八难 suffer from one ailment after another. ～番五次 several times; time and again; repeatedly
三百六十行 sānbǎi liùshí háng all trades and professions; all walks of life
三部曲 sānbùqǔ (名) trilogy
三岔路口 sānchà lùkǒu a fork in the road; a place where three roads meet; a junction
三长(長)两(兩)短 sāncháng-liǎngduǎn unexpected misfortune; sth. unfortunate, esp. death
三极(極)管 sānjíguǎn (名) triode: 晶体～ transistor
三角 sānjiǎo (名) 1 triangle 2 trigonometry
三脚架 sānjiǎojià (名) tripod
三教九流 sānjiào jiǔliú 1 various religious sects and academic schools 2 people of all sorts
三九天 sānjiǔtiān (名) the third nine-day period after the winter solstice — the coldest days of winter
三句话不离(離)本行 sānjùhuà bù lí běnháng can hardly open one's mouth without talking shop; talk shop all the time
三军 sānjūn (名) 1 the army 2 the three

armed services
三令五申 sānlìng-wǔshēn repeated injunctions
三六九等 sān-liù-jiǔděng minute distinction of grades and ranks
三轮(輪)车(車) sānlúnchē (名) tricycle; pedicab
三三两(兩)两 sānsānliǎngliǎng in twos and threes
三思而行 sān sī ér xíng think twice before you act
…三…四 …sān…sì [indicating dis-order]: 颠三倒四 incoherent; disorganized. 丢三落四 always be forgetting or mislaying things
三天两(兩)头(頭) sāntiān-liǎngtóu 〈口〉 almost every day
三围 sānwéi (名) chest, waist, and seat (or hip) measurements
三心二意 sānxīn-èryì 1 be of two minds; shilly-shally: 别～了. Don't shilly-shally. 2 half-hearted
三言两(兩)语 sānyán-liǎngyǔ in a few words; in one or two words: 我们怎能把这事的原委用～说清楚呢? How could we explain the whole thing in just a few words?
三月 sānyuè (名) 1 March 2 the third month of the lunar year; the third moon

叁 sān (数) three [used for the numeral 三 on cheques, etc. to avoid mistakes or alterations]

散 sǎn I (动) come loose; fall apart; not hold together: 把这些信捆好,别～了. Tie up these letters and see that they don't come loose. 包裹在运送到车站途中～了. The package got torn on the way to the station. II (形) scattered: 我们住得很～. We live rather far apart from one another.
see also sàn
散兵 sǎnbīng (名) skirmisher: ～壕 fire trench. ～坑 foxhole; pit. ～线 skirmish line. ～游勇 stragglers
散光 sǎnguāng (名) astigmatism: ～眼镜 astigmatic lenses
散货 sǎnhuò (名) bulk cargo: ～船 bulk freighter
散记 sǎnjì (名) random notes
散架 sǎnjià (动) fall apart; fall to pieces; break
散居 sǎnjū (动) live scattered
散乱(亂) sǎnluàn (形) in disorder
散漫 sǎnmàn (形) 1 undisciplined; careless and sloppy 2 unorganized; scattered
散文 sǎnwén (名) prose; essay
散装(裝) sǎnzhuāng (形) unpackaged; loose packed; in bulk

伞(傘) sǎn (名) 1 umbrella 2 sth. shaped like an umbrella: 降落～ parachute 3 protecting power: 核保护～ nuclear umbrella
伞兵 sǎnbīng (名) paratrooper; parachuter: ～部队 parachute troops; paratroops

散 sàn (动) 1 break up; disperse: 会议～了没有? Is the meeting over now? 2 distribute; disseminate; give out: ～传单 distribute leaflets 3 dispel; let out: 打开门窗～～这儿的空气. Please open the windows to let in fresh air.
see also sǎn
散布 sànbù (动) spread; disseminate; scatter; diffuse: ～谣言 spread rumours. 在这片原野上～着奇花异草. Exotic flowers are scattered here and there on this plain.
散步 sànbù (动) take a walk; go for a walk; go for a stroll
散场(場) sànchǎng (动) (of a theatre, cinema, etc.) empty after the show: 电影～了. The cinema emptied after the show. *or* The audience streamed out of the cinema after the show.
散发(發) sànfā (动) 1 give off; send forth; diffuse; emit: 花儿～着清香. The flowers sent forth wafts of delicate fragrance. 2 distribute; issue; give out: ～小册子 distribute brochures or booklets. 作为正式文件～ be circulated as an official document
散会(會) sànhuì (动) (of a meeting) be over; break up: 宣布～ declare the meeting over
散伙 sànhuǒ (动) (of a group, body or organization) dissolve; disband
散开(開) sànkāi (动) spread out or apart; disperse; scatter: 警察赶到现场时,人群已～了. The crowd had dispersed when the police rushed to the scene.
散失 sànshī (动) 1 scatter and disappear; be lost; be missing: ～的杂志已经找到. The missing magazines have been found. 2 (of moisture, etc.) be lost; evaporate; dissipate

S

丧(喪) sāng (名) funeral; mourning
see also sàng
丧礼(禮) sānglǐ (名) funeral
丧事 sāngshì (名) funeral arrangements
丧钟(鐘) sāngzhōng (名) death knell; knell: 敲响殖民主义的～ sound the death knell of colonialism
桑 sāng (名) white mulberry; mulberry
桑蚕(蠶) sāngcán (名) silkworm: ～丝 mulberry silk
桑拿浴 sāngnáyù (名) sauna: 洗～ have a sauna
桑梓 sāngzǐ (名)〈书〉one's native place
嗓 sǎng (名) **1** throat; larynx **2** voice
嗓门(門)儿(兒) sǎngménr (名) voice: 提高～ raise one's voice
嗓音 sǎngyīn (名) voice: 他～洪亮. His voice carries.
嗓子 sǎngzi (名) **1** throat; larynx: ～疼 have a sore throat **2** voice: 哑～ husky voice
丧(喪) sàng (动) lose: ～尽廉耻 lose all sense of shame
see also sāng
丧胆(膽) sàngdǎn (动) tremble with fear
丧魂落魄 sànghún-luòpò be scared out of one's wits
丧家之犬 sàng jiā zhī quǎn stray cur: 惶惶如～ flee helter-skelter
丧命 sàngmìng (动) get killed in an accident, etc.; meet a violent death
丧偶 sàng'ǒu (动) be bereaved of one's spouse (esp. one's wife); have lost one's wife or husband
丧气(氣) sàngqì (动) lose heart; be filled with despair: ～话 demoralizing words
丧气(氣) sàngqi〈口〉be unlucky; be out of luck; have bad luck
丧权(權)辱国(國) sàngquán-rǔguó humiliate the nation and forfeit its sovereignty
丧失 sàngshī (动) lose; forfeit: ～信心 lose confidence. ～时机 miss the opportunity. 不能～警惕 never relax one's vigilance. ～国籍 lose one's nationality
丧心病狂 sàng xīn bìng kuáng preposterous and unscrupulous
臊 sāo (名) the smell of urine; foul smell
see also sào

搔 sāo (动) scratch: ～首 scratch one's head
骚 sāo (动) disturb; upset: ～乱 disturbance; riot. ～扰 harass; molest
骚动(動) sāodòng I (名) disturbance; commotion; ferment II (动) be in a tumult; become restless
缫 sāo (动) reel silk from cocoons; reel
扫(掃) sǎo (动) **1** sweep; clear away: ～除街上的积雪 clear the streets of snow. ～清障碍 remove the obstacles **2** pass quickly along or over; sweep: 他向坐在大厅的人群～了一眼. His eyes swept over the people sitting in the hall.
see also sào
扫除 sǎochú (动) **1** do the cleaning; clean up: 大～ spring-cleaning **2** clear away; remove; wipe out: ～文盲 eliminate (or wipe out) illiteracy
扫荡(蕩) sǎodàng (动) mop up
扫地 sǎodì (动) **1** sweep the floor **2** (of honour, credibility, etc.) reach rock bottom: 名誉～ be thoroughly discredited
扫黄 sǎohuáng (形) anti-pornography
扫雷 sǎoléi (动) minesweeping
扫盲 sǎománg (动) eliminate (or wipe out) illiteracy
扫描 sǎomiáo (动) scan: ～器 scanner
扫墓 sǎomù (动) pay respects to a dead person at his tomb
扫清 sǎoqīng (动) clear away; get rid of: ～道路 clear the path; pave the way
扫射 sǎoshè (动) strafe
扫尾 sǎowěi (动) finish (the final part of task); wind up (the work)
扫兴(興) sǎoxìng (动) have one's spirits dampened; feel disappointed: 真叫人～! How disappointing!
嫂 sǎo (名) elder brother's wife; sister-in-law
臊 sào (形) shy; bashful: ～得脸通红 blush scarlet
see also sāo
扫(掃) sào
see also sǎo
扫帚 sàozhou (名) broom

S

涩(澀) sè (形) 1 puckery; astringent: 这些柿子太~,还不能吃. These persimmons make your mouth pucker. You can't eat them yet. 2 unsmooth; hard going 3 obscure; difficult to read
啬(嗇) sè (形) stingy; miserly
色 sè (名) 1 colour: 红~ red. 原~ primary colour 2 look; countenance; expression: 喜形于~ beaming with joy 3 kind; description: 各~人等 people of every description; all kinds of people 4 scene; scenery 5 woman's pretty looks
see also shǎi
色彩 sècǎi (名) colour; hue; tint; shade: 地方~ local colour. 文学~ literary flavour. ~鲜明 bright-coloured
色调 sèdiào (名) tone; hue
色狼 sèláng (名) lecher
色厉(厲)内荏 sè lì nèi rěn outwardly strong but inwardly weak
色盲 sèmáng (名) colour blindness
色情 sèqíng (名) pornographic: ~文学 pornography. ~狂 sex mania
森 sēn (形) 1 full of trees 2 dark; gloomy: 阴~~ gloomy; grim
森林 sēnlín (名) forest: ~火灾 forest fire. 原始~ primeval forests
森严(嚴) sēnyán (形) stern; strict; forbidding: 门禁~ heavily guarded entrance
僧 sēng (名) Buddhist monk; monk
僧多粥少 sēng duō zhōu shǎo little gruel and many monks — not enough to go around
僧侣 sēnglǚ (名) monks and priests; clergy
沙 shā I (名) 1 sand 2 sth. granulated or powdered: 豆~ bean paste II (形) (of voice) hoarse; husky
沙场(場) shāchǎng (名) battlefield; battleground: 久经~ be a seasoned soldier; be experienced
沙尘(塵)暴 shāchénbào sandstorm
沙袋 shādài (名) sandbag
沙发(發) shāfā (名) sofa
沙锅(鍋) shāguō (名) earthenware pot: ~豆腐 bean curd en casserole
沙坑 shākēng (名) jumping pit
沙拉 shālā (名) salad
沙里(裏)淘金 shālǐ táo jīn get small returns for great effort
沙砾(礫) shālì (名) grit
沙漠 shāmò (名) desert
沙漠化 shāmòhuà (动) desertification
沙滩(灘) shātān (名) sandy beach
沙土 shātǔ (名) sandy soil; sand
沙文主义(義) shāwén zhǔyì (名) chauvinism
沙哑(啞) shāyǎ (形) hoarse; husky; raucous
沙眼 shāyǎn (名) trachoma
沙子 shāzi (名) 1 sand; grit 2 small grains; pellets: 铁~ iron pellets; shot
鲨 shā (名) shark
鲨鱼(魚) shāyú (名) shark
砂 shā (名) sand; grit
砂布 shābù (名) emery cloth; abrasive cloth
砂糖 shātáng (名) granulated sugar
砂纸 shāzhǐ (名) abrasive paper; sandpaper
纱 shā (名) 1 yarn: 棉~ cotton yarn. ~厂 cotton mill 2 gauze; sheer: 铁~ wire gauze
纱布 shābù (名) gauze
纱橱 shāchú (名) screen cupboard
纱窗 shāchuāng (名) screen window
纱锭 shādìng (名) spindle
纱巾 shājīn (名) gauze kerchief
杀(殺) shā I (动) 1 kill; slaughter: ~人放火 commit murder and arson 2 fight; go into battle: ~出去 fight one's way out 3 weaken; reduce; abate: 风势稍~. The wind has abated. II (副) in the extreme; exceedingly: 闷~人 bored stiff
杀虫(蟲)剂(劑) shāchóngjì (名) insecticide; pesticide
杀风(風)景 shā fēngjǐng spoil the fun; spoil other people's pleasure
杀害 shāhài (动) murder; kill
杀鸡(鷄)取卵 shā jī qǔ luǎn kill the goose that lays the golden eggs
杀鸡(鷄)吓(嚇)猴 shā jī xià hóu kill the chicken to frighten the monkey — punish someone as a warning to others
杀菌 shājūn (动) disinfect; sterilize: ~剂 germicide; bactericide
杀戮 shālù (动) massacre; slaughter
杀人 shārén (动) murder: ~犯 murderer. ~越货 kill a person and seize his goods. ~不见血 kill (or harm) a person by invisible means
杀伤(傷) shāshāng (动) kill and wound;

inflict casualties on

杀身成仁 shā shēn chéng rén lay down one's life in the cause of justice

杀头(頭) shātóu (动) behead; decapitate

杀一儆百 shā yī jǐng bǎi execute one as a warning to a hundred

刹 shā (动) 1 put on the brakes; stop: 把车~住 stop (or brake) a car 2 check; curtail: ~住不正之风 check unhealthy tendencies
see also chà

刹车(車) shāchē I (动) put on the brakes II (名) brake

煞 shā (动) 1 stop; halt; check; bring to a close 2 tighten: ~一~腰带 tighten one's belt
see also shà

煞车(車) shāchē (动) see "刹车" shāchē

煞尾 shāwěi I (动) round off; wind up II (名) final stage; end; ending: ~这几句写得特别好. The concluding remarks are particularly well written.

啥 shá (代) what: 有~说~ say what one has to say; speak one's mind. 这没~了不起. This is nothing to speak of. 没~可怕 nothing to be afraid of

傻(儍) shǎ (形) 1 stupid; muddle-headed: 你真~, 借给他那一大笔钱. It was stupid of you to lend him such a large sum of money. 装~ pretend to be ignorant. 你别~乎乎的, 他什么也没有答应你. Don't be that naive. He hasn't promised you anything. 2 (think or act) mechanically: 别一个劲儿~干. Don't just keep slaving away at the job.

S

傻瓜 shǎguā (名) fool; blockhead; simpleton

傻呵呵 shǎhēhē (形) simple-minded; not very clever: 别看他~的, 在学校的成绩总是名列前茅. Maybe he doesn't look bright, but he is always among the best at school.

傻话 shǎhuà (名) stupid talk; nonsense; foolish words

傻劲(勁)儿(兒) shǎjìnr (名) 1 stupidity; foolishness 2 sheer enthusiasm; doggedness

傻笑 shǎxiào (动) laugh foolishly; giggle; smirk

傻眼 shǎyǎn (动) be dumbfounded; be stunned

傻子 shǎzi (名) fool; blockhead; simpleton

霎 shà (名) a very short time; moment; instant: ~时间 in a moment; in a twinkling; in a split second

厦 shà (名) a tall building; mansion: 高楼大~ tall buildings and large mansions

煞 shà I (名) evil spirit; goblin II (副) very
see also shā

煞费苦心 shà fèi kǔxīn cudgel one's brains; take great pains: ~地寻找借口 cudgel one's brains to find an excuse

煞有介事 shà yǒu jiè shì make a great fuss about sth. of little consequence; be ludicrously pompous

筛(篩) shāi I (名) sieve; sifter; screen II (动) sift; sieve; screen; riddle: ~面 sieve flour; sift flour. ~煤 screen coal. ~煤渣 sift cinders

筛分 shāifēn (名) screening; sieving: ~机 screening machine

筛选(選) shāixuǎn (动) select; choose

色 shǎi (名)〈口〉colour: 这布掉~吗? Will this cloth fade?
see also sè

色子 shǎizi (名) dice: 掷~ play dice

晒(曬) shài (动) 1 (of the sun) shine upon 2 dry in the sun; bask: ~粮食 dry grain in the sun. ~衣服 air one's clothes. 暑假他们去了海滩, 回来个个都~黑了. They went to the beach during the summer holidays and all came back with nice tans.

晒台(臺) shàitái (名) flat roof (for drying clothes, etc.)

晒太阳(陽) shàitàiyang sunbathe; bask in the sun

晒图(圖) shàitú (动) make a blueprint; blueprint

潸 shān〈书〉in tears: ~然泪下 shed tears

扇 shān (动) 1 (搧) fan: ~扇子 fan oneself 2 incite; instigate; fan up; stir up: ~起暴乱 incite a riot
see also shàn

扇动(動) shāndòng (动) 1 fan; flap: ~翅膀 flap the wings 2 instigate; incite; stir up; whip up: ~派性 incite factional strife

煽 shān (动) incite; instigate

煽风(風)点(點)火 shānfēng-diǎnhuǒ stir up trouble
煽情 shānqíng (动) 1 be tear-jerking 2 sensationalize

山 shān (名) 1 hill; mountain 2 anything resembling a mountain: 冰～ iceberg
山崩 shānbēng (名) landslide; landslip
山川 shānchuān (名) mountains and rivers; landscape
山村 shāncūn (名) mountain village
山地 shāndì (名) mountainous region; hilly area; hilly country
山顶 shāndǐng (名) the summit (or top) of a mountain; hilltop
山峰 shānfēng (名) mountain peak
山冈(岡) shāngāng (名) low hill; hillock
山歌 shāngē (名) folk song (sung in the fields during or after work)
山沟(溝) shāngōu (名) gully; ravine; (mountain) valley
山谷 shāngǔ (名) mountain valley
山洪 shānhóng (名) mountain torrents
山货 shānhuò (名) 1 produce of various kinds from a mountain region (such as haws, chestnuts and walnuts) 2 household utensils made of wood, bamboo, clay, etc.
山脊 shānjǐ (名) ridge (of a mountain or hill)
山涧 shānjiàn (名) mountain stream
山脚 shānjiǎo (名) the foot of a hill
山口 shānkǒu (名) mountain pass; pass
山林 shānlín (名) mountain forest; wooded mountain
山岭(嶺) shānlǐng (名) mountain ridge
山麓 shānlù (名) the foot of a mountain
山峦(巒) shānluán (名) chain of mountains
山脉(脈) shānmài (名) mountain range; mountain chain
山盟海誓 shānméng-hǎishì swear an oath of enduring fidelity
山坡 shānpō (名) hillside; mountain slope
山清水秀 shānqīng-shuǐxiù green hills and clear waters; picturesque scenery
山穷(窮)水尽(盡) shānqióng-shuǐjìn at the end of one's rope (or tether, resources); in desperate straits
山水 shānshuǐ (名) 1 scenery with hills and waters: 桂林～甲天下. The landscape of Guilin is among the finest under heaven. 2 traditional Chinese painting of mountains and waters; landscape painting
山头(頭) shāntóu (名) 1 hilltop; the top of a mountain 2 mountain stronghold; faction: 拉～ form a faction
山羊 shānyáng (名) goat
山腰 shānyāo (名) halfway up the mountain
山岳 shānyuè (名) lofty mountains
山楂 shānzhā (名) hawthorn: ～糕 haw jelly
山寨 shānzhài (名) mountain fastness; fortified mountain village
山珍海味 shānzhēn-hǎiwèi delicacies
山庄(莊) shānzhuāng (名) mountain villa

舢 shān
舢板 shānbǎn (名) sampan

衫 shān (名) unlined upper garment: 衬～ shirt. 汗～ undershirt

杉 shān (名) China fir

珊 shān
珊瑚 shānhú (名) coral: ～岛 coral island

删 shān (动) delete; leave out: 这一段可以～去. This paragraph can be left out. ～掉不必要的形容词 cut out the unnecessary adjectives
删除 shānchú (动) delete; strike (or cut, cross) out
删繁就简 shānfán-jiùjiǎn simplify literary writing by leaving out superfluous words
删改 shāngǎi (动) prune away; revise: 决议草案几经～才被通过. The draft resolution was revised several times before it was adopted.
删节(節) shānjié (动) abridge; abbreviate: 略加～ slightly abridged. ～本 abridged edition; abbreviated version. ～号 ellipsis; suspension points; ellipsis dots (…)

姗 shān
姗姗来(來)迟(遲) shānshān lái chí be slow in coming; arrive late

闪 shǎn I (动) 1 dodge; duck; get out of the way: ～到一边 dodge swiftly to one side; duck behind 2 twist; sprain: ～了腰 sprain one's back 3 flash; sparkle; shine: 一～而过 flash past. 脑子里～过一个念头. An idea flashed through one's mind. II (名) lightning: ～电 flashes of lightning
闪避 shǎnbì (动) dodge; sidestep

闪电(電) shǎndiàn (名) lightning: ~战 lightning war; blitzkrieg; blitz

闪光 shǎnguāng I (名) flash of light: ~灯 flashlight; photoflash II (动) gleam; glisten; glitter

闪开(開) shǎnkāi (动) get out of the way; jump aside ; dodge: 车队来了, 快~! Stand back! The motorcade is coming.

闪闪 shǎnshǎn (形) sparkle; glisten; glitter: 电光~. Lightning flashed.

闪身 shǎnshēn (动) 1 dodge 2 walk sideways: ~进去 walk in sideways

闪失 shǎnshī (名) accident; mishap: 不能有任何~ absolutely no mistake is allowed

闪烁(爍) shǎnshuò (动) 1 twinkle; glimmer; glisten: 星星在天空中~. Stars twinkled in the sky. 2 be evasive; be vague: ~其词 speak evasively

闪现 shǎnxiàn (动) flash before one

闪耀 shǎnyào (动) glitter; shine: 塔顶~着金光. The top of the tower is glittering.

擅 shàn I (副) do sth. on one's own authority: ~自提价 arbitrarily raise prices II (动) be good at: 不~应酬 be not particularly good at casual conversation

擅长(長) shàncháng (动) be good at; be expert in; be skilled in: 他~摄影. He is a good photographer.

擅离(離)职(職)守 shànlí zhíshǒu leave one's post without permission

擅自 shànzì (副) without authorization: ~决定 make a decision without proper authorization

善 shàn I (名) good deed: 行~ do good deeds II (形) 1 good and honest: 心怀不~ harbour evil intentions 2 wise; satisfactory; good: ~策 wise policy (or move) 3 friendly: 友~ on good terms 4 familiar: 面~ look familiar III (动) 1 be good at: 多谋~断 be resourceful and quick at making decisions 2 be apt to: ~忘 be forgetful 3 do well: 你做事必须~始~终. You must bring the matter to a successful conclusion since you did very well from the very start. IV (副) properly: ~自保重 look after yourself properly

善罢(罷)甘休 shànbà-gānxiū [often used in negative sentences] let the matter rest: 他们决不会~的. They will not take it lying down.

善本 shànběn (名) reliable text; good edition

善待 shàndài (动) treat nicely; show concern for

善后(後) shànhòu (动) properly handle the remaining problems: ~问题让我处理吧. Let me take care of the problems in the aftermath.

善款 shànkuǎn (名) funds raised; donation

善举(舉) shànjǔ (名) philanthropic act

善良 shànliáng (形) good and honest; kind-hearted

善始善终 shànshǐ-shànzhōng start well and end well; see sth. through

善心 shànxīn (名) mercy; kindness

善意 shànyì (名) goodwill; good intentions: ~的批评 a well-intentioned criticism

善于(於) shànyú (动) be good at; be adept in: ~歌舞 be good at singing and dancing. ~交际 be a good mixer; be good at socializing

善终 shànzhōng (动) die a natural death

膳 shàn (名) meals; board: 在学生食堂用~ have one's meals at the students' cafeteria

膳食 shànshí (名) meals; food

膳宿 shàn-sù (名) board and lodging

缮 shàn (动) 1 repair; be under repair: 房屋正在修~中. The house is under repair. 2 copy; write out: ~清 make a fair copy

缮写(寫) shànxiě (动) copy

禅(禪) shàn

see also chán

禅让(讓) shànràng (动) abdicate the throne (in favour of another person)

扇 shàn I (名) 1 fan: 电~ electric fan 2 leaf: 门~ door leaf. 隔~ partition II (量) [for a door or window]: 一~门 a door

see also shān

扇子 shànzi (名) fan

赡 shàn (动) support; provide for: ~养父母 support one's parents (of money paid to one's former wife). ~养费 alimony

讪 shàn I (动) mock; ridicule II (形) embarrassed: 脸上发~ look embarrassed

S

讪笑 shànxiào (动) ridicule; mock; deride

商 shāng I (动) discuss; consult: 有要事相～ have something important to discuss (with you) II (名) 1 trade; commerce; business: 经～ engage in trade; go into business; be in business 2 merchant; businessman: 皮货～ fur dealer 3 quotient: 智～ IQ (intelligence quotient)

商标(標) shāngbiāo (名) trade mark

商埠 shāngbù (名) commercial (or trading) port

商场(場) shāngchǎng (名) market; bazaar

商船 shāngchuán (名) merchant ship; merchantman

商店 shāngdiàn (名) shop; store

商定 shāngdìng (动) decide through consultation or discussion; agree

商队(隊) shāngduì (名) trade caravan

商贩 shāngfàn (名) small retailer; pedlar

商港 shānggǎng (名) commercial port

商行 shāngháng (名) trading company; commercial firm

商机(機) shāngjī (名) business opportunity: ～无限 limitless business opportunities

商检(檢) shāngjiǎn (名) commodity inspection

商量 shāngliang (动) consult; discuss; talk over: 我们得找校长～一下. We ought to talk it over with the principal of the school.

商品 shāngpǐn (名) commodity; goods; merchandise: ～粮 commodity grain; marketable grain. ～流通 commodity circulation. ～生产 commodity production

商洽 shāngqià (动) consult with sb.; take up (a matter) with sb.

商榷 shāngquè (动) discuss; deliberate: 这一点要进一步～. This point calls for further discussion.

商人 shāngrén (名) businessman; merchant; trader

商谈 shāngtán (动) exchange views; confer; discuss; negotiate: 就两校学术交流问题～ discuss the question of academic exchanges between the two institutions

商讨 shāngtǎo (动) discuss; deliberate over: 就发展两国关系进行～ hold discussions on developing relations between the two countries. 会议～了两国的经济合作问题. The meeting discussed the economic co-operation between the two countries.

商务(務) shāngwù (名) commercial affairs; business affairs: ～参赞 commercial counsellor. ～活动 commercial activity. ～行为 commercial act

商业(業) shāngyè (名) commerce; trade; business: ～部门 commercial departments. ～信贷 commercial credit. ～银行 commercial bank. ～区 commercial district

商酌 shāngzhuó (动) have consultations with

伤(傷) shāng I (名) wound; injury: 内～ internal injury. 轻～ slight injury II (动) 1 injure; hurt: 在一次事故中受～ be injured in an accident. ～感情 hurt sb.'s feelings; offend sb.'s sensibilities 2 be distressed: 哀～ feel grief 3 be harmful to; hinder: 无～大雅 not affect one's sense of propriety; not involve matters of principle 4 surfeit oneself with food, etc.: ～食 suffer from overeating

伤疤 shāngbā (名) scar

伤兵 shāngbīng (名) wounded soldier

伤病员 shāng-bìngyuán (名) the sick and wounded

伤风(風) shāngfēng (动) catch cold; have a cold

伤风(風)败俗 shāngfēng-bàisú offend public decency; lower the moral standard of the community

伤感 shānggǎn (形) distressed; sentimental

伤害 shānghài (动) injure; harm; hurt: 抽烟会～身体. Smoking is harmful to the health. ～自尊心 injure (or hurt) one's pride; hurt one's self-respect

伤寒 shānghán (名) typhoid fever; typhoid

伤痕 shānghén (名) scar; bruise: ～文学 trauma literature

伤口 shāngkǒu (名) wound; cut

伤脑(腦)筋 shāng nǎojīn knotty; troublesome; bothersome

伤神 shāngshén (动) overtax one's energies

伤势(勢) shāngshì (名) the condition of an injury (or wound): ～严重 be seriously wounded (or injured)

伤亡 shāng-wáng (名) casualties

伤心 shāngxīn (形) sad; grieved; brokenhearted: 看到他变得那么厉害,真叫我～. It grieves me to see him so changed.

赏 shǎng I (名) reward; award: 有～有罚. Give due rewards to good

people and mete out due punishments to evildoers. II (动) 1 grant a reward 2 admire; enjoy; appreciate: ~月 admire the full moon (particularly on the night of the Mid-autumn Festival). ~花 enjoy looking at the flowers. ~雪 enjoy a beautiful snow scene

赏赐 shǎngcì (动) grant (or bestow) a reward; award

赏光 shǎngguāng (动)〈套〉[used to request acceptance of an invitation]: 务请~ request the pleasure of your company

赏鉴(鑒) shǎngjiàn (动) appreciate (a work of art)

赏金 shǎngjīn (名) money reward; award

赏识(識) shǎngshí (动) recognize the worth of; appreciate: 教授很~这篇论文. The professor thinks highly of this dissertation.

赏玩 shǎngwán (动) admire; delight in; enjoy: ~大自然 enjoy the beauty of nature

赏心悦目 shǎngxīn-yuèmù be enchanted by beautiful scenery or feel overjoyed on a happy occasion

晌 shǎng (名) part of the day: 前半~儿 morning. 晚半~儿 dusk

晌午 shǎngwu (名)〈口〉midday; noon: ~饭 midday meal; lunch

尚 shàng I (副)〈书〉still; yet: 为时~早. It is still too early. 问题~未解决. The problem remains to be solved. II (动) esteem; value; set great store by: 崇~ uphold; advocate

尚且 shàngqiě (副) [used as an intensifier to indicate an extreme or hypothetical case] even: 大人~不易读懂,何况小孩子. Even adults find it difficult to read, to say nothing of children.

尚武 shàngwǔ (动) encourage a military or martial spirit

上 shàng I (形) 1 upper; up; upward: ~层阶级 upper class. 往~看 look up 2 higher; superior; better: ~等 superior quality. ~级机关 higher organization 3 first (part); preceding; previous: ~册 the first volume; Volume One; Book One II (动) 1 go up; mount; board; get on: ~公共汽车 get on a bus. ~飞机 board a plane. ~楼 go upstairs 2 go to; leave for: 你~哪儿去? Where are you going? ~街 go shopping (or window-shopping). 我~图书馆去. I'm going to the library. 3 submit; send in; present 4 forge ahead; go ahead 5 enter the court or field: 换人:三号下,四号~. Substitution: Player No. 4 for No. 3. 6 fill; supply; serve: 给锅炉~水 fill the boiler with water 7 place sth. in position; set; fix: ~螺丝 drive a screw in 8 apply; paint; smear: 给门~漆 have the door painted 9 be put on record; be carried (in a publication): 皇家婚礼的消息~了英国各大报纸. All major British papers carried a story about the royal wedding. 10 wind; screw; tighten: 表该~弦了. The watch needs winding. 11 be engaged (in work, study, etc.) at a fixed time: ~课 give or attend a lesson in class 12 up to; as many as: ~百人 some hundred people III 1 [used after a verb to indicate motion from a lower to a higher position]: 登~山顶 reach the summit 2 [used after a verb to indicate achievement of one's goal]: 穿~外衣 put on a coat. 考~大学 be admitted to a university 3 [used to indicate the beginning and continuity of an action]: 她爱~了司机的工作. She has come to love her job as a driver.

上班 shàngbān (动) go to work; start work; be on duty: 我们每天早上8点钟~. We start work at 8 every morning.

上报(報) shàngbào (动) 1 be reported in the press 2 report to a higher body

上辈 shàngbèi (名) 1 ancestors 2 the elder generation of one's family

上膘 shàngbiāo (动) (of animals) become fat; fatten

上宾(賓) shàngbīn (名) distinguished guest; guest of honour

上菜 shàngcài (动) serve the dishes (of food)

上策 shàngcè (名) the best policy; a very wise move

上层(層) shàngcéng (名) higher levels: ~领导 higher leadership

上层(層)建筑(築) shàngcéng jiànzhù superstructure

上场(場) shàngchǎng (动) 1 appear on the stage 2 enter the court or field; join in a contest

上乘 shàngchéng (形) first-class

上床(牀) shàngchuáng (动) go to bed

上蹿(躥)下跳 shàngcuān-xiàtiào run around on vicious errands

S

上当(當) shàngdàng (动) be taken in

上等 shàngděng (形) first-class; first-rate; superior: ～货 first-class goods; quality goods

上帝 shàngdì (名) God

上调 shàngdiào (动) transfer sb. to a post at a higher level

上颚 shàng'è (名) maxilla (of a mammal); the upper jaw

上方宝(寶)剑(劍) shàngfāng bǎojiàn the imperial sword (a symbol of high authority with which an official can act at his discretion)

上访 shàngfǎng (动) complain to the higher authorities about an injustice and request fair settlement

上风(風) shàngfēng (名) advantage; upper hand: 占～ get the upper hand

上岗 shànggǎng (动) go on duty; obtain a job

上告 shànggào (动) complain to the higher authorities or appeal to a higher court

上工 shànggōng (动) go to work; start work

上钩 shànggōu (动) rise to the bait; swallow the bait

上光 shàngguāng (动) glaze; polish

上好 shànghǎo (形) first-class; best-quality

上呼吸道 shànghūxīdào the upper respiratory tract: ～感染 infection of the upper respiratory tract

上火 shànghuǒ (动) get angry

上级 shàngjí (名) higher level; higher authorities: ～机关 higher authorities; a higher body. 老～ old boss; old chief

上将(將) shàngjiàng (名) (army; U. S. air force) general; (British air force) Air Chief Marshal; (navy) Admiral

上缴 shàngjiǎo (动) turn over (revenues, etc.) to the higher authorities

上进(進) shàngjìn (动) go forward; make progress: 力求～ strive to forge ahead. ～心 the desire for progress

上镜 shàngjìng I (动) be on camera II (形) telegenic

上课 shàngkè (动) **1** attend class; attend a lecture **2** conduct a class; give a lesson (or lecture)

上空 shàngkōng (名) in the sky; overhead

上口 shàngkǒu (动) **1** be able to read aloud poems or essays fluently **2** (of a poem or essay) make smooth reading

上来(來) shànglái (动) come up: 他还没～. He hasn't come upstairs yet.

上来(來) shànglái (动) **1** [used after a verb to indicate motion from a lower to a higher position or an action of coming nearer to the speaker]: 把箱子搬～吧. Bring those suitcases upstairs. **2** [used after a verb to indicate accomplishment]: 这个问题你一定答得～. You can of course answer this question.

上流 shàngliú (名) **1** upper reaches (of a river) **2** members of the upper circles: ～社会 high society; polite society

上路 shànglù (动) set out on a journey; start off

上马(馬) shàngmǎ (动) start (a project, etc.)

上门(門) shàngmén (动) come or go and see sb.; call; drop in; visit: 他好久没～了. It's a long time since he last called.

上面 shàngmian (名) **1** above; over; on top of; on the surface of: 小河～跨着一座石桥. A stone bridge spanned the stream. **2** above-mentioned; aforesaid; foregoing: ～列举了各种实例. Mentioned above are instances of diverse kinds. **3** the higher authorities; the higher-ups: ～有命令. There are orders from above. **4** aspect; respect; regard: 他在文学～下了很多功夫. He has put a lot of effort into literature.

上年纪 shàng niánji getting on in years

上品 shàngpǐn (名) high order; top grade

上气(氣)不接下气 shàngqì bùjiē xiàqì gasp for breath; be out of breath

上去 shàngqu (动) go up: 登着梯子～ go up (on) a ladder

上去 shàngqu (动) [used after a verb to indicate motion from a lower to a higher position or distance farther away from the speaker]: 走～ walk up. 把国民经济搞～ boost the national economy. 为了完成任务, 他把所有的力量都使～了. He has gone all out to make a success of his work.

上任 shàngrèn (动) take up an official post; assume office

上色 shàngshǎi (动) colour (a picture, map, etc.)

上上 shàngshàng (形) **1** the very best: ～策 the best policy **2** before last: ～星期 the week before last

上身 shàngshēn (名) **1** the upper part of the body **2** upper outer garment; shirt; blouse; jacket: 他～穿的是中山装. He is

S

wearing a Chinese-style jacket.

上升 shàngshēng (动) rise; go up; ascend: 气温~. The temperature is going up. 工厂产量稳步~. The output of the factory is rising steadily.

上声(聲) shàngshēng or shǎngshēng (名) falling-rising tone, one of the four tones in classical Chinese and the third tone in modern standard Chinese pronunciation

上市 shàngshì (动) go (or appear) on the market; be in season: 西红柿大量~. There are plenty of tomatoes on the market.

上市公司 shàngshì gōngsī listed company

上手 shàngshǒu I (名) left-hand seat; seat of honour II (动) start; begin: 今天的活一~就很顺利. Today's work started off quite smoothly.

上书(書) shàngshū (动) submit a written statement to a higher authority

上述 shàngshù (形) above-mentioned

上税 shàngshuì (动) pay taxes; pay duties

上司 shàngsi (名) superior; boss: 顶头~ one's immediate superior

上诉 shàngsù (动) appeal (to a higher court): 提出~ lodge an appeal

上算 shàngsuàn (形) more economical; worthwhile

上岁(歲)数(數) shàng suìshu 〈口〉 be getting on in years

上台(臺) shàngtái (动) 1 appear on the stage 2 assume power; come (or rise) to power

上天 shàngtiān I (名) Heaven; Providence; God II (动) go up to the sky: 我们又有一颗卫星~了. Another of our satellites has gone up.

S

上网 shàngwǎng (动) be on line; use the Internet; have access to the Internet

上文 shàngwén (名) foregoing paragraphs or chapters; preceding part of the text: 见~ see above

上午 shàngwǔ (名) forenoon; morning

上下 shàng-xià I (名) 1 high and low; old and young 2 relative superiority or inferiority: 不相~ equally matched; about the same; be on a par 3 from top to bottom; up and down: ~打量 look sb. up and down; size sb. up II (动) go up and down: 楼里安了电梯,顾客~很方便. With the instalment of an escalator, customers can easily go up and down. III (助) [used after a numeral or a numeral plus measure word] about: 四十岁~ about forty years old

上下文 shàng-xiàwén (名) context

上弦 shàngxián I (名) first quarter (of the moon) II (动) wind up a clock or watch

上限 shàngxiàn (名) upper limit; ceiling

上相 shàngxiàng (形) be photogenic; come out well in a photograph

上刑 shàngxíng (动) use torture (to extort a confession from sb.)

上行 shàngxíng (形) 1 up; upgoing: ~列车 up train 2 upriver; upstream: ~船 upriver boat

上行下效 shàng xíng xià xiào a bad example set by a person in power will be followed by his subordinates

上学(學) shàngxué (动)go to school

上旬 shàngxún (名) the first ten-day period of a month

上演 shàngyǎn (动) put on the stage; perform: 电影院今晚~什么片子? What's on at the cinema this evening?

上扬(揚) shàngyáng (动) go up (of price, cost, etc.)

上衣 shàngyī (名) upper garment; jacket

上瘾(癮) shàngyǐn (动) be addicted (to sth.); get into the habit (of doing sth.): 这种饮料喝多了会~. This soft drink is habit-forming.

上映 shàngyìng (动) show (a film): 今晚有部新片~. They are showing a new film tonight.

上游 shàngyóu (名) 1 upper reaches (of a river) 2 advanced position: 力争~ aim high

上谕 shàngyù (名) imperial edict

上涨(漲) shàngzhǎng (动) rise; go up: 物价~. The prices are spiralling.

上阵 shàngzhèn (动) go into battle; pitch into the work; play in a match

上肢 shàngzhī (名) upper limbs

上 shang 1 [used after nouns to indicate the surface of an object]: 墙~ on the wall. 脸~ in the face 2 [used after a noun to indicate the scope of sth.]: 会~ at the meeting. 事实~ in fact

烧(燒) shāo I (动) 1 burn: ~毁 burn down 2 cook; bake; heat: ~菜 cook food; prepare a meal. ~砖 bake bricks 3 stew after frying or fry after stewing: ~茄子 stewed eggplant. 红~肉 pork stewed in soy sauce **4** roast: ～鸡 roast chicken **5** run a fever: 她～得厉害. She has a very high fever. *or* She is running a high temperature. II (名) fever; temperature: 她～退了. Her temperature has come down.

烧饼 shāobing (名) sesame seed cake

烧饭 shāofàn (动) do the cooking; cook food; prepare a meal

烧火 shāohuǒ (动) make a fire; light a fire; tend the kitchen fire

烧毁 shāohuǐ (动) destroy by fire; burn up

烧酒 shāojiǔ (名) spirit usu. distilled from sorghum or maize

烧烤 shāokǎo (动、名) barbecue

烧伤(傷) shāoshāng (名) burn: 三度～ third-degree burns

烧香 shāoxiāng (动) burn joss sticks (before an idol)

烧灼 shāozhuó (动) burn; scorch; singe

鞘

shāo (名) whiplash

see also qiào

梢

shāo (名) tip; the thin end of a twig, etc.: 树～ the top of a tree

捎

shāo (动) take along sth. to or for sb.: ～个口信给他. Take a message to him.

捎脚 shāojiǎo (动) pick up passengers or goods on the way; give sb. a lift

稍

shāo (副) a little; slightly: ～加改动 make slight alterations. 请～等一会儿. Please wait a moment. ～纵即逝 transient; fleeting

稍稍 shāoshāo (副) a little; slightly: ～休息一下. Let's take a breather.

稍微 shāowēi (副) a little; slightly: 他感到～有点累. He felt a bit tired.

勺(杓)

sháo (名) spoon; ladle: 长柄～ ladle; dipper

勺子 sháozi (名) ladle; scoop

少

shǎo I (形) few; little: 留下吃饭的人很～. Only a few stayed for dinner. 他近来很～喝酒. He hardly ever drinks lately. 上海很～下雪. It seldom snows in Shanghai. II (动) **1** be short; lack: 我们还～几块钱. We're still short of a few yuan. **2** lose; be missing: 阅览室～了几本杂志. A few magazines are missing from the reading-room. **3** stop; quit: ～废话! Stop talking rubbish!

see also shào

少不得 shǎobude cannot do without; cannot dispense with: 学语言,一所设备完善的实验室是～的. We cannot dispense with a well-equipped laboratory in language study.

少不了 shǎobuliǎo **1** be bound to; be unavoidable: 这封信打得仓促, ～有些错误. The letter was typed in a hurry, so there are bound to be some errors. **2** considerable: 困难看来～. It looks as if there are going to be a lot of difficulties.

少而精 shǎo ér jīng fewer but better; small quantity, better quality

少见(見)多怪 shǎojiàn-duōguài childish curiosity or sheer ignorance

少量 shǎoliàng (形) a small amount; a little; a few

少数(數) shǎoshù (名) a small number: ～服从多数. The minority is subordinate to the majority.

少数(數)民族 shǎoshù mínzú minority nationality; ethnic group

少许 shǎoxǔ (形)〈书〉a little; a small quantity

哨

shào (名) **1** sentry post; post: 岗～ sentry post. 观察～ observation post. 放～ be on sentry duty; stand guard; stand sentry **2** whistle: 吹～ blow a whistle; whistle

哨兵 shàobīng (名) sentry; guard

哨所 shàosuǒ (名) sentry post; post

哨子 shàozi (名) whistle

少

shào I (形) young: 男女老～ men and women, old and young II (名) young master: 阔～ a profligate young man

see also shǎo

少妇(婦) shàofù (名) young married woman

少年 shàonián (名) **1** boyhood or girlhood; early youth (from ten to sixteen) **2** boy or girl of that age: ～犯罪 juvenile delinquency

少年老成 shàonián lǎochéng **1** an old head on young shoulders **2** a young but unenergetic person

少女 shàonǚ (名) young girl

少爷(爺) shàoye (名) young master of the house

少壮(壯) shàozhuàng (形) young and vigorous

奢

shē (形) **1** luxurious; extravagant: 穷～极欲 (wallow in) luxury **2** excessive; undue: ～望 extravagant hopes

奢侈 shēchǐ (形) luxurious; extravagant; wasteful: 生活~ live in luxury. ~品 luxury goods; luxuries

奢华(華) shēhuá (形) luxurious; extravagant: 陈设~ be luxuriously furnished

赊 shē (动) buy or sell on credit

赊购(購) shēgòu (动) buy on credit

赊欠 shēqiàn (动) buy or sell on credit; give or get credit

折 shé (动) 1 break; snap: 桌子腿撞~了. The table's legs are broken. 2 lose money in business

see also zhē; zhé

折本 shéběn (动) lose money in business

蛇 shé (名) snake; serpent

蛇头(頭) shétóu (名) trafficker in illegal immigrants; snakehead

蛇蝎 shéxiē (名) vicious people

舌 shé (名) 1 tongue 2 sth. shaped like a tongue: 火~ tongues of flame. 鞋~ the tongue of a shoe

舌敝唇焦 shébì-chúnjiāo talk till one is completely exhausted

舌尖 shéjiān (名) the tip of the tongue

舌苔 shétāi (名) coating on the tongue; fur

舌头(頭) shétou (名) tongue

舌战(戰) shézhàn (动) have a verbal battle with; argue heatedly with

舍(捨) shě (动) 1 give up; abandon: ~本逐末 attend to trivialities to the neglect of essentials 2 give alms

see also shè

S

舍得 shěde (动) be willing to give away; not grudge: ~花力气 stint no effort

舍己为(爲)人 shě jǐ wèi rén sacrifice one's own interests for the sake of others

舍近求远(遠) shějìn-qiúyuǎn search far and wide for what lies close at hand

舍车(車)保帅(帥) shějū-bǎoshuài make minor sacrifices to safeguard major interest

舍命 shěmìng (动) risk one's life

舍弃(棄) shěqì (动) give up; abandon

舍身 shěshēn (动) give one's life: ~救人 save sb.'s life at the cost of one's own

舍死忘生 shěsǐ-wàngshēng disregard one's own personal danger; risk one's life

涉 shè (动) 1 wade; ford: 远~重洋 travel across the oceans 2 go through; experience: ~世不深 have scanty knowledge of the world 3 involve

涉案 shè'àn (动) implicated (or involved) in a case

涉及 shèjí (动) involve; relate to; touch upon: 这事~重大原则问题. This involves matters of cardinal principle.

涉猎(獵) shèliè (动) do desultory reading; read cursorily: 有的书只要稍加~即可. There are books you have only to browse through.

涉世 shèshì (动) gain life experience: ~不深 have seen little of the world

涉嫌 shèxián (动) be suspected of being involved; be a suspect

社 shè (名) organized body; agency; society: 通讯~ news agency. 合作~ cooperative. 诗~ a poets' club. 出版~ publishing house

社保 shèbǎo (名) social security

社会(會) shèhuì (名) society: 人类~ human society. ~制度 social system. ~福利 social welfare. ~保险 social insurance. 国际~ international community

社会(會)保险(險) shèhuì bǎoxiǎn social security

社会(會)学(學) shèhuìxué (名) sociology: ~家 sociologist

社会(會)主义(義) shèhuìzhǔyì (名) socialism

社稷 shèjì (名) the state; the country

社交 shèjiāo (名) social intercourse; social activities

社论(論) shèlùn (名) editorial; leading article; leader

社区(區) shèqū community

设 shè I (动) 1 set up; arrange; found: ~宴 give a banquet 2 work out: ~计 work out a scheme II (连)〈书〉 if: ~有困难,当助一臂之力. I will do my best to help in case you have any difficulty.

设备(備) shèbèi (名) equipment; facilities: 旅馆~齐全. The hotel is provided with modern facilities.

设法 shèfǎ (动) think of a way; try; do what one can: 我们正在~筹集资金. We are trying to raise funds.

设防 shèfáng (动) set up defences; fortify; garrison: 不~的城市 an open city; an undefended city

设计 shèjì (名、动) design; plan: 毕业~ graduation project. ~一种新机器 design a new machine

设立 shèlì (动) establish; set up; found
设身处(處)地 shèshēn-chǔdì put oneself in sb. else's position; be considerate enough
设施 shèshī (名) installation; facilities: 军事～ military installations. 医疗～ medical facilities
设使 shèshǐ (连) if; suppose; in case
设想 shèxiǎng (动) 1 imagine; envisage; conceive; assume: 不堪～ too dreadful to contemplate 2 consider: 我们应该处处替国家～. We must always have the interest of the nation at heart.
设宴 shèyàn (动) give a banquet: ～招待 give a banquet in honour of sb.
设置 shèzhì (动) 1 set up; put up: ～专门机构 set up a special organization 2 install: 会场里～了扩音机. Loudspeakers are installed at the conference hall.

赦 shè (动) remit (a punishment): 大～ general pardon; amnesty. 特～ special pardon
赦免 shèmiǎn (动) remit (a punishment)

摄(攝) shè (动) 1 absorb; assimilate 2 take a photograph of; shoot
摄取 shèqǔ (动) 1 absorb; assimilate: ～营养 absorb nourishment 2 take a photograph of
摄像 shèxiàng (动) make a video recording
摄影 shèyǐng (动) 1 take a photograph; picture; have a picture taken: ～记者 press photographer; cameraman 2 shoot a film
摄影机(機) shèyǐngjī (名) camera
摄政 shèzhèng (动) act as regent: ～王 prince regent
摄制(製) shèzhì (动) produce (a film)

慑(懾) shè (动)〈书〉fear; be awed
慑服 shèfú (动) 1 submit to sb. out of fear; succumb 2 cow sb. into submission

舍 shè (名) house; shed; hut: 牛～ cowshed. 校～ school buildings
see also shě
舍亲(親) shèqīn (名)〈谦〉my relative

射 shè (动) 1 shoot; fire: ～箭 shoot an arrow. ～进一球 score a goal 2 discharge in a jet: 喷～ spout; spurt; jet. 注～ inject 3 send out (light, heat, etc.): 反～ reflect. 光芒四～ emit a brilliant light 4 allude to sth. or sb.; insinuate: 影～ insinuate; make innuendoes
射程 shèchéng (名) range (of fire): 有效～ effective range
射击(擊) shèjī I (动) shoot; fire II (名) shooting
射箭 shèjiàn I (动) shoot an arrow II (名) archery: ～手 archer
射门(門) shèmén (动) shoot (at the goal)
射频 shèpín (名) radio frequency
射手 shèshǒu (名) shooter; marksman; archer
射线(綫) shèxiàn (名) ray

麝 shè (名) 1 musk deer 2 musk
麝香 shèxiāng (名) musk

谁 shéi or shuí (代) 1 who: 你找～? Who are you looking for? 2 nobody: ～都不知道他. Nobody knows him. 3 anybody: 有～愿意跟我们一起去? Would anyone like to go with us?

深 shēn I (形) 1 deep: 一口～井 a deep well. 池～两米. The pool is two metres deep. 雪～过膝. The snow is knee-deep. 2 difficult; profound: 对他来讲,这本书太～了. The book is too difficult for him. 3thoroughgoing; penetrating; profound: 问题想得～ think deeply about a question. 我并没有～谈这个问题. I didn't go deeply into details about the matter. 影响很～ exert a profound influence 4 close; intimate: 他们俩交情很～. The two of them are just great friends. 5 dark; deep: ～蓝 dark blue. ～红 deep red; crimson. 颜色太～. The colour is too dark (or deep). 6 late: ～秋 late autumn. 夜～了. It was late at night. II (副) very; greatly; deeply: ～知 know very well; be fully aware of; be keenly alive to. ～感不安 feel very uneasy. ～信 be deeply convinced. ～受感动 be deeply moved
深奥 shēn'ào (形) abstruse; profound: ～的哲理 abstruse philosophy; a profound truth
深沉 shēnchén (形) 1 dark; deep: 暮色～. Dusk is deepening. 2 (of sound or voice) deep; dull: ～的声音 a deep voice; a dull sound 3 concealing one's real feelings: 这人很～. He's a deep person.
深仇大恨 shēnchóu-dàhèn deep-seated hatred; inveterate hatred
深处(處) shēnchù (名) depths; recesses: 在

S

密林～ in the depths of the forest. 在内心～ in the recesses of one's heart

深度 shēndù (名) 1 degree of depth; depth: 测量海水的～ determine the depth of the sea 2 profundity; depth: 他的文章缺乏～. His article lacks depth.

深更半夜 shēngēng-bànyè in the dead of night; in the middle of the night

深厚 shēnhòu (形) 1 deep; profound: ～的友谊 profound friendship 2 solid; deep-seated: ～的基础 a solid foundation

深呼吸 shēnhūxī deep breathing

深化 shēnhuà (动) deepen: 矛盾的～ intensification of a contradiction

深究 shēnjiū (动) go or look into sth. seriously

深居简出 shēnjū-jiǎnchū live a secluded life

深刻 shēnkè (形) deep; profound; deep-going: ～的印象 a deep impression

深谋远(遠)虑(慮) shēnmóu-yuǎnlǜ be far-sighted and capable of long-range planning; think carefully and plan deeply

深浅(淺) shēnqiǎn (名) 1 depth: 河的～ the depth of a river 2 proper limits (for speech or action); sense of propriety: 说话没～ speak carelessly and bluntly

深切 shēnqiè (形) heartfelt; profound: ～的同情 deep sympathy. ～地了解 deeply appreciate; be fully aware of

深情 shēnqíng (名) deep feeling; deep love: ～厚谊 profound sentiments of friendship

深秋 shēnqiū (名) late autumn

深入 shēnrù I (动) go deep into: ～人心 be highly popular II (形) thorough; penetrating: ～细致的分析 a carefully worked-out, in-depth analysis

深入浅(淺)出 shēnrù-qiǎnchū explain profound ideas in simple terms

深山 shēnshān (名) remote mountains

深深 shēnshēn (副) profoundly; deeply; keenly

深水 shēnshuǐ (名) deepwater: ～港 deep-water port

深思 shēnsī (动) think deeply: 好学～ study hard and think deeply

深思熟虑(慮) shēnsī-shúlǜ careful consideration

深邃 shēnsuì (形) 1 deep: ～的山谷 a deep valley 2 profound; abstruse: 哲理～ abstruse philosophical thinking

深谈 shēntán (动) discuss thoroughly; go deep into

深恶(惡)痛绝 shēnwù-tòngjué hate bitterly; detest; abhor

深信 shēnxìn (动) be deeply convinced; firmly believe

深夜 shēnyè (名) late at night

深渊(淵) shēnyuān (名) abyss: 苦难的～ in an abyss of misery

深远(遠) shēnyuǎn (形) profound and lasting; far-reaching

深造 shēnzào (动) take an advanced course of study or training: 送到国外～ be sent abroad for advanced study

深重 shēnzhòng (形) very grave; extremely serious

申

shēn (动) state; express; explain: 三令五～ give repeated instructions. 重～一贯政策 reiterate our consistent policy

申报(報) shēnbào (动) 1 report; submit to a higher body 2 declare sth. (to the Customs)

申辩(辯) shēnbiàn (动) defend oneself; argue (or plead) one's case: 被告有权～. The accused has the right to defend himself.

申斥 shēnchì (动) reprimand

申明 shēnmíng (动) declare; state; avow: ～理由 state one's reasons

申请 shēnqǐng (动) apply for: ～入(出)境签证 apply for an entry (exit) visa. ～书 application. ～调动 apply for a transfer; ask to be transfered to another job

申述 shēnshù (动) state; explain in detail: ～立场 state one's position. ～观点 expound one's views

申诉 shēnsù (动) appeal: 向上级提出～ appeal to the higher authorities.

申讨 shēntǎo (动) openly condemn; denounce

申冤 shēnyuān (动) 1 redress an injustice; right a wrong 2 appeal for redress of a wrong

呻 shēn

呻吟 shēnyín (动) groan; moan

伸

shēn (动) stretch; extend: ～出手来 stretch one's hand. ～大拇指 hold up one's thumb. 不要把头～出窗外. Don't put (or stick) your head out of the window (of a bus, etc.).

伸懒腰 shēn lǎnyāo stretch oneself

伸手 shēnshǒu (动) 1 stretch (or hold) out one's hand: 他～去拿字典. He reached for the dictionary. 2 ask for help, etc.: 虽

S

然困难，他们从不向国家～要援助. Though in great difficulties, they never asked the state for assistance.

伸缩 shēnsuō (动) 1 stretch out and draw back; expand and contract; lengthen and shorten: 镜头可以前后～. The lens of this camera can zoom in and out. 2 flexible; adjustable: 这些规定～性很大. These regulations are quite flexible. 留有～的余地 allow sb. some leeway

伸腿 shēntuǐ (动) 1 stretch one's legs 2 step in (to gain an advantage) 3 〈口〉 kick the bucket

伸腰 shēnyāo (动) straighten one's back; straighten oneself up

伸展 shēnzhǎn (动) extend; stretch: 把它的势力～到世界各处 extend its influence to different parts of the globe

伸张(張) shēnzhāng (动) uphold; promote: ～正气 promote healthy tendencies. ～正义 uphold justice

绅 shēn (名) gentry

绅士 shēnshì (名) gentleman; gentry

身 shēn I (名) 1 body: ～高 height. 上～ upper part of the body 2 life: 以～殉职 die a martyr at one's post 3 oneself; personally: 以～作则 set a good example for others 4 the main part of a structure; body: 车～ the body of a car. 机～ fuselage. 船～ hull II (量) [for clothing] suit: 一～新衣服 a new suit

身败名裂 shēnbài-mínglìè bring disgrace upon oneself and ruin one's reputation; be thoroughly discredited

身边(邊) shēnbiān (名) 1 at (or by) one's side: 他～有两名助手. He has two assistants working together with him. 2 (have sth.) on one; with one: ～没带钱 have no money on one. 她～总是带着一本词典. She always carries a dictionary with her.

身不由己 shēn bù yóu jǐ involuntarily; in spite of oneself

身材 shēncái (名) stature; figure; build

身长(長) shēncháng (名) 1 height (of a person) 2 length (of a garment from shoulder to hemline)

身段 shēnduàn (名) 1 (woman's) figure 2 (dancer's) posture

身份 shēnfen (名) 1 status; capacity; identity: ～证 identity card; ID card. 不合～ incompatible with one's status. 暴露～ reveal one's identity. 以官方～发言 speak in an official capacity 2 dignity: 有失～ be beneath one's dignity

身价(價) shēnjià (名) 1 social status: 抬高～ raise one's social status 2 the selling price of a slave

身教 shēnjiào (动) teach by one's own example

身临(臨)其境 shēn lín qí jìng be personally on the scene

身强力壮(壯) shēnqiáng-lìzhuàng (of a person) strong; tough; sturdy

身躯(軀) shēnqū (名) body; stature

身上 shēnshang (名) 1 on one's body; physically: 我～不舒服. I'm not feeling well. 2 (have sth.) on one; with one: ～没带笔. I haven't got a pen with me.

身世 shēnshì (名) one's life story; one's lot

身手 shēnshǒu (名) skill; talent: 大显～ fully display one's talents

身体(體) shēntǐ (名) 1 body 2 health: 注意～ look after one's health

身体(體)力行 shēntǐ-lìxíng earnestly practise what one advocates

身心 shēn-xīn (名) body and mind: ～健康 sound in body and mind

身孕 shēnyùn (名) pregnancy

身子 shēnzi (名) body: 光着～ be naked. ～不大舒服 not feel well

参 shēn (名) ginseng

see also cān; cēn

神 shén I (名) 1 god; deity 2 spirit; mind: 凝～ concentrate (or focus) one's attention 3 expression; look: 脸～ facial expression II (形) supernatural; magical: ～效 magical effect; miraculous effect

神采 shéncǎi (名) expression; look: ～奕奕 radiant with health and vigour

神出鬼没 shénchū-guǐmò (usu. of troop movement) appear and disappear mysteriously

神乎其神 shén hū qí shén mystifying; wonderful; miraculous: 说得～ laud sth. to the skies

神化 shénhuà (动) deify

神话 shénhuà (名) mythology; myth

神魂 shénhún (名) state of mind; mind: ～不定 be on tenterhooks

神机(機)妙算 shénjī-miàosuàn miraculous foresight

神经(經) shénjīng (名) nerve: ～紧张 be

S

nervous. ～官能症 neurosis. ～衰弱 neurasthenia. ～系统 nervous system

神经(經)病 shénjīngbìng (名) 1 neuropathy 2 mental disorder

神经(經)过(過)敏 shénjīng guòmǐn 1 neuroticism 2 oversensitive

神灵(靈) shénlíng (名) gods; deities; divinities

神秘 shénmì (形) mysterious

神明 shénmíng (名) gods; deities; divinities: 奉若～ worship sb. or sth.

神奇 shénqí (形) magical; mystical; miraculous: ～的效果 miraculous effect

神气(氣) shénqi I (名) expression; air; manner: 得意的～ an air of complacency. 他说话的～特别认真. He speaks in a very deliberate manner. II (形) 1 spirited; vigorous: 他看起来很～. He looks quite impressive. 2 putting on airs; cocky: 没有什么可～的. There is nothing to be cocky about. ～十足 looking triumphant; looking very dignified

神枪(槍)手 shénqiāngshǒu (名) crack shot; expert marksman

神情 shénqíng (名) expression; look: 露出愉快的～ look happy; wear a happy expression

神权(權) shénquán (名) 1 religious authority; theocracy 2 rule by divine right

神色 shénsè (名) expression; look: ～自若 look unruffled

神圣(聖) shénshèng (形) sacred; holy: ～职责 sacred duty. ～不可侵犯 sacrosanct; inviolable

神似 shénsì (形) be alike in spirit

神速 shénsù I (形) marvellously quick: 收效～ be miraculously effective II (名) amazing speed: 兵贵～. Speed is precious in military operations.

神态(態) shéntài (名) expression; carriage; bearing

神通 shéntōng (名) remarkable ability: ～广大 be immensely resourceful; have vast magic power

神童 shéntóng (名) child prodigy

神往 shénwǎng (动) be fascinated: 令人～ fascinating

神仙 shénxian (名) supernatural being; immortal

神像 shénxiàng (名) the picture or statue of a god or Buddha

神学(學) shénxué (名) theology

神医(醫) shényī (名) highly skilled doctor; miracle-making doctor

神职(職)人员 shénzhí rényuán clergy; clergymen

神志 shénzhì (名) consciousness; senses; mind: ～清醒 remain conscious; in full control of one's senses. ～昏迷 lose consciousness; go into a coma

什(甚) shén

see also shí

什么(麼) shénme (代) 1 [used to indicate interrogation]: 你说～? What did you say? *or* Beg your pardon? 2 [used to indicate sth. indefinite]: 我饿了,想吃点～. I'm hungry. I feel like having a bite. 我们好像在～地方见过. It seems that we've met somewhere before. 3 [used before 也 or 都 to indicate the absence of exceptions within the stated scope]: 他～也不怕. He is afraid of nothing. 4 [in a phrase or sentence with one 什么 preceding another, the 1st 什么 always determines the meaning of the 2nd 什么]: 有～就说～ speak freely; say all you have got to say. 你喜欢～,就拿～. You can take whatever you like. 5 [used to indicate surprise or displeasure]: 他是～人? What sort of person is he? 6 [used after a verb to indicate reproach or disapproval]: 你笑～? What's so funny? 急～,时间还早呢! What's the hurry? It's still early. 7 [used before parallel words or phrases to indicate enumeration]: ～乒乓球啊,羽毛球啊,篮球啊,排球啊,他都会. He can play table tennis, badminton, basketball, volleyball, and what not.

什么(麼)的 shénmede (代) and so on; and what not: 下班后,他总喜欢到酒吧间喝杯啤酒～. After work, he likes to go to the bar for a mug of beer or something like that.

审(審) shěn

审(審) shěn I (形) careful: ～视 look closely at; gaze at; examine II (动) 1 examine; go over: ～稿 go over a draft or make some editorial changes 2 interrogate; try: ～案 try a case. 公～ put sb. on public trial

审查 shěnchá (动) examine; investigate: ～计划 check a plan. ～属实 establish a fact after investigation

审处(處) shěnchǔ (动) 1 try and punish 2 deliberate and decide

审订 shěndìng (动) examine and revise: ～

课文 revise textbooks

审定 shěndìng (动) examine and approve: 该报告已由委员会～. The report has been studied and approved by the committee.

审核 shěnhé (动) examine and verify: ～预算 examine and approve a budget. ～经费 examine and verify the expenses

审计 shěnjì (动) audit: ～员 auditor

审校 shěnjiào I (动) check and revise II (名) reviser

审理 shěnlǐ (动) try; hear: ～案件 try a case; hear a case

审美 shěnměi (动) appreciate the beauty of: ～能力 aesthetic judgement

审判 shěnpàn (动) bring to trial; try: ～程序 judicial procedure. ～机关 judicial organ

审批 shěnpī (动) examine and approve: 报请领导～ be submitted to the leadership for examination and approval

审慎 shěnshèn (形) cautious; careful: 处理这个问题必须～. The matter has to be handled with great care.

审时(時)度势(勢) shěnshí-duóshì size up the current situation

审问 shěnwèn (动) interrogate

审讯 shěnxùn (动) interrogate; try

审议(議) shěnyì (动) consider; deliberate: 这个计划正在～中. The project is under discussion.

审阅 shěnyuè (动) examine carefully and critically

婶(嬸) shěn (名) 1 wife of father's younger brother; aunt 2 a form of address to a woman about one's mother's age; aunt; auntie

婶母 shěnmǔ (名) wife of father's younger brother; aunt

慎 shèn (形) careful; cautious: 谨小～微 overcautious

慎重 shènzhòng (形) cautious; careful; prudent; discreet: ～处理 handle with discretion. ～考虑 give careful consideration to

甚 shèn I (副) very; extremely: ～佳 very good. ～念 miss sb. very much II (动) surpass; exceed: 局势恶化, 日～一日. The situation is deteriorating with each passing day.

甚嚣尘(塵)上 shèn xiāo chén shàng arouse a public clamour; (of hostile political propaganda) spread far and wide

甚至 shènzhì (副) even; (go) so far as to; so much so that: 他很激动, ～连话都说不出来了. He was so excited that he couldn't utter a word. 他走得如此匆忙, ～都忘了说声再见. He left in such a hurry that he even forgot to say goodbye.

肾(腎) shèn (名) kidney

肾功能 shèngōngnéng (名) kidney function

肾结石 shènjiéshí (名) kidney stone

肾脏(臟) shènzàng (名) kidney

渗(滲) shèn (动) ooze; seep: 水都～到房子里去了. Water has seeped into the rooms.

渗漏 shènlòu (动) seep; leak

渗入 shènrù (动) 1 permeate; seep into: ～地下 seep into the ground 2 (of evil influence, ideas, etc.) infiltrate; pervade

渗透 shèntòu (动) 1 permeate; seep 2 infiltrate

声(聲) shēng I (名) 1 sound; voice: 雨～ the patter of rain (on a roof). 小～说话 speak in a low voice 2 tone: 四～ the four tones of a Chinese character 3 reputation: ～誉 reputation; fame; prestige II (动) make a sound: 不～不响 keep quiet; not utter a word III (量) [for frequency of utterance]: 我喊了他几～, 他都没有听见. I called him several times, but he didn't hear me.

声辩(辯) shēngbiàn (动) argue; justify

声波 shēngbō (名) sound wave; acoustic wave

声称(稱) shēngchēng (动) profess; claim; assert: ～已达成协议 claim to have reached an agreement

声带(帶) shēngdài (名) 1 vocal cords 2 sound track

声调 shēngdiào (名) 1 tone; note: ～低沉 in a low, sad voice 2 the tone of a Chinese character

声东(東)击(擊)西 shēng dōng jī xī make a feint to the east and attack in the west

声泪(淚)俱下 shēng-lèi jù xià shed tears while speaking: 他～地诉说了自己的不幸遭遇. Tears streamed down his cheeks as he recounted his misfortunes.

声名 shēngmíng (名) reputation: ～狼藉 become notorious; bring discredit on oneself

声明 shēngmíng I (动) state; declare; announce: 庄严～ solemnly state II (名)

statement; declaration: 发表～ issue a statement

声色 shēng-sè (名) the voice and countenance of a speaker: 不动～ maintain one's composure. ～俱厉 (speak) in a severe tone and with a severe look on one's face

声势(勢) shēngshì (名) impetuous force: 虚张～ bluff and bluster

声嘶力竭 shēngsī-lìjié shout oneself hoarse and suffer from exhaustion

声速 shēngsù (名) velocity of sound

声讨 shēngtǎo (动) denounce; condemn

声望 shēngwàng (名) popularity; prestige: 享有很高的～ enjoy great prestige; be held in high repute

声威 shēngwēi (名) renown; prestige: ～大震 add greatly to one's reputation and prestige

声息 shēngxī (名) 1 [often used in negative sentences] sound: 院子里静悄悄的,没有一点～. All was quiet and still, and not a sound was audible in the courtyard. 2 information: 互通～ keep in touch with each other

声响(響) shēngxiǎng (名) sound; noise

声学(學) shēngxué (名) acoustics: 建筑～ architectural acoustics

声讯 shēngxùn (名) audio information: ～电话 phone call that provides audio information

声音 shēngyīn (名) sound; voice

声誉(譽) shēngyù (名) reputation; fame; prestige

声援 shēngyuán (动) express support for; give vocal support to

声乐(樂) shēngyuè (名) vocal music

S

声张(張) shēngzhāng (动) make public; disclose: 不要～. Don't breathe a word of it.

生

shēng I (动) 1 give birth to; bear: ～孩子 give birth to a child 2 grow: ～芽 sprout 3 get: ～病 fall ill 4 light (a fire) II (形) 1 living: ～物 living things 2 unripe; green: 这些西瓜还是～的. The watermelons are not ripe yet. 3 raw; uncooked: ～肉 raw meat. 西红柿可以～吃. Tomatoes can be eaten raw. 4 unprocessed; unrefined; crude: ～铁 pig iron. ～皮 rawhide; (untanned) hide 5 unfamiliar; unacquainted; strange: ～词 new word 6 stiff; mechanical: ～凑 mechanically put together (disconnected words and phrases) III (副) [used before a few words to express emotion and sensation] extremely; very: ～疼 very painful IV (名) 1 existence; life: 一～ all one's life. 舍～取义 lay down one's life in the cause of justice 2 livelihood: 谋～ earn one's livelihood; make a living 3 pupil; student: 师～关系 teacher-student relationship

生搬硬套 shēngbān-yìngtào copy mechanically in disregard of specific conditions

生病 shēngbìng (动) fall ill

生菜 shēngcài (名) romaine lettuce; lettuce

生产(產) shēngchǎn I (动) 1 produce; manufacture: ～石油 produce oil 2 give birth to a child: 她快～了. She'll be having a baby soon. *or* She's expecting a baby. II (名) production: 发展～ develop production. ～成本 cost of production. ～定额 production quota. ～方式 mode of production. ～关系 relations of production. ～力 productive forces. ～率 productivity. ～资料 means of production. ～总值 total output value

生辰 shēngchén (名) birthday

生存 shēngcún (动) subsist; exist; live: ～竞争 struggle for existence. ～空间 living space

生动(動) shēngdòng (形) lively; vivid: ～的描写 vivid description. ～的语言 lively language

生动(動)活泼(潑) shēngdòng huópo lively; vivid and vigorous

生根 shēnggēn (动) take root; strike root

生活 shēnghuó I (名) 1 life: 日常～ daily life 2 livelihood: ～困难 be hard up II (动) live: 我们～得很幸福. We live a happy life. ～必需品 daily necessities. ～方式 way of life; life style. ～费用 living expenses; cost of living. ～水平 living standard. ～条件 living conditions. ～习惯 habits and customs

生火 shēnghuǒ (动) make a fire; light a fire

生冷 shēng-lěng (名) raw or cold food

生离(離)死别 shēnglí-sǐbié part never to meet again; part for ever

生理 shēnglǐ (名) physiology: ～学 physiology

生力军 shēnglìjūn (名) 1 fresh combatants 2 new young members of a group

生龙(龍)活虎 shēnglóng-huóhǔ bursting with energy; full of vim and vigour

生路 shēnglù (名) 1 means of livelihood 2 way out

生猛 shēngměng (形) live and fresh; strong: ～海鲜 fresh seafood. ～后生 strong young man
生米煮成熟饭 shēngmǐ zhǔchéng shúfàn what's done can't be undone
生命 shēngmìng (名) life: 月球上没有～. There is no life on the moon. ～线 lifeline; lifeblood
生命力 shēngmìnglì (名) vitality
生怕 shēngpà (动) fear; be afraid of: 我们在泥泞的路上小心地走着, ～滑倒了. We picked our way along a muddy road for fear we might slip and fall.
生僻 shēngpì (形) uncommon; rare: ～的字眼 rarely used words
生平 shēngpíng (名) life story; life
生气(氣) shēngqì I (动) take offence; get angry II (名) life; vitality: ～勃勃的人 a dynamic person
生前 shēngqián (名) before one's death; in one's lifetime: ～的愿望 unrealized wish (of a person who has passed away). ～友好 friends of the deceased
生擒 shēngqín (动) capture
生人 shēngrén (名) stranger
生日 shēngri (名) birthday
生色 shēngsè (动) add lustre to; give added significance to: 他的演出, 为酒会～不少. His performance made the cocktail party even more enjoyable.
生身父母 shēngshēn fù-mǔ one's own parents
生事 shēngshì (动) make trouble; create a disturbance: 造谣～ spread rumours and create disturbances
生手 shēngshǒu (名) sb. new to a job; novice; greenhorn
生疏 shēngshū (形) **1** not familiar: 人地～ be practically a stranger in a certain locality and have few friends there **2** out of practice; rusty: 他的英文有点～了. His English is a little rusty. **3** not as close as before: 分别多年, 我们的关系～了. We're not as close as we used to be, for we haven't been in touch for so many years.
生水 shēngshuǐ (名) unboiled water
生死 shēng-sǐ (名) life and death: ～与共 share life and death; through thick and thin. ～存亡的斗争 a life-and-death struggle. ～攸关的问题 a matter of vital importance
生态(態) shēngtài (名) ecology: ～平衡 ecological balance
生态(態)环(環)境 shēngtài huánjìng environment
生吞活剥 shēngtūn-huóbō accept uncritically other people's theory, method of doing things, etc.
生物 shēngwù (名) living things; living beings; organisms: ～化学 biochemistry. ～武器 biological weapon. ～学 biology. ～钟 biological clock
生物工程 shēngwù gōngchéng biological engineering
生息 shēngxī (动) live; exist; propagate: 休养～ live and multiply; rest and build up one's strength
生肖 shēngxiào (名) any of the twelve animals symbolizing the year in which one is born (The twelve animals are: the rat, the ox, the tiger, the rabbit, the dragon, the snake, the horse, the sheep, the monkey, the rooster, the dog and the pig.) (also as "属相" shǔxiang)
生效 shēngxiào (动) go into effect; become effective: 自签字之日起～ go into effect from the date of signature
生性 shēngxìng (名) natural disposition
生锈 shēngxiù (动) get rusty
生涯 shēngyá (名) career; profession: 教书～ the teaching profession
生疑 shēngyí (动) be suspicious
生意 shēngyi (名) business; trade: 做～ do business
生硬 shēngyìng (形) **1** stiff; rigid; harsh: 态度～ be stiff in manner **2** not natural; affected; forced: 这几个字用得很～. These words are not well-chosen.
生育 shēngyù (动) give birth to; bear: ～子女 bear children. 计划～ family planning. ～年龄 child-bearing age
生造 shēngzào (动) coin (words and expressions): ～词 coinage
生长(長) shēngzhǎng (动) **1** grow: 小麦～良好. The wheat is growing well. **2** grow up; be brought up
生殖 shēngzhí (动) reproduce: ～器 reproductive organs; genitals
生字 shēngzì (名) new word: ～表 (a list of) new words

甥 shēng (名) sister's son; nephew

甥女 shēngnǚ (名) sister's daughter; niece

牲 shēng (名) 1 domestic animal 2 animal sacrifice

牲畜 shēngchù (名) livestock; domestic animals

牲口 shēngkou (名) draught animals; beasts of burden

升 shēng I (动) 1 move upward: 上～ rise 2 promote: 被提～到负责岗位 be promoted to a position of responsibility II (量) 1 litre: 一～啤酒 a litre of beer 2 *sheng*, a unit of dry measure for grain (＝1 litre)

升格 shēnggé (动) promote; upgrade: 将外交关系～为大使级 upgrade diplomatic relations to ambassadorial level

升官 shēngguān (动) be promoted: ～发财 win promotion and get rich

升华(華) shēnghuá (动) 1 sublimate 2 raise things to a higher level

升级 shēngjí (动) 1 go up (one grade, etc.) 2 escalate: 战争～ escalation (of a war)

升降机(機) shēngjiàngjī (名) elevator; lift

升旗 shēngqí (动) raise (or hoist) a flag

升学(學) shēngxué (动) enter a higher school

升值 shēngzhí (动) revalue; appreciate

绳(繩) shéng I (名) rope; cord; string: 麻～ hemp rope. 钢丝～ steel cable; wire rope. ～梯 rope ladder II (动) restrict; restrain: ～以纪律 restrain (unruly people) by discipline. ～之以法 bring to justice

省 shěng I (动) 1 economize; save: ～钱 save money. ～时间 save time 2 omit; leave out: 这两个字不能～. These two words cannot be omitted. II (名) province: ～会 provincial capital
see also xǐng

省吃俭(儉)用 shěngchī-jiǎnyòng live frugally

省得 shěngde (连) so as to save (or avoid): 请准时来，～大家等你. Come on time so as not to keep us waiting.

省力 shěnglì (动) save effort; save labour

省略 shěnglüè (动) leave out; omit: ～句 elliptical sentence

省事 shěngshì (动) save trouble; simplify matters: 在食堂里吃饭～. Having meals in the canteen saves us a lot of trouble.

省心 shěngxīn (动) save worry

盛 shèng (形) 1 flourishing; prosperous: 全～时期 in the heyday of one's glory 2 vigorous; energetic: 火势很～. The fire is raging. 3 magnificent; grand: ～举 a grand occasion (or event) 4 abundant; plentiful: ～意 great kindness 5 popular; common; widespread: ～传 rumours go about that . . . 6 greatly; deeply: ～赞 praise profusely
see also chéng

盛产(產) shèngchǎn (动) abound in: ～石油 be rich in oil

盛传(傳) shèngchuán (动) be widely known; be widely rumoured

盛典 shèngdiǎn (名) grand ceremony

盛会(會) shènghuì (名) grand occasion; impressive gathering

盛举(舉) shèngjǔ (名) a grand event; a grand occasion

盛况 shèngkuàng (名) grand occasion; spectacular event: ～空前 an exceptionally grand occasion

盛名 shèngmíng (名) great reputation: ～之下，其实难副. While a person enjoys a high reputation, he may not be able to measure up to it.

盛气(氣)凌人 shèngqì líng rén domineering; arrogant; overbearing

盛情 shèngqíng (名) great kindness; boundless hospitality: 受到～款待 be accorded cordial hospitality

盛衰 shèng-shuāi (名) prosperity and decline; rise and fall; ups and downs

盛夏 shèngxià (名) the height of summer; midsummer

盛行 shèngxíng (动) be current (or rife, rampant); be in vogue: ～一时 be the rage for a time; prevail for a time

盛宴 shèngyàn (名) a grand banquet; a sumptuous dinner

盛意 shèngyì (名) great kindness: ～难却. It would be difficult to decline your kind offer.

盛誉(譽) shèngyù (名) great fame; high reputation

盛赞 shèngzàn (动) highly praise; pay high tribute to

盛装(裝) shèngzhuāng (名) splendid attire; Sunday best

剩 shèng (动) be left (over); remain: 还～多少? How much is left (over)? ～货 surplus goods. ～菜～饭 leftovers

剩下 shèngxià (动) be left (over); remain: ～多少钱? How much money is left? 别人都走了，就～我一个. The others have all gone; I'm the only one left here.

剩余(餘) shèngyú (名) surplus; remainder: ～价值 surplus value

胜(勝) shèng I (名) victory; success: 取～ win (victory) II (动) 1 defeat; conquer: 战～自然 conquer nature 2 surpass; be superior to: 事实～于雄辩. Facts speak louder than words. 3 be equal to; can bear: 力不能～ one's ability falls short of the task III (形) superb; wonderful; lovely: 引人入～ fascinating

胜败 shèng-bài (名) victory or defeat; success or failure: ～乃兵家常事. Victory or defeat is an ordinary experience for a soldier.

胜地 shèngdì (名) famous scenic spot: 避暑～ summer resort

胜负 shèng-fù (名) victory or defeat; success or failure: 战争的～ the outcome of a war

胜过(過) shèngguò (动) be better than; be superior to

胜迹 shèngjì (名) famous historical site

胜景 shèngjǐng (名) wonderful scenery

胜利 shènglì I (名) victory; triumph: 取得～ win victory. 从～走向～ from victory to victory. ～果实 fruits of victory. ～者 victor; winner II (副) successfully; triumphantly: ～完成任务 successfully carry out one's task

胜券 shèngquàn (名) the chances of success: 操～ be sure to succeed

胜任 shèngrèn (动) be competent; be qualified; be equal to: ～工作 prove equal to one's job; be competent at a job. 能～愉快 be able to fulfil the task with credit

胜似 shèngsì (动) be better than; surpass

胜诉 shèngsù (动) win a lawsuit

胜仗 shèngzhàng (名) victory: 打～ win a battle

圣(聖) shèng I (名) sage; saint II (形) 1 holy; sacred 2 of the emperor; imperial: ～上 His or Her Majesty

圣诞 shèngdàn (名) the birthday of Jesus Christ: ～老人 Santa Claus. ～节 Christmas Day. ～节前夕 Christmas Eve. ～卡 Christmas card; Xmas card

圣地 shèngdì (名) 1 the Holy Land 2 sacred place; shrine

圣洁(潔) shèngjié (形) holy and pure

圣经(經) shèngjīng (名) the Holy Bible; the Bible

圣灵(靈) shènglíng (名) the Holy Spirit; the Holy Ghost

圣人 shèngrén (名) sage

圣贤(賢) shèngxián (名) sages

圣谕 shèngyù (名) imperial decree

圣旨 shèngzhǐ (名) imperial edict

湿(濕) shī (形) wet; damp; humid: 他被雨淋～了. He got soaked in the rain.

湿度 shīdù (名) humidity

湿淋淋 shīlīnlīn (形) dripping wet; drenched: 身上浇得～的 get dripping wet

湿漉漉 shīlūlū (形) wet; damp

湿气(氣) shīqì (名) 1 moisture; dampness 2 fungus infection of hand or foot

湿润 shīrùn (形) moist: ～的土壤 damp soil. 空气～ humid air

湿透 shītòu (形) wet through; drenched: 汗水～ wet through with sweat

湿疹 shīzhěn (名) eczema

诗 shī (名) poetry; verse; poem

诗歌 shīgē (名) poems and songs; poetry

诗话 shīhuà (名) random notes on classical poets and poetry

诗集 shījí (名) collection of poems; poetry anthology

诗经(經) shījīng (名) *The Book of Songs*

诗句 shījù (名) verse; line

诗篇 shīpiān (名) 1 poem 2 inspiring story

诗人 shīrén (名) poet

诗兴(興) shīxìng (名) poetic inspiration: ～大发 have a strong urge to write a poem; be in poetic mood

诗意 shīyì (名) poetic atmosphere

诗韵(韻) shīyùn (名) 1 rhyme (in poetry) 2 rhyming dictionary

诗作 shīzuò (名) poetic works

师(師) shī (名) 1 teacher; master: 能者为～. Whoever knows the job will be the teacher. 2 model; example: 前事不忘,后事之～. Past experience, if remembered, is a guide for the future. 3 a person skilled in a certain profession: 工程～ engineer. 建筑～ architect. 技～ technician 4 of one's master or teacher: ～母 the wife of one's teacher or master 5 division: 装甲～ armoured division 6 troops; army: 正义之～ an army fighting for a just cause

师出无(無)名 shī chū wú míng dispatch

troops for war without cause
师范(範) shīfàn (名) teacher-training; pedagogical: ～学院 teachers-training college
师父 shīfu (名) **1** see "师傅" shīfu **2** a polite form of address to a Buddhist monk or nun or Taoist priest
师傅 shīfu (名) **1** master worker **2** a polite form of address to people who have skill or specialized knowledge: 老～ old master
师生 shī-shēng (名) teacher and student
师徒 shī-tú (名) master and apprentice
师长(長) shīzhǎng (名) **1** teacher **2** division commander
师资 shīzī (名) qualified teachers; teachers: 培养～ train teachers

狮(獅) shī (名) lion

狮子 shīzi (名) lion

嘘 shī (叹): ～, 别作声! Sh (or Hush)! Keep quiet!

失 shī I (动) **1** lose: 遗～ lose. 坐～良机 let slip a good opportunity; lose a good chance **2** fail to get hold of: ～手 drop. ～足 slip. 万无一～ one hundred percent safe **3** deviate from the normal: ～色 turn pale **4** break (a promise); go back on (one's word): ～信 break one's promise; fail to keep one's word **5** get lost: 迷～方向 lose one's bearings **6** fail to achieve one's end: ～望 be disappointed II (名) mishap; defect; mistake: ～之于烦琐. The fault is that it gives unwarranted attention to details.

失败 shībài I (动) fail; be defeated (in war, etc.): 他注定要～. He is doomed to fail. II (名) failure; defeat: ～是成功之母. Failure is the mother of success.
失策 shīcè I (动) make a wrong decision; miscalculate II (名) wrong move; unwise move
失常 shīcháng (形) abnormal; odd: 举止～ act oddly. 他今天有点～. He is not himself today.
失宠(寵) shīchǒng (动) be in disgrace; fall from grace
失传(傳) shīchuán (动) not be handed down from past generations: 一种～的艺术 a lost art
失聪(聰) shīcōng (动) become deaf
失措 shīcuò (动) be at a loss as to what to do: 仓皇～ unable to stay collected
失当(當) shīdàng (形) improper; inappropriate
失道寡助 shī dào guǎ zhù an unjust cause find little support
失地 shīdì (名) lost territory: 收复～ recover lost territory
失掉 shīdiào (动) **1** lose: ～信心 lose confidence. ～联系 lose contact **2** miss; fail to make use of: ～机会 miss a chance
失魂落魄 shīhún-luòpò be distracted: 吓得～ be scared out of one's wits
失火 shīhuǒ (动) catch fire; be on fire
失脚 shījiǎo (动) lose one's footing; slip
失节(節) shījié (动) **1** lose one's virginity **2** be disloyal
失控 shīkòng (动) be out of control
失口 shīkǒu (动) make a slip of the tongue
失礼(禮) shīlǐ (动) commit a breach of etiquette
失利 shīlì (动) suffer a setback (or defeat)
失恋(戀) shīliàn (动) suffer from unrequited love
失灵(靈) shīlíng (动) (of a machine, instrument, etc.) not work or not work properly: 机器～了. The machine is out of order.
失落 shīluò (动) lose
失密 shīmì (动) give away official secret due to carelessness; let out a secret
失眠 shīmián (动) suffer from insomnia
失明 shīmíng (动) lose one's sight; go blind
失陪 shīpéi 〈套〉 I must be leaving now
失窃(竊) shīqiè (动) have things stolen
失去 shīqù (动) lose: ～知觉 lose consciousness. ～时效 be no longer effective; cease to be in force
失散 shīsàn (动) lose touch with each other usually on account of some unfortunate incidents: 他找到了～多年的母亲. He has found his mother, with whom he was not in contact for many years.
失色 shīsè (动) **1** fade **2** turn pale: 大惊～ turn pale with fright
失声(聲) shīshēng (动) **1** cry out suddenly and unconsciously **2** be choked with tears **3** lose one's voice
失实(實) shīshí (动) be inconsistent with the facts: 传闻～. The rumour was unfounded.
失事 shīshì (动) have an accident
失势(勢) shīshì (动) lose power and influence; fall into disgrace
失守 shīshǒu (动) fall into enemy hands: 城市～ the fall of a city

S

失算 shīsuàn (动) miscalculate; misjudge
失调 shītiáo (动) 1 be out of balance: 供求～ imbalance of supply and demand 2 lack of proper care (after an illness, etc.): 产后～ lack of proper care after childbirth
失望 shīwàng (动) 1 lose hope or confidence 2 be disappointed
失误 shīwù (名) fault; mistake: 发球～ a serving fault
失陷 shīxiàn (动) (of cities, territory, etc.) fall; fall into enemy hands
失效 shīxiào (动) become invalid; be no longer in force; cease to be effective
失笑 shīxiào (动) cannot help laughing
失信 shīxìn (动) break one's promise; go back on one's word
失修 shīxiū (动) (of houses, etc.) be in bad repair; fall into disrepair
失言 shīyán (动) make a slip of the tongue; make an indiscreet remark: 酒后～ make an indiscreet remark under the influence of alcohol
失业(業) shīyè (动) lose one's job; be out of work; be unemployed
失业(業)保险(險) shīyè bǎoxiǎn unemployment insurance
失语 shīyǔ I (名) loss of ability to speak; aphasia II (动) remain silent
失约 shīyuē (动) fail to keep an appointment
失真 shīzhēn (动) 1 (of voice, images, etc.) lack fidelity; not be true to the original 2 distortion: 频率～ frequency distortion
失职(職) shīzhí (动) neglect one's duty; dereliction of duty
失重 shīzhòng (名) weightlessness
失主 shīzhǔ (名) owner of lost property
失踪(蹤) shīzōng (动) disappear; be missing
失足 shīzú (动) 1 lose one's footing; slip: ～落水 slip and fall into the water 2 commit a serious error in life (often of a moral nature): 一～成千古恨. One false step brings eternal regret.

施 shī (动) 1 put into practice: 实～ implement. 无计可～ no strong card to play 2 bestow; grant; hand out: ～恩 bestow favour. 己所不欲,勿～于人. Don't do to others what you don't want done to yourself. 3 exert; impose: ～加压力 exert pressure 4 use; apply: ～肥 apply fertilizer
施放 shīfàng (动) discharge; fire: ～催泪弹 fire tear-gas shells
施工 shīgōng (动) engage in construction: 正在～ be under construction
施加 shījiā (动) exert; bring to bear on: ～压力 bring pressure to bear on sb.; put pressure on sb. ～影响 exert one's influence over sb.
施礼(禮) shīlǐ (动) make a bow; salute
施舍(捨) shīshě (动) give alms; give in charity
施行 shīxíng (动) 1 put into force: ～责任制 implement a system of responsibility 2 perform: ～手术 perform a surgical operation
施展 shīzhǎn (动) put to good use; give free play to: ～本领 give full play to one's talent
施政 shīzhèng (名) administration: ～纲领 administrative programme
施主 shīzhǔ (名) 1 alms giver; benefactor 2 donor

尸(屍) shī (名) corpse; dead body: 政治僵～ political corpse
尸骨 shīgǔ (名) skeleton
尸体(體) shītǐ (名) corpse; dead body; remains: ～解剖 autopsy; post-mortem (examination)

虱(蝨) shī (名) louse
虱子 shīzi (名) louse

实(實) shí I (形) 1 solid: ～心车胎 solid rubber tyres 2 true; real; honest: 真心～意 sincere and honest II (名) 1 reality; fact: 名不副～. The name falls short of the reality. 2 fruit; seed: 开花结～ blossom and bear fruit
实报(報)实销 shíbào-shíxiāo reimburse the cost
实弹(彈) shídàn (名) live shell; live ammunition: ～演习 practice with live ammunition
实地 shídì (副) on the spot: ～考察 on-the-spot investigation
实干(幹) shígàn (动) get right on the job; do solid work: ～家 man of action
实话 shíhuà (名) truth: 说～ to tell the truth. ～实说 speak frankly; tell it like it is
实惠 shíhuì I (名) real benefit II (形) substantial
实际(際) shíjì I (名) reality; practice: 客观

～ objective reality. ～上 in fact; in reality; actually II (形) 1 practical; realistic: ～经验 practical experience 2 real; actual; concrete: ～情况 actual situation; reality. ～行动 concrete action. ～收入 real income

实践(踐) shíjiàn I (名) practice: ～出真知. Genuine knowledge comes from practice. II (动) put into practice; carry out: ～诺言 make good one's promise

实据(據) shíjù (名) substantial evidence; substantial proof: 真凭～ ironclad evidence

实况 shíkuàng (名) what is actually happening: 电视转播足球赛～ televise a football match; live telecast of a football match. ～转播 live broadcast; live telecast

实力 shílì (名) strength: ～地位 position of strength. 军事～ military strength. ～相当 match each other in strength

实例 shílì (名) instance; example

实情 shíqíng (名) the true state of affairs; the actual situation; truth

实权(權) shíquán (名) real power

实事求是 shí shì qiú shì seek truth from the facts; be down-to-earth: ～的态度 a realistic approach

实体(體) shítǐ (名) 1 substance 2 entity

实物 shíwù (名) 1 material object 2 in kind: ～交易 barter

实习(習) shíxí (名) practice; fieldwork; field trip: 去工厂～ go on a field trip to a factory. ～生 trainee

实现 shíxiàn (动) realize; achieve; bring about: ～改革 bring about a reform. 他的梦想～了. His dream has come true.

实效 shíxiào (名) actual effect; substantial results: 讲究～ stress on practical results

实行 shíxíng (动) put into practice (or effect); carry out; practise; implement: ～计划生育 practise family planning. ～对外开放政策 carry out the policy of opening to the outside world

实验(驗) shíyàn (名) experiment; test: 做～ do (or carry out) an experiment; make a test. ～动物 animal used as a subject of experiment. ～室 laboratory. ～小学 pilot school

实业(業) shíyè (名) industry and commerce; industry: ～家 industrialist

实用 shíyòng (形) practical; pragmatic: ～主义 pragmatism. 既美观又～ not only beautiful, but also practical

实在 shízài I (形) true; real; honest; dependable: ～的本事 real ability II (副) indeed; really; honestly: 我～不知道. I really don't know.

实战(戰) shízhàn (名) actual combat

实至名归(歸) shízhì-míngguī fame follows merit; reputation comes after real distinction

实质(質) shízhì (名) substance; essence: 这两种看法～上是一样的. These two views are virtually identical.

识(識) shí I (动) know: 不～字 be illiterate II (名) knowledge: 常～ general knowledge

识别 shíbié (动) distinguish; discern; spot: ～真假朋友 tell true friends from false ones

识大体(體) shídàtǐ have the overall interest at heart

识货 shíhuò (动) be able to tell good from bad; appreciate the true worth of sb.'s or sth.'s quality

识破 shípò (动) see through; penetrate: ～诡计 see through a plot

识途老马(馬) shí tú lǎomǎ an old horse who knows the way — a person of rich experience; an old stager

识相 shíxiàng (动) be sensible

识字 shízì (动) learn to read; become literate: ～班 literacy class

十 shí I (数) ten: ～倍 ten times; tenfold. II (形) topmost: ～足学究气 unadulterated pedantry

十恶(惡)不赦 shí è bù shè guilty of heinous crimes

十二月 shí'èryuè (名) 1 December 2 the twelfth month of the lunar year; the twelfth moon

十分 shífēn (副) very; fully; utterly; extremely: 天气～热. It's awfully hot. ～高兴 very pleased. ～难过 feel very sorry; feel very bad. ～赞赏 highly appreciate. ～有害 extremely harmful

十进(進)制 shíjìnzhì (名) the decimal system

十拿九稳(穩) shíná-jiǔwěn as good as assured

十全十美 shíquán-shíměi perfect; flawless; impeccable

十万(萬)火急 shíwàn huǒjí 1 post-haste 2 Most Urgent (mark on dispatches)

十项全能运(運)动(動) shí xiàng quánnéng yùndòng (名) decathlon

S

十一月 shíyīyuè (名) 1 November 2 the eleventh month of the lunar year; the eleventh moon

十月 shíyuè (名) 1 October 2 the tenth month of the lunar year; the tenth moon

十之八九 shí zhī bā-jiǔ in eight or nine cases out of ten; most likely

十字架 shízìjià (名) cross

十字街头(頭) shízì jiētóu busy streets

十字路口 shízì lùkǒu crossroads

十足 shízú (形) 100 per cent; out-and-out; sheer; downright: 干劲～ very energetic. ～的书呆子 a real bookworm

什 shí (形) assorted; varied; miscellaneous

see also shén

什锦 shíjǐn (形) assorted; mixed: ～饼干 assorted biscuits. ～奶糖 assorted toffees

什物 shíwù (名) articles for daily use; odds and ends

石 shí (名) 1 stone; rock 2 stone inscription: 金～ inscriptions on ancient bronzes and stone tablets

石板 shíbǎn (名) slabstone; flagstone

石沉大海 shí chén dàhǎi disappear like a pebble thrown into the sea; make no response

石雕 shídiāo (名) 1 stone carving 2 carved stone

石方 shífāng (名) cubic metre of stonework

石膏 shígāo (名) gypsum; plaster stone: ～像 plaster statue; plaster figure

石灰 shíhuī (名) lime: ～石 limestone

石匠 shíjiàng (名) stonemason; mason

石窟 shíkū (名) rock cave; grotto

石蜡(蠟) shílà (名) paraffin wax: ～油 paraffin oil

石棉 shímián (名) asbestos: ～瓦 asbestos shingle; asbestos tile

石墨 shímò (名) graphite

石器 shíqì (名) 1 stone implement; stone artefact 2 stone vessel; stoneware: ～时代 the Stone Age

石英 shíyīng (名) quartz: ～钟 quartz clock

石油 shíyóu (名) petroleum; oil: ～产品 petroleum products. ～化工厂 petrochemical works. ～勘探 petroleum prospecting

石子儿(兒) shízǐr (名) cobblestone; cobble; pebble: ～路 cobblestone street; cobbled road; macadam

拾 shí I (动) pick up (from the ground); collect: ～柴 collect firewood. ～麦穗 glean (stray ears of) wheat II (数) ten [used for the numeral 十 on cheques, banknotes, etc. to avoid mistakes or alterations]

拾掇 shíduo (动) 1 tidy up; put in order: 屋里～得整整齐齐的. The room is kept clean and tidy. 2 repair; fix: 这电视机有点毛病, 你给～一下好吗? Something is wrong with the TV set. Will you help me fix it?

拾金不昧 shí jīn bù mèi not pocket the money one picks up; return the money found

拾零 shílíng (名) sidelights; titbits

拾取 shíqǔ (动) pick up; collect

拾人牙慧 shí rén yáhuì pick up some irrelevant remarks from people and pass them off as a sample of one's own wit

拾遗 shíyí (动) pick up any lost article from the road: 路不～. No one pockets anything found on the road.

时(時) shí I (名) 1 time; times; days: 古～ ancient times 2 fixed time: 准～上班 get to work on time 3 hour: 报～ announce the hour; give the time signal. 上午八～ at 8 o'clock in the morning; at 8 a.m. 4 season: 四～ the four seasons. ～菜 delicacies of the season 5 opportunity; chance: 失～ lose the opportunity; miss the chance. 待～而动 bide one's time 6 tense: 过去～ the past tense II (形) current; present: ～事 current affairs III (副) 1 occasionally; from time to time: ～有出现 appear from time to time 2 now... now...; sometimes... sometimes...: ～断～续 intermittently; off and on. ～起～伏 constant rise and fall

时不我待 shí bù wǒ dài time and tide wait for no man

时差 shíchā (名) time difference; jet lag

时常 shícháng (副) often; frequently

时代 shídài (名) 1 times; age; era; epoch: 开创一个新～ usher in a new era. ～精神 the watchword of the time 2 a period in one's life: 少年～ childhood

时而 shí'ér (副) 1 from time to time; sometimes 2 now... now...; sometimes... sometimes...: 这几天～晴天, ～下雨. It has been sometimes fine and sometimes rainy these few days.

S

时光 shíguāng (名) 1 time: ～不早了. It's getting late. 2 times; years; days

时候 shíhou (名) 1 (the duration of) time: 你来这儿有多少～了? How long have you been here? 2 (a point in) time; moment: 现在是什么～了? What time is it? ～到了,该走了. It's time we left.

时机(機) shíjī (名) opportunity; an opportune moment: 等待～ bide one's time; wait for an opportunity. ～一到 when the opportunity arises; at the opportune moment. ～不成熟. Conditions are not ripe yet.

时间 shíjiān (名) 1 (the concept of) time: ～与空间 time and space 2 (the duration of) time: 办公～ office hours 3 (a point in) time: 北京～十九点正 19:00 Beijing time. ～表 timetable; schedule

时间性 shíjiānxìng (名) timeliness: 新闻报导～强. News reports must be timely.

时节(節) shíjié (名) 1 season: 秋收～ the autumn harvest season 2 time: 那～她才十二岁. She was only twelve then.

时局 shíjú (名) the current political situation

时刻 shíkè I (名) time; hour; moment: 关键的～ a critical moment II (副) constantly; always: ～准备保卫祖国 be ready to defend the country at any moment

时刻表 shíkèbiǎo (名) timetable; schedule: 火车～ railway timetable; train schedule

时髦 shímáo (形) fashionable; stylish; in vogue: 赶～ follow the fashion; be in the swim

时期 shíqī (名) period: 殖民统治～ the period of colonial rule

S

时区(區) shíqū (名) time zone

时尚 shíshàng I (形) trendy; fashionable II (名) fashion; vogue; fad

时时(時) shíshí (副) often; constantly

时事 shíshì (名) current events; current affairs

时势(勢) shíshì (名) the current situation; the trend of the times

时速 shísù (名) speed per hour

时态(態) shítài (名) tense

时下 shíxià (名) at present; right now

时鲜 shíxiān (形) (of vegetables, fruits, etc.) in season: ～水果 fresh fruits

时限 shíxiàn (名) time limit

时新 shíxīn (形) stylish; trendy: ～式样 up-to-date style

时兴(興) shíxīng (形) fashionable; in vogue; popular

时宜 shíyí (名) what is appropriate to the occasion: 不合～ be out of step with the time

时运(運) shíyùn (名) luck; fortune: ～不济 be out of luck; be dogged by misfortune; down on one's luck

时钟(鐘) shízhōng (名) clock

时装(裝) shízhuāng (名) fashionable dress; the latest fashion: ～表演 fashion show. ～模特儿 fashion model

食 shí I (动) eat: 不劳动者不得～. He who does not work, neither shall he eat. II (名) 1 meal; food: 废寝忘～ forget about his meals and rest. 主～ staple food 2 feed: 猪～ pig feed 3 eclipse: 日～ solar eclipse. 月～ lunar eclipse III (形) edible: ～油 edible oil; cooking oil

食道 shídào (名) oesophagus

食具 shíjù (名) eating utensils; tableware

食粮(糧) shíliáng (名) grain; foodstuff

食品 shípǐn (名) foodstuff; food; provisions: 罐头～ tinned (or canned) food. ～厂 bakery and confectionery; food products factory. ～工业 food industry. ～加工 food processing

食谱 shípǔ (名) recipes; cookbook

食宿 shí-sù (名) board and lodging

食堂 shítáng (名) dining room; mess hall; canteen

食物 shíwù (名) food

食言 shíyán (动) go back on one's word; break one's promise

食盐(鹽) shíyán (名) table salt; salt

食用 shíyòng (形) edible: ～植物油 edible vegetable oil

食欲 shíyù (名) appetite: ～不振 have a poor appetite. 促进～ stimulate the appetite; be appetizing

食指 shízhǐ (名) index finger; forefinger

蚀 shí I (动) 1 lose: 亏～ lose (money) in business 2 erode; corrode: 风雨侵～ weather-beaten II (名) eclipse: 日～ solar eclipse

蚀本 shíběn (动) lose one's capital: ～生意 a losing business; an unprofitable venture (or undertaking)

史 shǐ (名) history: 近代～ modern history. 编年～ annals. 国际关系～ history of international relations

史册 shǐcè (名) history; annals: 载入～ go down in history; go down in the annals

of...
史料 shǐliào (名) historical data; historical materials
史前 shǐqián (名) prehistoric: ～时代 prehistoric age (or times). ～学(考古) prehistory
史诗 shǐshī (名) epic
史实(實) shǐshí (名) historical facts
史书(書) shǐshū (名) history; historical records
史无(無)前例 shǐ wú qiánlì without precedent in history; unprecedented
史学(學) shǐxué (名) the science of history; historical science; historiography
使 shǐ I (动) 1 send; tell sb. to do sth.: ～人去收集经济信息 send sb. to collect economic information 2 use; employ; apply: ～化肥 apply chemical fertilizer 3 make; cause; enable: ～国家遭受巨大损失 cause enormous losses to the state. 这一批评～她大为生气. This criticism infuriated her. II (名) envoy; messenger: 特～ special envoy. 出～国外 be sent abroad as an envoy. 大～ ambassador
使不得 shǐbude 1 cannot be used; useless; unserviceable: 这支笔～了. This fountain pen is no longer serviceable. 2 impermissible; undesirable
使出 shǐchū (动) use; exert: ～浑身解数 do something for all one is worth. ～最后一点力气 spend the last bit of one's energy
使得 shǐde (动) 1 can be used 2 be workable; be feasible 3 make; cause; render
使馆 shǐguǎn (名) diplomatic mission; embassy: ～馆舍 premises of a diplomatic mission
使唤 shǐhuan (动) tell people to carry out orders: ～人 order people about; be bossy
使节(節) shǐjié (名) diplomatic envoy; envoy
使劲(勁) shǐjìn (动) exert all one's strength: 再使把劲 put on another spurt
使命 shǐmìng (名) mission: 历史～ historical mission
使用 shǐyòng (动) make use of; use; employ; apply: 合理～资金 rational utilization of capital. ～率 rate of utilization. ～寿命 service life. ～说明书 operation instructions
使者 shǐzhě (名) emissary; envoy; messenger
驶 shǐ (动) 1 drive; sail 2 (of a vehicle, etc.) speed: 急～而过 speed past
屎 shǐ (名) 1 excrement; dung; droppings: 鸡～ chicken droppings. 牛～ cow dung. 拉～ move the bowels; shit 2 secretion (of the eye, ear, etc.): 耳～ earwax
矢 shǐ I (名) arrow: 飞～ flying arrow II (动) vow; swear: ～忠 vow to be loyal
矢口否认(認) shǐkǒu fǒurèn flatly deny: 他～说过那句话. He categorically denied that he had ever made such a remark.
始 shǐ I (名) beginning; start: 自～至终 from beginning to end; from start to finish II (副) only then: 不断学习,～能进步. Only persistent study yields steady progress. III (动) start; begin: 自今日～ starting today
始末 shǐ-mò (名) the whole story: 事情的～ the whole story from beginning to end
始终 shǐzhōng (副) from beginning to end; from start to finish; all along; throughout: 他一生～保持谦虚谨慎的作风. He remained modest and prudent all his life. ～如一 constant; consistent
始终不渝 shǐzhōng bù yú unswerving; steadfast: 我们～地坚持和平共处五项原则. We unswervingly adhere to the five principles of peaceful coexistence.
室 shì (名) room: 休息～ waiting-room; lounge. 会客～ reception room. 办公～ office
室内 shìnèi (名) indoor; interior: ～运动 indoor sport. ～游泳池 indoor swimming pool. ～装饰 interior decoration
室外 shìwài (名) outdoor; outside: ～活动 outdoor activities
市 shì (名) 1 market: 菜～ food market. 上～ be on the market; be in season 2 city; municipality: 参观～容 go sightseeing in the city 3 pertaining to the Chinese system of weights and measures: ～尺 *chi*, a unit of length (=1/3 metre)
市场(場) shìchǎng (名) marketplace; market; bazaar: 国内～ domestic market. ～分析 market analysis. ～管理 market management. ～竞争 market competition. 贴现～ discount market. 投机～ speculative market. ～繁荣. The market

is brisk. 这种意见在学术界里没有什么～. This idea has received little support in academic circles.

市场(場)机(機)制 shìchǎng jīzhì market mechanism

市集 shìjí (名) 1 fair 2 small town

市价(價) shìjià (名) market price

市郊 shìjiāo (名) suburb; outskirts

市斤 shìjīn (名) *jin*, a unit of weight (= 1/2 kilogram)

市井 shìjǐng (名)〈书〉market-place; town: ～小人 philistine

市侩(儈) shìkuài (名) sordid merchant: ～习气 philistinism

市民 shìmín (名) residents of a city; townsfolk

市亩(畝) shìmǔ (名) *mu*, a unit of area (=0.0667 hectares)

市区(區) shìqū (名) city proper; urban district

市容 shìróng (名) the appearance of a city: 保持～整洁 keep the city clean and tidy

市长(長) shìzhǎng (名) mayor

市镇 shìzhèn (名) small towns; towns

柿

shì (名) persimmon

柿饼 shìbǐng (名) dried persimmon

柿子 shìzi (名) persimmon

式

shì (名) 1 type; style; fashion: 新～ new type. 旧～ old-fashioned 2 pattern; form: 程～ pattern 3 ceremony; ritual: 开幕～ opening ceremony 4 formula: 方程～ equation 5 mood; mode: 叙述～ indicative mood

式样(樣) shìyàng (名) style; type; model: 一排排的楼房,～都很美观. There are rows of buildings with graceful designs all around.

式子 shìzi (名) 1 posture 2 formula

试

shì I (动) try; test: ～一～ have a try. ～产 trial production. ～穿 try on (a garment, shoes, etc.) II (名) examination

试表 shìbiǎo (动)〈口〉take sb.'s temperature

试点(點) shìdiǎn I (动) make experiments; conduct tests at selected points; launch a pilot project II (名) a place where an experiment is made; experimental unit

试管 shìguǎn (名) test tube: ～婴儿 test-tube babies

试航 shìháng (名) trial voyage or flight

试金石 shìjīnshí (名) touchstone

试卷 shìjuàn (名) examination paper; test paper

试探 shìtàn (动) sound out; feel out; probe; explore: 我要～他一下. I'll sound him out.

试探性 shìtànxìng (形) trial; exploratory; probing: ～谈判 exploratory talks. ～气球 trial balloon

试题 shìtí (名) examination questions; paper: 数学～很不容易. The maths paper was quite stiff.

试图(圖) shìtú (动) attempt; try

试想 shìxiǎng (动) [used in a rhetorical question to imply mild reproach] just think: ～你这样下去结果会多糟. Just imagine what harm it will do you if you go on like this.

试销 shìxiāo (动) place goods on trial sale; trial sale

试行 shìxíng (动) try out: ～制造 trial produce

试验(驗) shìyàn I (名) trial; experiment; test II (动) test: ～新机器 try out the new machines. ～场 testing ground

试用 shìyòng (动) 1 try out 2 be on probation: ～人员 person on probation

试纸 shìzhǐ (名) test paper: 石蕊～ litmus paper

试制(製) shìzhì (动) trial produce

拭

shì (动) wipe away; wipe

拭目以待 shì mù yǐ dài look forward to the fulfilment of one's wish; wait and see

示

shì (动) show; notify; instruct: 出～证件 produce one's papers. 暗～ hint; drop a hint. 请～ ask for instructions

示范(範) shìfàn (动) set an example; demonstrate: ～机器操作 demonstrate how to operate the machine

示例 shìlì (动) give typical examples; give instances

示弱 shìruò (动) show signs of weakness

示威 shìwēi (动) 1 demonstrate; hold a demonstration: ～游行 demonstration; parade; march 2 put on a show of force; display one's strength

示意 shìyì (动) signal; hint; gesture: 以目～ wink at sb.; tip sb. the wink

示意图(圖) shìyìtú (名) sketch map

视

shì (动) 1 look at: 注～ look at closely 2 regard; look upon; treat: 一～同仁 treat everybody equally 3 inspect; watch: 巡～ go on an inspection tour

视察 shìchá (动) inspect: ～边防部队 inspect a frontier guard unit

视窗 shìchuāng (名) window; view-finder

视点(點) shìdiǎn (名) perspective: 独特的～ a unique perspective

视而不见(見) shì ér bù jiàn look but see not; turn a blind eye to: 对这些缺点,不能～. You can't just overlook these faults.

视觉(覺) shìjué (名) visual sense; vision; sense of sight

视力 shìlì (名) vision; sight: ～测验 eyesight test. ～好(差) have good (poor) eyesight

视频 shìpín (名) video; video CD

视死如归(歸) shì sǐ rú guī meet one's death like a hero

视听(聽) shì-tīng (名) 1 seeing and hearing; what is seen and heard 2 audio-visual: ～教具 audio-visual aids

视野 shìyě (名) field of vision

士 shì (名) 1 scholar 2 non-commissioned officer: 上～(英) staff sergeant; (美) sergeant first class. 中～ sergeant. 下～ corporal 3 a person trained in a certain field: 护～ nurse 4 (commendable) person: 烈～ martyr

士兵 shìbīng (名) rank-and-file soldiers; privates

士大夫 shìdàfū (名) court officials; scholar-officials (in feudal China); literati

士气(氣) shìqì (名) morale; fighting spirit: 鼓舞～ boost morale

士绅 shìshēn (名) gentry

士卒 shìzú (名) soldiers; privates: 身先～ (of an officer) fight at the head of his men; lead a charge

仕 shì (动) be an official

仕女 shìnǚ (名) 1 a bevy of beauties — a genre in traditional Chinese painting 2 maids of honour (in an imperial palace)

仕途 shìtú (名)〈书〉official career

恃 shì (动) rely on; depend on: 有～无恐 be fearless because one has powerful backing

恃才傲物 shì cái ào wù be contemptuous of others on the strength of one's own abilities; overweening

恃强凌弱 shì qiáng líng ruò bully the weak because one is backed by one's own strength

侍 shì (动) wait upon; attend upon; serve

侍从(從) shìcóng (动) attendants; retinue

侍奉 shìfèng (动) wait upon; attend upon; serve

侍候 shìhòu (动) wait upon; look after; attend

侍女 shìnǚ (名) maidservant; maid

侍卫(衛) shìwèi (名) imperial bodyguard

侍者 shìzhě (名) attendant; servant; waiter

世 shì (名) 1 lifetime; life: 一生一～ a lifetime 2 generation: ～交 a traditional friendly relationship which goes back to many generations 3 age; era: 当今之～ at present; nowadays 4 world: 举～闻名 well known all over the world; world-famous 5 epoch

世仇 shìchóu (名) 1 family feud 2 vendetta

世传(傳) shìchuán (动) be handed down through generations

世代 shìdài (名) for generations; from generation to generation; generation after generation: ～相传 pass on from generation to generation

世故 shìgù (名) the ways of the world; experience in human relationships: 老于～ experienced; worldly-wise

世故 shìgu (形) worldly-wise; crafty

世纪 shìjì (名) century

世家 shìjiā (名) aristocratic or noble family

世交 shìjiāo (名) friendship spanning two or more generations

世界 shìjiè (名) world: ～博览会 World's Fair. ～语 Esperanto. ～主义 cosmopolitanism

世界贸易组织(織) Shìjiè Màoyì Zǔzhī World Trade Organization; WTO

世面 shìmiàn (名) various aspects of society; society; world; life: 见过～ have seen the world

世人 shìrén (名) people at large

世上 shìshang (名) in the world; on earth: ～无难事,只怕有心人. Nothing in the world is difficult for one who is set to do it.

世事 shìshì (名) affairs of human life

世俗 shìsú I (名) common customs: ～之见 a philistine point of view II (形) secular; worldly

世态(態) shìtài (名) the ways of the world: ～炎凉 snobbery

世途 shìtú (名) experiences in life: ～坎坷 a life full of frustrations

世外桃源 shìwài táoyuán land of eternal peace far from the madding crowd

世袭(襲) shìxí (形) hereditary: ～制度 the hereditary system

世系 shìxì (名) pedigree; genealogy

事 shì I (名) 1 matter; affair; thing; business: 国家大～ state affairs 2 trouble; accident: 出～ have an accident. 惹～ make trouble; stir up trouble 3 job; work: 找～ look for a job 4 responsibility; involvement: 没有你的～了. This has nothing to do with you. II (动) be engaged in: 无所～～ doing nothing; loafing

事半功倍 shì bàn gōng bèi achieve twice the results for half the effort

事倍功半 shì bèi gōng bàn achieve half the result with twice the effort

事必躬亲(親) shì bì gōng qīn see (or attend) to everything oneself; take care of every single matter personally

事变(變) shìbiàn (名) 1 incident 2 emergency; exigency: 准备应付可能的突然～ be prepared against all possible emergencies

事出有因 shì chū yǒu yīn it is by no means accidental; there is a good reason for it

事端 shìduān (名) disturbance; incident: 挑起～ provoke incidents. 制造～ create disturbances

事故 shìgù (名) accident; mishap: 防止发生～ try to prevent accidents

事过(過)境迁(遷) shìguò-jìngqiān the affair is over and the situation has changed

事后(後) shìhòu (名) after the event; afterwards: ～诸葛亮 hindsight; be wise after the event

事迹 shìjì (名) deed; achievement: 模范～ exemplary deeds

事假 shìjià (名) leave of absence (to attend to private affairs); compassionate leave

事件 shìjiàn (名) incident; event

事理 shìlǐ (名) reason: 明白～ be sensible; be reasonable

事例 shìlì (名) example; instance: 典型～ a typical case. 有关～ a case in point

事前 shìqián (名) before the event; in advance; beforehand

事情 shìqing (名) affair; matter; thing; business: 今天我有许多～要做. I have a lot of work to attend to today. ～的真相 the truth of the matter. ～也真巧 as luck would have it

事实(實) shìshí (名) fact: ～胜于雄辩. Facts speak louder than words. ～如此. This is how things stand. 与～不符 not tally with the facts

事实(實)上 shìshíshang in fact; in reality; as a matter of fact; actually: ～的承认 de facto recognition

事态(態) shìtài (名) state of affairs; situation: ～严重. The situation is fairly grave.

事务(務) shìwù (名) 1 work; routine: ～繁忙 be tied up with a lot of work. ～工作 routine work. ～主义者 a person bogged down in the quagmire of routine matters 2 general affairs: ～员 office clerk

事物 shìwù (名) thing; object: 宇宙间的每一～ everything in the universe

事先 shìxiān (名) in advance; beforehand; prior: ～通知(他们). Notify them in advance. ～知道 prior knowledge. ～酝酿 prior deliberation; exchange of views in advance. ～警告 forewarn

事项 shìxiàng (名) item; matter: 注意～ points for attention. 议程～ items on the agenda

事业(業) shìyè (名) 1 cause; undertaking: 伟大而光荣的～ a great and glorious cause. 文化教育～ cultural and educational undertakings 2 enterprise; facilities: 公用～ public utilities. ～心 devotion to one's work; dedication

事宜 shìyí (名) matters concerned; relevant matters

事由 shìyóu (名) 1 the origin of an incident 2 main content

事与(與)愿(願)违(違) shì yǔ yuàn wéi things run counter to one's wishes

事在人为(爲) shì zài rén wéi all success hinges on human effort

誓 shì I (动) swear; vow; pledge: ～师 pledge mass effort II (名) oath; vow: 宣～ take the oath; be sworn in

誓不罢(罷)休 shì bù bàxiū swear not to stop; swear not to rest: 不达目的, ～. We'll never give up until we reach our goal.

誓词 shìcí (名) oath; pledge

誓死 shìsǐ (副) pledge one's life: ～保卫祖国 vow to fight to the death in defence of one's country

誓言 shìyán (名) oath; pledge: 履行～ fulfil a pledge

逝 shì (动) 1 pass: 时光易～. Time flies. 2 die; pass away: 病～ die of an illness

逝世 shìshì (动) pass away

势(勢) shì (名) 1 power; force; influence: 权～ (a person's) power and influence 2 momentum; impetus: 来～甚猛. The force with which things are moving is terrific. 3 the outward appearance of a nat-ural object: 地～ physical features of the land; terrain 4 situation; state of affairs; circumstances: ～所必然 inevitably 5 sign; gesture: 作手～ make a sign with the hand

势必 shìbì (副) certainly will; be bound to: 这商行～要破产. The business is bound to go bankrupt.

势不可当(當) shì bùkě dāng irresistible

势不两(兩)立 shì bù liǎng lì mutually exclusive; irreconcilable

势均力敌(敵) shìjūn-lìdí be evenly matched in strength; be in equilibrium

势力 shìli (名) force; power; influence: ～范围 sphere of influence. ～均衡 balance of power

势利 shìli (形) snobbish: ～小人 snob

势利眼 shìliyǎn (名) 1 snobbish attitude; snobbishness 2 snob

势如破竹 shì rú pò zhú win victory after victory without encountering any resistance; advance swiftly unhindered

势头(頭) shìtóu (名) impetus; momentum: ～越来越大 rise to a crescendo; gain momentum

势在必行 shì zài bì xíng be imperative; inevitable trend

是 shì I (动) 1 [used as the verb to be when the predicative is a noun]: 我～一个学生. I am a student. 2 [used for emphasis when the predicative is other than a noun]: 他～很努力的. He does work hard. 3 [used to indicate existence]: 前边不远～一家旅馆. There is a hotel not far ahead. 满身～汗 sweat all over 4 [used to indicate concession]: 这东西旧～旧, 可还能用. Yes, it's old, but it is still serviceable. 5 [placed before a noun to indicate fitness or suitability]: 这场雨下得～时候. It's raining just at the right time (for crops). 6 [used before a noun to indicate each and every one of the kind]: ～集体的事大家都要关心. Whatever concerns the collective concerns us all. ～有利于群众的事他都肯干. He is willing and ready to do whatever is of benefit to the masses. 7 [pronounced emphatically to indicate certainty]: 他～不知道. He certainly doesn't know. 8 [used in an alternative or negative question]: 你～坐火车, 还～坐飞机? Are you going by train or by air? 9 [used at the beginning of a sentence for the sake of emphasis]: ～谁告诉你的? Who told you this? 10 [used to answer in the affirmative] yes; right: ～, 我知道. Yes, I know. II (形) correct; right: 自以为～ consider oneself invariably correct

是非 shìfēi (名) 1 right and wrong; truth and falsehood: 明辨～ distinguish between right and wrong 2 quarrel; dispute: 搬弄～ tell tales; sow discord

是非曲直 shì-fēi qū-zhí rights and wrongs; truth and falsehood; merits and demerits

是否 shìfǒu (副) whether or not; whether; if: 他～能当选, 还不一定. It's not certain whether he will be elected or not.

嗜 shì (动) have a liking for; take to: ～酒 take to drinking too much

嗜好 shìhào (名) 1 hobby 2 addiction; habit

释(釋) shì (动) 1 explain; expound: ～义 explain the meaning (of a word, etc.) 2 clear up; dispel: ～疑 dispel misgivings; explain difficult points 3 let go; be relieved of: 如～重负 (feel) as if relieved of a heavy load 4 release; set free

释放 shìfàng (动) release; set free: ～俘虏 set war prisoners free; release war prisoners

释迦牟尼 Shìjiāmóuní (名) Sakyamuni, the founder of Buddhism

适(適) shì I (形) 1 fit; suitable; proper: ～于儿童 suitable for children 2 right; opportune: ～量 just the right amount 3 comfortable; well: 舒～ comfortable II (动) go; follow; pursue: 无所～从 not know what to do; not know whom to turn to

适才 shìcái (名) just now

适当(當) shìdàng (形) suitable; proper;

appropriate: ～的人选 suitable candidate. ～的调整 appropriate readjustment. ～的时机 an opportune moment

适得其反 shì dé qí fǎn turn out to be just the opposite of what one really wants; run counter to one's intentions

适度 shìdù (形) appropriate; moderate: 饮酒～ drink moderately

适逢其会(會) shì féng qí huì happen to be present on the occasion; turn up at the opportune moment

适合 shìhé (动) suit; fit: ～国情 be suited to domestic conditions. ～他的口味 suit his taste

适可而止 shìkě ér zhǐ refrain from going too far

适量 shìliàng (形) appropriate amount or quantity

适龄 shìlíng (形) of the right age: (入学)～儿童 children of school age

适时(時) shìshí (形) at the right moment; in good time; timely

适宜 shìyí (形) suitable; fit; appropriate: 他～做教师. He has the makings of a teacher. 她做这种工作很～. She is suitable for this job.

适意 shìyì (形) agreeable; enjoyable; comfortable

适应(應) shìyìng (动) suit; adapt; fit: ～新的环境 adapt oneself to a new environment. ～时代的需要 meet the needs of the times. 一切工作都应～经济改革的需要. All work should be geared to the needs of economic reform.

适用 shìyòng (形) suitable; applicable: 这个理论～于所有学科. This theory applies to every discipline.

适者生存 shìzhě shēngcún survival of the fittest

适中 shìzhōng (形) 1 moderate: 雨量～ moderate rainfall 2 (of place) well situated

似 shì

see also sì

似的 shìde (助) [indicating similarity]: 像雪～那么白 as white as snow. 他仿佛睡着了～. He seems to be dozing off. 他乐得什么～. He looks immensely happy.

氏 shì (名) family name; surname: 张～兄弟 the Zhang brothers

氏族 shìzú (名) clan: ～社会 clan society. ～制度 clan system

饰 shì I (名) decorations; ornaments: 服～ clothes and ornaments. 窗～ window decorations II (动) 1 adorn; dress up; polish; cover up: 把文章修～一下 polish an essay. 文过～非 cover up one's mistakes 2 play the role (or act the part) of a dramatic character

饰物 shìwù (名) 1 articles for personal adornment; jewelry 2 ornaments; decorations

收 shōu (动) 1 receive; accept: ～到一份电报 receive a telegram from sb. 请～下这件礼物. Please accept a small gift from us. 2 put away; take in: ～拾 tidy up. ～集 gather together 3 collect: ～税 collect taxes 4 harvest; gather in: ～庄稼 get in crops 5 bring to an end; stop: 时间不早,今天就～了吧. It's getting late. Let's call it a day. 6 (of emotion or action) restrain; control

收兵 shōubīng (动) withdraw (or recall) troops; call off a battle

收藏 shōucáng (动) collect; store up: ～古画 collect old paintings. ～粮食 store up grain

收场(場) shōuchǎng I (动) wind up; end up; stop: 草草～ hastily wind up a matter II (名) end; ending; denouement: 圆满的～ a happy ending

收成 shōucheng (名) harvest; crop: ～很好 a good harvest; a bumper crop

收存 shōucún(动) receive and keep

收到 shōudào (动) receive; get; achieve; obtain: ～良好效果 achieve good results

收发(發) shōufā I (动) receive and dispatch: ～室 office for incoming and outgoing mail II (名) dispatcher

收费 shōufèi (动) collect fees; charge

收复(復) shōufù (动) recover; recapture: ～失地 recover lost territory

收割 shōugē (动) reap; harvest; gather in: ～小麦 gather in the wheat. ～机 harvester; reaper

收工 shōugōng (动) stop work for the day

收购(購) shōugòu (动) purchase; buy: ～农副产品 purchase farm produce and sideline products

收回 shōuhuí (动) 1 take back; call in; regain; recall: ～主权 regain sovereignty. ～贷款 recall loans 2 withdraw; countermand: ～建议 withdraw a proposal. ～成命 countermand (or retract) an order; revoke a command

收获(獲) shōuhuò I (动) gather (or bring) in the crops; harvest II (名) results; gains: 学习～ gains of one's study. 一次很有～的旅行 a most rewarding trip

收集 shōují (动) collect; gather: ～信息 collect information

收监(監) shōujiān (动) take into custody; put in prison

收缴 shōujiǎo (动) take over; capture: ～敌人的武器 take over the enemy's arms

收据(據) shōujù (名) receipt

收敛(斂) shōuliǎn (动) 1 weaken or disappear: 她的笑容突然～了. The smile suddenly vanished from her face. 2 show restraint

收留 shōuliú (动) have sb. in one's care

收录(録) shōulù (动) 1 include: 这篇文章已～在他的选集里. This essay is included in his selected works. 2 receive and record: ～机 radio-recorder

收罗(羅) shōuluó (动) collect; gather; enlist: ～技术人才 recruit technical personnel. ～资料 collect data

收买(買) shōumǎi (动) 1 purchase; buy in: ～废铜烂铁 buy scrap iron 2 buy over; bribe: ～人心 court popularity; buy popular support

收盘(盤) shōupán (名) closing quotation (on the exchange, etc.): ～汇率 closing rate. ～价格 closing price

收讫 shōuqì (动) 1 payment received; paid 2 (on a bill of lading, an invoice, etc.) all the above goods received; received in full

收容 shōuróng (动) (of an organization) take in and provide for: ～伤员 admit wounded soldiers. ～难民 feed and house refugees; accept refugees

收入 shōurù I (名) income; revenue; earnings: 财政～ state revenue. ～和支出 revenue and expenditure II (动) take in; include: 修订版词典～许多成语. Many new idiomatic expressions are included in the revised edition of the dictionary.

收审(審) shōushěn (动) detain for interrogation

收拾 shōushi (动) 1 put in order; tidy up; clear away: ～东西 tidy things up. ～床铺 make the bed. ～残局 make the best of a messy situation 2 get things ready; pack: ～行李 pack one's luggage; pack up one's things 3 repair; mend: ～房子 give the house a facelift

收缩 shōusuō (动) 1 contract; shrink: 这种布要～. This kind of cloth shrinks. 2 concentrate one's forces; draw back

收条(條) shōutiáo (名) receipt

收听(聽) shōutīng (动) listen in: ～新闻广播 listen to the news broadcast

收尾 shōuwěi (名) 1 final phase of a project 2 concluding paragraph (of an article, etc.)

收效 shōuxiào (动) yield results; produce effects

收养(養) shōuyǎng (动) take in and bring up; adopt: ～孤儿 adopt an orphan

收益 shōuyì (名) (of an enterprise) income; profit

收音机(機) shōuyīnjī (名) radio (set)

收银台 shōuyíntái (名) cashier; cash register; check-out

收支 shōu-zhī (名) revenue and expenditure; income and expenses: ～平衡 revenue and expenditure in balance. ～逆差 unfavourable balance of payments

守 shǒu (动) 1 guard; defend: 把～ guard. ～住阵地 hold one's own position 2 keep watch; look after 3 observe; abide by: ～纪律 observe discipline. ～信用 keep one's promise

守备(備) shǒubèi (动) perform garrison duty; be on garrison duty; garrison

守财奴 shǒucáinú (名) miser

守法 shǒufǎ (动) abide by (or observe) the law; be law-abiding

守寡 shǒuguǎ (动) remain a widow; live as a widow

守候 shǒuhòu (动) 1 wait for; expect 2 keep watch

守旧(舊) shǒujiù (形) adhere to past practices; stick to old ways; be conservative

守口如瓶 shǒu kǒu rú píng keep one's mouth shut; be tight-lipped

守灵(靈) shǒulíng (动) keep vigil beside the coffin

守时(時) shǒushí (形) on time; punctual

守势(勢) shǒushì (名) defensive: 采取～ be on the defensive

守卫(衛) shǒuwèi (动) guard; defend

守夜 shǒuyè (动) keep watch at night

守约 shǒuyuē (动) abide by an agreement; keep an appointment

守则 shǒuzé (名) rules; regulations: 学生～ school regulations

守株待兔 shǒu zhū dài tù trust to chance and strokes of luck

首 shǒu I (名) 1 head: 昂~ hold one's head high 2 leader; head; chief: 祸~ chief culprit; arch-criminal II (量) [for poems or songs]: 一~歌 a song III (形) first: ~批 the first batch

首倡 shǒuchàng (动) initiate; start

首创(創) shǒuchuàng (动) initiate; originate; pioneer: ~精神 creative initiative; pioneering spirit

首次 shǒucì (名) for the first time; first

首当(當)其冲(衝) shǒu dāng qí chōng bear the brunt; be the first to be affected

首都 shǒudū (名) capital (of a country)

首恶(惡) shǒu'è (名) arch-criminal; principal culprit (or offender)

首发(發) shǒufā (动) first publication; launch: ~式 (publishing) launch

首富 shǒufù (名) the wealthiest family in the locality

首肯 shǒukěn (动) nod approval; approve; consent

首领 shǒulǐng (名) chieftain; leader; head

首脑(腦) shǒunǎo (名) head; leading personage: 政府~ head of government. ~会议 summit conference

首屈一指 shǒu qū yī zhǐ head the list; be second to none

首日封 shǒurìfēng (名) first-day cover

首饰 shǒushì (名) woman's personal ornaments; jewelry

首途 shǒutú (动)〈书〉set out on a journey

首尾 shǒu-wěi (名) 1 the first part and the last part; the opening and the concluding paragraph; the head and the tail 2 from beginning to end: 这次旅行,~经过了一个多月. This trip lasted over a month.

首席 shǒuxí I (名) seat of honour: 坐~ be seated at the head of the table II (形) chief: ~代表 chief representative

首先 shǒuxiān (副) 1 first: ~发言 be the first to take the floor 2 in the first place; first of all; above all: ~,让我代表全体师生向你表示热烈欢迎. On behalf of all the faculty members and students, let me, first of all, extend to you a warm welcome.

首相 shǒuxiàng (名) prime minister

首演 shǒuyǎn (名) first performance; première

首要 shǒuyào (形) of the first importance; first; chief: ~任务 the most important task. ~问题 a question of the first importance

手 shǒu I (名) 1 hand: ~背 the back of the hand. ~提包 handbag. ~织的花呢上衣 a hand-woven tweed jacket 2 a person doing (or good at) a certain job: 拖拉机~ tractor driver. 多面~ all-rounder. 能~ a skilled hand; crackerjack II (动) have in one's hand; hold: 人~一册. Everyone has a copy. III (形) handy; convenient: ~册 handbook; manual IV (量) [for skill or proficiency]: 他有一~好手艺. He's a real craftsman.

手笔(筆) shǒubǐ (名) sb.'s own handwriting or painting

手臂 shǒubì (名) arm

手边(邊) shǒubiān (名) on hand; at hand

手表(錶) shǒubiǎo (名) wristwatch

手不释(釋)卷 shǒu bù shì juàn be entirely engrossed in one's studies; be very studious

手册 shǒucè (名) handbook; manual: 教师~ teacher's manual

手抄本 shǒuchāoběn (名) handwritten copy

手电(電)筒 shǒudiàntǒng (名) electric torch; flashlight

手段 shǒuduàn (名) 1 means; medium; measure; method: 达到目的的一种~ a means to an end. 高压~ high-handed measures. 支付~ means of payment. 不择~ by fair means or foul; by hook or by crook; unscrupulous 2 trick: 耍~ play tricks

手法 shǒufǎ (名) 1 skill; technique: 夸张~ hyperbole. 艺术表现~ means of artistic expression 2 trick; gimmick: 卑劣的~ dirty tricks

手风(風)琴 shǒufēngqín (名) accordion

手稿 shǒugǎo (名) original manuscript; manuscript

手工 shǒugōng (名) 1 handwork: 做~ do handwork 2 by hand; manual: ~操作 done by hand; manual operations

手工业(業) shǒugōngyè (名) handicraft industry; handicraft

手工艺(藝) shǒugōngyì (名) handicraft art; handicraft: ~工人 craftsman. ~品 articles of handicraft art; handicrafts

手机(機) shǒujī (名) mobile phone

手迹 shǒujì (名) sb.'s original handwriting or painting

手脚 shǒujiǎo (名) 1 movement of hands or feet: ~利落 nimble; agile 2 underhand

S

method; trick: 从中弄～ play dirty tricks behind one's back

手巾 shǒujin (名) towel

手绢 shǒujuàn (名) handkerchief

手铐 shǒukào (名) handcuffs: 带上～ be handcuffed

手链(鏈) shǒuliàn (名) bracelet; wrist-chain

手令 shǒulìng (名) an order personally issued by sb. in command

手榴弹(彈) shǒuliúdàn (名) hand grenade

手忙脚乱(亂) shǒumáng-jiǎoluàn be in a tearing hurry

手气(氣) shǒuqì (名) luck at gambling

手枪(槍) shǒuqiāng (名) pistol; revolver

手巧 shǒuqiǎo (形) skilful with one's hands

手球 shǒuqiú (名) handball

手软 shǒuruǎn (形) too soft-hearted to act resolutely when severity is called for; lack firmness

手势(勢) shǒushì (名) gesture; sign; signal: 做～ make a gesture; gesticulate. ～语 sign language

手术(術) shǒushù (名) surgical operation; operation; ～室 operating room; operating theatre. ～台 operating table

手松(鬆) shǒusōng (形) (concerning money matters) free-handed; open-handed

手套 shǒutào (名) **1** gloves; mittens **2** baseball gloves; mitts

手提 shǒutí (形) portable: ～打字机 portable typewriter. ～箱 suitcase

手头(頭) shǒutóu (名) **1** on hand; at hand: ～工作很多 have a lot of work on hand **2** one's financial condition at the moment: ～紧 be short of money. ～宽裕 be quite well off at the moment

手推车(車) shǒutuīchē (名) handcart; wheelbarrow

手腕 shǒuwàn (名) skill; finesse; stratagem: 外交～ diplomatic skill. 政治～ political tactics

手无(無)寸铁(鐵) shǒu wú cùn tiě bare-handed; unarmed; defenceless

手舞足蹈 shǒuwǔ-zúdǎo dance for joy

手下 shǒuxià (名) **1** under the leadership of; under: 在他～工作 work under him **2** at hand: 东西不在～. I haven't got it with me.

手下留情 shǒuxià liú qíng show mercy to one's enemies or deal leniently with them

手心 shǒuxīn (名) **1** the palm of the hand **2** control: 这些罪犯逃不出警方的～. These criminals cannot escape the police net.

手续(續) shǒuxù (名) procedures; formalities: 办～ go through formalities

手艺(藝) shǒuyì (名) **1** craftsmanship; workmanship **2** handicraft; trade

手印 shǒuyìn (名) **1** an impression of the hand **2** thumb print; fingerprint

手语 shǒuyǔ (名) sign language; hand language; cheirology

手掌 shǒuzhǎng (名) palm

手杖 shǒuzhàng (名) walking stick; stick

手纸 shǒuzhǐ (名) toilet paper

手指 shǒuzhǐ (名) finger

手指甲 shǒuzhǐjia (名) fingernail

手镯 shǒuzhuó (名) bracelet

手足 shǒuzú (名) brothers: ～之情 brotherly affection

手足无(無)措 shǒu-zú wúcuò at a loss (as to) what to do; helpless

瘦 shòu (形) **1** thin **2** lean: ～肉 lean meat **3** tight: 这件上衣～了点. The coat is a bit tight.

瘦长(長) shòucháng (形) long and thin; tall and thin

瘦弱 shòuruò (形) thin and weak; fragile

瘦身 shòushēn (动) lose weight; diet; slim: ～广告 slimming ads. 运动～ stay slim through exercise

瘦小 shòuxiǎo (形) slight of stature

瘦削 shòuxuē (形) very thin; emaciated; haggard

瘦子 shòuzi (名) a lean or thin person

兽(獸) shòu (名) **1** beast; animal: 野～ wild animal **2** beastly; bestial: 人面～心 a beast in human shape

兽类(類) shòulèi (名) beasts; animals

兽行 shòuxíng (名) **1** brutality **2** bestial behaviour

兽性 shòuxìng (名) brutish nature; the beast in a man

兽医(醫) shòuyī (名) veterinary surgeon; veterinarian

兽欲 shòuyù (名) animal (or bestial) desire

寿(壽) shòu (名) **1** longevity **2** life; age: 长～ long life; longevity **3** birthday: 祝～ congratulate sb. on his birthday **4** for burial: ～木 coffin (prepared before one's death)

寿辰 shòuchén (名) birthday (of an elderly person)

寿礼(禮) shòulǐ (名) birthday present (for

an elderly person)

寿命 shòumìng (名) lifespan; life: 平均～ average lifespan (or life expectancy). 机器～ service life of a machine

寿星 shòuxing (名) 1 the god of longevity 2 an elderly person whose birthday is being celebrated

寿终正寝(寢) shòuzhōng-zhèngqǐn die in bed of old age; die a natural death

受 shòu (动) 1 receive; accept: ～教育 receive an education. ～礼 accept gifts 2 suffer; be subjected to: ～委屈 be wronged; suffer injustice. ～损失 suffer losses. ～监督 be subjected to supervision 3 stand; endure; bear: ～不了 not be able to bear; be unable to endure any longer

受潮 shòucháo (动) be made moist; become damp

受宠(寵)若惊(驚) shòu chǒng ruò jīng be overwhelmed by an unexpected favour (or a gracious offer)

受挫 shòucuò (动) be baffled; suffer a setback

受罚(罰) shòufá (动) be punished

受害 shòuhài (动) be injured or killed

受贿 shòuhuì (动) accept (or take) bribes

受奖(獎) shòujiǎng (动) be rewarded

受戒 shòujiè (动) be initiated into monkhood or nunhood

受惊(驚) shòujīng (动) be frightened; be startled

受精 shòujīng (动) be fertilized: 体内(外)～ internal (external) fertilization

受窘 shòujiǒng (动) be embarrassed

受苦 shòukǔ (动) suffer (hardships); have a rough time: ～受难 live in misery

受累 shòulěi (动) get involved; be incriminated

受累 shòulèi (动) be put to much trouble: 这么远来看我, 让您～了. It must have caused you a lot of bother to come all the way to see me.

受理 shòulǐ (动) accept and hear a case

受难(難) shòunàn (动) suffer a calamity or disaster; be in distress

受骗 shòupiàn (动) be deceived (fooled, cheated, or taken in)

受聘 shòupìn (动) accept an appointment

受气(氣) shòuqì (动) be bullied; be insulted

受屈 shòuqū (动) be wronged

受权(權) shòuquán (动) be authorized

受伤(傷) shòushāng (动) be injured; be wounded; sustain an injury

受审(審) shòushěn (动) stand trial; be tried; be on trial

受托 shòutuō (动) be commissioned; be entrusted (with a task)

受训 shòuxùn (动) receive training

受益 shòuyì (动) profit by; benefit from; be benefited

受用 shòuyòng (动) benefit from; profit by; enjoy: ～不尽 benefit from sth. all one's life

受援 shòuyuán (动) receive aid: ～国 recipient country

受灾(災) shòuzāi (动) be hit by a natural calamity: ～地区 disaster area; stricken (afflicted, or affected) area

受罪 shòuzuì (动) endure hardships or tortures; have a hard time

授 shòu (动) 1 award; vest; confer; give: ～权 authorize 2 teach; instruct: 函～ teach by correspondence; a correspondence course

授奖(獎) shòujiǎng (动) award (or give) a prize

授精 shòujīng (动) inseminate : 人工～ artificial insemination

授命 shòumìng (动) give orders: ～组阁 authorize sb. to form a cabinet

授受 shòu-shòu (动) give and accept: 私相～ offer and accept a gift privately for dubious purpose

授衔 shòuxián (动) confer a title or military rank

授勋(勳) shòuxūn (动) confer orders or medals; award a decoration

授意 shòuyì (动) get sb. to carry out one's plan; suggest

授予 shòuyǔ (动) confer; award

售 shòu (动) 1 sell: 出～ put on sale. ～货 sell goods 2 make (one's plan, trick, etc.) work; carry out (intrigues): 以～其奸 so as to carry out one's evil design

售货机(機) shòuhuòjī (名) vending machine

售货员 shòuhuòyuán (名) shop assistant; salesclerk: 女～ saleswoman

售价(價) shòujià (名) selling price; price

售票处(處) shòupiàochù (名) ticket office; booking office

售票员 shòupiàoyuán (名) ticket seller

狩 shòu〈书〉hunting (esp. in winter)

狩猎(獵) shòuliè (名) hunting

梳 shū I (名) comb: 木～ wooden comb II (动) comb one's hair, etc.

梳理 shūlǐ (动) comb; brush; sort out; straighten out

梳洗 shūxǐ (动) wash and dress: ～用具 toilet articles

梳妆(妝) shūzhuāng (动) dress and make up: ～打扮 be dressed up

梳子 shūzi (名) comb

疏 shū I (形) 1 thin; sparse; scattered: ～林 sparse woods. ～星 scattered stars 2 (of family or social relations) distant 3 not familiar with: 人地生～ be a complete stranger 4 scanty: 志大才～ have lofty aspiration but inadequate talent II (动) 1 dredge (a river, etc.) 2 neglect: ～于职守 be negligent of one's duties 3 disperse; scatter: ～散 evacuate

疏导(導) shūdǎo (动) dredge

疏忽 shūhu (名) carelessness; negligence; oversight

疏剪 shūjiǎn (动) prune (trees, branches)

疏浚 shūjùn (动) dredge: ～水道 dredge the waterways

疏漏 shūlòu (名) careless omission; slip; oversight

疏落 shūluò (形) sparse; scattered: ～的村庄 a straggling village

疏散 shūsàn I (形) sparse; scattered; dispersed II (动) evacuate: ～人口 evacuation

疏失 shūshī (名) careless mistake; remissness

疏通 shūtōng (动) 1 dredge 2 mediate between two parties

疏远(遠) shūyuǎn (动) drift apart; become estranged

蔬 shū (名) vegetables: 布衣～食 live simply; plain living

蔬菜 shūcài (名) vegetables; greens

蔬果 shūguǒ (名) vegetables and fruits

枢(樞) shū (名) pivot; hub; centre: 神经中～ nerve centre

枢纽 shūniǔ (名) pivot; hub; exis; key position: 交通～ a hub of communications

叔 shū (名) 1 father's younger brother; uncle 2 a form of address for a man about one's father's age; uncle 3 husband's younger brother

叔伯 shūbai (名) relationship between cousins of the same grandfather or great-grandfather

叔父 shūfù (名) father's younger brother; uncle

叔叔 shūshu (名) 1 father's younger brother; uncle 2 uncle (a child's form of address for any young man one generation its senior)

输 shū (动) 1 transport; convey: ～电 transmit electricity 2 lose; be beaten; be defeated: ～了一局 lose one game

输出 shūchū (动) 1 export 2 output

输电(電) shūdiàn (动) transmit electricity

输入 shūrù (动) 1 import 2 input

输送 shūsòng (动) carry; transport; convey: ～货物 deliver goods. ～带 conveyer belt. ～机 conveyer

输血 shūxuè (名) blood transfusion: ～者 blood donor

输氧 shūyǎng (名) oxygen therapy

输液 shūyè (名) infusion

输赢 shū-yíng (名) victory or defeat; winnings and losses

输油管 shūyóuguǎn (名) petroleum pipeline

殊 shū I (形) 1 different: 悬～ differ widely; be poles apart 2 outstanding; special: 待以～礼 treat sb. with unusual courtesy II (副) very much; extremely; really: ～难相信 very difficult to believe; hardly credible

殊死 shūsǐ (形) desperate; life-and-death: ～的搏斗 a life-and-death struggle

殊途同归(歸) shū tú tóng guī reach the same goal by different routes; all roads lead to Rome

抒 shū (动) express; give expression to; voice: 各～已见. Everybody may air his views.

抒发(發) shūfā (动) (of one's feelings) express; voice; give expression to

抒情 shūqíng (动) express (or convey) one's emotion: ～诗 lyric poetry; lyrics

舒 shū (动) 1 stretch; unfold 2 loosen; relax

舒畅(暢) shūchàng (形) happy; entirely free from worry: 心情～ feel happy

舒服 shūfu (形) 1 comfortable 2 be well: 她今天不大～. She isn't very well today.

舒适(適) shūshì (形) comfortable; cosy; snug: ～的生活 a comfortable life. ～的小房间 a cosy room

S

舒坦 shūtan (形) comfortable; at ease
舒展 shūzhǎn (动) 1 unfold; extend; smooth out 2 limber up; stretch: ～一下筋骨 stretch one's limbs

书(書) shū I (动) write II (名) 1 book 2 letter: 家～ a letter to or from home 3 document: 证～ certificate. 国～ letter of credence; credentials
书包 shūbāo (名) satchel; schoolbag
书报(報) shū-bào (名) books and newspapers
书本 shūběn (名) book: ～知识 book learning; book knowledge
书橱 shūchú (名) bookcase
书呆子 shūdāizi (名) bookworm
书店 shūdiàn (名) bookshop; bookstore
书法 shūfǎ (名) penmanship; calligraphy
书房 shūfáng (名) study
书画(畫) shū-huà (名) painting and calligraphy
书籍 shūjí (名) books; works
书记 shūji (名) secretary: 总～ general secretary. ～处 secretariat
书架 shūjià (名) bookshelf; bookcase
书刊 shū-kān (名) books and periodicals
书库 shūkù (名) stack room
书面 shūmiàn (形) written; in written form; in writing: ～通知 written notice. ～答复 written reply. ～声明 written statement. ～语 written language
书名 shūmíng (名) the title of a book
书目 shūmù (名) booklist; title catalogue: 参考～ bibliography
书皮 shūpí (名) book cover; dust jacket
书评 shūpíng (名) book review
书签(簽) shūqiān (名) bookmark
书生 shūshēng (名)〈旧〉 intellectual; scholar
书生气(氣) shūshēngqì (名) bookishness
书市 shūshì (名) book fair
书摊(攤) shūtān (名) bookstand
书写(寫) shūxiě (动) write: ～标语 write slogans; letter posters. ～纸 writing pad
书信 shūxìn (名) letter; written message: ～往来 correspondence
书桌 shūzhuō (名) desk

孰 shú (代)〈书〉 1 who; which: 人非圣贤，～能无过? Not everybody is a sage. Who can be entirely free from error? 2 what: 是可忍，～不可忍? If this can be tolerated, what cannot?

熟 shú (形) 1 ripe: 时机尚未成～. The time is not ripe yet. 2 (of food) cooked; done 3 processed: ～皮子 tanned leather 4 familiar: 听起来很～ sound familiar. 他们俩很～. They know each other quite well. 5 skilled; experienced; practised: ～手 practised hand; old hand 6 deep; sound: ～睡 be fast (or sound) asleep
熟谙 shú'ān (动)〈书〉 be familiar with; be good at
熟菜 shúcài (名) cooked food; prepared food
熟记 shújì (动) learn by heart; memorize
熟客 shúkè (名) frequent visitor
熟练(練) shúliàn (形) skilled; practised; proficient: ～工人 skilled worker
熟路 shúlù (名) familiar route: 他对这儿熟门～的. He knows his way around here.
熟能生巧 shú néng shēng qiǎo practice makes perfect
熟人 shúrén (名) acquaintance; friend
熟识(識) shúshi (动) be well acquainted with; know well
熟食 shúshí (名) prepared food; cooked food
熟视无(無)睹 shú shì wú dǔ pay no heed to; turn a blind eye to; ignore
熟睡 shúshuì (动) sleep soundly; be fast asleep
熟悉 shúxī (动) know sth. or sb. well; well acquainted with: ～情况 know the ropes
熟习(習) shúxí (动) have a good knowledge of; be versed in: ～业务 have an intimate knowledge of his own speciality. ～古典文学 be versed in classical literature
熟语 shúyǔ (名) idiom; idiomatic phrase
熟知 shúzhī (动) know very well; know intimately

赎(贖) shú (动) 1 redeem; ransom: 把抵押品～回来 redeem a mortgage 2 atone for (a crime)
赎金 shújīn (名) ransom money; ransom
赎买(買) shúmǎi (动) redeem; buy out
赎罪 shúzuì (动) atone for one's crime

数(數) shǔ (动) 1 count: 从一～到十 count from 1 to 10. ～～看，这班有多少学生. Count and see how many students there are in this class. 2 be particularly conspicuous by comparison: 全班～他功课好. He is considered

S

the best in the class. **3** enumerate; list: 历～其罪 enumerate sb.'s crimes
see also shù; shuò

数得着 shǔ de zháo be counted among the best: 她是中国～的电影演员. She is one of the best film actresses in China.

数典忘祖 shǔ diǎn wàng zǔ be well acquainted with many historical facts but entirely ignorant of the achievements of one's own ancestors; forget one's ancestral origin

数九寒天 shǔjiǔ hántiān the coldest day of the year

数一数二 shǔyī-shǔ'èr be among the very best; one of the best: 这所大学是全国～的高等学府. This university ranks as one of the most prestigious institutions of higher learning in the country.

暑 shǔ (名) heat; hot weather: 盛～ at the height of the summer. 中～ get sunstroke

暑假 shǔjià (名) summer vacation (or holidays)

暑天 shǔtiān (名) hot summer day; dog days

署 shǔ I (名) a government office; office: 专员公～ prefectural commissioner's office II (动) **1** arrange: 部～ make arrangements for sth. **2** act as deputy **3** sign; affix one's name to

署名 shǔmíng (动) sign; put one's signature to: 全体议员都在这封公开信上署了名. The open letter was jointly signed by all the congressmen. ～文章 a signed article

薯 shǔ (名) potato; yam: 白～ sweet potato

曙 shǔ (名)〈书〉daybreak; dawn

曙光 shǔguāng (名) first light of morning; dawn

黍 shǔ (名) millet

鼠 shǔ (名) mouse; rat

鼠辈 shǔbèi (名) mean creatures; scoundrels

鼠标(標) shǔbiāo (名) mouse

鼠窜(竄) shǔcuàn (动) scurry away

鼠目寸光 shǔmù cùn guāng be short-sighted

鼠疫 shǔyì (名) the plague

属(屬) shǔ I (名) **1** category: 金～ metals **2** genus: 亚～ subgenus **3** family members; dependents: 直系亲～ direct dependent II (动) **1** come within one's jurisdiction: 附～ be affiliated or attached to **2** belong to: 我们～于另外一个组织. We belong to another organization. **3** be: 查明～实 be verified
see also zhǔ

属地 shǔdì (名) possession; dependency

属相 shǔxiang (名)〈口〉see "生肖" shēngxiào

属性 shǔxìng (名) attribute; property

属于(於) shǔyú (动) belong to; be part of: 这个游泳池是～我们学校的. This swimming pool belongs to our school. 西沙群岛是～中国的. Xisha Qundao is part of China's territory.

树(樹) shù I (名) tree: 苹果～ apple tree II (动) **1** plant; cultivate: 十年～木,百年～人. It takes ten years to grow trees, but a hundred years to rear people. **2** set up; establish; uphold: ～典型 hold sb. up as a model

树碑立传(傳) shùbēi-lìzhuàn build up sb.'s prestige by an overdose of praise

树大招风(風) shù dà zhāo fēng a tall tree catches the wind — a person in a high position is liable to be attacked

树倒猢狲(猻)散 shù dǎo húsūn sàn when an influential person falls from power, his hangers-on disperse; a sinking ship is deserted by rats

树敌(敵) shùdí (动) make enemies

树干(幹) shùgàn (名) tree trunk; trunk

树冠 shùguān (名) crown (of a tree)

树立 shùlì (动) set up; establish: ～榜样 set an example

树林 shùlín (名) woods; grove

树苗 shùmiáo (名) sapling

树木 shùmù (名) trees

树皮 shùpí (名) bark

树阴(陰) shùyīn (名) shade (of a tree)

树枝 shùzhī (名) branch; twig

竖(豎) shù I (形) vertical; upright; perpendicular: ～线 a vertical line II (动) set upright; erect; stand: ～根柱子 erect a pole

竖井 shùjǐng (名) (vertical) shaft

竖立 shùlì (动) stand erect; stand: 宝塔～在山顶. The pagoda stands on the top of the hill.

竖琴 shùqín (名) harp

漱 shù (动) gargle; rinse

漱口 shùkǒu (动) rinse the mouth; gargle

S

庶 shù (形) multitudinous; numerous: 富～ rich and populous

庶民 shùmín (名)〈书〉the common people; the multitude

数(數) shù I (名) 1 number; figure: 人～ the number of people. 两位～ two-digit number. 心中有～ be aware how things stand 2 number (in grammar): 单(复)～ singular (plural) number II (数) several; a few: ～小时 several hours. ～十种 a few dozens
see also shǔ; shuò

数词 shùcí (名) numeral: 序～ ordinal number. 基～ cardinal number

数额 shù'é (名) number; amount

数据(據) shùjù (名) data: ～处理 data processing. ～库 data bank

数据(據)库 shùjùkù (名) database

数控 shùkòng (名) numerical control

数理逻(邏)辑 shùlǐ luójí (名) mathematical logic

数量 shùliàng (名) quantity; amount

数码 shùmǎ (名) 1 numeral: 阿拉伯～ Arabic numerals. 罗马～ Roman numerals 2 number; amount 3 digital: ～相机 digital camera

数目 shùmù (名) number; amount

数学(學) shùxué (名) mathematics

数字 shùzì (名) numeral; figure; digit: 天文～ astronomical figures. ～控制 numerical control

数字化 shùzìhuà (名) digitalization

墅 shù (名) villa

S

恕 shù (动) 1 forgive; pardon; excuse: 宽～ forgive 2 excuse me; beg your pardon: ～难从命. Forgive me for not complying with your wishes.

术(術) shù (名) 1 art; skill; technique: 医～ the art of healing. 美～ the fine arts. 不学无～的人 ignoramus 2 method; tactics: 战～ tactics. 权～ political manoeuvre

术语 shùyǔ (名) technical terms; terminology: 医学～ medical terminology

述 shù (动) state; relate; narrate

述评 shùpíng (名) review; commentary: 时事～ a critical review of current affairs

述说 shùshuō (动) state; recount; narrate

述职(職) shùzhí (动) report on one's work; report

束 shù I (动) 1 bind; tie: ～装就道 pack and start out on a journey 2 control; restrain: 无拘无～ uninhibited II (量) bundle; bunch; sheaf: 一～鲜花 a bunch of flowers; a bouquet

束缚 shùfù (动) tie; bind up; fetter: ～手脚 bind sb. hand and foot

束手待毙(斃) shùshǒu dài bì have no alternative but to wait for death; resign oneself to extinction

束手无(無)策 shùshǒu wú cè feel simply helpless

束之高阁 shù zhī gāogé lay aside and neglect; shelve; pigeon-hole: 他把我的建议～, 再也没有想过它. He put aside my proposal and never thought of it again.

戍 shù (动) defend; garrison: ～边 garrison the frontiers

刷 shuā I (动) 1 brush; clean: ～牙 brush one's teeth. ～地板 scrub the floor 2 daub; paste up: ～墙 whitewash a wall. ～标语 paste up posters 3 eliminate; remove II (象) swish; rustle: 风吹得树叶～～地响. The leaves rustled in the wind.
see also shuà

刷卡 shuākǎ (动) swipe a card; pay by credit card

刷新 shuāxīn (动) 1 renovate; refurbish: ～门面 repaint the front (of a shop, etc.); give (the shop, etc.) a facelift 2 break: ～纪录 set a new record 3 refresh: 电脑屏幕～ refresh the page on the computer screen

刷子 shuāzi (名) brush; scrub: 头发～ hair brush

耍 shuǎ (动) 1 play: 叫孩子们到别处～去. Tell the children to go and play elsewhere. 2 play (tricks): ～花招 play small tricks

耍赖 shuǎlài (动) act unreasonably and shamelessly

耍流氓 shuǎ liúmáng behave like a hoodlum; take liberties with women

耍脾气(氣) shuǎ píqi get into a huff; fly into a rage

耍态(態)度 shuǎ tàidu lose one's temper

耍威风(風) shuǎ wēifēng throw one's weight about; be overbearing

耍无(無)赖 shuǎ wúlài act shamelessly; act like a scoundrel

耍心眼儿(兒) shuǎ xīnyǎnr be too calculating

刷 shuà

see also shuā

刷白 shuàbái (形) white; pale: 他的脸立刻变得～. He turned pale instantly.

衰 shuāi (动) decline; wane: 兴～ rise and fall. 年老体～ weak with age

衰败 shuāibài (动) decline; wane; be at a low ebb

衰减 shuāijiǎn weaken; fail; diminish

衰竭 shuāijié (动) exhaust: 心力～ heart failure

衰老 shuāilǎo (形) aged; senile

衰落 shuāiluò (动) decline; be on the wane

衰弱 shuāiruò (形) weak; feeble: 神经～ suffer from neurasthenia

衰退 shuāituì (动) fail; decline: 视力～ failing eyesight. 经济～ economic recession

衰亡 shuāiwáng (动) become feeble and die; decline and fall; wither away

摔 shuāi (动) 1 fall; tumble; lose one's balance: 他～了一跤. He tripped over sth. and fell. 2 break: 他把腿～断了. He had his leg broken. 3 cast; throw; fling

摔打 shuāida (动) 1 beat; knock: 把扫帚上的泥～～. Beat the dirt off the broom. 2 temper oneself: 在困难环境中～出来 temper oneself in difficult circumstances

摔跟头(頭) shuāi gēntou 1 tumble; trip and fall 2 make a blunder

摔跤 shuāijiāo (动) 1 tumble; trip and fall 2 wrestle

甩 shuǎi (动) 1 move back and forth; swing: ～胳膊 swing one's arms 2 throw; fling; toss: ～手榴弹 throw a hand grenade 3 leave sb. behind; throw off: 公园里不得乱～废纸杂物. Don't leave litter in the park. 这个城市去年生产增加了一倍,把其他城市远远～到了后头. This city doubled its production last year, leaving all the other cities far behind.

甩掉 shuǎidiào (动) throw off; cast off; shake off; get rid of: ～包袱 get a load off one's back

甩手 shuǎishǒu (动) 1 swing one's arms 2 refuse to do; wash one's hands of: 每个人都该负责, 不能～不管. Nobody should refuse to do his or her duty.

率 shuài I (动) lead; command: ～队入场 lead the team into the arena II (形) 1 rash; hasty: 草～ careless. 轻～ rash 2 frank; straightforward: 坦～ frank. 直～ straightforward III (副) generally; usually: 大～如此. Such is the case, by and large.

see also lǜ

率领 shuàilǐng (动) lead; head; command: ～代表团 lead (or head) a delegation

率先 shuàixiān (副) take the lead in doing sth.; be the first to do sth.

率直 shuàizhí (形) frank and straightforward

帅(帥) shuài I (名) commander-in-chief: 元～ marshal. 挂～ take command II (形) beautiful; graceful; smart

帅哥 shuàigē (名) dashing young man; cute guy

闩 shuān I (名) bolt; latch: 门～ door bolt II (动) fasten with a bolt or latch: 把门～好 bolt the door

栓 shuān (名) 1 bolt; plug: 枪～ rifle bolt 2 stopper; cork

拴 shuān (动) tie; fasten: 把马～在树上 tie a horse to a tree

涮 shuàn (动) 1 rinse: 把衣服～一～. Rinse the clothes. 把这瓶子～一下. Give this bottle a rinse. 2 scald thin slices of meat in boiling water; quick boil: ～羊肉 dip-boiled mutton slices; rinsed mutton in Mongolian pot

霜 shuāng I (名) 1 frost 2 frostlike powder: 糖～ frosting; icing II (形) white; hoar: ～鬓 grey temples

霜冻(凍) shuāngdòng (名) frost

霜叶(葉) shuāngyè (名) red leaves; autumn leaves

孀 shuāng (名) widow

孀居 shuāngjū (动) live in widowhood

双(雙) shuāng I (形) 1 two; twin; both; dual: ～手 both hands. 成～成对 in pairs 2 even: ～数 even numbers 3 double; twofold: ～人床 double bed. ～人房间 double room II (量) pair: 一～筷(鞋等) a pair of chopsticks (shoes, etc.)

双胞胎 shuāngbāotāi (名) twins

双边(邊) shuāngbiān (形) bilateral: ～会谈 bilateral talks. ～贸易 bilateral trade

双层(層) shuāngcéng (形) double-deck; having two layers

双重 shuāngchóng (形) double; dual; twofold: ～标准 double standard. ～领导 dual leadership. ～国籍 dual nationality

双打 shuāngdǎ (名) doubles

S

双方 shuāngfāng (名) both sides; the two parties: 缔约～ both signatory states; the contracting parties. 劳资～ both labour and capital

双杠 shuānggàng (名) parallel bars

双关(關) shuāngguān (形) having a double meaning: 一语～ a phrase with a double meaning. ～语 pun

双管齐(齊)下 shuāng guǎn qí xià exert simultaneous efforts at both ends

双规 shuāngguī (动) quarantine and discipline: 他被～了 He is quarantined and under investigation.

双轨 shuāngguǐ (名) double track

双面 shuāngmiàn (形) two-sided; double-edged; double-faced; reversible: ～刀片 a double-edged razor blade. ～绣 double-faced embroidery

双亲(親) shuāngqīn (名) (both) parents; father and mother

双全 shuāngquán (形) enjoying a double blessing; possessing both complementary qualities: 智勇～ endowed with both wisdom and courage

双人床(牀) shuāngrénchuáng (名) double bed

双数(數) shuāngshù (名) even numbers

双休日 shuāngxiūrì (名) double-day weekend; weekend

双赢 shuāngyíng (名) win-win: ～谈判 a win-win negotiation. 取得～ have a win-win situation

双职(職)工 shuāngzhígōng (名) man and wife both employed

爽 shuǎng (形) 1 bright; clear; crisp: 秋高气～. The autumn weather is sunny and bright. *or* Autumn is beautiful and refreshing. 2 frank; straightforward; openhearted: 豪～ straightforward 3 feel well: 身体不～ be under the weather

爽口 shuǎngkǒu (形) tasty and refreshing

爽快 shuǎngkuai (形) 1 relaxed; refreshed 2 frank; straightforward; outright: 他说话极为～. He is very frank and outspoken.

爽朗 shuǎnglǎng (形) 1 bright and clear 2 hearty; candid; frank and open; straightforward: ～的笑声 peals of laughter

爽直 shuǎngzhí (形) frank; straightforward; candid

水 shuǐ (名) 1 water: 淡～fresh water. 自来～ running water. ～上公园 aquatic park 2 a general term for rivers, lakes, seas, etc.: 汉～ the Han River 3 a liquid: 墨～ ink. 桔子～ orangeade

水坝(壩) shuǐbà (名) dam

水泵 shuǐbèng (名) water pump

水表 shuǐbiǎo (名) water meter

水兵 shuǐbīng (名) seaman; sailor; bluejacket

水彩 shuǐcǎi (名) watercolour: ～画 watercolour (painting)

水草 shuǐcǎo (名) 1 pasture and water 2 waterweeds; water plants

水产(産) shuǐchǎn (名) aquatic product

水车(車) shuǐchē (名) 1 waterwheel 2 water wagon

水池 shuǐchí (名) pond; pool; cistern

水到渠成 shuǐ dào qú chéng when conditions are ripe, success is assured

水稻 shuǐdào (名) paddy (rice); rice

水滴石穿 shuǐ dī shí chuān dripping water wears through rock; little strokes fell great oaks

水电(電) shuǐ-diàn (名) water and electricity: ～供应 water and electricity supply

水电(電)站 shuǐdiànzhàn (名) hydroelectric (power) station; hydropower station

水分 shuǐfèn (名) 1 moisture 2 exaggeration

水沟(溝) shuǐgōu (名) ditch; drain; gutter

水垢 shuǐgòu (名) scale; incrustation

水管 shuǐguǎn (名) water pipe

水果 shuǐguǒ (名) fruit

水火 shuǐ-huǒ (名) 1 fire and water — two things diametrically opposed to each other: ～不相容 be absolutely irreconcilable 2 extreme misery: 拯救人民于～之中 save the people from the abyss of misery

水浇(澆)地 shuǐjiāodì (名) irrigated land

水晶 shuǐjīng (名) crystal; rock crystal

水井 shuǐjǐng (名) well

水坑 shuǐkēng (名) puddle; pool; water hole

水库 shuǐkù (名) reservoir

水涝(澇) shuǐlào (名) waterlogging: ～地 waterlogged land

水雷 shuǐléi (名) (submarine) mine: 敷设～ lay mines (in water)

水力 shuǐlì (名) waterpower; hydraulic power: ～资源 hydroelectric resources; waterpower resources

水利 shuǐlì (名) 1 water conservancy: ～设施 water conservancy facilities 2 irrigation works; water conservancy project: ～资源 water resources

水流 shuǐliú (名) 1 rivers; streams; waters 2 current; flow: ~湍急 rapid flow

水龙(龍)头(頭) shuǐlóngtóu (名) (water) tap; faucet; bibcock: 开(关)~ turn on (off) the tap

水陆(陸) shuǐ-lù (名) land and water: ~两用 amphibious. ~坦克 amphibious tank

水落石出 shuǐluò-shíchū when the water subsides the rocks emerge — the truth is out

水磨 shuǐmó (动) polish with a waterstone

水磨石 shuǐmóshí (名) terrazzo

水墨画(畫) shuǐmòhuà (名) ink and wash; wash painting

水泥 shuǐní (名) cement

水鸟(鳥) shuǐniǎo (名) aquatic bird; water bird

水牛 shuǐniú (名) (water) buffalo

水暖工 shuǐnuǎngōng (名) plumber

水泡 shuǐpào (名) 1 bubble 2 blister: 手上打了~ get blisters on one's hands

水平 shuǐpíng I (形) horizontal; level II (名) standard; level: 生活~ living standard

水禽 shuǐqín (名) aquatic bird

水渠 shuǐqú (名) ditch; canal

水乳交融 shuǐ-rǔ jiāoróng in complete harmony; in congenial company

水上运(運)动(動) shuǐshàng yùndòng aquatic sports; water sports

水生动(動)物 shuǐshēng dòngwù aquatic animal

水手 shuǐshǒu (名) seaman; sailor; boatswain

水塔 shuǐtǎ (名) water tower

水塘 shuǐtáng (名) pool; pond

水天一色 shuǐtiān yī sè the water and the sky blended in one colour

水田 shuǐtián (名) paddy field

水桶 shuǐtǒng (名) pail; bucket

水头(頭) shuǐtóu (名) flood peak; peak of flow

水土 shuǐtǔ (名) 1 water and soil: ~流失 soil erosion 2 natural environment and climate: ~不服 unaccustomed to the climate of a new place

水网(網) shuǐwǎng (名) a network of rivers

水位 shuǐwèi (名) water level

水文 shuǐwén (名) hydrology: ~站 hydrometric station

水系 shuǐxì (名) river system

水仙 shuǐxiān (名) narcissus

水箱 shuǐxiāng (名) water tank

水泄不通 shuǐ xiè bù tōng very crowded; packed with people

水性 shuǐxìng (名) 1 skill in swimming: 要参加海军必须懂~. You've got to be a good swimmer to join the navy. 2 the depth, currents and other characteristics of a river, lake, etc.

水银 shuǐyín (名) mercury; quicksilver

水源 shuǐyuán (名) 1 the source of a river; waterhead 2 source of water

水运(運) shuǐyùn (名) water transport

水灾(災) shuǐzāi (名) flood; inundation

水闸 shuǐzhá (名) sluice; watergate

水涨(漲)船高 shuǐ zhǎng chuán gāo when the river rises the boat goes up — things improve when the general situation improves

水蒸气(氣) shuǐzhēngqì (名) steam; water vapour

水中捞(撈)月 shuǐ zhōng lāo yuè fish for the moon — make impractical or vain efforts

水准(準) shuǐzhǔn (名) level; standard

水族 shuǐzú (名) aquatic animals: ~馆 aquarium

说 shuì (动) try to persuade: 游~ go around soliciting support for one's views; peddle an idea; canvass
see also shuō

税 shuì (名) tax; duty: 营业~business tax. 进口(出口)~ import (export) duty

税额 shuì'é (名) the amount of tax to be paid

税款 shuìkuǎn (名) tax payment; taxation

税率 shuìlǜ (名) tax rate; rate of taxation; tariff rate

税目 shuìmù (名) tax items; taxable items

税收 shuìshōu (名) tax revenue

税制 shuìzhì (名) tax system; taxation: 累进~ progressive taxation

睡 shuì (动) sleep: 他在沙发上躺了一会儿,但没~着. He lay on the sofa for a while, but didn't get a wink of sleep.

睡觉(覺) shuìjiào (动) sleep: 该~了. It's time to go to bed.

睡梦(夢) shuìmèng (名) sleep; dream: 从~中惊醒 be roused from sleep

睡眠 shuìmián (名) sleep: ~不足 not have enough sleep

睡衣 shuìyī (名) night clothes; pyjamas

吮 shǔn (动) suck

吮吸 shǔnxī (动) suck

瞬 shùn (名) wink; twinkling: 转～之间 in the twinkling of an eye

瞬时(時) shùnshí (形) instantaneous

瞬息 shùnxī (名) twinkling: ～万变的局势 the fast-changing situation

顺 shùn I (介) in the direction of; along: ～流而下 go downstream. ～河边走 walk along the river II (动) 1 arrange; put in order: 这篇文章还得～一～. This essay should be reorganized to make it more readable. 2 obey; yield to; act in submission to: 不能总是～着孩子. We can't always humour the child the way we do. 3 act at one's convenience: ～手关门 close the door after you. 4 suit: 不～他的意 not appeal to him

顺便 shùnbiàn (副) incidentally; in passing: 你去图书馆,～给我还这几本书. When you go to the library, please return these books for me if it doesn't give you too much inconvenience. ～说一句 by the way; incidentally. ～提到 mention in passing

顺差 shùnchā (名) favourable balance; surplus: 国际收支～ favourable balance of payments; balance of payments surplus

顺次 shùncì (副) in order; in succession; in proper sequence

顺从(從) shùncóng (动) be obedient to; submit to; yield to

顺当(當) shùndang (形) smoothly; without a hitch

顺耳 shùn'ěr (形) pleasing to the ear

顺访 shùnfǎng (动) visit a place on the way

顺风(風) shùnfēng have a favourable wind: 一路～ a pleasant journey; bon voyage

顺风(風)转(轉)舵 shùn fēng zhuǎn duò trim one's sails; chop around with the wind

顺口 shùnkǒu I (形) easy to read II (副) (say) offhandedly

顺理成章 shùn lǐ chéng zhāng (of a statement, argument, etc.) logical; well reasoned; follow a well mapped-out plan: 这显然是～的事. This is undoubtedly a matter of course.

顺利 shùnlì (形) smoothly; successfully: 进行～ get along pretty well. 手术进行得很～. It was a successful operation.

顺路 shùnlù I (副) on the way: 我昨天回家时～去看她. I dropped in on her on my way home yesterday. II (形) (of route) direct: 这么走不～. This is an indirect route.

顺势(勢) shùnshì (副) take advantage of a situation

顺手 shùnshǒu I (形) smoothly; without difficulty: 事情办得相当～. The work is proceeding smoothly. II (副) 1 conveniently; without lifting a finger 2 do sth. as a natural sequence: 我们扫完走廊,～把教室整理整理. Let's tidy up the classroom after sweeping the corridor.

顺水人情 shùnshuǐ rénqíng do sb. a favour without causing the slightest trouble to oneself

顺水推舟 shùnshuǐ tuī zhōu direct things on to their natural course

顺心 shùnxīn (形) satisfactory; gratifying

顺序 shùnxù I (名) sequence; order: 按年代～ in chronological order II (副) in proper order

顺延 shùnyán (动) postpone

顺眼 shùnyǎn (形) pleasing to the eye: 这图案看上去很～. This pattern is pleasant to look at.

顺应(應) shùnyìng (动) comply with; conform to: ～历史发展的潮流 go with the tide of historical development

说 shuō I (动) 1 speak; talk; say: ～好几国语言 speak several languages. 2 explain: 他得～几遍,才讲清楚. He had to explain several times to make himself understood. 3 scold: 他父亲～了他一顿. His father gave him a scolding. II (名) theory; teachings; doctrine: 著书立～ produce scholarly works to expound one's ideas

see also shuì

说不定 shuōbudìng perhaps; maybe: ～你是对的. Maybe you are right.

说不过(過)去 shuō bu guòqù cannot be justified; be unreasonable

说不好 shuōbuhǎo be unable to say for certain; not be certain; can't say

说不上 shuōbushàng 1 cannot say for sure 2 be not worth mentioning

说穿 shuōchuān (动) expose; disclose: ～某人真正用意 disclose sb.'s real intentions

说辞(辭) shuōcí (名) excuse; pretext

说…道… shuō … dào … [used before two parallel or similar adjectives or numerals]: 说三道四 make irresponsible remarks; gossip

说得过(過)去 shuōde guòqù be justifiable; be passable

S

说定 shuōdìng (动) settle; agree on: 这件事咱们就算～了. That's a deal we've made.

说法 shuōfa (名) 1 way of saying things; wording: 换一个～ put it in another way. 委婉的～ put it mildly 2 views; argument; version

说服 shuōfú (动) persuade; convince; bring round: 这个论点很有～力. This argument is very convincing. 需要做些～工作 require some persuading

说好 shuōhǎo (动) come to an agreement or understanding

说合 shuōhe (动) bring two (or more) parties together; talk over; discuss

说话 shuōhuà I (动) 1 speak; talk; say: 太激动了, 话都说不清楚了 be too excited to speak coherently. 我们～是算数的. We mean what we say. 2 chat; talk 3 criticize: 小心点, 人家也许会～. Be careful. Don't incite criticism. II (副) in a minute; right away: 我～就来. I'm coming.

说谎 shuōhuǎng (动) tell a lie; lie

说教 shuōjiào (动) preach [also used figuratively]

说客 shuōkè (名) a person sent to win sb. over or enlist his support through persuasion

说理 shuōlǐ (动) argue; reason things out: 咱们找他～去. Let's go and have it out with him.

说媒 shuōméi (动) act as matchmaker

说明 shuōmíng I (动) 1 explain; illustrate: ～理由 explain the cause 2 prove; demonstrate: 事实～这种做法是对的. Facts fully testify to the correctness of the approach. II (名) explanation; directions; caption: ～书 directions; synopsis (of a play or film)

说情 shuōqíng (动) plead for mercy for sb.

说妥 shuōtuǒ come to an agreement

说闲(閒)话 shuō xiánhuà (动) make critical or sarcastic remarks on the sidelines

说项 shuōxiàng (动) put in a good word for sb.

说笑 shuōxiào (动) chat and laugh

说一不二 shuō yī bù èr mean what one says; stand by one's word

数(數) shuò (副) frequently; repeatedly

see also shǔ; shù

数见(見)不鲜 shuò jiàn bù xiān common occurrence; nothing new

朔 shuò (名) 1 the first day of the lunar month 2 north: ～风 north wind

硕 shuò (形) large

硕果 shuòguǒ (名) rich fruits; great achievements

硕果仅(僅)存 shuòguǒ jǐn cún rare survival or survivor

硕士 shuòshì (名) Master: ～学位 Master's degree

烁(爍) shuò bright; shining: 闪～ twinkle; glimmer

斯 sī

斯文 sīwén (形) refined; gentle

厮 sī (副) with each other; together: ～打 come to blows; exchange blows

撕 sī (动) tear; rip: 从日历上～下一页 tear a page from the calendar. 上衣～了. The jacket is torn.

撕毁 sīhuǐ (动) tear up; tear to pieces: ～协定 tear up an agreement; tear an agreement to shreds

嘶 sī (形) hoarse

嘶哑(啞) sīyǎ (形) hoarse

思 sī I (动) 1 think; consider: 前～后想 weigh the ideas carefully 2 think of; long for: ～家 homesick. ～乡 think of one's native place with nostalgic longing II (名) train of thought

思潮 sīcháo (名) 1 trend: 文艺～ literary trends 2 thoughts: ～起伏 surging ideas

思考 sīkǎo (动) think deeply; ponder over; reflect on: ～问题 ponder a problem

思恋(戀) sīliàn (动) think fondly of; long for: ～故土 think fondly of one's native land

思量 sīliang (动) consider; turn sth. over in one's mind

思路 sīlù (名) train of thought; thinking: 打断～ interrupt one's train of thought

思虑(慮) sīlǜ (动) consider carefully; contemplate; deliberate

思慕 sīmù (动) think of sb. with respect; admire

思念 sīniàn (动) think of; long for; miss sb.

思索 sīsuǒ (动) think deeply; ponder: 反复～这个问题 turn the problem over and over in one's mind.

思维 sīwéi (名) thought; thinking: ～方式 mode of thinking

思乡(鄉) sīxiāng (动) be homesick

思想 sīxiǎng (名) thought; thinking; idea; ideology: 政治～ political thought. 有～准备 be mentally prepared. ～觉悟 political consciousness (or awareness). ～意识 ideology

思绪 sīxù (名) 1 train of thought; thinking: ～纷乱 confused thinking 2 mood: ～不宁 feel disquieted

私 sī (形) 1 personal; private: ～事 private affairs 2 selfish: 无～ unselfish; selfless 3 secret; private: 窃窃～语 whisper; exchange whispered comments 4 illicit; illegal: ～货 smuggled goods

私奔 sībēn (动) elope with sb.

私产(產) sīchǎn (名) private property

私仇 sīchóu (名) personal enmity

私房 sīfáng I (名) 1 a privately owned house or building; private residence 2 private savings: ～钱 private savings of a family member II (形) confidential: 谈～话 exchange confidences

私愤 sīfèn (名) personal spite: 泄～ vent personal spleen

私交 sījiāo (名) personal relationship

私立 sīlì (形) privately run; private: ～学校 private school

私利 sīlì (名) private (or selfish) interests; personal gain

私了 sīliǎo (动) settle privately; settle out of court

私囊 sīnáng (名) private purse: 中饱～ line one's pockets

私企 sīqǐ (名) private enterprise

私情 sīqíng (名) personal relationships: 不徇～ allow no consideration of personal relationships to interfere

私人 sīrén (形) private; personal: ～秘书 private secretary. ～企业 private enterprise. ～关系 personal relations

私生活 sīshēnghuó (名) private life

私生子 sīshēngzǐ (名) illegitimate child; bastard

私通 sītōng (动) 1 have secret communication with: ～敌人 have secret communication with the enemy 2 have illicit relations with

私下 sīxià (副) privately; in secret

私心 sīxīn (名) selfish motives (or ideas); selfishness: ～杂念 selfish ideas and ulterior motives

私刑 sīxíng (名) illegal punishment (meted out by a kangaroo court); lynching

私营(營) sīyíng (形) privately owned; privately operated; private: ～企业 private enterprise

私有 sīyǒu (形) privately owned; private: ～财产 private property. ～制 private ownership (of means of production)

私自 sīzì (副) privately; secretly; without permission: 事先不通知委员会就～决定 make a decision on one's own without the prior knowledge of the committee

司 sī I (动) take charge of; attend to; manage: 各～其事. Each has his own responsibilities. II (名) department (under a ministry)

司法 sīfǎ (名) administration of justice; judicature: ～部门 judicial departments. ～权 judicial powers. ～程序 legal proceedings; judicial procedure

司机(機) sījī (名) driver; chauffeur

司空见(見)惯 sīkōng jiàn guàn a common sight or occurrence; nothing to be surprised at

司令 sīlìng (名) commander; commanding officer: ～部 headquarters; command. 总～ commander-in-chief

司炉(爐) sīlú (名) stoker; fireman

司务(務)长(長) sīwùzhǎng (名) 1 mess officer 2 company quartermaster

司药(藥) sīyào (名) pharmacist; druggist; chemist

司仪(儀) sīyí (名) master of ceremonies

丝(絲) sī (名) 1 silk 2 a thread-like thing: 铜～ copper wire. 炒肉～ stir-fried shredded pork 3 a tiny bit; trace: 一～不差 not the slightest difference. 一～不挂 stark naked

丝绸 sīchóu (名) silk cloth; silk: ～之路 the Silk Road

丝瓜 sīguā (名) towel gourd; dishcloth gourd: ～络 loofah; vegetable sponge

丝毫 sīháo (名) the slightest amount or degree: ～不差 without the slightest discrepancy; tally in every detail

丝绵 sīmián (名) silk floss; silk wadding

丝绒 sīróng (名) velvet; velour

丝线(綫) sīxiàn (名) silk thread (for sewing); silk yarn

丝织(織)品 sīzhīpǐn (名) 1 silk fabrics 2 silk knit goods

S

死 sǐ I (动) die: 战～ be killed in action II (形) 1 dead: ～人 a dead person; the dead 2 to the death: ～战 fight to the death 3 extremely: 急～了 be worried to death. 渴～了 be parched 4 implacable; deadly: ～敌 sworn enemy 5 fixed; rigid; inflexible: ～规矩 a rigid rule 6 impassable; closed: ～胡同 a blind alley

死板 sǐbǎn (形) rigid; inflexible; stiff: 做事情不能太～. One must not be too inflexible in handling affairs.

死党(黨) sǐdǎng (名) sworn followers; diehard followers

死得其所 sǐ dé qí suǒ die a worthy death

死对(對)头(頭) sǐduìtou (名) deadly enemy; irreconcilable opponent

死鬼 sǐguǐ (名) [used to curse a person or crack a joke] devil: 你这～, 你干什么? You devil! What are you up to?

死胡同 sǐhútòng (名) blind alley; dead end

死灰复(復)燃 sǐhuī fù rán the embers are smouldering — revival of something that is not really dead

死活 sǐhuó I (名) life or death; fate II (副) 〈口〉 anyway; simply: 他～不肯去. He flatly refused to go.

死机(機) sǐjī (动) crash; dead (of computer)

死角 sǐjiǎo (名) 1 dead angle; dead space 2 a spot as yet untouched by a trend, political movement, etc.

死劲(勁)儿(兒) sǐjìnr (副) 〈口〉 with all one's strength (or might); for all one is worth: ～跑 run like crazy

死路 sǐlù (名) dead end; the road to ruin

死难(難) sǐnàn (动) die in an accident or a political incident

死气(氣)沉沉 sǐqì chénchén lifeless; spiritless; stagnant

死囚 sǐqiú (名) a convict sentenced to death

死去活来(來) sǐqù-huólái be half dead; be in deep pain; be mad with grief: 被打得～ be beaten half dead

死伤(傷) sǐshāng (名) the fatalities and injured persons; casualties

死尸(屍) sǐshī (名) corpse; dead body

死守 sǐshǒu (动) 1 defend to the last 2 rigidly adhere to

死亡 sǐwáng (动) die: ～率 death rate; mortality

死心 sǐxīn (动) give up the idea for ever; have no more illusions about sth.

死心塌地 sǐxīntādì be dead set: 他～要破坏这个计划. He is dead set on wrecking the plan.

死心眼儿(兒) sǐxīnyǎnr (形) stubborn; as obstinate as a mule

死刑 sǐxíng (名) death penalty; death sentence

死硬 sǐyìng (形) 1 stiff; inflexible 2 very obstinate; diehard: ～派 diehards

死有余(餘)辜 sǐ yǒu yú gū have committed more crimes than one could atone for by death

死于(於)非命 sǐ yú fēimìng die a violent death

死者 sǐzhě (名) the dead; the deceased; the departed

死症 sǐzhèng (名) incurable disease

肆 sì I (副) wantonly; unbridledly: 大～攻击 wantonly attack II (数) four [used for the numeral 四 on cheques, etc. to avoid mistakes or alterations]

肆无(無)忌惮(憚) sì wú jìdàn unbridled; brazen; unscrupulous: ～地攻击 launch an all-out attack

肆意 sìyì (副) wantonly; recklessly; wilfully: ～歪曲事实 wilfully distort the facts

寺 sì (名) temple: 清真～ mosque

寺院 sìyuàn (名) temple

四 sì (数) four

四…八… sì…bā… [used before two similar words to indicate various directions]: 四面八方 all quarters. 四通八达 extend in all directions

四边(邊) sìbiān (名) (on) four sides

四不像 sìbùxiàng nondescript; neither fish nor fowl

四处(處) sìchù (名) all around; everywhere: ～打听 make inquiries everywhere

四方 sìfāng I (名) all sides; all quarters: ～响应. Support came from every quarter. II (形) square; cubic: 一块～的手绢 a square handkerchief

四分五裂 sìfēn-wǔliè fall apart; be rent asunder

四个现代化 sìgè xiàndàihuà the Four Modernizations (i. e. of industry, agriculture, defence, and science and technology)

四海 sìhǎi (名) the four seas; the whole

country; the whole world: ～为家 make one's home no matter where one lives and works

四合院 sìhéyuàn (名) a compound with houses around a square courtyard; quadrangle

四季 sìjì (名) the four seasons: 一年有～. There are four seasons in a year.

四郊 sìjiāo (名) suburbs; outskirts

四邻(鄰) sìlín (名) one's near neighbours

四面 sìmiàn (名) (on) four sides; (on) all sides: 这座别墅的～都是树木. The villa is surrounded by trees on all sides.

四面楚歌 sìmiàn Chǔ gē be vulnerable to attack on all sides; be utterly isolated

四平八稳(穩) sìpíng-bāwěn 1 very steady; well balanced: 办事～be even-handed in the discharge of one's duty 2 be overcautious

四散 sìsàn (动) scatter (or disperse) in all directions

四声(聲) sìshēng (名) the four tones of the modern standard Chinese pronunciation

四野 sìyě (名) a vast expanse of country

四月 sìyuè (名) 1 April 2 the fourth month of the lunar year; the fourth moon

四肢 sìzhī (名) the four limbs; arms and legs

四周 sìzhōu (名) all around

驷 sì

驷马(馬) sìmǎ (名)〈书〉a team of four horses: 一言既出, ～难追. A word spoken is past recalling.

似 sì I (形) similar; like: 在这问题上, 我们的观点相～. We hold similar views on this matter. II (动) 1 seem; appear: ～应从速办理. It would seem necessary to act promptly. 2 surpass: 生活一年胜～一年. Life is getting better with each passing year.

see also shì

似…非… sì…fēi… [used to indicate both similarity and dissimilarity]: 似懂非懂 have only a hazy notion; not quite understand. 似笑非笑 a faint smile

似乎 sìhū (副) it seems; as if: 他～没有看过那本书. He doesn't seem to have read that book. ～要下雪了. It looks like snow.

似是而非 sì shì ér fēi apparently right but actually wrong; specious

俟 sì (动) wait: ～机进攻 wait for the right moment to attack

嗣 sì I (动) succeed; inherit: ～位 succeed to the throne II (名) heir; descendant

伺 sì (动) watch; await: ～机 bide one's time; watch for a chance

see also cì

饲 sì (动) raise; rear

饲料 sìliào (名) forage; fodder; feed: 猪～pig feed

饲养(養) sìyǎng (动) raise; rear: ～家禽 raise (or rear) poultry

松 sōng (名) pine: ～树 pine tree

松(鬆) sōng I (形) 1 loose; slack: 绑得太～loosely tied. 螺丝～了. The screw has come loose. 2 well off 3 light and crisp II (名) dried minced meat III (动) loosen; relax; slacken: ～腰带 loosen one's belt. ～一口气 heave a sigh of relief

松绑 sōngbǎng (动) 1 untie a person 2 free a person (or an organization) from unnecessary restrictions

松弛 sōngchí (形) 1 limp; flabby: 肌肉～flabby 2 lax: 纪律～ lax discipline

松动(動) sōngdòng I (形) less crowded II (动) 1 loose 2 show flexibility

松紧(緊) sōngjǐn (名) elasticity

松劲(勁) sōngjìn (动) relax one's efforts

松口 sōngkǒu (动) relent

松快 sōngkuai (形) relaxed

松软 sōngruǎn (形) soft; spongy; loose: ～的表土 spongy topsoil

松散 sōngsǎn (形) 1 loose; shaky 2 inattentive

松手 sōngshǒu (动) let go

松鼠 sōngshǔ (名) squirrel

松闲(閒) sōngxián (形) not busy; slack

松香 sōngxiāng (名) rosin; colophony

松懈 sōngxiè (形) absent-minded or sluggish

悚 sǒng

悚然 sǒngrán (形) terrified; horrified: 毛骨～ with one's hair standing on end

怂(慫) sǒng

怂恿 sǒngyǒng (动) instigate; incite; abet

耸(聳) sǒng (动) 1 tower: 高～入云 tower into the sky 2

alarm; attract (attention): 危言～听 give a horrible account of the situation just to scare the hearers

耸动(動) sǒngdòng (动) 1 shrug (one's shoulders) 2 create a sensation

耸肩 sǒngjiān (动) shrug one's shoulders

耸立 sǒnglì (动) rise like a tower

耸人听(聽)闻 sǒng rén tīngwén deliberately exaggerate facts so as to create a sensation; give a startling account of exaggerated facts

送 sòng (动) 1 deliver; carry: ～货到家 deliver goods to one's door 2 give as a present; give 3 see sb. off or out; accompany; escort: 到机场～人 see sb. off at the airport. 把客人～到门口 see a guest to the door

送别 sòngbié (动) see sb. off

送还(還) sònghuán (动) give back; return

送货 sònghuò (动) deliver goods: ～上门 deliver goods right to the doorstep of a customer; deliver to domicile

送客 sòngkè (动) see a visitor out

送礼(禮) sònglǐ (动) give sb. a present; present a gift to sb.

送命 sòngmìng (动) lose one's life; get killed

送人情 sòng rénqíng deliberately do sb. a good turn (sometimes by stretching a point) to curry his favour

送信 sòngxìn (动) send word; go and tell; deliver a letter by hand

送行 sòngxíng (动) 1 see sb. off; wish sb. bon voyage 2 give a send-off party

送葬 sòngzàng (动) join a funeral procession

送终 sòngzhōng (动) attend upon a dying senior member of the family; make arrangements for his funeral

诵 sòng (动) 1 read aloud; chant 2 recite

诵读(讀) sòngdú (动) read aloud; chant

讼 sòng (动) 1 bring a case to court: 诉～ lawsuit 2 dispute; argue: 聚～纷纭 a confused scene of people arguing among themselves

颂 sòng I (动) praise; extol; eulogize: 歌～sing the praises of II (名) song; ode; paean; eulogy: 《西风～》 *Ode to the West Wind*

颂词 sòngcí (名) congratulatory address or message; eulogy

颂歌 sònggē (名) song; ode

颂扬(揚) sòngyáng (动) extol; eulogize

搜 sōu (动) search

搜查 sōuchá (动) search; ransack; rummage: ～证 search warrant

搜肠(腸)刮肚 sōucháng-guādù rack one's brains (for a way out)

搜刮 sōuguā (动) extort; plunder; expropriate; fleece: ～钱财 extort money from

搜集 sōují (动) collect; gather: ～情报 collect information. ～意见 solicit opinions from. ～资料 collect data

搜罗(羅) sōuluó (动) collect; gather; recruit: ～人才 recruit qualified personnel

搜身 sōushēn (动) search the person; make a body search

搜索 sōusuǒ (动) search for; hunt for; hunt down: ～逃犯 hunt down an escaped convict

搜索枯肠(腸) sōusuǒ kūcháng rack one's brains (for fresh ideas or apt expressions)

搜寻(尋) sōuxún (动) search high and low for a missing person or article

搜腰包 sōu yāobāo search sb.'s pockets; search sb. for money and valuables

艘 sōu (量) [for boats or ships]: 两～鱼雷快艇 two torpedo boats

馊 sōu (形) sour; spoiled: 饭菜～了. The food has gone bad.

薮(藪) sǒu (名)〈书〉 1 a shallow lake overgrown with wild plants 2 a gathering place of fish or beasts 3 den; haunt

嗾 sǒu

嗾使 sǒushǐ (动) instigate; abet

叟 sǒu (名) old man: 智～ a wise old man

苏(蘇) sū (动) come to; become conscious again: 死而复～ come back to life

苏醒 sūxǐng (动) regain consciousness; come to: 当他～过来的时候,发现自己已躺在医院病房里. When he came to, he found himself lying in a hospital ward.

酥 sū I (形) 1 crisp 2 (of a person's limbs) limp; weak II (名) shortbread

酥脆 sūcuì (形) crisp: ～饼干 crisp biscuit

酥软 sūruǎn (形) limp; weak; soft

酥松(鬆) sūsōng (形) (of soil, etc.) loose; porous; (of pastries, etc.) flaky; crisp

酥油 sūyóu (名) butter: ～茶 buttered tea

S

俗 sú I (名) custom; convention: 陈规旧～ outdated customs. 入乡随～ When in Rome, do as the Romans do. II (形) 1 popular; common: 通～ popular 2 coarse; boorish: ～不可耐 hopelessly boorish 3 secular: 僧～ clergy and laity

俗话 súhuà (名) common saying; proverb: ～说 as the saying goes

俗气(氣) súqì (形) inelegant; in poor taste: 这间房子布置得太～. This room is arranged in poor taste.

俗套 sútào (名) conventional pattern; convention: 不落～ depart from the beaten track

宿 sù I (动) put up for the night: ～舍 dormitory; flat II (形) long-standing; old: ～愿 long-cherished wish see also xiǔ

宿仇 sùchóu (名) long-standing enmity

宿敌(敵) sùdí (名) an old enemy

宿命论(論) sùmìnglùn (名) fatalism

宿营(營) sùyíng (动) (of troops) take up quarters; camp

宿怨 sùyuàn (名) old grudge; old scores

溯 sù (动) 1 go against the stream: ～流而上 go upstream 2 trace back; recall: 回～ recall; reminisce

溯源 sùyuán (动) trace to the source: 追本～ taking into consideration the origin of the matter; get at the root of the problem

塑 sù (动) model; mould: ～像 mould a statue

塑钢(鋼) sùgāng (名) vinyl-coated steel

塑胶(膠) sùjiāo (名) plastic cement

塑料 sùliào (名) plastics: 泡沫～ foam plastics. ～炸弹 plastic bomb

塑像 sùxiàng (名) statue

塑造 sùzào (动) 1 model; mould 2 portray: 这本小说～一个典型的农村妇女的形象. The novel depicts a typical peasant woman.

诉 sù (动) 1 tell; relate; inform: 告～ tell. ～说 tell; recount 2 complain; accuse: 控～ accuse. 倾～ pour out (one's feelings, troubles, etc.). ～苦 vent one's grievances 3 appeal to; resort to: 上～ appeal to a higher court. ～诸武力 resort to force

素 sù I (名) 1 white: ～服 be dressed in white 2 vegetables: 吃～ have regular vegetarian meals; be a vegetarian 3 basic element; element: 毒～ poison. 维生～ vitamin II (形) 1 (of colours) plain 2 native: ～性 a person's disposition III (副) usually; always: ～不相识 not know sb. at all

素材 sùcái (名) source material (of literature and art); material

素菜 sùcài (名) vegetable dish

素来(來) sùlái (副) always; usually: 他～生活简朴. He always lives a plain life.

素昧平生 sù mèi píngshēng have never met before; have never had the pleasure of making sb.'s acquaintance

素描 sùmiáo (名) sketch

素食 sùshí (名) vegetarian food; vegetarian diet

素雅 sùyǎ (形) simple but in good taste

素养(養) sùyǎng (名) attainment: 艺术～ artistic attainment

素油 sùyóu (名) vegetable oil

素愿(願) sùyuàn (名) a long-cherished desire; wish; aspiration

素质(質) sùzhì (名) quality: 部队的军事～ the sterling military quality of the troops

素质(質)教育 sùzhì jiàoyù quality-oriented education; education for all-round development

速 sù I (形) fast; rapid; quick; instant: ～读 fast (speed) reading. ～效 quick results. ～溶咖啡 instant coffee II (名) speed; velocity III (动) invite: 不～之客 uninvited (or self-invited) guest

速成 sùchéng (动) complete quickly: ～班 crash course

速冻(凍) sùdòng (动) quick-freeze: ～饺子 quick-frozen dumplings

速记 sùjì (名) shorthand; stenography: ～员 stenographer

速决 sùjué (名) quick decision; quick solution: 速战～ get down to work right away and dispose of the problem promptly

速率 sùlǜ (名) speed; rate

速写(寫) sùxiě (名) 1 sketch 2 literary sketch

粟 sù (名) millet

夙 sù 〈书〉 I (名) early in the morning II (形) long-standing; old: ～愿 long-cherished wish

夙敌(敵) sùdí (名) an old enemy

夙兴(興)夜寐 sùxīng-yèmèi rise early and

retire late

肃(肅) sù (形) 1 respectful 2 solemn: 严～ solemn; serious; grave

肃静 sùjìng (形) solemn and silent

肃立 sùlì (动) stand at attention: ～默哀 stand in silent mourning

肃清 sùqīng (动) eliminate; clean up; mop up: ～官僚主义 eliminate bureaucracy

肃然起敬 sùrán qǐ jìng be filled with deep respect

酸 suān I (名) acid II (形) 1 sour; tart: ～牛奶 yogurt; sour milk 2 grieved; distressed: 心～ be sick at heart; feel sad 3 aching: 腰～背疼 have a pain in the back; have backache

酸菜 suāncài (名) pickled Chinese cabbage

酸辣汤(湯) suānlàtāng (名) vinegar-pepper soup

酸溜溜 suānliūliū (形) 1 sour 2 aching 3 feeling unhappy and ashamed

酸软 suānruǎn (形) aching and limp

酸甜苦辣 suān-tián-kǔ-là joys and sorrows of life

酸痛 suāntòng (形) aching: 浑身～ ache all over

酸味 suānwèi (名) tart flavour

酸雨 suānyǔ (名) acid rain

蒜 suàn (名) garlic: 一瓣～ a string of garlic

蒜泥 suànní (名) mashed garlic

蒜头(頭) suàntóu (名) the head (or bulb) of garlic

算 suàn I (动) 1 calculate: 心～: mental calculation 2 include; count: 把我也～上. Count me in. ～上伤病号,敌军只有百把人. There are only some one hundred enemy troops counting the sick and wounded. 3 plan; calculate: 失～ miscalculate; make an unwise move 4 consider; regard as; count as: 他～是我们这儿最好的厨师了. He is considered the best cook around here. 他说的不～. What he says doesn't count. 5 carry weight; count: 这样重要的事不能一人说了～. Such an important matter shouldn't be decided by any individual alone. 谁说了～? Who has the final say? 6 [followed by 了] forget it; let it pass: ～了,别说了. That's enough! Let's leave it at that. II (副) at long last; finally: 问题～解决了. The problem is finally solved.

算卦 suànguà (动) tell sb.'s fortune by using the Eight Trigrams

算计 suànji (动) 1 calculate; reckon: ～～一下,买这些东西要多少钱. Figure out how much all these things will cost. 2 consider; plan 3 expect; figure: 我～他明天到北京. I expect him to be in Beijing tomorrow. 4 secretly scheme against others

算旧(舊)账(賬) suàn jiùzhàng settle an old account; settle an old score

算命 suànmìng (动) tell one's fortune; fortune-telling: ～先生 fortune-teller

算盘(盤) suànpan (名) abacus

算是 suànshì (副) at last: 这一下你～猜着了. At last you've guessed right.

算术(術) suànshù (名) arithmetic

算数(數) suànshù (动) count; hold; stand: 我们说话是～的. We mean what we say.

算账(賬) suànzhàng (动) do account; balance the books

虽(雖) suī (连) though; although; while

虽然 suīrán (连) though; although

虽说 suīshuō (连)〈口〉 though; although

随(隨) suí (动) 1 follow: ～我去旧金山 follow me to San Francisco 2 comply with: ～顺 comply (with sb.'s wishes) 3 let (sb. do as he likes): ～你的便. Do as you please.

随笔(筆) suíbǐ (名) informal essay; random notes

随便 suíbiàn I (形) 1 casual; random; informal: ～聊天 chat; chitchat 2 do as one pleases: ～吃吧! Help yourselves. 3 careless; without thought: ～说话 speak casually II (连) anyhow; any: ～你怎么说,我是不会同意的. Whatever you may say about the matter, I won't agree with you.

随波逐流 suíbō-zhúliú drift with the tide (or current)

随从(從) suícóng I (动) accompany (one's superior); attend II (名) retinue; suite; entourage

随大溜 suídàliù drift with the stream; follow the general trend

随地 suídì (副) anywhere; everywhere: 随时～ at anytime and at any place. 不要～乱扔东西. Don't litter.

随风(風)倒 suífēngdǎo bend with the wind

随和 suíhe (形) amiable; obliging

随后(後) suíhòu (副) soon afterwards: 你先

S

走,东西～送到. You go ahead. The goods will be delivered right away.

随机(機)应(應)变(變) suíjī-yìngbiàn resourceful; act according to circumstances

随即 suíjí (副) immediately; presently

随口 suíkǒu (副) (speak) thoughtlessly or casually: ～说出 blurt out

随身 suíshēn (动) (carry) on one's person; (take) with one: ～行李 personal luggage; carry-on items; accompanying luggage

随声(聲)附和 suí shēng fùhè echo other people's views thoughtlessly

随时(時) suíshí (副) at any time; at all times: 有问题～可来找我. If you have any problem, come and see me at any time.

随手 suíshǒu (副) conveniently (when doing sth.); without extra trouble: ～关门. Shut the door after you.

随…随… suí…suí… [used before two verbs to indicate that one action is immediately followed by another]: 随叫随到 be available at any time; be on call at any hour

随同 suítóng (动) accompany

随心所欲 suí xīn suǒ yù follow one's bent; do as one pleases

随行人员 suíxíng rényuán entourage; suite; party: 总统及其～the President and his entourage

随意 suíyì (副) at will; as one pleases

随员 suíyuán (名) 1 anybody accompanying an important government official on his trip abroad 2 attaché

S

随着 suízhe I (介) along with; in the wake of: ～时间的推移 as time goes on; with the lapse (or passage) of time II(副) accordingly: 经济发展了,人们的生活也～改善了. With the economic development, the living conditions of the people have improved accordingly.

绥 suí I (形) peaceful II (动)pacify

绥靖 suíjìng (动) pacify; appease: ～政策 policy of appeasement

髓 suǐ (名) marrow: 脊～ spinal marrow (or cord)

碎 suì I (动) break to pieces; smash: 瓶～了. The bottle is smashed to pieces. II (形) 1 broken: ～玻璃 bits of broken glass. ～石 crushed stones 2 garrulous; gabby: 嘴太～ be too talkative; be a regular chatterbox

遂 suì (动) 1 satisfy; fulfil: ～愿 fulfilment of one's wish; a sense of fulfilment 2 succeed: 所谋不～ fail in an attempt

遂心 suìxīn (动) after one's own heart; to one's liking: ～如意 highly pleased; perfectly satisfied

遂意 suìyì (动) to one's liking

燧 suì (名) 1 flint 2 beacon fire

燧石 suìshí (名) flint

隧 suì

隧道 suìdào (名) tunnel; underground passage

岁(歲) suì (名) 1 year: ～末 the end of the year. ～入 annual income 2 year (of age): 三～女孩 a three-year-old girl

岁暮 suìmù (名) the close of the year

岁收 suìshōu (名) annual income (in a state budget); revenue

岁数(數) suìshu (名)〈口〉age; years: 您多大～了? How old are you? 上～ getting on in years

岁月 suìyuè (名) years: 艰苦的～ hard times. ～不居 cannot stay the flying tail of time; time flies

穗 suì (名) 1 the ear of grain; spike 2 tassel; fringe

穗子 suìzi (名) tassel; fringe

祟 suì (名) evil spirit; ghost: 作～ exercise evil influence; cause trouble

孙(孫) sūn (名) grandson

孙女 sūnnǚ (名) granddaughter

孙子 sūnzi (名) grandson

损 sǔn (动) 1 decrease; lose 2 harm; damage: 有益无～can only do good, not harm. ～公肥私 seek private gain at public expense

损害 sǔnhài (动) harm; damage; injure: ～声誉 damage one's reputation. ～健康 impair one's health; be harmful to one's health

损耗 sǔnhào (名) 1 loss; wear and tear 2 wastage: 减少～ reduce the wastage

损坏(壞) sǔnhuài (动) damage; have a harmful effect on

损人利己 sǔn rén lì jǐ harm others to benefit oneself

损伤(傷) sǔnshāng (动) 1 harm; damage; injure: 不要～群众的积极性. Make sure that the enthusiasm of the masses is not dampened. 2 suffer losses: 敌军兵力～很大. The enemy forces suffered heavy losses.

损失 sǔnshī I (动) lose: ～飞机五架 lose five planes II (名) loss; damage: 此事对我们公司是很大的～. It's a big loss to our firm.

笋(筍) sǔn (名) bamboo shoot: ～干 dried bamboo shoots

蓑 suō

蓑衣 suōyī (名) straw or palmbark rain cape

梭 suō (名) shuttle: 穿～外交 shuttle diplomacy

梭镖 suōbiāo (名) spear

唆 suō (动) instigate; abet: 教～ instigate; abet

唆使 suōshǐ (动) instigate; abet: ～者 instigator; abettor

缩 suō (动) 1 contract; shrink: 热胀冷～ expand with heat and contract with cold 2 draw back; withdraw; recoil: 退～ flinch; shrink. 他把身子一～. He shrank back (in shame, horror, etc.).

缩短 suōduǎn (动) shorten; curtail; cut down: ～距离 reduce the distance. ～期限 shorten the time limit

缩减 suōjiǎn (动) reduce; cut: ～军费 cut back military spending

缩手 suōshǒu (动) 1 draw back one's hand 2 shrink (from doing sth.): ～缩脚 be overcautious

缩水 suōshuǐ (动) (of cloth through wetting) shrink: ～率 shrinkage

缩头(頭)缩脑(腦) suōtóu-suōnǎo 1 be timid; be faint-hearted 2 shrink from responsibility

缩小 suōxiǎo (动) reduce; narrow (down): ～范围 narrow down the scope

缩写(寫) suōxiě I (名) abbreviation II(动) abridge: ～本 abridged edition

缩影 suōyǐng (名) epitome; miniature

索 suǒ I (名) large rope: 绳～ rope. 绞～ noose. II (动) 1 search: 遍～不得 look for sth. everywhere but in vain 2 demand; ask; exact: ～价 ask a price; charge III (形) lonely; depressed: 离群～居 live in solitude

索贿 suǒhuì (动) demand a bribe; ask for a bribe

索赔 suǒpéi (动) claim damages; claim an indemnity

索取 suǒqǔ (动) ask for; demand; exact; extort: 向大自然～财富 wrest wealth from nature

索然 suǒrán (形) depressed; in low spirits: 兴致～ feel low-spirited

索性 suǒxìng (副) without hesitation: 既然已经做了, ～就把它做完. Since you have started the work, you may as well go on till you are through with it.

索引 suǒyǐn (名) index: 卡片～ card index. 书名～ title index

琐 suǒ (形) trivial; petty

琐事 suǒshì (名) trifles; trivial matters: 家庭～ household chores

琐碎 suǒsuì (形) trifling; trivial

琐细 suǒxì (形) trifling; trivial

锁 suǒ I (名) lock: 弹簧～ spring lock. 枷～ shackles II (动) 1 lock up: ～门 lock a door 2 lockstitch: ～边 lockstitch a border

锁定 suǒdìng (动) lock on to; stay tuned to (a radio or television programme)

锁匠 suǒjiang (名) locksmith

锁链 suǒliàn (名) 1 chain 2 shackles; fetters; chains

锁钥(鑰) suǒyuè (名) key

所 suǒ I (名) 1 place: 住～ dwelling place 2 institute; office: 研究～ research institute II (量) [for buildings]: 一～房子 a house. 两～学校 two schools III (助) 1 [used together with 为 or 被 to indicate a passive construction]: 为人～笑 be laughed at 2 [used before a verb as the agent of the action]: 各尽～能 from each according to his ability. 闻～未闻 unheard of 3 [used before a verb which takes an object]: 我～认识的人 the people I know

所长(長) suǒcháng (名) what one is good at; one's strong point; one's forte

所得 suǒdé (名) income; earnings; gains: ～税 income tax

所属(屬) suǒshǔ (形) 1 what is subordinate to one or under one's command 2 what one belongs to or is affiliated with

所谓 suǒwèi (形) 1 what is called: ～民主,只是一种手段,不是目的. What is called democracy is only a means, not an

S

end. 2 so-called: ~"无核地区" the so-called "nuclear-free zones"

所向披靡 suǒ xiàng pīmǐ (of troops) carry all before one; be irresistible

所以 suǒyǐ I (连) [used to indicate cause and effect] so; therefore; as a result: 我和他一起工作过, ~对他比较熟悉. We used to be colleagues, so I know him quite well. II [used separately to indicate cause or reason]: ~呀, 要不然我怎么会这样说呢? That's just the point, otherwise I wouldn't have said it. III (名) [used in set phrases as an object]: 忘其~ forget oneself

所以然 suǒyǐrán (名) the reason why; the whys and wherefores: 知其然, 而不知~. Know the how but not the why.

所有 suǒyǒu I (动) own; possess II (名) possessions: 尽其~ give everything one has III (形) all: 把~的劲儿都使出来 exert all one's strength

所有制 suǒyǒuzhì (名) system of ownership; ownership

所在 suǒzài (名) place; location: 风景优美的~ a scenic spot. 问题~ the crux of the matter. ~多有 be found almost everywhere

所作所为(爲) suǒzuò-suǒwéi one's behaviour or conduct

T t

他 tā (代) 1 he 2 [any person, either male or female, when no distinction of sex is necessary or possible]: 一个人要是不努力, ~就将一事无成. Nobody can achieve anything of real significance unless he works very hard. 3 another; other; some other: ~乡 strange place. ~日 some day 4 [used between a verb and a numeral]: 再试~一次 have another try

他们 tāmen (代) they: ~俩 the two of them. ~学校离火车站不远. Their school is not far from the railway station.

他人 tārén (代) another person; other people; others

他杀(殺) tāshā (名) homicide

他乡(鄉) tāxiāng (名) a place away from home; a strange land: ~遇故知 meet an old friend in a distant land

她 tā (代) she

她们 tāmen (代) [indicating the female sex] they

它 tā (代) [neuter gender] it: 把~拿到厨房去. Take it to the kitchen.

它们 tāmen (代) they

塌 tā (动) 1 collapse; fall down; cave in: 椅子~了. The chair collapsed. 2 sink; droop: ~鼻梁 a flat nose 3 calm down: ~心 settle down

塌方 tāfāng (动) 1 cave in; collapse 2 landslide

塌实(實) tāshi (形) 1 down-to-earth; practical 2 feel relieved; feel at home: 事情办完就~了. You'll feel relieved when you've fulfilled your task. 睡得很~ have a sound sleep

塌陷 tāxiàn (动) subside; sink; cave in

塔 tǎ (名) 1 Buddhist pagoda 2 tower: 水~ water tower. 灯~ lighthouse; beacon. 蒸馏~ distillation column (or tower)

挞(撻) tà (动) flog; whip: 鞭~ flog; lash

拓 tà (动) make rubbings from inscriptions, pictures, etc. on stone tablets or bronze vessels
see also tuò

拓本 tàběn (名) a book of rubbings

榻 tà (名) couch; bed

沓 tà (形) 〈书〉 crowded; repeated: 纷至~来 come thick and fast; keep pouring in
see also dá

踏 tà (动) 1 step on; tread; stamp: 践~ trample. ~步 mark time 2 go to the spot (to make investigation or survey)

踏板 tàbǎn (名) 1 treadle; footboard; footrest 2 footstool (usu. placed beside a bed) 3 pedal (of a piano, etc.)

踏勘 tàkān (动) make an on-the-spot survey

踏青 tàqīng (动) walk on the green grass — go for an outing in early spring

胎 tāi (名) 1 foetus; embryo: 怀~ become or be pregnant 2 birth: 头~ first baby; firstborn 3 padding; stuffing; wadding 4 tyre: 内~ inner tube (of a tyre). 外~ outer cover (of a tyre); tyre

胎教 tāijiào (名) antenatal instruction (i.e. influencing the development of the foetus by maternal impressions)

胎生 tāishēng (名) viviparity: ～动物 viviparous animal; vivipara

台(臺) tái I (名) 1 platform; stage; terrace: 讲～ platform; rostrum. 检阅～ reviewing stand. 月～票 platform ticket 2 stand; support: 导弹发射～ missile launching pad 3 anything shaped like a platform, stage or terrace: 窗～ windowsill 4 (檯) table; desk: 写字～ (writing) desk. 梳妆～ dressing table 5 broadcasting station: 电视～ television broadcasting station 6 a special telephone service: 长途～ trunk call service II (量): 一～戏 a theatrical performance. 两～计算机 two computers

台布 táibù (名) tablecloth

台词 táicí (名) actor's lines

台灯(燈) táidēng (名) desk lamp; table lamp; reading lamp

台风(風) táifēng (名) typhoon

台阶(階) táijiē (名) a flight of steps

台历(曆) táilì (名) desk calendar

台球 táiqiú (名) 1 billiards 2 billiard ball

台柱子 táizhùzi (名) pillar; mainstay; backbone

台子 táizi (名) 1 platform; stage 2 table; desk 3 billiard table 4 ping-pong table

苔 tái (名) liver mosses

抬(擡) tái (动) 1 lift; raise: ～高物价 drive up prices 2 (of two or more people) carry: ～担架 carry a stretcher

抬杠 táigàng (动)〈口〉 argue

抬高 táigāo (动) raise; heighten; enhance: 打击别人，～自己 attack others so as to build oneself up

抬轿(轎)子 tái jiàozi carry sb. in a sedan chair—flatter (rich and influential people); sing the praises of; boost

抬举(舉) táiju (动) praise or promote one's subordinate: 不识～ fail to appreciate sb.'s kindness

抬头(頭) táitóu (动) 1 raise one's head 2 gain ground; look up; rise

泰 tài (形) 1 safe; peaceful; tranquil: ～然自若 feel or look composed; try to compose one's features 2 extreme; most: ～西 the West; the Occident

泰然 tàirán (形) calm; composed; self-possessed: ～处之 remain calm; take sth. calmly

泰山 Tàishān (名) Mount Taishan; Taishan Mountain

太 tài I (形) 1 highest; greatest; remotest: ～空 outer space. ～古 remote antiquity; ancient times 2 more or most senior: ～老伯 grand-uncle II (副) 1 excessively; too; over: ～晚 too late. 人～多了，会客室里坐不开. There are too many people for this reception room. *or* The reception room is too small to seat so many people. 2 extremely: 这着棋～妙了. This is an extremely wise move. 3 [used in negative sentences] very: 不～好 not very good; not good enough

太后 tàihòu (名) mother of an emperor; empress dowager; queen mother

太平 tàipíng (名) peace and tranquillity: ～门 exit. ～梯 fire escape. ～间 mortuary

太上皇 tàishànghuáng (名) 1 a title assumed by an emperor's father who abdicated in favour of his son 2 behind-the-scenes manipulator

太太 tàitai (名) 1 Mrs.; madame: 王～ Mrs. Wang; Madame Wang 2 madam 3 one's wife

太阳(陽) tàiyáng (名) 1 the sun: ～能 solar energy. ～系 the solar system 2 sunshine; sunlight

太阳(陽)镜 tàiyángjìng (名) sunglasses

太阳(陽)穴 tàiyángxué (名) the temples

太子 tàizǐ (名) crown prince

汰 tài (动) discard; eliminate: 淘～ eliminate

态(態) tài (名) 1 form; appearance; condition: 形～ shape; morphology. 姿～ posture; gesture. 事～的发展 the natural course of events; the latest developments 2 voice: 主动语～ the active voice

态度 tàidu (名) 1 manner; bearing; how one conducts oneself: ～和蔼 amiable; kindly 2 attitude; position: 工作～ attitude towards work. 服务～ service. 表明～ state one's position

坍 tān (动) collapse; fall; tumble: 墙～了. The wall has collapsed.

坍方 tānfāng (动) 1 cave in; collapse 2 landslide

坍塌 tāntā (动) cave in; collapse

T

贪 tān I (形) corrupt; venal: ~官污吏 corrupt officials II (动) 1 have an insatiable desire for: ~得无厌 be insatiably avaricious 2 covet; hanker after: ~小失大 seek small gains only to incur big losses

贪婪 tānlán (形)〈书〉avaricious; greedy; rapacious

贪恋(戀) tānliàn (动) be reluctant to part with; be greedy for

贪便宜 tān piányi eager to get things on the cheap; keen on gaining petty advantages

贪图(圖) tāntú (动) seek; hanker after; covet: ~便宜 seek advantage

贪玩 tānwán (动) be too fond of play

贪污 tānwū (名) corruption; graft: ~腐化 corruption and degeneration. ~分子 a person guilty of corruption; an official guilty of embezzling public funds

贪心 tānxīn I (名) greed; avarice; rapacity II (形) greedy; avaricious; insatiable; voracious: ~不足 insatiably greedy

贪赃(贜) tānzāng (动) take bribes

滩(灘) tān (名) 1 beach; sands: 海~ beach 2 shoal: 险~ dangerous shoals

瘫(癱) tān (动) be paralysed: 偏~ partial paralysis. 吓~了 be paralysed with fear

瘫痪 tānhuàn (动) 1 suffer from paralysis 2 be paralysed; break down: 交通运输陷于~. Transportation was paralysed.

摊(攤) tān I (动) 1 spread out: ~开地图 spread out a map 2 fry batter in a thin layer: ~鸡蛋 make an omelette 3 take a share in: 每人~五毛钱. Each will contribute 5 *mao*. II (名) vendor's stand; booth; stall: 水果~儿 fruit stall. 报~ newsstand III (量): 一~稀泥 a pool of mud

T

摊贩 tānfàn (名) street pedlar

摊牌 tānpái (动) lay one's cards on the table; have a showdown

摊派 tānpài (动) share out (costs, expenses, etc.)

摊子 tānzi (名) 1 vendor's stand; booth; stall 2 the structure of an organization; set-up: ~铺得太大 do sth. on too large a scale

痰 tán (名) phlegm; sputum: ~盂 spittoon

谈 tán I (动) talk, chat; discuss: 我们~得来. We are getting along very well. II (名) what is said or talked about: 纯系无稽之~ unadulterated nonsense. 奇~ strange talk; fantastic tale

谈何容易 tán hé róngyì easier said than done

谈虎色变(變) tán hǔ sè biàn turn pale at the bare mention of a dreadful experience or possibility

谈话 tánhuà I (动) talk; chat II (名) 1 conversation 2 statement: 发表书面~ make a written statement

谈论(論) tánlùn (动) discuss; talk about

谈判 tánpàn (名) negotiations; talk: 举行~ hold talks; hold negotiations. ~桌 negotiating table

谈天 tántiān (动) chat; have chit-chat

谈吐 tántǔ (名) style of conversation: ~不俗 talk in good taste

谈笑风(風)生 tánxiào fēng shēng brim with wit and humour

谈笑自若 tánxiào zìruò go on talking with gusto and composure

坛(壇) tán (名) 1 altar: 天~ the Temple of Heaven (in Beijing) 2 a raised plot of land for planting flowers, etc.: 花~ (raised) flower bed 3 platform; forum: 讲~ platform 4 circles; world: 文~ the literary world; literary circles

坛(罈) tán (名) (~子) earthern jar: 酒~ wine jug

昙(曇) tán

昙花一现 tánhuā yī xiàn be very ephemeral; be a flash in the pan; a transient success

檀 tán (名) sandalwood

檀香 tánxiāng (名) white sandalwood; sandalwood: ~木 sandalwood

潭 tán (名) deep pool; pond

弹(彈) tán (动) 1 shoot (as with a catapult, etc.); send forth 2 spring; leap 3 flick; flip: ~烟灰 flick the ash off a cigarette 4 fluff; tease: ~棉花 fluff cotton 5 play (a stringed musical instrument); pluck: ~钢琴 play the piano. 老调重~ harp on the same old tune 6 accuse; impeach: ~劾 impeach see also dàn

弹簧 tánhuáng (名) spring: ~床 spring bed.

～锁 spring lock

弹力 tánlì (名) elastic force; elasticity; resilience; spring

弹射 tánshè (动) launch (as with a catapult); catapult; shoot off; eject

弹性 tánxìng (名) elasticity; resilience; spring: 有～ springy

弹指之间 tánzhǐ zhījiān in a flash; in an instant

弹奏 tánzòu (动) play (a stringed musical instrument); pluck

毯 tǎn (名) (～子) blanket; rug; carpet: 毛～ woollen blanket. 地～ rug; carpet. 挂～ tapestry

忐 tǎn

忐忑 tǎntè (形) mentally disturbed: ～不安 feel uneasy; feel ill at ease; be fidgety

袒 tǎn (动) 1 wear nothing above one's waist; strip oneself naked to the waist: ～胸露臂 (of a woman) expose one's neck 2 shield; protect: ～护 shield; take sb. under one's wing

坦 tǎn (形) 1 level; smooth: 平～ (of land, etc.) level; smooth 2 completely at ease: ～然自若 calm and fearless

坦白 tǎnbái I (形) frank and straightforward II (动) confess; make a clean breast of sth.

坦陈(陳) tǎnchén (动) state frankly; own up

坦荡(蕩) tǎndàng (形) 1 (of a road, etc.) broad and smooth 2 broad-minded

坦克 tǎnkè (名) tank

坦然 tǎnrán (形) calm; unperturbed; having no misgivings

坦率 tǎnshuài (形) candid; frank; straightforward

探 tàn I (动) 1 try to find out; explore: 试～ sound out (sb.). 钻～ explore 2 visit; pay a call on 3 stretch forward: ～头～脑 peep from behind something II (名) scout; spy; detective: 敌～ enemy scout. 侦～ detective

探测 tàncè (动) survey; sound; probe: ～水深 take soundings

探访 tànfǎng (动) 1 go in search of: ～新闻 cover the news 2 pay a call on; visit

探监(監) tànjiān (动) visit a prisoner

探究 tànjiū (动) make a thorough inquiry; probe into: ～原因 look into the causes

探口气(氣) tàn kǒuqi ascertain (or find out) sb.'s opinions or feelings; sound sb. out

探亲(親) tànqīn (动) be on home leave

探身 tànshēn (动) lean forward

探视 tànshì (动) visit: ～病人 visit a patient

探索 tànsuǒ (动) explore; probe: ～各种可能性 explore all possibilities

探讨 tàntǎo (动) make an inquiry into: 从不同的角度对问题进行～ approach a subject from different angles

探听(聽) tàntīng (动) try and find out; make inquiries (usu. by indirect means)

探望 tànwàng (动) 1 look: 四处～ look around 2 visit

探问 tànwèn (动) 1 make cautious inquiries about 2 inquire after

探险(險) tànxiǎn (动) explore; make explorations: ～队 exploring (or exploration) party; expedition. ～家 explorer

探照灯(燈) tànzhàodēng (名) searchlight

叹(嘆) tàn (动) 1 sigh: ～一口气 heave a sigh 2 exclaim in admiration; acclaim; praise: 赞～ be full of praise; be filled with admiration for

叹词 tàncí (名) interjection; exclamation

叹服 tànfú (动) have nothing but admiration for: 令人～ compel one's admiration

叹气(氣) tànqì (动) sigh; heave a sigh

叹赏 tànshǎng (动) admire; praise: ～不绝 praise profusely

叹息 tànxī (动)〈书〉heave a sigh; sigh

炭 tàn (名) charcoal: 木～ charcoal. 烧～ make charcoal. ～火 charcoal fire

碳 tàn (名) carbon (C): ～化 carbonization. ～酸 carbonic acid

汤(湯) tāng (名) 1 hot water; boiling water: 赴～蹈火 go through fire and water 2 soup; broth: 鸡～ chicken broth 3 a liquid preparation of medicinal herb; decoction

蹚 tāng (动) wade; ford: ～水过河 wade across (a stream)

唐 táng

唐突 tángtū (动) be rude; offend: ～古人 show disrespect for ancient scholars

糖 táng (名) 1 sugar: 白～ refined sugar. 砂～ granulated sugar. 红～ brown sugar. 冰～ crystal sugar; rock candy. ～厂 sugar refinery 2 sweets; candy

T

糖果 tángguǒ (名) sweets; candy; sweetmeats
糖姜(薑) tángjiāng (名) sugared ginger; ginger in syrup
糖精 tángjīng (名) saccharin
糖尿病 tángniàobìng (名) diabetes
糖蒜 tángsuàn (名) garlic in syrup; sweetened garlic
塘 táng (名) 1 dyke; embankment: 河～ river embankment 2 pool; pond: 池～ pond 3 hot-water bathing pool: 洗澡～ public bath
搪 táng (动) 1 ward off; keep out: ～风 keep out the wind 2 evade: ～塞 stall sb. off with a vague answer; give vague answers 3 spread (clay, paint, etc.) over; daub: ～炉子 line a stove with clay
搪瓷 tángcí (名) enamel: ～茶缸 enamel mug. ～钢板 enamelled pressed steel. ～器皿 enamelware
堂 táng I (名) 1 the main room of a house 2 a hall (or room) for a specific purpose: 食～ dining hall. 纪念～ memorial hall 3 relationship between cousins, etc. of the same paternal grandfather or great-grandfather; of the same clan: ～兄 cousins on the paternal side; cousins II (量) [for classes]: 一～课 one class
堂皇 tánghuáng (形) grand; stately; imposing: 富丽～ beautiful and magnificent
堂堂 tángtáng (形) 1 dignified; impressive: 仪表～ dignified in appearance 2 (of a man) manly 3 awe-inspiring; formidable: ～正正 impressive or dignified in personal appearance; open and above-board
螳 táng (名) mantis
螳臂当(當)车(車) táng bì dāng chē court destruction for trying to withstand a far superior force
螳螂 tángláng (名) mantis
镗 táng (动) bore: ～床 boring machine; boring lathe; borer
膛 táng (名) thorax; chest: 胸～ chest
淌 tǎng (动) drip; shed; trickle: ～眼泪 shed tears. ～口水 drool; start drooling
倘 tǎng (连) if; supposing; in case
倘若 tǎngruò (连) if; supposing; in case
躺 tǎng (动) lie; recline: ～下歇歇 lie down and relax a while
躺椅 tǎngyǐ (名) deck chair
烫(燙) tàng I (动) 1 scald; burn: 小心～着! Watch out and don't get scalded. 2 heat up in hot water; warm: ～酒 heat wine (by putting the container in hot water) 3 iron; press: ～衣服 iron (or press) clothes II (形) very hot; scalding; boiling hot
烫发(髮) tàngfà (动) give or have a permanent wave; perm
烫伤(傷) tàngshāng (名) scald
趟 tàng (量) [for trip]: 到成都去了一～ make a trip to Chengdu
涛(濤) tāo (名) great waves; billows: 惊～骇浪 terrifying waves
掏 tāo (动) 1 draw out; pull out; fish out: 从床底下～出一双鞋来 fish out a pair of shoes from under the bed 2 dig (a hole, etc.); hollow out; scoop out: 在地上～一个洞 dig a hole in the ground 3 steal from sb.'s pocket: 他的皮夹子被～了. He had his wallet stolen.
滔 tāo (动) inundate; flood
滔滔 tāotāo (形) 1 torrential; surging: 白浪～, 无边无际 a vast expanse of white surging billows 2 letting loose a stream of words: 口若悬河, ～不绝 keep up a torrential flow of words
滔天 tāotiān (形) 1 (of billows, etc.) dashing to the skies: 波浪～ waves running mountains high 2 heinous; monstrous: ～罪行 monstrous crimes
韬(韜) tāo I (名) 1 sheath or bow case 2 the art of war II (动) hide; conceal
韬略 tāolüè (名) military strategy
逃 táo (动) 1 run away; escape; flee 2 evade; shirk
逃避 táobì (动) escape; evade; shirk: ～现实 escapism
逃遁 táodùn (动) flee; escape; evade: 仓皇～ flee in panic
逃荒 táohuāng (动) flee from famine; get away from a famine-stricken area
逃命 táomìng (动) run for one's life
逃难(難) táonàn (动) flee from a calamity; be a refugee
逃匿 táonì (动) make one's escape and go

into hiding
逃跑 táopǎo (动) run away; flee; take flight; take to one's heels
逃生 táoshēng (动) flee (or run) for one's life
逃税 táoshuì (动) evade a tax
逃亡 táowáng (动) make one's escape and go into hiding
逃逸 táoyì (动) hit and run: 撞车～者 hit-and-run driver
逃学(學) táoxué (动) play truant; cut class
逃之夭夭 táo zhī yāoyāo sneak away; slip out
逃走 táozǒu (动) take to one's heels
桃 táo (名) 1 peach 2 a peach-shaped thing: 棉～cotton boll
桃花 táohuā (名) peach blossom
桃李 táolǐ (名) one's pupils or disciples: ～满天下 have pupils everywhere under heaven
桃子 táozi (名) peach
淘 táo (动) 1 wash in a pan or basket: ～米 wash rice 2 clean out; dredge
淘金 táojīn (动) wash (for gold); pan: ～热 gold rush
淘气(氣) táoqì (形) naughty; mischievous: ～鬼 mischievous imp
淘汰 táotài (动) 1 supersede: 产品旧型号已经被～了. The products of old types have been superseded. 2 eliminate through selection or competition: ～赛 elimination series
陶 táo I (名) pottery; earthenware: 彩～ painted pottery II (动) 1 make pottery 2 educate; train: 熏～education; intellectual training
陶瓷 táocí (名) pottery and porcelain; ceramics
陶器 táoqì (名) pottery; earthenware
陶然 táorán (形) happy and carefree
陶冶 táoyě (动) 1 make pottery and smelt metal 2 exercise a healthy influence (on a person's character, etc.); mould one's personality
陶醉 táozuì (动) be drunk (with power, success, etc.): 我们不能～于已取得的成绩. We mustn't be carried away by our success.
讨 tǎo (动) 1 send a punitive expedition against 2 denounce; condemn: 声～ denounce 3 demand; ask for; beg for: ～饶 beg (for) forgiveness. ～教 solicit advice 4 incur; invite: ～厌 incur displeasure (or hatred). 自～苦吃 ask for trouble 5 discuss; study: 商～ discuss
讨伐 tǎofá (动) send armed forces to suppress; send a punitive expedition against
讨好 tǎohǎo (动) 1 ingratiate oneself with 2 [often used in negative sentences]: 这件事费力不～. It is a thankless task.
讨价(價)还(還)价 tǎojià-huánjià bargain; haggle
讨论(論) tǎolùn (动) discuss; talk over: 这件事我们得～～. We must talk it over. ～会 discussion; symposium
讨嫌 tǎoxián (形) disagreeable; annoying
讨厌(厭) tǎoyàn I (形) 1 disagreeable; disgusting; repugnant: 这人说话总是这么啰嗦, 真～! This chap is always talking at such great length. I'm bored stiff. 2 hard to handle; troublesome; nasty: 这是一个～的问题. This is a nasty problem. II (动) dislike; loathe; hate; be disgusted with
套 tào I (名) 1 case; cover: 枕～ pillowcase. 书～ dust jacket. 手～ gloves 2 harness: ～绳 lasso 3 that which covers something else: ～鞋 overshoes 4 cotton padding; batting: 被～ quilt padding 5 knot; loop; noose: 拴个～ tie a knot 6 convention; formula: ～语 polite formulas. 客～ banal civilities II (动) 1 put a ring round; tie: ～马 lasso a horse 2 copy: 这是从现成文章上～下来的. This is taken straight from someone else's work. 3 draw out: 想法儿～他的话. Let's try to draw the secret out of him. III (量) set; suit; suite: 一～制度 a set of regulations. 一～茶具 a teaset
套汇(匯) tàohuì (动) 1 buy foreign exchange by illegal means 2 engage in arbitrage (of foreign exchange); arbitrage
套间 tàojiān (名) a suite
套近乎 tào jìnhu try to be friendly with sb.; try to chum (or pal) up with sb.
套用 tàoyòng (动) apply mechanically
特 tè I (形) special; particular; unusual; exceptional: ～权 privilege. 奇～ peculiar. 奇～的人 an uncommon and singular man II (副) for a special purpose; specially III (名) secret agent; spy: 敌～ enemy agent
特别 tèbié I (形) special; particular; out of the ordinary: ～风味 an unusual flavour. ～的式样 special type II(副) 1 especially;

particularly:时间过得～快. The time sped quickly by. 2 going out of one's way to (do sth.); specially:我们～注意保障他们的安全. We made a special point of ensuring their safety.

特别行政区(區) tèbié xíngzhèngqū special administrative region: 香港～ Hong Kong Special Administrative Region

特产(産) tèchǎn (名) special local product; speciality

特长(長) tècháng (名) special skill; special work experience

特地 tèdì (副) for a special purpose; specially: 我们是～来看您的. We came specially to see you.

特点(點) tèdiǎn (名) characteristic; special feature; peculiarity

特定 tèdìng (形) 1 specially designated (or appointed) 2 specific; specified; given: 在～的条件下 under given (or specified) conditions

特级 tèjí (形) special grade (or class); superfine: ～茉莉花茶 superfine jasmine tea

特快 tèkuài (名) express (train)

特卖(賣) tèmài (动) red tag sale; sale

特派 tèpài (形) specially appointed: ～员 special representative

特权(權) tèquán (名) privilege; prerogative: ～阶层 privileged stratum

特色 tèsè (名) characteristic; distinguishing feature (or quality): 有中国～的社会主义 socialism with Chinese characteristics

特赦 tèshè (名) special pardon; amnesty

特使 tèshǐ (名) special envoy

特首 tèshǒu (名) Chief Executive (of Hong Kong or Macao Special Administrative Region)

特殊 tèshū (形) special; particular; peculiar; exceptional: ～化 become privileged. ～性 particularity; specific characteristics

特务(務) tèwu (名) special (or secret) agent; spy

特效 tèxiào (名)specially good effect; special efficacy: ～药 specific drug; specific; effective cure

特写(寫) tèxiě (名) 1 feature article or story; feature 2 close-up: ～镜头 close-up (shot)

特性 tèxìng (名) special property (or characteristic)

特许 tèxǔ (名) special permission: ～证 special permit

特异(異) tèyì (形) 1 exceptionally good; excellent; superfine 2 peculiar; distinctive: ～的风格 distinctive style

特约 tèyuē (动) engage by special arrangement: ～记者 special correspondent. ～评论员 special commentator

特征(徵) tèzhēng (名) characteristic; feature; trait

疼 téng (动) 1 ache; pain; sore: 头～ have a headache 2 love dearly; be fond of; dote on: 这孩子怪招人～的. How lovely the child is!

疼爱(愛) téng'ài (动) be very fond of; love very dearly

誊(謄) téng (动) copy in writing: 照底稿～一份 make a fair (or clean) copy of the draft

誊录(録) ténglù (动) copy out: ～文稿 copy out a manuscript

藤 téng (名) 1 cane; rattan: ～椅 cane chair; rattan chair 2 vine: 葡萄～ grapevine

腾 téng (动) 1 gallop; jump: 欢～ jump for joy 2 rise; soar: 升～ rise; ascend 3 make room; clear out; vacate: ～出时间 set aside some time. ～出房间 vacate the room. ～位置 make room for sb.

腾飞(飛) téngfēi (动) take off: 经济～ economic take-off

腾腾 téngténg (形) steaming; ascending: 烟雾～ fill with dense smoke

梯 tī (名) ladder; staircase: 电～ lift; elevator

梯队(隊) tīduì (名) echelon formation; echelon: 第二～ the second echelon

梯田 tītián (名) terraced fields

梯子 tīzi (名) ladder; stepladder

剔 tī (动) 1 pick: ～牙 pick one's teeth 2 reject: 挑～ pick holes in; find fault with

剔除 tīchú (动) reject; get rid of

踢 tī (动) 1 kick: ～开 kick away 2 play (football): ～足球 play football. ～进一个球 kick (or score) a goal

啼 tí (动) 1 cry; weep aloud: ～笑皆非 not know whether to laugh or cry 2 crow; caw: 鸡～. Cocks crow.

蹄 tí (名) hoof: 马～ horse's hoofs

题 tí I (名) topic; subject; title; problem: 讨论～ topic for discussion. 考～ examination questions; examination paper; paper. 文不对～ irrelevant II (动) inscribe: ～诗 inscribe a poem (on a painting, fan, wall, etc.)

题跋 tíbá (名) **1** preface and postscript **2** short comments, annotation, etc. on a scroll (of painting or calligraphy)

题材 tícái (名) subject matter; theme: 这是写电影的好～. This is good material for a film. *or* This is a good plot for a film scenario.

题词 tící I (动) write a few words of encouragement, appreciation or commemoration II (名) **1** inscription; dedication **2** foreword

题名 tímíng (动) inscribe one's name; autograph: ～留念 give one's autograph as a memento

题目 tímù (名) title; subject; topic: 辩论的～ subject (or topic) for a debate

题外话 tíwàihuà (名) digression

题字 tízì I (动) inscribe II (名) inscription; autograph: 作者亲笔～ the author's autograph

提 tí (动) **1** carry: 手里～着篮子 carry a basket in one's hand **2** lift; raise: ～升 promote. ～高生活水平 raise the standard of living **3** move up a date: 会议日期～前了. The date of the meeting has been advanced. **4** put forward; bring up; raise: ～意见 make suggestions. ～抗议 lodge a protest **5** draw (or take) out; extract: ～炼 extract; refine **6** mention; refer to; bring up: 旧事重～ bring up the matter again
see also dī

提案 tí'àn (名) motion; proposal

提拔 tíbá (动) promote: ～合格人员担任重要职务 promote qualified people to positions of responsibility

提包 tíbāo (名) handbag; shopping-bag; bag; valise

提倡 tíchàng (动) advocate; encourage: ～晚婚和计划生育 advocate late marriage and family planning. ～勤俭节约 advocate industry, economy and thrift

提成 tíchéng (动) set aside a percentage of the total amount of money for specific purposes

提出 tíchū (动) put forward; advance; pose; raise: 请～建议. Please feel free to make your suggestions.

提单(單) tídān (名) bill of lading (B/L): 联运～ through bill of lading

提法 tífǎ (名) the way sth. is put; formulation; wording: 这只是个～问题. This is just a matter of wording.

提干(幹) tígàn (动) **1** make sb. a cadre **2** promote a cadre to a higher position

提纲(綱) tígāng (名) outline

提纲(綱)挈领 tígāng-qièlǐng briefly mention the essential points; make a sketch of the plan (proposal, etc.)

提高 tígāo (动) raise; heighten; enhance; increase; improve: ～水位 raise the water level. ～警惕 enhance (or heighten) one's vigilance. ～工作效率 raise efficiency

提供 tígōng (动) provide; supply; furnish; offer: ～经济援助 provide financial assistance. ～意见 make recommendations. ～有关资料 provide relevant data

提货 tíhuò (动) pick up goods; take delivery of goods

提交 tíjiāo (动) submit (a problem, etc.) to; refer to: ～全会讨论 submit sth. to the plenary session for deliberation

提名 tímíng (动) nominate

提前 tíqián (动) **1** shift to an earlier date; move up (a date); advance **2** do sth. in advance or ahead of time: 请～通知他们. Please notify them in advance. ～释放战犯 release war criminals before their sentences expire

提琴 tíqín (名) the violin family: 小～ violin. 中～ viola. 大～ violoncello; cello. 低音～ double bass

提审(審) tíshěn (动) **1** bring a prisoner to court for trial; bring a detainee to trial **2** review a case tried by a lower court

提示 tíshì (动) point out; prompt

提问 tíwèn (动) put questions to; quiz

提携 tíxié (动) guide and support the younger generation

提心吊胆(膽) tíxīn-diàodǎn be terribly scared and worried; be on tenterhooks

提醒 tíxǐng (动) remind; warn; call attention to: 如果我忘了,请你～我一下. Please remind me in case I forget.

提要 tíyào (名) précis; summary; abstract; epitome; synopsis: 本书内容～ capsule summary (of the book)

提议(議) tíyì I (动) propose; suggest; move

II (名) proposal; motion

提早 tízǎo (动) advance; do sth. in advance: ~结束会议 bring the meeting to an earlier conclusion

体(體) tǐ I (名) 1 body; part of the body: ~高 height. ~重 weight 2 substance: 固~ solid. 液~ liquid 3 style; form: 文~ literary style; style of writing. 文~学 stylistics II (动) personally experience sth.; put oneself in another's position: ~谅 make allowances for

体裁 tǐcái (名) types or forms of literature

体操 tǐcāo (名) gymnastics

体察 tǐchá (动) observe and learn by experience

体格 tǐgé (名) physique; build: ~检查 physical examination; checkup

体会(會) tǐhuì (动) know (or learn) from experience; understand

体积(積) tǐjī (名) volume; bulk

体力 tǐlì (名) physical strength: 增强~ build up one's strength. ~劳动 physical (or manual) labour

体面 tǐmian I (名) dignity; face: 有失~ beneath one's dignity II (形) honourable; creditable

体能 tǐnéng (名) physical strength (as displayed in sports); stamina

体魄 tǐpò (名) physique: 强壮的~ strong (or powerful) physique

体态(態) tǐtài (名) poise; carriage; deportment: ~轻盈 good deportment; a graceful poise

体贴 tǐtiē (动) be full of thought for: ~入微 look after sb. with loving care

体统 tǐtǒng (名) code of ethics; propriety; decorum: 不成~ downright outrageous

体温 tǐwēn (名) (body) temperature: 量~ take someone's temperature

T

体无(無)完肤(膚) tǐ wú wán fū 1 beaten black and blue 2 thoroughly discredited or refuted

体系 tǐxì (名) system; set-up

体现 tǐxiàn (动) embody; incarnate; reflect; give expression to: 这个提案~了发展中国家的利益和要求. This proposal reflects the interests and demands of the developing countries.

体形 tǐxíng (名) bodily form; build

体型 tǐxíng (名) 1 type of build or figure 2 somatotype

体恤 tǐxù (动) show solicitude for

体验(驗) tǐyàn (动) learn through practice; learn through one's personal experience: ~生活 observe and learn from real life

体育 tǐyù (名) physical culture; physical training; sports: ~场 stadium. ~馆 gymnasium; gym

体制 tǐzhì (名) system of organization; system

体质(質) tǐzhì (名) physique; constitution

体重 tǐzhòng (名) (body) weight: ~增加 put on weight; gain weight. ~减轻 lose weight

涕 tì (名) 1 tears: 痛哭流~ cry piteously. 感激~零 weep tears of gratitude 2 nasal mucus

涕泣 tìqì (动)〈书〉 weep

剃 tì (动) shave: ~胡子 have a shave; shave oneself

剃刀 tìdāo (名) razor blade

替 tì I (动) take the place of; replace: 我~你洗衣服. I will do the washing for you. II (介) for; on behalf of: 大家~她难过. Everybody felt sorry for her.

替代 tìdài (动) replace; supersede

替身 tìshēn (名) 1 substitute; replacement 2 scapegoat

替罪羊 tìzuìyáng (名) scapegoat

惕 tì (形) cautious; watchful: 警~ be on the alert; be vigilant

嚏 tì (动) sneeze: 喷~ sneeze

天 tiān (名) 1 sky; heaven 2 day: 每~ every day. 前~ the day before yesterday 3 a period of time in a day: ~不早啦. It's getting late. 4 season: 春~ spring 5 weather: ~越来越冷了. It's getting colder and colder. 6 nature: 人定胜~. Man will prevail over nature. ~灾 natural calamity 7 God; Heaven: 谢~谢地! Thank Heaven!

天边(邊) tiānbiān (名) horizon; the ends of the earth; remotest places

天才 tiāncái (名) genius; talent; gift; endowment: 这孩子有语言~. The child has great aptitude for language.

天长(長)地久 tiāncháng-dìjiǔ enduring loyalty (in love)

天长(長)日久 tiāncháng-rìjiǔ in the course of time

天窗 tiānchuāng (名) skylight

天敌(敵) tiāndí (名) natural enemy

天地 tiāndì (名) 1 heaven and earth; world;

universe 2 field of activity; scope of operation: 别有～ a new level of understanding or appreciation

天鹅 tiān'é (名) swan: ～绒 velvet

天翻地覆 tiānfān-dìfù 1 causing tremendous changes: ～的变化 earth-shaking changes 2 turning everything upside down

天分 tiānfèn (名) endowments; gift; talent: ～高 gifted; talented

天赋 tiānfù I (形) inborn; innate; endowed by nature II (名) natural gift; talent; endowments

天高地厚 tiāngāo-dìhòu 1 debt of enduring gratitude 2 [often used in negative sentences] the immensity of heaven and earth: 不知～ overestimate one's own abilities to a ridiculous extent

天花板 tiānhuābǎn (名) ceiling

天花乱(亂)坠(墜) tiānhuā luànzhuì give an alarming but unrealistic description of sth.; describe vividly but with extravagance

天昏地暗 tiānhūn-dì'àn 1 clouds of dust darken the sky and obscure everything: 一阵～, 以后什么都记不起了. Everything went black. That's the last thing I can remember. 2 characterized by political decadence or social unrest; chaos

天机(機) tiānjī (名) 1 nature's mystery 2 secret: 泄漏～ give away a secret

天价(價) tiānjià (名) astronomical price; crazily high price

天经(經)地义(義) tiānjīng-dìyì indisputably correct

天空 tiānkōng (名) the sky; the heaven

天蓝 tiānlán (形) sky blue; azure

天良 tiānliáng (名) conscience: 丧尽～ have no conscience

天亮 tiānliàng (名) daybreak; dawn

天伦(倫) tiānlún (名) the natural relationships between members of a family: ～之乐 family happiness; domestic felicity

天罗(羅)地网(網) tiānluó-dìwǎng a tight encirclement; a dragnet

天南地北 tiānnán-dìběi 1 too far away from each other; far apart 2 different places or areas

天平 tiānpíng (名) balance; scales: 分析～ analytical balance

天气(氣) tiānqì (名) weather: ～多变 changeable weather. ～转晴. It's clearing up. ～预报 weather forecast

天堑 tiānqiàn (名) natural barrier: 长江～ the natural barrier of the Changjiang River

天桥(橋) tiānqiáo (名) over-line bridge; platform bridge; overhead walkway

天然 tiānrán (形) natural: ～气 natural gas. ～财富 natural resources

天壤 tiānrǎng (名) heaven and earth: ～之别 far removed (from); poles apart (from). 这两个词的意义有～之别. There is a world of difference in meaning between these two words.

天日 tiānrì (名) the sky and the sun; light: 重见～ be delivered from outer darkness

天色 tiānsè (名) time of the day; weather: ～已晚. It is getting late.

天生 tiānshēng (形) born; inborn; inherent; innate: 他真有学习语言的～才能吗? Has he really any aptitude for language?

天使 tiānshǐ (名) angel; cherub

天书(書) tiānshū (名) a book from heaven: 这对我是一部～. It's all Greek to me.

天堂 tiāntáng (名) paradise; heaven: 人间～ paradise on earth

天体(體) tiāntǐ (名) celestial body

天天 tiāntiān every day

天文 tiānwén (名) astronomy: ～数字 astronomical figure; enormous figure

天文馆 tiānwénguǎn (名) planetarium

天文台(臺) tiānwéntái (名) astronomical observatory

天下 tiānxià (名) 1 land under heaven: ～太平 peace reigns under heaven; the world (or the country) is at peace 2 state power: 打～ win state power

天仙 tiānxiān (名) 1 immortal; legendary goddess 2 a beauty

天险(險) tiānxiǎn (名) natural barrier

天线(綫) tiānxiàn (名) aerial; antenna

天性 tiānxìng (名) natural instincts; nature

天涯 tiānyá (名) the ends of the world: 远在～, 近在咫尺. It is as near as his hand and as remote as a star. ～海角 the ends of the earth; the remotest corners of the earth

天衣无(無)缝 tiānyī wú fèng flawless

天灾(災) tiānzāi (名) natural disaster (or calamity): ～人祸 natural and man-made calamities

天真 tiānzhēn (形) innocent; simple and unaffected; naive: ～的孩子 innocent

T

children. 他政治上太～了. He is politically naive.

天职(職) tiānzhí (名) bounden duty

天诛地灭(滅) tiānzhū-dìmiè suffer eternal perdition

天主教 tiānzhǔjiào (名) Catholicism: ～徒 Catholic

天资 tiānzī (名) natural gift; talent; natural endowments

天字第一号(號) tiān zì dìyī hào a thing of the greatest importance; a work of the highest order

添 tiān (动) add; increase: 增～光彩 add lustre to. ～衣服 put on more clothes

添枝加叶(葉) tiānzhī-jiāyè embellish the truth; embroider

甜 tián (形) 1 sweet; honeyed 2 sound: 睡得真～ sleep soundly; be sound asleep

甜美 tiánměi (形) 1 sweet: 味道～ taste sweet; have a sweet taste 2 pleasant; comfortable: 享受～的生活 enjoy comfort and ease in life

甜蜜 tiánmì (形) sweet; happy; honeyed: ～的笑容 sweet smiling face

甜食 tiánshí (名) sweet food; sweetmeats

甜丝(絲)丝 tiánsīsī (形) 1 pleasantly sweet: 这个菜～儿的, 很好吃. This dish is delicious, it has a sweet taste. 2 gratified; happy: 心里～的 feel happy and proud

甜头(頭) tiántou (名) 1 sweet taste 2 benefit: 给点～ give small favours to sb. (as an inducement)

甜言蜜语 tiányán-mìyǔ sweet and honeyed phrases; fine-sounding words

恬 tián (形)〈书〉1 quiet; tranquil: ～适 quiet and comfortable 2 carefree: ～不知耻 be lost to shame; be shameless

恬静 tiánjìng (形) quiet; peaceful; tranquil

填 tián (动) 1 fill; stuff: 义愤～膺 be filled with righteous indignation 2 write; fill in: ～表 fill in a form

填补(補) tiánbǔ (动) fill what is left vacant: ～缺额 fill a vacancy

填空 tiánkòng (动) fill a vacant position; fill a vacancy

填写(寫) tiánxiě (动) fill in; write: ～申请表 fill out an application form. 请在这里～你的姓名和职业. Please fill in the blanks here with your name and occupation.

田 tián (名) field; farmland: 稻～ rice field. 油～ oilfield

田地 tiándì (名) 1 field; farmland; cropland 2 wretched state

田间 tiánjiān (名) field; farm: ～管理 field management

田径(徑) tiánjìng (名) track and field: ～运动 track and field sports; athletics. ～运动员 athlete

田园(園) tiányuán (名) rural area; countryside: ～生活 idyllic life. ～诗 idyll; pastoral poetry

舔 tiǎn (动) lick

挑 tiāo I (动) 1 choose; select; pick: 我～我最喜欢的. I chose what I liked best. ～毛病 pick holes; find fault 2 carry; shoulder: ～水 carry water. ～重担 shoulder heavy responsibilities II (量) [for things which can be carried on a shoulder pole]: 一～水 two buckets of water
see also tiǎo

挑刺儿(兒) tiāocìr (动) find fault; pick holes: 他就爱～. He's much too fastidious.

挑肥拣(揀)瘦 tiāoféi-jiǎnshòu choose whichever is to one's personal advantage

挑剔 tiāoti (动、形) nit-pick; nit-picking

挑选(選) tiāoxuǎn (动) choose; select; pick out

挑字眼儿(兒) tiāo zìyǎnr carp at the wording

条(條) tiáo I (名) 1 twig: 柳～椅子 wicker chair 2 a long narrow piece; strip; slip: 布～ a strip of cloth. 便～ a note. 金～ gold bar 3 item; article: 逐～ item by item; point by point 4 order: 有～不紊 in perfect order; orderly II (量): 两～鱼 two fish. 三～船 three ships. 一～香烟 a carton of cigarettes. 四～建议 four proposals

条件 tiáojiàn (名) 1 condition; term; factor: 自然～ natural conditions. 在目前～下 under present circumstances. ～反射 conditioned reflex 2 requirement; qualification: 提出～ state the requirements

条款 tiáokuǎn (名) clause; article; provision: 最惠国～ most-favoured-nation clause. 法律～ legal provision

条理 tiáolǐ (名) proper arrangement or pre-

sentation; orderliness; method: ～分明 well-organized
条例 tiáolì (名) regulation; rules
条目 tiáomù (名) 1 clauses; subclauses 2 entry (in a dictionary)
条约 tiáoyuē (名) treaty; pact
条子 tiáozi (名) 1 strip: 纸～ a narrow strip of paper; a slip of paper 2 a short note
调 tiáo (动) 1 mix; adjust: ～匀 mix well; blend well 2 suit well: 风～雨顺 propitious weather for the crops. 饮食失～ live on an irregular diet 3 mediate: ～人 mediator; peacemaker
see also diào
调和 tiáohe (动) 1 be in harmonious proportion: 雨水～. Rainfall is well distributed. 2 mediate; reconcile: 从中～ mediate; act as mediator 3 compromise; make concessions
调剂(劑) tiáojì (动) 1 make up (or fill) a prescription 2 adjust; regulate: ～劳动力 redistribute labour power
调价(價) tiáojià (动) readjust (or modify) prices
调节(節) tiáojié (动) regulate; adjust: ～室温 regulate the room temperature. 空气～ air conditioning
调解 tiáojiě (动) mediate; make peace: ～纠纷 mediate a settlement
调控 tiáokòng (动) regulate; modulate; control: 宏观～ macro control. 对市场进行～ regulate the market
调理 tiáolǐ (动) 1 nurse one's health; recuperate 2 take care of; look after: ～牲口 look after livestock
调料 tiáoliào (名) condiment; seasoning; flavouring
调弄 tiáonòng (动) 1 make fun of; tease 2 arrange; adjust 3 instigate; stir up
调配 tiáopèi (动) mix; blend: ～颜色 mix colours
调皮 tiáopí (形) 1 naughty; mischievous 2 unruly; tricky
调情 tiáoqíng (动) flirt
调唆 tiáosuō (动) incite; instigate
调停 tiáotíng (动) mediate; intervene; act as an intermediary: 居间～ offer one's good offices between two parties
调味 tiáowèi (动) flavour; season: 加点生姜～ season food with some ginger
调戏(戲) tiáoxì (动) take liberties with (a woman); assail (a woman) with obscenities
调笑 tiáoxiào (动) make fun of; poke fun at; tease
调养(養) tiáoyǎng (动) be restored to health by taking nourishing food and tonics when necessary
调整 tiáozhěng (动) adjust; regulate; revise: ～价格 readjust prices
迢 tiáo (形) far; remote
迢迢 tiáotiáo (形) far away; remote: 千里～ come all the way from a distant place; come from afar
笤 tiáo
笤帚 tiáozhou (名) broom
挑 tiǎo (动) 1 raise: 把帘子～起来 raise the curtain 2 poke: ～火 poke a fire 3 stir up; instigate: ～事 stir up trouble; sow discord
see also tiāo
挑拨(撥) tiǎobō (动) instigate; incite: ～是非 foment discord. ～离间 sow dissension
挑动(動) tiǎodòng (动) provoke; stir up; incite: ～好奇心 excite one's curiosity
挑逗 tiǎodòu (动) provoke; tantalize
挑明 tiǎomíng (动) no longer keep it back; let it all out; bring it out into the open
挑唆 tiǎosuō (动) incite; abet; instigate
挑头(頭)儿(兒) tiǎotóur take the lead; be the first to do sth.:这是你～干的吧? You started all this, didn't you?
挑衅(釁) tiǎoxìn (动) provoke an incident
挑战(戰) tiǎozhàn (动) challenge: 接受～ accept a challenge. ～书 a letter of challenge; challenge
眺 tiào (动) look into the distance: 远～ enjoy a distant view
眺望 tiàowàng (动) enjoy a distant view from a height
跳 tiào (动) 1 jump; leap; spring; bounce: ～过一条沟 jump over a ditch. 高兴得直～ jump for (or with) joy 2 move up and down; beat: 他心～不规律. His heart beats irregularly. *or* His heartbeats are irregular. 3 skip (over): ～过了三页 skip over three pages
跳板 tiàobǎn (名) 1 gangplank 2 springboard; diving board
跳槽 tiàocáo (动) 1 (of a horse, etc.) leave its own manger to eat at another 2 throw up one job and take on another
跳高 tiàogāo (名) high jump: 撑竿～ pole vault
跳梁小丑 tiàoliáng xiǎochǒu a petty

T

scoundrel fond of playing tricks and creating trouble

跳水 tiàoshuǐ (动) dive: ～表演 diving exhibition

跳台(臺) tiàotái (名) diving tower; diving platform

跳舞 tiàowǔ (动) dance

跳远(遠) tiàoyuǎn (名) long jump; broad jump: 三级～ hop, step and jump

跳跃(躍) tiàoyuè (动) jump; leap; bound

跳蚤 tiàozao (名) flea

帖 tiē (形) submissive; obedient: 服～ docile and obedient
see also tiě; tiè

贴 tiē I (动) 1 paste; stick; glue: ～邮票 stick on a stamp 2 keep close to: 他～着墙走. He kept close to the wall and walked on. II (名) subsidy; allowance: 房～ housing allowance. 地区津～ weighting

贴边(邊) tiēbiān (名) hem (of a garment)

贴补(補) tiēbǔ (动) help (out) financially; subsidize

贴金 tiējīn (动) 1 gild 2 prettify

贴切 tiēqiè (形) (of words) apt; appropriate; proper: 比喻要用得～. A metaphor should be apt.

贴身 tiēshēn (形) 1 next to the skin: ～衣服 underclothes; underclothing 2 constantly accompanying: ～保镖 personal bodyguard

贴题 tiētí (形) relevant; pertinent; to the point: 着墨不多,但是十分～. The essay is terse but very much to the point.

贴现 tiēxiàn (名) discount (on a promissory note): ～率 discount rate

贴心 tiēxīn (形) intimate; close: ～朋友 bosom friend

帖 tiě I (名) 1 invitation: 请～ invitation 2 note; card: 字～儿 brief note II (量): 一～药 a dose (or draught) of herbal medicine
see also tiē; tiè

铁(鐵) tiě I (名) 1 iron (Fe): 生～ pig iron; cast iron. 废～ scrap iron. 趁热打～. Strike while the iron is hot. 打破"～饭碗" crack the "iron rice bowl" 2 arms; weapon: 手无寸～ bare-handed II (形) 1 hard or strong as iron: ～拳 iron fist 2 indisputable; unalterable: ～的事实 ironclad evidence

铁板 tiěbǎn (名) iron plate; sheet iron: ～钉钉 that clinches it; that's final; no two ways about it. ～一块 a monolithic bloc

铁饼 tiěbǐng (名) discus: 掷～ discus throw

铁窗 tiěchuāng (名) prison bars; prison: ～风味 prison life; life behind the bars

铁道 tiědào (名) railway; railroad: 地下～ underground (railway); tube; subway

铁饭碗 tiěfànwǎn (名) iron rice bowl—a secure job

铁匠 tiějiàng (名) blacksmith; smith

铁矿(礦) tiěkuàng (名) 1 iron ore 2 iron mine

铁链 tiěliàn (名) iron chain; shackles

铁路 tiělù (名) railway; railroad: ～运输 railway transportation

铁面无(無)私 tiěmiàn wú sī impartial and upright

铁器 tiěqì (名) ironware: ～时代 the Iron Age

铁锹 tiěqiāo (名) spade; shovel

铁青 tiěqīng (形) ashen; livid: 气得脸色～ turn livid with rage

铁石心肠(腸) tiěshí xīncháng be iron-hearted; have a heart of stone; be hard-hearted

铁丝(絲)网(網) tiěsīwǎng (名) 1 wire netting; wire meshes 2 wire entanglements: 有刺～ barbed wire entanglements

铁索 tiěsuǒ (名) cable; iron chain: ～吊车 cable car. ～桥 chain bridge

铁蹄 tiětí (名) enemy's cavalry—aggressor's cruel oppression

铁腕 tiěwàn (名) iron hand: ～人物 an iron-handed person; strong man

铁心 tiěxīn (动) be unshakeable in one's determination: ～务农 be a very determined farmer

铁证 tiězhèng (名) ironclad proof; irrefutable evidence: ～如山 irrefutable, conclusive evidence

帖 tiè (名) a book containing models of handwriting or painting for learners to copy: 碑～ a book of stone rubbings
see also tiē; tiě

厅(廳) tīng (名) 1 hall: 餐厅 dining hall; restaurant. 休息～ lounge; foyer. 会议～ conference hall. 音乐～ concert hall 2 office: 办公～ general office

听(聽) tīng (动) 1 listen; hear: ～音乐 listen to music. 我们

T

必须～～他的意见. We must hear what he has got to say. **2** heed; have a receptive ear for: 他不～. He refused to listen. **3** allow; let: ～任摆布 allow oneself to be twisted round sb.'s little finger

听便 tīngbiàn (动) do as one pleases; please yourself

听从(從) tīngcóng (动) accept; obey: ～劝告 accept sb.'s advice. ～指挥 obey orders

听候 tīnghòu (动) wait for (a decision, settlement, etc.)

听话 tīnghuà (形) obedient

听见(見) tīngjiàn (动) hear: 我～有人敲门. I heard a knock at the door.

听觉(覺) tīngjué (名) sense of hearing

听课 tīngkè (动) **1** visit (or sit in on) a class **2** attend a lecture

听力 tīnglì (名) **1** hearing (ability) **2** aural comprehension (in language learning)

听命 tīngmìng (动) take orders from: 俯首～ be at sb.'s beck and call

听凭(憑) tīngpíng (动) allow; let (sb. do as he pleases): ～别人的摆布 be at the mercy of others

听其自然 tīng qí zìrán let things take their own course

听取 tīngqǔ (动) listen to: ～汇报 listen to reports (from below)

听任 tīngrèn (动) allow; let (sb. do as he pleases): 这种事情不能～再度发生. This kind of thing should not be allowed to happen again.

听说 tīngshuō (动) be told; hear of; it is said: ～他要辞职了. It is said that he is going to resign.

听天由命 tīngtiān-yóumìng resign oneself to one's fate

听闻 tīngwén 〈书〉 I (动) hear: 骇人～ appalling; shocking II (名) what one hears

听信 tīngxìn (动) **1** wait for information **2** believe what one hears; believe: 不要～谣言. Don't believe such rumours.

听政会(會) tīngzhènghuì (名) hearing

听众(衆) tīngzhòng (名) audience; listeners

亭

tíng (名)(～子) pavilion; kiosk: 书～ bookstall. 报～ kiosk; news-stand. 凉～ wayside pavilion

亭亭 tíngtíng (形)〈书〉 erect; upright: ～玉立 (of a woman) slim and graceful; (of a tree, etc.) tall and erect

停

tíng (动) **1** stop; cease; halt; pause: 雨～了. It's stopped raining. 她～了一会儿,又接着讲下去. She paused a moment before she went on. **2** stop over; stay: 我在去纽约的途中在东京～了两天. On my way to New York, I stopped over in Tokyo for two days. **3** (of cars) be parked; (of ships) lie at anchor: 汽车～在哪儿? Where can we park the car?

停办(辦) tíngbàn (动) close down

停泊 tíngbó (动) anchor; berth: 这个码头可以～五十多艘轮船. The docks can berth over fifty vessels.

停产(產) tíngchǎn (动) stop production

停车(車) tíngchē (动) **1** stop; pull up: 下一站～十分钟. At the next station we'll have a ten-minute stop. **2** park: 此处不准～! No Parking! ～场 car park; parking lot; parking area

停当(當) tíngdang (形) ready; settled: 一切准备～. Everything's ready.

停电(電) tíngdiàn (动) cut off the power supply; have a power failure

停顿 tíngdùn (动) **1** stop; halt; pause: 陷于～状态 be at a standstill; stagnate **2** pause (in speaking)

停放 tíngfàng (动) park; place: 这里不准～车辆. Don't park in this area. *or* No Parking.

停工 tínggōng (动) stop work; shut down: ～待料 work being held up for lack of material

停火 tínghuǒ (动) cease fire: ～协议 cease-fire agreement

停刊 tíngkān (动) stop publication (of a newspaper, magazine, etc.)

停靠 tíngkào (动) (of a train) stop; (of a ship) berth

停留 tíngliú (动) stay; stop: 代表团在纽约作短暂～. The delegation had a brief stopover in New York.

停妥 tíngtuǒ (形) be done properly; be in order: 事情已商议～. The matter was settled after much deliberation.

停息 tíngxī (动) stop; cease: 雨～了. The rain has stopped.

停歇 tíngxiē (动) **1** stop doing business; close down **2** stop; cease **3** stop for a rest

停业(業) tíngyè (动) stop doing business; close down: 清理存货, 暂时～. Closed temporarily for stocktaking.

停战(戰) tíngzhàn (动) cease fire; stop fighting: ～协定 armistice; truce agreement

停职(職) tíngzhí (动) temporarily relieve sb. of his duties as a disciplinary action

停止 tíngzhǐ (动) stop; cease; halt; suspend; call off: ～敌对行动 cessation of hostilities. ～营业 business suspended

停滞(滯) tíngzhì (动) stagnate; be at a standstill: 经济～. The economy remains stagnant.

廷 tíng (名) the court of a feudal ruler; the seat of a monarchical government

庭 tíng (名) **1** front courtyard; front yard **2** law court: 民(刑)～ a civil (criminal) court

庭园(園) tíngyuán (名) flower garden; grounds

庭院 tíngyuàn (名) courtyard

挺 tǐng I (形) straight; erect; stiff: ～立 stand erect. 直～～地躺着 lie stiff. 笔～的衣服 well-pressed clothes II (动) **1** straighten up (physically): ～胸 square one's shoulders. ～起腰杆 straighten one's back **2** endure; stand; hold out: 你～得住吗? Can you hold out? III (副) very; rather; quite: ～好 very good. 今天～冷. It's rather cold today. IV (量) [for machine-guns]: 轻重机枪六十余～ over sixty heavy and light machine-guns

挺拔 tǐngbá (形) **1** tall and straight: ～的苍松 tall, straight pines **2** forceful (of handwriting): 笔力～ forceful strokes

挺进(進) tǐngjìn (动) (of troops) advance; press onward; push forward

挺立 tǐnglì (动) stand upright; stand firm: 几棵青松～在山坡上. Several pine trees stand erect on the hillside.

挺身 tǐngshēn (动) stand out (against sth.): ～而出 step forward bravely

T

铤 tǐng (形) (run) quickly: ～而走险 make a desperate effort; make a reckless move

艇 tǐng (名) a light boat: 汽～ steamboat. 炮～ gunboat. 登陆～ landing craft

通 tōng I (动) **1** lead to; go to: 四～八达 lead everywhere **2** open up or clear out by poking or jabbing: 把下水道～一下 clean the sewer **3** connect; communicate: 互～有无 supply each other's needs **4** notify; tell: ～个电话 give sb. a ring; call (or phone up) sb. **5** understand; know: 他～三种语言. He knows three languages. II (名) authority; expert: 日本～ an expert on Japan. 中国～ an old China hand; Sinologue III (形) **1** open; through: 电话打～了. The call has been put through. 这个主意行得～. This idea will work. **2** logical; coherent: 文理不～ ungrammatical and incoherent (writing) **3** general; common: ～称 a general term **4** all; whole: ～观全局 take an overall view of the situation see also tòng

通报(報) tōngbào I (动) circulate a notice: ～表扬 circulate a notice of commendation II (名) **1** circular **2** bulletin; journal:《科学～》*Science Bulletin*

通病 tōngbìng (名) common failing

通才 tōngcái (名) an all-round person; a man (or woman) of many talents

通常 tōngcháng (形) general; usual; normal: ～的方法 ordinary means. ～早起 usually get up early

通畅(暢) tōngchàng (形) **1** unobstructed; clear: 血液循环～. The blood circulation is normal. **2** easy and smooth: 文字～ make smooth reading

通车(車) tōngchē (动) **1** (of a railway or highway) be open to traffic **2** have transport service

通称(稱) tōngchēng I (动) be generally called; be generally known as II (名) a general term

通达(達) tōngdá (动) understand: ～人情 be sensible and considerate

通道 tōngdào (名) thoroughfare; passageway; passage

通电(電) tōngdiàn I (动) set up an electric circuit; electrify II (名) circular telegram

通牒 tōngdié (名) diplomatic note: 最后～ ultimatum

通风(風) tōngfēng I (形) well ventilated: 这里不～. It's very close in here. II (动) **1** ventilate: 把窗打开～. Open the windows to let in some fresh air. **2** leak out: ～报信 give sb. secret information

通告 tōnggào I (动) give public notice; announce II (名) public notice; announcement; circular

通共 tōnggòng (副) in all; altogether; all told

通过(過) tōngguò I (动) 1 pass through; pass: 路太窄,汽车不能～. The road is too narrow for cars. 2 adopt; pass; carry: 提案已一致～. The motion was carried unanimously. 以压倒多数～ be passed by an overwhelming majority II (介) 1 by means of; by way of; through: ～协商取得一致 reach unanimity through consultation. ～外交途径 through diplomatic channel 2 with the consent or approval of: 这个问题要～校方才能做出决定. No decision can be made on this matter until the school authorities have been consulted.

通航 tōngháng (动) be open to navigation or air traffic

通红 tōnghóng (形) very red; red through and through: 她羞得满脸～. She blushed scarlet.

通婚 tōnghūn (动) be (or become) related by marriage; intermarry

通货 tōnghuò (名) currency: ～膨胀 inflation. ～收缩 deflation

通缉 tōngjī (动) issue an order to search for an escaped convict

通奸 tōngjiān (动) commit adultery

通栏(欄)标(標)题 tōnglán biāotí banner (or streamer) headline; banner

通力 tōnglì (动) concerted effort: ～合作 make a concerted effort to cooperate

通例 tōnglì (名) general rule; usual practice

通令 tōnglìng I (名) circular order; general order II (动) issue a circular order: ～嘉奖 issue an order of commendation

通明 tōngmíng (形) well-illuminated; brightly lit: 灯火～ be ablaze with lights; be brightly lit

通盘(盤) tōngpán (形) overall; all-round; comprehensive: ～计划 overall planning

通气(氣) tōngqì (动) 1 ventilate 2 be in touch with each other: 这件事你得跟他通个气. You should keep him informed of the matter.

通情达(達)理 tōngqíng-dálǐ reasonable; appropriate

通权(權)达(達)变(變) tōngquán-dábiàn handle matters flexibly to meet the immediate needs of the situation

通融 tōngróng (动) stretch a point: 我想这事不好～. I don't think we can stretch a point in this case.

通商 tōngshāng (动) (of nations) have trade relations

通顺 tōngshùn (形) (of writing) clear and smooth: 文理～ grammatically correct and coherent

通俗 tōngsú (形) popular; common: ～易懂 simple and easy. ～读物 books for popular consumption; popular literature

通天 tōngtiān (形) 1 exceedingly high or great: ～的本事 exceptional ability; superhuman skill 2 having direct access to the highest authorities

通通 tōngtōng (副) all; entirely; completely: ～拿去吧. Take away the lot.

通宵 tōngxiāo (名) all night; throughout the night; round the clock: ～达旦 all night long

通晓(曉) tōngxiǎo (动) thoroughly understand; be well versed in; be proficient in: ～多种文字 know many languages

通信 tōngxìn (动) write to each other; correspond: ～处 mailing address

通行 tōngxíng I (动) pass (or go) through: 自由～ can pass freely; have free passage. 停止～. Closed to traffic. ～证 pass; permit; safe-conduct II (形) current; general: 这是全国～的办法. This is the current practice throughout the country.

通讯 tōngxùn (名) 1 communication: 无线电～ radio (or wireless) communication. 微波～ microwave communication 2 news report; news dispatch; correspondence; newsletter

通用 tōngyòng (形) 1 in common use; current; general: 当地民族～的语言 the language in common use among the local people 2 interchangeable: ～货币 currency

通则 tōngzé (名) general rule

通胀 tōngzhàng (名) inflation

通知 tōngzhī I (动) notify; inform: 你走以前～我一声. Let me know before you leave. II (名) notice; circular: 发出～ send out (or dispatch) a notice

童 tóng (名) 1 child: 牧～ shepherd boy. ～工 child labour. ～话 fairy tales. ～年 childhood 2 unmarried: ～女 maiden; virgin

童声(聲) tóngshēng (名) child's voice: ～合唱 children's chorus

瞳 tóng (名) pupil (of the eye)

T

瞳孔 tóngkǒng (名) pupil: 放大～ have one's pupils dilated

同 tóng I (形) same; alike; similar: ～工～酬 equal pay for equal work II (动) be the same as: ～上 ditto; idem III (副) together; in common: ～生死, 共患难 share weal and woe IV (介) with: 有事～群众商量. Consult with the masses when problems arise. V (连) and; as well as: 我～你一起去. I'll go with you.

同班 tóngbān I (动) be in the same class: ～同学 classmate II (名) classmate

同伴 tóngbàn (名) companion; pal

同胞 tóngbāo (名) 1 born of the same parents: ～兄弟(姐妹) brothers (sisters) 2 fellow countryman; compatriot

同辈 tóngbèi (动) of the same generation

同病相怜(憐) tóng bìng xiāng lián fellow sufferers sympathize with one another

同仇敌(敵)忾(愾) tóngchóu-díkài share a bitter hatred for the enemy

同窗 tóngchuāng I (动) study in the same school II (名) schoolmate

同等 tóngděng (形) of the same class, rank, or status; on an equal basis (*or* footing): ～重要 of equal importance

同甘共苦 tónggān-gòngkǔ share bitter and sweet

同归(歸)于(於)尽(盡) tóng guīyú jìn perish together; spell destruction for both or all

同行 tóngháng I (动) of the same profession II (名) a person of the same profession; one's colleague

同化 tónghuà I (动) assimilate (ethnic group) II (名) (in phonetics) assimilation

同伙 tónghuǒ I (动) work in partnership; collude (in doing evil) II (名) partner; cohort; confederate

同居 tóngjū (动) 1 live together 2 cohabit

同龄 tónglíng (动) of the same age or about the same age: 他和我～. He is my contemporary. ～人 contemporary

同流合污 tóngliú-héwū consort with evildoers

同盟 tóngméng (名) alliance; league: 结成～ form (*or* enter into) an alliance

同名 tóngmíng of the same title or name: 他与我～. He is my namesake.

同谋 tóngmóu I (动) conspire (with sb.) II (名) confederate; accomplice: ～犯 accomplice

同年 tóngnián (名) the same year

同情 tóngqíng (动) sympathize with; show sympathy for: 相互～和支持 sympathize with and support each other. 我很～你. I heartily sympathize with you. *or* I have every sympathy for you. ～心 sympathy; fellow feeling

同上 tóngshàng (名) ditto; idem

同声(聲)传(傳)译(譯) tóngshēng chuányì simultaneous interpretation

同时(時) tóngshí I (名) at the same time; simultaneously; meanwhile; in the meantime: ～存在 exist side by side; coexist II (连) moreover; besides; furthermore: 这是非常重要的任务, ～也是十分艰巨的任务. This is a very important task; moreover, it is a very arduous one.

同事 tóngshì I (动) work alongside; work together: 我们～已经多年. We've been working in the same department for years. II (名) colleague; fellow worker: 老～ an old colleague

同室操戈 tóng shì cāo gē internal strife; internecine feud

同岁(歲) tóngsuì of the same age: 我们两人～. We two are the same age.

同乡(鄉) tóngxiāng (名) a fellow villager, townsman or provincial

同心 tóngxīn (动) with one heart: ～协力 work with one heart and with concerted efforts; pull together. ～同德 be of one heart and one mind

同姓 tóngxìng of the same surname: 他与我～. He is my namesake.

同学(學) tóngxué I (动) study in the same school II (名) fellow student; schoolmate

同样(樣) tóngyàng (形) same; identical; similar: 用～的方法 by the same method. 我们持～的观点. We hold identical views.

同业(業) tóngyè (名) 1 the same trade or business 2 a person of the same trade or business

同一 tóngyī (形) same; identical: 向～目标前进 advance towards the same goal

同义(義)词 tóngyìcí (名) synonym

同意 tóngyì (动) agree; consent; approve

同志 tóngzhì (名) comrade
同舟共济(濟) tóng zhōu gòng jì pull together in times of trouble or crisis; stick together through thick and thin
同宗 tóngzōng of the same clan; have common ancestry
桐 tóng (名) a general term for paulownia, phoenix tree and tung tree
桐油 tóngyóu (名) tung oil
铜 tóng (名) copper (Cu): ~丝 copper wire. ~像 bronze statue
铜版 tóngbǎn (名) copperplate: ~画 copperplate; etching (or engraving)
铜管乐(樂)器 tóngguǎn yuèqì brass-wind instrument; brass wind
铜器 tóngqì (名) bronze, brass or copper ware: ~时代 the Bronze Age
铜墙(墻)铁(鐵)壁 tóngqiáng-tiěbì wall of bronze — impregnable fortress
筒 tǒng (名) 1 a section of thick bamboo: 竹~ a thick bamboo tube 2 a thick tube-shaped object: 笔~ brush pot. 邮~ pillar box; mailbox
桶 tǒng (名) pail; bucket; barrel: 水~ water bucket. 一~牛奶 a pail of milk
捅 tǒng (动) 1 poke; stab: ~了一刀 stab with a dagger. ~马蜂窝 stir up a hornets' nest 2 disclose; give away; let out: 谁把它给~出去了? Who gave it away (or let it out)?
捅娄(婁)子 tǒng lóuzi make a stupid move; make a blunder; get into trouble
统 tǒng I (名) interconnected system: 传~ tradition. 系~ system II (动) gather into one; unite: ~一指挥 unified command III (副) all; together
统称(稱) tǒngchēng I (动) be called by a joint name II (名) a general designation
统筹(籌) tǒngchóu (动) plan as a whole: ~兼顾 make overall planning by taking all factors into consideration
统共 tǒnggòng (副) altogether; in all
统计 tǒngjì I (名) statistics: 人口~ census; vital statistics. ~员 statistician II (动) add up; count: ~出席人数 count up the number of people present (at a meeting, etc.)
统率 tǒngshuài (动) command
统帅(帥) tǒngshuài I (名) commander-in-chief; commander II (动) command
统统 tǒngtǒng (副) all; completely; entirely; lock, stock and barrel: ~讲出来 own up
统辖 tǒngxiá (动) exercise jurisdiction over; govern
统一 tǒngyī I (动) unify; unite; integrate: ~行动 coordinate actions; act in unison II (形) unified; unitary: ~领导 unified leadership. 他们认识很不~. Their views are widely divergent.
统治 tǒngzhì (动) rule; dominate: ~阶级 ruling class. ~者 ruler
恸(慟) tòng 〈书〉 deep sorrow; grief
痛 tòng I (动) ache; pain: 头~ have a headache. 肚子~ have a stomachache. 嗓子~ have a sore throat II (名) sorrow: 哀~ sadness III (副) extremely; deeply; bitterly: ~哭 cry bitterly. ~骂 severely scold; roundly curse
痛斥 tòngchì (动) bitterly attack; sharply denounce
痛楚 tòngchǔ (名) anguish; agony
痛处(處) tòngchù (名) sore spot; tender spot: 触及~ touch sb.'s sore spot
痛定思痛 tòng dìng sī tòng recall or relieve a bitter experience
痛恨 tònghèn (动) hate bitterly; utterly detest
痛哭 tòngkū (动) cry (or weep) bitterly; wail: ~一场 have a good cry. 失声~ be choked with tears. ~流涕 weep bitter tears; cry one's heart out
痛苦 tòngkǔ I (名) pain; suffering; agony II (形) painful; sad; bitter
痛快 tòngkuai (形) 1 very happy; delighted; overjoyed: 心里感到~ feel happily relieved of a burden 2 to one's great satisfaction: 喝个~ drink one's fill. 玩个~ have a wonderful time 3 simple and direct; forthright; straightforward: 说话很~ speak frankly and directly; be outspoken. 他~地答应了. He readily agreed.
痛切 tòngqiè (形) with intense sorrow; most sorrowfully: ~反省 examine one's conscience with feelings of deep remorse
痛恶(惡) tòngwù (动) bitterly detest; abhor
痛惜 tòngxī (动) deeply regret; deplore
痛心 tòngxīn (形) pained; deeply grieved: 他对自己所犯的错误感到很~. He keenly regretted the mistake he had made.

痛心疾首 tòngxīn-jíshǒu detest; hate with very strong feeling

痛痒(癢) tòngyǎng (名) 1 sufferings; difficulties: ～相关 share a common lot 2 importance; consequence: 无关～ a matter of no consequence

通 tòng (量) [for repeated action]: 骂了他一～ give him a dressing down see also tōng

偷 tōu I (动) steal; pilfer: ～窃 steal; pilfer II (副) on the sly: ～看 steal a glance; peek; peep. ～听 eavesdrop

偷安 tōu'ān (动) seek temporary ease and comfort

偷空 tōukòng (动) take time off (from work to do sth. else); snatch a moment

偷懒 tōulǎn (动) loaf on the job; be lazy

偷梁换柱 tōuliáng-huànzhù make the story take on a different look by deliberately changing a few details; commit a fraud

偷拍 tōupāi (动) take photos secretly: 谨防～ beware of hidden cameras

偷窃(竊) tōuqiè (动) steal; pilfer

偷情 tōuqíng (动) have an affair; have an amour; have an illicit love affair

偷税 tōushuì (动) evade taxes

偷天换日 tōutiān-huànrì distort the truth by despicable means; perpetrate a gigantic fraud

偷偷 tōutōu (副) stealthily; secretly; on the sly: ～地溜走 sneak away. ～摸摸 furtively; surreptitiously; covertly

偷袭(襲) tōuxí (动) make a sneak attack; launch a surprise attack

偷闲(閒) tōuxián (动) snatch a moment of leisure: 忙里～ squeeze a little leisure from a busy programme; enjoy occasional leisure in a busy life

头(頭) tóu I (名) 1 head 2 hair or hair style: 梳～ comb the hair 3 top; end: 山～ hilltop. 桥～ the end of a bridge 4 beginning or end: 从～到尾 from start to finish 5 remnant; end: 铅笔～儿 pencil stub. 烟～ cigarette end 6 chief; head: 你们的～是谁? Who is the head of your section? 7 side; aspect: 两～落空 fall between two stools II (形) 1 first: ～等 first-class 2 leading: ～羊 lead sheep 3 [used before a numeral] first: ～一遍 the first time. ～三天 the first three days III (量) 1 [for domestic animals]: 三～牛 three head of cattle. 两～骡子 two mules 2 [for garlic]: 一～蒜 a bulb of garlic

头彩 tóucǎi (名) first prize in a lottery: 中～ win first prize in a lottery

头等 tóuděng (形) first-class; first-rate: ～大事 a matter of cardinal importance. ～舱 first-class cabin

头顶 tóudǐng (名) the top (or crown) of the head

头发(髮) tóufa (名) hair (on the human head): ～夹子 hairpin

头号(號) tóuhào (形) 1 number one; size one: ～敌人 arch-enemy 2 first-rate; top quality

头昏 tóuhūn dizzy; giddy: ～脑胀 feel giddy (or dizzy); feel one's head swimming

头奖(獎) tóujiǎng (名) first prize (in a contest, etc.)

头角 tóujiǎo (名) brilliance (of a young person); talent: 初露～ show one's talent for the first time

头里(裏) tóuli (名) 1 in front; ahead 2 in advance; beforehand: 咱们把话说在～. Let's make this clear from the very start.

头颅(顱) tóulú (名) head: 抛～,洒热血 lay down one's life in a just cause

头面人物 tóumiàn rénwù prominent figure; dignitary; VIP

头脑(腦) tóunǎo (名) 1 brain; mind: 她很有～. She has plenty of brains. ～简单 simple-minded. ～清醒 clear-headed 2 main threads; clue: 摸不着～ cannot make head or tail of sth.

头胎 tóutāi (名) firstborn

头条(條)新闻 tóutiáo xīnwén front-page headline

头痛 tóutòng (have a) headache: ～得厉害 have a bad headache. 这事真叫人～. This matter is a real headache.

头头儿(兒) tóutour (名)〈口〉head; chief; leader; boss

头头是道 tóutóu shì dào vividly; persuasively; methodically

头衔 tóuxián (名) title

头绪 tóuxù (名) main threads (of a complicated affair): 茫无～ be quite at a loss

头子 tóuzi (名) chieftain; chief; boss: 土匪～ bandit chief

头(頭) tou 1 [a suffix placed at the end of a noun, verb or adjective]: 木～ wood. 吃～ sth. worth eating. 甜～儿 a sweet foretaste 2 [at the end of nouns of locality] 上～ above. 下～ below

投 tóu (动) 1 throw; fling; hurl: ～篮 shoot. ～手榴弹 throw a hand-grenade 2 put in: ～票 cast a vote. ～资 invest 3 throw oneself into (a river, etc. to commit suicide): ～河 drown oneself in a river 4 project; cast: 树影～在窗户上. The tree cast its shadow on the window. 5 send; deliver: ～书 deliver a letter 6 go to; join: ～军 join the army 7 fit in with; agree with; cater to: ～其所好 cater to sb.'s likes

投案 tóu'àn (动) give oneself up (or surrender oneself) to the police

投保 tóubǎo (动) insure; take out an insurance policy

投奔 tóubèn (动) go and seek the assistance of a friend or relative

投标(標) tóubiāo (动) enter a bid; submit a tender: ～者 bidder

投产(產) tóuchǎn (动) go into operation; put into production

投诚 tóuchéng (动) (of enemy troops, rebels, etc.) surrender; cross over

投敌(敵) tóudí (动) defect to the enemy

投递(遞) tóudì (动) deliver: ～信件 deliver letters

投放 tóufàng (动) put (goods) on the market

投稿 tóugǎo (动) contribute (to a newspaper or magazine)

投合 tóuhé (动) 1 agree; get along: 他们俩很～. The two of them hit it off very well. 2 cater to: ～顾客的口味 cater to the tastes of the customers

投机(機) tóujī I (形) congenial; agreeable: 谈得很～ have a most agreeable chat II (动) 1 speculate: ～倒把 engage in speculation and profiteering 2 take advantage of every chance for personal gain: ～分子 opportunist

投井下石 tóu jǐng xià shí hit a man when he's down

投考 tóukǎo (动) sign up for an examination

投靠 tóukào (动) go and seek assistance from sb.; sponge on sb.

投票 tóupiào (动) vote; cast a vote: ～表决 decide by ballot; put sth. to the vote. ～箱 ballot box. 无记名～ secret ballot

投入 tóurù (动) throw into; put into: ～生产 go into operation

投射 tóushè (动) 1 throw (a projectile, etc.); cast 2 project (a ray of light); cast

投身 tóushēn (动) throw oneself into: ～到工作中去 throw oneself heart and soul into the work. ～到四个现代化建设事业中去 devote oneself to the cause of the four modernizations

投鼠忌器 tóu shǔ jì qì hesitate to hit out against an evildoer for fear of harming good people in the act

投诉 tóusù (动) 1 appeal: ～法院 appeal to a court 2 (of a customer) complain

投宿 tóusù (动) seek lodgings: ～客栈 put up at an inn for the night

投胎 tóutāi (动) reincarnation

投桃报(報)李 tóu táo bào lǐ exchange gifts; exchange visits

投降 tóuxiáng (动) surrender; capitulate

投掷(擲) tóuzhì (动) throw; hurl: ～标枪(铁饼、手榴弹) throw a javelin (discus, hand-grenade)

投资 tóuzī I (动) invest II (名) money invested; investment: 国家～ state investment

透 tòu I (动) 1 penetrate; soak through; seep through 2 tell secretly: ～个信儿 tip sb. off II (形) fully; thoroughly: 桃熟～了. The peaches are quite ripe. 你把道理说～了. You have fully explained the case. 没意思～了 as dull as ditchwater

透彻(徹) tòuchè (形) penetrating; thorough; in-depth: ～的分析 an in-depth analysis

透顶 tòudǐng (形) thoroughly; downright; in the extreme: 腐败～ rotten to the core

透风(風) tòufēng (动) 1 let in air 2 divulge a secret; leak: 这件事,他向我透了一点风. He gave me some tip about it.

透漏 tòulòu (动) divulge; leak; reveal: 消息～出去了. The news has leaked out.

透露 tòulù (动) divulge; leak; disclose; reveal: ～风声 leak (or disclose) information. 真相～出来了. The truth has come out.

透明 tòumíng (形) transparent: 不～ opaque. 半～ translucent

透明度 tòumíngdù (名) transparency

透辟 tòupì (形) penetrating; incisive; thorough

透气(氣) tòuqì (动) 1 ventilate: 开窗～ to open the windows and let some air in 2 breathe freely: 透不过气 feel suffo-

T

cated **3** leak (or disclose) information; drop a hint; tip off

透视 tòushì (名) **1** perspective **2** fluoroscopy

透析 tòuxī (名) **1** dialysis **2** thorough analysis

透支 tòuzhī (动) **1** (in banking) overdraw; make an overdraft **2** expenditure exceeds revenue; overspend **3** draw one's salary in advance

突 tū I (动) dash forward; charge: ~破 break through II (副) suddenly; abruptly: 气温~降. The temperature suddenly dropped. III (形) prominent; projecting

突变(變) tūbiàn (名) **1** sudden change **2** mutation

突出 tūchū I (形) **1** protruding; projecting: ~的前额 prominent forehead **2** outstanding; prominent: ~的成就 outstanding achievements II (动) give prominence to; stress; highlight: 他的文章没有~重点. In his essay he fails to give prominence to his main points.

突击(擊) tūjī (动) **1** make a sudden violent attack; assault: ~部队 shock-troops **2** concentrate one's effort to finish a job; do a crash job: ~他的工作 rush through his work

突破 tūpò (动) **1** break through; make (or effect) a break through: ~防线 break through a defence line. 医学上的~ a medical breakthrough **2** surmount; overcome: ~各种技术难关 surmount every technical difficulty. ~定额 overfulfil a quota

突起 tūqǐ (动) **1** break out; suddenly appear: 战事~. War broke out. 异军~. Quite unexpectedly, a new figure appeared on the scene. **2** rise high; tower: 峰峦~. Peaks suddenly begin to rise.

突然 tūrán (形) sudden; abrupt; unexpected: ~停止 suddenly stop; stop short. ~哭起来 burst into tears. ~袭击 launch a surprise attack

突如其来(來) tū rú qí lái come to sb. as a surprise

突突 tūtū (象): 她的心~地跳. Her heart thumped.

突围(圍) tūwéi (动) break out of an encirclement

凸 tū (形) protruding; raised: ~花银瓶 a silver vase with a raised floral design. ~面 convex

凸显(顯) tūxiǎn (动) show distinctively; prominent

秃 tū (形) **1** hairless; bald: 他的头开始~了. He's going baldish. **2** bare: 山是~的. The hill is bare. **3** blunt; without a point: 铅笔~了. The pencil is blunt. **4** incomplete; badly organized: 这篇文章的结尾显得有点~. This essay seems to end rather abruptly.

屠 tú (动) **1** slaughter (animals for food) **2** massacre; slaughter: 大~杀 mass massacre

屠杀(殺) túshā (动) massacre; slaughter

屠宰 túzǎi (动) butcher; slaughter: ~场 slaughter house

图(圖) tú I (名) **1** picture; drawing; chart; map: 地~ map **2** scheme; plan; attempt: 宏~ grand plan II (动) pursue; seek: ~私利 seek personal profit. ~省事 try to do things the easy way

图案 tú'àn (名) pattern; design

图表 túbiǎo (名) chart; diagram; graph: 统计~ statistical chart (or table)

图钉 túdīng (名) drawing pin; thumbtack

图画(畫) túhuà (名) drawing; picture; painting

图鉴(鑒) tújiàn (名) illustrated (or pictorial) handbook

图解 tújiě (名) diagram; graph; figure: 用~说明 explain through diagrams

图景 tújǐng (名) view; prospect: 壮丽的~ magnificent prospect

图谋 túmóu (动) plot; scheme; conspire: ~不轨 hatch a sinister plot

图片 túpiàn (名) picture; photograph: ~展览 photo (or picture) exhibition. ~说明 caption

图谱 túpǔ (名) a collection of illustrative plates: 历史~ atlas

图书(書) túshū (名) books: ~资料 books and reference materials. ~馆 library. ~目录 catalogue of books; library catalogue

图腾 túténg (名) totem

图像 túxiàng (名) picture; image

图样(樣) túyàng (名) pattern; design; draft; drawing

图章 túzhāng (名) seal; stamp

涂(塗) tú (动) **1** spread on; apply; smear: ~抹 apply **2** scribble; scrawl: 别在墙上乱

~. Don't scribble (or scrawl) on the wall. **3** blot out; cross out: ~掉几个字 cross out a few words

涂改 túgǎi (动) alter: ~无效 invalid if altered

涂抹 túmǒ (动) **1** daub; smear; paint **2** scribble; scrawl

涂饰 túshì (动) **1** cover with paint, lacquer, colour wash, etc. **2** daub (plaster, etc.) on a wall; whitewash

涂写(寫) túxiě (动) scribble; scrawl; doodle: 禁止~! No scribbling.

涂鸦 túyā (名) poor handwriting; scrawl; chicken tracks

途 tú (名) way; road; route: 沿~ along the way (or road). 半~而废 give up halfway

途径(徑) tújìng (名) way; channel: 通过外交~ through diplomatic channels

徒 tú I (形) empty; bare: ~手 bare-handed; unarmed II (副) **1** merely; only: ~有虚名 exist in name only **2** in vain; to no avail: ~费唇舌 waste one's breath III (名) **1** apprentice; pupil: 门~ pupil; disciple. 学~ apprentice **2** follower or believer: 佛教~ Buddhist **3** person; fellow: 无耻之~ shameless person. 赌~ gambler. 歹~ rascal; evildoer. 暴~ ruffian; thug

徒步 túbù (副) on foot: ~旅行 travel on foot

徒弟 túdì (名) apprentice; disciple

徒劳(勞) túláo (动) make a futile effort; work in vain: ~无功 all one's attempts proved futile

徒然 túrán (副) in vain; for nothing; to no avail: ~耗费精力 waste one's energy (or effort)

徒手 túshǒu (形) bare-handed; unarmed: ~操 free-standing exercises

徒刑 túxíng (名) imprisonment; (prison) sentence: 有期~ specified (prison) sentence. 无期~ life imprisonment

土 tǔ I (名) **1** soil; earth: 肥~ fertile (or good) soil. ~路 dirt road **2** land; ground: 国~ a country's territory; land. 领~ territory; domain II (形) **1** local; native: ~产 local product **2** homemade; crude: ~布 handwoven cloth **3** old-fashioned; unrefined; rustic; unenlightened: ~里~气 uncouth; boorish

土包子 tǔbāozi (名) clodhopper; (country) bumpkin

土崩瓦解 tǔbēng-wǎjiě crumble; fall apart; collapse like a house of cards

土产(產) tǔchǎn (名) local (or native) product

土地 tǔdì (名) land; soil; territory

土豆 tǔdòu (名)〈口〉potato

土匪 tǔfěi (名) bandit; brigand

土豪 tǔháo (名) local tyrant: ~劣绅 local tyrant and evil gentry

土话 tǔhuà (名) slang expression; local dialect

土皇帝 tǔhuángdì (名) local despot; local tyrant

土木 tǔmù (名) building; construction: 大兴~ build splendid houses on a grand scale

土壤 tǔrǎng (名) soil: ~改良 soil amelioration

土生土长(長) tǔshēng-tǔzhǎng local born and bred

土著 tǔzhù (名) original inhabitants; natives; aborigines

吐 tǔ (动) **1** spit: ~血 spit blood. ~痰 spit; expectorate **2** say; tell; pour out: ~实 tell the truth. ~怨气 air one's grievances
see also tù

吐露 tǔlù (动) reveal; tell: ~真情 reveal the truth

吐气(氣) tǔqì venting one's pent-up feelings: 扬眉~ feel happy and proud

吐 tù (动) **1** vomit; throw up: 要~ feel sick; feel like vomiting **2** give up unwillingly; disgorge: ~赃 disgorge ill-gotten gains
see also tǔ

兔 tù (名) (~子) hare; rabbit: 家~ rabbit. 野~ hare

兔死狐悲 tù sǐ hú bēi like grieves for like

湍 tuān〈书〉I (形) (of a current) rapid; torrential II (名) rapids; rushing water: 急~ a rushing current

湍急 tuānjí (形) (of a current) rapid; torrential: 水流~. The current is strong and rapid.

湍流 tuānliú (名) **1** swift current; rushing water; torrent; rapid **2** turbulent flow; turbulence

团(團) tuán I (形) round; circular: ~扇 round fan II (动) unite; conglomerate: ~结 unite with III (名) **1** group; society; organization: 剧～ drama troupe. 旅行～ a tourist group. 文工～ ensemble; art troupe. 代表～ delegation; mission; deputation **2** sth. shaped like a ball: 缩成一～ curl up. 汤～ boiled rice dumpling **3** regiment IV (量): 一～毛线 a ball of wool. 一～面 a lump of dough

团结 tuánjié (动) unite; rally: ～一致 unite as one. ～就是力量. Unity is strength.

团聚 tuánjù (动) gather together; reunite: 全家～ family reunion. 在中国,春节仍然是全家～的节日. The Spring Festival is still an occasion for family get-togethers in China.

团体(體) tuántǐ (名) organization; group; team: 群众～ mass organization. ～赛 team competition

团员 tuányuán (名) **1** member: 代表团～ a member of a delegation **2** a member of the Communist Youth League of China; League member

推 tuī (动) **1** push; shove: 把门～开 push the door open **2** plane: 用刨子把桌面～光 plane a table smooth **3** push forward; promote; advance: ～广 popularize. **4** infer; deduce: 类～ reason by analogy **5** decline (sth. offered) **6** push away; shirk; shift: 不要把责任～给人家. Don't shift the responsibility on to others. **7** put off; postpone: 动身日期要往后～. The departure date should be postponed. **8** elect; choose: ～他担任小组长 elect him group leader

推波助澜 tuībō-zhùlán add fuel to the flames; incite people to unrestrained anger or violence

推测 tuīcè (动) infer; conjecture; guess

推陈(陳)出新 tuī chén chū xīn weed through the old to bring forth the new

推迟(遲) tuīchí (动) put off; postpone; defer: ～两周付款 defer payment for two weeks

推崇 tuīchóng (动) attach great weight to: ～备至 hold sb. in very high esteem

推出 tuīchū (动) introduce; put out; present: ～新产品 put out a new product. ～一部新影片 present a new film

推辞(辭) tuīcí (动) decline (an appointment, invitation, etc.)

推倒 tuīdǎo (动) **1** push over; overturn **2** reverse; repudiate: 这不是一个错误的决定,不能予以～. This is not a wrong decision to be reversed.

推动(動) tuīdòng (动) promote; give impetus to; spur: 改革～进步. Reform spurs progress.

推断(斷) tuīduàn (动) infer; deduce

推度 tuīduó (动) infer; conjecture; guess

推翻 tuīfān (动) **1** overthrow; overturn; topple **2** repudiate; cancel; reverse: ～协议 repudiate an agreement

推广(廣) tuīguǎng (动) popularize; spread; extend: ～普通话 popularize common speech of the Chinese language. ～先进经验 spread advanced experience

推荐(薦) tuījiàn (动) recommend: ～她担任这个职务 recommend her for the post

推举(舉) tuījǔ (动) elect; choose

推理 tuīlǐ (名) inference; reasoning: 用～方法 by inference

推论(論) tuīlùn (名) inference; deduction; corollary

推敲 tuīqiāo (动) weigh; deliberate: ～词句 weigh one's words; choose one's words carefully

推求 tuīqiú (动) inquire into; ascertain

推却 tuīquè (动) refuse; decline; turn down

推让(讓) tuīràng (动) decline (a position, favour, etc.) out of modesty or politeness

推算 tuīsuàn (动) calculate; reckon; work out

推土机(機) tuītǔjī (名) bulldozer

推托 tuītuō (动) make an excuse (for not doing sth.): 她～嗓子坏了,怎么也不肯唱. She declined persistently to sing on the plea that she had nearly lost her voice.

推脱 tuītuō (动) evade; shirk: ～责任 evade (or shirk) responsibility; lay the blame on sb.

推委 tuīwěi (动) shift responsibility on to others; pass the buck

推想 tuīxiǎng (动) imagine; guess; reckon

推销 tuīxiāo (动) promote sales: ～员 salesman

推卸 tuīxiè (动) shirk (responsibility)

推心置腹 tuīxīn-zhìfù treat people sincerely: ～地交换意见 have a frank exchange of views

推行 tuīxíng (动) carry out; pursue; implement: ～新的政策 pursue a new policy. ～强权政治 practise power politics

推选(選) tuīxuǎn (动) elect; choose

推延 tuīyán (动) put off; postpone: 把会议～到明天 put off the meeting till tomorrow

推移 tuīyí (动) 1 (of time) elapse; pass: 随着时间的~ with the passage of time 2 (of a situation, etc.) develop; evolve: 时局的~ the march of events

颓 tuí (形) 1 ruined; dilapidated: ~垣断壁 a lot of debris 2 declining; decadent: 衰~ weak and degenerate; on the decline 3 dejected; dispirited: ~丧 dispirited; listless

颓败 tuíbài (形)〈书〉 declining; decadent

颓废(廢) tuífèi (形) dejected; decadent: ~派 the decadent school

颓势(勢) tuíshì (名) declining tendency

颓唐 tuítáng (形) dejected; dispirited

腿 tuǐ (名) 1 leg: 大~ thigh. 前~ foreleg. 后~ hindleg. ~肚子 calf (of the leg). ~勤 busy running about; tireless in running around 2 a leglike support: 桌子(椅子)~ legs of a table (chair) 3 ham: 火~ ham

腿脚 tuǐjiǎo (名) ability to walk: ~不灵便 have difficulty moving about

蜕 tuì I (动) slough off; exuviate II (名) exuviae: 蛇~ snake slough

蜕变(變) tuìbiàn (动) 1 change in quality (usu. for the worse) 2 decay: 自发~ spontaneous decay

蜕化 tuìhuà (动) 1 slough off; exuviate 2 (of person or thing) degenerate: ~变质分子 degenerate element; degenerate

退 tuì (动) 1 move back; retreat: 敌人已经~了. The enemy has retreated. 2 cause to move back; withdraw; remove: ~敌 repulse the enemy 3 withdraw from; quit: ~职 resign from office 4 decline; recede: ~烧了. The fever is gone. 水~了. The floods have subsided. 5 return: ~票 return a ticket one has bought and get a refund 6 cancel; break off: ~婚 break off an engagement. ~掉订货 cancel an order

退兵 tuìbīng (动) 1 beat a retreat 2 repulse the enemy

退步 tuìbù I (动) lag (or fall) behind; retrogress II (名) room for manoeuvre; leeway: 留个~ leave some room for manoeuvre; leave some leeway

退潮 tuìcháo (名) ebb tide; ebb

退出 tuìchū (动) withdraw from; secede; quit: ~会场 walk out of a meeting. ~组织 withdraw from an organization. ~政治舞台 retire from the political arena

退耕 tuìgēng (动) take land out of cultivation and return it to nature

退化 tuìhuà (动) degenerate; deteriorate

退换 tuìhuàn (动) exchange (or replace) a purchase

退回 tuìhuí (动) 1 return; send (or give) back: 把这篇稿子~给作者 return the article to its author 2 go (or turn) back

退居 tuìjū (动) 1 retire from a prominent position and take (a less important one) 2 be reduced to (a lower rank)

退路 tuìlù (名) 1 route of retreat: 切断敌军~ cut off the enemy's retreat 2 room for manoeuvre; leeway: 留个~ leave some leeway

退赔 tuìpéi (动) 1 return what one has unlawfully taken or pay compensation for it 2 refund

退却 tuìquè (动) 1 retreat; withdraw: 战略~ strategic retreat 2 hang back; shrink back; flinch

退让(讓) tuìràng (动) make a concession; yield; give in: 在原则问题上从不~ never compromise on matters of principle

退色 tuìshǎi (动) fade: 这种布~吗? Will this cloth fade?

退税 tuìshuì (动) duty drawback

退缩 tuìsuō (动) shrink back; flinch; cower: 在困难面前从不~ never flinch from difficulty

退位 tuìwèi (动) abdicate; give up the throne

退席 tuìxí (动) leave a banquet or a meeting; walk out: ~以示抗议 walk out in protest

退休 tuìxiū (动) retire: ~工人 retired workers. ~年龄 retirement age

退赃(贓) tuìzāng (动) give up (surrender, or disgorge) ill-gotten gains

退职(職) tuìzhí (动) resign or be discharged from office

吞 tūn (动) 1 swallow; gulp down: 把药丸~下去 swallow the pills 2 take possession of: 并~ annex

吞并(併) tūnbìng (动) annex; swallow up

吞没 tūnmò (动) 1 embezzle; misappropriate: ~公款 misappropriate public funds 2 swallow up; engulf: 这只小船给波涛汹涌的海洋~了. The small boat was engulfed by the stormy sea.

吞声(聲) tūnshēng (动)〈书〉 gulp down one's sobs; not dare cry out: 忍气~ swallow rude remarks and bottle up one's grievances

吞噬 tūnshì (动) swallow; gobble up; engulf

吞吐 tūntǔ (动) take in and send out in large quantities: ～量 handling capacity (of a harbour); the volume of freight handled

吞吞吐吐 tūntūntǔtǔ (speak) hesitantly and incoherently

屯 tún I (动) 1 collect; store up: ～粮 store up grain. ～聚 assemble; collect 2 station (troops); quarter (troops): ～兵 station troops II (名) village [often used in village names]

囤 tún (动) store up; hoard: ～货 store goods

see also dùn

囤积(積) túnjī (动) hoard for speculation: ～居奇 hoard for profiteering purposes; hoarding and speculation

臀 tún (名) buttocks: ～部 buttocks

脱 tuō (动) 1 (of hair, skin) peel off: 头发快～光了 going bald 2 take off; cast off: ～鞋(衣服) take off one's shoes (clothes) 3 escape from; get out of: ～险 be out of danger 4 miss out (words)

脱产(產) tuōchǎn (动) be temporarily released from one's regular work: ～学习 be temporarily released from work and sent on a study course

脱稿 tuōgǎo (动) (of a manuscript) be completed

脱钩 tuōgōu (动) break off relations; cut ties

脱节(節) tuōjié (动) come apart; be disjointed; dislocate: 理论与实践不能～. Theory must not be divorced from practice.

脱口而出 tuō kǒu ér chū say sth. without thinking; blurt out

脱口秀 tuōkǒuxiù (名) talk show

T

脱离(離) tuōlí (动) separate oneself from; break away from; be divorced from: ～实际 lose contact with reality; be divorced from reality. 病人～危险了. The patient is out of danger.

脱落 tuōluò (动) drop; fall off (or away); come off: 门的把手～了. The door handle has come off. 油漆～了. The paint is peeling off.

脱贫 tuōpín (动) shake off poverty; lift oneself out of poverty: ～致富 shake off poverty and build up a fortune

脱身 tuōshēn (动) get away: 我事情太多, 不能～. I have so much to attend to that I just can't get away.

脱手 tuōshǒu (动) 1 slip out of the hand 2 get off one's hands; dispose of

脱俗 tuōsú (形) free from philistinism; refined

脱胎 tuōtāi (动) 1 emerge from the womb of; be born out of: ～换骨 make a thoroughgoing change 2 a process of making bodiless lacquerware: ～漆器 bodiless lacquerware

脱逃 tuōtáo (动) run away; escape; flee: 临阵～ flee from battle; disappear just when one's service is most needed

脱险(險) tuōxiǎn (动) escape (or be out of) danger

脱销 tuōxiāo (动) be out of stock; be sold out

脱脂 tuōzhī (动) defat; degrease: ～棉 absorbent cotton. ～奶粉 defatted milk powder; nonfat dried milk

拖 tuō (动) 1 pull; drag; haul 2 delay; drag on: 不要再～了. Don't delay any more. 今天能做的不要～到明天. Don't put off today's work till tomorrow.

拖把 tuōbǎ (名) mop

拖车(車) tuōchē (名) trailer

拖船 tuōchuán (名) tugboat; tug; tow-boat

拖后(後)腿 tuō hòutuǐ hold sb. back; be a drag on sb.

拖拉 tuōlā (形) dilatory; slow; sluggish: ～作风 sluggishness

拖拉机(機) tuōlājī (名) tractor: 手扶～ walking tractor

拖累 tuōlěi (动) 1 encumber; be a burden on: 受家务～ be tied down by household chores 2 implicate; involve

拖泥带(帶)水 tuōní-dàishuǐ (of writing or work) messy; sloppy; slovenly

拖欠 tuōqiàn (动) fail to pay one's debts; be in arrears: ～债务 in debt

拖鞋 tuōxié (名) slippers

拖延 tuōyán (动) delay; put off; procrastinate: ～时间 play for time; stall (for time)

托 tuō I (名) sth. serving as a support: 枪～ the stock (or butt) of a rifle, etc. II (动) 1 support with the hand or palm: 她两手～着下巴. Her chin rested on her hands. 2 serve as a foil (or contrast); set off: 衬～ set off

3 ask; entrust: 把这项任务～付给他 entrust him with the task 4 plead; give as a pretext: ～病 pretend to be sick; plead illness. ～故不来 fail to show up on some pretext 5 rely upon; owe to: ～庇 owe all this to sb.'s kindness

托词 tuōcí I (动) find a pretext; make some excuse: ～谢绝 decline with some excuse II (名) pretext; excuse; subterfuge: 那不过是～. That was just an excuse.

托儿(兒)所 tuō'érsuǒ (名) nursery; day-care centre

托福 tuōfú 〈套〉[usu. used in returning sb.'s greetings] thanks to you: 托您的福,一切都还顺利. Everything is going fine, thank you.

托管 tuōguǎn (动) put under trusteeship: ～国 trustee. ～领土 trust territory

托盘(盤) tuōpán (名) (serving) tray

托人情 tuō rénqíng ask a favour through the good offices of sb.

托运(運) tuōyùn (动) consign for shipment; check: 将行李交付～ check in the luggage

鸵 tuó (名) ostrich

鸵鸟(鳥) tuóniǎo (名) ostrich: ～政策 ostrich policy; ostrichism

驼 tuó I (名) camel II (动) hunch

驼背 tuóbèi I (名) hunchback; humpback II (形) hunchbacked; humpbacked

驼峰 tuófēng (名) hump(of a camel)

驼绒 tuóróng (名) 1 camel's hair 2 camel-hair cloth

驮 tuó (动) carry (or bear) on the back

椭(橢) tuǒ

椭圆 tuǒyuán (名) ellipse; oval

妥 tuǒ (形) 1 appropriate; proper: 欠～ hardly proper; not quite appropriate 2 [used after a verb] ready; settled; finished: 事情基本上已办～了. The matter is as good as settled.

妥当(當) tuǒdang (形) appropriate; proper: 办得很～ well handled; quite well done

妥善 tuǒshàn (形) appropriate; proper; well arranged: ～安排 make appropriate arrangements. ～处理 careful and skilful handling of a problem

妥帖 tuǒtiē (形) appropriate; fitting and proper

妥协(協) tuǒxié (动) come to terms; compromise: 达成～ reach a compromise

拓 tuò (动) open up; develop

see also tà

拓荒 tuòhuāng (动) open up virgin soil; reclaim wasteland

唾 tuò I (名) saliva; spittle: ～沫 saliva; spittle II (动) spit: ～弃 spurn; cast aside

唾骂 tuòmà (动) reproach with contempt; revile

唾手可得 tuò shǒu kě dé be within easy reach

W w

挖 wā (动) dig; excavate: ～井 sink a well. ～洞 dig a hole. ～出 winkle out

挖掘 wājué (动) excavate; unearth: ～古物 excavate ancient relics. ～潜力 tap the potentialities

挖苦 wāku (动) speak sarcastically or ironically: ～一些人 make ironical remarks about some people

挖墙(墻)角 wā qiángjiǎo undermine sb.'s prestige; let sb. down

洼(窪) wā I (形) hollow; low-lying: ～地 depression; low-lying land II (名) low-lying area; depression: 水～儿 a waterlogged depression

洼陷 wāxiàn (动) (of ground) be low-lying

哇 wā (象) [sound of vomiting and crying]: ～的一声哭了起来 burst out crying

蛙 wā (名) frog: ～泳 breaststroke

娃 wá (名) 1 baby; child 2 newborn animal

娃娃 wáwa (名) baby; child

瓦 wǎ (名) 1 tile 2 made of baked clay: ～器 earthenware 3 watt

see also wà

瓦房 wǎfáng (名) tile-roofed house

瓦匠 wǎjiang (名) bricklayer; tiler; plasterer

瓦解 wǎjiě (动) fall apart; collapse;

crumble

瓦砾(礫) wǎlì (名) rubble; debris: 一片～ a lot of debris; a heap of rubble

瓦斯 wǎsī (名) gas

瓦特 wǎtè (名) watt: ～计 wattmeter

袜(襪) wà (名)(～子) socks; stockings

瓦 wà (动) cover (a roof) with tiles; tile

see also wǎ

歪 wāi (形) 1 askew; crooked; inclined; slanting: 他～戴帽子. He wore his hat askew. 2 inappropriate; unhealthy: ～风邪气 unhealthy tendencies and evil practices

歪门(門)邪道 wāimén-xiédào crooked ways; underhand means; dishonest practices

歪曲 wāiqū (动) distort; misrepresent; twist: ～事实 distort the facts

歪歪扭扭 wāiwāiniǔniǔ (形) irregular; shapeless and twisted; awry: 字写得～的 write awkwardly and carelessly; write a poor hand

歪斜 wāixié (形) crooked; aslant

外 wài 1 outside: ～表 exterior; surface. 课～活动 extra-curricular activities 2 other: ～省 other provinces 3 foreign; external: ～商 foreign merchant. 对～贸易 foreign trade 4 (relatives) of one's mother, sisters or daughters: ～孙 daughter's son; grandson. ～祖母 maternal grandmother 5 remotely related: ～人 a stranger; an outsider 6 unofficial: ～传 unofficial biography; anecdote 7 besides; in addition; beyond: 此～ besides

外包 wàibāo (动) outsource: ～业务 outsourced project. 软件～ software outsourcing

外币(幣) wàibì (名) foreign currency: ～汇票 foreign currency bill. ～申报单 foreign currencies declaration

外表 wàibiǎo (名) outward appearance; exterior; surface: ～美观 have a fine exterior; look nice. 从～看人 judge people by appearances

外宾(賓) wàibīn (名) foreign guest (or visitor)

外部 wàibù (名) 1 outside; external: ～世界 the external world 2 exterior; surface

外层(層)空间 wàicéng kōngjiān (名) outer space

外钞 wàichāo (名) foreign currencies

外电(電) wàidiàn (名) dispatches from foreign news agencies

外观(觀) wàiguān (名) outward appearance; exterior

外国(國) wàiguó (名) foreign country: ～朋友 foreign friends. ～人 foreigner. ～语 foreign language

外行 wàiháng I (名) layman; nonprofessional II (形) lay; not professional: ～话 remarks of a layman; amateurish remarks

外号(號) wàihào (名) nickname

外患 wàihuàn (名) foreign aggression: 内忧～ domestic unrest and foreign aggression

外汇(匯) wàihuì (名) foreign exchange: ～储备 foreign exchange reserve. ～兑换率 rate of exchange. ～行情 exchange quotations

外籍 wàijí (名) foreign nationality: ～工作人员 foreign personnel

外交 wàijiāo (名) diplomacy; foreign affairs: ～关系 diplomatic relations. ～部 the Ministry of Foreign Affairs; the Foreign Ministry. ～部长 Minister of (or for) Foreign Affairs; Foreign Minister. ～辞令 diplomatic language. ～官 diplomat. ～护照 diplomatic passport. ～交涉 diplomatic representation. ～礼节 diplomatic protocal. ～签证 diplomatic visa. ～生涯 diplomatic career. ～姿态 diplomatic gesture. ～豁免权 diplomatic immunities. ～使节 diplomatic envoy. ～使团 diplomatic corps. ～特权 diplomatic prerogatives (or privileges). ～信袋 diplomatic pouch; diplomatic bag. ～信使 diplomatic courier. ～政策 foreign policy

外界 wàijiè (名) 1 the external (or outside) world 2 outside: 向～征求意见 solicit comments and suggestions from people outside one's organization

外科 wàikē (名) surgical department: ～手术 surgical operation; surgery. ～医生 surgeon

外快 wàikuài (名) extra income

外来(來) wàilái (形) outside; external; foreign: ～户 a household from another place; non-native. ～语 word of foreign origin; loanword

外流 wàiliú (动) outflow; drain: 人材～ brain drain

外卖(賣) wàimài (名) takeaway: 叫～ order a takeaway
外貌 wàimào (名) appearance; exterior; looks
外面 wàimian (名) outside; out: 在～吃饭 eat (or dine) out
外企 wàiqǐ (名) foreign enterprise; foreign-owned business
外强中干(乾) wàiqiáng-zhōnggān outwardly strong but inwardly weak
外勤 wàiqín (名) 1 work done outside the office or in the field (as surveying, prospecting, news gathering, etc.) 2 field personnel
外人 wàirén (名) 1 stranger; outsider: 你说吧,这里没有～. Speak up. You're among friends. 2 foreigner; alien
外甥 wàisheng (名) sister's son; nephew
外甥女 wàishengnǚ (名) sister's daughter; niece
外事 wàishì (名) foreign affairs: ～活动 external public functions. 地方～办公室 office in charge of local foreign affairs
外孙(孫) wàisūn (名) daughter's son; grandson
外孙(孫)女 wàisūnnǚ (名) daughter's daughter; granddaughter
外套 wàitào (名) 1 overcoat 2 cape
外务(務) wàiwù (名) 1 things that are outside the scope of one's own job 2 foreign affairs
外乡(鄉) wàixiāng (名) another part of the country: ～口音 a non-local accent
外销 wàixiāo (动) for sale abroad or in another part of the country
外衣 wàiyī (名) 1 outer garment 2 semblance; appearance; garb
外因 wàiyīn (名) external cause
外用 wàiyòng (动) for external use
外语 wàiyǔ (名) foreign language
外援 wàiyuán (名) foreign aid
外在 wàizài (形) external; extrinsic: ～因素 external factor
外债 wàizhài (名) external debt; foreign debt
外资 wàizī (名) foreign capital: 引进～ absorb foreign capital. ～企业 foreign enterprise

豌 wān

豌豆 wāndòu (名) pea

剜 wān (动) cut out

剜肉补(補)疮(瘡) wānròu-bǔchuāng seek to save a desperate situation by resorting to harmful practice

蜿 wān

蜿蜒 wānyán (动) wind; zigzag; meander: 小溪～ a meandering stream

弯(彎) wān I (形) curved; crooked: 树枝都被厚雪压～了. The branches are weighed down by a heavy layer of snow. II (动) bend; flex: ～弓 bend a bow III (名) curve; corner: 拐～儿 go round curves; turn a corner

弯路 wānlù (名) a zigzag path; detour
弯曲 wānqū (形) winding; meandering; zigzag; crooked; curved: 一条～的山间小道 a path which zigzags up the hill

湾(灣) wān (名) 1 a bend in a stream: 河～ river bend 2 gulf; bay

完 wán I (形) intact; whole: ～好 in good condition; intact II (动) 1 run out; use up: 我们的汽油快用～了. We are running out of petrol. 2 finish: 我要说的话～了. That's all I wanted to say. 3 pay: ～税 pay taxes

完备(備) wánbèi (形) complete; perfect: 有不～的地方,请多提意见. Please feel free to make your suggestions if there is anything we have neglected.
完毕(畢) wánbì (动) finish; complete; end: 一切准备～. Everything is in order.
完成 wánchéng (动) accomplish; complete; fulfil; bring to success (or fruition): ～任务 accomplish a task
完蛋 wándàn (动)〈口〉be finished for good; be done for
完好 wánhǎo (形) intact; whole; in good condition: ～无缺 intact; undamaged
完婚 wánhūn (动)〈书〉(of a man) get married; marry
完结 wánjié (动) end; be over; finish: 事情并没有～. This is not the end of the story.
完了 wánliǎo (动) come to an end; be over
完满(滿) wánmǎn (形) satisfactory; successful: 问题已～解决了. We have found a satisfactory solution to the problem.
完美 wánměi (形) perfect; consummate: ～无缺 perfect; flawless
完全 wánquán I (形) complete; whole: 他话

W

没说～. He didn't tell the whole story. II (副) completely; fully; wholly; entirely; absolutely: ～不同 be totally different. ～合格 fully competent. ～正确 perfectly right; absolutely correct

完善 wánshàn (形) perfect; complete: 设备～ very well equipped

完事 wánshì (动) finish; get through; come to an end: 你～了没有? Are you finished?

完整 wánzhěng (形) complete; integrated; intact: 维护领土～ safeguard territorial integrity

玩 wán I (动) 1 play; have fun: 我们在东京～了几天. We spent a few days in Tokyo. 2 engage in some kinds of sports or recreational activities: ～牌 play cards. ～足球 play football 3 employ; resort to: ～手段 resort to crafty manoeuvres; play tricks 4 trifle with; treat lightly: ～世不恭 cynical 5 enjoy; appreciate II (名) object for appreciation: 古～ curio; antique

玩忽 wánhū (动) neglect; trifle with: ～职守 negligence (or dereliction) of duty

玩具 wánjù (名) toy; plaything

玩弄 wánnòng (动) 1 dally with: ～女性 play fast and loose with a woman's affections 2 play with; juggle with: ～两面派手法 resort to double-dealing tactics

玩儿(兒)不转(轉) wánrbuzhuàn can't handle; can't manage

玩儿(兒)命 wánrmìng 1 gamble (or play) with one's life; risk one's life needlessly 2 exerting the utmost strength; for all one is worth; with all one's might: ～地干 work like hell

玩儿(兒)完 wánrwán 1 be done for; be finished 2 dead

玩赏 wánshǎng (动) enjoy; take pleasure (or delight) in: ～风景 enjoy (or admire) the scenery

玩味 wánwèi (动) ponder; ruminate: 他的话很值得～. His words are worth pondering.

玩笑 wánxiào (名) joke; jest: 开～ play a joke (or prank) on; make jests

顽 wán (形) 1 stupid; ignorant 2 stubborn; obstinate 3 naughty; mischievous

顽固 wángù (形) 1 obstinate; stubborn; headstrong: ～不化 incorrigibly obstinate 2 bitterly opposed to change; diehard: ～分子 diehard; a stick-in-the-mud 3 (of illness) hard to cure: ～症 stubborn disease

顽抗 wánkàng (动) stubbornly resist

顽皮 wánpí (形) naughty; mischievous

丸 wán (名) 1 ball; pellet 2 pill; bolus: 药～ pill (of Chinese medicine)

纨 wán (名)〈书〉 fine silk fabrics

纨袴子弟 wánkù zǐdì profligate son of the rich; fop; dandy

宛 wǎn〈书〉 as if: 音容～在 as if the person were still alive. ～如 just like; as if. ～如昨日 as if it were yesterday

惋 wǎn (动)〈书〉 sigh

惋惜 wǎnxī (动) feel regret at sth.; condole with sb. over sth. unfortunate

碗 wǎn (名) bowl

婉 wǎn (形) 1 gentle; gracious; tactful: ～商 consult with sb. tactfully 2 graceful; elegant; lovely

婉拒 wǎnjù (动) (courteously) decline

婉言 wǎnyán (名) gentle words; tactful expressions: ～谢绝 tactfully decline; politely refuse. ～相劝 gently persuade; plead tactfully

婉转(轉) wǎnzhuǎn (形) 1 mild and indirect; tactful; in a roundabout way: 措词～ put it tactfully 2 sweet and agreeable: 歌喉～ a sweet voice; sweet singing

挽 wǎn (动) 1 draw; pull: 手～手 arm in arm. ～留 urge one to stay on. ～救一个垂危的病人 rescue a patient who is gravely ill 2 roll up: ～起袖子 roll up one's sleeves 3 coil up 4 lament sb.'s death: ～诗 elegy

挽回 wǎnhuí (动) retrieve; redeem: ～败局 retrieve a defeat. 无可～ irretrievable; irrevocable. ～面子 save face. ～名誉 rehabilitate sb. ～损失 retrieve a loss. ～影响 redeem one's reputation

挽联(聯) wǎnlián (名) elegiac couplet

晚 wǎn I (名) evening; night: 今～ this evening; tonight II (形) 1 far on in time; late: 起得～ get up late. 现在学还不～. It's still not too late to learn. 2 younger; junior

晚安 wǎn'ān〈套〉 good night

晚报(報) wǎnbào (名) evening paper
晚辈 wǎnbèi (名) the younger generation; one's juniors
晚餐 wǎncān (名) supper; dinner
晚点(點) wǎndiǎn (of a train, ship, etc.) late; behind schedule
晚饭 wǎnfàn (名) supper; dinner
晚会(會) wǎnhuì (名) soirée; evening party: 除夕～ New Year's Eve entertainment
晚节(節) wǎnjié (名) integrity cherished in old age: 保持～ maintain moral integrity to the end of one's days
晚年 wǎnnián (名) old age; one's remaining years: 过着幸福的～ spend one's evening of life in happiness
晚期 wǎnqī (名) later period: ～疾病 terminal illness. ～癌症 terminal cancer
晚上 wǎnshàng (名) (in the) evening; (at) night
晚霞 wǎnxiá (名) sunset glow; sunset clouds

万(萬) wàn I (数) 1 ten thousand 2 a very great number; myriad: ～物 all things on earth; all nature II (副) absolutely; by all means: ～不得已 out of sheer necessity; as a last resort

万(萬) wàn (数) ten thousand [used for the numeral 万 on cheques, etc. to avoid mistakes or alterations]

万般 wànbān I (名) all the different kinds II (副) utterly; extremely: ～无奈 have no alternative (but to)
万端 wànduān (形) multifarious: 感慨～ a myriad of thoughts passed through one's mind
万恶(惡) wàn'è (形) extremely evil; absolutely vicious
万分 wànfēn (形) very much; extremely: ～抱歉 be extremely sorry
万古 wàngǔ (名) through the ages; eternally; forever: ～长存 last forever; be everlasting. ～长青 remain fresh forever; be everlasting
万花筒 wànhuātǒng (名) kaleidoscope
万籁俱寂 wànlài jù jì all is quiet; silence reigns supreme
万里长(長)城 Wànlǐ Chángchéng the Great Wall
万难(難) wànnán (副) extremely difficult; utterly impossible: ～照办 extremely difficult to comply with your request
万能 wànnéng (形) 1 omnipotent; all-powerful 2 universal; all-purpose: ～工具机 all-purpose machine
万千 wànqiān (形) multifarious; myriad: 变化～ eternally changing; ever changing. 思绪～ be overwhelmed with a myriad of thoughts and feelings
万全 wànquán (形) perfectly sound; surefire: ～之计 a completely safe plan
万世 wànshì (名) all ages; generation after generation
万事 wànshì (名) all things; everything: ～大吉. Everything is just fine. ～亨通. Everything goes well. ～开头难. Everything's hard in the beginning.
万岁(歲) wànsuì I (动) long live: 全世界人民大团结～! Long live the great unity of the people of the world! II (名) the emperor; Your Majesty; His Majesty
万万 wànwàn I (副) [used in negative sentences] absolutely: 那是～不行的. That's absolutely out of the question. 这是～没有想到的. This is the last thing I expected. II (数) a hundred million
万无(無)一失 wàn wú yī shī no danger of anything going wrong; no risk at all; perfectly safe
万象 wànxiàng (名) every phenomenon on earth; all manifestations of nature: ～更新 everything looks fresh and gay
万幸 wànxìng (形) very lucky; by sheer luck
万一 wànyī I (连) just in case; if by any chance II (名) 1 contingency; eventuality: 防备～ be ready for all eventualities 2 one ten-thousandth; a very small percentage
万丈 wànzhàng (形) lofty or bottomless: ～深渊 a bottomless chasm; abyss. 怒火～ a towering rage
万众(衆) wànzhòng (名) millions of people; the multitude
万状(狀) wànzhuàng (形) in the extreme; extremely: 惊恐～ be frightened out of one's senses
万紫千红 wànzǐ-qiānhóng a riot (or blaze) of colour

腕 wàn (名)(～子) wrist

汪 wāng

汪汪 wāngwāng I (形) with tears gathering in one's eyes; tearful: 泪～的 tearful II (象) bark; yap; bow-wow: 狗～地叫. A dog is yapping.

汪洋 wāngyáng (形) (of a body of water) vast; boundless: 一片~ a vast expanse of water

亡 wáng (动) 1 flee; run away: 出~ flee one's country; live in exile 2 lose 3 die; perish: 阵~ be killed in action

亡故 wánggù (动) die; pass away

亡国(國) wángguó I (动) cause a state to perish II (名) a subjugated nation: ~之民 the people of a conquered nation

亡命 wángmìng (动) 1 flee; seek refuge; go into exile 2 become desperate: ~之徒 desperado

王 wáng I (名) king; prince: 国~ king II (形) grand; great: ~父 grandfather

王八 wángba (名) 1 tortoise 2 cuckold: ~蛋 bastard; son of a bitch

王朝 wángcháo (名) 1 imperial court; royal court 2 dynasty

王储 wángchǔ (名) crown prince

王法 wángfǎ (名) the law of the land; the law

王府 wángfǔ (名) mansion of a prince

王宫 wánggōng (名) (imperial) palace

王国(國) wángguó (名) 1 kingdom 2 realm; domain: 由必然~到自由~ from the realm of necessity to the realm of freedom

王后 wánghòu (名) queen consort; queen

王牌 wángpái (名) trump card

王室 wángshì (名) 1 royal family 2 imperial court; royal court

王位 wángwèi (名) throne

王子 wángzǐ (名) prince

枉 wǎng I (形) crooked; erroneous: 矫~ right a wrong; set things to rights II (动) 1 twist; pervert: ~法 pervert the law 2 treat unjustly; wrong: 冤~ bring false charges against sb. 被冤~ be wronged III (副) in vain; to no avail: ~活了半辈子 waste half a lifetime

枉费 wǎngfèi (动) waste; try in vain; be of no avail: ~唇舌 waste one's breath

枉然 wǎngrán (形) futile; in vain; to no purpose

罔 wǎng 〈书〉 1 deceive: 欺~ deceive; cheat 2 no; not: 置若~闻 take no heed of; turn a deaf ear to

惘 wǎng (形) disappointed

惘然 wǎngrán (形) frustrated; disappointed: ~若失 feel disappointed

网(網) wǎng I (名) 1 net: 鱼~ fishing net. 蜘蛛~ cobweb 2 network: 铁路~ railway network II (动) catch with a net; net: ~着了一条鱼 net a fish

网吧 wǎngbā (名) Internet bar; cybercafé

网虫(蟲) wǎngchóng (名) Internet geek

网兜 wǎngdōu (名) string bag

网罗(羅) wǎngluó I (名) a net for catching fish or birds; trap II (动) enlist the services of: ~人才 recruit talented people; employ qualified personnel

网络 wǎngluò (名) network; internet; the net

网迷 wǎngmí (名) Internet buff

网民 wǎngmín (名) cyber citizen; netizen

网球 wǎngqiú (名) 1 tennis 2 tennis ball

网上 wǎngshàng (副) online; on the internet: ~游戏 online games

网页 wǎngyè (名) web page

网友 wǎngyǒu (名) net friend

网站 wǎngzhàn (名) web site

网址 wǎngzhǐ (名) network address

往 wǎng I (动) go: 来~于上海南京之间 travel to and fro between Nanjing and Shanghai II (介) in the direction of; to; toward: 这趟车开~上海. The train is bound for Shanghai. ~左拐 turn to the left. ~前走 go straight on III (形) past; previous: ~事 past events

往常 wǎngcháng (名) habitually in the past: 他~不这样. He was not like that in the past.

往返 wǎngfǎn (动) move to and fro: ~于伦敦与华盛顿 shuttle between London and Washington

往后(後) wǎnghòu (名) from now on; in the future

往还(還) wǎnghuán (动) keep in contact: 常有书信~ be in constant correspondence

往来(來) wǎnglái I (动) come and go II (名) contact; dealings; intercourse: 贸易~ trade contacts; commercial intercourse. 友好~ exchange of friendly visits; friendly intercourse. 保持~ maintain contact; keep in touch

往事 wǎngshì (名) the past; past events: ~

历历. The past is still fresh in our memory.

往往 wǎngwǎng (副) often; frequently; more often than not

往昔 wǎngxī (名) in the past; in former times

忘 wàng (动) 1 forget: 他把这事全~了. He clean forgot all about it. 2 overlook; neglect: 别~了给我打电话. Don't forget to give me a ring.

忘恩负义(義) wàng'ēn-fùyì ungrateful

忘怀(懷) wànghuái (动) forget; dismiss from one's mind: 国庆那次游行情景我真不能~. I can hardly dismiss from my mind the moving scene of the parade on National Day.

忘记 wàngjì (动) 1 forget 2 overlook; neglect

忘年交 wàngniánjiāo (名) 1 friendship between generations 2 good friends despite great difference in age

忘却 wàngquè (动) forget

忘我 wàngwǒ (形) oblivious of oneself; selfless: ~地工作 work selflessly; work untiringly

忘形 wàngxíng (动) be beside oneself (with glee, etc.): 得意~ get dizzy with success

妄 wàng (形) 1 absurd; preposterous: 狂~ preposterous and arrogant 2 presumptuous; rash: ~加评论 make presumptuous comments

妄动(動) wàngdòng (动) take rash (or reckless, ill-considered) actions: 轻举~ act rashly

妄念 wàngniàn (名) fantastic idea

妄求 wàngqiú (动) vainly hope

妄图(圖) wàngtú (动) try in vain; make a futile attempt to

妄想 wàngxiǎng I (名) vain hope; wishful thinking II (动) attempt in vain

妄自菲薄 wàng zì fěibó make a humble estimate of one's abilities

妄自尊大 wàng zì zūndà swell with preposterous self-importance

望 wàng I (动) 1 look at: 登山远~ climb up a mountain and look far into the distance; climb to the mountain-top for a distant view 2 call on; visit: 看~ pay a call on sb. 3 hope; expect: 大喜过~ be overjoyed with the unexpectedly good result. ~准时出席. You are requested to be present on time. II (名) 1 reputation; prestige: 德高~重 enjoy high prestige and command great respect 2 full moon

望尘(塵)莫及 wàng chén mò jí be lagging too far behind to catch up

望而生畏 wàng ér shēng wèi awe-inspiring; forbidding

望梅止渴 wàng méi zhǐkě quench one's thirst by thinking of sour plums

望文生义(義) wàng wén shēng yì misinterpret words through superficial understanding

望眼欲穿 wàng yǎn yù chuān look forward to sth. with great eagerness

望洋兴(興)叹(嘆) wàng yáng xīngtàn be bitterly aware of one's inadequacy when confronted with a real challenge

望远(遠)镜 wàngyuǎnjìng (名) telescope; binoculars

望族 wàngzú (名)〈书〉distinguished family; a family of social distinction

旺 wàng (形) prosperous; flourishing; vigorous

旺季 wàngjì (名) busy season

旺盛 wàngshèng (形) vigorous; exuberant: 士气~ have high morale

威 wēi (名) impressive strength; might: 军~ the might of an army; military prowess. 示~ demonstrate; demonstration

威逼 wēibī (动) threaten by force; coerce; intimidate: ~利诱 resort to both intimidation and bribery

威风(風) wēifēng I (名) power and prestige: ~扫地 thoroughly discredited II (形) imposing; impressive; awe-inspiring: ~凛凛 majestic-looking

威吓(嚇) wēihè (动) intimidate; threaten; bully

威力 wēilì (名) power; might

威名 wēimíng (名) legendary heroism

威慑(懾) wēishè (动) terrorize with military force; deter: ~力量 deterrent force; deterrent

威望 wēiwàng (名) prestige

威武 wēiwǔ I (名) might; force; power: ~不能屈 not to be cowed by force II (形) powerful; mighty

威胁(脅) wēixié (动) threaten; menace; imperil: ~世界和平 threaten world peace. ~利诱 coercion and bribery; stick and carrot

威信 wēixìn (名) prestige; popular trust

威严(嚴) wēiyán I (形) majestic; awe-inspiring: ～的仪仗队 an impressive guard of honour II (名) prestige; dignity

煨 wēi (动) 1 cook over a slow fire; stew; simmer 2 roast (sweet potatoes, etc.) in fresh cinders

偎 wēi (动) snuggle up to; cling to

偎依 wēiyī (动) snuggle up to; nestle up: 那女孩子～着母亲. The girl nestled up to her mother.

微 wēi (形) 1 minute; tiny: 细～ minute; tiny. ～风 gentle breeze. ～笑 smile. 谨小慎～ be overcautious 2 profound; abstruse: 精～ subtle 3 declined: 衰～ on the decline

微波 wēibō (名) microwave

微波炉(爐) wēibōlú (名) microwave oven

微薄 wēibó (形) meagre; scanty: 收入～ have a meagre income

微不足道 wēi bù zú dào of no consequence; insignificant; negligible

微分 wēifēn (名) differential: ～学 differential calculus

微观(觀) wēiguān (形) microcosmic: ～经济学 microeconomics

微乎其微 wēi hū qí wēi hardly noticeable; negligible

微妙 wēimiào (形) delicate; subtle: ～的关系 subtle relations. 这个事情很～. This is a very delicate affair.

微弱 wēiruò (形) faint; feeble: 光线～ a faint light; a glimmer

微生物 wēishēngwù (名) microorganism; microbe

微微 wēiwēi (形) slight; faint: ～一笑 give a faint smile

微小 wēixiǎo (形) small; little: 极其～ infinitely small; infinitesimal. ～的希望 a slim chance

微笑 wēixiào (动) smile: ～服务 service with a smile

微型 wēixíng (形) miniature; mini-: ～汽车 minicar; mini. ～照相机 miniature camera; minicam

逶 wēi

逶迤 wēiyí (形) winding; meandering: ～的山路 a stretch of winding mountain path

巍 wēi (形) towering; lofty

巍峨 wēi'é (形) towering; lofty: ～的群山 sprawling lofty mountain

巍然 wēirán (形) towering; lofty; majestic: ～屹立 stand lofty and firm

巍巍 wēiwēi (形) towering; lofty

危 wēi I (名) danger; peril: 居安思～ think of danger while you live in peace II (动) endanger; imperil: ～及生命 pose a threat to human life III (形) 1 dangerous 2 dying: 病～ be critically ill 3 〈书〉 proper: 正襟～坐 sit up properly

危殆 wēidài (形)〈书〉(of one's life or situation) in great danger

危害 wēihài (动) harm; endanger; jeopardize: ～健康 be harmful to one's health

危机(機) wēijī (名) crisis: 经济～ economic crisis. ～四伏 beset with crises

危急 wēijí (形) critical; in imminent danger; in a desperate situation: ～关头 critical juncture

危难(難) wēinàn (名) danger and disaster; calamity: 处于～之中 be faced with danger

危如累卵 wēi rú lěi luǎn in a precarious situation

危亡 wēiwáng (名) danger of extinction

危险(險) wēixiǎn (名、形) danger; dangerous; perilous: 脱离～ out of danger. ～品 dangerous articles

危言耸(聳)听(聽) wēiyánsǒngtīng paint an alarming picture of the situation just to scare the audience

危在旦夕 wēi zài dànxī in imminent danger; on the verge of death or destruction: 生命～. Death is expected at any moment.

为(爲) wéi I (动) 1 do; act: 敢作敢～ bold in action. 青年有～ a young man of promise 2 act as; serve as: 以此～凭. This will serve as a proof. 3 become: 变沙漠～良田 turn the desert into arable land 4 be; mean: 一公里～二华里. One kilometer is equivalent to two *li*. II (介) [used together with 所 to indicate a passive structure]: ～人民所爱戴 be loved and respected by the people; enjoy popular support see also wèi

为非作歹 wéifēi-zuòdǎi do evil; perpetrate outrages

为难(難) wéinán (动) 1 feel embarrassed: 令人～ embarrass sb.; put sb. in an awkward situation 2 make things difficult for: 故意～ make things difficult for sb.; be deliberately hard on sb.

为期 wéiqī (to be completed) by a definite date: 以两周～ not exceeding two weeks. 课程～三个月. The course of study covers three months. ～不远. The day is not far off.

为人 wéirén behave; conduct oneself: ～正直 be upright

为人师(師)表 wéi rén shībiǎo be worthy of the name of teacher; be a paragon of virtue and learning

为生 wéishēng (动) make a living

为首 wéishǒu with sb. as the leader; headed (or led) by

为数(數) wéishù (动) amount to; number: ～不少 come up to a large number; amount to quite a good deal

为所欲为(爲) wéi suǒ yù wéi go to any length to achieve one's wicked purpose

为伍 wéiwǔ (动) associate with: 羞与～ would be ashamed of sb.'s company

为止 wéizhǐ up to; till: 迄今～ up to now; so far

违(違) wéi (动) 1 disobey; violate: ～令 disobey orders. ～约 violate the agreement 2 be separated: 久～了. I haven't seen you for ages.

违背 wéibèi (动) violate; go against; run counter to: ～规章制度 fail to abide by the rules and regulations. ～诺言 go back on one's word; violate one's commitment

违法 wéifǎ (动) break the law; defy the law: ～乱纪 violate the law and discipline

违反 wéifǎn (动) violate; run counter to: ～历史潮流 to against the trend of history

违犯 wéifàn (动) violate: ～宪法 act in violation of the constitution

违规 wéiguī (动) violate regulations: ～操作 operate contrary to the rules

违纪 wéijì (动) violate discipline: ～行为 breach of discipline

违禁 wéijìn (动) violate a ban: ～品 contraband goods

违抗 wéikàng (动) disobey; defy: ～命令 disobey orders

违宪(憲) wéixiàn (动) violate the Constitution; be unconstitutional

违心 wéixīn (动) against one's will; contrary to one's intentions; insincere

违章 wéizhāng (动) break rules and regulations: ～行驶 drive against traffic regulations. ～作业 work in a risky way in violation of the rules

围(圍) wéi (动) enclose; surround: 包～ besiege; surround; encircle. 突～ break out of an encirclement

围攻 wéigōng (动) 1 besiege; lay siege to 2 jointly attack sb.: 遭到～ come under attack from all sides

围观(觀) wéiguān (动) (of a crowd of people) watch; look on: ～的人群 a crowd of onlookers

围歼(殲) wéijiān (动) surround and annihilate

围巾 wéijīn (名) muffler; scarf

围困 wéikùn (动) besiege; hem in; pin down: 把敌人～起来 pin down the enemy

围拢(攏) wéilǒng (动) crowd around

围棋 wéiqí (名) *weiqi*; Go

围墙(牆) wéiqiáng (名) enclosure; enclosing wall

围裙 wéiqún (名) apron

围绕(繞) wéirào (动) 1 move; round: 地球～着太阳旋转. The earth moves round the sun. 2 centre on; revolve round: 全厂职工～着改进生产方法提出很多建议. The staff and workers of the factory made a number of proposals for revamping the method of production.

惟 wéi I (副) 1 only; alone: ～你是问. You alone will be held responsible. 2 〈书〉 but: 他工作努力，～注意身体不够. He works hard but takes too little care of himself. II (名) thinking; thought: 思～ thinking

惟独(獨) wéidú (副) only; alone: 大家都来了，～他没来. Everybody has come except him.

惟恐 wéikǒng (动) for fear that; lest: ～落后 for fear that one should lag behind. 我几次提醒他，～他忘了. I reminded him several times lest he should forget.

惟利是图(圖) wéi lì shì tú be bent solely on profit; be intent on nothing but profit; put profit-making first

惟妙惟肖 wéimiào-wéixiào remarkably true to life; absolutely lifelike

惟命是听(聽) wéi mìng shì tīng obey orders from the higher-up, whatever they are

惟我独(獨)尊 wéi wǒ dú zūn extremely conceited

惟一 wéiyī (形) only; sole: ~可能的解决办法 the only possible solution. ~出路 the only way out. ~合法政府 the sole legal government. ~可行办法 the only feasible way

唯 wéi (副) only; alone

see also wěi

唯物辩(辯)证(證)法 wéiwù biànzhèngfǎ (名) materialist dialectics

唯物史观(觀) wéiwù shǐguān (名) materialist conception of history; historical materialism

唯物主义(義) wéiwùzhǔyì (名) materialism

唯心史观(觀) wéixīnshǐguān (名) idealist conception of history; historical idealism

唯心主义(義) wéixīnzhǔyì (名) idealism

唯一 wéiyī see "惟一" wéiyī

帷 wéi (名) curtain

帷幕 wéimù (名) heavy curtain

帷幄 wéiwò (名)〈书〉army tent: 运筹~ devise strategies within a command tent; ponder over problems of military strategy at a command post

维 wéi (动) 1 link 2 maintain; safeguard; preserve

维持 wéichí (动) keep; maintain; preserve: ~秩序 keep order. ~现状 maintain the status quo. ~生活 support oneself or one's family; survive

维和 wéihé (动) peace-keeping: ~部队 peace-keeping force

维护(護) wéihù (动) safeguard; defend; uphold: ~团结 uphold unity. ~国家主权 defend state sovereignty. ~和平部队 peace-keeping force

维棉 wéimián (名) vinylon and cotton blend

维尼纶(綸) wéinílún (名) vinylon

维权(權) wéiquán (动) safeguard legal rights

维生素 wéishēngsù (名) vitamin

维新 wéixīn (名) reform; modernization: 日本明治~ the Meiji Reformation of Japan (1868)

维修 wéixiū (动) keep in (good) repair; service; maintain: 设备~ maintenance (or upkeep) of equipment

桅 wéi (名) mast: ~杆 mast. ~顶 masthead

桅灯(燈) wéidēng (名) 1 masthead light 2 barn lantern

伪(僞) wěi (形) 1 false; fake; bogus: 真~ true and false. ~钞 counterfeit (or forged) bank note 2 puppet: ~政权 puppet regime

伪钞 wěichāo (名) counterfeit (or forged) bank note

伪君子 wěijūnzǐ (名) hypocrite

伪善 wěishàn (形) hypocritical: ~的言词 hypocritical words

伪造 wěizào (动) forge; falsify; fabricate; counterfeit: ~证件 forge a certificate. ~账目 falsify accounts

伪装(裝) wěizhuāng I (动) pretend; feign: ~中立 pretend to be neutral II (名) 1 disguise; guise; mask 2 camouflage

苇(葦) wěi (名) reed

苇箔 wěibó (名) reed matting

苇席 wěixí (名) reed mat

伟(偉) wěi (形) big; great: 身体魁~ tall and of a powerful build

伟大 wěidà (形) great; mighty: ~的政治家 a great statesman. ~的事业 a great undertaking. ~的胜利 a signal victory

伟人 wěirén (名) a great man

纬(緯) wěi (名) 1 weft; woof 2 latitude

纬度 wěidù (名) latitude: 高(低)~ high (low) latitudes

纬线(綫) wěixiàn (名) 1 parallel 2 weft

唯 wěi〈书〉yea

see also wéi

唯唯诺诺 wěiwěinuònuò never say "no" to one's superior; be always ready to agree with one's leader; be obedient and docile

委 wěi I (动) 1 entrust; appoint: ~以重任 entrust sb. with an important task 2 throw away; cast aside: ~弃 discard 3 shift: ~过于人 shift the blame on to sb. else II (形) 1 indirect; roundabout: ~婉 mild and roundabout; tactful 2 listless; dejected: ~靡 listless; dispirited III (名) end: 原~ the beginning and the end; the whole story

委靡 wěimǐ (形) listless; dispirited; dejected: 精神~ listless; dispirited. ~不振 in low spirits; lackadaisical

委派 wěipài (动) appoint; designate

委曲求全 wěiqū qiú quán be forced to compromise; to avert a showdown or a head-on confrontation; compromise for the sake of the overall interest

委屈 wěiqu (动) 1 feel wronged; nurse a grievance: 诉说～ pour out one's grievances (or troubles) 2 do wrong to (sb.) 3 put sb. to great inconvenience; suffer great inconvenience: 你只好～一点. You'll have to put up with it.

委任 wěirèn (动) appoint: ～状 certificate of appointment

委实(實) wěishí (副) really; indeed: 我～不知道. I really haven't the faintest idea.

委托 wěituō (动) entrust; trust: ～他做这项工作 entrust him with the work. ～商店 commission shop. ～书 trust deed; a power of attorney

委婉 wěiwǎn (形) mild and roundabout; tactful: ～的语气 a mild tone. ～语 euphemism

委员 wěiyuán (名) committee member: ～会 committee; commission; council

萎

wěi (动) wither; wilt; fade

萎缩 wěisuō (动) 1 wither; shrivel 2 (of a market, economy, etc.) shrink; sag

萎谢 wěixiè (动) wither; fade

猥

wěi (形) 1 numerous; multifarious: ～杂 miscellaneous 2 base; obscene; salacious; indecent

猥亵(褻) wěixiè I (形) obscene; salacious II (动) behave indecently towards (a woman)

尾

wěi I (名) 1 tail: 牛～ ox-tail 2 end: 排～ a person standing at the end of a line 3 remaining part; remnant: 扫～工程 the final phase of a project II (量) [for fish]: 两～鱼 two fish

尾巴 wěiba (名) 1 tail 2 tail-like part: 飞机～ the tail of a plane 3 servile adherent; appendage

尾大不掉 wěi dà bù diào (of an organization) too cumbersome to be effective

尾气(氣) wěiqì (名) tail exhaust: ～超标 excess tail exhaust

尾声(聲) wěishēng (名) 1 coda 2 epilogue: 序幕和～ prologue and epilogue 3 end: 节目已接近～. The performance is drawing to an end.

尾数(數) wěishù (名) odd amount in addition to the round number (usually of a credit balance)

尾随(隨) wěisuí (动) tail behind; follow at sb.'s heels; shadow

尾追 wěizhuī (动) in hot pursuit; hot on the trail of

娓

wěi

娓娓 wěiwěi (形) (talk) tirelessly: ～动听 speak most interestingly

为(爲)

wèi (介) 1 [indicating the object of one's act of service]: ～人民服务 serve the people 2 [indicating an objective]: ～方便起见 for the sake of convenience

see also wéi

为此 wèicǐ to this end; for this reason (or purpose); in this connection

为何 wèihé why; for what reason

为虎作伥(倀) wèi hǔ zuò chāng act as cat's paw for an evildoer

为人作嫁 wèi rén zuò jià single-mindedly work for the good of another without ever thinking of oneself

为什(甚)么(麽) wèishénme why; why (or how) is it that

未

wèi (副) 1 have not; did not: 尚～恢复健康 have not yet recovered (from illness) 2 not: ～知可否 not know whether it will be all right

未必 wèibì (副) may not; not necessarily: 他～知道. He doesn't necessarily know.

未便 wèibiàn (副) not be in a position to; find it hard to: ～擅自处理 find it inappropriate to handle the matter on my own

未卜先知 wèi bǔ xiān zhī know beforehand without casting lots; foresee; have foresight

未曾 wèicéng (副) have not; did not: ～听说过 have never heard of it

未尝(嘗) wèicháng (副) 1 have not; did not: ～见过. We have never seen it before. 2 [used before a negative word to indicate a probable affirmative]: 那样也～不可. That should be all right.

未成年 wèichéngnián not yet of age; under age: ～人 minor

未定 wèidìng uncertain; undecided; undefined: 会议地点～. The venue of the conference is not yet fixed. ～稿 draft. ～之天 uncertainty; a toss-up

未婚 wèihūn (形) unmarried; single: ～夫 fiancé. ～妻 fiancée

未决 wèijué (形) unsettled; outstanding: 悬而～的问题 an outstanding issue; an open (or a pending) question

未可 wèikě cannot: ～乐观 have no cause for optimism; nothing to be optimistic about. 前途～限量 have a brilliant future

未可厚非 wèi kě hòu fēi can hardly be blamed; beyond reproach

未来(來) wèilái (名) 1 coming; approaching; next; future: ～的一个世纪 the coming century; next century 2 future; tomorrow: 美好的～ a glorious future

未老先衰 wèi lǎo xiān shuāi prematurely senile; get old before one's time

未了 wèiliǎo unfinished; outstanding: ～事宜 unsettled matters; unfinished business. ～的心愿 an unfulfilled wish

未免 wèimiǎn (副) rather; a bit too; truly: 这～太过分. This is really going too far. 他～太谦虚了. He is being too modest. 他～有点不够冷静了. He is not really as cool as he should be.

未遂 wèisuì (动) not accomplished; abortive: ～罪 attempted crime. 政变～. The coup d'état aborted. 心愿～. My wish remains unfulfilled.

未完 wèiwán unfinished: ～待续 to be continued

未详 wèixiáng (动) unknown: 出处～. The source is unknown.

未雨绸缪 wèi yǔ chóumóu provide for a rainy day; take precautions

未知数(數) wèizhīshù (名) 1 an unknown quantity 2 uncertainty: 他能否成功还是个～. It's still uncertain whether he will succeed.

味 wèi (名) 1 taste; flavour: 滋～ relish; gusto. 谈得津津有～ talk with relish 2 smell; odour: 香～ a sweet smell; fragrance; aroma 3 interest: 文笔艰涩无～. The style is difficult and dull.

W

味道 wèidào (名) taste; flavour: 这个菜～很好. This dish is very nice. 他的话里有点讽刺的～. There's a touch of irony in his remarks.

味精 wèijīng (名) monosodium glutamate; gourmet powder; MSG

味同嚼蜡(蠟) wèi tóng jiáo là it is like chewing wax; it's as dry as sawdust

畏 wèi (动) 1 fear: 不～艰险 fear neither hardships nor danger. 望而生～ forbidding 2 respect: 后生可～. The younger generation is full of promise and so deserves respect.

畏惧(懼) wèijù (动) fear; dread: 无所～ be fearless

畏难(難) wèinán (动) be afraid of difficulty

畏怯 wèiqiè (形) cowardly; chickenhearted

畏首畏尾 wèishǒu-wèiwěi be full of misgivings; be timorous and hesitant

畏缩 wèisuō (动) shrink (or flinch) from difficulty or danger: ～不前 hang back in fear

畏途 wèitú (名)〈书〉a dangerous road: 视为～ be regarded as a course which people fear to pursue; be regarded as a dangerous course to be avoided

畏罪 wèizuì (动) dread punishment for one's crime: ～潜逃 abscond

喂 wèi I (叹) [used in greeting or to attract attention] hello; hey: ～, 你哪儿去了? Hey, where have you been? II (动) feed: ～奶 breastfeed; suckle; nurse. 给病人～饭 feed a patient

喂养(養) wèiyǎng (动) feed; raise; keep: ～家禽 raise poultry

胃 wèi (名) stomach: ～病 stomach trouble

胃口 wèikǒu (名) 1 appetite: ～好 have a good appetite. 没有～ have no appetite 2 liking: 这种音乐合他的～. This kind of music appeals to him.

谓 wèi I (动) 1 say: 所～ what is called 2 be called: 何～人造卫星? What is meant by a man-made satellite? 何～平衡? What is meant by equilibrium? II (名) meaning; sense: 无～的话 twaddle; meaningless talk

谓语 wèiyǔ (名) predicate

位 wèi I (名) 1 place; location: 坐～ seat. ～次 seating arrangement 2 position: 名～ fame and position 3 throne: 即～ come to the throne. 篡～ usurp the throne II (数) place; figure; digit. 个～ unit's place. 十～ ten's place. 四～数 four-digit number III (量) [polite form]: 四～客人 four guests

位于(於) wèiyú (动) be located; be situated; lie: ～亚洲东部 be situated in the eastern part of Asia

位置 wèizhi (名) 1 seat; place 2 position

位子 wèizi (名) seat; place

慰 wèi (动) 1 console; comfort: ～勉 comfort and encourage 2 be relieved: 知你通过考试, 甚～. I am pleased to hear that you have passed the exam.

慰劳(勞) wèiláo (动) bring gifts to people or send one's best wishes to them in recognition of their services

慰问 wèiwèn (动) express sympathy for: ～信 a letter of sympathy; sympathy note

蔚 wèi

蔚蓝(藍) wèilán (形) azure; sky blue: ～的天空 an azure sky

蔚然成风(風) wèirán chéng fēng become prevalent; become the order of the day

蔚为(爲)大观(觀) wèi wéi dàguān afford a magnificent spectacle

卫(衛) wèi (动) defend; guard; protect: 自～还击 fight back in self-defence

卫兵 wèibīng (名) guard; bodyguard

卫道 wèidào (动) defend traditional moral principles: ～士 apologist

卫队(隊) wèiduì (名) squad of bodyguards; armed escort

卫生 wèishēng (名) hygiene; health; sanitation: 讲～ pay attention to hygiene. 公共～ public health. ～间 toilet. ～球 camphor ball; mothball. ～纸 toilet paper. 环境～ environmental sanitation

卫戍 wèishù (动) garrison

卫星 wèixīng (名) 1 satellite 2 artificial satellite; man-made satellite: 气象～ weather satellite. 通讯～ communication satellite. ～城 satellite town

卫星电(電)视 wèixīng diànshì satellite television

温 wēn I (形) warm; lukewarm: ～水 lukewarm water II (名) temperature: 体～ temperature (of the body) III (动) 1 warm up: 把酒～一下 warm up the wine 2 review; revise: ～课 review (or revise) one's lessons

温饱 wēnbǎo (名) have enough to eat and wear; be tolerably well off

温差 wēnchā (名) difference in temperature; range of temperature

温床(牀) wēnchuáng (名) 1 hotbed 2 breeding ground

温存 wēncún (形) 1 attentive; emotionally attached (usu. to a person of the opposite sex) 2 gentle; kind

温带(帶) wēndài (名) temperate zone

温度 wēndù (名) temperature: 室内(外)～ indoor (outdoor) temperature. ～计 thermograph

温度表 wēndùbiǎo (名) thermometer: 摄氏～ centigrade (or Celsius) thermometer. 华氏～ Fahrenheit thermometer

温故知新 wēngù-zhīxīn 1 restudy what you have learnt and you will gain fresh insights 2 look at the past in perspective and you will gain an understanding of the present

温和 wēnhé (形) 1 temperate; mild; moderate: 气候～ a temperate climate; mild weather 2 gentle; mild: 性情～ have a gentle disposition; be good-natured. 语气～ speak in a mild tone

温暖 wēnnuǎn (形) warm: 天气～ warm weather

温情 wēnqíng (名) tender feeling; tenderheartedness

温泉 wēnquán (名) hot spring

温柔 wēnróu (形) gentle and soft

温室 wēnshì (名) hothouse; greenhouse; glasshouse; conservatory: ～效应 greenhouse effect

温顺 wēnshùn (形) gentle and docile

温文尔(爾)雅 wēnwén-ěryǎ urbane; gentle and cultivated

温习(習) wēnxí (动) review; revise: ～功课 review one's lessons

温驯 wēnxùn (形) (of animals) docile; tame

瘟 wēn (名) acute communicable diseases

瘟疫 wēnyì (名) pestilence

文 wén I (名) 1 character; script; writing: 甲骨～ inscriptions on oracle bones 2 language: 英～ the English language 3 literary composition; writing: 散～ prose. 韵～ verse. ～如其人. The style is the man. 4 literary language 5 culture: ～物 cultural relics II (形) 1 civilian; civil: ～职 civilian service 2 gentle; refined: 举止～雅 refined in manner III (动) cover up; whitewash: ～过饰非 gloss over one's faults IV (量) [for coins in the old days]: 一～钱 one penny. 一～不值 not worth a farthing

文本 wénběn (名) text; version: 本合同两种～同等有效. Both texts of the contract are equally valid (or authentic).

文笔(筆) wénbǐ (名) style of writing: ～流利 write in an easy and fluent style

文不对(對)题 wén bù duì tí the answer is irrelevant to the question

文采 wéncǎi (名) 1 rich and bright colours

2 literary talent

文辞(辭) wéncí (名) diction; language: ～优美 The essay is written in an elegant style.

文牍(牘) wéndú (名) official paper: ～主义 red tape

文法 wénfǎ (名) grammar

文风(風) wénfēng (名) style of writing

文告 wéngào (名) proclamation; statement

文工团(團) wéngōngtuán (名) song and dance ensemble; art troupe

文官 wénguān (名) civil servant: ～政府 a civilian government

文豪 wénháo (名) literary giant; great writer

文化 wénhuà (名) 1 civilization; culture 2 education; culture; schooling; literacy: 学～ acquire an elementary education; acquire literacy; learn to read and write. ～交流 cultural exchange. ～遗产 cultural heritage. ～参赞 cultural counsellor. ～馆 cultural centre. ～程度 educational level. ～用品 stationery

文集 wénjí (名) collected works

文件 wénjiàn (名) documents; papers; instruments

文教 wénjiào (名) culture and education: ～事业 cultural and educational work

文静 wénjìng (形) gentle and quiet

文具 wénjù (名) stationery: ～店 stationer's; stationery shop

文科 wénkē (名) liberal arts: ～院校 colleges of arts

文理 wénlǐ (名) unity and coherence in writing: ～通顺 be well written and well organized

文盲 wénmáng (名) illiterate; illiteracy

文明 wénmíng I (名) civilization; culture: 物质～ material civilization. 精神～ spiritual values II (形) civilized: ～社会 civilized society. ～行为 civilized behaviour

文凭(憑) wénpíng (名) diploma

文人 wénrén (名) man of letters; scholar

文书(書) wénshū (名) 1 document; official dispatch 2 copy clerk

文思 wénsī (名) the train of thought as expressed in writing: ～敏捷 have a facile pen. ～枯竭 one's creative flow is drying up

文坛(壇) wéntán (名) the literary world (arena, or circles); the world of letters

文体(體) wéntǐ (名) literary form; style: ～学 stylistics

文物 wénwù (名) cultural relics; historical relics

文献(獻) wénxiàn (名) document; literature: 历史～ historical documents

文选(選) wénxuǎn (名) selected works; selected essays

文学(學) wénxué (名) literature: ～家 writer. ～批评 literary criticism. ～作品 literary works

文艺(藝) wényì (名) art and literature: ～复兴 the Renaissance

文娱 wényú (名) cultural recreation; entertainment: ～活动 recreational activities

文摘 wénzhāi (名) digest

文章 wénzhāng (名) 1 essay; article 2 literary works; writings 3 hidden meaning; implied meaning: 看来他话里还有些～. It seems he made innuendoes about something in his remarks.

文质(質)彬彬 wénzhì bīnbīn urbane; refined and courteous

文字 wénzì (名) 1 characters; script; writing: 拼音～ alphabetic writing 2 written language 3 writing (as regards form or style): ～通顺 make smooth reading

蚊 wén (名)(～子) mosquito

蚊香 wénxiāng (名) mosquito coil incense

蚊帐(帳) wénzhàng (名) mosquito net

纹 wén (名) lines: 脸上的皱～ wrinkles. ～理 veins; grain

闻 wén I (动) 1 hear: ～讯 hear the news. 耳～不如目见. Seeing is believing. 2 smell: 你～～这是什么味儿? Here, smell and tell me what it is. II (名) news; story: 要～ important news III (形) well-known; famous: ～人 well-known figure; celebrity

闻风(風)丧(喪)胆(膽) wén fēng sàng dǎn become terror-stricken (or panic-stricken) on hearing the news

闻名 wénmíng (形) well known; famous; renowned: ～全世界 enjoy a high reputation throughout the world

紊 wěn (形) disorderly; confused

紊乱(亂) wěnluàn (形) disorderly; chaotic; in confusion: 秩序～ chaotic

稳(穩) wěn (形) 1 steady; stable; firm: 站～ stand firm. 局面～定. The situation is in control. 2 sure; certain: 这事你拿得～吗? Are you quite sure of it? ～操胜券 have all assurance of success

稳步 wěnbù（副）with steady steps; steadily: ～前进 advance steadily; make steady progress

稳当(當) wěndang（形）reliable; secure; safe: 办事～ act prudently

稳定 wěndìng I（形）stable; steady: 物价～. Prices remain stable. ～的多数 a stable majority II（动）stabilize; steady: ～物价 stabilize commodity prices

稳固 wěngù（形）firm; stable: ～的基础 a firm (or solid) foundation

稳健 wěnjiàn（形）firm; steady: 迈着～的步子 walk with steady steps; stride vigorously ahead

稳妥 wěntuǒ（形）safe; reliable: 我们要～一些. We have to be on the safe side.

稳重 wěnzhòng（形）(of speech, manner) calm and steady; unruffled

刎 wěn（动）cut one's throat: 自～ cut one's own throat; commit suicide

吻 wěn I（名）1 lips 2 an animal's mouth II（动）kiss

吻合 wěnhé（动）be identical; coincide; tally: 意见～ hold identical views

问 wèn（动）1 ask; inquire: ～事处 inquiry desk. 不懂就～. Don't hesitate to ask when you don't understand. 2 ask after; inquire after: 他每次信里都～起你. He always asks after you in his letters. 请替我～她好. Please send her my best regards. 3 interrogate; cross-examine: 审～ interrogate 4 hold responsible: 出了事唯你是～. If anything goes wrong, we'll hold you responsible for it. *or* You will be answerable for anything that may happen.

问安 wèn'ān（动）pay one's respects (usu. to elders); wish sb. good health

问道于(於)盲 wèn dào yú máng take a blind man as one's guide; seek enlightenment from an ignoramus

问寒问暖 wènhán-wènnuǎn show solicitous concern about sb.'s health or welfare

问好 wènhǎo（动）send one's regards to: 他向您～. He sends you his greetings.

问号(號) wènhào（名）1 question mark; query 2 unknown factor; open question

问候 wènhòu（动）send one's respects (or regards) to; extend greetings to: 致以亲切的～ extend cordial greetings

问津 wènjīn（动）〈书〉make inquiries (as about prices): 无人～ nobody cares to make inquiries about it

问世 wènshì（动）be published for the first time; come out

问题 wèntí（名）1 question; problem; issue: 关键～ a key problem. 原则～ a question of principle. 悬而未决的～ an outstanding issue. 有个～我要责问他. I have a bone to pick with him. 2 trouble; mishap: 他又出～了. He has got into trouble again.

问讯 wènxùn（动）inquire; ask: ～处 inquiry office; information desk

问罪 wènzuì（动）denounce; condemn: 兴师～ denounce sb. publicly for his serious errors

翁 wēng（名）1 old man: 渔～ an old fisherman 2 father 3 father-in-law

嗡 wēng（象）drone; buzz; hum: 蜜蜂～～地飞. Bees are buzzing all around.

瓮(甕) wèng（名）urn; earthen jar: 菜～ a jar for pickling vegetables

瓮中之鳖 wèngzhōng zhī biē be bottled up or trapped: 已成～ have fallen into the trap

涡(渦) wō（名）whirlpool; eddy: 水～ eddies of water

涡流 wōliú（名）the circular movement of a fluid; whirling fluid; eddy

窝(窩) wō I（名）1 nest: 鸟～ bird's nest. 鸡～ hen-coop 2 lair; den: 贼～ thieves' den. 土匪～ bandits' lair 3 a hollow part of the human body; pit: 夹肢～ armpit. 酒～ dimple II（动）1 harbour; shelter: ～赃 harbour stolen goods 2 hold in; check: ～火 be filled with pent-up rage 3 bend III（量）[for animals] litter; brood: 一～十只小猪 ten piglets at a litter

窝藏 wōcáng（动）harbour; shelter; hide: ～罪犯 give shelter to (or harbour) a criminal

窝工 wōgōng（动）hold-up in the work

窝囊 wōnang（形）1 feel vexed; be annoyed: 受～气 be obliged to bottle up one's feelings 2 hopelessly stupid; chicken-hearted

窝棚 wōpeng（名）shack; shed; shanty

窝窝头(頭) wōwotóu（名）steamed bread of corn, sorghum, etc. (also as "窝头")

W

莴(萵) wō

莴笋(筍) wōsǔn (名) asparagus

蜗(蝸) wō (名) snail: ～牛 snail

喔 wō (象) cock's crow: ～～～! Cock-a-doodle-doo!

我 wǒ (代) **1** I **2** we: ～方 our side; we. ～军 our army **3** [used together with 你 to mean "everyone"]: 你也帮, ～也帮, 他很快就赶上同班了. With everybody ready to help, he soon caught up with the rest of the class. **4** self: 忘～精神 selfless spirit

我们 wǒmen (代) we

我行我素 wǒ xíng wǒ sù stick to one's old way of doing things

沃 wò I (形) fertile; rich: ～土 fertile soil; rich soil II (动) irrigate: ～田 irrigate farmland

斡 wò

斡旋 wòxuán I (动) mediate II (名) good offices

卧 wò (动) **1** lie: 仰～ lie on one's back. ～床不起 be laid up in bed; be bedridden **2** (of animals or birds) crouch; sit

卧车(車) wòchē (名) **1** sleeping car; sleeping carriage; sleeper **2** automobile; car; limousine; sedan

卧铺(舖) wòpù (名) sleeping berth

卧室 wòshì (名) bedroom

握 wò (动) hold; grasp: ～紧拳头 clench one's fist

握别 wòbié (动) shake hands at parting; part

龌 wò

龌龊 wòchuò (形) dirty; filthy: 卑鄙～ sordid; despicable

污 wū I (名) dirt; filth: 去～剂 detergent II (形) **1** dirty; filthy: ～泥 mud **2** corrupt: ～吏 corrupt official III (动) defile; smear: 玷～ sully; tarnish

污点(點) wūdiǎn (名) stain

污垢 wūgòu (名) dirt; filth

污泥 wūní (名) mud; mire: ～浊水 filth and mire

污染 wūrǎn (动) pollute; contaminate: 空气～ air pollution. 环境～ environmental pollution. 精神～ cultural contamination; ideological pollution

污染源 wūrǎnyuán (名) source of pollution

污辱 wūrǔ (动) **1** humiliate; insult **2** sully; taint

污水 wūshuǐ (名) foul (or waste) water; sewage; slops: 生活～ domestic sewage. ～处理 sewage disposal; sewage treatment

污浊(濁) wūzhuó (形) (of air, water, etc.) dirty; muddy; filthy

巫 wū (名) witch; wizard: ～婆 witch; sorceress. ～术 witchcraft; sorcery

诬 wū (动) falsely accuse

诬告 wūgào (动) bring a false charge against sb.

诬害 wūhài (动) do harm to sb. by spreading rumours about him or by trumping up a charge

诬赖 wūlài (动) falsely accuse sb. (of doing evil or saying wicked things): ～好人 incriminate innocent people

诬蔑 wūmiè (动) slander; vilify: ～不实之词 slander and libel. 造谣～ calumny and slander

诬陷 wūxiàn (动) frame a case against sb.

乌(烏) wū I (名) crow II (形) black; dark: ～云 black clouds; dark clouds

乌龟(龜) wūguī (名) **1** tortoise: ～壳 tortoiseshell **2** cuckold

乌合之众(衆) wūhé zhī zhòng a horde of rough, lawless persons; rabble; mob

乌黑 wūhēi (形) pitch-black; jet-black

乌亮 wūliàng (形) glossy black; jet-black

乌七八糟 wūqībāzāo in a horrible mess; at sixes and sevens

乌纱帽 wūshāmào (名) (symbol of) official post

乌鸦 wūyā (名) crow

乌烟瘴气(氣) wūyān-zhàngqì foul atmosphere; pestilential atmosphere

乌有 wūyǒu (名)〈书〉nothing; naught: 化为～ vanish like soup bubbles; melt into thin air

乌云(雲) wūyún (名) black clouds; dark clouds

呜(嗚) wū (象) toot; hoot; zoom: 汽笛～～地叫. The whistle kept hooting.

呜呼 wūhū I (叹)〈书〉alas; alack II (动) die: 一命～ breathe one's last

呜咽 wūyè (动) sob

W

钨(鎢) wū (名) tungsten; wolfram (W): ~丝 tungsten filament

屋 wū (名) 1 house 2 room: 外~ anteroom

屋子 wūzi (名) room

无(無) wú I (名) nothing; nil: 从~到有 start from scratch II (动) not have; there is not; without: ~一定计划 have no definite plan III (副) not: ~须多谈 need not go into details

无比 wúbǐ (形) incomparable; unparalleled; matchless: 英勇~ unrivalled in bravery. ~强大 incomparably powerful

无边(邊)无际(際) wúbiān-wújì boundless; limitless; vast: ~的大海 a boundless ocean

无病呻吟 wú bìng shēnyín 1 sigh with grief over imaginary misfortune 2 (of literary works) superficially sentimental; mawkish emotion

无不 wúbù all without exception; invariably: 大家~为之感动. None were untouched. 在场的人~为之掉泪. Everybody present was moved to tears.

无产(產)阶(階)级 wúchǎnjiējí (名) the proletariat

无偿(償) wúcháng (形) free; gratis; gratuitous: ~经济援助 free economic aid

无常 wúcháng (形) variable; changeable: 反复~ capricious

无耻 wúchǐ (形) shameless; brazen; impudent: ~谰言 shameless slander

无从(從) wúcóng (副) have no way (of doing sth.); not be in a position (to do sth.): 心中千言万语, 一时~说起. So many ideas crowded in upon my mind that for a moment I did not know how to begin.

无党(黨)派人士 wúdǎngpài rénshì people without party affiliation; non-party people

无敌(敵) wúdí (形) unmatched; invincible; unconquerable

无底洞 wúdǐdòng (名) a bottomless pit

无地自容 wú dì zì róng wish that one could disappear from the face of the earth; feel utterly ashamed

无动(動)于(於)衷 wú dòng yú zhōng remain indifferent or apathetic

无独(獨)有偶 wúdú-yǒu'ǒu another person or thing comparable in stupidity or notoriety

无度 wúdù (形) immoderate; excessive: 挥霍~ squander wantonly

无端 wúduān (副) for no reason: ~生气 flare up without provocation

无恶(惡)不作 wú è bù zuò stop at nothing in doing evil; be deeply steeped in iniquity

无法 wúfǎ (副) unable; incapable: ~应付 unable to cope with. ~分析 defy analysis

无法无天 wúfǎ-wútiān defy laws human and divine; be neither God-fearing nor law-abiding; trample law underfoot without batting an eyelid

无妨 wúfáng (副) there's no harm; may (or might) as well: 有意见~直说. Feel free to speak out if you have anything on your mind.

无非 wúfēi (副) nothing but; no more than; simply; only: 他谈的~是些日常琐事. What he says is nothing but the trivial of everyday life.

无风(風)不起浪 wú fēng bù qǐ làng there is no smoke without fire

无辜 wúgū I (形) innocent II (名) innocent persons

无故 wúgù (副) without cause or reason: 不得~缺席. Nobody may be absent without reason.

无关(關) wúguān (动) have nothing to do with: 此事与他~. It has nothing to do with him. ~宏旨 not a matter of cardinal principle. ~大局 not affecting the general situation; insignificant; of little account. ~紧要 of no importance; immaterial

无轨电(電)车(車) wúguǐ diànchē trackless trolley; trolleybus

无机(機) wújī (形) inorganic: ~肥料 inorganic fertilizer; mineral fertilizer. ~化学 inorganic chemistry

无稽 wújī (形) unfounded: ~之谈 unfounded rumour; sheer nonsense

无几(幾) wújǐ (形) very few; very little; hardly any

无济(濟)于(於)事 wú jì yú shì be of no avail; won't help matters

无家可归(歸) wú jiā kě guī wander about with no home to go to; be homeless: ~者 the homeless

无价(價)之宝(寶) wú jià zhī bǎo priceless treasure

W

无精打采 wújīng-dǎcǎi listless; crestfallen; in low spirits

无可奈何 wúkě nàihé it can't be helped

无孔不入 wú kǒng bù rù (of persons) seek every opportunity (to do evil)

无愧 wúkuì (动) have nothing to be ashamed of: 问心～ have no guilty conscience

无赖 wúlài I (形) rascally; scoundrelly; blackguardly: 耍～ act shamelessly II (名) rascal

无理 wúlǐ (形) unreasonable; unjustifiable: ～取闹 kick up a row

无量 wúliàng (形) immeasurable; boundless: 前途～ a boundless future

无聊 wúliáo (形) 1 falling in a vacant mood; bored 2 boring and silly; vapid

无论(論) wúlùn (连) no matter what, how, etc.; regardless of: ～是谁都不许无故缺席. Nobody should be absent without cause, no matter who he is.

无论(論)如何 wúlùn rúhé in any case; at any rate; whatever happens; at all events: ～, 我们也得在今天做出决定. We've got to make a decision today, whatever happens.

无名 wúmíng (形) 1 unknown: ～英雄 unknown hero; unsung hero 2 indescribable

无奈 wúnài I (形) cannot help but; have no alternative: 他出于～, 只得辞职了事. He had no choice but to hand in his resignation. II (连) but; however: 他本来想今天出去野餐的, ～天不作美, 下起雨来, 只好作罢. He meant to go on a picnic today, but he had to call it off because of wet weather.

无能 wúnéng (形) incompetent; incapable: 软弱～ weak and incapable

无能为(爲)力 wú néng wéi lì powerless; impotent: 在这种情况下, 他要帮忙也是～. He was in no position to help under such circumstances.

无期徒刑 wúqī túxíng life imprisonment

无情 wúqíng (形) merciless; ruthless; inexorable

无穷(窮) wúqióng (形) infinite; endless; boundless; inexhaustible: 言有尽而意～. The words may be limited but the message they convey is an inexhaustible source of inspiration.

无权(權) wúquán have no right: ～干预 have no right to interfere

无任所大使 wúrènsuǒ dàshǐ roving ambassador; ambassador-at-large

无日 wúrì [followed by 不, meaning "every day"]: ～不在渴望祖国的现代化早日实现 We constantly look forward to the early realization of the country's modernization.

无伤(傷)大雅 wú shāng dàyǎ not affect matters of major principle

无上 wúshàng (形) supreme; paramount; highest: ～光荣 the highest honour

无神论(論) wúshénlùn (名) atheism

无声(聲)无臭 wúshēng-wúxiù unknown; obscure

无绳电(電)话 wúshéng diànhuà cordless telephone

无时(時)无刻 wúshí-wúkè all the time; incessantly: 地球～不在运转. The earth is in constant motion.

无事忙 wúshìmáng busy oneself over nothing; make much ado about nothing

无事生非 wú shì shēng fēi make so much ado about nothing

无视 wúshì (动) ignore; disregard; defy: ～国家的法律 defy the laws of the country

无数(數) wúshù I (形) innumerable; countless: ～次 for the umpteenth time II (动) feel uncertain

无双(雙) wúshuāng (形) peerless; unrivalled: 盖世～ peerless in this human world

无私 wúsī (形) unselfish: ～的援助 disinterested assistance

无所事事 wú suǒ shì shì be at a loose end; fool about; idle away one's time

无所适(適)从(從) wú suǒ shì cóng not know how to behave; be at a loss what to do

无所谓 wúsuǒwèi 1 cannot be taken as: 会谈取得了一些进展, 但～什么突破. Some progress has been made in the talks, but it cannot be regarded as a breakthrough. 2 not matter: 他去不去～. It makes no difference whether he is going or not.

无条(條)件 wútiáojiàn unconditional; without preconditions: ～投降 unconditional surrender

无微不至 wú wēi bù zhì (of cares, concern) meticulous; in every possible way: ～的关怀 solicitous care

无味 wúwèi (形) 1 tasteless; unpalatable 2 dull; uninteresting: 枯燥～ dry like sawdust

无畏 wúwèi (形) fearless; dauntless

无谓 wúwèi (形) meaningless; pointless; senseless: ~的争吵 a futile quarrel

无…无… wú…wú… [used before two parallel words, similar or identical in meaning to emphasize negation]: 无穷无尽 inexhaustible; endless. 无忧无虑 carefree

无暇 wúxiá (动) have no time; be too busy: ~兼顾 have no time to attend to other things

无线(綫) wúxiàn (形) wireless: ~电话 radiophone. ~电报 wireless telegram; radiotelegram

无线(綫)电(電) wúxiàndiàn (名) radio: ~通讯 radio communication. ~传真 radiofacsimile

无限 wúxiàn (形) infinite; limitless; boundless; immeasurable: ~光明的未来 a future of infinite brightness; infinitely bright prospects

无效 wúxiào (形) of (or to) no avail; invalid; null and void: 宣布合同~ declare a contract invalid (or null and void)

无懈可击(擊) wú xiè kě jī unassailable; invulnerable: 他的论点是~的. His argument is unassailable.

无心 wúxīn I (动) not be in the mood for: 他心里有事,~去看电影. He was not in the mood to go to the movies. II (形) not intentionally; unwittingly; inadvertently: 他~伤害你的感情. He did not mean to hurt your feelings.

无形 wúxíng I (形) invisible: ~的枷锁 invisible shackles II (副) imperceptibly; virtually

无休止 wúxiūzhǐ ceaseless; endless: ~地争论 argue on and on

无须 wúxū (副) need not; not have to: ~操心 need not worry

无烟煤 wúyānméi (名) anthracite

无恙 wúyàng (形)〈书〉 in good health; well; safe: 安然~ safe and sound

无业(業) wúyè 1 be out of work; be unemployed: ~游民 vagrant 2 have no property

无疑 wúyí (形) beyond doubt; undoubtedly: 确凿~ well established and irrefutable

无意 wúyì I (动) have no intention (of doing sth.); not be inclined to: 他既然~参加,你就不必勉强他了. There is no point in pressing him to join since he has no inclination to do so. II (形) inadvertently; accidentally: 对这件事他~中露了一句. He dropped a remark about it inadvertently.

无意识(識) wúyìshí (形) unconscious: ~的动作 an unconscious act (or movement)

无垠 wúyín (形) boundless; vast: 一望~ boundless beyond the horizon

无与(與)伦(倫)比 wú yǔ lúnbǐ incomparable; unparalleled; unique; without equal

无缘无故 wúyuán-wúgù without rhyme or reason; for no reason at all

无政府主义(義) wúzhèngfǔzhǔyì (名) anarchism

无知 wúzhī (形) ignorant: 出于~ out of ignorance

无中生有 wú zhōng shēng yǒu out of this air; purely fictitious; fabricated

无足轻(輕)重 wú zú qīng-zhòng of little importance (or consequence); insignificant

无阻 wúzǔ without let or hindrance

无罪 wúzuì (形) innocent; not guilty: ~释放 set a person free with a verdict of "not guilty"

芜(蕪) wú 〈书〉I (形) 1 overgrown with weeds: 荒~ lie waste 2 mixed and disorderly II (名) grassland: 平~ open grassland

芜杂(雜) wúzá (形) mixed and disorderly

吾 wú (代)〈书〉 I or we: ~辈 we. ~国 my or our country

毋 wú (副)〈书〉 no; not: ~妄言. Don't talk nonsense.

毋宁(寧) wúnìng (副) rather... (than); (not so much...) as

毋庸 wúyōng (副) need not: ~讳言 no need for reticence; frankly speaking

武 wǔ (形) 1 military 2 connected with martial arts 3 valiant

武打 wǔdǎ (名) acrobatic fighting in Chinese opera or film

武断(斷) wǔduàn (形) arbitrary

武官 wǔguān (名) 1 military officer 2 military attaché: 海(空)军~ naval (air) attaché

武库 wǔkù (名) arsenal; armoury

武力 wǔlì (名) 1 force 2 military force; armed strength; force of arms: 诉诸~ resort to force

武器 wǔqì (名) weapon; arms: 常规~ conventional weapons. 核~ nuclear weapons

武术(術) wǔshù (名) *wushu*, martial arts

武装(裝) wǔzhuāng I (名) **1** arms; military equipment; battle outfit: 全副～ (in) full battle gear; armed to the teeth **2** armed forces: 人民～ the armed forces of the people. ～部队 armed forces. ～冲突 armed clash. ～干涉 armed intervention. ～起义 armed uprising II (动) equip (or supply) with arms; arm: ～到牙齿 be armed to the teeth

妩(嫵) wǔ

妩媚 wǔmèi (形) lovely; charming

五

wǔ (数) five: ～十 fifty. ～倍 fivefold; quintuple. ～分之一 one fifth. ～十年代 the fifties

五彩 wǔcǎi I (名) the five colours (blue, yellow, red, white and black) II (形) multicoloured: ～缤纷 colourful; a riot of colour

五谷(穀) wǔgǔ (名) **1** the five cereals (rice, two kinds of millet, wheat and beans) **2** food crops: ～丰登 an abundant harvest of grain

五官 wǔguān (名) **1** the five sense organs (ears, eyes, lips, nose and tongue) **2** facial features: ～端正 have regular features

五光十色 wǔguāng-shísè **1** multicoloured; bright with all kinds of colours **2** of great variety; of all kinds; multifarious

五湖四海 wǔhú-sìhǎi all corners of the land

五花八门(門) wǔhuā-bāmén variegated; kaleidoscopic

五金 wǔjīn (名) **1** the five metals (gold, silver, copper, iron and tin) **2** metals; hardware: ～店 hardware store

五年计(計)划(劃) wǔnián jìhuà Five-Year Plan

五体(體)投地 wǔ tǐ tóu dì have nothing but the greatest admiration for sb.

五味 wǔwèi (名) **1** the five flavours (sweet, sour, bitter, pungent and salty) **2** all sorts of flavours

五星红旗 wǔxīng hóngqí the Five-Starred Red Flag (the national flag of the People's Republic of China)

五言诗 wǔyánshī (名) a poem with five characters to a line

五一 wǔyī (名) May Day: ～国际劳动节 International Labour Day; May Day

五月 wǔyuè (名) **1** May **2** the fifth month of the lunar year; the fifth moon: ～节 the Dragon Boat Festival (the 5th day of the 5th lunar month)

五岳 wǔyuè (名) the Five Mountains, namely, Taishan Mountain (泰山) in Shandong, Hengshan Mountain (衡山) in Hunan, Huashan Mountain (华山) in Shaanxi, Hengshan Mountain (恒山) in Shanxi and Songshan Mountain (嵩山) in Henan

五脏(臟) wǔzàng (名) the five internal organs (heart, liver, spleen, lungs and kidneys): ～六腑 the internal organs of the body; the viscera

伍

wǔ I (数) five [used for the numeral 五 on cheques, banknotes, etc. to avoid mistakes or alterations] II (名) **1** army; ranks: 入～ join the army **2** company: 羞与为～ feel ashamed of sb.'s company

捂

wǔ (动) seal; cover; muffle: ～鼻子 cover one's nose (with one's hand). ～盖子 keep the lid on; cover up the truth

午

wǔ (名) noon; midday

午饭 wǔfàn (名) midday meal; lunch

午时(時) wǔshí (名) the period of the day from 11 a.m. to 1 p.m.

午睡 wǔshuì I (名) afternoon nap II (动) take (or have) a nap after lunch

午夜 wǔyè (名) midnight

舞

wǔ I (名) dance: 集体～ group dance II (动) **1** dance **2** move about as in a dance: 手～足蹈 jump for joy **3** dance with sth. in one's hands: ～剑 perform a sword-dance **4** flourish; wield; brandish: 挥～大棒 brandish the big stick

舞弊 wǔbì (名) fraudulent practices; malpractices

舞蹈 wǔdǎo (名) dance: ～动作 dance movement. ～家 dancer

舞剧(劇) wǔjù (名) dance drama; ballet

舞弄 wǔnòng (动) wave; wield; brandish: ～刀枪 brandish swords and spears

舞台(臺) wǔtái (名) stage; arena: 在国际～上 in the international arena. ～监督 stage director. ～设计 stage design

舞文弄墨 wǔwén-nòngmò indulge in rhetorical flourishes; twist legal phraseology for dishonest purposes

侮

wǔ (动) insult; bully: 外～ foreign aggression

侮辱 wǔrǔ (动) insult; humiliate; subject

sb. to indignities

误 wù I (名) mistake; error: 失~ error. 笔~ a slip of the pen II (动) **1** miss: ~了回家的最后一趟公共汽车 miss the last bus home **2** harm: ~人子弟 fail to give proper guidance to; exercise a harmful influence on the younger generation III (形) unintentionally; by accident: ~伤 accidentally hurt sb.; give unintentional offence to sb.

误差 wùchā (名) error: 平均~ mean error; average error

误点(點) wùdiǎn (动) late; overdue; behind schedule: 火车~十分钟. The train was ten minutes late (or behind schedule).

误会(會) wùhuì I (动) misunderstand; mistake; misconstrue: 你~了我的意思. You misunderstand me. II (名) misunderstanding: 消除~ dispel (or remove) misunderstanding

误解 wùjiě I (动) misread; misunderstand II (名) misunderstanding

误诊 wùzhěn (动) make a wrong diagnosis: ~病例 missed case

恶(惡) wù (动) loathe; dislike; hate: 好逸~劳 dislike work and love ease and comfort. 可~ loathsome; abominable
see also ě; è

悟 wù (动) realize; awaken: 执迷不~ persist in one's erroneous course

悟性 wùxìng (名) power of understanding; comprehension

晤 wù (动) meet; interview; see: 会~ meet with. ~谈 meet and talk; have a talk; interview

务(務) wù I (名) affair; business: 外~ foreign affairs. 公~ official business. 任~ task; job II (动) be engaged in; devote one's efforts to: ~农 go in for agriculture. 不~正业 neglect one's proper duties

务必 wùbì (副) must; be sure to

务实(實) wùshí (动) deal with concrete matters relating to work; be pragmatic: ~的政治家 a pragmatic politician

雾(霧) wù (名) **1** fog: 薄~ mist **2** fine spray: 喷~器 sprayer; inhaler

雾气(氣) wùqì (名) fog; mist; vapour

勿 wù (副) [indicating prohibition]: 请~入内. No admittance. 请~吸烟. No smoking.

物 wù (名) **1** thing; matter: 废~ waste matter. 公~ public property. 地大~博 vast in territory and rich in resources **2** the outside world; other people: 待人接~ one's conduct in social intercourse **3** content; substance: 空洞无~ totally void of substance

物产(產) wùchǎn (名) products; produce

物换星移 wùhuàn-xīngyí change of the seasons

物极(極)必反 wù jí bì fǎn things will develop in the opposite direction when they reach the limit

物价(價) wùjià (名) (commodity) price: ~波动 price fluctuation. ~指数 price index

物件 wùjiàn (名) thing; article

物理 wùlǐ (名) **1** innate laws of things **2** physics

物理学(學) wùlǐxué (名) physics

物力 wùlì (名) material resources

物流 wùliú (名) logistics; distribution

物品 wùpǐn (名) article; goods: 贵重~ valuables. 个人~ personal effects

物色 wùsè (动) look for; select: ~人才 look for qualified personnel

物业(業) wùyè (名) **1** property; real estate **2** property management: ~公司 real estate (or property) management company

物以类(類)聚 wù yǐ lèi jù birds of a feather flock together

物议(議) wùyì (名) public criticism or censure

物证 wùzhèng (名) material evidence

物质(質) wùzhì (名) matter; substance; material: ~生活 material life. ~刺激 material incentive

物质(質)文明 wùzhì wénmíng material civilization

物资 wùzī (名) goods and materials: ~交流 interflow of commodities

坞(塢) wù (名) a depressed place: 船~ dock. 花~ sunken flower bed

骛 wù (动) go after; seek for: 好高~远 set too high a demand on oneself; set one's sights too high

X x

曦 xī (名)〈书〉sunlight [usu. referring to that in early morning]: 晨～ early morning sunlight

熹 xī (名)〈书〉break of day

熹微 xīwēi (形)〈书〉(usu. of morning sunlight) faint; feeble

嘻 xī I (叹) a cry of surprise II (象) [sound of laughter]: ～～地笑 giggle

嬉 xī (动) play; sport

嬉皮笑脸 xīpí-xiàoliǎn give a merry roguish laugh; laugh roguishly and play the fool; be frivolous

嬉戏(戲) xīxì (动) play; sport

昔 xī (名) former times; the past: ～日 in former times

惜 xī (动) 1 cherish; treasure: 珍～ cherish; treasure 2 spare; stint; grudge: 不～代价 at any cost. 可～! It is a pity! 3 have pity on sb.

惜别 xībié (动) feel reluctant to part

熙 xī

熙熙攘攘 xīxīrǎngrǎng bustling with life; be a beehive of activity

析 xī (动) 1 divide; separate: 分崩离～ fall to pieces; come apart 2 analyse; dissect: 剖～ analyse; dissect

析出 xīchū (动) separate out

晰 xī (形) clear; distinct: 明～ clear; lucid. 清～ distinct

西 xī (名) west

西半球 xībànqiú (名) the Western Hemisphere

西餐 xīcān (名) Western-style food; European food: ～馆 a restaurant which serves Western food

西藏 Xīzàng (名) Xizang (Tibet)

西方 xīfāng (名) 1 the west 2 the West; the Occident: ～世界 the Western world

西服 xīfú (名) Western-style clothes (also as "西装")

西瓜 xīguā (名) watermelon: ～子 watermelon seed

西红柿 xīhóngshì (名) tomato

西化 xīhuà (动) westernize

西天 xītiān (名) (in Buddhism) Western Paradise

西洋 Xīyáng (名) the West; the Western world

西药(藥) xīyào (名) Western medicine

西医(醫) xīyī (名) 1 Western medicine 2 a doctor trained in Western medicine

牺(犧) xī

牺牲 xīshēng I (名) sacrifice II (动) lay down one's life: 英勇～ meet one's death like a hero

锡 xī (名) tin (Sn)

吸 xī (动) 1 inhale; breathe in: 深深～一口气 take a deep breath. ～了一口烟 take a puff at one's cigarettes 2 absorb: 宣纸～水性强. Rice paper is absorbent. 3 attract; draw to oneself

吸尘(塵)器 xīchénqì (名) vacuum cleaner

吸毒 xīdú (动) take drugs: ～者 drug addict

吸附 xīfù (名) absorption

吸力 xīlì (名) suction; attraction: 地心～ force of gravity

吸墨纸 xīmòzhǐ (名) blotting paper

吸纳 xīnà (动) absorb: ～农村剩余劳动力 absorb rural surplus manpower

吸取 xīqǔ (动) draw; assimilate: ～教训 learn (draw) a lesson

吸收 xīshōu (动) 1 absorb; assimilate; imbibe: ～营养 absorb nourishment 2 recruit; enrol; admit: ～入党 admit into the Party

吸铁(鐵)石 xītiěshí (名) magnet

吸血鬼 xīxuèguǐ (名) bloodsucker; vampire

吸烟 xīyān (动) smoke

吸引 xīyǐn (动) attract; draw; fascinate: ～注意力 attract attention. 大自然的美把我们～住了. We were fascinated by the beauty of nature.

奚 xī

奚落 xīluò (动) make gibes about; taunt

溪 xī (名) small stream; brook

希 xī I (动) hope: ～准时出席 Be sure to turn up on time. II (形) rare; uncommon

希罕 xīhan I (形) rare; uncommon: ～的动物 a rare animal II (动) value as a rarity; cherish: 我才不～他的帮助呢! I couldn't care for his offer of help. III (名) rare thing; rarity

希奇 xīqí (形) rare; curious: 这种事并不～. This is no rare occurrence. *or* There is nothing strange about it.

希望 xīwàng (动、名) hope; wish; expect: 他～当个医生. He hopes to become a doctor 有～的青年 a promising young man

稀 xī (形) 1 scarce; uncommon: 物以～为贵. Things become precious when they are scarce. 2 sparse; scattered: 地广人～ vast in area but sparsely populated 3 watery; thin: ～饭 porridge; gruel

稀薄 xībó (形) thin; rare: 空气～. The air is thin.

稀饭 xīfàn (名) rice or millet gruel; porridge

稀客 xīkè (名) rare visitor

稀烂(爛) xīlàn (形) completely smashed; smashed to pieces: 花瓶被打得～. The vase is smashed to smithereens.

稀里(裏)糊涂(塗) xīlihútu (形) muddleheaded

稀少 xīshǎo (形) few; rare; scarce

稀释(釋) xīshì (动) dilute

稀疏 xīshū (形) sparse; thin: 头发～ thin hair. 山区村落～. The villages are straggling in the mountainous area. 林木～. The woods are sparse.

悉 xī (动) know; learn: 熟～ be well acquainted with

息 xī I (名) 1 breath: 屏～ hold one's breath 2 news: 信～ news about sb. or sth.; information 3 interest: 利～ interest. 无～贷款 interest-free loan 4 rest: 安～ sleep. 作～时间表 timetable; programme II (动) stop; cease: 请～怒. Don't get excited. 经久不～的掌声 prolonged applause. 暴风雨已经平～. The storm has subsided.

息事宁(寧)人 xīshì-níngrén let the matter rest so as to annoy nobody

息息相关(關) xīxī xiāng guān be closely linked; be closely bound up

熄 xī (动) put out; extinguish: ～灯 lights-out

熄灭(滅) xīmiè (动) (of fire) go out; die out

夕 xī (名) sunset; evening: 除～ New Year's Eve. 命在旦～ on one's last legs

夕阳(陽) xīyáng (名) the setting sun

夕照 xīzhào (名) the glow of the setting sun

膝 xī (名) knee

膝盖(蓋) xīgài (名) knee

犀 xī (名) rhinoceros: ～牛 rhinoceros

犀利 xīlì (形) sharp; incisive: 文笔～ wield a trenchant pen

席 xí I (名) 1 mat 2 seat; place: 入～ take one's seat. 来宾～ seats for visitors. 在议会中取得三～ win three seats in Parliament 3 feast; banquet: 酒～ banquet II (量): 一～酒 a banquet. 一～话 a talk (with sb.); a conversation

席地 xídì (副) (sit or lie) on the ground: ～而坐 sit on the ground

席卷(捲) xíjuǎn (动) sweep across; engulf: 暴风雪～大草原. A blizzard swept across the vast grasslands.

席位 xíwèi (名) seat (at a conference, in a legislative assembly, etc.): 永久～ permanent seat

袭(襲) xí (动) 1 raid: 偷～敌军 make a sneak attack on the enemy. 寒气～人. There is a nip in the air. 2 follow the pattern of: 抄～ plagiarize

袭击(擊) xíjī (动) attack; raid: 这一带经常受到台风的～. This area is often hit by typhoons.

袭用 xíyòng (动) take over (sth. that has long been used in the past)

媳 xí (名) daughter-in-law

媳妇(婦) xífù (名) son's wife; daughter-in-law

媳妇(婦)儿(兒) xífur (名) 1 wife 2 a young married woman

习(習) xí I (动) 1 practise; exercise; review: 练～ practise. 复～ review (one's lessons). 实～ do field work. 实～医生 intern 2 be used to: 不～水性 be not good at swimming II (名) habit; custom; usual practice

习惯 xíguàn I (动) get used (or accustomed) to: 过几天你就会～这儿了. You'll get used to the place in a few days. II (名) habit; custom: 旧～ outmoded customs. ～成自然. Habit grows on a person as second nature. ～势力 force of habit

习气(氣) xíqì (名) custom; practice: 官僚～

bureaucratic practice
习染 xírǎn (动) contract (disease); be addicted to
习俗 xísú (名) custom; convention
习题 xítí (名) exercises (in school work)
习性 xíxìng (名) habits and acquired characteristics
习以为(爲)常 xí yǐ wéi cháng be used (or accustomed, inured) to sth.
习语 xíyǔ (名) idiom
习作 xízuò (名) an exercise in composition, drawing, etc.

喜 xǐ I (形) happy; pleased: 大～ highly pleased II (动) like; be fond of: ～新厌旧 be fickle in one's affections III (名) 1 happiness; happy event: 大～的日子 a day of great joy. 双～临门 be blessed with double happiness 2 pregnancy: 有～了 be expecting a baby
喜爱(愛) xǐ'ài (动) like; be fond of
喜报(報) xǐbào (名) a bulletin of glad tidings: 大红～ a report of happy tidings written on crimson paper
喜出望外 xǐ chū wàng wài be overjoyed at the unexpectedly good news; be pleasantly surprised
喜好 xǐhào (动) be fond of; be keen on: 他从小就～绘画. He has been fond of painting ever since his childhood.
喜欢(歡) xǐhuan (动) 1 like; love; be fond of 2 be happy; feel delighted
喜剧(劇) xǐjù (名) comedy
喜怒无(無)常 xǐ-nù wú cháng moody
喜气(氣)洋洋 xǐqì yángyáng in a happy mood
喜鹊 xǐquè (名) magpie
喜事 xǐshì (名) 1 a happy event; a joyous occasion: 瞧你这么高兴，有什么～? You look so happy. What's the good news? 2 marriage; wedding: 什么时候办～? When will the marriage (or wedding) take place?
喜闻乐(樂)见(見) xǐwén-lèjiàn love to see and hear; be enjoyed by
喜笑颜开(開) xǐxiào-yánkāi (of one's face) light up with pleasure; brighten up
喜形于(於)色 xǐ xíng yú sè be visibly pleased; beam with pleasure
喜讯 xǐxùn (名) happy news; good news
喜洋洋 xǐyángyáng (形) full of joy; jubilant
喜悦 xǐyuè (形) happy; joyous: 怀着无限～的心情 cherish a feeling of indescribable joy

洗 xǐ (动) 1 wash: ～衣服 wash clothes. 干～ dry-cleaning. ～衣粉 detergent. ～澡 take a bath; swim 2 kill and loot; sack: 血～ plunge (the inhabitants) in a bloodbath; massacre
洗尘(塵) xǐchén (动) give a dinner in honour of a visitor from afar
洗涤(滌) xǐdí (动) wash; cleanse
洗耳恭听(聽) xǐ ěr gōng tīng listen with respectful attention
洗发(髮)剂(劑) xǐfàjì (名) shampoo
洗劫 xǐjié (动) loot; sack
洗礼(禮) xǐlǐ (名) baptism
洗牌 xǐpái (动) shuffle (cards, etc.)
洗钱(錢) xǐqián (动) money laundering
洗染店 xǐrǎndiàn (名) laundering and dyeing shop
洗手 xǐshǒu (动) 1 wash one's hands: ～间 toilet; lavatory; washroom; rest room 2 refuse to have anything more to do with sth.: ～不干 wash one's hands of sth.
洗刷 xǐshuā (动) 1 wash and brush; scrub 2 wash off
洗心革面 xǐxīn-gémiàn thoroughly reform oneself; turn over a new leaf
洗雪 xǐxuě (动) wipe out (a disgrace); redress (a wrong)
洗衣 xǐyī (动) do washing; do laundry: ～机 washing machine. ～房 laundry; dry-cleaner
洗照片 xǐ zhàopiàn develop a film

铣 xǐ (动) mill; cut or shape (metal) with a rotating tool

玺(璽) xǐ (名) imperial or royal seal

隙 xì (名) 1 crack; chink: 墙～ a crack in the wall 2 loophole; chance: 无～可乘 leave or find no loophole that one could take advantage of

系 xì I (名) 1 system; series: 语～ (language) family. 太阳～ the solar system. 母～ matriarchy. 派～ faction 2 department (in a college); faculty II (动) 1 (係) be 〈书〉纯～揣测之事 be purely a matter of conjecture 2 (係) relate to: 成败所～ something on which success or failure hinges 3 (繫) tie; fasten: ～马 tether a horse
see also jì
系列 xìliè (名) set; series: 一～的问题 a series of problems
系统 xìtǒng (名) system: 灌溉～ irrigation

X

system. 卫生～ public health organizations. 作～的研究 make a systematic study

戏(戲) xì I (名) play; show: 京～ Beijing opera. 马～ circus show. 看～ go to the theatre; watch a play II (动) 1 play: ～水 play with water 2 make fun of; tease

戏法 xìfǎ (名) conjuring; magic; trick: 变～ conjure; juggle; perform tricks

戏剧(劇) xìjù (名) drama; play

戏弄 xìnòng (动) make fun of; play tricks on

戏曲 xìqǔ (名) traditional opera

戏说 xìshuō (动) render a playful version (of history); playful narrative

戏言 xìyán (名) joking remarks; pleasantries

戏院 xìyuàn (名) theatre

细 xì (形) 1 thin; slender 2 in tiny particles: ～沙 fine sand 3 fine; delicate: ～瓷 fine porcelain. 做工真～! What fine craftsmanship! 4 careful; meticulous; detailed: ～看 examine; scrutinize. ～问 make inquiries; ask about detailed information; interrogate 5 minute; trifling: ～节 minute details

细胞 xìbāo (名) cell

细节(節) xìjié (名) details; particulars

细菌 xìjūn (名) germs; bacteria

细粮(糧) xìliáng (名) fine food grain (usu. referring to wheat flour and rice)

细密 xìmì (形) fine and closely woven

细腻 xìnì (形) 1 fine and smooth 2 exquisite; minute: ～的描写 a minute description

细软 xìruǎn (名) jewelry, expensive clothing and other valuables

细水长(長)流 xìshuǐ cháng liú 1 economize on either human labour or natural resources to avoid running short 2 make a moderate but constant effort

细微 xìwēi (形) slight; fine; subtle: ～的区别 subtle difference

细小 xìxiǎo (形) tiny; fine; trivial: ～的事情 trivialities

细心 xìxīn (形) careful; attentive

细则 xìzé (名) detailed rules and regulations; by-laws

细致(緻) xìzhì (形) careful; meticulous: ～的安排 meticulous arrangement

瞎 xiā I (形) blind II (动) become blind: ～了左眼 blind in the left eye III (副) groundlessly; aimlessly: ～说 talk irresponsibly; speak groundlessly; talk nonsense. ～猜 make a wild guess. ～忙 work hard for nothing. ～闹 behave foolishly

瞎扯 xiāchě (动) talk irresponsibly; talk rubbish

瞎话 xiāhuà (名) lie: 说～ tell a lie; lie

瞎指挥 xiāzhǐhuī (动) issue confused orders; boss sb. around

瞎子 xiāzi (名) a blind person

虾(蝦) xiā (名) shrimp: 对～ prawn. 龙～ lobster. ～米 dried, shelled shrimps

呷 xiā (动) sip: ～一口茶 take a sip of tea

峡(峽) xiá (名) gorge: ～谷 gorge; canyon. 海～ strait

侠(俠) xiá

侠客 xiákè (名) (in old times) a chivalrous swordsman

侠义(義) xiáyì (形) chivalrous: ～行为 chivalrous conduct

狭(狹) xiá (形) narrow

狭隘 xiá'ài (形) narrow: 山路崎岖～. The mountain path is rugged and narrow. 心胸～ be narrow-minded

狭路相逢 xiálù xiāng féng (of adversaries) happen to meet on a narrow path; when two enemies meet, neither will yield

狭小 xiáxiǎo (形) narrow and small: 气量～ be narrow-minded

狭义(義) xiáyì (名) narrow sense: ～而言 strictly speaking

狭窄 xiázhǎi (形) 1 narrow; cramped: ～的楼梯 narrow staircase 2 narrow and limited: 心地～ be narrow-minded

辖 xiá (动) govern: ～区 region under one's jurisdiction

遐 xiá (形)〈书〉 far; distant

遐迩(邇) xiá'ěr (名)〈书〉 far and near: 闻名～ one's reputation spread far and wide

霞 xiá (名) morning or evening glow: 晚～ sunset clouds. 彩～ rosy clouds

瑕 xiá (名) flaw; defect

瑕疵 xiácī (名) flaw; blemish

暇 xiá (名) free time; leisure: 无～兼顾 have no time to attend to other matters

下 xià I (名) down; under; below: 往~走 go down. 楼~ downstairs. 桌~ under the table. 井~ at the bottom of a well. 地~宫殿 underground palace. 零~三度 three degrees below zero. 在他领导~ under his guidance II (形) 1 lower; inferior: ~级 lower rank; inferior. ~等 low grade 2 next: ~次 next time III (动) 1 descend; get off: ~楼 go downstairs. ~车 get off a bus. ~馆子 eat or dine out in a restaurant 2 (of rain, snow, etc.) fall: ~雨了. It's raining. 3 issue: ~命令 issue orders. ~通知 give notices. 4 put in: ~饺子 put dumplings in (boiling water). ~面条 cook noodles 5 form (an idea, opinion, etc.): ~决心 make up one's mind. ~结论 draw a conclusion. ~定义 give a definition 6 finish (work, etc.): ~班 go off duty; knock off. ~课了. Class is over. 7 (of animals) give birth to; lay: ~蛋 lay eggs. ~了四只小猫 give birth to four kittens 8 take off; dismantle: 把门~下来 take the door off. ~货 unload 9 put into use: ~笔 start writing. ~手 take action IV (量) [for the frequency of an action]: 敲了三~窗子 knock three times on the window. 突然亮了一~. There was a sudden flash.

下 xia [used after a verb as a complement] 1 [indicating movement from a higher place to a lower one]: 放~ put (sth.) down. 躺~ lie down 2 [indicating removal of sth. away from a position]: 脱~大衣 take off one's coat. 把那画拿~来 take that picture down 3 [used to indicate that there is enough space for sth.]: 这剧院坐得~2 000人. This theatre can seat 2,000 people. 碗太小装不~这汤. The bowl is too small for the soup. 4 [indicating the completion or result of an action]: 录~乐曲 have the music recorded. 打~基础 lay a foundation

下巴 xiàba (名) chin

下班 xiàbān (动) come off work; knock off

下半辈子 xiàbànbèizi the latter half of one's life; the rest of one's life

下半旗 xiàbànqí fly the flag at half-mast

下辈 xiàbèi (名) 1 future generations; offspring 2 the younger generation of a family

下辈子 xiàbèizi (名) the next life

下边(邊) xiàbian (名) see "下面" xiàmiàn

下不来(來)台(臺) xiàbuláitái be unable to get out of an embarrassing situation; be unable to back down with good grace; be on the spot: 给他一个~ put him on the spot

下策 xiàcè (名) very unwise move

下层(層) xiàcéng (名) lower levels; grassroots

下场(場) xiàchǎng (名) end: 遭到可耻~ come to a disgraceful end. 不会有好~ come to no good end

下地 xiàdì (动) 1 go to the fields 2 leave a sickbed; be up and about again

下毒手 xià dúshǒu lay murderous hands on sb.; deal sb. a deadly blow: 背后~ stab sb. in the back

下颚 xià'è (名) the lower jaw

下凡 xiàfán (动) (of gods or immortals) descend to the mortal world

下饭 xiàfàn (动) (of dishes) go with rice: 今天有什么菜~哇? What do we have to go with rice today?

下海 xiàhǎi (动) go into business; resign a government post and enter the private sector

下岗(崗) xiàgǎng (动) 1 come or go off sentry duty 2 (of a worker) be laid off; be made redundant: ~职工 redundant workers; laid-off workers

下工夫 xià gōngfu make painstaking effort

下跪 xiàguì (动) go down on one's knees

下贱(賤) xiàjiàn (形) low; degrading

下降 xiàjiàng (动) drop; fall; decline

下脚 xiàjiǎo I (动) get a foothold; plant one's foot II (名) leftover bits and pieces: ~料 leftover bits and pieces (of industrial material etc.); scrap

下来(來) xiàlái (动) come down

下来(來) xiàlái [used after a verb as a complement] 1 [indicating movement from a higher position to a lower one]: 眼泪顺着她脸颊流~. Tears streamed down her cheeks. 苹果掉~了. An apple has dropped. 他的体温降~了. His temperature has come down. 2 [indicating moving sth. away from a position]: 把牌子取~! Take off that plaque! 3 [indicating completion or result of an action]: 在这儿停~. Stop here. 她终于平静~了. She calmed down at last. 4 [indicating the continuation of an action]: 坚持~! Keep it up! 这个故事一代代流传

~. This legend has been handed down from generation to generation.

下列 xiàliè (名) following; listed below

下令 xiàlìng (动) give orders; order

下流 xiàliú (形) obscene; dirty: ~话 dirty words. ~的勾当 degrading behaviour

下落 xiàluò I (名) whereabouts: 打听某人的~ inquire about sb.'s whereabouts II (动)drop; fall

下马(馬) xiàmǎ (动) 1 get down from a horse 2 discontinue; back down

下马(馬)威 xiàmǎwēi (名) initial severity shown by a new official meant to establish his authority

下面 xiàmian (名) 1 below; under; underneath: 大桥~ under the bridge. 地毯~ underneath the carpet 2 next; following: ~只是几个例子. The following are but a few instances. 3 lower level; subordinate: 得到~的支持 win support from the grassroots

下坡路 xiàpōlù (名) downhill path; decline: 走~ go downhill; be on the decline

下铺(舖) xiàpù (名) lower berth

下棋 xiàqí (动) play chess

下情 xiàqíng (名) conditions at the lower levels; opinion of the masses

下去 xiàqù (动) 1 go down; descend 2 go on; continue: 他这样~将一事无成. If he goes on like this, he will accomplish nothing.

下去 xiàqù [used after a verb as a complement] 1 [used to indicate movement from a higher position to a lower one]: 洪水退~了. The flood has receded. 2 [used to indicate moving sth. or sb. away from somewhere]: 把犯人带~ take the prisoner away 3 [used to indicate the continuation of an action]: 不能再忍受~ can tolerate it no longer

下手 xiàshǒu I (动) start; set about: 不知从哪儿~ not know how to proceed II (名) assistant or subordinate

下属(屬) xiàshǔ (名) subordinate

下水 xiàshuǐ (动) 1 enter the water; be launched: 又一艘新船~了. Another new ship has been launched. 2 fall into evil ways: 给拖~了 be drawn into a gang of evil-doers

下水道 xiàshuǐdào (名) sewer; drainage

下榻 xiàtà (动) stay (at a place during a trip) :贵宾~的旅馆 the hotel where distinguished guests are staying

下台(臺) xiàtái (动) 1 step down from the stage 2 fall from grace; leave office 3 get out of an awkward position

下文 xiàwén (名) 1 the sentence, paragraph or chapter that follows 2 further development; follow-up: 那事还没有~呢! I haven't heard about any further development of that matter.

下午 xiàwǔ (名) afternoon

下限 xiàxiàn (名) the latest or minimum permissible; lower limit; prescribed minimum; floor level; floor

下旬 xiàxún (名) the last ten-day period of a month

下野 xiàyě (动) (of high officials) be compelled to resign

下意识(識) xiàyìshí (名) subconsciousness

下游 xiàyóu (名) 1 (of a river) lower reaches 2 backward position

下载(載) xiàzǎi (动) download

下肢 xiàzhī (名) lower limbs; legs

下种(種) xiàzhǒng (动) sow

吓(嚇) xià (动) frighten; scare; intimidate: ~坏了 be horrified

see also hè

吓唬 xiàhu (动) frighten

夏 xià (名) summer

夏季 xiàjì (名) summer

夏令营(營) xiàlìngyíng (名) summer camp

夏天 xiàtiān (名) summer

仙 xiān (名) celestial being; immortal

仙境 xiānjìng (名) fairyland

仙女 xiānnǚ (名) female immortal; female celestial; fairy maiden

仙人 xiānrén (名) celestial being; immortal

先 xiān 1 earlier; before; first; in advance: ~来~吃. First come, first served. 有言在~ make clear beforehand. 让他~说. Let him speak first. ~电话联系 contact sb. by telephone first 2 elder generation; ancestor: 祖~ ancestor; forefather

先辈 xiānbèi (名) elder generation

先导(導) xiāndǎo (名) guide; forerunner

先睹为(爲)快 xiān dǔ wéi kuài consider it a pleasure to be among the first to read (a poem, article, etc.) or see (a play, ballet, etc.)

先发(發)制人 xiān fā zhì rén gain the initia-

X

tive by striking first
先锋 xiānfēng (名) vanguard
先后(後) xiān-hòu I (名) priority; order: 这些项目都该分个～. These items should be taken up in order of priority. II (副) successively; one after another: 代表们～在会上发了言. The delegates spoke at the meeting one after another.
先见之明 xiān jiàn zhī míng foresight
先进(進) xiānjìn (形) advanced
先决 xiānjué (形) prerequisite: ～条件 precondition
先例 xiānlì (名) precedent: 开了～ set a precedent
先烈 xiānliè (名) martyr
先前 xiānqián (名) before; previously: 他～不是这样. He wasn't like this before.
先遣 xiānqiǎn (动) sent in advance: ～队 advance party
先驱(驅) xiānqū (名) pioneer; forerunner
先人 xiānrén (名) ancestor; forefather
先入为(爲)主 xiān rù wéi zhǔ first impressions are strongest; prejudices die hard
先声(聲)夺(奪)人 xiānshēng duó rén overawe one's opponent by a show of strength
先生 xiānsheng (名) 1 teacher 2 mister (Mr.); gentleman; sir: 总统～ Mr. President. 女士们, ～们 ladies and gentlemen
先天 xiāntiān (形) congenital; innate: ～不足 congenital deficiency; inborn weakness
先头(頭) xiāntóu (名) ahead; in front; in advance
先行 xiānxíng (动) go ahead of the rest: ～者 forerunner
先斩后(後)奏 xiān zhǎn hòu zòu take decisive action without asking for approval and only report it later as a fait accompli; act first, report later
先兆 xiānzhào (名) omen
先知 xiānzhī (名) prophet; person of foresight
鲜 xiān I (形) 1 fresh: ～花 fresh flower. 新～空气 fresh air. 2 bright-coloured; bright: 这条头巾颜色太～. This scarf is too gaudy. 3 delicious; tasty: 菜的味道真～! This dish is absolutely delicious! II (名) delicacy: 海～ seafood
鲜红 xiānhóng (形) bright red; scarlet
鲜美 xiānměi (形) delicious; tasty
鲜明 xiānmíng (形) 1 (of colour) bright: 色彩～ in bright colours. 2 clear-cut; distinct: ～的对比 a striking (or sharp) contrast. ～的立场 a clear-cut stand
鲜血 xiānxuè (名) (red) blood
鲜艳(豔) xiānyàn (形) bright-coloured: 颜色～ in gay colours. ～夺目 of dazzling beauty
掀 xiān (动) lift (a cover, etc.)
掀开(開) xiānkāi (动) open; lift; draw: ～锅盖 lift the lid off the pot
掀起 xiānqǐ (动) 1 surge: 大海里～起了巨浪. Big waves surged on the sea. 2 (of movement) set off; start: ～建设高潮 start an upsurge of construction
锨 xiān (名) shovel
纤(纖) xiān I (形) fine; minute II (名) fibre: 光～ optical fibre
纤弱 xiānruò (形) slim and fragile; delicate
纤维 xiānwéi (名) fibre: 人造～ synthetic fibre
纤细 xiānxì (形) slender; fine
涎 xián (名) saliva
舷 xián (名) the side of a ship: 左～ port. 右～ starboard
弦 xián (名) bowstring; string: ～乐器 stringed instrument
闲(閒) xián I (形) idle; unoccupied: ～不住 be unaccustomed to staying idle; always keep oneself busy II (名) spare time; leisure
闲工夫 xiángōngfu (名) spare time; leisure
闲逛 xiánguàng (动) saunter; stroll
闲话 xiánhuà (名) 1 idle chat 2 complaint; gossip
闲空 xiánkòng (名) free time; leisure
闲聊 xiánliáo (名) chat; chit-chat
闲气(氣) xiánqì (名) anger about trifles: 我可没工夫生这份～. I'm too busy to lose my temper over such a little thing.
闲情逸致 xiánqíng-yìzhì a leisurely and carefree mood
闲人 xiánrén (名) 1 person left idle; loafer 2 persons not concerned: ～免进. No admittance except on business.
闲散 xiánsǎn (形) 1 free and at leisure; at a loose end 2 unused; idle: ～资金 idle

capital. ～土地 scattered plots of unutilized land

闲事 xiánshì (名) other people's business: 别管～! Mind your own business!

闲谈 xiántán (动) chat; engage in casual conversation

闲暇 xiánxiá (名) leisure

闲置 xiánzhì (动) lie idle: 有些机器仍然～着. Some machines lie idle.

娴 xián (形) 1 refined 2 skilled

娴静 xiánjìng (形) gentle and refined

娴熟 xiánshú (形) adept; skilled

咸(鹹) xián (形) salty; salted: ～菜 pickles

贤(賢) xián (形) 1 virtuous; able 2 an able and virtuous person: 任人唯～ give positions to people with ability. 让～ relinquish one's post in favour of a better qualified person

贤惠 xiánhuì (形) (of a woman) capable; virtuous

贤良 xiánliáng (形) (of a man) able and virtuous

贤明 xiánmíng (形) wise and able

衔 xián I (动) hold in the mouth: ～着烟斗 hold a pipe between one's teeth II (名) rank; title: 军～ military rank. 头～ title. 大使～总领事 consul general with the rank of ambassador

衔接 xiánjiē (动) join; dovetail

嫌 xián I (动) dislike; mind: 一点也不～麻烦 not mind the bother at all. 他走了,～这儿太吵. He left because it was too noisy here. 我～她太啰嗦. I dislike her for being so grumpy. II (名) suspicion: 为了避～,我特意走开. I deliberately walked off to avoid suspicion.

嫌弃(棄) xiánqì (动) have the desire to stay away from sb.; give a wide berth to sb.

嫌恶(惡) xiánwù (动) detest; loathe

嫌疑 xiányí (名) suspicion: ～犯 suspect

显(顯) xiǎn I (动) show; display: ～身手 display one's abilities. 她很～老. She looks older than her age. II (形) obvious; noticeable: 成效不～. The result is not so marked.

显得 xiǎnde (动) look; seem; appear: 她～很高兴. She looks very happy.

显而易见(見) xiǎn ér yì jiàn obviously; evidently: ～, 这是一种错误的想法. Evidently, this is a mistaken idea.

显赫 xiǎnhè (形) illustrious; influential: 他曾～一时. He was a man of power and influence for a time.

显露 xiǎnlù (动) become visible

显然 xiǎnrán (形) obvious; evident

显示 xiǎnshì (动) show; demonstrate; manifest: ～出智慧和勇气 show both wisdom and courage

显示器 xiǎnshìqì (名) display; monitor

显微镜 xiǎnwēijìng (名) microscope

显现 xiǎnxiàn (动) appear; show: 在这困难的时刻,她～出坚强的个性. In this difficult hour, she revealed her strength of character.

显像管 xiǎnxiàngguǎn (名) kinescope

显眼 xiǎnyǎn (形) conspicuous; showy: ～的地方 a conspicuous place. 穿得太～ be loudly dressed

显要 xiǎnyào (形) powerful and influential: ～人物 a dignitary; VIP

显影 xiǎnyǐng (动) develop (a film)

显著 xiǎnzhù (形) marked; remarkable: 取得～的成效 gain remarkable success; achieve notable results

险(險) xiǎn I (形) 1 dangerous; risky: 真～哪! It was such a narrow escape (or a close shave)! 2 sinister; vicious: 阴～ sinister II (名) 1 a mountain or river which is so difficult to cross that it constitutes an almost impregnable barrier to an invading army: 天～ natural barrier 2 danger; risk: 脱～ be out of danger III (副) nearly: ～遭不测 escape death by a hair's breadth

险恶(惡) xiǎn'è (形) 1 dangerous; perilous: 处境～ be in a precarious position 2 sinister; vicious: ～用心 sinister intentions; evil motives

险境 xiǎnjìng (名) dangerous situation

险峻 xiǎnjùn (形) precipitous

险情 xiǎnqíng (名) dangerous state or situation: 雨水不断,大堤出现～. It keeps raining and the dam is threatened.

险些 xiǎnxiē (副) narrowly; nearly: 他～迷了路. He very nearly lost his way.

险要 xiǎnyào (形) strategically located and difficult of access

险诈 xiǎnzhà (形) sinister and crafty

险种(種) xiǎnzhǒng (名) insurance product

宪(憲) xiàn (名) constitution

宪兵 xiànbīng (名) military police; gendarme

宪法 xiànfǎ (名) constitution

宪章 xiànzhāng (名) charter: 联合国～ the United Nations Charter

宪政 xiànzhèng (名) constitutional government

羡 xiàn (动) admire; envy: ～慕 admire; envy

献(獻) xiàn (动) offer; present: ～策 offer advice; make suggestions. ～花 present bouquets. ～花圈 lay a wreath. ～血 donate blood. ～身 devote one's life to a cause

献丑(醜) xiànchǒu (动)〈谦〉[used when referring to one's own performance and writing] show one's poor skill

献词 xiàncí (名) congratulatory message: 新年～ New Year message

献计 xiànjì (动) offer advice; make suggestions

献礼(禮) xiànlǐ (动) present a gift

献媚 xiànmèi (动) butter up; resort to cheap undisguised flattery

献血 xiànxuè (动) donate blood

县(縣) xiàn (名) county

现 xiàn I (形) 1 now; present; current; existing: ～年 50 岁 be 50 years old now. ～阶段 the present stage. ～况 the current situation 2 (of money) on hand: ～钱 ready money; cash II (动) appear; reveal: ～原形 reveal one's true features. 她脸上～出一丝笑容. A faint smile appeared on her face.

现场(場) xiànchǎng (名) 1 scene (of an accident or crime): 保护～ keep the scene (of a crime or accident) intact 2 site; spot: ～会 on-the-spot meeting. ～表演 on-the-spot demonstration

现成 xiànchéng (形) ready-made: ～衣服 ready-made clothes

现存 xiàncún (形) in stock

现代 xiàndài I (名) modern times; the contemporary age II (形) modern; contemporary: ～派 modernist

现代化 xiàndàihuà I (名) modernization II (形) modern; modernized: ～设备 modern equipment

现房 xiànfáng (名) spot building

现货 xiànhuò (名) merchandise on hand; spots: ～交易 spot transaction; over-the-counter trading. ～市场 spot market

现金 xiànjīn (名) cash: ～付款 payment in cash

现款 xiànkuǎn (名) ready money; cash

现任 xiànrèn (形) currently in office; incumbent: ～总统 the incumbent president

现实(實) xiànshí I (名) reality: 脱离～ divorce oneself from reality; be unrealistic II (形) 1 real; actual: ～生活 real life 2 realistic; practical: ～的办法 practical measures. 采取～的态度 adopt a realistic attitude

现实(實)主义(義) xiànshízhǔyì (名) realism

现象 xiànxiàng (名) phenomenon: 罕见的～ rare phenomenon. 事物的～和本质 the appearance and essence of a matter

现行 xiànxíng (形) currently in effect: ～法令 decrees in effect; the current laws and decrees. ～政策 present policies

现役 xiànyì (名) active service: ～军人 serviceman

现在 xiànzài (名) now; today; at present

现状(狀) xiànzhuàng (名) present situation; existing state of affairs; status quo: 安于～ be content with things as they are

腺 xiàn (名) gland

馅 xiàn (名) filling; stuffing: 肉～儿 meat filling

陷 xiàn (动) 1 sink; get stuck: 越～越深 sink deeper and deeper. 车～进泥里了. The car got stuck in the mud. 眼窝深～ sunken eyes 2 (of a city) be occupied; fall 3 make false charges against sb.

陷阱 xiànjǐng (名) pitfall; trap: 布设～ lay a trap

陷落 xiànluò (动) 1 subside; cave in 2 (of territory) fall into enemy hands

陷入 xiànrù (动) 1 sink (or fall) into; land oneself in: ～困境 land oneself in a predicament. ～停顿状态 come to a standstill 2 be absorbed in: ～沉思 be lost in thought

限 xiàn I (动) limit; restrict: 数量不～ impose no restriction on quantity. 每券只～一人 each ticket entitles one person to admission. 不要～得这么死. Don't make such rigid restrictions. 公司～我半年完成这项设计工作. The firm allows me half a year to finish the designing. II (名) limit; bounds: 期～ time limit

限定 xiàndìng (动) set a limit to; restrict: ～范围 the prescribed limit

限度 xiàndù (名) limit; limitation: 我们的忍耐已经到了最后～. We have reached the limit of our patience.

限额 xiàn'é (名) norm; quota

限价(價) xiànjià I (动) fix the official price II (名) the (officially) fixed price: 最高～ the ceiling price. 最低～ the floor price

限量 xiànliàng (动) put a limit on quantity; set bounds to: 前途不可～ have boundless prospects; have a very bright future

限期 xiànqī I (动) set a time limit (for sth.): 你必须～把申请书交来. You must hand in your application before the deadline. II (名) time limit; deadline

限于(於) xiànyú (动) be limited to: ～篇幅, 不能刊载全文. As space is limited, it is impossible to publish the whole article. 本文讨论的范围～一些原则问题. The scope for the discussion of the present paper is confined to certain problems of principle.

限制 xiànzhì (动) restrict; limit; confine: 年龄～ age limit. 文章的字数不～. There is no restriction on the length of an article.

线(綫) xiàn I (名) 1 thread; string; wire: 丝～ silk thread. 毛～ knitting wool. 电～ electric wire. 2 line: 直～ straight line. 曲～ curved line. 光～ ray. 航～ airline. 流水～ assembly line. 边界～ boundary line. 海岸～ coastline. 政治路～ political line. 3 brink; verge: 在死亡～上 on the verge of death II (量) [for abstract matters, only after 一, 一 being the only numeral used before it]: 一～希望 a glimmer of hope. 一～光明 a gleam of light

线路 xiànlù (名) line; circuit: 电话～ telephone line

线圈 xiànquān (名) coil

线人 xiànrén (名) informer; inner connection; spy

线索 xiànsuǒ (名) clue

线条(條) xiàntiáo (名) (in drawing) line

襄 xiāng (动)〈书〉assist; help

镶 xiāng (动) 1 inlay; set; mount: ～金 inlaid with gold. ～牙 have a denture made 2 rim; edge; border: 给裙子～花边 edge a skirt with lace

镶嵌 xiāngqiàn (动) inlay; set

相 xiāng I (副) 1 each other; mutually: ～识 know each other. ～距甚远 be poles apart 2 [indicating how one party behaves towards the other]: 以礼～待 treat (sb.) with due courtesy. 另眼～看 look upon sb. with special respect; or in a different light II (动) see for oneself: ～女婿 take a look at prospective son-in-law

see also xiàng

相比 xiāngbǐ (动) compare: 二者～, 后者为佳. The latter is the better of the two.

相差 xiāngchà (动) differ: ～无几 The difference is negligible.

相称(稱) xiāngchèn (动) suit; match: 这种上衣跟你的年龄不～. This kind of jacket isn't particularly good for a man of your age.

相持 xiāngchí (动) be at a stalemate: 意见～不下 fail to reach agreement

相处(處) xiāngchǔ (动) get along (with one another): 不好～ difficult to get along with

相传(傳) xiāngchuán (动) 1 according to legend 2 pass on from one to another: 世代～ hand down from generation to generation

相当(當) xiāngdāng I (动) correspond to; be equal to: 得失～ The gains offset the losses. II (副) quite; considerably: ～成功 quite successful. ～艰巨 rather arduous. ～长时间 a considerably long time III (形) proper; suitable: 这个工作还没有找到～的人. We have not been able to find a proper person for the job yet.

相等 xiāngděng (动) be equal: 数量～ be equal in amount (or quantity, number)

相抵 xiāngdǐ (动) offset; counterbalance

相对(對) xiāngduì I (动) face each other: ～无言 look at each other in silence II (形) 1 relative [as opposed to "absolute"] 2 relatively; comparatively: ～稳定 relatively stable. ～地说 comparatively speaking

相反 xiāngfǎn (形) opposite; contrary: ～的方向 the opposite direction. 恰恰～ on the contrary; the other way round

相仿 xiāngfǎng (形) similar: 年纪～ be about the same age
相逢 xiāngféng (动) meet (by chance); come across
相符 xiāngfú (动) conform to; correspond to: 名实～ live up to one's reputation
相辅相成 xiāngfǔ-xiāngchéng complement each other
相干 xiānggān (动) [often used in a negative or interrogative sentence] have to do with; be concerned with: 这事跟你有什么～? What has this to do with you?
相隔 xiānggé (动) be separated by; be apart; be at a distance of: ～万里 be a long way away from each other. ～多年 after an interval of many years
相关(關) xiāngguān (动) be interrelated: 密切～ be closely related (or linked) to each other
相好 xiānghǎo (动) 1 be on very good terms 2 be intimate with or on intimate terms with [often referring to a sexual relationship]
相互 xiānghù (形) mutual; reciprocal: ～了解 mutual understanding. ～作用 interaction; interplay
相继(繼) xiāngjì (副) in succession; one after another: 代表们～发言. The delegates spoke in succession.
相近 xiāngjìn (形) 1 close; near: 比分～. The score was very close. 2 similar; about the same: 两人性格～. The two of them are similar in character.
相距 xiāngjù (动) apart; at a distance of
相连 xiānglián (动) be linked together; be joined
相劝(勸) xiāngquàn (动) persuade; offer advice
相识(識) xiāngshí I (动) be acquainted with each other II (名) acquaintance: 老～ an old acquaintance
相思 xiāngsī (动) (of parted lovers) be lovesick
相似 xiāngsì (形) similar
相提并论(論) xiāngtí-bìnglùn place on a par: 两者不能～. The two cannot be mentioned in the same breath.
相同 xiāngtóng (形) identical; the same
相投 xiāngtóu (动) be congenial: 兴趣～ have similar tastes and interests
相像 xiāngxiàng (形) similar; alike
相信 xiāngxìn (动) believe; have faith in
相形见绌 xiāng xíng jiàn chù be inferior by comparison; compare unfavourably with
相依 xiāngyī (动) be interdependent: 唇齿～ be dependent on each other like lips and teeth; be mutually dependent. ～为命 depend on each other for survival
相宜 xiāngyí (形) suitable; appropriate
相应(應) xiāngyìng (形) corresponding; relevant: 生产发展了,工人的生活水平也～提高了. The production has risen and the living standard of the workers has also gone up accordingly.
相映 xiāngyìng (动) set each other off: 湖光塔影,～成趣. The glimmering lake and the reflection of the pagoda on it set each other off and formed a delightful scene.
相遇 xiāngyù (动) meet: 我俩在电影院偶然～. We ran across each other in the cinema.
相撞 xiāngzhuàng (动) collide: 两车～. The two trains had a head-on crash.

厢 xiāng (名) 1 wing (of a one-storeyed house): ～房 wing-room 2 railway carriage or compartment; (theatre) box: 车～ carriage. 包～ box

箱 xiāng (名) box; case; trunk: 皮～ suitcase. 大～ trunk. 垃圾～ dustbin. 风～ bellows

香 xiāng I (形) 1 (of flowers, etc.) fragrant; scented 2 (of food) delicious; appetizing 3 with good appetite; with relish 4 (sleep) soundly II (名) 1 perfume; spice: 麝～ musk. 檀～ sandalwood 2 incense: ～炉 incense-burner
香肠(腸) xiāngcháng (名) sausage
香粉 xiāngfěn (名) face powder
香火 xiānghuǒ (名) 1 joss sticks and candles burning at a temple: ～甚盛 (of a temple) have many worshippers; attract a large number of pilgrims 2 temple attendant 3 ancestral sacrifices: 继～ continue the family line
香蕉 xiāngjiāo (名) banana
香精 xiāngjīng (名) essence
香客 xiāngkè (名) a worshipper at a Buddhist temple; a Buddhist pilgrim
香料 xiāngliào (名) 1 perfume 2 spice
香喷喷 xiāngpēnpēn (形) savoury; appetizing
香水 xiāngshuǐ (名) perfume
香甜 xiāngtián (形) 1 fragrant and sweet 2 (sleep) soundly
香烟 xiāngyān (名) cigarette

香油 xiāngyóu (名) sesame oil
香皂 xiāngzào (名) toilet soap
乡(鄉) xiāng (名) 1 countryside: 城～ urban and rural areas 2 native place: 思～ think of one's native place with nostalgic longing
乡村 xiāngcūn (名) village; countryside
乡亲(親) xiāngqīn (名) fellow villager; villagers; folks
乡思 xiāngsī (名) homesickness; nostalgia
乡土 xiāngtǔ (名) 1 native soil 2 of one's native land: ～风味 local flavour
乡下 xiāngxia (名) village; country; countryside
乡镇 xiāngzhèn (名) 1 villages and towns 2 small towns in general: ～企业 village and township enterprises
详 xiáng I (形) detailed II (动) know clearly: 作者生卒年月不～. The author's dates are unknown.
详尽(盡) xiángjìn (形) detailed; exhaustive: ～的记载 a detailed record
详情 xiángqíng (名) details; particulars
详细 xiángxì (形) detailed; minute: ～的报告 a detailed report
祥 xiáng (形) auspicious: 吉～ auspicious
翔 xiáng (动) circle in the air: 翱～ soar; hover
降 xiáng (动) 1 surrender: 宁死不～ rather die than surrender 2 tame; subdue
see also jiàng
降服 xiángfú (动) yield; surrender
享 xiǎng (动) enjoy
享福 xiǎngfú (动) live in ease and comfort
享乐(樂) xiǎnglè (动) indulge in material comfort; seek pleasure
享受 xiǎngshòu I (动) enjoy: ～公费医疗 enjoy free medical care II (名) enjoyment: 贪图～ seek ease and comfort
享有 xiǎngyǒu (动) enjoy (rights, prestige, etc.): ～崇高的威望 be held in high esteem. ～盛名 enjoy a high prestige
想 xiǎng (动) 1 think: 让我～一～. Let me think it over. ～办法 try to find a way (or solution). ～～后果 consider the consequences. ～问题 ponder over a problem 2 suppose; reckon: 你～他会来吗? Do you think he will come? 我～她还不知道此事. I don't think that she knows it yet. 我～是吧. I suppose so. 3 want to: ～试试吗? Would you like to have a try? 4 remember with longing; miss: 你～念他们吗? Do you miss them?
想必 xiǎngbì (副) presumably; most probably: 她怎么还没来? ～是火车误了点. Why hasn't she come yet? The train must have been late.
想不到 xiǎngbudào 1 unexpected: 真～你是这么三心二意. I never thought you were so half-hearted. 真～在这儿遇见你! Fancy meeting you here! 2 fail to give attention to: 这些事男人都～. A man never gives thought to these matters.
想不开(開) xiǎngbukāi take things too hard: 别为这事～! Don't take it to heart.
想当(當)然 xiǎngdāngrán assume sth. as a matter of course; take for granted: 你不能凭～办事. You can never take anything for granted whatever you do.
想得开(開) xiǎngdekāi take things philosophically
想法 xiǎngfa (名) idea; opinion: 我认为她的～都不对. I think her ideas are all mistaken.
想方设法 xiǎngfāng-shèfǎ try by every means possible
想家 xiǎngjiā be homesick: 我非常～. I'm awfully homesick.
想念 xiǎngniàn (动) think of sb. or sth. with nostalgic longing; miss
想起 xiǎngqǐ (动) remember; recall; call to mind: ～过去 recall the past. 我想不起在哪儿见过她. I can't remember where I last saw her.
想入非非 xiǎngrù fēifēi indulge in fantasy; daydream
想望 xiǎngwàng (动) desire; long for
想像 xiǎngxiàng I (动) imagine; visualize: 不可～ hard to imagine; inconceivable II (名) imagination: ～力 imaginative power
响(響) xiǎng I (动) sound; make a sound: 一声不～ without a word; keep silent. 电话铃～了. The telephone rang. II (名) sound; noise: 枪～ gun shot. 喇叭～ the blare of the horn III (形) loud; noisy: 电视机太～了, 拧低点儿! The TV is blaring; turn it down!
响彻(徹) xiǎngchè (动) resound through: 欢呼声～山谷. Cheers resounded throughout the valley.

响动(動) xiǎngdòng (名) sound of movement

响亮 xiǎngliàng (形) loud and clear; resounding; resonant

响声(聲) xiǎngshēng (名) sound; noise

响应(應) xiǎngyìng (动) respond; answer: ~政府的号召 answer the call of the government

饷 xiǎng (名) pay (for soldiers, policemen, etc.)

项 xiàng I (名) nape (of the neck) II (量) item: 造林是一~重大任务. Afforestation is a matter of vital importance.

项链 xiàngliàn (名) necklace

项目 xiàngmù (名) item

巷 xiàng (名) lane; alley

see also hàng

相 xiàng I (名) 1 looks; appearance: 长~儿 a person's appearance. 狼狈~ awkward look 2 〈书〉 prime minister 3 photograph: 照~ take a photo; have a photo taken II (动) look at and appraise: 人不可貌~. Never judge a person by his appearance.

see also xiāng

相册 xiàngcè (名) photo album

相机(機) xiàngjī (名) camera

相貌 xiàngmào (名) looks; appearance: ~端正 have regular features

相片 xiàngpiàn (名) photograph

相声(聲) xiàngsheng (名) cross talk

向 xiàng I (名) direction: 动~ trend. 风~ wind direction. 人心所~ popular sentiment II (动) 1 face: ~西 face west 2 side with (sb.): 你老~着他. You are always taking his part. III (介) to; towards: ~西前进 march west. ~我说明 explain it to me. ~别人学习 learn from others. ~纵深发展 develop in depth

向导(導) xiàngdǎo (名) guide

向来(來) xiànglái (副) always; all along ~如此. It has always been so.

向前 xiàngqián forward: 奋勇~ forge ahead. ~看 look to the future; look forward

向日葵 xiàngrìkuí (名) sunflower

向上 xiàngshàng upward; make progress

向上爬 xiàngshàngpá 1 climb (up) 2 seek personal advancement; be a social climber; be a careerist: 一心~ set one's mind on personal advancement

向往 xiàngwǎng (动) yearn for; look forward to

向阳(陽) xiàngyáng (动) (of a house) face south

象 xiàng (名) 1 elephant 2 appearance: 万~更新. Everything takes on a new look.

象棋 xiàngqí (名) (Chinese) chess

象形文字 xiàngxíng wénzì (名) pictograph; hieroglyph

象牙 xiàngyá (名) ivory: ~雕刻 ivory carving

象征(徵) xiàngzhēng I (动) symbolize; signify II (名) symbol; token

橡 xiàng (名) 1 oak 2 rubber tree

橡胶(膠) xiàngjiāo (名) rubber

橡皮 xiàngpí (名) 1 rubber eraser 2 rubber: ~膏 adhesive plaster. ~筋 rubber band

像 xiàng I (名) portrait; picture: 画~ portrait. 铜~ bronze statue. 雕~ sculpture II (动) 1 be like; resemble: 这孩子~他父亲. The child takes after its father. 我~不~个跳芭蕾舞的? Do I look like a ballet dancer? 2 look as if; seem: ~要下雨了. It looks as if it's going to rain. *or* It looks like rain. 3 like; such as: ~他这样的人真少见. People like him are rare.

像话 xiànghuà (形) reasonable; proper: 真不~! It's absolutely outrageous! 这才~. That's more like it.

像素 xiàngsù (名) pixel: 720~万的相机 camera with 7.2 megapixels. 图像的~分辨率达 6448 The icon image resolution is 64 by 48 pixels.

消 xiāo (动) 1 disappear; vanish: 雾已~了. The fog has lifted. 他的气~了. He has cooled (or calmed) down. 2 dispel; remove 3 pass the time in a leisurely way: ~夏 pass the summer in a leisurely way

消沉 xiāochén (形) low-spirited; downhearted

消除 xiāochú (动) eliminate; dispel; remove: ~顾虑 dispel misgivings. ~误会 clear up misunderstanding

消毒 xiāodú (动) disinfect; sterilize

消防 xiāofáng (名) fire control; fire fighting: ~队 fire brigade. ~车 fire engine

消费 xiāofèi (动) consume: ~品 consumer goods. ~城市 consumer-city. ~基金 funds for consumption. ~结构 consumption patterns. ~水平 level of con-

X

sumption. ～税 consumption tax. ～者 consumer. 保护～者权益 consumerism
消耗 xiāohào (动) consume; use up
消化 xiāohuà (动) digest: 好～ easy to digest; digestible. ～不良 indigestion
消极(極) xiāojí (形) 1 negative: ～因素 negative factor 2 passive; inactive: 态度～ appear inactive
消灭(滅) xiāomiè (动) 1 eliminate; wipe out: ～敌人 wipe out the enemy 2 perish; die out; become extinct
消磨 xiāomó (动) 1 sap; whittle away; wear off: ～志气 sap one's will. ～精力 whittle one's strength away 2 idle away; fritter away: ～岁月 idle (or fritter) away one's time
消遣 xiāoqiǎn I (动) kill time; amuse oneself II (名) diversion; pastime
消融 xiāoróng (动) (of ice, snow, etc.) melt
消散 xiāosàn (动) scatter and disappear; dissipate: 雾渐渐～了. The mist has gradually lifted.
消失 xiāoshī (动) disappear: 在黑夜里～ disappear into the night
消瘦 xiāoshòu (动) become thin
消亡 xiāowáng (动) wither away; die out
消息 xiāoxi (名) news; information: ～灵通人士 informed sources
消炎 xiāoyán (动) counteract inflammation
宵 xiāo (名) night: 通～ all night; throughout the night
宵禁 xiāojìn (名) curfew: 实行(解除)～ impose (lift) a curfew
逍 xiāo
逍遥 xiāoyáo (形) carefree
逍遥法外 xiāoyáo fǎ wài be at large
霄 xiāo (名) clouds: 耸入云～ towering into the sky
霄汉(漢) xiāohàn (名)〈书〉the sky; the firmament
硝 xiāo (名) nitre; saltpetre
硝烟 xiāoyān (名) smoke of gunpowder
削 xiāo (动) 1 peel with a knife: ～梨 peel a pear. ～铅笔 sharpen a pencil 2 (in table tennis) cut; chop: ～球 cut; chop
see also xuē
销 xiāo (动) 1 cancel; annul: 注～ write off. ～假 report back from leave of absence 2 sell; market: 产～ production and marketing. 畅～书 best-seller 3 spend: 开～ expenditure
销毁 xiāohuǐ (动) destroy by melting or burning: ～核武器 the destruction of nuclear weapons
销路 xiāolù (名) sale; market: ～很好 have a good market
销声(聲)匿迹 xiāoshēng-nìjì make no public appearances; lie low
销售 xiāoshòu (动) sell; market: ～量 sales volume
嚣 xiāo clamour; hubbub: 叫～ clamour
嚣张(張) xiāozhāng (形) arrogant; aggressive; rampant: ～一时 run rampant (or wild) for a time
萧(蕭) xiāo (形) desolate; dreary
萧瑟 xiāosè (形) 1 bleak; desolate: ～景象 bleak scene 2 rustle in the air: 秋风～. The autumn wind is soughing.
萧条(條) xiāotiáo I (形) bleak; desolate II (名) depression; slump: 经济～ economic depression; slump
潇(瀟) xiāo
潇洒(灑) xiāosǎ (形) casual and elegant: 举止～ act with grace and ease
潇潇 xiāoxiāo (形) (of rain or wind) whistling and pattering
淆 xiáo (动) confuse; mix up: 混～ confuse; obscure
晓(曉) xiǎo I (名) dawn; daybreak: 拂～ dawn II (动) 1 know: 家喻户～ known to every household 2 let sb. know; tell: ～以大义 enlighten one on the cardinal principle of justice
晓得 xiǎode (动) know: 天～! God knows!
小 xiǎo I (形) 1 small; little; petty; minor: ～姑娘 a little girl. ～溪 a small stream. ～声说话 talk in whispers. ～资产阶级 petty bourgeoisie. 2 young: ～儿子 the youngest son. ～猫 kitten 3 for a short time: ～憩 have a little rest. ～坐 sit for a while II (名) the young: 一家老～ the whole family
小本经(經)营(營) xiǎoběn jīngyíng do business with a small capital
小便 xiǎobiàn I (动) urinate; pass (or make) water II (名) urine
小菜 xiǎocài (名) pickles
小册子 xiǎocèzi (名) booklet; pamphlet

X

小产(產) xiǎochǎn (动) have a miscarriage
小车(車) xiǎochē (名) 1 wheelbarrow; pushcart 2 car
小吃 xiǎochī (名) snack; refreshments: ~店 snack bar
小丑 xiǎochǒu (名) clown; buffoon
小聪(聰)明 xiǎocōngming (名) cleverness in trivial matters: 耍~ play petty tricks
小道消息 xiǎodào xiāoxi a rumour on the grapevine
小调 xiǎodiào (名) 1 ditty 2 (in music) minor
小动(動)作 xiǎodòngzuò (名) 1 mean and petty action; little trick or manoeuvre: 搞~ get up to little tricks 2 fidgety movements (made by schoolchildren in class)
小恩小惠 xiǎo'ēn-xiǎohuì little or small favours; economic sops or bait
小儿(兒)科 xiǎo'érkē (名) paediatrics: ~医生 paediatrician
小贩 xiǎofàn (名) pedlar; vendor; hawker
小费 xiǎofèi (名) tip
小工 xiǎogōng (名) unskilled labourer
小广(廣)播 xiǎoguǎngbō spreading of hearsay information; the grapevine; bush telegraph
小鬼 xiǎoguǐ (名) little devil (a term of endearment in addressing a child)
小伙子 xiǎohuǒzi (名) lad; young fellow
小集团(團) xiǎojítuán (名) clique; faction
小家子气(氣) xiǎojiāziqì small-minded; petty
小轿(轎)车 xiǎojiàochē (名) sedan (car); limousine
小节(節) xiǎojié (名) small matter; trifle: 不拘~ not bother about petty formalities; not care about small matters; not be punctilious
小结 xiǎojié (名) brief summary
小姐 xiǎojie (名) 1 Miss 2 young lady
小看 xiǎokàn (动) look down upon; belittle
小康 xiǎokāng (形) moderately well off: ~之家 a moderately well-off family
小两(兩)口 xiǎoliǎngkǒu (名) young couple
小买(買)卖(賣) xiǎomǎimai (名) small business: 做~ do small business
小麦(麥) xiǎomài (名) wheat
小卖(賣)部 xiǎomàibù (名) 1 a small shop attached to a hotel, school, etc. 2 snack counter
小朋友 xiǎopéngyǒu (名) children
小便宜 xiǎopiányi (名) small gain; petty advantage
小品 xiǎopǐn (名) a short, simple piece of literary or artistic creation; essay; sketch
小气(氣) xiǎoqi (形) 1 mean; stingy 2 narrow-minded; petty
小巧玲珑(瓏) xiǎoqiǎo línglóng small and exquisite
小圈子 xiǎoquānzi (名) inner circle of people; clique: 搞~ engage in cliquish activities
小人 xiǎorén (名) 1 〈旧〉 a person of low position 2 a mean person; villain: ~得志 a case of a morally corrupt person holding sway
小人儿(兒)书(書) xiǎorénrshū (名) picture-story book
小商品 xiǎoshāngpǐn (名) small commodities: ~经济 small commodity economy
小时(時) xiǎoshí (名) hour
小时(時)工 xiǎoshígōng (名) helper paid by the hour; hourly-paid worker
小数(數) xiǎoshù (名) decimal
小说 xiǎoshuō (名) novel; fiction: 长篇~ novel. 中篇~ novelette. 短篇~ short story
小算盘(盤) xiǎosuànpan (名) selfish calculations
小提琴 xiǎotíqín (名) violin
小题大做 xiǎo tí dà zuò make a mountain out of a molehill; storm in a teacup
小偷 xiǎotōu (名) petty thief; pilferer; pickpocket
小偷小摸 xiǎotōu-xiǎomō pilfering
小腿 xiǎotuǐ (名) shank
小五金 xiǎowǔjīn (名) metal fittings (e. g. nails, wires, hinges, bolts, locks, etc.); hardware
小鞋 xiǎoxié (名) tight shoes—difficulties created by one's boss or superior when he cannot punish openly: 给某人穿~ deliberately make things hard for sb.
小型 xiǎoxíng (形) small-sized; miniature
小学(學) xiǎoxué (名) primary (or elementary) school
小意思 xiǎoyìsi (名) small token of kindly feelings; mere trifle
小资 xiǎozī (形) bourgeois; petty bourgeois: ~情调 bourgeois style
小子 xiǎozi (名)〈口〉 1 son; boy 2 〈贬〉 chap
小组 xiǎozǔ (名) group

校 xiào (名) 1 school 2 field officer

see also jiào

校官 xiàoguān (名) field officer

校舍 xiàoshè (名) school building

校友 xiàoyǒu (名) alumnus or alumna

校园(園) xiàoyuán (名) campus; school yard

校长(長) xiàozhǎng (名) head of a school (headmaster, principal, president, chancellor)

效 xiào I (名) effect: 见~ prove effective. 无~ be ineffective II (动) 1 imitate; follow the example of: 上行下~. The example set by the leading people will be followed by their subordinates. 2 devote to; render (a service)

效法 xiàofǎ (动) follow the example of; model oneself on

效果 xiàoguǒ (名) effect; result: 取得良好~ yield good results

效劳(勞) xiàoláo (动) offer one's services

效力 xiàolì I (动) render a service to: 为国~ serve one's country II (名) effect

效率 xiàolǜ (名) efficiency: ~高 efficient. ~低 inefficient

效命 xiàomìng (动) go all out to do one's duty regardless of personal danger

效益 xiàoyì (名) beneficial result; benefit: 经济~ economic results. 社会~ social effect

效忠 xiàozhōng (动) pledge loyalty or allegiance: ~祖国 devote oneself heart and soul to one's country

孝 xiào (名) 1 filial piety 2 mourning: 带~ be dressed in mourning

孝敬 xiàojìng (动) 1 give presents (to one's elders) 2 show filial piety

孝顺 xiàoshùn (动) show filial obedience

孝子 xiàozǐ (名) dutiful son

肖 xiào (动) resemble; be like: ~像 portrait; portraiture. 惟妙惟~ absolutely lifelike

哮 xiào 1 heavy breathing; wheeze: ~喘 asthma 2 roar; howl: 咆~ roar; thunder

啸(嘯) xiào (动) 1 whistle 2 howl; roar

笑 xiào (动) 1 smile; laugh: 微~ smile. 眉开眼~ beam. ~嘻嘻 grin. ~得合不拢嘴 grin from ear to ear. 站在那里傻~ stand there with a silly grin on one's face. 哈哈大~ roar with laughter. 窃~ laugh up one's sleeve 2 laugh at; ridicule: 他刚学,别~他. He's just started learning. Don't laugh at him.

笑柄 xiàobǐng (名) laughing stock

笑话 xiàohua I (名) joke: 说~ crack a joke. 闹~ make a fool of oneself; make a funny mistake II (动) laugh at; ridicule

笑里(裏)藏刀 xiàolǐ cáng dāo have murderous intent behind one's smiles

笑料 xiàoliào (名) laughing stock

笑眯眯 xiàomīmī (形) smilingly

笑面虎 xiàomiànhǔ (名) smiling villain

笑容 xiàoróng (名) smiling expression; smile: ~满面 be all smiles

笑颜 xiàoyán (名) smiling face

楔 xiē

楔子 xiēzi (名) 1 wedge 2 peg

些 xiē (量) 1 some: 这~ these. 好~ quite a few (or lot). 前~日子 recently. 写~信 write a few letters 2 a little; a bit: 好~了 (feel) a little better. 颜色深了~. The colour is a bit too dark.

蝎 xiē (名)(~子) scorpion

歇 xiē (动) have a rest; rest: ~口气 stop for a breather

歇脚 xiējiǎo (动) stop on the way for a rest

歇宿 xiēsù (动) put up for the night; make an overnight stop

歇息 xiēxi (动) 1 have a rest 2 go to bed

鞋 xié (名) shoes

鞋垫(墊) xiédiàn (名) shoe-pad; insole

鞋匠 xiéjiang (名) shoemaker; cobbler

鞋样(樣) xiéyàng (名) shoe pattern; outline of sole

鞋油 xiéyóu (名) shoe polish

挟(挾) xié (动) 1 hold sth. under the arm 2 coerce; force sb. to do one's bidding: 要~ intimidate. ~持 detain under duress

携 xié (动) 1 carry; take with: ~带 take along. ~款潜逃 abscond with funds 2 take sb. by the hand

谐 xié (形) 1 in harmony; in accord: 和~ harmonious 2 humorous: 诙~ humorous; jocular

谐和 xiéhé (形) harmonious

谐谑 xiéxuè (动) banter: 语带~ speak with raillery

谐音 xiéyīn (名) homophonic; homonymic

偕 xié (动) in the company of: ～行 travel together. ～同 accompanied by; along with

邪 xié (形) evil; heretical: 改～归正 give up one's evil ways and return to the right path. 歪风～气 unhealthy tendencies

邪道 xiédào (名) evil ways; infamous behaviour

邪恶(惡) xié'è (形) evil; wicked; vicious

邪乎 xiéhu (形)〈口〉 **1** extraordinary; abnormal; terrible: 疼得～. The pain is terrible. **2** fantastic; incredible: 他说得～. His story sounds incredible.

邪教 xiéjiào (名) (evil or dangerous) cult

邪路 xiélù (名) evil ways

邪门(門)歪道 xiémén-wāidào vicious pursuits; dishonest or evil practices

邪念 xiéniàn (名) wicked idea

邪说 xiéshuō (名) heresy; fallacy

斜 xié (形) slanting; inclined: ～线 slant (/); oblique line. ～着头 tilt one's head. ～眼看人 squint at sb. ～躺在沙发上 recline on a sofa

斜路 xiélù (名) wrong path: 走～ go astray

斜坡 xiépō (名) slope

协(協) xié **1** joint **2** assist

协定 xiédìng (名) agreement; accord: 贸易～ trade agreement

协会(會) xiéhuì (名) association; society

协力 xiélì (动) pull together; join in a common effort

协商 xiéshāng (动) consult; be in consultation with

协调 xiétiáo (动) harmonize; coordinate: 动作～ coordinated movement; coordination. 色彩～ well-matched colours

协同 xiétóng (动) cooperate with

协议(議) xiéyì (名) agreement: 达成～ reach (an) agreement

协助 xiézhù (动) assist

协奏曲 xiézòuqǔ (名) concerto

协作 xiézuò (名) cooperation; combined (or joint) efforts; coordination

胁(脅) xié (动) coerce; force: 威～ threaten. ～从 be an accomplice under duress

写(寫) xiě (动) write

写生 xiěshēng (动) paint from life; sketch

写实(實) xiěshí (动) write or paint realistically

写意 xiěyì (名) freehand brushwork in traditional Chinese painting

写照 xiězhào (名) portrayal; description

写字楼(樓) xiězìlóu (名) office building

写字台(檯) xiězìtái (名) writing desk; desk

写作 xiězuò (动) write: ～技巧 writing technique

血 xiě (名) blood: 献～ donate one's blood

see also xuè

亵(褻) xiè

亵渎(瀆) xièdú (动) blaspheme

泻(瀉) xiè (动) **1** (of river, rain, etc.) rush down; pour out **2** have loose bowels: 上吐下～ suffer from nausea and diarrhoea

泻肚 xièdù (动) have loose bowels; have diarrhoea

泻药(藥) xièyào (名) laxative

械 xiè (名) **1** tool; instrument: 机～ mechanism **2** weapon: 军～ weapons; arms **3** fetters, shackles, etc.

泄 xiè (动) let out; discharge; release; vent: ～洪 release flood water; flood discharge. ～私愤 give vent to one's personal spleen; give deliberate offence out of spite

泄漏 xièlòu (动) leak; let out: ～秘密 let the cat out of the bag

泄露 xièlòu (动) let out; reveal

泄密 xièmì (动) divulge a secret

泄气(氣) xièqì (动) lose heart; feel discouraged or deflated

卸 xiè (动) **1** unload: ～车 unload a truck. ～牲口 unhitch a draught animal **2** remove; strip: ～零件 remove parts from a machine

卸货 xièhuò (动) unload

卸装(裝) xièzhuāng (动) remove stage make-up and costume

谢 xiè (动) thank: 多～. Thanks a lot. 不用～. Don't mention it; not at all.

谢绝 xièjué (动) refuse politely; decline: 婉言～ politely decline. ～参观. Not open to visitors.

谢幕 xièmù (动) answer a curtain call

谢天谢地 xiètiān-xièdì thank God

谢谢 xièxie (动) thanks; thank you

谢意 xièyì (名) gratitude; thanks

谢罪 xièzuì (动) apologize for an offence

懈 xiè (形) slack; lax: 坚持不～ persistent. 作坚持不～的努力 make unremitting efforts. ～怠 slack and lazy; sluggish; lax

蟹 xiè (名) crab

屑 xiè I (名) bits; scraps; crumbs: 纸～ scraps of paper. 金属～ metal filings. 面包～ crumbs (of bread) II (动) [used negatively] to mind; to care: 不～ disdain to do sth.

辛 xīn 1 hard: 艰～ hardships 2 (of flavour) hot: ～辣 hot; pungent 3 suffering: 含～茹苦 endure suffering; bear hardships

辛苦 xīnkǔ I (形) hard; hardworking: 这个工作很～. It's a hard job. II (动) work hard; undergo hardships: 对不起,这事儿还得您再～一趟. I'm sorry to bother you, but you'll have to make another trip.

辛劳(勞) xīnláo I (形) painstaking; laborious II (名) pains; toil: 不辞～ spare no pains

辛勤 xīnqín (形) industrious; hard-working

辛酸 xīnsuān (形) sad; bitter; miserable: ～的往事 sad memories; bitter reminiscences

锌 xīn (名) zinc (Zn)

新 xīn (形) new; fresh; up-to-date: ～衣服 new clothes. ～技术 up-to-date technique. 最～消息 the latest news

新兵 xīnbīng (名) new recruit; recruit

新陈(陳)代谢 xīn-chén dàixiè metabolism

新房 xīnfáng (名) bridal bedroom.

新近 xīnjìn (名) recently; lately

新居 xīnjū (名) new home; new residence

新局面 xīnjúmiàn new situation; new dimension; fresh progress

新郎 xīnláng (名) bridegroom

新年 xīnnián (名) New Year: ～好! Happy New Year! ～献词 New Year message

新娘 xīnniáng (名) bride

新奇 xīnqí (形) novel; new; strange: ～的想法 a novel idea

新生 xīnshēng I (形) newborn; newly born: ～儿 newborn baby; infant baby. ～事物 newborn things II (名) 1 new life; rebirth 2 new student; freshman

新手 xīnshǒu (名) new hand; greenhorn

新闻 xīnwén (名) news: 头版～ front-page news (or story). 简明～ news in brief. ～公报 press communiqué. ～界 the press

新鲜 xīnxiān (形) fresh: ～空气 fresh air. ～牛奶 fresh milk

新兴(興) xīnxīng (形) newly risen; new and developing

新型 xīngxíng (形) new type; new pattern

新颖 xīnyǐng (形) novel and original: 题材～. The subject-matter is fresh and original. 式样～. The style is free from convention.

薪 xīn (名) 1 firewood; fuel 2 salary: ～水 salary; pay

心 xīn (名) 1 the heart: ～跳 heartbeats; palpitation 2 mind; feeling; intention: 善良的～ a kind heart. ～细 be meticulous. ～宽 be carefree. 伤～ sad. 好～ mean well; have good intentions. 小～! Be careful! *or* Watch out! 耐～ be patient 3 centre; core; middle: 问题的核～ the heart of the affair; the crux. 街～ the middle of a street. 轴～ axis. 中～ centre. 白菜～ the heart of a cabbage

心爱(愛) xīn'ài (形) beloved; treasured: ～的礼物 a treasured gift

心安理得 xīn'ān-lǐdé have an easy conscience; have no qualms about it

心病 xīnbìng (名) worry; anxiety

心不在焉 xīn bù zài yān absent-minded

心肠(腸) xīncháng (名) heart; intention: 热～ warm-hearted

心潮 xīncháo (名) a surge of emotion: ～澎湃 feel an onrushing surge of emotion

心得 xīndé (名) what one has learned from work or study

心地 xīndì (名) moral nature: ～善良 good-natured; kind-hearted

心烦 xīnfán (形) be vexed: ～意乱 be terribly upset

心服 xīnfú (动) be genuinely convinced

心浮 xīnfú (形) flighty and impatient

心腹 xīnfù I (名) trusted subordinate; henchman II (形) confidential: ～事 top secret. ～之患 a serious hidden trouble

心甘情愿(願) xīngān-qíngyuàn be most willing to; be perfectly happy to

心肝 xīngān (名) 1 conscience: 没～ heartless 2 [as a form of address] darling; deary

心寒 xīnhán (形) be bitterly disappointed

心狠 xīnhěn (形) cruel; merciless: ～手辣 wicked and merciless

心花怒放 xīnhuā nùfàng be transported with joy; be wild with joy

心怀(懷) xīnhuái I (动) harbour: ～叵测 harbour evil intentions. ～不满 nurse a grievance. ～鬼胎 have ulterior motives II (名) state of mind; mood

心慌 xīnhuāng (形) be flustered; be nervous: ～意乱 be perturbed; be put in a flurry

心灰意懒 xīnhuī-yìlǎn be in low spirits; be depressed

心机(機) xīnjī (名) scheming: 用尽～ rack one's brains. 枉费～ plot in vain

心计 xīnjì (名) scheming; calculation: 一个有～的女人 an intelligent woman

心焦 xīnjiāo (形) anxious; worried

心境 xīnjìng (名) mental state; mood: ～非常愉快 be in high spirits; be very happy

心静 xīnjìng (形) calm: ～自然凉. So long as one keeps calm, one doesn't feel the heat too much.

心坎 xīnkǎn (名) the bottom of one's heart: 我从～里感谢你. I thank you from the bottom of my heart.

心旷(曠)神怡 xīnkuàng-shényí relaxed and carefree

心理 xīnlǐ (名) psychology; mentality: 儿童～学 child psychology

心里(裏) xīnli (名) in the heart; at heart; in (the) mind: ～不痛快 feel bad about sth. ～有事 have sth. on one's mind

心里(裏)话 xīnlihuà (名) true words from the heart: 说～ speak one's mind

心灵(靈) xīnlíng I (形) clever; quick-witted: ～手巧 clever and deft II (名) soul; spirit: ～深处 deep down in one's heart

心领神会(會) xīnlǐng-shénhuì understand tacitly; take a hint

心乱(亂)如麻 xīn luàn rú má be upset by tangled thoughts and ideas; be utterly confused

心满(滿)意足 xīnmǎn-yìzú be perfectly contented with one's lot

心目 xīnmù (名) mind; mental view: 在某些人的～中 in some people's eyes

心平气(氣)和 xīnpíng-qìhé calm and good-natured

心切 xīnqiè (形) eager; impatient; anxious: 求胜～ be anxious to win

心情 xīnqíng (名) state of mind; mood: ～沉重 feel depressed or upset. ～舒畅 feel happy and gay

心神 xīnshén (名) mind; state of mind: ～不定 feel disturbed

心事 xīnshi (名) sth. weighing on one's mind; worry: ～重重 be laden with anxiety

心思 xīnsi (名) 1 thought; idea: 用～ give thought to sth. 2 state of mind; mood: 没有～下棋 not be in the mood to play chess

心酸 xīnsuān (形) feel sad

心疼 xīnténg (动) 1 (of children) love dearly 2 feel sorry to see sth. running to waste

心田 xīntián (名) heart

心头(頭) xīntóu (名) mind; heart: 记在～ bear in mind. ～肉 a dearly loved person or a treasured possession

心胸 xīnxiōng (名) breadth of mind: ～开阔 large-minded; unbiased. ～狭窄 narrow-minded; intolerant

心虚 xīnxū (形) 1 having a guilty conscience 2 lacking in self-confidence; diffident

心绪 xīnxù (名) state of mind: ～烦乱 be in a mental turmoil; eat one's heart out

心血 xīnxuè (名) painstaking effort: 费尽～ expend all one's energies

心血来(來)潮 xīnxuè lái cháo have a brainwave

心眼儿(兒) xīnyǎnr (名) 1 heart; mind: 小～ narrow-minded; petty. 打～里高兴 feel genuinely happy 2 intelligence; cleverness: 她这个人有～. She is intelligent and resourceful. 3 unnecessary misgivings: ～多 always have unwarranted misgivings.

心痒(癢) xīnyǎng (动) have an itch for sth.; have an itch to do sth.

心意 xīnyì (名) kindly feelings: 请收下这点礼物,那是我们大家的一点～. Please accept this small gift from us. We offer it to you as a token of our regard. 你可以放心,我不会辜负你的一片～. You may rest assured that I will not let you down.

心有余(餘)悸 xīn yǒu yújì have a residue of fear

心愿(願) xīnyuàn (名) wish; aspiration: 访问贵国是我多年的～. It is my long-cherished wish to visit your country.

心脏(臟) xīnzàng (名) the heart: ～病 heart disease; heart trouble

心直口快 xīnzhí-kǒukuài frank; outspoken

心智 xīnzhì (名) 1 intellect 2 mentality

心中有数(數) xīnzhōng yǒu shù have a pretty good idea of; know what's what

心醉 xīnzuì (动) be enchanted or fascinated

欣 xīn (形) happy; joyful: 欢～ happy; joyful

欣然 xīnrán (副) joyfully; with pleasure: ～接受 accept with pleasure

欣赏 xīnshǎng (动) enjoy; appreciate; admire

欣慰 xīnwèi (形) be gratified

欣喜 xīnxǐ (形) joyful; happy: ～若狂 be wild with joy

欣欣向荣(榮) xīnxīn xiàng róng thriving; flourishing; prosperours: 一派～的景象 a picture of growing prosperity

信 xìn I (名) 1 letter: 寄～ post a letter. 寄平～ by surface mail. 航空～ air mail. 介绍～ letter of introduction or recommendation 2 message; information: 口～ verbal message. 随时报～ keep sb. informed of sth. 3 trust; confidence: 守～ keep one's promise. 失～ break one's word (to someone); go back on one's word; break faith (with sb.) II (动) believe; trust: 我不～他有这么坏. I don't believe he is that bad. 我深～他的工作定会取得成功. I am deeply convinced that his task will be crowned with success.

信不过(過) xìnbuguò distrust; have no trust in: 你是～我, 所以不肯对我讲真话. You are not telling me the truth because you don't trust me.

信步 xìnbù (动) take a leisurely stroll

信贷 xìndài (名) credit: 长期～ long-term credit. ～额度 line of credit. ～资金 credit funds; funds for extending credit

信封 xìnfēng (名) envelope

信奉 xìnfèng (动) believe in: ～基督教 believe in Christianity; be a Christian

信服 xìnfú (动) believe and admire: 这些科学论据令人～. These scientific arguments carry conviction.

信号(號) xìnhào (名) signal

信笺(箋) xìnjiān (名) letter paper; writing pad

信件 xìnjiàn (名) letters; mail

信口开(開)河 xìnkǒu kāihé talk irresponsibly

信赖 xìnlài (动) trust; have faith in: 她是可以～的. She is trustworthy.

信念 xìnniàn (名) faith; belief; conviction

信任 xìnrèn (动) trust; have confidence in

信使 xìnshǐ (名) courier; messenger: 外交～ diplomatic courier

信誓旦旦 xìnshì dàndàn swear an oath in all solemnity

信手拈来(來) xìnshǒu niānlái write with facility

信守 xìnshǒu (动) abide by; stand by: ～诺言 keep a promise

信条(條) xìntiáo (名) article of faith; creed

信筒 xìntǒng (名) pillar box; mailbox

信徒 xìntú (名) believer; disciple; follower: 佛教～ Buddhist. 基督教～ Christian

信托 xìntuō (动) trust; entrust: ～公司 a trust company. ～商店 commission shop

信息 xìnxī (名) information; news: ～爆炸 information explosion. ～高速公路 information superhighway. ～不灵 have inadequate information facilities

信息产(產)业(業) xìnxī chǎnyè information industry; IT industry

信息高速公路 xìnxī gāosù gōnglù information superhighway

信箱 xìnxiāng (名) 1 mailbox 2 post office box (P.O.B.)

信心 xìnxīn (名) confidence; faith

信仰 xìnyǎng I (动) believe in II (名) faith; belief; conviction: 宗教～ religious belief. 不同的宗教～ different religious persuasions. 政治～ political conviction. ～危机 credibility crisis

信用 xìnyòng (名) 1 trustworthiness; credit: 讲～ keep one's word 2 credit: ～卡 credit card

信誉(譽) xìnyù (名) prestige; credit; reputation: 享有很高的国际～ enjoy high international prestige

信众(衆) xìnzhòng (名) (always plural) believers; followers (of a religion or cult)

衅(釁) xìn (名) quarrel; dispute: 挑～ provoke; provocation

兴(興) xīng (动) 1 prosper 2 become popular: 现在正～这个呢! That's all the vogue now. 我们那儿不～这一套. We don't go in for that sort of thing there. 3 promote; undertake: 大～土木 go in for large-scale construction. 百废俱～. All that was left undone is now being undertaken.
see also xìng

兴办(辦) xīngbàn (动) initiate; set up

兴奋(奮) xīngfèn (形) be excited

兴奋(奮)剂(劑) xīngfènjì (名) stimulant; dope: ～检测 dope-testing. 服用～ take dope

兴风(風)作浪 xīngfēng-zuòlàng stir up trouble; create disturbances

兴建 xīngjiàn (动) build; construct

兴利除弊 xīnglì-chúbì promote beneficial undertakings and abolish harmful practices

兴隆 xīnglóng (形) thriving; flourishing: 生意~ business is brisk

兴起 xīngqǐ (动) rise; spring up

兴盛 xīngshèng (形) prosperous

兴师(師)动(動)众(衆) xīngshī-dòngzhòng move troops and stir up people—draw in many people (to do sth.)

兴亡 xīng-wáng (名) rise and fall (of a nation)

兴旺 xīngwàng (形) prosperous; thriving: ~发达 grow and flourish; prosper

兴修 xīngxiū (动) start con struction; build

兴妖作怪 xīngyāo-zuòguài conjure up a host of demons to make trouble; stir up trouble

星 xīng (名) 1 star: 火~ Mars. 卫~ satellite 2 bit; particle: 一~半点 a tiny bit

星辰 xīngchén (名) stars

星斗 xīngdǒu (名) stars: 满天~. The sky is studded with numerous stars.

星火 xīnghuǒ (名) 1 spark: ~燎原. A single spark can start a prairie fire. 2 shooting star; meteor: 急如~ most urgent

星际(際) xīngjì (名) interplanetary: ~旅行 space travel. ~飞船 spaceship

星罗(羅)棋布 xīngluó-qíbù scattered all over like stars in the sky

星期 xīngqī (名) week: 今天~几? What day (of the week) is it today?

星球 xīngqiú (名) star: ~大战计划 star wars program

星探 xīngtàn (名) star spotter; star scout; casting agent

星座 xīngzuò (名) constellation

腥 xīng (形) having a fishy smell

猩 xīng

猩红 xīnghóng (形) scarlet; blood-red

猩猩 xīngxīng (名) orangutan: 大~ gorilla. 黑~ chimpanzee

形 xíng (名) 1 shape; form: 圆~ round; circular. 方~ square. 不成~ shapeless; amorphous 2 body; entity: 有~ tangible. 无~ intangible

形成 xíngchéng (动) take shape; form: ~了一种特殊的风格 have evolved a special style. ~习惯 form a habit; become a habitual practice. 一种新思想正在~. A new trend of thought is taking shape.

形而上学(學) xíng'érshàngxué metaphysics

形迹 xíngjì (名) a person's movements and expression: 不露~ betray nothing in one's countenance or behaviour. ~可疑 look suspicious

形容 xíngróng I (动) describe: 难以~ be difficult to describe; beggar description II (名)〈书〉appearance; countenance

形容词 xíngróngcí (名) adjective

形式 xíngshì (名) form: 内容与~的统一 unity of content and form

形势(勢) xíngshì (名) 1 situation; circumstances 2 terrain

形态(態) xíngtài (名) 1 form; shape; pattern 2 morphology

形体(體) xíngtǐ (名) 1 shape(of a person's body); physique 2 form and structure

形象 xíngxiàng (名) image; imagery: 国家的~ the image of a nation

形形色色 xíngxíngsèsè of all shades; of every description

形影不离(離) xíng-yǐng bùlí (of two people) be inseparable; on very close terms

形状(狀) xíngzhuàng (名) form; appearance; shape

刑 xíng (名) 1 punishment: 死~ capital punishment; the death penalty. 判处无期徒~ be sentenced to life imprisonment 2 torture; corporal punishment: 用~ put sb. to torture

刑场(場) xíngchǎng (名) execution ground

刑罚(罰) xíngfá (名) penalty; punishment

刑法 xíngfǎ (名) penal code; criminal law

刑事 xíngshì (名) criminal; penal: ~案件 criminal case

型 xíng (名) 1 model; type; pattern: 重~卡车 heavy truck. 血~ blood group 2 mould

型号(號) xínghào (名) model; type

行 xíng I (动) 1 walk; travel: 步~ go on foot; walk. ~程 distance of travel. 人~横道 pedestrian crossing. 2 prevail: 风~一时 be all the fashion 3 do; carry out: ~不通 be impracticable. 实~ put into effect. ~医 practise medicine 4 be all right: ~, 我马上就去. OK, I'll go straight away. 不~, 那不可以. No, that won't do. 我去~吗? Is it all right if I go? II (名) 1 trip: 欧洲之~ a trip to Europe 2 behaviour: 他言~一致. His actions match his words. III (形) capable;

competent: 我在这方面不～. I'm not good at these things. 他真～啊! He is really capable! 她现在还不～. She is not up to it yet.
see also háng
行刺 xíngcì (动) assassinate
行动(動) xíngdòng I (动) 1 move (or get) about: ～不便 have difficulty moving about 2 act; take action: ～起来 go into action II (名) action; operation: 军事～ military operations
行贿 xínghuì (动) bribe
行径(徑) xíngjìng (名) conduct; behaviour: 无耻～ shameless conduct; disgraceful behaviour
行军 xíngjūn (动) (of troops) march
行礼(禮) xínglǐ (动) salute
行李 xíngli (名) luggage; baggage: 手提～ hand-luggage. 超重～ excess luggage
行旅 xínglǚ (名) traveller: ～称便. Travellers find it convenient.
行骗 xíngpiàn (动) practise fraud; swindle; cheat
行期 xíngqī (名) date of departure: ～已近. The date of departure is drawing near. 推迟～ postpone one's trip
行乞 xíngqǐ (动) go begging
行人 xíngrén (名) pedestrian
行色 xíngsè (名) the circumstances in which people get things ready for a trip: ～匆匆 make hurried preparations for a trip
行善 xíngshàn (动) do charitable work; show mercy
行时(時) xíngshí (动) (of a thing) be in vogue
行使 xíngshǐ (动) exercise; perform: ～职权 exercise one's powers
行驶 xíngshǐ (动) (of a vehicle, ship, etc.) go; travel
行事 xíngshì (动) act; handle matters
行头(頭) xíngtou (名) (in traditional Chinese operas) stage costumes and properties
行为(爲) xíngwéi (名) behaviour; conduct; action: 报复～ an act of reprisals. 暴力～ an act of violence
行星 xíngxīng (名) planet
行凶 xíngxiōng (动) commit assault or manslaughter or murder
行医(醫) xíngyī (动) practise medicine (usu. on one's own)
行政 xíngzhèng (名) administration: ～部门 administrative department; executive branch. ～工作人员 administrative staff
行装(裝) xíngzhuāng (名) outfit for a journey; luggage
行踪(蹤) xíngzōng (名) whereabouts; sojourn: ～不定 be on a trip of no fixed destination

醒 xǐng (动) 1 wake up: 如梦初～ as if awakening from a dream. 去把他叫～. Go and wake him up. 2 regain consciousness; come to: 她终于～过来了. She has come to at last.
醒目 xǐngmù (形) striking: ～的标题 bold headlines
醒悟 xǐngwù (动) come to realize the truth; suddenly see the light

擤 xǐng (动) blow (one's nose): ～鼻涕 blow one's nose

省 xǐng (动) 1 examine one's own thoughts and feelings: 反～ make a self-examination 2 visit (one's seniors): ～亲 visit one's parents 3 be conscious: 不～人事 lose consciousness
see also shěng

兴(興) xìng (名) pleasure; urge; relish: 游～ the urge to go sightseeing. 诗～ poetic inspiration
see also xīng
兴冲冲 xìngchōngchōng (形) joyfully; gleefully; in high spirits
兴高采烈 xìnggāo-cǎiliè be filled with joy; jubilant
兴趣 xìngqù (名) interest: 我对下棋不感～. I take no interest in chess. 人们怀着极大的～听他讲话. The audience listened to him with great absorbing interest.
兴致 xìngzhì (名) interest: ～勃勃 (act) with great gusto

幸 xìng I (名) good fortune: 荣～ have the honour to II (副) fortunately
幸而 xìng'ér (副) luckily; fortunately
幸福 xìngfú I (名) happiness; well-being II (形) (of one's personal life) happy
幸好 xìnghǎo (副) fortunately; luckily
幸亏(虧) xìngkuī (副) fortunately; luckily
幸免 xìngmiǎn (动) escape by sheer luck; have a narrow escape
幸运(運) xìngyùn (形) fortunate; lucky: ～儿 child of fortune; a person born under a lucky star; lucky dog
幸灾(災)乐(樂)祸(禍) xìngzāi-lèhuò gloat over others' misfortune

杏 xìng (名) apricot: ~仁 almond

性 xìng I (名) 1 nature; character: 本~ true nature; inherent character. 他说谎成~. Lying has become his second nature. 她天~忧郁. She has a melancholy disposition. 2 sex: 男(女)~ the male (female) sex. ~教育 sex education 3 gender: 阳(阴)~ the masculine (feminine) gender II [a suffix indicating a property or characteristic]: 弹~ elasticity. 可行~ feasibility. 可能~ probability. 艺术~ artistic quality. 毁灭~的打击 a smashing blow. 决定~的胜利 a decisive victory

性爱 xìngài (名) sexual love; sex

性别 xìngbié (名) sexual distinction; sex: ~歧视 sexism; sexual discrimination; discrimination against women

性格 xìnggé (名) nature; character; temperament

性急 xìngjí (形) impatient

性交 xìngjiāo (动) sexual intercourse

性命 xìngmìng (名) life

性能 xìngnéng (名) function (of a machine, etc.); property; performance

性情 xìngqíng (名) temperament; temper: ~温柔 have a gentle disposition. ~暴躁 have a fiery temperament

性骚扰(擾) xìngsāorǎo sexual harrassment

性欲 xìngyù (名) sexual desire

性质(質) xìngzhì (名) nature; quality: 矛盾的~ the nature of the contradiction

性子 xìngzi (名) temper: 使~ get into a temper

姓 xìng (名) surname; family name: 他~王. His surname is Wang.

姓名 xìngmíng (名) surname and first name; full name

兄 xiōng (名) elder brother

兄弟 xiōngdì (名) 1 brothers: ~姐妹 siblings. ~阋墙 quarrel between brothers; internal quarrel 2 fraternal; brotherly: ~国家 fraternal countries

兄长(長) xiōngzhǎng (名) (a respectful form of address) elder brother; big brother

凶 xiōng I (形) 1 fierce; ferocious 2 terrible; fearful 3 inauspicious: ~多吉少 The chances of an auspicious outcome are much less than grim possibilities. II (名) act of violence

凶暴 xiōngbào (形) fierce and brutal

凶残(殘) xiōngcán (形) savage and ruthless

凶恶(惡) xiōng'è (形) ferocious and vicious; fiendish

凶狠 xiōnghěn (形) fierce and malicious

凶猛 xiōngměng (形) ferocious; violent

凶器 xiōngqì (名) tool or weapon used to perpetrate a criminal act

凶神恶(惡)煞 xiōngshén-èshà devilishly; fiendishly

凶手 xiōngshǒu (名) murderer; assassin

凶险(險) xiōngxiǎn (形) dangerous and dreadful: 病情~. The illness is critical.

凶相 xiōngxiàng (名) atrocious features; fierce look: ~毕露 reveal all one's ferocity

汹(洶) xiōng

汹汹 xiōngxiōng (形) 1 (of waves) roaring 2 violent; truculent: 气势~ blustering and truculent 3 heated; vociferous: 议论~ argue vociferously

胸 xiōng (名) 1 chest; bosom 2 mind; heart: ~无大志 cherish no lofty goal

胸怀(懷) xiōnghuái I (名) mind; heart: ~豁达 open-minded II (动) cherish; keep in one's heart: ~祖国 keep at heart the interest of one's own country

胸襟 xiōngjīn (名) breadth of mind

胸卡 xiōngkǎ (名) name tag

胸口 xiōngkǒu (名) the pit of the stomach; chest

胸脯 xiōngpú (名) chest

胸膛 xiōngtáng (名) chest

胸有成竹 xiōng yǒu chéngzhú have an overall consideration of sth. before any action is taken; have a well-thought-out plan

雄 xióng (形) 1 male: ~鸡 cock; rooster 2 grand; imposing: ~伟 magnificent; majestic 3 powerful; mighty: ~兵 a powerful army. ~辩 eloquence

雄才大略 xióngcái-dàlüè great wisdom coupled with bold strategy

雄厚 xiónghòu (形) rich; solid; abundant: 实力~ have an abundance of manpower and natural resources. 资金~ abundant funds

雄健 xióngjiàn (形) robust; powerful: ~的步伐 vigorous strides

雄师(師) xióngshī (名) powerful army

雄伟(偉) xióngwěi (形) grand; imposing;

magnificent
雄心 xióngxīn (名) great ambition: ～壮志 lofty aspirations and ideals
雄壮(壯) xióngzhuàng (形) powerful; majestic: 这首交响曲～非凡. The symphony is majestic and superb.

熊 xióng (名) bear

熊猫 xióngmāo (名) panda
熊市 xióngshì (名) bear market; down market
熊熊 xióngxióng (形) flaming; raging: ～烈火 raging flames

羞 xiū I (动) 1 be shy; be bashful: ～红了脸 blush scarlet 2 feel ashamed: 恼～成怒 be shamed into anger II (名) shame; disgrace: 遮～布 fig leaf

羞惭 xiūcán (形) ashamed: 满面～ blush with shame
羞耻 xiūchǐ (名) sense of shame; shame: 不知～ shameless; lost all sense of shame
羞答答 xiūdādā (形) coy; shy; bashful
羞愧 xiūkuì (形) feel both ashamed and sorry (for what one has done): ～难言 feel ashamed beyond words
羞怯 xiūqiè (形) shy; timid
羞辱 xiūrǔ I (名) disgrace; humiliation II (动) humiliate
羞涩(澀) xiūsè (形) shy; bashful

修 xiū (动) 1 repair: ～自行车 repair a bike. ～鞋 mend shoes 2 build: ～桥 build a bridge. ～大楼 put up a building 3 study; compile: ～哲学 study philosophy. ～县志 write county annals. 自～ study by oneself 4 trim; prune: ～指甲 trim one's fingernails. ～树枝 prune trees

修补(補) xiūbǔ (动) repair; patch up; tinker
修长(長) xiūcháng (形) slender; lanky
修辞(辭) xiūcí (名) rhetoric
修道院 xiūdàoyuàn (名) monastery; convent
修订 xiūdìng (动) revise: ～词典 revise a dictionary. ～版 a revised edition
修复(復) xiūfù (动) repair; restore; renovate
修改 xiūgǎi (动) revise; modify; amend; alter
修剪 xiūjiǎn (动) prune; trim
修建 xiūjiàn (动) build; construct
修理 xiūlǐ (动) repair; mend
修炼(煉) xiūliàn (动) (of Taoists) practise austerities; practise asceticism
修面 xiūmiàn (动) shave; have a shave
修女 xiūnǚ (名) nun (of a Christian religious order)
修配 xiūpèi (动) repair the damaged parts of a machine and supply replacements
修缮 xiūshàn (动) repair (buildings); renovate; revamp
修饰 xiūshì (动) 1 adorn; decorate 2 make up and dress up 3 polish; touch up
修行 xiūxing (动) practise Buddhism or Taoism
修养(養) xiūyǎng (名) 1 accomplishment; training: 文学或艺术～ literary or artistic accomplishment or attainment 2 good manners
修业(業) xiūyè (动) study in a school: ～证书 certificate showing courses attended
修整 xiūzhěng (动) 1 revamp 2 prune; trim
修正 xiūzhèng (动) revise; amend: ～草案 revise a draft. ～主义 revisionism
修筑(築) xiūzhù (动) build; construct

休 xiū (动) 1 stop; cease: 争论不～ argue endlessly 2 rest: 静～ complete rest

休会(會) xiūhuì (动) adjourn: 无限期～ adjourn indefinitely. ～期间 between sessions; during the recess
休假 xiūjià (动) have a holiday or vacation
休克 xiūkè I (名) shock II (动) go into shock
休息 xiūxi (动) rest: ～会儿 take a rest. 明天我～. Tomorrow is my day off. 课间～ break. 幕间～ intermission. ～室 common room (of faculty)
休闲 xiūxián (名) leisure time; relaxing time: ～旅游地 tourist resort. ～服 casual clothing
休想 xiūxiǎng (动) don't cherish any illusion that: 你～逃脱. Don't imagine you can get away with it.
休学(學) xiūxué (动) suspend one's schooling without losing one's status as a student
休养(養) xiūyǎng (动) recuperate: ～所 sanatorium; rest home
休战(戰) xiūzhàn (动) truce; armistice; ceasefire
休整 xiūzhěng (动) (of troops) rest and reorganize
休止 xiūzhǐ (动) stop; end: 无～的争论 argue endlessly; endless argument

宿 xiǔ (量) [used for counting nights]: 住一～ stay for one night
see also sù

朽 xiǔ (形) 1 rotten; decayed: 枯木～株 withered trees and rotten stumps 2 senile

袖 xiù I (名) sleeve: ～口 cuff (of a sleeve) II (动) tuck inside the sleeve: ～手旁观 look on with folded arms

袖珍 xiùzhēn (形) pocket-size; pocketable: ～字典 pocket dictionary

秀 xiù I (形) beautiful; elegant; graceful: 山清水～ beautiful scenery. ～外慧中 graceful and intelligent II 名 show: 做～ publicity stunt. 时装～ fashion show

秀才 xiùcai (名) scholar; intellectual; speechwriter

秀丽(麗) xiùlì (形) pretty; beautiful

秀美 xiùměi (形) graceful; elegant

秀气(氣) xiùqi (形) delicate; refined; graceful

锈 xiù I (名) rust II (动) become rusty

绣 xiù (动) embroider

绣花 xiùhuā (动) embroider; do embroidery

臭 xiù (名) odour; smell

see also chòu

嗅 xiù (动) smell; sniff; scent

嗅觉 xiùjué (名) (sense of) smell: ～很灵 have a keen sense of smell

需 xū (动) need; want: 急～ need badly. 必～品 necessaries; necessities

需求 xūqiú (名) requirement; demand

需要 xūyào I (动) need; require 这所房子～修理. The house wants repairing. II (名) needs: 满足读者的～ meet the needs of the readers

吁 xū (动) sigh: 气喘～～ pant for breath

see also yù

须 xū I (动) must; have to II (鬚) (名) beard; moustache: 留～ grow a beard

须知 xūzhī (名) the musts: 旅客～ notice to travellers; what tourists are required to bear in mind

虚 xū I (形) 1 empty; void; unoccupied: ～词 words of no semantic meaning; function word. 座无～席. All seats were occupied. 2 false: 徒有～名 have an ill-deserved reputation. ～情假意 a hypocritical show of friendship or affection 3 timid: 心里有点～ feel rather diffident 4 weak; in poor health: 气～ lacking in vital energy; sapless. 身体很～ be very weak physically II (副) to no avail; in vain: 弹不～发. Not a single shot missed its target.

虚报(報) xūbào (动) give a false report

虚词 xūcí (名) function word

虚度 xūdù (动) waste time: ～光阴 fritter away one's time

虚构(構) xūgòu (动) make up; fabricate: ～的情节 a fictitious plot

虚幻 xūhuàn (形) unreal; illusory

虚假 xūjiǎ (形) false; sham

虚惊(驚) xūjīng (名) false alarm

虚名 xūmíng (名) undeserved reputation

虚拟(擬) xūnǐ (形) 1 invented; fictitious 2 suppositional: ～语气 the subjunctive mood

虚拟(擬)现实(實) xūnǐ xiànshí virtual reality; VR

虚胖 xūpàng (名) puffiness

虚荣(榮) xūróng (名) vanity: ～心 vanity. 他的～心很强. He's a vain person.

虚弱 xūruò (形) 1 in poor health 2 weak; feeble: 兵力～ weak in military strength

虚实(實) xū-shí (名) the actual situation

虚岁(歲) xūsuì (名) nominal age (reckoned by the traditional method, i. e. considering a person one year old at birth and adding a year each lunar new year)

虚脱 xūtuō (名) collapse; prostration

虚伪(僞) xūwěi (形) hypocritical; false

虚心 xūxīn (形) open-minded; modest; modest and unassuming

虚张(張)声(聲)势(勢) xū zhāng shēngshì bluff and bluster

虚职(職) xūzhí (名) nominal position

墟 xū (名) ruins: 废～ ruins

许 xǔ I (动) 1 allow; permit: 我妈不～我抽烟. My mother doesn't allow me to smoke. 2 promise: 他～过我同我再谈一谈. He promised to have another talk with me. II (副) maybe; perhaps: 天这么黑,～是要下雨吧. It's so dark. Perhaps it's going to rain.

许多 xǔduō (形) many; much; a lot of

许久 xǔjiǔ (名) for a long time; for ages

许可 xǔkě (动) permit; allow

X

许可证 xǔkězhèng (名) licence; permit: 出口～ an export licence

许诺 xǔnuò (动) make a promise; promise

许愿(願) xǔyuàn (动) promise sb. a reward

栩 xǔ

栩栩 xǔxǔ (形) vivid; lively: ～如生 lifelike

畜 xù (动) raise (domestic animals)

see also chù

畜牧 xùmù (动) raise livestock or poultry: ～场 animal farm; livestock farm. ～业 animal husbandry

蓄 xù (动) 1 save up; store up: 水库的～水能力 the amount of water a reservoir can hold; the capacity of a reservoir 2 grow: ～须 grow a beard

蓄电(電)池 xùdiànchí (名) storage battery

蓄洪 xùhóng (动) store flood water

蓄谋 xùmóu (动) premeditate: ～已久 long premeditated

蓄意 xùyì (动) premeditate; harbour an (evil) intention: ～进行罪恶活动 have long harboured the intention of carrying out criminal activities

酗 xù

酗酒 xùjiǔ I (动) drink immoderately II (名) alcoholism

叙 xù (动) 1 chat: ～家常 engage in chit-chat 2 narrate; recount: ～事诗 narrative poem

恤 xù (动) 1 pity; sympathize: 怜～ have compassion on 2 give relief: 抚～ pay compensation

旭 xù

旭日 xùrì (名) the rising sun

序 xù I (名) 1 order; sequence: 顺～ keep in sequence. 程～ procedure. 井然有～ in good order 2 preface II (动) arrange in proper order: ～齿 be arranged in order of seniority in age

序幕 xùmù (名) prologue; prelude

序曲 xùqǔ (名) overture

序言 xùyán (名) preface; foreword

絮 xù I (名) 1 (cotton) wadding 2 sth. resembling cotton: 柳～ (willow) catkin II (动) wad with cotton: ～棉衣 line one's clothes with cotton

絮叨 xùdao (动) talk tediously at length; be a chatterbox; be long-winded

婿 xù (名) son-in-law

绪 xù (名) 1 thread; order in sequence: 头～ main threads (of a complicated affair). ～言 (or ～论) introduction (to book, etc.). 千头万～ a multitude of thoughts 2 task, undertaking: 续未竟之～ go on with the unfinished task

续(續) xù (动) continue; extend: 待～ to be continued. ～订 renew one's subscription (to a newspaper, etc.). ～假 extend one's leave of absence. ～弦 (of a man) remarry. ～集 continuation (of a book); sequel. 我断断～～在那里住了十年. I lived there off and on for ten years.

宣 xuān (动) declare; proclaim; announce: 不～而战 wage an undeclared war. 心照不～ have a tacit understanding

宣布 xuānbù (动) declare; proclaim; announce: ～独立 declare (or proclaim) independence. ～会议开始 declare a meeting open; call a meeting to order. ～一件事 make an announcement

宣称(稱) xuānchēng (动) assert

宣传(傳) xuānchuán I (动) 1 disseminate; publicize; propagate: ～交通规则 publicize traffic regulations. ～环境保护的重要性 make known the importance of environmental protection. 这个人很善于搞～. He is a very good PR man. 2 spread propaganda; propagandize: 两党都忙着～自己的政策. Both parties are busy propagandizing about their own policies. II (名) dissemination; propaganda: 电影里对战争恐怖的～太过分了. There has been too much propaganda about the horror of war.

宣读(讀) xuāndú (动) read out (in public) (a written statement, etc.)

宣告 xuāngào (动) declare; proclaim: ～成立 proclaim the founding of (a state, organization, etc.)

宣判 xuānpàn (动) pass judgment: ～有罪(无罪) pronounce sb. guilty (not guilty)

宣誓 xuānshì (动) swear; take an oath: ～就职 be sworn in

宣言 xuānyán (名) declaration; manifesto; proclamation

宣扬(揚) xuānyáng (动) propagate; advocate: 大力～经济体制改革的重要性. Give

wide publicity to the importance of restructuring the national economy.

宣战(戰) xuānzhàn (动) declare (or proclaim) war

喧 xuān (形) noisy: 锣鼓~天 a deafening sound of gongs and drums

喧宾(賓)夺(奪)主 xuān bīn duó zhǔ the person (or matter) of greater importance is relegated to the background; the person who plays second fiddle steals the limelight

喧哗(嘩) xuānhuá I (动) make a lot of noise: 请勿~. Quiet, please! II (名) confused noise; hubbub

喧闹 xuānnào I (形) noisy; full of noise; bustling II (动) make a lot of noise

喧嚣 xuānxiāo I (形) noisy II (动) clamour: ~一时 create quite a stir. ~鼓噪 make a clamour; stir up a commotion

轩 xuān (形)〈书〉 high; lofty

轩然大波 xuānrán dàbō a great disturbance; a big stir

旋 xuán (动) 1 circle; spin; revolve: 盘~ circle (in the sky) 2 return; come back: 凯~ return in triumph
see also xuàn

旋律 xuánlǜ (名) melody

旋钮 xuánniǔ (名) knob

旋绕(繞) xuánrào (动) curl up; drift about: 炊烟~ A wisp of smoke is curling up from a chimney.

旋涡(渦) xuánwō (名) whirlpool; eddy

旋转(轉) xuánzhuǎn (动) revolve; rotate; spin

玄 xuán (形) 1 profound; abstruse: ~理 metaphysical ideas 2 unreliable; incredible: 这话太~了. That's a pretty tall story.

玄妙 xuánmiào (形) mysterious; abstruse

玄虚 xuánxū (名) deceitful trick: 故弄~ deliberately juggle with false ideas to hide the truth

悬(懸) xuán I (动) 1 hang; suspend: ~空 suspended in midair. ~灯结彩 ornament (a building) with lanterns and festoons 2 feel anxious: 心~两地 have two worries at two places at the same time. ~念 be concerned about; be worried about 3 remain unsettled: ~而未决的问题 unsettled question; outstanding issue II (形) remote; widely different: ~隔 far apart. ~殊 a far cry from

悬案 xuán'àn (名) outstanding issue; unsettled question; pending care

悬挂(掛) xuánguà (动) (of portrait, flag, etc.) hang

悬赏 xuánshǎng (动) offer a reward (for sb.'s capture): ~缉拿某人 put a price on sb.'s head

悬崖 xuányá (名) cliff; precipice: ~勒马 rein in at the brink of the precipice; stop riding into imminent disaster

癣 xuǎn (名) tinea; ringworm

选(選) xuǎn I (动) 1 select; choose: 挑~ pick and choose 2 elect: 普(大)~ general election. 他当~为总统. He was elected president. II (名)selections: 诗~ selected poems

选拔 xuǎnbá (动) select or choose

选购(購) xuǎngòu (动) pick out and buy; choose

选集 xuǎnjí (名) selected works; selections; anthology

选举(舉) xuǎnjǔ I (动) elect; vote II (名) election: ~权 the right to vote

选美 xuǎnměi (名) beauty contest; beauty pageant

选民 xuǎnmín (名) (individually) voter; elector; (collectively) constituency; electorate

选派 xuǎnpài (动) select and appoint; detail

选票 xuǎnpiào (名) vote; ballot

选区(區) xuǎnqū (名) constituency; electoral district

选手 xuǎnshǒu (名) (of sports) selected contestant; player

选送 xuǎnsòng (动) select and recommend sb. (for a position or for admission to a school, etc.)

选修 xuǎnxiū (动) take as an elective course: ~课 elective (optional) course

选秀 xuǎnxiù (名) talent contest; talent show: NBA~ NBA draft

选择(擇) xuǎnzé (动) select; make a choice: 自然~ natural selection

旋 xuàn (动) 1 (鏇) turn sth. on a lathe; lathe 2 whirl: ~风 whirlwind
see also xuán

旋风(風) xuànfēng (名) whirlwind; tornado

泫 xuàn (动)〈书〉 drip; trickle

炫 xuàn (动) 1 dazzle 2 show off: ～耀 show off; make a display of

眩 xuàn (动) feel dizzy; feel giddy: 头晕目～ feel dizzy

绚 xuàn (形) gorgeous

绚丽(麗) xuànlì (形) gorgeous; magnificent: 文采～ ornate literary style. ～的鲜花 beautiful flowers

靴 xuē (名) boots: 马～ riding boots. 雨～ rubber boots; galoshes

削 xuē (动) cut; pare; peel

see also xiāo

削价(價) xuējià (动) cut prices

削减 xuējiǎn (动) cut (down); reduce

削弱 xuēruò (动) weaken; cripple

学(學) xué I (动) 1 study; learn: ～文化 learn to read and write. ～历史 study history; take a history course. 向他～ learn from him 2 imitate; mimic: 鹦鹉～舌 parrot II (名) 1 learning; knowledge: 才疏～浅 have little talent and less learning; be an indifferent scholar 2 subject of study; branch of learning: 数～ mathematics. 文～ literature. 3 school: 小～ primary school. 中～ high school. 大～ college; university. 上～ go to school

学报(報) xuébào (名) journal (of a college)

学潮 xuécháo (名) student strike

学费 xuéfèi (名) tuition fee; tuition

学风(風) xuéfēng (名) style of study

学府 xuéfǔ (名) institution of higher learning

学会(會) xuéhuì (动) learn; master: 这孩子～了走路. The child has learned to toddle.

学会(會) xuéhuì (名) association society; institute

学籍 xuéjí (名) one's status as a student

学究 xuéjiū (名) pedant: ～气 pedantry

学科 xuékē (名) branch of learning; discipline; subject

学历(歷) xuélì (名) a written account of one's education

学龄 xuélíng (名) school age: ～前 preschool age

学年 xuénián (名) school year

学派 xuépài (名) school of thought

学期 xuéqī (名) term; semester

学舌 xuéshé (动) 1 mechanically repeat other people's words; parrot; ape 2 wag one's tongue spreading hearsay

学生 xuésheng (名) pupil; student

学识(識) xuéshí (名) learning; knowledge; scholarly attainments: ～渊博 have great learning; be learned. ～浅薄 have little learning

学士 xuéshì (名) bachelor; B. A.

学术(術) xuéshù (名) academic research: ～交流 academic exchanges. ～论文 research paper; thesis. ～讨论会 symposium. ～界 academic circles

学说 xuéshuō (名) theory; doctrine

学徒 xuétú (名) apprentice

学位 xuéwèi (名) academic degree: 博士(硕士)～ doctoral (master's) degree

学问 xuéwen (名) learning; knowledge; scholarship: 做～ engage in intellectual pursuit. ～高深 be learned

学习(習) xuéxí (动) study; learn

学校 xuéxiào (名) school

学业(業) xuéyè (名) one's studies: ～成绩 school record

学院 xuéyuàn (名) college; institute

学者 xuézhě (名) scholar

学制 xuézhì (名) 1 term of study 2 school system (including the curriculum and other regulations)

穴 xué (名) 1 cave; den; hole: 洞～ cave. 虎～ tiger's lair. 匪～ bandits' den. 2 acupoint: ～位 acupuncture point

雪 xuě I (名) snow II (动) wipe out (a humiliation); avenge: ～耻 wipe out a disgrace. 昭～ rehabilitate

雪白 xuěbái (形) snow white

雪崩 xuěbēng (名) snowslide; avalanche

雪恨 xuěhèn (动) avenge: 报仇～ take revenge

雪花 xuěhuā (名) snowflake

雪花膏 xuěhuāgāo (名) vanishing cream

雪亮 xuěliàng (形) bright as snow; shiny: 把玻璃擦得～ polish the glass till it has a good shine

雪盲 xuěmáng (名) snow-blindness

雪泥鸿爪 xuění hóngzhǎo footprints left on the path of one's life; one's memorable events

雪橇 xuěqiāo (名) sled; sleigh

雪中送炭 xuě zhōng sòng tàn send help where it is badly needed; provide timely help

血 xuè (名) blood: 流～ shed blood. 出～ bleed

see also xiě
血案 xuè'àn (名) murder case
血管 xuèguǎn (名) blood vessel
血汗 xuèhàn (名) hard toil: ～工厂 sweatshop
血迹 xuèjì (名) bloodstain
血口喷人 xuèkǒu pēn rén venomously vilify; make unfounded and malicious attack upon sb.
血库 xuèkù (名) blood bank
血泪(淚) xuèlèi (名) tragic experience; sufferings
血淋淋 xuèlīnlīn (形) bloody
血泊 xuèpō (名) pool of blood
血气(氣) xuèqì (名) 1 vim and vigour 2 uprightness and staunchness of character: 有～的青年 a young man of strong will and moral integrity
血球 xuèqiú (名) blood cell
血肉 xuèròu (名) flesh and blood: ～关系 blood kinship
血色 xuèsè (名) redness of the skin; colour: 脸上没有～ look pale or off colour
血统 xuètǒng (名) blood lineage; blood relationship: 中国～的美国人 Americans of Chinese descent; Chinese Americans
血小板 xuèxiǎobǎn (名) (blood)platelet
血腥 xuèxīng (形) bloody; sanguinary
血型 xuèxíng (名) blood type
血压(壓) xuèyā (名) blood pressure: 高～ high blood pressure; hypertension. 我的～是正常的;低压 80 高压 120. My blood pressure is pretty normal, it's 120 over 80.
血液 xuèyè (名) blood
血缘 xuèyuán (名) blood relationship
血债 xuèzhài (名) debt of blood

勋(勳) xūn (名) merit: 功～ meritorious service
勋爵 xūnjué (名) (a title of nobility) Lord
勋章 xūnzhāng (名) medal; decoration

熏 xūn (动) 1 smoke; fumigate: 墙给烟～黑了. The wall was blackened by smoke. 2 treat (meat, fish, etc.) with smoke; smoke: ～鱼 smoked fish
熏染 xūnrǎn (动) contaminate; corrupt
熏陶 xūntáo (动) nurture; edify

循 xún (动) follow; abide by
循规蹈矩 xúnguī-dǎojǔ follow the beaten track; stick rigidly to rules and regulations
循环(環) xúnhuán (动) circulate; cycle: 血液～ blood circulation. 恶性～ vicious circle
循序渐进(進) xúnxù jiànjìn proceed systematically

旬 xún (名) 1 a period of ten days: 上(中、下)～ the first (second, last) ten days of month 2 a decade in a person's life (applied to old people alone)

询 xún (动) ask; inquire: 查～ make inquiries
询问 xúnwèn (动) ask about; inquire: ～健康情况 ask after sb.

巡 xún (动) patrol
巡查 xúnchá (动) go on a tour of inspection
巡航 xúnháng (动) cruise: ～导弹 cruise missile
巡回(迴) xúnhuí (动) make the rounds; go the rounds; tour; make a circuit of: ～大使 an ambassador-at-large. ～医疗队 mobile medical team
巡逻(邏) xúnluó (动) go on patrol; patrol
巡视 xúnshì (动) make an inspection tour
巡洋舰(艦) xúnyángjiàn (名) cruiser

寻(尋) xún (动) seek; search: ～欢作乐 seek pleasure. 我们到处～找她. We have been looking for her everywhere.
寻常 xúncháng (形) usual; common: 出国现在是很～的事了. Going abroad is a common occurrence nowadays.
寻短见(見) xún duǎnjiàn commit suicide; take one's own life
寻呼 xúnhū (动) page; bleep: ～机 pager; bleeper; beeper
寻开(開)心 xún kāixīn make fun of; joke
寻觅 xúnmì (动) seek; look for
寻求 xúnqiú (动) seek
寻思 xúnsi (动) think to oneself; think: 你～～这事该怎么办. Think over what to do about it.
寻味 xúnwèi (动) chew sth. over; think over: 耐人～ afford much food for thought; set one pondering
寻问 xúnwèn (动) inquire about: 不断有人来～这件事. People kept coming to inquire about that affair.
寻衅(釁) xúnxìn (动) pick a quarrel; provoke
寻找 xúnzhǎo (动) seek; look for

训 xùn I (动) lecture; teach; train: 受～ undergo training. ～他一顿 give him a lecture (or a dressing down) II (名) model; example: 不足为～. This should not be regarded as a criterion.

训斥 xùnchì (动) reprimand; dress down

训诂 xùngǔ (名) critical interpretation of an ancient text; exegesis

训练(練) xùnliàn (动) train; drill

训令 xùnlìng (名)〈旧〉instructions; directive

驯 xùn I (动) tame; subdue: ～马 break in a horse II (形) tame and docile: ～鹿 a tame deer

驯服 xùnfú I (动) tame; bring under control: ～烈马 tame a spirited horse II (形) obedient and docile

驯养(養) xùnyǎng (动) domesticate

汛 xùn (名) flood: 防～ flood control. ～期 flood season

讯 xùn I (动) interrogate; question: 审～ interrogate II(名) message; dispatch: 电～ dispatch

迅 xùn (形) fast; swift

迅猛 xùnměng (形) swift and violent

迅速 xùnsù (形) speedy; rapid: 动作～ be quick-moving. ～发展 rapid development. ～康复 speedy recovery. ～答复 prompt reply

逊(遜) xùn (形) 1 modest: 谦～ modest and unassuming. 出言不～ speak insolently 2 inferior

逊色 xùnsè (形) inferior: 稍有～ be slightly inferior by comparison

殉 xùn (动) 1 be buried alive with the deceased 2 lay down one's life for a cause

殉国(國) xùnguó (动) give one's life for one's country

殉难(難) xùnnàn (动) die (for a just cause)

殉葬 xùnzàng (动) be buried alive with the deceased

殉职(職) xùnzhí (动) die at one's post; die in line of duty

Y y

丫 yā (名) bifurcation; fork

丫杈 yāchà (名) fork (of a tree); crotch

丫头(頭) yātou (名) 1 girl 2 slave girl; maid

压(壓) yā (动) 1 press; push down; weigh down: ～扁 press flat; flatten. ～碎 crush (to pieces). 大雪把树枝～弯了. Heavy snow weighed the branches down. 2 keep under control; control: ～住心头怒火 keep one's temper 3 suppress: 镇～叛乱 suppress (or put down) a rebellion 4 approach: 敌军～境. Enemy troops are bearing down on the border. 5 shelve: 这份公文～在什么地方了. The document is being pigeonholed somewhere. see also yà

压倒 yādǎo (动) overwhelm; overpower; prevail over: ～多数 an overwhelming majority. 比赛中客队占～优势. The guest team dominated the game.

压低 yādī (动) lower; drop: ～声音说话 speak in a lowered voice. ～物价 keep the prices down

压服 yāfú (动) force sb. to submit; coerce sb. into submission: ～手段 coercive measure

压价(價) yājià (动) force price down: ～出售 sell at reduced prices

压力 yālì (名) 1 pressure: ～锅 pressure cooker 2 overwhelming force; pressure: 施加～ pressurize; bring pressure on sb. 屈于～ yield to pressure

压路机(機) yālùjī (名) road roller

压迫 yāpò (动) 1 oppress; repress 2 constrict

压岁(歲)钱(錢) yāsuìqián (名) money given to children as a lunar New Year gift

压缩 yāsuō (动) reduce; cut down; curtail: ～开支 cut down (or reduce) expenses

压抑 yāyì (动) contain; inhibit; depress: ～不住内心的激动 unable to contain one's excitement. 心情～ feel constrained

压榨 yāzhà (动) 1 press; squeeze 2 exploit; fleece; bleed sb. white

压制 yāzhì (动) suppress; stifle; inhibit: ～批评 gag criticism. ～反对的意见 suppress dissenting voices

压轴戏(戲) yāzhòuxì (名) the last item on a theatrical programme

呀 yā I (叹) [indicating surprise] ah; oh: ～, 下雪了! Oh, it's snowing! II (象) creak: 门～的一声开了. The door opened with a creak. *or* The door squeaked open.

鸦 yā (名) crow

鸦片 yāpiàn (名) opium

鸦雀无(無)声(聲) yā-què wú shēng it became so quiet that you could hear a butterfly

押 yā I (动) 1 give as security; mortgage; pawn: 抵~ leave sth. as security. ~房子借两万美元 mortgage a house for twenty thousand dollars 2 detain; take into custody: 在~犯 criminal in custody 3 escort: ~运 escort goods (on a train, truck, etc.) II (名) signature; mark made on a written statement in place of signature

押解 yājiè (动) send (a criminal or captive) under escort; escort

押金 yājīn (名) deposit; security

鸭 yā (名) duck

鸭绒 yāróng (名) duck's down; eiderdown: ~被 eiderdown quilt

涯 yá (名) margin; limit: 天~海角 the four corners of the earth; the end of the earth. 一望无~ boundless as far as the eye can reach

崖 yá (名) precipice; cliff: 悬~勒马 rein in on the edge of a precipice

牙 yá (名) 1 tooth 2 toothlike thing

牙齿(齒) yáchǐ (名) tooth

牙床(牀) yáchuáng (名) gum

牙雕 yádiāo (名) ivory carving

牙膏 yágāo (名) toothpaste

牙关(關) yáguān (名) mandibular joint: 咬紧~ clench (or grit) one's teeth

牙科 yákē (名) (department of) dentistry: ~医生 dentist

牙刷 yáshuā (名) toothbrush

牙痛 yátòng (名) toothache

牙龈 yáyín (名) gum

芽 yá (名) bud; sprout; shoot

衙 yá

衙门(門) yámen (名) *yamen*, government office in feudal China

哑(啞) yǎ (形) 1 mute; dumb: 又聋又~ deaf and dumb; deaf-mute 2 (of voice) hoarse; husky

哑巴 yǎba (名) a dumb person; mute

哑剧(劇) yǎjù (名) dumbshow; mime

哑谜 yǎmí (名) puzzling remark; enigma

雅 yǎ (形) 1 appropriate; proper; correct 2 refined; elegant: 古~ quaint 3〈敬〉 your: ~教 your esteemed instructions

雅观(觀) yǎguān (形) [often used in the negative] refined (in manner, etc.); in good taste: 很不~ inconsistent with the canons of good taste; boorish

雅思 yǎsī (名) IELTS

雅俗共赏 yǎ-sú gòng shǎng (of a work of art or literature) suit both refined and popular tastes; be enjoyed by both educated and ordinary people

雅兴(興) yǎxìng (名) aesthetic inclinations: 无此~ have no such poetic inspiration

雅致 yǎzhì (形) refined; elegant; tasteful: 陈设~ be furnished in good taste

亚(亞) yà (形) inferior; second: 不~于人 second to none; not inferior to anyone

亚健康 yàjiànkāng indifferent state of health (without being properly ill)

亚军 yàjūn (名) second place (in a sports contest)

亚麻 yàmá (名) flax: ~布 linen (cloth)

亚热(熱)带(帶) yàrèdài (名) subtropical zone; subtropics; semitropics

亚洲 Yàzhōu (名) Asia

压(壓) yà

see also yā

压根儿(兒) yàgēnr (副) [often used in the negative] from the start; in the first place; altogether: 他全忘了,好像~没有这回事. He clean forgot about it as if nothing of the kind had ever happened.

揠 yà (动)〈书〉 pull up

揠苗助长(長) yà miáo zhù zhǎng pull the shoots upward in a stupid effort to make them grow; spoil the show by ludicrous enthusiasm

轧 yà (动) 1 roll; run over: ~棉花 gin cotton 2 squeeze out; push out: 倾~ engage in political infighting

see also zhá

焉 yān〈书〉 1 here; herein: 心不在~ absent-minded 2 [often used in rhetorical questions] how: 如无大众支持, ~有今日? How could we fare so well without mass support?

淹 yān (动) flood; submerge; inundate: 庄稼被洪水～了. The crops were inundated.

淹死 yānsǐ (动) drown

阉 yān (动) castrate or spay: ～鸡 capon. ～猪 hog

阉割 yāngē (动) **1** castrate or spay **2** deprive a theory, etc. of its essence; emasculate

腌 yān (动) preserve in salt; salt; pickle: ～菜 pickled vegetables; pickles. ～鱼 salted fish
see also ā

烟 yān (名) **1** smoke **2** mist; vapour **3** tobacco or cigarette: 抽支～ have a cigarette; have a smoke

烟草 yāncǎo (名) tobacco

烟囱 yāncōng (名) chimney; funnel; stovepipe

烟斗 yāndǒu (名) (tobacco) pipe: ～丝 pipe tobacco

烟盒 yānhé (名) cigarette case

烟灰 yānhuī (名) cigarette ash: ～缸 ashtray

烟火 yānhuǒ (名) **1** smoke and fire: 建筑工地,严禁～. Lighting fires is strictly forbidden on the construction site. **2** fireworks: 放～put on a display of fireworks

烟煤 yānméi (名) bituminous coal; soft coal

烟幕 yānmù (名) smokescreen: ～弹 smoke shell; smoke bomb

烟丝(絲) yānsī (名) cut tobacco; pipe tabacco

烟雾(霧) yānwù (名) smoke; mist; vapour; smog: ～弥漫 full of smoke

烟消云(雲)散 yānxiāo-yúnsàn vanish like mist; melt into thin air

烟叶(葉) yānyè (名) tobacco leaf; leaf tobacco

咽 yān (名) pharynx
see also yàn

咽喉 yānhóu (名) **1** throat **2** vital passage: ～要地 a junction of strategic importance; key junction

颜 yán (名) **1** face; countenance: 和～悦色 look good-natured and obliging. 笑逐～开 one's face is wreathed in smiles **2** decency; face: 无～见人 feel ashamed to appear in public **3** colour: ～料 pigment; dyestuff. 五～六色 of all colours; multicoloured; colourful

颜面 yánmiàn (名) **1** face: ～神经 facial nerve **2** decency; face: 顾全～ save face

颜色 yánsè (名)〈口〉**1** colour **2** facial expression; countenance: 给他点儿～看看. Make him understand how to behave himself. *or* Teach him a lesson.

言 yán I (名) **1** speech; words: ～语 speech. 格～ maxim. 诺言 promise; pledge. ～外之意 the implication of a remark **2** character; word (in Chinese each character is called a word): 五～诗 a poem with five characters to a line II (动) say; talk; speak: 畅所欲～ speak freely. ～之有理. What one says is correct. *or* The remark sounds reasonable.

言不由衷 yán bù yóuzhōng speak insincerely; not speak one's mind

言传(傳)身教 yánchuán-shēnjiào teach by personal example as well as verbal instruction; set an example to the others in whatever one says or does

言辞(辭) yáncí (名) one's words; what one says: ～恳切 be sincere and earnest in what one says

言归(歸)于(於)好 yán guī yú hǎo become reconciled

言归(歸)正传(傳) yán guīzhèngzhuàn to come back to our story; to return to the subject

言过(過)其实(實) yán guò qí shí overstate the case

言和 yánhé (动) make peace

言简意赅 yánjiǎn-yìgāi brief and to the point; concise

言论(論) yánlùn (名) opinion on politics and other affairs: ～自由 freedom of speech

言听(聽)计从(從) yántīng-jìcóng act upon whatever sb. says; listen to all his counsel

言外之意 yán wài zhī yì what is actually meant; the real meaning; implication: 体会其～read between the lines

言行一致 yánxíng yīzhì consistency in words and deeds; the deeds match the words

言语 yányǔ (名) spoken language; speech

言语 yányu (动) speak; answer; reply: 你走的时候～一声儿. Don't just walk out without saying a word. 人家同你讲话呢,你怎么不～? Why did you make no response when people were speaking to you?

言之成理 yán zhī chéng lǐ sound reasonable

阎 yán

阎王 Yánwang (名) 1 Yama; King of Hell 2 an extremely cruel person

炎 yán I (形) scorching; extremely hot: ~夏 sweltering summer II (名) inflammation: 发~ inflammation. 支气管~ bronchitis

炎黄子孙(孫) Yán Huáng zǐsūn the Chinese people (supposed to be descendants of Yan Di and Huang Di)

炎凉 yánliáng (形) the way of behaving abjectly towards the rich and powerful and coldly towards the poor: 世态~ the way of the world follows the practice of playing up to the influential and giving the cold shoulder to the less fortunate

炎热(熱) yánrè I (形) scorching; blazing; burning hot II (名) the intense heat of summer: 冒着~ braving the sweltering heat

研 yán (动) 1 grind; pestle: ~成粉末 grind into fine powder 2 study: 钻~ study assiduously

研发(發) yánfā (动) research and development; R & D

研究 yánjiū (动) 1 study; research: 科学~ scientific research. ~生 postgraduate. ~员 research fellow 2 consider; discuss (problems, suggestions, applications, etc.)

研讨会(會) yántǎohuì (名) symposium; seminar

研制(製) yánzhì (动) research and manufacture; develop: ~新的武器 develop new weapons

妍 yán (形)〈书〉 beautiful; enchanting: 百花争~. A hundred flowers vie with each other in beauty.

盐(鹽) yán (名) salt: 精~ refined salt

盐碱土 yánjiǎntǔ (名) saline-alkali soil

盐田 yántián (名) salt pan

严(嚴) yán (形) 1 tight: 他嘴~,从来不乱说. He is too tight-lipped to let slip any careless remarks. 2 strict; severe; stern; rigorous: 治学谨~ adopt a rigorous approach in one's studies. 这位老师对学生管教很~. The teacher is very strict with his students. ~冬 severe winter. ~办 be dealt with severely

严惩(懲) yánchéng (动) punish severely: ~不贷 punish without leniency; punish with severity

严词 yáncí (名) in strong terms; in stern words: ~拒绝 give a stern rebuff; sternly refuse

严打 yándǎ (动) crack down; strike hard

严防 yánfáng (动) be strictly on guard against; take strict precautions against

严格 yángé (形) strict; rigorous; rigid: ~按规定办事 act strictly according to the regulations

严寒 yánhán (名) severe cold; bitter cold

严谨 yánjǐn (形) 1 rigorous; strict; careful and precise: 办事~ be meticulous and precise in one's work 2 compact; well-knit: 文章结构~. The essay is well-knit.

严禁 yánjìn (动) strictly forbid (or prohibit)

严峻 yánjùn (形) stern; severe; rigorous; grim: ~的考验 a severe test; a rigorous test

严酷 yánkù (形) 1 harsh; bitter; grim: ~的现实 harsh reality 2 cruel; ruthless: ~的压迫 cruel oppression. ~的剥削 ruthless exploitation

严厉(厲) yánlì (形) stern; severe: ~的批评 severe criticism

严密 yánmì (形) tight; close: ~监视 keep close watch over. ~注视形势的发展closely follow the development of the situation

严明 yánmíng (形) strict and impartial: 纪律~. Discipline is strictly observed.

严实(實) yánshi (形) 1 tight; close: 她的嘴~着呢! She has tight lips. 2 (hide) safely

严肃(肅) yánsù (形) serious; solemn; earnest: 他是个~的人,从来不苟言笑. He's a serious man and would never allow himself to make a frivolous remark.

严刑 yánxíng (名) cruel punishment

严阵以待 yán zhèn yǐ dài be fully on the alert for enemy attack; be fully prepared for any eventuality

严正 yánzhèng (形) solemn and just; serious and principled; stern: ~立场 solemn and just stand. ~声明 a solemn statement; solemnly declare

严重 yánzhòng (形) serious; grave; critical: 病情~. The patient's condition is serious. 局势~. The situation is grave.

岩(巖) yán (名) 1 rock 2 cliff; crag

岩层(層) yáncéng (名) rock stratum; rock formation

岩洞 yándòng (名) grotto

岩石 yánshí (名) rock
岩心 yánxīn (名) (drill) core
延 yán (动) 1 prolong; extend; lengthen: 蔓~spread. 苟~残喘 be at one's last gasp 2 postpone; delay: 会议~期了. The meeting is postponed.
延长(長) yáncháng (动) lengthen; prolong; extend: ~线 extension line. 这条铁路将~三百公里. The railway line will be extended (or prolonged) 300 kilometres.
延迟(遲) yánchí (动) delay; defer; postpone: 谈判~,但没有取消. The negotiation was postponed but not cancelled.
延缓 yánhuǎn (动) delay; postpone; put off
延年益寿(壽) yánnián-yìshòu (of tonics, etc.) prolong life; promise longevity
延期 yánqī (动) postpone; defer; put off: 比赛因天气不好~举行. The game was put off because of bad weather.
延伸 yánshēn (动) extend; stretch: 铁路一直~到国境线. The railway line stretches right to the frontier.
延误 yánwù (动) incur loss through delay: ~时日. Waste time on account of delay.
延续(續) yánxù (动) continue; go on; last: 会议~了三天. The session lasted for three whole days.
筵 yán (名) 1 〈书〉 a bamboo mat spread on the floor for people to sit on in ancient China 2 banquet; feast: 喜~ a wedding feast
筵席 yánxí (名) 1 seats arranged around a table at a banquet 2 banquet; feast
沿 yán I (介) along: ~街 along the streets. ~门求乞 beg from door to door. ~着河边走 take a stroll on the riverside II (动) follow (a tradition, pattern, etc.): 相~成习. The traditional practice has gradually become a social custom. III (名) edge; border
沿岸 yán'àn (名) along the bank or coast: 长江~城市 cities on both sides of the Changjiang River
沿革 yángé (名) the course of change and development; evolution: 社会风俗的~the evolution of social customs
沿海 yánhǎi (名) along the coast; coastal: ~地区 coastal areas. ~岛屿 offshore island. ~港口 maritime port
沿途 yántú (名) on the way; throughout a journey: 旅游团~受到热情接待. The tourist group was warmly received throughout its journey.
沿袭(襲) yánxí (动) carry on as before; follow: ~老规矩 tread the beaten track
沿用 yányòng (动) continue to use (an old method, etc.): ~原来的名称 still keep the old name
演 yǎn (动) 1 develop; evolve: ~进 improve through evolutionary process 2 elaborate: ~绎 deduce 3 drill; practise: ~算 make mathematical calculations 4 perform; play; act; put on: ~电影 show a film
演变(變) yǎnbiàn (动) develop; evolve: 历史~ historical evolution
演唱 yǎnchàng (动) sing (in a performance); act a part in Beijing opera or local opera
演出 yǎnchū (动) perform; show; put on a show: 首次~ the first performance or show; premiere (of a play, film, etc.). ~节目 programme. ~单位 producer
演化 yǎnhuà (名) evolution
演技 yǎnjì (名) acting
演讲(講) yǎnjiǎng I (动) give a lecture; make a speech II (名) lecture
演示 yǎnshì (动) demonstrate; show (using lab, experiment, charts, etc.)
演说 yǎnshuō I (动) deliver a speech; make an address II (名) speech
演算 yǎnsuàn (动) make mathematical calculations
演习(習) yǎnxí (动) manoeuvre; drill: 军事~ military manoeuvre or exercise
演戏(戲) yǎnxì (动) put on a play; act in a play
演艺(藝) yǎnyì (名) performing arts: ~界 performing artists
演绎(繹) yǎnyì (名) deduction: ~法 the deductive method
演员 yǎnyuán (名) actor or actress; ballet dancer or acrobatic performer
演奏 yǎnzòu (动) give an instrumental performance; play a musical instrument (in a performance)
偃 yǎn
偃旗息鼓 yǎnqí-xīgǔ 1 stop fighting; cease to criticize or attack others 2 be on a secret march
奄 yǎn 〈书〉 1 cover; overspread 2 suddenly; all of a sudden
奄奄 yǎnyǎn (形) (of breathing) feeble: 气息~ breathe feebly; be sinking fast; be dying. ~一息 at one's last gasp; on

one's last legs

掩 yǎn (动) 1 cover; hide: ～口而笑 laugh in one's sleeve. ～人耳目 hoodwink the public 2 shut; close: 虚～着门 with the door left ajar

掩蔽 yǎnbì I (动) cover; hide II (名) shelter; covered position

掩藏 yǎncáng (动) hide; conceal

掩耳盗铃 yǎn ěr dào líng bury one's head in the sand like an ostrich; engage in self-delusion

掩盖(蓋) yǎngài (动) cover; conceal: 不要～矛盾. Don't try to conceal the contradictions. 大雪～着田野. The fields are covered with a thick layer of snow.

掩护(護) yǎnhù (动) screen; shield; cover: ～进攻 screen an advance. 在黑夜的～下 under cover of night

掩埋 yǎnmái (动) bury

掩人耳目 yǎn rén ěr-mù deceive the public; hoodwink people

掩饰 yǎnshì (动) cover up; gloss over; conceal: ～错误 gloss over (or cover up) one's mistakes

掩眼法 yǎnyǎnfǎ (名) cover-up; camouflage

眼 yǎn I (名) 1 eye: 掩～术 conjuring device; sleight of hand 2 small hole: 针～eye of a needle. 炮～ muzzle of a gun (in a covered position) 3 key point: 节骨～儿 juncture II (量) [for wells]: 打一～井 sink a well

眼巴巴 yǎnbābā (副) 1 (expecting) eagerly; anxiously: 大家～地等着他回来. We were all anxiously waiting for his return. 2 helplessly (watching sth. unpleasant happen): 他～地看着老鹰把小鸡抓走了. He watched helplessly a hawk snatch away a chick.

眼馋(饞) yǎnchán (形) covetous; having a strong desire to possess sth.

眼福 yǎnfú (名) the good fortune of seeing sth. rare or beautiful: ～不浅 be lucky enough to enjoy such a wonderful view

眼高手低 yǎngāo-shǒudī set a high standard for every kind of work but fall far short of it himself; fastidious but incompetent

眼光 yǎnguāng (名) 1 eye: 大家都以怀疑的～望着他. Everyone eyed him with suspicion. 2 sight; foresight; insight; vision: ～远大 far-sighted. ～短浅 short-sighted

眼红 yǎnhóng (形) 1 covet; be envious; be jealous 2 furious: 仇人相见,分外～. When enemies meet, they will look daggers at each other.

眼花 yǎnhuā (形) have dim eyesight; have blurred vision: 令人头昏～ make one's head swim. ～缭乱 be dazzled

眼尖 yǎnjiān (形) be sharp-eyed; have sharp eyes; have keen sight

眼睑(瞼) yǎnjiǎn (名) eyelid

眼界 yǎnjiè (名) field of vision (or view); outlook: 扩大～ widen one's field of vision; broaden one's horizons

眼镜 yǎnjìng (名) glasses; spectacles

眼睛 yǎnjing (名) eye

眼看 yǎnkàn I (副) soon; in a moment: 天～就要亮了. The day is dawning. II (动) watch helplessly; look on passively: 咱们哪能～着庄稼被洪水冲走呢? How can we stand by and watch helplessly the crops in the fields being washed away by the flood?

眼科 yǎnkē (名) (department of) ophthalmology: ～医生 oculist; ophthalmologist

眼眶 yǎnkuàng (名) 1 eye socket; orbit: 她～里噙着泪水. Her eyes filled with tears. 2 rim of the eye

眼泪(淚) yǎnlèi (名) tears: ～汪汪 eyes brimming with tears; in tears

眼力 yǎnlì (名) 1 eyesight; vision: ～好(差) have good (poor) eyesight 2 judgement; discrimination

眼帘(簾) yǎnlián (名) eye: 映入～come into view

眼明手快 yǎnmíng-shǒukuài sharp-eyed and agile

眼前 yǎnqián (名) 1 before one's eyes: 他～是碧波万里. He found himself standing before a vast expanse of blue water. 2 at the moment; at present

眼球 yǎnqiú (名) eyeball

眼色 yǎnsè (名) wink: 使～give sb. a wink

眼神 yǎnshén (名) expression in one's eyes

眼熟 yǎnshú (形) look familiar: 这人看着很～,但我忘了在哪儿见过他. That person looks familiar but I don't remember where I met him.

眼下 yǎnxià (名) at the moment; at present; now: 这种裙子～不时兴了. These skirts are now out of fashion.

眼药(藥) yǎnyào (名) eye ointment or eyedrops

眼影 yǎnyǐng (名) eye shadow

眼睁睁 yǎnzhēngzhēng (副) (looking on) helplessly or unfeelingly
眼中钉 yǎnzhōngdīng (名) thorn in one's flesh (or side)
俨(儼) yǎn 〈书〉 majestic; solemn; dignified
俨然 yǎnrán 〈书〉 I (形) solemn; dignified: 望之～ appear dignified II (副) just like; as if: 这男孩说起话来～是个大人. The boy talks as if he were a grown-up.
衍 yǎn 〈书〉 1 spread out; develop; amplify 2 redundant; superfluous
衍变(變) yǎnbiàn (动) develop; evolve
衍生物 yǎnshēngwù (名) derivative
宴 yàn I (动) entertain at a banquet; fête: ～客 host a dinner in honour of the visitors II (名) feast; banquet: 盛～ banquet; sumptuous dinner. 便～ informal dinner
宴会(會) yànhuì (名) banquet; feast; dinner party
宴请 yànqǐng (动) entertain (to dinner); fête: ～贵宾 give a banquet in honour of the distinguished guests
谚 yàn (名) proverb; saying: 农～ peasants' proverb; farmers' saying
谚语 yànyǔ (名) proverb; saying
艳(艷) yàn (形) 1 bright; fresh and attractive: 娇～ pretty and charming 2 amorous: ～史 one's love affairs
艳丽(麗) yànlì (形) bright-coloured and beautiful; gorgeous: ～夺目 of dazzling beauty. 打扮得过于～ be loudly dressed
燕 yàn (名) (～子) swallow
燕麦(麥) yànmài (名) oats
燕尾服 yànwěifú (名) tailcoat
燕窝(窩) yànwō (名) edible bird's nest
厌(厭) yàn (动) 1 be disgusted with; detest: ～弃 detest and keep away from 2 be fed up with; be bored with: 这种书我看～了. I am tired of reading such books. 不～其烦 not mind taking all the trouble 3 be satisfied: 贪得无～ have an insatiable desire for gain
厌烦 yànfán (动) be sick of; be fed up with
厌倦 yànjuàn (动) be weary of; be tired of
雁 yàn (名) wild goose
赝 yàn (形) 〈书〉 counterfeit; spurious; fake
赝本 yànběn (名) spurious edition or copy
赝品 yànpǐn (名) counterfeit; fake; sham
唁 yàn (动) extend condolences
唁电(電) yàndiàn (名) telegram (or cable) of condolence; message of condolence
咽 yàn (动) swallow: 狼吞虎～ wolf down one's food
see also yān
咽气(氣) yànqì (动) breathe one's last; die
砚 yàn (名) inkstone; inkslab
砚台(臺) yàntái (名) inkstone; inkslab
焰 yàn (名) flame; blaze: 烈～ blazing (or raging) flames
焰火 yànhuǒ (名) fireworks
验(驗) yàn (动) 1 examine; check: ～护照 examine (or check) a passport. ～血 blood test 2 prove effective; produce the expected result: 灵～ effective
验明正身 yànmíng zhèngshēn verify the identity of a criminal before execution
验尸(屍) yànshī (动) postmortem; autopsy
验收 yànshōu (动) accept sth. as up to standard after a check
验证 yànzhèng (动) verify
央 yāng 1 entreat 2 centre
央告 yānggào (动) beg; implore
央求 yāngqiú (动) beg; entreat; implore: 我再三～, 他才答应. I kept pleading with him until he agreed.
殃 yāng I (名) calamity; disaster; misfortune: 遭～ meet with (or suffer) disaster II (动) bring disaster on: 祸国～民 bring calamity on the country and the people
秧 yāng (名) 1 seedling; sprout 2 rice seedling: 插～ transplant rice seedlings 3 vine 4 young; fry: 鱼～ young fish
秧歌 yānggē (名) yangko (dance), a popular rural folk dance
秧苗 yāngmiáo (名) rice shoots; rice seedlings
秧田 yāngtián (名) rice seedlings bed
羊 yáng (名) sheep: 绵～ sheep. 山～ goat
羊肠(腸)小道 yángcháng xiǎodào winding footpath
羊羔 yánggāo (名) lamb
羊倌 yángguān (名) shepherd

羊圈 yángjuàn (名) sheepfold; sheep-pen
羊毛 yángmáo (名) sheep's wool; fleece: ~衫woollen sweater; cardigan
羊皮 yángpí (名) sheepskin: 披着~的狼 a wolf in sheep's clothing
羊皮纸 yángpízhǐ (名) parchment
羊肉 yángròu (名) mutton: 烤~串 mutton cubes roasted on a skewer; shashlik
洋 yáng I (形) 1 vast; multitudinous 2 foreign: ~房 Western-style house 3 modern: ~办法 modern methods II (名) ocean: 太平~ the Pacific Ocean
洋白菜 yángbáicài (名) cabbage
洋葱 yángcōng (名) onion
洋灰 yánghuī (名) cement
洋为(爲)中用 yáng wéi Zhōng yòng make foreign things serve China
洋相 yángxiàng (名) [generally used in the set phrase 出洋相]: 出~make a spectacle of oneself
洋洋 yángyáng (形) numerous; copious: ~大观 spectacular; magnificent
洋溢 yángyì (动) be permeated with; brim with: 感情~brim with emotion
佯 yáng (动) pretend; feign; sham: ~作不知 pretend not to know. ~攻 feign (or simulate) attack; make a feint
阳(陽) yáng I (名) 1 (in Chinese philosophy, medicine, etc.) *yang*, the masculine or positive principle in nature 2 the sun: ~光 sunlight. ~历 solar calendar (as distinguished from the lunar calendar) II (形) 1 open; overt: ~奉阴违 agree in public but act differently in private 2 belonging to this world: ~间 in this human world 3 positive: ~极 positive pole; positive electrode
阳春 yángchūn (名) spring (season)
阳历(曆) yánglì (名) 1 solar calendar 2 the Gregorian calendar
阳伞(傘) yángsǎn (名) parasol; sunshade
阳台(臺) yángtái (名) balcony
阳性 yángxìng (名) 1 positive: ~反应 positive reaction 2 masculine gender
疡(瘍) yáng (名) sore: 溃~ ulcer
杨(楊) yáng (名) poplar
杨柳 yángliǔ (名) 1 poplar and willow 2 willow
杨树(樹) yángshù (名) poplar
扬(揚) yáng (动) 1 raise: ~手 wave one's hand (and beckon). ~长避短 make amends for one's weaknesses by exploiting one's strengths. 趾高气~ self-complacent and arrogant 2 spread; make known: 宣~ propagate; publicize. 名~四海 be known throughout the world
扬长(長)而去 yángcháng ér qù stalk off; stride out
扬帆 yángfān (动) hoist the sails; set sail
扬眉吐气(氣) yángméi-tǔqì hold one's head high; feel happy and proud
扬名 yángmíng (动) make a name for oneself; become famous: ~天下 become world-famous
扬声(聲)器 yángshēngqì (名) loudspeaker
扬水 yángshuǐ (动) pump up water: ~站 pumping station
扬言 yángyán (动) openly talk about taking aggressive action
扬扬 yángyáng (形) triumphantly; complacently: 得意~ look immensely complacent
痒(癢) yǎng (动) itch
痒痒 yǎngyang (动)〈口〉itch
氧 yǎng (名) oxygen (O)
氧吧 yǎngbā (名) oxygen bar
氧化 yǎnghuà (动) oxidize; oxidate: ~作用 oxidation
氧气(氣) yǎngqì (名) oxygen
养(養) yǎng I (动) 1 support; provide for: ~家 support a family 2 raise; keep; grow: ~鸭 raise ducks. ~花 grow flowers 3 give birth to: 她~了个儿子. She gave birth to a boy. 4 form; acquire; cultivate: ~成良好的习惯 form good habits 5 convalesce; recuperate: ~身体 recuperate 6 maintain; keep in good repair: ~路 maintain a road; road maintenance II (形) foster; adoptive: ~父(母) foster-father (mother). ~子(女) adopted son (daughter)
养病 yǎngbìng (动) recuperate
养虎遗患 yǎng hǔ yí huàn to rear a tiger is to court calamity; to appease an enemy is to invite disaster
养精蓄锐 yǎngjīng-xùruì conserve energy and build up strength
养老 yǎnglǎo (动) 1 provide for the aged

(usu. one's parents) **2** live in retirement: ~金 old-age pension. ~院 House of Respect for the Aged

养料 yǎngliào (名) nourishment

养神 yǎngshén (动) repose: 闭目~ sit in repose with one's eyes closed

养生 yǎngshēng (动) preserve one's health; keep in good health: ~之道 how to maintain good health; the formula for good health

养育 yǎngyù (动) bring up; rear: ~子女 bring up children

养殖 yǎngzhí (动) breed or cultivate (aquatics)

养尊处(處)优(優) yǎngzūn-chǔyōu enjoy high position and a life of ease and comfort

仰 yǎng (动) **1** face upward: ~望星斗 look at the stars **2** admire; respect: 信~ believe in. ~慕 hold sb. in high esteem **3** rely on; depend on: ~仗 look to sb. for help

仰面 yǎngmiàn face upward: ~朝天 lie on one's back. ~倒下 fall on one's back

仰人鼻息 yǎng rén bíxī be dependent on others and act slavishly; be at sb.'s beck and call

仰卧 yǎngwò (动) lie on one's back; lie supine

仰泳 yǎngyǒng (名) backstroke

恙 yàng (名)〈书〉ailment; illness: 安然无~ safe and sound

样(樣) yàng I (名) **1** appearance; shape: ~式 style; type. 模~ look; manner **2** sample; model; pattern: 货~ sample (goods). 鞋~ outline of a shoe; shoe pattern. 校~ proof sheet II (量) kind; type: 在他所选的课程里,他~~都是名列前茅. In each and every course he has chosen, he is always among the best.

样板 yàngbǎn (名) **1** sample plate **2** templet **3** model; prototype; example: 树立~ set an example

样本 yàngběn (名) **1** sample book **2** sample; specimen

样品 yàngpǐn (名) sample (product); specimen

样式 yàngshì (名) pattern; type; style; form: 各种~的帽子 hats in all styles

样子 yàngzi (名) **1** appearance; shape **2** manner; air **3** sample; model; pattern: 衣服~ clothes pattern **4** 〈口〉tendency; likelihood: 天像是要下雨的~. It looks like rain. 高高兴兴的~ look very happy

怏 yàng

怏怏 yàngyàng (形) disgruntled: ~不乐 look disgruntled and sad

要 yāo (动) **1** demand; ask **2** force; coerce

see also yào

要求 yāoqiú (动) ask for; demand; request: ~澄清 ask for clarification. ~出席 request one's presence. ~速予答复 demand a prompt reply

要挟(挾) yāoxié (动) coerce; put pressure on: 他们~他,要他俯首听命. They tried to coerce him into submission.

腰 yāo (名) **1** waist **2** waist (of a garment): 裤~ waist of trousers **3** middle: 半山~ halfway up a mountain; on a hillside

腰包 yāobāo (名) purse; pocket: 那样,我们都得掏~. In that case, we will all have to make a contribution.

腰缠万(萬)贯 yāochán wànguàn be loaded; be very rich

腰杆(桿)子 yāogǎnzi (名) **1** back: 挺起~ straighten one's back and square one's shoulders **2** backing; support: ~硬 have strong backing

腰身 yāoshēn (名) waistline; waist; waist measurement: 衣服的~ the waist of a dress

腰子 yāozi (名) kidney

夭 yāo (动) die young

夭亡 yāowáng (动) die young

夭折 yāozhé (动) **1** die young **2** come to a premature end: 谈判中途~. The negotiations broke down halfway.

妖 yāo I (名) goblin; demon; evil spirit II (形) **1** evil and bewitching: ~术 sorcery; witchcraft **2** coquettish; seductive

妖怪 yāoguài (名) monster; goblin; demon

妖魔鬼怪 yāomó-guǐguài demons and ghosts

妖魔化 yāomóhuà (动) demonize

妖孽 yāoniè (名) **1** person or event associated with evil or misfortune **2** evildoer

妖言 yāoyán (名) heresy; fallacy: ~惑众 spread fallacies to mislead the public; stir up public feeling by sophistry

邀 yāo (动) **1** invite; request: 特~代表 specially invited representative **2** gain; receive: 谅~同意. This will probably meet with your approval.

邀集 yāojí (动) invite a group of people to come and meet together

邀请 yāoqǐng (动) invite

肴 yáo (名) meat and fish dishes

肴馔 yáozhuàn (名) the courses at a banquet; dishes

窑(窯) yáo (名) 1 kiln: 砖～ brick kiln 2 cave dwelling

窑洞 yáodòng (名) cave dwelling

谣 yáo (名) 1 ballad; rhyme: 民～ ballad 2 rumour

谣传(傳) yáochuán I (动) rumour has it that II (名) the rumours that go about everywhere

谣言 yáoyán (名) rumour: 散布～ spread (or circulate) rumours

遥 yáo (形)〈书〉distant; remote; far

遥测 yáocè (名) telemetering: 空间～ space telemetry

遥感 yáogǎn (名) remote sensing

遥控 yáokòng (名) remote control; telecontrol

遥望 yáowàng (动) look into the distance

遥遥 yáoyáo (形) far away; remote: 在这方面～领先 be far ahead in this field. ～无期. It won't materialize in the foreseeable future. *or* The possibility is fairly remote.

遥远(遠) yáoyuǎn (形) distant; remote: ～的将来 the distant (or remote) future.

摇 yáo (动) shake; wave: ～头 shake one's head. ～旗 wave a flag. ～船 row a boat. ～铃 ring a bell

摇摆(擺) yáobǎi (动) sway; swing; rock; vacillate: 迎风～sway in the breeze. 在这个问题上,他们并没有～不定. There is no vacillation on their part on this question.

摇动(動) yáodòng (动) 1 wave; shake: 服用前请～瓶子. Shake the bottle before use. 2 rock; flail: 看见他们向我走近了,我就向他们～两臂. I flailed my arms at them when I saw them approach.

摇晃 yáohuàng (动) rock; sway; shake: 风浪大了,这只船开始有点～. When the sea gets rough, this boat begins to rock. 这椅子有点～. The chair is a bit rickety (or shaky).

摇篮(籃) yáolán (名) cradle: 我国古代文化的～ the cradle of ancient Chinese culture

摇旗呐喊 yáo qí nàhǎn beat the drum (for sb.); cheer and encourage

摇身一变(變) yáo shēn yī biàn assume an entirely different role in an instant

摇头(頭)摆(擺)尾 yáotóu-bǎiwěi assume an air of complacency

摇头(頭)丸 yáotóuwán (名) Ecstasy

摇尾乞怜(憐) yáo wěi qǐ lián wag the tail; fawn and beg for mercy

摇摇欲坠(墜) yáoyáo yù zhuì tottering; crumbling; teetering on the verge of collapse

摇曳 yáoyè (动) flicker; sway: ～的灯光 flickering light

窈 yǎo

窈窕 yǎotiǎo (形)〈书〉(of a woman) gentle and graceful

杳 yǎo (形)〈书〉too far away to be readily accessible: ～无踪迹 disappear without a trace; vanish like soap bubbles

杳无(無)音信 yǎo wú yīnxìn be absolutely no news about sb.; disappear for good

咬 yǎo (动) 1 bite; snap at: ～了一口 take a bite 2 (of a dog) bark: 鸡叫狗～cocks crow and dogs bark 3 incriminate another person: 反～一口 make a false countercharge against one's accuser 4 pronounce; articulate: 他字～不清楚. He can't enunciate clearly. 5 be nit-picking (about the use of words): ～字眼儿 be fastidious about words

咬文嚼字 yǎowén-jiáozì juggle with words like a pedant

咬牙切齿(齒) yǎoyá-qièchǐ gnash one's teeth

疟(瘧) yào (名)(～子)malaria

see also nüè

药(藥) yào I (名) 1 medicine; drug; remedy: 服～ take medicine. 良～苦口. Good medicine is bitter to taste. 2 certain chemicals: 火～ gunpowder II (动)〈书〉1 cure with medicine: 不可救～ incurable; beyond cure 2 kill with poison

药材 yàocái (名) medicinal materials; crude drugs

药草 yàocǎo (名) medicinal herbs

药店 yàodiàn (名) drugstore; chemist's shop
药方 yàofāng (名) prescription
药房 yàofáng (名) 1 drugstore; chemist's shop; pharmacy 2 hospital pharmacy; dispensary
药膏 yàogāo (名) ointment; salve
药棉 yàomián (名) absorbent cotton
药片 yàopiàn (名) (medicinal) tablet
药水 yàoshuǐ (名) 1 liquid medicine 2 lotion
药丸 yàowán (名) pill
药物 yàowù (名) medicines; pharmaceuticals; medicaments

要 yào I (形) important: 主～ principal. 紧～ imperative. ～点 gist. 险～ of strategic importance II (名) important substance: 摘～ abstract; précis. 纲～ outline III (动) 1 need; like to keep: 他～一个口琴. He needs a mouth organ. 2 ask; demand: ～账 demand payment of a debt. 她～我给她写一封介绍信. She asked me to write a letter of recommendation for her. 3 want; desire: 他～学游泳. He wants to learn swimming. 4 must; have to: 路很滑, 大家～小心. We have to be careful for the road is very slippery. 5 be going to: ～下雨了. It's going to rain. IV (连) 1 if: 明天～下雨, 我就不去了. If it rains tomorrow, I won't go. 2 either ... or ...: ～就去打篮球, ～就去溜冰, 别再犹豫了. You either go and play basketball or go skating. Don't hesitate any more.
see also yāo

要不 yàobù (连) (also as "要不然") otherwise; or else; or: 我得马上走, ～就要迟到了. I have to leave at once or I'll be late.
要不得 yàobude be no good; be intolerable: 这种干涉行为～. Such acts of interference are not to be tolerated.
要冲(衝) yàochōng (名) communications centre (or hub): 军事～ strategic point
要道 yàodào (名) thoroughfare: 交通～ important line of communications
要点(點) yàodiǎn (名) 1 main points; essentials; gist: 抓住～ grasp the main points 2 key stronghold
要饭 yàofàn (动) beg (for food or money): ～的 beggar
要害 yàohài (名) vital part; crucial point: ～部门 key department. 击中～ hit home; hit the nail on the head. ～部位 vital part
要好 yàohǎo (形) 1 be on good terms 2 eager to do well
要价(價) yàojià (动) ask a price; charge: 你～太高. You are asking too much.
要紧(緊) yàojǐn I (形) 1 important 2 be critical; be serious: 他的病～不～? Is his illness serious? II (动) be in a hurry to do sth.: 我～进城, 来不及和他细说. As I am in a hurry to go to town, I have no time to discuss the matter with him.
要领 yàolǐng (名) main points; essentials; gist: 不得～ fail to grasp the main points. 掌握～ grasp the essentials
要么(麽) yàome (连) or; either ... or...: 你～跟我们一起去, ～呆在家里, 随你的便. You can either go with us or stay at home. It's up to you.
要面子 yào miànzi be keen on face-saving; be anxious to keep up appearances
要命 yàomìng (动) 1 drive sb. to his death; kill 2 to an extreme degree: 好得～ awfully good. 挤得～ packed like sardines
要强 yàoqiáng (形) be eager to excel in whatever one does
要人 yàorén (名) very important person (VIP)
要塞 yàosài (名) fort; fortress; fortification
要是 yàoshì (连) if; suppose; in case
要死 yàosǐ extremely; awfully; terribly: 怕蛇怕得～ be terribly afraid of snakes
要素 yàosù (名) essential factor
要闻 yàowén (名) important news; front-page story
要言不烦 yào yán bù fán concise and succinct both in speech and writing
要职(職) yàozhí (名) important post: 身居～ hold an important post

钥(鑰) yào
see also yuè

钥匙 yàoshi (名) key: 一串～ a bunch of keys. 万能～ master key

耀 yào 1 shine; illuminate: 照～ shine on; illuminate 2 boast of: 他喜欢夸～自己的本领. He likes to boast about his own abilities. 3 honour; credit
耀武扬(揚)威 yàowǔ-yángwēi make a show of one's strength; sabre-rattling
耀眼 yàoyǎn (形) (of light) dazzling

耶 yē

耶稣 Yēsū (名) Jesus: ~基督 Jesus Christ. ~教 Protestantism

椰 yē (名) coconut palm; coconut tree; coco

椰子 yēzi (名) 1 coconut palm; coconut tree; coco 2 coconut

噎 yē (动) choke: 他吃得太快, ~住了. He started to choke as he was eating too fast. 因~废食 give up eating because of a hiccup

爷(爺) yé (名) 1 father: ~娘 father and mother 2 grandfather 3 a respectful form of address for a man of the older generation: 老大~ grandpa 4 〈旧〉a form of address for an official or rich man: 老~ lord; master

爷爷 yéye (名)〈口〉1 (paternal) grandfather 2 grandpa (a respectful form of address for an old man)

冶 yě (动) smelt (metal)

冶金 yějīn (名) metallurgy: ~工业 metallurgical industry

冶炼(煉) yěliàn (动) smelt: ~厂 smeltery

野 yě I (名) 1 open country: 旷~ open fields 2 limit; boundary: 分~ line of demarcation; watershed 3 not in power: 在~党 a party not in power; the opposition II (形) 1 wild; uncultivated; undomesticated: ~兽 wild animal. ~兔 hare. ~鸡 pheasant. ~花 wild flower 2 rude; rough: 说话太~ make rude remarks; be foulmouthed 3 unrestrained; unruly: 心~ unable to sit down and concentrate

野菜 yěcài (名) edible wild herbs

野餐 yěcān (名) picnic

野草 yěcǎo (名) weeds: ~丛生 be rank with weeds

野蛮(蠻) yěmán (形) 1 uncivilized; savage 2 atrocious; brutal

野人 yěrén (名) savage

野生 yěshēng (形) wild; uncultivated: ~动物 wildlife. ~植物 wild plant

野史 yěshǐ (名) unofficial history

野外 yěwài (名) open country; field: 在~工作 do fieldwork

野心 yěxīn (名) wild ambition; careerism: ~家 careerist

野战(戰) yězhàn (名) field operations: ~军 field army. ~医院 field hospital

也 yě I (副) 1 also; too; as well: 水库可以灌溉、发电, ~可以养鱼. A reservoir can be used to irrigate and generate power. It can also be used for raising fish. 2 [indicating concession]: 即使你不说, 我~知道. I am aware of the problem even if you say nothing. 3 [indicating resignation]: ~只好如此. Well, we will have to let it go at that. 4 [used together with 连 to indicate emphasis]: 连爷爷~乐得哈哈大笑. Even Grandpa was so amused as to roar with laughter. II (助)〈书〉1 [indicating judgement or explanation]: 非不能~, 是不为~. It is not a question of ability but one of readiness. 2 [indicating doubt or a rhetorical question]: 是可忍~, 孰不可忍~? If this can be tolerated, what cannot be tolerated?

也罢(罷) yěbà I [indicating tolerance or resignation]: ~, 你一定要走, 我送你上车. All right, if you insist on going now, I'll see you to the bus stop. II (助) whether ... or ...; no matter whether: 你去~, 不去~, 反正是一样. It makes no difference whether you are going or not.

也许 yěxǔ (副) perhaps; probably; maybe: 他~病了. Perhaps he's ill.

夜 yè (名) night; evening

夜班 yèbān (名) night shift

夜半 yèbàn (名) midnight

夜长(長)梦(夢)多 yècháng-mèngduō when the night is long, dreams are many—delay may lead to adversity

夜车(車) yèchē (名) 1 night train 2 [used with 开]: 开~ stay up late; burn the midnight oil

夜大学(學) yèdàxué (名) evening university

夜壶(壺) yèhú (名) chamber pot

夜间 yèjiān (名) at night: ~施工 carry on construction work at night

夜景 yèjǐng (名) night scene (or view)

夜郎自大 Yèláng zìdà ludicrous conceit stemming from pure ignorance

夜盲 yèmáng (名) night blindness

夜猫子 yèmāozi (名) 1 owl 2 a person who goes to bed late; night owl

夜幕 yèmù (名) gathering darkness; night: 在~中消失 disappear into the darkness

夜市 yèshì (名) night market

夜晚 yèwǎn (名) night

夜宵 yèxiāo (名) night snack

夜校 yèxiào (名) night (or evening) school
夜以继(繼)日 yè yǐ jì rì day and night; round the clock
夜莺(鶯) yèyīng (名) nightingale
夜总(總)会(會) yèzǒnghuì (名)nightclub
液 yè (名) liquid; fluid; juice
液化 yèhuà (名) liquefaction: ～天然气 liquefied natural gas (LNG)
液晶显示 yèjīng xiǎnshì liqnid crystal display; LCD
液态(態) yètài (名) liquid state
液体(體) yètǐ (名) liquid
液压(壓) yèyā (名) hydraulic pressure
腋 yè (名) axilla; armpit
谒 yè (动)〈书〉 call on (a superior or an elder person); pay one's respects to
谒见(見) yèjiàn (动) pay a call on (a superior or a senior person); have an audience with
页(頁) yè (名) leaf; page: 活～ loose leaf
页码 yèmǎ (名) page number
叶(葉) yè (名) 1 leaf 2 leaf-like thing: 百～窗 shutter; blind 3 page; leaf 4 part of a historical period:二十世纪中～ the middle of the twentieth century
叶落归(歸)根 yè luò guī gēn a person residing abroad will return to his ancestral home
叶子 yèzi (名) leaf
业(業) yè I (名) 1 trade; industry:旅游～tourism. 饮食～ catering trade. 各行各～ all trades and professions 2 occupation; profession: 就～ employment. 失～unemployed 3 course of study: 结～ complete a course of study. 毕～graduate 4 cause; enterprise: 创～ start an enterprise (or business) 5 estate; property:家～family property II (副) already:工程～已完竣. The project has already been completed.
业绩 yèjì (名) outstanding achievement; exemplary accomplishment
业内 yènèi (名) in the field; within the profession:～人士 people in the field
业务(務) yèwù (名) vocational work; professional work; business:～能力 professional competence. ～知识 professional knowledge; expertise. ～水平 professional competency; vocational level
业余(餘) yèyú (名) spare time; amateur: ～演员 an amateur actor. ～学校 after-hours school
业主 yèzhǔ (名) owner (of an enterprise or estate); proprietor
曳 yè (动) drag; haul; tug; tow
衣 yī (名) 1 clothing; clothes; garment 2 coating; covering: 糖～ sugar coating
衣钵 yībō (名) a Buddhist monk's mantle and alms bowl; legacy
衣橱 yīchú (名) wardrobe
衣服 yīfu (名) clothing; clothes
衣冠禽兽(獸) yīguān qínshòu a beast in human shape
衣柜(櫃) yīguì (名) wardrobe
衣架 yījià (名) 1 coat hanger; clothes rack 2 clothes tree; clothes stand
衣料 yīliào (名) dress material; cloth; coating; shirting
衣帽间 yīmàojiān (名) cloakroom
衣食住行 yī shí zhù xíng clothing, food, housing, and transport
依 yī I (动) 1 depend on:唇齿相～mutually dependent 2 comply with; listen to; yield to:劝他休息,他怎么也不～. He turned a deaf ear to our advice when we wanted him to take a breather. II (介) according to; in the light of; judging by: ～我看,这样办可以. In my opinion, this should be all right.
依次 yīcì (副) in proper order; successively
依从(從) yīcóng (动) comply with; yield to:在目前情况下,不可能～她自己的愿望办. There is no complying with her wishes under the present circumstances.
依存 yīcún (动) depend on each other for existence:相互～be interdependent
依法 yīfǎ according to law; in conformity with legal provisions
依附 yīfù (动) depend on; attach oneself to; become an appendage to
依旧(舊) yījiù (副) as before; still:别人都走了,他～坐在那里看书. While the others had left, he alone still sat reading there.
依据(據) yījù I (名) basis; foundation:为进一步研究提供科学～provide scientific basis for further research II (动) form a basis for action: 当时没有适当的条例可以～. There were no proper rules to go by.

依靠 yīkào I (动) rely on: ～自己的力量 depend on one's own strength II (名) backing; support

依赖 yīlài (动) depend on: 互为～ be mutually dependent; be interdependent

依恋(戀) yīliàn (动) have a sentimental attachment for

依然 yīrán (副) still; as before: 风景～如故. The landscape remains unchanged.

依顺 yīshùn (动) be docile and obedient

依稀 yīxī (形) vaguely; dimly: ～记得 vaguely remember; have a hazy notion. ～认识 faintly recognizable

依依不舍(捨) yīyī bù shě be reluctant to part; feel regret at parting from

依仗 yīzhàng (动) count on: ～权势 count on one's powerful connections for support; abuse one's power

依照 yīzhào (介) according to; in the light of: ～上级指示办事 act according to instructions from the higher level

一 yī I (数) **1** one: ～把椅子 a chair. 我见过他～次. I have met him once. **2** single; alone; only one: 她～个人去的. She went alone. **3** same: 这不是～码事. This is a different matter. **4** whole; all; throughout: 出了～身汗 sweat all over. 忙了～整天 be busy the whole day **5** each; per; every time: ～个月写～篇论文 write a paper each month **6** concentrated: ～心～意 single-minded; wholehearted **7** [indicating that the action occurs once or lasts for a short time]: 笑～笑 give a smile. 歇～歇 have a rest. 瞧～瞧 take a look **8** [used before a verb to indicate an action and its result]: 他～脚把球踢进了球门. He kicked the ball into the goal. II [used with certain words for emphasis]: 为害之甚, ～至于此! The damage done has reached such dimensions!

一把手 yībǎshǒu (名) **1** a participant in an activity **2** a capable person; a good hand **3** head of an enterprise or a government department

一败涂(塗)地 yī bài tú dì suffer a crushing defeat; be thoroughly defeated

Y

一般 yībān (形) **1** same as; just like: 他们俩～高. The two of them are of the same stature. 像狐狸～狡猾 as cunning as fox **2** general; ordinary; common: ～说来 generally speaking. 我～晚上10点睡觉. I usually go to bed at 10 in the evening. 这部电影很～. This film is just so-so.

一般化 yībānhuà vague generalization: ～地谈问题 talk in generalities (or in general terms)

一般见(見)识(識) yībān jiànshi (lower oneself to) the same level as sb.: 别跟他～. You don't want to bother yourself arguing with the likes of him.

一半 yībàn (名) one half; half

一辈子 yībèizi (名) all one's life; a lifetime

一本万(萬)利 yī běn wàn lì make big profits with a small capital

一本正经(經) yī běn zhèngjīng in all seriousness; in a matter-of-fact manner

一笔(筆)勾销 yī bǐ gōuxiāo write off (at one stroke); cancel

一臂之力 yī bì zhī lì a helping hand: 助我～ lend me a hand

一边(邊) yībiān I (名) one side: 站在我们～ stand together with us II (副) [indicating two simultaneous actions] at the same time; simultaneously: 他～往前走, ～拉开嗓子唱着歌儿. He strolled along, singing at the top of his voice.

一边(邊)倒 yībiāndǎo lean to one side; side with sb. without reservation

一并(併) yībìng (副) along with all the others; in the lump: ～付给 pay in a lump sum

一…不… yī…bù… **1** [used before two verbs to indicate that once an action is taken, it is irrevocable]: 一去不返 leave never to return. 一蹶不振 unable to recover after a setback **2** [used before a noun and a verb to form an emphatic expression]: 一言不发 be speechless. 一文不值 not be worth a farthing

一不做,二不休 yī bù zuò, èr bù xiū what we have started we will pursue to the end at any cost

一步登天 yī bù dēng tiān reach the pinnacle of power in one jump

一场(場)空 yīchǎngkōng be all in vain; be a futile effort; come to naught

一筹(籌)莫展 yī chóu mò zhǎn can find no way out; be absolutely helpless; be at one's wit's end

一触(觸)即发(發) yī chù jí fā may be triggered at any moment; be on the verge of breaking out; explosive

一次 yīcì for one time; once: 我做过～. I've done it once.

一蹴而就 yī cù ér jiù accomplish in one move; succeed without making the least effort

一旦 yīdàn I (名) in a single day; in a very short time: 毁于～ be destroyed in a single day II (副) once; in case; now that: ～这项研究计划完成,便可造福人类. Once this research project is completed, it will bring immense benefit to all mankind.

一刀两(兩)断(斷) yī dāo liǎng duàn sever for good and all

一刀切 yīdāoqiē find a single solution for diverse problems; impose uniformity without examining individual cases

一道 yīdào (副) together; side by side; alongside: 我们～走. Let's go together.

一等 yīděng (形) first-class; first-rate; top-grade

一点(點)儿(兒) yīdiǎnr a bit; a little: 我～都不知道. I have not the faintest idea. 只有那么～,够用吗? There is so little left. Is it enough for the present purpose?

一点(點)一滴 yīdiǎn-yīdī every little bit

一定 yīdìng I (形) 1 fixed; specified; definite; regular: ～的指标 fixed quota. ～的条件 specified conditions 2 given; particular; certain: 在～意义上 in a certain sense. 在～程度上 to a certain extent 3 proper; fair; due: 达到～水平 reach a fairly high level II (副) certainly; surely; necessarily: 他～会成功. He will surely succeed.

一肚子 yīdùzi a stomachful of; full of: ～委屈 be full of grievances. 他这人～坏水儿. He's full of evil ideas.

一度 yīdù once; on one occasion; for a time: 一年～ once a year; yearly; annually. 他～休学. He stopped going to school for a time.

一二 yī-èr one or two; just a few; just a little: 略知～ know a little about; have some idea about

一…二… yī…èr… [used before two morphemes of a disyllabic adjective to give emphasis]: 一清二楚 perfectly clear; crystal clear

一发(髮)千钧 yī fà qiān jūn hang by a thread; in imminent peril: 在这～的时刻 at this critical moment

一帆风(風)顺 yī fān fēng shùn plain sailing

一方面 yīfāngmiàn 1 one side: 这只是事物的～. This is only one side of the matter. 2 [often used reduplicatively]: on the one hand ..., on the other hand...; for one thing..., for another...

一风(風)吹 yīfēngchuī dismiss all things as of no significance

一概 yīgài (副) one and all; totally: ～拒绝 reject without exception

一概而论(論) yīgài ér lùn [usu. in the negative] lump things of different kinds together and treat them by the same inflexible criteria: 不能～ not to be lumped together

一干(乾)二净 yīgān-èrjìng thoroughly; completely: 忘得～ clean forget

一共 yīgòng (副) altogether; in all; all told: 三个小组～是十七个人. There are three groups consisting of seventeen people altogether.

一股劲(勁)儿(兒) yīgǔjìnr without a break; at one go; at a stretch: ～地干 do sth. without a break

一股脑(腦)儿(兒) yīgǔnǎor completely; lock, stock and barrel; root and branch

一贯 yīguàn (形) consistent; persistent; all along: ～政策 consistent policy. 我们～反对恐怖主义. We have always opposed terrorism.

一锅(鍋)粥 yīguōzhōu a pot of porridge — a complete mess; all in a muddle: 乱成～ in a mess; in utter confusion

一哄而起 yī hòng ér qǐ rush headlong into mass action

一哄而散 yī hòng ér sàn disperse without a trace all at once

一晃 yīhuàng (of time) in the twinkling of an eye

一回生,二回熟 yī huí shēng, èr huí shú 1 strangers at the first meeting, friends at the second 2 difficult at first, easy later on

一会(會)儿(兒) yīhuìr (名) 1 a little while 2 in a moment; presently: 我～就来. I won't be long. 3 now...now ...; one moment...the next ...: 他～出,～进,忙个不停. He is busily walking in and out at short intervals.

一技之长(長) yī jì zhī cháng professional skill; speciality

一家子 yījiāzi 1 a family: 我们不是～. We are not of the same family. 2 the whole family: ～都高兴极了. The whole family was overjoyed.

一见(見)如故 yī jiàn rú gù feel like old friends at the first meeting

一见(見)钟(鍾)情 yī jiàn zhōngqíng fall in

love at first sight

一箭双(雙)雕 yī jiàn shuāng diāo kill two birds with one stone

一经(經) yījīng (副) as soon as; once: 方案～批准, 我们就着手筹款. We will start to raise funds as soon as the plan is approved.

一…就… yī … jiù … no sooner ... than ...; the moment...; as soon as; once: 他一学就会. He learned the trick in a jiffy. 那张旧桌子轻轻一推就倒. The rickety old table collapsed with a slight push.

一举(舉) yījǔ I (名) an action that is soon to take place: 成败在此～. Success or failure hinges on this final effort. II (副) at one stroke: ～成名 become famous overnight

一举(舉)两(兩)得 yī jǔ liǎng dé kill two birds with one stone

一孔之见(見) yī kǒng zhī jiàn a parochial view

一口 yī kǒu 1 a mouthful; a bite: 吸～新鲜空气 have a breath of fresh air. 吃～苹果 take a bite at the apple 2 with certainty; readily; flatly: ～答应 readily agree

一口气(氣) yīkǒuqì 1 one breath: 只要我还有～, 就要为人民大众工作. As long as I breathe, I'll work for the people. 2 in one breath; at one go: ～干完 finish the work at one go

一块(塊)儿(兒) yīkuàir I (名) at the same place: 在～工作 work at the same place II (副) together: 他们～到上海游览. They went on a trip to Shanghai together.

一览(覽) yīlǎn (名) guidebook

一览(覽)表 yīlǎnbiǎo (名) table; schedule: 火车行车时刻～railway timetable

一揽(攬)子 yīlǎnzi (形) wholesale; package: ～交易 package deal. ～解决 package solution

一劳(勞)永逸 yī láo yǒng yì strive to get sth. done once and for all: 寻求～的解决办法 seek a permanent solution to the problem

一连 yīlián (副) in succession; on end; running: ～下了三天雨. It rained for three days on end.

一连串 yīliánchuàn (形) a succession of; a series of: ～的事件 a succession of events

一溜烟 yīliùyān (副) (runaway) swiftly: 他～就没影儿了. He vanished in an instant.

一路 yīlù I (名) all the way; throughout the journey: ～平安 have a pleasant journey; bon voyage. 他们～平安抵达纽约. They arrived in New York safe and sound. II (形) of the same kind: 他们俩是同～人: 性情相似, 学历相近. They are of the same type and similar both in temperament and in educational background.

一律 yīlǜ I (形) same; alike; uniform: 千篇～ stereotyped and monotonous II (副) all; without exception: 我国各民族～平等. All nationalities in our country are equal.

一落千丈 yī luò qiānzhàng decline rapidly; suffer a steep decline

一脉(脈)相承 yī mài xiāng chéng be inherited from the past; derive from the same origin

一毛不拔 yī máo bù bá even unwilling to give away a cent

一面 yīmiàn I (名) one side; one aspect: 住在学校宿舍里既有有利的～, 也有不利的～. Living in the college dormitory has its advantages and disadvantages. II (副) [indicating two simultaneous actions] at the same time; simultaneously: ～走, ～唱 sing while walking

一面之词 yīmiàn zhī cí the statement of one party to a dispute: 你不要听～. You mustn't listen to only one side of the story.

一鸣惊(驚)人 yī míng jīng rén (of an obscure person) amaze the world by one's successful maiden effort

一命呜(嗚)呼 yī mìng wūhū die; kick the bucket

一模一样(樣) yīmú-yīyàng exactly alike: 他长得跟他爸爸～. He is a chip off the old block.

一目了(瞭)然 yī mù liǎorán be clear at a glance

一念之差 yī niàn zhī chā make a wrong decision on the spur of the moment (often entailing unhappy results)

一瞥 yīpiē (名) 1 a quick glance 2 a glimpse of sth.

一贫如洗 yī pín rú xǐ impoverished; in utter destitution

一曝十寒 yī pù shí hán work by fits and starts; lack tenacity of purpose

一齐(齊) yīqí (副) at the same time; simultaneously: 全场～鼓掌 warm applause by the audience. 这次比赛足球迷～到场.

All the football fans turned out for the match.

一起 yìqǐ I (名) in the same place II (副) together

一气(氣)呵成 yīqì hē chéng get sth. done without any let-up

一窍(竅)不通 yī qiào bù tōng be utterly ignorant; be an ignoramus

一切 yīqiè (代) all; everything

一丘之貉 yī qiū zhī hé jackals from the same lair

一如既往 yī rú jìwǎng just as in the past; as before; as always: 我们将～坚决支持你们的正义斗争. We will, as always, firmly support your just struggle.

一身 yīshēn (名) 1 the whole body; all over the body: ～是劲 bursting with energy 2 a suit: ～新衣服 a new suit of clothes 3 a single person: 独自～ live all alone

一生 yīshēng (名) all one's life

一时(時) yīshí (名) 1 for a period of time: ～无出其右. Nobody proved better qualified for a time. 2 for a short while: ～还用不着 be of no use at the moment 3 accidentally: ～想不起他是谁. It happened I couldn't recall who he was. 4 [reduplicated use]: 高原上气候变化大, ～晴～雨, ～冷～热. On the plateau the weather is subject to frequent changes: it is clear for a while and then it starts to rain and it is often hot one moment and turns cold the next.

一事无(無)成 yī shì wú chéng accomplish nothing; fail to achieve anything of consequence

一视同仁 yī shì tóng rén treat people equally without discrimination

一手 yīshǒu I (名) proficiency; skill II (副) all by oneself; all alone: ～造成 be brought on all by oneself. ～包办 be manipulated all by oneself

一瞬 yīshùn (名) in the twinkling of an eye: 火箭飞行, ～千里. A rocket travels thousands of miles in a flash.

一丝(絲)不苟 yī sī bù gǒu be very scrupulous; be very meticulous

一丝(絲)不挂(掛) yī sī bù guà be stark-naked

一丝(絲)一毫 yīsī-yīháo a tiny bit; an iota: 没有～的诚意 without an iota of sincerity

一塌糊涂(塗) yītāhútú an awful mess; a dreadful state of affairs: 屋子乱得～. The room was a complete mess.

一体(體) yītǐ (名) 1 an organic (or integral) whole: 融成～merge into an organic whole 2 all people concerned: ～周知 be made known to all people concerned

一天到晚 yī tiān dào wǎn from morning till night; from dawn to dusk; all day long

一同 yītóng (副) together; (do sth. or take part in some activity) at the same time and place: ～欢度新年. Let us jointly celebrate New Year.

一头(頭) yītóu I (副) directly; headlong: ～扑进水里 plunge headlong into the water II (名) a head: 他比我高～. He is a head taller than I am.

一团(團)和气(氣) yī tuán héqì be always friendly with everybody on all occasions

一团(團)糟 yītuánzāo hopelessly chaotic; a complete mess

一碗水端平 yīwǎnshuǐ duānpíng hold a bowl of water level — be impartial: 你一定要～. You must be fair to both sides.

一网(網)打尽(盡) yī wǎng dǎjìn round up the whole gang at one fell swoop

一往无(無)前 yīwǎng wúqián press forward with an indomitable spirit

一味 yīwèi (副) simply; blindly: ～迁就解决不了任何问题. You can't solve any problem by simply making concessions.

一文不名 yī wén bù míng penniless

一问三不知 yī wèn sān bù zhī be entirely ignorant

一窝(窩)蜂 yīwōfēng like a swarm of bees: 孩子们～地拥上来. The children came swarming round.

一无(無) yīwú entirely without . . . : ～所知 know nothing; be ignorant. ～是处 have no merit to speak of. ～所有 be destitute or penniless

一五一十 yīwǔ-yīshí (narrate) systematically and in full detail: 他把发生的事情～地讲了一遍. He gave a full account of what had happened.

一系列 yīxìliè (形) a series of: ～问题 a whole series of questions. ～事件 a whole train of events

一下 yīxià I [used after a verb to indicate a brief action] one time; once: 让我看～. Let me have a look. 打听～make some inquiries II (副) in a short while; all at once; all of a sudden: 孩子们～都从屋里跑了出来. The children rushed out all at once.

一线(綫) yīxiàn (形) a ray of; a gleam of: ～希望 a gleam of hope

一相情愿(願) yī xiāng qíngyuàn one's own wishful thinking

一向 yīxiàng I (名) earlier on; lately II (副) consistently; all along

一笑置之 yīxiào zhì zhī dismiss with a laugh; laugh off

一些 yīxiē (量) a number of; certain; some; a few; a little: 只有这～了,怕不够吧? There's only so much left. I'm afraid it's not enough to go round. 他曾担任过～重要的职务. In the past he held some important posts.

一心 yīxīn I (副) wholeheartedly; heart and soul: ～为人民谋利益 devote oneself heart and soul to the welfare of the people II (形) of one mind: 关于这个问题,大家都是～一意的. We are all of one mind about this question.

一星半点(點) yīxīng-bàndiǎn a tiny bit; a very small amount

一行 yīxíng (名) a group travelling together; party: 代表团～十二人已于昨日起程. The twelve-person delegation left yesterday.

一言既出,驷马(馬)难(難)追 yī yán jì chū, sìmǎ nán zhuī a word spoken is past recalling

一言难(難)尽(盡) yī yán nán jìn it is hard to explain in a few words; it's a long story

一言以蔽之 yī yán yǐ bì zhī in a word; in a nutshell

一样(樣) yīyàng (形) the same; equally; alike: 哥儿俩相貌～,脾气也～. The two brothers are alike not only in appearance but also in temperament.

一一 yī yī (副) one by one; one after another

一…一… yī…yī… 1 [used before two nouns of the same kind] (**a**) [to indicate the whole]: 一生一世 all one's life (**b**) [to indicate a small amount] 一言一行 every word and deed. 一点一滴 every bit 2 [used before two verbs similar in meaning to indicate simultaneous action]: 一瘸一拐 hobble along 3 [used before two verbs opposite in meaning to indicate coordination or alternation of action]: 一问一答 a dialogue between two persons. 一起一落 rise and fall; ups and downs 4 [used before two corresponding words of locality to indicate opposite positions]: 一东一西 one east, one west; poles apart 5 [used before two adjectives opposite in meaning to indicate contrast]: 一长一短 one short, one long

一衣带(帶)水 yī yī dài shuǐ separated by a narrow strip of water

一意孤行 yī yì gū xíng act wilfully despite sb.'s advice to the contrary

一月 yīyuè (名) January

一再 yīzài (副) time and again; again and again; repeatedly: ～请求 request time and again. ～拖延 be postponed again and again

一早 yīzǎo (名)〈口〉early in the morning

一朝一夕 yīzhāo-yīxī overnight; in one day: 非～之功 not the work of a single day

一针见(見)血 yīzhēn jiàn xiě hit the nail on the head

一阵 yīzhèn (名) a burst; a fit; a peal: ～雷声 a peal of thunder. ～狂风 a gust of wind. ～笑声 an outburst of laughter

一知半解 yīzhī-bànjiě have an imperfect understanding of sth.; have a little learning

一直 yīzhí (副) 1 straight: ～走 go straight on 2 continuously; always; all along; all the way: 雨～下了一天一夜. It has been raining the whole day and night.

一纸空文 yī zhǐ kōngwén a mere scrap of paper

一致 yīzhì (形) identical; consistent

壹 yī (数) one [the complicated form of 一 used on cheques, banknotes, etc. to avoid mistakes or alterations]

医(醫) yī I (名) 1 doctor (of medicine): 牙～ dentist. 延～诊治 send for a doctor 2 medical science; medicine: 中～ traditional Chinese medicine. 他是学～的. He is a student of medicine. II (动) cure; treat: 把他的病～好 cure him of his illness

医保 yībǎo (名) medical insurance

医科 yīkē (名) medical courses in general; medicine

医疗(療) yīliáo (名) medical treatment: 公费～ public health services. ～器械 medical apparatus and instruments

医生 yīshēng (名) (medical) doctor: 内科～ physician; internist. 外科～surgeon. 主治～doctor in charge. 住院～resident doctor

医师(師) yīshī (名) (qualified) doctor; general practitioner

医术(術) yīshù (名) medical skill
医务(務) yīwù (名) medical matters
医药(藥) yīyào (名) medicine: ～费 medical expenses (or costs)
医院 yīyuàn (名) hospital: 综合性～ general hospital
医治 yīzhì (动) cure; treat; heal
医嘱(囑) yīzhǔ (名) doctor's advice (or orders)

伊 yī (代) he or she

伊斯兰(蘭)教 Yīsīlánjiào (名) Islam; Islamism: ～徒 Moslem

宜 yí I (形) suitable; appropriate; fitting: 适～ appropriate; fitting and proper. 老幼咸～ suitable for both young and old II (动) should; ought to: 不～操之过急. You should not act in haste. *or* It would not be inappropriate to restrain oneself from acting rashly.
宜人 yírén (形) pleasant; delightful: 气候～ the weather is mild and delightful

颐 yí (动) 〈书〉 keep fit; take care of oneself
颐和园(園) Yíhéyuán (名) the Summer Palace (in Beijing)
颐养(養) yíyǎng (动) 〈书〉 keep fit; take care of oneself

夷 yí I (形) safe: 化险为～ turn danger into safety II (动) raze: ～为平地 be razed to the ground

痍 yí (名) 〈书〉 wound; trauma: 满目疮～ There is more misery and desolation than meets the eye.

咦 yí (叹) [indicating surprise] well; why: ～, 这是怎么回事? Why, what is really the matter?

胰 yí (名) pancreas

姨 yí (名) **1** one's mother's sister; aunt **2** one's wife's sister; sister-in-law: 大～子 one's wife's elder sister. 小～子 one's wife's younger sister
姨表 yíbiǎo (名) maternal cousin: ～兄弟 male maternal cousins. ～姐妹 female maternal cousins
姨父 yífu (名) the husband of one's maternal aunt; uncle (also as "姨夫")
姨妈 yímā (名) 〈口〉 (married) maternal aunt; aunt
姨太太 yítàitai (名) 〈口〉 concubine

遗 yí I (动) **1** lose: ～失 lose **2** omit: ～忘 forget **3** leave behind; keep back; not give: 不～余力 spare no efforts **4** leave behind at one's death; bequeath; hand down: ～风 customs handed down from past generations. ～嘱 will; testament **5** involuntary discharge of urine, etc.: ～尿 bed-wetting II (名) sth. lost: 路不拾～. No one pockets anything found on the road.
遗产(產) yíchǎn (名) legacy; inheritance: 文化～ cultural heritage
遗臭万(萬)年 yí chòu wànnián leave a stinking name in human history
遗传(傳) yíchuán (名) heredity; inheritance: ～病 hereditary disease. ～学 genetics
遗传(傳)工程学(學) yíchuán gōngchéngxué (名) genetic engineering
遗稿 yígǎo (名) a manuscript left unpublished by the author at his death; posthumous manuscript
遗孤 yígū (名) orphan
遗憾 yíhàn (名、形) regret; pity: 对此表示～ express regret over the matter. 非常～, 事前有约会使我不能接受你的邀请. To my regret, a previous engagement prevents me from accepting your invitation.
遗迹 yíjì (名) historical remains
遗留 yíliú (动) leave over; hand down: 历史～下来的问题 questions left over by history
遗漏 yílòu (动) leave out by mistake
遗弃(棄) yíqì (动) abandon; forsake; leave uncared-for
遗容 yíróng (名) **1** remains (of the deceased): 瞻仰～ pay one's respects to the remains of sb. **2** a portrait of the deceased
遗孀 yíshuāng (名) widow
遗体(體) yítǐ (名) remains (of the dead): 向～告别 pay one's last respects to the remains
遗忘 yíwàng (动) forget
遗言 yíyán (名) words of the deceased; (a person's) last words
遗愿(願) yíyuàn (名) unfulfilled wish of the deceased; last wish; behest
遗址 yízhǐ (名) ruins; relics: 古城～ the ruins of an ancient city
遗志 yízhì (名) unfulfilled wish; behest: 继承先烈～ carry out the behest of the martyrs; continue the work left by the martyrs
遗嘱(囑) yízhǔ (名) testament; will

仪(儀) yí (名) 1 appearance; bearing: 威~ dignified bearing 2 ceremony; rite: 司~ master of ceremonies 3 present; gift: 贺~ present for a wedding, birthday, etc. 4 apparatus; instrument
仪表 yíbiǎo (名) 1 appearance; bearing: ~堂堂 look impressive and dignified 2 meter: ~厂 instrument and meter plant
仪器 yíqì (名) instrument; apparatus: 精密~precision instrument
仪式 yíshì (名) ceremony; rite: 签字~ signing ceremony
仪仗队(隊) yízhàngduì (名) guard of honour; honour guard: 三军~ a guard of honour of the three services
移 yí (动) 1 move; remove; shift: 迁~ move to another place 2 change; alter: ~风易俗 change established habits and social customs
移动(動) yídòng (动) move; shift: ~电话 cellular phone; mobile phone
移动(動)通信 yídòng tōngxìn mobile communication
移交 yíjiāo (动) 1 turn over; transfer; deliver into sb.'s custody 2 hand over one's job to a successor
移居 yíjū (动) move one's residence; migrate
移民 yímín I (动) migrate; emigrate; immigrate II (名) emigrant; immigrant
移植 yízhí (动) 1 transplant: ~秧苗 transplant seedlings 2 (in medicine) transplant; graft
疑 yí I (动) doubt; disbelieve; suspect: 坚信不~firmly believe. 无可置~ beyond doubt II (形)doubtful; uncertain: 存~leave the question open
疑案 yí'àn (名) doubtful case; open question; mystery
疑惑 yíhuò (动) feel uncertain; not be convinced: ~不解 feel puzzled
疑惧(懼) yíjù (名) apprehensions; misgivings
疑虑(慮) yílǜ (名) misgivings; doubt
疑难(難) yínán (形) difficult; knotty: ~问题 a knotty problem. ~病症 difficult and complicated cases (of illness)
疑神疑鬼 yíshén-yíguǐ be over-suspicious
疑团(團) yítuán (名) doubts and suspicions
疑问 yíwèn (名) query; question; doubt: 毫无~ doubtless; undoubtedly
疑心 yíxīn (名) suspicion: 起~ become suspicious
疑义(義) yíyì (名) doubt; doubtful point: 毫无~ no doubt; without doubt
怡 yí (形)〈书〉happy; pleased: 心旷神~ feel relaxed and happy
怡然 yírán (形) happy; contented: ~自得 happy and contented
贻 yí
贻害 yíhài (动) leave a legacy of trouble: ~无穷 entail endless trouble
贻误 yíwù (动) affect adversely; bungle: ~工作 affect the work adversely. ~青年 mislead the youth
贻笑大方 yíxiào dàfāng make a fool of oneself before professionals
椅 yǐ (名)(~子) chair
倚 yǐ I (动) 1 lean on or against; rest on or against: ~门而望 lean against the door and look expectantly into the distance 2 rely on; count on: ~势欺人 bully common people by abusing one's power and office II (形) biased; partial: 不偏不~ unbiased; even-handed; impartial
倚老卖(賣)老 yǐ lǎo mài lǎo be presumptuous because of one's seniority or old age
倚重 yǐzhòng (动) rely on sb. for counsel
蚁(蟻) yǐ (名) ant: ~巢 ants' nest
乙 yǐ (名) second: ~等 the second grade; grade B
乙醇 yǐchún (名) ethanol; alcohol
乙肝 yǐgān (名) hepatitis B; HBL
乙醚 yǐmí (名) ether
乙烯 yǐxī (名) ethylene: 聚~ polyethylene; polythene
已 yǐ I (动) stop; cease; end: 争论不~argue endlessly II (副) already: 问题~解决. The problem has already been solved. 雨季~过. The rainy season is over.
已故 yǐgù (形) deceased; late: ~总理 the late premier
已经(經) yǐjīng (副) already: 天~黑了,他们回来的影子都没有. It's already dark, but there is no sign of their coming back yet.
已往 yǐwǎng (名) before; in the past

以 yǐ I (动) use; take: 喻之～理 try to persuade one by reasoned argument. ～攻为守 the most effective defence is offence. ～其人之道,还治其人之身 give someone a taste of his own medicine II (介) **1** according to: ～级别高低为序 in order of seniority **2** because of: 不～人废言 not reject a piece of advice because the speaker is a person of no significance **3** in: ～失败而告终 end in failure III [indicating purpose] in order to; so as to: ～应急需 to meet an urgent need. ～待时机 to bide one's time IV [used together with a word of locality]: 二十岁～下 below the age of 20. 县级～上 above county level. 三日～后 in three days

以便 yǐbiàn (连) so that; in order to; so as to; with the aim of; for the purpose of: 每个学生都要掌握一门外语,～工作得更好. Every student is required to master a foreign language so that he or she will be better able to work in future.

以诚相待 yǐ chéng xiāng dài treat sb. with all sincerity

以德报(報)怨 yǐ dé bào yuàn return good for evil

以毒攻毒 yǐ dú gōng dú use poison as remedy for malignant disease; use poison as an antidote for poison; set a thief to catch a thief

以讹传(傳)讹 yǐ é chuán é pass on a wrong verbal message from one to another till it is grossly distorted

以后(後) yǐhòu (名) after; afterwards; later; hereafter: 从今～ from now on. ～,我们还要研究这个问题. We will go into it later.

以及 yǐjí (连) as well as; along with; and

以来(來) yǐlái (名) since: 自二次世界大战～ since World War II. 三年～ in the past three years

以理服人 yǐ lǐ fú rén convince by reasoning; persuade by sound arguments

以卵投石 yǐ luǎn tóu shí throw an egg against a rock; court disaster by immoderately overestimating one's own strength

以免 yǐmiǎn (连) in order to avoid or prevent: ～产生误会 to avoid or prevent misunderstanding

以内 yǐnèi (名) within; less than: 百码～ within a hundred yards

以前 yǐqián (名) before; formerly; previously: 三年～ three years ago. 1949 年～ before 1949

以权(權)谋私 yǐquán móusī seek private profit by taking advantage of administrative powers

以上 yǐshàng (名) **1** more than; above: 五十人～ over fifty people. 十岁～的孩子 children of ten and over **2** the above; the above-mentioned

以身试法 yǐ shēn shì fǎ defy the law

以身殉职(職) yǐ shēn xùn zhí die at one's post

以身作则 yǐ shēn zuò zé set a good example by one's conduct

以外 yǐwài (名) **1** beyond; outside: 办公室～ outside the office **2** in addition; into the bargain: 除此～,还有一件事你要记住. There's another thing I would like you to bear in mind.

以往 yǐwǎng (名) before; formerly; in the past: 这里～是一片荒野. This place used to be a vast expanse of wasteland.

以为(爲) yǐwéi (动) think; consider: 不～然 I beg to differ; I don't think so

以下 yǐxià (名) below; under: 他们的建议可以归纳为～几点. Their proposal can be summed up as follows. 气温已降到零度～. The temperature has dropped below zero.

以销定产(產) yǐ xiāo dìng chǎn plan production according to sales

以眼还(還)眼,以牙还(還)牙 yǐ yǎn huán yǎn, yǐ yá huán yá an eye for an eye and a tooth for a tooth

以怨报(報)德 yǐ yuàn bào dé return evil for good

以致 yǐzhì (连) [indicating an unpleasant result] with the result that; consequently: 他事先没有充分调查研究,～做出了错误的结论. He had not looked carefully into the matter so that he drew an erroneous conclusion.

矣 yǐ (助)〈书〉[used at the end of a sentence to indicate completion of an action like 了 in colloquial Chinese]: 悔之晚～. It's too late to repent.

意 yì (名) **1** meaning; idea: 同有此～ have identical views; be in agreement about sth. **2** wish; desire; intention: 好～ a good intention **3** expectation: 出其不～ take one by surprise; run counter to one's expectations. 如无～外 barring the unexpected **4** hint; trace; suggestion: 春～盎然. Spring is in the air.

意会(會) yìhuì (动) sense: 只可～,不可言传 can be fully understood but not in tangible terms

意见(見) yìjiàn (名) **1** idea; view; opinion: 交换～ exchange view **2** objection; complaint: 我对这种方法有～. I feel strongly about this approach to things. ～簿 comment book

意境 yìjìng (名) feeling or mood as expressed by art or literature; artistic conception: 这幅油画～深远. This painting gives expression to a high level of artistic conception.

意料 yìliào (动) anticipate; expect: 这是～中的事. That's what is to be expected.

意念 yìniàn (名) idea; thought

意气(氣) yìqì (名) **1** will and spirit: ～高昂 in high morale **2** temperament: ～相投 temperamentally compatible **3** personal feelings (or prejudice): ～用事 allow oneself to be swayed by personal feelings

意识(識) yìshí I (名) consciousness II (动) [often used with 到] be aware of; realize: ～到自己责任的重大 be conscious of the gravity of one's responsibilities

意识(識)形态(態) yìshí xíngtài ideology

意思 yìsi (名) **1** meaning; idea: 文章的中心～ the central theme **2** opinion; wish; desire: 大家的～ the consensus of opinion **3** a token of affection, appreciation, gratitude, etc.: 这件小礼品不过是我的一点儿～. This little gift is but a token of my appreciation. **4** suggestion; hint; trace: 他脸上露出忿怒的～. There is a suggestion of anger in his face. **5** interest; fun: 有～ interesting; enjoyable.

意图(圖) yìtú (名) intention; intent

意外 yìwài I (形) unexpected; unforeseen: 感到～ come to one as a surprise II (名) accident; mishap: 以防～ so as to prevent accidents

意味 yìwèi (名) **1** meaning; implication: ～深长的一笑 a meaning or knowing smile **2** interest; overtone; flavour: 他的文章中含有讽刺的～. There is touch of sarcasm in his article.

意想 yìxiǎng (动) imagine; expect: ～不到 unexpected; beyond all expectations

意向 yìxiàng (名) intention; purpose: ～书 letter of intent

意义(義) yìyì (名) meaning; sense; significance: 在某种～上 in a sense

意译(譯) yìyì (动) paraphrase; free translation

意愿(願) yìyuàn (名) wish; desire; aspiration

意志 yìzhì (名) will; will power: ～坚强 strong-willed

意中人 yìzhōngrén (名) the person one is in love with

癔 yì

癔病 yìbìng (名) hysteria

臆 yì **1** chest **2** subjectively

臆测 yìcè (动) conjecture; guess; make certain assumptions

臆断(斷) yìduàn (动) make an arbitrary decision; draw an arbitrary conclusion

臆造 yìzào (动) fabricate (a story, reason, etc.); invent

亦 yì (副)〈书〉also; too: 反之～然 and vice versa

亦步亦趋(趨) yìbù-yìqū ape sb. sedulously; follow sb.'s move slavishly

亦即 yìjí that is; namely

奕 yì

奕奕 yìyì (形) radiating health and vitality: 神采～ glow with health; look hale and hearty

裔 yì (名) descendants; posterity: 华～美国人 an American of Chinese descent

益 yì I (名) benefit; profit; advantage: 受～匪浅 benefit greatly from it. 公～ public welfare. 权～ rights and interests II (形) beneficial: ～虫 beneficial insect. ～鸟 beneficial bird. III (副) increasingly: 精～求精 keep improving; make even better progress

益处(處) yìchu (名) benefit; advantage

益友 yìyǒu (名) helpful friend; friend and mentor

溢 yì I (动) overflow; brim: 洋～ be overflowing II (形) excessive: ～美 undeserved praise

溢出 yìchū (动) spill over; overflow

缢 yì (动)〈书〉hang: 自～ hang oneself

谊 yì (名) friendship: 深情厚～ profound friendship

抑 yì (动) restrain; repress; curb

抑制 yìzhì I (动) restrain; control: ~愤怒 contain one's anger. ~感情 control one's emotion II (名) inhibition

易 yì I (形) 1 easy: 轻~ easily. 来之不~ hard-won 2 amiable: 平~近人 amiable and easy of access II (动) 1 change: ~手 change hands 2 exchange: ~货贸易 barter

易如反掌 yì rú fǎnzhǎng be simple and easy; can be easily accomplished

义(義) yì I (名) 1 justice; righteousness: 深明大~ have a strong sense of justice 2 human relationship: 无情无~ heartless and faithless 3 meaning; significance: 词~转换 semantic transfer. 一词多~ polysemy II (形) adopted; adoptive: ~女 adopted daughter. ~母 adoptive mother

义不容辞(辭) yì bùróng cí be duty-bound

义齿 yìchǐ (名) false tooth; denture

义愤 yìfèn (名) righteous indignation

义愤填膺 yìfèn tián yīng be filled with (righteous) indignation

义工 yìgōng (名) volunteer

义卖(賣) yìmài (名) a sale of goods (usu. at high prices) for charity or other worthy causes; charity bazaar

义气(氣) yìqì (名) personal loyalty

义务(務) yìwù I (名) duty; obligation: ~教育 compulsory education II (形) volunteer; voluntary: ~演出 benefit performance. ~劳动 volunteer labour

义演 yìyǎn (名) charity show

议(議) yì I (名) opinion; view: 异~ disagreement. 提~ proposal; motion II (动) consult; discuss: 自报公~ submit one's own request for public appraisal

议案 yì'àn (名) proposal; motion

议程 yìchéng (名) agenda: 列入~ place on the agenda; include in the agenda

议定书(書) yìdìngshū (名) protocol: 贸易~ trade protocol

议和 yìhé (动) negotiate peace

议会(會) yìhuì (名) parliament; legislative assembly

议价(價) yìjià I (动) negotiate a price II (名) negotiated price

议论(論) yìlùn (动) comment; talk; discuss: 随便~ make irresponsible comments. ~不休 argue endlessly. ~纷纷 all sorts of comments; widespread comment. ~文 argumentation

议事 yìshì (动) discuss official business: ~规则 rules of procedure; rules of debate. ~日程 agenda; order of the day

议题 yìtí (名) subject under discussion; topic for discussion

议员 yìyuán (名) member of a legislative assembly; Member of Parliament (MP); Congressman or Congresswoman

议院 yìyuàn (名) legislative assembly; parliament; congress

议长(長) yìzhǎng (名) the Speaker; president

刈 yì (动) mow; cut down: 刈草机 mower

轶 yì (动) 1 be lost 2 excel

轶事 yìshì (名) anecdote

屹 yì (形)〈书〉 towering like a mountain peak

屹立 yìlì (动) stand towering like a giant; stand erect

屹然 yìrán (形) towering; majestic: ~不动 stand rock-firm

诣 yì (名) (academic or technical) attainments: 学术造~ scholastic attainments

逸 yì I (名) ease; leisure: 有劳有~ alternate work with rest II (动) escape; flee: 逃~ escape

逸事 yìshì (名) anecdote (esp. about a famous person)

肄 yì (动) study

肄业(業) yìyè (动) study in school or at college: 他曾在大学~两年. He was in college for two years.

毅 yì (形) firm; resolute; 刚~ fortitude

毅力 yìlì (名) willpower; will; stamina: 惊人的~ amazing willpower

毅然 yìrán (副) resolutely; firmly; determinedly

疫 yì (名) epidemic disease; pestilence: 鼠~ the plague. 防~ epidemic prevention

疫病 yìbìng (名) epidemic disease

疫苗 yìmiáo (名) vaccine

役 yì I (名) 1 labour; service: 劳~ forced labour. 兵~ military service 2 servant: 仆~ servant; flunkey 3 battle: 滑铁卢之~ the Battle of Waterloo II

(动) use as a slave: 奴～ enslave

忆(憶) yì (动) recall; recollect

亿(億) yì (数) a hundred million

亿万(萬) yìwàn (数) hundreds of millions; millions upon millions: ～富翁 billionaire

艺(藝) yì (名) 1 skill: 球～ skill in a ball game 2 art: 文～ art and literature

艺人 yìrén (名) 1 actor or artist (in local drama, storytelling, acrobatics, etc.) 2 artisan; handicraftsman

艺术(術) yìshù I (名) 1 art: ～风格 artistic style. ～品 work of art 2 skill; technique; craft II (形) artistic; in good taste

艺苑 yìyuàn (名) the realm of art and literature; art and literary circles

呓(囈) yì (名) talk in one's sleep

呓语 yìyǔ (名) 1 talk in one's sleep 2 ravings

译(譯) yì (动) translate; interpret: 笔～ written translation. 口～ oral interpretation

译本 yìběn (名) translation

译文 yìwén (名) translated text; translation

译员 yìyuán (名) interpreter

译者 yìzhě (名) translator

译制(製) yìzhì (动) dub: ～片 dubbed film

驿(驛) yì (名) post

驿站 yìzhàn (名) post (where formerly couriers changed horses or rested)

翌 yì (形)〈书〉immediately following in time; next: ～日 next day. ～年 next year; the following year

异(異) yì (形) 1 different: 大同小～ identical in general terms though different on minor issues. ～父(母)兄弟 half brothers 2 unusual: ～乎寻常 out of the ordinary 3 strange: 深以为～ came to me as a big surprise

异常 yìcháng I (形) unusual; abnormal: ～现象 abnormal phenomena II (副) extremely; exceedingly; particularly: ～激动 get extremely excited

异端 yìduān (名) heterodoxy; heresy: ～邪说 heretical beliefs; unorthodox opinions

异国(國) yìguó (名) foreign country (or land): 远适～ reside far away in a foreign land

异乎寻(尋)常 yì hū xúncháng unusual; extraordinary: ～地热心 unusually enthusiastic

异化 yìhuà (名) alienation

异己 yìjǐ (名) dissident; alien: 在派性斗争中排除～ get rid of dissidents in factional strife

异教 yìjiào (名) paganism; heathenism: ～徒 pagan; heathen

异口同声(聲) yìkǒu-tóngshēng speak with one voice

异曲同工 yìqǔ-tónggōng different in approach and diction but equally outstanding in the overall effect

异乡(鄉) yìxiāng (名) foreign land; strange place (town or province) away from home

异想天开(開) yì xiǎng tiān kāi give free rein to one's fantasy

异性 yìxìng (名) the opposite sex

异样(樣) yìyàng (形) unusual; different: 他今天有一些～. He is not quite himself today.

异议(議) yìyì (名) objection; dissension: 提出～ raise an objection; take exception to; challenge

异族 yìzú (名) a different race or nation: ～通婚 mixed marriages

翼 yì (名) the wing of a bird, aeroplane, etc.

翼翼 yìyì (形) cautiously: 小心～ act with exceptional caution; act very cautiously

音 yīn (名) 1 sound: 噪～ noise 2 news; tidings: ～信 news; tidings

音标(標) yīnbiāo (名) phonetic symbol; phonetic transcription

音调 yīndiào (名) tone

音符 yīnfú (名) note

音阶(階) yīnjiē (名) scale

音节(節) yīnjié (名) syllable

音量 yīnliàng (名) volume (of sound)

音色 yīnsè (名) tone colour; timbre

音素 yīnsù (名) phoneme

音速 yīnsù (名) velocity (or speed) of sound: 超～ supersonic

音响(響) yīnxiǎng (名) sound; acoustics: ～效果 sound effects; acoustics

音译(譯) yīnyì (动) transliterate; transliteration

音乐(樂) yīnyuè (名) music: ～会 concert. ～家 musician

音质(質) yīnzhì (名) 1 tone quality 2 acoustic fidelity

因 yīn I (介) 1 on the basis of; in the light of: ～人而异 vary from person to person 2 because of; as a result of: ～母病请假 ask for a leave of absence on account of one's mother's illness. 会议～故改期. The meeting has been postponed for some reason. ～工负伤 work-related injuries II (名) cause; reason: 近～ immediate cause. 前～后果 cause and effect; the cause-effect relationship. 事出有～. There is no smoke without fire.

因材施教 yīn cái shī jiào impart knowledge to pupils according to their varying mental make-up

因此 yīncǐ (连) therefore; for this reason; consequently

因地制宜 yīn dì zhì yí adopt measures in the light of the realities of specific regions; suit measures to local conditions

因而 yīn'ér (连) thus; as a result; with the result that

因果 yīnguǒ (名) 1 cause and effect 2 karma; preordained fate

因陋就简 yīn lòu jiù jiǎn (do things) on the basis of the existing conditions no matter how simple and crude

因人设事 yīn rén shè shì create a job to accommodate a person

因势(勢)利导(導) yīn shì lì dǎo guide properly the trend in the development of events

因素 yīnsù (名) factor; element: 积极～ positive factors

因特网(網) yīntèwǎng (名) Internet

因为(爲) yīnwèi (连) because; for; on account of

因循 yīnxún (动) carry on as usual: ～守旧 stick to old ways; follow the beaten track

因缘 yīnyuán (名) 1 principal and subsidiary causes; cause 2 predestined relationship

茵 yīn (名) mattress: 绿草如～ a carpet of green grass

姻 yīn (名) 1 marriage: 联～ be connected by marriage 2 relation by marriage

姻亲(親) yīnqīn (名) relation by marriage: ～关系 relationship by marriage

姻缘 yīnyuán (名) predestined matrimonial affinity

殷 yīn (形) 1 earnest; ardent: 期望甚～ entertain ardent hopes 2 hospitable: 招待甚～ extend lavish hospitality

殷切 yīnqiè (形) ardent; earnest: ～的期望 earnest expectations

殷勤 yīnqín (形) eagerly attentive; warm: 受到～的接待 be accorded warm hospitality

阴(陰) yīn I (名) 1 (in Chinese philosophy, medicine, etc.) *yin*, the feminine or negative principle in nature 2 the moon: ～历 lunar calendar 3 shade: 树～ the shade of a tree 4 back: 碑～ the back of a stone tablet 5 private parts (esp. of the female) II (形) 1 cloudy; overcast 2 hidden: 阳奉～违 agree in public but object in secret 3 negative: ～离子 negative ion; anion

阴沉 yīnchén (形) cloudy; overcast; gloomy; sombre: 天色～. The sky is cloudy (or grey). 脸色～ have a sombre countenance; look glum

阴错阳(陽)差 yīncuò-yángchā an error caused by a strange coincidence

阴电(電) yīndiàn (名) negative electricity

阴沟(溝) yīngōu (名) sewer

阴魂 yīnhún (名) ghost; spirit; apparition: ～不散 the ghost lingers on — the evil influence remains

阴间 yīnjiān (名) the nether world; the Hades

阴冷 yīnlěng (形) (of weather) raw

阴历(曆) yīnlì (名) lunar calendar: ～正月 the first month of the lunar year

阴凉 yīnliáng I (形) shady and cool II (名) cool place; shade

阴谋 yīnmóu (名) plot; scheme; conspiracy: ～集团 a conspiratorial clique (or group). ～家 schemer; intriguer; conspirator

阴森 yīnsēn (形) (of a place, atmosphere, expression, etc.) gloomy; ghastly: ～的树林 a dense, dark wood

阴私 yīnsī (名) a secret act of dishonour

阴险(險) yīnxiǎn (形) look amiable but with evil intent at heart; insidious

阴性 yīnxìng (名) negative: ～反应 negative reaction

阴阳(陽)怪气(氣) yīnyáng guàiqì 1 (of one's manner of speaking) deliberately enigmatic or ambiguous 2 eccentric;

queer：他这个人～的. He's exasperatingly eccentric.

阴影 yīnyǐng (名) shadow：树木的～ shadow cast by a tree

阴雨 yīnyǔ (形) overcast and rainy：～连绵 drizzle continuously

阴郁(鬱) yīnyù (形) gloomy; dismal：心情～ feel gloomy (or depressed)

阴云(雲) yīnyún (名) dark clouds

荫(蔭) yīn (名) shade

see also yìn

荫蔽 yīnbì (动) be shaded or hidden by foliage

淫 yín (形) 1 excessive：～雨 excessive rains 2 lax; wanton：骄奢～逸 wallow in luxury and pleasure 3 licentious 4 obscene：～书 pornographic book

淫荡(蕩) yíndàng (形) lewd; lascivious; licentious

淫秽(穢) yínhuì (形) obscene; salacious

淫乱(亂) yínluàn (形) (sexually) promiscuous

淫威 yínwēi (名) abuse of power

吟 yín (动) chant; recite：～诗 recite or compose poetry

吟诵 yínsòng (动) chant; recite

吟咏 yínyǒng (动) recite a poem or literary essay rhythmically

垠 yín (名)〈书〉boundary; limit：一望无～ stretch beyond the horizon; boundless

龈 yín (名) gum

银 yín 1 silver 2 relating to currency：～行 bank 3 silver-coloured：～灰 silver grey. 她的头发已有点儿变为～灰色了. Her hair is already touched with grey.

银币(幣) yínbì (名) silver coin

银行 yínháng (名) bank：～存款 bank deposit. 外汇指定～ authorized bank for dealing in foreign exchange

银河 yínhé (名) the Milky Way

银幕 yínmù (名) (motion-picture) screen

银牌 yínpái (名) silver medal

银器 yínqì (名) silverware

银圆 yínyuán (名) silver dollar

饮 yǐn (动) 1 drink：～酒适量 drink moderately 2 feel keenly; nurse：～恨 nurse a grievance; feel eternal regret

饮料 yǐnliào (名) drink; beverage

饮品 yǐnpǐn (名) drink

饮泣 yǐnqì (动)〈书〉swallow one's tears; weep in silence：～吞声 choked with tears

饮食 yǐnshí (名) food and drink：～业 catering trade

饮水思源 yǐn shuǐ sī yuán don't forget about the source of the water you are drinking; one should keep in mind the source of one's joy while in happiness

饮用水 yǐnyòngshuǐ (名) drinking water

饮鸩止渴 yǐn zhèn zhǐ kě drink poison to quench thirst; seek temporary relief regardless of the imminent danger

引 yǐn (动) 1 lead; guide：～路 lead the way. ～航 pilot 2 leave：～避 keep away from sb. ～退 withdraw; retire 3 lure; attract：～人注目 attract people's attention 4 cause; make：～出麻烦 cause trouble 5 quote; cite：～某人说过这番话 quote sb. as saying something to this effect

引爆 yǐnbào (动) ignite; detonate

引导(導) yǐndǎo (动) guide; lead：主人～记者参观了几个主要车间. The host showed the journalists around several principal workshops.

引渡 yǐndù (动) extradite

引发(發) yǐnfā (动) initiate; touch off; spark off; trigger off：那个事件～了一场暴乱. The incident touched off a riot.

引号(號) yǐnhào (名) quotation marks

引火 yǐnhuǒ (动) light a fire：～烧身 draw fire against oneself

引见(見) yǐnjiàn (动) present (a person) to another; introduce：他把我～给部长. He presented me to the minister.

引荐(薦) yǐnjiàn (动) recommend

引进(進) yǐnjìn (动) 1 recommend 2 introduce from elsewhere：～技术装备 import technology and equipment

引经(經)据(據)典 yǐnjīng-jùdiǎn quote the classics or any other authoritative works (to support one's argument)

引咎 yǐnjiù (动)〈书〉take the blame：～自责 hold oneself answerable for a serious mistake and make a self-criticism

引狼入室 yǐn láng rù shì invite a dangerous foe or wicked person in

引力 yǐnlì (名) gravitation：万有～ universal gravitation

引领 yǐnlǐng (名) usher in; lead

引起 yǐnqǐ (动) give rise to; lead to; cause;

arouse: ～同情 arouse one's sympathy. ～争论 give rise to controversy
引擎 yǐnqíng (名) engine
引人入胜(勝) yǐn rén rù shèng (of scenery, literary works, etc.) fascinating; enchanting; absorbing
引入 yǐnrù (动) lead into; draw into; introduce from elsewhere: ～圈套 lure into a trap; ensnare
引申 yǐnshēn (动) extend (the meaning of a word, etc.)
引水 yǐnshuǐ (动) draw or channel water; divert: ～工程 diversion works
引文 yǐnwén (名) quoted passage; quotation
引信 yǐnxìn (名) detonator; fuse
引言 yǐnyán (名) foreword; introduction
引以为(爲)戒 yǐn yǐ wéi jiè take warning from a previous error
引用 yǐnyòng (动) quote; cite
引诱 yǐnyòu (动) lure; seduce: 物质～ material enticements
引证 yǐnzhèng (动) quote or cite as proof or evidence
引资 yǐnzī (动) attract funds (or investment) from outside
引子 yǐnzi (名) 1 an actor's opening words 2 introductory music 3 introductory remarks; introduction

隐(隱) yǐn I (动) hide; conceal: ～匿 hide from view II (形) latent; hidden: ～患 hidden danger (or trouble)
隐蔽 yǐnbì (动) conceal; take cover
隐藏 yǐncáng (动) go into hiding; lie low
隐含 yǐnhán (动) imply
隐患 yǐnhuàn (名) hidden trouble; hidden danger; snake in the grass: 消除～ remove a hidden peril
隐讳(諱) yǐnhuì (动) hush up; cover up; gloss over
隐晦 yǐnhuì (形) obscure; veiled: 文字写得很～. The language is obscure and ambiguous.
隐居 yǐnjū (动) live (esp. in former times) as a hermit and refuse to get involved in politics
隐瞒(瞞) yǐnmán (动) conceal; hide; hold back: ～事实 withhold the truth; hide (or hold back) the facts
隐情 yǐnqíng (名) facts one prefers not to disclose
隐忍 yǐnrěn (动) bear patiently; forbear
隐射 yǐnshè (动) insinuate; hint; throw out innuendoes
隐私 yǐnsī (名) private matters one wants to hush up or refrains from talking about: ～权 rights of privacy; privacy; the individual's right to privacy
隐痛 yǐntòng (名) painful traumatic experience
隐现 yǐnxiàn (动) be dimly visible
隐形眼镜 yǐnxíng yǎnjìng contact lens
隐隐 yǐnyǐn (形) indistinct; faint: 青山～. The blue mountains are faintly visible.
隐忧(憂) yǐnyōu (名) the worries that lie deep down in one's heart
隐约 yǐnyuē (形) indistinct; faint: 歌声～可以听见. The songs are faintly audible. 远处的高楼～可见. The tall apartments appear indistinct in the distance. ～其词 use ambiguous language; speak in equivocal terms

瘾(癮) yǐn (名) 1 addiction; craving; urge: 吸毒上～ be addicted to drugs; be a drug addict 2 strong interest (in a sport or pastime): 他看电视看上～了. He has developed a penchant for television programmes.

荫(蔭) yìn (形) shady; damp and chilly
see also yīn
荫凉 yìnliáng (形) shady and cool

印 yìn I (名) 1 seal; stamp; chop: 盖～ affix one's seal 2 print; mark: 脚～ footprint II (动) 1 print; engrave: ～广告 print advertisements 2 tally; conform: 心心相～ be deeply attached to each other
印发(發) yìnfā (动) print and distribute; distribute
印花 yìnhuā (名) 1 printing: ～丝绸 printed silk 2 revenue stamp; stamp: ～税 stamp duty; stamp tax
印鉴(鑒) yìnjiàn (名) a specimen seal impression for checking when making payments
印泥 yìnní (名) red ink paste used for seals
印染 yìnrǎn (名) printing and dyeing (of textiles)
印刷 yìnshuā (动) print: 这本书正在～中. The book is now in press. ～错误 misprint; typographical error. ～厂 printing house
印象 yìnxiàng (名) impression: 给人留下深刻的～ leave a deep impression on sb.

印证 yìnzhèng (动) confirm; corroborate; verify

应(應) yīng (动) 1 answer; respond: 喊他他不～. When I called him, he made no reply. 2 agree (to do sth.); promise; accept: 这事是我～下来的,由我负责吧. This is what I promised to do, and I will do it myself. 3 should; ought to: ～尽的义务 one's bounden duty. 他罪有～得. He fully deserves the punishment for the crime he has committed.
see also yìng

应该 yīnggāi (动) should

应有尽(盡)有 yīngyǒu-jìnyǒu have everything that one expects to find: 这家铺子货物～. The shop has much to offer.

应允 yīngyǔn (动) assent; consent: 点头～ nod assent (or approval)

膺 yīng 〈书〉 I (名) breast: 义愤填～ become very indignant at the gross injustice II (动) bear; receive: ～此重任 hold this post of responsibility

鹰 yīng (名) hawk; eagle

鹰犬 yīngquǎn (名) falcons and hounds — lackeys; hired thugs

英 yīng (名) 1 a person of outstanding talent or wisdom: ～豪 heroes 2 flower: 落～ fallen flowers

英俊 yīngjùn (形) 1 highly talented; brilliant 2 handsome and young

英名 yīngmíng (名) celebrated name

英明 yīngmíng (形) wise; brilliant: ～远见 brilliant foresight

英雄 yīngxióng (名) hero: 女～ heroine. ～气概 heroic spirit. ～所见略同. Great minds think alike.

英勇 yīngyǒng (形) valiant; brave: ～善战 be a valiant and seasoned soldier

英语 Yīngyǔ (名) English (language)

英姿 yīngzī (名) proud bearing

罂 yīng

罂粟 yīngsù (名) opium poppy

婴 yīng (名) baby; infant

婴儿(兒) yīng'ér (名) baby; infant

樱 yīng (名) 1 cherry 2 oriental cherry

樱花 yīnghuā (名) oriental cherry

樱桃 yīngtáo (名) cherry

鹦 yīng

鹦哥 yīnggē (名) parrot

鹦鹉 yīngwǔ (名) parrot

鹦鹉学(學)舌 yīngwǔ xuéshé repeat the words of others without thinking or understanding; parrot

缨 yīng (名) 1 tassel: 红～枪 red-tasselled spear 2 ribbon

赢 yíng (动) 1 win; beat: 足球比赛结果,甲队～了. Team A won in the football match. 2 gain (profit)

赢得 yíngdé (动) win; gain: ～全场欢呼喝彩 draw the cheers and applause of all the spectators

赢利 yínglì (名) profit; gain

赢余(餘) yíngyú (名) surplus; profit

荧(熒) yíng (形)〈书〉 1 glimmering 2 dazzled; perplexed

荧光 yíngguāng (名) fluorescence; fluorescent light: ～灯 fluorescent lamp. ～屏 fluorescent screen

萤(螢) yíng (名) firefly; glowworm

萤火虫(蟲) yínghuǒchóng (名) firefly; glowworm

营(營) yíng I (动) 1 seek: ～救 rescue 2 operate; own; run: 国～ state-run. 私～ private-owned II (名) 1 camp; barracks: 安～ pitch a camp 2 battalion: ～长 battalion commander

营房 yíngfáng (名) barracks

营火 yínghuǒ (名) campfire

营救 yíngjiù (动) save; rescue

营垒(壘) yínglěi (名) 1 barracks and the enclosing walls 2 camp

营利 yínglì (动) seek profits

营生 yíngshēng (动) earn (or make) a living

营生 yíngsheng (名) job: 找个～ look for a job

营私 yíngsī (动) seek private gain; feather one's nest: ～舞弊 embezzle; engage in fraudulent practices; be guilty of graft and corruption

营销 yíngxiāo (名) marketing

营养(養) yíngyǎng (名) nutrition; nourishment: ～不良 malnutrition; undernourishment. ～学 dietetics

营业(業) yíngyè (动) do business: ～时间 business hours. ～税 business tax; transactions tax. ～执照 business licence

营运(運) yíngyùn (名) operation: 投入～ go

into operation

萦(縈) yíng（动）〈书〉entangle; encompass

萦怀(懷) yínghuái（动）be on one's mind

萦回(迴) yínghuí（动）linger about

萦绕(繞) yíngrào（动）linger on

蝇(蠅) yíng（名）fly

蝇头(頭) yíngtóu（形）tiny：～微利 petty profits

蝇营(營)狗苟 yíngyíng-gǒugǒu seek personal gain everywhere without a sense of shame

盈 yíng（动）**1** be full of; be filled with：恶贯满～. The cup of iniquity is full to the brim. **2** have a surplus of

盈亏(虧) yíng-kuī（名）profit and loss：自负～(of an enterprise) be solely held economically responsible

盈利 yínglì（名）profit; gain

盈余(餘) yíngyú（名）surplus; net profit

迎 yíng（动）**1** greet; welcome：去机场～外宾 go to the airport to meet foreign guests **2** move towards; face：他～上前去和来访者握手. He went forward and shook hands with the visitors.

迎宾(賓) yíngbīn（动）receive visitors：～曲 a tune of welcome

迎风(風) yíngfēng **1** against the wind **2** with the wind：～风招展 (of a flag) flutter in the breeze

迎合 yínghé（动）cater to; pander to：～社会需要 cater to social needs

迎候 yínghòu（动）await the arrival of; meet：他们站在国宾馆门口～贵宾. They stood at the entrance to the State Guest House to wait for the arrival of the distinguished guests.

迎击(擊) yíngjī（动）(despatch troops to) fight the approaching enemy

迎接 yíngjiē（动）meet; greet：～国际劳动节! Greet International Labour Day!

迎面 yíngmiàn head-on; in one's face：西北风～刮来. The north-westerly wind was right in our faces. 他～走过去打招呼. He stepped across to greet them.

迎刃而解 yíng rèn ér jiě (of a problem) be readily solved

迎头(頭)赶(趕)上 yíngtóu gǎnshàng try hard to catch up

迎新 yíngxīn（动）**1** see the New Year in：送旧～ ring out the Old Year and ring in the New **2** welcome new arrivals

影 yǐng（名）**1** shadow; reflection **2** vague impression **3** photograph; picture：合～ group photo (or picture) **4** motion picture; film; movie：～院 cinema. ～迷 film (or movie) fan

影集 yǐngjí（名）photograph (or picture, photo) album

影片 yǐngpiàn（名）film; movie

影响(響) yǐngxiǎng I（名）influence; effect：产生巨大～ exercise a great influence II（动）affect; influence：～健康 affect one's health. ～威信 have an adverse effect on one's prestige

影星 yǐngxīng（名）movie star; film star

影印 yǐngyìn（动）photocopy; photostat; xerox

影子 yǐngzi（名）**1** shadow; reflection：～内阁 shadow cabinet **2** trace; sign; vague impression：这人连～都不见了. He has vanished without a trace. 那件事我连点儿～也记不得了. I haven't even the haziest notion of it.

颖 yǐng（形）intelligent

颖慧 yǐnghuì（形）(of a teenager) bright; intelligent

颖悟 yǐngwù（形）(of a teenager) brilliant; intelligent

应(應) yìng（动）**1** respond：答～ answer. 呼～ echo **2** comply with; promise：～邀 upon invitation. 以～读者的需要 meet the needs of the reading public **3** suit; respond to：～景 say or write sth. to celebrate the occasion **4** deal with; cope with：～付想像不到的困难任务 cope with incredibly difficult task

see also yīng

应变(變) yìngbiàn（动）prepare for an eventuality (or contingency)：～措施 emergency measure

应承 yìngchéng（动）agree (to do sth.); promise; consent：这件事他总算～下来了. He promised at last to get the work done as requested.

应酬 yìngchou I（动）engage in social activities：不善～ not skilled at socializing; not very good at casual conversation II（名）dinner party：今天晚上有个～. I've a social engagement this evening. ～话 commonplace civilities

应答 yìngdá（动）reply; answer：～如流

reply with facility

应付 yìngfu (动) 1 deal with; cope with; handle: ～自如 handle a situation with ease. 事情太复杂,难于～. The work is too complicated to be easily manageable. 2 do sth. perfunctorily: ～差事 do it half-heartedly according to routine; hurry through an assignment 3 make do with sth.

应急 yìngjí (动) meet an urgent need: ～措施 emergency measures

应接不暇 yìngjiē bù xiá unable to attend to too many visitors or too much business on special occasions

应景 yìngjǐng (动) do sth. for the occasion: ～诗 occasional verses

应诺 yìngnuò (动) agree or undertake (to do sth.); promise

应聘 yìngpìn (动) accept an offer of employment

应时(時) yìngshí I (形) seasonable; in season: ～小菜 small dishes of the season II (副) at once; immediately

应验(驗) yìngyàn (动) (of prediction, presentiment, etc.) tally with what happens later: 他的预言～了. His prediction has come true.

应用 yìngyòng (动) apply; use: ～新技术 make use of advanced technology. ～科学 applied science. ～文 practical writing (as in official documents, notices, receipts, etc.)

应运(運)而生 yìngyùn ér shēng come into being at the opportune historic moment

应战(戰) yìngzhàn (动) 1 engage the enemy 2 accept (or take up) a challenge

应召 yìngzhào (动) respond to a call or summons

应征(徵) yìngzhēng (动) 1 be recruited: ～入伍 be conscripted for service in the armed forces 2 send an article to a magazine in response to the editor's call for open competition or regular contributions

硬 yìng I (形) 1 hard; stiff; tough: 坚～ tough. ～水 hard water 2 strong; firm; obstinate: 心肠～ hard-hearted. 提出强～的抗议 lodge a strong protest 3 (of quality) good; (of a person) able: 货色～ goods of high quality. 功夫～ superb skill II (副) manage to do sth. with difficulty: ～撑着干 struggle through the work

硬邦邦 yìngbāngbāng (形) very hard; very stiff

硬币(幣) yìngbì (名) coin; specie

硬骨头(頭) yìnggǔtou (名) a dauntless person

硬化 yìnghuà I (动) harden II (名) sclerosis

硬件 yìngjiàn (名) hardware (of a computer)

硬盘 yìngpán (名) hard disk; hard drive

硬碰硬 yìng pèng yìng 1 counter toughness with toughness 2 (of a job) very stiff and demanding: 这是～的事,只有有真才实学的人才能完成. As the work is very demanding, only people of true worth can accomplish it.

硬说 yìngshuō (动) assert; allege: 他～一切没问题. He asserted that nothing was wrong.

硬通货 yìngtōnghuò (名) hard currency

映 yìng (动) reflect; mirror; shine

映衬(襯) yìngchèn (动) set off: 红墙碧瓦,互相～. The red walls and green tiles set each other off.

映照 yìngzhào (动) shine upon

哟 yō (叹) [an expression of mild surprise]: ～,你踩我的脚了. Oh! You have trodden on my foot.

哟 yo (助) [used at the end of a sentence to indicate the imperative mood]: 大家一起用力拉～! Let's all put in some more effort, pull!

庸 yōng I (形) 1 commonplace; mediocre: ～言～行 banal remarks and trivial matters 2 inferior; second-rate II (动)〈书〉[used in the negative] need: 无～细述. This needs no further elaboration. *or* There is no need to go into details.

庸才 yōngcái (名) mediocre person; mediocrity

庸碌 yōnglù (形) mediocre: ～无能 mediocre and incompetent

庸人 yōngrén (名) mediocre person

庸人自扰(擾) yōngrén zì rǎo feel hopelessly worried or get into trouble for imaginary fears

庸俗 yōngsú (形) vulgar; philistine; low: ～化 vulgarize; debase

庸医(醫) yōngyī (名) quack; charlatan

雍 yōng〈书〉harmony

雍容 yōngróng (形) natural, graceful and

poised: ～华贵 elegant and poised; distingué. 态度～ have a dignified bearing

壅 yōng (动) 1 stop up; obstruct 2 heap soil or fertilizer over and around the roots (of plants and trees): ～土 hilling. ～肥 heap fertilizer around the roots

壅塞 yōngsè (动) clog up; jam; congest: 水道～. The waterway is blocked up.

臃 yōng

臃肿(腫) yōngzhǒng (形) 1 too fat and clumsy to move; obese 2 (of an organization) cumbersome and overstaffed

拥(擁) yōng (动) 1 gather around: 一群青年～着一个老教师走出来. An old teacher came out, followed by a group of young people. 2 (of a crowd) rush in: 一～而入 crowd in 3 support; boost: ～戴 give support to

拥抱 yōngbào (动) embrace; hug

拥戴 yōngdài (动) support (sb. as leader): 受到人民的～ enjoy popular support

拥护(護) yōnghù (动) support; uphold; endorse: 我们～这个决定. We support this decision.

拥挤(擠) yōngjǐ I (动) crowd; push and squeeze II (形) crowded; be packed like sardines

拥有 yōngyǒu (动) possess; have; own: ～核武器 possess nuclear weapons

佣(傭) yōng I (动) hire (a labourer): 雇～ employ; hire II (名) servant: 女～ woman servant; maid
see also yòng

佣工 yōnggōng (名) hired labourer; servant

永 yǒng (副) perpetually; forever; always: ～不变心 remain loyal till one's dying day

永别 yǒngbié (动) say goodbye to sb. forever; part forever

永垂不朽 yǒng chuí bù xiǔ be immortal; eternal glory to

永垂青史 yǒng chuí qīng shǐ go down in history

永恒 yǒnghéng (形) eternal; everlasting: ～的真理 eternal truth

永久 yǒngjiǔ (形) permanent; perpetual; everlasting; forever; for good (and all): ～居留 permanent residence

永生 yǒngshēng I (名) 1 eternal life 2 all one's life: ～难忘 will never forget it for the rest of one's life II (形) immortal

永世 yǒngshì (名) forever: ～永世 for ever and ever

永远(遠) yǒngyuǎn (副) always; forever; ever

泳 yǒng (名) swim: 仰～ backstroke. 蛙～ breaststroke

泳装 yǒngzhuāng (名) swimsuit

涌 yǒng (动) 1 gush; well; pour; surge: 风起云～. The wind rose and the clouds began to gather. 2 rise; surge; emerge: 雨过天晴,～出一轮明月. The sky was cloudless after a passing shower, and there emerged a bright moon.

涌现 yǒngxiàn (动) (of people and events) emerge in large numbers

踊(踴) yǒng (动) leap up; jump up

踊跃(躍) yǒngyuè I (动) leap; jump: ～欢呼 leap and cheer II (形) eagerly; enthusiastically: ～参加 participate enthusiastically; take an active part

俑 yǒng (名) earthen human figures buried with the dead in ancient times; figurines: 兵马～ terracotta warriors

勇 yǒng (形) brave; valiant; courageous: 智～双全 possess both wisdom and courage

勇敢 yǒnggǎn (形) brave; courageous: 机智～ resourceful and courageous. ～善战 intrepid and warlike

勇猛 yǒngměng (形) full of valour; intrepid

勇气(氣) yǒngqì (名) courage; nerve: 鼓起～ pluck up (or muster up) one's courage

勇往直前 yǒng wǎng zhí qián advance bravely

勇于(於) yǒngyú (动) be ready to; never hesitate to; have the courage to: ～负责 be ready to shoulder responsibilities. ～进行经济改革 never hesitate to undertake any economic reform

用 yòng I (动) 1 use; employ; apply: ～脑子 use one's brain. 大材小～ put a man of talent to trivial use 2 [used in the negative] need: 东西都准备好了,您不～操心. Everything is OK. You don't have to worry. II (名) 1 expenses; outlay: 家～ family expenses 2 usefulness: 有～ useful. 没～ useless; worthless

用兵 yòngbīng (动) plan or direct the movements of military forces: 善于～ be a master of strategy
用场(場) yòngchǎng (名) use: 派～ be put to use
用处(處) yòngchu (名) advantage: 水库的～很大. A reservoir has many advantages.
用法 yòngfǎ (名) use; usage: ～说明 directions (for use).《英语～词典》*A Dictionary of English Usage*
用费 yòngfèi (名) expense; cost
用工 yònggōng (动) recruit and use (workers): ～制度 the system of recruitment
用功 yònggōng (形) hardworking; diligent; studious: ～读书 study diligently; work hard
用户 yònghù (名) consumer; user: 征求～意见 solicit consumers' opinions
用具 yòngjù (名) utensil; apparatus; appliance: 炊事～ kitchen (or cooking) utensils
用力 yònglì (动) exert one's strength: ～喊叫 shout for all one is worth
用品 yòngpǐn (名) articles for use: 日常生活～ articles for daily use; daily necessities
用人 yòngrén (动) choose a person for a job: ～不当 not choose the proper person for the job
用事 yòngshì (动) act (when swayed by one's feelings): 感情～ act impetuously
用途 yòngtú (名) use: 电脑的～很广. Computers are used extensively in our life.
用武 yòngwǔ (动) 1 use force 2 display one's abilities or talents: 大有～之地. There's ample scope for one's abilities.
用心 yòngxīn I (形) attentively; intently: ～学习 study diligently II (名) motive; intention: 别有～ have ulterior motives
用心良苦 yòngxīn liángkǔ have really given much thought to the matter; much considered
用意 yòngyì (名) intention; purpose: 我说这话的～,只是想劝告她一下. The drift of what I am saying is merely to give her a word of advice.
用语 yòngyǔ (名) 1 choice of words; wording: ～不当 inapt wording 2 phraseology; term: 专业～ technical term

Y

佣

yòng (名) commission

see also yōng

佣金 yòngjīn (名) commission; brokerage; middleman's fee

忧(憂)

yōu I (动) worry: ～虑 be worried or anxious II (名) sorrow; anxiety: 高枕无～ be free from anxieties and sleep soundly. 无～无虑 carefree
忧愁 yōuchóu (形) depressed; sad
忧患 yōuhuàn (名) suffering; misery
忧惧(懼) yōujù (形) apprehensive
忧虑(慮) yōulǜ (形) worried; concerned: 对他的健康状况深感～ feel very concerned about her health
忧伤(傷) yōushāng (形) sad; distressed; in deep sorrow
忧心 yōuxīn (名)〈书〉worry; anxiety: ～忡忡 heavy-hearted; laden with grief

优(優)

yōu (形) excellent; outstanding

优待 yōudài (动) give preferential treatment
优等 yōuděng (形) high-class; first-rate; excellent
优点(點) yōudiǎn (名) merit; strong (or good) point; virtue: ～和缺点 strong and weak points; strengths and weaknesses; advantage and disadvantage
优厚 yōuhòu (形) good; munificent: 待遇～ excellent pay and fringe benefits
优化 yōuhuà (动) optimize: ～经济结构 optimize the economic structure. ～组合 optimization grouping or regrouping
优惠 yōuhuì (形) preferential; favourable: ～贷款 loan on favourable terms. ～价格 preferential price. ～待遇 preferential treatment; favoured treatment
优良 yōuliáng (形) fine; good: ～的传统 a good tradition
优美 yōuměi (形) graceful; fine; exquisite: 风景～. The scenery is beautiful and exquisite.
优盘 yōupán (名) USB disk; flash disk
优柔寡断(斷) yōuróu guǎduàn characterized by hesitation and indecision; indecisive
优生学(學) yōushēngxué (名) eugenics
优胜(勝) yōushèng (形) superior in contest or in academic record
优势(勢) yōushì (名) superiority; dominant position: 占～ occupy a dominant position; gain the upper hand
优先 yōuxiān (形) have priority; take precedence: ～发展这种类型的产品 give priority to the development of this type of product
优秀 yōuxiù (形) outstanding; excellent;

splendid: ～作品 outstanding work of art or literature

优雅 yōuyǎ (形) graceful; elegant; in good taste

优异(異) yōuyì (形) excellent; outstanding; exceedingly good: 考试成绩～ get excellent examination results

优裕 yōuyù (形) affluent; abundant: 生活～ be comfortably off; live in comfort

优越 yōuyuè (形) superior; advantageous: ～的条件 superior conditions. ～感 superiority complex

优越性 yōuyuèxìng (名) superiority; advantage

优质(質) yōuzhì (名) high (or top) quality; high grade: ～名牌产品 high-quality famous-brand products. 提供～服务 provide good service

幽 yōu (形) 1 deep and remote; secluded: ～静 quiet 2 quiet; tranquil; serene 3 of the nether world: ～魂 ghost

幽暗 yōu'àn (形) dim; gloomy

幽会(會) yōuhuì (名) a lovers' rendezvous

幽静 yōujìng (形) quiet and secluded; peaceful

幽灵(靈) yōulíng (名) ghost; spectre; spirit

幽默 yōumò (形) humorous: ～感 sense of humour

幽深 yōushēn (形) (of woods, palaces, etc.) deep and serene; deep and quiet

幽雅 yōuyǎ (形) (of a place) quiet and in elegant taste

悠 yōu (形) 1 remote in time 2 leisurely

悠长(長) yōucháng (形) long; long-drawn-out: ～的岁月 long years

悠久 yōujiǔ (形) long; long-standing; age-old: 历史～ have a long history. ～的文化传统 age-old cultural tradition

悠然 yōurán (形) 1 carefree and leisurely: ～自得 be carefree and content 2 long; distant; far away: ～神往 thoughts turn to things distant

悠闲(閒) yōuxián (形) leisurely and carefree: ～自在 completely free and at ease

悠扬(揚) yōuyáng (形) (of music etc.) melodious

游 yóu I (动) 1 swim 2 wander about; travel; tour: 周～世界 travel round the world 3〈书〉associate with: 交～甚广 have a wide acquaintanceship among all sorts of people II (名) part of a river; reach: 上～ the upper reaches (of a river)

游伴 yóubàn (名) travel companion; fellow traveller

游船 yóuchuán (名) pleasure-boat

游荡(蕩) yóudàng (动) loaf about; loiter; wander

游击(擊) yóujī (名) guerrilla warfare

游记 yóujì (名) travel notes; travels

游客 yóukè (名) tourist; sightseer

游览(覽) yóulǎn (动) go sightseeing; be on a tour; visit: ～长城 visit the Great Wall

游乐(樂) yóulè (动) make merry; amuse oneself: ～场所 places of recreation. ～园 amusement park; pleasure ground (or garden)

游历(歷) yóulì (动) travel for pleasure; tour

游民 yóumín (名) vagrant; vagabond: 无业～ vagrant

游牧 yóumù (动) move about in search of pasture: ～部落 nomadic tribe

游山玩水 yóushān-wánshuǐ travel from one beauty spot to another; visit various scenic spots

游手好闲(閒) yóushǒu-hàoxián loaf about without a decent occupation

游玩 yóuwán (动) 1 play games 2 stroll about

游戏(戲) yóuxì I (名) recreation; game: 做～ play games II (动) play

游戏(戲)机(機) yóuxìjī (名) video game player; TV game player

游行 yóuxíng (名) parade; march: 国庆～ National Day parade. 反战～示威 anti-war demonstration

游移 yóuyí (动) (of attitude, policy, etc.) vacillate

游弋 yóuyì (动) cruise; ply

游艺(藝) yóuyì (名) entertainment; recreation: ～室 recreation room

游泳 yóuyǒng (动) swim: ～池 swimming pool. ～裤 bathing (or swimming) trunks

游资 yóuzī (名) floating capital

尤 yóu I (副) particularly; especially: 这一点～为重要. This is particularly important. II (动) have a grudge against; blame: 他这个人怨天～人. He blames everyone but himself for what has happened.

尤其 yóuqí (副) especially; particularly: 我喜欢图画，～是国画. I am fond of painting, particularly traditional Chinese painting.

犹(猶) yóu I (动)〈书〉just as; like: 虽死～生. He lives among us though he is dead. II (副) still: 记忆～新 be still fresh in one's memory; remain vivid in one's memory

犹如 yóurú (动) just as; like; as if: ～为虎添翼 like adding wings to a tiger

犹太教 Yóutàijiào (名) Judaism

犹太民族 Yóutài mínzú Jewish people

犹豫 yóuyù (动) hesitate; waver: ～不决 hesitate

由 yóu I (名) cause: 理～ reason; ground II (介) **1** because of; due to: 咎～自取 have only oneself to blame **2** by; through: ～此入内. This way in. **3** by; to: 这次会将～他主持. This meeting will be chaired by him. 这事～我处理. Leave it to me. **4** from: ～此可知 as may be inferred from this. ～北京出发 set out from Beijing III (动) follow; obey: 我们将～别人牵着鼻子走吗? Shall we allow others to lead us by the nose?

由不得 yóubude **1** not be up to sb. to decide: 这件事～我. I've no say in the matter. **2** cannot help: ～笑起来 can't help laughing

由来(來) yóulái (名) origin; root; cause

由来(來)已久 yóulái yǐ jiǔ long-standing

由于(於) yóuyú (介) due to; owing to; thanks to; as a result of

由衷 yóuzhōng (形) sincere; heartfelt: 表示～的感激 extend one's heartfelt thanks. 这种表扬有点儿言不～. This is somewhat insincere praise.

油 yóu I (名) oil; fat: 植物～ vegetable oil. 猪～ lard II (动) be stained with grease: 衣服～了. The coat has got stains on it. III (形) oily; glib

油泵 yóubèng (名) oil pump

油层(層) yóucéng (名) oil reservoir; oil layer

油船 yóuchuán (名) (oil) tanker; oil carrier

油膏 yóugāo (名) ointment

油管 yóuguǎn (名) **1** oil pipe: 铺设～ lay oil pipes **2** oil tube

油光 yóuguāng (形) glossy; shiny; varnished

油滑 yóuhuá (形) insincere; unctuous; slippery

油画(畫) yóuhuà (名) oil painting

油井 yóujǐng (名) oil well: 钻一口～ drill (or bore) a well

油库 yóukù (名) oil depot; tank farm

油料作物 yóuliào zuòwù oil-bearing crops; oil crops

油码头(頭) yóumǎtou (名) oil jetty; oil wharf; tanker (loading) terminal

油门(門) yóumén (名) **1** throttle **2** accelerator

油墨 yóumò (名) printing ink

油泥 yóuní (名) greasy filth; grease

油腻 yóunì I (形) grease; oily; heavy II (名) greasy or oily food

油漆 yóuqī I (名) paint: ～未干 wet paint II (动) cover with paint; paint

油腔滑调 yóuqiāng-huádiào glib; unctuous: 说起话来～ speak glibly; have a glib tongue

油砂 yóushā (名) oil sand

油田 yóutián (名) oil field

油头(頭)粉面 yóutóu-fěnmiàn loudly dressed and made up

油头(頭)滑脑(腦) yóutóu-huánǎo sly and flippant

油印 yóuyìn (名) mimeograph

油脂 yóuzhī (名) oil; fat

邮(郵) yóu I (动) post; mail II (形) relating to postal affairs: ～局 post office

邮包 yóubāo (名) postal parcel; parcel

邮戳 yóuchuō (名) postmark

邮袋 yóudài (名) mailbag; postbag; (mail) pouch

邮递(遞) yóudì I (动) send by post (or mail) II (名) postal delivery: ～员 postman; mailman

邮电(電) yóudiàn (名) post and telecommunications: ～局 post office

邮购(購) yóugòu (动) mail order

邮汇(匯) yóuhuì (动) remit by post

邮寄 yóujì (动) send by post; post

邮件 yóujiàn (名) postal matter; post; mail: 挂号～ registered post. 航空～ air mail

邮票 yóupiào (名) postage stamp; stamp: 纪念～ commemorative stamps

邮筒 yóutǒng (名) pillar box; postbox; mailbox

邮箱 yóuxiāng (名) postbox; mailbox

邮政 yóuzhèng (名) postal service: ～编码 postcode; Zip code. ～信箱 post office box (P. O. B.). ～储蓄 postal savings deposit

邮资 yóuzī (名) postage: ～已付 postage paid; postpaid. 国内～ postage paid for inland mail. 国外～ postage paid for overseas mail

莠 yǒu (名) 1 green bristlegrass 2 bad people: 良～不齐. Both good and bad people are intermingled.

有 yǒu (动) 1 have; possess 2 there is; exist: 这里边什么东西都没～. There is nothing whatever in here. 3 [indicating probability or comparison]: 他～他哥哥那么高了. He is probably as tall as his elder brother. ～话就直说. Speak straight out what you think. 4 [indicating that sth. has happened or appeared]: 形势～了很大的变化. A great change has taken place in the situation. 5 [indicating "many", "much", "advanced", etc.]: ～学问 be very learned. ～了年纪 get on in years 6 [somewhat like "certain"]: ～人这么说，我可没看见. Some say so, but I haven't seen it myself. 7 [meaning certain "people", "occasions" or "localities"]: 近来他～时显出心不在焉的样子. Recently, he has sometimes appeared absent-minded. 8 [used in certain set phrases to indicate politeness]: ～劳费神 sorry to have put you to such bother

有碍(礙) yǒu'ài (动) be a hindrance to; get in the way of; obstruct: ～交通 hinder traffic. ～观瞻 be unsightly; offend the eye; be an eyesore

有板有眼 yǒubǎn-yǒuyǎn rhythmical; measured; orderly: 他说话～. Whatever he says is well presented.

有备(備)无(無)患 yǒubèi-wúhuàn preparedness is a protection against danger

有偿(償) yǒucháng (形) with compensation; compensated; paid: ～技术转让 compensated transfer of technology. ～服务 paid services

有待 yǒudài (动) remain (to be done); await: ～解决 remain to be solved. 推行这些新办法～上级批准. We have to wait for the approval of the higher level to implement these new measures.

有的是 yǒudeshì have plenty of; there's no lack of: 别着急，～时间. Don't worry. We have plenty of time.

有底 yǒudǐ (动) know how things stand and feel confident of handling them; be fully prepared for what is coming: 他心里～，一点不慌. He was not at all nervous, for he knew what to expect.

有的放矢 yǒu dì fàng shǐ shoot the arrow at the target; speak or act with something definite in view

有点(點)儿(兒) yǒudiǎnr I (形) some; a little: 看来还～希望. It looks there is still a gleam of hope. II (副) somewhat; rather; a bit: 今天他～不大高兴. He looks somewhat displeased today.

有方 yǒufāng (形) with the proper method; in the right way: 领导～ exercise effective leadership

有份儿(兒) yǒufènr have a share; have taken a part in

有关(關) yǒuguān I (动) have sth. to do with; relate to; concern: 这件事与他～. This matter has something to do with him. II (形) relevant: ～部门 the department concerned

有鬼 yǒuguǐ there's something fishy: 这里面～. There is something fishy about it.

有过(過)之无(無)不及 yǒu guò zhī wú bùjí 〈贬〉 surpass; outdo: 在这方面，他比他的前任～. In this respect he even surpassed his predecessors.

有害 yǒuhài (形) harmful; pernicious; detrimental: 对健康～ harmful to one's health

有机(機) yǒujī (形) organic: ～肥料 organic fertilizer. ～化学 organic chemistry

有机(機)可乘 yǒu jī kě chéng a loophole to exploit

有价(價)证券 yǒujià zhèngquàn negotiable securities; securities

有奖(獎)储蓄 yǒujiǎng chǔxù lottery-attached deposit

有救 yǒujiù (of a disease) can be cured or remedied

有口皆碑 yǒu kǒu jiē bēi win popular acclaim

有口难(難)分 yǒu kǒu nán fēn find it difficult to explain oneself

有赖 yǒulài (动) depend on; rest on: ～于大家的共同努力 depend very much on the concerted effort of all people

有理 yǒulǐ (形) reasonable; justified; in the right

有力 yǒulì (形) strong; powerful; energetic; vigorous: ～的回击 (make) a vigorous counter-attack. 这篇文章写得简短～. This essay is concise and forceful.

有利 yǒulì (形) beneficial; advantageous: 在

～情况下 under favourable circumstances

有利可图(圖) yǒu lì kě tú be profitable

有门(門)儿(兒) yǒuménr 1 find the beginning of a solution; be hopeful (of success) 2 get the hang:这工作他试了几次,现在～了. After several trials, he began to get the hang of the work.

有名 yǒumíng (形) well known; famous; renowned; celebrated

有名无(無)实(實) yǒumíng-wúshí in name only; nominal; titular

有目共睹 yǒu mù gòng dǔ be universally acknowledged; be clear to all

有钱(錢) yǒuqián rich; wealthy: ～能使鬼推磨. Money makes the mare go.

有趣 yǒuqù (形) interesting; fascinating; amusing

有色 yǒusè (形) coloured: ～金属 non-ferrous metal. ～人种 coloured race

有生力量 yǒushēng lìliàng effective strength; effectives

有生以来(來) yǒu shēng yǐlái ever since one's birth; since one was born

有声(聲)有色 yǒushēng-yǒusè vivid and dramatic: 故事讲得～ bring the story to life

有始无(無)终 yǒushǐ-wúzhōng fail to carry sth. through to the end

有事 yǒushì 1 have a job; be employed; be occupied; be busy: 她现在～了,待遇还不错. She's got a job now, and is pretty well paid, too. 2 have sth. happen; meet with an accident; get into trouble: 别担心,我看不会～的. Don't worry, I don't think there'll be any trouble. 3 have sth. on one's mind; be anxious; worry: 他心里一定～. There must be something weighing on his mind.

有恃无(無)恐 yǒushì-wúkǒng fearless of what might happen because one has strong backing

有数(數) yǒushù I (动) know exactly what one is doing: 两个人心里都～儿. The two of them know exactly how things stand. II (形) not many; only a few: 离开学只剩下～的几天了. There are only a few days left before school starts.

有条(條)不紊 yǒutiáo-bùwěn in an orderly way; methodically; systematically

有为(爲) yǒuwéi (形) promising: 年轻～ young and promising

有…无… yǒu…wú… [used to indicate a case in which there is only one thing and not the other]: 有己无人 absolutely selfish. 有口无心 frank and straight forward. 有勇无谋 be brave but not resourceful. 有害无益 do only harm and no good

有喜 yǒuxǐ (动) be pregnant; be expecting

有线(綫) yǒuxiàn (形) wired: ～广播 wire (or wired) broadcasting. ～电报 telegraph; cable

有限 yǒuxiàn (形) limited; finite: 为数～ limited in number

有效 yǒuxiào (形) effective; efficient; valid: 采取～措施 take effective measures. 这张车票三日内～. This train ticket is good for three days.

有效期 yǒuxiàoqī (名) term (or period) of validity; expiry date

有心 yǒuxīn I (动) set one's mind on II (副) intentionally; on purpose

有心人 yǒuxīnrén (名) a person who is ambitious or tenacious of purpose

有言在先 yǒu yán zài xiān make clear at the beginning; forewarn

有益 yǒuyì (形) profitable; beneficial; useful

有意 yǒuyì I (动) be inclined to II (副) deliberately; on purpose: ～刁难 deliberately make things difficult for sb.

有意思 yǒu yìsi 1 significant; meaningful: 他说的话很～. What he said was significant. 2 interesting; enjoyable: 今天的晚会很～. The evening was most enjoyable.

有…有… yǒu…yǒu… 1 [used with two nouns or verbs with opposite meanings to indicate possession of both qualities]: 有利有弊 have both advantages and disadvantages 2 [used for emphasis before two nouns or verbs with identical or similar meanings]: 有凭有据 backed by evidence. 有说有笑 talk cheerfully

有余(餘) yǒuyú (动) have enough and to spare: 绰绰～ have more than enough

有种(種) yǒuzhǒng have guts; be plucky; be gritty: ～的跟我来! Let anyone who has guts follow me!

有助于(於) yǒuzhùyú (动) contribute to; be conducive to; conduce to: ～增进两国人民之间的友谊 be conducive to the promotion of the friendship between our two peoples

友 yǒu I (名) friend: 好~ close friend. 战~ comrade-in-arms II (形) friendly

友爱(愛) yǒu'ài (名) friendly affection; fraternal love

友邦 yǒubāng (名) friendly nation (or country)

友好 yǒuhǎo I (名) close friend; friend II (形) friendly; amicable: ~访问 friendly visit

友情 yǒuqíng (名) friendly sentiments; friendship

友人 yǒurén (名) friend: 国际~ friends from abroad

友谊 yǒuyì (名) friendship: 深厚的~ profound friendship

黝 yǒu (形) black; dark: ~黑 dark; swarthy

诱 yòu (动) 1 guide; teach: 循循善~ be good at giving instruction and guidance; teach with patience 2 lure; seduce; entice: ~敌 lure the enemy in

诱导(導) yòudǎo (动) guide; lead; induce

诱饵 yòu'ěr (名) bait

诱发(發) yòufā (动) bring out (sth. potential or latent); induce; cause to happen

诱惑 yòuhuò (动) 1 entice; tempt; seduce; lure 2 attract; allure: 窗外是一片~人的景色. Outside the window stretches a vista of enchanting beauty.

诱骗 yòupiàn (动) trap; trick

右 yòu (名) 1 the right side; the right: 靠~走 keep to the right 2 the Right: ~倾思想 Rightist thinking

右边(邊) yòubian (名) the right (or right-hand) side; the right

右倾 yòuqīng (名) Right deviation

右首 yòushǒu (名) the righthand side; the right

右翼 yòuyì (名) 1 right wing; right flank 2 the Right; the right wing

又 yòu (副) 1 [indicating repetition or continuation]: 读了~读 read again and again. 一年~一年 year after year 2 [indicating the simultaneous existence of several conditions or characteristics]: ~高~大 tall and big. 效率~高,管理~好 efficient and well-managed 3 [indicating additional ideas or afterthought]: 冬季日短,~是雪天,夜色早已笼罩了整个市镇. Days are short in winter. And it was a snowy day, so the whole town was already enveloped in a thick mist of dusk. 4 [indicating two contradictory ideas]: 她~想去,~不想去,拿不定主意. She was not sure whether she was to go and could not make up her mind. 5 [used in negative sentences or rhetorical questions for the sake of emphasis]: 他~不是什么生客,还用你老陪着吗? He is not a rare visitor. Do you have to keep him company all the time?

幼 yòu I (形) young; under age: ~畜 young animal; young stock II (名) children; the young: 扶老携~ bringing along the old and the young

幼虫(蟲) yòuchóng (名) larva

幼儿(兒) yòu'ér (名) infant; toddler: ~教育 pre-school education. ~园 kindergarten

幼苗 yòumiáo (名) seedling

幼年 yòunián (名) childhood; infancy

幼小 yòuxiǎo (形) immature

幼稚 yòuzhì (形) 1 young 2 childish; naive

柚 yòu (名)(~子) shaddock; pomelo; grapefruit

釉 yòu (名) glaze: 青~瓷器 blue glazed porcelain

淤 yū I (动) become silted up: 水渠里~了很多泥沙. The channel has silted up. II (名) silt: 河~ sludge from a riverbed

淤积(積) yūjī (动) silt up; deposit

淤泥 yūní (名) silt; sludge; ooze

淤塞 yūsè (动) silt up; be choked with silt

迂 yū (形) 1 roundabout: ~道访问 make a detour to call on sb. 2 pedantic: ~论 pedantic talk

迂腐 yūfǔ (形) trite; hackneyed; pedantic: ~的见解 pedantic ideas

迂回(迴) yūhuí I (形) circuitous; tortuous; roundabout: ~曲折 full of twists and turns; tortuous. ~前进 advance by a roundabout route II (动) outflank: 向敌人左侧~ outflank the enemy on the left

于(於) yú (介) 1 [similar to 在]: 生~1920年 be born in 1920. 闻名~世界 famous all over the world 2 [similar to 给]: 光荣归~英雄的人民. The credit goes to the heroic people. 3 [similar to 对 or 对于]: 忠~祖国 be loyal to one's country. 这样~你自己不利. It won't do you any good. 4 [similar to 从]: 出~无知 out of sheer ignorance. 出~

自愿 of one's own accord

于今 yújīn 1 up to the present; since 2 nowadays; today; now

于是 yúshì (连) thereupon; hence; consequently; as a result

盂 yú (名) a broad-mouthed receptacle for holding liquid; jar: 痰～ spitton

舆 yú I (名) 1 carriage; chariot 2 sedan chair 3 area; territory: ～地 territory II (形) public; popular: ～论 public opinion

舆论(論) yúlùn (名) public opinion: ～工具 mass media; the media. ～界 the media; press circles

舆情 yúqíng (名) public sentiment; popular feelings

虞 yú I (名)〈书〉1 supposition; prediction: 以备不～ be prepared for any contingency 2 anxiety; worry: 水旱无～ have no worries about drought or flood II (动) deceive; cheat; fool: 尔～我诈 each trying to cheat the other; mutual deception

娱 yú I (动) give pleasure to; amuse: 聊以自～ just to enjoy oneself II (名) joy; pleasure; amusement

娱乐(樂) yúlè (名) amusement; entertainment; recreation: ～场所 place of entertainment

愚 yú I (形) foolish; stupid: ～人 fool II (动) fool; dupe: 为人所～ be duped by sb. III (代)〈谦〉I: ～以为不可 in my opinion this wouldn't seem correct

愚笨 yúbèn (形) dull-witted; stupid; clumsy

愚蠢 yúchǔn (形) stupid; foolish; idiotic

愚昧 yúmèi (形) ignorant: ～无知 pure ignorance. ～落后 ignorant and backward

愚弄 yúnòng (动) deceive; hoodwink; make a fool of; dupe

余(餘) yú I (形) 1 surplus; spare; remaining: ～钱 spare money. ～年 the remaining years of one's life 2 more than; odd; over: 五十～年 fifty-odd years II (名) beyond; after: 工作之～ after work; in one's spare time

余波 yúbō (名) aftermath: 纠纷的～ the aftermath of the dispute

余存 yúcún (名) remainder; balance

余地 yúdì (名) leeway; room; latitude: 回旋～ room for manoeuvre. 还有改进的～. There is still room for improvement. 在这方面我们给他留有相当的～. In this respect we allow him considerable latitude.

余毒 yúdú (名) residual poison; pernicious influence

余额 yú'é (名) remaining sum; balance

余悸 yújì (名) lingering fear: 心有～ have a lingering fear after the incident

余粮(糧) yúliáng (名) surplus grain

余热(熱) yúrè (名) 1 surplus energy: 利用～取暖 use surplus energy for heating purposes 2 old people's capacity for work: 发挥～ do what one can in one's old age

余暇 yúxiá (名) spare time; leisure time; leisure

余兴(興) yúxìng (名) 1 lingering interest 2 entertainment after a meeting or a dinner party

余音 yúyīn (名) the residue of sound which remains in the ears of the hearer

渝 yú (动) (of one's attitude or feeling) change: 始终不～ remain faithful

愉 yú (形) pleased; happy: 不～ displeased; annoyed

愉快 yúkuài (形) happy; joyful; cheerful: 心情～ be in a happy mood

瑜 yú

瑜珈 yújiā (名) yoga

逾 yú (动) exceed; go beyond: ～限 exceed the limit. 年～六十 over sixty years old

逾期 yúqī (动) exceed the time limit

逾越 yúyuè (动) exceed; go beyond: ～权限 overstep one's authority. 不可～的障碍 an insurmountable obstacle (or barrier)

谀 yú (动)〈书〉flatter: 阿～ flatter and toady

鱼(魚) yú (名) fish

鱼翅 yúchì (名) shark's fin

鱼肚 yúdǔ (名) fish maw

鱼饵 yú'ěr (名) (fish) bait

鱼肝油 yúgānyóu (名) cod liver oil

鱼竿 yúgān (名) fishing rod

鱼钩 yúgōu (名) fish-hook

鱼贯 yúguàn (副) one following the other; in single file: ～而入 file in

鱼雷 yúléi (名) torpedo: ～快艇 torpedo boat

鱼鳞 yúlín (名) fish scale

鱼龙(龍)混杂(雜) yú-lóng hùnzá good and bad people mixed up

鱼目混珠 yúmù hùn zhū pass off fish eyes as pearls; pass off the sham as the

genuine
鱼水情 yú-shuǐqíng (名) close relationship (usu. between the military and civilians)
鱼网(網) yúwǎng (名) fishnet; fishing net
鱼子 yúzǐ (名) roe: ~酱 caviare
渔 yú I (名) fishing: ~船 fishing boat. ~翁 fisherman II (动) seek by unfair means: ~利 seek unfair gains
渔产(產) yúchǎn (名) aquatic products
渔场(場) yúchǎng (名) fishing ground; fishery
渔民 yúmín (名) fisherman; fisherfolk
渔业(業) yúyè (名) fishery: ~资源 fishery resources
宇 yǔ (名) 1 building; house: 庙~ temple 2 space; globe: ~宙 universe; cosmos. ~宙飞船 spacecraft
宇宙航行 yǔzhòu hángxíng astronavigation; space travels: ~员 astronaut; spaceman
语 yǔ I (名) 1 language; tongue; words: 汉~ the Chinese language. 本族~ mother tongue; native language. 甜言蜜~ sweet words 2 non-linguistic means of communicating ideas; semiology: 旗~ flag signal. 手~ sign language II (动) speak; say: 不言不~ be speechless; keep silent
语病 yǔbìng (名) faulty wording; unhappy choice of words
语词 yǔcí (名) words and phrases
语法 yǔfǎ (名) grammar
语汇(彙) yǔhuì (名) vocabulary
语气(氣) yǔqì (名) 1 tone; manner of speaking: ~友好 a friendly tone 2 mood: 祈使~ imperative mood
语态(態) yǔtài (名) voice: 主动(被动)~ the active (passive) voice
语文 yǔwén (名) 1 (oral and written) language: ~程度 one's reading and writing ability 2 language and literature
语无(無)伦(倫)次 yǔ wú lúncì speak incoherently; be totally disorganized in one's speech; talk inarticulately
语系 yǔxì (名) family of languages; language family
语序 yǔxù (名) word order
语焉不详 yǔ yān bù xiáng not go into details; not elaborate
语言 yǔyán (名) language: ~隔阂 language barrier. ~学 linguistics. 工作~ working language. 正式~ official language
语音 yǔyīn (名) pronunciation: ~学 phonetics
语源学(學) yǔyuánxué (名) etymology
语重心长(長) yǔzhòng-xīncháng sincere advice and earnest wishes; earnest exhortations
雨 yǔ (名) rain: 大~ a heavy rain. 暴~ storm; downpour. 毛毛~ drizzle
雨点(點) yǔdiǎn (名) raindrop
雨过(過)天晴 yǔ guò tiān qíng the sun shines again after the rain
雨后(後)春笋(筍) yǔ hòu chūnsǔn (spring up like) bamboo shoots after a spring rain
雨季 yǔjì (名) rainy season
雨具 yǔjù (名) rain gear (i. e. umbrella, raincoat, etc.)
雨量 yǔliàng (名) rainfall
雨伞(傘) yǔsǎn (名) umbrella
雨水 yǔshuǐ (名) rainwater; rainfall; rain: ~足 adequate rainfall
雨鞋 yǔxié (名) rubber boots; galoshes
雨衣 yǔyī (名) raincoat
与(與) yǔ I (动) 1 give; offer: 赠~ give sth. to sb. as a gift. ~人方便 be of help to others 2 help; support: ~人为善 sincerely help people to improve; be well intentioned II (介) with; to: ~困难作斗争 grapple with difficulties. ~世浮沉 swim with the tide III (连) and: 买方~卖方 buyer and seller. 战争~和平 war and peace
see also yù
与其 yǔqí (连) [used in the context of making a decision after weighing the pros and cons]: ~扬汤止沸, 不如釜底抽薪. It would be better to find a permanent solution in a slow process than to seek temporal relief by drastic measures.
与日俱增 yǔ rì jù zēng grow with each passing day; be steady on the increase
与时(時)俱进(進) yǔ shí jù jìn move with the times; keep abreast with the times
与世长(長)辞(辭) yǔ shì chángcí depart from the world; pass away
与世无(無)争 yǔ shì wú zhēng stand aloof from worldly strife
屿(嶼) yǔ (名) small island; islet: 岛~ islands and islets; islands
羽 yǔ (名) feather; plume
羽毛 yǔmáo (名) feather; plume: ~丰满 become full-fledged
羽毛球 yǔmáoqiú (名) 1 badminton 2 shuttlecock
羽毛未丰(豐) yǔmáo wèi fēng still young

and immature; fledgling

予 yǔ (动) give: 免～处分 no disciplinary action will be taken against one; be exempted from disciplinary action. ～人口实 give sb. a handle

予以 yǔyǐ (动) give; grant: ～优待 give one preferential treatment. ～批评 pass criticism

育 yù (动) 1 give birth to: 生儿～女 have children. 节～ birth control; family planning 2 rear; raise; bring up: ～秧 grow rice seedlings 3 educate: 教书～人 impart knowledge and educate people. 德～ moral education

育种(種) yùzhǒng (名) breeding: 杂交～ cross-breeding. 作物～ crop breeding

玉 yù I (名) jade II (形)〈书〉pure; handsome; beautiful: 亭亭～立 fair, slender and graceful

玉帛 yùbó (名)〈书〉jade objects and silk fabrics, used as state gifts in ancient China

玉成 yùchéng〈敬〉kindly help secure the success of sth.: 深望～此事. It is earnestly hoped that you will help arrange the matter successfully.

玉米 yùmǐ (名) maize

玉器 yùqì (名) jade article; jade object; jadeware

玉石俱焚 yù-shí jù fén destruction of all people good and bad alike

玉蜀黍 yùshǔshǔ (名) maize; corn

玉玺(璽) yùxǐ (名) imperial jade seal

芋 yù (名) 1 taro 2 tuber crops: 洋～ potato. 山～ sweet potato

吁(籲) yù (动) appeal; plead: 呼～ petition. ～请 plead with sb.; appeal to sb.

see also xū

域 yù (名) land within certain boundaries; territory; region: 领～ territory; field; area. 核物理学里的一个新领～ a new area of nuclear physics

域名 yùmíng (名) domain name

郁 yù (形) 1 strongly fragrant 2 (鬱) luxuriant; lush 3 (鬱) gloomy; depressed: 忧～ feel depressed or frustrated

郁闷 yùmèn (形) gloomy; unhappy: 有～之感 be in the doldrums

郁血 yùxuè (名) stagnation of the blood; venous stasis

郁郁 yùyù (形)〈书〉1 lush; luxuriant: ～葱葱 green and luxuriant 2 gloomy; melancholy; depressed

与(與) yù (动) take part in; participate in

see also yǔ

与会(會) yùhuì (动) attend a meeting: ～国 participating countries

与闻 yùwén (动) participate in the discussion of: ～其事 be a participant in the matter

誉(譽) yù I (名) reputation; fame: ～满全球 of world renown; famous the world over II (动) praise; eulogize

寓 yù I (动) 1 reside; live: ～居 stay in lodgings 2 imply; contain: 这个故事～有深意. This story conveys a profound message. II (名) residence: 公～ apartment house. 客～ lodgings

寓居 yùjū (动) reside abroad or in a place away from one's home town

寓所 yùsuǒ (名) residence; accommodation

寓言 yùyán (名) fable; allegory; parable

寓意 yùyì (名) implied meaning; message: ～深刻 be pregnant with meaning

遇 yù I (动) 1 meet: 不期而～ meet by chance; run across 2 treat; receive: 优～ treat sb. with special consideration II (名) chance; opportunity: 机～ favourable circumstances; opportunity

遇害 yùhài (动) be murdered; be killed

遇见(見) yùjiàn (动) meet: 在昨天的招待会上我～一位老朋友. I met an old friend at yesterday's reception.

遇救 yùjiù (动) be rescued

遇难(難) yùnàn (动) 1 be killed in an accident 2 be murdered

遇险(險) yùxiǎn (动) meet with a mishap; be in trouble

浴 yù (名、动) bath; bathe: 淋～ shower bath

浴场(場) yùchǎng (名) outdoor bathing place: 海滨～ bathing beach

浴池 yùchí (名) public bathhouse; public bath

浴盆 yùpén (名) bathtub

浴室 yùshì (名) bathroom

裕 yù (形) abundant; plentiful: 富～ abundant; affluent; well-to-do

欲 yù I (名) desire; longing; wish: 食～ appetite. 求知～ thirst for knowledge II (动) wish; want; desire: 畅所～

言 say all that one has to say; speak freely III (副) about to; on the point of: 摇摇~坠 teeter on the edge of collapse; tottering

欲罢(罷)不能 yù bà bùnéng be compelled to go ahead by force of circumstances, though against one's will

欲盖(蓋)弥(彌)彰 yù gài mí zhāng try to cover up the truth only to make it more glaring

欲壑难(難)填 yùhè nán tián the desire for gain is insatiable

欲加之罪,何患无(無)词 yù jiā zhī zuì, hé huàn wú cí if you are out to condemn sb., you can always trump up a charge

欲速则不达(達) yù sù zé bù dá haste makes waste; more haste, less speed

欲望 yùwàng (名) desire; wish; lust: 对权力的~ a lust for power

愈 yù I (动) recover; become well: 病~ recover from an illness II (副) [the more ... the more ...]: ~多~好 the more the better. 山路~来~陡. The mountain path becomes more and more steep.

愈合 yùhé (动) heal: 战争的创伤不久就~了. The wound of war soon healed.

愈加 yùjiā (副) all the more; even more; further: 矛盾变得~尖锐. The contradiction has become even more acute.

喻 yù I (动) 1 explain; illustrate: ~之以理 try to make sb. see reason 2 understand; know: 家~户晓 known to every household II (名) analogy: 比~ analogy; metaphor

御 yù I (形) of an emperor; imperial: ~花园 imperial garden II (禦)(动) resist; keep out; ward off: ~敌 resist the enemy; ward off an enemy attack. ~寒 keep out the cold

御用 yùyòng 1 for the use of an emperor 2 serve as a tool: ~文人 hack writer

狱(獄) yù (名) 1 prison; jail: 入~ be imprisoned; be put in jail 2 lawsuit; case: 文字~ literary inquisition

狱吏 yùlì (名) warder; prison officer; jailer

预 yù (副) in advance; beforehand: 勿谓言之不~也. Don't say you have not been forewarned.

预案(報) yù'àn (名) pre-arranged plan; emergency plan: 紧急~ contingency plan

预报(報) yùbào (动) forecast: 天气~ weather forecast

预备(備) yùbèi (动) prepare; get ready: ~再试一试 be prepared to make another effort. ~金 reserve fund. ~役 reserve duty (or service)

预测 yùcè (动) calculate; forecast

预产(産)期 yùchǎnqī (名) expected date of childbirth

预订 yùdìng (动) subscribe; book; place an order

预定 yùdìng (动) arrange in advance; schedule: 按~计划 on schedule

预防 yùfáng (动) prevent; take precautions against; guard against: 采取~措施 take preventive measures. ~胜于治疗. Prevention is better than cure.

预付 yùfù (动) pay in advance: ~费用 advanced charges. ~货款 cash before delivery. ~款项 advance payment

预感 yùgǎn I (名) premonition; presentiment: 不祥的~ an ominous presentiment II (动) sense: 大家都~到将要下一场大雨. We all felt that a heavy rain was to come.

预告 yùgào I (动) announce in advance II (名) advance notice; prepublication notice

预购(購) yùgòu (动) place an order or purchase in advance: ~合同 forward purchasing contract

预计 yùjì (动) calculate in advance; estimate: ~到达时间 estimated time of arrival (E. T. A.)

预见(見) yùjiàn I (动) foresee; predict: 这是可以~到的. This can be predicted. II (名) foresight; prevision: 英明的~ brilliant foresight

预料 yùliào (动) expect; predict; anticipate

预谋 yùmóu (动) premeditate; plan beforehand: ~杀人 premeditated murder

预期 yùqī (动) expect; anticipate: 达到~的效果 achieve the desired results

预示 yùshì (动) presage; betoken; indicate: 灿烂的晚霞~明天又是好天气. The rosy evening clouds presage another fine day tomorrow.

预算 yùsuàn (名) budget: ~赤字 budget deficit. ~外资金 extra-budgetary funds. ~内拨款 budgetary appropriations

预先 yùxiān (副) in advance; beforehand: ~通知 notify in advance. ~警告 forewarn

预想 yùxiǎng (动) anticipate; expect

预言 yùyán I (动) prophesy; predict; foretell II (名) prophecy; prediction: ～家 prophet

预演 yùyǎn (动) give a preview of (a film, a performance, etc.)

预约 yùyuē (动) make an appointment (with a doctor, etc.)

预兆 yùzhào (名) omen; sign; harbinger: 吉祥的～ an auspicious omen; a good sign

预支 yùzhī (动) 1 pay in advance 2 get payment in advance

预制(製) yùzhì (形) prefabricated: ～构件 prefabricated components

鹬 yù (名) sandpiper; snipe

妪(嫗) yù (名)〈书〉old woman

驭 yù (动) drive (a carriage): 驾～ drive; control

渊(淵) yuān I (名) deep pool: 深～ a deep pool; abyss. 天～之别 a world of difference. 罪恶的～薮 a sink of iniquity II (形) deep: ～博 erudite

渊源 yuānyuán (名) origin; source: 家学～ the intellectual background of the family

冤 yuān (名) 1 wrong; injustice: 不白之～ a gross injustice; an unrighted wrong 2 feeling of bitterness; hatred; enmity: ～～相报 reprisal breeds reprisal

冤仇 yuānchóu (名) rancour; enmity: 结～ feel rancour against sb.

冤大头(頭) yuāndàtóu (名) a person who spends money wastefully and foolishly; squanderer; wastrel

冤家 yuānjiā (名) enemy; foe

冤屈 yuānqū I (动) wrong; treat unjustly II (名) injustice: 受～ be wronged; suffer an injustice

冤枉 yuānwang I (动) wrong; treat unjustly: ～好人 wrong an innocent person. II (形) not worthwhile: 这钱花得真～. We shouldn't have spent our money so thoughtlessly. 走～路 take a roundabout way; go the long way round

冤狱(獄) yuānyù (名) an unjust charge or verdict; a miscarriage of justice; frame-up: 平反～ reverse an unjust verdict

鸳 yuān

鸳鸯 yuānyāng (名) 1 mandarin duck 2 an affectionate couple

元 yuán (名) 1 first; primary: ～旦 New Year's Day. ～月 first lunar month 2 chief; principal: 国家～首 head of state. ～帅 marshal. ～凶 arch-criminal 3 basic; fundamental: ～素 element. ～音 vowel 4 basic substance or element: 一～论 monism. 二～论 dualism

元件 yuánjiàn (名) part; component; cell

元老 yuánlǎo (名) senior statesman; founding member (of a political organization, etc.)

元气(氣) yuánqì (名) vitality; vigour: ～旺盛 full of vitality. 恢复～ regain one's strength (or health, vigour)

元宵 yuánxiāo (名) 1 the night of the 15th of the 1st lunar month 2 sweet dumplings made of glutinous rice flour (for the Lantern Festival)

元勋(勳) yuánxūn (名) a man who has rendered the most meritorious services to the state; founding father: 开国～ founders of a state

园(園) yuán (名) 1 a piece of land for growing flowers, vegetables, trees, etc.: 菜～ vegetable garden. 果～ orchard. 葡萄～ vineyard 2 a place for public recreation: 公～ park. 动物～ zoological garden; zoo. 植物～ botanical garden

园地 yuándì (名) 1 garden plot 2 field; scope (for certain activities): 文艺～ literary column

园丁 yuándīng (名) gardener

园艺(藝) yuányì (名) horticulture; gardening

猿 yuán (名) ape: 类人～ anthropoid ape

猿猴 yuánhóu (名) apes and monkeys

猿人 yuánrén (名) apeman: 北京～ Peking man

原 yuán I (形) 1 primary; original; former: ～始 primitive. ～意 original intention. ～文 original text 2 unprocessed; raw: ～矿石 raw ore. ～油 crude oil II (动) excuse; pardon: 情有可～. This is pardonable. III (名) level, open country: 平～ plain. 高～ plateau. 草～ grasslands. ～野 an expanse of open country

原版 yuánbǎn (名) original edition (of a book, etc.)

原材料 yuán-cáiliào (名) raw and other materials

原封 yuánfēng (形) untouched; intact: ～不动 be left intact; remain unchanged

原稿 yuángǎo (名) original manuscript; master copy

原告 yuángào (名) (of a civil case) plaintiff; (of a criminal case) prosecutor

原籍 yuánjí (名) ancestral home; native place; original domicile

原来(來) yuánlái I (形) original; former: ～的想法 original idea II (副) [indicating discovery of the truth]: 我说他今天为什么不来,～他是病了. So he is ill! I was just wondering why he was absent today.

原理 yuánlǐ (名) principle; tenet

原谅 yuánliàng (动) excuse; forgive; pardon

原煤 yuánméi (名) raw coal

原生态 yuánshēngtài (名) original ecology; primitive nature: ～旅游 eco-tourism ～文化保护 cultural conservation

原始 yuánshǐ (形) 1 original; firsthand: ～记录 original record 2 primeval; primitive: ～森林 primeval forest. ～社会 primitive society

原委 yuánwěi (名) ins and outs of a case; the whole story; all the details

原文 yuánwén (名) 1 the original (from which a translation is made) 2 original text

原先 yuánxiān (形) former; original: ～的计划 original plan

原形 yuánxíng (名) true features: ～毕露 show one's true colours (or features)

原因 yuányīn (名) cause; reason: 由于健康～ on health grounds

原油 yuányóu (名) crude oil

原原本本 yuányuánběnběn (relate) from beginning to end: 我把这件事～讲给他们听了. I told them everything down to the smallest detail.

原则 yuánzé (名) principle: ～上同意这个计划 agree to the plan in principle

原著 yuánzhù (名) original work; original: 读莎士比亚的～ read Shakespeare in the original

原状(狀) yuánzhuàng (名) original state; status quo ante

原子 yuánzǐ (名) atom: ～尘 fallout. ～能 atomic energy. ～反应堆 atomic reactor

源 yuán (名) 1 source (of a river); fountainhead: 发～ originate 2 source; cause: 资～ resources. 财～ source of income

源流 yuánliú (名) origin and development

源泉 yuánquán (名) source; fountainhead: 团结就是力量的～. Unity is the source of strength.

源源 yuányuán (副) in a steady stream; continuously: ～而来 come in an endless stream

源远(遠)流长(長) yuán yuǎn liú cháng a distant source and a long stream—of long standing and well established

员 yuán I (名) 1 a person engaged in some field of activity: 炊事～ cook. 售货～ shop assistant 2 member: 党～ Party member. 工会会～ member of a trade union II (量) [for military officers in the past]: 一～大将 an able general

员工 yuángōng (名) staff; personnel: 师生～ teachers, students and workers

圆 yuán I (形) 1 round; circular; spherical: ～桌 round table 2 tactful; satisfactory: 这人做事很～. He shows tact in handling matters. II (动) make plausible; justify: 自～其说 make one's statement sound plausible; try to justify oneself III (名) 1 circle 2 a coin of fixed value and weight: 银～ silver dollar

圆场(場) yuánchǎng (动) mediate; help to effect a compromise

圆规 yuánguī (名) compasses

圆滑 yuánhuá (形) smooth; unctuous; slick

圆寂 yuánjì (动) (of Buddhist monks or nuns) pass away; die

圆满(滿) yuánmǎn (形) satisfactory: ～的答案 a satisfactory solution; a correct answer

圆圈 yuánquān (名) circle; ring

圆通 yuántōng (形) flexible; accommodating

圆舞曲 yuánwǔqǔ (名) waltz

圆心 yuánxīn (名) the centre of a circle

圆形 yuánxíng (形) circular; round

圆周 yuánzhōu (名) circumference

圆珠笔(筆) yuánzhūbǐ (名) ballpoint pen; ball-pen

圆柱 yuánzhù (名) cylinder

圆桌 yuánzhuō (名) round table: ～会议 round-table conference

援 yuán (动) 1 pull by hand; hold: 攀～ climb up by holding on to sth. 2 quote; cite: ～例 cite a precedent 3 help; aid: 支～ support; give support to. 增～ reinforce

援救 yuánjiù (动) rescue; deliver from danger

援军 yuánjūn (名) reinforcements

援款 yuánkuǎn (名) aid fund

援外 yuánwài (动) give aid to foreign countries: ～物资 materials in aid of a foreign country

援引 yuányǐn (动) 1 quote; cite; invoke: ～例证 cite an example 2 recommend or appoint one's close associates

援助 yuánzhù (动、名) help; support; aid: 经济～ economic assistance; financial aid

缘 yuán I (名) 1 reason; cause: 无～无故 without rhyme or reason; for no reason at all 2 edge; fringe; brink: 外～ outer fringe (or edge) II (介) along: ～溪而行 walk along the stream

缘分 yuánfèn (名) predestined lot; fate; luck

缘故 yuángù (名) cause; reason

缘木求鱼 yuán mù qiú yú climb a tree to catch fish — resort to a futile approach

缘由 yuányóu (名) reason; cause

远(遠) yuǎn I (形) 1 far; distant; remote: ～古 the remote past. ～景规划 long-range planning 2 (of blood relationship) remote: ～亲 distant relative; remote kinsfolk 3 (of degree of difference) great II (动) keep away from: 敬而～之 keep sb. at a respectful distance

远程教育 yuǎnchéng jiàoyù distance learning

远大 yuǎndà (形) bright; lofty; ambitious: 眼光～ far-sighted. 前程～ (of a person) have bright prospects; have a bright future

远道 yuǎndào (名) a long way: ～而来 come all the way from afar

远东(東) Yuǎndōng (名) the Far East

远方 yuǎnfāng (名) distant place

远见(見) yuǎnjiàn (名) foresight; vision: ～卓识 far-sightedness and bold vision

远郊 yuǎnjiāo (名) outer suburbs

远近 yuǎnjìn (名) far and near: ～闻名 be well known far and wide

远虑(慮) yuǎnlǜ (名) foresight; long view

Y

远视 yuǎnshì (名) long sight; long-sightedness

远销 yuǎnxiāo (动) sell goods to distant places: ～海外 find a market abroad

远洋 yuǎnyáng (名) ocean: ～航行 ocean-going voyage

远征 yuǎnzhēng (动) go on an expedition: ～军 expeditionary army (or force)

远走高飞(飛) yuǎnzǒu-gāofēi soar; be off to a distant place

远足 yuǎnzú (动) make an excursion; go on a hike; go on a walking tour

院 yuàn (名) 1 courtyard; compound 2 a designation for certain government offices and public places: 法～ law court. 科学～ the academy of sciences

院士 yuànshì (名) academician

院外集团(團) yuàn wài jí tuán lobby

愿(願) yuàn I (名) 1 hope; wish; desire: 如～以偿 attain one's goal 2 promise: 许～ make promises II (动) be willing; be ready

愿望 yuànwàng (名) desire; wish; aspiration: 他有出国学习医学的强烈～. He has a strong desire to study medicine abroad.

愿意 yuànyì (动) 1 be willing; be ready 2 wish; like; want: 他们～你留在这里. They would like you to stay here.

怨 yuàn I (名) resentment; enmity: 结～ incur hatred II (动) blame; complain: 事情没办好只能～我自己. I have only myself to blame for I haven't really done the job well. 没有抱～的理由 no cause for complaint

怨愤 yuànfèn (名) discontent and indignation; bitterness

怨恨 yuànhèn I (动) have a grudge against sb. II (名) ill will; grudge; hatred

怨气(氣) yuànqì (名) grudge; complaint; resentment: 出～ air one's grievances; vent one's resentment

怨声(聲)载道 yuànshēng zài dào there is widespread discontent among the mass of the people

怨天尤人 yuàntiān-yóurén blame everyone and everything but oneself

曰 yuē (动)〈书〉1 say 2 call; name

约 yuē I (动) 1 make arrangements for: ～定 make an appointment with sb. 2 invite: 我已经～她来吃晚饭. I have asked her to come for dinner. II (名) pact; agreement; appointment: 立～ make a contract III (形) simple; brief: ～言之 to put it in a nutshell; in brief; in a word IV (副) about; around; approximately: ～五十人 some fifty people

约定 yuēdìng (动) agree to; appoint; arrange：大家～明天在公园会面．We all agreed to meet in the park tomorrow．在～的时间 at the appointed time

约会(會) yuēhuì (名) appointment; engagement; date; rendezvous：抱歉今天不能来,因为我已经有个～了．Sorry I won't be able to come today for I have a previous engagement．

约计 yuējì (动) count roughly; come roughly to

约见(見) yuējiàn (动) make an appointment to meet

约略 yuēlüè (形) rough; approximate：～的估计 a rough (or approximate) estimate

约莫 yuēmo (副) about; roughly：～有二十个人参加这次演说竞赛．Some twenty people participated in this speech contest．

约请 yuēqǐng (动) invite; ask

约束 yuēshù (动) keep within bounds; restrain; bind：有～力 have binding force

悦 yuè I (形) happy; pleased; delighted:不～ displeased．和颜～色 amiable and polite in manner II (动) please; delight：取～于人 try to please sb．

悦耳 yuè'ěr (形) pleasing to the ear; melodious

悦目 yuèmù (形) pleasing to the eye; pleasant to the eye

阅 yuè (动) 1 read; go over:～报 read newspapers．～卷 go over examination papers 2 review; inspect：～兵 review troops 3 experience; pass through：试行已～三月．Three months have passed since we started to try this out．

阅读(讀) yuèdú (动) read：～杂志 read magazines

阅览(覽) yuèlǎn (动) read：～室 reading room

阅历(歷) yuèlì I (动) experience：～过很多事 have seen much of the world II (名) knowledge of the world; personal experience：～浅 with little experience in the world

阅世 yuèshì (动)〈书〉see the world：～渐深 gradually become worldly-wise; gradually become experienced in life

越 yuè (动) 1 get over; jump over:～墙而逃 climb over the wall and make one's escape 2 exceed; overstep：～出职权 overstep one's authority．～界 cross the boundary

越发(發) yuèfā (副) 1 all the more; even more:过了中秋,天气～凉快了．After the Mid-autumn Festival, the weather becomes even cooler．2 [same as 越…越… when used with 越 or 越是]:观众越多,他们演得～卖力气．The bigger the audience, the more enthusiastic they will become in their performance．

越轨 yuèguǐ (动) exceed the bounds：行为～ overstep the bounds of correct behaviour

越过(過) yuèguò (动) cross; surmount; pass over：～障碍 surmount obstacles

越级 yuèjí (动) bypass the immediate leadership：～申诉 bypass the immediate leadership and appeal to higher levels

越境 yuèjìng (动) cross the boundary illegally; sneak in or out of a country

越权(權) yuèquán (动) exceed (or overstep) one's power or authority; ultra vires

越野 yuèyě (形) cross-country：～赛跑 cross-country race

越狱(獄) yuèyù (动) escape from prison:～犯 prison breaker

越…越… yuè…yuè… the more... the more...：～多～好 the more the better

越俎代庖 yuè zǔ dài páo overstep one's powers to handle affairs within other people's jurisdiction

跃(躍) yuè (动) leap; jump：一～而起 get up with a jump; jump to one's feet．～过 leap over

跃跃欲试 yuèyuè yù shì (动) be eager for a try; itch to have a try

岳 yuè (名) 1 high mountain 2 wife's parents

岳父 yuèfù (名) wife's father; father-in-law

岳母 yuèmǔ (名) wife's mother; mother-in-law

月 yuè (名) 1 the moon：新～ a new moon; crescent 2 month：～底 at the end of the month．～产量 monthly output

月报(報) yuèbào (名) 1 monthly magazine; monthly 2 monthly report

月饼 yuèbǐng (名) moon cake (esp. for the Mid-autumn Festival)

月份 yuèfèn (名) month：上～ last month

月光 yuèguāng (名) moonlight; moonbeam

月经(經) yuèjīng (名) menses; menstruation; period

月刊 yuèkān (名) monthly magazine; monthly

月亮 yuèliàng (名) the moon

月票 yuèpiào (名) monthly ticket (for going

by bus or underground railway)
月球 yuèqiú (名) the moon
月嫂 yuèshǎo (名) postnatal care maid
月色 yuèsè (名) moonlight
月食 yuèshí (名) lunar eclipse
月台(臺) yuètái (名) railway platform: ~票 platform ticket
月薪 yuèxīn (名) monthly pay
月子 yuèzi (名) month of confinement after childbirth: 坐~ be in confinement

钥(鑰) yuè (名) key
see also yào

乐(樂) yuè (名) music: 器~ instrumental music. 声~ vocal music
see also lè

乐池 yuèchí (名) orchestra pit; orchestra
乐队(隊) yuèduì (名) orchestra; band: 交响~ symphony (or philharmonic) orchestra. 军~ military band
乐谱 yuèpǔ (名) music score
乐器 yuèqì (名) musical instrument; instrument: 管~ wind instrument. 弦~ stringed instrument. 打击~ percussion instrument
乐曲 yuèqǔ (名) musical composition; composition; music
乐团(團) yuètuán (名) philharmonic society; philharmonic orchestra
乐章 yuèzhāng (名) movement

晕 yūn (动) 1 feel dizzy; feel giddy: 有点头~ feel a bit dizzy (or giddy). 头~目眩 have a dizzy spell 2 swoon; faint: ~了过去 lose consciousness; faint
see also yùn

晕倒 yūndǎo (动) fall down in a fainting fit
晕头(頭)转(轉)向 yūntóu zhuànxiàng confused and disoriented

云 yún (动)〈书〉say: 不知所~ not know what one is talking about; not know what one is driving at

云(雲) yún (名) cloud

云彩 yúncai (名) cloud
云层(層) yúncéng (名) cloud layer
云集 yúnjí (动) come together from different places; gather; converge
云雾(霧) yúnwù (名) cloud and mist; mist
云霞 yúnxiá (名) rosy clouds
云消雾(霧)散 yúnxiāo-wùsàn melt into thin air; vanish without a trace

耘 yún (动) weed: ~田 weed the fields

芸 yún

芸豆 yúndòu (名) kidney bean
芸芸众(衆)生 yúnyún zhòngshēng (in Buddhism) all living things

匀 yún I (形) even: 请把颜色涂~. Please spread the colour evenly. II(动) 1 even up; divide evenly 2 spare: 可以~给你们一些. We can spare you some.

匀称(稱) yúnchèn (形) well proportioned; well balanced; symmetrical
匀整 yúnzhěng (形) neat and well spaced; even and orderly

陨 yǔn (动) fall from the sky or outer space

陨落 yǔnluò (动) (of a meteorite, etc.) fall from the sky or outer space
陨石 yǔnshí (名) aerolite; stony meteorite

允 yǔn I (动) permit; allow; consent: 应~ consent. ~从 comply II (形) fair; just: 公~ fair; equitable

允诺 yǔnnuò (动) promise; consent; assent: 欣然~ readily consent
允许 yǔnxǔ (动) permit; allow

韵(韻) yùn (名) 1 rhyme: 押~ be in rhyme 2 charm: 风~ personal charm; graceful bearing

韵律 yùnlǜ (名) 1 metre (in verse) 2 rules of rhyming
韵母 yùnmǔ (名) simple or compound vowel (of a Chinese syllable)
韵文 yùnwén (名) literary composition in rhyme; verse

晕 yùn I (动) feel dizzy; feel giddy; faint II (名) halo: 月~ lunar halo
see also yūn

晕车(車) yùnchē (动) be carsick
晕船 yùnchuán (动) be seasick

运(運) yùn I (动) 1 carry; transport: 货~ freight transport. 空~ air transport; airlift 2 use; wield; utilize: ~笔 set pen to paper II (名) fortune; luck; fate: 好~ good luck. 不走~ be out of luck

运筹(籌)帷幄 yùnchóu wéiwò devise strategies at the headquarters
运筹(籌)学(學) yùnchóuxué (名) operations research
运动(動) yùndòng (名) 1 motion; movement 2 sports; athletics; exercise: 户外

~ outdoor exercise **3** (political) movement; campaign; drive

运动(動)会(會) yùndònghuì (名) sports meet; athletic meeting; games: 全国~ national games

运费 yùnfèi (名) transportation expenses: ~单 freight note. ~免付 carriage free. ~已付 freight (or carriage) paid. ~预付 freight prepaid

运河 yùnhé (名) canal

运气(氣) yùnqi (名) fortune; luck: 碰~ try one's luck

运输 yùnshū (名) transport; carriage; conveyance: 陆上(水路)~ land (water) transport. ~工具 means of transport. ~量 freight volume. ~业 transport service; carrying trade; transportation

运输机(機) yùnshūjī (名) transport plane; airfreighter

运送 yùnsòng (动) transport; ship; convey

运算 yùnsuàn (名) calculation; operation

运行 yùnxíng (动) move; be in motion: ~轨道 orbit (of a satellite). 列车已在~了. The train was already in motion.

运营(營) yùnyíng (动) (of buses, ships, etc.) run; ply

运用 yùnyòng (动) utilize; wield; apply; put to use: ~自如 handle with ease

运载工具 yùnzài gōngjù means of delivery

运载火箭 yùnzài huǒjiàn carrier rocket

运转(轉) yùnzhuǎn (动) **1** revolve; turn round **2** work; operate: 机器~正常. The machine is in good operation.

酝(醞) yùn

酝酿(釀) yùnniàng (动) **1** brew; ferment: 他当时意识到某种灾难正在~. He sensed that some sort of trouble was brewing. **2** have a preliminary informal discussion; deliberate on: ~协商 deliberations and consultations

蕴 yùn (动)〈书〉accumulate; hold in store; contain: ~涵 contain

蕴藏 yùncáng (动) hold in store; contain: 我国各地~着丰富的矿物资源. There are rich deposits of mineral resources in different parts of our land.

孕 yùn (名) pregnancy: 怀~ be pregnant; be conceived. 避~ contraception

孕妇(婦) yùnfù (名) pregnant woman

孕育 yùnyù (动) be pregnant with; breed: ~着危险 pregnant with danger

熨 yùn (动) iron; press: ~衣服 iron (or press) clothes

熨斗 yùndǒu (名) flat iron; iron: 电~ electric iron

Z z

扎(紮) zā (动) tie; bind: 把这个小包裹用绳子~起来. Tie the small parcel with a piece of string.

see also zhā

砸 zá (动) **1** pound; tamp: 把肉~成泥 pound the meat into a paste. ~了脚 have one's foot squashed **2** break; smash: ~核桃 crack walnuts. 杯子~了. The glass is broken. **3** fail; be bungled: 事情办~了 bungle a job

杂(雜) zá I (形) miscellaneous; mixed: ~活儿 odd jobs. ~费 miscellaneous expenses. ~七~八的东西 odds and ends II (动) mix; mingle: 夹~ be mingled with

杂拌儿(兒) zábànr (名) **1** mixed sweetmeats **2** mixture; miscellany

杂草 zácǎo (名) weeds

杂货 záhuò (名) sundry goods; groceries: 日用~ various household supplies. ~店 grocery

杂技 zájì (名) acrobatics

杂家 zájiā (名) an eclectic; a jack of all trades

杂交 zájiāo (动) cross-breed; hybridize

杂粮(糧) záliáng (名) coarse grain (e.g. maize, barley, millet, etc.)

杂乱(亂) záluàn (形) in disorder; in a jumble: ~无章 in a mess; jumbled

杂念 zániàn (名) selfish considerations: 私心~太重 too calculating

杂牌 zápái (形、名) a less known and inferior brand: ~货 goods of an inferior brand

杂税 záshuì (名) miscellaneous levies

杂文 záwén (名) satirical essay

杂务(務) záwù (名) odd jobs; sundry duties

杂音 záyīn (名) noise

杂院儿(兒) záyuànr (名) a compound occupied by many households

杂志 zázhì (名) magazine

杂质(質) zázhì (名) impurity

杂种(種) zázhǒng (名) **1** hybrid; crossbreed 2 bastard; son of a bitch

咋 zǎ (代) how; why: ~办? What is to be done? 情况~样? How are things? 你~不去? Why don't you go?

灾(災) zāi (名) 1 disaster; calamity: 天~ natural disaster. 水~ flood. 旱~ drought. 虫~ plague of insects 2 misfortune; adversity: 招~惹祸 court trouble

灾害 zāihài (名) calamity; disaster

灾荒 zāihuāng (名) famine

灾祸(禍) zāihuò (名) catastrophe

灾民 zāimín (名) victims of a natural calamity; people in an afflicted area

灾难(難) zāinàn (名) catastrophe; suffering: ~深重 long-suffering

灾情 zāiqíng (名) the damage caused by a disaster

灾区(區) zāiqū (名) afflicted area

栽 zāi (动) 1 plant; grow: ~树 plant trees. ~花 grow flowers 2 impose sth. on sb.: ~上罪名 trump up a charge against sb. 3 tumble; fall: ~倒 fall down; trip and fall

栽跟头(頭) zāi gēntou 1 trip and fall 2 suffer a setback

栽培 zāipéi (动) 1 cultivate; grow: ~果树 grow fruit trees 2 foster; train (qualified personnel)

栽赃(贜) zāizāng (动) 1 plant stolen or banned goods on sb. 2 make false charges against sb.

栽种(種) zāizhòng (动) plant; grow

哉 zāi (助)〈书〉1 [indicating exclamation]: 呜呼! 哀~! Alas! 2 [used together with an interrogative to express doubt or form a rhetorical question]: 有何难~? What's so difficult about it?

宰 zǎi I (动) 1 slaughter; butcher: ~牛 slaughter an ox 2 be in charge of; head: 主~ be in actual control of; have the final say in II (名) government official (in ancient China)

宰割 zǎigē (动) oppress and exploit

宰客 zǎikè (动) swindle money out of customers; rip off; overcharge

宰杀(殺) zǎishā (动) slaughter; butcher

宰相 zǎixiàng (名) prime minister (in feudal China); chancellor

载 zǎi I (名) year: 三~ three years II (动) record: ~入史册 go down in history. 刊~ record; publish (in the press)

see also zài

载 zài I (动) 1 carry; hold: ~客 carry passengers. ~货 carry goods. 轮船满~着大米. The ship is fully loaded with rice. 2 (the road) be filled with: 怨声~道. Popular grievances are openly voiced everywhere. II (副)〈书〉and; as well as; at the same time: ~歌~舞 singing and dancing

see also zǎi

载波 zàibō (名) carrier wave; carrier: ~电话机 carrier telephone

载荷 zàihè (名) load

载货 zàihuò (动) carry cargo (or freight): ~吨位 cargo tonnage

载体 zàitǐ (名) carrier

载运(運) zàiyùn (动) convey by vehicles, ships, etc.; transport; carry

载重 zàizhòng (名) load; carrying capacity: ~卡车 heavy-duty truck. ~汽车 truck; lorry

再 zài (副) 1 again; once more: ~说一遍. Say it again, please. 一而~, ~而三 again and again; time and again; over and over (again) 2 [to a greater extent or degree]: 这篇文章还得~改一次. The essay will have to be further polished. 3 [indicating continuation of time or action]: ~不走我们开会就要迟到了. We'll be late for the meeting if we stay any longer. 4 [indicating that one action takes place after the completion of another]: 你吃完晚饭~出去. Eat your supper before you go out. 5 [indicating additional information]: ~则 moreover; besides. 他对这件事不清楚, ~说, 他也不想插手. He doesn't know anything about the matter; besides, he doesn't want to get involved. 6 continue; return: 良机难~. Opportunity knocks but once.

再版 zàibǎn I (名) second edition II (动) reprint

再出口 zàichūkǒu re-export

再次 zàicì (副) once more; a second time; once again: ~登门拜访 pay sb. another visit. ~道谢 extend one's thanks to sb. again

再度 zàidù (副) once more; a second time; once again: ~当选 be re-elected

再分配 zàifēnpèi redistribute

再嫁 zàijià (动) (of a woman) remarry

再见(見) zàijiàn〈套〉goodbye; see you again (also as "再会")

再接再厉(厲) zàijiē-zàilì make persistent efforts; persevere

再生 zàishēng (动) 1 come to life again 2 regenerate 3 recycle

再生产(產) zàishēngchǎn reproduction

再说 zàishuō I (动) not consider or tackle a problem until some other time: 这事先搁两天～. Let's put the matter aside for a couple of days. II (连) what's more; besides: 现在去找他太晚了,～他也不一定在家. It's too late to go and see him now; besides, he may not be at home at the moment.

再投资 zàitóuzī reinvest; plough back

在 zài I (动) 1 exist: 这问题还～, 并没有解决. The problem still remains to be solved. 2 [indicating the position of a person or thing]: 你的钱包～桌子上. Your wallet is on the table. 3 remain: ～职 occupy a post 4 rest with; depend on: 事情的成败～你自己的努力. The success or failure of the matter depends on your own effort. II (介) [indicating time, place, condition, scope, etc.]: ～会上发言 speak at a meeting. ～理论上 in theory; theoretically. ～这种情况下 under such circumstances. 在全国范围内 throughout the country III (副) [indicating an action in progress]: 她～起草一个决议. She is drafting a resolution. IV [在 and 所 go together, usually followed by 不, thus forming an emphatic expression]: ～所不惜 regardless of the cost or sacrifice. ～所不免 be hardly avoidable

在场(場) zàichǎng (动) be on the scene; be on the spot

在岗(崗) zàigǎng (形) being employed

在行 zàiháng (形) be a professional: 她对这种工作很～. This sort of work is very much in her line.

在乎 zàihu (动) [often but not always used in the negative] care about; mind; take to heart: 满不～ couldn't care less. 对于这种批评他很～. He took this kind of criticism very much to heart.

在家 zàijiā (动) be at home; be in

在理 zàilǐ (形) reasonable; sensible; right: 这话说得～. That's a sensible comment.

在世 zàishì (动) live: 他～的时候 in his lifetime

在所不辞(辭) zài suǒ bù cí will not decline under all circumstances: 为国捐躯,～. I would not hesitate to lay down my life for my country.

在逃 zàitáo (动) has escaped; be at large: ～犯 escaped criminal; criminal at large; fugitive

在望 zàiwàng (动) 1 be visible: 隐隐～ indistinctly discernible 2 will soon materialize; be in the offing; be round the corner: 胜利～. Victory is in sight. *or* Success is round the corner.

在握 zàiwò (动) be in one's hands; be within one's grasp: 大权～ be in the saddle. 胜利～ Victory is within our grasp.

在线 zàixiàn (副) on line

在押 zàiyā (动) be under detention; be in custody; be in prison: ～犯 criminal in custody; prisoner

在野 zàiyě (动) be out of office; be in the opposition

在意 zàiyì (动) [usu. used in the negative] care about; mind; take to heart: 这些小事他是不会～. He won't mind such trifles.

在于(於) zàiyú (动) 1 lie in; consist in: 这项计划的好处就～简单易行. The beauty of the plan consist in its simplicity. 2 be determined by; depend on; rest with: 最后决定～我们自己. Final decision rests with us. 去不去～你们自己. It's up to you to decide whether you will go or not.

在职(職) zàizhí (动) be on the job; be employed: ～训练 in-service training. ～期间 during one's tenure of office

在座 zàizuò (动) be present (at a meeting, banquet, etc.)

簪 zān (名) hairpin

簪子 zānzi (名) hair clasp

咱 zán (代) 1 we [including both the speaker and the person or persons spoken to] 2 I

咱们 zánmen (代) we [including both the speaker and the person or persons spoken to]

攒 zǎn (动) accumulate; hoard; save: ～钱 save (or scrape) up money. 她把～的钱都买了衣服. She spent all her savings on clothes.

暂 zàn I (形) of short duration: 生命是短～的. Life is short (or brief). II (副) temporarily; for the time being; for the moment: ～行条例 provisional regulations. ～不答复 put off replying

暂定 zàndìng（动）arrange for the time being; temporarily decide: ～措施 tentative measure. ～议程 tentative agenda

暂缓 zànhuǎn（动）put off; defer: ～作出决定 put off making a decision

暂且 zànqiě（副）for the time being; for the moment: 此事～不谈，以后再议. Let's drop the matter for the time being. We can take it up later.

暂时(時) zànshí（形）temporary; transient: ～困难 temporary difficulties. ～现象 transient phenomenon

暂停 zàntíng I（动）suspend: ～付款 suspend payment. 讨论～，明天继续举行. Let us put off the discussion till tomorrow. II（名）(in sports) time-out: 要求～ ask for time-out

暂行 zànxíng（形）provisional; temporary: ～规定 temporary provisions. ～条例 provisional (or interim) regulations

赞 zàn I（动）1 support; assist: ～助 support; assist 2 praise; commend: 盛～ highly praise II（名）eulogy

赞不绝口 zàn bù jué kǒu give sb. lavish praise

赞成 zànchéng（动）approve of; assent; agree with; give one's blessing to: 我不太～他的意见. I don't quite agree with him. 他不～有些人小题大做. He doesn't approve of some people making a fuss about such trifles.

赞美 zànměi（动）eulogize; praise

赞赏 zànshǎng（动）appreciate; admire: 对他们这一友好举动大家表示～. We all appreciate this friendly act on their part. 我们非常～他们的才能. We are filled with admiration for their talents.

赞颂 zànsòng（动）extol; eulogize

赞叹(嘆) zàntàn（动）marvel at; highly praise: 运动员们的高超技艺令人～不已. The spectators all marvelled at the superb skill of the players.

赞同 zàntóng（动）approve of; endorse: 这一动议得到与会者的普遍～. This motion met with the general approval of the participants. 全厂职工一致～这项改革. The administrative personnel and workers of the factory unanimously endorsed this reform.

赞许 zànxǔ（动）praise; commend: 值得～ deserve commendation; be praiseworthy

赞扬(揚) zànyáng（动）speak in glowing terms of; pay tribute to

赞助 zànzhù（动）support; give assistance to; aid

赃(贜) zāng（名）stolen goods; booty; spoils: 退～ disgorge the spoils

赃物 zāngwù（名）1 stolen goods 2 bribes

脏(髒) zāng（形）dirty; filthy: ～衣服 dirty clothing; laundry. 你把书弄～了. You've soiled the book.

see also zàng

脏字 zāngzì（名）dirty word; swearword

葬 zàng（动）bury; inter: 火～ cremation. ～地 burial ground; grave

葬礼(禮) zànglǐ（名）funeral rites; funeral

葬身 zàngshēn（动）be buried: 敌机～海底. The enemy plane was shot down, plunging into the sea.

葬送 zàngsòng（动）ruin; put an end to: ～前途 ruin one's future

藏 zàng（名）1 storing place; depository: 宝～ hidden treasures; valuable (mineral) deposits 2 Buddhist or Taoist scriptures: 道～ Taoist scriptures

see also cáng

藏青 zàngqīng（形）dark blue

藏族 Zàngzú（名）the Zang (Tibetan) nationality

脏(臟) zàng（名）internal organs of the body; viscera: 心～ heart. 肾～ kidneys

see also zāng

糟 zāo（形）1 be pickled with grains or in wine: ～鱼 pickled fish 2 rotten; worn out; poor: 他身体很～，我有些担心. I am rather worried about his health. 3 in a wretched state; in a mess: 你把这件事弄～了. You've made a mess of the matter.

糟糕 zāogāo（形）in a terrible mess; bad luck; too bad: 真～！下起雨来了. It's too bad. It's raining.

糟粕 zāopò（名）dross; dregs: 弃其～，吸取精华 reject the dross and assimilate the essence

糟蹋 zāota（动）1 waste; ruin; spoil: ～粮食 waste grain 2 trample on; ravage: 这一村子曾被侵略军～得不成样子. This village was once badly ravaged by the invading troops. 3 violate (a woman)

遭 zāo I（动）meet with (disaster, misfortune, etc.); sustain; suffer:

～难 some misfortune befell one. 惨～毒手 be killed in cold blood II (量) round; time; turn: 走一～ make a trip. 看他如此发火,还是第一～. It's the first time that I have seen him flare up.

遭逢 zāoféng (动) meet with; encounter: ～盛世 live in an age of prosperity. ～不幸 meet with a misfortune

遭受 zāoshòu (动) suffer; be subjected to; sustain; undergo: ～损失 sustain losses. ～损害 suffer damage. ～耻辱 be subjected to indignities

遭殃 zāoyāng (动) suffer disaster or calamity

遭遇 zāoyù I (动) meet with; encounter: ～许多挫折 meet with many setbacks II (名) (bitter) experience; (hard) lot: 童年的～ one's unhappy childhood experience

遭罪 zāozuì (动) endure hardships, tortures, rough conditions, etc.; have a hard time

凿(鑿) záo I (名) 1 chisel 2 mortise II (动) cut a hole; chisel or dig: ～冰 make a hole in the ice. ～个窟窿 bore a hole III (形)〈书〉 certain; authentic; irrefutable: 确～ authentic; conclusive

凿井 záojǐng (动) dig (or sink, bore) a well

凿子 záozi (名) chisel

枣(棗) zǎo (名) jujube; (Chinese) date

枣脯 zǎofǔ (名) dried dates preserved in honey

枣红 zǎohóng (形) purplish red

枣树(樹) zǎoshù (名) jujube tree

早 zǎo I (名) morning: 从～到晚 from morning till night. 清～ early in the morning II (形) 1 long ago; as early as; for a long time: 他～走了. He left long ago. 2 early: ～春 early spring. ～稻 early rice. ～期 early stage; early phase. ～熟 premature; precocious III〈套〉 good morning

早安 zǎo'ān〈套〉 good morning

早操 zǎocāo (名) morning exercises

早产(產) zǎochǎn (名) premature delivery

早晨 zǎochén (名) (early) morning

早点(點) zǎodiǎn (名) (light) breakfast

早饭 zǎofàn (名) breakfast

早年 zǎonián (名) in one's early years

早日 zǎorì (副) at an early date; early; soon: 希望～完工. Hope you'll fulfil your task as soon as possible. 祝你～恢复健康. I wish you a speedy recovery.

早上 zǎoshang (名) early morning

早市 zǎoshì (名) 1 morning market 2 morning business

早退 zǎotuì (动) leave earlier than is required according to the regulations; leave early

早晚 zǎowǎn I (名) morning and evening: 他每天～都练拳术. He practises shadow boxing every day both in the morning and in the evening. II (副) sooner or later: 像他这样的人,～要倒霉的. People like him will come to grief sooner or later.

早先 zǎoxiān (名) previously; in the past: ～人们常来这儿散步. People used to come here for a walk.

早已 zǎoyǐ (副) long ago; for a long time: 他们～离婚了. They got divorced long ago.

早早儿(兒) zǎozǎor (副) as soon as possible; at an early date: 决定了,就～办. Let's get the work done as soon as possible if you have made up your mind.

澡 zǎo (名) bath: 洗～ take a bath; bathe

澡盆 zǎopén (名) bathtub

澡堂 zǎotáng (名) public baths; bathhouse

藻 zǎo (名) 1 algae 2 aquatic plants

藻类(類)植物 zǎolèi zhíwù algae

蚤 zǎo (名) flea: 水～ water flea

灶(竈) zào (名) 1 place for cooking; kitchen range; cooking stove 2 kitchen; mess; canteen: 学生～ students' cafeteria or canteen

燥 zào (形) dry: ～热 hot and dry; sultry

噪 zào (动) make an uproar; clamour: 名～一时 be enormously popular for a time

噪音 zàoyīn (名) noise: ～污染 noise pollution

躁 zào (形) rash; impetuous; restless: 戒骄戒～ guard against arrogance and rashness. 性子急～ quick-tempered; hot-tempered

造 zào (动) 1 make; build; create: ～汽车 make cars. ～房子 build a house. ～舆论 create public opinion 2 in-

Z

vent; cook up; concoct: 捏～ fabricate; concoct. ～谣言 start a rumour; cook up a story **3** train; educate: 可～之才 a person of promise

造反 zàofǎn (动) rise in rebellion; rebel; revolt

造福 zàofú (动) bring benefit to; benefit: 为后代～ benefit future generations

造化 zàohua (名) good fortune; good luck: 有～ be born under a lucky star; be lucky

造价(價) zàojià (名) cost (of building or manufacture)

造就 zàojiù I (动) bring up; train: ～人才就是智力投资. To train competent personnel is a kind of intellectual investment. II (名) achievements; attainments (usu. of young people)

造句 zàojù (动) make sentences

造林 zàolín (名) afforestation

造孽 zàoniè (动) do evil; commit a sin

造势 zàoshì (动) build up the atmosphere; create momentum; sensationalize: ～大会 mass rally. 新闻～ news spin

造物 zàowù (名) the divine force that created the universe

造型 zàoxíng (名) model; mould: ～优美 graceful in shape. ～艺术 plastic arts

造谣 zàoyáo (动) cook up a story and spread it around; start a rumour: ～惑众 fabricate rumours to mislead people. ～生事 start a rumour to create trouble. ～诬蔑 calumny and slander

造诣 zàoyì (名) (academic or artistic) attainments: ～很深 of great attainments

皂 zào (名) soap: 香～ toilet soap. 药～ medicated soap

责 zé I (名) duty; responsibility: 尽～ do one's duty. 爱护公物,人人有～. It is everybody's duty to take good care of public property. II (动) **1** demand; require: 求全～备 nit-pick **2** question closely; call sb. to account **3** reproach; blame; reprove: 斥～ reprimand; denounce. 痛～ rebuke severely **4** punish: 笞～ punish by flogging

责备(備) zébèi (动) reproach; blame; censure; take sb. to task

责成 zéchéng (动) instruct a person or an organization to fulfil an assigned task

责怪 zéguài (动) blame: 这事只能～他自己. He has nobody to blame but himself.

责令 zélìng (动) order; instruct: ～主管部门采取有力措施 instruct the department in charge to take effective measures

责骂 zémà (动) scold; rebuke; dress down: 把他们～一顿 give them a dressing down

责难(難) zénàn (动) censure; blame: 受到别人的～ bring the blame of others upon oneself

责任 zérèn (名) **1** duty; responsibility: 尽～ do one's duty. ～感 sense of responsibility (or duty). 承包～制 system of contracted responsibility. 岗位～制 system of job responsibility **2** responsibility for a fault or wrong; blame: 我愿意承担这个事故的～. I am ready to take the blame for the accident. 推卸～ shift the blame on to others; shirk responsibility

责问 zéwèn (动) ask reprovingly; call sb. to account: 我有件事要～他. I have a bone to pick with him.

责无(無)旁贷 zé wú páng dài be one's unshirkable responsibility; be duty-bound

则 zé I (名) **1** standard; norm; criterion: 以身作～ set an example by one's own conduct **2** rule; regulation: 章～ rules and regulations. 法～ law; rule II (量) item; paragraph: 新闻一～ an item of news. 寓言四～ four fables III (副)〈书〉[indicating cause and effect or condition]: 欲速～不达. Haste makes waste. IV [indicating concession or contrast]: 好～好,只是太贵. It's good indeed but too expensive. V [used together with 一, 二, 三 to enumerate causes or reasons]: 我想今天不去了,一～我有点累,二～我去过好几趟了. I don't think I am going today. First, I am feeling a bit tired; secondly, I have been there several times before.

泽(澤) zé I (名) **1** pool; pond: 沼～ marsh; swamp. 湖～ lakes **2** lustre (of metals, pearls, etc.): 光～ lustre; gloss; sheen II (形) damp; moist: 润～ moist; wet

择(擇) zé (动) select; choose; pick: 没有选～余地. This is Hobson's choice.

see also zhái

择善而从(從) zé shàn ér cóng choose and follow what is good; accept what is good

择业(業) zéyè (动) select a job; make a

career choice

择优(優)录(録)取 zéyōu lùqǔ enrol (or admit) on the basis of competitive selection

仄 zè

仄声(聲) zèshēng (名) oblique tones, i.e., the falling-rising tone (上声), the falling tone (去声) and the entering tone (入声), as distinct from the level tone (平声) in classical Chinese pronunciation

贼 zéi I (名) **1** thief; burglar **2** traitor; enemy: 卖国～ traitor (to one's country). 工～ scab; blackleg II (形) wicked; evil; crafty; sly; cunning: 真～ really cunning. ～眉鼠眼 look like a sly old fox; wear a thievish expression

贼喊捉贼 zéi hǎn zhuō zéi a thief crying "Stop thief"

贼头(頭)贼脑(腦) zéitóu-zéinǎo thievish; stealthy; furtive

贼心 zéixīn (名) evil designs or intentions: ～不死 still harbour evil intentions; cannot suppress evil thoughts

怎 zěn (代) why; how: 你～才来呀? Why are you so late?

怎么(麼) zěnme (代) **1** [interrogative pronoun]: 你～啦? What's wrong with you? 请问, 去车站～走? Excuse me, but how can I get to the railway station? 你～没去开会? Why didn't you attend the meeting? 这个词～拼? How do you spell the word? **2** [indicating the nature, condition and manner in general]: 你愿意～办就～办. Do as you please. **3** [used in the negative to indicate inadequacy]: 这个地方我不～熟悉. I am not quite familiar with the place.

怎么(麼)样(樣) zěnmeyàng (代) **1** how [used as a predicative or complement]: 跟我们一起去～? How about going there together with us? **2** [used in the negative]: 这旅馆并不～. This hotel is not so good as we expected. 他画得也并不～. He is not a particularly good painter.

怎么(麼)着 zěnmezhe (代) **1** [used to inquire about an action or state]: 我们都去, 你打算～? We are all going. What about you? 她今天不大做声, 是生气了还是～? She was quiet today. Was she angry or what? **2** in any case; whatever happens: ～也得把试验搞下去. The experiment must be carried on whatever happens.

怎样(樣) zěnyàng (代) **1** how [same as "怎么" zěnme]: 这件事你～向她解释? How are you going to explain this to her? **2** how [same as "怎么样" zěnmeyàng]: 你近来～? How have you been keeping?

曾 zēng (形) relationship between great-grandchildren and great-grand-parents

see also céng

曾孙(孫) zēngsūn (名) greatgrandson

曾祖 zēngzǔ (名) (paternal) great-grandfather

憎 zēng (动) hate; detest; abhor: 面目可～ look repulsive; repellent

憎恨 zēnghèn (动) hate; detest

憎恶(惡) zēngwù (动) detest; abhor; loathe

增 zēng (动) increase: ～产节约 increase production and practise economy. 产量与日俱～. Output has increased with each passing day.

增补(補) zēngbǔ (动) increase; supplement: 人员略有～. The staff has been slightly expanded.

增订 zēngdìng (动) revise and enlarge (a book)

增光 zēngguāng (动) do sb. credit; add to the prestige of: 这件事不会为他的声望～. This affair will not add to his prestige.

增加 zēngjiā (动) increase; raise; add: ～品种 increase the variety of types or patterns. ～收入 increase income. ～体重 put on weight

增进(進) zēngjìn (动) enhance; promote; further: ～友谊 promote friendship. ～健康 improve one's health

增强 zēngqiáng (动) strengthen; heighten; enhance: ～信心 gain fresh confidence. ～团结 strengthen unity; close one's ranks

增收节(節)支 zēngshōu-jiézhī increase revenue and reduce expenditure

增添 zēngtiān (动) add; increase: ～麻烦 put sb. to much inconvenience. ～光彩 bring added lustre to (organization, activity, etc.). ～设备 order additional equipment

增援 zēngyuán (动) reinforce: ～部队 reinforcements; reinforcing units

增长(長) zēngzhǎng (动) increase; rise; grow: 经济～ economic growth. 在实践中～才干 develop one's abilities in practice. ～知识和经验 add to one's knowledge and

experience
增值 zēngzhí 1 rise (or increase) in value; appreciation; increment 2 value added: ～税 value added tax (V.A.T.)
赠 zèng (动) give as a present; present as a gift: 捐～ donate; present. ～送仪式 presentation ceremony
赠款 zèngkuǎn (名) donation
赠言 zèngyán (名) words of advice spoken or written, offered to a friend at parting: 临别～ parting advice
赠阅 zèngyuè (动) (of publisher) give publications to others free of charge: ～本 complimentary copy
渣 zhā (名) 1 dregs; sediment; residue 2 small pieces: 面包～ crumbs
渣滓 zhāzǐ (名) dregs; sediment; residue: 社会～ dregs of society
扎 zhā (动) 1 prick: ～了手 prick one's finger 2 plunge into: 扑通一声,他就～进水里去了. He plunged into the water with a splash. *or* He jumped splash into the water. 3 (紮) pitch (a tent, etc.)
see also zā
扎根 zhāgēn (动) take root; strike root: ～、开花、结果 take root, blossom and bear fruit
扎啤 zhāpí (名) draught beer
扎实(實) zhāshi (形) solid; sound; down-to-earth: 他在基层做了出色而又～的工作. He has done remarkable, solid work at grass-roots level. 他有～的学问. He is a man of sound scholarship.
扎手 zhāshǒu I (动) prick the hand: 留神～. Mind the thorns. II (形) difficult to handle; thorny: 这事真～. This is a knotty problem.
扎眼 zhāyǎn (形) 1 garish; loud: 颜色～ garish colours 2 very showy
扎营(營) zhāyíng (动) pitch a tent or camp; encamp
闸 zhá (名) 1 sluice 2 brake: 踩～ step on the brake
闸口 zhákǒu (名) sluice gate; sluice valve
闸门(門) zhámén (名) floodgate
炸 zhá (动) fry in deep fat or oil; deep-fry: ～鸡腿 fried chicken legs
see also zhà
札 zhá (名) 1 thin pieces of wood used for writing on in ancient China 2 〈书〉 letter
札记 zhájì (名) reading notes or commentary
轧 zhá (动) roll (steel)
see also yà
轧钢(鋼) zhágāng (名) steel rolling: ～机 rolling mill. ～厂 steel rolling mill
眨 zhǎ (动) blink (one's eyes); wink: 眼睛也不～一～ without even batting an eyelid
眨眼 zhǎyǎn (动) wink: 一～的工夫 in the twinkling of an eye
栅 zhà (名) railings; bars: 铁～ iron bars
栅栏(欄) zhàlan (名) railings; fence
乍 zhà (副) 1 first; for the first time: 老朋友分别多年了,～一见面有说不出的高兴. On meeting quite unexpectedly an old friend I haven't seen for years, I was almost transported with joy. 2 suddenly; abruptly: ～变 change suddenly
炸 zhà (动) 1 explode; burst: 爆～ explode. 这瓶子一灌开水就～了. This glass bottle will break the moment it is filled with boiling water. 2 blow up; blast; bomb: ～桥 blow up a bridge. 轰～ bombardment 3 fly into a rage: 他一听就气～了. He flew into a towering rage when he heard it.
see also zhá
炸弹 zhàdàn (名) bomb: 定时～ time bomb
炸窝(窩) zhàwō (动) flee in terror
炸药(藥) zhàyào (名) explosive (charges); dynamite; TNT
诈 zhà (动) 1 cheat; swindle 2 pretend; feign: ～死 feign death. 兵不厌～. All is fair in war. 3 bluff sb. into giving information: 他是拿话～我,我一听就知道. I knew from the beginning that what he said was all bluff.
诈唬 zhàhu (动) bluff; bluster
诈骗 zhàpiàn (动) defraud; swindle
诈降 zhàxiáng (动) pretend to surrender; feign surrender
蚱 zhà
蚱蜢 zhàměng (名) grasshopper
榨 zhà I (动) press; extract; squeeze out: ～甘蔗 press sugar cane. ～油 extract oil II (名) a press for extracting juice, oil, etc.
榨菜 zhàcài (名) hot pickled mustard tuber

榨取 zhàqǔ (动) squeeze; extort

斋(齋) zhāi I (名) 1 vegetarian diet adopted by Buddhists and Taoists: 吃～ live on a vegetarian diet 2 room or building: 书～ study II (动) give alms (to a monk)

斋戒 zhāijiè (动) abstain from meat, wine, etc. (when offering sacrifices to gods or ancestors); fast

斋月 zhāiyuè (名) Ramadan; month of fast

摘 zhāi (动) 1 pick; pluck; take off: ～苹果 pick apples. ～花 pluck flowers. 把眼镜～下来 take off one's glasses 2 select; make extracts from: ～要 abstract; excerpts; précis

摘除 zhāichú (动) excise; remove: ～肿瘤 have a tumour removed

摘记 zhāijì I (动) take notes II (名) extracts; excerpts

摘录(録) zhāilù I (动) take passages; make extracts II (名) extracts; excerpts

摘帽子 zhāi màozi 1 take off one's hat or cap 2 cast off (or remove) a label: 摘掉落后帽子 cast off the label of "backwardness"; catch up with the others

摘要 zhāiyào I (动) make a summary II (名) summary; abstract; précis

宅 zhái (名) residence; mansion

宅院 zháiyuàn (名) a mansion with a courtyard; house

宅子 zháizi (名)〈口〉residence; house

择(擇) zhái (动) select; choose; pick

see also zé

择不开(開) zháibukāi 1 unravel: 线乱成了一团,怎么也～了. The skein of wool is so tangled that it is simply impossible to unravel it. 2 cannot get away from: 一点工夫也～ have no time to spare

窄 zhǎi (形) 1 narrow: ～道 narrow path 2 petty; narrow: 心眼儿～ narrow-minded 3 not well off; hard up

寨 zhài (名) 1 stockade 2 camp: 营～ military camp 3 mountain stronghold

债 zhài (名) debt: 欠～ run or get into debt; incur a debt; be in debt. 还～ pay (or repay, pay back) one's debt. 借～ ask for a loan; borrow money

债户 zhàihù (名) debtor

债权(權) zhàiquán (名) creditor's rights. ～国 creditor nation. ～人 creditor

债券 zhàiquàn (名) bond: ～持有人 bondholder

债台(臺)高筑(築) zhàitái gāo zhù be heavily in debt; be head over ears in debt; be saddled with huge debts

债务(務) zhàiwù (名) debt; liabilities: ～人 debtor

债主 zhàizhǔ (名) creditor

占 zhān (动) practise divination

see also zhàn

占卜 zhānbǔ (动) practise divination; divine

占卦 zhānguà (动) divine by means of the Eight Trigrams

占星 zhānxīng (动) divine by astrology; cast a horoscope: ～术 astrology

沾 zhān (动) 1 moisten; wet 2 be soiled with: ～上了泥 there are mud stains on sth. 3 touch: 烟酒不～ abstain from smoking and drinking 4 benefit from some sort of social relationship: ～光 benefit from one's association with sb. or sth.

沾边(邊) zhānbiān (动) 1 touch on only lightly: 这项工作他还没～儿. He has scarcely worked on the project. 2 be fairly close to the truth: 他讲的一点也不～. There is not a grain of truth in his statement.

沾光 zhānguāng (动) benefit from association with sb. or sth.

沾染 zhānrǎn (动) be infected by (or with); be contaminated by (or with): 不要～官僚主义习气. Don't allow yourself to be contaminated with bureaucratic style of work.

沾手 zhānshǒu (动) 1 touch with one's hand 2 have a hand in

沾沾自喜 zhānzhān zì xǐ feel smug or complacent; have smug complacency

粘 zhān (动) glue; stick; paste

粘连 zhānlián (名) adhesion

粘贴 zhāntiē (动) paste; stick: ～布告 put up a notice

毡(氈) zhān (名) felt: ～帽 felt hat

毡子 zhānzi (名) felt; felt rug; felt blanket

瞻 zhān (动) look forward or upwards

瞻念 zhānniàn (动) consider; think of: ～前途 think of the future

瞻前顾(顧)后(後) zhānqián-gùhòu 1 be

overcautious and indecisive **2** think twice before taking any action

瞻望 zhānwàng (动) look forward; look far ahead: 抬头～ raise one's head and look into the distance

瞻仰 zhānyǎng (动) look at with reverence: ～遗容 pay one's respects to sb.'s remains

盏(盞) zhǎn I (名) small cup: 酒～ small wine cup II (量) [for lamp]: 一～灯 a lamp

斩 zhǎn (动) cut; chop: ～断 chop off. 快刀～乱麻 cut the Gordian knot

斩草除根 zhǎncǎo-chúgēn pull the grass up by its roots; eradicate the root of trouble; root up all evil

斩钉截铁(鐵) zhǎndīng-jiétiě resolute and decisive

斩首 zhǎnshǒu (动) behead; decapitate

崭 zhǎn

崭新 zhǎnxīn (形) brand new; completely new

展 zhǎn I (动) **1** open up; spread out; unfold: ～翅高飞 soar into the sky. 愁眉不～ knit one's brows in anxiety **2** put to good use; give free play to: 一筹莫～. All his plans have come to naught. *or* He is simply helpless. **3** postpone; extend; prolong: ～期 postpone II (名) exhibition: 预～ preview

展出 zhǎnchū (动) put on display; be on show (or view); exhibit

展开(開) zhǎnkāi (动) **1** spread out; unfold; open up: 把地图～ unfold the map **2** launch; unfold; develop; carry out: ～攻势 launch an offensive. ～争论 start arguing

展览(覽) zhǎnlǎn (动、名) put on display; exhibit; show: ～馆 exhibition centre (or hall). ～会 exhibition. ～品 exhibit; item on display

展品 zhǎnpǐn (名) exhibit; item on display: 请勿抚摸～. Please do not touch the exhibits. *or* Hands off the exhibits.

展示 zhǎnshì (动) open up before one's eyes; reveal; show; lay bare: ～光明的前景 open up bright prospects

展望 zhǎnwàng I (动) look into the distance: ～未来 look into the future; look ahead II (名) forecast; prospect: 21世纪的～ prospects for the 21st century

展销 zhǎnxiāo (动) display and sell (goods): ～会 commodities fair; sales exhibition

辗 zhǎn

辗转(轉) zhǎnzhuǎn (动) **1** toss about in bed: ～不眠 lie in bed wide awake, tossing about from time to time. **2** pass through different hands or places: 故事～流传，成为一部传奇. The story passed from place to place and gradually developed into a legend.

湛 zhàn (形) profound; deep: 精～ consummate

蘸 zhàn (动) dip in (ink, sauce, etc.)

栈(棧) zhàn (名) **1** warehouse: 货～ warehouse; storehouse **2** inn: 客～ inn

栈道 zhàndào (名) a plank road built along the face of a cliff

栈房 zhànfáng (名) **1** warehouse; storehouse **2** inn

占(佔) zhàn (动) **1** occupy; seize; take: 霸～ forcibly occupy; seize. 攻～ occupy **2** constitute; hold; make up; account for: ～多数 constitute the majority. ～上风 gain the upper hand. ～优势 hold a dominant position. ～世界第一位 rank first in the world. ～世界人口的四分之一 account for a quarter of the world's population
see also zhān

占据(據) zhànjù (动) occupy; hold: ～重要的战略要地 capture a place of strategic importance. 在学术界～相当重要的地位 occupy a position of no small importance in the academic world

占领 zhànlǐng (动) capture; occupy; seize: ～邻国领土 occupy the territory of a neighbouring country. ～军 occupation army. ～市场 dominate the market

占便宜 zhàn piányi **1** gain advantage by unfair means; profit at other people's expense **2** enjoy an advantage

占线(綫) zhànxiàn (动) (of a telephone line) in use: 电话～. the line's busy (or engaged).

占有 zhànyǒu (动) **1** own; possess; have: ～第一手资料 have first-hand information **2** occupy; hold: ～重要地位 occupy an important place

站 zhàn I (动) **1** stand; be on one's feet: ～起来 stand up; rise to one's feet. 交通警～在十字路口指挥来往车辆. The traffic policeman stands at the crossroads to direct the passing vehicles. **2** stop; halt: 这是特快,中途不～. This is a non-stop express. 车还没～稳,别着急下车. There is no hurry getting off. The bus hasn't quite stopped yet. II (名) station; stop: 火车～ railway station. 公共汽车～ bus stop. 终点～ terminal; terminus. 服务～ service centre

站得高,看得远(遠) zhàn de gāo, kàn de yuǎn stand higher and look farther; be far-sighted

站队(隊) zhànduì (动) line up; fall in; stand in line; queue up

站岗(崗) zhàngǎng (动) stand (or mount) guard; be on sentry duty; stand sentry

站柜(櫃)台(臺) zhàn guìtái serve as a shop assistant; serve behind the counter

站台(臺) zhàntái (名) platform (in a railway station): ～票 platform ticket

站住 zhànzhù (动) **1** stop; halt **2** stand firmly on one's feet **3** stand (or hold) one's ground; consolidate one's position **4** hold water; be tenable

站住脚 zhànzhùjiǎo **1** stop; halt **2** stand (or hold) one's ground; consolidate one's position **3** stay put **4** hold water; be tenable

战(戰) zhàn I (名) war; warfare; battle; fight: 游击～ guerrilla war. 持久～ protracted war II (动) **1** fight: 不宣而～ wage an undeclared war **2** shiver; tremble; shudder: 胆～心惊 scared out of one's wits

战败 zhànbài (动) **1** be defeated; suffer a defeat; lose (a battle or war): ～国 vanquished (or defeated) nation **2** defeat; vanquish; beat

战备(備) zhànbèi (名) war preparedness; combat readiness

战场(場) zhànchǎng (名) battlefield; battleground; battlefront

战地 zhàndì (名) battlefield; battleground; combat zone: ～记者 war correspondent. ～指挥部 field headquarters

战斗(鬥) zhàndòu I (动) fight; combat: 英勇～ put up a heroic fight II (名) battle; action: 投入～ go into battle III (形) militant; fighting: ～的友谊 militant friendship. ～部队 combat forces. ～意志 will to fight. ～英雄 combat hero

战斗(鬥)力 zhàndòulì (名) combat effectiveness (or strength, capability); fighting capacity

战犯 zhànfàn (名) war criminal

战俘 zhànfú (名) prisoner of war (P. O. W.)

战功 zhàngōng (名) meritorious military service; outstanding military exploit; battle achievement

战鼓 zhàngǔ (名) battle drum

战果 zhànguǒ (名) results of battle; victory: ～辉煌 the splendid results of battle

战壕 zhànháo (名) trench; entrenchment

战火 zhànhuǒ (名) flames of war

战绩 zhànjì (名) military successes (or exploits, feats); combat gains

战舰(艦) zhànjiàn (名) warship

战局 zhànjú (名) war situation

战况 zhànkuàng (名) progress of a battle

战利品 zhànlìpǐn (名) spoils of war; captured equipment; war trophies (or booty)

战栗(慄) zhànlì (动) tremble; shiver; shudder: 吓得全身～ tremble all over with fear

战略 zhànlüè (名) strategy: 全球～ global strategy. ～核武器 strategic nuclear weapons. ～观点 strategic point of view. ～优势 strategic superiority

战胜(勝) zhànshèng (动) defeat; triumph over; vanquish; overcome: ～敌人 defeat (or vanquish) the enemy. ～困难 overcome (or surmount) difficulties

战士 zhànshì (名) **1** soldier; man **2** champion; warrior; fighter

战术(術) zhànshù (名) (military) tactics: ～核武器 tactical nuclear weapons. ～演习 tactical manoeuvre

战无(無)不胜(勝) zhàn wú bù shèng invincible; ever-victorious; all-conquering

战线(綫) zhànxiàn (名) battle line; battlefront; front

战役 zhànyì (名) campaign; battle

战友 zhànyǒu (名) comrade-in-arms; battle companion

战战兢兢 zhànzhànjīngjīng **1** quivering with fear **2** cautiously; with caution

战争 zhànzhēng (名) war; warfare: ～状态 state of war. 消除～ eliminate war. 挑起～ provoke war. ～狂人 war maniac

颤 zhàn (动) tremble; shiver; shudder
see also chàn

颤栗(慄) zhànlì (动) tremble; shiver; shudder

绽 zhàn (动) split; burst

章 zhāng (名) 1 chapter; section 2 order: 杂乱无~ disorganized or chaotic 3 rules; regulations; constitution: 规~ rules and regulations 4 seal; stamp: 盖~ affix one's seal 5 badge; medal: 领~ collar badge (or insignia). 奖~ medal; decoration. 袖~ armband

章程 zhāngchéng (名) rules; regulations; constitution

章法 zhāngfǎ (名) 1 presentation of ideas; art of composition 2 orderly ways; methodicalness: 他办事很有~. He is quite methodical in his work.

章节(節) zhāngjié (名) chapters and sections

樟 zhāng (名) camphor tree

樟脑(腦) zhāngnǎo (名) camphor: ~丸 camphor ball; mothball. ~油 camphor oil

樟树(樹) zhāngshù (名) camphor tree

张(張) zhāng I (动) 1 open; spread; stretch: ~嘴 open one's mouth. ~翅膀儿 spread the wings 2 look: 东~西望 peer (or look) around 3 magnify; exaggerate: 虚~声势 exaggerate one's military strength to deceive the enemy 4 [of a business] start: 开~ start a business II (量): 一~桌子 a table. 两~床 two beds. 一~纸 a piece of paper

张榜 zhāngbǎng (动) put up a notice; post a notice

张本 zhāngběn (名) seemingly casual remark foreshadowing the development of events

张挂(掛) zhāngguà (动) hang up (a picture, curtain, etc.)

张冠李戴 Zhāng guān Lǐ dài mistake one person or thing for another

张皇 zhānghuáng (形) 〈书〉 alarmed; scared: ~失措 be panicky

张口结舌 zhāngkǒu-jiéshé be tongue-tied; remain speechless

张力 zhānglì (名) 1 tension: 表面~ surface tension 2 pulling force

张罗(羅) zhāngluo (动) 1 take care of; get busy about: 这事交给我来~. I'll take care of that. 2 raise (funds): ~一笔钱 raise a sum of money 3 greet and entertain (guests); attend to (customers, etc.): 她正忙着~客人. She's busy attending to the guests.

张贴 zhāngtiē (动) put up (a notice, poster, etc.): ~通告 post (or put up) a notice

张望 zhāngwàng (动) 1 peep through a crack, etc. 2 look around

张牙舞爪 zhāngyá-wǔzhǎo fierce and quarrelsome

张扬(揚) zhāngyáng (动) publicize unnecessarily; make public (what should not be made known to the public): 四处~ spread the story around. 这事须严格保密, 请勿~出去. This is strictly confidential. On no account should you spread it around.

张嘴 zhāngzuǐ (动) 1 open one's mouth (to say sth.); be on the point of saying sth. 2 ask for a loan or a favour: 她想在此过夜,但又不好意思~. She would like to put up here for the night, but found it embarrassing to ask.

掌 zhǎng I (名) 1 palm (of hand) 2 (of certain animals and farmyard birds) bottom surface of foot; pad; paw: 鸭~ duck's webs. 熊~ bear's paw 3 shoe sole or heel: 给鞋子打前后~ have a shoe soled and heeled 4 horseshoe II (动) 1 strike with the palm of the hand; slap: ~嘴 slap sb. on the face 2 hold in control of; be in charge of: ~财权 have control over financial affairs

掌舵 zhǎngduò (动) be at the helm; operate the rudder; steer a boat

掌故 zhǎnggù (名) anecdotes

掌管 zhǎngguǎn (动) be in charge of; handle; administer: ~一个部门 be in charge of a department

掌柜(櫃) zhǎngguì (名) shopkeeper; manager (of a shop)

掌控 zhǎngkòng (动) manage and control

掌权(權) zhǎngquán (动) be in power; wield power; exercise control

掌声(聲) zhǎngshēng (名) clapping; applause: ~雷动 thunderous applause

掌握 zhǎngwò (动) 1 grasp; master; know well: ~技术 master a technique. ~问题实质 grasp the essence of the problem 2 control: ~会议 preside over a meeting. ~政权 wield political power. ~主动权

take the initiative in one's own hands

长(長) zhǎng I (形) 1 older; elder; senior: 比他年～ older than him 2 eldest; oldest: ～兄 eldest brother. ～女 eldest daughter II (名) chief; head: 科～ section chief. 代表团团～ head of a delegation III (动) 1 grow; develop: 孩子～大了,这件衣服穿不下了. The child has outgrown this jacket. 那里连草都不～. Even no grass would grow there. 2 come into being; begin to grow; form: ～锈 get rusty. 树木都～叶子了. The trees are coming into leaf. 3 acquire; enhance; increase: ～见识 gain one's knowledge and experience
see also cháng

长辈 zhǎngbèi (名) elder member of a family; one's senior

长大 zhǎngdà (动) grow up; be brought up

长进(進) zhǎngjìn (名) progress made in one's intellectual or moral education

长势(勢) zhǎngshì (名) (of crops) the condition of growth: 作物～良好. The crops are doing well.

长相 zhǎngxiàng (名)〈口〉features; appearance: 从他们的～看,他们像是兄弟俩. They are probably brothers, judging from their physical likeness.

长者 zhǎngzhě (名) 1 one's senior 2 a noble-minded person of advanced age; venerable elder

涨(漲) zhǎng (动) (of water level, prices, etc.) rise; go up: 价格上～. The prices have gone up.
see also zhàng

涨潮 zhǎngcháo (名) rising tide; flood tide

涨风(風) zhǎngfēng (名) the trend of prices going up

瘴 zhàng (名) miasma

障 zhàng I (动) hinder; obstruct II (名) barrier; block: 路～ barricade

障碍(礙) zhàng'ài (名) obstacle; impediment: ～物 obstacle; obstruction; barrier. 扫除～ remove obstacles. 制造～ create obstacles; erect barriers. ～赛跑 obstacle race; steeplechase

障眼法 zhàngyǎnfǎ (名) cover-up; camouflage: 玩弄～ throw dust into people's eyes

丈 zhàng I (量) *zhang*, a unit of length (= $3\frac{1}{3}$ metres) II (动) measure (land)

丈夫 zhàngfū (名) true man: ～气概 manliness

丈夫 zhàngfu (名) husband

丈量 zhàngliáng (动) measure (land): ～土地 measure land; take the dimensions of a field

丈母娘 zhàngmuniáng (名) mother-in-law

丈人 zhàngren (名) father-in-law

杖 zhàng (名) 1 cane; stick: 扶～而行 walk with a cane. 手～ (walking) stick 2 rod or staff used for a specific purpose: 擀面～ rolling pin

仗 zhàng I (动) 1 hold (a sword) 2 rely on; depend on: 狗～人势 act savagely like a dog owned by a powerful master II (名) battle; war: 打胜～ win a battle; win the war

仗势(勢)欺人 zhàng shì qī rén bully people by reliance on one's powerful connections or position

仗义(義)疏财 zhàng yì shū cái act in the cause of justice and make light of one's financial possessions; stand for justice and despise wealth

仗义(義)执(執)言 zhàng yì zhí yán speak out from a strong sense of justice

涨(漲) zhàng (动) 1 swell after absorbing water, etc. 2 (of the head) be swelled by a rush of blood: 他的脸～得通红. His face flushed scarlet. 头昏脑～ feel giddy
see also zhǎng

帐(帳) zhàng (名) curtain; tent: 蚊～ mosquito net

帐篷 zhàngpeng (名) tent: 搭～ pitch (or put up) a tent

账(賬) zhàng (名) 1 account: 记～ keep accounts. 结～ settle accounts 2 debt; credit: 赊～ buy or sell on credit

账簿 zhàngbù (名) account book; ledger

账房 zhàngfáng (名) 1 accountant's office 2 accountant

账户 zhànghù (名) account: 开立(结束)～ open (close) an account with a bank

账目 zhàngmù (名) items of an account; accounts

胀(脹) zhàng (动) 1 expand: 热～冷缩 expand when heated and contract when cooled. 人口膨～ expansion of population 2 (of body) feel tight: 肚子发～ have a feeling of tightness (or constriction) in the stomach

着 zhāo (名) 1 a move in chess: 走错一~ make a false move 2 trick; device; move: 使花~ play a trick
see also zháo; zhe; zhuó

朝 zhāo (名) 1 early morning; morning: ~阳 morning sun 2 day: 今~ today; the present
see also cháo

朝不保夕 zhāo bù bǎo xī precarious

朝晖 zhāohuī (名) the rays of the morning sun

朝令夕改 zhāo lìng xī gǎi make frequent changes in policy

朝气(氣) zhāoqì (名) youthful vigour; vitality: ~蓬勃 full of youthful vigour

朝三暮四 zhāosān-mùsì play fast and loose; chop and change: 这个人~,玩弄那姑娘的感情. This chap is playing fast and loose with that girl's feelings.

朝夕 zhāoxī (名) 1 every day; all the time 2 a very short time: 只争~ seize the day, seize the hour; seize every minute

朝霞 zhāoxiá (名) rosy clouds of dawn; rosy dawn

朝阳(陽) zhāoyáng (名) the rising sun; the morning sun

招 zhāo I (动) 1 beckon: 他把手一~,要我跟上. He beckoned me to follow. 2 recruit; enlist; enrol: ~工 recruit workers. ~生 enrol students 3 attract; incur; court: ~灾 court disaster; invite calamity 4 confess; own up: 被迫~认 make a confession under duress II (名) same as "着" zhāo

招标(標) zhāobiāo (动) invite tenders (or bids)

招兵买(買)马(馬) zhāobīng-mǎimǎ enlarge an army; recruit personnel

招待 zhāodài (动) entertain; serve (customers): 设宴~ give a dinner (or banquet) in honour of sb. ~客人 entertain guests. ~会 reception. ~所 guest house; hostel. 记者~会 press conference

招风(風) zhāofēng (动) attract notice and thus invite trouble

招供 zhāogòng (动) make a confession of one's crime; own up

招股 zhāogǔ (动) raise capital by floating shares

招呼 zhāohu (动) 1 call: 那边有人~你. Someone over there is calling you. 2 hail; greet; say hello to: 含笑~来宾 greet guests with a smile 3 notify; tell: 你要是想去,事先打个~. Let me know in advance if you want to go. 到站请~我一下. Remind me to get off at the stop.

招架 zhāojià (动) resist; ward off: 来势凶猛,难以~. The force was too great to resist.

招考 zhāokǎo (动) admit (students, applicants, etc.) by examination

招徕(徠) zhāolái (动) solicit: ~顾客 solicit customers

招揽(攬) zhāolǎn (动) solicit: ~顾客 solicit customers

招领 zhāolǐng (动) announce the finding of lost property: 失物~处 Lost and Found

招募 zhāomù (动) recruit; enlist

招牌 zhāopai (名) shop sign; signboard

招聘 zhāopìn (动) advertise for (workers, teachers, etc.)

招惹 zhāorě (动) provoke; incur; court: ~是非 court trouble

招认(認) zhāorèn (动) confess one's crime; own up; plead guilty

招商 zhāoshāng (动) invite outside investment

招生 zhāoshēng (动) enrol new students; recruit students: ~制度 enrolment system; admissions system. ~简章 school admission brochure

招收 zhāoshōu (动) recruit; take in: ~新学生 admit new students

招手 zhāoshǒu (动) beckon; wave: ~致意 wave one's greetings

招贴 zhāotiē (名) poster; placard; bill: ~画 pictorial poster (or placard)

招贤(賢) zhāoxián (动) recruit qualified personnel; scout about for talents

招摇 zhāoyáo (动) show off; put on airs: ~过市 swagger down the street. ~撞骗 behave under false pretences

招引 zhāoyǐn (动) attract; induce

招展 zhāozhǎn (动) flutter; wave

招致 zhāozhì (动) 1 recruit (personnel) 2 incur; give rise to: ~意外损失 incur unexpected losses. ~各种揣测 give rise to all sorts of speculation

招租 zhāozū (动) (house) for rent: 此屋~. Room to let.

昭 zhāo (形) clear; obvious

昭然若揭 zhāorán ruò jiē abundantly clear; as clear as daylight: 事实已~. The facts have come into the open.

昭雪 zhāoxuě (动) rehabilitate: 冤案得到了~. The wrong has been righted. *or* The person wronged has been rehabilitated.

昭彰 zhāozhāng (形) clear; manifest; evident: 罪恶~ be guilty of flagrant crimes

昭著 zhāozhù (形) clear; evident; obvious: 成绩~ have achieved remarkable successes. 臭名~ be notorious

着 zháo (动) **1** touch: 上不~天, 下不~地 be suspended in midair **2** feel; catch: ~凉 catch cold **3** burn: 灯点~了. The lamp is burning. 把烟点~了 light a cigarette **4** [used after a verb to indicate accomplishment or result]: 蒙~了 make a lucky guess **5** fall asleep; go to sleep: 他一上床就~了. He fell asleep as soon as he went to bed.

see also zhāo; zhe; zhuó

着慌 zháohuāng (动) feel worried; get alarmed

着火 zháohuǒ (动) catch fire

着急 zháojí (动) feel worried: 别~. Don't worry.

着迷 zháomí (动) be fascinated; be held spellbound

沼 zhǎo (名) natural pond

沼气(氣) zhǎoqì (名) marsh gas; biogas; methane

沼泽(澤) zhǎozé (名) marsh; swamp

找 zhǎo (动) **1** look for; try to find; seek: ~工作 look (or hunt) for a job. ~答案 seek a solution **2** want to see; call on: 早晨有位叫史密斯的先生~过你. A certain Mr. Smith wanted to see you this morning. 你该去~导师出个主意. You should go and ask your tutor for advice. **3** return the balance of money: 他~我三元. He gave me three *yuan* change.

找茬儿(兒) zhǎochár (动) find fault with

找出路 zhǎo chūlù find a way out

找对象 zhǎo duìxiàng look for a partner (in marriage)

找事 zhǎoshì (动) **1** look (or hunt) for a job **2** pick a quarrel with sb.; look for trouble

找死 zhǎosǐ (动) invite death; head for an accident or certain destruction

找寻(尋) zhǎoxún (动) look for; seek

爪 zhǎo (名) claw; talon

see also zhuǎ

爪牙 zhǎoyá (名) cat's paw

肇 zhào (动) 〈书〉 **1** start; commence; initiate **2** cause (trouble, etc.)

肇事 zhàoshì (动) cause trouble; create a disturbance: 追查~者 find out the troublemakers

罩 zhào I (动) cover; wrap: 用毕请把打字机~好. Please cover the typewriter after use. 天空~满乌云. Dark clouds covered the sky. II (名) cover; shade; hood; housing: 口~ mask. 灯~ lampshade. 发动机~ the engine housing

罩衫 zhàoshān (名) overall; dustcoat

兆 zhào I (名) sign; omen; portent: 吉祥之~ an auspicious omen II (数) **1** million; mega- **2** a million millions; billion III (动) portend; foretell: 瑞雪~丰年. A timely snow promises a good harvest.

兆头(頭) zhàotou (名) sign; omen; portent

兆周 zhàozhōu (量) megacycle

召 zhào (动) call together; convene; summon; send for

召唤 zhàohuàn (动) call; beckon: 工作在~着我们, 我们不能等了. Work beckons to us and we can't afford to wait.

召回 zhàohuí (动) recall: ~大使 recall an ambassador

召集 zhàojí (动) call together; convene: 把所有雇员~到一起 call all the employees together. ~会议 call (or convene) a conference. ~人 convener

召见(見) zhàojiàn (动) **1** call in (a subordinate) **2** summon (an envoy) to an interview

召开(開) zhàokāi (动) convene; convoke: ~一次首脑会议 hold a summit conference

召之即来(來) zhào zhī jí lái be at sb.'s beck and call

诏 zhào 〈书〉 I (动) instruct II (名) imperial edict

诏书(書) zhàoshū (名) imperial edict

照 zhào I (动) **1** shine; illuminate; light up: 他用手电筒~了我一下. He shone the torch at me. 日光灯把大厅~得通明. The hall was brightly lit by fluorescent lamps. **2** reflect; mirror: 湖面如镜, 把岸上树木~得清清楚楚. The water of the lake mirrored all the trees on the bank. **3** take a picture; photograph; film; shoot: ~一张团体相 have a group picture taken. 这是我在罗马~的几张相片.

These are a few snapshots I took in Rome. **4** take care of; look after: ～料 look after; attend to; keep an eye on **5** contrast: 对～ contrast; check against. 请对～原文. Please check this against the original. **6** understand: 心～不宣 have a tacit understanding II (介) **1** in the direction of; towards: ～这个方向走. Go in this direction. **2** according to; in accordance with: ～章办事 act according to regulations. ～我看 in my opinion III (名) **1** photograph; picture: 剧～ stage photo. 彩～ colour picture **2** licence; permit: 禁止无～行车. It is forbidden to drive without a licence. 护～ passport

照搬 zhàobān (动) mechanically copy

照办(辦) zhàobàn (动) act accordingly; do as one is told; comply with sb.'s request; follow sb.'s instructions

照本宣科 zhào běn xuān kē read mechanically from a prepared text

照常 zhàocháng (形) as usual: 天下着大雪,但孩子们～上学. In spite of the heavy snow, the children went to school as usual.

照抄 zhàochāo (动) copy word for word: 这封推荐信请你～一份. Please make a fair copy of this letter of recommendation.

照发(發) zhàofā (动) **1** issue as before **2** [used as a written instruction on an official document, etc.] approved for distribution

照顾(顧) zhàogù (动) **1** give consideration to; show consideration for; make allowance for: ～全局 take the entire situation into account. ～当地条件 take the local conditions into account **2** look after; care for; attend to: ～病人 look after the patients. 给予特别～ give preferential treatment

照管 zhàoguǎn (动) look after; tend; be in charge of: ～孩子 look after the children. 这件事由他～. He will take charge of the matter.

照会(會) zhàohuì I (动) present (or deliver, address) a note to (a government) II (名) note: 交换～ exchange notes. 普通～ verbal note. 正式～ personal note

照旧(舊) zhàojiù (形) as before; as usual; as of old: 体例～ follow the traditional stylistic rules

照看 zhàokàn (动) look after; attend to; keep an eye on: 请帮我～一下行李. Will you please keep an eye on my luggage?

照例 zhàolì (副) as a rule; as usual; usually: 她～每礼拜天去教堂. As a rule, she goes to church every Sunday.

照料 zhàoliào (动) take care of; attend to: 她不在期间把房子托给邻居～. She left the house in the care of a neighbour while she was away.

照明 zhàomíng (名) illumination; lighting: 舞台～ stage illumination. ～装置 lighting installation

照片 zhàopiàn (名) photograph; picture: 加印～ make copies of a print. 放大～ have the picture enlarged

照射 zhàoshè (动) shine; illuminate; light up; irradiate: 用紫外线～ irradiate with ultraviolet rays

照相 zhàoxiàng (动) take a picture (or photograph); photograph: ～复制 photocopy. ～馆 photostudio. ～簿 photo album

照相机(機) zhàoxiàngjī (名) camera

照样(樣) zhàoyàng (副) **1** after a pattern or model **2** in the same old way; as before

照耀 zhàoyào (动) shine; illuminate

照应(應) zhàoyìng (动) coordinate; correlate

照应(應) zhàoying (动) look after; take care of: 代表们受到东道国的很好～. All delegates were well looked after by the host country. 一路上他们互相～. They looked after each other all the way.

遮

zhē (动) **1** hide from view; cover; screen: 美丽的葡萄园给小山～住了. The beautiful vineyard was hidden from view by the hills. **2** keep out: ～风挡雨 keep out wind and rain

遮蔽 zhēbì (动) hide from view; obstruct; shelter: 一片森林～了我们的视线,看不到远处的村庄. The woods blocked our view of the distant villages.

遮丑(醜) zhēchǒu (动) gloss over one's blemishes; hide one's shame; cover up one's defect

遮挡(擋) zhēdǎng (动) shelter oneself from; keep out: ～寒风 keep out the cold wind

遮盖(蓋) zhēgài (动) **1** cover; overspread: 山路全给大雪～住了. The mountain paths were all covered by snow. **2** conceal; gloss over; cover up: ～缺点 gloss over one's shortcomings

遮羞 zhēxiū (动) hush up a scandal: ～解嘲

try to console oneself by putting on one's scandal a veneer of respectability. ～布 fig leaf

遮掩 zhēyǎn (动) **1** cover; overspread; envelop **2** cover up; hide; conceal: ～错误，不是正确的态度. It's not the right attitude to cover up one's mistakes.

折 zhē (动)〈口〉roll over; turn over: ～个跟斗 turn a somersault
see also shé; zhé

折腾 zhēteng (动)〈口〉**1** turn from side to side; toss about: 他～了好几个钟头才睡着. He tossed about in bed for hours before he fell asleep. **2** do sth. over and over again: 他把自行车拆了装，～了一个上午. He spent the whole morning dismantling and assembling the bike. **3** cause physical or mental suffering; get sb. down: 这种噪声真～人. The noise is getting on my nerves.

谪 zhé (动)〈书〉**1** demote a high official by assigning him a minor post in an outlying district (as a form of punishment in feudal times): ～居 live in exile **2** criticize; blame: 众口交～ be the target of public censure; be criticized by everybody

折 zhé I (动) **1** break; snap: ～断腿 fracture (or break) one's leg **2** suffer the loss of; lose: 损兵～将 suffer heavy casualties **3** bend; twist: 曲～ twists and turns. 百～不挠 remain unshaken in spite of all setbacks **4** turn back; change direction: 他本想出去散步，但到了门口又～了回来. He meant to go out for a stroll, but he turned back as soon as he reached the gate. **5** be convinced: 心～ be deeply convinced **6** convert into; amount to: 把瑞士法郎～成美元 convert Swiss francs into dollars **7** (摺)fold: 内有照片，请勿～叠! Photos, don't bend! II (名) **1** discount; rebate: 打八～ give a 20% discount **2** (摺) folder; passbook: 存～ deposit book; bankbook
see also shé; zhē

折叠 zhédié (动) fold: 把报纸～好 fold up the newspaper. ～椅 folding chair; camp chair. ～扇 folding fan

折服 zhéfú (动) **1** subdue; bring into submission: 强词夺理，不能～人. As you are arbitrary and unreasonable, you cannot expect anybody to give in. **2** convinced or fill sb. with admiration: 令人～ compel admiration

折合 zhéhé (动) convert into; amount to; be equivalent to: 一英镑～成人民币是多少? How much is a pound in terms of *yuan*?

折价(價) zhéjià (动) convert into money; evaluate in terms of money: ～退赔 pay compensation at the market price

折旧(舊) zhéjiù (名) depreciation: ～费 depreciation charge

折扣 zhékòu (名) discount; rebate: 打～ at a discount

折磨 zhémó (动) cause physical or mental suffering; torment

折射 zhéshè (名) refraction

折算 zhésuàn (动) convert: 把人民币～成美元 convert Renminbi into US dollars. ～率 conversion rate

折中 zhézhōng (动) compromise; make mutual concession; strike a balance (also as "折衷")

折衷主义(義) zhézhōngzhǔyì (名) eclecticism

哲 zhé I (形) wise; sagacious II (名) wise man; philosopher; sage: 先～ the sages of old

哲理 zhélǐ (名) philosophy

哲人 zhérén (名)〈书〉sage; philosopher

哲学(學) zhéxué (名) philosophy: ～家 philosopher

蛰(蟄) zhé

蛰居 zhéjū (动) live in seclusion

辙 zhé (名) **1** the track of a wheel; rut **2** [usu. used in the negative] way; idea: 没～ can find no way out; be at the end of one's rope

褶 zhě (名) pleat; crease: 百～裙 pleated skirt; accordion-pleated skirt. 熨平衬衫上的～儿 iron the wrinkles out of the skirt

褶皱(皺) zhězhòu (名) **1** fold **2** wrinkle

者 zhě **1** [used after an adjective or verb as a substitute for a person or a thing]: 老～ old man. 弱～ the weak. 读～ reader. 出版～ publisher **2** [used after 工作，主义 to indicate a person engaged in a certain profession or believe in a doctrine]: 医务工作～ medical worker. 唯物主义～ materialist **3** [used to indicate things mentioned above]: 二～必居其一. It must be one or the other.

赭 zhě (形) reddish brown; burnt ochre

这(這) zhè (代) 1 this: ～地方 this place. ～一回 this time 2 this moment; now: 我～就走. I'm leaving right now.

这般 zhèbān (代) such; so; like this: ～大小 this size; this big. 如此～ thus and thus; so on and so forth

这边(邊) zhèbiān (代) this side; here: 正义在我们～. Justice is on our side. 到～来. Come over here.

这次 zhècì (代) this time; present; current: ～会议 the present session. ～英国大选 the current British general elections

这儿(兒) zhèr (代) here; now; then: 打～起我就要天天锻炼了. From now on I'm going to do physical exercises every day.

这个(個) zhège (代) this one; this: 你要告诉我们的就是～呀! So this is what you wanted to tell us.

这里(裏) zhèlǐ (代) here

这么(麼) zhème (代) so; such; this way; like this: 事情不会～简单. The matter wouldn't be as simple as that. 这间屋子～大哪! This room is so big! ～多人,有地方吗? Is there enough room for so many people?

这么(麼)着 zhèmezhe (代) like this; so: ～好. It's better this way. 要是～,那我就留下不去了. In that case, I'll stay behind.

这些 zhèxiē (代) these: ～书 these books. ～日子 these days

这样(樣) zhèyàng (代) so; such; like this; this way: 别走～快. Don't walk so fast. 情况就是～. That's how things stand.

蔗 zhè (名) sugar cane

蔗糖 zhètáng (名) 1 sucrose 2 cane sugar

着 zhe (助) 1 [indicating an action in progress]: 他们正开～会呢. They are at a meeting. 他含～眼泪说. He said this with tears in his eyes. 2 [stressing the tone in an imperative sentence]: 你听～! You just listen. 快～点儿. Be quick. 3 [used after a verb to form a preposition]: 沿～ along. 挨～ next to. 朝～ towards

see also zhāo; zháo; zhuó

榛 zhēn (名) hazel

臻 zhēn (动)〈书〉attain (a happy state): 交通运输日～便利. The means of transportation are becoming better and better.

斟 zhēn (动) pour (tea or wine)

斟酌 zhēnzhuó (动) consider; deliberate: ～字句 weigh the words and phrases. 再三～ think the matter over

砧 zhēn (名) hammering block; anvil: ～杵 anvil and pestle

甄 zhēn (动)〈书〉distinguish after examination: ～选 select

甄别 zhēnbié (动) 1 examine and distinguish; screen 2 assess; appraise; verify

真 zhēn I (形) 1 true; real; genuine: ～事 a true story. ～心诚意 genuine desire; sincerity 2 clearly; unmistakably: 黑板上的字你看得～吗? Can you see the words on the board clearly? II (副) really; truly; indeed: 他～信了. He sincerely believed it. 他～是个了不起的学者. He is indeed a great scholar.

真才实(實)学(學) zhēncái-shíxué real talent and sound scholarship; professionally competent; well qualified or well trained

真诚 zhēnchéng (形) sincere; genuine; true: ～的愿望 sincere wish

真格的 zhēngéde real; true: 动～ start a shooting war; do sth. in real earnest

真话 zhēnhuà (名) the truth: 你必须说～. You must tell the truth.

真迹 zhēnjì (名) authentic work (of painting or calligraphy)

真假 zhēn-jiǎ (形) true or false; genuine or sham: 辨别～ tell the true from the false

真金不怕火炼(煉) zhēnjīn bù pà huǒ liàn true gold can be tried in the fire

真空 zhēnkōng (名) vacuum: 我们不是生活在～里. We do not live in a vacuum. ～地带 no man's land. ～吸尘器 vacuum cleaner

真理 zhēnlǐ (名) truth: 坚持～ uphold the truth

真面目 zhēnmiànmù true features; true colours: 认清～ see sb. in his true colours; know sb. for what he is. 露出～ reveal one's true colours

真凭(憑)实(實)据(據) zhēn-píng-shíjù conclusive evidence; true evidence

真切 zhēnqiè (形) vivid and truthful; clear; distinct

真情 zhēnqíng (名) **1** the real situation; the actual state of affairs **2** genuine feelings; true sentiments: ～的流露 a revelation of one's true sentiments

真人真事 zhēnrén-zhēnshì real people and real events; true story

真善美 zhēn-shàn-měi (名) truth, goodness and beauty

真实(實) zhēnshí (形) true; real; actual; authentic: 那儿的～情况不是人人都知道的. Not everyone knows the real situation there.

真是 zhēnshi [expressing arrogance]: 你也～,怎么来得这么晚? What a shame! Why are you so late?

真相 zhēnxiàng (名) the real (or true) situation; the real (or actual) facts; the actual state of affairs; truth: 弄清事实的～ acquaint oneself with the truth of the matter

真心 zhēnxīn (形) wholehearted; heartfelt; sincere: ～拥护 give wholehearted support to. ～话 true words from the heart

真正 zhēnzhèng (形) genuine; true; real: 患难之交才是～的朋友. A friend in need is a friend indeed.

真知 zhēnzhī (名) genuine (or real) knowledge; correct understanding

真知灼见(見) zhēnzhī-zhuójiàn penetrating knowledge and insight

真挚(摯) zhēnzhì (形) sincere; cordial: ～的友谊 sincere friendship

真主 zhēnzhǔ (名) Allah

贞 zhēn I (形) loyal; faithful II (名) (of women) chastity or virginity

贞操 zhēncāo (名) **1** chastity or virginity **2** loyalty; moral integrity

贞节(節) zhēnjié (名) chastity

贞洁(潔) zhēnjié (形) chaste; pure and undefiled

侦 zhēn (动) detect; scout; investigate

侦查 zhēnchá (动) investigate (a crime)

侦察 zhēnchá (动) reconnoitre; scout: ～敌情 gather intelligence about the enemy. ～兵 scout. ～机 reconnaissance plane

侦缉 zhēnjī (动) track down and arrest (a criminal)

侦探 zhēntàn (名) detective; spy: ～小说 detective story

侦听(聽) zhēntīng (动) intercept (enemy radio communications); monitor

箴 zhēn

箴言 zhēnyán (名) admonition; exhortation; maxim

珍 zhēn I (名) treasure: 山～海味 delicacies of great variety. 奇～异宝 rare treasure II (形) precious; valuable; rare: ～禽异兽 rare birds and animals

珍爱 zhēn'ài (动) treasure; love dearly

珍宝(寶) zhēnbǎo (名) jewellery; treasure: 如获～ as if one had come upon a rare treasure

珍藏 zhēncáng (动) collect (rare books, art treasures, etc.)

珍贵 zhēnguì (形) valuable; precious: ～物品 the valuables. ～的历史文物 precious historical relics

珍品 zhēnpǐn (名) treasure: 艺术～ art treasure

珍奇 zhēnqí (形) rare: ～的动物 rare animals

珍视 zhēnshì (动) value; prize; cherish; treasure

珍惜 zhēnxī (动) treasure; value; cherish: ～时间 fully recognize the value of time

珍重 zhēnzhòng (动) **1** highly value; treasure; set great store by: ～这个良好机会 set great store by this opportunity **2** take good care of yourself

珍珠 zhēnzhū (名) pearl: ～贝 pearl shell; pearl oyster

针 zhēn (名) **1** needle: 毛线～ knitting needle **2** stitch: 伤口缝了四～ sew the edges of a wound with four stitches. **3** anything like a needle: 松～ pine needle. 时～ hour hand. 别～ safety pin

针对(對) zhēnduì (动) **1** be directed against; be aimed at: 这些话不是～什么人说的. These remarks were not directed against anybody in particular. **2** in the light of; in accordance with; in connection with: ～儿童特点组织活动 organize activities for children in accordance with their special characteristics

针锋相对(對) zhēnfēng xiāng duì give tit for tat; be diametrically opposed to: 进行～的斗争 wage a tit-for-tat struggle

针剂(劑) zhēnjì (名) injection

针灸 zhēnjiǔ (名) acupuncture

针线(綫) zhēnxiàn (名) needlework: ～包 sewing kit. ～活 needlework; stitching; sewing

针眼 zhēnyǎn (名) **1** the eye of a needle

2 pinprick

针织(織) zhēnzhī (名) knitting: ~外套 knitted (or knit) coat. ~品 knit goods; knitwear; hosiery

枕 zhěn I (名) pillow: ~巾 pillowcase cover II (动) rest the head on: ~着胳臂睡觉 sleep with one's head resting on one's arm

枕戈待旦 zhěn gē dài dàn sleep with one's sword ready; be ready for battle

枕木 zhěnmù (名) sleeper; tie

枕套 zhěntào (名) pillowcase

枕头(頭) zhěntou (名) pillow

缜 zhěn

缜密 zhěnmì (形) careful; meticulous; deliberate: ~的分析 a careful thoroughgoing analysis

疹 zhěn (名) rash: 荨麻~ nettle rash

疹子 zhěnzi (名) measles

诊 zhěn (动) examine (a patient)

诊断(斷) zhěnduàn (动) diagnose: ~书 medical certificate

诊疗(療) zhěnliáo (名) diagnosis and treatment: ~室 consulting room. ~所 clinic; dispensary

诊脉(脈) zhěnmài (动) feel the pulse

鸩 zhèn (名) 1 a legendary poisonous bird, whose feathers can turn wine into poison 2 poisoned wine: 饮~止渴 drink poisoned wine to quench thirst; seek temporary relief regardless of consequences

震 zhèn (动) 1 shake; shock; vibrate; quake: 地~ earthquake. 防~ shockproof 2 greatly excited; deeply astonished; shocked: ~骇 shocked; astounded

震颤 zhènchàn (动) tremble; quiver

震荡(蕩) zhèndàng (动) shake; shock: ~全球 shake the world

震动(動) zhèndòng (动) quiver; cause sth. to quiver or tremble or vibrate: 引起了广泛的~ arouse widespread repercussions. 春雷~着山谷. The spring thunder rumbled in the valleys. *or* The spring thunder made the valleys vibrate.

震耳欲聋(聾) zhèn ěr yù lóng deafening; ear-splitting

震撼 zhènhàn (动) shake; shock; vibrate: ~人心的大事 a soul-stirring event

震惊(驚) zhènjīng (动) shock; amaze; astonish: ~中外 astonish the country and rest of the world; have a tremendous impact on people both at home and abroad

震怒 zhènnù (形) be enraged; be furious

震源 zhènyuán (名) focus (of an earthquake)

震中 zhènzhōng (名) epicentre

振 zhèn (动) 1 shake; flutter; flap: ~翅 flutter its wings up and down; flap its wings 2 invigorate; animate; brace up: 食欲不~ lose one's appetite. 他想到自己这次考得不错,精神为之一~. He felt excited when he thought that he had done very well at the exams this time.

振荡(蕩) zhèndàng (名) 1 vibration 2 oscillation

振动(動) zhèndòng (名) vibration: ~频率 vibration frequency

振奋(奮) zhènfèn (动) 1 feel invigorated; be filled with enthusiasm 2 inspire; stimulate: ~人心 inspire popular enthusiasm. 令人~的消息 heartening news

振兴(興) zhènxīng (动) develop vigorously; promote: ~中华 revitalize (or rejuvenate) China. ~工业 vigorously develop industry

振振有辞(辭) zhènzhèn yǒu cí speak plausibly and at great length

振作 zhènzuò (动) display vigour: ~起来 bestir oneself; brace up

赈 zhèn

赈济(濟) zhènjì (动) relieve; aid: ~灾民 relieve victims in afflicted (or stricken) areas; bring relief to refugees; feed the hungry

赈灾(災) zhènzāi (动) relieve the people scourged by natural disaster

镇 zhèn I (动) 1 press down; keep down; ease: ~痛 ease pain 2 guard; garrison: ~守 guard (a strategic region) 3 cool with cold water or ice: 冰~啤酒 iced beer II (形) calm; tranquil: ~定 calm and composed III (名) 1 garrison post: 军事重~ strategic post 2 town

镇静 zhènjìng (形) calm; cool; composed; unruffled: ~剂 sedative; tranquillizer

镇痛 zhèntòng I (动) ease pain: ~片 pain killer II (名) analgesia: 针刺~ acupuncture analgesia

镇压(壓) zhènyā (动) 1 suppress; repress;

put down: ～叛乱 put down a rebellion 2 〈口〉 execute (a criminal)

镇长(長) zhènzhǎng (名) town head

阵 zhèn I (名) 1 battle array (or formation): 严～以待 combat ready 2 position; front: 上～杀敌 off to fight at the front line 3 a period of time: 病了一～ be ill for some time II (量): 一～风 a gust of wind. 一～寒潮 a cold spell. 一～笑声 outbursts of laughter

阵地 zhèndì (名) position; front: 前沿～ a forward position. ～战 positional warfare

阵脚 zhènjiǎo (名) 1 front line 2 position; situation; circumstances: 稳住～ stand one's ground. 乱了～ be thrown into confusion

阵容 zhènróng (名) 1 battle array (or formation) 2 line-up: ～强大 have a strong line-up

阵势(勢) zhènshì (名) 1 battle array (or formation) 2 situation; condition; circumstances

阵亡 zhènwáng (动) be killed in action; fall in battle

阵线(綫) zhènxiàn (名) front; ranks; alignment

阵营(營) zhènyíng (名) camp

阵雨 zhènyǔ (名) shower

正 zhēng

see also zhèng

正月 zhēngyuè (名) the first month of the lunar year: ～初一 the lunar New Year's Day

症(癥) zhēng

see also zhèng

症结 zhēngjié (名) crux; crucial reason: 问题的～ the crux of a problem

征 zhēng (动) 1 go on a long journey 2 go on an expedition: ～讨 go on a punitive expedition

征(徵) zhēng I (动) 1 levy (troops); call up; draft: 应～入伍 enlist 2 levy (taxes); collect; impose: ～敛 levy and collect taxes 3 ask for; solicit: ～稿 solicit contributions (to a magazine etc.) II (名) sign; portent

征兵 zhēngbīng (动) conscript; draft; call up: ～法 conscription (or draft) law. ～年龄 conscription age; age for enlistment

征调 zhēngdiào (动) requisition; call up: ～物资和人员 requisition supplies and enlist personnel

征服 zhēngfú (动) conquer; subjugate: ～自然 conquer nature (or conquest of nature). ～黄河 tame (or harness) the Huanghe (Yellow) River

征购(購) zhēnggòu (动) requisition by purchase

征候 zhēnghòu (名) sign: 病人已有康复的～. The patient shows signs of recovery.

征集 zhēngjí (动) 1 collect; gather: ～签名 collect signatures (for an appeal) 2 draft; call up; recruit: ～新兵 recruitment

征募 zhēngmù (动) enlist; recruit

征聘 zhēngpìn (动) invite applications for jobs; advertise for a vacant position

征求 zhēngqiú (动) solicit; seek; ask for: ～意见 solicit opinions; seek counsel; ask for advice. ～订户 solicit (or canvass for) subscriptions

征收 zhēngshōu (动) levy; collect; impose: ～进口税 impose import duties

征税 zhēngshuì (动) levy (or collect) taxes; raise money by taxes: ～货物 dutiable goods

征途 zhēngtú (名) journey: 踏上～ embark (or set out) on a journey

征询 zhēngxún (动) seek the opinion of; consult

征用 zhēngyòng (动) expropriate; requisition; commandeer

征战(戰) zhēngzhàn (动) go on an expedition

征召 zhēngzhào (动) call up; enlist; draft; conscript: ～入伍 enlist in the army

征兆 zhēngzhào (名) sign; omen; portent

争 zhēng (动) 1 contend; vie; compete; strive: ～冠军 compete for championship. ～分夺秒 race (or work) against time; seize the moment 2 argue; dispute: 他们为修建新路的事情～了半天. They disputed for hours about whether to build a new road. 这是意气之～. The dispute was a display of personal feelings.

争霸 zhēngbà (动) contend (or struggle) for hegemony; vie (with each other) for supremacy

争辩(辯) zhēngbiàn (动) argue; debate; contend: 无休止的～ an endless debate

争吵 zhēngchǎo (动) quarrel; wrangle; squabble: 激烈的～ fierce (or bitter)

wrangling

争端 zhēngduān (名) controversial issue; dispute; conflict: 边界～ a border dispute

争夺(奪) zhēngduó (动) fight (or contend, scramble) for; vie with sb. for sth.: ～优势 fight for supremacy. ～冠军 compete for championship

争光 zhēngguāng (动) win honour (or glory) for: 为国～ win honour for or bring credit to one's country

争论(論) zhēnglùn I (动) argue; dispute II (名) controversy; dispute; debate; contention: 激烈的～ a heated argument. ～之点 the point at issue

争鸣 zhēngmíng (动) contend: 百家～. A hundred schools of thought contend.

争气(氣) zhēngqì (动) work hard to win honour for; try to bring credit to

争取 zhēngqǔ (动) strive for; fight for; win over: ～胜利 strive for victory. ～选票 canvass (for votes). ～主动 take the initiative. ～中立派 win over the neutral elements

争权(權)夺(奪)利 zhēngquán-duólì jockey for power and scramble for profit

争先 zhēngxiān (动) try to be ahead of others; try to be among the first: ～恐后 push ahead for fear of lagging behind

争议(議) zhēngyì (名) dispute; controversy: 有～的领土 disputed territory. 有～的问题 controversial issue. 引起很大～ give rise to a good deal of controversy

争执(執) zhēngzhí (动) disagree; dispute; stick to one's position (or guns): ～不下. Opinions differ and the issue remains undecided.

挣 zhēng

see also zhèng

挣扎 zhēngzhá (动) struggle: 垂死～ put up a last-ditch struggle

睁 zhēng (动) open (the eyes): ～开眼睛,好好看看. Open your eyes and take a closer look.

峥 zhēng

峥嵘(嶸) zhēngróng (形) 1 lofty and steep; towering 2 outstanding; extraordinary

狰 zhēng

狰狞(獰) zhēngníng (形) ferocious; savage; hideous: ～面目 ferocious features

蒸 zhēng (动) 1 evaporate 2 steam: ～饭 steam rice

蒸发(發) zhēngfā (动) evaporate

蒸馏 zhēngliú (名) distillation: ～水 distilled water

蒸气(氣) zhēngqì (名) vapour

蒸汽 zhēngqì (名) steam: ～机 steam engine. ～浴 steam bath; sauna

蒸蒸日上 zhēngzhēng rì shàng becoming more prosperous every day; flourishing; thriving

整 zhěng I (形) 1 whole; complete; full; entire: ～夜 the whole night; all night long. ～学期 a full term. 七点～ (of time) seven sharp 2 in good order; neat; tidy: 衣冠不～ untidy in dress; not properly dressed II (动) 1 put in order; rectify: ～改 reform. ～装待发 pack and get ready to go 2 repair; mend; renovate: ～修 renovate 3 make sb. suffer; punish; fix: ～人 give sb. a hard time

整队(隊) zhěngduì (动) line up: ～入场 file in

整顿 zhěngdùn (动) rectify; consolidate; reorganize: ～城市治安 improve public order in the cities. ～规章制度 re-establish rules and regulations

整风(風) zhěngfēng (动) rectify the incorrect style of work

整改 zhěnggǎi (动) rectify; make corrections: 责令立即～ request immediate corrections

整个(個) zhěnggè (形) whole; entire: ～上午 the whole morning. ～世界 the whole world. ～中国 the whole of China

整合 zhěnghé (动) integrate

整洁(潔) zhěngjié (形) clean and tidy; neat; trim: 衣着～ clean and tidy in dress

整理 zhěnglǐ (动) put in order; straighten out; arrange; sort out: ～房间 tidy up a room. ～资料 sort out the data. ～家务 straighten out one's domestic affairs

整流 zhěngliú (名) rectification: ～器 rectifier

整齐(齊) zhěngqí (形) 1 in good order; neat; tidy: ～划一 uniform and standardized 2 even; regular: 五官～ (have) regular features. 一排排～的住宅 rows of neatly arranged houses. 阵容～ a well-balanced line-up

整容 zhěngróng I (动) 1 tidy oneself up (i.e. have a haircut, a shave, etc.)

2 improve one's look by plastic surgery II (名) face-lifting

整数(數) zhěngshù (名) 1 integer; whole number 2 round number (or figure)

整套 zhěngtào (名) a complete (or whole) set of: ～设备 a complete set of equipment. ～行动计划 a series of plans for action

整体(體) zhěngtǐ (名) whole; (the situation) as a whole; entirety: ～方案 an overall plan. 考虑人民的～利益 consider the overall interests of the people

整形 zhěngxíng (动) plastic: ～手术 plastic operation. ～外科 plastic surgery

整修 zhěngxiū (动) renovate; repaint or restyle

整整 zhěngzhěng (形) whole; full: ～两天 two whole days. 到北京已～三年了. It is three full years since I came to Beijing.

整治 zhěngzhì (动) 1 renovate; repair; dredge (a river, etc.) 2 punish; fix

拯 zhěng (动) save; rescue; deliver

拯救 zhěngjiù (动) save; rescue; deliver

郑(鄭) zhèng

郑重 zhèngzhòng (形) serious; solemn; earnest: ～声明 solemnly declare. ～其事 seriously; in earnest

正 zhèng I (形) 1 straight; upright: 把这幅画放～ put the picture straight. ～北 due north 2 situated in the middle; main: ～门 main entrance 3 (of time) punctually; sharp: 九点～ at nine o'clock sharp 4 obverse; right: 胶卷的～面 the right side of the film 5 honest; upright: 他为人～直. He is an upright man. 6 appropriate; right: ～当 legitimate. 不～之风 unhealthy tendencies 7 (of colour or flavour) pure; right: 味儿不～ not the proper flavour 8 principal; chief: ～驾驶员 first pilot. ～教授 full professor. ～本 original text (or copy) 9 positive; plus: ～离子 positive ion II (动) rectify; correct; set right: ～音 correct one's pronunciation III (副) 1 just; right; precisely; exactly: ～是如此 exactly so. 这～是我们的想法. This is exactly what we think. 2 [indicating an action in progress]: ～下着雨呢. It's raining. 他～吃着饭呢. He is having dinner.

see also zhēng

正版 zhèngbǎn (名) legal copy (as opposed to pirated version)

正比 zhèngbǐ (名) direct ratio

正餐 zhèngcān (名) 1 a regular meal served in a restaurant 2 dinner

正常 zhèngcháng (形) normal; regular: ～速度 normal speed. 恢复～ return to normal. 关系～化 normalization of relations

正大 zhèngdà (形) upright; honest; aboveboard: ～光明 open and aboveboard

正当(當) zhèngdāng (动) just when; just the time for: ～委员会在日内瓦再次开会之际 when the committee met again in Geneva

正当(當) zhèngdàng (形) proper; appropriate; legitimate: ～权益 legitimate rights and interests. 通过～途径 through proper channels

正点(點) zhèngdiǎn (形) (of ships, trains, etc.) on schedule; on time; punctually: ～运行 running on schedule

正电(電) zhèngdiàn (名) positive electricity

正法 zhèngfǎ (动) execute (a criminal): 就地～ execute (a criminal) on the spot

正反 zhèng-fǎn positive and negative: ～两方面的看法 the pros and cons

正规 zhèngguī (形) regular; standard: ～部队 regular troops; regulars

正轨 zhèngguǐ (名) correct path: 纳入～ lead one onto the correct path

正好 zhènghǎo I (形) just in time; just right; just enough: 你来得～. You've come just in the nick of time. 这双鞋我穿～. This pair of shoes fits me superbly. II (副) happen to; chance to; as it happens: 我～与你同路. I happen to go in the same direction.

正经(經) zhèngjing (形) 1 decent; respectable; honest: ～人 a decent person 2 serious: ～事 serious matter

正面 zhèngmiàn I (名) 1 front; frontage; facade: 大楼的～ the facade of a building. ～进攻 frontal attack 2 the obverse side; the right side: 硬币的～ the obverse side of a coin II (形) 1 positive: ～教育 positive education 2 directly; openly: ～提出问题 raise a question directly and openly

正派 zhèngpài (形) upright; decent: ～人 an honourable person; a decent chap

正品 zhèngpǐn (名) quality products

正气(氣) zhèngqì (名) healthy trends (or

tendencies)

正巧 zhèngqiǎo I (副) as it happens: ～我也到那里去. I happened to be going there too. II (形) just at the right time: 你来得～. You've turned up at the opportune time.

正确 zhèngquè (形) correct; right

正人君子 zhèngrén-jūnzǐ a man of honour; a man of noble character; a noble-minded man

正式 zhèngshì (形) formal; official; regular: ～工作人员 a regular member of the staff. ～宴会 a formal dinner party. ～访问 official visit. ～文本 official text

正事 zhèngshì (名) one's proper business; no joking matter

正视 zhèngshì (动) face squarely; face up to: ～缺点 give serious thought to one's inadequacies

正数(數) zhèngshù (名) positive number

正题 zhèngtí (名) subject (or topic) of a talk or essay: 离开～ digress (from the subject)

正统 zhèngtǒng (形) orthodox: ～观念 orthodox ideas

正文 zhèngwén (名) main body (of a book, etc.); text

正午 zhèngwǔ (名) high noon

正误表 zhèngwùbiǎo (名) errata; corrigenda

正眼 zhèngyǎn look straight: 他和我说话时不敢～看着我. He did not dare look me straight in the face when he spoke.

正业(業) zhèngyè (名) a decent job; proper duties: 不务～ neglect one's own duties; engage in dubious work

正义(義) zhèngyì I (名) justice: 主持～ uphold justice II (形) just; righteous: ～的事业 a just cause. ～感 sense of justice

正在 zhèngzài (副) [to indicate an action in progress] in process of; in course of: 情况～变好. The situation is getting better. 他们～开会. They are at a meeting.

正直 zhèngzhí (形) upright; fair-minded: 一切～的人们 all fair-minded people

正职(職) zhèngzhí (名) the position of the chief of an office, department, etc.

正中 zhèngzhōng (名) middle; centre

正中下怀(懷) zhèng zhòng xiàhuái exactly as one wishes or hopes for

正宗 zhèngzōng (名) orthodox school

症 zhèng (名) disease; illness: 急～ acute disease. 不治之～ incurable disease. 对～下药 treat a sick person on the basis of a correct diagnosis

see also zhēng

症候 zhènghou (名) symptom

症状 zhèngzhuàng (名) symptom

证 zhèng I (动) prove; demonstrate: ～实 confirm; verify; bear testimony to; bear witness to II (名) evidence; certificate: 出生～ birth certificate. 身份～ identity card. 许可～ permit

证词 zhèngcí (名) testimony

证件 zhèngjiàn (名) credentials; certificate; papers

证据(據) zhèngjù (名) evidence; proof; testimony: ～确凿. The evidence is conclusive.

证明 zhèngmíng I (动) prove; testify; bear out II (名) certificate; identification; testimonial: 医生～ medical certificate

证券 zhèngquàn (名) negotiable securities: ～交易所 stock exchange

证人 zhèngren (名) witness: ～席 witness-box; witness-stand

证实(實) zhèngshí (动) confirm; verify; bear out: 有待～ remain to be confirmed

证书(書) zhèngshū (名) certificate; credentials: 毕业～ diploma. 结婚～ marriage certificate

证章 zhèngzhāng (名) badge

政 zhèng (名) **1** politics; political affairs: ～党 political party. ～策 policy. ～变 coup d'état. **2** certain administrative aspects of government: 民～ civil administration

政敌(敵) zhèngdí (名) political opponent

政法 zhèngfǎ (名) politics and law

政府 zhèngfǔ (名) government

政见(見) zhèngjiàn (名) political views

政界 zhèngjiè (名) political circles; government circles

政局 zhèngjú (名) political situation; political scene: ～稳定. The political situation is stable.

政客 zhèngkè (名) politician

政论(論) zhènglùn (名) political criticism: ～文 political essay

政权(權) zhèngquán (名) political power

政体(體) zhèngtǐ (名) form (or system) of government

政委 zhèngwěi (名) political commissar

政务(務) zhèngwù (名) government affairs

政治 zhèngzhì (名) politics; political affairs: ～避难 political refuge. ～磋商

political consultation. ～家 statesman; politician. ～觉悟 political consciousness. ～派别 political faction

政治局 zhèngzhìjú (名) the Political Bureau

挣 zhèng (动) **1** struggle to get free: ～脱枷锁 shake off the shackles (or fetters) **2** earn; make: ～钱 earn a living; make money. ～100 块钱 earn (or make) a hundred *yuan*

see also zhēng

汁 zhī (名) juice: 桔子～ orange juice

之 zhī I (代) **1** [used as object]: 求～不得的好机会 a welcome opportunity. 无不为～高兴 Everybody feels excited about it. **2** [without actual reference]: 久而久～ with the passage of time II (助) [used to connect the modifier and the word modified]: 千岛～国 country of a thousand islands. 无价～宝 a priceless treasure. 缓兵～计 stalling tactics

之后(後) zhīhòu (名) after; afterwards; later: 天黑～他们才能回来. They'll be back only after dark. 我们吵了一架,从那～我俩再没说过话. We had a quarrel and since then we have not spoken to each other.

之乎者也 zhī-hū-zhě-yě pedantic terms; archaisms

之前 zhīqián (名) ago; before; prior to: 五一～我不能走. I can't leave before May Day. 动身～ prior to one's departure

芝 zhī

芝麻 zhīma (名) sesame; sesame seed: ～酱 sesame paste. ～油 sesame oil

支 zhī I (动) **1** prop up; support: 把帐篷～起来 put up a tent **2** sustain; bear: 体力不～ too tired to go on doing sth.; too weak physically to stand it. 吃这么一点怎么～得了一天? How can such a light meal sustain us through the day? 她疼得真有点～不住. She could hardly bear the pain any more. **3** send away; order about: 把她～开! Put her off (or send her away) with some excuses! 你自己做吧,别总是～别人. Do it yourself. Don't always order people about! **4** pay out or withdraw (money): ～款 pay out or withdraw cash II (名) branch: 分～ branch. ～局 branch bureau. ～店 branch store III (量) **1** [for stick-like things, songs, army units, etc.]: 五～蜡烛 five candles. 三～铅笔 three pencils. 一～歌 a song. 两～队伍 two (army) units **2** watt: 60～光的灯泡 a 60 watt bulb. **3** (of textiles) count: 60～纱 60-count yarn

支部 zhībù (名) branch (of a party)

支撑 zhīchēng (动) prop up; shore up; sustain: 力图～一个摇摇欲坠的政权 try to shore up a tottering regime

支持 zhīchí I (动) support; back; espouse: ～他们的正义斗争 support their just struggles. 我们～这种理论. We espouse this theory. II (名) support; backing: 这项建议赢得广大群众的～. This proposal enjoys the support of the popular masses.

支出 zhīchū I (动) pay; expend; disburse II (名) expenses; expenditure; outlay

支点(點) zhīdiǎn (名) fulcrum

支付 zhīfù (动) pay; defray: ～手段 means of payment

支架 zhījià (名) support; stand; trestle

支解 zhījiě (动) dismember

支离(離)破碎 zhīlí-pòsuì torn to pieces; shattered

支流 zhīliú (名) **1** tributary **2** minor aspects

支配 zhīpèi (动) **1** allocate; arrange: 合理地～时间 arrange one's time properly. ～劳动力 allocate the work force **2** control; determine: 思想～行动. Thinking determines action.

支票 zhīpiào (名) cheque; check: 旅行～ traveller's cheque

支使 zhīshi (动) order about: ～人 order people about. 把他～走 give sb. to understand that his presence is no longer desirable; send sb. away with an excuse

支吾 zhīwú (动) equivocate; hum and haw: ～其词 speak equivocally. 一味～ be evasive throughout

支援 zhīyuán (动、名) support; aid

支柱 zhīzhù (名) pillar; prop; mainstay

枝 zhī I (名) branch; twig: 树～ branches of a tree II (量) [for stick-like things or for flowers with a branch]: 一～步枪 a rifle. 一～樱花 a spray of cherry blossoms

枝节(節) zhījié (名) **1** side issue; minor aspect: ～问题 minor issue; side issue; minor problem **2** unexpected complications: 横生～ deliberately complicate an issue

肢 zhī (名) limb: 四～ the four limbs (of the human body)

肢解 zhījiě (动) see “支解” zhījiě
肢体(體) zhītǐ (名) limbs
只(隻) zhī (量) 1 [for one of a pair]: 一～手 one hand. 两～耳朵 two ears. 一～鞋 one shoe 2 [for certain animals, boats or containers]: 一～鸡 one chicken. 两～羊 two sheep. 一～小船 a small boat. 两～箱子 two suitcases
see also zhǐ
只身 zhīshēn (副) alone; by oneself: ～在外 be alone and far away from home; all by oneself
只言片语 zhīyán-piànyǔ a few isolated words and phrases
织(織) zhī (动) weave; knit: 纺～ spinning and weaving; textile. ～毛衣 knit a sweater. 钩～ crochet
织布 zhībù (动) weave cotton cloth
织锦 zhījǐn (名) brocade; picture-weaving in silk
知 zhī I (动) 1 know; be aware of: 这话不～是谁说的. I don't know who said this. 2 inform; notify; tell: 通～ notify II (名) knowledge: 求～欲 thirst for knowledge
知彼知己 zhī bǐ zhī jǐ know the enemy and know yourself
知道 zhīdào (动) know; be aware of; realize: 我不～这件事. I know nothing about it. 你的意思我～. I know what you mean. 那时我不～事情会有这么严重. I didn't realize that things could be so serious.
知法犯法 zhī fǎ fàn fǎ knowingly violate the law; deliberately break the law
知己 zhījǐ (名) a person for whom one has profound friendship built on mutual understanding
知交 zhījiāo (名) bosom (or intimate) friend: 他和我父亲是～. He is an intimate friend of my father's.
知觉(覺) zhījué (名) 1 consciousness: 失去～ lose consciousness; go into a coma 2 perception
知名 zhīmíng (形) well-known; famous: ～人士 well-known personage; public figure; celebrity. ～度 popularity
知情 zhīqíng (动) know the inside story; have inside information: ～人 insider; a person who knows the details of a criminal activity
知趣 zhīqù (形) know how to behave in a delicate situation; be tactful
知人之明 zhī rén zhī míng unusual ability to appreciate a person's intelligence and moral character
知识(識) zhīshi (名) knowledge: ～渊博 have profound and encyclopedic knowledge; be learned. 技术～ technical know-how. ～分子 intellectual. ～界 intellectual circles; the intelligentsia
知识(識)产(產)权(權) zhīshi chǎnquán intellectual property rights
知识(識)经(經)济(濟) zhīshi jīngjì knowledge economy
知晓(曉) zhīxiǎo (动) know; understand
知心 zhīxīn (形) intimate; understanding: ～朋友 bosom friend. ～话 true words from the heart
知音 zhīyīn (名) a person who is deeply appreciative of sb.'s talents
知足 zhīzú (形) be content with one's lot
蜘 zhī
蜘蛛 zhīzhū (名) spider: ～网 cobweb
脂 zhī (名) 1 fat; grease: 油～ fat 2 rouge: 胭～ rouge
脂肪 zhīfáng (名) fat: 动物～ animal fat
脂粉 zhīfěn (名) cosmetics
职(職) zhí (名) 1 duty; job: 尽～ fulfil one's duty. 辞～ resign. 免～ be relieved of one's post 2 post; office: 撤～ be removed (or dismissed) from office. 就～ assume office
职(職)称 zhíchēng (名) professional title
职工 zhígōng (名) workers and staff members
职能 zhínéng (名) function: ～部门 functional institution; functional department
职权(權) zhíquán (名) authority of office: 行使～ exercise one's functions and powers. 超越～ overstep one's authority. ～范围 terms of reference; limits of one's functions and powers
职务(務) zhíwù (名) post; duty
职业(業) zhíyè (名) occupation: ～运动员 professional sportsman. ～外交官 career diplomat. ～学校 vocational school
职员 zhíyuán (名) office worker; staff member
职责 zhízé (名) duty; responsibility; obligation
直 zhí I (形) 1 straight: ～线 straight line 2 straightforward: 有话～说

speak out what you have to say. 心～口快 frank and out spoken **3** vertical **4** just; upright: 正～ upright. 是非曲～ rights and wrongs II (动) straighten: ～起腰来 straighten one's back III (副) **1** directly; straight: 一～走 go straight ahead. ～飞北京 fly non-stop to Beijing **2** continuously: 他～按汽车喇叭. He kept honking the horn. 我～到半夜才睡觉. I didn't go to bed until midnight.

直播 zhíbō I (名) **1** direct seeding **2** live radio or TV transmission II (动) broadcast a radio or TV programme live

直肠(腸) zhícháng (名) rectum

直达(達) zhídá (形) through; non-stop: 开往上海的～火车 a through train to Shanghai

直到 zhídào (动) until; up to: ～现在 up to now. ～上星期我才收到她的信. I didn't hear from her until last week.

直观(觀) zhíguān (形) directly perceived through the senses; audio-visual: ～教具 audio-visual aids

直角 zhíjiǎo (名) right angle

直接 zhíjiē (形) direct; immediate: ～联系 direct contact. ～去檀香山 go straight to Honolulu

直截了当(當) zhíjié-liǎodàng straightforward; come straight to the point

直径(徑) zhíjìng (名) diameter

直觉(覺) zhíjué (名) intuition

直率 zhíshuài (形) frank; candid

直升机(機) zhíshēngjī(名) helicopter

直属(屬) zhíshǔ (动) be directly under: ～外交部 be directly affiliated to the Foreign Ministry

直爽 zhíshuǎng (形) forthright

直挺挺 zhítǐngtǐng (形) straight and stiff

直系亲(親)属(屬) zhíxì qīnshǔ next of kin; immediate dependent

直辖 zhíxiá (形) directly under the jurisdiction of: ～市 municipality directly under the Central Government

直线(綫) zhíxiàn I (名) straight line II (副) sharp (rise or fall): 产量～上升. The output has shot up.

直销 zhíxiāo (动) direct sale; direct marketing

直性子 zhíxìngzi (名) straightforward person

直言 zhíyán (动) speak bluntly: ～不讳 call a spade a spade

直译(譯) zhíyì (动) literal translation

直至 zhízhì (动) until; up to: ～此时 up to this moment

植 zhí (动) plant; grow: 移～ transplant

植被 zhíbèi (名) vegetation

植树 zhíshù (动) plant trees: ～造林 afforestation

植物 zhíwù (名) plant; flora: ～检疫 plant quarantine. ～学 botany. ～园 botanical garden. ～油 vegetable oil. ～人 human vegetable; vegetable; vegetative patient

殖 zhí (动) breed: 生～ breed; reproduce. 繁～ reproduce; multiply

殖民 zhímín (动) colonize: 非～化 decolonize. ～统治 colonial rule. ～扩张 colonial expansion

殖民地 zhímíndì (名) colony

殖民主义(義) zhímínzhǔyì (名) colonialism: ～者 colonialist

值 zhí I (名) value: 价～ cost; value. 币～ currency value II (动) **1** be worth: 这车不～5 000美元. This car is not worth 5,000 dollars. 不～一提 not worth mentioning **2** happen to: 我们到时适～雨季. We happened to arrive there in the rainy season. **3** be on duty: ～夜 be on the night shift

值班 zhíbān (动) be on duty

值得 zhíde (动) **1** be worth the money **2** be of value: 不～ not worthwhile. 这些事～牢记. These facts are worth bearing in mind.

值钱(錢) zhíqián (形) costly; valuable

值勤 zhíqín (动) (of soldiers, policemen, etc.) be on duty

值日 zhírì (动) (of school children, etc.) be on duty for the day

执(執) zhí (动) **1** hold; grasp: ～笔 do the writing **2** take charge of; manage **3** persist: 各～一词. Different people tell different stories. *or* Different people hold different views.

执笔(筆) zhíbǐ (动) write; do the actual writing: 这报告是经小组讨论,由老王～的. The report was discussed in the group, but Lao Wang did the actual writing.

执法 zhífǎ (动) enforce the law

执迷不悟 zhí mí bù wù persist in pursuing a wrong course; refuse to mend one's ways

执拗 zhíniù (形) stubborn; wilful

执勤 zhíqín (动) be on duty

执行 zhíxíng (动) carry out; execute; implement: ～命令 carry out an order. ～政策 implement a policy. ～机构 executive body

执意 zhíyì (动) insist on: ～不肯 obstinately refuse

执照 zhízhào (名) licence; permit: 驾驶～ driver's licence

执政 zhízhèng (动) be in power; be in office: ～党 the party in power; the ruling party

侄 zhí (名) nephew (brother's son)

侄女 zhínǚ (名) niece

侄子 zhízi (名) nephew

止 zhǐ I (动) 1 stop: 中～ stop halfway; suspend. ～血 stop bleeding. ～渴 quench one's thirst 2 to; till: 到目前为～ to date; up to now II (副) only: 不～一次,而是多次 not just once, but many times

止步 zhǐbù (动) halt; stop: ～不前 stand still; mark time. 请～ out of bounds

止境 zhǐjìng (名) limit; boundary: 学无～. Learning is without limit.

止痛 zhǐtòng (动) relieve (or stop) pain: ～片 painkiller

址 zhǐ (名) location; site: 校～ the location of the school. 地～ address

趾 zhǐ (名) toe

趾高气(氣)扬(揚) zhǐgāo-qìyáng arrogant; haughty

趾甲 zhǐjiǎ (名) toenail

只 zhǐ (副) only; merely: 屋里～有我一个人. I was alone in the room.

see also zhī

只不过(過) zhǐ bùguò (副) only; just; merely: 我～是开个玩笑. I was only joking.

只得 zhǐdé (副) have to; be obliged to

只顾(顧) zhǐgù (副) be absorbed in; merely; simply: 你俩～说话,连我们到这儿干什么都忘了. The two of you are talking non-stop, even forgetting what we are here for.

只管 zhǐguǎn (副) by all means: 你有话～说吧! Feel free to say what you will.

只好 zhǐhǎo (副) have to: 时间到了,这个问题～下次再谈. Time is up. We'll have to discuss it again next time.

只是 zhǐshì I (副) 1 merely; only; just: 没什么,我～有点好奇而已. Oh, nothing particular. I was being a little curious. 2 simply: 他～摇头,不回答. He simply shook his head and refused to say a thing. II (连) but; however: 这件大衣样式很好,～颜色太鲜了一点. This coat is very stylish, only the colour is a little too bright.

只要 zhǐyào (连) so long as; provided: ～记住这点,就不会出问题. As long as you remember this, there will be no problem.

只有 zhǐyǒu (连) only; alone: ～你亲自跟他说,他才会同意去. He won't agree to go unless you talk to him personally.

只争朝夕 zhǐ zhēng zhāo-xī seize every minute; seize the day, seize the hour; race against the time

纸 zhǐ (名) paper: 一张白～ a blank sheet of paper

纸板 zhǐbǎn (名) cardboard

纸币(幣) zhǐbì (名) paper money; note

纸浆 zhǐjiāng (名) paper pulp; pulp

纸巾 zhǐjīn (名) tissue; paper towel

纸老虎 zhǐlǎohǔ (名) paper tiger

纸牌 zhǐpái (名) playing cards

纸上谈兵 zhǐshàng tán bīng be an armchair strategist; talk glibly about generalities without getting down to specific problems

纸烟 zhǐyān (名) cigarette

纸张(張) zhǐzhāng (名) paper

纸醉金迷 zhǐzuì-jīnmí a life of luxury and dissipation

旨 zhǐ (名) purport; purpose: 要～ main idea; gist. 宗～ purpose; aim. 会议通过了一系列～在进一步加强两国科学技术合作的决议. The meeting adopted a series of resolutions aimed at further strengthening the cooperation between our two countries in the field of science and technology.

旨意 zhǐyì (名) decree; order

指 zhǐ I (名) finger: 屈～可数 can be counted on one's fingers: 首屈一～的当代作家 a modern writer of the first water II (动) 1 point at; point to: 他～着远处的一座村落. He pointed to a distant village. 2 indicate; point out: ～出缺点 point out the shortcomings 3 depend on; count on: 单～望一个人是不能把事情做好的. You can't just count upon one single person to get the work done properly.

指标(標) zhǐbiāo (名) target; quota; norm: 生产～ production target. 质量～ quality index

指导(導) zhǐdǎo (动) guide; direct: ～思想 guiding principle. ～性计划 guidance planning

指点(點) zhǐdiǎn (动) instruct; give directions (or advice)

指定 zhǐdìng (动) appoint; assign; name: 到～的地方集合 assemble at the appointed meeting place

指挥 zhǐhuī I (动) command; direct; conduct: ～部队 command the armed forces. ～作战 direct operations. ～乐队 conduct an orchestra. ～所 command post II (名) commander; director; conductor

指挥部 zhǐhuībù (名) headquarters

指甲 zhǐjia (名) nail: 手～ fingernail. 脚～ toenail. ～刀 nail clippers. ～油 nail polish

指教 zhǐjiào (动) give advice: 望不吝～. Feel free to give your suggestions.

指控 zhǐkòng (动) accuse (sb. of); charge (sb. with)

指令 zhǐlìng (名) order; instruction: ～性计划 mandatory planning

指名 zhǐmíng (动) mention by name: 我不愿～道姓. I don't want to name names. ～攻击 attack sb. by name

指明 zhǐmíng (动) point out; show clearly: ～事情的严重性 point out the serious nature of the matter

指南 zhǐnán (名) guide; guidebook

指南针 zhǐnánzhēn (名) compass

指派 zhǐpài (动) appoint; designate

指日可待 zhǐ rì kě dài can soon be expected: 计划的完成～. The completion of the project is soon to be expected.

指桑骂槐 zhǐ sāng mà huái make innuendoes

指使 zhǐshǐ (动) incite; instigate: 受人～ act on sb.'s instigation

指示 zhǐshì I (动) 1 indicate; point out: ～剂 indicator. ～灯 pilot lamp 2 instruct; order II (名) order; instruction

指示器 zhǐshìqì (名) indicator

指手画(畫)脚 zhǐshǒu-huàjiǎo talk excitedly with wild gestures; make unwarranted remarks

指数(數) zhǐshù (名) index number; index: 生活费～ cost of living index. 综合～ composite index. 道琼斯股票～ Dow-Jones index

指头(頭) zhǐtou (名) 1 finger 2 toe

指望 zhǐwang I (动) look forward to; count on; expect: ～今年有好收成. We expect a good harvest this year. II (名) hope: 他的事还有～吗? Is there still hope of his eventual success?

指纹 zhǐwén (名) fingerprint

指引 zhǐyǐn (动) guide

指责 zhǐzé (动) censure; criticize: 横加～ make savage criticisms. 她的行为是无可～的. Her conduct is above reproach.

指摘 zhǐzhāi (动) nitpick

指战(戰)员 zhǐzhànyuán (名) officers and men

指针 zhǐzhēn (名) 1 (needle) indicator; pointer 2 guiding principle; guideline

指正 zhǐzhèng (动) correct; make a comment or criticism: 有不对的地方请大家～. Don't hesitate to criticize us for our inadequacies and errors.

滞(滯) zhì (形) stagnant; sluggish

滞留 zhìliú (动) be detained; be held up

滞销 zhìxiāo (动) not readily marketable: 这种货物～. There is little market for such goods.

滞胀(脹) zhìzhàng (名) stagflation

治 zhì (动) 1 rule; govern 2 harness; control: ～水 harness a river. ～沙 control sand 3 treat; cure: ～病 treat an illness 4 punish: 大家决定～～他. We've decided to teach him a lesson.

治安 zhì'ān (名) public order or security: 维持～ maintain law and order

治病救人 zhìbìng-jiùrén cure the sickness to save the patient; criticize a person in order to help him

治家 zhìjiā (动) manage a household

治理 zhìlǐ (动) 1 administer; govern: ～国家 run a state 2 harness; bring under control: ～河流 harness (or tame) a river

治疗(療) zhìliáo (动) treat; cure

治丧(喪) zhìsāng (动) make funeral arrangements: ～委员会 funeral committee

治外法权(權) zhìwài fǎquán (名) extraterritoriality; extrality

治学(學) zhìxué (动) pursue scholarly work: ～严谨 rigorous scholarship

治罪 zhìzuì (动) punish sb. (for a crime)

志 zhì (名) 1 will; aspiration: 雄心壮～ have lofty aspirations. 胸怀大～ cherish noble ambitions. 立～ dedicate oneself to a cause 2 records; annals: 县

～ annals of a county **3** mark; sign: 标～ mark

志哀 zhì'āi (动) show signs of mourning: 下半旗～ fly a flag at half-mast as a sign of mourning

志大才疏 zhì dà cái shū have high aspirations but little ability

志气(氣) zhìqì (名) aspiration; ambition: 长自己～,灭敌人威风 boost our morale and dampen the enemy's spirit

志士 zhìshì (名) person of ideals and integrity

志同道合 zhìtóng-dàohé have a common goal

志向 zhìxiàng (名) ideal; ambition: ～远大 have high aspirations

志愿 zhìyuàn I (名) ideal; wish II (动) volunteer: 他身体并不强壮,但他～献血. He volunteers to donate his blood although he is far from strong physically.

痣
zhì (名) mole

痔
zhì (名) haemorrhoids; piles

峙
zhì (动) stand erect; tower: 对～局面 confrontation

至
zhì I (动) to; until: 自始～终 from beginning to end. 会议开～下午五点钟. The meeting lasted until five o'clock in the afternoon. II (副) extremely; most: 欢迎之～ most welcome. ～感 (I am) deeply grateful

至诚 zhìchéng (形) sincere: ～的朋友 a sincere friend

至迟(遲) zhìchí (副) at (the) latest: 我～星期天回家. I'll be home on Sunday at the latest.

至高无(無)上 zhìgāo-wúshàng supreme

至交 zhìjiāo (名) best friend: 多年～ a very good friend of long standing

至今 zhìjīn (副) so far; up to now

至亲(親) zhìqīn (名) next of kin; closest relative; very close relative: ～好友 very close relatives and friends

至上 zhìshàng (形) supreme; the highest

至少 zhìshǎo (副) at (the) least: ～你应该给我来个电话. You should at least give me a call. ～可以说,他将加快改革的步伐. He will speed up the reform, to say the least.

至于(於) zhìyú I (连) as for; as to: ～具体时间,现在还没决定. As for the exact time, we have made no decision yet. II (副) go so far as to: 她不～对她母亲这样吧? She wouldn't go so far as to treat her mother like this, would she?

窒
zhì

窒息 zhìxī (动) stifle; suffocate: 屋里的空气令人～. It's very close in here. 浓烟几乎使他～. He was very nearly suffocated by the smoke.

桎
zhì

桎梏 zhìgù (名) fetters and handcuffs; shackles

致
zhì I (动) **1** send; extend (respects, greetings, etc.): ～以热烈的祝贺 extend warm congratulations. ～电 send a telegram; cable **2** result in; incur: 招～不满 incur sb.'s dislike **3** concentrate: ～力于 concentrate on; be devoted to II (连) so that; as a result: 措词晦涩,～使人误解本意. The wording is so ambiguous that it leads to misinterpretations. III (名) interest: 故事曲折有～. The plot is intricate and full of interest.

致(緻)
zhì (形) precise; meticulous; refined

致癌 zhì'ái cause (or produce) cancer; be carcinogenic: ～物质 carcinogen; carcinogenic substance

致词 zhìcí (动) make (or deliver) a speech

致敬 zhìjìng (动) salute: 鸣礼炮二十一响～ fire a 21-gun salute

致力 zhìlì (动) be devoted to

致命 zhìmìng (形) fatal: ～的弱点 fatal weakness; Achilles' heel

致谢 zhìxiè (动) extend thanks to

致意 zhìyì (动) give one's regards to; extend greetings to

掷(擲)
zhì (动) throw; cast: ～标枪 javelin throw. 孤注一～ risk everything on a single throw; put all one's eggs in one basket

挚(摯)
zhì (形) sincere; earnest: 诚～ sincere. 真～的友谊 true friendship

挚友 zhìyǒu (名) close friend

帜(幟)
zhì (名) flag; banner

置
zhì (动) **1** place; put: 安～ find a place for; help sb. to settle down. 搁～ put aside; shelve. 漠然～之 be indifferent to the matter **2** buy; equip: 添～衣服 buy some clothes. ～家具 buy some

furniture 3 set up: 装～ fix; install. 设～ establish; set up
置办(辦) zhìbàn (动) buy; purchase
置产(産) zhìchǎn (动) buy property (esp. an estate)
置评 zhìpíng (动) comment on; discuss: 不予～ give no comment
置若罔闻 zhì ruò wǎng wén turn a deaf ear to; pay no heed to: 对我的忠言,他都～. All my words of advice fell on deaf ears.
置身 zhìshēn (动) place oneself; stay: ～事外 stand aloof from the affair; refuse to get involved in the matter
置信 zhìxìn (动) believe: 难以～ hard to believe
置业 zhìyè (动) buy property
置疑 zhìyí (动) doubt: 不容～ allow of no doubt; undoubtedly
置之不理 zhì zhī bù lǐ ignore; pay no attention to
置之度外 zhì zhī dù wài give no thought to 把个人安危～ regardless of personal danger
制 zhì I (动) 1 (製) make; manufacture: 机～ machine-made. 仿～ imitate; copy. 复～品 reproduction 2 control; restrict: 控～ control. 限～ restrict II (名) system: 公～ the metric system. 私有～ private ownership
制版 zhìbǎn (名) plate making
制裁 zhìcái (动) sanction; punish: 实行～ impose sanctions (upon). 受法律～ be punished by law
制成品 zhìchéngpǐn (名) finished products; manufactured goods; manufactures
制订 zhìdìng (动) formulate; work out
制定 zhìdìng (动) lay down; formulate: ～宪法 draw up a constitution. ～法律 make laws. ～政策 formulate a policy. ～计划 work out a plan
制动(動) zhìdòng (动) apply the brake: ～器 brake
制度 zhìdù (名) system; institution: 社会～ social system. 规章～ rules and regulations
制服 zhìfú (名) uniform
制高点(點) zhìgāodiǎn (名) commanding height
制革 zhìgé (动) process hides; tan: ～厂 tannery
制冷 zhìlěng (动) freeze (to preserve)
制品 zhìpǐn (名) products; goods: 奶～ dairy products
制胜(勝) zhìshèng (动) get the upper hand of: ～敌人 subdue the enemy
制图(圖) zhìtú (动) make maps; chart: ～学 cartography
制药(藥) zhìyào pharmacy: ～学 pharmaceutics
制约 zhìyuē (动) restrict; restrain: 互相～ condition each other; interact
制造 zhìzào (动) 1 make; manufacture: 中国～ made in China. 手工～ hand-made 2 create; fabricate: ～紧张局势 create tension. ～谣言 fabricate rumours. ～借口 create a pretext
制止 zhìzhǐ (动) check; stop; curb: ～通货膨胀 halt inflation. ～这类事件再次发生 prevent the occurrence of similar incidents
制作 zhìzuò (动) make; manufacture: 精心～ made with meticulous care
秩 zhì (名) order
秩序 zhìxù (名) order; sequence: 维持社会～ maintain social order. ～井然 in good order
智 zhì (名) wisdom; intelligence; wit: 足～多谋 wise and resourceful. 斗～ a battle of wits
智慧 zhìhuì (名) wisdom: 集体～ collective wisdom
智力 zhìlì (名) intelligence; intellect: ～测验 intelligence test. ～开发 tap intellectual resources
智谋 zhìmóu (名) wit; resourcefulness: 人们十分钦佩他的～. People greatly admire him for his resourcefulness.
智囊 zhìnáng (名) brain truster; think tanker: ～团 brain trust; think tank
智取 zhìqǔ (动) take (a fort, town, etc.) by strategy
智商 zhìshāng (名) intelligence quotient; IQ
智育 zhìyù (名) intellectual development
智者千虑(慮),必有一失 zhìzhě qiān lǜ, bì yǒu yī shī even the wise are not always free from error; nobody is infallible
稚 zhì (形) young; childish: 幼～ childish
质(質) zhì I (名) 1 nature; character: 性～ nature; character. 本～ innate character; essence 2 quality: 优～产品 high-quality goods 3 matter; substance: 银～奖杯 silver

cup. 流～食物 liquid food II (动) question: ～疑 call in question
质变(變) zhìbiàn (名) qualitative change
质地 zhìdì (名) texture; grain
质量 zhìliàng (名) 1 quality 2 mass
质朴(樸) zhìpǔ (形) simple; unaffected
质问 zhìwèn (动) question; interrogate
质疑 zhìyí (动) call in question; query
质子 zhìzǐ (名) proton
炙 zhì I (动) broil; roast II (名)〈书〉roast meat
炙手可热(熱) zhì shǒu kě rè very powerful and exceedingly arrogant
中 zhōng (名) 1 centre; middle: 居～ in the centre 2 in; among: 园～ in the garden. 家～ at home. 学生～ among the students 3 between two extremes: ～年 middle age. ～秋 mid-autumn. ～产阶级 middle class 4 medium: ～号 medium size. ～级 intermediate level 5 China: 洋为～用 make foreign things serve China
see also zhòng
中波 zhōngbō (名) medium wave
中不溜儿(兒) zhōngbùliūr (形)〈口〉mediocre; middling
中部 zhōngbù (名) middle part
中餐 zhōngcān (名) Chinese food
中草药(藥) zhōngcǎoyào (名) Chinese herbal medicine
中层(層) zhōngcéng (名) middle-level
中程 zhōngchéng (名) (of aircraft, missile, etc.) intermediate range
中等 zhōngděng (形) average; moderate: ～城市 medium-sized city. ～教育 secondary school education
中断(斷) zhōngduàn (动) suspend; break off; discontinue
中队(隊) zhōngduì (名) squadron
中饭 zhōngfàn (名) lunch
中共 Zhōng Gòng〈简〉(中国共产党) the Communist Party of China (CPC)
中古 zhōnggǔ (名) 1 the middle ancient times in Chinese history 2 medieval times
中国(國)共产(產)党(黨) Zhōngguó Gòngchǎndǎng the Communist Party of China; the Chinese Communist Party
中国(國)共产(產)主义(義)青年团(團) Zhōngguó Gòngchǎnzhǔyì Qīngniántuán the Communist Youth League of China
中国(國)科学(學)院 Zhōngguó Kēxuéyuàn the Chinese Academy of Sciences
中国(國)人民解放军 Zhōngguó Rénmín Jiěfàngjūn the Chinese People's Liberation Army
中国(國)人民政治协(協)商会(會)议(議) Zhōngguó Rénmín Zhèngzhì Xiéshāng Huìyì the Chinese People's Political Consultative Conference
中国(國)社会(會)科学(學)院 Zhōngguó Shèhuì Kēxuéyuàn the Chinese Academy of Social Sciences
中华(華) Zhōnghuá (名) China: 振兴～ rejuvenate (or revitalize) China
中级 zhōngjí (名) middle level; intermediate
中坚(堅) zhōngjiān (名) nucleus; backbone: ～力量 backbone force
中间 zhōngjiān (名) 1 among; between: 我们～他最年轻. He is the youngest among us. 2 centre; middle: ～派 middle-of-the-roaders; middle elements
中立 zhōnglì (形) neutral: ～国 neutral state
中流砥柱 zhōngliú dǐzhù mainstay
中篇小说 zhōngpiān xiǎoshuō novelette
中期 zhōngqī (名) middle period: ～选举 mid-term election
中秋节(節) zhōngqiūjié (名) the Mid-autumn Festival (15th day of the 8th lunar month)
中人 zhōngrén (名) middleman; go-between
中山装(裝) zhōngshānzhuāng (名) Chinese tunic suit
中世纪 zhōngshìjì (名) Middle Ages; Medieval times
中式 zhōngshì (形) Chinese style
中枢(樞) zhōngshū (名) centre: 神经～ nerve centre
中途 zhōngtú (名) halfway; midway: ～在东京停留两小时 stop over in Tokyo for two hours
中外 Zhōng-wài (名) China and foreign countries: ～合资企业 a Chinese-foreign joint venture
中文 zhōngwén (名) the Chinese language
中午 zhōngwǔ (名) noon; midday
中心 zhōngxīn (名) centre; heart: 研究～ research centre. 问题的～ the heart of the matter
中性 zhōngxìng (形) neutral
中学(學) zhōngxué (名) middle (high) school
中旬 zhōngxún (名) the middle ten days of a month
中央 zhōngyāng (名) centre; middle: ～政府

the central government
中央集权(權) zhōngyāng jíquán centralization (of authority)
中药(藥) zhōngyào (名) traditional Chinese medicine
中叶(葉) zhōngyè (名) middle period: 19 世纪～ mid-19th century
中医(醫) zhōngyī (名) traditional Chinese medical science
中庸 zhōngyōng (名) the golden mean (of the Confucian school)
中用 zhōngyòng (形) useful; be of use: 不～ be of no use; good for nothing
中游 zhōngyóu (名) **1** middle reaches (of a river) **2** the state of being mediocre
中止 zhōngzhǐ (动) discontinue; suspend: ～学习 discontinue one's studies. ～谈判 suspend (break off) negotiations
中专(專) zhōngzhuān (名) polytechnic school
中转(轉) zhōngzhuǎn (动) change trains: ～站 transfer station
中子 zhōngzǐ (名) neutron

衷 zhōng (名) inner feelings; heart: 无动于～ not be moved in the least. 言不由～ speak insincerely. ～心拥护 give wholehearted support to

忠 zhōng (形) loyal; devoted
忠臣 zhōngchén (名) loyal court official
忠诚 zhōngchéng (形) loyal; faithful
忠告 zhōnggào (名) sincere advice; exhortation
忠厚 zhōnghòu (形) honest and sincere
忠实(實) zhōngshí (形) faithful; reliable: ～朋友 devoted friend. ～信徒 faithful disciple. ～可靠 reliable
忠心 zhōngxīn (名) loyalty; devotion: 赤胆～ ardent loyalty. ～耿耿 faithful and devoted. 为教育事业～耿耿 be committed to the teaching profession
忠言逆耳 zhōngyán nì ěr good advice is not always pleasing to the ear
忠于(於) zhōngyú (动) be true to; be loyal to: ～祖国 be loyal to one's country
忠贞 zhōngzhēn (形) loyal and steadfast: ～不渝 be unswervingly loyal; loyal and unyielding

钟(鐘) zhōng (名) **1** bell **2** clock: 闹～ alarm clock **3** time as measured in hours and minutes: 几点～啦? What time is it? 三点～ three o'clock. 一分～ one minute

钟(鍾) zhōng (动) concentrate (one's affection, etc.)
钟爱(愛) zhōng'ài (动) love dearly; cherish
钟摆(擺) zhōngbǎi (名) pendulum
钟表(錶) zhōngbiǎo (名) clocks and watches; timepiece
钟点(點) zhōngdiǎn (名) time; hour
钟点(點)工 zhōngdiǎngōng (名) labourer paid by the hour; hourly-paid worker
钟情 zhōngqíng (动) be deeply in love: 一见～ fall in love at first sight
钟头(頭) zhōngtóu (名) hour

终 zhōng I (名) **1** end; finish: 年～ end of the year. 自始至～ from beginning to end **2** death; end: 临～ on one's deathbed; when one is dying II (副) eventually; in the end
终点(點) zhōngdiǎn (名) end point; destination: ～站 terminus; terminal
终端 zhōngduān (名) terminal
终归(歸) zhōngguī (副) eventually; in the end; after all: 这问题～会解决的. This problem will be solved in the end. 他～是你的亲戚. He is after all your relative.
终结 zhōngjié (动) come to an end
终究 zhōngjiū (副) after all; in the end
终年 zhōngnián(名) **1** throughout the year: ～努力工作 be hard-working all the year round **2** the age at which one dies: 他～78 岁. He died at the age of seventy-eight.
终身 zhōngshēn (名) all one's life: ～制 lifelong tenure. ～伴侣 lifelong companion (referring to one's husband or wife). ～大事 a great event in one's life (usu. referring to marriage). ～职业 lifelong job
终生 zhōngshēng (名) one's lifetime: ～难忘的教训 a lesson for life
终于(於) zhōngyú (副) at last; in the end
终止 zhōngzhǐ (动) stop; put an end to; terminate

冢 zhǒng (名) tomb; grave: 古～ ancient tomb

种(種) zhǒng I (名) **1** seed: 稻～ rice seeds. 播～ sow seeds **2** breed; strain: 良～ fine breed. 杂～ cross-breed **3** species **4** race: 黄～人 the yellow race II (量) kind; type; sort: 这～行为 this kind of behaviour. 好几～颜色 different colours. 各～情况 various conditions
see also zhòng
种类(類) zhǒnglèi (名) category; pattern;

type：属于这一～ come under this category

种种 zhǒngzhǒng（形）all sorts of；a variety of：由于～原因 for various reasons. 想尽～办法 try every means possible

种子 zhǒngzi（名）seed：～选手 seeded player；seed

种族 zhǒngzú（名）race：～平等 racial equality. ～隔离 racial segregation；apartheid. ～歧视 racial discrimination. ～主义者 racist

肿(腫)

zhǒng（动）swell；be swollen

肿瘤 zhǒngliú（名）tumour：良性～ benign tumour. 恶性～ malignant tumour；cancer

踵

zhǒng（名）heel：接～而至 follow at one's heels

中

zhòng（动）**1** hit；fit exactly：打～了 hit the target. 猜～ guess right **2** be hit by；fall into；suffer：腿上～了一枪 be shot in the leg. ～埋伏 fall into an ambush. ～煤气 be gassed

see also zhōng

中标(標) zhòngbiāo（动）get（or win）the bid or tender

中彩 zhòngcǎi（动）win a prize in a lottery

中毒 zhòngdú（动）be affected by a kind of poison or toxin：食物～ food poisoning

中风(風) zhòngfēng（名）apoplexy

中计 zhòngjì（动）fall into a trap

中奖(獎) zhòngjiǎng（动）draw a prize-winning ticket in a lottery；get the winning number in a bond

中肯 zhòngkěn（形）（of remarks）sincere and pertinent

中伤(傷) zhòngshāng（动）slander；vilify：恶语～ slander sb. viciously

中暑 zhòngshǔ（动）suffer sunstroke

中选(選) zhòngxuǎn（动）be chosen；be selected

中意 zhòngyì（动）be to one's liking

种(種)

zhòng（动）grow；plant；cultivate：～花（菜等）grow flowers（vegetables，etc.）. ～树 plant trees

see also zhǒng

种地 zhòngdì（动）do farm work

种田 zhòngtián（动）do farm work

仲

zhòng **1** in the middle：～裁 arbitrate **2** second month in a season：～夏 mid-summer

众(衆)

zhòng I（形）many；numerous：寡不敌～ be outnumbered II（名）crowd；multitude：大～ the mass of the people；the masses. 观～ spectators；viewers；audience（watching a performance，TV show，etc.）. 听～ audience；listeners

众多 zhòngduō（形）numerous

众口难(難)调 zhòng kǒu nán tiáo it is difficult to please everybody

众目睽睽 zhòng mù kuíkuí in the public eye

众叛亲(親)离(離) zhòngpàn-qīnlí be opposed by the public and deserted by one's followers；be utterly isolated

众矢之的 zhòng shǐ zhī dì target of a thousand arrows；object of angry public criticism

众说纷纭 zhòng shuō fēnyún opinions vary

众所周知 zhòng suǒ zhōu zhī as is known to all；as everyone knows

众议(議)员 zhòngyìyuán（名）congressman；representative

众志成城 zhòng zhì chéng chéng united we stand；unity is strength；unity is the path to victory

重

zhòng I（形）**1** heavy：箱子很～. This box is very heavy. 你有多～？How much do you weigh？**2** important：事有轻～. We must draw a distinction between trivial and important matters. **3** serious：伤势不～ not seriously injured or wounded. 案情很～ a very serious case II（名）weight：净～ net weight. 举～ weightlifting III（动）regard as important：敬～ respect. 看～ value. 为人所～ be held in esteem

see also chóng

重办(辦) zhòngbàn（动）severely punish（a criminal）

重兵 zhòngbīng（名）massive forces：～把守 be heavily guarded

重酬 zhòngchóu I（动）generously reward II（名）a high（or handsome）reward

重大 zhòngdà（形）great；major；significant：～原则问题 a problem of major principle. 意义～ be of great significance

重担(擔) zhòngdàn（名）heavy burden；heavy（or great）responsibility

重地 zhòngdì（名）a place of importance which needs to be carefully guarded

重点(點) zhòngdiǎn（名）focal point；emphasis：～大学 key university. ～工程

major project. ～建设 key development project
重读(讀) zhòngdú (动) stress: ～音节 stressed syllable
重负 zhòngfù (名) heavy load (or burden): 如释～ feel as if relieved of a heavy load
重工业(業) zhònggōngyè (名) heavy industry
重活 zhònghuó (名) heavy work
重金 zhòngjīn (名) a huge sum (of money): ～购买 pay a high price for
重力 zhònglì (名) gravity
重量 zhòngliàng (名) weight
重任 zhòngrèn (名) important task; heavy responsibility: 肩负～ hold a position of great responsibility
重视 zhòngshì (动) attach importance to; pay attention to: ～教育 attach importance to education. ～某人 think highly of sb. ～这件事 take this matter seriously
重头(頭)戏(戲) zhòngtóuxì (名) traditional opera involving much singing and action
重托 zhòngtuō (名) great trust: 不负～ prove worthy of the great trust reposed in one
重心 zhòngxīn (名) 1 core; focus 2 centre of gravity
重型 zhòngxíng (形) heavy-duty: ～卡车 heavy-duty truck
重要 zhòngyào (形) important; significant; major: ～人物 VIP; important figure; dignitary. ～关头 critical juncture. ～政策 major policy. ～因素 key factor
重音 zhòngyīn (名) stress; accent: 词的～ word stress
重用 zhòngyòng (动) put sb. in a key position

州 zhōu (名) an administrative division (state, prefecture, etc.)

洲 zhōu (名) continent

洲际(際) zhōujì (名) intercontinental: ～导弹 intercontinental missile

舟 zhōu (名) boat: 轻～ a light boat. 泛～ go boating

周 zhōu I (名) 1 circumference; circuit: 圆～ circumference. 环行一～ make a circuit of. 地球绕太阳一～是一年. It takes the earth one year to move around the sun. 飞机在上空盘旋三～才降落. The plane circled around in the sky three times before landing. 2 week: 上～ last week. 三～ three weeks II (形) 1 all over; all around: 众所～知 as is known to all 2 thoughtful: 考虑不～ not be thoughtful enough
周波 zhōubō (名) cycle
周长(長) zhōucháng (名) circumference; perimeter
周到 zhōudào (形) thoughtful; considerate: 服务～ offer good service. 他考虑问题十分～. He is very considerate.
周刊 zhōukān (名) weekly publication
周密 zhōumì (形) careful; well conceived: ～的计划 a well-thought-out plan
周末 zhōumò (名) weekend
周年 zhōunián (名) anniversary
周期 zhōuqī (名) period; cycle
周全 zhōuquán (形) thorough; comprehensive
周身 zhōushēn (名) all over the body
周岁(歲) zhōusuì (名) one full year of life: 今天孩子满～. Today is the child's first birthday.
周围(圍) zhōuwéi (名) around; round; about: 楼房～ around the building. ～环境 surroundings; environment. ～的居民 the neighbourhood
周详 zhōuxiáng (形) careful; complete
周旋 zhōuxuán (动) deal with; contend with
周游 zhōuyóu (动) travel round: ～世界 travel round the world
周折 zhōuzhé (名) twists and turns: 几经～ after many setbacks
周转(轉) zhōuzhuǎn I (名) turnover: 现金～ cash flow. ～率 turnover rate II (动) have enough to meet the need: ～不开 have not enough to go round

粥 zhōu (名) gruel; porridge

轴 zhóu (名) 1 axis 2 axle; shaft: 车～ axle 3 spool; rod: 线～儿 spool. 画～ roller for a scroll of Chinese painting
轴承 zhóuchéng (名) bearing: 滚珠～ ball bearing
轴心 zhóuxīn (名) 1 axle centre 2 axis: ～国 Axis powers; the Axis

肘 zhǒu (名) elbow

帚 zhǒu (名) broom

咒 zhòu I (动) curse; damn: 诅～ curse bitterly II (名) incantation: 念～ chant incantations
咒骂 zhòumà (动) curse; abuse; swear

皱(皺) zhòu (动、名) wrinkle; crease: 上了年纪,脸上就会起~. When a person gets on in years, his face begins to wrinkle. 别把我的书弄~了. Take care not to crumple my book.
皱眉头(頭) zhòu méitóu knit one's brows; frown
皱纹 zhòuwén (名) wrinkles; lines: 满额~ a furrowed brow. 鱼尾~ (at the corner of one's eyes) crow's-feet. ~纸 crepe paper; tissue paper
皱褶 zhòuzhě (名) (of clothing) fold
绉(縐) zhòu (名) (textile material) crape; crepe
昼(晝) zhòu (名) daytime
昼夜 zhòu-yè (名) day and night; round the clock
骤 zhòu (形) sudden; abrupt: 一阵~雨 a passing shower. 天气~变. The weather suddenly changed.
骤然 zhòurán (副) suddenly; abruptly: ~枪声四起. We heard a burst of gunfire from all around.
诸 zhū (形) all; various
诸侯 zhūhóu (名) dukes or princes under an emperor
诸如 zhūrú (动) such as: ~此类 so on and so forth
诸位 zhūwèi (代) 〈敬〉: ~如果同意,我不反对. If you are agreeable among yourselves, I have no objection.
猪 zhū (名) pig; hog; swine: 小~ pigling; piglet. 母~ sow. 公~ boar
猪圈 zhūjuàn (名) pigsty; hogpen
猪肉 zhūròu (名) pork
猪食 zhūshí (名) pigwash; swill
猪油 zhūyóu (名) lard
猪鬃 zhūzōng (名) (hog) bristles
朱 zhū (形) vermilion
朱红 zhūhóng (形) vermilion; bright red
朱门(門) zhūmén (名) vermilion gates (red-lacquered gates of wealthy people's mansions)
诛 zhū (动) 〈书〉 put (a criminal) to death: 口~笔伐 denounce (a guilty person) both in writing and in speech
珠 zhū (名) bead; pearl: 珍~ pearl. 露~ dewdrops. 泪~儿 teardrop
珠宝(寶) zhūbǎo (名) pearls and jewels: ~商 jeweller
珠算 zhūsuàn (名) calculation with an abacus
株 zhū (量) [for plants and trees]: 四~桑树 four mulberry trees
株连 zhūlián (动) involve; implicate
蛛 zhū (名) spider
蛛丝(絲)马(馬)迹 zhūsī-mǎjì clues; traces (of a secret)
蛛网(網) zhūwǎng (名) spider web; cobweb
侏 zhū
侏儒 zhūrú (名) dwarf
烛(燭) zhú (名) candle: 蜡~ (wax) candle
烛光 zhúguāng (名) candlelight
烛台(臺) zhútái (名) candlestick
逐 zhú 1 pursue: 追~ pursue; chase 2 drive out; expel: ~出门外 drive out of the door 3 one by one: ~月增加 increase month by month
逐步 zhúbù (副) step by step: ~加以解决 settle sth. step by step. ~减少 phase down; wind down. ~升级 escalate
逐渐 zhújiàn (副) gradually: 他~习惯这里的气候了. He's getting used to the climate here.
逐项 zhúxiàng (副) item by item; on an individual basis
逐字逐句 zhú zì zhú jù word by word; verbatim
竹 zhú (名) bamboo: ~林 groves of bamboo
竹帛 zhúbó (名) bamboo slips and silk (used for writing on in ancient times)
竹竿 zhúgān (名) bamboo pole; bamboo
竹简 zhújiǎn (名) bamboo slip (used for writing on in ancient times)
竹笋(筍) zhúsǔn (名) bamboo shoots
主 zhǔ I (名) 1 owner; master: 一家之~ head of a family. 房~ landlord. 奴隶~ slave owner. 2 person or party concerned: 买~ buyer. 卖~ seller. 3 host: 宾~ host and guest 4 God; Lord 5 definite view: 心里没~ feel uncertain about sth. II (形) principal; main: 预防为~ put prevention first III (动) 1 be in charge of: 谁在这里~事? Who's in charge here? 2 hold a definite view; advocate: ~和 advocate a peaceful solution
主办(辦) zhǔbàn (动) sponsor
主编 zhǔbiān (名) chief editor: 报纸的~ the

editor-in-chief of a newspaper

主持 zhǔchí (动) 1 be in charge of; manage: ～日常工作 be in charge of the day-to-day work 2 preside over: ～会议 chair a conference. ～宴会 host a banquet 3 uphold: ～正义 uphold justice

主创(創) zhǔchuàng (动) principal creator: ～人员 principal staff and cast

主次 zhǔ-cì (名) primary and secondary: 分清～ distinguish between the primary and the secondary

主从(從) zhǔ-cóng (名) principal and subordinate

主打 zhǔdǎ (形) leading

主导(導) zhǔdǎo (形) guiding; leading; dominant: 起～作用 play a leading role. ～原则 guiding principle

主动(動) zhǔdòng (名) initiative: 争取～ try to gain the initiative. 尽量发挥别人的～性 give full play to other people's initiative

主犯 zhǔfàn (名) prime culprit

主妇(婦) zhǔfù (名) housewife; hostess

主攻 zhǔgōng (名) main attack

主顾(顧) zhǔgù (名) customer; client

主观(觀) zhǔguān (形) subjective: ～愿望 wishful thinking. ～努力 subjective efforts

主管 zhǔguǎn I (动) be in charge of; be responsible for II (名) person in charge

主婚 zhǔhūn (动) preside over a wedding ceremony

主机 zhǔjī (名) host computer; server; mainframe

主见(見) zhǔjiàn (名) one's own judgement; definite view: 她很有～. She is her own boss.

主教 zhǔjiào (名) bishop: 大～ archbishop. 红衣～ cardinal

主角 zhǔjué (名) leading role: 这部电影是她演～. She starred in this film.

主课 zhǔkè (名) main subject; major

主力 zhǔlì (名) main force

主流 zhǔliú (名) 1 main stream 2 essential aspect; main trend

主谋 zhǔmóu (名) chief instigator; chief plotter

主权(權) zhǔquán (名) sovereign rights; sovereignty: ～国 a sovereign state. 领土～ territorial sovereignty

主人 zhǔrén (名) 1 master; owner 2 host: 女～ hostess

主人公 zhǔréngōng (名) hero or heroine (in a literary work)

主人翁 zhǔrénwēng (名) master of one's own country

主任 zhǔrèn (名) director; head

主食 zhǔshí (名) staple food

主题 zhǔtí (名) theme; subject: ～歌 theme song

主体(體) zhǔtǐ (名) main body; main part

主席 zhǔxí (名) chairman; chairperson: ～团 presidium. ～台 rostrum; platform

主心骨 zhǔxīngǔ (名) backbone; pillar

主修 zhǔxiū (动) 1 specialize (in a subject); major: ～科目 major subjects 2 be responsible for the repair or overhaul (of a machine)

主演 zhǔyǎn (动) act the leading role (in a play or film)

主要 zhǔyào (形) main; major; chief; principal: ～原因 chief cause. ～目的 main objective

主页 zhǔyè (名) home page

主义(義) zhǔyì (名) doctrine; -ism: 唯物～ materialism. 唯心～ idealism

主意 zhǔyi (名) idea; plan; decision: 出～ give advice. 这个～不错. This is a very good idea.

主语 zhǔyǔ (名) subject

主宰 zhǔzǎi (动) dominate; dictate; control: ～世界 dominate the whole world. ～自己的命运 decide one's own destiny; be master of one's own fate

主战(戰) zhǔzhàn (动) advocate war: ～派 war party

主张(張) zhǔzhāng I (动) hold; maintain; advocate: ～开放政策 advocate a policy of opening to the outside world II (名) view; stand; proposition: 我赞成你的～. I am for your proposal. 我们一贯的～ our consistent stand

主旨 zhǔzhǐ (名) purport; substance; gist: 文章的～ the gist of the article

主治医(醫)生 zhǔzhì yīshēng (名) physician-in-charge; doctor in charge of a case

主子 zhǔzi (名) boss

煮 zhǔ (动) boil; cook

属(屬) zhǔ (动) 〈书〉 1 join; combine: ～文 compose a piece of prose writing 2 concentrate one's mind: ～望 look forward to

see also shǔ

属意 zhǔyì (动) fix one's mind on (sb. or sth.)

Z

嘱(囑) zhǔ (动) enjoin; advise; urge

嘱咐 zhǔfù (动) enjoin; exhort: 再三～ exhort again and again

嘱托 zhǔtuō (动) entrust: 人家～她好好照顾这个孤儿. She was entrusted with the task of taking good care of the orphan.

瞩(矚) zhǔ (动) gaze; look steadily: 高瞻远～ show foresight; be a person of vision. ～目 fix one's eyes upon

贮(貯) zhù (动) store; keep; reserve

贮藏 zhùcáng (动) store up; lay in: ～过冬的大白菜 lay in cabbages for the winter. 矿产～丰富 be rich in mineral resources

贮存 zhùcún (动) store; stock

注 zhù I (动) **1** pour: 大雨如～. The rain poured down. **2** concentrate: 全神贯～ concentrate on **3** annotate: 批～ make comments and annotations II (名) notes: 脚～ footnote

注册 zhùcè (动) register: ～处 registrar's office. ～商标 registered trademark

注定 zhùdìng (动) be doomed; be destined: ～灭亡 be doomed to destruction

注脚 zhùjiǎo (名) explanatory note; footnote

注解 zhùjiě I (动) annotate; explain with notes II (名) explanatory note; annotation

注明 zhùmíng (动) give clear indication of: ～出处 give sources (of quotations, etc.)

注目 zhùmù (动) fix one's eyes on: 引人～ eye-catching

注射 zhùshè (动) inject: ～器 syringe

注视 zhùshì (动) look attentively at; gaze at

注释(釋) zhùshì (名) explanatory note; annotation

注销 zhùxiāo (动) write off; cancel: 账已～. The account has been written off. ～登记 nullify the registration

注意 zhùyì (动) pay attention to; take notice of: ～台阶! Mind the steps! 过街要～! Be careful while crossing the road! ～力 attention

注重 zhùzhòng (动) lay stress on; emphasize

柱 zhù (名) post; pillar; column

柱石 zhùshí (名) pillar; mainstay

蛀 zhù (动) (of moths, etc.) eat into

蛀虫(蟲) zhùchóng (名) moth or any other insect that eats books, clothes or wood

住 zhù I (动) **1** live; reside; stay: 我在南方～了三年. I lived in the South for three years. ～旅馆 stay at a hotel **2** stop; cease: 雨～了. The rain has stopped. II [used after some verbs as a complement indicating a halt, standstill, etc.]: 站～! Halt! 接～! Catch it! 忍受不～了 can no longer stand it. 记～ remember; bear in mind

住处(處) zhùchù (名) residence; lodging: 你～在什么地方? Where do you live?

住房 zhùfáng (名) housing; lodgings; accommodation: ～问题 housing problems

住户 zhùhù (名) household

住口 zhùkǒu (动) shut up

住手 zhùshǒu (动) stop (doing sth.)

住宿 zhùsù I (名) accommodation: 安排～ try to find accommodation for sb. II (动) stay for the night

住院 zhùyuàn (动) be in hospital; be hospitalized: 我母亲～了. My mother is in hospital now. ～病人 in-patient. ～处 admission office (in a hospital). ～医生 resident (physician)

住宅 zhùzhái (名) residence

住址 zhùzhǐ (名) address

住嘴 zhùzuǐ (动) stop talking: ～,不许胡说! Stop talking nonsense!

驻 zhù (动) stay; be stationed: 我国～英大使 our ambassador to Britain. ～京记者 resident correspondent in Beijing

驻地 zhùdì (名) place where troops, etc. are stationed: 边防军～ frontier guard station

驻防 zhùfáng (动) be on garrison duty

驻军 zhùjūn I (动) station troops at a place II (名) stationed troops; garrison

驻守 zhùshǒu (动) garrison; defend

驻在国(國) zhùzàiguó (名) state to which a diplomatic envoy is accredited

驻扎(紮) zhùzhā (动) (of troops) be stationed

祝 zhù (动) offer good wishes; wish: ～你健康. I wish you good health. ～你一路顺风. Have a pleasant journey. *or* Bon voyage! ～你们成功! Good luck! Wish you success!

祝贺 zhùhè (动) congratulate: ～你们提前完成任务. We congratulate you on the fulfilment of the task ahead of schedule. 向您～! Congratulations!

祝捷 zhùjié (动) celebrate a victory
祝酒 zhùjiǔ (动) drink a toast; toast: 致~辞 propose a toast
祝寿(壽) zhùshòu (动) congratulate (an elderly person) on his or her birthday
祝愿(願) zhùyuàn (动) wish: ~您健康长寿! Wish you good health and longevity!
著 zhù I (动) write; compose: ~书 be a writer II (形) marked; outstanding: 显~的成就 marked success
著称(稱) zhùchēng (动) be noted for: 波士顿以红叶~. Boston is noted for its maple leaves.
著名 zhùmíng (形) famous; well-known: 一个~的医生 a well-known doctor
著作 zhùzuò (名) works; writings
助 zhù (动) help; assist; aid: 互~ help each other. 帮~ help. ~我一把 give me a hand. ~人为乐 find it a pleasure to help others
助词 zhùcí (名) auxiliary word; particle
助动(動)词 zhùdòngcí (名) auxiliary verb
助教 zhùjiào (名) assistant (of a college faculty): ~职务 assistantship
助理 zhùlǐ (名) assistant: ~编辑 assistant editor
助手 zhùshǒu (名) assistant; helper; aide
助听(聽)器 zhùtīngqì (名) hearing aid
助威 zhùwēi (动) cheer (for)
助兴(興) zhùxìng (动) add to the fun
助学(學)金 zhùxuéjīn (名) (student) grant
助长(長) zhùzhǎng (动) encourage: 这只能~他的骄气. This could only add to his arrogance.
筑(築) zhù (动) build: ~坝 build a dam. ~路 construct a road
铸(鑄) zhù (动) cast
铸工 zhùgōng (名) 1 foundry work 2 founder
铸件 zhùjiàn (名) casting
铸造 zhùzào (动) cast
抓 zhuā (动) 1 seize; catch; grab; grasp: ~住手臂 grab sb. by the arm. ~住良机 seize a golden opportunity. ~住讲话的重点 grasp the main points of a speech 2 arrest: 他被~起来了. He was arrested. ~住一名正在作案的窃贼 catch a thief red-handed 3 attract: 剧一开始就~住了观众. The play gripped the audience soon after it started. 4 take charge of: 他是~业务的副校长. He is a vice-president for academic affairs. 5 scratch: ~耳挠腮 scratch one's head
抓辫(辮)子 zhuā biànzi seize on sb.'s mistake; use sb.'s mistake to one's own advantage
抓差 zhuāchāi (动) draft sb. for a particular task; press sb. into service
抓紧(緊) zhuājǐn (动) keep a firm grasp on: ~时间 make the best use of the time. 你必须~治疗. You need an early and timely treatment.
抓阄(鬮)儿(兒) zhuājiūr draw lots
抓权(權) zhuāquán (动) grab power
抓瞎 zhuāxiā (动) be in a rush and muddle
抓药(藥) zhuāyào (动) have a prescription (of Chinese herbal medicine) made up
爪 zhuǎ (名) claw

see also zhǎo
拽 zhuài (动) drag: ~住衣袖 pull sb. by the sleeve
专(專) zhuān I (形) special: ~款 special fund. ~挑别人的毛病 be fond of nit-picking II (名) speciality: 一~多能 be expert in one thing and good at many; be a versatile person as well as a specialist III (动) monopolize: ~权 monopolize power
专长(長) zhuāncháng (名) special skill or knowledge; speciality: 学有~ have sound scholarship
专程 zhuānchéng (副) make a special trip to a certain place
专断(斷) zhuānduàn (动) make one's own decisions without consulting with others
专横 zhuānhèng (形) tyrannical; imperious: ~跋扈 despotic
专机(機) zhuānjī (名) special plane
专集 zhuānjí (名) special edition
专辑 zhuānjí (名) album
专家 zhuānjiā (名) expert; specialist
专科学(學)校 zhuānkē xuéxiào vocational training school
专栏(欄) zhuānlán (名) special column: ~作家 columnist
专利 zhuānlì (名) patent: ~权 patent right; patent. ~法 patent law
专卖(賣)店 zhuānmàidiàn (名) franchised store: 耐克~ a franchised Nike store
专门(門) zhuānmén (形) special; specialized: ~机构 special organ (or agency). ~术语 technical terms. ~知识

specialized knowledge; expertise
专人 zhuānrén (名) person specially assigned for a task
专题 zhuāntí (名) special subject (or topic)
专心 zhuānxīn (形) be attentive; be absorbed: ～致志 wholehearted devotion
专业(業) zhuānyè (名) special field of study: ～课 specialized courses. ～学校 vocational school
专业(業)户 zhuānyèhù (名) a rural family that goes in for a special kind of production; specialized household
专一 zhuānyī (形) single-minded: 心思～ give one's undivided attention
专用 zhuānyòng (动) for a special purpose
专员 zhuānyuán (名) (administrative) commissioner: ～公署 prefectural commissioner's office
专政 zhuānzhèng (名) dictatorship
专职(職) zhuānzhí (名) full-time job: ～人员 full-time personnel
专制 zhuānzhì (名) autocracy: 君主～ an autocratic monarchy
专注 zhuānzhù (形) absorbed; with one's attention fully held

砖(磚) zhuān (名) brick: 砌～ lay bricks
砖头(頭) zhuāntóu (名) brick
砖窑(窰) zhuānyáo (名) brick kiln

转(轉) zhuǎn (动) 1 turn; change: ～身 turn round. 好～ turn for the better 2 transfer
see also zhuàn
转包 zhuǎnbāo (动) subcontract
转变(變) zhuǎnbiàn (动) change; transform
转播 zhuǎnbō (动) relay (a radio or TV broadcast)
转产(產) zhuǎnchǎn (动) (of a factory) switch to the manufacture of another line of products; change the line of production
转车(車) zhuǎnchē (动) change trains or buses
转达(達) zhuǎndá (动) pass on; convey (one's message)
转动(動) zhuǎndòng (动) turn; move; turn round
转岗(崗) zhuǎngǎng (动) change one's job; transfer (of job or employment)
转告 zhuǎngào (动) pass on a message (to sb.)
转化 zhuǎnhuà (动) transform: 向反面～ change into the reverse
转换 zhuǎnhuàn (动) change; transform
转会(會) zhuǎnhuì (动) transfer (of professional sports player) from one club to another
转机(機) zhuǎnjī (名) a turn for the better: 形势有了～. The situation is improving.
转基因 zhuǎnjīyīn genetically modified; GM: ～水果 GM fruit
转嫁 zhuǎnjià (动) shift; transfer: 把罪责～给他人 shift the blame onto others
转交 zhuǎnjiāo (动) pass on; forward
转口 zhuǎnkǒu transit: ～贸易 entrepot trade; transit trade
转念 zhuǎnniàn (动) think over: 他刚想开口说话,但一～,觉得还是暂时不提为好. He was just going to speak when, on second thoughts, he felt it better not to bring up the matter for the time being.
转让(讓) zhuǎnràng (动) transfer one's right in sth.: 票不能～. This ticket is not transferable. 技术～ technological transaction; technical transfer
转入 zhuǎnrù (动) change over to: 从人类学～语言学学习 switch from anthropology to linguistics
转身 zhuǎnshēn (动) (of a person) turn round
转手 zhuǎnshǒu (动) 1 pass on 2 sell what one has bought
转述 zhuǎnshù (动) tell or report sth. as told by another; retell
转瞬间 zhuǎnshùnjiān in the twinkling of an eye
转弯(彎) zhuǎnwān (动) make a turn; turn a corner: 到下一个红绿灯就向右～. Turn right when you get to the next traffic lights.
转弯(彎)抹角 zhuǎnwān-mòjiǎo 1 full of twists and turns 2 speak in a roundabout way: 有话直说,别～的. Say what you want to, but don't beat about the bush.
转危为(爲)安 zhuǎn wēi wéi ān turn danger into safety; pull through a crisis
转向 zhuǎnxiàng (动) change direction
转型 zhuǎnxíng (动) 1 change the line of production 2 transformation (of society)
转学(學) zhuǎnxué (动) (of a student) transfer to another school: ～生 transfer student
转眼 zhuǎnyǎn (副) in the twinkling of an

eye; soon: ～又是秋天了. It'll be autumn before we are aware of it.

转业(業) zhuǎnyè (动) (of an officer) be transferred to civilian work

转移 zhuǎnyí (动) **1** shift; transfer: ～当地居民 evacuate the local people. ～重点 shift focus (onto...) **2** divert: ～视线 divert sb.'s attention **3** change: ～社会风气 bring about a change in social trends

转载 zhuǎnzǎi (动) reprint what has been published elsewhere

转战(戰) zhuǎnzhàn (动) fight the enemy successively in different localities

转账(賬) zhuǎnzhàng (动) transfer accounts: ～凭单 transfer document. 通过银行～结算 make settlement by means of transfer between bank accounts

转折 zhuǎnzhé (名) a turn in the course of events: 历史的～点 a historical turning point

转(轉)

zhuàn I (动) **1** turn; revolve; rotate; spin: 地球每24小时自～一周. The earth rotates once in every 24 hours. 轮子～得太慢. The wheel turns too slowly. **2** stroll: 出去～一～好吗? Do you feel like a stroll? II (量) revolution: 每秒钟一千～ 1,000 revolutions per second

see also zhuǎn

转动(動) zhuàndòng (动) turn; revolve; rotate; spin

转炉(爐) zhuànlú (名) converter

转速 zhuànsù (名) rotational speed

转向 zhuànxiàng (动) lose one's bearings; get lost: 晕头～ get totally confused

传(傳)

zhuàn (名) **1** biography **2** story (usu. in a historical style)

see also chuán

传记 zhuànjì (名) biography

传略 zhuànlüè (名) short biography; biographical sketch

赚

zhuàn (动) make a profit; gain: ～钱 make money

撰

zhuàn (动) write; compose: ～稿 contribute to newspapers, magazines, etc.

撰写(寫) zhuànxiě (动) write; compose

装(裝)

zhuāng I (名) clothing; outfit: 服～ garment. 西～ Western-style suit. 戏～ stage costume II (动) **1** pretend; feign: 不要～出什么都懂. Don't pretend to know everything there is to know. ～病 malinger. ～疯 feign madness **2** play the part: ～老太太 play the part of an old lady **3** install; fit: ～收音机 assemble a radio. ～电话 have a telephone installed **4** fill; load: 把书～进箱子 put the books in the box. ～行李 pack a suitcase. ～车 load a truck or a train

装扮 zhuāngbàn (动) dress up; disguise; masquerade

装备(備) zhuāngbèi I (动) equip; furnish; fit out II (名) equipment; installation

装裱 zhuāngbiǎo (动) mount

装订 zhuāngdìng (动) bind (books)

装潢 zhuānghuáng I (动) decorate: ～门面 decorate the shop front II (名) decoration

装货 zhuānghuò (动) load (cargo): ～单 shipping order

装甲 zhuāngjiǎ (形) armoured: ～车 armoured car

装门(門)面 zhuāng ménmian put up a front; maintain an outward show; keep up appearances

装模作样(樣) zhuāngmú-zuòyàng behave affectedly

装配 zhuāngpèi (动) assemble (a machine, etc.)

装腔作势(勢) zhuāngqiāng-zuòshì put on a pose

装饰 zhuāngshì (动) decorate; adorn: ～品 ornament; decoration. 室内～ interior decoration

装束 zhuāngshù (名) dress; attire

装蒜 zhuāngsuàn (动)〈口〉pretend not to know; feign ignorance

装卸 zhuāngxiè (动) **1** load and unload **2** assemble and disassemble: ～工 loader; stevedore

装修 zhuāngxiū (动) fix up: ～门面 give a building a facelift

装样(樣)子 zhuāng yàngzi put on an act

装置 zhuāngzhì I (动) install; fit II (名) installation; device

妆(妝)

zhuāng I (动) make up: 梳～ dress one's hair and apply make-up II (名) trousseau

妆饰 zhuāngshì (动) adorn; dress up; deck out

庄(莊)

zhuāng (名) village

庄户 zhuānghù (名) peasant household

庄家 zhuāngjiā (名) **1** banker (in gambling)

2 investor who tries to sway a stock price
庄稼 zhuāngjia (名) crops
庄严(嚴) zhuāngyán (形) solemn; stately; imposing
庄园(園) zhuāngyuán (名) manor; estate
庄重 zhuāngzhòng (形) sober; serious
桩(樁) zhuāng I (名) stake; pile; post II (量) [for events, matters, etc.]: 一～买卖 a business transaction. 小事一～ a trifling matter; it's nothing
幢 zhuàng (量) [for buildings]: 两～大楼 two big buildings
see also chuáng
壮(壯) zhuàng I (形) 1 strong; stout; healthy: 身体健～ be powerfully built; be physically strong 2 grand: 雄～ magnificent II (动) strengthen
壮大 zhuàngdà (动) grow in strength; expand; strengthen
壮胆(膽) zhuàngdǎn (动) do or say sth. intended to fill sb. with courage; boost sb.'s courage
壮观(觀) zhuàngguān (名) magnificent sight
壮举(舉) zhuàngjǔ (名) great undertaking; an act of heroism
壮阔 zhuàngkuò (形) immense and magnificent
壮丽(麗) zhuànglì (形) magnificent and enchanting; majestic: ～的诗篇 a splendid poem
壮烈 zhuàngliè (形) brave; heroic: ～牺牲 die a martyr
壮年 zhuàngnián (名) prime of life
壮士 zhuàngshì (名) hero; warrior
壮实(實) zhuàngshi (形) sturdy; robust
壮志 zhuàngzhì (名) lofty ideal; great aspiration: ～未酬 with one's noble ambitions unfulfilled
状(狀) zhuàng (名) 1 form; shape: 奇形怪～ grotesque; strange-shaped 2 condition; state of affairs: 现～ status quo. 症～ symptom 3 written complaint: 告～ sue sb. for; bring a lawsuit against sb. 4 certificate: 奖～ certificate of commendation. 委任～ certificate of appointment; commission
状况 zhuàngkuàng (名) condition; state: 目前的～ present state of affairs. 经济～ financial (or economic) situation. 历史～ historical conditions
状态(態) zhuàngtài (名) state of affairs; appearance: 心理～ psychology; state of mind. 呈透明～ be transparent
状语 zhuàngyǔ (名) adverbial
状元 zhuàngyuan (名) 1 the scholar who headed the successful candidates at the imperial examination 2 the very best (in any field)
锥 zhuī (名) 1 awl 2 cone
追 zhuī (动) 1 pursue; give chase: ～上他们 catch up with them 2 seek: 一生～求浮名而毫无成就 pursue transient fame all his life but accomplish nothing 3 get to the bottom of: ～究事情的根源 trace the root cause of the incident
追捕 zhuībǔ (动) pursue (a criminal)
追查 zhuīchá (动) trace; investigate: ～一项罪案 investigate a crime
追悼 zhuīdào (动) mourn sb.'s death: ～会 memorial meeting
追赶(趕) zhuīgǎn (动) run after
追怀(懷) zhuīhuái (动) recall: ～往事 recall the past
追回 zhuīhuí (动) recover: ～赃物 recover stolen goods
追悔 zhuīhuǐ (动) repent; regret: ～莫及 too late to repent
追击(擊) zhuījī (动) pursue the fleeing enemy
追加 zhuījiā (动) make an additional allocation for
追究 zhuījiū (动) look into; get to the roots of (a matter, etc.): ～事故的责任 make an investigation of the accident to find out who is to be held accountable
追求 zhuīqiú (动) 1 seek; pursue; go after: ～名誉地位 seek fame and position. ～真理 seek truth 2 woo; court
追认(認) zhuīrèn (动) 1 recognize retroactively 2 confer posthumously
追溯 zhuīsù (动) trace back to: 这座古老的建筑物可以～到第七世纪. This old building dates back to the 7th century.
追随(隨) zhuīsuí (动) follow: ～者 follower; adherent. 有人数众多的～者 have a large following
追问 zhuīwèn (动) inquire in great detail about; investigate
追星族 zhuīxīngzú (名) groupie
追寻(尋) zhuīxún (动) track down; search
追忆(憶) zhuīyì (动) look back; recall
追逐 zhuīzhú (动) 1 chase; pursue 2 seek:

～高额利润 seek exorbitant profits

追踪(蹤) zhuīzōng (动) track; be on sb.'s track

赘 zhuì (形) superfluous: 不待～言. Any further statement of the matter would seem superfluous.

赘述 zhuìshù (动) give unnecessary details; say more than is needed: 不必一一～. It is unnecessary to go into details.

赘疣 zhuìyóu (名) 1 wart 2 anything superfluous or useless

缀 zhuì (动) embellish; decorate: 点～ embellish; adorn

坠(墜) zhuì I (动) 1 fall; drop: ～马 fall off a horse 2 weigh down: 苹果把树枝～得弯弯的. The apples weighed the branches down. II (名) weight; pendant: 玉～儿 a jade pendant

坠毁 zhuìhuǐ (动) (of a plane, etc.) crash

坠落 zhuìluò (动) fall; drop

谆 zhūn

谆谆 zhūnzhūn (形) (of advice, instruction, etc.) earnest and tireless: ～告诫 repeatedly exhort. 言者～, 听者藐藐. Earnest words of advice fell on deaf ears.

准 zhǔn (动) allow; permit: 不～小孩入内. Children are not allowed in. 批～ approve. 获～ obtain permission. 不～张贴. No billing.

准(準) zhǔn I (名) standard; criterion: 高标～ high standard. 评选的标～ criterion for the selection. 外交～则 diplomatic norms II (形) 1 accurate: 他发音不～. His pronunciation is not accurate. 2 para-: ～军事组织 paramilitary organization III (副) definitely: 她～没去. She didn't go for sure. 这人～是她丈夫. This man must be her husband.

准备(備) zhǔnbèi (动) 1 prepare: ～发言稿 prepare a speech. 大家都～好了吗? Is everybody ready? 作最坏的～ prepare for the worst. ～出发 get ready to go 2 plan; intend: 我～明年春天到乡下走一趟. I plan to make a trip to the countryside next spring. 我今天不～讲了. I don't think I'll take the floor today.

准确(確) zhǔnquè (形) precise; accurate; exact: 给一个～的回答 give a precise answer

准儿(兒) zhǔnr (名)〈口〉certainty: 心里没～ feel uncertain

准绳(繩) zhǔnshéng (名) criterion; yardstick

准时(時) zhǔnshí (形) punctual; on time: ～平安抵达 arrive on time safe and sound

准星 zhǔnxīng (名) front sight (of a gun)

准许 zhǔnxǔ (动) permit; allow

准予 zhǔnyǔ (动) grant; approve: ～给假二日 grant a leave of two days absence

准则 zhǔnzé (名) norm; standard; criterion: 行为～ code of conduct.

捉 zhuō (动) 1 catch; arrest: 活～ capture alive 2 hold firmly; grasp: ～住 get hold of sth. or sb.

捉襟见(見)肘 zhuō jīn jiàn zhǒu find oneself confronted with difficulties too numerous to tackle all at once; have too many difficulties to cope with

捉迷藏 zhuō mícáng hide-and-seek

捉摸 zhuōmō (动) conjecture; predict: ～不定 unpredictable; elusive; difficult to conjecture

捉拿 zhuōná (动) arrest; catch: ～归案 bring sb. to justice

捉弄 zhuōnòng (动) tease; play pranks

拙 zhuō (形) clumsy; awkward

拙笨 zhuōbèn (形) clumsy; unskilful

拙见 zhuōjiàn (名)〈谦〉my humble opinion

拙劣 zhuōliè (形) clumsy and inferior: ～表演 a clumsy (or poor) performance

桌 zhuō I (名) table; desk: 餐～ dining table. 书～ writing desk II (量): 两～佳肴 two tables of delicious dishes

桌面儿(兒)上 zhuōmiànrshang on the table; aboveboard: 有话摆到～ put one's cards on the table; be aboveboard

浊(濁) zhuó (形) 1 muddy: ～水 muddy water. 污～ dirty; filthy 2 (of voice) deep and thick

浊音 zhuóyīn (名) voiced sound

卓 zhuó (形) remarkable; outstanding

卓绝 zhuójué (形) unsurpassed; extreme: 艰苦～ extreme hardships

卓识(識) zhuóshí (名) outstanding insight: 远见～ foresight and vision

卓有成效 zhuó yǒu chéngxiào highly effective; fruitful

卓越 zhuóyuè (形) brilliant; outstanding: ～的成就 remarkable achievements. ～的外交家 an outstanding diplomat

镯 zhuó (名) bracelet

着 zhuó (动) 1 apply; use: ～色 apply colour 2 touch; come into contact with: 不～边际 irrelevant; not to the point; neither here nor there 3 wear: 穿～体面 be decently dressed
see also zhāo; zháo; zhe

着陆(陸) zhuólù (动) (of airplane) land; touch down

着落 zhuóluò (名) 1 assured source: 这笔经费还没有～. We still don't know where to look for the money. 2 whereabouts: 那只失踪的船还没有～. The whereabouts of the boat is still unknown. 3 result: 他的工作还没～. He still hasn't got a definite job.

着手 zhuóshǒu (动) begin; set about: ～准备工作 get down to the preparations

着想 zhuóxiǎng (动) consider (the interests of sb. or sth.): 为他人～ have other people's interests at heart

着眼 zhuóyǎn (动) take as the basis: ～于人才培养 take the training of professional people as the starting point

着重 zhuózhòng (动) stress; emphasize: ～指出 point out emphatically

灼 zhuó I (动) burn; scorch II (形) luminous

灼见(見) zhuójiàn (名) penetrating insight

灼热(熱) zhuórè (形) scorching hot

酌 zhuó (动) 1 drink (wine) 2 weigh and consider

酌量 zhuóliàng (动) consider; deliberate

酌情 zhuóqíng (动) take the circumstances into consideration: ～处理 settle a matter fairly and reasonably; act at one's discretion

茁 zhuó

茁壮(壯) zhuózhuàng (形) sturdy; healthy and strong

琢 zhuó (动) chisel; carve
see also zuó

琢磨 zhuómó (动) 1 carve and polish (jade) 2 polish (literary works); refine

啄 zhuó (动) peck

啄木鸟(鳥) zhuómùniǎo (名) woodpecker

咨 zī

咨文 zīwén (名) 1 official communication 2 report delivered by the head of government on affairs of state: (美国的)国情～ State of the Union Message

咨询 zīxún (动) seek advice; consult: ～机构 advisory body

资 zī I (名) capital; fund: 投～ invest. 工～ pay; wages; salary. 川～ travelling expenses. 合～ joint venture II (动) provide: 可～借鉴 can serve as an example

资本 zīběn (名) capital: ～家 capitalist. ～主义 capitalism. ～市场 capital market. ～周转 turnover of capital. ～转移 capital transfer

资产(產) zīchǎn (名) assets; property; estate; capital: 固定(流动)～ fixed (liquid) assets. 无形～ intangible assets. ～冻结 freezing of assets

资产阶(階)级 zīchǎnjiējí (名) the bourgeoisie: 小～ petty bourgeoisie

资格 zīgé (名) 1 qualifications: 有～ be qualified. 代表～审查委员会 credentials committee 2 seniority: 摆老～ flaunt one's seniority

资金 zījīn (名) fund: ～外流 capital outflow. ～筹集 fund raising

资历(歷) zīlì (名) qualifications (including academic and work experience); credentials; record of service

资料 zīliào (名) information; data

资深 zīshēn (形) senior: ～教授 senior professor

资讯 zīxùn (名) information

资源 zīyuán (名) natural resources

资助 zīzhù (动) give financial aid

姿 zī (名) 1 looks; appearance: ～色 (of a woman) good looks 2 posture

姿势(勢) zīshì (名) gesture; posture; position: 站立～ (be) in a standing position

姿态(態) zītài (名) 1 posture; carriage: ～优美 elegant carriage 2 attitude; pose: 以和事佬的～出现 assume the role of a peacemaker. 高～ magnanimous. 保持低～ maintain (or cut) a low profile. 作出强硬～ take a strong posture; show intransigence

滋 zī

滋补(補) zībǔ (动) nourish: ～食品 nutritious food. ～药品 tonic

滋润 zīrùn (动) moisten

滋生 zīshēng (动) breed; flourish

滋味 zīwèi (名) taste; flavour

滋长(長) zīzhǎng (动) grow; develop: ～了骄傲情绪 become conceited

滋养(養) zīyǎng (动) nourish

髭 zī (名) moustache

吱 zī (象) 1 (of mice) squeak 2 (of birds, etc.) chirp; peep

吱声 zīshēng (动) utter; speak: 一直不～ keep one's mouth shut; remain silent or speechless

孜 zī

孜孜不倦 zī zī bù juàn diligently; assiduously

紫 zǐ (形) purple

紫罗(羅)兰(蘭) zǐluólán (名) violet

紫外线(綫) zǐwàixiàn (名) ultraviolet ray

紫药(藥)水 zǐyàoshuǐ (名) gentian violet

姊 zǐ (名) elder sister

姊妹 zǐmèi (名) sisters

子 zǐ I (名) 1 son: 母～ mother and son. ～女 sons and daughters; children 2 seed; egg: 瓜～ melon seeds. 鱼～ (fish) roe; caviar. 精～ sperm 3 sth. small and hard: 石头～儿 pebble. 棋～儿 chessman; piece 4 person: 女～ woman. 男～ man II (形) young; tender: ～鸡 chick. ～姜 tender ginger

子 zi [noun suffix]: 房～ house. 车～ vehicle. 镜～ mirror. 骗～ swindler; double dealer. 矮～ dwarf

子弹(彈) zǐdàn (名) bullet

子弟 zǐdì (名) 1 sons, younger brothers, nephews, etc.: 纨袴～ profligate sons of the rich; dandies 2 younger generation: 人民的～兵 the people's own army

子宫 zǐgōng (名) uterus; womb

子公司 zǐgōngsī (名) subsidiary company

子粒 zǐlì (名) seed; grain: ～饱满 full grains

子女 zǐnǚ (名) sons and daughters; children; offspring

子孙(孫) zǐsūn (名) children and grandchildren; descendants: ～后代 descendants; posterity

子午线(綫) zǐwǔxiàn (名) meridian

子夜 zǐyè (名) midnight

籽 zǐ (名) (of vegetables, etc.) seed

籽棉 zǐmián (名) unginned cotton

仔 zǐ (形) (of domestic animals and fowls) young: ～猪 piglet. ～鸡 chick

仔细 zǐxì (形) careful; attentive: ～观察 observe closely. ～听 listen attentively or carefully. ～研究 in-depth study

字 zì (名) 1 character; word: 汉～ Chinese character. 文～ writing system; writing. 象形文～ hieroglyph 2 form of a written or printed character: 斜体～ italicized word. 黑体～ boldface 3 calligraphy: ～画 calligraphy and painting 4 name: 签～ sign one's name

字典 zìdiǎn (名) dictionary

字迹 zìjì (名) handwriting: ～潦草 sloppy or illegible handwriting

字句 zìjù (名) words and expressions; writing: ～通顺 make easy and smooth reading

字据(據) zìjù (名) signed paper; receipt; contract

字里(裏)行间(間) zìlǐ-hángjiān between the lines: ～的意思不难看清. The implication is clear if we read between the lines.

字面 zìmiàn (名) literal: ～上的意思 literal meaning of a word

字母 zìmǔ (名) letters (of an alphabet): 汉语拼音～ the Chinese phonetic alphabet. 英语～ the English alphabet. 大写～ a capital letter

字幕 zìmù (名) caption (of film, video, etc.); subtitles

字体(體) zìtǐ (名) 1 style of calligraphy 2 typeface

字条(條)儿(兒) zìtiáor (名) brief note

字帖 zìtiè (名) copybook (for calligraphy)

字眼 zìyǎn (名) wording; diction: 玩弄～ play with words; wordplay

字纸篓(簍) zìzhǐlǒu (名) waste-paper basket

恣 zì (动) do as one pleases

恣意 zìyì (副) unscrupulously; recklessly; wilfully: ～践踏 wilfully trample on

自 zì I (代) oneself; one's own: ～问 ask oneself. ～画像 self-portrait. ～食其果 reap what one has sown; lie on the bed you have made for yourself II (副) naturally; certainly: ～当如此. It should be so as a matter of course. 我～有办法. I know how to handle it. III (介) since; from: ～古以来 since ancient times. ～小 from childhood. 来～大西洋彼岸 coming from the other side of the Atlantic

自爱(愛) zì'ài (名) self-respect

自拔 zìbá (动) free oneself (from pain or evildoing): 不能～ unable to extricate oneself from a difficult or embarrassing situation

自白 zìbái I (名) confession: ~书 a written confession II (动) vindicate oneself

自暴自弃(棄) zìbào-zìqì give oneself up for lost

自卑 zìbēi (形) have inferiority complex: ~感 inferiority complex; a sense of inferiority

自便 zìbiàn (动) at one's convenience; as one pleases: 听其~. Let him do as he pleases. 请~. Please do as you like.

自惭形秽(穢) zì cán xíng huì feel small; feel inferior to others

自称(稱) zìchēng (动) claim to be: ~作家 claim to be a writer

自持 zìchí (动) exercise self-restraint

自筹(籌) zìchóu (动) collect or raise (funds, etc.) independently: ~资金 raise funds independently; funds raised independently

自吹自擂 zìchuī-zìléi blow one's own trumpet; brag

自从(從) zìcóng (介) since; from

自大 zìdà (形) self-important; arrogant

自得 zìdé (形) self-satisfied: 洋洋~ smug; complacent. ~其乐 derive pleasure from sth.

自动(動) zìdòng (形) **1** automatic **2** voluntarily; of one's own accord

自动(動)扶梯 zìdòng fútī (名) escalator

自动(動)化 zìdònghuà (名) automation

自发(發) zìfā (形) spontaneous

自费 zìfèi (形) at one's own expense

自封 zìfēng (动) **1** proclaim oneself: ~的专家 a self-styled (or self-appointed) expert **2** confine oneself: 故步~ be complacent and conservative

自负 zìfù I (动) hold oneself responsible for sth.: ~盈亏 be held economically responsible II (形) conceited; be puffed up

自高自大 zìgāo-zìdà arrogant; self-important

自告奋(奮)勇 zì gào fènyǒng volunteer to undertake (a difficult task)

自给 zìjǐ (动) be self-sufficient: ~自足 self-sufficiency

自顾(顧)不暇 zì gù bù xiá be unable even to shift for oneself (much less look after others)

自豪 zìháo (形) be proud of; take pride in: ~感 sense of pride

自己 zìjǐ (代) **1** oneself: 你~做吧! Do it yourself! **2** closely related; own: ~的一间房子 a room of one's own

自己人 zìjǐrén (名) one of us: 今晚都是~. You are among friends tonight.

自荐(薦) zìjiàn (动) offer oneself as a candidate for a position

自尽(盡) zìjìn (动) commit suicide

自居 zìjū (动) call oneself: 以功臣~ consider oneself a war hero

自决 zìjué (名) self-determination

自觉(覺) zìjué I (动) be conscious of II (形) of one's own free will: 大家很~,都不在这里抽烟. Everyone consciously refrains from smoking here.

自夸(誇) zìkuā (动) sing one's own praises

自来(來)水 zìláishuǐ (名) running water; tap water

自理 zìlǐ (动) take care of oneself; provide for oneself; make one's own arrangements

自立 zìlì (动) stand on one's own feet

自力更生 zìlì gēngshēng self-reliance; rely on one's own effort

自量 zìliàng (动) estimate one's own ability: 不知~ unable to make a sober estimate of one's abilities or strengths; fail to understand one's own limitations

自流 zìliú (动) (of a thing) take it's own course: 听其~ let things drift along; let people do whatever they like without giving them proper guidance

自留地 zìliúdì (名) private plot

自满(滿) zìmǎn (形) self-satisfied; smug: ~情绪 complacency; self-satisfaction. 骄傲~ arrogant and complacent; conceited and self-satisfied

自鸣得意 zì míng déyì be pleased with one's temporary or insignificant success; talk with relish about what one regards as one's master stroke

自命不凡 zìmìng bù fán consider oneself head and shoulders above the ordinary run; pretentious

自欺欺人 zì qī qī rén try to make people believe something which even the person himself does not have any faith in: 这是~之谈. This is a hoax, pure and simple.

自取灭(滅)亡 zì qǔ mièwáng court destruction; take the road to one's doom

自然 zìrán I (名) nature: ~规律 law of nature. ~风光 natural scenery. ~淘汰 natural selection II (副) **1** in due course;

Z

naturally：过几天你～就会习惯的．You'll get used to it in a couple of days．到时候他～会明白的．He'll understand it when the time comes．**2** of course；naturally：～应该是我去啰！Naturally I am to go, aren't I？你～不用担心．Of course you should not worry about it．

自然 zìrɑn（形）unaffected；natural：表情～ look unaffected

自然主义(義) zìrán zhǔyì（名）naturalism

自认(認)晦气(氣) zì rèn huìqì look upon a piece of bad luck with resignation

自如 zìrú（形）〈书〉smoothly；with facility：运用～ handle（a tool）with skill；use with ease

自杀(殺) zìshā（动）commit suicide

自食其力 zì shí qí lì earn one's own living；earn one's bread

自始至终 zì shǐ zhì zhōng from beginning to end

自首 zìshǒu（动）surrender oneself to the police or judicial department

自私 zìsī（形）selfish；self-centred；egoistic

自讨苦吃 zì tǎo kǔ chī ask for trouble

自卫(衛) zìwèi（名）self-defence

自我 zìwǒ（代）self：～批评 self-criticism．～欣赏 self-admiration

自习(習) zìxí（动）（of students）study by oneself outside of class

自相残(殘)杀(殺) zì xiāng cánshā kill each other among members of the same group

自相矛盾 zì xiāng máodùn contradict oneself；be self-contradictory

自新 zìxīn（动）turn over a new leaf：改过～ correct past errors and start a new life

自信 zìxìn（动）be confident：～心 self-confidence

自行 zìxíng（副）**1** by oneself：～安排 arrange by oneself．～解决 settle a problem by oneself **2** of one's own accord

自行车(車) zìxíngchē（名）bicycle；bike

自修 zìxiū（动）study by oneself

自选(選) zìxuǎn（动）select by oneself：～动作 optional exercise．～项目 self-select items．～市场 supermarket

自学(學) zìxué（动）study by oneself：～教材 teach-yourself books．～成材 become educated without a master；be a self-made man

自言自语 zìyán-zìyǔ talk to oneself

自以为(爲)是 zì yǐ wéi shì be cocksure and impervious to criticism；be opinionated

自缢 zìyì（动）hang oneself

自由 zìyóu I（名）freedom；liberty：言论～ freedom of speech．新闻～ freedom of information．～党 Liberal Party II（形）free：～竞争 free competition．～关税区 tariff-free zone．～汇率 free exchange rate．～泛滥（erroneous ideas）spread unchecked．～散漫 easy-going and reluctant to observe discipline．～自在 happy-go-lucky

自圆其说 zì yuán qí shuō make one's argument sound plausible：不能～ cannot offer an acceptable explanation

自愿(願) zìyuàn（动）volunteer：～做某事 volunteer to do sth．～捐献 volunteer a donation．自觉～ willingly；of one's own free will．～退出 opt out

自在 zìzai（形）comfortable；at ease：感到不～ feel ill at ease；be embarrassed

自找 zìzhǎo（动）suffer from one's own actions：这是你～的！You asked for it．

自知之明 zìzhī zhī míng the wisdom of knowing one's own limitations；self-knowledge

自治 zìzhì（名）autonomy；self-government：～区 autonomous region．～权 autonomy

自主 zìzhǔ（动）be the master of one's own fate：～权 the power to make independent decisions．不由～ involuntarily

自助 zìzhù（形）self-service：～餐厅 cafeteria

自传(傳) zìzhuàn（名）autobiography

自尊 zìzūn（名）self-respect；pride；self-esteem：伤了她的～心 injure her self-esteem；hurt her feelings

自作聪(聰)明 zì zuò cōngmíng think oneself clever and act rashly

自作自受 zìzuò-zìshòu whatever a man sows, that he will also reap；be stewed in one's own juice

渍 zì（名）stain；sludge：油～ oil sludge．汗～ sweat stain

宗 zōng I（名）**1** ancestor：祖～ ancestor **2** faction；school：正～ orthodox school **3** purpose：万变不离其～．All changes, no matter how many, centre on one purpose．II（量）：一～心事 a cause for worry．大～款项 a large sum of money

宗教 zōngjiào（名）religion：～信仰 religious belief．～仪式 religious rites；ritual

宗派 zōngpài（名）faction；sect：～斗争 factional strife

宗旨 zōngzhǐ (名) aim; purpose: 联合国的~和原则 purposes and principles of the United Nations

宗族 zōngzú (名) clan

鬃 zōng (名) hair (on the neck of a pig, horse, etc.): 马~ horse's mane. 猪~ pig's bristles

棕 zōng (名) palm

棕榈 zōnglǘ (名) palm

棕色 zōngsè (名) brown

踪(蹤) zōng (名) track; trace; footprint: 跟~ be on the track of; shadow

踪迹 zōngjì (名) trace; track

踪影 zōngyǐng (名) trace; sign

综 zōng

综合 zōnghé (动) synthesize; bring into a state of balance: ~考察 comprehensive survey. ~性大学 a comprehensive university. ~报道 news round-up.

综合征 zōnghézhēng (名) syndrome

综述 zōngshù (动) summarize

综艺(藝) zōngyì (名) variety of art forms: ~节目 a variety show

总(總) zǒng I (动) sum up; put together: ~起来说 to sum up. 汇~ put (or gather) together II (形) 1 general; total: ~罢工 general strike. ~产量 total output. ~开关 master switch 2 chief: ~经理 general manager. ~编辑 editor-in-chief. ~公司 head company III(副) 1 always, invariably: 她~是迟到. She is always late. 他这人~能找到借口. He would invariably find some excuses. 2 eventually; sooner or later: 他的希望~会实现的. His wish will eventually come true. 你~会明白的. You will understand sooner or later. 这种事~是会发生的. These things will inevitably happen. 3 at least: 她~不会当面对他这样讲吧? At least she wouldn't say this to his face? 他走了~有一个星期吧. He's been away for at least a week. 4 anyway; after all: 他~是你的儿子. He is after all your son.

总得 zǒngděi (动) have to; must

总督 zǒngdū (名) governor-general; governor

总额 zǒng'é (名) total (amount)

总而言之 zǒng ér yán zhī in a word; in short

总共 zǒnggòng (副) altogether; in all: ~有一千人. There are altogether 1,000 people. 这几本书~要多少钱? How much do all these books come to?

总管 zǒngguǎn (名) person in overall charge

总归(歸) zǒngguī (副) eventually; after all: 这个问题~会得到解决的. This problem will eventually be solved. 他~是这个村子的人. After all, he is from our village.

总和 zǒnghé (名) sum; total; sum total

总机(機) zǒngjī (名) telephone exchange; switchboard

总计 zǒngjì (动) add up to; amount to; total

总结 zǒngjié I (动) sum up; summarize: ~经验 sum up one's experience II (名) summary: 做~ make a summary. ~报告 final report

总理 zǒnglǐ (名) premier; prime minister

总领事 zǒnglǐngshì (名) consul general: ~馆 consulate-general

总路线(綫) zǒnglùxiàn (名) general line

总数(數) zǒngshù (名) total; sum total

总算 zǒngsuàn (副) 1 finally; at last: 他最后~找到了一个满意的工作. He succeeded in finding a good job. 2 can almost be regarded as; on the whole

总体(體) zǒngtǐ (名) totality: ~规划 overall plan. ~设想 general idea. ~外交 total diplomacy. ~战略 total strategy

总统 zǒngtǒng (名) president (of a republic)

总务(務) zǒngwù (名) general affairs; general service

总之 zǒngzhī (连) in a word; in short

纵(縱) zòng I (形) vertical; longitudinal II (动) 1 let go; set free: 不能~虎归山. Don't set free a tiger. *or* Don't let an evildoer go unpunished. 2 indulge; not restrain: ~情歌唱 sing to one's heart's content. 3 jump; leap: 猫~身跳上围墙. The cat jumped onto the wall. III (连) 〈书〉even if; though

纵队(隊) zòngduì (名) column; file: ~队形 column formation

纵横 zòng-héng (形) vertically and horizontally; in length and breadth: ~交错 criss-cross. ~捭阖 manoeuvre among various states; tactics of a skilled diplomat

纵火 zònghuǒ (动) commit arson: ～犯 arsonist
纵情 zòngqíng (副) to one's heart's content: ～欢呼 cheer heartily
纵容 zòngróng (动) connive; wink at: 在某人～下 with the connivance of sb.
纵深 zòngshēn (名) depth: 向～发展 develop in depth
纵欲 zòngyù (动) indulge in sensual pleasures

走 zǒu (动) 1 walk; go: ～路去 go on foot; walk. ～一～ take a walk. ～进房间 go into the room 2 move: 这钟怎么不～啦! Why, the clock has stopped! 你这步棋～坏了. You have made a wrong move. 3 leave; depart: 她～了. She has left. 我该～了. It's time I left. *or* I must go now. 4 pay a visit to: ～亲戚 call on one's relatives 5 leak; leak out; let out: ～漏风声 let out a secret. 说～了嘴 make a slip of the tongue 6 depart from the original: ～调了 out of tune. 茶叶～味了. The tea has lost its flavour.
走动(動) zǒudòng (动) 1 walk about; stretch one's legs 2 socialize; visit each other
走访 zǒufǎng (动) interview; pay a visit to
走狗 zǒugǒu (名) running dog; lackey
走光 zǒuguāng (动) accidentally reveal parts of one's body
走过(過)场(場) zǒu guòchǎng make a gesture to give an impression of doing sth.
走红 zǒuhóng (动) become famous; gain popularity: 一夜～ suddenly have one's moment
走后(後)门(門) zǒu hòumén get in by the back door; secure advantage through influence; a back-door deal
走廊 zǒuláng (名) corridor; passage
走路 zǒulù (动) 1 walk: 这孩子已经学会～了. The child has learned to walk. 2 leave; get away
走马(馬)看花 zǒu mǎ kàn huā gain a superficial understanding through cursory observation
走南闯北 zǒunán-chuǎngběi journey north and south; travel extensively
走失 zǒushī (动) 1 get lost; wander away: 在人群中小孩～了. The child got lost among the crowd. 2 alter or lose its original meaning: 译文～了原意. The translation loses much of the original meaning.
走兽(獸) zǒushòu (名) beast
走私 zǒusī (动) smuggle
走投无(無)路 zǒu-tóu wú lù be in an impasse: 逼得～ be driven to the wall
走弯(彎)路 zǒu wānlù take a roundabout route; go astray; depart from the right course
走下坡路 zǒu xiàpōlù go downhill; be on the decline
走向 zǒuxiàng I (名) (of ore veins, mountain ranges, etc.) run; trend; alignment II (动) move towards; head for: ～反面 turn into one's opposite. ～胜利 advance toward victory. ～衰落 be on the decline
走穴 zǒuxué (动) moonlight (of performers)
走样(樣) zǒuyàng (动) deviate from the original model
走运(運) zǒuyùn (动) be lucky
走着瞧 zǒuzheqiáo wait and see: 咱们～! Let's wait and see.
走卒 zǒuzú (名) pawn; lackey; stooge

奏 zòu (动) 1 play (music): 独～ (instrumental) solo. 伴～ accompaniment 2 present a memorial to an emperor
奏效 zòuxiào (动) prove effective
奏乐(樂) zòuyuè (动) play music; strike up a tune

揍 zòu (动) beat; hit; strike: 把他～一顿 beat him up; manhandle him. 挨～ get a thrashing

租 zū (动) rent; hire; lease; let: ～电影院 rent a cinema. ～船 hire a boat. 房屋招～. Room to let.
租佃 zūdiàn (动) (of a landlord) rent out land to renants
租界 zūjiè (名) concession; leased territory
租借 zūjiè (动) rent; hire; lease: ～地 leased territory
租金 zūjīn (名) rent; rental
租赁 zūlìn (动) rent; lease; hire
租约 zūyuē (名) lease

卒 zú (名) soldier

族 zú (名) 1 race; nationality: 少数民～ national minority; ethnic group. 种～ race 2 clan 3 a class of things with common features: 水～ aquatic animals

足 zú I (名) foot: 赤～ barefoot II (形) 1 enough; ample: 丰衣～食 have plenty of food and clothing. 资金不～ inadequate funds 2 [often used in the neg-

ative] enough; sufficient: 微不～道 insignificant; negligible
足够 zúgòu (动) be enough; be sufficient
足迹 zújì (名) footprint; footmark; track
足球 zúqiú (名) soccer; football
足以 zúyǐ (副) enough; sufficient: 这些事实～说明问题. These facts suffice to illustrate the question in point.
足智多谋 zúzhì-duōmóu resourceful

诅 zǔ

诅咒 zǔzhòu (动) curse

祖 zǔ (名) 1 ancestor 2 originator

祖辈 zǔbèi (名) forefathers; ancestry; forebears
祖传(傳) zǔchuán (形) handed down from one's ancestors: ～秘方 a family prescription handed down from generation to generation
祖父 zǔfù (名) grandfather
祖国(國) zǔguó (名) motherland
祖母 zǔmǔ (名) grandmother
祖师(師) zǔshī (名) founder (of a school of learning, a religious sect, etc.)
祖孙(孫) zǔ-sūn (名) grandparent and grandchild: ～三代 three generations
祖先 zǔxiān (名) forefathers; ancestors
祖宗 zǔzong (名) ancestry
祖祖辈辈 zǔzǔbèibèi for generations

阻 zǔ (动) block; hinder; obstruct

阻碍(礙) zǔ'ài (动) hinder; impede: ～交通 block the traffic. ～生产的发展 hinder the development of production
阻挡(擋) zǔdǎng (动) stop; stem; resist: 不可～的洪流 an irresistible trend
阻击(擊) zǔjī (动) block; check: ～战 blocking action
阻拦(攔) zǔlán (动) stop; bar the way: 他一定要去,我们最好不去～. As he was bent on going, we had better not try to stop him.
阻力 zǔlì (名) obstruction; resistance: 冲破各种～ break through all kinds of obstructions. ～大 meet with no small resistance
阻挠(撓) zǔnáo (动) obstruct; stand in the way
阻塞 zǔsè (动) block; clog: ～交通 hold up traffic
阻止 zǔzhǐ (动) stop; prevent; hold back: ～谣言的散布 prevent the rumours spreading. ～事态恶化 prevent the situation from deteriorating

组 zǔ I (名) group: 分～讨论 be divided into groups for discussion II (动) organize: 改～ reorganize; reshuffle III (量) group; set: 两～人 two groups of people

组成 zǔchéng (动) make up; compose; consist of: ～部分 component part; component. 五十人～的代表团 a delegation composed of fifty people. 这个球队由二十名运动员～. This team consists of twenty players.
组阁 zǔgé (动) 1 form a cabinet 2 handpick people to set up a leading group
组合 zǔhé (动) make up; compose; combine
组织(織) zǔzhī I (动) organize: ～一次会议 organize a meeting. 这次展览会～得很好. This exhibition is well organized. ～内阁 form (or set up) a cabinet. ～演出 get up a performance II (名) 1 organization: ～处理 organizational measures; disciplinary measures. ～观念 sense of organization 2 tissue: 肌肉～ muscle tissue

钻(鑽) zuān (动) 1 drill; bore: ～孔 drill a hole 2 go through; make one's way into: ～山洞 go into a mountain cave. ～到水里 disappear into the water 3 make a thorough study of; dig into: ～研 make a persistent effort to learn. ～书本 bury oneself in books

see also zuàn

钻空子 zuān kòngzi exploit a loophole to one's own advantage: 不要让他～. Do not let him take advantage of this loophole.
钻牛角尖 zuān niújiǎojiān waste time and effort trying to solve an unimportant or insoluble problem: 喜欢～ be fond of hair-splitting
钻探 zuāntàn (动) drill (for exploratory purposes)
钻研 zuānyán (动) dig into; make a careful study of: 努力～业务知识 work hard to gain professional knowledge. ～技术 perfect one's skill; master the technique
钻营(營) zuānyíng (动) curry favour with sb. in authority for personal gain

攥 zuàn (动) grip; clasp

钻(鑽) zuàn I (动) drill; bore II (名) diamond

see also zuān

钻床(牀) zuànchuáng (名) drilling machine; driller

钻机(機) zuànjī (名) (drilling) rig

钻井 zuànjǐng (名) well drilling

钻石 zuànshí (名) diamond

钻头(頭) zuàntóu (名) bit (of a drill)

嘴 zuǐ (名) mouth: 闭~! Shut up! 光~上说 pay lip service. 瓶~儿 the mouth of a bottle. 烟~儿 cigarette holder

嘴巴 zuǐba (名) mouth

嘴唇 zuǐchún (名) lip

嘴紧(緊) zuǐjǐn (形) tight-lipped

嘴快 zuǐkuài (形) have a loose tongue

嘴脸(臉) zuǐliǎn (名)〈贬〉look; features

嘴皮子 zuǐpízi (名)〈口〉lips (of a glib talker): 耍~ talk glibly

嘴碎 zuǐsuì (形) garrulous

嘴甜 zuǐtián (形) fond of honeyed words

嘴硬 zuǐyìng (形) reluctant or unwilling to admit error or defeat

醉 zuì (形) 1 drunk; inebriated: 烂~ be dead drunk. 他有点儿~. He's tipsy. 2 (of certain food or fruits) liquor-saturated: ~枣 liquor-saturated dates

醉鬼 zuìguǐ (名) drunkard

醉汉(漢) zuìhàn (名) drunken man; drunkard

醉生梦(夢)死 zuìshēng-mèngsǐ lead an aimless and often dissipated life

醉翁之意不在酒 zuìwēng zhī yì bù zài jiǔ the drinker's mind is occupied with sth. other than wine — have ulterior motives

醉心 zuìxīn (动) be bent on; be engrossed in: ~于数学的研究 be engrossed in the study of mathematics

醉醺醺 zuìxūnxūn (形) tipsy; drunk

醉意 zuìyì (名) signs of getting drunk: 有几分~ be a bit tipsy

最 zuì (副) [indicating the superlative degree]: ~好 the best. ~小 the smallest. ~美丽 the most beautiful. ~能说明问题 can best illustrate this problem

最初 zuìchū (名) initial; first: ~阶段 the initial stage. ~印象 first impressions

最低工资 zuìdī gōngzī minimum wage or salary

最多 zuìduō (副) at most: 我在那儿~能呆三天. I can stay there for at most three days.

最好 zuìhǎo I (形) best; first-rate: ~的办法 the best way II (副) had better; it would be best: 你~先别告诉他. You'd better not tell him now.

最后(後) zuìhòu (名) last; final; at last; eventually: ~定本 final text. ~的结论 the final conclusion. 作~挣扎 make a last-ditch struggle

最后(後)通牒 zuìhòu tōngdié ultimatum

最惠国(國) zuìhuìguó most-favoured-nation; MFN: 给以~待遇 accord (a country) most-favoured-nation treatment

最近 zuìjìn (名) 1 recently; lately; of late: ~几年 in the last few years. ~的消息 the latest news 2 soon; in the near future

最终 zuìzhōng (形) final; ultimate: ~目的 the ultimate aim. ~的回答 the final answer

罪 zuì (名) 1 guilt; crime: 有~ be guilty of a crime 2 fault; blame: 归~于某人 lay the blame on sb. 3 suffering; hardship: 受~ suffer; have a hard time

罪大恶(惡)极(極) zuìdà-èjí be guilty of the most heinous crimes

罪恶(惡) zuì'è (名) crime; evil: ~滔天 be guilty of monstrous crimes

罪犯 zuìfàn (名) criminal; culprit

罪过(過) zuìguò (名) fault; offence; sin

罪魁祸(禍)首 zuìkuí huòshǒu chief criminal; arch-criminal

罪名 zuìmíng (名) charge; accusation

罪孽 zuìniè (名) sin: ~深重 be steeped in iniquity

罪行 zuìxíng (名) crime; offence

罪责 zuìzé (名) responsibility for an offence: ~难逃 cannot get away with (the crime)

罪证 zuìzhèng (名) evidence of a crime

罪状(狀) zuìzhuàng (名) criminal acts

尊 zūn (动) respect; esteem

尊称(稱) zūnchēng (名) respectful form of address

尊敬 zūnjìng I (动) respect; esteem; revere: ~父母 show respect to one's parents II (形) honourable; distinguished

尊严(嚴) zūnyán (名) dignity; honour: 法制的~ dignity of the legal system. 保持~ maintain one's dignity

尊长(長) zūnzhǎng (名) elders and betters
尊重 zūnzhòng (动) treat with respect; value: ～主权和领土完整 respect one's sovereignty and territorial integrity. ～知识 respect knowledge

遵 zūn (动) abide by; obey; observe

遵从(從) zūncóng (动) follow; comply with
遵命 zūnmìng (动)〈敬〉obey your instructions: 当～办理 will act in compliance with your instructions
遵守 zūnshǒu (动) observe; abide by; adhere to; comply with: ～公共秩序 observe public order. ～时间 be punctual. ～法律 abide by the law. ～诺言 honour one's commitment
遵循 zūnxún (动) follow; adhere to (principle, political line, etc.)
遵照 zūnzhào (动) act in accordance with; conform to; comply with

作 zuō

see also zuò
作坊 zuōfang (名) workshop

琢 zuó

see also zhuó
琢磨 zuómo (动) turn sth. over in one's mind; ponder

昨 zuó (名) yesterday

昨天 zuótiān (名) yesterday

左 zuǒ I (名) the left; the left side II (形) queer; unorthodox: ～嗓子 out-of-tune voice. ～道旁门 heterodoxy
左边(邊) zuǒbian (名) the left side
左派 zuǒpài (名) 1 the left wing 2 Leftist 3 progressive
左撇子 zuǒpiězi (名) left-handed person
左倾 zuǒqīng (名) "Left" deviation: ～错误 "Left"-deviationist errors
左舷 zuǒxián (名) port (of a ship)
左翼 zuǒyì (名) left wing; left flank
左右 zuǒyòu I (名) the left and right sides: ～摇晃 swing (from left to right); vacillate II (助) about; more or less: 五点钟～ about five o'clock. 两个月～ two months or so III (动) control; influence: ～局势 take the situation in hand. 被别人～ be swayed by sb. in one's attitude or views
左…右… zuǒ… yòu… [used to emphasize repetition of an action]: 左思右想 keep turning sth. over in one's mind. 左一个问题,右一个问题 one question cropping up after another
左右逢源 zuǒ-yòu féng yuán gain advantage from both sides; be able to achieve success one way or another
左右手 zuǒyòushǒu (名) one's right-hand man; valuable assistant
左右为(爲)难(難) zuǒ-yòu wéinán be in a dilemma

撮 zuǒ (量) [used for a bunch of hair] tuft: 一～儿白毛 a tuft of white hair

坐 zuò (动) 1 sit: 请～! Please sit down! ～在椅子上 sit in a chair. ～在板凳上 sit on a bench 2 go by; travel by: ～公共汽车 ride in a bus. ～火车 ride on a train. ～飞机 travel by plane 3 put (a pot, kettle, etc.) on a fire: 在炉子上～一壶水 put the kettle (of water) on the fire 4 (of guns) recoil; kick
坐标(標) zuòbiāo (名) (mathematics) coordinate
坐吃山空 zuò chī shān kōng sit idle and eat, and sooner or later your whole fortune will vanish
坐等 zuòděng (动) sit back and wait
坐垫(墊) zuòdiàn (名) cushion
坐井观(觀)天 zuò jǐng guān tiān see the sky from the bottom of a well — have a very narrow view
坐冷板凳 zuò lěngbǎndèng 1 hold a title with little or no duties 2 wait long for an appointment 3 be out in the cold
坐立不安 zuò-lì bù ān be restless; be fidgety; be on pins and needles; be on tenterhooks
坐落 zuòluò (动) (of a building, a house, etc.) be situated; be located
坐山观(觀)虎斗(鬥) zuò shān guān hǔ dòu sit on top of the mountain to watch the fight between two tigers — watch the struggle without being involved, then reap third party profit
坐失良机(機) zuò shī liángjī let slip a golden opportunity
坐视 zuòshì (动) sit by and watch; look on with folded arms
坐位 zuòwèi (名) seat
坐享其成 zuò xiǎng qí chéng enjoy the fruits of others' labour
坐以待毙(斃) zuò yǐ dài bì anticipate certain death without putting up a struggle
坐月子 zuò yuèzi be confined (in childbirth)

座 zuò I (名) **1** seat; place: 入～ take one's seat. ～无虚席 has a full house; be packed **2** stand; base; pedestal: 花瓶～儿 vase stand. 塑像～儿 pedestal for a statue II (量) [for large and solid thing]: 一～山 a mountain. 一～桥 a bridge. 一～铜像 a bronze statue

座上客 zuòshàngkè (名) guest of honour

座谈 zuòtán (动) have an informal discussion: ～会 informal discussion; forum; symposium

座位 zuòwèi (名) seat

座右铭 zuòyòumíng (名) motto; maxim

座钟(鐘) zuòzhōng (名) desk clock

作 zuò (动) **1** make; write; compose: ～画 paint a picture. **2** pretend; affect: 故～惊讶 feign surprise. 忸怩～态 be affectedly shy **3** regard as: 她把我当～亲生女儿. She treats me as her own daughter.

see also zuō

作案 zuò'àn (动) commit a crime

作罢(罷) zuòbà (动) cancel; drop; give up: 这事只好～. Well, the matter will have to be dropped.

作弊 zuòbì (动) practise fraud; cheat

作对(對) zuòduì (动) set oneself against; be antagonistic to

作恶(惡) zuò'è (动) do evil: ～多端 perpetrate numerous crimes

作法 zuòfǎ (名) way of doing things; method; practice

作废(廢) zuòfèi (动) become invalid: 过期～ become invalid after a specified date. 宣布条约～ declare a treaty null and void

作风(風) zuòfēng (名) style of work; way of life: 工作～ style of work. 生活～ way of life; life-style. ～正派 be honest and upright; have moral integrity. 实事求是的～ a practical and realistic way of doing things

作梗 zuògěng (动) obstruct; hinder; impede

作怪 zuòguài (动) make trouble

作家 zuòjiā (名) writer

作价(價) zuòjià (动) fix a price for sth.; evaluate

作料 zuòliao (名) condiments; seasoning

作孽 zuòniè (动) commit a sin

作呕(嘔) zuò'ǒu (动) feel sick (or nausea); feel like vomiting: 真是令人～! It's really disgusting!

作陪 zuòpéi (动) be invited to be present at a banquet given in honour of a distinguished guest

作品 zuòpǐn (名) works (of literature and art)

作曲 zuòqǔ (动) compose (music)

作数(數) zuòshù (动) be valid: 旧协定已经不～了. The old agreement is no longer binding.

作祟 zuòsuì (动) make mischief; cause trouble: 一定有人从中～. There must be someone trying to stir up (or create) trouble.

作威作福 zuòwēi-zuòfú ride roughshod over others; abuse one's power

作为(爲) zuòwéi I (名) **1** conduct; action: 他的～证明了他的品质高尚. His conduct bears unmistakable testimony to his noble-mindedness. **2** accomplishment: 无所～ do little and achieve nothing. 有所～ be ambitious and able to display one's talent II (动) **1** use as; regard as: 把它～跳板 use it as a springing board **2** as: ～你的母亲, 我不能视而不见. As your mother, I can't turn a blind eye to this.

作文 zuòwén (名) (student's) composition; essay

作物 zuòwù (名) crop: 夏季～ summer crops

作息 zuò-xī (动) work and rest: 按时～ work and rest according to schedule. ～(时间)表 timetable; work schedule

作秀 zuòxiù (动) put on a show: 他这是在～. He did this just for the show.

作业(業) zuòyè (名) **1** school assignment: 做～ do one's homework **2** work; task; operation: 水下～ underwater operation. 野外～ field work

作用 zuòyòng I (名) **1** role; function: 这一新机构的～ the function of this new organization. 他在文学界起了很大的～. He played an important role in literary circles. **2** action; effect: 化学～ chemical action. 反～ reaction. 副～ side effect II (动) affect; produce an effect on

作战(戰) zuòzhàn (动) fight a battle; fight: 英勇～ fight bravely

作者 zuòzhě (名) author; writer

作证 zuòzhèng (动) testify; give evidence; bear witness: 在法庭上～ bear witness in a lawcourt

作主 zuòzhǔ (动) **1** decide; have the final say: 这事她作不了主. She is in no position to decide. *or* It is not up to her to decide. **2** back up; support: 只要有你～, 我就干下去. I'll persist as long as you can back me up.

做 zuò (动) **1** do: ～家务事 do household chores. ～生意 do business **2** make: ～衣服 make clothes. ～文章 write an essay. ～饭 cook a meal **3** be; become: ～个好孩子. Be a good child. 他后来～了医生. He became a doctor later. ～朋友 make friends; be friends **4** celebrate (someone's birthday): ～生日 celebrate sb.'s birthday. ～寿 celebrate an elderly person's birthday **5** be used as: 这块布可以～一对枕套. This piece of cloth can be used to make a pair of pillowcases.

做伴 zuòbàn (动) keep sb. company

做到 zuòdào (动) accomplish; achieve: 说到～. One's word is one's bond. ～仁至义尽 do what is humanly possible to help

做东(東) zuòdōng (动) play the host

做法 zuòfǎ (名) way of doing things; practice

做工 zuògōng I (动) do (manual) work: 在纱厂～ work in a textile mill II (名) **1** labour involved in making things: 这件衣服～多少钱? How much is the tailoring of this jacket? **2** workmanship: ～精美 of exquisite workmanship

做官 zuòguān (动) be an official: ～当老爷 act as bureaucrats and overlords

做活儿(兒) zuòhuór do (manual) labour

做绝 zuòjué (动) leave no leeway; give no latitude: 把事情～ push things to the extreme

做客 zuòkè (动) be a guest

做礼(禮)拜 zuò lǐbài go to church (on sundays)

做媒 zuòméi (动) try to arrange matches for young people; be a matchmaker

做梦(夢) zuòmèng (动) dream: 白日～ daydream

做人 zuòrén (动) conduct oneself; behave: 不会～ not know how to behave tactfully in society. 重新～ turn over a new leaf

做文章 zuò wénzhāng **1** write an article **2** make an issue of: 别在这件事上～! Don't you try to make an issue of this matter!

做戏(戲) zuòxì (动) **1** act in a play **2** put on a show

做学(學)问 zuò xuéwen engage in scholarship; do research

做贼心虚 zuò zéi xīnxū have a guilty conscience

做作 zuòzuo (形) affected; artificial

附　录
APPENDICES

（一）汉语拼音声母韵母和国际音标对照表

Consonants and vowels of the Chinese phonetic alphabet and their corresponding international phonetic symbols

汉语拼音	国际音标	汉语拼音	国际音标
b	[p]	ê	[ɛ]
p	[p']	er	[ər]
m	[m]		
f	[f]	ai	[ai]
d	[t]	ei	[ei]
t	[t']	ao	[au]
n	[n]	ou	[əu]
l	[l]	an	[an]
g	[k]	en	[ən]
k	[k']	ang	[aŋ]
h	[x]	eng	[əŋ]
j	[tɕ]	ong	[uŋ]
q	[tɕ']	ia	[ia]
x	[ɕ]	ie	[iɛ]
z	[ts]	iao	[iau]
c	[ts']	iu, iou	[iəu]
s	[s]	ian	[ian]
zh	[tʂ]	in	[in]
ch	[tʂ']	iang	[iaŋ]
sh	[ʂ]	ing	[iŋ]
r	[ʐ]	iong	[yŋ]
		ua	[ua]
y	[j]	uo	[uə]
w	[w]	uai	[uai]
		ui, uei	[uei]
a	[a]	uan	[uan]

o	[o]	un, uen	[uən]
e	[ə]	ueng	[uəŋ]
i	[i]	uang	[uaŋ]
u	[u]	üe	[yε]
ü	[y]	üan	[yan]
-i	[ɿ][ʅ]*	ün	[yn]

* [ɿ]用于 z c s 后，[ʅ]用于 zh ch sh r 后。

（二）中国各省、自治区、直辖市的名称、简称及其人民政府所在地

Names and abbreviations of China's provinces, autonomous regions and municipalities directly under the central authority and their seats of people's government

名　称 Name	简　称 Abbreviation	人民政府所在地 Seat of the people's government
北京市 Beijing Shi	京 Jing	北京市 Beijing Shi
天津市 Tianjin Shi	津 Jin	天津市 Tianjin Shi
河北省 Hebei Sheng	冀 Ji	石家庄市 Shijiazhuang Shi
山西省 Shanxi Sheng	晋 Jin	太原市 Taiyuan Shi
内蒙古自治区 Nei Mongol Zizhiqu	内蒙古 Nei Mongol	呼和浩特市 Huhhot Shi
辽宁省 Liaoning Sheng	辽 Liao	沈阳市 Shenyang Shi
吉林省 Jilin Sheng	吉 Ji	长春市 Changchun Shi
黑龙江省 Heilongjiang Sheng	黑 Hei	哈尔滨市 Harbin Shi
上海市 Shanghai Shi	沪 Hu	上海市 Shanghai Shi
江苏省 Jiangsu Sheng	苏 Su	南京市 Nanjing Shi
浙江省 Zhejiang Sheng	浙 Zhe	杭州市 Hangzhou Shi
安徽省 Anhui Sheng	皖 Wan	合肥市 Hefei Shi
福建省 Fujian Sheng	闽 Min	福州市 Fuzhou Shi
江西省 Jiangxi Sheng	赣 Gan	南昌市 Nanchang Shi
山东省 Shandong Sheng	鲁 Lu	济南市 Jinan Shi
河南省 Henan Sheng	豫 Yu	郑州市 Zhengzhou Shi
湖北省 Hubei Sheng	鄂 E	武汉市 Wuhan Shi
湖南省 Hunan Sheng	湘 Xiang	长沙市 Changsha Shi
广东省 Guangdong Sheng	粤 Yue	广州市 Guangzhou Shi
广西壮族自治区 Guangxi Zhuangzu Zizhiqu	桂 Gui	南宁市 Nanning Shi
海南省 Hainan Sheng	琼 Qiong	海口市 Haikou Shi
重庆市 Chongqing Shi	渝 Yu	重庆市 Chongqing Shi
四川省 Sichuan Sheng	川 Chuan 蜀 Shu	成都市 Chengdu Shi
贵州省 Guizhou Sheng	黔 Qian 贵 Gui	贵阳市 Guiyang Shi
云南省 Yunnan Sheng	滇 Dian 云 Yun	昆明市 Kunming Shi

（续表）

名　称 Name	简　称 Abbreviation	人民政府所在地 Seat of the people's government
西藏自治区 Xizang Zizhiqu	藏 Zang	拉萨市 Lhasa Shi
陕西省 Shaanxi Sheng	陕 Shan 秦 Qin	西安市 Xi'an Shi
甘肃省 Gansu Sheng	陇 Long 甘 Gan	兰州市 Lanzhou Shi
青海省 Qinghai Sheng	青 Qing	西宁市 Xining Shi
宁夏回族自治区 Ningxia Huizu Zizhiqu	宁 Ning	银川市 Yinchuan Shi
新疆维吾尔自治区 Xinjiang Uygur Zizhiqu	新 Xin	乌鲁木齐市 Ürümqi Shi
台湾省 Taiwan Sheng	台 Tai	

中国的特别行政区的名称、简称

Names and abbreviations of China's Special Administrative Regions

名　称 Name	简　称 Abbreviation
中华人民共和国香港特别行政区 Hong Kong Special Administrative Region of the People's Republic of China	Hong Kong SAR
中华人民共和国澳门特别行政区 Macao Special Administrative Region of the People's Republic of China	Macao SAR

(三)普通话简介

About Mandarin Chinese

Mandarin is the world's most widely spoken language. It is the official language of the People's Republic of China, and one of the official languages of Singapore. Overseas Chinese communities around the world also often speak Mandarin.

With so many mutually unintelligible dialects of Chinese—including Cantonese, Wu, Hokkien (Min Nan) and Hakka—spoken around China, Mandarin has been promoted for almost a century as a Chinese *lingua franca*. Indeed, the Chinese word for Mandarin—*putonghua*—means "common speech".

Mandarin is based on the dialect of Beijing, though the pronunciation of the vast majority of speakers is also influenced by the speaker's native dialect. True Standard Mandarin is the preserve of television newsreaders, who receive rigorous elocution training.

Surveys have shown that within the People's Republic, around 53% of people are fluent in Mandarin. Fluency is more common among the young and those living in urban areas, where around 66% of people are fluent. Those who do not speak Mandarin well are often able to at least understand it. In Hong Kong and Macao, where Cantonese is still dominant, competency in Mandarin is rising, driven by closer integration with the Mainland.

Chinese who do not speak a common dialect are still united by the written language. A few variations in structure and vocabulary aside, formal written Chinese is largely the same across the Chinese-speaking world—only the pronunciation of the characters changes dramatically between dialects.

This situation has been complicated by the emergence of simplified characters. Simplified characters are used in Mainland China and most overseas Chinese communities, while traditional, or orthodox, characters are used in Hong Kong, Macao, and Taiwan. Educated Mainland Chinese can usually read traditional characters, though may not be able to write them. Chinese from other regions sometimes have trouble reading simplified characters.

The People's Republic of China uses the *hanyu pinyin* (or simply *pinyin*) system of romanization. *Pinyin* is a phonetic system used to teach Standard Mandarin pronunciation in Chinese schools, and for rendering of Chinese names in most foreign publications. Other regions make use of a variety of romanization systems.

Mandarin has a reputation as a difficult language to learn. The tonal system—whereby tones as well as consonants and vowels are used to differentiate words—is a challenge to those whose own languages are not tonal. Chinese characters are also a challenge to memorize. It is often said that knowledge of 3000 characters is enough to read a newspaper, but most educated Chinese are reckoned to know around 8000 characters. However, there is some good news for the foreign learner: grammar is fairly simple compared to many European languages, and verbs do not change.

(四)日常用语

Useful everyday expressions

yes/no = shì/bù 是/不
thank you = xièxie 谢谢
sorry = duìbuqǐ 对不起
excuse me = láojià 劳驾
I'm sorry, I don't understand = duìbuqǐ, wǒ tīng bù dǒng 对不起，我听不懂

Meeting people
hello/hi = nǐ hǎo 你好
How are you? = Nǐ hǎo ma? 你好吗?
Welcome! = Huānyíng, huānyíng! 欢迎，欢迎!
nice to meet you, pleased to meet you = rènshi nǐ zhēn hǎo 认识你真好

Going
Goodbye! = Zàijiàn! 再见!
Bye! = Zàijiàn! 再见!
Cheers! (British English)
(goodbye) = Zàijiàn! 再见!
(thank you) = Xièxie! 谢谢!
See you soon! = Xīwàng hěn kuài jiàndào nǐ! 希望很快见到你!
See you [later/tomorrow/next week]! = [Huítóu/míngtiān/xiàzhōu] jiàn! [回头/明天/下周]见!
See you around! = Huítóu jiàn! 回头见! (in informal situations)
(Have a) safe journey! = Yīlù píng'ān! 一路平安!
All the best! = Zhù nǐ yíqiè shùnlì! 祝你一切顺利!
= Zhù nǐ yìfān fēng shùn! 祝你一帆风顺!

Asking questions
Do you speak English/Chinese? = Nǐ jiǎng Yīngwén/Zhōngwén ma? 你讲英文/中文吗?
What's your name? = Nǐ jiào shénme míngzi? 你叫什么名字?
Where are you from? = Nǐ cóng nǎli lái? 你从哪里来?
How much is it? = Zhè yào duōshǎo qián? 这要多少钱?
Where is ...? = …zài shénme dìfang? …在什么地方?
Can I ...? = Wǒ néng bù néng…? 我能不能…?
Would you like ...? = Nǐ xiǎng bù xiǎng…? 你想不想…?

Statements about yourself
my name is ... = wǒ jiào…我叫…
I'm English/I'm American. = Wǒ shì Yīngguórén/Měiguórén. 我是英国人/美国人。
I don't speak Chinese. = Wǒ bù jiǎng Zhōngwén. 我不讲中文。
I live near Beijing/Chester. = Wǒ zhù Běijīng/Qièsītè fùjìn. 我住北京/切斯特附近。

I'm a student. = Wǒ shì yíge xuéshēng. 我是一个学生。
I work in an office. = Wǒ zaì bàngōngshì gōngzuò. 我在办公室工作。

When things are going well
Well done! = Gàn de hǎo! 干得好！
Congratulations! = Zhùhè nǐ! 祝贺你！
Excellent!, brilliant! = Tài hǎo le! 太好了！(in informal situations)

When things are not so good
Hard luck!, bad luck! = Zhēn bù zǒuyùn! 真不走运！
Too bad! = Zhēn zāogāo! 真糟糕！
Cheer up!, chin up! = Dǎqǐ jīngshén lai! 打起精神来！
Oh, dear! = Ā, tiān na! 啊，天哪！(in informal situations)
Damn! = Zāogāo! 糟糕！(in informal situations)
Blast! = Gāisǐ! 该死！(may be considered offensive)
Good luck! (you'll need it) = Zhù nǐ shí lái yùn zhuǎn! 祝你时来运转！
Get well soon! = Zhù nǐ zǎo rì kāngfù! 祝你早日康复！

Wishing someone well
Have a nice day! = Zhù nǐ dùguo měihǎo de yì tiān! 祝你度过美好的一天！
Have a good weekend! = Zhōumò kuàilè! 周末快乐！
Have a great holiday/vacation! = Jiàqī kuàilè! 假期快乐！
Have a good time! Enjoy yourself! = Zhù nǐ wánr de kuàihuo! 祝你玩儿得快活！
Have a good trip! = Zhù nǐ lǚtú yúkuài! 祝你旅途愉快！

Special greetings
Happy birthday! = Zhù nǐ shēngri kuàilè! 祝你生日快乐！
Merry Christmas! = Shèngdàn kuàilè! 圣诞快乐！
Happy New Year! = Xīnnián kuàilè! 新年快乐！
Happy Chinese New Year! = Gōngxǐ fācái! 恭喜发财！

In reply to "thank you"
You're very welcome. = Bú kèqi 不客气。
Don't mention it. = Bú yòng xiè 不用谢。
Not at all. = Bú xiè 不谢 (in informal situations)。

Eating and drinking
Help yourself! = Qǐng suíbiàn chī! 请随便吃！
Enjoy your meal! = Xīwàng nǐmen chī de kāixīn! 希望你们吃得开心！
Cheers! (as a toast) = Gānbēi! 干杯！

Sleeping
Good night! = Wǎn'ān! 晚安！
Sleep well! = Zhù nǐ shuì ge hǎo jiào! 祝你睡个好觉！

Emergencies
Can you help me, please? = Nǐ néng bāng wǒ yíxià ma? 你能帮我一下吗？
I'm lost. = Wǒ mílù le. 我迷路了。
I'm ill. = Wǒ shēngbìng le. 我生病了。
call an ambulance = jiào jiùhùchē 叫救护车

Reading signs

no entry	= jìnzhǐ rùnèi 禁止入内
no smoking	= jìnzhǐ xīyān 禁止吸烟
fire exit	= fánghuǒmén 防火门
for sale	= dàishòu 待售

THE CLOCK

What time is it?

Excuse me, what time is it?	= Qǐng wèn, jǐ diǎn le 请问，几点了？
It's exactly four o'clock.	= Zhènghǎo sì diǎn 正好四点。

There is no Chinese equivalent of "it is ..." in expressions of time. Usually, **xiànzài** 现在 (= now) is used at the beginning of the Chinese sentence to indicate the time.

it is ...	**xiànzài**… 现在…
4 o'clock	sì diǎn 四点
4 o'clock in the morning/4 am	zǎochén sì diǎn 早晨四点
4 o'clock in the afternoon/4 pm	xiàwǔ sì diǎn 下午四点
4:10/ten past four	sì diǎn shí fēn 四点十分
4:15	sì diǎn shíwǔ fēn 四点十五分
a quarter past four	sì diǎn yí kè 四点一刻
4:20	sì diǎn èrshí fēn 四点二十分
4:25	sì diǎn èrshíwǔ fēn 四点二十五分
4:30	sì diǎn sānshí fēn 四点三十分
half past four	sì diǎn bàn 四点半
4:35	sì diǎn sānshíwǔ fēn 四点三十五分
twenty-five to five	chà èrshíwǔ fēn wǔ diǎn 差二十五分五点
4:40	sì diǎn sìshí fēn 四点四十分
twenty to five	chà èrshí fēn wǔ diǎn 差二十分五点
4:45	sì diǎn sìshíwǔ fēn 四点四十五分
a quarter to five	chà yí kè wǔ diǎn 差一刻五点
4:50	sì diǎn wǔshí fēn 四点五十分
ten to five	chà shí fēn wǔ diǎn 差十分五点
4:55	sì diǎn wǔshíwǔ fēn 四点五十五分
five to five	chà wǔ fēn wǔ diǎn 差五分五点
5 o'clock	wǔ diǎn 五点
16:15	shíliù diǎn shíwǔ fēn 十六点十五分
8 o'clock in the evening/8 pm	wǎnshàng bā diǎn 晚上八点
12:00	shí'èr diǎn 十二点
12 noon	zhōngwǔ shí'èr diǎn 中午十二点
12 midnight	bànyè shí'èr diǎn 半夜十二点， wǔyè shí'èr diǎn 午夜十二点

In timetables etc. the twenty-four hour clock is used. For example, 4 pm is **shíliù diǎn** 十六点. In ordinary usage, one says **xiàwǔ sì diǎn** 下午四点.

When?

Chinese never drops the word **diǎn** 点; **at five** is **wǔ diǎn** 五点 and so on. It is not necessary to translate the word **at** into Chinese, but other prepositions or adverbs are still necessary.

At what time *will he come*? = Tā __ jǐ diǎn lái 他__几点来?
He'll come at *four*. = Tā __ sì diǎn lái 他__四点来。
He'll come at about *five*. = Tā __ **dàyuē** wǔ diǎn lái 他__**大约**五点来。
It must be ready by *ten*. = Shí diǎn **yǐqián** yídìng yào zhǔnbèihǎo 十点**以前**一定要准备好。
closed from *1* to *2 pm* = cóng xiàwǔ yì diǎn **dào** liǎng diǎn guānmén 从下午一点**到**两点关门
I'll go after *6*. = Wǒ liù diǎn **yǐhòu** qù 我六点**以后**去。

FORMS OF ADDRESS (Miss, Mr. , Mrs.)

The order of the given name, surname, and title in Chinese
Unlike the order in English names, Chinese surnames precede given names. For example, in the Chinese name below, **Wáng** 王 is the surname and **Tiěshān** 铁山 is the given name:
Wáng Tiěshān 王铁山

In Chinese, the title follows the surname or the full name:
Mr. Wang = Wáng xiānsheng 王先生
Mr. Tieshan Wang = Wáng Tiěshān xiānsheng 王铁山先生

Titles frequently used in addressing people
Miss Jones = Qióngsī xiǎojiě 琼斯小姐
Mr. Smith = Shǐmìsī xiānsheng 史密斯先生
Mrs. Davis = Dàiwéisī tàitai 戴维斯太太
Ms. Lambert = Lánbótè nǚshì 兰伯特女士
Professor Hull = Hè'ěr jiàoshòu 赫尔教授
Dr. Brown (medical) = Bùlǎng dàifu 布朗大夫
Dr. Brown (academic) = Bùlǎng bóshì 布朗博士

Titles frequently used in addressing people in China
Comrade Wang = Wáng tóngzhì 王同志
Teacher Wang = Wáng lǎoshī 王老师
Master (master worker) Wang = Wáng shīfu 王师傅
Master (schoolmaster) Wang = Wáng xiàozhǎng 王校长
Manager Wang = Wáng jīnglǐ 王经理

The following two forms are also frequently used by Chinese friends and colleagues in addressing each other:
Little Wang (to a person younger than the speaker) = Xiǎo Wáng 小王
Old Wang (to a person older than the speaker) = Lǎo Wáng 老王

GAMES AND SPORTS

In Chinese, the verb *dǎ* 打 is used for ball games played with the hand.
to play tennis = dǎ wǎngqiú 打网球
to play basketball = dǎ lánqiú 打篮球
to play volleyball = dǎ páiqiú 打排球
to play table tennis = dǎ pīngpāngqiú 打乒乓球

Chinese uses the verb *tī* 踢 for football, *xià* 下 for chess, *dǎ* 打 for cards and mahjong.

to play football = tī zúqiú 踢足球
to play chess = xià qí 下棋
to play cards = dǎ púkè 打扑克
to play mahjong = dǎ májiàng 打麻将

Players and events

a tennis player = yíge wǎngqiú yùndòngyuán 一个网球运动员
a tennis champion = yíge wǎngqiú guànjūn 一个网球冠军
to win a basketball game = yíng yìchǎng lánqiú bǐsài 赢一场篮球比赛
to lose a volleyball game = shū yìchǎng páiqiú bǐsài 输一场排球比赛
to draw in a football game = zài yìchǎng zúqiú bǐsài zhōng tīpíng 在一场足球比赛中踢平
the Olympic Games = Àolínpǐkè Yùndònghuì 奥林匹克运动会
the World Cup = Shìjiè Bēi Sài 世界杯赛
a world champion = yíge shìjiè guànjūn 一个世界冠军
a national champion = yíge quánguó guànjūn 一个全国冠军

LENGTH AND WEIGHT MEASUREMENTS

Length measurements

1 inch = 2.54 cm
1 foot = 30.48 cm
1 yard = 91.44 cm
1 mile = 1.61 km

Length

How long is the rope? = Zhègēn shéngzi yǒu duō cháng? 这根绳子有多长?
it's ten metres long = yǒu shí mǐ cháng 有十米长
the rope is three metres too short = zhègēn shéngzi duǎnle sān mǐ 这根绳子短了三米

Height

People: *how tall is he?* = tā (yǒu) duō gāo? 他(有)多高?
he's six feet tall = tā (yǒu) liù yīngchǐ gāo 他(有)六英尺高
he's taller/smaller than I am = tā bǐ wǒ gāo/ǎi 他比我高/矮
Things: *how high is the tower?* = nàzuò tǎ yǒu duō gāo? 那座塔有多高?
it's 100 metres high = yǒu yìbǎi mǐ gāo 有一百米高
A is higher than B = A bǐ B gāo A 比 B 高
A is lower than B = A bǐ B ǎi/dī A 比 B 矮/低

Distance

How far is it from your home to your school? = Nǐde jiā lí nǐde xuéxiào (yǒu) duō yuǎn? 你的家离你的学校(有)多远?
it's about 5 miles = dàyuē (yǒu) wǔ yīnglǐ 大约(有)五英里

Width/breadth

How wide is the river? = Zhètiáo hé yǒu duō kuān? 这条河有多宽?
it's seven metres wide = yǒu qī mǐ kuān 有七米宽

Depth

How deep is the lake? = Zhège hú yǒu duō shēn? 这个湖有多深?
it's four metres deep = yǒu sì mǐ shēn 有四米深

Note that a construction with **de 的** always comes before the noun it describes:
a street two kilometres long = yìtiáo liǎng gōnglǐ cháng **de** mǎlù 一条两公里长的马路
a 100-metre-high tower = yízuò yìbǎi mǐ gāo **de** tǎ 一座一百米高的塔
a river 50 metres wide = yìtiáo wǔshí mǐ kuān **de** hé 一条五十米宽的河

Weight measurements

1 ounce = 28.35 g (grammes)
*1 pound** = 453.60 g
1 stone = 6.35 kg (kilos)
1 ton = 1016.05 kg
* **a pound** (£1) is translated as **yì yīngbàng 一英镑**, and **a pound** (**1 lb**) is translated as **yí bàng 一磅.**

People: *how much does he weigh?* = Tā yǒu duō zhòng? 他有多重?
he weighs 82 kilos = tā (yǒu) bāshí'èr gōngjīn zhòng 他有八十二公斤重
Things: *what does the parcel weigh?* = Zhège bāoguǒ yǒu duō zhòng? 这个包裹有多重?
How heavy is it? = Zhè yǒu duō zhòng? 这有多重?
it weighs 10 kilos = yǒu shí gōngjīn zhòng 有十公斤重
A weighs more than B = A bǐ B zhòng A 比 B 重
sold by the kilo = àn gōngjīn chūshòu 按公斤出售

ILLNESSES, ACHES AND PAINS

Where does it hurt?

Where does it hurt? = Nǎr téng? 哪儿疼?
his leg hurts = tāde tuǐ téng 他的腿疼
he has a pain in his leg = tāde tuǐ téng 他的腿疼
Note that **his leg hurts** and **he has a pain in his leg** share the same Chinese translation.

Aches

he has [a headache/a sore throat/a stomach ache ...] = tā [tóuténg/sǎngzi téng/dùzi téng…] 他[头疼/嗓子疼/肚子疼…]

Note that **have** is not translated into Chinese.

Accidents

she broke her *leg* = tā shuāiduànle __ tuǐ 她摔断了__腿
I twisted my *ankle* = wǒ niǔshāngle __ jiǎobózi 我扭伤了__脚脖子
Note that, unlike English, Chinese doesn't require a possessive before the part of the body.

Being ill

to have/to catch [flu/measles/cold ...] = dé [liúgǎn/mázhěn/gǎnmào…]

得[流感/麻疹/感冒…]

to have cancer = dé áizhèng 得癌症

Treatment

to be treated for rabies = yīn kuángquǎnbìng ér jiēshòu zhìliáo 因狂犬病而接受治疗

to take tablets for indigestion = yīn xiāohuà bùliáng ér chī yào 因消化不良而吃药

to be operated on for cancer = yīn áizhèng ér zuò shǒushù 因癌症而做手术

（五）中文书信范例

Chinese model letters

应聘信 Accepting a job

尊敬的卜力先生：

感谢您9月8日的来信，并给了我一个在施耐得公司工作的机会。我非常乐意成为施耐得的一名编辑。

我将会按要求于12月15日前来报到上班。请问公司对员工的着装是否有具体的要求？

非常期待与您和您的团队见面。

此致

敬礼！

洪巧云

2007年9月10日

求职信 Applying for a job

尊敬的先生/女士：

我在4月16日的《卫报》上看到了你们的招聘广告，并想应聘客户服务经理一职。随信附上了我的个人简历。

我目前就职于宁波顺通货运，主要专注于对公司大客户的服务。我非常希望能有机会在英国工作。从我的简历上您能看到，我具有良好的专业教育背景，并在货运行业中有丰富的经验；具有良好的组织、沟通能力，思维活跃、有积极进取的精神和善于接受挑战的性格；具有良好的敬业精神和团队精神。

我随时可以通过电话参加面试。4月29日后随时可以前往英国进行面试。

期待您的回复。

此致

敬礼！

朱敏

2007年11月19日

简历 Curriculum Vitae

Foreign nationals would replace 民族 (ethnic group) with 国籍 (nationality) eg. 国籍：英国

简　历

姓名：王洛平　　性别：男
民族：汉
学历：工商管理硕士　　专业：风险管理
地址：北京朝阳区酒仙桥79号　　邮编：100000
电子邮件：cocoku@hotmail.com　　手机：13901085439

工作经历

2002 年 10 月至今　**开咨询有限公司：**
主要负责公司上市风险评估，制定融资方案，主要客户包括宝洁、上海通用、中国石化等。

2000 年 1 月—2002 年 8 月　**上海融通公关公司**
负责全球大客户部每日销售报表统计与分析，销售人员绩效评估。成功策划、组织并完成了“几内亚矿运”项目。

学历

1998 年 9 月—2000 年 9 月　**工商管理硕士(成绩优异)**
格拉斯哥大学，英国

1994 年 9 月—1998 年 7 月　**经济学学士(优秀毕业生)**
北京大学，中国

特长

语言
- 中文　母语
- 英语　流利
- 法语　流利

独立工作能力
- 具有严谨的工作作风和积极乐观的工作态度
- 具有丰富的项目运作能力和经验
- 具有跨文化、跨企业的沟通能力

团队精神
- 将公司的事业与个人的前途和紧密联系在一起；善于和同事进行业务沟通，在完成自身任务的同时，为实现团队目标积极协助其他同事工作
- 具有较强的亲和力和良好的社会交往能力

明信片 Postcard

100000

中国北京市西城区仙虞胡同 3 门

珍妮 收

浙江省杭州市湖跑路 39 号信源宾馆
叶清扬
310002

亲爱的珍妮：

我正坐在西湖边的茶馆里，一边喝着龙井茶，一边给你写明信片。

秋天的杭州非常美丽，到处飘着桂花的香味。今天我和雪莉沿着西湖骑自行车去植物园。沿途都是公园，草地上还有灰色的小松鼠在啃松果！植物园里有一家不起眼的小餐馆，但是饭菜很有特色，大多是以茶叶为原料做的。

杭州的生活非常悠闲自在，当地人也很友善，是个不错的休闲去处。

我后天坐火车回北京。周末我们聚一聚吧。

叶清扬

祝贺信 Chinese New Year wishes

亲爱的 is used when addressing friends

亲爱的爸爸妈妈：

春节快乐！

很久没有回家了，你们身体都还好吗？苏州已经很冷了吧？爸爸早上不要再那么早出去晨练，还是等天亮以后再去爬山吧。

时间过得真快，搬到北京都快半年了。我非常喜欢现在的工作，虽然非常忙，常常睡眠不足，但是很充实，和同事相处也比较融洽。我特别感谢同一个办公室的两位男同事，虽然他们都是老烟枪，烟瘾非常大，但是他们总是去办公室外抽烟。过去与我们合作的大多是中国和希腊的客户，现在我正在努力和迪拜的船东建立业务联系。

这是我结婚后的第一个春节，得去东北的婆家过年，没法回家和你们一起过大年三十，真是对不起。不过等过了大年初三我就回杭州探望您二老。

最后，恭祝二老身体安康！

The closing line is typically a wish for good health, or success in work. Where the addressees are elderly, wishing good health is more common.

女儿 毛毛
2007年11月20日

The date always follows the author's name, even in informal correspondence.

（六）英文书信范例

English model letters

应聘信 Accepting a job

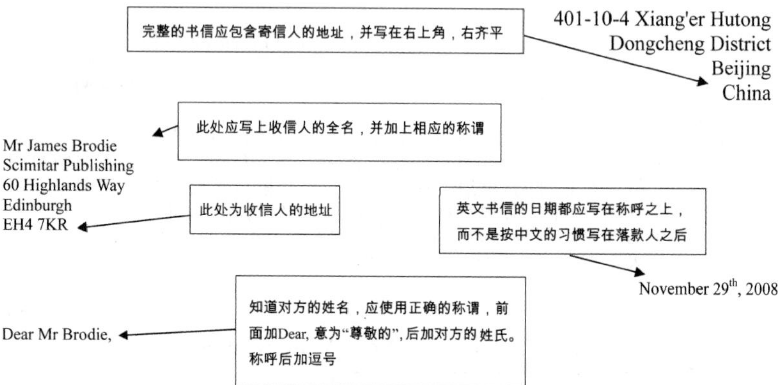

完整的书信应包含寄信人的地址，并写在右上角，右齐平

401-10-4 Xiang'er Hutong
Dongcheng District
Beijing
China

此处应写上收信人的全名，并加上相应的称谓

Mr James Brodie
Scimitar Publishing
60 Highlands Way
Edinburgh
EH4 7KR

此处为收信人的地址

英文书信的日期都应写在称呼之上，而不是按中文的习惯写在落款人之后

November 29th, 2008

Dear Mr Brodie,

知道对方的姓名，应使用正确的称谓，前面加Dear, 意为“尊敬的”，后加对方的姓氏。称呼后加逗号

Many thanks for your letter of November 28th offering me the position of editor at Scimitar. I am delighted to accept the offer.

I confirm that I will be able to start on December 15th. Could you please let me know the company's dress code?

I look forward to meeting up with you and the team soon.

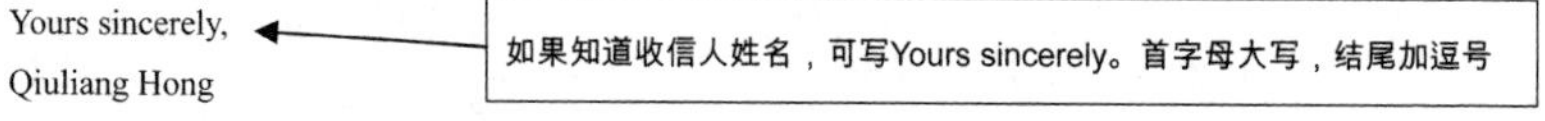

Yours sincerely,
Qiuliang Hong

如果知道收信人姓名，可写Yours sincerely。首字母大写，结尾加逗号

求职信 Applying for a job

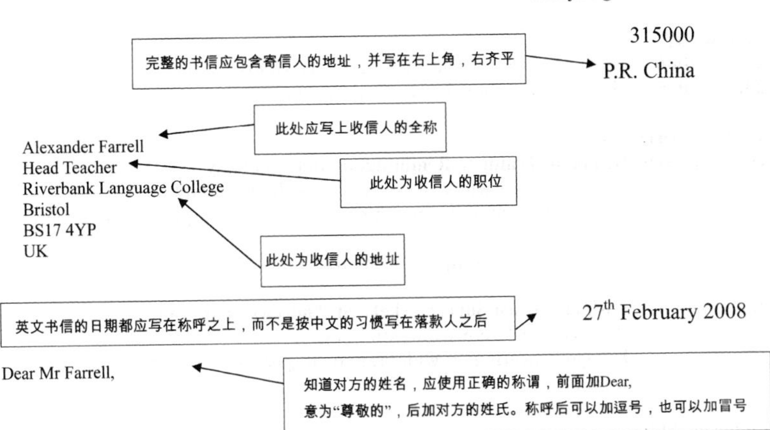

Flat 2511
Bibo Huayuan Gongyu
20 Zhongshan Lu
Yinzhou District
Ningbo City
Zhejiang Province

315000
P.R. China

Alexander Farrell
Head Teacher
Riverbank Language College
Bristol
BS17 4YP
UK

27th February 2008

Dear Mr Farrell,

完整的书信应包含寄信人的地址，并写在右上角，右齐平
此处应写上收信人的全称
此处为收信人的职位
此处为收信人的地址
英文书信的日期都应写在称呼之上，而不是按中文的习惯写在落款人之后
知道对方的姓名，应使用正确的称谓，前面加Dear,
意为“尊敬的”，后加对方的姓氏。称呼后可以加逗号，也可以加冒号

I am writing to express an interest in the vacancy for a Chinese teacher at your college advertised on Interlanguages.com.

I have over ten years experience of teaching Chinese to foreign students at various universities across China, and I would now like to teach in the UK. My work has given me insights into a variety of cultures, which I feel will help me rise to the challenge of working in a foreign country. You can find full details of my work history on the enclosed CV.

I am available for telephone interview at any time, and could travel to the UK for a face-to-face interview from 7th March.

I look forward to hearing from you soon.

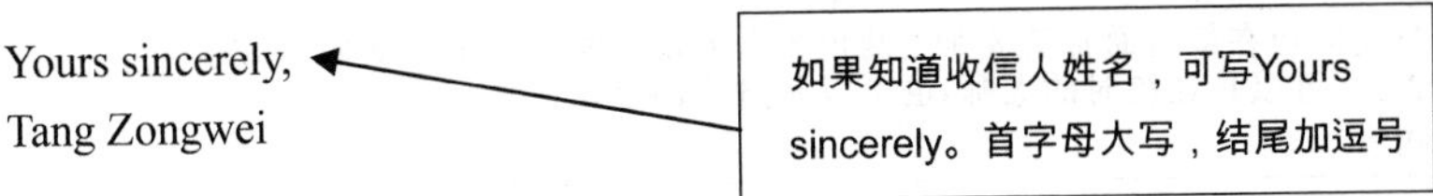

Yours sincerely,
Tang Zongwei

如果知道收信人姓名，可写Yours
sincerely。首字母大写，结尾加逗号

简历 Curriculum Vitae

Name: Shaoping Huang
Address: 17 Hartley Drive
London NW11 9JQ
Nationality: Chinese
Telephone: 020 8562 9853
Email: huangsp@freemail.com

Education:

2005—2006	University of St Andrews (UK) Business Studies	MA
2001—2005	Shanghai Jiaotong University Economics	BA

Work Experience:

2006—present Graduate Trainee, Remmington and Company
Worked in a variety of roles across the company
Managed a small team which successfully implemented a new IT system
Captain of the company football team

2005—2006 Cashier, Tesco Supermarket, St Andrews (part-time)
Worked part-time while studying
Enjoyed meeting a wide range of people and improving my oral English

Language Skills:

Mandarin	Native
Cantonese	Fluent
English	Fluent

Interests:

Travel (interrailing with British friends, summer 2006); swimming

References:

Mr Oliver Bashfor
Manager, Graduate Training Programme
Remmington and Company
London W1 4PQ

Dr John Yardley
Dept. of Business Studies
St Andrews University
St Andrews
Fife KY16 9AJ

英文简历在最后通常需要加上两位推荐人及其联系方式,可以是在校时的老师,也可以是过去的上司或同事

圣诞新年祝贺信 Christmas and New Year wishes

64 Argyle Gardens
London SE7 5FL

私人信件中不需要加收信人的地址

3rd January 2009

Dear Shirley and Brian,

英文中段落的区分有两种：一. 段首空两格，段落间不空行；二. 段首顶格，段落之间空一行

Merry Christmas and all the best for the New Year to you and your family! I hope you're all well and that Brian is enjoying his new job. My company is probably going to send me to Bristol for two months early in the year, so hopefully we'll have a chance to meet up again soon.

This year seems to have flown by—I don't know where all the time has gone! My mum was ill over the summer so I spent a lot of time looking after her, and apart from that I've been snowed under at work. I did get a chance to go to Greece for a holiday though. It was absolutely wonderful!

Next time you're in London, you must let me know and we can all go for dinner. A lovely little Italian has opened up just around the corner, and I know how Brian loves his Italian food!

All the very best to you both,
Julie

明信片 Postcard

Doug Pearman
14 Abbot Road
Dublin 6
IRELAND

收信人应在地址之前。英文地址的写法与中文相反，从小到大：先是门牌号，具体的街道，然后是城市，最后是国家。

Dear Doug,
Greetings from London! The weather has been great since we got here, which is good because there's so much to do. We spent three days just looking around the museums and galleries, which was fascinating but tiring! Today we're taking a well-earned break just sitting in the sunshine on Hampstead Heath. It's beautiful here.
See you back in Dublin again soon!
Xiaoqing

（七）中国节假日

Calendar of Chinese festivals and holidays

1st of the first lunar month

Chūnjié 春节（Spring Festival）
The most important festival in the Chinese calendar, Spring Festival, or Chinese New Year, occurs on the first day of the traditional Chinese lunar year (falling between the end of January and the end of February in the Gregorian calendar). People return home to be with their families. Traditions include cleaning the home; wearing new clothes; presenting gifts; pasting up auspicious couplets (duìlián 对联) on either side of the front door; giving children small amounts of money in red envelopes (hóngbāo 红包); in the North, making and eating boiled dumplings (jiǎozi 饺子) together; and letting off firecrackers and fireworks. In business, all debts should be cleared at New Year. Celebrations can start late in the preceding month, and go on till the following Lantern Festival. The official holiday, however, is just three days, sometimes extended to a week.

15th of the first lunar month

Yuánxiāojié 元宵节（Lantern Festival）
The Lantern Festival falls on the first full moon of the lunar year. The main activity is watching lanterns, and guessing the 'lantern riddles' written on them. The traditional food is round glutinous rice dumplings (yuánxiāo 元宵). The Lantern Festival marks the end of the New Year period.

8 March

Sānbā fùnǚ jié 三八妇女节（International Women's Day）
This celebratory day gives women a half or whole day's holiday.

12 March

Zhíshù jié 植树节（Tree-planting Day）
Begun in 1979, this is a day for addressing concerns about soil erosion.

early (between 4th and 6th) April

Qīngmíngjié 清明节（Qingming Festival）
Linked to the early Chinese solar calendar, the traditional Qingming Festival marked an important transition to warmer weather in the agricultural year. It is now an official one-day holiday, which is sometimes extended to three days. The main activity is 'sweeping the tombs' of the ancestors. At gravesides people conduct a symbolic sweeping with new willow fronds; offer food, gifts and flowers; and burn incense and paper money. It is also a festival for spring outings and kite flying.

1 May

Wǔyī guójì láodòng jié 五一国际劳动节 (International Labour, (*US*) Labor Day)
As in other parts of the world, May Day has been denoted a day for workers. There is an official three-day holiday at this time of year.

4 May

Wǔsì qīngnián jié 五四青年节 (Youth Day)
This day commemorates the May 4th Movement of 1919, when students in Beijing and across China demonstrated for nationalism and modernization.

8th of the fourth lunar month

Fódànjié 佛诞节 (Buddha's Birthday)
Buddha's Birthday is more popular in Hong Kong, and is especially celebrated in Buddhist temples.

1 June

Liùyī értóng jié 六一儿童节 (Children's Day)
On this day children are presented with gifts, and get free entrance to various kinds of entertainment.

5th of the fifth lunar month

Duānwǔjié 端午节 (Dragon Boat Festival)
A traditional festival, ostensibly commemorating the poet Qu Yuan (340-278 BC) of the state of Chu. Qu Yuan wrote long, mystical, seemingly patriotic poems. On hearing the news of the defeat of Chu by Qin, he is said to have committed suicide by jumping into the Miluo River. The traditions of dragon-boat racing and eating glutinous rice pyramids (zòngzi 粽子) are meant to mark Qu Yuan's death, since supposedly at the time local people threw rice into the river to divert the fish from eating his body.

1 July

Qīyī jiàndǎngjié 七一建党节 (Founding of the Chinese Communist Party)
The CCP was founded in Shanghai in 1921.

1 August

Bāyī jiànjūn jié 八一建军节 (Army Day)
A ceremonial day, it commeorates the founding of the People's Liberation Army and also emphasizes collaboration between the People's Liberation Army and the people.

7th of the seventh lunar month

Qīxījié 七夕节 (Double Seventh Festival)
This festival is associated with the traditional love story of the mortal Cowherd and celestial Weaving Girl. According to the story, the couple fell in love and she

came down to earth to marry him. However, they were discovered by the Queen of Heaven, who separated them by creating the Milky Way and took the Weaving Girl back to heaven. Subsequently, magpies took pity on the pair and once a year form themselves into a bridge between heaven and earth so that the Cowherd and Weaving Girl can be reunited. In contemporary China the festival is a day for lovers.

15th of the seventh lunar month

Zhōngyuánjié 中元节 (Hungry Ghost Festival)
Traditionally, the whole of the seventh month is Ghost Month, when spirits wander the earth. At the Hungry Ghost Festival, which is officially a one-day holiday but is sometimes extended to three days, ritual food offerings are made and paper money burnt to appease these spirits. This festival is more popular in Hong Kong.

10 September

Jiàoshī jié 教师节 (Teachers' Day)
The new official day for honouring teachers.

15th of the eighth lunar month

Zhōngqiūjié 中秋节 (Mid-Autumn Festival)
A traditional festival when the moon is full. On this day people enjoy the moon, set out food, and in particular eat moon cakes (yuèbǐng 月饼). It is timed to celebrate the harvest.

28 September

Kǒngzǐ dànshēng rì 孔子诞生日 (Confucius' Birthday)
Confucius is now increasingly popular as a national figure. His birthday is particularly celebrated at the Confucian temple in the city of Qufu, but also at other Confucian temples around the country.

1 October

Shíyī guóqìngjié 十一国庆节 (National Day)
This was the day that Chairman Mao proclaimed the founding of the People's Republic of China in 1949. Today, it is celebrated with grand processions of school children, workers, minority representatives and troops, and displays of military hardware. There are three days' official holiday, sometimes extended to a week.

9th of the ninth lunar month

Chóngyángjié 重阳节 (Double Ninth Festival)
The number nine symbolizes Yang (yáng 阳), the positive principle in nature. So, on the 9th day of the 9th month, this principle is at its strongest. Traditionally, people climb mountains on this day. The chrysanthemum is also symbolic of the festival.

mid-Winter (22nd or 23rd December)

Dōngzhì 冬至 (Winter Solstice)
As the turning point away from winter, it marks the time in the year when the Yang (yáng 阳) principle is at its lowest. Various kinds of dumplings are eaten, to build up strength.

25 December

Shèngdànjié 圣诞节 (Christmas Day)
A foreign import, but increasingly celebrated in a small way. It is particularly important in Hong Kong.

1 January

Yuándàn 元旦 (New Year's Day)
Though it does not have traditional significance, this day is an official holiday in China.